-wərds] *adv* hacia

.put E/S

ıal Olympic Com-

ın] *n no pl* yodo *m*

ıt, brought> *vt*
...
use to happen) pro-
.

‹eıt] *vt* ...

. .

ɔgrafío> ...

ˌ, -iest> ...

rgonzado, -a ...

ˈson) mudo, -a *m, f*
us poner sordina a

ʋnstream; ~ **arriba**
* **oro** to have a gold-
ʌ for a penny, in for a
for a sheep as for a
evuelto to fish in
el ~ suena, algo
moke, there's fire

sə'lektər] *n* **1.** SPORTS
ı) *m(f)* **2.** TECH selec-

ʼe) brave **2.** (*bueno*)
mal, persona) wild;
ugged ...

stool; (*para los pies*)
pavement *Brit,* side-

ı *m*

catequesis *f inv*
m (*Brit:* 4,55 *l, Am:*

ːrtʃ] *n* marzo *m; s. a.*

ədj seventeenth; *v.t.*

All entries (words, .compounds, variant spellings, cross-references) appear in alphabetical order and are printed in bold type.

English phrasal verbs come directly after the base verb and are signalled by ◆.

Arabic superscripts indicate **homographs** (identically spelt words with different meanings).

The IPA (International Phonetic Alphabet) is used for all **phonetic transcriptions, including American pronunciations.**

Angle brackets are used to show **irregular plural forms** and, **forms of irregular verbs and adjectives.**

Feminine forms of nouns and adjectives are shown unless they are identical to the masculine form. Spanish nouns are followed by their gender.

Roman numerals are used for the **grammatical divisions** of a word, and Arabic numerals for **sense divisions.**

The **swung dash** represents the entry word in examples and idioms. The ► sign introduces **a block of set expressions, idioms and proverbs.** Key words are underlined as a guide.

Various kinds of **meaning indicators** are used to guide users to the required translation:

- **areas of specialization**

- **definitions** or **synonyms**, typical **subjects** or **objects** of the entry

- **Regional vocabulary and variants** are shown both as headword and translations

- **Language registers**

When a word or expression has no direct translation, there is an **explanation** or a **cultural equivalent** (≈). Where a translation may be unclear, it is followed by an explanation in brackets.

s. a. and *v.t.* invites the reader to consult a **model entry** for further information.

DICCIONARIO

Cambridge
Klett
Compact

Español – Inglés
English – Spanish

CAMBRIDGE
UNIVERSITY PRESS

PUBLISHED BY THE PRESS SYNDICATE OF THE UNIVERSITY OF CAMBRIDGE
The Pitt Building, Trumpington Street, Cambridge, United Kingdom

CAMBRIDGE UNIVERSITY PRESS
The Edinburgh Building, Cambridge CB2 2RU, UK
40 West 20th Street, New York, NY 10011–4211, USA
477 Williamstown Road, Port Melbourne, VIC 3207, Australia
Ruiz de Alarcón 13, 28014 Madrid, Spain
Dock House, The Waterfront, Cape Town 8001, South Africa

http://www.cambridge.org

First published 2002
Fifth printing 2004

Printed in Italy by LEGO S.p.A.

Typeface: Univers Black, Weidemann

A catalogue record for this book is available from the British Library

Library of Congress Cataloguing in Publication data applied for

ISBN 0521 802989 paperback
ISBN 0521 752981 paperback + CD-ROM
ISBN 0521 540240 hardback + CD-ROM

Editorial Management: Marîa Teresa Gondar Oubiña, Anke Müller

Contributors: Peter Bereza, Alexander Burden, Roser Calvet i Riera, Anne Choffrut,
Majka Dischler, Maite Ferré Simó, Susan Frisbie Rabelo, Laura García Codony,
Concepción, Gil Bayo, Tim Gutteridge, Stephen John Hackett, Kay Hollingsworth,
Melva Josefina Márquez Rojas, Matthew C. Maxwell, Ana María Peris Moreno,
Josep Ràfols i Ventosa, Carlos Gerado Rodríguez Penagos, James Robert Gurney Salter,
Judith Santolaria Antolín, Anja Tauchmann, Stephen Alan Trott, Eduardo Vallejo,
Sandra Vilamitjana Parellada, Tessa Wigley

Typesetting: Dörr und Schiller GmbH, Stuttgart
Data processing: Andreas Lang, conTEXT AG für Information und Kommunikation, Zürich

Índice

Contents

Introducción

El *Diccionario Cambridge Klett Compact* es un diccionario bilingüe completamente nuevo destinado a estudiantes de inglés de habla española y a estudiantes de español de habla inglesa. En su confección y edición ha participado un gran número de hablantes nativos de ambas lenguas, lo que lo convierte en una herramienta lingüística amplia y actualizada.

En el diccionario se halla reflejado tanto el inglés británico como el inglés americano y proporciona, de esta manera, una guía fiable del inglés como lengua internacional. Al mismo tiempo ofrece una amplia cobertura tanto del español peninsular como del español de América Latina y constituye, por tanto, una herramienta útil de aprendizaje para cualquier estudiante de español en cualquier país de lengua española.

El diccionario incluye, además, una ayuda complementaria para el aprendizaje de aquellos aspectos que acostumbran a resultar más dificultosos a los estudiantes; por ejemplo, modelos de conjugaciones de los dos idiomas y una sección especial dedicada a los 'falsos amigos' que pueden confundir al estudiante.

Le deseamos que la consulta de este diccionario y el aprendizaje del nuevo idioma le reporten unos momentos agradables.

Este diccionario se puede adquirir con o sin CD-ROM. Si desea obtener más información, visítenos en nuestra dirección:

dictionary.cambridge.org

Introduction

The *Diccionario Cambridge Klett Compact* is a completely new bilingual dictionary for Spanish-speaking learners of English and English-speaking learners of Spanish. It has been written and edited by a large team of native speakers of both languages so that it provides an up-to-date and comprehensive language tool.

It covers British English and American English, so that it provides a reliable guide to English as an international language. It also has good coverage of the Spanish from Spain and Spanish from Latin America so that for learners of Spanish it can help them in all of the Spanish-speaking world.

The dictionary provides extra help with many areas that learners find difficult. For example, there is full information about the verb patterns of the the two languages and there is a special section on the 'false friends' that can be confusing for learners.

We hope that you enjoy using this book and that you enjoy learning your new language.

You can buy this book with or without a CD-ROM and you can find out more information on our website at:

dictionary.cambridge.org

La pronunciación del español
Spanish pronunciation

Remarkable differences can be observed in Spanish pronunciation, both within the various regions of the Iberian Peninsula and also in the individual countries where Spanish is spoken. Contrary to general opinion, these differences are stronger within Spain than between the various Spanish-speaking countries in America. In bilingual regions of the Iberian Peninsula like Catalonia, Valencia, the Balearic Islands, the Basque Provinces and Galicia, the pronunciation of Spanish is strongly influenced by the native languages of these areas. In other regions, on the other hand, the phonetic features of a range of dialects have been mixed into spoken Spanish. A particularly characteristic and autonomous note is evident in Andalusian pronunciation, for instance in the case of this dialect's own special **ceceo: s, z** and **c** are pronounced with an interdental fricative /th/(**káza**, as opposed to *casa* **kása**).

Generally, Castilian pronunciation is considered the standard pronunciation as it represents the closest approximation to the written form. This is also the pronunciation on which the following descriptions are based.

Vowels

Symbol	Graphic representation	Examples
[a]	a	san, acción
[e]	e	pez, saber
[i]	i	sí, mirar
[o]	o	con
[u]	u	tú, dibujo

Semi-vowels resp. semi-consonants

Symbol	Graphic representation	Examples	Notes
[i̯]	i, y	baile, hoy, despreciéis	*occurs in the diphthongs ai, ei, oi resp. ay, ey, oy and as the final element in triphthongs*
[j]	i	bieldo, apreciáis	*when i is pronounced as the first element in diphthongs and triphthongs*
[u̯]	u	auto, causa	*occurs in the diphthongs au, eu, ou*
[w]	u	bueno, cuerda	*when u is pronounced as the first element in diphthongs or triphthongs*

Consonants

Symbol	Graphic representation	Examples	Notes
[p]	p	pato	
[b]	b, v	vacío, hombre	*plosive: pronounced in the absolute initial sound after a pause and in the medial after a preceding nasal*
[β]	b, v	objeto, pueblo	*fricative: pronounced when it does not occur in the absolute initial sound or after m, n.*
[m]	m, n	mamá, convivir	*every non-word-final m and n before [p] [b]*
[mg]	n	enfermo, infusión	*every n which comes before f*

[n]	n	nadie, entre	
[n̦]	n	quince, conciencia	*n together with a following* [θ]
[n̦]	n	condenar, cantar	*dentalised n: together with a following* [t] *or* [d]
[ŋ]	n	cinco, fingir	*syllable-final n together with a following velar consonant*
[ɲ]	ñ, n	viña, concha	*ñ in the initial sound of the syllable and in syllable-final n before a palatal consonant*
[f]	f	café	
[k]	k, c, q	kilo, casa, que, actor	*occurs in the groupings c + a,o,u and qu + e,i and with syllable-final c*
[g]	g, gu	garra, guerra,	*plosive: occurs in the absolute initial sound or in the medial sound with preceding nasal in the groupings g + a,o,u and gu + e,i*
[x]	j, g	rojo, girar, gente	*equivalent to j and to the groupings g + e,i*
[ɣ]	g, gu	agua, alegre, estigma	*fricative: occurs in the groupings g + a,o,u and gu + e,i, when it does not come in the absolute initial sound or follow n*
[t]	t	letra, tío	*plosive: equivalent to d in the absolute initial sound or after n or l*
[d]	d	dedo, conde, caldo	*plosive: equivalent to d when it occurs in the absolute initial sound or follows n or l*
[ð]	d,t	cada, escudo, juventud	*fricative: equivalent to d when it does not occur in the absolute initial sound or follow n or l*
[θ]	c, z	cero, zarza, cruz	*occurs in the groupings c + e,i and z + a,o,u and in the final sound*
[l]	l	libro, bloque, sal	
[l̦]	l	alce	*interdental l: occurs together with a following* [θ]
[l̦]	l	altura, caldo	*dental l: occurs together with a following* [t] *or* [d]
[ʎ]	ll, l	llueve, colcha	*equivalent to ll and syllable-final l before a palatal consonant*
[s]	s	así, coser	
[r]	r	caro, prisa	*equivalent to the letter r when it occurs at the beginning of a word or follows n, l, s*
[rr]	r, rr	roca, honrado	*equivalent to -rr- and r-, -r- at the beginning of a word or at the beginning of a syllable after n, l, s*
[tʃ]	ch	chino	
[ɟ]	y, hi	cónyuge, inyección, yunque	*palatal affricate: fricative when y, hi occurs in the initial sound of a syllable*
[<ʃ>]	sh	shock	*like English shock, show*

Hispano-American pronunciation bears the closest similarity to that of the Andalusian region. Among the phonetic peculiarities to be encountered in the Hispano-American linguistic areas, the following phenomena are the most prominent:

yeismo
The **ll** is pronounced like a **y** (**yovér**, as opposed to *llover* **llovér**). This phonetic phenomenon is usual not only in Spanish-speaking areas of America but also in various regions of Spain like Andalusia, the Canary Islands, Extremadura, Madrid and Castilian subregions. The assumption that the **yeísmo** is a phonetic feature of all Hispano-American countries is false. The standard pronunciation of **ll** is maintained in subregions of Chile, Peru, Columbia and Ecuador.

A further peculiarity is the pronunciation of **y** as a dʒ (**adʒér**, as opposed to *ayer* **aɟér**) in Argentina, Uruguay and subregions of Ecuador and Mexico.

seseo
z and **c** (θ) are pronounced like **s** (**sínko**, as opposed to *cinco* θ**ínko**). This dialectal peculiarity is widespread not only in Hispano-America but also in subregions of Andalusia and on the Canary Islands.
In the vernacular pronunciation of some areas of Spain and Hispano-America, one also encounters aspiration of the **s** in the final sound (**lah kása**, as opposed to *las casas* – **las kásas**), which may even disappear altogether (**mímo**, as opposed to *mismo* **mísmo**). Both phenomena are considered vulgar and should therefore be avoided.

Símbolos fonéticos del inglés
English phonetic symbols

[ɑː]	plant, farm, father	[m]	man, am
[aɪ]	life	[n]	no, manner
[aʊ]	house	[ɒ]	not, long
[æ]	man, sad	[ɔː]	law, all
[b]	been, blind	[ɔɪ]	boy, oil
[d]	do, had	[p]	paper, happy
[ð]	this, father	[r]	red, dry
[e]	get, bed	[ʴ]	amateur *(Brit)*
[eɪ]	name, lame	[ɚ]	amateur *(Am)*
[ə]	ago, better	[s]	stand, sand, yes
[ɛː]	bird, her	[ʃ]	ship, station
[eə]	there, care	[t]	tell, fat
[ʌ]	but, son	[ʈ]	anesthetist *(Am)*
[f]	father, wolf	[tʃ]	church, catch
[g]	go, beg	[ʊ]	push, look
[ŋ]	long, sing	[uː]	you, do
[h]	house	[ʊə]	poor, sure
[ɪ]	it, wish	[v]	voice, live
[iː]	bee, me, beat, belief	[w]	water, we, which
[ɪə]	here	[z]	zeal, these, gaze
[j]	youth	[ʒ]	pleasure
[k]	keep, milk	[dʒ]	jam, object
[l]	lamp, oil, ill	[θ]	thank, death

A

A, a *f* A, a; ~ **de Antonio** A for Andrew *Brit,* A for Abel *Am*

a *prep* **1.** (*dirección*) to; **ir** ~ **Barcelona/Suiza** to go to Barcelona/Switzerland; **llegar** ~ **Madrid** to arrive in Madrid; **ir** ~ **casa de alguien** to go to sb's house; **ir** ~ **la escuela/~l cine** to go to school/to the cinema **2.** (*posición*) at; **estar sentado** ~ **la mesa** to be sitting at the table; **esperar** ~ **la puerta de la casa** to wait at the front door; ~ **la derecha** on the right; ~l **sur** (**de**) to the south (of); ~l **sol** in the sun **3.** (*distancia*) ~ **10 kilómetros de aquí** 10 kilometres (away) from here **4.** (*tiempo*) at; (*hasta*) until; ~ **las tres** at three o'clock; ~ **mediodía** at noon; ~ **los veinte años** at (the age of) twenty; ~l **poco rato** shortly after; ¿~ **cuántos estamos?** what's the date? **5.** (*modo*) ~ **pie** on foot; **ir** ~ **pie** to walk; ~ **mano** by hand; ~ **oscuras** in the dark; **tortilla a la española** Spanish omelette **6.** (*precio*) ¿~ **cómo está?** how much is it?; ~ **2 euros el kilo** (at) 2 euros a [*o* per] kilo **7.** (*relación*) **el partido terminó dos** ~ **dos** the game ended two all **8.** (*complemento indirecto*) to; **dio su fortuna** ~ **los pobres** he/she gave his/her fortune to the poor **9.** (*complemento directo*) **he visto** ~ **tu hermano** I've seen your brother **10.** (*con infinitivo*) to; **empezó** ~ **correr** he/she began to run **11.** (*complemento de verbo*) **oler** ~ **gas** to smell of gas; **jugar** ~ **los dados** to play dice ▶¡~ **que llueve mañana!** I bet it'll rain tomorrow!; ~ **Pedro le gusta mucho nadar,** ¿~ **que sí, Pedro?** Pedro likes swimming a lot; don't you, Pedro?

abacado *m AmL* BOT (*aguacate*) avocado, alligator pear *Am*

abacorar *vt AmL* (*acosar*) to hound

abad(esa) *m(f)* abbot *m,* abbess *f*

abadía *f* abbey

abajeño, -a *adj AmL* coastal

abajo I. *adv* **1.** (*movimiento*) down; **calle** ~ down the street; **cuesta** ~ downhill; **de arriba** ~ from top to bottom **2.** (*estado*) down (below); (*en casa*) downstairs; **boca** ~ face down; **hacia** ~ down, downwards; **el** ~ **firmante** the undersigned; **de veinte para** ~ twenty or under; **véase más** ~ see below **II.** *interj* ¡~ **el dictador!** down with the dictator!

abalanzarse <z→c> *vr* ~ **a la ventana** to dash (over) to the window; ~ **sobre** [*o* **contra**] **algo** to pounce on sth

abalear *vt Col* (*disparar*) to shoot

abanderado, -a *m, f* **1.** (*en actos públicos*) standard-bearer **2.** (*pionero*) champion

abandonado, -a *adj ser* (*descuidado*) neglected; (*desaseado*) slovenly

abandonar I. *vi* DEP to withdraw **II.** *vt* **1.** (*dejar*) to leave; (*desamparar*) to abandon;

niño abandonado abandoned baby; **le** ~**on sus fuerzas** his/her strength deserted him/her; **estar abandonado a sí mismo** to be left to one's own devices **2.** (*renunciar*) to give up **3.** INFOR (*interrumpir*) to leave **III.** *vr:* ~**se** **1.** (*entregarse*) to give oneself over **2.** (*ir desaliñado*) to let oneself go

abandono *m* **1.** (*abandonamiento*) abandonment; ~ **de servicio** giving-up work; ~ **de la víctima** denial of assistance **2.** (*renuncia*) renunciation; (*de una empresa, idea*) giving-up **3.** (*descuido*) neglect; **en un momento de** ~ in a moment of weakness

abanicar <c→qu> **I.** *vt* to fan **II.** *vr:* ~**se** to fan oneself

abanico *m* fan; **en** (**forma de**) ~ fan-shaped; **un** ~ **de posibilidades** a range of possibilities

abaratar I. *vt* (*bienes*) to make cheaper; (*precios*) to lower; ~ **costes** to cut costs **II.** *vr:* ~**se** to become cheaper

abarca *f* sandal

abarcar <c→qu> *vt* **1.** (*comprender*) to include; ~ **con la vista** to take in; ~ **muchas cosas a la vez** to have one's work cut out **2.** (*contener*) to contain ▶**quien mucho abarca poco** **aprieta** *prov* don't bite off more than you can chew

abarquillarse *vr* (*papel*) to crinkle; (*madera*) to warp

abarrotado *adj* completely full; ~ **de gente** crowded

abarrotar *vt* ~ **algo de algo** to pack sth with sth

abarrote *m* **1.** NÁUT stop-gap **2.** *Cuba, Méx* (*tienda*) grocery store **3.** *pl, Cuba, Méx* (*comestibles*) groceries *pl*

abarrotería *f* **1.** *AmL* (*ferretería*) ironmonger's *Brit,* hardware store *Am* **2.** *Guat* (*abacería*) retail grocery

abastecedor(a) *m(f)* supplier

abastecer *irr como crecer* **I.** *vt* (*proveer*) ~ **de** [*o* **con**] **algo** to provide with sth; COM to supply with sth **II.** *vr:* ~**se** ~**se de** [*o* **con**] **algo** to provide oneself with sth

abastecimiento *m* **1.** (*provisión*) ~ **de** [*o* **con**] **algo** provision of sth; ~ **de aguas** water supply **2.** COM ~ **de** [*o* **con**] **algo** supply of sth

abastero *m* **1.** *Chile* (*de carne*) wholesale livestock dealer **2.** *Méx* (*de artículos de consumo*) purveyor

abasto *m* **1.** (*abastecimiento*) supply **2.** (*provisiones*) provisions *pl* ▶**no dar** ~ **con algo** to be unable to cope with sth

abatí *m sin pl* **1.** *Arg* (*maíz*) maize *Brit,* corn *Am* **2.** *Arg, Par* (*bebida*) maize liquor

abatible *adj* **asiento** ~ folding seat

abatido, -a *adj* **1.** (*desanimado*) dejected **2.** (*mercancía*) depreciated

abatimiento *m* **1.** (*desánimo*) dejection **2.** (*derribo*) demolition **3.** (*desmontaje*) dismantling

abatir I. *vt* **1.** (*muro, casa*) to demolish; (*árbol*) to fell, to chop down *Am;* (*velas*) to lower; (*avión*) to shoot down; ~ **el respaldo** to recline the back-rest **2.** (*desmontar*) to dismantle **3.** (*humillar*) to humiliate **4.** (*debilitar*) to lay low **II.** *vr:* ~**se 1.** (*desanimarse*) to become dejected **2.** (*precipitarse*) ~**se sobre algo** to pounce on sth **3.** (*ceder*) to yield

abdicación *f* abdication; ~ **al trono** abdication from the throne

abdicar <c→qu> *vt* **1.** (*monarca*) to abdicate; **la reina abdicó la corona en su hija** the queen abdicated in favour of her daughter; ~ **la presidencia** to resign the presidency **2.** (*ideales*) to renounce

abdomen *m* abdomen

abdominal I. *adj* abdominal **II.** *m* DEP press-up *Brit,* sit-up *Am*

abecé *m* ABC, alphabet; **el** ~ **de la matemática** the fundamentals of mathematics ►**no saber el** ~ not to have a clue; **ser el** ~ **de algo** to be the basis of sth

abecedario *m* alphabet

abedul *m* (*madera, árbol*) birch

abeja *f* bee; ~ **reina** queen bee; ~ **obrera** worker (bee) ►**estar como** ~ **en flor** to be in top form; **ser como una** ~ to be a hard worker

abejón *m* drone

abejorro *m* **1.** (*insecto*) bumblebee **2.** (*escarabajo*) cockchafer ►**ser un** ~ to be a pain (in the neck)

aberración *f* **1.** (*desviación*) aberration; ~ **mental** mental aberration **2.** (*disparate*) absurdity **3.** *AmL* (*error*) mistake

aberrante *adj* **1.** (*anormal*) aberrant **2.** (*disparatado*) crazy

abertura *f* **1.** (*acción*) opening **2.** (*hueco*) hole **3.** (*franqueza*) openness

abeto *m* fir; ~ **rojo** spruce

abiertamente *adv* **1.** (*francamente*) openly **2.** (*patentemente*) clearly

abierto *m* DEP ~ **de tenis** tennis open championship

abierto, -a I. *pp de* **abrir II.** *adj* **1.** (*no cerrado*) open; ~ **a nuevas ideas** open to new ideas; **en campo** ~ in the open country; **un libro** ~ an open book **2.** (*persona*) open-minded; **la gente aquí es muy abierta** people here are very open-minded

abigarrado, -a *adj* many-coloured *Brit,* many-coloured *Am*

abismado, -a *adj* **1.** (*absorto*) engrossed **2.** (*sorprendido*) amazed

abismal *adj* enormous; (*odio*) profound

abismar I. *vt* **1.** (*sumir*) to cast down; ~ **a alguien en la desesperación** to plunge sb into despair **2.** (*confundir*) to confuse **II.** *vr:* ~**se 1.** (*hundirse*) to sink **2.** *AmL* (*asombrarse*) to be amazed

abismo *m* **1.** GEO abyss **2.** (*infierno*) hell **3.** (*diferencia*) chasm; **entre tus opiniones y las mías hay un** ~ there's a world of difference between our opinions

abjurar *vi, vt* ~ (**de**) **algo** to renounce sth

ablandar I. *vi* (*viento*) to drop; (*frío*) to become less severe **II.** *vt* **1.** (*poner blando*) to soften **2.** (*calmar*) to soothe **III.** *vr:* ~**se 1.** (*ponerse blando*) to soften **2.** (*persona*) to relent

abnegación *f* self-denial; **con** ~ selflessly

abnegado, -a *adj* selfless

abobado, -a *adj* silly

abocado, -a *adj* (*vino*) smooth

abocar <c→qu> **I.** *vt* (*líquido*) to pour **II.** *vr:* ~**se** (*reunirse*) to meet up

abocetar *vt* to sketch

abochornar I. *vt* **1.** (*calor*) to oppress; **este calor me abochorna** I'm suffocated by this heat; **estoy abochornado** I'm stifled **2.** (*avergonzar*) to embarrass **II.** *vr:* ~**se 1.** (*avergonzarse*) ~**se de** [*o* **por**] **algo** to be embarrassed by sth **2.** (*plantas*) to wilt

abofetear *vt* to slap

abogacía *f* legal profession; **ejercer la** ~ to practise *Brit* [*o* practice *Am*] law

abogado, -a *m, f* **1.** JUR lawyer; (*notario*) solicitor *Brit,* lawyer *Am;* (*en tribunal*) barrister, attorney *Am;* ~ **defensor** defending counsel, defense lawyer; ~ **divorcista** divorce lawyer; ~ **de oficio** court-appointed counsel, duty solicitor **2.** (*defensor*) advocate ►**ser un** ~ **de las causas perdidas** to be a champion of lost causes

abogar <g→gu> *vi* (*apoyar*) ~ **por** [*o* **en favor de**] **algo** to advocate sth

abolengo *m* ancestry; **de rancio** ~ of noble descent

abolición *f* abolition

abolir *irr vt* to abolish

abolladura *f* dent

abollar *vt* to dent

abolsarse *vr* **1.** (*tela*) to become baggy **2.** (*deformarse*) to become deformed; (*pared*) to bulge

abombado, -a *adj* **1.** (*combado*) bulging **2.** *AmS* (*atontado*) dopey

abombar I. *vt* to make convex **II.** *vr:* ~**se 1.** (*abultarse*) to bulge **2.** *CSur, Ecua, Nic* (*alimentos*) to go bad

abominable *adj* abominable

abominación *f* abomination

abominar *vt, vi* **1.** (*aborrecer*) to loathe **2.** (*renegar*) ~ **de alguien** to condemn sb

abonable *adj* **1.** (*cantidad*) payable **2.** (*letra de cambio*) due

abonado, -a *m, f* (*a revistas, espectáculo, al teléfono*) subscriber; (*a electricidad, gas*) customer

abonar I. *vt* **1.** (*garantizar*) to guarantee **2.** (*pagar*) to pay; ~ **en cuenta** to credit to an account; **para** ~ **en cuenta** A/C payee only **3.** (*terreno*) to fertilize **4.** PREN to subscribe to; ~ **a alguien a una revista** (*convencer*) to persuade sb to take out a subscription to a magazine; (*como regalo*) to take out a subscription to a magazine for sb **II.** *vr:* ~**se** to subscribe; ~**se a la temporada de ópera** to buy a season ticket to the opera

abono *m* **1.** TEAT season ticket; **sacar un** ~ to buy a season ticket **2.** PREN subscription **3.** (*para transporte público*) season ticket; ~ **mensual** monthly ticket; ~ **de 10 viajes** 10-journey ticket **4.** (*pago*) payment; ~ **en cuenta** credit **5.** (*fertilizante*) fertilizer, manure; ~ **químico** chemical fertilizer **6.** (*de la tierra*) fertilizing

abordable *adj* **1.** (*persona*) approachable **2.** (*tema*) that can be discussed; **no** ~ taboo

abordaje *m* boarding; **tomar al** ~ to board

abordar **I.** *vt* **1.** (*barco*) to board (*in attack*); (*chocar*) to ram **2.** (*persona*) to approach **3.** (*tema*) to discuss; (*problema*) to tackle **II.** *vi* NÁUT to dock

aborigen **I.** *adj* aboriginal. **II.** *mf* aborigine

aborrecer *irr como crecer vt* **1.** (*sentir aversión*) to loathe; ~ **a alguien de muerte** not to be able to abide sb **2.** (*exasperar*) to infuriate **3.** (*aburrir*) to bore

aborrecible *adj* detestable; (*persona*) loathsome

aborrecimiento *m* **1.** (*aversión*) loathing **2.** (*antipatía*) dislike

abortar **I.** *vi* **1.** (*provocado*) to have an abortion **2.** (*espontáneo*) to have a miscarriage **3.** (*fracasar*) to fail **II.** *vt* (*provocar un aborto*) to abort; (*hacer fracasar*) to cause to fail

aborto *m* **1.** (*provocado*) abortion **2.** (*espontáneo*) miscarriage

abota(r)gado, -a *adj* bloated

abota(r)garse <g→gu> *vr* to become bloated

abotonar *vt* to button up

abovedar *vt* **1.** (*formar*) to vault **2.** (*cubrir*) to cover (with a vault)

abra *f* **1.** (*bahía pequeña*) cove **2.** AmL (*desmonte*) clearing

abrasador(a) *adj* (*calor*) scorching

abrasar **I.** *vi* (*sol*) to scorch; (*comida*) to be burning hot **II.** *vt* **1.** (*quemar*) to burn; (*ácidos*) to corrode; ¡cuidado!, **este café abrasa la lengua** take care not to burn your tongue on the coffee! **2.** (*plantas*) to dry up **3.** (*dolor*) to sear; (*estómago*) to irritate; **la sed me abrasa (la garganta)** I have a raging thirst **4.** (*odio*) to consume **III.** *vr:* ~se **1.** (*quemarse*) to burn (up) **2.** (*morirse*) *t. fig* ~**se en deseos de algo** to be desperate for sth; ~**se de impaciencia por algo** to be desperately impatient to do sth

abrasión *f* **1.** GEO, TÉC abrasion **2.** MED graze

abrasivo *m* abrasive

abrasivo, -a *adj* abrasive; **líquido** ~ abrasive liquid

abrazadera *f* **1.** TIPO bracket **2.** TÉC clamp

abrazar <z→c> **I.** *vt* **1.** (*persona*) to embrace **2.** (*contener*) to include; (*abarcar*) to take in **3.** (*doctrina*) to embrace; (*religión*) to adopt **II.** *vr:* ~se to embrace (each other)

abrazo *m* embrace; **dar un** ~ **a alguien** to give sb a hug; **un (fuerte)** ~ (*en cartas*) with best wishes

abreboca *m* **1.** *inf* (*aperitivo*) appetizer **2.** Arg (*persona distraída*) absent-minded person

abrebotellas *m inv* bottle opener

abrecartas *m inv* letter opener

abrelatas *m inv* tin opener, can opener *Am*

abrevadero *m* **1.** (*pila*) water trough **2.** (*lugar*) watering place

abrevar *vt* (*ganado*) to water

abreviación *f* **1.** (*abreviatura*) *t.* LING abbreviation **2.** (*de un texto*) abridgement

abreviado, -a *adj* abridged; (*corto*) short

abreviar **I.** *vt* **1.** (*acortar*) to shorten **2.** (*palabras*) to abbreviate **3.** (*texto*) to abridge **II.** *vi* to hurry

abreviatura *f* abbreviation

abridor *m* opener

abrigado, -a *adj* (*con ropa*) **estar** [*o* **ir**] ~ to be wrapped up warm

abrigar <g→gu> **I.** *vt* **1.** (*proteger: del viento, frío*) to protect **2.** (*cubrir*) to cover **3.** (*tener*) to hold; ~ **esperanzas** to cherish hopes; ~ **proyectos** to harbour *Brit* [*o* harbor *Am*] plans **II.** *vr:* ~se to wrap up (warm)

abrigo *m* **1.** (*prenda*) coat; ~ **de pieles** fur coat; **de** ~ warm **2.** (*refugio*) shelter; **al** ~ **de** protected by ▶ **ser de** ~ to be tough

abril *m* April; *v.t.* **marzo** ▶ **tener trece** ~**es** *inf* to be thirteen (years old)

abrillantado, -a *adj* **1.** AmL (*brillante*) shining **2.** Arg **fruta abrillantada** glazed fruit

abrillantar *vt* **1.** (*hacer brillar*) to polish **2.** (*piedras preciosas*) to cut and polish

abrir *irr* **I.** *vt* **1.** (*algo cerrado*) to open; (*paraguas*) to put up; (*grifo*) to turn on; (*con la llave*) to unlock; (*luz*) to turn on; (*silla plegable*) to open out; ~ **la cabeza a alguien** to split sb's head open; ~ **una calle al tráfico** to open a street to traffic; ~ **a golpes** to knock open; ~ **de par en par** to open wide; **a medio** ~ (*puerta*) half-open **2.** (*canal, túnel*) to dig; (*agujero*) to bore **3.** (*perspectivas, mercado*) to open up **4.** (*comenzar, inaugurar*) to open; (*curso*) to begin **5.** (*ir en cabeza*) to lead **II.** *vi* (*tiempo*) to brighten up ▶ **en un** ~ **y cerrar de ojos** in the twinkling of an eye **III.** *vr:* ~se **1.** (*puerta, herida*) to open; **la ventana se abre al jardín** the window opens (out) onto the garden **2.** (*confiar*) to confide **3.** (*perspectivas*) to open up **4.** *inf* (*irse*) to beat it

abrochar *vt* (*con broches*) to fasten; (*con hebillas*) to buckle; (*con botones*) to button (up); **abróchense los cinturones (de seguridad)** fasten your seat belts

abrogar <g→gu> *vt* to abrogate

abrojo *m* **1.** BIO thistle **2.** Ven (*urticaria*) rash

abroncar <c→qu> *vt inf* **1.** (*echar una bronca*) to tick off, to tell off *Am* **2.** (*abuchear*) to boo

abrumador(a) *adj* **1.** (*agobiador*) overwhelming **2.** (*apabullante*) crushing

abrumar *vt* **1.** (*agobiar*) to overwhelm **2.** (*con trabajo, elogios*) to wear out

abrupto, -a *adj* **1.** (*camino, abismo*) steep **2.** (*carácter*) abrupt

absceso *m* abscess

absentismo *m* absenteeism; ~ **laboral** absenteeism from work

ábside *m* ARQUIT apse

absolución *f* 1. JUR acquittal; ~ **por falta de pruebas** acquittal owing to lack of evidence 2. REL absolution; **dar la** ~ **a alguien** to give absolution to sb

absolutamente *adv* (*completamente*) absolutely, completely; **está** ~ **de acuerdo con nosotros** he/she completely agrees with us; ~ **nada** nothing at all; **es** ~ **posible** it's quite possible

absoluto, -a *adj* absolute ►**nada en** ~ nothing at all; **en** ~ not at all

absolver *irr como volver vt* 1. JUR to acquit 2. REL to absolve

absorbente *adj* 1. (*esponja, trapo*) absorbent 2. (*película, libro*) absorbing; (*trabajo, persona*) demanding

absorber *vt* 1. (*tierra, esponja*) *t.* FÍS to absorb 2. (*aspiradora*) to suck (up) 3. (*cautivar*) to engross 4. (*incorporar*) to incorporate; (*empresa*) to take over

absorción *f* 1. (*de líquidos*) *t.* FÍS absorption 2. ECON takeover

absorto, -a *adj* 1. (*pasmado*) amazed 2. (*entregado*) absorbed

abstemio, -a I. *adj* abstemious; (*completamente*) teetotal II. *m, f* teetotaller *Brit,* teetotaler *Am,* non-drinker *Am*

abstención *f t.* POL abstention

abstenerse *irr como tener vr* (*privarse de*) *t.* POL to abstain; ~ **de votar** to abstain; ~ **del tabaco** to refrain from smoking; **rogamos que se abstengan de realizar visitas** we request you to refrain from visiting

abstinencia *f* abstinence; (*de alcohol*) abstemiousness; (*completa*) teetotalism; ~ **de consumo** cutting down on consumption; **síndrome de** ~ withdrawl symptoms

abstinente *adj* abstinent; (*de alcohol*) abstemious; (*completamente*) teetotal

abstracción *f* abstraction

abstracto, -a *adj* abstract; **en** ~ in the abstract

abstraer *irr como traer* I. *vt* to abstract II. *vr* ~**se en algo** to be absorbed in sth; ~**se de algo** to detach oneself from sth; **consiguió** ~**se de los gritos en la calle** he/she managed not to be distracted by the shouting in the street

abstraído, -a *adj* lost in thought; **estar** ~ **en algo** to be preoccupied by sth

abstruso, -a *adj form* abstruse

absurdo *m* absurdity; **reducir algo al** ~ to reduce sth to absurdity [*o* absurdum]

absurdo, -a *adj* absurd

abubilla *f* hoopoe

abuchear *vt* to boo; (*silbando*) to hiss

abucheo *m* booing; (*silbidos*) hissing

abuelo, -a *m, f* 1. grandfather *m,* grandmother *f;* **los** ~**s** the grandparents 2. *fig* elderly person ►**éramos** <u>pocos</u> **y parió la abuela** *inf* that was all we needed

abulense I. *adj* of/from Avila II. *mf* native/inhabitant of Avila

abulia *f* apathy

abúlico, -a *adj* weak-willed

abultado, -a *adj* bulky; (*labios*) thick

abultar I. *vi* to take up a lot of room II. *vt* 1. (*aumentar*) to increase 2. (*exagerar*) to exaggerate

abundancia *f* (*cantidad*) abundance; (*de bienes*) plenty; **en** ~ in abundance; **nadar en la** ~ to be rolling in money; **vivir en la** ~ to be affluent

abundante *adj* abundant; ~ **en algo** abounding in sth; ~**s lluvias** heavy rains; **una cosecha muy** ~ a plentiful harvest

abundar *vi* to abound; ~ **en algo** to be rich in sth

aburrido, -a *adj* 1. *estar* (*harto*) bored; **estar** ~ **de algo** to be bored of [*o* with *Am*] sth; **tus chistes me tienen** ~ I'm tired of your jokes 2. *ser* (*pesado*) boring

aburrimiento *m* 1. (*tedio*) boredom 2. (*fastidio*) bore

aburrir I. *vt* 1. (*hastiar*) to bore 2. (*fastidiar*) to weary II. *vr:* ~**se** to be [*o* become] bored; ~**se de algo** to become bored of sth, to tire of sth *Am*

abusar *vi* 1. (*usar indebidamente*) ~ **de algo** to misuse sth; ~ **de su salud** to abuse one's health 2. (*aprovecharse*) ~ **de alguien** to take advantage of sb 3. (*sexualmente*) ~ **de alguien** to sexually abuse sb; (*violar*) to rape sb

abusivo, -a *adj* improper; (*precios*) outrageous

abuso *m* 1. (*de poder*) misuse; ~ **de autoridad** abuse of authority; ~ **deshonesto** indecent assault 2. (*cosa abusiva*) **este precio es un** ~ this is an outrageous price

abyección *f* wretchedness

abyecto, -a *adj* wretched

a.C. *abr de* **antes de Cristo** AD

a/c 1. *abr de* **a cuenta** on account 2. *abr de* **al cuidado de** c/o

acá *adv* here; ~ **y allá** here and there; **para** ~ over here; **¡ven** ~! come here!

acabado *m* TÉC finish

acabado, -a *adj* 1. (*completo*) finished 2. (*salud*) ruined 3. (*sin posibilidades*) finished off

acabar I. *vi* 1. (*terminar*) to end; ~ **bien/mal** to turn out well/badly; ~ **en punta** to end in a point 2. (*una acción*) ~ **de hacer algo** to have just done sth; **ella acaba de llegar** she's just arrived; **el libro acaba de publicarse** the book has just been published 3. (*destruir, agotar*) ~ **con algo** to finish sth off; ~ **con alguien** to put paid to sb; **este niño** ~**á conmigo** this child will be the death of me 4. (*finalmente*) ~**ás por comprenderlo** you'll understand it in the end; ~**ás por volverme loco** you'll end up driving me mad II. *vt* 1. (*terminar*) to finish 2. (*consumir*) to finish off; ~ **todas las ga-**

lletas to eat up all the biscuits **III.** *vr:* ~**se** to come to an end; **la mantequilla se ha acabado** there's no butter left; **todo se acabó** it's all over; **¡se acabó!** and that's that!

acabose *m inf* **¡esto es el** ~**!** that really is the limit!

acacia *f* acacia

academia *f* **1.**(*corporación*) academy **2.**(*colegio*) (private) school; ~ **militar** military academy

académico, -a *adj* academic

acaecer *irr como crecer vi* to happen

acaecimiento *m* happening, occurrence

acahual *m Méx* (*girasol*) sunflower

acalambrarse *vr AmL* to get a cramp; **se le acalambró una pierna** he/she got a cramp in his/her leg

acallar *vt* **1.**(*hacer callar*) to silence **2.**(*apaciguar*) to pacify; (*conciencia*) to assuage; (*hambre*) to satisfy

acalorado, -a *adj* heated

acalorar **I.** *vt* **1.**(*dar calor*) to heat **2.**(*enfadar*) to inflame **II.** *vr:* ~**se 1.**(*sofocarse*) **se acaloró al correr** he/she got hot (while) running **2.**(*apasionarse*) ~**se con algo** to get worked up over sth **3.**(*enfadarse*) ~**se por algo** to get angry about sth; **se acalora por nada** he/she gets all het up about nothing *inf*

acampar *vi* to camp; (*tropa*) to encamp

acanalar *vt* **1.**(*hacer canales*) to furrow **2.** TÉC to groove

acantilado *m* cliff

acantilado, -a *adj* steep

acaparar *vt* **1.**(*objetos*) to hoard **2.**(*apoderarse*) ~**se de algo** to lay claim to sth; ~ **todas las miradas** to captivate everyone's attention

acapillar *vt Méx* (*atrapar*) to seize

acaramelar **I.** *vt* to coat with caramel **II.** *vr:* ~**se** (*novios*) to be all over each other

acariciar *vt* **1.**(*persona, animal*) to caress **2.**(*idea, plan*) to toy with

acarrear *vt* **1.**(*transportar*) to transport **2.**(*ocasionar*) to cause

acarreo *m* **1.**(*transporte*) transport **2.**(*importe*) haulage

acartonado, -a *adj* **1.**(*persona*) wizened **2.**(*cutis*) shrivelled *Brit,* shriveled *Am*

acartonarse *vr* **1.**(*tela*) to become stiff **2.**(*persona*) to become wizened **3.**(*cutis*) to shrivel up

acaso **I.** *m* chance; **el** ~ **hizo que ...** +*subj* as chance would have it... **II.** *adv* maybe; **¿está** ~ **enfermo?** is he/she ill by any chance? ►**por si** ~ (*en caso de*) in case; (*en todo caso*) just in case

acatamiento *m* **1.**(*respeto*) respect **2.**(*de las leyes*) ~ **de algo** compliance with sth

acatar *vt* **1.**(*respetar*) to respect **2.**(*obedecer*) to obey **3.** Col, Guat, PRico (*caer en cuenta*) to realize

acatarrarse *vr* to catch a cold

acaudalado, -a *adj* well-off

acaudalar *vt* to acquire

acaudillar *vt* to lead

acceder *vi* **1.**(*consentir*) to agree; ~ **a una petición** to agree to a request **2.**(*tener acceso*) to gain access **3.**(*ascender*) to accede; ~ **a la presidencia** to assume the presidency; ~ **a un cargo** to fill an office; ~ **al trono** to succeed to the throne

accesible *adj* **1.**(*persona*) approachable **2.**(*lugar*) accessible **3.**(*precios*) affordable **4.**(*explicación*) comprehensible

accésit *m inv* consolation [*o* second *Am*] prize

acceso *m* **1.**(*a pie, en vehículo*) access; **de fácil** ~ (*easily*) accessible; **libre** ~ free access **2.**(*ataque*) attack **3.** INFOR access

accesorio *m* **1.**(*de vestidos*) accessory **2.**(*utensilio*) implement **3.** *pl* (*de máquinas*) spare parts *pl*

accesorio, -a *adj* accessory

accidentado, -a **I.** *adj* **1.**(*terreno*) rugged **2.**(*difícil*) difficult **II.** *m, f* injured person

accidental *adj* **1.**(*no esencial*) incidental **2.**(*casual*) casual

accidentarse *vr* to have an accident

accidente *m* **1.**(*suceso desgraciado*) accident; ~ **en cadena** pile-up; ~ **de circulación** traffic [*o* road] accident; **por** ~ by accident; **sufrir un** ~ to have an accident **2.** MED faint **3.**(*desnivel*) unevenness; ~**s geográficos** geographical features

acción *f* **1.**(*acto*) act; **¡**~**!** CINE action!; **un hombre de** ~ a man of action; **entrar en** ~ to go into action; **poner en** ~ to put into action **2.**(*influencia*) action; ~ **recíproca** interaction; **de rápida** ~ rapid-action; **de** ~ **retardada** (*bomba*) delayed-action **3.** MIL action **4.** FIN share; ~ **común** ordinary share *Brit,* common share *Am;* ~ **preferente** preference share *Brit,* preferred share *Am* **5.** JUR action; ~ **por daños y perjuicios** action for damages; ~ **popular** incidental action

accionamiento *m* TÉC operation, drive *Am*

accionar **I.** *vi* to gesticulate **II.** *vt* TÉC to operate; ~ **un cohete** to fire a rocket

accionista *mf* shareholder, stockholder

acebo *m* holly

acechar *vt* **1.**(*espiar*) to spy on **2.**(*esperar*) to lie in wait for

acecho *m* spying; **estar al** ~ to lie in wait

acecinar **I.** *vt* **1.**(*salar*) to salt **2.**(*ahumar*) to cure **II.** *vr:* ~**se** to get thinner

aceitada *f* **1.** *AmL* oiling **2.** *AmL, inf* (*soborno*) kickback

aceitar *vt* **1.**(*motor, gozne*) to oil **2.**(*ensalada*) to dress; (*pan*) to coat with oil

aceite *m* oil; ~ **bruto** crude oil; ~ **comestible** cooking oil; ~ **esencial** essential oil; ~ **lubrificante** lubricating oil ►**echar** ~ **al fuego** to add fuel to the flames

aceitera *f* **1.**(*recipiente*) oil-can **2.** *pl* (*vinagreras*) cruet

aceitoso, -a *adj* oily

aceituna *f* olive ►**llegar a las** ~**s** to arrive late

aceitunado, -a *adj* olive(-green)

aceituno *m* olive tree

aceleración *f* acceleration

acelerador *m* **1.** AUTO accelerator *Brit,* gas pedal *Am;* **pisar el ~** to step on the gas **2.** FÍS **~ de partículas** particle accelerator

acelerar I. *vi* to accelerate; **¡no aceleres tanto!** don't accelerate so hard!, don't go so fast! *Am* **II.** *vt* to accelerate; **~ el paso** to walk faster

acelga *f* chard

acémila *f* **1.** (*animal*) mule **2.** *pey* (*persona*) ass *Brit,* jackass *Am*

acento *m* **1.** (*prosódico*) stress; **el ~ cae en la primera sílaba** the stress falls on the first syllable **2.** (*pronunciación, signo*) accent; **hablar inglés sin ~** to speak English without any accent; **esta palabra se escribe sin ~** this word is written without an accent **3.** (*entonación*) tone **4.** (*énfasis*) emphasis; **poner especial ~ en algo** to put special emphasis on sth

acentuación *f* (*prosódica*) stress; (*ortográfica*) accentuation

acentuado, -a *adj* **1.** (*al pronunciar*) stressed; (*al escribir*) with an accent; **no ~** unstressed; (*sin tilde*) unaccented **2.** (*marcado*) marked

acentuar <*1. pres:* acentúo> **I.** *vt* **1.** (*al pronunciar*) to stress; (*al escribir*) to write with an accent **2.** (*resaltar*) to highlight **3.** (*aumentar*) to increase **II.** *vr:* **~se** *AmL* (*una enfermedad*) to become worse

aceña *f* water mill

acepción *f* sense, meaning

aceptable *adj* acceptable

aceptación *f* **1.** (*aprobación*) approval; **tener ~** to be popular [*o* successful] **2.** COM, JUR acceptance

aceptado *interj AmL* (*vale*) OK

aceptar *vt* **1.** (*recibir*) to accept **2.** (*aprobar, conformarse*) to approve; **~ un compromiso** to accept an agreement; **~ hacer algo** to agree to do sth

acequia *f* **1.** (*canal de riego*) irrigation ditch **2.** *Méx* (*albañal*) drain, gutter *Am*

acera *f* pavement *Brit,* sidewalk *Am* ▶ **ser de la ~ de enfrente** *inf* to be gay

acerado, -a *adj* **1.** (*de acero*) steel **2.** (*mordaz*) biting

acerbo, -a *adj* **1.** (*gusto*) sharp **2.** (*despiadado*) cruel; (*crítica, tono*) harsh

acerca *prep* **~ de** (*sobre*) about; (*en relación a*) concerning

acercamiento *m* approach

acercar <c→qu> **I.** *vt* **1.** (*poner más cerca*) to bring nearer; **acerca la silla a la mesa** draw the chair up to the table **2.** (*traer*) to bring over **3.** *inf* (*llevar*) to take, to bring **II.** *vr:* **~se 1.** (*aproximarse*) **~se a alguien/algo** to approach sb/sth **2.** (*ir*) to come [*o* go] round; **~se a la tienda a por patatas** to go round to the shop for potatoes

acerico *m* pincushion

acero *m* steel

acérrimo, -a I. *superl de* acre **II.** *adj* (*defensor, partidario*) staunch; (*enemigo*) bitter

acertado, -a *adj* **1.** (*correcto*) correct **2.** (*atinado*) accurate **3.** (*conveniente*) apt

acertar <e→ie> **I.** *vi* **1.** (*dar*) to hit; **~ al blanco** to hit the mark **2.** (*hacer con acierto*) to be right; **acertaste en protestar** you were right to protest **3.** (*por casualidad*) **~ a hacer algo** to happen to do sth **4.** (*conseguir*) **no acerté a encontrar la respuesta** I didn't manage to find the answer **5.** (*encontrar*) **~ con algo** to come across sth **II.** *vt* **1.** (*dar en el blanco*) to hit **2.** (*encontrar*) to find **3.** (*adivinar*) to get right

acertijo *m* riddle

acervo *m* store; **~ cultural** cultural heritage

acético, -a *adj* acetic

acetona *f* acetone

achacar <c→qu> *vt* to attribute

achachay *interj Col, Ecua* expressing cold, brrrrr

achacoso, -a *adj* sickly; **estar ~** to be ailing

achalay *interj Arg, Perú* wow

achantar I. *vt inf* to intimidate **II.** *vr:* **~se** *inf* to hide away; (*no atreverse*) to back down

achaparrado, -a *adj* **1.** (*persona*) stocky **2.** (*objeto*) squat

achaque *m* **1.** (*dolencia*) ailment **2.** (*excusa*) pretext

achatado, -a *adj* flattened; **nariz achatada** snub nose; (*como un boxeador*) boxer's nose

achatar I. *vt* to flatten; **~ la nariz a alguien** to break sb's nose **II.** *vr:* **~se** to become flat

achicar <c→qu> **I.** *vt* **1.** (*empequeñecer*) to make smaller **2.** (*intimidar*) to intimidate **3.** (*agua*) to bale out **II.** *vr:* **~se 1.** (*empequeñecerse*) to become smaller; (*ropa*) to shrink **2.** (*acoquinarse*) to take fright; (*no atreverse*) not to dare **3.** *AmL* (*humillarse*) to demean oneself

achicharrar I. *vt* **1.** (*calor*) to scorch; **estoy achicharrado** I'm boiling (hot) **2.** (*comida*) to burn **3.** (*atosigar*) to harass **II.** *vr:* **~se 1.** (*comida*) to get burnt **2.** (*persona*) to be sweltering; (*planta*) to be wilting (in the heat)

achichiguar *vt Méx* **1.** (*servir de niñera*) to babysit **2.** (*malcriar*) to cosset

achichinque *m Méx* (*adulador*) groupie

achicoria *f* chicory

achinado, -a *adj* **1.** (*rasgos*) oriental; **ojos ~s** slanting eyes **2.** *CSur* (*aplebeyado*) coarse

achiote *m AmC, Bol, Méx* **1.** BOT annatto tree **2.** (*pigmento*) annatto

achipolarse *vr Méx* **1.** (*personas*) to grow sad **2.** (*plantas*) to wither

achiquillado, -a *adj* **1.** *Méx* (*infantil*) childish **2.** *Chile* (*como un muchacho*) boyish

achira *f AmS* BOT canna

achís *interj* atishoo *Brit,* atchoo *Am*

achispar I. *vt* to cheer up **II.** *vr:* **~se** to become tipsy

acholado, -a *adj CSur, Perú, Bol* **1.** (*mestizo*)

mestizo (*of mixed Spanish American and American Indian descent*) **2.**(*acobardado*) intimidated

acholar I. *vt Chile, Perú, Bol* **1.**(*avergonzar*) to embarrass **2.**(*amilanar*) to scare **II.** *vr:* ~**se** *CSur, Perú, Bol* (*acobardarse*) to become intimidated

achuchado, -a *adj inf* **1.**(*duro*) tough **2.**(*de dinero*) broke **3.**(*débil*) feverish

achuchar *vt* **1.** *inf*(*persona*) to stir up; ~ **a un perro contra alguien** to set a dog on sb **2.** *inf* (*estrujar*) to crush **3.**(*atosigar*) to harass **4.** *inf* (*acariciar*) to caress; (*abrazar*) to embrace; (*manosear*) to fondle

achuchón *m inf* **1.**(*abrazo*) squeeze **2.**(*empujón*) shove **3.**(*achaque*) indisposition

achucutado, -a *adj* **1.** *AmL* (*abatido*) depressed **2.** *Ven, Hond, Guat*(*triste*) sad

achucutarse *vr Col, Ecua,* **achucuyarse** *vr AmC* **1.**(*humillarse*) to shame **2.**(*acobardarse*) to chicken out *inf*

achumado, -a *adj Ecua* drunk

achumarse *vr Ecua* to get drunk

achunchar *vt AmL* (*avergonzar, amedrentar*) to humiliate

achura *f AmS* (*despojos de res*) offal

achurar *vt CSur* **1.**(*res*) to gut **2.**(*persona*) to stab to death

achuras *fpl Arg* offal

aciago, -a *adj* ill-fated; **un día** ~ a fateful day

acíbar *m* **1.** BOT aloe **2.**(*amargura*) bitterness

acicalarse *vr* to get dressed up

acicate *m* **1.**(*espuela*) spur **2.**(*estímulo*) stimulus

acidez *f* acidity; ~ **de estómago** MED heartburn, acid indigestion *Am*

ácido *m* **1.** QUÍM acid; ~ **cianhídrico** hydrocyanic acid; ~ **clorhídrico** hydrochloric acid; ~**s grasos insaturados** unsaturated fatty acids **2.** *inf*(*droga*) acid

ácido, -a *adj* **1.**(*agrio*) sour **2.**(*mordaz*) sharp **3.** QUÍM acidic

acídulo, -a *adj* sharp-tasting

acierto *m* **1.**(*en el tiro*) accuracy **2.**(*éxito*) success; (*en la lotería*) right number; **el casarte ha sido un** ~ you did well to get married **3.**(*habilidad*) skill; **hacer algo con** ~ to do sth skilfully

acitrón *m Méx* GASTR candied citron

aclamación *f* **1.**(*aplauso*) applause **2.** POL **por** ~ by acclamation [*o* acclaim *Am*]

aclamar *vt* **1.**(*vitorear*) to cheer **2.** POL to acclaim

aclaración *f* **1.**(*clarificación*) clarification **2.**(*explicación*) explanation **3.**(*de un crimen*) solution; (*de un secreto*) revelation

aclarar I. *vt* **1.**(*hacer más claro*) to lighten; ~ **el bosque** [*o* thin out] the forest; ~ **la voz** to clear one's throat [*o* thin (down) **3.**(*la ropa*) to rinse **4.**(*explicar*) to explain **5.**(*crimen*) to solve; (*secreto*) to reveal **II.** *vr:* ~**se** **1.**(*problema, cuestión*) to be clarified **2.** *inf* (*entender*) to catch on; **no te**

aclaras contigo mismo you don't know what you want **III.** *vimpers* **está aclarando** it's brightening up

aclaratorio, -a *adj* explanatory

aclimatación *f* acclimatization *Brit,* acclimation *Am*

aclimatar I. *vt* to acclimatize *Brit,* to acclimate *Am* **II.** *vr:* ~**se** to get acclimatized *Brit* [*o* acclimated *Am*]

acné *m o f sin pl* acne

acobardar I. *vt* to frighten; (*con palabras*) to intimidate; **le acobarda el fuego** he/she is afraid of fire **II.** *vr:* ~**se** **1.**(*desanimarse*) ~**se ante** [*o* **frente a**] **algo** to flinch from sth **2.**(*intimidarse*) to be frightened; **se acobarda de sí misma** he is afraid of his own shadow

acogedor(a) *adj* welcoming, inviting

acoger <g→j> **I.** *vt* to welcome; (*recibir*) to receive **II.** *vr:* ~**se** **1.**(*refugiarse*) to take refuge **2.**(*ampararse*) to shelter **3.**(*basarse*) to resort; ~**se a algo** to avail oneself of sth

acogida *f* welcome; (*recibimiento*) reception; **encontrar una buena** ~ to be well received; **el cantante tuvo una buena** ~ the singer was received with applause; **el proyecto no tuvo una buena** ~ the project didn't meet with approval

acogotar *vt* **1.**(*matar*) to kill (*with a blow to the head*) **2.**(*intimidar*) to pressurize *Brit,* to pressure *Am* **3.**(*derribar*) to knock down

acojonado, -a *adj vulg* **1.**(*asustado*) frightened, scared shitless *Am;* (*acobardado*) intimidated; **ahora está** ~ he/she is frightened now **2.**(*impresionado*) impressed; (*asombrado*) amazed

acojonante *adj vulg* **1.**(*fantástico*) fantastic **2.**(*impresionante*) incredible

acojonar I. *vt vulg* **1.**(*asustar*) to frighten, to scare the shit out of *Am;* (*intimidar*) to intimidate **2.**(*impresionar*) to impress; (*asombrar*) to amaze **II.** *vr:* ~**se** *vulg* **1.**(*asustarse*) to become frightened, to be scared shitless *Am;* (*acobardarse*) to back down; **no** ~**se** not to be frightened **2.**(*asombrarse*) to be amazed

acolchar *vt* to quilt

acólito *m* **1.**(*monaguillo*) altar boy **2.** *pey* (*seguidor*) follower

acometer I. *vi* to attack **II.** *vt* **1.**(*embestir*) to attack **2.**(*emprender*) to undertake **3.**(*ataque de tos, fiebre*) to attack; (*risa, sueño*) to overcome; **lo acometió la risa** he was overcome by laughter

acometida *f* **1.**(*embestida*) attack **2.**(*acceso*) fit **3.** TÉC connection

acomodado, -a *adj* **1.**(*cómodo*) comfortable **2.**(*rico*) well-off; **tener una vida acomodada** to live comfortably **3.**(*apropiado*) suitable **4.**(*precio*) reasonable

acomodador(a) *m(f)* TEAT, CINE usher

acomodar I. *vt* **1.**(*adaptar*) to adapt **2.**(*colocar*) to place **3.**(*albergar*) to accommodate **4.**(*proporcionar empleo*) ~ **de algo** (**a alguien**) to take on (sb) as sth **5.**(*conciliar*) to reconcile **II.** *vi* **si te acomoda** if it suits you **III.** *vr:* ~**se** **1.** (*adaptarse*) to adapt oneself; ~**se con todo** to put up with everything **2.** (*ponerse cómodo*) to make oneself comfortable

acomodaticio, -a *adj* **1.** (*adaptable*) adaptable **2.** *pey* (*oportunista*) opportunistic

acomodo *m* **1.** (*arreglo*) arrangement **2.** (*acuerdo*) agreement **3.** (*ocupación*) employment, job, post *Brit;* **buscar** ~ to look for a job **4.** *AmL* (*soborno*) bribe

acompañado, -a *adj* accompanied; **bien/ mal** ~ in good/bad company; **iba acompañada por su padre** she was accompanied by her father

acompañamiento *m* **1.** *t.* MÚS accompaniment **2.** (*cortejo*) retinue **3.** TEAT extras *pl*, supporting cast *Am* **4.** (*de comidas*) accompaniment, side dish *Am*

acompañante *mf* **1.** (*de una dama*) escort **2.** (*en el coche*) passenger

acompañar *vt* **1.** (*ir con*) *t.* MÚS to accompany; ~ **a alguien a casa** to see sb home; ~ **a alguien en un viaje** to go with sb on a journey; ~ **a alguien de compras** to go shopping with sb; ~ **a alguien con la guitarra/al piano** to accompany sb on the guitar/on the piano; ~ **el pollo con arroz y verduras** to serve the chicken with rice and vegetables **2.** (*hacer compañía*) ~ **a alguien** to keep sb company **3.** (*adjuntar*) to enclose **4.** (*ir incluido*) **el informe acompaña a la carta** the report is enclosed with the letter

acompasado, -a *adj* **1.** MÚS rhythmic **2.** (*pausado*) measured

acompasar *vt* **1.** MÚS ~ **algo** to mark the rhythm of sth **2.** (*adaptar*) ~ **algo a** [*o* **con**] **algo** to fit sth in with sth

acomplejado, -a *adj* full of complexes

acomplejar **I.** *vt* to give a complex **II.** *vr:* ~**se** to get a complex

aconchar **I.** *vt* **1.** (*guarecer*) to shelter **2.** *Méx* (*reprender*) to tell off **II.** *vr:* ~**se** **1.** (*arrimarse*) to come alongside **2.** NÁUT to run aground **3.** *Chile, Perú* (*sedimentarse*) to settle; ~ **a alguien los meados** *inf* to chicken out **4.** *Chile, Perú* (*serenarse*) to calm down

acondicionado, -a *adj* **bien/mal** ~ in good/bad condition

acondicionador *m* **1.** (*de aire*) air-conditioner **2.** (*para el pelo*) conditioner

acondicionar *vt* **1.** (*preparar*) to prepare; (*arreglar*) to arrange **2.** (*equipar*) to equip **3.** (*climatizar*) to air-condition

acongojar *vt* to distress

aconsejable *adj* advisable

aconsejado, -a *adj* (*prudente*) sensible

aconsejar *vt* to advise; ~ **algo a alguien** to recommend sth to sb; **esto aconseja prudencia** this calls for caution

acontecer *irr como crecer vi* to happen

acontecimiento *m* event

acopiar *vt* to gather together

acopio *m* **1.** (*de comida, bienes*) store; **hacer** ~ **de algo** to stock up with [*o* on *Am*] sth; **hacer** ~ **de paciencia** to draw on all one's reserves of patience; **hacer** ~ **de valor** to muster one's courage **2.** (*compra*) stock

acoplado *m* *RíoPl* trailer

acoplamiento *m* **1.** (*de máquinas, vagones*) coupling **2.** ELEC connection

acoplar **I.** *vt* **1.** (*ajustar*) to adjust; (*juntar*) to join **2.** (*piezas, remolque*) to fit together **3.** ELEC to connect **4.** (*adaptar*) to adapt **II.** *vr:* ~**se** to adapt

acoquinar **I.** *vt* to intimidate **II.** *vr:* ~**se** to allow oneself to be intimidated, to chicken out *Am, inf*

acorazar <z→c> **I.** *vt* to armour-plate *Brit*, to armorplate *Am* **II.** *vr:* ~**se** to arm oneself

acorazonado, -a *adj* heart-shaped

acordar <o→ue> **I.** *vt* **1.** (*convenir*) to agree **2.** (*decidir*) to decide **3.** MÚS to tune **II.** *vr* ~**se de algo/alguien** to remember sth/sb; **si mal no me acuerdo** if my memory serves me right; **¡acuérdate de decírselo!** remember to tell him/her!

acorde **I.** *adj* **1.** (*conforme*) agreed; **estar** ~ **con alguien** to be in agreement with sb; ~ **con el medio ambiente** in keeping with the environment **2.** MÚS harmonious **II.** *m* MÚS chord; ~ **mayor/menor** major/minor chord; **a los** ~**s de un vals** to the strains of a waltz

acordeón *m* accordion

acordonar *vt* **1.** (*botas*) to lace up **2.** (*un sitio*) to cordon off

acorralar *vt* **1.** (*ganado*) to round up **2.** (*cercar*) to fence in **3.** (*intimidar*) to intimidate; (*con preguntas*) to corner

acortar **I.** *vt* to shorten; (*duración*) to cut down; (*distancia*) to reduce; ~ **camino** to take a short cut; ~ **un pantalón unos centímetros** to take up a pair of trousers by a few centimetres **II.** *vr:* ~**se** to become shorter

acosar *vt* **1.** (*perseguir*) to hound **2.** (*asediar*) to harass; ~ **a alguien a** [*o* **con**] **preguntas** to pester sb with questions

acosijar *vt* *Méx* (*acosar*) to hound

acoso *m* relentless pursuit; *fig* harassment; ~ **sexual** sexual harassment

acostar <o→ue> **I.** *vt* to put to bed **II.** *vr:* ~**se** **1.** (*descansar*) to lie down; **estar acostado** to be lying down **2.** (*ir a la cama*) to go to bed; ~**se con alguien** to go to bed with sb **3.** *AmC, Méx, Col* (*dar a luz*) to give birth

acostumbrado, -a *adj* accustomed; **mal** ~ spoilt

acostumbrar **I.** *vi* ~ **a hacer algo** to be used to doing sth; **como se acostumbra a decir** as they say **II.** *vt* ~ **a alguien a hacer algo** to get sb used to doing sth **III.** *vr:* ~**se a algo** to get accustomed [*o* used] to sth

acotación *f* **1.** (*nota*) margin note, annotation **2.** TEAT stage direction **3.** (*cota*) elevation mark

acotamiento *m* **1.** (*acotación*) fencing

2. *Méx* (*arcén*) hard shoulder, shoulder *Am*
acotar *vt* **1.** (*delimitar*) to delimit; **terreno acotado** private property **2.** (*un plano*) ~ **algo** to mark elevations on sth **3.** (*un texto*) to annotate
ácrata **I.** *adj* **1.** (*anárquico*) anarchic **2.** (*anarquista*) anarchistic **II.** *mf* anarchist
acre¹ *adj* <acérrimo> **1.** (*áspero*) bitter **2.** (*ácido*) sour **3.** (*mordaz*) scathing; (*tono*) harsh
acre² *m* (*medida de tierra*) acre
acrecentar <e→ie> *vt,* **acrecer** *irr como crecer vt* to increase
acreditado, -a *adj* (*reputado*) reputable
acreditar **I.** *vt* **1.** (*atestiguar*) to vouch for **2.** (*autorizar*) to authorize **3.** (*diplomático*) to accredit; ~ **como embajador** to accredit as ambassador **4.** (*dar reputación*) to do credit **5.** FIN to credit **II.** *vr:* ~**se** **1.** (*adquirir reputación*) to get a reputation **2.** (*dar crédito de uno mismo*) to prove one's worth
acreedor(a) **I.** *adj* **hacerse** ~ **a** [*o* **de**] **algo** to be worthy of sth **II.** *m/f* FIN creditor
acribillar *vt* **1.** (*abrir agujeros*) to riddle; **acribillado a balazos** riddled with bullets; **anoche me han acribillado los mosquitos** last night I was eaten alive by the mosquitoes **2.** (*importunar*) to pester; ~ **a alguien a preguntas** to pester sb with questions
acrílico, -a *adj* acrylic; **fibra acrílica** acrylic fibre
acrimonia *f v.* **acritud**
acriollarse *vr AmL* to go native
acritud *f* **1.** (*acrimonia*) acrimony; **contestar con** ~ to reply bitterly **2.** (*de un dolor*) harshness
acrobacia *f* acrobatics *pl;* ~ **aérea** aerobatics *pl,* stunt flying *Am*
acróbata *mf* acrobat
acrobático, -a *adj* acrobatic
acrónimo *m* acronym
acta *f* **1.** (*de una reunión*) minutes *pl;* **levantar** ~ **de algo** to draw up a document of sth; **hacer constar en** ~ to record in the minutes **2.** (*certificado*) certificate **3.** JUR act; ~ **de acusación** bill of indictment; **Acta Única Europea** Single European Act
actitud *f* **1.** (*corporal*) posture; ~ **de ataque** threatening stance; ~ **de extrema cautela en cuanto a algo** policy of extreme caution with regard to sth **2.** (*disposición*) attitude; **adoptar una** ~ **reservada** to adopt a reserved attitude **3.** (*comportamiento*) behaviour *Brit,* behavior *Am;* **adoptar una** ~ **incomprensible** to behave incomprehensibly
activamente *adv* actively
activar *vt* **1.** (*avivar*) to stimulate **2.** (*acelerar*) to speed up; ~ **la digestión** to aid digestion **3.** QUÍM, FÍS, INFOR to activate; ~ **una bomba** to detonate a bomb
actividad *f* **1.** (*general*) activity; (*ocupación*) occupation; ~ **profesional** profession; **las ~es artísticas de una país** the cultural activities of

a country [*o* city]; **en** ~ active; **volcán en** ~ active volcano; **entrar en** ~ to go into action **2.** (*diligencia*) diligence
activo *m* FIN assets *pl;* ~ **circulante** current assets; ~ **fijo** fixed assets
activo, -a *adj* active; (*sustancia, medicamento*) effective
acto *m* **1.** (*acción*) action; ~ **de cortesía** act of courtesy; ~ **jurídico** (*válido*) legal act; (*negocio*) legal transaction; ~ **penal** criminal act; ~ **sexual** sexual act; ~ **de violencia** act of violence; ~ **de voluntad** professed intention; **cometer ~s de gamberrismo** to commit acts of vandalism; **hacer** ~ **de presencia** to put in an appearance **2.** (*ceremonia*) ceremony; ~ **conmemorativo** commemoration; ~ **estatal** state occasion; ~ **necrológico** funeral service **3.** TEAT act ▶~ **seguido...** immediately after ...; **en el** ~ immediately, on the spot
actor, actriz *m, f* TEAT, CINE actor *m,* actress *f;* ~ **de cine** film actor; ~ **suplente** understudy; **primer** ~ principal actor, leading man
actor(a) *m(f)* plaintiff
actriz *f v.* **actor**
actuación *f* **1.** (*conducta*) conduct; **la** ~ **de la policía** the police action **2.** (*actividad*) activity; (*desempeño de un cargo*) performance **3.** TEAT, MÚS performance; ~ **en directo** live performance **4.** *pl* JUR legal proceedings *pl*
actual *adj* **1.** (*de ahora*) present **2.** (*corriente*) current
actualidad *f* **1.** (*presente*) present; **en la** ~ at present **2.** (*cualidad*) topicality, currentness; **de** ~ topical; **ser de gran** ~ to be topical
actualizar <z→c> *vt* to bring up to date
actualmente *adv* at the moment, currently
actuar <*1.* pres: actúo> *vi* **1.** (*obrar, hacer*) to work **2.** (*tener efecto*) ~ **sobre algo** to have an effect on sth **3.** TEAT to act; ~ **en directo** perform live; ~ **de Don Juan** to play Don Juan; **ella no actúa en esta función** she doesn't appear in this performance **4.** JUR to appear; ~ **contra alguien** to take legal proceedings against sb
acuache *m Méx* (*compinche*) mate *Brit,* pal *Am*
acuarela *f* watercolour *Brit,* watercolor *Am*
acuario *m* aquarium
Acuario *m* Aquarius
acuartelar *vt* **1.** MIL to billet **2.** (*dividir*) to divide into quarters
acuático, -a *adj* aquatic; **parque** ~ waterpark
acuchamarse *vr Ven* (*entristecerse*) to get depressed
acuchillar *vt* **1.** (*herir*) to knife; (*matar*) to stab to death **2.** (*parqué*) to sand down; (*muebles*) to scrape
acuciante *adj* urgent
acuciar *vt* **1.** (*dar prisa*) to hurry up **2.** (*incitar*) to urge
acuclillarse *vr* to squat
acudiente *m Col* (*tutor*) tutor
acudir *vi* **1.** (*ir*) to go; ~ **a una cita** to keep an

appointment; ~ **al trabajo/a la puerta** to go to work/to the door; ~ **a las urnas** to go to the polls; ~ **a la memoria de alguien** to come to sb's mind **2.**(*corriendo*) ~ **a alguien** to go to help sb; ~ **en socorro de alguien** to come to sb's aid **3.**(*recurrir*) ~ **a** to turn to

acueducto *m* aqueduct

acuerdo *m* **1.**(*convenio*) *t.* POL agreement; **Acuerdo General sobre Aranceles y Comercio** General Agreement on Tariffs and Trade; **Acuerdo Monetario Europeo** European Monetary Agreement; **llegar a un** ~ to reach an agreement **2.**(*decisión*) decision; **tomar un** ~ to pass a resolution **3.**(*conformidad*) agreement; **estar de** ~ **con alguien** to agree with sb; **ponerse de** ~ to come to an agreement; **sin ponerse de** ~ without reaching (an) agreement; **de común** ~ by mutual consent ►**¡de** ~**!** I agree!, OK!; **de** ~ **con** in accordance with

acuerpado, -a *adj Bol* (*corpulento*) hefty

acular *vt* AUTO to back

acullá *adv elev* **1.**(*lugar*) over there **2.**(*dirección*) yonder

acullicar *vi Arg, Bol, Chile, Perú* (*mascar coca*) to chew coca leaves

acullico *m Arg, Bol, Perú* (*bola de coca*) small ball of coca

acumuchar *vt Chile* (*acumular*) to pile up

acumulación *f* **1.**(*amontonamiento*) accumulation **2.**(*de cosas reunidas*) collection

acumulador *m* ELEC accumulator

acumular *vt* **1.**(*reunir*) to collect **2.**(*amontonar*) *t.* ELEC to accumulate

acunar *vt* to rock (to sleep)

acuñar *vt* **1.**(*monedas*) to mint **2.**(*palabras*) to coin **3.** TÉC to wedge

acuoso, -a *adj* watery; (*fruta*) juicy

acupuntura *f* acupuncture

acurí *m Col, Ven* ZOOL agouti, guinea pig

acurrucarse <c→qu> *vr* to curl up; (*agacharse*) to crouch; (*a causa del frío*) to huddle up; ~ **en un sillón** to curl up in an armchair

acusación *f* **1.**(*inculpación*) accusation; ~ **de corrupción** charge of corruption **2.** JUR (*en juicio*) charge; (*escrito*) indictment; ~ **constitucional** *charge concerning an infringement of the constitution;* ~ **particular** private prosecution

acusado, -a **I.** *adj* **1.**(*claro, evidente*) pronounced **2.**(*marcado*) marked **II.** *m, f* accused

acusador(a) *m(f)* accuser

acusar *vt* **1.**(*culpar*) to accuse; **lo acusan de asesinato** he is accused of murder **2.**(*en juicio*) to charge **3.**(*en la escuela*) to tell on **4.**(*traslucir*) to reveal; TÉC to register **5.** ECON to confirm; ~ **recibo de un pedido** to acknowledge receipt of an order

acusativo *m* LING accusative

acuse *m* ~ **de recibo** acknowledgement of receipt

acústica *f* **1.**(*ciencia*) acoustics *sing* **2.**(*de un sitio*) acoustics *pl*

acústico, -a *adj* acoustic

acutí *m Arg, Par, Urug* ZOOL agouti

adagio *m* **1.**(*proverbio*) adage **2.** MÚS adagio

adalid *m* **1.**(*caudillo*) leader **2.**(*defensor*) champion

adán *m* slovenly fellow; **vas hecho un** ~ you look a mess

Adán *m* Adam; ~ **y Eva** Adam and Eve

adaptable *adj* adaptable

adaptación *f* **1.**(*acomodación*) adaptation **2.** LIT, MÚS, TEAT adaptation; **la** ~ **de una obra de teatro al cine** the film version of a play

adaptador *m* TÉC adapter

adaptar **I.** *vt* **1.**(*acomodar*) to adapt; **bien adaptado al grupo** well adapted to the group **2.**(*edificio*) to convert; ~ **un piso para oficina** to convert a flat into an office **3.**(*ajustar*) to adjust; ~ **algo a algo** to adapt sth to sth **4.** LIT, MÚS, TEAT, CINE to adapt; ~ **una novela a la pantalla** to adapt a novel for the screen **II.** *vr:* ~**se** to adapt; **se han adaptado muy bien el uno al otro** they have fitted in very well with each other

adecentar **I.** *vt* to tidy up **II.** *vr:* ~**se** to tidy oneself up

adecuado, -a *adj* **1.**(*apto*) appropriate **2.**(*palabras*) fitting; (*conveniente*) suitable; **la decoración de tu casa es muy adecuada** your house is very well decorated

adecuar *vt, vr:* ~**se** to adapt

adefesio *m* **1.**(*prenda*) rag, ridiculous costume **2.**(*persona*) scarecrow; **estar hecho un** ~ to look a sight

a. de (J)C. *abr de* **antes de (Jesu)cristo** BC

adelantado, -a *adj* **1.**(*precoz*) precocious **2.**(*avanzado*) advanced; **estar muy** ~ to be very advanced ►**por** ~ in advance

adelantamiento *m* **1.**(*avance*) advance; (*progreso*) progress **2.**(*del coche*) overtaking *Brit*, passing *Am;* **realizar un** ~ to overtake *Brit*, to pass *Am*

adelantar **I.** *vi* **1.**(*reloj*) to be fast **2.**(*progresar*) to progress; **no adelanto nada en francés** I'm not making any progress in French **3.**(*coche*) to overtake *Brit*, to pass *Am* **II.** *vt* **1.**(*reloj*) to put forward **2.**(*avanzar*) to move forward; ~ **unos pasos** to go forward a few steps **3.**(*coche, persona*) to overtake *Brit*, to pass *Am* **4.**(*viaje, partida*) to bring forward **5.**(*idea*) to put forward **6.**(*paga*) to advance **7.**(*obtener ventaja*) to gain; **¿qué adelantas con esto?** where does that get you? **III.** *vr:* ~**se 1.**(*reloj*) to be fast **2.**(*avanzarse*) to go forward **3.**(*llegar antes*) to get ahead **4.**(*anticiparse*) to anticipate; **te has adelantado a mis deseos** you've anticipated my wishes

adelante *adv* forward, ahead *Am;* **llevar un plan** ~ to carry forward a plan, to go ahead with a plan *Am;* **sacar una familia** ~ to provide for a family; **¡~!** come in!; **seguir** ~ to go (straight) on; **véase más** ~ see below

adelanto *m* 1.(*progreso*) progress; ~s técnicos technical innovations 2.(*anticipo*) advance

adelgazar <z→c> I. *vi, vr:* ~se to lose weight II. *vt* 1.(*cosas*) to make thin 2.(*peso*) to reduce

además *m* 1.(*gesto*) gesture; **hacer** ~ **de salir** to make as if to leave 2.(*actitud*) attitude; **en** ~ **de** getting ready to

además *adv* besides, moreover

adenda *f* addendum

adentrarse *vr* 1.(*entrar*) ~ **en algo** to go into sth; (*penetrar*) to penetrate into sth 2.(*estudiar a fondo*) to study thoroughly

adentro *adv* (*lugar y movimiento*) inside; **mar** ~ out to sea; **tierra** ~ inland; **el grito le salió de muy** ~ his/her cry came from deep within

adentros *mpl* innermost being; **para sus** ~ inwardly; **guardar algo para sus** ~ to keep sth to oneself

adepto, -a *m, f* 1.(*afiliado*) follower 2.(*partidario*) supporter

aderezar <z→c> *vt* 1.(*preparar*) to prepare 2.(*guisar*) to stew 3.(*condimentar*) to season; (*ensalada*) to dress

aderezo *m* 1.(*de un guiso*) preparation 2.(*condimentación*) seasoning; (*de, para una ensalada*) dressing 3.(*joyas*) set of jewels

adeudar I. *vt* 1.(*deber*) to owe 2.(*cargar*) to charge; ~ **una cantidad en cuenta** to debit an account for a sum II. *vr:* ~se to run into debt; ~se **mucho** to get deep into debt

adherencia *f* 1.(*adhesión*) adherence; AUTO roadholding, road grip *Am* 2.(*conexión*) connection

adherir *irr como sentir* I. *vt* (*sello*) to stick II. *vr:* ~se 1.(*pegarse*) to adhere 2.(*a una opinión*) to adhere, to support 3.(*a un partido*) ~se **a un partido** to join a party

adhesión *f* 1.(*adherencia*) adhesion 2.(*a una opinión*) adherence, support 3.(*apoyo*) ~ **a alguien** support of sb 4.(*a una asociación*) ~ **a algo** membership of sth

adhesivo *m* 1.(*sustancia*) adhesive; ~ **multiuso** all-purpose adhesive 2.(*pegatina*) sticker

adhesivo, -a *adj* adhesive

adicción *f* addiction; ~ **a las drogas** drug addiction

adición *f* (*añadidura*) *t.* MAT addition

adicional *adj* additional

adicionar *vt* to add

adicto, -a I. *adj* 1.(*leal*) devoted 2.(*que tiene adicción*) addicted; ~ **a las drogas** addicted to drugs; ~ **a la televisión** *inf* addicted to television II. *m, f* 1.(*dependiente*) addict 2.*CSur* (*partidario*) ~ **a alguien** supporter of sb

adiestrar *vt* (*personas, animales*) to train

adifés I. *adj Guat* (*difícil*) difficult II. *adv Ven* (*adrede*) on purpose

adinerado, -a *adj* wealthy

adiós I. *interj* 1.(*despedida*) goodbye, bye 2.(*al pasar*) hello, hi II. *m* farewell; **decir** ~ **a alguien** to say goodbye to sb

adiposo, -a *adj* adipose; **tejido** ~ fatty tissue

aditamento *m* 1.(*añadidura*) addition 2.(*complemento*) complement

aditivo *m* additive

aditivo, -a *adj* additional

adivinanza *f* riddle

adivinar *vt* 1.(*el futuro*) to foretell 2.(*conjeturar*) to guess; (*acertar*) to guess correctly; **¡adivina cuántos años tengo!** guess how old I am! 3.(*vislumbrar*) to glimpse

adjetivo *m* adjective; ~ **numeral** numeral

adjudicación *f* 1.(*de un premio, un pedido, una beca*) award(ing) 2.(*en una subasta*) sale

adjudicar <c→qu> I. *vt* 1.(*premio, encargo, beca*) to award 2.(*en una subasta*) to knock down *Brit*, to sell at auction *Am* II. *vr:* ~se 1.(*apropiarse*) to appropriate 2.(*victoria, premio*) to win

adjuntar *vt* to enclose

adjunto, -a *adj* 1.(*junto*) enclosed 2.(*auxiliar*) assistant; **profesora adjunta** UNIV senior lecturer *Brit*, associate professor *Am*

administración *f* 1.(*dirección, organización, órgano*) administration; **la** ~ **española** the Spanish authorities; **la** ~ **de correos** the postal service; ~ **de una cuenta** managing [*o* running *Brit*] of an account; ~ **de fincas** property management; ~ **municipal** town/city council 2.(*de medicamentos, de sacramentos*) administering 3.*Arg* (*gobierno*) government

administrador(a) *m(f)* administrator; (*gerente*) manager; ~ **de la masa** receiver

administrar *vt* 1.(*dirigir, cuidar*) administer; ~ **justicia** to dispense justice 2.(*racionar*) to ration 3.(*suministrar*) to supply 4.(*medicamentos, sacramentos*) to administer

administrativo, -a I. *adj* administrative II. *m, f* clerk

admirable *adj* admirable

admiración *f* 1.(*respeto, adoración*) admiration 2.(*asombro*) amazement 3.(*signo*) exclamation mark [*o* point *Am*]; (*frase*) exclamation

admirado, -a *adj* amazed; **me quedé admirada de tus conocimientos** I was amazed at your knowledge

admirador(a) *m(f)* admirer

admirar *vt* 1.(*adorar, apreciar*) to admire 2.(*asombrar*) to amaze

admisible *adj* admissible

admisión *f* 1.(*en una asociación, universidad*) ~ **en algo** admission [*o* acceptance] to sth 2.TÉC inlet

admitir *vt* 1.(*en una asociación, universidad*) ~ **en algo** to admit to sth 2.(*aceptar*) to accept; ~ **los métodos de alguien** to accept sb's methods 3.(*reconocer*) to recognize 4.(*permitir*) to permit; ~ **una queja** JUR to accept a complaint; **el asunto no admite dilación** the matter allows no delay; **es cosa admitida que...** it is generally admitted that ... 5.(*tener capacidad*) to hold

admonición *f* admonition; ADMIN warning
ADN *m abr de* **ácido desoxirribonucleico**
DNA
adobar *vt* **1.** (*con salsa*) to marinade; (*carne*)
to pickle **2.** (*piel*) to tan **3.** *inf* (*amañar*) to
fiddle
adobe *m* adobe
adobo *m* **1.** (*salsa*) marinade **2.** (*con salsa*)
marinating; (*para conservar*) pickling **3.** (*de
pieles*) tanning
adocenado, -a *adj* mediocre
adoctrinar *vt* **1.** (*de ideas*) to indoctrinate
2. (*enseñar*) to instruct; ~ **a alguien sobre
algo** to instruct sb about sth
adolecer *irr como crecer vi* (*ponerse
enfermo*) to fall ill; (*padecer*) to suffer; **este
chico adolece de falta de imaginación** this
boy suffers from a lack of imagination
adolescencia *f* adolescence
adolescente I. *adj* adolescent **II.** *mf* teenager
adonde *adv* (*relativo*) where; **el pueblo ~
iremos es muy bonito** the village we'll go to
is very pretty
adónde *adv* (*interrogativo*) where
adondequiera *adv* ~ **que** + *subj* wherever
adopción *f* adoption
adoptar *vt* to adopt
adoptivo, -a *adj* **1.** (*personas*) adoptive,
foster *Am* **2.** (*cosas*) adopted, foster *Am*
adoquín *m* **1.** (*piedra*) cobblestone **2.** *inf* (*persona*) blockhead
adoquinado *m* (*suelo*) cobbles *pl*
adoquinar *vt* to cobble
adorable *adj* adorable
adorar *vt* to adore; (*idolatrar*) to worship
adormecer *irr como crecer* **I.** *vt* **1.** (*personas*) to make sleepy **2.** (*dolor*) to numb
II. *vr:* ~**se** to fall asleep
adormecido, -a *adj,* **adormilado, -a** *adj*
(*cansado*) sleepy
adormilarse *vr* to doze
adornar I. *vt* to adorn; (*con ornamentos*) to
decorate **II.** *vr:* ~**se** to adorn oneself
adorno *m* adornment; (*decoración*) decoration; (*ornamento*) ornament; **árbol de** ~ ornamental tree; **la lámpara sólo está de** ~ the
lamp is just for decoration; **estar de** ~ *fig* to be
for show
adosado, -a *adj* **casa adosada** semi-detached
house *Brit,* duplex *Am,* two-family house *Am*
adosar *vt* **1.** (*apoyar*) ~ **a algo** to lean against
sth **2.** ARQUIT ~ **a algo** to build onto sth
adquirir *irr vt* **1.** (*conseguir*) to acquire; ~ **un
hábito** to acquire a habit **2.** (*comprar*) to purchase
adquisición *f* acquisition; (*de una empresa*)
takeover; ~ **de lenguas** acquisition of languages; **este coche es una buena** ~ this car is
a good buy
adquisitivo, -a *adj* acquisitive; **poder** ~ purchasing power
adrede *adv* on purpose
adrenalina *f* adrenalin

adriático, -a *adj* Adriatic; **mar Adriático**
Adriatic (Sea)
Adriático *m* Adriatic
adscribir *irr como escribir vt* **1.** (*atribuir*) to
assign **2.** (*destinar*) to appoint
aduana *f* **1.** (*tasa*) customs duty; **declaración
de** ~**s** customs declaration; **despacho de** ~
customs clearance; **sin** ~ duty-free **2.** (*oficina*)
customs office; **pase por la** ~**, por favor** go
through customs, please **3.** (*juego*) dice game
aduanero, -a I. *adj* customs; **exento de
derechos** ~**s** duty-free; **sujeto a derechos** ~**s**
dutiable **II.** *m, f* customs officer
aducir *irr como traducir vt* (*razón, motivo*) to
put forward; (*prueba*) to provide
adueñarse *vr* to take possession; ~ **del poder**
to take over power; **el pánico se adueñó de
él** panic got the better of him
adulación *f* flattery
adulador(a) I. *adj* flattering **II.** *m(f)* flatterer
adular *vt* to flatter
adulterar *vt* to falsify; (*alimentos*) to adulterate
adulterio *m* adultery
adúltero, -a I. *adj* adulterous **II.** *m, f* adulterer
adulto, -a I. *adj* **1.** (*persona, animal*) adult
2. (*desarrollado*) mature **II.** *m, f* adult
adusto, -a *adj* **1.** (*persona*) stern **2.** (*paisaje*)
bleak **3.** (*región, casa*) austere **4.** (*clima*) harsh
advenedizo, -a I. *adj* **1.** (*forastero*) foreign
2. *pey* (*arribista*) upstart **II.** *m, f* **1.** (*forastero*)
newcomer **2.** *pey* (*arribista*) upstart
advenimiento *m* advent; (*de un monarca*)
accession; **esperar algo como el santo** ~ *inf*
to wait impatiently for sth
adverbial *adj* adverbial
adverbio *m* adverb; ~ **de modo/de lugar/
de tiempo** adverb of manner/of place/of time
adversario, -a *m, f* opponent
adversidad *f* **1.** (*contrariedad*) adversity
2. (*desgracia*) setback
adverso, -a *adj* adverse; (*enemigo*) hostile;
(*clima*) harsh
advertencia *f* **1.** (*amonestación*) warning
2. (*indicación*) advice
advertido, -a *adj* experienced; **estar** ~ **del
peligro** to be aware of the danger
advertir *irr como sentir vt* **1.** (*reparar*) to
notice; **advirtió mis intenciones** he/she
guessed my intentions **2.** (*indicar*) to point out
3. (*llamar la atención*) ~ **algo** to draw attention to sth **4.** (*avisar*) to warn; (*aconsejar*) to
advise
adviento *m* Advent
advocar <c→qu> *vt AmL* JUR to advocate
adyacencia *f RíoPl* (*proximidad*) proximity;
en las ~**s** in the vicinity
adyacente *adj* adjacent
aéreo, -a *adj* **1.** (*del aire*) aerial; (*tráfico*) air;
base aérea MIL airbase; **compañía aérea** airline (company); **por vía aérea** (by) airmail
2. (*ligero*) light
aeróbic *m* aerobics

aerobús m airbus
aerodeslizador m hovercraft
aerodinámico, -a adj aerodynamic; (vehículo) streamlined
aeródromo m aerodrome
aeroespacial adj aerospace
aerofaro m beacon
aerolínea f airline
aeromodelismo m construction of model airplanes
aeromoza f Méx, AmS (azafata) air hostess, stewardess Am
aeronauta mf aeronaut
aeronáutica f aeronautics
aeronave f airship; ~ **espacial** spaceship
aeroplano m aeroplane Brit, airplane Am
aeropuerto m airport
aerosol m 1. (suspensión) aerosol 2. (espray) spray 3. (recipiente) spray can
aerotrén m aerotrain
afabilidad f affability
afable adj affable
afamado, -a adj famous
afamar vt to make famous
afán m 1. (ahínco) eagerness 2. (ambición) ~ **de algo** urge for sth; ~ **de lucro** profit motive; **con** ~ eagerly; **poner mucho** ~ **en algo** to put a lot of effort into sth 3. (anhelo) ~ **de algo** longing for sth; ~ **de notoriedad** hunger for publicity
afanador(a) m(f) 1. Arg (carterista) pickpocket; (descuidero) sneak thief 2. Méx (para la limpieza) cleaner
afanar I. vi to work hard II. vt CSur, inf to steal, to pinch III. vr: ~**se** (esforzarse) to toil (away)
afano m Arg, inf theft
afanoso, -a adj 1. (trabajoso) laborious 2. (persona) industrious
afarolarse vr Chile, Perú, inf to get worked up
afear vt 1. (desfigurar) to disfigure 2. (censurar) to censure
afección f 1. MED condition 2. (inclinación) inclination
afeccionarse vr CSur ~ **de algo/alguien** to take a liking to sth/sb
afectación f affectation; **comportarse con** ~ to behave affectedly
afectado, -a adj (amanerado) affected
afectar I. vt 1. (influir) to concern 2. (dañar) to harm; MED to attack 3. (impresionar) to affect 4. (aparentar) to feign 5. AmL (girar) to transfer 6. AmL (destinar dinero) ~ **a algo** to set aside for sth II. vr: ~**se** AmL to fall ill
afectísimo, -a adj suyo ~ yours truly
afectivo, -a adj 1. (de afecto) affective 2. (sensible) emotional 3. (cariñoso) affectionate
afecto m 1. (pasión) emotion 2. (cariño) ~ **a algo/alguien** affection for sth/sb
afecto, -a adj 1. (inclinado) ~ **a algo/alguien** inclined towards sth/sb 2. (agregado)

attached 3. (sujeto) **estar** ~ **al pago de impuestos** to be taxable 4. (afectado) **estar** ~ **de algo** to be afflicted with sth
afectuoso, -a adj 1. (cariñoso) affectionate 2. (cordial) kind; **afectuosamente** yours affectionately
afeitada f Arg, **afeitado** m shave; **afeitado húmedo** wet shave
afeitar I. vt (persona) to shave; **máquina de** ~ (safety) razor II. vr: ~**se** to shave
afeite m 1. (cosmético) cosmetic(s), make-up 2. (adorno) embellishment
afelpado, -a adj velvety; **sillón** ~ plush-covered armchair
afeminado m 1. (como una mujer) effeminate man 2. pey (blando) softy
afeminado, -a adj effeminate
afeminar vt, vr: ~**se** 1. (hacer(se) afeminado) to become effeminate 2. (ablandarse) to become soft
aferrar I. vt to grasp II. vr: ~**se** 1. (agarrarse) ~ **a algo** to cling on [o to] sth 2. (obstinarse) to stand by
Afganistán m Afghanistan
afgano, -a adj, m, f Afghan
afianzamiento m 1. (sujeción) fastening 2. (aseguramiento) securing 3. (firmeza) strength 4. JUR surety
afianzar <z→c> I. vt 1. (sujetar) to fasten; (con clavos) to nail down; (con puntales) to prop up; (con tornillos) to screw on 2. (dar firmeza) to strengthen; (asegurar) to secure II. vr: ~**se** 1. (apoyarse) to lean 2. (afirmarse) to become established
afiche m AmL poster
afición f 1. (inclinación) liking; **cobrar** [o **tomar**] **una** ~ **por** [o **a**] **algo** to develop [o take] a liking for [o to] sth; **tener** [o **sentir**] **una** ~ **hacia** [o **a**] **algo** to be fond of sth 2. (pasatiempo) hobby; **de** ~ as a hobby; **hacer algo por** ~ to do sth as a hobby 3. (afecto) affection 4. (hinchada) fans pl
aficionado, -a I. adj 1. (que siente afición) **ser** ~ **a la arquitectura** to be keen on architecture; **ser** ~ **a tocar la flauta** to be fond of playing the flute 2. (no profesional) amateur II. m, f 1. (entusiasta) lover; DEP fan; ~ **a la ópera** opera lover 2. (no profesional) amateur
aficionar I. vt ~ **a alguien a algo** to get sb interested in sth II. vr ~**se a algo** (acostumbrarse) to take a liking to sth; ~**se a alguien** to become fond of sb
afilado, -a adj 1. (nariz) pointed; (dedos) long; (cara) thin; **tener uñas afiladas** inf to be light-fingered 2. (mordaz) biting; **lengua afilada** fig sharp tongue
afilalápices m inv pencil sharpener
afilar I. vt 1. (cuchillo, lápiz) to sharpen 2. (sentidos) to sharpen II. vr: ~**se** 1. (sentido) to get sharp 2. (cara) to grow thin
afiliación f (acto, pertenencia) affiliation; ~ **política** political affiliation
afiliado, -a I. adj affiliated II. m, f member; ~

a un sindicato trade union member
afiliar I. *vt* (*incorporar*) ~ **a algo** to admit into sth II. *vr:* ~**se** ~**se a algo** to join sth
afín *adj* related
afinar I. *vi* (*cantando*) to sing in tune; (*tocando*) to play in tune II. *vt* **1.** (*hacer más fino*) to refine; (*perfeccionar*) to perfect; ~ **la puntería** to sharpen one's aim **2.** (*lápiz*) to sharpen **3.** (*metales*) to purify **4.** MÚS to tune
afincado, -a I. *adj* **1.** (*que posee fincas*) landed **2.** (*establecido*) established; **desde hace tiempo están ~s en Salamanca** they settled in Salamanca some time ago II. *m, f* landowner
afincarse <c→qu> *vr* to become established
afinidad *f* **1.** (*semejanza*) similarity; ~ **de caracteres** relatedness of character **2.** (*por parentesco*) relationship; **son parientes por ~** they are related by marriage
afirmación *f* **1.** (*confirmación*) confirmation; (*de preguntas*) affirmation; **contestar algo con afirmaciones** to answer in the affirmative **2.** (*aseveración*) assertion
afirmar I. *vt* **1.** (*decir sí*) to affirm; (*dar por cierto*) to confirm; ~ **con la cabeza** to nod in agreement **2.** (*aseverar*) to state **3.** (*asentar*) to secure II. *vr:* ~**se 1.** (*confirmarse*) to be confirmed **2.** (*ratificarse*) ~**se en algo** to reaffirm sth
afirmativamente *adv* affirmatively; **responder ~** to respond affirmatively; **responder ~ a algo** to reply in the affirmative to sth
afirmativo, -a *adj* affirmative; **en caso ~** if so; **respuesta afirmativa** positive answer
aflicción *f* ~ **por algo/alguien** grief for sth/sb; **dar ~ a alguien** to cause sb worry
aflictivo, -a *adj*, **afligente** *adj AmL* upsetting
afligir <g→j> I. *vt* **1.** (*apenar*) to upset **2.** (*atormentar*) to afflict II. *vr:* ~**se** ~**se por** [*o* de] **algo** to get upset about [*o* over] sth
aflojar I. *vi* to slacken II. *vt* **1.** (*nudo*) to loosen **2.** (*cuerda*) to slacken (off) **3.** *inf* (*dinero*) to fork out **4.** (*velocidad*) to reduce; ~ **el paso** to slacken one's pace; **un tira y afloja** a tug-of--war III. *vr:* ~**se** to slacken
aflorar *vi* **1.** (*salir a la superficie*) to come to the surface; (*agua subterránea*) to emerge **2.** (*apuntar*) to appear
afluencia *f* **1.** (*gente*) crowd; ~ **de votantes** turnout (at the polls) **2.** (*abundancia*) abundance
afluente *m* tributary
afluir *irr como huir vi* **1.** (*río*) ~ **a algo** to flow into sth; (*calle*) to lead into sth **2.** (*gente*) to flock; ~ **a un concierto/a Madrid** to flock to a concert/to Madrid
afluxionarse *vr* **1.** *AmC* (*hincharse*) to swell **2.** *Col, Cuba* (*acatarrarse*) to catch cold
afonía *f* hoarseness; **tener ~** to be hoarse
afónico, -a *adj* hoarse
aforar *vt* **1.** (*cantidad*) to assess **2.** (*mercan-*

cía) to value **3.** (*instrumentos de medida*) to gauge
aforismo *m* aphorism
aforo *m* **1.** (*de una cantidad*) assessment **2.** (*en un estadio, teatro*) capacity; **la sala tiene un ~ de 300 personas** the hall can seat 300 people **3.** TÉC gauging
afortunado, -a *adj* fortunate; **¡qué afortunada eres!** how lucky you are!
afrenta *f* **1.** (*vergüenza*) affront **2.** (*ofensa*) insult; **hacer una ~ a alguien** to insult sb
afrentar I. *vt* to insult II. *vr:* ~**se** to take offence *Brit*, to take offense *Am*
afrentoso, -a *adj* **1.** (*ofensivo*) insulting **2.** (*vergonzoso*) outrageous
África *f* Africa
africano, -a *adj, m, f* African
afrodisiaco *m*, **afrodisíaco** *m* aphrodisiac
afrontar *vt* **1.** (*hacer frente*) to face up to; ~ **un problema** to tackle a problem **2.** (*enfrentar*) to confront
afrutado, -a *adj* fruity
afuera *adv* (*estado, movimiento*) outside; **la parte de ~** the outside; **¡~!** *inf* get out of here!
afueras *fpl* outskirts *pl*; ~ **de la ciudad** outskirts of the city
agachar I. *vt* (*cabeza*) to lower II. *vr:* ~**se 1.** (*encogerse*) to crouch **2.** *AmL* (*ceder*) to give in
agache *m* **1.** *Col* (*mentira*) fib **2.** *Cuba* **andar de ~** to be on the run **3.** *Ecua* (*de tapadillo*) **de ~** on the sly
agalla *f* (*de un pez*) gill; **tener ~s** *fig* to have guts
agarrada *f* *inf* row; **tener una ~** to have a row
agarradera *f* *AmL*, **agarradero** *m* **1.** (*asidero*) handle **2.** (*enchufe*) influence **3.** (*excusa*) excuse
agarrado, -a *adj* stingy
agarrador *m* (*para cosas calientes*) oven glove *Brit*, pot holder *Am*
agarrar I. *vi* **1.** (*echar raíces*) to take root **2.** (*comida*) to stick **3.** (*coche*) to grip the road; **agarró y salió** *inf* he/she upped and left II. *vt* **1.** (*tomar*) to take **2.** (*asir*) to grasp **3.** (*delincuente, oportunidad*) to seize **4.** (*enfermedad, rabieta*) to catch; ~ **una borrachera** to get drunk; ~ **una pulmonía** to catch pneumonia III. *vr:* ~**se 1.** (*asirse*) to hold on; **agárrate, que te voy a contar qué me pasó ayer** *inf* just hold on! Wait till you hear what happened to me yesterday **2.** (*reñir*) to have a fight **3.** (*comida*) to stick **4.** *inf* (*tomar como pretexto*) ~**se al retraso del tren para justificarse** to use the train's late arrival as an excuse **5.** *AmL* (*coger*) to catch; (*frutas*) to pluck
agarrotar I. *vt* **1.** (*entumecer*) to stiffen up **2.** (*atar*) to tie tight **3.** (*oprimir*) to squeeze tight II. *vr:* ~**se 1.** (*entumecerse*) to go numb **2.** (*por el miedo*) to go rigid with fear **3.** TÉC to seize up
agasajar *vt* **1.** (*recibir*) to receive in great style

2. (*con comida*) to wine and dine; **el embajador fue agasajado con un banquete** a banquet was given in the ambassador's honour **3.** (*con regalos*) to lavish

agasajo *m* **1.** (*recibimiento*) splendid reception **2.** (*con comida*) lavish hospitality **3.** (*regalo*) present

agatas *adv Par, RíoPl* **1.** (*con dificultad*) with great difficulty **2.** (*casi no*) hardly; ~ **sabe leer** he/she can barely read **3.** (*tan sólo, escasamente*) barely; ~ **hace una hora** barely an hour ago

agaucharse *vr AmS* to imitate or dress like a gaucho; **tras tantos años de vida en el campo se agauchó mucho** after so many years in the country he/she had become very gaucho-like

agazaparse *vr* **1.** *inf* (*agacharse*) to crouch **2.** (*esconderse*) to hide

agencia *f* **1.** (*empresa*) agency; ~ **de colocaciones** employment agency; ~ **inmobiliaria** estate agency; ~ **de noticias** news agency [*o* service]; ~ **de publicidad** advertising agency; ~ **de transportes** carriers; **Agencia Tributaria** tax office; ~ **de viajes** travel agency **2.** (*sucursal*) branch

agenciar **I.** *vt inf* to get **II.** *vr:* ~**se** to get hold of; **agenciárselas** to manage; **agénciatelas como puedas** try to get by as best you can

agenciero, -a *m, f* **1.** *Arg* (*de negocios*) representative; (*de lotería*) lottery vendor **2.** *Chile* (*prestamista*) pawnbroker

agenda *f* **1.** (*calendario*) diary, engagement book *Am;* ~ **de bolsillo** pocket diary; **tener una ~ apretada** to have a full agenda **2.** (*cuaderno*) notebook **3.** (*orden del día*) agenda

agente¹ *mf* **1.** (*representante*) representative; (*de un artista, escritor*) agent; (*corredor*) agent, broker; ~ **autorizado** authorized agent; ~ **de bolsa** stockbroker; ~ **exclusivo** exclusive agent; ~ **de la propiedad inmobiliaria** estate agent *Brit,* realtor *Am;* ~ **de transportes** carrier **2.** (*funcionario*) ~ **de aduanas** customs officer; ~ **judicial** bailiff; ~ **de policía** policeman **3.** (*espía*) secret agent

agente² *m t.* MED (*cosa*) agent

agigantado, -a *adj* gigantic; **a pasos ~s** by leaps and bounds

ágil *adj* **1.** (*de movimiento*) agile **2.** (*mental*) alert, quick-witted **3.** (*estilo*) lively

agilidad *f* **1.** (*física*) agility; ~ **de dedos** dexterity **2.** (*mental*) acumen

agilizar <z→c> *vt* to speed up

agitación *f* **1.** (*movimiento*) movement; (*de un líquido*) stirring **2.** *t.* POL (*intranquilidad*) agitation; (*excitación*) excitement

agitado, -a *adj* (*vida*) hectic

agitar **I.** *vt* **1.** (*mover*) to move; (*bandera, pañuelo*) to wave; (*botella*) to shake; **agítese antes de usarlo** shake well before use **2.** (*intranquilizar*) to worry; (*excitar*) to excite **3.** (*sublevar*) to rouse **II.** *vr:* ~**se 1.** (*moverse*) to move about; (*con el cuerpo*) to wriggle;

(*bandera*) to wave; (*mar*) to get rough **2.** (*excitarse*) to get excited; (*preocuparse*) to get upset

aglomeración *f* agglomeration; ~ **de gente** crowd of people; ~ **urbana** urban sprawl

aglomerar **I.** *vt* (*reunir*) to gather (together); (*amontonar*) to pile up **II.** *vr:* ~**se** to crowd (together)

aglutinar *vt* **1.** (*pegar*) to agglutinate **2.** (*unir*) to unite; *fig* to bring together

agnóstico, -a *adj, m, f* agnostic

agobiado, -a *adj* **1.** (*cansado*) exhausted; ~ **por los años** weighed down by the years **2.** *fig* **estar ~ de trabajo** to be overloaded with work; **estoy ~ de deudas** I'm burdened with debts

agobiante *adj* **1.** (*trabajo*) overwhelming **2.** (*persona*) tiresome **3.** (*silencio, calor*) oppressive

agobiar **I.** *vt* **1.** (*abrumar*) to overwhelm; ~ **a alguien con alabanzas** to overwhelm sb with praise; **¡no me agobies!** *inf* don't keep going on at me! **2.** (*calor*) to suffocate; (*tristeza*) to depress **II.** *vr:* ~**se 1.** (*sentirse abatido*) to feel overwhelmed **2.** (*atarearse*) to work hard **3.** (*angustiarse*) ~**se por algo** to be weighed down with sth

agobio *m* **1.** (*carga*) burden **2.** (*cansancio*) exhaustion; (*de trabajo*) overwork **3.** (*opresión*) oppression; (*angustia*) anxiety

agolpamiento *m* crowd

agolparse *vr* **1.** (*personas*) to crowd (together) **2.** (*líquido*) to stream; **se agolparon las lágrimas en sus ojos** tears welled up in his/her eyes **3.** (*sucesos, pensamientos*) to come in quick succession

agonía *f* **1.** (*del moribundo*) death throes *pl* **2.** (*angustia*) anguish **3.** (*de una civilización*) decline

agónico, -a *adj* **período ~** hour of death; **estar ~** to be dying

agonizar <z→c> *vi* **1.** (*morir*) to be dying **2.** (*terminar*) to come to an end

agorero, -a **I.** *adj* ominous **II.** *m, f* soothsayer

agostar **I.** *vt* **1.** (*plantas*) to wither **2.** (*malograr*) to ruin **II.** *vr:* ~**se** to dry up

agosto *m* **1.** (*mes*) August **2.** (*período*) harvest (time); **hacer su ~** to make a killing; *v.t.* **marzo**

agotado, -a *adj* **1.** (*producto*) out of stock **2.** (*persona*) exhausted

agotador(a) *adj* exhausting; **hace un calor ~** the heat is unbearable

agotamiento *m* exhaustion

agotar **I.** *vt* **1.** (*existencias*) to use up **2.** (*mercancía*) to deplete **3.** (*paciencia, tema, posibilidad*) to exhaust **4.** (*cansar*) to tire (out) **II.** *vr:* ~**se 1.** (*mercancía*) to run out; **esta edición se agotó enseguida** this edition sold out immediately **2.** (*pilas*) to run down [*o* out *Am*] **3.** (*fuerzas*) to give out; (*conversación*) to dry up **4.** (*cansarse*) to wear oneself out

agraciado, -a *adj* **1.** (*gracioso*) graceful

2.(*bien parecido*) attractive **3.**(*afortunado*) lucky; **salir ~ en la lotería** to win in the lottery

agraciar *vt* **1.**(*conceder*) to award; **fue agraciado con un premio** he/she was awarded a prize **2.**(*vestido, adorno*) to enhance; **este traje le agracia la figura** this dress flatters her figure

agradable *adj* **1.**(*ameno*) pleasant; **~ al paladar** tasty; **es ~ a la vista** it is pleasing to the eye **2.**(*persona*) **~ con alguien** pleasant to sb

agradar *vi* to please; **me agrada oír música** I like listening to music; **me agrada esta gente** I like these people; **quieres ~ a todos** you want to please everyone

agradecer *irr como crecer vt* to thank; **te agradezco la invitación** thanks for the invitation; **les agradezco que me lo hayan dicho** I'm grateful to you for having told me; **le ~ía mucho si** +*subj* I'd be very grateful if; **no sabes ~ mi trabajo** you don't appreciate my work; **el campo ha agradecido la lluvia** the rain has done the fields good

agradecido, -a *adj* **1.**(*que agradece*) **~ por algo** grateful for sth; **le estaría muy ~ que me contestara lo antes posible** I should be very grateful if you would reply as soon as possible; **le estoy sumamente ~** I am exceedingly grateful (to you); **le quedamos muy ~s** we are very grateful (to you) **2.**(*que compensa*) worthwhile

agradecimiento *m* gratitude

agrado *m* **1.**(*afabilidad*) affability; **tratar a alguien con ~** to treat sb kindly **2.**(*complacencia*) willingness; **decidir según su ~** to decide as one likes; **he recibido con ~ su carta** I was very pleased to receive your letter; **esto no es de mi ~** this isn't to my liking

agrandar **I.** *vt* to make bigger; **~ la importancia de algo** to exaggerate the importance of sth **II.** *vr:* **~se** to get bigger

agrario, -a *adj* agrarian; **crédito ~** agrarian credit; **población agraria** rural population

agravamiento *m* **1.** MED worsening **2.**(*recrudecimiento*) aggravation

agravante **I.** *adj* aggravating **II.** *m o f* aggravating factor

agravar **I.** *vt* (*enfermedad, situación*) to make worse, to aggravate **II.** *vr:* **~se** (*enfermedad, situación*) to worsen

agraviar **I.** *vt* **1.**(*ofender*) to offend **2.** JUR to harm **II.** *vr:* **~se** to be offended

agravio *m* **1.**(*ofensa*) offence *Brit,* offense *Am* **2.** JUR grievance; **~ material** material damage; **sufrir ~s** to suffer injustice

agraz *m* **1.**(*uva*) sour grape; **en ~** prematurely **2.**(*zumo*) sour grape juice **3.**(*amargura*) bitterness

agredir *vt* to attack; **~ a alguien de palabra** to attack sb verbally

agregación *f* adding; **~ de un municipio** incorporation

agregado *m* **1.**(*conglomerado*) aggregate

2.(*aditamento*) addition

agregado, -a *m, f* **1.**(*diplomático*) attaché; **~ comercial** commercial attaché; **~ militar** military attaché **2.**(*adjunto*) assistant **3.** UNIV assistant professor *Brit,* associate professor *Am*

agregar <g→gu> **I.** *vt* **1.**(*añadir*) to add **2.**(*persona*) to appoint **II.** *vr:* **~se** to join; **~se a alguien** to join sb

agremiar **I.** *vt* to unionize **II.** *vr:* **~se** to form a union

agresión *f* aggression

agresividad *f* aggressiveness

agresivo, -a *adj* aggressive

agresor(a) **I.** *adj* aggressor **II.** *m(f)* aggressor, assailant

agreste *adj* **1.**(*campestre*) country **2.**(*terreno*) rough **3.**(*vegetación*) wild **4.**(*persona*) uncouth

agriar **I.** *vt* **1.**(*alimentos*) to sour **2.**(*persona*) to make bitter **II.** *vr:* **~se 1.**(*alimentos*) to turn sour **2.**(*persona*) to become embittered [*o* bitter]

agrícola *adj* agricultural; **cooperativa ~** agricultural cooperative

agricultor(a) *m(f)* farmer

agricultura *f* agriculture

agridulce *adj* bittersweet; GASTR sweet-and-sour

agrietar **I.** *vt* to crack **II.** *vr:* **~se** to crack; (*tela, pared*) to become cracked; (*piel, labios*) to become chapped

agrimensor(a) *m(f)* surveyor

agrimensura *f* surveying

agringarse <g→gu> *vr AmL:* to imitate or adopt the customs of a foreigner

agrio, -a *adj* **1.**(*sabor*) sour **2.**(*crítica*) sharp **3.**(*carácter*) bitter

agripado, -a *adj Col, inf*(*griposo*) **estar ~** to have the flu

agro *m* farming

agronomía *f* agronomy

agrónomo, -a *m, f* agronomist

agropecuario, -a *adj* agricultural, farming

agroturismo *m* agrotourism

agrupación *f* **1.**(*agrupamiento*) grouping **2.**(*conjunto*) group; **~ de municipios** municipal association **3.**(*asociación*) society **4.** MIL unit

agrupar **I.** *vt* to group (together); **~ algo por temas** to group sth by subject **II.** *vr:* **~se** to form a group

agua *f* **1.**(*líquido*) water; **~ de colonia** eau de cologne; **~s depuradas** purified water; **~ con gas** sparkling water; **~ del grifo** tap water; **~ de mar** seawater; **~ de nieve** meltwater; **~ potable** drinking water; **¡hombre al ~!** man overboard!; **claro como el ~** crystal clear **2.**(*lluvia*) rain; **~ nieve** sleet; **esta noche ha caído mucha ~** it rained a lot last night **3.** *pl* (*mar, río, manantial*) waters *pl;* **~s interiores** inland waters; **~s jurisdiccionales** territorial waters; **~s residuales** sewage; **~s termales** thermal waters; **~s abajo/arriba** downstream/upstream **4.** *pl* (*orina*) urine; ~**s menores** urine; **hacer** ~**s** to urinate ▸ **quedar en** ~ **de** <u>borrajas</u> to come to nothing; **volver las** ~**s a su** <u>cauce</u> to go back to normal; **estoy con el** ~ **hasta el** <u>cuello</u> I'm up to my neck in it; **como** ~ **de** <u>mayo</u> very welcome; **no hallar** ~ **en el** <u>mar</u> to act stupid; **llevar el** ~ **a su** <u>molino</u> to turn things to one's advantage; ~ **pasada no mueve** <u>molino</u> *prov* it's no use crying over spilt milk; **sacar** ~ **a las** <u>piedras</u> to make something out of nothing; **no llegará el** ~ **al** <u>río</u> it won't go that far; **estar entre** <u>dos</u> ~**s** to be sitting on the fence; **es** ~ <u>pasada</u> that's water under the bridge; <u>hacer</u> ~ (*buque*) to take in water; (*negocio*) to founder; <u>tomar</u> **las** ~**s** to take the waters

aguacate *m* avocado, alligator pear *Am*

aguacero *m* downpour; **cayó un** ~ there was a cloudburst

aguachento, -a *adj AmL v.* **aguado**

aguachirle *f pey* dishwater

aguacil *m CSur* ZOOL dragonfly

aguada *f* **1.** (*lugar*) watering place **2.** (*provisión*) water supply

aguado, -a *adj* watered-down; (*fruta*) tasteless

aguafiestas *mf inv, inf* spoilsport, party pooper *Am*

aguafuerte *m* etching; **grabar al** ~ to etch

aguaitar *vt* **1.** *Arg, Cuba* (*acechar*) to lie in wait for **2.** *Col* (*esperar*) to wait; ~ **unos días** to wait a few days; ~ **algo/a alguien** to wait for sth/sb

aguamarina *f* aquamarine

aguamiel *f* **1.** (*bebida*) mead **2.** *AmL* (*jugo del maguey*) maguey juice

aguanieve *f* sleet

aguanoso, -a *adj* (*fruta*) watery; (*suelo*) waterlogged

aguantable *adj* bearable

aguantadero *m Arg, Urug* hide-out

aguantar I. *vt* **1.** (*sostener*) to hold; (*sujetar*) to hold tight **2.** (*soportar*) to bear; (*tolerar*) to put up with; **no aguanto más** I can't bear it any more; **no poder** ~ **a alguien** not to be able to stand sb; **esta película no se aguanta** this film is unbearable; ~ **la mirada de alguien** to hold sb's stare **3.** (*durar*) to last; **este abrigo** ~**á mucho** this coat will last for a long time **4.** (*contener*) to contain; ~ **la risa** to hold back one's laughter **II.** *vr:* ~**se 1.** (*contenerse*) to restrain oneself **2.** (*soportar*) to put up with it; (*tener paciencia*) to be patient **3.** (*conformarse*) to resign oneself **4.** (*sostenerse*) to support oneself; ~**se de pie** to stay standing

aguante *m* **1.** (*paciencia*) patience; **tener mucho** ~ to be very patient **2.** (*resistencia*) endurance; (*de persona*) stamina

aguar <gu→gü> **I.** *vt* **1.** (*mezclar con agua*) to water (down) **2.** (*frustrar*) to spoil **II.** *vr:* ~**se 1.** (*llenarse de agua*) to fill with water; **no pude evitar que se me** ~**an los ojos** I couldn't stop my eyes from watering; **nuestras vacaciones se** ~**on** our holidays were spoilt [*o* spoiled] by rain **2.** (*estropearse*) to be spoilt [*o* spoiled]

aguardar I. *vt* to wait for; ~ **unos días** to wait a few days; ~ **algo/a alguien** to await sth/sb **II.** *vr:* ~**se** to be awaited

aguardiente *m* brandy

aguarrás *m* turpentine

agudeza *f* **1.** (*del cuchillo, de la crítica*) sharpness; ~ **visual** keenness of sight **2.** (*perspicacia*) perspicacity **3.** (*ingenio*) wittiness

agudizar <z→c> **I.** *vt* **1.** (*hacer agudo*) to sharpen **2.** (*agravar*) to make worse **II.** *vr:* ~**se** (*situación, enfermedad*) to worsen

agudo, -a *adj* **1.** (*afilado*) sharp **2.** (*sagaz*) shrewd; **vista aguda** keen sight **3.** (*ingenioso*) witty; (*mordaz*) scathing **4.** (*intenso: dolor, enfermedad*) acute; (*olor*) pungent **5.** (*sonido*) piercing **6.** (*grave*) severe **7.** LING *stressed on the last syllable*

agüero *m* omen; **de mal** ~ ill-omened; **ser de buen** ~ to augur well

aguerrido, -a *adj* (*fuerte*) hardened

aguijar *vt* **1.** (*animales*) to goad **2.** (*estimular*) to urge on; ~ **el paso** to make haste

aguijón *m* **1.** (*punta*) goad **2.** ZOOL, BOT sting, stinger *Am* **3.** (*estímulo*) stimulus

aguijonear *vt* **1.** (*animales*) to goad **2.** (*estimular*) to spur on **3.** (*inquietar*) to upset

águila *f* **1.** (*animal*) eagle; ~ **real** golden eagle **2.** (*persona*) very clever; **ser un** ~ **para los negocios** to have a great deal of business acumen

aguileño, -a *adj* aquiline; **rostro** ~ angular face

aguinaldo *m* tip (*given at Christmas*)

agüita *f Perú, inf* dough

agüitado, -a *adj Méx* gloomy

aguja *f* **1.** (*general*) needle; ~ **de gancho** crochet hook; ~ **de punto** knitting needle; **buscar una** ~ **en un pajar** to look for a needle in a haystack **2.** (*de una jeringa*) hypodermic needle **3.** (*del reloj*) hand; (*de otros instrumentos de medición*) pointer **4.** NÁUT ~ (**de marear**) ship's compass **5.** FERRO point **6.** (*de una torre*) spire; ~ **de la iglesia** church steeple; **las torres de esa catedral terminan en** ~**s** the towers of that cathedral are topped with spires **7.** BOT pine needle **8.** GASTR **carne de** ~ fore rib *Brit*, rib roast *Am*

agujerear *vt* to make holes in; (*orejas*) to pierce

agujero *m* hole; ~ (**en la capa**) **de ozono** hole in the ozone layer; **tapar un** ~ to fill a hole

agujetas *fpl* stiffness

agusanarse *vr* to get maggoty

aguzado, -a *adj* (*puntiagudo, sagaz*) sharp

aguzar <z→c> *vt* **1.** (*afilar*) to sharpen **2.** (*avivar*) ~ **la atención** to heighten one's attention; ~ **los sentidos** to sharpen one's senses; ~ **la vista** to look more carefully

aherrumbrarse *vr* to rust

ahí I. *adv* (*lugar*) there; ~ **está** there he/she/it is; ~ **viene** there he/she/it comes; **llámame de** ~ call me from there; ~ **está el problema** that's the problem; **me voy por** ~ I'm going that way ►¡~ **es nada!** not bad!; ~ **me las den todas** *inf* I couldn't care less; **por** ~, **por** ~ something like that **II.** *conj* **de** ~ **que…** that is why …

ahijado, -a *m, f* **1.**(*del padrino*) godchild **2.** *fig* protégé *m*, protégée *f*

ahijar *irr como airar vt* to adopt

ahínco *m* **1.**(*afán*) zeal **2.**(*empeño*) effort **3.**(*insistencia*) insistence

ahíto, -a *adj* (*harto*) satiated

ahogado, -a *adj* **1.**(*persona*) drowned; (*sin ventilación*) stifling **2.**(*lleno*) **estar** ~ **de trabajo** to be snowed under with work

ahogar <g→gu> **I.** *vt* **1.**(*en el agua*) to drown **2.**(*estrangular*) to strangle **3.**(*asfixiar*) to suffocate **4.**(*angustiar*) to oppress **II.** *vr:* ~**se** **1.**(*en el agua*) to drown **2.**(*asfixiarse*) to suffocate; ~**se de calor** to be sweltering (in the heat) **3.**(*motor*) to flood ►~**se en un vaso de agua** to make mountains out of molehills

ahogo *m* **1.**(*sofocación*) breathlessness **2.**(*asfixia*) asphyxia **3.**(*angustia*) anguish **4.**(*apuro*) hardship; ~**s económicos** financial difficulties

ahondar **I.** *vi* **1.**(*raíces*) to put down roots **2.**(*tema, cuestión*) ~ **en algo** to go deeply into sth **II.** *vt* **1.**(*profundizar*) to deepen **2.**(*introducir*) to introduce **III.** *vr:* ~**se** to go in more deeply

ahora *adv* now; (*dentro de un momento*) very soon; ~ **bien** now then; **de** ~ **en adelante** from now on; **hasta** ~ up to now; **por** ~ for the present; ~ **ríe,** ~ **llora** laughing one minute, crying the next; ¡~ (**lo entiendo**)! now I've got it!; ¡~ **sí que hemos tenido suerte!** we were really lucky there!; ~ **mismo vengo** I'm just coming; **acaba de salir** ~ **mismo** he/she has just gone out; ¡**ven** ~ **mismo!** come right now!; ¿**y** ~ **qué?** what now?

ahorcado, -a *m, f* hanged person

ahorcar <c→qu> **I.** *vt* to hang; ~ **los libros** to give up one's studies **II.** *vr:* ~**se** to hang oneself

ahorita *adv AmL* (*ahora*) right away

ahorrador(a) **I.** *adj* thrifty **II.** *m(f)* saver

ahorrar *vt* to save; (*economizar*) to economize; ~ **fuerzas** to save [*o* conserve] one's energy; ~ **esfuerzos a alguien** to save sb the trouble; **ahórrame explicaciones** spare me your explanation **II.** *vr:* ~**se** (*evitar*) to save oneself

ahorrativo, -a *adj* thrifty

ahorrista *mf AmL* saver

ahorro *m* (*acción, cantidad*) saving

ahuecar <c→qu> **I.** *vt* **1.**(*vaciar*) to hollow out **2.**(*tierra*) to break up; (*colchón*) to plump up **II.** *vr:* ~**se** **1.**(*ave*) to ruffle (up) its feathers **2.**(*envanecerse*) to give oneself airs **3.**(*papel pintado*) to blister

ahuevarse *vr Col, vulg* (*acobardarse*) to

chicken out

ahulado *m* **1.** *AmC, Méx* (*mantel*) (oilcloth) table cover; **pon el** ~ **en la mesa** put the tablecloth on the table **2.** *pl, AmC* (*zapatos*) rubber shoes *pl*

ahumado, -a *adj* **1.**(*color*) smoky; (*cristal*) tinted **2.**(*salmón*) smoked

ahumar **I.** *vi* to smoke **II.** *vt* **1.** GASTR to smoke **2.**(*llenar de humo*) to fill with smoke; (*una colmena*) to smoke out **III.** *vr:* ~**se** **1.**(*ennegrecerse*) to become blackened **2.**(*un guiso*) to acquire a burnt taste

ahuyentar *vt* **1.**(*espantar*) to frighten off [*o* away] **2.**(*dudas*) to dispel

aindiado, -a *adj AmL* Indian-looking

airar *irr* **I.** *vt* to anger **II.** *vr:* ~**se** to get angry

airbag *m* airbag

aire *m* **1.**(*atmósfera*) air; ~ **acondicionado** air conditioning; **Ejército del Aire** air force; **al** ~ **libre** in the open air; **echar una moneda al** ~ to toss a coin (into the air); **tomar el** ~ to go for a stroll; **dejar una pregunta en el** ~ to leave a question open; **cambiar de** ~**s** to have a change of air; ¡~! *inf* beat it! **2.**(*viento*) wind; **corriente de** ~ draught *Brit*, draft *Am;* **corre** ~ it's draughty; **hoy hace** ~ it's windy today **3.**(*aspecto*) appearance; **no me gusta el** ~ **de este hombre** I don't like the look of this man; **tener** ~ **de despistado** to look absent-minded; **darse** ~**s de grandeza** to have pretensions of grandeur; **darse** ~**s de intelectual** to give oneself an intellectual air; ¡**tiene unos** ~**s!** he/she is always putting on airs! **4.**(*garbo*) elegance **5.** MÚS tune, air **6.** *Arg, Par* (*cuello*) stiff neck

aireado, -a *adj* (*lugar*) ventilated

airear **I.** *vt* to air **II.** *vr:* ~**se** **1.**(*ventilarse*) to air **2.**(*coger aire*) to get some fresh air; (*resfriarse*) to catch a chill

airón *m* **1.** ZOOL heron **2.**(*penacho, adorno*) crest

airoso, -a *adj* graceful; **salir** ~ **de algo** to acquit oneself well in sth

aislado, -a *adj* (*individual*) isolated

aislamiento *m* **1.**(*retiro*) isolation **2.** *t.* TÉC (*apartamiento*) insulation; ~ **acústico** sound-proofing

aislante **I.** *adj* insulating; **cinta** ~ insulating [*o* electrical *Am*] tape **II.** *m* insulator

aislar **I.** *vt* **1.**(*general*) to isolate **2.** TÉC to insulate; **aislado contra el ruido** soundproof **II.** *vr:* ~**se** to isolate oneself

ajá *interj* aha

ajado, -a *adj* (*persona*) worn out; (*cara*) wrinkled

ajamonarse *vr pey, inf* to acquire a middle age spread

ajar *vt* (*cosa, persona*) to wear out

ajardinado, -a *adj* landscaped

ajedrecista *mf* chessplayer

ajedrez *m sin pl* **1.** DEP chess **2.**(*tablero y figuras*) chess set

ajenjo *m* **1.** BOT wormwood **2.**(*bebida*)

absinthe

ajeno, -a *adj* **1.** (*de otro*) somebody else's; **la felicidad ajena** other people's happiness **2.** *ser* (*impropio*) inappropriate; **esto es ~ a su carácter** this is alien to his/her character **3.** *estar* (*ignorante*) ignorant; **estar ~ a** [*o* **de**] **algo** to be unaware of sth; **vivía ~ a todo lo que pasaba en el mundo** he/she lived unaware of what was happening in the world **4.** (*carente, exento*) **~ a** [*o* **de**] lacking; **~ de piedad** pitiless; **~ de preocupaciones** carefree; **él es ~ a todo eso** he is not involved in that

ajetrear I. *vt* to overwork **II.** *vr:* **~se** to tire oneself out; (*darse prisa*) to rush around

ajetreo *m* (*de personas*) drudgery; (*en un sitio*) bustle

ají *m AmS, Ant* **1.** (*arbusto*) pepper (plant) **2.** (*pimentón*) chilli *Brit*, chili *Am;* (*de las Indias*) cayenne (pepper)

ajilimoje *m,* **ajilimójili** *m* GASTR garlic and pepper sauce; **con todos sus ~s** with all the trimmings

ajillo *m* GASTR **al ~** with garlic

ajipa *f And* Jerusalem artichoke

ajo *m* **1.** BOT garlic; (*diente*) clove of garlic **2.** *inf* (*taco*) swearword ►**andar** **tieso como un ~** *inf* to be stuck-up; **andar** (**metido**) **en el ~** *inf,* **estar en el ~** *inf* to be mixed up in it

ajotar *vt* **1.** *AmC, Ant* (*azuzar*) to incite **2.** *Cuba* (*desdeñar*) to scorn

ajuar *m* **1.** (*de la novia*) trousseau **2.** (*de una casa*) furnishings *pl*

ajumarse *vr Col, Cuba, PRico, inf* to get drunk

ajuntarse *vr inf* to live together

ajustable *adj* adjustable; **sábanas ~s** fitted sheets

ajustado, -a *adj* **1.** (*ropa*) tight **2.** (*adecuado*) fitting

ajustar I. *vi* to fit **II.** *vt* **1.** (*adaptar*) *t.* TÉC to adjust; **~ un vestido** to take in a dress; **~ una correa** to adjust a strap **2.** (*una pieza dentro de otra*) to fit **3.** (*acordar*) to reconcile **III.** *vr:* **~se 1.** (*ponerse de acuerdo*) to come to an agreement **2.** (*adaptarse*) to adapt; **no ~se al tema** not to keep to the subject; **~se a la verdad** to stick to the truth

ajuste *m* **1.** (*adaptación*) adjustment; **~ financiero** financial adjustment **2.** (*graduación*) graduation; **~ de brillo** brightness control **3.** (*encaje*) fitting **4.** (*acuerdo*) compromise; **~ de cuentas** settling of scores

ajusticiar *vt* to execute

al = a + el *v.* a

ala *f* wing; (*de hélice*) propeller blade; (*de mesa*) leaf; (*de sombrero*) brim; (*del tejado*) eaves *pl* ►**tener** **demasiadas** **~s** to be overconfident; **estar** **tocado** **del ~** *inf* to be crazy; **ahuecar el ~** to get going; **cortar las ~s a alguien** to clip sb's wings; **dar ~s a alguien** to encourage sb; **le** **faltan** **~s para...** he/she lacks the courage to ...

Alá *m* Allah

alabanza *f* praise; **deshacerse en ~s para con alguien** to shower praises on sb; **hacer una ~ de alguien** to sing sb's praises

alabar I. *vt* **~ a alguien por algo** to praise sb for sth; **alabado sea el Señor** praise be to God **II.** *vr:* **~se** to boast

alabastro *m* alabaster

alabear I. *vt* to warp **II.** *vr:* **~se** (*madera*) to warp

alacena *f* larder

alacrán *m* **1.** ZOOL scorpion **2.** (*persona*) **ser un ~** to be a gossip **3.** (*gancho*) hook

alado, -a *adj* **1.** (*con alas*) winged **2.** (*ligero*) swift

ALALC *abr de* Asociación Latinoamericana de Libre Comercio LAFTA

alambicado, -a *adj* **1.** (*sutil*) subtle **2.** (*rebuscado*) convoluted

alambicar <c→qu> *vt* **1.** (*destilar*) to distil *Brit,* to distill *Am* **2.** (*una expresión*) to refine; (*el lenguaje*) to polish; **diálogos alambicados** polished dialogues

alambique *m* still

alambrada *f* (*valla*) wire fence; (*con espinas*) barbed wire fence; (*red*) wire netting; **~ eléctrica** electric fence

alambrado *m* (*red*) wire netting; (*valla*) wire fence

alambrar *vt* to wire

alambre *m* wire; **~ de espinas** barbed wire

alambrera *f* **1.** (*de ventana*) wire screen **2.** (*de brasero, chimenea*) fireguard **3.** (*de alimentos*) wire cover

alambrista *mf* tightrope walker

alameda *f* **1.** (*lugar*) poplar grove **2.** (*paseo*) avenue; (*de álamos*) tree-lined avenue

álamo *m* (*madera*) *t.* BOT poplar; **~ temblón** aspen

alarde *m* show; **hacer ~ de algo** to make a show of sth

alardear *vi* **~ de algo** (*presumir*) to boast about sth

alardeo *m Méx* (*alarde*) showing off

alargado, -a *adj* elongated

alargar <g→gu> **I.** *vt* **1.** (*la extensión*) to lengthen; **~ la pierna** to stretch one's leg; **~ el cuello** to crane one's neck; **~ la mano** to hold out one's hand **2.** (*la duración*) to prolong **3.** (*retardar, diferir*) to delay **4.** (*el dinero*) to spin out **II.** *vr:* **~se 1.** (*en la extensión*) to lengthen; **no te alargues** be brief; **~se en cumplidos** to be full of compliments **2.** (*retardarse*) to be delayed

alarido *m* shriek

alarife *m* **1.** (*arquitecto*) architect **2.** (*albañil*) bricklayer **3.** *Arg* (*persona lista*) smart customer *inf*

alarma *f* **1.** (*general*) alarm; **~ por ozono** ozone warning; **falsa ~** false alarm; **dar la ~** to raise the alarm; **ha saltado la ~ del banco** the alarm in the bank has gone off **2.** (*susto*) scare; (*inquietud*) worry; **~ social** social unrest

alarmar I. *vt* **1.** (*dar la alarma*) to alarm **2.** (*inquietar*) to worry; (*asustar*) to frighten; **noticia alarmante** terrible news II. *vr:* ~**se** (*inquietarse*) to get worried; (*asustarse*) to take fright

alarmista *mf* alarmist

alavés, -esa I. *adj* of/from Álava II. *m, f* native/inhabitant of Álava

alazán, -ana *adj* (*caballo*) sorrel

alba *f* dawn; **al rayar** [*o* **romper**] **el** ~ at daybreak

albacea *mf* executor

albaceteño, -a I. *adj* of/from Albacete II. *m, f* native/inhabitant of Albacete

albacora *f* Chile, Perú, Méx swordfish

albahaca *f* basil

albanés, -esa *adj, m, f* Albanian

Albania *f* Albania

albañal *m* **1.** (*conducto*) sewer **2.** (*lugar*) dung heap **3.** (*lugar sucio*) mess

albañil *mf* **1.** (*constructor*) builder **2.** (*artesano*) bricklayer

albañilería *f* **1.** (*profesión*) bricklaying **2.** (*materias*) brickwork; **obra de** ~ bricklaying [*o* mason *Am*] (work)

albarán *m* delivery note, invoice

albarda *f* packsaddle ▶~ **sobre** ~ again and again

albaricoque *m* apricot

albaricoquero *m* apricot tree

albatros *m inv* albatross

albazo *m* Perú (*serenata*) morning serenade

albear *vi* Arg to get up very early

albedrío *m* whim; **libre** ~ free will; **a** [*o* **según**] **mi** ~ just as I like

alberca *f* cistern, reservoir

albergar <g→gu> I. *vt* to house II. *vr:* ~**se** to lodge

albergue *m* (*refugio*) refuge; (*alojamiento*) lodging; ~ **juvenil** youth hostel; ~ **de montaña** mountain hut

albino, -a *adj, m, f* albino

albóndiga *f* (*de carne*) meatball; (*de pescado*) fish rissole

albor *m* **1.** (*luz, comienzo*) dawn **2.** (*blancor*) whiteness

alborada *f* **1.** (*alba*) dawn **2.** (*canción*) dawn song **3.** MIL reveille

alborear *vi t. fig* to dawn; **al** ~ **el día** at break of day

albornoz *m* (*de baño*) bathrobe

alborotado, -a *adj* **1.** (*excitado*) excited **2.** (*irreflexivo*) rash

alborotar I. *vi* (*armar jaleo*) to make a racket; (*niños*) to romp about II. *vt* **1.** (*excitar*) to excite **2.** (*desordenar*) to agitate **3.** (*sublevar*) to stir up III. *vr:* ~**se 1.** (*excitarse*) to get excited **2.** (*sublevarse*) to riot

alboroto *m* **1.** (*vocerío*) racket; (*ruido*) noise **2.** (*bulla*) uproar; (*disturbio*) disturbance **3.** (*inquietud, zozobra*) worry

alborozado, -a *adj* jubilant

alborozar <z→c> I. *vt* to delight II. *vr:* ~**se** to be overjoyed

alborozo *m* joy

albricias *fpl inf* ¡~! good news!, congratulations

albufera *f* lagoon

álbum *m* <álbum(e)s> album; ~ **infantil** picture book

albumen *m* albumen

albur *m* ZOOL bleak ▶ **correr un** ~ to run a risk; **al** ~ at random

alburear I. *vt* CRi to disturb II. *vi* **1.** Col (*recibir dinero*) to get money **2.** Cuba (*engañar*) to deceive **3.** Méx (*hacer juegos de palabras*) to play on words

alcachofa *f* **1.** BOT artichoke **2.** (*de ducha*) shower head; (*de regadera*) sprinkler

alcahuete, -a *m, f* **1.** (*trotaconventos*) pimp, procurer *m*, procuress *f* **2.** (*encubridor*) go-between **3.** (*chismoso*) gossip

alcahuetear *vi* **1.** (*servir, hacer de alcahuete*) to pimp, to procure; **¿por qué consientes que él alcahuetee entre ti y ese muchacho?** why do you allow him to pair you off with that guy? **2.** (*chismorrear*) to gossip

alcalde(sa) *m(f)* mayor

alcaldía *f* **1.** (*oficio*) post of mayor **2.** (*oficina*) mayor's office

álcali *m* alkali

alcalino, -a *adj* alkaline

alcamonero, -a *adj* Ven (*entrometido*) meddlesome; (*de novedades*) newsy

alcance *m* **1.** (*distancia*) range; **misil de corto** ~ short-range missile; **de** ~ **limitado** short-range; **al** ~ **de la mano** within reach; **al** ~ **de todos los bolsillos** within everybody's means; **tener la victoria a su** ~ to have victory within one's grasp **2.** (*importancia*) importance; **de mucho/poco** ~ of great/little importance **3.** (*déficit*) deficit ▶ **la noticia de último** ~ the latest news; **ser persona de pocos** ~**s** to be a person of limited talents; **dar** ~ **a alguien** to catch up with sb

alcancía *f* money box *Brit*, piggy bank *Am*

alcanfor *m* camphor

alcanforar I. *vt* **1.** (*untar*) to anoint **2.** (*mezclar*) to camphorate; **alcohol alcanforado** camphorated alcohol II. *vr:* ~**se 1.** Col, Ven (*evaporarse*) to vaporize **2.** Hond (*perderse*) to make oneself scarce *inf*

alcantarilla *f* **1.** (*cloaca*) sewer **2.** (*sumidero*) drain

alcantarillado *m* sewer system, drains *pl*

alcanzar <z→c> I. *vi* **1.** to reach; **este cañón alcanza 10 kilómetros** this gun has a range of 10 kilometres; **el dinero no alcanza para pagar la comida** the money's not enough to pay for the food; **no alcanzo a todo el trabajo** I can't manage to do all the work II. *vt* **1.** (*dar alcance*) to catch up (with); **el ladrón fue alcanzado** the thief was caught; **ve tirando, ya te** ~**é** keep going, I'll catch up with you **2.** (*llegar*) to reach; ~ **un acuerdo** to reach an agreement; **el disparo le alcanzó en la**

pierna the shot struck his leg; ~ **fama** to become famous **3.** (*entender*) to grasp **III.** *vr:* ~**se no se me alcanza qué intentas con ello** I can't figure out what you mean by that

alcaparra *f* caper

alcatraz *m* **1.** ZOOL gannet **2.** BOT arum

alcaucil *m* **1.** (*alcachofa*) artichoke **2.** *Arg* (*trotaconventos*) pimp

alcázar *m* **1.** (*palacio*) palace **2.** MIL fortress

alce *m* elk, moose

alcista **I.** *adj* **mercado** ~ **de la bolsa** bull [*o* bullish] market; **movimiento** ~ **de los precios** upward trend in prices **II.** *mf* speculator, bull

alcoba *f* bedroom

alcohol *m* alcohol; ~ **de quemar** methylated spirit; **bebida sin** ~ non-alcoholic drink; **no tomo** ~ I don't drink alcohol; **estar bajo los efectos del** ~ to be under the influence of alcohol

alcohólico, -a *adj, m, f* alcoholic

alcoholímetro *m* Breathalyzer® *Brit,* drunkometer *Am*

alcoholismo *m sin pl* alcoholism

alcoholista **I.** *adj Arg* drunk; **un hombre** ~ a drunken man **II.** *mf Arg* drunkard

alcoholizado, -a *adj* alcoholic

alcoholizar <z→c> **I.** *vt* to alcoholize **II.** *vr:* ~**se** to become an alcoholic

Alcorán *m* Koran

alcornoque *m* **1.** BOT cork oak **2.** (*persona*) (pedazo de) ~ idiot

alcotán *m* hobby

alcotana *f* pickaxe

alcurnia *f* ancestry; **de** ~ of noble birth

alcuza *f* cruet

aldaba *f* **1.** (*picaporte*) doorknocker **2.** (*para ventanas, puertas*) bolt ▶ **tener buenas** ~**s** *inf* to have influence

aldea *f* small village

aldeano, -a **I.** *adj* **1.** (*de la aldea*) village **2.** (*ignorante*) rustic **II.** *m, f* **1.** (*de la aldea*) villager **2.** (*inculto*) country bumpkin

aldehído *m* aldehyde

aleación *f* alloy; ~ **ligera** light alloy

alear *vt* to flutter ▶ **ir aleando** to be getting better

aleatorio, -a *adj* random, fortuitous

alebrestarse *vr Col, inf* (*alborotarse*) to become agitated

aleccionador(a) *adj* instructive

aleccionar *vt* to instruct; **esto te** ~**á para no volver a hacer lo mismo** this will teach you not to do the same thing again

aledaño, -a *adj* adjoining

aledaños *mpl* outskirts *pl*

alegación *f* **1.** JUR (*declaración*) declaration; (*escrito*) statement; ~ **de culpabilidad** plea of guilty **2.** *pl* (*objeciones*) objections *pl*

alegar <g→gu> **I.** *vt* to cite; (*pruebas*) to produce; ~ **dolor de cabeza** to claim to have a headache **II.** *vi AmL* (*discutir*) to argue

alegato *m* **1.** (*escrito*) bill of indictment;

(*oral*) plea **2.** *AmL* (*disputa*) argument

alegoría *f* allegory

alegrar **I.** *vt* **1.** (*a personas*) to make happy **2.** (*cosas*) to brighten up **II.** *vr:* ~**se 1.** (*sentir alegría*) ~**se de** [*o* **con**] **algo** to be glad about sth; **me alegro de verle de nuevo** I'm pleased to see you again; **nos alegramos de que haya aceptado la invitación** we're glad that he/she has accepted the invitation; **me alegro (por ti)** I'm so happy for you **2.** (*beber*) to get tipsy

alegre *adj* **1.** (*contento*) happy; (*divertido*) merry; (*color*) bright; (*habitación*) pleasant; **un espíritu/una cara** ~ a cheerful nature/face; **estoy** ~ **de que** +*subj* I'm pleased that; **estar más** ~ **que unas pascuas** to be pleased as Punch **2.** (*frívolo*) frivolous; **llevar una vida** ~ to lead a free-and-easy life **3.** *inf* (*achispado*) merry; **estar** ~ to be tipsy

alegría *f* **1.** (*gozo*) happiness; (*buen humor*) cheerfulness; (*alborozo*) merriment; **llevarse una gran** ~ to be very happy **2.** BOT (*ajonjolí*) sesame

alegrón *m inf* thrill; **con esta noticia me has dado un** ~ you've really delighted me with this news; **con esta noticia me he llevado un** ~ I've been thrilled by this news

alegrón, -ona *adj Arg* tipsy

alejamiento *m* removal; *fig* aloofness

alejar **I.** *vt* **1.** (*distanciar*) to remove **2.** (*ahuyentar*) to drive away; **aleja estos pensamientos de tu cabeza** banish these thoughts from your mind **II.** *vr:* ~**se** to move away; (*retirarse*) to withdraw; **todos se alejan de él** everyone avoids him

alelar **I.** *vt* to stupefy **II.** *vr:* ~**se** to be stupefied

aleluya **I.** *interj* hallelujah **II.** *m o f* REL hallelujah; **estar de** ~ to rejoice

alemán *m* (*lengua*) German; **alto** ~ High German, standard German; **decir algo en** ~ to say sth in German

alemán, -ana *adj, m, f* German

Alemania *f* Germany; **República Federal de** ~ Federal Republic of Germany

alentado, -a *adj* (*valiente*) brave

alentar <e→ie> **I.** *vi* **1.** (*respirar*) to breathe **2.** (*estar vivo*) to be alive **II.** *vt* to encourage **III.** *vr:* ~**se 1.** (*animarse*) to take heart **2.** *Hond, Méx, Col, Ecua* (*restablecerse*) to get well

alerce *m* larch

alergia *f* allergy; ~ **a la primavera** hay fever; ~ **alimentaria** food allergy; ~ **al polen** pollen allergy; **esto me da** ~ I'm allergic to this

alérgico, -a *adj* allergic; **es** ~ **a estos temas** *inf* he/she really isn't keen on these subjects

alergólogo, -a *m, f* allergist

alero *m* **1.** ARQUIT eaves *pl* **2.** AUTO wing, fender *Am* **3.** DEP winger

alerón *m* **1.** AVIAT aileron **2.** AUTO spoiler; ~ **delantero/trasero** front/back spoiler

alerta **I.** *adj* alert; **estar** ~ **de algo** to be alert to sth **II.** *f* alert; **dar la** ~ to give the alarm; **poner**

en ~ **a alguien** to put sb on the alert **III.** *interj* watch out

aleta *f* **1.** (*general*) wing **2.** (*de un buzo*) flipper; (*de un pez*) fin

aletargar <g→gu> **I.** *vt* to become drowsy **II.** *vr:* ~**se** to get drowsy

aletear *vi* **1.** (*ave*) to flutter **2.** (*pez*) to wriggle **3.** *inf* (*cobrar fuerza*) to regain one's strength

aleteo *m* **1.** (*de un ave*) fluttering (of the wings) **2.** (*de un pez*) wriggling

alevín *m* **1.** (*pez*) fry, young fish **2.** (*principiante*) beginner

alevosía *f* treachery; **con** ~ treacherously

alevoso, -a *adj* treacherous

alfa *f* alpha; ~ **y omega** *fig* the beginning and the end, Alpha and Omega

alfabético, -a *adj* alphabetic(al); **estar por orden** ~ to be in alphabetical order

alfabetizar <z→c> *vt* to teach to read and write

alfabeto *m* alphabet

alfalfa *f* alfalfa, lucerne

alfaque *m* sandbank

alfar *m* **1.** (*taller*) pottery **2.** (*arcilla*) clay

alfarería *f* (*obrador, oficio*) pottery

alfarero, -a *m, f* potter

alféizar *m* windowsill

alfeñique *m* (*persona*) wimp *inf*

alférez *m* MIL second lieutenant

alfil *m* (*en ajedrez*) bishop

alfiler *m* **1.** (*aguja*) pin **2.** (*broche*) brooch; ~ **de corbata** tiepin; ~ **de gancho** *CSur, Ecua, Perú* safety pin **3.** (*pinza*) pincers *pl* ▶ **llevo la lección prendida con** ~**es** I'm badly prepared for the exam; **ir de veinticinco** ~**es** to be dressed up to the nines; **no caber un** ~ to be bursting at the seams

alfiletero *m* needle case

alfombra *f* carpet; ~ **persa** Persian carpet

alfombrado *m AmL* (*alfombra*) carpeting

alfombrar *vt* to carpet

alfombrilla *f* **1.** (*estera*) mat; ~ **de baño** bath mat **2.** MED German measles **3.** INFOR mousemat *Brit,* mousepad *Am*

alforja *f* bag; (*de caballería*) saddlebag ▶ **sacar los pies de las** ~**s** to come out of one's shell

alga *f* alga

algarabía *f* **1.** (*gritería*) uproar **2.** (*lengua*) Arabic **3.** BOT broom

algarada *f* outcry

algarroba *f* **1.** BOT carob **2.** (*fruto del algarrobo*) carob bean

algarrobo *m* carob tree

algazara *f* clamour *Brit,* clamor *Am;* (*de alegría*) jubilation

álgebra *f* MAT algebra

álgido, -a *adj* **1.** (*culminante*) **el período** ~ **del Barroco** the high point of the Baroque period; **la crisis está en su momento más** ~ the crisis has reached a climax **2.** (*muy frío*) freezing; **fiebre álgida** MED shivering fit

algo I. *pron indef* (*en frases afirmativas*) something; (*en negativas, interrogativas y condicionales*) anything; ~ **es** ~ it's better than nothing; **¿quieres** ~? do you want anything?; **¿apostamos** ~? do you want to bet?; **esta película es** ~ **aparte** this film is something special; **me suena de** ~ it seems familiar to me; **se cree** ~ he/she thinks he/she is something; **por** ~ **lo habrá dicho** he/she must have had a reason for saying it **II.** *adv* a little; **aún falta** ~ **hasta llegar** there's still a bit to go; ~ **así como** something like

algodón *m* **1.** (*planta, tejido*) cotton; **una camisa de** ~ a cotton shirt; ~ **en rama** raw cotton **2.** (*cosmético*) cotton wool *Brit,* cotton *Am* **3.** (*dulce*) candy floss *Brit,* cotton candy *Am* ▶ **criado entre algodones** pampered

algodonero, -a I. *adj* cotton **II.** *m, f* **1.** (*comerciante*) cotton dealer **2.** (*cultivador*) cotton grower

alguacil *m* bailiff

alguien *pron indef* (*en frases afirmativas*) somebody, someone; (*en interrogativas y condicionales*) anybody, anyone; **¿hay** ~ **aquí?** is anybody [*o* anyone] there?; ~ **me lo ha contado** somebody [*o* someone] told me; **se cree** ~ he/she thinks he/she is somebody [*o* someone]

algún *adj v.* **alguno¹**

alguno, -a¹ *adj* <algún> **1.** (*antepuesto*) some; (*en frases negativas e interrogativas*) any; **¿alguna pregunta?** any questions?; **de alguna manera** somehow; **en algún sitio** somewhere; **alguna vez** sometimes; **algún día** some day **2.** (*postpuesto: ninguno*) no, not any; **en sitio** ~ nowhere; **persona alguna** no one

alguno, -a² *pron indef* somebody, someone; ~**s de los presentes** some of those present; ~**s ya se han ido** some have already gone; **¿tienes caramelos? – sí, me quedan** ~**s** do you have any sweets? – yes, I still have some left; **los niños han vuelto a hacer alguna de las suyas** the children have been up to their tricks again

alhaja *f* **1.** (*de piedras preciosas*) piece of jewellery [*o* jewelry *Am*]; (*de bisutería*) costume jewellery [*o* jewelry *Am*] **2.** (*objeto de valor*) treasure **3.** *inf* (*persona*) **¡esta chica es una** ~! this girl's a real gem; **¡menuda** ~, **este niño!** this boy's a fine one!

alhajado, -a *adj Col* (*rico*) wealth

alhajera *f Arg, Chile* jewel box

alharaca *f* fuss

alhelí *m* <alhelíes> wallflower

alheña *f* **1.** BOT privet **2.** (*polvo*) henna

aliado, -a I. *adj* allied **II.** *m, f* ally; **los** ~**s** POL the Allies

alianza *f* **1.** (*pacto*) alliance; **Alianza Atlántica** Atlantic Alliance, NATO **2.** (*anillo*) wedding ring

aliar <1. pres: alío> **I.** *vt* to ally **II.** *vr:* ~**se** to ally oneself

alias *adv, m inv* alias

alicaído, -a *adj* weak; (*deprimido*) dejected

alicantino, -a I. *adj* of/from Alicante II. *m, f* native/inhabitant of Alicante

alicates *mpl* pliers *pl;* ~ **universales** combination pliers

aliciente *m* incentive

alienación *f* alienation

aliento *m* 1. (*respiración, vaho*) breath; **mal** ~ bad breath; **sin** ~ out of breath; **cobrar** ~ to get one's breath back; **esto me quita el** ~ this takes my breath away; **tomar** ~ to take a breath 2. (*ánimo*) courage; **dar** ~ **a alguien** to encourage sb

aligátor *m* alligator

aligerar I. *vi* to hurry (up) II. *vt* 1. (*cargas*) to lighten 2. (*aliviar*) to alleviate 3. (*acelerar*) to quicken; ~ **el paso** to quicken one's pace

alimaña *f* 1. (*animal*) pest; ~**s** vermin 2. (*persona*) animal, brute

alimentación *f* 1. (*nutrición*) food; (*aprovisionamiento*) feeding; **industria de la** ~ food industry 2. (*de animales*) feeding 3. (*de un horno, una caldera*) stoking; (*de una máquina*) feeding; ~ **de energía** energy supply; ~ **de papel** INFOR sheetfeed

alimentador *m* TÉC feeder; ~ **de hojas sueltas** INFOR cut-sheet feed

alimentador(a) *adj* TÉC feeder

alimentar I. *vi* to be nourishing II. *vt* 1. (*nutrir*) to feed; ~ **el odio** to fuel hatred 2. (*horno, caldera*) to stoke; (*máquina*) to feed; ~ **la máquina con energía** to supply the machine with energy 3. INFOR ~ **un ordenador con datos** to feed data into a computer III. *vr* ~**se de algo** to live on sth

alimenticio, -a *adj* 1. (*nutritivo*) nourishing 2. (*alimentario*) food; **industria alimenticia** food industry; **pensión alimenticia** maintenance *Brit,* alimony *Am;* **productos** ~**s** foodstuffs *pl*

alimento *m* 1. (*sustancia*) food; **los** ~**s** foodstuffs *pl;* ~**s congelados** frozen food 2. (*alimentación*) nourishment; **de mucho/poco** ~ full of/lacking nutritional value 3. *pl* JUR (*asistencia financiera*) alimony

alimón *m* **al** ~ together

alineación *f,* **alineamiento** *m* 1. (*general*) alignment; **no** ~ POL non-alignment 2. DEP line-up

alinear I. *vt* 1. (*poner en línea*) to line up 2. DEP to select; (*para un partido*) to field 3. POL **país no alineado** non-aligned country II. *vr:* ~**se** 1. (*ponerse en fila*) to line up 2. POL to align oneself

aliñar *vt* 1. (*condimentar*) to season; (*ensalada*) to dress 2. (*preparar*) to prepare

aliño *m* 1. (*condimento*) seasoning; (*para ensalada*) dressing 2. (*acción*) preparation

alioli *m* sauce of garlic and olive oil

alisar *vt* 1. (*una superficie*) to smooth down; (*un terreno*) to level (off) 2. (*el pelo*) to smooth

alisio *adj* **vientos** ~**s** trade winds

aliso *m* (*madera*) *t.* BOT alder

alistado, -a *adj* 1. (*rayado*) striped 2. (*recluta*) enlisted

alistamiento *m* 1. (*inscripción*) enrolment 2. (*lista*) list 3. MIL enlistment

alistar I. *vt* 1. (*inscribir*) to enrol 2. (*enumerar*) to list 3. MIL to recruit; (*en la marina*) to enlist II. *vr:* ~**se** 1. (*inscribirse*) to enrol 2. MIL to enlist

aliteración *f* alliteration

aliviadero *m* overflow channel

aliviar I. *vi* to quicken one's pace II. *vt* 1. (*carga*) to lighten; **tienes que** ~ **la maleta** you'll have to reduce the weight of the suitcase 2. (*de una preocupación*) to relieve 3. (*dolor, pena*) to alleviate; ~ **un bloqueo económico** to relax an economic blockade III. *vr:* ~**se** 1. (*dolor, pena*) to ease off [*o* up] 2. (*de una enfermedad*) to recover

alivio *m* 1. (*aligeramiento*) relief 2. (*de una enfermedad*) recovery; (*mejoría*) improvement ►**ser de** ~ *inf* to be horrible; **pescar un catarro de** ~ *inf* to get an awful cold; **vestir de** ~ to be in mourning

aljaba *f* quiver

aljibe *m* 1. (*cisterna*) cistern 2. (*tanque*) tank 3. (*barco*) tanker

allá *adv* 1. (*lugar, dirección*) there; **el más** ~ REL the hereafter; **¿cuánto se tarda de aquí** ~**?** how long does it take to go there?; **ponte más** ~ move further over 2. (*tiempo*) back; ~ **por el año 1964** round about 1964; ~ **en tiempos de Maricastaña** in the olden days ►**¡**~ **tú!** *inf* that's your problem!

allanamiento *m* 1. (*de un terreno*) levelling *Brit,* leveling *Am* 2. (*de dificultades*) removal 3. JUR ~ **de morada** breaking and entering

allanar I. *vt* 1. (*terreno, camino*) to level (out) 2. (*construcción*) to demolish 3. (*dificultades*) to remove 4. JUR ~ **una casa** to break into a house II. *vr:* ~**se** to agree; **no se allana nunca** he/she never gives way

allegado, -a I. *adj* close II. *m, f* relative

allegar <g→gu> *vt* (*recursos*) to gather together; (*pruebas, datos*) to collect

allende *elev* I. *adv* on the other side; ~ **de ser guapa, es agradable** besides being pretty, she's pleasant as well II. *prep* beyond; ~ **las montañas** beyond the mountains

allí *adv* (*lugar, dirección*) there; ~ **cerca, por** ~ over there; **¡**~ **viene!** he's/she's just coming!; **hasta** ~ as far as that

alma *f* 1. (*espíritu, persona*) soul; **agradecer con el** ~ to thank with all one's heart; **me arranca el** ~ it's heartbreaking; **me llega al** ~ I'm deeply touched; **lo siento en el** ~ I'm terribly sorry; **no tener** ~ to be heartless; **fue el** ~ **de la fiesta** he/she was the life and soul of the party 2. (*ánimo*) spirit 3. TÉC core ►~ **de cántaro** simpleton; **como** ~ **que lleva el diablo** *inf* like a bat out of hell; **un** ~ **de Dios** a good soul; **estar con el** ~ **en un hilo** *inf* to have one's heart in one's mouth; ~ **en pena** lost soul; **¡**~ **mía!** my darling!; **se le cayó el** ~ **a**

los pies *inf* his/her heart sank

almacén *m* 1. (*depósito*) warehouse; ~ **al por mayor** wholesale warehouse; **franco en** ~ exworks; **tener en** ~ to have in stock 2. (*tienda*) **grandes almacenes** department store

almacenaje *m,* **almacenamiento** *m* 1. (*de mercancías*) *t.* INFOR storage; ~ **definitivo** permanent storage 2. (*tasa*) storage charge

almacenar *vt* (*mercancías*) *t.* INFOR to store; ~ **en disco duro** to store on the hard disk

almacenero, -a *m, f CSur* (*dueño*) grocer

almacenista *mf* wholesaler

almadreña *f* wooden shoe

almanaque *m* almanac

almeja *f* 1. ZOOL clam 2. *vulg* (*vagina*) cunt

almena *f* merlon

almendra *f* 1. (*fruta*) almond; ~**s garapiñadas** sugar almonds 2. (*semilla*) kernel 3. *inf* (*guijarro*) pebble

almendro *m* almond tree

almeriense I. *adj* of/from Almería II. *mf* native/inhabitant of Almería

almiar *m* hayrick *Brit,* haystack *Am*

almíbar *m* syrup; **melocotón en** ~ peach in syrup

almibarado, -a *adj* sugary

almibarar *vt* to preserve in syrup; ~ **a alguien** to butter sb up

almidón *m* starch; (*cola*) paste

almidonado, -a *adj* (*acicalado*) spruced up

almidonar *vt* to starch

alminar *m* minaret

almirantazgo *m* admiralty

almirante *m* admiral

almirez *m* mortar

almizcle *m* musk

almizclero *m* musk deer

almohada *f* 1. (*cojín*) cushion; (*de la cama*) pillow 2. (*funda*) pillowcase ► **consultar algo con la** ~ *inf* to sleep on sth

almohadilla *f* (*cojín*) small cushion; (*acerico*) pin cushion; ~ **de tinta** inkpad

almohadón *m* cushion; (*del sofá*) sofa cushion

almoneda *f* 1. (*subasta*) auction 2. (*saldo*) clearance sale

almorranas *fpl* piles *pl*

almorzar *irr como forzar* I. *vi* 1. (*a mediodía*) to have lunch 2. *reg* (*desayunar*) to have breakfast II. *vt* 1. (*a mediodía*) to have for lunch 2. *reg* (*desayunar*) to have for breakfast

almuerzo *m* 1. (*al mediodía*) lunch; ~ **de negocios** business lunch; **¿qué hay de** ~? what's for lunch? 2. *reg* (*desayuno*) breakfast

almuerzo-coloquio *m* <almuerzos-coloquio> working lunch

aló *interj AmC, AmS* TEL hello; ~, **¿quién es?** hello, who's speaking?

alocado, -a *adj* 1. (*loco*) crazy 2. (*imprudente*) reckless 3. (*revoltoso*) rebellious

alocución *f* speech

alojamiento *m* 1. (*lugar*) accommodation

2. (*acción*) housing; MIL billeting

alojar I. *vt* 1. (*albergar*) to accommodate 2. (*procurar alojamiento*) to house; (*tropa*) to billet 3. (*cosa*) to lodge II. *vr:* ~**se** 1. (*hospedarse*) to stay; MIL to be billeted 2. (*meterse*) ~**se en algo** to put up at sth

alondra *f* lark

alopatía *f* allopathy

alopecia *f sin pl* alopecia

alpaca *f* 1. (*tela*) *t.* ZOOL alpaca 2. (*aleación*) nickel silver, German silver

alpargata *f* espadrille ► **no tener ni para** ~**s** not to have a penny to one's name

Alpes *mpl* **los** ~ the Alps + *pl vb,* Alps

alpinismo *m sin pl* mountaineering, mountain climbing

alpinista *mf* mountaineer, mountain climber

alpino, -a *adj* Alpine; **refugio** ~ mountain refuge

alpiste *m* 1. BOT canary grass 2. (*para pájaros*) birdseed 3. *inf* (*alcohol*) **le gusta mucho el** ~ he's/she's a boozer ► **no tener para** ~ *inf* to be on one's uppers

alquería *f* farm

alquilado, -a *m, f PRico* (*sirviente*) hireling

alquilar I. *vt* 1. (*dejar*) to rent (out), to let 2. (*tomar en alquiler*) to rent II. *vr:* ~**se** (*destinado a ser alquilado*) to be let; **se alquila** to let *Brit,* for rent *Am*

alquiler *m* 1. (*acción*) renting, letting; ~ **de coches** car-hire *Brit,* car-rental *Am;* ~ **con opción de compra** leasing 2. (*precio*) rent, rental

alquimia *f* alchemy

alquimista *mf* alchemist

alquitrán *m* tar

alquitranar *vt* to tar

alrededor *adv* 1. (*local*) around; ~ **de la plaza** around the square; **un viaje** ~ **de la tierra** a round-the-world voyage 2. (*aproximadamente*) ~ **de** around

alrededores *mpl* surroundings *pl;* (*de una ciudad*) outskirts *pl*

Alsacia *f* Alsace; ~**-Lorena** Alsace-Lorraine

alsaciano, -a *adj, m, f* Alsatian

alta *f* 1. (*documento*) (certificate of) discharge; **dar el** ~ to discharge; **dar de** ~ **del hospital** to discharge from hospital 2. (*inscripción*) registration; (*ingreso*) membership; **darse de** ~ **en** (**el registro de**) **una ciudad** to register as being resident in a city; **darse de** ~ **en una asociación** to become a member of an association; **dar de** ~ **a alguien en un partido** to admit sb as a member to a party

altamente *adv* highly; ~ **contaminado** highly contaminated; ~ **cualificado** highly qualified

altanería *f* arrogance, haughtiness

altanero, -a *adj* arrogant, haughty

altar *m* altar; ~ **mayor** high altar ► **quedarse para adornar** ~**es** to be left on the shelf; **poner a alguien en los** ~**es** to put sb on a pedestal; **tener a alguien en los** ~**es** to be full of admiration for sb

altavoz *m* loudspeaker

alterable *adj* 1.(*plan*) alterable 2.(*alimento*) perishable 3.(*persona*) changeable

alteración *f* 1.(*de planes*) alteration, change; FIN fluctuation; ~ **del horario** change [*o* alteration] to the timetable 2.(*perturbación*) disturbance 3.(*turbación*) unrest 4.(*irritación*) irritation 5.(*altercado*) dispute 6.(*adulteración*) adulteration

alterado, -a *adj* upset

alterar I. *vt* 1.(*cambiar*) to alter 2.(*perturbar*) to disturb 3.(*turbar*) to upset; (*irritar*) to irritate 4.(*adulterar*) to adulterate II. *vr:* ~**se** 1. ~**se por algo** (*aturdirse*) to get upset over sth; (*irritarse*) to be irritated by sth 2.(*cambiar*) to alter 3.(*alimentos*) to go off [*o* bad]; (*leche*) to go sour

altercado *m* argument, altercation *form*

altercar <c→qu> *vi* to argue

alternar I. *vi* 1.(*turnarse*) to alternate; **los veranos cálidos han alternado con los lluviosos** warm summers have alternated with rainy ones; ~ **en el volante** to take turns at the wheel 2.(*tratar*) ~ **con alguien** to associate with sb; **es persona que alterna** he/she is a good mixer 3.(*en un club nocturno*) to go clubbing II. *vt* to alternate; ~ **el trabajo con la diversión** to alternate between periods of work and leisure III. *vr* ~**se en algo** to take turns at sth

alternativa *f* 1.(*opción*) alternative; **no le queda otra** ~ **que...** he/she has no other alternative than ... 2. TAUR *ceremony in which a novice becomes a fully-qualified bullfighter;* **dar la** ~ **a alguien para algo** *fig* to consider sb mature enough to do sth

alternativamente *adv* alternatively

alternativo, -a *adj* 1.(*opcional*) alternative 2.(*con alternación*) alternating

alterne *m* **chica de** ~ hostess; **bar de** ~ singles bar

alterno, -a *adj* alternate; **cultivo** ~ AGR crop rotation; **en días** ~**s** every other day

alteza *f* 1.(*tratamiento*) nobleness; **Su Alteza Real** His/Her/Your Royal Highness 2.(*calidad*) eminence

altibajos *mpl* 1.(*de un terreno*) undulations *pl* 2.(*cambios*) ups *pl* and downs; **es una persona con muchos** ~ **en su estado de ánimo** he's/she's very changeable

altillo *m* 1.(*piso*) mezzanine (floor) 2.(*desván*) attic

altiplanicie *f,* **altiplano** *m* high plateau

Altísimo *m* **el** ~ the Almighty

altisonante *adj* high-flown

altitud *f* height, altitude; **a una** ~ **de 1500 metros** at a height of 1,500 metres

altivez *f* arrogance, haughtiness

altivo, -a *adj* (*soberbio*) arrogant, haughty

alto I. *interj* halt; **¡~ el fuego!** cease fire! II. *m* 1.(*descanso*) stop; ~ **el fuego** ceasefire; **dar el** ~ to order to halt 2.(*altura*) height; **medir 8**

metros de ~ to be 8 metres high 3.(*collado*) hill 4. *pl* (*piso alto*) upstairs III. *adv* (*en un lugar elevado*) high (up); **ponlo en lo más** ~ put it as high up as possible; **de** ~ **abajo** from top to bottom ►**pasar por** ~ to ignore; **pasar una pregunta por** ~ to overlook a question; **pasar un saludo por** ~ to ignore a greeting; **por todo lo** ~ splendidly

alto, -a *adj* 1.(*en general*) high; **un** ~ **cargo** a high-ranking position; **la alta Edad Media** the high Middle Ages; **notas altas** MÚS high notes; **artículos de cuero de alta calidad** high-quality leather goods; ~**s funcionarios** high officials; **tener un** ~ **concepto de alguien** to have a high opinion of sb 2.(*persona, árbol*) tall; (*edificio*) high, tall 3.(*en la parte superior*) upper; **clase alta** upper class 4. GEO (*territorio, río*) upper; **la alta montaña** the high mountains; **el** ~ **Tajo** the Upper Tajo 5.(*idioma, época*) high 6.(*tiempo*) late; **a altas horas de la noche** late at night 7.(*río*) in spate *Brit,* swollen *Am;* (*mar*) rough; **el río está** ~ the river is swollen 8.(*sonido*) loud; **hablar en voz alta** to speak loudly

altoparlante *m AmL* loudspeaker

altozano *m* small hill

altramuz *m* lupin

altruismo *m sin pl* altruism

altruista I. *adj* altruistic II. *mf* altruist

altura *f* 1.(*altitud*) height; **de gran** ~ high; **de poca** ~ low; **a gran** ~ at a great height; **una montaña de 2000 metros de** ~ a 2000-metre-high mountain; **el avión pierde** ~ the plane is losing altitude 2.(*estatura*) height 3.(*de un sonido*) pitch 4.(*excelencia*) excellence 5. *pl* (*cielo*) heaven ►**estar a la** ~ **del betún** *inf* to look really stupid; **estar a la** ~ **de las circunstancias** to rise to the occasion; **estar a la** ~ **de Valencia** to be in the vicinity of Valencia; **a estas** ~**s** at this point

alubia *f* bean

alucinación *f* hallucination

alucinado, -a *adj inf* (*asombrado*) **miraba** ~ **a la chica** he looked at the girl in amazement; **me quedé** ~ **al leerlo en el periódico** I was stunned on reading it in the newpaper

alucinante *adj inf* 1.(*estupendo*) fantastic 2.(*increíble*) incredible

alucinar I. *vi inf* 1.(*hablando*) to hallucinate; **¡tú alucinas!** *fig* you're crazy! 2.(*quedar fascinado*) to be fascinated; **aluciné con sus conocimientos de chino** I was amazed by his/her knowledge of Chinese II. *vt inf* 1.(*pasmar*) to amaze 2.(*fascinar*) to fascinate

alud *m* 1.(*de nieve*) avalanche 2.(*de gente*) **un** ~ **de gente** a throng of people

aludir *vi* (*referirse*) to allude; (*mencionar*) to mention; **darse por aludido** (*ofenderse*) to take it personally; **no darse por aludido** not to take the hint

alumbrado *m* lighting; ~ **público** street lighting

alumbramiento *m* 1.(*iluminación*) lighting

2. (*parto*) childbirth
alumbrar I. *vi* **1.** (*iluminar*) to give off light; **la lámpara alumbra poco** the lamp doesn't give off much light **2.** (*parir*) to give birth **II.** *vt* **1.** (*iluminar*) to light (up); (*a alguien*) to shine a light on **2.** (*parir*) to give birth to **III.** *vr:* ~**se** *inf* to get tipsy
aluminio *m* aluminium *Brit,* aluminum *Am*
alumnado *m* (*de escuela*) pupils *pl;* (*de universidad*) students *pl*
alumno, -a *m, f* (*de escuela*) pupil; (*de universidad*) student
alunizaje *m* moon landing
alunizar <z→c> *vi* to land on the moon
alusión *f* **1.** (*mención*) ~ **a algo** mention of sth **2.** (*insinuación*) allusion; **hacer una** ~ **a algo** to allude to sth
alusivo, -a *adj* ~ **a algo** regarding sth; **dijo una frase alusiva a la situación** he/she said a few words about the situation
aluvión *m* **1.** (*inundación*) *t. fig* flood **2.** (*sedimento*) alluvium; **tierra de** ~ alluvial soil
álveo *m* riverbed
alveolo *m,* **alvéolo** *m* **1.** ANAT alveolus **2.** (*del panal*) cell
alza *f* **1.** (*elevación*) rise; ~ **abusiva de los precios** extortionate price rise; **ir** [*o* **estar**] **en** ~ (*precios*) to be rising; (*persona*) to be up- -and-coming **2.** (*de un zapato*) raised insole **3.** (*de un arma*) sight
alzada *f* **1.** (*de un caballo*) height **2.** JUR appeal
alzado *m* ARQUIT elevation
alzado, -a *adj* **1.** (*fijado*) fixed **2.** (*sublevado*) raised **3.** *AmL* (*montaraz*) wild; (*en celo*) on heat
alzamiento *m* uprising
alzar <z→c> **I.** *vt* **1.** (*levantar*) to lift (up); (*precio, voz*) to raise **2.** (*poner vertical*) to put up **3.** (*sostener*) to hold up **4.** (*quitar*) to remove; (*colcha, mantel*) to take off; (*mesa*) to put away; (*campamento*) to break **5.** (*construir*) to erect **6.** AGR (*cosecha*) to gather in **II.** *vr:* ~**se 1.** (*levantarse, destacar*) to rise (up); **allí se alza la universidad** the university buildings rise up over there **2.** JUR to appeal **3.** *AmL* (*animales*) to become wild **4.** *AmL* (*sublevarse*) to revolt **5.** *AmL* (*robar*) to steal; ~**se con la pasta** *inf* to make off with the money [*o* dough]
ama *f* (*dueña*) mistress; (*propietaria*) owner; ~ **de casa** housewife; ~ **de cría** wet nurse; ~ **de llaves** housekeeper
amabilidad *f* kindness; **tuvo la** ~ **de avisarme** he/she was kind enough to warn me; **le agradezco su** ~ thank you for your kindness
amable *adj* kind; **ser** ~ (**para**) **con alguien** to be kind to sb; **¿sería Ud. tan** ~ **de explicármelo?** would you be so kind as to explain it to me?
amadrinar *vt* ~ **algo** to act as sponsor to sth; ~ **a alguien** to be godmother to sb
amaestrar *vt* **1.** (*animales*) to train; (*caballos*) to break in **2.** *pey* (*niños*) to train

3. (*instruir*) to coach
amagar <g→gu> **I.** *vi* **1.** (*amenazar*) to threaten; **estaba amagando la guerra cuando...** war was threatening to break out when ... **2.** (*enfermedad*) to show the first symptoms **II.** *vt* **1.** (*indicar*) **amagó un golpe** he/she made as if to strike **2.** (*amenazar*) to threaten; ~ **a alguien con algo** to threaten sb with sth
amago *m* **1.** (*amenaza*) threat **2.** (*indicio*) hint **3.** DEP feint
amainar I. *vi* to abate **II.** *vt* NÁUT to shorten
amalaya *interj AmL* I wish
amalgama *f* **1.** QUÍM amalgam **2.** (*mezcla*) mixture
amalgamar I. *vt* **1.** TÉC to amalgamate **2.** (*mezclar*) to mix **3.** (*unir*) to unite **II.** *vr:* ~**se** to amalgamate
amamantar *vt* (*bebé*) to breastfeed; (*cachorro*) to suckle
amancebamiento *m* cohabitation
amancebarse *vr* to cohabit
amanecer I. *vimpers* to dawn; **está amaneciendo** it's getting light **II.** *irr como crecer vi* to wake up **III.** *m* dawn; **al** ~ at dawn
amanecida *f AmL* dawn
amanerado, -a *adj* **1.** (*persona*) affected **2.** (*estilo*) mannered
amanerarse *vr* (*persona*) to become affected
amanezquera *f Méx, PRico* (*alba*) dawn; **en la** [*o* **de**] ~ at daybreak
amansador *m Méx* (*domador*) horse breaker
amansar I. *vt* **1.** (*animal*) to tame **2.** (*persona*) to subdue; (*sosegar*) to calm down **II.** *vr:* ~**se** to become tame
amante I. *adj* **soy poco** ~ **de hablar en público** I don't like speaking in public **II.** *mf* (*querido, aficionado*) lover; **un** ~ **de la naturaleza** a nature-lover
amanuense *mf* **1.** (*secretario*) secretary **2.** (*copista*) copyist
amañar I. *vt* **1.** (*plan, asunto*) to fix; ~ **una solución** to cook up a solution **2.** (*resultado, documento*) to fake **II.** *vr* ~**se con alguien** to get along well with sb; **amañárselas** (**para todo**) to manage to get by (in everything)
amaño *m* skill; **con** ~ skilfully *Brit,* skillfully *Am*
amapola *f* poppy ▶ **ponerse como una** ~ to turn as red as a beetroot [*o* beet *Am*]
amar *vt* to love
amaraje *m* water landing; **efectuar el** ~ to splash down
amarar *vi* to land on water
amargar <g→gu> **I.** *vt* to make bitter; ~ **la vida a alguien** to make life difficult for sb **II.** *vi* to be bitter; **la verdad amarga** the bitter truth **III.** *vr:* ~**se** to become bitter
amargo, -a *adj* bitter
amargor *m,* **amargura** *f* bitterness; **llorar con** ~ to weep bitterly
amarillear *vi* to turn [*o* go] yellow
amarillento, -a *adj* yellowish; (*fotografía,*

papel) yellowed

amarillismo *m sin pl* sensationalism

amarillo, -a *adj* 1.(*color*) yellow 2.(*pálido*) pale

amarra *f* 1. NÁUT hawser 2. *pl* (*apoyo*) connections *pl*

amarradero *m* 1.(*poste*) post, bollard 2.(*argolla*) mooring ring 3. NÁUT berth

amarrado, -a I. *pp* de **amarrar** II. *adj Arg, Par, PRico, Urug* (*tacaño*) mean *Brit,* stingy *Am;* (*innoble*) ignoble

amarrar I. *vt* 1.(*atar*) to tie up 2. NÁUT to moor 3. *inf* (*empollar*) to swot *Brit,* to cram *Am;* **estar** [*o* ir] **amarrado** (*haber empollado*) to have crammed; (*tener enchufe*) to have good connections ▶**tener a alguien muy amarrado** *inf* to keep sb under tight control II. *vr:* ~**se** *AmL* to get married

amartelarse *vr* 1.(*enamorarse*) ~**se de alguien** to fall in love with sb 2.(*ponerse cariñoso*) to smooch *inf*

amartillar *vt* 1.(*arma*) to cock 2. *inf* (*negocio*) to secure

amartizaje *m* landing on Mars

amasandería *f Chile* bakery

amasar *vt* 1.(*masa*) to knead 2.(*fortuna*) to amass 3. *pey* (*tramar*) to concoct

amasiato *m Méx, CRi, Perú* (*concubinato*) concubinage

amasijar *vt AmL* (*dar paliza*) to give a beating; (*pegar brutalmente*) to beat to a pulp

amasijo *m* 1.(*para hacer pan*) dough 2.(*acción de amasar*) kneading 3.(*argamasa*) mortar 4. *inf* (*mezcla*) mixture 5. *inf* (*intriga*) scheme

amateur I. *adj* amateur II. *mf* <amateurs> amateur

amatista *f* amethyst

amatorio, -a *adj* amatory

amauta *m Bol, Perú* 1.(*mago y sabio de los incas*) Incan sage 2.(*autoridad en pueblo indio*) village elder

amazacotado, -a *adj* 1.(*colchón*) lumpy 2.(*recargado*) overloaded; **un informe ~ de datos** a report crammed with facts; **estuvimos ~s en el tranvía** we were packed into the tram like sardines

amazona *f* 1.(*mujer*) amazon 2. DEP rider 3.(*traje*) riding habit

ambages *mpl* **¡habla sin ~!** don't beat about the bush!

ámbar *adj, m inv* amber

Amberes *m* Antwerp

ambición *f* ambition; **~ de poder** hunger for power; **sin ambiciones** unambitious; **mi ~ en la vida es...** my ambition in life is ...

ambicionar *vt* to aspire to; **sólo ambiciono salud** I only want to be healthy

ambicioso, -a *adj* ambitious

ambientación *f* 1. CINE, LIT setting 2.(*ambiente*) atmosphere 3. RADIO sound effects *pl*

ambientador *m* air freshener

ambientar I. *vt* 1.(*novela*) to set; **~ la acción de una novela en el siglo pasado** to set a novel in the last century; **la novela está ambientada en Lima** the novel is set in Lima 2.(*fiesta*) to enliven II. *vr:* ~**se** 1.(*aclimatarse*) to adjust 2.(*en una fiesta*) to get into the mood

ambiente *m* 1.(*aire*) air 2.(*medio*) surroundings *pl;* **medio ~** environment; **nocivo para el medio ~** harmful to the environment 3.(*social*) milieu 4.(*atmósfera*) atmosphere; **dar ~** to create a favourable atmosphere; **no había ~ en la calle** there wasn't much happening in the street; **el ~ en la reunión estaba caldeado** the atmosphere at the meeting was very tense 5. *CSur, Perú* (*habitación*) room; **un departamento de cuatro ~s** a four-room flat

ambigüedad *f* ambiguity; **sin ~es** unambiguous

ambiguo, -a *adj* 1.(*de doble significado*) ambiguous 2. LING *having two genders*

ámbito *m* 1.(*contorno*) surroundings *pl* 2.(*espacio*) area; **en el ~ nacional** on a national level

ambivalente *adj* ambivalent

ambo *m Arg* two-piece suit

ambos, -as *adj* both

ambulancia *f* 1.(*vehículo*) ambulance 2. MIL field hospital 3. FERRO **~ de correos** mail wagon

ambulante I. *adj* walking; **circo ~** travelling circus; **vendedor ~** pedlar *Brit,* peddler *Am;* **venta ~** peddling II. *mf* **~ de correos** railway post-office employee

ambulatorio *m* outpatient department

ambulatorio, -a *adj* outpatient

ameba *f* amoeba *Brit,* ameba *Am*

amedrentar I. *vt* 1.(*asustar*) to scare 2.(*intimidar*) to intimidate II. *vr:* ~**se** 1.(*asustarse*) to get scared 2.(*intimidarse*) to be intimidated

amelcochar I. *vt Arg, Méx, Par* (*almíbar*) to thicken II. *vi* 1. *Cuba* (*enamorarse*) to fall in love 2. *Méx* (*reblandecerse*) to soften

amén I. *m* amen; **decir ~ a todo** to agree to everything; **no decir ni ~** not to say a word; **en un decir ~** *inf* in a flash II. *prep* **~ de** except for

amenaza *f* 1.(*intimidación*) threat; **bajo la ~ de violencia** under the threat of violence 2.(*peligro*) menace

amenazador(a) *adj* 1.(*tono*) threatening; **gesto ~** threatening gesture 2.(*que anuncia peligro*) menacing

amenazar <z→c> I. *vt* (*intimidar*) to threaten; **el jefe lo ha amenazado con despedirle** the boss has threatened him with dismissal II. *vi, vt* (*presagiar*) to threaten; **amenaza tormenta** there's a storm in the offing; **está amenazando lluvia** it's threatening to rain

amenidad *f* 1.(*carácter de lo agradable*)

pleasantness **2.** (*entretenimiento*) entertainment **3.** (*distracción*) enjoyment

amenizar <z→c> *vt* **1.** (*hacer agradable*) to make pleasant **2.** (*entretener*) to entertain **3.** (*conversación*) to liven up

ameno, -a *adj* **1.** (*agradable*) pleasant **2.** (*entretenido*) entertaining

América *f* America; ~ **Central** Central America; ~ **Latina** Latin America; ~ **del Norte/del Sur** North/South America ►**hacer las ~s** to make a fortune

Many Spaniards emigrated to Latin America in the 19th and 20th centuries. The expression "**hacer las Américas**" refers directly to this fact and more or less means to make one's fortune in the Americas.

americana *f* jacket

americanismo *m* LING Americanism

americanista *mf* Americanist

americano, -a **I.** *adj* (*de América del Sur*) South American; (*estadounidense*) American; **el estilo de vida** ~ the American way of life **II.** *m, f* (*de América del Sur*) South American; (*estadounidense*) American

amerindio, -a **I.** *adj* American Indian, Amerindian **II.** *m, f* American Indian, Amerindian

amerizar <z→c> *vi* to land on water

ametralladora *f* machine gun

ametrallar *vt* to machine-gun

amianto *m* asbestos

amigable *adj* friendly

amígdala *f* tonsil

amigdalitis *f inv* tonsillitis *Brit,* tonsilitis *Am*

amigo, -a **I.** *adj* **1.** (*que tiene la amistad, amistoso*) friendly; **es muy amiga mía** she's a good friend of mine; **somos** (**muy**) **~s desde la infancia** we've been close friends since our childhood **2.** (*aficionado, partidario*) **ser ~ de algo** to be fond of sth; **soy más ~ de veranear en el campo que en la costa** I prefer spending the summer in the country rather than at the seaside; **soy ~ de decir las cosas claras** I'm in favour of calling a spade a spade; **este tipo es muy ~ de lucir** this guy is a great one for showing off ►**¡y tan ~s!** and that's that! **II.** *m, f* **1.** (*general*) friend; ~ **de lo ajeno** thief; ~ **por correspondencia** penfriend *Brit,* penpal *Am;* **hacerse ~ de alguien** to make friends with sb; **poner a alguien cara de pocos ~s** to look grimly at sb **2.** (*amante*) lover **3.** (*adepto*) supporter

amiguete *m inf* pal, mate *Brit,* buddy *Am*

amilanar **I.** *vt* **1.** (*intimidar*) to intimidate **2.** (*desanimar*) to discourage **II.** *vr:* ~**se** **1.** (*acobardarse*) to become frightened **2.** (*abatirse*) to become discouraged

aminoácido *m* amino acid

aminorar **I.** *vi* to diminish **II.** *vt* to reduce; ~ **el paso** to slacken one's pace

amistad *f* **1.** (*entre amigos*) friendship; **tener ~ con alguien** to be friendly with sb; **trabar ~**

con alguien to become friends with sb; **hacer las ~es con alguien** to make it up with sb **2.** *pl* (*amigos*) friends *pl*

amistar **I.** *vi Méx* to befriend **II.** *vr:* ~**se** *CSur* to become friends

amistoso, -a *adj* (*persona, cosa*) friendly, amicable; **partido** ~ friendly match; **llegar a un acuerdo** ~ to come to an amicable agreement

amnesia *f sin pl* amnesia

amnistía *f* amnesty; **Amnistía Internacional** Amnesty International; **conceder ~ a alguien** to grant an amnesty to sb

amnistiar <1. *pres:* amnistío> *vt* to grant an amnisty

amo *m* **1.** (*de la casa*) head of the household **2.** (*propietario*) owner **3.** (*patrón*) boss; **ser el ~ en algo** to be the boss in sth ►**ser el ~ del cotarro** *inf* to be the top dog; **hacerse el ~** (**de una asociación**) to become the leader (of an association)

amodorrarse *vr* to become drowsy [*o* sleepy]

amojonar *vt* to mark the boundary of

amoldar **I.** *vt* **1.** (*ajustar al molde*) to adjust **2.** (*moldear*) to mould *Brit,* to mold *Am* **3.** (*acomodar*) to adapt **II.** *vr:* ~**se** to adapt oneself

amonarse *vr inf* to get tipsy

amonestación *f* **1.** (*advertencia*) warning; (*represión*) reprimand; **tarjeta de ~** DEP yellow card **2.** (*de los novios*) marriage banns *pl;* **correr las amonestaciones** to publish the banns

amonestar **I.** *vt* **1.** (*advertir*) to warn; (*reprender*) to reprimand **2.** (*los novios*) to publish the banns of **II.** *vr:* ~**se** to have the banns published

amoníaco *m* ammonia

amontonar **I.** *vt* **1.** (*tierra, heno*) to pile up **2.** (*conocimientos, dinero*) to accumulate; **los refugiados estaban amontonados en el transbordador** the refugees were crowded together on the ferry **II.** *vr:* ~**se** **1.** (*cosas*) to pile up **2.** (*personas*) to crowd together **3.** (*sucesos, noticias*) to accumulate

amor *m* love; ~ **al prójimo** love for one's neighbour; ~ **propio** self-esteem; ~ **a primera vista** love at first sight; **¡~ mío!** my love!; **mi gran ~ es el cine** my great passion is the cinema; **hacer el ~ con alguien** *inf* to make love with sb; **hacer algo con ~** to do sth lovingly ►**por ~ al arte** for nothing; **en ~ y compaña** in peace and harmony; **¡por ~ de Dios!** for God's sake!; **con** [*o* **de**] **mil ~es** with the greatest of pleasure; ~ **con ~ se paga** *prov* one good turn deserves another

amoratado, -a *adj* purple; **un ojo** ~ a black eye; **tengo los labios ~s de frío** my lips are blue with cold; **tengo el brazo ~ de la caída** my arm is bruised from the fall

amordazar <z→c> *vt* **1.** (*poner mordaza*) to gag **2.** (*hacer callar*) to silence, to gag

amorfo, -a *adj* shapeless, amorphous

amorío(s) *m(pl) pey* love affair

amoroso, -a *adj* **1.**(*de amor*) loving **2.**(*cariñoso*) ~ con/para con alguien affectionate to/towards sb **3.**(*tierra, tela*) soft **4.**(*tiempo*) mild

amorrar I. *vi inf* **1.**(*bajar la cabeza*) to hang one's head **2.**(*mostrar enfado*) to sulk **II.** *vr:* ~**se 1.** *inf* (*enfadarse*) to get angry **2.** *inf* (*al beber*) ~**se a la botella** to put the bottle to one's lips

amortiguador *m* AUTO shock absorber

amortiguar <gu→gü> *vt* (*sonido*) to muffle; (*golpe, caída*) to cushion; (*pena, dolor*) to soothe; (*sentimiento*) to deaden; ~ **los faros** AUTO to dim one's headlights

amortización *f* **1.**(*de una deuda*) repayment **2.**(*fiscal*) depreciation

amortizar <z→c> *vt* **1.**(*deuda*) to pay off **2.**(*fiscalmente*) to write off **3.**(*inversión*) to recover **4.**(*empleos*) to cut back on

amoscarse <c→qu> *vr;* **amostazarse** <z→c> *vr inf* to go into a huff

amotinado, -a I. *adj* rebel **II.** *m, f* rebel

amotinar I. *vt* to stir up **II.** *vr:* ~**se** to rebel

amparar I. *vt* to protect; ~ **a alguien** to shelter sb; **la constitución ampara la libertad de religión** the constitution guarantees religious freedom **II.** *vr:* ~**se** to seek protection; ~**se bajo algo** to shelter behind sth; **se ampara en una ley antigua** he/she has recourse to an old law; **el espía se amparó en la oscuridad para escapar** the spy escaped under cover of darkness

amparo *m* **1.**(*protección*) protection; **estar al** ~ **de alguien** to be under sb's protection; **al** ~ **de la oscuridad** under cover of darkness **2.**(*refugio*) shelter

amperio *m* amp

ampliación *f* **1.**(*engrandecimiento*) enlargement; (*de un número, el capital*) increase; (*de un territorio*) expansion; (*de un edificio, una carretera*) extension; ~ **del surtido** stock enlargement **2.**(*de conocimientos*) broadening **3.**(*de un sonido*) amplification; ~ **de RAM** INFOR RAM expansion

ampliamente *adv* **1.**(*cumplidamente*) amply **2.**(*extensamente*) extensively; **las condiciones han mejorado** ~ conditions have considerably improved

ampliar <*1. pres:* amplío> *vt* **1.**(*hacer más grande*) to enlarge; (*capital, número*) to increase; (*territorio*) to expand; (*edificio, carretera*) to extend; **edición ampliada** extended edition **2.**(*conocimientos*) to broaden **3.**(*sonido*) to amplify

amplificador *m* amplifier

amplificar <c→qu> *vt* to amplify

amplio, -a *adj* **1.**(*casa*) spacious; (*jardín, parque*) extensive **2.**(*vestido*) loose-fitting **3.**(*informe*) detailed; (*experiencia, poderes*) wide-ranging; (*red de comunicaciones*) extensive; (*interés*) broad; **una derrota amplia** a serious defeat; **amplias partes de la pobla-**

ción large sections of the population; **en un sentido más** ~ in a wider sense

amplitud *f* **1.**(*extensión*) extent; (*de conocimientos*) range; (*de un informe*) extensiveness; ~ **de miras** broad-minded; ~ **del surtido** ECON range of stock; **de gran** ~ wide-ranging **2.**(*de una casa*) roominess; (*de un jardín, parque*) extensiveness **3.** FÍS amplitude

ampolla *f* **1.**(*en la piel, burbuja*) blister; **tener** ~**s en los pies** to have blisters on one's feet **2.**(*garrafa*) flask **3.**(*para inyecciones*) ampoule *Brit,* ampule *Am* ▶ **levantar** ~**s** to get people's backs up

ampolleta *f Arg* lightbulb

ampuloso, -a *adj* pompous

amputar *vt* to amputate

amuchar *vt Arg, Bol, Chile* to multiply

amueblar *vt* to furnish

amuermado, -a *adj inf* **1.** *ser* boring **2.** *estar* bored

amuermar I. *vt inf* **1.**(*aburrir*) to bore **2.**(*calor*) to make drowsy **II.** *vr:* ~**se** *inf* to get bored

amularse *vr Méx* **1.**(*mercancía*) to become unsellable **2.**(*persona*) to get stubborn

amuleto *m* amulet

amurallar *vt* to wall

anabolizante *m* anabolic steroid

anacardo *m* **1.** BOT cashew tree **2.**(*fruto*) cashew (nut)

anaconda *f* anaconda

ánade *mf* duck

anagrama *m* anagram

anal *adj* anal

anales *mpl* **1.** HIST annals *pl* **2.**(*de una universidad, sociedad*) records *pl*

analfabetismo *m sin pl* illiteracy

analfabeto, -a *m, f* illiterate (person)

analgésico *m* painkiller

análisis *m inv* **1.**(*general*) *t.* MAT analysis; ~ **de sistemas** INFOR systems analysis; ~ **de la situación económica** analysis of the economic situation; **¿qué** ~ **haces de la situación?** what's your analysis of the situation? **2.** MED test; ~ **del grupo sanguíneo** blood test (*to determine blood group*)

analista *mf* **1.**(*de anales*) chronicler **2.**(*que analiza*) analyst; ~ **político** political analyst; ~ **de sistemas** INFOR systems analyst; **el médico mandó las pruebas al** ~ the doctor sent the samples to the laboratory

analítico, -a *adj* analytic(al)

analizar <z→c> *vt* **1.**(*examinar*) *t.* MED to analyse *Brit,* to analyze *Am* **2.** LING to parse

analogía *f* analogy; **por** ~ **con algo** on the analogy of sth

análogo, -a *adj* analogous

ananá(s) *m CSur* pineapple

anaquel *m* shelf

anaranjado, -a *adj* orange

anarquía *f* anarchy

anárquico, -a *adj* anarchic

anarquismo *m sin pl* anarchism
anarquista I. *adj* anarchist II. *mf* anarchist
anatema *m o f* 1. (*maldición*) curse; **lanzar ~s contra alguien** to hurl abuse at sb 2. (*condena*) condemnation 3. (*excomunión*) anathema
anatematizar <z→c> *vt* 1. (*maldecir*) to curse 2. (*condenar*) to condemn 3. (*excomulgar*) to anathematize
anatomía *f* anatomy
anatómico, -a *adj* 1. MED anatomical 2. (*adaptado al cuerpo*) anatomically designed
anca *f* 1. (*de animal*) haunch; **~s de rana** frogs' legs 2. (*cadera*) hip 3. *pl, inf* (*nalgas*) backside ▸ **montar a las ~s** to sit behind
ancestral *adj* 1. (*relativo a los antepasados*) ancestral 2. (*antiguo*) ancient
ancho *m* width; **~ de vía** AUTO, FERRO gauge *Brit,* gage *Am;* **tener** [*o* **medir**] **cinco metros de ~** to be five metres wide
ancho, -a *adj* (*vasto*) wide; (*vestidos*) loose-fitting; **~ de espaldas** broad-shouldered; **a lo ~** widthways; **un árbol tumbado a lo ~ de la calle** a tree lying across the street ▸ **estar a sus anchas** to feel at ease; **en este pueblo estoy a mis anchas** I feel at home in this village; **se queda tan ~ cuando dice tonterías** he doesn't turn a hair when he talks nonsense; **venir a alguien muy ~** to be too much for sb
anchoa *f* anchovy
anchura *f* width; (*de un vestido*) looseness
ancianidad *f* old age
anciano, -a I. *adj* old II. *m, f* old man
ancla *f* anchor; **echar ~s** to drop anchor; **levar ~s** to weigh anchor
ancladero *m* anchorage
anclar *vi, vt* to anchor; **estar anclado** to be anchored
áncora *f* anchor
ancuviña *f* Chile 1. (*sepelio*) burial 2. (*tumba*) grave; **cavar una ~** to dig a grave
andadas *fpl* **volver a las ~** to revert to [*o* to fall back into] old habits
ándale *interj Méx* (*adios*) bye; (*deprisa*) come on
Andalucía *f* Andalusia
andaluz(a) *adj, m(f)* Andalusian
andamiaje *m,* **andamio** *m* scaffolding
andanada *f* volley; **lanzar una ~ contra alguien** *fig* to give sb a dressing-down; **por ~s** *Arg* in excess
andante *adj* errant; **parecer un cadáver ~** to look like death (warmed up)
andanza *f* 1. (*aventura*) adventure 2. (*suerte*) **buena ~** good fortune; **mala ~** misfortune
andar *irr* I. *vi* 1. (*caminar*) to walk; **~ a caballo** to ride (a horse); **~ a gatas** to go on all fours; (*bebés*) to crawl; **~ con paso majestuoso** to strut; **~ de prisa** to go quickly; **~ detrás de algo** to be after sth; **desde la estación hay 10 minutos andando** it's 10 minutes walk from the station; **esta niña andaba ya a los ocho meses** this girl was already walking

at the age of eight months 2. (*reloj, coche*) to go *Brit,* to run *Am;* (*máquina*) to work 3. (*tiempo*) to pass 4. (*estar*) **¿dónde está el periódico? – ~á por ahí** where's the newspaper? – it'll be around here somewhere; **~ atareado** to be busy; **~ metido en un asunto** to be involved in a matter; **~ haciendo algo** to be doing sth; **anda mucha gente buscando empleo** there are a lot of people looking for a job; **te ando llamando desde hace una hora** I've been trying to call you for an hour; **~ con gente de bien** to mix with respectable people; **los precios andan por las nubes** prices are sky-high; **~ mal de dinero** to be short of money; **andar mal de inglés** to be poor in English; **~emos por los 30 grados** it must be about 30 degrees; **~ por los 30** to be about 30; **no andes en mi escritorio** don't go rummaging in my desk ▸ **dime con quien andas y te diré quien eres** *prov* your friends are a guide to your character; **~ a la que salta** to seize the opportunity; **¡anda!** good heavens! II. *vt* he andado toda la casa para encontrarte I've looked all over the house for you III. *m* walk, gait
andariego, -a I. *adj* fond of travelling II. *m, f* wanderer
andas *fpl* portable platform ▸ **llevar a alguien en ~** to treat sb with great respect
andén *m* 1. FERRO platform 2. (*de muelle*) quayside 3. (*corredor*) corridor 4. (*de un puente*) footpath
Andes *mpl* **los ~** the Andes + *pl vb,* Andes
andinismo *m sin pl, AmL* mountaineering, mountain climbing
andinista *mf AmL* mountaineer, mountain climber
andino, -a *adj* Andean
Andorra *f* Andorra

Andorra is a small democratic state (only 467 square kilometres in area) that has a parliamentary principality as its form of government. It borders France to the north and east and Spain to the west and south.

---

andorrano, -a *adj, m, f* Andorran
andrajo *m* rag
andrajoso, -a *adj* ragged
andurrial *m Arg, Ecua, Perú* (*paraje pantanoso*) muddy road
andurrial(es) *m(pl)* godforsaken place
anécdota *f* anecdote
anegar <g→gu> I. *vt* 1. (*inundar*) to flood 2. (*ahogar*) to drown; **~ una sublevación en sangre** to suppress a revolt with violence II. *vr:* **~se** 1. (*campo*) to flood 2. (*ahogarse*) to drown; **~se en lágrimas** to dissolve into tears
anejo *m* 1. (*edificio*) annexe *Brit,* annex *Am* 2. (*carta*) enclosure 3. (*libro, revista*) supplement 4. (*en un libro*) appendix 5. INFOR attachment 6. (*pueblo*) district
anejo, -a *adj* (a edificios) joined; (a cartas)

A

enclosed
anemia *f sin pl* anaemia *Brit,* anemia *Am*
anémona *f* anemone
anestesia *f* anaesthesia *Brit,* anesthesia *Am*
anestesiar *vt* to anaesthetize *Brit,* to anesthetize *Am*
anestésico *m* anaesthetic *Brit,* anesthetic *Am*
anestesista *mf* anaesthetist *Brit,* anesthetist *Am*
anexión *f* annexation
anexionar *vt* to annex
anexo *m v.* **anejo**
anexo, -a *adj v.* **anejo, -a**
anfibio *m* (*animal, vehículo*) amphibian; (*avión*) seaplane
anfibio, -a *adj* amphibious; **animal** ~ amphibious animal; **vehículo** ~ amphibious vehicle
anfiteatro *m* 1. (*local*) amphitheatre *Brit,* amphitheater *Am* 2. (*en la universidad*) lecture theatre *Brit,* lecture hall *Am*
anfitrión, -ona *m, f* host *m,* hostess *f*
ánfora *f* 1. (*cántaro*) amphora 2. *Méx* (*electoral*) ballot box
angarillas *fpl* 1. (*andas*) litter 2. (*vinagreras*) cruet
ángel *m* angel; ~ **de la guarda** guardian angel; **tener mucho** ~ to be very charming
angelical *adj* angelic(al); **rostro** ~ angelic face
angina *f* ~ **de pecho** angina (pectoris); ~**s** sore throat
anglicismo *m* anglicism
angoleño, -a *adj, m, f* Angolan
angosto, -a *adj* narrow
angostura *f* 1. (*estrechez*) narrowness 2. (*paso estrecho*) narrows *pl*
anguila *f* 1. ZOOL eel 2. NÁUT slipway
angula *f* elver
angular I. *adj* angular II. *m* 1. FOTO **gran** ~ wide-angle lens 2. (*herramienta*) angle iron 3. **piedra** ~ cornerstone
ángulo *m* 1. MAT angle; ~ **recto** right angle; **en** ~ angled; ~ **de tiro** DEP angle of fire 2. (*rincón*) corner 3. (*arista*) edge 4. (*de vista*) angle of vision
anguloso, -a *adj* 1. (*lugar*) full of twists and turns 2. (*cara*) angular
angurria *f AmL: inf* 1. (*ganas*) craving; (*hambre*) ravenous hunger; *pey* (*glotonería*) gluttony 2. (*codicia*) greed
angurriento, -a *adj AmL* 1. *pey* (*glotón*) gluttonous; (*hambriento*) greedy; *t. fig* (*devorador*) voracious 2. (*codicioso*) avaricious
angustia *f* 1. (*temor*) anguish; ~ **vital** angst 2. (*aflicción*) anxiety; **dar** ~ to make anxious 3. (*aprieto*) distress
angustiar I. *vt* 1. (*acongojar*) to distress 2. (*causar temor*) to frighten 3. (*afligir*) to worry II. *vr:* ~**se** 1. (*afligirse*) to get worried 2. (*atemorizarse*) to get scared
angustioso, -a *adj* 1. (*lleno de angustia*) anguished 2. (*inquietante*) worrying 3. (*sofocante*) distressing

anhelante *adj* (*ansioso*) longing; **estar** ~ **por algo** to be longing for sth
anhelar I. *vi* to pant II. *vt* to long for
anhelo *m* ~ **de algo** longing for sth
anidar I. *vi* 1. (*hacer nido*) to nest 2. (*morar*) to live II. *vt* to take in
anilla *f* 1. (*aro t. para pájaros*) ring; (*de puro*) band 2. *pl* DEP rings *pl*
anillo *m* ring; ~ **de boda** wedding ring; ~ (**de crecimiento**) BOT growth ring ▸**venir como** ~ **al** dedo to be just right; **ese vestido te viene como** ~ **al** dedo this dress suits you perfectly; **no se me** caen **los** ~**s por...** it's not beneath me to ...
ánima *f* soul ▸**a las** ~**s** in the evening
animación *f* 1. (*acción de animarse*) *t.* CINE, INFOR animation; **dar** ~ to animate 2. (*viveza*) liveliness 3. (*actividad*) activity; **había mucha** ~ **en la calle** the street was very busy
animado, -a *adj* 1. (*persona*) in high spirits; **no estar muy** ~ not to be very cheerful 2. (*lugar*) busy 3. (*actividad*) lively 4. (*tener ganas*) **estar** ~ **a hacer algo** to be keen on doing sth 5. INFOR ~ **por ordenador** computer--animated
animador(a) I. *adj* encouraging II. *m(f)* 1. (*artista*) entertainer 2. (*de turistas*) host *m,* hostess *f* 3. (*presentador*) presenter 4. DEP cheerleader
animadversión *f* hostility; **sentir** ~ **por alguien** to feel hostile towards sb
animal I. *adj* 1. (*relativo a los animales*) animal; **comportamiento** ~ animal behaviour 2. (*grosero*) rude; **el aspecto** ~ **del hombre** the animal side of man II. *m* 1. ZOOL animal; ~**es de caza** game; ~ **de compañía** pet; ~ **de presa** predator; **comer como un** ~ *inf* to eat like a horse 2. *pey* (*persona ignorante*) fool; (*bruta*) brute
animalada *f inf* 1. (*disparate*) (piece of) nonsense 2. (*barbaridad*) disgrace; **¡qué** ~**!** how outrageous! 3. (*cantidad*) massive amount
animar I. *vt* 1. (*infundir vida*) to liven up 2. (*alentar*) to encourage 3. (*persona triste*) to cheer up 4. (*habitación*) to brighten up; (*economía*) to stimulate II. *vr:* ~**se** 1. (*cobrar vida*) to liven up 2. (*atreverse*) to dare 3. (*decidirse*) to decide; **¡por fin te has animado a escribir** (**una carta**)**!** so you've finally decided to write (a letter)!; **¿te** animas**?** will you have a go? 4. (*alegrarse*) to cheer up
ánimo *m* 1. (*espíritu*) spirit; **no estoy con** ~**s de...** I don't feel like ... 2. (*energía*) energy; (*valor*) courage; **cobrar** ~ to take heart; **dar** ~ to encourage; **¡**~**!** cheer up! 3. (*intención*) intention; **con** ~ **de...** with the intention of ...; **sin** ~ **de lucro** non-profit-making; **sin** ~ **de ofender a nadie** without wishing to offend anyone
animosidad *f* (*animadversión*) animosity
animoso, -a *adj* (*valeroso*) brave
aniñado, -a *adj* childlike; *pey* childish
aniquilar I. *vt* 1. (*destruir*) to annihilate; ~

todas las esperanzas to destroy all hope
2. (*salud*) to ruin **3.** (*desanimar*) to shatter
II. *vr:* **~se 1.** (*desaparecer*) to be annihilated
2. (*deteriorarse*) to deteriorate
anís <anises> *m* **1.** (*planta*) anise; (*semilla*)
aniseed **2.** (*licor*) anisette
aniversario *m* anniversary; **~ de bodas** wedding anniversary; **~ de muerte de alguien**
anniversary of sb's death
ano *m* ANAT anus; **~ artificial** colostomy
anoche *adv* (*al atardecer*) last night; **antes de
~** the night before last; **~ no pude dormir** I
couldn't sleep last night
anochecer **I.** *irr como crecer vimpers*
anochece it's getting dark **II.** *irr como crecer
vi* anochecimos en Burgos we arrived in
Burgos at nightfall **III.** *m* nightfall; **al ~** at
nightfall
anodino, -a *adj* **1.** (*cosa*) insipid **2.** (*persona*)
bland **3.** MED anodyne
ánodo *m* anode
anomalía *f* anomaly
anonadar **I.** *vt* **1.** (*pasmar*) to astound;
(*maravillar*) to overwhelm; **la noticia me
dejó anonadado** I was astonished by the
news **2.** (*aniquilar*) to destroy **3.** (*descorazonar*) to discourage **II.** *vr:* **~se 1.** (*descorazonarse*) to be discouraged **2.** (*aniquilarse*) to
be destroyed
anonimato *m* anonymity; **mantener el ~** to
remain anonymous
anónimo *m* **1.** (*autor*) anonymous author;
(*escrito*) anonymous work **2.** (*anonimato*)
anonymity; **guardar el ~** to preserve one's
anonymity
anónimo, -a *adj* anonymous; **sociedad
anónima** ECON limited liability company *Brit,*
public corporation *Am*
anorak <anoraks> *m* anorak
anorexia *f* anorexia
anormal *adj* (*no normal*) abnormal; **~** (*físico*)
physically handicapped; **~** (*síquico*) mentally
handicapped
anotación *f* **1.** (*acción de anotar*) annotation;
(*en un registro*) record **2.** (*nota*) note **3.** FIN
entry; **~ de intereses** credit (entry)
anotar *vt* (*apuntar*) to note (down); (*en un
registro*) to record
anquilosamiento *m* paralysis
anquilosar **I.** *vt* to paralyze **II.** *vr:* **~se 1.** (*las
articulaciones*) to get stiff **2.** (*paralizarse*) to
become paralyzed **3.** (*mentalmente*) to ossify
ánsar *m* goose
ansia *f* **1.** (*angustia*) anguish **2.** (*intranquilidad*) anxiety **3.** (*afán*) longing; **~ de poder**
craving for power **4.** *pl* (*náusea*) nausea
ansiar <*1. pres:* ansío> *vt* to long for; **el
momento ansiado** the long-awaited moment;
lograr la tan ansiada copa to win the much-longed-for cup; **~ el regreso de alguien** to
long for sb's return
ansiedad *f* anxiety
ansiosamente *adv* esperamos **~** su visita

we eagerly await your visit; **la esperaba ~ en
la estación** he waited for her anxiously in the
station
ansioso, -a *adj* **1.** (*intranquilo*) anxious
2. (*anheloso*) eager **3.** (*impaciente*) impatient
4. (*codicioso*) greedy
antagónico, -a *adj* **1.** (*opuesto*) opposed
2. (*rival*) antagonistic
antagonismo *m* (*oposición*) opposition;
(*rivalidad*) antagonism
antagonista *mf* antagonist
antaño *adv* long ago
antártico, -a *adj* Antarctic; **el polo ~** the
South Pole; **Océano Glacial Antártico** Antarctic Ocean
Antártida *f* Antarctica
ante **I.** *m* **1.** ZOOL elk **2.** (*piel*) suede **II.** *prep*
1. (*posición, con movimiento*) before **2.** (*en
vista de*) in view of **3.** (*adversario*) faced with
anteanoche *adv* the night before last
anteayer *adv* the day before yesterday
antebrazo *m* ANAT forearm
antecámara *f* anteroom
antecedente **I.** *adj* foregoing **II.** *m* **1.** LING
antecedent **2.** *pl* (*circunstancias*) history; (*de
una persona*) background; **~s penales** criminal record; **estar en ~s de algo** to be well
informed about sth; **poner a alguien en ~s
de algo** to fill sb in about sth
anteceder *vt* to precede
antecesor(a) *m(f)* **1.** (*en un cargo*) predecessor **2.** (*antepasado*) ancestor
antedicho, -a *adj* aforementioned, above-mentioned
antediluviano, -a *adj* antediluvian
antelación *f* con **~** in advance; **con la
debida ~** in good time
antemano *adv* de **~** in advance; **calcular de
~** to calculate in advance
antena *f* **1.** ZOOL antenna **2.** (*de telecomunicaciones*) aerial *Brit,* antenna *Am;* **~ colectiva**
communal aerial; **~ interior** indoor aerial;
estar en ~ to be on the air; **el programa lleva
un año en ~** the programme [*o* program *Am*]
has been running for a year **3.** NÁUT lateen yard
►**estar con las ~s puestas** *irón* to be all
ears
anteojeras *fpl* blinkers *pl Brit,* blinders *pl Am*
anteojo *m* **1.** (*catalejo*) telescope **2.** *pl*
(*gemelos*) opera glasses *pl;* (*prismáticos*) binoculars *pl;* (*lentes*) spectacles *pl*
antepasado, -a *m, f* ancestor
antepecho *m* **1.** (*barandilla*) handrail **2.** (*pretil*) parapet
antepenúltimo, -a *adj* last but two *Brit,* third
from the last *Am*
anteponer *irr como poner* **I.** *vt* **1.** (*poner delante*) **~ algo a algo** to place sth in front of sth
2. (*dar preferencia*) to give priority to **II.** *vr:*
~se 1. (*ponerse delante*) **~se a alguien** to
stand in front of sb **2.** (*tener preferencia*) to be
preferred
anteproyecto *m* draft

anterior I. *adj* previous; **la noche ~ había llovido** the night before it had rained; **en la página ~** on the preceding [*o* previous] page; **el presidente ~** the previous president II. *prep* **~ a** prior to

anterioridad I. *f* anteriority II. *prep* **con ~ a** prior to, before

anteriormente *adv* before, previously

antes I. *adv* **1.** (*de tiempo*) before; (*hace un rato*) just now; (*antiguamente*) formerly; (*primero*) first; **poco ~** shortly before; **piénsate ~ lo que dices** think before you speak; **ahora como ~** still; **~ con ~, cuanto ~** as soon as possible; **~ de nada** first of all; **~ que nada** above all; **los cardenales van ~ que los obispos** cardinals come before bishops **2.** (*comparativo*) rather II. *prep* **~ de** before III. *conj* **1.** (*temporal*) before; **~ (de) que llegues** before you arrive **2.** (*adversativo*) no estoy satisfecho con el examen, **~ bien decepcionado** I'm not happy with the examination, on the contrary, I'm disappointed IV. *adj* **ya habíamos visto a esta chica el día ~** we had already seen this girl the previous day

antesala *f* anteroom; **hacer ~** to wait (to be received)

antiaéreo, -a *adj* MIL anti-aircraft **antialcohólico, -a** I. *adj* teetotal II. *m*, *f* teetotaller

antiatómico, -a *adj* **refugio ~** fall-out shelter **antibalas** *adj inv* bullet-proof

antibiótico *m* antibiotic

antibloqueo *m* **sistema ~ de frenos** anti-lock braking system

anticiclón *m* anticyclone

anticipación *f* **1.** (*de una fecha*) bringing forward *Brit,* moving up *Am* **2.** (*de un suceso*) anticipation **3.** COM advance; **con ~** (*pago*) in advance

anticipadamente *adv* in advance; **jubilar ~ a alguien** to retire sb early

anticipado, -a *adj* (*elecciones*) early; **pagar por ~** to pay in advance

anticipar I. *vt* **1.** (*fecha*) to bring forward *Brit,* to move up *Am* **2.** (*suceso*) to anticipate; **no anticipemos los acontecimientos** let's not anticipate events **3.** (*dinero*) to advance; **~ una paga sobre el sueldo** to give an advance on a salary II. *vr* **~se a alguien** to beat sb to it; **el verano se ha anticipado este año** summer is early this year; **los invitados se han anticipado** the guests have arrived early

anticipo *m* **1.** (*del sueldo*) advance; **~ sobre el sueldo** advance on a salary **2.** (*de un pago*) advance payment

anticonceptivo *m* contraceptive, birth control method

anticonceptivo, -a *adj* contraceptive, birth-control; **píldora anticonceptiva** contraceptive pill

anticongelante *m* antifreeze **anticonstitucional** *adj* unconstitutional **anticorrosivo** *m* anticorrosive

anticuado, -a *adj* old-fashioned

anticuario, -a *m*, *f* (*vendedor*) antique dealer

anticuarse *vr* to become old-fashioned

anticucho *m Perú* kebob

anticuerpo *m* antibody **antideportivo, -a** *adj* unsporting **antideslizante** *adj* (*superficie*) non-slip; (*neumático*) non-skid **antidoping** *adj inv* **control ~** drugs test

antídoto *m* antidote

antieconómico, -a *adj* uneconomic(al)

antier *adv AmL, inf* the day before yesterday

antiestético, -a *adj* unattractive

antifaz *m* mask

antifris *m inv, AmL* anti-freeze

antigás *adj inv* **máscara ~** gasmask

antigualla *f pey* **1.** (*objeto*) piece of junk **2.** (*costumbre, estilo*) relic

antiguamente *adv* once, long ago

antigubernamental *adj* anti-governmental

antigüedad *f* **1.** (*edad antigua*) antiquity; **la ~ clásica** classical antiquity **2.** (*objeto*) antique **3.** (*edad*) age; **tener una ~ de 100 años** to be 100 years old **4.** (*en una empresa*) seniority; **tengo 5 años de ~** (**en el trabajo**) I've been working for 5 years (in the job)

antiguo, -a *adj* <antiquísimo> **1.** (*de muchos años*) old; (*relación*) long-standing **2.** (*anticuado*) antiquated; (*muy anticuado*) ancient; **a la antigua** in the old-fashioned way; **está chapado a la antigua** he is old-fashioned **3.** (*de la antigüedad*) ancient **4.** (*anterior*) former **5.** (*en un cargo*) **es el más ~ en esta empresa** he's the most senior member of staff in this firm

antihigiénico, -a *adj* unhygienic **antiinflacionista** *adj* anti-inflationary; **lucha ~** fight against inflation **antiinflamatorio, -a** *adj* anti-inflammatory

antílope *m* antelope

antinatural *adj* unnatural

antinomia *f* antinomy

antiparras *fpl inf* specs *pl*

antipatía *f* antipathy; **~ a** [*o* contra] alguien antipathy for sb

antipático, -a *adj* unpleasant

antipirético *m* MED, **antipirina** *f AmL* MED antipyretic, antifebrile

antiquísimo, -a *adj superl de* **antiguo**

antirreglamentario, -a *adj* unlawful; **entrada antirreglamentaria** DEP foul **antirrobo** *m* anti-theft device **antisemita** I. *adj* anti-Semitic II. *mf* anti-Semite **antisemitismo** *m sin pl* anti-Semitism

antiséptico, -a *adj* antiseptic **antisísmico, -a** *adj* earthquake-proof **antisocial** *adj* anti-social **antiterrorista** *adj* antiterrrorist; **lucha ~** fight against terrorism

antítesis *f inv* antithesis

antojadizo, -a *adj* capricious

antojarse *vimpers* **1.** (*encapricharse*) **se le antojó comprarse un coche nuevo** he/she took it into his/her head to buy a new car; **se me antojó un helado** I fancied an ice cream;

hace siempre lo que se le antoja he/she always does as he/she pleases 2.(*tener la sensación*) se me antoja que no vas a venir I've a feeling that you're not going to come; se me antoja que va a nevar I think it's going to snow

antojitos *mpl Méx* GASTR appetizers *pl*

antojo *m* 1.(*capricho*) whim; a mi ~ as I please 2.(*de una embarazada*) craving; tener ~s (*ganas*) to have cravings; *CSur*(*estar embarazada*) to be pregnant 3.(*mancha*) birthmark 4. *Méx*(*apetito*) appetite

antología *f* anthology ►de ~ (*memorable*) excellent

antonomasia *f* por ~ par excellence

antorcha *f* torch

antro *m pey*(*local*) dive; un ~ de corrupción a den of iniquity

antropófago, -a *m, f* cannibal

antropología *f* anthropology

antropólogo, -a *m, f* anthropologist

anual *adj* 1.(*que dura un año, que sucede cada año*) annual, yearly; informe ~ annual report 2.(*planta*) annual

anualidad *f* annuity; ~ vitalicia life annuity

anualmente *adv* annually, yearly

anuario *m* yearbook

anubarrado, -a *adj* cloudy

anudar I. *vt* 1.(*hacer un nudo*) to knot 2.(*juntar*) to join II. *vr:* ~se to become knotted; ~se la voz to get a lump in one's throat

anulación *f* 1.(*de una ley*) repeal 2.(*de una sentencia*) overturning 3.(*de un matrimonio*) annulment 4.(*de un contrato, un pedido, una subscripción*) cancellation 5.(*de una decisión, un permiso*) revocation

anular I. *vt* 1.(*ley*) to repeal 2.(*sentencia*) to overturn 3.(*matrimonio*) to annul 4.(*contrato, pedido, subscripción, cita*) to cancel 5.(*decisión, permiso*) to revoke 6.(*tren, autobús*) to cancel 7. DEP (*gol*) to disallow 8.(*persona*) to subjugate II. *vr:* ~se (*persona*) to limit oneself III. *adj* 1.(*relativo al anillo*) annular 2.(*de forma de anillo*) ring-shaped

anunciación *f* announcement

anunciar I. *vt* 1.(*dar noticia de algo*) to announce; acaban de ~ la llegada del vuelo they've just announced the arrival of the flight 2.(*dar publicidad*) to advertise 3.(*presagiar*) to herald II. *vr:* ~se 1.(*hacerse publicidad*) to be advertised 2.(*el verano*) to be heralded

anuncio *m* 1.(*de una noticia*) announcement 2.(*publicidad: en la TV*) advertisement, commercial *Am;* (*publicidad: en un periódico*) advertisement, ad *inf;* ~ en internet banner; ~ por palabras classified advertisement

anverso *m* obverse

anzuelo *m* 1.(*para pescar*) (fish-)hook 2. *inf* (*aliciente*) bait, lure; echar el ~ to offer a bait; echar el ~ a alguien to lure sb; morder [*o* picar en] [*o* tragar] el ~ to take the bait

añadidura *f* addition; por ~ in addition

añadir *vt* 1.(*agregar*) to add; a esto hay que ~ que... there's also the fact that ... 2.(*alargar*) to lengthen; ~ dos centímetros a las mangas to lengthen the sleeves by two centimetres [*o* centimeters *Am*]

añagaza *f* 1.(*para aves*) decoy 2.(*ardid*) ruse

añares *mpl Arg* ages *pl*

añejo, -a *adj* old; (*vino*) mature

añicos *mpl* fragments *pl;* hacer algo ~ to smash sth up; estoy hecho ~ *inf* I'm shattered

añil *m* 1. BOT indigo 2.(*color*) indigo blue

año *m* year; ~ bisiesto leap year; ~ civil calendar year; ~ luz light year; ~ natural calendar year; ~ nuevo New Year; la víspera de ~ nuevo New Year's Eve; ~ de servicio year of service; los ~s 60 the sixties; por los ~s 60 in the sixties; en el ~ 1960 in 1960; el ~ de la pera the year one; cumplir ~s to have a birthday; cumplir 60 ~s to turn sixty; necesitar ~s to take years; ¿cuántos ~s tienes? how old are you?; Juan le saca cinco ~s a Pepe Juan is five years older than Pepe; los ~s no pasan en balde the years take their toll; los ~s corren que vuelan the years fly by ►estar de buen ~ (*saludable*) to look well; (*gordo*) to be plump; un hombre entrado en ~s an elderly man; por él no pasan los ~s he doesn't seem to get any older; quitarse ~s to be older than one admits; a mis ~s at my age

añoranza *f* yearning; (*morriña*) homesickness

añorar *vt* to yearn for; (*tener morriña*) to be homesick for; ~ los viejos tiempos to long for the old days

añoso, -a *adj* aged

aojada *f Col* (*tragaluz grande*) skylight; (*pequeña*) bull's eye

aojar *vt* (*hechizar*) to bewitch

aorta *f* aorta

aovado, -a *adj* oval

aovar *vi* to lay eggs

aovillarse *vr* to curl up

apabullante *adj* overwhelming

apabullar *vt* 1.(*achicar*) to intimidate; (*confundir*) to confuse; (*abatir*) to crush; me quedé apabullado cuando oí la noticia I was devastated when I heard the news 2.(*humillar*) to humiliate

apacentar <e→ie> *vt, vr:* ~se to graze

apacible *adj* 1.(*persona*) placid 2.(*temperamento*) even 3.(*tiempo*) mild 4.(*viento*) gentle

apaciguar <gu→gü> I. *vt* 1.(*persona*) to pacify 2.(*calmar*) to calm down; (*dolor*) to ease II. *vr:* ~se to calm down

apadrinar *vt* 1.(*ser padrino*) ~ a alguien (*en un bautizo*) to be sb's godfather; (*en una boda*) to be sb's best man 2.(*proteger*) to protect 3.(*patrocinar*) to sponsor

apagado, -a *adj* 1.(*volcán*) extinct 2.(*sonido*) muffled 3.(*persona*) lifeless 4.(*color*) dull

apagar <g→gu> I. *vt* 1.(*luz, cigarrillo, fuego*) to put out; ~ el fuego con una manta to put out [*o* to extinguish] the fire with a blanket **2.**(*sed*) to quench **3.**(*hambre*) to satisfy **4.**(*protesta, disturbio*) to suppress **5.**(*televisor, radio*) to switch off **6.**(*vela*) to snuff **7.**(*color*) to tone down ▸**estar apagado** (*persona*) to not be in form; **¡apaga y vámonos!** that's enough! **II.** *vr:* ~**se 1.**(*fuego, pipa, luz*) to go out **2.**(*sonido*) to die away **3.**(*color*) to fade

apagón *m* blackout; ELEC power cut

apaisado, -a *adj* landscape; **formato** ~ landscape format

apalabrar *vt* to arrange

apalancar <c→qu> **I.** *vt* to lever up *Brit,* to jack up *Am* **II.** *vr:* ~**se** *inf* to install oneself

apaleada *f Arg, Méx,* **apaleamiento** *m* **1.**(*zurra*) drubbing **2.**(*de una alfombra*) beating

apalear *vt* **1.**(*a alguien*) to thrash, to beat **2.**(*una alfombra*) to beat **3.** AGR to winnow; ~ **un árbol** to shake the branches of a tree; ~ **un manzano** to knock fruit from an apple tree

apalizar <z→c> *vt* to beat up; **el equipo fue apalizado** *fig* the team were thrashed

apancle *m Méx* irrigation ditch

apandorgarse *vr Perú* **1.**(*emperezarse*) to become lazy **2.**(*repantingarse*) to grow stout **3.**(*vaguear*) to be indolent

apantallado, -a *adj Méx* overwhelmed

apañado, -a *adj* **1.**(*hábil*) skilful *Brit,* skillful *Am* **2.**(*adecuado*) suitable **3.** *inf* **estás** ~ **si crees que te voy a ayudar** you're quite mistaken if you think I'm going to help you

apañar I. *vt* (*remendar*) to mend ▸**¡ya te** ~**é yo!** I'll give you what for! **II.** *vr:* ~**se 1.**(*darse maña*) to contrive to **2.**(*arreglárselas*) to manage; **no sé cómo te las apañas** I don't know how you manage; **¡apáñatelas como puedas!** get by as best you can!

apaño *m* **1.**(*acción de apañar*) mending **2.**(*remiendo*) patch **3.**(*chanchullo*) scam **4.**(*amorío*) affair ▸**encontrar un** ~ to find a solution

aparador *m* **1.**(*mueble*) sideboard **2.**(*escaparate*) shop window **3.**(*taller*) workshop

aparato *m* **1.**(*utensilio*) *t.* DEP apparatus; ~ **indicador** meter; ~ **de precisión** precision instrument; ~ **de televisión** television set; ~ **para la ventilación** ventilation system; **gimnasia de** ~**s** apparatus gymnastics **2.** TEL receiver; **ponerse al** ~ to come to the phone; **el señor X está al** ~ Mr X is on the phone **3.**(*avión*) plane **4.**(*vendaje*) bandage **5.** ANAT system; ~ **digestivo** digestive system **6.**(*ostentación*) pomp **7.** POL (*de un partido*) machine

aparatoso, -a *adj* **1.**(*ostentoso*) ostentatious **2.**(*desmedido*) excessive; **un accidente** ~ a spectacular accident

aparcamiento *m* **1.**(*acción*) parking **2.**(*lugar*) car park *Brit,* parking lot *Am*

aparcar <c→qu> *vt* **1.**(*coche*) to park **2.**(*decisión*) to put off

aparear I. *vt* **1.**(*animales*) to mate **2.**(*formar un par*) to pair; ~ **personas** to pair people off **II.** *vr:* ~**se 1.**(*animales*) to mate **2.**(*formar un par*) to form a pair

aparecer *irr como crecer* **I.** *vi* to appear; (*algo inesperado*) to turn up; ~ **ante la opinión pública** to appear in public; **han aparecido casos de difteria** some cases of diphtheria have appeared **II.** *vr:* ~**se** to appear

aparejado, -a *adj* (*adecuado*) suitable; **llevar** [*o* **traer**] ~ to entail

aparejador(a) *m(f)* foreman builder *m,* forewoman builder *f*

aparejo *m* **1.**(*arnés*) harness **2.**(*poleas*) block and tackle **3.**(*jarcia*) tackle **4.**(*imprimación*) sizing **5.**(*construcción*) bond **6.** *pl* (*utensilios*) equipment

aparentar *vt* to feign; **trata de** ~ **que es rico** he tries to make out that he's rich; ~ **estar enfermo** to pretend to be ill; **no aparentas la edad que tienes** you don't look your age

aparente *adj* **1.**(*que parece y no es*) apparent **2.**(*perceptible a la vista*) visible **3.**(*de buen aspecto*) attractive

aparentemente *adv* apparently, seemingly

aparición *f* **1.**(*acción*) appearance **2.**(*visión*) apparition

apariencia *f* appearance; **en** ~ apparently; **guardar las** ~**s** to keep up appearances ▸**las** ~**s engañan** appearances can be deceptive

aparragarse *vr* **1.** *Chile, Hond, Méx, Par* (*achaparrarse*) to remain stunted **2.** *Chile* (*agazaparse*) to crouch

apartado *m* **1.**(*cuarto*) spare room **2.**(*párrafo*) paragraph **3.** ADMIN ~ **de Correos** post office box

apartado, -a *adj* **1.**(*lugar*) isolated **2.**(*persona*) unsociable

apartamento *m* apartment, flat *Brit*

apartamiento *m* (*separación*) separation

apartar I. *vt* **1.**(*separar*) to separate **2.**(*poner a un lado*) to put aside; ~ **a alguien para decirle algo** to take sb aside to tell him/her sth; ~ **el plato** to push the plate aside; **¡aparta la mano del taladro!** take your hand off the drill! **3.**(*de un cargo*) to remove **4.**(*de un propósito*) to dissuade **5.**(*la vista*) to avert **6.**(*la atención*) to divert **II.** *vr:* ~**se 1.**(*separarse*) to separate **2.**(*de un camino*) to turn off; **¡apártate!** get out of the way! **3.**(*del tema*) to deviate

aparte I. *adv* (*en otro sitio*) apart; **por correo** ~ under separate cover; **he sumado los euros y,** ~**, los dólares** I've added up the euros and the dollars separately; **esta cuestión debe tratarse** ~ this question must be dealt with on its own **II.** *prep* **1.**(*separado*) **él estaba** ~ **del grupo** he was separated from the group **2.**(*además de*) ~ **de** apart from; **esta sopa** ~ **de mala está fría** besides tasting bad, this soup is cold as well; ~ **de esto, perdí las llaves** apart from that, I lost the keys **III.** *m* (*de un escrito*) paragraph; **punto y** ~ new paragraph **IV.** *adj inv* **1.**(*singular*) special **2.**(*separado*) separate; **en un plato** ~ on a separate plate

apasionado, -a I. *adj* **1.**(*con pasión, temperamento*) passionate **2.**(*entusiasta*) enthusiastic **II.** *m, f* enthusiast

apasionante *adj* exciting

apasionar I. *vt* to fill with enthusiasm **II.** *vr:* ~**se 1.**(*entusiasmarse*) ~**se por algo** to become enthusiastic about sth **2.**(*enamorarse*) ~**se por alguien** to fall passionately in love with sb

apatía *f* apathy

apático, -a *adj* apathetic

apátrida *adj* stateless

apatusco *m Ven* **1.**(*intriga*) intrigue **2.**(*fingimiento*) pretence *Brit,* pretense *Am*

Apdo. *abr de* **Apartado de Correos** PO Box

apeadero *m* **1.**(*poyo*) mounting block **2.** FERRO halt **3.**(*en un camino*) stopping place

apear I. *vt inf* (*disuadir*) to dissuade **II.** *vr:* ~**se** (*de un vehículo*) to get out; (*de un caballo*) to dismount

apechugar <g→gu> *vi* ~ **con** to put up with stoically; ~ **con las consecuencias** to suffer the consequences; ~ **con una tarea complicada** to take on a difficult task

apedrear I. *v impers* to hail **II.** *vt* to throw stones at; (*lapidar*) to stone (to death) **III.** *vr:* ~**se** (*cosecha*) to be damaged by hail

apegado, -a *adj* **estar** ~ **a alguien** to be attached to sb

apegarse <g→gu> *vr* to become attached

apego *m* attachment; **tener un gran** ~ **a algo** to be very attached to sth

apelación *f* **1.** JUR (*recurso*) appeal **2.** *fig* remedy; **esto no tiene** ~ there's nothing to be done

apelar *vi* **1.**(*invocar*) to appeal; (*referirse*) to refer **2.**(*recurrir: a alguien*) to turn; (*a algo*) to resort; ~ **a todos los medios** to try everything **3.** JUR (*recurrir*) to appeal; **la sentencia ha sido apelada** an appeal has been lodged against the judgement

apelativo *m* **1.**(*apellido*) name **2.**(*sobrenombre*) nickname; ~ **cariñoso** pet name **3.** LING common noun

apellidar I. *vt* to name **II.** *vr:* ~**se** to be called; **se apellida Martínez** his/her surname is Martínez

apellido *m* surname; ~ **de soltera** maiden name; **primer** ~ father's surname; **por el** ~ **no caigo** the name doesn't mean anything to me

Every Spaniard has two surnames (**apellidos**): the first one is the father's name and the second is the mother's. If, for example, Señora Iglesias Vieira and Señor González Blanco were to become parents, the child's surname would be González Iglesias.

apelmazar <z→c> **I.** *vt* to compress **II.** *vr:*

~**se 1.**(*colchón, cojín*) to become hard **2.**(*nieve*) to crust **3.**(*harina*) to become lumpy **4.**(*lana, pelo*) to become matted

apelotonar I. *vt* **1.**(*cosas*) to roll into a ball **2.**(*personas*) to crowd together **II.** *vr:* ~**se 1.**(*personas, cosas*) to mass, to crowd together; ~**se en la entrada** to throng at the entrance; **en esta calle se apelotonan los coches** the traffic gets snarled up in this street **2.**(*formarse grumos*) to become lumpy

apenar I. *vt* to sadden **II.** *vr:* ~**se 1.**(*afligirse*) ~**se por algo** to grieve over [*o* at] sth **2.** *AmC* (*sentir vergüenza*) ~**se por algo** to feel embarrassed about sth

apenas I. *adv* **1.**(*casi no*) hardly; ~ **había nadie** there was hardly anybody [*o* anyone] there **2.**(*tan solo*) just; (*escasamente*) barely; ~ **hace un mes que estudio alemán** I've been learning German for just a month; ~ **hace una hora** barely an hour ago; **tengo** ~ **10 libras en el bolsillo** I've just 10 pounds in my pocket **II.** *conj* (*tan pronto como*) as soon as; ~ **salí a la calle, se puso a llover** as soon as I went out into the street it began to rain

apéndice *m* **1.**(*de un libro*) appendix; (*tomo separado*) supplement **2.**(*complemento*) appendage **3.** ANAT appendix; ~ **vermiforme** veriform appendix

apendicitis *f inv* appendicitis

apensionarse *vr* **1.** *Arg, Chile, Méx* (*entristecerse*) to become sad **2.** *Col* (*inquietarse*) to become distressed

apercibimiento *m* **1.**(*acto*) preparation **2.**(*amonestación, advertencia*) warning

apercibir I. *vt* **1.**(*preparar*) to prepare **2.**(*avisar*) to warn **3.**(*amonestar*) ~ **a alguien por algo** to rebuke sb for sth **4.** JUR to warn; **lo han apercibido con el despido** they have threatened him with dismissal **II.** *vr:* ~**se 1.**(*prepararse*) ~**se a** [*o* para] **algo** to prepare for sth **2.**(*percatarse*) ~**se de algo** to notice sth; **me he apercibido de lo importante que es el examen** I've become aware of how important the examination is

aperitivo *m* **1.**(*bebida*) aperitif **2.**(*comida*) appetizer ► **¡y ésto es tan solo el** ~**!** and that's only the beginning!

aperos *mpl* (*utensilios*) farming equipment

apertura *f* **1.**(*reunión, teatro, cuenta, en ajedrez*) opening **2.**(*testamento*) reading; ~ **de un crédito** opening of a credit

apesadumbrar I. *vt* to sadden **II.** *vr* ~**se por algo** to grieve over [*o* at] sth

apestar I. *vi* ~ **a algo** to stink of sth **II.** *vt* ~ **algo** to stink sth out **III.** *vr:* ~**se** *AmL* (*contagiarse*) to become infected

apestoso, -a *adj* **1.**(*que apesta*) stinking, stinky *inf* **2.**(*fastidioso*) annoying

apetecer *irr como crecer vi* **1.**(*tener ganas de*) to feel like; **¿qué te apetece?** what would you like?; **¿un viaje?** – **sí, me apetece la idea** a trip? yes – the idea appeals to me; **me apetece un helado** I feel like an ice cream

2. (*gustar*) **una copa de vino siempre apetece** a glass of wine is always welcome; **este libro me apetece más** this book appeals to me more

apetecible *adj* attractive; (*objetivo*) desirable

apetencia *f* **1.** (*apetito*) appetite **2.** (*deseo*) ~ **de algo** desire for sth

apetito *m* **1.** (*de comida*) ~ **de algo** appetite for sth; **abrir el** ~ to whet one's appetite **2.** (*deseo*) ~ **de algo** desire for sth; ~ **sexual** sexual appetite

apetitoso, -a *adj* **1.** (*que despierta el apetito*) appetizing **2.** (*sabroso*) tasty **3.** (*deseable*) desirable

apiadar I. *vt* to move to pity; **su mala suerte apiada a sus vecinos** his/her misfortune moved his/her neighbours to pity **II.** *vr* ~**se de** to take pity on; **¡Dios, apiádate de nosotros!** may God have mercy on us!

ápice *m* **1.** (*punta*) apex **2.** (*cúspide*) top **3.** (*nada*) iota; **no ceder un** ~ not to yield an inch; **no entender un** ~ not to understand the slightest thing

apicultor(a) *m(f)* beekeeper

apicultura *f* beekeeping, apiculture

apilar I. *vt* to pile up **II.** *vr:* ~**se** to pile up

apiñar I. *vt* **1.** (*cosas*) to cram; **apiñó las cosas en el coche y partieron** he/she crammed the things into the car and they set off **2.** (*personas*) to crowd together; (*animales*) to herd together **II.** *vr:* ~**se** to crowd together

apio *m* celery

apirularse *vr Chile* to dress up

apisonadora *f* steamroller

apisonar *vt* to roll flat

aplacar <c→qu> **I.** *vt* **1.** (*persona*) to calm down **2.** (*dolor*) to soothe **3.** (*hambre*) to satisfy **4.** (*sed*) to quench **II.** *vr:* ~**se** to calm down

aplanamiento *m* **1.** (*allanamiento*) levelling *Brit,* leveling *Am* **2.** (*desánimo*) dejection

aplanar I. *vt* **1.** (*allanar*) to level **2.** (*aplastar*) to flatten **3.** (*desanimar*) to discourage **II.** *vr:* ~**se** to get discouraged

aplastante *adj* overwhelming; (*derrota*) crushing; (*lógica, prueba*) devastating

aplastar *vt* **1.** (*chafar*) to flatten; **el desprendimiento de piedras aplastó a dos personas** the rockfall crushed two people **2.** (*con la mano*) to squash; ~ **un cigarrillo** to stub out a cigarette **3.** (*con el pie*) to crush **4.** (*derrotar*) to overwhelm **5.** (*persona*) to devastate

aplatanarse *vr* **1.** (*entregarse a la indolencia*) to become lethargic **2.** *Cuba, PRico* (*adoptar las costumbres*) to go native

aplaudir I. *vi* to applaud, to clap; **el publico rompió a** ~ the audience burst into applause **II.** *vt* **1.** (*palmear, alabar*) to applaud **2.** (*aprobar*) to approve

aplauso *m* applause; **salva de** ~**s** storm of applause; **digno de** ~ *fig* worthy of applause

aplazamiento *m* **1.** (*fecha, viaje, partido*) postponement; (*reunión*) postponement,

adjournment **2.** (*decisión*) deferment

aplazar <z→c> *vt* **1.** (*fecha, viaje, partido*) to postpone; (*reunión*) to postpone, to adjourn (*after having begun*); ~ **el viaje una semana** to postpone the trip by one week; **la reunión se aplaza hasta nueva orden** the meeting is adjourned until further notice **2.** (*decisión*) to defer **3.** *AmL* (*suspender*) to fail

aplicación *f* **1.** (*de pintura, crema*) application **2.** (*utilización*) use; (*uso práctico*) application, use; **las múltiples aplicaciones del plástico** the various applications [*o* uses] of plastic

aplicado, -a *adj* (*trabajador*) hardworking

aplicar <c→qu> **I.** *vt* **1.** (*poner sobre: pintura, crema*) to apply; ~ **dando un ligero masaje** apply, massaging lightly; ~ **un lazo a un vestido** to sew a bow onto a dress; ~ **el oído a la puerta** to put one's ear to the door; **aplicado con regularidad...** applied regularly ... **2.** (*utilizar*) to use; ~ **una máquina para un trabajo** to use a machine for a job; ~ **el freno** to apply the break; ~ **un tipo de interés** to apply a rate of interest **3.** *JUR* ~ **una sanción** to impose; **la ley no se puede** ~ **en este caso** the law is not applicable in this case **II.** *vr:* ~**se 1.** (*esforzarse*) to apply oneself; ~**se al estudio** to apply [*o* to devote] oneself to one's studies **2.** (*emplearse*) to be used

aplique *m* **1.** (*lámpara*) wall lamp, sconce **2.** *TEAT* prop

aplomo *m* (*seguridad*) self-confidence, composure; **perder el** ~ to lose one's composure

apocamiento *m* timidity

apocar <c→qu> **I.** *vt* to intimidate **II.** *vr:* ~**se** to lose heart

apodar I. *vt* (*dar un sobrenombre*) to call; (*un apodo*) to nickname **II.** *vr* ~**se... (*tener el sobrenombre*) to be called ...; (*el apodo*) to be nicknamed ...

apoderado, -a *m, f* **1.** *JUR* proxy **2.** *COM* agent

apoderar I. *vt* **1.** (*en general*) to authorize **2.** *JUR* to grant power of attorney to **II.** *vr:* ~**se** to take possession; **el espía se apoderó del maletín** the spy seized the briefcase; ~**se de los clientes de la competencia** to woo customers away from competitors; ~**se del liderato** to go into the lead

apodo *m* nickname

apogeo *m* **1.** *ASTR* apogee **2.** (*cumbre*) summit; **estar en el** ~ **de su carrera** to be at the peak of one's career; **el** ~ **del Barroco** the height of the baroque period

apolillado, -a *adj* **1.** (*de polilla*) moth-eaten **2.** (*anticuado*) antiquated

apolillar I. *vt* to eat away **II.** *vr:* ~**se** to get moth-eaten

apolillo *m Arg* (*el dormir*) sleep

apolismado, -a *adj* **1.** *AmL* (*magullado*) damaged **2.** *Col, Méx, PRico* (*raquítico*) sickly **3.** *CRi* (*holgazán*) lazy **4.** *Méx, Ven* (*deprimido*) depressed **5.** *PRico* (*tonto*) stupid;

(*simple*) simple

apolítico, -a *adj* apolitical

apología *f* defence *Brit,* defense *Am*

apoltronarse *vr* 1.(*emperezarse*) to get lazy 2.(*repantigarse*) to lounge

apoplejía *f* stroke

apoquinar *vt inf* to fork out; **apoquina lo que me debes** pay up what you owe me

aporrear I. *vt* 1.(*dar golpes*) to beat; ~ **el piano** to bang on the piano; ~ **la máquina de escribir** to hammer away on the typewriter; ~ **la puerta** to bang [*o* hammer] on the door 2.(*molestar*) to bother; **esta música me aporrea los oídos** (*por estar muy alta*) this music is deafening; (*por ser mala*) this music is unbearable II. *vr:* ~**se** to toil

aportación *f* 1.(*contribución*) contribution; **hacer una** ~ **a un trabajo** to make a contribution to a job 2.(*donación*) donation 3. ECON (*capital*) investment; ~ **dineraria** cash contribution; ~ **en especie** contribution in kind

aportar I. *vt* 1.(*contribuir*) to contribute; **he aportado algo a la fiesta** I've made a contribution to the party; **no aporta nada ir a esa conferencia** it's not worth going to that conference 2.(*información, evidencia, testigos, pruebas*) to provide 3.(*traer*) to bring; ~ **al matrimonio** to bring to the marriage II. *vi* 1.(*llegar a puerto*) to reach port 2.(*recalar*) to show up; **hace tiempo que no aporta por aquí** he/she hasn't put in an appearance here for quite a while

aposentar I. *vt* to lodge, to put up II. *vr* ~**se en algo** to lodge [*o* put up] at sth; MIL to be billeted in sth

aposento *m* 1.(*hospedaje*) lodging; **nos dieron** ~ they put us up 2.(*cuarto*) room

aposición *f* apposition

apósito *m* (*vendaje*) dressing; (*adhesivo*) sticking plaster *Brit,* adhesive tape *Am*

aposta *adv* on purpose

apostar <o→ue> I. *vi* ~ **por algo/alguien** to back sth/sb; ~**las a** [*o* con] **alguien** to compete with sb II. *vt, vr:* ~**se** 1.(*hacer una apuesta*) to bet; **¿qué/cuánto apostamos?** what/how much shall we bet?; **¿qué te apuestas a que no lo hace?** I bet you he/she won't do it; ~ **doble contra sencillo que...** I bet you two to one that ...; **puedes** ~ **la cabeza que...** you can bet your life that ... 2.(*poner*) to position (oneself)

apóstata *mf* apostate

apostatar I. *vi* to apostatize; ~ **de la fe cristiana** to break with the Christian faith

a posteriori *adv* with hindsight

apostilla *f* marginal note

apóstol *m* apostle; **Hechos de los Apóstoles** Acts of the Apostles; **ser un buen** ~ *fig* to be a good disciple

apostrofar *vt* to apostrophize

apóstrofo *m* LING apostrophe

apostura *f* good looks *pl*

apoteósico, -a *adj* tremendous; **éxito** ~ tremendous success

apoteosis *f inv* 1.(*de un héroe*) apotheosis 2.(*de un espectáculo*) climax

apoyabrazos *m inv* armrest

apoyacabezas *m inv* headrest

apoyar I. *vt* 1.(*colocar sobre*) to rest; (*contra*) to lean 2.(*fundar*) to base; ~ (**con pruebas**) to support 3.(*confirmar*) to confirm 4.(*patrocinar*) to back; (*ayudar*) to stand by; ~ **una moción/un ascenso** to support a motion/a promotion; ~ **una reforma** to back a reform II. *vi* ARQUIT to rest III. *vr:* ~**se** 1.(*descansar sobre*) to rest; ~**se en** [*o* contra] **algo** to lean on sth; ~**se con los brazos** to prop oneself up with one's arms; ~**se con la mano** to support oneself with one's hand 2.(*fundarse*) to be based

apoyo *m* 1.(*sostén, soporte*) support 2.(*respaldo*) backing, support; (*ayuda*) help; **prestar** ~ **a un plan** to support [*o* back] a plan; **tener un** ~ **en alguien** to have sb's support [*o* backing]; **cuenta con mi** ~ you can rely on me; **en** ~ **de** in support of

apreciable *adj* 1.(*observable*) noticeable; ~ **al oído** audible 2.(*considerable*) considerable 3.(*digno de estima*) worthy

apreciación *f* 1.(*juicio*) assessment 2.(*de una moneda*) appreciation 3.(*de una casa*) valuation 4.(*del tamaño*) estimation 5.(*captación*) detection

apreciado, -a *adj* (*en cartas*) ~**s Sres** Dear Sirs

apreciar *vt* 1.(*estimar*) to appreciate; **aprecio los perros** I like dogs; **si aprecias tu vida, ¡desaparece de aquí!** if you value your life, get out of here!; **aprecio la libertad** I value my liberty 2.(*una moneda*) to appreciate 3.(*una casa*) to value 4.(*tamaño, distancia*) to estimate 5.(*captar*) to detect; **de lejos no se aprecia ningún sonido** no sound can be heard from afar; **este cronómetro aprecia centésimas de un segundo** this chronometer indicates hundredths of a second; **el médico apreció una contusión en el pecho** the doctor detected bruising in the chest 6.(*valorar*) to assess

aprecio *m* 1.(*afecto*) affection; **te tengo un gran** ~ I'm very fond of you 2.(*estima*) esteem; **gran** ~ high opinion; **tengo un gran** ~ **por este político** I hold this politician in high regard 3. FIN valuation

aprehender *vt* 1.(*coger*) to apprehend; (*botín, contrabando*) to seize 2.(*percibir*) to perceive 3.(*comprender*) to understand

aprehensión *f* 1.(*acción de coger*) apprehension; (*del botín*) seizure 2.(*percepción*) perception 3.(*comprensión*) understanding

apremiante *adj* pressing

apremiar I. *vt* 1.(*acuciar*) to urge (on) 2.(*compeler*) to compel II. *vi* (*urgir*) to be urgent; **el tiempo apremia** time is pressing

apremio *m* 1.(*situación apremiante*) urgent situation; **por** ~ **de tiempo** because time is short 2.(*coacción*) compulsion 3.JUR legal proceedings *pl*

aprender *vt* to learn; **fácil de** ~ easy to learn; ~ **a leer** to learn to read; ~ **de la historia** to learn from history; ~ **de memoria** to learn by heart; **¿dónde has aprendido estos malos modales?** where did you learn such bad manners?; **siempre se aprende algo nuevo** you live and learn

aprendiz(a) *m(f)* apprentice; **entrar de** ~ to become an apprentice; **trabajar de** ~ to work as an apprentice ▶**ser** ~ **de mucho, maestro de nada** *prov* to be jack of all trades and master of none *prov*

aprendizaje *m* 1.(*acción de aprender*) learning; ~ **en línea** internet-based learning 2.(*formación profesional*) apprenticeship; **contrato de** ~ contract of apprenticeship; **puesto** [*o* **tiempo**] **de** ~ apprenticeship

aprensión *f* 1.(*recelo*) apprehension; **me da** ~ **decírtelo** I daren't tell you 2.(*asco*) disgust; **he cogido** ~ **a la leche** I've taken a strong dislike to milk; **me da** ~ **beber de este vaso** I find it disgusting to drink from this glass 3.(*temor*) fear; (*impresión*) impression; **tener la** ~ **de que...** +*subj* (*temer*) to be afraid that ...; (*creer*) to have the impression that ... 4.(*figuración*) imagining; **son aprensiones suyas** those are just his/her strange ideas

aprensivo, -a *adj* overanxious; (*hipocondríaco*) hypochondriacal

apresar *vt* 1.(*hacer presa*) to seize 2.(*delincuente, nave*) to capture

aprestar I.*vt* 1.(*preparar*) to prepare 2.(*telas*) to size II.*vr:* ~**se** to prepare

apresurado, -a *adj* 1.(*con prisa*) hurried; **andar con paso** ~ to walk quickly 2.(*con excesiva prisa*) hasty

apresuramiento *m* hurry, haste

apresurar I.*vt* 1.(*dar prisa*) to hurry 2.(*acelerar*) to speed up; ~ **el paso** to quicken one's step; ~ **la salida del viaje** to depart hastily II.*vr:* ~**se** to hurry; **¡no te apresures!** take your time!

apretado, -a *adj* 1.(*oprimido*) oppressed 2.(*tapón, tornillo*) tight; (*vestido*) close-fitting, tight; (*cinta, cuerda*) taut 3.(*personas*) tight-fisted 4.(*difícil*) **un caso** ~ an awkward case; **verse** [*o* **estar**] **muy** ~ to be in a very difficult situation 5.(*apurado*) **estar** ~ **de dinero** to be short of money; **estar** ~ **de tiempo** to be short of time

apretar <e→ie> I.*vi* 1.(*calor*) to become oppressive; (*dolor*) to become intense; (*lluvia*) to become heavier 2.(*vestido*) to be too tight; **la americana me aprieta por detrás** the jacket is too tight around the back 3.(*deudas, problemas*) ~ **a alguien** to weigh heavily on sb 4.(*esforzarse*) **tenemos que** ~ **si queremos aprobar** we'll have to make more of an effort if we want to pass; **si aprietas un poco puedes ganar el partido** if you put more effort into it, you can win the game 5.(*exigir*)

este profesor aprieta mucho en los exámenes this professor demands a lot in the examinations II.*vt* 1.(*hacer presión*) to press; ~ **un botón** to press a button; ~ **algo contra el pecho** to press sth against one's chest; ~ **el tubo de la pasta de dientes** to squeeze the toothpaste tube; ~ **el acelerador** to step on the accelerator; ~ **la ropa en la maleta** to pack clothes into the suitcase 2.(*estrechar, sujetar fuertemente*) ~ **las cuerdas de la guitarra** to tighten the strings of the guitar; ~ **los dientes** to grit one's teeth; ~ **filas** to close ranks; ~ **las letras** to squeeze letters together; ~ **las manos** to clasp one's hands; ~ **el puño** to clench one's fist; ~ **un nudo/un tornillo** to tighten a knot/a screw III.*vr:* ~**se** 1.(*estrecharse*) to become narrower 2.(*agolparse*) to crowd together 3.(*ceñirse*) ~**se el cinturón** to tighten one's belt

apretón *m* 1.(*presión*) squeeze 2.(*sprint*) sprint 3.(*aprieto*) jam *inf* 4.(*apretura*) crush

apretujar I.*vt inf* to squeeze II.*vr:* ~**se** to squeeze together

apretura *f* 1.(*de gente*) throng 2.(*escasez*) shortage 3.(*aprieto*) jam *inf*

aprieto *m* jam, fix; ~ **económico** financial difficulties; **estar en un** ~ to be in a jam; **poner a alguien en un** ~ **con una pregunta** to embarrass sb with a question; **sacar a alguien de un** ~ to get sb out of a fix

a priori *adv* a priori

aprisa *adv* quickly

aprisionar *vt* 1.(*poner en prisión*) to imprison 2.(*sujetar con cadenas*) to shackle 3.(*atar*) to bind 4.(*inmovilizar*) to immobilize; (*pillar*) to catch; **quedarse aprisionado en el barro** to be trapped in the mud

aprobación *f* (*de una decisión, un proyecto, una moción*) approval; (*de una ley*) passing; **murmullo de** ~ murmur of approval; **encontrar la** ~ **de alguien** to meet with sb's approval

aprobado *m* ENS pass; **he sacado un** ~ **en historia** I've passed history

aprobar <o→ue> I.*vt* 1.(*decisión, propuesta, proyecto, moción*) to approve; (*ley*) to pass; ~ **las condiciones** to agree to the conditions; **la censura no aprobaba muchas películas** the board of censors didn't pass many films; **la solicitud fue aprobada** the application was approved 2.(*examen, a un alumno*) to pass II.*vi* ENS to pass

aproches *mpl* AmL 1.(*proximidad*) surrounding districts *pl* 2.(*parentesco*) relation 3.(*vía de acceso*) approaches *pl*

apronte *m* AmL preparation

apropiación *f* 1.(*apoderamiento*) appropriation; ~ **indebida** misappropriation 2.(*aplicación adecuada*) application 3.(*adaptación*) adaptation

apropiado, -a *adj* 1.(*adecuado*) ~ **a** [*o* **para**] **algo** suitable for sth 2.(*oportuno*) appropriate; (*precio*) reasonable

apropiar I. *vt* **1.** (*adaptar*) to adapt **2.** *AmL* (*premio, beca*) to award; (*encargo*) to assign **II.** *vr* ~**se de algo** to appropriate sth
aprovechable *adj* usable
aprovechado, -a *adj* **1.** (*alumno, trabajador*) hardworking **2.** (*calculador*) opportunistic
aprovechamiento *m* exploitation; ~ **del tiempo libre** use of one's leisure time
aprovechar I. *vi* **1.** (*valer*) to be of use **2.** (*progresar*) **mi hijo no aprovecha en los estudios** my son isn't making progress in his studies ▶ **¡que aproveche!** enjoy your meal! **II.** *vt* to make good use of; (*abusar*) to exploit; ~ **una idea** to exploit an idea; ~ **un invento** to capitalize on an invention; ~ **el máximo de algo** to get the most out of sth **III.** *vr:* ~**se 1.** (*sacar provecho*) ~**se de algo** to profit by [*o* from] sth; **ellos hacen el trabajo sucio y luego los otros se aprovechan** they do the dirty work and then others get the benefit **2.** (*abusar*) to take advantage; ~**se de una mujer** to take advantage of a woman **3.** (*explotar*) ~**se de alguien** to exploit sb
aprovisionar *vt* ~ **de** [*o* con] **algo** to supply with sth
aproximación *f* **1.** (*acercamiento*) approach **2.** (*en una lotería*) consolation prize
aproximado, -a *adj* approximate
aproximar I. *vt* to bring nearer; **aproxima la silla a la mesa** draw your chair up to the table; ~ **opiniones** to bring opinions closer together **II.** *vr:* ~**se** to approach; ~**se con la silla a la ventana** to move one's chair over to the window; ~**se a los 50** to be getting on for 50; **se aproxima a la realidad** it comes close to the truth; **se aproxima agosto** August is approaching; **las tropas se aproximan** the troops are getting closer
aptitud *f* **1.** (*talento*) aptitude; ~ **para algo** aptitude for sth **2.** (*conveniencia*) suitability; ~ **para algo** fitness for sth; ~ **para el servicio militar** fitness for military service; **tener ~es físicas para la natación** to have the physical requirements for swimming
apto, -a *adj* suitable; ~ **para algo** fit for sth; ~ **para el servicio militar** fit for military service; **la película no es apta para menores** the film is not suitable for minors
apuesta *f* **1.** (*juego*) bet; **corredor de ~s** bookmaker **2.** (*cantidad*) bid
apuesto, -a *adj* handsome
apuntador(a) *m(f)* TEAT prompter; **en esta película no se salva ni el ~** *fig* nobody is spared in this film
apuntalar *vt* to prop up
apuntar I. *vi* to appear; (*día*) to break; (*trigo*) to sprout; (*estación*) to come; **apunta la primavera** spring is coming; **la recuperación económica empieza a ~** economic recovery is starting **II.** *vt* **1.** (*con un arma*) ~ **a algo** to aim at sth; **¡apunten!** take aim! **2.** (*con el dedo*) ~ **a algo** to point at sth **3.** (*anotar*) to note (down) **4.** (*inscribir*) to enroll; (*en una*

lista) to enter **5.** (*naipes*) ~ **a algo** to stake on sth **6.** (*tela*) to darn **7.** (*dictar*) to dictate; TEAT to prompt **8.** (*insinuar*) to hint at; ~ **algo y no dar** to make a promise and fail to keep it **9.** (*indicar*) to point out; ~ **que...** to point out that ...; **todo apunta en esta dirección** everything points in this direction **III.** *vr:* ~**se 1.** (*inscribirse*) ~**se a algo** to enrol in sth; (*en una lista*) to enter one's name in sth; ~**se a un club** to join a club **2.** (*el vino*) to go sour **3.** (*éxito, tanto*) to score **4.** (*victoria*) to achieve
apunte *m* **1.** (*escrito*) note; **tomar ~s** to take notes; **¿me dejas los ~s de física?** can you lend me your physics notes? **2.** (*bosquejo*) sketch **3.** FIN entry
apuñalar *vt* to stab
apuradamente *adv* **1.** (*exactamente*) precisely **2.** (*con dificultad*) with difficulty
apurado, -a *adj* **1.** (*falto*) ~ **de dinero** hard up; ~ **de tiempo** short of time **2.** (*dificultoso*) difficult; **verse** ~ to be in a fix **3.** (*con esmero*) careful **4.** *AmL* (*apresurado*) hurried; **estar** ~ to be in a hurry; **hacer un trabajo a las apuradas** to do a job hurriedly
apurar I. *vt* **1.** (*vaso*) to drain; (*plato*) to finish off **2.** (*paciencia, reservas*) to exhaust; ~ **todos los medios** to try everything **3.** (*atosigar*) to harass; **¡no me apures, mi paciencia tiene un límite!** don't hassle me, my patience is limited!; **ya vendrás cuando te apure el hambre** you'll come when you're hungry **4.** (*investigación*) to examine thoroughly **5.** (*avergonzar*) to embarrass; **me apura decirle que no tengo dinero** I'm embarrassed to tell him/her that I don't have any money **6.** *AmL* (*dar prisa*) to hurry **II.** *vr:* ~**se 1.** (*preocuparse*) to worry; **¡no te apures por eso!** don't worry about that! **2.** *AmL* (*darse prisa*) to hurry up; **¡no te apures!** there's no hurry
apuro *m* **1.** (*aprieto*) fix; (*dificultad*) difficulty; **estar en un** ~ to be in a fix; **sacar a alguien de un** ~ to get sb out of a fix; **poner en** ~ to put in an awkward position **2.** (*estrechez*) financial need; **sufrir grandes ~s** to be in financial difficulties **3.** (*vergüenza*) embarrassment; **me da** ~ **pedirle el dinero** it's embarrassing for me to ask him/her for money **4.** *AmL* (*prisa*) hurry
aquejado, -a *adj* ~ **de** afflicted by
aquejar *vt* **1.** (*afligir*) to grieve **2.** (*enfermedad*) to afflict; **lo aquejaba una enfermedad grave** he suffered from a serious disease
aquel *m* **tener un** ~ to have a certain something
aquel, -ella I. *adj dem* <aquellos, -as> that, those *pl;* **aquella casa es nuestra** that house is ours; **¿qué fue del hombre ~?** what became of that man?; **¿estabais de acuerdo en ~ punto?** did you agree on that point?; **en aquellos tiempos** in those days **II.** *pron dem v.* **aquél, aquélla, aquello**

aquél, aquélla, aquello <aquéllos, -as> *pron dem* that (one), those (ones); ~ **me gusta, éste no** I like that one, not this one; **¿qué es aquello?** what's that?; **como decía** ~ as the former said; **sólo pueden participar ~s que sepan inglés** only those with a knowledge of English may participate; **esta teoría se diferencia de aquélla** this theory differs from that one; ~ **que colabore recibirá un premio** each person who contributes will receive a prize; **oye, ¿qué hay de aquello?** hey, how about it?

aquí *adv* **1.** (*lugar, dirección*) here; (**por**) ~ **cerca** around here; ~ **dentro** in here; **éste de** ~ this fellow here; **¡ah, ~ estás!** oh, there you are!; **andar de** ~ **para allá** to walk up and down; **mira** ~ **dentro** look in here; **de** ~ **hasta allí hay 10 minutos a pie** it's 10 minutes walk from here; **mejor ir por** ~ it's better to go this way **2.** (*de tiempo*) **de** ~ **en adelante** from now on; **de** ~ **a una semana** a week from now; **hasta** ~ up till now

aquietar **I.** *vt* **1.** (*apaciguar*) to calm (down) **2.** (*aliviar*) to allay **II.** *vr:* **~se** to calm down; **~se con una explicación** to be content with an explanation

ara¹ *f* altar ▶ **dar la vida en ~s de una idea** to sacrifice one's life for an idea; **en ~s de la paz** in the interests of peace; **acogerse a las ~s de alguien** to take refuge with sb

ara² *m AmL* parrot

árabe **I.** *adj* **1.** (*país*) Arab **2.** (*palabra*) Arabic **3.** (*península*) Arabian **4.** (*de los moros*) Moorish **II.** *mf* (*persona*) Arab **III.** *m* (*lengua*) Arabic

Arabia *f* Arabia; ~ **Saudita** Saudi Arabia

arábigo, -a *adj* Arab; (*número*) Arabic

arado *m* plough *Brit,* plow *Am*

Aragón *m* Aragon

aragonés, -esa *adj, m, f* Aragonese

arancel *m* (*tarifa*) tariff; (*impuesto*) duty

arancelario, -a *adj* tariff, customs

arándano *m* bilberry, blueberry *Am*

arandela *f* TÉC washer

araña *f* **1.** ZOOL spider; **tela de** ~ spider's web, spiderweb *Am* **2.** (*candelabro*) chandelier

arañar **I.** *vt* **1.** (*rasguñar*) to scratch **2.** *inf* (*reunir*) to scrape together; **con un poco de suerte ~é un aprobado** with a little luck I'll scrape a pass **3.** (*tocar*) to play; ~ **la guitarra** to play the guitar **II.** *vi* to scratch **III.** *vr:* **~se** to scratch oneself

arañazo *m* scratch; **dar un** ~ **a alguien** to scratch sb; **defenderse a** ~ **limpio** to defend oneself stubbornly

arar *vt* to plough *Brit,* to plow *Am*

arbitraje *m* **1.** (*juicio*) arbitration **2.** DEP (*en fútbol, etc*) refereeing; (*en tenis, etc*) umpiring

arbitral *adj* arbitral; **jurisdicción** ~ arbitral jurisdiction

arbitrar **I.** *vt* **1.** (*disputa*) ~ **algo** to arbitrate in sth **2.** (*medios, recursos*) to provide **3.** DEP (*en fútbol, etc*) to referee; (*en tenis, etc*) to umpire

II. *vi* to adjudge

arbitrariedad *f* **1.** (*cualidad*) arbitrariness **2.** (*acción*) arbitrary act

arbitrario, -a *adj* arbitrary

arbitrio *m* **1.** (*decisión de un juez*) adjudication **2.** (*voluntad*) free will; **estar al** ~ **de alguien** to be at sb's discretion; **dejar algo al** ~ **de alguien** to leave sth to sb's discretion **3.** (*salida*) way out **4.** *pl* (*impuesto*) **~s municipales** municipal taxes

árbitro, -a *m, f* **1.** (*mediador*) arbitrator **2.** (*fútbol, boxeo*) referee; (*tenis*) umpire

árbol *m* **1.** BOT tree; ~ **de Navidad** Christmas tree; ~ **de la ciencia** tree of knowledge; ~ **genealógico** family tree **2.** TÉC (*eje*) shaft **3.** NÁUT mast ▶ **los ~es no le dejan ver el bosque** he can't see the wood for the trees; **del ~ caído todos hacen leña** *prov* there are always those who will seek to benefit from another's misfortune

arbolado *m,* **arboleda** *f* woodland

arbóreo, -a *adj* **1.** (*relativo al árbol*) tree, arboreal *form;* **masa arbórea** tree population **2.** (*parecido*) tree-like

arboricultura *f* forestry

arbusto *m* shrub, bush

arca *f* chest; (*para dinero*) safe; **las ~s del estado** the treasury ▶ ~ **de la alianza** REL Ark of the Covenant; ~ **de Noé** Noah's Ark; ~ **del pan** *inf* stomach, breadbasket *inf;* **ser un** ~ **cerrada** to be very reserved

arcada *f* **1.** ARQUIT arcade **2.** *pl* (*náusea*) retching

arcaico, -a *adj* (*anticuado*) archaic

arcángel *m* archangel

arcano *m* mystery

arcano, -a *adj* arcane

arce *m* maple

arcén *m* edge; (*de carretera*) hard shoulder *Brit,* shoulder *Am*

archiconocido, -a *adj inf* very well-known

archimillonario, -a *m, f* multimillionaire

archipiélago *m* archipelago; **el** ~ **canario** the Canary Islands

archisabido, -a *adj inf* very well-known; **esto está ya** ~ this is a well-known fact

archivador *m* **1.** (*mueble*) filing cabinet **2.** (*carpeta*) file

archivador(a) *m(f)* archivist

archivar *vt* (*documentos*) to file; INFOR to store; (*asunto: por un tiempo*) to put on file; (*para siempre*) to close the file on

archivero, -a *m, f* archivist

archivo *m* **1.** (*lugar*) archive(s); ~ **fotográfico** picture library; **constar en los ~s** to be on record **2.** *pl* (*documentos*) archives *pl* **3.** INFOR file

arcilla *f* clay; ~ **de alfarería** potter's clay

arcilloso, -a *adj* clayey

arco *m* **1.** ARQUIT arc; ~ **de medio punto** round arch **2.** (*arma*) *t.* MÚS bow **3.** *t.* MAT, ELEC arc; ~ **iris** rainbow; ~ **parlamentario** political spectrum; ~ **voltaico** arc lamp **4.** *AmL* DEP goal

arcón *m* large chest

arder vi 1.(quemar, llamear) to burn; ~ con fuerza to blaze; ~ sin llama to smoulder; ~ por los cuatro costados to be ablaze; ~ de fiebre to have a very high temperature; ~ de pasión to be inflamed with passion; ~ de rabia to be mad with rage; me arde la garganta my throat is burning; la reunión está que arde things are getting heated at the meeting; estoy que ardo (enfadado) I'm furious 2.+ en, fig ardo en deseos de conocerte I'm dying to get to know you; Valencia arde en fiestas the festivities in Valencia are at their height; el país arde en guerra war is raging in the country

ardid m ruse

ardiente adj 1.(pasión, deseo, fiebre) burning 2.(sed) raging 3.(persona) passionate 4.(color) bright

ardilla f squirrel

ardor m 1.(calor) heat; ~ de estómago heartburn 2.(fervor) ardour Brit, ardor Am; el ~ de su mirada the ardour [o ardor Am] of his/her look; en el ~ del combate in the heat of battle

ardoroso, -a adj 1.(apasionado) ardent 2.(caliente) hot; (calor) burning

arduo, -a adj arduous

área f t. MAT area; un ~ de 200 metros cuadrados an area of 200 square metres [o meters Am]; ~ de descanso AUTO lay-by Brit, rest stop Am; ~ de castigo DEP penalty area; ~ metropolitana metropolitan area; ~ de no fumar no-smoking area

arena f 1.(materia) sand; ~s movedizas quicksand 2.(escenario) arena ▶ edificar sobre ~ to build upon sandy ground; sembrar en ~ to labour Brit [o labor Am] in vain

arenal m sandy area

arenga f 1.inf (discurso) harangue 2. Chile (disputa) argument

arengar <g→gu> vt to harangue

arenoso, -a adj sandy

arenque m herring; ~s ahumados kippers pl

arepa f AmL: cornmeal griddlecake

arequipa f Col, Méx: type of milk pudding

arete m earring

argamasa f mortar

Argel m Algiers

Argelia f Algeria

argelino, -a adj, m, f Algerian

Argentina f Argentina

> **Argentina** (official title: **República Argentina**) lies in the southern part of South America. It is the second largest country in South America after Brazil. The capital of Argentina is **Buenos Aires**. The official language of the country is Spanish and the monetary unit is the **peso argentino**.

argentino, -a adj, m, f Argentinian

argolla f 1.(anilla) ring 2. Chile, Col, Hond, Méx (alianza) wedding ring

argot <argots> m (marginal) slang; (profesional) jargon

argucia f 1.(argumento falso) fallacy 2.(truco) trick

argüende m Méx (chisme) gossip

argüir irr como huir I. vt 1.(alegar) to argue 2.(deducir) to deduce 3.(probar) to prove II. vi to argue

argumentación f line of argument

argumentar vi, vt to argue

argumento m 1.(razón) argument; (razonamiento) reasoning 2.LIT, CINE, TEAT plot 3. AmL (discusión) discussion; (alegato) argument

aria f aria

aridez f aridity

árido, -a adj (terreno) arid, dry; (tema) dry

Aries m inv Aries

ariete m MIL battering ram; DEP striker

ario, -a adj, m, f Aryan

arisco, -a adj (persona) surly, unfriendly; (animal) skittish

arista f edge

aristocracia f aristocracy

aristócrata mf aristocrat

aristocrático, -a adj aristocratic

aritmética f arithmetic

aritmético, -a adj arithmetical

arlequín m harlequin

arma f 1.(instrumento) weapon, arm; un ~ homicida a murder weapon; ~ blanca knife; ~ de fuego firearm; ~ reglamentaria regulation weapon; llegar a las ~s to become violent; pasar a alguien por las ~s to shoot sb; rendir las ~s to surrender [o to lay down] one's arms; tomar las ~s to take up arms; ¡apunten ~s! take aim!; ¡descansen ~s! order arms! 2.(sección del ejército) arm 3. pl (blasón) arms pl ▶ ser un ~ de doble filo to be a double-edged sword; ser de ~s tomar to be bold

armada f 1.(fuerzas navales) navy; un oficial de la ~ a naval officer 2.(escuadra) fleet; HIST armada

armadillo m armadillo

armado, -a adj armed; ~ de algo armed with sth

armador(a) m(f) shipowner

armadura f 1.(de caballero) armour Brit, armor Am; una ~ a suit of armour [o armor Am] 2.(de gafas) frame; (de cama) bedstead; (de edificio) framework

armamento m (de una persona) arms pl; (de un país) armaments pl

armar I. vt 1.(persona, ejército) to arm; ~ a alguien de [o con]... to arm sb with ... 2.(embarcación) to fit out 3.TÉC to assemble; (tienda de campaña) to pitch 4.inf (jaleo) to stir up; (ruido) to raise; ~ la to start a row ▶ ~ a alguien caballero to knight sb; ~ un Cristo inf to kick up a stink II. vr ~se de [o con] algo to arm oneself with sth ▶ ~se de paciencia to muster one's patience; ~se de valor to pluck up courage

armario *m* cupboard; ~ **empotrado** built-in cupboard; ~ **(ropero)** wardrobe

armatoste *m* monstrosity (*huge useless object*)

armazón *m o f* (*armadura*) frame; (*de edificio*) skeleton

Armenia *f* Armenia

armenio, -a *adj, m, f* Armenian

armería *f* **1.** (*tienda*) gunsmith's (shop) **2.** (*museo*) armoury *Brit,* armory *Am*

armero *m* gunsmith

armiño *m* **1.** (*animal*) stoat **2.** (*piel*) ermine

armisticio *m* armistice

armonía *f* harmony; **falta de** ~ (*entre personas*) discord; **su comportamiento no estuvo en** ~ **con la solemnidad del acto** his/her behaviour wasn't in keeping with the solemnity of the ceremony

armónica *f* harmonica, mouth organ

armónico, -a *adj* harmonic

armonio *m* harmonium

armonioso, -a *adj* harmonious

armonizar <z→c> **I.** *vi* to harmonize; ~ **con** (*colores*) to blend with; **estos dos objetos armonizan** these two objects go together **II.** *vt* to harmonize; ~ **colores** to harmonize colours; ~ **ideas** to reconcile ideas

arnés *m* **1.** (*armadura*) armour, armor *Am* **2.** *pl* (*caballería*) harness

árnica *f* arnica

aro *m* **1.** (*argolla*) ring; (*para jugar, hacer gimnasia*) hoop **2.** *Arg* (*arete*) earring **3.** *AmL* (*anillo de boda*) wedding ring ►**entrar** [*o* **pasar**] **por el** ~ to knuckle under

aroma *m* (*olor*) scent; (*de café*) aroma

aromático, -a *adj* aromatic

aromatizante *adj, m* aromatic

aromatizar <z→c> *vt* **1.** (*perfumar*) to scent **2.** GASTR to flavour *Brit,* to flavor *Am*

arpa *f* harp

arpía *f* harpy

arpón *m* harpoon

arquear **I.** *vt* **1.** (*doblar*) to bend; (*espalda*) to arch; **el gato arqueó su lomo** the cat arched its back **2.** (*cejas*) to raise **II.** *vr:* ~**se** (*doblarse*) to bend; (*espalda*) to arch

arqueo *m* **1.** (*de espalda*) *t.* ARQUIT arching **2.** COM cashing up **3.** NÁUT capacity

arqueología *f* archaeology, archeology *Am*

arqueológico, -a *adj* archaeological, archeological *Am*

arqueólogo, -a *m, f* archaeologist, archeologist *Am*

arquero, -a *m, f* **1.** archer **2.** *Arg* DEP goalkeeper

arquetípico, -a *adj* archetypal

arquetipo *m* archetype

arquitecto, -a *m, f* architect; ~ **interiorista** interior designer; ~ **técnico** quantity surveyor

arquitectónico, -a *adj* architectural

arquitectura *f* architecture

arrabal *m* (*periferia*) suburb; (*barrio bajo*)

slum area; **vivir en los** ~**es** to live on the outskirts

arrabalero, -a *adj* **1.** (*de periferia*) suburban; (*de un barrio bajo*) from the slums **2.** (*grosero*) vulgar **II.** *m, f* **1.** (*de barrio bajo*) slumdweller **2.** (*grosero*) vulgar person

arracachada *f Col* silliness; **no dijeron más que** ~**s** they said nothing but nonsense

arracimarse *vr* to bunch together

arraigado, -a *adj* deep-rooted

arraigar <g→gu> *vi, vr:* ~**se** *t. fig* to take root

arraigo *m t. fig* rooting; **de mucho** ~ deep-rooted

arramblar *vi* ~ **con** to make off with

arrancada *f* **1.** (*salida*) (sudden) start **2.** DEP (*en halterofilia*) snatch

arrancar <c→qu> **I.** *vt* **1.** (*planta, flor*) to pull up; **el viento arrancó el árbol** the wind uprooted the tree **2.** (*pegatina, póster*) to tear off; (*página*) to tear out **3.** (*muela*) to extract, to pull (out); (*clavo*) to pull out **4.** (*quitar con violencia*) to snatch (away); **le** ~**on el arma** they wrenched the weapon from him/her; **el ladrón le arrancó el bolso de la mano** the thief snatched her handbag from her hand; **la granada le arrancó un brazo** the grenade blew off his/her arm; **la corriente arrancó el puente** the current swept away the bridge **5.** (*vehículo, motor*) to start **6.** (*conseguir: aplausos*) to draw; ~ **aplausos al público** to draw applause from the audience; ~ **una promesa a alguien** to force a promise out of sb; ~ **un secreto a alguien** to worm a secret out of sb; ~ **una victoria** to snatch (a) victory **II.** *vi* **1.** (*vehículo, motor*) to start **2.** (*iniciar: persona*) ~ **a hacer algo** to start doing sth; ~ **a correr** to start running; ~ **a cantar** to burst out singing **3.** (*provenir*) to stem; (*comenzar*) to begin; **esto arranca del siglo XV** this goes back to the 15th century

arranque *m* **1.** (*comienzo*) start; **en el** ~ **de la temporada** at the start of the season **2.** AUTO starting; ~ **automático** self-starter **3.** (*arrebato*) outburst; **un** ~ **de cólera/celos** a fit of anger/jealousy; **en un** ~ impulsively **4.** (*prontitud*) promptness; (*decisión*) initiative; **tener** ~ **para hacer algo** to have initiative to do sth **5.** ARQUIT base **6.** INFOR start-up

arras *fpl* thirteen coins that the bridegroom gives the bride during the wedding

arrasar **I.** *vt* (*destruir: edificios*) to demolish; (*región*) to devastate **II.** *vi* to triumph; POL to sweep the board **III.** *vr:* ~**se** (*ojos*) to fill with tears

arrastrado, -a *adj* poor, wretched; **traer una vida arrastrada** to have a wretched life

arrastrar **I.** *vt* **1.** (*tirar de*) to pull; (*algo pesado*) to drag; ~**on la caja montaña arriba** they dragged the box up the mountain; **el agua arrastra las piedras** the water sweeps the stones along; **el viento arrastra las hojas** the wind sweeps away the leaves; ~ **los pies**

(al caminar) to drag one's feet 2. (*impulsar*) ~ a alguien a hacer algo to lead sb to do sth; lo pude ~ al cine I was able to drag him to the cinema; no te dejes ~ por ese problema don't get carried away by that problem 3. (*producir*) to have as a consequence; eso le arrastró dolores de cabeza that caused him/her to have headaches II. *vi* (*vestido, cortinas*) to trail on the ground III. *vr:* ~se 1. (*reptar*) to crawl; ~se por el suelo to crawl along; se arrastró hasta la habitación he/she dragged himself/herself to the room 2. (*humillarse*) to grovel

arrastre *m* (*de objetos, bultos*) dragging; (*en pesca*) trawling ▶ **estar para el** ~ *inf* (*cosa*) to be ruined; (*persona*) to be a wreck

arre *interj* gee up *Brit*, giddap *Am*

arreada *f Arg, Chile, Méx* rustling

arrear I. *vt* 1. (*ganado*) to drive 2. *inf* (*golpe*) to give II. *vi inf* to hurry along; ¡arrea! (*rápido*) get a move on!; (*atiza*) good heavens!

arrebañaduras *fpl* leftovers *pl*

arrebatado, -a *adj* 1. (*alocado*) hasty, violent 2. (*impetuoso*) rash 3. (*rostro*) flushed

arrebatar I. *vt* 1. (*arrancar*) to snatch (away); el viento le arrebató el sombrero the wind blew off his/her hat; fue arrebatado por la corriente he was swept away by the current; ~ la vida a alguien to take sb's life; ~ la victoria a alguien to snatch victory from sb 2. (*extasiar*) to captivate 3. (*conmover*) to move II. *vr:* ~se (*exaltarse*) to get carried away

arrebato *m* 1. (*arranque*) outburst; un ~ de cólera a fit of anger 2. (*éxtasis*) ecstasy

arrebujar I. *vt* 1. (*arrugar*) to crumple up 2. (*envolver*) to wrap up II. *vr:* ~se to wrap oneself up; ~se en una manta to wrap oneself up in a blanket

arrecho, -a *adj Col, inf* 1. (*vigoroso*) vigorous 2. (*cachondo*) horny, randy 3. (*enfadado*) angry

arrechucho *m inf* (*de salud*) indisposition; le dio un ~ he/she had a bad turn

arreciar *vi* 1. (*viento*) to get stronger; (*lluvia*) to get heavier 2. (*críticas*) to intensify

arrecife *m* reef

arredrar I. *vt* 1. (*hacer retroceder*) to drive back 2. (*asustar*) to frighten II. *vr:* ~se 1. (*echarse atrás*) ~se ante algo to draw back from sth; ~se ante alguien to shrink (away) from sb 2. (*asustarse*) to get scared; sin ~se without flinching

arreglado, -a *adj* 1. (*ordenado*) tidy; (*cuidado*) neat 2. (*elegante*) smart 3. (*moderado: precio*) reasonable ▶ ¡estamos ~s! now we're in trouble!; estás arreglado si crees que te ayudaré you're very much mistaken if you think I'm going to help you; ¡vas ~ si piensas que...! you're in for a big surprise if you think ...!

arreglar I. *vt* 1. (*reparar*) to repair; (*ropa, zapatos*) to mend; esta sopa te ~á el estómago this soup will do your stomach good

2. (*ordenar*) to tidy up; ~ la habitación to tidy up the room; ~ la habitación para los invitados to get the room ready for the guests; ~ una mesa con flores to adorn a table with flowers 3. (*preparar*) to get ready; ~ a los niños para salir to get the children ready for going out 4. (*pelo*) to do 5. (*resolver: asunto*) to sort out 6. (*acordar*) to arrange; ~ las cuentas con alguien to get even with sb 7. MÚS to arrange ▶ ¡ya te ~é yo! *inf* I'll sort you out! II. *vr:* ~se 1. (*vestirse, peinarse*) to get ready 2. (*componérselas*) to manage; no sé cómo te las arreglas I don't know how you manage; ¿cómo te has arreglado para convencerlo? how did you manage to convince him? 3. (*ponerse de acuerdo*) to come to an agreement; (*solucionarse*) to work out; al final todo se arregló everything worked out all right in the end 4. (*mejorar*) to get better; el tiempo se está arreglando the weather is getting better

arreglo *m* 1. (*reparación*) repair 2. (*solución*) solution; no tienes ~ you're a hopeless case; este trabajo ya no tiene ~ this job is completely botched 3. (*acuerdo*) agreement; llegar a un ~ to reach a settlement; con ~ a lo convenido as agreed; obré con ~ a las normas I worked in accordance with the regulations 4. MÚS arrangement

arrellanarse *vr* to settle comfortably; ~ en algo to settle oneself in sth

arremangar <g→gu> *vt, vr:* ~se to roll up; ~se la camisa to roll up one's sleeves; arremángate roll up your sleeves

arremeter *vi* 1. (*criticar*) to attack; ~ contra alguien to attack sb 2. (*embestir*) to charge

arremetida *f* 1. (*crítica*) attack 2. (*embestida*) charge

arremolinarse *vr* 1. (*hojas, polvo, agua*) to swirl around 2. (*gente*) to mill around

arrendador(a) *m(f)* (*de casa*) landlord *m*, landlady *f*; (*de terreno, negocio*) *t.* JUR lessor

arrendamiento *m* 1. (*alquiler*) rent; (*de terreno, negocio*) lease; ~ financiero leasing 2. (*contrato*) contract

arrendar <e→ie> *vt* (*propietario*) to rent, to let; (*inquilino*) to rent, to lease

arrendatario, -a *m, f* (*de una casa*) tenant; (*de un terreno, negocio*) *t.* JUR lessee, leaseholder

arreos *mpl* (*de caballerías*) harness

arrepentido, -a *adj* 1. (*lamentándose*) sorry; REL repentant; estar ~ de algo to be sorry about sth, to regret sth 2. (*delincuente*) reformed; un terrorista ~ a reformed terrorist

arrepentimiento *m* (*lamento*) regret; REL repentance

arrepentirse *irr como sentir vr* (*lamentar*) to regret; REL to repent; ~ de algo to regret sth; REL to repent of sth

arrestar *vt* to arrest; MIL to confine to barracks

arresto *m* 1. (*detención*) arrest; estar bajo ~ to be under arrest 2. (*reclusión*) imprisonment; MIL detention; ~ **domiciliario** house arrest **3.** *pl* (*arrojo*) daring; **tener ~s** to be bold

arrevesado, -a *adj CSur, PRico* complicated; **un crucigrama bastante** ~ a rather difficult crossword puzzle

arria *f AmL* train of pack animals

arriar <*l.pres:* arrío> *vt* **1.** (*bandera*) to lower **2.** (*cabo, cadena*) to loosen **3.** (*inundar*) to flood

arriba *adv* **1.** (*posición*) above; (*en una casa*) upstairs; **más** ~ higher up; **te espero** ~ I'll wait for you upstairs; **lo** ~ **mencionado** the aforementioned; **la habitación de** ~ (*de encima*) the room above; **el piso de** ~ (*el último*) the top floor; **de** ~ **abajo** from top to bottom; (*persona*) from head to foot; **ensuciarse de** ~ **abajo** to get dirty from head to foot [*o* toe]; **leer un libro de** ~ **abajo** to read a book from cover to cover; **¡manos** ~! hands up! **2.** (*dirección*) up, upwards; **río** ~ upstream; **¡~!** get up! **3.** (*cantidad*) **tener de 60 años para** ~ to be over 60; **precios de 100 euros para** ~ prices from 100 euros upwards **4.** *CSur* **de** ~ (*gratis*) free (of charge); (*sin merecerlo*) for no reason

arribar *vi* **1.** NÁUT to reach port **2.** *AmL* (*llegar*) to arrive

arribista *mf* arriviste; (*en sociedad*) social climber

arriendo *m v.* **arrendamiento**

arriesgado, -a *adj* **1.** (*peligroso*) risky, dangerous **2.** (*atrevido*) daring

arriesgar <g→gu> I. *vt* **1.** (*vida, reputación*) to risk **2.** (*en el juego*) to stake **3.** (*hipótesis, afirmación*) to venture II. *vr:* ~**se** to take a risk; ~**se a hacer algo** to risk doing sth

arrimar I. *vt* **1.** (*acercar*) to bring closer **2.** (*apoyar*) ~ **algo a** to lean sth against II. *vr:* ~**se 1.** (*acercarse*) to come close(r); ~**se a algo** to move closer to sth; ~**se al poder** to seek the protection of the authorities **2.** (*apoyarse*) ~**se a algo** to lean against sth; **el niño se arrimó a su madre** the child snuggled up to his mother

arrinconado, -a *adj* **1.** (*apartado*) remote **2.** (*desatendido*) neglected **3.** (*olvidado*) forgotten

arrinconar I. *vt* **1.** (*objeto*) to put in a corner **2.** (*enemigo*) to corner **3.** (*deshacerse de*) to get rid of **4.** (*rehuir*) to ignore II. *vr:* ~**se** to withdraw from the world

arriscado, -a *adj* **1.** (*arriesgado*) risky **2.** (*escabroso*) craggy **3.** (*atrevido*) bold

arroba *f* **1.** INFOR at **2.** (*unidad de peso*) ≈ 11,502 kg

arrobar I. *vt* to entrance II. *vr:* ~**se** to become entranced

arrobo *m* ecstasy; REL trance

arrocero, -a I. *adj* rice; **industria arrocera** rice industry II. *m, f* rice grower

arrodillarse *vr* to kneel (down)

arrogancia *f* arrogance

arrogante *adj* arrogant

arrogarse <g→gu> *vr* to assume; ~ **la facultad de juzgar a los demás** to presume to judge other people

arrojado, -a *adj* daring

arrojar I. *vt* **1.** (*lanzar*) to throw; **el caballo arrojó al jinete** the horse threw the rider **2.** (*emitir*) to emit, to give off [*o* out]; **la chimenea arroja humo** the chimney is giving off smoke; ~ **un mal olor** to give off a bad smell **3.** (*expulsar*) to throw out **4.** *AmL, inf* (*vomitar*) to throw up **5.** (*un resultado*) to produce; ~ **beneficios** to yield profits; ~ **fallos** to contain errors; **mi cuenta arroja un saldo de 800 euros** my account shows a balance of 800 euros II. *vr:* ~**se** to throw oneself; ~**se al agua** to jump into the water

arrojo *m* daring; **con** ~ boldly

arrollador(a) *adj* **1.** (*mayoría*) overwhelming; (*fuerza*) devastating **2.** (*carácter, vitalidad, optimismo*) irresistible

arrollar *vt* **1.** (*enrollar*) to roll up **2.** (*atropellar*) to run over **3.** DEP (*derrotar*) to crush **4.** (*riada, agua*) to sweep away

arropar I. *vt* **1.** (*abrigar*) to wrap up; (*en la cama*) to tuck in **2.** (*proteger*) to protect II. *vr:* ~**se** (*abrigarse*) to wrap oneself up; (*en la cama*) to tuck oneself up; **¡arrópate bien!** wrap up warm!

arrorró *m AmS* lullaby

arrostrar *vt* (*consecuencias*) to face up to; (*peligro*) to face

arroyo *m* **1.** (*riachuelo*) stream **2.** (*cuneta*) gutter; **salir del** ~ to climb out of the gutter

arroz *m* rice; ~ **con leche** rice pudding

arrozal *m* ricefield

arruga *f* **1.** (*en la piel*) wrinkle **2.** (*en papel, tela*) crease; **este vestido hace ~s** this dress creases

arrugar <g→gu> I. *vt* **1.** (*piel*) to wrinkle **2.** (*papel, tela*) to crease II. *vr:* ~**se 1.** (*piel*) to wrinkle, to get wrinkled **2.** (*papel, tela*) to crease, to get creased **3.** (*achicarse*) to get scared

arruinar I. *vt* **1.** (*causar ruina*) to ruin **2.** (*destruir*) to destroy **3.** (*fiesta, vacaciones*) to spoil; (*plan*) to wreck II. *vr:* ~**se** to be ruined

arrullar I. *vt* (*a un niño*) to lull to sleep II. *vi* (*paloma*) to coo III. *vr:* ~**se** to bill and coo

arrullo *m* **1.** (*para niños*) lullaby **2.** (*de paloma*) cooing

arrumbar *vt* **1.** (*cosa*) to discard **2.** (*persona*) to ignore

arsenal *m* **1.** (*de armas, municiones*) arsenal **2.** NÁUT dockyard

arsénico *m* arsenic

arte *m o f* (*m en sing, f en pl*) **1.** (*disciplina artística*) art; ~ **culinario** culinary art; ~ **dramático** drama; ~ **narrativo** narrative art; ~**s plásticas** visual arts; ~**s y oficios** arts and crafts; **bellas ~s** fine arts; **el séptimo** ~ the cinema *Brit*, the movies *Am* **2.** (*habilidad*) skill; **tener mucho** ~ **para la pintura** to be a really skilled painter **3.** (*maña*) trick; **conseguir algo por malas ~s** to obtain sth by trickery; **desplegó todas sus ~s para convencerlo** she used all her wiles to convince him ▶**como por ~ de magia** as if by magic; **no tener ~ ni parte en algo** to have nothing whatsoever to do with sth; **~s de pesca** fishing tackle

artefacto *m* (*aparato*) appliance; (*mecanismo*) device; **~ explosivo** explosive device

artemisa *f* mugwort

arteria *f* **1.** ANAT artery **2.** (*de tráfico*) thoroughfare

arterio(e)sclerosis *f inv* arteriosclerosis

artesa *f* trough

artesanal *adj* craft; **industria ~** craft industry

artesanía *f* **1.** (*arte*) craftsmanship; **jarrón de ~** handmade vase **2.** (*obras*) handicrafts *pl*

artesano, -a *m, f* artisan, craftsman *m,* craftswoman *f*

artesonado *m* coffered ceiling

artesonado, -a *adj* coffered

ártico *m* **1.** (*océano*) Arctic Ocean **2.** (*región*) Arctic

ártico, -a *adj* Arctic

articulación *f* **1.** ANAT, TÉC joint **2.** LING articulation

articulado, -a *adj* articulated; **camión ~** articulated lorry

articular **I.** *vt* **1.** TÉC to join together **2.** LING to articulate **II.** *adj* articular

articulista *mf* feature writer

artículo *m* **1.** (*objeto*) article; COM commodity; **~s de consumo** consumer goods; **~s de lujo** luxury goods; **~s de primera necesidad** basic commodities; **~s de tocador** toiletries **2.** PREN, JUR, LING article **3.** (*en un diccionario*) entry

artífice *mf* **1.** (*artista*) artist **2.** *fig* architect

artificial *adj* artificial

artificio *m* **1.** (*mecanismo*) device; (*aparato*) appliance **2.** (*habilidad*) skill; (*truco*) trick; **un ~ técnico** a technical contrivance **3.** *pey* (*afectación*) affectation; **hablar con ~** to speak affectedly

artillería *f* artillery

artillero *m* gunner

artilugio *m* gadget

artimaña *f* (sly) trick

artista *mf* **1.** (*de bellas artes*) artist **2.** (*de circo, teatro*) artist(e) *m(f)*; (*de cine*) actor *m,* actress *f* **3.** (*experto*) expert; **es un ~ en su especialidad** he's an expert in his field

artístico, -a *adj* artistic

artrítico, -a **I.** *adj* arthritic **II.** *m, f* person with arthritis

artritis *f inv* arthritis

artrosis *f inv* arthrosis

arzobispo *m* archbishop

as *m t. fig* ace; **un ~ del volante** an ace driver

asa *f* handle

asado *m* **1.** GASTR roast **2.** *Arg* (*comida*) barbecue

asador *m* **1.** (*pincho*) spit **2.** (*aparato*) spit roaster **3.** (*restaurante*) rotisserie

asadura *f* offal

asalariado, -a **I.** *adj* wage-earning **II.** *m, f* wage earner

asaltante *mf* attacker; (*de banco*) raider

asaltar *vt* **1.** (*fortaleza, ciudad*) to storm; (*banco*) to break into, to raid **2.** (*persona*) to attack, to assault; **~ a alguien con preguntas** to bombard sb with questions **3.** (*pensamiento*) to cross one's mind; (*duda*) to assail; **me asaltó una idea** I was struck by an idea; **me asaltó el pánico** I got into a panic

asalto *m* **1.** (*a una fortaleza, ciudad*) storming; **~ a algo** storming of sth; **tomar por [o al] ~** to take by storm **2.** (*a un banco*) raid; **~ a un banco/a alguien** raid on a bank/of sb **3.** (*a una persona*) attack, assault **4.** DEP (*en boxeo*) round; (*en esgrima*) bout

asamblea *f* assembly; (*reunión*) meeting; **~ general** general assembly; **~ plenaria** plenary meeting; **~ de trabajadores** workers' meeting

asambleísta *mf* assemblyman *m,* assemblywoman *f*

asar **I.** *vt* **1.** GASTR to roast; **~ a la parrilla** to grill **2.** (*a preguntas*) to pester **II.** *vr:* **~se** to roast; **en esta casa se asa uno vivo** *inf* it's absolutely roasting in this house

asbesto *m* asbestos

ascendencia *f* **1.** (*linaje*) ancestry, descent; **de ~ escocesa** of Scottish descent **2.** (*antepasados*) ancestors *pl* **3.** (*origen*) origin

ascendente **I.** *adj* ascending; **en orden ~** in ascending order; **la carrera ~ de un pistón** the up-stroke of a piston **II.** *m* ascendant

ascender <e→ie> **I.** *vi* **1.** (*subir*) to rise; DEP to go up; **el equipo asciende a primera** (*división*) the team goes up to the first division **2.** (*escalar*) to climb **3.** (*de empleo*) to be promoted **4.** COM **~ a** (*cuenta*) to come to; (*cantidad*) to amount to **II.** *vt* to promote

ascendiente[1] *mf* (*antepasado*) ancestor

ascendiente[2] *m* (*influencia*) influence

ascensión *f* **1.** (*a una montaña, al trono*) ascent **2.** (*de Cristo*) Ascension

ascenso *m* **1.** (*de precio, temperatura*) rise **2.** (*a una montaña*) ascent **3.** (*de equipo, empleado*) promotion; **el ~ a primera** (*división*) the promotion to the first division

ascensor *m* lift *Brit,* elevator *Am;* **tomar el ~** to take the lift

ascético, -a *adj* ascetic

asco *m* **1.** (*sensación*) disgust, loathing; **tomar ~ a algo** to get sick of sth; **este olor me da ~** this smell makes me feel sick; **las espinacas me dan ~** I loathe spinach; **este hombre me da ~** I really detest this man; **hacer ~s a algo** to turn up one's nose at sth; **¡qué ~ de gente!** *inf* what dreadful people!; **¡qué ~!** how awful! **2.** (*situación*) **estar hecho un ~** (*lugar*) to be a mess; (*persona*) to feel low; **estar muerto de ~** to be bored stiff; **ser un ~** to be disgusting

ascua *f* ember ▸ **arrimar el ~ a su sardina** to feather one's nest; **estar en** [*o* **sobre**] **~s** to be on tenterhooks; **pasar algo sobre ~s** to deal with sth superficially; **tener a alguien en ~s** to keep sb on tenterhooks

aseado, -a *adj* (*limpio*) clean, tidy; (*arreglado*) smart

asear I. *vt* to clean up II. *vr:* **~se** to tidy oneself up

asechanza *f* 1. (*trampa*) trap 2. *pl* (*intrigas*) intrigues *pl*

asediar *vt* 1. MIL to besiege 2. (*importunar*) to bother

asedio *m* 1. MIL siege 2. (*fastidio*) nuisance

asegurado, -a *adj, m, f* insured

asegurador(a) *m(f)* (*persona*) insurance agent

aseguradora *f* (*empresa*) insurance company

asegurar I. *vt* 1. (*fijar*) to secure; **~ una puerta con una cadena** to secure a door with a chain 2. (*afirmar*) to affirm; **asegura no haber dicho nada** she maintains that she did not say anything 3. (*prometer*) to assure; (*garantizar*) to ensure; **se lo aseguro** I assure you; **aseguró que no lo sabía** he/she assured that he/she didn't know 4. (*mediante un seguro*) to insure II. *vr:* **~se** 1. (*comprobar*) to make sure; **~se de que funciona** to make sure that it works 2. (*hacerse un seguro*) to insure oneself

asemejarse *vr* to be alike; **~ a algo** to resemble sth, to be like sth

asentaderas *fpl inf* behind

asentado, -a *adj* 1. (*juicioso*) sensible 2. (*estable*) settled; (*empresa*) established

asentar <e→ie> I. *vt* 1. (*poner*) to place; (*campamento*) to pitch; **~ los cimientos** to lay the foundations; **la lluvia ha asentado el polvo** the rain has caused the dust to settle 2. (*sentar*) to seat; **~ en el trono** to seat on the throne 3. (*población*) to found 4. (*estómago*) to settle 5. (*golpe*) to fetch 6. (*principios*) to lay down II. *vr:* **~se** to settle

asentimiento *m* assent

asentir *irr como sentir vi* to agree; **~ a algo** to agree to sth; **~ con la cabeza** to nod in agreement

aseo *m* 1. (*acción*) cleaning; (**cuarto de**) **~** bathroom 2. (*estado*) cleanliness; **~ personal** personal hygiene 3. *pl* (*servicios públicos*) toilets *pl Brit,* restrooms *pl Am*

aséptico, -a *adj* 1. MED aseptic 2. (*desapasionado*) dispassionate; (*frío*) cold

asequible *adj* 1. (*precio*) reasonable; **esta casa no es ~ para nosotros** this house is beyond our means 2. (*objetivo*) attainable; (*plan*) feasible 3. (*persona*) approachable

aserradero *m* sawmill

aserrar <e→ie> *vt* to saw

aserto *m* assertion

asesinar *vt* to murder; (*personaje público*) to assassinate

asesinato *m* murder; (*de personaje público*) assassination; **robo con ~** robbery with murder

asesino, -a I. *adj t. fig* murderous; **ballena asesina** killer whale II. *m, f* murderer; (*de personaje público*) assassin; **~ (a sueldo)** hit man

asesor(a) I. *adj* advisory II. *m(f)* 1. (*consejero*) adviser, consultant; **~ legal** legal adviser 2. JUR assessor

asesoramiento *f* advice

asesorar I. *vt* to advise II. *vr* **~se en algo** to take advice about sth; **~se con un médico/ abogado** to take medical/legal advice

asesoría *f* 1. (*oficio*) consultancy 2. (*oficina*) consultant's office

asestar *vt* (*propinar*) to deal; **~ una puñalada a alguien** to stab sb; **~ un tiro a alguien** to fire a shot at sb

aseveración *f* assertion

aseverar *vt* (*afirmar*) to affirm; (*asegurar*) to assure; (*con energía*) to assert

asfaltado *m* 1. (*acción*) asphalting 2. (*capa*) asphalt

asfaltar *vt* to asphalt

asfalto *m* asphalt

asfixia *f* suffocation, asphyxia

asfixiante *adj* suffocating; **una atmósfera ~** a stifling atmosphere; **hace un calor ~** the heat is suffocating

asfixiar I. *vt* (*persona*) to suffocate; (*humo, gas*) to asphyxiate II. *vr:* **~se** to suffocate

así I. *adv* 1. (*de este modo*) in this way; **lo hizo ~** he/she did it like this; **~ es como lo hizo** that's how he/she did it; **yo soy ~** that's the way I am; **no puedes decir esto ~ como ~** you just can't say that; **no puedes tomar esta decisión ~ como ~** you can't take [*o* make] this decision just like that; **¡~ es!** that's right!; **¡~ es la vida!** that's life; **¿no es ~?** isn't it?; **por ~ decirlo** so to speak 2. (*ojalá*) **¡~ revientes!** I hope you die! 3. (*de extrañeza*) **¿~ que me dejas?** so you're leaving me? 4. (*de esta medida, cantidad*) **~ de grande** this big; **era ~ de feo** he was that ugly 5. *elev* (*temporal*) **~ que se fueron, lavamos los platos** as soon as they left, we washed the dishes ▸ **y todo** even so; **o ~á** *inf* one way or another; **¿~ qué?** what now?; **~ ~** so-so II. *conj* 1. (*concesiva*) **~ se esté muriendo de frío...** even though he's/she's freezing ...; **~ lo ahorques no dará su brazo a torcer** no matter what you say to him, he won't back down 2. (*consecutiva*) **empezó a llover ~ que nos quedamos en casa** it began to rain, so we stayed indoors; **sólo hay una plaza libre, ~ (es) que decídete pronto** there's only one free seat, so make up your mind; **te esperaré en la calle; ~ pues, no te retrases** I'll wait for you in the street, so don't be late 3. (*comparativa*) **~ el uno como el otro** both one and the other; **~ en la tierra como en el cielo** on earth as it is in heaven III. *adj inv* like

this, like that; **un sueldo** ~ a salary of that amount; **una cosa** ~ something like that
Asia *f* Asia; ~ **menor** Asia Minor
asiático, -a *adj, m, f* Asian, Asiatic
asidero *m* 1.(*asa*) handle 2.(*pretexto*) pretext
asiduidad *f* 1.(*frecuencia*) frequency 2.(*regularidad*) regularity
asiduo, -a *adj* 1.(*frecuente*) frequent 2.(*regular*) regular; **un** ~ **cliente de este local** a regular in this bar
asiento *m* 1.(*silla*) seat; ~ **delantero** front seat; ~ **trasero** [*o* **de atrás**] rear seat; **tomar** ~ to take a seat 2.(*sitio*) site 3.(*de vasija, botella*) bottom 4.(*poso*) sediment 5.(*en una cuenta*) entry; ~ **de cierre** closing entry
asignación *f* 1.*t.* INFOR assignment; (*de recursos*) allocation; ~ **de una tecla** assignment of a key 2. FIN allowance
asignar *vt t.* INFOR to assign; (*recursos*) to allocate; (*subvención*) to award
asignatura *f* subject; ~ **pendiente** *subject which has to be retaken*
asilado, -a *m, f* POL political refugee
asilar I. *vt* POL to grant political asylum II. *vr:* ~**se** to take refuge; POL to seek political asylum
asilo *m* 1.POL asylum; **pedir/conceder** ~ to seek/to grant political asylum 2.(*refugio*) refuge, shelter 3.(*de ancianos*) (old people's) home 4.(*de huérfanos*) orphanage
asimetría *f* asymmetry
asimétrico, -a *adj* asymmetric(al)
asimilación *f* assimilation
asimilar *vt t.* BIO to assimilate
asimismo *adv* likewise, also
asir *irr* I. *vt* (*sujetar*) to seize II. *vr* ~**se a algo** to seize sth
asistencia *f* 1.(*presencia*) attendance, presence; **sin la** ~ **del presidente** in the president's absence 2.(*ayuda*) assistance, help; ~ **financiera** financial assistance; ~ **letrada** JUR legal aid; ~ **médica** medical care; ~ **social** social work
asistencial *adj* welfare; **servicios** ~**es** welfare services
asistenta *f* 1.(*ayudante*) assistant 2.(*para limpiar*) cleaning woman
asistente *mf* 1.(*ayudante*) assistant 2.(*persona presente*) **los** ~**s** those present ▶~ **social** social worker
asistido, -a *adj* assisted; ~ **por ordenador** computer-assisted; **dirección asistida** power(-assisted) steering; **fecundación/respiración asistida** artificial insemination/respiration
asistir I. *vi* 1.(*ir*) ~ **a algo** to attend sth; **no voy a** ~ I won't go 2.(*estar presente*) to be present; **asistieron unas 50 personas** some 50 people were present 3.(*presenciar*) ~ **a algo** to witness sth II. *vt* 1.(*estar presente en*) to attend 2.(*ayudar*) to help, assist; ~ **a un enfermo** to care for a patient
asma *f sin pl* asthma

asmático, -a *adj, m, f* asthmatic
asno *m* 1.ZOOL donkey, ass 2. *inf* (*persona*) ass
asociación *f* association; **siempre pienso en él en** ~ **con...** I always think of him in connection with ...; **Asociación Europea de Libre Cambio** European Free Trade Area; **Asociación de Padres de Alumnos** parent-teacher association; ~ **de vecinos** residents' association
asociado, -a I. *adj* associated; (*miembro*) associate II. *m, f* 1.(*socio*) associate 2.(*miembro*) member 3.(*de una empresa*) partner
asociar I. *vt* 1.*t.* POL to associate; **la asocio con alguien** I associate her with sb 2.(*juntar*) to join 3.COM to take into partnership II. *vr:* ~**se** to associate; COM to become partners, to form a partnership; ~**se con alguien** (*hacer compañía*) to join sb
asolar <o→ue> *vt* (*destruir*) to devastate
asoleada *f Col, Chile, Guat* (*insolación*) sunstroke
asomar I. *vt* 1.(*mostrar*) to show 2.(*parte del cuerpo*) to stick out; ~ **la cabeza por la ventana** to put one's head out of the window II. *vi* (*verse*) to show; (*aparecer*) to appear; **asoma el día** day is breaking III. *vr:* ~**se** 1.(*mostrarse*) to show up; ~**se al balcón** to come out onto the balcony; **¡asómate!** put your head out! 2.(*una parte del cuerpo*) to stick out 3.(*acercarse*) to pop in; **¿por qué no te asomas un rato?** why don't you pop in for a bit?
asombrar I. *vt* (*pasmar*) to amaze II. *vr* ~**se de algo** to be amazed at sth
asombro *m* amazement; **poner cara de** ~ to look amazed; **no salir de su** ~ not to get over one's amazement
asombroso, -a *adj* amazing
asomo *m* hint; **hay** ~**s de recuperación económica** there are signs of economic recovery; **no pienso en ello ni por** ~ I don't give it the slightest thought; **¿tienes miedo? – ni por** ~ are you afraid? – not in the slightest; **sin el menor** ~ **de...** without the slightest trace of ...
asonancia *f* assonance
asonante *adj* assonant
asorocharse *vr AmS* to get altitude sickness
aspa *f* 1.(*figura*) cross; **marcar con un** ~ to mark with a cross; **en forma de** ~ cross-shaped 2.(*de molino*) sail; (*de ventilador*) blade
aspamento *m Arg*, **aspaviento** *m* fuss; **hacer** ~**s** to make a fuss
aspecto *m* 1.(*apariencia*) appearance; **tener buen/mal** ~ to look/not to look well 2.(*punto de vista*) aspect; **bajo ese** ~ from that point of view
áspero, -a *adj* 1.(*superficie*) rough 2.(*terreno*) rugged 3.(*sabor*) sour 4.(*persona, voz, tono*) harsh; **tener un carácter** ~ to be bad-tempered 5.(*clima*) tough
aspersión *f* sprinkling; **riego por** ~ watering by sprinkler

aspersor *m* sprinkler
aspiración *f* 1.(*inspiración*) breathing in 2.(*pretensión*) aspiration; **tener grandes aspiraciones** to have great aspirations 3. LING aspiration
aspirador *m v.* **aspiradora**
aspiradora *f* vacuum cleaner, hoover *Brit;* **pasar la ~** to vacuum
aspirante *mf* aspirant; (*a un empleo*) applicant; POL candidate
aspirar I. *vt* 1.(*inspirar*) to breathe in, inhale; **salir a ~ aire fresco** to go out to get a breath of fresh air 2.(*aspirador*) to suck in 3. LING to aspirate II. *vi* 1.(*inspirar*) to breathe in 2.(*pretender*) to aspire; **~ a mucho en la vida** to have high aims in life
aspirina® *f* aspirin®
asquear I. *vt* 1.(*dar asco*) to disgust 2.(*fastidiar*) to bother II. *vr:* ~**se** to feel disgusted
asquerosidad *f* disgusting mess; **esta casa está hecha una ~** this house is filthy
asqueroso, -a *adj* disgusting; (*sucio*) filthy
asta *f* 1.(*de martillo, pincel*) handle; (*de bandera*) flagpole; **a media ~** at half mast 2.(*cuerno*) horn
asterisco *m* asterisk
asteroide *m* asteroid
astil *m* 1.(*mango*) handle 2.(*de la balanza*) beam
astilla *f* 1.(*esquirla*) splinter; **clavarse una ~** to get a splinter 2. *pl* (*para fuego*) firewood
astillar *vt, vr:* ~(**se**) to splinter
astillero *m* shipyard
astracán *m* astrakhan
astral *adj* astral
astringente *adj, m* astringent
astro *m t. fig* star; **~ de la pantalla** film star
astrofísica *f* astrophysics
astrología *f* astrology
astrólogo, -a *m, f* astrologer
astronauta *mf* astronaut
astronáutica *f* astronautics
astronave *f* spaceship
astronomía *f* astronomy
astronómico, -a *adj t. fig* astronomical
astrónomo, -a *m, f* astronomer
astucia *f* 1.(*sagacidad*) astuteness, shrewdness; **actuar con ~** to be crafty 2.(*ardid*) trick
asturiano, -a *adj, m, f* Asturian
Asturias *f* Asturias; **el Príncipe de ~** the Prince of Asturias (*Spanish crown prince*)
astuto, -a *adj* astute, shrewd; (*con malicia*) crafty
asueto *m* (*descanso*) time off; (*vacaciones*) holiday; (**día de**) **~** day off; **un rato de ~** a break
asumir *vt* 1.(*responsabilidad*) to assume, to take on; (*cargo*) to take over; (*actitud*) to adopt; (*gastos*) to agree to pay 2.(*suponer*) to assume; **la catástrofe está asumiendo proporciones espantosas** the catastrophe is assuming frightening proportions
asunción *f* assumption

Asunción *f* REL Assumption
asunto *m* 1.(*cuestión*) matter; **ir al ~** to get to the point; **el ~ es que...** the thing is (that) ...; **¡~ concluido!** that's the end of it!; **ocúpate de tus ~s** mind your own business 2.(*negocio*) business; **tener ~s en el extranjero** to have business dealings abroad; **el ministro está envuelto en un ~ sucio** the minister is mixed up in a dubious affair 3. LIT (*tema*) theme; (*argumento*) plot 4. ARTE subject 5.(*amorío*) affair 6. POL **Ministerio de Asuntos Exteriores** Foreign Office *Brit,* State Department *Am;* **Ministro de Asuntos Exteriores** Foreign Secretary *Brit,* Secretary of State *Am*
asustadizo, -a *adj* (*persona*) jumpy; (*animal*) easily startled
asustar I. *vt* to scare, to frighten; **la responsabilidad no me asusta** I'm not afraid of the responsibility II. *vr:* ~**se** to be scared, to be frightened; ~**se de algo** to be frightened at sth; **no te asustes** don't be frightened
atacante *mf* 1.(*agresor*) attacker, assailant 2. DEP striker
atacar <c→qu> I. *vt* 1.(*embestir, agredir, criticar*) to attack; **~ por la espalda** to attack from behind 2.(*sueño*) to overcome 3.(*problema*) to tackle II. *vi t.* DEP to attack; **~ por las bandas** to attack from the wings
ataché *m AmC, PRico* paper clip
atadijo *m,* **atado** *m* bundle
atadura *f* 1.(*acción*) tying 2.(*cuerda*) rope, string 3.(*entre personas*) tie, bond 4.(*obstáculo*) restriction
atajar I. *vi* to take a short cut; **por este camino atajamos mucho** this road cuts short our route considerably II. *vt* 1.(*detener*) to stop; (*agua*) to stem 2.(*cortar el paso*) to head off 3.(*discurso*) to interrupt
atajo *m* short cut; **ir por un ~** to take a short cut ►**echar por el ~** *inf* to take the easy way out
atalaya *f* 1.(*torre*) watchtower 2.(*lugar elevado*) vantage point
atañer <3. *pret:* atañó> *v impers* **eso no te atañe** that doesn't concern you; **por lo que atañe a tu empleo** as far as your job is concerned
ataque *m* 1.(*embestida, agresión crítica*) attack; **~ por sorpresa** surprise attack; **pasar al ~** to go on the offensive 2. *t.* MED attack, fit; **~ al** [*o* **de**] **corazón** heart attack; **~ de nervios** nervous breakdwon; **~ de tos** fit of coughing
atar I. *vt* 1.(*sujetar*) to tie; (*juntar*) to tie together; (*cerrar*) to tie up; (*cautivo*) to bind; **~ a alguien las manos a la espalda** to tie sb's hands behind his/her back; **~ al perro** to tie up the dog 2.(*comprometer*) **esta profesión te ata mucho** this profession ties you down a lot ►**dejar algo atado y bien atado** to finish sth off completely; **~ corto a alguien** to keep a tight rein on sb; **estar de ~** to be raving mad

II. *vr:* ~**se** to do up; ~**se los zapatos** to lace up one's shoes

atarazana *f* dockyard

atardecer I. *irr como crecer vimpers* **atardece** it's getting dark II. *m* dusk; **al** ~ at dusk

atareado, -a *adj* busy; **andar muy** ~ to be very busy

atarear I. *vt* to give a job to II. *vr:* ~**se** to work hard

atascar <c→qu> I. *vt* to block II. *vr:* ~**se** 1. (*cañería*) to get blocked (up); **el desagüe se ha atascado** the drain has got blocked (up) 2. (*coche*) to get stuck 3. (*mecanismo*) to jam 4. (*en un discurso*) to get stuck, to dry up *inf* 5. (*negociaciones*) to get bogged down

atasco *m* 1. (*de una cañería*) blockage 2. (*de un mecanismo*) blocking; ~ **de papel** INFOR paper jam 3. (*de tráfico*) traffic jam

ataúd *m* coffin

ataviar <1. *pres:* me atavío> *vt, vr:* ~**se** to dress up

atavío *m* attire

ate *m* Méx GASTR *fruit paste*

ateísmo *m* atheism

atejonarse *vr* Méx 1. (*agacharse*) to crouch; (*esconderse*) to hole up *inf* 2. (*volverse astuto*) to become sharp

atemorizar <z→c> I. *vt* to scare, to frighten II. *vr* ~**se** (**de algo**) to get scared (at sth)

atemperar *vt* 1. (*crítica*) to temper 2. (*cólera*) to curb 3. (*temperatura*) to moderate

Atenas *f* Athens

atenazar <z→c> *vt* 1. (*miedo*) to grip 2. (*duda*) to torment

atención *f* 1. (*interés*) attention; **falta de** ~ inattentiveness; **digno de** ~ noteworthy; **¡~, por favor!** your attention please!; **estamos llamando la** ~ we're attracting attention; **los coches no me llaman la** ~ I'm not very interested in cars; **llamar la** ~ **de alguien sobre** [*o* **a**] **algo** to draw sb's attention to sth; **mantener la** ~ **de alguien** to hold sb's attention; **prestar** ~ **a algo** to pay attention to sth; (*escuchar*) to listen to sth; **absorber la** ~ **de alguien** to command sb's attention; **en** ~ **a este hecho** in view of this fact 2. (*cuidado*) attention, care; ~ **médica** medical care 3. (*en cartas*) **a la** ~ **de...** for the attention of ... 4. (*cortesía*) kindness; **colmar a alguien de atenciones** to make a real fuss over [*o* of *Brit*] sb; **tener muchas atenciones con alguien** to be very nice to sb ►**llamar la** ~ **a alguien** to rebuke sb

atender <e→ie> I. *vt* 1. (*prestar atención a*) to pay attention to; (*escuchar*) to listen to 2. (*seguir: consejo, recomendación*) to heed; (*deseo, petición*) to comply with; ~ **una solicitud** to grant a request 3. (*cuidar*) ~ **a alguien** to care for sb 4. (*tratar*) to treat 5. (*despachar*) to serve; **¿lo atienden?** are you being served? 6. (*llamada*) to answer; ~ **el teléfono** to mind the telephone 7. (*tener en cuenta*) to take into account II. *vi* 1. (*prestar atención*) to

pay attention; (*escuchar*) to listen 2. (*tener en cuenta*) ~ **a algo** to take sth into account; **atendiendo a las circunstancias actuales** bearing in mind present circumstances 3. (*perro*) ~ **por...** to answer to the name of ...

atenerse *irr como tener vr* ~ **a** (*reglas*) to abide by; (*lo dicho*) to stand by, to keep to; ~ **a lo seguro** to play (it) safe; **me atengo a lo que dije antes** I'm sticking to what I said before; **saber a qué** ~ to know where one stands; (*en un futuro*) to know what to expect; **si no lo haces, atente a las consecuencias** if you don't do it, you'll bear the consequences

atentado *m* (*ataque*) attack, assault; (*crimen*) crime; ~ **contra alguien** assassination attempt on sb; ~ **terrorista** terrorist attack; **ser víctima de un** ~ to be the victim of an assassination attempt; **esta ley es un** ~ **contra la libertad de expresión** this law is a threat to freedom of speech

atentamente *adv* (*final de carta*) (**muy**) ~ (*si la carta empieza "Dear Sir"*) yours faithfully; (*si la carta empieza "Dear Mr X"*) yours sincerely *Brit*, sincerely yours *Am*

atentar *vi* 1. (*cometer atentado*) ~ **contra alguien** to make an attempt on sb's life 2. (*infringir*) ~ **contra la ley** to break the law

atento, -a *adj* 1. (*observador*) attentive; **estar** ~ **a la conversación** to follow the conversation closely; **estar** ~ **al peligro** to be aware of the danger 2. (*cortés*) kind; **es muy** ~ **de su parte** it's most kind of you; **estuvo muy** ~ **con nosotros** he was very considerate towards us; **es muy** ~ **con las mujeres** he's very gallant towards women

atenuación *f* 1. attenuation; (*del dolor*) easing 2. JUR extenuation

atenuante I. *adj* extenuating II. *f* 1. *pl* JUR extenuating circumstances *pl* 2. *AmL* (*perdón*) excuse

atenuar <1. *pres:* atenúo> I. *vt* 1. to attenuate; (*dolor*) to ease 2. JUR to extenuate II. *vr:* ~**se** 1. to be attenuated; (*dolor*) to ease 2. JUR to be extenuated

ateo, -a I. *adj* atheistic II. *m, f* atheist; **ser** ~ to be an atheist

aterciopelado, -a *adj* velvety

aterirse *irr como abolir vr* to become numb; **quedarse aterido** to be stiff with cold

aterrador(a) *adj* terrifying; **noticias** ~**as** terrible news

aterrar I. *vt* (*atemorizar*) to terrify; (*sobresaltar*) to startle II. *vr:* ~**se** (*sobresaltarse*) to be startled; (*tener miedo*) to be afraid

aterrizaje *m* landing; ~ **con daños** (**para el avión**) crash-landing; ~ **forzoso** forced landing; ~ **movido/suave** bumpy/soft landing

aterrizar <z→c> *vi* to land

aterrorizar <z→c> I. *vt* 1. POL, MIL to terrorize 2. (*causar terror*) to terrify; **me aterroriza volar** I'm terrified of flying II. *vr:* ~**se** (*tener miedo*) to be afraid; (*sobresaltarse*) to be startled

atesorar *vt* **1.** (*tesoros*) to store up; **este museo atesora pinturas de gran valor** this museum has a collection of very valuable paintings **2.** ECON to hoard **3.** (*virtudes*) to possess

atestado *m* ~ (**policial**) statement

atestar *vt* **1.** JUR to attest **2.** (*llenar*) ~ **de algo** to pack with sth; **la maleta está atestada** the suitcase is packed full; **el palacio de deportes estaba atestado de gente** the sports centre [*o* center *Am*] was crammed with people

atestiguar <gu→gü> *vt* to testify to

atiborrar **I.** *vt* to stuff **II.** *vr* ~**se de algo** to stuff oneself with sth

ático *m* attic; (*de lujo*) penthouse

atildado, -a *adj* elegant

atildar **I.** *vt* to tidy (up) **II.** *vr:* ~**se** to dress up

atinado, -a *adj* accurate

atinar **I.** *vi* **1.** (*acertar*) ~ **con algo** to hit on [*o* upon] sth; **no atiné con la respuesta** I didn't come up with the answer **2.** (*al disparar*) to hit the target **3.** (*encontrar*) ~ **con algo** to find sth **4.** (*lograr hacer*) ~ **a hacer algo** to manage to do sth **II.** *vt* to find

atípico, -a *adj* atypical

atisbar **I.** *vt* to spy on **II.** *vr:* ~**se** to be discerned

atisbo *m* spying; **un** ~ **de esperanza** a glimmer of hope; **en Marte hay** ~**s de vida** there are signs of life on Mars

atizar <z→c> **I.** *vt* **1.** (*fuego*) to poke **2.** (*pasión*) to rouse **3.** (*bofetada*) to give **II.** *vr* ~**se un trago** to take a drink **III.** *vi* ¡**atiza!** good heavens!

atlántico, -a *adj* Atlantic

Atlántico *m* **el** ~ the Atlantic

atlas *m inv* atlas

atleta *mf* athlete

atlético, -a *adj* athletic

atletismo *m sin pl* athletics

atmósfera *f* atmosphere

atole *m AmC: drink prepared with cornmeal gruel*

atolladero *m* **1.** (*atascadero*) mire **2.** (*apuro*) jam; **estar en un** ~ to be in a fix; **sacar a alguien de un** ~ to get sb out of a jam

atollar *vi, vr:* ~**se** to get bogged down

atolón *m* atoll

atolondrado, -a *adj* (*insensato*) bewildered; (*tonto*) stupid

atolondramiento *m* **1.** (*de los sentidos*) bewilderment **2.** (*por una desgracia*) consternation **3.** (*irreflexión*) thoughtlessness

atolondrar **I.** *vt* to stun **II.** *vr:* ~**se** *t. fig* to be stunned

atomía *f AmL* evil act; **decir** ~**s** (*decir tonterías*) to talk nonsense; (*injuriar*) to mouth off *inf*

atómico, -a *adj* atomic; **refugio** ~ fallout shelter

atomizador *m* spray

átomo *m* atom

atónito, -a *adj* amazed

átono, -a *adj* unstressed

atontado, -a *adj* **1.** (*tonto*) stupid **2.** (*distraído*) inattentive

atontar **I.** *vt* **1.** (*aturdir*) to stun **2.** (*entontecer*) to bewilder **II.** *vr:* ~**se 1.** (*aturdirse*) to be stunned **2.** (*entontecer*) to get bewildered

atorar **I.** *vt* to stop up **II.** *vr:* ~**se 1.** (*atascarse*) to get clogged [*o* stopped] up **2.** (*al hablar*) to falter

atormentar **I.** *vt* **1.** (*torturar*) to torture **2.** (*molestar*) to harass; (*mortificar*) to torment **II.** *vr:* ~**se** to torment oneself

atornillador *m* screwdriver

atornillar *vt* (*sujetar*) to screw down; (*fijar*) to screw on; (*juntar*) to screw together; ~ **en la pared** to screw into the wall; ~ **fuertemente** to screw tight

atorozarse *vr AmC* **1.** (*atascarse*) to block up **2.** (*al hablar*) to choke up

atorrante *mf CSur, inf* tramp

atosigar <g→gu> **I.** *vt* **1.** (*apremiar*) to harass **2.** (*importunar*) to pester **II.** *vr:* ~**se** to be harassed; **no te atosigues** don't get worked up

atracadero *m* mooring

atracador(a) *m(f)* bank robber

atracar <c→qu> **I.** *vi* NÁUT to berth **II.** *vt* **1.** NÁUT to moor **2.** (*asaltar*) to hold up **3.** *inf* (*atiborrar*) ~ **de algo** to stuff with sth **III.** *vr inf* ~**se de algo** to stuff oneself with sth

atracción *f* **1.** *t.* FÍS attraction; ~ **universal** gravity **2.** *pl* (*diversiones*) entertainment; **parque de atracciones** amusement park

atraco *m* hold-up; ~ **a un banco** bank robbery; ~ **a mano armada** armed robbery

atracón *m inf* blowout; **darse un** ~ **de dulces** to stuff oneself with sweets; **darse un** ~ **de televisión** to watch too much television

atractivo *m* attraction; ~ **sexual** sex appeal

atractivo, -a *adj* attractive

atraer *irr como traer* **I.** *vt* (*cautivar*) to attract; (*ganarse*) to win over; ~ **a los inversores** to attract investors; ~ **a alguien a su bando** to get sb on one's side; **el cebo atrae a los peces** the bait lures the fish; **sentirse atraído hacia alguien** to feel drawn towards sb **II.** *vr* (*ganarse*) to win; ~**se las simpatías de alguien** to win sb's affections; ~**se las iras del público** to incur public anger

atragantarse *vr* **1.** (*al comer*) ~ **con algo** to choke on sth; **me he atragantado con una espina** a fish bone has got stuck in my throat; **este profesor se me ha atragantado** *fig* I can't bear this teacher **2.** (*al hablar: atascarse*) to become tongue-tied; (*trabucarse*) to get mixed up

atrancar <c→qu> **I.** *vt* (*puerta*) to bolt **II.** *vr:* ~**se 1.** (*tubo*) to become blocked **2.** (*un coche, al hablar*) to get stuck

atrapar *vt* **1.** (*coger*) to trap; (*ladrón*) to catch; (*animal escapado*) to capture; **el portero atrapó la pelota** the goalkeeper caught the ball; ~**on al ladrón en plena faena** they caught the thief red-handed **2.** (*conseguir*) ~ **una novia** *inf* to get oneself a girlfriend; ~ **un empleo** to land a job

atrás *adv* **1.** (*hacia detrás*) back, backwards; **contar** ~ to count down; **dar un paso** ~ to take a step backwards [*o* back]; **ir marcha** ~ (**con el coche**) to reverse *Brit*, to back up *Am;* **quedar** ~ to fall behind; **volver** ~ to go back; **¡~!** get back! **2.** (*detrás*) back, behind; **rueda de** ~ rear wheel; **dejar** ~ **a los persegui-dores** to leave one's pursuers behind; **que-darse** ~ to remain behind; **sentarse** ~ to sit at the back **3.** (*de tiempo*) **años** ~ years ago; **la amistad venía de** ~ we/they had been friends for a long time ►**echarse** ~ **de un acuerdo** to back out of an agreement; **volverse** ~ to back down

atrasado, -a *adj* **1.** (*en el estudio, desarrollo*) behind; (*país*) backward; **viven 20 años ~s** they're 20 years behind the times **2.** (*pago*) overdue **3.** (*tarde*) late; **llegué** ~ **a la reunión** I arrived late for the meeting; **el reloj va** ~ the watch is slow

atrasar **I.** *vt* **1.** (*aplazar*) to postpone; **la his-toria atrasa unos años esta batalla** history fixes the date of this battle some years earlier **2.** (*reloj*) to put back **3.** (*progreso*) to slow down **II.** *vr:* **~se 1.** (*quedarse atrás*) to remain behind **2.** (*retrasarse*) to be late; **el tren se ha atrasado** the train is late; **~se en los plazos** to be behind in one's instalments

atraso *m* **1.** (*en una carrera*) slowness **2.** (*de un tren*) delay **3.** (*de un país*) backwardness **4.** FIN arrears *pl*

atravesar <e→ie> **I.** *vt* **1.** (*persona*) ~ **la calle/la frontera** to cross the street/the border; ~ **la sala/la ciudad** to cross the hall/the town; ~ **un río nadando** to swim across a river; **hemos atravesado Francia** (**con el coche**) we drove across France; ~ **un momento difícil** to go through a difficult time **2.** (*cuerpo*) ~ **algo con una aguja** to pierce sth with a needle; ~ **algo taladrando** to bore through sth; **la bala le atravesó el corazón** the bullet went through his/her heart; **el avión atraviesa las nubes** the plane breaks through the clouds; **la lluvia atravesó el abrigo** the rain penetrated the coat; **una cica-triz le atraviesa el pecho** a scar runs across his/her chest **3.** (*poner de través*) to lay across; ~ **un coche en medio de la calle** to park a car diagonally across the road **II.** *vr:* **~se 1.** (*ponerse entremedio*) **no te atravieses en mi camino** don't get in my way; **se me ha atravesado una miga en la garganta** a crumb has got stuck in my throat; **cuando estoy nervioso se me atraviesan las pala-bras** when I'm worked up, I get tongue-tied **2.** (*en una conversación*) **~se en algo** to butt into sth **3.** (*no soportar*) **se me atraviesa ese tipo** I can't stand that fellow

atrayente *adj* attractive

atreverse *vr* (*osar, insolentarse*) to dare; ~ **a**

hacer algo to dare to do sth; ~ **a afrontar un problema** to venture to tackle a problem; **¿cómo te atreves a hablarme así?** how dare you speak to me like that?; **¡no te atreverás!** you wouldn't dare!

atrevido, -a *adj* **1.** (*persona, vestido*) daring **2.** (*insolente*) insolent

atrevimiento *m* **1.** (*audacia*) boldness **2.** (*descaro*) cheek *Brit*, nerve *Am*

atribución *f* **1.** (*de un hecho*) attribution **2.** (*competencia*) authority; **atribuciones de un empleado** an employee's area of responsi-bility; **tiene atribuciones mías para llevar las negociaciones** I've authorized him/her to conduct the negotiations

atribuible *adj* attributable

atribuir *irr como huir* **I.** *vt* **1.** (*hechos, cua-lidades*) to attribute; ~ **la culpa de algo a al-guien** to blame sth on sb; ~ **a alguien grandes facultades** to attribute great capabil-ities to sb; **atribuye el accidente a un defecto de los frenos** he/she puts the acci-dent down to brake failure **2.** (*funciones*) to confer **II.** *vr:* **~se 1.** (*hechos, cualidades*) to claim for oneself **2.** (*facultades*) **~se todo el poder** to assume absolute power

atribular **I.** *vt* **1.** (*apesadumbrar*) to trouble **2.** (*atormentar*) to torment **II.** *vr:* **~se 1.** (*ape-narse*) **~se con** [*o* por] **algo** to grieve about sth **2.** (*atormentarse*) **~se con** [*o* por] **algo** to be tormented by sth

atributo *m* **1.** *t.* LING attribute **2.** (*emblema*) emblem

atril *m* **1.** MÚS music stand **2.** (*de mesa*) lectern

atrincherar *vt, vr:* **~se** to entrench (oneself)

atrio *m* atrium

atrocidad *f* **1.** (*cosa atroz*) atrocity **2.** (*dis-parate*) foolish remark; **¡no digas ~es!** don't talk nonsense!; **este artículo está lleno de ~es** this article is full of outrageous comments **3.** (*gran cantidad*) **tener una** ~ **de dinero** to be rolling in money

atronador(a) *adj* deafening; (*aplauso*) thun-derous

atropellar **I.** *vt* **1.** (*vehículo*) to run over; **por poco me atropellan** I was almost run over **2.** (*empujar*) to push past; (*derribar*) to knock down **3.** (*agraviar*) to insult **4.** (*leyes*) to viol-ate; ~ **la lengua** to murder the language **5.** (*un trabajo*) to do hurriedly **II.** *vi* ~ **por todo** to disregard everything **III.** *vr:* **~se** to rush

atropello *m* **1.** (*colisión*) collision; (*acci-dente*) accident **2.** (*empujón*) push; (*derribo*) knocking down **3.** (*insulto*) insult **4.** (*injusti-cia*) outrage; **¡esto es un ~!** this is preposter-ous! **5.** (*prisa*) rushing; **tomar una decisión sin prisas ni ~s** not to rush a decision

atroz *adj* **1.** (*horroroso*) atrocious **2.** (*cruel*) cruel **3.** (*inhumano*) inhuman **4.** (*muy grande*) huge

atuendo *m* (*atavío*) outfit

atufar **I.** *vt* **1.** (*marear*) to make feel sick **2.** (*enfadar*) to annoy **II.** *vr:* **~se 1.** (*marearse*)

to feel sick **2.**(*enfadarse*) to get annoyed
atún *m* tuna (fish)
aturdido, -a *adj* **1.**(*pasmado*) stunned
2.(*irreflexivo*) thoughtless
aturdimiento *m* **1.**(*por un golpe, por una mala noticia*) daze **2.**(*irreflexión*) thoughtlessness
aturdir I. *vt* **1.**(*los sentidos*) to stupefy **2.**(*pasmar*) to stun II. *vr:* ~**se** *t. fig* to be stunned
atur(r)ullar I. *vt* to confuse II. *vr:* ~**se** to get flustered
atusar I. *vt* **1.**(*el peinado*) to smooth **2.**(*el pelo, la barba*) to trim II. *vr:* ~**se** to do oneself up
audacia *f* boldness, audacity
audaz *adj* bold, audacious
audible *adj* audible
audición *f* **1.**(*acción, facultad*) hearing **2.**(*concierto*) concert **3.** TEAT audition; **pasar una** ~ (*actor, instrumentista, cantante*) to audition
audiencia *f* **1.** TEL, RADIO, POL audience; **nivel de** ~ viewing figures *pl* **2.** JUR (*sesión*) hearing; (*sala*) courtroom; (*tribunal*) court
audífono *m* **1.**(*para sordos*) hearing aid **2.** AmL (*auricular*) receiver
auditivo *m* TEL earpiece
auditivo, -a *adj* ANAT hearing
auditor(a) *m(f)* ECON, FIN auditor
auditorio *m* **1.**(*público*) audience **2.**(*sala*) auditorium
auge *m* **1.**(*cumbre*) peak; (*de una época*) heyday; **en el** ~ **de su belleza** at the height of her beauty **2.**(*mejora*) improvement
augurar *vt* to predict
augurio *m* prediction
aula *f* **1.**(*de escuela*) classroom **2.**(*de universidad*) lecture theatre *Brit,* lecture hall *Am;* ~ **magna** main lecture theatre
aullar *irr vi* (*animal*) to howl
aullido *m* howl
aumentable *adj* **1.**(*de tamaño*) expandable **2.**(*de cantidad*) capable of being increased
aumentar I. *vi* **1.**(*en general*) to increase; (*temperatura, precios*) to rise, to increase; ~ **de volumen** to increase in volume; ~ **de velocidad** to speed up; ~ **de altura** to become taller; ~ **de peso** to get heavier; **los disturbios aumentan** the disturbances are spreading **2.**(*en extensión*) to extend; ~ **mucho** to extend greatly II. *vt* **1.** to increase; (*multiplicar*) to multiply; (*precios*) to raise, to increase **2.**(*de extensión*) to extend; ~ **el poder/el dominio** to extend the power/the authority III. *vr:* ~**se** **1.**(*en cantidad*) to increase **2.**(*en extensión*) to extend
aumentativo *m* LING augmentative
aumento *m* **1.** increase; (*de la temperatura*) rise; (*de valor*) appreciation; ~ **de precio** price rise **2.**(*en la extensión*) expansion
aun I. *adv* even; ~ **así** even so; **ni** ~ not even II. *conj* ~ **cuando** even though; ~ **no comprando nada, no me llega el dinero** even

when I don't buy anything, I don't have enough money
aún *adv* still; ~ **más** even more; ~ **no** yet; ¿~ **no ha llegado?** hasn't he arrived yet?
aunar *irr como aullar* I. *vt* **1.**(*unir*) to unite; ~ **esfuerzos** to join forces **2.**(*unificar*) to unify **3.**(*armonizar*) to harmonize II. *vr:* ~**se** to unite
aunque *conj* **1.**(*concesiva: a pesar de que, incluso si*) even though; ~ **es viejo, aún puede trabajar** although he's old, he can still work; **la casa,** ~ **pequeña, está bien** the house is nice, even if it's small; **tengo que conseguirte** ~ **me cueste la vida** I must have you, even if it costs me my life; ~ **parezca extraño** however strange it may seem; **tengo que regalarle** ~ **sea un boli** I must give him/her a present, even if it's only a biro **2.**(*adversativa*) but
aúpa *interj* up, up you get ►**de** ~ *inf* tremendous
au pair *mf* au pair
aupar *irr como aullar vt* **1.**(*a un niño*) to lift up **2.**(*ayudar a subir*) to help up; ~ **a alguien a la presidencia** to help sb become president
aura *f* (*atmósfera*) aura; **tiene un** ~ **misteriosa** he/she has a mysterious aura
áureo, -a *adj* golden
aureola *f* (*de alguien*) halo
auricular I. *adj* (*de la oreja*) aural; **testigo** ~ ear-witness; **dedo** ~ little finger II. *m* **1.** TEL receiver; **coger/colgar el** ~ to pick up/put down the receiver **2.** *pl* (*de música*) headphones *pl*
aurora *f t. fig* dawn
auscultar *vt* **1.** MED **el médico lo auscultó** the doctor sounded his chest **2.**(*sondear*) to sound out
ausencia *f* **1.**(*estado de ausente*) absence **2.**(*falta*) lack; ~ **de interés** lack of interest; **en** ~ **de algo mejor** for want of something better **3.** PSICO mental blackouts ►**en** ~ **del gato bailan los ratones** *prov* when the cat's away the mice will play *prov;* **hacer a alguien buenas** ~**s** to speak kindly of sb in his/her absence; **tener buenas** ~**s** to have a good reputation; **brillar por su** ~ to be conspicuous by one's absence
ausentarse *vr* (*irse*) to go away; ~ **de la ciudad** to leave town
ausente *adj* **1.**(*no presente*) absent; **estar** ~ to be absent; **estar** ~ **del trabajo** to be off work **2.**(*distraído*) distracted
auspiciar *vt* **1.**(*presagiar*) to predict **2.**(*patrocinar*) to back
auspicios *mpl* **1.**(*protección*) protection **2.**(*presagio*) prediction **3.**(*patrocinio*) auspices *pl*
austeridad *f* austerity
austero, -a *adj* austere
austral *adj* southern
Australia *f* Australia
australiano, -a *adj, m, f* Australian

Austria *f* Austria
austriaco, -a, austríaco, -a *adj, m, f* Austrian
autenticar <c→qu> *vt* to authenticate
autenticidad *f* authenticity; **sobre la ~ de tus palabras tengo mis dudas** I have my doubts about the truth of your words; **no creo en la ~ de esta información** I don't believe that this information is reliable
auténtico, -a *adj* **1.** (*verdadero*) authentic; **un ~ fracaso** an absolute failure; **hacía un calor ~** it was really hot; **es un ~ maestro en su especialidad** he's an absolute expert in his field **2.** (*palabra*) credible **3.** (*información*) reliable
autista *adj* autistic
auto *m* **1.** (*resolución*) decision **2.** *pl* (*actas*) proceedings *pl* **3.** AUTO car ▶ **constar** en ~s to be proven; **estar** en ~s to be in the picture; **poner** en ~s to put in the picture
autoabastecerse *vr* ~ **de algo** to be self-sufficient in sth **autoadhesivo, -a** *adj* self-adhesive
autobiografía *f* autobiography **autobiográfico, -a** *adj* autobiographic(al)
autobús *m* bus
autocar <autocares> *m* coach *Brit*, bus *Am*
autocarril *m* *Bol, Chile, Nic* (*autovía*) dual carriageway *Brit*, divided highway *Am*
autocensura *f* self-censorship
autochoque *m* bumper car
autocine *m* drive-in cinema
autocracia *f* autocracy
autócrata *mf* autocrat
autocrático, -a *adj* autocratic
autocrítica *f* self-criticism
autóctono, -a *adj* indigenous
autodefensa *f* self-defence *Brit*, self-defense *Am* **autodeterminación** *f* self-determination **autodidacto, -a** I. *adj* self-taught II. *m, f* self-taught person **autodominio** *m* self-control
autoescuela *f* driving school
autoestop *m* **hacer ~** to hitch-hike
autoestopista *mf* hitch-hiker
autoevaluación *f* self-evaluation **autofinanciación** *f* self-financing **autogestión** *f* self-management **autogobierno** *m* self-government
autógrafo *m* (*firma*) autograph
autolavado *m* car wash
autómata *m* **1.** (*aparato*) automatic device **2.** (*robot*) robot **3.** *pey* (*persona*) automaton
automático *m* press stud *Brit*, snap fastener *Am*
automático, -a *adj* automatic; **dispositivo ~** automatic mechanism; **fusil ~** automatic rifle; **la puerta se cierra de modo ~** the door snaps shut; (*en un metro*) the door closes automatically; **su despido fue ~** he/she was dismissed without notice
automatización *f* automation
automatizar <z→c> *vt* to automate

automotivarse *vr* to motivate oneself
automóvil *m* car; ~ **de carreras** racing car; ~ **eléctrico** electrically powered car; ~ **todo terreno** all-terrain vehicle; **Salón del Automóvil** motor show
automovilismo *m* DEP motoring
automovilista *mf* motorist, driver
automovilístico, -a *adj* car; **parque ~** fleet of vehicles
autonomía *f* **1.** (*de una personal*) autonomy; ~ **colectiva** free collective bargaining; ~ **municipal** municipal self-administration; **en esta empresa no tengo ~ para tomar decisiones** in this company I've no scope for making my own decisions **2.** (*territorio*) autonomous region
autonómico, -a *adj* autonomous; **proceso ~** process leading to autonomy; **política autonómica** regional policy; **elecciones autonómicas** regional elections
autónomo, -a *adj* **1.** POL autonomous; **la comunidad autónoma de Galicia** the autonomous region of Galicia **2.** (*trabajador*) self-employed; **trabajar de ~** to be self-employed; **¿cuánto pagas de ~s?** how much do you pay for your private health insurance?
autopista *f* motorway *Brit*, freeway *Am;* ~ **de datos** INFOR data highway; ~ **de la información** INFOR information highway; ~ **de peaje** toll motorway *Brit*, turnpike *Am*
autopsia *f* MED autopsy
autor(a) *m(f)* **1.** LIT author; MÚS composer; **derechos de ~** royalties; **una novela de ~ desconocido** a novel by an anonymous author **2.** (*de un acto*) originator; (*de una conspiración*) conspirator; (*de un crimen*) perpetrator; (*de un atentado*) assassin **3.** (*de un invento*) inventor; (*de un descubrimiento*) discoverer
autoridad *f* **1.** (*en general*) authority; ~ **del estado** state official; ~ **judicial** jurisdiction; ~ **de los padres** parental authority; **estar bajo la ~ de alguien** to be under sb's control; **¡aquí soy yo la ~!** I make the decisions here! **2.** (*pl*) (*policía*) authorities *pl;* **desacato a la ~** contempt (of court) **3.** (*experto*) authority
autoritario, -a *adj* authoritarian
autorización *f* authorization; (*para vender alcohol*) licence *Brit*, license *Am;* ~ **de acceso** INFOR access privileges; ~ **para hacer algo** authorization to do sth
autorizado, -a *adj* **1.** (*facultado*) authorized; **persona no autorizada** unauthorized person; ~ **para firmar** authorized to sign; **de fuentes autorizadas** from approved sources **2.** (*oficial*) official
autorizar <z→c> *vt* **1.** (*consentir*) to approve; **mi jefe me ha autorizado para ausentarme** my boss has given me permission to be off **2.** (*facultar*) to authorize **3.** (*dar derecho*) to entitle; **que sea mi jefe no le autoriza para insultarme** even though you're my boss, it doesn't give you the right to insult me; **este hecho nos autoriza a pensar**

que... this fact gives us reason to believe that ...

autorretrato *m* self-portrait **autoservicio** *m* self-service

autostop *m* **hacer ~** to hitch-hike

autostopista *mf* hitch-hiker

autosuficiencia *f* self-sufficiency; *pey* smugness **autosuficiente** *adj* self-sufficient; *pey* smug

autosugestión *f* autosuggestion

autovía *f* (*carretera*) dual carriageway *Brit*, divided highway *Am*

auxiliar¹ I. *adj* assistant; **profesor ~** UNIV assistant professor; (*en la escuela*) supply teacher II. *mf* assistant; **~ administrativo** administrative assistant; **~ técnico sanitario** medical technician; **~ de vuelo** flight attendant III. *vt* 1. (*dar auxilio*) to help 2. REL to give the last rites to

auxiliar² *m* LING auxiliary verb

auxilio *m* help; **~s espirituales** REL last rites; **primeros ~s** first aid; **pedir ~** to ask for help; **pedir ~ a alguien** to ask for sb's help

avalancha *f* avalanche

avance *m* 1. *t.* MIL advance; **~ de los precios** price rise 2. (*avanzo*) balance 3. (*presupuesto*) estimate 4. CINE, TV **~ de algo** trailer for sth; **~ informativo** news summary

avanzado, -a *adj* advanced

avanzar <z→c> I. *vi* 1. (*seguir adelante*) *t.* MIL to advance; **~ por una calle** to go along a street; **~ hacia alguien** to go towards sb; **a medida que el tiempo avanzaba** as time went by 2. (*progresar*) to progress; **no ~ nada** not to make any headway; **esta tendencia está avanzando** this trend is gaining ground II. *vt* to advance; **~ un pie** to put a foot forward

avaricia *f* 1. (*codicia*) greed 2. (*tacañería*) avarice

avaricioso, -a *adj*, **avariento, -a** *adj* 1. (*codicioso*) greedy 2. (*tacaño*) avaricious

avaro, -a I. *adj* miserly; **ser muy ~ de algo** to be very mean with sth II. *m, f* miser

avasallar I. *vt* 1. (*subyugar*) to subjugate 2. (*atropellar*) to steamroller II. *vr:* **~se** to submit

avatares *mpl* **los ~es de la vida** life's ups and downs; **los ~es de la suerte** the vagaries of fortune

Avda. *abr de* **Avenida** Av(e).

ave *f* bird; **~s de corral** poultry; **~ de paso** migratory bird; **~ rapaz** [*o* **de rapiña**] bird of prey

AVE *m abr de* **Alta Velocidad Española** high-speed train

avecinarse *vr* to approach

avellana *f* hazelnut

avellano *m* hazel (tree)

avemaría *f* Hail Mary ►**saberse** algo como el **~** to know sth inside out; **al ~** at dusk; **en un ~** in the twinkling of an eye

avena *f* oats *pl*

avenencia *f* 1. (*acuerdo*) agreement 2. (*armonía*) harmony; **en buena ~** in harmony 3. JUR settlement

avenida *f* 1. (*de un río*) flood 2. (*calle*) avenue

avenido, -a *adj* **dos personas bien avenidas** two good friends; **una pareja mal avenida** an ill-matched couple

avenir *irr como* venir I. *vt* to reconcile II. *vr:* **~se** 1. (*entenderse*) to get on 2. (*ponerse de acuerdo*) **~se en algo** to agree on sth; **no ~se a...** not to agree to ...; **~se a dialogar** to agree to hold talks

aventajado, -a *adj* (*alumno*) outstanding; **de estatura aventajada** extremely tall

aventajar *vt* 1. (*ser mejor*) to surpass 2. (*en una carrera*) to overtake *Brit*, to pass *Am;* **~ a todos** to get ahead of everyone 3. (*anteponer*) to prefer

aventar <e→ie> I. *vt* 1. (*echar aire a algo*) to fan 2. (*dispersar el viento*) to blow away 3. (*el grano*) to winnow II. *vr:* **~se** 1. *inf* (*pirárselas*) to beat it 2. (*las velas*) to billow out

aventón *m Méx, inf* push; **dar un ~** to give a lift; **ir de ~** to ride free

aventura *f* 1. (*extraordinaria*) adventure; **espíritu de ~** spirit of adventure 2. (*arriesgada*) venture 3. (*amorosa*) affair

aventurado, -a *adj* risky

aventurar I. *vt* 1. (*arriesgar*) to venture 2. (*algo atrevido*) to dare II. *vr:* **~se** to dare; **perdieron dinero al ~se en el mundo editorial** they lost money when they went into publishing

aventurero, -a I. *adj* adventurous; **espíritu ~** thirst for adventure II. *m, f* adventurer

avergonzado, -a *adj* (*sonrisa*) embarrassed; **sentirse ~** to be ashamed

avergonzar *irr* I. *vt* to shame II. *vr:* **~se de** [*o* **por**] **algo/alguien** to be ashamed of sth/sb

avería *f* 1. AUTO breakdown 2. (*de una mercadería*) damage 3. TÉC fault 4. NÁUT average; **~ gruesa/simple** general/petty average

averiar <1. *pres:* averío> I. *vt* to damage II. *vr:* **~se** 1. AUTO to break down 2. TÉC to fail 3. NÁUT to be damaged

averiguación *f* 1. (*haciendo pesquisas*) inquiry 2. (*al dar con*) discovery

averiguar <gu→gü> *vt* 1. (*inquiriendo*) to inquire into 2. (*dar con*) to discover; **averigua a qué hora sale el tren** find out (at) what time the train leaves

averigüetas *m inv, Méx* busybody

aversión *f* aversion

avestruz *m* ostrich

avezado, -a *adj* accustomed; **~ en los negocios** business-minded

avezar <z→c> I. *vt* to accustom II. *vr:* **~se** to get used to

aviación *f* 1. AVIAT aviation; **compañía de ~** airline (company) 2. MIL air force

aviador(a) *m(f)* aviator

aviar <1. *pres:* avío> I. *vt* 1. (*maleta*) to pack;

(*comida*) to prepare; (*mesa*) to set **2.**(*dar*) to provide; ~ **de algo** to provide with sth **3.**(*apresurar*) ~ **a alguien** to hurry sb up; **diles que vayan aviando** tell them to get a move on; **estar aviado** (*en un apuro*) to be in a tight spot **4.** *AmS* (*prestar*) to lend **II.** *vr:* ~**se 1.**(*arreglarse*) to get ready **2.**(*espabilarse*) to get by

avícola *adj* poultry

avicultura *f* poultry farming

avidez *f* **1.**(*ansia*) eagerness; ~ **de algo** eagerness for sth **2.**(*codicia*) greed

ávido, -a *adj* **1.**(*ansioso*) eager; ~ **de algo** eager for sth **2.**(*codicioso*) greedy

avieso, -a *adj* **1.**(*objeto*) crooked **2.**(*persona*) wicked

avilés, -esa I. *adj* of/from Ávila **II.** *m, f* native/inhabitant of Ávila

avinagrarse *vr* **1.**(*vino*) to turn sour **2.**(*persona*) to become bitter

avío *m* **1.**(*apresto*) preparation **2.**(*provisión*) provision **3.** *AmS* (*de dinero, de utensilios*) loan **4.** *pl* (*utensilios*) ~**s de coser** sewing things; ~**s de escribir** stationery ▶**¡al** ~**!** get on with it!

avión *m* **1.** AVIAT aeroplane *Brit*, airplane *Am;* ~ **a reacción** jet (plane); **por** ~ (*correos*) by airmail; **ir en** ~ **a Mallorca** to fly to Majorca **2.** ZOOL martin

avioneta *f* light aircraft

avisado, -a *adj* **1.**(*prudente*) sensible **2.**(*sagaz*) informed; **mal** ~ ill-advised

avisador *m* ~ **de movimientos** movement sensor

avisar *vt* **1.**(*dar noticia*) to notify; **avísame cuando estés de vuelta** let me know when you're back; **nos avisó que venía a cenar** he/she told us that he/she was coming to dinner; **llegar sin** ~ to arrive unannounced **2.**(*poner sobre aviso*) to warn **3.**(*llamar*) to call

aviso *m* **1.**(*notificación*) notification; (*en una cartelera*) notice; (*por el altavoz*) announcement; ~ **de llegada** COM (acknowledgement of) receipt; ~ **de salida** FERRO departure announcement; ~ **de siniestro** accident report; **hasta nuevo** ~ until further notice; **sin previo** ~ without notice **2.**(*advertencia*) warning; ~ **de bomba** bomb warning; **estar sobre** ~ to be warned; **poner sobre** ~ to warn; **servir a alguien de** ~ to be a lesson to sb **3.**(*consejo*) advice **4.**(*prudencia*) prudence **5.** *AmL* (*en el periódico*) advertisement

avispa *f* wasp

avispado, -a *adj* sharp

avispero *m* **1.**(*nido*) wasps' nest **2.**(*avispas*) swarm of wasps ▶**meterse en un** ~ to get oneself into a mess

avispón *m* hornet

avistar *vt* to sight

avituallar *vt* to supply with food

avivar *vt* (*dar viveza*) to enliven; (*fuego*) to stoke; (*pasión*) to arouse; (*color, luz*) to

brighten; (*sentidos*) to sharpen; ~ **el paso** to increase one's pace

avizor *adj* **estar ojo** ~ to be alert

avizorar *vt* to spy on

axila *f* **1.** ANAT armpit **2.** BOT axillary bud

axioma *m* axiom

ay *interj* **1.**(*de dolor*) ouch **2.**(*de pena, de sorpresa*) oh **3.**(*de miedo*) oh, my God; **¡~, qué divertido!** oh, how funny! **4.**(*de amenaza*) **¡~ si vienes tarde!** you'll regret it if you come late!; ~ **del que...** +*subj* woe betide [*o* to] anyone who ...

ayer *adv* yesterday; ~ **(por la) noche** last night; ~ **hace una semana** a week ago yesterday; **de** ~ **acá** overnight; **¡parece que fue** ~**!** it seems like only yesterday!; **no he nacido** ~ I wasn't born yesterday

ayo, -a *m, f* tutor

ayuda[1] *f* **1.**(*auxilio*) help; **perro de** ~ watchdog; **eso no me sirve de ninguna** ~ that doesn't help me **2.**(*lavativa*) enema

ayuda[2] *m* helper

ayudado, -a *m, f Col* **1.**(*brujo*) witchdoctor; (*de tribu*) medicine man **2.**(*endemoniado*) possessed person

ayudante *mf* **1.**(*que ayuda*) helper **2.**(*cargo*) assistant; (*en una escuela*) supply teacher *Brit*

ayudar I. *vt* **1.**(*socorrer*) to help; ~ **a alguien en el trabajo** to help sb with his/her work; ~ **a alguien a levantarse** to help sb up; ~ **a alguien a salir del coche** to help sb to get out of the car; ~ **a alguien a pasar la calle** to help sb across the road; ~ **a misa** to serve at mass; **¡Dios me ayude!** God help me!; **¿le puedo** ~ **en algo?** can I help you with anything?; ~ **a conseguir un trabajo** to help to get a job **2.**(*temporalmente*) to help out **II.** *vr:* ~**se 1.**(*mutuamente*) to help each other **2.**(*valerse de*) to help oneself

ayunar *vi* to fast

ayunas *adv* **estar en** ~ to not have eaten anything; (*ignorante*) never to understand anything

ayuno *m* fast

ayuno, -a *adj* **estar** ~ **de experiencia** to have no experience; **estoy** ~ **de lo que aquí se dice** I've no idea what it's all about

ayuntamiento *m* **1.**(*corporación*) district council; (*de una ciudad*) town/city council **2.**(*edificio*) town/city hall

azabache *m* jet; **ojos de** ~ jet-black eyes

azada *f* hoe

azafata *f* **1.** AVIAT air hostess; ~ **de congresos** conference hostess **2.** *Chile, Col* (*bandeja*) tray

azafrán *m* saffron

azahar *m* orange blossom

azalea *f* azalea

azar *m* **1.**(*casualidad*) chance; **juegos de** ~ games of chance; **al** ~ at random; **por** ~ by chance **2.**(*imprevisto*) misfortune; **los** ~**es de la vida** life's ups and downs

azarar I. *vt* to shame **II.** *vr:* ~**se 1.**(*avergonzarse*) to be ashamed **2.**(*ruborizarse*) to blush

3.(*turbarse*) to get confused
azaroso, -a *adj* **1.**(*proyecto*) hazardous; **una vida azarosa** an eventful life **2.**(*persona*) unlucky
Azerbaiyán *m* Azerbaijan
azogue *m* mercury ▸**tener** ~ **en el cuerpo** to be fidgety; **ser uno como el** ~ to be restless; **temblar como** ~ to shake like a leaf
azor *m* goshawk
azoramiento *m* **1.**(*nerviosismo*) excitement; (*ante un acto público*) stage fright **2.**(*turbación*) confusion
azorar I. *vt* **1.**(*poner nervioso*) to excite **2.**(*turbar*) to confuse II. *vr:* ~**se 1.**(*alterarse*) to get upset; (*ante un acto público*) to get stage fright **2.**(*turbarse*) to get flustered
Azores *fpl* **las** ~ the Azores + *pl vb*
azoro *m* **1.**AmC (*fantasma*) ghost **2.**AmC (*aparición*) apparition **3.**Méx, Perú, PRico (*azoramiento*) bewilderment
azotaina *f* spanking; **dar una** ~ to spank
azotar *vt* **1.**(*con un látigo*) to whip; (*con nudos*) to scourge; (*con la mano*) to thrash, to spank; **el viento me azota (en) la cara** the wind is lashing my face **2.**(*producir daños*) to devastate; **una epidemia azota la región** an epidemic is causing havoc in the region
azote *m* **1.**(*látigo*) whip; (*con nudos*) scourge **2.**(*golpe*) lash; (*golpe en las nalgas*) spank
azotea *f* terrace roof ▸**estar mal de la** ~ *inf* to be off one's rocker
azteca I. *adj* Aztec; **el equipo** ~ (*en fútbol*) Mexico II. *mf* Aztec

---

The Indian tribe of the **aztecas** built up a vast and powerful empire between the 14th and 16th centuries in the southern and central part of Mexico, which was conquered by the Spanish in 1521. The language of the **aztecas** was **náhuatl**.

---

azúcar *m* sugar; ~ **de cortadillo** rock candy; ~ **en polvo** icing sugar; **tener el** ~ **muy alto** MED to have a very high blood-sugar level
azucarar I. *vt* to sugar II. *vr:* ~**se** (*cristalizarse*) to crystallize
azucarero *m* (*recipiente*) sugar basin, sugar bowl *Am*
azucena *f* Madonna lily
azufrar *vt* to sulphurize, to sulfurize *Am*
azufre *m* sulphur, sulfur *Am*
azul *adj* blue; ~ **celeste** sky blue; ~ **marino** navy blue; ~ **verdoso** greenish-blue
azulado, -a *adj* bluish
azulejo *m* **1.**(*para pared*) (glazed) tile **2.**ZOOL blue wrasse **3.**(*aciano*) cornflower
azulgrana *adj* blue and scarlet; **el equipo** ~ DEP Barcelona Football Club
azumbrado, -a *adj inf* tipsy
azuzar <z→c> *vt* to incite

B

B, b *f* B, b; ~ **de Barcelona** B for Benjamin *Brit*, B for Baker *Am*
baba *f* **1.**(*de la boca*) spittle; **caérse a alguien la** ~ **por alguien** to dote on sb **2.**(*del caracol*) slime
babasfrías *m inv*, Col, *inf* fool
babastibias *m inv*, Ecua fool
babear *vi* to dribble, to drool
babel *m o f* **1.**(*desorden*) confusion **2.**(*sitio*) bedlam
babero *m* bib
Babia *f* **estar en** ~ to be daydreaming
bable *m* dialect of Asturias
babor *m* NÁUT port; **a** ~ on the port side
babosa *f* **1.**ZOOL slug **2.**AmL (*tontería*) stupid thing
babosada *f* AmC, Méx (*bobería*) silliness
babosear *vi inf* to drool, to dribble
baboso, -a I. *adj* **1.**(*lleno de baba*) slimy **2.**(*zalamero*) fawning **3.**AmL (*tonto*) silly II. *m, f* **1.**(*joven*) brat **2.**(*zalamero*) fawning individual
babucha *f* slipper
babuino *m* baboon
baca *f* (*portaequipajes*) roof rack, luggage rack
bacalao *m* **1.**(*pez, pescado*) cod; (*salado*) salt cod **2.**MÚS techno music ▸**cortar el** ~ to run the show
bacán I. *m* AmL (*rico*) rich guy, sugar daddy II. *adj* Perú (*estupendo*) great
bacanal *f* bacchanalia; (*orgía*) orgy
bachata *f* RDom, PRico party
bachatear *vi* AmL to go out on the town
bache *m* **1.**(*en la calle*) pothole **2.**AVIAT air pocket **3.**(*en la producción*) slump **4.**(*psíquico*) bad patch
bacheado, -a *adj* bumpy
bachicha *mf* CSur, Perú, *pey* (*italiano*) dago, wop
bachiller *mf* school-leaver; **título de** ~ ≈ secondary graduate, ≈ highschool graduate *Am*
bachillerato *m* (*título*) certificate of secondary education; (*estudios*) high school education for 14–17-year-olds
bacía *f* **1.**(*recipiente*) basin **2.**(*para animales*) feeding trough
bacilo *m* bacillus
backup *m* <backups> INFOR backup
bacteria *f* bacteria
bactericida I. *adj* bactericidal II. *m* bactericide
bacteriológico, -a *adj* bacteriological
bacteriólogo, -a *m, f* bacteriologist
báculo *m* **1.**(*bastón*) staff **2.**(*del obispo*) crosier **3.**(*apoyo*) support
badajo *m* **1.**(*de campana*) clapper **2.** *inf*(*persona*) chatterbox
badajocense I. *adj* of/from Badajoz II. *mf* native/inhabitant of Badajoz
badana *f* sheepskin ▸**zurrar la** ~ **a alguien** to

tan sb's hide
badén *m* **1.**(*desnivel*) dip **2.**(*en carreteras*) drainage channel
badil *m* fire shovel
bádminton *m* DEP badminton
badulaquear *vi* **1.**(*hacer tonterías*) to act like a fool **2.** *Arg, Col, Chile, Perú*(*engañar*) to swindle
bafle *m* (loud)speaker
bagaje *m* **1.** MIL baggage **2.**(*saber*) ~ **cultural** cultural knowledge
bagatela *f* trifle
bagayo *m* **1.** *Arg, inf* (*equipaje*) baggage **2.** *Arg, inf* (*objetos robados*) stolen goods *pl* **3.** *Arg, inf*(*prostituta*) whore
bagre **I.** *adj* **1.** *Bol, Col* (*cursi*) coarse **2.** *Guat, Hond, ElSal* (*inteligente*) clever **II.** *m* **1.** *AmL* ZOOL catfish **2.** *And* (*antipático*) unpleasant person **3.** *And* (*mujer fea*) old bag **4.** *CRi* (*prostituta*) slut
bah *interj* **1.**(*incredulidad*) never **2.**(*desprecio*) that's nothing **3.**(*conformidad*) OK
Bahamas *fpl* **las** (**islas**) ~ the Bahamas
bahía *f* bay
bailable **I.** *adj* música ~ dance music **II.** *m* dance number
bailador(a) **I.** *adj* dancing **II.** *m(f)* dancer (of flamenco)
bailar **I.** *vi* **1.**(*danzar*) to dance **2.**(*caballo*) to prance **3.**(*objetos*) to move; (*peonza*) to spin; TÉC to have play; **hacer** ~ **una peonza** to spin a top ▸~ **con la más fea** to get the short end of the stick; **¡que me quiten lo bailado!** *inf* nobody can take away the good times I've had!; **otro que tal** ~ he/she is just as bad **II.** *vt* to dance
bailarín, -ina **I.** *adj* dancing **II.** *m, f* dancer; (*de ballet*) ballet dancer
baile *m* **1.**(*acto*) dancing **2.**(*danza*) dance **3.**(*fiesta*) dance party; (*de etiqueta*) ball **4.** MED ~ **de San Vito** St Vitus' dance
bailongo *m inf* dance
bailotear *vi* **1.**(*bailar*) to dance about **2.**(*brincar*) to leap about
baja *f* **1.**(*disminución*) decrease; (*de precio, de temperatura*) drop **2.**(*cese de trabajo*) vacancy; ~ **por maternidad** maternity leave; **darse de** ~ (*temporalmente*) to take time off; (*por enfermedad*) to be on sick leave; (*definitivamente*) to give up one's job; **estar de** ~ (**por enfermedad**) to be off sick **3.**(*en una asociación*) resignation; **dar de** ~ **a alguien** to expel sb **4.**(*documento*) discharge certificate; (*del médico*) sick note **5.** MIL casualty **6.** FIN slump
bajada *f* **1.**(*descenso*) descent; ~ **de tipos de interés** ECON fall in interest rates; ~ **de bandera** minimum fare **2.**(*camino*) way down **3.**(*pendiente*) slope
bajamar *f* low tide
bajar **I.** *vi* **1.**(*ir hacia abajo*) to go down; (*venir hacia abajo*) to come down; ~ **en ascensor** to go/come down in the lift; ~ **las escaleras** to go/come down the stairs **2.**(*apearse*) ~ **de** (*de*

un caballo) to dismount, to get down from; (*de un coche*) to get out of **3.**(*las aguas*) to fall **4.**(*disminuir*) to decrease; (*temperatura*) to drop; (*hinchazón*) to go down **5.**(*adelgazar*) to lose weight **II.** *vt* **1.**(*transportar*) to bring down; (*coger*) to take down; ~ **las persianas** to lower the blinds **2.**(*precios*) to lower **3.**(*voz*) to lower; (*radio*) to turn down **4.**(*ojos*) to drop **5.** INFOR to download **6.** *Cuba, inf*(*pagar*) pay **III.** *vr:* ~**se 1.**(*descender*) ~**se de** (*de un caballo*) to dismount; (*de un coche*) to get out of **2.**(*inclinarse*) to bend down **3.**(*humillarse*) to lower oneself
bajativo *m AmL* digestive
bajeza *f* **1.**(*acción humillante*) mean act; (*acción vil*) vile act **2.**(*carácter*) baseness **3.**(*humildad*) lowliness
bajío *m* **1.**(*banco de arena*) sandbank **2.** *AmL* (*terreno bajo*) lowland
bajista **I.** *adj* FIN bearish; **tendencia** ~ bearish tendency **II.** *mf* **1.** MÚS bass player **2.** FIN bear
bajo **I.** *m* **1.**(*instrumento*) bass **2.**(*persona*) bass player **3.** *pl* (*piso*) ground floor *Brit*, first floor *Am* **4.** *pl* (*banco de arena*) sandbank **5.** *pl* (*parte inferior*) underneath; (*de una prenda*) hemline **II.** *adv* **1.**(*posición*) below **2.**(*voz*) quietly **III.** *prep* **1.**(*colocar debajo*) below **2.**(*por debajo de*) underneath; ~ **llave** under lock and key; ~ **la lluvia** in the rain; ~ **fianza** on bail; ~ **la condición de que** +*subj* on condition that
bajo, -a <más bajo *o* inferior, bajísimo> *adj* **1.** estar (*en lugar inferior*) low **2.** ser (*de temperatura*) low; (*de estatura*) short; **baja tensión** ELEC low tension; **con la cabeza baja/los ojos** ~**s** with head/eyes lowered; **tener la moral baja** to be in poor spirits **3.**(*voz*) low; (*sonido*) soft **4.**(*color*) pale **5.**(*metal*) base **6.**(*comportamiento*) mean **7.**(*clase social*) humble **8.**(*calidad*) poor
bajón *m* **1.**(*descenso*) decline; (*de precios*) drop; FIN slump **2.**(*de la salud*) worsening **3.** MÚS bassoon
bakalao *m* MÚS techno music
bala *f* **1.**(*proyectil*) bullet; ~ **de fogueo** blank cartridge; **como una** ~ like a flash **2.**(*fardo*) bale
balacear *vt AmL* (*herir o matar*) to shoot; (*disparar contra*) to shoot at
balada *f* ballad
baladí *adj* <baladíes> trivial, worthless
baladronada *f* boast
balalaica *f* MÚS balalaika
balance *m* **1.**(*vaivén*) oscillation; (*en la danza*) rocking; NÁUT rolling **2.** COM (*resultado*) balance; **hacer un** ~ to draw up a balance **3.**(*comparación*) comparison; **hacer (el)** ~ to take stock of the situation **4.**(*vacilación*) hesitation
balancear **I.** *vt* **1.**(*mecer*) to sway; (*acunar*) to rock **2.**(*equilibrar*) to balance **II.** *vr:* ~**se 1.**(*columpiarse*) to swing **2.** NÁUT to roll
balanceo *m* **1.**(*vaivén*) swaying; NÁUT rocking

2. (*vacilación*) hesitation
balancín *m* **1.** (*de los equilibristas*) balancing pole **2.** (*columpio*) seesaw, teeter-totter *Am* **3.** (*silla*) rocking chair; (*en el jardín*) swing hammock **4.** (*yugo*) yoke
balandra *f* sloop
balandrista *m* yachtsman *m,* yachtswoman *f*
balandro *m* yacht
balanza *f* **1.** (*pesa*) scales *pl;* **inclinar el fiel de la** ~ *fig* to tip the scales **2.** COM balance; ~ **de pagos** balance of payments
Balanza *f* ASTR Libra
balar *vi* to bleat
balaustrada *f* balustrade
balazo *m* **1.** (*tiro*) shot **2.** (*herida*) bullet wound
balbucear *vi, vt v.* **balbucir**
balbuceo *m* stammering; (*de niños*) babbling
balbucir *vi, vt* to stammer; (*niño*) to babble
Balcanes *mpl* **los** ~ the Balkans
balcón *m* **1.** (*de casa*) balcony **2.** (*mirador*) observation point
balconada *f* row of balconies
balda *f* shelf
baldado, -a *adj* **1.** (*tullido*) crippled **2.** *inf* (*muy cansado*) knackered *Brit*
baldaquín *m* canopy
baldar *vt* **1.** (*paralizar*) to paralyze; (*lisiar*) to disable **2.** (*perjudicar*) to harm
balde *m* bucket ▶**obtener algo de** ~ to get sth for nothing; **en** ~ in vain
baldío *m* AGR wasteland, uncultivated land
baldío, -a *adj* **1.** (*terreno*) uncultivated **2.** (*inútil*) useless; (*en balde*) vain
baldón *m* **1.** (*acción*) insult **2.** (*situación*) disgrace
baldosa *f* paving stone, floor tile
baldosado *m Col, Chile* (*suelo*) tiled floor
baldosín *m* tile
balear **I.** *vt AmL* ~ **a alguien** (*disparar contra*) to shoot at sb; (*herir, matar*) to shoot sb **II.** *vr:* ~**se** *AmL* **1.** (*disparar*) to exchange shots **2.** (*disputar*) to argue **III.** *adj* Balearic **IV.** *mf* native/inhabitant of the Balearic Islands
Baleares *fpl* **las** (**islas**) ~ the Balearics
baleo *m AmL* (*disparo*) shot
balero *m AmL* (*juego*) cup and ball
balido *m* bleat
balín *m* **1.** (*bala*) small bullet **2.** (*bolita de plomo*) pellet
balística *f sin pl* ballistics
baliza *f* (*señal*) marker; NÁUT buoy; AVIAT beacon; FERRO signal; AUTO warning light
balizar <z→c> *vt* **1.** (*con boyas*) to mark with buoys **2.** (*iluminar*) to light
ball *f AmL* **1.** (*balón*) ball **2.** (*proyectil*) shell
ballena *f* whale
ballenero *m* **1.** (*barco*) whaling ship **2.** (*pescador*) whaler
ballesta *f* **1.** TÉC spring **2.** HIST crossbow
ballet <ballets> *m* ballet
balneario *m* **1.** (*baños*) spa **2.** (*estación*) health resort

balompié *m* football *Brit,* soccer *Am*
balón *m* **1.** DEP ball **2.** (*recipiente para gases*) bag **3.** (*botella esférica*) canister **4.** NÁUT spinnaker **5.** (*en los tebeos*) speech balloon **6.** METEO balloon ▶**echar balones fuera** to evade the question
baloncesto *m* basketball
balonmano *m* handball
balonvolea *m* volleyball
balotaje *m Méx* voting
balsa *f* **1.** (*charca*) pool; (*estanque*) pond **2.** NÁUT (*barca*) ferry; (*plataforma*) raft; ~ **neumática** rubber dinghy ▶**ser una** ~ **de aceite** (*mar*) to be as calm as a millpond
balsámico, -a *adj* **1.** (*vinagre*) balsamic **2.** (*tranquilizador*) soothing
bálsamo *m* balm
báltico, -a **I.** *adj* Baltic; **el mar** ~ the Baltic Sea; **los países** ~**s** the Baltic countries **II.** *m, f* native/inhabitant of the Baltic countries
baluarte *m* bastion; **un** ~ **de la libertad** a bulwark of freedom
balumba *f* **1.** (*montón*) heap; **una** ~ **de ropa** a bundle of clothes **2.** *AmS* (*barullo*) racket
bambalina *f* TEAT drop(-scene); **entre** ~**s** backstage
bambolear **I.** *vt* to swing, to sway **II.** *vr:* ~**se** to swing, to sway
bamboleo *m* swaying
bambolla *f* ostentation
bambú *m* bamboo
banal *adj* banal
banalidad *f* banality
banalizar <z→c> *vt* to trivialize
banana *f AmL* banana
bananero, -a *adj* banana; **república bananera** *pey* banana republic
banano *m AmL* banana tree
banasta *f* large basket
banca *f* **1.** (*en el mercado*) stall **2.** *AmL* (*asiento*) bench **3.** FIN banking; ~ **electrónica** electronic banking **4.** (*en juegos de azar*) bank **5.** *AmS* (*influencia*) influence; **tener** ~ to have pull
bancal *m* (*en un jardín*) patch; (*en una pendiente*) terrace
bancario, -a *adj* bank(ing); **cuenta bancaria** bank account
bancarrota *f* bankruptcy
banco *m* **1.** (*asiento*) bench **2.** FIN bank; ~ **en casa** home banking; **Banco Interamericano de Desarrollo** Inter-American Development Bank; **Banco Central Europeo** Central European Bank; **Banco Europeo de Inversiones** European Investment Bank; ~ **emisor** issuing bank; **Banco Mundial** World Bank **3.** TÉC bench, work table; ~ **de pruebas** test bed; *fig* testing ground **4.** GEO stratum **5.** (*de peces*) shoal ▶~ **de datos** INFOR databank; ~ **de sangre** bloodbank
banda *f* **1.** (*cinta*) band; (*franja*) strip; ~ **de frecuencia** RADIO frequency band; ~ **sonora** CINE soundtrack; **estar fuera de** ~ DEP to be

out **2.** GEO (*de montaña*) side; (*de río*) bank **3.** (*pandilla*) gang; ~ **terrorista** terrorist group **4.** (*de música*) band; (*de música moderna*) group **5.** FIN ~ **de fluctuación** fluctuation range **6.** (*billar*) cushion **7.** (*como insignia*) sash

bandada *f* **1.** (*de pájaros*) flock; (*de peces*) shoal **2.** (*de personas*) gang

bandazo *m* **1.** NÁUT lurch; **dar ~s** to roll from side to side **2.** (*cambio*) marked shift

bandear I. *vt* **1.** AmC (*perseguir a alguien*) to chase; (*herir de gravedad*) to seriously wound **2.** Arg, Par, Urug (*taladrar*) to drill **3.** Arg, Par, Urug (*un río*) to cross **4.** Guat (*pretender*) to court **5.** Urug (*herir con palabras*) to hurt; (*inculpar*) to charge **II.** *vr:* ~**se 1.** (*mecerse*) to rock **2.** (*en la vida*) to shift for oneself

bandeja *f* tray; ~ **de entrada** in-tray; ~ **de salida** out-tray; **pasar la** ~ to pass the hat around; **servir en** ~ to hand on a plate

bandera *f* flag ▶**estar hasta la** ~ *inf* to be packed full

banderazo *m* DEP starting signal

banderilla *f* **1.** TAUR banderilla (*short decorated lance*) **2.** (*tapa*) cocktail snack on a stick

banderillero *m* TAUR banderillero (*bullfighter who uses the banderillas*)

banderín *m* **1.** (*bandera*) small flag; (*triangular*) pennant **2.** (*persona*) flag-bearer

banderola *f* **1.** (*como señal*) signalling [*o* signaling *Am*] flag **2.** MIL pennant **3.** CSur (*ventana*) fanlight *Brit*, transom *Am*

bandido, -a *m, f* **1.** (*criminal*) bandit **2.** (*persona pilla*) rogue

bando *m* **1.** (*edicto*) edict **2.** (*proclama*) proclamation **3.** (*partido*) faction **4.** (*de pájaros*) flock; (*de peces*) shoal

bandolera *f* (*correa*) bandoleer

bandolerismo *m sin pl* banditry

bandolero, -a *m, f* bandit

bandolina *f* MÚS mandolin

bangladesí *adj, mf* Bangladeshi

banjo *m* MÚS banjo

banking *m sin pl* banking; ~ **electrónico** e-banking

banquero, -a *m, f* banker

banqueta *f* **1.** (*taburete*) stool; (*para los pies*) footstool **2.** AmC (*acera*) pavement *Brit*, sidewalk *Am*

banquete *m* banquet

banquetear I. *vi* to feast **II.** *vt* to banquet

banquillo *m* **1.** (*banco pequeño*) bench; (*para los pies*) footstool; JUR dock **2.** DEP bench

bañada *f* AmL (*baño*) swim; (*de pintura*) coat

bañadera *f* AmL bath *Brit*, bathtub *Am*

bañado *m* Arg, Bol, Par marshland

bañador *m* (*de mujer*) swimming costume *Brit*, swimsuit *Am;* (*de hombre*) swimming trunks

bañar I. *vt* **1.** (*lavar*) to bath *Brit*, to bathe *Am* **2.** (*sumergir*) to immerse **3.** (*mar*) to bathe **4.** (*recubrir*) to coat; **bañado en sudor** bathed in sweat **5.** (*iluminar*) to flood with light **II.** *vr:*

~**se 1.** (*lavarse*) to have a bath *Brit*, to bathe *Am* **2.** (*en el mar*) to bathe, to have a swim

bañera *f* bath, bathtub *Am*

bañero, -a *m, f* (swimming) pool attendant

bañista *mf* **1.** (*en una playa*) bather **2.** (*en un balneario*) patient at a spa

baño *m* **1.** (*acto*) bathing; ~ **de fijación** FOTO fixation; ~ (**de**) **María** GASTR bain-marie; ~ **de sangre** bloodbath **2.** (*cuarto*) bathroom; **ir al** ~ to go to the toilet **3.** (*capa de pintura*) coat; (*de chocolate*) coating **4.** *pl* (*balneario*) spa; ~**s termales** hot springs; **ir a los** ~**s** to go to the spa

baptista *mf* REL Baptist

baptisterio *m* **1.** (*pila bautismal*) font **2.** (*lugar*) baptistery

baqueta *f* **1.** MIL ramrod **2.** MÚS drumstick

baquetazo *m* (*golpe*) heavy blow; (*caída*) heavy fall

baquetear *vt* to annoy

bar *m* **1.** (*café*) café; (*tasca*) bar **2.** FÍS bar

barahúnda *f* uproar

baraja *f* pack [*o* deck *Am*] of cards; **una** ~ **de posibilidades** *fig* a range of possibilities

barajar *vt* **1.** (*los naipes*) to shuffle **2.** (*mezclar*) to mix up **3.** (*varias posibilidades*) to consider; **se barajan varios nombres** several names are being bandied about **4.** (*caballo*) to rein in **5.** CSur (*detener*) to catch

baranda *f* **1.** (*de balcón*) handrail **2.** (*de billar*) cushion

barandilla *f* **1.** (*de balcón*) handrail **2.** (*pasamanos*) banister

baratijas *fpl* cheap goods *pl; pey* junk

baratillo *m* **1.** (*tienda*) junk shop **2.** (*puesto*) junk stall **3.** (*mercadillo*) flea market **4.** (*artículos*) junk

barato I. *m* (*venta*) bargain sale **II.** *adv* cheap(ly)

barato, -a *adj* cheap

barba *f* **1.** (*mentón*) chin **2.** (*pelos*) beard; **dejarse** ~ to grow a beard; **por** ~ per head **3.** *pl* (*de peces*) barbels *pl* **4.** *pl* (*de papel*) ragged edges *pl* ▶**subirse a las** ~**s de alguien** to be disrespectful to sb

barbacoa *f* barbecue

barbado *m* **1.** (*plantón*) cutting **2.** (*hijuelo*) shoot

barbar *vi* **1.** (*hombre*) to grow a beard **2.** (*planta*) to take root

barbaridad *f* **1.** (*crueldad*) barbarity; **¡qué** ~! how terrible! **2.** (*temeridad*) rash act **3.** (*disparate*) nonsense **4.** *inf* (*cantidad*) loads *pl*

barbarie *f* savagery

bárbaro, -a I. *adj* **1.** (*cruel*) savage **2.** *inf* (*estupendo*) tremendous **3.** HIST barbarian **II.** *m, f* **1.** (*grosero*) brute **2.** HIST barbarian

barbear *vt* **1.** AmC, Par (*afeitar*) to shave **2.** AmC, Méx (*adular*) to fawn on

barbecho *m* fallow (land); **estar en** ~ to be fallow

barbería *f* barber's (shop)

barbero *m* barber

barbilampiño I. *adj* smooth-faced II. *m* novice

barbilla *f* 1.(*mentón*) chin 2.(*barba*) beard

barbitúrico *m* barbiturate

barbo *m* barbel

barbudo, -a *adj* bearded

barca *f* 1.(*embarcación*) (small) boat; **dar un paseo en** ~ to take a boat ride 2. *pl* (*columpio*) swing boat

barcaza *f* barge

Barcelona *f* Barcelona

barcelonés, -esa I. *adj* of/from Barcelona II. *m, f* native/inhabitant of Barcelona

barchilón, -ona *m, f AmL* (*curandero*) healer

barco *m* ship; ~ **cisterna** tanker; ~ **de pasajeros** passenger ship; ~ **de vapor** steamer; ~ **de vela** sailing ship

baremo *m* 1.(*tabla de cuentas*) table 2.(*de tarifas*) price list 3.(*escala de valores*) range of values

bargueño *m* small cabinet

bario *m* barium

barítono *m* MÚS baritone

barman *m* <bármanes> barman, bartender

barniz *m* 1.(*laca*) polish; (*para madera*) varnish 2.(*para loza*) glaze 3.(*cosa superficial*) gloss

barnizado *m* 1.(*efecto*) varnish 2.(*acción*) varnishing

barnizar <z→c> *vt* 1.(*pintar*) to put a gloss on; (*madera*) to varnish 2.(*loza*) to glaze

barómetro *m* barometer

barón, -onesa *m, f* baron *m*, baroness *f*

barquero, -a *m, f* (*en un bote*) boatman *m,* boatwoman *f*; (*en una barca de pasaje*) ferryman *m*, ferrywoman *f*

barquilla *f* 1.(*barca*) small boat 2.(*de un globo*) basket 3. NÁUT log 4. *AmC* (*galleta*) ice-cream cone

barquillo *m* wafer

barra *f* 1.(*pieza larga*) bar; ~**s asimétricas** DEP asymmetric bars; ~ **de ejercicios** DEP exercise bar; ~ **de labios** lipstick; **desodorante en** ~ deodorant stick 2.(*de pan*) loaf; (*de chocolate*) bar 3.(*en un bar*) bar; ~ **americana** singles bar 4.(*raya*) dash; (*signo gráfico*) slash; MÚS bar 5.(*barrera*) barrier 6.(*palanca*) lever 7.(*bajío estrecho*) sandbank 8. INFOR ~ **de comandos** taskbar; ~ **de desplazamiento** scroll bar; ~ **espaciadora** space bar; ~ **de inversa** backslash 9. *AmL* (*pandilla*) gang 10. *AmS* (*público*) public

barrabasada *f* dirty trick

barraca *f* 1.(*vivienda provisional*) cabin 2.(*choza*) hut 3. *reg* (*vivienda rústica*) thatched farmhouse 4. *AmL* MIL barracks 5. *AmL* (*almacén*) storage shed 6.(*barracón*) big hut

barracón *m* big hut

barracuda *f* barracuda

barranco *m* 1.(*despeñadero*) cliff 2.(*cauce*) ravine 3.(*dificultad*) obstacle

barredera *f* street-cleaning vehicle

barredor(a) *m(f)* streetsweeper

barreminas *m inv* MIL minesweeper

barrena *f* 1.(*taladrador*) drill 2. AVIAT spin

barrenar *vt* 1.(*perforar*) to drill 2.(*planes*) to foil; (*leyes*) to violate

barrendero, -a *m, f* sweeper

barreno *m* 1.(*barrena grande*) large drill 2.(*perforación*) borehole; (*lleno de pólvora*) blasthole

barreño *m* washing-up basin

barrer *vt* 1.(*habitación*) to sweep 2.(*un obstáculo*) to sweep aside 3. *inf* (*derrotar*) to defeat ▶~ **para** [*o* hacia] **dentro** to look after number one

barrera *f* 1.(*barra*) barrier; ~ **lingüística** language barrier; ~ **del sonido** sound barrier 2.(*valla*) fence 3. DEP wall 4. TAUR barrier

barriada *f* 1.(*barrio*) district 2. *AmL* (*barrio pobre*) shanty town

barricada *f* barricade

barriga *f* 1.(*vientre*) belly 2.(*de una vasija*) rounded part 3.(*de una pared*) bulge ▶**rascarse la** ~ to laze about, to twiddle one's thumbs

barrigón *m* big belly

barrigón, -ona I. *adj* pottbellied II. *m, f* potbellied individual

barril *m* 1.(*cuba*) barrel; **cerveza de** ~ draught beer 2. *AmL* (*cometa*) hexagonal kite

barrilete *m* 1.(*barril pequeño*) small keg 2.(*que usan los carpinteros*) clamp 3.(*en un revolver*) cylinder 4. *AmL* (*cometa*) hexagonal kite

barrio *m* 1.(*zona de una ciudad*) district, neighbourhood *Brit,* neighborhood *Am;* ~ **chino** red-light district; ~ **comercial** business quarter 2.(*arrabal*) suburb ▶**irse al otro** ~ *inf* to snuff it

barriobajero, -a *adj pey* 1.(*de un barrio bajo*) slum 2.(*vulgar*) coarse

barrizal *m* mire

barro *m* 1.(*lodo*) mud 2.(*arcilla*) clay; **de** ~ earthenware 3.(*granito*) pimple

barroco I. *m sin pl* baroque II. *adj* 1.(*del periodo barroco*) baroque 2.(*elaborado*) overelaborate, gaudy *pej*

barrote *m* 1.(*barra*) (heavy) bar; **entre** ~**s** *fig, inf* behind bars 2.(*para reforzar*) crosspiece

barruntar(se) *vt, vr* to conjecture

barrunto *m* 1.(*conjetura*) conjecture; (*sospecha*) suspicion 2.(*indicio*) sign

bartola *f inf* **tumbarse a la** ~ to be idle

bártulos *mpl* belongings *pl*

barullo *m inf* 1.(*ruido*) din 2.(*desorden*) confusion

basa *f* 1.(*de una columna*) base 2.(*base*) basis

basalto *m* basalt

basar I. *vt* 1.(*asentar*) to base 2.(*fundar*) to ground II. *vr* ~**se en algo** (*teoría*) to be based on sth; (*persona*) to base oneself on sth

basca *f* 1. MED (*espasmo*) nausea; **tener** ~**s** to

feel sick **2.** inf (arrebato) fit of rage **3.** (en animales) rabies **4.** inf (gentío) gang
bascosidad f **1.** (suciedad) filth **2.** Ecua (insulto) obscenity
bascoso, -a adj **1.** MED queasy **2.** Col, Ecua (nauseabundo) nauseating **3.** Col, Ecua (indigno) contemptible, vile **4.** Col, Ecua (obsceno) obscene
báscula f scales pl
bascular vi **1.** (inclinarse) to tilt **2.** (oscilar) to seesaw
base f **1.** (lo fundamental) basis; ~ de datos INFOR database; **elaborado a** ~ **de algo** drawn up on the basis of sth; **partir de la** ~ **de que...** to start with the idea that ... **2.** ARQUIT, MIL, DEP base **3.** POL rank and file **4.** MAT base; (superficie) area; (línea) base line ►a ~ de **bien** inf really well
básico, -a adj (t. quím) basic
Basilea f Basle, Basel
basílica f basilica
basilisco m **1.** (mito) basilisk **2.** AmL ZOOL iguana
basket m sin pl basketball
basta f **1.** (hilván) tacking Brit, basting Am **2.** AmL (bastilla) hem
bastante I. adj enough; **tengo** ~ **frío** I'm quite cold II. adv (suficientemente) sufficiently; (considerablemente) rather; **con esto tengo** ~ this is enough for me
bastar I. vi to be enough; **¡basta!** that's enough! II. vr ~**se** (uno) **solo** to be self-sufficient
bastardía f **1.** (degeneración) bastardy **2.** (bajeza) meanness
bastardilla f TIPO italics pl
bastardo, -a I. adj **1.** (hijo) bastard **2.** BOT hybrid **3.** (vil) wicked II. m, f bastard
bastedad f coarseness
bastidor m **1.** TÉC frame(work); (de coche) chassis inv **2.** (de ventana) frame **3.** TEAT wing; **entre** ~**es** behind the scenes
bastilla f hem
bastimento m **1.** (provisión) supply **2.** (embarcación) vessel
bastión m bastion
basto, -a adj **1.** (grosero) rude; (vulgar) coarse **2.** (superficie) rough **3.** (mal hecho) roughly made
bastón m **1.** (para andar) stick; (para esquiar) ski pole **2.** (de mando) baton; **empuñar el** ~ to take command
bastoncillo m diminutivo de **bastón** small stick; ~ **de algodón** cotton bud Brit, cotton swab Am, Q-tip® Am
bastos mpl clubs pl (in Spanish card pack) ►**pintan** ~ things are getting difficult
basura f **1.** (desperdicios) rubbish Brit, garbage Am; ~ **del hogar** domestic rubbish; **echar algo a la** ~ to throw sth away **2.** (lo despreciable) trash
basural m AmL rubbish dump Brit, garbage dump Am

basurear vt Arg, Urug **1.** vulg (tratar despectivamente) to treat like shit **2.** (vencer) to defeat
basurero m **1.** (vertedero) rubbish dump Brit, garbage dump Am **2.** (recipiente) dustbin Brit, trashcan Am
basurero, -a m, f dustman m Brit dustwoman f Brit, garbage collector Am
bata f **1.** (albornoz) dressing gown **2.** (guardapolvos) overalls pl Brit, coverall Am **3.** (de laboratorio) lab coat; (de hospital) white coat
batacazo m **1.** (golpe) thump **2.** (caída) heavy fall; **se pegó un** ~ inf he/she came a cropper **3.** CSur, PRico (golpe de suerte) stroke of luck
bataclán m AmL striptease show
bataclana f AmL chorus girl, stripper
batahola f inf rumpus
batalla f **1.** MIL (episodio bélico) battle; ~ **campal** pitched battle; fig bitter dispute **2.** (lucha interior) struggle **3.** AUTO wheelbase
batallar vi **1.** (con armas) to fight; ~ **por algo** to battle over sth **2.** (disputar) to quarrel
batallita f story
batallón m **1.** MIL battalion **2.** inf (grupo) group
batán m **1.** (máquina) fulling mill **2.** AmL (piedra lisa) millstone **3.** Chile (tintorería) dry cleaner's
batanear vt to beat
batata I. adj CSur (tímido) shy II. f **1.** (planta) sweet potato plant **2.** (tubérculo) sweet potato **3.** CSur (susto) shock **4.** CSur (vergüenza) embarrassment **5.** AmL ~ **de la pierna** calf
bate m DEP bat; ~ **de béisbol** baseball bat
bateador(a) m(f) DEP batter
batear vt DEP to bat
batería¹ f **1.** t. TÉC battery; ~ **de cocina** pots and pans; ~ **solar** solar panel; **aparcar en** ~ to park adjacent to the kerb [o curb Am] **2.** TEAT footlights **3.** MÚS (en orquesta) percussion; (en conjunto) drums pl
batería² mf, **baterista** mf drummer
batida f **1.** (de los cazadores) beat **2.** (de la policía) raid **3.** AmL (paliza) beating, thrashing
batido m **1.** (bebida) milk shake; ~ **de fresa** strawberry milk shake **2.** (masa) dough **3.** (de huevos) batter
batidor m **1.** (instrumento) whisk **2.** (en la caza) beater **3.** (explorador) scout
batidora f (de mano) whisk; (eléctrica) mixer, blender
batiente I. adj flapping II. m **1.** (marco de ventana) frame; (de puerta) jamb **2.** (hoja de ventana, puerta) leaf **3.** MÚS damper **4.** (roca) reef
batifondo m CSur, inf (alboroto) uproar; (disturbio) commotion; (zozobra) uneasiness
batín m (man's) dressing gown
batir I. vt **1.** (golpear) to beat; (el viento) to beat against; (las olas) to crash against; (la lluvia) to beat down on; ~ **palmas** to clap **2.** (metal) to beat **3.** (moneda) to mint

4. (*casa*) to knock down **5.** (*toldo*) to flap **6.** (*privilegio*) to do away with **7.** (*enemigo*) to defeat; ~ **un récord** to beat a record **8.** MIL to beat **9.** (*un terreno*) to comb **10.** *CSur* (*denunciar*) to inform on **II.** *vr:* ~**se 1.** (*combatir*) to fight **2.** (*en duelo*) to fight a duel

batista *f* cambric

batracio *m* batrachian

baturrillo *m* hotchpotch *Brit,* hodgepodge *Am*

baturro, -a I. *adj inf* (*rudo*) rough **II.** *m, f* Aragonese peasant

batuta *f* MÚS baton ►**llevar la ~** to be in charge

baúl *m* **1.** (*mueble*) trunk; ~ **de viaje** trunk **2.** *AmL* (*portamaletas*) boot *Brit,* trunk *Am* **3.** *inf* (*vientre*) belly

bausán, -ana I. *adj* **1.** (*tonto*) stupid **2.** *AmL* (*perezoso*) lazy **II.** *m, f* simpleton

bautismal *adj* baptismal; **pila ~** font

bautismo *m* baptism; ~ **de sangre** first combat

bautista *mf* Baptist; **San Juan Bautista** St John the Baptist

bautizar <z→c> *vt* **1.** REL to baptize; (*nombrar*) to christen **2.** *inf* (*mojar*) to drench **3.** *inf* (*leche*) to water; ~ **el vino** to water down the wine

bautizo *m* baptism; (*ceremonia*) christening; (*fiesta*) christening party

bauxita *f* bauxite

baya *f* berry

bayeta *f* **1.** (*para fregar*) washing-up cloth, dish cloth **2.** (*tela de lana*) baize

bayoneta *f* bayonet

bayoya *m* PRico, RDom uproar

baza *f* **1.** (*naipes*) trick; **meter ~ en algo** *inf* to butt in on sth **2.** (*provecho*) benefit; **sacar ~ de algo** to profit from sth

bazar *m* **1.** (*mercado*) bazaar **2.** (*gran almacén*) large shop

bazo *m* ANAT spleen

bazofia *f* **1.** (*comida*) pigswill **2.** (*restos de comida*) leftovers *pl* **3.** (*cosa*) filthy thing

bazuca *f* bazooka

be *f letter* B

beata *f inf* (*moneda*) one peseta

beatería *f* **1.** (*devoción exagerada*) sanctimoniousness **2.** (*devoción falsa*) affected piety

beatificación *f* beatification

beatificar <c→qu> *vt* to beatify

beatitud *f* beatitude

beato, -a I. *adj* **1.** (*piadoso*) devout **2.** (*beatificado*) beatified **3.** *elev* (*feliz*) blessed **II.** *m, f* **1.** (*hermano*) lay brother *m,* lay sister *f* **2.** (*persona beatificada*) beatified person **3.** (*exageradamente devota*) devout person

bebe, -a *m, f AmL* baby

bebé *m* baby

bebedera *f Méx* drinking spree

bebedero *m* **1.** (*para animales*) waterhole; (*para animales domésticos*) drinking trough **2.** (*de jarro*) spout

bebedizo *m* **1.** (*medicinal*) potion **2.** (*enamoradizo*) love potion

bebedor(a) I. *adj* given to drinking **II.** *m(f)* drinker

bebendurria *f AmL, inf* drinking binge

bebé-probeta *m* <bebés-probeta> test-tube baby

beber I. *vi, vt* **1.** (*líquido*) to drink; ~ **de la botella** to drink from the bottle; ~ **a sorbos** to sip; ~ **de un trago** to gulp **2.** (*información*) to absorb **II.** *vr:* ~**se** to drink up; **bebérselo todo** to drink it all up

bebible *adj* drinkable

bebida *f* drink, beverage *form;* ~ **alcohólica** alcoholic drink; ~ **energética** energy drink; **darse a la ~** to take to drink

bebido, -a *adj* (*borracho*) drunk

beca *f* (*de estudios*) grant; (*por méritos*) scholarship; **conceder una ~ a alguien** to award a grant to sb

becada *f* woodcock

becar <c→qu> *vt* to award a grant to

becario, -a *m, f* grant holder; (*por méritos*) scholarship holder

becerro *m* HIST register

becerro, -a *m, f* yearling calf; **el ~ de oro** the golden calf

bechamel *f* white sauce

bedel(a) *m(f)* beadle, proctor

beduino, -a I. *adj* Bedouin **II.** *m, f* Bedouin

befa *f* jeer

befarse *vr* ~ **de alguien/algo** to jeer at sb/sth

befo *m* lip (of horse)

befo, -a *adj* **1.** (*belfo*) thick-lipped **2.** (*zambo*) knock-needed

begonia *f* begonia

beicon *m sin pl* bacon

beige *adj* beige

béisbol *m sin pl* DEP baseball

bejuco *m* liana

Belcebú *m* Beelzebub

beldad *f elev* beauty

belduque *m AmL* pointed sword

belén *m* **1.** (*nacimiento*) crib, Nativity scene **2.** *inf* (*confusión*) confusion

Belén *m* Bethlehem

belfo *m* **1.** (*de animales*) lip **2.** (*de personas*) prominent lower lip

belga *adj, mf* Belgian

Bélgica *f* Belgium

Belgrado *m* Belgrade

Belice *m* Belize

beliceño, -a *adj, m, f* Belizean

belicista I. *adj* belligerent **II.** *mf* warmonger

bélico, -a *adj* warlike

belicosidad *f* aggressiveness

belicoso, -a *adj* (*población*) warlike; (*persona*) aggressive

beligerancia *f* belligerency

beligerante I. *adj* belligerent **II.** *mf* belligerent individual

bellaco, -a I. *adj* cunning **II.** *m, f* rascal

bellaquear *vi* **1.** (*persona*) to cheat **2.** *AmL*

(*caballo*) to shy
bellaquería *f* **1.**(*acción*) dirty trick **2.**(*cualidad*) cunning
belleza *f* beauty
bello, -a *adj* beautiful
bellota *f* **1.**(*fruto*) acorn **2.**(*capullo*) bud
bemba *f AmL, pey* lip
bembo, -a *adj AmL* thick-lipped
bembudo, -a *adj AmL* thick-lipped
bemol I. *adj* MÚS flat **II.** *m* MÚS flat ▶**tener** ~**es** to be difficult
benceno *m* benzene
bencina *f* benzine
bendecir *irr como decir vt* **1.**(*sacerdote*) to bless; ~ **la mesa** to say grace **2.**(*alabar*) to praise **3.**(*consagrar*) to consecrate **4.**(*una cosa*) to approve
bendición *f* **1.**(*acto*) blessing **2.**(*cosa magnífica*) marvel **3.** *pl* (*casamiento*) wedding ceremony
bendito, -a I. *adj* **1.** REL blessed; (*agua*) holy; (*santo*) saintly; **¡~ sea!** *inf* thank God! **2.**(*dichoso*) lucky **3.**(*simple*) simple-minded **II.** *m, f* kind soul
benedictino, -a *adj, m, f* REL Benedictine
benefactor(a) I. *adj* beneficient **II.** *m(f)* benefactor
beneficencia *f* **1.**(*organización*) charity **2.**(*virtud*) beneficience
beneficiado, -a *adj, m, f* beneficiary
beneficiar I. *vt* **1.**(*favorecer*) to benefit **2.**(*tierra*) to cultivate **3.**(*mina*) to work **4.**(*mineral*) to refine **5.** *AmL* (*animal*) to slaughter **II.** *vr:* ~**se 1.**(*sacar provecho*) ~**se de algo** to benefit from sth **2.** *pey* (*enriquecerse*) ~**se de algo** to take advantage of sth
beneficiario, -a *m, f* beneficiary; (*de una letra de crédito*) assignee; ~ **de la pensión** receiver of the pension
beneficio *m* **1.**(*bien*) good **2.**(*provecho*) profit; **a** ~ **de** for the benefit of **3.** FIN profit **4.**(*cargo eclesiástico*) living **5.** *AmL* (*matanza*) slaughter
beneficioso, -a *adj* **1.**(*favorable*) beneficial **2.**(*útil*) useful **3.**(*productivo*) profitable
benéfico, -a *adj* **1.**(*que hace bien*) beneficial **2.**(*caritativo*) charitable
benemérito, -a *adj* worthy; **la Benemérita** the Civil Guard
beneplácito *m* **1.**(*permiso*) approval **2.**(*consentimiento*) consent
benévolo, -a *adj* **1.**(*favorable*) benevolent **2.**(*clemente*) indulgent
bengala *f* flare; (*pequeña*) sparkler
benignidad *f* **1.**(*de una persona*) kindness **2.**(*del clima*) mildness **3.** MED benignancy
benigno, -a *adj* **1.**(*persona*) kind; **ser** ~ **con alguien** to be kind to sb **2.**(*clima*) mild **3.** MED benign
benjamín, -ina *m, f* **1.**(*hijo menor*) youngest child **2.**(*de un grupo*) youngest member
beodo, -a I. *adj* drunk **II.** *m, f* drunkard
berbén *m Méx* (*escorbuto*) scurvy

berberecho *m* cockle
berbiquí *m* brace and bit
bereber, beréber *adj, mf* Berber
berenjena *f* aubergine *Brit,* eggplant *Am*
berenjenal *m* **1.** aubergine bed *Brit,* eggplant patch *Am* **2.** *fig* (*lío*) mess; **meterse en un** ~ to get into a mess
bergante *m* scoundrel
berilio *m* beryllium
berilo *m* beryl
Berlín *m* Berlin
berlina *f* **1.**(*vehículo*) saloon (car) *Brit,* sedan *Am* **2.** *AmL* (*pastel*) jam doughnut *Brit,* jelly donut *Am*
berlinés, -esa I. *adj* Berlin **II.** *m, f* Berliner
bermejo, -a *adj* red; (*de animales*) reddish-brown
bermellón *m* vermilion
bermudas *mpl* Bermuda shorts *pl*
Berna *f* Berne
berrear *vi* **1.**(*animal*) to bellow; (*oveja*) to bleat **2.**(*llorar*) to howl **3.** *inf* (*cantar desentonadamente*) to howl **4.**(*chillar*) to screech
berrido *m* **1.**(*de animales*) bellow; (*de ovejas*) bleating **2.**(*lloro*) howl **3.** *inf* (*canto desentonado*) howling **4.**(*chillido*) screech
berrinche *m* *inf* **1.**(*llorera*) tantrum **2.**(*enfado*) rage
berrinchudo, -a *adj AmL* on heat
berro *m* watercress
berza *f* cabbage
berzal *m* cabbage patch
berzotas *mf inv, inf* chump
besar I. *vt* **1.**(*personas*) to kiss **2.** *inf* (*objetos*) to touch **II.** *vr:* ~**se 1.**(*personas*) to kiss each other **2.**(*tocarse dos objetos*) to touch; (*chocar*) to bump into each other
beso *m* **1.**(*entre personas*) kiss; **comerse a alguien a** ~**s** to smother sb with kisses **2.**(*entre objetos*) bump
bestia¹ I. *adj* stupid **II.** *mf* **1.**(*persona bruta*) brute; (*grosera*) boor **2.**(*ignorante*) ignoramus
bestia² *f* **1.** ZOOL animal **2.**(*animal salvaje*) (wild) beast
bestial *adj* **1.**(*propio de una bestia*) bestial **2.**(*muy brutal*) brutal **3.** *inf* (*muy intensivo*) tremendous; *Brit* (*muy grande*) huge; (*muy bueno*) marvellous *Brit,* marvelous *Am*
bestialidad *f* **1.**(*cualidad*) bestiality **2.**(*crueldad*) brutality **3.** *inf* (*gran cantidad*) huge amount
best seller *m inv,* **bestséller** *m inv* bestseller
besucón, -ona I. *adj* fond of kissing **II.** *m, f* **es una besucona** she's very fond of kissing
besugo *m* **1.** ZOOL bream; **ojos de** ~ *inf* bulging eyes **2.** *inf* (*persona*) idiot; **¡no seas** ~**!** don't be an idiot!
besuquear *vt* to cover with kisses
betabel *f Méx* (*remolacha*) beetroot *Brit,* beet *Am;* ~ **forrajera** fodder beet
betarraga *f AmL* beetroot *Brit,* beet *Am*
betún *m* **1.** QUÍM bitumen **2.**(*para el calzado*)

shoe polish; **negro como el** ~ as black as pitch
bezo *m* thick lip
biaba *f Arg, Úrug* (*cachetada*) slap; (*paliza*) beating; **dar la** ~ (*pegar*) to beat up; (*derrotar*) to defeat
bianual *adj* biannual; BOT biennial
biatlón *m* DEP biathlon
biberón *m* feeding bottle
Biblia *f* Bible
bíblico, -a *adj* biblical
bibliobús *m* mobile library
bibliófilo, -a *m, f* bibliophile, book lover
bibliografía *f* bibliography
bibliográfico, -a *adj* bibliographic(al)
biblioteca *f* 1. (*local*) library; ~ **de consulta** reference library 2. (*mueble*) bookcase 3. (*estantería*) bookshelves *pl*
bibliotecario, -a *m, f* librarian
bicameral *adj* POL bicameral
bicarbonato *m* bicarbonate; ~ **sódico** bicarbonate of soda, baking soda, sodium bicarbonate
bicéfalo, -a *adj* two-headed
bicentenario *m* bicentenary, bicentennial *Am*
bíceps *m inv* ANAT biceps *inv*
bicha *f* 1. *inf* (*serpiente*) snake 2. (*figura*) mermaid
bicharraco *m* 1. *pey* (*bicho*) ugly creature 2. (*persona*) odd creature
bicho *m* 1. (*animal*) (small) animal; (*insecto*) bug 2. TAUR bull 3. *inf* (*persona*) unpleasant person; ~ **raro** weirdo; **mal** ~ rogue 4. *vulg* (*pene*) prick
bici *f inf abr de* **bicicleta** bike
bicicleta *f* bicycle; ~ **de carreras** racing bike; ~ **estática** exercise bike; ~ **de montaña** mountain bike
bicoca *f* 1. *inf* (*ganga*) bargain 2. *inf* (*pequeñez*) trifle 3. *AmL* (*de eclesiásticos*) skull cap
bicolor *adj* two-colour *Brit,* two-color *Am*
bidé *m* <bidés>, **bidet** *m* <bidets> bidet
bidireccional *adj* two-way; INFOR bidirectional
bidón *m* steel drum
biela *f* 1. TÉC connecting rod 2. (*de la bicicleta*) crank
bieldo *m* winnowing fork
Bielorrusia *f* Belorussia
bielorruso, -a *adj, m, f* Belorussian
bien I. *m* 1. (*bienestar*) well-being 2. (*bondad moral*) good 3. (*provecho*) benefit 4. *pl* ECON goods *pl* 5. *pl* (*posesiones*) property; (*riqueza*) wealth; ~**es inmuebles** real estate; ~**es de la tierra** agricultural produce II. *adv* 1. (*de modo conveniente*) properly; (*correctamente*) well; ~ **mirado** well thought of; **estar** ~ **de salud** to be in good health; **estar** (**a**) ~ **con alguien** to get on well with sb; **hacer** **algo** ~ to do sth well; **hacer** ~ **en** +*infin* to do well to +*infin;* **¡pórtate** ~**!** behave yourself!; **tener a** ~ +*infin* to see fit to +*infin;* **te está** ~ that serves you right 2. (*con gusto*) willingly

3. (*seguramente*) surely 4. (*muy*) very; (*bastante*) quite; **es** ~ **fácil** it's very simple 5. (*asentimiento*) all right; **¡está** ~**!** OK! ▶**ahora** ~ however; ~ **que** **mal** one way or another III. *adj* well-off IV. *conj* 1. (*aunque*) ~ **que** although; **si** ~ even though 2. (*o...o*) ~...~... either ... or ... 3. (*apenas*) **no** ~...(**cuando...**) no sooner ... (than ...) V. *interj* well done
bienal I. *adj* biennial II. *f* biennial show
bienaventurado *adj* 1. REL blessed 2. (*feliz*) fortunate
bienaventuranza *f* 1. REL (*gloria*) bliss; **las** ~**s** the Beatitudes 2. (*felicidad*) happiness
bienestar *m* 1. (*estado, sentimiento*) well--being 2. (*riqueza*) prosperity; **estado del** ~ welfare state
bienhablado, -a *adj* well-spoken
bienhechor(a) I. *adj* beneficent II. *m(f)* benefactor
bienintencionado, -a *adj* well-meaning
bienio *m* two-year period
bienpensante *adj, mf* orthodox
bienquistar I. *vt* to reconcile II. *vr:* ~**se** (*hacer amistad*) to become friendly; ~ **con alguien** (*congraciar*) to win sb over
bienquisto, -a *adj* ~ **de** [*o* **por**] **alguien** well--liked by sb
bienvenida *f* welcome; **dar la** ~ **a alguien** to welcome sb
bienvenido, -a I. *interj* welcome; **¡**~ **a casa!** welcome home!; **¡**~ **a España!** welcome to Spain! II. *adj* welcome
bies cortar al ~ to cut on the bias
bifásico, -a *adj* ELEC two-phase
bife *m CSur* 1. (*carne*) steak 2. *inf* (*sopapo*) slap
bifocal *adj* bifocal
bifurcación *f* 1. (*de un camino*) fork 2. INFOR branch
bifurcarse <c→qu> *vr* to fork
bigamia *f* bigamy
bígamo, -a I. *adj* bigamous II. *m, f* bigamist
bigote *m* 1. (*de hombre*) moustache, mustache *Am;* **estar de** ~(**s**) *inf* to be terrific 2. *pl* (*de animal*) whiskers *pl* 3. *AmL* (*croqueta*) croquette
bigotudo, -a *adj* with a big moustache
bigudí *m* curler
bikini *m* bikini
bilateral *adj* bilateral
biliar *adj* biliary; **cálculo** ~ gallstone
bilingüe I. *adj* bilingual II. *mf* bilingual person
bilingüismo *m sin pl* bilingualism
bilis *f inv* 1. ANAT bile 2. (*cólera*) spleen; **no tuve más remedio que tragar** ~ I had no choice but to put up with it
billar *m* 1. (*juego*) billiards; ~ **americano** pool 2. (*mesa*) billiard table
billete *m* 1. (*pasaje*) ticket; ~ **de ida y vuelta** return ticket *Brit,* roundtrip ticket *Am;* **sacar un** ~ to get a ticket 2. FIN note *Brit,* bill *Am* 3. (*de lotería*) ticket; ~ **premiado** winning

ticket **4.** (*mensaje breve*) note

billetera *f,* **billetero** *m* wallet *Brit,* billfold *Am*

billón *m* billion *Brit,* trillion *Am*

billonario, -a *m, f* billionaire

bimba *f AmL* (*embriaguez*) **pegarse una** ~ to get drunk

bimensual *adj* twice-monthly

bimestral *adj* (*cada dos meses*) bi-monthly; (*que dura dos meses*) two-month

bimotor I. *adj* twin-engined II. *m* twin-engined plane

binario, -a *adj* binary

bingo *m* (*juego*) bingo; (*sala*) bingo hall

binoculares *mpl* binoculars *pl*

binóculo *m* pince-nez

bioactivo, -a *adj* bioactive

biobasura *f* biorefuse

biodegradable *adj* biodegradable

biodiversidad *f* biodiversity

bioenergía *f* bioenergy

biofísica *f* biophysics

biogenética *f* biogenetics

biografía *f* biography

biografiar < *1. pres:* biografío> *vt* ~ a alguien to write the biography of sb

biógrafo *m CSur* (*cine*) cinema

biógrafo, -a *m, f* (*persona*) biographer

biología *f* biology

biólogo, -a *m, f* biologist

biomasa *f* biomass

biombo *m* (folding) screen

biomecánica *f* biomechanics

biónico, -a *adj* bionic

biopsia *f* biopsy

bioquímica *f* biochemistry

biorritmo *m* biorhythm

biosfera *f* biosphere

biosistema *m* biosystem

biotecnología *f* biotechnology

biotipo *m* biotype

biótopo *m* biotope

bipartidismo *m* POL two-party system

bípedo, -a *adj, m, f* biped

biplano *m* biplane

biplaza *adj, m* two-seater

bipolaridad *f* Fís bipolarity

biquini *m* bikini

birlar *vt inf* (*hurtar*) to pinch *Brit,* to swipe *Am;* **Carlos me birló el lápiz** Carlos pinched my pencil

Birmania *f* Burma

birmano, -a *adj, m, f* Burmese

birome *m o f CSur* ballpoint ben, biro® *Brit*

birra *f inf* beer

birrete *m* **1.** (*de clérigos*) biretta **2.** (*de catedráticos, jueces*) cap

birria *f* **1.** (*persona*) drip; **el delantero centro es una** ~ the centre forward is useless; **va hecho una** ~ he looks really scruffy **2.** (*objeto*) rubbish, trash; **la película es una** ~ the film is rubbish

birriondo, -a *adj Méx* **1.** (*callejero*) street;

(*animales*) jumpy; **disturbios** ~**s** street riots *pl;* **perro** ~ mutt **2.** (*enamoradizo*) easily infatuated **3.** (*cachondo*) randy *inf*

biruje *m AmL,* **biruji** *m* cold wind

bis I. *interj* encore II. *m* MÚS encore III. *adv* **1.** MÚS bis **2.** (*piso*) 7 ~ 7A

bisabuelo, -a *m, f* great-grandfather *m,* great-grandmother *f*

bisagra *f* hinge

bisar *vt* MÚS to give as an encore, to repeat

bisbis(e)ar *vt inf* **1.** (*musitar*) to mutter **2.** (*cuchichear*) to whisper

biscote *m* rusk

bisel *m* bevel

bisexual *adj* bisexual

bisexualidad *f sin pl* bisexuality

bisiesto *adj* año ~ leap year

bisílabo, -a *adj* two-syllable

bismuto *m* bismuth

bisnieto, -a *m, f* great-grandson *m,* great-granddaughter *f*

bisonte *m* (*americano*) buffalo; (*europeo*) bison

bisoñé *m* toupée

bisoño, -a I. *adj* inexperienced II. *m, f* (*novato*) novice

bisté *m* <bistés>, **bistec** *m* <bistecs> steak

bisturí *m* scalpel

bisutería *f* costume jewellery [*o* jewelry *Am*]

bit *m* <bits> INFOR bit; ~ **de parada** stop bit

bíter *m* bitters

bitoque *m* **1.** (*tapón*) bung **2.** *AmC* (*cloaca*) sewer **3.** *AmL* (*cánula de jeringa*) cannula **4.** *Méx, RíoPl* (*grifo*) faucet

bizantino, -a I. *adj* **1.** (*de Bizancio*) Byzantine **2.** *fig* hair-splitting II. *m, f* Byzantine

bizarría *f* **1.** (*valentía*) bravery **2.** (*gallardía*) dash **3.** (*generosidad*) generosity

bizarro, -a *adj* **1.** (*valiente*) brave **2.** (*apuesto*) dashing **3.** (*generoso*) generous **4.** (*extravagante*) odd

bizco, -a *adj* cross-eyed; **dejar a alguien** ~ *fig* to leave sb speechless

bizcocho I. *adj Méx* (*cobarde*) cowardly II. *m* **1.** GASTR sponge cake **2.** NÁUT hardtack

biznieto, -a *m, f v.* **bisnieto**

bizquear *vi* to squint

bizquera *f AmL* (*estrabismo*) squint; **tener** ~ to have a squint

bla-bla-bla *m* bla-bla-bla

blanca *f* **1.** MÚS minim *Brit,* half note *Am* **2.** (*pieza de dominó*) double-blank ▶ **estar sin** ~ *inf* to be broke

Blancanieves *f* Snow White

blanco *m* **1.** (*color*) white; **película en** ~ **y negro** black and white film **2.** (*de animal*) white patch **3.** (*espacio en un escrito*) blank space; **cheque en** ~ blank cheque [*o* check *Am*] **4.** (*diana*) target; **dar en el** ~ *fig* to hit the mark ▶ **se me quedó la mente en** ~ my mind went blank; **pasar la noche en** ~ to have a sleepless night; ~ **del ojo** white of the eye;

quedarse en ~ to go blank
blanco, -a I. *adj* 1. (*de tal color*) white 2. (*tez*) pale II. *m, f* white man *m*, white woman *f*
blancura *f* whiteness
blandear I. *vt* to persuade II. *vi* to begin to yield
blandengue *adj pey* soft, mushy
blandir I. *vt* to brandish II. *vi, vr:* ~se to wave about
blando, -a *adj* 1. (*objeto*) soft; **créditos** ~s ECON soft credits 2. (*carácter: suave*) mild; (*blandengue*) soft; (*cobarde*) cowardly; ~ **de corazón** soft-hearted 3. (*constitución*) weak 4. (*clima*) mild 5. (*lluvia, tono*) gentle 6. (*luz*) soft
blandura *f* 1. (*de una cosa*) softness 2. (*del carácter: suavidad*) mildness; (*blandenguería*) softness 3. (*lisonja*) flattery 4. (*del aire*) mildness 5. (*emplasto*) plaster
blanquear I. *vi* to whiten II. *vt* 1. (*poner blanco*) to whiten 2. (*pared*) to whitewash 3. (*dinero*) to launder 4. (*tejido*) to bleach 5. (*metal*) to blanch
blanquecino, -a *adj* whitish
blanqueo *m* 1. (*el poner blanco*) whitening 2. (*de una pared*) whitewashing 3. (*de tejido*) bleaching 4. (*de dinero*) laundering
blasfemar *vi* 1. REL to blaspheme 2. (*maldecir*) ~ **de algo** to swear about sth
blasfemia *f* 1. REL blasphemy 2. (*injuria*) insult 3. (*taco*) swearword
blasfemo, -a I. *adj* blasphemous II. *m, f* blasphemer
blasón *m* 1. (*escudo de armas*) coat of arms 2. (*honor*) honour *Brit,* honor *Am;* (*gloria*) glory 3. *pl* (*abolengo*) noble ancestry
blasonar I. *vt* to emblazen II. *vi* ~ **de algo** to boast about sth
blázer *m* blazer
bledo *m* goosefoot ▶ (no) **me** importa **un** ~ I couldn't care less
blindado, -a *adj* MIL armour-plated *Brit,* armor-plated *Am;* **puerta blindada** reinforced door
blindaje *m* armour (plating) *Brit,* armor (plating) *Am*
blindar *vt* to armour(-plate) *Brit,* to armor(-plate) *Am*
bloc *m* <blocs> 1. (*cuaderno*) notepad 2. (*calendario*) calendar pad
blofear *vi AmL* (*engañar*) to bluff
blofero, -a *m, f,* **blofista** *mf AmC, PRico* braggart, bluffer
blonda *f* 1. (*encaje*) blond lace 2. (*de papel*) (paper) doily
bloque *m* 1. block; ~ **de viviendas** block of flats 2. POL bloc ▶ **en** ~ en bloc
bloquear I. *vt* 1. (*cortar el paso*) to block 2. (*aislar*) to cut off 3. TÉC to jam 4. MIL (*asediar*) to blockade 5. FIN to freeze 6. DEP to block 7. (*obstaculizar*) to obstruct 8. (*interrumpir*) to cut off II. *vr:* ~se 1. (*una cosa*) to jam 2. (*una persona*) to have a mental block
bloqueo *m* 1. (*de un paso*) blocking; ~

comercial COM trade embargo 2. (*aislamiento*) cutting off 3. TÉC (*de un mecanismo*) jamming 4. MIL blockade 5. DEP block 6. (*de un proceso: estancamiento*) deadlock; (*interrupción*) cutting off 7. (*mental*) block
bluff *m* <bluffs> 1. (*finta*) feint 2. *AmL* (*fanfarronería*) bluff
blusa *f* 1. (*de mujer*) blouse 2. (*bata*) smock
blusón *m* smock
boa *f* boa
boato *m* ostentation
bobada *f* silly thing; **decir** ~s to talk nonsense
bobalicón, -ona I. *adj* 1. (*tonto*) silly 2. (*simple*) simple(-minded) II. *m, f* 1. (*tonto*) fool 2. (*simplón*) simpleton
bobear *vi* 1. (*hacer bobadas*) to fool about 2. (*decir bobadas*) to talk nonsense
bobina *f* 1. ELEC coil 2. (*de película, hilo*) reel
bobinar *vt* to wind
bobo, -a I. *adj* 1. (*tonto*) silly 2. (*simple*) simple II. *m, f* 1. (*tonto*) fool 2. (*simplón*) simpleton
boca *f* 1. ANAT mouth; ~ **abajo** face down(ward); ~ **arriba** face up(ward); **estaba tumbada** ~ **abajo/arriba** she was lying on her stomach/on her back; **andar de** ~ **en** ~ to be the subject of gossip 2. (*abertura*) opening; ~ **de metro** underground entrance *Brit,* subway entrance *Am;* ~ **de riego** hydrant 3. (*agujero*) hole 4. (*de cañón*) muzzle 5. (*de río, volcán*) mouth 6. (*de vino*) taste 7. TÉC (*de herramienta*) cutting edge 8. MÚS mouthpiece 9. INFOR slot ▶ **echar por la** ~ **sapos y culebras** to swear black and blue, to rant and rave; **quedarse con la** ~ **abierta** to be dumbfounded; **a** **pedir de** ~ perfectly
boca a boca *m sin pl* mouth-to-mouth resuscitation
bocacalle *f* 1. (*entrada de una calle*) street entrance 2. (*calle secundaria*) side street
bocadillo *m* 1. (*sandwich*) sandwich 2. (*refrigerio*) snack 3. (*tira cómica*) balloon, bubble
bocadito *m* 1. *Cuba* (*cigarrillo*) cigarette (*wrapped in tobacco leaf*) 2. *Cuba, RíoPl:* coconut or sweet potato dessert
bocado *m* 1. (*mordisco*) mouthful; ~ **de Adán** Adamns apple 2. (*freno*) bit
bocajarro *adv* **a** ~ (*tirar*) point-blank; **decir algo a** ~ to say sth straight out
bocamanga *f* 1. (*abertura*) hole for the head (in a cape) 2. (*puño*) cuff
bocana *f* estuario
bocanada *f* 1. (*de humo*) puff 2. (*de comida, bebida*) mouthful; **echar** ~s *fig* to boast
bocatero, -a *m, f Ven, Hond, Cuba,* **bocaza(s)** *mf* (*inv*) loudmouth; (*fanfarrón*) boaster
bocera *f* 1. (*restos de comida*) crumbs *pl* on the mouth; (*restos de bebida*) smears *pl* on the mouth 2. (*pupa*) cold sore
boceras *mf inv* (*tonto*) fool; (*que habla mucho*) bigmouth
boceto *m* sketch

bocha *f* 1.(*bola*) bowl; (**juego de**) **las ~s** bowls, bowling *Am* 2.*AmL, inf*(*cabeza*) nut
bochar *vt inf* 1.*AmL* (*rechazar*) to reject 2.*Arg*(*fracasar*) to fail
boche *m* 1.(*hoyo*) hole in the ground 2.*Arg* (*alemán*) German 3.*CSur, inf*(*bronca*) telling--off 4.*AmL, inf*(*repulsa*) snub
bochinche *m* 1.(*tumulto*) uproar; (*alboroto*) riot 2.*AmL* (*chisme*) piece of gossip
bochorno *m* 1.METEO sultry weather 2.(*sofocación*) stifling atmosphere 3.(*vergüenza*) shame; **me da ~ que esté mirando** it embarrasses me that he/she is looking
bochornoso, -a *adj* 1.METEO sultry 2.(*vergonzoso*) shameful
bocina *f* 1.(*de gramófono, auto*) horn; **tocar la ~** to blow the horn 2.(*caracola*) large shell 3.MÚS trumpet 4.(*megáfono*) megaphone
bocinar *vi* 1.(*por el cuerno*) to trumpet 2.AUTO to blow the horn
bocinazo *m* 1.AUTO blast 2.*inf*(*grito*) bellow; **pegar un ~ a alguien** to yell at sb
bocio *m* goitre *Brit*, goiter *Am*
boda *f* 1.(*ceremonia*) wedding 2.(*fiesta*) wedding reception; **noche de ~s** wedding night
bodega *f* 1.(*depósito de vino*) wine cellar 2.(*tienda*) wine shop; (*taberna*) bar 3.(*despensa*) pantry 4.(*tienda*) grocery store 5.NÁUT (*en un puerto*) storeroom; (*en un buque*) hold
bodegón *m* 1.(*taberna*) bar 2.(*casa de comidas*) cheap restaurant 3.ARTE still life
bodeguero, -a *m, f* 1.(*en una bodega*) owner of a wine cellar 2.*Cuba* (*en una abacería*) grocer
bodoque *m* 1.(*en un bordado*) raised tuft 2.*Méx* (*chichón*) bump 3.*Méx* (*pelota de papel, de lana*) lump; (*de lodo, de masa*) gob 4.*Méx* (*cosa mal hecha*) badly made thing, sloppy job *inf* 5. *inf*(*persona tonta*) blockhead
bodrio *m* 1.*inf* (*cosa*) rubbish, trash; **esta película es un ~** this film is rubbish 2.*inf* (*comida*) hotchpotch; **la comida fue un ~** the meal was terrible 3.*AmL* (*confusión*) mess
body *m* <bodies> body
BOE *m abr de* **Boletín Oficial del Estado** ≈ Hansard *Brit*, ≈ The Congressional Record *Am*
bóer *adj, mf*<bóers> Boer
bofe *m* lung; **echar los ~s** (**por algo**) *inf* to slog one's guts out (for sth)
bofetada *f* cuff, smack *Am;* **dar una ~ a alguien** to slap sb
bofia *f inf*cops *pl*
boga *f* 1.NÁUT rowing 2.(*moda*) vogue; **estar en ~** to be in vogue
bogador(a) *m(f)* rower
bogar <g→gu> *vi* 1.(*remar*) to row 2.(*navegar*) to sail
bogavante *m* lobster
bogotano, -a I.*adj* of/from Bogotá II.*m, f* native/inhabitant of Bogotá
Bohemia *f* Bohemia

bohemio, -a *adj, m, f* bohemian
bohío *m AmL* rustic hut (*made of wood and branches, cane or straw*)
boicot <boicots> *m* boycott
boicotear *vt* to boycott
boicoteo *m* boycott
boina *f* beret
boj *m* (*arbusto*) box tree; (*madera*) boxwood
bol *m* 1.(*tazón*) bowl 2.(*red de pesca*) dragnet; (*lance de red*) casting 3.(*bolo*) skittle
bola *f* 1.(*cuerpo esférico*) ball; **~ del mundo** globe; **~ de nieve** snowball 2.(*canica*) marble; **jugar a las ~s** to play marbles 3.*inf* (*mentira*) fib; (*rumor*) rumour *Brit*, rumor *Am* 4. *pl, vulg* (*testículos*) balls *pl*, nuts *pl Am;* **en ~s** *inf* naked, in starkers *Brit, inf*, in the buff *Am, inf* ▶**no dar pie con ~** to be unable to do anything right; **ir a su ~** to go one's own way
bolada *f* 1.(*en los bolos*) throw; (*en el billar*) stroke 2.*AmL* (*suerte*) piece of luck
bolado *m AmL* (*asunto*) matter
bolazo *m CSur: inf*1.(*disparate*) twaddle *Brit*, bunk *inf*2.(*mentira*) lie, bull(shit) *vulg*
bolchevique *adj, mf*Bolshevik
boleadoras *fpl CSur* (*especie de lazo*) bolas *pl*
bolear I. *vi* 1.(*en el billar*) to play for fun 2. *inf* (*contar mentiras*) to tell fibs II. *vt* 1.(*la pelota*) to play 2.*CSur* (*cazar*) to hunt; (*atrapar*) to catch with a lasso 3.*Méx* (*zapatos*) to polish 4.(*alumno*) to fail
bolera *f* bowling alley
bolero *m* MÚS bolero
boleta *f* 1.(*entrada*) ticket 2.(*pase*) pass 3.(*libranza*) bill of exchange, draft *Am* 4.MIL billet 5.*AmL* (*documento*) permit 6.*AmL* (*para votar*) ballot (paper)
boletería *f AmL* (*taquilla*) ticket agency [*o* office]; TEAT box office
boletero, -a *m, f AmL* (*taquillero*) ticket clerk
boletín *m* 1.(*publicación*) bulletin; **~ informativo** news bulletin 2.(*informe*) report; **~ de noticias** news report 3.(*cédula*) form
boleto *m* 1.*AmL* (*entrada, billete*) ticket 2.(*de quiniela*) coupon 3.*Arg* (*mentira*) lie
boli *m inf abr de* **bolígrafo** (ballpoint) pen, biro®
boliche *m* 1.(*bola*) jack 2.(*juego de bochas*) bowls; (*de bolos*) skittles 3.(*bolera*) bowling alley 4.*AmL* (*establecimiento*) grocery shop 5.*Arg, inf*(*bar*) bar
bólido *m* 1.ASTR meteorite 2.AUTO racing car
bolígrafo *m* (ballpoint) pen, biro®
bolillo *m* 1.(*para hacer encajes*) bobbin; **trabajar al ~** to make lace by hand 2.*Col* (*de tambor*) drumstick 3.*Méx* (*panecillo*) bread roll
bolita *f* 1.*CSur* (*canica*) marble 2.*Chile* (*balota*) ballot
bolívar *m* bolivar
Bolivia *f* Bolivia

> **Bolivia** is the fifth largest country in South America. Although **Sucre** is the capital, the seat of government is in **La Paz**, the largest city in the country. In addition to Spanish, the official languages of Bolivia are **quechua** and **aimara** (also known as **aimará**). The monetary unit is the **boliviano**.

boliviano m (*moneda*) boliviano

boliviano, -a *adj, m, f* Bolivian

bollería f (*establecimiento*) baker's; (*bollos*) buns *pl*, baked goods *pl*

bollo m **1.** (*panecillo*) bun; (*pastelillo*) cake **2.** (*abolladura*) dent; (*chichón*) lump **3.** (*cosmética*) puff **4.** (*confusión*) mix-up **5.** CSur, inf (*puñetazo*) punch

bolo m **1.** DEP skittle; (**juego de**) ~**s** skittles **2.** (*píldora*) large pill **3.** (*tonto*) nitwit **4.** TEAT (*compañía*) travelling company Brit, road company Am; (*papel*) guest star; **el grupo hizo muchos ~s en verano** the company put on a lot of shows in the summer

bolsa f **1.** (*saco*) bag; ~ **de agua caliente** hot-water bottle **2.** (*bolso*) handbag, purse Am; ~ **de plástico** plastic bag; ~ **de la compra** shopping bag **3.** (*pliegue en la ropa*) crease **4.** (*caudal*) wealth; ~ **de estudios** educational grant **5.** FIN stock exchange; ~ **de trabajo** employment bureau; ~ **negra** AmL black market; ~ **de valores** stock exchange **6.** AmL (*bolsillo*) pocket **7.** pl ANAT ~**s de los ojos** bags under the eyes

bolsear vt AmC, Méx, inf ~ **a alguien** to pick sb's pocket; ~ **algo a alguien** to sponge sth off sb

bolsillo m **1.** (*en una prenda de vestir*) pocket; **edición de** ~ pocket edition **2.** (*monedero*) purse; **rascarse el** ~ inf to fork out

bolsista mf **1.** FIN stockbroker **2.** AmC (*carterista*) pickpocket

bolso m **1.** bag; (*bolsa pequeña*) handbag, purse Am **2.** (*en una vela*) bulge; **hacer** ~ to belly out

boludo, -a inf **I.** adj Arg, Urug (*imbécil*) stupid **II.** m, f Arg, Urug (*imbécil*) jerk

bomba **I.** f **1.** t. MIL bomb; ~ **de mano** hand grenade; ~ **de relojería** time bomb **2.** TÉC pump; ~ **neumática** air pump; **dar a la** ~ to pump **3.** (*de lámpara*) shade **4.** AmL (*bola*) ball **5.** AmL (*pompa*) bubble **6.** AmL, inf (*borrachera*) **pegarse una** ~ to get drunk ▶ **a prueba de ~s** bomb-proof; **estar** ~ inf (*mujer*) to be gorgeous; (*comida*) to be great **II.** adj inf astounding; **éxito** ~ great success; **pasarlo** ~ to have a great time

bombacha f CSur (*ropa interior*) knickers pl Brit, panties pl

bombacho adj **pantalón** ~ baggy trousers pl

bombardear vt **1.** MIL to bomb **2.** (*abrumar*) to overwhelm **3.** FÍS to bombard

bombardeo m **1.** MIL bombing; ~ **aéreo** air raid **2.** FÍS bombardment

bombardero m (*avión*) bomber

bombazo m **1.** (*explosión*) bomb explosion **2.** inf (*sensación*) bombshell

bombeador(a) m(f) Arg bomber

bombear **I.** vt **1.** MIL to shell **2.** (*un líquido*) to pump **3.** (*un balón*) to lob **4.** CSur (*explorar*) to reconnoitre, to reconnoiter Am **II.** vr: ~**se** **1.** (*persona*) to put on airs **2.** (*objeto*) to bulge

bombeo m **1.** (*de líquidos*) pumping **2.** (*convexidad*) bulging

bombero m **1.** (*oficio*) fireman **2.** pl (*cuerpo*) fire brigade; **coche de** ~**s** fire engine

bombilla f **1.** ELEC (light) bulb **2.** AmS (*caña*) drinking straw

bombillo m **1.** (*de una cerradura*) thief tube **2.** AmC (*bombilla*) light bulb

bombín m **1.** (*sombrero*) bowler hat **2.** (*bomba de aire*) bicycle pump

bombita f Arg (*bombilla*) bulb

bombo m **1.** MÚS (*tambor grande*) bass drum **2.** (*en un sorteo*) drum **3.** (*elogio*) exaggerated praise ▶ **tener la cabeza hecha un** ~ to have a splitting headache; **anunciar algo a** ~ **y platillo** to announce sth with a lot of hype

bombón m **1.** (*golosina*) chocolate **2.** inf (*mujer*) **es un** ~ she's gorgeous

bombona f **1.** (*vasija*) carboy **2.** (*de gas*) cylinder

bombonera f **1.** (*caja de bombones*) chocolate box **2.** (*vivienda*) cosy little place

bómper m AmC (*parachoques*) bumper

bonachón, -ona adj **1.** (*buenazo*) kindly **2.** (*crédulo*) naive **3.** (*cándido*) simple

bonaerense **I.** adj of/from Buenos Aires province **II.** mf native/inhabitant of Buenos Aires province

bonanza f **1.** NÁUT calm conditions pl **2.** MIN rich vein of ore **3.** (*prosperidad*) prosperity

bondad f **1.** (*cualidad de bueno*) goodness **2.** (*amabilidad*) kindness; **tenga la** ~ **de seguirme** be so kind as to follow me

bondadoso, -a adj good-natured, kind

bondi m Arg, inf (*bus*) bus

bonete m **1.** (*gorro*) cap **2.** ZOOL reticulum

bonetería f Méx (*mercería*) draper's shop

bóngalo m AmL (*casa pequeña*) bungalow

bongo m AmL (*canoa*) small canoe; (*balsa*) small raft

bongó <bongoes> m bongo (drum)

boniato m sweet potato

bonificación f **1.** (*abono*) improvement **2.** (*gratificación*) bonus **3.** (*rebaja*) discount

bonificar <c→qu> vt **1.** (*abonar*) to improve **2.** (*gratificar*) to discount

bonito **I.** m ZOOL bonito **II.** adv AmL nicely

bonito, -a adj pretty

bonitura f AmL (*hermosura*) beauty

bono m **1.** (*vale*) voucher **2.** COM bond

bonoloto f state-run lottery

bonsái m <bonsais> bonsai

bonzo m REL Buddhist monk

boñiga f, **boñigo** m cow pat

boqueada f gasp; **dar las** ~**s** to be dying

boquear **I.** vi **1.** (*abrir la boca*) to gape

2.(*estar muriéndose*) to be at death's door **3.**(*estar acabándose*) to be in its final stages **II.** *vt* (*palabras*) to utter

boquera *f* **1.**(*en un canal de riego*) sluice **2.**(*en un pajar*) hatch **3.**(*en los labios*) cold sore

boqueras *mf inv, inf* loudmouth

boquerón *m* **1.**(*abertura grande*) wide opening **2.** ZOOL (fresh) anchovy

boquete *m* (*abertura estrecha*) opening; (*en una pared*) hole

boquiabierto, -a *adj* **1.**(*con la boca abierta*) open-mouthed **2.**(*admirado*) astonished; **dejar a alguien ~** to astonish sb

boquilla *f* **1.** MÚS mouthpiece **2.**(*de cigarrillos*) cigarette holder; (*de pipa*) mouthpiece; **~ de filtro** filter tip **3.**(*de bolso*) clasp **4.**(*de lámpara*) lamp-holder **5.** TÉC nozzle ▶**decir algo de ~** to say sth without meaning it

borboll(e)ar *vi* to bubble

borbollón *m* borbotón

Borbón *m* HIST Bourbon

borbónico, -a *adj* Bourbon

borbotón *m* bubbling; **hablar a borbotones** to talk ten to the dozen; **salir a borbotones** (*agua*) to gush out

borda *f* **1.** NÁUT (*borde del costado*) gunwale; **motor fuera** (**de**) **~** outboard motor; **echar algo por la ~** *t. fig* to throw sth overboard **2.** NÁUT (*vela mayor*) mainsail **3.**(*choza*) hut

bordada *f* NÁUT tack; **dar ~s** (*un barco*) to tack; (*una persona*) to move to and fro

bordado *m* embroidery

bordado, -a *adj* **1.**(*adornado*) embroidered **2.**(*perfecto*) superbly executed

bordador(a) *m(f)* embroiderer *m*, embroideress *f*

bordar *vt* **1.**(*adornar*) to embroider; (*un motivo*) to decorate **2.**(*ejecutar con primor*) to do superbly

borde I. *adj* **1.**(*planta*) wild **2.**(*hijo*) illegitimate **3.** *inf* (*persona*) difficult, stroppy **II.** *m* **1.** (*de camino*) verge; (*de mesa*) edge **2.**(*de río*) bank **3.**(*de vestido*) hem; (*como adorno*) border **4.**(*de sombrero*) brim

bordear I. *vt* **1.**(*ir por el borde*) to skirt; (*en coche*) to drive along **2.**(*hallarse en el borde*) to border on **3.**(*aproximarse*) to verge on; **su comportamiento bordea la locura** his/her behaviour borders on madness **II.** *vi* NÁUT to tack

bordillo *m* kerb *Brit*, curb *Am*

bordo *m* **1.** NÁUT board; **ir a ~** to go on board **2.** *Méx* (*presa*) dam

bordón *m* **1.**(*bastón*) staff **2.**(*estribillo*) refrain; (*muletilla*) pet phrase **3.** MÚS (*cuerda*) bass string; (*de tripa*) gut

boreal *adj* northern; **hemisferio ~** northern hemisphere

borgoña *m* burgundy

borla *f* **1.**(*adorno*) tassel **2.**(*para empolvarse*) powder puff

borne *m* ELEC terminal

bornear I. *vt* (*dar vuelta*) to bend; (*torcer*) to twist; (*ladear*) to incline **II.** *vi* NÁUT to swing at anchor **III.** *vr:* **~se** to bulge

boro *m* boron

borona *f* *AmL* maize bread *Brit*, corn bread *Am*

borra *f* **1.**(*relleno*) stuffing **2.**(*pelusa*) fluff **3.**(*sedimento*) sediment **4.**(*palabras sin sustancia*) padding

borrachera *f* **1.**(*ebriedad*) drunkenness; **agarrar una ~** to get drunk **2.**(*juerga*) drinking binge **3.**(*exaltación*) intoxication **4.**(*disparate*) absurdity

borracho, -a I. *adj* **1.** *ser* (*alcohólico*) hard drinking **2.** *estar* (*ebrio*) drunk; **estar ~ como una cuba** *inf* to be as drunk as a lord **3.**(*exaltado*) **~ de algo** elated with sth **4.**(*pastel*) soaked in liqueur **II.** *m, f* drunk

borrador *m* **1.**(*primer escrito*) rough draft **2.**(*cuaderno*) scribbling pad **3.**(*para la pizarra: trapo*) duster; (*esponja*) board rubber, board eraser

borradura *f* crossing-out, erasure

borrajear *vi, vt* to scribble

borrar I. *vt* **1.**(*con goma de borrar*) to rub out, to erase; (*con esponja*) to wipe off **2.**(*tachar*) to cross out **3.** INFOR to delete **4.**(*huellas*) to remove **5.**(*difuminar*) to efface **II.** *vr:* **~se** **1.**(*volverse no identificable*) to blur **2.**(*retirarse*) **~se de algo** to resign from sth

borrasca *f* **1.**(*temporal*) squall; (*tempestad*) storm **2.**(*peligro*) hazard; (*riesgo*) risk; (*contratiempo*) setback **3.**(*orgía*) spree

borrascoso, -a *adj* **1.** METEO stormy; **Cumbres Borrascosas** Wuthering Heights **2.**(*desenfrenado*) tempestuous

borrego, -a *m, f* **1.**(*cordero*) lamb **2.**(*persona*) meek person **3.** *AmL* (*noticia falsa*) hoax

borregos *mpl* **1.**(*nubes*) fleecy clouds *pl* **2.**(*olas*) white horses *pl*

borreguil *adj* meek

borrico *m* TÉC sawhorse

borrico, -a *m, f* donkey

borrón *m* **1.**(*mancha*) stain **2.**(*defecto*) blemish **3.**(*borrador*) rough draft; (*de un cuadro*) sketch ▶**hacer ~ y cuenta nueva** to wipe the slate clean

borronear *vt* **1.**(*borrajear*) to scribble **2.**(*dibujar*) to doodle

borroso, -a *adj* **1.**(*escrito, dibujo*) smudgy; (*escritura*) unclear **2.**(*foto*) blurred

boruquear *vt* *Méx* to be rowdy

boscaje *m* **1.**(*bosque denso*) thicket **2.**(*pintura*) woodland scene

boscoso, -a *adj* wooded

Bósforo *m* Bosphorus

Bosnia Herzegovina *f* Bosnia and Herzegovina

bosnio, -a *adj, m, f* Bosnian

bosorola *f* *CRi, Méx* (*borra*) sediment

bosque *m* **1.**(*lugar*) wood; **~ de coníferas** coniferous woodland; **~ frondoso** broad-

leaved woodland; ~ **pluvial** rainforest
2. (*barba*) thick beard
bosquejar *vt* to sketch
bosquejo *m* sketch
bosta *f* dung, droppings *pl*
bostezar <z→c> *vi* to yawn
bostezo *m* yawn
bota I. *adj Méx* **1.** (*torpe*) dim **2.** (*borracho*)
drunk II. *f* **1.** (*calzado*) boot; **estar con las ~s**
puestas *fig* to be ready to go; **ponerse las ~s**
inf to strike it rich **2.** (*botella de cuero*) wineskin **3.** (*cuba*) large barrel
botado, -a I. *adj* **1.** *AmC* (*malgastador*) spendthrift **2.** *Ecua* (*resignado*) resigned; (*resuelto*)
resolute **3.** *Guat* (*tímido*) shy **4.** *Méx* (*barato*)
dirt cheap II. *m, f Méx* foundling
botador(a) *adj AmL* (*derrochador*) spendthrift
botadura *f* launching
botánica *f sin pl* botany
botánico, -a I. *adj* botanical II. *m, f* botanist
botar I. *vi* **1.** (*pelota*) to bounce **2.** (*persona*)
to jump **3.** (*caballo*) to rear (up) ►**estar (uno)**
que bota to be hopping mad II. *vt* **1.** (*lanzar*)
to throw; (*la pelota contra el suelo*) to bounce
2. NÁUT (*barco*) to launch; (*el timón*) to put
over **3.** *AmL* (*tirar*) to throw away **4.** *AmL*
(*expulsar*) to fire; **lo ~on del colegio** he was
expelled from school **5.** *AmL* (*derrochar*) to
squander **6.** *AmL* (*extraviar*) to lose III. *vr:* **~se**
(*caballo*) to buck
botaratada *f inf* wild scheme
botarate *m* **1.** (*hombre alborotado*) madcap
2. *AmL* (*derrochador*) spendthrift
bote *m* **1.** (*golpe*) blow **2.** (*salto*) jump; **pegar**
un ~ to jump **3.** (*de pelota*) bounce; **la pelota**
dio cuatro ~s the ball bounced four times
4. (*vasija*) jar; **~ de cuestación** collecting tin
5. (*en la lotería*) jackpot **6.** (*en los bares*) kitty
7. NÁUT boat; **~ salvavidas** lifeboat ►**a ~**
pronto (*adj*) sudden; (*adv*) suddenly; **chupar**
del ~ *inf* to feather one's nest; **darse el ~** *inf* to
beat it; **estar de ~ en ~** to be packed; **la tiene**
en el ~ *inf* he's got her in his pocket
botella *f* bottle; **~ de cerveza** bottle of beer;
cerveza de ~ bottled beer
botellero *m* **1.** (*fabricante*) bottler **2.** (*es-*
tantería) wine-rack
botepronto *m* DEP half-volley
botica *f* **1.** (*farmacia*) pharmacy, chemist's
Brit, drugstore *Am* **2.** (*tienda*) haberdashery
boticario, -a *m, f* chemist *Brit,* druggist *Am*
botija *f* **1.** (*vasija*) earthenware jug **2.** *inf* (*per-*
sona gorda) fat person **3.** *AmL* (*tesoro*) buried
treasure
botijo *m* **1.** (*vasija*) earthenware drinking jug
2. (*tren*) excursion train
botín *m* **1.** (*calzado*) high shoe **2.** MIL booty
botina *f* ankle boot
botiquín *m* **1.** (*en casa*) medicine chest **2.** (*de*
emergencia) first-aid kit
botón *m* **1.** (*en vestidos*) button **2.** ELEC knob;
~ de muestra sample; *fig* illustration; **~ de**

opciones INFOR option button **3.** (*en instru-*
mentos de viento) key **4.** BIO (*capullo*) bud; **~**
de oro buttercup **5.** *CSur, pey* (*policía*) cop
botonadura *f* (set of) buttons *pl*
botones *m inv* **1.** (*en un hotel*) bellboy **2.** *pey*
(*recadero*) errand boy
boutique *f* boutique
bóveda *f* **1.** ARQUIT vault; **~ celeste** firmament
2. (*cripta*) vault **3.** (*forma abombada*) dome
bovino, -a *adj* bovine
bovinos *mpl* bovines *pl*
box *m* **1.** (*para caballos*) stall **2.** *AmL* (*boxeo*)
boxing **3.** *AmC* (*postal*) postbox *Brit,* mailbox
Am **4.** *pl* AUTO pits *pl;* **entrar en ~es** to make a
pit-stop
boxeador(a) *m(f)* boxer
boxear *vi* to box
boxeo *m* boxing
boya *f* buoy; (*en una red*) float
boyante *adj* **1.** (*flotante*) buoyant; (*barco*)
high in the water **2.** (*próspero*) prosperous; **el**
negocio va ~ business is booming
boyar *vi* **1.** NÁUT to be afloat again **2.** *AmL* (*flo-*
tar) to float
boyero *m* **1.** (*cuidador*) cowherd **2.** *Col* goad
boy scout <boy scouts> *mf* boy scout
bozal *m* **1.** (*de perro*) muzzle **2.** *AmL* (*ca-*
bestro) halter; (*cuerda*) headstall
bozo *m* **1.** (*pelos*) down **2.** (*cabestro*) halter;
(*cuerda*) headstall
bracear *vi* **1.** (*mover los brazos*) to swing
one's arms **2.** (*nadar*) to swim **3.** (*esforzarse*)
to make an effort **4.** (*forcejear*) to struggle
5. NÁUT to measure in fathoms
bracero *m AmL* **1.** (*jornalero*) farmhand
2. (*peón*) labourer *Brit,* laborer *Am*
braga *f* **1.** (*de bebé*) nappy *Brit,* diaper *Am*
2. *pl* (*de mujer*) panties *pl* **3.** *pl* (*de hombre*)
breeches *pl* ►**dejar a alguien en ~s** *inf* to
leave sb penniless; **estar en ~s** *inf* to be broke
bragado, -a *adj* **1.** (*malintencionado*)
malicious **2.** (*decidido*) resolute
bragapañal *m* disposable nappy *Brit,* disposable diaper *Am*
bragazas *m inv* henpecked husband
bragueta *f* flies *pl Brit,* fly *Am*
braguetazo *m* marriage for money; **dar el ~**
to marry for money
braille *m* Braille
brainstorming *m sin pl* tormenta de ideas,
brainstorming
bramadero *m* **1.** (*del ciervo*) rutting ground
2. *AmL* (*estaca para atar animales*) tethering
post
bramante *m* twine
bramar *vi* **1.** (*animal*) to roar; (*ciervo*) to bellow **2.** (*persona*) to bluster; **está que brama**
he/she is furious **3.** (*viento*) to howl
4. (*oleaje*) to thunder
bramido *m* **1.** (*animales*) roar; (*ciervos*) bellow **2.** (*persona*) blustering **3.** (*viento*) howling **4.** (*oleaje*) thundering
brandy *m* brandy

branquia f gill
branquial adj branchial
brasa f ember; **a la ~** grilled
brasero m 1.(*como calefacción*) brazier
2.AmL (*fuego*) fireplace; (*hogar*) hearth
Brasil m (**el**) ~ Brazil
brasileño, -a adj, m, f Brazilian
brava f Cuba (*golpe*) punch; **dar una ~** to
intimidate; **a la ~, por las ~s** Arg, Cuba, Méx,
PRico by force
bravata f 1.(*amenaza*) threat 2.(*bravuconada*) piece of bravado
bravío m fierceness
bravío, -a adj 1.(*animal: salvaje*) wild; (*sin
domar*) untamed 2.(*planta*) wild 3.(*persona:
indómita*) impetuous; (*rústica*) uncouth
bravo I. interj well done II. m thug
bravo, -a adj 1.(*valiente*) brave 2.(*bueno*)
excellent 3.(*salvaje: animal, persona*) wild;
(*mar*) stormy; (*terreno*) rugged 4.(*áspero*)
rough 5.(*fanfarrón*) boastful 6.AmL (*picante*)
hot
bravucón, -ona I. adj boastful II. m, f braggart
bravuconada f boasting
bravura f 1.(*de los animales*) ferocity 2.(*de
las personas*) bravery 3. pey (*bravata*) boasting
braza f 1.NÁUT (*unidad de longitud*) fathom
(*1,80 m*); (*cabo*) brace 2.DEP breast stroke
brazada f 1.(*movimiento de los brazos*)
movement of the arms; (*al nadar*) stroke
2.(*cantidad*) armful
brazalete m 1.(*pulsera*) bracelet 2.(*banda*)
armband
brazo m 1.ANAT arm; ~ **derecho** fig right-hand
man; ~ **de gitano** GASTR Swiss roll, jelly roll
Am; **cruzarse de ~s** to fold one's arms; fig to
stand by and do nothing; **dar el ~ a torcer** to
give way; **ir cogidos del ~** to walk arm-in-
-arm; **recibir a alguien con los ~s abiertos**
to welcome sb with open arms 2.(*de una silla*)
arm 3.GEO (*del río*) branch; (*del mar*) sound
4.ZOOL foreleg 5.BIO limb 6.(*poder*) power
7. pl (*jornaleros*) workers pl 8. pl (*protec-
tores*) backers pl
brea f 1.(*alquitrán*) tar 2.(*pez*) pitch
breakdance m sin pl break dancing
brear vt 1.(*maltratar*) to abuse; ~ **a alguien a
golpes** to beat sb up 2.(*burlarse*) ~ **a alguien**
to make fun of sb
brebaje m 1.(*bebida*) brew 2.(*medicina*)
potion
brecha f 1.MIL breach 2.(*abertura*) opening;
(*en una pared*) gap 3.(*impresión*) impression
4.(*herida en la cabeza*) gash ▶**estar en la ~**
to be in the thick of things
brécol(es) m(pl) broccoli
brega f 1.(*riña*) quarrel 2.(*lucha*) struggle
3.(*trabajo duro*) slog
bregar <g→gu> vi 1.(*reñir*) to quarrel
2.(*luchar*) to struggle 3.(*trabajar duro*) to
slave away, to slog away Brit
bresca f honeycomb

Bretaña f Brittany; **Gran ~** Great Britain
brete m fetters pl; **estar en un ~** to be in a
jam; **poner a alguien en un ~** to put sb on
the spot
bretón, -ona adj, m, f Breton
breva f 1.(*higo*) early fig 2.(*cigarro*) flat cigar
3.AmL (*tabaco*) chewing tobacco 4.(*ganga*)
piece of luck; **¡no caerá esa ~!** no such luck!
breve I. adj 1.(*de duración*) brief; **en ~** shortly
2.(*de extensión*) short II. m PREN short news
item
brevedad f 1.(*corta duración*) brevity; **a la
mayor ~ posible** as soon as possible 2.(*corta
extensión*) shortness
brevete m 1.(*membrete*) letterhead 2.Perú
(*permiso de conducir*) driving licence Brit,
driver's license Am
breviario m 1.(*libro de rezos*) prayer book
2.(*compendio*) compendium
brezo m heather
briago, -a adj Méx, inf drunk
bribón, -ona I. adj 1.(*pícaro*) rascally
2.(*vago*) idle II. m, f 1.(*bellaco*) rogue
2.(*pícaro*) scoundrel 3.(*niño*) rascal
bribonada f piece of mischief
bricolaje m do-it-yourself
brida f 1.(*de la caballería*) bridle 2.(*del sombrero*) chinstrap 3.TÉC (*reborde*) flange; (*arandela*) clamp 4. pl MED adhesion
bridge m bridge
brigada[1] f 1.MIL brigade 2.(*de obreros*) gang
3.(*de policía*) squad
brigada[2] m MIL sergeant-major
brillante I. m diamond II. adj 1.(*luz, color*)
bright; (*joya, conversación*) sparkling 2.(*compañía*) brilliant
brillantez f t. fig brilliance
brillantina f brilliantine, hair cream
brillar vi to shine; ~ **por su ausencia** irón to
be conspicuous by one's absence
brillo m 1.(*cualidad*) shine; (*reflejo de luz*)
glow; **dar ~ a algo** to polish sth 2.(*gloria*)
splendour Brit, splendor Am 3.(*excelencia*)
brilliance
brincar <c→qu> vi 1.(*saltar*) to hop; (*hacia
arriba*) to jump 2.(*pasar de un tema a otro*) to
skip 3.(*alterarse*) to fly into a rage; ~ **de alegría** to jump for joy; ~ **de rabia** to dance with
rage
brinco m hop; **dar ~s** to hop; **de un ~** in one
bound
brindar I. vi (*levantar la copa*) to drink a toast;
~ **por alguien** to drink to sb II. vt 1.(*ofrecer*)
to offer 2.TAUR to dedicate III. vr ~**se a hacer
algo** to offer to do sth
brindis m inv 1.(*el levantar los vasos*) toast;
echar un ~ to drink a toast 2.(*frase con que
se brinda*) dedication
brío m 1.(*energía*) spirit 2.(*pujanza*) drive
3.(*garbo*) elegance
brioso, -a adj 1.(*con energía*) spirited 2.(*con
pujanza*) vigorous 3.(*con garbo*) elegant
brisa f breeze

británico, -a I. *adj* British; **Inglés Británico** British English II. *m, f* Briton *Brit,* Britisher *Am*
brit-pop *m* MÚS Brit-pop
brizna *f* 1.(*hebra*) strand 2. BOT blade; (*de judías*) string 3.(*porción diminuta*) scrap; **no tiene ni una ~ de humor** he/she has no sense of humour whatsover 4. *AmL* (*llovizna*) drizzle
broca *f* TÉC (*taladro*) bit
brocado *m* brocade
brocal *m* rim; (*de pozo*) mouth
brocha *f* 1.(*pincel grueso*) brush; **de ~ gorda** crudely painted; *fig* slapdash; **pintor de ~ gorda** house painter 2.(*de afeitar*) shaving brush 3. *inf*(*mal pintor*) dauber
brochazo *m* brush stroke
broche *m* 1.(*en la ropa*) clasp; (*de adorno*) brooch; **~ de oro** *fig* finishing touch 2. *AmL* (*sujetapapeles*) paper clip 3. *pl, AmL* (*gemelos*) cufflinks *pl*
brocheta *f* skewer
broker *m* FIN broker
broma *f* 1.(*gracia*) fun, kidding *Am* 2.(*tontería*) joke; **~ pesada** practical joke; **decir algo en ~** to be kidding; **gastar ~s a alguien** to play jokes on sb; **~s aparte...** joking apart ...; **estoy de ~** I'm not serious; **no estoy para ~s** I'm in no mood for jokes; **no hay que andar con ~s con él** he doesn't put up with any nonsense; **¡ni en ~!** no way!
bromear *vi* to joke, to kid *Am;* **¿bromeas?** are you kidding?
bromista I. *adj* fond of jokes II. *mf* joker
bromo *m* bromine
bromuro *m* bromide
bronca *f* 1.(*riña*) row; **se armó una ~ tremenda** there was a tremendous row 2.(*reprimenda*) ticking-off *Brit,* chewing-out 3.(*tumulto*) uproar 4. *AmL* (*enfado*) anger; **me da ~** it makes me mad
bronce *m* bronze
bronceado *m* 1.(*de un objeto*) bronze finish 2.(*de la piel: efecto*) tan; (*acción*) tanning
bronceado, -a *adj* 1.(*objeto*) bronze 2.(*piel*) tanned
bronceador *m* suntan lotion
broncear I. *vt* 1.(*un objeto*) to bronze 2.(*la piel*) to tan II. *vr:* **~se** to get a (sun)tan
bronco, -a *adj* 1.(*voz*) gruff 2.(*metal: tosco*) rough; (*quebradizo*) brittle 3.(*genio*) surly 4. *AmL* (*caballo*) untamed
bronquedad *f* 1.(*de la voz*) gruffness 2.(*tosquedad de metales*) roughness; (*delicadez*) brittleness 3.(*del genio*) surliness
bronquio *m* ANAT bronchial tube
bronquitis *f inv* MED bronchitis
broquel *m* t. *fig* (*escudo*) shield
broqueta *f* skewer
brotar I. *vi* 1. BOT to sprout; (*árbol*) to grow; (*semilla*) to germinate 2.(*agua*) to flow 3.(*enfermedad*) to break out II. *vt* (*terreno*) to bring forth; (*planta*) to sprout
brote *m* 1. BOT shoot; **~s de soja** bean sprouts

2.(*comienzo*) origin 3.(*erupción*) outbreak
broza *f* 1.(*hojas*) dead leaves *pl;* (*ramas*) brushwood 2.(*arbustos*) undergrowth 3.(*palabras inútiles*) padding
bruces *adv* **caer de ~** to fall headlong; **darse de ~ con alguien** (*chocar*) to crash into sb; (*hallar casualmente*) to run into sb
bruja *f* 1.(*hechicera*) witch 2.(*lechuza*) barn owl
Brujas *f* Bruges
brujería *f* witchcraft
brujo *m* 1.(*hechicero*) wizard 2. *AmL* (*curandero*) medicine man
brújula *f* 1.(*compás*) compass; (*aguja*) magnetic needle; **perder la ~** *fig* to lose one's bearings 2.(*mira*) guide
brulote *m* AmS (*taco*) swear word
bruma *f* mist
brumoso, -a *adj* misty
bruñido *m* 1.(*acto*) polishing 2.(*brillo*) polish
bruñir <3. *pret:* bruñó> *vt* 1.(*sacar brillo*) to polish 2. *inf* (*maquillar*) to make up 3. *AmL* (*molestar*) to pester
brusco, -a *adj* 1.(*repentino*) sudden; **un ~ aumento** a sharp increase 2.(*persona*) abrupt
Bruselas *f* Brussels
brusquedad *f* 1.(*de un suceso*) suddenness 2.(*de un comportamiento*) abruptness; **con ~** sharply
brutal *adj* 1.(*violento*) brutal 2.(*desconsiderado*) tactless 3. *inf*(*enorme*) huge 4. *inf*(*estupendo*) tremendous
brutalidad *f* 1.(*calidad de bruto*) brutality 2.(*acción violenta*) brutal act; (*cruel*) cruel act 3.(*cantidad excesiva*) huge amount 4.(*estupidez*) stupidity
bruto *adj* 1.(*tosco*) uncut; **diamante en ~** rough diamond 2.(*peso*) gross
bruto, -a I. *adj* 1.(*brutal*) brutal 2.(*rudo*) uncouth 3.(*estúpido*) ignorant II. *m, f* 1.(*persona brutal*) brute 2.(*idiota*) idiot
bucal *adj* (of the) mouth; **higiene ~** oral hygiene
búcaro *m* (*jarra*) clay pitcher; (*arcilla*) fragrant clay; (*florero*) vase
buceador(a) *m(f)* diver
bucear *vi* 1.(*nadar*) to dive 2.(*investigar*) **~ en algo** to delve into sth
buceo *m* diving
buchada *f* mouthful
buche *m* 1.(*en las aves*) crop 2. *inf* (*estómago*) belly 3.(*bocanada*) mouthful 4.(*pliegue en la ropa*) crease 5.(*lo más íntimo*) inner thoughts *pl;* **guardar algo en el ~** to keep sth hidden
bucle *m* 1.(*rizo de cabello*) curl 2.(*onda*) *t.* INFOR loop
bucólico, -a *adj* pastoral; LIT bucolic
buda *m* Buddha
budín *m* pudding
budismo *m sin pl* Buddhism
budista *adj, mf* Buddhist
buen *adj v.* **bueno**

buenamente *adv* **1.** (*fácilmente*) easily **2.** (*voluntariamente*) voluntarily

buenaventura *f* **1.** (*suerte*) good luck **2.** (*adivinación*) fortune; **echar la ~ a alguien** to tell sb's fortune

buenazo, -a I. *adj* good-natured II. *m, f* good-natured person

bueno *interj* OK

bueno, -a *adj* <mejor *o* más bueno, el mejor *o* bonísimo *o* buenísimo> *delante de un substantivo masculino:* buen **1.** (*calidad*) good; (*tiempo*) fine; (*constitución*) sound; (*decisión*) right; **~s días** good morning; **buenas tardes/noches** good afternoon/evening; **buen viaje** have a good journey; **hace ~** it's nice weather; **dar algo por ~** to accept sth; **estar de buenas** to be in a good mood; **lo que tiene de ~ es que...** the good thing about it is that ...; **por las buenas o por las malas** by fair means or foul **2.** (*apropiado*) suitable **3.** (*fácil*) easy; **el libro es ~ de leer** the book is easy to read **4.** (*honesto*) honest; (*bondadoso*) kindly; (*niño*) well-behaved; **es buena gente** he/she is a nice person **5.** (*sano*) healthy **6.** *inf* (*atractivo*) attractive; **está buenísima** she's hot stuff **7.** (*bonito*) fine; **¡buena la has hecho!** now you've done it now!; **¡estaría ~!** *fig* I should think not!

Buenos Aires *m* Buenos Aires

buey *m* **1.** ZOOL ox **2.** *AmC* (*cornudo*) cuckold

búfalo *m* buffalo

bufanda *f* scarf

bufar *vi* **1.** (*resoplar*) to snort; (*gato*) to spit; **está que bufa** he/she is really furious **2.** *AmL* (*oler mal*) to stink

bufé *m v.* **bufet**

bufeo *m Ant, Hond, Méx* (*delfín*) dolphin; (*tonina*) tuna

bufet *m AmL* **1.** (*aparador*) sideboard **2.** (*cena fría*) cold supper **3.** (*restaurante*) dining-room

bufete *m* **1.** (*escritorio*) desk **2.** (*de abogado*) lawyer's office; **abrir ~** to set up in practice **3.** (*clientela*) lawyer's clients *pl* **4.** (*aparador*) sideboard

bufido *m* **1.** (*resoplido*) snort **2.** (*exabrupto*) sharp remark **3.** (*gato*) hiss

bufón, -ona I. *adj* clownish II. *m, f* **1.** (*bromista*) joker **2.** TEAT buffoon

bufonada *f* **1.** (*burla*) joking **2.** TEAT comic piece

buganvilla *f* bougainvillea

buhardilla *f* **1.** (*ventana*) dormer window **2.** (*desván*) loft **3.** (*vivienda*) garret

búho *m* **1.** ZOOL owl **2.** (*persona*) unsociable person **3.** (*línea de autobús*) night bus

buhonería *f* pedlar's [*o* peddler's *Am*] wares *pl*

buhonero *m* pedlar *Brit,* peddler *Am*

buitre *m* **1.** ZOOL vulture, buzzard **2.** *inf* (*persona*) sponger

buitrear *vi* **1.** *AmL* (*cazar*) to kill **2.** *CSur* (*vomitar*) to throw up

bujía *f* **1.** (*vela*) candle **2.** (*candelero*) candle-

stick **3.** AUTO sparking plug *Brit,* spark plug *Am* **4.** FÍS candlepower

bula *f* (*papal*) bull

bulbo *m* bulb

bule *m Méx* BOT gourd

bulevar *m* boulevard

Bulgaria *f* Bulgaria

búlgaro, -a *adj, m, f* Bulgarian

bulimia *f sin pl* MED bulimia

bulla *f* **1.** (*ruido*) racket **2.** (*aglomeración*) mob **3.** (*confusión*) fuss **4.** *AmL* (*pelea*) brawl

bullabesa *f* GASTR fish soup, bouillabaisse

bullanguero, -a I. *adj* rowdy II. *m, f* troublemaker

bulldozer, bulldózer *m* bulldozer

bullicio *m* **1.** (*ruido*) uproar **2.** (*tumulto*) commotion

bullicioso, -a *adj* noisy

bullir <3. *pret:* bulló> I. *vi* **1.** (*hervir*) to boil; (*borbotar*) to bubble; **le bulle la sangre (en las venas)** *fig* he/she is a bundle of energy **2.** (*agitarse*) to move; (*moverse*) to stir **3.** (*pulular*) to swarm II. *vt* to move III. *vr:* **~se** to budge

bulo *m* false rumour *Brit,* false rumor *Am*

bulto *m* **1.** (*tamaño*) size; **a ~** roughly; **de ~** bulky; **escurrir el ~** *inf* to pass the buck **2.** (*importancia*) importance; (*esencia*) substance; **un error de ~** a major error **3.** (*cuerpo indistinguible*) mass **4.** (*fardo*) bundle **5.** (*paquete*) piece of luggage **6.** MED swelling

bumerán, bumerang *m* boomerang; **efecto ~** boomerang effect

bungaló *m,* **bungalow** *m* bungalow

búnker *m* MIL bunker

buñuelo *m* **1.** (*pastel*) doughnut *Brit,* donut *Am* **2.** (*chapuza*) botched job

BUP *m abr de* **Bachillerato Unificado Polivalente** *secondary studies for pupils aged 14–17, now supplanted by the ESO*

buque *m* **1.** (*barco*) ship; **~ de pasajeros** passenger ship; **~ de carga** freighter; **~ de guerra** warship; **~ insignia** flagship; **~ de vapor** steamer **2.** (*casco*) hull **3.** (*cabida*) tonnage

buqué *m* (*de vino*) bouquet

buque-cisterna *m* <buques-cisterna> tanker

buraco *m Arg, Par, Urug* hole

burata *f Ven, inf* cash, dough *Am, inf*

burbuja *f* bubble

burbujear *vi* to bubble

burdel *m* brothel

Burdeos *m* Bordeaux

burdo, -a *adj* (*tosco*) coarse; (*excusa*) clumsy

bureo *m* amusement; **ir de ~** to have a good time

burgalés, -esa I. *adj* of/from Burgos II. *m, f* native/inhabitant of Burgos

burgo *m* **1.** (*aldea*) hamlet **2.** HIST (*castillo*) castle

burgués, -esa I. *adj t. pey* bourgeois, middle-class II. *m, f t. pey* bourgeois *m,* bourgeoise *f*

burguesía *f* bourgeoisie

buril *m* engraver's chisel
Burkina Faso *f* Burkina-Faso
burla *f* 1. (*mofa*) taunt; **hacer ~ de alguien** to make fun of sb 2. (*broma*) joke; **~s aparte** joking apart 3. (*engaño*) hoax
burlador(a) I. *adj* mocking II. *m(f)* 1. (*mofador*) mocker 2. (*bromista*) practical joker 3. (*seductor*) seducer
burlar I. *vt* 1. (*mofarse*) to mock 2. (*engañar*) to cheat 3. (*frustrar*) to frustrate 4. (*eludir*) to evade; (*orden*) to disregard; (*bloqueo*) to run 5. (*seducir*) to seduce II. *vr:* **~se** to joke
burlesco, -a *adj* 1. (*jocoso*) comic 2. LIT burlesque
burlete *m* (*de la puerta*) draught excluder *Brit*, weather stripp(ing) *Am*
burlón, -ona I. *adj* mocking II. *m, f* 1. (*mofador*) mocker 2. (*guasón*) joker, wag *Brit*
buró *m* 1. (*escritorio*) bureau 2. *AmL* (*mesa de noche*) bedside table
burocracia *f* bureaucracy
burócrata *mf* bureaucrat
burocrático, -a *adj* bureaucratic
burocratización *f* bureaucratization
burocratizar <z→c> *vt* to bureaucratize
burrada *f* 1. *inf* (*disparate*) silly thing; **decir ~s** to talk nonsense 2. *inf* (*cantidad grande*) load 3. (*manada*) drove of donkeys
burro *m* 1. TÉC sawhorse 2. *AmC* (*escalera*) step ladder 3. *AmC* (*columpio*) swing
burro, -a I. *adj* 1. (*tonto*) stupid 2. (*obstinado*) obstinate II. *m, f* 1. ZOOL donkey; **~ de carga** *t. fig* beast of burden 2. (*persona tonta*) idiot; **~ cargado de letras** pompous ass 3. (*persona obstinada*) obstinate person 4. (*persona trabajadora*) hard worker ►**esto es un ~ con dos albardas** that's saying the same thing twice over; **apearse del ~** to recognize one's mistake; **no ver tres en un ~** to be as blind as a bat
bursátil *adj* stock exchange
bus *m t.* INFOR bus
busaca *f* 1. *Col, Ven* (*bolsa*) bag 2. *Ven* (*cartera*) satchel
busca¹ *f* search; **en ~ de alguien** in search of sb
busca² *m* bleeper *Brit,* beeper *Am*
buscabullas I. *adj* troublemaking II. *mf inv* troublemaker
buscador *m* INFOR searcher
buscapié *m* hint
buscapleitos *mf inv, AmL* troublemaker
buscar <c→qu> *vi, vt* to look for; **enviar a alguien a ~ algo** to send sb to fetch sth; **ir a ~ algo** to go and look for sth; **me viene a ~ a las 7** he/she is picking me up at 7; **él se lo ha buscado** he brought it on himself; **~ tres pies al gato** to complicate matters; **'se busca'** 'wanted'
buscatesoros *mf inv* treasure-seeker
buscavidas *mf inv* 1. (*curioso*) busybody 2. (*diligente*) hustler
buscona *f* whore

buseta *f Col, Ven* (*pequeño autobús*) minibus
busilis *m inv, inf* difficulty; **dar en el ~** to put one's finger on the spot
búsqueda *f t.* INFOR search
busto *m* bust
butaca *f* 1. (*silla*) armchair 2. (*de cine, de teatro*) stall *Brit*, seat *Am*
butacón *m* large armchair
butano I. *adj* orange II. *m* 1. QUÍM butane (gas) 2. (*color*) orange
butifarra *f* 1. (*salchicha*) Catalan sausage 2. *AmL* (*media*) (badly-fitting) stocking
butrón *m inf* break-in
buzo *m* 1. (*buceador*) diver 2. (*mono*) overalls *pl Brit*, coverall *Am*
buzón *m* (*de correos*) letterbox *Brit*, mailbox *Am;* **~** (**electrónico**) INFOR mailbox
byte *m* INFOR byte; **~ de control** control byte

C

C, c *f* C, c; **~ de Carmen** C for Charlie
C/ *abr de* **calle** St
cabal I. *adj* 1. (*completo*) complete 2. (*persona*) honest II. *m* **no estar en sus ~es** not to be in one's right mind
cábala *f* 1. REL cabbala 2. (*intriga*) intrigue 3. *pl* (*suposición*) supposition
cabalgadura *f* (*de montura*) mount; (*de carga*) beast of burden
cabalgar <g→gu> I. *vi* to ride II. *vt* 1. (*a caballo*) to ride 2. (*el macho a la hembra*) to mount
cabalgata *f* procession, cavalcade
caballa *f* mackerel
caballada *f* 1. (*manada*) drove of horses 2. *AmL* (*animalada*) asinine thing to say or do
caballerango *m Méx* groom
caballeresco, -a *adj* 1. HIST knightly 2. (*galante*) chivalrous
caballería *f* 1. (*montura*) mount 2. MIL cavalry
caballeriza *f* stable
caballerizo *m* groom
caballero *m* 1. (*señor, galán*) gentleman 2. HIST knight
caballerosidad *f* gentlemanliness
caballeroso, -a *adj* gentlemanly
caballete *m* 1. (*de mesa*) trestle 2. (*de cuadro*) easel
caballito *m* 1. ZOOL **~ de mar** sea horse 2. *pl* (*en una feria*) merry-go-round, carousel *Am*
caballo *m* 1. (*animal*) horse; **a ~** on horseback; **ir a ~** to ride; **~ de batalla** *fig* hobby horse 2. (*ajedrez*) knight 3. DEP **~** (**de saltos**) jumper 4. AUTO horsepower 5. (*naipes*) queen 6. *inf* (*heroína*) smack
cabaña *f* 1. (*choza*) cabin 2. AGR livestock
cabaré *m*, **cabaret** *m* <cabarets> cabaret

cabecear I. *vi* 1. (*mover la cabeza*) to shake one's head 2. (*dormitar*) to nod off II. *vt* DEP to head

cabecera *f* 1. (*de una cama, de la mesa*) head; (*plaza de honor*) seat of honour [*o* honor *Am*]; **médico de** ~ general practitioner 2. (*del periódico*) masthead

cabecilla *mf* ringleader

cabellera *f* 1. (*de la cabeza*) hair; (*abundante*) mane 2. ASTR tail (of a comet)

cabello *m* hair; **se le pusieron los** ~**s de punta** his/her hair stood on end; **traído por los** ~**s** far-fetched

cabelludo, -a *adj* hairy; BOT fibrous

caber *irr vi* 1. (*tener espacio*) ~ **en algo** to fit in [*o* into] sth; **no** ~ **en sí de...** to be beside oneself with ...; **esta falda no me cabe** this skirt doesn't fit me 2. (*ser posible*) to be possible

cabestrillo *m* MED sling

cabeza¹ *f* 1. *t.* ANAT, TÉC head; ~ **de ajo** bulb of garlic; ~ **atómica** atomic warhead; ~ **de lectura** INFOR read head; ~ **de partido** administrative centre [*o* center *Am*]; ~ **abajo** upside down; ~ **arriba** upright; **de** ~ headfirst; **por** ~ a head; **abrirse la** ~ to split one's head open; **asentir con la** ~ to nod (one's head); **negar con la** ~ to shake one's head; **se me va la** ~ I feel dizzy; **de la** ~ **a los pies** from head to toe; **estar mal de la** ~ *inf* to be out of one's mind; **jugarse la** ~ to risk one's life; **levantar** ~ to pull through; **métetelo en la** ~ get it into your head; **algo se le pasa a alguien por la** ~ sth crosses sb's mind; **quitarse algo de la** ~ to put sth out of one's mind; **sentar (la)** ~ to settle down; **tener la** ~ **dura** to be stubborn; **traer a alguien de** ~ to drive sb crazy; **este chico tiene** ~ this boy is clever; **tener** ~ **para los negocios** to be business-minded 2. (*extremo*) top; **ir en** ~ DEP to be in the lead 3. AGR (*res*) head

cabeza² *m* head; ~ **de familia** head of the family; ~ **rapada** skinhead

cabezada *f* blow on the head; **dar** [*o* echar] **una** ~ *inf* to have a nap

cabezazo *m* 1. (*golpe*) blow on the head; **darse un** ~ to bang one's head 2. DEP header

cabezón, -ona I. *adj* 1. (*de cabeza grande*) with a big head 2. *inf* (*obstinado*) pigheaded II. *m, f* pigheaded person

cabezonería *f inf* pigheadedness

cabezota *mf inf* pigheaded person

cabida *f* space

cabina *f* cabin; (*en la playa*) cubicle; ~ **de control** TÉC control room; ~ **del piloto** cockpit; ~ **de proyección** projection room; ~ **de teléfonos** telephone box *Brit*, phone booth *Am*

cabinera *f Col* air hostess, stewardess

cabizbajo, -a *adj* with head bowed; (*triste*) dejected

cable *m t.* ELEC (*telegrama*) cable; **se le cruzaron los** ~**s** *inf* he/she lost control; **echar un** ~

a alguien *inf* to help sb out

cablegrafiar < *I. pres:* cablegrafío> *vt* to cable

cabo *m* 1. (*extremo*) end; **al fin y al** ~ in the end; **de** ~ **a rabo** from beginning to end; **llevar a** ~ to carry out; **no dejar ningún** ~ **suelto** to leave no loose ends 2. GEO cape; **Ciudad del Cabo** Cape Town 3. MIL corporal 4. NÁUT rope ▸ **al** ~ **de** after

cabotaje *m* coastal shipping

cabra *f* goat; ~ **montés** wild goat; **estar como una** ~ *inf* to be off one's head

cabrear I. *vt inf* to infuriate; **estar cabreado** to be furious II. *vr:* ~**se** *inf* to get angry

cabrero, -a *m, f* goatherd

cabrestante *m* 1. TÉC winch 2. NÁUT capstan

cabrío, -a *adj* goatish

cabriola *f* caper; **hacer** ~**s** to caper about

cabritillo, -a *m, f* kid

cabro *m AmS* billy goat

cabrón *m* billy goat

cabrón, -ona *m, f vulg* bastard, bugger

cabronada *f vulg* dirty trick

cábula *f* 1. *Arg, Par* (*amuleto*) amulet 2. *Arg* (*cábala*) cabal 3. *Chile, Méx, Perú, PRico* (*ardid*) ruse

caca *f inf* 1. (*excremento*) pooh *Brit*, poop *Am*; (*lenguaje infantil*) number two 2. (*chapuza*) rubbish

cacahuate *m Méx* (*cacahuete*) peanut

cacahuete *m* peanut

cacalote *m AmC* 1. GASTR popcorn 2. *inf* (*disparate*) silly thing

cacao *m* 1. (*planta*) cacao 2. *inf* (*jaleo*) to-do; **pedir** ~ *AmL* to give in

cacarear I. *vi* 1. (*gallinas*) to cackle 2. *inf* (*presumir*) to brag II. *vt inf* (*presumir*) to brag about

cacarizo, -a *adj Méx* pitted

cacastle *m AmC, Méx* 1. (*esqueleto*) skeleton 2. (*armazón*) pack frame (*fitted on shoulders to aid in carrying loads*)

cacatúa *f* 1. ZOOL cockatoo 2. *inf* (*mujer*) old bag

cacería *f* 1. (*partida*) hunting 2. (*piezas*) bag

cacerola *f* saucepan

cachafaz *adj AmS* roguish

cachalote *m* sperm whale

cachar *vt* 1. *AmC, Col, Chile* (*cornear*) to gore 2. *Arg, Nic, Urug* (*asir*) to seize 3. *AmC* (*hurtar*) to steal 4. *Arg, Chile* (*agarrar*) to grab 5. *AmL* (*al vuelo*) to catch in mid-air 6. *Chile* (*sospechar*) to suspect 7. *AmS, inf* (*burlarse*) to make fun of

cacharpas *fpl AmS* odds *mpl* and ends

cacharro *m* 1. (*recipiente*) pot 2. *pey, inf* (*aparato*) gadget 3. *pey, inf* (*trasto*) piece of junk; **¡quita ese** ~ **de ahí!** get rid of that junk!

cachas¹ I. *adj inv* 1. *inf* (*fuerte*) strong 2. *vulg* (*sexy*) sexy II. *fpl inf* bottom

cachas² *mf inv, inf* (*hombre*) hunk; (*mujer*) muscular woman

cachaza *f* 1. (*lentitud*) slowness 2. (*flema*)

phlegm

cachazudo, -a *adj* **1.**(*lento*) slow **2.**(*flemático*) phlegmatic

cachear *vt* to frisk

cachemir *m* cashmere

cacheo *m* searching, frisking

cachete *m* **1.**(*golpe*) slap **2.**(*carrillo*) (fat) cheek

cachetear *vt AmL* to slap

cachetón, -ona *adj AmL* (*mofletudo*) chubby-cheeked

cachimba *f AmL* **1.**(*pipa*) pipe **2.**(*cartucho*) cartridge

cachiporra *f* truncheon

cachivache *m* junk; **tienes la cocina llena de ~s** your kitchen is full of junk

cachondear *vr:* **~se** *vulg* **~ de uno** to take the mickey out of sb

cachondeo *m* **1.** *inf* (*broma*) joke; (*juerga*) good time; **tomar algo a ~** to take sth as a joke; **esto es un ~** this is a joke **2.** *vulg*(*burla*) farce

cachondo, -a I. *adj* **1.** *vulg* (*sexual*) sexy, horny; **poner a alguien ~** to turn sb on **2.** *inf* (*gracioso*) funny **3.**(*perra*) on heat II. *m, f* **1.** *vulg* (*juerguista*) reveller **2.** *inf* (*gracioso*) joker; **es un ~** he's a real laugh

cachorro, -a I. *adj AmL* despicable II. *m, f* (*de tigre*) cub; (*de perro, lobo*) pup(py)

cachudo, -a *adj* **1.**AmL (*animal*) horned **2.***Méx*(*persona*) long-faced

cacique *m* **1.**(*jefe indio*) chief **2.**(*tirano*) tyrant

caciquismo *m pey:* system of petty tyranny run by the local political boss

caco *m inf*burglar

cacto *m* cactus

cada *adj* each; **~ uno/una** each one; **libros a 5 euros ~ uno** books at 5 euros each; **~ hora** hourly; **~ día** daily; **~ vez más/peor** more and more/worse and worse; **¿~ cuánto?** how often?

cadalso *m* **1.**(*tarima*) platform **2.**(*patíbulo*) scaffold

cadáver *m* (*de personas*) corpse; (*de animales*) carcass

cadavérico, -a *adj* **1.**(*muerto*) cadaverous **2.**(*pálido*) deathly pale

cadena *f* **1.** *t. fig* (*objeto, sucesión*) chain; **~ alimentaria** BIO food chain; **~ (antideslizante)** AUTO snow chain; **~ hotelera** hotel chain; **~ humana** human chain; **~ perpetua** JUR life imprisonment; **trabajo en ~** assembly--line work; **atar un perro con ~** to chain up a dog; **choque en ~** pile-up; **reacción en ~** chain reaction **2.** GEO mountain chain **3.** RADIO, TV network; **~ de sonido** sound system

cadencia *f* **1.**(*ritmo*) rhythm **2.** LING, MÚS cadence

cadera *f* hip

cadete *m* MIL cadet

cadmio *m* cadmium

caducar <c→qu> *vi* **1.**(*documento*) to expire; **este pasaporte está caducado** this passport has expired **2.**(*producto*) **la leche está caducada** the milk is past its sell-by date

caducidad *f* **1.**(*de un documento*) expiry; **fecha de ~** date of expiry **2.**(*de productos*) **fecha de ~** sell-by date

caduco, -a *adj* **1.**(*personas*) senile **2.**(*perecedero*) perishable **3.**(*árbol*) deciduous

caer *irr* I. *vi* **1.**(*objeto, persona*) to fall (down); (*fecha, precio*) to fall; **~ al suelo** to fall to the ground; **~ en manos de alguien** to fall into sb's hands; **dejarse ~** *inf*(*abandonarse*) to let oneself go; (*presentarse*) to show up; **tu amigo me cae bien/mal** *fig* I like/I don't like your friend; **estar al ~** *inf* to be about to happen **2.**(*presidente*) to fall from power **3.**(*comida*) **~ bien a** to agree with **4.**(*vestidos*) to suit **5.** *inf* (*encontrarse*) to be (located); **¿por dónde cae Jerez?** whereabouts is Jerez? **6.**(*atacar*) **~ sobre algo/alguien** to fall on sth/sb II. *vr:* **~se** (*desplomarse*) to collapse; (*un avión*) to crash; (*pelo, dientes*) to fall out; (*casa*) to fall down; **~se de culo** to fall on one's backside; **se me ha caído el pañuelo** I've dropped my handkerchief; **~se de sueño** to be ready to drop

café *m* **1.**(*bebida*) coffee; **~ con leche** white coffee; **~ solo** black coffee; **tomar un ~** to have a coffee **2.**(*local*) café **3.**(*planta*) coffee tree; (*semilla*) coffee bean

cafeína *f* caffeine

cafetal *m* coffee plantation

cafetera *f* **1.**(*jarra*) coffee pot; **~ eléctrica** coffeemaker **2.** *inf*(*vehículo*) old banger

cafetería *f* café

cafeto *m* coffee tree

cafre *mf pey, inf* moron

cagalera *f inf* tener **~** to have the runs

cagar <g→gu> I. *vi vulg* to have a shit II. *vt vulg* to mess up; **¡ya la hemos cagado!** now we're really in the shit! III. *vr:* **~se** *vulg* (*de miedo*) to shit oneself; **¡me cago en diez!** shit!

caída *f* **1.**(*bajada brusca, de un imperio*) fall; (*de aviones*) crash; **~ del cabello** hair loss; **~ de gobierno** fall of the government; **~ del sistema** INFOR system crash; **la ~ del muro de Berlín** the fall of the Berlin wall; **esta calle tiene mucha ~** this street is very steep; **las cortinas tienen una bonita ~** the curtains hang well **2.**(*de agua*) waterfall **3.** FIN fall in prices **4.**(*puesta*) **a la ~ del sol** at sunset

caído, -a I. *adj* (*flojo*) drooping; (*abatido*) crestfallen II. *m, f* **1.**(*persona*) person who has fallen **2.**(*en la guerra*) soldier killed in action; **los ~s** the fallen

caigo *1. pres de* **caer**

caimán *m* caiman

Cairo *m* **El ~** Cairo

caja *f* **1.**(*recipiente*) box; **~ fuerte** safe; **~ de herramientas** *t.* INFOR tool box; **~ de música** musical box; **~ negra** AVIAT black box **2.**(*carcasa*) case; **~ de cambios** AUTO gearbox; **~**

torácica ANAT thoracic cavity **3.** FIN fund; **Caja (Postal) de Ahorros** (Post Office) savings bank

cajero, -a *m, f* cashier; ~ **automático** cash dispenser

cajeta *f* **1.** *Arg* (*cepo*) trap **2.** *AmC* GASTR toffee-like sweet

cajetilla *f* (*caja pequeña*) small box; (*de cigarrillos*) packet of cigarettes *Brit,* pack of cigarettes *Am*

cajón *m* (*caja grande*) big box; (*de embalaje*) crate; (*deslizante*) drawer; ~ **de salida** DEP starting gate; **eso es de** ~ *inf* that goes without saying

cajuela *f Méx* AUTO boot, trunk *Am*

cake *m AmL* cake

cal *f* lime; **cerrar a** ~ **y canto** to shut firmly

cala *f* **1.** (*bahía*) cove **2.** NÁUT hold **3.** (*en el terreno*) probe

calabacín *m* courgette *Brit,* zucchini *Am*

calabaza *f* **1.** BOT pumpkin **2.** *pey* (*persona*) dummy ►**dar** ~**s a alguien** (*un suspenso*) to fail sb; (*una negativa*) to give sb the brush-off

calabozo *m* **1.** (*mazmorra*) dungeon **2.** (*celda*) (prison) cell

calada *f inf* puff; **¿me das una ~?** will you let me have a puff?

caladero *m* fishing ground

calado *m* **1.** (*bordado*) open work **2.** NÁUT draught

calaguasca *f Col* GASTR raw brandy

calamar *m* squid

calambrazo *m* attack of cramp

calambre *m* **1.** (*eléctrico*) electric shock **2.** (*muscular*) cramp; ~ **de estómago** stomach cramp

calamidad *f* **1.** (*catástrofe*) calamity; (*desastre*) disaster **2.** *inf* (*persona*) disaster

calamitoso, -a *adj* calamitous

calandria *f* **1.** ZOOL calandra lark **2.** (*máquina*) calender; (*para ropa*) mangle

calaña *f* **ser de mala ~** to be bad

calar **I.** *vi* **1.** (*líquido*) to soak in **2.** (*material*) to be permeable **II.** *vt* **1.** (*líquido*) to soak; **el chaparrón me ha calado la chaqueta** the downpour has drenched my jacket **2.** (*con un objeto*) to pierce **3.** (*afectar*) ~ **a alguien** to make an impression on sb **4.** (*una prenda*) to do openwork on **5.** (*cortar*) to cut a piece out of **6.** *inf* (*desenmascarar*) to see through **7.** (*motor*) to stall **8.** NÁUT to draw **III.** *vr:* ~**se** **1.** (*mojarse*) to get soaked **2.** (*motor*) to stall **3.** (*gorra*) to pull down

calato, -a *adj Perú* naked

calavera *f* skull

calcáneo *m* ANAT heel bone

calcañar *m* ANAT heel

calcar <c→qu> *vt* **1.** (*dibujar*) to trace **2.** (*imitar*) to copy; **es calcado a su padre** he's the spitting image of his father

calceta *f* knitting

calcetín *m* sock

calcificar <c→qu> **I.** *vt* to calcify **II.** *vr:* ~**se** to calcify

calcinar **I.** *vt* **1.** (*carbonizar*) to burn **2.** QUÍM to calcine **II.** *vr:* ~**se** to burn

calcio *m* calcium

calco *m* **1.** (*de dibujos*) tracing **2.** (*imitación*) imitation **3.** LING calque

calcomanía *f* transfer

calculador(a) *adj* calculating

calculadora *f* calculator; ~ **de bolsillo** pocket calculator

calcular *vt* **1.** (*computar*) to calculate **2.** (*aproximadamente*) to estimate; **calculo que llegaré sobre las diez** I reckon that I'll arrive around ten

cálculo *m* **1.** *t.* ECON (*matemático, cómputo*) calculation; ~ **diferencial** differential calculus; ~ **mental** mental arithmetic; ~ **de probabilidades** theory of probability; **hacer un** ~ **de algo** to calculate sth **2.** (*suposición*) conjecture **3.** MED stone

caldear **I.** *vt* **1.** (*calentar*) to heat (up) **2.** (*acalorar*) to inflame **II.** *vr:* ~**se** **1.** (*calentarse*) to heat up **2.** (*acalorarse*) to get heated

caldera *f* **1.** (*caldero*) cauldron *Brit,* caldron *Am* **2.** TÉC boiler

calderilla *f* small change

caldero *m* cauldron *Brit,* caldron *Am*

caldo *m* **1.** GASTR broth **2.** (*vino*) wine **3.** BIO ~ **de cultivo** culture medium; *fig* breeding ground

caldoso, -a *adj* soggy

calefacción *f* heating

calefactor *m* **1.** (*aparato*) heater **2.** (*persona*) heating engineer

calefón *m Arg* gas water heater

caleidoscopio *m* kaleidoscope

calendario *m* calendar; ~ **de taco** tear-off calendar; ~ **de trabajo** schedule

calentador *m* heater; (*para la cama*) bed-warmer

calentamiento *m* **1.** (*caldeamiento*) warming **2.** DEP warm-up

calentar <e→ie> **I.** *vi* (*dar calor*) to be warm **II.** *vt* **1.** (*caldear*) to heat (up); (*con calefacción*) to warm (up); ~ **al rojo vivo** to make red-hot **2.** (*enfadar*) to anger **3.** *vulg* (*sexualmente*) to turn on **4.** *inf* (*pegar*) to give a good hiding **III.** *vr:* ~**se** **1.** (*caldearse*) to heat up **2.** (*enfadarse*) to get angry **3.** DEP to warm up

calentura *f* **1.** (*fiebre*) fever **2.** (*en los labios*) cold sore

calenturiento, -a *adj* **1.** (*febril*) feverish **2.** (*exaltado*) rash **3.** (*indecente: pensamiento*) dirty

calesita *f Arg, Par* merry-go-round

caleta *f* **1.** (*cala*) cove **2.** *AmL* (*barco*) coaster

calibrar *vt* **1.** (*medir*) to gauge, to gage *Am;* TÉC to calibrate **2.** (*calcular*) to weigh up

calibre *m* **1.** (*diámetro*) calibre *Brit,* caliber *Am;* **eso es una mentira de ~** *inf* that's a whopping lie **2.** (*instrumento*) gauge, gage *Am*

caliche *m* **1.** (*pared*) flake of lime **2.** (*piedrecilla*) pebbly particle **3.** (*maca en la fruta*) bruise

calidad *f* 1.(*clase, característica*) quality; **de alta** ~ high-quality; **de primera** ~ top-quality; **en** ~ **de** as 2.(*prestigio*) importance

cálido, -a *adj* (*país*) hot; *fig* warm

caliente *adj* 1.(*cálido*) warm; (*ardiente*) hot 2.(*acalorado*) heated; **poner(se)** ~ *vulg* to get randy

califa *m* caliph

calificación *f* 1.(*denominación*) description; (*evaluación*) assessment 2.(*cualificación*) qualification; ~ **profesional** professional qualification 3.(*nota*) mark, grade

calificado, -a *adj* 1. *t.* JUR (*cualificado*) qualified 2.(*reconocido*) well-known

calificar <c→qu> *vt* 1.(*definir*) ~ **de algo** to describe as sth 2.(*evaluar*) to assess 3. ENS to mark, to grade

calificativo *m* description, qualifier

California *f* California

caligrafía *f* calligraphy

calina *f* 1.(*neblina*) mist 2.(*polución*) smog

cáliz *m* 1. REL chalice 2. BOT calyx

caliza *f* limestone

callado, -a *adj* 1. estar (*sin hablar*) silent; (*silencioso*) quiet 2. ser (*reservado*) quiet

callampa *f* 1. *Col, Chile, Perú* (*seta*) mushroom 2. *Chile* (*sombrero*) felt hat

callana *f* 1. *AmS* (*vasija*) earthenware pan 2. *Chile* (*reloj*) large pocket watch 3. *Perú* (*tiesto*) flowerpot

callar I. *vi, vr* ~**se de** [*o por*] **algo** (*no hablar*) to keep quiet because of sth; (*enmudecer*) to fall silent due to sth; **¡cállate de una vez!** just shut up! II. *vt* (*un asunto*) to keep quiet about; (*un secreto*) to keep; **hacer** ~ **a uno** to make sb keep quiet

calle *f* street; (*en la autopista*) *t.* DEP lane; ~ **comercial** shopping street; ~ **de dirección única** one-way street; ~ **peatonal** pedestrian street; ~ **sin salida** cul-de-sac; ~ **arriba/abajo** up/down the street; **hacer la** ~ *inf* to streetwalk; **quedarse en la** ~ *inf* to be out of a job

callejear *vi* to stroll around

callejero *m* street directory

callejón *m* alley; ~ **sin salida** cul-de-sac

callista *mf* chiropodist

callo *m* 1.(*callosidad*) callus; (*ojo de gallo*) corn; **dar el** ~ *inf* to slave away 2. *pl* GASTR tripe

calma *f* 1.(*tranquilidad, silencio*) calm; ~ **chicha** NÁUT dead calm 2.(*serenidad*) calmness; **¡(con)** ~**!** calm down! 3. *inf* (*indolencia*) indolence

calmante I. *adj* (*que tranquiliza*) sedative; (*para dolores*) soothing II. *m* (*tranquilizante*) tranquilizer *Brit*, tranquilizer *Am*; (*analgésico*) painkiller

calmar I. *vi* (*viento*) to abate II. *vt* 1.(*tranquilizar*) to calm (down) 2.(*dolor*) to relieve; (*hambre*) to satisfy III. *vr:* ~**se** 1.(*tranquilizarse*) to calm down 2.(*dolor*) to ease off

calmoso, -a *adj* 1.(*tranquilo*) calm 2. *inf*

(*indolente*) sluggish

caló *m* gipsy [*o* gypsy *Am*] slang

calor *m* 1.(*de un cuerpo, afecto*) warmth 2.(*clima*) heat; ~ **sofocante** stifling heat; **hace mucho** ~ it's very hot 3.(*entusiasmo*) passion

caloría *f* calorie; **bajo en** ~**s** low-calorie

calorífero, -a *adj* heat-producing, heat-emitting

calote *m RíoPl* swindle

caluma *f Perú* (*desfiladero*) Andean gorge

calumnia *f* slander

calumniar *vt* to slander

caluroso, -a *adj* 1.(*clima*) hot 2. *fig* warm; **un recibimiento** ~ a warm reception

calva *f* 1.(*en la cabeza*) bald patch 2.(*en un tejido*) worn spot

calvario *m* REL Stations *pl* of the Cross; **pasar un** ~ to suffer agonies

calvero *m* clearing

calvicie *f* baldness

calvo, -a I. *adj* 1.(*en la cabeza*) bald; **estar** ~ to be bald 2.(*tejido*) threadbare 3.(*sin vegetación*) bare II. *m, f* bald person

calza *f* 1.(*media*) stocking 2.(*cuña*) wedge

calzada *f* 1.(*carretera*) (paved) road 2.(*carril*) carriageway *Brit*, lane

calzado *m* footwear

calzador *m* shoehorn

calzar <z→c> I. *vt* 1.(*poner zapatos*) to put on; (*esquís*) to clip on 2.(*llevar puesto*) to wear 3.(*poner una cuña*) to wedge II. *vr:* ~**se** (*zapatos*) to put one's shoes on; (*esquís*) to clip one's skis on

calzón *m AmL* (*pantalón*) trousers *pl*

calzoncillo(s) *m(pl)* men's underpants *pl*

calzoneras *fpl Méx* (*pantalón de montar*) riding pants *pl*

cama *f* 1.(*mueble*) bed; ~ **elástica** trampoline; **caer en** ~ to fall ill 2.(*de animales*) lair

camada *f* 1.(*de animales*) litter 2. *pey* (*cuadrilla*) gang

camafeo *m* cameo

camaleón *m t. fig* chameleon

cámara¹ *f* 1. FOTO camera; ~ **de vídeo** video camera; **a** ~ **lenta** in slow motion 2.(*consejo*) house; **Cámara Alta** POL upper house; **Cámara Baja** POL lower house 3.(*receptáculo, en un arma*) chamber; ~ **frigorífica** cold-storage room

cámara² *mf* CINE cameraman *m*, camerawoman *f*

camarada *mf* 1. POL comrade 2.(*amigo*) companion

camaradería *f* comradeship

camarero, -a *m, f* 1.(*en restaurantes*) waiter *m*, waitress *f*; **¡~!** waiter! 2.(*en la barra*) barman *m*, barmaid *f* 3.(*de habitación*) room waiter *m*, room waitress *m* 4.(*en un barco*) steward *m*, stewardess *f*

camarilla *f t. pey* clique

camarín *m* dressing room

camarón *m* prawn, shrimp

camarote *m* NÁUT cabin, berth
camarotero *m AmL* (*camarero de barco*)
steward
camastro *m* hard old bed
cambalache *m* swap
cambiable *adj* **1.** COM exchangeable **2.** (*variable*) changeable
cambiador *m Chile* switchman
cambiante *adj* **1.** (*irisado*) iridescent **2.** (*inestable*) changeable **3.** *pey* (*veleidoso*) moody
cambiar **I.** *vi* (*transformarse, alterar*) to change; ~ **de casa** to move (house); ~ **de coche** to buy a new car; ~ **de marcha** AUTO to change gear **II.** *vt* **1.** (*trocar, algo comprado*) to (ex)change; ~ **dinero** to change money; ~ **unas palabras con alguien** to exchange a few words with sb **2.** (*variar*) to change; ~ **algo de lugar** to move sth **III.** *vr* **1.** (*transformarse*) ~ **en algo** to change [*o* turn] into sth **2.** (*de ropa*) to change; (*de casa*) to move; ~**se a otra ciudad** to move to another town
cambiavía *m AmL* switchman
cambiazo *m* big change ▶**dar** el ~ **a alguien** *inf* to pull a fast one on sb
cambio *m* **1.** (*alteración, sustitución, transformación*) change; ~ **de aceite** AUTO oil change; ~ **climático** climatic change; ~ **de domicilio** change of address; ~ **de marchas** gear lever, gear *Am;* ~ **de tendencia** new trend; **hay un** ~ **en el horario** there's a change in the timetable; **a las primeras de** ~ at the first opportunity; **en** ~ however **2.** (*intercambio, en un comercio*) exchange; ~ **de impresiones** exchange of views; **libre** ~ COM free trade; **a** ~ **de algo** in exchange for sth **3.** FIN exchange rate; ~ **de divisa** [*o* de moneda] foreign exchange; **al** ~ **del día** at the current exchange rate **4.** (*suelto*) change; **¿tiene** ~ **de 100 euros?** can you change 100 euros? **5.** TÉC gear change *Brit,* gearshift *Am;* ~ **de marchas** gearbox, transmission **6.** DEP substitution
cambista *mf* **1.** (*que cambia dinero*) money-changer **2.** (*en la banca*) foreign exchange clerk
Camboya *f* Cambodia
cambuto, -a *adj Perú* (*menudo y rechoncho*) small and chubby
camelar *vt inf* **1.** (*engañar*) to cajole **2.** (*seducir*) to seduce
camelia *f* camellia
camello, -a *m, f* **1.** ZOOL camel **2.** *inf* (*persona*) drug dealer
camelo *m inf* **1.** (*timo*) con **2.** (*adulación*) flattery
camerino *m* TEAT dressing room
Camerún *m* Cameroon
camilla *f* **1.** (*angarillas*) stretcher **2.** (*cama de hospital*) hospital bed
camillero, -a *m, f* stretcher-bearer
camilucho, -a *m, f AmL* Indian day labourer
caminar **I.** *vi* **1.** (*ir*) to go; (*a pie*) to walk

2. (*río*) to flow **3.** (*astro*) to move **4.** AmL (*funcionar*) to work **II.** *vt* (*distancia*) to cover
caminata *f* long walk
camino *m* **1.** (*senda*) path; (*más estrecho*) track; (*calle*) road; **a medio** ~ halfway (there); **de** ~ **a Londres** on the road to London; **abrirse** ~ to make one's way; **ponerse en** ~ to set out [*o* off]; **ir por buen/mal** ~ *fig* to be on the right/wrong track **2.** (*distancia*) way; **está a dos horas de** ~ it's two hours' journey away **3.** (*manera*) way **4.** INFOR path ▶**todos los** ~**s llevan a** Roma *prov* all roads lead to Rome; ~ **de rosas** bed of roses; **su vida no ha sido ningún** ~ **de rosas** his/her life has been no bed of roses

> **Santiago de Compostela**, the capital of Galicia has been an important place of pilgrimage for the Roman Catholic Church since the 9th century. The **Camino de Santiago** which leads to **Santiago de Compostela** is a route that is travelled every year by thousands of pilgrims from all over the world.

camión *m* AUTO lorry *Brit,* truck *Am;* ~ **de la basura** dustcart *Brit,* garbage truck *Am;* ~ **volquete** dumper, dumptruck *Am*
camionero, -a *m, f* lorry driver *Brit,* truck driver *Am*
camioneta *f* **1.** (*furgoneta*) van; ~ **de reparto** delivery van **2.** *AmL* (*autobús*) bus
camisa *f* **1.** (*prenda*) shirt; ~ **de fuerza** straitjacket; **cambiar de** ~ to change sides; **no me llegaba la** ~ **al cuerpo** *inf* I was scared stiff **2.** (*funda*) case; (*de disco*) sleeve **3.** (*de reptil*) slough ▶**meterse en** ~ **de once varas** to bite off more than one can chew
camisería *f* shirtmaker's (shop)
camiseta *f* **1.** (*exterior*) T-shirt **2.** (*interior*) vest *Brit,* undershirt *Am* **3.** DEP shirt
camisón *m* nightdress, nightgown *Am*
camomila *f* camomile
camorra *f* **1.** *pey, inf* (*escándalo*) row; **buscar** ~ to go looking for trouble **2.** (*mafia*) Camorra
camorrear *vi RíoPl* to quarrel
camorrista **I.** *adj* troublemaking **II.** *mf* troublemaker
camote *m AmL* **1.** (*batata*) sweet potato **2.** (*molestia*) nuisance **3.** (*amante*) lover
camotear *vi Méx* (*vagabundear*) to roam
campamento *m* camp; ~ **de veraneo** summer camp
campana *f* bell; ~ **extractora de humos** extractor hood; **el coche dio tres vueltas de** ~ the car turned over three times; **echar las** ~**s a vuelo** *inf* to let everybody know
campanada *f* chime; **dar la** ~ *fig* to cause a stir
campanario *m* bell tower
campanilla *f* **1.** (*campana pequeña*) small bell; (*de la puerta*) bell **2.** ANAT uvula **3.** BOT bellflower
campante *adj inf* **1.** (*tranquilo*) calm; **que-**

darse tan ~ not to bat an eyelid **2.** (*satisfecho*) (self-)satisfied

campaña *f* **1.** (*campo*) countryside; **tienda de** ~ tent **2.** MIL, POL campaign; AGR season; ~ **de acoso y derribo** smear campaign; ~ **antitabaco** anti-smoking campaign; ~ **electoral** electoral [*o* election] campaign **3.** COM sales drive

campar *vi* to camp

campear *vi* **1.** *AmL* (*ir de acampada*) to camp **2.** *inf* (*arreglárselas*) **ir campeando** to get by **3.** (*sobresalir*) to abound

campechana *f* **1.** *Méx, Cuba* (*bebida*) cocktail **2.** NÁUT fantail grating

campechano, -a *adj* **1.** (*llano*) straightforward **2.** (*cordial*) cheerful

campeón, -ona *m, f* champion

campeonato *m* championship; **de** ~ *inf* terrific

campera *f CSur* windcheater

campesino, -a I. *adj* **1.** (*del campo*) rural; (*de la gente del campo*) country **2.** *t. pey* (*de un labrador*) peasant **II.** *m, f* **1.** (*que vive, trabaja*) countryman *m*, countrywoman *f*; **los** ~**s** country people **2.** *t. pey* (*labrador*) peasant

camping *m* **1.** (*campamento*) camping site **2.** (*actividad*) camping; **hacer** ~ to go camping

campiña *f* (*campo*) countryside; (*de cultivo*) farmland

campirano, -a *adj* **1.** *AmL* (*patán, rural*) rustic **2.** *Méx* (*campesino*) peasant **3.** *Méx* (*entendido en el campo*) good at farming **4.** *Méx* (*que maneja bien caballos*) skilled at handling horses

campista *mf* **1.** (*en las vacaciones*) camper **2.** *Méx* MIN mine leaseholder

campo *m* **1.** (*opuesto a ciudad*) countryside; (*de cultivo*) field; **gente del** ~ country people; **ir al** ~ to go into the country; **tener** ~ **libre para hacer algo** *fig* to be free to do sth **2.** *t.* DEP, MIL (*terreno*) field; ~ **de tiro** firing range **3.** *t.* POL, MIL (*campamento*) camp; ~ **de concentración** HIST concentration camp; ~ **de trabajo** work camp **4.** *t.* FÍS, INFOR (*área del saber*) field; ~ **de actuación** field of activity; ~ **para entradas** INFOR input field; ~ **de opción** INFOR option field; ~ **visual** field of vision

camposanto *m* cemetery

campus *m inv* campus

camuflaje *m* camouflage

camuflar *vt t. fig* to camouflage

cana *f* **1.** (*pelo blanco*) white hair; **echar una** ~ **al aire** *fig* to let one's hair down **2.** *Arg, inf* (*policía*) police **3.** *Arg, inf* (*prisión*) jail

Canadá *m* (**el**) ~ Canada

canal *m* **1.** *t.* ANAT (*cauce artificial*) canal **2.** GEO (*paso natural*) channel; **el Canal de la Mancha** the English Channel; **el Canal de Panamá** the Panama Canal **3.** (*canalón*) gutter **4.** TV channel; ~ **de televisión** television channel

canalización *f* **1.** (*de un río*) canalization **2.** (*alcantarillado*) sewerage system

canalizar <z→c> *vt* **1.** (*un río*) to canalize **2.** (*encauzar*) to channel

canalla *mf pey* swine

canallada *f* mean thing (to do)

canalón *m* gutter

canana *f* **1.** (*cinturón*) cartridge belt **2.** *AmL, inf* (*canallada*) dirty trick

Canarias *fpl* **las Islas** ~ the Canary Islands

canario *m* canary

canario, -a I. *adj* of/from the Canary Islands **II.** *m, f* (*de Canarias*) native/inhabitant of the Canary Islands

canasta *f* basket

canastero, -a *m, f* **1.** (*que fabrica canastas*) basket maker **2.** *Chile* (*panadería*) baker's helper

canastilla *f* **1.** (*cestita*) small basket; ~ **de costura** sewing basket **2.** (*del bebé*) layette **3.** *Arg, PRico* (*de la novia*) hope chest

cancanear *vi* **1.** *inf* (*vagar*) to wander about **2.** *AmL* (*tartamudear*) to stutter; (*hablar entrecortadamente*) to speak haltingly

cancel *m* **1.** (*en la puerta*) inner door **2.** (*mampara*) folding screen

cancelación *f* **1.** (*anulación, de una cita*) cancellation **2.** FIN (*de una cuenta*) closing; (*de una deuda*) payment; (*de un cheque*) stopping; ~ **de un pedido** cancellation of an order

cancelar *vt* **1.** (*anular*) to cancel; ~ **una cita** to cancel an appointment **2.** (*rescindir*) to rescind **3.** FIN (*una cuenta*) to close; (*una deuda*) to pay (off); (*un cheque*) to stop

cáncer *m* **1.** *t. fig* MED cancer **2.** ASTR Cancer

cancerígeno, -a *adj* carcinogenic

canceroso, -a *adj* cancerous; **tumor** ~ cancerous tumour

cancha *f* **1.** DEP (*de deporte*) sports field; (*de tenis, baloncesto*) court **2.** *AmL* (*hipódromo*) racecourse *Brit*, racetrack *Am* **3.** *AmL* (*de un río*) broad part of a river **4.** *AmL* (*espacio*) space

canchero, -a *m, f Arg* groundsman

canciller *mf* **1.** POL chancellor **2.** *AmL* (*de Asuntos Exteriores*) foreign minister

cancillería *f* **1.** POL chancellery **2.** *AmL* (*Asuntos Exteriores*) foreign ministry

canción *f* song; ~ **de moda** pop song; ~ **popular** folk song; **(es) siempre la misma** ~ (it's) always the same old story

cancionero *m* **1.** MÚS songbook **2.** LIT anthology (of verse)

canco *m* **1.** *Bol* (*nalga*) buttocks *pl* **2.** *Chile* (*olla*) earthenware casserole **3.** *Chile* (*tiesto*) flowerpot

cancona I. *adj Chile* broad-hipped **II.** *f Chile* broad-hipped woman

candado *m* padlock

candela *f* candle

candelabro *m* candelabra

candelejón, -ona *adj Chile, Col, Perú* (*inocente*) naïve

candelero *m* candlestick; **estar en el** ~ *fig* to be in the limelight

candelilla *f* 1. MED catheter 2. BOT (*inflorescencia*) inflorescence 3. BOT (*amento*) ament, catkin 4. *CRi, Chile, Hond* (*luciérnaga*) glowworm 5. *Cuba* (*hilván*) overstitch

candente *adj* 1. (*al rojo*) red-hot 2. (*palpitante*) burning

candidato, -a *m, f* 1. (*aspirante*) applicant 2. POL candidate; ~ **al título** DEP contender for the title

candidatura *f* 1. (*presentación*) application; POL candidature 2. (*lista*) list of candidates 3. (*papeleta*) ballot paper

candidez *f v.* **candor**

cándido, -a *adj v.* **candoroso**

candil *m* 1. (*lámpara*) oil lamp 2. *AmL* (*candelabro*) candelabra

candilejas *fpl* TEAT footlights *pl*

candinga *f* 1. *Chile* (*necedad*) absurdity 2. *Hond* (*maraña*) mess

candonga *f* 1. *inf* (*mofa*) joking 2. *inf* (*mulo*) mule 3. NÁUT storm sail 4. *Col* (*pendiente*) earring

candor *m* 1. (*inocencia*) innocence 2. (*ingenuidad*) naivety *Brit,* naiveté *Am;* (*simplicidad*) simplicity

candoroso, -a *adj* 1. (*inocente*) innocent 2. (*ingenuo*) naive; (*simple*) simple

caneca *f* 1. (*licorera*) liquor bottle 2. *Col* (*basurero*) trash can 3. *Cuba* (*de agua caliente*) hot-water bottle 4. *AmL* (*barril*) drum; (*balde*) bucket

caneco, -a *adj Bol* (*embriagado*) tipsy

canela *f* cinnamon; **¡esto es ~ fina!** *fig* this is exquisite!

canelón *m* 1. (*desagüe*) (roof)gutter 2. *pl* GASTR cannelloni 3. (*carámbano*) icicle

canesú *m* 1. (*en una prenda*) bodice 2. *AmS* (*escote*) yoke

canfín *m AmC* (*petróleo*) petrol *Brit,* gasoline *Am*

cangrejo *m* (*crustáceo*) crab; ~ **de río** crayfish

cangrina *f Col* discomfort

cangro *m Col, Guat* MED (*cáncer*) cancer

canguro[1] *m* ZOOL kangaroo

canguro[2] *mf inf* (*persona*) baby-sitter

caníbal *adj, mf* cannibal

canica *f* marble

canícula *f* 1. (*período*) dog days *pl* 2. ASTR Sirius

canijo, -a *adj* 1. *pey* (*endeble*) feeble; (*pequeñajo*) puny 2. *AmL* (*malvado*) sly

canilla *f* 1. ANAT (*hueso alargado*) long bone; (*tibia*) shinbone 2. TÉC (*carrete*) bobbin 3. *Arg, Par, Urug* (*grifo*) tap

canillera *f AmL* 1. (*espinillera*) shin guard 2. (*temblor*) trembling

canillita *m AmS* newspaper vendor

canino *m* canine (tooth)

canje *m* 1. (*intercambio*) exchange 2. (*de un vale*) cashing (in)

canjear *vt* 1. (*intercambiar*) to exchange 2. (*cambiar*) to cash (in)

canoa *f* 1. *t.* DEP (*bote a remo*) canoe; (*tronco*) dugout (canoe); ~ **canadiense** Canadian canoe 2. (*a motor*) motor boat 3. *AmL* (*artesa*) feeding trough

canódromo *m* dog track

canon *m* 1. (*precepto*) rule 2. REL, ARTE, LIT canon 3. ECON levy

canónico, -a *adj* canonical

canónigo *m* REL canon

canonizar <z→c> *vt* REL to canonize

canoso, -a *adj* grizzled

cansado, -a *adj* 1. *estar* (*fatigado*) tired 2. *estar* (*harto*) tired 3. *ser* (*fatigoso*) tiring; **un viaje ~** a tiring journey 4. *ser* (*aburrido*) boring 5. *ser* (*molesto*) tiresome 6. *AmL* **a las cansadas** at long last

cansador(a) *adj Arg* 1. *ser* (*fatigoso*) tiring 2. *ser* (*aburrido*) boring 3. *ser* (*molesto*) tiresome

cansancio *m* 1. (*fatiga*) tiredness; (*agotamiento*) exhaustion; **estoy muerto de ~** I'm dead tired 2. (*hastío*) boredom

cansar I. *vi* 1. (*fatigar*) to tire 2. (*hastiar*) to be tiresome II. *vt* 1. (*fatigar*) to tire (out) 2. (*hastiar*) to bore III. *vr:* ~**se** 1. (*fatigarse*) to tire oneself out 2. (*hartarse*) ~**se de algo** to get tired of sth

cansera *f* 1. *inf* (*cansancio*) fatigue; (*enojo*) annoyance; **sus quejas me causan ~** his/her complaining annoys me 2. *Col* (*tiempo malgastado*) wasted effort

cansino, -a *adj* 1. (*cansado*) weary 2. (*lento*) slow

Cantabria *f* Cantabria

cantábrico, -a *adj* Cantabrian; **el Mar Cantábrico** the Bay of Biscay

cantaletear *vt AmL* to harp on

cantante I. *adj* singing; **llevar la voz ~** *fig* to call the tune II. *mf* singer

cantar I. *vi, vt* 1. (*personas, pájaros*) to sing; (*gallo*) to crow; (*grillo*) to chirp; (*ranas*) to croak; **en menos que canta un gallo** *inf* in no time at all 2. (*alabar*) to sing the praises of 3. *inf* (*confesar*) to talk 4. (*en el juego*) to declare 5. *inf* (*oler mal*) to stink II. *m* song; (*copla popular*) folksong

cántaro *m* pitcher; **estar lloviendo a ~s** to be raining cats and dogs

cantautor(a) *m(f)* singer-songwriter

cante *m* singing; ~ **jondo** Flamenco singing ►**dar el ~** to stand out

cantera *f* 1. (*pedrera*) quarry 2. DEP young local club players

cantero *m* 1. (*picapedrero*) stonemason 2. *AmL* (*sembradío*) flowerbed

cántico *m* REL canticle

cantidad I. *f* 1. (*porción*) quantity; (*número*) number; **una gran ~ de** lots of; **¿qué ~ necesitas?** how much do you need? 2. (*suma de dinero*) sum II. *adv inf* a lot

cantilena *f* song ►**la misma ~** *inf* the same old story

cantimplora *f* 1. (*botella de campaña*) water

bottle *Brit,* canteen *Am* **2.** (*sifón*) syphon
cantina *f* **1.** (*en estaciones*) buffet; (*en cuarteles*) canteen **2.** (*bodega*) wine cellar
cantinela *f v.* **cantilena**
canto *m* **1.** (*acción*) singing; (*canción*) song; ~ **gregoriano** Gregorian chant; ~ **de los pájaros** birdsong; **estudia** ~ he's/she's studying singing **2.** (*alabanza*) song of praise **3.** LIT hymn **4.** (*esquina*) corner; (*arista, borde*) edge; (*de un vestido*) hem **5.** (*en un cuchillo*) back; (*en un libro*) fore-edge; **poner de** ~ to put on end **6.** (*grosor*) thickness **7.** (*guijarro*) pebble
cantón *m* **1.** (*esquina*) corner **2.** ADMIN, POL canton **3.** MIL cantonment
cantonera *f* (*de un libro*) corner piece; (*de metal*) corner bracket; (*armario*) corner unit
cantor(a) I. *adj* singing; **los canarios son muy** ~**es** canaries sing a lot II. *m(f)* elev singer
canuto *m* **1.** (*tubo*) tube **2.** inf (*porro*) joint
caña *f* **1.** AGR, BOT, MÚS reed; (*tallo de cereal*) stalk; (*junco*) cane; ~ **de azúcar** sugar cane **2.** ANAT (*de la pierna*) shinbone; (*tuétano*) marrow **3.** (*de pescar*) (fishing) rod **4.** (*de un arma, una columna*) shaft **5.** (*en el calzado*) leg **6.** (*de cerveza*) glass
cañada *f* **1.** (*barranco*) gully, gulch *Am* **2.** AGR (*camino de ganado*) cattle track
cañamazo *m* **1.** (*arpillera*) sackcloth, burlap **2.** (*para bordar*) embroidery fabric
cáñamo *m* **1.** (*planta*) hemp **2.** (*tejido*) canvas; **de** ~ hempen
cañería *f* pipe; ~ **del agua** plumbing
cañizal *m,* **cañizar** *m* reedbed
caño *m* **1.** (*tubo*) tube; (*de la fuente*) spout; (*chorro*) jet **2.** (*desagüe*) drainpipe
cañón *m* **1.** (*tubo*) tube; ~ **de escopeta** barrel; **de dos cañones** double-barrelled *Brit,* double-barreled *Am* **2.** MIL cannon; (*artillería*) gun; ~ **de nieve** snow cannon; **carne de** ~ cannon fodder **3.** (*de una pluma*) quill **4.** GEO canyon; **el Cañón del Colorado** the Grand Canyon
cañonazo *m* **1.** (*disparo*) cannon shot **2.** inf (*en el fútbol*) powerful shot
cañonera *f* **1.** (*en una fortificación*) embrasure **2.** *AmL* (*pistolera*) holster
caoba I. *adj* (*color*) ~ mahogany II. *f* **1.** (*madera*) mahogany **2.** (*árbol*) mahogany tree
caos *m inv* chaos
caótico, -a *adj* chaotic
cap. *abr de* **capítulo** ch.
capa *f* **1.** *t.* TAUR (*prenda*) cape **2.** (*cobertura*) covering; (*recubrimiento*) layer; (*baño*) coating; ~ **aislante** insulating layer; ~ **de nieve** covering of snow **3.** (*estrato*) layer; ~ **de ozono** ozone layer **4.** GEO, MIN stratum ►**defender a** ~ **y** espada to defend with all one's might; **hacer de su** ~ **un** sayo to do as one pleases; **andar** [*o* **estar**] **de** ~ caída inf to be down in the mouth
capacho *m* (large) basket, hamper
capacidad *f* **1.** *t.* FÍS (*cabida*) capacity **2.** (*aptitud*) aptitude; ~ **adquisitiva** purchasing

power; ~ **negociadora** negotiating skills *pl;* ~ **de persuasión** persuasiveness **3.** JUR capacity **4.** *AmL* (*persona dotada*) talented person
capacitación *f* (*capacidad*) capacity; (*formación*) training; JUR (*habilitación*) capacitation
capacitado, -a *adj* ~ **para algo** to be qualified for [*o* to do] sth
capacitar I. *vt* **1.** (*formar*) to train; (*preparar*) to prepare **2.** *AmL* JUR (*habilitar*) to capacitate II. *vr:* ~**se** to qualify
capar *vt* **1.** inf (*un pollo*) to caponize; (*animal o persona*) to castrate **2.** (*limitar*) to curtail
caparazón *m t. fig* shell
capataz *m* foreman
capaz *adj* **1.** (*con cabida*) capacious **2.** (*apto*) fit **3.** (*en condiciones*) capable **4.** *AmL* (*tal vez*) perhaps
capazo *m* **1.** (*espuerta*) (large) basket **2.** (*de bebé*) carrycot
capcioso, -a *adj* (*engañoso*) deceitful; (*insidioso*) cunning
capea *f* bullfight with young bulls
capear *vt* **1.** TAUR to make passes with the cape **2.** (*engañar*) to take in **3.** (*esquivar*) to dodge
capellán *m* **1.** (*con capellanía*) chaplain **2.** (*clérigo*) clergyman
capelo *m* **1.** (*sombrero cardenalicio*) cardinal's hat **2.** (*dignidad eclesiástica*) cardinalate **3.** *Cuba, PRico, Ven* (*de doctor*) academic cap, mortarboard *Am*
caperuza *f* (pointed) hood
capi *m* **1.** *AmS* (*maíz*) maize *Brit,* corn *Am* **2.** *Bol* (*harina*) white cornflour
capicúa *m* **1.** (*número*) symmetrical [*o* reversible] number **2.** (*palabra*) palindrome
capilla *f* REL chapel; ~ **ardiente** funeral chapel
capisayo *m* **1.** REL bishop's mantelletta **2.** *Col* (*camiseta*) vest *Brit,* undershirt *Am*
capital[1] I. *adj* essential; **letra** ~ *AmL* capital letter(s); **pena** ~ capital punishment; **de** ~ **importancia** of prime importance II. *m* ECON, FIN capital; ~ **fijo** fixed capital; ~ **a plazo** fixed-term deposit; **bienes de** ~ capital goods
capital[2] *f* (*de país*) capital (city); (*de provincia*) provincial capital
capitalismo *m* capitalism
capitalista I. *adj* capitalist(ic) II. *mf* capitalist
capitalizar <z→c> *vt* **1.** ECON, FIN to capitalize **2.** (*copar*) to seize
capitán *m* **1.** MIL, NÁUT, DEP captain; ~ **general** MIL commander-in-chief **2.** AVIAT flight lieutenant *Brit,* captain *Am* **3.** (*de una banda*) leader
capitanear *vt* **1.** MIL to command **2.** (*dirigir*) to lead **3.** (*equipo*) to captain
capitel *m* ARQUIT capital
capitolio *m* capitol; **el Capitolio** the Capitol
capitulación *f* **1.** MIL surrender **2.** (*acuerdo*) agreement
capitular I. *adj* REL chapter II. *vi* **1.** (*acordar*) to agree to [*o* on] **2.** (*rendirse*) to surrender
capítulo *m t.* REL chapter
capo *m* (*jefe mafioso*) mob boss

capó *m* bonnet *Brit,* hood *Am*
capón I. *adj* castrated II. *m* **1.** (*pollo*) capon **2.** (*coscorrón*) rap on the head
caporal *m* **1.** MIL squadron leader, corporal *Am* **2.** (*jefe*) leader **3.** AGR foreman
capota *f* AUTO convertible roof *Brit,* convertible top *Am*
capote *m* **1.** (*abrigo sin mangas*) cloak; ~ **de monte** *AmL* poncho **2.** TAUR cape; **echar un** ~ **a alguien** *fig* to give sb a helping hand
capotera I. *adj* **aguja** ~ cloak needle II. *f Hond* (*percha*) clothes peg; (*perchero*) coat rack
capricho *m* **1.** (*antojo*) whim; **a** ~ as you/he/ she like; **darse un** ~ to allow oneself sth **2.** MÚS capriccio
caprichoso, -a *adj* **1.** (*antojadizo*) capricious **2.** *pey* (*inconstante*) moody **3.** *pey* (*arbitrario*) arbitrary
Capricornio *m* Capricorn
cápsula *f* **1.** *t.* ANAT, BOT (*receptáculo*) capsule; ~ **espacial** AVIAT space capsule **2.** (*tapón*) cap
captación *f* **1.** (*obtención*) obtaining **2.** (*registro*) registration; ~ **de datos** INFOR data capture **3.** (*atracción*) attraction
captar I. *vt* **1.** (*recoger*) to collect; (*capital*) to raise **2.** (*percibir*) to make out **3.** TEL to pick up **4.** CINE, FOTO to take **5.** INFOR to capture **6.** (*comprender*) to grasp II. *vr:* ~**se** to be obtained
captura *f* **1.** (*apresamiento*) capture **2.** (*detención*) arrest **3.** NÁUT seizure **4.** (*piezas cobradas*) catch
capturar *vt* **1.** (*apresar*) to capture **2.** (*detener*) to arrest **3.** NÁUT to seize **4.** (*cazar, pescar*) to catch
capucha *f* **1.** *v.* **capuchón 2.** TIPO circumflex (accent)
capuchino *m* (*café*) capuccino
capuchino, -a *adj, m, f* Capuchin
capuchón *m* **1.** (*para la cabeza*) hood **2.** (*tapa*) top, cap
capujar *vt Arg* (*captar al vuelo*) to catch in mid-air
capullo *m* **1.** BOT (*de flor*) bud **2.** ZOOL cocoon; **salir del** ~ to hatch out **3.** *inf* (*prepucio*) foreskin **4.** *vulg* (*canalla*) bastard
caqui I. *adj* khaki II. *m* **1.** (*color, tela*) khaki **2.** BOT persimmon
cara I. *f* **1.** (*rostro*) face; ~ **a** ~ face to face; **a** ~ **descubierta** openly; (**no**) **dar la** ~ **por alguien** (not) to come to sb's defense; **echar en** ~ to reproach; **hacer** [*o* **plantar**] ~ **a** to face up to; **partir** [*o* **romper**] **la** ~ **a alguien** *inf* to smash sb's face in **2.** (*expresión*) expression; ~ **de póker** *inf* poker face; **una** ~ **larga** a long face; **una** ~ **de pocos amigos** *inf* a sour look; **salvar la** ~ to save face **3.** (*aspecto*) look; **tener buena/mala** ~ to look good/bad **4.** (*lado*) side; (*de una moneda*) face; ~ **o cruz** heads or tails **5.** *inf* (*osadía*) nerve; **¡qué** ~! what cheek!; **tener mucha** ~ to have some nerve II. *prep* (*en dirección a*) (**de**) ~ **a** facing; **de** ~ **al futuro** with an eye to the future

III. *conj* **de** ~ **a** + *infin* in order to + *infin*
carabela *f* NÁUT caravel
carabina *f* **1.** (*fusil*) carbine **2.** *inf* (*acompañanta*) chaperon
carabinero *m* police officer
caracol *m* **1.** ZOOL snail **2.** (*concha*) conch (shell) **3.** ANAT cochlea **4.** (*de pelo*) curl
caracola *f* conch
caracolillo *m* **1.** (*caracol pequeño*) small snail **2.** *AmL* (*café*) high quality small-beaned coffee **3.** (*de pelo*) kiss-curl
carácter <*caracteres*> *m* **1.** *t.* TIPO, INFOR, BIO (*en general*) character; (**no**) **tiene** ~ he/ she has (no) character; **sin** ~ characterless; ~ **de separación** hyphen **2.** (*índole*) nature; **con** ~ **de** as **3.** *AmL* (*personaje*) character
característica *f* characteristic
característico, -a I. *adj* characteristic; **rasgo** ~ characteristic II. *m, f* CINE, TEAT character actor *m,* character actress *f*
caracterizar <*z→c*> I. *vt* **1.** (*marcar*) to characterize **2.** (*describir*) to describe **3.** TEAT to play II. *vr:* ~**se 1.** (*destacar*) to be characterized **2.** CINE, TEAT to play a role convincingly
caracú *m* *CSur* GASTR marrow
caradura *mf inf* shameless person
carajillo *m inf: coffee with a dash of brandy*
carajo *m vulg* prick ►**en el quinto** ~ miles away; **irse al** ~ to go to hell; (*estropearse*) to go to the dogs; **al** ~ **con...** to hell with ...; **¡~!** hell!
caramanchel *m* **1.** *Perú* (*cobertizo*) shed **2.** *Chile* (*taberna*) canteen
caramba *interj inf* **¡**(**qué**) ~! (*enfado*) damn!; (*extrañeza*) good heavens!
carámbano *m* icicle
carambola *f* **1.** *inf* (*trampa*) trick **2.** (*en el billar*) cannon; **de** [*o por*] ~ *inf* by pure chance **3.** BOT carambola
caramelo *m* **1.** (*azúcar quemado*) caramel; (**de**) **color** ~ caramel-coloured *Brit,* caramel-colored *Am* **2.** (*golosina*) sweet *Brit,* candy *Am*
carantoña *f* (*zalamería*) piece of flattery; **hacer** ~**s a uno** to butter sb up
caraota *f* *Ven* (*haba*) kidney bean
carapacho *m* **1.** ZOOL (*caparazón*) carapace, shell **2.** *Cuba* GASTR *shellfish cooked in the shell*
caraqueño, -a I. *adj* of/from Caracas II. *m, f* native/inhabitant of Caracas
carátula *f* **1.** (*careta*) mask **2.** *pey* (*farándula*) show-business people **3.** (*portada*) title page; (*de un disco*) album [*o* CD] cover
caravana *f* **1.** (*remolque*) caravan *Brit,* trailer *Am* **2.** (*embotellamiento*) tailback **3.** (*recua*) caravan
carbón *m* coal; ~ **de leña** [*o vegetal*] charcoal; **dibujo al** ~ ARTE charcoal drawing; **papel** ~ carbon paper
carbonato *m* carbonate
carbonera *f* **1.** (*horno*) charcoal kiln **2.** (*almacén*) coal cellar

carbonero, -a I. *adj* coal II. *m, f* 1. (*productor*) charcoal burner 2. (*vendedor*) coal merchant

carbonilla *f* 1. (*polvo de carbón*) coal dust 2. *AmL* (*carboncillo*) charcoal

carbonizar <z→c> I. *vt* 1. (*abrasar*) to char 2. QUÍM to carbonize II. *vr:* ~**se** to carbonize

carbono *m* carbon; **dióxido de** ~ carbon dioxide

carburador *m* TÉC carburettor *Brit,* carburetor *Am*

carburante *m* fuel

carburar I. *vt* to carburet II. *vi inf* (*funcionar*) to work

carburo *m* carbide

carcajada *f* guffaw; **reírse a** ~**s** to roar with laughter; **soltar una** ~ to burst out laughing

carcajear *vi, vr:* ~**se** 1. (*reírse a carcajadas*) to roar with laughter 2. *inf* (*no respetar*) ~**se de algo/alguien** to have a good laugh at sth/sb

carcasa *f* TÉC casing

cárcel *f* prison; ~ **de régimen abierto** open prison; **tres años de** ~ three years imprisonment; **estar en la** ~ to be in prison; **ir a parar a la** ~ to end up in prison

carcelero, -a *m, f* prison officer, jailer

carcinoma *m* MED carcinoma

carcoma *f* 1. ZOOL woodworm 2. (*polvillo*) wood dust (*left by woodworm*) 3. (*destrucción lenta*) slow destruction

carcomer I. *vt* 1. (*corroer*) to eat away [*o* into] 2. (*minar*) to undermine II. *vr:* ~**se** *fig* to decay

carcomido, -a *adj* 1. (*madera*) eaten away 2. *fig* decayed

cardar *vt* 1. (*proceso textil*) to card 2. (*el pelo*) to backcomb

cardenal *m* 1. REL, ZOOL cardinal 2. (*hematoma*) bruise

cárdeno, -a *adj* (*color*) purple; (*res*) black and white; (*agua*) opaline blue

cardiaco, -a *adj,* **cardíaco, -a** *adj* heart; MED cardiac; **ataque** ~ heart attack; **paro** ~ cardiac arrest

cardinal *adj* cardinal; **los cuatro puntos** ~**es** the four cardinal points; **número** ~ LING cardinal number

cardiología *f* MED cardiology

cardiólogo, -a *m, f* MED cardiologist

cardiovascular *adj* MED cardiovascular

cardo *m* 1. BOT thistle 2. *pey, inf* (*desabrido*) prickly character

cardume(n) *m* 1. (*banco de peces*) shoal [*o* school] of fish 2. *CSur, inf* (*abundancia*) great quantity

carear I. *vt* 1. JUR (*confrontar*) to bring face to face 2. (*cotejar*) to compare II. *vr:* ~**se** (*enfrentarse*) to confront; JUR to come face to face

carecer *irr como crecer vi* ~ **de algo** to lack sth; **carece de importancia/de sentido** it's not important/it doesn't make sense; **tu afirmación carece de lógica** your assertion is illogical

carencia *f* 1. (*falta*) lack 2. ECON (*escasez*) shortage, scarcity 3. MED ~ **de algo** deficiency in sth

carente *adj* ~ **de algo** lacking in sth, devoid of sth; ~ **de escrúpulos** unscrupulous; ~ **de interés** uninteresting

careo *m t.* JUR confrontation

carestía *f sin pl* 1. (*escasez*) scarcity 2. ECON (*encarecimiento*) high cost; **la** ~ **de la vida** the high cost of living

careta *f* mask; **quitar la** ~ **a alguien** *t. fig* to unmask sb

carga *f* 1. (*acto*) loading; **permitida** ~ **y descarga** loading and unloading 2. (*cargamento*) load; (*flete*) freight; **animal de** ~ pack animal; **buque de** ~ freighter 3. (*obligación*) obligation; **ser una** ~ **para alguien** to be a burden on sb 4. MIL, FIN charge; ~ **explosiva** exposive charge; ~ **policial** baton charge; **¡a la** ~**!** MIL charge!; ~ **fiscal** [*o* **impositiva**] tax burden

cargado, -a *adj* 1. (*con cargamento*) ~ **con** [*o* **de**] **algo** loaded with sth; (*lleno*) full of sth; ~ **de problemas** laden with problems 2. FÍS, TÉC **la batería está cargada** the battery is charged 3. (*pesado*) heavy; **un ambiente** ~ *fig* a tense atmosphere 4. (*fuerte*) strong; **un café muy** ~ very strong coffee 5. *inf* (*borracho*) drunk

cargador *m* 1. (*oficio*) loader 2. (*en un arma*) chamber

cargamento *m* (*acto*) loading; (*carga*) load, cargo

cargar <g→gu> I. *vi* 1. (*llevar*) ~ **con algo** to carry sth 2. MIL (*atacar*) ~ **contra** [*o* **sobre**] **alguien** to charge at sb 3. (*reposar*) to lie; ARQUIT to rest; ~ **en cuenta a uno** FIN to charge to sb's account II. *vt t.* MIL to load; ~ **las tintas** *fig* to lay it on thick 2. (*achacar*) to attribute; ~ **a alguien con las culpas** to put the blame on sb 3. FIN (*en una cuenta*) to charge 4. *inf* (*irritar*) to annoy; **este tipo me carga** this guy is getting on my nerves 5. *inf* (*suspender*) **a Paco le han cargado las mates** Paco has failed in maths 6. INFOR to load 7. *AmL* (*llevar*) to have; **¿cargas dinero?** do you have any money on you? III. *vr:* ~**se** 1. (*llenarse*) ~**se de algo** to fill up with sth 2. *inf* (*romper*) to smash up; **¡te la vas a** ~**!** *fig* you're in for it! 3. *inf* (*matar*) to do in

cargo *m* 1. FIN (*cantidad debida*) charge; ~ **a cuenta** debit; **con** ~ **a nosotros** at our expense 2. (*puesto*) post; **desempeñar un** ~ to hold a position 3. (*responsabilidad*) responsibility; (*deber*) duty; **estoy a** ~ **de las correcciones** I'm responsible for the corrections; ~ **de conciencia** feeling of guilt

carguero *m* NÁUT freighter; (*de contenedores*) container ship

cariar <1. *pres:* caríu> I. *vt* MED to cause to decay II. *vr:* ~**se** MED to decay

caribe I. *adj* 1. *AmL* (*caribeño*) Caribbean 2. *AmL* (*antropófago*) cannibalistic 3. *AmL* (*cruel*) cruel 4. *Ant* (*furioso*) furious II. *m* 1. (*indígena*) Carib 2. *AmL* (*cruel*) savage

Caribe *m* el (**Mar**) ~ the Caribbean (Sea)
caribeño, -a I. *adj* Caribbean II. *m, f* native/
inhabitant of the Caribbean area
caricatura *f* (*dibujo*) caricature, cartoon
caricaturista *mf* caricaturist, cartoonist
caricia *f* caress; **hacer ~s a alguien** to caress
sb
caridad *f* (*amor al prójimo, generosidad*)
charity; (*limosna*) alms *pl;* **hacer obras de ~**
to do works of charity; **¡una limosna, por ~!**
alms!
caries *f inv* MED tooth decay, caries
carillón *m t.* MÚS carillon
carimbo *m Bol* branding iron
Carintia *f* Carinthia
cariño *m* 1. (*afecto*) affection; (*amor*) love;
hacer algo con ~ to do sth lovingly; **sentir ~
por alguien** to be fond of sb 2. (*persona
querida*) **¡~** (**mío**)! (my) dear! 3. (*mimo*)
caress; **hacer ~s** *inf* to caress
cariñoso, -a *adj* ~ **con alguien** affectionate [*o*
tender] towards sb
carioca I. *adj* of/from Rio de Janeiro; (*brasileño*) Brazilian II. *mf* native/inhabitant of
Rio de Janeiro
carisma *m* charisma
caritativo, -a *adj* charitable
cariz *m* 1. (*aspecto*) look; **esto toma buen ~**
this is looking good 2. METEO outlook
carmelito, -a *adj AmL* (*marrón claro*) light
brown
carmesí *adj* crimson
carmín I. *adj* carmine II. *m* 1. (*color*) carmine
2. BOT dog rose 3. (*pintalabios*) (**barra de**) ~
lipstick
carnal *adj* 1. REL carnal; **trato ~** sexual intercourse 2. (*consanguíneo*) full; **somos primos
~es** we're first cousins
carnaval *m* carnival; REL shrovetide
carnaza *f* bait
carne *f* 1. (*del cuerpo, pulpa*) flesh; **echar ~s**
to put on weight; **ser uña y ~** to be inseparable; **los placeres de la ~** the pleasures of the
flesh 2. (*alimento, plato*) meat; ~ **asada** roast
meat; ~ **de cerdo/vacuna** pork/beef; ~
picada mince *Brit,* ground meat *Am* ►**poner
toda la ~ en el** *asador* to risk all; ~ **de gallina** gooseflesh; **ser de ~ y** *hueso* (*auténtico*)
to be real; (*humano*) to be quite human
carné *m* <carnés> identity card; ~ **de estu-
diante/de identidad** student/identity card;
~ **de conducir** driving licence *Brit,* driver's
license *Am*
carneada *f AmL* 1. (*matanza*) slaughter
2. (*matadero*) slaughterhouse
carnear *vt* 1. *CSur* (*matar: un animal*) to
slaughter; (*una persona*) to murder brutally
2. *Chile* (*engañar*) to cheat 3. *Méx* (*apuñalar*)
to stab (to death)
carnero *m* 1. ZOOL ram 2. *CSur* (*débil*) weakling; (*desertor de huelga*) blackleg
carnet *m* <carnets> *v.* **carné**
carnicería *f* 1. (*tienda*) butcher's (shop),

meatshop 2. (*masacre*) massacre
carnicero, -a I. *adj* 1. (*carnívoro*) carnivorous
2. (*sanguinario*) bloodthirsty II. *m, f* butcher
carnitas *fpl AmC* GASTR barbecued pork
carnívoro, -a *adj* carnivorous; **animal ~** carnivore
carnoso, -a *adj* fleshy
caro *adv* dear(ly) *Brit;* **esto nos costará ~** *fig*
this'll cost us dear
caro, -a *adj* (*costoso, querido*) expensive, dear
Brit
carótida *f* ANAT carotid (artery)
carozo *m CSur* stone (*of fruit*)
carpa *f* 1. ZOOL carp 2. (*entoldado gigante*)
marquee; ~ **del circo** big top 3. *AmL* (*tienda
de campaña*) tent 4. *AmL* (*puesto de mercado*) market stall
Cárpatos *mpl* **los** (**Montes**) ~ the Carpa-
thians
carpeta *f* 1. (*portafolios*) folder; ~ **de anillas**
ring binder 2. (*de un disco*) cover, sleeve
3. (*cubierta*) cover
carpincho *m AmL* ZOOL capybara
carpintería *f* carpentry
carpintero, -a *m, f* carpenter; **pájaro ~**
woodpecker
carpir *vt AmL* to hoe
carraca *f* 1. *pey* (*objeto*) piece of junk; (*vehículo*) (old) jalopy 2. (*carcamal*) wreck 3. (*matraca*) ratchet 4. ZOOL blue wrasse
carraspear *vi* to clear one's throat
carraspera *f* hoarseness
carrasposo, -a *adj* 1. (*ronco*) hoarse 2. *Col,
Ecua, Ven* (*áspero*) rough
carrera *f* 1. (*movimiento*) run 2. (*recorrido*)
journey; (*de un astro*) course 3. DEP (*competición*) race; ~ **de armamento** (**nuclear**)
(nuclear) arms race; ~ **de relevos** relay race;
coche de ~s racing car 4. (*profesión*) profession; ~ **profesional** career 5. (*estudios
superiores*) degree course; **persona de ~**
graduate; **hacer una ~** to study 6. (*calle*)
street; *AmL* (*avenida*) avenue; **hacer la ~** *inf*
to be on the game 7. (*en un tejido*) ladder
carreta *f* wagon
carrete *m t.* FOTO, TÉC (*bobina*) spool, reel; ~
de película roll of film
carretera *f* (main) road; ~ **de circunvalación**
ring road *Brit,* bypass *Am,* beltway *Am*
carretilla *f* wheelbarrow
carriel *m Col, inf* (*bolso de bandolera*)
shoulder-bag
carril *m* 1. (*en la carretera*) lane; ~ **de ade-
lantamiento/lento** fast/slow lane 2. *t.* TÉC
(*raíl*) rail
carrilano, -a *m, f Chile* 1. (*ferroviario*) railway worker 2. (*bandolero*) bandit
carrillo *m inf* cheek
carrilludo, -a *adj* chubby-cheeked
carrito *m* (*de supermercado*) trolley *Brit,*
shopping cart *Am*
carro *m* 1. (*vehículo*) cart; ~ **acorazado** [*o*
blindado] armoured [*o* armored *Am*] car; **el**

Carro Mayor/Menor ASTR the Big/Little Dipper; **¡para el ~!** *inf* hold your horses! **2.** *AmL* (*coche*) car **3.** (*de una máquina de escribir*) carriage

carrocería *f* bodywork

carromato *m* (*entoldado*) covered wagon; (*roulotte*) caravan *Brit,* trailer *Am; pey* (*coche*) old banger

carroña *f* carrion

carroza *f* carriage

carruaje *m* carriage; (*de caballos*) coach

carrusel *m* **1.** (*tiovivo*) merry-go-round, carousel *Am* **2.** (*ecuestre*) cavalcade

carta *f* **1.** (*misiva, escrito*) letter; **~ certificada** registered letter; **~s al director** letters to the editor; **~ de porte** bill of lading; **~ de presentación** [*o* **de recomendación**] letter of introduction; **echar una ~** to post [*o* mail *Am*] a letter **2.** *t.* JUR (*documento*) document; **~ credencial** letter of credence; **Carta Magna** Magna Carta; **tomar ~s en un asunto** to intervene in a matter **3.** (*naipes*) card; **jugar a las ~s** to play (at) cards; **echar las ~s a alguien** to tell sb's fortune **4.** GEO (*mapa*) map; **~ astral** ASTR astral chart **5.** (*menú*) menu **6.** TV **~ de ajuste** test card *Brit,* test pattern *Am*

cartabón *m* set square

cartapacio *m* **1.** (*cuaderno*) notebook **2.** (*carpeta*) folder **3.** (*en una mesa*) desk pad

cartearse *vr* to correspond

cartel *m* poster; (*rótulo*) sign; TEAT bill; **prohibido fijar ~es** bill posters will be prosecuted; **tener ~** *fig* to be well-known

cártel *m* ECON cartel

cartelera *f* **1.** (*en el periódico*) entertainment guide; **estar en ~** to be on **2.** (*tablón*) notice board; TEAT, CINE publicity board

cárter *m* **1.** TÉC housing **2.** AUTO sump *Brit,* oil pan *Am*

cartera *f* (*de bolsillo*) wallet; (*de mano*) handbag, purse *Am;* (*de herramientas*) toolbag; (*portafolios*) portfolio; (*escolar*) (school) satchel; **ministro sin ~** POL minister without portfolio; **~ de valores** FIN securities portfolio; **~ de pedidos** ECON order book

carterista *mf* pickpocket

cartero, -a *m, f* postman *m Brit,* postwoman *f Brit,* mailman *m Am,* mailwoman *f Am*

cartílago *m* cartilage

cartilla *f* **1.** (*catón*) first reader **2.** (*cuaderno*) notebook; **~ de ahorros** savings book; **~ sanitaria** health attention card, NHS card *Brit* **3.** *AmL* (*carnet*) identity card

cartografía *f* cartography

cartón *m* **1.** (*material*) cardboard; **caja de ~** cardboard box **2.** (*envase*) carton; **~ de leche** carton of milk; **un ~ de tabaco** a carton of cigarettes **3.** ARTE cartoon **4.** *AmL* (*en periódicos*) cartoon

cartonaje *m* cardboard packaging

cartuchera *f* (*canana*) cartridge belt; (*bolsa*) cartridge clip

cartucho *m* **1.** *t.* MIL cartridge; **~ de tinta** ink cartridge; **~ de fogueo** blank cartridge **2.** (*envoltura: en forma de cucurucho*) cone; (*en forma de tubo*) roll

cartuja *f* Carthusian monastery

cartulina *f* thin cardboard; **~ amarilla** DEP yellow card

casa *f* **1.** (*edificio*) house; **~ adosada** semi-detached house; **~ de campo** country house; **~ de citas** brothel; **venta de ~ en ~** door-to-door selling **2.** (*vivienda*) flat **3.** (*hogar, en un juego*) home; **ir a ~** to go home; **¿vienes a mi ~?** will you come (over) to my place?; **vengo de ~** I'm coming from home; **en ~** at home; **estoy en ~ de Paco** I'm at Paco's (place); **llevar la ~** to run the house; **no parar en ~** to be always on the go; **todo queda en ~** it'll stay in the family **4.** ECON (*empresa*) firm; **~ discográfica** record company; **~ editorial** publishing house **5.** (*estirpe*) **~ real** royal family ▶**echar** [*o* **tirar**] **la ~ por la ventana** *inf* to spare no expense

casabe *m AmL* GASTR cassava bread

casaca *f* (*de hombre*) frock coat; **~ de montar** hacking jacket

casadero, -a *adj* marriageable

casal *m* **1.** AGR (*de labranza*) farmhouse **2.** (*casa solariega*) country house **3.** *AmS* (*pareja*) couple; **un ~ de águilas** a pair of eagles

casamiento *m* **1.** (*matrimonio*) marriage **2.** (*boda*) wedding

casar **I.** *vi* **1.** *elev* (*casarse*) to marry **2.** (*combinar*) to match **II.** *vt* **1.** (*unir en matrimonio*) to marry; **estar** [*o* **ser**] **casado** to be married; **los recién casados** the newlyweds **2.** (*combinar*) to combine; (*piezas*) to join together **3.** JUR (*anular*) to annul **III.** *vr* **~se con alguien** to get married to sb; **~se en** [*o* **por**] **la Iglesia** to get married in church; **~se por lo civil** to get married in a registry office

cascabel *m* (little) bell; **serpiente de ~** rattlesnake ▶**poner el ~ al gato** to bell the cat

cascada *f* waterfall; (*artificial*) cascade

cascado, -a *adj* **1.** (*roto*) broken (down) **2.** (*decrépito*) decrepit **3.** (*voz*) hoarse

cascajo *m* **1.** (*pedazo*) (broken) piece **2.** (*persona*) wreck; (*cosa*) piece of junk; **~s** rubbish **3.** (*gravilla*) piece of gravel

cascanueces *m inv* nutcracker

cascar <c→qu> **I.** *vi* **1.** *inf* (*charlar*) to chatter **2.** *vulg* (*morir*) to kick the bucket **II.** *vt* **1.** (*romper*) to crack; **~ un huevo/una nuez** to crack an egg/a nut **2.** *inf* (*pegar*) to clout **III.** *vr:* **~se 1.** (*romperse*) to crack; (*estropearse*) to break **2.** *inf* (*envejecer*) to get old

cáscara *f* shell; **~ de huevo** eggshell; **~ de limón** lemon peel; **¡~s!** *fig, inf* wow!

cascarón *m* **1.** (*de huevo*) shell **2.** NÁUT cockleshell

cascarrabias *mf inv, inf* cantankerous person, grouch

cascarudo *m Arg* beetle

casco *m* **1.** (*para la cabeza*) helmet; **los ~s**

azules the blue helmets (*members of the U.N. peacekeeping force*) **2.** *inf* (*cabeza*) head; **ligero de** ~**s** featherbrained; **calentarse los** ~**s** to agonize over **3.** (*pezuña*) hoof **4.** (*de un barco*) hull **5.** (*botella*) (empty) bottle **6.** (*centro ciudad*) city centre *Brit,* downtown *Am;* **el** ~ **antiguo** the old part of the city **7.** (*cascote*) piece of rubble **8.** TÉC (*cuerpo*) casing; ~ **de presión** pressure casing **9.** *pl* (*auriculares*) headphones *pl*

cascote *m* piece of rubble; ~**s** rubble

caseína *f* casein

caserío *m* **1.** (*granja*) farmhouse **2.** (*aldea*) hamlet

casero, -a **I.** *adj* **1.** (*hecho en casa*) homemade; **cocina casera** plain [*o* home-style] cooking; **remedio** ~ household remedy **2.** (*hogareño*) home-loving **II.** *m, f* **1.** (*propietario*) landlord *m,* landlady *f* **2.** (*administrador*) caretaker

caseta *f* **1.** (*barraca*) hut; (*de feria*) booth; (*de muestras*) stand; ~ **del perro** kennel, doghouse *Am;* ~ **de tiro** shooting gallery **2.** (*cabina*) cabin

casete[1] *m o f* (*cinta*) cassette; ~ **de vídeo** video cassette

casete[2] *m* **1.** (*aparato*) cassette recorder **2.** (*pletina*) cassette deck

casi *adv* almost; ~ ~ very nearly

casilla *f* **1.** (*caseta*) hut; **sacar a alguien de sus** ~**s** *fig* to drive sb mad **2.** (*en la cuadrícula*) box **3.** (*en un tablero*) square **4.** (*en un casillero*) pigeonhole

casillero *m* set of pigeonholes

casimba *f AmL* (*hoyo*) well; (*manantial*) spring; (*barril*) bucket

casino *m* **1.** (*casa de juego*) casino **2.** (*club*) club

caso *m* **1.** *t.* JUR,LING (*hecho*) case; (*circunstancia*) circumstance; ~ **aislado** isolated case; ~ **de fuerza mayor** case of force majeure; **¡eres un** ~! *inf* you're a right one!; **yo, en tu** ~... if I were you ...; **en** ~ **de** +*infin* in the event of; **dado** [*o* **llegado**] **el** ~ if it comes to it; **dado el** ~ **de que** +*subj* supposing (that); **en** ~ **contrario** otherwise; **en cualquier** ~ in any case; **en ningún** ~ on no account; **en último** ~ as a last resort; **en tal** ~ in such a case; **en todo** ~ in any case **2.** (*atención*) notice; **hacer** ~ **a alguien** (*considerar*) to pay attention to sb; (*obedecer*) to obey sb; (*creer*) to believe sb

caspa *f* dandruff

Caspio *m* (**el**) **Mar** ~ (the) Caspian Sea

caspiroleta *f AmL* GASTR eggnog

casquete *m* **1.** (*casco*) helmet **2.** (*gorrilla*) cap; ~ **polar** polar cap

casquillo *m* **1.** (*de bala*) cartridge case **2.** (*de bombilla*) light fitting

cassette[1] *m o f v.* **casete**[1]

cassette[2] *m v.* **casete**[2]

casta *f* **1.** (*raza*) race; **de** ~ **le viene al galgo** *fig* it runs in the family **2.** (*linaje*) lineage **3.** (*clase social*) caste

castaña *f* **1.** (*fruto*) chestnut; ~**s asadas** roast chestnuts **2.** *inf* (*golpe*) blow; **darse una** ~ to give oneself a knock **3.** *inf* (*bofetada*) slap; (*puñetazo*) thump **4.** *inf* (*borrachera*) drunkenness; **coger una** ~ to get tight **5.** *inf* (*rápido*) **a toda** ~ flat out

castañal *m,* **castañar** *m* chestnut grove

castañetear *vi* **1.** (*dedos*) to snap; **me castañeteaban los dientes de frío** my teeth were chattering with cold **2.** (*tocar las castañuelas*) to play the castanets

castaño *m* chestnut tree

castaño, -a *adj* brown

castañuela *f* castanet

castellano *m* LING (*español*) Spanish; (*variedad*) Castilian

castellano, -a I. *adj* Castilian; **la lengua castellana** the Spanish language **II.** *m, f* Castilian

castellanohablante *adj* Spanish-speaking

castidad *f* chastity; **cinturón de** ~ chastity belt

castigar <g→gu> **I.** *vt* **1.** (*punir*) ~ **por algo** to punish for sth; **¡castigado sin postre!** as a punishment you'll go without dessert! **2.** (*físicamente*) to beat; *fig* to castigate **3.** (*seducir*) to seduce **II.** *vr:* ~**se** to castigate oneself

castigo *m* **1.** (*punición*) punishment **2.** (*aflicción*) affliction

Castilla *f* Castile

Castilla-La Mancha *f* Castile and La Mancha

Castilla-León *f* Castile and León

castillo *m t.* NÁUT (fore)castle; ~ **de arena** sandcastle; ~ **de naipes** house of cards; **hacer** ~**s en el aire** *fig* to build castles in the air

castizo, -a *adj* **1.** (*típico*) typical **2.** (*auténtico*) authentic

casto, -a *adj* chaste

castor *m* beaver

castración *f* **1.** AGR gelding **2.** *t.* MED castration

castrar *vt* **1.** AGR to geld **2.** *t.* MED to castrate

casual *adj* chance; **por un** ~ *inf* by chance

casualidad *f* chance; **de** [*o* **por**] ~ by chance; **¡qué** ~! what a coincidence!; **da la** ~ **que conozco a tu mujer** it so happens that I know your wife

casualmente *adv* by chance

casulla *f* chasuble

cata *f* sampling; ~ **de vinos** wine-tasting

cataclismo *m* cataclysm

catacumbas *fpl* catacombs *pl*

catador(a) *m(f)* **1.** (*catavinos*) taster **2.** (*entendido*) connoisseur

catadura *f* **1.** (*cata*) tasting **2.** (*aspecto*) look(s); **sujeto de mala** ~ nasty-looking character

catalán *m* (*lengua*) Catalan

catalán, -ana *adj, m, f* Catalan, Catalonian

catalejo *m* telescope

catalizador *m* **1.** *t.* QUÍM, TÉC catalyst **2.** AUTO catalytic converter

catalogar <g→gu> *vt* **1.** (*registrar*) to cata-

logue *Brit,* to catalog *Am* **2.** (*clasificar*) to class; ~ **a alguien de algo** to classify sb as sth
catálogo *m* catalogue *Brit,* catalog *Am;* ~ **de materias/por autores** subject/author index; **casa de ventas por** ~ mail-order company; **en** ~ available
Cataluña *f* Catalonia
catamarán *m* DEP catamaran
cataplasma *f* **1.** MED poultice **2.** *inf* (*pesado*) bore
catapulta *f* catapult
catapultar *vt* to catapult
catar *vt* **1.** (*probar*) to taste **2.** (*experimentar*) to experience
catarata *f* **1.** (*salto de agua*) waterfall; **las ~s del Niágara** the Niagara Falls **2.** MED cataract
catarro *m* (*enfriamiento*) cold; MED catarrh; ~ **de nariz** headcold
catarsis *f inv* catharsis
catastro *m* cadastre *Brit,* cadaster *Am;* **oficina del** ~ land registry
catástrofe *f* catastrophe
catastrófico, -a *adj* catastrophic; **zona catastrófica** disaster area
catastrofismo *m* alarmism
catchup *m* <catchups> ketchup
cate *m inf* **1.** (*suspenso*) **me han dado dos ~s** I've failed two subjects **2.** (*bofetada*) whack
catear *vt inf* (*suspender*) to fail, to flunk *Am*
catecismo *m* REL catechism
cátedra *f* **1.** ENS (*púlpito*) lectern **2.** ENS (*docencia*) chair; **sentar** ~ to lay down the law; *irón* to pontificate
catedral *f* cathedral; **como una** ~ *fig* massive; (*alto*) huge
catedrático, -a *m, f* ENS professor; ~ **de instituto** ≈ secondary-school teacher
categoría *f* **1.** *t.* FILOS (*clase*) category; ~ **fiscal** tax bracket **2.** (*calidad*) quality; **de primera** ~ first-class **3.** (*rango*) rank; **dar** ~ to lend prestige; **tener mucha/poca** ~ to be important/unimportant
catequesis *f inv* **1.** REL catechesis **2.** (*clase*) religious instruction
caterva *f pey* load(s); (*de personas*) bunch
catete *m* *Chile* **1.** GASTR pork-broth porridge **2.** (*diablo*) devil
catéter *m* MED catheter
cateto, -a *m, f* yokel
catolicismo *m* REL (Roman) Catholicism
católico, -a *adj, m, f* (Roman) Catholic
catón *m* reader, primer *Am*
catorce *adj inv, m* fourteen; *v.t.* **ocho**
catorceavo, -a, catorzavo, -a *adj, m, f* fourteenth; *v.t.* **octavo**
catre *m t. pey* plank bed; (*de campaña*) camp bed; *inf* (*cama*) bed, sack *inf;* **llevar a alquien al** ~ to lay sb *vulg*
Cáucaso *m* **el** ~ the Caucasus
cauce *m* **1.** GEO (*lecho*) river bed **2.** (*acequia*) irrigation channel **3.** (*camino*) channel, course; ~ **jurídico** [*o* **legal**] JUR legal action; ~ **reglamentario** official channel

cauchal *m AmL* rubber plantation
caucho *m* **1.** (*sustancia*) rubber; **árbol del** ~ rubber tree **2.** *AmL* (*neumático*) tyre *Brit,* tire *Am*
caución *f* **1.** (*cautela*) caution **2.** JUR security
caudal I. *adj* tail II. *m* **1.** (*de agua*) volume **2.** (*dinero*) fortune; **caja de ~es** safe **3.** (*abundancia*) abundance; **un** ~ **de conocimientos** a wealth of knowledge
caudaloso, -a *adj* **1.** (*río*) large **2.** (*rico*) rich **3.** (*cantidad*) abundant
caudillaje *m* **1.** *t.* POL leadership **2.** *Arg, Chile, Perú, pey* (*caciquismo*) bossism
caudillo *m* MIL, POL leader; **el Caudillo** *Franco's nickname during his dictatorship*
caula *f AmL* (*estratagema*) trick
causa *f* **1.** *t.* POL (*origen, ideal*) cause; (*motivo*) reason; **a** [*o* **por**] ~ **de** on account of; **la** ~ **de su despido** the reason for his/her dismissal; **morir por la** ~ to die for the cause **2.** JUR lawsuit; (*proceso*) trial; **entender en una** ~ to handle a case; **instruir una** ~ to initiate legal proceedings *pl*
causante I. *adj* causing II. *mf* originator; (*culpable*) person responsible
causar *vt* to cause; ~ **alegría** to make happy; ~ **daño** to cause damage; ~ **efecto** to have an effect; ~ **problemas** to cause problems; ~ **risa a alguien** to make sb laugh; ~ **trabajo** to make work
causeo *m Chile* GASTR snack
cáustico, -a *adj* caustic
cautela *f* (*precaución*) caution
cauteloso, -a *adj* (*prudente*) cautious
cauterizar <z→c> *vt* MED to cauterize
cautivador(a) *adj* captivating
cautivar *vt* **1.** (*apresar*) to capture **2.** (*fascinar*) to captivate **3.** (*seducir*) to seduce
cautiverio *m,* **cautividad** *f* captivity
cautivo, -a *adj, m, f* captive
cauto, -a *adj* cautious
cava *m* cava

Cava is referred to as the Spanish Champagne. This quality sparkling white wine is produced in champagne cellars in the northeast of Spain.

---

cavar *vi, vt* to dig
caverna *f* **1.** (*cueva*) cave; (*gruta*) cavern; **los hombres de las ~s** cavemen **2.** MED cavern
cavernícola *mf* **1.** (*troglodita*) cave dweller **2.** *inf* (*retrógrado*) reactionary
caviar *m sin pl* caviar
cavidad *f t.* MED cavity
cavilar *vt* ~ **algo** to ponder (on) sth
caviloso, -a *adj* suspicious
cayado *m* **1.** (*del pastor*) crook **2.** (*del prelado*) crozier
caza¹ *f* **1.** (*montería*) hunting; **ir de** [*o* **a la**] ~ to go hunting **2.** (*animales*) game; ~ **mayor** big game; **carne de** ~ game
caza² *m* MIL fighter plane

cazabombardero *m* MIL fighter-bomber
cazador(a) I. *adj* hunting II. *m(f)* (*persona*) hunter *m*, huntress *f*; ~ **furtivo** poacher
cazadora *f* bomber jacket; ~ **de piel** leather jacket
cazadotes *m inv* fortune hunter
cazar <z→c> *vt* 1. (*atrapar*) to hunt; (*perseguir*) to pursue; (*con una trampa*) to trap 2. (*coger*) to catch 3. (*conseguir*) to get 4. (*probar la culpabilidad*) to catch out; (*sorprender*) to surprise 5. *inf* (*engañar*) to take in
cazarrecompensas *mf inv* bounty hunter
cazatalentos *mf* 1. *inv* ECON headhunter 2. CINE, DEP talent spotter *Brit*, talent scout *Am*
cazavirus *adj inv* INFOR anti-virus; **programa** ~ anti-virus programme [*o* program *Am*]
cazo *m* 1. (*puchero*) saucepan 2. (*cucharón*) ladle 3. *inf* (*chulo*) pimp
cazuela *f* casserole
cazurro, -a I. *adj* 1. (*hosco*) sullen 2. (*obstinado*) stubborn 3. (*torpe*) slow-witted 4. (*grosero*) coarse II. *m*, *f* 1. (*hosco*) sullen person 2. (*obstinado*) stubborn person 3. (*patán*) boor
c.c., C.C., c/c *f* 1. COM *abr de* **cuenta corriente** C/A 2. ELEC *abr de* **corriente continua** D.C.
CC.OO. *fpl abr de* **Comisiones Obreras** *Spanish communist federation of trade unions*
CE¹ *f* HIST *abr de* **Comunidad Europea** EC
CE² *m abr de* **Consejo de Europa** Council of Europe
ceba *f* 1. (*engorde*) fattening 2. (*alimento*) feed 3. (*de un horno*) stoking
cebada *f* barley
cebar I. *vt* 1. (*engordar*) to fatten (up) 2. (*horno*) to stoke (up) 3. (*un arma*) to prime 4. (*el anzuelo, una trampa*) to bait 5. (*máquina*) to start; (*cohete*) to fire 6. (*esperanza*) to nourish; (*cólera*) to inflame II. *vr*: ~**se** 1. (*entregarse*) ~**se en algo** to devote oneself to sth 2. (*ira*) to vent one's anger; **se cebó en él** he/she vented his/her anger on him 3. (*alimentarse*) to feed
cebiche *m AmS* GASTR ceviche (*dish of raw fish marinated in lemon juice*)
cebo *m* 1. (*alimento*) feed 2. (*de un anzuelo*) bait; *t. fig* lure 3. (*en un arma*) primer 4. (*en un horno*) fuel
cebolla *f* 1. BOT (*comestible*) onion 2. BOT (*bulbo*) bulb 3. *inf* (*cabeza*) head
cebollar *m* field of onions
cebolleta *f* 1. BOT (*cebolla tierna*) spring onion *Brit*, scallion *Am* 2. BOT (*tallo fino, muy aromático*) chive 3. *vulg* (*pene*) prick
cebra *f* zebra; **paso de** ~ AUTO zebra crossing *Brit*, crosswalk *Am*
cebú *m* zebu
cecear *vi* to pronounce the Spanish 's' as 'z'
ceceo *m* 1. (*en algunas regiones*) pronunciation of the Spanish 's' as 'z' 2. (*defecto*) lisp

In certain regions, for example in certain areas of Andalusia, the Spanish 's' is pronounced as a 'z'. This linguistic phenomenon is referred to as **ceceo**, e.g. 'cocer' instead of 'coser'.

cedazo *m* 1. (*para cribar*) sieve 2. (*para pescar*) large net
ceder I. *vi* 1. (*renunciar*) to renounce; (*de una pretensión*) to give up 2. (*disminuir*) to diminish; **cedió la fiebre** the fever went down; **cedió la lluvia** the rain eased off 3. (*capitular*) ~ **a algo** to give in to sth 4. (*cuerda, rama, puente*) to give way; (*cuero*) to give II. *vt* 1. (*dar*) to hand over 2. (*transferir*) to transfer 3. DEP (*balón*) to pass 4. AUTO **"ceda el paso"** "give way" *Brit*, "yield" *Am*
cedro *m* cedar
cedrón *m AmS* BOT lemon verbena
cédula *f* certificate; ~ **de ahorro** savings certificate; ~ **de cambio** bill of exchange; ~ **de citación** summons; ~ **personal** identity card; ~ **real** royal charter
CEE *f* HIST *abr de* **Comunidad Económica Europea** EEC
céfiro *m* zephyr, west wind
cegar *irr como fregar* I. *vi* to go [*o* become] blind II. *vt* 1. (*quitar la vista*) to blind; **le ciega la ira** he/she is blinded by rage 2. (*ventana*) to wall up; (*con clavos*) to nail up; (*pozo*) to fill up III. *vr*: ~**se** 1. (*ofuscarse*) to be blinded; ~**se de ira** to be blinded by rage 2. (*tubo*) to get blocked up
cegatón, -ona *pey* I. *adj inf* (*corto de vista*) near-sighted II. *m*, *f inf* poor-sighted person
ceguera *f t. fig* blindness
Ceilán *m* Ceylon
ceja *f* 1. (*entrecejo*) eyebrow; **fruncir las** ~**s** to knit one's eyebrows; **tener a alguien entre** ~ **y** ~ *inf* to have it in for sb 2. (*borde*) rim 3. MÚS (*instrumento de cuerda*) nut; (*instrumento de teclado*) pressure bar 4. MÚS (*para elevar el tono*) capo
cejar *vi* 1. (*en discusiones*) to climb down 2. (*cesar*) to give up; **sin** ~ unceasingly
cejijunto, -a *adj* 1. (*fisonomía*) having eyebrows that meet (in the middle) 2. (*adusto*) severe
celada *f* 1. (*yelmo*) helmet 2. (*emboscada*) ambush 3. (*trampa*) trap
celador(a) *m(f)* watchman; (*de aparcamientos*) parking attendant; (*de cárcel*) prison warden *Brit*, prison guard *Am*; (*de escuela*) monitor
celaje *m* 1. METEO cloudy sky 2. *AmL* (*fantasma*) ghost
celar *vt* (*vigilar*) to keep a watchful eye on
celda *f* (*pequeño espacio, de colmena*) cell; (*en prisión*) prison cell; ~ **de castigo** solitary confinement; ~ **acolchada** padded cell
celdilla *f* 1. (*de colmena*) cell 2. ARQUIT niche 3. BOT seed capsule
celebérrimo, -a *adj superl de* **célebre**

celebración f 1.(acto, festividad) celebration; **la ~ de una misa** the celebration of a Mass 2.(aplausos) applause 3.(organización) holding
celebrar I. vt 1.(mérito, acontecimiento) to celebrate 2.(reuniones) to hold; **~ una subasta** to hold an auction 3.(alegrarse) to be delighted 4.(aplaudir) to applaud 5.(llegada) to welcome 6.(ventajas) to dwell on 7.(un chiste) to laugh at 8.(tratado) to conclude II. vi REL to celebrate [o to say] Mass III. vr: ~**se** 1.(fiesta) to be celebrated 2.(reunión, partido) to be held
célebre <celebérrimo> adj 1.(famoso) ~ **por algo** famous for sth 2. inf(gracioso) witty
celebridad f 1.(alguien ilustre) celebrity 2.(renombre) fame 3.(festejo) celebration
celeridad f swiftness
celeste adj 1.(célico) celestial; **cuerpos ~s** heavenly bodies 2.(color) sky blue
celestial adj 1.(del cielo) celestial, heavenly; (delicioso) heavenly 2. irón, inf (tonto) silly
celibato m 1. REL celibacy 2.(soltería) single state
célibe I. adj 1. REL celibate 2.(soltero) single II. mf unmarried person
celo m 1.(afán) zeal 2. pl (por amor) jealousy; **tener ~s** to be jealous 3. pl (sospecha) mistrust 4. pl (envidia) envy 5.(ciertos animales de caza: macho) rut; (hembra) heat; **estar en ~** (macho) to be in rut; (hembra) to be on heat 6.(autoadhesivo) adhesive tape Brit, Scotch® tape
celosía f 1.(rejilla) lattice 2.(contraventanas) slatted shutter; (persianas) (Venetian) blinds pl
celoso, -a adj 1.(con fervor) ~ **en algo** zealous in sth 2.(exigente) ~ **de algo** conscientious about sth 3.(con celos) jealous 4.(con envidia) envious 5.(con dudas) distrustful
celta I. adj Celtic II. mf Celt
célula f BIO, POL cell; ~ **fotoeléctrica** photoelectric cell
celular adj 1. BIO cellular 2.(cárcel) **prisión ~** solitary confinement; **coche ~** police van
celulitis f inv MED cellulitis
cementar vt TÉC to cement
cementerio m 1.(camposanto) cemetery; ~ **de coches** used-car scrapyard 2.(depósito) dump; ~ **nuclear** nuclear waste dump
cemento m ARQUIT, ANAT cement; ~ **armado** reinforced concrete
cena f supper; **la Última Cena** the Last Supper
cenáculo m 1.(tertulia) group; (reunión) meeting 2.(de literatura) literary group 3.(camarilla) clique 4. REL cenacle
cenador m 1.(comedor) dining room 2.(en el jardín) arbour Brit, arbor Am
cenaduría f Méx eating house (serving only at night)
cenagal m 1.(con cieno) bog 2. inf (problema) mess; **estar en un ~** to be in a fix

cenagoso, -a adj boggy
cenar I. vi to have supper [o dinner]; **hoy hemos cenado lentejas** we had lentils for supper [o dinner] today II. vt to have for supper [o dinner]
cencerrear vi 1.(con cencerros) to ring 2.(tocar mal) to play badly 3.(bisagras) to creak 4.(traquetear) to rattle; (golpetear) to knock; (estruendo) to make a noise
cencerro m (de res) cowbell; **estar como un ~** inf to be crazy
cenefa f 1.(adorno) border; (encaje de bolillos) pillow lace 2.(de techos, muros) frieze
cenicero m ashtray
cenicienta f, **Cenicienta** f Cinderella
ceniciento, -a adj ash-coloured [o colored Am]
cenit m zenith
ceniza f 1.(residuo de algo quemado) ash; **Miércoles de Ceniza** Ash Wednesday; **reducir algo a ~s** to reduce sth to ashes 2. pl (restos mortales) ashes pl
cenizo m 1. BOT goosefoot 2.(que trae mala suerte) jinx
cenobio m REL (monjes) monastery; (monjas) convent
censar I. vi to carry out a census II. vt to take a census of
censo m 1.(de habitantes, estadística) census; ~ **electoral** POL electoral roll 2. FIN (gravamen: sobre una finca) ground rent
censor(a) m(f) censor
censura f 1.(crítica) censorship; ~ **cinematográfica** film censorship; **someter a la ~** to censor 2.(entidad) censor's office 3. FIN ~ **de cuentas** auditing 4. POL **moción de ~** motion of censure 5.(vituperación) condemnation
censurar vt 1.(juzgar) to censure; **on todas las escenas violentas** all the violent scenes were taken out 2.(vituperar) to condemn
centauro m centaur
centavo m 1.(centésima parte) hundredth (part) 2.(del dólar) cent, penny Am 3. AmC, CSur FIN (moneda) centavo
centavo, -a adj hundredth; v.t. octavo
centella f 1.(rayo) flash of lightning 2.(chispa) spark 3.(destello) sparkle
centell(e)ar vi 1.(relámpago) to flash 2.(fuego) to spark 3.(estrella) to twinkle 4.(ojos, gema) to glitter
centelleo m 1.(del relámpago) flashing 2.(de las llamas) sparking 3.(de las estrellas) twinkling 4.(de los ojos, de una gema) glittering
centena f hundred
centenar m 1.(cien) hundred 2. AGR rye field
centenario m centenary Brit, centennial Am
centenario, -a adj, m, f centenarian
centeno m rye
centésimo m Chile, Pan, Urug FIN (moneda) centesimo
centésimo, -a I. adj (parte, numeración) hundredth; **la centésima parte de...** a hun-

dredth of ... **II.** *m, f* hundredth (part)
centígrado *m* centigrade; **grado** ~ degree centigrade
centigramo *m* centigram, centigramme *Brit*
centilitro *m* centilitre *Brit,* centiliter *Am*
centímetro *m* centimetre *Brit,* centimeter *Am*
céntimo I. *adj* hundredth **II.** *m* **1.** (*centésima parte*) hundredth part **2.** FIN (*moneda española*) hundredth part of a peseta; *CRi, Par, Ven* centimo; ~ **de euro** eurocent; **estar sin un** ~ to be broke
centinela *mf* **1.** (*de museo, banco*) guard **2.** MIL sentry
centollo *m* spider crab
centrado, -a *adj* **1.** (*en el centro*) centred *Brit,* centered *Am* **2.** (*forma de ser*) stable
central I. *adj* central; **Europa Central** Central Europe; **comité** ~ central committee; **estación** ~ main station **II.** *f* **1.** (*oficina*) head office; ~ **de Correos** general [*o* main] post office; ~ **telefónica** TEL telephone exchange; (*de una empresa*) (telephone) switchboard **2.** TÉC plant; ~ **depuradora** waterworks; ~ **eléctrica** electric power station; ~ **hidroeléctrica** hydroelectric power station; ~ **nuclear** nuclear power station; ~ **térmica** oil-fired power station
centralismo *m* POL centralism
centralista I. *adj* POL centralist **II.** *mf* **1.** POL advocate of centralism **2.** *AmC, Ant* (*del ingenio azucarero*) sugar-mill owner
centralita *f* TEL switchboard
centralización *f* centralization
centralizar <z→c> *vt* to centralize
centrar I. *vt* **1.** TÉC (*colocar*) to centre *Brit,* to center *Am* **2.** (*aunar esfuerzos*) to concentrate **3.** (*interés, atención*) to focus **II.** *vi, vt* DEP (*fútbol*) to centre *Brit,* to center *Am* **III.** *vr:* ~**se 1.** (*basarse*) to centre *Brit,* to center *Am* **2.** (*familiarizarse*) ~**se en algo** to get to know sth; (*en un trabajo*) to settle (down) to sth **3.** (*interés, atención, miradas*) to focus
céntrico, -a *adj t.* TÉC central; **punto** ~ focal point; **piso** ~ an apartment in the centre of town
centrifugación *f* **programa de** ~ spin-drying programme, program *Am*
centrifugadora *f* spin-dryer; TÉC centrifuge
centrifugar <g→gu> *vt* to spin-dry; TÉC to centrifuge
centrífugo, -a *adj* centrifugal; **fuerza centrífuga** centrifugal force
centrismo *m* POL centrism
centrista I. *adj* POL centrist; **partido** ~ centrist party **II.** *mf* POL centrist
centro *m* **1.** *t.* POL, DEP (*el medio*) centre *Brit,* center *Am;* (*de la ciudad*) town centre *Brit,* downtown *Am;* ~ **de gravedad** centre [*o* center *Am*] of gravity; ~ **industrial** industrial centre [*o* center *Am*] **2.** (*institución*) centre *Brit,* center *Am;* ~ **de computación** computer centre [*o* center *Am*]; ~ **de enseñanza** teach-

ing institution; ~ **comercial** shopping centre [*o* center *Am*], mall *Am* **3.** ANAT ~ **nervioso** nerve centre [*o* center *Am*]
centroafricano, -a *adj, m, f* Central African
Centroamérica *f* Central America
centroamericano, -a *adj, m, f* Central American
centrocampista *mf* DEP midfielder
Centroeuropa *f* Central Europe
centuplicar <c→qu> *vt* to increase a hundredfold
céntuplo *m* hundredfold
centuria *f* elev century
centurión *m* HIST centurion
ceñido, -a *adj* **1.** (*vestido*) tight-fitting, figure-hugging **2.** (*forma de expresión*) sparing
ceñir *irr* **I.** *vt* **1.** *t.* MIL (*rodear*) to surround **2.** (*ponerse*) to put on; (*cinturón*) to buckle on **3.** (*acortar*) to shorten **4.** (*abreviar*) to shorten **II.** *vr:* ~**se 1.** (*ajustarse*) to limit oneself; (*al hablar*) to be brief; ~**se al presupuesto** to keep to the budget **2.** (*vestido*) to be close-fitting **3.** (*ponerse*) to put on; **se ciñó el cinturón** he/she buckled on his/her belt
ceño *m* frown; **fruncir** [*o* arrugar] **el** ~, **mirar con** ~ (*disgustado, enojado*) to frown
ceñudo, -a *adj* **1.** (*mirada*) grim **2.** (*persona: disgustada*) frowning
cepa *f* **1.** *t.* BOT (*tronco*) stump; (*en la vid, origen*) stock; **de pura** ~ real **2.** MED strain
cepillar I. *vt* **1.** (*cabello, traje*) to brush **2.** TÉC (*madera*) to plane **3.** *inf* (*robar*) to rip off **4.** *AmL, inf* (*adular*) to butter up **5.** *inf* (*ganar*) to win **6.** (*suspender*) to fail, to flunk *Am* **II.** *vr:* ~**se 1.** *inf* (*robar*) to rip off **2.** *inf* (*devorar*) to polish off **3.** *inf* (*gastarse dinero*) to squander **4.** *inf* (*matar*) to bump off **5.** *vulg* (*seducir*) to make it with; ~**se a una chica** to screw a girl
cepillo *m* **1.** (*para el cabello*) brush; (*para un traje*) clothes brush; (*de limpiar*) scrubbing brush; ~ **de barrer** broom; ~ **de dientes** toothbrush; **pasar el** ~ to brush **2.** TÉC (*para madera*) plane **3.** (*en misa*) collection box
cepo *m* **1.** (*caza*) trap; **caer en el** ~ to fall into the trap **2.** (*grilletes*) stocks *pl* **3.** *pl* AUTO wheel clamp
ceporro, -a I. *adj inf* (*ignorante*) dim-witted **II.** *m, f inf* dimwit; **dormir como un** ~ to sleep like a log
cera *f* wax; (*de vela*) candle-wax; ~ **de los oídos** earwax; ~ **para suelos** wax polish; **museo de** ~ wax museum; **blanco como la** ~ white as a sheet
cerámica *f* ceramics *pl*
ceramista *mf* potter
cerbatana *f* blowpipe *Brit,* blowgun *Am*
cerca I. *adv* **1.** (*en el espacio*) near; **aquí** ~ near here; **mirar de** ~ to look closely at **2.** (*en el tiempo*) close **II.** *prep* **1.** (*lugar*) ~ **de** near **2.** (*cantidad*) about **III.** *f* fence
cercado *m* **1.** (*valla*) fence **2.** (*recinto*) enclosure
cercanía *f* **1.** (*proximidad*) closeness; (*vecin-*

dad) neighbourhood *Brit*, neighborhood *Am*
2. *pl* (*alrededores*) outskirts *pl*
cercano, -a *adj* near
cercar <c→qu> *vt* **1.** (*vallar*) to fence in;
(*rodear*) to enclose **2.** (*rodear*) to surround
3. MIL (*sitiar*) to besiege; (*rodear*) to encircle
cercenar *vt* **1.** (*mutilar*) to cut off **2.** MED
(*miembro*) to amputate **3.** (*sueldo*) to cut
(back)
cerciorar I. *vt* to convince **II.** *vr:* ~**se** to make
sure
cerco *m* **1.** (*círculo*) circle; (*anillo*) ring;
(*borde*) rim **2.** (*valla*) fence **3.** (*de barril*) hoop
4. ASTR, METEO halo **5.** MIL siege
cerda *f* **1.** ZOOL sow **2.** (*pelo*) bristle; ~ **de
cerdo** pigs bristle
cerdada *f pey* dirty trick
Cerdeña *f* Sardinia
cerdo, -a I. *adj* (*sucio*) dirty **II.** *m*, *f* **1.** ZOOL
pig; **carne de** ~ pork **2.** (*insulto*) swine
cereales *mpl* cereals *pl*, grain
cerebelo *m* ANAT cerebellum
cerebro *m* **1.** ANAT (*en su totalidad*) brain;
(*parte mayor*) cerebrum **2.** (*inteligencia*)
brains *pl*
ceremonia *f* **1.** (*acto, celebración, misa*) ceremony **2.** (*cortesía*) formality; **sin** ~**s** without
any fuss
ceremonial *adj*, *m* ceremonial
ceremonioso, -a *adj* **1.** (*solemne*) ceremonious; (*formal*) formal **2.** (*persona*) stiff
cereza *f* cherry
cerezo *m* **1.** (*árbol*) cherry tree **2.** (*madera*)
cherry wood
cerilla *f* **1.** (*fósforo*) match **2.** (*vela*) wax taper
3. (*cerumen*) earwax
cerillero *m AmL* (*cajita*) matchbox
cerillo *m* **1.** *Méx* (*fósforo*) match **2.** (*vela*)
wax taper
cerner <e→ie> **I.** *vt* **1.** (*cribar*) to sieve, to
sift **2.** (*observar*) to observe **II.** *vr* ~**se sobre
algo** to hover over sth
cernícalo *m* **1.** ZOOL kestrel **2.** (*persona*) boor
cernir *irr vt* **1.** (*cribar*) to sieve, to sift
2. (*observar*) to observe; (*cielo, horizonte*) to
scan
cero *m* **1.** *t.* MAT (*punto inicial, valor*) zero;
ocho (*grados*) **bajo/sobre** ~ eight below/
above zero; **partir de** ~ to start from scratch
2. *inf* (*coche policía*) police car
cerote *m* **1.** *inf* (*miedo*) panic **2.** TÉC (*cera y
pez*) shoemaker's wax **3.** *AmC, Méx, inf*
(*excremento*) stool; **estar hecho un** ~ to look
a mess
cerrado, -a *adj* **1.** *estar* (*no abierto*) closed;
(*con llave*) locked; **la puerta está cerrada** the
door is closed; **a puerta cerrada** behind
closed doors; **aquí huele a** ~ it smells stuffy in
here **2.** *estar* METEO (*cielo*) overcast **3.** *ser* (*actitud*) reserved **4.** *ser* (*espeso*) thick; (*denso*)
dense; **noche cerrada** dark night **5.** *ser* (*característico*) typical; (*acento*) broad **6.** LING
(*fonética*) closed **7.** *ser* (*curva*) sharp **8.** *ser*

(*lerdo*) thick; ~ **de mollera** *inf* very dense
cerradura *f* **1.** (*dispositivo*) lock; ~ **antirrobo**
steering(-wheel) lock **2.** (*acción*) closing; (*con
llave*) locking
cerrajería *f* **1.** (*taller*) locksmith's (shop)
2. (*oficio*) locksmith's craft
cerrajero, -a *m*, *f* locksmith
cerramiento *m* **1.** (*acción*) closing **2.** (*alrededor*) enclosure
cerrar <e→ie> **I.** *vt* **1.** (*paraguas, ojos*) to
close; (*carta*) to seal; ~ **los oídos** to turn a deaf
ear; ~ **el pico** *inf* to keep one's trap shut; ~
archivo INFOR to close a file **2.** (*con llave*) to
lock **3.** (*carretera, puerto, establecimiento*) to
close; ~ **el paso a alguien** to bar sb's way
4. (*agujero, brecha*) to block (up); (*agua*) to
turn off **5.** (*terreno*) to close off; (*con un
cerco*) to enclose **6.** (*actividad, ciclo, negociación*) to conclude **II.** *vi* **1.** (*puerta, ventana*) to
close **2.** (*acabar*) to end **3.** (*atacar*) ~ **contra
alguien** to attack sb **III.** *vr:* ~**se 1.** (*puerta*) **la
puerta se cerró sola** the door closed by itself
2. (*herida*) to heal (up) **3.** (*obstinarse*) to persist **4.** (*el cielo*) to become overcast **5.** (*ser
intransigente*) to close one's mind **6.** (*agruparse*) to crowd together
cerrazón *f* **1.** (*torpeza*) dimness **2.** (*obstinación*) stubbornness **3.** METEO (*nubes*) storm
clouds
cerril *adj* **1.** (*terreno*) rough **2.** (*obstinado*)
obstinate **3.** (*torpe*) dense **4.** (*tosco*) uncouth
5. (*caballerías*) wild
cerrilismo *m* **1.** (*tosquedad*) uncouthness
2. (*obstinación*) obstinacy
cerro *m* **1.** (*colina*) hill; (*peñasco*) crag; **irse
por los** ~**s de Úbeda** *inf* to go off on a tangent; (*decir tonterías*) to talk (a lot of) rubbish
2. ZOOL (*cuello*) neck; (*espinazo*) back
cerrojazo *m inf* **echar** ~ **a algo** to slam sth
shut; *fig* to put an end to sth
cerrojo *m* bolt; **echar el** ~ **a la puerta** to bolt
the door
certamen *m* competition
certero, -a *adj* **1.** (*acertado*) accurate **2.** (*diestro en tirar: tirador*) crack **3.** (*informado*) well-
informed
certeza *f* certainty
certidumbre *f* certainty
certificación *f* **1.** (*acción, documento*) certification **2.** JUR (*atestación*) attestation
certificado *m* certificate; ~ **de aptitud** testimonial; ~ **de asistencia** certificate of attendance; ~ **escolar** school report; ~ **médico**
medical certificate
certificado, -a *adj* **1.** JUR certified **2.** (*correos*)
registered; **carta certificada** registered letter
certificar <c→qu> *vt* **1.** *t.* JUR (*afirmar*) to
certify **2.** (*correos*) to register
certísimo, -a *adj superl de* **cierto**
cerumen *m* earwax
cervato *m* fawn
cervecería *f* **1.** (*bar*) pub *Brit*, bar **2.** (*fábrica*)
brewery

cervecero *m* brewer

cervecero, -a *adj* beer; (*industria*) brewing

cerveza *f* beer; ~ **de barril** draught beer; ~ **negra** dark beer, stout; ~ **rubia** lager beer

cervical *adj* **1.** ANAT neck **2.** MED cervical

Cervino *m* **el Monte** ~ the Matterhorn

cerviz *f* ANAT nape of the neck

cesación *f,* **cesamiento** *m* cessation; ~ **del fuego** ceasefire

cesante **I.** *adj* **1.** (*suspendido*) suspended **2.** (*parado*) unemployed **II.** *mf* laid-off civil servants

cesantía *f* **1.** (*situación*) redundancy; (*paro*) unemployment **2.** (*suspensión*) suspension **3.** (*paga*) severance pay

cesar **I.** *vi* **1.** (*parar*) to stop; **sin** ~ ceaselessly **2.** (*en una profesión*) ~ **en algo** to leave sth **II.** *vt* **1.** (*pagos*) to stop **2.** (*despedir*) to dismiss; (*funcionario*) to dismiss

cesárea *f* caesarean

cese *m* **1.** (*que termina*) cessation; (*interrupción*) suspension; ~ **de pagos** suspension of payments, temporary receivership *Brit* **2.** (*de obrero*) sacking; (*de funcionario*) dismisaal; ~ **en el cargo** to retire from office **3.** JUR (*proceso*) abandonment

cesio *m* caesium *Brit,* cesium *Am*

cesión *f* **1.** (*entrega*) transfer **2.** JUR cession

césped *m* grass; '**prohibido pisar el ~**' 'keep off the grass'

cesta *f* basket

cestería *f* **1.** (*tienda*) basketwork shop **2.** (*artesanía*) basketwork **3.** (*artículos*) basketwork articles

cestero, -a *m, f* **1.** (*que fabrica*) basketmaker **2.** (*que vende*) basket seller

cesto *m t.* DEP basket; ~ **de los papeles** wastepaper basket, wastebasket *Am*

cesura *f* caesura

ceta *f* Z

cetáceo *m* cetacean

cetrería *f* falconry

cetrino, -a *adj* **1.** (*amarillento, verdoso*) greenish-yellow **2.** (*melancólico*) melancholy

cetro *m* **1.** (*vara*) sceptre *Brit,* scepter *Am;* **empuñar el** ~ *elev* to ascend the throne **2.** (*supremacía*) rule **3.** DEP championship; **ostentar el** ~ to reign supreme

ceutí **I.** *adj* of/from Ceuta **II.** *mf* native/inhabitant of Ceuta

cf. *abr de* **compárese** cf.

chabacanería *f* vulgarity

chabacano, -a *adj* vulgar

chabola *f* **1.** (*casucha*) shack **2.** *pl* (*barrio*) shanty town

chabolismo *m* shanty-town conditions *pl,* slums *pl*

chacal *m* jackal

chacalín *m AmC* ZOOL shrimp

chácara *f Par, Nic, Bol* **1.** (*granja*) small farm **2.** MED ulcer

chacarero, -a *m, f AmL* farmer; (*trabajador*) farm labourer

chacha *f inf* (*niñera*) nursemaid; (*criada*) maid; (*de limpieza*) cleaning lady

cháchara *f inf* (*charla*) chatter; **andar** [*o* **estar**] **de** ~ to have a chat

chacharear *vi inf* to chatter

chacho, -a *m, f inf* (*muchacho, muchacha*) boy *m,* girl *f*

chacolotear *vi* to clatter

chacota *f* **1.** (*jolgorio*) merriment **2.** (*broma*) joke; **echar** [*o* **tomar**] **algo a** ~ to take sth as a joke

chacotearse *vr* ~ **de algo/alguien** to make fun of sth/sb

chacra *f AmL* (*granja*) small farm; (*finca*) country estate

Chad *m* Chad

chafar **I.** *vt* **1.** (*aplastar*) to flatten *fig,* to squelch; (*arrugar*) to crease; (*deshacer*) to mess up **2.** (*confundir*) to confuse; **quedar(se)** **chafado** to be speechless **3.** (*estropear*) to spoil; **le ~on sus proyectos** they spoiled his/her plans **II.** *vr:* ~**se** (*aplastarse*) to be flattened; (*deshacerse*) to be messed up; (*arrugarse*) to be creased

chafarrinón *m* **1.** (*mancha*) spot **2.** (*cuadro*) daub

chaflán *m* **1.** (*bisel*) bevel (edge) **2.** (*en una calle*) street corner; (*en un edificio*) house corner

chagra *mf Ecua* (*labriego*) peasant

cháguar *m AmS* BOT caraguata, Paraguayan sisal

chal *m* shawl

chalado, -a **I.** *adj inf* crazy; **estar** ~ **por alguien** to be crazy about sb **II.** *m, f inf* nutcase

chaladura *f inf* **1.** (*locura*) (piece of) madness **2.** (*enamoramiento*) infatuation

chalanear **I.** *vi* **1.** (*traficar*) to deal **2.** (*regatear*) to haggle (over) **II.** *vt AmL* (*un caballo*) to break in; (*adiestrar*) to train

chalar **I.** *vt inf* to drive crazy **II.** *vr:* ~**se** *inf* to go crazy; ~**se por alguien** to be crazy about sb

chalé *m* (*casa unifamiliar*) detached family home; (*de campo*) country house; (*villa*) chalet

chaleco *m* waistcoat *Brit,* vest *Am;* ~ **salvavidas** life jacket

chalina *f* **1.** (*pañuelo*) scarf **2.** *Arg, Col, CRi* (*chal*) narrow shawl

chalupa *f* NÁUT launch

chamaco, -a *m, f Cuba, Méx* **1.** (*muchacho*) boy; (*muchacha*) girl **2.** (*novio*) boyfriend; (*novia*) girlfriend

chamagoso, -a *adj Méx* (*mugriento*) filthy

chamaril(l)ero, -a *m, f* **1.** (*que vende objetos viejos*) secondhand dealer **2.** (*tahúr*) cardsharp

chambelán *m* chamberlain

chambón, -ona *adj inf* **1.** (*afortunado*) lucky **2.** (*descuidado*) slovenly

chamborote *adj Ecua* **1.** (*de nariz larga*) long-nosed **2.** (*loc*) **pimiento** ~ long white pepper

chamico *m AmL* BOT thorn apple
chamiza *f* **1.** (*planta*) thatch **2.** (*leña*) brushwood
chamizo *m* **1.** (*árbol*) charred tree; (*leño*) charred log **2.** (*choza*) thatched hut **3.** *pey* (*vivienda*) shack
champán *m*, **champaña** *m* champagne
Champaña *f* Champagne
champiñón *m* mushroom
champú *m* shampoo; ~ **anticaspa** anti-dandruff shampoo
chamuscado, -a *adj* **1.** (*quemado*) scorched **2.** *inf* (*receloso*) suspicious **3.** *inf* (*amoscado*) cross
chamuscar <c→qu> **I.** *vt* (*quemar*) to scorch; (*aves*) to singe **II.** *vr:* ~**se 1.** (*quemarse*) to get scorched **2.** *inf* (*ponerse receloso*) to become suspicious **3.** *inf* (*amoscarse*) to go into a huff
chamusquina *f* (*quemadura*) scorching; (*de aves*) singeing; **esto huele a** ~ *inf* (*sospechoso*) this smells fishy; (*peligroso*) there's trouble in store
chance *m o f AmC* (*oportunidad*) chance
chancear **I.** *vi* to joke **II.** *vr:* ~**se** to make fun
chancero, -a *adj* joking
chanchería *f AmL* pork butcher's shop
chanchero, -a *m, f* pork butcher
chancho *m AmL* pig
chancho, -a *adj AmL* **1.** (*marrano*) dirty **2.** (*desaseado*) slovenly
chanchullo *m inf* swindle, fiddle
chancla *f* **1.** (*zapato viejo*) old shoe **2.** (*zapatilla*) slipper **3.** (*de playa*) flip flop
chancleta *f* **1.** (*chinela*) slipper **2.** *AmL* (*bebé*) baby girl **3.** *inf* (*persona inepta*) fool **4.** *AmL, pey* (*mujer*) slut
chanclo *m* **1.** (*zueco*) clog **2.** (*zapato de goma*) (rubber) overshoe, galosh
chándal *m* <chándals> tracksuit
changa *f* **1.** *inf* (*trato*) (unimportant) business deal **2.** *Arg* (*ocupación*) trade **3.** *AmS* (*transporte*) portering **4.** *AmS, Cuba* (*broma*) joke
changador *m* **1.** *AmS* (*cargador*) carrier **2.** *Arg* (*temporero*) casual worker
changar <g→gu> *vt* (*romper*) to break; (*descomponer*) to split up; (*destrozar*) to destroy
chanta *mf Arg, inf* (*impostor*) fraud
chantaje *m* blackmail
chantajear *vt* to blackmail
chantajista *mf* blackmailer
chantar *vt* **1.** (*poste*) to drive in **2.** *inf* (*vestir*) to put on; ~ **el abrigo a alguien** to help sb on with his/her coat **3.** (*verdad, impertinencia*) **se lo he chantado** I told it to him/her straight to his/her face **4.** *Chile* (*golpe*) to deal
chanza *f* joke; **estar de** ~ to be joking
chapa *f* **1.** (*metal*) sheet **2.** (*lámina*) plate; (*de madera*) panel **3.** (*contrachapado*) plywood **4.** (*tapón*) (bottle)cap **5.** (*colorete*) rouge, blusher *Am;* (*chapeta*) flush (in the cheeks) **6.** (*placa*) shield *Brit,* badge *Am* **7.** *AmL* (*cerra-*

dura) lock **8.** *pl* (*juego*) game played with bottlecaps
chapar *vt* **1.** (*con un metal*) to plate; (*con oro*) to gold-plate; (*con madera*) to veneer; (*con baldosines*) to tile; **chapado a la antigua** old-fashioned **2.** (*comentario*) to come out with
chaparra *f* kermes oak
chaparreras *fpl Méx* (*pantalones para montar a caballo*) chaps *pl*
chaparro *m* dwarf oak
chaparro, -a **I.** *adj inf* squat **II.** *m, f inf* shorty
chaparrón *m* **1.** (*lluvia fuerte*) downpour; (*chubasco*) cloudburst **2.** *inf* (*cantidad grande*) barrage
chapeado *m* **1.** (*de metal*) metal plate; ~ **de oro** gold plate **2.** (*de madera*) veneer **3.** (*de baldosines*) tiling
chapeado, -a *adj* **1.** (*de metal*) metal-plated; (*de oro*) gold-plated **2.** (*de madera*) veneered **3.** (*de baldosines*) tiled
chapear **I.** *vt* **1.** (*con un metal*) to plate; (*con oro*) to gold-plate; (*con madera*) to veneer; (*con baldosines*) to tile **2.** *AmL* (*la tierra*) to weed **II.** *vi* (*chacolotear*) to clatter
chapero *m inf* **1.** (*prostituto*) male prostitute, rent boy *inf* **2.** (*homosexual*) queer
chapetón, -ona **I.** *adj AmL* newly arrived **II.** *m, f AmL* Spaniard in America
chapín, -ina *m, f* Guatemalan
chapisca *f AmC* AGR (*cosecha de maíz*) maize [*o* corn *Am*] harvest
chapista *mf* **1.** (*planchista*) tinsmith **2.** (*de carrocería*) panel beater
chapistería *f* **1.** (*planchistería*) tinsmith's forge **2.** (*de carrocería*) car-body works *pl*
chapitel *m* ARQUIT (*de una torre*) spire; (*de una columna*) capital
chapopote *m Ant, Méx* (*asfalto*) asphalt
chapotear **I.** *vi* (*persona*) to paddle; (*agua*) to splash (around) **II.** *vt* to moisten
chapucear *vt* (*hacer mal y rápido*) to botch
chapucero, -a **I.** *adj* **1.** (*mal y rápido*) shoddy **2.** (*embustero*) deceitful **II.** *m, f* **1.** (*chambón*) bungler **2.** (*embustero*) cheat
chapulín *m* **1.** *AmL* (*langosta*) large cicada **2.** *AmC* (*niño*) child
chapurr(e)ar *vt* **1.** (*idioma*) to speak badly **2.** *inf* (*bebidas*) to mix
chapuza *f* **1.** (*chapucería*) shoddy job **2.** (*trabajo*) odd job
chapuzar <z→c> **I.** *vt* to dive in **II.** *vi, vr:* ~**se** to dive in
chapuzón *m* dip; **darse un** ~ to go for a dip
chaqué *m* morning coat
chaqueta *f* (*cazadora*) jacket; **cambiar de** [*o* **la**] ~ *fig* to change sides
chaquetear *vi* **1.** (*cambiar de ideas*) to change sides **2.** (*acobardarse*) to go back on one's word
chaquetero, -a **I.** *adj* opportunistic **II.** *m, f* POL turncoat
chaquetilla *f* bolero
chaquetón *m* long jacket; (*cazadora*) wind-

cheater *Brit*, windbreaker *Am*

charada *f* charade

charanga *f* 1. (*banda*) brass band 2. *AmL* (*baile*) dance

charca *f* pond

charco *m* puddle, pool

charcón, -ona *adj Arg, Bol, Urug* (*flaco*) skinny

charcutería *f* 1. (*productos*) cooked or cured pork products *pl* 2. (*tienda*) ≈ delicatessen

charla *f* 1. (*conversación*) chat; **estar de** ~ to have a chat 2. (*conferencia*) talk

charlar *vi* 1. (*conversar*) to chat 2. (*parlotear*) to chatter

charlatán, -ana I. *adj* talkative II. *m, f* 1. (*hablador*) chatterbox 2. (*chismoso*) gossip 3. (*vendedor*) hawker 4. (*curandero*) charlatan

charlatanería *f* 1. (*locuacidad*) talkativeness 2. (*palabrería*) sales talk 3. (*curanderismo*) charlatanism

charnela *f* hinge

charol *m* 1. (*barniz*) varnish 2. (*cuero*) patent leather 3. *AmL* (*bandeja*) tray

charqui *m AmS* (*charque*) beef jerky

charrán *m* rascal

charretera *f* 1. (*insignia*) epaulette 2. (*liga*) garter

charro, -a I. *adj* 1. (*salmantino*) Salamancan 2. *pey* (*rústico*) rustic; (*habla*) coarse 3. (*de mal gusto*) in bad taste; (*chillón*) flashy II. *m, f* 1. (*persona*) native/inhabitant of Salamanca 2. *pey* (*tosco*) boor

chárter *adj inv* charter; **vuelo** ~ charter flight

chasca *f* 1. (*ramaje*) brushwood 2. *CSur* (*pelo*) mop of hair

chascar <c→qu> I. *vi* 1. (*con la lengua*) to click; (*con el látigo*) to crack; (*con los dedos*) to snap 2. (*madera*) to creak; (*fuego*) to crackle II. *vt* (*comida*) to gulp down

chascarrillo *m* funny story

chasco *m* 1. (*burla*) joke 2. (*decepción*) disappointment; (*fracaso*) failure

chasco, -a *adj CSur* crinkly

chasis *m inv* 1. AUTO chassis 2. FOTO plateholder

chasque *m AmS* (*mensajero*) Indian messenger

chasquear I. *vt* 1. (*burlar*) to play a trick on 2. (*decepcionar*) to disappoint 3. (*faltar*) to let down II. *vi* 1. (*con la lengua*) to click; (*con el látigo*) to crack; (*con los dedos*) to snap 2. (*madera*) to creak; (*fuego*) to crackle

chasqui *m AmS* (*chasque*) Indian courier

chasquido *m* 1. (*de lengua*) click; (*de látigo*) crack 2. (*de la madera*) creak

chatarra *f* 1. (*metal viejo*) scrap (metal) 2. (*trastos*) junk, lumber *Brit* 3. *inf* (*dinero*) change

chatarrería *f* scrap yard

chatarrero, -a *m, f* scrap merchant

chato, -a I. *adj* 1. (*nariz*) snub 2. (*persona*) snub-nosed 3. (*objeto*) blunt; (*aplastado*) flat-

tened II. *m, f inf* (*tratamiento cariñoso*) kid

chatre *adj Chile, Ecua* (*elegante*) elegantly dressed

chaucha *f AmS* 1. (*judía verde*) green bean 2. (*patata*) new potato 3. *pl* (*calderilla*) small change

chauchera *f Chile, Ecua* (*monedero*) purse

chauvinista I. *adj* chauvinist(ic) II. *mf* chauvinist

chaval(a) *m(f)* 1. *inf* (*chico, chica*) kid; (*joven*) young man *m*, young woman *f* 2. *inf* (*novio*) boyfriend *m*, girlfriend *f*

chaveta *f* 1. (*remache*) rivet 2. (*pasador*) pin; **estar mal de la** ~ *inf* to have a screw loose

che I. *interj AmS* hey II. *f* name of the former spanish letter 'ch'

chécheres *mpl Col, CRi* things *pl*

checo, -a I. *adj* Czech; **República Checa** Czech Republic II. *m, f* Czech

checo(e)slovaco, -a I. *adj* Czechoslovak(ian) II. *m, f* Czechoslovakian

cheli *m* Madrid slang

chelín *m* (*moneda*) shilling

chelista *mf* cellist

chelo *m* cello

chepa *f inf* hump ► **subirse a la** ~ **de alguien** to be disrespectful to sb

cheposo, -a I. *adj* hunchbacked II. *m, f pey, inf* hunchback

cheque *m* cheque, check *Am* ~ **bancario** bank cheque [*o* check *Am*]; ~ **en blanco** blank cheque [*o* check *Am*]; ~ **cruzado** crossed cheque [*o* check *Am*]; ~ **sin fondo** bounced cheque [*o* check *Am*]; ~ **de viaje** traveller's cheque [*o* check *Am*]; **cobrar un** ~ to cash a cheque [*o* check *Am*]; **librar** [*o* **extender**] **un** ~ to make out a cheque [*o* check *Am*]

chequear I. *vt AmL* (*comprobar*) to check II. *vr:* ~**se** to have a checkup

chequeo *m* (*de la salud*) checkup; (*de un mecanismo*) service

chequera *f AmL* cheque book *Brit*, checkbook *Am*

Chequia *f* Czech Republic

chévere I. *adj Ven, inf* terrific, smashing *Brit* II. *mf Cuba, PRico, Ven* braggart

chic I. *adj inv* chic II. *m sin pl* elegance

chica I. *adj* 1. (*pequeña*) small 2. (*joven*) young II. *f* 1. (*niña, tratamiento cariñoso*) girl 2. (*joven*) young woman 3. (*criada*) maid

chicano, -a *m, f* Chicano (*person of Mexican origin living in the USA*)

chicarrón, -ona I. *adj* sturdy II. *m, f* sturdy kid

chicha I. *f* 1. *inf* (*carne*) meat; **tener pocas** ~**s** (*delgado*) to be slim 2. *AmL* GASTR chicha (*alcoholic beverage made from corn, grape, pineapple, etc.*) ► **ni** ~ **ni limonada** neither chalk nor cheese *Brit*, neither fish nor fowl *Am* II. *adj* NÁUT **calma** ~ dead calm

chicharra *f* 1. ZOOL cicada 2. (*juguete*) rattle 3. ELEC buzzer

chicharrón *m* 1. (*carne*) piece of burnt meat

2. *inf* (*persona*) sunburnt person **3.** GASTR crackling (of pork)
chichi I. *adj AmC* (*fácil*) easy II. *m vulg* vagina, pussy *vulg*
chichón *m* bump
chicle *m* chewing gum
chico I. *adj* **1.** (*pequeño*) small **2.** (*joven*) young II. *m* **1.** (*niño, tratamiento cariñoso*) boy **2.** (*joven*) young man **3.** (*para los recados*) errand boy
chicote *m AmL* (*látigo*) whip
chiflado, -a I. *adj inf* crazy; **estar ~ por alguien** to be crazy about sb II. *m, f inf* nutcase
chifladura *f* **1.** (*locura*) craziness; (*empeño*) keenness **2.** (*antojo*) whim
chiflar I. *vt inf* (*gustar*) to be crazy about; **me chiflan las aceitunas** I love olives II. *vr: ~se inf* **1.** (*pirrarse*) **~se por alguien** to be crazy [*o* mad] about sb *Brit* **2.** (*volverse loco*) to go crazy
chiflón *m AmL* (*viento*) gale; (*corriente*) draught *Brit*, draft *Am;* **un ~ de aire** a blast of air
chigüín *m AmC* (*chavalín*) kid
chiíta *adj, mf* Shiite
chile *m* (*especia*) chilli, chili *Am*
Chile *m* Chile

The capital of **Chile** (official title: **República de Chile**) is **Santiago (de Chile)**. Running from north to south, the country is over four thousand kilometres in length with an average width of just one hundred and eighty kilometres. The official language of the country is Spanish and the monetary unit is the **peso chileno**.

---

chileno, -a *adj, m, f* Chilean
chillar *vi* **1.** (*persona*) to yell; **¡no me chilles!** don't shout at me! **2.** (*animal salvaje*) to howl; (*ave, frenos*) to screech **3.** (*puerta*) to creak **4.** (*colores*) to clash **5.** *AmL* (*sollozar*) to sob
chillido *m* **1.** (*de persona*) yell **2.** (*de animal salvaje*) howl; (*de ave, frenos*) screech **3.** (*puerta*) creak **4.** *AmL* (*sollozo*) sob
chillón, -ona I. *adj* **1.** (*persona*) loud **2.** (*voz*) shrill **3.** (*color*) gaudy II. *m, f* loudmouth
chilote *m Méx:* drink made of chilli and pulque
chilpayate *m Méx, inf* (*muchacho*) kid; **los ~s** the kids
chimenea *f* **1.** *t.* GEO (*de un edificio*) chimney **2.** (*hogar*) fireplace
chimpancé *mf* chimpanzee
china *f* **1.** (*piedra*) pebble **2.** *AmL* (*india*) Indian woman; (*mestiza*) half-caste woman **3.** *AmL* (*amante*) mistress
China *f* (la) ~ China
chinchar I. *vt* **1.** *inf* to pester **2.** *inf* (*matar*) to kill II. *vr: ~se inf* to get upset; **¡chínchate!** so there!, tough luck!
chinche¹ *m o f* ZOOL bedbug

chinche² *mf inf* (*pelmazo*) pain
chincheta *f* drawing pin *Brit*, thumbtack *Am*
chinchilla *f* chinchilla
chinchudo, -a *adj Arg, inf* **estar ~** to be angry
chincol *f AmS* ZOOL crown sparrow
chinela *f* slipper
chingado, -a *adj inf* **1.** (*frustrado*) annoyed **2.** (*estropeado*) lousy
chingar <g→gu> I. *vt* **1.** *vulg* (*joder*) to fuck **2.** *inf* (*molestar*) to annoy **3.** *inf* (*bebidas alcohólicas*) to drink II. *vr: ~se inf* **1.** (*emborracharse*) to get plastered **2.** *AmL* (*frustrarse*) to be a washout **3.** *AmL* (*fallar*) to fail
chingo, -a *adj* **1.** *AmC* (*animal sin rabo*) with a cropped tail **2.** *AmC, Ven* (*chato*) flat-nosed **3.** *AmC* (*corto*) short **4.** *CRi* (*desnudo*) naked **5.** *Ven* (*ansioso*) anxious **6.** *Col, Cuba* (*pequeño*) tiny **7.** *Nic* (*bajo*) short
chingue *m Chile* ZOOL skunk
chinita *f* **1.** (*piedrecita*) small stone; **poner ~s a alguien** *fig* to make trouble for sb **2.** *Chile* (*insecto*) ladybird *Brit*, ladybug *Am*
chino *m AmL* (*indio*) Indian; (*mestizo*) mestizo
chino, -a I. *adj* Chinese II. *m, f* Chinese man *m*, Chinese woman *f* ▶**engañar a alguien como a un ~** *inf* to take sb for a ride
chip *m* INFOR chip
chipichipi *m Méx* (*llovizna*) drizzle
Chipre *f* Cyprus
chipriota *adj, mf* Cypriot
chiqueo *m* **1.** *Cuba, Méx* (*mimo*) pampering **2.** *AmC* (*contoneo*) swagger
chiquillada *f* **1.** (*niñería*) childishness **2.** (*travesura*) childish prank
chiquillería *f* kids *pl*
chiquillo, -a I. *adj* young II. *m, f* (*niño*) (small) child; (*chico*) (little) boy; (*chica*) (little) girl
chiquito, -a I. *adj inf* very small II. *m, f inf* kid; **no andarse con chiquitas** (*actuar sin miramiento*) not to beat about the bush
chirigota *f* joke
chirimbolo *m inf* **1.** (*chisme*) thingummyjig **2.** *pl* things *pl*
chirimoya *f* custard apple
chiringuito *m* kiosk (*selling snacks and drinks*)
chiripa *f* **1.** *inf* (*suerte*) stroke of luck; (*casualidad favorable*) fluke **2.** (*en el juego*) lucky break
chirle *adj* **1.** (*soso*) tasteless **2.** *inf* (*sin interés*) dull; (*sin substancia*) wishy-washy
chirlo *m* **1.** (*herida*) gash **2.** (*cicatriz*) scar
chirola *f* **1.** *Arg* (*moneda*) old coin made of nickel **2.** *Chile* (*moneda*) silver 20 centavo coin **3.** *pl, Arg* (*calderilla*) small change
chirona *f inf* jail, clink *inf*
chirriar <*l. pres:* chirrío> *vi* **1.** (*metal*) to squeak; (*madera*) to creak **2.** (*pájaros*) to chirp
chirrido *m* **1.** (*del metal*) squeaking; (*de la madera*) creaking **2.** (*de los pájaros*) chirping
chis *interj* (*silencio*) sh; (*oye*) hey

chisme *m* **1.**(*habladuría*) piece of gossip; **andar** [*o* **ir**] **con** ~**s** to gossip **2.**(*objeto*) thingummyjig; **recoge esos** ~**s** put away those things

chismorrear *vi* to gossip

chismoso, -a I. *adj* gossiping II. *m, f* gossip

chispa *f* **1.** *t.* ELEC spark; **echar** ~**s** to give off sparks; *fig* to be hopping mad **2.**(*ingenio*) wit; **ser una** ~ to be (very) lively **3.**(*gota*) drop (of rain) **4.** *inf* (*borrachera*) drunkenness **5.**(*una pizca*) **una** ~ **de...** a bit of ...

chispazo *m t.* ELEC spark; (*descarga*) spark discharge

chispear I. *vi* **1.**(*centellear*) to spark **2.**(*brillar*) to sparkle II. *vimpers* (*lloviznar*) to drizzle

chisporrotear *vi* (*despedir chispas*) to throw off sparks; (*el fuego*) to crackle

chistar *vi* to speak; **no** ~ not to say a word

chiste *m* **1.**(*cuento*) funny story; (*broma*) joke; ~ **verde** dirty joke; **no tiene** ~ **la cosa** that's not at all funny **2.**(*gracia*) point

chistera *f* **1.**(*sombrero*) top hat **2.**(*cesta*) (fish) basket

chistoso, -a I. *adj* funny II. *m, f* joker

chita *f* ANAT anklebone; **a la** ~ **callando** *fig* on the sly

chitón *interj* ssh

chiva *f Col, inf* (*noticia*) (piece of) news

chivar *vr:* ~**se** *inf* **1.**(*hablar*) to grass **2.** *AmL* (*enojarse*) to get annoyed

chivatazo *m inf* tip-off; **dar el** ~ to give a tip-off

chivatear *vi* **1.** *Arg, Chile* (*chillar*) to shout **2.** *AmS* (*alborotar los niños*) to make a ruckus **3.** *inf* (*delatar*) to squeal; ~ **contra alguien** to squeal on sb

chivato, -a *m, f inf* (*informador*) grass *Brit,* stool pigeon *Am;* (*en la escuela*) tell-tale

chivo, -a *m, f* kid; ~ **expiatorio** scapegoat

choapino *m Chile* potato-beetle larva

chocante *adj* **1.**(*raro*) strange; (*sorprendente*) startling **2.**(*escandaloso*) shocking **3.** *AmL* (*fastidioso*) annoying; (*repugnante*) disgusting

chocar <c→qu> I. *vi* **1.**(*vehículos*) ~ **contra algo** to collide with sth; (*dar*) to crash into sth; (*coches*) to run into sth **2.**(*proyectil*) to smash **3.**(*encontrarse*) ~ **con alguien** to come across sb; (*personas*) to run into sb; (*discutir*) to have words with sb; **chocó con su jefe** he/she clashed with his/her boss II. *vt* **1.**(*entrechocar*) ~ **las copas** to clink glasses **2.**(*sorprender*) to surprise **3.**(*perturbar*) to startle; (*escandalizar*) to shock **4.** *AmL* (*repugnar*) to disgust; **me chocan sus opiniones** I can't stand his/her opinions

chocarrería *f* **1.**(*chiste*) coarse joke; (*dicho*) crude story **2.**(*acción*) crude act

chocarrero, -a *adj* coarse

chochear *vi* **1.**(*por vejez*) to dodder (around); *inf* (*atontar*) to become stupid **2.**(*sentir cariño*) to dote

chocho, -a I. *adj* **1.**(*senil*) doddering; *inf*

(*lelo*) stupid **2.**(*chiflado*) doting II. *m, f* **1.**(*dulce*) sweet **2.** *inf* (*follón*) **montar un** ~ to make a fuss **3.** *inf* (*montón*) load **4.** *vulg* (*coño*) cunt

choclo *m* **1.**(*zueco*) clog **2.** *AmS* (*maíz*) maize *Brit,* corn *Am;* (*mazorca tierna*) green ear of maize **3.** *AmS* GASTR sweet tamale

choclón *m Chile* POL rally

chocolate *m* **1.**(*para comer*) chocolate **2.** *inf* (*hachís*) dope, hash *inf*

chocolatera *f* **1.**(*vasija*) chocolate pot **2.** *inf* (*vehículo*) old crock

chocolatería *f* **1.**(*establecimiento*) *café specializing in hot chocolate drinks* **2.**(*fábrica*) chocolate factory

chocolatina *f* chocolate bar

chofer *m,* **chófer** *m* (*de un automóvil*) driver; (*personal*) chauffeur; (*de un camión*) lorry driver *Brit,* truck driver *Am*

chollo *m inf* **1.**(*suerte*) luck **2.**(*ganga*) bargain **3.**(*trabajo*) cushy job

cholo, -a *m, f AmL* **1.**(*indio*) Indian integrated into Creole society **2.**(*mestizo*) mestizo

chomba *f Arg* (*polo*) polo shirt

chongo *m* **1.** *Méx, inf* (*trenza*) braid; (*moño*) knot, bun **2.** *Chile* (*cuchillo*) blunt knife

chopera *f* poplar grove

chopo *m* black poplar

choque *m* **1.**(*impacto*) impact **2.**(*colisión*) crash; ~ **de frente** head-on collision **3.**(*encuentro*) clash; (*disputa*) conflict **4.** *t.* MED (*susto*) shock

choricear *vt inf* to swipe

chorizo *m* chorizo (*hard pork sausage*)

chorizo, -a *m, f inf* petty thief; (*carterista*) pickpocket

chorlito *m* plover; **cabeza de** ~ *fig* scatterbrain

choro *m* **1.** *Chile* (*mejillón*) large mussel **2.** *AmS, inf* (*ladrón*) thief

chorote *m Méx, Ven* (*chocolate*) chocolate drink

chorrada *f* **1.** *inf* (*tontería*) stupid remark **2.** *inf* (*cosa superflua*) trivial thing **3.**(*chorrillo*) extra drop

chorrear *vi* **1.**(*fluir*) to gush (out) **2.**(*gotear*) to drip **3.**(*concurrir lentamente*) to trickle in

chorrillo *m* (*de agua*) thin stream; (*de un ingrediente*) small drop

chorro *m* **1.**(*hilo*) trickle; (*porción*) squirt; (*de un ingrediente*) drop **2.**(*torrente*) stream; *t.* TÉC jet; **avión** ~ jet plane; **beber a** ~**s** to drink without putting one's lips to the bottle; **llover a** ~**s** to pour **3.** *Arg, inf* (*ladrón*) thief

chotear I. *vi* to romp II. *vr:* ~**se** *inf* to make fun

choteo *m* **1.**(*burla*) joke **2.**(*diversión*) amusement

choto, -a *m, f* **1.**(*cría de la cabra*) kid **2.**(*de la vaca*) calf

choza *f,* **chozo** *m* **1.**(*cabaña*) hut **2.**(*vivienda*) hovel

chubasco m 1.(aguacero) (heavy) shower 2.(contratiempo) setback
chubasquero m raincoat, windbreaker Am
chúcaro, -a adj Arg, inf 1.(poco amable) awkward 2.(huraño) shy
chuchería f 1.(bocado) titbit Brit, tidbit Am; (dulce) sweet 2.(menudencia) trinket
chucho m 1.inf(perro) mutt 2.AmL (escalofrío) shivers pl; (fiebre) fever
chucrú m, **chucrut** m, **chucruta** f sin pl sauerkraut
chueco, -a adj AmL 1.(pies) bow-legged 2.inf(torcido) crooked
chufa f tiger nut
chufla f joke
chulada f 1.(insolencia) impudence 2.inf (cosa estupenda) marvellous thing
chulear I. vi, vr: ~se (jactarse) to brag II. vr: ~se to make fun
chulería f 1.(jactancia) bragging 2.(frescura) boldness
chuleta I. f 1.(costilla) chop 2.inf (apunte) crib (sheet) 3.inf(bofetada) punch II. adj inf cheeky; **ponerse** ~ to get fresh
chuletón m T-bone steak
chulo m 1.(gandul) layabout; (mal educado) lout 2.inf (proxeneta) pimp 3.(dandi) dandy
chulo, -a I. adj 1.(jactancioso) boastful; (presumido) conceited 2.(fresco) cheeky; **ponerse** ~ to get cocky 3.inf (elegante) smart; (lindo) pretty II. m, f 1.(fanfarrón) flashy type 2.(exagerador) braggart
chumbera f prickly pear cactus
chumbo m (fruto) prickly pear
chunga f inf joke; **estar de** ~ to be in high spirits
chungo, -a adj inf 1.(malo) bad; (comida) spoiled, off Brit 2.(persona: rara) odd; (enfermiza) poorly
chunguearse vr 1.inf (bromear) to crack jokes 2.inf(embromar) to make fun
chuño m AmS (fécula de patata) potato starch
chupa f 1.HIST doublet; **poner a alguien como** ~ **de dómine** inf to wipe the floor with sb 2.(chaqueta) leather jacket; (chaleco) waistcoat Brit, vest Am 3.AmC (borrachera) drunkenness
chupa-chups® m inv lollipop
chupada f (paja) suck; (cigarrillo) puff
chupado, -a adj 1.(flaco) skinny; (consumido) emaciated 2.(vestido) tight 3.inf(fácil) dead easy Brit, a cinch Am 4.AmL (borracho) drunk
chupaflor m AmC zool hummingbird
chupamirto m Méx zool hummingbird
chupar I. vt 1.(extraer) to suck out; (aspirar) to suck in; (absorber) to absorb 2.(caramelo) to suck; (helado) to lick 3.(cigarrillo) to smoke, to puff on 4.(salud) to sap II. vi 1.inf (mamar) to suckle 2.(aprovecharse) to sponge; ~ **del bote** to line one's pocket 3.AmL, inf(beber) to booze; (fumar) to smoke

III. vr: ~se 1.(secarse) to get very thin 2.inf (aguantar) to sit out, to put up with
chupatintas m inv, pey 1.(oficinista) clerk 2.(escritor) penpusher
chupe m 1.inf(chupete) dummy Brit, pacifier Am; (chupador) sucker 2.CSur, Ecua, Perú GASTR spicy chowder
chupete m 1.(del bebé) dummy, pacifier Am; (del biberón) teat 2.AmL (pirulí) lollipop
chupetear vi, vt to lick
chupetón m 1.(chupada) suck 2.inf (marca de un beso) lovebite
chupo m Col (del biberón) teat
chupón, -ona I. adj 1.(chupador) sucking 2.(parásito) scrounging II. m, f scrounger
churrasco m 1.(carne) steak 2.(barbacoa) barbecue
churrete m spot
churro m 1.(fritura) slice of fried dough; ¡vete a freír ~s! get stuffed! 2.(chapuza) (piece of) shoddy work 3.(suerte) piece of luck 4.Col (persona atractiva) good looker

---

Churro is the term for fritters. The most typical of Spanish breakfasts comprises **chocolate** (hot chocolate) **con churros**. **Churros** can be obtained either in a **churrería**, in a **cafetería**, or they can be bought **en un puesto de churros** (at a kiosk in the street).

---

churro, -a adj 1.(lana) coarse 2.(cordero) one-year old
churumbel m (voz gitana) kid
chusco m crust (of bread)
chusco, -a I. adj droll II. m, f joker
chusma f rabble, riffraff
chutar I. vt to shoot; **esto va que chuta** inf it's going well II. vr: ~se inf to shoot up
chute m inf shot; (droga) fix
chuza f 1.Arg, Urug (lanza) pike 2.Arg (gallo) cock's spur 3.Méx (juego: bolos) strike 4.pl, Arg (pelo) rats' tails
chuzar <z→c> vt Col (punzar) to prick
chuzo m HIST pike; **caen** ~**s** fig (lluvia) to pour; (nieve) to snow heavily
Cía. abr de **compañía** Co.
cianuro m cyanide
ciática f sciatica
ciberbar m, **cibercafé** m cybercafé
ciberespacio m cyberspace
cibernauta mf cybernaut
cibernética f cybernetics pl
cibersexo m cybersex
cicatear vi inf to be stingy with
cicatería f stinginess
cicatero, -a I. adj stingy II. m, f skinflint
cicatriz f scar
cicatrizar <z→c> I. vi, vr: ~se to heal (up) II. vt to heal
ciclamen m cyclamen
ciclismo m DEP cycling
ciclista I. adj cycle II. mf t. DEP cyclist
ciclo m (en general) cycle; ~ **económico**

economic cycle; ~ **del rey Arturo** Arthurian cycle

ciclomotor *m* moped, motorbike

ciclón *m* cyclone

ciclope *m*, **cíclope** *m* Cyclops

ciclostil(o) *m* cyclostyle

cicloturismo *m* cycle touring

cicuta *f* hemlock

ciego, -a I. *adj* **1.** (*privado de la vista*) blind; **quedarse ~** to go blind **2.** (*taponado*) blocked II. *m, f* blind man *m*, blind woman *f* III. *adv* a **ciegas** blindly; **obrar a ciegas** to act thoughtlessly

cielo I. *m* **1.** (*atmósfera*) sky; **a ~ raso** in the open air; **el reino de los ~s** the Kingdom of Heaven; **como caído del ~** out of the blue **2.** (*apelativo cariñoso*) darling II. *interj* **¡~s!** good heavens!

ciempiés *m inv* centipede

cien *adj inv* a [*o* one] hundred; **al ~ por ~** one hundred per cent; *v.t.* **ochocientos**

ciénaga *f* swamp

ciencia *f* **1.** (*saber*) knowledge; **a** [*o* **de**] **~ cierta** for sure **2.** (*disciplina*) science; **~s físicas** physical science; **~s políticas** political science; **~s** (**naturales**) natural science(s)

ciencia-ficción *f sin pl* science fiction

cieno *m* mud

científico, -a I. *adj* scientific II. *m, f* scientist

ciento I. *adj* <cien> *inv* a [*o* one] hundred; *v.t.* **ochenta** II. *m* **~s de huevos** hundreds of eggs; **el cinco por ~** five per cent

cierre *m* **1.** *t.* ECON, FIN (*conclusión*) closing; (*clausura*) closure; PREN time of going to press; **~ del ejercicio** close of the financial year; **~ patronal** lockout; **hora de ~** closing time **2.** (*dispositivo*) closing device; **~ centralizado** AUTO central locking **3.** *Arg* (*cremallera*) zip fastener, zipper *Am*

cierro *m Chile* (*sobre*) envelope

ciertamente *adv* certainly

cierto *adv* certainly; **por ~** by the way

cierto, -a *adj* <certísimo> **1.** (*verdadero*) true; (*seguro*) sure; **una información cierta** a correct piece of information; **estar en lo ~** to be right; **lo ~ es que...** the fact is that ... **2.** (*alguno*) a certain; **~ día** one day

ciervo, -a *m, f* deer

cierzo *m* north wind

cifra *f* **1.** (*guarismo*) figure; **~ de negocios** ECON turnover; **~ de ventas** ECON sales figures **2.** (*clave*) code; **en ~** in code **3.** (*monograma*) monogram **4.** (*resumen*) summary

cifrar I. *vt* **1.** (*codificar*) to code **2.** (*calcular*) to reckon **3.** (*esperanza*) to place II. *vr* **~se en algo** to amount to sth

cigala *f* crayfish

cigarra *f* cicada

cigarrera *f* **1.** (*vendedora*) cigar seller **2.** (*que elabora*) cigar maker **3.** (*caja*) cigar box **4.** (*petaca*) cigar case

cigarrillo *m* cigarette

cigarro *m* cigar

cigüeña *f* **1.** (*ave*) stork **2.** (*manivela*) crank

cigüeñal *m* AUTO crankshaft

cilindrada *f* AUTO cubic capacity

cilindro *m* cylinder; (*en un reloj*) drum

cima *f t. fig* summit; **~ del árbol** tree top; **~ del monte** mountain peak

cimarrón, -ona *adj AmL* wild

cimbo(r)rio *m* ARQUIT dome

cimbrar, cimbrear I. *vt* **1.** (*agitar*) to shake **2.** (*golpear*) to beat **3.** (*doblar*) to bend II. *vr:* **~se 1.** (*agitarse*) to sway **2.** (*doblarse*) to bend

cimbreo *m* **1.** (*agitación*) swaying **2.** (*golpe*) blow

cimbronazo *m* **1.** (*golpe*) blow (with the flat of a sword) **2.** *AmL* (*temblor nervioso*) jolt **3.** *AmL* (*tirón del lazo*) yank **4.** *AmL* (*temblor de tierra*) earthquake

cimentación *f* **1.** (*fundamento*) foundations *pl* **2.** (*edificación*) laying of foundations

cimentar <e→ie> *vt* **1.** (*fundar*) to found **2.** (*fundamentar*) to lay the foundations of **3.** (*afinar oro*) to refine **4.** (*consolidar*) to strengthen

cimiento *m* foundation

cimpa *f Perú* braid

cinc *m* zinc

cincel *m* chisel

cincelar *vt* to chisel

cincha *f* (*caballo*) girth, cinch

cinchar *vt* (*caballo*) to girth, to cinch

cinco I. *adj inv* five ►**estar sin ~** to be broke II. *m* five; **¡choca esos ~!** give me five!; *v.t.* **ocho**

cincuenta *adj inv, m* fifty; *v.t.* **ochenta**

cincuentavo *m* fiftieth; *v.t.* **octavo**

cincuentavo, -a *adj* fiftieth; *v.t.* **octavo**

cincuentena *f* unit consisting of fifty parts; **una ~ de personas** about fifty people

cincuentenario *m* fiftieth anniversary

cine *m* **1.** (*arte*) cinema, movies *pl Am;* **~ mudo/sonoro** silent/talking films; **~ negro** film noir; **me gusta el ~** I like films **2.** (*sala*) cinema, movie theater *Am;* **~ de barrio** local cinema, local movie theater *Am;* **ir al ~** to go to the cinema

cineasta *mf* film-maker; (*director*) director; (*aficionado*) film buff

cineclub *m* <cineclubs> film club

cinema *m* cinema, movies *pl Am*

cinemateca *f* film library

cinematografía *f* cinematography

cinematógrafo *m* **1.** (*proyector*) projector **2.** (*cine*) cinema

cingalés, -esa *adj, m, f* Singhalese

cíngaro, -a *adj, m, f* gipsy *Brit,* gypsy

cínico, -a I. *adj* (*descarado*) shameless; (*escéptico*) cynical II. *m, f t.* FILOS cynic

cinismo *m* (*descaro*) shamelessness; (*escepticismo*) cynicism

cinta *f* **1.** (*tira*) band; **~ adhesiva** adhesive tape; **~ aislante** insulating tape; **~ métrica** tape measure; **~ del pelo** hair ribbon; **~ de vídeo** videotape; **~ virgen** blank tape; **~**

transportadora conveyor belt **2.**(*hilera de baldosas*) tile skirting **3.**(*red de pesca*) tuna fish net

cinto *m* **1.**(*cinturón*) belt **2.**(*cintura*) waist

cintura *f* waist; ~ **de avispa** wasp waist

cinturón *m* **1.**(*ceñidor, correa*) belt; ~ **salvavidas** lifebelt; **ponerse el** ~ to fasten one's seatbelt; **apretarse el** ~ *fig* to tighten one' belt **2.** ASTR ring **3.**(*de una ciudad*) belt

cipe *adj AmC* (*enfermizo*) sickly, runty

ciprés *m* cypress

circense *adj* circus

circo *m* **1.**(*arena*) circus; ~ **ambulante** travelling [*o* traveling *Am*] circus **2.** GEO cirque

circuito *m* **1.** *t.* ELEC circuit; ~ **integrado** integrated circuit; **corto** ~ short circuit **2.** DEP circuit, track

circulación *f* **1.** *t.* ECON (*ciclo*) circulation; ~ **sanguínea** (blood) circulation; **retirar de la** ~ to withdraw from circulation **2.**(*tránsito*) traffic

circular I. *adj* circular II. *vi* **1.**(*recorrer*) to circulate **2.**(*personas*) to walk (around); **¡circulen!** move along! **3.**(*vehículos*) to drive (around) III. *f* circular

circulatorio, -a *adj* MED circulatory

círculo *m* circle; ~ **de amistades** circle of friends; ~ **vicioso** vicious circle

circuncidar *vt* to circumcise

circuncisión *f* circumcision

circundar *vt* to surround

circunferencia *f t.* MAT circumference

circunlocución *f* circumlocution

circunnavegar <g→gu> *vt* to circumnavigate

circunscribir *irr como escribir* I. *vt t.* MAT to circumscribe II. *vr:* ~**se** to limit oneself

circunscripción *f* **1.**(*distrito*) electoral district **2.** *t.* MAT (*concreción*) circumscription

circunscrito, -a *pp de* **circunscribir**

circunspecto, -a *adj* circumspect

circunstancia *f* circumstance; **en estas** ~**s** in these circumstances

circunstancial *adj* circumstantial

circunvalación *f* **carretera de** ~ bypass

cirílico, -a *adj* Cyrillic

cirineo, -a I. *adj* of Cyrene II. *m, f* helper

cirio *m* **1.**(*vela*) candle **2.** *inf*(*jaleo*) row

cirro *m* cirrus

cirrosis *f inv* MED cirrhosis

ciruela *f* plum; ~ **pasa** prune

ciruelo *m* **1.**(*pruno*) plum tree **2.** *inf*(*tonto*) idiot

cirugía *f* MED surgery; ~ **estética** cosmetic surgery

cirujano, -a *m, f* MED surgeon

ciscar <c→qu> I. *vt inf* to dirty, to soil II. *vr:* ~**se** *inf* to do one's business

cisco *m* **1.**(*carbón*) coaldust; **estar hecho un** ~ *inf* to be a wreck **2.**(*jaleo*) row

Cisjordania *f* (the) West Bank

cisma *m* **1.** REL schism **2.**(*desacuerdo*) disagreement

cisne *m* swan

cister *m*, **císter** *m* REL Cistercian Order

cisterna I. *adj* tank; **barco** ~ tanker II. *f* cistern, tank *Am*

cisura *f* **1.**(*fisura*) crack **2.**(*cicatriz*) scar **3.**(*incisión*) incision

cita *f* **1.**(*convocatoria*) appointment **2.**(*encuentro*) meeting; (*romántico*) date; ~ **anual** annual meeting; ~ **a ciegas** blind date; **tener una** ~ **con alguien** to be meeting sb; (*romántico*) to have a date with sb **3.**(*mención*) quotation

citación *f* **1.** JUR summons **2.**(*el mencionar*) quotation

citar I. *vt* **1.**(*convocar*) to arrange to meet **2.**(*mencionar*) to quote **3.** JUR to summon II. *vr:* ~**se** to arrange to meet

cítara *f* MÚS zither

citología *f* cytologie; **hacer una** ~ to have a smear test

cítrico, -a *adj* citric

cítricos *mpl* citrus fruits *pl*

ciudad *f* town; (*más grande*) city; ~ **hermanada** twin town; ~ **industrial** industrial town [*o* city]; ~ **de origen** home town; ~ **universitaria** university campus; ~ **dormitorio** dormitory town

ciudadanía *f* **1.**(*nacionalidad*) citizenship **2.**(*conjunto de ciudadanos*) citizenry, citizens *pl* **3.**(*civismo*) civic responsibility

ciudadano, -a I. *adj* **1.**(*de la ciudad*) city **2.**(*del ciudadano*) civic II. *m, f* **1.**(*residente*) resident **2.**(*súbdito*) citizen

ciudad-estado <ciudades-estado> *f* city-state

ciudadrealeño, -a I. *adj* of/from Ciudad Real II. *m, f* native/inhabitant of Ciudad Real

cívico, -a *adj* **1.**(*de la ciudad, del ciudadano*) civic **2.**(*del civismo*) public-spirited

civil I. *adj* civil; **derecho** ~ civil law; **guerra** ~ civil war II. *m* **1.** *inf* (*persona*) civil guard **2.**(*paisano*) civilian

civilización *f* civilization

civilizar <z→c> *vt* to civilize

civismo *m* community spirit, civic-mindedness

cizalla *f* **1.**(*recorte*) metal clippings **2.** *pl* (*tijeras*) wire-cutters *pl*

cizallar *vt* to cut with wire cutters

cizaña *f* **1.** BOT darnel **2.**(*enemistad*) discord **3.**(*adversidad*) trouble

cizañero, -a I. *adj* scheming II. *m, f* **1.**(*intrigante*) troublemaker **2.**(*pendenciero*) quarrelsome person

cl *abr de* **centilitro** centilitre *Brit,* centiliter *Am*

clamar I. *vi* to cry out II. *vt* to demand

clamor *m* **1.**(*lamento*) lament **2.**(*toque de campana*) tolling, knell

clamoroso, -a *adj* **1.**(*acompañado de clamor*) **acogida clamorosa** rousing reception **2.**(*éxito*) resounding

clan *m* clan

clandestinidad *f* **1.**(*secreto*) secrecy **2.** POL

underground
clandestino, -a *adj* **1.** (*secreto*) secret; **reunión clandestina** secret meeting **2.** (*ilegal*) movimiento ~ underground movement
claqué *f* tap dancing
claqueta *f* CINE clapperboard
clara *f* **1.** (*del huevo*) white **2.** (*bebida*) shandy *Brit, Aus*
claraboya *f* skylight
claramente *adv* clearly
clarear I. *vi* **1.** (*amanecer*) to grow light; **al ~ el día** at dawn **2.** (*despejarse*) to clear up **3.** (*concretarse*) to become clear II. *vt* to brighten III. *vr:* **~se 1.** (*transparentarse*) to be transparent **2.** (*descubrirse*) to reveal oneself
clarete *m* rosé (wine)
claridad *f* **1.** (*luminosidad*) brightness **2.** (*lucidez*) clarity
clarificación *f* **1.** (*iluminación*) illumination **2.** (*aclaración*) clarification
clarificar <c→qu> *vt* **1.** (*iluminar*) to illuminate **2.** (*aclarar*) to clarify
clarín *m* **1.** (*instrumento*) bugle **2.** (*músico*) bugler
clarinete *m* **1.** (*instrumento*) clarinet **2.** (*músico*) clarinet(t)ist
clarividencia *f* **1.** (*perspicacia*) discernment **2.** (*instinto*) intuition **3.** (*percepción*) clairvoyance
clarividente I. *adj* **1.** (*perspicaz*) discerning **2.** (*que percibe*) clairvoyant II. *mf* clairvoyant
claro I. *interj* of course II. *m* **1.** (*hueco*) gap **2.** (*calvero*) clearing **3.** (*calva*) bald patch III. *adv* clearly
claro, -a *adj* **1.** (*iluminado*) bright; **azul ~** light blue **2.** (*ilustre*) famous **3.** (*evidente*) clear; **poner** [*o* **sacar**] **en ~** to clarify **4.** (*fino*) thin
claror *m* brightness
claroscuro *m* chiaroscuro
clase *f* **1.** (*tipo*) kind; **trabajos de toda ~** all kinds of jobs **2.** *t.* BIO (*categoría, grupo social*) class; **~ turista** tourist class; **~ media** middle class **3.** ENS class; (*aula*) classroom; **dar ~s** to teach
clasicismo *m* classicism
clásico, -a I. *adj* classical; *fig* classic II. *m, f* classic
clasificación *f* **1.** (*ordenación*) sorting; **~ en grupos** sorting into groups **2.** *t.* BIO classification
clasificador *m* **1.** (*archivador*) filing cabinet **2.** (*personal*) classifier **3.** (*carpeta*) ring binder
clasificar <c→qu> I. *vt* **1.** (*ordenar*) ~ **por algo** to sort according to sth **2.** BIO ~ **por algo** to classify under sth II. *vr:* **~se** to qualify
clasismo *m* class-consciousness
claudicación *f* **1.** (*de principios*) abandonment **2.** (*cesión*) giving way [*o* in]
claudicar <c→qu> *vi* **1.** (*principios*) ~ **de algo** to abandon sth **2.** (*ceder*) to give way [*o* in]
claustro *m* **1.** (*galería, convento*) cloister **2.** (*conjunto de profesores*) senate **3.** (*reunión*

de profesores) senate meeting
claustrofobia *f* PSICO claustrophobia
cláusula *f* JUR, LING clause; (*ley*) article
clausura *f* **1.** (*cierre*) closure; **sesión de ~** closing session **2.** (*en un convento*) cloister
clausurar *vt* to close
clavado, -a *adj* **1.** (*semejante*) very similar **2.** (*exacto*) **a las dos clavadas** (at) two sharp **3.** (*confuso*) astonished
clavar I. *vt* **1.** (*hincar*) to knock in **2.** (*enclavar*) to nail **3.** (*fijarse*) to fix; **tener la vista clavada en algo** to have one's eyes fixed on sth **4.** *inf* (*engañar*) to cheat **5.** (*engastar*) to set **6.** *inf* (*dar*) to give **7.** *inf* (*cobrar*) to rip off II. *vr* **~se una astilla en el dedo** to get a splinter in one's finger
clave I. *adj inv* key II. *f* **1.** (*secreto*) ~ **de algo** key to sth **2.** (*código*) code; ~ **de acceso** password; **en ~** coded **3.** ARQUIT keystone **4.** MÚS clef
clavel *m* carnation
clavetear *vt* **1.** (*clavar clavos*) to nail up **2.** (*terminar*) to conclude **3.** (*guarnecer*) to decorate with studs
clavicémbalo *m* harpsichord
clavicordio *m* clavichord
clavícula *f* collar bone
clavija *f* **1.** TÉC pin **2.** MÚS (*de guitarra*) peg **3.** (*enchufe*) plug ▸**apretar las ~s a alguien** to put the screws on sb
clavo *m* **1.** (*punta*) nail; **dar en el ~** to hit the nail on the head **2.** (*especia*) clove **3.** (*callo*) corn
claxon *m* horn
clemencia *f* mercy
clemente *adj* merciful
clementina *f* tangerine
cleptómano, -a I. *adj* PSICO kleptomaniac II. *m, f* PSICO kleptomaniac
clerical *adj* clerical
clérigo *m* clergyman; (*sólo iglesia católica*) priest
clero *m* clergy
clic *m* click
cliché *m* **1.** (*tópico*) cliché **2.** FOTO negative
cliente, -a *m, f* customer; (*de un abogado*) client; ~ **fijo** regular customer
clientela *f* customers *pl;* (*de un abogado*) clients *pl*
clima *m* **1.** (*atmósfera*) atmosphere **2.** GEO climate
climatización *f* air conditioning
climatizador *m* air conditioner
climatizar <z→c> *vt* to air-condition
climatología *f* climatology
clímax *m inv* climax
clínica *f* clinic
clínico *m* clinical
clip *m* **1.** (*sujetapapeles*) paper clip **2.** (*pinza*) clip **3.** TV video (clip)
clítoris *m inv* clitoris
cloaca *f* sewer; ZOOL cloaca
clon *m* **1.** BIO clone **2.** (*payaso*) clown

clonar *vt* to clone
clónico, -a *adj* clonal
cloquear *vi* to cluck
clorato *m* chlorate
cloro *m* chlorine
clorofila *f* chlorophyl(l)
cloruro *m* chloride
club <clubs *o* clubes> *m* club; ~ **de alterne** hostess bar; ~ **deportivo** sports club
clueca *f* broody hen
cm *abr de* centímetro cm.
coacción *f* coercion
coaccionar *vt* to coerce
coagulación *f* coagulation, clotting
coagular I. *vt* to coagulate II. *vr:* ~**se** to coagulate, to clot
coágulo *m* clot
coalición *f* coalition
coaligarse <g→gu> *vr* to form an alliance
coartada *f* alibi
coartar *vt* 1. (*libertad*) to restrict 2. (*persona*) to inhibit
coautor(a) *m(f)* co-author
coba *f* lie; **dar** ~ **a alguien** to suck up to sb
cobalto *m* cobalt
cobarde I. *adj* cowardly II. *m* coward
cobardía *f* cowardice
cobaya *m o f* guinea pig
cobertizo *m* 1. (*tejado*) canopy 2. (*cabaña*) shed
cobertor *m* bedspread, counterpane *Brit*
cobertura *f* 1. (*cobertor*) bedspread; (*que cubre*) cover 2. COM (*acción*) coverage
cobija *f* 1. (*cubierta*) cover 2. ARQUIT (*teja*) ridge-tile 3. *AmL* (*manta*) blanket 4. *pl, AmL* (*ropa de cama*) bedclothes *pl;* **pegárse a alguien las** ~**s** to oversleep
cobijar I. *vt* 1. (*cubrir*) to cover 2. (*proteger*) to shelter 3. (*acoger*) to give shelter to II. *vr:* ~**se** (*protegerse*) to take shelter
cobijo *m* shelter
cobo *m AmC, Ant* 1. ZOOL giant sea snail 2. (*persona*) unsociable person; **ser un** ~ to be shy
cobra *f* cobra
cobrador(a) *m(f)* 1. COM (*que cobra*) collector 2. (*de tranvía*) conductor
cobrar I. *vt* 1. (*recibir*) to receive; (*suma*) to collect; (*cheque*) to cash; (*sueldo*) to earn; **¿me cobra, por favor?** can I pay, please? 2. (*exigir*) to levy; (*intereses*) to charge; (*deudas*) to recover 3. (*conseguir*) ~ **ánimos** to pluck up courage; ~ **fama** to become famous 4. (*cuerda*) to haul in II. *vi* 1. (*sueldo*) to get one's wages 2. *inf* **recibir una paliza** to get a beating; **¡que vas a** ~**!** you're going to get it! III. *vr:* ~**se** to cash up; *fig* to claim
cobre *m* 1. QUÍM copper 2. *pl* MÚS brass 3. *AmL* (*moneda*) copper coin
cobrizo, -a *adj* coppery
cobro *m* 1. (*como fuente financiera*) takings *pl* 2. (*acto de cobrar*) recovery 3. FIN (*impuestos*) collection; (*pago*) payment; ~ **por ade-**

lantado advance payment; ~ **pendiente** outstanding payment; **llamar a** ~ **revertido** to reverse the charges 4. *pl* COM arrears *pl*
coca *f* 1. BOT coca 2. (*droga*) cocaine 3. (*de pelo*) coil, bun 4. *inf* (*cabeza*) nut *Brit,* noodle *inf* 5. *inf* (*refresco*) Coke®
cocaína *f* cocaine
cocainómano, -a *m, f* cocaine addict
cocción *f* 1. (*acto*) cooking 2. (*duración*) cooking time; (*en el horno*) baking time
cocear *vi* to kick
cocer *irr* I. *vt* 1. (*cocinar*) to cook; (*hervir*) to boil; (*al horno*) to bake 2. (*cerveza*) to brew; (*cerámica*) to fire II. *vi* 1. (*cocinar*) to cook 2. (*hervir*) to boil 3. (*fermentar*) to ferment III. *vr:* ~**se** 1. (*cocinarse*) to be cooked 2. (*tramarse*) to be going on 3. (*sufrir*) to suffer greatly 4. *inf* (*pasar calor*) to be sweltering
cocha *f* 1. MIN water tank 2. *AmS* (*laguna*) lagoon; (*charco*) puddle
cochambroso, -a *adj inf* (*sucio*) filthy; (*asqueroso*) disgusting; (*maloliente*) stinking
cochayuyo *m AmS* BOT rockweed
coche *m* 1. (*automóvil*) car; ~ **de bomberos** fire engine; ~ **de carreras** DEP racing car; ~ **de línea** coach *Brit,* bus *Am;* **ir en** ~ to go by car 2. (*de caballos*) coach, carriage; ~ **de equipajes** luggage van *Brit,* baggage car *Am*
coche-bomba <coches-bomba> *m* car bomb
coche-cama <coches-cama> *m* FERRO sleeping car
cochecito *m* pram *Brit,* baby carriage *Am*
coche-patrulla <coches-patrulla> *m* patrol car
cochera *f* garage; ~ **de tranvías** (*almacén*) tram depot
coche-restaurante <coches-restaurante> *m* FERRO dining car
coche-vivienda <coches-vivienda> *m* (large) caravan
cochinada *f,* **cochinería** *f inf* filthy thing
cochinilla *f* 1. ZOOL (*insecto*) cochineal insect 2. ZOOL (*crustáceo*) woodlouse
cochinillo *m* piglet; ~ **asado** roast suckling pig
cochino, -a I. *adj inf* filthy II. *m, f* 1. ZOOL (*macho*) pig; (*hembra*) sow 2. *inf* (*guarro*) swine
cocho *m Chile* 1. (*bebida*) hot maize drink 2. GASTR pudding made with toasted flour
cocido *m* stew (*made with chickpeas and meat*)
cociente *m* MAT quotient; ~ **intelectual** IQ
cocina *f* 1. (*habitación*) kitchen 2. (*aparato*) cooker, stove *Am* 3. (*arte*) cookery, cooking; **la** ~ **francesa** French cooking [*o* cuisine]; **libro de** ~ cookery book, cookbook *Am*
cocinar I. *vt* to cook II. *vi* 1. (*guisar*) to cook 2. *inf* (*inmiscuirse*) to meddle
cocinero, -a *m, f* cook
cocinilla *f* (*portátil*) camping stove; (*de gas*) gas stove

coco *m* 1. BOT (*fruto*) coconut 2. BOT (*árbol*) coconut palm 3. *inf* (*cabeza*) head; (*cerebro*) brain; **comerse el ~** to worry 4. *inf* (*ogro*) bogeyman 5. ZOOL (*larva*) grub 6. BIO (*bacteria*) coccus

cocodrilo *m* crocodile

cocoliche *m Arg, Urug* LING *pidgin Spanish of Italian immigrants*

cocotero *m* coconut palm

coctel <coctels> *m*, **cóctel** <cócteles> *m* cocktail

coctelera *f* cocktail shaker

cocuy *m AmL* 1. BOT agave 2. (*bebida alcohólica*) maize [*o* corn *Am*] liquor 3. ZOOL firefly

cocuyo *m AmL* 1. ZOOL firefly 2. AUTO rear light

codazo *m* nudge (with one's elbow)

codear I. *vi* to nudge; (*más fuerte*) to elbow II. *vr:* **~se** to rub shoulders [*o* elbows]

codera *f* elbow patch

códice *m* codex

codicia *f* 1. (*en general*) greed; **~ de algo** greed for sth 2. (*de posesiones ajenas*) covetousness

codiciar *vt* to covet

codicioso, -a *adj* covetous

codificación *f* 1. (*con señales*) coding; *t.* INFOR encoding 2. JUR codification

codificar <c→qu> *vt* 1. JUR to codify 2. (*con señales*) to code; *t.* INFOR to encode

código *m* code; **~ de circulación** highway code; **Código Civil** civil code; **~ de barras** bar code; **mensaje en ~** coded message; **~ bancario** bank sorting code; **~ postal** postcode *Brit*, zip code *Am*

codillo *m* 1. ZOOL elbow 2. GASTR knuckle of pork 3. (*de un árbol*) stump (of a branch) 4. TÉC (*doblez*) elbow joint

codo *m* 1. ANAT elbow; **~ de tenis** tennis elbow; **empinar el ~** *inf* to go on the booze; **trabajar ~ a ~** to work side by side; **hablar por los ~s** *inf* to talk nonstop 2. TÉC (*doblez*) elbow joint 3. (*de camino*) bend (in the road)

codorniz *f* quail

coeficiente *m* MAT coefficient

coercer <c→z> *vt* 1. (*obligar*) **~ a algo** to constrain to sth; *t.* JUR to coerce into sth 2. (*cohibir*) to restrain 3. (*coartar*) to restrict

coerción *f* constraint; *t.* JUR coercion

coetáneo, -a *adj, m, f* contemporary

coexistencia *f* coexistence

coexistir *vi* to coexist

cofia *f* cap

cofradía *f* 1. (*hermandad*) brotherhood 2. (*gremio*) guild 3. (*asociación*) association

cofre *m* 1. (*caja*) chest; (*baúl*) trunk 2. (*de joyas*) jewel case

cofundador(a) *m(f)* co-founder

cogedero *m* (*mango*) handle

cogedor *m* dustpan

coger <g→j> I. *vt* 1. (*agarrar*) to take hold, to seize; (*objeto caído*) to pick up; **le cogió del brazo** he/she took him by the arm; **le cogió en brazos** he/she picked him up in his arms 2. (*tocar*) to touch 3. (*quitar*) to take away; (*en la aduana*) to confiscate 4. (*atrapar*) to catch; (*apresar*) to capture 5. (*flores*) to pick; **~ la cosecha** to harvest 6. AUTO (*atropellar*) to knock down 7. (*trabajo*) to take (up) 8. (*hábito*) to acquire; **~ cariño a alguien** to get fond of sb; **~ el hábito de fumar** to start smoking 9. (*enfermedad*) to catch; **~ frío** to catch a cold; **ha cogido una gripe** he's/she's caught the flu 10. (*una noticia*) to receive 11. (*sorprender*) to find 12. (*obtener*) to get; **¿vas a ~ el piso?** are you going to take the flat? 13. RADIO to pick up 14. (*tomar*) to take; **~ el tren/autobús** to take the train/bus 15. *AmL, vulg* (*copular*) to screw II. *vi* 1. (*planta*) to take 2. (*tener sitio*) to fit 3. *AmL, vulg* (*copular*) to screw III. *vr* 1. (*pillarse*) catch; **~se los dedos en la puerta** to catch one's fingers in the door 2. *inf* (*robar*) to steal

cogestión *f* joint management

cogida *f* 1. TAUR goring 2. (*de frutas*) picking 3. *AmL, vulg* (*cópula*) screw

cognición *f* cognition

cognitivo, -a *adj* PSICO cognitive

cogollo *m* 1. (*de col, lechuga*) heart; (*de árbol*) top 2. (*brote*) bud 3. (*algo selecto*) best part 4. (*núcleo*) core

cogorza *f* **pillar una buena ~** *inf* to get plastered

cogote *m* 1. (*de la cabeza*) back of the head 2. (*nuca*) scruff of the neck; **estar hasta el ~** *inf* to have had enough

cogotudo *m AmL* self-made man

cohabitación *f t.* POL cohabitation

cohabitar *vi* 1. (*convivir*) to live together 2. *pey* (*amancebarse*) to cohabit

cohecho *m* bribery

coherencia *f* coherence

coherente *adj* coherent

cohesión *f* cohesion

cohesionar *vt* to unite

cohete *m* rocket

cohibición *f* 1. (*intimidación*) intimidation 2. (*inhibición*) inhibition 3. (*restricción*) restraint

cohibido, -a *adj* 1. (*intimidado*) intimidated 2. (*tímido*) shy 3. (*inhibido*) inhibited 4. (*refrenado*) restrained

cohibir *irr como prohibir* I. *vt* 1. (*intimidar*) to intimidate 2. (*incomodar*) to inhibit 3. (*refrenar*) to restrain II. *vr:* **~se** to feel inhibited

coima *f* 1. HIST concubine 2. *pey* (*amante*) mistress 3. (*puta*) whore 4. *And, CSur* (*soborno*) bribe; (*dinero*) rake-off

coimear *vt AmS* (*sobornar*) to bribe

coincidencia *f* 1. (*simultaneidad*) coincidence; **¡qué ~!** what a coincidence! 2. (*acuerdo*) agreement 3. (*concordancia*) concordance 4. (*encuentro*) meeting

coincidente *adj* 1. (*simultáneo*) coincidental 2. (*concordante*) concordant 3. (*en el mismo lugar*) meeting

coincidir *vi* 1. (*sucesos*) to coincide 2. (*to-*

parse) to meet; ~ **con alguien** to meet sb **3.**(*concordar*) to agree; ~ **con alguien** to agree with sb

coipo *m Arg, Chile* ZOOL coypu

coito *m* coitus, (sexual) intercourse

cojear *vi* (*persona, animal*) to limp; (*mueble*) to wobble; *fig* (*tener defecto*) to have a weak point; **saber de qué pie cojea alguien** to know sb's weaknesses

cojera *f* limp

cojín *m* cushion

cojinete *m* TÉC bearing

cojo, -a I. *adj* **1.**(*persona, animal*) lame; **a la pata coja** on one leg **2.**(*mueble*) wobbly II. *m, f* lame person

cojón *m vulg* **1.** *pl* (*testículos*) balls *pl* **2.** *pl* (*interjecciones*) **¡cojones!** God damn it!, bloody hell! *Brit;* **es una música de cojones** it's really cool music

cojonudo, -a *adj vulg* fantastic, fucking great *vulg*

cojudo, -a *adj AmL* (*tonto*) stupid

col *f* cabbage; **~es de Bruselas** Brussels sprouts

cola *f* **1.** ANAT (*rabo*) tail; (*de conejo*) scut **2.**(*de vestido*) train; **llevar la ~** to wear a train **3.**(*al esperar*) queue, line; **hacer ~** to queue (up), to line up; **ponerse a la ~** to join the queue [*o* line] **4.**(*de un cometa*) tail **5.**(*pegamento*) glue **6.** *vulg* (*pene*) prick **7.** *AmL, inf* **pedir ~** to ask for a lift

colaboración *f* collaboration; (*periódico*) contribution

colaboracionismo *m* POL collaboration

colaborador(a) I. *adj* collaborating II. *m(f)* collaborator; LIT contributor

colaborar *vi* **1.**(*cooperar*) to collaborate **2.** LIT to contribute

colación *f* **1.** JUR (*mención*) official mention **2.** *inf*(*mencionar*) **sacar algo a ~** to bring sth up **3.**(*comida*) light meal

colada *f* **1.**(*de ropa*) washing **2.**(*blanquear con lejía*) bleaching **3.** QUÍM lye **4.**(*montaña*) defile *liter*

coladera *f* **1.**(*pasador*) strainer **2.** *Méx* (*alcantarilla*) sewer

coladero *m* strainer, colander

colado, -a *adj inf*(*enamorado*) **~ por alguien** crazy about sb

colador *m* sieve, strainer

colapsar I. *vt* (*tráfico*) to bring to a standstill II. *vi, vr:* **~se 1.**(*tráfico*) to come to a standstill **2.** MED to collapse

colapso *m* **1.** MED collapse **2.**(*destrucción*) destruction; (*paralización*) standstill

colar <o→ue> I. *vt* **1.**(*filtrar*) to filter **2.**(*metal*) to cast **3.**(*ropa: blanquear*) to bleach; (*en remojo*) to soak **4.** *inf* (*en la aduana*) to slip through II. *vi* **1.**(*penetrar: líquido*) to seep (through); (*aire*) to get in **2.** *inf* (*información*) to be credible; **a ver si cuela** let's see if it comes off III. *vr:* **~se 1.** *inf* (*entrar*) to slip in **2.**(*en una cola*) to jump the

queue [*o* line] **3.** *inf*(*equivocarse*) to be wrong; **¡te colaste!** you're way out!

colcha *f* bedspread, counterpane *Brit*

colchón *m* mattress; **~ de agua** water bed

colchonería *f* store which sells mattresses

colchoneta *f* **1.**(*colchón neumático*) airbed; (*colchón isotermo*) foam mattress **2.** DEP (*gimnasia*) mat

colear *vi* **1.**(*la cola*) to wag **2.**(*durar*) to last

colección *f* collection

coleccionar *vt* to collect

coleccionista *mf* collector

colecta *f* **1.** REL (*en misa*) collect **2.**(*recaudación*) collection (for charity)

colectividad *f* group

colectivizar <z→c> *vt* to collectivize

colectivo *m* **1.** POL collective, group **2.** *Méx* (*microbús*) minibus

colectivo, -a *adj* **1.**(*todos juntos*) collective; **acción colectiva** joint action **2.**(*global*) comprehensive

colector *m* **1.** ELEC collector **2.**(*canalización*) (main) sewer

colega *mf* **1.**(*compañero*) colleague **2.**(*homólogo*) counterpart **3.** *inf* (*amigo*) pal, mate *Brit,* buddy

colegiado, -a I. *adj* collegiate II. *m, f* **1.**(*miembro*) member **2.** DEP (*árbitro*) referee

colegial(a) I. *adj* **1.**(*de un colegio*) school **2.**(*inexperto*) inexperienced II. *m(f)* **1.**(*alumno*) schoolboy *m,* schoolgirl *f* **2.**(*inexperto*) inexperienced person

colegiarse *vr* **1.**(*afiliarse*) to become a member of a professional association **2.**(*organizarse*) to form a professional association

colegio *m* **1.** ENS school; **ir al ~** to go to school **2.** *AmL* (*universidad*) college; **~ mayor** hall of residence **3.**(*corporación*) professional association; **~ de abogados** bar association

colegir *irr como* elegir *vt* **1.**(*juntar*) to collect **2.**(*deducir*) to gather

cólera[1] *m* MED cholera

cólera[2] *f* (*ira*) anger; **acceso de ~** fit of anger

colérico, -a I. *adj* **1.**(*de temperamento*) badtempered **2.**(*furioso*) furious II. *m, f* irascible person

colesterol *m* cholesterol

coletilla *f* **1.**(*peinado*) ponytail; TAUR bullfighter's pigtail **2.**(*de un escrito*) postscript **3.**(*palabra*) tag question

colgado, -a *adj* **1.**(*cuadro*) hung up; (*bandera*) hung out **2.**(*suspendido*) failed

colgador *m* (*en general*) hanger; (*gancho*) (coat)hook; (*percha*) coat-hanger

colgante I. *adj* hanging; **puente ~** (*entre dos lados*) suspension bridge; (*de castillo*) drawbridge II. *m* **1.** ARQUIT festoon **2.**(*joya*) pendant

colgar *irr* I. *vt* **1.**(*pender, ahorcar*) **~ algo** to hang sth; (*decorar*) to decorate with sth; **~ el teléfono** to put down the phone **2.**(*dejar*) **~ los libros** to abandon one's studies **3.** *inf*(*suspender*) to fail **4.**(*atribuir*) to attribute II. *vi* **1.**(*pender*) to hang; (*de arriba para abajo*) to hang down; (*lengua del perro*) to droop **2.** TEL (*auricular*) to hang up **III.** *vr:* ~**se** to hang oneself

colibrí *m* hummingbird
cólico *m* MED colic
coliflor *f* cauliflower
coligado, -a I. *adj* (*unido*) united; (*aliado*) allied **II.** *m, f* ally
coligarse <g→gu> *vr* to form an alliance
colilla *f* cigarette end, fag end, butt
colín *m* **1.** *AmC, Ant* ZOOL American bobwhite **2.** (*pan*) breadstick
colina *f* hill
colindar *vi* ~ **con algo** to adjoin sth
colirio *m* eye drops *pl*
colisión *f* collision
colisionar *vi* ~ **con** [*o* **contra**] **algo** to collide with sth; *fig* to conflict with sth
collado *m* **1.** (*colina*) hill **2.** (*puerto*) pass
collage *m* ARTE collage
collar *m* **1.** (*adorno*) necklace; ~ **de perlas** string of pearls; ~ **de perro** dog collar **2.** (*insignia*) chain (of office) **3.** TÉC (*aro*) collar
colmado *m* **1.** (*tienda*) grocer's shop, grocery **2.** (*restaurante*) snack bar
colmado, -a *adj* (*lleno*) full; (*repleto*) heaped; **un año** ~ **de felicidad** a very happy year
colmar I. *vt* **1.** (*vaso*) ~ **de algo** to fill to the brim with sth **2.** (*alabanzas*) ~ **de algo** to heap on sth **3.** (*esperanzas*) to fulfil *Brit,* to fulfill *Am* **II.** *vr:* ~**se** to be fulfilled
colmena *f* beehive
colmenar *m* apiary
colmenero, -a *m, f* beekeeper
colmillo *m* eyetooth; (*de elefante*) tusk; (*de perro*) fang; **enseñar los** ~**s** *fig* to show one's teeth
colmo *m* (*lo máximo*) height; **el** ~ **de la elegancia** the height of elegance ▶ **¡esto es el** ~**!** this is the last straw!; **para** ~ on top of everything
colocación *f* **1.** (*empleo*) job **2.** (*disposición*) placing **3.** COM (*inversión*) investment **4.** DEP (*posición*) position
colocado, -a *adj inf* (*bebido*) plastered, pissed *Brit;* (*drogado*) high, stoned
colocar <c→qu> I. *vt* **1.** (*emplazar*) to place; (*según un orden*) to arrange; (*poner*) to put; (*cuadro*) to hang; (*cartel*) to put up **2.** DEP (*balón*) to kick; (*flecha*) to shoot **3.** COM (*invertir*) to invest; (*mercancías*) to sell **4.** (*empleo*) to find a job for **5.** (*casar*) to marry off **6.** *inf* (*encarcelar*) to lock up **II.** *vr:* ~**se 1.** (*empleo*) to get a job **2.** (*sombrero, gafas*) to put on **3.** (*posicionarse*) to place oneself; (*sentarse*) to sit (down) **4.** *inf* (*alcohol*) to get plastered; (*drogas*) to get high; (*heroína*) to shoot up
Colombia *f* Colombia

> **Colombia** (official title: **República de Colombia**) lies in the northwestern part of South America, between the Caribbean and the Pacific Ocean. The capital (**Santa Fe de**) **Bogotá** is also the largest city in the country. The official language of **Colombia** is Spanish and the monetary unit is the **peso**.

colombiano, -a *adj, m, f* Colombian
colombicultura *f* pigeon breeding
colombino, -a *adj* of Columbus
colon *m* ANAT colon
Colón *m* **1.** (*Cristóbal*) Columbus **2.** (*moneda*) colon
colonia *f* **1.** BIO, POL (*aglomeración*) colony **2.** *pl* (*para niños*) holiday camp **3.** (*barrio*) suburb **4.** (*perfume*) cologne
Colonia *f* Cologne; **agua de** ~ eau de cologne
coloniaje *m* AmL **1.** (*período*) colonial period **2.** (*sistema*) system of colonial government **3.** *pey* (*esclavitud*) slavery
colonialismo *m* colonialism
colonialista *adj, mf* colonialist
colonización *f* **1.** POL (*conquista*) colonization **2.** (*población*) settling
colonizador(a) I. *adj* colonizing II. *m(f)* **1.** (*conquistador*) colonizer **2.** (*poblador*) settler
colonizar <z→c> *vt* **1.** (*conquistar*) to colonize **2.** (*poblar*) to settle
colono *m* **1.** (*de una colonia*) settler **2.** (*labrador*) tenant farmer
coloquial *adj* LING colloquial
coloquio *m* **1.** (*conversación*) conversation; (*científico*) colloquium **2.** (*congreso*) conference
color *m* **1.** (*en general*) colour *Brit,* color *Am;* **película en** ~ colour [*o* color *Am*] film; **un hombre de** ~ a coloured [*o* colored *Am*] man; **huevos de** ~ *AmL* brown eggs; **nuestros** ~**es** DEP our team; **mudar de** ~ (*palidecer*) to turn pale; (*ruborizarse*) to blush; **subido de** ~ risqué; **sacar los** ~**es a alguien** to embarrass sb **2.** (*sustancia*) dye **3.** POL (*ideología*) hue ▶ **verlo todo de** ~ **de rosa** to see everything through rose-tinted spectacles
coloración *f* **1.** (*acto*) colouring *Brit,* coloring *Am* **2.** (*resultado, carácter*) coloration
colorado, -a *adj* **1.** (*rojo*) red; **ponerse** ~ to blush **2.** (*coloreado*) coloured *Brit,* colored *Am*
colorante I. *adj* colouring *Brit,* coloring *Am* II. *m* colouring *Brit,* coloring *Am*
colorar *vt* to colour *Brit,* to color *Am*
colorear I. *vt* **1.** (*dar color*) to colour *Brit,* to color *Am;* (*pintar*) to paint; (*teñir*) to dye, to tint **2.** (*al relatar*) to portray in a favourable [*o* favorable *Am*] light II. *vi* **1.** (*frutos*) to redden **2.** (*tirar a rojo*) to be reddish
colorido *m* colour(ing) *Brit,* color(ing) *Am*
colosal *adj* colossal
coloso *m* **1.** (*estatua*) colossus **2.** (*persona*) giant; (*en un campo*) colossus
columbrar *vt* **1.** (*divisar*) to make out **2.** (*solución*) to begin to see
columna *f* **1.** *t.* MIL (*pilar, periódico*) column

2. ANAT ~ **vertebral** spinal column **3.** *fig* (*apoyo*) pillar

columnista *mf* columnist

columpiar I. *vt* **1.**(*balancear*) to swing (to and fro) **2.**(*mecer*) to push on a swing II. *vr:* ~**se** to swing

columpio *m* **1.**(*para niños*) swing **2.** *AmL* (*mecedora*) rocking chair

colza *f* rape

coma[1] *m* MED coma

coma[2] *f* LING comma

comadre *f* **1.** *inf* (*comadrona*) midwife **2.**(*madrina*) godmother **3.** *inf* (*vecina*) neighbour *Brit*, neighbor *Am* **4.** *inf* (*amiga íntima*) bosom friend **5.** *inf* (*chismosa*) gossip **6.** *inf* (*celestina*) go-between

comadrear *vi inf* to gossip

comadreja *f* weasel

comadrona *f* midwife

comandancia *f* **1.**(*mando*) command **2.**(*cuartel*) command headquarters **3.** MIL, NÁUT (*zona*) command

comandante *m* **1.** MIL commander; (*grado*) commanding officer **2.** NÁUT captain **3.** AVIAT squadron leader

comandar *vi, vt* to command

comando *m* **1.** MIL command **2.** INFOR ~ **de arranque** start command

comarca *f* (*zona*) area; (*región*) region

comba *f* **1.**(*curvatura*) bend; (*de madera*) warp; (*de una cuerda*) sag **2.**(*cuerda*) skipping rope; (*juego*) skipping; **saltar a la** ~ to skip

combar I. *vt* to bend; (*madera*) to warp II. *vr:* ~**se** to bend; (*madera*) to warp; (*cuerda*) to sag

combate *m* **1.**(*lucha*) combat; (*batalla*) battle **2.** DEP (*competición*) competition; (*partido*) match; ~ **de boxeo** boxing match; **fuera de** ~ out of action

combatiente *adj, mf* combatant

combatir I. *vi* to fight II. *vt* **1.**(*luchar*) to fight **2.**(*rebatir*) to combat

combativo, -a *adj* combative

combi *m* fridge-freezer, refrigerator-freezer *Am*

combinación *f* **1.**(*composición*) combination; *t.* MAT permutation; ~ **ganadora** winning combination **2.** QUÍM compound **3.**(*de transportes*) connection **4.**(*lencería*) slip

combinado *m* cocktail

combinar I. *vi* to go II. *vt* **1.**(*componer*) to combine **2.**(*unir*) to unite; ~ **ideas** to link ideas **3.**(*coordinar*) to coordinate **4.** MAT to permutate III. *vr:* ~**se** to combine; *pey* (*compincharse*) to band together

combustible I. *adj* combustible II. *m* fuel

combustión *f* combustion

comecocos *m inv* **1.** *inf* (*obsesión*) obsession **2.**(*juego*) Pacman

comedia *f* **1.** TEAT (*obra*) play; (*divertida*) comedy **2.** CINE comedy **3.** *inf* (*farsa*) farce; **hacer** ~ to pretend

comediante, -a *m, f* **1.** CINE, TEAT actor **2.**(*farsante*) fraud

comedido, -a *adj* **1.**(*moderado*) moderate; (*contenido*) restrained **2.** *AmL* (*servicial*) obliging

comedimiento *m* **1.**(*moderación*) moderation; (*contenimiento*) restraint **2.**(*modestia*) modesty **3.**(*cortesía*) courtesy **4.** *AmL* (*disposición*) willingness

comediógrafo, -a *m, f* playwright

comedirse *irr como pedir vr* **1.**(*moderarse*) to behave moderately; (*contenerse*) to show restraint **2.** *AmL* (*ofrecerse*) to offer

comedor *m* **1.**(*sala*) dining room; (*en una empresa*) canteen; ~ **universitario** refectory **2.**(*mobiliario*) dining-room furniture

comején *m AmL* **1.**(*termita*) termite **2.**(*zozobra*) nagging uneasiness

comensal *mf* fellow diner

comentador(a) *m(f)* commmentator

comentar *vt* **1.**(*hablar sobre algo*) to talk about; (*hacer comentarios*) to comment on; (*explicar*) to explain **2.**(*una obra: criticar*) to discuss, to review; (*interpretar*) to interpret **3.** *pey* (*cotillear*) ~ **algo** to gossip about sth **4.** *inf* (*contar*) to mention

comentario *m* **1.**(*general*) comment; (*análisis*) commentary **2.** *pl* (*murmuraciones*) gossip

comentarista *mf* commentator

comenzar *irr como empezar* I. *vi* to begin, to commence; ~ **por hacer algo** to begin by doing sth; ~ **a trabajar** to begin to work; **para** ~ to begin with II. *vt* to begin, to commence *form*

comer I. *vi* **1.**(*alimentarse*) to eat; **dar de** ~ **a un animal** to feed an animal; ~ **caliente** to have a warm meal **2.**(*almorzar*) to have lunch; **antes/después de** ~ before/after lunch ►~ **por siete** to eat like a horse II. *vt* **1.**(*ingerir*) to eat **2.** *fig* (*consumir*) to consume **3.**(*corroer*) to eat away **4.**(*colores*) to fade **5.**(*dilapidar*) to squander **6.**(*en juegos*) to take ►**sin** ~**lo ni beberlo** without asking for it; **me echaron la culpa a mí sin** ~**lo ni beberlo** I got blamed although I had nothing to do with it III. *vr:* ~**se 1.**(*ingerir*) to eat up; ~**se a alguien a besos** to smother sb with kisses; **está para comérsela** she looks a treat **2.**(*corroer*) to eat away **3.**(*colores*) to fade **4.**(*palabras*) to skip; (*al pronunciar*) to slur

comercial[1] I. *adj* commercial II. *mf* (*profesión*) sales representative

comercial[2] *m AmL* (*anuncio*) commercial

comercialización *f* **1.**(*de un producto*) marketing **2.**(*de un acontecimiento*) commercialization

comercializar <z→c> *vt* **1.**(*producto*) to market **2.**(*acontecimiento*) to commercialize

comerciante, -a *m, f* shopkeeper; (*negociante*) dealer

comerciar *vi* **1.**(*tener trato con*) ~ **con un país** to trade with a country **2.**(*traficar en*) ~ **en algo** to deal in sth

comercio *m* **1.**(*actividad*) trade; ~ **exterior**

foreign trade; ~ **al por mayor** wholesale trade **2.** (*tienda*) shop **3.** (*relaciones*) dealings *pl*
comestibles *mpl* foods; **tienda de** ~ grocer's (shop), grocery
cometa[1] *m* ASTR comet
cometa[2] *f* (*de papel*) kite
cometer *vt* **1.** *t.* JUR to commit; (*error*) to make **2.** COM to give commission
cometido *m* (*encargo*) assignment; (*tarea*) task; (*obligación*) commitment
comezón *f* **1.** (*picor*) itch **2.** (*malestar*) uneasiness
cómic *m* <cómics> comic
comicios *mpl* **1.** (*elecciones*) elections *pl* **2.** HIST comitia
cómico, -a I. *adj* (*relativo a la comedia*) comedy; (*divertido*) comical **II.** *m, f* comedian
comida *f* **1.** (*alimento*) food; (*plato*) meal; (*cocina*) cooking; ~ **de** [*o* **para**] **animales** pet food; ~ **basura** junk food; ~ **casera** plain [*o* homestyle] cooking; ~ **francesa** French cuisine; ~ **rápida** fast food; **cama y** ~ bed and board **2.** (*horario*) ~ **principal** main meal (of the day) **3.** (*almuerzo*) lunch; ~ **de negocios** business lunch **4.** *Col, Perú, Chile* (*cena*) supper
comidilla *f inf* special interest; **ser la** ~ **del pueblo** to be the talk of the town
comienzo *m* (*principio*) beginning; **al** ~ at first; **a** ~**s de mes** at the beginning of the month
comillas *fpl* inverted commas; **entre** ~ in inverted commas
comilona *f inf* feast, blowout *inf*
comino *m* cumin; **no valer un** ~ not to be worth anything
comisaría *f* **1.** (*edificio*) ~ **de policía** police station, precinct *Am* **2.** (*cargo*) commissioner-ship
comisariato *m AmL* company store; (*almacén*) warehouse
comisario, -a *m, f* **1.** (*delegado*) commissioner **2.** (*de policía*) superintendant, chief police inspector
comisión *f* **1.** (*cometido*) assignment **2.** (*delegación*) commission; (*comité*) committee; **Comisión Europea** European Commission; ~ **permanente** standing committee **3.** COM commission; **a** ~ on a commission basis **4.** ADMIN ~ **de servicios** secondment
comisionado, -a *m, f* commissioner
comisionar *vt* to commission
comisura *f* ANAT (*del cráneo*) commissure; ~ **de los labios** corner of the mouth
comité *m* committee; ~ **de empresa** works committee
comitiva *f* procession; ~ **fúnebre** cortège
como I. *adv* **1.** (*del modo que*) as, like; **hazlo** ~ **quieras** do it any way you like; ~ **quien** [*o* **aquel que**] **dice** so to speak; **blanco** ~ **la nieve** white as snow; **vivfa** ~ **un hermitaño** he lived like a hermit **2.** (*comparativo*) as; **es tan alto** ~ **su hermano** he's as tall as his

brother **3.** (*aproximadamente*) about; **hace** ~ **un año** about a year ago **4.** (*y también*) as well as **5.** (*en calidad de*) as; **trabaja** ~ **camarero** he works as a waiter **II.** *conj* **1.** (*causal*) as, since; ~ **no tengo tiempo, no voy** I'm not going because I haven't time; **lo sé,** ~ **que lo vi** I know because I saw it **2.** (*condicional*) if **3.** (*con "si" +subj o con "que"*) as if **4.** (*final*) ~ **para** in order to **5.** (*temporal*) as soon as
cómo I. *adv* **1.** (*modal, exclamativo*) how; **¿~ estás?** how are you?; **¿~** (*dice*)? sorry?, pardon?; **según y** ~ it all depends **2.** (*por qué*) why; **¿~** (**no**)? why not?; **¡~ no!** certainly! **II.** *m* **el** ~ the how
cómoda *f* chest (of drawers), dresser *Am*
comodidad *f* **1.** (*confort*) comfort **2.** (*conveniencia*) convenience
comodín *m* **1.** (*en juegos*) joker **2.** (*palabra*) all-purpose word **3.** INFOR wild card **4.** (*pretexto*) pretext
cómodo, -a *adj* **1.** *ser* (*cosa*) comfortable; (*conveniente*) convenient **2.** *ser* (*perezoso*) lazy **3.** *estar* (*a gusto*) comfortable; **¡ponte ~!** make yourself comfortable!
comoquiera I. *adv* somehow **II.** *conj* **1.** (*causal*) ~ **que** +*subj* since **2.** (*concesiva*) ~ **que** +*subj* in whatever way; ~ **que sea eso** however that may be
compact (**disc**) *m* compact disc
compacto *m* **1.** (*disco*) compact disc **2.** (*reproductor*) compact disc player **3.** (*equipo*) compact hi-fi system
compacto, -a *adj* **1.** (*textura, tamaño*) compact; (*denso*) dense; (*firme*) firm; **disco** ~ compact disc **2.** (*escritura*) close
compadecer *irr como crecer* **I.** *vt* to feel sorry for **II.** *vr* ~**se de alguien/algo** to (take) pity (on) sth/sb
compadre *m* **1.** (*padrino*) godfather **2.** (*amigo*) friend, mate *Brit*, buddy
compadrear *vi* **1.** (*de compadraje*) to be pals **2.** *CSur* (*presumir*) to show off
compadreo *m pey* chumminess
compadrito *m AmS* (*chulo, bravucón*) braggart
compaginación *f* **1.** (*compatibilización*) combining **2.** (*paginación*) page makeup
compaginar I. *vt* **1.** (*combinar*) to combine **2.** (*paginar*) to page up **II.** *vr:* ~**se 1.** (*combinar*) to combine **2.** (*armonizar*) to go together
compañerismo *m* companionship; (*camaradería*) comradeship; DEP team spirit
compañero, -a *m, f* **1.** (*persona*) companion; (*amigo*) friend; (*pareja*) partner; *t.* POL comrade; ~ **de clase** schoolmate; UNIV fellow student; ~ **de piso** flatmate, roommate; ~ **de trabajo** workmate **2.** (*cosa*) other one (of a pair)
compañía *f* company; **animal de** ~ pet; **hacer** ~ **a alguien** to keep sb company
comparación *f* comparison; **no hay ni punto de** ~ there's no comparison
comparar I. *vt* to compare **II.** *vr:* ~**se** to be

compared
comparativo *m* comparative
comparecencia *f* *t.* JUR appearance (in court); **no** ~ failure to appear
comparecer *irr como crecer* *vi* *t.* JUR to appear (in court)
comparsa *mf* **1.** TEAT extra **2.** (*desfile de carnaval*) group of people with float
compartimentar *vt* to compartmentalize
compartim(i)ento *m* compartment
compartir *vt* **1.** (*tener en común*) to share **2.** (*repartirse*) to share (out)
compás *m* **1.** (*en dibujo*) compass **2.** (*ritmo*) beat; MÚS time **3.** AVIAT, NÁUT (*brújula*) compass
compasión *f* ~ **de alguien** pity on sb, compassion [*o* sympathy] with sb; **sin** ~ pitiless(ly)
compasivo, -a *adj* compassionate, sympathetic
compatibilidad *f* compatibility
compatibilizar <z→c> *vt* to reconcile
compatible *adj* compatible
compatriota *mf* compatriot, fellow citizen
compeler *vt* to compel
compendiar *vt* to summarize
compendio *m* **1.** (*resumen*) summary; (*manual*) textbook **2.** (*epítome*) epitome
compenetración *f* (mutual) understanding; (*fusión*) interpenetration
compenetrarse *vr* **1.** QUÍM (*fusionarse*) to interpenetrate **2.** (*identificarse*) to reach an understanding
compensación *f* compensation
compensar *vt* ~ **de algo** to compensate for sth
competencia *f* **1.** *t.* COM, DEP (*competición*) competition; (*rivalidad*) rivalry; ~ **desleal** unfair competition **2.** *t.* LING competence **3.** (*responsabilidad*) responsibility; **esto (no) es de mi** ~ I'm not responsible for this
competente *adj* competent
competer *vi* (*corresponder*) ~ **a alguien** to be the responsibility of sb
competición *f* competition
competidor(a) **I.** *adj* competing **II.** *m(f)* *t.* ECON competitor
competir *irr como pedir* *vi* **1.** (*enfrentarse*) ~ **por algo** to compete for sth **2.** (*igualarse*) to rival each other
competitividad *f* competitiveness
competitivo, -a *adj* competitive
compilador *m* INFOR compiler
compilar *vt* *t.* INFOR to compile
compincharse *vr pey, inf* to team up
compinche *mf pey, inf* mate *Brit*, buddy
complacencia *f* **1.** (*agrado*) willingness; (*satisfacción*) satisfaction; (*placer*) pleasure **2.** (*indulgencia*) indulgence
complacer *irr como crecer* **I.** *vt* (*gustar*) to please; ~ **una petición** to grant a request **II.** *vr:* ~**se** (*gustar*) ~**se en algo** to be pleased to sth
complaciente *adj* **1.** (*servicial*) obliging **2.** (*indulgente*) ~ **para** [*o* **con**] **alguien** indul-

gent towards sb
complejidad *f* complexity
complejo *m* complex
complejo, -a *adj* complex
complementar **I.** *vt* to complement; (*completar*) to complete **II.** *vr:* ~**se** to complement each other
complemento *m* **1.** *t.* LING complement **2.** (*culminación*) culmination **3.** (*paga*) supplementary payment, bonus; (*recargo*) surcharge **4.** *pl* (*accesorio*) accessory
completamente *adv* completely
completar **I.** *vt* to complete **II.** *vr:* ~**se** to complete each other
completo, -a *adj* (*íntegro*) complete; (*perfecto*) perfect; (*total*) total; (*lleno*) full; (*cine, espectáculo*) sold out; **pensión completa** full board; **la obra completa de Lorca** the complete works of Lorca
complexión *f* **1.** (*constitución*) constitution, build **2.** *AmL* (*tez*) complexion
complicación *f* **1.** *t.* MED (*problema*) complication **2.** (*complejidad*) complexity
complicar <c→qu> **I.** *vt* **1.** (*dificultar*) to complicate **2.** (*implicar*) to involve **II.** *vr:* ~**se** **1.** (*dificultarse*) to get complicated **2.** (*embrollarse*) to get involved
cómplice *mf* *t.* JUR accomplice; **hacerse** ~ **de alguien/algo** to become sb's accomplice
complicidad *f* complicity
compló *m* <complós>, **complot** *m* <complots> conspiracy
componente *m* **1.** *t.* TÉC component; MAT, QUÍM constituent; ~**s lógicos** INFOR software **2.** (*miembro*) member
componer *irr como poner* **I.** *vt* **1.** (*formar*) to put together; (*organizar*) to organize **2.** (*constituir*) to make up **3.** *t.* MÚS to compose **4.** TIPO to set (up) **5.** (*recomponer*) to repair **6.** (*asear*) to arrange **7.** *AmL* (*castrar*) to castrate **8.** *AmL* (*hueso*) to set **II.** *vr:* ~**se** **1.** (*constituirse*) to consist **2.** (*arreglarse*) to tidy oneself up **3.** *AmL* (*mejorarse*) to get better
comportamiento *m* conduct, behaviour *Brit*, behavior *Am*; *t.* TÉC performance
comportar **I.** *vt* to involve; **esto (no) comporta que** +*subj* this (doesn't) mean(s) that **II.** *vr:* ~**se** to behave
composición *f* **1.** *t.* LIT, MÚS composition **2.** TIPO typesetting; **taller de** ~ composing room
compositor(a) *m(f)* composer
compost *m sin pl* compost
compostación *f,* **compostaje** *m* composting
compostura *f* **1.** (*realización*) composition **2.** (*corrección*) repair **3.** (*aspecto*) tidiness **4.** (*comedimiento*) composure
compota *f* compote
compra *f* purchase; ~**s** shopping; **ir de** ~**s** to go shopping
comprador(a) *m(f)* buyer; (*cliente*) customer
comprar **I.** *vt* **1.** (*adquirir*) to buy; ~ **al con-**

tado to pay cash; ~ **a plazos** to buy on hire-purchase, to buy on an installment plan **2.** (*corromper*) to buy off **II.** *vr:* ~**se** to buy

comprender *vt* **1.** (*entender*) to understand; **hacerse** ~ to make oneself understood; ~ **mal** to misunderstand **2.** (*contener*) to comprise; (*abarcar*) to take in; (*incluir*) to include

comprensible *adj* understandable, comprehensible

comprensión *f* **1.** (*capacidad*) understanding; (*entendimiento*) comprehension **2.** (*inclusión*) inclusion

comprensivo, -a *adj* **1.** (*benévolo*) understanding **2.** (*tolerante*) tolerant **3.** (*inclusivo*) comprehensive

compresa *f* **1.** *t.* MED (*apósito*) compress **2.** (*higiénica*) sanitary towel *Brit,* sanitary napkin *Am*

compresión *f* compression

compresor *m* compressor

comprimido *m* pill

comprimir **I.** *vt* **1.** *t.* FÍS, TÉC to compress **2.** (*reprimir*) to restrain **II.** *vr:* ~**se** to control oneself

comprobación *f* **1.** (*control*) checking **2.** (*verificación*) verification; (*confirmación*) confirmation; (*prueba*) proof

comprobante **I.** *adj* (*justificante*) justifying; (*de control*) supporting **II.** *m* voucher, proof

comprobar <o→ue> *vt* **1.** (*controlar*) to check **2.** (*verificar*) to verify; (*confirmar*) to confirm; (*justificar*) to justify; (*probar*) to prove

comprometedor(a) *adj* compromising

comprometer **I.** *vt* **1.** (*implicar*) to involve **2.** (*exponer*) to endanger **3.** (*arriesgar*) to put at risk **4.** (*obligar*) to commit **II.** *vr:* ~**se** **1.** (*implicarse*) to compromise oneself **2.** (*obligarse*) to commit oneself; ~**se** (**en matrimonio**) to get engaged

compromiso *m* **1.** (*vinculación*) commitment; (*obligación*) obligation; **visita de** ~ formal visit; **sin** ~ without obligation; (**soltero y**) **sin** ~ free and single **2.** (*promesa*) promise; ~ **matrimonial** engagement **3.** (*acuerdo*) agreement **4.** (*aprieto*) awkward situation **5.** (*cita*) engagement

compuerta *f* (*de una presa*) sluice gate

compuesto *m t.* QUÍM compound

compulsa *f* certified copy

compulsar *vt* **1.** JUR to certify **2.** (*cotejar*) to compare

compulsivo, -a *adj* compulsive

compungido, -a *adj* **1.** (*contrito*) remorseful **2.** (*triste*) sad

compungir <g→j> **I.** *vt* to make remorseful **II.** *vr:* ~**se** (*sentir arrepentimiento*) to feel remorseful

computación *f* **1.** (*cálculo*) calculation **2.** INFOR computing

computador *m AmL* computer

computador(a) *adj* computer

computadora *f AmL* computer

computar *vt* **1.** (*calcular*) to calculate **2.** (*considerar*) to count

computerizar <z→c> *vt* to computerize

cómputo *m* calculation; ~ **de votos** count of votes

comulgar <g→gu> *vi* **1.** REL to take communion **2.** (*estar de acuerdo*) to agree

común **I.** *adj* common; **de** ~ **acuerdo** by common consent; **sentido** ~ common sense; **fuera de lo** ~ out of the ordinary; **poco** ~ unusual; **por lo** ~ usually **II.** *m* POL **los Comunes** the Commons *Brit*

comuna *f* **1.** *t.* HIST commune **2.** *AmL* (*municipio*) municipality

comunal *adj* ADMIN, POL communal; **elecciones** ~**es** municipal elections

comunicación *f* **1.** (*en general*) communication; **ponerse en** ~ **con alguien** to get in touch with sb **2.** (*comunicado*) message; (*ponencia*) paper **3.** (*conexión*) connection; ~ **telefónica** telephone call **4.** (*transmisión*) transmission **5.** (*de transporte*) link **6.** *pl t.* TEL communications *pl*

comunicado *m* communiqué; ~ **de prensa** press release

comunicar <c→qu> **I.** *vi* **1.** (*estar unido*) to be joined; (*estar en contacto*) to be connected **2.** (*conectar*) to connect **3.** (*teléfono*) to be engaged [*o* busy *Am*] **II.** *vt* **1.** (*informar*) to inform **2.** (*transmitir*) to communicate **3.** (*unir*) to connect; (*contactar*) to contact **4.** (*al teléfono*) to put through **III.** *vr:* ~**se** **1.** (*entenderse*) to communicate **2.** (*relacionarse*) to be connected

comunicativo, -a *adj* communicative

comunidad *f* community; ~ **de vecinos** residents' association; ~ **autónoma** autonomous region

comunión *f* communion

comunismo *m* POL communism

comunista **I.** *adj* POL communist(ic) **II.** *mf* POL communist

comunitario, -a *adj* **1.** (*colectivo*) communal **2.** (*municipal*) community **3.** POL (*Comunidad Europea*) Community

con **I.** *prep* **1.** (*compañía, instrumento, modo*) with; **estar** ~ **la gripe** to have the flu; ~ **el tiempo...** with time ... **2.** MAT **3** ~ **5** 3 point 5 **3.** (*actitud*) (**para**) ~ to, towards **4.** (*circunstancia*) ~ **este tiempo...** in this weather ... **5.** (*a pesar de*) in spite of **II.** *conj* + *infin* if; ~ **que** +*subj* as long as; ~ **sólo que** +*subj* if only

conato *m* **1.** (*intento*) attempt **2.** (*empeño*) effort

concatenación *f* (*acción*) linking

concatenar *vt* to link together

concavidad *f* concavity

cóncavo, -a *adj* concave

concebir *irr como pedir* **I.** *vi* to conceive **II.** *vt* to conceive; ~ **esperanzas** to have hopes

conceder *vt* **1.** (*otorgar*) to grant; (*asignar*) to give; ~ **la palabra a alguien** to give sb the floor; ~ **un premio** to award a prize **2.** (*admi-*

tir) to concede

concejal(a) *m(f)* town [*o* city] councillor *Brit,* councilman *m Am,* councilwoman *f Am*

concejo *m* council

concelebrar *vt* REL to concelebrate

concentración *f* concentration; ~ **pacífica** peaceful demonstration

concentrado *m* (*extracto*) concentrate

concentrar I. *vt* to concentrate II. *vr:* ~**se** 1. (*reunirse*) to assemble; (*agruparse*) to gather together 2. (*centrarse*) to concentrate

concepción *f* conception

concepto *m* 1. (*noción*) notion; (*plan*) concept 2. (*opinión*) opinion 3. (*motivo*) **bajo** [*o* **por**] **ningún** ~ on no account 4. (*calidad*) **en** ~ **de** by way of

conceptual *adj* conceptual

conceptualizar <z→c> *vt* to conceptualize

concernir *irr como cernir vi* to concern; **en** [*o* **por**] **lo que concierne a alguien...** as far as sb is concerned ...

concertación *f* coordination; ~ **social** social harmony

concertar <e→ie> I. *vi* t. LING to agree II. *vt* 1. (*arreglar*) to arrange 2. MÚS (*afinar*) to tune 3. (*armonizar*) to harmonize III. *vr:* ~**se** 1. (*ponerse de acuerdo*) to come to an agreement 2. *pey* (*compincharse*) to band together

concertista *mf* MÚS soloist

concesión *f* 1. *t.* COM concession 2. (*de una beca, de un premio*) awarding

concesionario, -a *m, f* dealer

concha *f* 1. (*del molusco*) shell; (*de tortuga*) tortoiseshell 2. TEAT prompt box 3. *AmL* (*descaro*) nerve 4. *AmL, vulg* (*vulva*) cunt ▶**tener más ~s que un galápago** *inf* to be a slippery customer

conchabar I. *vt* 1. (*mezclar*) to mix 2. *AmL* (*contratar*) to hire II. *vr:* ~**se** *inf* to plot; **estar conchabado con alguien** to be in league with sb

conchudo, -a *adj* 1. (*con conchas*) conchiferous 2. *AmL, inf* (*sinvergüenza*) shameless 3. *Méx, Col, inf* (*indolente*) sluggish

conciencia *f* 1. (*conocimiento*) awareness; **tomar** ~ **de algo** to become aware of sth 2. (*moral*) conscience; **a** ~ conscientiously; **libertad de** ~ freedom of worship; **(sin) cargo de** ~ (without) remorse; **me remuerde la** ~ my conscience is pricking me

concienciar I. *vt* 1. (*persuadir*) to persuade 2. (*sensibilizar*) to make aware II. *vr:* ~**se** 1. (*convencerse*) to convince oneself 2. (*sensibilizarse*) to become aware

concienzudo, -a *adj* conscientious

concierto *m* 1. MÚS (*función*) concert; (*obra*) concerto 2. (*disposición*) order 3. (*armonía*) harmony 4. *t.* ECON (*acuerdo*) agreement

conciliación *f* (*reconciliación*) reconciliation; ~ **laboral** arbitration

conciliador(a) *adj* conciliatory

conciliar I. *vt* 1. (*reconciliar*) to reconcile; (*armonizar*) to harmonize 2. *fig* ~ **el sueño** to

get to sleep II. *vr:* ~**se** (*reconciliarse*) to be reconciled

concilio *m t.* REL council

concisión *f* concision

conciso, -a *adj* concise

concitar *vt* to arouse

conciudadano, -a *m, f* fellow citizen

conclave *m,* **cónclave** *m* 1. REL conclave 2. (*reunión*) meeting

concluir *irr como huir* I. *vi* to end; **¡asunto concluido!** that's settled! II. *vt* 1. (*terminar*) to complete; (*negocio*) to conclude 2. (*deducir*) ~ **de algo** to conclude from sth III. *vr:* ~**se** to end

conclusión *f* conclusion; **en** ~ (*en suma*) in short; (*por último*) in conclusion; **llegar a la** ~ **de que...** to come to the conclusion that ...

concluyente *adj* conclusive; (*determinante*) decisive, unequivocal

concomitante *adj* concomitant

concordancia *f* 1. (*correspondencia*) concordance 2. LING agreement

concordar <o→ue> I. *vi* 1. (*coincidir*) to coincide 2. LING to agree II. *vt* 1. (*armonizar*) to reconcile 2. LING to make agree

concordia *f* harmony

concreción *f* 1. (*precisión*) sticking 2. (*acumulación*) agglomeration 3. MED stone

concretar I. *vt* 1. (*precisar*) to put in concrete form 2. (*limitar*) to limit II. *vr:* ~**se** to limit oneself

concretizar <z→c> *vt v.* **concretar**

concreto, -a *adj* concrete; **en** ~ specifically

concubina *f* concubine

conculcar <c→qu> *vt* to violate

concurrencia *f* 1. (*coincidencia*) coincidence 2. (*asistencia*) attendance 3. (*público*) audience 4. (*competencia*) competition

concurrido, -a *adj* crowded

concurrir *vi* 1. (*coincidir en el lugar*) to come together; (*en el tiempo*) to coincide 2. (*concursar*) ~ **por algo** to compete for sth 3. (*participar*) to take part 4. (*presenciar*) ~ **en algo** to attend sth

concursante *mf* 1. (*aspirante*) candidate 2. (*participante*) competitor, contestant

concursar I. *vi* to compete II. *vt* JUR ~ **a alguien** to declare sb bankrupt [*o* insolvent]

concurso *m* 1. *t.* DEP competition 2. (*oposición*) (public) competition 3. (*coincidencia*) coincidence 4. (*ayuda*) help

condado *m* 1. (*título*) countship 2. (*territorio*) county, shire *Brit;* HIST earldom

conde(sa) *m(f)* count *m,* countess *f*

condecoración *f* MIL decoration

condecorar *vt* MIL to decorate

condena *f* sentence, conviction; **cumplir una** ~ to serve a sentence

condenado, -a I. *adj inf* condemned II. *m, f* 1. (*reo*) convicted person, convict 2. REL **los ~s** the damned 3. *inf* (*endemoniado*) wretch 4. *inf* (*niño*) rascal

condenar I. *vt* 1. (*sentenciar, reprobar*) to

condemn **2.** REL to damn **3.** (*tapiar*) to wall up **II.** *vr:* ~**se 1.** REL to be damned **2.** (*acusarse*) to confess

condensador *m* ELEC condenser

condensar I. *vt* to condense **II.** *vr:* ~**se** to condense

condesa *f v.* **conde**

condescendencia *f* **1.** (*dignación*) condescension **2.** (*transigencia*) ~ **con algo/alguien** acquiescence to [*o* in] sth/sb

condescender <e→ie> *vi* **1.** (*avenirse*) ~ **con algo/alguien** to agree to st/with sb **2.** (*rebajarse*) to condescend

condescendiente *adj* **1.** (*benévolo*) kind **2.** (*complaciente*) obliging **3.** (*arrogante*) condescending

condición *f* **1.** (*índole de una cosa*) nature **2.** (*estado, requisito*) condition; **a** ~ **de que** +*subj* on condition that, providing **3.** (*situación*) position **4.** (*clase*) social class

condicional I. *adj t.* LING conditional **II.** *m* LING conditional

condicionar *vt* **1.** (*supeditar*) ~ **a algo** to make conditional on sth **2.** (*acondicionar*) to condition

condimentar *vt* to season, to flavour *Brit,* to flavor *Am*

condimento *m* seasoning, flavouring *Brit,* flavoring *Am*

condolencia *f* condolence, sympathy

condolerse <o→ue> *vr* ~**se de algo** to sympathize with sth

condón *m* condom

condonación *f* (*de una deuda*) writing off

condonar *vt* (*deuda*) to write off

cóndor *m* condor

conducción *f* **1.** (*transporte*) transport(ation) **2.** (*coche*) driving; ~ **temeraria** reckless driving **3.** (*conducto, administración*) management

conducir *irr como traducir* **I.** *vt* **1.** (*llevar*) to take; (*transportar*) to transport **2.** (*guiar*) to guide **3.** (*arrastrar*) to lead **4.** (*pilotar*) to drive **5.** (*mandar*) to direct **II.** *vi* **1.** (*dirigir*) to lead **2.** (*pilotar*) to drive **III.** *vr:* ~**se** to behave

conducta *f* **1.** (*comportamiento*) conduct, behaviour *Brit,* behavior *Am* **2.** (*mando*) management

conductismo *m* PSICO behaviourism *Brit,* behaviorism *Am*

conducto *m* **1.** (*tubo*) pipe **2.** MED canal; ~ **auditivo** ear canal **3.** (*mediación*) channels *pl*

conductor *m* FÍS conductor

conductor(a) I. *adj* conductive; **hilo** ~ conductor wire **II.** *m(f)* **1.** (*chófer*) driver **2.** (*jefe*) leader

conectar I. *vt* **1.** (*enlazar*) to connect **2.** (*enchufar*) to plug in **II.** *vi* to communicate

conejera *f* **1.** (*madriguera*) burrow, warren *fig,* overcrowded room **2.** *t. fig* den

conejillo *m* ~ **de Indias** *t. fig* guinea pig

conejo, -a *m, f* rabbit

conexión *f* **1.** *t.* TEL connection **2.** *pl* (*amis-*

tades) connections *pl*

confabularse *vr* to plot

confección *f* making; (*de vestidos*) dressmaking

confeccionar *vt* to make; (*plan*) to draw up

confederación *f* confederation

confederar I. *vt* to confederate **II.** *vr:* ~**se** to form a confederation

conferencia *f* **1.** (*charla*) lecture **2.** (*encuentro*) conference **3.** (*plática*) talk **4.** (*llamada telefónica*) call

conferenciante *mf,* **conferentista** *mf AmL* lecturer

conferir *irr como sentir vt* to confer

confesar <e→ie> **I.** *vt* **1.** (*admitir*) to confess **2.** REL (*declarar*) to confess; ~ **a alguien** to confess, to hear sb's confession **II.** *vr:* ~**se** to confess; ~**se culpable** to admit one's guilt

confesión *f* confession

confes(i)onario *m* confessional (box)

confesor *m* confessor

confeti *m* confetti

confiado, -a *adj* **1.** *ser* (*crédulo*) trusting **2.** *estar* (*presumido*) vain; (*de sí mismo*) self-confident

confianza *f* **1.** (*crédito*) trust; **amiga de** ~ close friend **2.** (*esperanza*) confidence **3.** (*en uno mismo*) self-confidence **4.** (*familiaridad*) familiarity **5.** *pl* (*familiaridad excesiva*) familiarities *pl*

confiar <1. *pres:* confío> **I.** *vi* ~ **en algo/alguien** to trust in sth/sb **II.** *vt* to entrust **III.** *vr* ~**se a alguien** to confide in sb

confidencia *f* secret

confidencial *adj* confidential

confidente *mf* **1.** (*cómplice*) confidant *m,* confidante *f* **2.** (*espía*) informer

configuración *f* **1.** (*formación*) shaping **2.** (*forma*) shape **3.** INFOR configuration

configurar I. *vt* **1.** (*formar*) to shape **2.** INFOR to configure **II.** *vr:* ~**se** to take shape

confín I. *adj* bordering **II.** *m* **1.** (*frontera*) border **2.** (*final*) limit

confinar I. *vi* ~ **con algo** to border on sth **II.** *vt* to confine

confirmación *f t.* REL confirmation

confirmar I. *vt t.* REL to confirm **II.** *vr:* ~**se** to be confirmed

confiscación *f* confiscation

confiscar <c→qu> *vt* to confiscate

confitar *vt* (*en almíbar*) to preserve in syrup; (*con azúcar*) to candy

confitería *f* cake [*o* pastry] shop, sweet shop *Brit,* candy shop *Am*

confitura *f* jam

conflagración *f* war

conflictividad *f* disputes *pl*

conflicto *m* conflict

confluencia *f* confluence

confluir *irr como huir vi* (*ríos, calles*) to meet

conformación *f* shape

conformar I. *vt* **1.** (*contentar*) to satisfy **2.** (*formar*) to shape **3.** (*ajustar*) to adjust **II.** *vi*

to agree **III.** *vr:* ~**se 1.** (*contentarse*) to be satisfied **2.** (*ajustarse*) to adjust
conforme I. *adj* (*adecuado*) **estar** ~ **con algo** to be satisfied with sth **II.** *prep* according to **III.** *conj* (*como*) as
conformidad *f* **1.** (*afinidad*) similarity **2.** (*aprobación*) approval
confort *m sin pl* comfort
confortable *adj* comfortable
confortar I. *vt* **1.** (*vivificar*) to strengthen **2.** (*alentar*) to encourage; (*consolar*) to comfort **II.** *vr:* ~**se 1.** (*reanimarse*) to regain one's strength **2.** (*consolarse*) to take comfort
confraternizar <z→c> *vi* to fraternize
confrontación *f* **1.** (*comparación*) comparison **2.** (*enfrentamiento*) confrontation
confrontar I. *vt* **1.** (*comparar*) to compare **2.** (*enfrentar*) to confront **II.** *vr* ~**se con alguien** to face up to sb
Confucionismo *m* FILOS Confucianism
confundir I. *vt* **1.** (*trastocar*) to mistake **2.** (*mezclar*) to mix up **3.** (*embrollar*) to confuse **II.** *vr:* ~**se 1.** (*mezclarse*) to mix **2.** (*embrollarse*) to get confused
confusión *f* confusion
confuso, -a *adj* confused
congelación *f* **1.** (*solidificación*) freezing; ~ **salarial** pay freeze **2.** frostbite; MED
congelador *m* **1.** (*electrodoméstico*) freezer **2.** (*compartimento en la nevera*) ice [*o* freezer] compartment
congelar I. *vt t. fig* to freeze **II.** *vr:* ~**se 1.** (*solidificarse*) to freeze **2.** (*helarse*) to get frostbitten
congénere *mf* **el ladrón y sus** ~**s** the thief and others like him, the likes of the thief
congeniar *vi* **congeniar con** to get on [*o* along] with
congénito, -a *adj* congenital
congestión *f t.* MED congestion
congestionar I. *vt t.* MED to congest **II.** *vr:* ~**se** *t.* MED to become congested
conglomerar I. *vt* to conglomerate **II.** *vr:* ~**se** to conglomerate
Congo *m* **el** ~ the Congo
congoja *f* **1.** (*pena*) sorrow **2.** (*desconsuelo*) anguish
congola *f* Col (*pipa de fumar*) pipe
congoleño, -a, congolés, -esa *adj, m, f* Congolese
congraciar I. *vt* to win over **II.** *vr:* ~**se** to ingratiate oneself
congratular I. *vt* to congratulate **II.** *vr* ~**se de** [*o* **por**] **algo** to congratulate oneself on sth
congregación *f* **1.** (*reunión*) meeting **2.** REL congregation
congregar <g→gu> **I.** *vt* to bring together **II.** *vr:* ~**se** to gather
congresal *mf AmL* member of a congress
congresista *mf* **1.** POL delegate, congressman *m*, congresswoman *f* **2.** (*asisitente a un congreso*) congress member
congreso *m* **1.** POL congress **2.** (*reunión*) congress, convention

congrio *m* conger eel
congruencia *f* **1.** (*coherencia*) coherence **2.** MAT congruence
cónico, -a *adj* conical
conífera *f* conifer
conjetura *f* conjecture
conjeturar *vt* to speculate
conjugación *f* conjugation
conjugar <g→gu> *vt* **1.** (*combinar*) to combine **2.** LING to conjugate
conjunción *f* conjunction
conjuntamente *adv* jointly; ~ **con** together with
conjuntar I. *vi* to match; ~ **con** to go with **II.** *vt* to harmonize **III.** *vr:* ~**se** to come together
conjuntivitis *f inv* conjunctivitis
conjunto *m* **1.** (*unido*) unit **2.** (*totalidad*) whole; **en** ~ as a whole **3.** (*en representaciones artísticas*) ensemble **4.** (*ropa*) outfit **5.** MAT set
conjura *f,* **conjuración** *f* conspiracy
conjurar I. *vi* to conspire **II.** *vt* **1.** (*invocar*) to beseech **2.** (*alejar*) to ward off **III.** *vr:* ~**se** to conspire
conllevar *vt* **1.** (*implicar*) to involve **2.** (*soportar*) to bear
conmemoración *f* commemoration
conmemorar *vt* to commemorate
conmemorativo, -a *adj* commemorative
conmigo *pron pers* with me
conminar *vt* **1.** (*amenazar*) to threaten **2.** JUR to warn
conmiseración *f* commiseration
conmoción *f* **1.** MED concussion **2.** *fig* shock
conmocionar *vt* **1.** MED to concuss **2.** *fig* to shake
conmovedor(a) *adj* **1.** (*conmocionando*) stirring **2.** (*sentimental*) moving
conmover <o→ue> **I.** *vt* **1.** (*emocionar*) to move **2.** (*sacudir*) to shake **II.** *vr:* ~**se 1.** (*emocionarse*) to be moved **2.** (*sacudirse*) to be shaken
conmutación *f t.* LING commutation
conmutador *m* ELEC switch
conmutar *vt* **1.** (*cambiar*) to exchange **2.** (*una pena*) ~ **por algo** to commute to sth **3.** ELEC to switch
connaturalizar <z→c> **I.** *vt* to accustom **II.** *vr* ~**se con algo** to get accustomed to sth
connivencia *f* collusion
cono *m* cone; **Cono Sur** GEO *Argentina, Chile, Paraguay and Uruguay*

> The economic union between the four countries in the most southerly part of Latin America, **Argentina, Chile, Paraguay** and **Uruguay** is referred to as **Cono Sur**.

conocedor(a) I. *adj* ~ **de algo** knowledgeable about sth **II.** *m(f)* expert
conocer *irr como crecer* **I.** *vt* **1.** (*saber, tener*

trato) to know; ~ **de vista** to know by sight; **dar a** ~ to make known **2.** (*reconocer*) to recognize **3.** (*descubrir*) to get to know **4.** (*por primera vez*) to meet; **les conocí en una fiesta** I met them at a party **II.** *vi* ~ **de algo** to know about sth **III.** *vr:* ~**se 1.** (*tener trato*) to know each other **2.** (*persona*) to know oneself

conocido, -a I. *adj* (well-)known **II.** *m, f* acquaintance

conocimiento *m* **1.** (*saber*) knowledge **2.** (*entendimiento*) understanding **3.** (*consciencia*) consciousness **4.** *pl* (*nociones*) knowledge

conque *conj inf* so

conquense I. *adj* of/from Cuenca **II.** *mf* native/inhabitant of Cuenca

conquista *f* conquest

conquistador(a) I. *adj* conquering **II.** *m(f)* **1.** conqueror **2.** *pl* (*de América*) conquistadores

conquistar *vt* to conquer

consagración *f* **1.** REL consecration **2.** (*dedicación*) dedication

consagrar I. *vt* **1.** REL to consecrate **2.** (*dedicar*) to dedicate **II.** *vr:* ~**se 1.** (*dedicarse*) to devote oneself **2.** (*acreditarse*) to distinguish oneself

consanguíneo, -a I. *adj* related by blood **II.** *m, f* blood relation

consciencia *f* consciousness

consciente *adj* conscious; **estar** ~ MED to be conscious; **ser** ~ **de algo** to be aware of sth

conscripción *f* Arg (*servicio militar*) conscription

conscripto *m AmS* (*quinto*) recruit, conscript

consecución *f* attainment

consecuencia *f* **1.** (*efecto*) consequence; **a** ~ **de** as a result of **2.** (*coherencia*) consistency

consecuente *adj* consistent

consecuentemente *adv* **1.** (*por consiguiente*) consequently **2.** (*con consistencia*) consistently

consecutivo, -a *adj* consecutive

conseguido, -a *adj* successful

conseguir *irr como seguir vt* **1.** (*obtener*) to get **2.** (*tener éxito*) ~ **obtener una beca** to succeed in obtaining a grant

consejero, -a *m, f* **1.** (*guía*) adviser, counselor, consultant **2.** (*miembro de un consejo*) member; ~ **delegado** managing director **3.** (*de una autonomía*) minister

consejo *m* **1.** (*recomendación*) piece of advice **2.** (*organismo*) council; **Consejo Europeo** Council of Europe **3.** (*reunión*) meeting

consenso *m* consensus

consensuar <*1. pres:* consensúo> *vt* to reach a consensus on

consentido, -a *adj* **1.** (*mimado*) spoiled **2.** (*tolerante*) complaisant

consentimiento *m* ~ **para algo** consent to sth

consentir *irr como sentir* **I.** *vi* (*admitir*) ~ **en**

algo to agree to sth **II.** *vt* **1.** (*autorizar*) to allow; (*tolerar*) to tolerate **2.** (*mimar*) to spoil **3.** (*aguantar*) to put up with

conserje *mf* **1.** (*encargado*) caretaker *Brit,* janitor *Am* **2.** (*hotel*) concierge, receptionist **3.** (*portero*) (hall) porter

conserjería *f* **1.** (*cargo*) job of caretaker **2.** (*oficina*) caretaker's office **3.** (*hotel*) reception (desk)

conserva *f* **1.** (*enlatado*) tinned food *Brit,* canned food *Am* **2.** (*conservación*) preserving

conservación *f* **1.** (*mantenimiento*) maintenance **2.** (*guarda*) conservation **3.** (*conserva*) preserving

conservador(a) I. *adj* conservative **II.** *m(f)* **1.** (*guardador*) curator **2.** POL conservative, Tory *Brit*

conservante *m* preservative

conservar I. *vt* **1.** (*mantener*) to maintain **2.** (*guardar*) to conserve **3.** (*hacer conservas*) to can **4.** (*continuar la práctica*) to preserve **II.** *vr:* ~**se** to survive; (*mantenerse*) to keep

conservatorio *m* conservatory

considerable *adj* considerable

consideración *f* **1.** (*reflexión*) consideration; **en** ~ **a** in consideration of **2.** (*respeto*) respect

considerado, -a *adj* **1.** (*tener en cuenta*) considered **2.** (*apreciado*) respected **3.** (*atento*) considerate

considerar I. *vt* to consider **II.** *vr:* ~**se** to consider oneself

consigna *f* **1.** MIL motto **2.** POL instruction **3.** (*depósito de equipajes*) left-luggage (office) *Brit,* checkroom *Am*

consignar *vt* **1.** (*asignar*) to assign **2.** (*protocolar*) to record **3.** (*poner en depósito*) to deposit in left-luggage [*o* baggage-check *Am*] **4.** COM to dispatch

consignatario, -a *m, f* **1.** (*destinatario*) addressee **2.** COM consignee

consigo *pron pers* **tiene el libro** ~ he/she has the book with him/her; **llévatelo** ~ take it with you

consiguiente *adj* resulting; **por** ~ consequently

consistencia *f* consistency

consistente *adj* consistent; (*argument*) sound; GASTR thick; ~ **en** consisting of

consistir *vi* **1.** (*componerse*) ~ **en algo** to consist of sth **2.** (*radicar*) ~ **en algo** to lie in sth

consistorio *m* **1.** REL consistory **2.** ADMIN town council

consola *f* **1.** (*mesa*) console table **2.** ELEC console; (*de videojuegos*) video console

consolación *f* consolation

consolador *m* (*vibrador*) vibrator, dildo *vulg*

consolar <o→ue> **I.** *vt* to console **II.** *vr:* ~**se** to console oneself

consolidación *f* consolidation

consolidar I. *vt* to consolidate **II.** *vr:* ~**se** to be consolidated

consomé *m* consommé

consonancia *f* **1.** (*rima*) rhyme **2.** (*armonía*)

harmony; **en ~ con** in keeping with
consonante I. *adj* **1.** (*que rima*) rhyming **2.** (*armonioso*) harmonious **II.** *f* LING consonant
consorcio *m* consortium
consorte *mf* **1.** (*partícipe*) partner **2.** (*cónyuge*) spouse **3.** *pl* JUR accomplices *pl*, co-litigants *pl* **4.** *pey, inf* (*compinche*) mate *Brit*, buddy
conspicuo, -a *adj* eminent
conspiración *f* conspiracy
conspirar *vi* to conspire
constancia *f* **1.** (*firmeza*) constancy **2.** (*perseverancia*) perseverance **3.** (*certeza*) certainty **4.** (*prueba*) proof; **dejar ~ de algo** to show evidence of sth
constante *adj* constant
Constanza *f* Constance; **Lago de ~** Lake Constance
constar *vi* **1.** (*ser cierto*) to be clear **2.** (*figurar*) to be on record; **hacer ~ algo** to put sth on record **3.** (*componerse*) to consist
constatar *vt* to confirm
constelación *f* constellation
consternación *f* consternation
consternar I. *vt* to dismay **II.** *vr: ~se* to be dismayed
constipado *m* cold
constipado, -a *adj* **estar ~** to have a cold
constipar *vr: ~se* to catch a cold
constitución *f* **1.** *t.* POL constitution **2.** (*establecimiento*) setting-up **3.** (*composición*) make-up
constitucional *adj* constitutional
constituir *irr como* huir **I.** *vt* **1.** (*formar*) to constitute **2.** (*ser*) to be **3.** (*establecer*) to establish **4.** (*designar*) **~ en algo** to designate as sth **II.** *vr: ~se* (*convertirse*) **~se en algo** to become sth
constitutivo, -a *adj* constituent
constreñimiento *m* constraint
constreñir *irr como* ceñir *vt* **1.** (*obligar*) to constrain **2.** MED to constrict **3.** (*cohibir*) to restrict
constricción *f* constriction
construcción *f* **1.** (*acción*) construction **2.** (*sector, edificio*) building; **~ aneja** annexe
constructivo, -a *adj* constructive
constructor(a) *m(f)* builder
construir *irr como* huir *vt* **1.** (*casa*) to build; (*erigir*) to erect **2.** LING to construe
consubstancial *adj v.* **consustancial**
consuelo *m* consolation
cónsul *mf* consul
consulado *m* **1.** (*lugar*) consulate **2.** (*cargo*) consulship
consulta *f* **1.** (*acción*) consultation **2.** (*de un médico*) surgery; **horas de ~** surgery hours **3.** (*asesoramiento*) **~ popular** POL referendum
consultar *vt* to consult
consultor(a) I. *adj* consulting; **empresa ~a** consultancy firm **II.** *m(f)* consultant
consultoría *f* consultancy; (*empresa*) con-

sultancy (firm)
consultorio *m* **1.** (*establecimiento*) consultancy; (*de un médico*) surgery **2.** (*en la radio*) phone-in
consumación *f sin pl* consummation
consumar *vt* to carry out; **~ el matrimonio** JUR to consummate the marriage
consumición *f* **1.** (*bar*) drink; **~ mínima** minimum charge **2.** (*agotamiento*) consumption
consumidor(a) *m(f)* consumer
consumir I. *vt* **1.** (*gastar, destruir*) to consume **2.** (*acabar*) to use **3.** (*comer*) to eat **4.** (*afligir*) to wear out **II.** *vr: ~se* **1.** (*persona*) to waste away **2.** (*gastarse*) to be consumed
consumismo *m* consumerism
consumo *m* consumption; **bienes de ~** consumer goods; **sociedad de ~** consumer society
consustancial *adj* consubstantial
contabilidad *f* **1.** (*sistema*) accounting **2.** (*profesión*) accountancy
contabilizar <z→c> *vt* to enter
contable I. *adj* countable **II.** *mf* accountant
contactar *vi, vt* **~ con alguien** to contact sb
contacto *m* **1.** (*tacto, persona*) contact **2.** AUTO ignition **3.** FOTO contact print
contado *m* **pagar al ~** to pay (in) cash
contador *m* (*del agua, de la luz*) meter
contados, -as *adj* (*raro*) scarce; **tiene los días ~** his/her days are numbered
contagiar I. *vt* to transmit, to infect **II.** *vr ~se de algo* to become infected with sth
contagio *m* contagion
contagioso, -a *adj* contagious; **tener una risa contagiosa** to have a contagious laugh
contaminación *f* pollution; **~ acústica** noise pollution; **~ ambiental** environmental pollution
contaminante I. *adj* polluting **II.** *m* pollutant
contaminar I. *vt* **1.** (*infestar*) to pollute **2.** (*contagiar*) to infect **3.** (*corromper*) to corrupt **II.** *vr: ~se* **1.** (*infectarse*) to become contaminated **2.** (*contagiarse*) to become infected **3.** (*corromperse*) to be corrupted
contante *adj* **~ y sonante** in hard cash
contar <o→ue> **I.** *vi* **1.** (*hacer cuentas, valer*) to count **2.** (+ *con: confiar*) **~ con alguien/algo** to rely on sth/sb **3.** (+ *con: tener en cuenta*) **~ con algo** to expect sth **II.** *vt* **1.** (*numerar, incluir*) to count; **sin ~ con** without taking into account **2.** (*narrar*) to tell; **¿qué cuentas?** (*saludo*) how's it going? **III.** *vr: ~se* to be counted
contemplación *f* **1.** (*observación*) contemplation **2.** REL meditation **3.** *pl* (*miramientos*) indulgence
contemplar *vt* **1.** (*mirar*) to look at **2.** (*considerar*) to consider **3.** (*complacer*) to spoil **4.** REL to meditate
contemplativo, -a *adj* contemplative
contemporáneo, -a *adj, m, f* contemporary
contemporizar <z→c> *vi* **~ con algo/alguien** to be accommodating towards sth/sb

contención *f* (*de agua, etc*) containment
contender <e→ie> *vi* ~ **por algo** to contend for sth
contendiente *mf* contender
contenedor *m* **1.** (*general*) container **2.** (*basura*) bin container *Brit*, (trash) dumpster *Am* **3.** (*escombros*) skip *Brit*, dumpster *Am*
contener *irr como* tener **I.** *vt* **1.** (*encerrar*) to contain **2.** (*refrenar*) to hold back; (*respiración*) to hold **II.** *vr:* ~**se** to contain oneself
contenido *m* **1.** (*incluido, significado*) contents *pl* **2.** (*concentración*) content
contentar **I.** *vt* to satisfy **II.** *vr:* ~**se** to be contented
contento, -a *adj* **1.** (*alegre*) happy **2.** (*satisfecho*) content
contestación *f* **1.** (*respuesta*) answer **2.** (*protesta*) protest
contestador *m* answerphone, answering machine
contestar **I.** *vt* (*responder*) to answer **II.** *vi* **1.** (*responder*) to answer **2.** (*replicar*) to answer back
contestatario, -a *m, f* rebel
contexto *m* context
contienda *f* **1.** (*disputa*) dispute **2.** (*batalla*) conflict
contigo *pron pers* with you; **me siento** ~ I'll sit beside you
contiguo, -a *adj* adjoining
continencia *f* continence
continental *adj* continental
continente *m* **1.** GEO continent **2.** (*aspecto*) air; (*compostura*) bearing **3.** (*cosa*) container
contingencia *f* **1.** (*eventualidad*) eventuality **2.** *t.* FILOS contingency **3.** (*riesgo*) risk
contingentar *vt* to establish quotas for
contingente **I.** *adj* possible **II.** *m* **1.** ECON quota **2.** MIL contingent
continuación *f* continuation; **a** ~ (*después*) next; (*en un escrito*) as follows
continuar <*1. pres:* continúo> **I.** *vi* to continue; ~**á** to be continued **II.** *vt* to continue
continuidad *f* continuity
continuo, -a *adj* continuous; **movimiento** ~ perpetual motion
contonearse *vr* to swing one's hips, to wiggle
contorno *m* **1.** (*de una figura*) outline **2.** (*de la cintura*) waist measurement **3.** (*pl*) (*territorio*) surrounding area
contra¹ **I.** *prep* against; **tener algo en** ~ to object **II.** *m* **los pros y los** ~**s** the pros and the cons
contra² *f* **1.** (*dificultad*) snag **2.** (*oposición*) **llevar la** ~ **a alguien** to contradict sb **3.** (*guerilla*) contra
contraataque *m* MIL counterattack
contrabajo *m* **1.** (*instrumento*) double bass **2.** (*músico*) double-bass player
contrabandista *mf* smuggler; ~ **de armas** gunrunner
contrabando *m sin pl* **1.** (*comercio*) smuggling; **pasar algo de** ~ to smuggle sth in **2.** (*mer-*

cancía) contraband
contracción *f* **1.** (*pl*) MED contractions *pl* **2.** *t.* LING contraction
contrachapado *m* plywood
contrachapado, -a *adj* plywood; **mesa contrachapada** plywood table; **madera contrachapada** plywood
contracorriente *f sin pl* crosscurrent
contractual *adj* contractual
contracultura *f sin pl* alternative society
contradecir *irr como* decir **I.** *vt* to contradict **II.** *vr:* ~**se** (*persona*) to contradict oneself
contradicción *f* contradiction
contradictorio, -a *adj* contradictory
contraer *irr como* traer **I.** *vt* **1.** (*encoger*) to contract **2.** (*adquirir: deudas*) to contract; (*enfermedad*) to catch, to contract *form* **3.** (*limitar*) to limit **II.** *vr:* ~**se** **1.** (*encogerse*) to contract **2.** (*limitarse*) to limit oneself
contraespionaje *m* counterespionage
contrafuerte *m* **1.** ARQUIT buttress **2.** (*zapato*) heel stiffener **3.** GEO spur
contrahecho, -a *adj* **1.** (*deforme*) deformed; (*persona*) hunchbacked **2.** (*falsificado*) counterfeit
contraindicación *f* MED contraindication
contralor *m AmL* FIN treasury inspector
contraloría *f AmL* treasury inspector's office
contraluz *m o f* back light(ing)
contramanifestación *f* counter-demonstration
contramedida *f* countermeasure
contraofensiva *f* counteroffensive
contraoferta *f* counteroffer
contraorden *f* countermand *form*
contrapartida *f* **1.** (*compensación*) compensation **2.** (*contabilidad*) balancing entry
contrapelo *adj* **a** ~ *t. fig* the wrong way
contrapesar *vt* to counterbalance, to offset
contrapeso *m* counterweight
contraponer *irr como* poner **I.** *vt* **1.** (*comparar*) to compare **2.** (*oponer*) to contrast **II.** *vr:* ~**se** to be contrasted
contraportada *f* back cover [*o* page]
contraposición *f* comparison
contraprestación *f* consideration
contraproducente *adj* counterproductive
contrapunto *m* MÚS counterpoint
contrariar <*1. pres:* contrarío> *vt* **1.** (*oponerse*) to oppose; (*plan*) to thwart **2.** (*disgustar*) to upset
contrariedad *f* **1.** (*inconveniente*) obstacle **2.** (*disgusto*) annoyance
contrario, -a **I.** *adj* (*opuesto*) contrary; (*perjudicial*) harmful; **al** ~ on the contrary; **en caso** ~ otherwise; **de lo** ~ or else; **llevar la contraria a alguien** to oppose [*o* contradict] sb **II.** *m, f* opponent
contrarreembolso *m* C.O.D., cash on delivery
contrarreforma *f sin pl* HIST Counter-Reformation
contrarrestar *vt* **1.** (*neutralizar*) to counter-

act **2.** DEP to return
contrasentido *m* **1.** (*contradicción*) contra-diction **2.** (*disparate*) piece of nonsense
contraseña *f* **1.** (*santo y seña*) password **2.** (*marca*) countermark
contrastar I. *vi* to contrast II. *vt* **1.** (*oro*) to hallmark **2.** (*peso*) to verify
contraste *m* **1.** *t.* FOTO contrast **2.** MED contrast medium **3.** (*persona*) inspector of weights and measures; (*oficina*) weights and measures office **4.** (*señal*) hallmark
contratación *f* contracting; ~ **bursátil** FIN trading (*on the stock exchange*)
contratar *vt* **1.** (*trabajador*) to hire; (*artista*) to sign up **2.** (*encargar*) to contract
contratiempo *m* setback
contratista *mf* contractor
contrato *m* contract; ~ **de alquiler** lease; ~ **colectivo** wage agreement
contravención *f* JUR contravention; ~ **de contrato** breach of contract
contravenir *irr como venir* *vt* to contravene
contraventana *f* shutter
contravidriera *f* double window
contrayente I. *adj* contracting II. *mf* contracting party; (*de un matrimonio*) bridegroom *m*, bride *f*
contribución *f* **1.** (*aportación*) contribution; **aportar una** ~ **a algo** to make a contribution to sth **2.** (*impuesto*) tax; ~ **municipal** council tax, local tax
contribuir *irr como huir* I. *vi* **1.** (*ayudar*) to contribute **2.** (*tributar*) to pay taxes II. *vt* (*aportar*) to contribute; (*pagar*) to pay
contribuyente *mf* taxpayer
contrición *f sin pl* contrition
contrincante *mf* opponent
contrito, -a *adj* contrite
control *m* control; (*inspección*) inspection; ~ **al azar** spot check; ~ **a distancia** TÉC remote control
controlador *m* INFOR driver; ~ **de la impresora** printer driver
controlador(a) *m(f)* controller; ~ **de vuelo** [*o* **de tráfico aéreo**] air traffic controller
controlar I. *vt* (*confirmar*) to check; (*regir*) to control II. *vr:* ~**se** to control oneself
controversia *f* controversy
controvertido, -a *adj* controversial
controvertir *irr como sentir* I. *vi* to argue II. *vt* to discuss
contumacia *f sin pl* **1.** (*porfía*) obstinacy **2.** JUR contempt (of court)
contumaz *adj* (*obstinado*) obstinate
contundencia *f sin pl* force
contundente *adj* **1.** (*objeto*) contusive **2.** *fig* convincing; **prueba** ~ conclusive proof
conturbación *f sin pl* perturbation
conturbar I. *vt* (*intranquilizar*) to trouble; (*turbar*) to perturb II. *vr:* ~**se** (*intranquili-zarse*) to be troubled; (*turbarse*) to become perturbed
contusión *f* MED bruise

contusionar *vt* to bruise
convalecencia *f* convalescence
convalecer *irr como crecer* *vi* ~ **de algo** to convalesce after sth
convaleciente *mf* convalescent
convalidación *f* **1.** (*de un título*) (re)vali-dation **2.** (*confirmación*) confirmation, recog-nition
convalidar *vt* **1.** (*título*) to (re)validate **2.** (*confirmar*) to confirm, to recognize
convencedor(a) *adj* convincing
convencer <c→z> I. *vt* **1.** (*persuadir*) to per-suade **2.** (*satisfacer*) **no me convence ese piso** I'm not at all sure about that flat II. *vr:* ~**se** to be convinced
convencido, -a *adj* sure
convencimiento *m sin pl* (*convicción*) con-viction; **tengo el** ~ **de que...** I'm convinced that ...
convención *f* convention
convencional *adj* conventional
conveniencia *f* **1.** (*provecho*) usefulness; **matrimonio de** ~ marriage of convenience **2.** (*acuerdo*) agreement **3.** (*oportunidad*) opportunity
conveniente *adj* **1.** (*adecuado*) suitable **2.** (*provechoso*) advisable; (*útil*) useful **3.** (*decente*) fitting
convenio *m* agreement
convenir *irr como venir* I. *vi* **1.** (*acordar*) to agree **2.** (*ser oportuno*) to be advisable **3.** (*co-rresponder*) to suit II. *vr* ~**se en algo** to agree on sth
convento *m* **1.** (*de monjes*) monastery **2.** (*de monjas*) convent
convergencia *f* convergence
convergente *adj* convergent
converger <g→j> *vi,* **convergir** <g→j> *vi* **1.** (*líneas*) to converge **2.** (*coincidir*) to coincide
conversación *f* conversation
conversador(a) *m(f)* conversationalist
conversar *vi* to talk
conversión *f* conversion
converso, -a *m, f* convert; HIST converted Jew or Moor
convertible *adj, m* convertible
convertir *irr como sentir* I. *vt* **1.** (*trans-formar*) ~ **en algo** to turn into sth **2.** *t.* REL to convert **3.** COM, TÉC to convert II. *vr:* ~**se** **1.** (*transformarse*) ~**se en algo** to turn into sth **2.** REL to convert
convexidad *f sin pl* convexity
convexo, -a *adj* convex
convicción *f* conviction
convicto, -a *adj* convicted
convidado, -a *m, f* guest
convidar I. *vt* to invite II. *vr:* ~**se** **1.** (*invitarse*) to invite oneself **2.** (*ofrecerse*) to offer one's services
convincente *adj* convincing
convite *m* **1.** (*invitación*) invitation **2.** (*ban-quete*) banquet

convivencia _f_ living together; _fig_ co-existence

convivir _vi_ to live together; _fig_ to coexist

convocar <c→qu> _vt_ **1.** (_citar para algo_) to summon; (_reunir_) to call (together); MIL to call up; **me ~on al examen** I was called for the examination **2.** (_concurso_) to announce **3.** (_reunión_) to call

convocatoria _f_ **1.** (_citación_) summons **2.** MIL call-up papers _Brit,_ draft papers _Am_ **3.** (_de un concurso_) official announcement **4.** (_de una conferencia_) notification

convoy _m_ **1.** MIL convoy **2.** _inf_ (_vinagreras_) cruet

convulsión _f_ **1.** MED convulsion **2.** POL upheaval **3.** GEO tremor

convulsionar _vt_ **1.** MED to produce convulsions in **2.** _t._ GEO, POL to convulse

conyugal _adj_ marital

cónyuge _mf form_ spouse; **los ~s** the married couple

coña _f vulg_ **1.** (_broma_) joking, piss-taking _Brit;_ **tomar algo a ~** to take sth as a joke; **¡ni de ~!** no way! **2.** (_lata_) annoyance; **eres la ~** you're a pain in the neck [_o ass Am_] **3.** (_estupidez_) rubbish

coñá _m,_ **coñac** _m_ <coñacs> cognac

coñazo _m vulg_ pain in the arse [_o ass Am_]; **¡esto es un ~!** this is a drag!

coñete _adj Chile, Perú, inf_ (_tacaño_) stingy, tight _inf_

coño I. _interj vulg_ damn, bloody hell _Brit_ II. _m vulg_ cunt, fanny _Brit,_ pussy _Am;_ **vive en el quinto ~** he/she lives in the back of beyond; **¿qué ~ te importa?** why the hell does it matter to you? III. _adj Chile, vulg:_ pejorative term for a Spaniard

cooperación _f_ cooperation

cooperador(a) _m(f)_ collaborator

cooperante _mf_ (overseas) voluntary worker

cooperar _vi_ **1.** (_juntamente_) to cooperate **2.** (_participar_) to collaborate

cooperativa _f_ cooperative, co-op

cooperativista _mf_ member of a cooperative

cooperativo, -a _adj_ cooperative

coordenada _f_ MAT coordinate

coordinación _f_ coordination

coordinador(a) I. _adj_ coordinating II. _m(f)_ coordinator

coordinar _vt_ to coordinate

copa _f_ **1.** (_vaso_) glass; **una ~ de vino** a glass of wine; **una ~ para el vino** a wine glass; **ir de ~s** to go out for a drink; **tener una ~ de más** to have had one too many **2.** (_de árbol_) top **3.** (_de sujetador_) cup **4.** (_de sombrero_) crown; **sombrero de ~** top hat **5.** DEP cup

copar _vt_ **1.** MIL (_rodear_) to surround; (_cortar la retirada_) to cut off **2.** (_acorralar_) to corner; **estar copado** to be stuck; (_negociaciones_) to be bogged down **3.** (_premios_) to win; **~ la banca** (_en un juego_) to sweep the board

copartícipe _mf_ (_codueño_) joint owner; (_socio_) partner

copatrocinar _vt_ to co-sponsor

cópec _m_ <copecks>, **copeca** _f_ kopeck

Copenhague _m_ Copenhagen

copete _m_ **1.** (_de persona_) tuft (of hair) **2.** (_de ave_) crest; (_de caballo_) forelock **3.** (_altanería_) haughtiness **4.** (_linaje_) **ser de alto ~** to be aristocratic

copetín _m_ **1.** _Méx_ (_copa de licor_) glass of liquor; (_aperitivo_) aperitif **2.** _Arg_ (_cóctel_) cocktail

copetón, -ona _adj Col_ tipsy; **estar ~** to be slightly drunk

copia _f_ **1.** (_de un escrito_) copy; (_al carbón_) carbon copy; **~ en limpio** fair copy; **~ de seguridad** INFOR back-up copy **2.** ARTE (_imagen_) copy; (_réplica_) replica **3.** FOTO print **4.** CINE, TIPO copy

copiadora _f_ photocopier, xerox® _machine Am_

copiar _vt_ **1.** (_general_) to copy **2.** (_fotocopiar_) to photocopy, to xerox® _Am_

copiloto, -a _m, f_ AVIAT copilot; AUTO co-driver

copioso, -a _adj_ (_exuberante_) copious; (_abundante_) abundant

copista _mf_ copyist

copla _f_ **1.** LIT verse **2.** MÚS popular song

copo _m_ flake; **~ de nieve** snowflake; **~s de maíz** cornflakes

copón _m_ REL ciborium; **del ~** _inf_ tremendous

copresidente, -a _m, f_ joint president

coprocesador _m_ INFOR co-processor

coproducir _vt_ CINE to co-produce

coproductor(a) _m(f)_ CINE co-producer

copropietario, -a _m, f_ co-owner

copucha _f Chile_ **1.** (_mentira_) lie **2.** (_vejiga de animal_) bladder

cópula _f_ **1.** BIO copulation **2.** LING copula

copulación _f_ copulation

copular _vi, vr:_ **~se** to copulate

coque _m_ MIN coke

coqueta _f_ **1.** (_chica, mujer_) flirt **2.** (_mueble_) dressing table

coquetear _vi_ to flirt

coquetería _f_ coquetry

coqueto, -a _adj_ **1.** (_que coquetea_) flirtatious **2.** (_encantador_) charming **3.** (_vanidoso_) vain **4.** (_objeto_) pretty

coracha _f AmL_ leather bag

coraje _m_ **1.** (_valor_) courage; **tener ~** to be courageous **2.** (_ira_) anger; **dar ~** to make angry

coral I. _adj_ **1.** (_color_) coral **2.** MÚS choral II. _m_ **1.** _t._ ZOOL coral **2.** (_composición_) chorale III. _f_ (_coro_) choir

Corán _m_ REL Koran

coraza _f_ **1.** MIL cuirass **2.** NÁUT armour-plating _Brit,_ armor-plating _Am_ **3.** ZOOL shell **4.** _fig_ shield

corazón _m_ **1.** _t._ _fig_ ANAT heart; **blando de ~** soft-hearted; **duro de ~** hard-hearted; **de todo ~** with all one's heart; **con el ~ en la mano** with one's heart on one's sleeve; **hacer algo de ~** to do sth willingly; **tener un ~ de oro** to have a heart of gold; **no tener ~** to be heartless **2.** BOT core **3.** (_coraje_) **hacer de tripas ~** to pluck up courage **4.** (*apelativo cariñoso*) ~ (**mío**) darling

corazonada *f* **1.** (*presentimiento*) hunch **2.** (*impulso*) sudden impulse **3.** (*acto*) impulsive act

corbata *f* tie

corbatín *m* bow tie

corbeta *f* NÁUT corvette

Córcega *f* Corsica

corcel *m* LIT steed

corchea *f* quaver

corchete *m* **1.** (*broche*) hook and eye; (*pieza*) hook **2.** TIPO square bracket

corcho I. *m* **1.** (*material, tapón*) cork **2.** (*en la pesca*) float II. *interj* for heaven's sake

corcovado, -a I. *adj* hunchbacked II. *m, f* hunchback

corcovar *vt* to bend

corcovear *vi* **1.** (*caballo*) to buck **2.** (*gato*) to arch its back

cordaje *m* **1.** (*de un instrumento, de una raqueta*) strings *pl* **2.** (*de una embarcación*) rigging

cordel *m* **1.** (*cuerda delgada*) cord **2.** (*cañada*) cattle track

corderillo *m* (*piel*) lambskin

cordero *m* **1.** (*carne*) mutton, lamb **2.** (*piel*) lambskin

cordero, -a *m, f* lamb

cordial I. *adj* **1.** (*persona*) cordial **2.** MED tonic II. *m* cordial

cordialidad *f* cordiality

cordillera *f* mountain range

cordillerano, -a *adj AmL* GEO Andean

córdoba *m Nic* (*moneda*) cordoba

Córdoba *f* Cordova [*o* Cordoba]

cordobés, -esa *adj, m, f* Cordovan

cordón *m* **1.** (*cordel*) cord; (*del uniforme*) braid; (*de zapatos*) shoelace; ~ **umbilical** ANAT umbilical cord **2.** ELEC flex *Brit*, cord *Am* **3.** NÁUT strand **4.** MIL cordon **5.** *CSur* (*de la acera*) kerb *Brit*, curb *Am*

cordura *f* **1.** (*razón*) good sense **2.** (*juicio*) wisdom **3.** (*prudencia*) prudence

Corea *f* Korea

coreano, -a *adj, m, f* Korean

corear *vt* **1.** (*cantando*) to chant **2.** (*asentir*) to echo **3.** *fig* (*aclamar*) to applaud

coreografía *f* choreography

coreógrafo, -a *m, f* choreographer

coriáceo, -a *adj* leathery

corintio, -a *adj, m, f* Corinthian

corinto I. *adj inv* maroon II. *m* Corinth

corista[1] *mf* MÚS chorister

corista[2] *f* TEAT chorus girl

cornada *f* **1.** (*golpe*) butt **2.** (*herida*) goring

cornamenta *f* **1.** (*de animales*) horns *pl*; (*de ciervos*) antlers *pl* **2.** (*del marido*) cuckold's horns *pl*

córnea *f* cornea

cornear *vt* **1.** (*golpear*) to butt **2.** (*herir*) to gore

corneja *f* crow

córner *m* DEP corner

corneta *f* **1.** (*instrumento*) cornet; (*en el ejército*) bugle; **hacer algo a toque de** ~ *fig* to do sth on command **2.** (*música*) cornet player **3.** (*de los sordos*) ear trumpet

corneta *m* **1.** (*músico*) cornet player **2.** MIL bugler

cornisa *f* cornice; **la** ~ **cantábrica** the Cantabrian Coast

cornucopia *f* **1.** (*cuerno*) cornucopia **2.** (*espejo*) ornamental mirror

cornudo I. *adj* (*marido*) cuckolded II. *m* cuckold

cornudo, -a *adj* (*animal*) horned

coro *m* ARQUIT, MÚS choir; **a** ~ in unison; **hacer** ~ **a alguien** to back sb up

corola *f* corolla

corolario *m* corollary

corona *f* **1.** *t.* POL (*adorno*) crown **2.** (*de flores*) garland, wreath **3.** (*de eclesiásticos*) tonsure **4.** (*de santos*) halo **5.** (*de los dientes*) crown **6.** ASTR corona

coronación *f* **1.** (*de un rey*) coronation **2.** (*de una acción*) culmination **3.** ARQUIT crown

coronar *vt* to crown; **para ~lo...** *fig* to crown it all ...

coronario, -a *adj* coronary

coronel(a) *m(f)* colonel

coronilla *f* crown (of the head); **estar hasta la** ~ **de algo** *inf* to be fed up to the back teeth with sth

corotos *mpl AmL* (*bártulos*) things *pl*

corpiño *m* bodice; *CSur* (*sujetador*) bra

corporación *f* **1.** *t.* COM corporation; ~ **de estudiantes** students' society **2.** HIST guild

corporal *adj* physical

corporativo, -a *adj* corporate

corpóreo, -a *adj* bodily

corpulencia *f* **1.** (*de alguien*) heftiness **2.** (*de algo*) massiveness

corpulento, -a *adj* **1.** (*persona*) hefty **2.** (*cosa*) massive

corpus *m sin pl* LING corpus

Corpus *m sin pl* REL Corpus Christi

corpúsculo *m* corpuscle

corral *m* **1.** (*cercado*) yard; (*redil*) stockyard; (*para la pesca*) fish weir; (*para gallinas*) chicken run **2.** HIST, TEAT open-air theatre **3.** (*lugar sucio*) pigsty **4.** (*para niños*) playpen

corralón *m* **1.** (*patio*) large yard **2.** (*casa de vecindad*) tenement **3.** *CSur* (*maderería*) lumberyard

correa *f* **1.** (*tira*) strap **2.** (*cinturón*) belt **3.** TÉC ~ **de transmisión** driving belt, drive **4.** (*afilador*) strop **5.** (*perro*) lead, leash **6.** (*elasticidad*) elasticity **7.** *inf* (*aguante*) **tener** ~ to be long-suffering

correaje *m t.* TÉC belts *pl*

corrección *f* **1.** TIPO proofreading; (*de ruta*) course correction **2.** (*represión*) rebuke **3.** (*cualidad*) correctness; (*comportamiento*) courtesy, (good) manners *pl*

correccional *m* reformatory

correctivo *m* corrective

correcto, -a *adj* correct

corrector(a) I. *adj* correcting II. *m(f)* TIPO proofreader

corredera *f* 1. TÉC slide; **puerta de** ~ sliding door 2. (*pista*) racetrack 3. (*cucaracha*) cockroach 4. *inf*(*alcahueta*) procuress *form*

corredizo, -a *adj* **nudo** ~ slipknot; **puerta corrediza** sliding door

corredor *m* corridor

corredor(a) *m(f)* 1. DEP (*a pie*) runner; ~ **de coches** racing driver; ~ **de fondo** long-distance runner 2. COM agent; ~ **de fincas** estate agent *Brit,* real estate broker *Am*

correduría *f* 1. (*oficio*) brokerage 2. (*comisión*) commission

corregible *adj* correctable

corregir *irr como* **elegir** I. *vt* 1. *t.* TIPO to correct 2. (*reprender*) to rebuke II. *vr:* ~**se** 1. (*en la conducta*) to change one's ways 2. (*al expresarse*) to correct oneself

correlación *f* correlation

correlacionar *vi, vt* to correlate

correlativo, -a *adj form* correlative

correligionario, -a *m, f* 1. REL coreligionist 2. POL fellow supporter

correntada *f AmL* (*rápido*) rapids *pl*

correo *m* 1. (*persona*) courier 2. (*correspondencia*) post *Brit,* mail *Am;* ~ **aéreo** airmail; ~ **certificado** registered [*o* certified] mail; ~ **electrónico** e-mail; ~ **urgente** special delivery; **a vuelta de** ~ by return post [*o* mail *Am*]; **echar al** ~ to post *Brit,* to mail *Am* 3. (*barco*) mail boat; (*tren*) mail train

Correos *mpl* post office; **ir a** ~ to go to the post office

correoso, -a *adj* tough

correr I. *vi* 1. (*caminar*) to run; **echarse a** ~ (*partir*) to start to run; (*escaparse*) to run off; **salir corriendo** to run out 2. (*apresurarse*) to rush; **a todo** ~ at top speed 3. (*conducir*) to go fast 4. (*tiempo*) to pass (quickly); **el mes que corre** this month; **en los tiempos que corremos...** at the present time ... 5. (*líquido*) to flow 6. (*viento*) to blow 7. (*camino*) to run 8. (*moneda*) to be valid 9. (*rumor*) to circulate 10. (*estar a cargo de*) **eso corre de** [*o* **por**] **mi cuenta** (*gastos*) I'm paying for that; (*un asunto*) I'm responsible for that ►**el que no corre, vuela** ≈ opportunity knocks but once *prov* II. *vt* 1. (*un mueble*) to move; (*una cortina*) to draw; (*un cerrojo*) to slide 2. (*un nudo*) to undo 3. (*un lugar*) to travel over; ~ **mundo** to travel widely 4. MIL to overrun 5. (*un caballo*) to race 6. (*la caza*) to chase 7. (*avergonzar*) to embarrass 8. (*tener*) ~ **la misma suerte** to suffer the same fate; **corre prisa** it's urgent ►**dejar** ~ **algo** not to worry about sth; ~**la** to make a night of it III. *vr:* ~**se** 1. (*moverse*) to move 2. (*avergonzarse*) to get embarrassed 3. *vulg* (*eyacular*) to come 4. (*colores*) to run 5. (*excederse*) to go too far

correría *f* 1. MIL raid 2. *pl* (*recorridos*) travels *pl*

correspondencia *f* 1. (*correo*) post *Brit,* mail *Am;* (*de cartas*) correspondence; **curso por** ~ correspondence course; **llevar la** ~ to attend to the correspondence 2. (*equivalente*) correspondence 3. (*conformidad*) agreement 4. (*entre medios de transporte*) connection

corresponder I. *vi* 1. (*equivaler*) to correspond 2. (*armonizar*) to match 3. (*convenir*) to tally 4. (*contestar*) to respond 5. (*pertenecer*) to belong 6. (*incumbir*) to concern; **no me corresponde criticarlo** it's not for me to criticize him 7. (*comunicar*) to communicate; (*medios de transporte*) to connect II. *vr:* ~**se** 1. (*ser equivalente, escribirse*) to correspond; (*armonizar*) to match; (*convenir*) to agree 2. (*comunicarse*) to communicate with each other

correspondiente *adj* 1. (*oportuno*) corresponding 2. (*apropiado*) appropriate 3. (*respectivo*) respective

corresponsabilizar <z→c> *vt* to make jointly responsible

corresponsable *adj* jointly responsible

corresponsal *mf* correspondent

corretaje *m* 1. (*negocio*) brokerage 2. (*comisión*) commission

corretear *vi* 1. (*vagar*) to stroll around 2. (*niños*) to run about

corrida *f* 1. TAUR bullfight 2. (*carrera*) run; **decir algo de** ~ to reel off sth from memory 3. *vulg* (*orgasmo*) orgasm

corrido, -a *adj* 1. ARQUIT (*sin interrupción*) continuous 2. (*cantidad: larga*) large; **un quilo** ~ a good kilo 3. *estar* (*avergonzado*) embarrassed; (*confuso*) confused 4. *ser* (*astuto*) astute

corriente I. *adj* 1. (*fluente*) running 2. (*actual*) current; (*moneda*) valid; **estar al** ~ **de algo** to be aware of sth; **ponerse al** ~ **de algo** to get to know about sth 3. (*ordinario*) ordinary 4. (*normal*) normal II. *f* 1. (*de agua, electricidad*) current; ~ **de aire** draught *Brit,* draft *Am;* ~ **alterna** alternating current; **hace** ~ there's a draught [*o* draft *Am*]; **ir contra la** ~ to swim against the tide; **seguir** [*o* **llevar**] **la** ~ **a alguien** to play along with sb 2. ARTE, LIT (*tendencia*) tendency

corrimiento *m* 1. (*movimiento*) movement 2. GEO slipping; ~ **de tierras** landslide 3. (*vergüenza*) embarrassment; (*timidez*) shyness

corro *m* 1. (*círculo*) circle; **hacer** ~ (*hacer un círculo*) to form a circle; (*hacer sitio*) to make room 2. AGR plot 3. (*juego*) ring-a-ring-a-roses

corroboración *f* corroboration

corroborar *vt* to corroborate

corroer *irr como* **roer** I. *vt* 1. (*un material*) to corrode 2. (*una persona*) consume; **el remordimiento lo corroe** he's consumed by remorse II. *vr:* ~**se** to corrode

corromper I. *vt* 1. (*descomponer*) to rot; (*un texto*) to corrupt 2. (*sobornar*) to bribe 3. (*enviciar*) to debauch; (*pervertir*) to corrupt

4. *inf* (*enojar*) to annoy **II.** *vi* to smell bad **III.** *vr:* ~**se 1.** (*descomponerse*) to rot; (*alimentos*) to go bad **2.** (*degenerar*) to become corrupted

corronchoso, -a *adj* AmL (*basto*) coarse

corrosca *f* Col broad-brimmed straw hat

corrosión *f* corrosion

corrosivo, -a *adj* **1.** (*sustancia*) corrosive **2.** (*estilo*) caustic

corrupción *f* **1.** (*descomposición*) decay **2.** (*de la moral, de un texto*) corruption **3.** (*soborno*) bribery, graft **4.** (*seducción*) seduction

corrupto, -a *adj* corrupt

corruptor(a) I. *adj* corrupting **II.** *m(f)* corrupter

corsario *m* HIST corsair

corsé *m* corset

corso, -a *adj, m, f* Corsican

cortacésped *m* lawnmower

cortada *f* **1.** (*rebanada*) slice **2.** AmL (*herida*) cut

cortado *m* GASTR *coffee with only a little milk*

cortado, -a *adj* **1.** (*leche: mala*) sour; (*cuajada*) curdled **2.** (*persona: tímida*) shy; (*avergonzada*) self-conscious, embarrassed **3.** (*estilo*) abrupt

cortafuegos *m inv* **1.** AGR firebreak, firebreak *Brit,* fire lane *Am* **2.** ARQUIT firewall

cortapisa *f* **1.** (*restricción*) restriction **2.** (*obstáculo*) obstacle; **hablar sin ~s** to talk freely; **poner ~s a alguien** to put obstacles in sb's path **3.** (*gracia*) wit

cortaplumas *m inv* penknife

cortar I. *vt* **1.** (*tajar*) to cut; (*por el medio*) to cut through; (*en pedazos*) to cut up; (*quitar*) to cut off; (*un traje*) to cut out; (*un árbol*) to cut down; (*la carne*) to carve; (*leña*) to chop; (*el césped*) to mow; (*pelo*) to trim; INFOR to cut; **~ al rape** to cut close; **¡corta el rollo!** that's enough! **2.** DEP (*la pelota*) to slice **3.** (*una bebida, una película, cartas*) to cut **4.** (*el agua*) to cut off; (*la corriente*) to switch off **5.** (*una carretera*) to cut **6.** (*la comunicación*) to cut off **II.** *vi* **1.** (*tajar*) cut **2.** (*romper*) **ha cortado con su novio** she has split up with her boyfriend **III.** *vr:* ~**se 1.** (*persona*) to cut oneself **2.** (*turbarse*) to become embarrassed; **no se cortó ni un pelo** he/she wasn't embarrassed in the least **3.** (*leche*) to turn; (*cuajarse*) to curdle **4.** (*piel*) to get chapped **5.** TEL to get cut off

cortaúñas *m inv* nailclippers *pl*

corte¹ *m* **1.** (*herida, tajo, de un traje*) cut **2.** (*de pelo*) haircut **3.** TÉC section; **~ transversal** cross section **4.** (*de un libro*) edge **5.** ELEC **~ de corriente** power cut ►**hacer a alguien un ~ de mangas** ≈ to give sb the V-sign; **dar ~** to embarrass; **¡qué ~!** how embarrassing!

corte² *f* court

cortedad *f* **1.** (*pequeñez*) smallness; (*escasez*) shortness **2.** (*timidez*) bashfulness **3.** (*de poco entendimiento*) stupidity

cortejar *vt* to court

cortejo *m* **1.** (*halago*) courtship **2.** (*séquito*) retinue **3.** (*desfile*) procession

Cortes *fpl* POL Spanish parliament

cortés *adj* polite

cortesana *f* courtesan

cortesano, -a *adj* **1.** (*palaciego*) court **2.** (*cortés*) courteous

cortesano *m* courtier

cortesía *f* **1.** (*cortesanía*) courtesy; (*gentileza*) politeness; **fórmula de ~** polite expression **2.** (*en una carta*) concluding formula

corteza *f* **1.** (*de un tronco*) bark; (*del queso*) rind; (*de una fruta*) peel; (*del pan*) crust; **la ~ terrestre** GEO the earth's crust **2.** (*exterioridad*) outward appearance; (*rusticidad*) roughness

cortijo *m* **1.** (*finca*) country estate **2.** (*casa*) country house

cortina *f* curtain; **~ de humo** MIL smokescreen; **correr/descorrer la ~** to draw/to draw back the curtain

corto, -a *adj* **1.** (*pequeño*) short; **~ de oído** hard of hearing; **~ de vista** short-sighted; **se ha casado de ~** she got married in a short dress; **a la corta o a la larga...** sooner or later ... **2.** (*breve*) brief **3.** (*de poco entendimiento*) slow **4.** (*tímido*) shy

cortocircuito *m* ELEC short circuit

cortometraje *m* CINE short

coruñés, -esa I. *adj* of/from Corunna **II.** *m, f* native/inhabitant of Corunna

corva *f* ANAT back of the knee

corzo, -a *m, f* roe deer

cosa *f* **1.** (*en general*) thing; **la trata como una ~** he treats her like an object; **eso es ~ tuya/mía** that's your/my affair; **¿sabes una ~?** do you know what?; **no me queda otra ~ que...** I have no alternative but ...; **ser una ~ nunca vista** to be unique; **no valer gran ~** not to be worth much; **tal como están las ~s...** as things stand ...; **como si tal ~** as if nothing had happened; **esas son ~s de Inés** that's typical of Inés **2.** *pl* (*pertenencias*) things *pl*

cosaco *m* Cossack ►**beber como un ~** to drink like a fish

coscacho *m* AmS, *inf* (*capón*) rap on the head

coscorrón *m* **1.** (*golpe*) bump on the head **2.** (*contratiempo*) setback

cosecha *f* **1.** AGR harvest **2.** (*conjunto de frutos*) crop; **de ~ propia** home-grown

cosechadora *f* combine harvester

cosechar *vi, vt* to harvest

cosechero, -a *m, f* harvester

coser I. *vt* **1.** (*un vestido*) to sew; (*un botón*) to sew on; (*un roto*) to sew up; **~ a alguien a balazos** to riddle sb with bullets **2.** MED to stitch (up) **II.** *vi* to sew; **esto es ~ y cantar** this is child's play **III.** *vr* ~**se con** [*o* **contra**] **alguien** to snuggle up to sb

cosido *m* sewing
cosmética *f* cosmetics *pl*
cosmético, -a *adj* cosmetic
cósmico, -a *adj* cosmic
cosmografía *f* ASTR cosmography
cosmología *f* ASTR cosmology
cosmonauta *mf* cosmonaut
cosmonave *f* spaceship
cosmopolita *adj, mf* cosmopolitan
cosmos *m sin pl* cosmos
coso *m* 1.(*plaza*) festival ground 2. *reg* (*calle principal*) main street 3. TAUR ~ **taurino** bullring
cosquillas *fpl* hacer ~ to tickle; **tener** ~ to be ticklish; **buscar las** ~ **a alguien** *fig* to try to stir sb up
cosquillear *vt* to tickle
cosquilleo *m* tickling
costa *f* 1. GEO coast; **Costa Azul** Côte d'Azur; **Costa de Marfil** Ivory Coast 2. FIN cost; **a toda** ~ at any price 3. *pl* JUR costs *pl*

Costa del Sol is the name of a coast in southern Spain, running from **Tarifa** (in the west) to **Almería** (in the east). It incorporates the following four **provincias: Cádiz, Málaga, Granada** and **Almería.** The coast of **Málaga** is probably the most well known (especially **Marbella** and **Fuengirola**) and is where Spanish celebrities particularly like taking their holidays.

costado *m* 1.(*lado*) side; **por los cuatro** ~s through and through 2. MIL flank; **entrar de** ~ to come in sideways
costal *m* sack; **eso es harina de otro** ~ *fig* that's something quite different
costalearse *vr* Chile 1.(*recibir un costalazo*) to fall heavily 2. *fig* (*sufrir una decepción*) to be disappointed
costanera *f* 1.(*repecho*) steep slope 2. *pl* (*maderos*) rafters *pl* 3. *Arg* (*paseo marítimo*) jetty
costar <o→ue> *vi, vt* 1.(*valer*) to cost; ~ **caro** to be expensive; **esto te va a** ~ **caro** this is going to cost you dear; **cueste lo que cueste** cost what it may 2.(*resultar difícil*) **me cuesta convencerlo** I find it difficult to persuade him
Costa Rica *f* Costa Rica

Costa Rica lies in Central America and borders the countries Nicaragua and Panama as well as the Pacific and the Caribbean. The capital of **Costa Rica** is **San José.** Spanish is the official language of the country and the monetary unit is the **colón.**

costarriqueño, -a *adj, m, f* Costa Rican
coste *m* 1.(*costo*) cost; ~ **de la vida** cost of living 2.(*precio*) price
costear I. *vt* 1.(*pagar*) to pay for 2. NÁUT to sail along the coast of II. *vr:* ~**se** to cover the

expenses
costeño, -a I. *adj* coastal II. *m, f* coastal dweller
costero, -a *adj* coastal
costilla *f* 1. *t.* ANAT, ARQUIT rib 2. GASTR chop 3. *irón* (*mujer*) better half
costillar *m* 1.(*costillas*) ribs *pl* 2. *inf* (*tórax*) ribcage
costo *m* 1.(*coste*) cost 2. *AmL* (*esfuerzo*) effort
costoso, -a *adj* 1.(*en dinero*) expensive 2.(*en esfuerzo*) difficult
costra *f* 1. MED scab 2.(*corteza*) crust
costumbre *f* 1.(*hábito*) habit; **de** ~ **se levanta bastante tarde** he/she usually gets up rather late; **como de** ~ as usual 2.(*tradición*) custom 3. *pl* (*conjunto de tradiciones*) customs *pl*
costura *f* 1. *t.* MED seam 2.(*coser*) sewing, needlework 3.(*confección*) dressmaking; **alta** ~ haute couture
costurera *f* (*modista*) dressmaker; (*zurcidora*) seamstress
costurero *m* sewing box
cota *f* 1.(*armadura*) doublet 2. GEO height above sea level
cotejar *vt* to compare
cotejo *m* comparison
cotidiano, -a *adj* daily
cotilla *mf inf* gossip
cotillear *vi inf* to gossip
cotilleo *m inf* gossip
cotillo, -a *adj inf* gossipy
cotización *f* 1.(*de acciones*) price 2.(*pago de una cuota*) contribution
cotizar <z→c> I. *vt* 1. FIN ~ **a algo** to stand at sth 2.(*estimar*) to value II. *vi* (*pagar*) to pay contributions III. *vr:* ~**se** 1. FIN ~ **a algo** to sell at sth 2.(*ser popular*) to be valued
coto *m* 1.(*vedado*) ~ **de caza** game [*o* hunting] preserve 2.(*mojón*) boundary stone 3.(*límite*) limit
cotorra *f* 1.(*papagayo*) parrot 2.(*urraca*) magpie 3. *inf* (*persona habladora*) chatterbox 4. *pey, inf* (*chivato*) telltale *Brit,* tattletale *Am*
cotorrear *vi inf* to chatter
cototo *m AmL, inf* (*chichón*) bump
COU *m abr de* **Curso de Orientación Universitaria** *one-year pre-university course*
covacha *f* 1.(*cueva*) small cave 2. *pey* (*vivienda*) dump
coxis *m inv* ANAT coccyx
coyote *m* coyote
coyuntura *f* 1. ANAT joint 2.(*oportunidad*) opportunity 3.(*situación*) situation, circumstances *pl* 4. ECON current economic situation
coyuntural *adj* ECON current
coz *f* 1.(*patada*) kick; **dar coces** to kick 2.(*culatada*) recoil 3.(*retroceso del agua*) backward flow 4.(*grosería*) rude remark
crack *m* 1. ECON crash 2.(*droga*) crack
cráneo *m* ANAT skull
crápula¹ *m* rake

crápula² *f* **1.**(*embriaguez*) drunkenness **2.**(*libertinaje*) licentiousness

craso, -a *adj* **1.**(*gordo*) fat **2.**(*burdo*) coarse

cráter *m* crater

creación *f* creation; *fig* the world

creador(a) I. *adj* creative II. *m(f)* creator; Dios ~ God, the Creator

crear I. *vt* **1.**(*hacer*) to create **2.**(*fundar*) to establish **3.** INFOR ~ **archivo** to make a new file II. *vr:* ~**se** to be created

creatividad *f* creativity

creativo, -a *adj* creative

crecer *irr* I. *vi* **1.**(*aumentar*) to grow, to increase **2.**(*relativo a la luna*) to wax **3.**(*relativo al agua*) to rise II. *vr:* ~**se** (*persona*) to grow more confident

creces *fpl* **1.**(*aumento*) increase **2.**(*exceso*) con ~ fully

crecida *f* **1.**(*riada*) flood **2.**(*crecimiento*) (sudden) growth

creciente *adj* growing, increasing

crecimiento *m* **1.** *t.* ECON growth **2.**(*moneda*) appreciation

credencial I. *adj* accrediting II. *fpl* credentials

credibilidad *f* credibility

crédito *m* **1.** FIN (*préstamo*) credit; ~ **puente** bridging loan; **dar a** ~ to loan; **pedir un** ~ to ask for a loan **2.**(*fama*) reputation **3.**(*confianza*) **dar** ~ **a algo/alguien** to believe in sth/sb

credo *m* **1.**(*creencias*) beliefs *pl* **2.**(*oración, dogma*) creed

credulidad *f* credulity

crédulo, -a *adj* credulous

creencia *f* belief; REL faith

creer *irr como leer* I. *vi* ~ **en Dios/alguien** to believe in God/sb II. *vt* **1.**(*dar por cierto*) to believe; **¡quién iba a** ~**lo!** who would have believed it!; **no te creo** I don't believe you; **hacer** ~ **algo a alguien** to make sb believe sth **2.**(*pensar*) **¡ya lo creo!** I should think so! III. *vr:* ~**se 1.**(*tener por probable*) to believe **2.**(*considerarse*) to believe oneself to be; **¡qué te has creído!** what do you take me for?

creíble *adj* credible, believable

creído, -a *adj* **1.** ser *inf* (*vanidoso*) conceited **2.** estar (*seguro*) sure

crema I. *adj* cream II. *f* **1.** cream; ~ **antiarrugas** anti-wrinkle cream **2.**(*natillas, pasta*) custard; **la** ~ **y la nata** *fig* the crème de la crème **3.** LING diaeresis *Brit*, dieresis *Am*

cremación *f* **1.**(*incineración*) cremation **2.**(*combustión de desechos*) incineration

cremallera *f* **1.**(*cierre*) zip fastener *Brit*, zipper *Am* **2.** TÉC rack; **tren de** ~ rack [*o* cog] railway

cremat ístico, -a *adj* financial

crematorio *m* crematorium

crematorio, -a *adj* **horno** ~ crematorium

cremosidad *f* creaminess

cremoso, -a *adj* creamy

crencha *f* parting *Brit*

crep¹ *m* (*tela*) crepe

crep² *f* GASTR crêpe

crepé *m* **1.**(*suela, tejido*) crepe **2.**(*postizo*) hairpiece

crepería *f* creperie

crepitación *f* crackling

crepitar *vi* to crackle

crepuscular *adj* twilight

crepúsculo *m* twilight, dusk; ~ **matutino** dawn

cresa *f* **1.**(*huevos*) eggs *pl* (*of queen bee*) **2.**(*gusano*) maggot

creso *m* Croesus

crespo, -a *adj* **1.**(*rizado*) curly **2.**(*irritado*) irritated **3.**(*estilo*) involved

crespón *m* (*tela*) crepe

cresta *f* **1.**(*del gallo*) (cocks)comb **2.**(*de una ola, de una montaña*) crest **3.**(*plumas*) crest **4.**(*cabello*) tuft

creta *f* chalk

Creta *f* Crete

cretense *adj, mf* Cretan

cretino, -a *m, f t. fig* cretin

cretona *f* cretonne

creyente *mf* believer

cría *f* **1.**(*el criar*) rearing, raising **2.**(*cachorro*) baby animal **3.**(*camada*) litter **4.**(*pájaro*) brood

criadero *m* **1.**(*plantel*) nursery **2.**(*vivero*) breeding ground **3.** MIN vein

criadero, -a *adj* fertile

criado, -a *m, f* servant

criador *m* (*Dios*) **el Criador** the Creator

criador(a) *m(f)* **1.**(*de animales*) breeder **2.**(*de vinos*) wine grower

criandera *f AmL* wet nurse

crianza *f* **1.**(*lactancia*) lactation **2.**(*educación*) upbringing **3.**(*vinos*) maturing

criar < *1. pres:* **crío**> I. *vt* **1.**(*alimentar*) to feed; (*mamíferos*) to suckle **2.**(*reproducir y cuidar*) to breed **3.**(*ser propicio*) to produce **4.**(*educar*) to bring up **5.**(*referente al vino*) to mature II. *vi* (*animal*) to have young III. *vr:* ~**se** to grow up

criatura *f* **1.** *t. fig* creature **2.**(*niño*) child **3.**(*feto*) foetus

criba *f* **1.**(*tamiz*) sieve **2.** *fig* (*proceso*) selection process

cribar *vt* to sieve

cric *m* jack

Crimea *f* Crimea

crimen *m* crime

criminal *adj, mf* criminal

criminalidad *f* criminality

criminalista *mf* criminal lawyer

criminología *f* criminology

crin *f* **1.**(*cerda*) mane **2.**(*filamento*) esparto grass

crío, -a *m, f inf* kid

criollo, -a *adj, m, f* Creole

cripta *f* crypt

críptico, -a *adj* cryptic

criptografía *f* cryptography

criptograma *m* cryptogram
criptón *m* krypton
crisálida *f* chrysalis
crisantemo *m* chrysanthemum, chrysanth
crisis *f inv* crisis; ~ **nerviosa** nervous breakdown
crisma¹ *m* REL chrism
crisma² *f inf* (*cabeza*) head
crisol *m* 1.(*recipiente*) crucible; *fig* melting pot 2.(*prueba*) test
crispación *f* 1.(*contracción*) contraction 2.(*irritación*) tension
crispar I. *vt* 1.(*contraer*) to contract 2.(*exasperar*) to exasperate II. *vr:* ~**se** 1.(*contraerse*) to contract 2.(*exasperarse*) to become exasperated
cristal *m* 1.(*cuerpo*) crystal 2.(*vidrio*) glass 3. *elev* (*agua*) water 4.(*ventana*) window
cristalera *f* 1.(*aparador*) glass cabinet 2.(*puertas*) French windows *pl*
cristalería *f* 1.(*empresa*) glassworks *pl* 2.(*objetos*) glassware
cristalero, -a *m, f* 1.(*colocador*) glazier 2.(*limpiador*) window cleaner
cristalino *m* MED crystalline lens
cristalino, -a *adj* 1.(*de cristal*) crystalline 2.(*transparente*) crystal-clear
cristalizar <z→c> I. *vi, vr:* ~se to crystallize II. *vt* to crystallize
cristiandad *f* Christendom
cristianismo *m* Christianity
cristianizar <z→c> *vt* to Christianize
cristiano *m inf* 1.(*persona*) person 2.(*castellano*) Spanish; **hablar en** ~ *fig* to speak plainly
cristiano, -a *adj, m, f* Christian
cristo *m* 1.(*crucifijo*) crucifix 2. *inf* (*persona*) **todo** ~ everyone
Cristo *m* Christ ►**donde** ~ **perdió el gorro** *inf* in the middle of nowhere; **donde** ~ **dio las tres voces** *inf* in the back of beyond
criterio *m* 1.(*norma*) criterion 2.(*discernimiento*) judgement 3.(*opinión*) opinion
crítica *f* 1.(*juicio*) criticism 2.(*prensa*) review, write-up; **tener buenas** ~**s** to get good reviews; (*análisis*) critique
criticable *adj* reprehensible *form*
criticar <c→qu> I. *vt* to criticize II. *vi* to gossip
crítico, -a I. *adj* critical II. *m, f* critic
criticón, -ona *m, f* faultfinder
Croacia *f* Croatia
croar *vi* (*rana*) to croak
croata *adj, mf* Croat(ian)
croché *m* 1.(*ganchillo*) crochet; **hacer** ~ to crochet 2. DEP hook
crol *m* crawl
cromar *vt* to chromium-plate
cromo *m* 1. QUÍM chromium 2.(*estampa*) (picture) card; ~**s de béisbol** baseball cards; **estar** [*o* **ir**] **hecho un** ~ to look wonderful *iron*
cromosfera *f* chromosphere
cromosoma *m* chromosome

crónica *f* 1. HIST chronicle 2.(*prensa*) (feature) article; (*reportaje*) report
crónico, -a *adj t.* MED chronic
cronista *mf* 1. HIST chronicler 2.(*periodista*) journalist
crono *m* DEP 1.(*tiempo*) time; ~ **personal** personal best time 2.(*cronómetro*) stopwatch
cronología *f* chronology, sequence of events
cronológico, -a *adj* chronological
cronometrador(a) *m(f)* DEP timekeeper
cronometraje *m* DEP timekeeping
cronometrar *vt* to time
cronómetro *m* chronometer; DEP stopwatch
croquet *m* croquet
croqueta *f* ≈ croquette
croquis *m inv* sketch, outline
cross *m inv* DEP cross-country running
crótalo *m* 1. ZOOL rattlesnake 2.(*instrumento*) castanet
cruasán *m* croissant
cruce *m* 1.(*acción*) crossing 2.(*intersección*) crossing, intersection 3.(*mezcla*) crossing, cross; ~ **de peatones** pedestrian crossing 4.(*interferencia*) interference 5. BIO cross
cruceiro *m* FIN cruzeiro
crucero *m* 1. ARQUIT transept 2.(*cruciferario*) crossbearer 3. NÁUT (*buque*) cruiser 4.(*viaje*) cruise
cruceta *f* 1. NÁUT crosstree 2.(*en la labor*) cross-stitch
crucial *adj* 1.(*en forma de cruz*) cross-shaped 2.(*decisivo*) crucial
crucificado *m* **el Crucificado** Christ
crucificar <c→qu> *vt* to crucify
crucifijo *m* crucifix
crucifixión *f* crucifixion
cruciforme *adj* cross-shaped
crucigrama *m* crossword (puzzle)
crudelísimo, -a *adj superl irr de* **cruel**
crudeza *f* 1.(*rigor*) harshness 2.(*rudeza*) coarseness 3.(*crueldad*) cruelty
crudo *m* crude oil
crudo, -a *adj* 1.(*sin cocer, natural*) raw 2.(*aplicado al tiempo*) harsh 3.(*blanco-amarillento*) yellowish-white 4.(*despiadado*) cruel 5.(*de difícil digestión*) difficult to digest
cruel *adj* <crudelísimo> ~ **con alguien** cruel to sb
crueldad *f* ~ **con alguien** cruelty to sb
cruento, -a *adj* bloody
crujía *f* ARQUIT bay; (*iglesia*) *passage between choir and altar*
crujido *m* 1.(*de papel*) rustling 2.(*de dientes*) grinding 3.(*de madera*) creaking
crujiente *adj* 1.(*dientes*) grinding 2.(*pan tostado*) crunchy
crujir *vi* 1.(*papel, hojas*) to rustle 2.(*dientes*) to grind 3.(*madera*) creak 4.(*huesos*) crack
crup *m* MED croup
crupier *m* croupier
crustáceo *m* crustacean
cruz *f* 1.(*aspa, crucifijo*) cross; ~ **gamada** swastika; **Cruz Roja** Red Cross 2.(*de una*

moneda) reverse; ¿**cara o ~?** heads or tails? **3.**(*de un árbol*) top of trunk where branches begin **4.**(*de un animal*) withers *pl* **5.** ASTR (Southern) Cross **6.**(*suplicio*) burden; **llevar una ~** to have a cross to bear

cruzada *f* crusade

cruzado *m* crusader

cruzado, -a *adj* **1.** BIO **animal ~** crossbred animal **2.**(*ropa*) **chaqueta cruzada** double-breasted jacket

cruzamiento *m* BIO crossing

cruzar <z→c> I. *vt* **1.**(*atravesar*) to cross; **~ los brazos/las piernas** to cross one's arms/legs; **~ algo con una raya** to cross out sth **2.** BIO to cross **3.**(*condecorar*) to decorate II. *vi* to cross III. *vr:* **~se 1.**(*caminos*) to cross **2.**(*encontrarse*) to meet; **~se con alguien** to pass sb **3.** *t.* MAT to intersect

CTNE *f abr de* **Compañía Telefónica Nacional de España** *former name of the Spanish national telephone company*

cu *f* (name of the letter) q

cuácara *f* **1.** *Col, Ven* (*levita*) frock coat **2.** *Chile* (*camisa ordinaria*) workman's blouse; (*chaqueta*) jacket

cuaderna *f* NÁUT frame (rib)

cuaderno *m* notebook; **~ de bitácora** NÁUT logbook

cuadra *f* **1.**(*de caballos*) stable **2.**(*conjunto de caballos*) stables *pl* **3.**(*lugar sucio*) pigsty **4.**(*sala*) hall; (*para dormir*) large room **5.** *AmL* (*manzana de casas*) block (of houses)

cuadrada *f* MÚS breve

cuadradillo *m* **1.**(*regla*) square ruler **2.**(*pieza de tela*) gusset

cuadrado *m* **1.** *t.* ASTR square; **elevar al ~** to square **2.**(*regla*) ruler **3.**(*trozo de tela*) gusset **4.**(*barra*) die

cuadrado, -a *adj* **1.**(*forma*) square; **tener la cabeza cuadrada** to be pigheaded **2.**(*macizo*) solid; **tenerlos ~s** *inf* to have balls *vulg* **3.**(*corpulento*) hefty

cuadragenario, -a I. *adj* forty-year-old II. *m, f* forty-year-old (person)

cuadragésimo, -a *adj, m, f* fortieth; *v.t.* octavo

cuadrangular *adj* quadrangular

cuadrángulo *m* quadrangle

cuadrante *m* **1.** ASTR, MAT quadrant **2.**(*reloj de sol*) sundial **3.** RADIO dial

cuadrar I. *vi* **1.**(*ajustarse, convenir*) to fit in **2.**(*coincidir*) to tally II. *vt t.* MAT to square III. *vr:* **~se 1.** MIL to stand to attention **2.**(*pararse un caballo*) to stand stock-still **3.** *inf* (*plantarse*) to dig one's heels in

cuadratura *f* ASTR, MAT quadrature

cuadrícula *f* grid squares *pl;* **papel de ~** squared [*o* gridded] paper

cuadricular I. *adj* squared II. *vt* to divide into squares

cuadriga *f* four-in-hand; (*en la antigua Roma*) quadriga

cuadrilátero *m* **1.**(*polígono*) quadrilateral

2. DEP ring

cuadrilla *f* **1.**(*brigada*) squad **2.**(*de amigos*) group **3.**(*de trabajo*) work team **4.** *pey* (*de maleantes*) gang

cuadro *m* **1.**(*cuadrado*) square; **a ~s** plaid, chequered *Brit,* check(er)ed *Am* **2.**(*pintura*) painting **3.**(*marco*) frame **4.**(*bancal*) flowerbed **5.**(*escena*) scene **6.**(*descripción*) description **7.**(*gráfico*) **~ sinóptico** synoptic chart **8.** MIL officers *pl* **9.** TÉC panel

cuadrúpedo *m* quadruped

cuádruple I. *adj* quadruple, four-fold II. *m* quadruple

cuadruplicar <c→qu> *vt, vr:* **~se** to quadruple

cuádruplo *m* quadruple

cuádruplo, -a *adj* quadruple

cuajada *f* curd

cuajar I. *vi* **1.**(*espesarse*) to thicken; (*la nieve*) to lie **2.** *inf* (*realizarse*) to come off II. *vt* **1.**(*leche*) to curdle **2.**(*cubrir*) to cover III. *vr:* **~se 1.**(*coagularse*) to coagulate **2.**(*llenarse*) **~se de algo** to fill (up) with sth **3.**(*leche*) to curdle IV. *m* fourth stomach

cuajo *m* **1.**(*sustancia*) rennet **2.** *fig* phlegm **▶de ~** completely

cual *pron rel* **1.**(*relativo explicativo*) **el/la ~** (*persona*) who, whom; (*cosa*) which; **lo ~** which; **los/las ~es** (*personas*) who, whom; (*cosas*) which; **cada ~** everyone **2.**(*relativo correlativo*) **hazlo tal ~ te lo digo** do it just as I tell you (to); **sea ~ sea su intención** whatever his/her intention may be

cuál I. *pron interrog* which (one); **¿~ es el tuyo?** which is yours? II. *pron indef* **1.**(*distributivo*) **~ más ~ menos** some more, some less **2.**(*ponderativo*) **tengo tres hermanas a ~ más bella** I've three sisters, each more beautiful than the other

cualesquier(a) *pron indef pl de* **cualquiera**

cualidad *f* quality

cualificación *f* **1.**(*calificación*) qualification **2.**(*clasificación*) rating

cualificar <c→qu> *vt* to qualify

cualitativo, -a *adj* qualitative

cualquiera I. *pron indef* (*delante de un substantivo: cualquier*) any; **en un lugar ~** anywhere; **a cualquier hora** at any time; **cualquier cosa** anything; **de cualquier modo** whichever way; (*de todas maneras*) anyway; **¡~ lo puede hacer!** anybody can do it! II. *mf* **ser una ~** *pey* to be a whore

cuan *adv* how; **cayó ~ largo era** he/she fell his/her whole length

cuando *conj* **1.**(*presente, pasado*) when; **de ~ en ~** from time to time **2.**(*futuro; +subj*) when; **~ quieras** when(ever) you want **3.**(*relativo*) **el lunes es ~ no trabajo** I don't work on Mondays **4.**(*condicional*) if; **~ más** [*o* mucho] at (the) most; **~ menos** at least **5.**(*aunque*) **aun ~** even if

cuándo *adv* when

cuantía *f* **1.**(*suma*) amount **2.**(*importancia*)

importance

cuántica *f* FÍS quantum theory

cuantificación *f* quantification

cuantificar <c→qu> *vt* 1.(*expresar numér-icamente*) to quantify 2. FÍS to quantize

cuantioso, -a *adj* substantial

cuantitativo, -a *adj* quantitative

cuanto I. *adv* ~ antes as soon as possible; ~ antes mejor the sooner the better; ~ más que... all the more that ...; ~ más lo pienso, menos me gusta the more I think about it, the less I like it II. *prep* (*por lo que se refiere a*) en ~ a as regards III. *conj* 1. (*temporal*) en ~ (que) as soon as 2. (*puesto que*) por ~ que inasmuch as IV. *m* FÍS quantum

cuanto, -a I. *pron rel* 1. (*neutro*) all that (which); tanto...~ as much ... as; dije (todo) ~ sé I said all that I know 2. *pl* all those that; la más hermosa de cuantas conozco the most beautiful of those I know II. *pron indef* unos ~s/unas cuantas some, several

cuánto *adv* 1. (*interrogativo*) how much 2. (*exclamativo*) how; ¡~ llueve! how hard it's raining!

cuánto, -a I. *adj* ¿~ vino? how much wine?; ¿~s libros? how many books?; ¿~ tiempo? how long?; ¿cuántas veces? how often? II. *pron interrog* how much [*o* many]; ¿~ hay de aquí a Veracruz? how far is it from here to Veracruz?

cuarenta I. *adj inv* forty II. *m* forty; *v.t.* ochenta ▶cantar las ~ a alguien to give sb a piece of one's mind

cuarentavo *m* fortieth; *v.t.* octavo

cuarentavo, -a *adj* fortieth; *v.t.* octavo

cuarentena *f* 1. (*aislamiento*) quarantine 2. (*cuarenta unidades*) una ~ de veces about forty times

cuarentón, -ona I. *adj* fortyish II. *m, f* forty--year-old

cuaresma *f* REL Lent

cuarta *f* 1. (*cuarta parte*) quarter 2. (*medida*) span 3. MÚS fourth

cuartear I. *vt* 1. (*dividir en cuartos*) to quarter 2. (*zigzaguear*) to zigzag up [*o* down] II. *vr:* ~se to crack

cuartel *m* 1. (*cuarta parte*) quarter 2. MIL (*acuartelamiento*) encampment; ~ general headquarters *pl* 3. MIL (*edificio*) barracks *pl* 4. (*perdón*) mercy

cuartelero, -a *adj* barracks

cuartelillo *m* (*de policía*) police station

cuarteo *m* 1. (*división*) division 2. (*grieta*) crack

cuarteto *m* MÚS quartet

cuartilla *f* (*hoja*) sheet of paper

cuarto *m* 1. (*habitación*) room; ~ de aseo lavatory; ~ de baño bathroom; ~ de estar living room; ~ trastero lumber room 2. (*pl*), *inf* (*dinero*) money, dough *inf;* tener cuatro ~s to have to watch every penny 3. (*de un ca-ballo*) ~s delanteros/traseros forequarters *pl* hindquarters *pl*

cuarto, -a I. *adj* fourth II. *m, f* quarter; ~ cre-ciente/menguante first/last quarter; ~ de final DEP quarterfinal; un ~ de hora a quarter of an hour; es la una y/menos ~ it's a quarter past/to one; *v.t.* octavo

cuartucho *m pey* poky room

cuarzo *m* quartz

cuate, -a *m, f* 1. *Méx* (*gemelo*) twin 2. *Guat, Méx* (*amigo*) mate *Brit,* buddy

cuaternario *m* GEO el ~ the Quaternary (period)

cuaternario, -a *adj* quaternary

cuatrero, -a *m, f* rustler

cuatrienal *adj* 1. (*repetición*) four-yearly 2. (*duración*) four-year

cuatrienio *m* four-year period

cuatrillizo, -a *m, f* quadruplet

cuatrimestre *m* four-month period

cuatrimotor *adj* four-engined

cuatro *adj inv, m* four; *v.t.* ocho

cuatrocientos, -as *adj* four hundred; *v.t.* ochocientos

cuatrojos *mf inv, inf* four-eyes

cuba *f* (*tonel*) barrel; estar como una ~ *inf* (*borracho*) to be plastered

Cuba *f* Cuba

> **Cuba** (official title: **República de Cuba**) is the largest of the West Indian Islands. The capital and also the largest city in Cuba is **La Habana**. The official language of the country is Spanish and the monetary unit is the **peso cubano**.

cubano, -a *adj, m, f* Cuban

cubata *f* GASTR rum and coke

cubertería *f* cutlery, silverware

cubeta *f* 1. (*cubo*) pail 2. FOTO tray 3. (*de un termómetro*) bulb

cubicar <c→qu> *vt* MAT 1. (*multiplicar*) to cube 2. (*medir el volumen*) to measure the vol-ume of

cúbico, -a *adj t.* MAT cubic

cubículo *m* cubicle

cubierta *f* 1. (*cobertura*) cover; (*de un libro*) jacket; (*de una rueda*) tyre *Brit,* tire *Am;* ~ de cama bedspread 2. NÁUT deck 3. ARQUIT roof 4. (*pretexto*) pretext

cubierto *m* 1. *t.* GASTR (*servicio de mesa*) place setting; poner un ~ to set a place 2. (*cubertería*) set of cutlery; los ~s the cut-lery, the silverware *Am* 3. (*techumbre*) ponerse a ~ to take cover

cubierto, -a I. *pp de* cubrir II. *adj* 1. (*cielo*) overcast 2. FIN cheque no ~ bounced cheque

cubil *m* lair

cubilete *m* 1. (*en juegos*) cup 2. (*molde*) mould *Brit,* mold *Am* 3. GASTR pie

cubismo *m* ARTE cubism

cubitera *f* ice tray

cubito *m* ~ de hielo ice cube

cúbito *m* ANAT ulna

cubo *m* 1. (*recipiente*) bucket; ~ de basura

dustbin *Brit,* trashcan *Am* **2.** (*de una rueda*) hub **3.** *t.* MAT cube

cubrecama *m* bedspread

cubrimiento *m* (*de un acontecimiento*) coverage

cubrir *irr como abrir* **I.** *vt* **1.** (*tapar*) to cover **2.** *t. fig* DEP, MIL, ZOOL, PREN to cover **3.** (*vacante*) to fill **4.** (*deuda*) to repay **II.** *vr:* ~**se 1.** (*taparse*) to cover oneself **2.** (*ponerse el sombrero*) to put on one's hat **3.** (*el cielo*) to become overcast **4.** MIL to take cover **5.** (*protegerse*) to cover oneself

cuca *f* **1.** (*chufa*) tiger nut **2.** (*oruga*) caterpillar **3.** *inf* (*jugadora*) compulsive gambler **4.** *vulg* (*pene*) prick **5.** *pl, inf* (*dinero*) dough

cucar <c→qu> *vt* (*guiñar*) to wink

cucaracha *f* cockroach

cuchara *f* spoon; ~ **de palo** wooden spoon; ~ **sopera** soup spoon; **meter** (**su**) ~ (*entrometerse*) to meddle

cucharada *f* (*porción*) spoonful; **una** ~ **grande/pequeña** a tablespoonful/teaspoonful; **a** ~**s** in spoonfuls; **meter su** ~ *fig* to meddle

cucharadita *f* (*cuchara*) teaspoon; (*medida*) teaspoonful

cucharilla *f* teaspoon

cucharón *m* ladle

cuchichear *vi* to whisper

cuchicheo *m* whispering

cuchilla *f* **1.** (*de afeitar*) razor blade **2.** (*de cocina*) kitchen knife; (*de carnicero*) cleaver **3.** (*hoja*) blade

cuchillada *f* **1.** (*navajazo*) slash; (*corte*) cut **2.** (*herida*) stab wound; **andar a** ~**s con alguien** *fig* to be bitterly hostile to sb

cuchillería *f* knife shop, cutler's *Brit*

cuchillero *m* **1.** (*persona*) cutler **2.** (*abrazadera*) bracket

cuchillo *m* **1.** (*para cortar*) knife; ~ **de bolsillo** pocket knife; ~ **de cocina** kitchen knife; ~ **de monte** hunting knife; **pasar a** ~ to put to the sword **2.** (*de la ropa*) gore **3.** ARQUIT support

cuchitril *m* **1.** (*pocilga*) pigsty **2.** *fig* (*habitación*) hole

cuchuco *m Col* GASTR pork and barley soup

cuchufleta *f* joke

cuclillas *fpl* **estar en** ~ to be squatting

cuclillo *m* cuckoo

cuco *m* cuckoo

cuco, -a *adj* **1.** (*astuto*) crafty **2.** (*bonito*) pretty

cucufato, -a **I.** *adj Bol, Perú* sanctimonious **II.** *m, f Bol, Perú* hypocrite

cucurucho *m* **1.** (*de papel*) cone **2.** (*de helado*) ice-cream cone **3.** (*gorro cónico*) pointed hat

cuello *m* **1.** ANAT neck; ~ **uterino** cervix; **alargar el** ~ to crane one's neck; **estar con el agua al** ~ to be in a tight spot **2.** (*de una prenda*) collar; ~ **alto** polo neck *Brit,* turtleneck *Am;* ~ **de pico** V-neck; ~ **redondo** crew

neck **3.** (*de un recipiente*) neck; ~ **de botella** *fig* bottleneck

cuenca *f* **1.** GEO basin; ~ **del río** river basin **2.** (*región*) valley **3.** (*recipiente*) wooden bowl **4.** (*de los ojos*) socket

cuenco *m* **1.** (*vasija*) bowl **2.** (*concavidad*) hollow

cuenta *f* **1.** (*cálculo*) counting; (*calculación final*) calculation; ~ **atrás** countdown; ~**s atrasadas** outstanding debts *pl;* **rendición de** ~**s** balance; **Tribunal de Cuentas** National Audit Office; **por** ~ **del Estado** at the public expense; **pagar la** ~ to pay the bill; **trabajar por** ~ **propia** to be self-employed; **establecerse por su** ~ to set up one's own business; **a** ~ **de alguien** on sb's account; **echar** ~**s** to reflect; **dar** ~ **de algo** to report on sth; **ajustar las** ~**s a alguien** to get even with sb; **ajuste de** ~**s** act of revenge; **caer en la** ~ to catch on; **hablar más de la** ~ to talk too much; **a fin de** ~**s** after all; **en resumidas** ~**s** in short; **perder la** ~ to lose count **2.** (*en el banco*) account; ~ **corriente** [*o de giros*] current account; ~ **de crédito** loan account; **abonar en** ~ to credit; **abrir una** ~ to open an account; **girar a una** ~ to transfer to an account **3.** (*consideración*) **tener en** ~ to bear in mind; **tomar en** ~ to take into consideration; **darse** ~ **de algo** to realize sth **4.** (*de un collar*) bead ▶**hacer la** ~ **de la vieja** to count on one's fingers

cuentagotas *m inv* dropper; **con** [*o a*] ~ *fig* bit by bit

cuentakilómetros *m inv* (*de velocidad*) speedometer, odometer *Am*

cuentarrevoluciones *m inv* tachometer

cuentista *mf* **1.** (*chismoso*) gossip **2.** (*fanfarrón*) braggart **3.** (*narrador*) storyteller; LIT short-story writer

cuento *m* **1.** LIT (*historieta*) story; ~ **chino** *inf* tall story; ~ **de hadas** fairy tale [*o story*]; ~ **de nunca acabar** never-ending story; **tener mucho** ~ *inf* (*presumir*) to boast a lot; (*exagerar*) to exaggerate everything; **dejarse de** ~**s** to stop beating about the bush **2.** ARQUIT, TÉC brace ▶**eso es como el** ~ **de la lechera** don't count your chickens before they're hatched; **venir a** ~ to matter; **no venir a** ~ to be beside the point

cuerda *f* **1.** (*gruesa*) rope; (*delgada*) string; ~ **floja** tightrope; ~ **métrica** tape measure; **andar en la** ~ **floja** *fig* to be in an unstable position; **ser de la misma** ~ *fig* to be cast in the same mould [*o mold Am*]; **bajo** ~ secretly **2.** (*del reloj*) spring; **dar** ~ **al reloj** to wind up one's watch; **dar** ~ **a alguien** to encourage sb **3.** ANAT ~**s vocales** vocal chords **4.** (*de instrumentos*) string; ~ **metálica** steel string; ~ **de tripa** gut string; **juego de** ~**s** set of strings; **apretar las** ~**s** *fig* to tighten up

cuerdo, -a *adj* **1.** (*de juicio sano*) **estar** ~ to be sane **2.** (*razonable*) sensible

cueriza *f AmL* (*zurra*) beating

cuerno *m* **1.** MÚS, ZOOL horn; ~ **de la abun-**

dancia horn of plenty, cornucopia; **poner a alguien los ~s** *inf* to be unfaithful to sb **2.** *inf* (*exclamativo*) **¡y un ~!** my foot!; **irse al ~** to be ruined; (*plan*) to fall through; **¡que se vaya al ~!** he/she can go to hell!

cuero *m* **1.** (*piel*) leather; **~ cabelludo** scalp; **~ curtido** tanned hide; **estar en ~s** *inf* to be stark naked; **dejar a alguien en ~s** *inf* to fleece sb **2.** (*recipiente*) wineskin

cuerpear *vi* *Arg, Urug, inf* (*esquivar*) to dodge

cuerpo *m* **1.** (*del hombre o del animal*) body; (*sólo el tronco*) trunk; (*de una mujer*) figure; (*cadáver*) corpse, cadaver; **a ~ descubierto** unarmed; **una foto de ~ entero** a full-length photo(graph); **luchar ~ a ~** to fight hand-to-hand; **dar con el ~ en tierra** to fall down; **tomar ~** to take shape; **estar de ~ presente** to lie in state; **hacer de(l) ~** to relieve oneself; **haz lo que te pida el ~** do what you feel like doing **2.** *t.* FÍS (*objeto*) body **3.** (*corporación, colección*) body; **~ de bomberos** fire brigade *Brit,* fire department *Am;* **~ diplomático** diplomatic corps; **~ docente** teaching staff **4.** (*grosor*) thickness; **~ de letra** TIPO point size; **tener poco ~** to be thin **5.** (*parte principal*) main body; (*de iglesia*) nave ▶**vivir a ~ de rey** to live like a king

cuervo *m* raven, crow; **cría ~s y te sacarán los ojos** *prov* a dog bites the hand that feeds it *prov*

cuesta *f* slope; **~ abajo/arriba** downhill/uphill; **un camino en ~** an uphill road; **llevar a alguien/algo a ~s** to carry sb/sth on one's back; **la ~ de enero** January (*when, following Christmas spending, people are often short of money*)

cuestación *f* charity collection

cuestión *f* question, matter; **~ de confianza** POL vote of confidence; **~ de gustos** question of taste; **~ secundaria** minor matter; **eso es otra ~** that's another matter; **la ~ es pasarlo bien** the main thing is to enjoy oneself

cuestionable *adj* questionable

cuestionar *vt* to question

cuestionario *m* questionnaire

cuete *m* *Méx* **1.** (*loncha de carne*) slice of meat **2.** (*borrachera*) drunken spree; **traer un ~** to be plastered

cueva *f* cave; (*sótano*) cellar; **~ de ladrones** *fig* den of thieves

cuidado *m* care; **¡~!** careful!; **¡~ con el escalón!** mind the step!; **¡anda con ~!** watch your step!; **de ~** serious; **eso me tiene sin ~** I couldn't care less about that; **salir de ~** (*mejorar*) to be out of danger; (*dar a luz*) to give birth

cuidador(a) *m(f)* caregiver; *Arg* nurse

cuidadora *f* *Méx* nanny

cuidadoso, -a *adj* careful

cuidar **I.** *vi* to take care **II.** *vt* to look after **III.** *vr:* **~se** to look after oneself; **~se mucho de (no) hacer algo** to take good care not to do

sth; **¡cuídate!** take care!

cuita *f* worry

cuitado, -a *adj* worried

culata *f* **1.** (*del fusil*) butt; **salir el tiro por la ~** to backfire **2.** (*del caballo*) croup, hindquarters *pl*

culebra *f* snake

culebrón *m* **1.** *aumentativo de* **culebra** big snake **2.** TV soap opera **3.** (*hombre cazurro*) wily character **4.** (*mujer intrigante*) scheming woman

culera *f* seat (of trousers)

culinario, -a *adj* culinary

culminación *f* **1.** (*lo máximo*) culmination **2.** ASTR zenith

culminante *adj* **punto ~** high point

culminar *vi* to culminate

culo *m* **1.** (*trasero*) bottom, backside *Brit;* **caer de ~** to fall on one's backside; *fig* to be amazed; **lamer el ~ a alguien** *vulg* to lick sb's arse; **ser ~ de mal asiento** *inf* to be restless; **tonto del ~** berk *Brit;* **¡vete a tomar por el ~!** *vulg* piss off! **2.** (*de vaso o botella*) bottom

culpa *f* fault; JUR guilt; **echar la ~ a alguien** to blame sb; **y ¿qué ~ tengo yo?** and how am I to blame (for that)?

culpabilidad *f* guilt

culpabilizar <z→c> *vt* to blame

culpable **I.** *adj* guilty; **declarar ~** to find guilty **II.** *mf* culprit

culpar **I.** *vt* **~ de** [*o* por] **algo** to blame for sth **II.** *vr* **~se de** [*o* por] **algo** to be to blame for sth

cultismo *m* (*palabra culta*) learned word

cultivable *adj* arable, cultivable

cultivador(a) *m(f)* **1.** (*persona*) grower; **~ de vino** wine grower **2.** (*instrumento*) cultivator

cultivar *vt* **1.** *t. fig* AGR to cultivate; **~ la tierra** to farm the land **2.** (*bacterias*) to culture

cultivo *m* **1.** AGR (*acto*) cultivation; (*resultado*) crop; **~ de regadío** irrigated crop **2.** (*de bacterias*) culture

culto *m* **1.** (*veneración*) worship; **~ de la personalidad** personality cult **2.** REL **~ divino** divine service

culto, -a *adj* (*persona*) educated, cultured

cultura *f* culture; **~ ambiental** environmental conservation; **~ general** general knowledge

cultural *adj* cultural

culturismo *m* body-building

culturista *mf* body-builder

culturización *f* education

culturizar <z→c> *vt* to educate

cuma *f* **1.** *AmC* (*machete*) long knife **2.** *Perú* (*comadre*) godmother

cumbre *f* **1.** (*cima*) summit **2.** (*reunión*) summit meeting **3.** (*culminación*) height

cumiche *m* *AmC* baby of the family

cumpleaños *m inv* birthday

cumplido *m* compliment; **visita de ~** formal [*o* courtesy] visit; **hacer algo por ~** to do sth out of courtesy

cumplido, -a *adj* **1.** (*acabado*) completed; **¡misión cumplida!** mission accomplished!

2.(*abundante*) plentiful **3.**(*cortés*) courteous **4.**(*con el servicio militar finalizado*) **un soldado** ~ an ex-serviceman

cumplidor(a) I. *adj* reliable II. *m(f)* reliable person

cumplimentar *vt* **1.**(*felicitar*) to congratulate **2.**(*visita de cumplido*) to pay one's respects to **3.**(*una orden*) to carry out **4.**(*un impreso*) to complete

cumplimiento *m* **1.**(*observación*) fulfilment; ~ **de un deber** performance of a duty; **no** ~ non-fulfilment **2.**(*cumplido*) compliment

cumplir I. *vi* **1.**(*hacer su deber*) ~ **con su deber/su promesa** to do one's duty/to keep one's promise; **hacer algo sólo por** ~ to do sth as a matter of form; ~**é por ti** I'll act on your behalf **2.**(*soldado*) to finish one's military service **3.**(*plazo*) to end II. *vt* **1.**(*una orden*) to carry out **2.**(*una promesa*) to keep **3.**(*un plazo*) to keep to **4.**(*el servicio militar*) to do **5.**(*una prestación*) to make **6.**(*una pena*) to serve **7.**(*las leyes*) to observe **8.**(*años*) **en mayo cumplo treinta años** I'm thirty years old in May III. *vr:* ~**se** to be fulfilled

cúmulo *m* **1.**(*amontonamiento*) heap **2.** METEO cumulus

cuna *f* cradle; **canción de** ~ lullaby

cundir *vi* **1.**(*dar mucho de sí*) to be productive; (*el arroz*) to swell; **esta comida cunde mucho** this food is very nourishing **2.**(*un trabajo*) to go well **3.**(*mancha, epidemia, un rumor, una noticia*) to spread

cuneco, -a *m, f Ven* baby of the family

cuneta *f* ditch

cuña *f* **1.**(*traba*) wedge **2.** *fig* (*enchufe*) influence **3.** MED bedpan

cuñado, -a *m, f* brother-in-law *m*, sister-in-law *f*

cuño *m* **1.**(*troquel*) die stamp **2.** *t. fig* stamp; **de nuevo** ~ (*palabra*) newly-coined

cuota *f* **1.**(*porción*) quota; (*de una deuda*) instalment; ~ **de crecimiento** rate of increase; ~ **de mercado** market share **2.**(*contribución*) fee; ~ **de socio** membership fee

cupé *m* AUTO coupé

cupido *m* **1.**(*de la mitología romana*) Cupid **2.** *fig* (*mujeriego*) womanizer

cupo I. *3. pret de* **caber** II. *m* **1.** ECON quota **2.** MIL draught *Brit*, draft *Am*

cupón *m* coupon; (*de lotería*) lottery ticket; ~ **de descuento** discount coupon

cupón-respuesta *m* <cupones-respuesta> reply coupon

cuprífero, -a *adj* copper

cúpula *f* **1.**(*media esfera*) dome **2.**(*máximos dirigentes*) leading members *pl;* ~ **dirigente** top management **3.** BOT cup **4.** NÁUT turret

cura[1] *m* priest

cura[2] *f* **1.**(*curación*) cure **2.**(*tratamiento*) treatment; ~ **para adelgazar** diet; ~ **de almas** REL cure of souls; ~ **de deshabituación** cure for drug addiction [*o* alcoholism]; **primera** ~ first aid

curable *adj* curable

curación *f* (*tratamiento*) treatment

curado, -a *adj* **1.**(*sanado*) cured **2.**(*endurecido*) hardened **3.**(*salado, ahumado*) cured **4.** *AmL* (*borracho*) drunk

curanderismo *m* folk healing; *pey* quack medicine

curandero, -a *m, f* **1.**(*mago*) witch doctor **2.**(*charlatán*) quack (doctor)

curar I. *vi* to recover II. *vt* **1.**(*a un enfermo: tratar*) to treat; (*sanar*) to cure **2.**(*ahumar, salar*) to cure **3.**(*pieles*) to tan **4.**(*madera*) to season **5.**(*hilos y lienzos*) to bleach III. *vr:* ~**se** to recover; ~**se en salud** to take precautions

curare *m* curare

curativo, -a *adj* curative

curcuncho, -a *adj AmL* (*corcovado*) hunchbacked

curda *f inf* drunkenness; **agarrar una** ~ to get tight

curdo, -a I. *adj* Kurdish II. *m, f* Kurd

curia *f* **1.** REL Curia **2.**(*tribunal*) bar

curiosear *vi* to look round; (*fisgar*) to snoop

curiosidad *f* **1.**(*indiscreción, objeto*) curiosity; **despertar la** ~ **de alguien** to arouse sb's curiosity **2.**(*pulcritud*) neatness

curioso, -a I. *adj* **1.**(*indiscreto, interesante*) curious; **estar** ~ **por saber algo** to be curious to know sth; **¡qué** ~**!** how curious! **2.**(*aseado*) neat II. *m, f* **1.**(*indiscreto*) busybody, snoop **2.**(*mirón*) onlooker, bystander **3.** *AmL* (*curandero*) quack doctor

currante *mf inf* worker

currar *vi inf,* **currelar** *vi inf* to work

currículo *m* curriculum

curriculum (**vitae**) *m,* **currículum** (**vitae**) *m* curriculum vitae

curro *m inf* (*trabajo*) job

currutaco, -a *adj inf* flashy

curry *m* curry

cursar *vt* **1.**(*cursos*) to take; (*asignatura*) to study **2.**(*tramitar*) to file; (*una orden*) to issue; (*un telegrama, un mensaje*) to send; (*una solicitud*) to pass on **3.**(*frecuentar*) to frequent

cursi I. *adj inf* **1.**(*una persona*) affected, twee *Brit* **2.**(*una cosa*) kitschy, tasteless II. *mf inf* affected person

cursilada *f inf,* **cursilería** *f inf* **1.**(*acción cursi*) pretentious act **2.**(*calidad de cursi*) affectation

cursillista *mf* member (*of a short course*)

cursillo *m* short course; ~ **de socorrismo** life-saving classes

cursiva *f* italics *pl*

cursivo, -a *adj* cursive

curso *m* **1.**(*transcurso*) course; ~ **de agua** watercourse; **estar en** ~ to be going on; **en el** ~ **del año** in the course of the year; **tomar un** ~ **favorable** to go favourably; **dar** ~ **a una solicitud** to deal with an application **2.**(*de enseñanza*) course; ~ **acelerado** crash course; **asistir a un** ~ to take part in a course; **perder el** ~ to fail a subject **3.** FIN (*circulación*)

estar en ~ to be in circulation
cursor *m* 1. INFOR cursor 2. TÉC slide
curtido *m* 1. (*cuero*) tanned hide 2. (*acción*) tanning 3. *fig* experienced
curtido, -a *adj* 1. *fig* hardened 2. (*cuero*) tanned
curtidor(a) *m(f)* tanner
curtiduría *f* tannery
curtiembre *f* AmL 1. (*taller*) tannery 2. (*acción*) tanning
curtir I. *vt* 1. (*tratar pieles, broncearse*) to tan 2. (*acostumbrar a la vida dura*) to harden II. *vr:* ~se 1. (*ponerse moreno*) to become tanned 2. (*acostumbrarse a la vida dura*) to become inured
curva *f* curve
curvar *vt, vr:* ~se to bend
curvatura *f* curvature
curvilíneo, -a *adj* MAT curvilinear
curvo, -a *adj* curved
cusca *f* 1. *Méx* (*prostituta*) whore 2. *Col* (*embriaguez*) drunkenness 3. *Col* (*colilla de cigarro*) butt ►hacer la ~ a alguien *inf* to play a dirty trick on sb
cuscurro *m* (*de pan*) crust
cuscús *m inv* couscous
cusma *f* AmS coarse woollen Indian shirt
cúspide *f* 1. MAT apex 2. *fig* pinnacle
custodia *f* 1. (*guarda*) custody; **bajo** ~ in custody; **estar bajo la ~ de alguien** to be in sb's care 2. (*ostensorio*) monstrance
custodiar *vt* to guard
custodio, -a *m, f* guardian
cususa *f* AmC uncured rum
cutáneo, -a *adj* skin
cutícula *f* cuticle
cutis *m inv* skin, complexion
cutre I. *adj* 1. (*tacaño*) stingy, mean *Brit* 2. (*sórdido*) seedy, grotty, crummy *inf;* **ropa** ~ cheap clothes *pl* II. *mf* miser
cutrería *f,* **cutrez** *f* 1. (*tacañería*) stinginess, meanness *Brit* 2. (*sordidez*) seediness, shabbiness
cuyo, -a *pron rel* whose; **por cuya causa** for which reason
C.V. 1. *abr de* **curriculum vitae** CV 2. *abr de* **caballos de vapor** HP, h.p.

D

D, d *f* D, d; ~ **de Dolores** D for David *Brit,* D for dog *Am*
D. *abr de* **Don** Mr
Dª *abr de* **Doña** Mrs
dactilar *adj* **huellas** ~es fingerprints *pl*
dádiva *f* (*regalo*) gift
dadivoso, -a *adj* generous
dado¹ *m* 1. (*cubo*) die; ~s dice *pl;* **tirar el** ~ to throw a die 2. *pl* (*juego*) dice; **jugar a los** ~s

to play dice; **jugarse una cerveza a los** ~s to play dice for a glass of beer
dado² *conj* 1. (*ya que*) ~ **que llueve...** given that it's raining ... 2. (*supuesto que*) ~ **que sea demasiado difícil...** supposing it's too difficult ...
dado, -a *adj* (*supuesto, determinado*) given; **dada la coyuntura actual...** given the current situation ...; **en el caso** ~ in this particular case ►**no ser** ~ *Méx* to be brave; **ser** ~ **a algo** to be given to sth
daga *f* dagger; PRico (*machete*) machete
daiquiri *m Cuba* daiquiri
dalia *f* dahlia
dálmata *m* dalmatian
daltónico, -a *adj* colour-blind *Brit,* color-blind *Am*
dama *f* 1. (*señora*) lady; ~ **de honor** (*de la reina*) lady-in-waiting; (*de la novia*) bridesmaid; **primera** ~ POL first lady 2. *pl* (*juego*) (**juego de**) ~s draughts *Brit,* checkers *pl Am*
damajuana *f* demijohn
damasco *m* 1. (*tejido*) damask 2. AmL (*fruta*) damson
damnificar <c→qu> *vt* (*persona*) to injure; (*cosa*) to damage
danés *m gran* ~ Great Dane
danés, -esa I. *adj* Danish II. *m, f* Dane
danta *f* Ven, Col ZOOL tapir
Danubio *m* Danube
danza *f* dance ►**en** ~ *inf* on the go
danzar <z→c> I. *vi* 1. (*bailar, girar*) to dance 2. (*moverse*) to run about II. *vt* to dance
danzarín, -ina *m, f* dancer
dañar I. *vi* to harm II. *vt* (*cosa*) to damage; (*persona*) to injure; ~ **la imagen** to ruin the image III. *vr:* ~se to get damaged; (*fruta, cosecha*) to go bad
dañero, -a *adj* Ven (*embaucador*) misleading
dañino, -a *adj* harmful
daño *m* 1. (*perjuicio*) damage; ~ **material** physical damage; ~s **ecológicos** environmental harm; ~s **y perjuicios** JUR damages 2. (*dolor*) hurt; **hacer** ~ **a alguien** to hurt sb; **hacerse** ~ to hurt oneself; **no hace** ~ it doesn't hurt
dar *irr* I. *vt* 1. (*entregar*) to give; ~ **una patada a alguien** to kick sb; ~ **un abrazo a alguien** to hug sb; **¿a quién le toca** ~ (**las cartas**)? whose turn is it to deal?; ~ **forma a algo** to shape sth; ~ **permiso** to give permission; ~ **importancia a algo** to consider sth important 2. (*producir*) **la vaca da leche** the cow yields milk; **este árbol da naranjas** this tree bears oranges 3. (*celebrar*) to give; ~ **clases** to teach; ~ **una conferencia** to give a talk; ~ **una fiesta** to give a party 4. (*causar*) ~ **gusto** to please; ~ **miedo** to be frightening; **me das pena** I feel sorry for you 5. (*presentar*) ~ **una película** to show a film; **¿dónde dan la película?** where's the film showing?; **¿qué dan en la ópera?** what's showing at the opera house? 6. (*expresar*) ~ **las buenas noches** to

say goodnight; ~ **la enhorabuena a alguien** to congratulate sb; ~ **el pésame a alguien** to give one's condolences to sb; ~ **recuerdos** to send one's regards **7.** (*comunicar: una noticia, un mensaje*) to give **8.** (*hacer*) ~ **un paseo** to go for a walk; **no da golpe** *inf* he/she is bone-idle *Brit* **9.** (*encender*) to turn on; ~ **el agua** to turn the water on; ~ **la luz** to turn the light on **10.** (*sonar*) **el reloj ha dado las dos** the clock has chimed two o'clock **11.** (*aplicar: crema*) to apply **12.** (+ *'de'*) ~ **a alguien de alta** MED to discharge sb; MIL to pass sb as fit; ~ **a alguien de baja** MED to put sb on sick leave; MIL to discharge sb; (*miembro*) to expel sb **13.** (+ *'a'*) ~ **a conocer algo** to let sth be known; ~ **a entender algo a alguien** to let sb know sth ▶**dale que te** <u>pego</u> *inf* on and on; **estar dale que dale con un mismo tema** *inf* to keep going on about the same topic **II.** *vi* **1.** (+ *'a'*) **el balcón da a la calle/al norte** the balcony faces the street/north; **la ventana da al patio** the window opens onto the courtyard **2.** (+ *'con'*) ~ **con alguien en la calle** to run into sb in the street; ~ **con la solución** to find the solution **3.** (+ *'contra'*) ~ **contra algo** to hit sth; **la piedra ha dado contra el cristal** the stone hit the glass **4.** (*caer*) ~ **de espaldas/de narices en el suelo** to land on one's back/on one's face on the ground; ~ **en la trampa** to fall into the trap **5.** (*acertar*) ~ **en el blanco** *fig* to hit the target; ~ **en el clavo** *fig* to hit the nail on the head **6.** (+ *'para'*) **esta tela da para dos vestidos** this cloth will be enough for two dresses; **da para vivir** it's enough to live on **7.** (+ *'por'* + *adjetivo*) ~ **a alguien por inocente** to assume sb is innocent; ~ **a alguien por muerto** to take sb for dead; ~ **por concluido algo** to treat sth as concluded; ~ **el libro por leído** to assume that the book has been read **8.** (+ *'por'* + *verbo*) **le ha dado por dejarse el pelo largo** he/she has decided to grow his/her hair long **9.** (+ *'que'* + *verbo*) ~ **que decir** to give cause for comment; ~ **que hablar** to be the topic of conversation; ~ **que hacer** to be a lot of work; ~ **que pensar** to give cause for thought ▶**¡qué** <u>más</u> **da!** *inf* what does it matter?; ~ **de sí** (*jersey*) to stretch **III.** *vr:* ~**se 1.** (*suceder*) to happen **2.** (*frutos*) to grow **3.** (+ *'a': consagrarse*) to devote oneself; (*entregarse*) to surrender; ~**se a la bebida** to give oneself over to drink **4.** (+ *'contra'*) ~**se contra algo** to hit sth **5.** (+ *'por'* + *adjetivo: creerse*) ~**se por algo** to believe oneself to be sth; ~**se por aludido** to take the hint; ~**se por vencido** to give up; ~**se por enterado** to show that one has understood **6.** (+ *'a'* + *verbo*) ~**se a conocer** (*persona*) to make oneself known; (*noticia*) to become known; ~**se a entender** to hint **7.** (+ *'de'*) ~**se de baja** to sign off; ~**se de alta** to sign up; ~**se de alta en Hacienda** to register with the Inland Revenue; **dárselas de valiente** *inf* to pretend to be brave **8.** (+ *sus-*

tantivo) ~**se un baño** to have a bath; ~**se cuenta de algo** to realize sth; ~**se prisa** to hurry up; ~**se un susto** to get a fright

dardo *m* **1.** (*arma*) spear **2.** (*del juego*) dart; **jugar a los** ~**s** to play darts **3.** (*pulla*) cutting remark

dársena *f* dock

datar *vi*, *vt* to date

dátil *m* date

dativo *m* dative

dato *m* **1.** (*circunstancia*) fact; ~**s personales** personal details **2.** (*cantidad*) figure **3.** (*fecha*) date **4.** *pl* INFOR data *pl*; ~**s de entrada/de salida** input/output data; ~**s fijos** fixed data; **elaborar** ~**s** to compile data

dcha. *abr de* **derecha** rt.

d. de J.C. *abr de* **después de Jesucristo** AD

de *prep* **1.** (*posesión*) **el reloj** ~ **mi padre** my father's watch; **los hijos** ~ **Ana** Ana's children **2.** (*origen*) from; **ser** ~ **Italia/**~ **Lisboa** to come from Italy/from Lisbon; ~ **Málaga a Valencia** from Malaga to Valencia; **el avión procedente** ~ **Lima** the plane from Lima; **un libro** ~ **Goytisolo** a book by Goytisolo; ~ **ti a mí** from you to me **3.** (*material, cualidad*) of; ~ **oro** of gold, gold; ~ **madera** of wood, wooden; **un hombre** ~ **buen corazón** a good-hearted man **4.** (*temporal*) from; ~ **niño** as a child **5.** (*finalidad*) **máquina** ~ **escribir** typewriter; **hora** ~ **comer** mealtime **6.** (*causa*) of, from **7.** (*condición*) ~ **haberlo sabido no habríamos ido** if we had known we wouldn't have gone **8.** (*partitivo*) **dos platos** ~ **sopa** two bowls of soup; **un vaso** ~ **agua** a glass of water **9.** (+ *nombre propio*) **la ciudad** ~ **Cuzco** the city of Cuzco; **el tonto** ~ **Luis lo ha roto** that idiot Luis broke it; **pobre** ~ **mí** poor me

deambular *vi* to wander around

debajo I. *adv* underneath **II.** *prep* ~ **de** (*local*) below, under; (*con movimiento*) under; **pasar por** ~ **del puente** to go under the bridge

debate *m* **1.** POL debate **2.** (*charla*) discussion

debatir I. *vt* **1.** POL to debate **2.** (*considerar*) to discuss **II.** *vr:* ~**se** to struggle; ~**se entre la vida y la muerte** to hover between life and death

debe *m* debit

deber I. *vi* (*suposición*) **debe de estar al llegar** he/she should arrive soon; **deben de ser las nueve** it must be nine o'clock **II.** *vt* **1.** (*estar obligado*) to have to; **no** ~**ías haberlo dicho** you shouldn't have said it **2.** (*tener que dar*) to owe **III.** *vr:* ~**se 1.** (*tener por causa*) ~**se a algo** to be due to sth; (*agradeciendo algo*) to be thanks to sth **2.** (*estar obligado*) to have a duty; **se debe a su profesión** his/her job is his/her vocation **IV.** *m* **1.** (*obligación*) duty; ~ **de conciencia** moral duty **2.** *pl* (*tareas*) homework; **tener muchos** ~**es** to have a lot of homework; **dar muchos** ~**es** to set a lot of homework

debido *prep* ~ **a** due to
debido, -a *adj* (*conveniente, necesario*) proper; **como es** ~ as is proper
débil *adj* weak; (*sonido*) faint; (*luz*) dim
debilidad *f* ~ **por algo** weakness for sth
debilitar *vt* to weaken
debitar *vt AmL* to debit
débito *m* debt; (*debe*) debit; ~ **conyugal** marital duty
debocar <c→qu> *vi Arg, Bol* to vomit
debut <debuts> *m* debut; **hacer su** ~ to make one's debut; (*teatro*) opening, first performance
debutar *vi* to make one's debut
década *f* decade; **la** ~ **de los 40** the 40s
decadencia *f* **1.** (*decaimiento*) decay; ~ **moral** decadence **2.** (*de un imperio*) decline
decadente *adj* (*en declive*) declining; (*moralmente*) decadent
decaer *irr como caer vi* to decline; ~ **en fuerza** to lose strength; ~ **el ánimo** to get [*o* become] discouraged; **decae de ánimo** he/she is losing heart
decaído, -a *adj* **1.** (*abatido*) downhearted **2.** (*débil*) weak
decaimiento *m* **1.** (*afligimiento*) dejection **2.** (*debilidad*) weakness
decálogo *m* REL Decalogue
decano, -a *m, f* UNIV dean
decapitar *vt* to decapitate
decatlón *m* decathlon
decena *f* ten; ~**s** MAT tens; ~**s de miles** tens of thousands; **una** ~ **de huevos** ten eggs
decencia *f* decency
decenio *m* decade
decente *adj* **1.** (*decoroso*) decent **2.** (*honesto*) upright **3.** (*respetable*) respectable
decepción *f* disappointment; **llevarse una** ~ to be disappointed
decepcionar *vt* to disappoint
deceso *m* death, decease *form*
decibel(io) *m* decibel
decididamente *adv* **1.** (*resueltamente*) resolutely **2.** (*definitivamente*) decidedly
decidido, -a *adj* determined
decidir I. *vi* to decide II. *vt* **1.** (*determinar, acordar*) to decide **2.** (*mover a*) to persuade III. *vr* ~**se por/en contra de algo** to decide in favour [*o* favor *Am*] of/against sth
décima *f* tenth ►**tener** ~**s** to have a slight temperature
decimal *adj* decimal; **número** ~ decimal number
décimo *m* (*de lotería*) tenth share of a lottery ticket
décimo, -a I. *adj* tenth II. *m, f* tenth; (*de lotería*) tenth share of a lottery ticket; *v.t.* octavo
decimoctavo, -a *adj* eighteenth; *v.t.* octavo
decimocuarto, -a *adj* fourteenth; *v.t.* octavo
decimonono, -a *adj,* **decimonoveno, -a** *adj* nineteenth; *v.t.* octavo
decimoquinto, -a *adj* fifteenth; *v.t.* octavo
decimoséptimo, -a *adj* seventeenth; *v.t.*

octavo
decimosexto, -a *adj* sixteenth; *v.t.* octavo
decimotercero, -a *adj,* **decimotercio, -a** *adj* thirteenth; *v.t.* octavo
decir *irr* I. *vi* **1.** (*expresar*) ~ **algo de alguien** to say sth about sb; ~ **que sí** to say yes; **diga** [*o* **dígame**] TEL hello; **es** [*o* **quiere**] ~ in other words; **¡no me digas!** *inf* really!; ~ **por** ~ to talk for talking's sake; **por** ~**lo así** to put it like that; **el qué dirán** what people will say; **¡quién lo diría!** who would have thought it!; **y que lo digas** you can say that again; **y no digamos** not to mention; **dicen de él que es un buen profesor** they say he is a good teacher **2.** (*contener*) to say; **la regla dice lo siguiente:...** the rule says the following: ... **3.** (*armonizar*) to suit; ~ **con algo** to go with sth II. *vt* **1.** (*expresar*) to say; (*comunicar*) to tell; ~ **algo para sí** to say sth to oneself; **¡no digas tonterías!** *inf* don't talk rubbish!; **dicho y hecho** no sooner said than done; **como se ha dicho** as has been said **2.** (*mostrar*) to show; **su cara dice alegría** he/she has a happy face ►**no es muy guapa, que digamos** she's not exactly pretty III. *vr* **¿cómo se dice en inglés?** how do you say it in English?; **¿cómo se dice 'ropa' en inglés?** how do you say 'ropa' in English? IV. *m* saying ►**ser un** ~ to be a manner of speaking
decisión *f* **1.** (*resolución*) resolution; (*acuerdo*) decision; **tomar una** ~ to take [*o* make] a decision **2.** (*firmeza*) determination; **tener** ~ to be determined
decisivo, -a *adj* decisive
declamar *vt* to declaim; (*versos*) to recite
declaración *f* **1.** (*a la prensa*) declaration; **hacer declaraciones** to make a statement **2.** JUR statement; ~ **final** closing statement; **prestar** ~ to give evidence; **tomar** ~ **a alguien** to take sb's statement **3.** (*de bienes, impuestos*) ~ **de la renta** income-tax return; **hacer una** ~ **de valor de algo** to declare the value of sth
declarar I. *vi* **1.** (*testigo*) to testify, to give evidence **2.** (*a la prensa*) to make a statement II. *vt* **1.** (*manifestar*) to declare; ~ **abierta la reunión** to declare the meeting open; ~ **a alguien culpable/inocente** to convict/acquit sb **2.** (*ingresos, a aduanas*) to declare III. *vr:* ~**se 1.** (*aparecer*) to break out **2.** (*manifestarse*) to declare oneself; ~**se en huelga** to go on strike; ~**se inocente** to plead innocent; ~**se en quiebra** to declare oneself bankrupt
declinación *f* **1.** (*disminución*) decline **2.** LING declension
declinar I. *vi* **1.** (*disminuir*) to decline **2.** (*extinguirse*) to come to an end II. *vt* (*rechazar*) *t. fig* to decline
declive *m* **1.** (*del terreno*) slope; **en** ~ sloping; **en fuerte** ~ steeply sloping **2.** (*decadencia*) decline; **en** ~ in decline
decodificar *vt* to decode
decolaje *m AmL* take-off

decolar *vi AmL* to take off

decolorar I. *vt* 1. QUÍM to discolour *Brit,* to discolor *Am* 2. (*el sol*) to bleach II. *vr:* ~se to fade

decomisar *vt* to confiscate

decoración *f* 1. (*adorno*) decoration 2. (*con muebles*) furnishing 3. TEAT scenery

decorado *m* TEAT set

decorador(a) *m(f)* decorator; TEAT set designer; ~ **de interiores** interior designer [*o* decorator]; ~ **de escaparates** window-dresser

decorar *vt* 1. (*adornar*) to decorate 2. (*con muebles*) to furnish; ~ **con moqueta** to carpet

decorativo, -a *adj* decorative

decoro *m* 1. (*dignidad*) dignity; **con** ~ with dignity; **vivir con** ~ to live with dignity 2. (*respeto*) respect; **guardar el** ~ to show respect 3. (*pudor*) decency; **con** ~ decently

decoroso, -a *adj* 1. (*decente*) decent 2. (*digno*) dignified

decrecer *irr como crecer vi* to decrease; (*nivel, fiebre*) to fall; ~ **en intensidad** to diminish in intensity

decrépito, -a *adj* 1. (*persona*) decrepit 2. (*cosa*) battered 3. (*sociedad*) declining

decretar *vt* to decree

decreto *m* decree; ~ **gubernamental** government decree

decúbito *m* position; ~ **prono/supino** prone/supine position

dedal *m* thimble

dédalo *m* 1. (*laberinto*) labyrinth 2. (*lío*) mess

dedear *vt Méx* to finger

dedicación *f* 1. (*consagración*) consecration 2. (*entrega*) dedication, commitment; ~ **plena** (*en el trabajo*) full-time 3. (*dedicatoria*) dedication

dedicar <c→qu> I. *vt* 1. (*destinar*) to dedicate 2. (*consagrar*) to consecrate II. *vr:* ~se to devote oneself; ~**se a algo** (*profesionalmente*) to work as sth; ~**se a la enseñanza** to be a teacher; **¿a qué se dedica Ud.?** what do you do?

dedicatoria *f* dedication

dedillo *m inf* **saberse algo al** ~ to know sth inside out

dedo *m* (*de mano*) finger; (*de pie*) toe; ~ **anular** ring finger; ~ **corazón** middle finger; ~ **gordo** big toe; ~ **índice** index finger, forefinger; ~ **meñique** little finger *Brit,* pinkie *Am;* ~ **pulgar** thumb; **chuparse el** ~ *inf* to suck one's thumb; **señalar a alguien con el** ~ to point sb out ►**no tener dos** ~**s de frente** *inf* to be as thick as two short planks; **estar a dos** ~**s de algo** to be within an inch of sth; **estar para chuparse los** ~**s** *inf* to be absolutely delicious; **¿crees que me chupo el dedo?** do you think I was born yesterday?; **hacer** [*o* **ir a**] ~ to hitch-hike; **no mover un** ~ to not lift a finger; **pillarse los** ~**s** to get one's fingers burnt; **nombrar a** ~ to hand-pick; **poner el** ~ **en la llaga** to touch a nerve

deducción *f* 1. (*derivación*) deduction 2. ECON deduction; (*fiscal*) allowance, deduc-

tion; ~ **estándar** basic allowance; ~ **por hijo** child tax allowance

deducir *irr como traducir vt* 1. (*derivar*) to deduce 2. (*descontar*) to deduct

defecación *f* defecation

defecar <c→qu> *vi* to defecate

defecto *m* 1. (*carencia*) lack; **en** ~ **de** in the absence of; **en su** ~ (*cosa*) if it is unavailable; (*persona*) in his/her absence 2. (*falta*) defect; ~ **físico** physical defect; ~ **genético** genetic defect

defectuoso, -a *adj* faulty, defective

defender <e→ie> I. *vt* 1. (*ideas, contra ataques*) *t.* JUR to defend 2. (*proteger*) to protect II. *vr:* ~se 1. (*contra ataques*) to defend oneself 2. (*arreglárselas*) to get by; **¿hablas francés? – me defiendo** do you speak French? – I can get by

defendible *adj* defensible

defensa¹ *f* 1. (*contra ataques*) *t.* JUR, DEP defence *Brit,* defense *Am;* **en legítima** ~ JUR in self-defence; **acudir en** ~ **de alguien** to come to sb's defence 2. *pl t.* BIO defences *pl Brit,* defenses *pl Am;* **tener** ~**s** to have resistance 3. *Méx* (*paragolpes*) bumper *Brit,* fender *Am*

defensa² *mf* DEP defender

defensiva *f* defensive; **a la** ~ on the defensive

defensivo, -a *adj* defensive

defensor(a) I. *adj* defending II. *m(f)* defender; ~ **de la naturaleza** environmental campaigner

deferencia *f* (*consideración*) deference; (*cortesía*) courtesy; **por** ~ **a algo** in deference to sth; **tener la** ~ **de...** +*infin* to be so kind as to ...

deferente *adj* deferential

deferir *irr como sentir vi* to defer

deficiencia *f* 1. (*insuficiencia*) lack 2. (*defecto*) deficiency

deficiente I. *adj* 1. (*insuficiente*) lacking 2. (*defectuoso*) deficient II. *mf* ~ **mental** mentally handicapped person

déficit *m inv* 1. FIN deficit; ~ **presupuestario** budget deficit 2. (*escasez*) shortage

deficitario, -a *adj* (*empresa*) loss-making; (*cuenta*) in deficit

definición *f* (*aclaración*) *t.* TV definition; **por** ~ by definition

definido, -a *adj* (*claro*) *t.* LING definite

definir I. *vt* to define II. *vr:* ~se to take a stand

definitivo, -a *adj* 1. (*irrevocable*) final 2. (*decisivo*) decisive ►**en definitiva** in short

deforestación *f* deforestation

deformación *f* 1. (*alteración*) distortion 2. (*desfiguración*) deformation; ~ **física** physical deformity

deformar I. *vt* 1. (*alterar*) to distort 2. (*desfigurar*) to deform II. *vr:* ~se to become deformed; (*jersey*) to lose its shape

deforme *adj* 1. (*imagen*) distorted 2. (*cuerpo*) deformed

deformidad *f* MED deformity

defraudar *vt* 1. (*estafar*) to cheat; ~ **a Ha-**

cienda to evade one's taxes **2.** (*decepcionar*) to disappoint

defunción *f* death; **certificado de** ~ death certificate

degeneración *f* **1.** (*proceso*) degeneration **2.** (*estado*) degeneracy

degenerar *vi* to degenerate

deglutir *vt* to swallow

degolladero *m* **1.** (*cuello*) throat **2.** (*matadero*) slaughterhouse **3.** (*cadalso*) scaffold

degollar <o→ue> *vt* **1.** (*matar*) ~ **un animal** to slit an animal's throat; ~ **a alguien** (*decapitar*) to behead sb; (*cortar la garganta*) to slit sb's throat **2.** *inf* (*malograr*) to make a hash of

degradación *f* **1.** (*humillación*) humiliation **2.** (*en el cargo*) demotion **3.** (*deterioro*) deterioration; ~ **del medio ambiente** environmental damage **4.** (*en pintura*) ~ **de color** colour gradation

degradante *adj* demeaning

degradar I. *vt* **1.** (*en el cargo*) to demote **2.** (*calidad*) to worsen; ~ **el medio ambiente** to damage the environment **3.** (*humillar*) to humiliate **4.** (*color*) to tone down **II.** *vr* to degrade [*o* demean] oneself

degüello *m* **1.** (*degolladura*) slaughter **2.** (*decapitación*) beheading ▶**tirar a alguien a** ~ *inf* to have it in for sb

degustación *f* tasting; ~ **de vinos** wine tasting

degustar *vt* to taste

dehesa *f* pasture

deidad *f* (*dios*) deity

deificar <c→qu> *vt* **1.** (*divinizar*) to deify **2.** (*ensalzar*) to idolize

dejadez *f* **1.** (*falta de aseo*) slovenliness **2.** (*pereza*) laziness **3.** (*negligencia*) neglect

dejado, -a *adj* **1.** *ser* (*descuidado*) slovenly **2.** *estar* (*abatido*) dejected

dejar I. *vi* ~ **de hacer algo** to stop doing sth; **no dejes de escribirles** don't fail to write them; **¡no deje de venir!** make sure you come! **II.** *vt* **1.** (*en general*) to leave; ~ **el libro sobre la mesa** to leave the book on the table; ~ **acabado** to finish; ~ **caer** to drop; ~ **claro** to make clear; ~ **constancia de algo** to put sth on record; ~ **a deber** to owe; ~ **en libertad** to set free; ~ **algo para mañana** to leave sth for tomorrow; ~ **a alguien en paz** to leave sb in peace; **¡déjanos en paz!** leave us alone!; ~ **mucho que desear** to leave a lot to be desired; ~ **algo sin lavar** to not wash sth; ~ **triste** to sadden **2.** (*abandonar*) to leave; ~ **la carrera** to drop out of university **3.** (*ganancia*) to give **4.** (*permitir: algo*) to allow, to let; **no me dejan salir** they won't let me go out **5.** (*entregar*) to give; (*prestar*) to lend; (*en herencia*) to leave; ~ **un recado** to leave a message; ~ **algo en manos de alguien** to leave sth in sb's hands ▶**¡déjalo ya!** forget about it! **III.** *vr:* ~**se 1.** (*descuidarse*) to neglect oneself

2. (*olvidar*) to forget ▶~**se caer** to hint; ~**se llevar** to let oneself get carried away; ~**se querer** to let oneself be loved

deje *m* hint; **se te nota un** ~ **catalán** you have a slight Catalan accent

dejo *m* **1.** (*entonación*) inflection; (*acento*) accent **2.** (*regusto*) *t. fig* aftertaste

del *v.* = de + el *v.* **de**

delación *f* delation, accusation

delantal *m* apron, pinafore *Brit*

delante I. *adv* **1.** (*ante, en la parte delantera*) in front; **de** ~ from the front; **abierto por** ~ open at the front **2.** (*enfrente*) opposite **II.** *prep* ~ **de** in front of; ~ **mío** [*o* **de mí**] in front of me

delantera *f* **1.** (*parte anterior*) front (part) **2.** (*primera fila*) front row **3.** (*distancia*) lead; **coger la** ~ **a alguien** to gain a lead on sb; **llevar la** ~ **a alguien** to have a lead over sb **4.** DEP forward line

delantero *m* **1.** (*parte anterior*) front (part) **2.** DEP forward; ~ **centro** centre [*o* center *Am*] forward

delantero, -a *adj* front

delatar I. *vt* **1.** (*denunciar*) to inform on **2.** (*manifestar*) to reveal **II.** *vr:* ~**se** to give oneself away

delegación *f* **1.** (*atribución, comisión*) delegation; ~ **de poderes** delegation; **actuar por** ~ **de alguien** to act on behalf of sb **2.** (*oficina*) local office; (*filial*) branch; **Delegación de Hacienda** (local) tax office **3.** *Méx* (*comisaría*) police station; (*ayuntamiento*) council

delegado, -a *m, f* delegate; ~ **gubernamental** government representative

delegar <g→gu> *vt* **1.** (*encargar*) ~ **algo en alguien** to delegate sth to sb **2.** (*transferir*) to transfer

deleitar I. *vt* to delight **II.** *vr* ~**se con** [*o* **en**] **algo** to delight in sth

deleite *m* delight; **con** ~ with pleasure

deletrear *vt* to spell

deleznable *adj* **1.** (*frágil*) fragile **2.** (*inconsistente*) weak; (*despreciable*) contemptible

delfín *m* dolphin

delgado, -a *adj* thin; (*esbelto*) slender

deliberado, -a *adj* **1.** (*tratado*) considered **2.** (*intencionado*) deliberate

deliberar *vi, vt* **1.** (*reflexionar*) to deliberate **2.** (*discutir*) ~ **sobre** [*o* **acerca de**] **algo** to discuss sth

delicadeza *f* **1.** (*finura*) delicacy; **con** ~ delicately **2.** (*debilidad*) weakness **3.** (*miramiento*) attentiveness; **tener la** ~ **de...** to be thoughtful enough to …

delicado, -a *adj* **1.** (*fino, frágil*) delicate **2.** (*exquisito*) fine **3.** (*atento*) thoughtful **4.** (*enfermizo*) frail; **ser** ~ **de salud** to suffer from poor health **5.** (*asunto*) delicate **6.** (*exigente*) demanding

delicia *f* delight

delicioso, -a *adj* (*persona, cosa*) delightful; (*comida*) delicious

delictivo, -a *adj* criminal; **acto** ~ criminal act
delimitar *vt* **1.** (*terreno*) to mark out **2.** (*definir*) to define
delincuencia *f* crime, delinquency; ~ **juvenil** juvenile delinquency
delincuente I. *adj* criminal **II.** *mf* criminal; ~ **reincidente** persistent offender
delineante *mf* draughtsman *m Brit,* draughtswoman *f Brit,* draftsman *m Am,* draftswoman *f Am*
delinear *vt* to draw
delinquir <qu→c> *vi* to commit an offence [*o* offense *Am*]
delirante *adj* **1.** *t.* MED delirious **2.** (*idea*) crazy
delirar *vi* **1.** (*desvariar*) to be delirious **2.** (*disparatar*) to talk nonsense
delirio *m* **1.** (*enfermedad*) delirium **2.** (*ilusión*) delusion; ~ **de grandezas** delusions of grandeur
delito *m* crime; ~ **contra los derechos humanos** human rights violation; ~ **de guerra** war crime; **cuerpo del** ~ corpus delicti; ~ **común** common offence
delta *m* **1.** GEO delta **2.** DEP **ala** ~ (*aparato*) hang-glider; (*actividad*) hang-gliding
demacrarse *vr* to become haggard
demagogia *f* demagogy, demagogism *pej*
demanda *f* **1.** (*petición*) request; ~ **de empleo** job application; ~ **de extradición** JUR extradition request; **en** ~ **de algo** in search of sth **2.** COM ~ **de algo** demand for sth; ~ **adicional** surplus demand; ~ **agregada** total demand; ~ **energética** energy demands *pl;* **tener mucha** ~ to be in great demand **3.** JUR action, lawsuit; **presentar una** ~ **contra alguien** to bring an action against sb
demandado, -a I. *adj* (*solicitado*) requested **II.** *m, f* JUR defendant
demandante I. *adj* JUR **parte** ~ plaintiff **II.** *mf* claimant; JUR plaintiff
demandar *vt* **1.** (*pedir*) to ask for; (*solicitar*) to request **2.** JUR ~ **por algo** to sue [*o* file a suit] for sth
demarcación *f* **1.** (*delimitación*) demarcation; **línea de** ~ line of demarcation **2.** (*terreno*) area
demás I. *adj* other; ...**y** ~... (*y otros*) ... and other ...; **y** ~ (*etcétera*) and so on; **por lo** ~ otherwise **II.** *adv* besides, moreover; **por** ~ more; **está por** ~ **que** +*subj* there is no point (in)
demasía *f* **1.** (*exceso*) excess; **en** ~ in excess **2.** (*insolencia*) insolence
demasiado *adv* (+ *adj*) too; (+ *verbo*) too much; **comió** ~ he/she ate too much
demasiado, -a *adj* (*singular*) too much; (*plural*) too many; **hace** ~ **calor** it's too hot; **demasiado vino** too much wine; **demasiados libros** too many books
demencia *f* **1.** MED dementia; ~ **senil** senile dementia **2.** (*locura*) madness, insanity
demencial *adj,* **demente** *adj* insane, mad
demérito *m* **1.** (*falta de mérito*) fault **2.** (*per-*

juicio) disadvantage; **obrar en** ~ **de alguien** to count against sb
democracia *f* democracy
demócrata I. *adj* democratic **II.** *mf* democrat
democratacristiano, -a I. *adj* Christian Democrat(ic) **II.** *m, f* Christian Democrat
democrático, -a *adj* democratic
democratizar <z→c> **I.** *vt* to democratize **II.** *vr:* ~**se** to become democratic
demográfico, -a *adj* demographic; **explosión demográfica** population explosion; **estadísticas demográficas** vital statistics
demoledor(a) *adj* (*ataque*) devastating; (*argumento*) overwhelming; (*crítica*) merciless
demoler <o→ue> *vt* **1.** (*edificio*) to demolish **2.** *fig* (*destruir*) to destroy
demonio *m* **1.** (*espíritu*) demon **2.** (*diablo*) devil; **ser el mismísimo** ~ to be a real devil ►**tener el** ~ **en el cuerpo** to never stop; **de mil** ~**s** dreadful; **saber a** ~**s** to taste awful; **tentar al** ~ to tempt fate; **¡véte al** ~! go to hell!; **cómo/dónde/qué** ~**s...** how/where/what the hell ...; **como un** ~ like a madman; **ponerse como un** ~ to go mad; **ese** ~ **de mujer/de niño...** that devil of a woman/of a child ...; **¡**~**(s)!** damn!
demora *f* delay
demorar I. *vt* to delay **II.** *vr:* ~**se 1.** (*retrasarse*) ~**se en hacer algo** to delay in doing sth **2.** (*detenerse*) to be held up
demostración *f* **1.** (*prueba*) test **2.** (*argumentación*) proof **3.** (*explicación*) explanation **4.** (*exteriorización*) display **5.** (*exhibición*) exhibition, demonstration
demostrar <o→ue> *vt* **1.** (*probar*) to demonstrate **2.** (*mostrar, exhibir*) to show **3.** (*explicar*) to explain **4.** (*expresar*) to express
demostrativo, -a *adj* **1.** (*probatorio*) evidential; **documento** ~ **del pago** document showing proof of payment **2.** LING demonstrative; **pronombre** ~ demonstrative pronoun
demudado, -a *adj* (*pálido*) pale
demudar I. *vt* **1.** (*variar*) to alter; **la mala noticia le demudó el rostro** he/she was visibly distressed by the bad news **2.** (*desfigurar*) to distort **II.** *vr:* ~**se 1.** (*de color*) to go pale **2.** (*desfigurarse*) to change
denegar *irr como fregar vt* **1.** (*negar*) to deny; ~ **un derecho a alguien** to deny sb a right **2.** (*rechazar*) to refuse; ~ **una solicitud** to reject a request
denigrar *vt* **1.** (*humillar*) to denigrate **2.** (*calumniar*) to vilify **3.** (*injuriar*) to insult
denominación *f* **1.** (*nombre*) name **2.** (*acción*) naming; **Denominación de Origen** guarantee of region of origin of wine or food **3.** FIN denomination
denominador *m* MAT denominator; **reducir a un común** ~ *t. fig* to reduce to a common denominator
denominar I. *vt* (*llamar*) to name **II.** *vr:* ~**se**

to be called

denotar vt (significar) to denote

densidad f density

denso, -a adj 1. (compacto) dense 2. (espeso) thick 3. (pesado) heavy

dentado, -a adj toothed; (filo) serrated; BOT dentate; **rueda dentada** TÉC cog(wheel)

dentadura f teeth pl; ~ **postiza** false teeth

dental adj dental

dentellada f 1. (mordisco) bite; **comer algo a ~s** to wolf sth down; **matar a alguien a ~s** (fiera) to tear sb to bits; **pelearse a ~s** to fight tooth and nail 2. (herida) toothmark

dentera f **dar ~ a alguien** (dar grima) to set sb's teeth on edge; inf (dar envidia) to make sb jealous

dentición f 1. (aparición) teething 2. (dientes) teeth

dentífrico m toothpaste

dentífrico, -a adj **pasta dentífrica** toothpaste

dentista I. adj dental II. mf dentist

dentro I. adv inside; **a ~** inside; **desde ~** from within; **por ~** inside II. prep 1. (local) ~ **de** inside 2. (con movimiento) ~ **de** into; **mirar ~ de la habitación** to look into the room 3. (temporal) ~ **de** within; ~ **de poco** soon ▸ ~ **de lo que cabe** all things considered; ~ **de lo posible** as far as possible

denuncia f 1. (acusación) accusation; **hacer una ~ ante alguien por algo** to make [o file] a complaint to sb about sth; **hacer una ~ por falta de pago** to make an official complaint due to non-payment 2. (de una injusticia) denunciation; **ser una ~ de algo** to expose sth 3. (tratado) cancellation

denunciar vt 1. (acusar) ~ **a alguien por algo** to accuse sb of sth 2. (delatar) to betray 3. (hacer público) to expose; **oficial, quiero ~ un robo** officer, I want to report a robbery 4. (tratado) to cancel

denuncio m And (denuncia) report

Dep. abr de **departamento** department

D.E.P. abr de **descanse en paz** R.I.P.

deparar vt to bring; **nunca se sabe lo que a uno le ~á el destino** you never know what fate has in store for you

departamento m 1. (de un establecimiento) t. UNIV department; ~ **de contabilidad** accounts department 2. (de un objeto) compartment 3. (ministerio) ministry 4. (distrito) district 5. FERRO compartment 6. AmL (apartamento) flat Brit, apartment Am

departir vi to converse

dependencia f 1. (sujeción) dependency; **vivir en ~ de alguien** to be dependent on sb 2. (sucursal) branch 3. (empleados) personnel 4. (sección) section 5. pl (habitaciones) rooms pl

depender vi depender **de algo/alguien** to depend on sth/sb; **¡depende!** it depends!; **depende de ti** it's up to you

dependiente adj ~ **de algo/alguien** depend-

ent on sth/sb

dependiente, -a m, f dependant Brit, dependent Am; (de una tienda) shop assistant

depilación f hair removal; ~ **a la cera** waxing

depilar I. vt to remove hair from II. vr ~**se las cejas** to pluck one's eyebrows; ~**se las piernas** (con cera) to wax one's legs; (con maquinilla) to shave one's legs

depilatorio m hair remover

depilatorio, -a adj depilatory

deplorable adj deplorable; **espectáculo ~** dreadful scene

deplorar vt 1. (lamentar) to regret deeply 2. (condenar) to deplore

deponer irr como poner I. vt 1. (destituir) to remove; (monarca) to depose; ~ **de un cargo** to remove from a position 2. (deshacerse de) to set aside; ~ **las armas** to lay down one's weapons II. vi to give evidence, to testify

deportación f deportation

deportar vt to deport

deporte m sport; ~ **de (alta) competición** competitive sport; ~ **hípico** equestrian sport; ~**s de invierno** winter sports; **hacer ~** to practise [o practice Am] sports

deportista I. adj sporty II. mf sportsman m, sportswoman f; ~ **aficionado** amateur sportsman m, amateur sportswoman f; ~ **profesional** professional sportsman m, professional sportswoman f

deportividad f DEP sportsmanship

deportivo m 1. (club) sports club 2. (automóvil) sports car

deportivo, -a adj sporting; **noticias deportivas** sports news; (zapatillas) **deportivas** sports shoes, trainers pl Brit

depositar I. vt to put; FIN to deposit; (cadáver) to lay out; ~ **su confianza en alguien** to place one's trust in sb II. vr: ~**se** to settle

depósito m 1. (acción de guardar) keeping; **en ~** bonded 2. (acción de poner al cuidado) depositing 3. (depósito) warehouse; ~ **de armas** weapons store; ~ **de cadáveres** morgue, mortuary; ~ **de equipajes** FERRO left-luggage office Brit, checkroom Am; ~ **judicial** police morgue; ~ **de objetos perdidos** lost property office Brit, lost-and-found Am 4. (del wáter) cistern, tank Am 5. AUTO petrol tank Brit, gas tank Am 6. t. FIN deposit; **hacer un ~** to make a deposit

depravar I. vt to corrupt II. vr: ~**se** to become depraved

depre f inf **estar con la ~** to be feeling down

depreciación f (desvalorización) depreciation; ~ **monetaria** devaluation

depreciar I. vt (desvalorizar) to depreciate; (moneda) to devalue II. vr: ~**se** to depreciate

depredación f (saqueo) pillage

depredador(a) I. adj 1. ZOOL predatory 2. (saqueador) pillaging II. m(f) predator

depredar vt (saquear) to pillage

depresión f 1. (tristeza) depression 2. GEO

hollow **3.** ECON, METEO depression; ~ **cíclica** cyclical depression; ~ **económica** recession, slump

depresivo, -a adj **1.** (que deprime) depressing **2.** (propenso a) depressive

deprimir I. vt (abatir) to depress II. vr: ~se (abatirse) to become depressed

deprisa adv fast, quickly; ~ **y corriendo** in a rush

depuración f purification; POL purge

depurado, -a adj (estilo) polished

depuradora f (de agua) water-treatment plant; ~ **de aguas residuales** sewage plant

depurar vt **1.** (purificar) to purify; ~ **el estilo** to polish one's style **2.** POL to purge

derecha f **1.** (diestra) right **2.** (lado) right-hand side; **a la** ~ (estar) on the right; (ir) to the right; **doblar a la** ~ to turn right; **tengo a mi madre a la** ~ my mother is on my right; **rebasar por la** ~ to go down to the right **3.** POL right (wing); **de** ~(**s**) right-wing

derechamente adv **1.** (directamente) directly **2.** (correctamente) rightly

derechista I. adj POL right-wing II. mf POL right-winger

derecho I. adv straight II. m **1.** (legitimidad) right; ~ **de asociación** freedom of association; ~ **de libertad de conciencia y culto** right to freedom of conscience and worship; ~**s de pago de indemnización** right to receive compensation; ~**s de propiedad intelectual** intellectual property rights; ~ **de sufragio** right to vote; **con** ~ **a** with the right to; **miembro de pleno** ~ full member; **estar en su (perfecto)** ~ to be within one's rights; **hacer uso de un** ~ to exercise one's right; **por** ~ **propio** in one's own right; **tener** ~ **a** to have the right to; **el** ~ **al pataleo** inf the right to complain **2.** (jurisprudencia, ciencia) law; ~ **criminal** criminal law; ~ **político** political law; **estudiar** ~ to study law; **conforme a** ~ lawful; **de** ~ by right **3.** (de un papel, una tela) right side **4.** pl (impuestos) duties pl; ~**s de exportación** export duties; **libre de** ~**s** duty-free; **sujeto a** ~**s** subject to duty **5.** pl (honorarios) fee(s); ~**s de mediación** intermediary fee; ~**s de autory** royalties, copyright ▶**¡no hay** ~! inf it's not fair!

derecho, -a adj **1.** (diestro) right; **lado** ~ right-hand side **2.** (recto) straight **3.** (erguido) upright; **ponerse** ~ to stand up straight **4.** (justo) honest; **a derechas** fairly **5.** (directo) direct

derivación f **1.** t. LING derivation; MAT derivative; ~ **a tierra** ELEC earth connection **2.** FERRO branch **3.** (de agua) channel

derivado m derivative

derivar I. vi **1.** (proceder) to derive **2.** (tornar) ~ **hacia algo** to turn towards sth **3.** NÁUT to drift II. vt **1.** t. MAT, LING (deducir) to derive **2.** (desviar) to divert; ~ **una conversación hacia otro tema** to move on to another topic **3.** ELEC to shunt III. vr ~**se de algo** to come

from sth

dermatólogo, -a m, f dermatologist

dérmico, -a adj skin, dermal

dermoprotector(a) adj kind to the skin, skin-friendly

derogación f **1.** (de una ley) repeal **2.** (disminución) decrease

derogar <g→gu> vt (una ley) to repeal

derramamiento m spilling; (de sangre, lágrimas) shedding

derramar I. vt **1.** (verter) to pour; (sin querer) to spill; (lágrimas, sangre) to shed **2.** (repartir) ~ **un gasto** to share out an expense II. vr: ~se **1.** (esparcirse: líquidos) to spill; (otros) to scatter **2.** (desaguar) ~ **en algo** to leak onto sth **3.** (diseminarse) to spread

derrame m **1.** v. **derramamiento 2.** (desbordamiento) overflow **3.** MED haemorrhage Brit, hemorrhage Am; ~ **cerebral** brain haemorrhage Brit, brain hemorrhage Am

derrapar vi to skid

derredor m surroundings; **en** ~ around

derrengado, -a adj **1.** (deslomado) broken **2.** (torcido) twisted **3.** (exhausto) exhausted

derretir irr como pedir I. vt **1.** (deshacer) to melt **2.** (derrochar) to squander II. vr: ~se **1.** (deshacerse) to melt **2.** inf (consumirse) ~se **de calor** to be boiling hot; **estar derretido (de amor) por alguien** to be crazy about sb

derribar vt **1.** (edificio) to demolish, to knock down, to tear down; (puerta) to batter down; (árbol) to fell; (avión) to shoot down **2.** (jinete) to knock off; (boxeador) to knock down **3.** (del cargo, poder) to remove; (gobierno) to overthrow **4.** (humillar) to humiliate

derribo m **1.** (caída provocada) knocking down; (de un avión) downing; (de un futbolista) trip **2.** (demolición) demolition **3.** (escombros) rubble

derrocar <c→qu> vt **1.** (despeñar: persona) to knock over; (edificio) to knock down, to tear down **2.** (destituir) to remove

derrochador(a) adj, m(f) spendthrift

derrochar vt **1.** (despilfarrar) to squander **2.** inf (tener en abundancia) to be brimming with

derroche m **1.** (despilfarro) waste **2.** (exceso) profusion

derrota f **1.** (fracaso) defeat **2.** NÁUT course **3.** (senda) path

derrotado, -a adj **1.** (vencido) defeated **2.** (harapiento) ragged **3.** (deprimido) despondent

derrotar I. vt **1.** (vencer) to defeat **2.** (desmoralizar) to demoralize II. vr: ~se NÁUT to drift off course

derrotero m (rumbo) course; **ir por nuevos** ~**s** fig to follow a new course

derrotista mf defeatist

derruir irr como huir vt **1.** (derribar) to knock [o tear] down **2.** (destruir) to destroy

derrumbamiento m 1.(*de un edificio*) demolition 2.(*de una persona*) collapse 3.(*de tierras*) landslide

derrumbar I. *vt* 1.(*despeñar, derruir*) to knock [*o* tear] down 2.(*moralmente*) to devastate II. *vr:* ~**se** 1.(*edificio*) to fall down 2.(*esperanzas*) to collapse

desabastecido, -a I. *adj* without supplies

desaborido, -a *adj* insipid II. *m, f* bore

desabotonar *vt, vr:* ~**se** to unbutton

desabrido, -a *adj* 1.(*comida*) insipid 2.(*tiempo*) bad 3.(*persona*) disagreeable

desabrigado, -a *adj* unprotected; **estar** ~ (*persona*) to be too lightly dressed

desabrochar *vt, vr:* ~**se** (*botones, hebillas, ganchos*) to undo, to unfasten; (*cordones*) to untie

desacatar *vt* to disobey

desacato m ~ **a algo** disrespect for sth; JUR contempt (of court)

desacertado, -a *adj* 1.(*equivocado*) mistaken 2.(*inapropiado*) unfortunate

desacierto m mistake

desaconsejado, -a *adj* not advised

desaconsejar *vt* to advise against; ~ **algo a alguien** to advise sb against sth

desacorde *adj* 1.MÚS discordant 2.(*opinión*) conflicting; **estar** ~ **con algo/alguien** to not agree with sb/sth

desacostumbrado, -a *adj* (*fuera de la rutina*) unaccustomed; (*no común*) unusual

desacostumbrar I. *vt* ~ **a alguien de algo** to break sb of the habit of sth II. *vr* ~**se a** [*o* **de**] **hacer algo** (*perder el hábito*) to get out of the habit of doing sth; (*perder la rutina*) to become unused to sth

desacreditar I. *vt* to discredit II. *vr:* ~**se** to become discredited

desactivar *vt* (*explosivos*) to defuse

desacuerdo m (*discrepancia*) disagreement; **estar en** ~ to disagree

desafiador(a) I. *adj* defiant II. *m(f)* challenger

desafiar <1. *pres:* desafío> I. *vt* 1.(*retar*) to challenge 2.(*hacer frente a*) to defy II. *vr:* ~**se** to challenge each other

desafilado, -a *adj* blunt

desafinado, -a *adj* (*tono*) out of tune

desafinar *vi* MÚS (*al cantar*) to sing out of tune; (*al tocar*) to play out of tune; (*instrumento*) to be out of tune

desafío m 1.(*reto, prueba*) challenge 2.(*duelo*) duel

desaforado, -a *adj* 1.(*fuera de la ley*) lawless 2.(*desmedido*) excessive

desafortunado, -a *adj* unlucky

desafuero m outrage

desagradable *adj* unpleasant; **ser** ~ **al tacto/gusto** to feel/taste unpleasant

desagradar *vi* to displease; **me desagrada...** I don't like ...

desagradecido, -a *adj* ungrateful

desagrado m displeasure

desagraviar I. *vt* 1.(*excusarse*) to apologize

2.(*compensar*) to compensate II. *vr* ~**se de algo** to make amends for sth

desagravio m amends *pl*; (*compensación*) compensation; **en** ~ **de** as amends for

desaguar <gu→gü> I. *vi* 1.(*desembocar*) to flow 2.(*verterse*) to spill II. *vt* (*desecar*) to drain; ~ **el sótano** to pump water out of the cellar III. *vr:* ~**se** (*verterse*) to spill

desagüe m plughole, drain *Am*

desaguisado m 1.(*agravio*) offence *Brit*, offense *Am* 2.*inf* (*lío*) mess

desaguisado, -a *adj* 1.(*ilegal*) illegal 2.(*escandaloso*) outrageous

desahogado, -a *adj* 1.(*lugar*) spacious; (*prenda*) loose 2.(*adinerado*) well-off 3.(*descarado*) shameless

desahogar <g→gu> I. *vt* 1.(*aliviar*) to relieve 2.(*consolar*) to console II. *vr:* ~**se** 1.(*desfogarse*) to let off steam 2.(*confiarse*) ~**se con alguien** to tell one's troubles to sb; ~**se de un disgusto con alguien** to get sth off one's chest by talking to sb 3.(*recuperarse*) to recover

desahogo m 1.(*alivio*) relief 2.(*reposo*) rest 3.(*holgura económica*) comfort 4.(*descaro*) brazenness

desahuciado, -a *adj* 1.(*enfermo*) hopeless 2.(*inquilino*) dispossessed

desahuciar I. *vt* 1.(*enfermo*) to declare past saving 2.(*inquilino*) to evict 3.(*quitar la esperanza*) to deprive of hope II. *vr:* ~**se** to lose all hope

desahucio m eviction

desairado, -a *adj* 1.(*humillado*) insulted 2.(*desgarbado*) clumsy 3.(*ropa*) shabby

desairar *irr como* airar *vt* 1.(*humillar*) to insult 2.(*desestimar*) to slight 3.(*rechazar*) to snub

desaire m 1.(*humillación*) insult 2.(*desprecio*) disdain 3.(*desatención*) discourtesy

desajustar I. *vt* 1.(*desordenar*) to put out of balance; (*aparato*) to put out of order 2.(*aflojar*) to loosen II. *vr:* ~**se** 1.(*desavenir*) to break down 2.(*aflojarse*) to come loose

desajuste m 1.(*desorden*) imbalance 2.(*desconcierto*) confusion 3.(*de aparatos*) breakdown

desalentador(a) *adj* discouraging

desalentar <e→ie> I. *vt* (*desesperanzar*) to discourage II. *vr:* ~**se** to lose heart

desaliento m 1.(*falta de valor*) dismay 2.(*de fuerzas*) weakness

desaliñado, -a *adj* shabby

desaliño m shabbiness

desalmado, -a I. *adj* heartless II. *m, f* swine

desalojar I. *vi* to move out II. *vt* (*abandonar: casa*) to vacate; (*puesto*) to leave; (*persona*) to eject; (*cosa*) to dislodge

desalquilar I. *vt* (*dejar libre*) to stop renting II. *vr:* ~**se** to remain vacant

desamor m 1.(*falta de amor*) indifference 2.(*aborrecimiento*) dislike

desamparado, -a I. *adj* 1.(*persona*) defence-

less *Brit,* defenseless *Am* **2.**(*vagabundo*) homeless **3.**(*lugar*) exposed **4.**(*casa*) abandoned **II.** *m, f* **los ~s** the poor and homeless
desamparar *vt* **1.**(*dejar*) to abandon **2.**(*desasistir*) to fail to help
desamparo *m* **1.**(*falta de protección*) defencelessness *Brit,* defenselessness *Am* **2.**(*abandono*) abandonment
desamueblado, -a *adj* unfurnished
desamueblar *vt* **~ algo** to remove the furniture from sth
desandar *irr como andar vt* **~ lo andado** to retrace one's steps; *fig* to go back to square one; **no se puede ~ lo andado** *prov* it's no use crying over spilt milk *prov*
desangrar I. *vt* **1.**(*animales*) to bleed **2.**(*pantanos*) to drain **3.**(*arruinar*) to bleed dry **II.** *vr:* **~se 1.**(*perder mucha sangre*) to bleed heavily **2.**(*morirse*) to bleed to death
desanimado, -a *adj* **1.**(*persona*) downhearted **2.**(*lugar*) lifeless
desanimar I. *vt* to discourage **II.** *vr:* **~se** to lose heart
desánimo *m* dejection
desanudar *vt* (*nudo*) to untie
desapacible *adj* unpleasant
desaparecer *irr como crecer vi* to disappear; **~ del mapa** to vanish off the face of the earth; (*en guerra*) to go missing, to be missing in action
desaparecido, -a I. *adj* missing **II.** *m, f* missing person
desaparición *f* (*el perderse*) disappearance
desapego *m* indifference
desapercibido, -a *adj* **1.**(*inadvertido*) unnoticed; **pasar ~** to go unnoticed **2.**(*desprevenido*) unprepared; **coger ~** to catch unawares [*o* off guard]
desaplicado, -a *adj* lazy
desaprensivo, -a *adj* unscrupulous
desaprobar <o→ue> *vt* **1.**(*conducta*) **algo** to disapprove of sth **2.**(*solicitud*) to reject
desaprovechado, -a *adj* **1.**(*infructuoso*) fruitless **2.**(*malogrado*) wasted
desaprovechar *vt* to waste
desarmador *m* **1.**(*gatillo*) trigger **2.** *Méx* (*destornillador*) screwdriver
desarmar I. *vi* POL to disarm **II.** *vt* **1.**(*dejar sin armas*) to disarm; (*argumentos*) to confound **2.**(*desmontar*) to take apart
desarme *m* POL disarmament
desarraigar <g→gu> *vt* **1.**(*árbol, persona*) to uproot **2.**(*costumbre, creencia*) to eradicate
desarraigo *m* **1.**(*de árbol, persona*) uprooting **2.**(*de costumbre, creencia*) eradication
desarreglado, -a *adj* (*cuarto, persona*) untidy; (*vida*) disorganized
desarreglar *vt* **1.**(*desordenar*) to mess up **2.**(*perturbar*) to disturb
desarreglo *m* **1.**(*desorden: cuarto, persona*) untidiness; (*vida*) confusion **2.**(*desperfecto, molestia*) problem; (*en el coche*) trouble
desarrollar I. *vt* **1.**(*aumentar*) to develop; **~**

relaciones comerciales to develop trade relations **2.**(*tratar en detalle*) to expound **3.**(*desenrollar*) to unroll **II.** *vr:* **~se 1.**(*progresar*) to develop **2.**(*tener lugar*) to take place
desarrollo *m* **1.** *t.* FOTO development; **ayuda al ~** development aid; **país en vías de ~** developing country **2.**(*crecimiento*) growth; **~ profesional** professional development
desarrugar <g→gu> *vt* to smooth out
desarticular I. *vt* **1.**(*mecanismo*) to dismantle **2.**(*articulación*) to dislocate **3.**(*grupo*) to break up **II.** *vr:* **~se 1.**(*mecanismo*) to come apart; (*piezas*) to come loose **2.**(*articulación*) to become dislocated **3.**(*grupo*) to break up
desaseado, -a *adj* (*sucio*) dirty; (*desordenado*) untidy
desasir *irr como asir* **I.** *vt* **~ algo** to let go of sth **II.** *vr:* **~se 1.**(*desprenderse*) to come off **2.**(*desacostumbrarse*) to let go
desasosegar *irr como fregar* **I.** *vt* to worry **II.** *vr:* **~se** to become uneasy
desasosiego *m* unease
desastrado, -a *adj* **1.**(*desaliñado*) untidy; (*harapiento*) shabby **2.**(*infortunado*) unlucky, wretched
desastre *m* disaster; **ser un ~** *inf* (*alguien*) to be hopeless; (*algo*) to be a flop
desastroso, -a *adj* disastrous
desatado, -a *adj* **1.**(*desligado*) untied **2.**(*desenfrenado*) wild; **estar ~** to be out of control
desatar I. *vt* **1.**(*soltar*) to untie; (*nudo, paquete, zapatos*) to undo **2.**(*causar*) to unleash **II.** *vr:* **~se 1.**(*soltarse*) to untie oneself; (*nudo*) to come undone **2.**(*desligarse*) to free oneself **3.**(*desencadenarse: tormenta*) to break; (*crisis*) to erupt **4.**(*perder la contención*) **~se en improperios** to let loose a stream of abuse
desatascar <c→qu> *vt* **1.**(*desobstruir*) to unblock **2.**(*sacar del atascadero*) to pull out **3.**(*activar*) to get going
desatención *f* **1.**(*distracción*) inattention **2.**(*descortesía*) discourtesy
desatender <e→ie> *vt* **1.**(*desoír*) to ignore **2.**(*abandonar*) to neglect
desatento, -a *adj* **1.**(*distraído*) inattentive; (*negligente*) careless **2.**(*descortés*) **~ con alguien** impolite to sb
desatinado, -a *adj* **1.**(*desacertado*) foolish **2.**(*irreflexivo*) rash
desatinar *vi* (*conducta*) to act foolishly; (*palabras*) to say stupid things
desatino *m* **1.**(*error*) mistake; (*torpeza*) blunder **2.**(*tontería*) rubbish
desatornillador *m* AmL screwdriver
desatornillar *vt* to unscrew; **~ un tornillo** to remove a screw
desatracar <c→qu> *vi* NÁUT to cast off
desatrancar <c→qu> *vt* **1.**(*puerta*) to unbolt **2.**(*desatascar*) to unblock
desautorizado, -a *adj* unauthorized
desautorizar <z→c> *vt* (*inhabilitar*) to

deprive of authority; (*prohibir*) to ban; (*desmentir*) to deny

desavenencia *f* 1.(*desacuerdo*) disagreement 2.(*discordia*) friction

desavenir *irr como venir* I. *vt* to cause to fall out II. *vr:* ~se to fall out

desaventajado, -a *adj* 1.(*poco ventajoso*) unfavourable *Brit,* unfavorable *Am* 2.(*inferior*) inferior

desayunar I. *vi* to have [*o* eat] breakfast; ~ **fuerte** to eat a large breakfast II. *vt* ~ **algo** to have sth for breakfast

desayuno *m* breakfast

desazón *f* 1.(*desasosiego*) unease 2.(*malestar*) discomfort 3.(*picor*) itch

desazonar I. *vt* 1.(*enfadar*) to annoy 2.(*inquietar*) to worry II. *vr:* ~se 1.(*enfadarse*) to get annoyed 2.(*inquietarse*) to worry

desbancar <c→qu> *vt* to oust

desbandarse *vr* 1.MIL to disband 2.*fig* to scatter

desbarajuste *m* chaos; ¡esto es un ~ total! this is a total mess!

desbaratar I. *vt* 1.(*desunir, dispersar*) to break up 2.(*desmontar*) to take apart 3.(*arruinar*) to ruin II. *vr:* ~se 1.(*separarse*) to break up 2.(*estropearse*) to break down 3.(*fracasar*) to fail

desbloquear I. *t.* POL to unblock 2.FIN to unfreeze

desbocado, -a *adj* 1.(*herramienta*) worn 2.(*escote*) wide 3.(*persona: deslenguado*) foulmouthed; (*enloquecida*) mad 4.(*caballo*) runaway

desbocar <c→qu> I. *vt* 1.(*cacharro*) to chip 2.(*enloquecer*) to drive mad [*o* crazy] II. *vr:* ~se 1.(*enloquecer*) to go mad [*o* crazy] 2.(*caballo*) to bolt

desbordamiento *m* overflowing; INFOR overflow; *fig* outbreak

desbordante *adj* (*alegría, entusiasmo*) boundless; ~ **de alegría** brimming with happiness

desbordar I. *vr:* ~se 1.(*líquido*) to overflow; (*río*) to overflow, to burst its banks *Brit* 2.(*vicio*) to get out of control II. *vi* to overflow; ~ **de alegría** to be brimming with happiness; ~ **de emoción** to be full of emotion III. *vt* (*exceder*) to exceed; **esto desborda mi paciencia** this is the final straw

desbravar *vt* 1.(*domar*) to tame; (*caballo*) to break (in) 2.(*dominar*) to bring under control

descabalgar <g→gu> *vi* to dismount

descabellado, -a *adj* preposterous

descabellar *vt* 1.TAUR to give the coup de grâce to (*to kill the bull by sticking a sword in its neck*) 2.(*desgreñar*) to ruffle

descabezado, -a *adj* headless

descabezar <z→c> *vt* 1.(*decapitar*) to behead 2.(*podar*) to top, to cut the tops off 3.~ **un sueñecito** to have a nap

descafeinado, -a *adj* 1.(*café*) decaffeinated 2.*fig* (*falto de fuerzas*) watered-down

descalabrar I. *vt* ~ **a alguien** to injure sb on the head ►**salir descalabrado** to come off badly II. *vr:* ~se (*en la cabeza*) to injure one's head

descalabro *m* 1.(*herida*) serious injury 2.(*revés*) setback; **sufrir un** ~ (*derrota*) to suffer a defeat

descalcificar <c→qu> *vt* decalcify

descalificación *f* disqualification

descalificar <c→qu> *vt* to disqualify

descalzar <z→c> I. *vt* ~ **a alguien** to take sb's shoes off II. *vr:* ~se (*alguien*) to take one's shoes off

descalzo, -a *adj* 1.(*sin zapatos*) barefoot 2.*fig* (*indigente*) destitute

descambiar *vt inf* to swap, to change back, to exchange

descaminar I. *vt* to misdirect ►**ir descaminado** to be on the wrong track II. *vr:* ~se 1.(*perderse*) to get lost 2.(*descarriarse*) to go astray

descampado *m* piece of open ground; **en** ~ in the open

descansado, -a *adj* 1.estar (*bien dormido*) rested 2.ser (*cómodo*) restful

descansar I. *vi* 1.(*reposar*) to rest; **descanse en paz** (*difunto*) rest in peace 2.(*recuperarse*) to recover 3.(*dormir*) to sleep; ¡**que descanses!** sleep well! 4.(*apoyar*) to rest 5.(*confiar*) to trust II. *vt* 1.(*apoyar*) to rest 2.(*aliviar*) to relieve III. *vr:* ~se (*confiarse*) to trust (*en in*)

descansillo *m* landing

descanso *m* 1.(*reposo*) rest; **día de** ~ day of rest, day off 2.(*recuperación*) recovery 3.(*tranquilidad*) peace 4.(*pausa*) *t.* DEP break; (*alto*) pause; **sin** ~ without a break 5.(*alivio*) relief 6.(*apoyo*) support 7.(*descansillo*) landing

descapotable I. *adj* **coche** ~ convertible II. *m* convertible

descarado, -a *adj* 1.(*desvergonzado*) shameless 2.(*evidente*) blatant

descararse *vr* (*insolentarse*) ~ **con alguien** to be impudent [*o* cheeky *Brit*] to sb

descarga *f* 1.(*de mercancías*) unloading 2.(*disparo*) discharge; (*disparos*) volley; **una** ~ **de golpes** a hail of blows 3.ELEC, FÍS, FIN discharge; ~ **eléctrica** (*calambre*) electric shock

descargar <g→gu> I. *vi* 1.(*desembocar*) to flow 2.(*tormenta*) to break II. *vt* 1.(*carga*) to unload; ~ **el vientre** to move one's bowels 2.ELEC, FÍS to discharge; (*corriente*) to use up 3.(*disparar*) to fire; ~ **un golpe sobre...** to land a blow on ... 4.(*desahogar*) to vent; ~ **su mal humor con** [*o* sobre] **alguien** to vent one's bad temper on sb 5.(*aliviar*) to relieve; FIN to discharge 6.JUR (*absolver*) to acquit (*de* of); (*librar*) to release 7.INFOR to download III. *vr:* ~se 1.(*vaciarse*) to empty; ELEC, FÍS to discharge; (*pila*) to go flat, to run out 2.(*librarse*) to unburden oneself 3.(*desahogarse*) to let off steam

descargo *m* 1.(*descarga*) unloading 2. FIN discharge 3.(*liberación*) release 4.(*justificación*) excuse; **en mi** ~ in my defence [*o* defense *Am*] 5.(*absolución*) acquittal; **testigo de** ~ witness for the defence [*o* defense *Am*]

descarnado, -a *adj* 1.(*sin carne*) scrawny; (*huesudo*) bony; (*flaco*) thin 2.(*acre*) brutal 3.*fig* bare

descaro *m* cheek

descarriar <*l. pres:* descarrío> I. *vt* 1.(*animal*) to separate from the herd 2.(*descaminar*) to misdirect II. *vr:* ~**se** 1.(*perderse*) to get lost 2.(*descaminarse*) to go astray

descarrilamiento *m* derailment

descarrilar *vi* to be derailed

descartar I. *vt* (*propuesta*) to reject; (*posibilidad*) to rule out II. *vr:* ~**se** (*naipes*) to discard

descascarar I. *vt* (*pelar*) to peel; (*nuez*) to shell II. *vr:* ~**se** to chip

descascarillarse *vr* (*loza*) to chip; (*pintura*) to peel

descendencia *f* descendents *pl;* **tener** ~ to have offspring

descendente *adj* 1.(*en caída*) descending 2.(*en disminución*) diminishing

descender <e→ie> I. *vi* 1.(*ir abajo*) to descend; (*a un valle, una mina*) to go down 2.(*disminuir*) to diminish 3.(*proceder*) to be descended II. *vt* 1.(*llevar*) to take down 2.(*una escalera*) to go down

descendiente *mf* descendant

descenso *m* 1.(*bajada*) descent; **carrera de** ~ DEP downhill race 2.(*cuesta, pendiente*) slope 3.(*disminución, caída*) decline; ECON downturn

descentralizar <z→c> *vt* to decentralize

descerrajar *vt* 1.(*puerta*) to force 2.(*tiro*) ~ **a alguien** to fire at sb

descifrar *vt* (*mensaje, código*) to decipher; (*problema*) to figure out

descocado, -a *adj* 1.(*descarado*) impudent 2.(*indecente*) brazen

descoco *m* 1.(*descaro*) impudence 2.(*indecencia*) brazenness

descodificador *m* decoder

descodificar <c→qu> *vt* to decode

descojonante *adj inf* hilarious

descojonarse *vr inf* (*reír*) ~**se de alguien/algo** to piss oneself laughing

descolgar *irr como* colgar I. *vt* 1.(*quitar*) to take off 2.(*teléfono*) to pick up 3.(*bajar*) to take down ▸ **andar descolgado** *inf* to be left out II. *vr:* ~**se** 1.(*bajar*) to come down 2.(*aparecer*) to turn up 3.(*dejar caer*) to drop

descollar <o→ue> *vi* to stand out; **Goya descolló en la pintura de su tiempo** Goya stands out among the artists of his time

descolorar *vt, vr;* **descolorir** *vt, vr:* ~**se** *v.* **decolorar**

descomedido, -a *adj* 1.(*excesivo*) excessive 2.(*insolente*) rude

descomedirse *irr como* pedir *vr* to go too far

descompaginar *vi* to upset

descompasado, -a *adj* 1.(*sin proporción*) out of all proportion 2. MÚS out of time

descompensar I. *vt* to unbalance; **estar descompensado** to be unbalanced II. *vr:* ~**se** to unbalance

descomponer *irr como* poner I. *vt* 1.(*desordenar*) to mess up 2.(*separar*) to take apart 3.(*corromper*) *t.* QUÍM to decompose 4.(*enfurecer*) to anger II. *vr:* ~**se** 1.(*desmembrarse*) to come apart 2.(*corromperse*) to decay 3.(*enfermar*) to become ill 4.(*encolerizarse*) to lose one's temper

descomposición *f* 1.(*separación*) separation; QUÍM decomposition 2.(*corrupción*) decay 3.(*diarrea*) ~ (**de vientre**) diarrhoea *Brit,* diarrhea *Am*

descompostura *f* 1.(*desarreglo*) disorder 2.(*descomedimiento*) rudeness

descompuesto, -a I. *pp de* descomponer II. *adj* 1.(*desordenado*) untidy 2.(*podrido*) rotten 3.(*alterado*) upset; **ponerse** ~ **de rabia** to lose one's temper 4.(*enfermo*) ill

descomunal *adj* enormous

desconcertar <e→ie> *vt* 1.(*desbaratar*) to ruin; (*planes*) to upset 2.(*pasmar*) to confuse; **estar desconcertado** to be disconcerted

desconchado *m* (*de loza*) chip; (*en la pared*) *place where paint has come off*

desconcierto *m* 1.(*desarreglo*) disorder 2.(*desorientación*) confusion

desconectar I. *vi, vt* to disconnect; (*radio, tele*) to switch off; (*desenchufar*) to unplug II. *vi inf* to switch off

desconfiado, -a *adj* distrustful

desconfianza *f* distrust

desconfiar <*l. pres:* desconfío> *vi* ~ **de alguien/algo** to mistrust sb/sth

descongelar I. *vt* 1.(*comida*) to thaw out; (*el frigorífico*) to defrost 2. FIN to unfreeze; ~ **los salarios** to lift a wage freeze II. *vr:* ~**se** (*comida*) to thaw out; (*el frigorífico*) to defrost

descongestionar *vt* to unblock; MED to clear

desconocer *irr como* crecer *vt* 1.(*ignorar*) ~ **algo** to be unaware of sth 2.(*subestimar*) to underestimate 3.(*no conocer*) to not know; (*no reconocer*) to not recognize 4.(*no aceptar*) to deny; ~ **la paternidad** to disown one's paternity

desconocido, -a I. *adj* unknown; (*correos*) address unknown; **estar** ~ (*cambiado*) to be unrecognizable II. *m, f* stranger; **un completo** ~ a total stranger

desconocimiento *m* 1.(*ignorancia*) ignorance; **por** ~ **de los hechos** without full knowledge of the facts 2.(*ingratitud*) ingratitude

desconsiderado, -a *adj* inconsiderate

desconsolado, -a *adj* (*triste*) grief-stricken; (*inconsolable*) unconsolable

desconsolar <o→ue> I. *vt* to distress II. *vr:* ~**se** to lose hope

desconsuelo *m* distress; **daba** ~ **verlo** it was sad to see him like that

descontado, -a adj (descartado) discounted ►**dar** algo por ~ to take sth for granted; **por** ~ of course

descontar <o→ue> vt **1.**(restar) to take away **2.**(letras) to discount **3.**(descartar) to disregard; **descontando que fuera...** +subj assuming that it was not ...

descontento m dissatisfaction

descontento, -a adj dissatisfied

descontrol m loss of control

descontrolarse vr (máquina) to go out of control; (persona) to go wild

descorazonar I. vt to discourage II. vr: ~se to lose heart

descorchador m corkscrew

descorchar vt (botella) to uncork

descorrer I. vt to draw; (cortinas, cerrojo) to draw back; ~ **el cerrojo** to unbolt the door II. vr: ~se to open

descortés adj impolite

descortesía f discourtesy

descoser I. vt (costura) to unpick Brit, to unstitch; **tengo la manga descosida** my sleeve is coming apart at the seam II. vr: ~se **1.**(costura) to come apart at the seam; **se me ha descosido un botón** one of my buttons has come off **2.** inf to fart

descosido, -a adj **como un** ~ (loco) like mad; **hablar como un** ~ to talk one's head off

descoyuntar vt **1.**(dislocar) to dislocate **2.**(falsear) to distort ►**estar descoyuntado** inf to be dead beat

descrédito m discredit; **caer en** ~ to fall into disrepute

descreído, -a adj sceptical Brit, skeptical Am

descremar vt (leche) to skim

describir irr como escribir vt **1.**(explicar) to describe **2.**(trazar) to trace

descripción f description; JUR statement, particulars pl

descuajaringar <g→gu> I. vt to break into pieces II. vr: ~se inf (cansarse) to be knackered; ~ **de risa** to laugh one's head off

descuartizar <z→c> vt to cut up; (en cuatro) to quarter

descubierto m **1.**(lugar) **al** ~ in the open; MIN opencast **2.**(bancario) overdraft; **al** [o **en**] ~ (cuenta, cheque) overdrawn; **quedarse en** ~ to be overdrawn **3.**(en evidencia) **poner algo al** ~ to bring sth into the open; **quedar al** ~ to be revealed

descubierto, -a I. pp de **descubrir** II. adj open; (sin techo) open-air; (cielo) clear; (cabeza) uncovered; (paisaje) bare

descubridor(a) m(f) discoverer

descubrimiento m **1.**(tierras, invento) discovery **2.**(revelación) disclosure; JUR detection

descubrir irr como abrir I. vt **1.**(destapar) to uncover **2.**(encontrar) to discover **3.**(averiguar) to find out **4.**(inventar) to invent **5.**(revelar) to reveal **6.**(desenmascarar) to unmask II. vr: ~se **1.**(salir a la luz) to come out **2.**(traicionarse) to give oneself away

3.(desenmascararse) to reveal oneself **4.**(saludo) to raise one's hat

descuento m **1.**(deducción) discount **2.**(rebaja) reduction; COM discount; ~ **por pago al contado** cash discount; ~ **por cantidad** quantity discount; ~ **al por mayor** discount on bulk purchase; ~ **por not tener siniestros** no claims bonus **3.**(de letras de cambio: acción) discounting; (cantidad) discount **4.** DEP injury time

descuidado, -a adj **1.** ser (falto de atención) inattentive; (de cuidado) careless; (imprudente) negligent; (desaseado) slovenly; (desaliñado) untidy **2.** estar (abandonado) neglected; (desprevenido) unprepared; **aspecto** ~ untidiness; **coger** ~ **a alguien** to catch sb off his/her guard

descuidar I. vi ¡descuida! don't worry! II. vt **1.**(desatender) to neglect **2.**(ignorar) to overlook III. vr: ~se **1.**(abandonarse) to neglect oneself, to let oneself go **2.**(distraerse) to be distracted

descuidero, -a m, f pickpocket

descuido m **1.**(falta de atención) inattentiveness; (de cuidado) carelessness; (imprudencia) negligence **2.**(error) oversight; **por** ~ inadvertently

desde I. prep **1.**(temporal: pasado) since; (a partir de) from; ~...**hasta**... from ... until ...; ~ **ahora** (**en adelante**) from now on; ¿~ **cuándo?** since when?; ¿~ **cuándo vives aquí?** how long have you lived here (for)?; ~ **entonces** since then; ~ **hace un mes** for a month; ~ **hace poco/mucho** for a short/long time; ~ **hoy/mañana** from today/tomorrow; ~ **el principio** from the beginning; ~ **ya** from now on **2.**(local) from; **te llamo** ~ **el aeropuerto** I'm calling from the airport II. adv ~ **luego** (por supuesto) of course; ¿**vienes con nosotros?** - ¡~ **luego!** are you coming with us? - of course I am!; **hace un tiempo horroroso** - ¡~ **luego!** the weather is dreadful - absolutely! III. conj ~ **que** since

desdecir irr como decir I. vi to be unworthy; ~ **de los suyos** to let one's family down II. vr: ~se **de algo** to withdraw sth, to take sth back; ~se **de una promesa** to go back on a promise

desdén m disdain

desdentado, -a adj toothless

desdeñable adj **1.**(insignificante) insignificant; **nada** ~ far from negligible **2.**(despreciable) despicable

desdeñar vt **1.**(despreciar) to scorn **2.**(rechazar) to spurn

desdeñoso, -a adj disdainful; (soberbio) contemptuous

desdibujar I. vt to blur II. vr: ~se to become blurred

desdicha f **1.**(desgracia) misfortune; (suceso) calamity **2.**(miseria) misery

desdichado, -a adj unfortunate; **es un** ~ he is an unfortunate wretch

desdoblar I. vt **1.**(desplegar) to unfold;

(*extender*) to open out, to spread out **2.** (*dividir*) to divide **3.** (*duplicar*) to double **II.** *vr:* **~se 1.** (*abrirse*) to open out **2.** (*dividirse*) to divide **3.** (*duplicarse*) to double

desdoro *m* dishonour *Brit,* dishonor *Am*

deseable *adj* desirable

desear *vt* to want; (*sexualmente*) to desire; *~* **suerte a alguien** to wish sb luck; **hacerse ~** to play hard to get; **¿desea algo más?** would you like anything else?; **dejar mucho que ~** to leave a lot to be desired

desecar <c→qu> **I.** *vt* (*pantano*) to dry out; (*alimentos, aire*) to dry **II.** *vr:* **~se** to dry up

desechable *adj* **1.** (*de un solo uso*) disposable; **guantes ~s** disposable gloves; **botellas ~s** non-returnable bottles **2.** (*despreciable*) despicable; **nada ~** far from negligible

desechar *vt* **1.** (*tirar*) to throw away **2.** (*descartar*) to rule out; (*desestimar*) to reject **3.** (*desdeñar*) to scorn

desecho(s) *m(pl)* (*restos*) remains *pl;* (*residuos*) residue; (*basura*) waste; **~s tóxicos** toxic waste; **de ~** waste; **el ~ de la sociedad** the dregs of society

desembalar *vt* to unpack

desembarazado, -a *adj* **1.** (*expedito*) free **2.** (*desenvuelto*) free and easy

desembarazar <z→c> **I.** *vt* **1.** (*desocupar*) to empty **2.** (*despejar*) to clear; (*librar*) to free **II.** *vr:* **~se** to free oneself **III.** *vi Chile* (*dar a luz*) to give birth

desembarazo *m* **1.** (*despejo*) clearing **2.** (*desenvoltura*) ease

desembarcadero *m* landing stage; (*puente*) jetty, wharf

desembarcar <c→qu> **I.** *vi* **1.** (*descargar*) to disembark **2.** (*una escalera*) to lead to **II.** *vt* **1.** (*descargar*) to unload **2.** (*transportar*) to transport

desembarco *m* (*arribada*) landing

desembargar <g→gu> *vt* **~ algo** to lift the embargo on sth

desembarque *m* **1.** (*arribada*) landing **2.** (*descarga*) unloading

desembarrancar <c→qu> *vt* to refloat

desembocadura *f* **1.** (*de un río*) mouth **2.** (*desagüe*) outlet

desembocar <c→qu> *vi* **1.** (*río*) **~ en** to flow into **2.** (*situación*) **~ en** to result in

desembolsar *vt* **1.** (*sacar*) **~ algo** to take sth out of one's pocket **2.** (*pagar*) to pay, to pay out *Brit;* (*gastar*) to spend

desembolso *m* **1.** (*pago*) payment **2.** (*gasto*) expense

desembozar <z→c> **I.** *vt* **1.** (*descubrir*) to uncover **2.** (*desatrancar*) to unblock **II.** *vr:* **~se 1.** (*descubrirse*) to uncover oneself **2.** (*desatrancarse*) to become unblocked

desembragar <g→gu> *auto* **I.** *vi* to release the clutch **II.** *vt* to release

desembrollar *vt inf* **1.** (*madeja*) to disentangle **2.** (*asunto*) to sort out

desembuchar **I.** *vi inf* (*confesar*) to come

clean; **¡desembucha de una vez!** out with it! **II.** *vt* **~ algo** to come clean about sth

desempacar <c→qu> *vt* to unpack

desempapelar *vt* (*paquete*) to unwrap; **~ una habitación** to strip the wallpaper of a room

desempaquetar *vt* to unwrap

desempatar *vi* to break the tie

desempate *m* breakthrough

desempeñar *vt* **1.** (*préstamo*) to pay off **2.** (*cargo*) to hold; (*trabajo*) to carry out; **~ un papel** to play a role

desempeño *m* **1.** (*de un préstamo*) repayment **2.** (*ejercicio*) fulfilment *Brit,* fulfillment *Am;* (*realización*) performance

desempleado, -a **I.** *adj* unemployed **II.** *m, f* unemployed person

desempleo *m* unemployment

desempolvar *vt* **1.** (*limpiar*) to dust **2.** (*lo olvidado*) to revive, to brush up

desencadenar **I.** *vt* **1.** (*soltar*) to unleash **2.** (*provocar*) to trigger **II.** *vr:* **~se** to break loose

desencajar **I.** *vt* (*sacar*) to dismantle; *med* to dislocate; (*cara*) to distort **II.** *vr:* **~se** (*salirse*) to come apart; *med* to dislocate

desencantar **I.** *vt* **1.** (*desilusionar*) to disillusion; (*decepcionar*) to disappoint **2.** (*desembrujar*) **~ algo** to break the spell on sth **II.** *vr:* **~se** to become disillusioned

desencanto *m* **1.** (*decepción*) disappointment **2.** (*desilusión*) disillusion

desenchufar *vt* to unplug

desencoger <g→j> **I.** *vt* **1.** (*extender*) to spread out **2.** (*estirar*) to stretch **II.** *vr:* **~se 1.** (*extenderse*) to spread out **2.** (*estirarse*) to stretch **3.** (*desempacharse*) to come out of one's shell

desencolarse *vr* to come unstuck

desencuadernar **I.** *vt* (*libro*) to remove the binding from **II.** *vr:* **~se** *t. fig* to fall apart

desenfadado, -a *adj* **1.** (*desenvuelto*) self-assured **2.** (*carácter*) easy-going **3.** (*ropa*) casual

desenfado *m* openness; (*sin inhibiciones*) naturalness

desenfocado, -a *adj* foto out of focus

desenfrenado, -a *adj* frantic

desenfreno *m* lack of restraint

desenganchar **I.** *vt* **1.** (*gancho*) to unhook **2.** (*soltar*) to take off; (*caballos*) to unhitch **3.** ferro to uncouple **II.** *vr:* **~se** *inf* (*de la droga*) to get off drugs

desengañar **I.** *vt* (*desilusionar*) to disillusion; **~ a alguien** (*abrir los ojos*) to shatter sb's illusions **II.** *vr:* **~se** (*decepcionarse*) to be disappointed; **pronto te ~ás** (*verás claro*) you'll soon see the truth

desengaño *m* disillusion; **sufrir un ~ amoroso** to have an unhappy love affair

desengrasar *vt* to remove the grease from

desenlace *m* outcome; **la película tiene un ~ feliz** the film has a happy ending

desenlazar <z→c> **I.** *vt* **1.** (*desatar*) to untie

2. (*resolver*) to clear up **II.** *vr:* ~**se** (*resolverse*) to be resolved; TEAT to end

desenmarañar *vt* **1.** (*desenredar*) to untangle **2.** (*desentrañar*) to figure out

desenmascarar I. *vt* to unmask; *fig* to expose **II.** *vr:* ~**se** to remove one's mask; *fig* to reveal oneself

desenredar I. *vt t. fig* to unravel; (*pelo*) to untangle **II.** *vr:* ~**se** *inf* (*librarse*) to extricate oneself

desenroscar <c→qu> *vt* **1.** (*abrir, sacar de la rosca*) to unscrew **2.** (*desenrollar*) to unwind

desentenderse <e→ie> *vr* **1.** (*despreocuparse*) ~ **de algo** to want nothing to do with sth; ~ **de un problema** to wash one's hands of a problem **2.** (*fingir ignorancia*) ~ **de algo** to pretend to not know about sth; **hacerse el desentendido** to turn a deaf ear

desenterrar <e→ie> *vt* **1.** to dig up, to disinter *form;* (*cadáver*) to exhume **2.** (*encontrar*) to find; ~ **viejos recuerdos** to rake up old memories

desentonar *vi* **1.** (*cantar*) to sing out of tune; (*tocar*) to play out of tune **2.** (*no combinar*) to not go [*o* match]; **con esa ropa desentonas en la fiesta** with those clothes you'll be out of place at the party

desentorpecer *irr como crecer vt* **1.** (*desembarazar*) to clear **2.** (*desentumecer*) to loosen up **3.** (*afinar*) to polish up

desentrañar *vt* (*descubrir*) to unravel

desentumecer *irr como crecer vt* to loosen up; DEP to warm up

desenvoltura *f* self-confidence; (*descaro*) cheek, gall

desenvolver *irr como volver* **I.** *vt* **1.** (*desempaquetar*) to unwrap **2.** (*desenrollar*) to unwind; (*desdoblar*) to unfold **3.** (*descubrir*) to discover **4.** (*desarrollar*) to develop **II.** *vr:* ~**se 1.** (*llevarse*) to get on with **2.** (*manejarse*) to handle oneself

desenvuelto, -a I. *pp de* **desenvolver II.** *adj* (*resuelto*) self-assured; (*descarado*) impudent

deseo *m* **1.** (*anhelo*) wish; ~ **imperioso** burning desire; **tener ~s de venganza** to want to get one's revenge; **tengo grandes ~s de que vengan** I really hope they come; **formular un** ~ to make a wish **2.** (*necesidad*) need **3.** (*ansia*) longing **4.** (*sexual*) desire **5.** (*impulso*) whim

deseoso, -a *adj* **estar** ~ **de hacer algo** (*ansioso*) to be eager to do sth; **estoy** ~ **de conocerlo** I'm dying to meet him

desequilibrado, -a *adj* unbalanced; (*trastornado*) (mentally) disturbed

desequilibrar I. *vt* **1.** (*descompensar*) to unbalance **2.** (*trastornar*) to disturb **II.** *vr:* ~**se 1.** (*descompensarse*) to unbalance **2.** (*psíquicamente*) to become disturbed

desequilibrio *m* **1.** (*falta de equilibrio*) lack of balance; (*descompensación, desproporción*) imbalance **2.** (*trastorno*) disturbance; ~

mental mental instability

desertar *vi* **1.** MIL to desert; ~ **de** to desert from; ~ **a** to go over to **2.** *fig* (*abandonar*) to abandon

desértico, -a *adj* desert

desertor(a) *m(f)* deserter

desesperación *f* **1.** (*desmoralización*) desperation, despair; **con** ~ desperately; **caer en la** ~ to become desperate **2.** (*enojo*) exasperation **3.** (*que desespera*) **ser una** ~ to be a cause of despair; **tu manera de trabajar es mi** ~ the way you work exasperates me

desesperado, -a *adj* **1.** (*desmoralizado*) desperate; (*situación*) hopeless; **correr/gritar como un** ~ to run/shout like mad; **hacer algo a la desesperada** to do sth as a last resort **2.** (*enojado*) exasperated

desesperante *adj* **1.** (*sin esperanza*) hopeless; **resulta ~...** there is no point ...; **¡eres ~!** you're a disaster! **2.** (*exasperante*) exasperating; **tu comportamiento es** ~ your behaviour drives me to despair

desesperar I. *vt* **1.** (*quitar la esperanza*) ~ **a alguien** to cause sb to lose hope **2.** (*exasperar*) to exasperate **II.** *vi* to despair; **no desesperes de que sigan vivos** don't lose hope, they're still alive **III.** *vr:* ~**se 1.** (*perder la esperanza*) to give up hope; **¡no te desesperes!** don't give up hope **2.** (*lamentarse*) ~ **por algo** of sth **3.** (*despecharse*) to despair

desestimar *vt* **1.** (*despreciar*) ~ **algo** to have a low opinion of sth **2.** (*rechazar*) to reject; ~ **una demanda/una reclamación** to reject a demand/a claim

desfachatez *f* cheek

desfalcar <c→qu> *vt* (*dinero*) to embezzle

desfalco *m* embezzlement

desfallecer *irr como crecer* **I.** *vi* **1.** (*debilitarse*) to weaken **2.** (*colapsar*) to collapse; (*desmayarse*) to faint **3.** (*perder el ánimo*) to lose heart; **después de una hora empezó a** ~ after an hour he/she began to flag **II.** *vt* **1.** (*debilitar*) to weaken **2.** (*desanimar*) to discourage

desfallecimiento *m* **1.** (*debilidad*) weakening **2.** (*desmayo*) faint; (*colapso*) collapse; ~ **de ánimo** loss of heart; ~ (**de las fuerzas**) loss of strength; **poco antes de llegar a la meta le sobrevino el** ~ just before reaching the end, he/she collapsed

desfasado, -a *adj* **1.** (*anticuado: persona*) old-fashioned; (*cosa*) antiquated; **estar** ~ to be behind the times **2.** TÉC out of phase

desfase *m* (*diferencia*) gap; ~ **con la realidad** lack of realism; **íque ~!** *inf* wild!

desfavorable *adj* unfavourable *Brit,* unfavorable *Am*

desfavorecer *irr como crecer vt* **1.** (*perjudicar*) to discriminate against **2.** (*sentar mal*) **este clima me desfavorece** this climate doesn't suit me **3.** (*oponerse*) to be against

desfigurar *vt* **1.** (*afear: las facciones*) to disfigure; (*el cuerpo, el tipo*) to deform

2. (*deformar*) to deface; (*una imagen, la realidad*) to distort; (*un texto*) to mutilate **3.** (*disfrazar*) to disguise **4.** (*ocultar*) to hide

desfiguro *m* Méx (*cosa ridícula*) silly stunt; **hacer un** ~ to make a fool of oneself

desfiladero *m* GEO gorge

desfilar *vi* **1.** (*marchar en fila*) *t.* MIL to walk in file; **desfilaron ante la reina** they paraded before the queen **2.** (*salir*) to file out

desfile *m* **1.** (*acción*) marching; (*de tropas*) march-past; (*parada*) parade; POL march; (*en una fiesta*) procession; ~ **de modelos** fashion show **2.** (*personas*) procession; **participar en el** ~ to join the procession

desflorar *vt* **1.** (*a una mujer*) to deflower **2.** (*estropear*) to spoil; (*gastar*) to use up

desfogar <g→gu> I. *vt* **1.** (*un sentimiento*) to vent; ~ **su ira** to vent one's anger; ~ **su mal humor en** [*o* con] **alguien** to take it out on sb **2.** (*un fuego*) to fan II. *vi* (*tormenta*) to break III. *vr:* ~**se** to let off steam; ~**se en** [*o* con] **alguien** (*ira*) to take one's anger out on sb; (*frustración*) to take one's frustration out on sb

desgajar I. *vt* **1.** (*arrancar*) to tear off; (*romper*) to break; (*ramas*) to snap off; ~ **una página de un libro** to tear a page out of a book **2.** (*separar*) to tear apart **3.** (*despedazar*) to tear to pieces II. *vr:* ~**se** (*desprenderse*) to come off; (*romperse*) to break off; (*rama*) to snap off

desgana *f* **1.** (*inapetencia*) lack of appetite; **comer con** ~ to eat without appetite **2.** (*falta de interés*) lack of enthusiasm; **con** ~ without enthusiasm

desganado, -a *adj* **estar** ~ (*sin apetito*) to have no appetite; (*sin entusiasmo*) to have lost one's enthusiasm

desgañitarse *vr* (*gritar*) to shout one's head off; (*enronquecerse*) to shout oneself hoarse

desgarbado, -a *adj* **1.** (*sin garbo*) ungainly **2.** (*larguirucho*) gangling

desgarrador(a) *adj* heartrending

desgarrar I. *vt* **1.** (*partir*) to tear; (*en muchos pedazos*) to tear to pieces; ~ **un paquete** to tear open a parcel **2.** (*causar pena*) **esto me desgarra el corazón** this breaks my heart; **estas imágenes desgarran el corazón** these pictures are heartbreaking II. *vr:* ~**se 1.** (*romperse*) to tear **2.** (*anímicamente*) **se me desgarra el corazón al pensar que no voy a verte nunca más** it breaks my heart to think I'll never see you again

desgarro *m* **1.** (*rotura*) tear **2.** (*descaro*) cheek; **contestar con** ~ to answer insolently, to talk back **3.** AmL (*esputo*) spittle

desgastar I. *vt* **1.** (*estropear*) to wear out; **este pantalón está desgastado por las rodillas** these trousers are worn at the knees **2.** (*consumir*) to use up **3.** (*cansar*) to wear out II. *vr:* ~**se 1.** (*consumirse*) to wear out; (*color*) to fade **2.** (*acabarse*) to run out **3.** (*debilitarse*) to wear oneself out

desgaste *m* **1.** (*fricción*) wear; ~ **natural** wear and tear **2.** (*consumo*) consumption

desglosar *vt* **1.** (*una hoja*) to detach **2.** (*una cuestión*) to treat separately; ~ **los gastos** to itemize expenses

desgobernar <e→ie> *vt* **1.** (*un país*) to misgovern; (*de una institución*) to mismanage; ~ **un asunto** to mishandle an affair **2.** (*los huesos*) to dislocate **3.** (*perturbar*) to disturb

desgobierno *m* **1.** (*de un país*) misgovernment; (*una institución*) mismanagement **2.** (*desorden*) disorder

desgracia *f* **1.** (*suerte adversa*) bad luck; **por** ~ unfortunately; **este año estoy de** ~ this year I've had nothing but bad luck; **tuve la** ~ **de perder todo mi dinero en el bingo** I was unlucky enough to lose all my money at bingo; **tiene la** ~ **de ser sordo** he has the misfortune of being deaf; **he tenido la** ~ **de...** I've been unlucky enough to ...; **para mayor** ~ to top it off **2.** (*acontecimiento*) misfortune; **llevar una temporada de** ~**s** to have one disaster after another; **en el accidente no hubo** ~**s personales** in the accident nobody was hurt; **es una** ~ **que...** +*subj* it's a terrible shame that ...; **eres una verdadera** ~ you're an absolute disgrace **3.** (*pérdida de gracia*) disgrace; **caer en** ~ to fall from grace, to fall into disgrace ▶ ~ **compartida, menos sentida** *prov* misery loves company *prov;* **las** ~**s nunca vienen solas** *prov* it never rains but it pours *prov*

desgraciadamente *adv* unfortunately

desgraciado, -a I. *adj* **1.** (*sin suerte*) unlucky; **ser** ~ (*tener mala suerte*) to be unlucky; (*no llegar a nada*) to be a disaster **2.** (*infeliz*) miserable **3.** (*que implica desgracia*) unfortunate; **fue una intervención desgraciada** it was an unfortunate intervention **4.** (*pobre*) poor II. *m, f* **1.** (*sin suerte*) unlucky person **2.** (*infeliz*) **es un** ~ he's a poor wretch **3.** (*pobre*) poor person **4.** (*persona sin valor*) **ser un** ~ to be worthless **5.** *pey* (*miserable*) scoundrel, rotter

desgraciar I. *vt* **1.** (*estropear*) to ruin **2.** (*disgustar*) to displease II. *vr:* ~**se** (*malograrse*) to be ruined

desgranar *vt* **1.** (*maíz, trigo*) to thresh; (*habas*) to shell; ~ **(las cuentas de) un rosario** to tell one's beads **2.** (*repetir*) ~ **insultos/palabrotas** to reel off a stream of abuse/obscenities; ~ **mentiras** to tell a string of lies

desgravable *adj* tax-deductible

desgravación *f* **1.** (*reducción de un impuesto*) tax allowance, tax deduction **2.** (*de un gasto*) tax relief; ~ **sobre bienes de capital** capital allowance; ~ **por cargas familiares** tax allowance [*o* deduction] for dependants

desgravar *vt* **1.** (*suprimir: un impuesto, un derecho*) to exempt from **2.** (*reducir*) ~ **el tabaco** (*bajar el impuesto*) to reduce the tax on tobacco; (*el arancel*) to reduce the duties on tobacco **3.** (*deducir*) to deduct

desgreñado, -a *adj* dishevelled

desguace *m* **1.** (*lugar*) scrapyard *Brit*, breaker's yard **2.** (*acción*) scrapping *Brit*, wrecking **3.** (*materiales*) scrap ►**estar para el ~** *inf* to have had it

desguazar <z→c> *vt* **1.** (*desmontar*) to take to pieces **2.** (*reducir a chatarra*) to scrap *Brit*, to break up, to wreck; **~ algo** (*quitar las partes útiles*) to use sth for scrap

deshabitado, -a *adj* (*edificio*) empty; **ciudad deshabitada** ghost town; **una región muy deshabitada** a very sparsely populated region

deshabitar *vt* **1.** (*un edificio*) to abandon; **~ una casa** to vacate a house **2.** (*despoblar*) to empty

deshacer *irr como hacer* **I.** *vt* **1.** (*un paquete*) to unwrap; (*una costura*) to unpick; (*un nudo*) to undo; (*la cama*) to mess up; (*un aparato*) to dismantle; (*una maleta*) to unpack; **~ los puntos** to unpick [*o* undo] the stitches; **~ un error** to rectify a mistake **2.** (*romper*) to break; (*en pedazos*) to tear apart; (*cortar*) to cut up; (*una res*) to butcher; (*una tela*) to tear to pieces; (*a golpes*) to knock to pieces **3.** (*arruinar*) to ruin; (*plan*) to spoil, to thwart *form* **4.** (*disolver*) to dissolve; (*hielo*) to melt; (*contrato, negocio*) to dissolve; **~ una casa** *fig* to move home **5.** MIL to rout ►**no intentes ~ lo hecho** what's done can't be undone; **ser el que hace y deshace** to be the boss **II.** *vr:* **~se 1.** (*descomponerse*) to come apart; (*hielo*) to melt; (*desaparecer*) to disappear; **se me ha deshecho el helado** my ice cream has melted; **~se en cumplidos** to be full of praise; **~se de impaciencia** to be dying of impatience; **~se en lágrimas** to burst into tears; **~se en llanto** to cry one's heart out; **~se de nervios** to be a nervous wreck; **~se por algo** to try one's hardest to do sth; **se deshace por complacernos** he/she does everything possible to please us; **~se a trabajar** to work oneself into the ground; **~se empollando** to tire oneself out studying **2.** (*romperse*) to break; (*costura, nudo*) to come undone; (*pastel*) to fall apart; (*silla*) to fall to pieces **3.** (*desprenderse*) to come away; **~se de algo** (*venderlo*) to offload sth; **~se de alguien** (*librarse de, asesinar*) to get rid of sb; (*despedir*) to say goodbye to sb

desharrapado, -a *adj* ragged

deshecho, -a **I.** *pp de* **deshacer** **II.** *adj* **1.** (*deprimido*) devastated; **dejar a alguien ~** to leave sb shattered **2.** (*cansado*) tired; **estar ~** to be exhausted **3.** (*tormenta*) violent; (*lluvia*) heavy

deshelar <e→ie> **I.** *vt* (*hielo, nieve*) to melt; (*una nevera*) to defrost **II.** *vr:* **~se** (*hielo*) to melt; (*nieve*) to thaw; (*nevera*) to defrost

desheredar *vt* to disinherit

deshidratar **I.** *vt* to dry; (*cuerpo*) to dehydrate **II.** *vr:* **~se** to dry out; (*cuerpo*) to dehydrate

deshielo *m* **1.** (*el deshelar*) thawing; (*de la nevera*) defrosting **2.** (*clima*) *t.* POL thaw

deshilachar *vt, vr:* **~se** to fray

deshilvanado, -a *adj* (*discurso*) disjointed

deshinchar **I.** *vt* **1.** (*sacar el aire*) to deflate **2.** (*una inflamación*) to reduce **3.** (*cólera*) to vent **II.** *vr:* **~se 1.** (*perder aire*) to deflate; **se me ha deshinchado la rueda de la bici** my bicycle tyre [*o* tire *Am*] is flat **2.** (*una inflamación*) to go down **3.** *inf* (*deponer la vanidad*) to get down off one's high horse

deshojado, -a *adj* **1.** (*árbol*) leafless **2.** (*libro*) **un libro ~** a book with pages missing

deshojar **I.** *vt* **1.** BOT to strip the leaves from; **~ una flor** to pull the petals off a flower **2.** (*un libro*) to tear the pages out of **II.** *vr:* **~se 1.** BOT (*un árbol*) to lose its leaves; (*una flor*) to lose its petals **2.** (*un libro*) to lose its pages

deshollinar *vt* **1.** (*la chimenea*) to sweep **2.** (*limpiar*) to clean off soot **3.** (*curiosear*) to take a close look at

deshonesto, -a *adj* **1.** (*inmoral*) indecent **2.** (*tramposo*) dishonest

deshonor *m* (*afrenta*) dishonour *Brit*, dishonor *Am*

deshonra *f* (*afrenta*) disgrace; **ser una ~ para la empresa** (*desacreditar*) to be a disgrace to the company; **tener algo a ~** (*como insulto*) to take offence [*o* offense *Am*] at sth; (*como humillante*) to think sth is beneath one

deshonrar *vt* to disgrace; (*ofender*) to offend; (*humillar*) to humiliate; **~ a alguien** (*desacreditar*) to bring disgrace on sb

deshonroso, -a *adj* **1.** (*que causa deshonra*) disgraceful **2.** (*poco honroso*) dishonest

deshora *f* inconvenient time; **hablar a ~(s)** to interrupt; **venir a ~(s)** (*en un momento inconveniente*) to come at a bad moment; (*demasiado tarde*) to arrive too late; **dormir a ~s** to sleep at odd hours

deshuesado, -a *adj* **1.** (*fruta*) stoned **2.** (*carne*) boned

desidia *f* **1.** (*descuido*) carelessness; **me molesta tu ~ en el trabajo** I don't like your lack of attention to your work **2.** (*pereza*) laziness

desierto *m* **1.** GEO desert **2.** (*lugar despoblado*) wasteland; **predicar en el ~** *fig* to preach to the winds

desierto, -a *adj* **1.** (*sin gente*) deserted **2.** (*como un desierto*) desert **3.** (*sin participantes*) **una subasta desierta** an auction without bidders; **el premio fue declarado ~** the prize was not awarded; **dar por ~ un concurso** to declare a competition void

designación *f* **1.** (*nombramiento*) appointment; **~ de candidatos** selection of candidates **2.** (*nombre*) name; **~ del contenido** contents

designar *vt* **1.** (*dar un nombre*) to designate; **~ a alguien con un apodo** to give sb a nickname **2.** (*destinar*) to assign; (*elegir*) to choose; (*fecha*) to set; (*nombrar*) to appoint (*para* to); **~ un abogado** to appoint a lawyer; **~ un candidato** to select a candidate; **~ un representante** to nominate a representative

designio *m* **1.** (*plan*) plan **2.** (*propósito*) intention **3.** (*deseo*) wish; **su ~ es conver-**

tirse en multimilionario his/her ambition is to be a multimillionaire

desigual *adj* **1.**(*distinto*) unequal; **ser muy ~** to be very different **2.**(*injusto*) unfair **3.**(*irregular*) uneven **4.**(*inconstante*) inconsistent

desigualdad *f* **1.**(*diferencia*) inequality **2.**(*injusticia*) unfairness **3.**(*irregularidad*) unevenness **4.**(*del carácter*) inconsistency; (*del tiempo*) changeability

desilusión *f* **1.**(*desengaño*) disappointment; **sufrir una ~** to be disappointed **2.**(*desencanto*) disillusion

desilusionante *adj* (*que desencanta*) disillusioning

desilusionar **I.** *vt* **1.**(*quitar la ilusión*) to disillusion **2.**(*decepcionar*) to disappoint **II.** *vr:* **~se 1.**(*perder la ilusión*) to become disillusioned; (*ver claro*) to see things for what they are **2.**(*decepcionarse*) to be disappointed

desinencia *f* ending; **~ nominal** noun ending

desinfectante *m* disinfectant

desinfectar *vt* to disinfect

desinflado, -a *adj* (*rueda*) flat

desinflar **I.** *vt* (*sacar el aire*) to deflate **II.** *vr:* **~se** (*perder aire*) to go down; **se me ha desinflado la rueda de atrás** my back tyre [*o* tire *Am*] is flat

desintegración *f* **1.**(*de una cosa*) disintegration; (*debido al clima*) erosion; FÍS fission; QUÍM decomposition **2.**(*de un territorio, un grupo*) breakup

desintegrar **I.** *vt* **1.**(*disgregarse*) to disintegrate; (*una piedra*) to erode; FÍS to split; QUÍM to decompose **2.**(*un grupo, un país*) to break up **II.** *vr:* **~se 1.**(*disgregarse*) to disintegrate; (*edificio, muro*) to fall down; FÍS to split; QUÍM to decompose **2.**(*grupo*) to break up; (*partido*) to fall apart

desinterés *m* **1.**(*indiferencia*) indifference; **sentir ~ por algo** to not be interested in sth **2.**(*altruismo*) altruism; (*generosidad*) generosity; **hacer algo con ~** to do sth without thinking about personal gain

desinteresado, -a *adj* **1.**(*indiferente*) indifferent; (*en un conflicto*) impartial **2.**(*altruista*) altruistic; (*generoso*) generous

desintoxicación *f* detoxification

desintoxicar <c→qu> **I.** *vt* to detoxify **II.** *vr:* **~se 1.**to undergo detoxification; (*de alcohol*) to dry out **2.**fig to get away from it all

desistir *vi* **1.**(*de un proyecto*) **~ de algo** to give up sth; **no ~é de convencerte** I'll do my best to persuade you; **no hay manera de hacerles ~ de su propósito** there is no way of getting them to back down **2.**(*renunciar a*) **~ de un derecho** to waive a right; **~ de un cargo** to resign from a post; **~ de una petición** to withdraw a request; **~ de un contrato** to withdraw from a contract

deslavazado, -a *adj* **1.**(*lacio*) limp; **este traje te queda ~** this dress doesn't really suit

you **2.**(*incoherente*) disjointed **3.**(*insulso*) insipid

desleal *adj* (*infiel*) disloyal; (*traidor*) treacherous; **competencia ~** unfair competition; **publicidad ~** misleading advertising; **ser ~ a su patria** to betray one's country; **ser ~ con su partido** to betray one's party; **has sido ~ a tu familia** you have been disloyal to your family; **ten cuidado con lo que le cuentes, es una persona muy ~** be careful what you tell him/her, he/she isn't very trustworthy; **ser ~ con** [*o* a] **alguien** (*injusto*) to treat sb unfairly

deslealtad *f* **1.**(*infidelidad*) disloyalty **2.**(*injusticia*) unfairness

desleír *irr como reír* **I.** *vt* (*disolver*) to dissolve **II.** *vr:* **~se** to dissolve

deslenguado, -a *adj* **1.**(*desvergonzado*) foul-mouthed; **ser ~** to be foul-mouthed **2.**(*chismoso*) gossipy; **ser ~** to be a gossip; **¡no seas ~!** don't be such a gossip!

desliar <*I. pres:* deslío> **I.** *vt* to undo **II.** *vr:* **~se** to come undone

desligar <g→gu> **I.** *vt* **1.**(*un nudo*) to undo; (*un enredo*) to untangle; (*una persona*) to untie **2.**(*un asunto*) to clear up **3.**(*separar*) to separate; **~ intereses particulares de los de la empresa** to separate private interests from those of the company **4.**(*de un compromiso*) to release **II.** *vr:* **~se 1.**(*un nudo*) to come undone; (*persona*) to get out of; (*un enredo*) to unravel **2.**(*un asunto*) to be resolved **3.**(*de un compromiso*) to be released; **no poder ~se de algo** to be unable to get out of sth

deslindar *vt* **1.**(*un lugar*) to demarcate; **~ una finca** to mark the boundary of a farm; **~ dos provincias** to mark the boundary between two provinces **2.**(*determinar*) to outline; **~ dos temas** to distinguish between two topics

desliz *m* **1.**(*error*) slip; (*indiscreción*) indiscretion **2.**(*adulterio*) affair

deslizante *adj* **1.**(*que desliza, que hace deslizar*) slippery, slippy **2.**(*corredizo*) sliding

deslizar <z→c> **I.** *vt* **1.**(*pasar*) **~ la mano sobre algo** to run one's hand over sth; **~ un sobre por debajo de una puerta** to slip an envelope under the door **2.**(*incluir con disimulo*) to slip; **~ algo en una conversación** to slip sth into a conversation **II.** *vi* to slip **III.** *vr:* **~se 1.**(*resbalar*) **~ sobre algo** to slide over sth; **~se por un tobogán** to go down a slide; **las lágrimas se deslizaban por sus mejillas** the tears slid down his/her cheeks; **con la tormenta se han deslizado algunas tejas** the storm has blown a few tiles off **2.**(*escaparse*) to slip away; **el ladrón se deslizó entre los clientes** the thief slipped away through the customers **3.**(*el tiempo*) to slip away **4.**(*cometer un error*) to slip up; (*una indiscreción*) to slip out

deslomar **I.** *vt* **1.**(*dañar*) **~ a alguien** to break sb's back **2.**(*agotar*) to exhaust **II.** *vr:*

~se 1. (*dañarse*) to do one's back in **2.** (*trabajar*) to work oneself to death

deslucido, -a *adj* **1.** (*ropa*) shabby **2.** (*actuación*) lacklustre *Brit*, lackluster *Am* **3.** (*sin gracia*) dull

deslucir *irr como lucir* **I.** *vt* **1.** (*estropear*) to ruin; **la lluvia deslució la procesión** the rain ruined the parade **2.** (*quitar el lustre: metal*) to tarnish; (*una prenda, un tejido, colores*) to fade **3.** (*desacreditar*) to discredit **II.** *vr:* **~se 1.** (*fracasar*) to fail **2.** (*perder el lustre*) to lose one's shine; (*colores*) to fade; (*metal*) to become dull **3.** (*desacreditarse*) to be discredited

deslumbrador(a) *adj,* **deslumbrante** *adj* (*impresionante*) dazzling; (*mujer*) stunning

deslumbrar *vt* to dazzle

deslustrar *vt* **1.** (*quitar el brillo*) to tarnish **2.** (*gastar*) to wear out; (*una prenda, un tejido, colores*) to fade **3.** (*estropear*) to ruin **4.** (*un vidrio*) to frost **5.** (*desacreditar*) to discredit

desmadrado, -a *adj* (*desenfrenado*) wild

desmadrarse *vr inf* (*desenfrenarse*) to go wild; (*alocarse*) to go mad; **¡no te desmadres!** don't go over the top!

desmadre *m* **1.** (*comportamiento*) outrageous behaviour [*o* behavior *Am*]; **la policía acabó con el ~ entre los hinchas** the police put an end to the mayhem between the fans **2.** (*caos*) chaos; **tus fiestas acaban siendo un ~** your parties are always completely wild

desmalezar <z→c> *vt AmL* to weed, to clear brush

desmán *m* **1.** (*salvajada*) outrage; **cometer desmanes contra alguien** to commit outrages against sb **2.** (*exceso*) excess; **debido a sus desmanes con la bebida** due to his/her excessive drinking **3.** (*desgracia*) misfortune; **he sufrido muchos desmanes** a lot of bad things have happened to me

desmandado, -a *adj* **1.** (*rebelde*) rebellious; (*caballo*) runaway **2.** (*violento*) violent **3.** (*desmadrado*) wild

desmandarse *vr* **1.** (*rebelarse*) to rebel; (*descontrolarse*) to get out of control; (*un caballo*) to bolt **2.** (*insolentarse*) to be insolent; (*insultar*) to be rude; (*cometer actos violentos*) to become violent **3.** (*apartarse*) to go off on one's own; **~ del rebaño** to stray from the flock

desmano *m* **a ~** out of the way

desmantelar *vt* **1.** (*derribar*) to knock down; (*un edificio*) to demolish **2.** (*desmontar*) to take apart; (*bomba*) to dismantle; (*escenario*) to take down **3.** (*abandonar*) to abandon; (*liquidar*) to liquidate **4.** NÁUT (*desarbolar*) to unmast

desmañado, -a **I.** *adj* clumsy; **es muy ~ para trabajos manuales** he's very clumsy with his hands **II.** *m, f* **ser un ~** (*torpe*) to be clumsy; (*chapucero*) to be shoddy

desmaquillador *m* make-up remover

desmaquillador(a) *adj* **leche ~a** make-up remover

desmaquillarse *vr* to take one's make-up off

desmayado, -a *adj* **1.** (*sin conocimiento*) unconscious **2.** (*sin fuerza*) exhausted; (*color*) faded

desmayar **I.** *vi* (*desanimarse*) to lose heart **II.** *vr:* **~se** (*desvanecerse*) to faint; **se desmayó en mis brazos** he/she fainted in my arms

desmayo *m* **1.** (*desvanecimiento*) faint; **hablar con ~** to speak in a small voice **2.** (*desánimo*) dismay **3.** (*debilidad*) weakness

desmedido, -a *adj* excessive; **tener un apetito ~** to have an enormous appetite; **afición desmedida por la bebida** excessive drinking

desmedirse *irr como pedir* *vr* **1.** (*excederse*) to go too far; **~ en la bebida** to drink to excess **2.** (*insolentarse*) to be insolent; (*insultar*) to be rude

desmedrado, -a *adj* (*flaco, débil*) puny

desmejorar **I.** *vt* (*estropear*) to ruin; (*gastar*) to wear out **II.** *vi* to deteriorate; **con la gripe has desmejorado mucho** the flu has really weakened you **III.** *vr:* **~se 1.** (*estropearse*) to be ruined; (*gastarse*) to wear out, to go downhill *inf* **2.** (*perder la salud*) to deteriorate

desmelenado, -a *adj* (*despeinado*) tousled

desmembrar <e→ie> **I.** *vt* **1.** (*desunir*) to break up; (*una institución*) to dismantle; (*un cuerpo*) to dismember; **la bomba le desmembró la mano** the bomb took his/her hand off **2.** (*escindir*) to separate **II.** *vr:* **~se 1.** (*desunirse*) to break up **2.** (*escindirse*) to separate (*de* from)

desmentir *irr como sentir* **I.** *vt* **1.** (*negar*) to deny; **~ a alguien** (*contradecir*) to contradict sb; (*decir que miente*) to accuse sb of lying; **el artículo desmiente la historia** the article disproves the story **2.** (*demostrar que es falso*) to refute; **~ una sospecha** to refute an accusation; **las pruebas desmienten tus palabras** the evidence contradicts what you have said **3.** (*desdecir*) **~ algo/a alguien** to be unworthy of sth/sb; **con su comportamiento desmiente a su familia** with this behaviour [*o* behavior *Am*] he/she is letting down his/her family; **este vino desmiente su marca** this wine doesn't do justice to its label **II.** *vi* to be out of line **III.** *vr* **~se** to contradict oneself

desmenuzable *adj* crumbly

desmenuzar <z→c> **I.** *vt* **1.** (*deshacer*) to break into small pieces; (*fish*) to flake; (*con un cuchillo*) to chop up; (*con los dedos*) to crumble; (*raspar*) to grate; (*moler*) to grind; (*papel*) to tear up **2.** (*analizar*) to scrutinize **II.** *vr:* **~se** to crumble

desmerecer *irr como crecer* **I.** *vt* (*no merecer*) to not deserve; **desmereces mi amor** you don't deserve my love **II.** *vi* **1.** (*decaer*) to decline; (*belleza*) to lose one's looks **2.** (*ser inferior*) **~ de alguien/algo** to be worse than sb/sth; **~ en talento de alguien** to be less talented than sb; **tu último libro no**

desmerece de los anteriores your latest book maintains the standard of the previous ones; **desmereces de tu familia** your family are too good for you

desmesurado, -a *adj* **1.** (*enorme*) enormous **2.** (*excesivo*) excessive; (*ambición*) boundless; (*pretensiones*) exaggerated; **beber de una forma desmesurada** to drink to excess **3.** (*desvergonzado*) shameless; (*descortés*) rude; (*ofensivo*) offensive

desmesurarse *vr* **1.** (*excederse*) to go too far **2.** (*atreverse*) to be daring **3.** (*insultar*) to be rude

desmigajar **I.** *vt* to crumble **II.** *vr:* ~**se** to crumble

desmilitarizar <z→c> *vt* to demilitarize

desmirriado, -a *adj* (*flaco*) skinny; (*raquítico*) puny

desmochar *vt* **1.** (*despuntar*) to cut the top off; (*plantas*) to pollard **2.** (*mutilar*) to mutilate

desmontable *adj* (*que se puede quitar*) detachable; (*sacar*) removable; (*deshacer*) that can be taken apart; (*doblar*) foldable

desmontar **I.** *vt* **1.** (*un mecanismo*) to disassemble **2.** (*una pieza: quitar*) to detach; (*sacar*) to remove **3.** (*una estructura, un edificio*) to take down **4.** (*un bosque*) to cut down **5.** (*un terreno*) to clear **6.** (*un montón de tierra*) to level **7.** (*una pistola*) to uncock **8.** (*de un caballo, de una moto*) to throw **II.** *vi* (*de un caballo*) to dismount; (*de una moto*) to help get down from **III.** *vr:* ~**se** (*bajarse*) to dismount

desmonte *m* **1.** (*de un terreno*) levelling *Brit*, leveling *Am* **2.** (*de un bosque*) clearance, cut *Brit* **3.** (*escombros*) heap of soil **4.** *pl* AGR clearing

desmoralizador(a) *adj* **1.** (*que desanima*) demoralizing **2.** (*que corrompe*) corrupting

desmoralizar <z→c> **I.** *vt* **1.** (*desanimar*) to demoralize; **la crítica la ha desmoralizado mucho** the criticism has really got [*o* gotten *Am*] to her **2.** (*corromper*) to corrupt **II.** *vr:* ~**se 1.** (*desanimarse*) to lose heart; (*perder la confianza*) to lose one's confidence; **las tropas se iban desmoralizando** the soldiers were gradually becoming demoralized **2.** (*corromperse*) to be corrupted

desmoronamiento *m* **1.** (*arruinamiento*) ruin; (*de un edificio*) collapse **2.** (*disminución: de un imperio, una ideología*) decline; (*de una persona*) breakdown; (*de un sentimiento*) weakening; **la crisis económica produjo el** ~ **de mi fortuna** the economic crisis used up all my wealth

desmoronar **I.** *vt* (*deshacer*) to wear away; (*edificio*) to ruin; GEO to erode **II.** *vr:* ~**se 1.** (*deshacerse*) to fall to pieces; (*un edificio, un muro*) to fall down; QUÍM to decay **2.** (*disminuir*) to decline; (*sentimiento*) to weaken **3.** (*persona*) to fall apart

desnatar *vt* (*la leche*) to skim; **leche sin ~** whole milk

desnaturalizado, -a *adj* **1.** (*alimentos*) adulterated **2.** (*hijo*) ungrateful; **madre desnaturalizada** uncaring mother **3.** QUÍM denatured

desnaturalizar <z→c> **I.** *vt* **1.** (*expatriar*) to denaturalize **2.** (*desvirtuar*) to denature; (*aspecto*) to spoil; (*carácter*) to ruin; ~ **la competencia** to distort the marketplace **3.** QUÍM to denature **II.** *vr:* ~**se** (*expatriarse*) to abandon one's country

desnivel *m* **1.** (*diferencia de altura*) drop; (*pendiente*) slope **2.** (*desequilibrio*) imbalance; (*disparidad*) inequality; ~ **cultural** cultural difference [*o* gap] **3.** (*altibajo*) unevenness

desnivelar **I.** *vt* **1.** (*un terreno*) to make uneven **2.** (*desequilibrar*) to unbalance; (*balanza*) to tip **II.** *vr:* ~**se 1.** (*torcerse*) to twist; (*calle*) to become uneven **2.** (*perder el equilibrio*) to become unbalanced

desnucar <c→qu> **I.** *vt* **1.** (*herir*) ~ **a alguien** to break sb's neck **2.** (*matar*) to kill; ~ **una gallina** to wring a chicken's neck; ~ **el conejo de un golpe en el cogote** to kill the rabbit with a blow to its neck **II.** *vr:* ~**se** to break one's neck

desnuclearizado(a) *adj* nuclear-free

desnudar **I.** *vt* **1.** (*desvestir*) to undress **2.** (*descubrir*) to strip **II.** *vr:* ~**se** (*desvestirse*) to undress

desnudez *f* **1.** (*persona*) nudity **2.** *fig* bareness

desnudo *m* ARTE nude

desnudo, -a *adj* **1.** (*desvestido*) naked, nude; ~ **de (la) cintura para arriba/abajo** naked from the waist up/down **2.** (*con poca ropa*) half-naked **3.** (*despojado*) bare **4.** (*pobre*) penniless; **este mes me he quedado ~** *inf* this month I haven't got a penny **5.** (*claro*) clear; **al** ~ clearly; **decir a alguien la verdad desnuda** to tell sb the plain truth **6.** (*desprovisto*) ~ **de algo** devoid of sth

desnutrición *f* malnutrition, undernourishment

desnutrido, -a *adj* undernourished

desobedecer *irr como crecer* *vi, vt* to disobey

desobediencia *f* disobedience; MIL insubordination

desobediente *adj* disobedient; MIL insubordinate

desocupación *f* **1.** (*desembarazo*) ease; (*evacuación*) vacation **2.** (*paro*) unemployment **3.** (*ociosidad*) leisure

desocupado, -a **I.** *adj* **1.** (*parado*) unemployed **2.** (*vacío*) empty; (*vivienda*) vacant; (*paso, plaza*) clear; (*ocioso*) idle; **estoy ~** I'm not busy **II.** *m, f* unemployed person

desocupar **I.** *vt* **1.** (*desembarazar*) to clear; (*evacuar*) to evacuate; ~ **una vivienda** to vacate a property **2.** (*vaciar*) to empty **II.** *vr:* ~**se 1.** (*de una ocupación*) to get away; **cuando pueda ~me** when I'm free **2.** (*quedarse vacante*) to be vacant **III.** *vi* AmL (*parir*) to give birth

desodorante **I.** *adj* (*para el hogar*) deodorizing; (*para el cuerpo*) deodorant; **espray** ~ (*para el cuerpo*) deodorant spray; (*para el hogar*) air freshener spray **II.** *m* (*para el cuerpo*) deodorant; ~ **en barra** stick deodorant; ~ **antitranspirante** antiperspirant

desoír *irr como oír vt* ~ **algo** to not listen to sth

desolación *f* **1.** (*devastación*) desolation **2.** (*desconsuelo*) distress

desolado, -a *adj* **1.** (*desierto*) desolate **2.** (*desconsolado*) devastated

desolar <o→ue> **I.** *vt* (*destruir, afligir*) to devastate **II.** *vr:* ~**se** to be devastated

desolladero *m* slaughterhouse

desollar <o→ue> *vt* **1.** (*quitar la piel*) to flay, to skin; ~ **a alguien vivo** *fig* to fleece sb, to skin sb alive **2.** (*causar daño económico*) to fleece; (*engañar*) to deceive **3.** (*maltratar*) to mistreat **4.** (*criticar*) to lambast

desorbitado, -a *adj* **1.** (*ojos*) bulging, bug-eyed *inf* **2.** (*exagerado*) exaggerated; (*desmedido*) exhorbitant

desorbitar I. *vt* (*exagerar*) to exaggerate; (*dar demasiada importancia*) to blow out of proportion **II.** *vr:* ~**se** (*asunto*) to get out of control; **se le ~on los ojos** *fig* he/she was flabbergasted

desorden *m* **1.** (*desarreglo*) mess; (*confusión*) chaos; ~ **público** public disturbance; **la casa está en** ~ the house is in a mess **2.** (*exceso*) excess **3.** *pl* (*alboroto*) disorders *pl* **4.** MED disorder

desordenado, -a *adj* **1.** (*desorganizado*) jumbled; (*persona, cosa*) messy; (*vida*) chaotic **2.** (*excesivo*) excessive

desordenar *vt* (*turbar*) to mess up; (*mezclar*) to mix up; (*pelo*) to ruffle

desorganización *f* lack of organization; **en esta empresa llevan una** ~ **increíble** this company is completely disorganized

desorganizar <z→c> **I.** *vt* to disrupt; (*planes*) to disturb **II.** *vr:* ~**se** (*persona, empresa*) to be disorganized

desorientación *f* **1.** (*extravío*) disorientation **2.** (*confusión*) confusion **3.** (*falta de orientación*) loss of direction

desorientar I. *vt* **1.** (*extraviar*) to lose one's bearings, to disorientate *Brit*, to disorient *Am* **2.** (*confundir*) to confuse **II.** *vr:* ~**se 1.** (*extraviarse*) to become disorientated *Brit*, to become disoriented *Am* **2.** (*confundirse*) to become confused

desovar *vi* (*pez, anfibio*) to spawn; (*insecto*) to lay eggs

despabilado, -a *adj* **1.** (*listo*) smart **2.** (*despierto*) alert

despabilar I. *vt* **1.** (*despertar*) to wake up **2.** (*avivar*) to sharpen up; **en la mili ya lo ~án** in the army they'll soon show him what's what; **es muy perezosa, pero en el colegio ya la ~án** she's very lazy, but at school they'll soon make her sharpen up **3.** (*acabar deprisa*) to finish off; (*fortuna*) to squander; (*comida*) to

eat up **4.** (*robar*) to steal **5.** (*matar*) to kill **II.** *vi* **1.** (*darse prisa*) to hurry up **2.** (*avivarse*) **si quieres empezar a trabajar por tu cuenta, tienes que** ~ if you want to work for yourself, you'll have to get your act together **III.** *vr:* ~**se 1.** (*sacudir el sueño*) to waken up **2.** (*darse prisa*) to hurry up **3.** (*avivarse*) to get one's act together; **se ha despabilado desde que va al colegio** he/she has really come to life since starting school **4.** *AmL* (*marcharse*) to leave

despachante *mf RíoPl* COM customs officer

despachar I. *vt* **1.** (*enviar*) to send, to ship; (*mercancías*) to dispatch **2.** (*concluir*) to finish off; (*buque*) to clear out **3.** (*resolver*) to decide; (*discutir*) to discuss **4.** (*atender*) to serve, to wait on **5.** (*vender*) to sell **6.** (*matar*) to kill **7.** (*comer, beber*) to polish off **8.** *inf* (*despedir*) to dismiss, to sack *Brit*, to fire *Am* **II.** *vi* **1.** (*acabar*) to finish **2.** (*atender*) to do business; **por las tardes no despachan en esta tienda** this shop doesn't open in the evenings **3.** (*conversar*) ~ **con alguien** to consult with sb **III.** *vr:* ~**se 1.** (*darse prisa*) to hurry up **2.** (*desahogarse*) to let off steam; ~**se a** (**su**) **gusto con alguien** to speak frankly to sb **3.** (*desembarazarse*) ~**se de alguien** to rid oneself of sb

despacho *m* **1.** (*oficina*) office; (*en casa*) study; ~ **de abogado** lawyer's office; ~ **de aduana** customs office; ~ **de patentes** patent office; **mesa de** ~ desk **2.** (*envío*) sending **3.** (*de un asunto*) resolution; (*entrevista*) consultation **4.** (*de clientes*) service; **sólo tenemos** ~ **por las mañanas** we only see clients in the morning **5.** (*venta*) sale; **géneros sin** ~ unsaleable [*o* unsellable *Am*] goods; **no tener buen** ~ to sell slowly; **tener buen** ~ to sell well **6.** (*despido*) dismissal **7.** (*de un pedido*) dispatch, shipping; (*de la correspondencia, el equipaje*) sending; (*de un buque*) clearance **8.** (*muebles*) office furniture; **comprarse un** ~ **nuevo** to refurnish one's office **9.** (*taquilla*) ticket office; (*tienda*) shop; ~ **de billetes** [*o* **boletos** *AmL*] FERRO ticket office; ~ **de localidades** TEAT, CINE box [*o* ticket] office **10.** (*parte*) message; (*telegrama*) telegram; (*entre gobiernos*) dispatch; ~ **judicial** legal dispatch

despachurrar I. *vt* **1.** (*aplastar*) to squash; (*reventar*) to burst **2.** (*embrollar*) to mix up; **despachurras todos los chistes** you're dreadful at telling jokes **3.** (*apabullar*) to silence; **me dejó despachurrado** I was left speechless; **lo despachurró con sus argumentos** he/she silenced him with his/her arguments **II.** *vr:* ~**se** to flatten; (*fruta*) to squash

despacio I. *adv* **1.** (*lentamente*) slowly; **por allí viene caminando** ~ here he/she comes, walking slowly; **en esta oficina las cosas van** ~ in this office things move slowly **2.** (*calladamente*) quietly **II.** *interj* take it easy

despampanante *adj* (*mujer*) stunning

despancar <c→qu> *vt AmS* (*maíz*) to husk

desparejado, -a *adj* odd; **este calcetín está**

~ this is an odd sock; **estos calcetines están ~s** these socks don't match

desparpajo m **1.** (*desenvoltura*) self-confidence; (*en el hablar*) ease; **con ~** confidently **2.** (*habilidad*) skill; **con ~** skilfully **3.** (*frescura*) cheek; **con ~** cheekily

desparramar I. vt **1.** (*dispersar*) to scatter; **~ los juguetes sobre el suelo** to scatter the toys across the floor; **~ su atención** to allow one's attention to wander **2.** (*un líquido*) to spill **3.** (*malgastar*) to waste **4.** (*una noticia*) to spread **5.** *Arg, Méx, PRico* (*diluir*) to dilute **II.** vr: **~se 1.** (*dispersarse*) to scatter; **el rebaño se desparramó por el campo** the flock spread out across the field; **al pasar el coche los pájaros se ~on** when the car went past the birds scattered **2.** (*un líquido*) to spill **3.** (*divertirse*) to enjoy oneself **4.** (*dispersar su atención*) to allow one's attention to wander

desparramo m **1.** *Chile, Cuba* (*desparramiento*) scattering **2.** *Chile, Urug* (*desbarajuste*) disorder

despatarrado, -a adj **1.** (*espatarrado*) **estar ~** to have one's legs wide apart; (*en un sofá*) to sprawl **2.** (*pasmado*) astonished **3.** (*asustado*) frightened

despatarrar I. vt **1.** (*asombrar*) to astonish **2.** (*asustar*) to frighten **II.** vr: **~se 1.** (*espatarrarse*) to open one's legs wide; **se despatarró sobre la cama** he/she sprawled on the bed **2.** (*pasmarse*) to be astonished **3.** (*caerse*) to go sprawling; **~se de risa** to split one's sides laughing **4.** inf (*una mujer*) to spread one's legs

despavorido, -a adj terrified

despechar I. vt (*indignar*) to anger **II.** vr **~se contra alguien** to get angry with sb

despecho m **1.** (*animosidad*) spite, rancour *Brit*, rancor *Am* **2.** (*desesperación*) despair **3.** **a ~ de algo** in spite of sth

despectivo, -a adj **1.** (*despreciativo*) contemptuous; (*desdeñoso*) disdainful; (*tono*) derogatory; **tratar de manera despectiva** to treat with a lack of respect **2.** LING pejorative

despedazar <z→c> I. vt (*romper*) to smash; (*en mil pedazos*) to tear to pieces; (*con un cuchillo, una tijera*) to cut up; (*con las manos*) to tear up; (*el corazón*) to break; **la bomba le despedazó la mano** the bomb blew his/her hand off **II.** vr: **~se 1.** (*romperse*) to smash; (*en mil pedazos*) to fall to pieces; (*muro*) to fall down; (*cristal*) to shatter; (*globo*) to burst **2.** (*apenar*) **se me despedazó el alma cuando vi tanta miseria** *fig* seeing such misery broke my heart

despedida f **1.** (*separación*) goodbye, farewell **2.** (*acto oficial*) send-off; (*fiesta*) leaving party; **~ de soltero** stag night [o party]; **~ de soltera** hen night [o party]; **cena de ~** farewell dinner; **mañana le dan la ~ en el palacio** tomorrow they are giving her a send-off in the palace **3.** (*en una carta*) close

despedir *irr como pedir* **I.** vt **1.** (*decir adiós*) to say goodbye; **~ a alguien con una fiesta** to

give sb a leaving party; **salió a ~me a mi coche** he/she came out to the car to say goodbye to me; **vinieron a ~me al aeropuerto** they came to the airport to see me off **2.** (*echar*) to throw out; (*de un empleo*) to dismiss, to sack *Brit*, to fire *Am* **3.** (*difundir*) to give off; (*emitir*) to emit; **el volcán despide fuego** the volcano gives off flames **4.** (*lanzar*) to launch; (*flecha*) to fire **5.** (*apartar de sí*) to get rid of **II.** vr: **~se 1.** (*decir adiós*) to say goodbye **2.** (*dejar un empleo*) to leave; **~se de un trabajo** to leave a job **3.** (*de obtener, conseguir algo*) **despídete de ese dinero** goodbye to that money; **despídete este mes de salir por las noches** this month you can forget about going out in the evening

despegado, -a adj **1.** (*poco cariñoso*) distant **2.** (*áspero*) unfriendly **3.** (*suelto*) unstuck

despegar <g→gu> **I.** vt to unstick; **~ dos hojas** to separate two pages; **sin ~ los labios** without a word **II.** vi to take off; **la economía no despega** the economy is stagnant **III.** vr: **~se 1.** (*desprenderse*) to come off; (*deshacerse*) to come apart **2.** (*perder el afecto*) **~se de alguien** to lose one's feelings for sb

despego m **1.** (*falta de cariño*) coldness **2.** (*falta de afecto*) lack of feeling; **sentir ~ por alguien** to feel nothing for sb **3.** (*falta de interés*) indifference

despegue m AVIAT, ECON take-off; (*cohete*) blast-off, lift-off

despeinado, -a adj unkempt

despeinar I. vt to ruffle **II.** vr **me despeiné** I ruffled my hair

despejado, -a adj **1.** (*sin nubes, obstáculos*) clear **2.** (*ancho*) wide; (*habitación*) spacious **3.** (*listo*) smart **4.** (*despierto*) alert; (*cabeza*) clear

despejar I. vt **1.** (*un lugar, una mesa*) to clear; (*sala*) to tidy up; **~ la calle de nieve** to clear the street of snow **2.** (*una situación*) to clarify; (*un misterio*) to clear up **3.** (*una persona*) **el aire fresco despejó mi mente** the fresh air cleared my mind **4.** DEP to clear; **~ el tiro a córner** to concede a corner **II.** vr: **~se 1.** (*cielo, misterio*) to clear up **2.** (*despabilarse*) to wake up; (*mentalmente*) to sharpen one's wits **3.** (*adquirir desenvoltura*) to gain self-confidence **4.** (*un enfermo*) to improve; **se ha despejado un poco** he/she is feeling a bit better

despeje m (*en fútbol, hockey*) clearance

despejo m **1.** (*de un lugar*) clearing **2.** (*en el trato*) self-confidence **3.** (*entendimiento*) understanding

despellejar I. vt **1.** (*desollar*) to flay, to skin **2.** inf (*criticar*) to lambast *form*, to cut to bits, to skin alive **3.** inf (*desvalijar*) to fleece **II.** vr: **~se** to peel

despelotarse vr inf **1.** (*desnudarse*) to strip off, to strip down **2.** (*de risa*) to split one's sides

despeluzar <z→c> vt, vr v. **despeluznar**

despeluznante adj terrifying

despeluznar I. *vt* 1.(*causar miedo*) to terrify 2.(*pelo*) to ruffle 3.*Cuba* (*desplumar*) to pluck II. *vr* to be terrified; **se despeluz(n)ó** (**del miedo que tenía**) it made his/her hair stand on end
despensa *f* 1.(*fresquera*) larder, pantry 2.(*provisiones*) provisions *pl* 3.(*comestibles*) groceries 4. *Arg* (*almacén*) shop
despeñadero *m* 1. GEO precipice 2.(*riesgo*) danger; **meterse en un** ~ to get into danger
despeñadero, -a *adj* sheer
despeñar I. *vt* to throw down; ~ **a alguien por un precipicio** to throw sb over a cliff II. *vr:* ~**se** to throw oneself down; **el motorista se despeñó por el talud** the driver went headlong down the slope
desperdiciar *vt* to waste; (*ocasión*) to miss
desperdicio *m* 1.(*residuo*) rubbish *Brit,* garbage *Am;* ~**s biológicos** biological waste 2.(*malbaratamiento*) waste; **no tener** ~ *irón* to be good from start to finish *iron*
desperdigar <g→gu> *vt, vr:* ~**se** to scatter
desperezarse <z→c> *vr* to stretch
desperfecto *m* 1.(*deterioro*) damage 2.(*defecto*) fault, defect; **esta máquina tiene un pequeño** ~ this machine has a slight defect
despertador *m* (*reloj*) alarm clock
despertar <e→ie> I. *vt* to wake up II. *vr:* ~**se** to wake up III. *m* awakening
despiadado, -a *adj* (*inhumano*) ruthless; (*cruel*) cruel
despichar *vi inf* to peg out, to bite the dust
despido *m* (*descontratación*) dismissal, sack; ~ **colectivo** wholescale redundancies
despierto, -a *adj* 1.(*insomne*) awake 2.(*listo*) smart; **mente despierta** sharp mind
despilfarrador(a) I. *adj* wasteful; (*con dinero*) spendthrift II. *m(f)* wasteful person; (*con dinero*) spendthrift
despilfarrar *vt* to waste; (*dinero*) to squander
despilfarro *m* (*derroche*) waste; (*de dinero*) squandering
despintar I. *vt* 1.(*colores*) to wash out 2.(*la realidad*) to misrepresent 3. *Chile, PRico* ~ **a alguien** (*apartar la mirada*) to look away from sb; (*perder de vista*) to lose sight of sb II. *vr:* ~**se** 1.(*borrarse*) to fade; ~**se con el sol** to fade with the sunlight 2. *inf* (*de la memoria*) **este asunto no se me despinta** I can't forget what happened
despiojar *vt* to delouse
despistado, -a I. *adj* absent-minded II. *m, f* **eres un** ~ you're absent-minded
despistar I. *vt* (*confundir*) to confuse; (*desorientar*) to mislead II. *vr:* ~**se** 1.(*perderse*) to get lost 2.(*desconcertarse*) to become confused
despiste *m* 1.(*distracción*) confusion 2.(*error*) slip; **un** ~ **lo tiene cualquiera** anyone can make a mistake
desplante *m* rude remark
desplazado, -a *adj* (*no integrado*) out of

place; (*trasladado*) displaced
desplazamiento *m* 1.(*traslado*) displacement 2.(*remoción*) removal
desplazar <z→c> *vt* 1.(*mover*) to move 2.(*suplantar*) to displace
desplegable *adj* folding; **silla** ~ folding chair
desplegar *irr como fregar vt* 1.(*abrir*) to open out; (*desdoblar*) to unfold; (*bandera*) to unfurl 2. MIL to deploy 3.(*desarrollar*) to develop; ~ **toda su fantasía** to give free rein to one's imagination
despliegue *m* 1.(*desdoblamiento*) unfolding 2. MIL deployment
desplomarse *vr* 1.(*casa, persona*) to collapse 2.(*desviarse*) to go off course
desplumar *vt* 1.(*plumas*) to pluck 2.(*robar*) to fleece; ~ **a alguien jugando a las cartas** to clean sb out at cards
despoblación *f* depopulation
despoblado *m* (*yermo*) deserted place
despoblado, -a *adj* depopulated
despoblar <o→ue> *vt* 1.(*de habitantes*) to depopulate 2.(*un bosque*) to clear; **el huracán despobló la zona de árboles** the hurricane blew down all the trees in the area
despojar I. *vt* to strip; **la** ~**on de todo** they took everything she had; ~ **de un derecho a alguien** to deprive sb of a right II. *vr:* ~**se** 1.(*desistir*) ~**se de algo** to give up sth 2.(*quitar*) ~ **de algo** to remove sth; (*ropa*) to take off
despojo *m* 1.(*presa*) spoils *pl;* ~ **del mar** flotsam and jetsam 2. *pl* (*restos*) leftovers *pl;* (*del matadero*) offal; (*escombros*) rubble; (*mortales*) mortal remains
desposado, -a *adj* (*recién casado*) newly wed
desposar I. *vt* to marry II. *vr:* ~**se con** to get married to
desposeer *irr como leer* I. *vt* 1.(*expropiar*) to dispossess 2.(*no reconocer*) to not recognize; **la desposeyeron de sus derechos** they deprived her of her rights 3.(*destituir*) to oust; ~ **a alguien de su cargo** to remove sb from his/her position 4.(*desplumar*) ~ **a alguien de algo** to fleece sb of sth II. *vr:* ~**se** 1.(*renunciar*) ~**se de algo** to give up sth 2.(*desapropiarse*) ~**se de algo** to relinquish sth
desposorio(s) *m(pl)* 1.(*esponsales*) engagement, betrothal *form* 2.(*matrimonio*) marriage
despostar *vt AmS* to joint meat
déspota *mf* despot
despótico, -a *adj* despotic
despotismo *m* despotism
despotricar <c→qu> *vi inf* 1.(*chochear*) to be senile 2.(*maldecir*) ~ **de algo/alguien** to rant and rave about sth/sb
despreciable *adj* contemptible; **nada** ~ to not be sneered at
despreciar I. *vt* 1.(*menospreciar*) to despise 2.(*rechazar*) to spurn; (*oferta*) to turn down II. *vr:* ~**se** to run oneself down
despreciativo, -a *adj* disdainful

desprecio *m* contempt

desprender I. *vt* 1.(*soltar*) to release 2.(*olor, gas*) to give off 3.(*deducir*) to deduce; **de su aviso desprendemos que...** from his/her warning we can deduce that ... II. *vr:* ~**se** 1.(*soltarse*) to untie oneself 2.(*deshacerse*) to come undone; (*desembarazarse*) to rid oneself of; ~**se de cualquier duda** to get rid of any doubts; (*renunciar*) to part with 3.(*deducirse*) **de tu comportamiento se desprende que...** from your behaviour [*o* behavior *Am*] one can see that ...

desprendido, -a *adj* (*generoso*) generous; (*altruista*) disinterested

desprendimiento *m* 1.(*separación*) separation; ~ **de tierras** landslide; ~ **de retina** detached retina 2.(*generosidad*) generosity

despreocupación *f* 1.(*indiferencia*) indifference 2.(*insensatez*) carelessness

despreocupado, -a *adj* 1.(*negligente*) careless 2.(*tranquilo*) unconcerned

despreocuparse *vr* 1.(*tranquilizarse*) to stop worrying 2.(*desatender*) ~**se de algo** to neglect sth

despresar *vt AmS* to carve

desprestigiar I. *vt* to discredit II. *vr:* ~**se** 1.(*rebajarse*) to fall into discredit 2.(*perder reputación*) to see one's reputation suffer

desprevenido, -a *adj* unprepared; **coger a alguien** ~ to catch sb unawares [*o* off guard]

desproporción *f* disproportion

desproporcionado, -a *adj* disproportionate

despropósito *m* stupid remark; **decir** ~**s** to make stupid remarks

desproveer *irr como proveer vt* to deprive

desprovisto, -a *adj* ~ **de** lacking; **el estadio está** ~ **de las normas de seguridad necesarias** the stadium lacks the necessary safety provisions

después I. *adv* 1.(*tiempo*) after; ~ **de la cena** after supper; **una hora** ~ an hour later 2.(*espacio*) ~ **de la torre** behind the tower 3.(*concesivo*) ~ **de todo** after all II. *conj* ~ (**de**) **que** after

despuntar I. *vt* (*gastar la punta*) to blunt; (*quitarla*) to remove the tip of II. *vi* 1.(*flor*) to bud; (*planta*) to sprout 2.(*amanecer*) to dawn; **al** ~ **la aurora** at the break of dawn 3.(*distinguirse*) to stand out; **despunta en inglés** he/she excels at English III. *vr:* ~**se** (*gastarse*) to become blunt

desquiciado, -a *adj inf* disturbed

desquiciar I. *vt* 1.(*desencajar*) to unhinge 2.(*alterar*) to disturb II. *vr:* ~**se** to become unstable

desquitar *vt, vr:* ~**se** 1.(*resarcir*) to win back; ~**se de una pérdida** to make good a loss 2.(*desagraviar*) ~ **de algo** to make up for sth 3.(*vengar*) to get even with

desquite *m* 1.(*satisfacción*) satisfaction 2.(*venganza*) revenge; **tomar(se) el** ~ to avenge oneself

desrielar *vi AmL* to derail

destacable *adj* outstanding

destacado, -a *adj* outstanding

destacamento *m* MIL detachment, detail

destacar <c→qu> I. *vi* to stand out; ~ **en el deporte** to excel at sports II. *vt* (*realzar*) to emphasize III. *vr:* ~**se** (*descollar*) to stand out

destajo *m* piecework; **trabajar a** ~ to do piecework; *fig* to work hard; **hablar a** ~ *inf* to talk nineteen to the dozen; **a** ~ *Arg, Chile* (*a ojo*) by guesswork

destapar I. *vt* 1.(*abrir*) to open; ~ **la olla** to take the lid off the pot 2.(*desabrigar*) to uncover 3.(*secretos*) to reveal II. *vr:* ~**se** 1.(*perder la tapa*) to lose its lid 2.(*desabrigarse*) to be uncovered 3. *inf* (*desnudarse*) to strip off, to strip down 4.(*descubrirse*) to be revealed 5.(*desahogarse*) ~**se con** [*o* **haciendo**] **algo** to let off steam by doing sth

destaponar *vt* 1.(*una botella*) to uncork 2.(*obstrucción*) to unplug 3. *Perú* (*abrir*) to open

destartalado, -a *adj* ramshackle

destellar *vi* to sparkle

destello *m* 1.(*rayo*) ray 2.(*reflejo*) glint 3.(*resplandor*) sparkle 4.(*indicio*) glimmer

destemplado, -a *adj* 1.(*sonido*) out of tune 2.(*voz*) harsh 3.(*tiempo*) unpleasant 4.(*persona*) bad-tempered

destemplanza *f* 1.(*inmoderación*) excess; **con** ~ excessively 2.(*tiempo*) unsettledness 3.(*malestar*) indisposition

destemplar I. *vt* 1.(*sonido*) to be out of tune 2.(*perturbar*) to disturb II. *vr:* ~**se** 1.(*alterarse*) to get upset 2.(*indisponerse*) to become ill

desteñido, -a *adj* (*descolorido*) faded; (*manchado*) discoloured *Brit*, discolored *Am*

desteñir *irr como ceñir* I. *vi* (*descolorarse*) to fade; (*despintar*) to run II. *vt* 1.(*descolorar*) to fade; QUÍM to bleach 2.(*manchar*) to stain III. *vr:* ~**se** (*descolorarse*) to fade; (*despintar*) to run, to bleed

desternillarse *vr* ~ **de risa** to laugh one's head off

desterrar <e→ie> *vt* 1.(*exiliar*) to exile; ~ **a alguien del país** to exile sb from the country 2.(*alejar*) to banish

destetar *vt* to wean

destiempo *m* **a** ~ at the wrong moment

destierro *m* 1.(*pena*) exile 2.(*lugar*) (place of) exile 3.(*lugar muy alejado*) remote place

destilación *f* (*alcohol*) distillation; (*petróleo*) refining

destilar I. *vi* to distil *Brit*, to distill *Am* II. *vt* 1.(*alambicar*) to distil *Brit*, to distill *Am* 2.(*filtrar*) to filtrate 3.(*soltar*) to give off 4.(*sentimiento*) to exude; **la crítica destila mala leche** the criticism is full of spite

destilería *f* distillery; ~ **de petróleo** oil refinery

destinar *vt* 1.(*dedicar*) to dedicate; (*asignar*) to assign 2.(*enviar*) to send 3.(*designar*) to appoint; ~ **a alguien para Ministro de**

Defensa to appoint sb as Minister of Defence [*o* Defense *Am*] **4.** MIL to post

destinatario, -a *m*, *f* (*correo*) addressee; (*mercancía*) consignee

destino *m* **1.** (*hado*) fate; **tuvo un ~ muy triste** he/she met an unhappy end **2.** (*empleo*) job, post *Brit;* **pedir un importante ~ en el gobierno** to apply for an important position in the government **3.** (*destinación*) destination; **estación de ~** destination station; **puerto de ~** destination port; **el barco sale con ~ a México** the boat is bound for Mexico **4.** (*finalidad*) purpose

destitución *f* dismissal; **~ del cargo** removal from one's post [*o* office *Am*]

destituir *irr como huir vt* **1.** (*despedir*) to dismiss; **~ al jefe de gobierno** to remove the head of the government **2.** *elev* (*privar*) **~ a alguien de algo** to deprive sb of sth

destornillador *m* **1.** (*herramienta*) screwdriver, turnscrew *Brit;* **~ de estrella** crosspoint screwdriver *Brit,* Philips screwdriver *Am* **2.** GASTR screwdriver

destornillar *vt* to unscrew

destrabar I. *vt* to untie **II.** *vr:* **~se** to come undone

destral *m* hatchet

destreza *f* skill; **~ manual** dexterity; **con ~** skilfully *Brit,* skillfully *Am*

destripador(a) *m(f)* *fig* murderer; **Jack el ~** Jack the Ripper

destripar *vt* **1.** (*despanzurrar: persona, animal*) to disembowel; (*pez*) to gut **2.** (*despachurrar*) *t. fig* to crush **3.** (*estropear*) to ruin

destrísimo, -a *adj superl de* **diestro**

destrozar <z→c> *vt* **1.** (*despedazar*) to smash; (*libro*) to rip up; (*ropa*) to tear up; **~ un vehículo** (*conduciendo*) to smash up a vehicle **2.** (*moralmente*) to shatter; **estar destrozado** to be an emotional wreck **3.** *inf* (*físicamente*) to shatter; **el viaje me ha destrozado** I'm absolutely exhausted from the journey; **he trabajado todo el día y estoy destrozado** I've been working all day and now I'm knackered **4.** (*planes*) to ruin **5.** (*enemigo, cosecha*) to destroy

destrozo *m* **1.** (*daño*) damage **2.** (*acción*) destruction

destrozón, -ona *adj, m, f inf* destructive; **este niño es un ~** this child leaves a trail of destruction in his wake

destrucción *f* destruction

destructivo, -a *adj* destructive

destruir *irr como huir vt* **1.** (*destrozar*) to destroy **2.** (*física o moralmente*) to shatter **3.** (*aniquilar*) to annihilate

desubicado, -a *adj AmL* out of place; *fig* disorientated *Brit,* disoriented *Am*

desuncir <c→z> *vt* to unyoke

desunión *f* **1.** (*separación*) separation **2.** (*discordia*) disunity

desunir I. *vt* **1.** (*separar*) to separate **2.** (*enemistar*) **~ a dos personas** to cause discord

between two people **II.** *vr:* **~se 1.** (*separar*) to separate **2.** (*enemistar*) to fall out

desusado, -a *adj* **1.** (*anticuado*) old-fashioned **2.** (*insólito*) unusual

desuso *m* **caer en ~** to fall into disuse; (*máquina*) to become obsolete

desvaído, -a *adj* **1.** (*colores*) faded **2.** (*persona*) dull; **es una mujer desvaída** she's a bit insipid

desvalido, -a *adj* needy

desvalijar *vt* to clean out *inf*

desvalimiento *m* destitution

desvalorización *f* depreciation; **~ monetaria** monetary devaluation

desvalorizar <z→c> *vt* to devalue

desván *m* loft, attic

desvanecer *irr como crecer* **I.** *vt* **1.** (*color*) to tone down **2.** (*dudas*) to dispel; **~ las sospechas de alguien** to allay sb's suspicions **II.** *vr:* **~se 1.** (*desaparecer*) to disappear; (*alcohol*) to evaporate; (*colores, esperanzas*) to fade; (*enojo*) to abate; **el entusiasmo se desvaneció rápidamente** the enthusiasm soon abated **2.** (*desmayarse*) to faint

desvanecimiento *m* **1.** (*desaparición*) disappearance **2.** (*mareo*) faint; **tener un ~** to faint

desvariar < *l. pres:* desvarío> *vi* (*delirar*) to be delirious; (*decir incoherencias*) to talk nonsense

desvarío *m* **1.** (*locura*) madness; **los ~s de una imaginación enfermiza** the crazed imaginings of a sick mind **2.** (*delirio*) delirium **3.** (*monstruosidad*) monstrosity

desvelar I. *vt* **1.** (*sueño*) **~ a alguien** to keep sb awake **2.** (*revelar*) to reveal **II.** *vr:* **~se 1.** (*no dormir*) to stay awake **2.** (*esmerarse*) **~se por algo/alguien** to devote oneself to sth/sb

desvelo *m* **1.** (*insomnio*) insomnia **2.** (*despabilamiento*) alertness **3.** (*pl*) (*celo*) jealousy **4.** (*pl*) (*atención*) efforts *pl*

desvencijado, -a *adj* dilapidated

desvencijar I. *vt* to break **II.** *vr:* **~se** to fall to pieces

desventaja *f* disadvantage, drawback

desventajoso, -a *adj* disadvantageous; (*condiciones*) unfavourable *Brit,* unfavorable *Am;* **apariencia desventajosa** unprepossessing appearance

desventura *f* misfortune

desventurado, -a *adj* unfortunate; **una familia desventurada** an ill-fated family

desvergonzado, -a *adj* **1.** (*sinvergüenza*) shameless **2.** (*descarado*) brazen

desvergonzarse *irr como avergonzar vr* to lose all sense of shame; **~ con alguien** to be rude to sb

desvergüenza *f* shamelessness

desvestir *irr como pedir vt, vr:* **~se** to undress

desviación *f* **1.** (*torcedura*) deviation; **~ de la columna vertebral** curvature of the spine; **~ jurídica** miscarriage of justice **2.** (*del tráfico*) diversion, detour; (*bocacalle*) turning

3.(*aberración*) deviance
desviado, -a *adj* (*diferente*) deviant
desviar <*l. pres:* desvío> I. *vt* (*del camino, dinero*) to divert; (*de un propósito*) to distract; ~ **una cuestión** to avoid a problem II. *vr:* ~**se** **1.**(*del camino*) to be diverted; (*del tema*) to be distracted; (*de una idea, intención*) to be put off; **la brigada se desvió hacia la izquierda** the brigade turned towards the left **2.**(*extraviarse*) to get lost
desvincular I. *vt* to dissociate II. *vr:* ~**se** to dissociate oneself
desvío *m* **1.**(*desviación*) deviation **2.**(*carretera*) detour; (*temporal*) diversion, detour **3.**(*despego*) indifference
desvirgar <g→gu> *vt* to deflower
desvirtuar <*l. pres:* desvirtúo> *vt* (*argumento, prueba*) to undermine; (*rumor*) to scotch; ~ **la competencia** to distort the marketplace
desvivirse *vr* **1.**(*chiflarse*) ~ **por alguien** to be crazy about sb; **se desvive por ella** he's head over heels in love with her **2.**(*afanarse*) ~ **con** [*o* **por**] **alguien** to be utterly devoted to sb; **se desvivió por conseguir este documento** he/she went to every length imaginable to get this document
detallado, -a *adj* detailed; **una lista detallada** an itemized list
detallar *vt* **1.**(*pormenorizar*) to detail, to itemize **2.**COM to retail
detalle *m* **1.**(*pormenor*) detail; **en** [*o* **al**] ~ in detail; **venta al** ~ retail sales; **entrar en** ~**s** to go into details **2.**(*finura*) nice gesture; **has tenido un** ~ **regalándome las flores** it was very kind of you to give me the flowers
detallista I. *adj* precise; *pey* pedantic II. *mf* **1.**(*minucioso*) perfectionist **2.**COM retailer **3.**(*considerado*) thoughtful person
detectable *adj* detectable
detectar *vt* to detect
detective *mf* detective
detector *m* detector; ~ **de humo** smoke detector
detención *f* **1.**(*parada*) stopping; (*de la correspondencia*) withholding; ~ **del crecimiento** inhibition of growth **2.**JUR arrest; ~ **ilegal** false imprisonment; ~ **preventiva** preventive detention, remand in custody; ~ **domiciliaria** house arrest **3.**(*dilación*) delay; **sin** ~ without delay **4.**(*prolijidad*) detail; **describir con** ~ to describe in detail; **ha corregido el examen con** ~ he/she took great care in marking the exam
detener *irr como* tener I. *vt* **1.**(*parar*) to stop; (*correspondencia*) to withhold; ~ **los progresos de una enfermedad** to halt the evolution of a disease **2.**JUR to arrest **3.**(*retener*) ~ (**en su poder**) to keep (in one's power) II. *vr:* ~**se** **1.**(*pararse*) to stop **2.**(*entretenerse*) ~**se en algo** to pass one's time doing sth
detenidamente *adv* thoroughly, carefully
detenido, -a I. *adj* **1.**(*minucioso*) thorough

2.(*arrestado*) arrested **3.**(*apocado*) timid **4.**(*escaso*) insufficient II. *m, f* person under arrest
detenimiento *m* **1.**(*minuciosidad*) care; **con** ~ thoroughly **2.**(*tardanza*) delay; **con** ~ late **3.**JUR arrest
detentar *vt* to hold unlawfully
detergente I. *adj* detergent II. *m* detergent; ~ **para lavar la ropa** washing powder *Brit*, laundry detergent *Am;* ~ **lavavajillas** washing-up liquid *Brit*, dish liquid *Am*
deteriorar I. *vt* **1.**(*empeorar*) to worsen **2.**(*romper*) to break **3.**(*gastar*) to wear out II. *vr:* ~**se** **1.**(*empeorarse*) to worsen **2.**(*estropearse*) to spoil; **mercancía deteriorada** spoiled goods
deterioro *m* **1.**(*desmejora*) deterioration; ~ **de calidad** decline in quality **2.**(*daño*) damage; **sin** ~ undamaged; ~ **debido al almacenamiento** damaged in storage **3.**(*desgaste*) wear and tear **4.**(*echarse a perder*) spoiling; **sujeto a** ~ perishable; **de fácil** ~ easily spoilt
determinación *f* **1.**(*fijación*) establishment; ~ **de los daños** ascertainment of damages; ~ **de objetivos** setting of objectives **2.**(*decisión*) decision; **tomar una** ~ to take [*o* make] a decision; **con** ~ determinedly **3.**(*audacia*) determination
determinado, -a *adj* **1.**(*cierto*) *t.* LING definite **2.**(*atrevido*) determined **3.**(*preciso*) specific
determinante I. *adj* decisive; **palabra** ~ LING determiner II. *m* decisive factor; MAT determinant
determinar I. *vt* **1.**(*fijar*) to establish; (*plazo*) to fix **2.**(*decidir*) to decide; JUR to settle; ~ **un pleito** to adjudicate a (court) case **3.**(*causar*) to determine **4.**(*motivar*) ~ **a alguien a hacer algo** to determine sb to do sth II. *vr:* ~**se por algo** to decide in favour [*o* favor *Am*] of sth; ~**se a hacer algo** to decide to do sth
detestable *adj* loathsome
detestar *vt* to detest, to loathe
detonación *f* **1.**(*acción*) detonation **2.**(*ruido*) explosion
detonador *m* detonator
detonante I. *adj* **1.**(*explosivo*) explosive **2.**AmL (*que molesta*) discordant II. *m* (*causa*) cause
detonar I. *vi* to detonate, to set off II. *vt* to detonate
detractor(a) I. *adj* denigrating II. *m(f)* detractor
detrás I. *adv* **1.**(*local*) behind; **allí** ~ over there, behind that; **entrar por** ~ to come in through the back; **me asaltaron por** ~ they attacked me from behind **2.**(*en el orden*) **el que está** ~ the next one; **primero estás tu y** ~ **van mis amigos** *fig* you're more important to me than my friends II. *prep* **1.**(*local: tras*) ~ **de** behind; ~ **de la carta** on the back of the letter; **quedar** ~ **de los otros** to be behind the others; **ir** ~ **de alguien** to be looking for sb;

hablar mal (por) ~ **de alguien** to criticize sb behind his/her back **2.** (*en el orden*) **uno ~ de otro** one after another

detrimento *m* **1.** (*daño*) harm; **causa ~ de la salud** it damages your health **2.** (*perjuicio*) detriment; **en ~ de alguien** to sb's detriment; **en ~ de su salud** at cost to his/her health

deuda *f* **1.** (*débito*) debt; ~ **activa** productive debt; ~ **contraída** debt; ~ **del Estado** Treasury notes/bonds; ~ **externa** foreign debt; ~ **interna** internal debt; ~ **pública** national debt; ~ **a pagar** debt due; ~ **pendiente** outstanding debt; ~ **vencida** mature debt; **cargado de ~s** burdened with debt; **contraer ~s** to get into debt; **sin ~s** free of debt **2.** (*moral*) debt; **estar en ~ con alguien** to be indebted to sb; **lo prometido es ~** a promise is a promise **3.** (*pecado*) **y perdónanos nuestras ~s...** and forgive us our trespasses ...

deudor(a) I. *adj* indebted; **saldo ~** debit balance II. *m(f)* debtor; ~ **solidario** joint debtor

devaluación *f* devaluation

devaluar <*I. pres:* devalúo> *vt* to devalue

devanar I. *vt* to wind II. *vr:* ~**se** *Cuba* (*reírse mucho*) to split one's sides laughing **2.** ~**se los sesos** to rack one's brains

devaneo *m* **1.** (*amorío*) flirtation **2.** (*distracción*) distraction **3.** (*locura*) delusion

devastación *f* devastation

devastar *vt* to devastate

devengar <g→gu> *vt* **1.** (*salario*) to earn **2.** (*intereses*) to yield; **interTs devengado** accrued interest

devenir *irr como* **venir** *vi* **1.** (*acaecer*) to occur **2.** (*convertirse*) ~ **en algo** to become sth

devoción *f* **1.** (*religión*) religious belief; **fingir ~** to feign belief **2.** (*oración*) devotion **3.** (*respeto*) devotion; **rezar con ~** to pray devoutly **4.** (*obediencia*) obedience; **estar a la ~ de alguien** to be at sb's disposal **5.** (*fervor*) fervour *Brit,* fervor *Am;* **amar con ~** to love devotedly; **hacer con ~** to do with great devotion; **tener ~ a un santo** to venerate a saint **6.** (*afición*) attachment

devocionario *m* prayer book

devolución *f* return; ~ **a origen** return to sender; FIN refund; ~ **de impuestos** tax refund, tax return; **'no se admiten devoluciones'** 'no refunds'

devolver *irr como* **volver** I. *vt* **1.** to return; *fig* to restore; ~ **bien por mal** to repay evil with good; ~ **un favor** to return a favour [*o* favor *Am*]; ~ **la visita** to return a visit; **devuélvase al remitente** (*en cartas*) return to sender; **esta máquina no devuelve cambio** this machine does not give change; ~ **la pelota al defensa** to pass the ball back to the defender **2.** (*vomitar*) to throw up II. *vr:* ~**se** *AmL* (*volver*) to return; ~**se a casa** to go back home

devorador(a) *adj* **hambre ~a** ravenous hunger

devorar *vt* to devour; ~ **la comida** to wolf down one's food; **la enfermedad devoró sus**

fuerzas the illness consumed his/her strength; **me devora la impaciencia** I am consumed with impatience

devoto, -a I. *adj* **1.** (*religioso*) devout **2.** (*adicto*) devoted; ~ **admirador de los Beatles** loyal [*o* keen *Brit*] fan of the Beatles II. *m, f* **1.** (*creyente*) devotee **2.** (*admirador*) enthusiast

deyección *f* **1.** (*volcán*) ejecta **2.** (*defecación*) defecation **3.** *pl* (*heces*) faeces *pl Brit,* feces *pl Am*

DGT *f* **1.** (*turismo*) *abr de* **Dirección General de Turismo** *Spanish department for tourism* **2.** (*tráfico*) *abr de* **Dirección General de Tráfico** *Spanish department for traffic*

día *m* day; ~ **de año nuevo** New Year's day; ~ **de cumpleaños** birthday; **el ~** D D-day; ~ **de descanso** rest day; ~ **de los difuntos** All Souls' Day; ~ **festivo** holiday; ~ **hábil** [*o* **laborable**] working day; **el ~ del juicio final** Judgement Day; ~ **lectivo** school day; ~ **libre/de baja** day off; ~ **de Reyes** Epiphany; ~ **del santo** saint's day; **cambio del ~** today's exchange rate; **al abrir el ~** at the break of day; **al caer el ~** at the close of day; **al otro ~** by the next day; **antes del ~** before the break of day; **de hoy en ocho ~s** eight days from now; **de un ~ a otro** from one day to the next; **cualquier ~** any day; **durante ~s enteros** for days at a time; **una diferencia como del ~ a la noche** as different as you can get; **un ~ sí y otro no,** ~ **por medio** *AmL* every other day; ~ **y noche** day and night; **el ~ de hoy** nowadays; **el ~ de mañana** in the future; **el ~ menos pensado** one fine day; **el ~ que...** the day that ...; **el otro ~** the other day; **en su ~** in his/her day; **hoy (en) ~** nowadays; **un buen ~** one fine day; **un ~ de estos** one of these days; **un ~ u otro** some day; **hace buen ~** it's nice weather; **a ~s** at times; **de ~** by [*o* during the] day; **del ~** today's; ~ **a ~** day by day; ~ **tras** [*o* por] ~ day after day; **de ~ en ~** from day to day; **¡buenos ~s!** hello; (*por la mañana*) good morning; **¡hasta otro ~!** until another day; ►**hay más ~s que longanizas** *inf* there will be other days; **mañana será otro ~** tomorrow is another day; **tiene los ~s contados** his/her days are numbered; **entrado en ~s** getting on; **¡no en mis ~s!** over my dead body!; **un ~ y otro** again and again; **todo el santo ~** the whole day long; **alcanzar a alguien en ~s** to outlive sb; **dar a alguien el ~** to ruin sb's day; **estar al ~** to be up to date; **no pasar los ~s** por alguien to not look a day older; **un ~ es un ~** it's just one day; **tener ~s** (*viejo*) to be old; (*de mal humor*) to be bad-tempered; **vivir al ~** to live from day to day

diabetes *f inv* diabetes

diabético, -a *adj, m, f* diabetic

diablo *m* devil; **ser un ~ de hombre** to be an absolute devil; **tener el ~ en el cuerpo** to be a little devil; **abogado del ~** devil's advocate; **duele como el ~** it hurts like hell ►**¡con mil**

~s! hell!; de mil ~s hellish; **aquí hay** mucho ~ *inf* there is something fishy going on here; **más sabe el ~ por viejo que por** sabio *prov* the older, the wiser *prov;* **anda el ~** suelto *inf* there's trouble brewing; **aquí** anda **el ~** everything is going wrong; **dar de** comer **al ~** *inf* to curse; dar **al ~** *inf* to send to hell; darse **al ~** *inf* to blow one's top; **¡vete al ~!** go to hell!; **¿cómo ~s...?** how on earth ...?; **¡qué ~s!** hell!; **¿qué ~s pasa aquí?** what the hell is going on here?; **¡~s!** damn!

diablura *f* prank

diabólico, -a *adj* 1.(*maligno*) diabolic(al) 2.(*complicado*) fiendish

diadema *f* (*corona*) diadem; (*joya*) tiara; (*del pelo*) hairband

diáfano, -a *adj* 1.(*transparente*) transparent 2.(*translúcido*) translucent 3.(*claro*) clear; **un argumento ~** a clear argument

diafragma *m* 1.FOTO, ANAT diaphragm 2.(*anticonceptivo*) (Dutch) cap *Brit,* diaphragm *Am*

diagnosis *f inv* diagnosis

diagnosticar <c→qu> *vt* to diagnose

diagnóstico *m* 1.(*diagnosis*) diagnosis; **~ precoz** early diagnosis 2.(*análisis*) analysis

diagonal I. *adj* diagonal; **en ~** diagonally II. *f* diagonal

diagrama *m* diagram; **~ de bloques** block diagram; **~ esquemático** schematic diagram; **~ de puntos** scatter diagram; **~ de flujo** flowchart

dial *m* dial; **~ de velocidad** AUTO speedometer

dialectal *adj* dialect

dialéctica *f* dialectics *pl*

dialecto *m* dialect

diálisis *f inv* dialysis

dialogar <g→gu> *vi* (*hablar*) to talk; **~ con alguien** to have a conversation with sb; **escrito en forma dialogada** written in the form of a dialogue [*o* dialog *Am*]

diálogo *m* 1.(*conversación*) conversation 2.LIT dialogue *Brit,* dialog *Am*

diamante *m* diamond; **bodas de ~** diamond wedding; **~ brillante** brilliant; **~ (en) bruto** rough [*o* uncut] diamond

diametralmente *adv* diametrically; **~ opuesto** diametrically opposed

diámetro *m* diameter

diana *f* 1.MIL reveille; **a toque de ~** *fig* highly disciplined 2.(*objeto*) target 3.(*del blanco*) bull's-eye; **hacer ~** to hit the bull's-eye

diantre *interj inf* damn

diapasón *m* MÚS range; **~ normal** standard pitch; (*objeto*) tuning fork; (*de voz*) pitch-pipe; (*guitarra*) fingerboard; **bajar/subir el ~** *inf* to turn the volume up/down

diapositiva *f* slide

diariero, -a *m, f AmS* paperboy, newspaper vendor

diario *m* 1.(*periódico*) (daily) newspaper; **~ de avisos** classified advertising newspaper 2.(*dietario*) journal; **~ de navegación** NÁUT log 3.(*memorias*) diary 4.(*gastos*) daily expenses

diario, -a *adj* daily; **a ~** daily; **de ~** everyday; **uniforme de ~** service uniform

diarismo *m AmL* (*periodismo*) journalism

diarrea *f* diarrhoea *Brit,* diarrhea *Am*

dibujante *mf* (*lineal*) draughtsman *m,* draughtswoman *f;* **~ proyectista** architectural draughtsman *m,* architectural draughtswoman *f;* (*de bocetos*) sketcher; (*de caricaturas, dibujos animados*) cartoonist

dibujar I. *vt* 1.(*trazar*) to draw; **~ copiando** to draw from a copy; **~ según modelo** to draw from a model; **~ a pulso** to draw freehand; **~ a lápiz** to draw in pencil 2.(*describir*) to describe II. *vr:* **~se** to be outlined

dibujo *m* 1.(*acción*) drawing 2.(*resultado*) drawing; **~ acotado** contour drawing; **~s animados** cartoons 3.(*muestra*) illustration; **con ~s** illustrated 4.(*estampado*) pattern

dicción *f* 1.(*declamación*) declamation 2.(*pronunciación*) diction; (*estilo*) eloquence

diccionario *m* dictionary; **~ de artes y ciencias** dictionary of art and science; **~ enciclopédico** encyclopaedic [*o* encyclopedic *Am*] dictionary; **~ de inglés-español** English-Spanish dictionary

dicha *f* (*suerte*) luck; **~ conyugal** marital bliss; **por ~** fortunately; **nunca es tarde si la ~ es buena** *prov* better late than never *prov*

dicharachero, -a I. *adj* funny II. *m, f* joker

dicho *m* 1.(*ocurrencia*) observation 2.(*refrán*) saying 3. *pl* (*al casarse*) vows *pl;* **tomarse los ~s** to take one's vows ►**del ~ al** hecho **hay mucho trecho** *prov* it's easier said than done *prov*

dicho, -a I. *pp de* decir II. *adj* **dicha gente** the said people; **~ y hecho** no sooner said than done

dichoso, -a *adj* 1.(*feliz*) **~ de algo** happy to sth 2. *irón* (*maldito*) blessed

diciembre *m* December; *v.t.* marzo

dictado *m* 1.(*escuela*) dictation 2. *fig* (*inspiración*) dictate; **seguir los ~s de la conciencia** to follow one's conscience

dictador(a) *m(f)* dictator

dictadura *f* dictatorship

dictáfono *m* Dictaphone®

dictamen *m* 1.(*peritaje*) opinion; **~ en juicio** legal opinion; **dar ~** to give advice 2.(*informe*) report; **~ facultativo** medical report 3.(*opinión*) opinion; **tomar ~ de alguien** to consult with sb 4.JUR **~ judicial** legal judgment

dictaminar *vi* to pronounce judgement

dictar *vt* 1.(*un dictado*) to dictate 2.(*una sentencia*) to pass 3.(*una ley*) to enact 4.(*un discurso*) to give 5.*AmS* (*clases*) to teach 6. *fig* (*sugerir*) to suggest

didáctico, -a *adj* didactic; **material ~** teaching material

diecinueve *adj inv, m* nineteen; *v.t.* ocho

dieciocho *adj inv, m* eighteen; *v.t.* ocho

dieciséis *adj inv, m* sixteen; *v.t.* ocho

dieciseisavo, -a *adj, m, f* sixteenth; *v.t.* octavo

diecisiete *adj inv* seventeen; *v.t.* ocho

diecisieteavo, -a *adj, m, f* seventeenth; *v.t.* octavo

diente *m* 1. (*de la boca*) tooth; ~ **canino** canine (tooth); ~ **incisivo** incisor; ~ **de leche** milk tooth; ~ **molar** molar; ~s **postizos** false teeth; ~ **picado** tooth with caries; **armado hasta los** ~s armed to the teeth; **daba** ~ **con** ~ his/her teeth were chattering 2. TÉC tooth; (*de horquilla*) prong; **de dos** ~s two-pronged 3. BOT ~ **de ajo** clove of garlic; ~ **de león** dandelion ▶ **decir** algo **entre** ~s to mumble sth; **poner los** ~s **largos** a alguien to make sb green with envy; **pelar el** ~ *AmL, inf* to smile flirtatiously; **tener buen** ~ to have a healthy appetite; **volar** ~ *AmL* (*comer*) to stuff one's face

diesel *m* diesel

diestro *m* (*torero*) matador

diestro, -a <destrísimo *o* diestrísimo> *adj* 1. (*a la derecha*) right; **a** ~ **y siniestro** *fig* left, right and centre [*o* center *Am*] 2. (*hábil*) skilful *Brit*, skillful *Am* 3. (*astuto*) cunning 4. (*que usa la mano derecha*) right-handed

dieta *f* 1. (*para adelgazar*) diet; ~ **absoluta** starvation diet; **estar a** ~ to be on a diet; **poner alguien a** ~ to put sb on a diet 2. (*alimentación*) ~ **alimenticia** diet; ~ **básica** staple diet 3. (*asamblea*) diet 4. *pl* (*retribución*) allowance, expenses *pl*; (*de diputados*) salary

dietético, -a *adj* dietary; **régimen** ~ diet; **médico** ~ dietician

diez *adj inv, m* ten; *v.t.* ocho

diezmar *vt* (*aniquilar*) to decimate

difamación *f* defamation; (*escrita*) libel; (*oral*) slander

difamar *vt* to defame; (*por escrito*) to libel; (*hablando*) to slander

difamatorio, -a *adj* defamatory; (*escrito*) libellous *Brit*, libelous *Am*; (*hablando*) slanderous

diferencia *f* 1. (*desigualdad*) difference; ~ **de los tipos de interés** interest differential/margin; **a** ~ **de algo** unlike [*o* in contrast with] sth 2. (*desacuerdo*) disagreement; **arreglar** (**las**) ~s to settle one's differences 3. MAT difference; ~ **de caja** cash deficit

diferencial[1] I. *adj* 1. (*variable*) variable 2. MAT differential II. *f* MAT differential

diferencial[2] *m* AUTO differential (gear)

diferenciar I. *vi* to differentiate II. *vt* 1. (*distinguir*) to distinguish 2. MAT to differentiate III. *vr*: ~**se** to differ

diferendo *m AmS* (*disputa*) dispute

diferente I. *adj* different; ~s **veces** several times; **España es** ~ Spain is different II. *adv* differently; **piensa muy** ~ he/she has a very different way of thinking

diferir *irr como sentir* I. *vi* to differ; ~ **de algo** to be different from sth II. *vt* to postpone; ~ **el**

pago to delay payment; **transmisión en diferido** pre-recorded broadcast

difícil *adj* difficult; ~ **de explicar** difficult to explain; **de** ~ **acceso** hard to get to

difícilmente *adv* with difficulty; **un material** ~ **soluble** a substance which is hard to dissolve; (*apenas*) hardly

dificultad *f* difficulty; **estar en** ~es to be in difficulty; **expresarse con** ~ to express oneself with difficulty; **poner** ~es **a alguien** to put sb in a difficult position; **ahí está la** ~ that's where the problem lies

dificultar *vt* to hinder; ~ **la circulación** to obstruct the traffic

dificultoso, -a *adj* difficult; (*laborioso*) heavy-going

difteria *f* diphtheria

difuminar *vt* (*dibujo*) to stump, to blur; (*luz*) to diffuse

difundir I. *vt* to spread; (*gas*) to give off; ~ **por la radio** to broadcast on the radio II. *vr*: ~**se** to spread; **la niebla se difundió por todo el valle** the fog spread right across the valley; **la novedad se ha difundido por toda la ciudad** the news has spread throughout the city

difunto, -a I. *adj* deceased; **el** ~ **presidente** the late president II. *m, f* deceased person; **día de** ~s All Souls' Day; **misa de** ~s Requiem (mass)

difusión *f* 1. (*expansión, divulgación*) dissemination; TV, RADIO broadcast; ~ **de productos** distribution of products 2. (*prolijidad*) lengthiness

difuso, -a *adj* 1. (*extendido*) widespread 2. (*vago, prolijo*) diffuse

digerir *irr como sentir vt* 1. (*la comida*) to digest 2. (*a una persona*) to stomach; (*noticia, libro*) to absorb

digestión *f* (*de alimentos*) digestion; **tener mala** ~ to have stomach problems; **corte de** ~ stomach cramp

digestivo, -a *adj* digestive; **aparato** ~ ANAT digestive system

digital I. *adj* 1. (*dactilar*) finger; **huellas** ~es fingerprints 2. INFOR, TÉC digital; **ingreso** ~ digital input; **ordenador** ~ digital computer II. *m* foxglove

digitalizar <z→c> *vt* to digitize *Brit*, to digitalize *Am*

dígito I. *adj* digital II. *m* MAT, INFOR digit; ~ **de verificación** verification number; ~ **de control** check bit

dignarse *vr* ~ **hacer algo** to condescend to do sth; **se dignaron invitarnos a su fiesta** *irón* they deigned to invite us to their party

dignatario, -a *m, f* dignitary

dignidad *f* 1. (*respeto*) dignity; **con** ~ with dignity 2. (*decencia*) decency 3. (*cargo*) office

digno, -a *adj* 1. (*merecedor*) deserving; ~ **de compasión** worthy of sympathy; ~ **de confianza** trustworthy; ~ **de fe** worth believing in; ~ **de mención** worth mentioning; ~ **de ver** worth seeing 2. (*adecuado*) fitting

3. (*noble*) noble **4.** (*con gravedad*) dignified
digresión *f* (*del tema*) digression
dije *m* (*colgante*) charm; **ser un** ~ *inf* (*persona*) to be a treasure [*o* jewel]
dilación *f* (*aplazamiento*) postponement; (*retraso*) delay; **sin** ~ without delay
dilapidar *vt* to squander; ~ **una fortuna** to squander a fortune
dilatación *f* **1.** (*ampliación*) expansion; MED dilation; ~ **del mercado** COM expansion of the market **2.** (*desahogo*) calm
dilatado, -a *adj* **1.** (*pupila*) dilated **2.** (*extenso*) extensive
dilatar **I.** *vt* **1.** (*extender*) to expand; MED to dilate **2.** (*aplazar*) to postpone; ~ **la reunión** to postpone the meeting **3.** (*retrasar*) to delay **4.** (*prolongar*) to prolong **II.** *vr:* ~**se 1.** (*extenderse*) to expand **2.** *AmL* (*demorar*) to delay
dilatorio, -a *adj* dilatory
dilema *m* dilemma; **encontrarse en un** ~ to be in a dilemma
diligencia *f* **1.** (*esmero*) diligence **2.** (*agilidad*) skill **3.** (*trámite*) paperwork; ~**s policiales** police proceedings; **evacuar una** ~ to resolve a matter; **hacer** ~**s** to do business **4.** (*asunto administrativo*) procedure; ~ **judicial/policial** legal/police procedures; ~**s preparatorias** initial proceedings; ~**s de prueba** taking of evidence **5.** (*nota oficial*) communication; ~ **de notificación** official notification **6.** (*carreta*) stagecoach
diligente *adj* **1.** (*cuidadoso, aplicado*) diligent **2.** (*ágil*) able
dilucidar *vt* to elucidate
dilución *f* **1.** (*de líquidos, colores*) dillution **2.** (*de sólidos*) dissolving
diluir *irr como huir* **I.** *vt* **1.** (*líquidos, colores*) to dilute; **sin** ~ undiluted **2.** (*sólidos*) to dissolve; **dejar** ~ **en la boca** to allow to dissolve in one's mouth **II.** *vr:* ~**se** to dissolve
diluviar *v impers* to pour with rain
diluvio *m* **1.** (*lluvia*) downpour **2.** *inf* (*abundancia*) shower; ~ **de balas** hail of bullets
dimanar *vi* to emanate; **tu éxito dimana de tu constancia** your success stems from your perseverance
dimensión *f* (*extensión, tamaño, medida*) dimension; *fig* magnitude; **de dos dimensiones** in two dimensions; **la** ~ **cultural** the cultural aspect; **una edificio de grandes dimensiones** a large building; **un escándalo de grandes dimensiones** a major scandal; **este asunto está alcanzando dimensiones inesperadas** this affair is turning out to be bigger than people expected
dimes *mpl* ~ **y diretes** *inf* tittle-tattle; **andar en** ~ **y diretes** to quibble
diminutivo *m* LING diminutive
diminutivo, -a *adj* diminutive; **lente diminutiva** diminishing lens
diminuto, -a *adj* tiny
dimisión *f* resignation; **presentar la** ~ to resign

dimitir *vt, vi* to resign; ~ **de un cargo** to resign (from) a position; **dimitió de presidente del club** he/she resigned as club president
Dinamarca *f* Denmark
dinamarqués, -esa **I.** *adj* Danish **II.** *m, f* Dane
dinámica *f* dynamics *pl*
dinámico, -a *adj* dynamic
dinamismo *m* (*energía*) dynamism
dinamita *f* dynamite
dinamitar *vt* to dynamite
dinamizar *vt* to vitalize
dinamo *f,* **dínamo** *f* dynamo
dinastía *f* dynasty
dineral *m* fortune; **costar un** ~ *inf* to cost a fortune
dinero *m* money; ~ **blanco** silver coins; ~ **en caja** cash in hand; ~ **electrónico** e-cash; ~ **metálico** [*o* **contante y sonante**] hard [*o* ready] cash; ~ **de rescate** ransom money; ~ **de curso legal** legal tender; ~ **negro** undeclared money; ~ **en reserva** cash reserve; ~ **suelto** loose change; **hacer** ~ to make money; **pagar en** ~ to pay in cash; **estar mal de** ~ to be short of money; **ser alguien de** ~ to be rich ►~ **en manos de necio como agua se va** *prov* a fool and his money are soon parted *prov;* **los** ~**s del sacristán cantando se vienen y cantando se van** *prov* easy come, easy go; ~ **ahorrado,** ~ **ganado** *prov* a penny saved is a penny earned *prov*
dinosaurio *m* dinosaur
dintel *m* ARQUIT lintel
diñar *vt inf* to give; ~**la** *inf* to kick the bucket
dio 3. *pret de* **dar**
diócesis *f inv* diocese
diodo *m* diode
dioptría *f* dioptre *Brit,* diopter *Am*
dios(a) *m(f)* god *m,* goddess *f*
Dios *m* God; ~ **Hombre** Jesus Christ; ~ **mediante** God willing; ~ **te bendiga** God bless you; **¡**~ **nos libre!** Heaven help us!; **¡**~ **sabe!** God knows!; ~ **sabe que estuve ahí** I swear I was there; ~ **tenga en su gloria** God rest his/her soul; **¡alabado sea** ~**!** praise the Lord!; **así** ~ **me asista** JUR so help me God; ~ **lo llamó** he/she went to meet his/her maker; **¡**~ **mío!** my God!; **¡ay** ~**!** oh dear!; **¡santo** ~**!** my God! ►**costar** ~ **y ayuda** to take a lot of work; **a la buena de** ~ at random; **armar la de** ~ **es Cristo** *inf* to raise a hell of a row; **a** ~ **rogando y con el mazo dando** *prov* trust in God but keep your powder dry *prov;* **como** ~ **le trajo al mundo** stark naked; **¡**~ **nos coja confesados!** Lord help us!; **todo** ~ everyone; ~ **aprieta pero no ahoga** *prov* God strikes not with both hands *prov;* ~ **los cría y ellos se juntan** *prov* birds of a feather flock together *prov;* ~ **dirá** time will tell; **hacer algo como** ~ **manda** to do sth properly; **si** ~ **quiere** God willing; **¡sabe** ~**!** God only knows!; **que sea lo que** ~ **quiera** if it is meant to be; **¡válgame** ~**!** good God!; **¡vaya por** ~**!** for Heaven's sake;

venga ~ **y lo vea** I'll eat my hat; **¡vive ~!** I swear to God!; **vivir como** ~ to live like a lord; **¡a ~!** goodbye!; **¡por ~!** for God's sake!

dióxido *m* dioxide

dioxina *f* dioxin

diploma *m* diploma; ~ **de asistencia** attendance certificate; ~ **de bachiller(ato)** school-leaving certificate equivalent to A-levels in the UK and high school graduation in the USA; ~ **de capitán** captain's commission; ~ **de maestría** teaching certificate; ~ **de reconocimiento** official diploma; ~ **universitario** university title

diplomacia *f* 1.(*política, tacto*) diplomacy 2.(*cuerpo*) diplomatic corps 3.(*carrera*) diplomatic career

diplomado, -a *adj* qualified; **traductora diplomada** qualified translator

diplomático, -a I. *adj* diplomatic II. *m, f* diplomat

diptongo *m* diphthong

diputación *f* 1.(*delegación*) deputation; ~ **permanente de Cortes** standing committee of the Spanish parliament; ~ **provincial** provincial delegation of government 2.(*personas*) delegation 3.(*cargo*) post of member of parliament 4. *Méx* (*edificio*) town hall

diputado, -a *m, f* member of parliament; ~ **en** [*o a*] **Cortes** member of the Spanish parliament; ~ **independiente** independent (member)

dique *m* 1.(*rompeolas*) dike; ~ **de abrigo** breakwater 2. NÁUT dry dock; ~ **flotante** floating dock 3.(*freno*) brake; **poner un ~ a algo** to restrain sth

dirección *f* 1.(*rumbo*) direction; ~ **de la circulación** direction of traffic; ~ **única** one-way; ~ **prohibida** no entry; ~ **de marcha** gear control; ~ **visual** viewing direction; **en** ~ **longitudinal** lengthwise; **en** ~ **opuesta** in the opposition direction; **el viento soplaba en** ~ **oeste** the wind was blowing from the east; **salir con** ~ **a España** to leave for Spain 2.(*administración, mando*) direction; ~ **central** central control; ~ **general** head office; ~ **comercial** business management; ~ **del Estado** state control; ~ **política** political control; ~ **regional** regional government; **alta** ~ senior management 3.(*guía*) direction; ~ (*artística*) TEAT artistic direction; ~ **de personal** personnel management; **bajo la** ~ **de** directed by 4.(*señas*) address; ~ **comercial** business address; ~ **de correo electrónico** e-mail address 5. AUTO steering; ~ **asistida** power steering

directa *f* AUTO top gear; (*coche automático*) drive ▶**poner la** ~ *inf* to go all out

directiva *f* 1.(*dirección*) board (of directors) 2.(*instrucción*) directive

directivo, -a I. *adj* managing; **junta directiva** managing committee II. *m, f* 1.(*ejecutivo*) director; (*manager*) manager 2.(*de la junta directiva*) member of the board of directors

directo *m* 1. FERRO through train 2. DEP straight (punch)

directo, -a *adj* 1.(*recto*) straight 2.(*inmediato, franco*) direct; **transmisión en** ~ live broadcast; **un tren** ~ a through train; **seguir el camino más** ~ to take the shortest route

director(a) I. *adj* managing II. *m(f)* director; (*jefe*) manager; ~ **accidental** [*o* en funciones] acting director; ~ **administrativo** administrative director; ~ **de departamento** department manager; ~ (**de escena**) CINE, TEAT director; ~ (**de escuela**) headmaster *m Brit*, headmistress *f Brit*, principal *mf Am*; ~ **de fábrica** factory manager; ~ **general** managing director; ~ **de la obra** project manager; ~ **de orquesta** conductor; ~ **invitado** guest conductor; ~ **de sucursal** branch manager; ~ **técnico** technical director; ~ **de la tesis** doctoral advisor

directorio *m* 1.(*junta*) governing body 2.(*manual*) directory 3.(*agenda*) address book 4. INFOR directory; ~ **raíz** root [*o* parent] directory 5.(*guía de teléfonos*) telephone directory *Brit*, phonebook *Am*

directriz *f* 1.(*orientación*) guideline 2. MAT directrix

dirigente *mf* leader; **los ~s** the leadership; **preparar a los ~s** to train the leadership

dirigible I. *adj* steerable II. *m* (*globo*) airship

dirigido, -a *adj* (*sistemas*) remote-controlled

dirigir <g→j> I. *vt* 1.(*un coche, un buque*) to steer 2.(*el tráfico*) to direct 3.(*un envío, palabras*) to address 4.(*la vista*) to turn; ~ **todas sus atenciones a algo** *fig* to focus all one's effort on sth 5.(*una nación*) to lead; (*empresa*) to manage; (*finca*) to run; (*orquesta, debate*) to conduct; ~ **una casa** to run a household 6.(*por un camino*) to lead 7. CINE, TEAT, TV to direct; **una película dirigida por...** a film directed by... II. *vr:* ~**se** 1.(*a un lugar*) ~**se a** to head for/towards 2.(*a una persona*) ~**se a alguien** to address sb

dirimir *vt* 1.(*contrato, matrimonio*) to annul 2.(*asunto, disputa*) to settle; ~ **los empates** to break a tie

discapacitado, -a *adj* disabled, handicapped

discernimiento *m* 1.(*acción de distinguir*) differentiation; (*capacidad de distinguir*) discernment 2.(*juicio*) discrimination; **obrar sin** ~ to behave indiscriminately

discernir *irr como* cernir *vt* (*diferenciar*) to differentiate; ~ **entre lo bueno y lo malo** to distinguish between good and bad

disciplina *f* discipline

disciplinado, -a *adj* disciplined

disciplinar *vt* 1.(*someter*) to discipline 2.(*enseñar*) to instruct

disciplinario, -a *adj* disciplinary; **sanción disciplinaria** disciplinary measure

discípulo, -a *m, f* 1.(*alumno*) pupil 2.(*seguidor*) disciple

disc-jockey <dis yoqueis> *mf* DJ, disc jockey

disco *m* **1.** (*lámina circular*) disc *Brit,* disk *Am;* (*en el teléfono*) dial; ~ **de freno** brake disc [*o* disk *Am*]; ~ **de horario** parking permit; ~ **de señales** FERRO signal (disc) **2.** MÚS record; ~ **de larga duración** LP; **siempre pones el mismo** ~ *inf* you always go on about the same thing; **¡cambia el** ~ **ya!** *inf* give it a break! **3.** DEP discus **4.** (*semáforo*) traffic light **5.** INFOR disk; ~ **de arranque** boot disk; ~ **duro** hard disk; ~ **flexible** floppy (disk)
discográfico, -a *adj* record
díscolo, -a *adj* disobedient
disconforme *adj* **1.** (*persona*) in disagreement **2.** (*cosa*) incompatible
disconformidad *f* **1.** (*con algo, entre personas*) disagreement; **se te nota tu** ~ **con la decisión** you obviously disagree with the decision **2.** (*de cosas*) incompatibility
discontinuidad *f* **1.** (*inconstancia*) discontinuity **2.** (*interrupción*) interruption
discontinuo, -a *adj* **1.** (*inconstante*) discontinuous **2.** (*interrumpido*) interrupted
discordancia *f* **1.** (*disconformidad*) disagreement; **hubo** ~**s a la hora de elegir un representante** there was a clash over the choice of representative **2.** MÚS discordance, dissonance
discordante *adj* **1.** (*opinión*) conflicting **2.** MÚS discordant, dissonant
discordar <o→ue> *vi* **1.** (*cosas*) to clash **2.** (*personas*) to disagree **3.** (*instrumento*) to be out of tune
discorde *adj* **1.** (*persona*) in disagreement **2.** MÚS discordant
discordia *f* discord
discoteca *f* **1.** (*local*) disco(thèque) **2.** (*discos*) record collection
discreción *f* discretion; ~ **absoluta** strict privacy; **a** ~ at one's discretion; **bajo** ~ confidentially; **con** ~ tactfully; **entregarse a** ~ MIL to surrender unconditionally
discrecional *adj* discretional; **cuestión** ~ optional matter; **parada** ~ request stop
discrepancia *f* **1.** (*entre cosas*) discrepancy **2.** (*entre personas*) disagreement
discrepante *adj* divergent
discrepar *vi* **1.** (*diferenciarse*) to differ **2.** (*disentir*) to dissent; **discrepo de lo que Ud. piensa sobre eso** I disagree with what you think about that
discreto, -a *adj* (*reservado*) discreet; (*cantidad*) modest
discriminación *f* **1.** (*perjuicio*) discrimination **2.** (*diferenciación*) differentiation; **de difícil** ~ difficult to distinguish between
discriminar *vt* **1.** (*diferenciar*) to differentiate (between) **2.** (*perjudicar*) to discriminate against
discriminatorio, -a *adj* discriminatory
disculpa *f* **1.** (*perdón*) apology; **admitir una** ~ to accept an apology; **pedir** ~**s** to apologize; **eso no tiene** ~ there is no excuse for it **2.** (*pretexto*) excuse; **¡qué** ~ **más tonta!** what a stupid excuse!; **¡no valen** ~**s!** no excuses!

disculpable *adj* pardonable
disculpar **I.** *vt* **1.** (*perdonar*) to forgive; **discúlpame por no haberte escrito** forgive me for not writing to you **2.** (*justificar*) to justify; **tu inexperiencia no disculpa ese comportamiento** your inexperience does not excuse such behaviour [*o* behavior *Am*] **II.** *vr:* ~**se** to apologize; ~**se con alguien por algo** to apologize to sb for sth
discurrir **I.** *vi* **1.** (*pensar*) ~ **sobre algo** to ponder on sth **2.** (*andar*) to roam; **los niños discurrían por la feria** the children wandered around the fair **3.** (*río*) to flow **4.** (*transcurrir*) to pass **II.** *vt* to come up with
discurso *m* **1.** (*arenga*) speech; ~ **de clausura** closing speech; ~ **de recepción** opening speech; ~ **solemne** formal speech; **pronunciar un** ~ to make a speech **2.** (*plática*) talk **3.** (*disertación escrita*) dissertation; (*oral*) presentation **4.** (*raciocinio*) reasoning **5.** (*transcurso*) passing
discusión *f* **1.** (*debate*) discussion; ~ **del presupuesto** POL budget debate; ~ **pública** public debate **2.** (*riña*) argument; **entablar una** ~ to start an argument; **sin** ~ without argument [*o* question]
discutible *adj* **1.** (*disputable*) debatable **2.** (*dudoso*) doubtful
discutido, -a *adj* controversial
discutir **I.** *vi, vt* **1.** (*hablar*) to discuss; ~ **un asunto** to discuss sth; ~ **un plan a fondo** to discuss a plan in detail; ~ **el recorte del presupuesto** to debate the budget cut; ~ **sobre el precio** to argue about the price **2.** (*opinar diferentemente*) ~ **de** [*o* **sobre**] **algo** to argue about [*o* over] sth **II.** *vt* (*contradecir*) **siempre me discutes lo que digo** you always contradict what I say
disecar <c→qu> *vt* **1.** ANAT to dissect **2.** (*preparar un animal muerto*) to stuff **3.** (*secar una flor*) to press
disección *f* ANAT dissection
diseminar **I.** *vt* **1.** (*semillas*) to disperse **2.** (*noticias*) to spread **II.** *vr:* ~**se** to spread
disensión *f* **1.** (*desavenencia*) disagreement **2.** (*riña*) quarrel
disentería *f* MED dysentery
disentimiento *m* disagreement
disentir *irr como sentir vi* to dissent; **disiento de tu opinión** I disagree with you; **en religión disentimos profundamente** we have deep differences regarding religion
diseñador(a) *m(f)* **1.** (*dibujante*) artist **2.** (*decorador*) designer
diseñar *vt* **1.** (*crear*) to design **2.** (*dibujar*) to draw; (*delinear*) to draught *Brit,* to draft *Am* **3.** (*proyectar*) to plan
diseño *m* **1.** (*dibujo*) drawing; (*boceto*) sketch; (*esbozo*) outline; ~ **de construcción** construction plan; ~ **de página** *t.* INFOR page design **2.** (*forma*) design; ~ **ergonómico** ergonomic design **3.** (*en tejidos*) pattern **4.** (*descripción*) description

disertación f (escrita) dissertation; (oral) presentation

disertar vi (por escrito) to write a dissertation; (oralmente) to give a presentation, to expound

disfraz m 1.(para engañar) disguise; (para la cara) mask; (traje) fancy dress, costume; MIL camouflage 2.(disimulación) pretence Brit, pretense Am; **presentarse sin** ~ to be frank

disfrazar <z→c> I. vt 1.(enmascarar) to disguise; (la cara) to cover with a mask; MIL to camouflage 2.(escándalo) to cover up; (voz) to disguise; (sentimiento) to hide; ~ **su embarazo** to conceal one's pregnancy; ~ **su tristeza con una sonrisa** to hide one's sadness behind a smile II. vr: ~**se de** (enmascararse) to disguise oneself as

disfrutar vi, vt 1.(gozar) ~ **de algo** to enjoy sth; ~ **de excelente salud** to enjoy excellent health; ~ **de licencia** to be on leave 2.(poseer) ~ **de algo** to have sth (de); **este coche disfruta de muchas comodidades** this car has a number of features for your added comfort 3.(utilizar) to have the use; (sacar provecho) to have the benefit

disfrute m 1.(goce) enjoyment 2.(aprovechamiento) benefit

disgregación f disintegration; Fís splitting; GEO, METEO erosion

disgregar <g→gu> I. vt 1.(materia) to disintegrate; Fís to split 2.(gente) to disperse II. vr: ~**se** 1.(gente) to disperse; **el público se disgregó al terminar el espectáculo** the audience dispersed when the show ended 2.(materia) to disintegrate; Fís to split

disgustar I. vt 1.(desagradar) to displease; **me disgusta** I don't like it 2.(enfadar) to anger; (ofender) to offend II. vr: ~**se** 1.(enfadarse) ~**se por** [o **de**] **algo** to get angry about sth 2.(ofenderse) ~**se por algo** to be offended about sth; **se ha disgustado por tus comentarios** he/she took offence [o offense Am] at your comments 3.(reñir) ~**se con alguien** to quarrel with sb

disgusto m 1.(desagrado) displeasure; (repugnancia) repulsion; **estar a** ~ to be ill at ease 2.(aflicción) suffering; (molestia) annoyance; (enfado) anger; **dar un** ~ **a alguien** (afligir) to cause sb suffering; (causar molestias) to annoy sb 3.(pelea) quarrel

disidencia f 1.(desavenencia) disagreement 2. POL dissent

disidente adj, mf dissident

disimulación f 1.(fingimiento) pretence Brit, pretense Am 2.(ocultación) concealment 3.(tolerancia) tolerance

disimulado, -a I. adj 1.(fingido) feigned 2.(encubierto) concealed 3.(engañoso) misleading; (hipócrita) hypocritical II. m, f 1.(hipócrita) hypocrite 2. **hacerse el** ~ to feign ignorance

disimular I. vi to pretend II. vt 1.(ocultar) to conceal; ~ **el miedo** to hide one's fear; **no** ~

algo to not hide sth; **la falda disimulaba su barriga** the skirt made her stomach look smaller 2.(paliar) to make better 3.(tolerar) to tolerate; ~ **algo a alguien** to tolerate sth from sb

disimulo m 1.(fingimiento) pretence Brit, pretense Am; (engaño) deceit; **con** ~ furtively 2.(tolerancia) tolerance

disipación f 1.(desvanecimiento) dispelling; (volatilización) dispersal; fig scattering 2.(libertinaje) dissipation 3.(derroche) waste

disipado, -a adj 1.(libertino) dissipated 2.(que derrocha) wasteful

disipador(a) I. adj wasteful II. m(f) spendthrift

disipar I. vt 1.(nubes, niebla) to disperse; (dudas) to dispel; **el sol disipa las nieblas** the sun disperses the clouds; ~ **el cansancio** to dispel one's tiredness 2.(derrochar) to squander II. vr: ~**se** to disperse; (dudas) to vanish; ~**se en humo** (desaparecer) to vanish into thin air; (fracasar) to go up in smoke

dislate m 1.(absurdo) absurdity 2.(disparate) nonsense

dislexia f dyslexia

disléxico, -a adj, m, f dyslexic

dislocación f 1. MED dislocation 2.(desplazamiento) displacement; GEO fault 3.(desfiguración) dismemberment

dislocar <c→qu> I. vt 1. MED to dislocate 2.(desplazar) to displace 3.(desfigurar) to dismember II. vr: ~**se** 1.(deshacerse) to come apart 2.(desarticularse) to be dislocated

disminución f decrease; ~ **de los gastos** fall in spending; ~ **de la natalidad** decline in the birth rate; ~ **de la pena** JUR remission of sentence; ~ **de peso** weight loss; ~ **de los precios** fall in prices; ~ **de la presión** TÉC loss of pressure; ~ **de la producción** fall in production; ~ **de riesgo** risk reduction; ~ **de tamaño** reduction in size; ~ **de la tensión** reduction of tension; ~ **del valor** depreciation; ~ **de las ventas** fall in sales; **ir en** ~ to diminish

disminuir irr como huir I. vi (en intensidad) to diminish; (número) to decrease; (existencias) to decline; ~ **de tamaño** to shrink II. vt to diminish; (precio, sueldo) to lower; (velocidad) to reduce; ~ **de tamaño** to make smaller; ~ **en duración** to make shorter; ~ **la ganancia** to reduce profits

disnea f MED laboured [o labored Am] breathing

disociación f separation

disociar vt, vr: ~**se** to separate

disoluble adj 1.(contrato) rescindible 2. QUÍM soluble

disolución f 1.(dilución) dissolution; (de la familia) break-up; (de las costumbres) dissoluteness; ~ **de contrato** rescission of a contract 2. QUÍM solution

disoluto, -a I. adj dissolute II. m, f debauchee

disolvente m QUÍM solvent; (para pintura) thinner

disolver *irr como volver vt, vr:* ~**se** (*manifestación*) to dissolve; (*reunión*) to break up

disonancia *f* **1.** MÚS dissonance **2.** (*desproporción*) difference **3.** (*discordancia*) discord

dispar *adj* dissimilar

disparado, -a *adj salir* ~ to rush off

disparador *m* **1.** (*de un arma*) trigger; **poner en el** ~ *inf* to drive to distraction **2.** FOTO shutter release; ~ **automático** automatic shutter release

disparar **I.** *vt* (*un proyectil, el arma*) to fire; ~ **un tiro/flechas a** [o **contra**] **alguien** to fire a shot/arrows at sb; ~ **una piedra contra alguien** to throw a stone at sb **II.** *vi* **1.** (*tirar*) to fire; ~ **contra alguien** to fire at sb; **esta pistola no dispara bien** this pistol doesn't fire well **2.** *AmL* (*caballo*) to bolt **III.** *vr:* ~**se 1.** (*arma*) to go off **2.** (*precios*) to shoot up **3.** (*salir corriendo*) to rush off; (*caballo*) to bolt **4.** (*desbocarse*) to blow one's top

disparatado, -a *adj* **1.** (*absurdo*) nonsensical **2.** *inf* (*desmesurado*) outrageous

disparatar *vi* (*hablar*) to talk nonsense; (*obrar*) to act foolishly

disparate *m* **1.** (*insensatez: acción*) foolish act; (*comentario*) foolish remark; (*idea*) foolish idea **2.** *inf* (*mucho*) **me gusta un** ~ I really love him/her/it; **costar un** ~ to cost a fortune

disparidad *f* disparity; ~ **de precios** ECON difference in prices

disparo *m* **1.** (*el disparar*) firing **2.** (*tiro*) shot; ~ **al aire** shot into the air; ~ **de partida** firing of starting pistol

dispendio *m* (*derroche*) waste; (*de dinero*) squandering

dispensa *f* (*excepción*) exemption; REL dispensation; ~ **de edad** JUR exemption on grounds of age

dispensable *adj* (*impedimento*) dispensable; (*error*) forgivable

dispensador *m*, **dispensadora** *f* (*aparato*) dispenser

dispensar *vt* **1.** (*otorgar*) to give out; ~ **cuidados a alguien** to care for sb; ~ **favores/atención a alguien** to lavish favours/attention on sb; ~ **ovaciones/elogios a alguien** to shower sb with acclaim/praise; **le** ~**on un tratamiento privilegiado** they gave him/her special treatment **2.** (*librar*) to release; (*de molestias*) to relieve; ~ **a alguien de su cargo** to relieve sb of his/her position; ~ **a alguien del servicio militar** to exempt sb from military service; **me** ~**on del castigo** they let me off being punished **3.** (*excusar*) to forgive; **dispénseme que le interrumpa** forgive me for interrupting

dispensario *m* dispensary; ~ **sanitario** (health) clinic

dispepsia *f* dyspepsia

dispersar **I.** *vt* to spread; (*personas, animales*) to disperse; MIL to put to flight; (*una manifestación*) to break up; (*light*) to diffuse; FÍS to scatter; ~ **sus energías** to divide one's

energy **II.** *vr:* ~**se** (*semillas*) to be dispersed; (*personas, animales*) to disperse; MIL to spread out

dispersión *f* dispersion; FÍS diffusion; ~ **de la luz** diffusion of light; ~ **de la nubosidad** dispersion of the clouds; **pintura de** ~ emulsion paint; **la** ~ **de las tropas** the dispersal of the troops; **la** ~ **de los manifestantes** the breaking up of the demonstration

disperso, -a *adj* scattered; MIL in disarray

displicencia *f* **1.** (*desagrado*) displeasure; **tratar con** ~ to treat with contempt **2.** (*desaliento*) indifference

displicente *adj* contemptuous

disponer *irr como poner* **I.** *vi* to have the use; **puede** ~ **de mí cuando Ud. quiera** I am at your disposal; ~ **de tiempo** to have time **II.** *vt* **1.** (*colocar*) to place; ~ **las sillas en círculo** to set out the chairs in a circle **2.** (*preparar*) to prepare; (*la mesa*) to lay; ~ **las camas para los huéspedes** to make the beds for the guests **3.** (*determinar*) to stipulate; ~ **en testamento** to dispose of in a will **III.** *vr:* ~**se 1.** (*colocarse*) to position oneself **2.** (*prepararse*) to get ready; **me disponía a escribir la carta cuando...** I was getting ready to write the letter when ...

disponibilidad *f* **1.** (*disposición*) availability **2.** *pl* (*dinero*) resources *pl;* **nuestras** ~**es no nos permitirán nunca comprar una casa** it will never be within our means to buy a house

disponible *adj* available

disposición *f* **1.** (*colocación*) arrangement; ~ **del espacio** organization of space **2.** (*de ánimo, salud*) disposition **3.** (*para algún fin*) preparation; ~ **de servicio** service provision; **estar en** ~ **de hacer algo** to be ready to do sth **4.** (*disponibilidad*) availability; **de libre** ~ freely available; **estoy a su** ~ I am at your disposal; **poner a** ~ to make available **5.** (*talento*) aptitude; **tener** ~ **para la música** to have an aptitude for music **6.** (*resolución*) agreement; ~ **legal** legal provision; **última** ~ last will and testament; **tomar las disposiciones precisas** to take the appropriate measures

dispositivo *m* device; ~ **de alarma** burglar alarm; ~ **antirrobo** anti-theft device; ~ **de cambio de velocidades** AUTO gears *pl;* ~ **sensitivo** TÉC sensor; ~ **de televisión** video security system; ~ **de visualización** INFOR monitor; ~ **táctico** MIL plan of action; ~ **intrauterino** MED intrauterine device

dispuesto, -a **I.** *pp de* **disponer** **II.** *adj* **1.** (*preparado*) ready; ~ **para el uso** ready to use; **estar** ~ **para salir** to be ready to go out; **estar** ~ **a trabajar/a negociar** to be prepared to work/to negotiate **2.** (*habilidoso*) capable **3.** (*de buen cuerpo*) well-built **4.** (*de ánimo, salud*) **estar bien** ~ (*ánimo*) to be in a good frame of mind; (*de salud*) to be well; **estar mal** ~ (*ánimo*) to be in a poor frame of mind; (*de salud*) to be indisposed

disputa *f* (*pelea*) fight; (*conversación*) argu-

ment; ~ **legal** legal dispute; **sin** ~ without argument [*o* question]; **en** ~ at issue
disputable *adj* disputable
disputado, -a *adj* hard-fought
disputar I. *vi* to argue II. *vt* **1.** (*controvertir*) to dispute **2.** (*competir*) to compete for; ~ **una carrera** to contest a race III. *vr:* ~**se** to compete with one another (for); **todos se disputan la foto** they all want the photograph
disquete *m* INFOR floppy disk; ~ **de arranque** start-up disk; ~ **de destino** destination drive; ~ **para instalación** setup disk
disquetera *f* disk drive
disquisición *f* treatise
distancia *f t. fig* distance; ~ **focal** FÍS focal length; ~ **entre ruedas** AUTO inter-wheel spacing; ~ **de seguridad** safe distance; ~ **visual** visibility; **a** ~ (*lejos*) far away; (*desde lejos*) from a distance; **¿a qué** ~**?** how far?; **acortar** ~**s** to close the gap; **cubrir** ~**s** to cover a lot of ground; **guardar las** ~**s** *fig* to keep one's distance; **tener a alguien a** ~ to keep sb at arm's length
distanciado, -a *adj t. fig* distant; **están** ~**s** *fig* they have drifted apart
distanciamiento *m fig* distance
distanciar I. *vt* to distance II. *vr:* ~**se 1.** (*de una persona*) to drift apart **2.** (*de un lugar*) to move away
distante *adj t. fig* distant
distar *vi* to be distant; **disto mucho de creerlo** that's very hard for me to believe
distender <e→ie> *vt* **1.** (*estirar*) to stretch **2.** (*aflojar*) to loosen; *fig* to relax
distensión *f* **1.** (*relajación*) easing of tension; POL détente; TÉC slackening **2.** MED strain
distinción *f* **1.** (*diferenciación*) distinction; **a** ~ **de algo** in contrast to sth; **no hacer** ~ to make no distinction; **sin** ~ de irrespective of **2.** (*claridad*) clarity **3.** (*honor*) distinction **4.** (*elegancia*) refinement; (*educación*) good manners *pl*
distinguible *adj* **1.** (*diferenciable*) distinguishable **2.** (*visible*) visible
distinguido, -a *adj* **1.** (*ilustre*) distinguished **2.** (*elegante*) refined **3.** (*en cartas*) Dear; ~ **amigo:...** Dear Sir, ...
distinguir <gu→g> I. *vt* **1.** (*diferenciar*) to distinguish; **no** ~ **lo blanco de lo negro** *inf* to not be able to tell left from right **2.** (*señalar*) to single out **3.** (*divisar*) to make out **4.** (*condecorar*) to honour *Brit*, to honor *Am;* (*tratar mejor*) to favour *Brit,* to favor *Am;* ~ **a alguien con su confianza** to honour [*o* honor *Am*] sb with one's trust II. *vr:* ~**se 1.** (*poder ser visto*) to be noticeable **2.** (*ser diferente*) to be different
distintivo *m* emblem
distintivo, -a *adj* **característica distintiva** distinguishing characteristic
distinto, -a *adj* **1.** (*diferente*) different; **es** ~ **a** [*o* de] **los demás** he is different from the others; **operaciones distintas a la actividad**

de la empresa activities which are different from the company's usual business **2.** (*nítido*) distinct **3.** *pl* (*varios*) various
distorsión *f* **1.** MED sprain **2.** FÍS distortion **3.** (*falseamento*) distortion; **distorsiones de competencia** distortion of the market
distorsionar I. *vt* to distort II. *vr:* ~**se** MED to sprain
distracción *f* **1.** (*entretenimiento*) pastime **2.** (*falta de atención*) distraction **3.** JUR ~ **de fondos** embezzlement
distraer I. *vt* **1.** (*entretener*) to entertain **2.** (*dinero*) to embezzle **3.** (*desviar*) to divert II. *vr:* ~**se 1.** (*entretenerse*) to amuse oneself; **el niño se distrae sólo** the child amuses himself **2.** (*no atender*) to be distracted
distraído, -a I. *adj* **1.** (*desatento*) distracted **2.** (*entretenido*) entertaining **3.** *Chile, Méx* (*mal vestido*) badly dressed II. *m, f* **hacerse el** ~ to pretend to not notice
distribución *f* **1.** (*repartición, disposición*) distribution; (*de correo*) delivery; ~ **de agua** water distribution; ~ **de equipajes** baggage reclaim; ~ **del espacio** spatial distribution; ~ **de funciones** division of functions; ~ **de información** distribution of information **2.** COM distribution; ~ **exclusiva** exclusive distribution; ~ **mayorista** wholesale distribution **3.** FIN sharing out; ~ **de beneficios** profit breakdown **4.** CINE, TÉC distribution; **armario de** ~ ELEC connection cabinet
distribuidor *m* **1.** TÉC distributor; ~ **automático** automatic dispenser; ~ **automático de billetes** ticket dispenser **2.** COM dealer
distribuidor(a) *m(f)* distributor; ~ **exclusivo** exclusive distributor; ~ **industrial** industrial retailer; ~ **oficial** official dealer
distribuir *irr como huir* I. *vt* **1.** (*repartir*) to distribute; (*disponer*) to arrange; (*una tarea*) to allocate; (*el correo*) to deliver **2.** COM to distribute **3.** FIN to share out II. *vr:* ~**se** to divide up
distributivo, -a *adj* distributive; **justicia distributiva** retributive justice (*branch of law dealing with redistribution of incomes through taxation*)
distrito *m* district; ~ **electoral** constituency; ~ **industrial** industrial area; ~ **judicial** jurisdiction; ~ **de policía** police district
disturbio *m* disturbance, riot
disuadir *vt* to dissuade; ~ **a alguien de algo** to dissuade sb from sth
disuasión *f* dissuasion; POL, MIL deterrence
disuasivo, -a *adj* dissuasive; POL, MIL deterrent; **poder** ~ deterrent
disuelto, -a *pp de* **disolver**
disyuntiva *f* choice
disyuntivo, -a *adj* disjunctive; **conjunción disyuntiva** LING disjunctive (conjunction)
dita *f* **1.** AmC, *Chile* debt **2.** ECON (*cosa*) bond; (*persona*) bondsman
DIU *m* MED *abr de* **dispositivo intrauterino** IUD

diurético, -a *adj* diuretic
diurno, -a *adj* daily; **trabajo** ~ day work; **luz diurna artificial** artificial daylight
diva *f* diva
divagación *f* 1. (*desviación*) digression 2. *pl* (*sin concierto*) ramblings *pl*
divagar <g→gu> *vi* 1. (*desviarse*) to digress 2. (*hablar sin concierto*) to ramble
diván *m* divan
divergencia *f* divergence
divergente *adj* divergent; **opiniones ~s** differing opinions
divergir <g→j> *vi* t. MAT to diverge; (*opiniones*) to differ; (*personas*) to disagree
diversidad *f* diversity
diversificación *f* 1. (*variedad*) diversity 2. ECON diversification
diversificar <c→qu> I. *vt* to diversify; ~ **los horizontes** to broaden one's horizons II. *vr:* ~**se** to diversify
diversión *f* 1. (*entretenimiento*) entertainment 2. (*pasatiempo*) pastime 3. MIL diversion
diverso, -a *adj* 1. (*distinto*) distinct; (*desemejante*) dissimilar 2. (*variado*) diverse 3. ~**s** (*varios*) various; (*muchos*) many
divertido, -a *adj* 1. (*alegre*) amusing 2. (*que hace reír*) funny 3. AmL (*achispado*) tipsy
divertir *irr como sentir* I. *vt* 1. (*entretener*) to amuse; **sus bromas me divierten** his/her jokes are funny 2. (*apartar*) to divert II. *vr:* ~**se** 1. (*alegrarse*) to amuse oneself (*en* with); **¡que te diviertas!** enjoy yourself! 2. (*distraerse*) to be distracted
dividendo *m* dividend; **arrojar** ~**s** to pay dividends
dividir I. *vt* 1. (*partir*) to divide; ~ **por la mitad** to divide in two 2. (*distribuir*) to distribute 3. (*separar*) to separate; **divide y vencerás** *prov* divide and conquer *prov;* (*sembrando discordia*) to disunite 4. (*agrupar*) to divide up 5. MAT ~ **algo entre** [*o por*] **dos** to divide sth by two II. *vr:* ~**se** 1. (*partirse*) to divide 2. (*agruparse*) to divide up into 3. (*enemistarse*) to fall out
divieso *m* MED boil
divinidad *f* 1. (*ser divino*) divinity 2. (*deidad*) deity 3. *inf* (*preciosidad*) **esta mujer es una** ~ that woman is absolutely divine
divinizar <z→c> *vt* 1. (*deificar*) to deify 2. (*santificar*) to sanctify 3. (*glorificar*) to exalt
divino, -a *adj* divine, heavenly
divisa *f* 1. (*insignia*) emblem 2. (*mote*) motto 3. (*en el escudo*) device 4. *pl* (*moneda*) (foreign) currency
divisar *vt* (*percibir*) to make out; **divisé a lo lejos un vehículo** in the distance I made out a vehicle
divisible *adj* divisible; **ser** ~ **por dos** to be divisible by two
división *f* 1. (*partición*) t. MAT division 2. (*separación*) separation 3. (*parte*) portion 4. MIL division 5. (*desavenencia*) disagreement 6. (*de un discurso*) part 7. LING hyphen

divisor *m* MAT divisor; **máximo común** ~ highest common factor
divisoria *f* 1. dividing lines 2. GEO watershed
divisorio, -a *adj* dividing; **línea divisoria de las aguas** watershed
divorciado, -a I. *adj* divorced II. *m, f* divorcee
divorciar I. *vt* to divorce II. *vr:* ~**se** to get divorced; **ella se divorció de él** she divorced him
divorcio *m* 1. (*separación*) divorce 2. (*discrepancia*) disagreement; ~ **de opiniones** difference of opinions
divulgación *f* disclosure; (*publicación*) publication; **libro de** ~ popularizing book
divulgar <g→gu> I. *vt* (*propagar*) to spread; (*dar a conocer*) to make known; (*popularizar*) to popularize II. *vr:* ~**se** (*propagarse*) to spread; (*conocerse*) to become known
Dn. *abr de* **don** ≈ Mr *Brit,* ≈ Mr. *Am* (*used with the forename*)
DNI *m abr de* **Documento Nacional de Identidad** ID
Dña. *abr de* **doña** ≈ Mrs *Brit,* ≈ Mrs. *Am*
do <does> *m* (*de la escala diatónica*) C; (*de la solfa*) doh; ~ **bemol** C flat; ~ **de pecho** high C; **dar el** ~ **de pecho** *fig* to make a great effort; ~ **sostenido** C sharp
dobladillo *m* (*pliegue*) hem; (*del pantalón*) turn-up, cuff
doblador(a) *m(f)* CINE dubbing actor *m,* dubbing actress *f*
doblaje *m* CINE dubbing
doblar I. *vt* 1. (*arquear*) to bend 2. (*plegar*) to fold; **no** ~ do not bend 3. (*duplicar*) to be twice as much as; **mi madre me dobla en edad** my mother is twice my age 4. (*una película*) to dub 5. (*rodear*) to go round; ~ **la esquina** to turn the corner 6. (*convencer*) to convince II. *vi* 1. (*redoblar*) to double 2. (*torcer*) to turn (*a* towards) 3. (*hacer dos papeles*) to play two roles 4. (*campanas*) to toll III. *vr:* ~**se** 1. (*inclinarse*) to bend down 2. (*ceder*) to give in
doble[1] I. *adj inv* 1. (*duplo*) double; ~ **clic** double click; **contabilidad por partida** ~ double-entry bookkeeping; **tener** ~ **nacionalidad** to have dual nationality; ~ **personalidad** split personality 2. (*hipócrita*) two-faced; **Pedro es muy** ~ Pedro is very two-faced II. *mf* t. CINE double
doble[2] *m* 1. (*duplo*) double 2. (*pliegue*) fold 3. (*toque de campanas*) knell 4. (*tenis*) (**partido de**) ~**s** doubles (match)
doble[3] *f* doubles *pl*
doblegar <g→gu> I. *vt* 1. (*torcer*) to 2. (*persuadir*) to persuade II. *vr:* ~**se** 1. (*torcerse*) to twist 2. (*someterse*) to give in; **se doblegó a mis súplicas** he/she gave in to my pleas
doblez[1] *m* (*pliegue*) fold
doblez[2] *m o f* (*hipocresía*) duplicity
doce *adj inv, m* twelve; *v.t.* **ocho**

doceavo, -a *adj* twelfth; *v.t.* **octavo**
docena *f* dozen; **una ~ de huevos** a dozen eggs; **la ~ del fraile** baker's dozen
docencia *f* teaching; **dedicarse a la ~** to be a teacher
doceno, -a *adj* twelfth; *v.t.* **octavo**
docente I. *adj* teaching **II.** *mf* teacher; UNIV lecturer *Brit,* professor *Am*
dócil *adj* **1.** (*sumiso*) obedient **2.** (*manso*) docile **3.** (*metal*) ductile
docilidad *f* **1.** (*sumisión*) obedience **2.** (*mansedumbre*) docility **3.** (*del metal*) ductability
docto, -a *adj* learned; **~ en leyes** well-versed in the law
doctor(a) *m(f)* doctor
doctorado *m* **1.** (*grado*) doctorate **2.** (*estudios*) **curso de ~** doctoral course
doctoral *adj* UNIV doctoral; **tesis ~** doctoral thesis
doctorando, -a *m, f* PhD student
doctorar *vt, vr:* **~se** to gain one's doctorate [*o* PhD]; **~se en historia** to do a doctorate [*o* PhD] in history
doctrina *f* **1.** (*teoría*) doctrine **2.** (*sabiduría*) learning **3.** (*catecismo*) catechism
documentación *f* **1.** (*estudio*) information **2.** (*documentos*) documentation; (*del coche*) vehicle documents *pl,* car papers *pl*
documentado, -a *adj* **1.** (*identificado*) documented; (*personas*) with papers **2.** (*informado*) informed
documental *adj, m* documentary
documentar I. *vt* **1.** (*probar*) to document **2.** (*instruir*) to inform **II.** *vr:* **~se** to inform oneself
documento *m* document; **~s de envío** dispatch documents; **Documento Nacional de Identidad** ID, identity card
dodotis® *m inv* nappy *Brit,* diaper *Am,* pampers® *Am*
dogal *m* (*de animal*) halter; (*de verdugo*) noose
dogma *m* dogma
dogmático, -a *adj* dogmatic
dogo *m* bulldog
dólar *m* dollar
dolencia *f* ailment; **~ respiratoria** respiratory complaint
doler <o→ue> **I.** *vi* to hurt; **me duele la cabeza** I have a headache **II.** *vr:* **~se 1.** (*quejarse*) **~se de algo** to complain about sth **2.** (*arrepentirse*) to regret (*de*)
dolido, -a *adj* hurt; **estoy ~ por tus palabras** I feel hurt by your remarks
doliente *adj* **1.** (*enfermo*) ill **2.** (*afligido*) sorrowful
dolo *m* **1.** (*engaño*) fraud **2.** JUR **con ~** under false pretences [*o* pretenses *Am*]
dolor *m* pain; **~ de cabeza** headache; **estar con ~es** to have labour [*o* labor *Am*] pains; **retorcerse de ~** to writhe in pain; **tengo ~ de barriga** I have (a) stomach ache
dolorido, -a *adj* **1.** (*dañado*) painful; **tener la**

rodilla dolorida to have hurt one's knee **2.** (*apenado*) sad
doloroso, -a *adj* **1.** (*lastimador*) painful **2.** (*lamentable*) regrettable
doloso, -a *adj* fraudulent
doma *f* taming; (*de caballos*) breaking-in
domable *adj* (*animal*) tamable; (*caballo*) breakable
domador(a) *m(f)* (*de circo*) tamer
domar *vt,* **domeñar** *vt* to tame
domesticado, -a *adj* **animal ~** domestic animal
domesticar <c→qu> *vt* **1.** (*animales*) to domesticate **2.** (*personas*) to bring under control
doméstico, -a I. *adj* domestic; **vuelo ~** national flight; **animal ~** pet; **gastos ~s** household expenses **II.** *m, f* (domestic) servant
domiciliación *f* (*orden permanente*) standing order; (*de recibos*) direct debit; (*de una letra de cambio*) bank transfer
domiciliar I. *vt* **1.** (*un recibo*) to pay by direct debit; **~ el alquiler** to pay the rent by standing order; **~ la nómina** to pay the salary direct into sb's account **2.** (*dar domicilio*) to house **II.** *vr:* **~se** to reside
domiciliario, -a *adj* home; **arresto ~** JUR house arrest
domicilio *m* (*de alguien*) residence; (*una empresa*) address; **reparto a ~** home delivery; **~ social** registered office
dominación *f* **1.** (*el dominar*) domination **2.** (*poder*) power
dominante *adj* dominant; **~ en el mercado** dominant in the marketplace
dominar I. *vi* **1.** (*imperar*) to rule **2.** (*sobresalir*) to stand out **3.** (*predominar*) to predominate **II.** *vt* **1.** (*conocer*) to have a good knowledge of; (*idioma*) to have a good command of **2.** (*reprimir*) to control; **~ el odio** to overcome one's hatred **3.** (*sobresalir*) to dominate **4.** (*divisar*) to look out over **III.** *vr:* **~se** to control oneself
domingas *fpl inf* boobs *pl*
domingo *m* Sunday; **~ de Resurrección** Easter Sunday; **~ de Ramos** Palm Sunday; *v.t.* **lunes**
dominguero, -a I. *adj* Sunday **II.** *m, f pey* Sunday driver
dominical I. *adj* Sunday; **descanso ~** Sunday off; **oración ~** Lord's Prayer **II.** *m* PREN Sunday supplement
dominicano, -a *adj, m, f* GEO, REL Dominican
dominio *m* **1.** (*dominación*) control; **~ de sí mismo** self-control **2.** (*poder*) authority **3.** (*territorio*) domain **4.** (*campo*) subject **5.** (*posesión*) ownership; **ser del ~ público** *fig* to be common knowledge
dominó <dominós> *m* (*juego*) dominoes *pl*
don *m* gift; **tener ~ de gentes** to have a way with people; **tener el ~ de palabra** to have a way with words
don, doña *m, f* ≈ Mr *m,* Mrs *f Brit,* ≈ Mr. *m,*

≈ Mrs. *f Am* (*used in combination with the forename*)

donación *f* donation; JUR gift

donador(a) *m(f)* donor

donaire *m* 1.(*gracia*) grace 2.(*chiste*) witticism

donante *mf* donor

donar *vt* to donate

donativo *m* donation

doncella *f* 1.(*criada*) maid 2. *elev* (*muchacha*) maiden

donde *adv* where; **a** [*o* hacia] ~... where ... to; **de** ~... where ... from; **en** ~ where; **la calle** ~ **vivo** the street where I live; **estuve** ~ **Luisa** I was at Luisa's

dónde *pron interrog, rel* where; **¿a** [*o* hacia] ~**?** where to?; **¿de** ~**?** where from?; **¿en** ~**?** where?; **¿~ se habrá enterado?** where can he/she have found out?

dondequiera *adv* 1.(*en cualquier parte*) anywhere 2.(*donde*) wherever; ~ **que estés** wherever you are

donjuán *m* womanizer

donoso, -a *adj* graceful

donostiarra I. *adj* of/from San Sebastian II. *mf* native/inhabitant of San Sebastian

donosura *f* 1.(*garbo*) grace 2.(*gracia*) wit

donut *m* <donuts> doughnut *Brit,* donut *Am*

doña *f v.* **don**

dopar *vt, vr:* ~**se** DEP to take drugs

doping *m sin pl* drug-taking

dorada *f* (*pez*) gilthead bream

dorado, -a *adj* golden

dorar I. *vt* 1.(*sobredorar*) to gild 2.(*tostar*) to brown 3.(*suavizar*) to sweeten; ~ **la píldora** to sugar the pill II. *vr:* ~**se** to go brown

dormilón, -ona *m, f inf* sleepyhead

dormir *irr* I. *vi* 1.(*descansar*) to sleep; ~ **a pierna suelta** [*o* sound] asleep; ~ **de un tirón** to sleep right through the night; ~ **sobre algo** *fig* to sleep on sth; **quedarse dormido** to fall asleep 2.(*pernoctar*) to spend the night; ~ **en casa de alguien** to sleep at sb's house 3.(*reposar*) to rest 4.(*descuidarse*) to let things slide II. *vt* (*a un niño*) to get to sleep; (*a un paciente*) to put to sleep; ~ **la borrachera/mona** *inf* to sleep off one's hangover; ~ **la siesta** to have a siesta [*o* nap]; **¡no hay quien duerma a este niño!** it's impossible to get this child to sleep!; **esta monotonía me duerme** this monotony is sending me to sleep III. *vr:* ~**se** 1.(*adormecerse*) to fall asleep; **se me ha dormido el brazo** I've got pins and needles in my arm; ~**se en los laureles** to rest on one's laurels 2.(*descuidarse*) to not pay attention

dormitar *vi* to doze

dormitorio *m* 1.(*en una casa*) bedroom; (*muebles*) bedroom furniture [*o* set] 2.(*en un colegio*) dormitory

dorsal I. *adj* ANAT dorsal; **espina** ~ backbone II. *m* DEP number

dorso *m* (*reverso*) *t.* ANAT back; ~ **de la mano**

back of the hand; **véase al** ~ please turn over

dos I. *adj inv* two; ~ **puntos** colon; **de** ~ **en** ~ two by two; **están a** ~ DEP it's two-all ▶**cada** ~ **por tres** all the time; **en un** ~ **por tres** in a flash II. *m* two; **los/las** ~ both ▶**como** ~ **y** ~ **son cuatro** as sure as night follows day; *v.t.* **ocho**

doscientos, -as *adj* two hundred; *v.t.* **ochocientos**

dosel *m* (*baldaquín*) canopy; **cama con** ~ four-poster (bed)

dosificar <c→qu> *vt* to measure out

dosis *f inv* dose; **una buena** ~ **de paciencia** a lot of patience; (*drugs*) fix *inf*

dotación *f* 1.(*equipamiento*) equipping 2.(*personal: de un buque*) crew; (*de una fábrica*) workforce; (*de una oficina*) staff 3.(*financiación*) endowment 4.(*donación*) donation 5.(*ajuar*) dowry

dotado, -a *adj* 1.(*con talento*) gifted 2.(*hombre: genitales*) endowed

dotar *vt* 1.(*constituir dote*) to give as a dowry 2.(*equipar*) ~ **de** [*o* con] **algo** to equip with sth 3.(*señalar bienes*) to endow 4.(*financiar*) to provide funds for 5.(*con sueldo*) to provide

dote¹ *m o f* (*ajuar*) dowry

dote² *f* (*aptitud*) gift; ~ **de mando** leadership ability

doy 1. *pres de* **dar**

Dpto. 1. *abr de* **departamento** (*sección*) department 2. *AmL abr de* **departamento** (*distrito*) administrative district

Dr(a). *abr de* **doctor(a)** Dr *Brit,* Dr. *Am*

draga *f* dredge

dragaminas *m inv* minesweeper

dragar <g→gu> *vt* to dredge

dragón *m* 1.(*monstruo*) dragon 2.(*reptil*) flying dragon; ~ **marino** (*pez*) weever fish

drama *m* drama; TEAT play

dramático, -a *adj* dramatic; **autor** ~ playwright

dramatismo *m* dramatism

dramatizar <z→c> *vt* dramatize

dramaturgo, -a *m, f* playwright

dramón *m inf* melodrama, tear-jerker *Am*

drapear *vt* to drape

drástico, -a *adj* drastic

drenaje *m* drainage

drenar *vt* to drain

driblar *vi, vt* DEP to dribble; ~ **a un contrario** to dribble round an opponent

dril *m* (*tela*) drill, duck

droga *f* drug, dope *inf;* ~ **sintética** synthetic drug

drogadicto, -a I. *adj* addicted to drugs II. *m, f* drug addict

drogado, -a *adj* **estar** ~ to be drugged

drogar <g→gu> I. *vt* to drug II. *vr:* ~**se** to take drugs

drogata *mf* pey, *inf* junkie

drogodelincuencia *f* drug-related crime

drogodependencia *f* drug addiction

droguería *f* shop selling soap, shampoo,

cleaning materials etc.
dromedario *m* dromedary
drupa *f* drupe
dublinés, -esa I. *adj* of/from Dublin II. *m, f* Dubliner
ducado *m* (*territorio*) duchy
ducal *adj* ducal
ducha *f* 1. (*para ducharse*) shower 2. MED douche ▸**recibir una ~ de agua fría** to receive a shock
duchar I. *vt* to shower II. *vr:* ~**se** to have [o take] a shower
ducho, -a *adj* skilled
dúctil *adj* 1. (*condescendiente*) easy going 2. (*dilatable*) stretchable; (*flexible*) pliable
duda *f* (*indecisión, incredulidad*) doubt; **salir de ~s** to dispel one's doubts; **sin ~** (**alguna**) without a doubt; **no cabe la menor ~** there is not the slightest doubt; **poner algo en ~** to question sth
dudable *adj* doubtful
dudar I. *vi* 1. (*desconfiar*) ~ **de algo** to doubt sth 2. (*vacilar*) to hesitate II. *vt* to doubt
dudosamente *adv* doubtfully
dudoso, -a *adj* 1. (*inseguro*) doubtful 2. (*indeciso*) undecided 3. (*sospechoso*) dubious
duelo *m* 1. (*desafío*) duel; **retar a** ~ to challenge to a duel 2. (*pesar*) grief 3. (*funerales*) mourning 4. (*cortejo*) funeral procession
duende *m* 1. (*espíritu*) elf; (*fantasma*) ghost 2. **tener** ~ to have charm
dueño, -a *m, f* 1. (*propietario*) owner; (*amo*) boss; ~ **y señor** lord and master; **hacerse ~ de algo** (*apropiarse*) to take possession of sth; (*dominar*) to take command of sth; **ser ~ de sí mismo** (*empresario*) to be one's own boss; **no ser ~ de sí mismo** (*dominarse*) to not be in control of oneself; **poner a alguien como no digan dueñas** *inf* to call sb every name under the sun 2. (*de familia*) head
duermevela *m o f* (*sueño ligero*) light sleep; (*sueño agitado*) restless sleep
dulce I. *adj* 1. (*referente al sabor*) sweet 2. (*suave*) soft 3. (*agradable*) pleasant 4. (*metal*) soft 5. (*agua*) fresh II. *m* 1. (*postre*) dessert 2. (*almíbar*) syrup 3. (*golosina*) sweet *Brit,* candy *Am;* **a nadie le amarga un ~** *inf* gifts are always welcome
dulcificar <c→qu> *vt* 1. (*azucarar*) to sweeten 2. (*suavizar*) to soften; (*hacer más grato*) to sugar
dulzor *m,* **dulzura** *f* 1. (*sabor*) sweetness 2. (*suavidad*) softness 3. (*bondad*) goodness
duna *f* dune
dundera *f* AmL (*bobada*) stupidity
dundo, -a *adj* AmL (*bobo*) silly
dúo *m* duet; **cantar a** ~ to sing a duet
duodécimo, -a *adj* twelfth; *v.t.* octavo
duodenal *adj* MED **úlcera** ~ duodenal ulcer
duodeno *m* ANAT duodenum
dúplex *m* ARQUIT duplex
duplicado *m* duplicate; **por** ~ in duplicate

duplicar <c→qu> *vt, vr:* ~**se** to duplicate
duplicidad *f* (*falsedad*) duplicity
duplo *m* double
duplo, -a *adj* double
duque(sa) *m(f)* duke, duchess *m, f*
durabilidad *f* durability
durable *adj* durable; (*producto*) long-lasting
duración *f* duration, length; (*de un préstamo*) term; **de larga ~** long-term
duradero, -a *adj* long-lasting
durante *prep* during; **hablar ~ una hora** to talk for an hour
durar *vi* 1. (*extenderse*) to last; ~ **todo el día** to last the whole day 2. (*permanecer*) to stay 3. (*resistir*) to last
durazno *m* AmL (*fruta*) peach; (*árbol*) peach tree
dureza *f* 1. (*rigidez*) hardness; ~ **de vientre** constipation 2. (*callosidad*) hard skin
durmiente I. *adj* sleeping; **la Bella Durmiente** Sleeping Beauty II. *mf* sleeper
duro I. *m* five-peseta coin II. *adv* hard ▸**¡dale ~!** *inf* go at it!; (*a personas*) hit him/her as hard as you can!; **quedarse ~** *Arg, inf* to be amazed
duro, -a *adj* hard; ~ **de corazón** hard-hearted; ~ **de oído** hard of hearing; **a duras penas** barely; **estoy contigo a las duras y las maduras** I'll stick with you through thick and thin
DVD *abr de* **videodisco digital** DVD

E

E, e *f* E, e; ~ **de España** E for Edward *Brit,* E for easy *Am*
e *conj* (*before 'hi' or 'i'*) **madres ~ hijas** mothers and daughters
E *abr de* **Este** E
ea *interj* (*animando*) come on
ebanista *mf* cabinetmaker, woodworker
ébano *m* ebony
ebrio, -a *adj elev* 1. (*borracho*) inebriated 2. (*extasiado*) ~ **de** beside oneself with; (*ciego*) blind with
ebullición *f* 1. (*de líquidos*) boiling 2. (*agitación*) turmoil
eccema *m* MED eczema
echado, -a *adj* 1. (*postrado*) lying down; **estar** ~ to be lying down; ~ **para adelante** *inf* pushy 2. *Nic, CRi* (*indolente*) idle
echar I. *vt* 1. (*tirar*) to throw; (*carta*) to post *Brit,* to mail *Am;* (*a la basura, al suelo*) to throw out; **la suerte está echada** the die is cast 2. (*verter*) to pour; ~ **en algo** to pour into sth 3. (*expulsar*) to throw out; (*despedir*) to sack *Brit,* to fire *Am* 4. *inf* (*crecer: pelo*) to grow; (*hojas, flores*) to sprout 5. (*emitir*) to give off; ~ **humo** to let out smoke 6. (*tumbar*) to lie down 7. (*proyectar*) to show; TEAT to

stage; **en el cine echan 'Titanic'** 'Titanic' is on at the cinema [*o* movie theater *Am*] **8.** (*calcular*) **te echo 30 años** I reckon you're 30 **9.** (*tiempo, esfuerzo*) **eché dos horas en acabar** it took me two hours to finish **10.** *Perú* (*emborracharse*) ~**le** to get drunk **11.** *Chile* (*echar a correr*) ~**las** to beat it **II.** *vi* **1.** (*lanzar*) to throw **2.** (*verter*) to pour **3.** (*empezar*) to begin; ~ **a correr** to break into a run **III.** *vr:* ~**se 1.** (*postrarse*) to lie down; **me eché en la cama** I lay down in bed **2.** (*lanzarse*) to jump; ~**se sobre algo/alguien** to fall upon sth/sb; ~**se a los pies de alguien** to throw oneself down before sb; ~**se atrás** *fig* to have second thoughts **3.** (*empezar*) to begin; ~**se a llorar** to burst into tears; ~**se a la bebida** to take to drink **4.** *inf* (*iniciar una relación*) ~**se un novio** to get a boyfriend

echarpe *m* stole; *AmL* (*chal*) shawl
echón, -ona *Ven* **I.** *adj* conceited **II.** *m, f* braggart
eclesiástico *m* clergyman
eclesiástico, -a *adj* ecclesiastical
eclipsar I. *vt* **1.** ASTR to eclipse **2.** (*oscurecer*) to darken **3.** *fig* to outshine **II.** *vr:* ~**se 1.** (*sufrir un eclipse*) to be eclipsed **2.** (*decaer*) to decline
eclipse *m* eclipse; ~ **solar** solar eclipse
eco *m* **1.** *t. fig* echo; **hacer** ~ *fig* to have an impact; **tener** ~ *fig* to arouse interest; ~**s de sociedad** PREN gossip column **2.** (*repercusión*) consequence
ecografía *f* ultrasound scan
ecología *f* ecology
ecológico, -a *adj* ecological; **daños** ~**s** environmental damage; **producción ecológica** AGR organic farming
ecologismo *m sin pl* green movement, environmentalism
ecologista I. *adj* ecological **II.** *mf* ecologist, environmentalist
economato *m* cooperative store
economía *f* **1.** (*situación, sistema*) economy; ~ **de desechos** recycling industry; ~ **forestal** forestry sector; ~ **sumergida** black economy; ~ **de escala** economy of scale; ~ **de oferta** supplyside economy **2.** (*ciencia*) economics; ~ **de la empresa** business economics; ~ **política** political economics **3.** (*ahorro*) saving **4.** (*moderación*) thrift(iness) **5.** (*cosa ahorrada*) savings *pl;* **hacer** ~**s** to economize
económico, -a *adj* **1.** ECON economic; **año** ~ financial year; **estudiar Ciencias Económicas** to study economics **2.** (*barato*) cheap; (*ahorrador*) economical; (*persona*) thrifty
economista *mf* economist
economizar <z→c> *vi, vt* to economize; **no** ~ **esfuerzos** to spare no effort; ~ **esfuerzos** to save one's efforts
ecosistema *m* ecosystem
ecotest *m* ecotest
ecu, ECU *m abr de* **European Currency Unit** ecu, ECU

ecuación *f* equation
ecuador *m* equator; **paso del** ~ half-way point
Ecuador *m* Ecuador

Ecuador lies in the northwestern part of South America. It borders Colombia to the north, Peru to the east and south and the Pacific Ocean to the west. The capital is **Quito**. The official language of the country is Spanish and the monetary unit of **Ecuador** is the **sucre**.

ecuánime *adj* **1.** (*justo*) fair; (*imparcial*) impartial **2.** (*sereno*) level-headed
ecuanimidad *f* **1.** (*imparcialidad*) impartiality **2.** (*calma*) composure
ecuatorial *adj* equatorial
ecuatoriano, -a I. *adj* of/from Ecuador **II.** *m, f* native/inhabitant of Ecuador
ecuestre *adj* equestrian
ecuménico, -a *adj* universal
eczema *m* MED eczema
edad *f* **1.** (*años*) age; ~ **para jubilarse** retirement age; ~ **del pavo** adolescence; **mayor de** ~ adult; **menor de** ~ minor; **ser mayor/menor de** ~ to be of/under age; **a la** ~ **de...** at the age of ...; **¿qué** ~ **tiene?** how old is he/she?; **de mi** ~ of my age; **de cierta** ~ getting on in years; **llegar a la mayoría de** ~ to come of age; **de mediana** ~ middle-aged; **la tercera** ~ old [*o* retirement] age **2.** (*época*) age, era; **la Edad Media** the Middle Ages; **la** ~ **de piedra** the Stone Age
edema *m* oedema
edén *m* Eden; *fig* (*paraíso*) paradise
edición *f* **1.** (*impresión, conjunto de ejemplares*) edition; ~ **de bolsillo** paperback edition **2.** (*de un acontecimiento*) **la presente** ~ **del Festival de Cine** this year's Film Festival
edicto *m* **1.** (*aviso*) announcement **2.** JUR edict
edificable *adj* with planning permission
edificación *f* (*construcción*) construction
edificante *adj* edifying
edificar <c→qu> *vt* **1.** (*construcción*) to build **2.** (*moral*) to edify
edificio *m* building
edil(a) *m(f)* town councillor *Brit*, councilman *m Am*, councilwoman *f Am*
Edimburgo *m* Edinburgh
editar *vt* **1.** (*publicar*) to publish **2.** (*preparar*) to edit
editor *m* INFOR editor
editor(a) *m(f)* **1.** (*que publica*) publisher **2.** (*que prepara textos*) editor
editorial¹ I. *adj* **1.** (*publicar*) publishing **2.** (*preparar*) editing; **casa** ~ publishing house; **éxito** ~ best-seller **II.** *f* publisher
editorial² *m* editorial
editorialista *mf* leader writer
Edo. *Méx, Ven abr de* **Estado** State
edredón *m* eiderdown; ~ **nórdico** duvet,

quilt *Brit,* comforter *Am*

educación *f* **1.**(*instrucción*) education, teaching; ~ **de adultos** adult education; ~ **ambiental** environmental education; ~ **física** ENS physical education; ~ **a distancia** distance learning; ~ **permanente** permanent education; **Educación General Básica** HIST education for children aged 6 to 14; **Educación preescolar** nursery school education; ~ **vial** road education; **Ministerio de Educación y Ciencia** Ministry of Education and Science **2.**(*comportamiento*) manners *pl;* **este niño no tiene** ~ this child has no manners **3.**(*crianza*) upbringing

educado, -a *adj* **1.**(*culto*) cultured, cultivated **2.**(*cortés*) (**bien**) ~ polite; **mal** ~ rude

educar <c→qu> *vt* **1.**(*dar instrucción*) to educate **2.**(*criar*) to bring up; **los padres educan a los hijos** children are brought up by their parents **3.**(*facultades*) to improve; **debes ~ tu oído** you should train your ear

educativo, -a *adj* (*instructivo*) educational

edulcorante *m* sweetener

edulcorar *vt* to sweeten

edutenimiento *m sin pl* edutainment

EEB *f abr de* **encefalopatía espongiforme bovina** MED BSE

EE.UU. *mpl abr de* **Estados Unidos** USA

efe *f* (*letra*) f; **la letra ~** the letter f

efectista *adj* for effect

efectivamente *adv* in fact

efectividad *f* effectiveness

efectivo *m* (*dinero*) cash; ~ **electrónico** electronic cash; **en ~** (in) cash

efectivo, -a *adj* **1.**(*que hace efecto*) effective **2.**(*auténtico*) real; **un éxito ~** a real success; **hacer ~** to put into action; (*cheque*) to cash **3.**(*no interino*) fixed

efecto *m* **1.** effect; ~ **boomerang** boomerang effect; ~ **invernadero** greenhouse effect; ~ **retardado** delayed reaction; **~s secundarios** side effects; **hacer ~** to have an effect; **hacer buen ~** (*impresión*) to make a good impression; **tener ~** to take effect; **llevar a ~** to carry out; **en ~** indeed; **para los ~s** effectively; **con ~s retroactivos** retroactively **2.** COM asset

efectuar <*1. pres:* efectúo> **I.** *vt* to carry out; (*viaje*) to go on; ~ **una compra** to make a purchase; ~ **una llamada** to make a phone call **II.** *vr:* **~se** (*tener lugar*) to take place; (*realizarse*) to be carried out

efemérides *fpl* PREN list of the day's anniversaries

efervescente *adj* (*líquido*) fizzy; **pastilla ~** soluble pill

eficacia *f* **1.**(*de persona*) efficiency; (*de medida*) effectiveness; ~ **económica** economic efficiency; **con ~** effectively; **sin ~** useless **2.** TÉC efficiency

eficaz *adj* (*persona*) efficient; (*medida*) effective

eficiencia *f* (*persona*) efficiency; (*medida*) effectiveness

eficiente *adj* (*persona*) efficient; (*medida*) effective

efusión *f* **1.**(*cordialidad*) effusion; **con gran ~** very effusively **2.**(*derramamiento*) spillage

efusivo, -a *adj* effusive

EGB *f* HIST *abr de* **Educación General Básica** education for children aged 6 to 14

Egeo *m* Aegean; **el mar ~** the Aegean Sea

egipcio, -a *adj, m, f* Egyptian

Egipto *m* Egypt

eglefino *m* haddock

ego *m* PSICO ego

egocéntrico, -a *adj* egocentric, self-centred *Brit,* self-centered *Am*

egoísmo *m sin pl* selfishness, egoism

egoísta **I.** *adj* selfish, egoistical; **ser un ~** to be very selfish **II.** *mf* selfish person, egoist

egregio, -a *adj* eminent, illustrious

egresado, -a **I.** *adj* graduate **II.** *m, f Arg, Chile* (*universidad, escuela*) graduate

egresar *vi Arg, Chile* (*escuela*) to finish school; (*universidad*) to graduate

eh *interj* **1.**(*advertencia*) OK; **no vuelvas a hacerlo, ¿~?** don't do it again, OK? **2.**(*susto, incomprensión*) **¿~?** eh?

ej. *abr de* **ejemplo** example

eje *m* **1.** TÉC, MAT axle; ~ **anterior** front axle **2.**(*centro*) ~ **de la conversación** core of the conversation; **ser el ~ de atención** to be the centre [*o* center *Am*] of attention; **el Eje** HIST the Axis

ejecución *f* execution; (*de proyectos*) implementation; ~ **de un pedido** carrying out of an order; ~ **de la sentencia** JUR execution of sentence; **poner en ~** to carry out

ejecutar *vt* to execute; (*ley*) to enforce

ejecutiva *f* executive (body)

ejecutivo, -a **I.** *adj* **1.**(*que decide*) *t.* JUR executive; **comité ~** executive [*o* administrative] committee; **poder ~** executive power **2.**(*urgente*) urgent **II.** *m, f* (*en cargo directivo*) executive; (*empleado*) manager; ~ **de marketing** marketing executive, executive [*o* administrative] committee

ejemplar **I.** *adj* exemplary; **un alumno ~** a model student **II.** *m* (*ejemplo*) example; (*de libro*) copy; (*de revista*) issue; ~ **de muestra** sample

ejemplarizar <z→c> *vi AmL* to serve as an example

ejemplificar <c→qu> *vt* to exemplify

ejemplo *m* example; **dar buen ~** to set a good example; **poner por ~** to give as an example; **por ~** for example; **sin ~** unprecedented; **predicar con el ~** to practise what one preaches; **tomar por ~** to take as an example

ejercer <c→z> **I.** *vt* (*profesión*) to practise *Brit,* to practice *Am;* (*derechos*) to exercise **II.** *vi* (*como abogado, médico*) to practise *Brit,* to practice *Am;* (*de profesor*) to work

ejercicio *m* **1.**(*de una profesión*) practice; **en ~** practising *Brit,* practicing *Am* **2.** DEP exercise; (*entrenamiento*) training; **el médico me**

recomendó hacer ~ my doctor advised me to take [*o* do] exercise; **tener falta de** ~ to be out of practice **3.** ENS (*para practicar*) exercise; (*prueba*) test **4.** MIL ~ **de las armas** weapons training; ~ **de combate** combat exercise **5.** ECON ~ **contable** tax year; ~ (**económico**) financial year

ejercitar I. *vt* **1.** (*profesión*) to practise *Brit,* to practice *Am;* (*actividad*) to carry out; ~ **la cirugía** to work as a surgeon **2.** (*desarrollar*) to develop **3.** (*adiestrar*) to train **II.** *vr:* ~**se** to train; ~**se en natación** to do swimming training

ejército *m* MIL (*tropas*) army; (*fuerzas armadas*) armed forces; ~ **del aire** air force

ejote *m AmC, Méx* string bean

el, la, lo <los, las> *art def* **1.** the; **el perro** the dog; **la mesa** the table; **los amigos/las amigas** the friends; **prefiero** ~ **azul al amarillo** I prefer the blue one to the yellow one **2.** **lo** + *adj* **lo bueno/malo** the good/bad thing; **lo antes** [*o* **más pronto**] **posible** as soon as possible; **hazlo lo mejor que puedas** do it the best you can **3.** + *nombres geográficos* **el Canadá** Canada; **la China/India** China/India **4.** + *días de semana* **llegaré el domingo** I'll arrive on Sunday; **los sábados no trabajo** I don't work on Saturdays **5.** + *nombre propio, inf* **he visto a la Carmen** I saw Carmen **6.** + *que* **lo que digo es...** what I'm saying is ...; **lo que pasa es que...** the thing is that ... **7.** *como interj* **¡la de gente que vino!** so many people came!

él *pron pers, 3. sing m* **1.** (*sujeto*) he **2.** (*tras preposición*) him; **el libro es de** ~ (*suyo*) the book is his

elaboración *f* **1.** (*fabricación*) manufacture; (*tratamiento*) treatment **2.** (*de comidas*) preparation; **de** ~ **casera** home-made **3.** (*de una idea*) development; (*de una obra*) construction

elaborar *vt* **1.** (*fabricar*) to manufacture; (*preparar*) to prepare **2.** (*una idea*) to develop; (*una obra*) to construct

elación *f AmL* elation, exaltation

elasticidad *f* elasticity

elástico *m* elastic

elástico, -a *adj* elastic; (*concepto*) ambiguous; (*horario, persona*) flexible; (*tela*) stretch

Elba *m* **1.** (*río*) **el** ~ the (river) Elbe **2.** (*isla*) Elba

ele *f* L, l; **la letra** ~ the letter l

elección *f* (*selección*) choice; *t.* POL election; **elecciones legislativas** general election; ~ **parcial** by-election; ~ **de la profesión** career choice; **lo dejo a su** ~ the choice is yours

electo, -a *adj* elect

elector(a) I. *adj* electing **II.** *m(f)* voter; **los** ~**es** the electorate

electorado *m* electorate

electoral *adj* electoral; **colegio** ~ electoral college

electricidad *f* to electricity

electricista I. *adj* electrical **II.** *mf* electrician

eléctrico, -a *adj* (*que usa electricidad*) electric; (*relacionado*) electrical; **máquina eléctrica** electrical appliance

electrificar <c→qu> *vt* to electrify

electrizar <z→c> *vt t. fig* to electrify

electrocardiograma *m* electrocardiogram

electrocución *f* electrocution

electrocutar *vt* to electrocute

electrodo *m* electrode; ~ **positivo/negativo** positive/negative electrode

electrodoméstico *m* household [*o* electrical] appliance

electroimán *m* electromagnet

electromagnético, -a *adj* electromagnetic

electrón *m* electron

electrónica *f* electronics

electrónico, -a *adj* electronic; **microscopio** ~ electron microscope; **correo** ~ e-mail

electrotecnia *f* electrical engineering

electrotécnico, -a *adj* related to electrical engineering

elefante, -a *m, f* elephant *m;* ~ **marino** elephant seal ▶**ver** ~**s volando** to believe anything

elegancia *f* elegance; (*buen gusto*) tastefulness

elegante *adj* elegant; (*con buen gusto*) tasteful

elegantoso, -a *adj inf* posh *Brit*

elegir *irr* **I.** *vi, vt* (*escoger*) to choose; **a** ~ **entre** to be chosen from **II.** *vt* POL to elect

elementado, -a *adj Chile, Col* (*alelado*) bewildered

elemental *adj* basic; **conocimientos** ~**es** basic knowledge

elemento *m* **1.** (*componente, persona*) element; ~ **base** basic element; **tener** ~**s de juicio** to be able to judge; ~ **decisivo** crucial factor **2.** *pl* (*fuerzas naturales*) elements *pl* **3.** *pl* (*nociones fundamentales*) ~**s de matemáticas** basic mathematics *pl* **4.** *pl* (*medios*) resources *pl*

elenco *m* **1.** (*catálogo*) list, catalogue *Brit,* catalog *Am* **2.** TEAT cast **3.** *AmL* (*personal*) staff **4.** *Chile, Perú* (*equipo*) team

elepé *m* LP, album

elevación *f* **1.** (*subida*) rise **2.** GEO elevation

elevado, -a *adj* (*alto*) elevated; (*nivel, estilo*) refined; MAT raised to the power of

elevador *m* **1.** *AmC* (*ascensor*) lift *Brit,* elevator *Am* **2.** *Arg* (*para cargas*) goods [*o* freight] elevator

elevalunas *m inv* AUTO electric window-winder, automatic windows

elevar I. *vt* **1.** (*subir*) to raise; ~ **al trono** to put on the throne **2.** MAT ~ **a** to raise to the power of; **tres elevado a cuatro** three to the power of four **3.** (*enviar*) to present; ~ **una protesta** to lodge a complaint **II.** *vr:* ~**se 1.** (*tener altura*) to rise **2.** (*tener precio*) ~**se a** to amount to; (*cotización*) to stand at **3.** (*hallarse*) to stand

eliminación *f* **1.**(*supresión, de errores*) elimination; (*de aranceles*) abolition; (*de basura, residuos*) disposal **2.** MED discharge **3.** DEP elimination

eliminar *vt* **1.**(*suprimir, matar*) to eliminate; ~ **la competencia** to eliminate the competition **2.** DEP to knock out; **fueron eliminados en la cuarta prueba** they went out in the fourth round

eliminatoria *f* **1.**(*competición*) knockout competition *Brit*, playoff **2.**(*vuelta*) qualifying round; (*atletismo*) heat

elipse *f* ellipse

elipsis *f inv* ellipsis

elite *f*, **élite** *f* elite; **de** ~ top-class

elitista *adj* elitist

elixir *m* elixir

ella *pron pers, 3. sing f* **1.**(*sujeto*) she **2.**(*tras preposición*) her; **el abrigo es de** ~ (*suyo*) the coat is hers

ellas *pron pers, 3. pl f* **1.**(*sujeto*) they **2.**(*tras preposición*) them; **el coche es de** ~ (*suyo*) the car is theirs

ello *pron pers, 3. sing neutro* **1.**(*sujeto*) it **2.**(*tras preposición*) it; **para** ~ for it; **por** ~ that is why; **estar en** ~ to be doing it; **¡a** ~! let's do it!

ellos *pron pers, 3. pl m* **1.**(*sujeto*) they **2.**(*tras preposición*) them; **estos niños son de** ~ (*suyos*) these children are theirs

elocuencia *f* eloquence; **con** ~ eloquently

elocuente *adj* eloquent; **las pruebas son** ~**s** *fig* the evidence speaks for itself

elogiar *vt* to eulogize *form*, to praise

elogio *m* eulogy, praise; **hacer** ~**s** to eulogize; **recibir** ~**s** to be praised; **digno de** ~ praiseworthy

elote *m AmC* maize [*o* corn *Am*] cob

eludir *vt* (*evitar*) to elude; (*preguntas*) to evade; ~ **su responsabilidad** to shirk one's responsibility

emanar **I.** *vi* **1.**(*escaparse*) ~ **de** to emanate from *form*; (*líquido*) to ooze from **2.**(*tener su origen*) ~ **de** to stem from **II.** *vt* to give off

emancipación *f* emancipation

emancipar **I.** *vt* (*liberar*) to free; (*feminismo*) to emancipate **II.** *vr:* ~**se** to become emancipated

embadurnar **I.** *vt* **1.**(*manchar*) ~ **algo de** [*o* con] **algo** to smear sth with sth **2.**(*pintar*) to daub **II.** *vr* ~**se de** [*o* con] **algo** to be smeared with sth

embajada *f* embassy

embajador(a) *m(f)* ambassador

embalaje *m* (*envoltorio*) packaging; (*acción*) packing

embalar **I.** *vt* to pack **II.** *vr:* ~**se 1.**(*correr*) to dash off **2.** *inf* (*hablar mucho*) to talk nineteen to the dozen

embalsamar *vt* **1.**(*cadáveres*) to embalm **2.**(*perfumar*) to perfume

embalsar *vt* to dam

embalse *m* **1.**(*pantano*) reservoir **2.**(*acción*)

damming **3.** *Arg* (*presa*) dam

embarazada **I.** *adj* (*encinta*) pregnant; **estar** ~ **de seis meses** to be six months pregnant; **quedarse** ~ to become [*o* get] pregnant **II.** *f* pregnant woman

embarazado, -a *adj* (*cohibido*) awkward

embarazar <z→c> *vt* **1.**(*estorbar*) to get in the way **2.**(*cohibir*) ~ **a alguien** to make sb feel awkward **3.**(*dejar encinta*) ~ **a alguien** to get sb pregnant

embarazo *m* **1.**(*gravidez*) pregnancy; **interrupción del** ~ abortion **2.**(*cohibición*) awkwardness; **causar** ~ **a alguien** to make sb feel awkward **3.**(*impedimento*) obstacle

embarazoso, -a *adj* awkward

embarcación *f* (*barco*) vessel; ~ **de recreo** pleasure craft

embarcadero *m* pier, wharf

embarcar <c→qu> **I.** *vi* to go on board; (*avión*) to board **II.** *vt* **1.**(*en barco*) to stow **2.**(*avión*) to put on board **3.**(*en un asunto*) to involve **III.** *vr:* ~**se 1.**(*en barco*) to embark **2.**(*avión*) to board **3.**(*en un asunto*) to become involved

embargar <g→gu> *vt* **1.**(*retener*) to confiscate **2.**(*absorber*) to overcome **3.**(*molestar*) to bother

embargo **I.** *m* **1.** COM embargo **2.**(*retención*) confiscation **II.** *conj* **sin** ~ however

embarque *m* **1.**(*de material*) loading **2.**(*de personas*) boarding; **tarjeta de** ~ boarding card

embarrada *f Cuba, PRico, And* **1.**(*desliz*) blunder **2.**(*tontería*) foolishness, stupid act

embarrancar <c→qu> **I.** *vi* (*barco*) to run aground; *fig* to get stuck **II.** *vr:* ~**se** to run aground

embarullar **I.** *vt inf* to mix up **II.** *vr:* ~**se** *inf* to get mixed up

embate *m* **1.**(*del mar*) pounding **2.**(*acometida*) onslaught

embaucador(a) **I.** *adj* deceitful **II.** *m(f)* cheat

embaucar <c→qu> *vt* to cheat

embeber **I.** *vi* to shrink **II.** *vt* **1.**(*absorber*) to absorb **2.**(*empapar*) to soak up **3.**(*contener*) to contain **III.** *vr:* ~**se 1.**(*empaparse*) ~**se de algo** to be soaked in sth **2.**(*enfrascarse*) to become absorbed

embejucarse *vr Col, inf* (*disgustarse*) to get upset; (*encolerizarse*) to get angry

embelesar **I.** *vi, vt* to captivate **II.** *vr* ~**se de** [*o* con] **algo** to be captivated by sth

embellecer *irr como crecer vt* **1.**(*hacer más bonito*) to beautify **2.**(*idealizar*) to idealize

embestida *f* onslaught

embestir *irr como pedir* **I.** *vi* to charge **II.** *vt* **1.**(*atacar*) to attack; (*coche*) to crash into **2.** *inf* (*pidiendo*) to ask for money

emblema *m* emblem; (*de marca*) logo

embobar **I.** *vt* (*asombrar*) to amaze; (*fascinar*) to fascinate **II.** *vr* ~**se en** [*o* con] **algo** to be amazed by sth; (*de fascinación*) to be fascinated by sth

embocadura *f* **1.** (*entrada*) entrance; (*de un río*) mouth **2.** (*vino*) taste **3.** MÚS mouthpiece

embocar <c→qu> *vt* (*enfilar*) ~ algo to slip into sth; **embocó la bola** he/she putted the ball

embolador *m Col, inf* shoeshine

embolar **I.** *vt Col, inf* (*zapatos*) to shine **II.** *vr:* ~se *AmC* to get drunk

embolia *f* embolism; ~ cerebral brain clot

émbolo *m* TÉC piston

embolsar *vt* to pocket

emboquillado *m* filter

emborrachar **I.** *vt* **1.** (*a alguien*) to make drunk **2.** GASTR ~ con algo to soak in sth **II.** *vr:* ~se **1.** (*beber*) to get drunk **2.** (*los colores*) to run

emborrascarse <c→qu> *vr* **1.** METEO to cloud over **2.** (*negocio*) to falter

emborronar *vt* **1.** (*de tachaduras*) to cover with blots and smudges **2.** (*escribir*) to scribble

emboscada *f* ambush; **tender una ~ a alguien** to lay an ambush for sb

emboscarse <c→qu> *vr* (*para atacar*) to lie in ambush

embotellado, -a *adj* (*bebida*) bottled; **vino ~** bottled wine

embotellamiento *m* **1.** (*de vino*) bottling **2.** (*de tráfico*) jam

embotellar **I.** *vt* **1.** (*líquido*) to bottle **2.** (*tráfico*) to block **3.** *inf* (*lección*) to swot up *inf* **II.** *vr:* ~se **1.** (*tráfico*) to get congested **2.** *inf* (*lección*) to swot

embozar <z→c> **I.** *vt* **1.** (*rostro*) to cover **2.** (*hecho*) to hide **II.** *vr:* ~se (*rostro*) to cover one's face

embragar <g→gu> AUTO **I.** *vi* to engage the clutch **II.** *vt* to engage

embrague *m* AUTO clutch

embriagar <g→gu> **I.** *vi, vt* **1.** (*emborrachar*) to inebriate **2.** (*enajenar*) to hypnotize; **este perfume embriaga** this perfume is intoxicating **II.** *vr:* ~se (*emborracharse*) to get drunk

embriaguez *f* **1.** (*borrachera*) inebriation; **en estado de ~** inebriated **2.** (*enajenación*) delight

embrión *m* BIO embryo; (*idea*) beginnings *pl*

embrionario, -a *adj* embryonic

embrollar **I.** *vt* **1.** (*liar*) to mess up; **embrollas todo lo que tocas** you mess everything up; **lo embrollas más de lo necesario** you're overcomplicating things **2.** *CSur* (*engañar*) to deceive **II.** *vr:* ~se to get tangled up; ~se en algo to get involved in sth

embrollo *m* **1.** (*lío*) mess; (*de hilos*) tangle; **meterse en un ~** to get into a mess **2.** (*embuste*) swindle; **no me vengas con ~s** don't try and fool me **3.** (*chanchullo*) dodgy business; **este negocio seguro que es un ~** I'm sure that's a dodgy business

embromado, -a *adj AmL: inf* **1.** (*difícil*) hard **2.** (*molesto*) annoyed

embromar *vt* **1.** (*gastar una broma*) to play a joke on **2.** (*engatusar*) to wheedle **3.** *AmL* (*fastidiar*) to annoy

embroncarse <c→qu> *vr Arg, inf* to get angry

embrujado, -a *adj* bewitched; **casa embrujada** haunted house

embrujar *vt* **1.** (*haciendo brujería*) to captivate **2.** (*embelesar*) to hypnotize

embuchado *m* **1.** GASTR sausage **2.** (*para ocultar*) decoy **3.** POL electoral fraud

embudo *m* **1.** (*aparato*) funnel; **en forma de ~** funnel-shaped; **aplicar la ley del ~** to apply one-sided rule **2.** (*trampa*) deceit **3.** (*de tráfico*) bottleneck

embuste *m* **1.** (*mentira*) lie **2.** (*estafa*) swindle

embustero, -a **I.** *adj* lying; **¡qué tío más ~!** what a swindler! **II.** *m, f* **1.** (*mentiroso*) liar **2.** (*estafador*) swindler

embute *m Méx, inf* (*soborno*) bribe

embutido *m* sausage

embutir **I.** *vt* **1.** to pack; ~ lana en un cojín to pack wool into a cushion; **íbamos embutidos en el tranvía** in the tram we were packed in like sardines **2.** (*el embutido*) to stuff **II.** *vr* ~se de algo to stuff oneself with sth

eme *f* M, m; **la letra ~** the letter m; **mandar a alguien a la ~** *inf* (*mierda*) to tell sb to eff off

emergencia *f* **1.** (*acción*) appearance **2.** (*suceso*) emergency; **estado de ~** state of emergency; **plan de ~** emergency plan; **declarar el estado de ~ en una zona** to declare a state of emergency in an area

emergente *adj* **país ~** emergent country

emerger <g→j> *vi* **1.** (*del agua*) to emerge; **mi jefe emergió de la nada** my boss is a self-made man **2.** (*de la superficie*) to surface

emeritense **I.** *adj* of/from Mérida **II.** *mf* native/inhabitant of Mérida

emigración *f* emigration; (*animales*) migration

emigrado, -a *m, f,* **emigrante** *mf* emigrant; POL emigré

emigrar *vi* to emigrate; (*animales*) to migrate

eminencia *f* **1.** (*talento*) expert; **ser una ~ en su campo** to be an expert in one's field; **ser una ~ en literatura contemporánea** to be a specialist in contemporary literature **2.** GEO height **3.** (*título*) Eminence

eminente *adj* **1.** (*sobresaliente*) outstanding **2.** (*elevado*) high

emisión *f* **1.** TV, RADIO (*difusión*) broadcast; (*en directo*) live broadcast; (*programa*) programme *Brit*, program *Am* **2.** (*de radiación, calor, luz*) emission; **emisiones contaminantes** pollution **3.** FIN issue

emisor(a) *adj* **1.** TV, RADIO broadcasting **2.** FIN **banco ~** issuing bank

emisora *f* broadcasting station; ~ clandestina pirate station; ~ de radio radio station; ~ de televisión television station

emitir *vt* **1.** TV, RADIO to broadcast; (*en directo*) to broadcast live **2.** (*luz, calor, olor, radiación*) to emit, to give off; (*humo*) to let off **3.** (*grito*) to let out **4.** (*dictamen*) to give **5.** FIN to issue

emoción *f* **1.** (*sentimiento*) emotion; (*conmoción*) excitement; **lleno de emociones** full of thrills; **palabras llenas de ~** words full of emotion; **llorar de ~** to cry with emotion; **sin ~** without emotion; **sentir una honda ~** to feel a deep emotion; **dar rienda suelta a sus emociones** to give free rein to one's emotions **2.** (*turbación*) excitement

emocional *adj* emotional

emocionante *adj* **1.** (*excitante*) exciting, thrilling **2.** (*conmovedor*) moving

emocionar I. *vt* **1.** (*apasionar*) to excite; **este libro no me emociona** this book doesn't do anything for me; **sólo la idea ya lo emocionaba** the idea alone was enough to excite him **2.** (*conmover*) to move; **los espectadores estaban emocionados** the spectators were moved; **tus palabras me ~on** I found your words very moving **II.** *vr:* **~se 1.** (*conmoverse*) to be moved **2.** (*turbarse*) to get flustered; (*alegrarse*) to get excited

emolumentos *mpl* salary; (*de un libro*) royalties *pl;* (*honorarios*) fees *pl*

emoticón *m* emoticon, smiley

emotivo, -a *adj* **1.** (*persona*) emotional **2.** (*palabras*) moving

empacar <c→qu> **I.** *vi* AmL to pack **II.** *vt* to pack

empachado, -a *adj* **estoy ~** (*indigestado*) I've got indigestion; (*harto*) I'm so full I feel sick

empachar I. *vt* **1.** (*indigestar*) to give indigestion **2.** (*turbar*) to bother; **para decirlo no me empacha que estés delante** I don't mind saying it in front of you **II.** *vr:* **~se 1.** (*indigestarse*) to get indigestion; (*comer demasiado*) to eat too much **2.** (*turbarse*) to get flustered; **no ~se de expresar sus sentimientos** not to be afraid of showing one's feelings

empacho *m* **1.** (*indigestión*) indigestion; **tengo un ~ de dulces** I've eaten too many sweets; **tengo un ~ de televisión** I'm sick of watching television **2.** (*turbación*) fluster; **no tengo ~ en...** I don't mind ...

empadronamiento *m* registration in local census bureau; **oficina de ~** register office

empadronar I. *vt* to register (for a census) **II.** *vr:* **~se** to register (for a census)

empalagar <g→gu> **I.** *vt* **1.** (*alimento*) to be oversweet **2.** (*persona*) to cloy upon; **tanta cortesía me empalaga** I find all this politeness cloying; **esta película empalaga** this film is too treacly **II.** *vr* **~se de** [*o* con] algo (*hastiarse*) to get sick of sth

empalagoso, -a *adj* **1.** (*alimento*) oversweet **2.** (*persona*) cloying **3.** (*película*) treacly

empalmar I. *vi* **1.** (*dos trenes*) to link up **2.** (*dos caminos, ríos*) **~ con algo** to meet sth; **esta carretera empalma con la nacional** this road joins up with the national highway **II.** *vt* (*maderos, tubos*) to fit together;

(*cables, película*) to splice; (*teléfono*) to connect; **~ a puerta** DEP to shoot on goal **III.** *vr:* **~se** (*sexualmente*) to get a hard-on

empalme *m* **1.** (*acción: de maderos, tubos*) fitting together; (*de cable, película*) splice; (*del teléfono*) connection **2.** (*punto: de maderos, tubos*) join; (*del teléfono*) connection; (*estación*) FERRO transfer station **3.** (*erección*) hard-on

empanada *f* **1.** GASTR pie (*usually containing meat or tuna*); **~ mental** *inf* complete mix-up **2.** (*timo*) swindle

empanadilla *f* small pasty

empanar *vt* **1.** (*rebozar*) to coat in breadcrumbs **2.** (*rellenar*) to fill

empantanarse *vr* (*terreno*) to flood; *fig* to get bogged down

empañarse *vr* (*ventana*) to mist up; (*ojos*) to fill with tears; (*reputación*) to become tainted

empañetar *vt* AmL (*encalar*) to plaster

empapar I. *vt* **1.** (*mojar*) to soak; **la lluvia ha empapado el suelo** the rain has soaked the floor; **el vendaje está empapado de sangre** the bandage is soaked with blood **2.** (*absorber*) to soak up **II.** *vr:* **~se 1.** (*mojarse*) to get soaked **2.** (*un tema*) **~se de algo** to become versed in sth

empapelar I. *vi, vt* (*las paredes*) to (wall)paper **II.** *vt* **1.** (*objeto*) to wrap up **2.** *inf* (*encausar*) to prosecute

empaque *m* **1.** (*gravedad*) portentousness; **andaba con gran ~** he/she walked with great pomp **2.** (*semblante*) air; (*del rostro*) expression; **su ~ era grave** he/she had a severe expression **3.** (*el empaquetar*) packing **4.** AmL (*desfachatez*) cheek

empaquetador(a) *m(f)* packer

empaquetar *vt* **1.** (*objetos*) to pack **2.** (*personas*) **~ en algo** to fit into sth **3.** MIL to punish

emparedado *m* sandwich

emparejar I. *vi* **1.** (*ponerse al lado*) **~ con alguien** to catch up with sb **2.** (*ponerse al nivel*) to draw level **II.** *vt* **1.** (*juntar*) to pair up; **ya estoy emparejado** I've already got a partner; **me quieren ~ con ella** they want to pair me up with her **2.** (*nivelar*) to level **3.** (*ventana*) to leave slightly open **III.** *vr:* **~se** (*formar pareja*) to make a pair; (*parejas*) to pair up; **en el siguiente partido quedé emparejado con Juan** in the next game I was Juan's partner

emparentado, -a *adj* **~ con algo** related to sth; **está bien ~** he married into an important family

emparentar <e→ie> *vi* **~ con una familia** to marry into a family

empastador(a) *m(f)* AmL (book)binder

empastar *vt* **1.** (*rellenar*) to fill; (*cubrir*) to cover; **~ un diente** to have a tooth filled; **~ la cara con crema** to cover one's face with cream **2.** (*libro*) to bind

empaste *m* **1.** MED filling; **tengo dos muelas con ~** I've got fillings in two of my back teeth **2.** (*relleno*) filling; (*cubrir*) covering

empatar I. *vi* **1.** DEP to draw; ~ **a uno** to draw one-all; **estar empatados a puntos en la clasificación** to have the same points in the league table **2.** POL to tie **II.** *vt* **1.** *AmL* (*cuerdas*) to tie together; ~ **mentiras** to tell one lie after another **2.** *CRi, PRico* (*amarrar*) to moor **3.** *Ven, Col* (*importunar*) to annoy

empate *m* **1.** DEP draw; **gol del** ~ the equalizer **2.** POL tie

empatía *f* empathy

empavonar I. *vt AmL* (*pringar*) to grease **II.** *vr:* ~**se** *AmC* to get dressed up

empecinarse *vr* ~ **en algo** to be stubborn about sth

empedernido, -a *adj* **1.** (*incorregible*) incorrigible; **bebedor** ~ hardened drinker; **fumador** ~ chain smoker; **solterón** ~ confirmed bachelor **2.** (*insensible*) unfeeling

empeine *m* instep

empelotado, -a *adj* **1.** (*confuso*) confused **2.** *AmL, inf* (*desnudo*) starkers **3.** *Méx* (*colado por alguien*) infatuated

empelotarse *vr* **1.** *inf* (*enredarse*) to get into a wrangle **2.** *AmL, inf* (*desnudarse*) to strip

empeñado, -a *adj* **1.** (*obstinado*) **estar** ~ (**en hacer algo**) to be determined (to do sth); **lo vi** ~ **en invitarme** I realized that he was set on inviting me **2.** (*discusión*) heated

empeñar I. *vt* (*objetos*) to pawn; ~ **la palabra** to give one's word **II.** *vr:* ~**se 1.** (*insistir*) to insist; **se empeña en hablar contigo** he/she insists on speaking to you; **no te empeñes** don't go on about it; **si te empeñas en beber este vino asqueroso...** if you insist on drinking this disgusting wine ... **2.** (*endeudarse*) to get into debt **3.** (*mediar*) to mediate

empeño *m* **1.** (*afán*) determination; **con** ~ determinedly; **tengo** ~ **por** [*o* **en**] **sacar la mejor nota** I'm determined to get the highest mark; **pondré** ~ **en...** I will try my best to ... **2.** (*compromiso*) commitment **3.** (*de objetos*) pawning; **casa de** ~**s** pawnbroker's

empeorar I. *vt* to make worse; **con tus palabras lo has acabado de** ~ what you've said has just made it worse **II.** *vi, vr:* ~**se** to worsen

empequeñecer *irr como crecer* *vt* **1.** (*disminuir*) to make smaller **2.** (*quitar importancia*) to trivialize

emperador *m* **1.** POL emperor **2.** ZOOL swordfish

emperatriz *f* empress

emperrarse *vr inf* (*obstinarse*) to be bent [*o* dead set] on

empezar *irr vi, vt* to begin, to start; **empezó de la nada** he/she started with nothing; **¡no empieces!** don't start!; ~ **con buen pie** to get off to a good start; **para** ~ **me leeré el periódico** to begin with, I'll read the newspaper; **para** ~ **no tengo dinero y, además, no tengo ganas** first of all, I have no money, and what's more, I don't feel like it

empiezo *m Col, Ecua, Guat* (*comienzo*) beginning

empinado, -a *adj* **1.** (*pendiente*) steep **2.** (*edificio*) high

empinar I. *vt* **1.** (*poner vertical*) to stand up **2.** (*alzar*) to raise; ~ **una botella** to raise a bottle (*in order to drink*); ~ **la cabeza** to raise one's head; ~ **el codo** *inf* to have a drink, to booze *inf* **II.** *vr:* ~**se 1.** (*persona*) to stand on tiptoes; (*animal*) to stand on its hind legs **2.** (*un edificio*) to tower

empipada *f AmL* binge; **darse una** ~ **de chocolate** to have a chocolate binge

empiparse *vr AmL* to have a binge

empírico, -a *adj* empirical

emplaste *m* plaster

emplasto *m* poultice

emplazamiento *m* **1.** (*lugar, situación*) location **2.** JUR summons *pl* **3.** MIL emplacement

emplazar <z→c> *vt* **1.** (*citar*); JUR to summon; **le emplazo para darme una respuesta mañana** you have until tomorrow to give me an answer **2.** (*situar*) to locate; MIL to emplace; **este monumento no está bien emplazado aquí** this isn't the best place for this monument

empleado, -a *m, f* employee; ~ **de oficina** office worker; ~ **de ventanilla** clerk; **los** ~**s de una empresa** company personnel [*o* staff]

empleador(a) *m(f) AmL* employer

emplear I. *vt* **1.** (*usar: medio, técnica, método*) to use; (*tiempo*) to spend; **¡podrías** ~ **mejor el tiempo!** you could use your time better!; **¡ya te está bien empleado!** it serves you right!; **dar algo por bien empleado** to be satisfied at the results of sth **2.** (*dinero*) to invest; **he empleado todo el dinero en la casa** I've put all my money into the house **3.** (*colocar*) to employ; (*ocupar*) to engage; **en estos momentos no estoy empleado** I'm unemployed at the moment **II.** *vr:* ~**se 1.** (*colocarse*) ~**se de** [*o* **como**] **algo** to be employed as sth **2.** (*usarse*) to be used **3.** (*esforzarse*) ~**se a fondo** to put everything into sth

empleo *m* **1.** (*trabajo*) job, post *Brit;* (*ocupación*) employment; **pleno** ~ full employment; **no tener** ~ to be out of work; **crear** ~ to create employment; **solicitud de** ~ job application **2.** (*uso, técnica, método*) use; (*tiempo*) spending; **modo de** ~ instructions for use; **el** ~ **de materias primas y energía** the use of raw materials and energy

emplomadura *f* **1.** (*cubrimiento*) lead covering **2.** (*precinto*) leading **3.** (*plomo*) leadwork **4.** *AmL* (*empaste*) filling

emplomar *vt* **1.** (*cubrir*) to cover with lead **2.** (*precintar*) to seal with lead **3.** *AmL* (*empastar*) to fill **4.** *Col, Guat* (*enredar*) to entangle

emplumar *vt inf* to stick sb with sth

empobrecer *irr como crecer* **I.** *vt* to impoverish; **la edad empobrece los reflejos** age slows one's reflexes **II.** *vi, vr:* ~**se** to become poorer; **este terreno se ha empobrecido** this soil has become less fertile

empobrecimiento *m* 1.(*depauperación*) impoverishment 2.(*empeoramiento*) worsening

empollar I. *vi* 1. *inf* (*estudiante*) to swot 2. *AmL* (*ampollar*) to blister II. *vt* 1.(*ave*) to brood 2. *inf* (*lección*) to swot up; **estar empollado de algo** to have swotted up on sth

empollón, -ona *m*, *f inf* swot

empolvar I. *vt* to cover with dust II. *vr:* ~**se** (*el rostro*) to powder

emponchado, -a *adj* 1. *AmL* (*astuto*) sharp, crafty 2. *Arg, Ecua, Perú, Urug* (*con poncho*) wearing a poncho 3. *Arg, Bol, Perú* (*sospechoso*) suspicious

emponzoñar *vt* to poison

emporio *m* 1.(*ciudad*) trading place; (*centro comercial*) shopping centre [*o* center *Am*], (shopping) mall *Am* 2.(*centro cultural*) cultural centre [*o* center *Am*] 3. *AmC* (*almacén*) store

empotrado, -a *adj* fitted, built-in

empotrar *vt* 1.(*en una pared*) to fit *Brit,* to build in 2.(*chocar*) to crash

empotrerar *vt AmL* to put out to pasture

emprendedor(a) *adj* resourceful, enterprising

emprender *vt* 1.(*trabajo*) to begin; (*negocio*) to set up; ~ **la marcha** to set out; ~ **la vuelta** to go back; ~ **el vuelo** to take off; **al anochecer la emprendimos hacia la casa** at nightfall we set off back to the house 2. *inf* (*principiar una acción*) ~**la con alguien** to take it out on sb; ~**la a insultos con alguien** to begin insulting sb

empresa *f* 1. ECON enterprise; (*compañía*) company; ~ **de mensajería** courier company; **mediana** ~ medium-sized company; **pequeña** ~ small company; ~ **matriz** parent company; ~ **privada** private enterprise; ~ **pública** state-owned company 2.(*iniciativa*) resourcefulness 3.(*operación*) task

empresarial *adj* 1.(*del empresario*) entrepreneurial 2.(*de la empresa*) business; (*compañía*) company

empresario, -a *m*, *f* 1. ECON businessman *m*, businesswoman *f*; **pequeño** ~ small businessman 2. TEAT impresario

empréstito *m* loan; ~ **público** government loan

empujar *vi, vt* 1.(*dar empujón*) to push; (*con violencia*) to shove; (*multitud*) to elbow, to shoulder; **me empujó hacia atrás** he/she pushed me back; **me empujó contra la pared** he/she pushed me against the wall 2.(*empleado*) to dismiss 3.(*instar*) to urge; **su familia le empuja a que se case** his family is urging him to get married 4.(*intrigar*) to intrigue

empuje *m* 1.(*acción*) pushing 2. FIS force; ~ **ascensional** upward force 3.(*energía*) energy; (*resolución*) drive; **persona de ~** pushy person; **no tienes el ~ suficiente para llevar la empresa** you don't have enough

drive to run the company

empujón *m* push; (*violento*) shove, shove; **dar un ~ a alguien** to give sb a shove; **entrar en un local a empujones** to push one's way into a place; **si no le damos un ~ al trabajo no lo acabaremos** if we don't push ahead with it we won't finish it

empuntar I. *vi* 1.(*irse*) to go away 2. *Col, inf* ~**las** to beat it *inf* II. *vt* 1. TAUR (*empitonar*) to gore 2. *Col, Ecua* (*encarrilar*) to direct towards III. *vr:* ~**se** *Ven* (*obstinarse*) to dig one's heels in

empuñadura *f* (*puño*) handle; (*de un bastón*) grip; **de una espada** hilt

empuñar *vt* 1.(*tomar*) to take; (*asir*) to grip; ~ **las armas** to take up arms 2.(*un puesto*) to land 3. *Chile* (*la mano*) to clench

empurrarse *vr AmC* to get irritated

emú *m* emu

emulación *f* 1.(*imitación*) emulation 2.(*competencia*) competition

emular *vt* 1.(*imitar*) to emulate 2.(*competir*) ~ **algo** to compete with sth

émulo, -a *m*, *f* 1.(*imitador*) imitator 2.(*oponente*) competitor

emulsión *f* emulsion

en *prep* 1.(*lugar: dentro*) in; (*encima de*) on; (*con movimiento*) in, into; **el libro está ~ el cajón** the book is in the drawer; **pon el libro ~ el cajón** put the book in the drawer; **he dejado las llaves ~ la mesa** I've left the keys on the table; **coloca el florero ~ la mesa** put the vase on the table; ~ **la pared hay un cuadro** there is a painting on the wall; **pon el póster ~ la pared** put the poster on the wall; **estar ~ el campo/~ la ciudad/~ una isla** to be in the countryside/in the city/on an island; ~ **Escocia** in Scotland; **vacaciones ~ el mar** holidays at the seaside; **jugar ~ la calle** to play in the street; **vivo ~ la calle George** I live in George Street; **estoy ~ casa** I'm at home; **estoy ~ casa de mis padres** I'm at my parents' house; **trabajo ~ una empresa japonesa** I work in a Japanese company 2.(*tiempo*) in; ~ **el año 2005** in 2005; ~ **mayo/invierno/el siglo XIX** in may/winter/the 19th century; ~ **otra ocasión** on another occasion; ~ **aquellos tiempos** in those times [*o* days]; ~ **un mes/dos años** in a month/two years; **lo terminaré ~ un momento** I'll finish it in a moment; ~ **todo el día** all [*o* the whole] day 3.(*modo, estado*) ~ **absoluto** not at all; ~ **construcción** under construction; ~ **flor** in flower; ~**venta** for sale; ~ **vida** while living; ~ **voz alta** aloud; **de dos ~ dos** two at a time; **decir algo ~ español** to say something in Spanish; **pagar ~ libras** to pay in pounds 4.(*medio*) **papá viene ~ tren/~ coche** dad is coming by train/by car; **he venido ~ avión** I came by air [*o* plane]; **lo reconocí ~ la voz** I recognised him by his voice 5.(*ocupación*) **doctor ~ filosofía** Ph.D in Philosophy; **trabajo ~ ingenie-**

ría **genética** I work in genetic engineering; **estar** ~ **la policía** to be in the police force; **estar** ~ **la mili** to be doing military service; **trabajar** ~ **Correos/** ~ **una fábrica** to work in the postal service/in a factory **6.**(*con verbo*) **pienso** ~ **ti** I am thinking of you; **no confío** ~ **él** I don't trust him; **ingresar** ~ **un partido** to join a party; **ganar** ~ **importancia** to gain in importance **7.**(*cantidades*) **aumentar la producción** ~ **un 5%** to increase production by 5%; **me he equivocado sólo** ~ **3 euros** I was only wrong by 3 euros **8.** ECON ~ **fábrica** ex-works; **franco** ~ **almacén** ex-store

enagua(s) *f(pl)* underskirt

enajenación *f* **1.**(*de una propiedad*) transfer **2.**(*de la mente*) derangement; ~ **mental** insanity **3.**(*embeleso*) delight **4.**(*distracción*) distraction **5.**(*entre personas*) estrangement

enajenar I. *vt* **1.**(*una posesión*) to transfer **2.**(*enloquecer*) to drive mad **3.**(*turbar*) to disturb; (*fascinar*) to fascinate II. *vr:* ~**se 1.**(*de una posesión*) ~**se de algo** to transfer sth **2.**(*enloquecer*) to go mad **3.**(*de alguien*) to become estranged

enaltecer *irr como crecer vt* **1.**(*ensalzar*) to praise **2.**(*dignificar*) to ennoble

enamoradizo, -a *adj* romantic; **es un joven** ~ he is a young romantic

enamorado, -a I. *adj* ~ (de alguien/algo) in love (with sb/sth); **estuvimos un tiempo** ~**se** we were in love for a time II. *m, f* lover *m, f;* **día de los** ~**s** St Valentine's Day

enamorar I. *vt* (*conquistar*) to win the heart of; **mi profesora me ha enamorado** I've fallen in love with my teacher II. *vr* ~**se (de alguien/algo)** to fall in love (with sb/sth)

enanito, -a *m, f* Blancanieves y los siete ~s Snow White and the Seven Dwarfs

enano, -a I. *adj* tiny II. *m, f* **1.**(*persona*) dwarf **2.** *inf* (*criatura*) kid; **disfrutar como un** ~ *inf* to have a whale of a time; **te vengaste como un** ~ *inf* you really got your own back

enarbolar *vt* (*bandera*) to hoist; (*cartel*) to stick up; (*espada*) to wield

enarcar <c→qu> I. *vt* **1.**(*arquear*) to bend; (*las cejas*) to arch **2.**(*tonel*) to hoop II. *vr:* ~**se 1.**(*arquearse*) to arch **2.**(*encogerse*) to shrink **3.** *Méx* (*caballo*) to rear

enardecer *irr como crecer* I. *vt* **1.**(*personas*) to fire with enthusiasm; (*pasiones*) to kindle; ~ **los ánimos** to raise spirits **2.**(*enfervorizar*) to inflame **3.**(*sexualmente*) to arouse II. *vr:* ~**se 1.**(*pasiones*) to be kindled **2.**(*entusiasmarse*) ~**se por algo** to become enthusiastic about sth **3.** MED (*inflamarse*) to become inflamed **4.**(*sexualmente*) to be aroused

encabezado *m Guat, Méx* (*titular*) heading

encabezamiento *m* **1.**(*de un escrito, libro, artículo*) heading **2.**(*de una carta: parte superior*) letterhead; (*tratamiento*) form of address; (*primeras líneas*) opening

encabezar <z→c> *vt* **1.**(*lista, grupo*) to head; (*institución*) to be the head of **2.**(*un escrito*) to be at the top of; (*un artículo*) to be the title of; ~ **un libro con una cita** to open a book with a quotation **3.**(*una carta: la parte superior*) to head; (*el tratamiento*) to title; (*las primeras líneas*) to open

encabritarse *vr* **1.**(*animal, vehículo*) to rear up **2.**(*persona*) to lose one's temper

encadenar *vt* **1.**(*poner cadenas*) to chain (up) **2.** *fig* (*unir*) to connect, to link up; (*atar*) to tie down

encajar I. *vi* **1.** *t.* TÉC to fit; (*cerradura*) to bolt; **la puerta encaja mal** the door doesn't fit properly; **esta puerta no encaja con este marco** this door doesn't fit into this frame **2.**(*datos, hechos*) to fit in; **las dos declaraciones encajan** the two statements fit together; **¡ves como todo encaja!** see how everything fits!; **este chiste no encaja aquí** this joke is out of place here II. *vt* **1.** *t.* TÉC to fit; ~ **en algo** to clamp into sth; ~ **dos piezas** to fit two pieces together; ~ **la ventana en el marco** to fit the window into the frame; ~ **el sombrero en la cabeza** to stick a hat on one's head; ~ **la funda en la máquina** to put the covering over the machine **2.** *inf* ~ **un tiro a alguien** to shoot sb; ~ **un golpe a alguien** to hit sb **3.** *inf* (*aceptar*) to take; **no** ~ **la muerte de alguien** not to take sb's death well; **no sabes** ~ **una broma** you don't know how to take a joke **4.**(*gol*) to let in **5.** *inf* (*soltar*) to come out with; ~ **una reprimenda a alguien** to give sb a talking-to; **nos encajó todas sus vacaciones** we had to listen to him/her telling us all about his/her holidays **6.** *inf* (*endilgar*) to palm off on sb; ~ **una tarea a alguien** to palm a task off on sb **7.**(*insertar*) to fit; **tenemos que** ~ **esta historia en la edición de mañana** we have to fit this story into tomorrow's edition III. *vr:* ~**se 1.**(*empotrarse*) ~**se en algo** to crash into sth **2.** AmL, *inf* (*aprovecharse*) to go too far **3.**(*atascarse*) to jam

encaje *m* **1.**(*acción*) fitting **2.**(*tejido*) lace

encajonar I. *vt* **1.**(*en cajones*) to put in a drawer; (*en cajas*) to box (up) **2.**(*a la fuerza*) to cram; **estábamos encajonados en el coche** we were crammed into the car **3.** *fig* (*cortar la salida*) to box in II. *vr:* ~**se 1.**(*apretarse*) ~**se en algo** to squeeze into sth **2.**(*un río*) to narrow down

encalambrarse *vr AmL* **1.**(*calambre*) to cramp up **2.**(*de frío*) to become numb

encalar *vt* to whitewash

encallar *vi* **1.**(*barco*) to run aground **2.**(*asunto*) to founder; (*negociaciones*) to break down

encallecer *irr como crecer* I. *vi, vr:* ~**se** (*piel*) to harden II. *vr:* ~**se** (*persona*) to become inured

encalmarse *vr* to calm down

encaminar I. *vt* **1.**(*orientar*) to guide; **¿me puede** ~ **al pueblo más próximo, por favor?** can you tell me how to get to the nearest village, please?; **estar bien encaminado**

to be on the right track **2.**(*dirigir*) to direct; ~ sus pasos hacia el pueblo to head towards the village; ~ la mirada/la conversación hacia un punto to direct one's gaze/the conversation towards a point; ~ los esfuerzos hacia una meta to focus one's efforts on a goal; medidas encaminadas a reducir el paro measures intended to reduce unemployment; ~ los negocios hacia algo to steer one's business towards sth **II.** *vr* ~se a/hacia algo to head for/towards sth; ~se a la meta to focus on the goal

encamotarse *vr AmL, inf* ~ de alguien to fall in love with sb

encandilar I. *vt* to dazzle; tu belleza lo encandiló your beauty captivated him; escuchar encandilado to listen in raptures **II.** *vr:* ~se **1.** *fig* (*luz, emociones*) to light up **2.** *AmL* (*asustarse*) to be scared **3.** *PRico* (*enfadarse*) to get angry

encanecer *irr como crecer vi, vr:* ~se **1.** (*pelo*) to go grey *Brit*, to go gray *Am;* pelo encanecido grey hair *Brit*, gray hair *Am* **2.** (*persona*) to get old

encantado, -a *adj* **1.** (*satisfecho*) delighted; estar ~ de [o con] algo/alguien to be delighted with sth/sb; ¡~ (de conocerle)! pleased to meet you!; estoy ~ con mi nuevo trabajo I love my new job; estoy ~ de la vida I am thrilled **2.** (*distraído*) estar ~ to have one's head in the clouds **3.** (*embrujado*) haunted

encantador(a) I. *adj* **1.** (*persona*) charming; (*bebé*) lovely, adorable **2.** (*fiesta, lugar*) lovely **3.** (*música*) beautiful **II.** *m(f)* charmer; ~ de serpientes snake charmer

encantamiento *m* spell

encantar *vt* **1.** (*hechizar*) to bewitch; (*serpientes*) to charm **2.** (*gustar*) me encanta viajar I love to travel; me encantan los dulces I love sweet things; me encanta que te preocupes por mí I love the fact that you care about me **3.** (*cautivar*) to captivate; (*fascinar*) to fascinate

encanto *m* **1.** (*hechizo*) spell; romper el ~ to break the spell **2.** (*atractivo*) charm; ¡es un ~ de niño! what an adorable child!

encañado *m* **1.** (*tubos*) drain **2.** (*cañas*) pipes *pl;* (*plantas*) trellis

encapotarse *vr* (*cielo*) to become overcast [o cloudy]

encapricharse *vr* **1.** (*con una cosa*) ~se con algo to be taken by sth **2.** (*con una persona*) to become infatuated, to have a crush on; te has encaprichado con ella you're infatuated with her

encapuchado, -a *adj* hooded

encaramar I. *vt* **1.** (*alzar*) to raise; ~ a alguien a la fama mundial to make sb world-famous **2.** (*alabar*) to praise **II.** *vr:* ~se **1.** (*subir*) ~se a un árbol to climb a tree; ~se a una escalera to climb a staircase **2.** (*de categoría*) to rise; ~se a lo más alto de la

empresa to rise to the top of the company

encarar I. *vt* **1.** (*persona, cosa*) to bring face to face **2.** (*riesgo*) to face up to **3.** (*fusil*) ~ a algo/alguien to aim at sth/sb **II.** *vr:* ~se **1.** (*dos personas*) to be face to face **2.** (*a una dificultad*) ~se a algo to face up to sth **3.** *inf* (*a un superior*) ~se a alguien to stand up to sb

encarcelación *f*, **encarcelamiento** *m* imprisonment

encarcelar *vt* to imprison; estar encarcelado to be in prison

encarecer *irr como crecer vt* **1.** com to raise the price of **2.** (*alabar*) to praise **3.** (*subrayar*) to emphasize; encareció la necesidad de aprender idiomas he/she stressed the need to learn languages **4.** (*insistir*) to urge; me encareció que no dejara de visitarla she urged me not to stop visiting her

encarecidamente *adv* strongly; le ruego ~... I have to insist ...

encarecimiento *m* **1.** com price increase; el ~ de la vida the increase of the cost of living **2.** (*acentuación*) emphasis **3.** (*insistencia*) con ~ insistently

encargado, -a I. *adj* in charge **II.** *m, f* person in charge; ~ de negocios chargé d'affaires; ~ de campo groundsman; ~ de curso course director; ~ de obras site manager; ~ de prensa press officer

encargar <g→gu> **I.** *vt* **1.** (*encomendar*) to put in charge; lo ~on del departamento de ventas they put him in charge of the sales department; encargó a su hija a una vecina he asked a neighbour [o neighbor *Am*] to look after his daughter **2.** (*comprar*) to order **3.** (*mandar*) to ask; me han encargado que ocupe la presidencia I have been asked to take over the presidency **4.** jur to commission **II.** *vr* ~se de algo to take responsibility for sth; tengo que ~me aún de un par de cosas I still have to get a couple of things done

encargo *m* **1.** (*pedido*) order; ~ por anticipado advance order; hacer un nuevo ~ to make another order **2.** (*trabajo*) job; traje de ~ tailor-made suit; de ~ to order; por ~ de at the request of; hacer ~s to run errands; tener ~ de hacer algo to be commissioned to do sth; este vestido te viene como hecho de ~ this dress really suits you

encariñado, -a *adj* estar ~ con algo to be very attached to sth; estar ~ con alguien to be fond of sb

encariñarse *vr* ~ con algo to get attached to sth; ~ con alguien to grow fond of sb; el niño se ha encariñado con su tía the child has become attached to his aunt

encarnación *f* incarnation; la ~ del horror the embodiment of horror

encarnado, -a *adj* **1.** (*color carne*) flesh coloured [o colored *Am*]; (*rosado*) pink; (*rojo*) red **2.** (*persona*) incarnate; era el diablo ~ it was the devil incarnate

encarnar I. *vi* rel to incarnate **II.** *vt* (*represen-*

tar) to represent; ~ **a** CINE, TEAT to play the role [*o* part] of

encarnizado, -a *adj* **1.** (*lucha*) bloody **2.** (*herida*) sore; (*ojo*) bloodshot **3.** (*persona*) cruel

encarnizamiento *m* cruelty; (*de la lucha*) fury; (*ensañamiento*) bloodthirstiness

encarpetar *vt* to file away; (*encuadernar*) to bind; *AmL* (*dar carpetazo*) to shelve

encarrilar *vt* **1.** FERRO to put on rails; **ir encarrilado** to be on the right track **2.** (*dirigir*) to guide

encartar *vt* JUR to summon

encasillado *m* (*de un crucigrama*) grid

encasillar I. *vt* **1.** (*meter en casillas*) to pigeonhole **2.** (*clasificar*) to classify **3.** (*considerar*) to consider; **me ~on como un comunista** they considered me a communist **4.** CINE, TEAT to typecast II. *vr* **~se en algo** to limit oneself to sth, to be classified as sth

encasquetar I. *vt* **1.** (*sombrero*) to put on firmly **2.** (*dar*) **~ un golpe a alguien** to hit sb **3.** (*una idea*) to get into one's head **4.** (*endilgar*) to lumber with; **nos ~on la parte peor** we were lumbered [*o* stuck] with the worst part; **me encasquetó un rollo tremendo** I had to listen to him going on and on II. *vr:* **~se 1.** (*sombrero*) to put on one's head **2.** (*idea*) **se te ha encasquetado esa idea** you've got this idea into your head

encausar *vt* JUR to prosecute; (*acusar*) to accuse

encauzar <z→c> *vt* (*corriente*) to channel; (*debate*) to lead; **~ su vida** to sort out one's life

encéfalo *m* MED brain

encefalopatía *f* encephalopathy; **~ espongiforme bovina** bovine spongiform encephalopathy, mad cow disease *inf*

encenagarse <g→gu> *vr* **1.** (*con barro*) to get covered in mud **2.** (*pervertirse*) to become corrupt

encendedor *m* lighter

encender <e→ie> I. *vi* (*fuego*) to catch fire; (*motor*) to fire II. *vt* **1.** (*cigarrillo*) to light; **~ un conflicto** to stir up a conflict **2.** (*conectar*) to switch on **3.** (*pasiones*) to arouse **4.** AUTO, TÉC to ignite III. *vr:* **~se 1.** (*desencadenarse*) to break out **2.** (*inflamarse*) to ignite **3.** (*luz*) go come on; (*ruborizarse*) to blush

encendido *m* AUTO, TÉC ignition; **~ automático** automatic ignition; **~ defectuoso** faulty ignition

encendido, -a *adj* **1.** (*conectado*) **estar ~** to be on; **la luz está encendida** the light is on **2.** (*ardiente*) burning; (*cigarrillo*) lighted; (*apasionado*) passionate; **estar ~** to be lit **3.** (*rojo*) red

encerado *m* blackboard

encerar *vt* to wax; (*lustrar*) to polish

encerrar <e→ie> I. *vt* **1.** (*depositar, recluir*) to lock in [*o* up]; **~ entre paréntesis** to put in brackets **2.** (*contener*) to contain; **la oferta encerraba una trampa** the offer held a trap

II. *vr:* **~se** to lock oneself in; *fig* to cut oneself off

encerrona *f* trap; **preparar una ~ a alguien** to frame [*o* lay a trap for] sb

encestar *vi* DEP to score a basket

enchastrar *vt* *CSur* to dirty

enchilada *f* *AmC* enchilada

enchilado, -a *adj* *Méx* **1.** (*bermejo*) ruddy **2.** (*colérico*) angry; (*rabioso*) furious

enchilar I. *vt* *AmC* **1.** GASTR to season with chilli **2.** (*molestar*) to annoy **3.** (*decepcionar*) to disappoint II. *vr:* **~se** *AmC* (*enfurecerse*) to blow one's top

enchinar I. *vt* *Méx* (*enrizar*) to curl II. *vr:* **~se** *Méx* **1.** (*ponerse carne de gallina*) to get gooseflesh **2.** (*acobardarse*) to be frightened

enchinchar I. *vt* **1.** *Guat, RDom* (*incomodar*) to annoy **2.** *Méx* **~ a alguien** (*hacer perder el tiempo*) to waste sb's time II. *vr:* **~se 1.** *Arg* (*malhumorarse*) to be in a bad mood; **¿estás enchinchado?** are you in a bad mood? **2.** *Guat, Méx, Perú, PRico* (*llenarse de chinches*) to be infested with bugs

enchironar *vt* *inf* to throw in jail

enchivarse *vr* *Col, Ecua* to get furious

enchufar *vt* **1.** ELEC to plug in **2.** TÉC (*conectar*) to connect **3.** (*acoplar*) to couple **4.** *inf* (*persona*) **~ a alguien** to get a job for sb (by pulling strings)

enchufe *m* **1.** (*clavija*) plug **2.** (*toma*) socket **3.** *inf* (*contactos*) **tener ~** *inf* to have connections **4.** (*trabajo*) good job (*which has been obtained by pulling strings*) **5.** INFOR plug-in

enchutar *vt* *AmC* **1.** (*embutir*) **~ de algo** to fill with sth **2.** (*introducir*) to introduce

encía *f* ANAT gum

enciclopedia *f* encyclopaedia *Brit,* encyclopedia *Am;* **~ en ocho volúmenes** an eight-volume encyclopedia; **ser una ~ viviente** to be a walking encyclopedia

enciclopédico, -a *adj* encyclopaedic *Brit,* encyclopedic *Am;* **diccionario ~** encyclopedic dictionary

encierro *m* **1.** (*reclusión*) confinement; (*prisión*) imprisonment; (*aislamiento*) isolation; (*como protesta*) sit-in **2.** (*lugar*) quiet spot; (*cercado*) enclosure **3.** TAUR *running of bulls in the San Fermín festival in Pamplona*

Strictly speaking, **encierro** a term from *tauromaquia* (art of bullfighting), refers to the following two processes: the bulls are first driven into the arena pens and then locked up in the **toril** (bull cage). For many people this represents the actual **fiesta** (public festival).

encima I. *adv* **1.** (*arriba: con contacto*) on top; (*sin tocar*) above **2.** *fig* **echarse ~ de alguien** to attack sb; **se nos echa el tiempo ~** time is running out; **quitarse algo de ~** (*librarse*) to get sth off one's back; **quitar a alguien un peso de ~** to take a weight off sb's mind; **se me ha quitado un peso de ~** that's a weight

off my mind; **tener algo** ~ to be saddled with sth; **ya tenemos bastante** ~ we've got enough on our plate; **llevaba mucho dinero** ~ he/she had a lot of money on him/her **3.** (*además*) besides; **te di el dinero y** ~ **una botella de vino** I gave you the money and a bottle of wine as well **4.** (*superficialmente*) **por** ~ superficial(ly) **II.** *prep* **1.** (*local: con contacto*) ~ **de** on top of; **con queso** ~ with cheese on top; **el libro está** ~ **de la mesa** the book is on the table; **estar** ~ **de alguien** *fig* to be on sb's case [*o* back] **2.** (*local: sin contacto*) (**por**) ~ **de** above; **viven** ~ **de nosotros** they live above us; **por** ~ **de todo** above all; **por** ~ **de la media** above average **3.** (*con movimiento*) (**por**) ~ **de** over; **pon esto** ~ **de la cama** put this over the bed; **cuelga la lámpara** ~ **de la mesa** hang the light above the table; **¡por** ~ **de mí!** *fig* over my dead body!; **ése pasa por** ~ **de todo** *fig* he only cares about himself **4.** (*más alto*) **el rascacielos está por** ~ **de la catedral** the skyscraper is higher than the cathedral **5.** (*en contra de*) **por** ~ **de alguien** against one's will
encimera *f* worktop, counter *Am*
encina *f* holm oak
encinta *adj* pregnant; **dejar** ~ **a alguien** to get sb pregnant
enclave *m* enclave
enclenque *adj* (*enfermizo*) sickly; (*débil*) weak; (*flaco*) puny
encocorar I. *vt inf* to irritate **II.** *vr:* ~**se** *inf* to get annoyed
encoger <g→j> **I.** *vi* (*tejido*) to shrink **II.** *vt* **1.** (*contraer*) to contract **2.** (*reducir*) to shrink **3.** (*desalentar*) to depress; **verlo así me encoge el ánimo** it depresses me to see him like this **III.** *vr:* ~**se 1.** (*contraerse*) to contract; (*persona*) to cringe; ~**se de hombros** *fig, inf* to shrug one's shoulders **2.** (*reducirse*) to shrink **3.** (*acobardarse*) to get scared
encolar *vt* to glue
encolerizar <z→c> **I.** *vt* to incense **II.** *vr:* ~**se** to be incensed
encomendar <e→ie> **I.** *vt* **1.** (*recomendar*) to recommend **2.** (*confiar*) ~ **algo a alguien** to entrust sth to sb **II.** *vr:* ~**se** to commend; ~**se a Dios** to commend one's soul to God
encomendería *f Perú* COM grocery store
encomiar *vt* to praise
encomienda *f* **1.** (*encargo*) assignment **2.** (*encomio*) praise **3.** (*recomendación*) recommendation **4.** (*beneficio*) payment **5.** (*recado*) errand **6.** *AmL* (*postal*) parcel
encomio *m* praise; **digno de** ~ praiseworthy
enconar I. *vt* **1.** (*agravar*) to worsen; (*agudizar*) to intensify; (*espolear*) to spur on **2.** (*exasperar*) to exasperate **3.** (*inflamar*) to inflame **II.** *vr:* ~**se 1.** (*inflamarse*) to become inflamed **2.** (*agravarse*) to worsen; (*agudizarse*) to intensify **3.** (*ensañarse*) ~**se con alguien** to vent one's rage on sb
encono *m* (*rencor*) spite

encontradizo, -a *adj* **hacerse el** ~ to contrive a meeting
encontrado, -a *adj* (*opuesto*) opposite; **opiniones encontradas** conflicting opinions
encontrar <o→ue> **I.** *vt* **1.** (*hallar*) to find **2.** (*coincidir con*) to come across **3.** (*considerar*) to find; (*notar*) to be conscious of **II.** *vr:* ~**se 1.** (*estar*) to be **2.** (*sentirse*) to feel **3.** (*citarse*) ~**se con alguien** to meet sb **4.** (*coincidir*) ~**se con alguien** to run [*o* bump] into sb **5.** (*hallar*) to find; ~**se con algo** to come across sth; **me encontré con que el coche se había estropeado** I found that the car had broken down; ~**se con un problema** to come up against a problem; ~**se con una sorpresa desagradable** to have a nasty surprise; **no sé lo que me** ~**é cuando llegue** I don't know what I'll find when I arrive; ~**se todo hecho** *inf* to be born with a silver spoon in one's mouth
encontronazo *m inf* crash; **darse un** ~ to have a collision; **tener un** ~ **con alguien** to quarrel with sb; (*enfrentamiento*) to clash with sb
encorvado, -a *adj* hunched; **un viejecito** ~ a stooped old man
encorvar I. *vt* (*cosa*) to bend; (*cuerpo*) to stoop **II.** *vr:* ~**se** (*cosa*) to become bent; (*madera*) to warp; (*persona*) to become hunched
encrespar I. *vt* **1.** (*rizar*) to frizz; **el viento encrespó las aguas** the wind churned up the waters **2.** (*erizar*) to stand on end **3.** (*irritar*) to annoy; (*excitar*) to excite **II.** *vr:* ~**se 1.** (*rizarse*) to curl **2.** (*erizarse*) to stand on end **3.** (*irritarse*) to get annoyed
encrucijada *f* (*cruce*) crossroads *inv*, intersection; **estar en una** ~ *fig* to be at a crossroads [*o* turning point]
encuadernación *f* **1.** (*encuadernado*) binding **2.** (*cubierta*) cover; ~ **en pasta** hardback; ~ **en rústica** paperback **3.** (*taller*) bookbinder's
encuadernador(a) *m(f)* bookbinder
encuadernar *vt* to bind; **encuadernado en rústica** paperback; **encuadernado en pasta** hardback; **sin** ~ unbound
encuadrar *vt* **1.** *t.* CINE, FOTO, TV (*enmarcar*) to frame **2.** (*encajar*) to insert **3.** (*incluir*) to include
encubierto, -a I. *pp de* **encubrir II.** *adj* **tus palabras son una acusación encubierta** what you've said is a veiled accusation
encubridor(a) *m(f)* JUR accessory after the fact
encubrir *irr como* **abrir** *vt* **1.** (*cubrir*) to cover **2.** (*ocultar*) to hide; (*silenciar*) to hush up; (*escándalo, crimen*) to cover up; (*un delincuente*) to harbour *Brit*, to harbor *Am*
encuentro *m* **1.** (*acción*) encounter; **ir al** ~ **de alguien** to go to meet sb **2.** (*cita, reunión*) meeting **3.** (*encontronazo*) confrontation; MIL encounter **4.** DEP match, game; ~ **amistoso** DEP

friendly match [*o* game]

encuerado, -a *adj Cuba, Méx* **1.**(*desharrapado*) shabby **2.**(*desnudo*) naked

encuerar *vt, vr:* ~**se** *AmL* to undress, to strip

encuerista *mf AmL* stripper

encuesta *f* **1.**(*sondeo*) opinion poll; ~ **estadística** statistical survey; ~ **no oficial** straw poll; **hacer una** ~ to carry out an opinion poll **2.**(*investigación*) inquiry; ~ **judicial** judicial inquiry

encularse *vr Arg: inf* **1.**(*ofenderse*) ~**se por algo** to get pissed off about sth **2.**(*enojarse*) to get angry

enculebrado, -a *adj Col, inf* (*endeudado*) indebted

encumbrar **I.** *vt* **1.**(*levantar*) to raise **2.**(*socialmente*) to elevate; ~ **a alguien a la fama** to make sb famous **3.**(*exaltar*) to praise **II.** *vr:* ~**se** **1.**(*elevarse*) to rise **2.**(*engrandecerse*) to be ennobled **3.**(*envanecerse*) to be vain

ende *adv* **por** ~ therefore

endeble *adj* **1.**(*débil*) weak; (*enfermizo*) sickly **2.**(*inconsistente*) flimsy

endémico, -a *adj* **1.** MED endemic **2.**(*continuo*) constant

endemoniado, -a *adj* **1.**(*poseso*) possessed **2.**(*malo*) bad **3.** *inf* (*difícil, tremendo*) awful; **tienes un genio** ~ you've got a terrible temper; **tengo un hambre endemoniada** I'm dying of hunger **4.** *inf* (*travieso*) naughty; ¡~**s chiquillos!** damn kids! *inf*

endenantes *adv AmL, inf* a bit before

enderezar <z→c> *vt* **1.**(*poner derecho*) to straighten **2.**(*corregir*) to straighten out

endeudarse *vr* to get into debt; (*favor*) to be indebted, to owe a favour [*o* favor *Am*]

endiablado, -a *adj v.* **endemoniado**

endibia *f* chicory *Brit*, endive *Am*

endilgar <g→gu> *vt inf* **1.**(*cargar*) ~ **algo a alguien** to offload sth onto sb; **me** ~**on sus opiniones moralistas** they inflicted their moralistic opinions on me **2.**(*una tarea*) **me** ~**on el trabajo sucio** I got stuck with the dirty work **3.**(*encaminar*) to guide

endomingarse <g→gu> *vr* to put on one's Sunday best; **ir endomingado** to wear one's Sunday best

endosar *vt* FIN to endorse; (*traspasar*) to pass on; ~ **una letra** to endorse a document

endoso *m* endorsement; ~ **de una letra** endorsement of a document; **sin** ~ unendorsed

endovenoso, -a *adj* intravenous; **por vía endovenosa** intravenously

endrina *f* sloe

endrino *m* blackthorn

endrino, -a *adj* bluish-black

endrogarse <g→gu> *vr* **1.** *AmL* (*drogarse*) to take drugs **2.** *Méx, Perú* (*endeudarse*) to get into debt

endulzar <z→c> *vt* **1.**(*poner dulce*) to sweeten **2.**(*suavizar*) to soften

endurecer *irr como crecer* **I.** *vt* **1.**(*poner*

duro) to harden; TÉC to chill; ANAT to stiffen **2.**(*mente*) to toughen; (*persona*) to inure **3.**(*hacer resistente*) to strengthen **II.** *vr:* ~**se** **1.**(*ponerse duro*) to get tough; (*sentimientos*) to become hardened **2.**(*hacerse resistente*) to be strengthened **3.**(*agudizarse*) to become more intense

endurecimiento *m* **1.**(*dureza*) hardness **2.**(*proceso*) hardening; ~ **de las arterias** hardening of the arteries **3.**(*resistencia*) harshness **4.**(*terquedad*) stubbornness

ene **I.** *adj inv* MAT x; ~ **veces** x times **II.** *f* (*letra*) N, n; **la letra** ~ the letter n

enebrina *f* juniper berry

enebro *m* juniper

eneldo *m* dill

enema *m* (*lavado*) enema; **poner un** ~ **a alguien** to give sb an enema

enemigo, -a <enemicísimo> **I.** *adj* enemy; (*hostil*) hostile; **país** ~ hostile country **II.** *m, f* enemy; (*contrario*) opponent; ~ **acérrimo** sworn enemy; ~**s mortales** mortal enemies *pl*; **ser** ~ **de algo** to be opposed to sth

enemistad *f* enmity; (*hostilidad*) animosity

enemistar **I.** *vt* to make enemies of **II.** *vr:* ~**se** to become enemies

energético, -a *adj* energy; **fuentes energéticas** sources of energy; **valor** ~ (*de alimentos*) calories *pl*

energía *f t.* FÍS energy; (*fuerza*) force; ~ **nuclear** nuclear energy; ~ **eólica** wind power; **con** ~ *fig* forcefully; **con toda su** ~ with all one's force; **sin** ~ *fig* feebly; **la glucosa da** ~ glucose gives you energy; **emplear todas las** ~**s en algo** to put all one's energies into sth

enérgico, -a *adj* **1.**(*fuerte*) energetic **2.**(*decidido*) firm **3.**(*estricto*) tough; **ponerse** ~ **con alguien** to get tough with sb **4.**(*efectivo*) effective

energúmeno, -a *m, f inf* lout, boor; **se puso a gritar como un** ~ he started shouting like a maniac

enero *m* January; **la cuesta de** ~ the post-Christmas slump; *v.t.* **marzo**

enervante *adj* (*irritante*) annoying

enervar **I.** *vt* **1.**(*debilitar*) to enervate **2.** *inf* (*poner nervioso*) to irritate **II.** *vr:* ~**se** **1.**(*debilitarse*) to be enervated **2.** *inf* (*ponerse nervioso*) to get flustered

enésimo, -a *adj* MAT nth; **por enésima vez** *inf* for the thousandth [*o* umpteenth] time

enfadar **I.** *vt* **1.**(*irritar*) to anger; **estar enfadado con alguien** to be angry [*o* mad] with sb **2.** *AmL* (*aburrir*) to bore **II.** *vr:* ~**se** to get angry; ~**se con alguien** to get angry [*o* mad] with sb

enfado *m* (*enojo*) anger; (*molestia*) annoyance

énfasis *m inv* emphasis; (*insistencia*) insistence; **poner** ~ **en algo** to emphasize sth

enfático, -a *adj* emphatic; (*insistente*) insistent

enfatizar <z→c> **I.** *vt* to emphasize **II.** *vt* to emphasize

enfermar I. *vi, vr* ~(se) de algo to get ill [*o* sick] with sth II. *vt* to make ill [*o* sick]

enfermedad *f* illness; (*específica*) disease; ~ del hígado liver disease; ausencia por ~ sickness [*o* sick] leave; costar una ~ *fig* to take its toll

enfermera *f* nurse

enfermería *f* infirmary

enfermero *m* male nurse; (*camillero*) stretcher-bearer

enfermizo, -a *adj* 1.(*de mala salud*) sickly 2.(*morboso*) sick

enfermo, -a I. *adj* ill, sick; ~ del corazón suffering heart disease; ~ de gravedad seriously ill; caer ~ de algo to come down with sth; ponerse ~ to get ill; esta situación me pone ~ this situation is really getting me down II. *m, f* ill person; (*paciente*) patient

enfervorizar <z→c> I. *vt* to enthuse II. *vr:* ~se to become enthused

enfilar I. *vi* to head II. *vt* 1.(*poner en fila*) to put in a row 2.(*enhebrar*) to string 3.(*poner en linea*) to line up 4.(*ruta*) to take; enfilamos la carretera we went down the road

enfisema *m* MED emphysema

enflaquecer *irr como crecer* I. *vi, vr:* ~se to become thin II. *vt* to make thin

enfocar <c→qu> *vt* 1.(*ajustar*) to focus; mal enfocado out of focus 2.(*iluminar*) ~ algo to shine light upon sth 3.(*una cuestión*) to approach; (*considerar*) to consider; no enfocas bien el problema you're not addressing the issue properly

enfoque *m* 1.(*punto de vista*) opinion, stance 2.(*planteamiento*) approach; (*concepción*) conception

enfrascar <c→qu> I. *vt* to bottle II. *vr* to get wrapped up in; ~se en la lectura to immerse oneself in reading

enfrentamiento *m* confrontation; (*encontronazo*) collision; (*pelea*) fight; ~s callejeros street-fighting

enfrentar I. *vt* 1.(*encarar*) to bring face to face; (*confrontar*) to confront 2.(*hacer frente*) to face up to; ~ los hechos to face the facts II. *vr:* ~se 1.(*encararse*) to come face to face 2.(*afrontarse*) ~se con alguien to face up to sb 3.(*pelearse*) to fight; los manifestantes se ~on con la policía the demonstrators clashed with the police 4.(*confrontar*) to confront 5.(*oponerse*) to oppose; estar enfrentado a alguien to be up against sb

enfrente I. *adv* 1.(*en el lado opuesto*) opposite; allí ~ over there; la casa de ~ the house opposite 2.(*en contra*) tendrás a tu familia ~ your family will be against you II. *prep* (*local: frente a*) ~ de opposite; ~ de mí opposite me; ~ del teatro opposite the theatre; vivo ~ del parque I live opposite the park; ponerse ~ alguien *fig* to be opposed to sb

enfriamiento *m* 1.(*pérdida de temperatura*) cooling; ~ económico economic slowdown

2.(*resfriado*) cold; pillar un ~ *inf* to catch a cold [*o* chill]

enfriar <1. *pres:* enfrío> I. *vi* to cool (down) II. *vt* to cool; *fig* to cool down; ~ el vino to chill the wine III. *vr:* ~se 1.(*perder calor*) to cool (down) 2.(*refrescar, apaciguarse*) to cool off 3.(*acatarrarse*) to catch a cold

enfundar I. *vt* (*espada, cuchillo*) to sheathe; pistola to put back in the holster II. *vr:* ~se (*ropa*) to put on

enfurecer *irr como crecer* I. *vt* to enrage II. *vr:* ~se 1.(*encolerizarse*) to be furious 2.(*mar*) to become rough

enfurruñar *vr:* ~se to get in a huff

engajado, -a *adj* Col, CRi curly

engalanar I. *vt* (*decorar*) to decorate; (*adornar*) to embellish II. *vr:* ~se to do oneself up, to get dressed up

enganchar I. *vt* 1.(*sujetar*) to hook; (*remolque*) to hitch up; (*caballerías*) to harness 2.(*prender*) to catch on; TAUR to impale 3. *inf* (*atrapar*) to catch; (*convencer*) to persuade 4. MIL to recruit 5. FERRO, TÉC to couple II. *vr:* ~se 1.(*sujetarse*) ~se de algo to get hooked on sth 2.(*prenderse*) ~se de [*o* con] algo to get caught on sth 3.(*enredarse*) to get caught up; ~se en una pelea to get caught up in a fight 4. MIL to sign up for the army 5. *inf* (*drogarse*) ~se a to get hooked on; estar enganchado to be hooked

enganche *m* 1.(*gancho*) hook 2.(*acto*) hooking 3. MIL recruitment, enlistment *Am*

engañabobos *mf inv, inf* (*timador*) con artist, conman *m,* conwoman *f*

engañar I. *vi* to deceive; las apariencias engañan appearances can be deceptive II. *vt* 1.(*desorientar*) to confuse 2.(*mentir*) to deceive; (*estafar*) to cheat; ~ a alguien (*ser infiel*) to cheat on sb; (*burlarse*) to laugh at sb; ~ el hambre to stave off one's hunger; dejarse ~ to fall for it *inf* III. *vr:* ~se 1.(*equivocarse*) to be wrong 2.(*hacerse ilusiones*) to get excited; ¡no te engañes con esta oferta! don't get all excited about this offer!

engañifa *f inf,* **engañifla** *f Chile* trap

engaño *m* 1.(*mentira*) deceit 2.(*truco*) trick 3.(*error*) mistake 4.(*ilusión*) illusion

engañoso, -a *adj* 1.(*persona*) deceitful 2.(*algo: falaz*) false; (*equívoco*) incorrect; publicidad engañosa false advertising

engaratusar *vt AmC, Col* (*engatusar*) to coax

engarce *m* 1.(*engarzado*) setting 2.(*montura*) mount(ing) 3.(*unión*) coupling

engarzar <z→c> I. *vt* 1.(*trabar*) to join together 2.(*montar*) to set II. *vr:* ~se *AmL* to get caught up

engastar *vt* to set

engaste *m* 1.(*engastado*) setting 2.(*montura*) set

engatusar *vt* to sweet-talk; ~ a alguien para que haga algo to coax sb into doing sth

engavetar vt Guat to pigeon-hole; ~ **a alguien** to shelve sb

engendrar vt **1.**(concebir) to beget liter **2.**(causar) to give rise to; **la pobreza engendra violencia** poverty gives rise to violence

engendro m **1.**(persona fea) freak **2.**(idea) piece of claptrap

englobar vt **1.**(incluir) to include, to comprise **2.**(reunir) to bring together **3.**(resumir) to summarize

engolillarse vr **1.** Cuba (contraer deudas) to get into debt **2.** Perú (encolerizarse) to lose one's temper

engolosinar I. vt ~ **a alguien** (atraer) to entice sb; (engatusar) to beguile sb II. vr ~**se con algo/alguien** to be attracted to sth/sb; (encariñarse) to be taken by sth/sb

engomar vt **1.**(con cola) to put glue on **2.**(cabello) to put gel on

engordar I. vi **1.**(ponerse gordo) to get fat **2.**(aumentar de peso) to gain weight; **he engordado tres kilos** I've gained three kilos **3.**(poner gordo) to be fattening **4.** inf (enriquecerse) to get rich II. vt AGR to fatten

engorro m **1.**(impedimento) snag **2.**(molestia) nuisance

engorroso, -a adj awkward; (molesto) bothersome

engranaje m **1.**TÉC gear; (mecanismo) cogs pl **2.**(sistema) gearing

engranar I. vi to interlock II. vt **1.**(endentar) to fit **2.**(enlazar) to connect

engrandecer irr como crecer vt **1.**(aumentar) to increase; (acrecentar) to enlarge; (elevar) to ennoble **2.**(exagerar) to exaggerate **3.**(enaltecer) to praise

engrasar vt **1.**(con grasa) to grease; (enaceitar) to oil **2.**AUTO, TÉC (lubricar) to lubricate **3.**(manchar) to stain

engrase m **1.**(engrasado) greasing; AUTO, TÉC lubrication **2.**(grasa) grease; (lubricante) lubrication

engreído, -a adj **1.**(envanecido) conceited **2.** AmL (mimado) spoilt

engreír irr como reír I. vt **1.**(envanecer) to make arrogant **2.**AmL (mimar) to pamper II. vr: ~**se 1.**(envanecerse) to become vain; (presumir) to boast **2.**AmL (hacerse mimado) to become spoilt

engrifarse vr **1.** Col (volverse altivo) to become arrogant **2.** Méx (irritarse) ~**se** to get annoyed; (malhumorarse) to lose one's temper

engrosar <o→ue> I. vi, vr: ~**se 1.**(engordar) to become fatter **2.**(aumentar) to increase II. vt **1.**(engordar) to fatten **2.**(aumentar) to increase; (multiplicar) to multiply

engrudo m paste

engualichar vt Arg **1.**(endemoniar) ~ **a alguien** to put a spell on sb **2.**(al amante) ~ **a alguien** to have power over sb

enguandocar vt Col (adornar) to adorn; (recargar) to overload

enguaraparse vr AmC (fermentar) to ferment

enguatar vt to fill (with padding), to quilt

engubiar vt Urug to defeat

engullir <3. pret: **engulló**> vt **1.**(tragar) to swallow **2.**(atropelladamente) to devour **3.** pey (comer) to gobble down

enharinar vt (rebozar) to coat with flour; (espolvorear) to sprinkle with flour

enhebrar vt **1.**(pasar hebra) to thread **2.**(ensartar) to string together

enhiesto, -a adj **1.**(derecho) straight; (erguido) upright **2.**(alto) high

enhorabuena f congratulations pl; **dar la ~ a alguien** to congratulate sb; **estar de ~** to be on top of the world; **¡~!** congratulations!

enigma m enigma; **descifrar/plantear un ~** to unravel/to pose an enigma

enigmático, -a adj enigmatic; (misterioso) mysterious

enjabonar vt **1.**(al lavar) to soap **2.** inf (dar coba) to butter up, to sweet talk **3.** inf (regañar) to tick off

enjalbegar <g→gu> vt to whitewash

enjambre m **1.**(de abejas) swarm **2.**(muchedumbre) throng

enjaular vt (encerrar) to lock up; (en una jaula) to cage

enjetarse vr Arg, Méx **1.**(enojarse) to get angry **2.**(ofenderse) to take offence [o offense Am]

enjuagar <g→gu> vt to rinse

enjuague m **1.** t. TÉC rinse **2.**(manejo) rinsing **3.**(líquido) ~ **bucal** mouthwash

enjugamanos m inv, AmL hand-towel

enjugar <g→gu> I. vt **1.**(secar) to dry; (limpiar) to wipe (off) **2.**(una deuda) to write off II. vr: ~**se 1.**(secarse) to dry **2.**(adelgazar) to lose weight

enjuiciar vt **1.**(juzgar) to analyze; (censurar) to criticize **2.**(procesar) to prosecute; (sentenciar) to sentence

enjutarse vr Guat, Ven **1.**(enflaquecerse) to become thin **2.**(achicarse) to get smaller; (encogerse) to shrink

enjuto, -a adj scrawny; ~ **de carnes** thin

enlace m **1.**(conexión) connection **2.** t. ELEC, FERRO (empalme) link; (unión) join; ~ **ferroviario** railroad link **3.**(entrelazado) joining **4.**(boda) wedding **5.**(contacto) link; ~ **policial** police informer **6.**QUÍM bond; (sistema) bonding **7.**INFOR link

enlatados mpl Col (comestibles en latas) tinned Brit [o canned Am] food

enlatar vt to tin Brit, to can Am; **programa enlatado** TV prerecorded programme [o program Am]

enlazar <z→c> I. vi (transporte) to link up II. vt **1.**(atar) to tie; (unir) to join; (entrelazar) to interlink **2.** t. ELEC, TÉC (empalmar) to connect III. vr: ~**se** (casarse) to marry

enloquecedor(a) adj maddening

enloquecer irr como crecer I. vi, vr: ~**se** to go

out of one's mind, to go mad; ~ **de dolor** to be in terrible pain; ~ **de rabia** to be raging mad; ~ **por alguien** to be mad [*o* crazy] about sb **II.** *vt* to madden, to drive crazy; **me enloquecen los pasteles** I'm mad [*o* crazy] about cakes

enlozado *m AmL* enamel finish, glaze

enlozar <z→c> *vt AmL* to enamel, to glaze

enlucido *m* plaster

enlucir *irr como lucir vt* **1.** (*con yeso*) to plaster **2.** (*lustrar*) to polish

enlutar **I.** *vt* **1.** (*en el vestir*) to dress in mourning; **mujeres enlutadas** women dressed in mourning **2.** (*ensombrecer*) to darken; (*entristecer*) to sadden **II.** *vr:* ~**se** to wear black

enmadrar *vr:* ~**se** to be tied to one's mother's apron strings

enmarañar **I.** *vt* **1.** (*enredar*) to mix up **2.** (*confundir*) to confuse; (*complicar*) to complicate **II.** *vr:* ~**se** **1.** (*enredarse*) to get mixed up **2.** (*confundirse*) to get confused; (*complicarse*) to get complicated

enmarcar <c→qu> *vt* to frame; (*encajar*) to place

enmascarar **I.** *vt* **1.** (*poner máscara*) to mask; (*disfrazar*) to disguise **2.** (*ocultar*) to hide; (*encubrir*) to cover up **II.** *vr:* ~**se** **1.** (*con una máscara*) to wear a mask; (*disfrazarse*) to disguise oneself **2.** (*encubrirse*) to cover one's tracks

enmendar <e→ie> **I.** *vt* **1.** (*corregir*) to correct; ~ **la plana a alguien** to find fault with sb **2.** (*modificar*) to modify; (*una ley*) to amend **II.** *vr:* ~**se** to mend one's ways

enmicar <c→qu> *vt Méx* (*cubrir con plástico*) to cover in plastic

enmienda *f* **1.** (*corrección*) correction; **no tener** ~ *fig* to be beyond repair **2.** (*modificación*) modification; (*de una ley*) amendment **3.** (*indemnización*) compensation

enmohecer *irr como crecer vi, vr:* ~**se** **1.** (*cubrirse de moho*) to go mouldy *Brit,* to go moldy *Am;* (*pudrirse*) to rot **2.** (*caer en desuso*) to become rusty

enmudecer *irr como crecer* **I.** *vi* **1.** (*perder el habla*) to be struck dumb; ~ **de miedo** to be struck speechless with fear **2.** (*callar*) to go silent **II.** *vt* to silence

ennegrecer *irr como crecer* **I.** *vt* **1.** (*poner negro*) to blacken **2.** (*oscurecer*) to darken; (*ensombrecer*) to sadden **II.** *vr:* ~**se** **1.** (*ponerse negro*) to blacken **2.** (*oscurecerse*) to darken; (*ensombrecer*) to sadden

ennoblecer *irr como crecer vt* **1.** (*conceder el título*) to ennoble **2.** (*mejorar*) to enhance; (*refinar*) to refine **3.** (*enaltecer*) to exalt; **nos ennoblece su presencia** we are honoured [*o* honored *Am*] by your presence

enojar **I.** *vt* **1.** (*enfadar*) to anger **2.** (*molestar*) to annoy **II.** *vr:* ~**se** **1.** (*enfadarse*) to get angry **2.** (*molestarse*) to get cross

enojo *m* **1.** (*enfado*) anger; **con** ~ angrily **2.** (*molestia*) annoyance

enojón, -ona **I.** *adj Chile, Ecua, Méx* (*enoja-*

dizo) touchy **II.** *m, f Chile, Ecua, Méx* (*enojadizo*) a quick-tempered person

enojoso, -a *adj* **1.** (*enfadoso*) vexing **2.** (*molesto*) annoying **3.** (*complicado*) complicated; (*trabajoso*) strenuous

enorgullecer *irr como crecer* **I.** *vt* to fill with pride **II.** *vr:* ~**se** to be proud

enorme *adj* enormous; (*gigantesco*) huge; (*desmedido, extraordinario*) remarkable, monstrous *pej*

enormidad *f* **1.** (*tamaño*) enormity; *fig* lot; **trabajó una** ~ he/she worked a lot **2.** (*cantidad*) great number; **una** ~ **de dinero** a lot of money

enrabiar **I.** *vt* to enrage **II.** *vr:* ~**se** to get angry

enraizado, -a *adj* rooted; **una costumbre muy enraizada** a deep-seated tradition

enraizar *irr vi* to set [*o* put] down roots

enrastrojarse *vr AmL* to get dirty

enredadera *f* climbing [*o* trailing] plant

enredar **I.** *vi* (*niño*) to get into mischief; **¡no andes enredando con las cerillas!** don't play with the matches! **II.** *vt* **1.** (*liar*) to mix up; (*confundir*) to confuse **2.** (*enemistar*) to make enemies of **III.** *vr:* ~**se** **1.** (*cuerda, asunto*) to get mixed up **2.** (*planta*) to climb **3.** *inf* (*amancebarse*) to have an affair

enredo *m* **1.** (*de alambres*) tangle **2.** (*mentira*) troublemaking **3.** (*asunto*) muddle **4.** (*intriga*) intrigue **5.** (*engaño*) deceit **6.** (*amorío*) affair **7.** *pl, inf* (*trastos*) stuff

enrejado *m* (*de hierro*) grating; (*de caña*) fence

enrejar *vt* (*ventana*) to put a grating over; (*huerta*) to fence in

enrevesado, -a *adj* (*intrincado*) complicated; (*camino, carretera*) winding; (*difícil*) difficult

enriquecer *irr como crecer* **I.** *vt* **1.** (*hacer rico, engrandecer, metal, tierra*) to enrich **2.** (*adornar*) to embellish **II.** *vr:* ~**se** to get rich; ~**se** (**a costa ajena**) to get rich (at other people's expense)

enriquecimiento *m* enrichment; ~ **injusto** *JUR* embezzlement

enrocar *vi* (*ajedrez*) to castle

enrojecer *irr como crecer* **I.** *vi* to blush; ~ **de ira** to go red with anger; (*con fiebre*) to flush **II.** *vt* (*cielo*) to redden **III.** *vr:* ~**se** (*persona*) to blush; (*cielo*) to redden

enrolar *vt* **1.** NÁUT to enrol *Brit,* to enroll *Am* **2.** MIL to enlist

enrollar **I.** *vt* (*cartel*) to roll up; (*cuerda*) to coil **II.** *vr:* ~**se** *inf* **1.** (*extenderse demasiado*) to go on and on; ~**se como una persiana** to talk the hind leg off a donkey **2.** (*ligar*) ~**se con alguien** to take up with sb **3.** (*saber estar*) to get on well

enronquecer *irr como crecer* **I.** *vt* to make hoarse **II.** *vi, vr:* ~**se** to go hoarse

enroscar <c→qu> **I.** *vt* **1.** (*enrollar*) to wind; ~ **el hilo en el palo** to wind the thread around the stick **2.** (*tornillo*) to screw in **3.** (*tapa*) to twist on **II.** *vr:* ~**se** to curl up; **la**

serpiente se enroscó en la rama the snake coiled itself round the branch
enrostrar *vt AmL* to throw in one's face
enrular *vt CSur* to curl

Anyone who visits **Mallorca** brings **ensaimadas** with them, at least every Spanish tourist does. An **ensaimada** is a light spiral-shaped pastry that can be filled with sweet **cabello de ángel**, a type of mashed pumpkin filling.

---

ensalada *f* 1.salad; ~ **de frutas** fruit salad 2.(*confusión*) mix-up
ensaladera *f* salad bowl

Ensaladilla rusa: Take jacket potatoes, cooked vegetables (carrots, green beans, peas), olives, and hard-boiled eggs. Finely chop all these ingredients (similar to potato salad), then add tuna and dress the dish with mayonnaise and a little vinegar.

---

ensalmo *m* (*conjuro*) charm; (**como**) **por** ~ as if by magic
ensalzar <z→c> I. *vt* (*dignificar*) to dignify; (*alabar*) to praise II. *vr:* ~**se** to boast
ensamblar *vt* to assemble
ensanchar I. *vt* to widen II. *vr:* ~**se** to widen
ensanche *m* 1.(*ampliación*) enlargement; (*de anchura*) widening 2.(*ciudad*) suburb; **zona de** ~ area for urban development
ensangrentar <e→ie> *vt* to cover in blood
ensartar *vt* 1.(*perlas*) to string 2.(*pinchar*) to skewer 3.(*hablar*) to reel off
ensayar I. *vt* 1.TEAT to rehearse 2.(*probar*) to test; (*examinar*) to examine II. *vr* ~**se en algo** to rehearse sth
ensayo *m* 1.TEAT rehearsal; ~ **general** dress rehearsal 2. LIT essay 3. (*prueba*) test; (*experimento*) experiment; **tubo de** ~ test tube
enseguida *adv* at once, straight [*o* right] away
ensenada *f* 1.(*mar*) inlet 2.*Arg* (*corral*) meadow
enseña *f* insignia; (*estandarte*) standard
enseñante *mf* teacher
enseñanza *f* 1.(*sistema*) education; ~ **primaria** primary education; ~ **privada** private education; ~ **pública** public education; ~ **secundaria** secondary education; ~ **superior** higher education 2.(*docencia*) teaching; ~ **a distancia** distance learning; ~ **universitaria** university education; **método de** ~ teaching method; **dedicarse a la** ~ to be a teacher 3.(*lección*) lesson; **de lo ocurrido en el pasado no has sacado ninguna** ~ you haven't learned anything from past events
enseñar *vt* 1.(*instruir, dar clases*) to teach; (*explicar*) to explain; **él me enseñó la poca química que sé** he taught me the little I know about chemistry; **ella me enseñó a tocar la**

flauta she taught me how to play the flute; **hay que** ~ **con el ejemplo** you have to lead by example; **¡la vida te** ~**á!** life is the best teacher!; **¡ya te** ~**é yo a obedecer!** I'll teach you a bit of obedience! 2.(*mostrar*) to show; **te enseñé a hacer las camas** I showed you how to make beds; ~ **el camino a alguien** to show sb the way 3.(*dejar ver*) to show; (*presentar*) to present; (*exhibir*) to exhibit
enseñorearse *vr* ~ **de algo** to take over sth
enseres *mpl* belongings *pl;* (*útiles*) tools *pl;* (*mobiliario*) goods *pl*
ensillar *vt* to saddle
ensimismarse *vr* 1.(*absorberse*) to become absorbed; ~ **en recuerdos/una lectura** to become engrossed in one's memories/reading 2. Col, Chile (*engreírse*) to become vain
ensoberbecerse *irr como crecer vr* (*persona*) ~ **de algo** to boast about sth
ensombrecer *irr como crecer* I. *vt* (*oscurecer*) to darken; (*ofuscar*) to cast a shadow over II. *vr:* ~**se** 1.(*entristecerse*) to become sad 2.(*oscurecerse*) to darken
ensoñación *f* daydream
ensopar I. *vt AmS* (*empapar*) to soak II. *vr:* ~**se** *AmS* to get soaked
ensordecedor(a) *adj* deafening
ensordecer *irr como crecer* I. *vi* (*quedarse sordo*) to go deaf II. *vt* (*ruido*) to deafen
ensortijado, -a *adj* curly
ensortijar *vt* (*pelo*) to curl
ensuciar I. *vt* to dirty II. *vr:* ~**se** 1.(*mancharse*) to get dirty; ~**se de algo** to be stained with sth 2.(*reputación*) to tarnish 3. *inf* (*excremento*) to soil oneself
ensueño *m* dream; **de** ~ fantastic
entablar *vt* 1.(*conversación*) to strike up; (*negociaciones*) to begin; (*amistad*) to establish; (*juicio*) to file; ~ **relaciones comerciales** to establish trade links 2.(*suelo*) to put floorboards on 3.(*ajedrez*) to set up
entablillar *vt* to splint
entallado, -a *adj* taken in at the waist
entallar I. *vt* (*vestido*) to take in at the waist II. *vi, vr:* ~**se** to fit; **la chaqueta entalla bien** the jacket fits well
entarimado *m* floorboards *pl*
ente *m* 1.FILOS being 2.(*autoridad*) body; **el Ente Público** the public sector 3.(*persona*) geek
entecarse <c→qu> *vr Chile* (*emperrarse*) to be stubborn
enteco, -a *adj* sickly
entendederas *fpl inf* brains *pl;* **es muy corto de** ~ he's pretty dim [*o* dumb]
entendedor(a) *m(f)* expert ►**a buen** ~, **con pocas palabras bastan** *prov* a word to the wise is sufficient *prov*
entender <e→ie> I. *vi* 1.(*comprender*) to understand; **si entiendo bien Ud. quiere decir que...** am I right in saying that what you mean is that ... 2.(*saber*) ~ **mucho de algo** to know a lot about sth; **no** ~ **nada de**

algo to know nothing about sth **II.** *vt* **1.** (*comprender*) to understand; **dar a ~ que...** to imply that ...; **dar a ~ a alguien que...** to give sb to understand that ...; **lo entendieron mal** they misunderstood it; **¿qué entiende Ud. por 'acuerdo'?** what do you understand by 'agreement'?; **ellos ya se harán ~** they'll soon make themselves understood; **no ~ ni jota/papa** *inf* not to understand a thing; **no entiende una broma** he/she can't take a joke **2.** (*creer*) to think; **yo entiendo que sería mejor si** +*subj* I think it would be better if; **yo no lo entiendo así** that's not the way I see it; **tengo entendido que...** (*según creo*) I believe that ...; (*según he oído*) I've heard that ... **III.** *vr:* **~se 1.** (*llevarse*) to get on **2.** (*ponerse de acuerdo*) to agree; **para el precio entiéndete con mi socio** as regards the price, reach an agreement with my partner **3.** *inf* (*liarse*) to have an affair **4.** *inf* (*desenvolverse*) to manage; **no me entiendo con este lío de cables** I can't manage with this tangle of leads; **¡que se las entienda!** let him/her get on with it! **5.** (*expresiones*) **¡yo me entiendo!** I know what I'm doing!; **pero ¿cómo se entiende?** *inf* but what does it mean?; **eso se entiende por sí mismo** this is self-explanatory **IV.** *m* opinion; **a mi ~** the way I see it

entendido, -a I. *adj* **1.** (*listo*) clever, smart **2.** (*experto*) **~ en algo** expert on sth; **no se dio por ~** he pretended he hadn't heard **3.** (*claro*) **queda ~ que...** it is clear that ...; **queda ~ que te acompaño a casa** of course I'll take you home; **bien ~ que...** on the understanding that ... **II.** *m, f* expert; (*vinos*) connoisseur; **es un gran ~ en informática** he's a real expert on computers; **hacerse el ~** to act smart

entendimiento *m sin pl* **1.** (*razón*) reason; (*facilidad de comprensión*) understanding; **obrar con ~** to go about things reasonably; **un hombre de mucho ~** a very reasonable man **2.** (*acuerdo*) agreement

enterado, -a *adj* **~ de algo** (*iniciado*) aware of sth; (*conocedor*) knowledgeable about sth; **yo ya estaba ~ del incidente** I already knew about the incident; **no se dio por ~** he pretended not to have understood

enteramente *adv* wholly

enterar I. *vt* **1.** (*informar*) **~ de algo** to tell about sth **2.** *Méx, CRi, Hond* COM to pay **II.** *vr* **~ de algo** (*descubrir*) to find out about sth; (*saber*) to hear about sth; **me enteré de la explosión por la radio** I heard about the explosion on the radio; **no me enteré de nada hasta que me lo dijeron** I wasn't aware of anything until they told me; **pasa las hojas sin ~se de lo que lee** he/she spends hours reading without taking anything in; **¡para que se entere!** *inf* that'll teach him/her/you!; **para que te enteres...** for your information ...

entereza *f sin pl* **1.** (*determinación*) strength of mind **2.** (*aplomo*) aplomb **3.** (*integridad*) integrity; **a la muerte de su madre demostraron mucha ~** they showed great fortitude when their mother died

enterizo, -a *adj* in one piece

enternecer *irr como crecer* **I.** *vt* **1.** (*ablandar*) to soften **2.** (*conmover*) to move; (*hacer ceder*) to make relent **II.** *vr:* **~se** (*conmoverse*) to be touched; (*ceder*) to relent

entero, -a *adj* **1.** (*completo*) *t.* MAT whole, entire; **por ~** completely; **se pasa días ~s sin decir ni una palabra** he/she goes for days at a time without speaking; **el espejo salió ~ de aquí** when the mirror left here it was in one piece; **la comisión entera se declaró a favor** the whole committee declared themselves to be in favour [*o* favor *Am*]; **el juego de café no está ~** some of the coffee service is missing **2.** (*persona íntegra*) honest

enterrador(a) *m(f)* (*sepulturero*) gravedigger

enterramiento *m* (*funeral*) burial; (*tumba*) grave

enterrar <e→ie> **I.** *vt* **1.** (*a un muerto*) to bury; **¡ésa nos ~á a todos!** *inf* she will outlive the lot of us! **2.** (*un objeto*) to bury; (*no muy profundo*) to cover up **3.** (*ilusiones, esperanzas*) to abandon **II.** *vr:* **~se** (*recluirse*) to hide oneself away

enterratorio *m AmS* (*cementerio*) Indian burial ground

entibiar I. *vt* (*líquido*) to cool; *fig* to soften **II.** *vr:* **~se** (*líquido*) to become lukewarm; *fig* to soften

entidad *f* **1.** (*asociación*) organization; **~ aseguradora** insurance firm; **~ crediticia** credit company; **~ jurídica** legal entity; **~ bancaria** bank **2.** (*importancia*) importance

entierro *m* **1.** (*inhumación*) burial; **¡no pongas esa cara de ~!** don't look so glum! **2.** (*funeral*) funeral **3.** (*comitiva*) funeral procession

entintar *vt* (*manchar*) to stain; (*teñir*) to dye; TIPO to ink

entonación *f* LING, MÚS intonation

entonar I. *vi* **1.** (*canción*) to sing in tune **2.** (*armonizar*) to go well; **los colores de las cortinas no entonan con los de la pared** the colours [*o* colors *Am*] of the curtains don't go well with the walls **II.** *vt* **1.** (*canción*) to sing **2.** (*fortalecer*) to liven up

entonces *adv* **1.** (*temporal*) then; **desde ~** from then on; **hasta ~** until then; **en** [*o* por] **aquel ~** at that time **2.** (*modal*) then; **¿y qué pasó?** and what happened next?; **¿pues ~ por qué te extraña si no vienen?** then why are you surprised that they don't come?; **¡~!** I should think so!; **si lo amas ¿~ por qué no se lo dices?** if you love him, then why don't you tell him?

entontecer *irr como crecer* **I.** *vi, vr:* **~se** to become a moron **II.** *vt* to stupefy

entornar *vt* (*puerta*) to leave slightly open

entorno *m* surroundings *pl;* (*medio ambiente*) environment; (*mundillo*) world, sphere

entorpecer *irr como crecer vt* **1.**(*movimiento*) to make slow [*o* clumsy]; (*frío*) to numb; **el frío me entorpecía los dedos** the cold numbed my fingers **2.**(*dificultar*) to hamper; (*retrasar*) to slow down **3.**(*sentidos*) to dull

entrabar *vt AmS* to interfere

entrada *f* **1.**(*puerta*) entrance; (*para coche*) door; ~ **a la autopista** motorway slip road *Brit,* (entry) ramp *Am;* ~ **trasera** back door **2.**(*acción*) entrance; **hacer una** ~ to make an entrance; **se prohibe la** ~ no entry [*o* admittance] **3.**(*comienzo*) entry; (*en un cargo*) start; ~ **en funciones** starting date; ~ **en vigor** coming into force; **de** ~ right from the start; **así de** ~ **tu idea no me pareció mal** at first your idea didn't strike me as bad **4.**(*cine, teatro*) ticket; ~ **gratuita** free entry [*o* admission] **5.**(*público*) audience; **en el estreno hubo una gran** ~ a great number of people were at the première **6.**GASTR first course, entrée **7.** *pl* (*pelo*) **tiene** ~s his/her hair is receding **8.**MÚS entry; **dar la** ~ to enter **9.**(*en diccionario*) entry **10.**(*depósito*) deposit; **ya hemos dado la** ~ **para el coche** we've already paid the deposit [*o* down payment] for the car **11.**COM income; ~ **de pedidos** orders *pl* **12.**FIN ~s **y salidas** income and costs **13.**INFOR input **14.** DEP tackle

entrado, -a *adj* **un señor** ~ **en años** an elderly gentleman; **llegamos entrada la noche** we arrived when it was already dark; **hasta muy** ~ **el siglo XVII** until well into the seventeenth century

entrador(a) *adj* **1.**AmS (*animoso*) spirited; (*atrevido*) daring **2.***Arg* (*simpático*) friendly **3.***AmL* (*enamoradizo*) romantic **4.***Chile* (*entremetido*) interfering **5.***Guat, Nic* (*compañero*) companionable

entrampar *vt* **1.**(*animal*) to trap **2.**(*engañar*) to deceive **3.** *inf* (*embrollar*) to mess up **4.** *inf*(*deudas*) to indebt *form* **II.** *vr:* ~**se** to get into debt

entrante¹ *adj* (*próximo*) next; **a primeros del mes** ~ at the start of next month

entrante² *m* GASTR first course, starter

entraña *f* **1.** *pl* (*órganos*) entrails *pl;* **echar las** ~s *inf*to throw up; **¡hijo de mis** ~s! *inf*my darling child!; **por mis hijos doy las** ~s *inf*I'd give anything for my children **2.**(*lo esencial*) core **3.** *pl* (*carácter*) nature; **de buenas** ~s good-natured **4.** *pl* (*interior*) core; **las** ~s **de la tierra** the bowels of the earth

entrañable *adj* (*amistad*) intimate; (*película, persona*) endearing; (*recuerdo*) fond

entrañar *vt* to involve; ~ **graves peligros** to entail serious dangers

entrar **I.** *vi* **1.**(*pasar*) to enter; ~ **por la ventana** to come in through the window; ~ **por la fuerza** to break in; **el tren entra en la esta-**ción the train enters the station; **me entró por un oído y me salió por otro** it went in one ear and out the other; ~ **con buen pie** to start off on the right foot; **¡entre!** come in! **2.**(*caber*) to fit; ~ **en el armario** to fit into the wardrobe [*o* closet *Am*]; **no me entra el anillo** I can't get the ring on; **el corcho no entra en la botella** the cork won't fit into the bottle; **por fin he hecho** ~ **el tapón** I've finally got the lid on **3.**(*penetrar*) to go in; **el clavo entró en la pared** the nail went into the wall; **¡no me entra en la cabeza cómo pudiste hacer eso!** I can't understand how you could do this! **4.**(*empezar*) to begin; ~ **en relaciones** to start a relationship; **el verano entra el 21 de junio** summer begins on the 21st of June; **después entré a trabajar en una casa más rica** afterwards I started working in a wealthier household; **cuando entró de alcalde** when he/she was elected mayor; **no** ~ **en detalles** not to go into details; ~ **en calor** to warm up; ~ **en vigor** to come into force; **me entró la tentación** I was tempted; **me entró un mareo** I became dizzy; **me entró el sueño** I became sleepy; **me entró el hambre** I became hungry **5.**(*como miembro*) ~ **en algo** to become a member of sth; ~ **en la Academia de Ciencias** to be admitted to the Royal Academy of Science **6.**(*formar parte*) **en un kilo entran tres panochas** you can get three corncobs to the kilo; **eso no entraba en mis cálculos** I hadn't reckoned on this; **en esta receta no entran huevos** there are no eggs in this recipe **7.**MÚS to come in **8.**DEP to tackle **9.**INFOR to access **10.**(*dar*) **esperemos que no te entre la gripe** we hope you don't get the flu; **le ha entrado la costumbre de...** he/she's got into the habit of ... **11.**inf (*entender*) **las matemáticas no me entran** I can't get the hang of mathematics **12.**inf (*soportar*) **su hermano no me entra** I can't stand his/her brother **13.**inf(*relacionarse, tratar*) **no sabe** ~ **a las chicas** he doesn't know how to chat up [*o* pick up] girls; **a él no sabes como** ~le you don't know how to deal with him **14.**(*opinar*) **yo en eso no entro** [*o* ni **entro ni salgo**] *inf*I've got nothing to do with this **II.** *vt* to put; ~ **el coche en el garaje** put the car into the garage

entre *prep* **1.**(*dos cosas*) between; (*más de dos cosas*) among(st); **salir de** ~ **las ramas** to emerge from among(st) the branches; **pasar por** ~ **las mesas** to go between the tables; ~ **semana** during the week; **ven** ~ **las cinco y las seis** come between five and six; ~ **tanto** meanwhile; **lo cuento** ~ **mis amigos** I consider him as one of my friends; **un ejemplo** ~ **muchos** one of many examples; **el peor** ~ **todos** the worst of the lot; **llegaron veinte** ~ **hombres y mujeres** twenty men and women arrived; **se la llevaron** ~ **cuatro hombres** she was carried off by four men; **lo hablaremos** ~ **nosotros** we'll speak about it among(st) ourselves; ~ **el taxi y la entrada me quedé sin dinero** what with the taxi and the ticket I had no money left; **lo dije ~ mí** I was speaking to myself; **¡guárdalo ~ los libros!** keep it amongst your books; **me senté ~ los dos** I sat down between the two of them **2.** MAT **ocho ~ dos son cuatro** eight divided by two is four

entreabierto, -a adj ajar

entreabrir irr como abrir vt to open slightly

entreacto m (intermedio) interval

entrecano, -a adj greying Brit, graying Am

entrecejo m (ceño) brow; **fruncir el ~** to frown

entrecomillar vt to put in inverted commas Brit, to put in quotes [o quotation marks]

entrecortado, -a adj (respiración) uneven, laboured Brit, labored Am; (voz) halting; **con la voz entrecortada por los sollozos** with a voice broken with sobs

entrecruzar <z→c> vt, vr: ~**se** to interweave; (miradas) to cross; (cintas) to interlace

entredicho m 1. (prohibición) ban 2. (duda) **poner algo en ~** to put sth in question; **poner en ~ la veracidad** to question the truth

entrega f 1. (dedicación) dedication 2. (fascículo) instalment Brit, installment Am; **novela por ~s** serialized novel 3. (de documentos) delivery; (ceremonia) giving; ~ **de premios** prizegiving; ~ **de títulos** UNIV graduation ceremony; **hacer ~ de algo** to hand sth over 4. COM delivery; ~ **a domicilio** home delivery; **talón de ~** delivery sheet; **pagadero a la ~** payable on delivery; ~ **contra reembolso** collect on delivery 5. MIL surrender; (de prisioneros) release

entregar <g→gu> I. vt 1. (dar) to give, to hand over [o in]; ~**la** inf to kick the bucket 2. (carta) to deliver 3. MIL to surrender; (prisioneros) to hand over II. vr: ~**se** 1. (desvivirse) to take to; ~**se a la bebida** to take to drink 2. (delincuente) to give oneself up 3. MIL to surrender 4. (sexo) to yield

entrelazar <z→c> vt, vr: ~**se** to join, to (inter)weave

entremedias adv 1. (local) between; (más de dos cosas) amongst; ~ **de...** somewhere between ... 2. (temporal) meanwhile

entremeses mpl hors d'oeuvres pl, appetizers pl Am

entremeterse vr to interfere, to butt in inf

entremetido, -a I. adj interfering II. m, f busybody

entremezclar vt to intermingle

entrenador(a) m(f) DEP coach

entrenamiento m 1. DEP training session 2. (práctica) training

entrenar vt, vr: ~**se** to train

entrepierna f 1. (muslo, pantalón) crotch; **esto se me pasa por la ~** vulg I don't give a shit about this 2. Chile (de baño) swimsuit

entreplanta f mezzanine

entresacar <c→qu> vt 1. (escoger) to pick

out; (elegir) to choose 2. (pelo) to thin out

entresijo m fig secret; **los ~s** the ins and outs

entresuelo m mezzanine, first floor

entretanto adv meanwhile

entretecho m CSur (desván) attic

entretejer vt 1. (meter) to weave in 2. (entrelazar) to interweave

entretela f inner lining

entretener irr como tener I. vt 1. (divertir) to entertain; **sabe cómo ~ a los niños** he/she knows how to entertain the children 2. (apartar la atención) to distract 3. (asunto) to delay; ~ **a alguien con excusas** to keep giving sb excuses 4. (detener) to hold up II. vr: ~**se** 1. (pasar el rato) to amuse oneself; ~**se con revistas** to amuse oneself by reading magazines 2. (tardar) to delay; **¡no te entretengas!** don't dilly dally! 3. (apartar la atención) to be distracted

entretenido, -a adj entertaining

entretenimiento m 1. (diversión) entertainment; (pasatiempo) activity; **en el bosque hay mucho ~ para los niños** children can have a great time in the forest 2. (conservación) upkeep

entretiempo m sin pl between season; (primavera) spring; (otoño) autumn

entrever irr como ver vt 1. (objeto) to glimpse 2. (sospechar) to surmise; (intenciones) to guess

entreverar I. vt to intermingle II. vr: ~**se** Arg, Perú to jumble together

entrevero m CSur 1. (confusión) jumble 2. (riña) brawl 3. (escaramuza) skirmish

entrevista f 1. (inteviú) interview; **hacer una ~ a alguien** to interview sb; ~ **de trabajo** job interview 2. (reunión) meeting

entrevistar I. vt to interview II. vr: ~**se** (entrevista) to be interviewed; (reunión) to have a meeting

entristecer irr como crecer I. vt to sadden II. vr: ~**se** to be saddened

entrometerse vr to interfere

entrometido, -a adj, m, f v. **entremetido**

entroncar <c→qu> vi 1. (tener parentesco) ~ **con alguien** to be related to sb 2. AmL (tren) to connect

entronque m 1. (parentesco) relations pl 2. AmL (tren) connection

entrucharse vr Méx 1. (entremeterse) ~ **en algo** to interfere with sth 2. (enamorarse) ~ **de alguien** to fall in love with sb

entuerto m (agravios) wrongdoing, offence Brit, offense Am

entumecerse irr como crecer vr (frío) to go numb; (músculo) to stiffen; (hinchazón) to swell

entumecido, -a adj (frío) numb; (pierna, rígido) stiff; (hinchado) swollen

enturbiar vt to darken

entusiasmar I. vt to enthuse II. vr: ~**se** to get enthusiastic

entusiasmo m sin pl enthusiasm

entusiasta I. *adj* enthusiastic II. *mf* enthusiast
entusiástico, **-a** *adj* enthusiastic
enumeración *f* enumeration
enumerar *vt* to enumerate; (*escrito*) to set down
enunciado *m* 1. (*de problema*) setting out 2. (*texto*) summary 3. LING statement
enunciar *vt* (*explicar*) to set out; (*expresar*) to state
enunciativo, **-a** *adj* oración enunciativa declarative sentence
envalentonar I. *vt* to spur II. *vr:* ~se to become brave
envanecer *irr como crecer* I. *vt* to make vain II. *vr:* ~se 1. (*enorgullecerse*) to become proud 2. (*engreírse*) to become vain
envasar *vt* to package; (*en latas*) to tin *Brit,* to can *Am;* (*en botellas*) to bottle
envase *m* 1. (*paquete*) package; (*recipiente*) container; (*botella*) bottle 2. (*casco*) bottle; ~ sin retorno non-returnable bottle 3. (*acción*) packing; ~ al vacío vacuum packing
envejecer *irr como crecer vt, vr:* ~se to age
envenenar *vt* to poison
envergadura *f* (*importancia*) magnitude; (*alcance*) scope; de gran ~ far-reaching
envés *m* back
enviado, **-a** *m, f* envoy; ~ especial PREN, TV, RADIO special correspondent
enviar <*1. pres:* envío> *vt* to send; ~ por correo to post *Brit,* to mail *Am*
envidia *f* envy; tener ~ a alguien to envy sb; tener ~ de algo to be jealous of sth; daba ~ verlo de lo guapo que iba it made me envious to see how handsome he looked; lo corroe la ~ he is eaten up by jealousy
envidiable *adj* enviable
envidiar *vt* to envy; ¡mucho tienes tú que ~le a ella! *irón* you've got no reason to be jealous of her!
envidioso, **-a** *adj* envious
envío *m* sending; (*expedición*) issue; ~ a domicilio home delivery; ~ contra reembolso cash on delivery; ~ urgente urgent delivery; ~ con valor declarado declared value delivery; gastos de ~ postage and packing *Brit,* shipping and handling *Am*
enviudar *vi* to be widowed; (*una mujer*) to become a widow; (*un hombre*) to become a widower
envoltorio *m* 1. (*lío*) bundle 2. (*embalaje*) wrapping 3. (*caramelo*) wrapper
envoltura *f* (*capa exterior*) covering; (*embalaje*) wrapping
envolver *irr como volver* I. *vt* 1. (*en papel*) to wrap; ~ con [*o* en] algo to wrap up in sth 2. (*empaquetar, ropa*) to pack; ~ con [*o* en] algo to pack in sth; (*para regalo*) to gift-wrap 3. (*implicar*) to involve 4. (*rodear*) to envelop II. *vr* to get involved; el policía se envolvió en un asunto sospechoso the policeman got mixed up in a shady business
envuelto, **-a** *pp de* **envolver**

enyesar *vt* to plaster
enzarzar *vr:* ~se en to get involved [*o* entangled] in
enzima *m o f* enzyme
eñe *f* Ñ, ñ; la letra ~ the letter ñ
eólico, **-a** *adj* wind; central eólica wind power plant
EP *f abr de* Educación Primaria primary education
epa *interj AmL* (*saludo*) hi!; (*llamar la atención*) hey!; (*accidente*) (wh)oops!
épica *f* epic
epicentro *m* epicentre *Brit,* epicenter *Am*
épico, **-a** *adj* epic; poema ~ epic poem
epidemia *f* epidemic
epidermis *f inv* epidermis
epifanía *f* Epiphany, Twelfth Night
epígrafe *m* 1. (*título*) title 2. (*inscripción*) epigraph
epilepsia *f* epilepsy
epiléptico, **-a** *adj, m, f* epileptic
epílogo *m* (*de libro*) epilogue *Brit,* epilog *Am*
episcopal *adj* episcopal; sede ~ bishop's palace
episodio *m* 1. *t.* MÚS, LIT, TV episode 2. (*etapa*) stage 3. (*suceso*) incident
epitafio *m* epitaph
época *f* 1. HIST epoch, age; coches de ~ classic cars *pl;* muebles de ~ antique furniture; trajes de ~ historical [*o* period] costumes *pl;* un invento que hizo ~ an epoch-making invention 2. (*tiempo*) time; ~ de las lluvias rainy season; es la ~ más calurosa del año it is the hottest time of the year; en aquella ~ at that time
epopeya *f* LIT epic
equidad *f sin pl* 1. (*justicia*) fairness 2. (*de precios*) equity
equilátero, **-a** *adj* MAT equilateral
equilibrado, **-a** *adj* balanced; (*sensato*) sensible
equilibrar *vt, vr:* ~se to balance
equilibrio *m* 1. (*en general*) balance; mantener el ~ to keep one's balance; perder el ~ to lose one's balance; para llegar a fin de mes tengo que hacer muchos ~s *fig* I have to do a juggling act to make my money last until the end of the month 2. (*contrapeso*) counterweight 3. (*armonía, mesura*) balance
equilibrista *mf* tightrope artist
equino, **-a** *adj* equine
equinoccio *m* equinox
equipaje *m* (*maletas*) baggage, luggage *Am;* entrega de ~s baggage check-in; exceso de ~ excess baggage; registro de ~ baggage inspection; hacer el ~ to pack; ~ de mano hand baggage [*o* luggage *Am*]
equipal *m Méx* 1. (*silla de mimbre*) rustic wicker chair 2. (*silla de cuero*) leather chair
equipamiento *m* ~ de serie AUTO standard equipment
equipar *vt* to equip; (*de ropa*) to fit out
equiparable *adj* comparable

equiparar *vt* **1.**(*igualar*) to put on the same level **2.**(*comparar*) to compare, to liken

equipo *m* **1.**(*grupo*) team; (*turno*) shift; ~ **gestor** management team; ~ **de investigadores** research team; **trabajo en** ~ teamwork **2.** DEP team; **carrera por** ~**s** team race; **caerse con todo el** ~ *inf* to completely fluff [*o* blow] it; **el** ~ **de casa/de fuera** the home/visiting team **3.**(*utensilios*) equipment; ~ **de alta fidelidad** hi-fi system; ~ **productivo** productive equipment; **bienes de** ~ capital goods *pl*

equis I. *adj inv* X; ~ **euros** X number of euros; **el señor** ~ Mr X II. *f inv* **1.**(*letra*) X, x; **la letra** ~ the letter x **2.** *Col* (*serpiente*) snake

equitación *f sin pl* horseriding; **escuela de** ~ horseriding [*o* riding] school

equitativamente *adv* equitably

equitativo, -a *adj* equitable; **hicieron un reparto** ~ **de las ganancias** they shared out the profits equally

equivalencia *f* equivalence

equivalente I. *adj* equivalent; **una cantidad** ~ **a diez dólares** an amount equivalent to ten dollars II. *m* equivalent; **el** ~ **a diez días de trabajo** the equivalent of ten days' work

equivaler *irr como valer vi* to be equivalent; **la negativa equivaldría a la ruptura de las negociaciones** saying no would mean the breakdown of negotiations; **lo que equivale a decir que...** which is the same as saying that ...

equivocación *f* mistake; (*error*) error; (*malentendido*) misunderstanding; (*confusión*) mix-up; **por** ~ by mistake

equivocadamente *adv* by mistake

equivocado, -a *adj* mistaken; **número** ~ wrong number

equivocar <c→qu> I. *vt* **1.**(*confundir*) to get wrong; **equivoqué los sobres de las cartas** I mixed up the envelopes for the letters **2.**(*desconcertar*) to throw II. *vr:* ~**se** to be wrong; ~**se en** [*o* de] **algo** to be wrong about sth; ~**se de camino** to take the wrong way; ~**se al escribir/al hablar** to make a mistake (when) writing/when speaking; ~**se al hacer una cuenta** to make a mistake in one's calculations; ~**se al leer** to misread; ~**se de número** (**de teléfono**) to dial the wrong number; ~**se de tranvía** to take the wrong tram; ~**se de puerta** to take the wrong door

equívoco *m* (*doble sentido*) ambiguity; (*malentendido*) misunderstanding

equívoco, -a *adj* **1.**(*con dos sentidos*) ambiguous **2.**(*dudoso*) doubtful

era¹ *f* **1.**(*período*) era; ~ **postcomunista** the post-communist era; ~ **terciaria** tertiary era **2.**(*para trigo*) threshing floor

era² **3.** *imp de* **ser**

erario *m* revenue; **el** ~ **público** the public treasury

ere *f* R, r; **la letra** ~ the letter r

erección *f* **1.**(*del pene*) erection **2.**(*de monumentos*) building

erecto, -a *adj* (*tieso*) erect; (*cuerpo*) upright

eremita *mf* hermit

eres **2.** *pres de* **ser**

erguido, -a *adj* (*derecho*) upright

erguir *irr* I. *vt* to raise; ~ **el cuello** to straighten one's neck; **con la cabeza erguida** with one's head held high II. *vr:* ~**se** **1.**(*ponerse de pie*) to stand up straight; (*en una silla*) to sit up (straight); **el perro se irguió sobre las patas traseras** the dog rose up on its hind legs **2.**(*engreírse*) to boast

erial I. *adj* fallow II. *m* fallow field

erigir <g→j> I. *vt* **1.**(*construir*) to build; ~ **un andamio** to put up scaffolding **2.**(*fundar*) to establish **3.**(*nombrar*) to appoint; **la erigieron presidente** she was named president II. *vr:* ~**se** **1.**(*declararse*) ~**se en algo** to declare oneself to be sth **2.**(*hacer de*) ~**se en algo** to act as sth

erizado, -a *adj* **1.** BOT prickly **2.**(*pelo*) on end

erizar <z→c> I. *vt* **1.**(*el pelo*) to make stand on end; **el frío me erizó el vello** the cold gave me goose pimples; **el miedo me erizó los cabellos** I was so frightened my hair stood on end **2.**(*un asunto*) to complicate; **estar erizado de dificultades** to be full of problems; **la vida está erizada de espinas** life is full of difficulties; **el camino está erizado de obstáculos** the way is littered with obstacles II. *vr:* ~**se** **1.**(*pelo*) to stand on end; **mis cabellos se** ~**on del susto** I was so shocked my hair stood on end; **se me erizó el vello de tanto frío** it was so cold I had goose pimples **2.**(*persona*) to stiffen

erizo *m* **1.**(*mamífero*) hedgehog **2.**(*pez*) globefish **3.**(*del castaño*) burr, shell **4.**(*de mar*) sea urchin **5.** *inf* (*persona*) grouch **6.**(*defensa*) spike

ermita *f* hermitage

ermitaño *m* hermit crab

ermitaño, -a *m, f* hermit

erogación *f* **1.** *Arg, Méx, Par* (*pago*) costs *pl* **2.** *Ven, Col* (*donativo*) contribution

erogar <g→gu> *vt Arg, Col* (*pagar*) to pay; (*bienes*) to distribute

erógeno, -a *adj* erogenous

erosión *f* **1.**(*desgaste*) wearing away, wear and tear; (*desaparición*) disappearance; ~ **monetaria** gradual devaluation **2.** GEO erosion **3.**(*de la piel*) graze **4.**(*de alguien*) decline; **sufrir** ~ to go into decline; (*perder influencia*) to lose influence; (*perder prestigio*) to lose prestige

erosionar I. *vt* **1.**(*desgastar*) to wear away **2.** GEO to erode; **el agua erosiona las rocas** water erodes rocks **3.**(*la piel*) to abrade **4.**(*a alguien*) to harm; **el artículo erosionó al partido** the article damaged the party II. *vr:* ~**se** to decline; (*perder prestigio*) to lose prestige; (*perder influencia*) to lose influence

erótico, -a *adj* erotic

erotismo *m* eroticism, erotism

errabundo, -a *adj* (*sin orientación*) wandering; (*vagabundo*) vagrant

erradicar <c→qu> *vt* to eradicate; (*una planta*) to uproot; (*una institución*) to abolish; (*una enfermedad*) to stamp out

errar *irr* I. *vi* 1.(*equivocarse*) to err; ~ **en algo** to make a mistake in sth; ~ **en la respuesta** to give the wrong answer; ~ **en el camino** to take the wrong road; *fig* to make the wrong choice 2.(*andar vagando*) to wander; (*vagabundear*) to live on the streets; ~ **por algo** to roam around sth; **ir errando por las calles** to wander the streets II. *vt* (*no acertar*) to miss; ~ **la vocación** to choose the wrong career III. *vr* ~**se en algo** to make a mistake in sth

errata *f* errata

erre *f* RR, rr; **la letra** ~ the letter rr; ~ **que** ~ *inf* stubbornly; **él está,** ~ **que** ~, **empeñado en subir a la montaña** he absolutely insists on going up the mountain

erróneo, -a *adj* erroneous; **decisión errónea** wrong decision

error *m* 1.(*falta*) fault; ~ **de cálculo** miscalculation; ~ **de operación** INFOR operative error; ~ **ortográfico** spelling mistake; ~ **freudiano** Freudian slip; **cometer un** ~ to make a mistake; **has cometido un** ~ **muy grave** you have made a very serious mistake 2.(*equivocación*) mistake; (*descuido*) oversight; **estar en el** ~ to be wrong; **por** ~ by mistake 3.FÍS, MAT (*diferencia*) error 4.(*conducta reprochable*) misconduct 5.JUR ~ **judicial** miscarriage of justice 6.TIPO ~ **de imprenta** misprint

eructar *vi* to belch, to burp

eructo *m* belch, burp

erudición *f* erudition; (*sabiduría*) wisdom

erudito, -a I. *adj* 1.(*persona*) erudite; ~ **a la violeta** *pey* pseudo-intellectual; (*sabio*) wise 2.(*obra*) scholarly; **conocimientos** ~**s** extensive knowledge II. *m, f* scholar; (*sabio*) man of learning; (*experto*) expert; **es un** ~ **en filosofía** he is a philosophy scholar

erupción *f* 1.GEO eruption; ~ **volcánica** volcanic eruption 2.MED rash

es *3. pres de* **ser**

esa(s) *adj, pron dem v.* **ese, -a**

ésa(s) *pron dem v.* **ése**

esbeltez *f* 1.(*delgadez*) slenderness 2.(*altura*) height 3.(*gracia*) grace 4.(*elegancia*) elegance

esbelto, -a *adj* 1.(*delgado*) slender 2.(*alto*) tall 3.(*grácil*) graceful 4.(*elegante*) elegant; **un hombre** ~ a well-proportioned man

esbirro *m* 1.*pey*(*que comete actos violentos*) henchman, goon *inf*; (*sicario*) assassin 2.(*alguacil*) constable 3.(*de las autoridades*) representative

esbozar <z→c> *vt* 1.(*dibujo*) to sketch 2.(*un tema*) to outline; ~ **un discurso** to summarize a speech 3.(*una sonrisa*) **esbozó una sonrisa** a smile formed upon his/her lips

esbozo *m* 1.(*dibujo*) sketch 2.(*de un proyecto*) outline

escabechar *vt* 1.GASTR to marinate 2. *inf*(*sus-*

pender) to fail 3. *inf*(*matar*) to do in

escabeche *m* 1.(*adobo*) marinade; **atún en** ~ pickled tuna; **poner en** ~ to marinade 2.(*alimento: pescado*) pickled fish; ~ **de pollo** marinated chicken

escabechina *f* 1. *inf*(*en un examen*) **en el examen hubo gran** ~ lots of people failed the exam 2.(*destrozo*) damage; (*carnicería*) bloodbath; **hacer una** ~ to wreak havoc

escabel *m* (*taburete*) stool; (*para los pies*) footstool

escabroso, -a *adj* 1.(*áspero*) rough; (*terreno*) uneven 2.(*asunto*) thorny 3.(*indecente*) obscene

escabullirse <3. pret: se escabulló> *vr* 1.(*desaparecer*) to slip away; ~ (**por**) **entre la multitud** (*o* sneak off) through the crowd 2.(*escurrirse*) to slip through; **la trucha se me escabulló** (**de entre las manos**) the trout slipped through my fingers

escacharrar I. *vt* 1.(*objeto*) to break 2.(*plan, proyecto*) to spoil; **la lluvia nos escacharró la fiesta** the rain spoilt the party; **escacharró nuestros planes** it wrecked our plans II. *vr:* ~**se** 1.(*objeto*) to break; **se me ha escacharrado la escultura** my sculpture has broken 2.(*plan, proyecto*) to be spoilt; **nuestros planes se** ~**on por culpa de la lluvia** our plans were spoilt by the rain

escafandra *f* diving (*o* wet) suit; ~ **autónoma** scuba diving outfit; ~ **espacial** space suit

escala *f* 1. *t.* MÚS (*serie, proporción, de mapa*) scale; ~ **de colores** range of colours (*o* colors *Am*], colour (*o* color *Am*] scale; ~ **de cuotas** payment scale; ~ **de descuentos** range of discounts; ~ **de grados** degree scale; ~ **impositiva** tax bracketing; ~ **de reproducción** scale of reproduction; ~ **de Richter** Richter scale; ~ **de salarios,** ~ **de valores** set of values, salary scale; **a** ~ to scale; **hacer** ~**s** to do scales; **un mapa a** ~ **1:100.000** a map with a 1:100,000 scale; ~ **milimétrica** millimetre scale 2.(*medida*) level; **a** ~ **mundial** on a world scale; **a** ~ **nacional** on a national scale; **en gran** ~ on a large scale; **comprar en gran** ~ to buy in bulk; **fabricación en gran** ~ large-scale production; **ser de mayor** ~ to be on a large scale 3.(*parada, puerto*) stop; **escala** stopover; ~ **forzada** forced landing; **el avión tuvo que hacer** ~ **en París** the plane had to land in Paris; **hacer** ~ **en un puerto** to make a stop at a port 4.(*escalera*) ladder; ~ **de cuerda** rope ladder

escalada *f* 1.(*subida*) climb, ascent; ~ **libre** free climbing; ~ **en roca** rock climbing 2.(*a una posición, cargo*) promotion 3.(*aumento*) increase; (*de un conflicto, la violencia*) escalation

escalafón *m* (*de cargos*) ranking; (*de sueldos*) salary scale; **subir en el** ~ to move up in the ranking

escalar I. *vi* 1.(*en las montañas, socialmente*) to climb 2.(*profesionalmente*) to rise

II. *vt* **1.**(*subir*) to go up; (*una montaña*) to climb; **has escalado las cimas del poder** you have reached the summit of power **2.**(*ladrón*) to break into; ~**on la habitación por la ventana** they got into the room through the window **3.**(*una posición*) to rise to; **escaló el cargo más alto de la empresa** he/she rose to the highest position in the company **4.** MIL to escalate

escaldado, -a *adj* **1.**(*quemado*) scalded **2.**(*escarmentado*) cautious; **salir ~ to** learn one's lesson

escaldadura *f Arg* (*lastimadura*) chafing

escaldar I. *vt* **1.**(*metal*) to make red hot **2.** MED to scald; (*inflamar*) to inflame **II.** *vr:* ~**se 1.**(*persona*) to be scalded **2.**(*piel*) to become chafed

escalera *f* **1.**(*escalones*) staircase, stairs; AVIAT stairway; ~ **abajo** downstairs; ~ **arriba** upstairs; ~ **de caracol** spiral staircase; ~ **mecánica** [*o* **automática**] escalator; ~ **de servicio** service stairs **2.**(*escala*) ladder; ~ **de bomberos** firemen's ladder; ~ **de cuerda** rope ladder; ~ **doble** stepladder; ~ **de incendios** fire escape; ~ **de mano** ladder; ~ **de tijera** stepladder; **subir la ~** to go up the ladder **3.**(*naipes*) run; ~ **de color real** royal flush

escalfar *vt* to poach

escalinata *f* main staircase; (*fuera*) outside steps *pl*

escalofriante *adj* **1.**(*pavoroso*) chilling; **película** ~ scary film *Brit,* scary movie *Am* **2.**(*asombroso*) hair-raising

escalofrío *m* **1.**(*sensación*) chill; **al abrir la ventana sentí** ~**s** I felt a chill when I opened the window; **el libro me produjo** ~**s** the book sent shivers down my spine; **cierra la puerta, tengo** ~**s** close the door, I feel chilly **2.** MED shiver

escalón *m* **1.**(*de una escala*) rung; ~ **lateral** side step **2.**(*nivel*) step; **subir un** ~ (*profesionalmente*) to move up the ladder; **este libro es un** ~ **hacia el éxito** this book is a stepping stone on the way to success; **descender un** ~ **en la opinión pública** to go down in the eyes of the public **3.** MIL echelon

escalonado, -a *adj* **1.**(*terreno*) terraced **2.**(*precio*) graded; **tarifa escalonada** graded fare **3.**(*horario, vacaciones*) staggered **4.**(*pelo*) layered

escalonar *vt* **1.**(*situar*) to spread out; ~ **puestos de vigilancia** to set look-out posts at regular intervals **2.**(*terreno*) to terrace **3.**(*precio*) to grade **4.**(*horarios, vacaciones*) to stagger **5.**(*pelo*) to layer

escalope *m* escalope; ~ **a la vienesa** Wiener schnitzel

escalpelo *m* scalpel

escama *f* **1.**(*placa*) *t.* ZOOL, BOT scale; ~**s de jabón** soap flakes; **tener más** ~**s que un besugo** *fig* to be impossible to resolve **2.** *inf* (*recelo*) suspicion; **le salieron** ~**s** he/she began to have doubts

escamado, -a *adj* **1.**(*piel, superficie*) scaly **2.** *inf* (*receloso*) cautious

escamar I. *vt* **1.**(*el pescado*) to scale **2.** *inf* (*inquietar*) to make suspicious **II.** *vr:* ~**se** *inf* to smell a rat; **me escamé al oír la noticia** I was worried when I heard the news; **me escamé de tu respuesta** I was suspicious of your response

escamocha *f Méx* (*sobras*) leftovers *pl*

escamoso, -a *adj* scaly; (*piel*) flaky

escamotear *vt* **1.**(*ilusionista*) to whisk out of sight **2.**(*quitar*) to remove; (*robar*) to palm **3.**(*ocultar*) to hide; (*información*) to withhold; ~ **la verdad/un asunto** to cover up the truth/a matter

escampar *vimpers* **espera hasta que escampe** wait until it clears

escanciar *vt* to pour

escandalizar <z→c> **I.** *vi* to cause an upset **II.** *vt* **1.**(*indignar*) to scandalize **2.**(*horrorizar*) to horrify **3.**(*impactar*) to shock **4.**(*alborotar*) **ayer por la noche escandalizaste la casa con tus gritos** last night you woke up the whole house with your shouting **III.** *vr:* ~**se 1.**(*indignarse*) ~**se de** [*o* por] **algo** to be scandalized by sth **2.**(*estar horrorizado*) ~**se de** [*o* **por**] **algo** to be horrified at sth

escándalo *m* **1.**(*ruido*) uproar; **armar un** [*o* **dar el**] ~ to make a scene; **se armó un** ~ there was a terrible uproar **2.**(*hecho inmoral*) scandal; ~ **público** public scandal; **causar** ~ to cause a scandal; **la piedra del** ~ the root of the scandal; **estos precios son un** ~ these prices are outrageous; **tu comportamiento es un** ~ your behaviour [*o* behavior *Am*] is a disgrace; **de** ~ scandalous **3.**(*pasmo*) **¡qué** ~**!** can you believe it?

escandaloso, -a *adj* **1.**(*ruidoso*) noisy; (*alborotado*) uproarious **2.**(*inmoral, irritante*) scandalous; **precios** ~**s** outrageous prices **3.**(*revoltoso*) unruly; **esta clase es escandalosa** this class is rowdy [*o* out of control]

Escandinavia *f* Scandinavia

escandinavo, -a *adj, m, f* Scandinavian

escanear *vt* to scan

escáner *m* scanner

escaño *m* **1.**(*banco*) bench **2.** POL (*acta de diputado*) seat

escapada *f* (*huida*) escape; (*viaje*) short trip

escapar I. *vi* **1.**(*de la cárcel, de un peligro*) to escape; (*de un encierro*) to evade; **logré** ~ I managed to escape; **es imposible** ~ **a esta ley** it is impossible to dodge this law **2.**(*deprisa, ocultamente*) to get away; ~ **de casa** to run away from home; **el ladrón escapó por la ventana** the thief got away through the window **II.** *vr:* ~**se 1.**(*de la cárcel, de un peligro*) to escape; (*de un encierro*) to evade **2.**(*deprisa, ocultamente*) to get away; ~**se de casa** to run away from home; **el ladrón se escapó por la ventana** the thief got away through the window; **algunas cosas se escapan al poder de la voluntad** some things are beyond one's power **3.** (*agua, gas*) to leak **4.** (*decir*) to come out; **se me ha escapado que te vas a casar** I let it slip that you were getting married **5.** (*soltarse*) to get away; **se escapó un tiro** a shot was let loose; **se me ha escapado su nombre** I've forgotten your name; **se me ha escapado el autobús** I've missed the bus; **se me ha escapado la mano** my hand slipped; **se me ha escapado la risa** I couldn't help laughing; **se me escapó un suspiro** I let out a sigh **6.** (*pasar inadvertido*) to go unnoticed; **no se te escapa ni una** you don't miss a thing

escaparate *m* **1.** (*de una tienda*) shop window; **estar en el ~** *fig* to be in the limelight **2.** (*estantería*) bookcase **3.** *AmL* (*armario*) dresser **4.** *inf* (*pecho*) cleavage; **tener mucho ~** to have a big cleavage

escaparatista *mf* window dresser [*o* decorator]

escapatoria *f* **1.** (*lugar*) escape; **no hay ~** *fig* there's no way out **2.** (*excusa*) excuse **3.** (*solución*) way out; **es la única ~ que tienes** it's your only way out; **no tener ~** to have no way out; (*cláusula*) loophole

escape *m* **1.** (*de un gas, líquido*) leak **2.** (*solución*) way out; **no tenía ~** (*de una amenaza*) there was no way out; **no había ningún ~ a la situación** there was no way out of the situation **3.** (*rápidamente*) **a ~** like a shot; **dame a ~ las tijeras** quickly, pass me the scisssors

escápula *f* shoulder blade

escaquearse *vr inf* to skive off

escarabajo *m* beetle

escaramujo *m* wild [*o* dog] rose

escaramuza *f* **1.** (*lucha*) skirmish **2.** (*discusión*) row

escarapelar **I.** *vt* **1.** *Col, CRi, Méx* (*descascarar*) to peel **2.** *Col* (*manosear*) to handle; (*ajar*) to wear out **II.** *vr:* **~se** *Méx, Perú* **1.** (*atemorizarse*) to be scared **2.** (*temblar*) to shudder

escarbar **I.** *vi* **1.** (*en la tierra*) **~ en algo** to dig sth **2.** (*escudriñar*) **~ en algo** to investigate sth; (*entremeterse*) to pry into sth **II.** *vt* **1.** (*la tierra*) to dig up; **~ la arena** to dig up sand **2.** (*la lumbre*) to poke **3.** (*tocar*) **~ algo** to pick at sth **4.** (*limpiar*) to clean; **~ los dientes** to pick one's teeth **5.** (*investigar*) to investigate; (*entremeterse*) to pry into **III.** *vr:* **~se** to pick; **no te escarbes la herida** don't pick at the sore; **~se las orejas** to scratch [*o* pick] one's ears

escarceo *m* **1.** *pl* (*divagaciones*) distractions *pl*; **~s políticos** political comings and goings; **sin ~s** without hesitation; **~ amoroso** fling **2.** *pl* (*vueltas*) prancing; **el caballo dio ~s** the horse pranced about **3.** (*oleaje*) ripple

escarcha *f* frost

escarchar **I.** *vt* (*frutas*) to crystallize **II.** *vimpers* **ha escarchado** it's frosty

escarlata *adj* scarlet

escarlatina *f* MED scarlet fever

escarmentar <e→ie> **I.** *vi* **1.** (*desenga-*

ñarse) to realize the truth; **~ en cabeza ajena** to learn from sb else's mistakes **2.** (*enmendarse*) to learn one's lesson **II.** *vt* **1.** (*castigar*) to punish **2.** (*reprender*) to reprimand **3.** (*desengañar*) to teach a lesson; **quedar** [*o* estar] **escarmentado de algo** to learn one's lesson from sth

escarmiento *m* **1.** (*lección*) lesson; **me sirvió de ~** it taught me a lesson **2.** (*penalización*) punishment; (*pena*) sentence

escarnecer *irr como crecer vt* (*burlarse*) to mock; (*ridiculizar*) to deride

escarnio *m* scorn; **con ~** scornfully

escarola *f* curly endive

escarpado, -a *adj* (*terreno*) rugged; (*montaña*) steep and craggy

escarpia *f* hook

escasamente *adv* scarcely; **hace ~ dos horas que se han ido** they left only two hours ago

escasear **I.** *vi* **1.** (*faltar*) to be scarce; **escasea la leche** milk is scarce **2.** (*ir a menos*) to diminish **II.** *vt* (*dar con escasez*) to skimp on

escasez *f* **1.** (*insuficiencia*) shortage; **comprar con ~** to spend sparingly **2.** (*falta*) shortage; **~ de lluvias** lack of rain; **~ de viviendas** housing shortage; **una región con ~ de agua** a region with scarce rainfall **3.** (*pobreza*) neediness; **vivir con ~** to live in need

escaso, -a *adj* **1.** (*insuficiente*) insufficient, scant(y); (*tiempo*) little; **~ de palabras** of few words; **viento ~** light wind; **andar ~ de dinero** to be short of money; **estar ~ de tiempo** to be short of time; **tener escasas posibilidades de ganar** to have little chance of winning; **en dos horas escasas** in only two hours **2.** (*mezquino*) mean

escatimar *vt* to skimp; **no ~ gastos/medios** not to skimp on costs/means; **~ el aplauso a alguien/algo** to be sparing in the applause for sb/sth; **me escatimó parte del dinero** he/she didn't give me some of the money

escayola *f* **1.** (*yeso*) plaster **2.** MED plaster; **¿cuándo te quitan la escayola?** when are they taking the plaster off? **3.** (*estuco*) stucco

escayolar *vt* MED to put a plaster-cast on; **llevar el brazo escayolado** to have an arm in plaster

escena *f* **1.** (*parte del teatro*) stage; **aparecer en ~** to appear on stage; **poner en ~** to stage; **puesta en ~** staging; **salir a la ~** to go on stage; **salir de la ~** to go off stage **2.** (*lugar, parte de una obra*) scene; **~ final** final scene; **cambio de ~** change of scene; **~ del crimen** scene of the crime; **desaparecer de ~** (*marcharse*) to leave the scene; (*morirse*) to pass on; **poner en ~** to put on stage; **salir a ~** (*aparecer*) to make an appearance **3.** (*arte*) theatre *Brit*, theater *Am*; **dedicarse a la ~** to devote oneself to the stage **4.** LIT scene **5.** (*suceso, reproche*) scene; **~ de celos** display of jealousy; **hacer una ~ ridícula** to make a ridiculous scene

escenario *m* **1.** (*parte del teatro*) stage **2.** (*lugar, situación*) scene; ~ **del crimen** scene of the crime; **un cambio de** ~ a change of scene

escénico, -a *adj* scenic; **efectos** ~**s** stage effects *pl;* **escuela de arte** ~ drama school; **palco** ~ stage

escenografía *f* **1.** (*decoración*) set design **2.** (*decorados*) set

escenógrafo, -a *m, f* set designer

escepticismo *m sin pl* (*desconfianza*) scepticism *Brit,* skepticism *Am*

escéptico, -a I. *adj* (*desconfiado*) sceptical *Brit,* skeptical *Am;* **ser** ~ **respecto a algo** to be sceptical [*o* skeptical *Am*] about sth II. *m, f* sceptic *Brit,* skeptic *Am;* **es un** ~ **de la homeopatía** he doesn't take homoepathy seriously

escindir I. *vt* **1.** (*dividir*) to divide; (*partido*) *t.* Fís to split **2.** (*separar*) to separate **3.** (*cortar*) to split II. *vr:* ~**se 1.** (*dividirse*) ~**se en algo** to divide into sth; (*partido*) to split into sth **2.** (*separarse*) to separate

escisión *f* **1.** (*división*) division; (*de un partido*) split; *t.* Fís splitting **2.** (*separación*) separation; MED excision

esclarecer *irr como crecer vt* **1.** (*explicar*) to clear up; (*un crimen, misterio*) to shed light upon; ~ **un asunto** to clear up a matter **2.** (*iluminar*) to illuminate **3.** (*afamar*) ~ **a alguien** to make sb famous

esclarecido, -a *adj* **1.** (*ilustre*) great; (*famoso*) famous **2.** (*lugar*) clear

esclarecimiento *m* **1.** (*explicación*) explanation **2.** (*fama*) fame **3.** (*iluminación*) illumination

esclavitud *f* **1.** (*sistema*) slavery, servitude; **someter a la** ~ to submit to slavery **2.** (*dependencia*) dependence

esclavizar <z→c> I. *vt* **1.** (*cautivar*) to enslave **2.** (*dominar*) to control; ~ **a alguien** (*hacer depender*) to make sb dependent; **la empresa te ha esclavizado** you're a slave to the company II. *vr:* ~**se** to become a slave

esclavo, -a I. *adj* **1.** (*cautivo*) slave **2.** (*dominado*) dependent; (*obediente*) obedient; **eres esclava de tu familia** you do everything your family wants; **ser** ~ **del alcohol** to be a slave to alcohol II. *m, f* slave; **ser el** ~ **de alguien** (*obedecer*) to be sb's slave; (*estar enamorado*) to be at sb's command; **ser un** ~ **de algo** *fig* to be dependent on sth; **eres un** ~ **del alcohol** you can't live without alcohol

esclerosis *f inv* sclerosis; ~ **múltiple** multiple sclerosis

esclusa *f* **1.** (*recinto*) lock; TÉC sluice **2.** (*puerta*) lock gate

escoba *f* **1.** (*para barrer*) broom, brush *Brit;* **no vender ni una** ~ *inf* to be completely useless; (*de bruja*) broomstick **2.** BOT broom **3.** *inf* (*mujer*) frump

escobazo *m* **1.** (*golpe*) knock [*o* smack] with a brush; **echar a alguien a** ~**s** *inf* to throw sb out **2.** *Arg, Chile* (*barredura*) **dar un** ~ **al**

---

suelo to give the floor a quick sweep

escobilla *f* **1.** (*cepillo*) *t.* ELEC brush; (*de baño*) toilet brush **2.** (*escoba*) broom **3.** (*brezo*) heather **4.** (*cardencha*) teasel **5.** (*del limpiaparabrisas*) windscreen wiper pad *Brit,* windshield wiper blade *Am* **6.** (*plumero*) feather duster

escobillar I. *vi AmL* (*zapatear*) to tap or shuffle the feet II. *vt* to brush

escocedura *f* **1.** (*picor*) smarting, stinging **2.** (*irritación*) inflammation; (*ampolla*) blister

escocer *irr como cocer* I. *vi* **1.** (*picar*) to sting **2.** (*ofender*) to be offended; (*irritar*) to be annoyed; **no me escuece que no me hayan invitado** I'm not annoyed at not being invited II. *vr:* ~**se 1.** (*inflamarse*) to redden **2.** (*dolerse*) to be sore; (*enfadarse*) to get angry

escocés *m* **1.** (*lengua*) (Scottish) Gaelic **2.** (*tela*) tartan **3.** (*bebida*) Scotch

escocés, -esa I. *adj* Scottish; **cuadros escoceses** tartan; **falda escocesa** kilt; (*para mujeres*) tartan skirt II. *m, f* Scot, Scotsman *m,* Scotswoman *f*

Escocia *f* Scotland

escoger <g→j> I. *vi* to choose; **no has sabido** ~ you've made the wrong choice II. *vt* **1.** (*elegir, seleccionar*) to choose **2.** (*decidirse*) to decide

escogido, -a *adj* **1.** *ser* (*selecto*) finest; (*persona*) upper class; **mercancías escogidas** top quality goods **2.** *estar* (*elegido*) taken; **estos plátanos están ya muy** ~**s** all the good bananas have gone

escolar I. *adj* academic; **curso** ~ academic year; **edad** ~ school-going age II. *mf* schoolboy *m,* schoolgirl *f*

escolaridad *f* (*en una escuela*) schooling, education; **libro de** ~ reports *pl;* **la** ~ **es obligatoria** education is compulsory; **perder la** ~ not to be eligible to take an exam

escolarización *f* education; ~ **obligatoria** compulsory education; **esta región tiene una tasa de** ~ **muy baja** this area has a very low enrolment [*o* enrollment *Am*]

escolarizar <z→c> *vt* to educate; ~ **una región** to educate a region

escolero, -a *m, f Perú* (*escolar*) schoolboy *m,* schoolgirl *f*

escollar *vi* **1.** (*barco*) to hit a reef **2.** *Arg, Chile* (*proyecto*) to fail

escollo *m* **1.** (*peñasco*) rock; (*dificultad*) difficulty **2.** (*riesgo*) pitfall; **sortear un** ~ to overcome an obstacle

escolta *f* **1.** MIL (*acompañante*) escort; **buque de** ~ escort ship; **dar** ~ **a alguien** to escort sb **2.** (*acompañamiento*) escort **3.** (*guardaespaldas*) bodyguard; (*guardia*) guard

escoltar *vt* to escort

escombrera *f* tip *Brit,* dump *Am*

escombro(s) *m(pl)* rubble; **hacer** ~ *Arg* to exaggerate

esconder I. *vt* (*ocultar*) to hide; (*tapar*) cover

up; **su comportamiento esconde alguna intención** his/her behaviour [o behavior *Am*] is trying to hide something; **el fondo del mar esconde muchas riquezas** the ocean bed has many secret treasures **II.** *vr:* ~**se** (*persona, cosas*) to hide

escondidas *adv* **a** ~ secretly; **a** ~ **del profesor** behind the teacher's back

escondido, -a *adj* **1.** (*secreto*) hidden; **en** ~ hidden away **2.** (*retirado*) remote

escondido(s) *m(pl) AmL* hide and seek

escondite *m* **1.** (*juego*) hide and seek; **jugar al** ~ to play hide and seek **2.** (*lugar*) hiding place

escondrijo *m* hideout

escopeta *f* (*arma*) shotgun; ~ **de aire comprimido** air rifle [o gun *Am*]; ~ **de cañones recortados** sawn-off shotgun

escopetear *vt* **1.** *Méx* (*con indirectas*) to be snide about **2.** *Ven* (*contestar mal*) to give an unpleasant reply to

escorbuto *m* scurvy

escorchar *vt Arg* (*molestar*) to annoy; (*enfadar*) to anger; ¡**no me escorches la paciencia!** don't try my patience!

escoria *f* **1.** (*residuo mineral*) slag **2.** (*hez*) dregs *pl* **3.** (*despreciable*) scum; **la** ~ **de la sociedad** the scum of society

Escorpio *m* Scorpio

escorpión *m* (*alacrán*) scorpion

Escorpión *m* Scorpio

escotado *m* neckline

escotado, -a *adj* with a low neckline; **lleva un vestido muy** ~ she's wearing a dress with a plunging neckline

escotadura *f* (*cortadura*) cut; (*en el cuello*) neckline

escotar **I.** *vt* **1.** (*cortar un escote*) to cut **2.** (*ajustar*) to cut to fit **3.** (*pagar*) to pay one's share **II.** *vi* ~ **entre todos** to club together (to buy sth)

escote *m* **1.** (*en el cuello*) neckline; ~ **en pico** V-neck **2.** (*busto*) bust **3.** (*dinero*) share; **pagar a** ~ to split the price; **pagaron la cena a** ~ they went Dutch on the dinner bill

escotilla *f* hatchway

escozor *m* **1.** (*picor*) burning **2.** (*resentimiento*) resentment **3.** (*pena*) pain

escrachar *vt* **1.** *AmL* (*tachar*) to strike out, to eliminate **2.** *PRico* (*estropear*) to ruin **3.** *Arg, inf* (*arruinar*) to wreck

escracho *m RíoPl* **1.** (*cara fea*) mug *inf* **2.** (*esperpento*) fright

escribanía *f* **1.** (*juego*) writing set **2.** (*mueble*) desk **3.** *AmL* (*notaría*) notary

escribano *m* **1.** (*notario*) notary **2.** (*secretario judicial*) court clerk **3.** (*amanuense*) scribe **4.** *ZOOL* bunting

escribiente *mf* scribe

escribir *irr* **I.** *vi, vt* write; ~ **algo a mano** to write sth by hand; ~ **algo a máquina** to typewrite sth; **escrito a mano** handwritten; **escrito a máquina** typewritten; ¿**cómo se**

escribe tu nombre? how do you spell your name? **II.** *vr:* ~**se** to write (to each other); **se escriben mucho** they write to each other a lot; **estaba escrito que acabarían casándose** it was in their stars to get married

escrito *m* **1.** (*carta*) letter; (*nota*) note **2.** (*literario, científico*) text; *JUR* brief, writ **3.** *pl* (*obras*) writings *pl*; **los** ~**s de Oscar Wilde** Oscar Wilde's works

escrito, -a **I.** *pp de* escribir **II.** *adj* written; **por** ~ in writing; **con la emoción escrita en su cara** with excitement written all over his/her face

escritor(a) *m(f)* writer

escritorio *m* **1.** (*mesa*) desk **2.** (*oficina*) office **3.** *INFOR* desktop

escritura *f* **1.** (*acto*) writing **2.** (*signos*) script; ~ **fonética** phonetic script **3.** (*documento*) deed; ~ **de propiedad** title deeds; ~ **de hipoteca** mortgage deeds; ~ **de seguro** insurance certificate; ~ **social** company registration; **mediante** ~ in writing; **las Sagradas Escrituras** *REL* the Holy Scriptures

escriturar *vt* to put down in deed

escroto *m* scrotum

escrúpulo *m* **1.** (*duda*) scruple; ~**s de conciencia** pangs of conscience; **ser una persona sin** ~**s** to be completely unscrupulous; **no tener** ~**s en hacer algo** to have no qualms about doing sth **2.** (*escrupulosidad*) scrupulousness **3.** (*asco*) disgust; **me da** ~ **beber de latas** I think it's disgusting to drink out of cans

escrupulosidad *f* scrupulousness

escrupuloso, -a *adj* **1.** (*meticuloso*) scrupulous **2.** (*honrado*) principled **3.** (*quisquilloso*) fussy

escrutar *vt* **1.** (*mirar*) to scrutinize **2.** (*recontar*) to count

escrutinio *m* **1.** (*examen*) scrutiny **2.** (*recuento*) count **3.** (*votación*) vote

escuadra *f* **1.** (*para dibujar*) set square; ~ **de delineante** draughtsman's [o draftsman's *Am*] square; **a** ~ at right angles **2.** (*de apoyo, fijación*) bracket **3.** *MIL* (*de infantería*) squad; (*de naves, aviones*) squadron **4.** *MIL* (*cargo*) (squad) corporal **5.** (*cuadrilla*) team **6.** *DEP* corner (of the net)

escuadrilla *f AVIAT* squadron

escuadrón *m MIL* squadron

escuálido, -a *adj* (*flaco*) scrawny; (*maciento*) emaciated

escualo *m* shark

escucha¹ *m MIL* scout

escucha² *f* (*de conversaciones*) listening; ~ **telefónica** telephone tapping; **servicio de** ~ monitoring service; **estar a la** ~ to be listening; ~ **electrónica** electronic surveillance

escuchar **I.** *vi* **1.** (*atender*) to listen **2.** (*en secreto*) to eavesdrop **3.** (*obedecer*) to pay attention **II.** *vt* **1.** (*oír*) to listen to; (*seguir*) to follow; (*en secreto*) to eavesdrop; ~ **un concierto** to listen to a concert; ~ **una conversación telefónica** to tap into a telephone conversation; ~ (**la**) **radio** to listen to the radio **2.**(*prestar atención*) to pay attention; **¡escúchame bien!** pay attention to what I'm saying! **III.** *vr:* ~**se** to like the sound of one's own voice

escuchimizado *adj inf* puny

escudar I. *vt* (*proteger*) to shield **II.** *vr* **1.**(*excusarse*) ~**se en algo** to use sth as an excuse **2.**(*ampararse*) ~**se con algo** to take refuge in sth

escudería *f* DEP racing car team

escudilla *f* bowl

escudo *m* **1.**(*arma*) shield **2.**(*amparo*) defence *Brit*, defense *Am;* (*persona*) protector **3.**(*emblema*) ~ (**de armas**) coat of arms **4.**(*moneda*) escudo (*monetary unit of Chile and Portugal*)

escudriñar I. *vt* **1.**(*examinar*) to scrutinize; (*una habitación*) to search **2.**(*mirar*) to scour; ~ **el cielo en busca de aviones** to scour the skies in search of planes **II.** *vi* ~ **en la intimidad de alguien** to invade sb's privacy

escuela *f* **1.**(*institución, edificio*) school; (*de enseñanza primaria*) primary school, elementary school; **Escuela de Bellas Artes** School of Fine Arts; ~ **de conducir** driving school; ~ **de idiomas** language school; ~ **normal** teacher training college; ~ **de párvulos** nursery school; ~ **superior técnica** polytechnic; ~ **taller** workshop **2.**(*método de enseñanza*) method **3.**(*conocimientos*) teaching; **ha tenido buena** ~ he/she has been well taught; **la vida es la mejor** ~ life is the best teacher **4.**(*estilo, seguidores*) school; **la** ~ **holandesa/de Durero** the Dutch school/the Dürer school; **su ejemplo ha hecho** ~ his/her work has set an example **5.**(*doctrina*) belief

escueto, -a *adj* **1.**(*sin adornos*) bare **2.**(*lenguaje*) concise; *pey* curt; **explicar algo de forma escueta** to explain sth briefly **3.**(*desembarazado*) frank

escuincle *m Méx, inf* (*chiquillo*) baby, kid

esculcar <c→qu> *vt AmC, Col, Méx* (*registrar*) to go through

esculpir *vt* **1.**(*modelar*) to sculpt; ~ **a cincel** to sculpt using a chisel; ~ **en madera** to carve in wood; ~ **una figura en mármol** to sculpt a figure in marble **2.**(*grabar*) to engrave

escultor(a) *m(f)* sculptor *m*, sculptress *f;* ~ **de madera** wood carver

escultura *f* sculpture; ~ **de madera** wood carving

escultural *adj* **1.**(*escultórico*) sculptural; **arte** ~ sculpture **2.**(*bello*) statuesque; **esta chica tiene medidas** ~**es** this girl has got beautiful curves

escupidera *f* **1.**(*para escupir*) spittoon **2.** *AmL* (*orinal*) chamberpot

escupir I. *vi* **1.**(*por la boca*) to spit **2.** *inf* (*contar*) to spit it out **II.** *vt* **1.**(*por la boca*) to spit out; ~ **sangre** to spit blood **2.**(*pagar*) to cough up **3.**(*arrojar*) to give out; ~ **fuego** to belch smoke; **el volcán escupe lava** the volcano

spits lava **4.**(*tratar mal*) to abuse; ~ **a alguien** to insult sb **5.** *inf* (*decir*) to spit out; **escupe lo que sabes** spill the beans

escupitajo *m* gob of spit

escurreplatos *m inv* plate rack

escurridizo, -a *adj* slippery; (*idea*) elusive; **lazo** ~ slipknot

escurrido, -a *adj* **1.**(*flaco*) thin; ~ **de caderas** slim-hipped; ~ **de pecho** flat-chested **2.**(*ropa*) tight **3.** *Méx, PRico* (*avergonzado*) embarrassed

escurridor *m* **1.**(*colador*) drainer, colander **2.**(*escurreplatos*) dish drainer, plate rack *Brit* **3.**(*de una lavadora*) wringer

escurrir I. *vi* (*gotear, ropa*) to drip; (*verdura*) to drain **II.** *vt* **1.**(*ropa*) to wring out; (*platos, verdura*) to drain **2.**(*deslizar*) to slip; ~ **la mano por encima de algo** to run one's hand over sb; **escurrió el dinero en mi bolsillo** he/she slipped the money into my pocket **3.**(*una vasija*) to empty; ~ **la** (**botella de**) **cerveza** to empty the bottle of beer **III.** *vr:* ~**se 1.**(*resbalar*) to slip **2.**(*escaparse*) to slip out; **el pez se me escurrió de** (**entre**) **las manos** the fish slipped out of my hands; ~**se por un agujero** to slip through a hole; ~ **el bulto** *inf* to dodge the issue **3.**(*desaparecer*) to slip away; ~**se** (**por**) **entre la gente** to slip away in the crowd **4.**(*gotear*) to drip; (*lágrima*) to trickle **5.** *inf* (*dar*) to overdo

esdrújulo, -a *adj* with the accent falling on the third-last syllable: *e.g., 'esdrújulo', 'número'*

ese *f* S, s; **la letra** ~ the letter s; **ir haciendo** ~**s** *inf* to stagger [*o* reel] from side to side

ese, -a I. *adj* <**esos, -as**> that; **¿**~ **coche es tuyo?** is that car yours?; **esas sillas están en el medio** those chairs are in the way; **el chico** ~ **no me cae bien** I don't like that boy **II.** *pron dem v.* **ése, ésa, eso**

ése, ésa, eso <**ésos, -as**> *pron dem* that, that one; **me lo ha dicho ésa** that girl told me; **¿por qué no vamos a otro bar?** – ~ **no me gusta** why don't we go to another bar? – I don't like that one; **llegaré a eso de las doce** I'll arrive at about twelve o'clock; **estaba trabajando, en eso** (**que**) **tocaron al timbre** I was working when I heard the bell; **¡a** ~**!** get him!; **¡no me vengas con ésas!** come off it!; **me ofrecieron mucho dinero pero, ¡ni por ésas!** they offered to pay me a lot, but not on your life!; **eso mismo te acabo de decir** that's what I've just said; **aun con eso prefiero quedarme en casa** even so, I'd rather stay at home; **lejos de eso** just the opposite; **no es eso** it's not that; **por eso** (**mismo**) that's why; **¿y eso?** what do you mean?; **¿y eso qué?** so what?; **¡eso sí que no!** definitely not!; *v.t.* **ese, -a**

esencia *f* **1.**(*naturaleza*) essence; **se dice que el irlandés es por** ~ **hablador** it is said that the Irish are talkative by nature **2.**(*fondo*) base; **ser de** ~ to be very pure; **en** ~ in essence

E

3. QUÍM essence; ~ **de café** coffee essence; ~ **de rosas** essence of roses **4.** (*colmo*) height; **ser la ~ de la arrogancia** to be the height of arrogance
esencial *adj* **1.** (*sustancial*) fundamental; **elemento ~** essential element; **lo ~** the main thing **2.** (*indispensable*) essential; **alimento/ aceite ~** essential food/oil
esencialmente *adv* essentially
esfera *f* **1.** MAT sphere **2.** (*del reloj*) face, dial **3.** (*ámbito*) *t.* ASTR field; ~ **de actividad** area of activity; ~ **de influencia** sphere of influence **4.** (*clase*) class; **las altas ~s de la sociedad** the upper classes
esférico *m* DEP ball
esférico, -a *adj* spherical
esferográfico *m* AmS (*bolígrafo*) ball-point pen
esfinge *f* **1.** (*animal fabuloso*) sphinx; **ser una ~** *fig* to be inscrutable **2.** ZOOL hawk moth
esfínter *m* ANAT sphincter
esforzado, -a *adj* courageous
esforzar *irr como* forzar I. *vt* **1.** (*forzar*) to force; (*vista, voz*) to strain; ~ **demasiado la vista** to strain one's eyes **2.** (*dar ánimo*) to encourage II. *vr:* ~**se** (*moralmente*) to strive; (*físicamente*) to make an effort
esfuerzo *m* **1.** (*acción de esforzarse*) effort; **sin ~** effortlessly; **hacer un ~** to make an effort; **me ha costado muchos ~s conseguirlo** it took me a lot of effort to manage it **2.** (*económico*) strain; **hacer un ~** to tighten one's belt **3.** (*valor*) courage **4.** (*vigor*) energy **5.** TÉC stress
esfumar I. *vt* (*contornos*) to blur; (*colores*) to tone down II. *vr:* ~**se 1.** (*desaparecer*) to fade away; (*contornos*) to blur **2.** *inf* (*marcharse*) to beat it; **¡esfúmate!** beat it!
esgrima *f* fencing; **practicar la ~** to do fencing
esgrimir *vt* **1.** (*blandir*) to wield **2.** (*argumento*) to use
esgrimista *mf* AmL fencer
esguince *m* **1.** MED sprain; **hacerse un ~ en el tobillo** to sprain one's ankle **2.** (*movimiento*) sidestep **3.** (*gesto*) frown
eslabón *m* **1.** (*de una cadena*) link **2.** (*entre acontecimientos*) step; **el ~ perdido** the missing link
eslalon *m* slalom
eslavo, -a *adj, m, f* Slav
eslogan *m* slogan
eslora *f* NÁUT length of a ship
eslovaco, -a I. *adj* Slovakian II. *m, f* Slovak
Eslovaquia *f* Slovakia
Eslovenia *f* Slovenia
esloveno, -a *adj, m, f* Slovenian
esmaltar *vt* **1.** (*metal, cerámica*) to enamel **2.** (*adornar de colores*) to paint **3.** (*embellecer*) to beautify
esmalte *m* **1.** (*barniz*) varnish; (*sobre metal, porcelana*) enamel; ~ **de laca** lacquer enamel; **sin ~** unenamelled *Brit*, unenameled *Am*

2. (*de uñas*) nail polish [*o* varnish *Brit*] **3.** (*labor*) enamelling *Brit*, enameling *Am* **4.** (*color*) smalt **5.** (*de los dientes*) enamel **6.** (*lustre*) shine **7.** (*adorno*) embellishment
esmerado, -a *adj* **1.** (*persona*) painstaking **2.** (*obra*) professional
esmeralda I. *adj* emerald II. *f* emerald; ~ **oriental** corundum
esmerarse *vr* **1.** (*obrar con esmero*) to take pains; ~ **en la limpieza** to clean conscientiously **2.** (*esforzarse*) ~ **en algo** to make an effort with sth **3.** (*lucirse*) to make a good impression; **hoy te has esmerado en la comida** today's lunch was wonderful
esmeril *m* (*roca*) emery; **papel de ~** emery paper
esmerilar *vt* to polish using emery
esmero *m* care; **con ~** with great care
esmirriado, -a *adj* (*flaco*) scrawny; (*raquítico*) puny
esmoquin *m* dinner jacket *Brit*, tuxedo *Am*
esnifar *vt inf* (*cocaína*) to snort; (*pegamento, pintura*) to sniff
esnob I. *adj* snobbish II. *mf* snob
esnobismo *m* snobbery
eso *pron dem v.* **ése**
ESO *f abr de* **Educación Secundaria Obligatoria** (compulsory) secondary education up to age sixteen
esófago *m* oesophagus *Brit*, esophagus *Am*
esos *adj v.* **ese**
ésos *pron dem v.* **ése**
esotérico, -a *adj* esoteric
esoterismo *m sin pl* esoteric nature
espabilada *f* Col (*parpadeo*) blink; **en una ~** in a second
espabilado, -a *adj* **1.** (*listo*) smart **2.** (*despierto*) awake
espabilar I. *vi* **1.** (*darse prisa*) to hurry up **2.** (*avivarse*) to liven up; **si quieres empezar a trabajar por tu cuenta, tienes que ~** if you want to be self-employed, you'll have to shake up II. *vt* **1.** (*despertar*) to wake up **2.** (*avivar*) to get one's act together *inf*, to shake up; **en la mili ya lo ~án** he's having to shake up in the army; **es muy perezosa, pero en el colegio ya la ~án** she's very lazy, but when she gets to school she'll have to change her act **3.** (*acabar deprisa*) to hurry; (*fortuna*) to squander; (*comida*) to wolf down **4.** (*robar*) to swipe **5.** (*matar*) to bump off III. *vr:* ~**se 1.** (*sacudir el sueño*) to wake oneself up; (*la pereza*) to get busy; **tómate un café para ~te** have a coffee to wake yourself up **2.** (*darse prisa*) to hurry up **3.** (*avivarse*) **se han espabilado desde que van al colegio** they've livened up since they started school **4.** AmL (*marcharse*) to head off
espachurrar *inf* I. *vt* to squash II. *vr:* ~**se** to get squashed
espaciador *m* space bar
espacial *adj* space; **estación ~** space station
espaciar I. *vt* (*sillas*) to separate; (*alumnos*) to

distribute; (*letras*) to space out; ~ **las visitas** to spread out [*o* to stagger] the visits; ~ **los árboles** to space out the trees **II.** *vr:* ~**se** (*en un discurso*) to go on at length, to expatiate *form*

espacio *m* **1.** (*área*) *t.* ASTR space; (*superficie*) area; (*trayecto*) distance; ~ **sideral** outer space; ~ **vacío** empty space; ~ **verde** green belt; ~ **virtual** cyberspace; ~ **vital** living space; ~ **web** web site; **a doble** ~ double-spaced **2.** (*que ocupa un cuerpo*) room, space; **este armario ocupa demasiado** ~ this wardrobe takes up too much space **3.** (*de tiempo*) period; **en el** ~ **de dos meses** in a period of two months; **por** ~ **de tres horas** for a three hour period **4.** (*programa*) programme *Brit,* program *Am;* ~ **informativo** news bulletin; ~ **publicitario** advertising spot

espacioso, -a *adj* (*lugar*) spacious, roomy

espada¹ *m* **1.** TAUR bullfighter **2.** ZOOL swordfish

espada² *f* **1.** (*arma*) sword; ~ **negra** foil; **desnudar la** ~ to unsheathe one's sword; **el despido era mi** ~ **de Damocles** the possibility of losing my job hung over me like a sword of Damocles; **tu respuesta es una** ~ **de dos filos** [*o* **de doble filo**] your answer is a double-edged sword; **de capa y** ~ cloak-and-dagger **2.** (*naipes*) spade; **pintan** ~**s** spades are trumps ►**estar entre la** ~ **y la pared** to be between the devil and the deep blue sea

espadachín *m* **1.** (*esgrimidor*) swordsman **2.** (*fanfarrón*) loudmouth; (*pendenciero*) troublemaker

espadaña *f* **1.** (*campanario*) bell tower [*o* gable] **2.** BOT bullrush

espagueti(s) *m/(pl)* spaghetti; ~**s a la boloñesa** spaghetti bolognese

espalda *f* **1.** ANAT back; **ancho de** ~**s** broad-shouldered; **ser cargado de** ~**s** to be hunched; **andar de** ~**s** to walk backwards; **con las manos en la** ~ with one's hands clasped behind one's back; **estar a** ~**s de alguien** to be behind sb; **estar de** ~**s a la pared** to have one's back to the wall; **atacar por la** ~ to attack from the rear; **coger a alguien por la** ~ *fig* to take sb by surprise; **doblar la** ~ *fig* to put one's back into a task; **volver la** ~ **a alguien** *fig* to turn one's back on sb; **hablar a** ~**s de alguien** to talk behind sb's back; **me caí de** ~**s al oír eso** *inf* I was astonished to hear that; **tener las** ~**s muy anchas** *fig* to put up with a lot; **tener las** ~**s bien guardadas** *inf* to have friends in high places; **la responsabilidad recae sobre mis** ~**s** the responsibility is on my shoulders; **vivir de** ~**s a la realidad** to live in the clouds **2.** DEP backstroke; **100 metros** ~ 100 metres [*o* meters *Am*] backstroke; **¿sabes nadar** ~? do you know how to swim backstroke?; **nadar de** ~**s va bien para la columna** swimming backstroke is good for your spine **3.** (*de un edificio*) back **4.** (*de un animal*) back; (*para el consumo*) shoulder

espaldero *m* Ven **1.** (*guardaespaldas*) bodyguard **2.** (*asistente de un militar*) henchman

espaldilla *f* **1.** (*de una res*) shoulder **2.** ANAT shoulder blade

espanglis *m* Spanglish

espantadizo, -a *adj* **1.** (*persona*) jittery **2.** (*caballo*) skittish

espantajo *m* **1.** (*espantapájaros*) scarecrow; **tal como vas vestido pareces un** ~ dressed like that, you look a fright [*o* like a scarecrow] **2.** (*fantoche*) bogeyman

espantamoscas *m inv* fly-swatter

espantapájaros *m inv* scarecrow

espantar **I.** *vt* **1.** (*dar susto*) to shock; (*dar miedo*) to frighten **2.** (*ahuyentar a un animal*) to shoo away; (*asustándolo*) to frighten off **3.** (*asombrar*) to awe **II.** *vr:* ~**se 1.** (*personas*) ~**se de** [*o* **por**] **algo** to be scared of sth **2.** (*animales*) to be shooed away; (*asustándolos*) to be frightened off

espanto *m* **1.** (*miedo*) fright; **¡qué** ~! how awful!; **hace un calor de** ~ it's terribly hot; **los precios son de** ~ prices are outrageous; **estar curado de** ~**s** *inf* to have been around a few years **2.** (*terror*) horror **3.** (*enfermedad*) shock **4.** AmL (*fantasma*) ghost

espantosidad *f* AmC, Col, PRico (*horror*) horror

espantoso, -a *adj* **1.** (*horroroso*) horrible **2.** (*feo*) hideous **3.** (*asombroso*) awesome

España *f* Spain

español *m* Spanish; **clases de** ~ Spanish classes; **aprender** ~ to learn Spanish; **traducir al** ~ to translate into Spanish

español(a) **I.** *adj* Spanish; **a la** ~**a** Spanish-style **II.** *m/(f)* Spaniard

esparadrapo *m* adhesive [*o* medical] tape

esparcimiento *m* **1.** (*acción*) spreading **2.** (*diversión*) fun

esparcir <c→z> **I.** *vt* **1.** (*cosas*) to spread out; (*líquido*) to spill; **el viento ha esparcido los papeles de la mesa** the wind has blown the papers off the table **2.** (*mancha*) to spread over **3.** (*noticia*) to spread **4.** (*distraer*) ~ **el ánimo** to amuse oneself **II.** *vr:* ~**se 1.** (*cosas*) to spread out **2.** (*noticias*) to spread **3.** (*distraerse*) to relax; **¿qué haces para** ~**te?** what do you do for fun?

espárrago *m* asparagus; ~ **triguero** wild asparagus; **¡vete a freír** ~**s!** *inf* get lost!; **estar hecho un** ~ *fig* to be as thin as a rake; **ser un**

~ **to be a wet blanket**
esparraguera *f* asparagus plant
espartano, -a *adj* spartan
espartillo *m AmL*, **esparto** *m* esparto
espasmo *m* spasm
espasmódico, -a *adj* spasmodic
espatarrarse *vr* to sprawl out
espátula *f* 1. TÉC trowel 2. (*manualidades*) palette [*o* putty] knife 3. MED spatula
especia *f* spice
especial *adj* 1. (*no habitual*) special; (*adecuado*) perfect; **edición/comisión/escuela** ~ special edition/committee/school; **en** ~ in particular; **¿qué has hecho hoy? – nada en** ~ what did you do today? – nothing special; **no pensaba en nada en** ~ I wasn't thinking of anything in particular; **él es para mí alguien muy** ~ he means a lot to me 2. (*raro*) peculiar
especialidad *f* 1. (*de un restaurante, una empresa*) speciality *Brit*, specialty *Am* 2. (*rama*) field; DEP speciality *Brit*, specialty *Am*
especialista *mf* 1. (*experto*) specialist 2. (*médico*) specialist 3. CINE stuntman *m*, stuntwoman *f*
especialización *f* specialization; **mi** ~ **es la física cuántica** my field is quantum physics
especializar <z→c> *vi, vr:* ~**se** to specialize; **personal especializado** skilled staff
especialmente *adv* (*específicamente*) specially; **lo he hecho** ~ **para ti** I made it specially for you; (*particularmente, sobre todo*) especially
especie *f* 1. *t.* BOT, ZOOL (*clase*) species *inv;* ~ **amenazada de extinción** endangered species; **la** ~ **animal** animals *pl;* **ese es una** ~ **de cantante** he's a kind of singer; **gente de todas las** ~**s** all kinds of people; **un hombre de mala** ~ an unpleasant man 2. COM **pagar en** ~**s** to pay in kind 3. (*rumor*) rumour *Brit*, rumor *Am;* **corre la** ~ **que...** people are saying that ...
especificación *f* 1. (*precisión*) specification; **especificaciones técnicas** technical specifications 2. (*explicación*) explanation
especificar <c→qu> *vt* 1. (*explicar*) to explain; **el ministro especificó los problemas actuales de la economía** the minister spelled out the present economic problems; **no – los pormenores de las negociaciones** not to give details of the negotiations 2. (*citar*) to specify; (*enumerar*) to enumerate
específico, -a *adj* specific; **el significado** ~ **de una palabra** the specific meaning of a word
espécimen *m* <especímenes> 1. (*ejemplar*) specimen; ~ **de lujo** prime example 2. (*muestra*) sample
espectacular *adj* spectacular
espectáculo *m* 1. TEAT show; (*de variedades*) variety show; ~ **de circo** circus; ~ **deportivo** sporting event 2. (*visión*) sight 3. *inf* (*escándalo*) **dar el** ~ to make a spectacle [*o* scene]
espectador(a) *m(f)* spectator

espectro *m* 1. (*fantasma*) phantom, spectre *Brit*, specter *Am* 2. FÍS spectrum
especulación *f* speculation
especulador(a) *m(f)* speculator
especular *vi* 1. *t.* FIN (*conjeturar*) to speculate; ~ **en la Bolsa** to speculate on the stock market 2. (*meditar*) to speculate
especulativo, -a *adj* 1. (*que especula*) speculative 2. (*teórico*) theoretical
espejado *m AmL* mirror-like
espejismo *m* 1. (*óptico*) mirage 2. (*de la imaginación*) illusion
espejo *m* mirror; ~ **retrovisor** car mirror, rearview mirror; **mirarse al** ~ to look at oneself in the mirror; **el cine es el** ~ **de la vida** the cinema reflects real life
espeluznante *adj* horrific
espera *f* 1. (*acción, duración*) wait; **tuvimos dos horas de** ~ we had a two-hour wait; **estoy a la** ~ **de recibir la beca** I'm waiting to hear about the grant; **esta** ~ **me saca de quicio** this waiting around is really getting to me 2. (*estado*) waiting; **lista de** ~ waiting list; **en** ~ **de su respuesta** (*final de carta*) looking forward to hearing from you; **en** ~ **de tu carta, te mando el paquete** I'm sending you the parcel and look forward to hearing from you 3. (*paciencia*) patience 4. (*plazo*) period; **no tener** ~ to be urgent; **sin** ~ immediate; **quien espera, desespera** *prov* a watched pot never boils *prov*
esperanza *f* hope; ~ **de vida** life expectancy; **no tener** ~**s** to have no hope; **abrigar** ~**s** to foster hopes; **estar en estado de buena** ~ to be pregnant [*o* expecting]; **poner las** ~**s en algo** to put one's hopes into sth; **tener** ~**s de conseguir un puesto de trabajo** to have hopes of getting a job; **veo el futuro con** ~ I'm hopeful about the future; **con** ~ **no se come** *prov* who lives by hope will die by hunger
esperanzador(a) *adj* hopeful
esperanzar <z→c> I. *vt* to give hope to II. *vr* ~**se en algo** to become hopeful about sth
esperar I. *vi* 1. (*aguardar*) to wait; ~ **al aparato** (*teléfono*) to stay on the line; **hacerse** ~ to keep people waiting; **es de** ~ **que** +*subj* it is to be expected that; **esperemos y veamos cómo evolucionan las cosas** let's wait and see how things develop; **¡que se espere!** let him wait!; **¿a qué esperas?** what are you waiting for?; **espera, que no lo encuentro** hold on, I can't find it; **ganaron la copa tan esperada** they won the long-awaited cup; **uno sólo tiene que** ~ **a que las cosas lleguen** all things come to those who wait 2. (*confiar*) to hope; ~ **en alguien** to place one's hope in sb II. *vt* 1. (*aguardar*) to wait for; **hace una hora que lo espero** I've been waiting for you for an hour; **hacer** ~ **a alguien** to keep sb waiting; **la respuesta no se hizo** ~ the answer was not long in coming; **te espero mañana a las nueve** I'll be waiting for you tomorrow at nine

o'clock; **me van a ~ al aeropuerto** they're meeting me at the airport; **nos esperan malos tiempos** there are bad times in store for us; **espero su decisión con impaciencia** (*final de carta*) I'm looking forward to hearing from you; **te espera una prueba dura** a hard test awaits you **2.** (*un bebé, recibir, pensar*) to expect; **ya me lo esperaba** I expected it **3.** (*confiar*) to hope; **espero que nos veamos pronto** I hope to see you soon; **esperando recibir noticias tuyas...** looking forward to hearing from you **...**; **espero sacar grandes ganancias de este negocio** I hope to make a lot of profit out of this business; **espero que sí** I hope so

esperma *m* sperm

espermatozoide *m* spermatozoid

esperpéntico, -a *adj* grotesque

esperpento *m* **1.** (*persona*) fright **2.** (*desatino*) piece of nonsense **3.** (*estilo literario*) literary style coined by Valle Inclán

espesar I. *vt* (*líquido*) to thicken **II.** *vr*: **~se** (*bosque*) to become denser

espeso, -a *adj* **1.** (*cabello, niebla, bosque, líquido*) thick **2.** (*persona*) untidy **3.** *Arg, Perú, Ven* (*molesto*) bothersome

espesor *m* **1.** (*grosor*) thickness; (*nieve*) depth **2.** (*densidad*) density

espesura *f* **1.** (*del cabello, bosque*) thickness; (*de un líquido*) density **2.** (*bosque*) thicket

espetar *vt* **1.** (*ave, objeto*) to skewer **2.** *inf* (*de repente*) to come out with; **~ una bronca a alguien** to give sb a telling-off; **~ un sermón a alguien** to give sb a talking-to; **~ cuatro verdades a alguien** *fig* to give sb a piece of one's mind

espía *mf* spy; (*de la policía*) informer; (*infiltrado*) infiltrator; **~ doble** double agent

espiantar I. *vi, vr*: **~se** *CSur, inf* (*alejarse*) to head off; (*huir*) to escape **II.** *vt* *CSur* (*hurtar*) to steal

espiar <**1.** *pres*: **espío**> **I.** *vi* (*hacer espionaje*) to spy **II.** *vt* to spy on; (*para la policía*) to inform on

espichar *vt* *Col, inf* (*aplastar*) to squash

espiga *f* **1.** BOT ear; **dibujo de ~** herringbone **2.** (*madera*) dowel

espigado, -a *adj* **1.** (*forma*) tall **2.** (*maduro*) ripe **3.** (*árbol*) tall; (*persona*) lanky

espigarse <g→gu> *vr* to shoot up

espigón *m* **1.** (*dique*) mole; (*rompeolas*) breakwater **2.** (*espiga*) ear **3.** (*de un clavo*) point **4.** (*aguijón*) sting

espina *f* **1.** (*de pescado*) bone **2.** BOT thorn **3.** (*astilla*) splinter **4.** ANAT **~** (*dorsal*) spine **5.** (*inconveniente*) problem; **esto me da mala ~** *inf* I don't like the look of this **6.** (*pesar*) frustration; **sacarse una ~** *inf* (*desquitarse*) to get even; (*desahogarse*) to let it all out; **tener una ~ clavada** to have sth hanging over one

espinaca *f* spinach

espinal *adj* spinal; **médula ~** spinal chord

espinazo *m* ANAT spinal column; **doblar el ~** *fig* to work hard

espinilla *f* **1.** ANAT shin; **dar a alguien una patada en la ~** to kick sb in the shin **2.** (*grano*) blackhead; **sacarse una ~** to get rid of a blackhead

espino *m* **1.** BOT **~ albar** hawthorn **2.** TÉC **alambre de ~** barbed wire

espinoso, -a *adj*, **espinudo, -a** *adj* *AmC, CSur* **1.** (*planta*) thorny; (*pescado*) bony **2.** (*problema*) tricky

espionaje *m* espionage; **~ industrial** industrial espionage; **servicio de ~ británico** British secret service

espira *f* spiral

espiración *f* MED exhalation

espiral I. *adj* spiral; **escalera ~** spiral staircase **II.** *f* spiral

espirar I. *vi* (*aire*) to exhale **II.** *vt* (*olor*) to give off

espiritismo *m sin pl* spiritualism; **sesión de ~** seance

espiritista *adj* spiritualist

espíritu *m* spirit; (*alma*) soul; (*inteligencia*) mind; (*idea principal*) essence, nature; **~ de compañerismo** brotherly spirit; **~ de contradicción** contrariness; **~ emprendedor** hard-working nature; **~ deportivo** sportsmanship; **~ de la época** spirit of the age; **~ de observación** (*don*) gift of observation; **el Espíritu Santo** REL the Holy Spirit; **~ de solidaridad** spirit of solidarity; **pobre de ~** mean-spirited; **exhalar el ~** to breathe one's last; **cobrar ~** to take shape; **levantar el ~ a alguien** to lift sb's spirits; **tener un ~ de rebelión** to have a spirit of rebellion; **hacer algo con ~ alegre** to go about sth cheerfully; **evocar los ~s** to call upon the spirits

espiritual *adj* spiritual; **vida ~** spiritual life; **mantenemos una relación puramente ~** we have a purely Platonic relationship

espita *f* **1.** (*de una cuba*) tap *Brit*, faucet *Am*; (*del gas*) gas-tap *Brit*, gas spigot *Am*; () **2.** (*palmo*) span **3.** *inf* (*borracho*) drunk

esplendidez *f* **1.** (*generosidad*) generosity **2.** (*magnificencia*) splendour *Brit*, splendor *Am*

espléndido, -a *adj* **1.** (*generoso*) generous **2.** (*aspecto*) splendid; (*día*) beautiful; (*comida*) lovely; (*ocasión, idea, resultado*) excellent

esplendor *m* splendour *Brit*, splendor *Am*

esplendoroso, -a *adj* splendid

espliego *m* lavender

esplín *m* (*melancolía*) spleen

espolear *vt* **1.** (*al caballo*) to spur **2.** (*a alguien*) to spur on

espoleta *f* (*de bomba*) fuse

espolvorear *vt* to sprinkle

esponja *f* **1.** (*para lavar*) *t.* ZOOL sponge; **~ de baño** bath sponge; **beber como una ~** *inf* to drink like a fish; **¡pasemos la ~!** *inf* let's forget about it! **2.** (*persona*) sponger *Brit*, sponge *Am*, leech *Am*

esponjoso, **-a** *adj* (*masa*) fluffy; (*pan*) light
espontáneamente *adv* spontaneously
espontaneidad *f* spontaneity
espontáneo *m* TAUR *bullfight spectator who enters the ring to participate*
espontáneo, **-a** *adj* spontaneous; (*saludo*) natural; **curación espontánea** spontaneous healing
espora *f* spore
esporádico, **-a** *adj* sporadic
esportivo, **-a** *adj* AmL **1.** (*deportivo*) sporting **2.** (*afectando descuido*) casual
esposar *vt* to handcuff
esposas *fpl* (*manillas*) handcuffs *pl;* **colocar las ~ a alguien** to handcuff sb
esposo, **-a** *m*, *f* spouse; (*marido*) husband; (*mujer*) wife; **le presento a mi esposa** this is my wife; **salude a su ~** give my regards to your husband; **los ~s** the bride and groom
espray *m* **1.** (*líquido*) spray **2.** (*envase*) aerosol
esprint *m* sprint
esprintar *vt* to sprint
esprínter *mf* sprinter
espuela *f* **1.** (*de caballo*) spur; **poner las ~s a alguien** to spur sb on **2.** *inf* (*la última copa*) one for the road; **tomar la ~** to have one for the road
espuerta *f* carrier; **a ~s** in sackloads
espuma *f* (*burbujas*) foam; (*de las olas*) spray; (*de jabón*) lather; (*de cerveza*) head; **~ de afeitar** shaving foam; **crecer como la ~** *inf* (*persona*) to shoot up; (*cosa*) to grow very quickly
espumadera *f* skimmer
espumarajo *m* **1.** *pey* (*espuma*) froth **2.** (*de la boca*) foam; **echar ~s por la boca** *fig* to be foaming at the mouth
espumilla *f* **1.** (*tejido*) gauzy fabric **2.** AmL GASTR (*merengue*) meringue
espumillón *m* tinsel
espumoso, **-a** *adj* (*masa*) foamy; (*líquido*) sparkling; **vino ~** sparkling wine
espurio, **-a** *adj* **1.** (*falso*) spurious **2.** (*persona*) illegitimate
esputo *m* spit(tle); MED sputum
esqueje *m* cutting
esquela *f* **1.** (*nota*) notice of death **2.** (*necrológica*) ~ (**mortuoria**) obituary notice; **publicar una ~** to publish an obituary
esquelético, **-a** *adj* **1.** ANAT skeletal **2.** (*persona*) scrawny
esqueleto *m* **1.** ANAT skeleton; **después de la operación quedé hecho un ~** after the operation I was so thin I looked like a skeleton; **esta noche vamos a mover el ~** *inf* tonight we're going to dance **2.** (*de un avión, barco*) shell; (*de un edificio*) framework
esquema *m* **1.** (*gráfico*) sketch; **en ~** in rough **2.** (*de una clase*) summary; **tengo que hacer el ~ del discurso** I have to make an outline for the speech **3.** (*idea*) idea; **romper los ~s** to

shake up sb's ideas
esquemático, **-a** *adj* schematic
esquematizar *vt* to outline
esquí *m* **1.** (*patín*) ski; **~ de fondo** cross--country ski **2.** (*deporte*) skiing; **~ acuático** water-skiing
esquiador(a) *m(f)* skier; **~ de fondo** cross--country skier
esquiar < *1. pres:* esquío> *vi* to ski
esquila *f* **1.** (*cencerro*) cowbell; (*campanilla*) small bell **2.** (*esquileo*) shearing
esquilar *vt* **1.** (*ovejas*) to shear; (*perros*) to clip; **esta tarde iré a que me esquilen** *inf* this afternoon I'm going to get my hair cut **2.** (*timar*) to rip off
esquileo *m* (*acción*) shearing
esquilmar *vt* **1.** (*frutos*) to harvest **2.** (*la tierra*) to exhaust **3.** (*explotar*) to exploit
esquimal **I.** *adj* Eskimo; **perro ~** husky **II.** *mf* Eskimo
esquina *f* corner; **casa que hace ~** house on the corner; **hacer un saque de ~** DEP to take a corner; **a la vuelta de la ~** around the corner; **doblar la ~** to turn the corner
esquinar **I.** *vi* to be on the corner **II.** *vt* **1.** (*objetos*) to turn round **2.** (*maderos*) to square **III.** *vr:* **~se** to have a quarrel
esquinazo *m* *inf* corner; **dar ~ a alguien** (*dejar plantado*) to stand sb up; (*rehuir*) to avoid sb
esquirla *f* splinter, chip
esquirol *mf* scab, blackleg
esquivar **I.** *vt* **1.** (*golpe*) to dodge **2.** (*problema*) to shirk **3.** (*encuentro*) ~ **algo** to get out of sth **4.** (*a alguien*) to avoid **II.** *vr:* **~se** to back out
esquivo, **-a** *adj* **1.** (*huidizo*) evasive **2.** (*arisco*) aloof
esquizofrenia *f* schizophrenia
esquizofrénico, **-a** *adj*, *m*, *f* schizophrenic
esta *adj v.* **este, -a**
ésta *pron dem v.* **éste**
estabilidad *f* stability; (*de una amistad*) firmness; (*del carácter*) steadiness, stability; **~ de los precios** price stability
estabilización *f* stability
estabilizar <z→c> **I.** *vt* to stabilize; (*amistad*) to establish **II.** *vr:* **~se** to stabilize
estable *adj* stable; (*trabajo*) steady; (*carácter*) steadfast, stable
establecer *irr como* crecer **I.** *vt* **1.** (*fundar*) to establish; (*grupo de trabajo*) to set up; (*sucursal, tienda*) to open; (*principio, récord*) to set; (*orden, escuela*) to found **2.** (*colocar*) to place; (*campamento*) to set up; (*colonos*) to settle; (*conexión*) to establish **II.** *vr* **~se de algo** (*instalarse*) to set oneself up as sth
establecimiento *m* **1.** (*fundación, relaciones*) establishment; (*de un grupo de trabajo*) setting-up; (*de una sucursal*) opening; (*de un principio, récord*) setting; (*del orden, de una escuela*) founding **2.** (*de colonia*)

settlement

establo *m* **1.**(*cuadra*) stable, barn; **esta casa es un ~** *fig* this house is a pigsty **2.** *Cuba* (*cochera*) depot; (*para alquilar*) garage

estaca *f* (*palo*) post; (*para tienda*) peg; (*garrote*) stick

estacada *f* fence; **dejar a alguien en la ~** to leave sb in the lurch; **quedarse en la ~** to be left in the lurch

estación *f* **1.**(*año, temporada*) season; **~ de las lluvias** rainy season **2.** *t.* RADIO, TV, FERRO station; (*parada*) stop; **~ de autobuses** bus station; **~ central** central station; **~ de destino** destination; **~ de metro** underground station *Brit*, subway station *Am* **3.**(*centro*) *t.* REL station, centre *Brit*, center *Am;* **~ meteorológica** weather station; **~ orbital** orbiting space station; **~ de servicio** service [*o* gas *Am*] station

estacionamiento *m* **1.** AUTO (*acción*) parking; (*espacio*) parking place [*o* space]; (*lugar*) car park **2.**(*colocación*) placing **3.** MIL (*posición*) positioning **4.**(*estabilización*) stabilization

estacionar I. *vt* **1.** AUTO to park **2.**(*colocar*) to place **3.** MIL to position II. *vr:* **~se 1.** AUTO to park **2.**(*alguien*) to stabilize **3.**(*parar*) to stabilize; **la producción se ha estacionado** production has stabilized

estacionario, -a *adj* stable

estada *f* *AmL*, **estadía** *f* **1.**(*estancia*) stay **2.**(*de un modelo*) session **3.** COM (*tiempo*) demurrage; (*tarifa*) cost of such a delay

estadía *f* *AmL* (*estancia*) stay

estadio *m* **1.** DEP stadium **2.** MED stage

estadística *f* statistics *pl*

estadístico, -a I. *adj* statistical II. *m, f* statistician

estado *m* **1.**(*condición*) condition; (*situación*) state; **~ de alarma** state of alert; **~ civil** marital status; **~ de las cosas** (*general*) state of affairs; **~ de gracia** state of grace; **~ de la economía** state of the economy; **~ de derecho** constitutional state; **~ de emergencia** state of emergency; **~ financiero** financial situation; **~ gaseoso** gaseous state; **~ de guerra** state of war; **el cuarto ~** (*periodismo*) the press; **~ de necesidad** JUR state of necessity; **en buen ~ de conservación** in a good state of upkeep; **en ~ de embriaguez** in a state of inebriation; **estar en ~ interesante** [*o* **de buena esperanza**] to be pregnant; **en ~ de merecer** marriageable **2.** POL state; **~ comunitario** community state; **~ miembro** member state; **presupuestos del ~** state budget; **~ totalitario** police state **3.** MIL **~ mayor** (general) staff; **~ de sitio** martial law **4.** FIN **~ de cuentas** balance statement; **~ de los gastos** statement of expenses

Estados Unidos *mpl* United States *pl* of America

estadounidense I. *adj* of/from the United States, American II. *mf* native/inhabitant of the United States, American

estafa *f* swindle

estafador(a) *m(f)* swindler

estafar *vt* to swindle; **la cajera me ha estafado el cambio** the checkout assistant has shortchanged me

estafeta *f* (*correos*) sub-post office *Brit*, branch post office *Am*

estafilococo *m* MED staphylococcus

estagnación *f* *AmC* stagnation

estaje *m* *AmL* piecework

estajear *vi* *AmL* to do as piecework

estajero, -a *m, f* *AmL* pieceworker, freelancer

estalactita *f* stalactite

estalagmita *f* stalagmite

estallar *vi* **1.**(*globo, neumático*) to burst; (*bomba*) to explode, to go off; (*cristales*) to shatter; (*látigo*) to crack; **estalló una ovación** applause broke out; **me estalla la cabeza** I have a splitting headache **2.**(*revolución, incendio*) to break out; (*tormenta*) to break; **al ~ la guerra** when the war broke out **3.**(*risa*) to burst out; **~ en llanto** to burst into tears; **estaba enfadado y al final estalló** he was angry and he finally snapped

estallido *m* **1.**(*ruido*) explosion; (*de un globo*) bursting **2.**(*de una revolución*) outbreak; **~ de cólera** outbreak of cholera

Estambul *m* Istanbul

estampa *f* **1.**(*dibujo*) illustration; **~ de la Virgen** image of the Virgin Mary **2.**(*huella*) imprint **3.**(*impresión*) impression; (*aspecto*) appearance; **un caballo de magnífica ~** a splendid-looking horse; **tienes mala ~** you look terrible; **¡maldita sea tu ~!** damn you!; **ser la viva ~ de la pobreza** to be the incarnation of poverty; **ser la viva ~ de su padre** *inf* to be the spitting image of one's father

estampado *m* **1.**(*tejido*) print; **no me gusta este ~** I don't like this design **2.**(*metal*) engraving

estampado, -a *adj* printed

estampar I. *vt* **1.**(*en papel, tela*) to print; (*con relieve*) to stamp; **~ un dibujo en una camiseta** to print a design on a T-shirt **2.** TÉC (*una chapa*) to press; (*un motivo en una chapa*) to stamp; **se me quedó estampado en la cabeza** *fig* it imprinted itself on my memory **3.**(*huella*) to imprint; **~ una firma** to sign one's name; **~ la firma al pie del documento** to sign at the foot of the document **4.** *inf* (*arrojar*) to hurl **5.** *inf* (*dar*) to give; **~ una bofetada a alguien** to give sb a slap; **~le un beso a alguien en la cara** to plant a kiss on sb's face II. *vr* **~se con algo** *inf* to crash into sth

estampida *f* stampede

estampido *m* bang; **~ del trueno** peal of thunder; **dar un ~** to bang

estampilla *f* **1.**(*sello*) rubber stamp **2.** *AmL* (*de correos*) stamp

estancamiento *m* **1.**(*del agua*) stagnation **2.**(*de una mercancía*) monopolization **3.**(*de *los negocios*) breakdown; (*de un proceso*) deadlock; ~ **coyuntural** matrimonial deadlock **4.** ECON recession

estancar <c→qu> **I.** *vt* **1.**(*un río*) to stagnate; **aguas estancadas** stagnant water **2.**(*mercancía*) to monopolize **3.**(*proceso*) to hold up **II.** *vr:* ~**se 1.**(*río*) to be held back **2.**(*negocio*) to falter; **quedarse estancado** to get stuck; **me he estancado en los estudios** I've got bogged down in my studies

estancia *f* **1.**(*permanencia*) stay; ~ **en un hospital** stay in hospital **2.**(*habitación*) room **3.** *AmL* (*hacienda*) estate **4.** *Cuba, Ven* (*quinta*) smallholding **5.**(*poesía*) stanza

estanciera *f Arg* (*furgoneta*) station wagon

estanciero, -a *m, f CSur, Col, Ven* **1.**(*de ganado*) cattle farmer **2.**(*de latifundios*) landowner

estanco *m* **1.**(*establecimiento*) tobacconist's (*also selling stamps*) **2.**(*monopolio*) monopoly

estanco, -a *adj* **1.** NÁUT watertight **2.**(*separado*) independent

estándar I. *adj* standard; **tipo** ~ standard version **II.** *m* standard

estandarizar <z→c> *vt* to standardize

estandarte *m* banner

estanque *m* **1.**(*en un parque*) pool, pond **2.**(*para el riego*) tank

estanquero, -a *m, f* tobacconist

estanquillo *m* **1.** *Ecua* (*taberna*) tavern **2.** *Méx* (*tienda*) small shop or stall

estante *m* **1.**(*tabla*) shelf; (*para libros*) bookshelf **2.**(*estantería para libros*) bookcase

estantería *f* shelves *pl;* (*para libros*) bookcase

estañar *vt Ven* **1.**(*herir*) to wound **2.** TEC to tin; (*soldar*) to solder

estaño *m* tin; ~ **para soldar** solder

estar *irr* **I.** *vi* **1.**(*hallarse*) to be; (*un objeto: derecho*) to stand; (*tumbado*) to lie; (*colgando*) to hang; **Valencia está en la costa** Valencia is on the coast; **¿está Pepe?** is Pepe there?; **¿dónde estábamos?** where were we?; **como estamos aquí tú y yo** as you and I are here; **ya lo hago yo, para eso estoy** I'll do it, that's why I'm here; **¿está la comida?** is lunch ready? **2.**(*sentirse*) to be; **¿cómo estás?** how are you?; **ya estoy mejor** I'm better; **hoy no estoy bien** today I'm not well **3.**(*+ adjetivo, participio*) to be; ~ **asomado al balcón** to be looking out over the balcony; ~ **cansado** to be tired; ~ **sentado** to be sitting; ~ **ubicado** *AmL* to be located; ~ **viejo** to be old; **el asado está rico** the roast is delicious; **está visto que...** it is obvious that ... **4.**(*+ bien, mal*) ~ **mal de azúcar** to be running out of sugar; ~ **mal de la cabeza** to be off one's head; ~ **mal de dinero** to be short of money; **eso te está bien empleado** *inf* it serves you right; **esa blusa te está bien** that blouse suits you; **este peinado no te está bien** this hairstyle doesn't suit you **5.**(*+ a*) ~ **al caer** (*persona*) to be about to arrive; (*suceso*) to be about to happen; **están**

al caer las diez it's almost ten o'clock; ~ **al día** to be up to date; **estamos a uno de enero** it's the first of January; **¿a qué estamos?** what day is it?; **las peras están a 2 euros el kilo** pears cost 2 euros a kilo; **el cuadro está ahora a 8.000 libras** the painting now costs 8,000 pounds; **las acciones están a 12 euros** the shares are at 12 euros; **Sevilla está a 40 grados** it is 40 degrees in Seville; **el termómetro está a diez grados** the thermometer shows ten degrees; **están uno a uno** they're drawing one-all; ~ **a examen** to be under examination; **estoy a lo que decida la asamblea** I will follow whatever the assembly decides; **estoy a oscuras en este tema** I'm in the dark about this matter **6.**(*+ con*) to be; **estoy con mi novio** I'm with my boyfriend; **en la casa estoy con dos más** I share the house with two others; **estoy contigo en este punto** I agree with you on that point **7.**(*+ de*) to be; ~ **de broma** to be joking; ~ **de charla** to be chatting; ~ **de mal humor** to be in a bad mood; ~ **de parto** to be in labour [*o* labor *Am*]; ~ **de pie** to be standing; ~ **de suerte** to be lucky; ~ **de secretario** to be working as a secretary; ~ **de viaje** to be travelling [*o* traveling *Am*]; **en esta reunión estoy de más** I'm not needed in this meeting; **esto que has dicho estaba de más** there's no call for what you've just said **8.**(*+ en*) **el problema está en el dinero** the problem is the money; **yo estoy en que él no dice la verdad** I believe he's not telling the truth; **no estaba en sí cuando lo hizo** he/she wasn't in control of himself/herself when he/she did it; **siempre estás en todo** you don't miss a thing; **estoy en lo que tú dices** I agree with you **9.**(*+ para*) ~ **para morir** to feel like dying; **hoy no estoy para bromas** today I'm in no mood for jokes; **el tren está para salir** the train is about to leave **10.**(*+ por*) **estoy por llamarle** I think we should call him/her; **eso está por ver** we don't know that yet; **la historia de esta ciudad está por escribir** the history of this city has not been written yet; **este partido está por la democracia** this party believes in democracy **11.**(*+ gerundio*) to be; **¿qué estás haciendo?** what are you doing; **estoy haciendo la comida** I'm making lunch; **siempre estás viendo la tele** you're always watching television; **he estado una hora esperando el autobús** I've been waiting for the bus for an hour; **estoy escribiendo una carta** I'm writing a letter; **¡lo estaba viendo venir!** I saw it coming!; **este pastel está diciendo cómeme** this cake is crying out to be eaten **12.**(*+ que*) **estoy que no me tengo** I can hardly stand up I'm so tired; **está que trina** he/she's furious **13.**(*+ sobre*) **estáte sobre este asunto** look after this matter; **siempre tengo que ~ sobre mi hijo para que coma** I always have to force my son to eat; **ser una persona que siempre está**

sobre sí (*serena*) to always be in control of oneself **14.**(*entendido*) **a las 10 en casa, ¿estamos?** 10 o'clock at home, OK? **II.** *vr:* ~**se 1.**(*hallarse*) to be **2.**(*permanecer*) to stay; ~**se de charla** to be chatting; **te puedes** ~ **con nosotros** you can stay with us; **me estuve con ellos toda la tarde** I spent the whole afternoon with them; **¡estáte quieto!** keep still; **¡estáte callado!** shut up!

estarcir *vt* to stencil

estárter *m* choke

estatal *adj* state

estática *f sin pl* statics

estático, -a *adj* static; (*pasmado*) rooted to the spot

estatua *f* statue

estatuaria *f* statues *pl*

estatuilla *f* statuette; CINE Oscar

estatura *f* stature; (*altura*) height; **¿qué ~ tienes?** how tall are you?; **es un hombre de ~ pequeña** he's a short man; **su ~ política** his/her political stature

estatus *m inv* status

estatutario, -a *adj* statutory

estatuto *m* **1.**(*de una sociedad*) rule **2.** JUR, POL statute; (*de autonomía*) statute of autonomy; **~ de los trabajadores** employment legislation

este *m* **1.**(*punto*) east; **Alemania del Este** East Germany **2.**(*viento*) easterly

este, -a I. *adj* <estos, -as> this; **~ perro es mío** this dog is mine; **esta casa es nuestra** this house is ours; **estos guantes son míos** these gloves are mine **II.** *pron dem v.* **éste, ésta, esto**

éste, ésta, esto <éstos, -as> *pron dem* him, her, this; **(a) éstos no los he visto nunca** I've never seen them; **~ se cree muy importante** this guy thinks he's very important; **antes yo también tenía una camisa como ésta** I used to have a shirt like this before, too; **(estando) en esto** [*o* **en éstas**], **llamaron a la puerta** and then, someone called at the door; **¡ésta sí que es buena!** *irón* that's a good one!, that's brilliant!; **te lo juro, por ésta(s)** I swear to God!; *v.t.* **este, -a**

estela *f* **1.** NÁUT wake **2.**(*de avión*) slipstream, vapour [*o* vapor *Am*] trail **3.**(*rastro*) trail; **dejar una ~ de recuerdos** to leave a lot of memories in one's wake **4.** ARQUIT stele

estelar *adj* **1.** ASTR stellar; **sistema ~** stellar system **2.**(*extraordinario*) **invitado ~** star guest; **programa ~** TV star programme *Brit,* star program *Am*

estelaridad *f* Chile (*popularidad*) stardom; **tener una gran ~** to be a star

estenografía *f* shorthand

estenografiar <1. pres: estenografío> *vt* to take down in shorthand

estentóreo, -a *adj* (*voz, risa*) booming

estepa *f* **1.** GEO steppe **2.** BOT rockrose

estera *f* matting

estercolero *m* **1.**(*montón*) dunghill **2.**(*lu-*

gar) rubbish tip *Brit,* garbage heap *Am*

estéreo I. *adj inf* stereo **II.** *m* **1.**(*estereofonía*) stereophonics **2.**(*equipo*) stereo

estereofónico, -a *adj* stereophonic

estereotipado, -a *adj* stereotyped; **frase estereotipada** hackneyed expression

estereotipo *m* stereotype

estéril *adj* **1.**(*persona*) sterile; (*mujer*) infertile **2.**(*tierra*) barren **3.**(*trabajo*) mundane; (*esfuerzo*) useless; (*discusión*) pointless

esterilidad *f* **1.**(*de una persona*) sterility **2.**(*tierra*) barrenness

esterilizar <z→c> *vt* to sterilize

esterilla *f* **1.**(*estera*) mat; **~ eléctrica** electric blanket; **~ del camping** camping mat **2.** Ecua (*rejilla*) **silla de ~** wicker chair

esterlina *adj* **libra ~** pound sterling

esternón *m* MED sternum, breastbone

estero *m* **1.** AmL (*pantano*) bog **2.** Cuba (*ría*) estuary **3.** Chile, Ecua (*arroyo*) stream **4.** Ven (*aguazal*) pool; **estar en el ~** to be up the creek without a paddle

esteroide *m* steroid

estertor *m* (*respiración*) rasp; (*de la muerte*) death rattle

esteta *mf* aesthete

estética *f* aesthetics *Brit,* esthetics *Am*

esteticien *mf* beautician, aesthetician *Brit,* esthetician *Am*

estético, -a *adj* aesthetic *Brit,* esthetic *Am;* **cirugía estética** plastic [*o* cosmetic] surgery; **no ~** unaesthetic *Brit,* unesthetic *Am*

estetoscopio *m* stethoscope

estiaje *m* (*nivel*) low water

estibador *m* stevedore, docker *Brit,* longshoreman

estibar *vt* **1.**(*cargar*) to load **2.**(*distribuir*) to trim

estiércol *m* manure; **sacar el ~** *fig* to do the dirty work

estigma *m* stigma; (*en el cuerpo*) mark; REL stigmata *pl*

estigmatizar <z→c> *vt* to stigmatize; REL to mark with stigma

estilar I. *vt* to usually do; **estila levantarse pronto** he/she usually gets up early **II.** *vr:* ~**se** to be in fashion; **ya no se estila llevar pantalones acampanados** it's no longer in fashion to wear bell bottoms

estilista *mf* **1.** LIT stylist **2.**(*diseño*) designer, stylist

estilístico, -a *adj* stylistic

estilizar <z→c> *vt* to stylize; (*adelgazar*) to make slim

estilo *m* **1.** *t.* ARTE, LIT (*modo*) style; **~ de la fuente** INFOR font style; **al ~ de** in the style of; **~ de vida** lifestyle; **por el ~** like that; **¿estás mal?, pues yo estoy por el ~** are you not feeling well? neither am I; **algo por el ~** something similar; **ya me habían dicho algo por el ~** I'd already been told something like that **2.** DEP style; **~ libre** freestyle **3.** LING **~ directo/indirecto** direct/indirect speech

4. BOT style
estilográfica *f* fountain pen
estima *f* esteem; **tener a alguien en mucha** ~ to hold sb in high esteem
estimación *f* **1.** (*aprecio*) esteem; ~ **propia** self-esteem **2.** (*evaluación*) estimate; ~ **de ventas** sales forecast
estimado, -a *adj* **1.** (*apreciado*) respected **2.** (*en cartas*) ~ **Señor** Dear Sir
estimar I. *vt* **1.** (*apreciar*) to apppreciate, to value; ~ **mucho a alguien** to appreciate sb a lot; ~ **poco a alguien** not to think much of sb; ~ **en demasía** to overrate **2.** (*tasar*) to estimate **3.** (*valorar*) ~ **en algo** to value at sth **4.** (*juzgar*) to judge; **lo estimó oportuno** he/she considered it appropriate; ~ **que...** to consider that ... **5.** JUR (*una demanda*) to admit II. *vr:* ~**se 1.** (*apreciarse*) to value each other **2.** (*calcularse*) ~**se en algo** to be valued at sth
estimulante *m* stimulant
estimular *vt* **1.** (*excitar*) to stimulate; (*en la sexualidad*) to excite, to turn on *inf* **2.** (*animar*) to encourage; ECON to stimulate
estímulo *m* **1.** (*incentivo*) incentive; ECON boost; ~ **de la exportación** an export incentive **2.** MED stimulus
estío *m elev* summer
estipendio *m* stipend
esti(p)tiquez *f AmL* (*estreñimiento*) constipation
estipulación *f* **1.** (*convenio*) agreement **2.** JUR stipulation
estipular *vt* **1.** (*acordar*) to stipulate **2.** (*fijar*) to fix
estirado, -a *adj* (*adusto*) severe; (*engreído*) haughty, snooty *inf*
estirar I. *vi* to stretch; **no estires más que se rompe la cuerda** if you stretch it any more the rope will break II. *vt* **1.** (*alargar*) to stretch out; (*suma*) to spin out; (*un discurso*) to draw out; ~ **el bolsillo** to spin out one's resources **2.** (*alisar*) to smoothe; ~ **la masa** to roll out the dough; **aún tengo que** ~ **la cama** I still have to make the bed **3.** (*extender*) to stretch **4.** (*tensar*) to tighten; ~ **la piel** to have a face-lift **5.** (*piernas, brazos*) to stretch out; **voy a salir a** ~ **un poco las piernas** I'm going to stretch my legs a little; ~ **demasiado un músculo** to overstretch a muscle; ~ **el cuello** to crane (one's neck); ~ **la pata** *inf* to kick the bucket *inf* **6.** (*alambre*) to draw III. *vr:* ~**se** to stretch; (*crecer*) to shoot up
estirón *m* **1.** (*tirón*) pull **2.** (*crecimiento*) **dar un** ~ *inf* to shoot up
estirpe *f* stock; JUR heirs *pl*
estival *adj* summer
esto *pron dem v.* **éste**
estocada *f* **1.** *t.* TAUR swordthrust **2.** (*herida*) stab wound
Estocolmo *m* Stockholm
estofa *f pey* (*calidad*) class; **gente de baja** ~ lower class people
estofado *m* (meat) stew

estofar *vt* **1.** (*guisar*) to stew **2.** (*enguatar*) to quilt
estoico, -a *adj* stoical
estola *f* stole
estólido, -a I. *adj* dim-witted II. *m, f* dullard
estomacal *adj* stomach; **trastorno** ~ stomach upset
estómago *m* stomach; **dolor de** ~ stomach-ache; **tener buen** ~ *fig* to be tough; **tener a alguien sentado en el** ~ *fig* not to like sb; **se me revolvió el** ~ it turned my stomach
Estonia *f* Estonia
estonio, -a *adj, m, f* Estonian
estoque *m* **1.** (*espadín*) rapier; **estar hecho un** ~ *fig* to be as thin as a rake **2.** BOT gladiolus
estorbar I. *vi* **1.** (*obstaculizar*) to get in the way **2.** (*molestar*) to be annoying II. *vt* **1.** (*impedir*) to stop **2.** (*obstaculizar*) to hinder **3.** (*molestar*) to bother
estorbo *m* **1.** (*molestia*) nuisance; **sal de casa, que sólo eres un** ~ leave the house, you're only getting in the way **2.** (*obstáculo*) obstacle
estornino *m* starling
estornudar *vi* to sneeze
estornudo *m* sneeze
estos *adj v.* **este, -a**
estrabismo *m sin pl* squint
estrado *m* dais; ~ **del testigo** JUR witness box; **citar a alguien para** ~**s** to subpoena [*o* call as a witness]
estrafalario, -a *adj inf* **1.** (*ropa*) shabby **2.** (*extravagante*) outlandish; (*ridículo*) preposterous
estragar <g→gu> *vt* **1.** (*dañar*) to damage **2.** (*embotar*) to numb; (*gusto*) to pervert
estrago *m* damage; **hacer grandes** ~**s en la población civil** to wreak havoc upon the civil population
estragón *m* tarragon
estrambótico, -a *adj* eccentric
estramonio *m* thorn apple
estrangulación *f t.* MED strangulation; ~ **de intestinos** strangulation of the intestines
estrangulador *m* AUTO ~ **de aire** choke; TEC throttle
estrangulador(a) *m(f)* (*asesino*) strangler
estrangulamiento *m* **1.** (*de persona*) strangulation **2.** (*estorbo*) blockage **3.** (*estrechamiento*) bottleneck
estrangular I. *vt* **1.** (*asesinar*) to strangle **2.** MED to strangulate **3.** TÉC to throttle II. *vr:* ~**se** to be strangled
estraperlista *mf* black marketeer
estraperlo *m* **1.** (*tráfico*) black market; **adquirir algo de** ~ to buy sth on the black market **2.** (*mercancía*) black market goods *pl*
Estrasburgo *m* Strasbourg
estratagema *m* **1.** (*artimaña*) ploy **2.** MIL strategy
estratega *mf* strategist
estrategia *f* strategy
estratégico, -a *adj* strategic

estrato *m t.* GEO stratum; ~ **social** social stratum

estrechamente *adv* **1.**(*pobremente*) in austerity; **vivimos** ~ we barely make ends meet **2.**(*íntimamente*) closely **3.**(*rigurosamente*) strictly

estrechar I. *vt* **1.**(*angostar*) to narrow; (*ropa*) to take in **2.**(*abrazar*) to hug; (*la mano*) to shake **3.**(*amistad*) to deepen; **hemos estrechado nuestra relación** our relationship has become closer **4.**(*obligar*) to oblige II. *vr:* ~**se 1.**(*camino*) to become narrower **2.** *inf*(*en un asiento*) to squeeze in **3.**(*dos personas*) to become close; ~**se las manos** to shake hands **4.**(*amistad*) to deepen **5.**(*económicamente*) to live on a minimum; ~**se el cinturón** *inf* to tighten one's belt

estrechez *f* **1.**(*espacial*) narrowness; ~ **de espíritu** mean-spiritedness **2.**(*rigidez*) strictness **3.**(*de amistad*) deepening **4.**(*escasez*) shortage; (*apuro*) jam; ~ **de dinero** lack of money **5.** *pl* (*económicamente*) neediness

estrecho *m* GEO strait; ~ **de Gibraltar** strait of Gibraltar

estrecho, -a *adj* **1.**(*angosto*) narrow; **él es muy** ~ **de caderas** he's got very narrow hips; **hacérselas pasar estrechas a alguien** *inf* to give sb a hard time **2.**(*amistad*) close **3.**(*ropa, lugar*) tight **4.**(*rígido*) strict **5.** *inf* (*sexualmente*) prudish

estregar *irr como fregar* I. *vt* **1.**(*frotar*) to rub; (*cepillar, para limpiar*) to scrub **2.**(*sacar brillo*) to shine II. *vr:* ~**se** to rub

estrella *f* **1.** ASTR, CINE star; ~ **fija** fixed star; ~ **fugaz** shooting star; ~ **de Venus** the planet of Venus; **una nueva** ~ **del teatro** a new star of the stage; **querer contar las** ~**s** *fig* to aim for the moon; **poner a alguien por las** ~**s** to praise sb to the skies; **ver las** ~**s** (**de dolor**) *fig* to see stars **2.**(*destino*) fate; **haber nacido con buena** ~ to have been born under a lucky star; **tener buena/mala** ~ to be lucky/unlucky **3.** TIPO asterisk **4.** ZOOL ~ **de mar** starfish

estrellado, -a *adj* **1.**(*esteliforme*) star-shaped **2.**(*noche, cielo*) starry; **cielo** ~ starry sky **3.**(*avión*) crashed

estrellar I. *adj* star II. *vt* (*romper*) to smash; (*arrojar*) to hurl; ~ **huevos en una sartén** to break eggs in a frying pan III. *vr:* ~**se 1.**(*chocar*) ~**se contra** [*o* **en**] **algo** to crash into sth; ~**se con alguien** *fig* to bump into sb **2.**(*avión*) to crash; (*barco*) to break up; (*globo*) to burst; ~**se contra** [*o* **en**] **algo** to collide with sth **3.**(*fracasar*) to fail

estrellato *m* stardom

estremecedor(a) *adj* **1.**(*emoción*) moving **2.**(*horrible*) harrowing

estremecer *irr como crecer* I. *vt* **1.**(*conmover*) to move **2.**(*hacer tiritar*) to make tremble II. *vr:* ~**se 1.**(*por un suceso, de un susto*) to be shocked; **se estremecieron sus creencias** their beliefs were rocked **2.**(*tem-*

blar) to shiver

estremecimiento *m* **1.**(*emoción*) shock **2.**(*de cañonazo, terremoto*) rumble **3.**(*de frío, miedo*) shivering **4.**(*de susto*) shock

estrenar I. *vt* **1.**(*usar*) to use for the first time; (*ropa*) to wear for the first time; (*edificio*) to inaugurate; ~ **un piso** to move into a new flat; **sin** ~ brand new; **estos guantes están sin** ~ these gloves are brand new **2.** CINE, TEAT to première **3.**(*trabajo*) to start; ~ **un cargo** to have one's first day in a job [*o* post *Brit*] II. *vr:* ~**se 1.**(*carrera artística*) to make one's debut **2.** CINE, TEAT to be premièred **3.**(*trabajo*) to open, to start work

estreno *m* **1.**(*uso*) first use; (*edificio*) opening; ~ **de piso** showing of new flat *Brit,* house-warming *Am;* **ser de** ~ to be brand new **2.**(*de un actor, un músico*) debut; (*de una obra*) première

estreñido, -a *adj* constipated

estreñimiento *m* constipation

estreñir *irr como ceñir vt* (*comida*) to constipate; **las judías me estriñen** green beans give me constipation

estrépito *m* **1.**(*ruido*) din; **reírse con** ~ to laugh loudly **2.**(*ostentación*) fanfare; **con gran** ~ ostentatiously

estrepitoso, -a *adj* (*risa, aplausos*) loud; (*fracaso*) spectacular

estreptococo *m* MED streptococcus

estrés *m* stress; **producir** ~ to be stressful

estresante *adj* stressful

estresar *vt* to stress

estría *f* **1.** ARQUIT flute **2.** *pl* (*rayas*) grooves *pl;* ~**s del embarazo** stretchmarks *pl* from pregnancy

estriado, -a *adj* **1.** ARQUIT fluted **2.**(*con rayas*) ribbed

estribación *f* GEO foothills *pl*

estribar *vi* to lie; **nuestro éxito estriba en nuestra larga experiencia** our success is due to our lengthy experience; **la dificultad estriba en la falta de práctica** the problem lies in the lack of practice

estribillo *m* **1.** MÚS chorus **2.** LIT refrain **3.**(*frase*) catchphrase; **siempre** (**con**) **el mismo** ~ *fig* always the same old story

estribo *m* **1.**(*de jinete*) stirrup; **estar sobre los** ~**s** *fig* to be careful; **perder los** ~**s** *fig* to fly off the handle **2.**(*del coche*) running board; (*de moto*) footrest **3.**(*entibo*) buttress **4.**(*respaldo*) grip

estribor *m* NÁUT starboard

estricnina *f* strychnine

estricto, -a *adj* **1.**(*severo*) strict **2.**(*exacto*) exact

estridente *adj* shrill; (*vestir*) loud

estripazón *m* AmC **1.**(*apertura*) opening **2.**(*destrozo*) mutilation

estrofa *f* (*de poema*) stanza; (*de canción*) verse

estrógeno *m* oestrogen *Brit,* estrogen *Am*

estroncio *m sin pl* strontium

estropajo *m* **1.** (*de fregar*) scourer; **poner a alguien como un ~** to lay into sb; **servir de ~** *fig* to work like a slave **2.** BOT loofah

estropajoso, -a *adj* **1.** (*seco*) dry; (*carne*) tough **2.** (*pelo*) straw-like **3.** (*tartajoso*) slurring **4.** (*andrajoso*) ragged

estropear I. *vt* **1.** (*deteriorar: planes, comida*) to spoil; (*televisor*) to break; (*cosecha*) to ruin; **con lo que dijiste, lo has estropeado todo** by saying that, you have ruined everything **2.** (*aspecto*) to spoil; **desde la muerte de su mujer está muy estropeado** since his wife died he looks terrible; **está muy estropeado por la enfermedad** the disease has had a very bad effect on him II. *vr:* ~**se 1.** (*deteriorarse*) to spoil **2.** (*averiarse*) to break down; (*comida*) to go off; (*planes*) to be spoilt

estropicio *m* **1.** (*destrozo*) mess **2.** (*alboroto*) uproar

estructura *f* structure; (*edificio*) framework

estructural *adj* structural; **problemas ~es** structural [*o* organizational] problems *pl*

estructurar I. *vt* to structure; (*clasificar*) to classify II. *vr:* ~**se** to be structured

estruendo *m* **1.** (*ruido*) din **2.** (*alboroto*) uproar **3.** (*ostentación*) ostentation

estruendoso, -a *adj* deafening; (*aplauso*) thunderous

estrujar I. *vt* **1.** (*apretar, naranja*) to squeeze **2.** (*machacar*) to crush; (*papel*) to crumple up **3.** (*al saludar*) to hug II. *vr:* ~**se 1.** (*entre mucha gente*) to push **2.** (*apretujarse*) to squeeze together; ~**se los sesos** *inf* to rack one's brains

estucar <c→qu> *vt* to plaster, to stucco

estuche *m* case; (*cajita*) little box; ~ **de gafas** spectacle [*o* glasses] case; ~ **de joyas** jewel box; ~ **de violín** violin case

estuco *m* plaster, stucco

estudiado, -a *adj* (*amanerado*) affected

estudiante *mf* **1.** (*de universidad*) student; ~ **de ciencias** science student **2.** (*de escuela*) pupil

estudiantil *adj* student; **movimiento ~** student movement

estudiar I. *vi, vt* **1.** (*aprender, observar*) to study; ~ **para médico** to study to be a doctor; **dejar de ~** to drop out **2.** (*analizar*) to analyze, to study II. *vt* **1.** (*reflexionar*) to think about; **lo ~é** I'll think about it **2.** (*obra de teatro*) to learn

estudio *m* **1.** (*trabajo intelectual*) studying; **dedicarse tres horas todos los días al ~** to devote three hours every day to studying **2.** (*ensayo, obra*) study; (*informe*) report; (*investigación*) research; ~ **de impacto ambiental** environmental impact study; **estar en ~** to be under study **3.** MÚS étude **4.** ARTE, TV studio; ~ **cinematográfico** cinema studio; ~ **radiofónico** radio studio; ~ **de registro de sonido** sound studio **5.** MED (*prueba*) test **6.** (*taller*) studio **7.** (*piso*) bedsit **8.** *pl* (*carrera*) studies *pl;* **cursar ~s** to study; **no se me dan**

bien los ~s I'm not good at studying; **tener ~s** to have studied

estudioso, -a I. *adj* studious II. *m, f* scholar

estufa *f* heater; ~ **eléctrica** electric fire [*o* heater]

estulticia *f elev* inanity

estupefacción *f* **1.** (*asombro*) amazement; (*sorpresa*) surprise **2.** (*espanto*) fright **3.** MED stupefaction

estupefaciente *m* MED narcotic; (*droga*) drug

estupefacto, -a *adj* **1.** (*atónito*) amazed **2.** (*espantado*) shocked

estupendo, -a *adj* fantastic; ¡~! great!

estupidez *f* stupidity

estúpido, -a I. *adj* stupid II. *m, f* idiot

estupor *m* **1.** (*asombro*) amazement **2.** (*espanto*) shock **3.** MED stupor

estupro *m* rape (*of a minor*)

esturión *m* sturgeon

esvástica *f* swastika

ETA *abr de* **Euzkadi Ta Askatasuna** ETA (*radical Basque separatist movement*)

etapa *f* (*fase*) stage; (*época*) phase; **por ~s** in stages; **quemar ~s** *fig* to come along quickly; **quemar ~s con el coche** *fig* to speed along

etarra I. *adj* **un comando ~** an ETA cell II. *mf* ETA member

etc. *abr de* **etcétera** etc.

etcétera etcetera

éter *m* ether

etéreo, -a *adj* ethereal

eternidad *f* eternity; **tardar una ~** to take a lifetime

eternizar <z→c> I. *vt* to make last forever; *pey* (*alargar*) to spin out II. *vr:* ~**se** to take ages; ~**se en algo** to take ages doing sth

eterno, -a *adj* eternal; (*discurso*) long-winded

ética *f* **1.** *t.* FILOS (*moral*) ethics; ~ **profesional** professional code of conduct **2.** (*decencia*) decency; **no tener ~** to have no sense of decency

ético, -a *adj* ethical

etílico, -a *adj* **1.** QUÍM ethyl **2.** (*alcohólico*) alcoholic; **borrachera etílica** drunkenness; **en estado ~** drunk

etimología *f sin pl* etymology

etimológico, -a *adj* etymological

etíope *adj, mf* Ethiopian

Etiopía *f* Ethiopia

etiqueta *f* **1.** (*rótulo*) label; ~ **del precio** price tag **2.** (*convenciones*) etiquette; ~ **de la red** netiquette; ~ **de palacio** court etiquette; **de ~** (*solemne*) formal; (*ceremonioso*) ceremonial; **función de ~** formal function; **traje de ~** formal [*o* evening] dress; **ir de ~** *inf* to be dressed up

etiquetar *vt* to label; (*encasillar*) to stereotype

etnia *f* (*pueblo*) ethnic group

étnico, -a *adj* ethnic

etnología *f sin pl* ethnology

etnólogo, -a *m, f* ethnologist

eucalipto *m* eucalyptus

eucaristía _f_ Eucharist
eufemismo _m_ euphemism
euforia _f_ euphoria
eufórico, -a _adj_ euphoric
eunuco _m_ eunuch
Eurasia _f_ Eurasia
euro _m_ euro
eurocheque _m_ eurocheque _Brit,_ eurocheck _Am_
eurocomisario, -a _m, f_ POL Eurocommissioner
eurocracia _f_ POL eurocracy
eurodiputado, -a _m, f_ member of the European Parliament, MEP
euroescéptico, -a _m, f_ eurosceptic
Europa _f_ Europe
europarlamentario, -a _m, f_ member of the European Parliament, MEP
europeidad _f_ Europeanness
europeísmo _m sin pl_ Europeanism
europeísta _adj, mf_ pro-European
europeizar _irr como enraizar vt_ to Europeanize
europeo, -a I. _adj_ European; **Consejo Europeo** Council of Europe **II.** _m, f_ European
eurotúnel _m_ Channel tunnel
euscaldún, -una _adj_ Basque-speaking
Euskadi _m_ Basque Country
euskera _m,_ **eusquera** _m_ Basque
eutanasia _f_ euthanasia, mercy killing
evacuación _f_ 1.(_personas, edificios_) evacuation 2. MED excretion
evacuar _vt_ 1.(_ciudad, población_) to evacuate 2.(_diligencias, trámites_) to carry out; (_deber_) to fulfil _Brit,_ to fulfill _Am;_ (_consulta_) to perform; (_negocio, trato_) to conclude 3. MED ~ (**el vientre**) to have a bowel movement
evadir I. _vt_ (_evitar: problema, persona_) to avoid; (_peligro, riesgo_) to avert; ~ **la mirada de alguien** to avoid sb's gaze **II.** _vr:_ ~**se** to get away
evaluación _f_ 1.(_valoración_) valuation 2. ENS assessment; (_examen_) exam(ination)
evaluar < _l. pres:_ evalúo> _vt_ 1.(_valorar_) to value 2.(_apreciar_) ~ **en algo** to price at sth 3.(_analizar_) _t._ ENS to assess
evangélico, -a I. _adj_ evangelical **II.** _m, f_ evangelist
evangelio _m_ Gospel; **el Evangelio según San Mateo** the Gospel according to St Matthew; **decir el** ~ _fig_ to speak the truth
evaporación _f_ evaporation
evaporar I. _vt_ (_convertir en vapor_) to evaporate **II.** _vr:_ ~**se** 1.(_convertirse en vapor_) to evaporate 2.(_desaparecer_) to vanish; (_persona_) to disappear into thin air
evasión _f_ evasion; ~ **de impuestos** ECON tax evasion; (_fuga_) escape; **lectura de** ~ escapist literature; ~ **de la realidad** escape from reality
evasiva _f_ 1.(_rodeo_) evasions _pl;_ **dar** ~**s** to hedge 2.(_pretexto_) excuse 3.(_escapatoria_) way out
evasivo, -a _adj_ evasive; (_ambiguo_) ambigu-

ous, non-committal
evento _m_ 1.(_incidente_) incident, event; **a todo** ~ in any event; ~ **social** social event 2. DEP meeting
eventual _adj_ 1.(_posible_) possible; (_accidental_) fortuitous; (_provisional_) temporary; **trabajo** ~ casual job 2.(_adicional_) extra; **ingresos** ~**es** extra income
eventualidad _f_ 1.(_cualidad_) contingency 2.(_inseguridad_) insecurity 3.(_hecho_) eventuality
eventualmente _adv_ fortuitously; (_tal vez_) possibly
evidencia _f_ (_certidumbre_) evidence; **poner algo en** ~ (_probar_) to prove sth; (_hacer claro_) to make sth clear; **poner a alguien en** ~ to make sb look bad
evidenciar _vt_ (_demostrar_) to show; (_patentizar_) to indicate
evidente _adj_ evident; (_pruebas_) manifest
evidentemente _adv_ evidently; ¡~! of course!
evitar _vt_ 1.(_prevenir_) to prevent; (_molestias, disgustos_) to avoid; **no pude** ~ **que declarasen** I couldn't keep [_o_ prevent] them from testifying; **pude** ~ **mayores estragos** I was able to prevent further damage 2.(_rehuir_) to avoid; **antes de los exámenes evito salir por la noche** I try not to go out at night before the exams **II.** _vr:_ ~**se** 1.(_cosas_) to avoid 2.(_personas_) to avoid each other
evocación _f_ 1.(_de espíritus_) invocation 2.(_recuerdo_) evocation
evocar <c→qu> _vt_ 1.(_espíritus_) to invoke 2.(_recordar_) to evoke; (_revivir_) to relive; **estuvimos toda la tarde evocando nuestra niñez** we spent the whole afternoon remembering our childhood; **tu presencia evocó en mí el recuerdo de tu madre** your being there made me remember your mother
evolución _f_ 1. _t._ MED (_desarrollo_) progress 2.(_cambio_) transformation; **experimentar una** ~ to undergo a transformation 3. BIO evolution 4. MIL manoeuvre _Brit,_ maneuver _Am_ 5. _pl_ (_vueltas_) turns _pl_
evolucionar _vi_ 1.(_desarrollarse_) to progress 2.(_cambiar_) to transform 3. MED to evolve 4.(_dar vueltas_) to turn 5. MIL to manoevre _Brit,_ to maneuver _Am_
ex I. _adj_ ~ **novia** ex-girlfriend **II.** _mf inf_ ex
exacción _f_ (_cobro_) collection; (_impuesto_) tax(ation)
exacerbar I. _vt_ 1.(_dolor_) to intensify; (_crisis_) to deepen, to exacerbate 2.(_irritar_) to aggravate **II.** _vr:_ ~**se** 1.(_dolor_) to intensify; (_crisis_) to deepen 2.(_irritarse_) to become irritated
exactitud _f_ 1.(_precisión_) accuracy 2.(_veracidad_) exactitude 3.(_puntualidad_) punctuality
exacto, -a _adj_ 1.(_con precisión_) accurate; (_al copiar algo_) faithful 2.(_correcto_) correct; **eso no es del todo** ~ that's not exactly true 3.(_puntual_) punctual
exageración _f_ exaggeration
exagerado, -a I. _adj_ exaggerated; (_publici-_

dad) distorted; (*precio*) steep; (*en los gestos*) theatrical **II.** *m, f* **¡eres un ~!** don't exaggerate!

exagerar *vi, vt* **1.**(*sobrepasarse*) to exaggerate; **~ los precios** to charge excessive prices; **~ los gestos** to behave theatrically; **pienso que ese paso sería ~** I think such a step would be going too far **2.**(*al relatar*) to exaggerate; **¡anda, anda, no exageres tanto!** *inf* come on, stop exaggerating!

exaltación *f* **1.**(*gloria*) exaltation **2.**(*entusiasmo*) enthusiasm; (*pasión*) fervour *Brit,* fervor *Am;* (*excitación*) excitement

exaltado, -a I. *adj* **1.**(*sobreexcitado*) over-excited; (*apasionado*) passionate; (*entusiasmado*) enthusiastic **2.**(*violento*) extreme **3.**(*radical*) radical **II.** *m, f* **1.**(*nervioso*) excitable person **2.** POL extremist **3.**(*loco*) lunatic

exaltar I. *vt* **1.**(*elevar*) to exalt **2.**(*realzar*) **~ a alguien** to praise sb **II.** *vr* **~se con algo** (*apasionarse*) to become excited about sth; (*obsesionarse*) to become obsessed with sth

examen *m* **1.**(*prueba, reflexión*) examination; **~ de conciencia** soul-searching; **~ de conducir** driving test; **~ de ingreso** entrance exam; **~ de selectividad** *Spanish university entrance exam;* **presentarse a un ~** to sit for an exam; **tribunal de exámenes** examination board; **aprobar/suspender un ~** to pass/fail an exam **2.**(*médico*) examination; **someterse a un ~** to have a check-up **3.** TÉC test; AUTO check **4.**(*estudio*) examination; (*indagación*) research

examinador(a) *m(f)* examiner

examinar I. *vt* **1.** *t.* MED (*poner un examen, reflexionar*) to examine **2.** TÉC, AUTO to inspect **3.**(*estudiar*) to study, to examine; (*observar*) to observe **4.** ADMIN, JUR to examine; **para ~lo** for examination; **al ~lo** upon examination **II.** *vr:* **~se** (*en una prueba*) to sit [*o* take] an exam; **mañana me examino de francés** tomorrow I've got my French exam; **volver a ~se** to resit [*o* retake] an exam

exangüe *adj* **1.**(*desangrado*) bloodless **2.**(*agotado*) exhausted **3.**(*muerto*) lifeless

exánime *adj* **1.**(*inánime*) lifeless **2.**(*debilitado*) weak

exasperación *f* (*ira*) exasperation

exasperante *adj* exasperating

exasperar I. *vt* to exasperate **II.** *vr:* **~se** to get exasperated

excarcelar *vt* to release from prison

excavación *f* excavation; (*arqueológica*) dig

excavadora *f* excavator

excavar *vt* to excavate; (*en arqueología*) to dig

excedencia *f* (*laboral*) leave

excedente I. *adj* **1.**(*sobrante*) surplus **2.**(*funcionario*) redundant; (*temporalmente*) on (extended) leave **II.** *m* surplus; **~ en la balanza comercial** trade surplus

exceder I. *vi* to be greater; **~ de algo** to exceed sth **II.** *vt* (*aventajar: persona*) to outdo; (*cosa*) to be better than **III.** *vr:* **~se 1.**(*sobre-*

pasar) **~se en algo** to excel at sth; **~se a sí mismo** to outdo oneself **2.**(*pasarse*) to go too far; **has vuelto a ~te** you've overstepped the mark again; **te excedes en el uso de tacos** you swear too much

excelencia *f* **1.**(*exquisitez*) excellence; **por ~ par** excellence **2.**(*cargo*) Excellency

excelente *adj* excellent

excelentísimo, -a *adj* honourable *Brit,* honorable *Am;* **el ~ Ayuntamiento de Cádiz** the Cadiz city council; **el ~ señor Presidente** his excellency, the President

excelso, -a *adj* **1.** *elev* (*muy eminente*) illustrious **2.**(*excelente*) excellent

excentricidad *f* eccentricity; **estoy harta de tus ~es** I've had it up to here with your eccentric behaviour [*o* behavior *Am*]

excéntrico, -a *adj, m, f* eccentric

excepción *f* exception; **~ de la regla** exception to the rule; **con ~ de algunos casos** with a few exceptions; **sin ~** (**ninguna**) without exception; **de ~** unique; **un vino de ~** an exceptionally good wine; **a** [*o* con] **~ de** with the exception of; **todo el mundo a** [*o* con] **~ de mí** everybody except me ►**la ~ confirma la regla** (*prov*) it is the exception which proves the rule

excepcional *adj* (*extraordinario*) exceptional; (*raro*) unusual

excepto *adv* except; **todo el mundo ~ yo** everybody except me; **~ algunos casos** with the exception of some cases

exceptuar < *I. pres:* **exceptúo** > *vt* to except; **~ de un deber** to release sb from a duty

excesivo, -a *adj* excessive; **exposición excesiva** FOTO over-exposure

exceso *m* **1.**(*abuso, demasía*) excess; **~ de alcohol** excessive drinking; **~ de capacidad** overcapacity; **~ de demanda** excess demand; **~ de deudas** too many debts; **~ de equipaje** excess baggage; **~ de peso** excess weight; **~ de velocidad** speeding; **en ~** in excess; **comer con** [*o* en] **~** to overeat; **solía beber hasta el ~** he/she used to drink to excess **2.** FIN surplus **3.** *pl* (*libertinaje*) indulgence; **en su juventud cometió muchos ~s** in his youth he indulged in a lot of excess **4.** *pl* (*desorden*) chaos

excitable *adj* excitable; (*irritable*) temperamental; **muy ~** very highly-strung

excitación *f* **1.**(*exaltación*) excitement; (*sexual*) arousal **2.**(*irritación*) nervousness **3.**(*incitación*) stimulation

excitar I. *vt* **1.**(*incitar*) to incite; (*apetito*) to stimulate **2.**(*poner nervioso*) to put on edge **3.**(*sexualmente*) to arouse **II.** *vr:* **~se 1.**(*enojarse*) to become agitated, to get all worked up *inf* **2.**(*sexualmente*) to become aroused

exclamación *f* **1.**(*frase*) exclamation; **signo de ~** exclamation mark **2.**(*grito*) cry; **lanzar una ~ de sorpresa** to cry out in surprise

exclamar *vi, vt* **1.**(*declamar*) to exclaim

2. (*gritar*) to cry

excluir *irr como huir* *vt* **1.** (*expulsar, eliminar*) to exclude; (*descartar*) to rule out **2.** (*rechazar*) to reject

exclusión *f* **1.** (*eliminación*) exclusion; **con ~ de** excluding; **con ~ de la prensa** press-free **2.** (*expulsión*) expulsion **3.** (*rechazo*) rejection

exclusiva *f* **1.** (*privilegio*) sole rights *pl* **2.** (*monopolio*) monopoly **3.** PREN exclusive; (*primicia*) scoop

exclusivamente *adv* exclusively

exclusive *adv* exclusively; **cerrado hasta el 27 de agosto ~** closed up to and including the 26th of August

exclusivo, -a *adj* exclusive; **contrato/ modelo ~** exclusive contract/model

excma. *adj abr de* **excelentísima** honourable *Brit,* honorable *Am*

excmo. *adj abr de* **excelentísimo** honourable *Brit,* honorable *Am*

excombatiente *mf* ex-serviceman *m Brit,* ex-servicewoman *f Brit,* veteran *Am*

excomulgar <g→gu> *vt* REL to excommunicate

excomunión *f* REL excommunication

excoriación *f* graze

excoriar *vt* to graze

excrecencia *f* outgrowth

excremento *m* excretion

exculpar **I.** *vt* JUR to acquit **II.** *vr:* **~se** to be acquitted

excursión *f* **1.** (*paseo*) excursion, trip; **~ a pie** hike; **ir de ~** to go on an excursion [*o* outing] **2.** (*de estudios*) field trip

excursionista *mf* daytripper, excursionist; (*a pie*) hiker; (*turista*) sightseer

excusa *f* **1.** (*pretexto*) excuse **2.** (*disculpa*) apology; **presentar sus ~s** to apologize **3.** (*justificación*) justification

excusable *adj* justifiable

excusado *m* toilet

excusar **I.** *vt* **1.** (*justificar*) to justify **2.** (*disculpar*) to excuse **3.** (*eximir*) to let off **4.** (*evitar*) to avoid **5.** (+ *inf*) **excusas venir** you don't have to come **II.** *vr* **~se de algo** to apologize for sth

execrable *adj* loathsome

exención *f* exemption; **~ de derechos de aduana** exemption from import/export duty; **~ de impuestos** tax exemption; **~ del servicio militar** exemption from military service

exento, -a *adj* exempt, free; **~ de aranceles** duty-free; **~ de averías** free of breakdowns; **~ de impuestos** tax free; **~ de mantenimiento** free of maintenance; **rentas exentas del impuesto** tax-free income; **estar ~ de la jurisdicción local** to be beyond local jurisdiction

exequias *fpl* funeral rites *pl*

exfoliante *m* exfoliating cream/lotion

exfoliar **I.** *vt* to exfoliate; **la falta de humedad exfolia la piel** lack of moisture dries out

the skin **II.** *vr:* **~se** (*pintura*) to peel; (*corteza*) to flake

exhalación *f* **1.** (*aire*) exhalation **2.** (*suspiro*) sigh **3.** (*rayo*) flash of lightning; **pasar corriendo como una ~** to go past like a streak of lightning **4.** (*estrella*) shooting star

exhalar **I.** *vt* **1.** (*aire*) to exhale, to breathe out **2.** (*emanar*) to give off **3.** (*suspiros, quejas*) to let out **II.** *vr* **~se** to hurry

exhaustivo, -a *adj* exhaustive; **de forma exhaustiva** thoroughly

exhausto, -a *adj* exhausted, knackered *inf*

exhibición *f* **1.** (*ostentación*) display **2.** (*exposición*) exhibition **3.** (*presentación*) show; **~ cinematográfica** film festival; **~ deportiva** sports festival

exhibicionismo *m sin pl* **1.** (*sexual*) indecent exposure, flashing *inf* **2.** (*deseo de exhibirse*) showing-off

exhibicionista *mf* **1.** (*sexual*) flasher **2.** (*presuntuoso*) show-off

exhibir **I.** *vt* **1.** (*mostrar*) to exhibit **2.** (*ostentar*) to show off **3.** JUR to show **II.** *vr:* **~se** to put on a show; **~se en público** to expose oneself

exhortación *f* **1.** (*ruego*) exhortation **2.** (*amonestación*) warning

exhortar *vt* **1.** (*rogar*) to exhort **2.** (*amonestar*) to warn

exhumar *vt* **1.** (*cadáver*) to exhume **2.** (*recordar*) to relive

exigencia *f* **1.** (*demanda*) demand; **tener ~s** *inf* to be very demanding **2.** (*requisito*) requirement

exigente *adj* demanding

exigible *adj* (*obligación*) enforceable; JUR payable on demand

exigir <g→j> *vt* **1.** (*solicitar*) to ask for, to demand; **el docente exige demasiado** the teacher is asking for too much **2.** (*reclamar, pedir*) to demand; **la carta exige contestación** the letter needs to be answered

exiguo, -a *adj* meagre *Brit,* meager *Am*

exil(i)ado, -a **I.** *adj* exiled **II.** *m, f* exile

exil(i)ar **I.** *vt* to exile **II.** *vr:* **~se** to go into exile; **muchos chilenos se ~on en España** many Chilean people sought exile in Spain

exilio *m* exile

eximio, -a *adj elev* illustrious; **un ejemplo ~** a paramount example

eximir **I.** *vt* to exempt; **~ de obligaciones** to free from obligations; **~ de responsabilidades** to release from responsibilities **II.** *vr:* **~se** to be exempted

existencia *f* **1.** (*vida*) existence **2.** *pl* COM stock; **en ~** in stock; **liquidacion de ~s** stock liquidation; **renovar las ~s** to renew stocks; **en tanto haya ~s** as soon as stocks are in

existencial *adj* existential

existente *adj* **1.** (*que existe*) existing **2.** COM in stock

existir *vi* to exist, to be; **existen numerosas actividades** there are many activities; **cree que existen ovnis** he believes that UFOs exist

exitazo *m inf* howling success, smash hit

éxito *m* success; ~ **de taquilla** box office hit; ~ **de ventas** sales success; **con** ~ successfully; **sin** ~ without success; **tener** ~ to be successful

exitoso, -a *adj* successful

éxodo *m* exodus; ~ **rural** rural depopulation; ~ **urbano** urban depopulation; (*de técnicos, científicos, etc.*) brain drain

exonerar *vt* 1.(*eximir*) to exempt 2.(*culpa*) to exonerate 3.(*relevar*) to relieve; ~ **a alguien de su cargo** to remove sb from his/her position

exorbitante *adj* 1.(*excesivo*) excessive; (*precio*) exorbitant 2.(*exagerado*) exaggerated

exorcismo *m* exorcism

exornar *vt* to enhance; LIT to embellish

exótico, -a *adj* exotic

exotismo *m* exoticism

expandir I. *vt* 1.(*dilatar*) to expand 2.(*divulgar*) to spread II. *vr:* ~**se** 1.(*dilatarse*) to expand 2.(*extenderse, divulgarse*) to spread

expansión *f* 1.(*dilatación*) expansion; POL enlargement 2.(*extensión*) extension 3.(*crecimiento*) growth 4.(*difusión*) spread 5.(*diversión*) recreation

expansionarse *vr* 1.(*dilatarse*) to expand 2.*inf* (*sincerarse*) to talk openly 3.*inf* (*divertirse*) to relax

expansivo, -a *adj* 1.(*dilatable*) expansive 2.(*comunicativo*) open

expatriar <1.*pres:* expatrío> I. *vt* 1.(*exiliar*) to exile 2.(*quitar la ciudadanía*) to deprive of citizenship II. *vr:* ~**se** 1.(*exiliarse*) to go into exile 2.(*renunciar a la ciudadanía*) to renounce one's citizenship

expectación *f* 1.(*expectativa*) expectation; **con** ~ expectantly 2.(*emoción*) excitement

expectante *adj* (*atento*) expectant

expectativa *f* 1.(*expectación*) expectation; **estar a la** ~ **de algo** to be on the lookout for sth 2.(*perspectiva*) prospect; ~ **de vida** life expectancy

expectorante *adj* MED expectorant

expectorar *vt* to expectorate

expedición *f* 1.(*viaje*) expedition; ~ **científica** scientific expedition; ~ **militar** military expedition 2.(*grupo*) expedition 3.(*remesa*) shipment; (*acción*) shipping; (**empresa de**) ~ shipping agent; **oficina de** ~ issuing [*o* shipping] office 4.(*documento*) issue

expedicionario, -a I. *adj* expeditionary II. *m, f* member (of an expedition)

expediente *m* 1.(*asunto judicial*) proceedings *pl;* **instruir un** ~ to open proceedings 2.(*legajo*) file; (*sumario*) record; ~ **académico** academic [*o* student] record 3.(*administrativo*) file 4.(*trámite*) requirement; **cubrir el** ~ *inf* to keep up appearances

expedir *irr como* pedir *vt* 1.(*carta*) to send; (*pedido*) to ship; ~ **por avión** to send by air mail; ~ **por correo** to send by post [*o* mail *Am*]; ~ **por vía marítima** to send by sea

2.(*documento*) to issue

expeditar *vt* 1.*AmL* (*acelerar*) to speed up 2.*AmC, Méx* (*despachar*) to send

expedito, -a *adj* 1.(*desembarazado*) free 2.(*rápido*) swift

expeler *vt* (*sangre, excreto*) to expel; (*aire, humo*) to give out

expendedor *m* ~ **automático** vending machine; ~ **de bebidas/cigarrillos** soft drink/cigarette vending machine

expendedor(a) I. *adj* **máquina** ~**a de billetes/tabaco** ticket/cigarette vending machine II. *m(f)* vendor

expendio *m And, Méx, Ven* (*estanco*) shop

expensas *fpl* costs *pl;* **a** ~ **de** at the expense of; **vivir a** ~ **de alguien** to live off sb

experiencia *f* 1.(*práctica, vivencia*) experience; ~ **docente** teaching experience; **falta de** ~ **laboral** lack of work experience; **tener mucha/poca** ~ to have a lot of/little experience; **saber algo por** ~ **propia** to know sth from experience 2.(*experimento*) experiment

experimentado, -a *adj* 1.(*con experiencia*) experienced 2.(*comprobado*) tested; **no** ~ **en animales** (*en etiquetas*) not tested on animals

experimental *adj* experimental

experimentar I. *vi* to experiment II. *vt* 1.(*sentir*) to experience 2.(*hacer experimentos*) to experiment with; (*probar*) to test 3.(*sufrir*) to register; ~ **un alza** to register a rise; ~ **un aumento** to register an increase; ~ **una caída** to register a fall; ~ **una pérdida** to register a loss

experimento *m* experiment

experto, -a I. *adj* expert II. *m, f* 1.(*conocedor*) expert 2.(*perito*) specialist

expiación *f* 1.(*purgación*) expiation 2.(*castigo*) serving

expiar <1.*pres:* expío> *vt* 1.(*purgar*) to expiate 2.(*pena*) to serve

expirar *vi* 1.(*morir*) to expire; (*cultura*) to die out 2.(*plazo*) to expire; **antes de** ~ **el mes** before the end of the month

explanada *f* (*espacio*) flat area

explanar *vt* 1.(*allanar*) to level, to grade 2.(*explicar*) to explain

explayar I. *vt* to extend; ~ **la mirada** to look around II. *vr:* ~**se** 1.(*extenderse*) to spread 2.(*expresarse*) to speak at length; ~**se con alguien** (*confiarse*) to talk openly to sb 3.(*divertirse*) to enjoy oneself

explicable *adj* 1.(*que se puede explicar*) explicable, explainable 2.(*comprensible*) understandable

explicación *f* 1.(*aclaración*) explanation; **pedir explicaciones** to ask for explanations 2.(*motivo*) reason; **sin dar explicaciones** without giving reasons 3.(*interpretación*) interpretation 4.*pl* (*excusas*) reason; **dar explicaciones** to justify

explicar <c→qu> I. *vt* 1.(*manifestar*) to tell 2.(*aclarar, exponer*) to explain 3.(*interpretar*) to interpret 4.(*justificar*) to justify II. *vr:* ~**se**

E

1.(*comprender*) to understand; **no me lo explico** I don't understand it **2.**(*disculparse*) to apologize **3.**(*articularse*) to express oneself; **¿me explico?** do I make myself clear?; **ella se explica muy bien** she expresses herself very clearly

explicativo, -a *adj* explanatory

explícito, -a *adj* explicit

exploración *f* **1.** MIL reconnaissance (mission) **2.** MED examination **3.**(*investigación*) exploration

explorador(a) I. *adj* **1.** MIL reconnaissance **2.**(*investigador*) explorative II. *m(f)* **1.** MIL scout **2.**(*scout*) Boy Scout *m*, Girl Guide *f* Brit, Girl Scout *f* Am **3.**(*investigador*) explorer

explorar *vt* **1.** MIL to reconnoitre Brit, to reconnoiter Am **2.** MED to analyze **3.**(*investigar*) to explore

explosión *f* **1.**(*estallido*) explosion, boom; ~ **demográfica** population boom; **gran** ~ Fís big bang; **motor de** ~ internal combustion engine; **hacer** ~ to explode **2.**(*detonación*) detonation; (*voladura*) blasting; ~ **fallida** undetonated explosive **3.**(*arrebato*) outburst; ~ **de carcajadas** guffaws

explosionar *vi, vt* to explode

explosivo *m* explosive

explosivo, -a *adj* explosive; **artefacto** ~ explosive device

explotación *f* **1.**(*aprovechamiento*) exploitation; AGR plantation; MIN working; ~ **abusiva** exploitation; ~ **a cielo abierto** opencast mining; ~ **de la energía** harnessing of energy; ~ **minera** mine **2.**(*empresa*) management **3.**(*abuso*) exploitation

explotar I. *vi* **1.**(*estallar*) to explode; ~ **en carcajadas** to burst out laughing **2.**(*tener un arrebato*) to blow up *inf* II. *vt* **1.**(*recursos, terreno*) to exploit; AGR to cultivate; MIN to exploit; ~ **pozos petrolíferos** to exploit oil wells **2.**(*empresa*) to manage **3.**(*abusar*) to exploit

expoliar *vt* to ransack

expolio *m* **1.**(*acción*) ransacking **2.**(*botín*) loot **3.** *inf*(*alboroto*) din

exponente *m* **1.**(*ejemplo*) example; (*índice*) index **2.** MAT exponent

exponer *irr como* **poner** I. *vt* **1.**(*mostrar*) to show, to display **2.**(*hablar*) to set out **3.**(*exhibir*) to exhibit **4.**(*proponer*) to put forward **5.**(*explicar*) to explain **6.**(*arriesgar*) to endanger **7.**(*abandonar*) to abandon **8.** FOTO to expose II. *vr:* ~**se 1.**(*descubrirse*) to expose oneself **2.**(*arriesgarse*) to endanger oneself

exportación *f* export

exportador(a) I. *adj* exporting II. *m(f)* exporter

exportar *vt* to export

exposición *f* **1.**(*explicación*) explanation **2.**(*informe*) report **3.**(*exhibición*) exhibition; ~ **universal** world('s) fair **4.** FOTO exposure

expósito, -a I. *adj* abandoned II. *m, f* abandoned child, foundling *liter*

expositor(a) *m(f)* **1.**(*que exhibe*) exhibitor **2.**(*que aclara*) exponent **3.**(*mueble*) display case

exprés I. *adj inv* express; **café** ~ espresso; **olla** ~ pressure cooker II. *m* (*tren*) express

expresamente *adv* **1.**(*literalmente*) clearly **2.**(*deliberadamente*) expressly

expresar I. *vt* to express II. *vr:* ~**se** to express oneself

expresión *f* **1.** expression; **reducir a la mínima** ~ to reduce to the bare minimum **2.** *pl* (*saludos*) greetings *pl*

expresionismo *m sin pl* ARTE expressionism

expresionista *adj, mf* expressionist

expresivo, -a *adj* **1.**(*vivo*) expressive **2.**(*revelador*) revealing **3.**(*significativo*) meaningful **4.**(*afectuoso*) affectionate

expreso I. *m* **1.**(*tren*) express **2.**(*correo*) special delivery II. *adv* express

expreso, -a *adj* **1.**(*explícito*) express **2.**(*claro*) clear **3.**(*rápido*) express; **tren** ~ express train; **enviar una carta por** (**correo**) ~ to send a letter by special delivery

exprimidor *m* squeezer

exprimir *vt* **1.**(*frutas*) to squeeze; ~ **a alguien para que hable** *fig* to put pressure on sb to talk **2.**(*ropa*) to wring **3.**(*persona*) to exploit, to bleed (dry) *inf*

expropiación *f* expropriation; ~ **forzosa** compulsory purchase

expropiar *vt* to expropriate

expuesto, -a I. *pp de* **exponer** II. *adj* **1.**(*peligroso*) risky **2.**(*sin protección*) exposed **3.**(*sensible*) vulnerable; ~ **a perturbaciones** vulnerable to disturbances; (~ **a la vista**) on display

expugnar *vt* to conquer

expulsar *vt* **1.**(*a alguien*) to expel, to kick out *inf*; (*del país*) to deport; (*excluir*) to bar; ~ **a alguien de la escuela** to expel sb from school; ~ **a alguien del campo de juego** DEP to send sb off the pitch [*o* field]; ~ **de la sala** to eject from the room **2.**(*emitir*) to give off, to expel

expulsión *f* **1.**(*de alguien*) expulsion; (*del país*) deportation; DEP sending off Brit, expulsion; ~ **de la escuela** expulsion from school **2.**(*emisión*) expulsion

expurgar <g→gu> *vt* **1.**(*purificar*) to clean out **2.**(*censurar*) to expurgate

exquisitez *f* exquisiteness; (*manjar*) delicacy

exquisito, -a *adj* exquisite; (*comida*) delicious

éxtasis *m inv* ecstacy

extemporáneo, -a *adj* **1.**(*a destiempo*) unseasonable; **son unas temperaturas extemporáneas para esta altura del año** these are unusual temperatures for this time of year **2.**(*inoportuno*) inopportune; (*inadecuado*) inappropriate

extender <e→ie> I. *vt* **1.**(*papeles, mantequilla, pintura*) to spread **2.**(*desplegar*) to unfold; ~ **la mano** to reach out one's hand

3. (*ensanchar*) to widen; (*agrandar*) to enlarge; ~ **la vista** to look around **4.** (*propagar*) to spread **5.** (*escribir*) to write out; (*documento*) to draw up **II.** *vr:* ~**se 1.** (*terreno*) to extend; (*en la cama*) to stretch out **2.** (*prolongarse*) to last **3.** (*difundirse, expresarse*) ~**se por algo** to extend over sth; ~**se en discusiones interminables** to get bogged down in endless discussions

extendido, -a *adj* **1.** (*amplio*) widespread; **un parentesco muy** ~ a far-reaching set of family relations **2.** (*prolongado*) long **3.** (*conocido*) well-known; **estar muy** ~ to be very well-known **4.** (*detallado*) extensive **5.** (*mano, brazos*) outstretched

extensible *adj* **1.** (*ampliable*) extensible; **cable** ~ extension lead *Brit,* extension cord *Am* **2.** (*desplegable*) folding; **mesa** ~ folding table **3.** (*elástico*) elastic **4.** (*plazo*) extendible

extensión *f* **1.** (*dimensión*) extent; (*longitud*) length; **en toda la** ~ **de la palabra** in all senses of the word; **por** ~ by extension **2.** (*difusión*) spreading **3.** (*duración*) length **4.** (*ampliación*) enlargement; ~ **hacia el este** POL enlargement towards the east; ~ **eléctrica** extension lead *Brit* [o cord *Am*] **5.** TEL extension

extensivo, -a *adj* extensive; **hacer extensiva una invitación a alguien** to extend an invitation to sb; **hacer** ~**s sus saludos a alguien** to offer one's greetings to sb

extenso, -a *adj* **1.** (*amplio*) extensive **2.** (*dilatado*) lengthy, drawn-out

extenuar <*1.pres:* extenúo> *vt* **1.** (*agotar*) to exhaust **2.** (*debilitar*) to weaken

exterior I. *adj* **1.** (*de fuera*) external, exterior; **aspecto** ~ external appearance; **espacio** ~ outer space **2.** (*extranjero*) foreign; **Ministerio de Asuntos Exteriores** Foreign Office *Brit,* State Department *Am;* **relaciones** ~**es** external relations *pl* **II.** *m* **1.** (*parte de afuera, apariencia*) exterior **2.** *pl* CINE location shots *pl*

exteriorizar <z→c> *vt* (*manifestar*) to show; (*revelar*) to reveal

exteriormente *adv* externally, outwardly

exterminar *vt* **1.** (*aniquilar*) to exterminate **2.** (*devastar*) to destroy

exterminio *m* **1.** (*aniquilación*) extermination **2.** (*devastación*) destruction

externo, -a *adj* external; **consultorios** ~**s** outpatients' department; **de uso** ~ MED external use only

extinción *f* **1.** (*apagado*) extinguishing; ~ **de incendios** fire extinguishing **2.** ECOL extinction; **en vías de** ~ threatened by extinction **3.** (*de obligación, derecho*) end; (*de contrato*) termination

extinguir <gu→g> **I.** *vt* **1.** (*apagar*) to extinguish **2.** (*finalizar*) to terminate **II.** *vr:* ~**se 1.** (*apagarse*) to be extinguished **2.** (*finalizar*) to be terminated; ECOL to become extinct

extinto, -a I. *adj* **1.** (*especie, volcán*) extinct **2.** (*fuego*) extinguished **3.** *AmS, Méx* (*muerto*) deceased **II.** *m, f AmS, Méx* deceased

extintor *m* ~ **de incendios** fire extinguisher

extirpación *f* **1.** MED extraction; (*de un miembro*) amputation **2.** (*erradicación*) eradication **3.** (*desarraigo*) extirpation

extirpar *vt* **1.** MED to extract; (*miembro*) to amputate **2.** (*erradicar*) to eradicate **3.** (*arrancar*) to extirpate

extorsión *f* **1.** (*chantaje*) extorsion **2.** (*molestia*) nuisance; **ser una** ~ to be a pain *inf*

extorsionar *vt* **1.** (*chantajear*) to extort **2.** (*molestar*) to bother

extra¹ I. *adj* **1.** (*adicional*) extra; **horas** ~**s** overtime; **paga** ~ bonus **2.** (*excelente*) extra special; **de calidad** ~ top quality **II.** *prep* ~ **de** in addition to **III.** *m* **1.** (*complemento*) extra; (*en periódico, revista*) special supplement **2.** (*paga*) bonus

extra² *mf* **1.** CINE, TV extra **2.** (*ayudante*) helper

extracción *f* **1.** (*sacar*) removal; (*de un diente*) extraction; ~ **de sangre** extraction [o drawing] of blood **2.** (*lotería*) draw **3.** *t.* MIN (*origen*) extraction

extraconyugal *adj* extramarital

extractar *vt* to extract; (*resumir*) to summarize

extracto *m* **1.** (*resumen*) summary **2.** (*pasaje*) extract; ~ **impreso** INFOR printed extract **3.** QUÍM extract

extractor *m* ~ **de humo** extractor fan

extradición *f* extradition

extraditar *vt* to extradite

extraer *irr como traer vt* **1.** (*sacar*) to remove; (*dientes*) to extract; ~ **de un libro** to extract from a book **2.** QUÍM, MIN to extract **3.** MAT to extract

extraescolar *adj* extracurricular

extrafino, -a *adj* top quality **extrajudicial** *adj* extrajudicial

extralimitarse *vr* to go too far; ~ **en sus funciones** to overstep one's bounds; ~ **en sus esfuerzos** to make a superhuman effort

extranjería *f* status of aliens; **ley de** ~ immigration law

extranjero *m* abroad

extranjero, -a I. *adj* foreign; **lengua extranjera** foreign language **II.** *m, f* foreigner

extrañamente *adv* strangely

extrañar I. *vt* **1.** (*desterrar*) to deport **2.** (*sorprender*) to surprise; **¡no me extraña!** I'm not surprised! **3.** (*echar de menos*) to miss **II.** *vr* ~**se de algo** to find sth strange

extrañeza *f* **1.** (*rareza*) strangeness; **causar** ~ to cause surprise **2.** (*perplejidad*) surprise

extraño, -a I. *adj* **1.** (*raro, forastero*) strange, odd; (*extranjero*) foreign **2.** (*peculiar*) peculiar; (*extraordinario*) remarkable **II.** *m, f* (*forastero*) outsider, stranger; (*extranjero*) foreigner

extraoficial *adj* unofficial; **una declaración** ~ an off-the-record statement

extraordinario *m* PREN special supplement

extraordinario, -a *adj* **1.** (*fuera de lo nor-*

mal) extraordinary; (*muy bueno*) fantastic **2.**(*por añadidura*) special **3.**(*raro*) strange **4.**(*sorprendente*) surprising

extraparlamentario, -a *adj* extraparliamentary

extrarradio *m* outskirts *pl*

extrasensorial *adj* extrasensory **extraterrestre** I. *adj* extraterrestrial II. *mf* extraterrestrial, alien

extravagancia *f* **1.**(*rareza*) strangeness **2.**(*excentricidad*) eccentricity

extravagante I. *adj* **1.**(*raro*) odd **2.**(*excéntrico*) eccentric II. *mf* eccentric

extraviado, -a *adj* **1.**(*cosa*) lost **2.**(*animal*) stray

extraviar <*l. pres:* extravío> I. *vt* **1.**(*despistar*) to confuse **2.**(*perder*) to lose; (*dejar*) to leave II. *vr:* ~se **1.**(*errar el camino*) to get lost **2.**(*perderse*) to get lost; (*carta*) to go missing *Brit,* to get lost in the mail *Am* **3.**(*descarriarse*) to stray; *fig* to go astray

extremado, -a *adj* **1.**(*excesivo*) excessive **2.**(*exagerado*) extreme

Extremadura *f* Extremadura

extremar I. *vt* to carry to extremes; ~ **la prudencia** to be extremely cautious; **la policía extremó las medidas de seguridad** the police tightened security measures II. *vr* ~**se en algo** to put a lot of work into sth

extremaunción *f* REL extreme unction

extremeño, -a I. *adj* of/from Extremadura II. *m, f* native/inhabitant of Extremadura

extremidad *f* **1.**(*cabo*) end; (*punta*) tip **2.** *pl* ANAT limb

extremismo *m* extremism; (*religioso*) fundamentalism; ~ **derechista** right-wing extremism

extremista *adj, mf* extremist

extremo *m* **1.**(*cabo*) end; **a tal** ~ to such an extreme; **con** [*o* **en**] ~ a lot; **en último** ~ in the last resort; **pasar de un** ~ **a otro** to go from one extreme to another; **los** ~**s se tocan** opposite ends of the spectrum meet up **2.**(*asunto*) matter; **en este** ~ on this point **3.**(*punto límite*) extreme; **esto llega hasta el** ~ **de...** this goes so far as ... **4.** *pl* (*aspavientos*) **hacer** ~**s** to go wild

extremo, -a I. *adj* **1.**(*intenso*) extreme **2.**(*distante*) furthest; **los barrios más** ~**s** the outermost areas **3.**(*límite*) extreme II. *m, f* DEP winger, outside forward; ~ **derecho** right winger, right outside forward

extrínseco, -a *adj* (*externo*) extrinsic(al); **circunstancias extrínsecas** extrinsic circumstances

extrovertido, -a *adj* PSICO outgoing

exuberancia *f* exuberance

exuberante *adj* exuberant; (*vegetación*) lush

exultar *vi* to exult

eyaculación *f* ejaculation

eyacular *vi* to ejaculate

F

F, f *f* F, f; ~ **de Francia** F for Frederick *Brit,* F for Fox *Am*

fa *m inv* MÚS F; ~ **sostenido** F sharp

fabada *f* bean stew (*typical dish of Asturias prepared with pork products*)

fábrica *f* **1.**(*lugar de producción*) factory; ~ **de cerveza** brewery; **en** [*o* **ex**] ~ ex-works *Brit* **2.**(*de ladrillo, piedra*) masonry; **obra de** ~ stonework **3.**(*invención*) fabrication; ~ **de mentiras** pack [*o* tissue] of lies **4.**(*edificio*) building

fabricación *f* manufacturing; ~ **en masa** mass production

fabricante *mf* **1.**(*que fabrica*) manufacturer **2.**(*dueño*) factory owner

fabricar <c→qu> *vt* **1.**(*producir*) to manufacture; ~ **cerveza** to brew beer **2.**(*construir*) to build **3.**(*inventar*) to fabricate

fabril *adj* industrial; (*de la fabricación*) manufacturing

fábula *f* **1.** LIT fable **2.** *inf* (*invención*) tale **3.**(*relato mitológico*) myth **4.** ¡**de** ~! terrific!, smashing!

fabulador(a) *m(f)* **1.**(*fabulista*) writer of fables **2.**(*que inventa cosas fabulosas*) storyteller

fabuloso, -a *adj* **1.**(*inventado*) fabulous; **personaje** ~ ficticious character **2.**(*extraordinario*) fabulous

facción *f* **1.**(*banda*) guerrilla band **2.**(*de un partido*) faction **3.** *pl* (*rasgos*) (facial) features *pl*

faccioso, -a I. *adj* rebellious II. *m, f* **1.**(*rebelde*) rebel **2.**(*de un partido*) member of a faction

faceta *f* facet; (*aspecto*) aspect, side

faceto, -a *adj Méx* **1.**(*chistoso*) facetious **2.**(*presuntuoso*) cocksure

facha[1] I. *adj pey, inf* fascist II. *mf pey, inf* fascist

facha[2] *f inf* appearance, look; **tener una** ~ **sospechosa** to look suspicious; **estar hecho una** ~ to look a sight

fachada *f* **1.**(*de un edificio*) façade **2.**(*apariencia*) façade, front; **su buen humor es pura** ~ his/her good humour is pure pretence [*o* pretense *Am*]

fachendear *vi inf* to swank *inf*

fachendoso, -a I. *adj inf* swanky *inf* II. *m, f* **fachero** *m Arg, inf* nice-looking man

fachinal *m Arg* marshland

facial *adj* facial

fácil *adj* **1.**(*sin dificultades*) easy, simple; **la ventana es** ~ **de abrir** the window is easy to open; **es más** ~ **de decir que de hacer** *prov* easier said than done *prov* **2.**(*cómodo*) undemanding **3.**(*probable*) probable; **es** ~ **que** +*subj* it is likely that; **es** ~ **que nieve** it may well snow **4.**(*carácter*) easy-going **5.**(*mujer*)

loose *pej*
facilidad *f* 1. (*sin dificultad*) ease 2. (*dotes*) facility; **tener ~ para algo** to have an ability for sth; **tener ~ para los idiomas** to have a flair for languages 3. *pl* (*de pago*) facilities *pl*; **ofrecer** [*o* dar] **~es a alguien para algo** to offer [*o* give] sb facilities for sth
facilitar *vt* 1. (*favorecer*) to facilitate; (*posibilitar*) to make possible 2. (*suministrar*) to furnish, to supply
fácilmente *adv* 1. (*sin dificultad*) easily 2. (*con probabilidad*) probably
facineroso, -a *m, f* 1. (*delincuente*) criminal 2. (*malvado*) wicked person
facistol *m* lectern
facón *m RíoPl:* gaucho's knife
facsímil(e) *m* 1. (*reproducción*) facsimile 2. TEL fax
factibilidad *f* feasibility
factible *adj* feasible, viable
fáctico, -a *adj* factual; **los poderes ~s** the institutions holding effective control
factor *m t.* MAT (*causa*) factor; **~ de riesgo** risk factor
factoría *f* factory
factótum *m inf* factotum
factura *f* 1. (*cuenta*) bill; (*recibo*) receipt; **pasar ~** to render an account; **su holgazanería le pasa ahora ~** *inf* he/she is now having to pay the price for his/her idleness 2. (*hechura*) **esta chaqueta es de buena ~** this jacket is well made
facturación *f* 1. (*elaboración de una factura*) invoicing 2. FERRO registration 3. COM turnover 4. (*equipaje*) check-in
facturar *vt* 1. (*cobrar*) to bill; **~ los gastos de transporte** to bill for transport costs 2. COM (*ganar*) to earn; **nuestra compañía factura tres millones de euros al mes** our company is bringing in three million euros a month 3. FERRO to register 4. AVIAT **~ (el equipaje)** to check in
facultad *f* 1. (*atribuciones*) authority; **tener ~ para hacer algo** to have the authority to do sth; **conceder ~es a alguien (para hacer algo)** to authorize sb (to do sth) 2. (*aptitud*) faculty; **recobró sus ~es** he/she recovered his faculties 3. UNIV faculty 4. *pl* (*dotes*) faculties *pl*
facultar *vt* to authorize; **este título me faculta para ejercer la abogacía** this qualification entitles me to practise [*o* practice] law *Am*
facultativo, -a I. *adj* 1. (*potestativo*) optional 2. UNIV faculty 3. (*del médico*) medical II. *m, f* doctor
facundia *f* 1. (*verbosidad*) verbosity *form* 2. (*locuacidad*) talkativeness
facundo, -a *adj* 1. (*verboso*) verbose *form* 2. (*locuaz*) talkative
fado *m* MÚS fado
faena *f* 1. (*tarea*) task; **~s domésticas** chores *pl* 2. *inf* (*mala pasada*) dirty trick; **hacer una**

~ a alguien to play a dirty trick on sb 3. TAUR bullfighter's performance, especially with the cape
faenar I. *vi* 1. (*pescar*) to fish 2. (*laborar*) to work II. *vt* (*matar reses*) to slaughter animals
faenero, -a *m, f Chile* field worker
fagot¹ *mf* MÚS bassoonist
fagot² *m* MÚS bassoon
fagotista *mf* MÚS bassoonist
failear *vt AmC, RíoPl* COM (*documentos*) to file; (*en una carpeta*) to put in a folder
faíno, -a *adj Cuba* simple
fair play *m sin pl* DEP fair play
faisán *m* pheasant
faja *f* 1. (*para ceñir*) corset, girdle; (*para abrigar*) sash 2. (*distintivo honorífico*) sash 3. (*franja*) strip 4. (*de libros*) promotional band
fajada *f* 1. *Ant* (*ataque*) attack, assault 2. *Arg, inf* (*paliza*) beating; **le han dado una buena ~** they gave him a hell of a beating 3. *Ven* (*chasco*) disappointment
fajar I. *vt* 1. (*envolver*) to wrap; (*periódicos*) to put a wrapper on 2. *AmL* (*golpear*) to strike II. *vr:* **~se** 1. (*ponerse una faja*) to put on a girdle [*o* sash] 2. *AmL* (*pelearse*) to fight III. *vi* **~ con alguien** to fight with sb
fajilla *f AmL* wrapper
fajín *m* 1. *diminutivo de* **faja** 2. (*de generales, funcionarios*) sash
fajina *f* 1. (*en la era*) rick 2. (*de leña*) faggots *pl Brit*, fagots *pl Am*
fajita *f* GASTR appetizer of grilled meat wrapped in a corn tortilla
fajo *m* 1. (*papeles*) bundle; **~ de billetes** *inf* wad of dough *inf* 2. *pl* (*de bebé*) baby's swaddling clothes
falacia *f* deceit
falange *f* 1. MIL, HIST, ANAT phalanx 2. POL **la Falange (Española)** the (Spanish) Falange
falangista *adj, mf* Falangist
falaz *adj* false; **apariencia ~** deceptive appearance
falca *f* wedge
falcado, -a *adj* sickle-shaped
falcar <c→qu> *vt reg* to secure with wedges
falda *f* 1. (*vestido*) skirt; **~ pantalón** culottes; **~ plisada** pleated skirt; **~ tubo/recta** straight skirt; **estar pegado a las ~s de una mujer** to be under a woman's thumb; **se ha criado bajo las ~s de mamá** he/she has been brought up tied to his/her mother's apron strings 2. (*regazo*) lap 3. (*de una mesa camilla*) table cover 4. (*de una montaña*) lower slope 5. GASTR brisket 6. (*de sombrero*) brim 7. *inf* (*mujer*) **es asunto de ~s** it is to do with women; **le tiran mucho las ~s** he is a real ladies' man
faldellín *m Ant, Ven* christening robe
faldeo *m Arg, Chile* (*ladera*) mountainside
faldero, -a *m* 1. (*hombre*) womanizer 2. (*animal*) **perro ~** lapdog
faldón *m* 1. (*de una camisa*) (shirt-)tail 2. (*de una funda*) flap 3. ARQUIT gable 4. (*de la chi-*

menea) fireplace
falencia *f Col* bankruptcy, insolvency
falibilidad *f* fallibility
falible *adj* (*erróneo*) fallible; (*engañoso*) deceitful
fálico, -a *adj* phallic
falla *f* 1.(*defecto*) defect; (*en un sistema*) fault 2. GEO fault 3. *Col* ENS day's absence (*from school*)
fallar I. *vi* 1. JUR to pronounce sentence 2.(*malograrse: proyecto*) to fail; (*plan, intento*) to miscarry 3.(*no funcionar*) to go wrong; **le ~on los nervios** his/her nerves let him/her down; **algo le falla** there is sth wrong with him/her; **no falla nunca** (*cosa*) it never fails; (*persona*) you can always count on her/him 4.(*romperse*) to break 5.(*no cumplir con su palabra*) ~ **a alguien** to let sb down; (*en una cita*) to stand sb up II. *vt* 1. JUR to pronounce sentence on; ~ **la absolución** to acquit; ~ **un pleito** to rule on a case 2.(*premio*) to award 3. DEP to miss 4.(*en el juego de naipes*) to trump

> The **Fallas** is the name of the largest public festival in Valencia on March 19th, which is **día del padre** (Father's Day) in Spain. **Fallas** are figures made from papier-mâché that are humorous caricatures, mainly of well-known public figures. They are burned during the "**noche del fuego**" on March 19th.

fallecer *irr como crecer vi* to pass away, to die
fallecido, -a I. *adj* deceased, late II. *m, f* deceased
fallecimiento *m* death
fallero, -a *m, f person who participates in las Fallas*
fallido, -a I. *adj* 1.(*proyecto*) unsuccessful; (*intento*) abortive 2. COM (*deuda*) bad 3.(*en quiebra*) bankrupt II. *m, f* irrecoverable loan
fallo *m* 1. JUR sentence 2.(*error*) error; (*omisión*) omission; ~ **humano** human error; **este asunto solo tiene un pequeño ~** this matter only has one small shortcoming [*o* hitch] 3.(*certamen*) decision 4. TÉC breakdown 5.(*en el juego de naipes*) void 6.(*fracaso*) failure 7. MED ~ **cardíaco/renal** heart/kidney failure
falluto, -a *adj RíoPl, inf* (*en el comportamiento*) unreliable; (*en el modo de ser*) two-faced, hypocritical
falo *m elev* phallus
falocracia *f* male chauvinism
falopa *f Arg, inf* (*droga*) drugs *pl*
falopero, -a *m, f Arg, inf* (*adicto*) addict
falsario, -a I. *adj* counterfeit II. *m, f* (*mentiroso*) liar
falseable *adj* falsifiable, forgeable
falseador(a) *m(f)* forger
falseamiento *m* forgery
falsear I. *vi* 1.(*flaquear*) to weaken 2. MÚS to be out of tune II. *vt* 1.(*adulterar al referir*) to

misrepresent; (*verdad*) to distort 2.(*falsificar materialmente*) to counterfeit
falsedad *f* (*en el carácter*) falseness; (*hipocresía*) hypocrisy
falsete *m* MÚS falsetto; **cantar en** ~ to sing falsetto
falsificación *f* (*acto, objeto*) forgery; ~ **de billetes** counterfeiting of banknotes
falsificador(a) *m(f)* (*de documentos*) forger; (*de moneda*) counterfeiter
falsificar <c→qu> *vt* to forge, to falsify; ~ **la verdad** to distort the truth
falso *adv* **en** ~ (*falsamente*) falsely; **jurar en** ~ to commit perjury; **coger a alguien en** ~ to catch sb out [*o* in a lie]; **dar un golpe en** ~ (*movimiento*) to miss the mark; **dar un paso en** ~ (*tropezar*) to stumble; (*equivocarse*) to make a mistake; **sonar** ~ to ring false
falso, -a I. *adj* 1.(*no cierto, no auténtico*) false; **¡~!** not true! 2.(*no natural*) artificial; (*pseudo*) pseudo; **llave falsa** fake key; **puerta falsa** false door 3.(*caballería*) vicious II. *m, f* (*mentiroso*) liar; (*hipócrita*) hypocrite
falta *f* 1.(*carencia*) lack; (*ausencia*) absence; ~ **de dinero** shortage of money; ~ **de educación** lack of education; ~ **de liquidez** liquidity problem; **echar en** ~ **algo/a alguien** to miss sth/sb; **me hace** ~ **dinero** I need money; **¡ni** ~ **que hace!** there is absolutely no need! 2.(*equivocación*) error; ~ **ortográfica** spelling error; **sin ~s** with no mistakes; **sin** ~ without fail 3. DEP foul 4. JUR default; (*omisión censurable*) misdemeanour *Brit,* misdemeanor *Am* ►**a** ~ **de pan, buenas son tortas** *prov* half a loaf is better than none *prov*
faltar *vi* 1.(*no estar*) to be missing; (*persona*) to be absent; ~ **a clase** to miss class; ~ **a una cita** not to turn up at an appointment; **me faltan mis llaves** my keys are missing 2.(*necesitarse*) ~ (*por*) **hacer** to be still to be done; **nos falta dinero para...** we do not have enough money to ...; **me falta tiempo para hacerlo** I need time to do it; **no falta quien...** there is always sb who ...; **falta** (**por**) **saber si...** we need to know if ...; **¡no ~ía** [*o* faltaba] **más!** it is the limit!; (*respuesta a agradecimiento*) you are welcome!; (*asentir amablemente*) of course!; **por si algo faltaba...** as if it were not enough already ...; **¡lo que faltaba!** that is the last straw! 3.(*temporal: quedar*) to be left; **faltan cuatro días para tu cumpleaños** your birthday is in four days; **falta mucho para que vengan** they won't be here for a long time yet; **falta poco para las doce** it is nearly twelve o'clock; **faltan diez para las nueve** *AmL* it is ten to nine; **poco le faltó para llorar** he/she was on the verge of tears 4.(*no cumplir*) ~ **a una promesa** to break a promise; **nunca falta a su palabra** he/she never goes back on his/her word 5.(*ofender*) to be rude; ~ **a alguien** to be disrespectful [*o* rude] to sb 6.(*cometer una falta*) ~ **en algo** to make a mistake 7. *elev*

(*morir*) to expire

falto, -a *adj* (*escaso*) ~ **de algo** short of sth; (*desprovisto*) lacking in sth; ~ **de recursos** lacking in resources; **estar** ~ **de cariño** to be in need of love [*o* lacking affection]

faltón, -ona *adj inf* **1.** (*que falta a su palabra*) unreliable, fly-by-night *inf* **2.** (*negligente*) negligent, remiss **3.** *AmL* (*vago*) idle, do-nothing **4.** (*grosero*) rude

faltriquera *f* pocket; (*a la cintura*) a pouch tied around the waist and under the apron or skirt

fama *f* **1.** (*gloria*) glory; (*celebridad*) fame; **tener** ~ to be famous; **dar** ~ **a algo/alguien** to make sth/sb famous; **unos tienen la** ~ **y otros cardan la lana** *prov* some do all the work while others get all the glory *prov* **2.** (*reputación*) reputation; **tener** ~ **de fanfarrón** to have a reputation of being boastful; **ser de mala** ~ to have a bad reputation **3.** (*rumor*) rumour *Brit*, rumor *Am*; **corre la** ~ **de que** there is a rumour [*o* rumor *Am*] going round that

famélico, -a *adj* starving

familia *f* **1.** (*pareja e hijos*) family; (*que comparten una casa*) household; ~ **numerosa** large family (*for administrative purposes, a family with three or more children*); **cabeza de** ~ head of the household **2.** (*parentela*) relatives *pl*; ~ **política** in-laws *pl*; **libro de** ~ book recording the details of a family, including births, deaths, marriages, etc.; **de buena** ~ from a good family; **eso viene de** ~ that runs in the family; **en** ~ with the family; **ser de la** ~ to be one of the family; **acordarse de la** ~ **de alguien** *inf* to insult sb **3.** (*hijos*) family

familiar **I.** *adj* **1.** (*íntimo*) intimate; **asunto** ~ personal matter; **economía** ~ domestic economy **2.** (*conocido*) familiar **3.** LING colloquial **II.** *mf* (*pariente*) relative

familiaridad *f* (*confianza*) intimacy; (*trato familiar*) familiarity

familiarizar <z→c> **I.** *vt* (*acostumbrar*) to familiarize **II.** *vr:* ~**se** to familiarize oneself, to get to know; ~**se con un sistema nuevo** to familiarize oneself with a new system

famoso, -a *adj* **1.** (*conocido*) ~ **por algo** famous for sth **2.** *inf* (*sonado*) talked-of

fan *mf* <fans> (*admirador*) fan; (*de fútbol*) supporter

fanático, -a **I.** *adj* fanatical **II.** *m, f* **1.** *inf* (*hincha*) fan; **es una fanática del rock** she is crazy about rock **2.** *pey* (*extremista*) fanatic

fanatismo *m sin pl* fanaticism

fané *adj AmL, inf* (*arrugado*) crumpled, rumpled; (*marchito*) withered

fanfarria *f* **1.** *inf* (*jactancia*) bragging **2.** MÚS (*banda*) (military [*o* brass]) band; (*música*) fanfare

fanfarrón, -ona *inf* **I.** *adj* (*chulo*) swanky **II.** *m, f* (*bravucón*) braggart, swank

fanfarronada *f inf* brag, baloney

fanfarronear *vi inf* to brag

fangal *m* quagmire

fango *m* **1.** (*lodo*) mud; **baños de** ~ MED mudbath **2.** (*deshonra*) dishonour *Brit*, dishonor *Am*

fangoso, -a *adj* muddy

fantasear **I.** *vi* **1.** (*soñar*) to fantasize **2.** (*presumir*) to boast, to pose **3.** (*soñar despierto*) to daydream **II.** *vt* to invent

fantaseo *m* fantasizing

fantasía *f* **1.** (*imaginación*) imagination; (*cosa imaginada*) fantasy; **joyas de** ~ imitation jewellery; **¡déjate de** ~**s!** come down to earth! *inf* **2.** LIT fantastic tale **3.** MÚS fantasia

fantasioso, -a **I.** *adj* **1.** (*inventado*) fanciful; **idea fantasiosa** fanciful idea **2.** (*fachendoso*) swanky *inf* **II.** *m, f* poseur *form*, show-off

fantasma **I.** *m* **1.** (*aparición*) ghost; **andar como un** ~ to be lifeless; **aparecer como un** ~ to appear from [*o* out of] nowhere **2.** (*visión*) phantom **3.** *inf* (*fanfarrón*) boaster, poseur *form* **II.** *adj* ghost; **empresa** ~ dummy company

fantasmada *f inf* pose

fantasmagoría *f* phantasmagoria; TEAT optical illusion

fantasmagórico, -a *adj* phantasmagorical; TEAT with optical illusion

fantasmal *adj* phantom, illusory

fantasmón, -ona **I.** *adj inf* posey **II.** *m, f* poseur *form*, show-off

fantástico, -a *adj* **1.** (*irreal*) fantastic, imaginary **2.** *inf* (*fabuloso*) fantastic, fabulous

fantochada *f* **1.** (*fantasmada*) pose **2.** (*tontería*) silly act [*o* remark]

fantoche *m* **1.** (*títere*) puppet **2.** (*mamarracho*) sight **3.** (*fantasmón*) poseur; *form* phony *inf*

fañoso, -a *adj Ven* twanging

FAO *f* **1.** *abr de* **Organización de las Naciones Unidas para la Agricultura y la Alimentación** FAO **2.** *abr de* **fabricación asistida por ordenador** CAM

FAQ *abr de* **frequently asked questions** FAQ

faquir *m* fakir

faralá *f* <faralaes> **1.** (*volante*) flounce **2.** *inf* (*oropel*) frills *pl*, frippery

farallón *m* (*mar, lago*) out-jutting rock

faramallear *vi Chile, Méx* to brag

farándula *f* **1.** (*farsa*) farce **2.** TEAT the stage, theatre [*o* theater *Am*] world **3.** *inf* (*palabrería*) blarney, bamboozling *inf*

faraón *m* Pharaoh

faraónico, -a *adj* pharaonic

fardada *f inf* showing off

fardar *vi inf* (*presumir*) to boast; (*impresionar*) to make an impression

fardo *m* **1.** (*bulto*) package; (*de ropa*) bundle **2.** *inf* (*beso*) podge *Brit*, tub *Am*

fardón, -ona *adj inf* **1.** (*chulo*) swanky *inf*, boastful **2.** (*vistoso*) showy; (*coche*) swish, flashy *inf*

farero, -a *m, f* lighthouse keeper

farfullar I. *vi inf* (*balbucear*) to splutter II. *vt inf* (*chapucear*) to botch
farfullero, -a *m, f inf* 1. (*tartamudo*) splutterer 2. (*chapucero*) botcher
farináceo, -a *adj* floury, farinaceous
faringe *f* ANAT pharynx, throat
faringitis *f inv* MED pharyngitis
fariña *f AmS* coarse cassava flour
farisaico, -a *adj* 1. (*fariseo*) Pharisaic(al) 2. (*falso*) hypocritical
fariseo, -a *m, f* 1. (*de la secta judía*) Pharisee 2. (*hipócrita*) hypocrite
farmacéutico, -a I. *adj* pharmaceutical; **industria farmacéutica** pharmaceutical industry; **productos ~s** pharmaceutical products II. *m, f* chemist *Brit,* druggist *Am*
farmacia *f* 1. (*tienda*) chemist's *Brit,* drugstore *Am;* ~ **de guardia** all-night chemist's [*o* drugstore *Am*] 2. (*ciencia*) pharmacy
fármaco *m* medicine, drug
farmacodependencia *f* drug dependence
farmacólogo, -a *m, f* pharmacologist
faro *m* 1. AUTO headlight; ~ **antiniebla** fog light [*o* lamp] 2. NÁUT lighthouse
farol *m* 1. (*lámpara*) lamp; (*de papel*) Chinese lantern; ~ (**de calle**) streetlight 2. DEP bluff 3. *inf* (*fanfarronada*) idle boast, swank *inf;* (*patraña*) tall story; **tirarse un** ~ to show off 4. *pl AmL* (*ojos*) eyes; **¡adelante con los ~es!** *inf* go for it!
farola *f* street light [*o* lamp]; (*poste*) lamppost
farolazo *m AmC, Méx* swig of liquor
farolear *vi inf* to brag, to swank *inf*
farolero, -a I. *adj inf* bragging II. *m, f* 1. (*oficio*) lamplighter 2. (*fanfarrón*) show-off
farolillo *m* Chinese lantern; ~ **rojo** *inf* team [*o* competitor] in last place
farra *f* **estar** [*o* **ir**] **de** ~ *inf* to party
fárrago *m* jumble, hotch-potch *Brit,* hodge-podge *Am*
farragoso, -a *adj* jumbled-up
farrear I. *vi CSur, inf* to paint the town red II. *vr:* ~**se** *RíoPl* (*dinero*) to squander, to blow *inf*
farrista I. *adj CSur* fun-loving; **mi hija es muy** ~ my daughter is always out living it up II. *mf CSur* (*que le gusta ir a fiestas*) party-loving
farruco, -a I. *adj* defiant; **ponerse** ~ **con alguien** to get cocky with sb II. *m, f RíoPl:* Galician or Asturian immigrant
farruto, -a *adj Bol, Chile* puny
farsa *f* 1. TEAT (*farándula*) theatre *Brit,* theater *Am;* (*sainete*) farce 2. (*engaño*) sham
farsante I. *adj inf* sham II. *mf inf* charlatan
FAS *fpl* MIL *abr de* **Fuerzas Armadas** the (armed) forces
fascículo *m* 1. ANAT fascicle 2. (*de libro*) instalment *Brit,* installment *Am*
fascinación *f* fascination; **sentir** ~ **por algo** to be fascinated by [*o* drawn to] sth
fascinador(a) *adj,* **fascinante** *adj* fascinating; (*persona*) captivating; (*libro*) enthralling

fascinar I. *vi, vt* (*encantar*) to fascinate; (*libro*) to enthral *Brit,* enthrall *Am* II. *vr:* ~**se** to be fascinated
fascismo *m* fascism
fascista I. *adj* fascist(ic) II. *mf* fascist
fascistoide *adj* fascist-like
fase *f* 1. (*período, estado*) phase 2. ELEC, FÍS, QUÍM phase; **de tres** ~**s** three-phase; (*nave espacial*) stage
fast food *m o f sin pl* fast food
fastidiado, -a *adj inf* 1. (*enfermo*) unwell 2. (*molesto*) annoyed 3. (*estropeado*) broken; **andar ~ de...** to have a bad ...; **ando ~ de dinero/tiempo estos días** I don't have enough money/time these days; **anda ~ de la rodilla** he has a bad knee
fastidiar I. *vt* 1. (*molestar*) to annoy; **¡no te fastidia!** *inf* you must be joking! 2. *inf* (*estropear*) ruin 3. (*causar hastío*) to sicken 4. (*aburrir*) to bore II. *vr:* ~**se** *inf* 1. (*enojarse*) to get cross; **¡fastídiate!** stuff it! *inf;* **¡hay que ~se!** it's unbelievable! 2. (*aguantarse*) to put up with it 3. *AmL* (*perjudicarse*) to harm
fastidio *m* 1. (*disgusto*) bother; **¡vaya ~!** what a nuisance; (*mala suerte*) misfortune 2. (*aburrimiento*) bore 3. (*hastío*) repugnance
fastidioso, -a *adj* 1. (*molesto*) annoying 2. (*aburrido*) boring 3. (*pesado*) dull; **persona fastidiosa** a bore
fasto *m* 1. (*pompa*) pomp 2. *pl* (*anales*) annals *pl*
fastuosidad *f* lavishness
fastuoso, -a *adj* (*casa, boda*) sumptuous; (*persona*) flashy
fatal I. *adj* 1. (*inevitable*) unavoidable; **el momento** ~ the inevitable [*o* fateful moment] 2. (*desagradable*) disagreeable 3. (*funesto*) fatal; (*mortal*) mortal; **mujer** ~ femme fatale 4. JUR not extendable 5. *inf* (*muy mal*) awful II. *adv inf* awfully; **el examen me fue** ~ my exam was a disaster
fatalidad *f* 1. (*desgracia*) misfortune 2. (*destino*) fate
fatalismo *m sin pl* fatalism
fatalista I. *adj* fatalistic II. *mf* 1. (*que sigue el fatalismo*) fatalist 2. *inf* (*pesimista*) pessimist
fatídico, -a *adj* 1. (*que predice el futuro*) prophetic 2. *inf* (*algo*) fateful 3. (*terrible*) horrible
fatiga *f* 1. (*cansancio*) weariness, fatigue *form;* ~ **visual** eye strain 2. (*sofocos*) shortness of breath 3. TÉC fatigue 4. *pl* (*sacrificios*) hardship
fatigado, -a *adj* 1. (*agotado*) worn-out 2. (*sofocado*) short of breath 3. TÉC with fatigue
fatigador(a) *adj* (*que cansa*) tiring; (*que molesta*) annoying
fatigar <g→gu> I. *vt* 1. (*cansar*) to tire, to fatigue *form* 2. (*molestar*) to annoy; (*importunar*) to pester II. *vr:* ~**se** 1. (*agotarse*) to wear oneself out; (*ojos*) to strain 2. (*esforzararse*) to exert oneself 3. (*sofocarse*) to get short of

breath
fatigoso, -a *adj* **1.**(*trabajo*) tiring **2.**(*persona*) tiresome; (*jadeante*) panting
fatuidad *f* (*vanidad*) conceit; (*inmodestia*) immodesty
fatuo, -a *adj* **1.**(*presumido*) conceited; (*jactancioso*) boastful **2.**(*necio*) fatuous
fauces *fpl* **1.**ZOOL fauces *pl* **2.**AmL (*dientes*) teeth
fauna *f* fauna
fauno *m* faun
fausto *m* (*lujo*) sumptuousness; (*ostentación*) ostentation
fausto, -a *adj* fortunate
favela *f* AmL **1.**(*casucha*) shanty **2.** *pl* (*barrio*) shanty town
favor *m* **1.**(*servicio*) favour *Brit,* favor *Am;* (*ayuda*) good turn; **por ~** please; **hacer un ~ a alguien** to do sb a favour; **¡hágame el ~ de dejarme en paz!** would you please leave me alone!; **te lo pido por ~** I am begging you; **hagan el ~ de venir puntualmente** please be punctual; **~ con ~ se paga** *prov* one good turn deserves another *prov* **2.**(*gracia*) favour *Brit,* favor *Am;* **a** [*o* **en**] **~ de alguien** in sb's favour; **tener a alguien a su ~** to have sb on your side; **a ~ del viento/de la corriente** with the wind/the current **3.**(*beneficio*) **voto a ~** vote for; **estar a ~ de algo** to be in favour of sth; **votar a ~ de alguien** to vote for sb
favorable *adj* **1.**(*propicio*) favourable *Brit,* favorable *Am* **2.**(*optimista*) promising **3.**(*benévolo*) kind
favorecedor(a) *adj* becoming; **es un vestido muy ~ para ti** the dress is very becoming on you
favorecer *irr como crecer* **I.** *vt* **1.**(*beneficiar*) to benefit **2.**(*ayudar*) to help **3.**(*dar preferencia*) to favour *Brit,* to favor *Am* **4.**(*prendas de vestir*) to become **II.** *vr:* **~se** to benefit
favorecido, -a *adj* **1.**(*propiciado*) favoured *Brit,* favored *Am* **2.**(*fotografía*) **has salido ~ en la foto** you have come out well in the photo
favoritismo *m* (*nepotismo*) nepotism; (*parcialidad*) favouritism *Brit,* favoritism *Am*
favorito, -a **I.** *adj* favourite *Brit,* favorite *Am;* **plato ~** favourite dish **II.** *m, f* **1.**(*del rey*) favourite *Brit,* favorite *Am;* **~ del público** the public's darling; **la favorita del rey** the king's mistress **2.**DEP (the) favourite *Brit,* (the) favorite *Am*
fax *m inv* fax; **mandar un ~ a una empresa/a Suecia** to send a fax to a company/to Sweden
faxear *vt* to fax
fayuca *f Méx, inf* black market; **tabaco de ~** contraband tobacco
fayuquero, -a *m, f Méx, inf* smuggler
faz *f* **1.** *elev* (*rostro*) face **2.**(*anverso*) obverse
FCC *abr de* **fluorclorocarbonados** CFC
fe *f* **1.**(*religión*) faith; **~ en Dios** faith in God; **doy profesión de ~** I profess my faith **2.**(*con-*

fianza) faith; **digno de ~** worthy of trust; **dar ~ a algo/alguien** to vouch for sth/sb; **dar ~ de algo** to certify sth; **tener ~ en alguien** to believe in sb; **de buena/mala ~** in good/bad faith **3.**(*lealtad*) fidelity **4.**(*certificado*) certificate; **~ de bautismo/de matrimonio** certificate of baptism/marriage certificate; **~ de erratas** errata
fealdad *f* **1.**(*monstruosidad*) ugliness **2.**(*indignidad*) indignity
febrero *m* February; *v.t.* **marzo**
febril *adj* (*fiebre*) feverish; **acceso ~** sudden temperature; (*actividad*) hectic
fecal *adj* faecal *Brit,* fecal *Am;* **sustancias ~es** faecal matter
fecha *f* **1.**(*data*) date; (*señalada*) day; **~ de caducidad** expiry [*o* expiration] date; (*de comida*) sell-by date; **~ de cierre** closing date; **~ clave** decisive day; **~ de las elecciones** Polling day *Brit,* Election day *Am;* **~ de entrega** date of delivery; **~ límite** [*o* **tope**] deadline; **sin ~** undated; **en la ~ fijada** on the agreed day; **hasta la ~** until now, so far; **adelantar/atrasar la ~ de algo** to bring forward/put back the date of sth; **¿cuál es la ~ de hoy?** what is the date today? **2.**ECON date; **a 30 días ~** at 30 days' sight **3.** *pl* (*época*) days *pl;* **en estas ~s** around this time
fechable *adj* datable
fechado, -a *adj* (*en cartas*) **~ el...** dated ...
fechador *m* date-stamp
fechar *vt* to date
fechoría *f* **1.**(*delito*) misdemeanour *Brit,* misdemeanor *Am* **2.**(*travesura*) prank
fécula *f* starch
fecundación *f* fertilization
fecundar *vt t.* BIO to fertilize
fecundidad *f* **1.**(*fertilidad*) fertility **2.**(*abundancia*) abundance **3.**(*productividad*) productiveness
fecundizar <z→c> *vt* to fertilize
fecundo, -a *adj* **1.**(*prolífico*) prolific **2.**(*tierra*) fertile; (*campo*) productive **3.**(*creador*) fertile
FED *m* POL *abr de* **Fondo Europeo de Desarrollo** EDF
fedatario *m* (public) notary
federación *f* federation
federado, -a *adj* federate; **estado ~** federate state
federal **I.** *adj* federal; (*partidario del federalismo*) federalist; **estado ~** federal state; **república ~** federal republic **II.** *mf* federalist
federalismo *m sin pl* federalism
federalista *adj, mf* federalist
federalizar <z→c> **I.** *vt* to federalize **II.** *vr:* **~se** to form a federation
federar **I.** *vt* (*aliarse*) to unite; (*federalizar*) to federate **II.** *vr:* **~se** (*unirse*) to become a member; (*federalizarse*) to form a federation
federativo, -a *adj* federative
fehaciente *adj* indisputable; JUR irrefutable; **copia ~** certified true copy

felación *f* fellatio

felicidad *f* **1.** (*alegría*) happiness **2.** (*dicha*) good fortune; ¡~es! (*boda, nacimiento, etc*) congratulations!; (*Navidad*) Merry Christmas; (*cumpleaños*) happy birthday; **te deseamos muchas ~es** we wish you all the best

felicitación *f* **1.** (*enhorabuena*) congratulation **2.** (*tarjeta*) greetings card

felicitar I. *vt* ~ **a alguien por algo** to congratulate sb on sth **II.** *vr* ~**se por algo** to be glad about sth; ~**se de que** +*subj* to be glad that

feligrés, -esa *m, f* parishioner, church member

felino, -a *adj* feline

feliz *adj* **1.** (*dichoso*) happy; ¡~ **Navidad!** merry Christmas!; ¡~ **viaje!** have a good journey [*o* trip]! **2.** (*exitoso*) fortunate, successful

felón, -ona I. *adj* **1.** (*traidor*) treacherous **2.** (*infame*) wicked **II.** *m, f* **1.** (*traidor*) traitor **2.** (*infame*) villain

felonía *f* **1.** (*deslealtad*) disloyalty **2.** (*infamia*) infamy *form* **3.** *AmL* JUR serious offence *Brit*, felony *Am*

felpa *f* **1.** (*peluche*) plush **2.** *inf* (*paliza*) beating, licking **3.** *inf* (*reprimenda*) telling-off

felpeada *f Arg, Urug, CSur, inf* dressing-down

felpudo *m* doormat

felpudo, -a *adj* (*tela*) plushy; (*moqueta*) shaggy

femenino *m* LING feminine

femenino, -a *adj* **1.** (*de sexo femenino*) female; **equipo** ~ women's team **2.** (*afeminado*) effeminate **3.** LING feminine

feminidad *f* femininity

feminismo *m sin pl* (*doctrina*) feminism; (*movimiento*) feminist movement

feminista *adj, mf* feminist

fémur *m* ANAT femur, thigh-bone *inf*

fenecer *irr como crecer vi* **1.** (*morirse*) to die **2.** *elev* (*acabarse*) to end

fenicio, -a *adj, m, f* Phoenician

fénix *m* phoenix

fenomenal I. *adj* **1.** (*extraordinario*) incredible; (*estupendo*) terrific **2.** *inf* (*tremendo*) tremendous **3.** (*fenoménico*) phenomenal **II.** *adv inf* terrifically

fenómeno I. *adj inv, inf* marvellous *Brit*, marvelous *Am*; ¡~! terrific! **II.** *m* **1.** *t.* FILOS, MED (*suceso*) phenomenon; (*maravilla*) marvel **2.** (*genio*) genius **3.** (*monstruo*) freak **III.** *adv* marvellously *Brit*, marvelously *Am*

feo I. *m inf* **1.** (*grosería*) insult; **hacer un ~ a alguien** to snub [*o* slight] sb **2.** (*aspecto*) ugly person **II.** *adv inf* bad, badly

feo, -a *adj* **1.** (*espantoso*) ugly; **dejar ~ a alguien** *fig* to show sb up [*o* in a bad light]; **tener las cartas muy feas** *fig* to have very bad cards; **la cosa se está poniendo fea** things aren't looking too good **2.** (*reprobable*) bad; **está muy ~ lo que hiciste** what you did was really nasty [*o* rotten] ▶**ser más ~ que Picio** to be (as) ugly as sin; **le tocó bailar con**

la **más fea** he/she drew the short straw

feracidad *f* fertility

feraz *adj* fertile

féretro *m* coffin

feria *f* **1.** (*exposición*) fair, show; ~ **de muestras** trade fair **2.** (*fiesta*) festival **3.** (*verbena*) fair; **puesto de** ~ stand

feriado, -a *adj AmL* holiday; **día** ~ bank [*o* legal] holiday

ferial I. *adj* (*de exposición*) fair, show; **recinto** ~ trade fair pavilion **II.** *m* fair; (*lugar*) fairground

feriante *mf* **1.** (*que exhibe*) exhibitor; (*en la verbena*) stall holder **2.** (*que compra*) fairgoer

feriar I. *vi* to take time off **II.** *vt* **1.** (*mercar*) buy **2.** (*vender*) to sell **3.** (*permutar*) to exchange, to barter

fermentación *f* fermentation

fermentar I. *vi* **1.** (*vino*) to ferment **2.** (*agitarse*) to get in a state, to work oneself up **II.** *vt* to ferment

fermento *m* **1.** (*sustancia*) fermenting agent **2.** (*origen*) cause

ferocidad *f* **1.** (*salvajismo*) ferocity **2.** (*crueldad*) savagery

feroz *adj* **1.** (*salvaje*) fierce **2.** (*cruel, violento*) savage **3.** *inf* (*muy grande*) huge

férreo, -a *adj* **1.** (*de hierro, tenaz*) iron **2.** (*del ferrocarril*) railway *Brit*, railroad *Am*

ferrería *f* foundry

ferretería *f* **1.** (*tienda*) ironmonger's, hardware store **2.** (*ferrería*) ironworks *pl*

ferretero, -a *m, f* ironmonger, hardware dealer

férrico, -a *adj* ferrous

ferrocarril *m* **1.** (*vía*) railway line *Brit*, railroad *Am* **2.** (*tren*) railway; ~ **de cremallera** rack railway *Brit*, rack railroad *Am*; ~ **de vía ancha** wide-gauge railway *Brit*, wide-gauge railroad *Am*; **por** ~ by rail

ferrocarrilero, -a *adj AmL, inf* (*ferroviario*) railway *Brit*, railroad *Am*; **el transporte** ~ rail transport

ferroviario, -a I. *adj* railway *Brit*, railroad *Am* **II.** *m, f* railway worker *Brit*, railroad worker *Am*

ferruginoso, -a *adj* **1.** (*agua, mineral*) ferrous **2.** (*color*) rust-coloured *Brit*, rust-colored *Am*

ferry *m* ferry

fértil *adj* **1.** (*tierra*) fertile; **estar en edad** ~ to be of reproductive age **2.** (*rico*) rich

fertilidad *f* fertility; (*t. de tierra*) productiveness

fertilización *f* (*de tierra*) fertilization; ~ **in vitro** in vitro fertilization

fertilizante *m* fertilizer

fertilizar <z→c> *vt* to fertilize

férula *f* **1.** (*palmeta*) cane **2.** (*cirugía*) splint **3.** (*poder abusivo*) tyranny

férvido, -a *adj elev* **1.** (*hirviente*) fervid **2.** (*sentimiento*) ardent

ferviente *adj* fervent

fervor *m* **1.** *t.* REL fervour *Brit*, fervor *Am*

2. (*calor*) intense heat **3.** (*entusiasmo*) enthusiasm; **con ~** ardently

fervoroso, -a *adj* fervent

festejar I. *vt* **1.** (*celebrar*) to celebrate **2.** (*galantear*) to court, to woo **3.** *AmL* (*azotar*) to beat **II.** *vr:* **~se** to enjoy oneself

festejo *m* **1.** (*conmemoración*) celebration **2.** (*galanteo*) courtship **3.** *pl* (*actos públicos*) festival, public festivities *pl*

festín *m* **1.** (*celebración*) celebration **2.** (*banquete*) feast

festinar *vt AmC* **1.** (*agasajar*) to wine and dine **2.** (*arruinar*) to ruin **3.** (*apremiar*) to hasten

festival *m* festival; **~ de cine** film festival

festividad *f* **1.** (*conmemoración*) festivity **2.** (*día*) feast

festivo, -a *adj* **1.** (*de fiesta*) festive, celebratory; **día ~** bank holiday **2.** (*humorístico*) humorous, entertaining; (*persona*) witty

festón *m* **1.** (*guirnalda*) garland **2.** (*remate cosido*) scallop

festonear *vt* **1.** (*bordar*) to scallop **2.** (*adornar*) to festoon

feta *f Arg* slice

fetal *adj* foetal *Brit,* fetal *Am*

fetén I. *adj inv, inf* **1.** (*auténtico*) authentic **2.** (*excelente*) smashing **II.** *f inf* (*verdad*) truth

fetiche *m* fetish

fetichismo *m sin pl* fetishism

fetichista I. *adj* fetishistic **II.** *mf* fetishist

fetidez *f* fetidness *form*

fétido, -a *adj* fetid *form;* **bomba fétida** stink bomb

feto *m* **1.** MED foetus *Brit,* fetus *Am* **2.** *inf* (*feo*) ugly sod *inf*

feúcho, -a *adj inf* unattractive, plain

feudal *adj* feudal, manorial; **señor ~** feudal lord

feudalismo *m sin pl* **1.** (*sistema*) feudalism **2.** (*época*) feudal era

feudo *m* fief; **este pueblo es un ~ de los socialistas** this town is a socialist stronghold

fiabilidad *f* **1.** (*de una persona*) trustworthiness **2.** (*de una empresa, de datos*) reliability

fiable *adj* **1.** (*persona*) trustworthy **2.** (*empresa*) reliable

fiaca *f Arg, inf* (*pereza*) laziness

fiado, -a *adj* trusting; **comprar al ~** to buy on credit

fiador *m* (*de puerta*) catch; (*de pistola*) safety catch

fiador(a) *m(f)* backer, bondsman; **salir ~ por alguien** to stand surety [*o* bail] for sb

fiambre I. *adj* **1.** GASTR cold **2.** *inf* (*noticia*) stale; (*discurso*) old hat **II.** *m* **1.** GASTR cold meat **2.** *inf* (*cadáver*) stiff; **ese está ~** that one is stone-dead

fiambrera *f* (*cesta*) picnic basket; (*para el almuerzo*) lunch pail [*o* box]; (*caja*) Tupperware® container

fianza *f* **1.** (*depósito*) deposit **2.** (*garantía*) security **3.** (*fiador*) surety, bail; **en libertad bajo ~** free [*o* out] on bail

fiar <*1. pres:* fío> **I.** *vi* **1.** (*al vender*) to give credit; **en esa tienda no fían** that shop does not give credit **2.** (*confiar*) to trust; **es de ~** he/she is trustworthy **II.** *vt* **1.** (*garantizar*) to stand surety [*o* bail] for **2.** (*dar crédito*) to sell on credit **3.** (*confiar*) to entrust **III.** *vr* **~se de algo/alguien** to trust sth/sb; **no te fíes de lo que dice** don't trust what he/she says

fiasco *m* fiasco

fibra *f* **1.** *t.* BIO, MED (*filamento*) fibre *Brit,* fiber *Am;* **~ muscular** muscle fibre [*o* fiber *Am*]; **~ de vidrio** fibreglass *Brit,* fiberglass *Am* **2.** (*vigor*) energy; **no tiene ~ suficiente para llevar la empresa** he/she has not got enough drive run the business

fibroso, -a *adj t.* MED fibrous

ficción *f* **1.** (*simulación*) simulation **2.** (*invención*) invention; **~ novelesca** fiction

ficha *f* **1.** (*de ruleta*) chip; (*de dominó*) domino; (*de ajedrez*) piece, man **2.** (*para una máquina*) token; (*de teléfono*) telephone token; (*de guardarropa*) cloakroom [*o* checkroom *Am*] token **3.** (*tarjeta informativa*) (index) card; (*en el trabajo*) card; **~ perforada** INFOR punched card; **~ policial** police record; **~ técnica** technical specifications **4.** DEP signing **5.** (*bribón*) rascal

fichaje *m* DEP signing (up)

fichar I. *vi* **1.** DEP to sign **2.** (*en el trabajo*) to clock in **II.** *vt* **1.** (*registrar*) to enter; **~ a alguien** (*la policía*) to open a file on sb; **estar fichado** to have a police record **2.** *inf* (*desconfiar*) to mistrust **3.** DEP to sign up **4.** (*anotar informaciones*) to record

fichero *m* **1.** (*archivador*) filing-cabinet; (*caja*) box file **2.** INFOR file

ficticio, -a *adj* ficticious

ficus *m* rubber plant

fidedigno, -a *adj* reliable

fideicomiso *m* trust

fidelidad *f* **1.** (*lealtad*) fidelity, faithfulness **2.** (*precisión*) precision; **alta ~** high fidelity

fideo *m* **1.** GASTR fine noodle **2.** *inf* (*persona*) beanpole

fiduciario, -a I. *adj* fiduciary **II.** *m, f* trustee

fiebre *f* fever; **~ del heno** hay fever; **~ del juego** compulsive gambling; **~ del oro** gold rush; **~ palúdica** malaria; **tener poca ~** to have a slight temperature

fiel I. *adj* **1.** (*persona*) faithful; **ser ~ a una promesa** to keep a promise; **siempre me han sido ~es** they have always been loyal to me **2.** (*retrato*) faithful **3.** (*memoria*) accurate **II.** *m* **1.** (*seguidor*) faithful **2.** (*de una balanza*) needle, pointer; **él podría inclinar el ~ de la balanza** he could tip the scales [*o* balance] **3.** *pl* REL the faithful

fieltro *m* felt

fiera *f* **1.** ZOOL wild animal **2.** TAUR bull **3.** (*persona*) animal; **llegó hecho una ~** *inf* he arrived in a furious state; (*persona astuta*) wizard, whizz *Brit,* whiz *Am*

fiereza f 1.(*de un animal*) ferocity, ferociousness 2.(*de una persona*) cruelty
fiero, -a adj 1.(*feroz*) fierce 2.(*cruel*) cruel 3.(*feo*) ugly 4.(*fuerte*) terrible
fierro m AmL 1.(*hierro*) iron 2.(*del ganado*) branding iron
fiesta f 1.(*día*) holiday; ¡Felices Fiestas! Merry Christmas and a Happy New Year!; **hoy hago** ~ I have taken the day off today 2.(*celebración*) celebration; ~ (**mayor**) festival; **aguar la** ~ *inf* to be a wet blanket 3. *pl* (*caricias*) **hacer** ~**s a alguien** to caress sb 4. *inf* (*humor*) **estar de** ~ to be in a very cheerful mood 5. *inf* (*asunto*) **tengamos la** ~ **en paz** let's agree to differ
fifí m AmL (*señorito*) playboy, man-about-town
fifiriche adj AmL (*enclenque*) weak
fig. abr de figurativo fig
figura f 1. *t.* ARTE, MAT (*de un cuerpo*) figure; ~ **decorativa** (*persona*) formal figure; **un vestido que realza la** ~ (*que adelgaza*) a dress which enhances the figure; (*que modela*) a dress which moulds [*o* molds *Am*] the figure 2.(*cara, mueca*) face; (*aspecto*) countenance 3.(*imagen*) image; **se distinguía la** ~ **de un barco** you could make out the shape of a boat 4. TEAT character 5.(*personaje*) figure; **las grandes** ~**s del deporte** great sporting [*o* sports *Am*] figures 6.(*ilustración*) illustration 7.(*de la baraja*) *court card* 8. MÚS note
figuración f 1. ARTE representational art 2.(*imaginación*) imagination 3. CINE extras *pl*
figurado, -a adj 1.(*lenguaje*) metaphorical 2.(*uso*) figurative; **en sentido** ~ in a figurative sense
figurante mf CINE, TEAT extra
figurar I. vi 1.(*encontrarse*) to figure; **no figura en la lista** it is not on the list; **figura en el puesto número tres** he appears in third place 2.(*destacar*) to stand out 3.(*aparentar*) to pose; **le gusta un montón** ~ he loves putting on airs II. vt 1.(*representar*) to represent 2. TEAT to appear 3.(*simular*) to pretend; **figuró no haber oído el comentario** he pretended not to have heard the comment III. vr: ~**se** to imagine; ¡**figúrate!** just think!; **no vayas a** ~**te que...** don't go thinking that ...
figurativo, -a adj figurative; **no** ~ non-figurative
figurín m 1.(*dibujo*) fashion design [*o* drawing]; (*modelo*) model 2.(*persona*) flashy person 3.(*revista*) fashion magazine
figurita f Arg picture card
figurón m inf pompous person, stuffed shirt inf
figuroso, -a adj Chile, Méx (*extravagante en el vestir*) loud-dressing
fija f 1. CSur (*en una apuesta*) sure bet 2. Arg (*arpón*) harpoon
fijación f 1.(*sujeción*) fixation; (*con chinchetas*) sticking up; (*con cuerdas*) tying up; (*con cola*) gluing on; (*con clavos*) nailing; (*con cadenas*) chaining; (*con tornillos*) screwing on 2.(*de precio, regla*) fixing 3.(*de la mirada*)

fixedness 4.(*de esquíes*) ski binding 5.(*obsesión*) **tener una** ~ **por alguien** to have a fixation with [*o* on] sb
fijado m FOTO fixing
fijador m 1.(*para el pelo*) hair gel 2.(*de pintura*) fixative 3. FOTO fixer
fijar I. vt 1.(*sujetar*) to fix; (*con cuerdas*) to tie up; (*con cola*) to glue on; (*con clavos*) to nail; (*con cadenas*) to chain; (*con tornillos*) to screw on; ~ **con chinchetas** to stick up with drawing pins; ~ **una placa en la pared** to fix a plaque on the wall; **prohibido** ~ **carteles** bill posters prohibited 2.(*la mirada*) to fix; ~ **la atención en algo** to concentrate on sth 3.(*residencia, precio*) to establish 4. *t.* QUÍM to fix II. vr: ~**se** 1.(*en un lugar*) to establish oneself 2.(*atender*) to pay attention; **no se ha fijado en mi nuevo peinado** he/she has not noticed my new hairdo; **ese se fija en todo** nothing escapes him; **fíjate bien en lo que te digo** listen carefully to what I have to say 3.(*mirar*) to notice; **no se fijó en mí** he/she did not notice me
fijeza f 1.(*seguridad*) certainty 2.(*persistencia*) persistence; **mirar con** ~ **a alguien** to stare fixedly at sb
fijo, -a I. adj 1.(*estable*) stable; **cliente** ~ regular client; **precio** ~ fixed price 2.(*idea*) fixed 3.(*mirada*) steady 4.(*trabajador*) permanent II. adv with certainty; **saber algo de** ~ to know sth for sure
fila f 1.(*hilera*) row; ~ **de coches** line of cars; **en** ~ **india** in single file; **aparcar en doble** ~ to double-park; **en** ~ in line; **salir de la** ~ to step out of line 2. MIL rank; ¡**en** ~**s!** fall in!; ¡**rompan** ~**s!** fall out!; **llamar a** ~**s** to call up *Brit,* to draft *Am* 3. *inf* (*tirria*) dislike 4. MAT row 5. *pl* (*de un partido*) ranks *pl*
filamento m 1.(*de un tejido*) thread 2. ELEC filament 3. BOT fibre *Brit,* fiber *Am*
filantropía f *sin pl* philanthropy
filántropo mf philanthropist
filarmónico, -a adj Philharmonic; **orquesta filarmónica** Philharmonic Orchestra
filatelia f philately, stamp collecting
filatelista mf philatelist, stamp collector
filete m 1. GASTR (*solomillo*) steak; (*lonja*) fillet *Brit,* filet *Am* 2.(*ribete*) edging 3. ARQUIT, TIPO fillet 4.(*tornillo*) thread 5. TÉC border
filetear vt 1.(*un vestido*) to hem 2. GASTR to fillet *Brit,* to filet *Am* 3.(*tornillo*) to thread 4. TÉC to edge
filfa f inf 1.(*mentira*) lie 2.(*engañifa*) fraud
filiación f 1.(*origen*) filiation; (*de ideas*) relation 2.(*datos personales*) particulars *pl* 3.(*en un partido*) affiliation
filial I. adj filial; **equipo** ~ DEP sister club II. f 1. COM subsidiary 2. REL dependency
filibustero m HIST buccaneer; POL filibuster
filigrana f 1.(*de orfebrería*) filigree 2.(*en un papel*) watermark
Filipinas fpl **las** ~ the Philippines
filipino, -a adj, m, f Philippine

filisteo, -a *adj, m, f* HIST Philistine
film *m* CINE, FOTO film *Brit,* movie *Am;* ~ **transparente** Cling wrap® *Brit,* Saran wrap® *Am*
filmación *f* **1.** (*de reportaje*) footage **2.** (*rodaje*) filming, shooting
filmadora *f* camera
filmar *vt* to film, to shoot
filme *m* film *Brit,* movie *Am*
fílmico, -a *adj* film *Brit,* movie *Am*
filmina *f* slide
filmografía *f* films, movies *Am*
filmoteca *f* film archive
filo *m* **1.** (*de cuchillo*) blade; **un arma de dos ~s** *fig* a double-edged sword **2.** (*entre dos partes*) dividing line **3.** *AmC* (*hambre*) hunger ▶ **al ~ del amanecer** dot on dawn; **al ~ de la medianoche** at the stroke of midnight
filología *f* philology; ~ **germánica** Germanic language and literature; ~ **hispánica** Hispanic language and literature
filólogo, -a *m, f* philologist
filón *m* **1.** MIN seam **2.** (*negocio*) gold mine
filoso, -a *adj AmL* (*afilado*) sharp
filosofar *vi* to philosophize
filosofía *f* **1.** (*disciplina*) philosophy **2.** (*serenidad*) calm; **tomar las cosas con** ~ to be philosophical about things
filosófico, -a *adj* philosophical
filósofo, -a *m, f* philosopher
filoxera *f* (*insecto*) phylloxera
filtración *f* **1.** (*de un líquido*) leak, seepage; (*de la luz*) filtration **2.** (*de información*) leak
filtrador *m* filter
filtrar I. *vi* **1.** (*líquido*) to leak (out), to seep; (*luz*) to filter **2.** (*tubería*) to leak **II.** *vt* **1.** (*por un filtro*) to filter; (*llamadas*) to screen **2.** (*datos*) to leak **3.** (*noticia*) to percolate **III.** *vr:* ~**se 1.** (*líquido*) to seep; (*luz*) to filter **2.** (*noticia*) to percolate **3.** (*dinero*) to dwindle
filtro *m* **1.** (*tamiz*) filter; **cigarrillo con** ~ filter tip cigarette; ~ **solar** sunscreen **2.** (*poción*) philtre *Brit,* philter *Am*
filudo, -a *adj AmL* sharp
fin *m* **1.** (*término*) end; ~ **de semana** weekend; **a ~(es) de mes** at the end of the month; **algo toca a su** ~ sth is coming to an end; **poner** ~ **a algo** to put an end to sth; **sin** ~ neverending; **al** ~ **y al cabo, a** ~ **de cuentas** after all **2.** (*propósito*) aim; ~**es deshonestos** immoral purposes; **a** ~ **de que** +*subj* so that ▶ **el** ~ **justifica los medios** *prov* the end justifies the means *prov*
finado, -a *m, f* deceased
final¹ I. *adj* (*producto, resultado*) end; (*fase, examen*) final; (*solución*) ultimate; **el juicio** ~ REL the Final [*o* last] Judgement; **palabras ~es** last words **II.** *m* end; (*de un libro*) ending; MÚS finale; **película con** ~ **feliz** film with a happy ending; **al** ~ **no nos lo dijo** in the end he did not tell us
final² *f* DEP (*partido*) final; (*ronda*) finals *pl*
finalidad *f* purpose; FILOS finality
finalista *mf t.* FILOS finalist

finalización *f* finalization; ~ **de contrato** completion of a contract
finalizar <z→c> **I.** *vi* to finish; (*plazo*) to end **II.** *vt* to end; (*discurso*) to conclude
finalmente *adv* finally, at last
financiación *f* financing, funding; ~ **de los partidos** political party financial backing
financiador(a) *m(f)* financial backer
financiar *vt* to finance
financiera *f* finance company
financiero, -a I. *adj* financial **II.** *m, f* financier
financista *mf AmL* **1.** (*experto en finanzas*) financial expert **2.** (*el que financia*) financier
finanzas *fpl* finances *pl*
finar *vi* to die
finca *f* (*urbana*) (town) property, urban real estate *Am;* (*rústica*) (country) property [*o* real estate *Am*]
finés, -esa I. *adj* Finnish **II.** *m, f* Finn
fineza *f* **1.** (*delgadez*) fineness **2.** (*suavidad*) softness **3.** (*de calidad*) excellence **4.** (*cumplido*) compliment **5.** (*regalo*) gift **6.** (*primor*) exquisiteness
fingido, -a *adj* fake, make-believe; (*persona*) false
fingidor(a) *m(f)* (*de una enfermedad*) person who pretends to be ill; (*de sentimientos*) person who feigns a feeling
fingimiento *m* **1.** (*de una enfermedad*) pretence *Brit,* pretense *Am;* (*de un sentimiento*) feigning **2.** (*engaño*) trick; (*hipocresía*) hypocrisy
fingir <g→j> **I.** *vi* to pretend **II.** *vt* to pretend; (*sentimiento*) to feign
finiquitar *vt* **1.** (*cuenta*) to settle **2.** *inf* (*asunto*) to wind up
finiquito *m* settlement, acquittance; (*documento*) final discharge
finisecular *adj* turn-of-the-century, fin-de--siècle *liter*
finito, -a *adj* finite; **número** ~ MAT finite number
finlandés, -esa I. *adj* Finnish **II.** *m, f* Finn
Finlandia *f* Finland
fino *m* dry sherry
fino, -a *adj* **1.** (*delgado*) fine; **lluvia fina** fine rain **2.** (*liso*) smooth, even **3.** (*de calidad*) excellent; **oro** ~ refined gold; **tener un paladar** ~ to have a discriminating palate **4.** (*sentido*) acute **5.** (*cortés*) polite; **modales ~s** refined manners **6.** (*astuto*) shrewd **7.** (*metal*) precious
finolis I. *adj inv, inf* la-di-da, hoity-toity **II.** *mf inv, inf* affected person
finta *f t.* DEP feint; **hacer una** ~ to feint
finura *f* **1.** (*delgadez*) fineness **2.** (*suavidad*) smoothness **3.** (*calidad*) excellence **4.** (*cortesía*) refinement **5.** (*astucia*) shrewdness
fiordo *m* fjord, fiord
fique *m Col* BOT sisal
firma *f* **1.** (*en documentos*) signature **2.** (*de un acuerdo*) signing **3.** (*empresa*) firm
firmamento *m* firmament

firmante *mf* signatory, signer; **el/la abajo ~** the undersigned

firmar *vi, vt* to sign; **~ autógrafos** to sign autographs; **~ un cheque** (*para pagar*) to sign a cheque [*o* check *Am*]; (*para cobrar*) to endorse a cheque [*o* check *Am*]; **~ un tratado / acuerdo** to sign [*o* subscribe to] a treaty/an agreement

firme I. *adj* (*fijo*) firm; (*estable*) steady; (*seguro*) secure; (*carácter*) resolute; (*postura corporal*) straight; (*amistad*) strong; **con mano ~** with a firm hand; **esta mesa no está ~** this table is unsteady; **es ~ en sus propósitos** he/she is resolute in his/her intentions; **¡~s!** MIL attention! II. *m* 1. (*de la carretera*) road surface 2. (*de guijo*) roadbed III. *adv* de ~ (*fuertemente*) strongly; (*sin parar*) steadily; **estudiar de firme** to study hard; **el calor aprieta de ~** the heat is intense

firmeza *f* 1. (*solidez*) solidity; (*de un mueble*) sturdiness 2. (*de una creencia*) firmness; **~ de carácter** resolution 3. (*perseverancia*) perseverance

firulete *m* 1. *CSur* (*adorno*) cheap adornment 2. *RíoPl* (*paso de tango*) tango step

fiscal I. *adj* 1. (*del fisco*) fiscal 2. (*de los impuestos*) tax II. *mf* 1. JUR public prosecutor *Brit,* district attorney *Am;* **Fiscal General del Estado** Attorney General 2. (*interventor*) auditor, inspector

fiscalía *f* office of the public prosecutor *Brit,* district attorney's office *Am*

fiscalidad *f* taxation

fiscalización *f* audit; (*de impuestos*) tax inspection

fiscalizador(a) *m(f)* auditor; (*de impuestos*) tax inspector

fiscalizar <z→c> *vt* to audit; (*lo fiscal*) to inspect

fisco *m* exchequer, treasury

fisgar <g→gu> I. *vi* (*indagar*) **~ en algo** to snoop into [*o* about] sth; **le encanta ~ en mis asuntos** she loves prying into my affairs II. *vt* 1. (*pescar*) to harpoon 2. (*con el olfato*) to sniff out

fisgón, -ona *m, f pey* 1. (*que indaga*) nosy Parker 2. (*que se burla*) mocker

fisgonear *vi pey* **~ en algo** to pry into sth

física *f* physics *pl*

físicamente *adv* physically

físico *m* physique; **tener un buen ~** (*cuerpo*) to have a good physique; (*aspecto general*) to be good-looking

físico, -a I. *adj t.* FÍS physical; **educación física** ENS physical education II. *m, f* physicist

fisiología *f* physiology

fisiólogo, -a *m, f* physiologist

fisión *f* FÍS, BIO fission

fisionar *vt* to undergo fission

fisionomía *f v.* **fisonomía**

fisioterapeuta *mf* physiotherapist

fisioterapia *f* physiotherapy

fisonomía *f* 1. (*general*) physiognomy 2. (*del rostro*) face 3. (*aspecto*) appearance 4. (*rasgos*) features *pl*

fisonomista *mf* physiognomist; **¿eres un buen ~?** do you have a good memory for faces?

fístula *f* 1. MED fistula 2. (*tubo*) tube

fisura *f* 1. (*grieta*) fissure, crack 2. MED (*en un hueso*) hairline fracture 3. MED (*en el ano*) fissure

flac(c)idez *f* 1. (*de las carnes*) flabbiness 2. (*de la piel*) flaccidity

flác(c)ido, -a *adj* 1. (*carnes*) flabby 2. (*piel*) flaccid 3. (*vestiduras*) loose

flaco *m* weak point [*o* spot]

flaco, -a *adj* 1. (*delgado*) thin; **los años de las vacas flacas** the lean years 2. (*escaso*) poor; **rendimientos ~s** poor performance 3. (*débil*) weak; **punto ~** weak spot

flacucho, -a *adj pey, inf* skinny

flagelar I. *vt* 1. (*azotar*) to flog; REL to flagellate 2. (*verbalmente*) to censure II. *vr:* **~se** to flagellate oneself

flagelo *m* whip; (*azote*) scourge

flagrante I. *adj* (*evidente*) flagrant II. *adv* **en ~** red-handed

flamante *adj inf* 1. (*vistoso*) flamboyant 2. (*nuevo*) brand-new

flamear I. *vi* 1. (*llamear*) to flame 2. (*bandera*) to flap II. *vt* 1. GASTR to flambé 2. MED to disinfect (*using a flame*)

flamenco *m* 1. ZOOL flamingo 2. (*cante*) flamenco 3. (*lengua*) Flemish

---

The **flamenco**, a very traditional form of song and dance from **Andalucía**, is known the world over. The origins of the **flamenco** can be found in the rich traditions of three national groups: the Andalusians, the Moors and the Gypsies. The song and dance movements (solo or duet) are always accompanied by a rhythmic clapping of hands and clicking of fingers together with various cries.

---

flamenco, -a I. *adj* 1. (*andaluz*) flamenco; **cante ~** flamenco 2. (*de Flandes*) Flemish 3. (*chulo*) cocky II. *m, f* Fleming

flan *m* crème caramel; **estar hecho un ~** to be shaking like a leaf

flanco *m* flank, side

Flandes *m* Flanders

flanquear *vt* 1. (*estar al lado*) to flank 2. MIL to outflank

flaquear *vi* 1. (*fuerzas*) to flag; (*salud*) to decline 2. (*en un examen*) to be poor 3. (*demanda*) to slacken 4. (*edificio*) to be on the point of giving way 5. (*ánimo*) to lose heart

flaqueza *f* 1. (*de flaco*) thinness 2. (*debilidad*) weakness

flas *m,* **flash** *m inv* 1. FOTO flash 2. (*noticia*) newsflash

flato *m* 1. MED flatulence 2. *AmC* (*melancolía*) melancholy

flatoso, -a *adj AmL* (*miedoso*) apprehensive

flatulencia *f* MED flatulence

flauta[1] *f* ~ (**dulce**) recorder; ~ (**travesera**) flute

flauta[2] *mf*, **flautista** *mf* flautist *Brit*, flutist *Am*

flebitis *f inv* MED phlebitis

flecha *f* 1. (*arma*) arrow; **ser rápido como una** ~ *fig* to be as quick as lightning 2. (*de torre*) spire 3. (*de viga*) rise

flechar I. *vi* to have the bow drawn II. *vt* 1. (*un arco*) to draw 2. *inf* (*enamorar*) to sweep sb off his/her feet

flechazo *m* 1. (*de flecha*) arrow shot 2. *inf* (*de amor*) **lo nuestro fue un** ~ ours was love at first sight

fleco *m* 1. (*adorno*) fringe 2. (*del pelo*) fringe 3. *pl* (*de vestido*) frayed edges *pl* 4. *pl fig* (*asunto*) final [*o* small] details *pl*

fleje *m* iron hoop

flema *f* 1. (*calma*) imperturbability 2. (*mucosidad*) phlegm

flemático, -a *adj* I. *adj* phlegmatic II. *m, f* phlegmatic person

flemón *m* 1. MED conjunctivitis 2. (*dental*) gumboil

flequillo *m* fringe; ()

fleta *f AmC* 1. (*friega*) rubbing 2. (*zurra*) thrashing; (*castigo*) spanking

fletador(a) *m(f)* 1. (*de avión*) charterer 2. COM freighter 3. (*pasajeros*) carrier

fletamento *m* 1. (*de avión*) charter 2. COM (*apelocción*) fringe, freightage 3. (*contrato*) freight 4. (*pasajeros*) carrier

fletán *m* halibut

fletar I. *vt* 1. (*avión*) to charter 2. COM to freight 3. *AmL* (*vehículo*) to hire, to rent 4. *CSur* (*despedir*) to fire II. *vr*: ~**se** *AmC* (*fastidiarse*) to get annoyed

flete *m* 1. (*carga*) cargo, freight 2. COM (*tasa*) freight 3. *AmL* (*tarifa*) hire charge

flexibilidad *f* 1. (*de palo*) flexibility; (*de músculo*) suppleness 2. (*de una persona*) flexibility; ~ **de precios** price flexibility

flexibilizar <z→c> *vt* to make (more) flexible

flexible *adj* 1. (*palo*) flexible; (*músculo*) supple 2. (*persona*) flexible; **horario** ~ flexitime

flexión *f* 1. (*del cuerpo*) flexion, bending; (*plancha*) press-up; ~ **de brazos en la espaldera** pull-up 2. LING inflection 3. GEO monoclinal fold

flexionar *vt* to flex, to bend

flexo *m* flexible table lamp

flipado, -a *adj inf* freaked *inf*; (*drogado*) stoned, high

flipante *adj inf* amazing, far-out *inf*, awesome *inf*; (*drogas*) mind-bending

flipar I. *vt inf* **este actor me flipa** I love this actor II. *vi, vr*: ~**se** *inf* (*drogas*) to be spaced-out [*o* on a high], to get high [*o* stoned]

flipper *m* pinball machine

flirt *m* <flirts> flirt

flirtear *vi* to flirt

flirteo *m* flirtation

flojear *vi* 1. (*disminuir*) to diminish; (*calor*) to ease up 2. (*en una materia*) ~ **en algo** to be poor at sth

flojedad *f* 1. (*debilidad*) weakness 2. (*pereza*) slackness

flojera *f inf* 1. (*debilidad*) weakness; **cogió** ~ **de piernas** his legs went weak 2. (*pereza*) slackness

flojo, -a *adj* 1. (*cuerda*) slack; (*nudo*) loose 2. (*vino, café, argumento*) weak; (*viento*) light; (*luz*) feeble; ~ **de carácter** spineless; **estoy** ~ **en inglés** I am weak in English; **la política me la trae floja** *vulg* I don't give a damn about politics 3. (*cosecha*) poor 4. (*obrero*) slack 5. *AmL* (*cobarde*) cowardly

floppy *m* INFOR floppy disk

flor *f* 1. BOT (*planta*) flowering plant; (*parte de la planta*) flower, bloom; **estar en** ~ to be in flower [*o* bloom]; **camisa de** ~**es** flowery shirt 2. (*lo más selecto*) flower; **la** ~ **y nata de la sociedad** the cream of society; **la** ~ **de la canela** *fig* the best; **la** ~ **de la vida** the prime of life 3. (*piropo*) compliment 4. (*de los metales*) iridescence 5. (*de las pieles*) grain 6. (*virginidad*) virginity 7. (*del vino*) lees *pl* 8. (*nivel*) **pasó volando a** ~ **de tierra** the plane skimmed over the ground; **tengo los nervios a** ~ **de piel** my nerves are frayed

flora *f* flora

floración *f* 1. (*acción*) flowering 2. (*tiempo*) flowering season

florear I. *vi* 1. (*la espada*) to flourish 2. MÚS to play a trill [*o* appogiatura] 3. *AmL* (*florecer*) to flower II. *vt* 1. (*adornar*) to adorn with flowers 2. (*harina*) to sift 3. (*naipes*) to stack 4. (*piropear*) to compliment

florecer *irr como crecer* I. *vi* 1. (*planta*) to flower, to bloom 2. (*industria*) to flourish II. *vr*: ~**se** to grow mould *Brit*, to grow mold *Am*

floreciente *adj* 1. (*planta*) flowering 2. (*industria*) flourishing

florecimiento *m* 1. (*de una planta*) flowering 2. (*de una industria*) flourishing

Florencia *f* Florence

florentino, -a *adj, m, f* Florentine

floreo *m* 1. (*conversación*) empty talk 2. MÚS ornament

florería *f CSur, Bol, Perú* (*floristería*) florist's, flower shop

florero *m* 1. (*jarrón*) vase; **estar de** ~ *fig* to be just for decoration 2. (*maceta*) flowerpot

floresta *f* 1. (*bosque*) wood, forest 2. (*de poemas*) anthology

florete *m* DEP foil

floricultor(a) *m(f)* floriculturist

floricultura *f* floriculture

florido, -a *adj* 1. (*con flores*) flowery; (*floreciente*) flowering; **árbol** ~ tree in flower [*o* bloom] 2. (*selecto*) select 3. (*lenguaje*) florid

florín *m* florin

floripondio *m pey* 1. (*flor*) large flower

2. (*adorno*) gaudy adornment, frippery *Brit*

florista *mf* florist

floristería *f* florist's, flower shop

floritura *f* heavy ornamentation

flota *f* fleet

flotación *f* **1.** floating, flotation, floatation; **línea de** ~ NÁUT waterline **2.** TÉC buoyancy **3.** FIN flotation, floatation

flotador *m* **1.** TÉC (*de pesca*) float **2.** (*en barcos*) float; (*para niños*) rubber ring **3.** (*cisterna*) ballcock **4.** *RíoPl inf* (*michelines*) roll of fat

flotar *vi* **1.** (*en agua: activamente*) to stay afloat; (*pasivamente*) to be suspended; (*en aire*) to float **2.** (*bandera*) to wave **3.** FIN to float

flote *m* **estar a** ~ to be afloat; **mantenerse a** ~ *t. fig* to manage to keep one's head above water; **sacar a** ~ **una empresa** to get a business going

fluctuación *f* **1.** (*oscilación*) fluctuation **2.** (*irresolución*) uncertainty

fluctuante *adj* fluctuating

fluctuar <*l. pres:* fluctúo> *vi* to fluctuate; **estoy fluctuando entre comprarme un coche o no** I can't decide whether to buy a car or not

fluidez *f* **1.** (*de líquido*) fluidity **2.** (*de expresión*) hablar con ~ **un idioma extranjero** to speak a foreign language fluently

fluido *m* **1.** (*líquido*) fluid **2.** ELEC current **3.** (*expresión*) fluent

fluido, -a *adj* **1.** (*alimento*) liquid; **es** ~ **de palabra** he speaks with ease **2.** (*tráfico*) free-flowing

fluir *irr como huir vi* **1.** (*correr*) to run; (*brotar*) to flow **2.** (*palabras*) to flow

flujo *m* **1.** (*de un líquido*) flow; ~ **de datos** *t.* INFOR data flow; ~ **de palabras** stream [*o* flood] of words **2.** (*de la marea*) rising tide **3.** MED discharge; ~ **de vientre** diarrhoea *Brit*, diarrhea *Am;* ~ **menstrual** menstrual flow

fluminense **I.** *adj* of/from Rio de Janeiro **II.** *mf* native/inhabitant of Rio de Janeiro

flúor *m* fluorine

fluorescencia *f* fluorescence

fluorescente **I.** *adj* fluorescent; **tubo** ~ fluorescent tube **II.** *m* fluorescent light

flus *m* **1.** *Ant, Col, Ven* (*terno*) suit of clothes **2.** *ElSal* (*racha de buena suerte*) lucky streak

fluvial *adj* fluvial; **puerto** ~ river port

FM *f abr de* **Frecuencia Modulada** FM

FMI *m abr de* **Fondo Monetario Internacional** IMF

fobia *f* **1.** MED phobia **2.** (*aversión*) aversion

foca *f* **1.** ZOOL seal **2.** (*piel*) sealskin **3.** *pey* (*gordo*) whale

focal *adj* focal; **distancia** ~ focal length

focalizar <z→c> *vt* to focus on

foche **I.** *adj Chile* (*maloliente*) smelly **II.** *mf Chile* (*persona corrompida*) corrupt person, rotten apple *inf*

foco *m* **1.** FÍS, MAT focus **2.** (*centro*) focal point; ~ **de infección** source of infection **3.** (*lám-*

para) light; (*estadio*) floodlight; (*teatro*) spotlight **4.** *AmL* (*bombilla*) light bulb

fofo, -a *adj* flabby; **estoy** ~ I am flabby

fogaje *m Arg, Col, PRico, Ven* (*bochorno*) stifling heat

fogata *f* (*en el campo*) bonfire; (*de alegría*) blaze; (*como baliza*) flare

fogón *m* **1.** (*de la cocina*) stove **2.** (*de máquinas de vapor*) furnace; FERRO firebox **3.** (*de un cañón*) vent **4.** *AmL* (*fogata*) fire

fogonazo *m* **1.** (*de arma*) flash **2.** (*de pólvora*) flare

fogonero *m* stoker

fogosidad *f* **1.** (*de pasión*) passion **2.** (*de persona*) ardour *Brit,* ardor *Am* **3.** (*de debate*) animation

fogoso, -a *adj* **1.** (*pasión*) passionate **2.** (*persona*) ardent **3.** (*debate*) animated **4.** (*caballo*) spirited

fogueado, -a *adj AmL* expert

foguear **I.** *vt* **1.** (*un arma*) to fire a blank (cartridge) **2.** MIL to get used to gunfire **3.** (*a penalidades*) to harden **II.** *vr:* ~**se** to become hardened

fogueo *m* **bala de** ~ blank (cartridge)

foguerear **I.** *vt Chile, Cuba* (*quemar*) to burn off **II.** *vi* (*hacer una hoguera*) to make a fire

foja *f AmL* sheet; ~ **de servicios** record

folclor(e) *m* folklore

folclórico, -a **I.** *adj* traditional **II.** *m, f* singer of flamenco

folclorista *mf* folklore specialist

fólder *f AmL* (*carpeta*) folder

foliación *f* foliation

foliar **I.** *adj* foliar **II.** *vt* TIPO to foliate

folio *m* **1.** (*hoja de papel*) sheet (of paper) **2.** (*de un libro*) leaf

folk *m sin pl* MÚS folk music

follador *m* **1.** (*que afuella*) bellows operator **2.** *vulg* (*fornicador*) shagger *Brit*

follaje *m* **1.** (*de árbol, bosque*) foliage **2.** (*adorno*) decoration of branches and leaves **3.** (*en un texto, al hablar*) waffle, wordiness

follar[1] **I.** *vi vulg* to fuck **II.** *vt* **1.** *vulg* (*coitar*) to fuck **2.** *vulg* (*fastidiar*) to bug *inf* **3.** (*deshacer*) to destroy

follar[2] <o→ue> **I.** *vt* **1.** (*soplar*) to blow with bellows **2.** *inf* (*suspender*) to screw up **II.** *vr:* ~**se** *vulg* to silently fart, the butler's revenge *inf*

folletín *m* newspaper serial; **novela de** ~ pulp novel

folletinesco, -a *adj* pulp

folleto *m* pamphlet; ~ **publicitario** advertising leaflet, flier

follón *m inf* **1.** (*alboroto*) row; **armar un** ~ to cause a commotion **2.** (*asunto enojoso*) trouble

follón, -ona *adj* **1.** (*chulo*) swaggering **2.** (*holgazán*) lazy

follonero, -a *m, f* troublemaker

fome *adj Chile* (*aburrido*) boring; **más** ~ **que jugar solo a la escondida** duller than playing hide-and-seek by yourself

fomentar *vt* 1. (*empleo*) to promote; (*economía*) to boost 2. (*discordias*) to foment

fomento *m* 1. (*del empleo*) promotion; (*de la economía*) boosting; **Banco Internacional de Reconstrucción y Fomento** International Bank for Reconstruction and Development 2. (*de discordias*) fuelling *Brit*, fueling *Am*

fonda *f* inn

fondeadero *m* anchorage

fondeado, -a *adj AmL* well-off, well-heeled *Am*

fondear I. *vi* NÁUT to anchor II. *vt* 1. (*anclar*) to anchor 2. (*sondear*) to sound 3. (*registrar*) to search; (*una cuestión*) to examine thoroughly; ~ **un asunto** to examine a matter thoroughly

fondeo *m* 1. NÁUT anchoring; (*sondeo*) sounding 2. (*registro*) search

fondillos *mpl* (*pantalones*) seat; (*trasero*) behind

fondista *mf* 1. (*de una fonda*) innkeeper 2. DEP long-distance runner

fondo *m* 1. (*de un cajón*) back; (*del río*) bed; (*de un valle*) bottom; **los bajos ~s** the underworld [*o* low life]; **en el ~ de su corazón** in his/her heart of hearts; **en este asunto hay mar de ~** there are underlying issues in this matter; **tocar ~** ECON to hit bottom 2. (*de un edificio*) depth; **al ~ del pasillo** at the end of the corridor; **mi habitación está al ~ de la casa** my bedroom is at the back of the house 3. (*lo esencial*) essence; **artículo de ~** editorial; **en el ~** at bottom; **ir al ~ de un asunto** to go to the heart of the matter; **tratar un tema a ~** to seriously discuss a subject; **hay un ~ de verdad en lo que dices** there is sth of truth in what you say; **su carta tiene un ~ amargo** his/her letter had a bitter undertone to it 4. (*índole*) nature, disposition; **persona de buen ~** a good person at heart; **tiene un buen ~** he/she has a happy disposition 5. (*de un cuadro*) background; (*de una tela*) background colour [*o* color *Am*]; **ruido/música de ~** background noise/music 6. (*conjunto de cosas, biblioteca*) collection 7. DEP long-distance; **corredor de ~** long-distance runner; **esquiador de ~** cross-country skier 8. FIN, POL fund; ~ **común** kitty; **Fondo Monetario Internacional** International Monetary Fund; **Fondo Social Europeo** European Social Fund; **a ~ perdido** non-recoverable 9. *pl* (*medios*) funds *pl*; ~**s públicos** public funds; **cheque sin ~s** bad cheque *Brit*, bad check *Am* 10. NÁUT sea bed; **tocar ~** to touch bottom; **irse a ~** to sink

fondón, -ona *adj pey, inf* big-bottomed

fonema *m* LING phoneme

fonética *f* phonetics *pl*

fono *m Chile* (*auricular del teléfono*) receiver

fonógrafo *m* FÍS phonograph

fonología *f* LING phonology

fonoteca *f* sound archive, sound [*o* music] library

fontanería *f* 1. (*acción, conducto*) plumbing 2. (*establecimiento*) plumber's

fontanero, -a I. *adj* (*natural*) spring; (*artificial*) fountain II. *m*, *f* plumber

footing *m sin pl* jogging; **hacer** ~ to jog

forajido, -a I. *adj* outlawed II. *m*, *f* outlaw, bandit

foral *adj* 1. (*de los privilegios*) referring to the privileges obtained by the granting of charters in the Middle Ages to certain towns 2. (*de la jurisdicción*) jurisdictional 3. (*de las leyes*) statutory

foráneo, -a *adj* 1. (*de otro lugar*) outside 2. (*extraño*) alien

forastero, -a I. *adj* 1. (*de otro lugar*) outside; (*extranjero*) foreign 2. (*extraño*) alien II. *m*, *f* stranger; (*extranjero*) foreigner

forcejear *vi* 1. (*esforzarse*) to struggle 2. (*resistir*) to resist

forcejeo *m* 1. (*esfuerzo*) struggle 2. (*resistencia*) resistance

fórceps *m inv* forceps *pl*

forense I. *adj* forensic; **médico** ~ forensic surgeon II. *mf* pathologist

forestal *adj* forest, woodland; **camino** ~ forest track; **repoblación** ~ afforestation; **guarda** ~ forester *Brit*, forest ranger *Am*

forestar *vt* to afforest

forfait *m* 1. COM fixed price 2. (*esquiar*) ski pass

forfaiting <forfaitings> *m* COM price fixing

forja *f* 1. (*fragua*) forge 2. (*ferrería*) ironworks *pl* 3. (*creación*) forging 4. (*argamasa*) mortar

forjar I. *vt* 1. (*metal*) to forge 2. (*muro*) to build; (*revocar*) to render 3. (*inventar*) to invent 4. (*crear*) to forge; (*imperio*) to build II. *vr*: ~**se** 1. (*imaginarse*) to imagine; ~ **ilusiones** to build castles in the air 2. (*crear*) to make

forma *f* 1. (*figura*) form, shape; **las ~s de una mujer** a woman's curves; **en ~ de gota** in the shape of a drop; **dar ~ a algo** (*formar*) to shape sth; (*precisar*) to spell out 2. (*manera*) way; ~ **de comportamiento** way of behaviour [*o* behavior *Am*]; ~ **de pago** method of payment; **defecto de** ~ JUR defect of form; **tiene una extraña ~ de andar** he/she has a strange way of walking; **de ~ libre** freely; **en ~ escrita** written; **en (buena y) debida** ~ duly; **de ~ que** so that; **de todas ~s,...** anyway, ...; **lo haré de una ~ u otra** I will do it one way or another; **no hay ~ de abrir la puerta** this door is impossible to open 3. (*comportamiento*) manners *pl* 4. (*molde*) mould *Brit*, mold *Am* 5. (*condición*) **estar en** ~ to be fit [*o* in good shape] 6. DEP form

formación *f* 1. (*creación*) creation; (*de una sociedad*) formation; ~ **del balance** establishment of the balance sheet; ~ **de humo** forming of smoke 2. *t.* MIL (*de personas*) formation; ~ **política** political group; ~ **de tropas** military force; **desfilar en** ~ **cerrada** to march past in close formation 3. (*educación*) edu-

cation; ~ **de adultos** adult education; ~ **escolar** school education; ~ **profesional** vocational training **4.** GEO formation **5.** (*forma*) form
formal *adj* **1.** (*relativo a la forma*) formal; **requisito** ~ formal requirement **2.** (*serio*) serious; (*educado*) educated; (*cumplidor*) reliable **3.** (*oficial*) official; **una invitación** ~ a formal invitation; **tiene novio** ~ she has a steady boyfriend
formalidad *f* **1.** (*seriedad*) seriousness; (*exactitud*) correctness **2.** *pl* ADMIN, JUR formalities *pl* **3.** (*norma de comportamiento*) formality
formalismo *m* formalism
formalizar <z→c> I. *vt* **1.** (*dar forma*) to formalize **2.** (*solemnizar*) to solemnize; ~ **un noviazgo** (*comprometerse*) to become engaged; (*casarse*) to marry **3.** JUR to formalize; ~ **un contrato** to formalize a contract; ~ **una solicitud** to formalize a motion II. *vr:* ~**se 1.** (*formarse*) to be formalized **2.** (*volverse formal*) to grow up
formar I. *vi* **1.** MIL to fall in **2.** (*figurar*) to figure II. *vt* **1.** (*dar forma*) to form, to shape **2.** (*constituir*) to form; MIL to form up; ~ **parte de** to form part of **3.** (*educar*) to train; (*enseñar*) to teach III. *vr:* ~**se 1.** (*crearse*) to form; MIL to fall in **2.** (*ser educado*) to be educated; **se ha formado a sí mismo** he is self-taught **3.** (*desarrollarse*) to develop **4.** (*hacerse*) to form; ~**se una idea de algo** to form an impression of sth
formatear *vt* INFOR to format
formateo *m* INFOR formatting
formativo, -a *adj* **1.** *t.* LING (*que da forma*) formative **2.** (*educativo*) educational; (*instructivo*) instructive
formato *m* format; (*tamaño*) size; ~ **de datos** INFOR data format; ~ **de texto** INFOR text format; ~ **vertical** vertical format
formica® *f sin pl* Formica®
formidable *adj* **1.** *inf* (*estupendo*) fantastic **2.** (*enorme*) enormous **3.** (*temible*) awesome
formón *m* **1.** (*escoplo*) chisel **2.** (*sacabocados*) punch
fórmula *f* **1.** *t.* MAT, QUÍM formula; ~ **de despedida** (*carta*) closing formula, close; **coche de ~ 1** DEP Formula One car **2.** *AmL* MED prescription
formulación *f* **1.** (*de una idea*) formulation; ~ **de balances** drawing up of the balance; ~ **de la propuesta** drawing up of a proposal **2.** FÍS formula
formular I. *adj* formulaic II. *vt* **1.** (*expresar con una fórmula*) to express with a formula **2.** (*manifestar*) to formulate; ~ **demanda** to file a claim [*o* suit]; ~ **denuncia** to lodge a complaint **3.** (*recetar*) to prescribe
formulario *m* **1.** (*impreso*) form; ~ **para giro postal** postal order form **2.** (*colección de fórmulas*) formulary; (*de recetas*) recipe book
formulario, -a *adj* **1.** (*cortés*) formal **2.** (*formular*) formulaic

formulismo *m* formalism; (*burocrático*) red tape
fornicar <c→qu> *vi* **1.** (*realizar el acto sexual*) to fornicate **2.** (*cometer adulterio*) to commit adultery
fornido, -a *adj* well-built, husky
foro *m* **1.** (*plaza*) forum; ~ **romano** Roman forum **2.** JUR (*lugar*) court of law **3.** JUR (*curia*) the Bar **4.** TEAT upstage area; **irse por el ~** *inf* to slip away unnoticed
forofo, -a *m, f* fan, buff
forrado, -a *adj* **1.** (*con forro*) lined **2.** *inf* (*rico*) stinking rich *inf*
forraje *m* **1.** (*pasto*) hay; (*verde*) grass; *AmL* (*seco*) feed **2.** *inf* (*fárrago*) hotchpotch *Brit*, hodgepodge *Am*
forrar I. *vt* (*el exterior, una pared*) to face; (*el interior, una prenda*) to line; (*una butaca*) to upholster; (*un libro*) to cover; ~ **con algodón** to cover with cotton II. *vr:* ~**se** *inf* **1.** (*enriquecerse*) to make a packet **2.** (*hartarse*) ~**se de algo** to stuff oneself with sth
forro *m* **1.** (*exterior, de una pared*) facing; (*interior, de una prenda*) lining; (*de una butaca*) upholstery; (*de un libro*) cover **2.** NÁUT sheathing **3.** AUTO ~ **de freno** brake lining **4.** *inf* (*en absoluto*) **ni por el** ~ at all **5.** *AmL, vulg* (*preservativo*) condom, rubber *Am*; (*gilipollas*) asshole *vulg*
fortachón, -ona *adj* *inf* beefy
fortalecedor(a) *adj* **1.** (*vigorizador*) invigorating **2.** (*que da ánimo*) encouraging **3.** (*reforzante*) fortifying, revitalizing
fortalecer *irr como crecer* I. *vt* **1.** (*vigorizar*) to invigorate **2.** (*animar*) to encourage **3.** (*reforzar*) to fortify II. *vr:* ~**se 1.** (*vigorizarse*) to fortify oneself **2.** (*volverse más fuerte*) to become stronger
fortalecimiento *m* **1.** (*de una cosa*) fortifying **2.** (*del cuerpo*) toughening **3.** (*del ánimo*) encouragement
fortaleza *f* **1.** (*fuerza*) strength; **de poca** ~ not very tough **2.** (*virtud*) fortitude **3.** (*robustez*) robustness **4.** MIL fortress, stronghold
fortificación *f* **1.** (*fortalecimiento*) strengthening **2.** MIL (*acción*) fortifying **3.** MIL (*obra*) fortification
fortificar <c→qu> I. *vt* **1.** (*fortalecer*) to strengthen **2.** MIL to fortify II. *vr:* ~**se 1.** (*fortalecerse*) to fortify oneself **2.** MIL to build fortifications
fortín *m* **1.** (*fuerte*) fort **2.** (*defensa*) bunker
fortísimo, -a *adj* *superl de* **fuerte**
fortuito, -a *adj* fortuitous, chance
fortuna *f* **1.** (*suerte*) fortune; **por** ~ (*afortunadamente*) fortunately; (*por casualidad*) luckily; **probar** ~ to try one's luck **2.** (*destino*) fate **3.** (*capital*) fortune; **su voz era su** ~ her voice was her asset
fórum *m* forum
forúnculo *m* MED boil, furuncle
forzado *m* **1.** (*presidiario*) convict **2.** (*galeote*) galley slave

forzado, -a *adj* 1. (*artificial*) forced; **trabajos ~s** hard labour [*o* labor *Am*] 2. (*ocupado*) occupied
forzar *irr* I. *vt* 1. (*obligar*) to force 2. (*un acontecimiento*) to bring about 3. (*violar*) to rape 4. (*esforzar*) to force; (*voz*) to strain 5. (*obligar a entrar*) to push in; (*a abrirse*) to force open II. *vr:* ~**se** 1. (*obligarse*) to force oneself 2. (*esforzarse*) to push oneself
forzosamente *adv* (*inevitablemente*) unavoidablly; (*obligatoriamente*) necessarily
forzoso, -a *adj* forced, necessary; **aterrizaje ~** forced landing; **venta forzosa** compulsary sale
forzudo, -a *adj* strong
fosa *f* 1. (*hoyo*) pit; (*alargado*) MIL, GEO trench; **~ séptica** septic tank 2. (*sepultura*) grave; **~ común** common grave 3. ANAT fossa; **~ nasal** nostril
fosfato *m* phosphate
fosforecer *irr como crecer vi* to phosphoresce
fosforescencia *f* phosphoresence
fosforescente *adj* phosphorescent; **pintura ~** luminous paint
fósforo *m* 1. QUÍM phosphorus 2. (*cerilla*) match
fósil I. *adj* 1. GEO fossil 2. *inf* (*anticuado*) antiquated II. *m* fossil
fosilizado, -a *adj* GEO fossilized
fosilizarse <z→c> *vr* 1. GEO to fossilize 2. *inf* (*persona*) to turn into an old fossil
foso *m* 1. (*hoyo*) hole; (*alargado*) ditch; MIL trench; (*fortaleza*) moat 2. MÚS, TEAT orchestra pit 3. DEP pit 4. (*en un garaje*) inspection pit
foto *f* photo; **~** (**tamaño**) **carnet** passport photo
fotocopia *f* photocopy
fotocopiadora *f* photocopier
fotocopiar *vt* to photocopy
fotoeléctrico, -a *adj* photoelectric
fotogénico, -a *adj* photogenic
fotografía *f* 1. (*imagen*) photograph; **~ aérea** aerial photograph; **~ en color** colour [*o* color *Am*] photograph; **~** (**tamaño**) **carnet** passport photograph; **álbum de ~s** photo(graph) album 2. (*arte*) photography
fotografiar < *l. pres:* fotografío> I. *vi* to photograph II. *vt* 1. (*hacer fotos*) to photograph 2. (*describir*) to describe in detail III. *vr:* ~**se** to have one's photo taken
fotográfico, -a *adj* photographic; **máquina fotográfica** camera; **papel ~** photographic paper
fotógrafo, -a *m, f* photographer
fotograma *m* 1. CINE still 2. FOTO photogram
fotomatón *m* 1. (*mecanismo*) photo automaton 2. (*cabina*) photo booth 3. (*foto*) passport-size photo
fotomodelo *mf* photographic model
fotomontaje *m* photomontage
fotonovela *f* photostory
fotoquímica *f* photochemistry

fotorreportaje *m* report with photographs, illustrated feature
fotosíntesis *f sin pl* photosynthesis
fotovoltaico, -a *adj* photovoltaic
FP *f abr de* **Formación Profesional** vocational training, technical education
frac *m* <fracs *o* fraques> tails *pl*
fracasar *vi* 1. (*no tener éxito*) to fail; **la película fracasó** the film was a flop; **~ en un examen** to fail an exam 2. NÁUT to break up
fracaso *m* 1. (*acción*) failure 2. (*fiasco*) fiasco 3. (*desastre*) disaster
fracción *f* 1. (*división*) division; (*ruptura*) rupture; (*de una cantidad*) splitting up 2. (*parte*) fraction; (*de un objeto*) fragment; (*de una organización*) splinter group; **~ parlamentaria** parliamentary faction 3. MAT, QUÍM fraction
fraccionamiento *m* 1. (*división*) division; (*ruptura*) rupturing; (*de una cantidad*) splitting up; (*de una organización*) splintering 2. QUÍM fractionation
fraccionar I. *vt* 1. (*dividir*) to divide; (*romper*) to break up; (*una cantidad*) to split up; **~ el pago** to pay in instalments [*o* installments *Am*]; (*una organización*) to break away 2. QUÍM to fractionate II. *vr:* ~**se** to fractionalize; (*grupo*) to split up
fraccionario, -a *adj* 1. MAT fractional; **número ~** fraction 2. POL factional 3. (*incompleto*) incomplete
fractura *f* 1. (*rotura*) break; MED fracture; **~ simple/complicada** closed/compound fracture 2. GEO (*falla*) fault
fracturar I. *vt* to break; (*una caja fuerte*) to force II. *vr:* ~**se** to fracture
fragancia *f* fragrance; (*perfume*) perfume; (*vino*) bouquet
fragata *f* 1. NÁUT frigate 2. ZOOL frigate bird
frágil *adj* 1. (*objeto*) fragile 2. (*constitución, salud*) delicate; (*anciano*) frail 3. (*carácter*) weak; **tener una memoria ~** to have a bad memory
fragilidad *f* 1. (*de un objeto*) fragility 2. (*de la constitución, salud*) delicacy; (*de un anciano*) frailty 3. (*del carácter*) weakness
fragilizar <z→c> *vt* to weaken
fragmentación *f* fragmentation; (*en muchos pedazos*) breaking up; (*de un cristal*) shattering
fragmentar I. *vt* (*dividir*) to fragment, to divide; (*en muchos pedazos*) to break up; (*romper*) to break; (*una roca*) to split II. *vr:* ~**se** (*cristal*) to shatter; (*roca*) to split
fragmentario, -a *adj* 1. (*compuesto*) compound 2. (*incompleto*) fragmentary
fragmento *m* 1. (*parte*) fragment; (*de un cristal*) splinter; (*de una roca*) chip; (*de un tejido*) remnant; (*de un papel*) scrap 2. LIT, MÚS (*parte*) fragment, excerpt
fragor *m* din
fragoroso, -a *adj* deafening
fragosidad *f* 1. (*de un monte*) ruggedness

2. (*de un camino*) unevenness **3.** (*lugar*) roughness; (*lleno de arbustos*) denseness

fragoso, -a *adj* **1.** (*áspero*) rough **2.** (*ruidoso*) noisy

fragua *f* forge

fraguar <gu→gü> **I.** *vi* **1.** (*cemento*) to set **2.** (*idea*) to devise **II.** *vt* (*metal*) to forge; **¿qué estás fraguando?** *fig* what are you scheming?

fraile *m* **1.** REL friar **2.** (*en un vestido*) accidental turn-up **3.** TIPO *part of a page which fails to be printed*

frambuesa *f* raspberry

frame *m* INFOR frame

francés, -esa I. *adj* French; **tortilla francesa** plain omelette **II.** *m, f* Frenchman *m,* Frenchwoman *f*

Francfort *m* Frankfurt

franchute *mf pey* Frog, Frenchy

Francia *f* France

franciscano, -a I. *adj* **1.** REL Franciscan **2.** AmL (*pardo*) dun **II.** *m, f* Franciscan

francmasonería *f* freemasonry

franco *m* **1.** (*moneda francesa, belga, suiza*) franc **2.** (*lengua*) Frankish

franco, -a I. *adj* **1.** (*sincero*) frank **2.** (*generoso*) generous **3.** (*libre*) free; **puerto** ~ free port; ~ **a bordo** free on board; ~ **de derechos** duty-free; ~ **en fábrica** ex-factory **4.** (*claro*) patent **5.** HIST Frankish **6.** (*francés*) French **II.** *m, f* Frank

francófilo, -a *adj* Francophile

francófono, -a I. *adj* francophone, French-speaking **II.** *m, f* French-speaking person

francotirador *m* **1.** (*guerrillero*) guerrilla; (*tirador emboscado*) sniper **2.** (*persona aislada*) loner; **ser un** ~ to be a loner

franela *f* **1.** (*tejido*) flannel **2.** AmL (*camiseta*) T-shirt

franelear *vi* Arg, *inf* to pet

franja *f* **1.** (*guarnición*) border **2.** (*tira*) strip; **en la misma** ~ **horaria** in the same time zone

frankfurt *m* GASTR frankfurter, hot dog *inf*

franquear I. *vt* **1.** (*carta*) to pay postage on; **a** ~ **en destino** postage paid at destination **2.** (*desobstruir*) to clear **3.** (*río*) to cross; ~ **el paso** to open the way; (*obstáculo*) to get round **4.** (*conceder*) to grant **5.** (*dar libertad*) to free **II.** *vr:* ~**se** to have a heart-to-heart talk

franqueo *m* **1.** (*sellos*) postage; **sin** ~ without stamps **2.** (*acción: de una carta*) franking **3.** (*de una salida*) opening

franqueza *f* **1.** (*sinceridad*) frankness; **admitir algo con** ~ to openly admit sth **2.** (*generosidad*) generosity **3.** (*familiaridad*) intimacy **4.** (*exención*) exemption

franquicia *f* **1.** (*de franqueo*) exemption; ~ **postal** free postage **2.** ECON franchise

franquiciador(a) I. *adj* COM franchise **II.** *m(f)* COM franchiser

franquismo *m sin pl* **1.** (*régimen*) Franco's regime **2.** (*movimiento*) Francoism

franquista I. *adj* Francoist **II.** *mf* Francoist

fraques *pl de* **frac**

frasco *m* **1.** (*botella*) flask; (*de perfume*) perfume bottle; ~ **pulverizador** sprayer **2.** AmL: *measurement of liquids, 2.37 litres*

frase *f* **1.** (*oración*) sentence **2.** (*locución*) expression; (*refrán*) saying; (*expresión famosa*) well-known phrase; ~ **hecha** idiom; ~ **proverbial** proverb **3.** (*sin valor*) cliché **4.** (*estilo*) style **5.** MÚS phrase

fraseología *f* **1.** LING phraseology **2.** (*verbosidad*) verbiage

fraternal *adj* fraternal, brotherly

fraternidad *f* fraternity

fraternizar <z→c> *vi* **1.** (*unirse*) to mingle with; POL to sympathize with **2.** (*alternar*) to fraternize

fratricidio *m* fratricide

fraude *m* fraud; ~ **fiscal** tax fraud [*o* evasion]; **cometer** ~ to commit a fraudulent act

fraudulento, -a *adj* fraudulent; **publicidad fraudulenta** misleading advertising

fray *m* REL Brother

frazada *f* AmL blanket; (*de lana*) woollen blanket

frecuencia *f t.* FÍS frequency; **con** ~ frequently

frecuentar *vt* **1.** (*lugar*) to frequent **2.** (*a alguien*) to be in touch with **3.** (*acción*) to do sth frequently

frecuente *adj* **1.** (*repetido*) frequent **2.** (*usual*) common

fregadero *m* (kitchen) sink

fregado *m* **1.** (*limpieza*) cleaning; (*de los platos*) washing-up *Brit,* dishes *Am* **2.** *inf* (*enredo*) mess **3.** *pey* (*pelea*) brawl

fregado, -a *adj* **1.** AmL (*descarado*) cheeky; (*fastidioso*) tiresome **2.** AmL (*astuto*) sly **3.** AmC (*severo*) strict

fregador *m* **1.** (*fregadero*) sink **2.** (*estropajo*) scourer

fregar *irr vt* **1.** (*frotar*) to rub **2.** (*limpiar: el suelo*) to scrub; (*con fregona*) to mop; (*los platos*) to wash up **3.** AmL, *inf* (*molestar*) to annoy

fregona *f* **1.** (*utensilio*) mop **2.** *pey* (*sirvienta*) drudge, skivvy *Brit* **3.** *pey* (*mujer ordinaria*) common woman

freidora *f* fryer

freír *irr* **I.** *vt* **1.** (*guisar*) to fry; (*en mucho aceite*) to deep-fry; **mandar a alguien a** ~ **espárragos** *inf* to tell sb to get lost **2.** *inf* (*molestar*) to annoy **3.** *inf* (*matar*) to bump off *inf;* ~ **a balazos** to shoot dead **II.** *vr:* ~**se** **1.** (*alimento*) to fry **2.** *inf* (*persona*) to find it hot; **aquí te fríes** it's boiling here

fréjol *m* Perú BOT, GASTR (*frijol*) bean

frenada *f* Arg, Chile (*frenazo*) sudden braking

frenar I. *vt* **1.** (*hacer parar*) to stop **2.** (*un impulso, persona*) to restrain; (*un desarrollo*) to check, to curb **II.** *vi* to brake; ~ **en seco** to slam on the brakes **III.** *vr:* ~**se en algo** to restrain oneself from (doing) sth

frenazo *m* **1.** AUTO sudden braking; **pegar un** ~ to step on the brakes **2.** (*del desarrollo*) curb; **sufrir un** ~ *fig* to suffer a setback

frenesí *m* **1.** (*exaltación*) frenzy **2.** (*locura*) wildness; (*delirio furioso*) passion

frenético, -a *adj* **1.** (*exaltado*) frenzied; aplauso ~ frenzied applause **2.** (*loco*) wild **3.** (*furioso*) furious

freno *m* **1.** TÉC brake; ~ **de mano** handbrake *Brit,* emergency brake *Am* **2.** (*para un caballo*) bit **3.** (*contención*) curb; **tirar del** ~ **a alguien** to hold sb back; **no tener** ~ not to hold back

frente¹ *f* **1.** (*parte de la cara*) forehead; **fruncir la** ~ to frown **2.** (*cara*) face; ~ **a** ~ face to face; **bajó la** ~ he/she bowed his/her head

frente² I. *m* **1.** (*delantera*) front; (*de un edificio*) façade, face; **al** ~ (*dirección*) ahead; (*lugar*) in front; **de** ~ head-on; **¡de** ~! MIL forward march!; **estar al** ~ **de algo** to be in charge of sth; **hacer** ~ **a alguien** to stand up to sb; **hacer** ~ **a algo** to face up to sth; **no tener dos dedos de** ~ *inf* to be as thick as two short planks; **ponerse al** ~ to take charge **2.** POL, METEO, MIL front; **un** ~ **frío** a cold front **3.** (*de un escrito*) top margin II. *prep* **1.** ~ **a** (*enfrente de*) opposite; (*delante de*) in front of; (*contra*) as opposed to; (*ante*) in the face of **2.** **en** ~ **de** opposite

fresa I. *adj* strawberry-coloured [*o* colored *Am*] II. *f* **1.** BOT strawberry **2.** TÉC milling cutter, drill

fresadora *f* milling machine, rotary tool

fresal *m* strawberry bed

fresar *vt* to mill

fresco *m* **1.** (*frescor*) freshness, cool air; (*frío moderado*) coolness; (*viento*) cool; **salir a tomar el** ~ to go out to get some fresh air; **hoy hace** ~ it is cool today **2.** ARTE fresco **3.** *AmL* (*refresco*) soft drink

fresco, -a I. *adj* **1.** (*frío*) cool; (*prenda*) lightweight, cool; (*cutis*) fresh, rosy **2.** (*reciente*) fresh; **noticia fresca** up-to-date news; **queso** ~ cottage cheese **3.** (*descansado*) fresh **4.** *inf* (*desvergonzado*) fresh, cheeky **5.** (*impasible*) cool **6.** (*equivocado*) **estar** ~ *inf* to be wrong II. *m, f inf* cheeky person

frescor *m* **1.** (*frío moderado*) coolness; (*frescura*) freshness **2.** ARTE colour of flesh *Brit,* color of flesh *Am*

frescura *f* **1.** (*frescor*) freshness, cool air; (*frío moderado*) coolness **2.** *inf* (*desvergüenza*) cheek **3.** (*desembarazo*) naturalness; **con** ~ freely

fresno *m* ash

fresquera *f* food safe *Brit*

fresquería *f* *AmL: establishment where drinks are made and sold*

frialdad *f* **1.** (*frío*) coldness **2.** (*despego*) coolness; **me trató con** ~ he/she was cool towards me **3.** (*impasibilidad*) coolness **4.** (*falta de sentimientos*) indifference; (*frigidez*) frigidity **5.** (*estilo*) impersonality; (*del ambiente*) lack of warmth

fricandó *m* GASTR fricandeau

fricasé *m* GASTR fricassee

fricción *f* **1.** (*resistencia*) friction **2.** (*del cuerpo*) rub; (*con linimento*) massage

3. (*desavenencia*) friction; (*disputa*) fight

friccionar *vt* (*en seco*) to rub; (*con linimento*) to massage

friega *f* **1.** (*fricción*) rub **2.** *AmL* (*molestia*) bother **3.** *inf* (*zurra*) beating

friegaplatos *m inv* dishwasher

frigidez *f* frigidity

frígido, -a *adj* frigid

frigorífico *m* **1.** (*nevera*) fridge, refrigerator **2.** (*local*) cold store

frigorífico, -a *adj* refrigeratory; **camión** ~ refrigerator lorry *Brit,* refrigerator truck *Am*

frijol *m,* **fríjol** *m AmL* bean

frío *m* cold; **hace** ~ it is cold; **hace un** ~ **que pela** it is bitterly cold; **coger** ~ to catch cold; **tener** ~ to be cold; **no dar a alguien ni** ~ **ni calor** to leave sb indifferent

frío, -a *adj* **1.** (*no caliente*) cold **2.** (*relación*) cool **3.** (*falto de sentimientos*) indifferent; (*frígida*) frigid **4.** (*impasible*) impassive **5.** (*inexpresivo*) inexpressive; (*ambiente*) impersonal

friolento, -a *adj AmL* (*friolero*) sensitive to the cold

friolera *f* **1.** *irón* (*insignificante*) trifle; **ganaron la** ~ **de 50 millones** in the lotto they won a mere fifty million in the lottery **2.** *inf* (*montón*) pile

friolero, -a *adj* sensitive to the cold

frisa *f* **1.** (*tela*) woolen fabric **2.** *Arg, Chile* (*pelo*) nap **3.** *PRico, RDom* (*manta*) blanket **4.** MIL palisade **5.** NÁUT weatherstripping

frisar I. *vi* to border II. *vt* (*tejido*) to frizz

friso *m* **1.** ARQUIT frieze **2.** (*de la pared*) wainscot

frisón, -ona *adj, m, f* Frisian

fritanga *f pey* (*comida frita*) (greasy) fried food; **hueles a** ~ you reek of fried food

frito *m* fry

frito, -a I. *pp de* **freír** II. *adj* **1.** (*comida*) fried **2.** *inf* (*dormido*) **quedarse** ~ to fall fast asleep **3.** *inf* (*muerto*) dead; **quedarse** ~ to kick the bucket; **dejar a alguien** ~ to snuff sb **4.** *inf* (*harto*) **estar** ~ **con algo** to be fed up with sth; **me tienen** [*o* traen] **frito con sus preguntas** I am fed up with their questions

frivolidad *f* **1.** (*ligereza*) frivolity **2.** (*coquetería*) coquetry **3.** (*trivialidad*) triviality **4.** (*sensualidad*) sensuality

frívolo, -a *adj* **1.** (*ligero*) light **2.** (*coqueto*) coquettish **3.** (*superficial*) frivolous, superficial **4.** (*sensual*) sensual

fronda *f* **1.** (*hoja*) frond **2.** *pl* (*follaje*) foliage

frondosidad *f* **1.** (*de una planta*) leafiness; (*de un bosque*) luxuriance **2.** (*follaje*) foliage

frondoso, -a *adj* (*planta, árbol*) leafy; (*bosque*) lush

frontal I. *adj* **1.** ANAT frontal **2.** (*relativo al frente*) front **3.** (*de frente*) head-on II. *m* **1.** ANAT frontal bone **2.** REL frontal

frontera *f* **1.** (*límite*) border; **atravesar la** ~ to cross the frontier **2.** (*frontispicio*) frontispiece; (*de un edificio*) façade

fronterizo, -a *adj* (*en la frontera*) frontier; (*país*) border(ing); **paso** ~ border post

frontero *adj* opposite, facing

frontis *m inv* (*frontispicio*) frontispiece; (*de un edificio*) façade

frontispicio *m* **1.** (*delantera*) front; (*de un edificio*) façade **2.** (*de un libro*) frontispiece **3.** ARQUIT pediment **4.** (*cara*) face

frontón *m* **1.** (*juego*) pelota **2.** (*pared*) wall (*used to play pelota*) **3.** (*pista*) pelota court; (*edificio*) building in which pelota is played **4.** ARQUIT frontispiece, pediment

frotación *f*, **frotadura** *f* **1.** (*acción*) rubbing; (*con cepillo*) brushing **2.** (*efecto*) friction

frotamiento *m* (*acción de frotar*) rubbing; (*con cepillo*) brushing

frotar I. *vt* to rub; (*con cepillo*) to brush; (*con un estropajo*) to scrub **II.** *vr:* ~**se** to rub oneself; ~**se con una toalla** to rub oneself with a towel

frotis *m* MED smear

fructífero, -a *adj* fruitful

fructificación *f* **1.** (*de una planta*) fruitfulness **2.** (*de un esfuerzo*) fruition

fructificar <c→qu> *vi* **1.** (*planta*) to bear fruit **2.** (*esfuerzo*) to come to fruition

frugal *adj* frugal

frugalidad *f* frugality

fruición *f* delight

frunce *m* gather, shirr

fruncimiento *m* **1.** (*pliegue*) pleat, shirring **2.** (*arrugamiento*) puckering *pl* **3.** (*de los labios*) pursing; (*de la frente*) wrinkling; (*del entrecejo*) frowning

fruncir <c→z> **I.** *vt* **1.** (*tela*) to gather, to shirr; (*arrugar*) to pucker **2.** (*labios*) to purse; (*frente*) to wrinkle; ~ **el entrecejo** to frown **II.** *vr:* ~**se** to affect modesty

fruslería *f* **1.** (*baratija*) trifle **2.** *inf* (*bagatela*) nothing **3.** *inf* (*tontería*) silly thing

frustración *f* **1.** (*de planes*) thwarting; (*fracaso*) failure; (*de una esperanza*) frustration **2.** (*desilusión*) disappointment

frustrado, -a *adj* (*persona*) frustrated; (*intento*) failed

frustrar I. *vt* **1.** (*estropear*) to thwart; ~ **las esperanzas de alguien** to frustrate sb's hopes **2.** (*decepcionar*) to discourage **II.** *vr:* ~**se** **1.** (*plan*) to fail **2.** (*esperanzas*) to be disappointed

fruta *f* fruit; ~ **de Aragón** passion fruit; ~ **del tiempo** seasonal fruit; ~**s tropicales** tropical fruits; **de postre comimos** ~ we had fruit for dessert

frutal I. *adj* fruit **II.** *m* fruit tree

frutería *f* greengrocer's

frutero *m* **1.** (*recipiente*) fruit bowl **2.** ARTE still life

frutero, -a I. *adj* fruit; **es muy** ~ he eats a lot of fruit **II.** *m, f* fruit seller, fruiterer *Brit*

fruticultura *f* fruit growing

frutilla *f* **1.** (*cuenta*) rosary bead **2.** *AmL* (*fresón*) strawberry

fruto *m* **1.** BOT fruit **2.** (*hijo*) offspring **3.** (*rendi*-

miento) fruit; (*resultado*) result **4.** (*ganancia*) profit; *t.* JUR (*provecho*) benefit

fucsia¹ **I.** *adj* (*color*) fuschia-coloured [*o* colored *Am*] **II.** *m* fuschia

fucsia² *f* BOT fuschia

fue 1. *3. pret de* **ir 2.** *3. pret de* **ser**

fuego *m* **1.** fire; **¿me das** ~? can you give me a light?; ~**s artificiales** fireworks *pl;* **a** ~ **lento** GASTR over a low heat; *fig* little by little; **prender** [*o* **pegar**] ~ **a algo** to set sth alight [*o* on fire]; **echar** ~ **por los ojos** to look daggers at sb **2.** MIL firing; **estar entre dos** ~**s** to be caught in the crossfire [*o* middle]; **arma de** ~ firearm **3.** (*ardor*) ardour *Brit*, ardor *Am;* **en el** ~ **de la discusión** in the heat of the discussion

fuel *m* refined oil

fuelle *m* **1.** (*instrumento, de una cámara*) bellows *pl* **2.** (*de un vestido*) fold **3.** (*de un carruaje*) folding top **4.** *inf* (*pulmones*) lungs *pl;* (*aguante*) stamina **5.** *inf* (*soplón*) telltale *Brit*, tattletale *Am*

fuente *f* **1.** (*manantial*) spring **2.** (*construcción*) fountain **3.** (*plato llano*) platter; (*plato hondo*) (serving) dish **4.** (*origen*) source; ~**s bien informadas** reliable sources

fuera I. *adv* **1.** (*lugar*) outside; **por** ~ on the outside; **de** ~ from the outside; **el nuevo maestro es de** ~ the new teacher is not from here; **estar** ~ **de lugar** to be irrelevant [*o* out of place] **2.** (*dirección*) out; **¡~!** out!; **¡~ con esto!** no way!; **¡~ de mi vista!** out of my sight!; **echar a alguien** ~ to throw sb out; **hacia** ~ outwards; **salir** ~ to go out **3.** (*tiempo*) out; ~ **de plazo** past the deadline **4.** *inf* (*de viaje*) away; **me voy** ~ **una semana** I am going away for a week **II.** *prep* **1.** *t. fig* (*local*) out of; **estar** ~ **de casa** to be away from home; ~ **de juego** DEP offside; ~ **de serie** exceptional **2.** (*excepto*) ~ **de** outside of **III.** *conj* ~ **de que** +*subj* apart from the fact that **IV.** *m* boo

fueraborda *m* **1.** (*motor*) outboard motor **2.** (*embarcación*) outboard motor boat

fuereño, -a I. *adj AmL, inf* (*forastero*) outside, foreign **II.** *m, f AmL, inf* (*forastero*) outsider

fuero *m* **1.** (*privilegio*) privilege **2.** (*jurisdicción*) jurisdiction; **en mi** ~ **interno** inwardly **3.** (*código*) code

fuerte I. *adj* <fortísimo> **1.** (*resistente*) strong; (*robusto*) tough; **caja** ~ safe; **hacerse** ~ to entrench oneself; **ser** ~ **de carácter** to be strong-willed **2.** (*musculoso*) strong; (*gordo*) fat **3.** (*intenso*) intense; (*sonido*) loud; (*comida, golpe*) heavy; (*abrazo, beso*) big; **un vino** ~ a full-bodied wine **4.** (*valiente*) brave **5.** (*sólido*) solid; (*duro*) hard; (*tela*) thick **6.** (*genio*) **tener un carácter** [*o* **genio**] **muy** ~ to be quick-tempered **7.** (*poderoso*) powerful **8.** (*versado*) **estar** ~ **en matemáticas** to be good at mathematics **9.** (*considerable*) considerable **10.** (*violento*) disturbing; (*expresión*) nasty; **palabra** ~ rude word **11.** (*terreno*) rough **12.** LING (*vocal*) the Spanish

vowels a, e, o; (*forma*) when the word stress falls on the word stem **13.** MIL fortified **II.** *m* **1.** (*de una persona*) strong point **2.** MIL fort **3.** MÚS forte **4.** (*auge*) zenith **III.** *adv* **1.** (*con fuerza*) strongly; (*con intensidad*) intensely **2.** (*en voz alta*) aloud **3.** (*en abundancia*) copiously; **desayunar** ~ to have a large breakfast
fuerza *f* **1.** *t.* FÍS (*capacidad física*) strength; *t.* FÍS (*potencia*) force; ~ **de ánimo** strength of mind; ~ **de voluntad** willpower; **tiene más ~ que yo** he/she is stronger than I am; **sin ~s** weak, drained; **se le va la ~ por la boca** he/she is all talk [*o* hot air] **2.** (*capacidad de soportar*) toughness; (*eficacia*) effectiveness **3.** (*poder*) power; ~ **de disuasión** powers of dissuasion; ~ **mayor** act of God, force majeure **4.** (*violencia*) force; **a** [*o* **por**] **la** ~ willy-nilly; **por** ~ (*por necesidad*) out of necessity; (*con violencia*) by force; **recurrir a la** ~ to resort to violence **5.** (*intensidad*) intensity **6.** (*expresividad*) expressiveness **7.** *pl* POL political groups *pl;* MIL forces *pl;* ~**s del orden público** forces of law and order **8.** ELEC power **9.** (*usando*) **a** ~ **de** by means of; **lo ha conseguido todo a** ~ **de trabajo** he/she has achieved everything through hard work
fuete *m AmL* (*látigo*) whip
fuga *f* **1.** (*huida*) flight; (*de la cárcel*) escape; **darse a la** ~ to escape, to run away; ~ **de capital** flight of capital; ~ **de cerebros** brain drain **2.** (*en tubos*) leak; (*de líquido*) leakage; (*de gas*) escape; **la cañería tiene una** ~ the pipe has a leak; **hubo una** ~ **de gas/petróleo** there was a gas/oil leak **3.** MÚS fugue **4.** (*auge*) peak
fugacidad *f* brevity; (*caducidad*) transitoriness
fugarse <g→gu> *vr* to flee; (*de casa*) to run away; (*para casarse*) to elope; ~ **de la cárcel** to escape from prison
fugaz *adj* fleeting; (*caduco*) short-lived; **estrella** ~ shooting star
fugitivo, -a **I.** *adj* fugitive; (*belleza*) transitory **II.** *m, f* fugitive; (*de la cárcel*) escapee
fulana *f pey* whore
fulano, -a *m, f* **1.** (*evitando el nombre*) so--and-so **2.** (*persona indeterminada*) guy, Joe Bloggs *Brit,* John Doe *Am;* **no me importa lo que digan** ~ **y mengano** I do not care what Tom, Dick or Harry say **3.** (*amante*) lover
fular *m* **1.** (*tela*) fine silk **2.** (*pañuelo*) foulard, silky scarf
fulcro *m* fulcrum
fulero, -a *adj inf* **1.** (*embustero*) lying **2.** (*chapucero*) **eres muy** ~ you are a bungler
fulgor *m* (*resplandor*) radiance; (*centelleo*) sparkle; (*de una superficie*) gleam
fulgurante *adj* **1.** (*rápido*) rapid; **su carrera fue** ~ he/she rose rapidly in his/her career **2.** (*dolor*) intense
fulgurar *vi* (*resplandecer*) to shine; (*centellear*) to sparkle; (*espejear*) to gleam
fullería *f* **1.** (*trampa*) trick; (*en el juego*)

cheating; **hacer** ~**s** to cheat **2.** (*treta*) ruse
fullero, -a **I.** *adj* **1.** (*tramposo*) tricky **2.** *inf* (*astuto*) crafty **II.** *m, f* **1.** (*tramposo*) trickster; (*en el juego*) cheat, cardsharper **2.** *inf* (*astuto*) crafty individual
fulminación *f* **1.** (*aniquilación*) destruction **2.** (*de un explosivo*) fulmination **3.** (*emisión*) emission; (*de amenazas*) threatening **4.** (*de una sentencia*) sentencing
fulminante **I.** *adj* **1.** *t.* MED (*inesperado*) sudden **2.** (*explosivo*) explosive **3.** (*mirada*) withering **II.** *m* gunpowder
fulminar **I.** *vi* to explode **II.** *vt* **1.** (*dañar*) to strike down; (*aniquilar*) to destroy; (*matar*) to electrocute; **un rayo/el cáncer lo fulminó** he was struck down by lightning/cancer **2.** (*arrojar*) to hurl **3.** (*imponer*) to impose; ~ **una censura** to impose censorship **4.** (*amenazar*) to threaten angrily
fumadero *m* smoking room; ~ **de opio** opium den
fumador(a) **I.** *adj* **zona de no** ~**es** no-smoking area **II.** *m/f* (*fumar*) smoker; **no** ~ non-smoker
fumar **I.** *vi, vt* to smoke **II.** *vr:* ~**se 1.** (*fumar*) to smoke **2.** *inf* (*gastar*) to squander **3.** *inf* (*faltar*) to cut; ~**se la clase** to skive off school
fumigar <g→gu> *vt* to fumigate
fumista *mf* stove installer [*o* maker]
funambulesco, -a *adj* **1.** (*extravagante*) extravagant **2.** (*relativo al funámbulo*) acrobatic; (*como un funámbulo*) like a tightrope walker
funámbulo, -a *m, f* tightrope walker
función *f* **1.** *t.* BIO, MAT (*papel*) function; **el precio está en** ~ **de la calidad** the price depends on the quality **2.** (*cargo*) office; (*tarea*) duty; **entrará en** ~ **mañana** he/she will take up her duties tomorrow; (*cargo*) he/she will enter into office tomorrow; **el ministro en funciones** acting minister **3.** (*acto formal*) function; CINE showing; TEAT performance; ~ **doble** double feature; ~ **de noche** late show
funcional *adj* functional
funcionalidad *f* functionality
funcionamiento *m* **1.** (*marcha*) running; ~ **administrativo** running of the administration; ~ **del mercado** market organization; **poner en** ~ to bring into operation **2.** (*rendimiento*) performance; (*manera de funcionar*) operation; **en estado de** ~ in working order; (*máquina*) working
funcionar *vi* to function; (*estar trabajando*) to be working; **el coche no funciona bien** the car is not going properly; **la televisión no funciona** the television does not work; **No Funciona** (*cartel*) out of order
funcionario, -a *m, f* (*de una organización*) employee; (*del Estado*) civil servant
funda *f* (*cubierta*) cover; (*para gafas*) glasses case; (*de libro*) (dust) jacket; (*de almohada*) pillowcase; (*de butaca*) loose cover; (*de revólver*) holster; ~ **nórdica** duvet
fundación *f* **1.** (*creación*) foundation, found-

F

ing **2.** (*institución*) foundation **3.** (*justificación*) foundation, fundament **4.** (*de una estructura*) foundations *pl*
fundado, -a *adj* well-founded
fundador(a) I. *adj* founder, founding II. *m(f)* founder
fundamental *adj* **1.** fundamental; (*esencial*) essential; (*básico*) basic; **argumento** ~ key argument; **conocimientos** ~**es** rudimentary knowledge **2.** MAT cardinal
fundamentalismo *m sin pl* fundamentalism
fundamentalista *adj, mf* fundamentalist
fundamentar *vt* **1.** ARQUIT to lay the foundations of **2.** (*basar*) to base **3.** (*establecer*) to establish
fundamento *m* **1.** ARQUIT foundations *pl* **2.** (*base*) basis **3.** (*motivo*) grounds; **sin** ~ groundless **4.** (*formalidad*) sensibleness; (*seriedad*) seriousness; **hablar sin** ~ not to talk seriously **5.** *pl* (*conocimientos*) fundamentals *pl*
fundar I. *vt* **1.** (*crear*) to found **2.** TÉC to found **3.** (*basar*) to base; (*justificar*) to found II. *vr:* ~**se** **1.** (*basarse*) to base oneself; (*tener su justificación*) to be founded **2.** (*asentarse*) to be established
fundición *f* **1.** (*de un metal*) smelting **2.** (*en una forma*) casting **3.** (*de ideas*) fusion **4.** (*taller*) foundry **5.** (*hierro*) cast iron **6.** TIPO font
fundidor *m* founder
fundillo *m* **1.** AmL (*fondillos*) seat of trousers **2.** Méx (*trasero*) bottom
fundir I. *vt* **1.** (*deshacer*) to melt **2.** (*dar forma*) to found, to cast **3.** (*bombilla*) to fuse; (*plomo*) to blow **4.** (*unir*) to unite; (*empresas*) to merge **5.** *inf* (*gastar*) to squander II. *vr:* ~**se** **1.** (*deshacerse*) to melt **2.** (*bombilla*) to fuse; (*plomo*) to blow **3.** (*unirse*) to unite; (*empresas*) to merge **4.** *inf* (*arruinarse*) to become ruined; (*negocio*) to go bankrupt
fundo *m* Chile, Perú (*finca*) country property
fúnebre *adj* **1.** (*triste*) mournful **2.** (*sombrío*) gloomy **3.** (*de los difuntos*) funerary; **coche** ~ hearse; **pompas** ~**s** (*ceremonia*) funeral; (*empresa*) undertaker's
funeral I. *adj* funerary, funereal II. *m* **1.** (*entierro*) burial **2.** *pl* (*misa*) funeral, obsequies *pl*
funeraria *f* funeral parlour
funerario, -a *adj* funeral
funesto, -a *adj* **1.** (*aciago*) ill-fated **2.** (*desgraciado*) terrible **3.** *inf* (*sin talento*) inept
fungible *adj* ECON consumable
fungicida I. *adj* fungicidal II. *m* fungicide
fungir <g→j> *vi* **1.** AmL (*un cargo*) to hold the post **2.** AmC (*presumir*) to give oneself airs
funicular I. *adj* funicular; (*de cable aéreo*) cable; **tren** ~ cable [*o* funicular] railway II. *m* funicular; ~ **aéreo** cable car
furcia *f* pey whore, tart *inf*
furgón *m* **1.** (*carro*) wagon; (*camioneta*) van **2.** FERRO (*para el equipaje*) luggage van Brit, baggage car Am; (*para mercancías*) wagon

Brit, freight car Am; ~ **de cola** train rear wagon Brit, caboose Am
furgoneta *f* van
furia *f* **1.** (*ira, ímpetu*) fury **2.** (*persona*) estaba hecha una ~ she was furious **3.** *inf* (*energía*) energy **4.** (*auge*) zenith
furibundo, -a *adj* **1.** (*furioso*) furious **2.** *inf* (*entusiasta*) enthusiastic; (*extremado*) extreme
furioso, -a *adj* **1.** (*furibundo*) furious **2.** (*loco*) beside oneself **3.** (*violento*) violent; (*tempestad*) raging **4.** (*tremendo*) tremendous; (*sentimiento*) intense
furor *m* **1.** (*ira*) fury **2.** (*ímpetu*) impulse **3.** (*energía*) drive **4.** (*auge*) craze; **hacer** ~ to be the (latest) thing **5.** (*afición*) passion **6.** (*locura*) frenzy **7.** MED ~ **uterino** nymphomania
furtivo, -a *adj* furtive; **cazador** ~ poacher
furúnculo *m* MED boil
fusa *f* MÚS demisemiquaver Brit, thirty-second note Am
fuselaje *m* AVIAT fuselage
fusible I. *adj* fusible II. *m* fuse
fusil *m* rifle
fusilamiento *m* **1.** (*ejecución*) execution (by firing squad) **2.** *inf* (*de textos*) cribbing
fusilar *vt* **1.** (*ejecutar*) to execute, to shoot **2.** *inf* (*copiar*) to crib
fusilería *f* **1.** (*fusiles*) rifles **2.** (*soldados*) fusiliers **3.** (*fuego*) gunfire
fusilero *m* fusilier, rifleman
fusión *f* **1.** (*fundición*) fusion **2.** (*unión*) union; ECON merger
fusionar I. *vi* to fuse II. *vt* **1.** (*deshacer*) to fuse **2.** (*unir*) to fuse; (*empresas*) to merge III. *vr:* ~**se** to fuse; (*empresas*) to merge
fusta *f* **1.** (*látigo*) riding whip **2.** (*leña*) brushwood **3.** (*tejido*) woollen cloth
fustán *m* AmL (*combinación*) lady's slip
fuste *m* **1.** (*madera*) wood **2.** (*vara*) pole; (*de una lanza*) shaft **3.** ARQUIT shaft **4.** (*importancia*) importance; (*sustancia*) solidity; (*de una persona*) consequence **5.** (*arzón*) pommel
fustigar <g→gu> *vt* **1.** (*azotar*) to whip **2.** (*reprender*) to reprimand
fútbol *m* football Brit, soccer Am; ~ **americano** American football, football Am
futbolín *m* table football
futbolista *mf* DEP football player Brit, soccer player Am
futbolístico, -a *adj* footballing, football Brit, soccer Am
fútbol-sala *m sin pl* DEP indoor football, five--a-side football Brit
fútil *adj* trivial
futileza *f* Chile (*pequeñez*) trifle
futilidad *f* triviality
futre *m* AmL, pey stuck-up person, toff
futurible I. *adj* possible; (*acontecimiento*) likely; (*persona*) potential II. *mf* potential candidate
futurismo *m sin pl* Futurism

futuro *m* 1. *t.* LING (*tiempo*) future 2. FIN **compra de ~s** purchase of futures

futuro, -a I. *adj* future **II.** *m, f inf* intended

futurólogo, -a *m, f* futurologist

G

G, g *f* G, g; **~ de Granada** G for George

gabacho, -a *m, f pey* (*francés*) Froggy

gabán *m* overcoat

gabardina *f* 1. (*tela*) gabardine 2. (*prenda*) raincoat

gabarra *f* NÁUT (*para carga y descarga*) barge; (*más pequeña*) lighter; (*remolcada*) tug

gabela *f* tax

gabinete *m* 1. (*estudio*) study; (*salita*) private sitting room; **~ de prensa** press office 2. POL cabinet 3. (*tocador*) dressing room 4. (*museo*) museum 5. (*de médico*) office

Gabón *m* Gabon

gabonés, -esa *adj, m, f* Gabonese

gacela *f* gazelle ▶ **correr como una ~** to run like the wind

gaceta *f* 1. (*publicación*) gazette 2. *inf* (*persona*) gossip, grapevine

gacetilla *f* 1. (*de un periódico*) news-in-brief section; (*notas de sociedad*) gossip column 2. (*noticia*) news item

gacetillero, -a *m, f* journalist; (*de chismorreo*) gossip columnist

gacha *f* 1. *pl* (*comida*) ≈ porridge 2. *inf* (*barro*) mud

gachí <gachís> *f inf* bird, chick

gacho, -a *adj* drooping; **orejas gachas** floppy ears; **sombrero ~** slouch hat; **con las orejas gachas** with one's tail between one's legs

gachó *m inf* guy, bloke

gachumbo *m Col, Ecua* hollowed-out fruit shell

gaditano, -a I. *adj* of/from Cadiz **II.** *m, f* native/inhabitant of Cadiz

gaélico, -a *adj* Gaelic

gafa *f* 1. *pl* (*anteojos*) glasses *pl;* **~s de bucear** diving mask; **llevar ~s** to wear glasses; **ponerse las ~s** to put one's glasses on 2. (*varilla*) earpiece 3. TÉC (*grapa*) staple 4. TÉC (*abrazadera*) clamp

gafar *vt* 1. *inf* (*mala suerte*) to jinx 2. (*con las uñas*) to claw 3. (*con grapas*) to staple

gafe *m* 1. (*cenizo*) jinx 2. (*aguafiestas*) partypooper, wet-blanket

gag *m* <gags> gag

gago, -a I. *adj AmL* stuttering **II.** *m, f* stutterer

gaita *f* 1. MÚS (*gallega*) bagpipes *pl;* (*zamorana*) hurdy-gurdy 2. *inf* (*cuello*) neck 3. *inf* (*lata*) **vaya ~** what a pain; **tener que hacer eso** having to do that is a real pain ▶ **estar** _hecho_ **una ~** to be in a bad way

gaitero, -a *m, f* (*de gaita gallega*) (bag)piper;

(*de gaita zamorana*) hurdy-gurdy player

gajes *mpl* fees *pl* ▶ **~ del** _oficio_ *irón* occupational hazards; **son ~ del oficio** it's all in a day's work

gajo *m* 1. (*de naranja*) segment 2. (*racimo*) bunch 3. (*rama*) branch

gala *f* 1. (*fiesta*) gala 2. (*garbo*) elegance 3. (*selecto*) best 4. *pl* (*vestido*) finery, (fine) clothes *pl* ▶ **hacer ~ de algo** to take pride in sth

galáctico, -a *adj* galactic

galaico, -a *adj* Galician

galaicoportugués, -esa *adj* Galician-Portuguese

galán *m* 1. (*hombre*) handsome man 2. (*novio*) beau 3. TEAT (*papel*) leading man 4. (*mueble*) (clothes) valet

galante *adj* 1. (*atento*) gallant 2. (*mujer*) flirtatious 3. (*historia*) risqué

galanteador(a) *adj* flirtatious

galantear *vt* to woo

galantería *f* 1. (*hacia una mujer*) gallantry 2. (*amabilidad*) politeness 3. (*generosidad*) generosity 4. (*cumplido*) compliment

galápago *m* turtle

galardón *m* prize

galardonar *vt* to award a prize to; **~ a alguien con un título** to confer a title on sb

galaxia *f* (*universo*) galaxy

galbana *f inf* laziness

galena *f* MIN galena, lead sulphide *Brit,* lead sulfide *Am*

galeno *m inf* doctor, physician *Am*

galeón *m* NÁUT galleon

galeote *m* galley slave

galera *f* 1. NÁUT galley 2. ZOOL mantis shrimp 3. TIPO galley 4. MAT dividing line 5. *AmL* (*cobertizo*) shed 6. *AmL* (*sombrero: de copa*) top hat; (*de hongo*) bowler hat

galerada *f* galley proof

galería *f* 1. (*corredor, de arte*) gallery 2. *pl* (*grandes almacenes*) department store; (*centro comercial*) shopping centre *Brit,* shopping center *Am,* mall *Am* 3. *pl* (*bulevar*) arcade 4. MIN, TEAT gallery; **hablar para la ~** to play to the gallery

galerista *mf* art gallery owner

galerón *m* 1. *AmS* (*romance*) ballad 2. *Col, Ven* MÚS folkdance and song 3. *CRi, ElSal* (*cobertizo*) shed

galés, -esa I. *adj* Welsh **II.** *m, f* Welshman *m,* Welshwoman *f*

Gales *m* (**el País de**) **~** Wales

galgo, -a *m, f* greyhound; **~ inglés** whippet

galguerías *fpl Col* (*golosinas*) sweets *pl Brit,* candies *pl Am*

Galia *f* Gaul

Galicia *f* Galicia

galicismo *m* French loan word(s), Gallicism

galimatías *m inv* 1. (*lenguaje*) gibberish 2. (*enredo*) jumble

gallardear *vi* 1. (*ostentar gallardía*) to act with self-assurance 2. (*presumir*) to show off, to strut

gallardía f 1.(apostura) poise 2.(garbo) style, elegance 3.(valentía) bravery

gallardo, -a adj 1.(de aspecto) elegant 2.(garboso) dashing 3.(valiente) brave 4.(generoso) noble

gallear I. vi 1.(fanfarronear) to brag 2.(alzar la voz) to shout 3.(creerse importante) to strut around II. vt (el gallo a la gallina) to tread

gallego, -a I. adj Galician II. m, f 1.(habitante) Galician 2. AmS, pey (español) Spaniard

galleguismo m word or phrase of Galician origin

galleta f 1.(dulce) biscuit Brit, cookie Am; (salada) cracker 2. inf (bofetada) slap, smack 3. MIN anthracite briquet [o briquette], nuts pl

galletero m biscuit tin Brit, cookie tin Am

gallina f 1.(hembra del gallo) hen; ~ clueca brooding hen 2. inf (cobarde) chicken 3.(juego) jugar a la ~ ciega to play blind man's buff ▶~ en corral ajeno fish out of water; acostarse con las ~s to go to bed very early

gallinazo m turkey buzzard

gallinero m 1.(corral) chicken coop, henhouse 2. TEAT inf gallery, gods pl Brit

gallito m inf ser un ~ to be a tough guy; ponerse ~ to act tough

gallo m 1.(ave) cock, rooster Am; ~ de pelea fighting cock; ~ silvestre capercaillie 2.(pez) (John) dory 3.(engreído) show-off 4. MÚS false note; soltar un ~ to let out a squeak 5.(esputo) phlegm 6. AmL (hombre fuerte) tough guy ▶alzar el ~ to put on airs; en menos que canta un ~ in an instant [o flash]; si el dinero fuera mío, otro ~ nos cantara inf if it was my money, it would be another story

galo, -a I. adj 1.(de la Galia) Gaulish 2.(francés) French II. m, f 1.(de la Galia) Gaul 2.(francés) Frenchman m, Frenchwoman f

galón m 1.(cinta) braid 2. MIL (distintivo) stripe, decoration 3.(medida inglesa) gallon

galopada f gallop

galopante adj galloping

galopar vi to gallop

galope m gallop

galopín m 1.(golfillo) urchin 2.(granuja) rascal 3.(granujilla) ragamuffin, whippersnapper

galpón m AmL shed

galuchar vi Col, Cuba, PRico, Ven to gallop

galvanismo m sin pl FÍS galvanism

galvanización f 1. MED galvanization 2. TÉC electroplating

galvanizar <z→c> vt 1. TÉC to electroplate 2.(una institución) to galvanize

gama f 1. MÚS gamut; (escala) scale 2.(escala) range; una ~ amplia/reducida de productos a wide/narrow range of products

gamada adj cruz ~ swastika

gamba f prawn, shrimp

gamberrada f act of hooliganism; hacer ~s to horse around inf

gamberro, -a m, f hooligan, yobbo inf

gambeta f AmL 1.(distensión) swerve 2.(evasiva) dodge 3.(fútbol) dummy; hacer ~s to dribble

gamín, -ina m, f Col (pilluelo) urchin

gamma f gamma

gamo m fallow deer

gamonal m AmL: local political boss

gamonalismo m AmL caciquism

gamuza f 1.(animal) chamois 2.(piel) chamois (leather) 3.(paño) duster

gana f desire; tener ~s de hacer algo to feel like doing sth; tengo ~s de irme de vacaciones I feel like going on holiday; son ~s de fastidiar inf they're just trying to be difficult; de buena/mala ~ willingly/unwillingly; me quedé con las ~s de verlo I wish I'd been able to see him; no me da la (real) ~ inf I can't be bothered; venir en ~ to feel like; no me viene en ~ I don't feel like it; este es feo con ~s inf he's bloody ugly

ganadería f 1.(ganado) livestock 2.(crianza) livestock farming 3.(comercio) livestock trade

ganadero, -a I. adj livestock II. m, f 1.(criador: de vacas) cattle farmer; (de cerdos) pig farmer; (de ovejas) sheep farmer 2.(tratante: de vacas) cattle merchant; (de cerdos) pig merchant; (de ovejas) sheep merchant

ganado m 1.(reses) livestock pl; ~ bovino [o vacuno] cattle pl; ~ cabrío goats pl; ~ ovino sheep inv; ~ porcino pigs pl 2. AmL (~ vacuno) cattle pl 3. inf (de personas) crowd

ganador(a) I. adj winning II. m(f) winner

ganancia f 1.(beneficio) profit 2.(sueldo) earnings pl

ganancial adj pertaining to earnings or profit; bienes ~es property acquired during marriage

ganancioso, -a adj 1.(que da ganancia) profitable 2.(beneficiado) salir ~ de algo to make a profit from sth

ganapán m 1. pey (trabajador) odd-job man 2.(rudo) lout

ganar I. vi 1.(vencer) to win 2.(mejorar) ~ en algo to improve at sth; ~ en condición social to better oneself socially con esto sólo puedes salir ganando you can't lose with this; no gana para sustos with her it is one thing after another II. vt 1.(trabajando) to earn; con ese negocio consiguió ~ mucho dinero he/she made a lot of money out of that business 2.(jugando) win; (a alguien) to beat; le he ganado 30 euros I won 30 euros from him/her 3.(adquirir) to gain; (libertad) to win; ~ conocimientos de algo to acquire knowledge of sth; ~ experiencia to gain experience; ~ peso to put on weight; ¿qué esperas ~ con esto? what do you hope to gain by that?; 4.(llegar a) to reach; ~ la orilla to reach the shore 5.(aventajar) ~ a alguien en algo to be better than sb at sth 6. MIL (ciudad) to take 7.(convencer) to win over III. vr:

~se 1. (*dinero*) to earn; **si no me sale, me la gano** *inf* if I don't get it right, I'm in trouble; **¡te la vas a ~!** *inf* you're for it **2.** (*a alguien*) to win over

ganchillo *m* **1.** (*gancho*) hook **2.** (*labor*) crochet; **hacer ~** to crochet

gancho *m* **1.** (*instrumento*) hook **2.** DEP (*boxeo*) hook; (*baloncesto*) hook shot **3.** (*de árbol*) stump **4.** (*algo que atrae*) bait **5.** *AmL* (*horquilla*) hairpin **6.** (*garabato*) scrawl **7.** (*atractivo*) **tener ~** to be attractive **8.** (*persona*) decoy

ganchudo, -a *adj* hooked

gandido, -a *adj Col, pey* (*glotón*) gluttonous

gandinga *f* **1.** (*mineral*) fine washed ore **2.** *Cuba, PRico* GASTR offal [*o* liver] stew

gandul(a) I. *adj* lazy **II.** *m(f)* layabout

gandulear *vi* to loaf about

gandulería *f* loafing

ganga *f* **1.** (*oferta*) bargain; **a precio de ~** at a bargain price; **¡menuda ~ este nuevo jefe!** *irón* we've got our work cut out with the new boss **2.** ZOOL sandgrouse **3.** MIN slag

ganglio *m* ANAT ganglion; **~ linfático** lymph gland

gangosear *vi* to speak through one's nose

gangoso, -a I. *adj* nasal **II.** *adv* **hablar ~** to speak through one's nose

gangrena *f* MED gangrene

gangrenarse *vr* to become gangrenous

gángster *mf* gangster

ganguear *vi* to speak through one's nose

gangueo *m* twang

gansada *f inf* silly thing; **hacer ~s** to clown about; **decir ~s** to talk nonsense

gansear *vi inf* **1.** (*hacer gansadas*) to clown about, to goof around *Am* **2.** (*decir gansadas*) to talk nonsense

ganso, -a *m, f* **1.** (*ave: hembra*) goose; (*macho*) gander **2.** *inf* (*perezoso*) lazybones *inv* **3.** *inf* (*estúpido*) ninny, gubbins; **hacer el ~** to clown about

Gante *m* Ghent

ganzúa¹ *f* (*llave*) picklock

ganzúa² *m* (*ladrón*) burglar

gañán *m* **1.** (*mozo*) farmhand **2.** (*tosco*) brute

gañido *m* (*de animal, persona*) howl; (*de perro*) yelp; (*de ave*) squawk

gañir <3. *pret:* gañó> *vi* (*animal, persona*) to howl; (*perro*) to yelp; (*ave*) to squawk

gañote *m* throat

garabatear I. *vt* (*al escribir*) to scribble; (*dibujando*) to doodle **II.** *vi* **1.** TÉC to use a hook **2.** (*al escribir*) to scribble **3.** (*andar con rodeos*) to beat around the bush

garabato *m* **1.** (*gancho*) hook **2.** (*al escribir*) scribble **3.** (*atractivo*) appeal **4.** (*al dibujar*) doodle

garaje *m* garage

garambaina *f* **1.** (*adorno*) frippery **2.** *pl* (*tonterías*) nonsense **3.** *pl* (*ademanes*) mannerisms **4.** *pl* (*garabatos*) scrawl

garandumba *f AmS* flat river boat

garante I. *adj* responsible **II.** *mf* guarantor

garantía *f* **1.** (*seguridad*) guarantee; **sin ~** (*en la lotería*) no liability assumed **2.** FIN (*aval*) guarantee, collateral; (*caución*) surety **3.** COM guarantee; **~s constitucionales** POL constitutional rights

garantir *irr como abolir vt v.* **garantizar**

garantizador(a) *m(f)* guarantor

garantizar <z→c> *vt* **1.** (*asegurar*) to guarantee; **no está garantizado que él sea el orador** it's not certain that he'll be the speaker **2.** JUR to act as guarantor for

garañón *m* **1.** (*asno*) stud jackass [*o* donkey]; (*camello*) stud camel **2.** *AmL* (*caballo semental*) stud

garapiña *f* **1.** (*galón*) braid **2.** GASTR sugar icing [*o* coating]

> In Latin America **garapiña** (or **garrapiña**) is a refreshing drink, which is prepared from pineapple rinds, water and milk.

garapiñar *vt* to coat with sugar

garbancero, -a I. *adj* chickpea **II.** *m, f* chickpea seller

garbanzo *m* chickpea ▶**por un ~ no se descompone la olla** *prov* nobody is irreplaceable *prov*; **ser el ~ negro (de la olla)** to be the black sheep of the family; **ganarse los ~s** *inf* to earn one's living

garbear I. *vi* **1.** (*afectar garbo*) to put on airs **2.** (*trampear*) to cheat (for a living) **II.** *vt* **1.** (*garbas*) to bind into sheaves **2.** (*robar*) to steal **III.** *vr:* **~se** to go for a stroll

garbeo *m* stroll

garbillar *vt* to sieve, to sift

garbillo *m* **1.** (*criba*) sieve **2.** MIN screen

garbo *m* **1.** (*elegancia*) elegance; (*de movimiento*) grace(fulness) **2.** (*brío*) dash **3.** (*generosidad*) generosity **4.** (*de un escrito*) style

garboso, -a *adj* **1.** (*elegante*) elegant **2.** (*brioso*) dashing **3.** (*generoso*) generous

garceta *f* **1.** (*ave*) egret **2.** (*pelo*) sidelock

gardenia *f* gardenia

garduña *f* marten

garete *inf* **ir(se) al ~** (*proyecto*) to go down the tubes; NÁUT to go adrift

garfa *f* claw

garfio *m* hook

gargajear *vi* to spit phlegm

gargajo *m* phlegm, gob *inf*

garganta *f* **1.** (*gaznate*) throat; (*cuello*) neck; (*empeine*) instep; **tener buena ~** to have a good voice; **se me hizo un nudo en la ~ de lo nervioso que estaba** I was so nervous I had a lump in my throat **2.** (*de un objeto*) neck **3.** GEO (*quebrada*) gorge, ravine; (*angostura*) narrow pass **4.** TÉC, ARQUIT neck

gargantilla *f* **1.** (*collar*) (short) necklace; (*de perlas*) string of pearls **2.** (*cinta*) choker

gárgaras *fpl* gargles *pl*; **hacer ~** to gargle; **¡vete a hacer ~!** *inf* get lost!

gargarear *vi Chile, Guat, Perú* (*barbotear*) to

gargle

gargarizar <z→c> *vi* to gargle

gárgola *f* ARQUIT gargoyle

garita *f* 1.(*de centinelas*) sentry box 2.(*de portero*) lodge 3. FERRO signal box 4.(*de fortificación*) lookout post, watch tower

garito *m* 1.(*local*) nightclub; (*de juego*) gambling den; (*antro*) dive, joint 2.(*ganancia*) winnings *pl*

garlar *vi inf* to chatter

garlito *m* trap; **caer en el ~** *fig* to fall into the trap

garlopa *f* jack [*o* long] plane

garnacha *f* 1.(*uva*) garnacha (*purplish grape*) 2.(*vino*) garnacha (*sweet wine made from garnacha grapes*)

garra *f* 1.(*de animal*) claw; **caer en las ~s de alguien** to fall into sb's clutches; **la policía le echó la ~** the police got hold of him 2. *pey* (*mano*) paw 3. NÁUT hook 4. *pl, AmL* (*harapos*) rags, tatters *pl* 5. *inf* (*brío*) **tener ~** to be compelling [*o* appealing]; **este equipo tiene ~** this team has real class

garrafa *f* (*pequeña*) carafe; (*más grande*) demijohn; **vino de ~** cheap wine

garrafal *adj* (*muy grande*) enormous; (*muy malo*) terrible

garrapata *f* tick

garrapatear *vi, vt* to scribble, to scrawl

garrapiña *f v.* **garapiña**

garrapiñar *vt v.* **garapiñar**

garrido, -a *adj* 1.(*gallardo*) smart 2.(*atractivo: hombre*) handsome; (*mujer*) pretty

garrocha *f* TAUR goad

garronear *vi Arg* to goad

garrotazo *m* blow with a stick [*o* club]

garrote *m* 1.(*palo*) stick 2.(*ligadura*) tourniquet 3.(*de ejecución*) garotte

garrotillo *m sin pl* MED croup

garrucha *f* pulley

garrulería *f* chatter

gárrulo, -a *adj* 1.(*pájaro*) twittering 2.(*persona*) talkative 3.(*arroyo*) babbling; (*viento*) howling

garúa *f AmL* (*llovizna*) drizzle

garuar *vimpers AmL* (*lloviznar*) to drizzle

garza *f* heron

garzón, -ona *m, f AmL* (*camarero*) waiter *m*, waitress *f*

gas *m* 1.(*fluido*) gas; **~ natural** natural gas; **bombona de ~** gas cylinder; **cartucho de ~** gas cartridge; **cocina de ~** gas cooker *Brit*, gas stove *Am*; **agua con ~** carbonated water; **agua sin ~** still water 2. *inf* AUTO **dar ~** to accelerate; **ir a todo ~** to go at full speed; **quedarse sin ~** *fig* to run out of steam 3. *pl* (*en el estómago*) **~es** wind

gasa *f* 1.(*tela*) gauze; **~ hidrófila** surgical gauze 2. MED lint 3.(*pañal*) nappy liner *Brit*, diaper liner *Am* 4.(*de luto*) crêpe

gascón, -ona I. *adj* of/from Gascony II. *m, f* Gascon

gasear *vt* 1.(*agua*) to carbonate 2. QUÍM to

gasify 3.(*matar*) to gas

gaseiforme *adj* gaseous

gaseosa *f* lemonade, soda

gaseoso, -a *adj* 1.(*bebida*) fizzy 2.(*gaseiforme*) gaseous

gasfitería *f AmL* plumbing

gasificación *f* 1.(*de bebida*) carbonation 2. QUÍM gasification

gasificar <c→qu> *vt* 1.(*bebida*) to carbonate 2. QUÍM (*transformar en gas*) to gasify

gasista *m* gasman

gasoducto *m* gas pipeline

gasógeno *m* gasogene

gasoil *m*, **gas-oil** *m* diesel

gasóleo *m* diesel

gasolina *f* petrol *Brit*, gas(oline) *Am*; **~ sin plomo** unleaded petrol *Brit* [*o* gasoline *Am*]; **~ súper** three-star petrol *Brit* [*o* gasoline *Am*]; **echar ~** to fill up with petrol *Brit* [*o* gasoline *Am*]

gasolinera *f* 1.(*establecimiento*) petrol station *Brit,* gas station *Am* 2.(*lancha*) motorboat

gastado, -a *adj* 1.(*vestido, zapato*) worn out; (*cuello*) frayed; (*talón*) worn down; (*suelo*) worn; (*neumático*) bare; (*pilas*) used up 2.(*expresión*) hackneyed 3.(*persona*) worn out

gastador *m* 1. MIL (*zapador*) sapper 2.(*condenado*) convict

gastador(a) I. *adj* extravagant, lavish II. *m(f)* spendthrift

gastar I. *vt* 1.(*dinero*) to spend 2.(*vestido, zapato, neumático*) to wear out; (*talón, suelo*) to wear down 3.(*tiempo*) to spend 4.(*electricidad*) to use 5.(*consumir, usar*) use; **¿qué talla/número gastas?** what size are you? 6.(*tener*) **~ mal/buen humor** to be bad/good-humoured *Brit*, to be bad/good-humored *Am* 7.(*poseer*) to have II. *vr:* **~se** 1.(*dinero*) to spend 2.(*vestido*) to wear out 3.(*consumirse*) to run out

Gasteiz *m* Vitoria

gasto *m* 1. *pl* (*de dinero*) spending; (*en un negocio*) costs *pl*; ECON, COM (*desembolso*) expenditure; (*costos adicionales*) expenses *pl*; **~s adicionales** extra charges; **~s pagados** all expenses paid; **~s corrientes** running costs; **~s de inscripción** inscription charges *pl;* **~s de personal** staff costs *pl;* **~s generales** overhead (expenses); **el ~ público** public expenditure; **~s de representación** expenses *pl* 2.(*de fuerza*) expenditure; **no merece el ~ de tanto tiempo** it's not worth spending so much time on it 3.(*consumo*) consumption 4.(*de una fuente*) flow

gástrico, -a *adj* gastric

gastritis *f inv* MED gastritis

gastroenteritis *f inv* MED gastroenteritis

gastronomía *f sin pl* (*arte culinaria*) gastronomy

gastronómico, -a *adj* gastronomic

gastrónomo, -a *m, f* 1.(*que trabaja en gas-*

tronomía) gastronome **2.**(*gourmet*) gourmet
gata *f* **1.**(*hembra del gato*) (she-)cat **2.**(*nube-cilla*) hill cloud **3.**(*madrileña*) woman from Madrid
gatas andar a ~ to crawl
gateado, -a *adj* feline; **marmol** ~ veined marble
gatear I. *vi* **1.**(*trepar*) to climb, to clamber **2.**(*ir a gatas*) to crawl **3.***AmL* (*enamorar*) to seduce II.*vt* **1.**(*arañar*) to scratch **2.***inf* (*robar*) to swipe
gatera *f* **1.**(*de gatos*) catflap **2.**NÁUT cat hole **3.***AmL* (*verdulera*) vegetable seller
gatillo *m* **1.**(*percusor*) trigger; **apretar el** ~ to pull the trigger **2.**(*de dentista*) forceps *pl* **3.**(*de cuadrúpedo*) nape (of neck) **4.**(*ratero*) petty thief
gato *m* **1.**(*félido*) cat; (*macho*) tomcat **2.**(*astuto*) fox **3.**(*madrileño*) man from Madrid **4.**TÉC (*de coche*) jack; (*de carpintero*) vice **5.**(*para dinero*) moneybag ►**llevarse el** ~ **al agua** *inf* to bring [o pull] it off; **el Gato con Botas** Puss in Boots; **dar** ~ **por liebre a alguien** *inf*to rip sb off; **cuando el** ~ **no está los ratones bailan** when the cat's away, the mice will play; **éramos cuatro ~s** *inf* there was hardly anyone else there; **aquí hay** ~ **encerrado** *inf* there's something fishy going on here; ~ **escaldado del agua fría huye** *prov* once bitten twice shy; **de noche todos los ~s son pardos** all cats are grey [o gray *Am*] in the night; **ser** ~ **viejo** to be an old hand
GATT *m* abr de **Acuerdo General sobre Aranceles y Comercio** GATT
gatuno, -a *adj*feline, catlike
gatuperio *m* **1.**(*mezcla*) hotchpotch *Brit*, hodgepodge *Am* **2.**(*embrollo*) dirty business
gauchaje *m CSur* gauchos *pl*
gauchear *vi* **1.***Arg, Urug* (*vivir como un gaucho*) to live as a gaucho **2.***Arg* (*errar*) to rove
gaucho *m AmL* **1.**(*campesino*) gaucho **2.**(*jinete*) skilled horseman

Gauchos were the cattle drovers or "cow-boys" of the South American **Pampa**.

gaucho, -a *adj* **1.**(*de gaucho*) gaucho **2.***AmL* (*grosero*) coarse **3.***AmL* (*astuto*) cunning
gaveta *f* drawer
gavia *f* **1.**(*zanja*) ditch **2.**NÁUT (*vela*) topsail
gavilán *m* **1.**(*ave*) sparrow hawk **2.**(*de pluma*) nib **3.**(*de espada*) quillon **4.**(*del cardo*) thistle flower
gavilla *f* **1.**(*fajo*) bundle, sheaf **2.**(*cuadrilla*) band
gaviota *f* (sea)gull
gay *m* gay
gazapera *f* **1.**(*madriguera*) warren **2.**(*de mala gente*) den **3.**(*riña*) brawl
gazapo *m* **1.**(*conejo*) young rabbit **2.**(*en un periódico*) misprint **3.** *inf*(*al hablar*) slip
gazmoñería *f* **1.**(*mojigatería*) prudishness

2.(*hipocresía*) hypocrisy
gazmoño, -a *adj* **1.**(*mojigato*) prudish **2.**(*hipócrita*) hypocritical
gaznápiro, -a *m, f* simpleton
gaznatada *f AmL* blow to the throat
gaznate *m* gullet
gazpacho *m* GASTR gazpacho

Gazpacho, a cold vegetable soup made from **tomates** (tomatoes), **pepinos** (cucumbers), **pimientos** (peppers), **aceite de oliva** (olive oil) and a little **pan** (bread), is prepared in summer, especially in the south of Spain, in **Andalucía** and **Extremadura**.

GB *m* **1.** abr de **gigabyte** GB **2.** abr de **Gran Bretaña** GB
Gbit *m* abr de **gigabit** Gbit
Gbyte *m* abr de **gigabyte** GB
géiser *m* geyser
geisha *f* geisha
gel *m* gel
gelatina *f* **1.**(*sustancia*) gelatine, gelatin *Am* **2.**GASTR jelly
gelatinoso, -a *adj* **1.**(*como la gelatina*) gelatinous **2.**(*de gelatina*) jelly
gélido, -a *adj*icy
gema *f* **1.**(*piedra preciosa*) gem, jewel **2.**BOT bud, gemma
gemebundo, -a *adj* groaning, moaning
gemelo, -a I. *adj* twin; **hermanos ~s** twin brothers II. *m, f* (*mellizo*) twin
gemelos *mpl* **1.**(*anteojos*) binoculars *pl*; ~ **de teatro** opera glasses **2.**(*de la camisa*) cufflinks *pl* **3.**ASTR **Gemelos** Gemini **4.**ANAT calves *pl*
gemido *m* **1.**(*de dolor*) groan; (*de pena*) moan; (*al llorar*) wail **2.**(*de animal*) whimper
geminación *f* **1.**(*duplicación*) duplication **2.**LING gemination
Géminis *m* Gemini
gemir *irr como pedir vi* **1.**(*de dolor*) to groan; (*de pena*) to moan **2.**(*animal*) to whine
gen *m* BIO gene
genciana *f* gentian
gendarme *m* policeman
genealogía *f* genealogy
genealógico, -a *adj* genealogical; **árbol** ~ family tree
generación *f* **1.**(*producción*) generation; **instrucción de** ~ INFOR generative instruction **2.**(*descendientes*) generation
generacional *adj* generational
generador *m* ELEC generator
generador(a) *adj* **1.**(*productivo*) productive; **medidas ~as de empleo** employment creation measures **2.**ELEC generating
general I. *adj* **1.**(*universal*) general; **cuartel** ~ headquarters; **cultura** ~ general knowledge; **junta** ~ (**extraordinaria**) (extraordinary) general meeting; **regla** ~ general rule; **de uso** ~ (*para todo uso*) multi-purpose, all-purpose; (*para todo el mundo*) for general use; **por lo**

~, **en** ~ in general, generally; **por regla** ~ as a (general) rule; **en** ~ **me siento satisfecho** overall, I'm satisfied; **en** ~ **hace mejor tiempo aquí** generally speaking, the weather is better here **2.** (*vago*) general; **tengo una idea** ~ **del tema** I have a general idea about the subject **II.** *m* general; ~ **en jefe** supreme commander

generalato *m* **1.** MIL (*grado*) generalship; (*oficiales*) generals *pl* **2.** REL generalship

generalidad *f* **1.** (*calidad general, validez general*) generality; **en la** ~ **de los casos** in most cases **2.** (*vaguedad*) respondió con una ~ he/she gave a vague reply; **hablar de** ~**es** to talk about nothing in particular **3.** *pl* (*conocimientos generales*) basic knowledge

Generalitat *f regional government of Catalonia*

generalización *f* **1.** (*universalización*) generalization **2.** (*difusión*) spread

generalizador(a) *adj* generalizing

generalizar <z→c> *vt* **1.** (*hacer general*) to generalize **2.** (*difundir*) to spread

generalmente *adv* **1.** (*en general*) generally **2.** (*ampliamente*) widely **3.** (*habitualmente*) generally

generar *vt* **1.** (*producir*) to generate; ~ **beneficios** to generate profits **2.** (*provocar*) to create; ~ **un clima de confianza** to create a climate of trust

generativo, -a *adj* generative

generatriz *f* **1.** FÍS generator **2.** MAT generatrix

genérico, -a *adj* **1.** (*de la especie*) generic; **medicamentos** ~**s** generic drugs **2.** LING **nombre** ~ common noun

género *m* **1.** BIO genus; ~ **humano** mankind, human race **2.** (*clase*) type, sort; **¿qué** ~ **de hombre es?** what sort of man is he?; **sin ningún** ~ **de dudas** without a shadow of a doubt; **tomar todo** ~ **de precauciones** to take every possible precaution **3.** LING gender **4.** LIT, ARTE genre; **el** ~ **novelístico** fiction; **el** ~ **lírico** lyric poetry **5.** COM (*artículo*) article; (*mercancía*) merchandise, goods *pl*; (*tela*) cloth; ~**s de punto** knitwear **6.** MÚS **el** ~ **lírico** opera; **el** ~ **chico** light opera, zarzuela **7.** (*manera*) manner

generosidad *f* **1.** (*dadivosidad*) generosity **2.** (*magnanimidad*) magnanimity

generoso, -a *adj* **1.** (*dadivoso*) generous; **ser** ~ **con** [*o* **para con**] **alguien** to be generous to sb **2.** (*magnánimo*) magnanimous **3.** (*abundante*) generous

génesis *f inv* genesis

Génesis *m* Genesis

genética *f sin pl* BIO genetics

genético, -a *adj* genetic

genial *adj* **1.** (*idea*) brilliant **2.** (*gracioso*) funny **3.** (*estupendo*) great

genialidad *f* **1.** (*cualidad*) genius **2.** (*acción*) stroke of genius

genio *m* **1.** (*carácter*) character; **tener mal** ~ to be bad-tempered; **tener mucho** ~ to be

very temperamental **2.** (*persona*) genius; **el** ~ **de Cervantes** Cervantes the genius **3.** (*empuje*) drive **4.** (*de una época*) spirit **5.** (*ser fabuloso*) genie **6.** ARTE genius

genista *f* broom

genital *adj* genital

genitales *mpl* genitals *pl*

genitivo *m* LING genitive

genocidio *m* genocide

Génova *f* Genoa

gente *f* **1.** (*personas*) people *pl*; ~ **de armas** men at arms; **la** ~ **joven/mayor** young/old people; ~ **menuda** (*niños*) children; **a este partido le preocupa la** ~ this party cares about people; **tienes que tratar más con la** ~ you should spend more time with other people; **¿qué dirá la** ~**?** what will people say?; **tener don de** ~**s** to have a way with people **2.** (*personal*) staff **3.** MIL (*tropa*) troop; NÁUT crew **4.** *inf* (*parentela*) family; **¿qué tal tu** ~**?** how are your folks? **5.** *AmL* (*honrado*) honest people

gentil **I.** *adj* **1.** (*pagano*) pagan **2.** (*apuesto*) dashing; (*elegante*) elegant **3.** (*amable*) considerate **II.** *mf* pagan, heathen

gentileza *f* **1.** (*garbo*) elegance **2.** (*cortesía*) kindness; **¿tendría Ud. la** ~ **de ayudarme?** would you be so kind as to help me?

gentilicio, -a *adj* **nombre** ~ *noun describing people from a particular place*

gentío *m sin pl* crowd

gentuza *f pey* rabble; **¡qué** ~**!** what a rabble!

genuflexión *f* genuflection

genuino, -a *adj* (*persona*) genuine; (*manuscrito*) authentic; (*amor*) true; **es un caso** ~ **de histeria** it is a genuine case of hysteria

geodesia *f* geodesy

geografía *f sin pl* geography

geográfico, -a *adj* geographical

geógrafo, -a *m, f* geographer

geología *f sin pl* geology

geológico, -a *adj* geological

geólogo, -a *m, f* geologist

geometría *f sin pl* geometry

geométrico, -a *adj* geometri(cal)

geopolítico, -a *adj* geopolitical

Georgia *f* Georgia

georgiano, -a *adj, m, f* Georgian

geranio *m* geranium

gerencia *f* (*de una empresa, un teatro*) management; (*de un banco*) directors *pl*

gerente *mf* (*de una gran empresa*) director, general manager; (*de una pequeña empresa*) manager; (*de un departamento*) head

geriatra *mf* geriatrician

geriatría *f sin pl* geriatrics *pl*

geriátrico, -a *adj* geriatric; **clínica geriátrica** geriatric hospital

gerifalte *m* **1.** (*persona*) bigwig **2.** (*halcón*) gerfalcon [*o* gyrfalcon]

germánico, -a **I.** *adj* **1.** (*de Germania*) Germanic **2.** (*de Alemania*) German **II.** *m, f* German

germanio *m* germanium

germanismo *m word or phrase of German origin*

germanista *mf* Germanist, German scholar

germanización *f* Germanization

germanizar <z→c> *vt* to Germanize, to make German

germano, -a *adj, m, f v.* **germánico**

germanófilo, -a *adj* Germanophilic

germanófobo, -a *adj* Germanophobic

germanooccidental *adj, mf* West German

germanooriental *adj, mf* East German

germen *m* 1. BIO germ; ~ **de trigo** wheatgerm 2. (*origen*) origin

germicida *m* germicide

germinación *f* germination

germinar *vi* 1. BOT to germinate 2. (*sospechas*) to arouse; ~ **en** to give rise to

gerontocracia *f* POL gerontocracy

gerontología *f sin pl* gerontology

gerundense I. *adj* of/from Gerona II. *mf* native/inhabitant of Gerona

gerundio *m* LING gerund

gesta *f* heroic deed, exploit; LIT epic poem or narrative

gestación *f* 1. (*de una persona, un animal*) gestation 2. (*de un plan, proyecto*) preparation; (*de un complot*) hatching; **el proyecto está en** ~ the project is at the planning stage

gestar I. *vt* to gestate II. *vr:* ~**se** (*proceso*) to develop; (*plan, proyecto*) to be prepared; (*complot*) to be hatched

gesticulación *f* 1. (*con las manos*) gesticulation 2. (*con la cara*) face-pulling; (*de dolor*) grimace

gesticular *vi* 1. (*con las manos*) to gesticulate 2. (*con la cara*) to pull faces; (*de dolor*) to grimace

gestión *f* 1. (*diligencia*) measure; **hacer gestiones** to take measures [*o* steps] 2. (*de una empresa*) management; **la** ~ **del gobierno** the government's management of the country; **la** ~ **al frente de la escuela** school management 3. INFOR ~ **de ficheros** file management

gestionar *vt* 1. (*asunto*) to conduct 2. (*negocio*) to manage

gesto *m* 1. (*con el cuerpo*) movement; (*con la mano*) gesture; (*con el rostro*) expression; **torcer el** ~ to scowl 2. (*semblante*) face 3. (*acto*) gesture; **un** ~ **de apoyo** a gesture of support

gestor(a) I. *adj* managing II. *m(f) person who handles official matters on the behalf of his/her client*

gestoría *f agency handling official matters*

gestual *adj* gestural; **lenguaje** ~ body language

gestualidad *f* (*del rostro*) expressiveness; (*del cuerpo*) body language

ghanés, -esa *adj, m, f* Ghanese

GHz *abr de* **gigahertz** GHz

giba *f* 1. (*chepa*) hump, hunch 2. (*bulto*) lump

3. (*molestia*) nuisance

gibar *vt* 1. (*concorvar*) to bend 2. *inf* (*jorobar*) to bother, to hassle

gibón *m* gibbon

gibosidad *f* hump

Gibraltar *m* Gibraltar

gibraltareño, -a *adj, m, f* Gibraltarian

Giga *m* Giga

gigabyte *m* gigabyte; ~**s por segundo** gigabytes per second

gigante I. *adj* giant, gigantic II. *m* 1. (*ser*) giant 2. (*en fiesta popular*) *papier maché giant* ► **un** ~ **con pies de barro** an idol with feet of clay

gigantesco, -a *adj* gigantic

gigantismo *m sin pl* MED giantism [*o* gigantism]

gigoló *m* gigolo

gilipollas *mf inv, vulg* jerk, wanker

gilipollez *f vulg* bullshit; **decir gilipolleces** to talk rubbish

gimnasia *f* 1. DEP gymnastics *pl;* ~ **rítmica** rhythm gymnastics; **hacer** ~ to do gymnastics 2. ENS gym 3. (*ejercicio*) **hacer** ~ to do exercises

gimnasio *m* gymnasium; ~ (**de musculación**) gym

gimnasta *mf* gymnast

gimnástico, -a *adj* gymnastic

gimotear *vi* 1. *pey* (*gemir*) to groan 2. (*lloriquear*) to whimper, to whine

gimoteo *m* 1. (*gemidos*) groan 2. (*lloriqueo*) whimper, whining

ginebra *f* gin

Ginebra *f* Geneva

ginebrino, -a I. *adj* of/from Geneva II. *m, f* native/inhabitant of Geneva

ginecología *f sin pl* gynaecology *Brit,* gynecology *Am*

ginecológico, -a *adj* gynaecological *Brit,* gynecological *Am*

ginecólogo, -a *m, f* gynaecologist *Brit,* gynecologist *Am*

ginesta *f* broom

gingivitis *f inv* MED gingivitis

gira *f* 1. (*de un día*) (day)trip, excursion; (*más larga*) tour 2. (*de un artista*) tour; **estar de** ~ to be on tour

girado, -a *m, f* FIN drawee

giralda *f* weathervane; (*en forma de gallo*) weathercock

girar I. *vi* 1. (*dar vueltas*) to revolve; (*con rapidez*) to spin 2. (*conversación*) ~ **en torno a algo** to revolve around sth 3. (*beneficios*) **este negocio gira mucho** this business has a big turnover 4. (*torcer*) to turn II. *vt* 1. (*dar la vuelta*) to turn; ~ **la vista** to look round 2. COM (*dinero*) to send; ~ **a cargo de alguien** (*letra*) to draw on sb

girasol *m* sunflower

giratorio, -a *adj* revolving

giro *m* 1. (*vuelta, cariz*) turn; **un** ~ **de volante** a turn of the steering wheel; **tomar un** ~

favorable/negativo to take a turn for the better/worse; **me preocupa el ~ que toma este asunto** I don't like the way this issue is developing **2.** LING (*locución*) expression **3.** COM (*letra*) draft; **~ postal** money order **4.** COM (*de una empresa*) business turnover
gitanada *f* **1.** (*engaño*) contemptible trick **2.** (*zalamería*) wheedling
gitanear *vi inf* to wheedle
gitanería *f* **1.** *inf* (*halago*) wheedling praise **2.** (*grupo*) band of gipsies [*o* gypsies *Am*] **3.** (*vida*) gipsy [*o* gypsy *Am*] way of life **4.** (*acción*) gipsy [*o* gypsy *Am*] saying
gitano, -a I. *adj* **1.** (*de los gitanos*) gipsy *Brit*, gypsy *Am* **2.** *inf* (*zalamero*) wheedling **II.** *m*, *f* **1.** (*calé*) gipsy *Brit*, gypsy *Am*; **ir hecho un ~** *inf* to look like a tramp **2.** *inf* (*estafador*) swindler **3.** GASTR **brazo de ~** Swiss roll *Brit*, jelly roll *Am*
glaciación *f* glaciation
glacial *adj* **1.** (*helado*) icy cold; **zona ~** polar region **2.** (*persona*) cold
glaciar *m* GEO glacier
gladiador *m* gladiator
gladiolo *m*, **gladíolo** *m* gladiolus
glande *m* ANAT glans penis
glándula *f* ANAT gland
glandular *adj* glandular
glasé *m* glacé silk
glasear *vt* (*alimentos, papel*) to glaze; (*tarta*) to ice
glaucoma *m* MED glaucoma
glicerina *f* glycerine *Brit*, glycerin *Am*
global *adj* **1.** (*total*) overall; **valoración ~** total value **2.** (*cantidad*) total **3.** (*informe*) comprehensive **4.** (*mundial*) global
globalidad *f* totality
globalización *f* **1.** (*de un problema*) overall treatment **2.** (*generalización*) generalization **3.** (*mundialización*) globalization
globalizante *adj* generalizing
globalizar <z→c> *vt* **1.** (*problema*) to give an overall view of **2.** (*generalizar*) to generalize **3.** (*mundializar*) to globalize
globo *m* **1.** (*esfera*) sphere; **~ de una lámpara** (round) lampshade; **~ ocular** eyeball **2.** (*tierra, mapa*) globe **3.** (*para niños*) balloon; **~** (**aerostático**) hot-air balloon **4.** *inf* (*borrachera*) **tener un ~** to be plastered **5.** *inf* (*enfado*) anger **6.** *inf* (*preservativo*) condom, johnny *Brit*, rubber *Am* **7.** DEP (*tenis*) lob **8.** (*comics, tebeos*) speech balloon [*o* bubble] ▶**en** ~ as a whole
globular *adj* **1.** (*de globo*) spherical **2.** (*de glóbulo*) globular
globulina *f* BIO globulin
glóbulo *m* ANAT corpuscle **~ blanco/rojo** white/red corpuscle
gloria¹ *f* **1.** (*fama*) glory; **Goya es una ~ nacional** Goya is a national treasure **2.** (*paraíso*) heaven; **conseguir la ~** to go to heaven; **estar en la ~** *inf* to be in seventh heaven **3.** (*esplendor*) glory ▶**sin pena ni ~**

whitout any ado; **oler/saber a ~** to smell/taste delicious
gloria² *m* REL gloria, doxology
gloriarse <*1. pres:* me glorío> *vr* **1.** (*presumir*) **~se de algo** to boast about sth **2.** (*complacerse*) **~se de** [*o* en] **algo** to glory in sth
glorieta *f* **1.** (*cenador*) arbour *Brit*, arbor *Am* **2.** (*plazoleta*) (small) square **3.** (*rotonda*) roundabout
glorificación *f* glorification
glorificar <c→qu> **I.** *vt* to glorify **II.** *vr* **~se de algo** to boast about sth
glorioso, -a *adj* **1.** *t.* REL glorious **2.** (*jactancioso*) boastful
glosa *f* **1.** **~ a algo** (*aclaración*) explanation on sth; (*anotación*) note on sth; (*comentario*) comment on sth **2.** LIT gloss **3.** MÚS variation
glosar *vt* **1.** (*anotar*) to annotate **2.** (*comentar*) to comment on; LIT to gloss **3.** (*tergiversar*) to deliberately misinterpret
glosario *m* glossary
glotis *f sin pl* ANAT glottis
glotón *m* glutton
glotón, -ona I. *adj* gluttonous, greedy **II.** *m*, *f* glutton, gannet *inf*
glotonear *vi* to be gluttonous
glotonería *f* gluttony
glucemia *f* MED glycaemia *Brit*, glycemia *Am*
glucosa *f* glucose
gluten *m* **1.** (*cola*) glue **2.** BOT gluten
glúteo *m* ANAT gluteous *pl*, buttocks *pl*
glutinoso, -a *adj* glutinous
gnomo *m* gnome
gnosis *f inv* REL gnosis
gnosticismo *m sin pl* REL gnosticism
gobernabilidad *f sin pl* governability
gobernable *adj* **1.** (*país*) governable **2.** (*nave*) steerable
gobernación *f* government
gobernador(a) I. *adj* governing **II.** *m(f)* governor
gobernanta *f* *AmL* **1.** (*niñera*) nanny **2.** (*institutriz*) governess **3.** (*ama de llaves*) housekeeper
gobernante *mf* ruler
gobernar <e→ie> *vt* **1.** POL (*mandar*) to govern **2.** (*dirigir*) to manage; (*nave*) to steer; **~ una casa** to run a household **3.** (*máquina*) to handle, to run **4.** (*a una persona*) to rule
gobierno *m* **1.** POL government; **~ autonómico** regional government; **~ central** central government; **en círculos afines al ~** in the corridors of power **2.** (*ministros*) cabinet; **~ en la sombra** shadow cabinet **3.** (*del gobernador*) governorship; (*residencia*) governor's residence **4.** (*dirección*) management **5.** (*de una nave*) steering **6.** (*de una máquina*) handling
goce *m* pleasure, enjoyment
godo, -a I. *adj* Gothic **II.** *m*, *f* **1.** HIST Goth **2.** *AmC, pey* (*español*) Spaniard
gofre *m* waffle
gol *m* DEP goal; **~ del empate** equalizer;

meter un ~ to score (a goal) ▶**meter un** ~ **a alguien** *inf* to put one over [*o* pull a fast one] on sb

gola *f* **1.**(*gorguera*) ruff **2.**(*garganta*) throat

golazo *m* DEP great goal

goleador(a) *m(f)* DEP goalscorer

golear *vt* DEP to score a lot of goals against, to hammer

goleta *f* NÁUT schooner

golf *m sin pl* DEP golf

golfa *f* **1.** *inf*(*puta*) slut, hussy **2.** *v.* **golfo, -a**

golfear *vi* to loaf about

golfista *mf* DEP golfer

golfo *m* GEO gulf

golfo, -a **I.** *adj* (*niño*) naughty **II.** *m, f* **1.**(*pilluelo*) urchin **2.**(*vagabundo*) tramp **3.**(*sinvergüenza*) scoundrel

gollería *f* delicacy

gollete *m* **1.** ANAT (*garganta*) throat **2.**(*de vasija*) neck

golondrina *f* **1.**(*pájaro*) swallow **2.** *reg* (*barca*) motorboat

golondrino *m* **1.**(*pájaro*) young swallow **2.**(*vagabundo*) drifter, rolling stone

golosina *f* **1.**(*manjar*) delicacy **2.**(*dulce*) sweet *Brit,* candy *Am* **3.**(*deseo*) fancy *Brit,* desire **4.**(*cosa apetitosa*) titbit *Brit,* tidbit *Am*

golosinear *vi* to nibble at sweets [*o* candy *Am*]

goloso, -a **I.** *adj* **1.**(*de dulces*) sweet-toothed **2.**(*apetitoso*) appetizing; **es una oferta muy golosa** it's a very tempting offer **II.** *m, f* **ser un** ~ to have a sweet tooth

golpe *m* **1.**(*impacto*) blow; (*choque*) bump; ~ **de Estado** coup (d'état); ~ **de pincel** brushstroke; **un** ~ **de tos** a fit of coughing; **andar a** ~**s** to be always fighting; **abrirse de** ~ (*door, window*) to fly open; **cerrar la puerta de** ~ to slam the door shut; **dar un** ~ to strike; **me he dado un** ~ **en la cabeza** I've banged my head; **parar un** ~ to stop a blow; **me lo tragué de un** ~ I downed it in one go [*o* all at once] **2.**(*ruido*) bang **3.**(*ocurrencia*) witty remark **4.**(*atraco*) hold-up **5.**(*gran cantidad*) crowd; ~ **de gente** lots of people **6.** TÉC (*pestillo*) spring bolt **7.**(*sorpresa*) shock **8.**(*de vestido*) flap **9.**(*en el boxeo*) punch; ~ **bajo** punch below the belt; ~ **franco** free kick ▶**de** ~ (**y porrazo**) (*al mismo tiempo*) at the same time; (*de repente*) suddenly; **a** ~ **de vista** at a glance; **no pegó ni** ~ *inf* he didn't lift a finger

golpear **I.** *vi* **1.**(*dar un golpe*) to hit **2.**(*latir*) to throb, to beat **3.** TÉC (*motor*) to knock **II.** *vt* to hit; (*puerta*) to knock on **III.** *vr* ~**se la cabeza** to bang one's head

golpetear **I.** *vi* **1.**(*dar golpes*) to hammer **2.**(*traquetear*) to rattle **II.** *vt* to hammer

golpista *mf* participant in a coup (d'état)

goma *f* **1.**(*sustancia*) rubber; ~ **de borrar** rubber *Brit,* eraser *Am;* ~ **elástica** (*sustancia*) rubber; (*objeto*) elastic band; ~ **de pegar** glue **2.** *inf* (*preservativo*) condom, johnny *Brit,*

rubber *Am* **3.** *AmL* (*resaca*) hangover

goma-dos *f sin pl* plastic explosive

gomaespuma *f* foam rubber

gomería *f* *Arg* COM tyre [*o* tire *Am*] dealer, tyre [*o* tire *Am*] workshop

gomero *m* *AmL* (*árbol*) rubber tree

gomina® *f* hair [*o* styling] gel

gominola *f* winegum *Brit,* gumdrop *Am*

gomosidad *f* **1.**(*elasticidad*) elasticity **2.**(*adherencia*) stickiness

gomoso *m* sticky

gónada *f* ANAT gonad

góndola *f* **1.**(*de Venecia*) gondola **2.** *AmL* bus

gondolero *m* gondolier

gong *m* <gongs>, **gongo** *m* gong

gonorrea *f* MED gonorrhoea *Brit,* gonorrhea *Am*

gordo *m* **1.**(*grasa*) fat **2.**(*lotería*) **el** ~ first prize (in the lottery), the jackpot; **sacar el** ~ *fig* to bring home the bacon

gordo, -a **I.** *adj* **1.**(*persona*) fat; (*comida*) fatty; (*tejido*) thick **2.**(*suceso*) important; (*salario*) big; **una mentira gorda** a big lie; **ha pasado algo muy** ~ sth serious has happened ▶**se armó la gorda** *inf* all hell broke loose; **me cae** ~ I don't like him **II.** *m, f* fat man, fat woman *m, f*

gordura *f* (*obesidad*) fatness; (*corpulencia*) corpulence; (*tejido adiposo*) fat

gorgojo *m* **1.**(*insecto*) weevil **2.** *inf* (*persona*) midget

gorgoritear *vi inf* to warble

gorgotear *vi* **1.**(*hacer ruido*) to gurgle; (*arroyo*) to babble **2.**(*burbujear*) to bubble

gorgoteo *m* **1.**(*ruido*) gurgle; (*de un arroyo*) babbling **2.**(*borboteo*) bubbling

gorguera *f* **1.**(*gola*) ruff **2.**(*de la armadura*) gorget

gorila *m* **1.**(*animal*) gorilla **2.** *inf* (*portero*) bouncer **3.** *inf* (*guardaespaldas*) bodyguard **4.** *inf*(*matón*) thug

gorjear **I.** *vi* **1.**(*personas*) to twitter **2.**(*pájaros*) to chirp **II.** *vr:* ~**se 1.**(*niño*) to gurgle **2.** *AmL* (*burlarse*) to make fun of

gorjeo *m* **1.**(*de personas*) twittering; (*de bebés*) gurgling **2.**(*de pájaros*) chirping

gorra *f* **1.**(*prenda*) cap; ~ **de visera** peaked cap *Brit,* baseball cap *Am* **2.**(*para niños*) bonnet ▶**de** ~ *inf* (*gratis*) free; **andar** [*o* **vivir**] **de** ~ *inf* to sponge

gorrear *vi, vt inf* to scrounge; **¿te puedo** ~ **un cigarrillo?** can I cadge a cigarette off you?

gorrero *m inf* scrounger

gorrinada *f* (*acción injusta*) dirty trick

gorrinera *f* pigsty

gorrino, -a *m, f* **1.**(*cochinillo*) suckling pig; (*cerdo*) pig; (*cerda*) sow **2.** *pey* (*persona*) pig

gorrión *m* **1.**(*pardal*) sparrow **2.** *AmC* (*colibrí*) hummingbird

gorro *m* hat; (*de uniforme*) cap; ~ **para bebés** baby's bonnet; ~ **de natación** bathing cap; ~ **de papel** paper hat ▶**estar hasta el** ~ **de algo**

to be fed up with sth
gorrón *m* **1.**(*piedra*) pebble, cobblestone **2.** TÉC pivot
gorrón, -ona *m, f* **1.** *inf* (*aprovechado*) scrounger **2.** *AmC* (*egoísta*) selfish person
gorronear *vi v.* **gorrear**
gorronería *f inf*scrounging
gota *f* **1.**(*de líquido*) drop; **café con unas ~s de ron** coffee with a dash of rum; **el agua salía ~ a ~ del grifo** the water dripped out of the tap; **apurar el vaso hasta la última ~** to drain the glass to the last drop; **parecerse como dos ~s de agua** to be like two peas in a pod **2.**(*pizca*) drop; **no queda ni ~ de agua** there's not a drop of water left; **no tiene ni una ~ de paciencia** he/she doesn't have an ounce of patience **3.** METEO **~ fría** cold front **4.** MED (*enfermedad*) gout **5.**(*gotero*) **el ~ a ~ the drip ►la ~ que colma el vaso** the last straw; **sudar la ~ gorda** *inf* to sweat blood
gotear I. *vi* **1.**(*líquido*) to drip; (*escurrir*) trickle **2.**(*salirse*) to leak II. *vimpers* **está goteando** it's drizzling, it's spitting (with rain) *Brit*
goteo *m* **1.**(*gotear*) drip(ping) **2.** MED drip *Brit*
gotera *f* **1.**(*filtración, grieta*) leak; **hay una ~ en el baño** there's a leak in the bath(room) **2.**(*mancha*) stain **3.**(*achaque*) complaint **4.** *pl, AmL* (*afueras*) outskirts *pl*
gotero *m* **1.** MED drip **2.** *AmL* (*cuentagotas*) dropper
gótico, -a *adj* Gothic
gotoso, -a I. *adj* MED gouty II. *m, f* MED goutsufferer
gozada *f inf*delight
gozar <z→c> I. *vi* **1.**(*complacerse*) to enjoy oneself **2.**(*disfrutar*) **~ de algo** to enjoy sth; **~ de una increíble fortuna** to be incredibly wealthy II. *vt* **1.**(*disfrutar*) to enjoy **2.**(*poseer carnalmente*) to possess III. *vr:* **~se** to enjoy oneself; **~se en** to take pleasure in
gozne *m* hinge
gozo *m* **1.**(*delicia*) delight; (*placer*) pleasure **2.**(*alegría*) joy **3.**(*del fuego*) flame ►**mi ~ en un pozo** all for nothing
gr. *abr de* gramo g.
grabación *f* **1.**(*de disco*) recording **2.** TV (*de una serie*) shooting **3.** INFOR copying
grabado *m* **1.** ARTE (*acción*) engraving **2.** ARTE (*copia*) print; **~ al agua fuerte** etching; **~ en madera** woodcut **3.**(*ilustración*) illustration
grabador(a) *m(f)* engraver
grabadora *f* TÉC tape recorder
grabadura *f* (*acción, efecto*) recording; (*en piedra*) engraving; (*en madera*) cutting
grabar I. *vt* **1.** ARTE to engrave; (*en madera*) to cut **2.**(*disco*) to record **3.** INFOR to copy **4.**(*fijar*) to engrave II. *vr:* **~se** to become engraved
gracejo *m* wit, humour *Brit*, humor *Am*
gracia *f* **1.** *pl* (*agradecimiento*) **¡~s!** thanks!; **¡muchas ~s!** thanks a lot!; **¡~s a Dios!** thank

God!; **te debo las ~s** I owe you my thanks; **no me ha dado ni las ~s** he/she didn't even say "thank you"; **~s a tus esfuerzos lo conseguí** thanks to your efforts, I managed it **2.** REL grace **3.**(*perdón*) mercy **4.**(*favor*) favour *Brit*, favor *Am* **5.**(*agrado*) **me cae en ~** I like him/her **6.**(*garbo*) elegance; **está escrito con ~** it's elegantly written **7.**(*chiste*) joke; **no tiene (ni) pizca de ~** it's not in the least bit funny; **no me hace nada de ~** I don't find it funny in the least; **si lo haces se va la ~** if you do it it loses its charm; **este cómico tiene poca ~** this comedian isn't very funny; **la ~ es que...** the funny thing is that ...; **no estoy hoy para ~s** I'm not in a mood for jokes today **8.** *irón* (*ocurrencia*) **hoy ha hecho otra de sus ~s** he/she has been up to his/her tricks again
grácil *adj* graceful
gracilidad *f* gracefulness
gracioso, -a I. *adj* **1.**(*atractivo*) attractive **2.**(*chistoso*) funny; **para mí no fue nada ~** I didn't find it at all funny **3.**(*gratis*) free II. *m, f* TEAT comic character; **algún ~ me ha escondido las llaves** some joker has hidden my keys; **no te hagas el ~ conmigo** don't try to play the clown with me
grada *f* **1.**(*de un estadio*) tier; **las ~s** the terraces **2.**(*peldaño*) step **3.** AGR harrow **4.** NÁUT slipway **5.** *pl* (*escalinata*) steps *pl* **6.** *pl, AmL* (*atrio*) courtyard
gradación *f* **1.**(*escalonamiento*) gradation **2.** MÚS gradation **3.**(*retórica*) climax
gradería *f*, **graderío** *m* **1.**(*de un estadio*) terraces *pl* **2.** *fig* crowd
grado *m* **1.**(*nivel*) degree; **~ de confianza** degree of trust; **quemaduras de primer ~** MED first-degree burns; **en ~ sumo** greatly, highly **2.**(*parentesco*) degree **3.** ENS year; **~ elemental** basic level **4.** UNIV degree; **~ de doctor** doctorate **5.** MAT degree; **~ centígrado** degree centigrade **6.** LING **~ comparativo** degree of comparison **7.** MIL (*rango*) rank **8.**(*de alcohol*) degree
graduable *adj* adjustable
graduación *f* **1.**(*regulación*) adjustment **2.**(*en grados*) graduation; (*en niveles, de personas*) grading; (*de precios*) regulation **3.**(*de un vino*) strength; **~ alcohólica** alcohol content **4.** MIL rank **5.** UNIV graduation
graduado, -a I. *adj* graduate(d) II. *m, f* **1.** UNIV graduate; **~ en ingeniería** engineering graduate **2.** ENS **~ escolar** school-leaving certificate
gradual *adj* gradual
gradualmente *adv* **1.**(*en grados*) by degrees **2.**(*progresivamente*) gradually
graduar <1. *pres:* gradúo> I. *vt* **1.**(*regular*) to regulate **2.** TÉC to graduate; **~ la vista a alguien** to test sb's eyesight **3.**(*en niveles*) to classify; (*precios*) to regulate **4.** UNIV to confer a degree on **5.** MIL to confer a rank on; **~ a alguien de coronel** to confer the rank of colonel on sb II. *vr:* **~se** to graduate; **se graduó en económicas** he/she graduated in economics

grafía f (*escritura*) writing; (*ortografía*) spelling

gráfica f graph

gráfico m graph; ~ **de tarta** pie chart; **tarjeta de ~s** INFOR graphics card

gráfico, -a adj 1.(*de la escritura*) written 2.(*del dibujo*) illustrated; **diccionario** ~ visual dictionary 3.(*claro*) graphic 4.*fig* expressive

grafismo m 1.(*grafía*) handwriting 2.(*aspecto estético*) vivid writing style 3. INFOR computer graphics

grafista mf graphic artist [o designer]

grafito m MIN graphite

grafología f sin pl graphology

grafólogo, -a m, f graphologist

gragea f MED (sugar-coated) pill

grajear vi 1.(*el grajo*) to caw 2.(*un bebé*) to gurgle

grajilla f jackdaw

grajo m 1.(*ave*) rook 2.(*charlatán*) chatter-box 3. *AmL* (*sobaquina*) body odour *Brit*, body odor *Am*

gral. adj abr de **general** gen.

gramática f LING grammar; ~ **generativa** transformational grammar ►**tener mucha ~ parda** inf to be worldy-wise

gramatical adj grammatical; **regla** ~ grammatical rule

gramático, -a m, f grammarian

gramilla f AmL (*hierba*) lawn, grass

gramo m gramme *Brit*, gram *Am*

gramófono m gramophone *Brit*, phonograph *Am*

gramola f 1.(*gramófono*) gramophone *Brit*, phonograph *Am* 2.(*en un bar*) jukebox

gran adj v. **grande**

grana I. adj (*color*) scarlet II. f 1.(*acción*) seeding 2.(*semilla*) seed 3.(*cochinilla*) cochineal

granada f 1.(*fruto*) pomegranate 2.(*proyectil: de mano*) grenade; (*de artillería*) shell

granadilla f 1.(*fruto*) passion fruit 2. AmC (*planta*) passionflower

granadino, -a I. adj of/from Granada II. m, f native/inhabitant of Granada

granado m pomegranate tree

granado, -a adj 1.(*ilustre*) distinguished 2.(*maduro*) mature 3.(*alto*) tall

granar vi to seed

granate I. adj burgundy II. m MIN garnet

Gran Bretaña f Great Britain

grancanario, -a I. adj of/from Grand Canary II. m, f native/inhabitant Grand Canary

grande I. adj <más **grande** o **mayor**, **grandísimo**> (*precediendo un substantivo singular: gran*) 1.(*de tamaño*) big; (*número, cantidad*) large; **gran ciudad** big city; **una habitación ~** a large room; **una gran suma de dinero** a large sum of money; **una gran mentira** a big lie; **gran velocidad** high speed; **vino gran cantidad de gente** a lot of people came; **tengo un gran interés por...** I'm very interested in ...; **no me preocupa gran cosa** I'm not very worried about it 2. *inf* (*de edad*) grown-up 3.(*moralmente*) great; **un gran hombre** a great man; **una gran idea** a great idea ►**ir** ~ **a alguien** to be too much for sb; **pasarlo en** ~ to have a great time; **vivir a lo** ~ to live in style II. m 1.(*prócer*) great; **los ~s de la industria** the major industrial players 2.(*título*) **Grande de España** Spanish Grandee

grandemente adv (*mucho*) greatly; (*extremadamente*) extremely

grandeza f 1.(*tamaño*) size; **delirio de** ~ delusions of grandeur 2.(*excelencia de cosas, de personas*) greatness 3.(*de un Grande*) status of grandee

grandilocuencia f grandiloquence

grandilocuente adj grandiloquent

grandiosidad f impressiveness, grandeur

grandioso, -a adj impressive; (*rimbombante*) grandiose

grandullón, -ona adj oversized

granear vt 1.(*semilla*) to sow 2.(*pólvora*) to sieve 3. ARTE to grain

granel carga a ~ bulk order; **a** ~ (*sin envase*) loose; (*líquido*) by volume; (*en abundancia*) in abundance

granero m granary; (*de granja*) barn; **Castilla es el** ~ **de España** Castile is the granary of Spain

granítico, -a adj 1.(*de granito*) granite 2.(*parecido al granito*) granitic

granito m MIN granite

granizada f 1.(*pedrisco*) hailstorm 2.(*de balas*) hail

granizado m iced drink; ~ **de café** ≈ iced coffee

granizar <z→c> v impers to hail

granizo m hail

granja f 1.(*finca*) farm 2.(*establecimiento*) dairy store

granjear I. vt 1.(*ganado*) to farm 2.(*adquirir*) to earn II. vr: ~**se** to earn

granjero, -a m, f farmer

grano m 1.(*de cereales, sal, arena*) grain; (*de café*) bean; (*de mostaza*) seed; ~**s** grain; ~ **de uva** grape 2.(*de piel*) spot, pimple 3. TÉC grain; **de** ~ **duro** coarse-grained; **de** ~ **fino** fine-grained ►**aportó su** ~ **de arena** he/she did his/her bit; **de un** ~ (**de arena**) **hace una montaña** he/she always makes a mountain out of a molehill; **apartar el** ~ **de la paja** to separate the wheat from the chaff; **ir al** ~ to get to the point

granoso, -a adj grainy

granuja[1] m 1.(*pilluelo*) rascal 2.(*bribón*) scoundrel; **el muy** ~ **me ha engañado** that scoundrel has cheated me

granuja[2] f 1.(*uva*) grapes pl 2.(*de las frutas*) seeds pl

granujada f 1.(*travesura*) prank 2.(*bribonada*) dirty trick

granujería f 1.(*travesura*) prank 2.(*bribonada*) dirty trick 3.(*de pillos*) bunch of raga-

muffins **4.**(*de bribones*) bunch of scoundrels
granujiento, -a *adj* **1.**(*cara*) spotty, pimply **2.**(*superficie*) grainy
granulación *f* granulation
granulado *m* granules *pl*
granular I. *adj* grainy II. *vt* to granulate
granuloso, -a *adj* grainy
grapa *f* **1.**(*para papeles, madera*) staple **2.**(*licor*) grappa
grapadora *f* stapler
grapar *vt* to staple
grasa¹ *f* **1.** ANAT fat; ~ **de cerdo** pork fat; **cocinar sin** ~ to cook without fat [*o* grease]; **tener mucha** ~ **en los muslos** to have fat thighs **2.** TÉC (*lubricante*) oil, grease **3.**(*mugre*) grime **4.** MIN **las ~s** slag
grasa² *Arg* I. *adj inf, pey* common II. *m inf, pey* **ser un** ~ to be common
grasiento, -a *adj* fatty; (*de aceite*) greasy
graso, -a *adj* **1.**(*grasiento*) fatty; **piel grasa** oily skin; **pelo graso** greasy hair **2.**(*gordo*) fat
gratén *m* GASTR **al** ~ au gratin
gratificación *f* **1.**(*recompensa*) reward; (*sobre objetos perdidos*) compensation **2.**(*del sueldo*) bonus; ~ **de Navidad** Christmas bonus **3.**(*propina*) tip **4.**(*satisfación*) gratification
gratificante *adj* gratifying
gratificar <c→qu> *vt* **1.**(*recompensar*) ~ **a alguien por algo** to reward sb for sth; **se ~á a quien lo encuentre** there is a reward for the finder **2.**(*en el trabajo*) ~ **a alguien** to give sb a bonus **3.**(*complacer*) to gratify
gratinador *m* grill
gratinar *vt* GASTR to cook au gratin, to brown on top
gratis *adv* free
gratitud *f* gratitude
grato, -a *adj* **1.**(*agradable*) pleasant; ~ **al paladar** tasty; **tu novio me ha dado una grata impresión** your boyfriend seems very nice; **tu visita me es muy grata** I'm very glad you could come **2.**(*en una carta*) **me es ~ comunicarle que...** I am pleased to inform you that ...
gratuidad *f* **1.**(*de gratis*) **reclamar la ~ de la enseñanza/la sanidad** to demand free education/health services **2.**(*arbitrariedad*) arbitrariness **3.**(*algo infundado*) unjustified remark
gratuito, -a *adj* **1.**(*gratis*) free **2.**(*arbitrario*) arbitrary **3.**(*infundado*) groundless; **es una acusación gratuita** the accusation is groundless; **este rumor es** ~ this rumour [*o* rumor *Am*] is without foundation; **lo que has hecho ha sido bastante** ~ what you did was quite unnecessary
grava *f* gravel
gravable *adj* taxable
gravamen *m* **1.**(*carga*) burden **2.**(*de los ingresos*) tax
gravar *vt* **1.**(*cargar*) to burden **2.** FIN to tax; ~ **algo con un impuesto** to impose a tax on sth

grave *adj* **1.**(*objeto*) heavy **2.**(*enfermedad*) serious; **está** ~ he/she is very ill **3.**(*persona, situación*) serious; **este es un momento ~ para la industria** this is a difficult time for the industry **4.**(*estilo*) solemn **5.**(*sonido*) deep **6.** LING **acento** ~ grave accent; **palabra** ~ word whose stress falls on the penultimate syllable
gravedad *f* **1.** FÍS gravity; **centro de** ~ centre of gravity **2.** MED seriousness; **estar herido de** ~ to be seriously injured **3.** MÚS (*de los sonidos*) depth **4.**(*de un estilo*) solemnity **5.**(*de una situación, de un asunto*) seriousness
gravidez *f elev* pregnancy
grávido, -a *adj* **1.**(*mujer*) pregnant **2.** *elev* (*cargado*) ~ **de algo** laden with sth
gravilla *f* gravel
gravitación *f* FÍS gravitation
gravitar *vi* **1.** FÍS to gravitate **2.**(*un cuerpo*) ~ **sobre algo** to rest on sth **3.**(*recaer*) ~ **sobre** to loom over
gravitatorio, -a *adj* gravitational
gravoso, -a *adj* **1.**(*pesado*) burdensome **2.**(*costoso*) expensive
graznar *vi* (*cuervo*) to caw; (*ganso*) to honk; (*pato*) to quack
graznido *m* (*de cuervo*) caw; (*de ganso*) honk; (*de pato*) quack
greca *f* **1.**(*adorno*) frieze **2.** *AmL* (*cafetera eléctrica*) coffee machine
Grecia *f* Greece
grecolatino, -a *adj* Greco-Latin
grecorromano, -a *adj* Greco-Roman
greda *f* **1.**(*arcilla*) clay **2.**(*para desengrasar*) fuller's earth
gredal *m* claypit
gregal *adj* gregarious
gregario, -a *adj* **1.**(*persona*) gregarious **2.**(*soldado*) common
gregarismo *m sin pl* gregariousness
gregoriano, -a *adj* Gregorian
greguería *f* uproar, hullabaloo
gremial I. *adj* **1.**(*de una asociación*) relating to an association **2.**(*de un sindicato*) relating to a trade union **3.** HIST guild II. *mf* **1.**(*de una asociación*) association member **2.**(*de un sindicato*) union member
gremialismo *m sin pl* **1.**(*mundo de*) system of associations **2.**(*doctrina*) collectivism **3.**(*tendencia*) tendency to form associations
gremio *m* **1.**(*asociación*) association **2.**(*sindicato*) trade union **3.** HIST guild
greña *f* mop [*o* mat] of hair, rats' tails *pl* ►**andar a la ~ con alguien** to squabble [*o* bicker] with sb
greñudo, -a *adj* (*pelo*) tangled, matted
gres *m* **1.**(*arcilla*) potter's clay **2.**(*producto*) earthenware
gresca *f* **1.**(*bulla*) uproar, racket **2.**(*riña*) quarrel
grial *m* grail
griego, -a *adj, m, f* Greek
grieta *f* **1.**(*en la pared, una taza*) crack; (*en la piel*) chap **2.**(*desacuerdo*) rift

grifa f hash, dope, pot

grifo m 1. TÉC tap Brit, faucet Am; **agua del ~** tap water; **abrir/cerrar el ~** to turn the tap on/off; **he dejado el ~ abierto** I've left the tap running 2.(mitología) griffon 3. Perú, Ecua, Bol (gasolinera) petrol station Brit, gas station Am

grifo, -a adj inf stoned, high (on dope)

grillarse vr 1. inf (persona) to go nuts 2.(tubérculo) to sprout

grillera f 1.(agujero) cricket hole 2.(jaula) cricket cage 3. inf (lugar) **esto es una ~** this place is a madhouse 4.(de la policía) police van

grillete m 1.(cepo) shackle, fetter 2. NÁUT shackle

grillo m 1.(insecto) cricket 2.(de tubérculo) shoot 3. pl (grilletes) shackles pl

grima f **me da ~** (asco) it's disgusting; (dentera) it sets my teeth on edge

grimillón m Chile multitude

gringada f AmL: inf 1.(truco sucio) dirty trick 2.(grupo de gringos) group of gringos

gringo m inf gibberish; **hablar en ~** to talk double Dutch

gringo, -a m, f AmL: inf 1.(persona) gringo (North American or North European) 2.(de EE.UU.) Yank(ee)

gripa f AmL flu, influenza

gripal adj MED flu, influenza

griparse vr TÉC to seize up

gripe f MED flu, influenza

griposo, -a I. adj MED **estar ~** to have the flu II. m, f flu patient

gris I. adj 1.(color) grey Brit, gray Am; **~ marengo** charcoal grey Brit, charcoal gray Am; **de ojos ~es** grey-eyed Brit, gray-eyed Am 2.(persona) boring II. m 1.(color) grey Brit, gray Am 2.(viento) cold wind 3. HIST (policía) member of Spanish National Police

grisáceo, -a, adj greyish Brit, grayish Am

grisma f Chile, Guat, Hond (pizca) pinch

grisú m <grisúes o grisús> MIN firedamp

gritadera f Col, Ven (griterío) loud shouting

gritar I. vt 1.(dar gritos) to shout at; **¡a mí no me grites!** don't you shout at me! 2.(reprender) to tell off 3.(en un concierto) to boo II. vi to shout, to yell

griterío m uproar

grito m shout; **~ de protesta** cry of protest; **pegar un ~** to shout, to yell; **me lo dijo a ~s** he/she told me in a very loud voice; **a ~ limpio** [o **pelado**] at the top of one's voice; **la región está pidiendo a ~s ayuda internacional** the region is crying out for international support ▶ **poner el ~ en el cielo por algo** to raise hell about sth; **ser el último ~** to be the (latest) rage

groenlandés, -esa I. adj Greenland II. m, f Greenlander

Groenlandia f Greenland

grogui adj groggy, half-asleep

grosella f (red)currant

grosería f 1.(descortesía) rudeness 2.(ordinariez) vulgarity 3.(tosquedad) crudeness 4.(estupidez) stupidity 5.(observación) rude comment; (palabrota) swearword

grosero, -a adj 1.(descortés) rude 2.(ordinario) vulgar 3.(tosco) crude

grosor m thickness

grotesco, -a adj grotesque

grúa f 1.(máquina) crane 2.(vehículo) tow truck, breakdown van Brit, wrecker Am

gruesa f (cantidad) gross

grueso m 1.(espesor) thickness 2.(parte principal) main part 3. MED (intestino) large intestine 4. COM **vender en ~** to sell in bulk 5. TIPO downstroke

grueso, -a adj 1.(persona) stout 2.(objeto, tela) thick 3.(mar) **mar gruesa** heavy seas 4.(broma) crude

grulla f crane

grumete m NÁUT cabin boy

grumo m 1.(coágulo) lump; **~ de sangre** blood clot 2.(de lechuga) heart 3.(de planta) shoot

grumoso, -a adj lumpy

gruñido m 1.(de cerdo, persona) grunt 2.(del perro) growl 3. fig (queja) grumble 4.(de puerta) creak

gruñir <3. pret: gruñó> vi 1.(cerdo, person) to grunt 2.(perro) to growl 3. fig (quejarse) to grumble 4.(puerta) to creak

gruñón, -ona I. adj inf grumbling, whingeing II. m, f inf grumbler; **es un viejo ~** he's a grumpy old man

grupa f hindquarters pl; **volver ~s** MIL to turn around

grupal adj group

grupo m 1.(conjunto) group; **~ (industrial)** COM corporation; **~ parlamentario** POL parliamentary group; **~ de presión** POL pressure group; **~ principal** INFOR main group; **trabajo en ~** groupwork 2. TÉC unit

grupúsculo m POL small group

gruta f (artificial) grotto; (natural) cave

guaca f AmL 1.(tumba) tomb 2.(tesoro) buried treasure 3.(hucha) money box; **hacer ~** to make money

guacal m AmC, Col, Ven (calabaza, jícara) gourd

guacamayo m macaw

guacamol(e) m AmL GASTR guacamole

guacamote m Méx manioc

guachada f AmL, inf (canallada) dirty trick

guachimán m AmL (vigilante) watchman

guacho, -a m, f AmS (huérfano) orphan; (expósito) abandoned child

guadal m Arg sandy bog

guadalajareño, -a I. adj of/from Guadalajara II. m, f native/inhabitant of Guadalajara

guadaña f 1.(herramienta) scythe 2.(muerte) **la Guadaña** the Grim Reaper

guadañar vt to scythe

guagua f 1. AmC (autobús) bus 2. CSur (bebé) baby 3.(trivialidad) trifle

guajiro, -a I. *adj* peasant II. *m, f Cuba* white peasant

gualdo, -a *adj* yellow; **la bandera roja y gualda** the Spanish flag

guamazo *m Méx* punch

guamúchil *m Méx* (*planta*) camachile

guanábano *m AmL* (*árbol*) soursop tree; (*fruta*) custard apple

guanaco *m* (*mamífero*) guanaco

guanaco, -a I. *adj AmL* (*tonto*) simple; (*lento*) slow II. *m, f* 1. *AmL* (*tonto*) simpleton 2. *AmC, pey* native of El Salvador

guanajo, -a *m, f Cuba, PRico* 1. (*pavo*) turkey 2. (*bobo*) fool, idiot

guanche *m* 1. (*persona*) original inhabitant of the Canary Islands 2. HIST (*lengua*) language of the original inhabitants of the Canary Islands

guandoca *f Col* (*cárcel*) prison

guango, -a *adj Méx* baggy

guano *m* 1. (*excrementos*) guano 2. *CSur* (*estiércol*) dung

guantada *f* slap; **dar una ~ a alguien** to slap sb

guantazo *m v.* **guantada**

guante *m* glove; **~ cibernético** INFOR data glove ▸ **colgar los ~s** (*boxeador*) to hang up one's gloves; (*futbolista*) to hang up one's boots; **le echaron el ~ al ladrón** they caught the thief; **ir** [*o* **sentar**] **como un ~** to fit like a glove; **recoger el ~** to take up the challenge

guantear *vt AmL* (*abofetear*) to slap (around)

guantelete *m* gauntlet

guantera *f* AUTO glove box [*o* compartment]

guantero, -a *m, f* glovemaker

guapear *vi inf* 1. (*ostentar*) to dress showily 2. (*fanfarronear*) to boast about, to swank *Brit*

guaperas I. *adj inf* good-looking II. *m inv, inf* heart-throb; **va de ~** he thinks he's a real heart-throb

guaperío *m* **el ~** the jet set

guapeza *f* 1. (*aspecto: en general*) good looks *pl*; (*de mujer*) prettiness; (*de hombre*) handsomeness 2. (*en los vestidos*) elegance 3. (*valentonería*) bravery; *pey* bravado 4. *pey* flashiness

guapo *m* 1. (*galán*) handsome man 2. *AmL, pey* (*pendenciero*) bully

guapo, -a *adj* 1. (*atractivo: en general*) good-looking; (*de mujer*) pretty; (*de hombre*) handsome 2. (*en el vestir*) **estar** [*o* **ir**] **~** to look smart 3. *AmL* (*valiente*) brave

guaquero, -a *m, f AmL* graverobber; (*ilegal*) plunderer (*person who digs for ancient Indian archaeological valuables*)

guaraca *f AmL* (*honda*) catapult; (*látigo*) whip

guaraná *f PRico* BOT guaraná, paullinia

guarangada *f AmL* (*grosería*) rude comment

guaraní *adj, m* Guaraní

guarapo *m AmL* (*jugo*) sugar-cane juice; (*bebida*) sugar-cane liquor

guarapón *m AmS* broad-brimmed hat

guarda¹ *mf* guard; **~ forestal** forester *Brit,* forest ranger *Am;* (*cuidador*) custodian, keeper; **~ jurado** security guard

guarda² *f* 1. (*acto*) guarding, safekeeping 2. (*protección*) protection 3. (*de un libro*) flyleaf 4. (*de la ley*) observance 5. *pl* (*de llave*) guard; (*de cerradura*) ward 6. *pl* (*de abanico*) outer ribs *pl*

guardabarrera *mf* crossing [*o* gate] keeper

guardabarros *m inv* mudguard *Brit,* fender *Am*

guardabosque(s) *mf* (*inv*) 1. (*de caza*) gamekeeper 2. (*guarda forestal*) forester *Brit,* forest ranger *Am*

guardacostas *m inv* coastguard

guardaespaldas *mf inv* bodyguard

guardagujas *mf inv* FERRO pointsman *m,* pointswoman *f Brit,* switchman *m,* switchwoman *m Am*

guardameta *mf* DEP goaltender, goalkeeper

guardapolvo *m* (*mono*) overalls *pl*

guardar I. *vt* 1. (*vigilar*) to guard 2. (*proteger*) to protect 3. (*ley*) to observe 4. (*conservar*) to keep; **~ un sitio** to keep a place; **~ un trozo de pastel a alguien** to save a piece of cake for sb; **guárdame esto, que ahora vengo** keep this for me, I'll be back soon [*o* right back] 5. (*poner*) **¿dónde has guardado las servilletas?** where did you put the serviettes?; **~ el dinero en el banco** to keep money in the bank; **~ algo en el bolsillo** to put sth in one's pocket 6. (*quedarse con*) to keep 7. (*ahorrar*) to save; **~ las fuerzas** to save one's strength 8. INFOR to save II. *vr:* **~se** 1. (*evitar*) **~se de hacer algo** to be careful not to do sth 2. (*protegerse*) **~se de algo/alguien** to be on one's guard against sth/sb

guardarropa¹ *m* 1. (*cuarto*) cloakroom *Brit,* checkroom *Am* 2. (*armario*) wardrobe

guardarropa² *mf* 1. (*de vestuario*) cloakroom attendant *Brit,* checkroom attendant *Am* 2. TEAT (*guardarropía*) wardrobe

guardarropía *f* 1. TEAT (*accesorios*) props *pl* 2. TEAT (*cuarto*) wardrobe ▸ **de ~** make-believe

guardería *f* (*centro educativo*) nursery; (*en hipermercado*) crèche

guardia¹ *f* 1. (*vigilancia*) duty; **¿cuál es la farmacia de ~?** which chemist is on the emergency rota? *Brit,* which pharmacy is open 24 hours? *Am;* **estar de ~** to be on duty; MIL to be on guard duty 2. (*protección*) **estar en ~** to be on one's guard; **poner a alguien en ~** to put sb on his/her guard 3. DEP guard; **bajar la ~** to lower one's guard; **en ~** (*esgrima*) en garde 4. (*instituciones*) **la Guardia Civil** the Civil Guard; **~ municipal** [*o* **urbana**] local police

guardia² *mf* **~ civil** civil guard; **~ municipal** [*o* **urbano**] local policeman; **~ de tráfico** traffic policeman *m,* traffic policewoman *f*

guardián, -ana *m, f* 1. (*protector*) guardian; **perro ~** watchdog 2. (*en el zoo*) (zoo)keeper

guardilla *f* 1. (*habitación*) attic room 2. (*ven-*

tana) attic window **3.** (*buhardilla*) attic, garret

guarecer *irr como crecer* **I.** *vt* **1.** (*proteger*) to protect **2.** (*albergar*) to shelter; **lo guarecí en mi casa** I took him in **3.** (*curar*) to cure **II.** *vr:* ~**se** (*cobijarse*) to take refuge; ~**se de la lluvia** to take shelter from the rain

guarida *f* **1.** (*de animales*) den, lair **2.** (*refugio*) hideout

guarismo *m* MAT numeral; (*cifra*) cipher

guarnecer *irr como crecer* *vt* **1.** (*adornar*) ~ **algo con** [*o* **de**] **algo** to adorn sth with sth; GASTR to garnish sth with sth; (*vestido*) to trim sth with sth **2.** MIL (*ciudad*) to garrison **3.** (*equipar*) ~ **con** [*o* **de**] **algo** to equip with sth; (*proveer*) to provide with sth

guarnición *f* **1.** GASTR *accompaniment to a main dish;* (*adorno*) garnish; **chuletas de cordero con** ~ (**de patatas y ensalada**) lamb chops served with salad and potatoes **2.** (*adorno*) adornment; (*en vestido*) trimming; (*en joya*) setting **3.** MIL garrison **4.** *pl* (*arreos*) harness

guarrada *f inf* **1.** (*mala pasada*) dirty trick **2.** (*palabras*) swear [*o* dirty] word(s) **3.** (*asquerosidad*) **ser una** ~ (*sucio*) to be filthy; (*asqueroso*) to be disgusting; **¡qué ~ de baño!** what a filthy bathroom!; **¡qué ~ de fotografía!** what a disgusting photograph!

guarrería *f v.* **guarrada**

guarro, -a I. *adj* **1.** (*cosa*) disgusting; **chiste ~** dirty joke **2.** (*persona*) dirty; (*moralmente*) smutty **II.** *m, f* pig

guasa *f* **1.** (*burla*) joke; **estar de ~** to be joking; **tiene ~ que...** +*subj* it's ironic that ... **2.** (*sosería*) dullness

guasanga *f AmL* (*bullanga*) hubbub

guasca *f AmL* (*látigo*) whip

guasearse *vr* to joke; ~ **de alguien/algo** to make fun of sb/sth

guasería *f Arg, Chile* (*grosería*) rudeness, obscenity

guaso, -a *adj CSur* **1.** (*rústico*) peasant **2.** (*tosco*) coarse

guasón, -ona *m, f* joker

guata *f* **1.** (*algodón*) cotton padding **2.** *AmL* (*barriga*) belly

guate *m AmC, Méx: maize stalks used for fodder*

Guatemala *f* Guatemala

> **Guatemala** (official title: **República de Guatemala**) lies in Central America. The capital is also called **Guatemala**. The official language of the country is Spanish and the monetary unit of **Guatemala** is the **quezal**.

guatemalteco, -a *adj, m, f* Guatemalan

guateque *m inf* party

guatero *m Chile* hot-water bottle

guau *interj* (*perro*) woof, bow-wow; (*persona*) wow

guay *adj inf* great, cool

guayaba *f* **1.** (*fruto*) guava **2.** (*jalea*) guava jelly **3.** *AmL* (*mentira*) lie

guayabo *m* guava tree

guayacán *m AmL* BOT lignum-vitae tree

Guayana *f* Guyana

guayanés, -esa *adj, m, f* Guyanese

guayar I. *vt Ant* to grate **II.** *vr:* ~**se** *PRico* to get drunk

gubernamental *adj* **1.** (*relativo a*) governmental **2.** (*partidario*) loyalist

gubernativo, -a *adj* governmental; **policía gubernativa** national police

gubia *f* TÉC gouge

guepardo *m* cheetah

güero, -a I. *adj AmL* (*rubio: pelo, persona*) blond(e); (*tez*) fair **II.** *m, f AmL* (*rubio*) blond *m,* blonde *f*

guerra *f* war; **la ~ civil española** the Spanish Civil War; **la ~ de las galaxias** star wars; ~ **de precios/tarifas** price/tariff war; ~ **santa** holy war; **la Primera/Segunda Guerra Mundial** the First/Second World War; ~ **química/psicológica/biológica** chemical/psychological/biological warfare; **ir a la ~** to go to war; **estar en pie de ~** to be on a war footing; **tener la ~ declarada a alguien** *inf* to have it in for sb; **dar mucha ~** *inf* to be a real handful; **en ~** at war

guerrear *vi* **1.** (*hacer guerra*) to wage war **2.** (*resistir*) to resist

guerrera *f* trench coat

guerrero, -a I. *adj* **1.** (*de guerra*) warlike **2.** (*travieso*) naughty **3.** (*revoltoso*) rebellious **II.** *m, f* warrior

guerrilla *f* **1.** (*guerra*) guerrilla warfare **2.** (*partida*) guerrilla band

guerrillear *vi* to wage guerrilla warfare

guerrillero, -a *m, f* guerrilla (fighter)

gueto *m* ghetto

guía¹ *mf* (*de un grupo*) guide; ~ **turístico** tourist guide

guía² *f* **1.** MIL scout **2.** (*manillar*) handlebar

guía³ *f* **1.** (*pauta*) guidance, guideline **2.** (*persona*) guide **3.** (*manual*) handbook; ~ **comercial** trade directory; ~ **de ferrocarriles** railway [*o* railroad *Am*] timetable; ~ **telefónica** telephone directory, phone book *Am;* ~ **turística** travel guide(book) **4.** (*de planta*) main stem **5.** TÉC guide **6.** (*del bigote*) end **7.** *PRico* (*volante*) steering wheel **8.** *pl* (*riendas*) reins *pl*

guiar <*1. pres:* guío> **I.** *vt* **1.** (*a alguien*) to guide **2.** (*conversación*) to direct **3.** (*planta*) to train **II.** *vr* ~**se por algo** to be guided by sth; **me guío por mi instinto** I follow my instincts

guija *f* pebble

guijarro *m* **1.** (*canto*) pebble **2.** *pl* (*en playa*) pebbles *pl*

guijo *m* gravel

guillarse *vr inf* **1.** (*chiflarse*) to go nuts **2.** (*irse*) **guillárselas** to beat it

guillotina *f* **1.** (*de ejecución, para papel*) guillotine **2.** TÉC **ventana de ~** sash window

guillotinar *vt* to guillotine

guinda *f* **1.**(*fruta*) morello cherry **2.**NÁUT (*de arboladura*) height **3.** *inf*(*remate*) **poner la ~ a algo** to top sth off; **y la ~ fue que...** and the best bit was that ...

guindilla *f* GASTR chilli pepper *Brit*, chili pepper *Am*

guindo *m* (*árbol*) (morello) cherry tree ▸**caerse del ~** *inf* to catch [*o* cotton] on; **subirse al ~** *inf* to have one's head in the clouds

guineo *m AmL* (*banana*) banana

guiñapo *m* **1.**(*trapo*) rag **2.**(*andrajoso*) bedraggled person; **estar hecho un ~** to be a wreck **3.**(*degradado*) down-and-out **4.**(*debilucho*) weakling

guiñar I. *vt* **~ el ojo a alguien** to wink at sb **II.** *vi* **1.**(*con el ojo*) to wink **2.**NÁUT to yaw

guiño *m* wink; **hacer un ~ a alguien** to wink at sb

guiñol *m* **1.**(*teatro*) puppet show **2.**(*títere*) puppet

guión *m* **1.**CINE, TV script **2.**(*de una conferencia*) outline **3.**LING (*de compuesto, al fin de renglón*) hyphen; (*en diálogo*) dash **4.**(*persona*) scriptwriter **5.**(*real*) standard **6.**(*de procesión*) banner

guionista *mf* CINE screenwriter; TV scriptwriter

guipar *vt inf* **1.**(*ver*) to see, to spot **2.**(*entender*) to catch on to, to see through

guipuzcoano, -a I. *adj* of/from Guipuzcoa **II.** *m, f* native/inhabitant of Guipuzcoa

guiri *mf* *pey* **1.**(*extranjero*) foreigner **2.**(*guardia*) civil guard

guirigay *m* <guirigayes *o* gurigáis> *inf* **1.**(*lenguaje*) gibberish **2.**(*griterío*) uproar **3.**(*barullo*) hubbub

guirlache *m* (hard) nougat

guirnalda *f* garland

guisa *f* **a ~ de** like; **de tal ~** in such a way; **no puedes hacerlo de esta ~** you can't do it like that

guisado *m* stew

guisante *m* pea

guisar I. *vt* **1.**(*cocinar*) to cook; (*con salsa*) to stew, to braise **2.**(*tramar*) to prepare **II.** *vr:* **~se** to cook; **se está guisando** it's cooking; **tú te lo guisas, tú te lo comes** *prov* as you make your bed so must you lie in it *prov*

guiso *m* **1.**(*plato*) dish **2.**(*en salsa*) stew

guisote *m pey* poor quality stew, concoction

güisqui *m* whisky *Brit*, whiskey *Am*

guita *f* **1.**(*cuerda*) twine, packthread **2.** *inf* (*dinero*) dough, curd

guitarra *f* (*instrumento*) guitar ▸**venir como una ~ en un entierro** to be completely out of place; **chafar la ~ a alguien** to mess it up for sb

guitarrero, -a *m, f* **1.**(*fabricante*) guitar maker **2.**(*guitarrista*) guitarist

guitarrista *mf* guitarist

güito *m* **1.** *inf* (*sombrero*) hat **2.**(*de albaricoque*) stone

gula *f* gluttony

gulasch *m* goulash

guripa *m inf* **1.**(*soldado*) soldier **2.**(*guardia*) policeman, cop *Am* **3.**(*golfo*) rogue

gurrumino *m* henpecked husband

gurrumino, -a *adj* **1.**(*tacaño*) stingy, mean *Brit* **2.**(*pequeño*) puny

gurú *m* guru

gusanillo *m* worm ▸**entrarle a uno el ~ de algo** *inf* to get the bug [*o* an irresistible urge] for sth; **matar el ~** *inf*(*comiendo*) to kill one's hunger; (*bebiendo*) to quench one's thirst

gusano *m* **1.**(*lombriz*) worm; **~ de tierra** earthworm; **~ de luz** glow-worm **2.**(*oruga*) caterpillar **3.**(*larva de mosca*) maggot **4.** *fig* (*persona despreciable*) worm

gustar I. *vi* **1.**(*agradar*) **me gusta nadar/el helado** I like swimming/ice cream; **me gustan estos zapatos** I like this shoes; **¿te gusta estar aquí?** do you like it here?; **¡así me gusta!** well done!; **como Ud. guste** as you wish; **cuando guste** whenever you like [*o* want] **2.**(*apasionarse*) **~ de** +*infin* to enjoy **3.**(*atraer*) **me gusta tu hermano** I fancy your brother **4.**(*querer*) **me gustas** I like you **5.**(*condicional*) **me ~ía saber...** I would like to know ... **II.** *vt* (*probar*) to taste

gustativo, -a *adj* taste

gustazo *m* **1.**(*placer*) great pleasure; **tuve el ~ de darle la mano** I had the great pleasure of shaking his/her hand; **darse el ~ de algo** to treat oneself to sth **2.**(*ante una desgracia*) satisfaction

gustillo *m* **1.**(*sabor*) aftertaste, tang **2.**(*sensación*) kick; **da ~ ver que le regañan a ella también** I get a kick out of seeing her criticised for a change

gusto *m* **1.**(*sentido*) taste; **una broma de mal ~** a joke in bad taste; **no hago nada a su ~** nothing I do pleases him/her; **lo ha hecho a mi ~** he/she did it to my satisfaction; **sobre ~s no hay nada escrito** there's no accounting for tastes **2.**(*sabor*) taste, flavour *Brit*, flavor *Am;* **~ a algo** taste of sth; **huevos al ~** eggs cooked to order **3.**(*placer*) pleasure; **con ~** with pleasure; **~s caros** expensive tastes *pl;* **coger ~ a algo** to take [*o* develop] a liking to sth; **encontrar ~ en algo** to find enjoyment in sth; **derretirse de ~** to swoon with pleasure; **estar a ~** to feel comfortable; **tanto ~ en conocerla – el ~ es mío** pleased to meet you – the pleasure is all mine; **hago lo que me viene en ~** I do what I please; **cantan que da ~** they sing wonderfully

gustoso, -a *adj* **1.**(*sabroso*) tasty, savoury *Brit*, savory *Am* **2.**(*con gusto*) **te acompañaré ~** I'd be glad to accompany you **3.**(*agradable*) pleasant

gutapercha *f* gutta-percha

gutural *adj* guttural, throaty

gym-jazz *m* DEP jazz gymnastics *pl*

gymkhana *f* gymkhana

H

H, h *f* H, h; ~ **de Huelva** H for Harry *Brit,* H for How *Am*

ha *interj* ah, ha; ¡~, ~! Ha, ha!

haba *f* broad bean ►**son ~s** contadas there's no doubt about it; **en todas partes** cuecen **~s** *prov* it's the same the world over

Habana *f* **La ~** Havana

habanero, -a *adj, m, f* Havanan

habano *m* (*cigar*) Havana cigar

haber *irr* **I.** *aux* **1.** (*en tiempos compuestos*) to have; **ha ido al cine** he/she has gone to the cinema; **he comprado el periódico** I've bought the newspaper **2.** (*de obligación*) ~ **de hacer algo** to have to do sth; **has de hacerlo** (*sin falta*) you must do it; **han de esforzarse más** they must make more of an effort **3.** (*futuro*) **han de llegar pronto** they will [*o* should] be here soon **4.** (*imperativo*) **no tengo sitio** − ¡~ **venido antes!** there's no room − you should have come earlier! **II.** *vimpers* **1.** (*ocurrir*) **ha habido un terremoto en Japón** there has been an earthquake in Japan; **¿qué hay?** what's the news?; **¿qué hay, Pepe?** how's it going, Pepe? **2.** (*efectuarse*) to take place; **hoy no hay cine** the cinema is closed today; **ayer hubo reunión** there was a meeting yesterday; **después habrá baile** there'll be a dance afterwards **3.** (*existir*) **aquí no hay agua** there is no water here; **eso es todo...** ¡**y ya no hay más!** that's all ... and nothing more!; **¿hay algo entre tú y ella?** is there something going on between you two?; **hay poca gente que...** there are few people who ...; **hay quien cree que...** some people think that ...; **¡muchas gracias!** − **no hay de qué** thanks a lot! − not at all; **no hay quien me gane al ping-pong** nobody can beat me at table tennis **4.** (*hallarse, estar*) **hay un cuadro en la pared** there is a painting on the wall; **había un papel en el suelo** there was a piece of paper on the floor; **no hay leche/platos en la mesa** there is no milk/there are no plates on the table; **¿había mucha gente?** where there many people? **5.** (*tiempo*) **había una vez...** once there was ... **6.** (*obligatoriedad*) **¡hay que ver cómo están los precios!** my God! look at those prices!; **hay que trabajar más** we have to work harder; **no hay que olvidar que...** we must not forget that ... **III.** *vt* **compra cuantos sellos pueda** − buy as many stamps as you can **IV.** *vr* **habérselas con alguien** to be up against sb **V.** *m* **1.** (*capital*) assets *pl;* **tener algo en su ~** *fig* to have sth to one's credit **2.** (*en cuenta corriente*) balance, account; **pasaré la cantidad a tu ~** I'll pay the amount into your account **3.** *pl* (*emolumentos*) assets *pl*

habichuela *f* (kidney) bean; (*judía blanca*) haricot bean

hábil *adj* **1.** (*diestro*) skilled; **ser ~ para algo**

to be skilled at sth **2.** (*en el oficio*) **ser ~ en algo** to be good at sth **3.** (*astuto*) shrewd; **una respuesta ~** a clever response **4.** JUR working; **días ~es** working days

habilidad *f* **1.** (*destreza*) skill; **no tengo gran ~ con las manos** I'm not very skilful with my hands **2.** (*facultad*) ability **3.** (*astucia*) shrewdness **4.** (*gracia*) grace; **se mueve con ~** she moves gracefully

habilidoso, -a *adj* **1.** (*diestro*) skilful, able **2.** (*astuto*) shrewd **3.** (*gracioso*) graceful

habilitación *f* **1.** JUR (*de personas*) ~ **para algo** entitlement to sth **2.** (*de empleo*) paymaster's duties **3.** (*oficina*) paymaster's office **4.** (*de un espacio*) fitting out

habilitar *vt* **1.** (*a personas*) to train, to teach; JUR to entitle, to empower; (*documentos*) to authorize **2.** COM (*dar capital*) to fund, to finance **3.** (*proveer*) ~ **de algo** to provide with sth; ~ **horas de visita** to provide with visiting hours **4.** (*espacio*) to fit out

habiloso, -a *adj AmL* **1.** (*hábil*) skilled, skilful *Brit,* skillful *Am* **2.** (*astuto*) shrewd

habitabilidad *f sin pl* habitability

habitable *adj* liveable

habitación *f* **1.** (*cuarto*) room; (*dormitorio*) bedroom; ~ **individual** single room **2.** (*vivienda*) dwelling **3.** (*acción*) living

habitáculo *m* **1.** (*vivienda*) dwelling **2.** ECOL (*espacio*) habitat **3.** AUTO interior

habitante *mf* inhabitant; **¿cuántos habitantes tiene Madrid?** what is the population of Madrid?

habitar **I.** *vi* to live **II.** *vt* to live in; **hace tiempo que habita en Escocia** he/she has been living in Scotland for some time now

hábitat *m* <hábitats> habitat

hábito *m* **1.** (*costumbre*) habit; **he dejado el ~ de fumar** I gave up smoking **2.** REL (*sotana*) habit; (*orden*) insignia ►**el ~ no hace al** monje *prov* clothes don't make the man

habitual *adj* regular; **cliente ~** regular client; **bebedor ~** habitual drinker; **lo dijo con su ironía ~** he said it with his customary irony

habituar <1. *pres:* habitúo> *vt, vr* ~**(se) a algo** to get used to sth

habla *f* **1.** (*facultad*) speech, diction; **quedarse sin ~** to be left speechless **2.** (*acto*) speech; **un país de ~ inglesa** an English-speaking country; **¡Juan al ~!** TEL Juan speaking! **3.** (*manera, dialecto*) way of speaking

hablado, -a *adj* spoken; **bien ~** well-spoken; **el francés ~** spoken French; **ser mal ~** to be foul-mouthed

hablador(a) **I.** *adj* talkative **II.** *m(f)* **1.** (*cotorra*) chatterbox **2.** (*chismoso*) gossip

habladuría *f* rumour *Brit,* rumor *Am;* **~s** gossip

hablante *mf* speaker

hablantina *f Col, Ven* talkative

hablar **I.** *vi* **1.** (*decir*) to speak, to talk; **~ a gritos** to shout; **~ alto/bajo** to speak loudly/ softly; **~ entre dientes** to mutter; **déjeme**

terminar de ~ let me finish; ~ **claro** to speak frankly; **el autor no habla de este tema** the author does not address this topic; **la policía le ha hecho** ~ the police have made him talk; **los números hablan por sí solos** the figures speak for themselves; **¡no ~ás en serio!** you must be joking!; **por no ~ de...** not to mention ...; **¡y no se hable más!** and that's an end to it; **¡ni ~!** no way! **2.** (*conversar*) ~ **con alguien** to talk to sb; ~ **con franqueza** to talk sincerely; ~ **por teléfono** to talk on the telephone; **no he podido** ~ **con él** I haven't managed to speak to him; ~ **por los codos** *inf* to talk nineteen to the dozen **II.** *vt* **1.** (*idioma*) to speak **2.** (*decir*) to say; ~ **a alguien** (*de algo/ alguien*) to talk to sb (about sth/sb); **no me habló en toda la noche** he/she didn't say a word all night **3.** (*asunto*) **lo hablaré con tu padre** I'll talk about it with your father **III.** *vr:* **~se** to talk to each other; **no se hablan** they are not on speaking terms; **no se habla con su madre** he/she doesn't talk to his/her mother; **nos hablamos de tú** we are on familiar terms

hablilla *f* rumour *Brit,* rumor *Am*

hablista *mf* elegant speaker

hacedero, -a *adj* practicable, feasible

hacedor(a) *m(f)* **1.** (*creador*) maker, creator; **el Hacedor** REL the Maker **2.** (*de una hacienda*) administrator

hacendado, -a I. *adj* landowning **II.** *m, f* **1.** (*de una hacienda*) landowner **2.** *AmS* (*de ganado*) livestock farmer, rancher *Am*

hacendoso, -a *adj* hard-working

hacer *irr* **I.** *vt* **1.** (*producir*) to make; (*coche,*) to manufacture; **la casa está hecha de madera** the house is made of wood; **Dios hizo al hombre** God created man **2.** (*realizar*) to do; (*libro*) to write; **¿qué hacemos hoy?** what shall we do today?; ~ **una llamada** to make a phone call; **demuestra lo que sabes** ~ show us what you can do; **hazlo por mí** do it for me; **a medio** ~ half-finished; **hicimos la trayectoria en tres horas** we did the journey in three hours; **¡Dios mío, qué has hecho!** my God! what have you done?; **lo hecho, hecho está** there's no use crying over spilt milk; **puedes** ~ **lo que quieras** you can do whatever you want; **¿qué haces por aquí?** what are you doing round here?; **¡me la has hecho!** you've let me in for it; **la ha hecho buena** he's/she's really messed things up **3.** (*pregunta*) to ask; (*observación*) to make; (*discurso*) to make, to give **4.** (*ocasionar: ruido*) to make; (*daño*) to cause; ~ **destrozos** to wreak havoc; ~ **sombra** to cast a shadow; **no puedes** ~**me esto** you can't do this to me **5.** (*construir*) to build **6.** (*procurar*) to make; **¿puedes** ~**me sitio?** can you fit me in? **7.** (*transformar*) ~ **pedazos algo** to smash sth up; **estás hecho un hombre** you're a man now; **¿quién te hace el pelo?** who does your hair? **8.** (*conseguir: dinero, amigos*) to make

9. (*llegar*) ~ **puerto** to enter harbour *Brit* [*o* harbor *Am*]; ~ **noche en...** to spend the night in ... **10.** (*más sustantivo*) ~ **el amor** to make love; ~ **caso a alguien** to pay heed to sb; ~ **cumplidos** to pay compliments; ~ **deporte** to do sport; ~ **frente a algo/alguien** to face up to sth/sb; ~ **la maleta** to pack; ~ **uso de algo** to make use of sth **11.** (*más verbo*) ~ **creer algo a alguien** to make [*o* have] sb believe sth; ~ **venir a alguien** to make sb come; **hazle pasar** let him in; **no me hagas contarlo** don't make me say it **12.** (*limpiar*) **hacer las escaleras** *inf* to do the steps **13.** TEAT ~ **una obra** to do [*o* put on] a play; ~ **el papel de Antígona** to play the role of Antigone **14.** ENS (*carrera*) to study, to do; **¿haces francés o inglés?** are you doing French or English? **15.** GASTR (*comida, pastel*) to make; (*patatas*) to do; **quiero la carne bien hecha** I want the meat well done **II.** *vi* **1.** (*convenir*) **eso no hace al caso** that's not relevant **2.** (*oficio*) ~ **de algo** to work as sth **3.** (*con preposición*) **por lo que hace a Juan...** as regards Juan ...; **hizo como que no me vio** he pretended he hadn't seen me **III.** *vr:* ~**se 1.** (*volverse*) to become; ~**se del Madrid** to become a Madrid supporter **2.** (*crecer*) to grow **3.** (*simular*) to pretend; **se hace a todo** he's always pretending; **hacerse el sueco** to pretend not to hear; ~**se la víctima** to act like a victim **4.** (*habituarse*) ~**se a algo** to get used to sth **5.** (*dejarse hacer*) ~**se una foto** to have one's picture taken **6.** (*conseguir*) ~**se respetar** to instill respect; ~**se con el poder** to seize power **7.** (*resultar*) to be; **se me hace muy difícil creer eso** it's very difficult for me to believe that **IV.** *vimpers* **1.** (*tiempo*) **hace frío/calor** it is cold/hot; **hoy hace un buen día** it's a nice day today **2.** (*temporal*) **hace tres días** three days ago; **no hace mucho** not long ago; **desde hace un día** since yesterday

hacha *f* **1.** (*herramienta*) axe, hatchet **2.** (*antorcha*) torch **3.** (*vela*) large candle ▸**ser un** ~ **en algo** to be brilliant [*o* an ace] at sth

hachazo *m* stroke of the axe

hache *f* H, h; **la** ~ the letter h ▸**por** ~ **o por be** for one reason [*o* thing] or another

hachear *vt* to cut (with an axe), to chop

hachero *m* **1.** (*candelero*) torch stand, candleholder **2.** (*persona*) woodcutter, lumberjack

hachís *m* hashish

hacia *prep* **1.** (*dirección*) towards, to; **el pueblo está más** ~ **el sur** the village lies further to the south; **el pueblo está yendo** ~ **Valencia** the village is on the way to Valencia; **fuimos** ~ **allí** we went that way; **vino** ~ **mí** he/she came towards me **2.** (*cerca de*) near **3.** (*respecto a*) regarding

hacienda *f* **1.** (*finca*) country estate **2.** (*bienes*) ~ **pública** public finance

Hacienda *f* (*ministerio*) the Treasury, the Exchequer *Brit;* (*administración*) the Inland Revenue; **el Ministro de Economía y** ~ the

Chancellor of the Exchequer; **¿pagas mucho a ~?** do you pay a lot of tax?

hacinamiento *m* 1.(*de haces*) piling 2.(*de objetos*) stacking; (*de personas*) (over)crowding

hacinar I. *vt* to pile II. *vr:* ~**se** (*personas*) to (over)crowd; (*objetos*) to stack

hacker *mf* (*pirata informático*) hacker

hada *f* fairy; **cuento de ~s** fairy tale; **~ madrina** fairy godmother

hado *m* fate

Haití *m* Haiti

haitiano, -a *adj, m, f* Haitian

hala *interj* 1.(*sorpresa*) well, well 2.(*prisa*) come on

halagador(a) *adj* flattering

halagar <g→gu> *vt* to flatter

halago *m* 1.(*acción*) flattery 2.(*palabras*) flattering words *pl*, compliment

halagüeño, -a *adj* 1.(*halagador*) flattering 2.(*prometedor*) encouraging

halcón *m* 1. ZOOL falcon 2. POL hawk

halconero, -a *m, f* falconer

hálito *m* 1.(*aliento*) breath 2.(*vapor*) steam 3. *elev* (*viento*) breeze

hall *m* hall

hallar I. *vt* 1.(*encontrar*) to find; (*sin buscar*) to come across 2.(*inventar*) to invent 3.(*averiguar*) to check 4.(*darse cuenta*) to realize 5.(*tierra*) to discover II. *vr:* ~**se** 1.(*sitio*) to be 2.(*estado*) to feel; **no me hallo a gusto aquí** I don't feel comfortable here; **se halló con la resistencia de su partido** he met opposition from his party

hallazgo *m* 1. discovery 2. *pl* findings *pl*

halo *m* halo

halógeno *m* halogen

haltera *f* DEP weight, dumbbell

halterofilia *f* DEP weightlifting

halterófilo, -a *m, f* DEP weightlifter

hamaca *f* 1.(*cama*) hammock 2.(*tumbona*) deckchair 3. *AmL* (*mecedora*) rocking chair

hamacar <c→qu> *vt, vr:* ~(**se**) *AmS, Guat* to rock

hambre *f* 1.(*apetito*) hunger; **huelga de ~** hunger strike; **matar el ~** to kill one's hunger; **me ha entrado** (el) **~** I'm getting hungry; **morirse de ~** to die of hunger; **tener ~** to be hungry 2.(*de la población*) starvation 3.(*deseo*) **~ de algo** longing for sth; **~ de poder** hunger for power ►**a buen ~ no hay pan duro** *prov* hunger is the best sauce; **ser más listo que el ~** to be no fool

hambrear *vi AmL* 1.(*hacer pasar hambre*) to starve 2.(*mendigar*) to be hungry

hambriento, -a *adj* 1.(*con hambre*) hungry 2.(*muerto de hambre*) starving 3.(*deseoso*) **estar ~ de poder** to be hungry for power

hambrón, -ona *m, f pey* glutton

hambruna *f AmL* famine

hamburguesa *f* GASTR hamburger; **~ con queso** cheeseburger

hamburguesería *f* hamburger bar

hampa *f* 1.(*gente*) underworld 2.(*modo de vida*) criminal class

hampón *m* 1.(*maleante*) crook 2.(*valentón*) thug

hamster *m* hamster

handicap *m* handicap

hangar *m* AVIAT hangar

haragán, -ana *m, f* loafer

haraganear *vi* to loaf around

haraganería *f* loafing around

harakiri *m* hara-kiri

harapiento, -a *adj* ragged, in tatters

harapo *m* rag

hardware *m* hardware

harem *m*, **harén** *m* harem

harina *f* 1. GASTR flour; **~ integral** wholemeal [*o* wholewheat *Am*] flour; **~ de trigo** wheat flour 2.(*polvo*) powder ►**esto es ~ de otro costal** this is a horse of a different colour *Brit* [*o* color *Am*]

harinear *vimpers Ven* to drizzle

harinoso, -a *adj* 1.(*parecido a la harina*) floury 2.(*con harina*) with flour

harmonía *f* harmony

harnero *m* sieve

hartar *irr* I. *vt* 1.(*saciar*) **~ a alguien** to give sb their fill 2.(*fastidiar*) **me harta con sus chistes** I'm getting sick of his/her jokes II. *vr:* ~**se** 1.(*saciarse*) to eat one's fill; (*en exceso*) to eat too much 2.(*cansarse*) to get fed up; ~**se de reír** to laugh oneself silly; **me he hartado del tiempo que hace en Escocia** I'm sick of [*o* fed up with] this weather in Scotland

hartazgo *m* glut; **darse un ~** (**de dulces**) to have a binge (on the sweets); **tengo un ~ de televisión** I've been watching too much television

harto, -a I. *adj* 1.(*repleto*) full; (*en exceso*) too full 2.(*sobrado*) **tengo hartas razones** I have plenty of reasons 3.(*cansado*) **estar ~ de alguien/algo** to be sick of [*o* fed up with] sb/sth II. *adv* (*sobrado*) (more than) enough; (*muy*) a lot of

hartura *f* (over)abundance

hasta I. *prep* 1.(*de lugar*) to; **te llevo ~ la estación** I'll give you a lift to the station; **volamos ~ Madrid** we're flying to Madrid; **~ cierto punto** to a certain degree, up to a point 2.(*de tiempo*) until, up to until; **~ ahora** up to now; **~ el próximo año** up until next year 3.(*en despedidas*) **¡~ luego!** see you later!; **¡~ la vista!** see you again!; **¡~ la próxima!** until next time! II. *adv* even III. *conj* **~ cuando** come lee el periódico he/she even reads the newspaper while he's/she's eating; **no consiguió un trabajo fijo ~ que cumplió 40 años** he/she didn't get a steady job until he/she was forty

hastiar <1. *pres:* hastío> I. *vt* 1.(*aburrir*) to bore 2.(*hartar, repugnar*) to sicken II. *vr* ~**se de alguien/algo** to get fed up with sb/sth

hastío *m* 1.(*tedio*) boredom; **¡qué ~!** what a bore! 2.(*repugnancia*) disgust

hatajo *m* 1. (*de ganado*) small herd 2. (*de personas*) bunch, cluster

hatillo *m* belongings *pl*; (*de ropa*) bundle

hato *m* 1. (*de ropa*) belongings 2. (*de ganado*) small group of livestock animals 3. (*montón*) a whole lot

Hawai *m* Hawaii

hawaiano, -a *adj, m, f* Hawaian

haya *f* 1. (*árbol*) beech 2. (*madera*) beechwood

Haya *f* La ~ the Hague

hayal *m* beech grove

hayuco *m* beech nut

haz *m* 1. (*hato*) bunch; (*de papeles*) sheaf 2. Fís face; **sobre el ~ de la tierra** on the face of the earth

haza *f* plot of cultivable land

hazaña *f* feat, exploit

hazmerreír *m inv* laughing stock; **es el ~ de la gente** he's the butt of everyone's jokes

HB *m abr de* **Herri Batasuna** *Basque nationalist political coalition*

he *1. pres de* **haber**

hebilla *f* buckle

hebra *f* 1. (*hilo*) thread 2. (*fibra*) fibre; **tabaco de ~** loose tobacco

hebreo *m* 1. (*lengua*) Hebrew 2. *inf* (*mercader*) merchant 3. *inf* (*usurero*) usurer

hebreo, -a *adj, m, f* Hebrew

hebroso, -a *adj* fibrous

hecatombe *f* hecatomb

hechicería *f* 1. (*arte*) witchcraft 2. (*hechizo*) spell

hechicero, -a *m, f* 1. (*brujo*) sorcerer 2. (*de tribu*) witch doctor

hechizar <z→c> *vt* 1. (*encantar*) to cast a spell on 2. (*captivar*) captivate, to enchant

hechizo *m* spell; **romper el ~** to break the spell

hecho *m* 1. (*circunstancia*) fact 2. (*acto*) action, deed; **~ delictivo** criminal act; **los Hechos de los Apóstoles** the Acts of the Apostles 3. (*suceso*) event; JUR deed; **exposición de los ~s** statement of events; **lugar de los ~s** scene of the crime; **los ~s que causaron el incendio** the events that gave rise to the fire ▶ **de ~** in fact

hecho, -a *adj* 1. (*maduro*) mature; **vino ~** mature wine 2. (*cocido*) cooked; **me gusta la carne hecha** I like meat well done; **el pollo está demasiado ~** the chicken is overcooked 3. (*acabado*) finished; **frase hecha** idiom; **traje ~** ready-made suit 4. (*adulto*) **un hombre ~ y derecho** a real man

hechura *f* 1. (*factura*) making; **de buena ~** well-made 2. (*de un vestido*) tailoring 3. (*obra*) work; (*de Dios*) creation 4. (*del cuerpo*) shape

hectárea *f* hectare

hectogramo *m* hectogramme *Brit,* hectogram *Am*

hectolitro *m* hectolitre *Brit,* hectoliter *Am*

hectómetro *m* hectometre *Brit,* hectometer

Am

heder <e→ie> *vi* ~ **a algo** to stink of sth

hediondez *f* stench

hediondo, -a *adj* 1. (*fétido*) fetid 2. (*repugnante*) repulsive 3. (*obsceno*) obscene

hedonismo *m sin pl* hedonism

hedonista I. *adj* hedonistic II. *mf* hedonist

hedor *m* stench; ~ **a huevos podridos** stench of rotten eggs

hegemonía *f* hegemony

hegemónico, -a *adj* hegemonic

helada *f* frost; **las primeras ~s del año** the first frosts of the year; **anoche cayó una ~** there was a frost last night

heladera *f* (*nevera*) refrigerator, fridge; **este sitio es una ~** it's absolutely freezing here

heladería *f* ice cream parlour *Brit* [*o* parlor *Am*]

heladero, -a *m, f* ice cream seller

helado *m* 1. (*postre*) ice cream 2. (*sorbete*) sorbet

helado, -a *adj* 1. (*frío*) freezing; (*congelado*) frozen; **estoy ~** I'm freezing; **el lago está ~** the lake is frozen; **las cañerías están heladas** the pipes are frozen 2. (*pasmado*) **me quedé ~** I was left speechless; (*de miedo*) I was petrified 3. (*altivo*) aloof

helador, -a *adj* (*viento*) freezing

heladora *f* 1. (*nevera*) ice-box, refrigerator 2. (*para helados*) ice cream maker [*o* machine]

helaje *m Col* intense cold, frost

helar <e→ie> I. *vt* 1. (*congelar*) to freeze 2. (*pasmar*) to astonish II. *vimpers* to freeze III. *vr:* **~se** 1. (*congelarse*) to freeze; **el lago se ha helado** the lake has frozen over 2. (*morir*) to freeze to death 3. (*pasar frío*) to be frozen [*o* ice cold]; **~se de frío** to get chilled to the bone

helecho *m* fern, bracken

helénico, -a *adj* 1. (*antiguo*) Hellenic 2. (*actual*) Greek

helenista *mf* Hellenist

hélice *f* 1. TÉC propeller 2. ANAT, MAT helix; **la doble ~** the double helix

helicoidal *adj* helicoidal

helicóptero *m* helicopter

helio *m* helium

heliocéntrico, -a *adj* heliocentric

helipuerto *m* heliport

helvético, -a *adj, m, f* Swiss

hematíe *m* MED red blood cell [*o* corpuscle]

hematoma *m* bruise; MED haematoma *Brit,* hematoma *Am*

hembra *f* 1. *t.* ZOOL, ELEC female 2. TÉC female; (*tornillo*) nut

hembraje *m AmS* 1. (*de ganado*) herd of female animals 2. *pey* (*de mujeres*) gaggle

hemeroteca *f* newspaper archive

hemiciclo *m* 1. (*semicírculo*) semicircle 2. (*sala*) semicircular hall; (*parlamento*) floor 3. POL (*en España, Congreso de Diputados*) Parliament chamber

hemiplejia *f,* **hemiplejía** *f* MED hemiplegia,

semi-paralysis

hemipléjico, -a I. *adj* hemiplegic, semi-paralysed *Brit*, semi-paralyzed *Am* II. *m, f* hemiplegic, person suffering partial paralysis

hemisférico, -a *adj* hemispherical

hemisferio *m* hemisphere

hemofilia *f* MED haemophilia *Brit*, hemophilia *Am*

hemoglobina *f* BIO haemoglobin *Brit*, hemoglobin *Am*

hemograma *m* MED blood count

hemorragia *f* MED haemorrhage *Brit*, hemorrhage *Am*

hemorroides *fpl* haemorrhoids *pl Brit*, hemorrhoids *pl Am*

hemostático *m* MED haemostatic *Brit*, hemostatic *Am*

henar *m* (*terreno*) hay field; (*pajar*) hayloft

henchir *irr como pedir* I. *vt* to fill; ~ **los pulmones de aire** to fill one's lungs with air II. *vr:* ~**se** (*hartarse de comida*) to stuff oneself

hender <e→ie> I. *vt* 1. (*algo de madera*) to split; (*algo de plástico*) to cut 2. (*abrirse paso*) to make one's way through 3. (*mar*) to plough; **el barco hendía las aguas** the ship ploughed the waves II. *vr:* ~**se** to split

hendidura *f* 1. (*raja*) split; (*en la pared, en un jarrón*) crack 2. (*de una guía*) groove

hendija *f AmL* (*rendija*) crack

hendimiento *m* splitting

hendir *irr como cernir vt v.* **hender**

henequén *m AmL* henequen (*plant and fabric derived from it*)

henil *m* hayloft

heno *m* hay; **fiebre del** ~ hay fever

hepático, -a *adj* hepatic; **cirrosis hepática** cirrhosis of the liver

hepatitis *f inv* MED hepatitis

heptágono I. *adj* heptagonal II. *m* heptagon

heptatlón *m* DEP heptathlon

heráldica *f sin pl* heraldry

heráldico, -a *adj* heraldic

herbáceo, -a *adj* 1. (*de hierba*) herbaceous 2. (*de hierbas medicinales*) homeopathic

herbajar I. *vi* to graze II. *vt* to put out to pasture

herbaje *m* 1. (*lugar*) pasture 2. (*comida*) grass

herbario I. *adj* herbal II. *m* herbalist

herbicida *m* herbicide

herbívoro *m* herbivore

herbolario *m* health food shop

herbolario, -a *m, f* herbalist

herboristería *f v.* **herbolario**

herborizar <z→c> *vi* to collect herbs

hercio *m* FÍS hertz

hercúleo, -a *adj* Herculean; **una empresa hercúlea** a Herculean task

heredable *adj* able to be inherited

heredad *f* 1. (*finca*) estate 2. (*terreno*) piece of land

heredar *vt* to inherit; **propiedad heredada** inherited property; **problemas heredados del franquismo** problems handed down from

Franco's time

heredero, -a *m, f* heir; **el** ~ **del trono** the heir to the throne; **el príncipe** ~ the crown prince

hereditario, -a *adj* hereditary; **enfermedad hereditaria** hereditary disease

hereje *mf* REL heretic

herejía *f* 1. REL heresy 2. (*calumnia*) insult 3. (*fechoría*) evil deed 4. (*rebeldía*) rebellion

herencia *f* 1. JUR inheritance 2. (*legado*) legacy; **una** ~ **de la antigüedad** a legacy of the past

herético, -a *adj* heretical

herida *f* 1. (*lesión*) wound; **tocar a alguien en la** ~ *fig* to find somebody's weak [*o* sore] spot 2. (*ofensa*) affront

herido, -a I. *adj* 1. (*lesionado*) injured; MIL wounded; ~ **de gravedad** seriously injured; MIL mortally wounded 2. (*ofendido*) hurt, offended II. *m, f* injured person; MIL wounded soldier; **los** ~**s** the wounded; **en el atentado no hubo** ~**s** nobody was wounded in the attack

herir *irr como sentir* I. *vt* 1. (*lesionar*) to injure; MIL to wound 2. (*golpear*) to hit 3. (*flecha*) to sink into 4. MÚS (*instrumento de cuerda*) to pluck; (*instrumento de tecla*) to strike 5. (*sol*) to beat down 6. (*ofender*) to hurt, to offend; **no quisiera** ~ **susceptibilidades** I wouldn't want to hurt anybody's feelings 7. (*acertar*) to hit II. *vr:* ~**se** to be injured

hermafrodita *adj, m* hermaphrodite

hermana *f* sister; *v.t.* **hermano**

hermanado, -a *adj* twinned; **ciudad hermanada** twinned city

hermanamiento *m* 1. (*de ciudades*) twinning 2. (*acción*) joining

hermanar I. *vt* (*unir*) to join; (*de ciudades*) to twin; **Santiago está hermanada con...** Santiago is twinned with ... II. *vr:* ~**se** to be twinned

hermanastro, -a *m, f* stepbrother *m,* stepsister *f*

hermandad *f* (*de hombres*) brotherhood; (*de mujeres*) sisterhood; REL religious association

hermano, -a *m, f* (*pariente*) brother *m,* sister *f*; ~ **de padre** half-brother (*on the father's side*); ~ **político** brother-in-law; ~ **de leche** foster brother; ~**s siameses** Siamese twins; **mi** ~ **mayor/pequeño** my elder/younger brother; **tengo tres** ~**s** (*sólo chicos*) I have three brothers; (*chicos y chicas*) I have three brothers and sisters; **medio** ~ half-brother; **lenguas hermanas** sister tongues

hermético, -a *adj* hermetic(al); (*al aire*) airtight; (*al agua*) watertight

hermetismo *m* secrecy; **el** ~ **entre las personas de su confianza es absurdo** it's absurd for people he/she trusts to behave so secretively

hermetizar <z→c> *vt* to seal (hermetically)

hermosear *vt* 1. (*a una persona*) to beautify 2. (*a una cosa*) to embellish, to adorn

hermoso, -a adj **1.** (paisaje, mujer) beautiful; (hombre) handsome **2.** (día) lovely **3.** (niño) pretty; (sanote) robust **4.** (persona) good **5.** (gesto) nice

hermosura f beauty

hernia f MED hernia

herniarse vr to rupture oneself; irón to work very hard; ¡no te herniarás, no! irón don't burst a blood vessel!

héroe m hero; (protagonista) main character

heroicidad f **1.** (hazaña) feat (of heroism) **2.** (cualidad) heroic qualities

heroico, -a adj heroic

heroína f **1.** (de héroe) heroine; (protagonista) main character **2.** (droga) heroin

heroinómano, -a m, f heroin addict

heroísmo m sin pl heroism

herpes m o f inv MED herpes

herrador m (black)smith, farrier

herradura f **1.** (de caballo) horseshoe; camino de ~ bridle path **2.** ZOOL horseshoe bat

herraje(s) m(pl) ironwork

herramienta f tool; ~ agrícola agricultural machinery; caja de (las) ~s tool box

herrar <e→ie> vt **1.** (caballo) to shoe **2.** (a un animal) to brand

herrería f blacksmith's, smithy

herrerillo m tit

herrero m blacksmith; en casa del ~, cuchillo de palo prov the shoemaker's wife is always worst shod

herrete m (metal) tip

herrumbre f rust

herrumbroso, -a adj rusty

hertz m FÍS hertz

hervidero m **1.** (manantial) hot spring; un ~ de intrigas a hotbed of intrigue **2.** (multitud) throng

hervido m **1.** (de los alimentos, líquidos) boiling; (a fuego lento) simmering **2.** (burbujeo) bubbling **3.** AmS (cocido) stew

hervidor m **1.** (de cocina, para el agua) kettle; (de cocina, para la leche) milk pan **2.** TÉC boiler

hervir irr como sentir I. vi **1.** (alimentos) to boil; (a fuego lento) to simmer **2.** (burbujear) to bubble **3.** (el mar) to be choppy **4.** (persona) to get angry; ~ en cólera to lose one's temper; le hierve la sangre his/her blood is boiling **5.** (abundar) esta calle hierve en rumores the street is a hotbed of rumours [o rumors Am] II. vt **1.** (bullir) to boil **2.** (desinfectar) to sterilize

hervor m **1.** (acción) boil; dar un ~ a algo to bring sth to the boil; levantar el ~ to come to the boil; le falta un ~ fig he's got a screw loose **2.** (burbujeo) bubbling **3.** (de la juventud) fervour Brit, fervor Am

heterodoxo, -a adj heterodox

heterogeneidad f heterogeneity

heterogéneo, -a adj heterogeneous

heterosexual adj, mf heterosexual

heterosexualidad f sin pl heterosexuality

hexadecimal adj hexadecimal

hexaedro m MAT hexahedron

hexagonal adj hexagonal

hexágono m hexagon

hez f **1.** (poso) sediment **2.** pl (escoria) dregs pl **3.** pl (excrementos) faeces pl Brit, feces pl Am

hibernación f **1.** ZOOL hibernation **2.** MED deep sleep

hibernal adj **1.** (temporada) winter **2.** ZOOL hibernating

hibernar vi to hibernate

hibisco m hibiscus

hibridación f hybridization

híbrido m BIO hybrid

híbrido, -a adj hybrid; computador ~ hybrid computer

hidalgo m HIST nobleman

hidalgo, -a adj **1.** (de los nobles, noble) noble **2.** (generoso) gentlemanly

hidra f **1.** (pólipo) hydra **2.** (en la mitología) Hydra

hidratante adj moisturizing; crema ~ moisturizer

hidratar vt **1.** QUÍM to hydrate **2.** (piel) to moisturize

hidrato m hydrate

hidráulica f hydraulics pl

hidráulico, -a adj hydraulic

hídrico, -a adj **1.** (relativo al agua) water **2.** (que contiene agua) hydric

hidroavión m seaplane

hidrocarburo m hydrocarbon

hidrodinámico, -a adj hydrodynamic

hidroeléctrico, -a adj hydroelectric; central hidroeléctrica hydroelectric power station

hidrófilo, -a adj QUÍM hydrophilic

hidrofobia f **1.** MED (fobia al agua) hydrophobia **2.** (rabia) rabies

hidrófobo, -a adj **1.** QUÍM hydrophobic **2.** (rabioso) rabid

hidrófugo, -a adj water-resistant

hidrogenar vt to hydrogenize

hidrógeno m hydrogen

hidrografía f sin pl hydrography

hidrográfico, -a adj hydrographic

hidrológico, -a adj hydrological

hidropesía f MED dropsy

hidrópico, -a adj dropsical

hidroplano m **1.** AVIAT seaplane **2.** NÁUT hydroplane

hidrosfera f GEO hydrosphere

hidrosoluble adj water-soluble

hidrostático, -a adj hydrostatic

hidroterapia f MED hydrotherapy

hidróxido m hydroxide

hiedra f ivy

hiel f **1.** (bilis) bile **2.** (amargura) bitterness; echar la ~ to sweat blood **3.** pl (adversidades) troubles pl

hielera f **1.** Chile, Méx (nevera portátil) ice chest **2.** Arg (cubitera) icecube tray

hielo m **1.** (del agua) ice; ~ en la carretera

black ice; ~ **picado** crushed ice; **el barco ha quedado aprisionado en el** ~ the ship is trapped in the ice; **capa** [*o* **manta**] **de** ~ icecap **2.** *pl* (*helada*) frost, cold spell **3.** (*frialdad*) coldness; **romper el** ~ to break the ice ▶**quedarse de** ~ to be stunned

hiena *f* hyena

hierático, -a *adj* hieratic

hierba *f* **1.** (*planta*) grass; *t.* MED herb; ~ **medicinal** medicinal herb; **infusión de** ~**s** herbal tea; **mala** ~ weed; **tenis sobre** ~ lawn tennis; **está jugando mejor sobre** ~ **esta temporada** his grass court game has improved this season **2.** *inf* (*droga*) grass ▶**y otras** ~**s** *irón* and such like; **mala** ~ **nunca muere** *prov* the Devil looks after his own; **como la mala** ~ like wildfire; **segar la** ~ **en verde** to cut the grass while it's green

hierbabuena *f* mint

hierbajo *m* weed

hierra *f* AmL branding

hierro *m* **1.** (*metal*) *t.* DEP iron; **edad del** ~ Iron Age; **salud de** ~ iron constitution; **voluntad de** ~ iron will **2.** (*del ganado*) branding iron **3.** (*para marcar*) brand **4.** (*de lanza*) tip of spear **5.** (*arma*) weapon **6.** (*herramienta, golf*) iron **7.** *pl* (*grilletes*) shackles *pl* **8.** *pl* (*cadenas*) chains *pl* ▶**quitar** ~ **a un asunto** to play sth down

hifi *adj* hi-fi

hígado *m* **1.** ANAT liver **2.** *pl* (*valor*) guts *pl* ▶**me pone del** ~ it really gets on my nerves

higiene *f* hygiene; ~ **personal** personal cleanliness [*o* hygiene]

higiénico, -a *adj* hygienic; **compresa higiénica** sanitary towel *Brit,* sanitary napkin *Am;* **papel** ~ toilet paper

higienización *f* cleaning

higienizar <z→c> *vt* to clean

higo *m* **1.** (*fruto*) fig; ~ **chumbo** prickly pear **2.** *inf* (*cosa sin valor*) **esto me importa un** ~ I don't give a toss; **esto no vale un** ~ this is a load of rubbish **3.** (*algo arrugado*) **estar hecho un** ~ (*persona*) to be wizened; (*ropa*) to be crumpled

higrómetro *m* hygrometer

higuera *f* fig tree ▶**estar en la** ~ to have one's head in the clouds

hijastro, -a *m, f* stepson *m,* stepdaughter *f*

hijo, -a *m, f* **1.** (*parentesco*) son *m,* daughter *f;* ~ **adoptivo** adopted son; **un** ~ **de papá** Daddy's boy; ~ **político** son-in-law; ~ **predilecto** (**de una ciudad**) favourite [*o* favorite *Am*] son; ~ **de puta** *vulg* bastard; ~ **único** only child; **pareja sin** ~**s** childless couple; **como cualquier** ~ **de vecino** just like everybody else; **es** ~ **de Madrid** he's from Madrid **2.** *pl* (*descendencia*) children *pl,* offspring

híjole *interj Méx, inf* (*caramba*) Jesus

hijuela *f* **1.** (*de camino*) track **2.** (*de herencia*) part of an inheritance **3.** (*de una institución*) branch

hijuelar *vt Chile* to parcel

hila *f* **1.** (*acción*) spinning **2.** *pl* (*hebras*) fibre *Brit,* fiber *Am*

hilacha *f,* **hilacho** *m* ravelled [*o* raveled *Am*] thread

hilada *f* **1.** (*hilera*) line **2.** ARQUIT course

hilado *m* **1.** (*acción*) spinning **2.** (*hilo*) thread; (*en la industria*) yarn; **fábrica de** ~**s** yarn factory

hilador(a) *m(f)* spinning machine

hiladora *f* spinner

hilandería *f* **1.** (*actividad, arte*) spinning **2.** (*fábrica*) textile mill

hilandero *m* (*lugar*) spinner's

hilandero, -a *m, f* spinner

hilar *vt* **1.** (*hilo, araña*) to spin **2.** (*inferir*) to work out **3.** (*cavilar*) to ponder; ~ **fino** *fig* to split hairs

hilarante *adj* hilarious; **gas** ~ laughing gas

hilaridad *f* hilarity; **esta comedia provoca la** ~ **del público** this comedy has the audience in stitches

hilatura *f* **1.** (*fábrica*) textile [*o* spinning] mill **2.** (*fabricación*) spinning

hilaza *f* **1.** (*hilo*) thread **2.** (*en la industria*) yarn

hilera *f* **1.** (*fila, de cosas iguales*) row, line; MIL file; **colocarse en la** ~ to get into line **2.** TÉC drawplate **3.** ARQUIT ridgepiece

hilo *m* **1.** (*para coser*) thread; (*más resistente*) yarn; (*para bordar*) floss; ~ **bramante** twine; ~ **dental** dental floss; ~ **de perlas** string of pearls; **cortar el** ~ **de la vida a alguien** *fig* to cut short sb's life; **mover los** ~**s** *fig* to pull the strings; **pender de un** ~ *fig* to hang by a thread **2.** (*tela*) linen **3.** TÉC wire; ~ **conductor** thread; **telegrafía sin** ~**s** wireless telegraphy **4.** (*de un discurso*) gist; **no sigo el** ~ **de la película** I'm not following this film; **perder el** ~ (**de la conversación**) to lose the thread (of the conversation); **recoger el** ~ **de la historia** to pick up the thread of the story **5.** (*de un líquido*) trickle **6.** MÚS ~ **musical** piped music

hilván *m* **1.** (*costura*) tacking, basting *Am* **2.** (*hilo*) tacking [*o* basting *Am*] thread

hilvanado *m* tacking, basting *Am*

hilvanar *vt* **1.** (*vestido*) to tack, to baste *Am* **2.** (*frases*) to weave together; **un discurso mal hilvanado** an incoherent speech

himen *m* ANAT hymen

himeneo *m* nuptials *pl*

himno *m* hymn; ~ **nacional** national anthem

hincapié *m* hold; **hacer** ~ **en algo** to emphasize sth

hincar <c→qu> I. *vt* **1.** (*clavar*) to stick; ~ **el diente en algo** *fig, inf* to get one's teeth into sth **2.** (*pie*) to get a strong foothold, to stand firmly II. *vr* ~**se de rodillas** to kneel down

hincha¹ *mf* (*seguidor*) fan

hincha² *f inf* (*tirria*) grudge

hinchable *adj* inflatable; **colchón** ~ inflatable mattress; **muñeca** ~ blow-up doll

hinchada *f* supporters *pl*

hinchado, -a *adj* **1.** (*pie, madera*) swollen

2. (*estilo*) wordy, verbose **3.** (*persona*) pompous

hinchamiento *m* swelling

hinchar I. *vt* **1.** (*globo*) to blow up; (*neumático*) to inflate; (*estómago*) to swell; ~ **la bici** to inflate the bike tyres [*o* tires *Am*] **2.** (*exagerar*) to exaggerate; ¡no lo hinches! come off it! **3.** (*río*) to swell **4.** *AmL* (*molestar*) to bother **II.** *vr:* ~se **1.** (*pierna*) to swell; se me ha hinchado mucho el pie my foot's really swollen **2.** (*engreírse*) to become conceited **3.** *inf* (*de comer*) ~se (de algo) to stuff oneself (with sth) **4.** (*hacer mucho*) ~se a mirar/a escuchar algo to look at/to listen to sth non-stop; ~se a insultar a alguien to go overboard insulting sb

hinchazón *f* **1.** (*del pie, madera*) swelling; (*del río*) flooding **2.** (*soberbia*) conceit **3.** (*de un estilo*) pomposity

hindi *m* hindi

hindú *mf* **1.** (*indio*) Indian **2.** (*del hinduismo*) Hindu

hinduismo *m sin pl* REL Hinduism

hinojo *m* **1.** (*planta*) fennel **2.** HIST (*rodilla*) knee; **de** ~s on one's knees; **ponerse de** ~s to get down on one's knees

hipar *vi* **1.** (*tener hipo*) to have hiccups **2.** (*perros*) to pant **3.** (*fatigarse*) to get tired **4.** (*sollozar*) to whine **5.** (*desear*) ~ **por algo/alguien** to long for sth/sb

hiper *m inf* superstore, hypermarket *Brit*

hiperacidez *f* hyperacidity

hiperactividad *f* hyperactivity

hiperactivo, -a *adj* hyperactive

hipérbola *f* MAT hyperbola

hipérbole *f* LIT hyperbole

hiperbólico, -a *adj* MAT hyperbolic

hipercrítico, -a *adj* hypercritical, overcritical

hiperenlace *m* hyperlink

hiperinflación *f* COM hyperinflation

hipermercado *m* superstore, hypermarket *Brit*

hipermétrope *adj* MED long-sighted

hipermetropía *f* MED long-sightedness

hiperrealismo *m sin pl* hyperrealism

hipersensibilidad *f sin pl* hypersensitivity

hipersensible *adj* hypersensitive, oversensitive

hipertensión *f* MED high blood pressure

hipertenso, -a I. *adj* suffering from high blood pressure **II.** *m, f* person with high blood pressure; **mi padre es** ~ my father has high blood pressure

hipertexto *m* hypertext

hipertrofia *f* MED hypertrophy

hipertrofiarse *vr* to grow out of all proportion

hípica *f sin pl* (*general*) horsemanship; (*montar*) riding; (*carreras*) horse racing

hípico, -a *adj* equestrian, horse

hipido *m* whimper, sob

hipnosis *f inv* hypnosis

hipnótico *m* MED sedative

hipnótico, -a *adj* hypnotic

hipnotismo *m* hypnotism

hipnotización *f* hypnotizing

hipnotizador(a) *m(f)* hypnotizer

hipnotizar <z→c> *vt* to hypnotize

hipo *m* **1.** (*fisiológico*) hiccup; **tener** ~ to have (the) hiccups **2.** (*deseo*) ~ **de algo** longing for sth; ...que quita el ~ *fig* ... that takes your breath away **3.** (*tirria*) grudge

hipocondría *f* MED hypochondria

hipocondríaco, -a *adj, m, f* hypochondriac

hipocrático, -a *adj* Hippocratic; el juramento ~ the Hippocratic oath

hipocresía *f* hypocrisy

hipócrita I. *adj* hypocritical **II.** *mf* hypocrite

hipodérmico, -a *adj* MED hypodermic

hipódromo *m* DEP racecourse, racetrack *Am*

hipófisis *f inv* ANAT pituitary gland

hipogastrio *m* ANAT hypogastric

hipopótamo *m* hippopotamus

hipoteca *f* mortgage

hipotecable *adj* mortgageable

hipotecar <c→qu> *vt* to mortgage; si haces eso ~ás tu libertad if you do that you're signing away your freedom

hipotecario, -a *adj* mortgage; **crédito** ~ mortgage loan

hipotensión *f* MED low blood pressure

hipotenso, -a I. *adj* suffering from low blood pressure **II.** *m, f* ser ~ to have low blood pressure

hipotenusa *f* MAT hypotenuse

hipotermia *f* MED hypothermia; **muerte por** ~ death from hypothermia

hipótesis *f inv* hypothesis

hipotético, -a *adj* hypothetical; es totalmente ~ que... we cannot be at all sure that ...

hipotónico, -a *adj, m, f* hypotonic

hippie, hippy I. *adj* hippy; **moda** ~ hippy style **II.** *mf* hippy

hiriente *adj* hurtful

hirsuto, -a *adj* **1.** (*pelo*) hairy, shaggy **2.** (*planta*) bristly **3.** (*carácter*) surly, brusque

hirviente *adj* boiling

hisopear *vt* to sprinkle (with holy water)

hisopo *m* **1.** (*planta*) hyssop **2.** (*de iglesia*) aspergillum

hispalense I. *adj* of/from Seville **II.** *mf* native/inhabitant of Seville

hispánico, -a *adj* **1.** (*de España*) Spanish **2.** (*de Hispania*) Hispanic; **Filología Hispánica** Spanish Language and Literature

hispanidad *f sin pl* **1.** (*calidad*) Spanishness **2.** (*conjunto*) Spanish-speaking world

hispanismo *m* UNIV Hispanism

hispanista *mf* foreign expert on Spanish history and culture

hispanizar <z→c> *vt, vr:* ~se to take on Spanish customs

hispano, -a I. *adj* **1.** (*español*) Spanish **2.** (*en EE.UU.*) Hispanic **II.** *m, f* **1.** (*español*) Spaniard **2.** (*en EE.UU.*) Hispanic

Hispanoamérica *f* Spanish America

> **Hispanoamérica** is a generic term that includes all countries of Central and South America, where Spanish is (officially) spoken. There are nineteen states in total:**Argentina, Bolivia, Chile, Colombia, Costa Rica, Cuba, Ecuador, El Salvador, Guatemala, Honduras, México, Nicaragua, Panamá, Paraguay, Perú, Puerto Rico, República Dominicana, Uruguay** and **Venezuela.** In contrast, the collective term **Latinoamérica** (or **América Latina**) applies to all those countries of Central and South America that were colonised by the Spaniards, Portugese and French.

hispanoamericano, -a *adj, m, f* Spanish American
hispanohablante I. *adj* Spanish-speaking; **los países ~s** Spanish-speaking countries II. *mf* Spanish speaker
histeria *f* hysteria
histérico, -a I. *adj* hysterical II. *m, f* hysterical person
histerismo *m* hysteria
histología *f* MED histology
historia *f* 1. (*antigüedad*) history; **~ natural** natural history; **~ universal** universal [*o* world] history; **pasar a la ~** (*ser importante*) to go down in history; (*no ser actual*) to be out of date 2. *t. inf* story; **cuenta la ~ completa** tell the whole story; **ésa es la misma ~ de siempre** it's the same old story; **eso sólo son ~s** that doesn't prove anything; **ya sabes la ~** you know what I'm talking about; **¡déjate de ~s!** stop fooling around; **¡no me vengas con ~s!** come off it
historiador(a) *m(f)* historian
historial I. *adj* historical II. *m* 1. (*antecedentes*) file, record; **~ delictivo** police record 2. (*currículo*) curriculum vitae; **~ profesional** professional background; **este hecho no empañará el ~ de esta institución** this will not tarnish the reputation of this institution; **él tiene un ~ intachable** he has an impeccable record
historiar *vt* 1. (*contar*) to tell the story of 2. ARTE to paint 3. *AmL* (*enmarañar*) to complicate
historicismo *m* historicism
histórico, -a *adj* (*que tiene que ver con la historia*) historical; (*acontecimiento*) historic; **un miembro ~ del partido** a longstanding party member
historieta *f* 1. (*anécdota*) anecdote 2. (*con viñetas*) comic strip
historiografía *f sin pl* historiography
historiógrafo, -a *m, f* historiographer
histrión *m* 1. HIST histrion 2. (*actor*) actor 3. (*payaso*) clown 4. (*efectista*) playactor
histriónico, -a *adj* histrionic
histrionismo *m* 1. (*teatralidad*) acting

2. (*efectismo*) histrionics *pl*
hitleriano, -a *adj* Hitlerian
hito *m* (*mojón*) milestone ▶**mirar a alguien de ~ en ~** to stare at sb
hit-parade *m* (*los cuarenta*) top forty
hobby *m* <hobbies> hobby
hocicar <c→qu> I. *vt* (*hozar*) **~ algo** to root about [*o* around] in sth II. *vi* 1. (*caerse*) to fall flat on one's face 2. *inf* (*dificultad*) to run into trouble 3. NÁUT (*amorrar*) to pitch 4. (*dar de bruces*) to run [*o* bump] into III. *vt, vi* (*tocar(se)*) to nuzzle
hocico *m* 1. (*morro*) muzzle; (*de cerdo*) snout 2. *inf* (*cara*) mug; **caer de ~s** to fall on one's face; **estar de ~s** to be in a bad mood; **meter el ~ en todo** *fig* to stick one's nose in everything 3. *vulg* (*boca*) rubber lips *pl*
hocicudo, -a *adj AmL* 1. (*persona*) thick-lipped 2. (*animal*) long-snouted
hockey *m sin pl* hockey; **~ sobre hielo/hierba** ice/field hockey
hogar *m* 1. (*casa*) home; **~ del pensionista** old people's home; **~ de adopción** foster home; **artículos para el ~** household items; **persona sin ~** homeless person 2. (*familia*) family; **la vida del ~** family life; **crear un ~** to start a family 3. (*de cocina, de tren*) boiler; (*de chimenea*) hearth; (*de fundición*) furnace
hogareño, -a *adj* 1. (*ambiente*) family 2. (*persona*) homeloving
hogaza *f* large loaf of bread
hoguera *f* 1. (*en un campamento*) bonfire; (*de alegría*) blaze 2. HIST (*ejecución*) stake; **morir en la ~** to be burnt at the stake
hoja *f* 1. (*de una planta*) leaf; (*pétalo*) petal; **~s del bosque** forest leaves; **árbol sin ~s** leafless tree; **los árboles vuelven a echar ~s** the leaves on the trees are sprouting again 2. (*de papel*) sheet; **~ de lata** tinplate; **~ volante** leaflet, flyer *Am;* **~ de una mesa** (*extensible*) table flap; **pasar la ~** to turn the page; **~ de movilización** MIL call-up paper; **no hay [*o* tiene] vuelta de ~** *fig* there's no doubt about it 3. (*formulario*) form; **~ de estudios** educational record; **~ de pedido** order form; **~ de servicios** service record; **tener una buena ~ de servicios** to have a good record 4. (*de arma*) blade; **~ de afeitar** razor blade 5. (*de ventana*) pane
hojalata *f* tinplate
hojalatería *f* (*local*) tinsmith's; (*mercancía*) tinware
hojalatero *m* tinsmith, tin worker
hojaldre *m* puff pastry; **pastel de ~** puff
hojarasca *f* 1. (*hojas*) fallen [*o* dead] leaves 2. (*estilo*) waffle; **tus promesas son ~** your promises don't mean a thing
hojear *vt* to browse through
hojoso, -a *adj* leafy
hojuela *f* 1. (*hoja*) small leaf 2. GASTR pancake; (*aceitunas*) crushed olives 3. *AmC* (*hojaldre*) puff pastry
hola *interj* hello

holán m AmC (lienzo) canvas
holanda f cheese; (tela) fine linen
Holanda f the Netherlands
holandés, -esa I. adj Dutch; **la escuela holandesa** ARTE the Dutch school II. m, f Dutchman m, Dutchwoman f
holding m <holdings> COM holding company; **el ~ de empresas fiduciarias** the holding of fiduciary companies
holgado, -a adj 1.(vestido) loose 2.(espacioso) spacious; **en este coche se va ~** there's lots of space in this car; **ir ~ de tiempo** to have plenty of time
holganza f 1.(ociosidad) leisure; (agradable) rest 2.(diversión) enjoyment; (regocijo) merriment
holgar irr como colgar I. vi 1.(sobrar) to be unnecessary; **huelgan las palabras** what can you say?; **huelga decir que...** needless to say that ... 2.(descansar) to relax II. vr: ~se 1.(alegrarse) ~se de [o con] algo to be pleased with sth 2.(divertirse) ~se de algo to have a good time with sth
holgazán, -ana m, f layabout
holgazanear vi to laze [o loaf] arodun
holgazanería f laziness
holgorio m v. jolgorio
holgura f 1.(de vestido) looseness 2.TÉC play 3.(bienestar) **vivir con ~** to live comfortably
holladura f 1.(acción) treading 2.(huella) footprint
hollar <o→ue> vt 1.(pisar) to step on; (dejar huellas) to leave footprints 2.(despreciar) to trample on
hollejo m skin (of grape or olive)
hollín m soot
holocausto m 1.(genocidio) holocaust 2.REL sacrifice
holografía f holography
hológrafo, -a adj holograph
holograma m hologram
hombracho m, **hombrachón** m strong man; pey brute
hombrada f feat of prowess, manly act
hombradía f v. hombría
hombre I. m 1.(varón) man; **el ~ de la calle** fig the man in the street; **~ de las cavernas** caveman; **~ de confianza** right-hand man; **~ de estado** statesman; **~ del montón** nobody special; **~ de negocios** businessman; **~ de paja** front man; **el ~ medio** the average man; **el ~ del saco** the bogeyman Brit, the boogeyman Am; **ser ~ de dos caras** to be two-faced; **el ~ del tiempo** the weatherman; **el defensa fue al ~** DEP the defender went for the man; **¡está hecho un ~!** he's become a man!; **hacer un ~ de alguien** to make a man out of sb; **se comportó como un ~** he behaved like a man; **¡~ al agua!** man overboard! 2.(especie humana) **el ~** mankind 3. inf (marido) man II. interj (sorpresa) well, well; (duda) well...; **¡~!, ¿qué tal?** hey! how's it going?; **¡cállate, ~!** give it a rest, eh!; **¡pero, ~!** but, come on!;

¡sí, ~! yes, of course!
hombre-anuncio m <hombres-anuncio> sandwich man
hombrear I. vi to play the man II. vr **quiere ~se con su padre** he wants to play at being a man with his father
hombrecillo m little man; (sin importancia) insignificant man
hombre-lobo m <hombres-lobo> werewolf
hombre-mono m <hombres-mono> apeman
hombrera f 1.(almohadilla) shoulder pad 2.(de uniforme) epaulet(te) 3.(de armadura) shoulder plate
hombre-rana m <hombres-rana> frogman
hombría f 1.(conducta) uprightness 2.(comportamiento) manliness; **un acto de ~** a worthy action
hombro m 1.ANAT shoulder; **ancho de ~s** broad-shouldered; **cargado de ~s** round-shouldered; **encogerse de ~s** to shrug one's shoulders; **llevar algo a ~s** carry sth on one's shoulders 2.TIPO part of typographical letter that does not leave a mark ▶**arrimar el ~** to lend a hand; **echarse al ~** to put one's shoulder to the wheel; **mirar a alguien por encima del ~** to look down one's nose at sb
hombruno, -a adj mannish; **mujer hombruna** mannish woman
homenaje m 1.(el honrar) tribute; **hacer una fiesta en ~ de alguien** to celebrate in honour [o honor Am] of sb; **rendir ~ a alguien** to pay homage to sb 2.HIST obedience, allegiance
homenajear vt to pay tribute to
homeópata mf homeopath
homeopatía f sin pl homeopathic medicine
homeopático, -a adj homeopathic
homicida I. adj homicidal; **el arma ~** the murder weapon II. mf (planeado) murderer m, murderess f; (no planeado) person guilty of manslaughter
homicidio m homicide; (planeado) murder; (no planeado) manslaughter; **~ frustrado** attempted murder; **brigada de ~s** murder squad
homínido m BIO hominid
homo adj inf gay
homogeneidad f sin pl homogeneity
homogeneización f homogenization
homogeneizar <z→c> vt 1. t. QUÍM to homogenize 2.(uniformar) to standardize
homogéneo, -a adj homogeneous, uniform
homógrafo m homograph
homógrafo, -a adj homographic
homologable adj equivalent; **el récord no es ~** the record cannot be accepted
homologación f 1.(de una escuela) validation, accreditation 2.DEP (de un récord) official recognition 3.TÉC (de un casco) authorization 4.JUR (de un arreglo) confirmation; (de

un convenio) ratification

homologar <g→gu> I. *vt* 1.(*escuela*) to validate 2. DEP (*récord*) to recognize officially 3. TÉC to authorize; **homologar un casco to** authorize a helmet 4. JUR (*arreglo*) to confirm; (*convenio*) to ratify II. *vr:* ~**se** to be officially recognized

homólogo, -a I. *adj* equivalent II. *m, f* counterpart; **el presidente mejicano y su ~ francés** the Mexican president and his French counterpart

homónimo *m* namesake

homónimo, -a I. *adj* homonymous II. *m, f* homonym

homosexual *adj, mf* homosexual

homosexualidad *f sin pl* homosexuality

honda *f* sling

hondo *m* depth

hondo, -a *adj* deep; **en lo ~ del valle** in the depths of the valley; **respirar ~** to breathe deeply; **cante ~** *purist Flamenco musical style*

hondonada *f* GEO depression, hollow

hondura *f* depth; **meterse en ~s** *fig* to get into deep water

Honduras *f* Honduras

Honduras lies in Central America and borders **Nicaragua**, **El Salvador** and **Guatemala** as well as the Caribbean and the Pacific Ocean. The capital is **Tegucigalpa**. Spanish is the official language of the country and the monetary unit of **Honduras** is the **lempira**.

---

hondureño, -a *adj, m, f* Honduran

honestidad *f sin pl* honesty

honesto, -a *adj* honest

hongo *m* 1. BOT fungus; (*comestible*) mushroom 2.(*sombrero*) bowler (hat) ►**estar solo como un ~** to be as lonely as a cloud

honor *m* honour *Brit,* honor *Am;* **cuestión de ~** matter of honour; **¡palabra de ~!** word of honour!; **¡por mi ~!** on my honour!; **hacer ~ a su nombre** to honour his/her name; **es para mí un gran ~** it is a great honour for me; **hacer los ~es** to do the honours

honorabilidad *f* honour *Brit,* honor *Am*

honorable *adj* honourable *Brit,* honorable *Am*

honorario, -a *adj* honorary; **cónsul ~** honorary consul

honorarios *mpl* fees *pl*

honorífico, -a *adj* honorary

honra *f* 1.(*honor, reputación*) honour *Brit,* honor *Am;* **¡a mucha ~!** I'm proud of it! 2. REL **~s fúnebres** funeral proceedings

honradez *f* (*honestidad*) honesty; (*integridad*) integrity; **falta de ~** lack of integrity

honrado, -a *adj* (*íntegro, moral*) honourable *Brit,* honorable *Am;* (*decente*) upright; **llevar una vida honrada** to lead an honourable [*o* honorable *Am*] life

honrar I. *vt* to honour *Brit,* to honor *Am;* **nos honra con su presencia** he honours [*o* hon-

ors *Am*] us with his presence II. *vr* ~**se con** [*o* **de**] **algo** to be an honour [*o* honor *Am*] for sb

honrilla *f* self-esteem

honroso, -a *adj* honourable *Brit,* honorable *Am*

hontanar *m* spring

hopo *m* 1.(*rabo*) bushy tail 2.(*mechón*) tuft

hora *f* 1.(*de un día*) hour; ~**s de consulta** surgery hours; ~**s extraordinarias** overtime; **~ feliz** happy hour; ~(**s) punta** rush hour; **un cuarto de ~** a quarter of an hour; **media ~** half an hour; **una ~ y media** an hour and a half; **a última ~** at the last minute; **a primera/última ~ de la tarde** in the early/late afternoon; **noticias de última ~** last-minute news; **el pueblo está a dos ~s de camino** the village is two hours' walk away; **estuve esperando ~s y ~s** I was waiting for hours and hours; **a la ~** on time 2.(*del reloj*) time; **¿qué ~ es?** what time is it?, what's the time?; **¿a qué ~ vendrás?** what time are you coming?; **adelantar la ~** to put [*o* set] the clock forward; **poner el reloj en ~** to set one's watch; **retrasar la ~** to put [*o* set] the clock back; **me ha dado** [*o* **tengo**] **~ para el martes** I've got an appointment for Tuesday 3.(*tiempo*) time; **a la ~ de la verdad...** when it comes down to it ...; **comer entre ~s** to eat between meals; **estar en ~s bajas** to be feeling down; **no lo dejes para última ~** don't leave it till the last minute; **tener (muchas) ~s de vuelo** *fig* to be (very) experienced; **ven a cualquier ~** come at any time; **ya va siendo ~ que tomes tus propias decisiones** it is about time that you made your own decisions 4. REL prayer 5. *pl* (*mitología*) **las ~s** the seasons

horadar *vt* to perforate

hora-hombre <horas-hombre> *f* ECON man-hour; **con las huelgas se pierden al año miles y miles de horas-hombre** thousands and thousands of man-hours are lost every year as a result of strikes

horario *m* 1.(*escolar, de medio de transporte*) timetable, schedule *Am;* (*de consulta*) surgery hours; **~ de atención al público** opening hours; **~ flexible** flexitime; **~ de oficina** office hours; **¿qué ~ hacen?** what hours do they work?; **tenemos ~ de tarde** we work evenings 2.(*manecilla del reloj*) hour hand

horario, -a *adj* hourly

horca *f* 1.(*para colgar*) gallows *pl* 2.(*bieldo*) winnowing fork 3.(*horquilla*) pitchfork

horcajadas a ~ astride

Horchata is a refreshing drink from Valencia made with **chufas** (a specific type of almond), **azúcar** (sugar) and **agua** (water).

---

horda *f* 1.(*de salvajes*) horde 2.(*banda*) violent group

horizontal I. *adj* horizontal II. *f* horizontal

position
horizontalidad *f sin pl* horizontality
horizonte *m* horizon
horma *f* **1.** TÉC (*molde*) mould *Brit,* mold *Am* **2.** (*muelle*) ~ **de zapatos** shoetree ▸**encontrar la ~ de su** <u>zapato</u> *inf* to meet one's match
hormiga *f* ant; ~ **blanca** white ant; **ser una ~** *fig* to be always working
hormigón *m* concrete; ~ **armado** reinforced concrete
hormigonera *f* concrete mixer
hormiguear *vi* **1.** (*picar*) to tingle, to itch **2.** (*gente, insectos*) to swarm; ~ **de algo** to seethe [*o* teem] with sth
hormigueo *m* **1.** (*picor*) pins and needles; **tengo un ~ en la espalda** my back is itching **2.** (*multitud*) swarming
hormiguero *m* **1.** (*de hormigas*) anthill **2.** (*de gente*) swarm; **la plaza era un ~ de gente** the square was seething with people
hormiguero, -a *adj* related to ants; **oso ~** anteater
hormona *f* hormone
hormonal *adj* hormone, hormonal
hormonar *vt* to treat with hormones
hornacina *f* ARQUIT (vaulted) niche
hornada *f* **1.** (*de horno*) batch, ovenload **2.** (*conjunto*) **una ~ de médicos** a whole lot of doctors
hornalla *f AmL* **1.** (*parrilla*) barbecue **2.** (*del fogón*) hotplate **3.** (*horno*) oven
hornear *vt* to bake
hornero, -a *m, f* baker
hornillo *m* (*cocina*) stove; (*de una cocina*) ring; ~ **de gas** gas ring; ~ **portátil** portable cooker
horno *m* **1.** (*cocina*) oven; ~ **microondas** microwave oven; **recién salido del ~** straight from [*o* out of] the oven; **asar al ~** to oven roast **2.** TÉC furnace; ~ **crematorio** cremation furnace; **alto ~** blast furnace; (*para cerámica*) kiln ▸**no está el ~ para** <u>bollos</u> this is not the right time
horóscopo *m* horoscope
horqueta *f* **1.** (*horca*) winnowing fork **2.** (*horquilla*) pitchfork **3.** (*de un árbol*) fork
horquilla *f* **1.** (*del pelo*) hairclip *Brit,* bobby pin *Am;* (*de moño*) hairpin **2.** (*de bicicleta, árbol*) fork **3.** TÉC yoke
horrendo, -a *adj v.* **horroroso**
hórreo *m* raised granary
horrible *adj* **1.** (*horroroso*) horrible; **un crimen ~** a ghastly crime; **una historia ~** a horrible story **2.** (*muy feo*) grotesque
horripilante *adj* horrifying
horripilar **I.** *vt* **1.** (*erizar*) ~ **a alguien** to make one's hair stand on end; **estas historias me horripilan** I'm horrified by these stories **2.** (*horrorizar*) to horrify **II.** *vr:* ~**se** to be horrified
horrísono, -a *adj* dreadful; **un griterío ~** a frightful clamour [*o* clamor *Am*]

horror *m* **1.** (*miedo, aversión*) horror; **tener ~ a algo** to have a horror of sth; **siento ~ a la oscuridad** I'm terrified of the dark; **me da ~ verte con esta corbata** you look terrible with that tie on; **el diseño moderno me parece un ~** I don't like modern design at all; **¡qué ~!** *inf* how horrible! **2.** *pl* (*actos*) **los ~es de la guerra** the atrocities of war **3.** *inf* (*mucho*) **ganar un ~ de dinero** to earn a lot of money; **hoy hace un ~ de frío** it's hellishly cold today; **me cuesta ~es** it's very hard for me; (*me gusta ~es el regalo*) I absolutely love the gift
horrorizar <z→c> **I.** *vt* to horrify; **me horrorizó ver el accidente** I was horrified by the accident **II.** *vr* ~**se de algo** to be horrified [*o* terrified] by sth
horroroso, -a *adj* horrifying; **una escena horrorosa** a terrible scene; **su última novela es horrorosa** his last novel is awful
hortaliza *f* vegetable
hortelano, -a *m, f* market gardener *Brit,* truck gardener *Am;* ~ **aficionado** amateur gardener
hortensia *f* hydrangea
hortera[1] *inf* **I.** *adj* vulgar, tasteless, tacky **II.** *m* vulgar person
hortera[2] *f* wooden bowl
horterada *f inf* tasteless thing; **este vestido es una ~** this dress is completely tasteless; **esta película es una ~** this film is so tacky
hortícola *adj* horticultural; **productos ~s** horticultural produce
horticultor(a) *m(f)* gardener
horticultura *f sin pl* horticulture
hortofrutícola *adj* fruit and vegetable gardening
hortofruticultura *f sin pl* fruit and vegetable growing
hosco, -a *adj* **1.** (*persona*) gruff **2.** (*ambiente*) unpleasant, hostile
hospedaje *m* **1.** (*acción, situación*) residence; **dar ~ a alguien** to put sb up **2.** (*coste*) rent
hospedar **I.** *vt* to accommodate **II.** *vr:* ~**se** to stay
hospedería *f* **1.** (*fonda*) inn **2.** (*en convento*) hospice
hospedero, -a *m, f* innkeeper
hospiciano, -a *m, f* **1.** (*niño*) orphan **2.** (*pobre*) poor person
hospicio *m* **1.** (*para niños*) children's home **2.** (*para pobres, en un monasterio*) hospice
hospital *m* hospital; ~ **militar** military hospital
hospitalario, -a *adj* **1.** (*acogedor*) welcoming, hospitable **2.** (*de hospital*) hospital
hospitalidad *f sin pl* hospitality
hospitalización *f* **1.** (*envío*) hospitalization **2.** (*estancia*) stay in hospital
hospitalizar <z→c> *vt* to hospitalize; **ayer ~on a mi madre** yesterday my mother went into hospital; **estoy hospitalizado desde**

el domingo I've been in hospital since Sunday

hosquedad *f* **1.**(*de una persona*) gruffness **2.**(*de un lugar*) dismalness

hostal *m* cheap hotel

hostelería *f* **1.**ECON hotel business **2.**ENS hotel management; **escuela superior de ~** school of hotel management

hostelero, -a I. *adj* hotel II. *m, f* hotelier

hostería *f* inn

hostia I.*f* **1.**REL host; (*sin consagrar*) wafer **2.** *vulg* (*bofetada*) clout, smack; (*golpe*) bash; **darse una ~** (*chocar*) to smash **3.** *vulg* (*uso hiperbólico*) **¡me cago en la ~!** for fuck's sake; **¡este examen es la ~!** fucking hell! what an exam!; **hace un tiempo de la ~** (*malo*) the weather's really shitty; (*bueno*) the weather's fantastic; **iba a toda ~** he was going full speed II. *interj vulg* Jesus

hostiar *vt vulg* (*bofetada, golpe*) to belt

hostigador(a) *adj* annoying

hostigamiento *m* **1.**(*fustigación*) whipping **2.**(*molestia*) annoyance **3.**(*apremio*) harrassment

hostigante *adj Col* (*sabor*) sickly; (*persona*) annoying

hostigar <g→gu> *vt* **1.**(*fustigar*) to whip **2.**(*molestar*) to bother; (*con observaciones*) to harrass **3.**(*incitar*) to incite **4.**MIL to make small attacks

hostigoso, -a *adj Chile, Guat, Perú* cloying

hostil *adj* hostile; **le hicieron un recibimiento ~** he was given a hostile reception

hostilidad *f* hostility

hostilizar <z→c> *vt* **1.**(*hostigar*) to annoy **2.**MIL to attack

hostión *m vulg* heavy clout

hotel *m* **1.**(*establecimiento*) hotel; **~ residencia** boarding house, guesthouse **2.**(*casa*) country house, villa; (*mansión*) mansion

hotelero, -a I. *adj* hotel; **industria hotelera** hotel business II. *m, f* hotelier, hotelkeeper

hotelito *m* (*casa*) house; (*de vacaciones*) holiday home

hovercraft *m* <hovercrafts> hovercraft

hoy *adv* today; **~ (en) día** nowadays; **llegará de ~ a mañana** it will arrive any time now; **de ~ en adelante** from now on; **los niños de ~ (en día)** children nowadays; **llegará de ~ a mañana** it will arrive today or tomorrow

hoya *f* **1.**(*hoyo*) hollow **2.**(*sepultura*) grave **3.** GEO (*hondonada*) plain

hoyo *m* **1.**(*concavidad*) hollow **2.**(*agujero*) hole **3.**(*sepultura*) grave

hoyuelo *m* dimple

hoz *f* **1.**AGR sickle **2.**GEO (*desfiladero*) defile; (*garganta*) gorge

hozar <z→c> I. *vi* to root around II. *vt* to root around in

huacal *m And, Méx:* wooden box

huachafoso, -a *adj Perú* affected, pretentious

huaico *m Perú* landslide

huarache *m Méx* **1.**(*sandalia*) sandal **2.**GASTR

corn dough filled with fried beans

huarmi *f AmS* **1.**(*mujer muy trabajadora*) hardworking woman **2.**(*ama de casa*) housewife

huasca *f AmL* (*látigo*) whip

huaso, -a I. *adj AmS* (*campesino*) peasant II. *m, f AmS* (*campesino*) peasant

hubo *3. pret de* **haber**

hucha *f* **1.**(*alcancía*) moneybox, piggy bank **2.**(*ahorros*) savings

hueco *m* **1.**(*agujero*) hole; **~ del ascensor** lift well *Brit,* elevator shaft *Am;* **~ de la mano** hollow of the hand; **~ de la ventana** window space **2.**(*lugar*) space; **hazme un ~** move over **3.**(*tiempo*) time; **hazme un ~ para mañana** make time for me tomorrow

hueco, -a *adj* **1.**(*ahuecado*) hollow; (*vacío*) empty **2.**(*sonido*) resonant **3.**(*tierra*) soft **4.**(*palabras*) empty **5.**(*persona*) vain; **ponerse ~** to become vain; **tener la cabeza hueca** *pey* to be thick **6.**(*estilo*) trite

huecograbado *m* TIPO photogravure

huelga *f* strike; **~ de advertencia** warning strike; **~ de brazos caídos** sit-down strike; **~ general** general strike; **~ de hambre** hunger strike; **~ salvaje** wildcat strike; **convocar una ~** to call a strike; **declararse en** [*o* **hacer**] **~** to go on strike; **en esta fábrica estamos en ~** we're on strike in this factory

huelguista *mf* striker

huelguístico, -a *adj* strike

huella *f* **1.**(*señal*) mark; **~ de un animal** animal track; **~ dactilar** fingerprint **2.**(*vestigio*) trace; (*pasos*) footsteps; **seguir las ~s de alguien** to follow sb's footsteps

huelveño, -a I. *adj* of/from Huelva II. *m, f* native/inhabitant of Huelva

huérfano, -a I. *adj* orphan; **ser ~ de padre** to have no father; **quedarse ~** to become an orphan; **la ciudad se queda huérfana en invierno** the city empties in winter II. *m, f* orphan

huero, -a *adj* (*discurso*) trite; (*huevo*) rotten; **la cosa ha salido huera** it was a bit of a disaster

huerta *f* (*frutales*) orchard; (*hortalizas*) market garden *Brit,* truck garden *Am*

huertero, -a *adj* *m, f Arg, Nic, Perú* market gardener *Brit,* truck gardener *Am*

huerto *m* (*hortalizas*) vegetable patch; (*frutales*) orchard; **~ familiar** allotment ▶ **llevar a alguien al ~** *inf* (*engaño*) to lead sb up the garden path; (*sexo*) to seduce sb [*o* have sex with]

huesa *f* shallow grave

huesera *f Chile* ossuary

hueso *m* **1.**ANAT bone; **carne sin ~** boneless meat; **te voy a romper los ~s** *inf* I'm going to kick your face in; **estar en los ~s** to be a rack of bones **2.**(*de fruto*) stone, pit *Am* **3.**(*faena*) task; **un ~ duro de roer** a hard nut to crack; **este profesor es un ~** this teacher's really strict **4.**AmL (*trabajo*) hard work ▶ **dar con**

sus ~s en la cárcel to end up in jail; **calado hasta los ~s** soaked to the skin; **dar en ~** inf to come a cropper

huésped m t. BIO host

huésped(a) m(f) guest

hueste f 1. HIST (ejército) host 2. (de un partido) supporters

huesudo, -a adj 1. (persona) big-boned 2. (carne) bony

hueva f roe

huevada f AmL, inf (estupidez) stupid thing

huevear vi AmS, inf (hacer tonterías) to fool around

huevera f egg cup; (cartón) egg crate

huevería f shop that sells eggs

huevero m (que fabrica) egg producer

huevero, -a m, f (que vende) egg seller

huevo m 1. BIO egg; **~ duro** hard-boiled egg; **~s fritos** fried eggs; **~ pasado por agua** soft-boiled egg; **~s revueltos** scrambled eggs; **clara de ~** egg white; **ir pisando ~s** to go very slowly and/or carefully; **poner un ~** to lay an egg; vulg to have [o take] a shit 2. AmL (valor) guts pl 3. vulg (testículo) ball; **¡estoy hasta los ~s!** I've had it up to here!; **me importa un ~** I don't give a shit; **¡tiene ~s la cosa!** that's quite something!; **poner algo a alguien a ~** to make sth very easy for sb; **me costó un ~** (de dinero) it cost loads; (de dificultades) it was damn difficult; **¡y un ~!** like hell!

huevonear vi Méx, vulg to piss around

huida f flight; **~ del lugar del accidente** flight from the scene of the accident; **no hay ~ posible** there's no way out

huidizo, -a adj 1. (persona) elusive 2. (momento) fleeting

huido, -a m, f escaped prisoner

huir irr I. vi (escapar) to flee; **~ de casa** to run away from home; **el tiempo huye** time flies; **pudieron ~ de sus perseguidores** they managed to give their pursuers the slip II. vt, vi (evitar) **~ (de) algo** to keep away from sth; **~ (de) alguien** to avoid sb

huiro m AmS (alga) seaweed

hule m 1. (para la mesa) tablecloth 2. (tela) oilcloth 3. AmL (caucho) rubber

hulero, -a m, f AmL rubber tapper

hulla f fossil coal; **~ blanca** hydroenergy

hullero, -a adj coal; **período ~** GEO Carboniferous period

humanamente adv humanly; **hacer todo lo ~ posible** to do everything humanly possible

humanidad f 1. (género humano) la ~ mankind; **un crimen contra la ~** a crime against humanity 2. (naturaleza, caridad humana) humanity 3. inf (corpulencia) fatness 4. pl (letras) arts

humanismo m sin pl humanism

humanista mf humanist

humanístico, -a adj humanistic

humanitario, -a adj humanitarian; **organización humanitaria** humanitarian organization

humanitarismo m sin pl humanitarianism

humanización f sin pl 1. (dignificación) humanization 2. ARTE humanizing

humanizador(a) adj humanizing

humanizar <z→c> I. vt (dignificar, arte) to humanize II. vr: **~se** to become human

humano, -a adj 1. (del hombre) human 2. (manera de ser) humane

humanoide m humanoid

humareda f cloud of smoke

humazo m thick smoke

humear I. vi 1. (humo) to smoke 2. (vapor) to steam 3. (enemistad) to linger on, to smolder 4. (engreírse) to act vain II. vr: **~se** to give oneself airs

humectador m humidifier

humectante adj moisturizing

humedad f humidity; (agradable) moisture; (desagradable) dampness

humedal m wetland

humedecer irr como crecer vt to moisten

húmedo, -a adj (mojado) wet; (agradable) moist; (desagradable) damp; (con vapor) humid; (aire) muggy

húmero m ANAT humerus

humidificar <c→qu> vt to humidify

humildad f 1. (modestia) humility, humbleness 2. (religiosa) meekness 3. (social) lowliness

humilde adj 1. (modesto) humble; **un ~ trabajador** a humble worker 2. (en sentido religioso) meek 3. (condición social) poor; **ser de orígenes ~s** to be of humble origin

humillación f 1. (degradación) humiliation 2. (vergüenza) shame

humillante adj humiliating

humillar I. vt 1. (degradar) to humiliate 2. (avergonzar) to shame II. vr: **~se** to lower oneself

humo m 1. (de combustión) smoke; **señal de ~** smoke signal; **en ese bar siempre hay ~** it's always smoky in that bar; **la chimenea echa ~** the chimney pours out smoke; **tragar el ~ al fumar** to inhale cigarette smoke 2. (vapor) steam 3. (al cocinar) smoke, steam 4. pl (vanidad) conceit; **bajar los ~s a alguien** to take sb down a peg; **subírse los ~s a la cabeza** to put on airs; **tener muchos ~s** to be very conceited

humor m 1. (cualidad, humorismo) humour Brit, humor Am; **~ negro** gallows humour Brit [o humor Am]; **¡pero no tienes sentido del ~ o qué!** have you got no sense of humour Brit [o humor Am]? 2. (ánimo) mood; **estar de buen/mal ~** to be in a good/bad mood; **no estoy de ~ para bailar** I'm not in the mood for dancing 3. MED (líquido) humour Brit, humor Am

humorada f (dicho, broma) witticism; **dejémonos de ~s** let's stop beating around the bush

humorado, -a adj **bien/mal ~** (por un momento) in a good/bad mood; (carácter)

even-tempered/bad-tempered
humorismo *m sin pl* comedy
humorista *mf* comic, humorist; (*dibujante*) cartoonist
humorístico, -a *adj* comic
humus *m sin pl* humus
hundido, -a *adj* 1. (*ojos*) deep-set; (*techo*) collapsed 2. (*persona*) downcast, demoralized
hundimiento *m* 1. (*de un barco*) sinking 2. (*de un edificio*) *t.* ECON collapse 3. GEO (*depresión*) hollow
hundir I. *vt* 1. (*barco*) to sink 2. (*sumergir*) ~ **la mano en el agua** to put one's hand in the water; ~ **los pies en el barro** to sink one's feet into the mud 3. (*suelo*) to cave in 4. (*arruinar*) to ruin; (*proyecto*) to cause to fail; (*empresa*) to bankrupt; (*esperanzas*) to destroy; **la crisis económica ha hundido a muchos empresarios** the economic crisis has ruined many businessmen II. *vr:* ~**se** 1. (*barco*) to sink 2. (*edificio*) to collapse; (*suelo*) to cave in; **el rublo se hunde** the rouble is plummeting 3. (*fracasar*) to fail, to lose it; **me he hundido en el tercer set** I lost it in the third set
húngaro, -a *adj, m, f* Hungarian
Hungría *f* Hungary
huno, -a I. *adj* HIST Hun II. *m, f* HIST Hun
huracán *m* hurricane; **las tropas pasaron como un ~ por la ciudad** the troops stampeded through the city; (*persona*) whirlwind of energy
huracanado, -a *adj* tempestuous; **vientos ~s** hurricane winds
huraño, -a *adj* 1. (*insociable*) unsociable 2. (*hosco*) surly
hurgar <g→gu> I. *vt, vi* 1. (*remover*) ~ **en algo** to poke about in sth; ~ **el fuego** to poke the fire 2. (*fisgonear*) ~ **en algo** to look [*o* rummage] through sth II. *vr* ~**se la nariz** to pick one's nose
hurgón *m* (*de fuego*) poker
hurgonear *vt* to jab, to poke
hurguetear *vt AmL* ~ **algo** rummage about in sth
hurí *f* houri
hurón, -ona *m, f* 1. (*animal*) ferret 2. *inf* (*husmeador*) nosy parker 3. *inf* (*huraño*) unsociable
huronear *vi* 1. (*cazar*) to hunt with ferrets 2. (*fisgonear*) to nose around, to snoop
huronera *f* 1. (*madriguera*) ferret hole 2. (*escondrijo*) hiding place; (*de ladrones*) den; (*escondite*) hideout
hurra *interj* hooray
hurtadillas a ~ secretly; **lo hizo a ~ de su novia** he did it behind his girlfriend's back
hurtar I. *vt* 1. (*robar*) to steal; (*en tiendas*) to shoplift 2. (*con el peso*) to give sb short measure 3. (*mar*) to eat away 4. (*cuerpo*) to avoid 5. (*ocultar*) to hide II. *vr* ~**se a algo** to keep away from sth
hurto *m* 1. (*acción*) stealing; (*en tiendas*)

shoplifting 2. (*cosa*) stolen property
húsar *m* MIL hussar
husmear I. *vt* (*perro*) to sniff II. *vi* (*perro*) to sniff around; (*fisgonear*) to nose around
husmeo *m* 1. (*de un perro*) sniffing 2. (*fisgoneo*) nosing around, snooping
huso *m* 1. (*textil*) spindle 2. GEO ~ **horario** time zone
huy *interj* 1. (*de dolor*) ow 2. (*de asombro*) wow

I

I, i *f* I, i; ~ **de Italia** I for Isaac *Brit,* I for Item *Am;* ~ **griega** y
ibérico, -a *adj* Iberian; **Península Ibérica** Iberian Peninsula
Iberoamérica *f* Latin America
iberoamericano, -a *adj, m, f* Latin American
ibicenco, -a I. *adj* of/from Ibiza II. *m, f* native/inhabitant of Ibiza
Ibiza *f* Ibiza
iceberg *m* <icebergs> iceberg; **la punta del ~** the tip of the iceberg
icono *m,* **ícono** *m* REL, INFOR icon
iconoclasta I. *adj* iconoclastic II. *mf* iconoclast
iconografía *f* iconography
ictericia *f sin pl* MED jaundice
ictiología *f sin pl* ichthyology
I+D *abr de* **Investigación y Desarrollo** R & D
ida *f* departure; **billete de ~** single (ticket); **billete de ~ y vuelta** return (ticket)
idea *f* 1. *t.* FILOS idea; ~ **fundamental** basic idea; **ni ~** no idea; **dar a alguien (una) ~ de algo** to give sb an idea of [*o* about] sth; **tener la ~ de hacer algo** to have the idea of doing sth 2. (*propósito*) intention; **tener ~ de hacer algo** to have the intention of doing sth; **llevar ~ de hacer algo** to intend to do sth 3. *pl* (*convicciones*) ideas *pl*
ideal *adj, m* ideal
idealismo *m* idealism
idealista I. *adj* idealistic II. *mf* idealist
idealización *f* idealization
idealizar <z→c> *vt* to idealize
idear *vt* 1. (*concebir*) to conceive 2. (*inventar*) to think up 3. (*trazar un proyecto*) to design; (*un plan*) to devise
ideario *m* 1. (*conjunto de ideas*) doctrine 2. (*ideología*) ideology
ídem *pron* ditto
idéntico, -a *adj* 1. (*igual*) identical; **es ~ a su madre** he/she is just like his/her mother 2. (*semejante*) same
identidad *f* 1. (*personalidad*) identity; **carné de ~** identity card; **no pude probar mi ~** I was unable to prove my identity 2. (*coinciden-*

cia) sameness

identificable *adj* identifiable

identificación *f* **1.** (*de alguien*) identification **2.** INFOR password

identificar <c→qu> I. *vt* **1.** (*reconocer*) to recognize; (*establecer la identidad*) to identify **2.** (*equiparar*) to categorize II. *vr:* ~**se 1.** (*demostrar la identidad*) to identify **2.** (*solidarizarse*) to sympathize **3.** (*compenetrarse*) ~**se con alguien/algo** to identify oneself with sb/sth

ideología *f* ideology

ideólogo, -a *m, f* ideologist, idealogue

idílico, -a *adj* idyllic

idilio *m* **1.** LIT idyll **2.** (*relación amorosa*) love affair

idioma *m* language; **hablar el mismo** ~ *fig* to be on the same wavelength

idiomático, -a *adj* idiomatic

idiosincrasia *f* idiosyncrasy, quirk

idiota I. *adj* idiotic, stupid II. *mf* **1.** MED subnormal person **2.** (*estúpido*) idiot

idiotez *f* **1.** *t.* MED imbecility **2.** (*estupidez*) idiocy

ido, -a *adj* **1.** *inf* (*mal de la cabeza*) crazy **2.** (*despistado*) absent-minded **3.** AmC (*borracho*) drunk

idólatra I. *adj* **1.** (*que rinde culto*) idolatrous **2.** (*que ama excesivamente*) adoring II. *mf* **1.** (*quien rinde culto*) idolater *m,* idolatress *f* **2.** (*quien ama una persona o cosa*) adorer

idolatrar *vt* **1.** (*rendir culto*) to worship **2.** (*adorar*) to adore; (*amar*) to idolize

idolatría *f* **1.** (*culto*) idolatry **2.** (*adoración*) adoration

ídolo *m* **1.** (*persona*) idol **2.** *pey* (*divinidad*) idol, deity; (*efigie*) graven image

idoneidad *f* **1.** (*aptitud*) suitability **2.** (*capacidad*) aptitude

idóneo, -a *adj* apt

iglesia *f* church; **casarse por la** ~ to have a church wedding

iglú *m* igloo

ígneo, -a *adj* igneous

ignición *f* **1.** (*combustión*) combustion; (*incandescencia*) incandescence **2.** (*inicio de una combustión*) ignition

ignífugo, -a *adj* (*que protege contra el fuego*) fireproof; (*que no se quema*) noninflammable *Brit,* nonflammable *Am*

ignominia *f* ignominy, disgrace

ignominioso, -a *adj* ignoble, ignominious

ignorancia *f* **1.** (*desconocimiento*) ignorance **2.** (*incultura*) lack of culture [*o* education]; **la** ~ **es atrevida** *prov* a little learning [*o* knowledge] is a dangerous thing

ignorante I. *adj* **1.** (*desconocedor*) ~ **de algo** ignorant about [*o* of] sth **2.** (*inculto*) uncultured, uneducated II. *mf pey* dunce, ignoramus

ignorar *vt* **1.** (*desconocer, no saber*) ~ **algo** to be ignorant of sth **2.** (*no hacer caso*) to ignore

igual¹ I. *adj* **1.** (*idéntico*) identical; (*seme-*

jante) same; **nunca he visto cosa** ~ I've never seen anything like it **2.** (*llano*) flat **3.** (*constante: temperaturas, clima*) stable; (*ritmo*) steady **4.** MAT equal **5.** (*lo mismo*) **a mí me pasó** ~ the same (thing) happened to me; **habla** ~ **que su padre** he/she speaks just like his/her father; **¡es** ~! it doesn't matter ►**al** ~ **que...** as well as ... II. *mf* equal; **no tiene** ~ he/she has no equal III. *adv inf* (*quizá*) ~ **no viene** he/she might not come

igual² *m* MAT equal(s) sign

igualación *f* **1.** (*igualamiento*) equalization; (*equiparación*) matching **2.** (*allanamiento*) flattening **3.** (*nivelación*) levelling *Brit,* leveling *Am* **4.** (*ajuste*) adjustment **5.** (*convenio*) agreement; (*pago*) retainer

igualada *f* equalizer

igualado, -a *adj* **1.** (*parecido*) similar **2.** (*empatado*) level

igualar I. *vt* **1.** (*hacer igual*) to equalize; (*equiparar*) to match **2.** (*allanar*) to flatten (out) **3.** (*nivelar*) to level **4.** (*ajustar*) to even out II. *vi* **1.** (*equivaler*) to be equal **2.** (*combinar*) to match III. *vr:* ~**se 1.** (*parecerse*) ~**se a** [*o* con] **alguien** to be similar to sb **2.** (*compararse*) to equate **3.** (*ponerse al igual*) to make equal, to equate

igualdad *f* **1.** equality; (*uniformidad*) sameness, uniformity; ~ **de derechos** equal rights; **en** ~ **de condiciones** all things (being) equal; **estar en** ~ **de condiciones** to be on an equal footing **2.** (*semejanza*) similarity **3.** (*regularidad*) steadiness; (*de superficie*) smoothness

igualitario, -a *adj* egalitarian

igualitarismo *m sin pl* egalitarianism

igualmente I. *interj* and the same to you II. *adv* equally

iguana *f* iguana

ijada *f* **1.** ANAT abdominal cavity **2.** (*dolor*) pain in the side, stitch

ikurriña *f* flag of the Basque Country

ilegal *adj* illegal, unlawful

ilegalidad *f* illegality

ilegible *adj* **1.** (*la letra*) illegible **2.** (*el contenido*) unreadable

ilegitimar *vt* **1.** (*asunto*) to invalidate **2.** (*hijo*) to disinherit

ilegitimidad *f* **1.** (*asunto*) illegality **2.** (*hijo*) illegitimacy

ilegítimo, -a *adj* **1.** (*asunto*) illegal **2.** (*hijo*) illegitimate; (*relación*) adulterous **3.** (*exigencia*) illegitimate

ileso, -a *adj* unharmed, unhurt; **salir** [*o* **resultar**] ~ to be unscathed

iletrado, -a *adj* **1.** (*inculto*) uncultured **2.** (*analfabeto*) uneducated

ilícito, -a *adj* illegal, illicit

ilimitado, -a *adj* unlimited

ilocalizable *adj* **el médico está** ~ the doctor cannot be found

ilógico, -a *adj* illogical

iluminación *f* **1.** (*el alumbrar*) *t.* ARTE illumination **2.** (*alumbrado*) lighting; (*como adorno*) illuminations *pl* **3.** REL enlightenment

iluminado, -a *adj* **1.** (*un lugar*) *t.* ARTE illuminated; (*un monumento*) lit up **2.** REL enlightened

iluminar *vt* **1.** (*alumbrar*) *t.* ARTE to illuminate; (*un monumento*) to light up **2.** *fig* to enlighten, to illuminate

ilusión *f* **1.** (*alegría*) excitement; **ese viaje me hace mucha** ~ I'm excited about the journey **2.** (*esperanza*) hope; **no te hagas ilusiones** do not get your hopes up **3.** (*sueño*) illusion **4.** (*espejismo*) (optical) illusion

ilusionante *adj* exciting

ilusionar **I.** *vt* **1.** (*entusiasmar*) to excite; **estar ilusionado con algo** to be excited about sth; **me ilusiona mucho hacer ese viaje** I'm very excited about that journey **2.** (*hacer ilusiones*) to raise false hopes **3.** (*engañar*) to delude **II.** *vr:* ~**se 1.** (*alegrarse*) to be excited **2.** (*esperanzarse*) **el proyecto le ilusiona mucho** the project has got his hopes up

ilusionismo *m* illusionism, conjuring

ilusionista *mf* illusionist

iluso, -a **I.** *adj* gullible **II.** *m, f* dreamer

ilusorio, -a *adj* **1.** (*engañoso*) illusory **2.** (*de ningún efecto*) ineffective

ilustración *f* **1.** (*imagen, instrucción*) illustration; ~ **gráfica** graphic illustration; (*explicación*) explanation **2.** HIST **la Ilustración** the Enlightenment

ilustrado, -a **I.** *adj* **1.** (*con imágenes*) illustrated **2.** (*instruido*) enlightened **3.** (*de la Ilustración*) pertaining to the Enlightenment **II.** *m, f* learned [*o* erudite] person

ilustrador(a) **I.** *adj* **1.** (*ilustrativo, aclarativo*) illustrative **2.** (*instructivo*) enlightening **II.** *m(f)* illustrator

ilustrar **I.** *vt* **1.** (*con imágenes, aclarar*) to illustrate **2.** (*instruir*) to enlighten **II.** *vr:* ~**se** to enlighten oneself

ilustrativo, -a *adj* **1.** (*aclarador*) illustrative **2.** (*sintomático*) representative

ilustre *adj* (*famoso*) illustrious; (*egregio*) distinguished

imagen *f* **1.** (*representación mental, fama*) image; **ser la viva** ~ **de alguien** to be the spitting [*o* living] image of sb **2.** TV picture **3.** (*escultura sagrada*) idol, graven image; (*pintura*) icon

imaginable *adj* imaginable

imaginación *f* (*imaginativa, fantasía*) imagination; **ni por** ~ on no account

imaginar **I.** *vt* to imagine; ~ **fantasmas** to imagine things **II.** *vr:* ~**se 1.** (*representarse*) to imagine oneself; **me lo imagino** I can imagine [*o* picture] it **2.** (*figurarse*) to imagine, to suppose

imaginario, -a *adj t.* MAT imaginary, unreal

imaginativo, -a *adj* imaginative

imán *m* **1.** *t. fig* (*hierro*) magnet **2.** REL imam

iman(t)ar *vt* to magnetize

imbatibilidad *f sin pl* invincibility

imbatible *adj* unbeatable

imbebible *adj* undrinkable

imbécil *adj, mf t.* MED imbecile

imbecilidad *f t.* MED imbecility, subnormality

imberbe *adj* **1.** (*sin barba*) clean-shaven **2.** *pey* (*inmaduro*) beardless

imborrable *adj* **1.** (*lápiz, tinta*) indelible **2.** (*acontecimiento*) unforgettable

imbricación *f* **1.** ARQUIT imbrication **2.** (*superposición*) overlapping; (*entrecruzamiento*) criss-crossing

imbricar <c→qu> **I.** *vt* to imbricate **II.** *vr:* ~**se 1.** (*superponerse*) to overlap **2.** (*entrecruzarse*) to criss-cross **3.** (*entrelazarse*) to interlace

imbuido, -a *adj* imbued; ~ **de algo** imbued with sth

imbuir *irr como huir* **I.** *vt* **1.** (*inculcar*) to imbue **2.** (*transmitir*) to infuse **II.** *vr* ~**se de algo** to imbibe sth

IME *m abr de* **Instituto Monetario Europeo** EMI

imitable *adj* imitable

imitación *f* **1.** (*copia, reproducción*) imitation; **a** ~ **de...** as an imitation of ... **2.** (*como falsificación*) imitation; **perlas de** ~ imitation pearls **3.** (*parodia*) impression

imitado, -a *adj* **1.** (*copiado*) imitated **2.** (*falso*) imitation

imitador(a) *m(f)* (*copista*) imitator; (*parodista*) impersonator

imitar *vt* to imitate, to copy; (*parodiar*) to impersonate; ~ **una firma** to forge a signature; (*asemejarse*) to imitate

impaciencia *f* impatience

impacientar **I.** *vt* to make impatient **II.** *vr:* ~**se** to become impatient

impaciente *adj* impatient; **estamos** ~**s por empezar** we are eager to start

impactar *vt* **1.** (*un acontecimiento*) to make an impact **2.** (*un proyectil*) to strike

impacto *m* **1.** (*choque de un proyectil*) impact; (*huella*) damage; *fig* repercussions *pl* **2.** AmL (*en el boxeo*) punch **3.** (*golpe emocional*) shock, impact; ~ (**medio**)**ambiental** environmental impact **4.** INFOR hit

impagable *adj* **1.** (*no pagable*) unpayable **2.** (*inapreciable*) priceless

impago *m* non-payment; ~ **de impuestos** non-payment of taxes

impalpable *adj* **1.** (*intocable, intangible*) impalpable **2.** (*sutil*) tenuous

impar **I.** *adj* **1.** (*número, sin par*) odd **2.** ANAT single **3.** (*sin igual*) unique, peerless **II.** *m* odd number

imparable *adj* unstoppable

imparcial *adj* **1.** (*sin tomar partido, justo*) impartial **2.** (*sin prejuicios*) unbiased

imparcialidad *f* (*falta de parcialidad, de prevención*) impartiality, fairness

impartir *vt* **1.** (*dar, comunicar*) to give **2.** (*conferir*) to impart *form*

impasibilidad *f* impassiveness

impasible *adj* impassive

impavidez *f* sangfroid, intrepidness

impávido, -a *adj* self-possessed, intrepid

impecable *adj* **1.** *ser* (*correcto*) impeccable **2.** *estar* (*nuevo*) **el motor del coche está ~** the car's engine is in perfect condition

impedido, -a I. *adj* disabled; **estar ~ para algo** to be incapacitated for sth **II.** *m, f* disabled person

impedimento *m* **1.** (*que imposibilita algo*) restraint **2.** (*obstáculo*) impediment, hindrance; (*acerca del matrimonio*) impediment **3.** MED handicap

impedir *irr como pedir vt* **1.** (*imposibilitar*) to prevent, to keep from **2.** (*obstaculizar*) to impede, to hinder **3.** (*estorbar*) to impede

impeler *vt* **1.** (*empujar, impulsar*) to impel, to drive **2.** (*incitar*) to urge; **fue impelido a robar por sus amigos** he was pushed into stealing by his friends

impenetrabilidad *f* **1.** (*inaccesibilidad, incomprensibilidad*) impenetrability **2.** (*impermeabilidad*) imperviousness

impenetrable *adj* **1.** (*inaccesible, incomprensible*) impenetrable **2.** (*impermeable*) impervious

impenitencia *f* impenitence

impenitente *adj* (*empedernido*) impenitent; (*incorregible*) incorrigible

impensable *adj* unthinkable

impensado, -a *adj* **1.** (*repentino*) sudden **2.** (*imprevisto*) unforeseen; (*inesperado*) unexpected

impepinable *adj inf* unquestionable

imperar *vi* to reign; *fig* to prevail

imperativo *m* **1.** LING imperative **2.** *pl* (*necesidad*) imperative

imperativo, -a *adj* **1.** (*autoritario*) imperative; (*imperioso*) imperious **2.** (*exigente*) demanding; (*obligatorio*) imperative

imperceptible *adj* **1.** (*inapreciable*) imperceptible **2.** (*minúsculo*) minute

imperdible I. *adj* unlosable **II.** *m* safety pin

imperdonable *adj* unpardonable, inexcusable

imperecedero, -a *adj* imperishable; *fig* everlasting

imperfección *f* imperfection, flaw

imperfecto *m* LING imperfect

imperfecto, -a *adj* imperfect, flawed

imperial *adj* imperial

imperialismo *m* POL imperialism

impericia *f* **1.** (*ineptitud*) inaptitude **2.** (*inexperiencia*) inexperience **3.** (*torpeza*) ineptitude

imperio *m* **1.** (*territorio*) empire; *t. fig* realm **2.** (*mandato*) reign **3.** (*autoridad*) sovereignty **4.** (*altanería*) imperiousness

imperioso, -a *adj* **1.** (*autoritario*) imperious **2.** (*urgente, forzoso*) imperative

impermeabilidad *f* impermeability

impermeabilizar <z→c> *vt* **1.** (*un tejido*) to waterproof **2.** (*una abertura*) to make watertight

impermeable I. *adj* impermeable **II.** *m* raincoat

impersonal *adj t.* LING impersonal

impertérrito, -a *adj* (*impávido*) imperturbable; (*sin miedo*) fearless

impertinencia *f* **1.** (*insolencia, descaro*) impertinence, impudence **2.** (*inoportunidad*) inappropriateness

impertinente I. *adj* **1.** (*insolente, descarado*) impertinent, impudent **2.** (*inoportuno*) inopportune **3.** (*pesado*) exacting **II.** *mf* impertinent person

imperturbabilidad *f* imperturbability

imperturbable *adj* imperturbable

ímpetu *m* **1.** (*vehemencia*) vehemence **2.** (*brío*) impetus, energy **3.** (*violencia*) impetus, force

impetuosidad *f* impetuousity

impetuoso, -a *adj* **1.** (*temperamento*) impetuous **2.** (*movimiento*) hasty; (*fuerza*) vehement **3.** (*acto*) impetuous, rash

impiedad *f* **1.** (*falta de fe*) impiety **2.** (*de piedad*) pitilessness

impío, -a I. *adj* **1.** (*irreligioso, irrespetuoso*) impious **2.** (*inclemente*) pitiless **II.** *m, f* non--believer, infidel

implacable *adj* **1.** (*imposible de ablandar*) implacable **2.** (*riguroso*) relentless

implantación *f* **1.** MED implant **2.** (*introducción*) implantation **3.** (*asentamiento*) settlement **4.** (*generalización*) establishment

implantar I. *vt* **1.** *t.* MED to implant **2.** (*asentar*) to establish **3.** (*instituir*) to found, to institute **4.** (*introducir*) to introduce **II.** *vr:* **~se** to become established

implementar *vt AmL* **1.** (*un método*) to introduce **2.** (*un plan*) to implement; (*una orden, un deber*) to carry out

implemento *m AmL* (*utensilio*) tool; (*accesorio*) implement; **~s agrícolas** farming equipment

implicación *f* **1.** (*inclusión*) inclusion **2.** (*en un delito*) implication **3.** (*consecuencia*) implications *pl* **4.** (*significado*) significance

implicar <c→qu> **I.** *vt* **1.** (*incluir*) to involve **2.** (*significar*) to imply; **eso implica que...** this means that ... **II.** *vr:* **~se** to be [*o* become] involved

implícito, -a *adj* **1.** (*incluido*) implicit **2.** (*sobreentendido*) understood **3.** (*tácito*) tacit

implorar *vt* (*a alguien*) to implore; (*algo*) to beg; **~ (el) perdón** to beg forgiveness

impoluto, -a *adj* immaculate

imponderable *adj* imponderable

imponderables *mpl* imponderables *pl*

imponente I. *adj* **1.** (*impresionante*) imposing **2.** (*que infunde respeto*) awesome **3.** (*inmenso*) enormous; (*grandioso*) great **4.** *inf* (*atractivo*) gorgeous **II.** *mf* FIN depositor

imponer *irr como poner* **I.** *vt* **1.** (*idea, sanciones*) to impose; **~ a** [*o* **sobre**] **alguien** (*carga, impuestos*) to impose on [*o* upon] sb

2. (*nombre*) to give **3.** (*respeto*) to command **4.** FIN to levy, to tax; (*invertir*) to deposit **II.** *vi* to impress **III.** *vr:* ~**se 1.** (*hacerse necesario*) to become necessary; (*hacerse ineludible*) to become unavoidable **2.** (*hacerse obedecer*) **se impuso a los demás** he/she made his/her authority felt **3.** (*prevalecer*) ~**se a algo** to prevail over sth **4.** (*tomar como obligación*) **me impuse una hora de ejercicio diario** I imposed an hour's daily exercise on myself

imponible *adj* **1.** FIN taxable; **no** ~ tax free, tax exempt *Am* **2.** (*importación*) dutiable **3.** *inf* (*ropa*) unwearable

impopular *adj* unpopular

impopularidad *f* unpopularity

importación *f* **1.** (*acción*) importation **2.** (*producto*) import

importador(a) **I.** *adj* importing **II.** *m(f)* importer

importancia *f* **1.** (*interés*) importance; **sin** ~ unimportant; **restar** [*o* **quitar**] ~ **a algo** to play sth down **2.** (*extensión*) scope, magnitude **3.** (*trascendencia*) significance **4.** (*prestigio, influencia*) importance; **se daba** ~ **ante los demás** he gave himself airs in front of everyone else

importante *adj* **1.** (*de gran interés*) important; **lo** ~ **es** +*infin* the important thing is +*infin* **2.** (*dimensión*) considerable **3.** (*cantidad*) significant **4.** (*calidad*) high **5.** (*situación*) good **6.** (*persona influyente*) important

importar **I.** *vt* **1.** (*mercancía*) to import **2.** (*precio*) to cost, to amount to; (*valer*) to be worth **3.** (*traer consigo*) to imply, to involve **II.** *vi* to matter, to mind; **no importa la hora que sea** it doesn't matter what time it is; **¿a ti qué te importa?** what has it got to do with you?; **¿te importa esperar?** do you mind waiting?; **me importa un pepino** *inf* I couldn't care less

importe *m* (*cuantía*) value; (*total*) amount

importunar *vt* (*incomodar, molestar*) to pester, to importune *form*

importunidad *f* **1.** (*incomodidad, molestia*) importunity **2.** (*indiscreción*) tactlessness

importuno, -a *adj* **1.** (*incómodo, molesto*) importunate **2.** (*indiscreto*) tactless **3.** (*inoportuno*) inopportune

imposibilidad *f* impossibility

imposibilitado, -a *adj* **1.** (*impedido*) disabled; (*paralítico*) paralytic **2.** (*de acudir*) **el despegue se vio** ~ **por la niebla** the take-off was impeded by the fog

imposibilitar *vt* (*impedir*) to impede, to make impossible; (*evitar*) to prevent

imposible **I.** *adj* **1.** (*irrealizable*) impossible **2.** *inf* (*insoportable*) impossible, unbearable **3.** *AmL* (*repugnante*) horrid **II.** *m* **lo** ~ the impossible

imposición *f* **1.** (*de una carga, condena, condiciones*) imposition **2.** (*de impuestos*) taxation **3.** (*de un nombre*) giving **4.** REL ~ **de manos** laying-on of hands **5.** FIN deposit

impositiva *f AmL* tax office

impositivo, -a *adj* **1.** FIN tax **2.** *CSur* (*imperativo*) imperative

impostergable *adj* that cannot be postponed

impostor(a) **I.** *adj* **1.** (*difamador*) slanderous **2.** (*tramposo*) fraudulent **II.** *m(f)* **1.** (*difamador*) slanderer **2.** (*tramposo*) impostor, imposter

impostura *f* **1.** (*calumnia*) slander **2.** (*trampa*) imposture, fraud

impotencia *f* **1.** (*falta de poder*) *t.* MED impotence **2.** (*incapacidad*) incapacity **3.** (*indefensión*) helplessness

impotente *adj* **1.** (*sin poder*) impotent, powerless **2.** (*incapaz*) incapable **3.** (*desvalido*) helpless **4.** MED impotent

impracticable *adj* **1.** (*irrealizable*) unfeasible **2.** (*intransitable*) impassable

imprecación *f* curse, imprecation *form*

imprecar <c→qu> *vt* to curse, to imprecate *form*

imprecisión *f* **1.** (*falta de precisión*) inexactness **2.** (*falta de determinación*) vagueness

impreciso, -a *adj* **1.** (*no preciso*) imprecise **2.** (*indefinido*) vague

impredecible *adj* unpredictable; (*suceso*) unforeseeable

impregnar **I.** *vt* **1.** (*empapar, un tejido*) to impregnate, to saturate **2.** (*penetrar*) to penetrate **3.** (*influir*) **el derecho romano impregna nuestras leyes** Roman law influences our laws **II.** *vr:* ~**se** to become impregnated

impremeditado, -a *adj* **1.** (*impensado*) unpremeditated **2.** (*irreflexivo*) unintentional **3.** (*involuntario*) inadvertent

imprenta *f* **1.** (*técnica, arte*) printing **2.** (*taller*) printer's **3.** (*impresión*) print **4.** BIO ~ **genética** genetic imprint **5.** (*máquina*) press

imprescindible *adj* (*ineludible*) essential; (*obligatorio*) necessary; (*insustituible*) indispensable

impresentable **I.** *adj* unpresentable **II.** *mf* embarrassment

impresión *f* **1.** (*huella*) imprint **2.** TIPO printing, impression **3.** INFOR print-out **4.** FOTO print **5.** (*grabación*) recording **6.** (*sensación, opinión*) impression; **cambiar impresiones** to compare notes

impresionable *adj* **1.** (*fácil de impresionar*) impressionable **2.** (*sensible*) susceptible **3.** TIPO, INFOR printable

impresionante *adj* **1.** (*emocionante, de gran efecto*) impressive, striking **2.** (*magnífico*) magnificent

impresionar **I.** *vt* **1.** (*emocionar, inculcar*) to impress; (*conmover*) to move **2.** FOTO to print **3.** (*grabar*) to cut **II.** *vr:* ~**se** (*emocionarse*) to be impressed; (*conmoverse*) to be moved

impresionismo *m* ARTE impressionism

impreso *m* **1.** (*hoja*) sheet **2.** (*formulario*) form **3.** (*envío*) printed matter; ~ **publicitario** leaflet, flyer *Am*

impreso, -a *pp de* **imprimir**
impresor, -a I. *adj* printing II. *m, f* printer
impresora *f* INFOR printer; ~ **de inyección de tinta** ink-jet printer; ~ **láser** laser printer
imprevisible *adj* unforeseeable; (*persona*) unpredictable
imprevisión *f* 1.(*despreocupación*) thoughtlessness; (*descuido*) carelessness 2.(*ligereza*) imprudence
imprevisto *m* 1.(*algo inesperado*) contingency, sth unexpected 2. *pl* (*gastos*) unexpected expenses
imprevisto, -a *adj* (*no previsto*) unforeseen; (*inesperado*) unexpected
imprimir *irr vt* 1. TIPO, INFOR to print 2.(*editar*) to publish 3.(*reproducir*) to reproduce 4. *t. fig* (*un sello*) to stamp 5.(*inculcar*) to instil
improbabilidad *f* improbability, unlikelihood
improbable *adj* improbable, unlikely
ímprobo, -a *adj* 1. *elev* (*inmoral*) immoral 2.(*esfuerzo*) huge, tremendous; (*trabajo*) mammoth
improcedente *adj* 1.(*inoportuno*) inopportune; (*extemporáneo*) ill-timed 2.(*inadecuado*) inappropriate 3.(*antirreglamentario*) irregular; JUR inadmissable
improductividad *f* 1.(*falta de productividad, rendimiento*) unproductiveness 2.(*falta de rentabilidad*) unprofitability
improductivo, -a *adj* 1.(*no productivo, sin rendimiento*) unproductive 2.(*antieconómico*) unprofitable
impronta *f* 1.(*impresión*) impression 2.(*molde*) mould *Brit,* mold *Am* 3.*fig* mark
impronunciable *adj* unpronounceable
improperio *m* (*ofensa*) offense; (*insulto*) insult
impropiedad *f* 1.(*inexactitud en el lenguaje*) impropriety; (*incorrección*) incorrectness 2.(*inoportunidad*) inappropriateness 3.(*ineptitud*) ineptitude
impropio, -a *adj* 1.(*inoportuno*) improper, unfitting; **ese comportamiento es ~ en él** that behaviour is not usual in [*o* not worthy of] him 2.(*inadecuado*) inappropriate
improrrogable *adj* 1.(*no prolongable*) non--extendable, non-extendible 2.(*no aplazable*) that cannot be postponed
improvisación *f* improvisation
improvisado, -a *adj* impromptu, improvised
improvisar *vt* to improvise; TEAT to ad-lib
improviso, -a *adj* unexpected; **de ~** unexpectedly; **coger a alguien de ~** to surprise sb
imprudencia *f* 1.(*irreflexión, descuido*) imprudence, carelessness 2.JUR negligence; ~ **temeraria** criminal negligence; (*conducir*) reckless driving
imprudente *adj* 1.(*irreflexivo*) imprudent; (*insensato*) unwise 2.(*incauto*) incautious 3.(*indiscreto*) indiscreet 4.JUR negligent
impudicia *f* (*desvergüenza*) shamelessness
impúdico, -a *adj* indecent, immodest; (*obsceno*) lewd

impudor *m* (*desvergüenza*) shamelessness
impuesto *m* FIN tax; ~ **sobre la renta** income tax; ~ **sobre la propiedad** property tax; ~ **sobre el Valor Añadido** Value Added Tax; **libre de ~s** tax-free, duty-free; **sujeto a ~s** taxable, dutiable
impugnación *f* 1. *t.* JUR contest(ation); ~ **de un testamento** probate action 2.(*negación*) refutation 3.(*objeción*) counterargument
impugnar *vt* 1. *t.* JUR to contest 2.(*combatir*) to dispute; (*una teoría*) to challenge
impulsar *vt* 1.(*empujar*) to impel 2.(*incitar*) to incite 3.(*estimular*) to motivate; (*promover*) to instigate
impulsión *f* 1.TÉC drive 2. *elev* (*empuje*) impetus
impulsivo, -a I. *adj* impulsive II. *m, f* impulsive person
impulso *m* 1.(*empujón*) push 2.(*estímulo*) impulse, stimulus; ~ **sexual** sex drive 3.(*empuje*) drive 4.FÍS momentum
impulsor(a) I. *adj* **fuerza ~a** driving force II. *m(f)* catalyst
impune *adj* unpunished
impunidad *f* impunity
impureza *f* 1. *t.* REL impurity 2.(*obscenidad*) foulness
impuro, -a *adj* 1. *t.* REL impure 2.(*obsceno*) lewd
imputabilidad *f* imputability
imputable *adj* imputable, attributable
imputación *f* 1.(*insinuación*) insinuation 2.(*acusación*) imputation
imputar *vt* 1.(*atribuir*) to impute 2.(*cargar*) to charge 3.COM to impute
inabarcable *adj* impossible to encompass; (*inmenso*) vast
inacabable *adj* never-ending, interminable
inaccesibilidad *f* inaccessibility
inaccesible *adj* 1.(*objeto, razonamiento*) ~ **para alguien** inaccessible to sb 2.(*persona*) inaccessible, unapproachable 3.(*inalcanzable*) beyond one's reach
inacción *f* 1.(*inactividad*) inaction 2.(*ociosidad*) idleness
inaceptable *adj* unacceptable
inactividad *f* 1.(*inacción, de una sustancia*) inactivity; (*desocupación*) unemployment 2.MED inactivity
inactivo, -a *adj* 1.(*persona*) inactive; (*desocupado*) jobless 2.(*funcionamiento, sustancia*) *t.* MED inactive 3.(*volcán*) dormant
inadaptable *adj* unadaptable
inadaptación *f* inability to adapt
inadecuación *f* inadequacy
inadecuado, -a *adj* inadequate
inadmisible *adj* inadmissible
inadvertencia *f* inadvertence, oversight
inadvertido, -a *adj* 1.(*descuidado*) inadvertent; **me cogió ~** it caught me unprepared 2.(*desapercibido*) unnoticed
inagotable *adj* inexhaustible; (*persona*) tire-

less

inaguantable *adj* unbearable, intolerable

inalámbrico, -a *adj* TEL cordless, wireless

inalcanzable *adj* unattainable, beyond one's reach

inalienable *adj* inalienable

inalterable *adj* 1. (*invariable, permanente*) unalterable 2. (*imperturbable*) impassive

inalterado, -a *adj* unchanged

inamovible *adj* fixed, immovable

inanición *f* starvation

inanidad *f* inanity

inanimado, -a *adj,* **inánime** *adj* inanimate

inapelable *adj* 1. JUR unappealable, not open to appeal 2. (*inevitable*) definitive

inapetencia *f* loss [*o* lack] of appetite

inaplazable *adj* 1. (*impostergable*) that can't be postponed, undeferable 2. (*urgente*) urgent, pressing

inaplicable *adj* inapplicable

inapreciable *adj* 1. (*imperceptible*) inappreciable 2. (*de gran valor*) priceless

inaprensible *adj* 1. (*inasible*) elusive 2. (*incomprensible*) incomprehensible

inasequible *adj* out of reach; **esa casa es ~ para nuestro bolsillo** that house is beyond our means

inaudible *adj* inaudible

inaudito, -a *adj* 1. (*sin precedente*) unprecedented 2. (*vituperable*) outrageous

inauguración *f* 1. (*puente, exposición*) opening 2. (*estatua*) unveiling 3. (*comienzo*) inauguration

inaugural *adj* inaugural

inaugurar *vt* 1. (*puente*) to open 2. (*estatua*) to unveil 3. (*comenzar*) to inaugurate

inca *adj, m* Inca

The **incas** were a small Indian tribe, who lived in **Perú**. In the 15th century, however, they expanded their empire, which ultimately covered present-day Colombia, Ecuador, Peru and Bolivia, and extended south into the northern part of Argentina and Chile.

---

incaico, -a *m, f* Inca

incalculable *adj* 1. (*invalorable, no cuantificable*) incalculable 2. (*comportamiento*) invaluable

incalificable *adj* 1. (*indecible*) inexpressible, indescribable 2. (*reprobable*) reproachable

incanato *m Chile, Perú* HIST Incan period

incandescente *adj* 1. FÍS (*metal*) incandescent 2. (*temperamento, pasión*) fiery

incansable *adj* tireless

incapacidad *f* 1. (*ineptitud*) incompetence 2. (*psíquica*) incapacity; (*física*) disability 3. (*falta de abilidad*) inability, incapability

incapacitación *f* (*minusvalía*) t. JUR incapacitation

incapacitado, -a I. *adj* 1. (*incapaz*) incapacitated 2. (*incompetente*) incompetent 3. (*para negocios*) unemployable II. *m, f* 1. (*minus-*

válido) disabled person 2. JUR (*para negocios*) incapacitated person

incapacitar *vt* 1. JUR to disqualify; (*para negocios*) to incapacitate 2. (*impedir*) to impede

incapaz *adj* 1. (*inepto*) incapable 2. JUR (*sin capacidad legal*) incapacitated, incompetent 3. (*sin talento*) inept

incasable *adj* 1. (*imposible de casar*) unmarriageable 2. JUR *unable to marry without legal autorization*

incautación *f* seizure, confiscation

incautarse *vr* 1. (*confiscar*) ~**se de algo** to confiscate sth 2. (*adueñarse*) ~**se de algo** to appropriate sth

incauto, -a *adj* 1. (*sin cautela*) incautious; (*confiado*) credulous 2. (*ingenuo*) naive

incendiar I. *vt* ~ **algo** (*sin intención*) to unintentionally set sth on fire; (*intencionalmente*) to set fire to sth, to commit arson II. *vr:* ~**se** to catch fire

incendiario, -a *adj, m, f* incendiary

incendio *m* fire; ~ **intencionado** arson

incentivar *vt* to motivate, to offer incentives to

incentivo *m* incentive

incertidumbre *f* 1. (*inseguridad*) incertitude 2. (*duda*) incertitude, uncertainty

incesante *adj* incessant

incesto *m* incest

incestuoso, -a *adj* incestuous

incidencia *f* 1. *t.* MAT incidence 2. (*consecuencia*) repercussion 3. (*efecto*) impact

incidente I. *adj* incidental II. *m* incident

incidir *vi* 1. (*consecuencias*) ~ **en algo** to impinge on [*o* affect] sth 2. *elev* (*falta*) ~ **en un error** to fall into error 3. FÍS ~ **en algo** to incise; ~ **en algo** to incise in sth 4. (*tema*) ~ **en algo** to touch on sth 5. MED ~ **en algo** to make an incision in sth

incienso *m* incense

incierto, -a *adj* (*dudoso*) doubtful, uncertain; (*falso*) untrue

incineración *f* incineration; (*de personas*) cremation

incinerador *m* 1. TÉC incinerator 2. (*para cadáveres*) crematorium

incinerador(a) *adj* 1. TÉC incinerating 2. (*para cadáveres*) crematory

incineradora *f* 1. *v.* **incinerador(a)** 2. (*para basuras*) incinerator

incinerar *vt* 1. TÉC to incinerate 2. (*cadáveres*) to cremate

incipiente *adj* incipient

incisión *f t.* MED incision

inciso *m* 1. TIPO subsection 2. LING (*paréntesis*) parenthesis; (*coma*) comma 3. (*al relatar*) aside 4. (*en documentos*) interpolation

incitación *f* 1. (*instigación*) incitement 2. (*ánimo*) animation

incitante *adj* 1. (*instigador*) inciting 2. (*que anima*) animating

incitar *vt* 1. (*instigar*) to incite 2. (*animar*) to

animate
incívico, **-a** *adj* antisocial
incivil *adj*, **incivilizado**, **-a** *adj* 1.(*inculto*) uncivilised 2.(*rudo*) uncivil
inclemencia *f* 1.(*falta de clemencia*) inclemency, unmercifulness 2.(*clima*) inclemency; (*invierno*) harshness; (*paisaje*) bleakness; **las ~s del tiempo** the inclemency of the weather
inclinación *f* 1.(*declive*) slope 2.(*reverencia, con la cabeza*) bow 3.(*afecto*) ~ **por alguien/algo** inclination for [*o* to] sb/sth 4.(*tendencias*) propensity, tendency
inclinado, **-a** *adj* 1.(*ángulo, de cuerpo*) inclined 2.(*dispuesto*) ~ **a algo** inclined to [*o* towards] sth
inclinar I. *vt* to incline II. *vr:* **~se** 1.(*reverencia*) to bow; (*árboles*) to bend 2.(*propender*) to incline 3.(*preferir*) **~se por algo** to have a penchant for sth
incluir *irr como huir* *vt* 1.(*comprender, contener*) to include, to enclose, to contain; **todo incluido** all-inclusive 2.(*formar parte*) to include
inclusa *f* ≈ orphanage (*home for abandoned children*)
inclusión *f* inclusion; **con ~ de...** with the inclusion of
inclusive *adv* inclusively
incluso I. *adv* inclusively II. *prep* including; **habéis aprobado todos, ~ tú** you have all passed, even you
incluso, **-a** *adj* included
incoar *vt* 1.(*comenzar*) to initiate 2. JUR (*proceso*) to institute proceedings
incógnita *f* 1. MAT (*magnitud*) variable 2.(*enigma*) enigma; (*secreto*) secret; **despejar la ~** (*enigma*) to solve the enigma; (*secreto*) to disclose the secret
incógnito, **-a** *adj* incognito
incoherencia *f* incoherence
incoherente *adj* incoherent
incoloro, **-a** *adj* colourless *Brit*, colorless *Am*
incólume *adj* intact, unscathed
incombustible *adj* incombustible
incomible *adj* inedible, uneatable
incomodar I. *vt* to inconvenience, to incommode *form* II. *vr:* **~se** 1.(*molestarse*) **no se incomodes, que abro yo** don't trouble yourself, I'll open the door 2. *CSur* (*enfadarse*) to become angry
incomodidad *f*, **incomodo** *m* 1.(*inconfortable*) uncomfortableness, discomfort 2.(*molestia*) inconvenience, uneasiness
incómodo, **-a** *adj* 1.(*inconfortable*) uncomfortable; **estar ~** to be uncomfortable 2.(*molesto*) tiresome
incomparable *adj* incomparable
incompatibilidad *f* incompatibility; **~ de oficios** job incompatibility
incompatible *adj* incompatible
incompetencia *f* incompetence
incompetente *adj* incompetent
incompleto, **-a** *adj* incomplete

incomprensible *adj* 1.(*no inteligible*) incomprehensible 2.(*inexplicable*) inexplicable
incomprensión *f* 1.(*no querer comprender*) unwillingness to understand 2.(*no poder comprender*) incomprehension
incomunicación *f* 1.(*aislamiento*) isolation 2.(*en prisión*) solitary confinement 3.(*falta de comunicación*) lack of communication
incomunicado, **-a** *adj* 1.(*aislado*) incommunicado 2.(*en prisión*) **el preso estuvo 6 días ~** the prisoner spent 6 days in solitary confinement
incomunicar <c→qu> *vt* 1.(*aislar*) to isolate 2.(*bloquear*) to cut off
inconcebible *adj* 1.(*inimaginable*) inconceivable 2.(*inadmisible*) unacceptable
inconciliable *adj* irreconcilable
inconcluso, **-a** *adj* unfinished
inconcreción *f* imprecision
inconcreto, **-a** *adj* imprecise
incondicional I. *adj* unconditional II. *mf* 1.(*amigo*) faithful [*o* steadfast] friend 2.(*servil*) devoted person, yes man *pej*
inconexo, **-a** *adj* unconnected
inconformista *mf* nonconformist
inconfundible *adj* unmistakable
incongruencia *f* (*incoherencia*) incongruity
incongruente *adj* (*contradictorio*) incongruous
inconmensurable *adj* 1.(*que no puede medirse*) incommensurate 2.(*enorme*) immense
inconmovible *adj* 1.(*cosas*) immutable 2.(*personas*) steadfast
inconsciencia *f* 1.(*desmayo*) unconsciousness 2.(*insensatez*) senselessness; (*irresponsabilidad*) thoughtlessness; (*ignorancia*) unawareness
inconsciente *adj* 1. **estar** (*desmayado*) unconscious 2. **ser** (*insensato*) senseless; (*irresponsable*) thoughtless; (*ignorante*) unaware 3. **ser** (*gesto*) involuntary
inconsistencia *f* flimsiness
inconsistente *adj* 1.(*irregular*) uneven 2.(*poco sólido*) flimsy; (*argumento*) weak
inconsolable *adj* inconsolable, broken-hearted
inconstancia *f* inconstancy
inconstante *adj* 1.(*irregular*) inconstant 2.(*caprichoso*) changeable
inconstitucionalidad *f* unconstitutionality
incontable *adj* 1.(*innumerable*) countless 2.(*inenarrable*) unmentionable; LING uncountable
incontenible *adj* 1.(*irrefrenable*) unrestrainable 2.(*fuera de control*) uncontrollable 3.(*risa, júbilo, impulso*) irrepressible
incontestable *adj* 1.(*innegable*) incontestable 2.(*pregunta*) unanswerable
incontinencia *f* t. MED incontinence
incontrolado, **-a** I. *adj* 1.(*que no puede controlarse*) uncontrolled 2.(*que no puede verifi-*

carse) unverified **3.** (*violento*) violent **II.** *m, f* unruly [o uncontrolled] person

incontrovertible *adj* incontrovertible

inconveniencia *f* **1.** (*descortesía*) discourtesy **2.** (*disparate*) absurd remark **3.** (*no adecuado*) inappropriateness

inconveniente I. *adj* **1.** (*descortés*) discourteous; (*disparate*) absurd **2.** (*no adecuado*) inappropriate **3.** (*no aconsejable*) unadvisable **II.** *m* **1.** (*desventaja*) disadvantage **2.** (*obstáculo*) inconvenience

incordiar *vt* to bother; ¡deja de ~! stop being so irritating!

incordio *m inf* (*molestia*) bother, pest

incorporación *f* **1.** (*al enderezarse*) straightening up; (*al sentarse*) sitting up **2.** (*integración, en un equipo*) incorporation; ~ a filas MIL induction

incorporar I. *vt* **1.** (*a un grupo*) ~ a [o en] algo to incorporate in [o into] sth **2.** (*a una persona*) to include **II.** *vr:* ~se **1.** (*enderezarse*) to sit up **2.** (*en el trabajo*) mañana me incorporo al nuevo trabajo tomorrow I start my new job **3.** (*agregarse*) ~se a [o en] algo to join sth **4.** MIL (*a filas*) to join up

incorrección *f* **1.** (*no correcto*) inaccuracy **2.** (*falta*) error, mistake **3.** (*descortesía*) discourtesy

incorrecto, -a *adj* **1.** (*erróneo*) erroneous **2.** (*descortés*) impolite

incorregible *adj* incorrigible

incorruptible *adj* incorruptible

incorrupto, -a *adj* **1.** (*personas*) undefiled **2.** (*cosas*) uncorrupted

incredibilidad *f* unbelievability

incredulidad *f* **1.** (*desconfianza*) incredulity **2.** REL (*sin fe*) lack of faith

incrédulo, -a I. *adj* **1.** (*desconfiado*) incredulous **2.** REL (*sin fe*) unbelieving **II.** *m, f* **1.** (*desconfiado*) incredulous person **2.** REL (*sin fe*) unbeliever; (*escéptico*) sceptic *Brit,* skeptic *Am*

increíble *adj* incredible

incrementar I. *vt* to increase; (*intensificar*) to intensify **II.** *vr:* ~se to increase

incremento *m* **1.** (*aumento*) increment **2.** (*crecimiento*) increase

increpar *vt* to rebuke

incriminar *vt* JUR to incriminate

incruento, -a *adj* bloodless

incrustación *f* **1.** (*proceso*) embedding **2.** ARTE inlaying **3.** MED incrustation **4.** (*costra*) incrustation

incrustar I. *vt* ARTE (*con madera*) to inlay **II.** *vr:* ~se **1.** (*introducirse*) to embed itself **2.** MED to encrust

incubación *f* incubation (period)

incubadora *f* incubator

incubar *vt, vr:* ~se to incubate

incuestionable *adj* unquestionable

inculcar <c→qu> **I.** *vt* **1.** (*enseñar*) to instil, to instill *Am;* ~ a sus hijos la fe religiosa to instill [o to inculcate] the religious beliefs in [o into] his children **2.** (*infundir*) to inculcate; **el nuevo entrenador ha inculcado un espíritu nuevo en el equipo** the new coach has inculcated the team with a new spirit **II.** *vr:* ~se to be obstinate; ~ en algo to be obstinate about sth

inculpación *f* accusation

inculpar *vt* ~ a alguien de algo to accuse sb of sth; JUR to charge sb with sth

inculto, -a *adj* **1.** (*sin instrucción*) uneducated **2.** (*comportamiento*) unrefined, uncouth **3.** AGR (*sin cultivar*) uncultivated

incultura *f* lack of education [o culture]

incumbencia *f* responsibility, incumbency *form;* no es de tu ~ it's none of your business

incumbir *vi* **1.** (*atañer*) to concern **2.** ADMIN (*ser de la competencia*) ~ a alguien to be incumbent on [o upon] sb

incumplimiento *m* non-compliance; ~ de contrato breach of contract

incumplir *vt* to break, to fail to fulfil [o fulfill *Am*]

incurable I. *adj* **1.** (*enfermedad*) incurable **2.** (*sin esperanza*) hopeless **II.** *mf* incurable person

incurrir *vi* **1.** (*situación mala*) incurrió en el desprecio de su jefe he brought on his boss's scorn; ~ en una falta to commit an error; ~ en viejas costumbres to go back to old habits **2.** (*odio*) to incur

incursión *f* incursion, strike

indagación *f* investigation, enquiry *Brit,* inquiry *Am*

indagar <g→gu> *vt* ~ algo to investigate, to look into sth

indebido, -a *adj* **1.** (*cantidades*) wrong **2.** (*injusto*) wrongful; (*ilícito*) illicit; respuesta indebida inappropriate reply

indecencia *f* **1.** (*persona*) indecency; (*obscenidad*) obscenity **2.** (*acción*) indecency, outrage; (*dicho*) unseemliness

indecente *adj* **1.** (*inadecuado*) improper **2.** (*obsceno*) indecent; (*sin vergüenza*) shameless **3.** (*guarro*) filthy, indecent

indecisión *f* **1.** (*irresolución*) iresolution **2.** (*vacilación*) hesitation, indecision

indeciso, -a *adj* **1.** (*irresoluto*) irresolute **2.** (*que vacila*) indecisive **3.** (*resultado*) inconclusive

indecoroso, -a *adj* **1.** (*indecente*) indecent **2.** (*incorrecto*) indecorous

indefendible *adj* indefensible

indefensión *f* defencelessness *Brit,* defenselessness *Am*

indefenso, -a *adj* defenceless *Brit,* defenseless *Am*

indefinible *adj* indefinable, undefinable

indefinidamente *adv* indefinitely

indefinido, -a *adj t.* LING indefinite

indeformable *adj* that keeps its shape

indelicadeza *f* **1.** (*vulgaridad*) vulgarity **2.** (*desconsideración*) indelicacy

indelicado, -a *adj* indelicate

indemne *adj* 1. (*persona*) unharmed 2. (*cosa*) undamaged

indemnización *f* indemnity, indemnification; ~ **de despido** unemployment compensation, severance pay

indemnizar <z→c> *vt* 1. (*daños y perjuicios*) to indemnify; ~ **de** [*o* **por**] **algo** to indemnify for sth 2. (*gastos*) to reimburse

independencia *f* independence; **con** ~ **de algo** independently of sth

independentismo *m* POL independence movement

independiente *adj* 1. (*libre*) independent; **un piso** ~ an individual flat 2. (*profesión, sin partido*) independent 3. (*soltero*) single

independización *f* (*liberación*) liberation; (*adolescente*) emancipation

independizar <z→c> I. *vt* to make independent II. *vr:* ~**se** 1. (*liberarse*) to become independent 2. (*adolescente*) to become independent [*o* emancipated]

indescifrable *adj* indecipherable

indescriptible *adj* indescribable

indeseable I. *adj* undesirable II. *mf* undesirable [*o* despised] person

indestructible *adj* indestructible

indeterminación *f* 1. (*inconcreción*) indeterminacy 2. (*indecisión*) indecision

indeterminado, -a *adj* 1. (*inconcreto*) indeterminate 2. (*indeciso*) indecisive

indexación *f* 1. indexation 2. INFOR indexing

indexar *vt* INFOR to index

India *f* **la** ~ India; **las** ~**s** the Indies

indiada *f* AmL: a group of Indians

indicación *f* 1. (*señal*) indication; (*por escrito*) observation; ~ **de las fuentes** source reference 2. MED (*síntoma*) symptom; (*en recetas*) directions *pl* 3. (*consejo*) advice; **por** ~ **de...** on the advice of ... 4. *pl* (*instrucciones*) instructions *pl*

indicado, -a *adj* 1. (*aconsejable*) advisable; (*adecuado*) indicated; **eso es lo más** ~ that is the most suitable 2. MED (*tratamiento*) recommended

indicador *m* indicator; TÉC gauge, gage *Am;* ECON index; ~ **de carretera** roadsign; ~ **de gasolina** fuel gauge [*o* gage *Am*]

indicar <c→qu> *vt* 1. TÉC (*aparato*) to register 2. (*señalar, sugerir*) to indicate; (*mostrar*) to show 3. MED to prescribe

indicativo, -a *adj t.* LING indicative

índice *m* 1. (*biblioteca, catálogo*) index, catalogue, catalog *Am;* (*libro*) table of contents 2. (*dedo*) index finger, forefinger 3. (*estadísticas*) rate; ~ **de audiencia** audience ratings; ~ **de paro** unemployment rate; ~ **de Precios al Consumidor** Retail Price Index 4. TÉC pointer; (*de reloj*) hand

indicio *m* 1. (*señal*) sign 2. JUR indication 3. (*vestigio*) trace

indiferencia *f* indifference

indiferente *adj* indifferent; **me es** ~ it doesn't make any difference to me

indígena I. *adj* indigenous, native; (*en Latinoamérica*) Latin American II. *mf* native; (*en Latinoamérica*) Latin American

indigencia *f* poverty

indigente I. *adj* destitute II. *mf* destitute person

indigestar I. *vt* to cause indigestion to II. *vr:* ~**se** 1. (*empacharse*) ~**se de** [*o* **por**] **algo** to get indigestion from sth 2. *inf* (*hacerse antipático*) to be detestable 3. AmL (*inquietarse*) to worry

indigestión *f* MED indigestion; **contraer una** ~ to get indigestion

indigesto, -a *adj ser* indigestible, hard to digest

indignación *f* indignation

indignado, -a *adj* ~ **por algo** indignant about [*o* at] sth

indignante *adj* infuriating, outrageous

indignar I. *vt* to infuriate, to outrage II. *vr* ~**se por algo** to become indignant [*o* infuriated] about sth

indignidad *f* indignity

indigno, -a *adj* 1. (*desmerecedor*) unworthy; ~ **de confianza** unworthy of trust 2. (*vil*) contemptible

índigo *m* indigo

indio, -a I. *adj* 1. (*de la India*) Indian 2. (*de América*) American Indian. II. *m, f* 1. (*de la India*) Indian 2. (*de América*) American Indian ►**hacer el** ~ (*tonterías*) to fool around [*o* about]; (*el ridículo*) to act the fool

indirecta *f inf* hint, insinuation; **lanzar** [*o* **soltar**] **una** ~ to drop a hint

indirecto, -a *adj* indirect; **complemento** ~ LING indirect object

indisciplina *f* indiscipline, lack of discipline

indisciplinado, -a I. *adj* (*falto de disciplina*) undisciplined; (*desobediente*) disobedient; (*insumiso*) insubordinate II. *m, f* (*desobediente*) disobedient person; (*insumiso*) insubordinate person

indiscreción *f* 1. (*no guardar un secreto*) indiscretion 2. (*observación*) faux pas, gaffe 3. (*curiosidad*) nosiness

indiscreto, -a *adj* 1. (*imprudente*) imprudent 2. (*que no guarda secretos*) indiscreet

indiscriminado, -a *adj* indiscriminate

indiscutible *adj* indisputable

indisociable *adj* inseparable; QUÍM indissoluble

indispensable *adj* indispensable; **lo** (**más**) ~ the most essential; **el requisito** ~ **es...** the key requisite is ...

indisponer *irr como* poner I. *vt* 1. (*enemistar*) ~ **a uno contra otro** to set one person against another 2. (*de salud*) to indispose II. *vr:* ~**se** 1. (*enemistarse*) to quarrel 2. (*ponerse mal*) to become indisposed

indisposición *f* (*de salud, desgana*) indisposition

indispuesto, -a *adj* 1. (*enfermizo, con desgana*) indisposed 2. (*enemistado*) at odds

3.(*reacio*) unwilling

indistintamente *adv* **1.**(*indiscriminada-mente*) indiscriminately; **se aplica a todos los niños** ~ it applies to all the children without distinction **2.**(*irreconocible*) indistinctly

indistinto, -a *adj* **1.** *elev* (*indiferenciado*) undifferentiated **2.**(*igual*) indistinguishable **3.**(*difuso*) vague; (*poco claro*) indistinct

individual *adj* **1.**(*personal*) personal; (*peculiar*) individual **2.**(*simple*) single **3.** *CSur* (*idéntico*) identical

individualista **I.** *adj* individualistic **II.** *mf* individualist

individualizar <z→c> *vt* to individualize; (*diferenciar*) to single out

individuo *m* **1.**(*espécimen*) individual **2.**(*miembro*) member **3.** *pey* (*sujeto*) individual, character

indivisible *adj* indivisible

indócil *adj* **1.**(*desobediente*) unruly **2.**(*cabezota*) wilful *Brit,* willful *Am*

indoctrinar *vt AmL* to indoctrinate; *fig* to brainwash

indocumentado, -a *adj* **1.** *ser* (*no registrado*) unregistered **2.** *estar* (*sin documentos*) without papers [*o* means of identification]

índole *f* nature, kind

indolencia *f* **1.**(*apatía*) apathy **2.**(*indiferencia*) indifference **3.**(*desgana*) indolence

indolente *adj* **1.**(*apático*) apathetic **2.**(*indiferente*) indifferent **3.**(*con desgana*) indolent

indomable *adj* **1.**(*que no se somete*) indomitable **2.**(*indomesticable*) untameable **3.**(*fuera de control*) unmanageable

indómito, -a *adj* **1.**(*indomable*) indomitable **2.**(*rebelde*) rebellious

Indonesia *f* Indonesia

indonesio, -a *adj, m, f* Indonesian

inducción *f* **1.** ELEC, FILOS induction **2.**(*instigación*) inducement

inducir *irr como traducir vt* **1.** ELEC (*corriente*) to induce **2.**(*instigar*) to induce; ~ **a error** to lead astray, to mislead **3.** FILOS (*razonar*) to induce; **de todo esto induzco que...** from all this I induce that ...

inductor(a) *adj* **1.** ELEC (*corriente*) inductor **2.**(*instigador*) inducer

indudable *adj* undeniable; **es ~ que...** it is certain that ...

indulgencia *f* **1.** REL (*pecados*) indulgence, remission **2.** *elev* (*cualidad*) indulgence; **proceder sin ~ contra...** to proceed without leniency against ...

indultar *vt* **1.** JUR (*perdonar*) to pardon; (*después del proceso*) to reprieve; ~ **a alguien de la pena de muerte** to grant sb a reprieve from the death penalty **2.**(*eximir*) to exempt

indulto *m* **1.**(*perdón total*) pardon **2.**(*perdón parcial*) remission **3.**(*exención*) exemption

indumentaria *f* **1.**(*ropa*) clothing, clothes *pl;* (*vestir*) dress **2.** HIST (history of) costume [*o* apparel]

industria *f* **1.** COM industry; ~ **del automóvil** car [*o* automobile *Am*] industry **2.**(*empresa*) business; (*fábrica*) factory **3.**(*dedicación*) industry **4.**(*maña*) adeptness; (*pericia*) expertise

industrial **I.** *adj* industrial; **nave** ~ industrial warehouse; **planta** ~ industrial plant; **polígono** ~ industrial estate, industrial park **II.** *mf* industrialist; (*fabricante*) manufacturer

industrialización *f* industrialization

industrializar <z→c> *vt, vr:* ~**se** to industrialize

industrioso, -a *adj* **1.**(*trabajador*) industrious **2.**(*mañoso*) dexterous, dextrous

inédito, -a *adj* **1.**(*no publicado*) unpublished **2.**(*desconocido*) unknown **3.**(*nuevo*) original, new

inefable *adj* ineffable, inexpressible

inefectivo, -a *adj* **1.**(*sin resultado*) ineffective, ineffectual **2.** COM (*no rentable*) unprofitable

ineficacia *f* **1.**(*sin resultado*) ineffectiveness **2.** COM (*sin rentabilidad*) lack of profitability **3.**(*de una persona*) inefficiency

ineficaz *adj* **1.**(*cosa*) ineffective **2.**(*persona*) ineffectual

ineficiente *adj* inefficient

INEM *m abr de* **Instituto Nacional de Empleo** *national employment agency*

inenarrable *adj* indescribable

inepcia *f AmL* **1.**(*ineptitud*) ineptitude **2.**(*necedad*) imbecility

ineptitud *f* **1.**(*incapacidad*) ineptitude; ~ **para algo** ineptitude in sth **2.**(*incompetencia*) incompetence; ~ **para algo** incompetence in sth

inepto, -a *adj* **1.**(*incapaz*) inept; ~ **para algo** inept at sth **2.**(*incompetente*) incompetent; ~ **para algo** incompetent at sth

inequívoco, -a *adj* unequivocal; (*inconfundible*) unmistakable

inercia *f t.* FÍS inertia; **por** ~ mechanically

inerme *adj* **1.**(*desarmado*) unarmed **2.** BIO (*sin aguijón*) without a sting; (*sin púas*) without spines **3.**(*indefenso*) defenceless

inerte *adj* **1.**(*sin vida*) inanimate **2.**(*inmóvil*) inert

inescrutable *adj elev* inscrutable

inesperado, -a *adj* unexpected

inestabilidad *f* **1.**(*fragilidad*) *t.* TÉC fragility **2.**(*variabilidad*) instability

inestable *adj* **1.**(*frágil*) *t.* TÉC fragile **2.**(*variable*) unstable

inestimable *adj* inestimable

inevitable *adj* inevitable, unavoidable

inexactitud *f* **1.**(*no exacto*) inexactitude, inaccuracy **2.**(*error*) incorrection

inexacto, -a *adj* **1.**(*no exacto*) inexact **2.**(*erróneo*) inaccurate

inexcusable *adj* **1.**(*ineludible*) unavoidable **2.**(*sin disculpa*) inexcusable

inexistencia *f* non-existence

inexistente *adj* non-existent

inexorable *adj elev* inexorable

inexperiencia *f* inexperience
inexperto, -a *adj* inexpert; (*sin experiencia*) inexperienced
inexplicable *adj* inexplicable
inexpresivo, -a *adj* 1.(*cara, mirada*) impassive, inexpressive 2.(*cosa*) inexpressive
inexpugnable *adj* 1.(*inconquistable*) impregnable 2.(*irreductible*) unyielding
inextricable *adj* 1.(*enmarañado*) inextricable 2.(*complicado*) intricate
infalible *adj* infallible
infamante *adj* shameful
infamar *vt* to defame
infame *adj* 1.(*vil*) wicked 2.(*muy malo*) vile
infamia *f* 1.(*canallada*) infamy 2.(*deshonra*) dishonour *Brit,* dishonor *Am*
infancia *f* 1.(*niñez, niños*) childhood; **enfermedades de la** ~ childhood illnesses 2.(*etapa inicial*) infancy
infante, -a *m, f* 1. *elev* (*niño, niña*) infant; **jardín de** ~**s** *AmL* nursery school *Brit,* preschool *Am* 2.(*príncipe, princesa*) infante *m,* infanta *f* 3.(*soldado*) infantryman, foot soldier
infantería *f* MIL infantry
infanticida I. *adj* **madre** ~ infanticidal mother II. *mf person who commits infanticide*
infantil *adj* 1.(*referente a la infancia*) infant; **trabajo** ~ child labour *Brit,* child labor *Am;* **sonrisa** ~ child's smile 2. *pey* (*ingenuo*) infantile
infarto *m* heart attack
infatigable *adj* tireless
infausto, -a *adj* unfortunate
infección *f* MED 1.(*contaminación*) contagion 2.(*afección*) infection
infeccioso, -a *adj* MED infectious; **enfermedad infecciosa** contagious illness
infectar I. *vt* 1. MED (*contagiar*) to transmit 2. *inf* (*contaminar*) to infect 3.(*corromper*) to corrupt II. *vr:* ~**se** 1.(*contagiarse*) ~**se de SIDA** to catch AIDS 2.(*inflamarse*) to become infected
infecto, -a *adj* 1.(*contagiado*) ~ **de algo** infected with sth 2.(*nauseabundo*) nauseating 3.(*corrupto*) corrupt, tainted
infecundidad *f* infertility
infelicidad *f* 1.(*falta de felicidad*) unhappiness 2.(*suerte adversa*) misfortune
infeliz I. *adj* 1.(*no feliz*) unhappy 2. *inf* (*ingenuo*) ingenuous II. *mf inf* 1.(*desgraciado*) wretch 2.(*buenazo*) kind-hearted person
inferior I. *adj* 1.(*debajo*) lower; **labio** ~ lower lip 2.(*de menos calidad*) inferior 3.(*menos*) ~ **a algo** lesser than sth 4.(*subordinado*) subordinate II. *mf* inferior
inferioridad *f* inferiority; **estar en** ~ **de condiciones** to be at a disadvantage
inferir *irr como sentir* I. *vt* 1.(*deducir*) to infer; ~ **de** [*o* **por**] **algo** to infer from sth 2.(*ocasionar*) to occasion 3.(*causar*) to cause II. *vr:* ~**se** to be deducible
infernal *adj* infernal; **ruido** ~ infernal din

infértil *adj* infertile
infertilidad *f sin pl* infertility
infestar *vt* 1.(*inundar*) ~ **de algo** to overrun with sth 2.(*infectar*) ~ **de algo** to infect with sth 3.(*causar*) to ravage 4.(*corromper*) ~ **de algo** to corrupt with sth
inficionar *vt* 1.(*contaminar*) to infect 2.(*envenenar*) to poison 3. *form* (*corromper*) to corrupt
infidelidad *f* 1.(*deslealtad*) infidelity, unfaithfulness 2.(*incredulidad*) unbelief
infiel I. *adj* <infidelísimo> 1.(*desleal*) unfaithful 2.(*pagano*) heathen 3.(*inexacto*) imprecise II. *mf* pagan
infiernillo *m* camp(ing) [*o* portable] stove
infierno *m* 1. *t.* REL hell; **me mandó al** ~ he/she told me to go to hell 2.(*en la mitología*) underworld
infiltración *f t.* POL infiltration
infiltrar I. *vt* 1.(*penetrar*) to infiltrate, to penetrate 2.(*inculcar*) to imbue II. *vr:* ~**se en algo** 1.(*penetrar*) to penetrate sth 2.(*introducirse*) to infiltrate sth
ínfimo, -a *adj* 1.(*muy bajo*) very low 2.(*mínimo*) minimal 3.(*vil*) vile
infinidad *f* 1.(*cualidad de infinito*) infinity 2.(*gran número*) enormous quantity
infinitivo *m* infinitive
infinito *m t.* MAT infinity
infinito, -a *adj* 1.(*ilimitado*) limitless; (*cosas no materiales*) boundless 2.(*incontable*) infinite
infinitud *f sin pl* infinitude
inflable *adj* inflatable
inflación *f* 1. *t.* ECON inflation 2.(*exceso*) excess
inflacionista *adj* ECON inflationist
inflamable *adj* (in)flammable
inflamación *f* 1. *t.* MED inflammation 2. TÉC ignition; **punto de** ~ ignition point
inflamar I. *vt* 1.(*encender*) to ignite 2.(*excitar*) *t.* MED to inflame II. *vr:* ~**se** *t.* MED to become inflamed
inflamatorio, -a *adj* MED inflammatory
inflar I. *vt* 1.(*llenar de aire*) to inflate 2.(*exagerar*) to exaggerate II. *vr* 1.(*hincharse*) ~**se de algo** to swell with sth 2. *inf* (*de comida*) to stuff oneself
inflexibilidad *f* 1.(*rigidez*) inflexibility 2.(*firmeza*) firmness
inflexible *adj* 1.(*rígido*) inflexible 2.(*firme*) firm
inflexión *f* 1.(*de la voz*) *t.* MAT, LING inflection, inflexion 2.(*torcimiento*) bend
infligir <g→j> *vt* (*dolor*) to inflict; ~ **un castigo** to inflict a punishment; ~ **daño** to cause injury
influencia *f* influence; **tener** ~ to be influential
influenciar *vt* to influence **dejarse** ~ to be influenced
influir *irr como huir* I. *vi* 1.(*contribuir*) ~ **en** [*o* **sobre**] **algo** to have a hand in sth 2.(*actuar*)

~ **en algo** to have an influence on sth **II.** *vt* to influence

influjo *m* influence

influyente *adj* influential

información *f* **1.** information **2.** (*noticias*) news + *sing vb* **3.** MIL intelligence **4.** TEL directory enquiries *pl Brit*

informador(a) *m(f)* **1.** (*informante*) informant; (*de policía*) informer **2.** (*periodista*) reporter

informal *adj* **1.** (*desenfadado*) informal, casual; **lenguaje** ~ informal language **2.** (*no cumplidor*) unreliable

informalidad *f* informality

informante *mf* informant

informar I. *vt* **1.** (*comunicar*) to inform; (*periodista*) to report **2.** *elev* (*fundamentar*) to found **II.** *vi* JUR to plead **III.** *vr* ~**se de algo** to find out about sth

informática *f* computer [*o* computing] science

informático, -a I. *adj* **fallo** ~ computer error **II.** *m, f* computer expert

informativo *m* news broadcast, news programme *Brit,* news program *Am;* **el** ~ **de las nueve** the nine o'clock news

informativo, -a *adj* informative; **boletín** ~ (*por escrito, radial*) (news) bulletin

informatización *f* computerization

informatizar <z→c> *vt* to computerize

informe I. *adj* **1.** (*sin forma*) shapeless **2.** (*indefinido*) undefined **II.** *m* report

infortunado, -a *adj* unfortunate

infortunio *m* misfortune, adversity

infotainment *m* infotainment

infracción *f* infraction; (*administrativa*) breach; ~ **de tráfico** traffic offence [*o* offense *Am*]

infractor(a) I. *adj* offending **II.** *m(f)* infractor, offender

infraestructura *f* **1.** (*construcción*) foundations *pl* **2.** (*medios*) infrastructure

infrahumano, -a *adj* subhuman

infranqueable *adj* impassable, insurmountable *fig*

infrarrojo, -a *adj* infrared

infrautilización *f* underuse

infrautilizar <z→c> *vt* to underuse

infravalorar *vt* to undervalue, to underestimate

infrecuencia *f* infrequency

infrecuente *adj* infrequent

infringir <g→j> *vt* to infringe; ~ **la ley** to break the law

infructuoso, -a *adj* fruitless; (*fracasado*) unsuccessful

ínfula *f pl* (*soberbia*) pretensions *pl;* **darse** ~**s** to put on airs (and graces)

infundado, -a *adj* unfounded

infundio *m* lie

infundir *vt* (*deseo*) to infuse; (*respeto*) to command; (*temor*) to intimidate; (*sospechas*) to instil

infusión *f* infusion; (*de hierbas*) herb(al) tea

ingeniar I. *vt* to devise **II.** *vr:* ~**se** to contrive, to manage

ingeniería *f* engineering; **escuela de** ~ school of engineering

ingeniero, -a *m, f* engineer

ingenio *m* **1.** (*inventiva*) ingenuity, ingeniousness **2.** (*talento para contar*) wit **3.** (*persona*) gifted person, genius **4.** (*maña*) aptitude **5.** (*máquina*) device

ingenioso, -a *adj* **1.** (*hábil*) skilful *Brit,* skillful *Am* **2.** (*listo*) ingenious

ingente *adj* enormous; ~ **cantidad** huge quantity

ingenuidad *f* **1.** (*inocencia*) ingenuousness, candour *Brit,* candor *Am* **2.** (*torpeza*) naivety

ingenuo, -a *adj* ingenuous, candid

ingerir *irr como sentir vt* **1.** (*referente a medicamentos*) to take **2.** (*beber, comer*) to ingest

ingestión *f* **1.** (*referente a medicamentos*) taking, intake **2.** (*el beber, comer*) ingestion, consumption

Inglaterra *f* England

ingle *f* ANAT groin

inglés, -esa I. *adj* English **II.** *m, f* Englishman *m,* Englishwoman *f*

inglete *m* **1.** MAT forty-five degree angle **2.** (*ensambladura*) mitre joint *Brit,* miter joint *Am*

ingobernable *adj* **1.** (*no gobernable*) ungovernable **2.** (*no dirigible*) unmanageable

ingratitud *f* ingratitude

ingrato, -a *adj* ungrateful; ~ (**para**) **con alguien** ungrateful to sb; (*tarea*) thankless

ingravidez *f* weightlessness, lack of gravity

ingrávido, -a *adj* **1.** (*falta de gravedad*) lacking in gravity, weightless **2.** (*ligero*) light

ingrediente *m* **1.** (*sustancia*) ingredient **2.** (*elemento*) element

ingresar I. *vi* **1.** (*inscribirse*) ~ **en algo** to become a member of sth **2.** (*hospitalizarse*) to be admitted to hospital **II.** *vt* **1.** FIN (*cheque*) to pay in, to deposit **2.** (*hospitalizar*) to hospitalize **3.** (*percibir*) to earn

ingreso *m* **1.** (*inscripción*) entry; **examen de** ~ entrance exam **2.** (*ceremonia*) initiation **3.** (*alta*) incorporation **4.** (*en una cuenta*) deposit **5.** *pl* (*retribuciones*) income

íngrimo, -a *adj AmL* (*solitario*) solitary

inhábil *adj* **1.** (*persona: torpe*) clumsy; (*incompetente*) inept **2.** JUR **día** ~ non-working day

inhabilidad *f* ineptitude

inhabilitar *vt* JUR **1.** (*incapacitar*) ~ **para algo** to incapacitate for sth **2.** (*prohibir*) ~ **a** (**hacer**) **algo** to disqualify from (doing) sth

inhabitable *adj* uninhabitable

inhabitado, -a *adj* uninhabited

inhabitual *adj* unusual

inhalador *m* MED inhaler

inhalar *vt t.* MED to inhale, to breathe in

inherente *adj* inherent; ~ **a algo** inherent in

sth

inhibición *f* 1.(*represión*) repression 2.(*abstención*) abstention 3. MED, JUR inhibition

inhibir I. *vt* 1.(*reprimir*) to repress 2. BIO, JUR to inhibit II. *vr* ~se de algo to abstain from sth; ~se de hacer algo to refrain from doing sth

inhibitorio, -a *adj* JUR inhibitive

inhospitalario, -a *adj* inhospitable, unfriendly

inhóspito, -a *adj* inhospitable

inhumación *f* inhumation, burial

inhumano, -a *adj* (*no humano*) inhuman; (*sin compasión*) inhumane

inhumar *vt elev* to inhume, to bury

INI *m abr de* Instituto Nacional de Industria *national industry institute*

iniciación *f* 1.(*comienzo*) beginning, commencement 2.(*introducción*) ~ a [*o* en] algo initiation to sth 3.(*de un novato*) initiation

iniciado, -a I. *adj* initiated II. *m, f* initiate

iniciador(a) *m(f)* initiator, pioneer

inicial I. *adj* inital; fase ~ initial phase II. *f* (*letra*) initial

iniciar I. *vt* 1.(*comenzar*) to begin 2.(*introducir*) to initiate 3. INFOR to log in [*o* on]; ~ el funcionamiento del ordenador to log in [*o* on] to a computer II. *vr:* ~se 1.(*comenzar*) to begin 2.(*introducirse en*) ella sola se inició en la lectura she taught herself to read

iniciativa *f* initiative; ~ privada ECON private enterprise

inicio *m* beginning

inigualable *adj* incomparable, unrivalled *Brit,* unrivaled *Am*

inimaginable *adj* unimaginable

ininteligible *adj* unintelligible; (*escritura*) illegible

ininterrumpido, -a *adj* uninterrupted

iniquidad *f* 1.(*injusticia*) iniquity 2.(*infamia*) wickedness

injerencia *f* interference

injerir *irr como sentir* I. *vt* 1.(*introducir*) to introduce; ~ en algo to introduce into sth 2.(*injertar*) to graft II. *vr:* ~se to interfere

injertar *vt* (*plantas*) *t.* MED to graft

injerto *m* 1.(*acción de injertar*) grafting 2.(*brote*) *t.* MED graft

injuria *f* (*con palabras*) insult, affront; (*con acciones*) harm; JUR slander

injuriar *vt* (*con palabras*) to insult; (*con acciones*) to injure

injurioso, -a *adj* injurious

injusticia *f* injustice, unfairness

injustificado, -a *adj* unjustified

injusto, -a *adj* 1.(*no justo*) unjust, unfair 2.(*injustificado*) *t.* JUR inequitable

inmaculado, -a *adj* 1.(*limpísimo*) immaculate 2.(*impecable*) impeccable

inmadurez *f* sin pl immaturity

inmaduro, -a *adj* immature

inmediaciones *fpl* surroundings *pl,* vicinity

inmediatamente *adv* 1.(*sin demora*) immediately 2.(*directamente*) directly

inmediato, -a *adj* 1.(*sin demora*) immediate; de ~ immediately, right away 2.(*directo*) direct 3.(*próximo*) adjacent

inmejorable *adj* unbeatable, excellent

inmemorable *adj,* **inmemorial** *adj* immemorial; desde tiempos ~es since [*o* from] time immemorial

inmensidad *f* 1.(*extensión*) immensity 2.(*cantidad*) vastness

inmenso, -a *adj* immense

inmerecido, -a *adj* undeserved

inmersión *f* (*sumersión*) *t.* ASTR immersion

inmerso, -a *adj* immersed; *fig* involved

inmigración *f* immigration

inmigrante *mf* immigrant

inmigrar *vi* to immigrate

inmigratorio, -a *adj* immigratory

inminente *adj* imminent

inmiscuir *irr como huir* I. *vt* to put in II. *vr:* ~se to interfere, to meddle

inmisericorde *adj* hard-hearted

inmobiliaria *f* 1.(*construcción*) construction company 2.(*venta, alquiler*) estate agency *Brit,* real estate office [*o* agency] *Am*

inmobiliario, -a *adj* property

inmoderado, -a *adj* immoderate

inmodestia *f* immodesty

inmodesto, -a *adj* immodest

inmolación *f* immolation, sacrifice

inmolar *vt, vr:* ~(se) Jesús se inmoló por los hombres Jesus sacrificed himself for mankind

inmoral *adj* immoral; (*en cuestiones sexuales*) indecent

inmoralidad *f* 1.(*indignidad*) immorality 2.(*indecencia*) indecency

inmortal *adj* immortal

inmortalidad *f* immortality

inmortalizar <z→c> I. *vt* to immortalize II. *vr:* ~se to be immortalized

inmóvil *adj* immobile; (*inamovible*) unmovable; (*quieto*) still, motionless

inmovilidad *f* immobility

inmovilización *f* 1.(*incapaz de moverse*) paralysis; MED, MIL immobilization 2. COM lock-up

inmovilizar <z→c> *vt* 1.(*paralizar*) to paralyse; ~ a alguien to put sb out of action 2. MED to immobilize 3. COM to lock up

inmueble *adj, m* property

inmundicia *f* 1.(*suciedad*) filth 2.(*indecencia*) immorality 3.(*basura*) rubbish *Brit,* garbage *Am*

inmundo, -a *adj* filthy; (*asqueroso*) disgusting

inmune *adj* 1. MED immune 2.(*exento*) ~ de algo exempt from sth

inmunidad *f* immunity

inmunizar <z→c> I. *vt* to immunize; (*vacunar*) to vaccinate II. *vr:* ~se to safeguard oneself

inmunodeficiencia *f* MED immunodeficiency; síndrome de ~ adquirida Acquired

Immune Deficiency Syndrome
inmunología *f* MED immunology
inmutabilidad *f* 1.(*inmodificable*) immutability 2.(*imperturbable*) impassivity
inmutable *adj* 1.(*inmodificable*) immutable 2.(*imperturbable*) imperturbable
inmutar I. *vt* 1.(*afectar*) to affect 2.(*variar*) to alter II. *vr:* ~**se** to be affected; **sin** ~**se** without turning a hair [*o* batting an eye], impassively
innato, -a *adj* innate, inborn; **tiene un talento** ~ he has an natural talent
innavegable *adj* 1.(*aguas*) unnavigable 2.(*embarcación*) unseaworthy
innecesario, -a *adj* unnecessary
innegable *adj* undeniable
innoble *adj* ignoble
innovación *f* innovation
innovador(a) I. *adj* innovative, novel II. *m(f)* innovator
innovar *vt* to innovate
innumerable *adj* innumerable; **un gentío** ~ countless people
inobservancia *f* non-observance
inocencia *f* 1.(*falta de culpabilidad, ingenuidad*) innocence 2.(*falta de malicia*) harmlessness, candour *Brit,* candor *Am*
inocentada *f* 1.(*tontada: comentario*) naive remark; (*acción*) naive action 2.(*broma*) ≈ *April fool joke, in Spain played on 28th December;* **gastar una** ~ **a alguien** to play a practical joke on sb
inocente *adj* 1.(*sin culpa*) innocent 2.(*sin malicia*) harmless 3.(*ingenuo*) innocent, ingenuous
inocuidad *f sin pl* innocuousness, harmlessness
inocular *vt* 1.MED to inoculate 2.(*serpientes*) to administer an antitoxin
inocuo, -a *adj* innocuous, harmless
inodoro *m* toilet
inodoro, -a *adj* odourless *Brit,* odorless *Am*
inofensivo, -a *adj* inoffensive
inoficioso, -a *adj* AmL useless, idle
inolvidable *adj* unforgettable
inoperante *adj* ineffective
inopinado, -a *adj* unexpected
inoportunidad *f* 1.(*fuera de lugar*) inappropriateness 2.(*fuera de tiempo*) inopportuneness, untimeliness
inoportuno, -a *adj* 1.(*fuera de lugar*) inappropriate 2.(*fuera de tiempo*) inopportune, untimely
inorgánico, -a *adj* 1.(*no viviente*) inorganic 2.(*no organizado*) disorganized
inoxidable *adj* rustproof; (*acero*) stainless
input *m* <inputs> INFOR input
inquebrantable *adj* (*decisión*) unwavering; (*cosa*) unbreakable
inquietante *adj* (*preocupante*) worrying; (*perturbador*) disturbing
inquietar I. *vt* to worry II. *vr* ~**se con** [*o* **por**] **algo** to worry about sth
inquieto, -a *adj* 1. estar (*intranquilo*) anxious

2. *ser* (*desasosegado*) restless
inquietud *f* 1.(*intranquilidad*) anxiety 2.(*desasosiego*) restlessness 3.(*preocupación*) worry 4. *pl* (*anhelos*) aspirations *pl*
inquilino, -a *m, f* tenant, lessee
inquina *f* aversion
inquirir *irr como adquirir vt* to enquire *Brit,* to inquire *Am*
inquisición *f* investigation
Inquisición *f* Inquisition, The Holy Office
inquisidor *m* inquisitor
inquisidor(a) *adj* inquisitive
inri *m* REL INRI; **para más** ~ *fig* to make matters worse
insaciable *adj* insatiable; (*sed*) unquenchable
insalubre *adj* unhealthy, insalubrious *form*
insalubridad *f* unhealthiness
insalvable *adj* unsalvageable; (*obstáculo*) insuperable
insanable *adj* incurable
insano, -a *adj* 1.(*insalubre*) unhealthy 2.(*loco*) insane
insatisfacción *f sin pl* dissatisfaction
insatisfactorio, -a *adj* unsatisfactory
insatisfecho, -a *adj* dissatisfied
inscribir *irr como escribir* I. *vt* 1.(*registrar*) to register; **a los dos días de nacer la inscribieron en el registro civil** two days after she was born they registered her birth 2.(*grabar*) to inscribe; ~ **en algo** to inscribe on sth 3.(*alistar*) to enrol *Brit,* to enroll *Am;* ~ **en algo** to enrol for [*o* on] sth 4.MAT to inscribe II. *vr:* ~**se** 1.(*registrarse*) to register; **se inscribió en la oficina de empleo** he registered at the Job Centre 2. *t.* UNIV (*alistarse*) to enrol *Brit,* to enroll *Am;* ~**se en algo** to enrol for [*o* on] sth
inscripción *f* 1.(*registro*) registration 2.(*alistamiento*) *t.* UNIV enrolment *Brit,* enrollment *Am;* ~ **en la universidad** enrolment at university; ~ **en un curso** enrolment on a course 3.(*escrito grabado*) inscription
inscrito, -a *pp de* **inscribir**
insecticida *m* insecticide
insecto *m* insect
inseguridad *f* insecurity
inseguro, -a *adj* insecure
inseminación *f* insemination
inseminar *vt* to inseminate
insensatez *f* 1.(*falta de sensatez*) foolishness 2.(*disparate*) stupidity
insensato, -a *adj* foolish
insensibilidad *f* 1.(*física o afectiva*) insensitivity 2.(*resistencia*) immunity
insensibilizar <z→c> I. *vt* to render insensitive; MED to desensitize II. *vr:* ~**se** 1.(*no sentir*) to become insensitive 2.(*resistir*) to become immune
insensible *adj* 1.(*física o afectivamente*) insensitive 2.(*resistente*) immune 3.(*imperceptible*) imperceptible
inseparable *adj* inseparable
inserción *f* 1.(*inclusión*) inclusion; ~ **social**

social insertion **2.** MED implant

insertar I. *vt* **1.** (*llave, moneda, texto*) to insert **2.** (*anuncio*) to place II. *vr:* ~**se 1.** (*músculo*) to be attached **2.** (*tumor*) ~**se en algo** to invade sth

inservible *adj* useless

insidia *f* **1.** (*asechanzas, trampa*) trap **2.** (*engaño*) deception, trick **3.** (*mala pasada*) treacherous act

insidioso, -a I. *adj* **1.** (*intrigante*) scheming **2.** (*capcioso*) treacherous **3.** (*enfermedad*) insidious II. *m*, *f* **1.** (*intrigante*) schemer **2.** (*capcioso*) treacherous person

insigne *adj* (*personaje público*) distinguished; (*científico*) eminent

insignia *f* **1.** (*de asociación*) badge; (*honorífica*) decoration; (*militar*) insignia **2.** (*bandera*) flag, ensign

insignificancia *f* **1.** (*pequeñez, no importancia*) insignificance **2.** (*no significancia*) triviality

insignificante *adj* **1.** (*pequeño, no importante*) insignificant **2.** (*no significante*) trivial

insinceridad *f* insincerity

insincero, -a *adj* (*no sincero*) insincere

insinuación *f* **1.** (*alusión*) allusion **2.** (*engatusamiento*) insinuation

insinuante *adj* **1.** (*palabras*) insinuating **2.** (*comportamiento*) ingratiating **3.** (*seductor*) suggestive

insinuar <*1. pres:* insinúo> I. *vt* **1.** (*dar a entender*) to insinuate; **¿qué estás insinuando?** what are you insinuating? **2.** (*hacer creer*) **¿quién te ha insinuado eso?** who has put that into your head? II. *vr:* ~**se 1.** (*engatusar*) ~**se a alguien** to get in with sb **2.** *inf* (*amorosamente*) ~**se a alguien** to flirt with sb **3.** (*cosa*) to be discernible

insipidez *f* **1.** (*de comida*) insipidness **2.** (*de persona: aburrida*) dullness; (*sin espíritu*) listlessness

insípido, -a *adj* **1.** (*comida*) insipid **2.** (*persona: aburrida*) dull; (*sin espíritu*) listless

insistencia *f* **1.** (*perseverancia*) persistence **2.** (*énfasis*) insistence; **pedir algo con** ~ to press for sth

insistente *adj* **1.** (*perseverante*) persistent; (*machacón*) insistent **2.** (*con énfasis*) pressing

insistir *vi* **1.** (*perseverar*) to persist; ~ **en algo** to persist in sth **2.** (*exigir, recalcar*) to insist; ~ **en algo** to insist on sth

insobornable *adj* incorruptible

insociable *adj*, **insocial** *adj* unsociable

insolación *f* **1.** METEO *period of unbroken sunshine* **2.** MED sunstroke

insolencia *f* **1.** (*impertinencia*) impertinence, disrespect **2.** (*arrogancia*) arrogance

insolentarse *vr* to become insolent; ~ **con alguien** to be insolent to sb

insolente *adj* **1.** (*impertinente*) impertinent **2.** (*arrogante*) insolent

insolidario, -a *adj* unsupportive; (*egoísta*) selfish

insólito, -a *adj* **1.** (*inhabitual*) unusual, uncommon **2.** (*extraordinario*) unwonted *form*

insoluble *adj* **1.** (*no soluble*) insoluble **2.** (*insolucionable*) insoluble

insolvencia *f* bankruptcy; ECON insolvency

insolvente I. *adj* bankrupt; ECON insolvent II. *mf* insolvent

insomnio *m* MED insomnia, sleeplessness

insondable *adj* bottomless, unfathomable *fig*

insonorización *f* soundproofing

insonorizar <z→c> *vt* to soundproof

insoportable *adj* unbearable

insoslayable *adj* unavoidable, inevitable

insospechable *adj* **1.** (*imprevisible*) unforeseeable **2.** (*sorprendente*) surprising

insospechado, -a *adj* **1.** (*no esperado*) unexpected **2.** (*no sospechado*) unsuspected, unforeseen

insostenible *adj* unsustainable

inspección *f* **1.** (*reconocimiento*) inspection; **Inspección de Trabajo** Inspectorate **2.** (*de equipaje*) check **3.** (*de trabajo*) supervision **4.** (*de una máquina*) *t.* TÉC inspection; **Inspección Técnica de Vehículos** ≈ MOT test

inspeccionar *vt* **1.** (*reconocer*) *t.* TÉC to inspect **2.** (*equipaje*) to check **3.** (*trabajo*) to supervise

inspector(a) *m(f)* **1.** (*controlador*) inspector **2.** ENS school inspector

inspiración *f* **1.** (*de aire*) inhalation **2.** (*ideas*) inspiration

inspirar I. *vt* **1.** (*aire*) to inhale **2.** (*ideas, confianza*) to inspire II. *vr:* ~**se ~se en algo/alguien** to be inspired by sth/sb

instalación *f* **1.** (*acción*) installation; (*de baño*) plumbing **2.** (*lo instalado*) TÉC fitting; (*objeto fijo*) fixture; (*objetos movibles*) fittings *pl Brit*, furnishings *pl Am* **3.** *pl* (*edificio*) installation; **instalaciones deportivas** sports facilities *pl*

instalador(a) *m(f)* installer, fitter

instalar I. *vt* **1.** (*calefacción, teléfono*) to install, to instal *Am;* (*baño*) to plumb, to fit **2.** (*alojar*) to accommodate **3.** (*en un cargo*) to install, to instal *Am* II. *vr:* ~**se 1.** (*en una ciudad*) to settle; **me instalé en un sillón** I installed myself in an armchair **2.** (*negocio*) to set up

instancia *f* **1.** (*acción de instar*) urging **2.** (*solicitud*) application; (*petición formal*) petition **3.** JUR instance; **en última** ~ *fig* as a last resort

instantánea *f* FOTO snapshot

instantáneo, -a *adj* instantaneous; (*efecto, café*) instant; **la muerte fue instantánea** death was instantaneous

instante *m* instant; **al cabo de un** ~ the next instant; **en un** ~ in an instant; **pienso en ti a cada** ~ I think of you constantly; **¡un** ~**!** one moment!

instar *vi, vt* (*pedir*) to urge; ~ **a algo** to press for sth; **le** ~**on a que aceptara el puesto** they

urged him to accept the post
instauración f 1. (*de imperio*) foundation 2. (*de democracia*) establishment 3. (*de plan*) implementation
instaurar vt 1. (*imperio*) to found 2. (*democracia*) to establish 3. (*plan*) to implement
instigación f 1. instigation; (*a algo malo*) incitement 2. (*de las masas*) rousing
instigador(a) I. adj 1. instigating; (*a algo malo*) inciting 2. (*de las masas*) rousing II. m(f) instigator; (*a algo malo*) inciter
instigar <g→gu> vt 1. to instigate; (*a algo malo*) to incite 2. (*a las masas*) to rouse
instintivo, -a adj instinctive
instinto m instinct; ~ de supervivencia survival instinct
institución f 1. (*social*) institution; ~ penitenciaria prison 2. (*fundación*) foundation 3. (*establecimiento: de comité*) setting-up; (*de derecho*) institution; (*de beca*) creation; (*de norma, de horario*) introduction
institucional adj institutional
institucionalizar <z→c> vt to institutionalize
instituir irr como huir vt 1. (*fundar*) to found 2. (*establecer: comisión*) to set up; (*derecho*) to institute; (*beca*) to create; (*norma*) to introduce
instituto m 1. ENS (*de bachillerato*) secondary school, high school Am 2. (*científico*) institute; Instituto Monetario Europeo European Monetary Institute; Instituto Nacional de Empleo Employment Service 3. REL order 4. (*establecimiento*) ~ de belleza beauty salon
institutriz f governess
instrucción f 1. (*enseñanza*) teaching; (*en una máquina*) instruction 2. (*conocimientos*) knowledge; (*formación*) training 3. pl (*órdenes*) instructions pl, directions pl; (*directrices*) guidelines pl 4. JUR (*proceso*) proceedings pl
instructivo, -a adj instructive, educational
instructor(a) I. adj juez ~ JUR examining magistrate Brit II. m(f) (*en escuela*) teacher; (*en empresa*) t. MIL instructor
instruido, -a adj educated
instruir irr como huir vt 1. (*enseñar*) to teach; (*en una máquina*) to instruct; (*en tarea específica*) to train 2. (*informar*) to inform 3. JUR (*proceso*) to prepare
instrumentación f instrumentation
instrumental I. adj t. MÚS instrumental II. m 1. LING instrumental case 2. (*de médico*) t. MÚS instruments pl
instrumentalizar <z→c> vt to use as an instrument
instrumentar vt t. MÚS to orchestrate, to arrange, to score
instrumentista mf 1. (*músico*) instrumentalist 2. (*fabricante*) maker of musical instruments 3. (*de quirófano*) member of the surgical staff in charge of the instruments

instrumento m instrument
insubordinación f insubordination
insubordinar I. vt to rouse to rebellion, to stir up II. vr: ~se to rebel
insubsanable adj 1. (*daño*) irreparable 2. (*deficiencia*) unrectifiable 3. (*dificultad*) insurmountable
insuficiencia f 1. (*cualidad*) insufficiency 2. (*escasez*) deficiency; (*falta*) lack 3. (*incompetencia*) incompetence 4. MED failure
insuficiente I. adj insufficient; (*conocimientos*) inadequate II. m ENS fail; he sacado un ~ en inglés I got a fail in English
insuflar vt 1. MED to pump into 2. (*ánimo*) to raise
insufrible adj insufferable
insular adj insular
insulina f MED insulin
insulso, -a adj 1. (*comida*) insipid, tasteless 2. (*persona, película*) dull
insultante adj insulting; (*de modo grosero*) rude
insultar vt 1. (*con insultos*) to insult 2. (*con injurias*) to abuse
insulto m 1. (*palabra gruesa*) insult 2. (*injuria*) abuse
insumisión f 1. (*de un pueblo*) rebelliousness 2. MIL refusal to do military service 3. (*intransigencia*) intransigence
insumiso m one who refuses to do military service or its alternative
insuperable adj 1. (*dificultad*) insuperable, insurmountable; (*persona*) unrivalled Brit, unrivaled Am 2. (*resultado*) unbeatable
insurgente I. adj insurgent II. mf insurgent
insurrección f insurrection; ~ militar mutiny
insustancial adj 1. (*sin sustancia*) insubstantial 2. (*sin interés*) uninteresting 3. (*no importante*) unimportant, insignificant 4. (*superficial*) superficial
insustituible adj irreplaceable
intachable adj irreproachable; (*comportamiento*) faultless
intacto, -a adj 1. (*no tocado*) untouched 2. (*no dañado*) intact 3. (*puro*) pure 4. (*no tratado*) untreated
intangible adj 1. (*inviolable*) inviolable 2. (*intocable, inmaterial*) intangible
integración f integration
integrador m integrator
integral I. adj 1. (*completo*) integral, full 2. (*pan*) wholemeal, wholegrain; (*arroz*) brown rice 3. (*elemento*) integral, intrinsic 4. MAT integral; cálculo ~ integral calculus II. f MAT integral
integrar I. vt 1. (*constituir*) to constitute, to comprise 2. (*en conjunto*) t. MAT to integrate II. vr: ~se to integrate
integridad f 1. (*totalidad*) entirety 2. (*honradez*) integrity 3. (*física*) physical well-being
integrismo m 1. (*ideológico*) fundamentalism 2. (*católico*) orthodoxy

integrista *mf* 1.(*ideológico*) fundamentalist 2.(*católico*) orthodox catholic

íntegro, -a *adj* 1.(*completo*) whole 2.(*persona*) honest, upright

intelecto *m* intellect

intelectual I. *adj* intellectual; (*interés*) studious; (*facultad*) intelligent, scholarly II. *mf* intellectual

inteligencia *f* 1.(*capacidad*) intelligence 2.(*comprensión*) comprehension 3.(*acuerdo*) understanding 4. POL intelligence; **servicio de** ~ MI5 *Brit*, CIA *Am*

inteligente *adj* intelligent

inteligibilidad *f sin pl* intelligibility

inteligible *adj* 1.(*comprensible*) comprehensible 2.(*sonido*) *t.* FILOS intelligible

intemperancia *f* 1.(*intolerancia*) intolerance 2.(*intransigencia*) intransigence 3.(*falta de moderación*) intemperance, excess

intemperante *adj* 1.(*intolerante*) intolerant 2.(*intransigente*) intransigent 3.(*no moderado*) intemperate

intemperie *f* 1.(*el aire libre*) **a la** ~ out in the open; **dormir a la** ~ to sleep outdoors 2.(*del clima*) harsh climate; (*mal tiempo*) inclement weather

intempestivo, -a *adj* 1.(*observación*) inopportune 2.(*visita*) ill-timed

intención *f* 1.(*propósito*) intention; (*propósito firme*) resolution; **sin** ~ unintentionally; **con** ~ deliberately; **tener segundas intenciones** to have an ulterior motive; **tener buenas intenciones** to mean well 2.(*idea*) idea 3.(*objetivo*) intent

intencionado, -a *adj* intentional; JUR premeditated; **bien** ~ (*acción*) well-meant; (*persona*) well-meaning; **mal** ~ unkind; (*persona*) malicious

intencionalidad *f* intention; JUR premeditation

intendencia *f* 1. MIL service corps, quartermaster corps *Am* 2.(*dirección*) management 3. *CSur* (*distrito*) district

intendente *m* 1. MIL quartermaster-general 2.(*de empresa*) manager 3. *CSur* (*de un distrito*) mayor

intensidad *f* 1.(*fuerza*) *t.* FÍS intensity; (*de tormenta*) severity 2.(*de palabras*) vehemence 3.(*de viento*) force 4.(*de luz*) brightness

intensificación *f sin pl* intensification

intensificar <c→qu> I. *vt* to intensify II. *vr:* ~**se** (*tensión*) to heighten; (*tráfico, calor*) to increase; (*conflicto*) to intensify

intensivo, -a *adj* intensive

intenso, -a *adj* 1.(*fuerza, olor*) strong 2.(*palabras*) vehement 3.(*tormenta*) severe 4.(*frío, calor*) intense

intentar *vt* 1.(*probar*) to attempt, to try 2.(*proponerse*) to intend, to mean

intento *m* 1.(*lo intentado*) attempt, try 2.(*propósito*) aim

intentona *f inf* reckless attempt

interacción *f* interaction

interactivo, -a *adj* interactive

intercalación *f* insertion; ~ **de líneas** insert

intercalar I. *adj elev* interpolated; (*día*) intercalary II. *vt* (*en un periódico*) to insert

intercambiar I. *vt* to interchange; (*opiniones*) to exchange; (*cosas*) to swap; ~ **correspondencia con alguien** to correspond with sb II. *vr:* ~**se** (*lugares*) to exchange places

intercambio *m* exchange

interceder *vi* to intercede; ~ **en favor de alguien** to intercede on behalf of sb

interceptar *vt* 1.(*comunicaciones*) to cut off; (*el paso de algo, pelota*) to intercept; (*tráfico*) to hold up, to stop 2.(*mensaje, conversación telefónica*) to intercept 3.(*calle*) to block off

intercesión *f* 1.(*en favor de alguien*) intercession 2.(*en secuestro*) intervention

intercomunicador *m* intercom

intercomunicar <c→qu> *vt* to intercommunicate

intercontinental *adj* intercontinental

intercultural *adj* intercultural

interdisciplinar *adj*, **interdisciplinario, -a** *adj* interdisciplinary

interés *m* 1.(*importancia*) concern 2.(*deseo, atención*) interest; **tengo mucho** ~ **en que...** it is of interest to me that ...; **tengo** ~ **por saber...** I'm interested in knowing ...; **no poner** ~ **en algo** to show [*o* to take] no interest in sth 3.(*provecho*) interest; **el** ~ **público** the public's interest; **esto redunda en** ~ **tuyo** this redounds to your credit 4. FIN interest; (*rendimiento*) yield; **un 10 % de** ~ 10 % interest; **dar mucho** ~ to give a lot of interest

interesadamente *adv* selfishly; **actuar** ~ (*por propio interés*) to act selfishly; (*por interés material*) to act in one's own interest

interesado, -a I. *adj* 1.(*con interés*) interested 2.(*parcial*) biased, prejudiced 3.(*egoísta*) selfish, self-seeking II. *m, f* 1. the interested party, the person concerned 2.(*egoísta*) selfish person

interesante *adj* interesting; **hacerse el** ~ to show off [*o* play to the gallery]

interesar I. *vi* to be of interest; **este tema no me interesa** this subject is of no interest to me II. *vt* 1.(*inspirar interés*) to interest 2.(*atraer*) to attract, to appeal III. *vr:* ~**se** 1.(*mostrar interés*) ~**se por algo** to become interested in sth 2.(*preguntar por*) ~**se por algo** to ask about sth; ~**se por la salud de alguien** to ask after sb's health

interface *m* INFOR interface

interfecto, -a I. *adj* murdered II. *m, f* 1. JUR murder victim 2. *inf* (*susodicho*) the person mentioned [*o* in question]

interferencia *f t.* FÍS, LING interference

interferir *irr como sentir* *vi t.* FÍS to interfere; ~ **en algo** to interfere with [*o* in] sth; **eso no interfiere en mi decisión** that does not influence my decision

interfono *m* intercom

intergubernamental *adj* intergovernmental

interinidad *f* **1.** (*cualidad*) temporariness; **estar en situación de** ~ to be in a temporary job **2.** (*de un cargo*) duration

interino, -a I. *adj* **1.** (*funcionario, plaza*) temporary **2.** POL interim II. *m, f* **1.** (*suplente*) stand-in **2.** (*funcionario*) temporary [*o* acting] incumbent; (*maestro*) supply teacher

interior I. *adj* interior; **decoración** ~ interior decoration; (*sin costa*) inland; **mercado** ~ COM (*de la UE*) internal market; (*de Inglaterra*) home [*o* domestic] market; **ropa** ~ underwear; **la vida** ~ **de una persona** a person's inner life II. *m* **1.** (*lo de dentro*) interior; **el** ~ **de un país** the interior of a country; **Ministerio del Interior** POL Home Office *Brit*, Department of the Interior *Am;* **en el** ~ **de...** inside ... **2.** DEP inside-forward

interiores *mpl* **1.** (*entrañas*) insides *pl* **2.** *inf* (*de una cosa*) innards *pl* **3.** ARQUIT house interiors *pl* **4.** CINE (*secuencias*) interior shots *pl;* (*decorados*) film sets *pl* **5.** Col (*calzoncillos*) men's underpants *pl*

interioridad *f* **1.** (*cualidad*) inwardness **2.** *pl* (*de alguien*) intimacies *pl;* (*de una familia*) family secrets *pl*

interiorista *mf* **1.** (*arquitecto*) interior designer **2.** (*diseñador*) interior decorator [*o* designer]

interiorizar <z→c> *vt* to internalize; (*emociones*) to repress

interiormente *adv* **1.** (*en su interior*) inside **2.** (*internamente*) internally

interjección *f* LING interjection, exclamation

interlocutor(a) *m(f)* speaker, interlocutor *form;* ~**es sociales** ECON management and workers' representatives

intermediario, -a I. *adj* intermediary II. *m, f* **1.** (*mediador*) mediator, intermediary; (*enlace*) go-between **2.** (*comerciante*) middleman

intermedio *m* interval

intermedio, -a *adj* **1.** (*capa*) intermediate **2.** (*período de tiempo*) intervening **3.** (*calidad*) **mandos** ~**s** middle management; (*tamaño*) medium

interminable *adj* interminable, endless

intermitencia *f* **1.** (*calidad*) intermittency **2.** MED intermittence **3.** AUTO indicator

intermitente *m* intermittence; AUTO indicator *Brit,* turn signal *Am*

internación *f v.* **internamiento**

internacional *adj* international; **derecho** ~ JUR international law; **partido** ~ DEP international game

internacionalidad *f* international nature

internacionalización *f* internationalization

internacionalizar <z→c> *vt* to internationalize

internado *m* boarding school

internado, -a I. *adj* boarding II. *m, f* **1.** (*alumno*) boarder **2.** (*demente*) inmate

internamiento *m* **1.** (*en hospital*) admission, confinement; ~ **en algo** admission to sth **2.** MIL internment; ~ **en algo** internment in sth

internar I. *vt* **1.** (*penetrar*) to lead inland **2.** (*ingresar*) ~ **en** (*hospital*) to admit to; (*asilo*) to commit to **3.** MIL to intern II. *vr:* ~**se** **1.** (*penetrar*) *t.* DEP to enter **2.** (*en tema*) ~**se en algo** to delve into sth

internauta *mf* INFOR Internet user

internet *f sin pl* INFOR Internet

interno, -a I. *adj* internal; **régimen** ~ (*de una empresa*) internal management; (*de un partido*) internal affairs II. *m, f* (*en colegio*) boarder; (*en cárcel*) inmate; MED resident doctor, houseman

interpelación *f* POL interpellation; JUR appeal, plea

interpolación *f* MAT interpolation

interponer *irr como poner* I. *vt* **1.** (*entre varias cosas*) to interpose; (*entre dos cosas: silla*) to place; (*papel*) to insert; (*alguien*) to come **2.** (*en un asunto*) to intervene **3.** JUR to bring, to lodge II. *vr:* ~**se** to intervene

interposición *f* **1.** (*entre varias cosas*) interposition; (*de una silla*) placing between; (*de un papel*) insertion; (*de alguien*) coming between **2.** (*en un asunto*) intervention **3.** JUR bringing, lodging

interpretable *adj* (*texto*) interpretable; MÚS, TEAT performable

interpretación *f* **1.** (*de texto*) interpretation; (*traducción oral*) interpreting **2.** TEAT performance; MÚS rendering; **escuela de** ~ TEAT stage [*o* acting] school

interpretar *vt* **1.** (*texto, traducir oralmente*) to interpret **2.** TEAT to perform; MÚS to render

interpretativo, -a *adj* interpretative, interpretive; **fuerza interpretativa** interpretive ability

intérprete¹ *mf* **1.** (*de texto*) scholar **2.** (*actor*) performer **3.** (*traductor*) interpreter, translator

intérprete² *m* INFOR interpreter

interprofesional *adj* **Salario Mínimo Interprofesional** minimum wage

interpuesto, -a *pp de* **interponer**

interregional *adj* interregional

interrelacionado, -a *adj* interrelated

interrelacionar *vt* to interrelate

interrogación *f* **1.** (*de policía*) interrogation, questioning **2.** (*signo*) question mark

interrogador(a) I. *adj* questioning II. *m(f)* **1.** (*que pregunta*) questioner **2.** (*policía*) interrogator, cross-examiner

interrogante¹ I. *adj* questioning II. *m* question

interrogante² *m o f* questioner

interrogar <g→gu> *vt* **1.** (*hacer preguntas*) to question **2.** (*policía*) to interrogate

interrogativo, -a *adj* **1.** (*mirada*) questioning **2.** LING (*pronombre, oración*) interrogative

interrogatorio *m* interrogation, (cross-)examination

interrumpir *vt* **1.** (*cortar*) to interrupt; (*brus-*

camente al hablar) to break; (*tráfico*) to hold up **2.**(*estudios*) to terminate; ~ **las vacaciones** (*por unos días*) to temporarily interrupt one's holidays; (*definitivamente*) to cut short one's holidays

interrupción *f* **1.**(*corte*) break; (*del tráfico*) stoppage, hold-up; **sin** ~ uninterruptedly **2.**(*de los estudios*) termination

interruptor *m* ELEC switch, socket *Am*

intersección *f* intersection, crossing, junction

intersticio *m* (*espacio*) *t.* BIO interstice; (*en pared*) crack; (*entre placas*) fissure

interurbano, -a *adj* intercity; **conferencia interurbana** TEL intercity call

intervalo *m*, **intérvalo** *m* (*lapso de tiempo*) *t.* MÚS interval; **a ~s** at intervals

intervención *f* **1.**(*participación*) participation **2.**(*en conflicto*) intervention; (*en temas familiares*) involvement **3.**(*mediación*) mediation **4.** POL intervention **5.** MED operation **6.**(*del teléfono*) tapping; (*del correo*) interception

intervencionismo *m* POL interventionism

intervenir *irr como venir* **I.** *vi* **1.**(*tomar parte*) to participate **2.**(*en conflicto*) to intervene **3.**(*mediar*) to mediate **4.**(*suceder*) to occur **II.** *vt* **1.** MED to operate on **2.**(*incautar*) to seize **3.**(*teléfono*) to tap; (*correo*) to intercept **4.** COM to audit

interventor(a) *m(f)* **1.** COM auditor **2.** POL supervisor

interviú *m o f* interview

intestinal *adj* intestinal

intestino *m* **1.** ANAT intestine; **el ~ grueso** the large intestine; **el ~ delgado** the small intestine **2.** *pl* (*tripas*) intestines *pl,* bowels *pl*

intestino, -a *adj* internal; **luchas intestinas** (*en un país*) domestic disputes *pl;* (*en un partido*) internal wrangling

íntimamente *adv* **1.**(*estrechamente*) closely **2.**(*en lo íntimo*) intimately

intimar **I.** *vi* to become intimate [*o* friendly] **II.** *vt* to require

intimidación *f* intimidation

intimidad *f* **1.**(*personal*) heart of hearts **2.** *pl* (*sexuales*) private parts *pl;* (*asuntos*) personal matters *pl;* (*privacidad*) privacy **3.**(*vida privada*) private life

intimidar **I.** *vt* to intimidate **II.** *vr:* ~**se** to be intimidated

intimidatorio, -a *adj* intimidating

íntimo, -a *adj* **1.**(*interior, interno*) inner, innermost **2.**(*amigo*) intimate, close **3.**(*velada*) intimate **4.**(*conversación*) private

intocable **I.** *adj* untouchable **II.** *mf* untouchable

intolerable *adj* intolerable

intolerancia *f* intolerance

intolerante *adj* intolerant

intoxicación *f* (*alimentos*) food poisoning; (*alcohol*) intoxication

intoxicar <c→qu> *vt, vr:* ~(**se**) to poison

intracomunitario, -a *adj* intra-EU

intraducible *adj* untranslatable

intragable *adj* unpalatable, unbearable *fig*

intranet *f sin pl* INFOR Intranet

intranquilidad *f sin pl* uneasiness

intranquilizador(a) *adj* worrying

intranquilizar <z→c> *vt, vr:* ~(**se**) to worry

intranquilo, -a *adj* **1.**(*nervioso*) edgy **2.**(*preocupado*) worried, uneasy **3.**(*excitado*) agitated, restless

intransferible *adj* untransferable

intransigencia *f* **1.**(*falto de condescendencia*) intransigence **2.**(*intolerancia*) intolerance

intransigente *adj* **1.**(*no condescendiente*) intransigent **2.**(*intolerante*) intolerant

intransitable *adj* impassable

intransitivo, -a *adj* LING intransitive

intrascendencia *f sin pl* triviality

intrascendente *adj* trivial

intratable *adj* **1.**(*persona*) impossible **2.**(*material*) unusable **3.**(*asunto*) intractable **4.**(*enfermedad*) untreatable

intrepidez *f* intrepidity, fearlessness

intrépido, -a *adj* intrepid

intriga *f* **1.**(*maquinación*) intrigue **2.**(*de una película*) suspense

intrigante **I.** *adj* **1.**(*persona*) scheming **2.**(*película*) gripping **II.** *mf* schemer

intrigar <g→gu> **I.** *vi* to scheme **II.** *vt* to intrigue

intrincado, -a *adj* (*bosque*) thick; (*camino*) twisting; (*nudo*) intricate; (*situación*) complicated

intrincar <c→qu> *vt* (*hilos*) to tangle; (*asunto*) to complicate

intrínseco, -a *adj* **1.**(*interior*) intrinsic; **valor ~** intrinsic value **2.**(*propio*) inherent **3.**(*esencial*) intrinsic

introducción *f* **1.**(*de una llave, de un disquete*) insertion, introduction; (*de clavo*) hammering in; (*de medidas*) introduction; INFOR (*de datos*) input **2.**(*de moda*) introduction; (*de mercancías*) launching **3.**(*de libro*) preface **4.** MÚS overture, prelude

introducir *irr como traducir* **I.** *vt* **1.**(*llave, disquete*) to insert, to put in; (*clavo*) to hammer in; (*medidas*) to introduce; INFOR (*datos*) to enter, to input **2.**(*moda*) to introduce **3.**(*discordia*) to sow **II.** *vr:* ~**se** **1.**(*meterse*) to get in(to) **2.**(*en un ambiente*) ~ **en algo** to enter into sth **3.**(*moda*) to be introduced **4.**(*entrometerse*) to interfere

introductorio, -a *adj* introductory; **capítulo ~** introduction

intromisión *f* interference

introspección *f* introspection

introversión *f* introversion

introvertido, -a *adj* introverted

intrusión *f* trespass; (*en la vida privada*) intrusion

intruso, -a **I.** *adj* intrusive **II.** *m, f* **1.** intruder; (*en reunión*) interloper **2.**(*en fiesta*) gatecrasher

intuición *f* intuition; **saber algo por** ~ to know sth intuitively

intuir *irr como huir vt* **1.** (*reconocer*) to intuit form **2.** (*presentir*) to sense; **intuyo que...** I have a hunch that ...

intuitivo, -a *adj* intuitive

inundación *f* flood(ing)

inundar *vt* to flood

inusitado, -a *adj* **1.** (*inhabitual*) unusual, uncommon **2.** (*extraordinario*) unwonted **3.** (*raro*) uncommon

inusual *adj* **1.** (*inhabitual*) unusual **2.** (*extraordinario*) unwonted

inútil I. *adj* **1.** (*que no sirve*) useless; MIL unfit **2.** (*esfuerzo*) vain **3.** (*sin sentido*) futile **II.** *mf* (*torpe*) incompetent person

inutilidad *f* uselessness; (*laboral*) incapacity; MIL unfitness

inutilizar <z→c> *vt* **1.** (*objeto*) to render useless; (*sello*) to cancel; (*instalaciones*) to render unusable **2.** (*al enemigo*) to defeat

invadir *vt* **1.** MIL (*país*) to invade **2.** (*entrar en gran número*) to overrun; **los hinchas invadieron el campo** the fans invaded the pitch [*o* field] **3.** (*plaga*) to infest **4.** (*tristeza, dudas*) to assail **5.** (*jurisdicción*) to encroach on; (*privacidad*) to intrude on

invalidar *vt* (*anular*) to invalidate; (*declarar nulo*) to declare null and void; JUR (*matrimonio, contrato*) to annul; (*acuerdo, ley*) to rescind

invalidez *f* **1.** invalidity; (*nulidad*) nullity; JUR (*de matrimonio*) annulment; (*de acuerdo, ley*) rescindment **2.** MED disability; **pensión de** ~ disability allowance

inválido, -a I. *adj* **1.** MED disabled **2.** (*acuerdo*) invalid; JUR null and void **II.** *m, f* disabled person, invalid

invariable *adj t.* MAT invariable

invasión *f* **1.** *t.* MIL, MED invasion **2.** (*de plaga*) plague **3.** (*en jurisdicción*) encroachment; (*en privacidad*) intrusion **4.** MED spreading, infestation

invasor(a) I. *adj* invasive **II.** *m(f)* invader

invectiva *f* invective

invencible *adj* **1.** (*inderrotable*) invincible **2.** (*insuperable*) unbeatable **3.** (*obstáculo*) unsurmountable

invención *f* invention; (*mentira*) lie

invendible *adj* unsaleable; COM unmarketable

inventar *vt* to invent

inventariar <*1. pres:* inventarío> *vt* to make an inventory of

inventario *m* **1.** (*recuento*) stocktaking, inventory **2.** (*lista*) inventory, list

inventiva *f* inventiveness

invento *m* invention

inventor(a) *m(f)* inventor

inverificable *adj* unverifiable

invernada *f* **1.** *elev* (*estación*) winter season **2.** (*hibernación*) hibernation **3.** CSur (*invernadero*) winter pasture **4.** Méx (*cosecha*) winter crop **5.** Ven (*aguacero*) heavy rainstorm

invernadero *m* greenhouse, hothouse; **el efecto** ~ the greenhouse effect

invernal *adj* winter; (*tiempo*) wintry; **sueño** ~ ZOOL winter sleep, hibernation

invernar <e→ie> *vi* ZOOL to winter; (*los que duermen*) to hibernate

inverosímil *adj* **1.** (*increíble*) implausible **2.** (*que no parece verdad*) improbable, hard to believe

inverosimilitud *f* **1.** (*falta de credibilidad*) implausibility **2.** (*falta de probabilidad*) improbability

inversión *f* **1.** COM, FIN (*dinero*) investment **2.** (*efecto de invertir*) inversion

inversionista *mf* investor

inverso, -a *adj* inverse, opposite; **a la inversa** inversely; **y a la inversa** vice versa; **en orden** ~ in reverse order

inversor(a) *m(f)* investor

invertebrado, -a *adj* **1.** ZOOL (*sin columna vertebral*) invertebrate **2.** (*débil*) spineless

invertido, -a I. *adj* **1.** (*al revés*) inverted; (*volcado*) upside-down **2.** (*sexualmente*) homosexual **II.** *m, f* homosexual

invertir *irr como sentir vt* **1.** (*orden*) to invert **2.** (*volcar*) to turn upside down **3.** (*dinero*) to invest

investidura *f* (*en un cargo*) investiture; REL ordination

investigación *f* **1.** (*indagación*) investigation; (*averiguación*) enquiry *Brit,* inquiry *Am;* ~ **de mercado** market research **2.** (*ciencia*) research **3.** (*estudio*) study

investigador(a) I. *adj* investigative; **comisión** ~**a** investigatory commission **II.** *m(f)* investigator, researcher; ~ **privado** private detective

investigar <g→gu> *vt* **1.** (*indagar*) to investigate; (*averiguar*) to enquire *Brit,* to inquire *Am* **2.** (*en la ciencia*) to research

investir *irr como pedir vt* (*en un cargo*) to confer; **la invistieron doctor honoris causa por la Universidad de Salamanca** she was given an honorary PhD from the University of Salamanca

inveterado, -a *adj* (*costumbre*) inveterate, long-standing

inviabilidad *f sin pl* non-viability

inviable *adj* non-viable, unfeasible

invicto, -a *adj* unbeaten

invidencia *f* blindness

invidente I. *adj* blind **II.** *mf* blind person

invierno *m* **1.** (*estación*) winter **2.** AmL (*lluvias*) rainy season **3.** AmC (*aguacero*) shower

inviolabilidad *f* POL (*de derechos*) inviolability

inviolable *adj* POL (*derechos*) inviolable

invisibilidad *f* invisibility

invisible *adj* invisible

invitación *f* **1.** (*a una fiesta, una acción*) invitation **2.** (*tarjeta*) invitation card

invitado, -a I. *adj* invited **II.** *m, f* guest; ~ **de honor** guest of honour [*o* honor *Am*]

invitar I. *vt* 1. (*convidar*) to invite 2. (*instar*) to press; (*rogar*) to beg; (*tentar*) to be inviting [*o* tempting] II. *vi* to invite; **esta vez invito yo** this time it's on me

invocación *f* invocation

invocar <c→qu> *vt* 1. (*dirigirse*) to invoke; (*suplicar*) to implore, to appeal 2. (*alegar*) to allege 3. JUR (*apoyarse en una ley*) to invoke

involución *f* 1. POL reaction 2. BIO involution, regression

involucionista *adj, mf* POL reactionary

involucrar I. *vt* to involve II. *vr:* ~**se** 1. (*inmiscuirse*) to interfere 2. (*intervenir*) to become [*o* get] involved

involuntariedad *f* 1. (*por obligación*) involuntariness 2. (*falta de voluntad*) unwillingness 3. (*sin querer*) unintentionality

involuntario, -a *adj* 1. (*sin querer*) unintentional 2. (*por obligación*) involuntary

involutivo, -a *adj* regressive

invulnerabilidad *f* 1. (*que no puede ser herido*) invulnerability 2. (*insensibilidad*) insensitiveness

invulnerable *adj* 1. (*que no puede ser herido*) invulnerable 2. (*insensible*) insensitive; **es** ~ **a las críticas** he/she is insensitive to the criticism

inyección *f* 1. MED injection 2. TÉC fuel injection; **motor de** ~ fuel-injected engine

inyectable I. *adj* MED injectable II. *m* MED injection

inyectar *vt* to inject

inyector *m t.* TÉC injector

ion *m* ion

ionosfera *f* ionosphere

IPC *m* ECON *abr de* Índice de Precios al Consumo RPI

ir *irr* I. *vi* 1. (*general*) to go; **¡voy!** I'm coming!; **¡vamos!** let's go!, come on!; ~ **a pie** to go on foot; ~ **en bicicleta** to go by bicycle; ~ **a caballo** to go on horseback; **tengo que** ~ **a París** I have to go to Paris; ~ **detrás de una chica** to chase after a girl 2. (*ir a buscar*) **iré por el pan** I'll go and get the bread 3. (*progresar*) to go; **¿cómo va la tesina?** how is the dissertation going?; **¿cómo te va?** how are things?; **va para médica** she is a budding doctor [*o* studying to be a doctor]; **en lo que va de año** so far this year; ~ **de culo** *vulg* to be headed straight for disaster 4. (*diferencia*) **de dos a cinco van tres** two from five leaves three 5. (*referirse*) **eso no va por ti** I'm not referring to you; **¿tú sabes de lo que va?** do you know what it is about? 6. (*interj: sorpresa*) **¡vaya coche!** what a car!; **¡qué va!** of course not! 7. (*con verbo*) **iban charlando** they were chatting; **voy a hacerlo** I'm going to do it 8. (*edad*) ~ **para viejo** to be getting on II. *vr:* ~**se** 1. (*marcharse*) to leave 2. (*dirección*) to go; ~**se para el sur** to go southwards; ~**se por las ramas** to beat about the bush 3. (*resbalar*) to slip 4. (*perder*) to leak

ira *f* anger, wrath *form*

iracundo, -a *adj* irate

Irán *m* Iran

iraní *adj, mf* Iranian

Iraq *m* Iraq

iraquí *adj, mf* Iraqi

irascible *adj* irascible

irgo *1. pres de* **erguir**

irguió *3. pret de* **erguir**

iridio *m* iridium

iridiscente *adj* iridescent

iris *m inv* ANAT iris; **arco** ~ rainbow

irisar I. *vi* to be iridescent II. *vt* to make iridescent

Irlanda *f* Ireland

irlandés, -esa I. *adj* Irish II. *m, f* Irishman *m*, Irishwoman *f*

ironía *f* irony; ~ **del destino** quirks of fate

irónico, -a I. *adj* ironic II. *m, f* ironic person

ironizar <z→c> *vt* to be ironic

IRPF *m abr de* **Impuesto sobre la Renta de las Personas Físicas** personal income tax

irracional *adj* (*contra la razón*) irrational; (*contra la lógica*) illogical; **número** ~ MAT irrational number; **ser** ~ to be unreasonable

irracionalidad *f sin pl* irrationality

irradiación *f* 1. (*de material nuclear*) radiation 2. MED (*tratamiento*) radiotherapy; (*dolor*) diffusion

irradiar I. *vt* 1. (*emitir*) to radiate 2. (*difundir*) to diffuse 3. (*tratamiento*) to irradiate II. *vi* to radiate III. *vr:* ~**se** to be diffused, to be disseminated *form*

irrazonable *adj* irrational

irreal *adj* unreal

irrealidad *f* unreality

irrealizable *adj* unrealizable, unfeasible

irrebatible *adj*, **irrechazable** *adj* irrefutable

irreconciliable *adj* irreconcilable

irreconocible *adj* unrecognizable

irrecuperable *adj* irretrievable

irreductible *adj* uncompromising

irreflexión *f* recklessness, thoughtlessness

irreflexivo, -a *adj* 1. (*acción*) reckless 2. (*persona*) rash 3. (*precipitado*) hasty

irrefrenable *adj* 1. (*desarrollo*) uncontrollable 2. (*persona*) irrepressible

irrefutable *adj* irrefutable

irregular *adj* 1. (*desigual*) irregular, uneven 2. (*contra las reglas*) irregular; (*sin reglas*) without rules; (*anómalo*) anomalous *form*

irregularidad *f* 1. (*desigualdad, del terreno*) irregularity, unevenness 2. (*contra las reglas*) irregularity; (*sin reglas*) absence of rules

irrelevante *adj* irrelevant

irremediable *adj* 1. (*inevitable*) inevitable 2. (*irreparable*) irremediable 3. (*daño físico*) irreversible

irremisible *adj* 1. (*falta*) unpardonable 2. (*pérdida*) irretrievable

irrenunciable *adj* 1. (*imprescindible*) indispensable 2. (*destino*) inescapable

irreparable *adj* 1. (*que no se puede reparar*)

irreparable; (*incompensable*) which cannot be compensated **2.** (*daño físico*) irreversible
irrepetible *adj* unique
irreprimible *adj* irrepressible
irreprochable *adj* irreproachable
irreproducible *adj* **1.** (*irrepetible*) unrepeatable **2.** (*que ya no se puede fabricar*) irreplaceable
irresistible *adj* **1.** (*atractivo*) irresistible **2.** (*inaguantable*) unbearable
irresoluble *adj* unsolvable
irresolución *f* **1.** (*indecisión*) indecisiveness **2.** (*vacilación*) irresolution
irresoluto, -a *adj* **1.** (*indeciso*) indecisive **2.** (*vacilante*) irresolute **3.** (*problema*) unsolved
irrespetuoso, -a *adj* disrespectful
irrespirable *adj* **1.** (*por tóxico*) unbreathable **2.** (*aire*) stale, suffocating
irresponsabilidad *f* **1.** (*falta de responsabilidad*) absence of responsibility; (*por minoría de edad*) absence of legal responsibility (*as a minor*) **2.** (*desconsideración*) irresponsibility **3.** COM (*sociedades*) absence of liability
irresponsable I. *adj* **1.** (*no responsable*) irresponsible; ~ **de algo** not responsible for sth **2.** COM (*sociedades*) ~ **de algo** not liable for sth **II.** *mf* irresponsible person
irreverencia *f* irreverence
irreverente *adj* irreverent
irreversible *adj* irreversible
irrevocable *adj* **1.** (*no revocable*) irrevocable; (*firme*) firm **2.** (*inamovible*) unalterable
irrigación *f* **1.** AGR (*regadío*) irrigation **2.** MED (*del recto*) administration of an enema; (*vagina*) douching
irrigar <g→gu> *vt* **1.** AGR (*regar*) to irrigate **2.** MED (*la sangre*) to oxygenate
irrisorio, -a *adj* derisory; **a precios ~s** at ridiculous [*o* ridiculously low] prices
irritabilidad *f sin pl* irritability
irritable *adj* irritable
irritación *f* **1.** MED (*órgano*) inflammation; (*de piel*) irritation **2.** (*enfado*) irritation
irritante *adj* **1.** (*enojar, molesto*) irritating **2.** MED (*órgano*) inflamed
irritar I. *vt* **1.** (*enojar, molestar*) to irritate **2.** MED (*órgano*) to inflame **II.** *vr*: ~**se 1.** (*enojarse*) to become irritated **2.** MED (*órgano*) to become inflamed
irrompible *adj* **1.** (*material*) unbreakable **2.** (*amistad*) solid
irrumpir *vi* ~ **en algo** to burst into sth
irrupción *f* **1.** (*entrada*) irruption **2.** MIL (*invasión*) invasion; (*ataque*) raid
IRTP *m abr de* **Impuesto sobre el Rendimiento del Trabajo Personal** PAYE
isla *f* island
Islam *m* REL Islam
islámico, -a *adj* Islamic
islamización *f* Islamization
islandés, -esa I. *adj* Icelandic **II.** *m, f* Icelander

Islandia *f* Iceland
isleño, -a I. *adj* island **II.** *m, f* islander
islote *m* islet
isobara *f*, **isóbara** *f* METEO isobar
isotónico, -a *adj* isotonic
Israel *m* Israel
israelí *adj*, *mf* Israeli
israelita *adj*, *mf* Israelite
istmo *m* GEO isthmus
itacate *m Méx* (*provisión*) travel(ling) provisions
Italia *f* Italy
italiano, -a *adj*, *m, f* Italian
itálico, -a HIST **I.** *adj* Italic **II.** *m, f* Italic; (*letra*) italics *pl*
itinerante *adj* itinerant, traveling *Brit,* travelling *Am*
itinerario *m* **1.** (*ruta*) itinerary **2.** FERRO (*horario*) timetable *Brit,* schedule *Am* **3.** AVIAT (*vuelo*) route
ITV *f abr de* **Inspección Técnica de Vehículos** MOT test
IVA *m abr de* **Impuesto sobre el Valor Añadido** VAT
izada *f AmL* raising
izar <z→c> *vt* NÁUT to hoist
izcuinche *m Méx* **1.** (*perro callejero*) mangy stray dog **2.** (*niño callejero*) street urchin
izda. *adj*, **izdo.** *adj abr de* **izquierda, izquierdo** left
izquierda *f* **1.** (*mano*) left hand **2.** POL left **3.** (*lado*) left side; **a la ~** to the left
izquierdista I. *adj* POL left-wing, leftist **II.** *mf* POL left-winger, leftist
izquierdo, -a *adj* left; *fig* crooked; (*zurdo*) left-handed; **levantarse con el pie ~** to get up on the wrong side of the bed

J

J, j *f* J, j; ~ **de Juan** J for Jack *Brit,* J for Jig *Am*
ja *interj* ha
jabalí *m* <jabalíes> wild boar
jabalina *f* **1.** ZOOL female wild boar **2.** DEP javelin
jabato *m* **1.** ZOOL young wild boar **2.** (*hombre*) daredevil; **luchar como un ~** to fight like a lion
jabato, -a *adj* brave
jabón *m* **1.** (*para lavar*) soap; **pastilla de ~** bar of soap **2.** *PRico, Arg* (*susto*) fright ▶ **dar ~ a alguien** to soft-soap sb; **dar un ~ a alguien** to give sb a hard time
jabonar *vt* **1.** (*con jabón*) to soap **2.** *inf* (*reprender*) to tell off
jaboncillo *m* **1.** (*de tocador*) (bar of) toilet soap **2.** (*de sastre*) French chalk
jabonera *f* **1.** (*para depositar jabón*) soapdish **2.** BOT soapwort

jabonoso, -a *adj* soapy
jabugo *m* type of Spanish ham (*from Jabugo*)
jaca *f* **1.** (*yegua*) mare **2.** *pey* (*caballo*) nag **3.** *AmL* (*gallo*) (fighting) cock
jacal *m Méx, Ven* hut
jacalear *vi Méx* to spread rumours [*o* rumors *Am*]
jacarandá *m AmL* BOT jacaranda
jacarandoso, -a *adj* merry
jacarero, -a *m, f inf* joker
jacinto *m* hyacinth
jaco *m* **1.** (*caballo pequeño*) small horse **2.** *pey* (*caballo*) nag
jactancia *f* boasting, boastfulness
jactancioso, -a **I.** *adj* boastful **II.** *m, f* boaster
jactarse *vr* **jactarse de algo** to boast of [*o* about] sth
jaculatoria *f* short prayer
jacuz(z)i® *m* Jacuzzi®
jade *m* jade
jadear *vi* to pant
Jaén *m* Jaen
jaenero, -a, jaenés, -esa **I.** *adj* of/from Jaen **II.** *m, f* native/inhabitant of Jaen
jaez *m* **1.** (*de caballo*) harness **2.** (*clase, condición*) kind, ilk; **persona de mal ~** bad type; **no te fíes de gente de ese ~** don't trust that sort of people
jaguar *m* jaguar
jagüel *m,* **jagüey** *m AmL* (*balsa*) pool; (*cisterna*) cistern
jaiba **I.** *adj* **1.** *Ant, Méx* (*astuto*) cunning **2.** *Cuba* (*perezoso*) lazy **II.** *f AmL* (*cangrejo*) crab
jáibol *m Méx* whisky and soda, highball *Am*
jalada *f Méx, Ven: inf* **1.** (*exageración*) exaggeration **2.** (*reprimenda*) ticking-off
jalado, -a *adj* **1.** *Méx, Ven* (*exagerado*) exaggerated **2.** *AmL* (*demacrado*) emaciated **3.** *AmL* (*obsequioso*) obliging **4.** *AmL* (*borracho*) drunk
jalar **I.** *vt* **1.** *AmL* (*una cuerda*) to pull **2.** *AmL* (*una persona*) to attract **3.** *inf* (*comer*) to guzzle, to wolf down **II.** *vi Bol, PRico, Urug, Ven* (*largarse*) to clear off **III.** *vr:* **~se** *AmL* (*emborracharse*) to get drunk
jalea *f* jelly
jalear *vt* (*animar*) to encourage
jaleo *m* **1.** (*barullo*) commotion; **armar ~ to** kick up a row [*o* fuss] **2.** (*desorden*) confusion; **me he armado un ~ con los nombres** *inf* I've got the names all mixed up **3.** (*riña*) quarrel
jalón *m* **1.** (*vara*) pole **2.** (*hito*) landmark, milestone
jalonar *vt* **1.** (*un terreno*) to stake out **2.** (*marcar*) to mark
jamar **I.** *vt inf* (*comer*) to hoover *Brit,* to scarf (down) *Am* **II.** *vr:* **~se** *inf* (*atracarse*) to stuff oneself
jamás *adv* never; **~ de los jamases** never in your life; **~ había tenido la oportunidad** I'd/he'd/she'd never had the chance; **¿habías**

leído ~ algo parecido? had you ever read anything like it?; **nunca digas nunca ~** never (ever) say never; **nunca ~** never again
jamba *f* (*de la ventana*) reveal, window post; (*de la puerta*) door post
jamelgo *m inf* (*caballo*) nag
jamón *m* ham; **~ dulce** [*o* **de York**] boiled ham; **~ serrano** cured ham ▶ **¡y un ~!** *inf* get away!
Japón *m* Japan
japonés, -esa *adj, m, f* Japanese
jaque *m* **1.** DEP check; **~ mate** checkmate; **dar ~ to** check **2.** *inf* (*perdonavidas*) big talker ▶ **tener a alguien en ~** *fig* to keep sb in check
jaquear *vt* DEP to check
jaqueca *f* (severe) headache, migraine; **este tipo me da ~** *inf* this guy's getting to me
jara *f* **1.** BOT rockrose **2.** *Guat, Méx* (*flecha*) arrow
jarabe *m* syrup; (*para la tos*) cough mixture [*o* syrup] ▶ **dar ~ de palo a alguien** *inf* to give sb a thrashing; **~ de pico** *inf* empty talk
jarana *f* **1.** *inf* (*juerga*) spree; **ir de ~** *inf* to go on a spree **2.** *Méx* MÚS small guitar **3.** *AmL* (*burla*) joke **4.** *AmC* (*deuda*) debt **5.** *Col* (*embuste*) trick
jaranear **I.** *vi inf* (*ir de copas*) to go out on the town; (*divertirse*) to live it up **II.** *vt Col* (*importunar*) to pester
jaranero, -a *m, f* **ser un ~** to be a reveller [*o* reveler *Am*]
jarcia *f* NÁUT rigging
jardín *m* (*césped*) garden; (*flores, plantas*) garden; **~ de infancia** (*hasta los tres años*) creche *Brit,* nursery school; (*a partir de tres años*) kindergarten; **los jardines de una ciudad** the municipal parks; **trabajar en el ~ to** garden
jardinear *vt AmL* to garden
jardinera *f* **1.** (*profesión*) (woman) gardener **2.** (*maceta*) window box ▶ **a la ~** à la jardiniere
jardinería *f* gardening
jardinero, -a *m, f* gardener
jareta *f* **1.** (*para ceñir*) casing; **cinturón de ~** drawstring waist **2.** (*dobladillo*) hem; (*pliegue*) tuck **3.** *CRi, Par* (*bragueta*) trouser fly, zip *Brit,* zipper *Am*
jarocho, -a *adj* **1.** (*rudo, insolente*) boorish, uncouth **2.** *AmL* (*natural de Veracruz*) native of Veracruz
jarra *f* jar; (*de agua*) jug, pitcher *Am* ▶ **ponerse de** [*o* **en**] **~s** to stand with arms akimbo
jarro *m* jug, pitcher; (*de agua*) pitcher; **echar un ~ de agua fría** *fig* to pour cold water on
jarrón *m* vase
jartón, -ona *m, f AmC, Méx* (*comilón*) greedy-guts *inf*
jaspeado, -a *adj* speckled; (*tela, lana*) variegated
jauja *f* earthly paradise; **¡pero te crees que esto es Jauja!** where do you think you are?;

para ti la vida es Jauja you're living in clover
jaula *f* (*para animales*) cage
jauría *f* pack of hounds
jazmín *m* jasmine
jazz *m sin pl* MÚS jazz; **tocar** ~ to jazz
J.C. *abr de* Jesucristo J.C.
jebe *m* 1. (*alumbre*) alum 2. *AmL* (*caucho*) rubber
jeep *m* <jeeps> jeep
jefatura *f* 1. (*cargo*) leadership 2. (*sede*) ~ del gobierno seat of government; ~ de policía police headquarters
jefazo *m inf* big boss
jefe, -a *m, f* (*de una organización, empresa*) head, boss; (*de un departamento*) head; (*de una banda*) leader; ~ **de filas** DEP team captain; ~ **de gobierno** head of the government; ~ **de(l) Estado** head of state; ~ **de partido** party leader; **redactor** ~ editor-in-chief; **en mi casa no soy yo el** ~, **sino mi mujer** it's my wife who wears the trousers [o pants], not me
jengibre *m* ginger
jeque *m* sheik(h)
jerarca *mf* high official
jerarquía *f* hierarchy
jerárquico, -a *adj* hierarchical
jerez *m* sherry
jerga *f* (*lenguaje*) jargon
jergón *m* 1. (*colchón*) rough mattress, pallet 2. *inf* (*persona*) oaf
jeribeque *m* hacer ~s to make faces
jerigonza *f* 1. (*galimatías*) gibberish 2. (*jerga*) jargon
jeringa *f* (*instrumento*) syringe
jeringar <g→gu> *vt* 1. (*con la jeringa*) to syringe 2. *inf* (*molestar*) to pester
jeringuilla *f* syringe
jeroglífico *m* 1. (*signo*) hieroglyph(ic) 2. (*pasatiempo*) rebus, puzzle
jeroglífico, -a *adj* hieroglyphic
jersey *m* pullover, jumper *Brit*; ~ **de cuello alto** roll-neck *Brit* [o turtleneck *Am*] sweater
Jerusalén *m* Jerusalem
Jesucristo *m* Jesus Christ
jesuita *adj, m* Jesuit
Jesús *m* Jesus ▶ **en un** (**decir**) ~ in a flash; **¡**~**!** (*al estornudar*) bless you!; (*interjección*) good heavens!
jet¹ *m* <jets> (*avión*) jet
jet² *f sin pl* (*alta sociedad*) jet set
jeta *f* 1. *inf* (*cara*) mug, dial; **ése tiene una** ~ **increíble** *fig* what incredible cheek that guy has 2. (*labios*) lips 3. (*del cerdo*) snout
ji *interj* ha
jíbaro, -a *adj* 1. *AmL* (*campesino*) country, peasant; (*costumbres, vida*) rural 2. *AmL* (*planta, animal*) wild 3. *Ant, Méx* (*huraño*) shy
jibia *f* cuttlefish
jícama *f Méx* BOT edible tuber
jícaro *m AmC* (*árbol*) calabash tree
jicotera *f AmC, Méx* wasps' nest
jienense, -a I. *adj* of/from Jaen II. *m, f*

native/inhabitant of Jaen
jijona *m* soft nougat (*made in Jijona*)
jilguero *m* goldfinch
jincho, -a *adj Col, inf* (*borracho*) drunk
jineta *f* genet
jinete *m* (*persona*) horseman; (*profesional*) rider
jinetear *vt AmL* (*domar*) to break in (horses)
jinetera *f Cuba, inf* prostitute
jiote *m Méx* MED impetigo
jipa *f Col* Panama hat
jira *f* 1. (*jirón*) strip of cloth 2. (*picnic*) picnic 3. (*excursión*) outing
jirafa *f* 1. ZOOL giraffe 2. (*para el micro*) boom
jirón *m* shred; **hacer algo jirones** to tear sth to shreds
jitazo *m Méx* hit
jitomate *m Méx* (*tomate*) tomato
JJ.OO. *abr de* **Juegos Olímpicos** Olympic Games
jo *interj* 1. (*so*) whoa 2. (*sorpresa*) **¡**~**!** well, well!
jobillo *m PRico, inf* irse de ~s to play truant
jockey *m* jockey
jocosidad *f* 1. (*cualidad*) humour *Brit,* humor *Am* 2. (*chiste*) joke
jocoso, -a *adj* humourous, jocular
jocundo, -a *adj* jovial
joda *f Arg, vulg* (*broma*) joke; **lo dije en** ~ I was only joking
joder I. *vt vulg* 1. (*copular*) to fuck, to screw 2. (*fastidiar*) to piss off; **¡no me jodas!** piss off! 3. (*echar a perder*) to fuck up 4. (*robar*) to pinch II. *vi vulg* to fuck III. *vr:* ~**se** *vulg* 1. (*fastidiarse*) to get pissed off; **¡jódete!** piss [o fuck] off!; **¡hay que** ~**se!** to hell with it!; **¡no te jode!** you must be off your head! 2. (*echar a perder*) **nuestra amistad se ha jodido** our friendship's gone down the drain [o tubes *Brit*]; **la tele se ha jodido** the telly's buggered IV. *interj vulg* shit
jodido, -a I. *pp de* joder II. *adj vulg* 1. (*cansado*) buggered; **estoy** ~ I'm buggered 2. (*difícil*) fucking difficult; **es** ~ **tener que trabajar tanto** it's damned hard [o bloody tough *Brit*] having to work so much
jodón, -ona I. *adj Méx, inf* fucking [o bloody *Brit*] annoying II. *m, f Méx, inf* pain in the neck
joint-venture, joint venture *f* ECON joint venture
jojoba *f AmL* BOT jojoba
jolgorio *m* merriment
jolín *interj,* **jolines** *interj* sugar
jopé *interj* sugar
Jordania *f* Jordan
jordano, -a *adj, m, f* Jordanian
jornada *f* 1. (*de trabajo*) working day; (*tiempo trabajado*) hours of work; ~ **continua** continuous timetable without lunch break, finishing early; ~ **partida** split shift; **trabajo media** ~ I work half a day [o part-time] 2. (*viaje*) day's journey; (*andando*) day's march

[*o* walk]; **este pueblo está a dos ~s de viaje** this village is two days' journey away **3.** *pl* (*congreso, simposio*) conference

jornal *m* (*paga*) day's wage [*o* pay]; **trabajar a ~** to be paid by the day

jornalero, -a *m, f* day labourer *Brit,* day laborer *Am*

joroba *f* **1.** (*de persona*) hunched back **2.** (*de camello*) hump **3.** *inf* (*molestia*) nuisance

jorobado, -a I. *adj* hunchbacked II. *m, f* hunchback

jorobar I. *vt inf* to annoy II. *vr:* **~se** *inf* **1.** (*enojarse*) to get annoyed **2.** (*aguantar*) to put up with it; **si no le gusta, ¡que se jorobe!** if he doesn't like it, he can lump it!

jorongo *m Méx* poncho

joropo *m Col: popular dance of the Colombian lowlanders*

jota *f* **1.** (*letra*) j **2.** (*baile*) *Aragonese dance* ►**no entender** [*o* **saber**] **ni ~** *inf* not to have a clue; **no ver ni ~** *inf* not to see a thing

joto *m* **1.** *Col* (*paquete*) bundle **2.** *Méx, pey* (*homosexual*) queer

joven I. *adj* young; **de muy ~** in early youth II. *mf* young man *m,* young woman *f;* **los jóvenes** young people

jovial *adj* cheerful, jovial

joya *f* **1.** (*alhaja*) jewel; (*piedra*) gem; **las ~s** jewellery, jewelry *Am* **2.** (*persona, cosa*) gem; **esta mujer de la limpieza es una ~** this cleaning lady is a real treasure; **este niño es una ~** this child is a little gem

joyería *f* **1.** (*joyas*) jewellery *Brit,* jewelry *Am* **2.** (*tienda*) jeweller's shop *Brit,* jeweler's shop *Am*

joyero *m* jewel case

joyero, -a *m, f* jeweller *Brit,* jeweler *Am*

juanete *m* (*del pie*) bunion

jubilación *f* **1.** (*acción*) retirement; **~ anticipada** early retirement **2.** (*pensión*) pension

jubilado, -a *m, f* pensioner, retiree; **aquí viven muchos ~s** lots of retired people live round here

jubilar I. *vt* **1.** (*a alguien*) to pension off **2.** *inf* (*un objeto*) to take out of circulation; **~ algo** to get rid of sth II. *vr:* **~se 1.** (*retirarse*) to retire **2.** *AmC* (*hacer novillos*) to play truant

júbilo *m* joy, jubilation

jubiloso, -a *adj* jubilant; **estar ~** to be joyful

judaico, -a *adj* Jewish, Judaic

judas *m* traitor

judía *f* **1.** (*mujer*) Jewess **2.** bean; **~ verde** green bean

judicatura *f* **1.** (*cargo*) office of judge, judgeship **2.** (*de un país*) judicature, judiciary **3.** **~ del trabajo** ≈industrial law

judicial *adj* judicial

judío, -a I. *adj* Jewish II. *m, f* Jew

judo *m* DEP judo

juego *m* **1.** (*diversión*) game; **~ de mesa** board game; **~ de los roles** role-playing; **hacer ~s malabares** to juggle; **tengo mal ~** I've a bad hand; **perder dinero en el ~** to

gamble money away **2.** DEP play; **~ en blanco** nil draw; **~ limpio** fair play; **~ sucio** foul play; **fuera de ~** (*persona*) offside; (*balón*) out of play; **entrar/poner en ~** to come/to bring into play **3.** (*conjunto*) set; **~ de café** coffee set; **~ de mesa** dinner service; **hacer ~** to match **4.** TÉC play; **esta llave no hace ~ con la cerradura** this key doesn't turn in the lock ►**desgraciado en el ~, afortunado en** <u>amores</u> *prov* lucky at cards, unlucky in love *prov;* **hacer el ~ a alguien haciendo algo** to play into one's rival's hands by doing sth; **tomarse algo a ~** to take sth as a joke; **vérsele a alguien el ~** to know what sb is up to

juerga *f* spree; **ayer estuve de ~** *inf* I was (out) partying [*o* on a spree] yesterday; **anoche se armó una ~ increíble en ese bar** *inf* there was a real party going on in that bar last night; **correrse unas cuantas ~s** *inf* to go out at night quite a bit

jueves *m inv* Thursday; **Jueves Santo** Maundy Thursday ►**no es** <u>nada</u> **del otro ~** it's nothing to write home about; *v.t.* **lunes**

juez *mf t.* JUR judge; **~ de instrucción** JUR examining magistrate; **~ de paz** justice of the peace; **ser ~ y parte** to be biased; **~ de línea** [*o* **de banda**] DEP linesman

jugada *f* **1.** DEP play; **~ de ajedrez** chess move; **~ antirreglamentaria** foul play; **las ~s de Michael Jordan encandilaban al público** the audience loved Michael Jordan's plays; **Ronaldo hizo una ~ genial** Ronaldo made a great move **2.** (*jugarreta*) bad turn; **hacer** [*o* **gastar**] **una ~ a alguien** to play a dirty trick on sb

jugador(a) I. *adj* **mi marido es muy ~** my husband like to gamble a lot II. *m(f) t.* DEP player

jugar *irr* I. *vi* **1.** (*a un juego, deporte*) to play; **~ limpio/sucio** to play fair/unfairly; **¿quién juega?** (*juego de mesa*) whose move it?; (*partido en la TV, radio*) who's playing?; **¿puedo ~?** can I join in?; **¿a qué juegas?** *fig* what are you playing at? **2.** (*bromear*) to play about; **hacer algo por ~** to do sth for fun **3.** (*en un negocio*) to speculate; **~ a la bolsa** to speculate on the stock exchange **4.** (*hacer juego*) to match II. *vt* **1.** (*un juego, una partida*) to play **2.** (*apostar*) to gamble; **~ fuerte** to play for high stakes **3.** (*una carta*) to play; (*una torre*) to move III. *vr:* **~se 1.** (*la lotería*) to be drawn **2.** (*apostar*) **~se algo** to gamble [*o* to bet] on sth; **¿qué te juegas que...?** (do you) want to bet that ...? **3.** (*arriesgar*) to risk; **~se el todo por el todo** to stake one's all ►**jugársela a alguien** to take sb for a ride

jugarreta *f inf* **1.** (*jugada*) bad move **2.** (*trampa*) dirty trick; **hacer una ~ a alguien** to pull a fast one on sb

juglar *m* HIST, LIT, MÚS minstrel

jugo *m* **1.** (*de fruta, carne*) juice; **~s gástricos**

gastric juices **2.** (*esencia*) essence; **declaraciones con mucho** ~ *fig* important declarations ▶**sacar el** ~ **a alguien** to squeeze sb dry

jugoso, -a *adj* (*fruta, carne*) juicy

juguete *m* **1.** (*objeto*) toy; **el barco era un** ~ **de las olas** *fig* the boat was at the mercy of the waves **2.** *pl* COM toys *pl*

juguetear *vi* **1.** (*con las llaves, una pelota*) to play **2.** (*los niños*) to romp

juguetería *f* toyshop

juguetón, -ona *adj* playful

juicio *m* **1.** (*facultad para juzgar*) reason **2.** (*razón*) sense; **falta de** ~ lack of common sense; **recobrar el** ~ to come to one's senses; **tú no estás en tu sano** ~ you're not in your right mind **3.** (*opinión*) opinion; **a mi** ~ to my mind; **emitir un** ~ **sobre algo** to pass judgement on sth **4.** JUR trial; ~ **criminal** criminal proceedings; **llevar a alguien a** ~ to take sb to court; **el** (**día del**) **Juicio final** REL the Last Judgement

juicioso, -a *adj* (*sensato*) sensible; (*acertado*) fitting

juil *m Méx* ZOOL Mexican lake trout; **si el** ~ **no abriera la boca, no lo pescarían** *prov* silence is golden *prov*

julepe *m* **1.** (*castigo*) punishment; (*reprimenda*) telling-off; **dar** ~ **a alguien** (*castigar*) to punish sb; (*dar una reprimenda*) to give sb a dressing-down **2.** *AmL* (*miedo*) scare **3.** *AmL* (*ajetreo*) drudgery; **dar un** ~ **a alguien** *inf* to make sb sweat

julia *f* **1.** ZOOL snakefish **2.** *Méx, inf* (*coche celular*) police van, paddy wagon *Am*

julio *m* **1.** (*mes*) July; *v.t.* **marzo 2.** FÍS joule

juma *f AmL, inf* drunkenness

jumado, -a *adj AmL, inf* drunk

jumarse *vr Col, Cuba* to get drunk

jumento *m* donkey

jumo *m PRico* drunkenness

jumo, -a *adj AmL* (*borracho*) drunk

juncal *adj* (*gallardo*) slim

junco *m* **1.** BOT reed **2.** (*bastón*) (walking) stick, cane **3.** (*embarcación*) junk

jungla *f* jungle

junio *m* June; *v.t.* **marzo**

júnior *m* <juniors> junior

junta *f* **1.** (*comité*) committee; (*consejo*) council; ~ **calificadora** ENS examining board; ~ **directiva** COM board of directors; ~ **militar** MIL military junta; ~ **municipal** POL district council **2.** (*reunión*) meeting; ~ **general** general meeting; **celebrar** ~ to hold a board meeting; ~ **de accionistas** shareholders' meeting **3.** TÉC (*de dos ladrillos, tablas*) joint; (*de dos tubos*) junction; (*sellado*) seal

juntar I. *vt* **1.** (*aproximar*) ~ **la mesa a la pared** to move the table over to the wall; ~ **las sillas** to put the chairs together **2.** (*unir*) to join **3.** (*reunir: personas*) to assemble; (*objetos*) to put together; (*dinero*) to collect **4.** (*puerta, ventana*) to pull to **II.** *vr:* ~**se**

1. (*reunirse*) to meet **2.** (*unirse*) to come together **3.** (*aproximarse*) to come closer **4.** (*vivir juntos*) to move in (together); **se han juntado** they've started living together

junto I. *adv* **hablaba por teléfono y trabajaba en el ordenador, todo** ~ he/she was on the phone and at his/her computer at the same time **II.** *prep* **1.** (*local*) ~ **a** near to; **¿quién es el que está** ~ **a ella?** who's the man at her side?; **estábamos** ~ **a la entrada** we were at the entrance; **pasaron** ~ **a nosotros** they walked past us **2.** (*con movimiento*) ~ **a** beside; **he puesto la botella** ~ **a las otras** I've put the bottle beside the others; **pon la silla** ~ **a la mesa** put the chair next to the table **3.** (*con, en compañía de*) ~ **con** together with

junto, -a *adj* joined; **nos sentamos todos** ~**s** we all sat together; **me las pagarás todas juntas** you'll pay for that

juntura *f* TÉC (*de dos ladrillos, tablas*) joint; (*de dos tubos*) junction; (*sellado*) seal

jupiarse *vr AmC* to get drunk

jura *f* oath; (*acto*) swearing in

juraco *m AmL* hole

jurado *m* **1.** JUR (*miembro*) juror; (*tribunal*) jury **2.** (*de un examen*) qualified examiner **3.** (*de un concurso*) panel member

jurado, -a *adj* qualified; **intérprete** ~ sworn interpreter

juramentar I. *vt* to swear in **II.** *vr:* ~**se** to be sworn in

juramento *m* **1.** *t.* JUR (*jura*) oath; **falso** ~ perjury; **estar bajo** ~ to be on oath; **tomar** ~ **a alguien** to swear sb in **2.** (*blasfemia*) swearword

jurar *vt, vi* to swear; ~ **por alguien** to swear by sb; ~ **en falso** to commit perjury; ~ **por todos los santos** to swear blind; **jurársela(s) a alguien** *inf* to swear vengeance on sb

jurel *m* horse mackerel

jurero, -a *m, f Chile, Ecua* (*testigo falso contratado*) false witness

jurídico, -a *adj* legal, lawful

jurisdicción *f* **1.** JUR (*potestad*) jurisdiction; ~ **militar** military law; **ese caso no está dentro de la** ~ **de este tribunal** that case does not come within the jurisdiction of this court **2.** (*territorio*) administrative district

jurisdiccional *adj* jurisdictional, judicial; **no** ~ **extrajudicial; aguas** ~**es** territorial waters

jurisperito, -a *m, f* legal expert

jurisprudencia *f* **1.** (*legislación*) jurisprudence **2.** (*ciencia*) science of law

jurista *mf* jurist

jurungar <g→gu> *Ven* **I.** *vt* to bore **II.** *vr:* ~**se** to get bored

justamente *adv* **1.** (*con justicia*) justly **2.** (*precisamente*) precisely **3.** (*ajustadamente*) **este vestido viene** ~ **al cuerpo** this dress is close-fitting

justicia *f* **1.** (*cualidad, poder judicial*) justice; **en** ~, **él merece ganar el premio** in all fairness, he deserves to win the prize; **hacer** ~ **a**

alguien to do sb justice **2.** (*derecho*) law; **administrar** ~ to administer justice
justiciero, -a *adj* (*justo*) just; (*severo*) strict
justificable *adj* justifiable
justificación *f* **1.** (*disculpa*) justification; **no hay** ~ **para lo que has hecho** there's no excuse for what you've done **2.** (*prueba*) proof, evidence; (*documento*) document
justificante *m* supporting evidence; (*de ausencia*) note of absence
justificar <c→qu> **I.** *vt* **1.** (*disculpar*) to justify; **mi desconfianza es justificada** my distrust is vindicated **2.** (*probar*) to prove; (*con documentos*) to substantiate **II.** *vr:* ~**se** to justify oneself
justipreciar *vt* (*apreciar*) to assess; (*tasar*) to evaluate
justiprecio *m* (*aprecio*) assessment; (*tasación*) valuation, appraisal
justo I. *adv* **1.** (*exactamente*) right; **llegué** ~ **a tiempo** I arrived just in time **2.** (*escasamente*) scarcely; **tengo** ~ **para vivir** I've just enough to live on **II.** *mpl* the just
justo, -a *adj* **1.** (*persona, decisión*) just **2.** (*exacto*) exact; (*acertado*) correct; **el peso** ~ the correct weight; **¿tiene el dinero** ~**?** **es que no tengo cambio** do you have the exact amount (of money)? I don't seem to have any change **3.** (*escaso*) **ha venido muy justo el dinero** money's been very tight **4.** (*ajustado*) close-fitting; **este abrigo me viene** ~ this coat is rather tight for me
juvenil I. *adj* youthful, young **II.** *mf* DEP **juego con los** ~**es** I'm in the junior team
juventud *f* **1.** (*edad*) youth **2.** (*estado*) early life **3.** (*jóvenes*) young people
juzgado *m* **1.** (*jueces, local*) court; ~ **de guardia** police court; ~ **de lo penal** criminal court **2.** (*territorio*) juridical district
juzgar <g→gu> **I.** *vt* **1.** (*juez: decidir*) to judge; (*condenar*) to sentence **2.** (*opinar sobre*) to judge; (*considerar*) to consider, to deem; ~ **mal a alguien** to misjudge sb; **juzgo necesario avisarle** I consider it necessary to inform him/her/you; **le** ~**on de maleducado** they considered him ill-mannered; **no te juzgo capaz de hacerlo** I don't think you're capable of doing it **II.** *vi* **1.** (*juez*) to judge **2.** (*opinar*) ~ **sobre apariencias** to judge by appearances; **a** ~ **por como me mira, debe conocerme** judging by how he/she is looking at me, he/she must know me

kartin(g) *m* <kartin(g)s> DEP go-carting
katiuska *f* gumboot, Wellintons *pl*
kayac *m* <kayacs> DEP kayak
Kazajistán *m* Kazakhstan
KB *m* INFOR *abr de* **kilobyte** KB
kéfir *m* kefir (*type of yoghurt*)
keniano, -a *adj, m, f* Kenyan
keniata *adj, mf* Kenyan
kerosén *m* AmS kerosene
keroseno *m* kerosene, paraffin
ketchup *m* <ketchups> ketchup
kg *abr de* **kilogramo** kg
kibutz *m* <kibutzs> kibbutz
kikirikí *m* cock-a-doodle-doo
kilo *m* kilo
kilocaloría *f* kilocalorie
kilociclo *m* kilocycle
kilogramo *m* kilogramme *Brit*, kilogram *Am*
kilohercio *m* kilohertz
kilolitro *m* kilolitre *Brit*, kiloliter *Am*
kilometraje *m* **1.** AUTO mileage *Brit*, milage *Am* **2.** (*distancia*) distance in kilometres *Brit* [*o* kilometers *Am*]; **hay que recorrer un buen** ~ we've got a fair bit of distance to cover
kilometrar *vt* to measure in kilometres *Brit* [*o* kilometers *Am*]
kilométrico, -a *adj* **1.** (*en kilómetros*) kilometric **2.** (*muy largo*) very long; (*escrito*) lengthy
kilómetro *m* kilometre *Brit*, kilometer *Am*
kilotón *m* kiloton
kilovatio *m* kilowatt
kilovatio-hora *m* <kilovatios-hora> kilowatt hour
kínder *m inv*, **kindergarten** *m inv*, *AmL* kindergarten, nursery school
kit *m* <kits> kit
kl *abr de* **kilolitro** kl
kleenex® *m inv*, **klínex** *m inv* Kleenex®, tissue
km *abr de* **kilómetro** km.
km/h *abr de* **kilómetro por hora** km/h
K.O. *adj abr de* **knock-out** knock-out; **dejar** ~ **a alguien** to knock sb out
Kremlin *m* Kremlin
Kurdistán *m* Kurdistan
kurdo, -a I. *adj* Kurdish **II.** *m, f* Kurd
Kuwait *m* Kuwait
kuwaití *adj, mf* Kuwaiti
kv *abr de* **kilovatio** kw
kv/h *abr de* **kilovatio-hora** kw/h

K

K, k *f* K, k; ~ **de Kenia** K for King
kaki *adj* khaki
karaoke *m* karaoke
karate *m*, **kárate** *m* DEP karate
kart *m* <karts> go-cart

L

L, l *f* L,l; ~ **de Lisboa** L for Lucy *Brit*, L for Love *Am*
l *abr de* **litro(s)** l
I. 1. *abr de* **libro** bk **2.** *abr de* **ley** l
L. 1. *abr de* **Ley** l **2.** *abr de* **lira(s)** L, l

la I. *art def v.* **el, la, lo** II. *pron pers, f sing* **1.** *objeto directo: f sing* her; (*cosa*) it; ¡tráeme~! bring her/it to me!; **mi bicicleta y ~ tuya** my bicycle and yours **2.** (*con relativo*) **~ que...** the one that ...; **~ cual** which III. *m* MÚS A; **en ~ bemol menor** in A flat minor

laberíntico, -a *adj* labyrinthine; *fig* rambling

laberinto *m* **1.** (*lugar*) labyrinth, maze **2.** (*maraña*) tangle

labia *f inf* glibness; **tener mucha ~** to be a smooth talker

labial *adj* labial

lábil *adj* **1.** *t.* QUÍM (*carácter*) labile **2.** (*frágil*) frail

labio *m* **1.** (*boca*) lip; **~ leporino** harelip; **cerrar los ~s** to close one's mouth; **morderse los ~s** *fig* to keep back what one thinks; **estar sin despegar los ~s** to not say a word **2.** (*borde*) rim **3.** *pl* (*vulva*) labia *pl*

labioso, -a *adj* Ecua (*adulador*) honey-tongued

labor *f* work; (*de coser*) needlework; (*labranza*) ploughing *Brit,* plowing *Am;* **no estoy por la ~** I don't feel like it; **~ de ganchillo** crochet work; **ocupación: sus ~es** occupation: housewife; **hacer ~es** to do needlework

laborable *adj* **1.** AGR arable **2.** (*de trabajo*) **día ~** working day

laboral *adj* labour *Brit,* labor *Am*

laborar I. *vi* **1.** (*gestionar*) **~ por** [o en favor de] algo to strive for sth **2.** (*intrigar*) to scheme II. *vt v.* **labrar**

laboratorio *m* laboratory, lab

laborear *vt* **1.** *v.* **labrar 2.** MIN to work

laboreo *m* **1.** AGR farm work **2.** MIN working

laboriosidad *f* diligence, industriousness

laborioso, -a *adj* **1.** (*trabajador*) hard-working, industrious **2.** (*difícil*) arduous

laborismo *m* POL Labour Movement

laborista I. *adj* **partido ~** Labour Party II. *mf* member of the Labour Party

labrado *m* **1.** (*acción*) working; AGR tillage **2.** (*resultado*) result; (*dibujo*) fine detail; (*de un cristal*) etching **3.** (*campo*) cultivated land **4.** *pl* (*tierra*) ploughed fields *pl Brit,* plowed fields *pl Am*

labrado, -a *adj* **1.** (*telas*) embroidered; (*objetos*) wrought; (*madera*) carved; (*cristal*) etched **2.** AGR tilled; **campo ~** ploughed field

labrador(a) *m(f)* farmhand

labrantío *m* land for cultivation

labrantío, -a *adj* **1.** (*cultivado*) sown **2.** (*cultivable*) arable

labranza *f* **1.** (*cultivo*) tillage **2.** (*trabajo*) work **3.** (*hacienda*) farm

labrar *vt* **1.** (*trabajar un material*) to work; (*un dibujo*) to draw; (*cristal*) to etch; **sin ~** plain **2.** (*cultivar, en jardín*) to work; (*arar*) to plough *Brit,* to plow *Am* **3.** MIN to work **4.** (*coser*) to sew; (*bordar*) to embroider **5.** (*acuñar*) to coin **6.** (*causar gradualmente*) to bring about; **~ la felicidad de alguien** to

make sb happy; **~ la perdición de alguien** to bring sb to ruin

labriego, -a *m, f* farmworker

laburante *mf Arg, Urug, inf* worker

laburar *vi Arg, Urug, inf* to work

laburo *m Arg, Urug, inf* work

laca *f* **1.** (*pintura*) lacquer, shellac **2.** (*para el pelo*) hairspray; (*para las uñas*) nail varnish, nail polish

lacayo *m* **1.** (*criado*) footman **2.** *pey* (*adulador*) lackey

lacerante *adj* cutting; (*dolor*) searing; (*grito*) piercing

lacerar *vt* **1.** (*herir*) to injure; **~ el alma** to wound the soul **2.** (*magullar*) to bruise **3.** (*la honra*) to damage

lachear *vt Chile* to chat up

lacho I. *adj Chile, Perú* (*hombre enamoradizo*) easily enamored; (*acostumbrado a galantear*) womanizing II. *m Chile, Perú* (*enamorado*) lover; (*pisaverde*) dandy

lacio, -a *adj* **1.** (*marchito*) withered **2.** (*flojo*) limp; (*cabello*) straight, lank

lacón *m* ham

lacónico, -a *adj* brief; (*persona*) laconic

lacra *f* **1.** (*de una enfermedad*) mark; (*cicatriz*) scar **2.** (*vicio*) blight

lacrar *vt* **1.** (*cerrar*) to seal **2.** (*contagiar*) to impair the health of **3.** (*perjudicar*) to blight

lacre *m* sealing wax

lacrimógeno, -a *adj* (*de lágrimas*) tear; **gas ~** tear gas; (*sentimental*) soupy; **película lacrimógena** *pey* tearjerker

lacrimoso, -a *adj* **1.** (*lloroso*) tearful **2.** (*lastimoso*) sorrowful **3.** (*quejumbroso*) whining

lactancia *f* **1.** (*acción*) nursing, breastfeeding **2.** (*período*) pre-weaning period

lactante I. *adj* still on milk II. *mf* unweaned infant

lactar I. *vt* to nurse, to breastfeed II. *vi* to nurse

lacteado, -a *adj* milk; **papilla lacteada** milk-baby formula

lácteo, -a *adj* milk, dairy; *fig* milky; **vía láctea** ASTR Milky Way

láctico, -a *adj* lactic

lactosa *f* lactose

lacustre *adj* lacustrine; **construcciones ~s** lake dwellings

ladeado, -a *adj* tilted; **el cuadro está ~** the picture is lopsided

ladear I. *vt* **1.** (*inclinar*) to slant; (*un sombrero*) to tip **2.** (*desviar*) to skirt; **~ un problema** to get around a problem II. *vi* (*caminar*) to walk lopsided; (*desviarse*) to turn off III. *vr:* **~se 1.** (*inclinarse*) to lean **2.** *Chile* (*enamorarse*) **~se de alguien** to fall in love with sb

ladera *f* slope, hillside

ladilla *f* crab louse

ladino, -a *adj* (*taimado*) cunning

lado *m* **1.** *t.* MAT side; **a ambos ~s** on both sides; **por el ~ materno** on the mother's side;

ir de un ~ a otro to go back and forth; **dormir del ~ izquierdo** to sleep on ones left side; **por todos ~s** everywhere; **al ~** nearby; **la casa de al ~** the house next-door; **al ~ de** (*junto a*) beside, next to; **al ~ mío, a mi ~** next to me, by my side; **por un ~..., y por el otro ~...** on the one hand..., and on the other hand... **2.** (*borde*) edge; (*extremo*) end; (*parte*) side **3.** (*lugar*) **por el ~ del río** by the river; **ir a algún otro ~** to go somewhere else; **~ a ~** side by side **4.** (*punto de vista*) side; **por el ~ ecológico** on the ecological side; **el ~ bueno de la vida** the good side of life; **su ~ débil** his weak spot **5.** (*camino*) direction; **tomar por otro ~** to go another way **6.** (*partido*) **me puse de tu ~** I sided with you ▶**dejar de ~ a alguien** to ignore sb; **mirar de ~ a alguien** to look out of the corner of one's eye at sb

ladrar *vi* (*perro*) to bark; (*amenazar*) to growl ▶**perro que ladra no muerde** *prov* his bark is worse than his bite

ladrido *m* **1.** (*perro*) bark **2.** *pey* (*calumnia*) slander

ladrillo *m* **1.** (*de construcción*) brick **2.** *inf* **ser un ~** (*película, libro*) to be deadly dull

ladrón *m* (*enchufe*) multiple socket

ladrón, -ona **I.** *adj* thieving **II.** *m, f* (*bandido*) thief, robber; **~ cuatrero** treacherous thief ▶**piensa el ~ que todos son de su condición** *prov* we all judge others by our own standards; **la ocasión hace al ~** *prov* opportunity makes the thief *prov*

ladronzuelo, -a *m, f* (*ratero*) petty thief

lagar *m* **1.** (*aceite*) oil press; (*vino*) winepress **2.** (*edificio*) press house

lagartear **I.** *vt* **1.** *Chile* to pinion **2.** *Col* (*hacer chanchullos*) to finagle **II.** *vi* *Guat, Méx* (*cazar lagartos*) to catch lizards

lagartija *f* small lizard

lagarto **I.** *m* **1.** (*reptil*) lizard **2.** *AmL* (*caimán*) alligator **II.** *interj* touch wood! *Brit*, knock on wood! *Am*

lagarto, -a **I.** *adj* sly **II.** *m, f* (*persona*) crafty fellow

lagartón, -ona **I.** *adj* shrewd; *pey* sly **II.** *m, f* sharp fellow; *pey* sly devil *m*, sly bitch *f*

lago *m* lake

lágrima *f* **1.** (*del ojo*) tear **2.** (*de vino*) drop ▶**llorar ~s de sangre por algo** to shed bitter tears for sth; **llorar a ~ viva** to weep bitterly; **deshacerse en ~s** to burst into tears

lagrimal **I.** *adj* lachrymal **II.** *m* corner of the eye

lagrimear *vi* **1.** (*llorar*) to cry easily **2.** (*ojos*) to water

lagrimoso, -a *adj* **1.** (*triste*) tearful **2.** (*ojos*) watery

laguna *f* **1.** (*agua salada*) lagoon; (*dulce*) small lake **2.** (*omisión*) gap; **~ en la memoria** memory lapse

laicado *m* laity

laicalización *f Chile* secularization

laicalizar <z→c> *vt Chile* to secularize

laico, -a **I.** *adj* lay **II.** *m, f* layman *m*, laywoman *f*

> The term **laísmo** refers to the incorrect usage of **la(s)** as the indirect object instead of **le(s)**, e.g. "**La regalé una novela de Borges**" instead of "**Le regalé una novela de Borges**". Such use is commonly accepted in certain regions but not accepted by most Spanish speakers.

laja *f* flat stone; **~ de pizarra** slate slab

lama *f* **1.** (*cieno*) silt **2.** (*de metal*) slat

lambiche *adj Méx, vulg* (*adulador*) arse-licking *Brit*, ass-kissing *Am*

lameculos *mf inv, vulg* arselicker *Brit*

lamedura *f* licking

lamentable *adj* regrettable

lamentación *f* **1.** (*acción*) lamentation **2.** (*expresión*) lament

lamentar **I.** *vt* to regret; **lo lamento** I'm sorry **II.** *vr* ~**se de algo** to complain about sth

lamento *m* lament

lameplatos *mf inv* **1.** *inf* (*goloso*) glutton **2.** (*pobre*) scrounger

lamer **I.** *vt* **1.** (*pasar la lengua*) to lick **2.** (*tocar*) to lap; **las olas lamen las arenas** the waves lap against the shore ▶**mejor lamiendo que mordiendo** it's easier to catch a bear with honey than with vinegar **II.** *vr:* ~**se** to lick oneself; ~**se de gusto** to lick one's lips

lamido *m* licking

lamido, -a *adj* **1.** (*flaco*) scrawny **2.** (*pálido*) pale **3.** (*relamido*) affected **4.** (*gastado*) worn out

lámina *f* **1.** (*hojalata*) tin plate; (*hoja de metal*) sheet; (*segmento*) lamina; **~ para proyector** projector plate **2.** TIPO plate **3.** (*ilustración*) print; **con ~s** illustrated

laminador *m* (*empresa*) rolling mill

laminar **I.** *adj* **1.** (*en forma de lámina*) laminar **2.** (*formado de láminas*) laminated **II.** *vt* **1.** (*cortar*) to split **2.** (*guarnecer*) to laminate

lampa *f And* (*pala*) shovel; (*azada*) pick

lámpara *f* **1.** (*luz*) lamp, light; **~ de alarma** warning light; **~ fluorescente** fluorescent lamp; **~ de pie** standard lamp **2.** TV, RADIO valve *Brit*, tube *Am* **3.** (*mancha*) grease stain

lamparazo *m Col* drink

lamparilla *f* (*luz*) small lamp

lamparón *m* **1.** (*mancha*) grease stain **2.** MED scrofula

lampiño, -a *adj* (*sin barba*) beardless; (*sin pelo*) hairless

lana *f* **1.** (*material, tela*) wool; **~ esquilada** fleece; **perro de ~s** poodle **2.** *Méx, inf* (*dinero*) dough; **tienen mucha ~** they're loaded ▶**unos cardan la ~ y otros cobran la fama** some do all the work and others get all the credit; **cardar la ~ a alguien** to give sb a good telling off

lanar *adj* wool-bearing; **ganado ~** sheep

lance *m* **1.** (*acción*) throw; (*red*) cast

2. (*trance*) critical moment **3.** (*pelea*) quarrel; ~ **de honor** duel **4.** (*juego*) move **5.** *inf* (compra) secondhand; **comprar de** ~ to buy secondhand; **de** ~ at a bargain price **6.** (*episodio*) ~ **de amor** love afair; ~ **de fortuna** stroke of luck

lancha *f* **1.** (*piedra*) flat stone; ~ **de pizarra** slate slab **2.** (*bote*) motorboat; ~ **a remolque** barge; ~ **de salvamento** lifeboat

lanchar *vi Ecua* **1.** (*nublarse*) to become overcast **2.** (*helar*) to freeze

lancinante *adj* (*dolor*) stabbing

landa *f* moorland

lanero, -a *adj* wool

langosta *f* **1.** (*insecto*) locust; **por esta nevera ha pasado la** ~ *inf* sb has polished off everything in the fridge **2.** (*crustáceo*) lobster

langostino *m* prawn

langucia *f AmL* hunger

languidecer *irr como crecer vi* (*debilitarse*) to languish; (*persona*) to languish (away); (*flores*) to droop; (*fuego*) to die down; ~ **de amor** to pine; **la conversación languideció** the conversation flagged

languidez *f* **1.** (*debilidad*) weakness **2.** (*espíritu*) listlessness

lánguido, -a *adj* **1.** (*débil*) weak **2.** (*espíritu*) languid

lanilla *f* (*pelillo*) nap

lanolina *f* lanolin

lanoso, -a *adj*, **lanudo, -a** *adj* woolly, wooly *Am;* (*oveja*) wool-bearing

lanza *f* **1.** (*arma*) lance **2.** (*carro*) pole ▶ **quebrar** ~**s** to cross swords, to argue; **romper una** ~ **en favor de alguien** to stick up for sb

lanzabengalas *m inv* flare gun

lanzacohetes *m inv* rocket launcher

lanzada *f* (*golpe*) spear thrust; (*herida*) lance wound

lanzadera *f* shuttle; (*plataforma*) platform, launch(ing) pad

lanzado, -a *adj* **1.** (*decidido*) determined; (*emprendedor*) enterprising **2.** (*impetuoso*) impetuous; (*fogoso*) forward

lanzador(a) *m(f)* thrower; (*beisbol*) bowler, pitcher

lanzallamas *m inv* flamethrower

lanzamiento *m* throw; ~ **de bombas** dropping of bombs; ~ **comercial** commercial promotion, product launch; ~ **espacial** space launch; ~ **de peso** DEP shot put

lanzamisiles *m inv* missile-launcher

lanzar <z→c> **I.** *vt* **1.** (*arrojar*) ~ **a algo/alguien** to throw at [o to] sth/sb; ~ **peso** to put the shot **2.** (*al mercado*) to launch **II.** *vr* ~**se a/ sobre algo/alguien** to throw oneself at/ against sth/sb; ~**se a correr** to break into a run; ~**se al agua** to dive into the water; ~**se en paracaídas** to parachute; ~**se en picado** to nosedive; ~**se a algo** to undertake sth

lanzaroteño, -a I. *adj* of/from Lanzarote **II.** *m, f* native/inhabitant of Lanzarote

laña *f* (*grapa*) clamp

lapa *f* **1.** ZOOL limpet **2.** *inf* (*persona*) nuisance; **pegarse como una** ~ to stick like a leech

La Paz *f* La Paz

lapicera *f Arg, Urug* (*pluma*) ballpoint pen

lapicero *m* **1.** (*lápiz*) pencil **2.** (*recipiente*) penholder

lápida *f* stone tablet; ~ **conmemorativa** memorial tablet; ~ **mortuoria** gravestone

lapidar *vt* to stone

lapidario, -a *adj* **1.** (*piedras preciosas*) lapidary **2.** (*categórico*) categorical, scathing; **frase lapidaria** memorable phrase

lápiz *m* pencil; ~ **de labios** lipstick; ~ **de ojos** eye pencil; ~ **de color** crayon, wax crayon *Brit;* ~ **de pizarra** chalk

lapón, -ona I. *adj* Lapp **II.** *m, f* (*habitante*) Lapp, Laplander

Laponia *f* Lapland

lapso *m* **1.** (*período*) ~ (**de tiempo**) lapse **2.** *v.* **lapsus**

lapsus *m inv* blunder; ~ **linguae** slip of the tongue

laquear *vt* to lacquer

lar *m* **1.** (*fuego*) hearth **2.** (*hogar*) home

lardo *m* **1.** (*tocino*) lard **2.** (*grasa*) animal fat

largar <g→gu> **I.** *vt* **1.** (*soltar*) to release **2.** *inf* (*golpe*) to land; (*bofetada*) to let fly **3.** *inf* (*discurso*) to give **4.** *inf* (*deshacerse de*) ~ **algo a alguien** to unload sth on sb; **siempre larga el trabajo a los demás** he/she is always unloading work on others **5.** (*revelar*) to tell; **si te lo digo, lo ~ás a todos** if I tell you, you'll go and tell everyone **II.** *vr:* ~**se 1.** (*irse*) to leave; (*de casa*) to leave home **2.** *AmL* (*comenzar*) to begin; ~**se a hacer algo** to start to do sth **III.** *vi inf* to talk a lot, to yack

largo I. *adv* (*en abundancia*) plenty; **tenemos comida para** ~ we've got plenty of food; ~ **y tendido** at length ▶ **a lo** ~ **de la playa** along the beach; **a lo** ~ **del día** throughout the day; **¡**~ (**de aquí**)**!** clear off! **II.** *m* (*longitud*) length; **nadar tres** ~**s** to swim three lengths of the pool; **diez metros de** ~ ten metres long

largo, -a *adj* **1.** (*tamaño, duración*) long; **a** ~ **plazo, a la larga** in the long term [o run]; **a la larga o a la corta** sooner or later; **a lo** ~ **de los años** throughout the years; **dar largas a algo** to put off doing sth; **el pantalón te está** ~ your trousers are too long for you; **ir de** ~ to be in a long dress; (*de gala*) to be in formal dress; **pasar de** ~ to pass by; *fig* to ignore; **tener cincuenta años** ~**s** to be well past 50; **tener las manos largas** (*pegar*) to be free with one's hands; (*robar*) to be light-fingered **2.** (*extensivo*) lengthy; (*mucho*) abundant; **por** ~ for a long time **3.** *inf* (*astuto*) shrewd

largometraje *m* full-length [o feature] film

larguero *m* **1.** (*carpintería*) long beam **2.** DEP crossbar

largueza *f* **1.** (*largura*) length **2.** (*generosidad*) largesse **3.** (*liberalidad*) liberality

larguirucho, -a *adj inf* lanky

largura *f* length
laringe *f* larynx
laringitis *f inv* laryngitis
larva *f* larva
larvado, -a *adj* latent
las I. *art def v.* el, la, lo II. *pron pers f pl*
1. (*objeto directo*) them; ¡míra~! look at
them! 2. (*con relativo*) ~ que... the ones that
...; ~ cuales those which 3. (*laísmo*)
*improper use of 'la' and 'las' as indirect
objects instead of 'le' and 'les'*
lascar <c→qu> *vt* 1. NÁUT to pay out 2. *Méx*
(*lastimar*) to bruise
lascivia *f* 1. (*lujuria*) lasciviousness 2. (*indecencia*) lewdness 3. (*sensualidad*) lust
lascivo, -a *adj* 1. (*sensual*) lustful 2. (*lujurioso*) lascivious 3. (*indecente*) lewd
láser *m* laser
lasitud *f* lassitude
laso, -a *adj* 1. (*cansado*) weary 2. (*pelo*) lank
3. (*cuerda*) slack
lástima *f* 1. (*compasión*) pity; dar [*o* causar]
~ to inspire pity; me da mucha ~ I feel very
sorry for him/her; su último libro da ~ his/
her latest book is pathetic; de [*o por*] ~ out of
pity; estar hecho una ~ to be a sorry sight;
¡qué ~! what a pity! 2. (*lamentación*) complaint
lastimadura *f* injury
lastimar I. *vt* 1. (*herir*) to hurt; las botas me
han lastimado los pies my feet hurt from my
boots 2. (*agraviar*) to offend II. *vr:* ~se 1. (*herirse*) to hurt oneself 2. (*quejarse*) ~se de
algo to complain about sth
lastimero, -a *adj*, **lastimoso, -a** *adj*
1. (*daño*) harmful 2. (*lástima*) pitiful
lastra *f* flagstone
lastrar *vt* 1. (*poner peso*) to ballast 2. (*subrayar*) to emphasize
lastre *m* 1. (*cantera*) gravel 2. NÁUT ballast
3. (*estorbo*) dead weight; ser un ~ to be a
burden
lata *f* 1. (*metal*) tin 2. (*envase*) tin *Brit*, can
Am 3. (*conversación*) long boring conversation 4. *inf* (*pesadez, aburrido*) bore; dar la ~
to be a nuisance; ¡vaya ~! (*fastidio*) what a
pain!
latazo *m inf* 1. (*tontería*) foolishness 2. (*pesadez*) pain; ser un ~ (*pesado*) to be a drag; (*fastidioso*) bother; (*aburrido*) bore; dar el ~ to be
a nuisance
latear *vi AmL* 1. (*aburrir a alguien*) to bore
2. (*parlotear*) se pasa el día lateando he/she
spends all day blabbing away
latente *adj* latent
lateral *adj* 1. (*lado*) lateral 2. (*secundario*) secondary
latería *f* 1. (*conjunto de latas*) cans *pl* of pre-
serves; la ~ de su despensa the canned goods
in her pantry 2. *AmL* (*hojalatería*) tinsmith's
shop
latido *m* 1. (*corazón*) heartbeat; (*herida, arteria*) throbbing 2. (*perro*) yelp

latifundio *m* large landed estate
latifundista *mf* owner of a large estate
latigazo *m* 1. (*golpe*) whiplash 2. (*chasquido*) crack of a whip 3. (*destino*) stroke of
fate 4. (*reprimenda*) tongue lashing 5. *inf*
(*trago*) swig
látigo *m* whip
latiguear I. *vi* to crack a whip II. *vt AmL* to
flog
latiguillo *m* 1. (*efectismo*) hamming
2. (*muletilla*) catchphrase; (*expresión*) platitude
latín *m* Latin; saber (mucho) ~ *inf* to know
what's what, to know a thing or two
latino, -a I. *adj* Latin; América Latina Latin
America II. *m, f* Latin; *AmL* (*latinoamericano*)
Latin American
Latinoamérica *f* Latin America
latinoamericano, -a *adj, m, f* Latin American
latir *vi* 1. (*corazón*) to beat; (*arteria, herida*) to
throb 2. (*perros*) to yelp
latitud *f* 1. GEO, ASTR latitude 2. (*extensión*)
breadth
lato, -a *adj* (*amplio*) broad; (*extendido*) extensive; en sentido ~ in the broad sense
latón *m* brass
latoso, -a *adj* bothersome
latrocinio *m* larceny
laúd *m* MÚS lute
laudable *adj* praiseworthy
laudatorio, -a *adj* laudatory; discurso ~
eulogistic speech
laudo *m* decision
laureado, -a *adj* 1. (*coronado*) crowned with
laurel 2. (*premiado*) laureate, prize-winning
laurear *vt* 1. (*coronar*) to crown with laurel
2. (*premiar*) to award
laurel *m* 1. (*árbol*) laurel 2. (*condimento*) bay
leaf 3. *pl* (*honor*) honour *Brit*, honor *Am;* dormirse en los ~es to rest on one's laurels
lauro *m* 1. (*laurel*) laurel 2. (*gloria*) glory
lava *f* (*volcán*) lava
lavable *adj* washable; (*color*) colourfast *Brit*,
colorfast *Am*
lavabo *m* 1. (*pila*) washbasin *Brit*, sink *Am*
2. (*cuarto*) toilet *Brit*, bathroom *Am*
lavacoches *m inv* (*instalación*) car wash
lavacristales *mf inv* window cleaner
lavadero *m* (*de ropa*) laundry; (*en el río*)
washing place
lavado *m* wash; ~ en seco dry-cleaning; MED
lavage; ~ de cerebro *fig* brainwashing; ~ de
cara *fig* facelift
lavadora *f* washing machine
lavafaros *m inv* AUTO headlamp washer
lavanda *f* lavender
lavandería *f* laundry, launderette *Brit*, laun-
dromat *Am*
lavaplatos *m inv* 1. (*electrodoméstico*) dishwasher 2. *Col, inf* (*fregadero*) (kitchen) sink
lavar I. *vt* (*limpiar*) to wash; ~ la cabeza to
wash one's hair; ~ los platos to wash up II. *vr:*

~**se** to wash; ~**se los dientes** to brush [*o* clean *Brit*] one's teeth

lavarropas *f inv, Arg* (*lavadora*) washing machine

lavativa *f* **1.** (*enema*) enema **2.** (*instrumento*) enema bag

lavatorio *m* **1.** MED lotion, wash **2.** REL maundy; ~ **del Jueves Santo** feet-washing on Maundy Thursday **3.** *AmL* (*lavabo*) lavatory *Brit*, washroom *Am*

lavavajillas *m inv* **1.** (*electrodoméstico*) dishwasher **2.** (*detergente*) washing-up liquid

lavotear I. *vt* to wash quickly and badly **II.** *vr:* ~**se** *inf* to wash quickly

laxante *m* laxative

laxar *vt* **1.** (*relajar*) to relax **2.** (*vientre*) to loosen up

laxitud *f* laxity

laxo, -a *adj* **1.** (*flojo*) slack **2.** (*moral*) lax

lazada *f* (*de zapato*) bow

lazareto *m* (*de contagiosos*) quarantine station

lazo *m* **1.** (*nudo*) bow **2.** (*para caballos*) lasso; (*para conejos*) snare **3.** (*cinta*) ribbon **4.** (*vínculo*) tie; ~**s afectivos** emotional bonds

lda., ldo. *abr de* **licenciado, -a** graduate

le *pron pers* **1.** *objeto indirecto: m sing* him; *f sing* her; *forma cortés* you; **¡da~ un beso!** give him/her a kiss!; **si Ud. quiere, ~ puedo llamar el lunes** if you like, I can phone you on Monday **2.** *reg, objeto directo: m sing* him **3.** *forma cortés* you

leal *adj* loyal

lealtad *f* loyalty

lebrel *m* greyhound

lección *f* **1.** (*lectura*) reading **2.** (*pl*) (*enseñanza escolar*) lessons *pl;* **tomar lecciones de matemáticas** to take mathematics classes **3.** UNIV lecture **4.** (*tema a estudiar*) lesson; **¿te tomo la ~?** *inf* should I test you? **5.** (*advertencia*) warning; **dar una ~ a alguien** to teach sb a lesson; **¡que te sirva de ~!** let that be a lesson to you!

lechada *f* **1.** (*para blanquear*) whitewash **2.** (*argamasa*) grout

lechal I. *adj* (*cachorro*) suckling; **cordero ~** suckling lamb **II.** *m* (*cordero*) baby lamb

lechar *adj* **1.** (*cachorro*) suckling; **corzo ~** unweaned fawn, *of roe deer* **2.** (*productor*) **vaca ~** milk [*o* milch *Brit*] cow

leche *f* **1.** (*líquido*) milk; ~ **en polvo** powdered milk; ~ **entera** whole milk; ~ **desnatada** skimmed milk; ~ **semidesnatada** low fat milk; ~ **desmaquillante** cleansing milk **2.** *vulg* (*esperma*) spunk **3.** *inf* (*golpe*) blow; **¡te doy una ~!** I'm going to belt you one! **4.** *inf* (*hostia*) **¡~s!** damn it!; **ser la ~** to be too much; **estar de mala ~** to be in a foul mood; **tener mala ~** to be vindictive; **a toda ~** at full speed

lechera *adj, f v.* **lechero**

lechería *f* dairy

lechero, -a I. *adj* milk **II.** *m, f* milkman *m,* milkwoman *f*

lechigada *f* litter

lecho *m* bed; (*río*) riverbed

lechón, -ona *m, f* **1.** (*animal*) suckling pig **2.** *pey* (*persona*) fat slob

lechosa *f AmL* BOT papaya

lechoso, -a *adj* milky

lechuga *f* lettuce ▶**como una ~** as fresh as a daisy; **ser más fresco que una ~** *inf* to have a lot of nerve

lechuguino, -a *m, f pey* (*presumido*) dandy

lechuza *f* barn owl

lectivo, -a *adj* **ciclo ~** ENS school cycle; UNIV academic cycle; **día ~** school day

lector *m* INFOR reader

lector(a) *m(f)* **1.** (*que lee*) reader; (*en voz alta*) lector **2.** (*profesor*) conversation assistant **3.** (*aparato*) player; ~ **de CD** CD player

lectorado *m* assistantship

lectura *f* **1.** *t.* INFOR (*acción de leer, instrumento*) reading; (*disertación*) dissertation; ~ **(en voz alta)** reading aloud; **el portavoz dio ~ al comunicado** the spokesman read the communiqué **2.** (*obra*) reading material **3.** (*conocimientos*) knowledge; **ser de mucha ~** to be well-read **4.** (*perspectiva*) interpretation

leer *irr vt* **1.** (*percibir, instrumento*) to read; ~ **en voz alta** to read aloud **2.** (*interpretar*) to interpret; ~ **en la cara de alguien** to see from sb's expression

legación *f* legation

legado *m* **1.** POL legacy; REL legate **2.** (*herencia*) legacy

legajo *m* dossier

legal *adj* **1.** (*determinado por la ley*) legal; **medicina ~** forensic medicine **2.** (*conforme a la ley*) lawful **3.** (*fiel*) trustworthy

legalidad *f* legality; **al filo de la ~** semi-legal; **fuera de la ~** unlawful

legalista *adj* legalistic

legalización *f* **1.** (*autorización*) legalization, legalisation *Brit* **2.** (*atestamiento*) authentication

legalizar <z→c> *vt* **1.** (*autorizar*) to legalize **2.** (*atestar*) to authenticate

légamo *m* (*cieno*) mud

legaña *f* sleep, rheum; **tienes ~s** you have sleep in your eyes

legar <g→gu> *vt* **1.** (*legado*) to bequeath **2.** (*enviar*) to delegate

legendario, -a *adj* legendary; (*famoso*) renowned

legible *adj* legible

legión *f* **1.** MIL legion **2.** (*multitud*) crowd; **hay comida para una ~** there's enough food to feed an army

legionario, -a I. *adj* legionary **II.** *m, f* legionnaire

legionella *f* MED Legionnaire's disease

legislación *f* **1.** (*acción*) lawmaking **2.** (*leyes*) legislation

legislador(a) I. *adj* legislative **II.** *m(f)* **1.** (*que* *legisla*) legislator **2.** *AmL* (*parlamentario*) member of parliament

legislar *vi* to legislate

legislativo, -a *adj* legislative; **poder** ~ legislative power

legislatura *f* **1.** (*período*) term of office **2.** *AmL* (*parlamento*) legislative body

legitimación *f* **1.** (*legalización*) authentication **2.** (*habilitación*) recognition **3.** (*hijo*) legitimization, legitimisation *Brit*

legitimar I. *vt* **1.** (*dar legitimidad*) to authenticate **2.** (*habilitar*) to recognize **3.** (*hijo*) to make legitimate **II.** *vr:* ~**se** to establish one's title

legítimo, -a *adj* **1.** (*legal*) legitimate; **defensa legítima** self-defense **2.** (*verdadero*) genuine **3.** (*hijo*) legitimate

lego, -a I. *adj* **1.** (*no eclesiástico*) lay **2.** (*ignorante*) uninformed **II.** *m, f* lay brother *m*, lay sister *f;* **ser un ~ en el tema** to know nothing about the subject

legua *f* league; **a la ~** miles away; **se ve a la ~ que no dicen la verdad** it's obvious that they're lying

leguleyo, -a *m, f pey* pettifogging lawyer, shyster

legumbre *f* **1.** (*planta*) legume **2.** (*fruta seca*) pulse; (*fruta fresca*) vegetable; **frutas y ~s** fruit and vegetables

leíble *adj* readable

leído, -a *adj* **1.** (*persona*) well-read **2.** (*revista*) widely-read

The term **leísmo** refers to the incorrect or perhaps non-standard usage of **le(s)** as the direct object instead of **lo(s)** or **la(s)**, e.g. "**Les visité ayer, a mis hermanas**" instead of "**Las visité ayer, a mis hermanas**." Such use is commonly accepted in certain regions but not accepted by most Spanish speakers.

lejanía *f* distance

lejano, -a *adj* faraway; (*parentesco*) distant; **en un futuro no muy ~** in the not-so-distant future

lejía *f* **1.** QUÍM lye **2.** (*para lavar, decolorar*) bleach

lejos I. *adv* far; ~ **de algo** far from sth; **a lo ~** in the distance; **de ~** from afar; **ir demasiado ~** *t. fig* to go too far; **es de ~ la mejor soprano** she is by far the best soprano; **llegar ~** *fig* to go far; **sin ir más ~** *fig* to take an obvious example **II.** *prep* ~ **de** far from; **está muy ~ de mí hacer algo** *fig* I have no intention of intervening in sth

lelo, -a I. *adj inf* **1.** **ser** (*tonto*) silly, goofy *Am* **2.** **estar** (*pasmado*) stunned; (*mareado*) dizzy **II.** *m, f* (*persona*) dolt, gubbins, dork *Am*

lema *m* **1.** (*tema*) theme; (*mote*) motto **2.** (*contraseña*) watchword

lencería *f* **1.** (*telas*) linen; (*ropa de cama*) bed linen **2.** (*tienda de telas*) draper's shop; (*de ropa interior*) lingerie shop; ~ **de un almacén** linen room **3.** (*ropa interior*) underwear

lengón, -ona *adj Col* (*deslenguado*) outspoken

lengua *f* **1.** ANAT tongue; **lo tengo en la punta de la ~** I have it on the tip of my tongue; **morderse la ~** *t. fig* to bite one's tongue; **¿te ha comido alguien la ~?** has the cat got your tongue?; **sacar la ~ a alguien** to stick ones tongue out at sb; **se me trabó la ~** I got tongue-tied; **tener la ~ demasiado larga** *fig* to talk too much **2.** LING tongue; ~ **materna** mother tongue; ~ **oficial** official language **3.** (*forma*) tongue; ~ **de agua** tongue of water ▶**tener la ~ de trapo** *inf* to stutter and stammer; **estar con la ~ fuera** to be out of breath; **tener una ~ viperina** to be a backbiter; **atar la ~ a alguien** to silence sb; **dar a la ~** to gab; **desasir la ~ a alguien** to loosen sb's tongue; **aquí alguien se ha ido de la ~** sb here has spilled the beans; **tirar a alguien de la ~** to pump sb for information; **volar ~** *AmC* (*hablar*) to gossip

lenguado *m* sole

lenguaje *m* language; ~ **técnico** technical language

lenguaraz *adj* talkative

lenguaz *adj* garrulous

lengüeta *f* **1.** (*zapato*) tongue; (*balanza*) pointer **2.** MÚS reed

lengüetear *vi AmL, inf* to stick one's tongue out

lengüilargo, -a *adj inf* impudent

lengún, -ona I. *adj AmL* (*calumniador*) backbiting; (*chismoso*) gossipy **II.** *m, f AmL* (*calumniador*) backbiter; (*chismoso*) gossip

lenidad *f sin pl* lenience

lenificar <c→qu> *vt* to soothe

lenitivo, -a *adj* alleviating

lente *t.* FOTO (*cristal*) lens; ~ **convergente** converging lens; ~ **de aumento** magnifying glass

lenteja *f* lentil; **dar algo por un plato de ~s** *fig* to sell sth of value for sth worthless; **ganarse las ~s** *fig* to earn one's daily bread

lentejuela *f* sequin, spangle

lentes *mpl* eyeglasses *pl*; **llevar ~** to wear glasses

lenticular *adj* lenticular

lentilla *f* contact lens

lentitud *f* slowness; *fig* slow-wittedness; **con ~** slowly

lento, -a *adj* slow; *fig* slow-witted; (*enfermedad*) lingering; **a cámara lenta** in slow motion; **a paso ~** slowly; **cocinar a fuego ~** to cook over low heat [*o* a low flame]; **quemar a fuego ~** *fig* to burn slowly

leña *f sin pl* **1.** (*madera*) firewood; **echar ~ al fuego** to add more firewood; *fig* to add fuel to the flames **2.** (*castigo*) beating; **¡~ con él!** let him have it!; **dar ~** to give a beating; **repartir ~** to dish out blows; **recibir ~** to get beaten up ▶**hacer ~ del árbol caído** to kick somebody when he is down; **llevar ~ al <u>monte</u>** to carry coals to Newcastle

leñador(a) *m(f)* woodcutter, lumberjack

leñazo *m inf* bash; **¡qué ~ se pegó con su coche!** he/she really crashed his car!; **darse un ~ en la cabeza** to bash one's head

leñe *interj* damn it!

leño *m* **1.** (*de árbol*) log **2.** (*tonto*) blockhead

leñoso, -a *adj* woody

Leo *m* Leo

león *m* lion; *AmL* (*puma*) puma, cougar *Am;* **~ (marino)** sea lion ►**no es tan <u>fiero</u> el ~ como lo pintan** *inf* it's not as bad as it looks

leonado, -a *adj* tawny

leonera *f* **1.** (*jaula*) lion's cage **2.** (*habitación*) messy room

leonés, -esa **I.** *adj* of/from León **II.** *m, f* native/inhabitant of León

leonino, -a *adj* **1.** (*animal*) leonine **2.** (*contrato*) unfair

leontina *f* watch chain

leopardo *m* leopard

leotardo(s) *m(pl)* leotards *pl,* tights *pl*

Lepe saber más que ~ to be very sharp

lépero, -a **I.** *adj* **1.** *AmC* (*grosero*) coarse; (*vil*) rotten **2.** *Cuba* (*perspicaz*) shrewd **3.** *Ecua, inf* (*arruinado*) broke **II.** *m, f AmC* pauper

leporino, -a *adj* harelike; **labio ~** harelip

lepra *f MED sin pl* leprosy

leprosario *m Méx* leper colony

leproso, -a **I.** *adj* leprous **II.** *m, f* leper

lerdear *vi AmC, Arg* **1.** (*hacer algo con pesadez*) to be sluggish **2.** (*demorarse*) to take a long time; (*llegar tarde*) to be late

lerdo, -a *adj* slow, sluggish

leridano, -a **I.** *adj* of/from Lérida **II.** *m, f* native/inhabitant of Lérida

les *pron pers* **1.** *m pl, reg* (*objeto directo*) them; (*forma cortés*) you **2.** *mf pl* (*objeto indirecto*) them; (*forma cortés*) you

lesbiana *f* lesbian

lésbico, -a *adj* lesbian

lesear *vi Chile* to fool around

lesera *f AmL* stupidity

lesión *f* injury; **~ cardiaca** heart damage

lesionar **I.** *vt* **1.** (*herir*) to injure **2.** (*dañar*) to damage **II.** *vr:* **~se** to get hurt

lesivo, -a *adj* harmful

leso, -a *adj* injured

letal *adj elev* lethal

letanía *f* litany; **¡ya está éste con su ~!** there he/she goes again with his usual story

letárgico, -a *adj* lethargic

letargo *m* lethargy

letón, -ona **I.** *adj* Latvian, Lettish **II.** *m, f* Latvian, Lett

Letonia *f* Latvia

letra *f* **1.** (*signo*) letter; **~s de molde** block letters; **~ mayúscula/minúscula** capital/small letter; **con ~ mayúscula/minúscula** in capitals/small letters; **al pie de la ~** to the letter; **~ por ~** word for word; **poner cuatro**

~s a alguien to drop sb a line; **tener las ~s gordas** *fig* to be perfectly clear **2.** (*escritura*) handwriting; **de su puño y ~** in his own handwriting **3.** *pl* (*saber*) learning, letters; *UNIV* arts *pl;* **aprender las primeras ~s** *fig* to learn one's ABC; **hombre de ~s** man of letters **4.** *MÚS* lyrics *pl* **5.** *COM* ~ **(de cambio)** bill of exchange; **~ al portador** draft payable to the bearer; **~ a la vista** sight draft; **girar una ~ a cargo de alguien** to draw a bill on sb

letrado, -a **I.** *adj* learned **II.** *m, f* lawyer

letrero *m* notice, sign

leucemia *f sin pl MED* leukaemia *Brit,* leukemia *Am*

leucocito *m* leucocyte *Brit,* leukocyte *Am*

leva *f* **1.** *MIL* levy **2.** (*barco*) weighing anchor

levadizo, -a *adj* **puente ~** drawbridge

levadura *f* **1.** (*masa*) leavening yeast; **~ en polvo** baking powder **2.** (*hongo*) yeast

levantamiento *m* **1.** (*amotinamiento*) uprising **2.** (*alzar*) lifting; **~ del cadáver** removal of the corpse

levantar **I.** *vt* **1.** (*alzar*) to lift, to raise; (*del suelo*) to pick up; (*algo tumbado, inclinado*) to straighten; (*polvo, telón*) to raise; (*cartel*) to take down; (*un campamento*) to strike; (*las anclas*) to weigh; **~ el vuelo** to take off; **después del fracaso ya no levantó cabeza** he never recovered from the fiasco **2.** (*despertar, provocar*) to awaken; **no queremos ~ sospechas** we don't want to arouse suspicion; **~ polémica** to give rise to controversy **3.** (*construir*) to build; (*monumento*) to erect; (*muro*) to put up **4.** (*suprimir*) to remove; (*embargo, castigo*) to lift **5.** (*mapa*) to draw up; **~ acta de algo** to draw up a report on sth **6.** (*voz*) to raise; **~ la voz a alguien** to raise one's voice to sb **7.** (*mirada, mano*) to raise **8.** (*caza*) to flush out **II.** *vr:* **~se 1.** (*de la cama*) to get up; **~se con el pie izquierdo** *fig* to get out of bed on the wrong side **2.** (*sobresalir*) to stand out **3.** (*sublevarse*) to rebel; **se ~on pocas voces críticas** very few protested **4.** (*viento*) to rise **5.** *inf* (*robar*) to swipe, to pinch **6.** (*telón*) to rise **7.** (*sesión*) to adjourn; **se levanta la sesión** the meeting is closed, court is adjourned

levante *m sin pl* **1.** (*Este*) east **2.** (*viento*) east wind

levantisco, -a *adj* rebellious

levar *vt* **~ (las) anclas** to weigh anchor

leve *adj* (*enfermedad*) mild; (*peso, sanción*) light; (*error*) slight; (*pecado*) venial

levedad *f sin pl* lightness

levitar *vi* to levitate

lexicalizar <z→c> *vt* to lexicalize

léxico *m* **1.** (*diccionario*) lexicon **2.** (*vocabulario*) vocabulary

lexicón *m* lexicon

ley *f* **1.** *JUR, REL, FÍS* law; **~ del embudo** *inf* one--sided law; **Ley Fundamental** Fundamental Law; **Ley General Tributaria** Tax Law; **~ marcial** martial law; **~ orgánica** constitu-

tional law; **la ~ de la oferta y demanda** the law of supply and demand; **~ de prescripción** statute of limitations; **la ~ seca** the Prohibition; **la ~ de la selva**, **la ~ del más fuerte** the law of the jungle; **fuerza de ~** force of law; **proyecto de ~** bill; **hacer algo con todas las de la ~** to do sth properly; **hecha la ~, hecha la trampa** every law has its loophole; **respetar las ~es del juego** to follow the rules of the game; **regirse por la ~ del embudo** to have one law for oneself, and one for everyone else; **según la ~ vigente** in accordance with the law currently in force; **se le aplicó la ~ de la fuga al reo** the prisoner was shot while trying to escape; **ser de ~** *inf* to be reliable **2.** *pl* (*estudio*) Law **3.** (*oro*) legal standard of fineness; (*monedas*) genuine; **oro de ~** standard gold; **ser de buena ~** *fig* to be genuine
leyenda *f* **1.** LIT, REL legend **2.** (*plano*) caption **3.** (*moneda*) inscription
lezna *f* awl
liana *f* liana
liar *< l. pres:* **lío** > **I.** *vt* **1.** (*fardo*) to tie up; (*paquete*) to wrap up; **~ el petate** *inf* to pack up and go **2.** (*cigarrillo*) to roll **3.** *inf* (*engañar*) to take in; (*enredar*) to mix up; **¡ahora sí que la hemos liado!** we've really done it now! **II.** *vr:* **~se 1.** *inf* (*juntarse*) to become lovers **2.** (*embarullarse*) to get complicated; **~se la manta a la cabeza** *inf* to throw caution to the winds [*o* take the plunge] **3.** (*ponerse a*) **~se a golpes con alguien** to start fighting with sb
libanés, -esa *adj, m, f* Lebanese
Líbano *m* **El ~** Lebanon
libar *vi* (*abeja*) to suck
libelo *m* libel
libélula *f* dragonfly
liberación *f* liberation, release
liberal I. *adj t.* POL liberal; (*generoso*) generous **II.** *mf* Liberal
liberalidad *f* (*generosidad*) generosity
liberalización *f* liberalization
liberalizar <z→c> *vt* to liberalize
liberar *vt* to liberate, to set free; (*eximir*) to exempt
liberiano, -a *adj, m, f* Liberian
líbero *m* DEP sweeper
libérrimo, -a *adj superl de* **libre**
libertad *f* **1.** (*libre arbitrio*) liberty; **~ de culto** freedom of worship; **~ de expresión** freedom of speech; **~ de prensa** freedom of the press; **en ~ bajo fianza** on bail; **en ~ condicional** on parole; **poner en ~** to set free; **tomarse demasiadas ~es** to take too many liberties **2.** (*naturalidad*) familiarity
libertar *vt* to liberate
libertario, -a *adj, m, f* libertarian
libertinaje *m* libertinage
libertino, -a *adj* dissolute **II.** *m, f* libertine
Libia *f* Libya
libidinoso, -a *adj* lustful
libido *f sin pl* libido
libio, -a *adj, m, f* Libyan

libra *f* pound; **~ esterlina** pound sterling; **una ~ de judías** a pound of beans
Libra *f* Libra
librado, -a *adj* **salir bien ~ de algo** to come out of sth unscathed, to be successful in sth; **salir mal ~** to come out the worse for wear, to fail
libramiento *m*, **libranza** *f* order of payment; (*de un cheque*) payment
librar I. *vt* **1.** **~ de algo/alguien** (*dejar libre*) to free from sth/sb; (*salvar*) to save from sth/sb; **¡líbreme Dios!** God [*o* Heaven] forbid!; **y líbranos del mal** and deliver us from evil **2.** COM to draw; **~ una letra a cargo de alguien** to draw a draft on sb **II.** *vi inf* (*tener libre*) **hoy libro** I have today off **III.** *vr* **~ de algo/alguien** (*deshacerse*) to get rid of sth/sb; (*salvarse*) to escape from sth/sb; **~se de una buena** to have a narrow escape
libre <libérrimo> *adj* **1.** (*en general*) free; (*independiente*) independent; **zona de ~ cambio** free trade area; **~ de franqueo** no postage necessary; **dar vía ~** to give the green light; **estar ~ de preocupaciones** to be free from worries; **la imaginación es ~** imagination is free to wander; **eres bien ~ de hacerlo** you are quite free to do so **2.** (*soltero*) single **3.** (*descarado*) forward
librea *f* (*traje*) livery
librecambio *m sin pl* free trade
librería *f* **1.** (*tienda*) bookshop; **~ de depósito** book warehouse; **~ de ocasión** secondhand bookshop **2.** (*papelería*) stationer's **3.** (*estantería*) bookcase
librero, -a *m, f* bookseller
libreta *f* **1.** (*cuaderno*) notebook; (*para notas*) notepad **2.** (*de ahorros*) bank book
libro *m* (*escrito*) book; (*volumen*) volume; **~ de bolsillo** paperback; **~ blanco** white paper; **~ científico** science book; **~ de cocina** cookery book *Brit*, cookbook *Am;* **~ de consulta** reference book; **~s de contabilidad** account book; **~ de escolaridad** school record; **~ de familia** *official booklet in which details of one's marriage and children's birth-dates, etc. are registered;* **~ ilustrado** picture book; **~ de reclamaciones** complaints book; **los Libros Sagrados** the Holy Scriptures; **~ de texto** textbook ▶**hablar como un ~ abierto** to express oneself clearly; **hablar como un ~ cerrado** not to express oneself clearly; **colgar los ~s** to abandon one's studies
licencia *f* **1.** (*permiso*) licence *Brit,* license *Am;* (*para un libro*) authorization; **~ de conducir** *Méx, Cuba* driving licence *Brit,* driver's licence *Am;* **~ de obras** building permit; **~ de pesca/de armas** fishing/gun licence **2.** (*soldado*) **estar tres días de ~** to be on leave for three days **3.** (*libertad*) liberty
licenciado, -a *m, f* **1.** (*estudiante*) graduate; **~ en economía** Economics graduate **2.** (*soldado*) discharged soldier
licenciar I. *vt* (*despedir*) to dismiss; (*soldado*)

to discharge **II.** *vr:* **~se** to graduate; **se licenció en psicología** he got a degree in psychology

licenciatura *f* **1.**(*título*) degree **2.**(*carrera*) university studies *pl*

licencioso, -a *adj* (*persona*) licentious; (*conducta*) dissolute

liceo *m* **1.**(*sociedad*) literary society **2.** *AmL* (*colegio*) secondary school

licitación *f* **1.**(*concurso*) tender; **sacaron el proyecto a ~** the project was put out to tender **2.**(*subasta*) bidding

licitador(a) *m(f)* bidder

licitar *vt* to bid

lícito, -a *adj* **1.**(*permitido*) allowed **2.**(*justo*) fair **3.**(*legal*) lawful

licitud *f sin pl* legality

licor *m* liquor; (*de frutas*) liqueur

licra® *f* Lycra®

licuadora *f* (*batidora*) blender; (*para fruta*) liquidizer

licuar <*l. pres:* licúo> *vt* **1.** fís to liquate **2.**(*fruta*) to liquefy **3.** min to eliquate

líder *m/f* leader; **la empresa ~** the leading company

liderar *vt* **1.**(*ser el primero*) to lead; **el equipo que lidera la clasificación** the team at the top of the table **2.**(*dirigir*) to head

liderato *m*, **liderazgo** *m sin pl* leadership; **capacidad de ~** leadership capability

lidia *f* fight; taur bullfight

lidiar *vt, vi* to fight; **~ con los niños** *fig* to contend with the kids

liebre *f* hare; **~ marina** sea hare ▶**levantar la ~** to let the cat out of the bag; **donde menos se piensa salta la ~** things always happen when you least expect them to

lienzo *m* **1.**(*tela*) cloth; (*para cuadros*) canvas **2.**(*óleo*) painting

liga *f* **1.**(*alianza*) league **2.**(*prenda*) suspender, garter **3.** dep league

ligadura *f* **1.**(*lazo*) bond **2.** *fig* (*traba*) tie **3.** mús ligature

ligamento *m* anat ligament

ligar <g→gu> **I.** *vi inf* (*tontear*) to flirt; **~ con alguien** (*conocer*) to get off with sb, to pick sb up **II.** *vt* **1.**(*atar*) to tie **2.**(*metal*) to alloy **3.**(*unir*) to join **4.** mús (*notas*) to slur **III.** *vr:* **~se 1.**(*unirse*) to join **2.** *inf* (*tontear*) to flirt

ligazón *f* (*unión*) link

ligerear *vi Chile* (*apresurarse*) to walk quickly

ligereza *f* **1.**(*rapidez*) swiftness **2.**(*levedad*) lightness **3.**(*error*) thoughtless act; (*indiscreción*) indiscretion

ligero, -a *adj* **1.**(*leve, ingrávido*) light; (*ruido*) soft; **ir muy ~ de ropa** to be lightly clad **2.**(*ágil*) nimble ▶**hacer algo a la ligera** to do sth without thinking; **tomarse algo a la ligera** to not take sth seriously

lignito *m* min lignite

ligón *m* womanizer; **ser un ~** to be a Don Juan

ligona *f* flirt

ligue *m inf* **1.**(*acción*) pick-up; **dicen que tiene un ~ con el director** they say she's having an affair with the director **2.**(*persona*) chat-up, pick-up

liguero *m* suspender belt, garter belt *Am*

liguero, -a *adj* dep league; **competición liguera** league competition

lija *f* **1.**(*papel*) sandpaper; **~ esmeril** emery paper; (*piel*) shagreen **2.** zool dogfish

lijadora *f* sander

lijar *vt* to sand

lijoso, -a *adj Cuba* stuck-up

lila¹ I. *adj* lilac coloured *Brit*, lilac colored *Am* **II.** *f* bot lilac

lila² *m* (*color*) lilac

lile *adj Chile* weak

liliputiense *adj*, *m/f* Lilliputian

lima *f* **1.**(*instrumento*) file; **rebajar con la ~** to file down **2.** bot (*fruta*) lime; (*árbol*) lime tree ▶**comer como una ~** *inf* to eat like a horse

limadura *f* **1.**(*pulido*) polishing **2.** *pl* (*partículas*) filings

limar *vt* **1.**(*pulir*) to file; *fig* to perfect **2.**(*consumir*) to wear down

limaza *f* slug

limbo *m* **1.** rel limbo; **estar en el ~** (*distraído*) to be distracted; (*atontado*) to be bewildered; (*no enterarse*) to be oblivious **2.**(*de vestido*) hem

limeño, -a I. *adj* of/from Lima **II.** *m, f* native/inhabitant of Lima

limitación *f* limitation; (*de una norma*) restriction; **sin limitaciones** unlimited; **el plan tiene sus limitaciones pero ha sido eficaz** despite its shortcomings, the plan has been effective

limitado, -a *adj* **1.**(*poco*) scant; (*medios*) limited; **un número ~** a limited number **2.**(*tonto*) slow-witted

limitar I. *vi* **~ con algo** to border on sth **II.** *vt* to limit; (*libertad*) to restrict; (*definir*) to fix the boundaries of **III.** *vr:* **~se** to confine oneself

límite *m* limit; **~ de crédito** credit limit; **situación ~** extreme situation; **sin ~s** limitless; **la fecha ~ para entregarlo es el...** the deadline for turning it in is ...

limítrofe *adj* bordering; **países ~s** neighbouring *Brit* [*o* neighboring *Am*] countries

limo *m* mud

limón *adj, m* lemon

limonada *f* lemonade; **~ de vino** sangria (*type of sangria made of wine and lemonade*)

limonar *m* **1.** agr lemon grove **2.** *Guat* (*limonero*) lemon tree

limonero *m* lemon tree

limosna *f* alms *pl;* **pedir ~** to beg

limosnear *vi* to beg

limosnero, -a I. *adj* charitable **II.** *m, f AmL* (*pedigüeño*) beggar

limoso, -a *adj* muddy

limpiabarros *m inv* footscraper

limpiabotas *m/f inv* bootblack

limpiachimeneas *mf inv* chimney sweep
limpiacristales[1] *mf inv* (*persona, producto*) window cleaner
limpiacristales[2] *m inv* (*producto*) window cleaning fluid
limpiador *m* cleaner
limpiador, -a I. *adj* cleaning; **leche ~a** cleansing milk II. *m, f* cleaner
limpiamuebles *m inv* furniture polish
limpiaparabrisas *m inv* windsreen wiper, windshield wiper *Am*
limpiar I. *vt* 1.(*suciedad*) to clean; (*dientes*) to brush; (*chimenea*) to sweep; **~ el polvo** to dust; **~ en seco** to dry-clean 2.(*librar*) to clear; **~ de culpas** to exonerate 3. *inf* (*robar*) to nick II. *vi* (*quitar la suciedad*) to clean III. *vr:* **~se** to clean; (*nariz*) to wipe; (*dientes*) to brush
límpido, -a *adj elev* (*limpio*) limpid
limpieza *f* 1.(*lavar*) washing; (*casa, zapatos*) cleaning; **~ de cutis** facial; **~ a fondo** thorough cleaning; **hacer la ~** to do the cleaning; **señora de la ~** cleaning lady 2.(*estado*) cleanness, cleanliness 3.(*eliminación*) cleansing; POL purge 4.(*habilidad*) skill, precision
limpio *adv* (*sin trampas*) fairly; **jugar ~** to play fair ▶**escribir en ~** to make a clean copy; **¿qué has sacado en ~ de todo este asunto?** what do you make of all this?; **en ~** (*dinero*) net
limpio, -a *adj* 1.(*cocina, persona, agua*) clean; (*aire*) pure; (*almendra*) shelled 2.*fig* honorable ▶**lo dejaron ~** *inf* (*sin dinero*) they cleaned him out; **no sacar nada en ~ de algo** to make neither head nor tail of sth
limpión *m* 1.(*lavado*) wash; **dar un ~ a alguien** to give sth a wipe 2.*AmL* (*trapo*) dishcloth
limusina *f* AUTO limousine
linaje *m* lineage; **de rancio ~** of ancient descent
linaza *f* flax seed; **aceite de ~** linseed oil
lince *m* lynx; **tener ojos de ~** to be sharp-eyed; **ser un ~** *fig* to be very sharp
linchamiento *m* lynching
linchar *vt* to lynch
lindar *vi* **~ con algo** to border on sth
linde *m o f*, **lindero** *m* boundary; (*camino*) edge
lindeza *f* 1.(*bonito*) prettiness 2.(*gracioso*) witty remark 3. *pl, irón* (*insulto*) insult; **me llamó "idiota" y otras ~s parecidas** he called me an "idiot" and other such compliments
lindo, -a *adj* pretty; (*niño*) lovely, cute; **divertirse a lo ~** to have a great time
línea *f* 1. *t.* MAT, MIL, ECON (*raya*) line; **~ de intersección** intersecting line; **~ de meta** DEP (*fútbol*) goal line; (*atletismo*) finishing line; **~ recta** straight line; **fracasar en toda la ~** to fail completely 2.(*renglón*) line; **~ en blanco** blank line; **leer entre ~s** to read between the lines; **te pongo cuatro ~s para...** I'm writing

you just a few lines to ... 3.(*de transporte*) line; (*trayecto*) route; **~ aérea** airline; **~ férrea** railway [*o* railroad *Am*] line; **coche de ~** coach *Brit,* long-distance bus *Am* 4. TEL telephone line; **~ para el fax** fax line; **~ roja** hotline; **no hay ~** the line is dead [*o* down] 5.(*pariente*) line; **por ~ materna** on his mother's side 6.(*tipo*) figure; **guardar la ~** to watch one's figure 7.(*directriz*) policy 8.(*fábrica*) **~ de montaje** assembly line
lineal *adj t.* MAT, ARTE linear
linfa *f* BIO lymph
linfático, -a *adj* lymphatic; **gánglio ~** lymph node
lingotazo *m inf* swig; **pegarse un ~** to take a swig
lingote *m* ingot; (*de acero*) pig
lingüista *mf* linguist
lingüística *f* linguistics
lingüístico, -a *adj* linguistic
linier *m* <liniers> DEP linesman
linimento *m* liniment
lino *m* 1. BOT flax 2.(*tela*) linen
linóleo *m* linoleum
linterna *f* 1.(*de mano*) torch, flashlight 2.(*farol*) lantern; **~ mágica** magic lantern 3.(*faro*) lighthouse
lío *m* 1.(*embrollo*) mess; **¡déjame de ~s!** don't come to me with your problems!; **me hago un ~ con tus explicaciones** I'm getting all confused by your explanation; **¡me meto en cada ~!** I always get myself in such scrapes!; **no entiendo ese ~** I can't make anything of that mess 2.(*de ropa*) bundle 3. *inf* (*relación*) affair; **sé que tienes un ~ por ahí** I know you're having an affair
liofilizar <z→c> *vt* to freeze-dry, to lyophilize
lioso, -a *adj* (*difícil*) complicated; **persona liosa** troublemaker
lipidia *f* 1. *AmC* (*pobreza*) poverty; (*miseria*) misery 2. *Cuba, Méx* (*impertinencia*) impertinence
lipidiar *vt Cuba, Méx, PRico* to annoy
lipotimia *f* blackout
liquelique *m Col, Ven* white linen jacket
liquen *m* lichen
liquidación *f* 1.(*de una mercancía*) sale; **~ por fin de temporada** (*invierno*) end of season sale; (*verano*) summer sale; **~ total** clearance sale 2.(*de una empresa*) liquidation 3.(*de una factura*) payment; (*cuenta*) settlement
liquidar *vt* 1.(*licuar*) to liquefy 2. *inf* (*acabar*) to liquidate; (*matar*) to kill; **lo ~on** *inf* they bumped him off 3.(*mercancía*) to sell; **~ las existencias** to sell off all merchandise 4.(*cerrar*) to close 5.(*factura*) to settle
liquidez *f* 1.(*agua*) fluidity 2. COM liquidity
líquido *m* 1.(*agua*) liquid; **~ amniótico** amniotic fluid; **~ de frenos** brake fluid 2.(*saldo*) cash; **~ imponible** taxable income
líquido, -a *adj* 1.(*material, consonante*)

liquid **2.** (*dinero*) cash; **renta líquida** disposable income

lira *f* **1.** (*moneda*) lira **2.** (*instrumento*) lyre

lírica *f* poetry

lírico, -a **I.** *adj* **1.** LIT lyric(al) **2.** MÚS lyrical **II.** *m, f* utopian; *AmL* lyric poet

lirio *m* lily; ~ **de los valles** lily of the valley

lirismo *m sin pl* **1.** LIT lyricism **2.** (*sentimentalismo*) emotionalism

lirón *m* dormouse; **dormir como un** ~ to sleep like a log

Lisboa *f* Lisbon

lisboeta **I.** *adj* of/from Lisbon **II.** *mf* native/inhabitant of Lisbon

lisiado, -a **I.** *adj* crippled **II.** *m, f* cripple

lisiar **I.** *vt* (*lesionar*) to injure; (*mutilar*) to maim **II.** *vr:* ~**se** to become disabled

liso, -a *adj* **1.** (*superficie*) smooth; (*pelo*) straight; **los 100 metros** ~**s** the 100 metre flat race **2.** (*tela, vestido*) plain

lisonja *f* flattery

lisonjear *vt* to flatter

lisonjero, -a **I.** *adj* flattering **II.** *m, f* flatterer

lista *f* **1.** (*enumeración*) list; ~ **de la compra** shopping list; ~ **del censo electoral** electoral roll; ~ **única** slate (*list of party candidates on a single ticket*)*;* **estar en la** ~ **de espera** to be on the waiting list; **pasar** ~ (*leer*) to take roll call; (*controlar siempre*) to check on **2.** (*tira, de madera*) strip; (*estampado*) stripe; **a** ~**s** striped

listado *m* list

listado, -a *adj* striped

listar *vt* to list

listillo, -a *m, f* smart aleck, clever cloggs

listín *m* (*de teléfonos*) directory

listo, -a *adj* **1.** *ser* (*inteligente*) clever; (*sagaz*) shrewd; (*hábil*) skilful; **pasarse de** ~ to be too clever by half **2.** *estar* (*preparado*) ready; ~ **para enviar** *t.* INFOR ready to send; ~ **para el envío/para el tiraje** ready to ship/print; ~ **para despegar** ready for takeoff; **estás** ~ **si crees que...** *inf* you've got another think coming if you think that …

listón *m* (*madero*) lath; **poner el** ~ **muy alto** *fig* to set very high standards

lisura *f* **1.** (*llano*) evenness **2.** *AmL* (*frescura*) impudent remark **3.** *fig* (*ingenuidad*) naivety; (*franqueza*) frankness

litera *f* (*cama*) bunk; FERRO couchette; NÁUT berth

literal *adj* literal

literario, -a *adj* literary; **lenguaje** ~ literary language

literato, -a *m, f* man *m* of letters, woman *f* of letters

literatura *f* literature; ~ **barata** pulp fiction; ¡**eso es sólo hacer** ~! that's only words, but no action!

litigante *adj, mf* litigant

litigar <g→gu> *vt* **1.** *t.* JUR (*disputar*) to dispute **2.** (*llevar a juicio*) to be in dispute

litigio *m* **1.** (*disputa*) dispute; **en caso de** ~ in the case of dispute; **en** ~ in dispute **2.** (*juicio*) lawsuit

litografía *f* **1.** ARTE (*proceso*) lithography **2.** (*grabado*) lithograph

litoral **I.** *adj* coastal **II.** *m* (*costa*) coast; (*playa*) shore

litri *adj* *inf* pretentious, hoity-toity

litro *m* litre *Brit,* liter *Am;* **un** ~ **de leche** a litre *Brit* [o liter *Am*] of milk

litrona *f* *inf* litre bottle of beer *Brit,* liter bottle of beer *Am*

Lituania *f* Lithuania

lituano, -a *adj, m, f* Lithuanian

liturgia *f* liturgy

liviandad *f* (*frivolidad*) triviality

liviano, -a *adj* **1.** (*trivial*) light **2.** (*ligero*) light; (*error*) trivial

lividez *f* lividness

lívido, -a *adj* **1.** (*amoratado*) livid; ~ **de frío** livid with cold **2.** (*pálido*) ashen

llaga *f* **1.** (*herida*) wound; (*úlcera*) ulcer; (*ampolla*) sore **2.** (*pena*) sorrow

llagar <g→gu> **I.** *vt* (*herir*) to wound; (*rozar*) to cause a sore **II.** *vr:* ~**se** **1.** (*ulcerarse*) to get a sore **2.** (*herirse*) to get hurt; ~**se** (**los pies**) to get sores (on your feet)

llama *f* **1.** (*fuego*) flame; *fig* burning passion **2.** ZOOL llama

llamada *f* **1.** (*voz*) call; ~ **al orden** call to order; ~ **del programa** INFOR program call **2.** (*de teléfono*) phonecall; ~ **urbana** local call; ~ **a cobro revertido** reverse charge call **3.** (*gesto*) gesture **4.** (*a la puerta golpeando*) knock; (*con el timbre*) ring **5.** (*en un libro*) reference mark **6.** MIL call-up, conscription *Brit,* draft *Am*

llamado, -a *adj* (*conocido como*) called; (*supuesto*) so-called

llamado *m AmS v.* **llamamiento**

llamador *m* **1.** (*picaporte*) doorknocker **2.** (*timbre*) doorbell

llamamiento *m* **1.** (*exhortación*) appeal; (*soldado*) call-up; **hacer un** ~ **a todos** to issue an appeal to all **2.** MIL ~ **a filas** call to arms **3.** JUR (*citación*) summons, subpoena

llamar **I.** *vt* **1.** (*voz*) to call; (*por teléfono*) to telephone, to ring up *Brit;* ~ **a declarar a alguien** to call on sb to testify; ~ **a filas** MIL to call up *Brit,* to draft *Am;* **te llaman al teléfono** you're wanted on the phone; ~ **a capítulo a alguien** to tell sb off; ~ **al perro con un silbido** to whistle to the dog **2.** (*denominar*) to call; **lo llamé idiota a la cara** I called him an idiot to his face **3.** (*despertar*) to wake up; ~ **la atención** (*reprender*) to reprimand; (*ser llamativo*) to attract attention; ~ **la atención sobre algo** to draw attention to sth **II.** *vi* **1.** (*a la puerta golpeando*) to knock; (*con el timbre*) to ring; ¿**quién llama?** who is it? **2.** *inf* (*gustar*) to appeal; **el chocolate no me llama nada** chocolate just doesn't appeal to me **III.** *vr:* ~**se** to be called; ¿**cómo te llamas?** what's your name?; ¡**como me llamo David,**

que lo harás! *inf* you will do it, as sure as my name is David!

llamarada *f* 1. (*llama*) blaze 2. (*rubor*) sudden flush

llamarón *m Chile, Col, Ecua* sudden blaze

llamativo, -a *adj* (*traje*) flashy; (*color*) loud

llamear *vi* to blaze

llana *f* (*herramienta*) trowel

llanca *f Chile* MIN bluish-green copper ore

llaneza *f sin pl* simplicity

llanito, -a *m, f inf* Gibraltarian

llano *m* plain

llano, -a *adj* 1. (*liso*) flat; (*terreno*) level 2. (*campechano*) straightforward 3. LING paroxytone 4. (*sencillo*) **el pueblo** ~ the common people

llanta *f* 1. *AmL* (*rueda*) tyre *Brit,* tire *Am* 2. (*cerco*) (metal) rim; ~ **de aleación** alloy wheel

llantería *f sin pl, AmL* weeping and wailing

llantina *f inf* uninterrupted weeping

llanto *m* crying

llanura *f* plain

llapa *f AmS* extra

llave *f* 1. *t. fig* (*instrumento*) key; ~ **de contacto** AUTO ignition key; ~ **maestra** master key; **ama de** ~**s** housekeeper; ~ **en mano** (*coche*) on the road; ~**s en mano** (*casa*) available for immediate occupancy; **echar la** ~ to lock; **estar bajo** ~ to be under lock and key; **la** ~ **no entra** the key doesn't fit; **la** ~ **para descubrir el secreto** the key to the secret; **meter/sacar la** ~ to put in/pull out the key 2. MÚS (*trompeta*) valve; (*órgano*) stop; (*instrumentos de viento*) key 3. (*grifo*) tap *Brit,* faucet *Am* 4. (*tuerca*) spanner; ~ **inglesa** adjustable spanner, monkey wrench 5. (*interruptor*) switch 6. TIPO bracket 7. DEP hold, armlock

llavero *m* (*utensilio*) key ring

llegada *f* 1. (*al destino*) arrival 2. (*meta*) finishing line

llegar <g→gu> I. *vi* 1. (*al destino, el correo*) to arrive; (*avión*) to land; (*barco*) to dock; ~ **a la meta** DEP to reach the finishing line; **estar al** ~ to be about to arrive; ~ **a Madrid/al hotel** to arrive in Madrid/at the hotel; ~ **tarde** to be late; **¡todo llegará!** all in good time!; **¡hasta ahí podíamos** ~**!** that's the limit! 2. (*recibir*) **no me ha llegado el dinero** I haven't received the money 3. (*durar*) to live; ~ **a viejo** to live to old age; ~ **a los ochenta** to reach the age of eighty; **el enfermo no** ~**á a la primavera** the patient won't make it to spring; **este gobierno no** ~**á a 2 años** this government won't last two years 4. (*ascender*) to amount to; **la cinta no llega a tres metros** the ribbon is less than 3 m long; **no llega a 20 euros** it's less than 20 euros 5. (*lograr*) **ese** ~**á lejos** that fellow will go far; ~ **a ser muy rico** to become very rich; **llegamos a recoger 8.000 firmas** we managed to get 8,000 signatures; ~ **a ministro** to succeeding in becoming a minister; **nunca** ~**é a entenderte** I'll never

understand you 6. (*ser suficiente*) to be enough 7. (*tocar*) ~ **a** [*o* hasta] **algo** to reach sth; **el niño no llega a los productos de limpieza** the child can't get at the cleaning products; **no me llegas ni a la suela de los zapatos** you can't hold a candle to me II. *vr:* ~**se** (*ir*) to go; ~**se por casa de alguien** to stop by [*o* to go round *Brit*] sb's house

llenador(a) *adj Chile* filling; **esta fruta es muy** ~**a** this fruit is very filling

llenar I. *vt* 1. (*atestar*) to fill; ~ **de algo** to fill with sth; **es necesario** ~ **esa laguna** *fig* this gap must be filled; **los niños** ~**on el suelo de papeles** the children littered the floor with papers; ~**se los bolsillos de caramelos** to fill one's pockets with sweets *Brit* [*o* candy *Am*] 2. (*cumplimentar*) to fill in [*o* out] 3. (*colmar*) ~ **de algo** to overwhelm with sth; **nos llenó de regalos** we were showered with gifts 4. (*satisfacer*) to satisfy 5. (*agradecer*) to be grateful for II. *vi* (*comida*) to be filling; **la pasta llena mucho** pasta is very filling III. *vr:* ~**se de algo** *inf* 1. (*comida*) to stuff oneself with sth 2. (*irritarse*) to be fed up with sth

lleno *m* (*teatro, auditorio*) full house

lleno, -a *adj* (*recipiente*) full; **luna llena** full moon; ~ **de** full of, filled with; **a la planta le da el sol de** ~ the plant is directly in the sun; **el autobús iba** ~ the bus was full; **estoy** ~ *inf* I'm full; **el escritorio estaba** ~ **de papeles** the desk was covered with papers

llevadero, -a *adj* bearable

llevar I. *vt* 1. (*a un destino, acompañar*) to take; (*transportar*) to transport; (*en brazos*) to carry; (*viento*) to blow; (*comida*) to take out; ~ **a alguien en el coche** to give sb a lift; ~ **algo a alguien** to take sth to sb; **dos pizzas para** ~, **por favor** two pizzas to take away, please 2. (*exigir, cobrar*) to charge; (*costar*) to cost; **me llevó un dineral reparar el tejado** it cost me a fortune to fix the roof; **este trabajo lleva mucho tiempo** this work takes a lot of time 3. (*tener*) ~ **consigo** to be carrying, to have 4. (*conducir*) to lead; ~ **de la mano** to lead by the hand; ~ **consigo** [*o* **aparejado**] to include; **esto no lleva a ninguna parte** this isn't getting us anywhere 5. (*ropa*) to wear 6. (*coche*) to drive 7. (*finca*) to run 8. (*estar*) to have been; ~ **estudiando tres años** to have been studying for three years; **llevo cuatro días aquí** I've been here for four days 9. (*gestionar*) to manage; ~ **las cuentas** to manage the accounts; **el abogado que lleva el caso** the lawyer handling the case 10. (*inducir*) ~ **a algo** to lead to sth, to induce sth; **me llevó a pensar que...** it led me to think that ... 11. (*exceder*) to exceed; **te llevo dos años** I'm two years older than you; **me llevas dos centímetros** you are two cm taller than me 12. (*tener como ingrediente*) **esta receta lleva 12 huevos** this recipe calls for 12 eggs; **¿lleva picante?** does it have hot pepper? ▶ **dejarse** ~ **por algo** to be carried away with sth;

dejarse ~ **por alguien** to let sb influence you; ~ **las de perder** to look like losing; **¿qué tal lo llevas?** how are you holding up? **II.** *vr:* ~**se 1.** (*coger*) to take; **la riada se llevó (por delante) el puente** the flood washed away the bridge; ~**se dos años** to be two years older **2.** (*ganar*) to win; ~**se la mayor/peor parte** to get the best/worst of it **3.** (*estar de moda*) to be in fashion; **ya no se llevan los zapatos de plataforma** platform shoes are no longer in fashion **4.** (*soportarse*) to get along; **mi jefe y yo nos llevamos bien** my boss and I get along well; ~**se a matar** to hate each other ▶...**y me llevo cuatro** MAT ... and carry four

lliclla *f Bol, Ecua, Perú* blanket (*carried on the back by Indian women*)

llicta *f Bol* GASTR potato meal cake (*type of hard cake eaten while chewing coca to give flavour to the coca ball*)

llorar I. *vi* **1.** (*lágrimas*) to cry, to weep; **desahogarse llorando** to relieve one's feelings by crying; **la película te hacía** ~ the film made you cry; **me lloran los ojos** my eyes are watering; ~ **de alegría** to cry for joy; **de** ~ enough to make one cry; **lloramos de risa** we laughed till we cried **2.** (*vid, árbol*) to bleed ▶**quien no llora no mama** *inf* if you don't ask, you don't get **II.** *vt* **1.** (*lágrimas*) ~ **por algo/alguien** to cry over sth/sb; *fig* ~ **la muerte de alguien** to mourn sb's death **2.** (*quejarse*) to whine **3.** (*lamentar*) to bemoan

llorera *f inf* fit of crying, blubbering

llorica *mf inf* crybaby, whiner

lloriquear *vi* to whimper, to snivel

lloriqueo *m* whimpering

lloro(s) *m(pl)* crying; **con estos** ~**s no conseguirás nada** this crying won't get you anywhere

llorón, -ona I. *adj* always crying; **sauce** ~ weeping willow **II.** *m, f* crybaby, whiner

lloroso, -a *adj* tearful

llovedizo, -a *adj* (*techo*) leaky; **agua llovediza** rainwater

llover <o→ue> *vi, vt, vimpers* to rain; **está lloviendo** it's raining; **llueve a mares** [*o a cántaros*] it's pouring; **siempre llueve sobre mojado** it never rains but it pours; **como llovido del cielo** heaven sent; **llueven las malas noticias** it's one piece of bad news after another; **me escucha como quien oye** ~ *inf* it's water off a duck's back to him/her, in one ear and out the other; **ya ha llovido mucho desde entonces** *fig* a lot has happened since then

llovida *f AmL* rain; **¡qué** ~**!** what a downpour!

llovizna *f* drizzle

lloviznar *vimpers* **está lloviznando** it's drizzling

lluqui *adj Ecua* (*zurdo*) left-handed

lluvia *f* **1.** (*chubasco*) rain; ~ **de estrellas** meteor shower; **época de las** ~**s** rainy season; ~ **ácida** acid rain; ~ **radiactiva** fallout

2. (*cantidad*) shower; **hubo una** ~ **de protestas** there was a shower of protests **3.** *AmL* (*ducha*) shower

lluvioso, -a *adj* rainy; **tiempo** ~ rainy weather

lo I. *art def v.* **el, la, lo II.** *pron pers m y neutro sing* **1.** (*objeto: masculino*) him; (*neutro*) it; **¡llámo~!** call him!; **¡haz~!** do it! **2.** (*con relativo*) ~ **que...** what; ~ **cual** which; ~ **que quiero decir es que...** what I mean is that ...

loa *f* (*alabanza*) praise

loable *adj* commendable

loar *vt* to praise

lobato *m* **1.** (*lobo*) wolf cub **2.** (*cachorro*) cub

lobezno *m* wolf cub

lobisón *m Arg, Par, Urug* werewolf

lobo, -a *m, f* wolf; ~ **cerval** lynx; ~ **de mar** old salt; ~ **marino** seal; **en esa ocasión le vimos las orejas al** ~ that time we saw his/her true colours *Brit* [*o colors Am*]; **meterse en la boca del** ~ to go into the lion's den; **ser un** ~ **con piel de oveja** to be a wolf in sheep's clothing; **tener un hambre de** ~**s** to be as hungry as a wolf

lóbrego, -a *adj* gloomy

lóbulo *m* ANAT lobe; ~ **de la oreja** earlobe

local I. *adj* local; **periódico** ~ local newspaper **II.** *m* locale; COM premises *pl;* ~ **público** public building

localidad *f* **1.** (*municipio*) town **2.** (*entrada*) ticket; (*asiento*) seat

localismo *m* regionalism; *pey* (*chovinismo*) provincialism, parochialism

localista *adj pey* parochial, of local interest; **escritor** ~ parochial writer

localización *f* **1.** (*búsqueda*) finding; AVIAT tracking **2.** (*posición*) location

localizar <z→c> *vt* **1.** (*encontrar*) to find; ~ **por teléfono** to get in touch by phone **2.** (*limitar*) to localize; AVIAT to track; (*fuego, epidemia*) to confine

locería *f AmL* crockery

loche *m Col* ZOOL loach

loción *f* **1.** (*líquido*) lotion; ~ **capilar** hair lotion; ~ **tónica** after-shave **2.** (*crema*) lotion; ~ **bronceadora** suntan lotion; ~ **hidratante** moisturizing cream **3.** (*fricción*) massage

loco, -a I. *adj* **1.** (*chalado*) mad, crazy; **a lo** ~, **a tontas y a locas** any old way; **estar** ~ **atar** to be raving [*o stark staring*] mad; **estar** ~ **por la música** to be crazy about music; **estar** ~ **con la bicicleta** to be wild about one's bike; **estar** ~ **de contento** to be elated; **estar medio** ~ to be not all there **2.** (*maravilloso*) tremendous; **tener una suerte loca** to be incredibly lucky **II.** *m, f* madman; **casa de** ~**s** *t. fig* madhouse; **cada** ~ **con su tema** to each his own!; **hacerse el** ~ to act dumb; **hacer el** ~ to act the fool; **tener una vena de** ~ to have a streak of madness

locomoción *f* locomotion

locomotor, -a *adj* locomotive

locomotora *f* locomotive

locomotriz *adj* locomotive
locro *m AmS: meat and vegetable stew*
locuacidad *f* talkativeness
locuaz *adj* loquacious; (*charlatán*) talkative
locución *f* (*expresión*) phrase; ~ **prepositiva** prepositional phrase
locura *f* 1. (*enajenación mental*) madness; **querer con** ~ to be madly in love with; **una casa de** ~ a dream house 2. (*disparate*) crazy thing; **andar haciendo** ~**s** to be doing foolish things
locutor(a) *m(f)* speaker
locutorio *m* 1. (*claustro*) locutory 2. TEL telephone box *Brit*, telephone booth *Am*
lodazal *m* mudhole
lodo *m* mud
logia *f* 1. ARQUIT loggia 2. (*reunión*) lodge
lógica *f* logic
lógico, -a *adj* logical; (*normal*) natural
logística *f* logistics *pl*
logístico, -a *adj* logistic
logopeda *mf* speech therapist
logopedia *f* speech therapy
logotipo *m* (*distintivo*) logotype; (*de una empresa, un producto*) logo
logrado, -a *adj* successful, well done; **te ha quedado muy** ~ **el cuadro** you've done a wonderful job on that painting
lograr I. *vt* to achieve; (*premio*) to win; **logré convencerla** I managed to convince her II. *vr:* ~**se** to be successful
logrero, -a *m, f* moneylender
logro *m* achievement
logroñés, -esa I. *adj* of/from Logroño II. *m, f* native/inhabitant of Logroño
loma *f* hill
lomada *f AmS* hill
lombriz *f* worm; ~ **intestinal** tapeworm; ~ **de tierra** earthworm
lomo *m* 1. (*espalda*) back; **agachar el** ~ *inf* to work very hard; **sobar el** ~ **a alguien** *inf* to butter sb up; **ser un mentiroso de tomo y** ~ to be an out-and-out liar 2. (*solomillo*) loin 3. (*de libro*) spine 4. (*de cuchillo*) back
lona *f* canvas
loncha *f* slice; (*beicon*) rasher
lonchería *f AmC, Méx* lunch counter
londinense I. *adj* London II. *mf* Londoner
Londres *m* London
longanimidad *f sin pl, elev* forbearance
longánimo, -a *adj elev* forbearing
longaniza *f spicy pork sausage;* **hay mas días que** ~**s** there's all the time in the world
longevidad *f sin pl* longevity
longevo, -a *adj* (*que dura*) long-lived; (*viejo*) very old
longitud *f* length; **salto de** ~ DEP long jump; **cuatro metros de** ~ four metres [*o* meters *Am*] long; **cincuenta grados** ~ **este/oeste** fifty degrees longitude east/west; **estar en la misma** ~ **de onda** *fig* to be on the same wavelength
longitudinal *adj* **corte** ~ longitudinal section

longitudinalmente *adv* longitudinally, lengthwise
longui(s) *mf inv* **hacerse el** ~ *inf* to play dumb
lonja *f* 1. COM public exchange 2. (*loncha*) slice
lonjear *vt* 1. *Arg* (*cortar*) to slice 2. *Arg, inf* (*azotar*) to give a good thrashing to
loor *m elev* praise; **en** ~ **de la Virgen María** in praise of the Virgin Mary
loquear *vi inf* to clown around
loquera *f* 1. (*manicomio*) madhouse 2. *AmL* (*locura*) madness
lora *f Col* (*loro*) parrot
Lorena *f* Lorraine
loro *m* 1. ZOOL parrot; **repetir como un** ~ to repeat parrot fashion; **hablar como un** ~ to talk non-stop 2. *pey, inf* (*mujer*) old hag
los I. *art def v.* **el, la, lo** II. *pron pers m y neutro pl* 1. (*objeto directo*) them; **¡lláma~!** call them! 2. (*con relativo*) ~ **que...** the ones that ...; ~ **cuales** which
losa *f* 1. (*piedra*) slab; (*lápida*) gravestone 2. (*baldosa*) tile
lote *m* 1. (*parte*) share; COM lot 2. (*toqueteo*) **darse** [*o* **pegarse**] **el** ~ to get off with
lotería *f* lottery; ~ **primitiva** weekly lottery; **administración de** ~ office selling lottery tickets; **a Juan le tocó la** ~ John won the lottery; **un décimo de la** ~ a tenth share of a lottery number; **¡con ese hijo te tocó la** ~**!** you really struck gold with that son of yours!; **jugar a la** ~ to play the lottery
loto¹ *m* 1. (*planta*) lotus 2. (*flor*) lotus flower
loto² *f inf* lottery
Lovaina *f* Louvain
loza *f* earthenware; (*vajilla*) crockery; ~ **fina** china
lozanía *f sin pl* 1. (*vegetación*) lushness 2. (*persona: robustez*) vigour *Brit*, vigor *Am*; (*salud*) healthiness
lozano, -a *adj* 1. (*planta*) lush 2. (*persona: robusta*) vigorous; (*saludable*) healthy
lubina *f* sea bass
lubricante *m* lubricant
lubricar <c→qu> *vt* to lubricate
lúbrico, -a *adj* (*obsceno*) lewd
lubrificante *m* lubricant
lubrificar <c→qu> *vt* to lubricate
Lucayas *fpl* **islas** ~ the Bahamas
lucense I. *adj* of/from Lugo II. *mf* native/inhabitant of Lugo
Lucerna *f* Lucerne
lucernario *m* skylight
lucero *m* 1. (*estrella*) bright star 2. (*en la frente de cuadrúpedos*) star
lucha *f* fight; DEP wrestling; ~ **cuerpo a cuerpo** hand-to-hand fighting [*o* combat]; ~ **contra la droga** the fight against drugs
luchador(a) *m(f)* fighter; DEP wrestler
luchar *vi* ~ **por algo** to fight for sth, to struggle for sth
luche *m Chile* 1. (*juego*) hopscotch 2. BOT

GASTR sea lettuce

lucidez *f sin pl* **1.** (*estado*) lucidity; **antes de morir tuvo todavía un momento de** ~ before dying he had one last moment of lucidness **2.** (*clarividencia*) clarity; (*sagacidad*) clear-headedness

lucido, -a *adj* **1.** (*brillante*) outstanding **2.** (*selecto*) select

lúcido, -a *adj* **1.** (*clarividente*) clear-sighted; (*sagaz*) astute **2.** (*sobrio*) clear-headed

luciérnaga *f* firefly

lucio *m* pike

lucir *irr* I. *vi* **1.** (*brillar*) to shine; **esa lámpara luce muy poco** this lamp gives off very little light **2.** (*compensar*) to compensate; (*verse*) to look good; **el vestido no le luce** the dress doesn't look good on her; **es un trabajo pesado y que no luce** it's hard work, though it doesn't look it; **ese collar luce mucho con el vestido rojo** that necklace goes really well with the red dress; **este jersey hecho a mano no luce** this handmade sweater doesn't look much; **me he pasado la mañana recogiendo, pero no me luce** I've spent the whole morning tidying though you'd never know it; **no te luce el dinero que tienes** no one would ever know you are wealthy II. *vt* (*exhibir*) to display; **lucía un bronceado impecable** he/she was showing off her perfect tan III. *vr:* ~**se 1.** (*exhibirse*) to display **2.** (*destacarse*) to stand out; **¡ahora sí que nos hemos lucido!** *irón* now we've really made a mess of it!

lucrarse *vr* to profit

lucrativo, -a *adj* lucrative; **no** ~ not profitable; **sin fines** ~**s** non-profit making

lucro *m* profit; **con ánimo de** ~ for profit; **organización sin ánimo de** ~ non-profit organisation

luctuoso, -a *adj* sorrowful

lúdico, -a *adj* ludic; **el aspecto** ~ **de la vida** the fun side of life

luego I. *adv* **1.** (*después*) later; **¡hasta** ~! see you later! **2.** (*entonces*) then **3.** (*por supuesto*) **desde** ~ of course II. *conj* **1.** (*así que*) and so **2.** (*después de*) ~ **que** as soon as

lugar *m* **1.** (*sitio, localidad, situación*) place; **el** ~ **de autos** the scene of the incident; **en primer/segundo** ~ first/second; **tener** ~ to take place; **en algún** ~ **de la casa** somewhere in the house; **hacerse una composición de** ~ to consider the pros and cons; **la observación está fuera de** ~ that comment is out of place; **en** ~ **de** instead of; **yo en** ~ **de usted...** if I were you ... **2.** (*motivo*) **no des** ~ **a que te reprendan** don't give them any cause for reproach; **dar** ~ **a un escándalo** to give rise to a scandal

lugareño, -a *adj, m, f* local

lugarteniente *m* deputy

lúgubre *adj* (*sombrío*) gloomy

lugués, -esa I. *adj* of/from Lugo II. *m, f* native/inhabitant of Lugo

lujo *m* luxury; **permitirse el** ~ **de... to treat oneself to the luxury of ...; un** ~ **asiático** the ultimate in luxury; **con gran** ~ **de detalles** with a wealth of detail; **darse el** ~ **de** to give oneself the pleasure of

lujoso, -a *adj* luxurious

lujuria *f* lechery, lust

lujurioso, -a I. *adj* lecherous II. *m, f* lecher

lulo *m Chile* (*bulto cilíndrico*) small cylindrical bundle

lumbago *m* MED lumbago

lumbar *adj* lumbar

lumbre *f sin pl* (*llamas*) fire; (*brasa*) glow; **¿me das** ~? can you give me a light?; **sentados al amor de la** ~ sitting by the fireside; **poner a la** ~ to put on the stove

lumbrera *f* **1.** (*claraboya*) skylight **2.** (*talento*) leading light

luminarias *fpl* (*para fiestas*) decorative lights

luminosidad *f* luminosity; (*astro, día*) brightness

luminoso, -a *adj* **1.** (*brillante*) bright, luminous; (*día*) light; **anuncio** ~ illuminated [*o* neon] sign; **potencia luminosa** illuminating power **2.** (*excelente*) brilliant

luna *f* **1.** ASTR moon; (*luz*) moonlight; ~ **creciente/menguante** waxing/waning moon; ~ **llena/nueva** full/new moon; ~ **de miel** honeymoon; **media** ~ half moon; **a la luz de la** ~ in the moonlight; **estar en la** ~ to be daydreaming; **pedir la** ~ to ask for the moon; **tener** ~**s** *fig* to have whims **2.** (*cristal*) plate glass; (*espejo*) mirror; ~**s del coche** car windows ▶ **quedarse a la** ~ **de** Valencia to be disappointed

lunar I. *adj* lunar II. *m* **1.** (*en la piel*) mole **2.** (*en una tela*) polka-dot **3.** (*mancha*) stain

lunarejo, -a I. *adj AmL* **1.** (*persona con lunares*) with moles on the face **2.** (*animal con lunares*) spotted II. *m, f AmL* (*persona con lunares*) person with moles

lunático, -a *adj* lunatic

lunes *m inv* Monday; ~ **de carnaval** the last Monday before Lent; ~ **de Pascua** Easter Monday; **el** ~ on Monday; **el** ~ **pasado** last Monday; **el** ~ **que viene** next Monday; **el** ~ **por la noche/al mediodía/por la mañana/por la tarde** Monday night/at midday/morning/afternoon; (*todos*) **los** ~ every Monday, on Mondays; **en la noche del** ~ **al martes** in the small hours of Monday; **el** ~ **entero** all day Monday; **cada dos** ~ (*del mes*) every other Monday; **hoy es** ~, **once de marzo** today is Monday, March 11th; **pasar de ir al trabajo el** ~ not to go to work on Monday

luneta *f* **1.** (*adorno*) crescent-shaped ornament **2.** (*anteojo*) lens

lunfardismo *m Arg* slang word

lupa *f* magnifying glass; **mirar con** ~ to examine meticulously

lupanar *m* brothel

lúpulo *m* **1.** BOT hop plant **2.** (*cerveza*) hops

lustrabotas *mf inv, AmL* shoeshine

lustrador *m Arg, Nic* shoeshine boy

lustrar *vt* to polish; (*zapatos*) to shine

lustre *m* **1.** (*brillo*) lustre *Brit,* luster *Am;* sacar ~ a los zapatos/a los muebles to polish shoes/furniture; tener ~ *fig* to be famous or noble **2.** *AmL* (*betún*) shoe polish

lustrín *m Chile* shoeshine stall

lustrina *f Chile* (*betún*) shoe polish

lustro *m* lustrum; en el último ~ *elev* in the last five years

lustroso, -a *adj* shiny; estar ~ *fig* to be radiant

luto *m* mourning; (*vestido*) mourning clothes; ir de ~ to wear mourning; estar de ~ por alguien to be in mourning for sb; declarar día de ~ nacional to declare a day of national mourning

luxación *f* MED dislocation

Luxemburgo *m* Luxembourg

luxemburgués, -esa **I.** *adj* of/from Luxembourg **II.** *m, f* native/inhabitant of Luxembourg

luz *f* **1.** (*resplandor*) light; ~ corta dipped headlights; ~ larga full beam; ~ natural natural light; ~ trasera rear light, tail light *Am;* traje de luces bullfighter's suit; a la ~ del día in daylight; a media ~ in subdued light; claro como la ~ del día crystal clear; dar a ~ to give birth; ¡~ de mis ojos! the apple of my eye!; sacar a la ~ *fig* to bring to light; salir a la ~ *fig* to come to light; arrojar ~ sobre un asesinato to shed light on the murder; a la ~ de los nuevos datos... in the light of the new data ... **2.** (*energía*) electricity; ¡da la ~! turn on the light!; se fue la ~ the power went off **3.** (*fuente de luz*) light source; (*lámpara*) light; apagar/encender la ~ to turn off/on the light **4.** ARQUIT aperture **5.** *pl* (*inteligencia*) intelligence; el Siglo de las Luces the Age of Enlightenment; ser de pocas luces to be dim-witted; tener pocas luces to be stupid; a todas luces evidently

M

M, m *f* M, m; ~ de María M for Mary *Brit,* M for Mike *Am*

Mᵃ *abr de* **María** abbreviation for the name Mary

maca *f* (*daño*) damage; (*en un mueble*) defect; (*fruta*) bruise; (*del carácter*) blemish

macabí *m Cuba* cunning person, shark *fig*

macabro, -a *adj* macabre

macaco, -a **I.** *adj Cuba, Chile* (*feo*) ugly **II.** *m, f* **1.** ZOOL macaque **2.** *AmL, pey* Chink

macagua *f* **1.** *AmS* (*ave*) laughing falcon **2.** *Ven* (*serpiente*) large poisonous snake **3.** *Cuba* BOT macaw-tree

macana *f* **1.** (*tontería*) piece of nonsense

2. (*mentira*) lie **3.** ECON unsaleable goods *pl* **4.** *AmL* (*porra*) baton, truncheon *Brit*

macaneador(a) *m(f) Arg, inf* fibber

macanear **I.** *vi CSur* **1.** (*disparatar*) to act rashly **2.** (*hacer tonterías*) to act foolishly; (*decir tonterías*) to talk nonsense **3.** (*mentir*) to lie **II.** *vt inf* (*chapucear*) to botch

macanudo, -a *adj AmL, inf* fantastic, super

macarra *m inf* **1.** (*chorizo*) lout, roughneck *Am* **2.** (*chulo*) pimp

macarrón *m* **1.** *pl* (*pasta*) macaroni **2.** (*bollo*) macaroon

macedonia *f* ~ (*de frutas*) fruit salad

macerar **I.** *vt* **1.** (*con golpes*) to macerate **2.** GASTR to marinate **3.** (*mortificar*) to mortify **II.** *vr:* ~se to mortify oneself

maceta *f* **1.** (*tiesto*) flowerpot **2.** *Chile* (*ramo*) bunch of flowers **3.** (*martillo*) mallet

macetero *m* flowerpot stand; *AmL* flowerpot

machacar <c→qu> **I.** *vt* **1.** (*triturar*) to pound **2.** (*insistir*) to insist on, to harp on **3.** *inf* (*estudiar*) to swot up **4.** *inf* (*destruir*) to crush **II.** *vr:* ~se *inf* to wear oneself out; machacársela *vulg* to have a wank *Brit,* to jerk off

machacón, -ona *adj pey* insistent; ¡no seas ~! (*no insistas*) stop going on and on!

machamartillo a ~ very firmly; creer algo a ~ to firmly believe sth; repetir algo a ~ to repeat sth ad nauseam

machete *m* **1.** machete **2.** *Arg, Urug, Col, inf* (*chuleta*) crib (sheet)

machetear **I.** *vt, vi Arg, Col, inf* (*copiar*) to copy **II.** *vr:* ~se *Méx* (*trabajar*) to work; *inf* (*empollar*) to swot

machetero, -a *m, f* **1.** cutter **2.** (*que corta la caña de azúcar*) cane-cutter **3.** *Arg, inf* (*copión*) copycat **4.** *Méx* (*empollón*) plodder

machismo *m* male chauvinism; (*virilidad*) manliness, masculinity

machista *adj* (male) chauvinistic

macho **I.** *m* **1.** ZOOL (*masculino*) male; ~ cabrío billy goat **2.** *inf* (*machote*) tough guy **3.** (*pieza*) male part **4.** ARQUIT buttress **II.** *adj* **1.** (*masculino*) male **2.** (*fuerte*) macho

machona *f AmL, inf* butch

machote **I.** *m* **1.** *inf* (*hombre*) (tough) guy **2.** *AmL* (*borrador*) (rough) draft; (*modelo*) model **II.** *adj inf* **1.** (*viril*) manly **2.** (*valiente*) brave

machucar <c→qu> *vt* **1.** (*golpear*) to pound **2.** (*destruir*) to destroy; (*aplastar*) to crush

machucho, -a *adj* **1.** estar *pey* (*viejo*) old; ¡qué ~! how old he is! **2.** *ser* (*tranquilo*) serene

macilento, -a *adj* **1.** (*pálido*) wan; (*cansado*) haggard **2.** (*flaco*) gaunt **3.** (*triste*) sombre *Brit,* somber *Am*

macizo *m* **1.** (*masa*) solid mass; (*trozo*) chunk **2.** GEO massif **3.** (*plantas*) flowerbed **4.** ARQUIT section **5.** *pl* GASTR soused sardines *pl*

macizo, -a *adj* **1.** (*oro, puerta*) solid; de plata maciza of solid silver **2.** (*persona*) robust; estar ~ to be robust; un tío ~ a well-built guy

3. (*sólido*) solid **4.** (*mujer*) stacked *inf;* (*hombre*) well-built

macramé *m* macramé

macroinstrucción *f* INFOR macro

mácula *f* **1.** (*mancha*) spot; *fig* stain; **sin** ~ *fig* pure **2.** *inf* (*engaño*) trick

macuto *m* **1.** (*mochila*) rucksack *Brit,* backpack *Am;* MIL kit bag **2.** *inf* (*joroba*) hump **3.** *Ven* (*de los mendigos*) begging basket

madama *f RíoPl* (*patrona de burdel*) madame

madeja *f* **1.** (*de hilo*) skein, hank; **enredar la** ~ *fig* to complicate matters **2.** (*cabello*) mat **3.** *pey* (*hombre dejado*) slob; (*perezoso*) layabout

madera *f* **1.** (*de los árboles*) wood; ~ **prensada** particle board, chipboard; (*cortada*) timber, lumber *Am;* **de** ~ wooden; **tocar** ~ to touch [*o* knock on *Am*] wood; **¡toca** ~! touch [*o* knock on *Am*] wood!; **ser de la misma** ~ to be just the same; **tener** ~ **de** to have the makings of; **tener** [*o* **ser de**] **buena/mala** ~ (not) to have what it takes **2.** *inf* (*policía*) **la** ~ the law **3.** MÚS (*instrumentos*) woodwinds *pl*

maderaje *m,* **maderamen** *m* timbers *pl;* ~ **de techo** roof timbers

maderería *f* timber yard, lumber yard *Am*

madero *m* **1.** (*viga*) beam; (*tablón*) board **2.** (*persona*) oaf

madona *f* Madonna

madrastra *f* **1.** (*pariente*) stepmother **2.** *pey* (*mala madre*) bad mother

madraza *f inf* mother hen *fig;* **es una verdadera** ~ she is a really devoted mother

madre *f* **1.** (*de familia*) mother; ~ **de alquiler** surrogate mother; ~ **de leche** wet nurse; ~ **política** mother-in-law; **futura** ~ mother-to-be; **¡**~ (**mía**)**!** goodness me!; **¡**~ **de Dios!** Holy Mary!; **como su** ~ **lo/la parió** *inf* in his/her birthday suit; **¡la** ~ **que lo parió!** *vulg* the bastard!; **¡la** ~ **que te parió!** *vulg* you bastard!; **¡viva la** ~ **que te parió!** *inf* well done!; **¡tu** ~**!** *inf* up yours! *vulg;* **de puta** ~ *vulg* (fucking) great! *vulg;* **el ciento y la** ~ *inf* (all) the world and his wife *Brit,* everyone and his brother *Am;* **sacar a alguien de** ~ *inf* to drive sb mad [*o* nuts]; **los alquileres se están saliendo de** ~ *inf* rents are becoming ridiculously high **2.** REL **la** ~ **Teresa** Mother Theresa; ~ **superiora** Mother Superior **3.** (*origen*) cradle; ~ **patria** mother country; **ahí está la** ~ **del cordero** *inf* that is the crux of the matter **4.** GEO river bed **5.** TÉC wooden support **6.** GASTR dregs *pl*

madrear *vt* **1.** *Méx* (*romper a golpes*) to bash up **2.** *Méx, vulg* (*pegar fuerte*) to beat up

madrejón *m Arg* watercourse

madreperla *f* mother of pearl

madreselva *f* honeysuckle

Madrid *m* Madrid

madriguera *f* **1.** (*guarida*) den; (*de conejo*) burrow; (*de ratón*) hole; (*de zorro*) earth; (*de tejón*) set **2.** (*escondrijo*) lair

madrileño, -a I. *adj* of/from Madrid; **las noches madrileñas** the Madrid nights II. *m,*

f native/inhabitant of Madrid

madrina *f* **1.** (*de bautismo*) godmother **2.** (*de boda*) ~ (**de boda**) maid of honour *Brit* [*o* honor *Am*] **3.** (*de un artista, una asociación*) patroness

madrugada *f* **1.** (*alba*) dawn; **en la** [*o* **de**] ~ in the early morning; **salimos de viaje de** ~ we set off in the early hours; **a las cinco de la** ~ at five in the morning **2.** (*madrugón*) **pegarse una** ~ to get up very early

madrugador(a) I. *adj* **1.** (*que se levanta pronto*) **ser muy** ~ to be an early riser [*o* earlybird] **2.** *inf* (*astuto*) smart II. *m(f)* early riser

madrugar <g→gu> *vi* to get up early; **tienes que** ~ **más para ganarme** *fig* you will have to be quicker off the mark to beat me ►**a quien madruga, Dios le ayuda** *prov* the early bird catches the worm *prov;* **no por mucho** ~ **amanece más temprano** *prov* ≈ everything will happen at its appointed time

madrugón *m* **darse un** ~ to get up very early

maduración *f* (*de fruta*) ripening; (*de persona*) maturing

madurar I. *vt* **1.** (*hacer maduro: fruta*) to ripen; (*persona*) to mature **2.** (*reflexionar sobre*) to think over II. *vi, vr:* ~**se** (*volverse maduro: fruta*) to ripen; (*persona*) to mature

madurez *f* (*de fruta*) ripeness; (*de persona*) maturity; (*de un plan*) readiness; **estar en la** ~ to be middle-aged

maduro, -a *adj* (*fruta*) ripe; (*persona: prudente*) mature; (*mayor*) adult; (*plan*) ready; **una manzana demasiado madura** an overripe apple; **en la edad madura** middle-aged; **estar a las duras y a las maduras** to take the bad with the good

maestría *f* **1.** (*habilidad*) mastery; **con** ~ skilfully *Brit,* skillfully *Am* **2.** (*título*) Master's degree

maestro, -a I. *adj* **1.** (*principal*) master **2.** (*con gran conocimiento*) master; **obra maestra** masterpiece **3.** (*animal*) trained II. *m, f* **1.** (*profesor*) teacher **2.** (*persona de gran conocimiento*) master **3.** (*capataz*) overseer; ~ **de cocina** master chef; ~ **de obras** foreman **4.** (*lo que enseña*) school; **la vida es la mejor maestra** life is the best school **5.** MÚS master

mafia *f* **la Mafia** the Mafia

mafioso, -a I. *adj* of the Mafia II. *m, f* mafioso

maganzón, -ona I. *adj Col, CRi* lazy II. *m, f Col, CRi* lazybones *inv inf*

magdalena *f* (*pastel*) sweet muffin ►**estar como una Magdalena** to be inconsolable; **llorar como una Magdalena** to cry like a child

magia *f* magic; **como por arte de** ~ as if by magic

mágico, -a I. *adj* **1.** (*misterioso*) magic; **varita mágica** magic wand **2.** (*maravilloso*) marvellous *Brit,* marvelous *Am* II. *m, f* magic

magín *m inf* creativity

magisterio *m* **1.** (*labor*) teaching; **dedicarse al** ~ to be a teacher **2.** (*profesión*) teaching; **estudiar** ~ to study to become a teacher

3. (*maestros*) teachers *pl*

magistrado, -a *m, f* **1.** (*funcionario superior*) senior civil servant **2.** JUR (*juez*) magistrate; (*miembro del Tribunal Supremo*) Supreme Court judge

magistral *adj* **1.** ENS teaching **2.** (*con maestría*) masterly **3.** (*tono*) affected

magistratura *f* **1.** (*oficio*) magistracy, judgeship **2.** (*jueces*) magistracy, judges **3.** (*funcionarios*) senior civil servants *pl*

magma *m* magma

magnanimidad *f* magnanimity

magnánimo, -a *adj* magnanimous

magnate *m* tycoon; ~ **de las finanzas** finance magnate; ~ **de la prensa** press baron

magnesio *m* magnesium

magnético, -a *adj* magnetic; *fig* (*que atrae*) attractive

magnetismo *m* magnetism; **ejercer un intenso** ~ **sobre alguien** to have a lot of influence over sb

magnetizar <z→c> *vt* **1.** (*un cuerpo*) to magnetize **2.** (*hipnotizar*) to hypnotize **3.** (*entusiasmar*) to enthuse; (*retener la atención*) to captivate

magnetofón *m* tape recorder

magnetofónico, -a *adj* recording; **cinta magnetofónica** (recording) tape

magnetófono *m* tape recorder

magnificencia *f* **1.** (*esplendor*) magnificence **2.** (*liberalidad*) lavishness

magnífico, -a *adj* **1.** (*lujoso*) sumptuous; (*valioso*) valuable **2.** (*excelente*) magnificent **3.** (*liberal*) lavish **4.** (*título*) **Magnífico Señor Rector** Chancellor *Brit*, Rector *Am*

magnitud *f* magnitude; **la** ~ **de este problema es alarmante** the magnitude of this problem is alarming

magno, -a *adj* (*importante*) great; **Alejandro Magno** Alexander the Great; **aula magna** main hall

magnolia *f* magnolia

magnolio *m* magnolia

mago, -a *m, f* magician; **los Reyes Magos** the Magi, the Three Wise Men

magra *f* slice of ham

magrear *vt vulg* to feel up

magro *m* (*como el lomo*) tenderloin; *inf* (*carne magra*) lean meat

magro, -a *adj* lean

magua *f Cuba, PRico, Ven* (*contrariedad*) setback

magüey *m AmL* BOT maguey

magulladura *f,* **magullamiento** *m* bruising

magullar *vt* to bruise

mahometano, -a *adj, m, f* Muslim, Mohammedan

mahonesa *f* mayonnaise

maicena® *f* cornflour *Brit,* cornstarch *Am*

maicillo *m* AGR maize *Brit,* corn *Am*

maíz *m* sweetcorn *Brit,* corn *Am*

maizal *m* maize field *Brit,* cornfield *Am*

majada *f* **1.** (*aprisco*) fold **2.** (*estiércol*) dung, cowpat

majaderear *vt AmL* to annoy

majadería *f* **1.** (*tontería*) idiocy; **¡no hagas caso a sus** ~**s!** don't pay any attention to his idiocies! **2.** (*imprudencia*) foolishness

majadero, -a I. *adj* **1.** (*insensato*) silly **2.** (*porfiado*) pestering **3.** (*imprudente*) foolish; (*loco*) crazy II. *m, f* **1.** (*imbécil*) idiot **2.** (*porfiador*) pest

majagua *f Cuba* **1.** (*árbol*) *type of linden tree* **2.** (*chaqueta*) suit jacket

majamama *f Chile* jumble

majar *vt* **1.** (*en un mortero*) to crush **2.** (*en la era*) to thresh **3.** (*molestar*) to pester **4.** *inf* (*azotar*) to smack

majara, majareta I. *adj inf* crazy, nuts II. *mf inf* crackpot

majarete *m* **1.** *Cuba* (*galanteador*) Don Juan **2.** *PRico* (*confusión*) commotion **3.** *Ant, Ven* (*postre*) blancmange (*made with corn, milk and sugar*)

maje I. *adj Méx, inf* gullible II. *mf Méx, inf* sucker

majestad *f* **1.** (*título*) Majesty; **Su Majestad** Your Majesty **2.** (*majestuosidad*) majesty

majestuosidad *f* majesty

majestuoso, -a *adj* majestic

majo, -a *adj* **1.** (*bonito*) lovely; (*guapo*) attractive **2.** (*agradable*) pleasant **3.** (*ataviado*) stylish, smart *Brit;* **ponte maja para la fiesta** dress up for the party

mal I. *adj v.* **malo** II. *m* **1.** (*daño*) harm; (*injusticia*) wrong; (*sufrimiento*) suffering; **la caída del dólar le ha hecho mucho** ~ the fall of the dollar has done him a lot of harm **2.** (*lo malo*) bad thing; **el** ~ **menor** the lesser evil; **decir** ~ **de alguien** to talk badly of sb; **menos** ~ thank goodness **3.** (*inconveniente*) problem; **el** ~ **está en que...** the problem is that ... **4.** (*enfermedad*) illness; ~ **de montaña** mountain sickness; ~ **de vientre** stomach complaint **5.** (*desgracia*) misfortune ►**el** ~ **de ojo** the evil eye; **bien vengas,** ~**, si vienes solo** *prov* it never rains but it pours; **no hay** ~ **que por bien no venga** *prov* every cloud has a silver lining; **no te preocupes, no hay** ~ **que por bien no venga** don't worry, it's an ill wind that blows nobody any good; **el que escucha su** ~ **oye** *prov* those who listen at doors never hear good of themselves III. *adv* **1.** (*de mala manera, insuficientemente*) badly; **dejar** ~ **a alguien** to show sb in a bad light; **estar** ~ **de dinero** to be badly off; **esto acabará** ~ this will end badly; **vas a acabar** ~ you are going to come to a bad end; **este chico va de** ~ **en peor** this boy is going from bad to worse; **me sentó** ~ **que te fueras sin despedirte** I was hurt that you went without saying goodbye; **mi nueva compañera de trabajo me cae** ~ I don't like my new workmate **2.** (*equivocadamente*) wrongly **3.** (*difícilmente*) ~ **podrás ganar con esta moto** you'll be hard-pressed to win with this motorbike **4.** (+ *a mal*) **tomarse algo a** ~ to take sth badly; **tomarse a** ~ **un consejo** to take a piece of advice badly; **¡no te lo tomes tan a** ~**!** don't take it so badly!; **estoy a** ~ **con mi vecino** I'm on bad terms with my neighbour **5.** (*mal que bien*) ~ **que bien, el negocio sigue funcionando** better or worse, the business is still working; ~ **que bien, tendré que ir al dentista este mes** whether I like it or not, I will have to go to the dentist this month; **aprobar los exámenes más** ~ **que bien** to scrape through the exams

malabarismo *m* (*juegos malabares*) juggling; **hacer** ~**s para mantener su puesto de trabajo** *fig* to do a balancing act to keep one's job

malabarista *mf* (*artista*) juggler

malaconsejar *vt* to badly advise; **actuar malaconsejado** to act on bad advice

malacostumbrado, -a *adj* **estar** ~ (*mimado*) to be spoilt; (*sin modales*) to be badly brought-up; (*vicioso*) to have bad habits

malacostumbrar I. *vt* **1.** (*mimar*) to spoil **2.** (*educar mal*) to bring up badly **3.** (*viciar*) ~ **a algo** to get into the bad habit of sth **II.** *vr:* ~**se** to get into a bad habit

Málaga *f* Malaga ▶**salir de** ~ **para entrar en Malagón** to jump out of the frying pan into the fire, to go from bad to worse

malagradecido, -a *adj* ungrateful

malagueño, -a I. *adj* of/from Malaga **II.** *m, f* native/inhabitant of Malaga

malandante *adj* unfortunate; **persona** ~ unfortunate person

malandanza *f* (*desgracia*) misfortune; (*golpe*) blow

malandrín, -ina I. *adj* roguish **II.** *m, f* rogue

malanga I. *adj* *Cuba* cowardly **II.** *f* **1.** (*sombrero de paja*) straw hat **2.** *RDom* (*pelo*) **pelar a alguien la** ~ to cut sb's hair **3.** *AmC, Méx* (*planta*) taro

malapata *mf* (*patoso*) clumsy oaf; **tener** ~ (*poca destreza*) to be maladroit; (*malas intenciones*) to have wicked intentions; (*mala suerte*) to be unlucky; **la cosa tiene** ~ *fig* it is ill-starred [*o* fated]

malaria *f* malaria

Malasia *f* Malaysia

malasombra I. *adj* **1.** (*desastrado*) scruffy **2.** (*malvado*) wicked **II.** *mf* **1.** (*desastre*) disaster **2.** (*mala persona*) wicked person

malaventura *f* **1.** (*desgracia*) unhappiness; (*golpe*) blow **2.** (*mala suerte*) misfortune

malayo, -a *adj, m, f* Malay, Malayan

malbaratar *vt* **1.** (*vender barato*) to sell at too low a price **2.** (*malgastar*) to squander; **malbarató toda la herencia en sólo un año** he/she squandered the entire inheritance in just one year

malcarado, -a *adj* **1.** (*repulsivo*) repulsive **2.** (*enfadado*) cross; (*furioso*) furious; (*malhumorado*) grumpy

malcomer *vi* **1.** (*poco, cosas de mala cualidad*) to eat badly; **el dinero sólo da para** ~ the money isn't sufficient to eat properly **2.** (*sin ganas*) to eat without appetite

malcriadez *f AmC, AmS* ill-breeding; (*descortesía*) rudeness

malcriado, -a *adj* (*mal educado*) spoilt; (*descortés*) rude

malcriar <*1. pres:* malcrío> *vt* to bring up badly; (*mimar*) to spoil

maldad *f* evil, wickedness

maldecir *irr* **I.** *vt* to curse, to damn; **¡te maldigo!** I curse you! **II.** *vi* **1.** (*jurar*) to swear **2.** (*hablar mal*) to speak ill; (*difamar*) to speak evil **3.** (*quejarse*) ~ **de algo/alguien** to complain about sth/sb

maldición *f* **1.** (*imprecación*) curse; **parece que le ha caído una** ~ he/she seems to be cursed; **en el mismo año le cayó la** ~ **del mago** that same year the curse the magician had put on him/her was fulfilled **2.** (*juramento*) swear word; **soltar una** ~ **contra alguien** to swear at sb

maldito, -a I. *pp de* maldecir **II.** *adj* **1.** (*endemoniado*) damned; **¡maldita sea!** *inf* damn (it)!; **¡**~ **seas!** *vulg* damn you!; **maldita la idea que tengo del tema** *inf* I don't have a clue about the subject; ~ **el caso que me hacen** *inf* they aren't taking a blind bit of notice of me; **no vale la maldita pena** *inf* there's absolutely no bloody point; **¡maldita la gracia (que me hace)!** I don't find it in the least bit funny!; **¡malditas las ganas (que tengo)!** I haven't the slightest wish to! **2.** (*maligno*) wicked; **¡vete,** ~**!** go away, you blasted nuisance!; **soltar la maldita** to talk nineteen to the dozen

maldoso, -a *adj Méx* wicked

maleable *adj* **1.** (*forjable*) malleable **2.** (*flexible*) pliable **3.** (*dócil*) pliant

maleante I. *adj* **1.** (*delincuente*) delinquent; **gente** ~ delinquents **2.** (*maligno*) miscreant **II.** *mf* **1.** (*delincuente*) delinquent **2.** (*persona maligna*) miscreant

malear I. *vt* **1.** (*pervertir*) to pervert **2.** (*dañar: a alguien*) to harm; (*algo*) to spoil; (*perjudicar*) to harm **II.** *vr:* ~**se** to go to the dogs

malecón *m* **1.** (*dique*) dyke **2.** (*rompeolas*) breakwater **3.** FERRO embankment **4.** (*embarcadero*) jetty

maledicencia *f* (evil) talk

maleducado, -a *adj* **1.** (*sin modales*) ill-mannered; (*niño*) ill-bred; **tu amigo es muy** ~ your friend is very ill-mannered **2.** (*descortés*) rude **3.** (*mimado*) spoilt

maleducar *vt* to spoil

maleficio *m* **1.** (*hechizo*) curse **2.** (*daño*) harm

maléfico, -a I. *adj* **1.** (*perjudicial*) harmful **2.** (*que hechiza*) who casts spells; **poder** ~ evil power **II.** *m, f* sorcerer

malentendido *m* misunderstanding

malestar *m* **1.** (*físico*) malaise **2.** (*espiritual*) uneasiness

maleta¹ *f* suitcase; **hacer la** ~ to pack one's suitcase

maleta² *m* (*diletante*) dilettante; DEP amateur; **este fontanero es un** ~ this plumber is an amateur

maletera *f Col, Méx,* **maletero** *m* AUTO boot *Brit,* trunk *Am*

maletero, -a *m, f* **1.** (*en las estaciones*) porter **2.** *Chile* (*ladrón*) thief

maletín *m* (*de aseo*) toilet bag; (*para herramientas*) tool box; (*en una bici*) pannier; ~ (*de viaje*) overnight bag

malevaje *m Arg* ruffians *pl*

malevolencia *f* **1.** (*malignidad*) malevolence **2.** (*animosidad*) animosity; **no me trates con** ~ do not treat me with animosity

malévolo, -a *adj* malevolent

maleza *f* **1.** (*hierbas malas*) weeds *pl;* **el jardín se está llenando de** ~ the garden is becoming overrun with weeds **2.** (*matorral*) thicket

malgastador(a) **I.** *adj* wasteful **II.** *m(f)* spendthrift

malgastar *vt* to waste; ~ **todo el dinero en tabaco** to squander all the money on cigarettes; ~ **dinero en el bingo** to waste money on bingo; **con él no haces más que** ~ **tu paciencia** with him you are only wasting your patience; ~ **el tiempo charlando** to waste time chatting; ~ **una oportunidad** to waste an opportunity

malhadado, -a **I.** *adj* (*desventurado*) ill-fated **II.** *m, f* ill-fated person; **ha sido toda su vida un** ~ he has been unlucky all his life

malhechor(a) **I.** *adj* delinquent **II.** *m(f)* delinquent, wrongdoer

malherir *irr como sentir vt* to seriously injure

malhumorado, -a *adj* **1.** *ser* bad-tempered **2.** *estar* **estar** ~ to be in a bad mood

malicia *f* **1.** (*intención malévola*) malice; **hacer todo con** ~ to do everything with malice **2.** (*maldad*) wickedness **3.** (*picardía*) mischievousness; **tener mucha** ~ to be full of mischief **4.** (*interpretación maliciosa*) distrust **5.** *inf* (*sospecha*) suspicion; **tengo mis** ~**s** I have my suspicions; **no tener** ~ to be very trusting

maliciar *vt, vr:* ~**se 1.** (*sospechar*) to suspect; **no malicies de cualquiera** do not distrust just anyone; ~ **de todo** to be suspicious of everything **2.** (*pervertir*) to pervert

malicioso, -a *adj* **1.** (*con intención malévola*) malicious **2.** (*maligno*) malign **3.** (*que sospecha malicia*) suspicious

malignidad *f* **1.** (*de persona*) evilness **2.** MED malignance

maligno, -a *adj* (*pernicioso*) malign; (*persona*) spiteful; (*sonrisa*) malicious; MED malignant

malinchista **I.** *adj Méx* preferring foreign things **II.** *mf Méx* person who prefers foreign things

malintencionado, -a *adj* unkind

malinterpretar *vt* to misinterpret

malla *f* **1.** (*de un tejido*) mesh, weave; **de** ~(**s**) **ancha(s)/estrecha(s)/fina(s)** open/close/ fine weave; **caer en las** ~**s de alguien** *fig* to fall prey to sb **2.** (*tejido*) cloth **3.** (*vestido*) leotard **4.** *pl* (*pantalones*) leggings *pl* **5.** *AmL* (*de baño*) swimming costume *Brit,* swimsuit *Am*

mallo *m* **1.** (*mazo*) mallet **2.** (*juego*) croquet; (*terreno para este juego*) croquet field **3.** *Chile* (*guiso de patatas*) potato stew

Mallorca *f* Majorca

mallorquín, -ina **I.** *adj* of/from Majorca **II.** *m, f* native/inhabitant of Majorca

malnutrido, -a *adj* malnourished

malo, -a **I.** *adj* <peor, pésimo> (*precediendo un sustantivo masculino: mal*) **1.** (*en general*) bad; **mala gestión** mismanagement; **malas palabras** bad words; **tengo mala cabeza para los números** I am no good with numbers; **eres** ~ **de entender** you are difficult to understand; **fumar es** ~ **para la salud** smoking is bad for your health; **de mala gana** unwillingly; **me gusta la casa, lo** ~ **es que es demasiado cara** I like the house, the problem is that it is too expensive; **tener mala mano para algo** to have no talent for sth; **siempre anda con malas mujeres** he is always with flighty women; **se casó sin decirnos ni una mala palabra** he/she got married without saying a single word to us; **es** ~ **para madrugar** he is bad at getting up early; ~ **sería si no llegáramos a una solución** it would be really bad if we did not find a solution; **tener mala suerte** to be unlucky; **hace un tiempo malísimo** the weather is really bad; **el trabajo en las minas es muy** ~ the work in the mines is very hard; **me vino de malas** it happened at a very inconvenient time for me; **la chapa de este coche es mala** the bodywork of this car is poor; **hacer un trabajo de mala manera** to do a job badly **2.** *ser* (*falso*) false **3.** *ser* (*malévolo*) nasty; **tener mal genio** to have a bad temper; **una mala persona** a nasty person; **venir de malas** to have a hostile attitude **4.** *estar* (*enfermo*) ill; **caer** ~ to become ill **5.** *ser* (*travieso*) naughty **6.** *estar* (*estropeado*) spoilt; (*leche*) off *Brit,* gone bad [*o* sour]; (*ropa*) worn-out ▶ **más vale** ~ **conocido que** <u>bueno</u> **por conocer** *prov* better the devil you know **II.** *adv* **si no pagas voluntariamente tendré que intentarlo por las malas** if you don't pay voluntarily I will have to take steps to force you to; **hoy te llevo al dentista aunque sea por las malas** today I am taking you to the dentist even if I have to drag you there; **podemos llegar a un acuerdo por las buenas o por las malas** we can reach an agreement by fair means or foul; **estoy a malas con mi jefe** I am at daggers drawn with my boss; **se pusieron a malas por una tontería** they fell out with each other over an insignificance; **andar a malas** to be on bad terms; **han vuelto a fallar un penalti, hoy están de** ~**s** they have

malograr I. *vt* 1.(*desaprovechar*) to waste; has malogrado la ocasión you have wasted the occasion 2.(*frustrar*) to frustate 3.(*estropear*) to ruin II. *vr:* ~se 1.(*fallar*) to fail; se han malogrado mis esperanzas my hopes have come to nothing 2.(*estropearse*) to be ruined 3.(*desarrollarse mal*) to turn out badly 4.(*morir demasiado pronto*) to die an untimely death; (*morir en un accidente*) to die in an accident 5.(*interrumpirse*) to be interrupted
failed to score a penalty again, today they are out of luck III. *m, f* (*persona*) bad man *m*, bad woman *f;* CINE baddie; los ~s de la peli the bad guys

maloliente *adj* foul-smelling; me molestan tus cigarros ~s your smelly cigarettes annoy me

malparar *vt* (*persona*) to come off badly; salió malparado de la pelea he came off worse in the fight; salir malparado de un asunto to come off badly in a matter

malparir *vi* to have a miscarriage

malpensado, -a *adj* evil-minded; no seas tan ~ don't be so cynical

malquerencia *f* 1.(*antipatía*) antipathy; sentir mucha ~ hacia alguien to feel great antipathy towards sb 2.(*mala voluntad*) ill will; sentir ~ hacia alguien to bear sb ill will

malquistar I. *vt* to set against; me has malquistado con tu familia you have set your family against me II. *vr:* ~se to fall out

malsano, -a *adj* 1.(*insano, enfermizo*) unhealthy 2.(*moralmente*) unwholesome

malsonante *adj* (*sonido*) jarring; (*palabra*) nasty; (*doctrina*) dangerous; ruidos ~s jarring noises

malta *f* 1. *t.* AGR malt 2. *Arg* (*cerveza*) beer

maltés, -esa *adj, m, f* Maltese

maltón, -ona I. *adj AmS* overgrown II. *m, f AmS* overgrown youth

maltraído, -a *adj Bol, Chile, Perú* disheveled

maltratar *vt* 1.(*tratar mal, causar daño físico, psíquico*) to maltreat 2.(*insultar*) ~ (de palabra) to abuse (verbally) 3.(*estropear*) to damage

maltrato *m* 1.(*físico, psíquico*) maltreatment, abuse 2.(*insulto*) (verbal) abuse 3.(*de una cosa*) misuse

maltrecho, -a *adj* 1.(*golpeado*) battered 2.(*deprimido*) low

malura *f Chile* pain or discomfort

malva I. *adj* mauve II. *f* mallow; estar criando ~s *inf* to be pushing up daisies; ser (como) una ~ *inf* to be meek and mild

malvado, -a I. *adj* wicked; una persona malvada a wicked person II. *m, f* wicked person

malvavisco *m* marsh mallow

malvender *vt* to sell at a loss

malversar *vt* to misappropriate, to embezzle

malversión *f* embezzlement, misappropriation

Malvinas *fpl* Falkland Islands *pl*

malvís *m inv* song thrush

malvón *m Arg, Méx, Par, Urug* BOT geranium

mama *f* 1.(*pecho*) breast; (*ubre*) udder 2. *inf* (*mamá*) mummy *Brit,* mommy *Am*

mamá *f inf* mummy *Brit,* mommy *Am*

mamada *f* 1.(*acción*) breastfeeding; el bebé se queda dormido después de cada ~ the baby always falls asleep after breastfeeding 2.(*cantidad mamada*) breastfeed 3. *AmL* (*ganga*) bargain; ¡vaya ~! what a bargain! 4. *vulg* (*felación*) blow job; dar una ~ a alguien to give sb a blow [*o* French] job, to go down on sb

mamadera *f AmL* (*biberón*) baby bottle

mamar I. *vt, vi* 1.(*en el pecho*) to breastfeed; no le des de ~ tanto al niño don't breastfeed the baby so much 2.(*adquirir*) has mamado la pereza (con la leche) you acquired your laziness at your mother's breast 3. *inf* (*comer*) to wolf (down) 4. *vulg* mamársela a alguien to give sb a blow job II. *vr:* ~se *vulg* (*emborracharse*) to get sloshed

mamario, -a *adj* mammary

mamarracho *m* 1.(*persona que viste mal*) sight; (*ridícula*) ridiculous person 2.(*cosa mal hecha*) botch; (*fea*) hideous thing; (*sin valor*) piece of junk 3.(*persona despreciable*) despicable person

mameluco *m* 1.(*bobo*) idiot 2. *AmL* (*de bebé*) romper suit

mamífero I. *adj* mammalian II. *m* mammal

mamila *f* 1. ANAT (*mujer*) mammilla 2. ANAT (*hombre*) nipple 3. *Méx* (*biberón*) baby bottle

mamografía *f* MED mammogram, mammograph

mamón, -ona *m, f* 1. *vulg* jerk; (*hombre*) prick; (*mujer*) bitch 2. *AmL, inf* (*borracho*) drunk

mamonear *vt Guat, Hond* 1.(*golpear*) to beat 2.(*retardar*) to postpone 3.(*pasar el tiempo con futilezas*) to waste time

mamotreto *m pey* 1.(*libro*) hefty tome 2.(*armatoste*) cumbersome object; esta butaca es un ~ this armchair is a cumbersome piece of furniture

mampara *f* screen (door), (room) divider

mamporro *m inf* clout; darse un ~ contra algo to bash oneself against sth; con el hielo me pegué un ~ en medio de la calle I went sprawling on the ice in the middle of the street

mampostería *f* 1.(*obra*) rubblework; ~ de ladrillos en bruto brickwork 2.(*oficio*) dry-stone walling

mamúa *f Arg, Urug, vulg* (*borrachera*) agarrarse una ~ to get smashed

mamut <mamuts> *m* mammoth

manada *f* (*rebaño de vacas, ciervos*) herd; (*de ovejas, aves*) flock; (*de peces*) shoal; (*de lobos*) pack; ~ de gallinas brood of hens; ~ de gente crowd of people; una ~ de curiosos a crowd of onlookers; llegaron en [*o* a] ~s al concierto people arrived at the concert in droves; pasamos la frontera en ~ we crossed

over the border en masse
Managua m Managua
manantial I. adj running **II.** m **1.** (fuente natural) spring; ~ **caliente** hot spring; ~ **medicinal** health spa **2.** (fuente artificial) fountain
3. (origen) source
manar I. vt to flow with; **la fuente mana
agua fría** the fountain flows with cold water;
la herida no paraba de ~ **sangre** the wound
wouldn't stop flowing with blood **II.** vi **1.** (surgir) to well; **el agua manaba sucia de la
fuente** dirty water welled from the fountain
2. (fluir fácilmente) to flow; **las palabras
manaban de su boca** the words flowed from
his/her mouth
manatí m manatee
manazas mf inv, inf clumsy person, klutz Am;
ser un ~ to be clumsy
mancha f **1.** (en la ropa, piel) dirty mark; (de
tinta) stain; (salpicadura) spot; (de maquillaje) smudge **2.** (toque de color) fleck; **este
perro es blanco con** ~**s negras** this dog is
white with black patches; **la corbata tiene** ~**s
azules y blancas** the tie has splashes of blue
and white **3.** (boceto) sketch **4.** (deshonra)
stain; **sin** ~ stainless
Mancha f **canal de la** ~ the (English) Channel
manchado, -a adj **1.** (ropa, mantel) stained
2. (cara, fruta) dirty **3.** (caballos, vacas)
dappled; (salpicado) spotted
manchar I. vt **1.** (ensuciar) to dirty **2.** (desprestigiar) to sully **II.** vr: ~**se** (ensuciarse) to
get dirty
manchego, -a I. adj of/from la Mancha **II.** m,
f native/inhabitant of la Mancha
mancilla f stain; **sin** ~ pure
mancillar vt to sully
manco, -a I. adj **1.** (de un brazo) one-armed;
(de una mano) one-handed; **es** ~ **de la mano
izquierda/derecha** (le falta) he/she lacks a
left/right hand; (la tiene inutilizada) his/her
left/right hand is useless; **no ser (cojo ni)** ~
(ser hábil) to be dexterous; (ser largo de
manos) to be light-fingered **2.** (defectuoso)
faulty; (incompleto) incomplete **II.** m, f (con
un brazo) one-armed man; (con una mano)
person who is missing a hand
mancomunar I. vt to join together **II.** vr: ~**se**
to unite
mancomunidad f **1.** (comunidad) community **2.** JUR joint ownership [o responsibility]
mancornas fpl Col, Chile cuff links pl
mancuernillas fpl Méx cuff links pl
manda f legacy, bequest
mandadero, -a m, f messenger; (de recados)
errand boy m, errand girl f; (de oficina) office
boy m, office girl f
mandado m (encargo) errand; (orden) order;
(compra) purchase; **hacer un** ~ to run an
errand
mandamás mf pey, inf big shot
mandamiento m **1.** (orden) order; ~ **de**

detención arrest warrant; ~ **judicial** court
order **2.** (precepto) precept **3.** REL commandment
mandar I. vt **1.** (ordenar) to order; ~ **a alguien que** +subj to order sb to; **lo que Ud.
mande** whatever you say **2.** (prescribir) to
prescribe **3.** (dirigir) to lead; (gobernar) to govern **4.** (encargar) ~ **buscar/hacer/venir** to
ask to fetch/do/come **5.** (enviar) to send; ~ **al
cuerno** inf to send to hell **6.** TÉC to control;
mandado a distancia remote controlled
II. vr: ~**se** to manage alone
mandarín m **1.** (idioma) Mandarin **2.** pey, inf
(funcionario) mandarin
mandarina f mandarin, tangerine
mandatario, -a m, f agent; **primer** ~ POL
head of state; JUR attorney
mandato m **1.** (orden) order; (prescripción)
prescription; (delegación) delegation; ~ **judicial** injunction; ~ **de pago** warrant for payment; **por** ~ **de las leyes** by law **2.** POL mandate; ~ **internacional** international mandate;
~ **parlamentario** parliamentary mandate
mandíbula f **1.** ANAT jaw; **reír(se) a** ~
batiente to laugh one's head off **2.** TÉC clamp;
~ **prensora** vice; ~ **de sujeción** clamp
mandil m **1.** (delantal) apron; (de cuero)
leather apron **2.** AmL (de caballería) cloth
(used to rub down a horse)
mandilón m pey, inf wimp
mandinga m **1.** AmL, inf (diablo) devil
2. Arg, inf (muchacho) scamp
mando m **1.** (poder) control; MIL command;
(del presidente) term of office; **don de** ~
leadership qualities; **estar al** ~ **de** to be in
command of; **estar bajo el** ~ **de alguien** to be
under sb's command; **tener el** ~ **y el palo** inf
to rule the roost **2.** (quien lo tiene) ~**s intermedios de una empresa** middle manage-
ment of a business; **alto** ~ MIL high command
3. TÉC control; ~ **a distancia** remote control; ~
manual manual control; **botón de** ~ control
button
mandolina f MÚS mandolin
mandón, -ona I. adj bossy **II.** m, f bossy person
manducar <c→qu> vi, vt inf to gobble, to
scarf Am
manecilla f **1.** (del reloj) hand **2.** (broche)
clasp **3.** TÉC pointer **4.** (signo) sign (clenched
fist with extended index finger to draw attention to sth)
manejable adj **1.** (objeto) user-friendly
2. (persona) tractable **3.** AUTO manoeuvrable
Brit, maneuverable Am
manejar I. vt **1.** (usar) to use; (máquina) to
operate; fig to handle; ~ **un cuchillo** to use a
knife; **manejas bien las cifras** you are good
with numbers; **saber** ~ **el dinero** to know
how to handle money; **'¡manéjese con cuidado!'** 'handle with care!' **2.** INFOR to use
3. (dirigir) to handle; ~ **intereses** to manage
interests **4.** (a alguien) to manage; **maneja al**

marido a su antojo she can twist her husband round her little finger **5.** *AmL* (*un coche*) to drive **II.** *vr:* ~**se** to manage; **saber ~se en la vida** to know how to get on in life; **manejárselas** *inf* to get by

manejo *m* **1.** (*uso*) use; (*de una máquina*) operation; (*fig* handling; ~ **de animales** handling of animals; ~ **a distancia** remote control **2.** INFOR management; ~ **de errores** error management; ~ **de la memoria** memory management; ~ **de información** information management **3.** (*trato*) handling **4.** (*de un negocio*) running **5.** *AmL* (*de un coche*) driving **6.** *pl* (*intrigas*) machinations *pl*

manera *f* **1.** (*forma, modo*) manner, way; ~ **de decir** way of saying; ~ **de obrar** way of doing things; ~ **de pensar** way of thinking; ~ **de proceder** way of acting; **es su ~ de ser** that's the way he/she is; ~ **de ver las cosas** way of seeing things; **a la ~ de sus abuelos** in the way their grandparents did; **a la ~ de la casa** in the habitual way; **a ~ de** a sort of; **a mi ~** my way; **a mi ~ de ver** to my way of looking at things; **de la ~ que sea** somehow or other; **de cualquier ~, de todas ~s** anyway; **de esta ~** that way; **de ~ que** (*finalidad*) so that; **mañana tienes que madrugar, de ~ que es mejor que te acuestes pronto** tomorrow you have to get up early, so you had better get to bed early; **¿de ~ que sacaste mala nota?** so you got a bad mark, did you?; **de ninguna ~** no way; **se echó a gritar de tal ~ que...** *inf* he/she started to shout in such a way that ...; **de una ~ o de otra** one way or another; **en cierta ~** in a way; **en gran ~** largely; **no hay ~ de...** there is no way that ...; **¡qué ~ de llover!** just look at the rain!; **sobre ~** a lot; **primero se lo dije de buena ~** first I said it to him nicely; **contestar de mala ~** to answer rudely; **hacer las cosas de mala ~** to do things badly **2.** *pl* (*modales*) manners *pl;* **¡estas no son ~s!** this is no way to behave!

maneto, -a *adj* **1.** *Hond* (*manos*) one-handed **2.** *Guat, Ven* (*piernas*) knock-kneed

manga *f* **1.** (*del vestido*) sleeve; **de ~s cortas/largas** short-/long-sleeved; **estar en ~s de camisa** to be in shirt-sleeves; **¡a buenas horas ~s verdes!** *inf* a bit late in the day!; **andar ~ por hombro** *inf* to be a mess; **poner algo ~ por hombro** *inf* to turn sth inside out; **sacarse algo de la ~** *fig* to come up with sth; **hacer un corte de ~s a alguien** to give sb the finger; **ser más corto que las ~s de un chaleco** *fig* to be as thick as two short planks; **tener (la)** [*o* **ser de**] ~ **ancha** *fig* to be lenient; **tienen algo en la manga** they are keeping sth up their sleeve **2.** (*tubo*) hose **3.** AVIAT ~ **de aire** windsock **4.** METEO ~ **de viento** tornado; ~ **de agua** waterspout **5.** GASTR (*filtro*) muslin strainer; (*pastelera*) pastry bag, icing bag *Brit* **6.** *inf* (*borrachera*) drunkenness **7.** *Arg, pey* (*grupo de personas*) mob ▶**hacer ~s y capirotes** to completely ignore; **tirar la ~** to ask for

a loan

manganeta *f Hond* trick

mangante *mf inf* **1.** (*ladrón*) thief **2.** (*holgazán*) loafer **3.** (*mendigo*) beggar

manganzón, -ona *m, f AmL* loafer

mangar <g→gu> *vt inf* to swipe, to nick; (*en tiendas*) to shoplift

mangle *m AmL* BOT mangrove tree

mango *m* **1.** (*puño*) knob; (*alargado*) handle; **tener la sartén por el ~** *fig* to hold the reins **2.** BOT mango tree **3.** (*fruta*) mango

mangoneador(a) *adj* **1.** (*entrometido*) meddlesome **2.** (*dominador*) dominating **3.** (*vago*) idle

mangonear *inf* **I.** *vi* **1.** (*entrometerse*) to meddle **2.** (*vaguear*) to loaf **II.** *vt* to wangle; **está mangoneando todo** he/she has got a finger in every pie

mangoneo *m inf* **1.** (*entremetimiento*) meddling **2.** (*vagancia*) idleness

manguear *vt Arg, inf* (*dinero*) to scrounge

manguera *f* (*tubo*) hose

mangueta *f* **1.** (*listón*) batten **2.** (*palanca*) lever **3.** (*retrete*) U-bend

manguito *m* **1.** (*mitón*) muff **2.** (*protección*) oversleeve **3.** (*cilindro hueco*) sleeve **4.** (*anillo*) hoop

maní *m* peanut

manía *f* **1.** (*locura*) mania **2.** (*extravagancia*) eccentricity, quirk **3.** (*obsesión*) obsession; **tener ~ por la moda** to be obsessed with fashion **4.** *inf* (*aversión*) aversion; **tener ~ a alguien** not to be able to stand sb; **coger ~ a alguien** to take a dislike to sb

maniaco, -a, maníaco, -a I. *adj* maniacal **II.** *m, f* maniac; ~ **sexual** sex maniac

maniatar *vt* ~ **a alguien** to tie sb's hands up; **lo ~on a la silla** they tied his hands to the chair

maniático, -a I. *adj* **1.** (*extravagante*) fussy **2.** (*loco*) manic **3.** (*obsesivo*) neurotic **II.** *m, f* **1.** (*extravagante*) fusspot **2.** (*loco*) maniac; **un ~ del fútbol** a football fanatic; **ser un ~ del cine** to be crazy about films; **un ~ de la limpieza** a cleaning maniac

manicomio *m* psychiatric hospital; *fig* (*casa de locos*) madhouse

manicura *f* manicure

manicuro, -a *m, f* manicurist

manido, -a *adj* **1.** (*alimentos*) off; (*fruta*) overripe **2.** (*objetos*) worn; (*libro*) tatty; (*ropa*) shabby **3.** (*trillado*) hackneyed **4.** (*oculto*) hidden

manifestación *f* **1.** (*expresión*) expression; **como ~ de cariño** as an expression of love **2.** (*reunión*) demonstration

manifestante *mf* demonstrator

manifestar <e→ie> **I.** *vt* **1.** (*declarar*) to declare **2.** (*mostrar*) to show **II.** *vr:* ~**se** **1.** (*declararse*) to declare oneself; ~**se a favor/en contra de algo** to declare oneself in favour *Brit* [*o* favor *Am*] of/against sth **2.** (*revelarse*) to show oneself **3.** (*política*) to demonstrate

manifiesto *m* manifesto

manifiesto, -a *adj* (*evidente*) manifest; **poner de** ~ (*revelar*) to show [*o* make clear]; (*expresar*) to declare

manigua *f Cuba* jungle

manija *f* handle

manilargo, -a I. *adj* **1.** (*hurtador*) light-fingered **2.** (*dadivoso*) generous II. *m, f* petty thief

manilla *f* **1.** *v.* **manija 2.** (*del reloj*) hand **3.** *pl* (*para prisioneros*) handcuffs *pl* **4.** (*pulsera*) bracelet

manillar *m* handlebars *pl*

maniobra *f* **1.** (*operación manual*) handling **2.** (*uso*) use **3.** (*ardid*) ploy; ~s **fraudulentas** fraudulent tactics **4.** MIL manoeuvre *Brit,* maneuver *Am;* **estar de** ~s to be on manoeuvres *Brit* [*o* maneuvers *Am*] **5.** (*vehículo*) manoeuvre *Brit,* maneuver *Am;* FERRO shunting; (*movimiento*) movement

maniobrable *adj* manoeuvrable *Brit,* maneuverable *Am;* **un vehículo fácilmente** ~ a highly manoeuvrable *Brit* [*o* maneuverable *Am*] car

maniobrar I. *vi* **1.** MIL to carry out manoeuvres *Brit* [*o* maneuvers *Am*] **2.** (*intrigar*) to scheme II. *vt* **1.** (*manejar*) to handle **2.** (*manipular*) to manipulate

manipulación *f* **1.** (*empleo*) use, handling **2.** (*elaboración*) making **3.** (*alteración*) manipulation

manipular *vt* **1.** (*maniobrar*) to manoeuvre *Brit,* to maneuver *Am;* (*máquina*) to operate **2.** (*elaborar*) to make **3.** (*alterar*) to manipulate **4.** (*interferir*) ~ **algo** to interfere with sth **5.** (*manosear*) ~ **algo** to fiddle with sth

maniquí <maniquíes> *m* **1.** (*modelo*) model **2.** (*muñeco*) puppet, dummy **3.** (*para ropa*) mannequin

manir *irr como abolir vt* (*carne*) to hang

manirroto, -a *adj* spendthrift

manitas: hacer ~ *inf* to canoodle, to snog *Brit;* **ser un** ~ *inf* to be dexterous, to be good with one's hands

manito *m Méx* mate *Brit,* pal

manivela *f* handle

manjar *m* **1.** (*comestible*) food **2.** (*exquisitez*) delicacy

mano *f* **1.** ANAT hand; **a** ~ **alzada** (*votación*) by a show of hands; **a** ~ **armada** armed; **a** ~**s llenas** in abundance; **nunca alcé la** ~ **contra mis hijos** I never raised my hand to my children; **apretón de** ~s handshake; **bajo** ~ underhand; **cargar las** ~s to overdo it; **coger a alguien con las** ~**s en la masa** to catch sb red-handed; **cogidos de las** ~s hand in hand; **comer de la** ~ **de alguien** *fig* to eat out of sb's hand; **me lo prometió con la** ~ **en el corazón** he promised me with his hand on his heart; **dar de** ~ (*al trabajo*) to leave work; **echar una** ~ **a alguien** to give sb a hand; **dejar algo en** ~s **de alguien** to leave sth in

sb's hands; **echar** ~ **de alguien** to make use of sb; **ser de** ~ **abierta/cerrada** *fig* to be generous/tight-fisted; **estar al alcance de la** ~ to be within (arm's) reach; **estar** ~ **sobre** ~ *fig* to be idle; **hecho a** ~ hand-made; **irse a las** ~s to come to blows; **su vida se le había ido de las** ~s his/her life has got out of hand; **se le ha ido la** ~ (*desmesura*) he/she has overdone it; (*violencia*) he/she has lost control; **se lavó las** ~s (**como Pilatos**) **en el asunto** he washed his hands of the matter; **llevar a alguien de la** ~ to lead sb by the hand; *fig* to guide sb; ~ **a** ~ *fig* hand in hand; **¡**~s **a la obra!** to work!; **meter** ~ to take action; **meter** ~ **a alguien** *inf* to touch sb up; **pedir la** ~ **de alguien** to ask for sb's hand in marriage; **no voy a poner las** ~s **en el fuego por nadie** I am not going to risk my neck for anyone; **si a** ~ **viene...** if it drops into my lap ...; **echar** ~ **de algo** to draw on sth; **traer algo entre** ~s to be up to sth; **tomarle la** ~ **a algo** *inf* to take sth up; **untar la** ~ **a alguien** to grease sb's palm; **¡venga esa** ~! let's shake on it! **2.** ZOOL (*de un mono*) hand; (*de un perro*) paw; ~ **de ave** bird's claw; ~ **de cerdo** pig's trotter **3.** (*reloj*) hand **4.** (*lado*) ~ **derecha/izquierda** right-/left-hand side; **a** [*o* **de**] **la** ~ **derecha** on the right(-hand side) **5.** (*capa*) coat; **una** ~ **de pintura** a coat of paint; **la pared necesita una** ~ **de pintura** the wall needs a coat of paint **6.** (*trabajador*) hand; ~ **de obra** labour *Brit,* labor *Am;* ~ **de obra especializada** skilled labour *Brit* [*o* labor *Am*] **7.** (*habilidad*) skill; **tener buena** ~ **para coser** to be good at sewing; **tener** ~ **izquierda** to be tactful; **tener** ~ **con** to have a way with; ~ **de santo** sure remedy **8.** (*de naipes*) hand; **ser** ~ to lead **9.** (*de ajedrez*) game ►**muchas** ~s **en un plato hacen mucho garabato** *prov* too many cooks spoil the broth

manojo *m* bunch; ~ **de llaves** bunch of keys; **ser un** ~ **de nervios** to be a bundle of nerves

manopla *f* **1.** (*guante*) mitten **2.** (*para lavarse*) flannel *Brit,* washcloth *Am*

manoseado, -a *adj* **1.** (*sobado*) worn **2.** (*trillado*) hackneyed

manosear *vt* to handle; *pey* to paw

manotazo *m* smack; **dar** ~s to smack

manoteador(a) I. *adj CSur* (*caballo piafador*) pawing II. *m(f)* **1.** *Arg, Méx* (*ratero*) thief **2.** (*que mueve mucho las manos*) gesticulator

manotear *vi* to gesticulate

manotón *m* slap

mansalva *adv* **a** ~ (*sobre seguro*) without risk; (*traidoramente*) point-blank; (*en gran cantidad*) in abundance

mansarda *f AmC, AmS* attic

mansedumbre *f* **1.** (*suavidad*) gentleness **2.** (*sumisión*) meekness

mansión *f* **1.** (*casa suntuosa*) mansion **2.** (*morada*) dwelling

manso, -a *adj* **1.** (*dócil*) docile **2.** (*animales*) tame **3.** (*aguas*) quiet **4.** (*aire*) still **5.** (*clima*) mild

manta¹ *f* **1.** (*de cama*) blanket; **a** ~ in abundance; **liarse la** ~ **a la cabeza** (*actuar con decisión*) to take it on oneself to do sth; (*de modo irreflexivo*) to recklessly decide to do sth; **tirar de la** ~ to let the cat out of the bag **2.** (*zurra*) beating **3.** ZOOL manta

manta² *mf* (*persona torpe*) oaf

manteca *f* **1.** (*grasa*) fat; ~ **de cerdo** lard **2.** *RíoPl* (*mantequilla*) butter; **como** ~ as soft as butter; **eso no se le ocurre ni al que asó la** ~ *inf* nobody in their right mind would do that

mantecado *m* **1.** (*bollo*) pastry cake (*type of shortbread*) **2.** (*helado*) icecream (*made from a custard base*)

mantecoso, -a *adj* **1.** (*de manteca*) greasy; (*sabor*) buttery **2.** (*consistencia*) soft; (*carne*) fatty

mantel *m* tablecloth; **comer a** ~**es** to dine formally; **estar a mesa y** ~ to have free board; **poner/levantar los** ~**es** *fig* to lay/clear the table

mantelería *f* table linen

mantener *irr como* tener **I.** *vt* **1.** (*conservar, relaciones*) to maintain; (*orden*) to keep; ~ **a punto** to keep in working order; **mantiene la línea** she keeps her figure; ~ **la calma** to keep calm **2.** (*perseverar*) ~ **algo** to keep sth up **3.** (*sustentar*) to maintain; ~ **correspondencia con alguien** to keep up a correspondence with sb **4.** (*sostener*) to support **5.** (*proseguir*) to continue; ~ **una conversación con alguien** to hold a conversation with sb **II.** *vr:* ~**se** **1.** (*sostenerse*) to support oneself **2.** (*continuar*) to continue **3.** (*perseverar*) to keep; **se mantiene en sus trece** *inf* he/she is sticking to his/her guns **4.** (*sustentarse*) to support oneself

mantenido, -a *adj* kept

mantenimiento *m* **1.** (*alimentos*) sustenance **2.** TÉC maintenance; ~ **de datos** INFOR database update; **sin** ~ maintenance-free **3.** (*de una propiedad*) upkeep

mantequilla *f* butter

mantequillera *f* *AmL:* butter dish

mantilla *f* **1.** (*de mujer*) mantilla **2.** (*de niño*) swaddling clothes *pl;* **el negocio está en** ~**s** *inf* the business is in its infancy; **estar en** ~**s sobre algo** *inf* to be in the dark about sth **3.** (*de caballo*) horse blanket

manto *m* **1.** (*prenda*) cloak; (*talar*) gown **2.** (*capa*) layer; **el** ~ **ácido de la piel** the acid layer of the skin **3.** (*velo*) veil **4.** MIN ~ seam **5.** GEO ~ **terrestre** earth's crust **6.** BOT ~ **vegetal** humus

mantón *m* shawl

mantudo, -a **I.** *adj* (*ave*) with droopy wings **II.** *m, f* *AmC* masked [*o* disguised] person

manual **I.** *adj* **1.** (*con las manos*) manual, hand; **trabajos** ~**es** handicrafts *pl* **2.** (*manejable*) user-friendly **II.** *m* manual, handbook; ~ **de referencia** reference book; ~ **de instruc-**

ciones instruction manual

manubrio *m* **1.** (*puño*) stock **2.** (*manivela*) handle; **piano de** ~ barrel organ

manufactura *f* **1.** (*acción, producto*) manufacture **2.** (*taller*) factory

manufacturar *vt* to manufacture

manuscrito *m* manuscript

manuscrito, -a *adj* handwritten

manutención *f* **1.** (*alimentos*) keep **2.** TÉC maintenance

manzana *f* **1.** (*fruta*) apple; **la** ~ **de la discordia** the bone of contention; **sano como una** ~ as fit as a fiddle **2.** (*conjunto de casas*) block; **dar la vuelta a la** ~ to go round the block **3.** *AmL* ANAT (*nuez*) Adam's apple

manzanilla *f* **1.** (*planta*) camomile **2.** (*flor*) camomile flower **3.** (*infusión*) camomile tea **4.** (*vino*) manzanilla (*type of dry sherry*)

manzano *m* apple tree

maña *f* **1.** (*habilidad*) skill, dexterity; **tener** ~ **para algo** to have a knack for sth **2.** (*astucia*) craftiness **3.** *pl* (*caprichos*) whims *pl;* **tiene** ~**s** he/she has his/her little whims ►**más vale** ~ **que fuerza** *prov* better brains than brawn

mañana¹ **I.** *f* (*temprano*) early morning; (*hasta el mediodía*) morning; **a las 5 de la** ~ at 5 a.m.; **de la noche a la** ~ overnight; **de** ~ in the early morning; **por la** ~ in the morning; **todas las** ~**s** every morning; **por la** ~ tomorrow morning **II.** *adv* **1.** (*día*) tomorrow; **¡hasta** ~**!** see you tomorrow!; ~ **será otro día** tomorrow is another day **2.** (*futuro*) tomorrow ►**no dejes para** ~ **lo que puedas hacer hoy** *prov* do not leave for tomorrow what you can do today

mañana² *m* tomorrow; **pasado** ~ the day after tomorrow; **el día de** ~ in the future

mañanero, -a **I.** *adj* **1.** (*madrugador*) early-rising **2.** (*de la mañana*) morning **II.** *m, f* early riser

mañanita *f* **1.** (*prenda*) bed jacket **2.** *Méx* (*canción*) serenade

mañero, -a *adj* *Arg, inf* fussy

maño, -a **I.** *adj* of/from Aragón **II.** *m, f* native/inhabitant of Aragón

mañosear *vi* **1.** *Chile, Perú* to act craftily **2.** *CSur, Méx* to be finicky

mañoso, -a *adj* **1.** (*hábil*) dexterous, handy **2.** (*sagaz*) guileful

mapa *m* map; ~ **astronómico** map of the stars; ~ **del tiempo** weather map; **borrar del** ~ (*matar*) to wipe off the map [*o* the face of the earth]; **desaparecer del** ~ to vanish into thin air; **no estar en el** ~ *fig* to be out of this world

mapache *m,* **mapachín** *m* *AmL* raccoon

maqueta *f* **1.** ARQUIT (*scale*) model **2.** (*formato*) format; (*de libro*) dummy

maquetación *f* layout

maquetar *vt* to lay out

maquiavélico, -a *adj* (*retorcido*) Machiavellian

maquillador(a) *m(f) t.* TEAT make-up artist

maquillaje *m* **1.** (*acción*) application of make-up **2.** (*producto*) make-up

maquillar I. *vt* 1.(*poner base de fondo*) to apply foundation to; (*con pinturas*) to apply make-up to 2.(*disimular*) to disguise II. *vr:* ~se (*con base de fondo*) to put on foundation; (*con pinturas*) to put on make-up

máquina *f* 1.(*artefacto*) machine; ~ de afeitar electric shaver [*o* razor]; ~ de coser/lavar sewing/washing machine; ~ fotográfica camera; ~ de escribir automática electric typewriter; ~ destructora de documentos paper-shredder; a toda ~ (at) full speed; escrito a ~ typed; hecho a ~ machine-made 2.(*aparato de monedas*) vending machine; ~ de tabaco cigarette dispenser; ~ tragaperras *inf* slot-machine 3.(*tren*) engine

maquinación *f* plot

maquinal *adj* mechanical, automatic

maquinar *vt* 1.(*urdir*) to scheme 2.(*trabajar*) to work

maquinaria *f* 1.(*máquinas*) machinery 2.(*mecanismo*) mechanism

maquinilla *f* (safety) razor

maquinista *mf* 1.(*conductor*) machinist; ~ de trenes train driver *Brit*, engineer *Am* 2.(*constructor*) engineer

maquinizar <z→c> *vt* to mechanize

mar *m o f* 1. GEO sea; Mar Antártico Antarctic Ocean; Mar de las Antillas Caribbean Sea; Mar Báltico Baltic Sea; Mar de Irlanda Irish Sea; Mar Mediterráneo Mediterranean Sea; Mar del Norte North Sea; en alta ~ offshore; ~ adentro high seas; ~ de fondo swell; ~ gruesa/picada/rizada heavy/rough/choppy sea; *fig* unrest; por ~ by sea; hacerse a la ~ to put out to sea; al otro lado del ~ overseas; arar en el ~ *fig* to labour *Brit* [*o* labor *Am*] in vain; arrojarse a la ~ *fig* to venture forth 2. *inf* la ~ de... there is an abundance of ...; llueve a ~es it is pouring with rain; lloró a ~es he/she cried his/her eyes out; sudar a ~es to pour with sweat; ser la ~ de aburrido to be excruciatingly boring; ser la ~ de bonita to be incredibly pretty ►quien no se <u>aventura</u> no pasa la ~ *prov* nothing ventured, nothing gained; echar <u>pelillos</u> al ~ to let bygones be bygones, to bury the hatchet *Am*

maraca *f* maraca

maraña *f* 1.(*maleza*) thicket 2.(*lío*) mess; ~ de cabello tangle of hair; ~ de hilo tangle of threads 3.(*embuste*) fabrication

marasmo *m* 1.(*debilitamiento*) weakening 2.(*inmovilidad*) paralysis

maratón *m o f* marathon; la reunión fue verdaderamente un ~ the meeting was a real marathon

maravilla *f* 1.(*portento*) marvel; a las mil ~s, de ~ marvellously *Brit*, marvelously *Am;* hablar ~s de alguien to speak extremely well of sb; hacer ~s *fig* to work wonders 2.(*admiración*) wonder 3. BOT (*caléndula*) marigold

maravillar I. *vt* to amaze II. *vr* ~se de algo to marvel at sth

maravilloso, -a *adj* marvellous *Brit*, marvelous *Am*

marbellí I. *adj* of/from Marbella II. *mf* native/inhabitant of Marbella

marca *f* 1.(*distintivo*) mark; ~ de agua watermark; ~ de ganado brand 2.(*de productos*) brand; ~ registrada registered trademark; ropa de ~ designer label; un idiota de ~ mayor a complete idiot 3.(*huella*) impression 4. DEP record 5.(*medida*) measurement 6. INFOR bookmark

marcadamente *adv* 1.(*claramente*) clearly 2.(*singularmente*) markedly 3.(*con énfasis*) emphatically

marcado, -a *adj* 1.(*señalado*) marked 2.(*evidente*) clear 3.(*singular*) singular 4.(*enfático*) emphatic

marcador *m* 1.(*tablero*) scoreboard; abrir el ~ to open the scoring; cerraron el ~ con tres tantos they finished the game with three goals 2. *Arg* (*rotulador*) marker pen

marcaje *m* DEP marking, cover(age)

marcapaso(s) *m* (*inv*) pacemaker

marcar <c→qu> I. *vt* 1.(*señalar*) to mark; (*ganado*) to brand; (*mercancías*) to label; ~ una época to denote an era; ~ el compás to beat time 2.(*resaltar*) to emphasize 3.(*teléfono*) to dial 4.(*cabello*) to style 5. DEP ~ un gol to score a goal; ~ un punto to score a point 6. DEP (*a un jugador*) to mark, to cover II. *vr:* ~se to show

marcha *f* 1.(*movimiento*) progress; poner en ~ to start 2.(*caminata*) hike 3.(*curso*) course; ~ de los negocios business trend; la ~ de los acontecimientos the course of events; sobre la ~ along the way 4.(*velocidad*) gear; ~ atrás reverse; a toda ~ at full speed 5. *t.* MIL, MÚS march; ~ silenciosa silent march 6.(*salida*) departure; ¡en ~! let's go! 7. *inf* (*acción*) action; ¡aquí hay mucha ~! this is where the action is!; ir de ~ to go out on the town; tener ~ to be full of go

marchamo *m* 1.(*aduanas*) customs stamp 2.(*embutidos*) tag

marchante I. *adj* commercial II. *mf* dealer; ~ de obras de arte art dealer

marchantía *f* *AmC, PRico, Ven* clientele

marchar I. *vi* 1.(*ir*) to go; ¡marchando! let's go! 2.(*funcionar*) to work; ~ sobre ruedas *fig* to go like clockwork II. *vr:* ~se 1.(*irse*) to leave; ¿os marcháis? are you leaving? 2.(*huir*) to flee; ~se del país to flee the country

marchitar I. *vi* 1.(*plantas*) to wither 2.(*personas*) to be on the wane II. *vr:* ~se to wither

marchito, -a *adj* withered

marchoso, -a *adj inf* 1.(*salidor*) fun-loving 2.(*elegante*) elegant

marcial *adj* martial; artes ~es martial arts; ley ~ martial law

marcianitos *mpl inf* little green men *pl*

marciano, -a *adj, m, f* Martian

marco *m* 1.(*recuadro*) frame; (*armazón*)

framework; **el ~ legal** the legal framework **2.**(*ambiente*) background **3.**(*moneda*) mark

marea *f* **1.**(*mar*) tide; **~ alta** high tide; **~ baja** low tide; **~ creciente** rising tide; **~ menguante** ebb tide; **~ negra** oil slick [*o* spill]; **~ viva** spring tide **2.**(*multitud*) flood; **una ~ humana** a flood of people

mareado, -a *adj* **1.**(*indispuesto*) sick; (*en el mar*) seasick; (*en el coche*) carsick; (*al viajar*) travel-sick; **estoy ~** I feel sick **2.**(*aturdido*) dizzy; *fig* confused **3.**(*bebido*) tipsy

marear I. *vt* **1.** *inf* (*molestar*) to pester **2.** MED to nauseate **3.**(*aturdir*) to make dizzy; *fig* to confuse **II.** *vr:* **~se 1.**(*enfermarse*) to feel sick; (*en el mar*) to get seasick; (*al viajar*) to get travel-sick **2.**(*quedar aturdido*) to become dizzy; *fig* to become confused **3.**(*emborracharse*) to get tipsy

marejada *f* swell; *fig* unrest

maremagno *m,* **maremágnum** *m inv* **1.**(*multitud*) multitude **2.**(*confusión*) commotion

maremoto *m* tidal wave; (*seísmo*) seaquake

mareo *m* **1.**(*malestar*) nausea; (*en el mar*) seasickness; (*al viajar*) travel-sickness, motion sickness **2.**(*vértigo*) dizziness; **¡qué ~ de hombre!** *inf* what a nuisance that man is!

marfil *m* **1.**(*elefante*) ivory **2.**(*dentadura*) dentine

marfileño, -a I. *adj* **1.**(*nacionalidad*) of/from the Ivory Coast **2.**(*material*) ivory-like **II.** *m, f* native/inhabitant of the Ivory Coast

margarina *f* margarine

margarita *f* **1.** BOT daisy; **deshojar la ~** to play 'she loves me, she loves me not' **2.**(*bebida*) margarita **3.** ZOOL periwinkle **4.**(*perla*) pearl; **echar ~s a puercos** to cast pearls before swine **5.** TIPO daisywheel

margen *m o f* **1.**(*borde*) edge; **el ~ del río** the riverside [*o* riverbank]; **al ~** apart; **dejar al ~** to leave out; **mantenerse al ~ de algo** *fig* to keep out of sth **2.**(*página*) margin **3.**(*libertad*) leeway; **dar ~** to give leeway **4.**(*ganancia*) profit margin; **~ de costos** margin of costs; **~ de seguridad** safety margin

marginado, -a I. *adj* **1.**(*excluido*) excluded, marginalized **2.**(*aislado*) isolated **II.** *m, f* outcast

marginal *adj* **1.**(*al margen*) apart **2.**(*secundario*) secondary

marginar *vt* **1.**(*ignorar algo*) to disregard; (*a alguien*) to marginalize **2.**(*acotar*) to annotate in the margin

maría *f* **1.** *inf* (*ama de casa*) housewife **2.** *inf* (*marihuana*) grass, pot **3.** *inf* ENS easy subject

mariachi *m Méx* mariachi musician

marica *m vulg* **1.**(*homosexual*) queer, poof *Brit,* fag *Am* **2.**(*cobarde*) sissy **3.**(*insulto grosero*) berk *Brit,* asshole *Am*

Maricastaña *f* **tiempos de ~** *inf* years ago; **desde los tiempos de ~** from the year dot; **este chiste es de los tiempos de ~** that joke is as old as the hills

maricón *m vulg v.* **marica**

mariconada *f vulg* **1.**(*acción malintencionada*) dirty trick; **hacer una ~ a alguien** to play a dirty trick on sb **2.**(*tontería*) silly [*o* poncy *Brit*] thing to do

marido *m* husband; **mi ~** my husband

mariguana, marihuana *f sin pl* marijuana, marihuana

marimacho *m inf* butch (woman); (*niña*) tomboy; *pey* (*lesbiana*) dyke

marimandón, -ona *m, f inf* bossy boots

marimba *f* **1.** MÚS (*de maderas*) marimba **2.** MÚS (*tambor*) African drum **3.** *Arg* (*paliza*) beating

marimorena *f inf* rumpus; **armar la ~** to kick up a fuss; **se armó la ~** all Hell broke loose

marina *f* **1.**(*flota*) navy; **la ~ mercante** the merchant marine **2.** ARTE seascape **3.** GEO coastal region

marinera *f* **1.**(*blusa*) middy blouse **2.** *And* (*baile*) popular folk dance

marinero *m* sailor; **~ de agua dulce** *irón* landlubber

marinero, -a *adj* **1.**(*relativo al mar*) marine; **buque ~** seagoing boat; **pueblo ~** coastal town; **pescado a la marinera** fish in a sauce with tomatoes, mussels and wine **2.**(*relativo a la marina*) marine; **nudo ~** sailor's knot

marino *m* (*navegante*) sailor, seaman

marino, -a *adj* marine

marioneta *f* **1.**(*títere*) puppet, marionette **2.** *pl* (*teatro*) puppet show

mariposa *f* **1.** ZOOL butterfly; **~ nocturna** moth **2.**(*lámpara*) lamp (*wick floating in oil*) **3.** DEP butterfly stroke **4.** *pey* (*afeminado*) pansy ►**¡a otra cosa ~!** let's talk about something else!

mariposear *vi* **1.**(*ser inconstante*) to be fickle **2.**(*flirtear*) to flirt **3.**(*rondar*) **~ a alguien** to dance attendance on sb

mariquita[1] *f* ZOOL **1.**(*insecto*) ladybird **2.**(*perico*) parakeet

mariquita[2] *m inf* poof *Brit,* fag *Am*

marisabidilla *f inf* know-all

mariscal *m* marshal

marisco *m* seafood

marisma *f* marsh

marisquería *f* **1.**(*tienda*) seafood shop **2.**(*restaurante*) seafood restaurant

marital *adj* marital; **vida ~** married life

maritatas *fpl Guat, Hond* junk

marítimo, -a *adj* maritime, marine; **ciudad marítima** seaside town; **seguro ~** marine insurance

marjal *m* fen

marmita *f* pot

mármol *m* marble; **frío como el ~** as cold as stone; **de ~** of marble

marmóreo, -a *adj* marble(-like)

marmota *f* **1.** ZOOL marmot; **~ de América** groundhog **2.** *inf* (*dormilón*) sleepyhead **3.** *pey* (*criada*) maid

maroma *f* **1.**(*cuerda*) rope **2.** *AmL* (*pirueta*) somersault **3.** *AmL* (*cambio de partido político*) change of political allegiance; (*de opinión*) change of opinion

maromo *m inf* guy, bloke *Brit*

marqués, -esa *m, f* marquis *m,* marquise *f*

marquesina *f* (glass) canopy, marquee

marquetería *f* marquetry; (*ebanistería*) cabinet-making

marrajo *m* shark

marrajo, -a *adj* (*toro*) vicious; (*persona*) crafty

marrana *f* **1.** (*cerda*) sow **2.** *pey, inf* (*mujer sucia*) slut; (*vil*) despicable woman

marranada *f inf* filthiness; (*acción*) a dirty trick

marrano *m* **1.** (*cerdo*) pig **2.** *pey, inf* (*hombre sucio*) dirty man; (*grosero*) rude man; (*vil*) despicable man

marrano, -a *adj* filthy

marrar *vi* **1.** (*errar*) to miss; ~ **el golpe** *fig* to miss the mark **2.** (*desviarse*) to stray

marras *adv* **tema de** ~ the same old subject; **la persona de** ~ the person in question; **lo de** ~ the same old thing

marrón **I.** *adj* brown **II.** *m* **1.** (*color*) brown **2.** *AmC* (*martillo*) hammer

marroquí *adj, mf* Moroccan

Marruecos *m* Morocco

marrullería *f* flattery; **déjate de** ~**s** cut the flattery; (*labia*) glibness

marrullero, -a **I.** *adj* flattering; (*con labia*) glib **II.** *m, f* flatterer

Marsella *f* Marseilles

marsellés, -esa *adj, m, f* Marseillaise

marsopa *f* porpoise

marsupial **I.** *adj* **animal** ~ marsupial **II.** *m* marsupial

marta *f* **1.** ZOOL marten; ~ **cebellina** sable **2.** (*piel*) sable

Marte *m* Mars

martes *m inv* Tuesday; ~ **y trece** Friday the thirteenth; *v.t.* **lunes**

martill(e)ar *vt* **1.** (*golpear*) to hammer **2.** (*atormentar*) to torment **3.** (*repetir*) to repeat

martilleo *m* hammering

martillero *m* *Arg, Chile* auctioneer

martillo *m* **1.** (*herramienta*) hammer; ANAT malleus; **creer algo a macha** ~ to firmly believe sth; **repetir algo a macha** ~ to repeat sth ad nauseam **2. pez** ~ hammerhead **3.** (*subasta*) gavel

martín *m* ~ **pescador** kingfisher; ~ **del río** heron

martinete *m* **1.** ZOOL heron **2.** MÚS (*macillo*) hammer **3.** (*mazo*) hammer; (*para clavar estacas*) sledgehammer

martingala *f inf* sly trick, dodge

mártir *mf* martyr

martirio *m* REL martyrdom; *fig* torture

martirizar <z→c> *vt* to torture

maruja *f pey, inf* housewife (*used to refer to women whose sole interests are their homes,*

family, personal appearance and gossip)

marxismo *m* Marxism

marxista *adj, mf* Marxist

marzo *m* March; **en** ~ in March; **a principios/a mediados/a fin(al)es de** ~ at the beginning/in the middle/at the end of March; **el 21 de** ~ the 21st of March; **el mes de** ~ **tiene 31 días** the month of March has 31 days; **el pasado** ~ **fue muy frío** last March was very cold

mas **I.** *m* manor **II.** *conj* LIT but, yet

más **I.** *adv* **1.** (*cantidad*) more; ~ **dinero/zapatos** more money/shoes **2.** (*comparativo*) more; ~ **inteligente/complicado** more intelligent/complicated; ~ **grande/pequeño** bigger/smaller; ~ **temprano/tarde** earlier/later; **correr** ~ to run more; **esto me gusta** ~ I like this better; ~ **acá** closer; ~ **adelante** (*local*) further forward [*o* on]; (*temporal*) later; **es** ~ **guapo que tú** he is more handsome than you; **cada día** [*o* **vez**] ~ more and more; **cuanto** ~ **mejor** the more the merrier; ~ **allá de esto** beyond this; ~ **de la cuenta** too much **3.** (*superlativo*) **el/la** ~ the most; **la** ~ **bella** the most beautiful; **el** ~ **listo de la clase** the cleverest in the class; **el modelo que** ~ **se lleva** the model that is most in fashion; **lo que** ~ **me gusta** what I most like [*o* like most]; **lo que** ~ **quieras** what you most want; **lo** ~ **probable es que llueva** it is likely to rain; **lo** ~ **pronto posible** as early as possible; ~ **que nunca** more than ever; **a lo** ~ at (the) most; **a** ~ **no poder** to the utmost; **a** ~ **tardar** at the latest; **todo lo** ~ at most **4.** (*con numerales, cantidad*) ~ **de treinta** more than thirty; **son** ~ **de las diez** it is after ten **5.** (*preferencia*) ~ **quiero la muerte que la esclavitud** I prefer death to slavery **6.** (*tan*) ¡**está** ~ **guapa!** you look so beautiful; ¡**qué tarde** ~ **apacible!** what a peaceful afternoon! **7.** (*con pronombre interrogativo, indefinido*) ¿**algo** ~? anything else?; **no, nada** ~ no, nothing else **8.** (*en frases negativas*) **no puedo** ~ I have had it; **nunca** ~ never again **9.** MAT plus; **tengo tres libros,** ~ **los que he prestado** I have three books, plus those I have lent **10.** (*a* **más**) **a** ~ **y mejor** really; **llueve a** ~ **y mejor** it is raining with a vengeance; **divertirse a** ~ **y mejor** to have a really good time **11.** (*de* **más**) **de** ~ spare, more than enough; **hay comida de** ~ there is food to spare; **estar de** ~ not to be needed; **de lo** ~ very **12.** (**más bien**) ~ **bien** rather; **no es muy delgado; es** ~ **bien gordo** he is not very thin; rather he is fat **13.** (**más o menos**) ¿**cómo te ha ido?** – ~ **o menos** how did it go? – so-so; ~ **o menos** (*aproximadamente*) more or less; **le va** ~ **o menos** he is doing so-so; **ni** ~ **ni menos** exactly **14.** (*por* **más** *que*) **por** ~ **que lo intento, no consigo dormirme** however hard I try, I cannot sleep ►**tener sus** ~ **y sus menos** to have one's good and one's bad points; **sin** ~ **acá ni** ~ **allá** without more ado; **el** ~ **allá** the beyond; **el que** ~ **y el que**

menos every single one; **quien ~ y quien menos** everyone; **es ~, ~ aún** what is more; **el no va ~** the last word; **el no va ~ (de la moda)** the latest fashion; **como el que ~** as well as the next man; **sin ~ ni ~** without more ado; **¿qué ~ da?** what difference does it make? II. *m* MAT plus sign

masa *f* **1.** (*pasta*) mixture; (*para hornear*) dough; **coger a alguien con las manos en la ~** to catch sb red-handed **2.** (*volumen, muchedumbre*) mass; **~ monetaria** money supply; **medios de comunicación de ~s** mass media; **en ~** en masse **3.** ELEC earth *Brit*, ground *Am*

masacrar *vt* to massacre

masacre *f* massacre

masaje *m* massage; **dar ~s** to massage; **darse ~s** to be massaged

masajista *mf* masseur *m*, masseuse *f*

masato *m AmS* GASTR **1.** (*mazamorra*) coconut sweet **2.** (*bebida*) *fermented maize or rice drink*

mascada *f* **1.** *AmL* (*tabaco*) *quid of chewing tobacco* **2.** (*boxeo*) uppercut **3.** *Col, Cuba, Chile* (*bocado*) bite **4.** *Méx* (*pañuelo*) silk kerchief

mascar <c→qu> *vt* **1.** (*masticar*) to chew **2.** (*mascullar*) to mumble **3.** (*presentir*) to have a premonition

máscara *f* **1.** (*careta*) mask; **traje de ~** fancy dress; **quitar la ~ a alguien** *fig* to unmask sb; **quitarse la ~** *fig* to reveal oneself **2.** *pl* (*fiesta*) fancy dress party **3.** (*enmascarado*) masquerade; (*de Carnaval*) carnival

mascarada *f* **1.** (*baile*) masquerade **2.** (*farsa*) farce

mascarilla *f* **1.** (*máscara*) mask **2.** (*protección*) face mask **3.** (*cosmética*) **~ exfoliante** face scrub; **~ facial** face pack **4.** (*molde*) cast

mascota *f* mascot; (*animal de compañía*) pet

masculinidad *f* masculinity

masculino *m* LING masculine

masculino, -a *adj* **1.** (*aspecto, rasgos*) masculine; **moda masculina** men's fashion **2.** LING **género ~** masculine form

mascullar *vt* to mumble

masía *f* manor house

masificación *f* overcrowding

masilla *f* putty

masita *f AmS* GASTR small cake

masivo, -a *adj* **1.** (*grande*) massive **2.** (*fuerte*) strong **3.** (*de masas*) mass

masón, -ona *m, f* Mason, Freemason

masoquista I. *adj* masochistic II. *mf* masochist

mastectomía *f* mastectomy

máster <másters> *m* master's degree

masticar <c→qu> *vt* **1.** (*mascar*) to chew **2.** (*meditar*) to ponder

mástil *m* **1.** NÁUT mast, spar **2.** (*poste*) post, pole **3.** MÚS (*guitarra, violín*) neck

mastín *m* mastiff

mastuerzo *m* **1.** BOT cress **2.** (*hombre*) idiot

masturbación *f* masturbation

masturbarse *vr* to masturbate

mata *f* **1.** (*matorral*) clump **2.** (*planta*) plant; (*arbusto*) bush **3.** *pl, inf* (*cabellera*) mop of hair

matadero *m* **1.** (*desolladero*) slaughterhouse; **ir al ~** *fig* to put one's life in danger; **llevar al ~** *fig* to send sb to his/her death **2.** (*fatiga*) strain

matador(a) I. *adj* **1.** (*que mata*) killer **2.** (*cansador*) killing **3.** *inf* (*ridículo*) ludicrous II. *m(f)* **1.** TAUR matador **2.** (*asesino*) killer

matamoscas *m inv* **1.** (*insecticida*) fly-spray **2.** (*objeto*) fly-swat **3.** (*trampa*) flypaper

matanza *f* **1.** (*el matar*) killing **2.** (*en batallas*) slaughter; **hacer una ~** to massacre **3.** (*carneada*) slaughter; **hacer la ~** to slaughter an animal **4.** GASTR cured pork products *pl*

matar I. *vt* **1.** (*quitar la vida*) to kill; **~ a golpes** to beat to death; **~ a palos** to club to death; **~ a puñaladas** to knife [*o* stab] to death; **~ a tiros** to shoot dead; **que me maten si yo esperaba una cosa así** *inf* I swear on my mother's grave that I didn't expect this **2.** (*carnear*) to slaughter **3.** (*saciar*) to assuage; (*hambre*) to satisfy; (*sed*) to quench **4.** (*luz, fuego*) to put out **5.** (*sellos*) to postmark **6.** (*redondear*) to round off **7.** (*naipes*) to top **8.** (*color, brillo*) to tone down **9.** (*acabar con alguien*) **~ a disgustos** to be the death of **10.** (*aniquilar*) to be the end of; (*el tiempo*) to kill; (*el aburrimiento, nerviosismo*) to alleviate **11.** (*molestar*) to annoy; **~ a preguntas a alguien** to drive sb mad with questions II. *vr:* **~se 1.** (*suicidarse*) to kill oneself **2.** (*aniquilarse*) **te estás matando trabajando así** you are wearing yourself out working like that **3.** (*trabajar sin descanso*) **~se a trabajar** to work oneself to death; **~se por algo** to go out of one's way to do sth

matarife *mf* butcher

matarratas *m inv* **1.** (*raticida*) rat poison **2.** *pey, inf* (*aguardiente*) firewater; (*alcohol de mala calidad*) rotgut, hooch

matasanos *mf inv, irón, inf* quack

matasellos *m inv* postmark

matasuegras *m inv, inf* party blower

matazón *m AmL* (*matanza*) massacre

match *m* match

mate I. *adj* dull II. *m* **1.** (*ajedrez*) mate; **jaque ~** checkmate **2.** (*acabado*) matte **3.** *pl inf* (*matemáticas*) maths *Brit*, math *Am* **4.** *AmS* (*bebida*) maté tea (*herbal infusion drunk from a gourd*)

In South America **mate** means: 1. The maté plant, 2. The leaves of the maté plant, from which tea is made, 3. The tea itself, and 4. A container in which the tea is kept.

matemáticas *fpl* mathematics

matemático, -a I. *adj* mathematical II. *m, f*

mathematician

materia *f* **1.** *t.* FÍS (*substancia*) matter; ~ **gris** ANAT grey matter; ~ **prima** raw material **2.** (*tema*) subject, matter; **en** ~ **de** in the matter of **3.** *t.* ENS (*disciplina*) subject; ~ **penal** JUR penal matter

material I. *adj* (*real*) tangible; **daño** ~ physical damage; **el autor** ~ **del hecho** the actual perpetrator of the deed **II.** *m* material; ~**es de construcción** building materials; ~ **de enseñanza** teaching material; ~ **de oficina** office equipment

materialismo *m* materialism

materialista I. *adj* materialistic **II.** *mf* materialist

materializar <z→c> **I.** *vt* **1.** (*hacer material*) to bring into being **2.** (*realizar*) to carry out **3.** (*hacer aparecer*) to produce **II.** *vr:* ~**se** to materialize

materialmente *adv* materially; **ser** ~ **posible** to be physically possible

maternal *adj* maternal, motherly

maternidad *f* **1.** (*el ser madre*) maternity **2.** (*hospital*) maternity hospital; (*sala*) maternity ward

materno, -a *adj* maternal; **abuelo** ~ maternal grandfather; **lengua materna** mother tongue

matero, -a I. *adj* AmS mate-drinking **II.** *m, f* mate-drinker

matinal *adj* morning; **sesión** ~ (*congreso, conferencia*) morning session; CINE, TEAT matinee

matiné *f* matinée

matiz *m* **1.** (*gradación*) shade **2.** (*toque*) touch **3.** (*sentido*) nuance

matizar <z→c> *vt* **1.** (*combinar colores o tonos*) to blend; ~ **de rojo** to tinge with red **2.** (*graduar*) to tint **3.** (*de un sentido*) to tinge; ~ **una frase de significado irónico** to give a sentence an ironical slant; (*concretar*) to specify

matón, -ona *m, f* **1.** (*chulo*) bully **2.** (*guardaespaldas*) bodyguard **3.** (*asesino*) murderer

matorral *m* thicket

matraca *f* **1.** (*carraca*) rattle, noisemaker **2.** *inf* (*fastidio*) **dar la** ~ to pester; **ser** ~ to be a bore

matraz *m* flask

matrero, -a *adj* **1.** (*astuto*) cunning **2.** (*receloso*) suspicious **3.** (*engañoso*) deceitful **4.** AmS (*fugitivo*) fugitive

matrícula *f* **1.** (*documento*) registration document **2.** (*inscripción*) enrolment *Brit,* enrollment *Am;* UNIV matriculation **3.** AUTO (*placa*) number plate *Brit,* license plate *Am;* **número de la** ~ registration number *Brit,* license number *Am* **4.** (*lista*) register **5.** (*conjunto de alumnos*) student enrolment *Brit,* enrollment *Am* **6.** ENS **aprobar con** ~ **de honor** to pass with distinction [*o* with highest honors *Am*] (*allowing student free enrolment in a subject for the following course*)

matricular I. *vt* to register; UNIV to enrol *Brit,* to enroll *Am* **II.** *vr* ~**se en la universidad** to enrol in the university

matrimonial *adj* matrimonial, marriage; **agencia** ~ dating agency; **vida** ~ married life

matrimonio *m* **1.** marriage; ~ **canónico** church wedding; ~ **civil** civil wedding; **consumar el** ~ to consummate the marriage; **contraer** ~ to marry **2.** (*marido y mujer*) married couple; **cama de** ~ double bed

matriz I. *f* **1.** (*útero*) womb **2.** (*molde*) cast **3.** TIPO, MAT matrix **4.** (*de un talonario*) stub **II.** *adj* **la casa** ~ **está en Sevilla** the parent company is in Seville; **lengua** ~ primal language

matrona *f* **1.** (*comadrona*) midwife **2.** (*de familia*) matron

maturrango, -a I. *adj* **1.** AmS (*mal jinete*) **ser** ~ to be a poor rider **2.** Chile (*tosco*) clumsy **II.** *m, f* AmS (*mal jinete*) poor horserider

matute *m* **1.** (*contrabando*) smuggling; **de** ~ *fig* clandestinely; **pasar de** ~ to pass clandestinely; **viajar de** ~ to travel clandestinely **2.** (*género*) contraband

matutino, -a *adj* morning; **periódico** ~ morning paper; **sesión matutina** morning session

maula¹ *mf* *inf* **1.** (*tramposo*) cheat **2.** (*inútil*) good-for-nothing

maula² *f* **1.** (*baratija*) a piece of junk; **este coche es una** ~ this car is a piece of junk **2.** (*engaño*) trick

maullar *irr como aullar vi* to miaow *Brit,* to meow *Am*

maullido *m* miaow *Brit,* meow *Am*

mauritano, -a *adj, m, f* Mauritanian

mausoleo *m* mausoleum

maxilar I. *adj* ANAT maxillary **II.** *m* jaw

máxima *f* maxim

máxime *adv* particularly

máximo, -a I. *adj* maximum; **rendimiento** ~ maximum output; **triunfo** ~ greatest triumph; **pon la radio al** ~ turn the radio as high as it goes **II.** *m, f* maximum; **como** ~ at most; (*temporal*) at the latest

maya¹ *f* BOT daisy

maya² *adj, m* Mayan

The **mayas** were an Indian race of people native to Central America (present-day Mexico, Guatemala and Honduras) with a civilisation that was highly advanced in many fields. The great number of ruins bears witness to this fact, such as the pyramids constructed from blocks of stone, numerous inscriptions and drawings, and not least the very accurate calendar that these people possessed.

---

mayestático, -a *adj* majestic; **plural** ~ the royal we

mayo *m* **1.** (*mes*) May; *v.t.* **marzo 2.** (*árbol*) maypole

mayonesa *f* mayonnaise

mayor I. *adj* **1.** (*tamaño*) bigger; **la** ~ **parte**

the majority, most; **el ~ barco** the largest boat; **mal ~** greater evil; **~ que** bigger than; **comercio al por ~** wholesale trade; **se repartieron palos al por ~** *fig* many blows were dealt **2.** (*edad*) older; **~ que** older than; **mi hermano ~** my older [*o* big] brother; **el ~ de mis hermanos** the eldest of my brothers and sisters; **ser ~** to be grown-up; **ser ~ de edad** to be an adult, to be of legal age; **persona ~** elderly person; **los ~es** the adults, the grown--ups; **ya es ~ para esos juguetes** he/she is too old for [*o* has outgrown] those toys **3.** MÚS major; **tono ~** major key; **tercera ~** major third; **escala en do ~** scale of C major **II.** *m* **1.** MIL major **2.** (*superior*) superior **3.** *pl* (*ascendientes*) ancestors *pl*

mayoral *m* (*capataz*) foreman

mayorcito, -a *adj inf* ¡si ya eres ~! what a big boy/girl you are now!; ¿no crees que ya eres mayor para eso? don't you think you are a little too old for that?

mayordomo, -a *m, f* administrator; (*de una mansión*) butler

mayoría *f* majority; **~ de edad** (age of) majority; **llegar a la ~ de edad** to come of age; **~ relativa** relative majority; **la ~ tiene un coche** most [*o* the majority] have a car

mayorista I. *adj* wholesale; **comercio ~** wholesale business **II.** *mf* wholesaler

mayoritariamente *adv* mainly, preponderantly *form*

mayoritario, -a *adj* majority; **tener el apoyo ~** to have majority support

mayormente *adv* especially, particularly

mayúscula *f* capital (letter); **escribirse con ~** to be written with a capital (letter)

mayúsculo, -a *adj* (*grande*) big; **letra mayúscula** capital letter

maza *f* **1.** (*porra*) club **2.** (*para machacar*) pestle **3.** (*percusor*) hammer

mazacote *m* **1.** (*hormigón*) concrete; **esta esponja está hecha un ~** this sponge is rock hard **2.** *inf* (*comida*) stodge

mazacotudo, -a *adj AmL* dense

mazapán *m* marzipan

mazazo *m* blow; **dar ~s a alguien** *fig* to hurt sb; **la muerte de su hijo fue un ~ para él** the death of his son was a terrible blow for him

mazmorra *f* dungeon

mazo *m* **1.** (*martillo*) mallet **2.** (*del mortero*) pestle; (*grande*) sledgehammer **3.** (*manojo*) bundle

mazorca *f* (*del maíz*) cob; (*del cacao*) pod; **~ de maíz** corncob, ear of corn

me I. *pron pers* **1.** (*objeto directo*) me; ¡míra~! look at me! **2.** (*objeto indirecto*) me; **da~ el libro** give me the book **II.** *pron reflexivo* **~ lavo** I wash myself; **~ voy** I am going; **~ he comprado un piso** I have bought myself a flat; **~ lavo el pelo** I wash my hair

meada *f* **1.** *inf* (*pis*) wee, pee; **echar una ~** to take a piss **2.** (*mancha de orina*) piss; **aquí hay una ~ de gato** a cat has pissed here

meadero *m vulg* bog *Brit*

meandro *m* (*curva*) meander

mear *vi, vr:* **~se** *inf* to piss; **el niño se ha meado en el pantalón** the boy has peed (in) his pants; **~se de risa** to die laughing

meato *m* ANAT meatus; **~ auditivo** auditory meatus; **~ urinario** urinary meatus

mecánica *f* mechanics

mecánico, -a I. *adj* mechanical **II.** *m, f* mechanic

mecanismo *m* mechanism; (*dispositivo*) device

mecanizar <z→c> *vt* **1.** (*automatizar*) to mechanize **2.** (*elaborar*) to shape

mecano® *m* (*juguete*) Meccano®

mecanografía *f* typewriting

mecanógrafo, -a *m, f* typist

mecate *m AmC, Col, Méx, Ven* (*cuerda*) rope

mecedora *f* rocking chair

mecenas *mf inv* patron

mecer <c→z> **I.** *vt* **1.** (*balancear*) to rock; (*columpiar*) to swing **2.** (*menear*) to move **II.** *vr:* **~se 1.** (*balancearse*) to rock; (*columpiarse*) to swing **2.** (*menearse*) to move

mecha *f* **1.** (*pabilo*) wick; (*de explosivos*) fuse **2.** (*gasa*) swab **3.** (*mechón*) tuft **4.** *pl* (*mechones teñidos*) highlights *pl*, streaks *pl*; **hacerse ~s** to have highlights [*o* streaks] put in **5.** (*tocino*) streak **6.** *inf* (*prisa*) **a toda ~** very fast **7.** *inf* (*fastidio*) **aguantar ~** to grin and bear it

mechero *m* **1.** (*encendedor*) lighter **2.** (*quemador*) burner

mechificar <c→qu> *vi AmS* to trick

mechón *m* tuft

mechudo, -a *adj AmL* (*desgreñado*) unkempt

meco, -a *adj* **1.** *Méx* (*grosero*) rude **2.** *Méx* (*bermejo con negro*) blackish red; **toro ~** blackish red bull

medalla *f* medal; **~ militar** military decoration

medallista *mf* (*ganador*) medal winner, medallist *Brit*, medalist *Am*

medallón *m* medallion

médano *m,* **medaño** *m* **1.** (*duna*) dune **2.** (*bajío*) sandbank

media *f* **1.** (*promedio*) average **2.** (*calceta*) stocking; *AmL* (*calcetín*) sock

mediacaña *f* bead

mediación *f* mediation

mediado, -a *adj* (*medio lleno*) half full; (*trabajo*) half-completed; **para ~s de semana** by the middle of the week [*o* by midweek]

mediador(a) *m(f)* mediator

mediana *f* **1.** AUTO central reservation *Brit,* median strip *Am* **2.** MAT median

medianero, -a I. *adj* (*en medio*) **pared medianera** party [*o* dividing] wall **II.** *m, f* (*intermediario*) mediator

medianía *f* **1.** (*término medio*) average **2.** (*mediocridad*) mediocrity **3.** (*persona*) **ser una ~** (*inteligencia*) to not be very bright

mediano, -a adj **1.** (calidad) average **2.** (tamaño) medium; **talla mediana** medium **3.** ECON medium-sized
medianoche f **1.** (hora) midnight; **a** ~ at midnight **2.** (panecillo) small soft roll
mediante I. adj Dios ~ God willing **II.** prep by means of; (a través de) through
mediar vi **1.** (intermediar) to mediate **2.** (interceder) ~ **por alguien** to intercede on behalf of sb **3.** (realizar hasta la mitad) to half do **4.** (interponerse) to intervene **5.** (transcurrir) to happen **6.** (existir) to exist; **entre tú y yo media un abismo** there is a world of difference between you and me
mediato, -a adj next but one
medicación f medication
medicamento m medicine
medicar <c→qu> **I.** vt to medicate; (recetar) to prescribe **II.** vr: ~**se** to take medicine
medicina f medicine; **la** ~ **naturista** natural remedies
medicinal adj medicinal; **balón** ~ medicine ball; **hierba** ~ medicinal plant
medición f measurement
médico, -a I. adj medical; **cuerpo** ~ medical corps **II.** m, f doctor; **Colegio de Médicos** Medical Association; ~ **de cabecera** general practitioner; ~ **forense** forensic surgeon; ~ **naturista** homeopath
medida f **1.** (medición) measurement **2.** (dimensión) measurement; **a la** ~ (ropa) made-to-measure; **tomar la(s)** ~**(s)** to take the measurement(s); **hasta cierta** ~ up to a point; **en la** ~ **de lo posible** as far as possible; **a** ~ **que** as **3.** LIT metre Brit, meter Am **4.** (prudencia) prudence; **con** ~ with care **5.** (moderación) moderation; **sin** ~ without moderation **6.** (acción) measure; **tomar** ~**s** to take measures ► **¡vaya** ~ **de pata!** AmL, inf what a clanger Brit [o blooper Am]!
medidor m **1.** (instrumento) gauge **2.** AmL (contador) meter
medidor(a) I. adj measuring; **reloj** ~ stopwatch **II.** m(f) gauge Brit, gage Am
medieval adj medieval
medio m **1.** (mitad) middle; **en** ~ **de** in the middle of; **en** ~ **de todo** in the middle of it all; **meterse por** ~ to intervene; **quitar de en** ~ to get rid of; **quitarse de en** ~ to get out of the way; **de** ~ **a** ~ smack on **2.** (instrumento) means; ~ **de transporte** means of transport; **por** ~ **de** by means of **3.** PREN, RADIO, TV medium; ~**s de comunicación** the media **4.** (entorno) surroundings pl; ~ **ambiente** environment **5.** DEP halfback **6.** Cuba (moneda) five cent coin **7.** pl (fuentes) sources pl **8.** pl (capital) means pl; **estar corto de** ~**s** to be hard-up
medio, -a I. adj **1.** (mitad) half; **a las cuatro y media** at half past four; **litro y** ~ one and a half litres Brit [o liters Am]; **mi media naranja** fig my other half **2.** (promedio) **ciudadano** ~ average person **II.** adv half; ~ **vestido** half

dressed; **a** ~ **asar** half done; ~ **dormido, dormido a medias** half asleep; **tomar a medias** to share; **ir a medias** to go halves
medioambiental adj environmental
mediocre adj mediocre
mediocridad f mediocrity
mediodía m **1.** (hora) midday; **al** ~ at noon **2.** (sur) south
medir irr como pedir **I.** vt **1.** (calcular) to measure; **¿cuánto mides?** how tall are you? **2.** (sopesar) to weigh; ~ **los riesgos** to weigh up the risks **3.** (moderar) to moderate **II.** vi to measure **III.** vr: ~**se** to be moderate; ~**se con alguien** to measure oneself against sb
meditabundo, -a adj meditative
meditación f meditation
meditar vt, vi to meditate
mediterráneo, -a adj Mediterranean; **isla mediterránea** Mediterranean island
Mediterráneo m Mediterranean
medrar vi **1.** (crecer) to grow **2.** (avanzar) to thrive
medroso, -a I. adj **1.** estar frightened **2.** ser apprehensive **II.** m, f coward
médula f **1.** ANAT marrow; ~ **espinal** spinal cord **2.** BOT pith **3.** (meollo) core; **hasta la** ~ to the core; **hay que llegar a la** ~ **de las cosas** you have to get to the core of the matter; **estar hasta la** ~ inf to be fed up
medular adj **1.** (tuétano) marrow; (médula espinal) spinal **2.** (esencial) essential; **parte** ~ fundamental part
medusa f jellyfish
mefítico, -a adj **1.** (dañino) contaminated, noxious **2.** (fétido) fetid
megaciclo m megacycle
megáfono m megaphone
megalomanía f megalomania
megalómano, -a adj megalomaniac
megavatio m megawatt
mejicano, -a adj, m, f Mexican
Méjico m Mexico
mejilla f cheek; **poner la otra** ~ to turn the other cheek
mejillón m mussel
mejor I. adj **1.** (compar) better; ~ **que** better than; **es** ~ **que no vayas** +subj it is better that you don't go; **cambiar a** ~ to change for the better; **pasar a** ~ **vida** to pass away **2.** (superl) **el/la/lo** ~ the best; **el** ~ **alumno** the best student; **la** ~ **nota** the best mark; ~ **postor** highest bidder; **el** ~ **día** the best day **II.** adv better; **a lo** ~ maybe; ~ **que** ~ better still [o yet]; **en el** ~ **de los casos** at best; ~ **quiero un coche viejo que una moto** I prefer to have an old car than a motorbike
mejora f **1.** (mejoramiento) improvement; ~ **salarial** (pay) rise Brit, (pay) raise Am **2.** (puja) higher bid
mejorable adj improvable
mejoramiento m improvement
mejorana f marjoram
mejorar I. vt **1.** (perfeccionar) to improve

2. (*superar*) to surpass; (*subasta*) to outbid **II.** *vi, vr:* ~**se 1.** (*enfermo*) to get better; **¡que se mejore!** I hope you get better soon! **2.** (*tiempo*) to improve

mejoría *f* improvement

mejunje *m* **1.** (*cosmético, medicamento*) mixture **2.** *pey* concoction

melancolía *f* melancholy

melancólico, -a I. *adj* melancholic **II.** *m, f* melancholic person

melanina *f* melanin

melanoma *m* MED melanoma

melena *f* **1.** (*crin*) mane **2.** (*pelo*) long hair (*shoulder-length or longer, worn loose*); **soltarse la** ~ *t. fig* to let one's hair down

melenudo, -a I. *adj* long-haired **II.** *m, f* long-haired person; *pey* (*haragán*) layabout

melifluo, -a *adj* mellifluous

melillense I. *adj* of/from Melilla **II.** *mf* native/inhabitant of Melilla

melindre *m* **1.** (*con miel y harina*) fried honeyed pastry; (*con mazapán*) marzipan sweet **2.** *pl* (*delicadeza exagerada*) mincing ways *pl;* (*afectada*) affectation; **hacer** ~**s** to affect

melindroso, -a I. *adj* (*delicado*) dainty; (*afectado*) affected **II.** *m, f* (*persona delicada*) dainty person; (*afectada*) affected person

melisa *f* lemon balm

mella *f* **1.** (*hendidura*) nick **2.** (*hueco*) gap **3.** (*merma*) decrease; **hacer** ~ to make an impression

mellar *vt* **1.** (*hacer mellas*) to nick **2.** (*disminuir*) to shrink

mellizo, -a I. *adj* **1.** (*gemelo*) twin **2.** (*igual*) identical **II.** *m, f* twin

melocotón *m* **1.** (*fruto*) peach **2.** *inf* (*borrachera*) **anoche cogí un melocotón** I got plastered last night

melocotonero *m* peach tree

melodía *f* melody

melódico, -a *adj* melodic

melodrama *m* melodrama

melodramático, -a *adj* melodramatic

melómano, -a *m, f* music lover

melón *m* **1.** (*fruto*) melon **2.** *inf* (*cabeza*) nut, noggin *Am* **3.** *pl vulg* (*pechos*) tits *pl*, boobs *pl*

melón, -ona *m, f inf* nutter

melopea *f inf* (*borrachera*) drunkenness

meloso, -a *adj* sweet

membrana *f* membrane; ~ **mucosa** mucous membrane

membrete *m* letterhead

membrillo *m* (*árbol*) quince tree; (*fruto*) quince; **carne** [*o* **dulce**] **de** ~ quince jelly

membrudo, -a *adj* brawny

memela *f Méx* GASTR thin maize tortilla

memo, -a I. *adj* idiotic **II.** *m, f* idiot

memorable *adj* memorable

memorándum *m* <memorandos> memorandum

memoria *f* **1.** (*facultad, recuerdo*) memory; **a la** [*o* **en**] ~ **de** in memory of; **de** ~ by heart;

flaco de ~ forgetful; **hacer** ~ to try and remember; **traer a la** ~ to bring to mind; **venir a la** ~ to come to mind **2.** (*informe*) report **3.** INFOR memory **4.** *pl* (*autobiografía*) autobiography

memorial *m* **1.** (*petición*) petition **2.** (*agenda*) notebook **3.** (*boletín*) newsletter

memorizar <z→c> *vt* **1.** (*aprender*) to memorize **2.** INFOR to store

mena *f* MIN ore

menaje *m* household furnishings *pl;* ~ **de cocina** kitchen utensils

mención *f* mention; **digno de** ~ worth mentioning; **hacer** ~ **de** to mention

mencionar *vt* to mention

menda I. *pron pers, inf* yours truly; **aquí el** [*o* **este**] ~ **no dijo nada** yours truly didn't say anything **II.** *pron indef, inf* **un** ~ a guy

mendicante I. *adj* mendicant **II.** *mf* beggar

mendicidad *f* begging; **vivir de la** ~ to live by begging

mendigar <g→gu> *vi, vt* ~ **algo** to beg for sth

mendigo, -a *m, f* beggar

mendrugo *m* **1.** (*trozo de pan*) crust **2.** *inf* (*torpe*) clodhopper

menear I. *vt* to move; (*cabeza*) to shake; ~ **la cola** to wag one's tail **II.** *vr:* ~**se 1.** (*moverse*) to move **2.** *inf* (*apresurarse*) to get a move on **3. meneársela** *vulg* to wank *Brit*, to jerk off *Am*

meneo *m* **1.** (*brusco*) jolt **2.** *inf* (*vapuleo*) beating; **dar un** ~ **a alguien** to give sb a beating

menester *m* **1.** (*necesidad*) need; **ser** ~ to be necessary; **haber** ~ **de algo** to need sth **2.** *pl* (*tareas*) jobs *pl*

menesteroso, -a I. *adj* needy **II.** *m, f* needy person

menestra *f* vegetable stew

menestral(a) *m(f)* artisan

mengano, -a *m, f* **fulano y** ~ so-and-so

mengua *f* **1.** (*disminución*) decrease; **sin** ~ **de** without a diminishing of; JUR without detriment to **2.** (*carencia*) lack; **sin** ~ sufficient **3.** (*descrédito*) discredit

menguante *f* **1.** (*marea*) ebb; (*estiaje*) low water level **2.** (*mengua*) decrease

menguar <gu→gü> **I.** *vi* to diminish **II.** *vt* to decrease; (*punto*) to reduce

meninge *f* ANAT meninx, meninges *pl;* **me estrujé las** ~**s** *inf* I racked my brains

meningitis *f inv* MED meningitis

menisco *m* ANAT meniscus

menopausia *f* MED menopause, change of life

menor I. *adj* **1.** (*tamaño*) smaller; ~ **que** smaller than; (*número*) smaller; **al por** ~ COM retail; **no dar la** ~ **importancia a algo** not to give sth the least importance; **Asia Menor** Asia Minor **2.** (*edad*) younger; ~ **que** younger than; ~ **de edad** underage; **el** ~ **de mis hermanos** the youngest of my brothers **3.** MÚS minor; **tono** ~ minor key; **tercera** ~ minor third **II.** *mf* (*persona*) minor; **esta película no**

es apta para ~es this film is not suitable for under-eighteens
Menorca f Minorca
menorista I. adj Chile, Méx retail II. mf Chile, Méx (minorista) retailer
menorquín, -ina adj, m, f Minorcan
menos I. adv 1.(contrario de más) less; **a ~ que** unless; **el/la ~** the least; **el coche (el) ~ caro** the least expensive car; **eso es lo de ~** that is the least important thing; **lo ~** the least; **al** [o por lo] **~** at least; **aún ~** even less; **cuanto ~... (tanto) más** the less ... the more; **de ~** short; **echar de ~** to miss; **en ~ de nada** in no time; **ir a ~** to decrease; **~ de 20 personas** fewer than 20 people; **~ de una hora** less than an hour; **~ mal** thank goodness; **¡ni mucho ~!** not at all!; **son las ocho ~ diez** it's ten minutes to eight; **cada vez ~ tiempo/casos** less and less time/fewer and fewer cases 2. MAT minus 3.(excepto) except; **todo ~ eso** anything but that II. m MAT minus
menoscabar vt 1.(disminuir) to diminish 2.(dañar) to impair; fig to damage 3.(desacreditar) to discredit
menoscabo m 1.(disminución) decrease 2.(daño) impairment; fig damage; **sufrir ~** to suffer damage
menospreciable adj despicable
menospreciar vt 1.(despreciar) to underrate 2.(desdeñar) to despise 3.(subestimar) to underestimate
menosprecio m 1.(desprecio) underrating 2.(desdén) scorn 3.(subestimación) underestimate
mensaje m message; **~ de error** INFOR error message; **~ (de) radio** radio communication; **~ de socorro** SOS message
mensajería f messenger [o courier] service
mensajero, -a I. adj messenger; **paloma mensajera** messenger [o carrier] pigeon II. m, f messenger
menso, -a adj Méx (necio) stupid
menstruación f menstruation
menstruar <1. pres: menstrúo> vi to menstruate
mensual adj monthly; **revista ~** monthly (magazine)
mensualidad f 1.(sueldo) monthly salary 2.(paga) monthly payment; (compra aplazada) monthly instalment Brit [o installment Am]; **~ del alquiler** month's rent
mensurar vt to measure
menta f 1.(planta) mint 2.(infusión) mint tea 3.(extracto) menthol; **caramelo de ~** mint
mentado, -a adj well-known; (mencionado) above-mentioned
mental adj mental; **cálculo ~** mental arithmetic
mentalidad f mentality
mentalizar <z→c> I. vt (preparar) to prepare (mentally); (concienciar) to make aware; **~ a alguien de algo** to make sb aware of sth II. vr: **~se** (prepararse) to prepare oneself

(mentally); (concienciarse) to make oneself aware
mentar <e→ie> vt to mention
mente f 1.(pensamiento) mind; **tener en (la) ~** to have in mimd; **no puedo quitarme esa idea de la ~** I cannot get that idea out of my head; **se me ha ido de la ~** the name has gone right out of my head; **tengo la ~ en blanco** my mind is a complete blank; **traer a la ~** to bring to mind 2.(intelecto) intellect
mentecato, -a I. adj silly II. m, f fool
mentir irr como sentir vi 1.(engañar) to lie; **miente más que habla** he/she is a compulsive liar; **¡miento!** I tell a lie!, I am wrong! 2.(inducir a error) to be misleading
mentira f (embuste) lie; **~ piadosa** white lie; **¡parece ~!** I can hardly believe it!
mentiroso, -a I. adj (persona) lying II. m, f liar
mentís m inv denial; **dar un ~ a algo** to deny sth
mentol m menthol
mentón m chin
mentor m mentor
menú m <menús> t. INFOR menu
menudear I. vi to be frequent II. vt to do frequently; **~ sus visitas** to make frequent visits
menudencia f 1.(pequeñez) trifle 2.(meticulosidad) meticulousness 3. pl (del cerdo) pork products pl
menudillos mpl (despojos) giblets pl
menudo, -a adj 1.(minúsculo) minuscule 2.(pequeño y delgado) slight 3.(fútil) futile 4.(exclamación) **¡menuda película!** what a film!; **¡~ lío has armado!** what a fuss you have created! 5. COM **por** [o a] **la menuda** retail ►**a ~** often
meñique I. m little finger, pinkie, pinky Am II. adj inf tiny
meollo m 1.(sesos) brains pl 2.(médula) marrow 3.(fundamento) essence, crux
mequetrefe m inf good-for-nothing
meramente adv merely
mercachifle m pey 1.(comerciante) hawker 2.(avaro) moneygrubber
mercader m merchant; **~ de grueso** wholesaler
mercadería f merchandise
mercadillo m street market, flea market
mercado m market; **~ de capitales** investment market; **~ de divisas** foreign exchange market; **~ exterior/interior** overseas/domestic market; **el ~ de Madrid** the Madrid market; **~ alcista/bajista** bull/bear market; **~ de trabajo** labour market; **~ único europeo** European Single Market; **~ de valores** securities market; **hay ~ los sábados** there is a market on Saturdays
mercancía f goods pl; **tren de ~s** goods [o freight] train
mercante I. adj mercantile II. mf (barco) merchantman

mercantil *adj* mercantile

merced *f* mercy; ~ **a** thanks to; **estar a ~ de alguien** to be at sb's mercy

mercenario, -a *adj, m, f* mercenary

mercería *f* 1. (*tienda*) haberdasher's shop *Brit,* notions store *Am* 2. (*artículos*) haberdashery *Brit,* notions *pl Am*

mercurio *m* mercury

Mercurio *m* Mercury

merecedor(a) *adj* deserving; **hacerse ~ de algo** to earn sth

merecer *irr como crecer* **I.** *vt* 1. (*ser digno de*) to deserve; **merece que lo ahorquen** he deserves to be hung; **merece respeto de nuestra parte** he/she deserves our respect; **este libro merece mención** this book deserves a mention 2. (*valer*) to be worthy of; **no merece la pena** it is not worth it **II.** *vi* ~ **bien de algo** to be deserving of sth **III.** *vr:* ~**se** to deserve

merecido *m* deserts *pl;* **se llevó su ~** he got his just deserts

merendar <e→ie> **I.** *vt* to have for tea, to have for an afternoon snack **II.** *vi* to have tea, to have an afternoon snack; (*en el campo*) to picnic **III.** *vr:* ~**se** *inf* to wangle; ~**se a alguien** to get the better of sb

merendero *m* picnic area

merengue *m* 1. (*dulce*) meringue 2. (*persona débil*) weakling 3. *CSur, inf* (*lío*) mess

meridiano *m* meridian

meridiano, -a *adj* 1. (*del mediodía*) midday 2. (*evidente*) clear

meridional **I.** *adj* south; **Andalucía está en la España ~** Andalucía is in southern Spain **II.** *mf* southerner

merienda *f* 1. (*comida por la tarde*) tea, afternoon snack 2. (*picnic*) picnic; **ir de ~** to go for a picnic; ~ **de negros** *fig* free-for-all

mérito *m* 1. (*merecimiento*) merit; **hacer ~s** to prove oneself worthy; **callarse sus ~s** to hide one's light under a bushel 2. (*valor*) worth; **de ~** (*obra*) excellent; (*persona*) worthy

meritorio, -a **I.** *adj* meritorious **II.** *m, f* (*aprendiz*) apprentice; (*empleado sin sueldo*) unpaid employee [*o* trainee]

merlo *m AmL* zool wrasse

merluza *f* 1. zool hake 2. *vulg* (*borrachera*) **coger una buena ~** to get sloshed; **estar (con la) ~** to be sloshed

merluzo, -a *adj inf* silly

merma *f* decrease; ~ **de peso** loss of weight

mermar **I.** *vt* to lessen; (*sueldo*) to cut; ~ **peso** to reduce weight **II.** *vi, vr:* ~**se** to decrease

mermelada *f* jam; ~ **de naranja** marmalade

mero **I.** *adv* 1. *AmC, Méx* (*pronto*) soon 2. *Méx* (*muy*) very 3. *Méx* (*precisamente*) precisely **II.** *m* 1. zool grouper 2. *Méx* (*jefe*) boss

mero, -a *adj* 1. (*sencillo*) simple 2. (*sin nada más*) mere; **la mera verdad** the plain truth 3. *Méx* (*preciso*) precise 4. *Méx* (*propio*) own

merodear *vi* to prowl; ~ **por un sitio** to hang about a place

merolico, -a *m, f Méx* 1. (*vendedor charlatán*) quack 2. (*persona charlatana*) chatterer

mes *m* 1. (*período*) month; **a principios/a mediados/a fin(al)es de** ~ at the beginning/ in the middle/at the end of the month; **5.000 pesetas al** ~ 5000 pesetas a month; **todos los** ~**es** every month; **el ~ corriente** this month; **el ~ que viene** next month; **el ~ pasado** last month; **hace un** ~ a month ago; **con un ~ de anticipo** a month's salary in advance 2. (*sueldo*) ~ (**de trabajo**) monthly salary 3. *inf* (*menstruación*) period; **tengo el** ~ I have my period

mesa *f* 1. (*mueble*) table; ~ **de despacho** office desk; ~ **de tertulia** coffee table; **vino de** ~ table wine; **bendecir la** ~ to say grace; **poner la** ~ to lay [*o* set] the table; **quitar la** ~ to clear the table; **en la** ~ (*comiendo*) at the table; **¡a la** ~**!** food's ready!; **servir una** ~ to serve a table; **tener a alguien a** ~ **y a mantel** to give sb free board; **vivir** [*o* **estar**] **a** ~ **puesta** to live a life of leisure 2. (*junta directiva*) board 3. pol ~ **electoral** *officials in charge of a polling station* 4. geo plateau 5. infor ~ **digitalizadora** digitizer 6. (*pensión*) board; ~ **y cama** board and lodging

mesar *vt, vr* ~**se los pelos,** ~ **sus pelos** to tear one's hair out

mesero, -a *m, f Méx* (*camarero*) waiter *m,* waitress *f*

meseta *f* geo plateau

mesías *m* Messiah

mesilla *f* small table; ~ **de noche** bedside table, nightstand *Am*

mesón *m* inn, tavern

mesonero, -a *m, f* innkeeper

mestizo, -a **I.** *adj* 1. (*entre blancos e indios*) mestizo 2. (*entre dos razas*) mixed-race **II.** *m, f* 1. (*entre blancos e indios*) mestizo 2. (*entre dos razas*) person of mixed race

---

A **mestizo** in Latin America means a person of mixed race whose parents were of white (i.e. European) and Indian origin. (In Brazil, **mestizos** are known as **mamelucos**.)

---

mesura *f* 1. (*moderación*) moderation 2. (*cortesía*) courtesy, civility 3. (*calma*) calm

meta[1] *f t. fig* winning post; (*portería*) goal; **la ~ de su vida** his/her aim in life; **fijarse una ~** to set oneself a goal

meta[2] *mf* (*portero*) goalkeeper *Brit,* goaltender *Am*

metabolismo *m* metabolism

metadona *f* methadon(e)

metafísica *f* filos metaphysics

metafísico, -a **I.** *adj* 1. filos metaphysical 2. (*difícil*) subtle **II.** *m, f* metaphysician

metáfora *f* metaphor

metafórico, -a *adj* metaphorical

metal *m* 1. (*material*) metal; ~ **noble** precious

metal; ~ **pesado** heavy metal **2.** (*de voz*)
timbre **3.** (*instrumento*) brass instrument
4. (*dinero*) **el vil** ~ filthy lucre
metálico *m* (*monedas*) coins *pl;* **en** ~ in cash;
premio en ~ cash prize
metálico, -a *adj* metallic; **tela metálica**
(metal) screening
metalurgia *f* metallurgy
metalúrgico, -a I. *adj* metallurgical; **industria metalúrgica** metallurgical industry II. *m,*
f metallurgist
metamorfosear I. *vt* to transform II. *vr:* ~**se**
to metamorphose
metamorfosis *f inv* **1.** ZOOL, GEO metamorphosis **2.** (*en una persona*) transformation
metano *m* methane
metástasis *f inv* MED metastasis
metedura *f* **¡vaya** ~ **de pata!** *inf* what a
clanger *Brit* [*o* blooper *Am*]!
metelón, -ona *adj Méx* meddling
meteórico, -a *adj* **1.** METEO meteorological
2. (*rápido*) meteoric
meteorismo *m* flatulence
meteorito *m* meteorite
meteoro *m* **1.** METEO meteorological phenomenon **2.** ASTR meteor
meteorología *f sin pl* meteorology
meteorológico, -a *adj* meteorological;
informe ~ weather forcast; **estación meteorológica** weather station
meteorólogo, -a *m, f* meteorologist; TV,
RADIO weather forecaster, weatherman
meter I. *vt* **1.** (*introducir*) to insert; (*poner*) to
put; ~ **en una caja** to put in a box; **¡mete el
enchufe!** put the plug in!; ~ **un clavo en la
pared** to hammer a nail into the wall; ~ **el
coche en el garaje** to put the car in the garage; ~ **a alguien en la cárcel** to put sb in jail
2. (*invertir*) to invest; ~ **en el banco** to put in
the bank **3.** (*en costura*) to take in **4.** DEP ~ **un
gol** to score a goal **5.** (*de contrabando*) to
smuggle **6.** *inf* (*encasquetar*) to palm off;
(*vender*) to sell; (*enjaretar*) to foist; **nos metió
una película aburridísima** he foisted a really
boring film on us; **le metieron tres meses de
cárcel** they gave him/her three months in jail
7. *inf* (*pegar*) ~ **un puñetazo a alguien** to
punch sb **8.** (*provocar*) ~ **miedo/un susto a
alguien** to frighten/startle sb; ~ **prisa a alguien** to hurry sb (up); ~ **ruido** to be noisy
9. (*hacer participar*) to involve; ~ **a toda la
familia en el asunto** to involve the whole
family in the matter **10.** (*emplear*) to employ;
~ **a alguien a fregar platos** to set sb to work
washing dishes; ~ **a una chica de peluquera**
to put a girl to work as a hairdresser ▶ **a todo** ~
inf as fast as possible II. *vr:* ~**se** **1.** (*introducirse*) to put; ~**se el dedo en la nariz** to stick
one's finger in one's nose; **se lo ha metido en
la cabeza que...** he/she has got it into his/
her head that ...; **¡métetelo donde te quepa!**
vulg go and stick it up your arse *Brit* [*o* ass *Am*]!
2. (*entrar en un lugar*) to enter; **lo vi** ~**se en**

un cine I saw him go into the cinema; ~**se
entre la gente** to mingle with the people; **se
metió en el armario** he/she got into the
wardrobe; **¿dónde se habrá metido?** where
has he/she got to?; ~**se para adentro** to go
inside **3.** (*entrar indebidamente*) to enter
unlawfully **4.** *inf* (*aceptar algo*) **¿cuándo se te
~á esto en la cabeza?** when will you get it
into your head? **5.** (*inmiscuirse*) to meddle;
¡no te metas donde no te llaman! mind
your own business! **6.** (*provocar*) ~**se con alguien** to provoke sb **7.** (*comenzar un oficio*)
~**se monja** to become a nun; ~**se a actor** to
become an actor
metiche *adj Méx* (*entrometido*) meddlesome
meticuloso, -a I. *adj* meticulous II. *m, f*
meticulous person
metida *f inf* (*avance*) **dar una** ~ **a algo** to give
sth a boost; **tengo que darle una buena** ~ **a
los estudios** I have to give my studies a real
boost
metido *m inf* (*reprimenda*) ticking off; **pegar
un** ~ **a alguien** to give sb a ticking off
metido, -a *adj* **1.** (*introvertido*) ~ **en sí
mismo** withdrawn **2.** (*envuelto*) involved;
sigue estando muy ~ **en el negocio a pesar
de su edad** he is still very involved in the business in spite of his age **3.** (*con abundantes*) ~
en carnes chubby; ~ **en años** elderly **4.** *inf*
(*relación*) **está muy** ~ **con esa chica** he is
very involved with that girl; **está muy** ~ **con
la dirección de la empresa** he is in with the
management of the company **5.** (*puesto*) **la
llave está metida** the key is in
metl *m Méx* (*agave*) agave
metódico, -a I. *adj* methodical II. *m, f*
methodical person
metodismo *m* Methodism
metodista *adj, mf* Methodist
método *m* **1.** (*sistema*) method; **proceder
con** ~ to proceed methodically **2.** (*libro*) manual; **un** ~ **de guitarra** a guitar manual
metodología *f* methodology
metomentodo I. *adj inv* nosy II. *mf inv, inf*
nosy parker; **ser un** ~ to be a real busybody
metraje *m* length; **película de largo** ~ feature-length film; **película de corto** ~ short
(film)
metralla *f* **1.** (*munición*) shell; **fuego de** ~
shellfire **2.** (*trozos*) shrapnel
metralleta *f* sub-machine gun, tommy gun
métrica *f* LIT metrics
métrico, -a *adj* metric
metro *m* **1.** (*unidad*) metre *Brit,* meter *Am;* ~
cuadrado square metre *Brit* [*o* meter *Am*]; ~
cúbico cubic metre *Brit* [*o* meter *Am*] **2.** (*para
medir*) ruler; ~ **de cinta** tape measure; ~
plegable folding ruler **3.** FERRO underground
Brit, subway *Am* **4.** *t.* MÚS (*poesía*) metre *Brit,*
meter *Am*
metrópoli *f* (*urbe*) metropolis; (*capital*) capital

metropolitano *m* FERRO underground *Brit,* subway *Am*
metropolitano, -a *adj* **1.**(*de la capital*) metropolitan **2.**(*de la urbe*) city
mexicano, -a *adj, m, f v.* **mejicano**
México *m* Mexico

> **México** or **Méjico** (official title: **Estados Unidos Mexicanos**) lies in Central America and borders the USA in the north. The capital, **Ciudad de México** (Mexico City), has almost twenty million inhabitants. Spanish is the official language of the country and the monetary unit is the **peso.** The original inhabitants of Mexico, the **aztecas** (Aztecs), referred to themselves as **mexica.**

mezcal *m Méx* BOT mescal
mezcla *f* **1.**(*sustancia*) mixture; ~ de carburantes blend of fuel; ~ **explosiva** *t. fig* explosive mixture **2.**(*acto*) mixing **3.**(*tela*) mixed fibres *Brit,* mixed fibers *Am; sin* ~ pure **4.**(*argamasa*) mortar
mezclar I. *vt* **1.**(*unir*) to blend; GASTR (*añadir*) to mix **2.**(*revolver*) to muddle; (*confundir*) to mix up **3.**(*involucrar*) to involve II. *vr:* ~se **1.**(*inmiscuirse*) to meddle **2.**(*en un grupo de personas*) ~se entre los espectadores to mingle with the spectators; ~se con gente de mucho dinero to mix with wealthy people **3.**(*revolverse*) to mix
mezcolanza *f pey* hotchpotch *Brit,* hodgepodge *Am*
mezquindad *f* **1.**(*tacañería*) stinginess, meanness *Brit* **2.**(*acto vil*) mean action
mezquino, -a I. *adj* **1.**(*tacaño*) stingy, mean *Brit* **2.**(*innoble*) ignoble **3.**(*insuficiente*) inadequate **4.**(*despreciable*) despicable **5.**(*miserable*) small-minded II. *m, f* miser
mezquita *f* mosque
mg. *abr de* **miligramo** mg
mi I. *adj* (*antepuesto*) my; ~ **amigo/casa** my friend/house; ~s **amigos** my friends II. *m inv* MÚS E; ~ **mayor** E major; ~ **menor** E minor
mí *pron pers* me; a ~ (*objeto directo*) me; (*objeto indirecto*) to me; para ~ for me; ¿y a ~ qué? so what?; para ~ (que)... I think (that) ...; por ~ as far as I'm concerned; por ~ que se quede as far as I'm concerned he/she can stay; por ~ mismo by myself; ¡a ~ con esas! don't give me that!; ¡a ~! (*¡socorro!*) help!
miaja *f* crumb
miau *m* miaow *Brit,* meow *Am*
mica *f* **1.** MIN mica **2.** And (*orinal*) chamber pot **3.** *AmC, inf* (*borrachera*) drunkenness
micción *f* urination
miche *m* **1.** CRi (*pendencia*) brawl **2.** Chile (*juego*) game of marbles
michelín *m* roll of fat, spare tyre *Brit* [*o* tire *Am*]
mico *m* **1.** ZOOL long-tailed monkey **2.** *inf* (*persona fea*) hideous person **3.** *inf* (*niño*) little monkey, tyke *Am* ▶ dar ~ a alguien *inf* (*dejar*

plantado) to stand sb up; dar el ~ a alguien *inf* (*engañar*) to take sb in; quedarse hecho un ~ *inf* (*avergonzado*) to be ashamed; volverse ~ para hacer algo *inf* to go mad [*o* crazy] trying to do sth
micro *m* (*micrófono*) mike
microbio *m* microbe
microbús *m* minibus **microchip** *m* microchip **microficha** *f* microfiche **microfilm** *m* <microfilm(e)s> microfilm
microfilmar *vt* to microfilm
micrófono *m* microphone
microonda *f t.* FÍS (*cocina*) microwave; horno (de) ~s microwave (oven) **microorganismo** *m* micro-organism
microscópico, -a *adj* microscopic; de tamaño ~ *inf* of microscopic size
microscopio *m* microscope; ~ de 60 aumentos microscope with x60 magnification; ~ electrónico electron microscope
microtenis *m inv, AmL* table tennis
miedo *m* **1.**(*angustia*) fear; por ~ a [*o* de] for fear of; por ~ de que +*subj* for fear that; meter ~ a alguien to frighten sb; dar ~ to be frightening; me entró [*o* dio] ~ I became frightened; morirse de ~ to be petrified; cagarse de ~ *vulg* to shit oneself (with fear) **2.** *inf* (*maravilloso*) de ~ terrific; el concierto estuvo de ~ the concert was terrific **3.** *inf* (*terrible*) de ~ dreadful; hace un frío de ~ it is dreadfully cold ▶al que mal vive, el ~ le sigue *prov* ≈ those who act badly always live in fear; a quien ~ han, lo suyo le dan *prov* ≈ fear is the tool of a tyrant
miedoso, -a I. *adj ser* fearful II. *m, f* apprehensive person, scaredy-cat *inf*
miel *f* (*de abeja*) honey; ~ blanca bees' honey; luna de ~ honeymoon; quedarse con la ~ en los labios to be left wanting more; si encima me pagan el viaje ¡~ sobre hojuelas! if they also pay for the trip it would be the icing on the cake!; hacerse de ~ to go all sugary ▶no hay ~ sin hiel *prov* there is no rose without a thorn; ~ sobre hojuelas even better; hazte de ~ y te comerán las moscas *prov* ≈ if you are too good people will take advantage of you
mielga *f* **1.** BOT alfalfa **2.** ZOOL dogfish
miembro I. *m* **1.** *pl* (*extremidades*) limbs *pl* **2.**(*pene*) ~ (viril) male member **3.** *t.* LING, MAT (*socio*) member; no ~ non-member; ~ de pleno derecho full member; hacerse ~ de to join **4.**(*parte*) component II. *adj* los Estados ~s the member states
mientes *fpl* thoughts *pl;* caer en (las) ~ to come to mind; parar [*o* poner] ~ en algo to give sth great thought; traer a las ~ to recall; todo se le vino a las ~ everything came back to him/her; ¡ni por ~! never!
mientras I. *adv* meanwhile; ~ (tanto) in the meantime II. *conj* ~ (que) while; ~ (que) +*subj* as long as; ~ se ríe no se llora you cannot laugh and cry at the same time; ~ más le

dan más pide el niño the more the child gets, the more he/she wants

miércoles *m inv* Wednesday; ~ de ceniza Ash Wednesday; ~ santo Easter Wednesday; *v.t.* lunes

mierda *f vulg* **1.** (*heces*) shit **2.** (*porquería*) muck **3.** (*persona, cosa despreciable*) el maestro nuevo es una ~ the new teacher is lousy; esta película es una ~ this film is a piece of shit; ¡2.000 pesetas, una ~! 2000 pesetas, that's peanuts!; es una ~ de coche the car is a piece of junk; no valer una ~ to be a load of crap; cubrirse de ~ to discredit oneself **4.** (*borrachera*) ¡vaya ~ que cogí ayer! God, I got sloshed yesterday! **5.** (*expresiones*) ¡~! shit!; ¡una ~! like hell!; ¡a la ~! to hell with it!; ¡¡vete) a la ~! get lost!; ¡eso te importa una ~! you don't give a damn about that!; mandar a alguien a la ~ to tell sb to go to hell; ¿qué ~ ocurre? what the hell is going on?; irse a la ~ to go to the dogs; no comerse ni (una) ~ to get absolutely nowhere

mies *f* **1.** (*cereal maduro*) (ripe) corn **2.** (*temporada*) harvest (time) **3.** *pl* (*campos*) cornfields *pl*

miga *f* **1.** (*pan*) bread (*not the crust*); (*trocito*) crumb; hacer buenas/malas ~s con alguien to get on well/badly with sb; hacer ~s a alguien to leave sb in a sorry state; estar hecho ~ (*cansado*) to be shattered; hacer ~s to destroy **2.** (*esencia*) essence; esto tiene su ~ there is something behind this

migaja *f* **1.** (*trocito*) crumb; una ~ de algo a scrap of sth **2.** *pl* (*sobras*) leftovers *pl*

migración *f* **1.** (*emigración*) emigration **2.** ZOOL migration

migraña *f* migraine

mijo *m* millet

mil **I.** *adj inv* thousand; dos ~ millones two billion; ya se lo he dicho ~ veces I have already told him/her hundreds of times **II.** *m* **1.** (*número*) thousand **2.** (*cantidad indefinida*) ~es thousands; a ~es by the thousand; ~es y ~es thousands and thousands; varios ~es de dólares several thousand dollars; a las ~ (y quinientas) very late; pasar las ~ y una to be a huge amount

milagro *m* miracle; hacer ~s to work wonders; contar la vida y ~s de alguien to tell all the gory details about sb's life; esta vez se escapó de ~ this time he/she had a lucky escape; si sales de ésta, solo saldrás de ~ if you get out of this, it will be a miracle; ~ (sería) que +*subj* it would be a miracle if

milagroso, -a *adj* **1.** miraculous **2.** (*maravilloso*) marvellous *Brit,* marvelous *Am*

Milán *m* Milan

milanés, -esa **I.** *adj* Milanese **II.** *m, f* Milanese

milanesa *f* breaded escalope

milano *m* red kite

milenario *m* millennium

milenario, -a *adj* millennial

milenio *m* millennium

milenrama *f* yarrow

mili *f inf* military service; ir a [o hacer] la ~ to do military service; ¿ya hiciste la ~? have you done your military service?; tener mucha ~ *inf* to be an old hand

milibar *m* FÍS millibar

milicia *f* **1.** (*tropa*) military; ~ nacional (*ciudadanos*) militia **2.** (*actividades militares*) military operation

miligramo *m* milligram **mililitro** *m* millilitre *Brit,* milliliter *Am* **milímetro** *m* millimetre *Brit,* millimeter *Am*

militante **I.** *adj* militant **II.** *mf* (*de un partido*) militant, active member

militar **I.** *vi* **1.** (*cumplir el servicio*) to serve **2.** (*en un partido*) to be an active member of; ~ en favor de/contra algo to campaign for/against sth **II.** *adj* military; los altos mandos ~es the military high command **III.** *m* soldier

milla *f* mile; ~ marina nautical mile

millar *m* thousand; protestaron a ~es they protested by the thousand

millo *m AmC, Méx* type of millet

millón *m* million; mil millones a billion; cuatro millones de habitantes four million inhabitants; un ~ de gracias a million thanks

millonada *f inf* (*muchísimo dinero*) fortune

millonario, -a *m, f* millionaire, millionairess *f*

milonga *f* **1.** MÚS popular dance **2.** *And, CSur* (*fiesta*) party **3.** *And, CSur, inf* (*trola, mentira*) tall story

milpa *f AmL* **1.** (*campo*) cornfield **2.** (*planta*) maize *Brit,* corn *Am*

milpiés *m inv* millipede

mimar *vt* **1.** (*consentir*) to indulge; (*excesivamente*) to spoil **2.** (*favorecer*) to favour *Brit,* to favor *Am*

mimbre *m* **1.** (*material*) wicker; de ~ wicker; muebles de ~ wicker furniture; silla de ~ wicker chair **2.** (*ramita*) piece of wicker

mimbrera *f* osier; (*sauce*) willow

mimeografiar < *1. pres:* mimeografío> *vt AmL* to mimeograph

mimeógrafo *m AmL* mimeograph

mimetismo *m* mimicry

mímica *f* **1.** (*facial*) mime **2.** (*señas*) sign language **3.** (*ademanes*) gesticulation

mímico, -a *adj* imitative; TEAT mimetic

mimo *m* **1.** (*actor*) mimic; hacer ~ de alguien to mimic sb **2.** (*caricia*) caress; necesitar mucho ~ to need a lot of affection **3.** (*condescencia*) spoiling; le dan demasiado ~ they spoil him **4.** (*con cariño*) realizo mi trabajo con ~ I carry out my work with love

mimosa *f* mimosa

mimoso, -a *adj* **1.** (*mimado*) spoilt **2.** *ser* (*cariñoso*) affectionate **3.** *estar* (*apegado*) clinging

mina *f* **1.** MIN mine; ~ de carbón coal mine; este negocio es una ~ this business is a gold mine **2.** (*pasillo subterráneo*) underground passage **3.** (*explosivo*) mine; ~ de mar under-

water mine; ~ **de tierra** landmine **4.** (*de lápiz, bolígrafo*) lead
minar I. *vt* **1.** (*excavar, colocar minas*) to mine **2.** (*debilitar*) to undermine **II.** *vr:* ~**se** *inf* (*hartarse*) to become fed up
minarete *m* minaret
mineral I. *adj* mineral; **agua** ~ mineral water **II.** *m* **1.** GEO mineral **2.** MIN ore
mineralogía *f sin pl* mineralogy
minería *f* mining
minero, -a I. *adj* mining **II.** *m, f* (*trabajador*) miner
minga I. *interj RíoPl, inf* no way!, like hell! **II.** *f And* communal work
mingaco *m Chile: communal work done by neighbours*
miniatura *f* miniature
minibús *m* minibus **minifalda** *f* miniskirt
minifundio *m* smallholding
minifundista *mf* smallholder
minigolf *m* minigolf
minimizar <z→c> *vt* **1.** (*simplificar*) to minimize **2.** (*subestimar*) to underestimate
mínimo *m* minimum; ~ **de presión** METEO trough of low pressure; **un** ~ **de respeto** a minimum of respect; **como** ~ (*cantidad*) as a minimum; **como** ~ **podrías llamar por teléfono** you could at least phone; **reducir al** ~ to reduce to the bare minimum
mínimo, -a *adj superl de* **pequeño** minimum; **las temperaturas mínimas** the minimum temperatures; **cifra mínima** minimum figure; **la mínima obligación posible** the slightest obligation possible; **sin el más** ~ **ruido** without the least noise; **no ayudar en lo más** ~ to be no help at all
minino, -a *m, f inf* pussy [*o* kitty] (cat)
miniprímer *m o f* hand blender
miniserie *f* miniseries
ministerial *adj* (*de minister*) ministerial; (*de gobierno*) governmental
ministerio *m* **1.** (*cartera, edificio*) ministry **2.** (*cargo*) ministerial office
ministro, -a *m, f* **1.** (*de un gobierno*) minister; **primera ministra** prime minister; ~ **sin cartera** minister without portfolio; **Ministro de Economía y Hacienda** Chancellor of the Exchequer *Brit,* Treasury Secretary *Am;* **Ministro de Educación y Ciencia** Education Minister *Brit,* Education Secretary *Am;* **Ministro del Interior** Home Secretary *Brit,* Secretary of the Interior *Am* **2.** JUR court official **3.** (*en la embajada*) diplomat
minivacaciones *fpl* short break **minivestido** *m* minidress
minoría *f* minority; ~ **de bloqueo** blocking minority; ~ **de edad** minority
minoridad *f* minority
minorista I. *adj* retail **II.** *mf* retailer
minoritario, -a *adj* minority
minucia *f* (*de poca importancia*) trifle
minuciosidad *f* meticulousness
minucioso, -a *adj* meticulous

minúscula *f* LING lower case; **en** ~**s** in lower case [*o* small] letters; **escribirse con** ~ to be written in lower case
minúsculo, -a *adj* **1.** (*muy pequeño*) minuscule, minute **2.** LING **letra minúscula** lower-case [*o* small] letter
minusvalía *f* **1.** (*física*) handicap, disability **2.** COM capital loss
minusválido, -a I. *adj* handicapped **II.** *m, f* handicapped person
minusvalorar *vt* to undervalue
minuta *f* **1.** (*cuenta*) lawyer's bill **2.** (*borrador*) rough draft; (*copia*) carbon copy **3.** (*apunte*) note **4.** (*menú*) menu
minutero *m* minute hand
minuto *m* minute; **sin perder un** ~ at once; **vuelvo en un** ~ I will be [*o* back in a minute] right back
mío, -a *pron pos* **1.** (*de mi propiedad*) mine; **el libro** ~ the book is mine; **la botella es mía** the bottle is mine; **¡ya es** ~**!** I have it! **2.** (*tras artículo*) **el** ~/**la mía** mine; **los** ~**s** (*cosas*) mine; (*parientes*) my family; **ésta es la mía** *inf* this is just what I want; **he vuelto a hacer una de las mías** I have been up to it again; **eso es lo** ~ that is my strong point **3.** (*tras substantivo*) of mine; **una amiga mía** a friend of mine; **¡amor** ~**!** my darling!; **(no) es culpa mía** it is (not) my fault
miocardio *m* ANAT myocardium
mioma *m* MED myoma, myogenic tumour *Brit* [*o* tumor *Am*]
miope I. *adj* myopic, short-sighted **II.** *mf* short-sighted person
miopía *f* myopia, short-sightedness
mira *f* **1.** (*para apuntar*) sight **2.** MIL watchtower; **estar en la** ~ **de alguien** to be in sb's sights **3.** (*mirada*) gaze; **pusieron la** ~ **en el cuadro/la chica** (*atención*) their gaze fixed on the picture/the girl; **he puesto la** ~ **en esa casa** (*aspirar*) I have set my sights on that house; **con amplias** ~**s** broad-minded; **de** ~**s estrechas** narrow-minded; **con** ~**s a** with a view to **4.** (*pl*) (*intención*) intention; **con** ~**s desinteresadas** disinterestedly
mirada *f* look; ~ **perdida** faraway look; **devorar con la** ~ to gaze hungrily at; **echar una** ~ **a algo** to glance at sth; **levantar la** ~ to look up; **apartar la** ~ to look away; **ser el blanco de las** ~**s** to be stared at; **volver la** ~ **atrás** to look back
mirado, -a *adj* **1.** (*respetuoso*) respectful **2.** *inf* (*delicado*) considerate **3.** (*cuidadoso*) discreet **4.** (*respetado*) **estar bien/mal** ~ (*persona*) to be well/badly thought of; **está mal** ~ **ir sin regalo** it is not the done thing to go without a present **5.** (*si bien se mira*) **bien** ~, ... all things considering [*o* considered], ...
mirador *m* **1.** (*balcón*) glassed-in balcony; (*ventana*) bay window **2.** (*atalaya*) viewpoint
miramiento *m* **1.** (*consideración*) consideration; **tener** ~ **con alguien** to have [*o* show] consideration for sb; **sin** ~ inconsiderately;

M

andar con ~s to tread carefully; sin ~s de without considering 2.(*cuidado*) discretion; sin ~ indiscreetly 3.(*timidez*) hesitation 4. *pl* (*cortesías*) civilities *pl*, courtesies *pl*
mirar I. *vt* 1.(*observar*) to observe; (*ver*) to look at; ~ fijamente a alguien to stare at sb; ~ algo por encima to give sth a quick look (over) 2.(*buscar*) to look for 3.(*prestar atención*) to watch; mira bien el dinero que te devuelven check the change they give you; ¡mira el bolso! keep an eye on the bag!; ¡pero mira lo que estás haciendo! but look what you are doing! 4.(*meditar*) to think about; mirándolo bien, bien mirado taking everything into consideration 5.(*tener en cuenta*) to take into account; siempre estás mirando tu porvenir you always have your future in mind; ~ el dinero to be careful of the money 6.(*estimar*) ~ bien/mal to have a good/poor opinion of; ~ con buena/mala cara to approve/disapprove of II. *vi* 1.(*dirigir la vista*) to look; ~ por la ventana to look out of the window; ~ por un agujero to look through a hole; ~ atrás to look back; ~ alrededor to look around 2.(*buscar*) to look for; siempre miramos por nuestros hijos we always look out for our children 3.(*dar*) la casa mira al este the house faces east; la ventana mira al mar the window overlooks [*o* gives on to] the sea 4.(*de aviso, exclamativo*) ¡mira! ya llega look! here he/she comes; mira, mira, con que tú también apareces por aquí well, well, so you're here too; mira, mira, déjate de tonterías that is enough, stop being silly; ¡pues, mira por donde...! surprise, surprise ...!; mire, ya se lo he explicado tres veces look, I have already explained it to him/her three times 5.(*tener en cuenta*) mira, que no nos queda mucho tiempo look, we do not have much time left; mira que si se cae este jarrón just imagine if the vase fell 6.(*ir a ver, considerar, afectar*) mira (a ver) si han llegado ya go and see if they have arrived yet; quedarse mirando (*sorprendido*) to stop and stare; por lo que mira a... as regards .... 7.(*mira que*) mira que es tonta, ¿eh? she really is silly, isn't she? ►ser de mírame y no me toques to be very delicate III. *vr*: ~se (*verse*) to look at oneself; ~se a los ojos to look into another's eyes; ~se en el espejo to look at oneself in the mirror; se mire como se mire however [*o* no matter how] you look at it; si bien se mira taking everything into consideration
mirasol *m* sunflower
miriápodo *m* myriapod
mirilla *f* (*en la puerta, pared*) peephole *Brit,* eyehole *Am;* FOTO viewer
miriñaque *m* 1.HIST (*crinolina*) hoop skirt 2. CSur FERRO cowcatcher
mirlo *m* 1.ZOOL blackbird 2. *inf* (*lengua*) debes aprender a achantar el ~ you have to learn to hold your tongue

mirón, -ona I. *adj* inquisitive II. *m, f* 1.(*espectador curioso*) onlooker; *pey* (*de intimidades*) snoop; (*voyeur*) peeping Tom 2. INFOR lurker
mirra *f* myrrh
misa *f* REL (*ceremonia*) mass; ~ de difuntos requiem mass; ~ del gallo midnight mass; ir a ~ to go to mass; ayudar a ~ to assist at mass; cantar ~ to sing mass; decir ~ to say mass ►no saber de la ~ la media [*o* la mitad] *inf* not to know the half [*o* the first thing] of it; no se puede estar en ~ y repicar you can't be in two places at once; eso va a ~ *inf* and that's a fact
misántropo, -a I. *adj* misanthropic II. *m, f* misanthrope
miscelánea *f* (*revoltijo*) miscellany
miserable I. *adj* 1.(*pobre*) poor 2.(*lamentable*) pitiful 3.(*tacaño*) stingy 4.(*poco, mísero*) miserable; un sueldo ~ a miserable wage II. *mf* 1.(*desdichado*) wretch; (*que da pena*) poor thing 2.(*canalla*) swine
miseria *f* 1.(*pobreza*) poverty; caer en la ~ to become impoverished; vivir en la ~ to live in poverty 2.(*poco dinero*) pittance 3.(*tacañería*) stinginess 4. *pl* (*infortunios*) misfortunes *pl*
misericordia *f* 1.(*compasión*) compassion 2.(*perdón*) forgiveness
misericordioso, -a *adj* 1.(*que siente*) compassionate 2.(*que perdona*) forgiving
mísero, -a *adj v.* **miserable**
misil *m* missile; ~ antiaéreo anti-aircraft missile
misión *f* mission; (*embajada*) embassy, legation; POL assignment
misionero, -a *m, f* missionary
mismamente *adv* 1.(*sólo*) only 2.(*literalmente*) literally 3.(*hasta*) even; da ~ escalofríos it sends shivers down your spine 4.(*en realidad*) actually 5. *inf* (*precisamente*) just; ayer ~ estuvimos hablando de ello only yesterday we were talking about it
mismo *adv* 1.(*incluso*) even; me duele sentado ~ it hurts me even when I am sitting down 2.(*manera*) así ~ in that way 3.(*justamente*) ahí ~ just there; aquí ~ right here; ayer ~ only yesterday 4.(*ejemplo*) nos podemos ver el miércoles ~ we could meet on Wednesday, say
mismo, -a *adj* 1.(*idéntico*) el/lo ~/la misma the same; al ~ tiempo at the same time; da lo ~ it does not matter; por lo ~ for that reason; lo ~ José como [*o* que] María both José and María; lo ~ que coma o no coma, sigo engordando (it makes no difference) whether I eat or not, I keep putting on weight; lo ~ no vienen they might not come; quedamos [*o* seguimos] en las mismas we are where we were 2.(*semejante*) el~/la misma/lo ~ the same; llevar la misma falda to wear an identical skirt 3.(*reflexivo*) myself; te perjudicas a ti ~ you harm yourself; yo

misma lo vi I myself saw him/it; **lo hizo por sí misma** she did it (all) by herself; **lo podemos hacer nosotros** ~**s** we can do it ourselves **4.**(*precisamente*) **este** ~ **perro fue el que me mordió** that very dog was the one which bit me; **¡eso** ~**!** exactly! **5.**(*hasta*) actual; **el** ~ **embajador asistió a la fiesta** the ambassador himself attended the party; **mi misma familia me abandonó** my own family abandonded me

miss *f* Miss; ~ **España** Miss Spain

misterio *m* (*enigma, secreto*) mystery; **obrar con** ~ to act mysteriously

misterioso, -a *adj* mysterious

mística *f sin pl* mysticism

místico, -a I. *adj* mystical II. *m, f* mystic

mistificar <c→qu> *vt* **1.**(*burlarse*) to hoax **2.**(*falsear*) to misrepresent

mistol *m Arg, Par* BOT jujube tree

mitad *f* **1.**(*parte igual*) half; ~ **hombre** ~ **bestia** half man, half beast; **a** ~ **de precio** at half price; **cara** ~ (*cónyuge*) other half; **mezcla harina y agua,** ~ **y** ~ mix flour and water, half and half [*o* in equal amounts]; **reducir a la** ~ to halve; **¿estás contenta? –** ~ **y** ~ are you happy?– so-so **2.**(*medio*) middle; **en** ~ **del bosque** in the middle of the forest; **cortar por la** ~ to cut in half **3.** DEP half

mítico, -a *adj* mythical, mythological

mitigar <g→gu> I. *vt* **1.**(*dolores*) to alleviate; (*sed*) to quench; (*hambre*) to take the edge off; (*temperamento*) to pacify; ~ **la inquietud de alguien** to set sb's mind at rest **2.**(*colores, luz*) to subdue; (*calor*) to mitigate II. *vr:* ~**se 1.**(*dolores*) to lessen **2.**(*color, luz*) to become subdued

mitin *m* political meeting, rally

mito *m* myth

mitología *f* mythology

mitológico, -a *adj* mythological

mitón *m* mitten

mitote *m Méx* **1.**(*jaleo*) uproar; (*caos*) riot **2.**(*danza*) ritual Aztec dance

mitra *f* mitre *Brit,* miter *Am*

mixto *m* (*fósforo*) match

mixto, -a *adj* mixed

mixtura *f* mixture

ml. *abr de* mililitro ml

mm. *abr de* milímetro mm

mobiliario *m* furniture

moca *m* **1.**(*café*) mocha **2.** *Ecua* (*ciénaga*) quagmire

mocasín *m* moccasin

mocedad *f* youth

mocetón, -ona *m, f* (*chico*) strapping lad; (*chica*) big girl

mochales *adj inv, inf* **estar** ~ to be crazy

mochila *f* rucksack *Brit,* backpack *Am;* (*de un soldado*) pack; (*de un estudiante*) satchel; (*para bebés*) baby carrier

mochilero, -a *m, f* backpacker; **ir de mochilera** to go backpacking

mocho, -a *adj* **1.**(*vaca*) hornless; (*árbol*) pol-

larded **2.**(*cabeza*) cropped **3.** *AmL* (*mutilado*) mutilated

mochuelo *m* **1.** ZOOL small owl **2.** *inf* (*carga*) burden; **cargar a alguien con el** ~ to stick sb with the dirty work; **siempre me toca cargar con el** ~ I am always stuck [*o* lumbered *Brit*] with the job; **cada** ~ **a su olivo** *fig* to each his own

moción *f t.* POL motion; **presentar una** ~ **de censura** to put forward a censure motion

moco *m* **1.**(*materia*) mucus; (*de la nariz*) snot; **limpiarse los** ~**s** to wipe one's nose **2.**(*del pavo*) wattle; **no es** ~ **de pavo** *fig* it's nothing to sneeze [*o* sniff] at **3.**(*de una mecha*) snuff; **a** ~ **de candil** by candlelight ▶**llorar a** ~ **tendido** *inf* to cry one's eyes out

moco, -a *adj inf* (*borracho*) plastered; (*drogado*) high

mocoso, -a I. *adj* runny-nosed II. *m, f pey* brat

moda *f* fashion; **vestido/peinado de** ~ fashionable dress/hairstyle; **estar de** ~ to be fashionable; **ponerse/pasar de** ~ to come into/go out of fashion; **ir a la (última)** ~ to follow the (latest) fashion

modal I. *adj* modal II. *mpl* manners *pl;* ~**es de la mesa** table manners; **¡qué** ~**es son estos!** what manners are these!; **¿has olvidado tus** ~**es?** have you forgotten your manners?

modalidad *f* form; ~**es de un contrato** types of contract

modelar *vt* to model; *fig* to fashion

modelo *mf* **1.**(*de modas*) model **2.** ARTE, FOTO model; ~ **vivo** live model

modelo *m* **1.**(*ejemplo*) model; **un político** ~ a model politician; **hacer algo según el** ~ to do sth according to the model; ~ **fuera de mercado** *t.* COM discontinued model **2.**(*esquema*) design

módem *m* INFOR modem

moderación *f* **1.**(*comedimiento*) moderation; **comer con** ~ to eat in moderation **2.** TV, RADIO presentation **3.**(*de un debate*) chairing

moderado, -a I. *adj* (*propuesta, persona, velocidad*) moderate; (*precio, petición*) reasonable; (*castigo*) light II. *m, f* POL moderate

moderador(a) I. *adj* moderating II. *m(f)* **1.** TV, RADIO presenter, moderator *Am* **2.**(*de un debate*) chairperson, moderator *Am*

moderar I. *vt* **1.**(*disminuir*) to moderate **2.** TV, RADIO to present **3.**(*debate*) to chair II. *vr:* ~**se** to calm down

modernismo *m* modernism

modernización *f* modernization

modernizar <z→c> I. *vt* to modernize II. *vr:* ~**se** to modernize oneself, to come up to date

moderno, -a *adj* modern; **edad moderna** present day; **historia moderna** modern history

modestia *f* **1.**(*humildad, sencillez*) modesty; ~ **aparte** modesty apart [*o* aside]; **vestir con** ~ to dress discreetly **2.**(*conformidad*) conformity **3.**(*de una mujer*) demureness

modesto, -a *adj* **1.**(*humilde, sencillo*) modest **2.** (*poco complicado*) simple **3.** (*mujer*) demure

módico, -a *adj* modest

modificación *f* (*de plan*) modification; (*de tema*) alteration; LING qualification; ~ **de estatutos** modification of statutes

modificar <c→qu> **I.** *vt* (*plan*) to modify; (*texto*) to revise; (*tema*) to alter; LING to qualify **II.** *vr:* ~**se** to adapt

modismo *m* idiom

modista *mf* dressmaker

modisto *m* fashion designer

modo *m* **1.** (*manera*) way; ~ **de andar/hablar/pensar** way of walking/talking/thinking; **hazlo a tu** ~ do it your way; **de este** ~ in this way; **de ningún** ~ no way; **hacer algo de cualquier** ~ to do sth any old how; **encontrar un** ~ **de resolver el problema** to find a way to solve the problem; **he encontrado el** ~ **de hacerlo** I have found the way to do it; **no es** ~ **de hablar a un superior** that is no way to speak to a superior; **de cualquier** ~ **no hubieran ido** anyway they would not have gone; **de** ~ **que lo has conseguido** so you have managed it; **utilizar el paraguas a** ~ **de espada** to use the umbrella as a sword; **en cierto** ~ in a way; **de un** ~ **u otro** one way or another; **de todos** ~**s no hubo heridos** at any rate no one was injured; **de todos** ~**s, lo volvería a intentar** anyway, I would try again; **de todos** ~**s es mejor que te vayas** in spite of everything it would be better for you to go **2.** LING mood **3.** INFOR mode; ~ **de operación** operational mode **4.** *pl* (*comportamiento*) manners *pl;* **tener buenos/malos** ~**s** to have good/bad manners; **decir algo con buenos/malos** ~**s** to say sth politely/rudely; **¿qué** ~**s son esos?** what manners are these?

modorra *f* drowsiness

modorro, -a *adj* **1.** (*somnoliento*) drowsy **2.** (*torpe*) lumbering **3.** (*atontado*) dazed **4.** (*fruta*) shrivelled *Brit,* shriveled *Am*

modoso, -a *adj* **ser** [*o* **estar**] ~ to be well--mannered

modular *vt, vi* to modulate

módulo *m* **1.** *t.* ARQUIT, ELEC (*de un mueble*) unit **2.** (*de una prisión*) wing **3.** ENS, INFOR module **4.** MÚS modulation **5.** AVIAT ~ **de mando** command module

mofa *f* mockery; **hacer** ~ **de algo** to scoff at sth

mofar *vi, vr* ~**se de algo/alguien** to scoff at sth/sb

mofeta *f* **1.** ZOOL skunk **2.** MIN noxious gas

moflete *m* chubby cheek

mofletudo, -a *adj* chubby-cheeked

mogolla *m Col* GASTR dark wholegrain bread

mogollón *m inf* **1.** (*cantidad*) load(s); **había** ~ **de gente en la fiesta** there were loads of people at the party; **había** ~ **de público en el pabellón** there were masses of spectators in the pavilion **2.** (*lío*) mess

mohín *m* face; **hacer un** ~ **gracioso** to pull a funny face

mohíno, -a *adj* **1.** (*enfadado*) sulky; (*de mal humor*) grumpy **2.** (*triste*) glum

moho *m* **1.** BOT mould *Brit,* mold *Am;* **no** (**dejar**) **criar** ~ (*alimentos*) to be eaten immediately; (*un objeto*) to be in constant use **2.** (*óxido*) rust **3.** (*desidia*) laziness

mohoso, -a *adj* **1.** (*de moho*) mouldy *Brit,* moldy *Am* **2.** (*oxidado*) rusty

mojama *f* salted dried tuna

mojar I. *vt* **1.** (*con un líquido*) to wet; (*ligeramente*) to moisten; (*para planchar*) to dampen **2.** (*el pan*) to dunk **3.** *inf* (*celebrar*) to celebrate **4.** *inf* (*apuñalar*) to stab **II.** *vi* (*en un asunto*) to get involved **III.** *vr:* ~**se 1.** (*con un líquido*) to get wet; **no te mojes los pies en el charco** do not get your feet wet in the puddle **2.** *inf* (*comprometerse*) to get involved

mojarra *f Arg* short broad knife

mojicón *m* **1.** GASTR sponge cake **2.** *inf* (*puñetazo*) punch in the face

mojigato, -a *adj* **1.** (*gazmoño*) prudish **2.** (*hipócrita*) hypocritical

mojón *m* **1.** (*hito*) boundary stone; ~ **kilométrico** milestone **2.** (*poste*) post

mol *m* mole

molar I. *adj* **1.** (*de muela*) **diente** ~ molar **2.** (*de moler*) grinding **II.** *m* molar **III.** *vi inf* **1.** (*gustar*) **este libro mola** this book is really cool; **me molan las rubias** I am into [*o* I go for] blonds; **me mola ese tío** I really like that guy **2.** (*llevarse*) to be in; **ahora mola llevar pelo corto** nowadays short hair is in

Moldavia *f* Moldavia

moldavo, -a *adj, m, f* Moldavian

molde *m* **1.** TÉC, GASTR mould *Brit,* mold *Am;* TIPO form; **pan de** ~ sliced bread; **letras de** ~ block letters; **romper** ~**s** to break the mould *Brit* [*o* mold *Am*] **2.** (*modelo*) model

moldeador *m* (*para el cabello*) perm

moldear *vt* **1.** (*formar*) to mould *Brit,* to mould *Am;* **diversas circunstancias han moldeado su vida** diverse circumstances have shaped his/her life **2.** (*vaciar*) to cast

moldura *f* **1.** (*listón*) trim **2.** ARQUIT moulding *Brit,* molding *Am*

mole¹ *f* (*masa*) mass

mole² *m Méx* GASTR **1.** (*salsa*) sauce; ~ **verde** green sauce **2.** (*guiso*) stew

---

Mole is the name given to a Mexican chilli sauce. Cayenne pepper from the chilli plant gives this sauce its characteristic sharp taste.

---

molécula *f* molecule

molecular *adj* molecular; **biología** ~ molecular biology

moler <o→ue> *vt* **1.** (*café, trigo*) to grind; (*aceitunas*) to press **2.** (*fatigar*) to exhaust; **estoy molido de la excursión** the trip has exhausted me **3.** (*molestar*) to bother **4.** (*estropear*) to ruin

molestar I. *vt* (*estorbar*) to inconvenience; (*fastidiar*) to bother; (*dolores*) to hurt; (*enfadar*) to annoy; **esta camisa me molesta** this shirt annoys me; **este dolor en la espalda me molesta** this pain in my shoulder bothers me **II.** *vr:* ~**se 1.** (*tomarse la molestia*) to bother; **ni siquiera te has molestado en comprobarlo** you haven't even taken the trouble to check it; **no te molestes en ir allí** don't bother to go there; **no te molestes por mí** don't put yourself out for me; **no tendrías que haberte molestado** you shouldn't have bothered **2.** (*ofenderse*) to take offence *Brit,* to take offense *Am;* **se ha molestado por tu comentario** he/she has taken offence *Brit* [*o* offense *Am*] at what you said

molestia *f* **1.** (*fastidio*) bother; (*por dolores*) discomfort; **ser una** ~ to be a nuisance; **no es ninguna** ~ it doesn't bother me **2.** (*inconveniente*) trouble; **no es ninguna** ~ **(para mí)** it is no trouble (for me); **tomarse la** ~ to take the trouble; **perdonen las** ~**s** we apologize for the inconvenience caused **3.** (*enfado*) annoyance **4.** (*dolor*) discomfort

molesto, -a *adj* **1.** *ser* (*desagradable*) unpleasant; (*fastidioso*) troublesome **2.** *estar* (*enfadado*) ~ **por algo** annoyed about sth; (*ofendido*) hurt by sth **3.** *estar* (*incómodo*) uncomfortable; **estoy** ~ **por el vendaje** the bandage is uncomfortable

molicie *f* **1.** *elev* (*blandura*) softness **2.** (*comodidad*) **vivir en la** ~ to live a life of luxury

molido, -a *adj inf* (*cansado*) **estoy** ~ I am worn out; **el trabajo me ha dejado** ~ the work has left me worn out

molinero, -a I. *adj* milling **II.** *m, f* miller

molinete *m* **1.** (*en una ventana*) ventilator **2.** (*juguete*) windmill *Brit,* pinwheel *Am*

molinillo *m* **1.** (*aparato*) ~ **de café** coffee grinder **2.** (*juguete*) windmill *Brit,* pinwheel *Am* **3.** (*para batir*) wooden stirrer

molino *m* **1.** (*máquina*) mill; ~ **de papel** paper mill **2.** (*inquieto*) restless person **3.** (*pesado*) irksome person

mollar *adj* **1.** (*fruta*) soft; (*carne*) tender **2.** (*persona*) gullible **3.** (*trabajo*) cushy

mollejas *fpl* sweetbreads *pl*

mollera *f* **1.** (*de la cabeza*) crown **2.** (*fontanela*) fontanelle *Brit,* fontanel *Am;* **la** ~ **se cierra** the fontanelle is closing; **tener la** ~ **cerrada** *fig* to be old enough to reason **3.** (*seso*) brain; **eso no me entra en la** ~ I just do not understand that; **ser duro de** ~ to be stubborn

mollete *m* **1.** (*pan*) muffin **2.** (*moflete*) plump cheek **3.** *Bol* GASTR *bread made quickly and poorly*

molo *m Chile* (*rompeolas*) breakwater; (*dique*) seawall

molón, -ona *adj* **1.** *inf* (*bonito*) pretty **2.** (*presumido*) vain **3.** *Guat, Ecua, Méx* (*fastidioso*) tiresome

molusco *m* mollusc

momentáneo, -a *adj* **1.** (*instantáneo*) momentary **2.** (*provisional*) provisional; **hacer un arreglo** ~ to find a provisional solution **3.** (*temporal*) temporary

momento *m* **1.** (*instante*) instant, moment; **¡espera un** ~! wait a moment!; **de un** ~ **a otro** at any time now; **al** ~ immediately; **en cualquier** [*o* **en todo**] ~ at any time; **el** ~ **decisivo** the moment of truth; **en el** ~ **adecuado** at the appropriate time; **en el** ~ **de la salida** when they were about to start; **en este** ~ **hay demasiado paro** at the moment there is too much unemployment; **en este** ~ **estaba pensando en ti** I was just thinking about you; **de** ~, **no te puedo decir nada** for the moment, I can't tell you anything; **de** ~ **leeré el periódico y luego...** for the time being I'll read the newspaper and then ...; **de** [*o* **por el**] ~ **no sé nada de él** for the moment I haven't heard from him; **en un** ~ **de flaqueza** in a moment of weakness; **la tensión aumentaba por** ~**s** the tension was growing ever stronger [*o* stronger and stronger]; **aparecer en el último** ~ to arrive at the last moment; **en todo** ~ **mantuvo la calma** at all times he/she remained calm; **no tengo un** ~ **libre** I do not have one free moment; **hace un** ~ **que ha salido** he/she left a moment ago; **este estudiante me pregunta a cada** ~ this student is always asking me questions **2.** (*período*) period; **atravieso un mal** ~ I am going through a bad patch **3.** (*actualidad*) present; **la música del** ~ present-day music **4.** (*situación*) moment **5.** Fís momentum

momia *f* **1.** (*egipcia*) mummy **2.** (*persona*) painfully thin person

momificar <c→qu> *vt* to mummify

momio *m inf* cushy job; **este trabajo es un** ~ this is a cushy job; **este traje es un** ~ this suit is a bargain; **de** ~ free

momio, -a *adj* lean

mona *f* **1.** ZOOL female monkey; (*especie*) Barbary ape **2.** *inf* (*borrachera*) drunken state; **coger una** ~ to get drunk; **estar como una** ~ to be drunk; **dormir la** ~ to sleep off a hangover **3.** GASTR ~ **de Pascua** Easter cake ►**aunque la** ~ **se vista de seda,** ~ **se queda** *prov* you can't make a silk purse from a sow's ear; **vete a freír** ~**s** *inf* go jump in the lake; **estar hecho una** ~ to feel mortified

Mónaco *m* Monaco

monada *f* **1.** (*zalamería*) flattery **2.** (*gracia*) antics *pl* **3.** *pl* (*amaneramiento*) affectation **4.** (*algo bonito*) **es una** ~ **de chica** that girl is a beauty; **¡qué** ~ **de vestido!** what a gorgeous dress!; **este bebé es una** ~ this baby is a cute little thing

monaguillo, -a *m, f* altar boy

monarca *mf* monarch

monarquía *f* monarchy

monárquico, -a I. *adj* **1.** (*de la monarquía*) monarchic **2.** (*partidario*) monarchist **II.** *m, f* monarchist

M

monasterio *m* monastery

monda *f* **1.** (*acción*) peeling **2.** (*peladura*) peel **3.** (*poda*) pruning ►**ser la** ~ *inf* to be terrific; **este pueblo es la** ~, **nadie sabe dónde está el cine** this village is the pits, nobody knows where the cinema is

mondadientes *m inv* toothpick

mondadura *f* **1.** (*acción*) peeling **2.** *pl* (*peladuras*) peelings *pl*

mondar I. *vt* **1.** (*plátano, patata, palo*) to peel; (*guisantes*) to shell; (*rama*) to pare **2.** (*árbol*) to prune II. *vr:* ~**se 1.** (*pelarse*) to peel **2.** (*limpiar*) ~**se los dientes** to clean one's teeth with a toothpick **3.** *inf* (*reírse*) ~**se** (**de risa**) *inf* to die laughing

mondo, -a *adj* **1.** (*cabeza*) shaven **2.** *inf* (*de dinero*) **quedarse** ~ (**y lirondo**) to be broke ►~ **y lirondo** *inf* plain, pure and simple

mondongo *m* **1.** entrails *pl*, innards *pl* **2.** (*carne*) sausage meat

moneda *f* **1.** (*pieza*) coin; ~ **de cinco peniques** five pence coin; ~ **de 5/10/25 centavos** nickel/dime/quarter; ~ **suelta** change; **teléfono de** ~**s** pay phone; **pagar a alguien con la misma** ~ *fig* to pay sb back tit for tat; **la otra cara de la** ~ the other side of the coin; **esto es** ~ **corriente** *fig* that is the norm; **si él me ofrece calidad, yo le pago en buena** ~ *fig* if he offers me quality, I'll see him right **2.** (*de un país*) currency; ~ **base** base currency; ~ **de curso legal** legal tender; ~ **extranjera** foreign currency; ~ **fuerte/débil** strong/weak currency; ~ **nacional** local currency; ~ **única europea** European single currency

monedero *m* **1.** (*bolsa*) purse **2.** (*persona*) ~ **falso** counterfeiter

monegasco, -a I. *adj* of/from Monaco II. *m, f* native/inhabitant of Monaco

monería *f* (*gracia*) antics *pl*

monetario, -a *adj* monetary; **institución monetaria** monetary institution; **tormentas monetarias** monetary turmoil

mongólico, -a I. *adj* MED of Down's syndrome II. *m, f* MED person with Down's syndrome; **ser un** ~ to have Down's syndrome

mongolismo *m sin pl* MED Down's syndrome

monigote *m* **1.** (*dibujo mal hecho*) childlike drawing; (*figura*) stick figure; **hacer** ~**s** (*figuras humanas*) to draw stick figures; (*borrones*) to doodle **2.** (*muñeco*) rag doll, paper doll **3.** (*persona*) spineless individual, wimp

monitor *m* TÉC, TV, INFOR monitor; (*pantalla*) screen

monitor(a) *m(f)* (*de un deporte*) coach, trainer; (*de un campamento*) camp leader; ~ **de natación** swimming instructor

monitorio, -a *adj* admonitory; **carta monitoria** admonitory letter

monja *f* nun, sister

monje *m* monk, brother

monjil I. *adj* nun-like; **llevar una vida** ~ *fig* to lead the life of a hermit; (*muy recatado*) prud-ish II. *m* nun's habit

mono *m* **1.** ZOOL monkey; **¿tengo** ~**s en la cara?** *inf* what are you staring at?; **hacer** ~**s a alguien** to make a sign to sb **2.** (*fantoche*) nobody; **en esta casa soy el último** ~ in this house I am a nobody **3.** (*traje*) overalls *pl*; (*de mecánico*) boiler suit *Brit*, coveralls *pl Am*; (*de calle*) jumpsuit *Am* **4.** *inf* (*de drogas*) withdrawal symptoms *pl*; **tener el** ~ to be suffering from withdrawal symptoms; **le entra el** ~ he gets withdrawal symptoms **5.** (*persona fea*) ugly devil **6.** (*joven tonto*) silly youth **7.** (*dibujo*) cartoon

mono, -a *adj* **1.** (*niño*) cute; (*chica*) pretty; (*vestido*) lovely **2.** *Col, inf* (*rubio*) blonde

monóculo *m* monocle

monocultivo *m* monoculture, singlecrop farming

monogamia *f sin pl* monogamy

monógamo, -a *adj* monogamous

monografía *f* monograph

monograma *m* monogram

monolingüe *adj* monolingual

monólogo *m* monologue; TEAT soliloquy

monopatín *m* skateboard

monopolio *m* monopoly

monopolizar <z→c> *vt* COM to monopolize, to corner (a market); ~ **la atención de alguien** to monopolize sb's attention

monosílabo *m* monosyllable; **responder con** ~**s** to answer in monosyllables

monosílabo, -a *adj* monosyllabic

monotonía *f* monotony

monótono, -a *adj* monotonous

monóxido *m* monoxide

monseñor *m* monsignor

monserga *f inf* **1.** (*lengua*) drivel; **¡no me vengas con** ~**s!** don't spout drivel at me! **2.** (*lata*) bore; **este trabajo es una** ~ this job is a bore

monstruo I. *m* **1.** (*ser fantástico*) monster **2.** (*persona fea*) hideous person **3.** (*persona perversa*) fiend **4.** (*artista*) superstar II. *adj inv* **una actuación** ~ a magnificent performance

monstruosidad *f* monstrosity; **eso que dices es una** ~ what you are saying is a monstrosity

monstruoso, -a *adj* **1.** (*desfigurado*) disfigured **2.** (*terrible*) monstrous; **es** ~ **tener que estudiar durante el verano** it is monstrous to have to study during the summer **3.** (*enorme*) huge

monta *f* **1.** (*de maquinaria*) assembly; (*de joyas*) setting **2.** (*de caballo*) mating season; (*acto*) mounting **3.** (*importe*) total **4.** (*importancia*) importance; **de poca** ~ unimportant

montacargas *m inv* (service) lift *Brit*, (freight) elevator *Am*

montador(a) *m(f)* **1.** TÉC (*de máquinas*) fitter, assembler **2.** CINE editor

montaje *m* **1.** TÉC assembly **2.** CINE editing; FOTO montage **3.** TEAT decor **4.** (*engaño*) set-up

montante *m* **1.** (*importe*) total **2.** (*de puerta*) jamb; (*de ventana*) mullion

montaña *f* **1.** GEO (*monte*) mountain; (*zona*) mountains *pl;* ~ **rusa** big dipper; **prefiero la ~ al mar** I prefer the mountains to the seaside; **la fe mueve ~s** faith will move mountains **2.** (*de cosas*) difficulty ▶ **hacer una ~ de un grano de arena** to make a mountain out of a mole-hill; grande **como una ~** as big as a house

montañero, -a *m, f* mountaineer

montañés, -esa I. *adj* **1.** (*de la montaña*) highlander **2.** (*de Santander*) of/from Santander II. *m, f* native/inhabitant of Santander

montañismo *m* mountaineering

montañoso, -a *adj* mountainous

montar I. *vi* **1.** (*subir a una bici, un caballo*) to get on; (*en un coche*) to get in; ~ **en** (*una bici, un caballo*) to get onto; (*en un coche*) to get into; **tanto monta que vaya como que no** *fig* it doesn't matter whether I go or not **2.** (*ir a caballo*) to ride; ~ **en bici** to ride a bycicle **3.** (*una cuenta*) ~ **a** to come to II. *vt* **1.** (*subir en un caballo*) to mount; **no montes al niño en el alféizar** don't sit the lad on the window-sill **2.** (*ir a caballo*) to ride **3.** (*acaballar, cubrir*) to cover **4.** (*máquina*) to assemble; (*tienda*) to open **5.** (*clara de huevo*) to beat; (*nata*) to whip **6.** (*casa*) to furnish **7.** (*negocio*) to set up **8.** TEAT to stage **9.** (*diamante*) to set **10.** (*arma*) to cock **11.** CINE to edit **12.** *inf* (*excursión*) to organize **13.** (*guardia, ejército*) to mount **14.** *inf* (*lío*) ~**la** to kick up a fuss; ~ **un número** to make a scene III. *vr:* ~**se 1.** (*subir*) to climb; **no te montes ahí** do not climb up there **2.** *inf* (*arreglárselas*) **¿cómo te lo montas con el trabajo?** how do you manage with the work?; **no nos lo montamos muy bien entre nosotros** we are not coping very well on our own; **me lo monto solo** I manage on my own

montaraz *adj* **1.** (*salvaje*) wild **2.** (*resistente*) tough **3.** (*tosco*) coarse **4.** (*arisco*) unsociable

monte *m* **1.** (*montaña*) mountain; **el ~ de los Olivos** the Mount of Olives **2.** (*bosque*) ~ **alto** woodland; ~ **bajo** scrub; **batir el ~** (*cazar*) to go hunting; (*buscar*) to beat the undergrowth; **echarse al ~** to take to the hills **3.** *pl* (*cordillera*) mountain range **4.** (*establecimiento*) ~ **de piedad** state-owned pawnshop ▶ **no todo el ~ es orégano** *prov* all that glitters is not gold

montepío *m* **1.** (*caja para viudas*) fund for widows; (*para huérfanos*) fund for orphans **2.** (*pensión de viuda*) widow's pension; (*de huérfano*) orphan's pension

montera *f* **1.** (*gorra*) cap; **ponerse el mundo por ~** *fig* not to be affected by the opinion of others **2.** (*de una galería*) glass roof

montería *f* hunting

montés, -esa *adj* wild; **cabra montesa** mountain goat; **gato ~** wildcat

montículo *m* mound

monto *m* total

montón *m* heap; **un ~ de ropa** a heap of

clothes; **había un ~ de gente** there were a lot of people; **tengo problemas a montones** *inf* I have loads of problems; **tomar montones de pastillas** *inf* to take loads of pills; **ser del ~** to be ordinary; **tener una cara del ~** to have a run-of-the-mill face; **la bomba atómica redujo Hiroshima a un ~ de escombros** the atomic bomb reduced Hiroshima to a pile of rubble

montura *f* **1.** (*arnés*) harness; (*silla*) saddle **2.** (*animal*) mount **3.** (*de gafas*) frame; (*de una joya*) setting

monumental *adj* **1.** (*grande, de importancia*) monumental; (*error*) tremendous **2.** (*de monumento*) **el Madrid ~** the sights of Madrid

monumento *m* memorial; (*grande*) monument; ~ **funerario** gravestone; ~ **de la literatura** literary work of art; **los ~s de una ciudad** the sights of a city; **esta casa es un ~ nacional** this house is a listed building; **esta chica es un ~** this girl is beautiful

monzón *m* monsoon

moña *f* **1.** (*lazo*) bow **2.** *inf* (*borrachera*) drunken state; **estar ~** to be drunk

moño *m* **1.** (*pelo*) bun **2.** (*lazo*) bow **3.** (*plumas*) crest **4.** *Col* (*capricho*) whim **5.** *Chile* (*pelo*) hair; (*copete*) forelock **6.** *pl* (*adornos*) frippery **7.** *inf* (*expresiones*) **quitar ~s a alguien** to bring sb down a peg (or two); **ponerse ~s** to put on airs (and graces); **estar hasta el ~ de algo** to be fed up to the back teeth with sth; **se me ha puesto en el ~ de...** I have taken it into my head to ...

MOPU *m abr de* **Ministerio de Obras Públicas y Urbanismo** *Spanish ministerial department in charge of public transport infrastructure and planning, now called Fomento*

moquear *vi* to have a runny nose

moqueta *f* fitted carpet, carpet *Am*

mora *f* **1.** BOT (*del moral*) mulberry; (*de la zarzamora*) blackberry **2.** JUR delay

morada *f* **1.** (*casa*) abode **2.** (*residencia*) residence **3.** (*estancia*) stay; **la eterna ~** heaven

morado, -a *adj* purple; **poner un ojo ~ a alguien** to give sb a black eye; **pasarlas moradas** to have a bad time; **ponerse ~ (comiendo)** *inf* to gorge [*o* stuff] oneself

moral I. *adj* **1.** (*ético*) moral; **código ~** code of ethics; **tengo la certidumbre ~** I have the moral conviction **2.** (*espiritual*) spiritual II. *f* morals *pl;* ~ **relajada** relaxed morals; **tú y yo no tenemos la misma ~** you and I do not have the same principles; **levantar la ~ a alguien** to boost sb's morale; **hay que tener ~ para hacer eso** you have to be sure of yourself to do that; **tener más ~ que el Alcoyano** to keep one's morale high in the face of overwhelming difficulties

moraleja *f* moral

moralidad *f* (*cualidad*) morality

moralista *mf* moralist

moralizar <z→c> I. *vi* to moralize II. *vt* to

improve the morals of

morapio *m inf* red (wine), red plonk

moratón *m* bruise

moratoria *f t.* FIN moratorium; ~ **nuclear** moratorium on nuclear weapons testing

mórbido, -a *adj* **1.** (*enfermo*) ill **2.** (*suave*) soft

morbo *m* **1.** (*enfermedad*) illness **2.** (*interés malsano*) morbid fascination; **este partido de fútbol tiene mucho** ~ this football game has created a lot of unhealthy interest; **el color negro me da** ~ I find black a morbid colour

morbosidad *f* morbidity

morboso, -a *adj* **1.** (*clima*) unhealthy **2.** (*placer, imaginación*) morbid

morcilla *f* **1.** GASTR black pudding, blood sausage **2.** TEAT improvisation **3.** *Cuba* (*mentira*) lie **4.** *inf* (*fastidiar*) **¡que te den** ~! *vulg* get stuffed!

morcillo *m* shin; (*carne*) shoulder

mordaz *adj* **1.** (*comentario*) caustic; (*crítica*) scathing **2.** (*sabor*) bitter **3.** (*corrosivo*) corrosive

mordaza *f* **1.** (*en la boca*) gag; **quieren ponerme una** ~ *fig* they want to shut me up **2.** TÉC clamp

mordedor(a) *adj* liable to bite; **perro ladrador, poco** ~ *prov* his bark is worse than his bite

mordedura *f* bite

morder <o→ue> I. *vt* **1.** (*con los dientes*) to bite; **te voy a hacer** ~ **el polvo** I am going to crush you; **está que muerde** *inf* he/she is furious **2.** (*corroer*) to corrode **3.** *AmL* (*estafar*) to cheat II. *vr:* ~**se** to bite; **¡no te muerdas las uñas!** don't bite your nails; **tuve que** ~**me la lengua** I had to bite my tongue; **no** ~**se la lengua** to say what one thinks

mordida *f* **1.** *Méx, inf* (*acción*) bite; (*dinero*) bribe **2.** *Arg v.* **mordisco**

mordisco *m* bite, nibble

mordisquear *vt* ~ **algo** to nibble at sth

morena *f* **1.** ZOOL moray eel **2.** (*pan*) wholemeal [*o* wholegrain] bread **3.** GEO moraine

moreno *m* mixture of ground coal and vinagre (*used by shearers to cure cuts*)

moreno, -a I. *adj* brown; (*de piel*) swarthy; (*de cabello*) dark-haired; (*de ojos*) brown-eyed II. *m, f* **1.** (*negro*) coloured person *Brit*, colored person *Am* **2.** *Cuba* (*mulato*) mulatto

morera *f* mulberry tree

morete *m AmC,* **moretón** *m inf* bruise

morfema *m* LING morpheme

morfina *f* morphine

morfinómano, -a I. *adj* addicted to morphine II. *m, f* morphine addict

morgue *f AmL* morgue

moribundo, -a I. *adj* dying II. *m, f* dying person

morigeración *f elev* moderation

morigerado, -a *adj elev* **1.** (*moderado*) moderate **2.** (*bien criado*) well brought-up **3.** (*de buenas costumbres*) well-behaved

morigerar *vt elev* to moderate

morir *irr* I. *vi* **1.** (*perecer*) to die; (*en catástrofe, guerra, accidente*) to be killed; ~ **de hambre/sed** to die of starvation/thirst; ~ **ahogado** (*en agua*) to drown; (*en humo*) to asphyxiate, to suffocate; ~ **de viejo** to die of old age; ~ **en un incendio** to die in a fire; ~ **a causa de las graves heridas** to die from serious wounds; **murió al pie del cañón** he died with his boots on **2.** (*tarde*) to draw to a close; (*luz*) to fade away; (*tradición*) to die out; (*camino*) to peter out; (*río*) to finish; (*sonido*) to die away II. *vr:* ~**se** **1.** (*perecer*) to die; (*planta*) to wither; **se le ha muerto su padre** his/her father has died; **¡así te mueras!** *inf* good riddance to you! **2.** (*con 'de'*) ~**se de hambre/de sed** to die of starvation/thirst; ~**se de frío** to freeze to death; ~**se de vergüenza** to die of shame; ~**se de risa** to die laughing; ~**se de pena** to pine away **3.** (*con 'por'*) **me muero por conocer a tu nueva novia** I am dying to meet your new girlfriend; **me muero (de ganas) por saber lo que te dijo** I am dying to know what she/he said to you; **me muero por ella** I am crazy about her **4.** (*miembro del cuerpo*) to become numb

mormón, -ona *adj, m, f* Mormon

moro, -a I. *adj* (*musulmán*) Muslim II. *m, f* Muslim; **ser un** ~ *inf* to be chauvinistic; **¡hay** ~**s en la costa!** *fig* watch out!; **¡no hay** ~**s en la costa!** *fig* the coast is clear!

morochos *mpl Ven* twins *pl*

morondo, -a *adj* bare

moroso, -a I. *adj* **1.** (*deudor*) slow to pay up **2.** *elev* (*lento*) slow; (*estilo*) drawn-out; **el río avanza de manera morosa** the river advances at a slow pace II. *m, f* debtor in arrears, defaulter

morral *m* **1.** (*de las caballerías*) nosebag **2.** (*zurrón*) knapsack

morralla *f* **1.** (*cosas*) trifles *pl* **2.** (*gente*) rabble **3.** (*pescados*) small fry

morrear *vt, vr:* ~**se** *vulg* to neck, to snog

morriña *f sin pl, inf* (*nostalgia*) homesickness

morro *m* **1.** ZOOL (*hocico*) snout **2.** (*de persona*) ~**s** (*labios*) lips; (*boca*) mouth; **beber a** ~ to drink straight from the bottle; **me caí de** ~**s** I fell flat on my face; **te voy a partir los** ~**s** *inf* I'm going to smash your face in; **estar de** ~(**s**) *fig* to be angry; **torcer el** ~ *fig* to pout; **tiene un** ~ **que se lo pisa** *inf* he/she has a real nerve; **lo hizo así, por el** ~ *inf* he/she did it like that, quite brazenly; **se quedó el dinero por (todo) el** ~ *inf* he brazenly kept all the money **3.** (*de pistola*) muzzle; (*de barco, avión, coche*) nose **4.** (*montículo*) hillock

morrocotudo, -a *adj inf* **1.** (*formidable*) terrific **2.** (*susto, disgusto*) dreadful

morrón I. *adj* pimiento ~ sweet red pepper II. *m inf* (*golpe*) blow

morsa *f* walrus

morse *m* Morse code; **señal** ~ Morse code signal

mortadela *f* mortadella, ≈ bologna

mortaja *f* **1.**(*sábana*) shroud; (*vestidura*) burial clothes *pl* **2.** *AmL* (*de cigarrillo*) cigarette paper

mortal I. *adj* **1.**(*sujeto a la muerte*) mortal; **los restos ~es** the mortal remains; **los ~es** mankind **2.**(*que la causa*) mortal, lethal; **pecado ~** mortal sin; **peligro ~** mortal danger; **tener un odio ~ a alguien** to have a deadly hatred of sb **3.**(*pesado*) deadly; (*aburrido*) dreary **II.** *mf* mortal

mortalidad *f* **1.**(*cualidad*) mortality **2.**(*número*) mortality rate

mortandad *f* loss of life; **el virus ébola causó una gran ~ en Zaire** Ebola fever caused a carnage in Zaire; **la ~ de la guerra en Ruanda** the bloodbath during the war in Rwanda

mortecino, -a *adj* (*luz*) dim; (*color*) muted; (*fuego*) dull

mortero *m* **1.** *t.* MIL (*cuenco*) mortar **2.**(*cemento*) cement, mortar

mortífero, -a *adj* deadly

mortificación *f* **1.**(*tormento*) torment **2.** *t.* REL (*humillación*) mortification

mortificar <c→qu> **I.** *vt* **1.**(*atormentar*) to torment **2.** *t.* REL (*humillar*) to mortify **II.** *vr:* **~se 1.**(*atormentarse*) to be tormented **2.** REL to mortify oneself **3.** *Méx* (*avergonzarse*) to be ashamed

mortuorio, -a *adj* death

moruno, -a *adj* Moorish; **pincho ~** spicy meat kebab

mosaico *m* mosaic

mosca *f* **1.** ZOOL fly; **por si las ~s** *inf* just in case; **tener la ~ detrás de la oreja** *inf* to be suspicious; **estar ~** *inf* (*receloso*) to be suspicious; (*enfadado*) to be cross; **no se oía el vuelo de una ~** you could have heard a pin drop; **papar ~s** *inf* to be spellbound; **¿qué ~ te ha picado?** what's bugging you?; **andar cazando ~s** to spend time on futile things **2.**(*barba*) goatee **3.**(*persona*) nuisance, bore; **~ cojonera** *vulg* fucking [*o* bloody *Brit*] pest; **~ muerta** hypocrite **4.** *inf* (*dinero*) dough, dosh; **aflojar la ~** to shell out

moscada *adj* **nuez ~** nutmeg

moscarda *f* blowfly, bluebottle

moscardón *m* **1.** ZOOL (*moscarda*) blowfly, bluebottle; (*tábano*) horsefly; (*avispón*) hornet **2.**(*persona*) pest

moscatel *m* Muscatel

moscón *m v.* **moscardón**

moscón, -ona *m, f* blowfly

moscovita *adj, mf* Muscovite

Moscú *m* Moscow

mosqueado, -a *adj* **1.** *inf* (*enfadado*) cross; **estar ~ con alguien** to be cross with sb **2.**(*moteado*) spotted; (*vaca*) mottled

mosquearse *vr inf* (*ofenderse*) to take offence *Brit*, to take offense *Am;* (*enfadarse*) to get angry

mosqueo *m* anger; **coger un ~ de aúpa** to fly into a rage

mosquetero *m* **1.**(*soldado*) musketeer **2.** *Arg, Bol* (*en una fiesta*) party-crasher

mosquetón *m* **1.**(*arma*) carbine **2.**(*anilla*) snap ring

mosquita *f* **~ muerta** hypocrite; **se hace la ~ muerta** he/she looks as if butter wouldn't melt in his/her mouth

mosquitero *m* mosquito net(ting)

mosquito *m* mosquito; (*pequeño*) gnat

mostaza *f* mustard; (*semilla*) mustard seed; (**de**) **color ~** mustard(-yellow)

mosto *m* grape juice

mostrador *m* **1.**(*tienda*) counter; (*escaparate*) shop window **2.**(*bar*) bar **3.**(*ventanilla*) window

mostrar <o→ue> **I.** *vt* (*enseñar*) to show; (*presentar*) to display; **¡no muestres tu miedo!** do not reveal your fear! **II.** *vr:* **~se** to appear; **~se amigo** to be friendly

mota *f* **1.**(*partícula*) speck; **~ (de polvo)** speak of dust **2.**(*mancha*) spot; (*lunar*) mole

mote *m* **1.**(*apodo*) nickname; **~ cariñoso** pet name **2.** *AmL* (*maíz*) boiled maize *Brit* [*o* corn *Am*]

moteado, -a *adj* (*ojos*) flecked; (*tela*) dotted; (*huevos*) speckled

motear *vt* to fleck, to speckle

motejar *vt* (*tildar*) to brand

motel *m* motel

motero, -a *m, f* biker

motete *m* **1.** MÚS motet **2.** *AmS* bundle

motín *m* uprising; (*militar*) mutiny; **un ~ en la cárcel** a prison riot

motivación *f* motivation

motivar *vt* **1.**(*incitar*) to motivate **2.**(*explicar*) to explain **3.**(*provocar*) to cause; **los puntos que motivan el presente contrato son...** the points which give rise to the present contract are ...

motivo *m* **1.**(*causa*) reason behind; (*crimen*) motive; **con ~ de...** on the occasion of ...; **por este ~** for this reason; **carecer de ~ alguno** to have no point whatsoever **2.**(*tela*) motif

moto *f inf* motorbike; **~ acuática** jet ski; **~ para la nieve** snowmobile; **ir en ~** to ride a motorbike; **iba como una ~** *inf* he/she was going like a bat out of hell; **estar como una ~** to be wound up; **ponerse como una ~** (*sexual*) to get horny; (*enfadado*) to get furious

motocicleta *f* motorcycle; **ir en ~** to go by motorcycle

motociclismo *m sin pl* motorcycling

motociclista *mf* motorcyclist

motoneta *f AmL* motor scooter

motor *m* **1.** *t. fig* motor; **~ de búsqueda** INFOR search engine; **~ de explosión** internal combustion engine; **~ de reacción** jet engine; **vehículo de ~** motor vehicle **2.**(*causa*) cause

motor(a) *adj* motor; **nervio ~** motor nerve

motora *f* motorboat

motorismo *m sin pl* motorcycling

motorista *mf* **1.** DEP motorcyclist **2.**(*chófer*)

motorist, driver **3.** (*policía*) motorized policeman

motorizar <z→c> *vt* to motorize; **estar motorizado** *inf* to have wheels [*o* a car]

motosierra *f* chain saw

motriz *adj* driving; **fuerza** ~ driving force

movedizo, -a *adj* **1.** (*móvil*) moving; **arenas movedizas** quicksand; *fig* dangerous ground **2.** (*inconstante*) changeable

mover <o→ue> **I.** *vt* **1.** (*desplazar*) to move; ~ **la cola** to wag one's tail; ~ **la cabeza** (*asentir*) to nod (one's head); (*negar*) to shake one's head **2.** (*ajedrez*) to move **3.** (*incitar*) to rouse; ~ **a alguien a compasión** to move sb; ~ **a alguien a lágrimas** to move sb to tears **4.** INFOR to move; ~ **archivo** move file **II.** *vr:* ~**se** to move; ¿**nos movemos o qué?** shall we make a move?; ¡**venga, muévete!** come on! get a move on!

movible *adj* **1.** (*pieza*) movable **2.** (*carácter*) changeable

movida *f* **1.** *inf* fuss; ¡**qué** ~! (*lío*) what a business! **2.** (*ambiente*) scene

movido, -a *adj* **1.** (*foto*) blurred **2.** (*activo*) active; (*vivo*) lively; **he tenido un día muy** ~ I have had a very busy day **3.** MÚS rhythmic

móvil **I.** *adj* mobile **II.** *m* **1.** (*para colgar*) mobile **2.** (*crimen*) motive **3.** TEL mobile (phone), cellphone *Am*

movilidad *f sin pl* mobility

movilización *f* **1.** (*recursos, tropas*) mobilization **2.** (*huelga*) industrial action **3.** (*dinero*) release

movilizar <z→c> *vt* **1.** (*ejército, recursos, fuerzas*) to mobilize **2.** (*dinero*) to release

movimiento *m* **1.** *t.* FÍS movement; ~ **vibratorio** vibratory movement; **hacer** ~**s** ARQUIT to subside; **poner en** ~ to put [*o* set] in motion; **había mucho** ~ **en las tiendas** the shops were busy **2.** (*ajedrez*) move **3.** MÚS (*velocidad*) tempo; (*tiempo*) movement **4.** HIST, LIT, POL movement; **el Movimiento (Nacional)** *ruling political organization in Francoist Spain* **5.** COM movement; ~**s bursátiles** stock-market movements

moza *f* (*chica*) girl; ¡**está ya hecha una** ~! she is a big girl now!

mozambiqueño, -a *adj, m, f* Mozambican

mozo *m* **1.** (*criado*) servant; ~ (**de café**) waiter; ~ (**de estación**) porter; ~ **de hotel** bellboy **2.** (*soldado*) recruit

mozo, -a **I.** *adj* **1.** (*joven*) young; **la gente moza** the youth **2.** (*soltero*) single **II.** *m, f* (*chico*) lad; (*chica*) girl; (*joven*) youth, young man; ¡**pero si estás hecho un** ~! (*a un chico*) what a strapping lad you are!; (*a un adulto*) you are nothing but a lad!

mu **I.** *interj* (*vaca*) moo **II.** *m* **no decir ni** ~ *inf* not to say a word

mucamo, -a *m, f AmL* (*criado*) servant; (*criada*) maid

muceta *f* (*del doctor, juez*) cape

muchacha *f* **1.** *v.* **muchacho 2.** (*criada*) maid

muchachada *f AmL* group of youths

muchacho, -a *m, f* (*chico*) boy; (*chica*) girl

muchedumbre *f* **1.** (*de cosas*) collection; **salió volando una** ~ **de pájaros** a flock of birds flew off **2.** (*de personas*) crowd

mucho, -a I. *adj* a lot of; ~ **vino** a lot of wine, much wine; ~**s libros** a lot of books, many books; **esto es** ~ **para ella** this is too much for her; **hace ya** ~ **tiempo que...** it has been a long time since ...; **muchas veces** lots of times; **eso me parece** ~ **decir** I think that is going a bit far ▸ **mal de** ~**s, consuelo de tontos** *prov* ≈ only a fool finds comfort in the fact that a misfortune is shared by others **II.** *adv* (*intensidad*) very; **trabajar/esforzarse** ~ to work/to try hard; (*cantidad*) a lot; (*mucho tiempo*) for a long time; (*muchas veces*) many times; (*a menudo*) often; **lo sentimos** ~ we are very sorry; **no hace** ~ **estuvo aquí** he was here not long ago; **es con** ~ **el más simpático** he is by far the most pleasant; ¡**pero que muy** ~! extremely!; **lo tenemos en** ~ we think highly of him; **por** ~ **que se esfuercen, no lo conseguirán** however hard they try, they will not manage it; **ni** ~ **menos** far from it; **como** ~ at (the) most

mucosa *f* mucus

mucosidad *f* (*moco*) mucosity

mucoso, -a *adj* mucous; **membrana mucosa** mucous membrane

muda *f* **1.** (*ropa interior*) change of underwear; (*cama*) change of sheets **2.** (*serpiente*) slough, shedding of skin **3.** (*pájaro, pelo*) moult *Brit*, molt *Am* **4.** (*voz*) **está de** ~ his voice is breaking

mudable *adj* changeable

mudanza *f* (*de casa*) move; **camión de** ~**s** removal van, moving van; **estar de** ~ to be moving house

mudar **I.** *vi, vt* **1.** (*cambiar*) to change; ~ (**de**) **pluma** to moult *Brit,* to molt *Am;* ~ (**de**) **piel** to slough, to shed; **los años le han mudado el** [*o* **del**] **carácter** the years have altered his/her character **2.** (*de ropa*) to change **II.** *vr:* ~**se 1.** (*casa*) to move (house); **nos mudamos** (**de aquí**) we are moving (from here); ~**se a Granada** to move to Granada; ~**se a una casa nueva** to move to a new house **2.** (*ropa*) ~**se** (**de ropa**) to change clothes

mudez *f sin pl* muteness, dumbness; (*silencio*) silence

mudo, -a I. *adj* dumb; **cine** ~ silent films *Brit,* silent movies *Am;* **quedarse** ~ **de asombro** to be speechless with amazement **II.** *m, f* mute [*o* dumb] person

mueble **I.** *m* **1.** (*pieza*) piece of furniture; ~ **bar** drinks cabinet; ~ **biblioteca** bookcase; **cama** ~ foldaway bed; ~ **zapatero** shoe cupboard; ~ **de cocina** kitchen unit **2.** *pl* furniture; **con/sin** ~**s** furnished/unfurnished; ~**s de cocina** kitchen units [*o* cabinets]; ~**s de época** period furniture; ~**s tapizados** upholstered furniture **II.** *adj* JUR **bienes** ~s movable goods, personal property

mueca *f* face; **hacer** ~s to pull faces; (*de dolor, disgusto*) grimace

muela *f* **1.** (*diente*) molar; ~s **del juicio** wisdom teeth; ~ **picada** molar with tooth decay; **dolor de** ~s toothache **2.** (*molino*) millstone **3.** (*para afilar*) grindstone

muelle **I.** *m* **1.** (*resorte*) spring; (*reloj*) mainspring **2.** (*puerto*) wharf; ~ **flotante** floating quay **3.** (*andén*) loading dock **II.** *adj* (*blando*) soft; (*cómodo*) comfortable

muérdago *m* mistletoe

muerte *f* **1.** (*acción de morir*) death; ~ **forestal** forest destruction; ~ **súbita** MED crib death; ~ **a traición** death by treachery; **pena de** ~ death penalty; **condenar a** ~ to condemn [*o* sentence] to death; **morir de** ~ **natural** to die of natural causes; **está luchando contra la** ~ he/she is fighting for his/her life; **estar enfermo de** ~ to be at death's door; **está en su lecho de** ~ he/she is on his/her deathbed; **hasta que la** ~ **os separe** (*matrimonio*) till death do you part **2.** (*asesinato*) murder **3.** (*destrucción*) destruction ▶**cada** ~ **de un obispo** once in a blue moon; **de mala** ~ lousy, crummy; **un hotel de mala** ~ a grotty hotel; **a** ~ to death; **a ese tipo lo odio a** ~ I detest that man; **llevarse un susto de** ~ to have a dreadful fright

muerto, -a **I.** *pp de* morir **II.** *adj* dead; **cal muerta** slaked [*o* hydrated] lime; **horas muertas** period of inactivity; **naturaleza muerta** still life; **estar** ~ (**de cansancio**) to be exhausted; **estar** ~ **de hambre/sed** to be ravenous/dying of thirst; **para mí esa está muerta** I disown her; **caerse** ~ to drop dead; **no tener dónde caerse** ~ *inf* to be penniless; **punto** ~ AUTO neutral **III.** *m, f* dead person; (*difunto*) deceased; (*cadáver*) corpse; (*víctima*) victim; **están tocando a** ~s the bells are tolling for a death; **ahora me cargan el** ~ **a mí** *inf* now they are laying the blame on me; **hacerse el** ~ (*callado*) to keep as quiet as a mouse; (*quieto, t. fig*) to play dead; (*nadando*) to float; **ser un** ~ **de hambre** to be a nobody

muesca *f* nick; (*ranura*) groove

muesli *m* muesli

muestra *f* **1.** (*mercancía*) sample; ~ **gratuita** free sample; **feria de** ~s trade fair **2.** (*prueba*) proof; ~ **de amistad** token of friendship **3.** (*demostración*) demonstration; **dar** ~(**s**) **de valor** to give a demonstration of courage; **de** ~, **un botón** one example will suffice **4.** (*de labores*) example; ~ **de bordado/punto** example of embroidery/knitting **5.** MED ~ **de sangre/orina** blood/urine sample [*o* specimen] **6.** (*rótulo*) sign ▶**por la** ~ **se conoce el paño** *prov* a friend in need is a friend indeed

muestrario *m* collection of samples

muestreo *m* sampling

mugido *m* **1.** (*vaca*) moo **2.** (*viento, mar*) roar

mugir <g→j> *vi* **1.** (*vaca*) to moo **2.** (*viento,*

agua) to roar

mugre *f sin pl* grime

mugriento, -a *adj* grubby

mujer *f* woman; ~ **de edad** elderly lady; ~ **fácil** loose woman; ~ **fatal** femme fatale; ~ **de la limpieza** cleaning lady; ~ **de la calle** prostitute; **una** ~ **de rompe y rasga** a woman who knows what she wants (and how to get it); **ser una** ~ **de su casa** to be a good housewife; **tomar** ~ to take a wife; **está hecha toda una** ~ she really is grown-up; **esto es cosa de** ~s this is women's stuff

mujerero, -a *adj* AmC, AmS (*mujeriego*) woman-chasing, skirt-chasing

mujeriego *m* womanizer

muladar *m* (*basurero*) rubbish dump *Brit,* trash dump *Am;* (*estiércol*) dunghill

mulato, -a **I.** *adj* (*mestizo*) mulatto; (*color*) brown-skinned **II.** *m, f* mulatto

mulero, -a *m, f* RíoPl **1.** *inf* (*mentiroso*) liar **2.** *inf* (*tramposo*) cheat

muleta *f* **1.** (*apoyo*) crutch; **andar con** ~s to walk with crutches **2.** TAUR *red cloth attatched to a stick used by a matador*

muletilla *f* (*coletilla*) tag; (*palabra*) pet word; (*frase*) catch phrase

mullido, -a *adj* soft

mullir <3. *pret:* mulló> *vt* **1.** (*almohada*) to fluff up **2.** (*tierra*) to dig over; (*cepas*) to hoe

mullo *m* **1.** ZOOL (*salmonete*) red mullet **2.** Ecua (*abalorio*) coloured *Brit* [*o* colored *Am*] bead

mulo *m, f* (*caballo y asna*) hinny; (*asno y yegua*) mule

multa *f* fine; **poner una** ~ **a alguien** to fine sb

multar *vt* to fine; **me han multado con 3.000 pesetas** I've been fined 3000 pesetas

multicines *mpl* multiplex

multicolor *adj* multicoloured *Brit,* multicolored *Am;* TIPO polychromatic

multicopista *f* duplicator

multiforme *adj* multifarious

multilingüe *adj* multilingual

multimedia *adj inv* multimedia; **programa** ~ **de computadora** multimedia computer program

multimillonario, -a *m, f* multimillionaire

multinacional *adj, f* multinational

múltiple *adj* multiple; (*variado*) multifarious; ~s **veces** numerous times

multiplicación *f t.* MAT multiplication

multiplicar <c→qu> **I.** *vi, vt* **1.** MAT ~ **por algo** to multiply by sth; **tabla de** ~ multiplication table **2.** (*reproducir, aumentar*) to multiply **II.** *vr:* ~**se** **1.** (*reproducirse*) to multiply; **¡creced y multiplicaos!** REL go forth and multiply! **2.** (*desvivirse*) to be everywhere at the same time

multiplicidad *f* multiplicity

múltiplo, -a *adj, m, f* multiple

multitud *f* **1.** (*cantidad*) multitude; **una** ~ **de flores** a great number of flowers **2.** (*gente*) multitude, crowd; (*vulgo*) masses *pl*

M

multitudinario, -a *adj* multitudinous
multiuso *adj inv* multi-purpose
mundanal *adj*, **mundano, -a** *adj* 1. (*del mundo*) of the world; (*terrenal*) worldly 2. (*extravagante*) society
mundial *adj* world; campeonato ~ de fútbol World Cup; guerra ~ world war; a nivel ~ worldwide
mundillo *m* 1. *inf* (*ambiente*) world; el ~ de la música the world of music; ella se maneja bien en ese ~ she gets on well in that circle 2. (*encaje*) lace pillow
mundo *m* 1. (*tierra*) earth; (*planeta*) planet; (*globo*) world; ~ profesional professional world; el ~ antiguo the ancient world; el otro ~ the next world; no sabemos si en los otros ~s hay vida we do not know if there is life on the other planets; dar la vuelta al ~ to go round the world; echar al ~ to give birth to; venir al ~ to be born; irse de este ~ to die; se bañaban como Dios los/las trajo al ~ they swam in the nude; ver ~ to travel a lot; andar por esos ~s de Dios *inf* (*estar de viaje*) to be travelling all over the place; (*estar perdido*) to be lost; recorrer medio ~ to visit many countries; con la mayor tranquilidad del ~ with the utmost calm; rápidamente se le cae el ~ encima he/she quickly gets discouraged; vive en otro ~ *fig* he/she lives in a world of his/her own; este ~ es un pañuelo it is a small world; desde que el ~ es ~ since the world began; ponerse el ~ por montera, reírse del ~ not to care what others think/say; hacer un ~ de algo to make a mountain out of a molehill; así va [*o* anda] el ~ that is the way things are; no es nada del otro ~ it is nothing out of this world; por nada del ~ not for the world; dejó el ~ y se metió monja she left this world and became a nun 2. (*humanidad*) todo el ~ everyone, everybody; a la vista de todo el ~ for the whole world to see; todo el ~ sabe que... everyone knows that ...; lo sabe medio ~ nearly everyone knows that ... 3. (*experiencia*) worldliness; Lola tiene mucho ~ Lola is worldly-wise
mundología *f sin pl, inf* worldly wisdom
Múnich *m* Munich
munición *f* (*de armas*) ammunition
municipal *adj* municipal; parque ~ municipal park; término ~ municipality
municipio *m* 1. (*población*) municipality, borough 2. (*ayuntamiento*) town hall 3. (*concejo*) town council
munificencia *f sin pl* munificence
munir I. *vt CSur* ~ de algo to provide with sth; ir munido de los documentos necesarios to have the necessary documents II. *vr CSur* ~se de algo to provide oneself with sth; ~se del equipo necesario to provide oneself with the necessary equipment; ~se de suficientes provisiones to equip oneself with sufficient provisions
muñeca *f* 1. (*brazo*) wrist 2. (*juguete*) doll

3. (*maniquí*) dummy; ~ hinchable inflatable doll 4. *fig* (*niña*) doll, cutie *Am*
muñeco *m* 1. (*juguete*) doll; ~ articulado jointed doll; ~ de nieve snowman 2. *pey* (*monigote*) puppet
muñequera *f* wristband
muñón *m* stump
mural I. *adj* wall II. *m* mural
muralla *f* wall
murciélago *m* bat
murga *f inf* (*banda*) street band; dar la ~ a alguien to bother sb; ¡deja de darme la ~! stop bothering [*o* bugging] me!
murmullo *m* 1. (*voz*) whisper; (*cuchicheo*) murmur 2. (*hojas*) rustling; (*agua*) murmur
murmuración *f* (*calumnia*) slander; (*cotilleo*) gossip
murmurar I. *vi*, *vt* (*entre dientes*) to mutter; (*susurrar*) to murmur; ~ al oído de alguien to whisper in sb's ear II. *vi* 1. (*gruñir*) to grumble 2. (*criticar*) to criticize; (*chismorrear*) to gossip 3. (*agua*) to murmur; (*hojas*) to rustle
muro *m* wall; ~ de contención retaining wall; Muro de las Lamentaciones the Wailing Wall; ~ medianero party [*o* dividing] wall
murria *f sin pl, inf* (*tristeza*) gloominess, blues
murrio, -a *adj* gloomy, blue
mus *m* card game
musa *f* muse; se le sopló la ~ he/she was inspired; (*en un juego*) he/she was on a lucky streak
musaraña *f* 1. ZOOL shrew 2. *fig* (*bicho*) small animal; (*insecto*) bug; pensar en las ~s *fig* to have one's head in the clouds 3. (*nubecilla*) film
muscular *adj* muscular
musculatura *f* musculature
músculo *m* muscle; ~ deltoide deltoid muscle; ser ~ puro to be all muscle
musculoso, -a *adj* muscular
muselina *f* muslin
museo *m* museum; ~ etnográfico museum of ethnography
musgo *m* moss
música *f* 1. (*sonido*) music; (*partituras*) score; ~ folclórica traditional music; ~ ratonera *inf* cabaret [*o* pub] music; ~ sacra sacred music; ~ de cámara chamber music; ~ ambiental muzak, canned [*o* piped] music; ~ ligera easy listening; banda de ~ band; caja de ~ music box; ¡véte con la ~ a otra parte! *inf* get out of here!; tus palabras nos sonaron a ~ celestial you were spouting nonsense; tener talento para la ~ to be musical 2. (*orquesta*) orchestra
musical I. *adj* musical; composición ~ musical composition II. *m* musical
músico, -a I. *adj* musical II. *m*, *f* musician; (*compositor*) composer; ~ ambulante itinerant musician
musicología *f sin pl* musicology
musicólogo, -a *m*, *f* musicologist
musitar *vi* 1. (*balbucear*) to mumble; (*susu-*

rrear) to whisper; ~ **al oído de alguien** to whisper in sb's ear **2.** (*hojas*) to rustle
muslo *m* (*persona*) thigh; (*animal*) leg
mustela *f* weasel
mustio, -a *adj* **1.** (*flores*) wilting **2.** (*triste*) low
musulmán, -ana *adj, m, f* Muslim
mutable *adj* mutable
mutación *f* **1.** (*transformación, genes*) mutation **2.** TEAT scene change **3.** METEO appreciable change
mutilado, -a *m, f* cripple; ~ **de guerra** disabled war veteran
mutilar *vt* **1.** (*cuerpo*) to mutilate **2.** (*recortar*) to cut
mutis *m inv* **1.** TEAT exit; ~ **por el foro** quick exit; **hacer** ~ to exit **2.** (*silencio*) ¡~! shh!
mutismo *m* silence; **no hay manera de sacarlo de su** ~ there is no way of making him break his silence
mutual I. *adj* mutual II. *f* CSur mutual benefit society
mutualidad *f* **1.** (*cooperativa*) mutual benefit society; ~ **de accidentes de trabajo** mutual insurance company; ~ **obrera** workers' mutual society **2.** (*reciprocidad*) mutuality
mutuo, -a *adj* mutual
muy *adv* very; **es** ~ **improbable que…** +*subj* it is very unlikely that …; ~ **a pesar mío** much to my dismay; ~ **de tarde en tarde** once in a blue moon; ~ **de mañana** in the very early morning; ¿**y qué ha hecho el** ~ **tunante?** and what has the little devil done?; **le saluda** ~ **atentamente,** (*en cartas*) yours faithfully [*o* sincerely]; ¡**dejarnos plantados: eso es** ~ **de María!** to leave us in the lurch: that is typical of María!; **es Ud.** ~ **libre de hacer lo que quiera** you are absolutely free to do what you like; ¡**guárdate** ~ **mucho de irlo contando por ahí!** *inf* be very careful not to go around talking about it!

N

N, n *f* N, n; ~ **de Navarra** N for Nelly *Brit,* N for Nan *Am*
naba *f* turnip
nabo *m* **1.** BOT turnip **2.** *vulg* (*pene*) cock **3.** ARQUIT main pillar
nácar *m* mother-of-pearl, nacre; **de** ~ nacreous, pearly
nacarado, -a *adj,* **nacarino, -a** *adj* nacreous, pearly
nacatamal *m AmC, Méx* GASTR pork tamale
nacer *irr como crecer vi* **1.** (*venir al mundo*) to be born; **nací el 29 de febrero** I was born on the 29th of February; **no nací ayer** I wasn't born yesterday; **haber nacido para la música** to be a natural for music; **volver a** ~ to have a

very narrow escape **2.** (*del huevo*) to hatch **3.** (*germinar*) to germinate **4.** (*astr*) to be created; **nace una estrella** a star is born **5.** (*día*) to rise; **al** ~ **el día** at the break of day **6.** (*originarse*) to stem; (*arroyo*) to begin; (*surgir*) to arise; **nació una duda en su mente** *elev* a doubt was sown in his/her mind ▶**nadie nace enseñado** *prov* we all have to learn; **no con quien naces, sino con quien** paces *prov* it's your environment that counts, not your birth
nacido, -a I. *pp de* nacer II. *adj* **bien** ~ (*origen*) born into a good family; (*comportamiento*) noble; ~ **de padres ricos** born into a well-off family III. *m, f* **recién** ~ newborn; **los** ~**s el 2 de abril** those born on the 2nd of April; **un mal** ~ a born villain
naciente¹ I. *adj fig* incipient, budding II. *m* (*oriente*) orient; (*este*) east
naciente² *f Arg, Par* spring
nacimiento *m* **1.** (*venida al mundo*) birth; **de** ~ by birth; **ciego de** ~ born blind; **lugar de** ~ birthplace; **partida de** ~ birth certificate; (*belén*) Nativity scene **2.** (*linaje*) family; **ser de humilde** ~ to be of humble birth **3.** (*comienzo*) beginning; ~ **del pelo** root (of hair)
nación *f* nation; (**la Organización de**) **las Naciones Unidas** the United Nations (Organization)
nacional *adj* national; **carretera** ~ (*en el Reino Unido*) A [*o* arterial] road; (*en los Estados Unidos*) highway; **moneda** ~ national currency; **producto** ~ national product; **renta** ~ national income; **vuelos** ~**es** domestic flights
nacionalidad *f* (*ciudadanía*) nationality, citizenship; **ser de** ~ **española** to have Spanish nationality, to be a Spanish national
nacionalismo *m* nationalism
nacionalista *adj, mf* nationalist
nacionalización *f* (*persona*) naturalization, nationalization; (*expropiación*) expropriation
nacionalizar <z→c> I. *vt* (*persona*) to naturalize, to nationalize II. *vr* ~**se español** to obtain Spanish nationality
naco *m* **1.** *AmC* (*cobarde*) coward **2.** *AmC* (*marica*) queer **3.** *Arg* (*miedo*) fear
nada I. *pron indef* nothing; ¡**gracias!** – ¡**de** ~! thank you! – not at all!; ¡**pues** ~! well all right then; **por** ~ **se queja** he/she complains about the slightest thing; **como si** ~ as if nothing had happened; **le costó** ~ **más y** ~ **menos que…** it cost him/her the fine sum of …; ~ **menos que el director** the director himself; **no servir para** ~ to be useless II. *adv* not at all; ~ **más** (*solamente*) only; (*no más*) no more; ¡~ **más!** enough!; ~ **de** ~ absolutely nothing; **no ser** ~ **difícil** not to be difficult at all; ¡~ **de eso!** none of that!; ¡**y** ~ **de llegar tarde!** no arriving late!; ¡**casi** ~! hardly anything!; **antes de** ~ (*sobre todo*) above all; (*primero*) first of all; **para** ~ not in the slightest III. *f* nothing, nothingness; **salir de la** ~ to appear out of

nowhere; **la ~ de nuestras vidas** *elev* the emptiness of our lives

nadador(a) *m(f)* swimmer

nadar *vi* to swim; **~ en deudas** to be swimming in debt

nadería *f* nothing important

nadie *pron indef* nobody, anybody, no one; **no ví a ~** I didn't see anybody, I saw nobody; **no vino ~** nobody came; **tú no eres ~ para decir...** who are you to say ...?; **un don ~ a** nobody; **tierra de ~** no man's land

nadita I. *f Ecua, Méx* **en ~ estuvo que lo mataran** they almost killed him II. *adv Méx* **in** no time

nado *adv* **a ~** afloat, swimming; **cruzar algo a ~** to swim across sth

nafta *f* 1. QUÍM naphtha 2. *CSur* (*gasolina*) petrol *Brit*, gasoline *Am*

nagual *f Méx, Hond* witch doctor

nagualear *vi* 1. *Méx* (*mentir*) to lie 2. *Méx* (*robar*) to swipe

naif *adj* naive; ARTE naive, primitive

nailon *m* nylon

naipe *m* 1. (*carta*) card 2. *pl* (*baraja*) pack of cards

najarse *vr inf* to beat it, to scram

nalga *f* buttock; **~s** bottom

namibio, -a *adj, m, f* Namibian

nana *f* 1. (*canción*) lullaby 2. (*niñera*) nanny

nanay *interj inf* no way!

napia(s) *f(pl) inf* conk

Nápoles *m* Naples

napolitano, -a *adj, m, f* Neapolitan

naranja I. *f* 1. BOT orange 2. ARQUIT **media ~ dome** ►¡~s (**de la China**)! no way!; **tu media ~** your better half II. *adj* (*de color*) ~ orange

naranjada *f* orangeade

naranjado, -a *adj* orangey

naranjal *m* orange grove

naranjo *m* orange tree

narcisismo *m sin pl* narcissism, egoism

narcisista *adj* narcissistic

narciso *m* 1. BOT daffodil, narcissus *inv* 2. (*persona*) narcissist

narco *m inf* drug dealer [*o* trafficker]

narcosis *f inv* MED narcosis

narcoterrorismo *m sin pl* drugs terrorism

narcótico *m* narcotic

narcótico, -a *adj* narcotic

narcotizar <z→c> *vt* to narcotize

narcotraficante *mf* drug dealer [*o* trafficker]

narcotráfico *m* drug dealing [*o* trafficking]

narigada *f Ecua* pinch of snuff

narigón *m inf* big nose

narigón, -ona *adj* big-nosed

narigudo, -a *adj* (*narigón*) big-nosed

nariz *f* 1. ANAT nose; **~ chata** flat nose; **~ ganchuda** hooked nose; **~ respingona** turned-up nose; **~ aguileña** aquiline nose; **dar a alguien con la puerta en las narices** to slam the door in sb's face; **darse de narices con alguien** *inf* to bump straight into sb; **sonarse/limpiarse la ~** to blow/wipe one's nose; **romper las**

narices a alguien to smash sb's face in; **no ver más allá de sus narices** *inf* to be short-sighted; **quedarse con un palmo de narices** *inf* to be let down 2. *inf* (*eufemismo por 'cojones'*) **estar hasta las narices** to have had it up to here; **hasta que se me hinchen las narices** until I lose my rag; **lo hizo por narices** he/she did it because he/she felt like it; **¡(qué) narices!** no way; **tener narices** to be too much; **¡tócate las narices!** would you believe it? 3. (*intuición*) suspicions *pl*; **me da en la ~ que...** I've got a funny feeling that...

narizudo, -a *adj Méx* (*narigudo*) large-nosed

narración *f* narration

narrador(a) *m(f)* narrator; (*que cuenta la historia*) storyteller

narrar *vt* 1. (*contar*) to narrate 2. (*informar*) to tell

narrativa I. *adj* narrative II. *f* literature

nasal *adj* nasal

nata *f* 1. (*producto*) cream; **~ montada** whipped cream 2. (*sobre un líquido*) film 3. (*lo más selecto*) the best; **la crema y ~ de la sociedad** the crème de la crème of society

natación *f* DEP swimming

natal *adj* native, home; **ciudad ~** home town; **país ~** native country [*o* land]

natalicio, -a *adj* birthday

natalidad *f* birth; **índice de ~** birth rate; **de fuerte/baja ~** with a high/low birth rate

natatorio, -a *adj* swimming; **vejiga natatoria** ZOOL swimming bladder

natillas *fpl* custard

natividad *f* nativity

nativo, -a I. *adj* 1. (*natal*) native, home; **lengua nativa** native [*o* mother] tongue; **profesor ~** native teacher 2. (*metal*) native II. *m, f AmL* native

nato, -a *adj* born; **un triunfador ~** a born winner

natural I. *adj* 1. (*no artificial, sencillo*) natural; **de tamaño ~** life-sized; **esto es lo más ~ del mundo** (*normal*) it is the most natural thing in the world; (*lógico*) makes perfect sense 2. (*nacido*) **ser ~ del Reino Unido** to be a British natural; **hijo ~** illegitimate child II. *m* native

naturaleza *f* 1. (*campo*) nature; **~ muerta** still life; **en plena ~** in the heart of the countryside 2. (*manera*) nature 3. (*índole*) type; **de ~ pública** of the public domain

naturalidad *f sin pl* naturalness; **lo dijo con mucha ~** he said it very naturally

naturalizar <z→c> I. *vt* to naturalize; **~ costumbres** to take on customs; **~ un animal** to acclimatize an animal II. *vr* **~se a algo** (*habituarse*) to get used to sth

naufragar <g→gu> *vi* 1. (*hundirse*) to sink 2. (*no hundir del todo*) to be wrecked; (*personas*) to be shipwrecked 3. (*fracasar*) to fall through

naufragio *m* 1. (*accidente*) shipwreck 2. (*fracaso*) failure; (*de negociaciones*) breakdown

náufrago, -a I. *adj* shipwrecked **II.** *m, f* shipwrecked sailor, castaway

nauseabundo, -a *adj* nauseating

náuseas *fpl* sick feeling; **tengo** ~ I feel sick; **dar** ~ **a alguien** to make sb feel sick

náutica *f sin pl* navigation

náutico, -a *adj* nautical; **club** ~ yacht club

nava *f* plain

navaja *f* **1.** (*cuchillo*) (pocket) knife; ~ **de afeitar** razor; ~ **automática** flick knife *Brit,* switchblade *Am* **2.** ZOOL (*molusco*) razor clam **3.** (*colmillo*) tusk; (*aguijón*) sting

navajada *f,* **navajazo** *m* **1.** (*golpe*) stabbing **2.** (*herida*) stab [*o* knife] wound, gash

navajero, -a *m, f* (*delincuente*) thug who carries a knife

naval *adj* naval

navarro, -a I. *adj* of/from Navarra **II.** *m, f* native/inhabitant of Navarra

nave *f* **1.** NÁUT ship, vessel **2.** AVIAT ~ (**espacial**) spaceship, spacecraft **3.** (*en una iglesia*) nave; ~ **central** main nave **4.** (*almacén*) warehouse **5.** (*fábrica*) factory unit ▶**quemar las** ~**s** to burn one's bridges

navegable *adj* navigable; **rutas** ~**s** navigable routes

navegación *f* navigation

navegador *m* INFOR browser

navegante *mf* navigator; ~ **de internet** Net surfer

navegar <g→gu> **I.** *vi, vt* to navigate; ~ **veinte nudos por hora** to sail at 20 knots an hour; ~ **contra la corriente** to go against the flow; ~ **por la web** to surf the net **II.** *vi* (*vagar*) to roam

Navidad *f* Christmas; **¡feliz** ~! merry Christmas!

navideño, -a *adj* Christmas; (*ambiente*) festive

naviero, -a I. *m, f* shipowner **II.** *adj* shipping

navío *m* ship

nazi *adj, mf* HIST Nazi

nazismo *m sin pl* Nazism

N. de la R. *abr de* **Nota de la Redacción** Ed.

N. del T. *abr de* **Nota del Traductor** T.N.

NE *abr de* **Nordeste** NE

neblina *f* mist; *fig* haze

neblinoso, -a *adj* **1.** (*nebuloso*) foggy **2.** (*brumoso*) misty

nebuloso, -a *adj* **1.** (*brumoso*) misty **2.** (*nuboso*) cloudy **3.** (*vago*) hazy **4.** (*oscuro*) obscure

necedad *f* stupidity; **no decir más que** ~**es** to talk a lot of nonsense

necesariamente *adv* necessarily

necesario, -a *adj* necessary; **es** ~ **que haya más acuerdo** there is a need for more agreement; **la lluvia hizo** ~ **quedarse en casa** the rain meant we had to stay at home

neceser *m* (*de aseo*) toilet bag; (*de costura*) sewing box; (*de afeitar*) shaving kit; (*de herramientas*) tool box; (*de maquillaje*) cosmetic bag

necesidad *f* **1.** (*ser preciso*) need, necessity; **de primera** ~ essential; **no tiene** ~ **de trabajar** there is no need for him/her to work **2.** (*requerimiento*) need; **tener** ~ **de algo** to be in need of sth **3.** (*apuro*) difficulty; (*penurias*) suffering **4.** *pl* (*evacuación corporal*) **hacer sus** ~**es** to relieve oneself

necesitado, -a I. *adj* (*pobre*) needy; **estar** ~ **de amor** to be in need of love **II.** *m, f* poor person; **los** ~**s** the poor

necesitar I. *vt* **1.** (*precisar*) to need; **se necesita piso** flat wanted *Brit,* apartment wanted *Am* **2.** (*tener que*) to need to; **necesitas comer algo** you've got to eat something **II.** *vi* (*precisar*) ~ **de algo** to need sth

necio, -a I. *adj* idiotic **II.** *m, f* idiot

nécora *f* fiddler crab

necrófago, -a I. *adj* necrophagous, carrion-eating **II.** *m, f* carrion-eater

necrología *f* **1.** (*biografía*) obituary **2.** (*nota*) list of deaths

necrológico, -a *adj* necrological

necrosis *f* MED necrosis; (*gangrena*) gangrene

néctar *m* nectar

nectarina *f* nectarine

neerlandés, -esa I. *adj* Dutch **II.** *m, f* Dutchman *m,* Dutchwoman *f*

nefando, -a *adj* abominable

nefario, -a *adj* terrible

nefasto, -a *adj* awful; (*día*) horrible

nefrítico, -a *adj* MED suffering from nephritis

nefritis *f* MED nephritis

negación *f* **1.** (*desmentir*) denial **2.** (*denegar*) refusal **3.** LING negative; **es la** ~ **del arte** it is anything but art

negado, -a I. *adj* ~ **para algo** useless at sth **II.** *m, f* **ser un** ~ **para las matemáticas** to be no good at maths *Brit* [*o* math *Am*]; **ser un** ~ **para las labores de la casa** to be useless at housework

negar *irr como* **fregar I.** *vt* **1.** (*desmentir*) to deny **2.** (*rehusar*) to refuse; (*rechazar*) to reject; ~ **con la cabeza** to shake one's head **II.** *vr:* ~**se** to refuse

negativa *f* (*negación*) denial; (*rehusamiento*) refusal; (*rechazo*) rejection

negativo *m* FOTO negative

negativo, -a *adj* negative; **tu respuesta fue negativa** your answer was negative

negligencia *f* **1.** (*descuido*) carelessness **2.** (*abandono*) neglect **3.** JUR negligence

negligente I. *adj* **1.** (*descuidado*) careless; **ser** ~ **en** [*o* **para**] **su trabajo** to be a careless worker **2.** JUR negligent **II.** *mf* JUR negligent party

negociable *adj* negotiable; **el precio es** ~ the price is open to negotiation

negociación *f* (*convenio*) negotiation; ~ **colectiva** collective bargaining; **entrar en negociaciones con alguien** to enter into negotiations with sb

negociado *m* **1.** (*dependencia*) section; **jefe de** ~ head of department **2.** *AmS* (*negocio*)

suspicious deal
negociador(a) I. *adj* negotiating II. *m(f)*
1. (*comerciante*) merchant 2. (*mediador*)
negotiator
negociante *mf* 1. (*comerciante*) dealer
2. *pey* moneygrubber
negociar I. *vi* (*comerciar*) to deal II. *vi, vt*
(*dialogar, concertar*) to negotiate
negocio *m* 1. (*comercio*) business; ~ al detalle retail business; hombre/mujer de ~s
businessman/businesswoman 2. (*asunto*)
matter; eso no es ~ mío it's none of my business ▶hacer un ~ redondo *inf* to do a good
bit of business
negra *f* MÚS crotchet *Brit,* quarter note *Am*
negrada *f Cuba* HIST slaves (*body of slaves
belonging to a plantation*)
negrero, -a *m, f* 1. (*que trata con esclavos*)
slave dealer 2. (*tirano*) slave driver 3. *CSur*
(*aprovechado*) parasite
negrilla *f,* **negrita** *f* TIPO bold face
negro, -a I. *adj* black; ~ del sol suntanned; ~
como la boca del lobo pitch-black; ~ como
el carbón as black as coal ▶estar/ponerse ~
inf to be/get furious; pasarlas negras *inf* to
have a terrible time; tener la negra *inf* to be
jinxed; verse ~ para hacer algo *inf* to have a
hard time doing sth; verse ~ [*o* pasarlas
negras] para encontrar algo *inf* to have a
hard time finding sth; verlo todo ~ to be very
pessimistic II. *m, f* 1. (*persona*) black; trabajar como un ~ *inf* to work like a slave
2. (*escritor*) ghost writer 3. *Arg, inf* (*cariño*)
darling
negrura *f* blackness
negruzco, -a *adj* blackish
neme *m Col* asphalt
nene, -a *m, f inf* (*niño*) baby; (*expresión de
cariño*) dear
nenúfar *m* water lily
neocapitalismo *m sin pl* ECON neocapitalism
neoclasicismo *m sin pl* neoclassicism
neoclásico, -a *adj* neoclassical
neófito, -a *m, f* 1. (*bautizado*) recently baptized person 2. (*iniciado*) novice
neolatino, -a *adj* LING Neo-Latin; lenguas
neolatinas Romance languages
neolítico *m* neolithic
neologismo *m* neologism
neón *m* neon
neoyorquino, -a I. *adj* of/from New York
II. *m, f* New Yorker
neozelandés, -esa I. *adj* of/from New Zealand II. *m, f* New Zealander
nepalés, -esa I. *adj* Nepalese II. *m, f* Nepalese person
nepotismo *m sin pl* nepotism
Neptuno *m* Neptune
nervadura *f* 1. ARQUIT ribs *pl* 2. BOT venation
3. BIO veins *pl*
nervio *m* 1. (*conductor*) nerve; ataque de ~s
nervous breakdown; crispar los ~s a alguien,

poner a alguien los ~s de punta *inf* (*enfadar*) to drive sb mad [*o* crazy]; (*poner nervioso*) to get on sb's nerves; ponerse de los
~s to get nervous [*o* flustered]; estar atacado
de los ~s to be a nervous wreck; ser un puro
~ *inf* to be a bundle of nerves; tener ~s de
acero to have nerves of steel 2. (*tendón*)
sinew 3. BOT vein 4. (*libro*) band 5. (*ímpetu*)
impetus; esta empresa tiene ~ this company
is dynamic
nerviosidad *f* 1. (*tensión*) tension 2. (*nerviosismo*) nervousness
nerviosismo *m* nervousness
nervioso, -a *adj* 1. ANAT nervous; el sistema
~ the nervous system 2. (*intranquilo*) excitable
nervudo, -a *adj* tough; (*apariencia*) sinewy,
wiry
neto, -a *adj* 1. (*claro*) clear 2. (*no bruto*) net
neumático I. *adj* pneumatic; martillo ~
pneumatic drill II. *m* tyre *Brit,* tire *Am*
neumonía *f* MED pneumonia
neura *f inf* obsession
neural *adj* neural
neurología *f sin pl* MED neurology
neurólogo, -a *m, f* MED neurologist
neurona *f* ANAT neuron, neurone *Brit*
neurosis *f inv* neurosis
neurótico, -a *adj, m, f* neurotic
neurotizar <z→c> *vt inf* ~ a alguien to
make sb neurotic
neutral *adj, mf* neutral
neutralidad *f* neutrality
neutralización *f* neutralization
neutralizar <z→c> I. *vt* to neutralize II. *vr:*
~se to be neutralized
neutro, -a *adj* 1. *t.* QUÍM neutral 2. ZOOL sexless
3. LING neuter; género ~ neuter gender
neutrón *m* FÍS neutron
nevada *f* snowfall; (*tormenta*) snowstorm
nevado, -a *adj* 1. (*cubierto*) snow-covered;
(*montaña*) snow-capped 2. (*blanco*) snow-white
nevar <e→ie> *vimpers* to snow
nevazón *f Arg, Chile, Ecua* METEO blizzard,
snowstorm
nevera *f* (*frigorífico*) fridge; (*portátil*) cool
box; este cuarto es una ~ this room is freezing
nevisca *f* light snowfall
neviscar <c→qu> *vimpers* to snow lightly
nexo *m* 1. nexus 2. LING connective
ni *conj* ~... ~... neither ... nor ...; no fumo ~
bebo I don't smoke or drink, I neither smoke
nor drink; ~ (siquiera) not even; ¡~ lo
pienses! don't even let it cross your mind!;
sin más ~ más without any further ado; ¡~
que fueras tonto! anyone would think you
were stupid!; ~ bien... *Arg* as soon as ...
nica *adj Nic, inf* Nicaraguan
Nicaragua *f* Nicaragua

Nicaragua lies in Central America, bordering Honduras to the north, Costa Rica to the south, the Caribbean to the east and the Pacific Ocean to the west. The capital of Nicaragua is **Managua**. The official language of the country is Spanish and the monetary unit is the **córdoba**.

nicaragüense *adj, mf* Nicaraguan
nicho *m* niche
nicotina *f* nicotine
nidada *f* **1.** (*huevos*) clutch (of eggs) **2.** (*polluelos*) brood
nidal *m* **1.** (*lugar*) nest **2.** (*huevo*) brooding egg **3.** (*escondite*) hiding place
nidificar <c→qu> *vi* ZOOL to nest
nido *m* **1.** (*lecho*) den; ~ **de ladrones** den of thieves; ~ **de discordias** hotbed of dissent; **caerse del** ~ *fig* to come down to earth with a bump **2.** (*nidal*) nest
niebla *f* fog; **hay** ~ it is foggy
nieto, -a *m, f* grandchild, grandson *m,* granddaughter *f;* **los nietos** the grandchildren
nieve *f* **1.** (*precipitación*) snow; ~ **carbónica** dry ice; **a punto de** ~ GASTR stiff; **copo de** ~ snowflake **2.** *inf* (*cocaína*) coke, snow **3.** *AmC* (*helado*) ice cream
NIF *m abr de* **Número de Identificación Fiscal** Fiscal Identity Number
nigeriano, -a *adj, m, f* Nigerian
nigua *f AmC* ZOOL jigger flea
Nilo *m* Nile
nilón *m* nylon
nimbo *m* METEO nimbus
nimiedad *f* (*insignificancia*) trifle
nimio, -a *adj* insignificant
ninfa *f* **1.** (*mitología*) nymph **2.** (*joven*) girl **3.** ZOOL nymph
ninfómana *f* nymphomaniac
ningún *adj indef v.* **ninguno**
ninguno, -a **I.** *adj indef* (*precediendo un substantivo masculino singular: ningún*) any; **por ningún lado** anywhere; **de ninguna manera** in no way; **ninguna vez** never; **en ningún sitio** nowhere; **no hay ningún peligro** there is no danger **II.** *pron indef* anything, nothing; (*personas*) anybody, nobody; **no quiso venir** ~ nobody wanted to come
niña *f* **1.** (*chica, persona no adulta*) girl **2.** ANAT pupil; **eres como las** ~**s de mis ojos** *fig* you are the apple of my eye
niñera *f* nanny; (*canguro*) babysitter
niñería *f* **1.** (*de niños*) childish act **2.** *inf* (*pequeñez*) triviality
niñez *f* childhood; *fig* infancy
niño *m* **1.** (*persona no adulta*) boy; ~ **bien** *inf* rich kid; ~ **de la bola** the baby Jesus; ~ **mimado** (*favorito*) spoilt child; ~ **de pecho** babe-in-arms; ~ **probeta** test tube baby; **¡no seas** ~**!** don't act like a child! **2.** *reg* (*joven*) young
nipón, -ona **I.** *adj* Japanese **II.** *m, f* native/inhabitant of Japan
níquel *m* nickel

niqui *m* (*camiseta*) T-shirt
nitidez *f* brightness; FOTO clarity
nítido, -a *adj* bright; FOTO clear
nitrato *m* nitrate; ~ **de plata** silver nitrate
nítrico, -a *adj* nitric; **ácido** ~ nitric acid
nitrito *m* nitrite
nitro *m* nitre, saltpetre
nitrógeno *m* nitrogen
nitroglicerina *f* nitroglycerine
nitroso, -a *adj* nitrous
nivel *m* **1.** (*estándar*) standard; ~ **de vida** standard of living; **estar al** ~ to come up to scratch; **estar al** ~ **de lo exigido** to rise to the occasion **2.** (*horizontalidad, grado, cota*) level; ~ **de burbuja** TÉC spirit level; ~ **estilístico** stylistic level; **paso a** ~ level crossing *Brit,* grade crossing *Am;* ~ **de la riada** flood level; **sobre el** ~ **del mar** above sea level
nivelación *f* levelling *Brit,* leveling *Am;* ~ **del presupuesto** balancing the budget
nivelado, -a *adj* level; (*horizontal*) horizontal
nivelar **I.** *vt* to level; (*parcela*) to level out **II.** *vr:* ~**se** to level out; ~**se con alguien** to catch up with sb
níveo, -a *adj elev* snowy, snow-white
nixtamal *m Méx* corn (*specially processed for tortilla-making*)
NO *abr de* **Noroeste** NW
no *adv* **1.** (*respuesta*) no; **¡que** ~**!** I tell you it isn't! **2.** + *adjetivo* non-; ~ **protegido** non-protected **3.** + *verbo* not; ~**... nada** not ... anything; ~**... nadie** not ... anyone; ~**... nunca** not ... ever, never; ~ **lo compró** he/she did not buy it; ~ **tal** not at all; ~ **ya** not only; **ya** ~ not any more, no longer; **hoy** ~ **tengo clase** I don't have class today; ~ **tiene más que un abrigo** he/she only has one coat; ~ **quedan más que dos botellas** there are only two bottles left; ~ **querer más hijos** not to want any more children; ~ **quiero hablar más de esto** I don't want to talk about this any more **4.** (*retórica*) **¿**~**?** isn't he/she?, don't we/they? ► ~ **bien** + *subj* as soon as; **el** ~ **va más** the best, the state-of-the-art; **tener un** ~ **sé qué** to have something special; **a** ~ **ser que** + *subj* unless; **¡a que** ~**!** do you want to bet?; **¿cómo** ~**?** of course; **o, si** ~ otherwise
n⁰ *abr de* **número** No.
nobiliario, -a *adj* noble
nobilísimo, -a *adj superl de* **noble**
noble **I.** *adj* <nobilísimo> **1.** *t.* QUÍM (*aristócrata*) noble **2.** (*bueno*) upright **3.** (*honesto*) honest **II.** *mf* nobleman *m,* noblewoman *f*
nobleza *f* **1.** (*linaje, hidalguía*) nobility **2.** (*bondad*) uprightness **3.** (*honestidad*) honesty
noche *f* **1.** (*contrario de día*) night; ~ **cerrada** complete darkness; **Noche Vieja** New Year's Eve, Hogmanay *Scot;* **buenas** ~**s** (*saludo*) good evening; (*despedida*) good night; **turno de** ~ night shift; **media** ~ midnight; **a media** ~ at midnight; **por la** ~ at night; **toda la** ~ all night long; **ayer** (**por la**) ~ last night; **hacerse**

de ~ to get dark; **hacer** ~ **en** to spend the night in **2.** (*tarde*) evening **3.** (*oscuridad*) darkness; **es de** ~ it's dark; **no veo más que** ~ **a mi alrededor** *elev* I am surrounded by darkness ▶ **ser como la** ~ **y el día** to be as different as night and day, to be like chalk and cheese *Brit;* **de la** ~ **a la mañana** overnight; **pasar una** ~ **en blanco** not to sleep a wink all night
Nochebuena *f* Christmas Eve; **en** ~ on Christmas Eve
nochecita *f AmL* dusk, nightfall
nocherniego, -a *adj, m, f v.* **noctámbulo**
nochero *m* **1.** *CSur* (*vigilante*) nightwatchman **2.** *Col* (*mesilla*) bedside table
Nochevieja *f* New Year's Eve, Hogmanay *Scot*
noción *f* **1.** (*idea*) idea; **perder la** ~ **del tiempo** to completely forget about the time **2.** *pl* (*fundamentos*) base; **tengo nociones de francés** I know a bit of French
nocividad *f* harmfulness
nocivo, -a *adj* harmful; ~ **para la salud** damaging to health
noctámbulo, -a **I.** *adj* (*trasnochador*) **ser** ~ to be a night-bird; (*salir*) to go out at night **II.** *m, f* (*trasnochador*) night worker; (*que sale*) night owl
nocturno *m* MÚS nocturne
nocturno, -a *adj* **1.** (*de noche*) night; **la vida nocturna** nightlife **2.** BOT, ZOOL nocturnal
nodo *m* node
nodriza *f* **1.** (*ama*) wet-nurse **2.** (*transporte*) **avión** ~ mother aeroplane *Brit,* mother airplane *Am;* **buque** ~ supply ship
nódulo *m* nodule
Noé *m* REL Noah; **el arca de** ~ Noah's ark
nogal *m,* **noguera** *f* walnut tree
nómada **I.** *adj* nomadic; **pueblo** ~ nomadic people **II.** *mf* nomad
nomás *adv AmL* **1.** (*solamente*) only; ~ **que** +*subj* unless; **¡pase** ~**!** come straight in! **2.** (*nada más*) and that was all **3.** (*apenas*) hardly
nombradía *f* (*reputación*) reputation; (*fama*) fame; **de gran** ~ of great repute
nombrado, -a *adj* **1.** (*que se nombra*) named **2.** (*fama*) famous
nombramiento *m* **1.** (*designación*) appointment; (*military*) commission **2.** (*documento*) title
nombrar *vt* **1.** (*citar*) to quote; (*mencionar*) to mention **2.** (*llamar*) to call **3.** (*designar*) to appoint; (*militar*) to commission
nombre *m* **1.** (*designación*) name; ~ **y apellido** name and surname, full name; ~ **de familia** surname *Brit,* last name *Am;* ~ **ficticio** false name; ~ **de pila, primer** ~ Christian [*o* first] name; ~ **del producto** product name; ~ **de soltera** maiden name; **de** ~, ~ **artístico** stage name, by name; **sin** ~ nameless; **en** ~ **de** on behalf of; **a su propio** ~ in his/her own name; **conocer a alguien de** ~ to know sb by name; **dar su** ~ to give one's name; **poner un**

~ **a alguien** to give sb a name; **llamar a las cosas por su** ~ *fig* to call a spade a spade; **tu conducta no tiene** ~ your behaviour *Brit* [*o* behavior *Am*] is a disgrace; **reservar a** ~ **de X** to book in X's name **2.** (*reputación*) reputation; **de** ~ famous **3.** LING noun; ~ **común** common noun; ~ **propio** proper noun
nomenclátor *m* catalogue of names
nomenclatura *f* nomenclature
nomeolvides *f inv* forget-me-not
nómina *f* **1.** (*lista*) list; (*de sueldos*) payroll **2.** (*haberes*) salary
nominación *f* appointment, nomination
nominal *adj* **1.** (*relativo al nombre*) nominal; **citación** ~ personal summons; **valor** ~ nominal value **2.** LING noun
nominalmente *adv* nominally
nominar *vt* to nominate
nominativo *m* LING nominative
nominativo, -a *adj* nominative
non **I.** *adj* odd **II.** *m* odd number; **de** ~ odd; **estar** [*o* **quedar**] **de** ~ *inf* to be the odd one out; **decir** (**que**) ~**es** *fig* to say no
nonada *f* trifle
nonagésimo, -a *adj* ninetieth; *v.t.* **octavo**
nonato, -a *adj* **1.** (*nacimiento*) born by caesarean [*o* cesarean *Am*] section **2.** (*no existente*) unborn
nono, -a *adj* ninth; *v.t.* **octavo**
noquear *vt* to knock out
nordeste *m* **1.** (*dirección*) North East **2.** (*viento*) northeasterly
nórdico, -a *adj* **1.** (*del norte*) northern, northerly; **la ciudad más nórdica de España** the most northerly city in Spain **2.** HIST Nordic **3.** (*escandinavo*) Scandinavian
noreste *m v.* **nordeste**
noria *f* **1.** (*para agua*) water wheel **2.** *inf* (*trabajo*) treadmill *fig;* **este trabajo es una** ~ this job is a pain in the neck **3.** (*columpio*) big wheel *Brit,* Ferris wheel *Am*
norirlandés, -esa **I.** *adj* Northern Irish **II.** *m, f* native/inhabitant of Northern Ireland
norma *f* **1.** (*regla*) rule; (*general*) norm, standard; ~**s de circulación** highway code; ~ **técnica** technical norm; **observar la** ~ to follow the rules; **como** ~ (**general**) as a rule **2.** (*escuadra*) set square
normal *adj* **1.** (*habitual*) normal; **gasolina** ~ two-star petrol *Brit,* regular gas *Am* **2.** (*según la norma*) regulation
normalizar <z→c> *vt* **1.** (*volver normal*) to normalize **2.** (*reglar*) to regulate
normalmente *adv* normally; (*habitualmente*) usually
normando, -a *adj, m, f* Norman
normativa *f* rules *pl;* ~ **comunitaria** POL Community regulations *pl;* **según la** ~ **vigente** according to current rules
normativo, -a *adj* normative
noroeste *m* **1.** (*dirección*) North West **2.** (*viento*) northwesterly
norte *m* **1.** (*punto cardinal*) north; **el** ~ **de**

España Northern Spain; **al ~ de** north of **2.**(*viento*) northerly **3.**(*polo ártico*) North Pole **4.**(*guía*) aim; **ha perdido el ~** *fig* he/she has lost his/her way; **sin ~** aimless **5.**(*objetivo*) objective

norteamericano, -a *adj, m, f* North American; (*de los EE.UU.*) American

nortear I. *vt* NÁUT to steer to the north **II.** *vi* **1.** NÁUT to veer northwards **2.**(*viento*) **nortea** the north wind is blowing **III.** *vr:* ~**se** *Méx* to get lost; **al dar la vuelta nos norteamos** we lost our way when we turned around

norteño, -a I. *adj* Northern **II.** *m, f* Northerner

nortino, -a *adj, m, f Chile, Perú* (*norteño*) northern

Noruega *f* Norway

noruego, -a *adj, m, f* Norwegian

nos I. *pron pers* us; **tu primo nos pegó** your cousin hit us; **nos escribieron una carta** they wrote a letter to us **II.** *pron reflexivo* ourselves, each other

nosocomio *m AmL* (*hospital*) hospital

nosotros, -as *pron pers, 1. pl* **1.**(*sujeto*) we **2.**(*tras preposición*) us

nostalgia *f* (*de lugar*) homesickness; (*del pasado*) nostalgia; ~ **de alguien** longing for sb; **tengo ~ de María** I'm longing to see María again

nostálgico, -a *adj* (*de un lugar*) homesick; (*del pasado*) nostalgic; ~ **de alguien** longing (for) sb; **sentimiento ~** sentimental longing; **estar ~** to be nostalgic

nota *f* **1.**(*anotación*) note; ~ **al pie de la página** footnote; ~ **preliminar** preliminary notes **2.**(*apunte*) note; **tomar ~** to take notes; **tomar (buena) ~ de algo** to take (good) note of sth **3.**(*aviso*) letter; ~ **circular** circular **4.**(*calificación*) mark *Brit*, grade *Am;* **sacar malas ~s** to get bad marks *Brit* [*o* grades *Am*] **5.**(*factura*) receipt; ~ **de caja** receipt **6.**(*cuenta*) bill **7.**(*detalle*) touch; **una ~ individual** a personal touch **8.** MÚS note ▶**dar la ~** to stand out (in a negative way); **dejar mala ~** to leave a bad impression; **forzar la ~** to go too far

notabilidad *f* **1.**(*importancia*) noteworthiness **2.**(*personalidad*) **es una ~** he/she's quite a character; **es una ~ en su género** he/she's an expert in his/her field

notable I. *adj* remarkable; (*suma*) considerable **II.** *m* **1.** ENS *in the Spanish education system the qualification equivalent to 7 or 8 on a scale of ten* **2.** *pl* (*personas importantes*) notables *pl*

notación *f* **1.**(*sistema*) notation; ~ **musical** musical notation; ~ **fonética** phonetic script **2.** MAT, QUÍM annotation

notar *vt* **1.**(*percibir*) to notice; (*calor*) to feel; **hacer ~** to point out; **hacerse ~** to stand out; **no se te nota nada** you wouldn't notice **2.**(*apuntar*) to write (a note)

notaría *f* **1.**(*profesión*) profession of notary **2.**(*despacho*) notary's office

notariado, -a *adj* profession of notary

notarial *adj* JUR legal; (*hecho por el notario*) notarial

notario, -a *m, f* notary

noticia *f* (piece of) news; **las ~s** the news; ~ **falsa** a false news item; ~ **de prensa** press report; ~ **bomba** bombshell; **ser ~** to be in the news; ~**s de última hora** latest news; **no tener ~ de alguien** to not have heard from sb; **tener ~ de algo** to have heard about sth; **andar atrasado de ~s** not to be up to date (with the news)

noticiario *m* RADIO, TV news report, newscast *Am;* ~ **deportivo** sports news

notificación *f* notification; ~ **de accidentes** accident report; ~ **por escrito** written notification; ~ **pública** public notification; ~ **de la sentencia** delivery of verdict

notificar <c→qu> *vt* to notify; **hacer ~** to let sb know

notoriedad *f* **1.**(*nombradía*) fame; **adquirir ~** to become well-known **2.**(*evidencia*) clarity

notorio, -a *adj* **1.**(*conocido*) well-known **2.**(*evidente*) obvious

novatada *f* **1.**(*broma*) prank, hazing *Am;* **gastar la ~ a alguien** to play a trick on sb; **pagar la ~** to learn the hard way **2.** *inf* (*complicación*) beginner's mistake

novato, -a *m, f* (*en un lugar*) new boy *m,* new girl *f;* (*en una actividad*) beginner

novecientos, -as *adj* nine hundred; *v.t.* **ochocientos**

novedad *f* **1.**(*acontecimiento*) new development; **¿hay alguna ~?** anything new?; **las últimas ~es** the latest; **el enfermo sigue sin ~es** the patient's condition is unchanged; **¡sin ~ en el frente!** all quiet on the front! **2.**(*cosa*) novelty; (*libro*) new publication

novedoso, -a *adj AmL* novel

novel I. *adj* new; (*sin experiencia*) inexperienced **II.** *mf* beginner

novela *f* novel; ~ **corta** novella; ~ **por entregas** serialized novel; ~ **policíaca** detective story; ~ **rosa** romance; **¡déjate de ~s!** stop dreaming!

novelar I. *vi* to write novels **II.** *vt* to make into a novel

novelesco, -a *adj* novel; *fig* amazing

novelista *mf* novelist

novelística *f sin pl* fiction

noveno, -a *adj, m, f* ninth; *v.t.* **octavo**

noventa *adj inv, m* ninety; *v.t.* **ochenta**

novia *f v.* **novio**

noviar *vi CSur* to go steady; ~ **con alguien** to be going out with sb

noviazgo *m* **1.**(*para casarse*) engagement **2.** *inf* (*relación*) relationship

novicio, -a *m, f* **1.** REL novice **2.**(*principiante*) beginner **3.**(*persona recatada*) shy person

noviembre *m* November; *v.t.* **marzo**

novillada *f* TAUR *bullfight with young bulls and less experienced bullfighters*

novillero, -a *m, f* **1.** (*torero*) apprentice bull-fighter **2.** (*escuela*) truant

novillo, -a *m, f* young bull ▶ **hacer** ~**s** to play truant

novio, -a *m, f* **1.** (*para casarse*) bridegroom *m*, bride *f*; **los** ~**s** (*en la boda*) the bride and groom; (*después de la boda*) the newly-weds; **viaje de** ~**s** honeymoon **2.** (*en relación amorosa*) boyfriend *m*, girlfriend *f*; **echarse novia** to get a girlfriend; **tontear con el** ~ to flirt with one's boyfriend ▶ **compuesta y sin** ~ all dressed up and nowhere to go

novísimo, -a *adj* brand new; (*noticia*) latest

nubarrón *m* storm cloud

nube *f* cloud; ~ **de humo y gases** cloud of smoke and chemicals; ~ **de mosquitos** cloud of mosquitos; ~ **de verano** *t. fig* passing cloud; (*pequeñez*) trifle; **descargar una** ~ to rain ▶ **bajar de las** ~**s** to come back down to earth; **estar por las** ~**s** (*precios*) to be sky-high; **poner a alguien por las** ~**s** to praise sb to the skies; **ponerse por las** ~**s** *inf* (*persona*) to go up the wall; **vivir en las** ~**s** to have one's head in the clouds

núbil *adj* nubile

nublado I. *adj* cloudy **II.** *m* METEO cloud cover

nublar I. *vt* **1.** (*nubes*) to cloud **2.** (*mente*) to get confused; (*ojos*) to mist over **II.** *vr:* ~**se** **1.** (*nubes*) to cloud over **2.** (*mente*) to get confused; (*ojos*) to mist over; **se me nubló la vista** my eyes clouded over

nubosidad *f* cloudiness

nuboso, -a *adj* cloudy

nuca *f* ANAT nape, back of the neck

nuclear *adj* nuclear; **energía** ~ nuclear energy [*o* power]

núcleo *m* **1.** QUÍM nucleus **2.** (*centro*) hub; ~ **de una idea** core of an idea; ~ **urbano** town

nudillo *m* ANAT knuckle

nudo *m* **1.** *t.* NÁUT (*atadura*) knot; ~ **corredizo** slipknot; **deshacer el** ~ to untie the knot; **hacer un** ~ **en la garganta** to get a lump in one's throat **2.** (*madera*) knot; ~ **de rama** fork in a branch; **sin** ~**s** smooth **3.** (*punto de reunión*) centre *Brit,* center *Am;* ~ **de comunicaciones** communications centre *Brit* [*o* center *Am*]; ~ **ferroviario** junction **4.** (*cosa que une*) **el** ~ **de la amistad** the ties of friendship **5.** (*dificultad*) **el** ~ **del problema es...** the crux of the problem is ... **6.** NÁUT (*velocidad*) knot

nudoso, -a *adj* knotty; (*madera*) gnarled

nuera *f* daughter-in-law

nuestro, -a I. *adj pos antepuesto* our; ~ **hijo/nuestra hija** our son/daughter; ~**s nietos** our grandchildren; **por nuestra parte** on our side **II.** *pron pos* **1.** (*propiedad*) **la casa es nuestra** the house is ours; **¡ya es** ~! *fig* we've got it! **2.** *tras artículo* **el** ~/**la nuestra/lo** ~ ours; **los** ~**s** our people; (*parientes*) our family; **¡eso es lo** ~! that's what we're good at!; **ésta es la nuestra** *fig, inf* this is our chance **3.** *tras substantivo* of ours, our; **una amiga nuestra** a

friend of ours; **es culpa nuestra** it is our fault

nueva *f* piece of news; **esto me coge de** ~**s** this is news to me; **no te hagas de** ~**s** don't pretend you didn't know; **la buena** ~ good tidings *pl*

nuevamente *adv* **1.** (*otra vez*) again **2.** (*últimamente*) recently

Nueva York *f* New York

Nueva Zelanda *f* New Zealand

nueve *adj inv, m* nine; *v.t.* **ocho**

nuevo, -a I. *adj* new; **de** ~ again; **sentirse como** ~ to feel like a new man; **¿qué hay de** ~? what's new?; **hasta** ~ **aviso** until our next communication **II.** *m, f* new person

nuez *f* **1.** BOT walnut; ~ **de anacardo** cashew nut; ~ **de coco** coconut; ~ **moscada** nutmeg; **cascar nueces** to crack nuts **2.** ANAT Adam's apple; **apretar la** ~ **a alguien** *inf* to wring sb's neck

nulidad *f* **1.** (*no válido*) nullity; **declarar la** ~ **de algo** to declare sth invalid **2.** *inf* (*persona*) nonentity; **ser una** ~ to be useless

nulo, -a *adj* **1.** (*inválido*) null; **declarar** ~ to declare invalid; **voto** ~ invalid vote **2.** (*incapaz*) useless; **soy** ~ **para el deporte** I'm no good at sports

núm. *abr de* **número** No.

numen *m elev* (*del artista*) inspiration

numeración *f* **1.** (*sistema*) numbering system; ~ **arábiga** Arabic numerals; ~ **correlativa** correlated sequence; ~ **decimal** decimal system **2.** (*acción*) numbering

numerador *m* **1.** MAT numerator **2.** (*aparato*) meter; (*sello*) stamp

numeral I. *adj* numeral **II.** *m* LING number

numerar *vt* **1.** (*poner números*) to number; ~ **correlativamente** to make a correlated sequence; (*páginar*) to paginate; **sin** ~ unnumbered **2.** (*contar*) to number off

numerario *m* cash

numerario, -a *adj* **1.** (*de números*) full **2.** (*fijo*) permanent; (*profesor*) tenured

numéricamente *adv* numerically

numérico, -a *adj* numerical

número *m* **1.** MAT number; ~ **cardinal** cardinal number; ~ **primo** prime number; ~ **quebrado** fraction; **en** ~**s redondos** in round numbers; **aprender de** ~**s** *inf* to learn one's sums; **hacer** ~**s** to do one's sums; **hacer** ~**s para ver si...** to calculate if ... **2.** (*cantidad*) number; ~ **de habitantes** number of inhabitants; **sin** ~ innumerable **3.** *t.* LING (*cifra, edición*) number; ~ **de matrícula** registration number *Brit,* license number *Am;* ~ **de identificación personal** PIN (personal identification number); ~ **de zapatos** shoe size; **es el** ~ **uno de la clase** he's the top of the class; ~ **suelto** odd number; **el** ~ **1000** number 1,000 **4.** (*ejemplar*) copy; ~ **atrasado** back issue **5.** (*actuación*) ~ **de baile** dance number; **montar un** ~ to make a scene

numeroso, -a *adj* numerous; **familia numerosa** large family

nunca *adv* never; ~ **jamás** never ever; **más que** ~ more than ever
nuncio *m* **1.** REL nuncio **2.** (*que anuncia*) messenger; *fig* harbinger
nupcial *adj* nuptial; **corona** ~ bridal wreath
nupcias *fpl* nuptials *pl;* **segundas** ~ remarriage; **posteriores** ~ later wedding
nurse *f AmL* **1.** (*niñera*) nanny; (*extranjera*) au-pair **2.** (*enfermera*) nurse
nutria *f* otter
nutricio, -a *adj* (*nutritivo*) nutritious
nutrición *f* nutrition
nutrido, -a *adj* **1.** (*alimentado*) fed; **bien** ~ well-fed; **mal** ~ undernourished **2.** (*numeroso*) ample; (*biblioteca*) well-stocked
nutrir I. *vt* **1.** (*alimentar*) to feed; (*piel*) to nourish **2.** (*fortalecer*) to strengthen II. *vr* ~**se de** [*o* con] **algo** to feed off sth
nutritivo, -a *adj* nutritious; **valor** ~ nutritional value

Ñ

Ñ, ñ *f* Ñ, ñ

The **eñe** is the trade mark of the Spanish **alfabeto**. Up until a few years ago the 'ch', - **la che** - (directly after the 'c') and the 'll' - **la elle** - (after the 'l') were also part of the alphabet, as they are both independent sounds in their own right. This had to be changed, however, in order to internationalise the Spanish alphabet, i.e. bring it into line with other languages.

ña *f AmC, AmS, inf* (*señora*) lady, Missis
ñácara *f Chile* sore, ulcer
ñandutí *m CSur* Paraguayan lace
ñangotarse *vr* **1.** *PRico, RDom* (*ponerse en cuclillas*) to squat **2.** *PRico* (*someterse*) to yield **3.** *PRico* (*perder el ánimo*) to lose heart
ñaña *f Chile, Perú* elder sister
ñapango, -a *adj Col* mestizo, half-breed
ñaque *m* junk
ñata *f AmL, inf* conk *Brit,* beak *Am*
ñato, -a I. *adj* **1.** *CSur* (*chato*) snub-nosed **2.** *Col* (*gangoso*) nasal II. *m, f AmL* guy
ñeque I. *adj AmC* strong II. *m* **1.** *Chile, Ecua, Perú* (*fuerza*) strength; (*energía*) vim **2.** *Perú* (*valor, coraje*) courage
ñire *m Chile* BOT antarctic beech
ño *m AmC, AmS, inf* (*señor*) abbreviated form of 'señor' used only before the first name
ñoco, -a *adj AmS* (*sin dedo*) missing a finger; (*sin mano*) missing a hand
ñoñería *f* **1.** (*simpleza*) inanity **2.** (*dengues*) silliness
ñoño, -a I. *adj inf* **1.** (*soso*) insipid; (*aburrido*) boring **2.** (*tonto*) inane **3.** (*remilgado*) prudish II. *m, f inf* **1.** (*tonto*) idiot **2.** (*aburrido*) bore
ñoqui *m* gnocchi
ñorbo *m Ecua, Perú* BOT passionflower
ñu *m* gnu
ñudo *m* knot; **al** ~ *AmL, inf* in vain
ñuto, -a *adj AmS, Arg, Perú* (*ablandado*) tenderized

O

O, o *f* O, o; ~ **de Oviedo** O for Oliver *Brit,* O for Oboe *Am* ▸**no saber hacer la 'o' con un canuto** not to know a thing
o, ó *conj* or; ~ **...,** ~ **...** either ..., or ...; ~ **sea** in other words; ~ **bien** or else; ~ **mejor dicho** or rather
O *abr de* **oeste** W
oasis *m inv* oasis
obcecación *f* stubborn insistence
obcecar <c→qu> I. *vt* to blind II. *vr:* ~**se** to be blinded, to stubbornly insist
obedecer *irr como crecer* I. *vt* (*orden, a alguien*) to obey; (*instrucciones*) to follow; **hacerse** ~ to make people obey II. *vi* (*provenir*) to be due; (*responder*) to respond
obediencia *f* obedience
obediente *adj* obedient
obelisco *m* obelisk
obertura *f* t. MÚS overture
obesidad *f* obesity
obeso, -a *adj* obese
óbice *m elev* **no ser** ~ **para que alguien** +*subj* not to prevent sb from
obispado *m* REL **1.** (*cargo*) bishopric **2.** (*diócesis*) diocese
obispo *m* REL bishop ▸**trabajar para el** ~ to work for nothing
óbito *m* demise *form*
obituario *m* **1.** (*libro*) register of deaths **2.** *AmL* (*defunción*) demise **3.** *AmL* (*del periódico*) obituary
objeción *f* objection; ~ **de conciencia** conscientious objection; **poner** ~ **a algo** to object to sth
objetar *vt* to object; **tengo algo que** ~ I have an objection
objetividad *f* objectivity
objetivo *m* **1.** (*finalidad*) goal; **tener como** ~ to have as one's goal **2.** FOTO lens **3.** (*blanco*) target
objetivo, -a *adj* objective
objeto *m* **1.** (*cosa*) object; ~ **de enseñanza** teaching aid; ~ **de lujo** luxury item; ~ **de valor** valuables *pl;* **la mujer** ~ woman as an object; ~**s perdidos** lost property **2.** (*motivo*) purpose; **el** ~ **de la presente es...** the purpose of this letter is ...; **con** (**el**) [*o* **al**] ~ **de...** in order to ...; **no tener** ~ to be pointless;

tener por ~ to have as one's aim **3.** LING object
objetor(a) *m(f)* dissenter; ~ **de conciencia** conscientious objector
oblea *f* **1.** (*hostia*) wafer; **estar hecho una** ~ *inf* to be as thin as a rake **2.** (*sello*) stamp
oblicuidad *f* obliquity
oblicuo, -a *adj* oblique, slanted
obligación *f* **1.** (*deber*) obligation; ~ **alimenticia** duty to provide maintenance; ~ **de comunicación** need to reply; ~ **de secreto** obligation to maintain confidentiality; **contraer una** ~ to undertake an obligation; **cumplir con una** ~ to fulfil *Brit* [*o* to fulfill *Am*] an obligation; **dedicarse a sus obligaciones** to devote oneself to one's duties; **faltar a sus obligaciones** to neglect one's duties; **tener la** ~ **de hacer algo** to be obliged to do sth **2.** (*deuda*) liability; (*documento*) bond
obligado, -a *adj* **1.** *estar* obliged **2.** *ser* (*imprescindible*) obligatory; **tema** ~ compulsory topic; **es** ~... one must ... **3.** *estar* (*agradecido*) grateful
obligar <g→gu> I. *vt* **1.** (*forzar*) to force; (*comprometer*) to oblige **2.** *Chile, Arg* (*invitar*) to invite to drink II. *vr:* ~**se** to commit oneself
obligatoriedad *f* obligation; **de** ~ **general** universally compulsory; ~ **de visado** visa requirement; ~ **del voto** requirement to vote
obligatorio, -a *adj* obligatory; **asignatura obligatoria** compulsory subject; **compromiso** ~ binding commitment; **no** ~ not compulsory; (*oferta*) not binding; **es** ~ **llevar puesto el casco** helmets must be worn
oblongo, -a *adj* oblong
obnubilación *f* **1.** (*trastorno*) confusion **2.** (*ofuscación*) fascination **3.** (*vista*) blurring
obnubilar *vt* **1.** (*trastornar*) to confuse **2.** (*ofuscar*) to fascinate
oboe *m* MÚS **1.** (*instrumento*) oboe **2.** (*músico*) oboist
obra *f* **1.** (*creación, labor*) work; ~ **de arte** work of art; ~ **benéfica** charitable act; ~**s completas** collected [*o* complete] works; ~ **de consulta** reference work; ~ **maestra** masterpiece; ~ **meritoria** commendable act; ~ **de teatro** play; **por** ~ (**y gracia**) **de** thanks to; **¡manos a la** ~**!** let's get to work! **2.** (*construcción*) building work; (*lugar en construcción*) construction site; (*edificio*) building; ~ **de caminos, canales y puertos** civil engineering; ~**s públicas** public works; ~ **de reforma** renovation; ~ **de romanos** *fig* Herculean task; ~ **vieja** old building; **mano de** ~ labour *Brit,* labor *Am;* **estar en** ~**s** to be under construction ▸~**s son amores y no buenas razones** *prov* actions speak louder than words; ~ **empezada, medio acabada** *prov* the hardest part is getting started *prov*
obradera *f Col, Guat, Pan* (*diarrea*) diarrhoea *Brit,* diarrhea *Am*
obrador *m* **1.** (*taller*) workshop **2.** (*de confitería*) bakery
obrador(a) I. *adj* working II. *m(f)* worker

obraje *m* **1.** *CSur* sawmill **2.** *Méx* butcher's shop
obrajero, -a *m, f* **1.** *AmL* (*propietario de un obraje*) sawmill owner **2.** *Arg, Par* (*peón de un obraje*) sawmill worker **3.** *AmL* (*artesano*) craftsman **4.** *Méx* (*carnicero*) pork butcher
obrar I. *vi* **1.** (*actuar*) to act; ~ **contra las buenas costumbres** to behave badly; ~ **a tontas y a locas** *inf* to act rashly **2.** *vulg* (*defecar*) to move one's bowels **3.** (*encontrarse*) to find oneself II. *vi, vt* **1.** (*hacer efecto*) to have an effect on; ~ **buen efecto** to be effective; ~ **sobre alguien/algo** to act on sb/sth **2.** (*construir*) to build **3.** (*hacer*) to do; (*trabajar*) to work; **sin** ~ unworked
obrerismo *m* **1.** POL labour movement *Brit,* labor movement *Am* **2.** (*conjunto*) working class movement
obrerista I. *adj* working-class II. *mf* labour *Brit* [*o* labor *Am*] movement activist
obrero, -a I. *adj* (*relativo al trabajo*) working; (*relativo al obrero*) working-class II. *m, f* worker; ~ **agrícola** agricultural labourer *Brit* [*o* laborer *Am*]; ~ **asalariado** labourer *Brit,* laborer *Am,* paid worker; ~ **eventual** temporary [*o* seasonal] worker; ~ **desocupado** unemployed worker; ~ **especializado** [*o* cualificado] skilled worker; ~ **fijo** permanent employee; **ser alguien** ~ **de su propia ruina** to be the author of one's own downfall
obscenidad *f* obscenity
obsceno, -a *adj* obscene
obscurecer *irr como* crecer *vt v.* **oscurecer**
obscuridad *f v.* **oscuridad**
obscuro, -a *adj v.* **oscuro**
obsequiar *vt* **1.** (*con atenciones*) to honour *Brit,* to honor *Am;* (*con bebidas*) to toast; (*con regalos*) to bestow **2.** (*agasajar*) to lavish attention on; (*festejar*) to celebrate; ~ **con su presencia** to honour *Brit* [*o* to honor *Am*] with one's presence; ~ **a alguien con un banquete** to hold a banquet in sb's honour **3.** *AmL* (*regalar*) to give
obsequio *m* **1.** (*regalo*) gift **2.** (*agasajo*) attention; **¡hágame Ud. este** ~**!** please do this favour *Brit* [*o* favor *Am*] for me!; **en** ~ **de alguien** in honour *Brit* [*o* honor *Am*] of sb
obsequioso, -a *adj* (*cortés*) attentive
observación *f* **1.** (*contemplación, vigilancia*) observation **2.** (*comentario*) remark; ~ **marginal** note **3.** (*observancia*) observance
observador(a) I. *adj* observant II. *m(f)* observer
observancia *f* observance
observante *adj* (*orden*) observant
observar *vt* **1.** (*contemplar, cumplir*) to observe **2.** (*orden*) to follow; (*normas, plazos*) to adhere to **3.** (*notar*) to notice; **hacer** ~ **algo a alguien** to bring sth to sb's attention
observatorio *m* observatory; ~ **astronómico** observatory; ~ **meteorológico** weather station
obsesión *f* obsession

obsesionado, -a *adj* obsessed; **está ~ con ella** he is obsessed with [*o* by] her

obsesionar I. *vt* to obsess; **el fútbol lo obsesiona** he is obsessed with [*o* by] football II. *vr:* **~se** to be obsessed; **~se con algo/alguien** to be obsessed by [*o* with] sth/sb

obsesivo, -a *adj* obsessive

obseso, -a I. *adj* obsessed II. *m, f* obsessive person; **~ del sexo** sex maniac

obsoleto, -a *adj* obsolete

obstaculizar <z→c> *vt* to hinder; **~ la carretera** to obstruct [*o* block] the road; **~ el progreso** to hinder progress

obstáculo *m* **1.** obstacle; **salvar un ~** to overcome an obstacle; **triunfar ante todos los ~s** to triumph in the face of great odds; **poner ~s a alguien** to hinder sb **2.** COM barrier; **~s comerciales** trade barriers **3.** DEP hurdle

obstante *adv* **no ~** nevertheless

obstar I. *vi* to stand in the way II. *vimpers* to be a hindrance; **eso no obsta para que...** +*subj* that does not prevent ...

obstetra *mf* MED obstetrician

obstetricia *f* MED obstetrics *pl*

obstinación *f* **1.** (*terquedad*) obstinacy **2.** (*tenacidad*) persistence

obstinado, -a *adj* **1.** (*terco*) obstinate **2.** (*tenaz*) persistent **3.** (*intransigente*) unyielding

obstinarse *vr* to persist; **~ en su silencio** to remain silent; **~ contra algo/alguien** to hold firm against sth/sb

obstrucción *f* obstruction; MED blockage; **~ de la autoridad** JUR ≈ obstruction of duty

obstruir *irr como huir* I. *vt* **1.** (*el paso, acción*) to obstruct **2.** (*una tubería*) to block II. *vr:* **~se** to get blocked

obtención *f* obtaining; QUÍM extraction; **~ de alimentos** food production; **~ de datos** data collection; **~ de la velocidad máxima** attainment of maximum speed

obtener *irr como tener vt* to obtain; QUÍM to extract; (*resultado, ventaja*) to gain; **~ un pedido** to receive an order; **difícil de ~** not easily obtainable

obtenible *adj* obtainable

obturación *f* **1.** (*cierre*) closure; (*bloqueo*) blockage **2.** (*de dientes*) filling

obturador *m* FOTO shutter

obturar *vt* **1.** (*cerrar*) to close; (*bloquear*) to block **2.** (*los dientes*) to fill

obtuso, -a *adj* **1.** (*cosa*) blunt **2.** (*persona*) obtuse

obús *m* **1.** (*artillería*) howitzer **2.** (*proyectil*) shell **3.** AUTO valve core

obviar I. *vi* (*ser un obstáculo*) to stand in the way II. *vt* **1.** (*evitar*) to avoid **2.** (*eliminar*) to remove; **~ un problema** to get round a problem

obvio, -a *adj* obvious; **es ~** it's obvious; **lo ~ del mensaje** the clarity of the message

oc *abr de* **ondas cortas** SW

oca *f* **1.** ZOOL goose; **¡es la ~!** *inf* it's the best! **2.** (*juego*) snakes *pl* and ladders **3.** BOT oxalis

ocasión *f* occasion; **coche de ~** second hand car; **libros de ~** bargain [*o* cut-price] books; **aprovechar la ~** to make the most of the opportunity; **desperdiciar la ~** to waste the opportunity; **en esta ~** on this occasion; **llegada la ~** when the occasion arises; **en ocasiones** sometimes; **en la primera ~** at the first opportunity; **con ~ de** on the occasion of; **dar a alguien ~ para quejarse** to give sb cause to complain ►**la ~ hace al ladrón** *prov* opportunity makes the thief *prov;* **la ~ la pintan calva** *prov* strike while the irón is hot *prov,* make hay while the sun shines *prov*

ocasional *adj* **1.** (*no habitual*) occasional; **trabajo ~** temporary work **2.** (*casual*) chance **3.** (*para una ocasión*) occasional **4.** (*causante*) causative; **enfermedad ~** underlying illness

ocasionar *vt* **~ algo** to cause sth, to bring sth about; **~ dolores de cabeza a alguien** to give sb a headache

ocaso *m* **1.** ASTR setting; (*del sol*) sunset; (*oeste*) west **2.** (*final*) end **3.** (*decadencia*) decline

occidental *adj* western; **potencias ~es** Western powers

occidente *m* GEO west; **el ~** the West

occipucio *m* MED occiput

occiso, -a *adj form* murdered

OCDE *f abr de* **Organización para la Cooperación y el Desarrollo Económicos** OECD

Oceanía *f* Oceania

océano *m* **1.** (*mar*) ocean; **Océano Austral** Southern Ocean; **Océano Boreal** Arctic Ocean **2.** *fig* (*cantidad*) sea; **un ~ de gente** a sea of people; **un ~ de sangre** a sea of blood; **un ~ de gente salía del concierto** a huge throng of people left the concert

oceanografía *f* oceanography

ocelote *m* ocelot

ochava *f AmL* (*chaflán*) corner house; (*de un edificio*) cant

ochenta I. *adj inv* **1.** eighty; **los años ~** the eighties; **un hombre de alrededor de ~ años** a man of about eighty years of age; **una mujer en sus ~** a woman in her eighties **2.** (*octogésimo*) eightieth II. *m* eighty

ocho I. *adj inv* eight; **jornada de ~ horas** eight-hour day; **~ veces mayor/menor que...** eight times bigger/smaller than ...; **a las ~** at eight (o'clock); **son las ~ y media de la mañana/tarde** it is half past eight in the morning/evening; **las ~ y cuarto/menos cuarto** a quarter past/to eight; **a las ~ en punto** at eight o'clock precisely [*o* on the dot]; **el ~ de agosto** the eighth of August; **dentro de ~ días** in a week's time; **de aquí a ~ días** a week from now ►**echar a alguien con los ~s y los nueves** to be blunt with sb; **ser más chulo que un ~** *inf* to be a right show off; **dar igual ~ que ~** not to care less II. *m* eight

ochocientos, -as *adj* eight hundred; **esta basílica fue construida hace ~ años** this

basilica was built eight hundred years ago; **vinieron más de ochocientas personas** more than eight hundred people came
ocio *m* leisure; ~ **anual** annual holidays *pl;* **horas de** ~ spare time; **entregarse al** ~ to lead a life of leisure
ociosear *vi AmS* to be at leisure, to loaf around *inf*
ociosidad *f* idleness ►**la** ~ **es la madre de todos los vicios** *prov* the devil makes work for idle hands *prov,* idleness is the root of all evil *prov*
ocioso, -a *adj* **1.** *estar* (*inactivo*) idle **2.** *ser* (*inútil*) useless; **palabras ociosas** talking for talking's sake
oclusión *f* LING, METEO occlusion
ocote *m Méx* BOT ocote pine
ocre *adj* ochre *Brit,* ocher *Am*
octagonal *adj* octagonal
octágono *m* octagon
octava *f* LIT, MÚS octave
octavilla *f* (*volante*) leaflet; ~ **difamatoria** defamatory leaflet
octavo, -a I. *adj* eighth; **en** ~ **lugar** in eighth place; (*enumeración*) eighth; **estoy en** ~ **curso** I am in eighth year; **la octava parte** an eighth II. *m, f* eighth
octeto *m* **1.** MÚS octet **2.** INFOR byte
octogésimo, -a *adj* eightieth; *v.t.* octavo
octubre *m* October; *v.t.* **marzo**
óctuplo, -a *adj* eightfold
ocular I. *adj* ocular; **examen** ~ eye test; **testigo** ~ eyewitness II. *m* eyepiece
oculista *mf* MED ophthalmologist
ocultación *f,* **ocultamiento** *m* concealment; ~ **fiscal** tax evasion
ocultar I. *vt* (*cosa*) to hide; (*información, delito*) to conceal; ~ **la cara entre** [*o* con] **las manos** to cover one's face with one's hands II. *vr:* ~**se** to hide
ocultismo *m* **el** ~ the occult
oculto, -a *adj* (*escondido*) hidden; (*secreto*) secret; **de** ~ incognito; **en** ~ in secret; **traerse algo** ~ to keep sth hidden
ocupación *f* **1.** (*trabajo*) occupation; ~ **lucrativa** well-paid job; ~ **del ocio** occupation of leisure time; ~ **temporal** temporary job; **sin** ~ unemployed **2.** (*apoderamiento*) *t.* MIL occupation; ~ **hotelera** hotel occupancy; **primera** ~ **de un apartamento** first occupation of a flat *Brit* [*o* apartment *Am*]; **zona de** ~ occupied zone
ocupacional *adj* occupational
ocupado, -a *adj* **1.** (*sitio*) occupied **2.** (*persona*) busy **3.** (*línea de teléfono*) engaged *Brit,* busy *Am*
ocupante I. *adj* MIL occupying II. *mf* **1.** (*de vehículo*) occupant; (*de tren, avión*) passenger **2.** (*de un edificio*) resident
ocupar I. *vt* **1.** (*lugar, teléfono*) *t.* MIL to occupy **2.** (*un cargo*) to hold; (*vacante*) to fill **3.** (*tiempo, espacio, asiento*) to take up **4.** (*vacante*) to fill **5.** (*a una persona*) to keep

busy **6.** (*tiempo, espacio*) to take up II. *vr* ~**se de** [*o* con] **algo** to busy oneself with sth; ~**se de alguien** (*cuidar*) to look after sb; **ella se ocupó de todo** she took care of everything
ocurrencia *f* **1.** (*idea*) idea; **¡qué** ~ **pensar que es mi culpa!** imagine saying that it was my fault!; **dijo que podía comerse 20 panecillos, ¡qué** ~**!** he/she said that he/she could eat 20 rolls, what nonsense!; **se bañó en el mar en pleno invierno, ¡qué** ~**!** he/she swam in the sea in the middle of winter, what a thing to do!; **tener la** ~ **de...** to have the bright idea of ... **2.** (*suceso*) occurrence
ocurrente *adj* witty
ocurrir I. *vi* to happen; **¿qué ocurre?** what's wrong?; **¿qué te ocurre?** what's the matter?; **lo que ocurre es que...** the thing is that ...; **cuida de que no vuelva a** ~ **algo semejante** make sure the same thing doesn't happen again II. *vr:* ~**se** to occur; **no se me ocurre nada** I can't think of anything; **no se le ocurre más que decir tonterías** he/she does nothing but talk nonsense; **¿cómo se te ocurrió esa tontería?** what on earth made you think of a stupid thing like that?; **nunca se me hubiese ocurrido pensar que...** I never would have imagined that ...
oda *f* LIT ode
odiar *vt* to hate; ~ **a alguien a muerte** to have an undying hatred for sb, to hate sb's guts *inf*
odio *m* hate, hatred; **hacer algo por** ~ **a alguien** to do sth out of hatred for sb
odiosidad *f* **1.** (*carácter*) hatefulness **2.** (*aversión*) odiousness **3.** *AmL* (*molestia*) irksomeness
odioso, -a *adj* **1.** (*hostil*) nasty **2.** (*repugnante*) horrible **3.** *AmL* (*fastidioso*) annoying
odisea *f* odyssey
odontología *f* MED dentistry
odontólogo, -a *m, f* MED dentist
odre *m* (*cuero*) wineskin
OEA *f abr de* **Organización de los Estados Americanos** OAS
oeste *m* **1.** (*punto*) west; **el lejano** ~ the wild [*o* far] west; **película del** ~ western; **hacia el** ~ westward(s); **al** ~ **de...** west of ... **2.** (*viento*) westerly
ofender I. *vt* **1.** (*humillar*) to offend; ~ **la vista** to be an eyesore; ~ **a Dios** to offend God; **hacerse el ofendido** to take offence *Brit* [*o* offense *Am*] **2.** (*herir*) to insult II. *vr:* ~**se** to take offence [*o* offense *Am*]; **¡no te ofendas conmigo!** don't get angry with me!
ofensa *f* offence, offense *Am;* **dicho sea sin** ~ **de nadie** I say this without wishing to offend anyone
ofensiva *f* offensive; **tomar la** ~ to go on the offensive
ofensivo, -a *adj* **1.** (*hiriente*) offensive **2.** (*dañino*) damaging; ~ **para el medio ambiente** environmentally damaging **3.** (*que ataca*) attacking
ofensor(a) *adj* (*de ofensa*) offending; (*de*

ataque) attacking

oferta *f* **1.** (*propuesta*) offer; ~ **de empleo** job offer; ~ **especial** special offer; **estar de** ~ to be on special offer; **este supermercado tiene muchas ~s** this supermarket has lots of special offers; **hacer mayor** ~ to outbid **2.** COM tender, bid **3.** ECON supply; ~ **y demanda** supply and demand; ~ **excesiva** oversupply

ofertar *vt* to offer; **invitar a alguien a** ~ to invite sb to bid

office *m small room adjoining the kitchen used as a dining area or utility room*

offset *m* offset

oficial *adj* official; **boletín** ~ official gazette

oficial(a) *m(f)* **1.** (*oficio manual*) (skilled) worker; (*administrativo*) clerk; ~ **de albañil** builder's mate; ~ **cervecero** brewery worker; ~ **de obra** building worker; **~a de peluquería** hairdresser; **~a** (**de secretaría**) secretary **2.** MIL officer; ~ **de complemento** reserve officer; ~ **marinero** ship's officer **3.** (*funcionario*) civil servant; ~ **del juzgado** court clerk; ~ **de la justicia** sheriff; ~ **del registro civil** registry clerk

oficialidad *f* **1.** (*carácter*) official nature **2.** MIL officers *pl*

oficialismo *m* **1.** *Arg* (*burocracia*) bureaucracy **2.** *AmL* (*del gobierno*) the government and its party members

oficialista **I.** *adj* **1.** *AmL* (*burocrático*) bureaucratic **2.** *AmL* (*del gobierno*) governmental **II.** *mf* *AmL: fervent follower of the government's policy*

oficializar <z→c> *vt* to make official

oficiar **I.** *vt* **1.** REL to celebrate **2.** (*comunicar*) to inform **II.** *vi* *inf* (*obrar*) to act; ~ **de intérprete** to act as interpreter

oficina *f* office; ~ **de asistencia social** social security office; ~ **de correos** post office; ~ **de cuenta** accounts *pl* office; ~ **de empleo** job centre *Brit,* job office *Am;* ~ **de información matrimonial** marriage advice office; ~ **de maquinaria** machine room; ~ **de matrícula** registration office; ~ **de objetos perdidos** lost property (office); ~ **de pasaportes** passport office

oficinista *mf* office worker

oficio *m* **1.** (*trabajo manual*) trade; ~ **de ebanista** cabinet-making; ~ **especializado** skilled trade; **ejercer un** ~ to have a trade; **sin** ~ **ni beneficio** out of work; **tomar algo por** ~ *fig* to do sth out of habit; **ser del** ~ *inf* to be on the game **2.** (*profesión*) profession; **de** ~ by trade; **gajes del** ~ occupational hazards; **son gajes del** ~ it's all in a day's work **3.** (*función*) function; **defensor de** ~ JUR defence counsel *Brit,* defense counsel *Am* (*paid for by the state*)*;* **de** ~ ex officio; **ofrecer sus buenos ~s** to offer one's services **4.** (*escrito*) official document **5.** REL service; ~ **de difuntos** funeral service; **Santo Oficio** Holy Office

oficioso, -a *adj* **1.** (*extraoficial*) unofficial; **mentira oficiosa** white lie **2.** (*activo*) diligent

3. (*servicial*) obliging

ofidios *mpl* snakes *pl*

ofimática *f* INFOR office automation

ofrecer *irr como crecer* **I.** *vt* to offer; ~ **un banquete** to give a meal; ~ **grandes dificultades** to present a lot of difficulties; ~ **un sacrificio** to offer up a sacrifice; **vamos a** ~ *inf* we're going for a drink **II.** *vr:* **~se** (*brindarse*) to offer oneself; **¿se le ofrece algo?** do you need anything?; **¿qué se le ofrece?** may I help you?

ofrecimiento *m* **1.** (*oferta*) offer **2.** REL offering

ofrenda *f* offering; (*sacrificio*) sacrifice

ofrendar *vt* to offer; (*sacrificar*) to sacrifice

oftalmía *f* MED ophthalmia

oftálmico, -a *adj* ophthalmic

oftalmología *f* MED ophthalmology

oftalmólogo, -a *m, f* MED ophthalmologist

ofuscación *f,* **ofuscamiento** *m* **1.** (*vista*) blindness **2.** (*de la mente*) confusion **3.** (*de alguien*) blinding

ofuscar <c→qu> **I.** *vt* **1.** (*cegar*) to blind **2.** (*la mente*) to confuse; ~ (**la mente**) **a alguien** to confuse sb **II.** *vr* **~se en algo** to insist on sth; **~se con una idea** to be obsessed by an idea

ogro *m t. fig* ogre

ohmio *m* FÍS ohm

oída *f* **conocer a alguien de ~s** to have heard about sb; **saber algo de ~s** to have heard about sth

oído *m* **1.** (*sentido*) hearing; **aprender de** ~ to learn by ear; **aplicar el** ~ to listen carefully; **aguzar el** ~ to prick up one's ears; **tener buen** ~ to have a good ear; **duro de** ~ hard of hearing **2.** ANAT ear; **cera de ~s** ear wax; ~ **interno/medio/externo** inner/middle/outer ear; **zumbido de ~s** buzzing in the ears; **me zumban los ~s** my ears are buzzing [*o* ringing]; **cerrar los ~s a algo** to turn a deaf ear to sth; **dar ~s a alguien** (*escuchar*) to listen to sb; (*creer*) to believe sb; **hacer ~s de mercader** to pretend not to hear; **ladrar a alguien al** ~ to yell into sb's ear; **llegar a ~s de alguien** to come to sb's notice [*o* attention]; **pegarse al** ~ to be catchy; **ser todo ~s** to be all ears ▶**¡~ al parche!** look out!; **regalar los ~s** to flatter

oír *irr* *vt* (*sentir*) to hear; (*escuchar*) to listen; **¡oye!** hey!; **¡oye, ven aquí!** come here!; **¿oyes?** do you understand?; **¡oiga!** excuse me!; **¡Dios te oiga!** may your prayers be answered!; **como lo oyes** believe it or not; **lo que hay que** ~ what next?; ~ **decir que...** to hear that ...; **parece que no has oído bien** you don't seem to have heard properly; **ya me oirá** he/she hasn't heard the last of me; **no se oye el vuelo de una mosca** you could hear a pin drop ▶~, **ver y callar** *prov* hear no evil, see no evil, speak no evil; ~ **como quien oye llover** not to be listening

ojal *m* **1.** (*para botones*) buttonhole **2.** (*ojete*) eyelet

ojalá *interj* I hope so, I wish; ¡~ **tuvieras razón!** if only you were right!

ojeada *f* glance; **echar una ~ a algo** to glance at sth; **¿puedes echar una ~ a mi maleta?** (*vigilar*) could you keep an eye on my suitcase?

ojear *vt* **1.** (*mirar con atención*) to stare at **2.** (*pasar la vista*) to glance at **3.** (*la caza*) to beat

ojeras *fpl* bags *pl* (under the eyes); **tener ~** to have dark circles under one's eyes

ojeriza *f* grudge; **tener ~ a alguien** to bear a grudge against sb

ojeroso, -a *adj* haggard, tired

ojete *m* **1.** (*ojal*) eyelet **2.** *vulg* (*ano*) arsehole *Brit*, asshole *Am* **3.** *Arg, Méx* (*vagina*) vagina

ojímetro *m inf* **a ~** at a rough guess

ojiva *f* ARQUIT (*arco*) pointed arch

ojival *adj* pointed

ojo I. *m* **1.** ANAT eye; **~ de buey** NÁUT porthole; **~ de gallo** *fig* corn; **~ morado** black eye; **~s rasgados** almond [*o* slanting] eyes; **~s saltones** [*o* **de rana**] bulging eyes; **a ~** by eye; **aguzar los ~s** to narrow one's eyes; **con ~s de cordero degollado** with a sad look; **los niños llenan antes los ~s que la barriga** children's eyes are always bigger than their stomachs; **mirar con buenos/malos ~s** to approve/disapprove of; **pasar los ~s por algo** to run one's eyes over sth; **¡qué ~ tienes!** you don't miss a thing!; **tener ~ clínico** to be a good diagnostician; *fig* to be very observant **2.** (*agujero*) hole; **~ de aguja** eye of a needle; **~ de cerradura** keyhole; **~ del huracán** eye of the storm; **~ de patio** opening; **~ de un puente** span of a bridge; **meterse por el ~ de una aguja** to be very sharp ▶**donde pone el ~, pone la bala** he/she is a good shot; **no parecerse ni en el blanco de los ~s** to be as different as chalk and cheese *Brit;* **poner los ~s en blanco** to roll one's eyes; **costar un ~ de la cara** to cost an arm and a leg; **no tener ~s en la cara** to be blind; **~s que no ven, corazón que no siente** *prov* out of sight, out of mind *prov;* **a ~ de buen cubero** roughly; **mirar con unos ~s redondos como platos** to look wide-eyed; **a ~s cerrados** without thinking; **con los ~s cerrados** with complete confidence; **andar con cien ~s** to be on one's guard; **cuatro ~s** *pey* four-eyes; **cuatro ~s ven más que dos** *prov* two heads are better than one *prov;* **poner delante de los ~s de alguien** to make clear to sb; **ser el ~ derecho de alguien** to be the apple of sb's eye; **¡dichosos los ~s que te ven!** *irón* it's great to see you after so long!; **estar entrampado hasta los ~s** to be up to one's neck in debt; **a ~s vistas** visibly; **en un abrir y cerrar de ~s** in a flash; **andar con ~** to be careful; **cerrar los ~s a algo** to shut one's eyes to sth; **clavar los ~s en algo** to lay eyes on sth; **comerse con los ~s** to devour with one's eyes; **echar el ~ a algo/alguien** to have one's eye on sth/sb;

echar un ~ a algo/alguien to take a look at sth/sb; (*vigilar*) to keep an eye on sth/sb; **meter algo a alguien por los ~s** to shove sth down sb's throat; **no pegar ~** to not sleep a wink; **no saber dónde poner los ~s** not to know which way to turn; **sacarle los ~s a alguien** to kill sb; **ser todo ~s** to give one's full attention; **tener ~** (*cuidado*) to be careful; **tiene mucho ~ con los turistas** he/she is good at dealing with tourists; **tener a alguien entre ~s** (*estar enfadado*) to be angry with sb; (*tener manía*) to have it in for sb; **¡mis ~s!** my darling!; **~ por ~** (**y diente por diente**) *prov* an eye for an eye (a tooth for a tooth) II. *interj* (be) careful, look out; ¡~ **con ese tipo!** watch out for that guy! ▶¡~ **al dinero que es el amor verdadero!** you can't live on thin air!

ojota *f AmL* (*sandalia*) sandal

okey I. *adj* okay II. *m AmL* okay; **dar el ~** to give the go ahead III. *adv* okay

okupa *mf inf* squatter

ola *f* wave; **~ de calor** heatwave; **~ de frío** cold spell

olé *interj* ≈ bravo

Olé (or **ole**) is not only a cry of encouragement during a bullfight or a Flamenco dance, but also a general cry of enthusiasm and joy. **¡Olé!** is associated worldwide with Spain and its folklore.

---

oleada *f t. fig* wave; **~ de gente** throng of people

oleaginoso, -a *adj* oily

oleaje *m* swell, surf

óleo *m* **1.** (*aceite*) oil **2.** ARTE oil paint; **cuadro al ~** oil painting; **pintar al ~** to paint in oil **3.** REL **administrar los ~s** to anoint sb with holy oil

oleoducto *m* pipeline

oleoso, -a *adj* oily

oler *irr* I. *vi* to smell; **~ a algo** to smell of sth; **~ bien** to smell good II. *vt* to smell; **~ una flor** to smell a flower; **~ el peligro** to smell danger

olfa *mf RíoPl* **1.** *inf* (*chupamedias*) bootlicker **2.** *inf* (*persona servil*) toady

olfatear I. *vt* **1.** (*oliscar*) to sniff **2.** (*husmear*) to smell out II. *vi* **1.** (*oliscar*) to sniff **2.** (*curiosear*) to nose about

olfativo, -a *adj* olfactory

olfato *m* sense of smell; **tener** (**buen**) **~** *fig* to have a good nose [*o* instinct]

oliente *adj* smelling; **mal ~** bad-smelling, smelly

oligarquía *f* oligarchy

oligofrenia *f* mental deficiency

oligofrénico, -a I. *adj* mentally deficient II. *m, f* mental retard

olimpiada *f,* **olimpíada** *f* Olympics + *pl vb*

olímpico, -a *adj* Olympic

oliscar <c→qu> *vi* **1.** (*oler*) to smell **2.** *v.* **olfatear**

olisquear *vt, vi v.* **olfatear**

oliva I. *adj* (**verde**) ~ olive (green) **II.** *f* **1.** BOT (*árbol*) olive tree; (*fruta*) olive **2.** (*color*) olive (green)

oliváceo, -a *adj* olive-green

olivarero, -a *adj* olive; **región olivarera** olive-growing region

olivo *m* olive tree; **el Monte de los Olivos** REL the Mount of Olives

olla *f* **1.** (*para cocinar*) pot; ~ **exprés** pressure cooker; ~ **de grillos** *inf* madhouse; **tengo la cabeza como una ~ de grillos** *inf* my head is buzzing **2.** GASTR stew

olmo *m* elm

olor *m* smell; **buen** ~ good smell; (*fragancia*) scent; ~ **corporal** body odour *Brit* [*o* odor *Am*]; **viene al ~ de tu dinero** he is after your money; **vivir en ~ de santidad** to lead the life of a saint; **tener ~ a** to smell of

olores *mpl Chile* (*especias*) spices *pl*

oloroso, -a *adj* fragrant

oloroso *m* GASTR full-bodied sherry

olote *m Méx* corncob

OLP *f abr de* **Organización para la Liberación de Palestina** PLO

olvidadizo, -a *adj* forgetful

olvidar *vt, vr:* ~**se** to forget; **no ~ que...** (*considerar*) to remember that ...; **dejar olvidado** to leave be; **se me ha olvidado tu nombre** I've forgotten your name

olvido *m* **1.** (*falta de memoria*) forgetfulness **2.** (*omisión*) oversight, forgetting; ~ **de sí mismo** self-neglect; **caer en (el)** ~ to sink into oblivion; **enterrar en el** ~ to forget forever

ombligo *m* **1.** ANAT navel, belly button *inf;* **se me encoge el** ~ *fig* I'm getting cold feet **2.** (*centro*) centre *Brit,* center *Am;* **el ~ del mundo** the centre *Brit* [*o* center *Am*] of the world; **contemplarse el** ~ to self-gratify

ombú *m Arg* BOT umbra tree, ombu

ominoso, -a *adj* despicable

omisión *f* **1.** (*supresión*) omission **2.** (*negligencia*) negligence; ~ **de auxilio** JUR failure to render assistance **3.** (*lapsus*) oversight

omiso, -a *adj* (*negligente*) negligent; **hacer caso ~ de algo** to take no notice of sth

omitir *vt* **1.** (*no hacer*) to fail to do; **no ~ esfuerzos** to spare no effort **2.** (*pasar por alto*) to omit

ómnibus *m* AUTO bus

omnímodo, -a *adj* all-embracing

omnipotencia *f* omnipotence

omnipotente *adj* almighty, omnipotent

omnipresencia *f* omnipresence

omnipresente *adj* ubiquitous

omnisciencia *f* omniscience

omnisciente *adj* omniscient, all-knowing

omnívoro, -a I. *adj* omnivorous **II.** *m, f* omnivore

omoplato *m,* **omóplato** *m* ANAT scapula, shoulder blade

OMS *f abr de* **Organización Mundial de la Salud** WHO

onagra *f* evening primrose; **aceite de** ~ evening primrose oil

once I. *adj inv* eleven ► **estar a las ~ y cuarto** to have a screw loose; **estar a las ~** (*ropa*) to be askew **II.** *m* eleven; *v.t.* **ocho**

ONCE *f abr de* **Organización Nacional de Ciegos Españoles** *Spanish national organization for the blind*

onceno, -a *adj* eleventh; *v.t.* **octavo** ► **el ~, no estorbar** *inf* don't get in the way

oncología *f* MED oncology

onda *f. t.* FÍS, RADIO wave; ~ **explosiva** [*o* **expansiva**] shockwave; ~**s del pelo** waves *pl* of hair ► **¡qué buena ~!** *inf* that's really cool!; **estar en la misma** ~ to be on the same wavelength; **estar en la ~ de algo** *inf* (*comprender*) to be on top of sth; (*seguir*) to keep up with sth

ondear *vi* (*formar*) to undulate; (*moverse*) to ripple; (*bandera*) to flutter

ondulación *f* **1.** (*movimiento*) undulation; (*de agua*) ripple **2.** (*formación*) wave; ~ **permanente** perm, permanent wave

ondulado, -a *adj* wavy; **cartón ~** corrugated cardboard

ondular I. *vi* (*formar ondas*) to ripple; (*moverse*) to undulate; (*bandera*) to flutter; (*culebra*) to slither **II.** *vt* to wave

ondulatorio, -a *adj* undulatory; **movimiento ~** wave motion

oneroso, -a *adj* **1.** (*molesto*) onerous; (*gravoso*) burdensome **2.** (*costoso*) costly **3.** (*remunerable*) remunerative

ONG *f abr de* **Organización No Gubernamental** NGO

onírico, -a *adj* oniric

onomástica *f* **1.** (*materia*) onomastics *pl* **2.** (*día*) name-day, saint's day

onomástico, -a *adj* onomastic; **fiesta onomástica** *party to celebrate a name-day*

ONU *f abr de* **Organización de las Naciones Unidas** UNO

onubense I. *adj* of/from Huelva **II.** *mf* native/inhabitant of Huelva

onza *f* ounce

opa *mf CSur* **1.** (*retrasado mental*) mental retard **2.** (*simple*) fool

opacar <c→qu> *vt* **1.** *AmL* (*hacer opaco*) to darken **2.** *Méx* (*superar*) to outshine; **su belleza opaca a las de las demás** her beauty eclipses that of all others

opacidad *f* opacity

opaco, -a *adj* **1.** (*no transparente*) opaque; **proyector de cuerpos ~s** overhead projector **2.** (*sin brillo*) dull; (*oscuro*) gloomy **3.** (*persona, voz*) gloomy

opalescente *adj* opalescent

ópalo *m* MIN opal

opción *f* **1.** (*elección*) choice; (*posibilidad*) option; ~ **del menú** INFOR menu option **2.** (*derecho*) right; ~ **al cambio** right to exchange **3.** ECON, JUR option; ~ **de compra** option to purchase

opcional *adj* optional

OPEP *f abr de* **Organización de Países Exportadores de Petróleo** OPEC

ópera *f* 1. MÚS opera; **teatro de la** ~ opera house 2. CINE, LIT ~ **prima** author's first work

operación *f* 1. MAT, MED operation; ~ **quirúrgica** surgical operation 2. (*actividad*) activity; (*negocio*) transaction; ~ **por acciones** share trading; ~ **de saneamiento** clean-up operation

operado, -a *adj* TÉC operated; ~ **a mano** hand-operated; ~ **por teclado** keyboard-controlled

operador(a) *m(f)* 1. CINE projectionist; ~ **de cámara** cameraman 2. INFOR, TEL operator 3. MED surgeon

operar I. *vi* 1. (*actuar*) *t.* MIL to operate 2. COM to do business; ~ **con bancos** to do business with banks 3. (*tener efecto*) to take effect II. *vt* 1. MED to operate on 2. (*producir un efecto*) to bring about; ~ **milagros** to work miracles III. *vr:* ~se to have an operation

operario, -a *m, f* worker; ~ **sin cualificar** unskilled worker

operativo, -a *adj* 1. (*efectivo*) operative 2. INFOR **sistema** ~ operating system

operatorio, -a *adj* MED operative

opereta *f* MÚS operetta

opinable *adj* (*discutible*) debatable; (*controvertido*) controversial

opinar I. *vi, vt* to think; ~ **bien/mal de algo/alguien** to have a good/bad opinion of sth/sb; **¿tú qué opinas de** [*o* **sobre**] **esto?** what do you think about this?; **¿qué opinas del nuevo jefe?** what's your opinion of the new boss? II. *vi* to give an opinion; **¿puedo** ~**?** can I say what I think?

opinión *f* opinion; (*postura*) stance; (*punto de vista*) viewpoint; **en mi** ~ in my opinion; **cambiar de** ~ to change one's opinion [*o* mind]; **dar su** ~ **(sobre algo)** to express an opinion (about sth); **ser de otra/la misma** ~ to be of a different/the same opinion; **ser de la** ~ **que...** to be of the opinion that ...; **tener buena/mala** ~ **de algo/alguien** to have a good/bad opinion of sth/sb

opio *m* opium

opíparo, -a *adj* sumptuous

oponente I. *adj* opposing II. *mf* opponent

oponer *irr como* **poner** I. *vt* 1. (*enfrentar*) to oppose; (*confrontar*) to confront 2. (*objetar*) to object; ~ **reparos** to raise objections; ~ **resistencia** to offer resistance II. *vr:* ~se 1. (*rechazar*) to object; ~se **a algo** to oppose sth 2. (*enfrentarse*) to oppose each other 3. (*obstaculizar*) to hinder 4. (*ser contrario*) to be opposed 5. (*estar enfrente*) to be opposite

oporto *m* GASTR port (wine)

oportunidad *f* 1. (*posibilidad*) chance; (*ocasión*) opportunity; **a la primera** ~ at the first opportunity; **una segunda** ~ a second chance; **aprovechar la** ~ to make the most of the opportunity; **(no) tener** ~ **de...** (not) to have the opportunity of ... 2. (*cualidad*) opportune-

ness; (*temporal*) timeliness; (*adecuación*) appropriateness 3. *pl* (*ofertas*) bargain buys *pl*

oportunismo *m* opportunism

oportunista *mf* opportunist

oportuno, -a *adj* 1. (*adecuado, apropiado*) appropriate; **es muy** ~ it is just what was needed; **en el momento** ~ at the right moment 2. (*propicio*) opportune 3. (*al caso*) relevant 4. (*permisible*) permissible

oposición *f* 1. (*resistencia*) *t.* POL opposition; **encontrar** ~ to meet opposition; **presentar** ~ to oppose 2. (*objeción*) objection 3. (*contraposición*) comparison 4. *(pl)* UNIV (competitive) examination (*for a public-sector job*); **por** ~ by examination; **presentarse a unas oposiciones** to sit an examination (*for a public-sector job*)

opositar *vi* ~ **a algo** to sit an examination for sth

opositor(a) I. *adj* opposing; **partido** ~ opposing party II. *m(f)* 1. (*oponente*) *t.* POL opponent 2. (*candidato*) candidate (*in examination for a public-sector job*)

opresión *f* 1. (*angustia*) anxiety 2. (*represión*) oppression 3. (*presión*) pressure; (*compresión*) compression

opresivo, -a *adj* 1. (*agobiante, represivo*) oppressive; (*constringente*) restrictive; (*aire*) suffocating 2. (*presionante*) pressing; (*comprimente*) compressive

opresor(a) I. *adj* oppressive II. *m(f)* oppressor

oprimir *vt* 1. (*presionar*) to press; (*comprimir*) to compress 2. (*agobiar*) to weigh down 3. (*reprimir*) to oppress; (*constreñir*) to restrict

oprobio *m* disgrace

oprobioso, -a *adj* disgraceful

optar *vi* 1. (*escoger*) ~ **por algo/alguien** to opt for sth/sb 2. (*aspirar*) to aspire 3. (*solicitar*) ~ **a algo** to apply for sth; ~ **a un cargo** to apply for a position 4. (*tener acceso*) to have access

optativo, -a *adj* optional; (*asignatura*) **optativa** optional subject

óptica *f* 1. FÍS optics *pl* 2. (*establecimiento*) optician's 3. (*punto de vista*) viewpoint; **bajo esta** ~ according to this point of view

óptico, -a I. *adj* 1. ANAT optic; **nervio** ~ optic nerve 2. FÍS optical II. *m, f* optician

optimar *vt* to optimize, to optimise *Brit*

optimismo *m* optimism

optimista I. *adj* optimistic II. *mf* optimist

optimizar *vt* to optimize

óptimo *m* optimum

óptimo, -a I. *superl de* **bueno** II. *adj* (very) best; (*excelente*) excellent

opuesto, -a I. *pp de* **oponer** II. *adj* 1. (*enfrente*) opposite; **al lado** ~ on the other side; **en dirección opuesta** in the opposite direction 2. (*diverso*) different; (*contrario, enfrentado*) opposing; **polo** ~ *t. fig* opposite pole; **el sexo** ~ the opposite sex 3. (*enemigo*) enemy

opulencia *f* 1. (*abundancia, exuberancia*)

opulence **2.** (*riqueza*) affluence

opulento, -a *adj* **1.** (*abundante, lujoso*) opulent **2.** (*rico*) affluent

oquedad *f* (*concavidad, vacío*) hollow

ora *conj elev* ~..., ~... now ..., now ..., either ..., or ...

oración *f* **1.** REL prayer; **decir una** ~ to say a prayer **2.** (*frase*) sentence; LING clause; (*discurso*) speech; ~ **coordinada** coordinate clause; ~ **subordinada** subordinate clause; **partes de la** ~ parts of speech; ~ **simple/ compuesta** simple/compound sentence

oráculo *m* oracle

orador(a) *m(f)* orator; (*portavoz*) spokesperson

oral *adj* oral; **sexo** ~ oral sex; **vista** ~ JUR hearing; **por vía** ~ MED orally

órale *interj Méx* (*animar*) come on; (*oiga*) hey; (*acuerdo*) OK, right

orangután *m* orang-utan

orar *vi elev* ~ **por algo** to pray for sth; (*rogar*) to plead for sth

oratoria *f* **1.** (*retórica*) oratory **2.** (*elocuencia*) eloquence

oratorio *m* REL chapel

oratorio, -a *adj* oratorical

orbe *m* **1.** (*círculo*) circle; (*esfera*) sphere; (*terráqueo*) globe **2.** (*mundo*) world

órbita *f* **1.** ASTR, FÍS orbit; ~ **planetaria** planetary orbit; ~ **terrestre** terrestrial orbit; **poner en** ~ to put into orbit; **estar en** ~ *fig* to be up to date; **estar fuera de** ~ *fig* to be out of touch **2.** (*ámbito*) sphere **3.** ANAT eye socket; **se me salían los ojos de las** ~**s** *fig* I couldn't believe my eyes

orca *f* killer whale

órdago *m* **de** ~ *inf* terrific

orden¹ <órdenes> *m* **1.** (*colocación, organización*) *t.* REL, ARQUIT order; **en** ~ in order; **alterar el** ~ to change the order; **llamar al** ~ to call to order; **poner en** ~ to put in order; **ser persona de** ~ to be orderly; *fig* to be upright; **sin** ~ **ni concierto** without rhyme or reason, any old way **2.** (*sucesión*) order; **en** [o **por**] **su** (**debido**) ~ in the right order; **por** ~ by order; **por** ~ **de antigüedad** in order of seniority **3.** (*categoría*) rank; **de primer/segundo** ~ first-rate/second-rate; **del** ~ **de** in the order of **4.** JUR ~ **constitucional** constitution; ~ **jurídico** judicial order

orden² <órdenes> *f* **1.** (*mandato*) order; ~ **de arresto** arrest warrant; ~ **ministerial** ministerial decree; ~ **de registro** search warrant; **órdenes son órdenes** orders are orders; **¡a** ~**!** yes, sir!; **contrario a las órdenes** against orders; **dar una** ~ to give an order; **cumplir una** ~ to obey an order; **estar a las órdenes de alguien** to be at sb's command; **hasta nueva** ~ until further notice; **tus deseos son órdenes para mí** *irón* your wish is my command; **estar a la** ~ **del día** *fig* to be the order of the day **2.** COM, REL order; ~ **de entrega** delivery order; ~ **de pago** payment order; ~

permanente standing order; **por** ~ by order; **por** ~ **de** to the order of; **entrar en una** ~ (**religiosa**) to join a religious order; ~ **de caballería** HIST order of knighthood **3.** *pl* REL (*sacramento*) orders *pl;* **las órdenes mayores/ menores** the major/minor orders

ordenación *f* **1.** (*disposición*) arrangement **2.** (*ordenanza*) order; (*regulación*) regulation; ~ **jurídica** legal system; ~ **territorial** regional development **3.** REL ordination

ordenado, -a **I.** *adj* **1.** *estar* (*en orden*) tidy, neat **2.** *estar* (*encaminado*) directed **3.** *ser* (*persona*) organized **II.** *m, f* REL ordained person

ordenador *m* computer; ~ **de a bordo** car computer; ~ **personal** personal computer; ~ **portátil** laptop computer; **asistido por** ~ computer-aided

ordenamiento *m* **1.** (*ordenación*) organization **2.** (*regulación*) legislation; ~ **constitucional** constitution; ~ **jurídico** judicial legislation

ordenancista *adj* strict

ordenanza¹ *f* **1.** (*ordenación*) organization **2.** (*medida*) order **3.** *pl* ADMIN, MIL regulations *pl*

ordenanza² *m* **1.** MIL orderly **2.** (*botones*) office assistant

ordenar **I.** *vt* **1.** (*arreglar*) to organize; (*habitación, armario*) to tidy; (*colocar*) to arrange; (*clasificar*) to order **2.** (*mandar*) to order **3.** REL to ordain **II.** *vr:* ~**se** REL to be ordained

ordeña *f* AmC, CSur, Méx milking

ordeñadora *f* milkmaid

ordeñar *vt* to milk

ordeñe *m Arg, Cuba* milking

ordinal *adj, m* ordinal

ordinariez *f* (*vulgaridad*) vulgarity

ordinario, -a *adj* **1.** (*habitual*) usual; **de** ~ usually **2.** (*grosero*) rude **3.** *t.* JUR (*regular*) ordinary

orear **I.** *vt* **1.** (*airear*) to air **2.** (*secar*) to dry **II.** *vr:* ~**se** *inf* to get a breath of fresh air

orégano *m* oregano

oreja *f* **1.** ANAT ear; **aguzar las** ~**s** to prick up one's ears; **calentar las** ~**s a alguien** to box sb's ears; *fig* to give sb a dressing-down; **ser todo** ~**s** to be all ears **2.** (*sentido*) hearing **3.** (*lateral*) flap; (*lengüeta*) tongue; (*del zapato*) eyelet tab; **sillón de** ~**s** wing chair ► **ver las** ~**s al lobo** to have a close shave; **con las** ~**s gachas** with one's tail between one's legs; **agachar las** ~**s** to lose heart; **¡no agaches las** ~**s!** don't give up!; **enseñar la** ~ to show one's true colours *Brit* [*o* colors *Am*]

orejera *f* **1.** (*en una gorra*) earflap **2.** *pl* (*en una cinta*) earmuffs *pl*

orejero, -a *m, f Chile, pey* telltale

orejón *m* GASTR dried apricot

orensano, -a **I.** *adj* of/from Orense **II.** *m, f* native/inhabitant of Orense

oreo *m* **1.** (*ventilación*) airing **2.** (*desecación*) drying

orfanato *m* orphanage
orfanatorio *m Méx* orphanage
orfandad *f* **1.** (*estado*) orphanhood **2.** (*pensión*) orphan's allowance
orfebre *mf* (*orífice*) goldsmith; (*platero*) silversmith
orfebrería *f* **1.** (*obra*) articles *pl* worked in precious metal; (*en oro*) articles *pl* worked in gold **2.** (*arte*) working of precious metals; (*en oro*) goldsmithing
orfelinato *m* orphanage
orfeón *m* MÚS choral society
orgánico, -a *adj* organic; **Ley Orgánica del Estado** basic law
organigrama *m* organization chart; ~ **del programa** INFOR flowchart
organillo *m* MÚS barrel organ
organismo *m* **1.** ANAT, BIO organism **2.** (*institución*) body; ~ **oficial** official body
organista *mf* MÚS organist
organización *f* organization; ~ **central** central organization; **Organización del Tratado del Atlántico Norte** North Atlantic Treaty Organization; **Organización No Gubernamental** Non-Governmental Organization
organizado, -a *adj* organized
organizador(a) **I.** *adj* organizing; **comité** ~ organizing committee **II.** *m(f)* (*de un evento*) organizer; ~ **de despacho** office organizer
organizar <z→c> **I.** *vt* to organize; (*una fiesta*) to hold **II.** *vr:* ~**se** **1.** (*asociarse*) to organize oneself **2.** (*surgir*) to break out; **¡menuda se organizó!** all hell broke loose!; **se organizó una pelea** a fight broke out **3.** (*ordenar*) to arrange; ~**se el tiempo** to organize one's time
organizativo, -a *adj* organizing
órgano *m* **1.** (*organismo*) *t.* ANAT organ; ~ **judicial** judicial body; ~**s rectores** governing board; ~**s sexuales** sexual organs **2.** MÚS organ; ~ **automático** automatic organ; ~ **electrónico** electric organ
orgasmo *m* orgasm
orgía *f* **1.** (*bacanal*) orgy **2.** (*desenfreno*) disinhibition
orgiástico, -a *adj* **1.** (*de bacanal*) orgiastic **2.** (*desenfrenado*) unrestrained
orgullo *m* **1.** (*satisfacción*) pride; ~ **por** [*o* **de**] **algo** pride in sth; ~ **profesional** professional pride; **sentir** ~ **por alguien/algo** to be proud of sb/sth; **tener el** ~ **de...** to be proud to ...; ~ **propio** self-respect **2.** (*soberbia*) arrogance
orgulloso, -a *adj* **1.** estar (*satisfecho*) proud; **sentirse** ~ **de algo/alguien** to feel proud of sth/sb **2.** ser proud; (*soberbio*) arrogant
orientación *f* **1.** (*situación*) situation **2.** (*posición*) position **3.** (*ajuste*) adjustment **4.** (*asesoramiento*) advice; (*dirección*) management; ~ **profesional** career [*o* vocational] guidance **5.** (*tendencia*) tendency; **tu** ~ **política** your political leanings
oriental **I.** *adj* **1.** (*del Este*) eastern; **Alemania Oriental** East Germany; **alfombra** ~ Persian

rug **2.** (*del Extremo Oriente*) oriental **II.** *mf* Oriental
orientar **I.** *vt* **1.** (*dirigir*) to direct; **orientado a la práctica** with a practical focus **2.** (*ajustar*) to adjust **3.** (*asesorar*) to advise **4.** (*dirigir*) to manage **II.** *vr:* ~**se** **1.** (*dirigirse*) to orientate oneself, to orient oneself *Am; fig* to find one's bearings; ~**se bien** to have a good sense of direction; **se orientó muy bien en el trabajo** he settled in well in the job **2.** (*tender*) to tend
oriente *m* **1.** GEO east; **el Oriente Próximo,** **el Cercano Oriente** the Near East; **el Extremo Oriente, el Lejano Oriente** the Far East **2.** (*viento*) easterly
orífice *m* goldsmith
orificio *m* **1.** (*agujero*) orifice **2.** (*abertura*) opening; ~ **de salida** outlet
origen *m* **1.** (*principio*) origin; **texto/idioma de** ~ source text/language **2.** (*causa*) cause; **dar** ~ **a algo, ser** ~ **de algo** to give rise to sth **3.** (*ascendencia*) descent **4.** (*procedencia*) origin; **de** ~ **español** of Spanish origin
original **I.** *adj* **1.** (*auténtico, creativo*) original; **versión** ~ original version; **el pecado** ~ original sin **2.** (*originario*) originating **3.** (*singular*) peculiar **II.** *m* original; **fiel al** ~ faithful to the original
originalidad *f* **1.** (*autenticidad, creatividad*) originality **2.** (*singularidad*) peculiarity
originar **I.** *vt* **1.** (*causar*) to cause **2.** (*provocar*) to provoke **II.** *vr:* ~**se** **1.** (*tener el origen*) to originate **2.** (*surgir*) to arise **3.** (*proceder*) ~**se en algo** to spring from sth
originario, -a *adj* **1.** (*oriundo*) native; **es** ~ **de Chile** he comes from Chile **2.** (*de origen*) **país** ~ country of origin **3.** (*original*) original; (*innato*) innate
orilla *f* **1.** (*borde*) edge **2.** (*ribera*) bank; **a** ~**s del Ebro** on the banks of the Ebro; ~ **de** *inf* on the edge of **3.** *pl, AmL* (*arrabales*) outskirts *pl*
orillar *vt* **1.** (*tela*) to hem; (*adornar*) to trim **2.** (*resolver*) to surmount **3.** (*sortear*) to skirt (around)
orillero, -a **I.** *adj AmL: pey* **1.** (*arrabalero*) low class **2.** (*grosero*) coarse **II.** *m, f AmL: pey* **1.** (*arrabalero*) common person **2.** (*grosero*) ill--bred person
orillo *m* selvage
orín *m* **1.** (*óxido*) rust; **cubierto de** ~ rusty **2.** (*pl*) (*orina*) urine
orina *f* <orines> urine
orinal *m* chamber pot; (*de niño*) potty
orinar **I.** *vi, vt* to urinate; ~ **sangre** to urinate blood; **ir a** ~ to go to the lavatory **II.** *vr:* ~**se** to wet oneself; ~**se en la cama** to wet the bed; **estoy orinándome** I need to urinate
oriundo, -a *adj* ~ **de** native to; **es** ~ **de Méjico** he comes from Mexico
orla *f* **1.** (*de tela*) edge; ~ **de luto** black border **2.** (*foto*) graduating-class photo [*o* picture]
orlar *vt* (*adornar*) to trim
ornamentación *f* adornment

ornamentar *vt* to adorn

ornamento *m* 1. (*adorno*) ornament 2. *pl* REL (*vestiduras*) vestments *pl*

ornar *vt* to adorn

ornato *m* adornment

ornitorrinco *m* duck-billed platypus

oro *m* 1. (*metal*) gold; ~ **de ley** fine gold; **bañado en** ~ gold-plated; **de** ~ gold; **color** ~ golden; **valer su peso en** ~ to be worth one's weight in gold 2. (*dinero*) money; **hacerse de** ~ to make one's fortune; **nadar en** ~ to be swimming in money ►**prometer a alguien el** ~ **y el moro** to promise sb the earth; **mi palabra es** ~ my word is my honour *Brit* [*o* honor *Am*]; **guardar como** ~ **en paño** to treasure; **no es** ~ **todo lo que reluce** *prov* all that glitters is not gold *prov*

orondo, -a *adj* 1. (*gordo*) fat 2. (*engreído*) smug

oropel *m* 1. (*latón*) imitation gold leaf 2. *t. pey* (*adorno*) tinsel

orquesta *f* MÚS orchestra

orquestar *vt t. fig* to orchestrate

orquestina *f* MÚS (*de baile*) (dance) band

orquídea *f* orchid

ortiga *f* nettle

orto *m* sunrise

ortodoncia *f* MED orthodontics *pl*

ortodoxo, -a I. *adj* orthodox; **ser católico** ~ to be a devout Catholic II. *m, f* orthodox

ortogonal *adj* right-angled

ortografía *f* spelling; **falta de** ~ spelling mistake

ortográfico, -a *adj* spelling; **reglas ortográficas** spelling rules; **reforma ortográfica** spelling reform

ortopeda *mf* MED orthopaedist *Brit,* orthopedist *Am*

ortopedia *f* MED orthopaedics *Brit,* orthopedics *Am*

ortopédico, -a MED I. *adj* orthopaedic *Brit,* orthopedic *Am;* **pierna ortopédica** artificial leg II. *m, f* orthopaedist *Brit,* orthopedist *Am*

ortopedista *mf* orthopaedist *Brit,* orthopedist *Am*

oruga *f* 1. ZOOL caterpillar 2. TÉC caterpillar track

orujo *m* 1. (*residuo*) marc 2. (*aguardiente*) *strong Spanish liqueur made from residue of grape skins after pressing*

orzuelo *m* MED stye

os I. *pron pers* (*objeto directo e indirecto*) you II. *pron reflexivo* yourselves; **¿~ marcháis?** are you leaving?

osa *f* 1. ZOOL she-bear 2. ASTR **la Osa Mayor/Menor** the Great/Little Bear ►**¡anda la ~!** *inf* good heavens!

osadía *f* daring; (*desfachatez*) boldness

osado, -a *adj* daring

osamenta *f* 1. (*esqueleto*) skeleton 2. (*restos mortales*) bones *pl*

osar *vi* to dare; **¿cómo osas decir esto?** how dare you say that!

oscense I. *adj* of/from Huesca II. *mf* native/inhabitant of Huesca

oscilación *f* 1. (*vaivén*) oscillation 2. (*variación*) fluctuation 3. (*indecisión*) indecision

oscilante *adj* 1. (*indeciso*) indecisive 2. (*que varía*) fluctuating

oscilar *vi* 1. (*en vaivén*) to oscillate 2. (*péndulo*) to swing 3. (*variar*) to fluctuate

oscilatorio, -a *adj* oscillatory

oscurecer *irr como crecer* I. *vimpers* to get dark II. *vt* 1. *t. fig* (*privar de luz*) to darken 2. (*confundir*) to confuse III. *vr*: ~**se** 1. *t. fig* (*volverse oscuro*) to darken 2. *t. fig* (*debilitarse*) to wane IV. *m* dusk; **al** ~ at dusk

oscurecimiento *m* (*t. fig*) darkening; (*anochecer*) nightfall

oscuridad *f* 1. (*falta de luz*) darkness; **en la** ~ in the dark 2. (*falta de claridad*) obscurity; **en la** ~ in obscurity

oscuro, -a *adj* dark; *fig* obscure; **azul** ~ dark blue; **a oscuras** in the dark; **de** ~ **origen** of obscure origin

óseo, -a *adj* bony; **restos** ~**s** skeletal remains

osezno, -a *m, f* bear cub

osificar <c→qu> *vt, vr*: ~**se** to ossify

osmosis *f sin pl,* **ósmosis** *f sin pl* osmosis

oso *m* bear; ~ **blanco** polar bear; ~ **de peluche** teddy bear; **fuerte como un** ~ as strong as an ox

ostensible *adj* obvious; **hacer** ~ to make evident

ostensivo, -a *adj* 1. (*manifiesto*) evident 2. (*ostentoso*) ostentatious

ostentación *f* display; (*jactancia*) ostentation; **hacer** ~ **de algo** to show sth; (*jactarse*) to flaunt sth

ostentar *vt* 1. (*mostrar*) to show; (*jactarse*) to flaunt 2. (*poseer*) to have; (*puesto, poder*) to hold

ostentoso, -a *adj* 1. (*jactancioso*) ostentatious 2. (*llamativo*) showy; (*provocativo*) provocative

ostra *f* oyster ►**aburrirse como una** ~ *inf* to be bored to death; **¡~s!** *inf* Jesus!

ostracismo *m* (*de la vida pública*) ostracism; (*exilio*) exile; **condenar al** ~ (*fig*) to ostracize

ostrogodo, -a I. *adj* Ostrogothic II. *m, f* Ostrogoth

otalgia *f* MED earache

OTAN *f abr de* **Organización del Tratado del Atlántico Norte** NATO

otario, -a *CSur* I. *adj* foolish II. *m, f* fool

otate *m Méx* BOT reed, rush

otear I. *vt* 1. (*ver*) to scan 2. (*escudriñar*) to scrutinize 3. (*observar*) to watch II. *vi* to look; (*desde un alto*) to look down on

otero *m* hillock

otitis *f sin pl* MED inflammation of the ear; ~ **media** inflammation of the middle ear

otomana *f* ottoman

otomano, -a *adj, m, f* Ottoman

otomía *f Arg, Col* atrocity

otoñal *adj* (*lugar, tiempo*) autumnal; **un amor**

~ *fig* late love

otoño *m* (*estación*) autumn, fall *Am;* **a fin(al)es de** ~ at the end of autumn [*o* fall *Am*]; **el ~ (de la vida)** the autumn (of one's life)

otorgamiento *m* **1.** (*concesión*) concession; JUR execution; (*de documento*) drawing up; (*de contrato*) award; (*de licencia*) grant; **~ de poder** bestowal of power **2.** (*consentimiento*) consent

otorgar <g→gu> *vt* **1.** (*conferir*) to confer; **~ poderes** to confer powers **2.** (*conceder*) to concede; (*ayudas*) to offer; **~ un plazo** to set a time limit **3.** (*expedir*) to issue; **~ licencia** to grant a license **4.** (*acceder*) **~ algo** to agree to sth; **~ su consentimiento** to give one's consent

otorrinolaringólogo, -a *m, f* MED ear, nose and throat specialist

otro, -a I. *adj* another, other; **al ~ día** the next day; **el ~ día** the other day; **en otra ocasión** another time; **la otra semana** the other week; **en ~ sitio** in another place, somewhere else; **otra cosa** another thing; **~ tanto** as much again; **otra vez** again; **¡otra vez será!** maybe another time!; **es ~ Mozart** he is another Mozart; **eso ya es otra cosa** that is much better; **¡hasta otra (vez)!** until the next time! **II.** *pron indef* **1.** (*distinto: cosa*) another (one); (*persona*) someone else; **~s** others; **el ~/la otra/lo ~** the other (one); **ninguna otra persona, ningún ~** nobody else; **de un sitio a ~** from one place to another; **no ~ que...** none other than ...; **ésa es otra** (*cosa distinta*) that is different; *irón* (*aún peor*) that is even worse **2.** (*uno más*) another; **otras tres personas** three more people; **¡otra, otra!** more!

otrora *adv* formerly

otrosí *adv* furthermore

ovación *f* ovation; **dar/recibir una ~** to give/receive an ovation

ovacionar *vt* to give an ovation

oval *adj*, **ovalado, -a** *adj* oval

óvalo *m* (*forma*) oval

ovario *m* ANAT ovary

oveja *f* sheep *inv*; (*hembra*) ewe; **la ~ negra de la familia** the black sheep of the family ▶**cada ~ con su pareja** *prov* birds of a feather flock together *prov*

ovejero, -a I. *adj* sheep; **perro ~** sheep dog **II.** *m, f* **1.** (*ganadero*) sheep breeder; (*pastor*) shepherd **2.** *AmL* (*perro*) sheep dog

overol *m* *AmL* overall

ovetense I. *adj* of/from Oviedo **II.** *mf* native/inhabitant of Oviedo

oviducto *m* oviduct

ovillar I. *vt* to wind into a ball; (*enrollar*) to wind up **II.** *vr:* **~se** to roll up into a ball

ovillo *m* ball; *fig* tangle; **hacerse un ~** (*enredarse*) to get tangled up; (*encogerse*) to curl up into a ball; (*al hablar*) to get all tangled up

ovino, -a I. *adj* sheep; **ganado ~** sheep *pl* **II.** *m, f* sheep *inv*

ovíparo, -a *adj* oviparous

ovni *m* UFO

ovoide I. *adj* ovoid, egg-shaped **II.** *m* **1.** MAT ovoid **2.** *AmL* (*pelota*) rugby ball

ovulación *f* ovulation

ovular *vi* to ovulate

óvulo *m* ANAT ovule

oxidable *adj* (*metal*) which rusts

oxidación *f* **1.** QUÍM oxidation **2.** (*metal*) rusting

oxidar I. *vt* **1.** QUÍM to oxidize **2.** (*metal*) to rust; **un hierro oxidado** a piece of rusty iron **II.** *vr:* **~se 1.** (*metal*) to rust; (*mente*) to go rusty; **~se de no moverse** to rust through lack of use **2.** QUÍM to oxidize

óxido *m* **1.** QUÍM oxide **2.** (*orín*) rust

oxigenar I. *vt* **1.** (*cabello*) to bleach; (**rubio**) oxigenado platinum [*o* peroxide] blond(e) **2.** QUÍM to oxigenate; **agua oxigenada** (hydrogen) peroxide **II.** *vr:* **~se** *inf* to get some fresh air

oxígeno *m* QUÍM oxygen

oyente *mf* listener; (**libre**) ~ UNIV unmatriculated student

ozono *m* QUÍM ozone; **el agujero en la capa de ~** the hole in the ozone layer

P

P, p *f* P, p; **~ de París** P for Peter

pabellón *m* **1.** (*tienda*) bell tent **2.** (*bandera*) flag **3.** ARQUIT pavillion **4.** ANAT **~ de la oreja** auricle, outer ear

pabilo *m*, **pábilo** *m* wick

pábulo *m* food; *fig* fuel; **dar ~ a rumores** to encourage rumours *Brit* [*o* rumors *Am*]

paca *f* (*fardo*) bale

pacato, -a *adj* **1.** (*mojigato*) prudish **2.** (*apacible*) gentle **3.** (*tímido*) shy

pacer *irr como crecer vi, vt* to graze

pacha *f* **1.** *Nic, Méx* (*botella aplanada*) flask **2.** *Nic* (*biberón*) baby's bottle

pachá *m* pasha; **vivir como un ~** *fig* to live like a lord

pachacho, -a *adj* *Chile* short-legged

pachaco, -a *adj* **1.** *AmC* (*aplastado*) flattened **2.** *CRi* (*inútil, enclenque*) feeble

pachamama *f* *And* (*Madre Tierra*) Mother Earth

pachamanca *f* *And* **1.** (*plato*) barbecued meat **2.** (*horno*) barbecue pit

pachanga *f* **1.** *Cuba* (*danza*) Cuban dance **2.** *Col, inf* (*fiesta*) party

pacho, -a *adj* **1.** (*indolente*) lazy **2.** *Nic* (*flaco*) skinny

pachón, -ona I. *adj* **1.** (*perro*) shaggy; **perro ~** shaggy dog **2.** *AmL* (*peludo*) hairy **II.** *m, f* **1.** ZOOL beagle **2.** *inf* (*persona*) calm quiet fellow

pachorra *f inf* slowness; **tener** ~ to be lackadaisical [*o* laid-back]

pachorriento, -a *adj AmS* phlegmatic, lackadaisical

pachucho, -a *adj* **1.** *inf* (*persona*) off-colour *Brit*, off-color *Am* **2.** (*fruta*) overripe

pachulí *m* patchouli

paciencia *f* patience; **se me ha acabado la** ~ I've run out of patience; **ése hace perder la** ~ **a un santo** he'd try the patience of a saint

paciente I. *adj* patient; **ser** ~ **con alguien** to be patient with sb II. *mf* patient

pacificación *f* pacification

pacificar <c→qu> I. *vi* to become peaceful II. *vt* (*apaciguar*) to pacify; (*reconciliar*) to reconcile III. *vr:* ~**se** to calm down; (*viento*) to abate

pacífico, -a *adj* peaceful; **carácter** ~ (*nación*) peacefulness

Pacífico *m* Pacific (Ocean)

pacifismo *m* pacifism

pacifista *adj, mf* pacifist

paco, -a *adj AmL* reddish

pacota *f Méx* (*pacotilla*) rabble

pacotilla *f* **1.** (*calidad inferior*) trashiness; **tienda de** ~**s** junk shop; **de** ~ (*mercancía*) shoddy; (*restaurante*) second-rate; **ser de** ~ to be shoddy **2.** *AmL* (*chusma*) rabble

pacotillero, -a I. *adj* second-rate; **tienda pacotillera** shop selling shoddy goods II. *m, f* **1.** (*vendedor*) street vendor **2.** *AmL* (*negociante que viaja*) street hawker

pactar I. *vi* to come to an agreement; **¡hay que** ~ **para sobrevivir!** you have to compromise if you want to get on! II. *vt* to agree on

pacto *m* agreement; (*contrato*) contract

padecer *irr como crecer* I. *vi* to suffer II. *vt* **1.** (*sufrir*) to suffer; ~ **algo** to suffer from sth; ~ **un error** to labour [*o* labor *Am*] under a misapprehension **2.** (*soportar*) to endure

padecimiento *m* **1.** (*sufrimiento*) suffering **2.** (*enfermedad*) ailment

padrastro *m* **1.** (*marido de madre*) stepfather **2.** (*mal padre*) cruel father **3.** (*pellejo*) hangnail

padrazo *m* **es un** ~ *inf* he's a great dad

padre I. *m* **1.** *t.* REL father; ~ **espiritual** confessor; **¡tu** ~**!** *inf* up yours! **2.** *pl* (*padre y madre*) parents *pl* **3.** *pl* (*antepasados*) forefathers *pl;* **dormir con sus** ~**s** to have passed away ▸ **tal** ~, **tal** hijo *prov* like father, like son II. *adj inf* tremendous; **un escándalo** ~ a huge scandal; **recibir una paliza de** ~ **y muy señor mío** to take one hell of a beating

padrenuestro *m* Lord's Prayer

padrillo *m CSur* stallion

padrinazgo *m* **1.** (*título*) godfathership **2.** (*protección*) patronage

padrino *m* (*de bautizo*) godfather; (*de boda*) best man; **tener buenos** ~**s** *fig* to know the right people

padrón *m* **1.** ADMIN (*registro*) (census) register **2.** *AmL* (*caballo*) stallion

padrote *m AmC, Méx* **1.** (*equino*) stallion; (*bovino*) breeding bull **2.** *inf* (*alcahuete*) pimp

paella *f* paella

Paella is a Spanish rice dish containing various types of meat and fish, **marisco** (seafood) and **azafrán** (saffron), which gives the rice its characteristic dark-yellow colour. Originally from **Valencia**, paella is known today throughout the world.

---

paellera *f* paella dish

pág. *abr de* página p.

paga *f* **1.** (*sueldo*) pay **2.** (*acto*) payment

pagadero, -a *adj* **1.** (*a pagar*) due **2.** (*pagable*) payable

pagado, -a *adj* paid; (*en aduana*) duty paid; ~ **de sí mismo** full of oneself

pagador(a) *m(f)* payer

pagaduría *f* payment office

paganismo *m sin pl* paganism

pagano, -a I. *adj* pagan II. *m, f* **1.** (*infiel*) pagan **2.** *inf* (*pagador*) payer; **hacer de** ~ to always end up footing the bill

pagar <g→gu> I. *vt* **1.** (*gastos*) to pay; (*una deuda*) to repay; ~ **un anticipo** to make an advance payment; **una cuenta sin** ~ an unpaid bill; ~ **una deuda a plazos** to pay off a debt in instalments [*o* installments *Am*] **2.** (*expiar*) to atone for; ~ **una condena** to serve a sentence; **¡me las** ~**ás!** you'll pay for this! **3.** (*recompensar*) to repay; (*una visita*) to return; **¡Dios se lo pague!** God will reward you! II. *vr* **1.** (*aficionarse*) ~**se de algo** to take a liking to sth **2.** (*presumir*) to boast; ~**se de algo** to boast about sth **3.** (*contentarse*) to be content

pagaré *m* promissory note, IOU

página *f* **1.** (*hoja*) page; **pasar la** ~ (**adelante**) to turn the page **2.** (*episodio*) chapter **3.** TEL ~**s blancas** telephone directory; ~**s amarillas** yellow pages **4.** INFOR ~ **web** web site

paginación *f* pagination

paginar *vt* to paginate

pago *m* **1.** (*reintegro*) payment; ~ **adicional** supplement; ~ **extraordinario** one-off payment, bonus; ~ **inicial** down payment; ~ **a plazos** payment by instalments [*o* installments *Am*]; **día de** ~ pay day; **anticipar el** ~ to pay in advance; **sujeto a** ~ subject to payment; ~ **contra entrega** payment on delivery **2.** (*salario*) pay; ~ **anticipado** advance payment; ~ **por hora** hourly pay; ~ **por incapacidad** sick pay **3.** *fig* (*recompensa*) reward; **¿éste es el** ~ **que me das?** is this how you repay me? **4.** (*heredad*) estate **5.** *Arg, Perú* (*de nacimiento*) home region

pai *m AmL* GASTR pie

paila *f AmL* (*sartén*) frying pan

país *m* GEO, POL country; ~ **comunitario** member state (*of the European Union*); ~ **industrializado** industrialized country; ~

limítrofe neighbouring [o neighboring *Am*] country; ~ **en vías de desarrollo** developing country; ~ **en vías de industrialización** industrializing country
paisa *m AmL v.* **paisano**
paisaje *m* landscape; (*campo*) countryside
paisajista *mf* ARTE landscape artist
paisanada *f CSur* peasants *pl*
paisano, -a *m, f* **1.** (*no militar*) civilian; **ir de** ~ to be in plain clothes **2.** (*compatriota*) compatriot **3.** (*campesino*) peasant
Países Bajos *mpl* Netherlands
paja *f* **1.** (*hierba, caña*) straw; **cama de** ~ straw bed; **no pesar una** ~ to be as light as a feather; **no dormirse en las** ~**s** *inf* to be alert **2.** *vulg* (*masturbación*) **hacerse una** ~ *vulg* to wank *Brit,* to jerk off *Am*
pajar *m* haystack; (*lugar*) hayloft; **buscar una aguja en un** ~ *fig* to search for a needle in a haystack
pájara *f* **1.** (*ave*) hen **2.** (*cometa*) kite **3.** *pey* (*mujer*) slyboots *inf* **4.** *inf* (*desfallecimiento*) **me entró la** ~ I fainted
pajarera *f* aviary
pajarero, -a I. *adj* **1.** (*de pájaros*) bird; **redes pajareras** bird nets **2.** (*persona*) perky, cheerful **3.** (*telas*) bright-coloured *Brit,* bright-colored *Am* **4.** *AmL* (*caballos*) skittish II. *m, f* (*cazador de pájaros*) bird catcher; (*criador de pájaros*) bird breeder; (*vendedor de pájaros*) bird dealer
pajarita *f* (*corbata*) bow tie
pájaro *m* bird; ~ **bobo** penguin; ~ **carpintero** woodpecker; ~ **mosca** hummingbird; ~ **de cuenta** *inf* wily bird; ~ **gordo** *fig* big shot; **tener la cabeza llena de** ~**s** to be scatterbrained; **voló el** ~ *inf* the chance has gone ▶**más vale** ~ **en mano** que **ciento volando** *prov* a bird in the hand is worth two in the bush
pajarón, -ona *adj Arg, Chile, inf* scatterbrained
pajarraco *m inf* (*pillo*) rogue
paje *m* (*criado*) page
pajero *m CSur, vulg* wanker *Brit,* jerk-off *Am*
pajita *f* (drinking) straw
pajizo, -a *adj* **1.** (*con, de paja*) straw **2.** (*color, cabello*) straw-coloured *Brit,* straw-colored *Am*
pajolero, -a *adj inf* damned
pajonal *m CSur* scrubland
pajuela *f* **1.** (*para encender*) straw taper **2.** *Bol* (*cerilla*) match **3.** *Bol, Col* (*mondadientes*) toothpick
pajuerano, -a *m, f Arg, Bol, Urug, pey* (*paleto*) country bumpkin, hick *Am*
Pakistán *m* Pakistan
pakistaní *adj, mf* Pakistani
pala *f* **1.** (*para cavar*) spade; (*cuadrada*) shovel; ~ **mecánica** mechanical shovel; *AmL* bulldozer **2.** (*del timón*) rudder **3.** (*raqueta*) racket; (*bate*) bat **4.** (*hélice*) blade **5.** (*del calzado*) upper
palabra *f* word; ~ **clave** *t.* INFOR keyword,

password; ~**s cruzadas** crossword; ~ **extranjera** foreign word; ~**s insultantes** rude words; ~ **de matrimonio** promise of marriage; ~**s mayores** strong words; ~ **técnica** technical term; **juego de** ~**s** pun, play on words; **libertad de** ~ freedom of speech; **bajo** ~ on one's word of honour *Brit* [*o* honor *Am*]; **buenas** ~**s** empty words; **de pocas** ~**s** quiet; **ahorrar** ~**s** not to waste one's words; **aprender las** ~**s** to learn one's lines; **beber las** ~**s a alguien** to hang on sb's every word; **coger a alguien la** ~ to take sb at his word; **cumplir la** ~ to be as good as one's word; **dirigir la** ~ **a alguien** to speak to sb; **faltar a la** ~ to go back on one's word; **llevar la** ~ to speak; **medir las** ~**s** to choose one's words carefully; **no entender** ~ not to understand a single word; **quitar a alguien la** ~ **de la boca** to take the words right out of sb's mouth ▶**dejar a alguien con la** ~ **en la boca** to interrupt sb; **a** ~**s necias oídos sordos** *prov* sticks and stones will break my bones, but names will never hurt me *prov;* **poner dos** ~**s a alguien** to write sb a short note; **hablar a medias** ~**s** to drop hints; **decir la última** ~ to have the last word; **de** ~ (*oral*) by word of mouth; (*que cumple sus promesas*) honourable *Brit,* honorable *Am*
palabrería *f* (empty) words, hot air
palabrero, -a I. *adj* wordy II. *m, f* gasbag *Brit, inf*
palabrota *f* swearword
palaciego, -a I. *adj* palace II. *m, f* courtier
palacio *m* palace; (*casa grande*) mansion; **Palacio de las Cortes** Spanish parliament building; **Palacio de Justicia** law courts; ~ **municipal** town hall
palada *f* **1.** (*de la pala*) shovelful **2.** (*de remo*) stroke
paladar *m* palate; ~ **blando** soft palate; **tener buen** ~ (*vino*) to be smooth on the palate; (*persona*) to have a discerning palate
paladear *vt* **1.** (*degustar*) to taste **2.** (*saborear*) to savour *Brit,* to savor *Am;* ~ **un dulce** to allow a sweet to dissolve in one's mouth
palanca *f* **1.** (*pértiga*) lever; (*palanqueta*) crowbar; ~ **de mando** AVIAT, INFOR joystick **2.** *AmL* (*influencia*) influence; **tener mucha** ~ to have a lot of influence **3.** (*en las piscinas*) rigid diving board **4.** AUTO ~ **de cambio** gear lever *Brit,* gearshift *Am*
palangana *f* washbasin
palanganear *vi AmL, inf* to brag
palanquear *vt AmL* **1.** (*apalancar*) to lever **2.** (*influenciar*) to influence
palanqueta *f* crowbar
palapa *f Méx* sunshade
palatal *adj* palatal
palatino, -a *adj* **1.** ANAT palatal; **hueso** ~ hard palate **2.** (*del palacio*) palace; **vida palatina** palace life
palco *m* TEAT box
palenque *m* **1.** (*palestra*) arena **2.** (*estacada*) fence

palenquear vt Arg, Urug to tether
paleontología f sin pl paleontology
Palestina m Palestine
palestino, -a adj, m, f Palestinian
paleta f **1.** (pala) (small) shovel; (del albañil) trowel **2.** (del pintor) palette **3.** (de turbinas) blade **4.** (omóplato) shoulder blade **5.** Col, inf (helado) ice lolly
paletada f shovelful; una ~ de yeso a shovelful of plaster
paletilla f (omóplato) shoulder blade
paleto m fallow deer
paleto, -a I. adj uncouth II. m, f yokel, hick Am
paliacate m Méx large brightly coloured [o colored Am] scarf
paliar <1. pres: palío, palio> vt **1.** (delito) to mitigate **2.** (enfermedad) to alleviate **3.** (restar importancia) to excuse
paliativo m palliative
paliativo, -a adj MED palliative; **remedio ~** palliative remedy
palidecer irr como crecer vi **1.** (persona) to turn pale **2.** (cosa) to fade
palidez f paleness
pálido, -a adj pale; (estilo) flat
palillo m **1.** (palo) (small) stick; **tener las piernas como ~s** fig to have legs like matchsticks; **tocar todos los ~s** inf to pull out all the stops **2.** (para los dientes) toothpick **3.** (para el tambor) drumstick
palio m (baldaquín) canopy; **recibir a alguien bajo ~** fig to roll out the red carpet for sb
palique m inf chat; **estar de ~ con alguien** to chat to sb
palisandro m rosewood
paliza¹ f **1.** (zurra) beating; **dar una buena ~** (pegar) to beat up; (derrotar) to thrash; **¡no me des la ~!** fig give me a break! **2.** inf (esfuerzo) slog; **¡qué ~ me he pegado subiendo la montaña!** climbing that mountain has exhausted me!
paliza² mf inv, inf (pesado) pain; **tu amigo es un ~(s)** your friend is a real bore
palma f **1.** (palmera) palm (tree); (hoja de palmera) palm leaf **2.** (triunfo) **llevarse la ~** to be the best **3.** ANAT palm; **conozco el barrio como la ~ de mi mano** inf I know the area like the back of my hand; **llevar a alguien en ~s** to treat sb with kid gloves **4.** pl (ruido) clapping; (aplauso) applause; **tocar las ~s** to clap; (aplaudir) to applaud
palmada f **1.** (golpe) pat **2.** pl (ruido) clapping; **~s de aplauso** applause; **dar ~s** to clap
palmar I. m palm grove; **ser más viejo que un ~** to be as old as the hills II. vi inf **~la** to kick the bucket
palmario, -a adj (evidente) clear
palmatoria f (candelero) candlestick
palmeado, -a adj **1.** (figura) palm-shaped **2.** ZOOL webbed
palmear vi (aplaudir) to clap

palmense I. adj of/from Las Palmas II. mf native/inhabitant of Las Palmas
palmera f palm (tree)
palmeral m palm grove
palmero, -a I. adj of/from the island of Palma II. m, f native/inhabitant of the island of Palma
palmípedas fpl web-footed birds pl
palmo m (hand)span; **con un ~ de la lengua fuera** inf with one's tongue hanging out ►**dejar a alguien con un ~ de narices** to disappoint sb badly; **~ a ~** inch by inch; **conocer algo ~ a ~** to know every inch of sth
palmotear vi to clap
palmoteo m (aplauso) clapping
palo m **1.** (bastón) stick; (vara) pole; (garrote) club; (estaca) post; **~ de la escoba** broomstick; **~ de hockey** hockey stick; **~ de la portería** goalpost **2.** NÁUT mast **3.** (madera) wood **4.** (paliza) beating; **andar a ~s** to be at each another's throats; **dar ~s de ciego** to thrash about wildly; fig to grope in the dark; **dar un ~ a alguien** fig to tear a strip off sb; (cobrar mucho) to rip sb off; **echar a alguien a ~s** to throw sb out; **liarse a ~s con alguien** to come to blows with sb; **moler a alguien a ~s** to beat sb black and blue ►**~ de agua** AmL downpour; **no dar un ~ al agua** not to do a stick of work; **de tal ~, tal astilla** prov like father, like son; **cada ~ que aguante su vela** prov everyone must face up to their responsibilities; **ser un ~** to be a setback
paloma f (ave) pigeon; (blanca, como símbolo) dove; **~ mensajera** carrier pigeon; **ser una ~ sin hiel** fig to be as gentle as a lamb
palomar m dovecote, pigeon loft
palomilla f **1.** ZOOL (mariposa nocturna) moth **2.** (tornillo) wing [o butterfly] nut
palomitas fpl GASTR popcorn
palomo m (cock) pigeon
palote m **1.** (palillo) drumstick **2.** (ejercicio) downstroke
palpable adj **1.** (tangible) palpable **2.** (evidente) clear
palpar vt **1.** (tocar) to touch **2.** inf (magrear) to touch up Brit, to feel up Am **3.** (percibir) to feel; **se palpaba el entusiasmo** you could feel the enthusiasm
palpitación f **1.** (del pulso) throb; (del corazón) beating; (por estar excitado) palpitation **2.** (estremecimiento) shudder
palpitante adj **1.** (corazón) throbbing **2.** fig (emocionante) exciting; (interés) burning; **un problema de ~ actualidad** a problem of the utmost relevance
palpitar vi **1.** (contraerse) to shudder; (corazón, pulso) to throb **2.** (manifestarse) **en sus palabras palpita la dulzura** his words are full of sweetness
pálpito m (corazonada) hunch
palta f AmS BOT avocado (pear)
palto m CSur BOT avocado pear tree

P

palúdico, -a *adj* MED malarial; **fiebre palúdica** malaria
paludismo *m* MED malaria
palurdo, -a I. *adj* uncouth II. *m, f* yokel, hick *Am*
palustre I. *adj* marsh; **planta** ~ marsh plant II. *m* trowel
pamela *f* broad-brimmed ladies' hat
pamema *f* *inf* 1. (*tontería*) silly thing 2. (*melindre*) flattery
pampa *f* GEO pampas + *sing/pl vb*

The **pampa** is a flat, treeless, grassy steppe in Argentina. It is a very fertile agricultural area with moist, sandy soil ideally suited to the cultivation of cereals.

---

pámpano *m* 1. (*vástago*) vine shoot; **echar ~s** to put out shoots 2. (*hoja*) vine leaf
pampear *vi* CSur to travel over the pampas
pampero, -a I. *adj* of/from the Pampas II. *m, f* native/inhabitant of the Pampas
pampino, -a I. *adj* Chile of/from the Chilean pampas II. *m, f* Chile native/inhabitant of the Chilean pampas
pamplina *f* *inf* (*pamema*) silly thing
pamplonés, -esa I. *adj* of/from Pamplona II. *m, f* native/inhabitant of Pamplona
pamplonica *adj, mf inf v.* **pamplonés**
pan *m* 1. (*alimento*) bread; ~ **de azúcar** sugar loaf; ~ **candeal** white bread; ~ **integral** wholemeal bread; ~ **con mantequilla** bread and butter; ~ **de molde** sliced bread; ~ **de munición** (army) ration bread; ~ **rallado** breadcrumbs *pl*; **estar a ~ y agua** to be on (a strict diet of) bread and water; **ganarse el ~** to earn one's living; **este año hay mucho ~** it's been a good harvest this year 2. (*pieza*) **un ~ de jabón** a bar of soap 3. (*laminilla*) gold leaf ▸**comer ~ con** <u>corteza</u> (*ser independiente*) to fend for oneself; (*recuperar la salud*) to be on the mend; **¡el ~ de cada día!** the same old thing!; **no sólo de ~ vive el** <u>hombre</u> man cannot live by bread alone; **ser un** <u>pedazo</u> **de ~**, **quien da ~ a** <u>perro</u> **ajeno, pierde ~ y pierde perro** *prov*: ≈ don't expect gratitude from strangers; **a falta de ~, buenas son** <u>tortas</u> *prov* half a loaf is better than none, beggars can't be choosers; (**llamar**) **al ~, ~ y al** <u>vino</u>, **vino** *inf* to call a spade a spade; **ser más** <u>bueno</u> **que el ~** to be very good-natured; **ser ~** <u>comido</u> *inf* to be dead easy; **con su ~ se lo** <u>coma</u> *inf* that's his lookout [*o* problem]; <u>comer</u> **el ~ de alguien** to live off sb; **no se le** <u>cuece</u> **el ~** he's/she's very impatient
pana *f* (*tejido*) corduroy
panacea *f* panacea, cure-all
panadería *f* bakery
panadero, -a *m, f* baker
panal *m* honeycomb
Panamá *m* Panama

Panamá is divided in two by the Panama Canal and links Central America to North America. The capital, which is also called **Panamá**, is the largest city in the country. Spanish is the official language of the country, although English is widely used. The monetary unit of Panama is the **balboa**.

---

panameño, -a *adj, m, f* Panamanian
pancarta *f* placard
pancho *m* Arg GASTR (*perrito caliente*) hotdog
pancho, -a *adj* (*tranquilo*) calm
pancista *mf* opportunist
pancita *f* Méx GASTR tripe
páncreas *m inv* pancreas
panda¹ *m* ZOOL panda
panda² *f v.* **pandilla**
pandear *vi, vr:* ~**se** (*pared*) to bulge; (*viga*) to warp
pandereta *f,* **pandero** *m* MÚS tambourine
pandilla *f* band; (*de amigos*) group; ~ **de ladrones** gang of thieves
pandorga *f* 1. (*cometa*) kite 2. *inf* (*mujer gorda*) fat woman 3. (*barriga*) paunch 4. Col (*chanza, diablura*) prank
panecillo *m* roll
panegírico *m* panegyric
panegírico, -a *adj* eulogizing
panel *m* 1. (*carpintería, téc*) panel; ~ **de control** control panel 2. (*encuesta*) panel 3. (*que discute en público*) discussion panel
panela *f* 1. (*bizcocho*) maize cake, corn cake *Am* 2. Col, CRi, Hond (*azúcar*) brown sugar loaf
panera *f* 1. (*para trigo*) grain store 2. (*cesto*) bread bin, breadbox *Am*
pánfilo, -a *adj* 1. (*fácil de engañar*) gullible 2. (*lento*) slow
panfleto *m* pamphlet; *fig* propaganda
pánico *m* panic; **entrar en** ~ to panic; **tener** ~ **a algo** to be terrified of sth
pánico, -a *adj* panic
panificar <c→qu> *vt* ~ **algo** to make bread from sth
panizo *m* millet
panocha *f,* **panoja** *f* 1. (*de maíz*) corncob 2. (*espiga*) ear of corn; (*racimo*) cornstalk
panoli *inf* I. *adj* idiotic II. *mf* idiot
panorama *m* panorama; *fig* outlook; **el ~ de cráteres en la luna** the landscape of craters on the moon
panqué *m* Cuba, Méx, **panqueque** *m* AmS GASTR pancake
pantagruélico, -a *adj* (*comidas*) enormous; **banquete** ~ lavish feast
pantaleta(s) *f(pl)* Méx, Ven (*bragas*) knickers *pl* Brit, panties *pl*
pantalla *f* 1. (*de la lámpara*) shade 2. (*protección*) screen; **servirse de alguien como** ~ to hide behind sb; **servir de** ~ (*testaferro*) to be a figurehead 3. INFOR, TV, CINE screen; ~ **com-**

pleta full-size screen; ~ **cromática** colour [*o color Am*] screen; ~ **panorámica** wide screen; **estrella de la** ~ screen star; **pequeña** ~ *inf* TV

pantalón *m* trousers *pl*, pair of trousers; ~ **bombacho** (*amplio*) baggy trousers; (*hasta la pantorrilla*) knickers *pl Brit;* ~ **de pinzas** pleated trousers; ~ **tejano** [*o* **vaquero**] jeans *pl;* **llevar los pantalones** *fig* to wear the trousers [*o* pants]

pantanal *m* marshland

pantano *m* 1.(*ciénaga*) marsh; (*laguna*) swamp 2.*fig* (*atolladero*) fix 3.(*embalse*) reservoir

pantanoso, -a *adj* marshy

panteón *m* 1.HIST pantheon 2.(*sepultura*) tomb; ~ **de familia** family vault 3.*AmL* (*cementerio*) cemetery

panteonero, -a *m, f AmL* gravedigger

pantera *f* panther

pantimedia(s) *f(pl) Méx* tights *pl Brit*, pantyhose

pantis *mpl inf* tights *pl Brit*, pantyhose

pantomima *f* pantomime

pantorrilla *f* calf

pantufla *f*, **pantuflo** *m* slipper

panucho *m Méx* meat and bean stuffed tortilla

panul *m CSur* BOT (*apio*) celery

panza *f* 1.(*barriga*) belly; (*de un recipiente*) bulge; **llenarse la** ~ to fill one's belly 2.ZOOL stomach; (*rumiantes*) rumen

pañal *m* nappy *Brit*, diaper *Am;* **dejar en** ~**es a alguien** *fig* to leave sb way behind; **estar aún en** ~**es** *fig* to be still in its infancy; **en física estoy en** ~**es** I haven't got a clue about physics

pañería *f* 1.(*comercio*) drapery *Brit*, dry goods *pl Am* 2.(*tienda*) draper's (shop) *Brit*, dry goods store *Am*

pañetar *vt Col* (*una pared*) to skim with plaster

paño *m* 1.(*tejido, trapo*) cloth; ~ **asargado** serge; ~ **de cocina** (*para fregar*) dishcloth; (*para secar*) tea towel *Brit*, dish towel *Am* 2.(*ancho de una tela*) width 3.(*mancha*) stain ▶ **ser el** ~ **de lágrimas de alguien** to be sb's shoulder to cry on; **andarse con** ~**s calientes** to do things by halves; **aplicar** ~**s calientes** to apply half measures; ~**s menores** underwear; **¡conozco el** ~**!** *inf* I know what's what!; **hay** ~ **que cortar** there's plenty to be getting on with

pañoleta *f* fichu

pañuelo *m* 1.(*moquero*) handkerchief; **el mundo es un** ~ it's a small world 2.(*pañoleta*) fichu; (*de cabeza*) headscarf, scarf

papa[1] *m* pope

papa[2] *f* 1.*reg, AmL* (*patata*) potato; **no entender ni** ~ not to understand a thing 2.*inf v.* **paparrucha** 3.*pl* (*comida*) purée

papá *m inf* 1.(*padre*) dad; **Papá Noel** Father Christmas 2.*pl* **los** ~**s** mum and dad

papachar *vt Méx* (*mimar*) to spoil

papada *f* (*de la persona*) double chin, jowl; (*del animal*) dewlap

papagayo *m* 1.(*loro*) parrot 2.(*hablador*) chatterbox; **hablar como un** ~ to be a real chatterbox 3.(*pez*) parrot fish

papal I. *adj* papal II. *m AmL* potato field

papalote *m Ant, Méx* paper kite

papamoscas *m inv* 1.ZOOL flycatcher 2.*inf* (*papanatas*) halfwit

papamóvil *m* popemobile

papanatas *m inv, inf* halfwit

paparrucha *f inf*, **paparruchada** *f inf* 1.(*noticia falsa*) piece of nonsense; (*patraña*) lie 2.(*obra sin valor*) piece of trash; **ese libro es una** ~ this book is trash

papaya *f* pawpaw, papaya

papayo *m* pawpaw (tree)

papel *m* 1.(*para escribir, material*) paper; (*hoja*) piece of paper; (*escritura*) piece of writing; ~ **de barba** untrimmed paper; ~ **de calcar** tracing paper; ~ **cebolla** onionskin (paper); ~ **continuo** continuous listing paper; ~ **de envolver** wrapping paper; ~ **de regalo** giftwrap; ~ **de estraza** brown paper; ~ **de aluminio** aluminium [*o* tin] foil; ~ **de seda** tissue paper; ~ **de fumar** cigarette paper; ~ **higiénico** toilet paper; ~ **de hilo** parchment paper; ~ **de lija** sandpaper; ~ **maché** papier mâché; ~ **moneda** banknotes *pl*, bills *pl Am;* ~ **de música** music paper; ~ **pautado** ruled paper; ~ **pintado** wallpaper; ~ **de plata** silver paper; ~ **reciclado** recycled paper; ~ **secante** blotting paper; ~ **de tornasol** litmus paper; ~ **mojado** *fig* worthless scrap of paper; **tus palabras fueron** ~ **mojado** your words were no more than empty promises; **ponerse más blanco que el** ~ to go as white as a sheet 2.(*rol*) role; ~ **protagonista** leading role; ~ **secundario** supporting role; **hacer su** ~ to play one's part; **hacer un** ~ **ridículo** to make a fool of oneself; **hacer buen/mal** ~ to make a good/bad impression; **hacer el** ~ **de malo en la película** to play the role of the baddy in the film; **repartir los** ~**es** to assign the parts 3.*pl* (*documentos*) documentation; (*de identidad*) identity papers *pl*

papela *f inf* ID papers *pl*

papeleo *m* (*trámites*) paperwork; ~ **burocrático** red tape

papelera *f* 1.(*cesto*) wastepaper basket; (*en la calle*) litter bin 2.(*fábrica*) paper mill 3.(*mueble*) desk

papelería *f* stationer's

papelerío *m AmL* mass of papers

papelero, -a I. *adj* paper II. *m, f* (*vendedor*) stationer

papeleta *f* (*cédula*) slip of paper; (*en el examen*) result slip; ~ **del monte de piedad** pawn ticket; ~ **de propaganda** flier *Brit*, flyer *Am;* **menuda** ~ **le ha tocado** that's a nasty problem he's got

papelón *m* 1.*pey* (*papel inútil*) scrap of paper 2.*inf* (*actuación*) embarrassing behaviour *Brit*,

embarrassing behavior *Am;* ¡qué ~! how embarrassing!; **hacer un** ~ to make a spectacle of oneself
papelote *m,* **papelucho** *m* 1. *pey* (*inútil*) scrap of paper 2. (*reciclable*) pulped paper
papera *f* MED 1. *pl* (*enfermedad*) mumps *pl* 2. (*bocio*) goitre *Brit,* goiter *Am*
papi *m inf* dad(dy)
papilla *f* baby food; **dar** ~ **a alguien** *fig* to con sb; **echar la** (**primera**) ~ *inf* to be as sick as a dog; **hacer** ~ **a alguien** *fig* to beat hell out of sb; **estar hecho** ~ *fig* to be smashed to a pulp
papiro *m* papyrus
papo *m* 1. (*buche: de animal*) dewlap; (*de ave*) crop; *inf* (*bocio*) goitre *Brit,* goiter *Am* 2. (*papada*) double chin, jowl
paquebote *m* packet boat
paquete *m* 1. *t. fig* (*atado*) packet; ~ **postal** parcel 2. *inf* (*castigo*) **meter un** ~ **a alguien** (*reprender*) to give sb a real telling-off; (*castigar*) to punish sb heavily 3. *inf* (*genitales*) bulge; **marcar** ~ to wear tight-fitting trousers
paquete, -a *adj Arg* smart
paquetear *vi Arg, Urug, inf: to show off how smartly dressed one is*
paquete-bomba *m* <paquetes-bomba> parcel bomb
paquetería *f* 1. (*paquete*) parcels *pl* 2. *Arg* (*vanidad*) vanity
paquidermo *m* pachyderm
paquistaní *adj, mf v.* **pakistaní**
par I. *adj* 1. (*número*) even; ~**es o nones** odds or evens 2. (*igual*) equal; **a la** ~ at the same time; **esta película entretiene a la** ~ **que instruye** this film is both entertaining and educational; **sin** ~ without equal ▶**de** ~ **en** ~ wide open; **abrir una ventana de** ~ **en** ~ to open a window wide II. *m* 1. (*dos cosas*) pair; **un** ~ **de zapatos/pantalones** a pair of shoes/trousers 2. (*algunos*) **un** ~ **de minutos** a couple of minutes 3. (*título*) peer
para I. *prep* 1. (*destino*) for; **asilo** ~ **ancianos** old people's home; **un regalo** ~ **el niño** a present for the child 2. (*finalidad*) for; **gafas** ~ **bucear** diving goggles; **servir** ~ **algo** to be useful for sth; **las frutas son buenas** ~ **guardar la línea** fruit is good for keeping in shape; **¿**~ **qué es esto?** what is this for? 3. (*dirección*) to; **voy** ~ **Madrid** I'm going to Madrid; **mira** ~ **acá** look over here 4. (*duración*) for; ~ **siempre** forever; **con esto tenemos** ~ **rato** with this we've got enough for quite a while; **vendrá** ~ **Navidad/finales de marzo** he/she will come for Christmas/towards the end of March; **estará listo** ~ **el viernes** it will be ready for [o by] Friday; **diez minutos** ~ **las once** *AmL* ten to eleven 5. (*contraposición*) for; **es muy activo** ~ **la edad que tiene** he is very active for his age 6. (*trato*) (con) with; **es muy amable** ~ **con nosotros** he/she is very kind to us 7. (+ *estar*) **estar** ~... (*disposición*) to be ready to ...; (*a punto de*) about to ...; **no estoy** ~ **bro-**

mas I'm in no mood for jokes; **está** ~ **llover** it's about to rain; **está** ~ **llegar** he/she is about to arrive; **quiere estar** ~ **sí** he/she wants to be alone 8. (*a juicio de*) ~ **mí, esto no es lo mismo** in my opinion, this is not the same; ~ **mí que va a llover** I think it's going to rain II. *conj* 1. + *infin* to; **he venido** ~ **darte las gracias** I've come to thank you 2. ~ **que** +*subj* so that; **te mando al colegio** ~ **que aprendas algo** I send you to school so that you learn sth
parabién *m* congratulations *pl;* **dar el** ~ **a alguien** to congratulate sb
parábola *f* 1. (*alegoría*) parable 2. MAT curve, parabola
parabólica *f* satellite dish
parabólico, -a *adj* 1. (*alegórico*) allegorical; **expresarse en sentido** ~ to speak allegorically 2. MAT parabolic 3. TÉC satellite
parabrisas *m inv* AUTO windscreen *Brit,* windshield *Am*
paraca *f AmL* strong breeze from the Pacific
paracaídas *m inv* parachute
paracaidismo *m sin pl* parachuting
paracaidista *mf* DEP parachutist; MIL paratrooper
parachoques *m inv* AUTO bumper, fender *Am*
parada *f* 1. (*de un autobús, tranvía*) stop; ~ **de taxis** taxi rank 2. (*acción de parar*) stopping; ~ **de una fábrica** factory stoppage; **estoy cansada, tenemos que hacer una** ~ I'm tired, we need to have a rest 3. DEP, MIL parade; **paso de** ~ marching step
paradero *m* (*de una persona*) whereabouts; (*de una cosa*) destination; **está en** ~ **desconocido** his whereabouts are unknown; **no logramos descubrir el** ~ **del paquete** we didn't manage to find out where the packet ended up
paradigma *m* (*ejemplo*) paradigm
paradisíaco, -a *adj* heavenly; **un placer** ~ a heavenly delight
parado, -a I. *adj* 1. (*que no se mueve*) stationary; **estar** ~ to be motionless; (*fábrica*) to be at a standstill; **quedarse** ~ to remain motionless; *fig* to be surprised; **me quedé tan** ~ **que no pude decir nada** I was so surprised I was left totally dumbstruck; **me has dejado** ~ you have really surprised me 2. (*sin empleo*) unemployed 3. (*remiso*) slow 4. (*tímido*) shy 5. *AmL* standing (up) ▶**salir bien/mal** ~ **de algo** to come out of sth well/badly; **ser el peor** ~ **en algo** to be the one who comes off worst in sth II. *m, f* unemployed person; **los** ~**s** the unemployed; ~ **de larga duración** long-term unemployed person
paradoja *f* paradox; **esto es una** ~ this is absurd
parador *m* 1. inn 2. (*en España*) state-run luxury hotel
paraestatal *adj* semi-official
parafina *f* paraffin
parafrasear *vt* to paraphrase

paráfrasis *f inv* paraphrase
paragolpes *m inv,* AmL bumper, fender *Am*
parágrafo *m* paragraph; ..., ~ **aparte** ..., new paragraph; *fig* ..., to change the subject
paraguas *m inv* umbrella
Paraguay *m* Paraguay

Paraguay lies in South America and borders Bolivia, Brazil and Argentina. It is a landlocked country. The capital of Paraguay is **Asunción**. The official languages of the country are Spanish and **guaraní**. The monetary unit of the country is also called the **guaraní**.

---

paraguayo, -a *adj, m, f* Paraguayan
paragüero *m* (*mueble*) umbrella stand
paraíso *m* 1. (*en el cielo*) heaven; ~ **terrenal** earthly paradise; **entrar en el** ~ to go to heaven 2. TEAT gods *pl* 3. *Méx* (*gallinero*) henhouse
paraje *m* 1. (*lugar*) place; (*punto*) spot 2. (*estado*) state
paralela *f* 1. MAT parallel 2. *pl* DEP parallel bars *pl;* ~**s asimétricas** asymmetric bars
paralelo *m* 1. (*comparación*) comparison; **establecer un** ~ **entre dos cosas** to compare two things; **estos libros no admiten** ~ these books cannot be compared 2. GEO parallel 3. ELEC **conexión en** ~ parallel connection; **conectado en** ~ connected in parallel
paralelo, -a *adj* parallel; **líneas paralelas** parallel lines; **las calles son paralelas** the streets are parallel; **seguir caminos** ~**s** to develop along similar lines
paralelogramo *m* parallelogram
parálisis *f inv* paralysis; ~ **infantil** infantile paralysis; **sufre** ~ **de las piernas** his/her legs are paralysed [*o* paralyzed *Am*]
paralítico, -a I. *adj* (*persona*) paralysed *Brit,* paralyzed *Am* II. *m, f* paralytic
paralización *f* 1. (*del cuerpo*) paralysis 2. (*de un proyecto, un proceso*) halting; ~ **de una obra** halting of a building job
paralizar <z→c> I. *vt* 1. (*persona*) to paralyse *Brit,* to paralyze *Am;* **el miedo/el frío la paralizó** she was paralysed [*o* paralyzed *Am*] by fear/the cold 2. (*cosa*) to stop; ~ **un transporte** to paralyse [*o* to paaralyze *Am*] a means of transport II. *vr* 1. (*persona*) to be paralysed [*o* paralyzed *Am*] 2. (*cosa*) to stop
paramento *m* 1. (*adorno*) ornament; (*vestidura*) vestment 2. (*para un caballo*) trappings *pl*
parámetro *m* parameter
paramilitar *adj* paramilitary; **fuerzas** ~**es** paramilitary forces
páramo *m* 1. (*terreno desierto*) wilderness; (*infértil*) wasteland; (*altiplano*) barren plateau 2. (*lugar desamparado*) exposed place
parangón *m* 1. (*comparación*) comparison; **sin** ~ incomparable 2. (*semejanza*) similarity
parangonar *vt* 1. (*comparar*) to compare

2. TIPO to justify
paraninfo *m* UNIV (*salón*) auditorium, assembly hall
paranoia *f* paranoia
paranoico, -a I. *adj* paranoid II. *m, f* paranoic
parapente *m* paragliding
parapetarse *vr* to protect oneself; ~ **tras una excusa** to hide behind an excuse; **se parapetó en el hecho de que no tenía dinero** he used the excuse that he didn't have any money
parapeto *m* 1. MIL parapet; (*barricada*) barricade 2. (*baranda*) railing
paraplejía *f* paraplegia
parapléjico, -a *adj, m, f* paraplegic
parapsicología *f* parapsychology
parar I. *vi* 1. (*detenerse, cesar*) to stop; **hablar sin** ~ to talk without stopping; **¿para el tren en este pueblo?** does the train stop in this town?; **a la vuelta paramos en casa de mi tía** on the way back we'll stop at my aunt's house; **la máquina funciona sin** ~ the machine works non-stop; **mis hijos no me dejan** ~ my kids never give me a break; **mis remordimientos de conciencia no me dejan** ~ my guilty conscience doesn't give me any peace; **ha parado de llover** it has stopped raining; **no para de quejarse** he/she never stops complaining; **no para (de trabajar)** he never stops (working) 2. (*acabar*) to finish; **si sigues así irás a** ~ **a la cárcel** if you carry on like this you'll end up in jail; **la maleta fue a** ~ **a Bilbao** the suitcase ended up in Bilbao; **por fin, el paquete fue a** ~ **a tus manos** the packet finally reached you; **¿dónde iremos a** ~? what's the world coming to?; **¿en qué irá a** ~ **esto?** where will it all end?; **salimos bien/mal parados del asunto** we came out of the affair well/badly; **¿dónde quieres ir a** ~? what are you getting at?; **siempre venimos a** ~ **al mismo tema** we always end up talking about the same thing 3. (*alojarse, estar*) to live; **no sé dónde para** I don't know where he/she lives; **nunca para en casa** he/she is never at home; **siempre para en el mismo hotel** he/she always stays at the same hotel; **¿paras mucho en este bar?** *inf* do you come to this bar often? 4. (*convertirse*) **la tienda paró en un restaurante** the shop was converted into a restaurant II. *vt* 1. (*detener*) to stop; (*un golpe*) to block; (*un gol*) to save; (*el motor*) to turn off; **cuando se enfada no hay quien lo pare** when he gets angry there's no stopping him 2. (*en el juego*) to bet III. *vr* 1. (*detenerse*) to stop; **el reloj se ha parado** the clock has stopped; ~**se a pensar** to stop and think; ~**se a descansar** to stop to rest 2. AmL (*levantarse*) to get up
pararrayos *m inv* lightning conductor
parásito, -a I. *adj t. fig* parasitic II. *m, f t. fig* parasite
parásitos *mpl* RADIO statics *pl,* interference
parasol *m* 1. (*quitasol*) sunshade 2. (*en el*

coche) sun visor **3.** (*umbela*) canopy
parcela *f* **1.** (*terreno*) plot; ~ **de cultivo** cultivated plot; ~ **edificable** building plot **2.** (*parte*) portion
parcelar *vt* **1.** (*dividir*) to parcel out **2.** (*medir*) to measure out
parche *m* **1.** (*pegote*) patch; (*para una herida*) (sticking) plaster, Bandaid®; **bolsillo de** ~ patch pocket; ~ **para el ojo** eye patch; **pegar un** ~ **a alguien** *inf* to put one over on sb; **poner un** ~ to patch up **2.** (*retoque*) makeshift remedy; (*de pintura*) dab; **poner** ~**s** to patch up; *fig* to paper over the cracks **3.** (*piel del tambor*) drumskin **4.** (*tambor*) drum
parchear *vt* **1.** (*poner parches*) to patch (up) **2.** (*manosear*) to touch up *Brit*, to feel up *Am*
parchís *m* (*juego*) ludo *Brit*, parcheesi *Am*
parcial I. *adj* **1.** (*incompleto*) partial; **la venta** ~ **del terreno** the partial sale of the land **2.** (*arbitrario*) biased **II.** *mf* supporter
parcialidad *f* **1.** (*preferencia*) bias, favoritism **2.** (*grupo*) faction
parco, -a *adj* **1.** (*moderado*) moderate; (*sobrio*) frugal **2.** (*escaso*) meagre *Brit*, meager *Am;* ~ **en palabras** of few words; **ser** ~ **en conceder favores** to be sparing with one's favours [*o* favors *Am*]
pardiez *interj* HIST good gracious
pardillo *m* linnet
pardillo, -a *inf* **I.** *adj* **1.** (*palurdo*) uncouth **2.** (*ingenuo*) simple **II.** *m, f* **1.** (*palurdo*) yokel **2.** (*ingenuo*) simpleton
pardo, -a I. *adj* (*color*) greyish-brown; **oso** ~ brown bear; **de ojos** ~**s** brown-eyed **2.** (*oscuro*) dark **3.** (*voz*) dull **II.** *m, f AmL* mulatto
pardusco, -a *adj* brownish
parear *vt* **1.** (*formar parejas*) to pair; (*atar*) to tie together; (*ropa*) to match up **2.** BIO to mate **3.** (*igualar*) to match
parecer I. *irr como crecer vi* (*tener cierto aspecto*) to seem; (*aparentar*) to appear; **a lo que parece** as far as one can tell; **tu idea me parece bien** I think your idea is a good one; **parece mayor de lo que es** he seems older than he is; **parece mentira que** +*subj* it seems incredible that; **aunque parezca mentira** though it may seem incredible; **me parece que no tienes ganas** I don't think you want to; **parece que va a llover** it looks like rain; **¿qué te parece?** what do you think?; **¿qué te parece el piso?** what do you think of the flat?; **si te parece bien,...** if you agree, ...; **me ha parecido oír un grito** I thought I heard a scream, if it's OK with you; **parecen hermanos** they look like brothers ▶ **quien no parece, perece** *prov* if you don't look after your own interests, nobody else will **II.** *irr como crecer vr* to look alike; **se parece a una estrella de cine** she looks like a film star; **te pareces mucho a tu madre** you look very much like your mother; **¡esto se te parece!** this looks like you! **III.** *m* **1.** (*opinión*) opinion;

(*juicio*) judgement; **a mi** ~ in my opinion; **arrimarse al** ~ **de la mayoría** to follow the opinion of the majority; **esto es cuestión de** ~**es** this is a matter of opinion **2.** (*aspecto, apariencia*) appearance; **ser de buen** ~ to be good-looking; **al** ~ apparently; **por el bien** ~ for the sake of appearances
parecido *m* similarity, likeness; **tienes un gran** ~ **con tu hermana** you and your sister look very alike
parecido, -a *adj* **1.** (*semejante*) similar **2.** (*de aspecto*) **ser bien/mal** ~ (*persona*) to be good/bad-looking; (*cosa*) to be appropriate/inappropriate
pared *f* **1.** (*tabique, muro*) wall; (*de una montaña*) face; (*separación*) partition; ~ **abdominal** stomach wall; ~ **maestra** (load-)bearing wall **2.** (*personas*) wall; (*cosas*) mountain ▶ **vivimos** ~ **por medio** we live next door; **estar blanco como la** ~ to be as white as a sheet [*o* ghost]; **entre cuatro** ~**es** cooped up; **dejar a alguien pegado a la** ~ to put sb on the spot; **quedarse pegado a la** ~ to be put on the spot; **hablar a la** ~ to talk to a brick wall; **¡cuidado, que estas** ~**es oyen!** careful, walls have ears!; **subirse por las** ~**es** to go up the wall; (*enfadarse*) to blow one's top; (*estar nervioso*) to [*o* go] stir crazy
paredón *m* thick wall; **llevar a alguien al** ~ to take sb before a firing squad
pareja *f* **1.** (*par*) couple; (*de la guardia civil*) pair of Civil Guards; ~ **de hecho** common law couple; ~**s mixtas** DEP mixed doubles; **hacen buena** ~ they make a good partnership [*o* couple]; **¿dónde está la** ~ **de este guante?** where is the other glove?; **su bondad y su modestia corrían** ~**s** his goodness was matched by his modesty; **no correr** ~**s** to be dissimilar **2.** (*compañero*) partner **3.** (*en los dados, los naipes*) pair
parejo, -a *adj* **1.** (*igual*) equal; (*semejante*) similar; **los caballos iban** ~**s** the horses were neck and neck **2.** (*llano*) smooth
parentela *f* relations *pl*
parentesco *m* relationship, kinship; ~ **por consanguinidad** blood relationship
paréntesis *m inv* **1.** (*signo*) bracket; **poner algo entre** ~ to put sth in brackets; **entre** ~ *fig* by the way; **abrir/cerrar el** ~ to open/close brackets; *fig* to introduce/finish a digression **2.** (*oración*) digression **3.** (*interrupción*) interruption; **hicimos un** ~ **para almorzar** we had a break for lunch
paridad *f* **1.** (*comparación*) comparison **2.** FIN, ECON parity; ~ **adquisitiva** parity of purchasing power; ~ (**de cambio**) exchange parity **3.** (*igualdad*) equality; (*semejanza*) similarity; ~ **de fuerzas** parity of strength; **competir a** ~ **de medios** to compete on an equal basis
pariente, -a I. *adj* **1.** (*de la misma familia*) related **2.** (*parecido*) similar **II.** *m, f* **1.** (*familiar*) relative; **los** ~**s** the relations, the relatives; ~ **mayor** direct ancestor; ~**lejano/**

cercano distant/close relative **2.** *inf* (*marido, mujer*) other half; **mi** ~ my missus, my old man

parihuela(s) *f/pl)* stretcher

paripé *m* show; **hacer el** ~ to put on a show; (*presumir*) to show off; (*fingir*) to pretend; (*fingir cariño*) to put on a show of affection

parir I. *vt* **1.** (*dar a luz*) to give birth to **2.** (*producir*) to produce; (*causar*) to cause **II.** *vi* **1.** (*dar a luz*) to give birth **2.** (*descubrirse*) to come to light **3.** (*expresarse*) to express oneself; ~ **sin dificultad** to express oneself well ▶poner a alguien a ~ *inf* to run sb down

París *m* Paris

parisiense *adj, mf* Parisian

paritario, -a *adj* equal; **comité** ~ joint committee

paritorio *m* **1.** (*sala*) delivery room **2.** *AmC* (*parto*) birth

parking *m* <parkings> car park, parking lot *Am*

parlamentar *vi* **1.** (*hablar*) to talk **2.** (*negociar*) to negotiate

parlamentario, -a I. *adj* parliamentary; **debate** ~ parliamentary debate **II.** *m, f* **1.** (*diputado*) member of parliament **2.** (*negociador*) negotiator

parlamento *m* **1.** (*cámara*) parliament; **Parlamento Europeo** European Parliament **2.** *t.* TEAT (*discurso*) speech **3.** (*negociaciones*) negotiations *pl*

parlanchín, -ina I. *adj inf* talkative **II.** *m, f inf* (*persona*) chatterbox; (*indiscreta*) gossip

parlotear *vi* to chatter

parloteo *m* chat

parné *m inf* (*dinero*) dough

paro *m* **1.** (*parar: una fábrica*) shutdown; (*de trabajar*) stopping **2.** (*huelga*) ~ **laboral** strike; (*por parte de los empresarios*) lockout **3.** (*desempleo*) unemployment; ~ **forzoso** unemployment; **estar en** ~ to be unemployed; **cobrar el** ~ to be on the dole **4.** ZOOL tit; ~ **carbonero** coal tit

parodia *f* parody; **hacer una** ~ **de algo** to parody sth

parodiar *vt* to parody

parpadear *vi* **1.** (*ojos*) to blink; **sin** ~ *fig* without a second thought **2.** (*luz, llama*) to flicker

parpadeo *m* **1.** (*de los ojos*) blinking **2.** (*de una luz, una llama*) flicker

párpado *m* eyelid

parque *m* **1.** (*jardín*) park; ~ **de atracciones** amusement park; ~ **natural** National Park; ~ **zoológico** zoo **2.** (*depósito*) depot; ~ **de bomberos** fire station, fire department *Am;* ~ **militar** military depot; ~ **temático** theme park **3.** (*conjunto*) collection; ~ **industrial** industrial park; ~ **de maquinaria** pool of machinery; ~ **móvil** fleet of (official) vehicles; ~ **de vehículos** fleet of vehicles, car pool **4.** (*para niños*) playpen

parqué *m* parquet

parqueadero *m AmL* car park, parking lot

parquear *vt AmL* to park

parquedad *f* frugality; **hablar con** ~ to be sparing with one's words

parquet *m* parquet

parquímetro *m* parking meter

parra *f* (*vid*) (grape)vine; **subirse a la** ~ (*enfadarse*) to hit the roof; (*darse importancia*) to get above oneself

párrafo *m v.* **parágrafo**

parral *m* **1.** (*parras*) vine; (*techo*) vine arbour *Brit*, vine arbor *Am* **2.** (*viña*) vineyard

parranda *f* spree; **ir de** ~ to go out on the town

parrilla *f.* **1.** (*para la brasa*) grill; (*de un horno*) oven rack **2.** (*establecimiento*) grill(room) **3.** DEP ~ (**de salida**) (starting) grid **4.** *AmL* AUTO roof-rack

parrillada *f* grill; ~ **de pescado** grilled fish; ~ **de carne** mixed grill

párroco I. *adj* parish **II.** *m* parish priest

parroquia *f* **1.** (*territorio, fieles*) parish **2.** (*iglesia*) parish church **3.** (*clientela*) customers *pl*

parroquial *adj* parish; **iglesia** ~ parish church

parroquiano, -a I. *adj* parish **II.** *m, f* **1.** (*feligrés*) parishioner **2.** (*cliente*) customer

parsimonia *f* **1.** (*calma*) calm; (*lentitud*) deliberation; **con** ~ calmly **2.** (*en los gastos*) economy **3.** (*prudencia*) care; (*moderación*) moderation

parsimonioso, -a *adj* **1.** (*tranquilo*) calm; (*flemático*) phlegmatic **2.** (*ahorrador*) economical **3.** (*prudente*) careful; (*moderado*) moderate

parte¹ *f* **1.** (*porción, elemento*) part; (*de repuesto*) spare (part); ~ **alícuota** proportion; ~ **constitutiva** component part; ~ **esencial** vital part; ~ **del león** lion's share; ~ **del mundo** part of the world; **una cuarta** ~ a quarter; **de varias** ~s of several parts; **en** ~ in part; **en gran** ~ largely; **en mayor** ~ for the most part; ~ **por** ~ bit by bit; **tomar** ~ **en algo** to be involved in sth **2.** (*repartición*) division; ~ **hereditaria** share of the inheritance; **tener** ~ **en algo** to have a share in sth; **dar** ~ **a alguien en algo** to give sb a part of sth; **llevarse la peor/mejor** ~ to come off (the) worst/best **3.** (*lugar*) place; **¿a qué** ~ **vas?** where are you going?; **a ninguna** ~ nowhere; **en ninguna** ~ nowhere; **en cualquier** ~ anywhere; **por todas (las)** ~s everywhere; **en otra** ~ somewhere else; **¿de qué** ~ **de España es tu familia?** which part of Spain is your family from?; **no llevar a ninguna** ~ *fig* to lead nowhere **4.** *t.* JUR (*bando*) party; (*en una discusión*) participant; ~ **contratante** contracting party; ~ **laboral** employee **5.** (*lado*) side; ~ **de delante/de atrás** front/back; **dale recuerdos de mi** ~ give him/her my regards; **somos primos por** ~ **de mi padre/de mi madre** we are cousins on my father's/mother's side; **por mi** ~ **puedes hacer lo que quieras** as far as I'm concerned you can do what you like; **estar de ~ de alguien** to be on sb's side; **ponerse de ~ de alguien** to take sb's side; **saber de buena ~** to know from a reliable source; **me tienes de tu ~** I'm on your side; **de ~ a ~** (*de un lado a otro*) from side to side; (*de arriba a abajo*) from top to bottom; **por otra ~** on the other hand; (*además*) what's more **6.**(*sección*) section; (*tomo*) volume; (*capítulo*) chapter **7.** TEAT, MÚS (*papel*) part **8.** *pl* (*genitales*) (private) parts *pl;* **me dio una patada en salva sea la ~** *inf* he gave me a kick in the you-know-whats **9.**(*temporal*) **de primeros de mes a esta ~** from the beginning of this month; **de unos cuantos días a esta ~** a few days from now ▶ **tomar** [*o* **echar**] **algo a mala ~** to take sth as an insult

parte² *m* **1.**(*comunicado*) message; **dar ~** to report; **tienes que dar ~ del robo a la policía** you have to report the theft to the police **2.** RADIO, TV report; **~ meteorológico** weather report

partero, -a *m, f* midwife *f,* male midwife *m;* (*médico*) obstetrician

parterre *m* flower bed

partición *f* **1.**(*acción de partir*) partition **2.** MAT division

participación *f* **1.**(*intervención*) participation; **~ en los beneficios** profit-sharing **2.**(*parte*) share **3.**(*billete*) lottery ticket (*which is shared between several people*); (*parte que se juega*) stake **4.**(*anuncio*) notice; (*aviso*) warning

participante *mf* participant

participar I. *vi* **1.**(*tomar parte*) to participate; **los países participantes** the participating countries; **~ en un juego** to take part in a game; **participo en tu alegría** I share your happiness **2.**(*tener parte*) to have a part; **~ en una herencia** to share in an inheritance **3.**(*tener en común*) **~ de algo** to share sth; **participamos de la misma opinión** we are of the same opinion II. *vt* (*comunicar*) to inform

partícipe I. *adj* involved II. *mf* participant; **~ de algo** person involved in sth; **hacer a alguien ~ de algo** (*compartir*) to share sth with sb; (*informar*) to inform sb of sth

participio *m* LING participle; **~ activo** [*o* **de presente**] present participle; **~ pasivo** [*o* **de pretérito**] past participle

partícula *f* **1.** *t.* FÍS, QUÍM particle; **~ elemental** fundamental particle; **~s de polvo** dust particles **2.** LING particle; **~ prepositiva** prefix

particular¹ I. *adj* **1.**(*propio*) peculiar; (*individual*) individual; (*típico*) typical; (*personal*) personal; **el sabor ~ del azafrán** the special flavour [*o* flavor *Am*] of saffron **2.**(*raro*) peculiar **3.**(*extraordinario*) unusual; **caso ~** unusual case; **en ~** in particular; **posee un talento ~ para dibujar** he has a special talent for drawing **4.**(*privado*) private; **envíamelo a mi domicilio ~** send it to my home address

5.(*determinado*) particular; **tenemos que concentrarnos en este problema ~** we must concentrate on this particular problem II. *mf* private individual; (*civil*) civilian

particular² *m* matter

particularidad *f* **1.**(*especialidad*) speciality *Brit,* specialty *Am;* (*singularidad*) distinctive feature; (*peculiaridad*) peculiarity; **la ~ de este método estriba en que...** the distinctive feature of this method is that ... **2.**(*rareza*) peculiarity **3.**(*detalle*) detail; (*circunstancia*) circumstance; **las ~es del crimen** the circumstances of the crime **4.**(*en el trato*) intimacy

particularizar <z→c> I. *vt* **1.**(*explicar*) to go into details about **2.**(*mostrar preferencia*) to favour *Brit,* to favor *Am* **3.**(*personalizar*) **~ en alguien** to make references to sb **4.**(*distinguir*) to distinguish; **sus saques particularizan su estilo de jugar** the distinctive feature of his/her style of play is his/her serve II. *vi* (*explicar*) to go into details

particularmente *adv* particularly

partida *f* **1.**(*salida*) departure **2.**(*envío*) consignment **3.** FIN item; **~ doble** double entry **4.**(*anotación*) entry; (*certificado*) certificate; **~ de defunción** death certificate **5.**(*juego*) game; **jugar una ~ de ajedrez** to play a game of chess **6.**(*grupo*) party; MIL faction; (*en un juego*) team; (*excursión*) trip; **~ de campo** excursion (to the country) **7.**(*muerte*) death **8.**(*lugar*) place

partidario, -a I. *adj* **1.**(*parcial*) biased **2.**(*seguidor*) **ser ~ de algo** to be in favour [*o* favor *Am*] of sth II. *m, f* **1.**(*seguidor*) follower; (*afiliado*) member; (*de un proyecto, una idea*) supporter **2.**(*guerrillero*) partisan

partidismo *m* **1.**(*parcialidad*) bias; (*a favor de un partido*) political bias, partisanism **2.** POL party loyalty

partido *m* **1.** POL party; **~ de clase media** middle-class party; **~ de derecha(s)/de izquierda(s)** left-wing/right-wing party; **~ obrero** worker's party; **~ pequeño** minority party; **~ popular** people's party; **sistema de ~ único** one-party system **2.**(*grupo*) group; **formar ~** to band together; **esta idea tiene mucho ~** this idea has a lot of supporters; **el candidato tenía cada vez menos ~** the candidate had less and less support; **la película tuvo mucho ~ en el extranjero** the film was very successful abroad **3.** DEP (*juego*) match; **~ amistoso** friendly **4.**(*equipo*) team **5.**(*para casarse*) match; **encontrar un buen ~** to make quite a catch **6.** ADMIN district; **~ judicial** administrative area; **cabeza de ~** administrative centre [*o* center *Am*] **7.**(*determinación*) determination; **tomar ~ a favor de algo/alguien** (*inclinarse*) to lean towards sth/sb; (*opinar*) to express an opinion on sth/sb; (*decidirse*) to choose sth/sb; **tomar ~** MIL to enlist **8.**(*provecho*) advantage; **de esto aún se puede sacar ~** sth can still be made of this;

no sacarás ~ de él you'll get nothing out of him/her; **saqué** ~ **del asunto** I profited from the affair **9.** *AmL* (*del pelo*) parting
partido, -a *adj* (*liberal*) generous
partidor *m* divider
partir I. *vt* **1.** *t.* MAT (*dividir*) to divide; ~ **por la mitad** to divide into two halves; **estar a ~ un piñon** to be thick as thieves **2.** (*romper*) to break; (*madera*) to chop; (*una nuez*) to crack; ~ **el pan** REL to break bread; ~ **la cabeza a alguien** to crack sb's head open **3.** (*repartir*) to share out; (*clasificar*) to classify **4.** (*compartir*) to share **5.** (*una baraja*) to cut **II.** *vi* **1.** (*tomar como base*) to start; **a ~ de ahora** from now on; **a ~ de mañana** from tomorrow; **a ~ de las seis** from six o'clock onwards; **a ~ de entonces** since then **2.** (*salir de viaje*) to leave; (*ponerse en marcha*) to start; **partimos de Cádiz a las cinco** we left Cadiz at five o'clock **III.** *vr* **1.** (*rajarse*) to split; (*cristal*) to crack **2.** *inf* (*de risa*) ~**se** (**de risa**) to split one's sides laughing
partisano, -a *m, f* partisan
partitivo, -a *adj* **1.** LING partitive **2.** (*que se puede partir*) divisible; (*que se puede romper*) breakable
partitura *f* MÚS score; (*hojas*) sheet music
parto *m* (*alumbramiento*) birth; ~ **prematuro** premature birth; **dolores de** ~ labour [*o* labor *Am*] pains *pl;* **estar de** ~ to be in labour [*o* labor *Am*]; **esto es el** ~ **de los montes** *fig* this is an anticlimax
parturienta *f* **1.** (*que está de parto*) woman in labour [*o* labor *Am*] **2.** (*que acaba de parir*) woman who has just given birth
parva *f* **1.** AGR unthreshed grain **2.** (*montón*) heap
parvedad *f* **1.** (*escasez*) scarcity; (*pequeñez*) smallness; (*poquedad*) fewness **2.** (*para comer*) morsel
parvo, -a *adj* (*pequeño*) small; (*escaso*) scarce
parvulario *m* kindergarten; (*educación preescolar*) nursery school, preschool *Am*
párvulo, -a *m, f* infant; **escuela de** ~**s** nursery school, preschool *Am;* **clase de** ~**s** nursery class
pasa *f* (*uva seca*) raisin; ~ **de Corinto** currant; **helado de ron y** ~**s** rum and raisin ice cream; **estar hecho una** ~ *inf* to be as shrivelled [*o* shriveled *Am*] as a prune
pasable *adj* passable
pasabocas *m inv,* *Col* (*tapas*) appetizer
pasacalle *m* MÚS passacaglia; (*marcha*) lively march
pasada *f* **1.** (*paso*) passing; **hacer varias** ~**s** to make several passes; **de** ~ when passing; *fig* in passing **2.** (*mano*) going-over; (*pintura*) coat; **dar una** ~ **a algo** to give sth another going-over; **dar otra** ~ **con agua limpia** to give another wipe with clean water **3.** *inf* (*comportamiento*) excess; **¡vaya** (**mala**) ~**!** what a thing to do!; **hacer una mala** ~ **a alguien** to play a dirty trick on sb **4.** *inf* (*exagera-*

ción) **¡es una** ~**!** it's way over the top! **5.** (*puntada*) tacking [*o* basting *Am*] stitch; (*costura*) row of stitches; **dar unas** ~**s a algo** to tack sth, baste sth *Am* **6.** (*con la plancha*) **sólo le voy a dar una** ~ I'm just going to give it a quick iron **7.** (*en un juego*) pass
pasadero, -a *adj* passable
pasadizo *m* (*pasillo*) corridor; (*entre dos calles*) alley; ~ **secreto** secret passageway
pasado *m* (*tiempo, vida*) past; LING past (tense); **en el** ~ in the past; **son cosas del** ~ it's all in the past
pasado, -a *adj* **1.** (*de atrás*) past; **el año** ~ last year; **la conferencia del año** ~ last year's conference; ~ **mañana** the day after tomorrow; ~**s dos meses** after two months; ~ **de moda** out of fashion; (*vestido*) unfashionable **2.** (*estropeado: alimentos*) bad; (*fruta*) overripe; (*leche*) off, sour; (*mantequilla*) rancid; (*ropa*) worn-out; (*flores*) wilted; **el yogur está** ~ **de fecha** the yogurt is past its sell-by date **3.** (*muy cocido*) overcooked; **¿quieres el filete muy** ~**?** do you want the steak very well done?; **un huevo** ~ **por agua** a soft-boiled egg
pasador *m* **1.** (*alfiler*) pin; (*imperdible*) safety pin; (*broche*) clip; (*de corbata*) tiepin **2.** (*para el cabello*) hairclip, slide *Brit*, barrette *Am* **3.** (*cerrojo*) bolt **4.** (*colador*) colander **5.** *pl* (*gemelos*) cufflinks *pl*
pasadores *mpl* **1.** (*botón*) cufflinks *pl* **2.** *Perú* (*cordones*) shoelaces *pl*
pasaje *m* **1.** (*acción de pasar*) passing; (*de una calle, un territorio*) crossing **2.** (*derecho*) toll **3.** (*en barco*) voyage **4.** (*billete de avión*) (plane) ticket; (*de barco*) (boat) ticket; (*precio*) fare **5.** (*pasajeros*) passengers *pl* **6.** (*pasillo*) passage; ~ **subterráneo** underground passage **7.** (*estrecho*) strait
pasajero, -a I. *adj* **1.** (*transitorio, breve*) passing; (*fugaz*) fleeting **2.** (*calle, plaza*) busy **II.** *m, f* (*viajero*) passenger; **tren de** ~**s** passenger train
pasamano(s) *m(pl)* handrail
pasamontañas *m inv* balaclava, ski mask *Am*
pasante I. *adj* (*viajante*) travelling *Brit*, traveling *Am* **II.** *mf* **1.** (*auxiliar*) assistant; (*de un abogado*) articled clerk; ~ **de pluma** clerk **2.** (*profesor*) tutor
pasapalos *m inv, Méx, Ven* (*tapas*) appetizer
pasaporte *m* (*para viajar*) passport; **dar** (**el**) ~ **a alguien** *inf* (*despedirlo*) to give sb their marching orders; (*matarlo*) to bump sb off
pasapuré(s) *m* (*inv*) vegetable mill; (*patatas*) potato masher
pasar I. *vi* **1.** (*por delante*) to pass; ~ **corriendo** to run past; ~ **desapercibido** to go unnoticed; ~ **de largo** to go past; **pásate un momento por mi casa** drop round to my house; **dejar** ~ (*por delante*) to allow to go past; ~ **por encima de** (*un obstáculo*) to overcome; (*una persona*) to overlook; **el avión pasó por encima de los Pirineos** the plane flew over the Pyrenees; ~ **por alto** *fig* to leave

out; **no dejes ~ la oportunidad** don't miss the opportunity **2.** (*por un hueco*) to go through; **el sofá no pasa por la puerta** the sofa won't go through the door; **el Ebro pasa por Zaragoza** the Ebro flows through Zaragoza; **~ por una crisis** to go through a crisis **3.** (*trasladarse*) to move; **pasemos al comedor** let's go to the dining room **4.** (*acaecer*) to happen; **¿qué pasa?** what's up?; **¿qué te pasa?** what's wrong?; **pase lo que pase** whatever happens; **dejar ~ algo** to allow sth to happen; **lo que pasa es que...** the thing is that ... **5.** (*acabar*) to pass; **ya ha pasado la tormenta** the storm has passed; **cuando pasen las vacaciones...** when the holidays are over ... **6.** (*el tiempo*) to pass; **han pasado dos semanas sin llover** we have had two weeks without rain; **lo pasado, pasado** what's done is done **7.** (*ser transferido*) to be transferred **8.** (*poder existir*) to get by; **vamos pasando** we manage **9.** (*aparentar*) to pass for; **pasa por nuevo** it looks new; **podrías ~ por inglesa** you could be taken for an Englishwoman; **hacerse ~ por médico** to pass oneself off as a doctor **10.** (*cambiar*) to go; **paso a explicar porqué** and now I will (go on to) explain why; **~ a mayores** to go from bad to worse **11.** (*ser admisible*) to pass; **arreglándolo aún puede ~** if we fix it it should still be okay; **~ por un control** to pass a checkpoint **12.** (*no jugar*) to pass **13.** *inf* (*no necesitar*) **yo paso de salir** I don't want to go out; **paso de esta película** I can't be bothered with this film; **pasa de todo** he/she couldn't care less about anything **II.** *vt* **1.** (*atravesar*) to cross; **~ el puente** to cross the bridge; **~ el semáforo en rojo** to go through a red light **2.** (*por un hueco*) to go through; **~ la tarjeta por la ranura** to swipe the card through the slot; **~ algo por debajo de la puerta** to slide sth under the door **3.** (*trasladar*) to transfer; **~ a limpio** to make a fair copy **4.** (*dar*) to pass; **~ la pelota** to pass the ball **5.** (*una temporada*) to spend; **~ el invierno en Mallorca** to spend the winter in Majorca; **~lo bien/mal** to have a good/bad time; **~lo en grande** to have a whale of a time; **¡que lo paséis bien!** enjoy yourselves! **6.** (*sufrir*) to experience; **~ hambre** to go hungry; **~ frío** to feel the cold; **has pasado mucho** you have been through a lot; **pasé un mal rato** I went through a difficult time **7.** (*transmitir*) to send; (*una película*) to show; (*una noticia*) to broadcast; (*dinero*) to give; **~ un recado** to pass on a message; **me has pasado el resfriado** you've given me your cold; **le paso a la Sra. Ortega** I'll put you through to Señora Ortega **8.** (*sobrepasar*) to exceed; (*cierta edad*) to be older than; **he pasado los treinta** I am over thirty; **te paso en altura** I am taller than you **9.** (*hacer deslizar*) **~ la mano por la mesa** to run one's hand over the table; **~ la aspiradora** to vacuum **10.** (*tolerar*) to allow to pass **11.** (*aprobar*) to

pass **12.** (*omitir*) to overlook **13.** (*leer sin atención*) to skim **14.** (*repasar*) to check; (*estudiar*) to study **15.** (*tragar*) to swallow; **no puedo ~me la pastilla** I can't swallow the pill **16.** (*colar*) to strain **17.** (*las hojas de un libro*) to turn **18.** (*géneros prohibidos*) to smuggle **III.** *vr* **1.** (*acabarse*) to pass; **se me han pasado las ganas** I don't feel like it any more; **ya se le ~á el enfado** his anger will soon subside; **~se de fecha** to miss a deadline **2.** (*exagerar*) to go too far; **~se de la raya** to go over the line; **~se de listo** to be too clever by half; **te has pasado de listo** you've been too clever for your own good; **te has pasado un poco con la sal** you've overdone the salt a bit **3.** (*por un sitio*) to visit; **me pasé un rato por casa de mi tía** I popped round to my aunt's house for a while; **se me pasó por la cabeza que...** it occurred to me that ...; **no se te pasará ni por la imaginación** you'll never be able to guess; **~se la mano por el pelo** to run one's hand through one's hair **4.** *t.* MIL (*cambiar*) to go over; **se ha pasado de trabajadora a perezosa** she has gone from being hard-working to being lazy **5.** (*olvidarse*) to be forgotten; **se me pasó tu cumpleaños** I forgot your birthday **6.** (*estropearse: alimentos, leche*) to spoil, to go off; (*fruta*) to overripen; (*mantequilla*) to go rancid; (*flores*) to wilt; **se ha pasado el arroz** the rice is overcooked; **~se de moda** to go out of fashion **7.** (*escaparse*) to be missed; **se me pasó la oportunidad** I missed my chance; **se me pasó el turno** I missed my turn

pasarela *f* **1.** (*para desfiles*) catwalk **2.** (*de un barco*) gangway **3.** (*puente provisional*) temporary bridge; (*para peatones*) walkway

pasarratos *m inv,* **pasatiempo** *m* **1.** (*diversión*) pastime; **los pasatiempos del periódico** the games and puzzles section of the newspaper **2.** (*hobby*) hobby

pascana *f* **1.** *AmS* (*etapa de un viaje*) stage **2.** *Arg, Bol, Perú* (*posada*) wayside inn

Pascua *f* **1.** (*de resurrección*) Easter; **~ Florida** Easter Sunday; **mona de ~** Easter cake; **de ~s a Ramos** once in a blue moon; **hacer la ~ a alguien** *inf* to do the dirty on sb **2.** (*fiesta judía*) Passover **3.** *pl* (*navidad*) Christmas time; **dar las ~s a alguien** to wish sb a merry Christmas **4.** *pl* (*pentecostés*) Whitsun ▶**tener cara de ~(s)** *inf* to be glowing with happiness; **¡y santas ~s!** and that's that!; **estar como una(s) ~(s)** to be over the moon

pascual *adj* **1.** (*relativo a la pascua cristiana*) Easter **2.** (*relativo a la pascua judía*) Passover **3.** (*navideño*) Christmas **4.** (*de pentecostés*) Whitsun

pase *m* **1.** (*desfile*) parade; (*de moda*) fashion show **2.** DEP pass **3.** CINE showing **4.** (*en los naipes*) pass **5.** *t.* MIL (*permiso*) pass; (*licencia*) licence *Brit,* license *Am;* (*para entrar gratis*) free pass; (*para viajar en tren*) rail pass; **~ (de transporte**) travel pass **6.** *AmL* (*pasaporte*) passport

paseandero, -a adj CSur fond of walking; **mi madre es a pesar de sus años muy paseandera** despite her age, my mother walks a lot
paseante mf walker; ~ (**en corte**) inf loafer
pasear I. vt **1.** (en coche) to take for a ride; (a pie) to take for a walk; ~ **al perro** to walk the dog; ~ **a un caballo** to exercise a horse **2.** (llevar a todas las partes) to take sb around **II.** vi, vr **1.** (a pie) to go for a walk; (en coche) to go for a drive; (a caballo) to ride **2.** (caballo) to trot **III.** vr (estar ocioso) to hang about
paseo m **1.** (a pie) walk; (en coche, a caballo) ride; (en barco) trip; **dar un** ~ to go for a walk; **¡vete a** ~**!** get lost!; **mandar a alguien a** ~ to tell sb to get lost **2.** (para pasear) avenue; ~ **marítimo** promenade, esplanade **3.** (distancia) short walk; **de aquí al colegio sólo hay un** ~ it's only a short walk from here to the school
pasillo m (corredor) passage; (entre habitaciones, pisos) corridor, hallway
pasión f **1.** (ardor) passion; ~ **de ánimo** melancholy; **con** ~ passionately; **sin** ~ without enthusiasm **2.** (afecto) passion; (preferencia) preference; **sentir** ~ **por el fútbol** to be passionate about football **3.** (de Jesucristo) Passion
pasional adj **1.** (ardiente) passionate; **crimen** ~ crime of passion **2.** REL Passion
pasionaria f **1.** (flor) passionflower **2.** (fruto) passion fruit
pasiva f LING passive
pasividad f passivity, passiveness
pasivo m **1.** (deuda) liabilities pl **2.** (en el balance) debit side **3.** (pensión) pension
pasivo, -a I. adj **1.** t. LING passive; **verbo** ~ passive verb; **voz pasiva** passive **2.** ECON **haber** ~ pension; **las clases** ~**s** pensioners **II.** m, f pensioner
pasmado, -a I. adj (asombrado) amazed; (torpe) slow **II.** m, f idiot
pasmar I. vt **1.** (asombrar) to astonish; **me has dejado pasmado** you have left me completely stunned; **no te quedes pasmado** don't just stand there **2.** (enajenar) to enthuse **3.** (aturdir) to bewilder **4.** (enfriar) to chill; **la helada ha pasmado las lechugas** the frost has spoilt the lettuces **II.** vr **1.** (asombrarse) to be astonished **2.** (quedar fascinado) ~**se ante algo** to be fascinated by sth **3.** (helarse) to freeze; (planta) to be affected by frost
pasmo m **1.** (asombro) astonishment; (admiración) wonder **2.** (objeto) marvel; **ser el** ~ **de alguien** inf (asombrar) to astonish sb
pasmoso, -a adj amazing
paso I. m **1.** (acción de pasar) passing; (en coche) overtaking; **al** ~ on the way; **me salió al** ~ **en el pasillo** he waylaid me in the corridor; **ceder el** ~ (a una persona) to make way; (en el tráfico) to give way, to yield Am; **estar de** ~ to be passing through; **al** ~ **que come ve la tele** when eating, he watches TV; **de** ~

(indirectamente) by the way; **de** ~ **que vas al centro, puedes llevarme a la estación** on your way to the centre [o center Am], you could take me to the station; **nadie salió al** ~ **de sus mentiras** nobody put a stop to his lies **2.** (movimiento) step; (progreso) progress; **bailar a** ~ **de vals** to dance a waltz; **ir al** ~ to keep in step; **llevar el** ~ **al ritmo de una melodía** to march in time to a tune; **marcar el** ~ to mark the rhythm [o time]; **a cada** ~ at every step; **a** ~ **llano** smoothly; ~ **a** ~ step by step; **contar los** ~**s a alguien** to watch sb's every move; **dar un** ~ **adelante/atrás** to take a step forwards/backwards; **dar un** ~ **en falso** to trip; fig to make a false move; **he dado un enorme** ~ **en mis investigaciones** I have made enormous progress in my research **3.** (velocidad) pace; **a** ~**s agigantados** with giant steps; fig by leaps and bounds; **a buen** ~ quickly; **a** ~ **de tortuga** at snail's pace; **a este** ~ **no llegarás** at this speed you'll never get there; **a este** ~ **no conseguirás nada** fig at this rate you won't achieve anything **4.** (sonido) footstep; (de un caballo) sound of horse's hooves **5.** (manera de andar) walk; **salir de su** ~ to change one's ways **6.** (pisada) footprint; (de un animal) track; **seguir los** ~**s de alguien** to follow sb; fig to follow in sb's footsteps; **volver sobre sus** ~**s** to retrace one's steps **7.** (distancia) pace; **vive a dos** ~**s de mi casa** he lives very near to my house **8.** (pasillo) passage; (en el mar) strait; (entre montañas) pass; ~ **subterráneo** underground passage; **abrirse** ~ to open up a path for oneself; fig to make one's way; **esta puerta da** ~ **al jardín** this door leads to the garden; **¡prohibido el** ~**!** (pasar) no throughfare! Brit, no thruway; (entrar) no entry!; **andar en malos** ~**s** to fall into bad ways; **con este dinero puedo salir del** ~ with this money I can solve my problems; **sólo lo has dicho para salir del** ~ you only did it to get out of a jam **9.** (para atravesar algo) crossing; ~ **de cebra** zebra crossing; ~ **a nivel** level crossing; **¡**~**!** make way!; ~ **de ecuador** halfway point **10.** (medida) step; **dar todos los** ~**s necesarios** to take all the necessary steps; **no dar** ~ not to do anything **11.** (de un contador) unit; **marcar los** ~**s** to count the units **12.** (de un escrito) passage **II.** adv gently
pasota I. adj inf apathetic **II.** mf inf drop-out; **es un** ~ **total** he/she doesn't give a damn about anything
paspadura f AmS chapped skin
pasquín m wall poster
pasta f **1.** (masa) paste; (para un pastel) pastry; (para paredes) filler; (para madera, ventanas) putty; ~ **de dientes** toothpaste **2.** (comida italiana) pasta **3.** (pastelería) pastries pl **4.** (encuadernación) cover; **de** ~ **dura/blanda** hardback/softback **5.** inf (dinero) dough **6.** (madera) pulp; **tener** ~ **para algo** to be cut out for sth; **tiene** ~ **para**

ser ministro he's got what it takes to be a minister; tener buena ~ to be good-natured

pastar *vt, vi* to graze

pastel *m* 1.(*tarta*) cake; (*bollo*) pastry; (*de carne, pescado*) pie 2.(*lápiz*) pastel crayon 3.(*pintura*) pastel 4.(*chapucería*) botch 5.(*asunto*) descubrir el ~ to catch on; vámonos antes de que se descubra el ~ let's go before we get found out

pastelear *vi* 1.(*contemporizar*) to stall 2.(*chanchullear*) to wangle

pastelería *f* 1.(*comercio*) pastry shop; (*arte*) pastrymaking 2.(*pasteles*) pastries *pl*

pastelero, -a *m, f* 1.(*repostero*) pastrycook 2.(*contemporizador*) staller; ser un ~ to go with the flow, to be spineless

pastelillo *m* (*dulce*) pastry; (*de carne, pescado*) pie

pastelón *m* 1.GASTR large meat pie 2.AmL (*loseta para pavimentar*) large paving stone

pasteurizar <z→c> *vt* to pasteurize

pastiche *m* pastiche

pastilla *f* 1.(*medicinal*) tablet; ~ contra el dolor painkiller; ~ para la garganta throat lozenge; ~ para la tos cough drop 2.(*dulce*) sweet, candy *Am;* ~ de café con leche coffee-flavoured sweet *Brit,* coffee-flavored candy *Am* 3.(*trozo*) piece; ~ de caldo stock cube; ~ de chocolate bar of chocolate; ~ de jabón bar of soap; ir a toda ~ *inf* to go at full pelt

pastizal *m* pasture

pasto *m* 1.(*pastura*) grazing 2.(*pastizal*) pasture 3.(*hierba*) grass; ~ seco fodder 4.(*alimento*) feed 5.(*materia, rumores*) food; ser ~ de las llamas to go up in flames; ser ~ de la murmuración to be the subject of gossip 6.(*en abundancia*) a todo ~ at full pelt; pudimos beber y comer a ~ we ate and drank our fill 7.(*vino*) de ~ ordinary; vino de ~ table wine

pastor *m* 1.REL minister; (*obispo*) bishop 2.ZOOL ~ alemán Alsatian *Brit,* German shepherd *Am;* perro ~ sheepdog

pastor(a) *m(f)* (*de ganado*) herdsman *m;* (*de ovejas*) shepherd

pastorear *vt* 1.(*cuidar el ganado*) to look after; (*llevarlo a los pastos*) to graze 2.REL to guide 3.AmC (*mimar*) to spoil 4.AmL (*atisbar*) to spy on

pastoreo *m* grazing

pastoso, -a *adj* 1.(*blando*) soft 2.(*pegajoso*) sticky; (*espeso*) thick; lengua pastosa furred tongue 3.(*voz*) mellow 4.AmL (*región*) grassy

pata *f* 1.*inf* ANAT leg; (*de un perro, un gato*) paw; (*de una silla, una mesa*) leg; ~ de gallo BOT goosefoot; (*dibujo*) check; ~s de gallo (*en el rostro*) crow's feet; ~ de palo wooden leg; mala ~ *inf* bad luck; estirar la ~ *inf* to kick the bucket; ir a ~ *inf* to go on foot; ~s arriba

upside down; la habitación está ~s arriba the room has been turned upside down; poner todo ~s arriba to turn everything upside down; a la ~ coja hopping; a (la) ~ llana simply; a cuatro ~s on all fours; meter la ~ *inf* (*cometer una indiscreción*) to put one's foot in it; poner a alguien de ~s en la calle *inf* to throw sb out 2.ZOOL (female) duck

patada *f* 1.(*contra algo*) kick; (*en el suelo*) stamp; dar una ~ contra la pared to kick the wall; dar ~s en el suelo to stamp one's feet; romper una puerta a ~s to kick a door down; dar la ~ a alguien to give sb the boot; me da cien ~s he/she really gets on my nerves; echar a alguien a ~s to kick sb out; tratar a alguien a ~s to treat sb like dirt; a ~s *fig* by the bucketload 2.*inf* (*paso*) step; (*de un caballo*) pace; esto me ha costado muchas ~s *fig* I've really had to work hard for this 3.(*huella de un pie*) footmark; (*de una pata*) pawprint

Patagonia *f* Patagonia; ir a la ~ to go to Patagonia

Patagonia lies in the southernmost part of Chile and Argentina, to the south of the Pampa. Unlike the Pampa, this vast, scantily cultivated, barren steppe is unsuited to the growth of cereals and is used mainly for rearing sheep.

---

patalear *vi* to kick; (*en el suelo*) to stamp one's feet; está que patalea he is furious; (*niño*) to throw a tantrum

pataleo *m* 1.(*acción de patalear*) kicking; (*en el suelo, ruido*) stamping 2.(*queja*) complaint; derecho al ~ *inf* right to complain

patán I. *adj* rustic; ser ~ *fig* to be uncouth II. *m* yokel, hick *Am*

patata *f* 1.potato; ~s fritas chips *pl Brit,* French fries *pl Am;* una bolsa de ~s fritas a bag of crisps *Brit,* a bag of potato chips *Am;* tortilla de ~ Spanish omelette [*o* omelet *Am*]; puré de ~(s) mashed potatoes 2.*inf* (*basura*) dud; este ordenador es una ~ this computer is a piece of junk ►no entender ni ~ *inf* (*palabra*) not to understand a single word; (*ser tonto*) to be completely stupid; ¡~! (*al hacer una foto*) cheese!

patatús *m inv, inf* (*desmayo*) faint; le dio un ~ he/she fainted; (*ataque*) fit

patear I. *vt* 1.(*dar golpes*) to kick; ~ el estómago a alguien to kick sb in the stomach 2.(*pisotear*) to trample 3.(*tratar rudamente*) to trample on II. *vi* 1.(*en el suelo*) to stamp; (*estar enfadado*) to be furious 2.(*andar mucho*) to tramp about; estar pateando todo el día to spend the whole day walking; tuve que ~ para tener este éxito I had to work really hard for this success

patentar *vt* to patent

patente I. *adj* 1.(*visible*) clear 2.(*evidente*)

patent; **hacer** ~ to establish; (*comprobar*) to prove; (*revelar*) to reveal **II.** *f* **1.** (*documento*) licence *Brit,* license *Am;* (*permiso*) permit; ~ **de comercio** trading permit [*o* license *Am*]; ~ **de sanidad** bill of health **2.** (*título*) title; ~ **de piloto** pilot's licence **3.** JUR patent; ~ **industrial** industrial patent; ~ **pendiente** patent pending; ~ **de privilegio** letters patent; **solicitar la** ~ to apply for a patent

patentizar <z→c> *vt* to make evident; (*comprobar*) to prove; (*revelar*) to reveal

patera *f* small boat

paternal *adj* paternal; **amor** ~ paternal [*o* fatherly] love

paternalismo *m* paternalism

paternidad *f* **1.** (*relación*) fatherhood; JUR paternity **2.** (*calidad*) fatherliness **3.** REL **Vuestra Paternidad** Father

paterno, -a *adj* paternal; **casa paterna** parental home; **mi abuelo** ~ my paternal grandfather

patero, -a **I.** *adj Chile* bootlicking **II.** *m, f Chile* bootlicker

patético, -a *adj* **1.** (*conmovedor*) moving; (*tierno*) tender; (*manifestando dolor*) painful **2.** *pey* (*exagerado*) pathetic

patibulario, -a *adj* **1.** (*relativo al patíbulo*) gallows; **horca patibularia** gallows *pl* **2.** (*terrible*) horrifying; **novela patibularia** horrifying novel

patíbulo *m* scaffold; (*horca*) gallows *pl*

patidifuso, -a *adj* stunned; (*de horror*) aghast; **me quedé** ~ I was aghast

patilla *f* **1.** (*de unas gafas*) sidepiece; (*de un madero*) peg **2.** *pl* (*pelo*) sideburns *pl*

patín *m* **1.** (*de hielo*) ice skate; (*de ruedas*) roller skate; **patines en línea** rollerblades **2.** (*patinete*) scooter **3.** (*de vela*) catamaran; (*de pedales*) pedal boat **4.** (*tabla*) skateboard **5.** TÉC shoe

patinador(a) **I.** *adj* skating **II.** *m(f)* (*de hielo*) (ice) skater; (*sobre ruedas*) (roller) skater; (*artístico sobre hielo*) ice dancer; (*sobre ruedas*) roller skate dancer; (*de velocidad*) speed skater

patinaje *m* **1.** (*sobre hielo*) (ice) skating; (*sobre ruedas*) (roller) skating; ~ **artístico** (*sobre hielo*) figure skating; (*sobre ruedas*) roller dancing *Brit;* ~ **de velocidad** speed skating **2.** (*deslizamiento*) slip; (*de un vehículo*) skid

patinar *vi* **1.** (*sobre patines de hielo*) to (ice) skate; (*sobre patines de ruedas*) to (roller) skate **2.** (*deslizarse*) to slip; (*un vehículo*) to skid **3.** (*equivocarse*) to slip up

patinazo *m* **1.** (*deslizamiento*) slip; (*de un vehículo*) skid **2.** *inf* (*equivocación*) blunder

patinete *m* scooter

patio *m* **1.** ARQUIT (*interior*) courtyard; (*entre dos casas*) back yard; ~ **de recreo** playground **2.** TEAT pit

patiperrear *vi Chile* to traipse around

patitieso, -a *adj* **1.** (*paralizado*) paralysed

Brit, Aus, paralyzed *Am;* (*de frío*) frozen stiff; **quedarse** ~ **de frío** to be frozen stiff **2.** (*sorprendido*) stunned; **quedarse** ~ to be struck dumb **3.** (*presumido*) stuck-up

patito, -a *adj AmL* primrose yellow

patizambo, -a *adj* knock-kneed and/or bow-legged

pato, -a *m, f* **1.** ZOOL duck; (*macho*) drake **2.** *inf* (*torpe*) clumsy person ▶ **estar hecho un** ~ (**de agua**) *inf* to be extremely dull; **pagar el** ~ *inf* to carry the can

patochada *f* (*tontería*) piece of nonsense; **decir** ~**s** to talk rubbish

patógeno, -a *adj* MED pathogen; **germen** ~ harmful germ

patojo, -a **I.** *adj* crooked-legged; (*como un pato*) waddling **II.** *m, f Col, Guat* kid *inf*

patología *f* MED pathology

patológico, -a *adj t. fig* pathological

patólogo, -a *m, f* MED pathologist

patoso, -a *adj* **1.** (*soso*) boring **2.** (*torpe*) clumsy

patraña *f* lie, pack of lies

patria *f* native land; ~ **adoptiva** adoptive homeland; ~ **celestial** heaven; **madre** ~ mother country; *AmL* Spain

patriada *f CSur* rising

patriarca *m t.* REL patriarch

patrimonial *adj* hereditary; **bien** ~ inheritance

patrimonio *m* **1.** (*herencia*) inheritance; ~ **cultural** cultural heritage **2.** (*riqueza*) wealth

patrio, -a *adj* **1.** (*relativo a la patria*) native **2.** (*relativo al padre*) paternal

patriota **I.** *adj* patriotic **II.** *mf* **1.** (*que ama a su patria*) patriot **2.** (*compatriota*) compatriot

patriotero, -a **I.** *adj* jingoistic **II.** *m, f* jingoist

patriótico, -a *adj* patriotic

patriotismo *m* **1.** (*del patriota*) patriotism **2.** (*del patriotero*) jingoism

patrocinador(a) *m(f) t.* DEP sponsor

patrocinar *vt t.* DEP to sponsor

patrocinio *m* **1.** (*protección*) patronage **2.** DEP sponsorship

patrón *m* **1.** (*modelo*) model; (*de costura*) pattern **2.** FIN ~ **monetario** monetary standard

patrón, -ona *m, f* **1.** (*que protege*) patron *m,* patroness *f* **2.** (*jefe*) boss **3.** (*de una casa*) head; (*de una pensión*) landlord *m,* landlady *f* **4.** (*santo*) patron saint

patronal **I.** *adj* (*empresario*) employers'; **cierre** ~ lockout **II.** *f* **1.** (*asociación*) employers' organization **2.** (*fiesta*) **fiesta** ~ patron saint's day

patronato *m* **1.** (*protección*) patronage **2.** ECON employers' organization **3.** (*fundación*) foundation **4.** (*junta directiva*) board

patrono, -a *m, f* **1.** (*jefe*) boss **2.** (*de un feudo*) landowner **3.** (*miembro del patronato*) board member **4.** REL patron saint

patrulla *f t.* MIL (*de policía*) patrol; **estar de** ~ to be on patrol

patrullar *vi, vt* to patrol

patucos mpl (*para bebés*) bootees pl; (*para mayores*) bedsocks pl

patuleco, -a adj AmC, AmS (*de pies*) lame; (*de piernas*) bow-legged

paturro, -a adj Col short and stocky

pauiar m (*pantano*) marsh

paulatinamente adv gradually

paulatino, -a adj gradual

paupérrimo, -a adj superl de **pobre**

pausa f pause; con ~ unhurriedly

pausado, -a adj deliberate

pauta f 1. (*modelo*) guide 2. (*normas*) standard; **marcar la** ~ to set the example [o standard] 3. (*falsilla*) lines pl (*on writing paper*) 4. (*regla*) rule

pautado, -a adj lined

pava f 1. ZOOL v. **pavo, -a** 2. AmL (*olla*) pot; (*tetera*) tea kettle 3. AmL (*sombrero*) straw hat 4. And, AmC (*flecos*) fringe ▸**pelar la** ~ inf (*los enamorados*) to court

pavada f 1. CSur (*disparate*) piece of foolishness 2. CSur (*poquísimo*) pittance 3. AmC (*mala suerte*) piece of bad luck

pavear I. vi 1. CSur (*hacer el tonto*) to fool about 2. CSur (*pelar la pava*) to court II. vt 1. And, CSur (*bromear*) to play a joke on 2. And (*asesinar*) to bump off

pavimentar vt (*con adoquín, con losas*) to pave; (*con asfalto*) to surface

pavimento m 1. (*recubrimiento: en una casa*) flooring; (*en la carretera*) surfacing 2. (*material: en una casa*) floor; (*en una carretera*) surface

pavo m inf (*un duro*) five pesetas; **¡dame diez ~s!** give me fifty pesetas!; (*dólar*) buck Am; **me debes diez ~s** you owe me ten bucks; **soltar el** ~ to pay up

pavo, -a I. m, f 1. ZOOL turkey; ~ **real** peacock 2. (*persona*) idiot; **estar en la edad del** ~ inf to be at an awkward stage (*of one's adolescence*); **comer** ~ inf to be a wallflower; **no es moco de** ~ inf it's not to be scoffed at [o sneezed]; **se me subió el** ~ inf I went as red as a beetroot [o beet Am]; **ir de** ~ AmL to travel for free II. adj idiotic

pavonearse vr to strut (about); ~**se de algo** to show off about sth

pavor m terror

pavoroso, -a adj terrifying

payada f CSur MÚS improvised gaucho minstrel song

payador m CSur gaucho minstrel

payasada f clowning; pey idiotic behaviour Brit [o behavior Am]; **hacer ~s** to clown about

payasear vi to clown about

payaso, -a m, f 1. (*del circo*) clown 2. (*bromista*) joker; **¡deja de hacer el ~!** stop fooling about!

payés, -esa m, f reg peasant farmer (*from Catalonia or the Balearic Isles*)

payo, -a m, f non-gipsy Brit, non-gypsy Am (*gypsy term to refer to people who are not gypsies*)

paz f peace; (*tratado*) peace treaty; **hacer las paces** to make up; **no dar** ~ **a la lengua** not to stop talking; **estar en** ~ **con alguien** to be quits with sb; **¡a la ~ de Dios!** God be with you!; **¡déjame en ~!** leave me alone!; **¡...y en ~!** ... and that's that!; **que en** ~ **descanse** may he/she rest in peace

pazguato, -a I. adj simple II. m, f simpleton

pazo m manor house (*in Galicia*)

PCE m abr de **Partido Comunista Español** Spanish Communist Party

P.D. abr de **posdata** P.S.

pe f p; **de** ~ **a pa** inf from A to Z

peaje m 1. (*de tránsito, de carretera*) toll 2. (*taquilla*) tollbooth

peana f (*pedestal*) pedestal

peatón, -ona m, f pedestrian

peca f freckle

pecado m sin; ~ **capital** deadly sin; ~ **original** original sin; **sin** ~ without sin; fig unblemished; **pagar sus ~s** to pay for one's sins; **sería un** ~ **rechazarlos** it would be a crying shame to reject them; **¡estos niños de mis ~s!** irón, inf these children of mine!; **¡ay, José de mis ~s!** irón, inf oh, my beloved José!

pecador(a) I. adj sinning II. m(f) sinner

pecar <c→qu> vi 1. REL to sin 2. (*errar*) to go astray 3. ~ **por exceso** to go too far; **peca por exceso de confianza** he/she is too confident by half; **éste no peca de hablador** he/she's not exactly talkative

pecarí m AmL ZOOL peccary

pecera f fish tank; (*en forma de globo*) fishbowl

pechada f 1. AmS (*empujón*) shove 2. Arg, inf (*sablazo*) touch for a loan

pechador(a) m(f) Arg, inf sponge(r), moocher Am

pechar vt 1. (*pagar*) to pay 2. (*empujar*) to push 3. Arg, inf (*pedir*) to sponge, to mooch Am; ~ **a alguien** to sponge off sb

pechazo m AmS, inf sponging, mooching Am

pecho m 1. ANAT breast, chest Am; **dar el** ~ **al bebé** to breastfeed the baby; **el bebé toma el** ~ the baby breastfeeds; **a** ~ **descubierto** (*sin armas*) unarmed; fig openly; **dar el** ~ **a alguien** fig to face up to sb; **gritar a todo** ~ to shout at the top of one's voice; **partirse el** ~ **por alguien** to slog one's guts out for sb 2. (*pulmones*) lungs pl 3. (*en la costura*) bust 4. (*conciencia*) heart; **abrir su** ~ **a alguien** to open one's heart to sb; **tomarse algo muy a** ~ to take sth to heart 5. (*coraje*) courage; **¡~ al agua!** courage!

pechuga f 1. (*pecho de ave*) breast; ~ **de pollo** chicken breast 2. inf (*de mujer*) bosom

pechugón, -ona adj 1. inf (*de mucho pecho*) busty 2. AmL (*descarado*) shameless 3. AmL (*franco*) outspoken

pecíolo m leaf stalk

pecoso, -a adj freckly

pectoral I. adj 1. ANAT pectoral 2. (*contra la tos*) cough II. m MED pectoral

pecuario, -a *adj* livestock
pecueca *f Col, Ecua, Ven* **1.** (*pezuña*) hoof **2.** (*olor*) smell of feet
peculiar *adj* **1.** (*especial*) distinctive **2.** (*raro*) peculiar
peculiaridad *f* **1.** (*singularidad*) peculiarity **2.** (*distintivo*) distinguishing feature
peculio *m* private money; **pagar de su ~ to** pay out of one's own money
pedagogía *f sin pl* pedagogy
pedagógico, -a *adj* pedagogical
pedagogo, -a *m, f* educator, teacher
pedal *m* pedal; MÚS (*sordina*) soft pedal; (*bajo*) pedal note; **pisar el ~** AUTO to accelerate
pedalear *vi* to pedal
pedante **I.** *adj* pretentious, pedantic **II.** *mf* pedant
pedantería *f* pedantry
pedazo *m* **1.** (*parte*) (big) piece; **~ de papel** piece of paper; **caerse a ~s** to fall apart, to fall to pieces; **estoy que me caigo a ~s** *inf* I'm absolutely exhausted; **hacerse ~s** to fall to pieces; **hacer ~s** to break; (*madera*) to smash up; (*un pastel*) to cut up; (*papel*) to tear up; (*con tijeras*) to cut to pieces **2.** (*persona*) **~ de mi alma** my darling; **ser un ~ de pan** to be very good-natured; **¡~ de alcornoque/animal!** *inf* you idiot!; **¡~ de bruto!** *inf* you brute!
pederasta *m* pederast
pedernal *m* flint
pedestal *m* **1.** (*cimiento*) pedestal; **poner a alguien en un ~** to put sb on a pedestal **2.** (*apoyo*) base
pedestre *adj* **1.** (*a pie*) pedestrian; **carrera ~** foot race **2.** (*chabacano*) vulgar
pediatra *mf* paediatrician *Brit,* pediatrician *Am*
pediatría *f sin pl* paediatrics *Brit,* pediatrics *Am*
pedicura *f* pedicure; **hacerse la ~** to have a pedicure
pedicuro, -a *m, f* chiropodist
pedida *f* **~ de mano** *asking for sb's hand in marriage*
pedido *m* COM (*de un servicio*) reservation; (*de un producto*) order; **~ suplementario** additional order; **enviar sobre ~** to supply on request; **a ~** to order; **a ~ de** at the request of
pedido, -a *adj* **1.** (*solicitado*) requested; **este anillo ya lo tiene ~ mi nieta** this ring has already been reserved for my granddaughter **2.** (*encargado*) ordered; **el armario ya está ~** the wardrobe has already been ordered
pedigrí *m* pedigree
pedigüeño, -a **I.** *adj* persistent **II.** *m, f* nuisance
pedilón, -ona *adj AmL* persistent
pedimento *m* (*petición*) request
pedinche *mf Méx* (*pedigüeño*) scrounger
pedir *irr vt* **1.** (*rogar*) to ask for; **~ algo a alguien** to ask sb for sth; **os pido que hagáis menos ruido** I'm asking you to make less noise; **~ prestado** to borrow; **a ~ de boca** just

right **2.** (*exigir, cobrar*) to demand; (*necesitar*) to need; (*solicitar, demandar*) to request; **~ a gritos algo** *fig* to be crying out for sth; **una paella que no hay más que ~** a sublime paella **3.** (*encargar*) to order **4.** (*para casarse*) **~ la mano de alguien** to ask for sb's hand in marriage; **~ en matrimonio a alguien** to propose to sb **5.** (*mendigar*) to beg; **~ limosna** to beg; **están pidiendo para la Cruz Roja** they are collecting for the Red Cross
pedo *m inf* **1.** (*ventosidad*) fart; **tirarse un ~** to fart **2.** (*borrachera*) drunkenness; **estar en ~** to be blind drunk; **ponerse en ~** to get blind drunk
pedofilia *f sin pl* paedophilia *Brit,* pedophilia *Am*
pedorrear *vi inf* to fart repeatedly
pedorreta *f inf* raspberry, Bronx cheer *Am;* **hacer una ~ a alguien** to blow a raspberry at sb
pedorro, -a **I.** *adj* (*de pedos*) farting; (*tonto*) stupid; (*pelma*) annoying **II.** *m, f* (*que tira pedos*) farter; (*tonto*) stupid fart; (*pelmazo*) bore, drag
pedrada *f* **1.** (*lanzar*) throw of a stone; **matar a alguien a ~s** to stone sb to death; **pegar una ~ a alguien** to throw a stone at sb **2.** (*ofensa*) wounding remark ▶**sentar algo como una ~** to take sth very badly; **venir como ~ en ojo de boticario** to be just what the doctor ordered
pedrea *f* **1.** (*lanzar pedradas*) stoning; (*pelea*) stone-throwing fight **2.** METEO hailstorm **3.** (*lotería*) small prizes *pl* (*in lottery*)
pedregal *m* stony [*o* rocky] ground
pedregoso, -a *adj* stony
pedregullo *m CSur* gravel
pedrera *f* stone quarry
pedrería *f* (*piedras*) precious stones *pl;* (*joyas*) jewellery *Brit,* jewelry *Am*
pedrisco *m* METEO hail
pedrusco *m* **1.** (*piedra*) lump of stone **2.** *AmL v.* **pedregal**
pedúnculo *m* stalk
pega *f* **1.** *inf* (*dificultades*) difficulty; **poner ~s a** to find fault with; (*desventaja*) drawback, snag **2.** (*pregunta*) trick question **3.** (*falso*) **de ~** fake **4.** *CSur, Méx, inf* (*trabajo*) job
pegada *f CSur* **1.** (*mentira*) lie **2.** (*suerte*) piece of luck
pegadizo, -a **I.** *adj* **1.** (*pegajoso*) sticky; (*enfermedad*) contagious; **melodía pegadiza** catchy tune **2.** (*postizo*) false **3.** (*gorrón*) sponging, freeloading *Am* **II.** *m, f* sponge(r), freeloader *Am*
pegajoso, -a *adj* **1.** (*adhesivo*) sticky, adhesive **2.** (*persona*) tiresome; (*niño*) clinging **3.** MED contagious
pegamento *m* glue; **~ en barra** stick glue; **~ de contacto** bonding cement
pegar <g→gu> **I.** *vt* **1.** (*aglutinar*) to stick; **~ un sello** to attach [*o* stick on] a stamp; **no ~ ojo** not to sleep a wink **2.** (*con hilo, grapa*) to

attach **3.**(*muebles*) ~ **la mesilla a la cama** to put the side table right next to the bed **4.**(*contagiar*) to give **5.**(*fuego*) ~ **fuego a algo** to set fire to sth **6.**(*golpear*) to hit; ~ **una paliza a alguien** to beat sb up **7.**(*un grito*) to let out; (*un tiro*) to fire; ~ **una patada** to kick; ~ **una bofetada** to slap; ~ **un salto** to jump; ~ **un susto a alguien** to frighten sb **8.** INFOR to paste **9.** *AmL, inf* (*tener suerte*) to be lucky; ~**la** to get what one wants **10.** *Méx* (*atar*) to tie **II.** *vi* **1.**(*hacer juego*) to go together; **te pegan bien los zapatos con el bolso** those shoes go really well with the bag; **esto no pega ni con cola** this really doesn't go **2.**(*rozar*) ~ **en algo** to brush against sth; (*tocar*) to touch sth **3.**(*golpear*) to beat; **¡cómo pega el sol hoy!** *inf* the sun is really hot today! **4.** *inf* (*currar*) to work hard; **no** ~ **golpe** [*o* **palo al agua**] not to do a thing **III.** *vr* **1.**(*impactar*) ~**se con algo** to bump into sth; ~**se con alguien** to fight with sb; ~**se un tortazo en el coche** *inf* to crash one's car **2.**(*quemarse*) to stick to the pot **3.**(*entrometerse*) ~**se a algo** to interfere in sth **4.**(*aficionarse*) ~**se a algo** to acquire a liking for sth **5.**(*acompañar siempre*) ~**se a alguien** to stick to sb (like glue); (*perseguir*) to follow sb; **siempre anda pegado a mí** he/she is always following me about **6.**(*contagiarse*) **finalmente se me pegó el sarampión** I finally caught the measles **7.** *inf* (*engañar*) **pegársela a alguien** *inf* to trick sb; **pegársela al marido/a la mujer** to cheat on one's husband/one's wife **8.** *inf* (*darse*) ~**se la gran vida** to live it up; ~**se un tiro** to shoot oneself; ~**se un tiro en la cabeza** to shoot oneself in the head
pegatina *f* sticker
pegote *m* **1.**(*emplasto*) plaster, Band-Aid® **2.** *pey, inf* (*guisote*) stodgy mess **3.** *inf* (*persona*) hanger-on **4.** *inf* (*chapuza*) botch **5.** *inf* (*añadido feo*) **esa corbata es un** ~ that tie just doesn't go **6.** *inf* (*farol*) **tirarse** ~**s** to show off
peinado *m* hairstyle, hairdo; **hacerse un** ~ to have one's hair done
peinado, -a *adj* combed
peinador *m* **1.**(*para peinar, afeitar*) robe **2.**(*tocador*) dressing table
peinar I. *vt* **1.**(*desenredar*) to comb **2.**(*acicalar*) to style **II.** *vr* to comb one's hair; (*arreglar el pelo*) to style [*o* to do] one's hair
peine *m* (*para peinarse*) comb; **¡te vas a enterar de lo que vale un** ~**!** *fig* you'll soon find out what's what!; **¡ya apareció el** ~**!** *fig* so that's it!
peineta *f* Spanish ornamental comb
peinilla *f* **1.** *Col, Ecua* (*peine*) dressing comb **2.** *Col, Ecua, Pan, Ven* (*especie de machete*) large machete
p.ej. *abr de* **por ejemplo** e.g.
pejiguera *f inf* nuisance
pela *f* **1.** *inf* (*dinero*) **no me queda ni una sola** ~ I'm completely broke; **no me quedan**

más ~**s** I've got no money left; ~ **larga** lots of dough **2.**(*estar pelando*) peeling
pelada *f* **1.**(*rapada*) haircut **2.** *CSur* (*calva*) bald head **3.** *AmL* (*error*) blunder
peladez *f* **1.** *And* (*pobreza*) poverty **2.** *Méx* (*palabrota*) obscenity
pelado *m inf* (*pobretón*) poor wretch
pelado, -a *adj* **1.**(*rapado*) shorn **2.**(*escueto, despojado*) bare **3.** *inf* (*números*) round; **esto vale las 5.000 peladas** this costs exactly 5000 **4.** *AmL, inf* (*sin dinero*) broke
peladuras *fpl* (*cáscaras*) peelings *pl*
pelagatos *m inv, inf* poor wretch
pelaje *m* **1.**(*piel*) coat, fur **2.** *pey* (*pinta*) appearance, looks *pl*
pelambre *m o f* **1.**(*pelo*) thick hair; (*de animales*) fur; (*pelambrera*) mop **2.**(*zona calva*) bald patch **3.** *AmL* (*habladurías*) rumours *pl*
pelambrera *f* **1.**(*pelo*) mop **2.**(*calvicie*) bald patch
pelandusca *f inf* floozie; (*puta*) whore
pelapatatas *m inv* potato peeler
pelar I. *vt* **1.**(*pelo*) to cut; (*rapar*) to shear; (*plumas*) to pluck; (*frutas, verduras*) to peel; (*animales*) to skin **2.**(*murmurar*) to criticize **3.**(*robar*) to fleece **4.**(*en el juego*) to clean out **5.**(*difícil*) **ser duro de** ~ to be a hard nut to crack **6.** *AmL, inf* (*dar una paliza*) to beat up **7.** *And, inf* (*morir*) ~**la** to kick the bucket **II.** *vi inf* **hace un frío que pela** it's freezing cold **III.** *vr* **1.**(*el pelo*) to have one's hair cut; **ir a** ~**se** to go for a haircut **2.**(*la piel*) to peel **3.** *vulg* (*masturbarse*) **pelársela** to have a wank *Brit*, to jerk off *Am* **4.** *inf* (*intensificador*) **corre que se las pela** she is a really fast runner; **pelárselas por algo** to be crazy about sth; **pelárselas por hacer algo** to do everything possible to do sth
pelaverduras *m inv* vegetable peeler
peldaño *m* step; (*escalera portátil*) rung
pelea *f* **1.**(*lucha*) fight **2.**(*verbal*) quarrel, argument; **buscar** ~ to be looking for trouble
pelear I. *vi* **1.**(*luchar*) to fight **2.**(*discutir*) to argue **3.**(*sufrir*) to suffer **4.**(*trabajar*) ~ **por algo** to struggle for sth **II.** *vr* **1.**(*con violencia*) ~**se por algo** to fight over sth **2.**(*verbal*) ~**se por algo** to argue about sth **3.**(*enemistarse*) to fall out
pelele *m* **1.**(*muñeco*) rag doll **2.**(*de bebés*) rompers *pl;* (*para dormir*) sleepsuit **3.** *inf* (*persona*) puppet
peleón *m inf* troublemaker
peleón, -ona *adj* quarrelsome; **vino** ~ cheap wine
peletería *f* **1.**(*costura*) furrier's; (*venta*) fur shop **2.** *AmC* (*zapatería*) shoe store
peliagudo, -a *adj* (*complicado*) tricky
pelícano *m,* **pelicano** *m* pelican
película *f* film, movie *Am;* ~ **en blanco y negro** black and white film; ~ **hablada** talkie; ~ **muda** silent film [*o* movie *Am*]; ~ **de suspense** thriller; ~ **de terror** horror film [*o* movie *Am*]; ~ **del oeste** western; **de** ~ *inf*

sensational; **como de** ~ like sth out of the movies; **un matrimonio como de** ~ a wedding like you see in the movies; **poner en** ~ to film; **echar una** ~ to show a film; **¡allí ~s!** it's nothing to do with me!; **no saber de qué va la** ~ not to have a clue

peligrar *vi* to be in danger; **hacer** ~ to endanger

peligro *m* danger; ~ **de incendio** fire risk; **puesta en** ~ endangering; **correr (un gran)** ~ to be at (great) risk; **correr** ~ **de hacer algo** to run the risk of doing sth; **estar en** ~ **de muerte** to be in mortal danger; **fuera de** ~ out of danger; **poner en** ~ to endanger; **poniendo en** ~ **su propia vida** risking his/her own life

peligroso, -a *adj* dangerous

pelillo *m inf* (*pequeñez*) trifle; **echar ~s a la mar** to make up; **¡~s a la mar!** let bygones be bygones!

pelirrojo, -a I. *adj* red-haired II. *m, f* redhead, carrot-top *inf*

pella *f* 1. (*masa*) lump; ~ **de algodón** ball of cotton wool 2. *inf* (*dinero*) dough

pelleja *f* 1. (*de animal*) hide 2. *inf* (*persona muy delgada*) skinny person; **ser una** ~ to be all skin and bones 3. *vulg* (*prostituta*) whore 4. *pey* (*vieja antipática*) old bag

pellejerías *fpl Chile* hard times *pl*

pellejo *m* 1. (*de animal*) hide 2. (*de persona*) skin; **no tener más que el** ~ to be all skin and bones; **no caber en su** ~ *fig* to be bursting with pride; **quitar el** ~ **a alguien** *fig* to criticize sb; **si yo estuviera en tu ~ …** *inf* if I were in your shoes … 3. *inf* (*vida*) **salvar(se) el** ~ to save one's skin; **arriesgar el** ~ to risk one's neck; **para esto yo no daría mi** ~ I wouldn't risk my neck for that; **pagar con el** ~ to pay with one's life; **perder el** ~ to lose one's life 4. (*odre*) wineskin 5. (*fruta*) peel; (*salchicha*) skin 6. (*de las uñas*) hangnail 7. *inf* (*ebrio*) drunkard

pellizcar <c→qu> I. *vt* 1. (*repizcar*) to pinch 2. *inf* (*pizcar algo*) to take a pinch of; (*comida*) to nibble II. *vr* to pinch oneself

pellizco *m* 1. (*pizco*) pinch; **dar un** ~ **a alguien** to pinch sb 2. (*poquito: de sal*) pinch; (*de bocadillo*) nibble

pelma *m inf*, **pelmazo** *m inf* (*pesado*) bore, drag

pelo *m* 1. (*cabello*) hair; (*de animal*) fur; (*de ave*) plumage; (*de barba*) whisker; **tener el** ~ **rubio** to have fair hair; **tirar el** ~ (*perro*) to moult *Brit*, to molt *Am;* **cortarse el** ~ to have one's hair cut; **soltarse el** ~ to take one's hair down; *fig* to let one's hair down 2. (*vello*) down; (*pelusa*) fluff; (*de alfombra*) pile 3. *inf* (*categoría*) **de** ~ wealthy; **la gente de medio** ~ the hoi polloi; **luce buen** ~ he/she is doing well 4. (+ *al*) **al** ~ perfectly; **todo irá al** ~ everything will be fine; **el traje ha quedado al** ~ the suit looks great; **venir al** ~ to be just right, to happen [*o* come] at just the right time; **sin venir al** ~ inconveniently 5. *inf* (*poco*)

por un ~ **te caes** you very nearly fell; **escaparse por un** ~ to escape by the skin of one's teeth; **no se mueve ni un** ~ **de aire** the air is completely still ►**cortar un** ~ **en el aire** (*cuchillo*) to be as sharp as a razor; (*listo*) to be very clever; **no tener ~s en la lengua** *inf* not to mince words; **un hombre de** ~ **en pecho** a real man; **ponerse a uno los ~s de punta** to make one's hair stand on end; **no tocar un** ~ (**de la ropa**) **a alguien** *inf* not to lay a finger on sb; **contar algo con ~s y señales** *inf* to describe sth in great detail; **colgado de un** ~ hanging from a thread; **no tener (un)** ~ **de tonto** *inf* to be nobody's fool; **agarrarse a un** ~ to clutch at straws; **estar hasta los ~s** *inf* to be fed up; **tomar el** ~ **a alguien** *inf* to pull sb's leg; **no se te ve el** ~, **¿por dónde andas?** *inf* I/we haven't seen you for ages, where have you been hiding?; **a** ~ (*la cabeza descubierta*) bare-headed; (*sin prepararse*) unprepared

pelón, -ona I. *adj* 1. (*calvo*) bald 2. (*rapado*) shaven-headed II. *m, f inf* (*pobre*) poor wretch

pelota[1] *f* 1. (*balón*) ball; **echar la** ~ **a alguien** *fig* to leave sb holding the baby; **devolver la** ~ **a alguien** (*argumentar*) to turn the tables on sb; (*vengarse*) to give sb a taste of their own medicine; **la** ~ **sigue en el tejado** *fig* things are still up in the air 2. (*juego*) pelota 3. *pl, vulg* (*testículos*) balls *pl*, ballocks *pl;* **tocar las ~s a alguien** to irritate sb; **y esto lo hago así porque me sale de las ~s, tocarse las ~s** to do absolutely nothing, I do it like this because I bloody well feel like it!; **¡fíjate, que tiene ~s!** I'll tell you one thing, he's got balls!; **¡y esto es así, por ~s!** that's how it is, and no arguing!; **de ~s** cool 4. *vulg* (*desnudo*) **en ~s** starkers; **dejar a alguien en ~s** (*juego*) to clean sb out; (*ropa*) to strip sb naked; **pillar a alguien en ~s** *fig* to catch sb with their trousers down ►**hacer la** ~ **a alguien** to suck up to sb

pelota[2] *m inf* crawler

pelotazo *m* 1. (*con el pie*) shot; (*tirando*) throw; (*con la raqueta*) stroke 2. *inf* (*bebida*) slug; **meterse un** ~ to have a drink

pelotear I. *vi* 1. (*tenis*) to knock up; (*fútbol*) to have a kick about 2. (*de un sitio al otro*) to throw back and forth II. *vt* (*cuentas*) to check

pelotera *f inf* fight

pelotón *m* 1. (*de gente*) crowd; (*en carreras*) pack; MIL squad; ~ **de ejecución** firing squad 2. (*enredo*) tangle

pelotudo, -a I. *adj CSur, vulg* idiotic II. *m, f CSur, vulg* jerk

peluca *f* wig; **usar** ~ to wear a wig

peluche *m* 1. (*tejido*) plush 2. (*juguete*) soft toy; **oso** ~ teddy bear

pelucón *m And, inf* bigwig

pelucón, -ona *adj And, inf* long-haired

peludo, -a *adj* 1. hairy; (*con una barba*) bearded 2. *AmC, inf* (*difícil*) tricky

peluquería *f* hairdresser's; ~ **de señoras/ señores** ladies'/gents'[*o* men's] hairdressers; **ir a la** ~ to go to the hairdresser's

peluquero, -a *m, f* hairdresser
peluquín *m* toupée; **¡ni hablar del ~!** it's out of the question!
pelusa *f* 1.(*vello*) down; (*tejido*) fluff 2.(*de polvo*) fluff 3. *inf*(*celos*) jealousy; **sentir ~ to be jealous** 4.(*envidia*) envy; **sentir ~ to be envious**
pelvis *f inv* pelvis
pena *f* 1.(*tristeza*) sorrow; **ahogar las ~s** to drown one's sorrows 2.(*lástima*) **ser una ~** to be a pity; **¡qué ~!** what a shame!; **me da mucha ~ el gato** I feel really sorry for the cat; **me da mucha ~ el tener que verlo así** it really upsets me to see him like this 3.(*sanción*) punishment; **~ de cadena perpetua** life sentence; **~ capital** capital punishment; **~ pecuniaria** fine 4.(*dificultad*) trouble; **pasar las ~s del purgatorio** to go through hell; **a duras ~s** with great difficulty; (*apenas*) scarcely; **sin ~ ni gloria** undistinguished; **valer la ~ to** be worth the effort [o the trouble]; **¡allá ~s!** it's not my problem! 5. *AmL* (*vergüenza*) shame; **tener ~ to** be ashamed ▶ **so ~ que** +*subj* under pain of
penable *adj* punishable
penacho *m* 1.(*de aves, adorno*) crest 2. *inf* (*vanidad*) pride
penado, -a I. *adj* 1.(*triste*) sad 2.(*difícil*) difficult 3. *AmL* (*tímido*) shy II. *m, f* convict
penal I. *adj* JUR penal; **antecedentes ~es** criminal record II. *m* 1.(*prisión*) prison 2. *AmL* (*falta*) foul (*inside the penalty area*) 3.(*penalti*) penalty; (*en baloncesto*) free throw
penalidad *f* 1.(*molestia*) hardship 2.(*sanción*) punishment
penalización *f* penalization
penalizar <z→c> *vt* to penalize
penalti *m* 1.(*falta*) foul (*inside the penalty area*); **área de ~s** penalty area 2.(*sanción*) penalty; (*en baloncesto*) free throw; **casarse de ~** *inf* to have a shotgun wedding
penar I. *vt* (*delincuente, delito*) to punish II. *vi* 1.(*padecer*) to suffer; **~ de amores** to be unhappy in love 2.(*ansiar*) **~ por algo** to long for sth
penca *f* 1.(*hoja*) fleshy leaf 2. *AmL* (*borrachera*) **agarrarse una ~** to get drunk 3. *And* (*atractivo*) **una ~ de hombre/de mujer** a really good-looking man/woman; **una ~ de casa** a gorgeous house
penco *m* 1.(*jamelgo*) nag 2. *And, inf* (*atractivo*) **un ~ de hombre/de mujer** a really good-looking man/woman 3. *inf* (*holgazán*) layabout; (*inútil*) waster; (*torpe*) clod
pendejada *f AmL, inf* 1.(*disparate*) foolishness; **¿cómo se te pudo ocurrir tal ~?** what ever made you think of such a stupid thing? 2.(*acto cobarde*) cowardly act 3.(*cualidad de cobarde*) cowardliness
pendejear *vi Col, inf* to mess around *inf*
pendejo, -a *m, f Arg, inf* (*necio*) fool
pendencia *f* fight; **armar ~** to start a fight

pendenciero, -a I. *adj* quarrelsome II. *m, f* troublemaker
pender *vi* 1.(*colgar*) to hang 2. JUR to be pending
pendiente¹ I. *adj* 1.(*colgado*) hanging 2.(*problema, asunto*) unresolved; (*cuenta, trabajo, pedido*) outstanding; **una cuenta ~ de pago** an outstanding account; **quedar ~ una asignatura** to have one subject left to pass (*as a resit or carried over to next year*) 3.(*ocupado*) **estate ~ del arroz** keep an eye on the rice; **¡tú estate ~ de lo tuyo!** mind your own business!; **estar ~ de los labios de alguien** (*estar atento*) to be hanging on sb's every word; **estoy ~ de si me conceden la beca o no** I'm waiting to see whether or not they'll give me the grant 4.(*depender*) **estamos ~s de lo que digan nuestros padres** it all depends on what our parents say II. *m* (*de oreja*) earring; (*de nariz*) nose ring
pendiente² *f* (*cuesta, del tejado*) slope; **de mucha ~** steep
péndola *f* 1.(*de reloj*) pendulum 2.(*reloj*) pendulum clock
pendón *m* 1.(*estandarte*) banner 2. *inf* (*buscona*) floozie
péndulo *m* pendulum
pene *m* penis
penetración *f* 1.(*acción*) penetration 2.(*comprensión*) insight; (*inteligencia*) intelligence
penetrante *adj* 1.(*profundo*) deep; (*dolor*) fierce 2.(*frío*) biting; (*hedor*) strong; (*olor*) pervasive 3.(*sonido*) penetrating; (*grito*) piercing
penetrar I. *vi* to penetrate II. *vt* 1.(*atravesar*) to penetrate 2.(*entender*) to understand; **~ un misterio** to unravel a mystery; **~ una intención** to fathom an intention; **~ los pensamientos de alguien** to penetrate sb's thoughts III. *vr* **~se de algo** to become imbued with sth
penicilina *f* MED penicillin
península *f* GEO peninsula; **la Península Ibérica** the Iberian Peninsula

The **Península Ibérica** (Iberian Peninsula) includes Spain and Portugal. The Spanish language makes use of this term (and the corresponding adjective **peninsular**, in order to differentiate between the Spanish mainland and the two Spanish island groups (**Baleares y Canarias**) as well as the country's territories in Africa (**Ceuta y Melilla**).

peninsular *adj* peninsular; **las temperaturas ~es** temperatures in the Iberian peninsula
penique *m* penny
penitencia *f* 1.(*pena*) punishment; **imponer una ~ a alguien** to impose a punishment on sb 2. REL penance; **hacer ~** to do penance 3.(*arrepentimiento*) penitence
penitenciaría *f* prison, penitentiary *Am*

penitenciario, -a *adj* **1.**(*relativo a la penitenciaría*) prison **2.**(*relativo a la penitencia*) penitentiary

penitente *adj, mf* penitent

penoso, -a *adj* **1.**(*arduo*) laborious **2.**(*dificultoso*) difficult **3.**(*con pena*) upset **4.** *AmL* (*vergonzoso*) shameful

pensado, -a *adj* **1.**(*reflexionado*) considered; **esto está poco ~** this hasn't been properly thought out; **lo tengo bien ~** I have thought it through thoroughly; **tener ~ hacer algo** to have it in mind to do sth; **el día menos ~ volverá** just when it's least expected he/she will return **2.**(*persona*) **ser un mal ~** to always be ready to think the worst

pensador(a) I. *adj* thinking **II.** *m/f* thinker

pensamiento *m* **1.**(*acción, idea, objeto*) thought; **ya el ~ solo me da risa** the very thought of it makes me laugh **2.**(*intención*) intention **3.**(*mente*) mind; **tengo un problema en el ~** there's sth on my mind; **¿cuándo te vino esa idea al ~?** when did that idea occur to you? **4.**(*apotegma*) maxim **5.**(*contenido*) thoughts *pl* **6.** BOT pansy

pensar <e→ie> **I.** *vi, vt* **1.**(*formar un juicio, reflexionar*) **~ (en) algo** to think (about) sth; **todo pasa cuando menos se piensa (en ello)** everything happens when you least expect it; **¡ni ~lo!** don't even think about it!; **¡no quiero ni ~lo!** I don't even want to think about it!; **nos dio mucho que ~ que no hubiera regresado aún** the fact that he/she hadn't returned yet gave us a lot to think about; **esto es algo para ~lo bien** we need to think carefully about this; **lo hicimos sin ~lo** we did it without thinking; **sin ~lo me dio una bofetada** he suddenly slapped me; **pensándolo bien** on reflection **2.**(*considerar*) to consider **II.** *vi* (*opinar, suponer*) to think; **pienso que deberíamos irnos** I think we should go; **~ muy mal de alguien** to think very badly of sb **III.** *vt* **1.**(*intención*) to think of; **pensábamos venir este fin de semana** we were thinking of coming this weekend; **lo pensó mejor y no lo hizo** he/she thought better of it and didn't do it **2.**(*inventar, tramar*) to think up

pensativo, -a *adj* thoughtful, pensive

pensión *f* **1.**(*paga*) pension; **~ recibida de la empresa** occupational pension; **~ de viudez** widow's pension; **~ alimenticia** maintenance; **aún no cobra la ~** (*no recibe la paga*) he/she doesn't get a pension yet; (*no tiene la edad*) he/she isn't a pensioner yet **2.**(*para huéspedes*) guesthouse **3.**(*precio por alojamiento*) (charge for) board and lodging; **~ completa** full board

pensionado *m* ENS boarding school

pensionado, -a *m, f* (*jubilado*) pensioner

pensionar *vt* to give a pension to

pensionista *mf* **1.**(*jubilado*) pensioner **2.**(*huésped*) guest (*at boarding house*) **3.**(*alumno*) boarder

pentagonal *adj* pentagonal

pentágono *m* pentagon

pentagrama *m* MÚS stave, staff

pentatlón *m* pentathlon

Pentecostés *m* REL **1.**(*cristiano*) Whitsun; **Pascua de ~** Whit Sunday **2.**(*judío*) Pentecost

penúltimo, -a *adj* penultimate, next-to-last

penumbra *f* semi-darkness; ASTR penumbra

penuria *f* **1.**(*escasez*) scarcity; **pasar muchas ~s** to suffer great hardship **2.**(*pobreza*) poverty

peña *f* **1.**(*roca*) crag **2.**(*grupo*) group; (*de aficionados*) club; (*tertulia*) circle; *inf* (*de jóvenes*) gang

peñasco *m* (*peña*) boulder

peñascoso, -a *adj* rocky

peñón *m* **1.**(*peñasco*) crag; **el Peñón** the Rock (of Gibraltar) **2.**(*monte*) mountain

peón *m* **1.**(*obrero*) unskilled labourer *Brit* [*o* laborer *Am*]; (*jornalero*) farmhand; *Méx* (*aprendiz*) apprentice **2.**(*en juegos*) piece; (*en ajedrez*) pawn

peonza *f* (*juguete*) spinning top

peor *adv, adj comp de* **mal(o)** worse; **en matemáticas soy ~ que tú** I am worse at maths than you are; **el ~ de la clase** the worst in the class; **el pequeño es el ~ de los dos** the little one is the worse of the two; **y verás, será ~ aún** you'll see, it will get even worse; **el ~ día, verás como te hablará** just when you least expect it, he/she will speak to you; **en el ~ de los casos** at worst; **si pasa lo ~** if worst comes to worst; **pero lo ~ de todo fue...** but the worst thing of all was ...; **vas de mal en ~** you're going from bad to worse; **~ es nada** it's better than nothing

pepa *f* **1.** *AmL* (*pepita*) seed **2.** *And* (*mentira*) fib

Pepa *f inf* **¡viva la ~!** (*indiferencia*) who cares!; (*regocijo*) hurrah!, hurray! *Am*

Pepe *m* **ponerse como un ~** *inf* to have a great time; **ver menos que ~ Leches** *inf* to be as blind as a bat

pepena *f* **1.** *Col* (*abanico*) fan **2.** *Méx* (*lo recogido*) collection; (*vísceras*) viscera

pepinillo *m* gherkin

pepino *m* **1.**(*para ensaladas*) cucumber; **eso me importa un ~** *inf* I don't give two hoots about that **2.**(*melón*) unripe melon

pepita *f* BOT seed

pepsina *f* pepsin

pequeñajo, -a I. *adj inf* small **II.** *m, f inf* kid

pequeñez *f* **1.**(*tamaño*) smallness **2.**(*minucia*) trifle

pequeño, -a I. *adj* small, little; **ya desde ~ solía venir a este sitio** I've been coming here since I was little; **esta camisa me queda ~** this shirt is too small for me **II.** *m, f* little one

pequeñoburgués, -esa *adj, m, f* petit bourgeois

pequinés *m* ZOOL Pekinese

pequinés, -esa *adj, m, f* Pekinese

pera I. *adj* posh; **niño** ~ posh brat *Brit,* little rich kid II. *f* 1. BOT pear 2. (*barba*) goatee 3. TÉC ~ **de goma** rubber bulb 4. *vulg* (*masturbación*) **hacerse una** ~ to wank *Brit,* to jerk off *Am* ►**pedir** ~**s al** <u>olmo</u> *inf* to ask for the impossible; **poner a alguien las** ~**s a** <u>cuarto</u> *inf* to tell sb a few home truths; **eso** <u>es</u> **la** ~ *inf* that's the limit; <u>tocarse</u> **la** ~ *vulg* to sit on one's backside

peral *m* pear tree

perca *f* perch

percance *m* (*contratiempo*) setback; (*por culpa propia*) blunder; (*de plan, proyecto*) hitch

per cápita *adv* per capita; **consumo** ~ per capita consumption

percatarse *vr* ~**se de algo** (*darse cuenta*) to notice sth; (*comprender*) to realize sth

percebe *m* goose barnacle

percepción *f* 1. (*acción*) perception 2. (*idea*) notion; (*impresión*) impression 3. FIN receipt

perceptible *adj* 1. (*que puede comprenderse*) perceptible 2. FIN payable

perceptivo, -a *adj* perceptive

perceptor(a) *m(f)* recipient

percha *f* 1. (*en el armario*) hanger 2. (*perchero*) coat stand; (*en la tienda*) clothes rail; **vestido de** ~ ready-made dress 3. *AmC* (*chaqueta*) jacket 4. *inf* (*tipo*) build; **tener buena** ~ to have a good figure

perchero *m* ~ **(de pared)** coat rack; ~ **(de pie)** coat stand

percibir *vt* 1. (*notar*) to perceive 2. (*darse cuenta*) to notice 3. (*comprender*) to realize 4. (*cobrar*) to receive

percusión *f* 1. (*golpeo*) striking 2. TÉC percussion; **barra de** ~ percussion bar 3. MÚS percussion; **instrumento de** ~ percussion instrument

percusionista *mf* (*de bongos, congas*) percussionist; (*de batería*) drummer

perdedor(a) I. *adj* losing II. *m(f)* loser

perder <e→ie> I. *vt* 1. (*en general*) to lose; ~ **la cuenta** to lose count; **he perdido mis gafas** I've lost my glasses; ~ **terreno** *fig* to lose ground 2. (*malgastar*) to waste 3. (*no aprovechar*) **si llego tarde al espectáculo pierdo la entrada** if I arrive late for the show my ticket will be wasted 4. (*peso, costumbre*) to lose 5. (*oportunidad, tren*) to miss 6. (*ocasionar daños*) to destroy; **el fuego perdió todo el edificio** the fire destroyed the whole building; **esa equivocación nos perdió** that mistake was our undoing; **el juego lo** ~**á** gambling will be his undoing; **el régimen lo llevo muy bien, lo que me pierde es ver comer a los demás** I don't have a problem with the diet, it's seeing other people eat which leads me astray 7. ENS (*suspender*) ~ **el curso** to fail the year II. *vi* 1. (*en general*) to lose; **Portugal perdió por 1 a 2 frente a Italia** Portugal lost 2–1 against Italy; **vas a salir perdiendo** you're going to come off worst; **llevar todas** las de ~ to be fighting a losing battle; **lo echó todo a** ~ he/she lost everything; **la comida se quemó y todo se echó a** ~ the food was burnt and everything was completely ruined; **cómete esos plátanos que si no se echan a** ~ eat these bananas, otherwise they'll just go to waste 2. (*decaer*) to decline; **por mi profesión he perdido mucho en salud** my job has been very bad for my health 3. (*desteñir*) to fade III. *vr* 1. (*extraviarse*) to get lost; **¡qué se le habrá perdido por allí?** *fig* what is he/she doing there? 2. (*bailando, leyendo*) to lose oneself; ~**se en palabrerías complicadas** (*hablando*) to get bogged down in complicated wordplay 3. (*desaparecer*) to disappear 4. (*arruinarse*) ~**se por algo/alguien** to be ruined by sth/sb 5. (*desperdiciarse*) to be wasted; **se pierde mucha agua por falta de conciencia ecológica** a lot of water is wasted through lack of environmental awareness 6. (*ocasión*) to miss out; **si no te vienes, tú te lo pierdes** if you don't come, you'll be the one who misses out 7. (*extinguirse*) to die out; **poco a poco la minifalda se va perdiendo** miniskirts are slowly going out of fashion 8. (*anhelar*) ~**se por algo/alguien** to be mad about sth/sb

perdición *f* 1. (*acción*) loss; (*daño*) ruin 2. (*moral*) perdition

pérdida *f* loss; ~ **de cabellos** hair loss; ~ **de conciencia** loss of consciousness; ~ **por fricción** wear; **esto es una** ~ **de tiempo** this is a waste of time; **es fácil de encontrar, no tiene** ~ it's easy to find, you can't miss it; **el edificio ha sufrido** ~**s enormes después del incendio** the building has been very badly damaged in the fire; **el coche tiene una leve** ~ **de aceite** the car has a slight oil leak; ~**s humanas** victims; **no hubo que lamentar** ~**s humanas** fortunately there were no lives lost

perdidamente *adv* 1. (*con exceso*) **estar** ~ **enamorado** to be madly in love 2. (*inútilmente*) pointlessly

perdido, -a I. *adj* 1. (*que no se encuentra*) lost; **dar a alguien por** ~ to give sb up for lost; **dar algo por** ~ to give sth up for lost; *fig* to give up on sth; **estar** ~ to be lost 2. (*vicioso, sin salida*) **estar loco** ~ *inf* to be completely insane [*o* mad *Brit*] 3. (*sucio*) **poner algo** ~ *inf* to make sth completely dirty; **ponerse** ~ **de pintura** *inf* to get covered in paint II. *m, f* 1. *inf* (*vago*) layabout; (*pobre*) poor wretch; **hacerse el** ~ *inf* to make oneself scarce 2. (*libertino*) waster

perdiz *f* partridge; **...y fueron felices y comieron perdices** ... and they lived happily ever after

perdón *m* 1. (*absolución, indulto*) pardon 2. (*disculpa*) **¡~!** sorry!; **¿~?** pardon?; **¡con ~!** if you'll excuse me!; **no cabe** ~ it's inexcusable; **pedir** ~ **a alguien** to ask for sb's forgiveness; (*disculparse*) to apologize to sb; **con** ~ **de la mesa, esto es una porquería** I hope you will excuse the expression at table, but this is a load of crap

perdonable *adj* forgivable

perdonar *vt* **1.** (*ofensa, deuda*) to forgive; (*pecado, pena*) to pardon; **no te perdono** I don't forgive you; **perdona que te interrumpa** forgive me for interrupting; **perdona, ¿puedo pasar?** excuse me, can I come through? **2.** (*obligación*) to let off; **te perdono los 20 euros** I'll forget about the 20 euros you owe me; **les he perdonado la tarde a mis empleados** I have given my employees the afternoon off **3.** (*dejar pasar*) **no ~ ningún esfuerzo** to spare no effort; **no ~ ningún medio** to use all possible means; **la guerra no perdona a nadie** war spares no-one

perdurable *adj* **1.** (*duradero*) long-lasting **2.** (*eterno*) everlasting

perdurar *vi* **1.** (*todavía*) to persist **2.** (*indefinidamente*) to last for ever; **su recuerdo ~á para siempre entre nosotros** his memory will always be with us

perecedero, -a *adj* **1.** (*pasajero*) transitory **2.** (*alimento*) perishable

perecer *irr como crecer vi* **1.** (*morir*) to perish; **~ de sed** to die of thirst **2.** (*daño, sufrimiento*) to suffer

peregrinación *f* REL pilgrimage; **ir en ~ to** make a pilgrimage

peregrinar *vi* **1.** REL to make a pilgrimage **2.** (*viajar: a pie*) to wander; (*con vehículo*) to drive around; **para matricularme tuve que ~ por cientos de oficinas** to register I had to trek round hundreds of offices

peregrino, -a I. *adj* **1.** (*persona*) wandering **2.** (*extraño*) strange **3.** (*raro*) unusual **4.** (*extraordinario*) extraordinary II. *m, f* pilgrim

perejil *m* **1.** BOT parsley **2.** *pl* (*adornos*) trimmings *pl*

perenne *adj* **1.** (*perpetuo*) everlasting; BOT perennial **2.** (*constante*) constant

perentorio, -a *adj* **1.** (*urgente*) pressing, peremptory *liter* **2.** (*pago*) due **3.** (*decisión*) definite; **plazo ~** fixed time limit

pereza *f* **1.** (*gandulería*) laziness **2.** (*de movimientos*) slowness; **me dio ~ ir y me quedé en casa** I couldn't be bothered going so I stayed at home

perezosa *f Arg, Perú, Urug* deckchair

perezoso, -a *adj* **1.** (*gandul*) lazy **2.** (*movimiento*) unhurried **3.** *fig* **y ni corto ni ~ me soltó un sopapo** *inf* without stopping to think he/she slapped me

perfección *f* perfection; **estilo de gran ~** highly polished style; **hacer algo a la ~** to do sth to perfection

perfeccionamiento *m* perfection; (*de técnica, sistema*) improvement; (*profesional*) further training

perfeccionar *vt* to perfect; (*de técnica, sistema*) to improve

perfeccionista *adj, mf* perfectionist

perfectamente *adv* perfectly; **sabes ~**

que... you know perfectly well that ...; **te entiendo ~** I understand you perfectly; **es ~ comprensible** it is perfectly understandable; **¡~!** exactly!

perfecto *m* LING perfect tense

perfecto, -a *adj* **1.** perfect; **nadie es ~** nobody is perfect; **habla un inglés ~** he/she speaks perfect English; **un ~ caballero** a perfect gentleman; **eres un ~ idiota** you are a complete idiot **2.** LING **pretérito ~** past perfect

perfidia *f* **1.** (*deslealtad*) disloyalty **2.** (*traición*) betrayal

pérfido, -a *adj* **1.** (*desleal*) disloyal **2.** (*traidor*) treacherous

perfil *m* **1.** *t.* TÉC (*de cara*) profile; **de ~** in profile; **~ genético** genetic profile **2.** (*contorno*) outline **3.** (*de personalidad, doctrina*) characteristics *pl*; **el ~ del candidato** the description of the candidate

perfilar I. *vt* **1.** (*retocar*) to touch up **2.** (*sacar perfil*) to outline; TÉC to streamline II. *vr* **1.** (*distinguirse*) to stand out **2.** (*tomar forma*) to take shape

perforación *f* **1.** (*con máquina*) drilling; (*de oreja*) piercing; (*de papel*) punching; (*con muchos agujeros*) perforation **2.** (*agujeros, línea*) perforation

perforar *vt* (*con máquina*) to drill; (*oreja*) to pierce; (*papel*) to punch; (*para decorar, arrancar*) to perforate

perfumador *m* (*utensilio*) perfume spray

perfumar I. *vt* to perfume; **las flores perfuman la habitación** the smell of flowers fills the room II. *vi* to be fragrant

perfume *m* **1.** (*sustancia*) perfume **2.** (*olor*) fragrance

perfumería *f* **1.** (*tienda*) perfume shop **2.** (*productos*) perfume

pergamino *m* parchment; **libro (con encuadernación) en ~** parchment-bound book; **familia de ~s** ancient family

pericia *f* **1.** (*habilidad*) expertise **2.** (*práctica*) skill

pericial *adj* expert; **informe ~** expert report

perico *m* **1.** ZOOL parakeet **2.** *inf* (*puta*) whore **3.** *inf* (*cocaína*) snow

periferia *f* periphery; (*de ciudad*) outskirts *pl*

perifollo *m* **1.** BOT chervil **2.** *inf* (*adornos*) trimmings *pl*

perífrasis *f inv* circumlocution, wordiness

perifrástico, -a *adj* circumlocutory, long-winded

perilla *f* (*barba*) goatee ▶**venir de ~s** to be just what was needed

perillán, -ana *m, f* **1.** (*niño*) rascal **2.** (*adulto*) rogue

perímetro *m* MAT perimeter

perineo *m* perineum

perinola *f* (*peonza*) (small) spinning top

periodicidad *f* frequency

periódico *m* (*diario*) newspaper

periódico, -a *adj* periodic; (*publicación*) periodical; **sistema ~** QUÍM periodic table

periodicucho *m pey* scandal sheet, rag
periodismo *m* (*profesión, estudios*) journalism
periodista *mf* journalist
periodístico, -a *adj* 1.(*de los periodistas*) journalistic 2.(*de los periódicos*) newspaper; **reportaje** ~ newspaper report
periodo *m*, **período** *m t.* MAT, FÍS, GEO (*tiempo, época, menstruación*) period; ~ **álgido** critical period; ~ **glacial** ice age; ~ **productivo** productive period; ~ **de prueba** trial period
peripecia *f* (*incidente*) vicissitude; **ha pasado por muchas ~s en esta vida** he/she has had many ups and downs in his/her life
peripuesto, -a *adj inf* dressed up to the nines; (*hombre*) all spruced up; (*mujer*) dolled up *Am*
periquete *m* **esto lo hago yo en un** ~ I can do that in no time; **estoy lista en un** ~ I'll be ready in a jiffy
periquito *m* parakeet
periscopio *m* periscope
perito, -a I. *adj* expert II. *m, f* 1.(*experto*) expert 2. UNIV graduate; ~ **agrónomo** agronomist; ~ **mercantil** accountant; **Escuela de Peritos** *professional training college*
peritoneo *m* peritoneum
perjudicar <c→qu> I. *vt* 1.(*causar daño*) to damage; (*naturaleza, intereses*) to harm; (*proceso, desarrollo*) to hinder; **fumar perjudica la salud** smoking is bad for your health 2.(*causar desventaja*) to disadvantage II. *vr* to harm oneself
perjudicial *adj* 1.(*que causa daño*) harmful; ~ **para la salud** harmful to health 2.(*desventajoso*) disadvantageous
perjuicio *m* 1.(*daño: de imagen, naturaleza*) harm; (*de objeto*) damage; (*de libertad*) infringement; **causar ~s** to cause harm; **sin ~ de que** +*subj* despite the fact that 2.(*detrimento*) detriment; **ir en ~ de alguien** to be to sb's detriment
perjurar *vi* 1.(*en falso*) to commit perjury 2.(*faltar al juramento*) to break one's oath
perjurio *m* 1.(*en falso*) perjury 2.(*faltar al juramento*) breaking one's word
perla *f* pearl; ~ **cultivada** cultured pearl; **eso viene de ~s** that is just what was needed
permanecer *irr como crecer vi* (*estar, seguir*) to remain; ~ **quieto** to keep still; ~ **invariable** to remain unchanged; ~ **dormido** to carry on sleeping; ~ **sentado** to remain seated
permanencia *f* 1.(*estancia*) stay; (*duración*) duration; **luchar para lograr la** ~ **en primera** DEP to fight to stay in the first division 2.(*persistencia*) persistence 3.(*continuación*) continuation
permanente I. *adj* permanent; **estado** ~ permanent state II. *f* perm
permeabilidad *f* permeability
permeable *adj* permeable; ~ **al agua** permeable to water

permisible *adj* permissible
permisión *f* permission
permisionario, -a *m, f AmL* official agent
permisividad *f* permissiveness
permisivo, -a *adj* permissive
permiso *m* 1.(*aprobación, autorización*) permission; **me dio** ~ **para hacerlo** he/she gave me permission to do it; **pedir** ~ **a alguien** to ask sb for permission 2.(*licencia*) permit; ~ **de conducir** driving licence *Brit*, driver's license *Am*; ~ **de residencia/de trabajo** residence/work permit 3.(*vacaciones*) leave; **pedir** ~ to request leave; **estar de** ~ MIL to be on leave
permitir I. *vt* 1.(*consentir*) to permit; **¿me permite pasar/entrar/salir?** may I get past/enter/leave?; **no está permitido fumar** smoking is not allowed; **si me permite la expresión** if you will excuse the phrase 2.(*autorizar*) to authorize 3.(*hacer posible, tolerar*) to allow; **esta máquina permite trabajar el doble** this machine allows you to do twice as much work; **no permito que me levantes la voz** I won't allow you to raise your voice to me II. *vr* to allow oneself
permuta *f* exchange
permutar *vt* to exchange
pernera *f* (*trouser*) leg
pernicioso, -a *adj* damaging; ~ **para algo/alguien** damaging to sth/sb
pernil *m* 1.(*del cerdo*) leg of ham 2.(*del pantalón*) (*trouser*) leg
pernio *m* hinge
perno *m* bolt
pernoctar *vi* to spend the night
pero I. *conj* but; (*sin embargo*) however; **¡~ si todavía es una niña!** but she is still only a child!; **¡~ si ya la conoces!** but you already know her!; **¿~ qué es lo que quieres?** what do you want? II. *m* (*objeción*) objection; **el proyecto tiene sus ~s** there are lots of problems with the project; **sin un** ~ no buts; **poner ~s a algo** to object to sth; **¡no hay ~ que valga!** there are no buts about it!; **poner ~s a todo** to object to everything
perogrullada *f* obvious truth
perol *m* (*metal*) cooking pot
peroné *m* fibula
peronista *adj, mf* Peronist
peroración *f* (*discurso*) speech
perorar *vi* 1.(*dar discurso*) to make a speech; *pey* to hold forth 2. *inf* (*hablar*) to ramble on 3.(*pedir*) to ask persistently
peróxido *m* peroxide
perpendicular *adj, f* perpendicular
perpetrar *vt* to perpetrate
perpetuar <1. *pres:* perpetúo> I. *vt* 1.(*recuerdo, memoria, nombre*) to preserve 2.(*situación, error, mentira*) to perpetuate II. *vr* to be perpetuated
perpetuidad *f* 1.(*continuidad*) continuity 2.(*eternidad*) perpetuity; **a** ~ in perpetuity; **condenar a** ~ to condemn to life imprison-

ment
perpetuo, -a *adj* **1.** (*incesante*) perpetual; **nieves perpetuas** permanent snow **2.** (*vitalicio*) life; **cadena perpetua** life sentence
perplejo, -a *adj* perplexed
perra *f* **1.** ZOOL bitch; *v.t.* **perro** I. **2.** (*obstinación*) obsession **3.** *inf* (*rabieta*) tantrum; **coger una** ~ to throw a tantrum **4.** *inf* (*modorra*) sleepiness; (*pereza*) laziness **5.** (*mujer malvada*) bitch **6.** *inf* (*dinero*) penny; **no tener una** ~ to be broke **7.** *inf* (*borrachera*) drunkenness; **cogerse una** ~ to get pissed
perramus *m inv, Arg, Bol, Urug* (*impermeable*) raincoat
perrera *f* (*casita*) kennel; (*de perros callejeros*) dog pound
perrería *f* (*vileza*) dirty trick
perrilla *f Méx* (*orzuelo*) snare
perrito *m* ~ **caliente** hot dog
perro, -a I. *m, f* (*macho*) dog; (*hembra*) bitch; ~ **callejero** stray dog; ~ **faldero** lapdog; ~ **lazarillo** guide-dog; **echar los** ~**s a alguien** *inf* to tear sb to shreds; **morir como un** ~ *inf* to die a lonely death ▶**se llevan como el** ~ **y el** gato *inf* they fight like cat and dog; **ser como el** ~ **del** hortelano to be a dog in the manger; **¡venga ya, a otro** ~ **con ese** hueso! *inf* pull the other one!; humor **de** ~**s** *inf* filthy mood; **a** ~ **flaco todo son** pulgas *prov* misfortunes never come singly; tiempo **de** ~**s** *inf* filthy weather; ~ ladrador, **poco mordedor** *prov* his bark is worse than his bite; **muerto el** ~ **se acabó la rabia** *prov* dead dogs don't bite; **ser** ~ viejo *inf* to be an old hand II. *adj* lousy; **llevar una vida perra** to lead a wretched life
persa I. *adj* Persian; **alfombra** ~ Persian rug II. *mf* Persian
persecución *f* **1.** (*seguimiento*) pursuit; ~ **en coche** car chase **2.** (*acoso*) persecution
perseguir *irr como* seguir *vt* to chase; (*contrato, chica*) to pursue; **la policía persigue al fugitivo** the police are pursuing the fugitive; **me persigue la mala suerte** I am dogged by bad luck; **me persiguen los remordimientos** I am tormented by remorse; **el jefe me persigue todo el día** the boss is always on my back; **¿qué persigues con esto?** what do you hope to achieve by this?
perseverancia *f* **1.** (*insistencia*) ~ **en algo** insistence on sth **2.** (*en trabajo, actividad*) ~ **en algo** perseverance in sth **3.** (*firmeza*) resolve
perseverante *adj* **1.** (*insistente*) insistent **2.** (*constante*) persevering **3.** (*firme*) determined
perseverar *vi* **1.** (*insistir*) to insist **2.** (*mantener*) ~ **en algo** to persevere in sth
Persia *f* Persia
persiana *f* blind
pérsico, -a *adj* Persian
persignarse *vr* to cross oneself
persistencia *f* **1.** (*insistencia*) insistence **2.** (*perduración*) persistence

persistente *adj* **1.** (*persona*) persistent **2.** (*acción, recuerdo*) lasting
persistir *vi* **1.** (*insistir*) to insist **2.** (*perdurar*) to persist
persona *f* person; ~ **de contacto** contact; ~ (**non**) **grata** persona (non) grata; **en** ~ in person; ~ **jurídica** legal entity; ~ **mayor** adult, grown-up; ~ **física** individual; **ser buena/ mala** ~ to be good/bad; **había muchas** ~**s** there were a lot of people; **no había ninguna** ~ **allí** there was nobody there; **se apareció en la** ~ **de...** he/she appeared in the form of ...; **ese es una** ~ **de cuidado** you need to be careful with him
personaje *m* **1.** (*personalidad*) personality; ~ **de culto** cult figure; **es todo un** ~ he/she is a real character **2.** TEAT, LIT character
personal¹ I. *adj* personal; **datos** ~**es** personal details; **pronombre** ~ personal pronoun II. *m* **1.** (*plantilla*) personnel; (*en empresa*) staff; ~ **de a bordo** AVIAT aircrew; ~ **docente** teaching staff; ~ **de tierra** AVIAT ground crew **2.** *inf* (*gente*) people *pl*
personal² *f* DEP foul
personalidad *f* personality
personalizar <z→c> *vt* **1.** (*hacer personal*) to personalize **2.** (*aludir*) to get personal
personarse *vr* to appear; ~ **en juicio** to appear before the court; **persónese ante el director** report to the director; **el lunes tengo que personarme en el INEM** on Monday I have to go to the job centre *Brit* [*o* center *Am*]
personero, -a *m, f AmL* government representative
personificar <c→qu> *vt* to personify; **personifica la maldad** he is evil personified
perspectiva *f* **1.** (*general*) perspective **2.** (*vista*) view **3.** *pl* (*posibilidad*) prospects *pl* **4.** (*distancia*) **aún no disponemos de la** ~ **adecuada para valorar este periodo** we are still too close to the period to be able to judge it
perspicacia *f* insight
perspicaz *adj* **1.** (*vista*) keen **2.** (*persona*) perceptive
persuadir I. *vt* **1.** (*inducir*) to encourage; **le** ~**é para que no haga el viaje** I will try to persuade him not to make the journey **2.** (*convencer*) to persuade II. *vr* to be persuaded
persuasión *f* **1.** (*acto*) persuasion; **emplear todo su poder de** ~ to use all one's powers of persuasion **2.** (*convencimiento*) belief
persuasivo, -a *adj* persuasive
pertenecer *irr como* crecer *vi* **1.** (*ser de*) to belong; **esta casa me pertenece** this house belongs to me; **esta cita pertenece a Hamlet** this is a quotation from Hamlet **2.** (*tener obligación*) **te pertenece a ti hacerlo** it is your duty to do it; **esto pertenece al Ministerio de Asuntos Exteriores** that's the Foreign Office's *Brit* [*o* State Department's *Am*] responsibility
perteneciente *adj* ~ **a** belonging to; **los países** ~**s a la ONU** the countries which are

members of the UN; **todo lo ~ al caso** everything which is relevant to the case; **un cuadro ~ a la colección de Thyssen** a picture which belongs to the Thyssen collection
pertenencia f 1.(acción) belonging; (afiliación) membership 2. pl (bienes) belongings pl 3. pl (accesorios) accessories pl
pértiga f t. DEP (vara) pole; **salto de ~** pole vault; **saltar con ~** to pole vault; **~ del trole** current-collecting pole, trolley pole
pertinacia f (de lluvia, persona) persistence
pertinaz adj (lluvia, tos, persona) persistent
pertinente adj 1.(oportuno) appropriate 2.(datos, pregunta, comentario) relevant, pertinent 3.(relativo) **en lo ~ a...** with regard to ...
pertrechar I. vt to supply II. vr ~**se de algo** (de alimentos) to supply oneself with sth; (de equipamiento) to equip oneself with sth
pertrechos mpl MIL supplies pl
perturbación f disturbance
perturbado, -a I. adj PSICO disturbed II. m, f ~ (mental) mentally disturbed person
perturbador(a) I. adj disturbing II. m(f) 1.(por hacer ruido) disturber of the peace 2.(por alborotar) troublemaker
perturbar vt to disturb; (confundir) to confuse
Perú m Peru

Perú lies in the western part of South America. It is the third largest country after Brazil and Argentina. The capital and also the largest city in Peru is **Lima**. Both Spanish and **quechua** are the official languages of the country and the monetary unit is the **sol**. The original inhabitants of Peru were the **incas**.

peruano, -a adj, m, f Peruvian
perversidad f 1.(maldad) wickedness 2.(sexual) perversity
perversión f 1.(acción) perversion; ~ **de menores** corruption of minors 2.(cualidad) perversity
perverso, -a adj 1.(malo) wicked 2.(moral) twisted 3.(sexual) perverse
pervertido, -a I. adj perverted II. m, f pervert
pervertir irr como sentir I. vt to corrupt II. vr 1.(en costumbres, ideología) to become corrupt 2.(depravarse) to become perverted
pesa f t. DEP weight; ~ **del reloj** clock weight; **hacer (entrenamiento de) ~s** to do weight training; **levantamiento de ~s** weightlifting
pesadez f 1.(de objeto) heaviness 2.(de movimiento) slowness, sluggishness 3.(de sueño) drowsiness 4.(de tarea) boring nature 5.(de persona) tiresome nature 6.(de viaje) tediousness 7.(de lectura) density, (aburrido) dullness 8.(de dibujo) over-elaboration 9.(de estómago) (acid) indigestion
pesadilla f nightmare
pesado, -a adj 1.(que pesa) heavy; **tengo la**

cabeza pesada my head feels rather stuffy; **tengo el estómago ~** my stomach is uncomfortably full 2.(lento) slow 3.(molesto) tiresome 4.(duro) hard; **hacer un diccionario es ~** writing a dictionary is hard work 5.(aburrido) boring 6.(sueño) deep; (tiempo) oppressive; (viaje) tedious; (lectura) heavy going; (dibujo) over-elaborate
pesadumbre f 1.affliction 2. elev heaviness
pésame m condolences pl; **dar el ~** to offer one's condolences; **reciba mi más sincero ~ por la muerte de su hermana** please accept my condolences for the loss of your sister
pesantez f gravity
pesar I. vi 1.(tener peso) to weigh; **esta caja pesa mucho** this box is very heavy; **pon encima lo que no pese** put the lightest things on top 2.(cargo, responsabilidad) ~ **sobre alguien** to weigh heavily on sb; (problemas) to weigh sb down 3.(hipoteca) to affect II. vt 1.(objeto, persona) to weigh; (cantidad concreta) to weigh out; **¿me puede ~ la fruta?** could you weigh this fruit for me? 2.(ventajas) to weigh up 3.(disgustar) **me pesa haberte mentido** I regret having lied to you; **mal que te pese...** much as you may dislike it ...; **pese a quien pese** come what may; **pese a que...** although ... III. m 1.(pena) sorrow; **muy a ~ mío** to my great sadness 2.(remordimiento) regret ►**a ~ de** in spite of; **a ~ de todo lo quiere intentar** in spite of everything, he/she wants to try it
pesaroso, -a adj 1.(afligido) sad; **está ~ por haberlo dicho** he really regrets having said it 2.(disgustado) upset 3.(preocupado) worried
pesca f 1.(acción, oficio, industria) fishing; **ir de ~** to go fishing; ~ **de altura** deep-sea fishing; ~ **de arrastre** trawling; ~ **de bajura** inshore fishing; **y toda la ~** fig, inf and all the rest of the crew 2.(captura) capture
pescadería f (tienda) fishmonger's Brit, fishmarket
pescadilla f whiting; **ser la ~ que se muerde la cola** inf to be a vicious circle
pescado m fish
pescador(a) m(f) (de caña) angler; (de mar) fisherman
pescar <c→qu> vt 1.(con caña, en barco) to fish for; **ir a ~ sardinas** to fish for sardines 2.(resfriado) to catch 3. inf (novio) to land 4. inf (entender) to understand 5.(sorprender) to catch out
pescuezo m (scruff of the) neck; **retorcer el ~ a alguien** inf to wring sb's neck; **sacar el ~** inf to be snooty; **salvar el ~** fig to save one's skin
pese adv ~ **a** in spite of, despite
pesebre m manger; (de Navidad) Nativity scene
pesero m Méx minibus
peseta f peseta; **cambiar la ~** inf to throw up
pesetero, -a m, f money-grubbing; **este comerciante es un ~** all this businessman

thinks about is money
pesimismo *m sin pl* pessimism
pesimista I. *adj* pessimistic II. *mf* pessimist
pésimo, -a *adj* dreadful
peso *m* 1. (*de objeto*) weight; **coger/perder**
~ to gain/lose weight; **¿qué ~ tiene?** how
much does it weigh?; **vender a ~** to sell by
weight; **eso cae por su propio ~** that goes
without saying 2. (*pesadez*) heaviness; **tener**
~ **en las piernas** to have heavy legs
3. (*importancia*) weight; **es un gran ~ dentro**
de la empresa he/she has a lot of influence
within the business; **tener una razón de ~** to
have a good reason 4. (*carga*) burden; **llevar**
el ~ de algo to bear the burden of sth; **me**
saco un ~ de encima that's taken a load off
my mind 5. DEP (*bola*) shot 6. DEP (*boxeo*) ~
gallo bantamweight 7. (*moneda*) peso ▶ **com-**
prar a ~ de oro to pay way over the odds;
pagar a ~ de oro to pay the earth
pespuntar *vt* to backstitch
pespunte *m* 1. (*acción, costura*) backstitch-
ing 2. (*puntada*) backstitch
pespuntear *vt* to backstitch
pesquero *m* fishing boat
pesquero, -a *adj* fishing
pesquisa¹ *f* inquiry; **hacer ~s** to make
inquiries
pesquisa² *m Arg, Ecua, Par* detective
pestaña *f* eyelash; **quemarse las ~s** *fig* to
burn the midnight oil
pestañ(e)ar *vi* to blink; **sin ~** without batting
an eyelid
pestañeo *m* blinking
peste *f* 1. *t.* MED (*plaga*) plague; ~ **bubónica**
bubonic plague 2. (*olor*) stench; **aquí hay una**
~ **increíble** it really stinks here 3. (*crítica*)
echar ~s de alguien to heap abuse on sb
pesticida *m* pesticide
pestífero, -a *adj* 1. (*fétido*) foul-smelling
2. (*pernicioso*) pernicious
pestilencia *f* 1. (*olor*) stench 2. MED pesti-
lence
pestilente *adj v.* **pestífero**
pestillo *m* (*de puerta, cerradura*) bolt; **echar**
el ~ to shoot the bolt; ~ **de golpe** spring bolt
petaca *f* 1. (*para cigarros*) cigarette case;
(*para tabaco*) tobacco pouch 2. (*para bebidas*)
hip flask 3. *AmL* (*caja*) box; (*baúl*) chest;
(*cesto*) basket 4. *AmC* (*joroba*) hump
petacón, -ona *adj AmL* tubby
pétalo *m* petal
petanca *f* DEP bowls, petanque
petardo *m* 1. (*de fiesta*) firecracker; **tirar ~s**
to let off firecrackers 2. (*estafa*) swindle; **pegar**
un ~ a alguien to take sb for a ride 3. *inf* (*persona o cosa mala*) **ser un ~** to be a pain
petate *m* (*de soldado, marinero*) kit bag; **liar**
el ~ *fig* to pack up and go
petatearse *vr Méx* (*morirse*) to peg out *inf*
petenera *f* MÚS *Andalusian song;* **salirse por**
~s to go off on a tangent
petición *f* 1. (*ruego, solicitud*) request; **a ~**

de... at the request of ...; **¿has hecho ya la ~**
de mano? have you asked her to marry you
yet? 2. (*escrito*) petition
peticionar *vt AmL* to petition
petirrojo *m* robin (redbreast)
petiso, -a I. *adj Arg, Urug* 1. (*pequeño*) small;
(*muy pequeño*) tiny 2. (*enano*) short II. *m, f*
short person
petisú *m* eclair
petitorio, -a *adj* petitionary
peto *m* 1. (*de armadura*) breastplate 2. (*de*
bebé, delantal) bib 3. (*pantalón*) overalls,
dungarees *pl Am*
pétreo, -a *adj* 1. (*como piedra, pedregoso*)
stony 2. (*duro*) rock-hard
petrificación *f* petrification
petrificar <c→qu> I. *vt t. fig* to petrify II. *vr:*
~se to turn to stone
petrodólar *m* ECON petrodollar
petróleo *m* 1. (*carburante*) petroleum,
(crude) oil 2. (*de lámpara*) paraffin
petrolero *m* (*barco*) oil tanker
petrolero, -a I. *adj* 1. (*del carburante*) petrol,
oil 2. (*de la lámpara*) paraffin II. *m, f* (*persona*) arsonist
petrolífero, -a *adj* oil-bearing; **campo ~** oilfield; **industria petrolífera** oil industry
petroquímica *f sin pl* petrochemistry
petulancia *f* 1. (*arrogancia*) arrogance
2. (*insolencia*) insolence 3. (*vanidad*) vanity
petulante *adj* 1. (*arrogante*) arrogant;
(*creído*) conceited 2. (*insolente*) insolent
petunia *f* petunia
peyorativo, -a *adj* pejorative; **un comenta-**
rio ~ a derrogatory remark
peyote *m AmL* BOT peyote cactus
pez¹ *m* ZOOL fish; **estar como (el) ~ en el**
agua to be in one's element; **estar ~ en**
español *inf* to have no idea of Spanish; **ese es**
un buen ~ he's a wily bird; **un ~ gordo** a big
shot
pez² *f* 1. (*betún*) pitch 2. (*excremento*) meco-
nium
pezón *m* 1. (*de mujer*) nipple 2. (*de animal*)
teat 3. BOT stalk
pezuña *f* 1. (*de vaca, oveja*) hoof 2. *pl, inf* (*de*
persona) feet *pl*
PHN *abr de* **Plan Hidrológico Nacional**
national water plan
pi *f* MAT pi
piadoso, -a *adj* 1. (*misericordioso*) merciful;
(*bondadoso*) compassionate 2. (*devoto*) pious
pialar *vt AmL* to lasso
pianista *mf* pianist
piano I. *m* piano; ~ **de cola** grand piano II. *adv*
MÚS piano
piar <*1. pres:* pío> *vi* 1. (*pájaro*) to chirp
2. (*clamar*) ~ **por algo** to cry out for sth
piara *f* herd (of pigs)
PIB *m abr de* **Producto Interior Bruto** GDP
pibe, -a *m, f Arg* (*chico*) boy; (*chica*) girl
pibil *m Méx* GASTR chili sauce
pica *f* 1. (*lanza*) pike 2. *pl* (*de cartas*) spades

pl

picacho *m* peak

picada *f* 1.(*de avispa*) sting; (*de serpiente*) bite 2.(*de pez*) bite 3. *CSur* (*tapas*) snack

picadero *m* 1.(*para adiestrar*) ring; (*escuela*) riding school 2. *inf* bachelor pad, diggings *pl*

picadillo *m* (*carne picada*) mince *Brit*, ground meat *Am*; (*para embutido, salchichas*) filling; **hacer ~ a alguien** *inf* to make mincemeat of sb

picado *m* (*de avión*) dive; **las acciones cayeron en ~** shares slumped; **su fama ha caído en ~** his reputation has plummeted

picado, -a *adj* 1.(*con picaduras: abrigo*) moth-eaten; (*fruta*) rotten; (*muela*) decayed; (*cara*) pockmarked 2.(*con agujeros*) perforated 3.(*mar*) choppy 4. *inf* (*enfadado*) annoyed

picador *m* 1.(*adiestrador*) horse-breaker 2. TAUR picador (*mounted bullfighter who goads the bull with a lance*) 3. MIN faceworker

picadura *f* 1.(*de insecto*) sting; (*de serpiente*) bite 2.(*en ropa, metal*) hole 3.(*tabaco*) cut tobacco 4.(*caries*) cavity

picaflor *m* 1. ZOOL hummingbird 2. *AmL* (*tenorio*) Don Juan

picante I. *adj* 1.(*comida*) spicy, hot 2. *fig* risqué II. *m* 1. GASTR spicy food 2.(*de comida*) spiciness 3.(*de expresión*) sauciness

picantería *f And* (*restaurante modesto*) small restaurant

picapica *f* (**polvos**) **~** (*de picores*) itching powder; (*de estornudos*) sneezing powder

picapleitos *m inv, pey* pettifogger, shyster

picaporte *m* 1.(*aldaba*) doorknocker 2.(*tirador*) door handle 3.(*pestillo*) latch

picar <c→qu> I. *vi* 1.(*sol, ojos*) to sting 2.(*chile, pimienta*) to be hot 3.(*pez, clientes*) to take the bait 4.(*de la comida*) to snack 5.(*tener picazón*) to itch; **me pica la espalda** my back is itchy 6.(*avión*) to dive 7.(*golpear*) **~ a la puerta** to knock on the door 8.(*aspirar*) **~ muy alto** to aim too high 9.(*ser*) **su actitud pica en valiente** his attitude is a brave one II. *vt* 1.(*con punzón*) to prick, to pierce 2.(*sacar*) **~ una aceituna de la lata** to fish an olive from the tin 3.(*insecto*) to sting; (*serpiente*) to bite 4.(*ave*) to peck 5.(*desmenuzar*) to chop up; (*carne*) to mince; (*tabaco*) to shred 6.(*caballo*) to spur on 7.(*papel, tela*) to perforate; (*billete*) to punch 8.(*ofender*) to irritate; **estar picado con alguien** to be annoyed with sb; **¿qué mosca te ha picado?** what's eating you? 9.(*incitar*) to goad 10. TIPO to insert 11. INFOR to click on III. *vr* 1.(*metal*) to rust; (*muela*) to decay; (*ropa*) to get moth-eaten; (*vino*) to turn sour; (*semillas*) to go off 2.(*mar*) to become choppy 3.(*ofenderse*) to become irritated; (*mosquearse*) to become angry; **~se por nada** to get irritated about the slightest thing; **siempre se pica cuando juega** he/she always becomes angry when playing 4. *AmL* (*embriagarse*) to get tipsy

picardear I. *vi* to get into mischief II. *vr* to fall into bad ways

picardía *f* 1.(*malicia*) roguishness; **lo dije con ~** I said it out of a sense of mischief 2.(*travesura*) naughty trick 3.(*broma*) joke

picaresco, -a *adj* 1.(*astuto*) cunning 2.(*comentario*) mischievous

pícaro, -a I. *adj* 1.(*granuja*) roguish 2.(*astuto*) cunning 3.(*comentario*) naughty II. *m, f* (*granuja*) rogue ▸**~ de siete suelas** *inf* out-and-out rogue

picarón *m AmL* (*buñuelo*) fritter

picatoste *m* crouton

picazón *f* 1.(*comezón*) itch 2.(*disgusto*) annoyance

picha *f vulg* (*pene*) dick, prick

pichanga *f* 1. *Arg* (*vino*) wine (*not fully fermented*) 2. *Bol* (*fácil*) **ser ~** to be a cinch *inf*

pichi *m* 1.(*falda*) pinafore 2. *CSur, inf* (*pipí*) pee, wee wee *childspeak*

pichicata *f Arg, inf* (*droga*) drugs *pl*

pichicatearse *vr Arg, inf* (*drogarse*) to take drugs

pichicatero, -a *m, f Arg, inf* (*adicto*) drug addict

pichicato, -a I. *adj AmC* stingy II. *m, f AmC* skinflint

pichichi *m* DEP top goal-scorer

pichín *m CSur, inf* (*pipí*) pee

pichincha *f* 1. *Arg* (*ganga*) bargain 2. *Chile* (*cantidad pequeña*) tiny bit; **con sólo una ~ de leche** with just a drop of milk

pichirre I. *adj Ven* (*tacaño*) stingy II. *mf Ven, inf* (*tacaño*) skinflint

pichón *m* young pigeon

pichón, -ona *m, f* (*querido*) darling

pichoso, -a *adj* 1. *Col* (*de ojos llorosos*) watery-eyed 2. *Ven* (*sucio*) dirty

pichula *f Chile, vulg* (*pene*) dick

pichulear *vt* 1. *Chile* (*engañar*) to cheat 2. *CSur* (*negociar*) to buy and sell (*on a small scale*)

picnic *m* picnic

pico *m* 1.(*pájaro*) woodpecker 2.(*del pájaro*) beak 3. *inf* (*boca*) mouth, gob *Brit*; **¡cierra el ~!** shut your trap!; **~ de oro** the gift of the gab; **tener un buen ~** to be a smooth talker; **¡él de ~ todo lo que quieras!** he's always promising the earth!; **alguien se fue del ~** sb let the cat out of the bag; **¡ese se perderá por el ~!** his big mouth will be the end of him! 4.(*herramienta*) pickaxe *Brit*, pickax *Am* 5.(*montaña*) peak; **cortado a ~** sheer 6.(*de jarra*) lip 7.(*cantidad*) **llegar a las cuatro y ~** to arrive just after four o'clock; **tiene cuarenta y ~ de años** he/she is forty-something; **salir por un ~** to cost a lot

picor *m* (*en la piel*) itching; (*en la boca*) stinging, burning

picota *f* 1.(*tortura*) pillory; **poner en la ~ a alguien** *fig* to pillory sb 2. BOT cherry

picotada *f,* **picotazo** *m* (*de ave*) peck; (*de insecto*) sting; (*de serpiente*) bite; **pegar una**

~ (*ave*) to peck; (*insecto*) to sting; (*serpiente*) to bite; **arrancar a ~s** to peck off
picotear I. *vi* 1. (*comer*) to nibble 2. (*hablar*) to chatter II. *vt* to peck III. *vr* 1. (*personas*) to squabble 2. (*pájaros*) to peck
pictórico, -a *adj* pictorial; **técnica pictórica** painting technique
picudo, -a *adj* 1. (*puntiagudo*) pointed; (*anguloso*) angular 2. (*charlatán*) gossipy
pie *m* 1. (*extremidad, medida*) foot; ~**s planos** flat feet; ~ **de atleta** MED athlete's foot; ~ **equino** clubfoot; **¿qué ~ calza Ud.?** what shoe size do you take?; **al ~ del árbol** at the foot of the tree; **al ~ de la carta** at the bottom of the letter; **a(l) ~ de (la) obra** on the spot; **a ~ on foot**; **a ~ firme** steadfastly; **quedarse de ~** to remain standing; **estar de ~** to be standing; **ponerse de ~** to stand up; **caer de ~s** to land on one's feet; **ya sabemos de qué ~ cojea** *fig* now we know his weak spot; **tener los ~s en el suelo** *fig* to be realistic; **echar ~ a tierra** (*salir de coche*) to get out; (*salir del tren, autobús*) to get off; **se marchó del hospital por su propio ~** he left hospital under his own steam; **no hacer ~** (*en una piscina*) to be out of one's depth; **perder ~** (*en una piscina*) to get out of one's depth; **estoy cansada: no me tengo en ~** I am so tired I can barely stand; **con buen ~** *fig* on the right footing; **estar en ~ de guerra** to be on a war footing; **en ~ de igualdad** on an equal footing; **este informe está hecho con los ~s** *inf* this report is a dreadful piece of work; **ya tiene un ~ en el hoyo** *inf* he/she already has one foot in the grave; **este nació de ~** *inf* this one was born lucky; **no le des ~ para que se queje de ti** don't give him/her a chance to complain about you 2. TIPO ~ **de imprenta** imprint; ~ **de página** foot of the page 3. (*planta*) stem; (*tronco*) trunk; ~ **de vid** vine stock 4. (*métrica*) foot 5. TEAT cue 6. (*trípode*) leg ►~ **de banco** *inf* stupid idea; **hoy no doy ~ con bola** I can't seem to do anything right today; **no tener ni ~s ni cabeza** to make no sense; **estar al ~ del cañón** to be ready for action; ~ **de fuerza** AmL armed forces; **buscar tres ~s al gato** (*daño*) to ask for trouble; (*complicaciones*) to complicate matters; **seguir algo al ~ de la letra** to follow sth to the letter; **andarse con ~s de plomo** to tread very carefully; **poner ~s en polvorosa** to cut and run; **creer a ~(s) juntillas** to believe unquestioningly; **parar los ~s a alguien** *inf* to put sb in his/her place; **~s, ¿para qué os quiero?** time to leave!; **salir por ~s** *inf* to beat it; **de a ~** ordinary
piedad *f sin pl* 1. REL piety; (*compasión*) pity; **¡ten ~ de nosotros!** have pity on us! 2. ECON **monte de ~** pawnshop
piedra *f* 1. GEO, MED stone; ~ **pómez** pumice stone; ~ **preciosa** precious stone; **cartón ~** papier-mâché; **Edad de Piedra** Stone Age; **poner la primera ~** to lay the foundation

stone; **lo saben hasta las ~s** the whole world knows; **lavado a la ~** stonewashed; ~ **angular** *fig* cornerstone; ~ **filosofal** *fig* philosopher's stone; ~ **de toque** *fig* touchstone; **no te quejes que menos da una ~** *fig* don't complain, it's better than nothing; **no dejar ~ por mover** *fig* to leave no stone unturned; **no dejar ~ sobre ~** to raze to the ground; **cuando lo supimos nos quedamos de ~** we were absolutely stunned when we found out about it; **tirar la ~ y esconder la mano** to play the innocent; **tirarse ~s a su propio tejado** to foul one's own nest; **pasar a alguien por la ~** *inf* to lay sb 2. (*granizo*) hail 3. (*mechero*) flint
piel *f* 1. (*de persona*) skin; **estos niños son de la ~ del diablo** these children are little devils; **en esa empresa se dejó la ~** *inf* he/she worked himself/herself into the ground for that company 2. (*de animal*) skin, hide; (*con pelo*) fur; (*cuero*) leather; **un abrigo de ~es** a fur coat 3. (*de fruta*) skin ►~ **de gallina** goose-pimples *pl*; **se me puso la ~ de gallina oyendo su historia** hearing his story made my flesh crawl
pienso *m* (*ganado*) fodder; ~ **completo** compound feed
pierna *f* (*extremidad*) leg; (*entre la rodilla y el pie*) lower leg; ~ **ortopédica** artificial leg; **estirar las ~s** to stretch one's legs; **con las ~s cruzadas** with one's legs crossed; **dormir a ~ suelta** to be fast asleep; **en ~s** bare-legged
pieza *f* 1. (*pedazo*) piece; (*parte*) part; (*reproducción*) copy; ~ **de artillería** artillery piece; ~ **de recambio** spare part; ~ **suelta** individual part; **un traje de dos ~s** a two-piece suit; ~ **por ~** piece by piece; **vender a ~s** to sell by the piece 2. (*caza*) specimen; (*pesca*) catch 3. MÚS, TEAT piece 4. (*damas, ajedrez*) piece 5. AmL (*habitación*) room 6. (*moneda*) coin, piece 7. *inf* (*malicioso*) **¡menuda ~ está hecho ese!** what a little rascal he is! ►**quedarse de una ~** to be absolutely dumbfounded
pifia *f* 1. (*error*) blunder 2. And (*escarnio*) mockery
pigmentación *f* pigmentation
pigmento *m* pigment
pignorar *vt* to pawn
pija *f* AmL, *vulg* (*pene*) dick
pijada *f inf* (*tontería*) piece of nonsense; **¡esos son ~s!** what a load of nonsense!
pijama *m* pyjamas *pl*, pajamas *pl* Am
pije *m* Chile, *inf* (*fanfarrón*) toff *inf*
pijo *m vulg* (*pene*) dick; **¡y un ~!** like hell!
pijo, -a *pey, inf* I. *adj* posh; **niño ~** upper-class twit II. *m, f* posh youth
pijotero, -a *adj* 1. *pey* (*fastidioso*) annoying 2. AmL (*tacaño*) stingy
pila *f* 1. (*recipiente*) basin; (*lavadero*) sink; (*fuente*) fountain; (*bautismal*) font; **nombre de ~** first name, Christian name 2. FÍS battery; ~ **reversible** reversible battery; **ponerse las ~s** *inf* to get one's act together 3. (*montón*)

pile; **una ~ de libros** a pile of books **4.** ARQUIT
pile **5.** INFOR **~ de discos** disk drive
pila-botón *f* <pilas-botón> (*batería*) watch
battery
pilar *m* **1.**(*columna*) pillar **2.**(*apoyo*) prop
3.(*en camino*) milestone
pilcha *f CSur, inf* (*prendas*) fine clothes *pl*
pilche *m And* wooden bowl
píldora *f* pill; **la ~** (**anticonceptiva**) the pill;
dorar la ~ a alguien *inf* to sweeten the pill;
me tragué la ~ *fig* I fell for it
pileta *f* **1.** *Arg* (*de cocina*) kitchen sink **2.** *Arg*
(*piscina*) swimming pool **3.** *RíoPl* (*abrevadero*)
water trough **4.** *Arg* **tirarse a la ~** to go headlong into sth
pilila *f inf* (*pene de niño*) willy *Brit*
pililo, -a *m, f CSur, pey* tramp
pillaje *m* pillage
pillapilla *m inf* **jugar al ~** to play tag
pillar *vt* **1.**(*atropellar*) to knock down, to run
over **2.**(*encontrar*) to find; (*en flagrante*) to
catch; **me pillas de buen humor** you've
caught me in a good mood; **la noche nos pilló
en el monte** when night came we were still
on the mountain; **eso no me pilla de sorpresa** that doesn't surprise me; **tu casa nos
pilla de camino** your house is on our way;
Correos no nos pilla cerca the Post Office
isn't very near; **aquí te pillo, aquí te mato** *fig*
to strike while the iron is hot **3.**(*entender*) to
grasp **4.**(*robar*) to steal **5.** *Arg* (*orinar*) to piss
pillastre *m inf* rascal
pillín, -ina I. *adj inf* crafty II. *m, f inf* little rascal
pillo, -a I. *adj inf* crafty II. *m, f inf* rascal
pilmama *f Méx* nanny
pilme *m Chile* ZOOL blister beetle
pilón *m* **1.**(*lavadero*) basin; (*abrevadero*)
drinking trough **2.**(*mortero*) mortar **3.**(*pesa*)
weight **4.** ARQUIT pillar
piloncillo *m Méx* brown sugar
piloso, -a *adj* hairy
pilotar *vt* (*barco*) to steer; (*coche*) to drive;
(*avión*) to fly
pilote *m* ARQUIT pile
pilotear *vt AmL* **1.**(*ayudar*) to guide **2.**(*negocio*) to run **3.** *Chile* (*explotar*) to exploit
piloto¹ I. *mf* **1.** NÁUT navigator; (*oficial*) first
mate; (*práctico*) (*harbour*) pilot **2.** AVIAT pilot;
poner el ~ automático to set the automatic
pilot **3.** AUTO driver; **~ de carreras** racing
driver II. *adj* (*de prueba*) test; (*de modelo*)
show, model; **piso ~** show flat *Brit*, model
apartment *Am;* **experiencia ~** test
piloto² *m* **1.**(*lámpara*) pilot light **2.** *Arg*
(*impermeable*) raincoat
piltrafa *f* **1.**(*comida*) scrap **2.**(*persona*)
wreck
pilucho, -a *adj Chile* naked
pimentero *m* **1.** BOT pepper plant **2.**(*vasija*)
pepper pot
pimentón *m* paprika
pimienta *f* pepper; **~ en grano** peppercorns

pl
pimiento *m* pepper; **~ encarnado** red
pepper; **me importa un ~ lo que él diga** I
couldn't care less what he says
pimpante *adj inf* **1.**(*elegante*) swish **2.**(*despreocupado*) unconcerned; **tan ~** as if nothing
had happened
pimpón *m sin pl* DEP ping-pong
pinacate *m Méx* ZOOL black stinkbug
pinacoteca *f* art gallery
pináculo *m* pinnacle
pinar *m* pine grove
pincel *m* (paint)brush; (*de maquillaje*)
make-up brush; **estar hecho un ~** to be styl-
ishly dressed
pincelada *f* brushstroke; **dar las últimas ~s**
fig to apply the finishing touches
pinchar I. *vi* **1.**(*rueda*) to puncture *Brit,* to
have a flat (tire) *Am* **2.**(*fracasar*) to fail ▸**ni ~
ni cortar** *inf* to not count for anything II. *vt*
1.(*alfiler*) to prick **2.**(*estimular*) to prod;
(*mortificar*) to wound **3.**(*inyección*) to give an
injection; **tengo que ir al médico para que
me pinche** I have to go the doctor's for an
injection **4.**(*teléfono*) to tap III. *vr* **1.**(*alfiler*)
to prick oneself **2.**(*rueda*) **se nos ha pin-
chado una rueda** one of our wheels has a
puncture **3.**(*insulina*) to give oneself an injection **4.** *inf* (*drogarse*) to shoot up
pinchazo *m* **1.**(*espina*) prick; **me dieron
unos ~s insoportables en el estómago** I
had some really horrible shooting pains in the
stomach **2.**(*neumático*) puncture, flat (tyre)
Brit, flat (tire) *Am;* **tuvimos un ~ tras la
curva** we had a puncture after the bend
pinche *mf* kitchen boy, cook's helper *Am*
pinchito *m* (*tapa*) snack; (*en un palillo*) aperitif on a cocktail stick
pincho *m* **1.**(*erizo*) sting; (*rosa*) thorn **2.** *v.*
pinchito
pinciano, -a I. *adj* of/from Valladolid II. *m, f*
native/inhabitant of Valladolid
pinedo *m AmC* pine grove
pinga *f Col, Méx, Perú, vulg* (*pene*) prick *vulg;*
¡**de ~!** unreal!
pingajo *m inf* rag
pingo *m* **1.** *inf* (*harapo*) rag **2.** *pey* (*mujer*) slut
3. *CSur* (*caballo*) horse ▸**ir de ~** to go out on
the town; **poner a alguien hecho un ~** to
run sb down
pingonear *vi inf* to loaf about
ping-pong *m sin pl* ping-pong
pingüe *adj* (*negocio*) lucrative; **~s beneficios**
fat profits
pingüino *m* penguin
pino *m* **1.**(*árbol, madera*) pine; **~ piñonero**
stone pine **2.** DEP handstand ▸**en el quinto ~**
in the back of beyond
pinol(e) *m AmC* pinole, (*aromatic powder to
mix in chocolate*)
pinta¹ I. *f. t.* ZOOL (*mancha*) spot; (*gota*) drop;
a ~s spotted **2.** *inf* (*aspecto*) appearance;
tener ~ de caro to look expensive; **tener**

buena ~ (*dish*) to look tasty; (*persona*) to be attractive; **sacar por la** ~ to recognize

pinta² *f* (*medida*) pint

pintada *f* **1.** ZOOL guinea fowl **2.** (*pared*) (piece of) graffiti

pintado, -a *adj* (*animal*) spotted; **papel** ~ wallpaper; **eso viene como** ~ that is just what was needed; **el traje te sienta que ni** ~ *inf* the suit really suits you; **no lo puedo ver ni** ~ *inf* I can't stand even the sight of him

pintalabios *m inv* lipstick

pintar I. *vi* **1.** ARTE to paint **2.** (*bolígrafo*) to write II. *vt* **1.** (*pared*) to paint; (*con dibujos*) to decorate; ~ **de azul** to paint blue; **¡recién pintado!** wet paint! **2.** (*cuadro*) to paint; **¿qué pinta eso aquí?** *fig* what's that doing here?; **no** ~ **nada** *fig* (*persona*) to have no influence; (*asunto*) to be completely irrelevant **3.** (*describir*) to describe III. *vr* to do one's make-up

pinto, -a *adj* spotted

pintor(a) *m(f)* painter

pintoresco, -a *adj* picturesque, colourful *Brit*, colorful *Am*

pintura *f* **1.** (*arte*) painting; ~ **a la aguada** watercolour *Brit*, watercolor *Am*; ~ **al óleo** oil painting; ~ **rupestre** cave painting; **voy a clases de** ~ I go to painting classes **2.** (*cuadro*) painting; **no lo puedo ver ni en** ~ *inf* I can't stand him **3.** (*color*) paint; **caja de** ~**s** paintbox; **dar una capa de** ~ **a algo** to give sth a coat of paint

pinturero, -a I. *adj* fashion-conscious II. *m, f* dandy

pinza(s) *f(pl)* **1.** (*tenacilla*) tongs *pl;* TÉC pincers *pl* **2.** (*para la ropa*) (clothes) peg, (clothes) pin *Am* **3.** (*para depilar*) tweezers *pl* **4.** (*costura*) pleat **5.** (*de cangrejo*) claw

pinzón *m* finch

piña *f* **1.** (*pino*) pine cone **2.** (*fruta*) pineapple

piñón *m* **1.** (*pino*) pine nut; **estar a partir un** ~ **con alguien** *inf* to be thick as thieves **2.** TÉC pinion

pío *m* cheep; **no decir ni** ~ not to say a word; **¡~, ~, ~!** tweet, tweet!

pío, -a *adj* (*piadoso*) pious; (*bondadoso*) compassionate; **monte** ~ benefit fund; **obra pía** charitable deed

piocha *adj Méx, inf* (*magnífico*) great

piojo *m* louse; **estar como** ~**s en costura** *inf* to be packed in like sardines

piojoso, -a I. *adj* **1.** (*con piojos*) louse-infested; (*miserable*) lousy, crummy; (*sucio*) grotty **2.** *pey* (*mezquino*) mean II. *m, f pey* scoundrel

piola I. *adj Arg, inf* (*astuto*) clever II. *f AmS* (*cuerda*) cord

piolet *m* ice axe

piolín *m AmS* twine

pionero, -a *m, f* pioneer

pipa *f* **1.** (*fumador*) pipe; **preparar la** ~ to fill one's pipe; **fumar en** ~ to smoke a pipe **2.** (*tonel*) barrel **3.** (*de fruta*) pip, seed **4.** CRi, *inf* (*cabeza*) head **5.** *inf* (*pistola*) rod **6.** *pl* (*de*

girasol) sunflower seed **7.** *inf* (*muy bien*) **lo pasamos** ~ we had a great time

pipe *m AmC* (*camarada*) buddy

pipeta *f* pipette

pipí *m inf* pee, wee wee *childspeak*

pipil *adj AmC* Mexican

pipiolo, -a *m, f* **1.** *irón* (*novato*) novice, greenhorn **2.** *Méx* (*niño*) kid

pipón, -ona I. *adj Ant, Arg, Ecua, inf* (*barrigón*) pot-bellied; (*harto*) stuffed II. *m, f PRico, inf* (*niño*) boy; (*niña*) girl

pique *m* **1.** (*rivalidad*) rivalry; **menudo** ~ **se traían entre ellos** they really hate each other **2.** *Arg, Par, Nic* (*camino*) trail **3.** (*hundirse*) **irse a** ~ (*barco*) to sink; (*plan*) to fail

piqueta *f* pickaxe *Brit*, pickax *Am*

piquete *m* **1.** (*huelga*) (strike) picket **2.** MIL squad

pira *f* (*hoguera*) pyre; ~ **funeraria** funeral pyre

pirado, -a I. *adj inf* crazy II. *m, f inf* nutcase

piragua *f* canoe

piragüismo *m* canoeing

piramidal *adj* pyramidal

pirámide *f* pyramid

piraña *f* piranha

pirarse *vr inf* to clear off; ~ **de la clase** to skip class

pirata I. *mf* pirate; ~ **aereo** hijacker; INFOR hacker II. *adj* pirate; **emisora** ~ pirate radio station

pirca *f AmC* stone wall

pirco *m Chile* GASTR succotash

pirenaico, -a *adj* Pyrenean; **el Aneto es el pico** ~ **más elevado** Aneto is the highest mountain in the Pyrenees

Pirineos *mpl* Pyrenees

piripi *adj inf* tipsy

pirómano, -a *m, f* pyromaniac

piropear *vt inf* to make flirtatious comments to

piropo *m* **1.** *inf* (*lisonja*) flirtatious comment; **echar** ~**s** to make flirtatious comments **2.** (*granate*) garnet

pirotecnia *f sin pl* pyrotechnics

pirrarse *vr inf* ~**se por alguien** to be crazy about sb

pirueta *f* pirouette

piruja *f Méx, inf* hooker

piruleta *f*, **pirulí** *m* <pirulís> lollipop

pis *m inf* piss

pisa *f* **1.** (*acción de pisar*) treading **2.** *inf* (*paliza*) beating

pisada *f* **1.** (*acción*) footstep **2.** (*huella*) footprint; **seguir las** ~**s de alguien** *fig* to follow in sb's footsteps **3.** (*patada*) stamp of the foot

pisapapeles *m inv* paperweight

pisar *vt* **1.** (*poner el pie*) to tread; **¡no pises las flores!** don't tread on the flowers!; **me han pisado en el bus** sb trod on my foot on the bus; **ir pisando huevos** *fig* to tread carefully; ~ **los talones a alguien** *fig* to follow on sb's heels; ~ **fuerte** *fig* to make a big impact **2.** (*entrar*) to enter **3.** (*uvas, aceitunas*) to tread; (*tierra*) to tread down **4.**(*humillar*) to walk all over **5.** *inf* (*planes*) to pre-empt; **con su proyecto me pisan el terreno** their plan has beaten me to it; **me han pisado el tema** they have stolen my topic

piscicultura *f* fish farming

piscina *f* swimming pool; ~ **cubierta** indoor swimming pool

Piscis *m inv* Pisces

pisco *m* **1.**(*aguardiente*) *strong Peruvian liquor;* ~ **sour** *cocktail made with pisco, lemon and sugar* **2.** *Col, Ven* (*pavo*) turkey **3.** *Col, pey* (*hombre*) bloke *Brit,* guy

piscolabis *m inv, inf* snack

piso *m* **1.**(*pavimento*) floor; (*calle*) surface **2.**(*planta*) floor, storey *Brit,* story *Am;* **de dos** ~**s** with two floors **3.**(*vivienda*) flat *Brit,* apartment *Am* **4.**(*zapato*) sole **5.** MIN layer (*of workings*)

pisotear *vt* to trample; *fig* to walk all over

pisotón *m* stamp; **dar un** ~ **a alguien** to tread on sb's foot

pispear *vt Arg* (*birlar*) to nick *Brit,* to swipe

pista *f* **1.**(*huella*) trail; (*indicio*) clue; **estar sobre la buena** ~ to be on the right lines; **seguir la** ~ **a alguien** to follow sb's trail **2.**(*de circo*) ring; (*para atletismo, coches*) track; (*de tenis*) court; (*de baile*) floor; ~ **de aterrizaje** runway; ~ **de esquí** ski slope; ~ **de hielo** ice rink **3.**(*camino*) trail **4.** INFOR track

pistache *m* **1.** GASTR (*helado*) pistachio ice cream; (*dulce*) pistachio sweet **2.** *Méx* (*pistacho*) pistachio

pistacho *m* pistachio

pistero *m* (*taza*) cup with spout

pistilo *m* pistil

pisto *m* **1.**(*caldo*) chicken broth **2.**(*fritada*) vegetable stew (*made with tomato, onion, pepper and courgette*) **3.**(*mezcla*) hotchpotch *Brit,* hodgepodge *Am* **4.** *AmC* (*dinero*) dough ▶ **darse** ~ to show off

pistola *f* **1.**(*arma*) pistol **2.**(*del pintor*) spray gun

pistolera *f* **1.**(*funda*) holster **2.** *pl inf* ANAT *fat accumulated on hips*

pistolero *m* gunman

pistoletazo *m* pistol shot; ~ **de salida** *fig:* starting signal

pistón *m* **1.**(*émbolo*) piston **2.**(*de arma*) percussion cap **3.** MÚS key

pistonudo, -a *adj inf* great

pita *f* **1.** BOT agave, century plant **2.** *inf* (*gallina*) hen; ¡~, ~, ~! tweet, tweet!, cluck! cluck!

pitada *f Arg, inf* (*calada*) puff; **¿me das una ~?** will you let me have a puff?

pitanza *f* **1.**(*ración*) daily ration; *inf* (*alimentos*) grub **2.**(*precio*) price

pitar I. *vt, vi* **1.**(*claxon*) to blow; **me pitan los oídos** my ears are buzzing **2.**(*pagar*) to pay **3.** *AmS* (*fumar*) to smoke **4.** *Chile* (*engañar*) to cheat **II.** *vi* **1.** *inf* (*funcionar*) to work **2.** *inf* (*deprisa*) **salir pitando** to rush off **3.** *inf* (*ser*

suficiente) **¡con la mitad vas que pitas!** half of it should be more than enough!

pitido *m* whistle

pitillera *f* (*estuche*) cigarette case

pitillo *m* cigarette

pitiminí *m* BOT miniature rose; (*persona*) finicky person

pitiyanqui *m PRico* Yankee-lover

pito *m* **1.**(*silbato*) whistle; (*claxon*) horn; **tocar** ~**s** to click one's fingers; **entre** ~**s y flautas** *inf* what with one thing and another; **por** ~**s o por flautas** *inf* for one reason or another; **tomar a alguien por el** ~ **del sereno** *inf* to take no notice of sb; **no me importa un** ~ *inf* I don't give a damn about it; **no valer un** ~ *inf* to be completely worthless **2.**(*canica*) marble; **jugar a los** ~**s** to play marbles **3.**(*cigarro*) cigarette **4.**(*de vasija*) spout **5.**(*abucheo*) booing **6.** *inf* (*pene*) dick

pito, -a *adj inf* smart; **iba todo** ~ he looked really smart

pitón *m* **1.** ZOOL python **2.**(*cuerno*) budding horn; (*de toro*) horn **3.**(*pitorro*) spout

pitonisa *f* fortune teller

pitopausia *f inf* midlife crisis in males

pitorrearse *vr inf* to make fun

pitorreo *m inf* joking; **¡esto es un** ~! this is a joke!

pitorro *m* spout

pituco, -a I. *adj CSur* **1.**(*cursi*) affected, snooty **2.**(*muy acicalado*) overdressed **3.**(*nuevo rico*) nouveau riche **II.** *m, f CSur* **1.**(*cursi*) snob, toff *Brit* **2.**(*nuevo rico*) nouveau riche

pitufo *m inf* titch *Brit,* shrimp *Am*

pituita *f* mucus

pituitario, -a *adj* pituitary; **glándula pituitaria** pituitary gland

pivote *m* TÉC pivot

píxel *m* INFOR pixel

piyama *m AmL* pyjamas *pl,* pajamas *pl Am*

pizarra *f* **1.**(*roca*) slate **2.**(*encerado*) blackboard

pizarrín *m* slate pencil

pizarrón *m AmL* (*encerado*) blackboard

pizca *f* **1.** *inf* (*poco*) pinch, little bit; **una** ~ **de sal** a pinch of salt; **no tienes ni** ~ **de vergüenza** you have no shame whatsoever **2.** *Méx* (*cosecha*) harvest

pizcar <c→qu> *vt Méx* to pick

pizco *m* **1.**(*poco*) little bit **2.** *inf* (*pellizco*) pinch

pizpireta *adj* (*mujer*) vivacious

pizza *f* pizza

placa *f* **1.**(*lámina, plancha*) sheet; FOTO plate; INFOR board; ~ **base** INFOR motherboard; ~ **giratoria** FERRO turntable **2.**(*cartel*) plaque; ~ **conmemorativa** commemorative plaque **3.** AUTO number plate *Brit,* license plate *Am* **4.** MED ~ **dental** (dental) plaque

placar *m,* **placard** *m Arg, Urug* (*armario empotrado*) built-in cupboard, built-in closet *Am*

placebo *m* MED placebo

pláceme *m* congratulations *pl;* **dar el ~ a alguien** to congratulate sb

placenta *f* placenta

placentero, -a *adj* pleasant

placentino, -a I. *adj* of/from Plasencia II. *m, f* native/inhabitant of Plasencia

placer I. *m* 1. (*goce*) pleasure; **con sumo ~** with great pleasure; **casa de ~** brothel 2. (*arena*) sandbank II. *irr como crecer vi* to please; **¡haré lo que me plazca!** I will do as I please!

placero, -a *m, f AmL* (*vendedor*) street trader

plácet *m form* approval; **dar el ~ a un embajador** to accept an ambassador's credentials

placidez *f* calmness

plácido, -a *adj* calm

plaga *f* 1. AGR plague 2. (*calamidades*) disaster; (*lacra*) blight 3. (*abundancia*) glut; **este año hemos tenido una ~ de cerezas** this year we've had a glut of cherries

plagado, -a *adj* infested; **el texto estaba ~ de faltas** the text was full of mistakes; **la casa está plagada de cucarachas** the house is infested with cockroaches

plagar <g→gu> I. *vt* to infest; **~ de algo** to fill with sth; **~on la ciudad de carteles** they covered the city with posters II. *vr:* **~se** to become infested; **el pueblo se plagó de ratas** the village became infested with rats

plagiar *vt* 1. (*copiar*) to plagiarize 2. *AmL* (*secuestrar*) to kidnap

plagio *m* 1. (*copia*) plagiarism 2. *AmL* (*secuestro*) kidnapping

plan *m* 1. (*proyecto*) plan; **~ de emergencia** emergency plan; **si no tienes ~ para esta noche paso a buscarte** if you don't have anything planned for tonight I'll come round and fetch you 2. *inf* (*ligue*) date 3. *inf* (*actitud*) **esto no es ~** it's just not on; **en ~ de... as ...; está en un ~ que no lo soporto** I can't stand him when he behaves like this

plana *f* 1. (*folio*) page; **a toda ~** full-page; **un artículo en primera ~** a front-page article 2. (*caligrafía*) writing exercise 3. (*planicie*) plain 4. (*en una organización*) **la ~ mayor del partido** the party leadership

plancha *f* 1. (*lámina*) sheet; TIPO plate 2. (*para ropa*) iron 3. NÁUT gangway 4. *inf* (*desacierto*) blunder; **hacer** [o **tirarse**] **una ~** to put one's foot in it 5. GASTR grill; **a la ~** grilled 6. DEP (*gimnasia*) press-up

planchado *m* (*acción, ropa*) ironing

planchado, -a *adj* 1. *AmC* (*acicalado*) neat, smart *Brit* 2. (*anonadado*) flattened; **lo dejé ~** *inf* I left him speechless

planchar *vt* to iron

plancton *m sin pl* BIO plankton

planeador *m* AVIAT glider

planear I. *vi* (*ave*) to hover; AVIAT to glide II. *vt* to plan

planeta *m* planet

planetario *m* planetarium

planetario, -a *adj* planetary

planicie *f* plain

planificación *f* planning; **~ regional** local planning

planificar <c→qu> *vt* to plan

planilla *f* 1. ECON (*personal*) payroll 2. (*impreso*) form; **~ de cálculo** INFOR spreadsheet 3. *AmL* (*nómina*) payroll

planisferio *m* planisphere

plano *m* 1. MAT plane; **~ inclinado** inclined plane 2. (*mapa*) map; **levantar un ~** to draw a map 3. CINE **primer ~** close-up; **en primer ~** (*delante*) in the foreground 4. (*totalmente*) **de ~** directly; (*negar*) flatly; **aceptó de ~ nuestra propuesta** she accepted our suggestion straight away

plano, -a *adj* flat; **superficie plana** flat surface

planta *f* 1. BOT plant; **~ anual** annual; **~ de interior** houseplant; **~ medicinal** medicinal plant; **~ trepadora** climbing plant 2. (*pie*) sole 3. (*fábrica*) plant; **~ de abastecimientos de agua** waterworks; **~ de energía atómica/ hidráulica** atomic/hydraulic power station; **~ incineradora** incineration plant; **~ de reciclaje de basuras** recycling plant; **~ siderúrgica** steel plant 4. (*piso*) floor, storey *Brit,* story *Am;* **~ alta** top floor; **~ baja** ground floor *Brit,* first floor *Am* 5. ARQUIT ground plan; (*proyecto*) building plan 6. (*aspecto*) **tener buena ~** to be good-looking

plantación *f* 1. (*acción*) planting 2. (*finca, terreno*) plantation

plantado, -a *adj inf* **bien ~** (*atractivo*) good-looking

plantar I. *vt* 1. (*bulbo*) to plant; **han plantado el monte** they have planted trees on the hillside 2. (*clavar*) to stick in; **~ una tienda de campaña** to pitch a tent 3. *inf* (*golpe*) to land; **~ un tortazo a alguien** to slap sb 4. *inf* (*cita*) to stand up; **desapareció y me dejó plantado** he/she disappeared and left me standing; **dejó plantada a su novia** he stood his girlfriend up; **lo ~on en la calle** they chucked him out 5. (*abandonar*) to abandon II. *vr:* **~se** 1. (*resistirse*) **~se ante algo** to stand firm in the face of sth 2. (*asno, perro*) to refuse to move 3. (*aparecer*) to get to; **se ~on en mi casa en un periquete** they arrived at my house in no time 4. (*negarse*) to refuse 5. (*en los naipes*) to stick; **aquí me planto** I'm sticking

planteamiento *m* 1. (*enfoque*) approach; **tu ~ de la cuestión no me parece el adecuado** your approach to the question strikes me as incorrect 2. MAT solution

plantear I. *vt* 1. (*asunto, problema*) to approach; **este problema está mal planteado** this problem has been incorrectly formulated 2. (*causar*) to cause; (*discusión*) to provoke 3. (*proponer*) to put forward, to pose II. *vr* 1. (*reflexionar*) to think about 2. (*cuestión*) to ask oneself; **ahora me planteo si...** now I ask myself whether ...

plantel *m* **1.** (*conjunto*) group **2.** (*vivero*) nursery **3.** *Arg* (*plantilla*) staff

planteo *m Arg* demand

plantificar <c→qu> **I.** *vt* (*golpe*) to land; (*beso*) to plant **II.** *vr* to get there; **se plantificó allí al poco tiempo** he got there almost straight away

plantilla *f* **1.** (*empleados*) staff; ~ **de profesores** teaching staff **2.** (*de zapato*) insole **3.** (*zapatero*) sole **4.** (*patrón*) pattern **5.** (*equipo*) squad

plantío *m* **1.** (*acción de plantar*) planting **2.** (*terreno*) plot, patch **3.** (*lo plantado*) field of crops

plantón *m* **1.** (*planta*) seedling; (*rama*) cutting **2.** *inf* (*espera*) long wait; **dar un** ~ **a alguien** to stand sb up; **y ahora estoy de** ~ I've been left waiting around

plañir <3. *pret:* plañó> *vi* to wail

plaqué *m* (*de oro*) gold-plating; (*de plata*) silver-plating

plaqueta *f* MED platelet

plasma *m* plasma

plasmar *vt* **1.** (*moldear*) to mould *Brit,* to mold *Am* **2.** (*representar*) to represent

plasta[1] *mf pey* bore, drag

plasta[2] *f* **1.** (*mal hecha*) botch **2.** (*blanda*) soft mass

plástica *f* plastic arts *pl;* (*escultura*) sculpture

plasticidad *f* plasticity; *fig* expressiveness

plástico *m* plastic; (*para envolver*) cling film *Brit,* plastic wrap *Am*

plástico, -a *adj* **1.** (*materia*) plastic **2.** (*expresivo*) expressive; **las artes plásticas** the plastic arts

plastificar <c→qu> *vt* to laminate

plastilina® *f* plasticine *Brit,* modelling clay *Brit,* modeling clay *Am*

plata *f* **1.** (*metal*) silver; ~ **labrada** silverwork; ~ **de ley** sterling silver; **bodas de** ~ silver anniversary; (*de matrimonio*) silver wedding anniversary **2.** (*moneda*) silver coins *pl* **3.** *AmL* (*dinero*) money; **¡adiós mi** ~! *CSur, inf* what a disaster! ▸**hablar en** ~ to talk bluntly

plataforma *f* **1.** (*estrado*) platform **2.** (*tranvía*) platform; (*vagón*) flatbed truck; ~ **giratoria** turntable; ~ **petrolífera** oil rig; ~ **de lanzamiento** launch pad *Am* **3.** POL platform **4.** GEO ~ **continental** continental shelf

platal *m AmL* (*dineral*) fortune

plátano *m* **1.** (*árbol frondoso*) plane tree **2.** (*árbol frutal tropical*) banana tree; (*fruta*) banana; ~ **guineo** plantain

platea *f* stalls *pl Brit,* orchestra *Am*

plateado, -a *adj* (*con plata*) silver-plated; (*color*) silver

platear *vt* to silver-plate

platense *adj* **1.** (*de La Plata*) of/from La Plata **2.** (*de Río de La Plata*) native/inhabitant of the River Plate region

platería *f* **1.** (*tienda*) jeweller's *Brit,* jeweler's *Am* **2.** (*taller*) silversmith's **3.** (*vajilla*) silverware

platero, -a *m, f* silversmith; (*joyero*) jeweller *Brit,* jeweler *Am*

plática *f* **1.** (*conversación*) chat; **estar de** ~ to be chatting **2.** (*sermón*) sermon

platicar <c→qu> *vi inf* to chat

platija *f* flounder

platillo *m* **1.** (*de una taza*) saucer **2.** (*de una balanza*) pan **3.** MÚS cymbal

platina *f* **1.** (*de microscopio*) slide **2.** TYPO platen **3.** (*de tocadiscos, casete*) deck

platino *m* **1.** QUÍM platinum **2.** *pl* AUTO contact points *pl*

plato *m* **1.** (*vajilla*) plate; (*para taza*) saucer; **tiro al** ~ DEP clay pigeon shooting; **ahora tengo que pagar los** ~**s rotos** *fig* now I've got to pay the consequences; **tener cara de no haber roto un** ~ **en la vida** *inf* to look as if butter wouldn't melt in one's mouth; **comer en un mismo** ~ *fig* to be bosom pals **2.** (*comida*) dish; ~ **combinado** *dish usually consisting of meat or fish and vegetables;* ~ **fuerte** main dish; *fig* main part; **hoy hay** ~ **único** today there is only one dish; **nos sirvieron tres** ~**s y postre** we were served three courses and dessert **3.** (*de balanza*) pan

plató *m* CINE (film) set

platón *m AmL* serving dish

platónico, -a *adj* platonic

platudo, -a *adj AmL* well-heeled

plausible *adj* **1.** (*loable*) laudable **2.** (*admisible*) acceptable

playa *f* **1.** (*mar*) beach; ~ **naturista** nudists' beach **2.** *AmL* (*espacio*) open space; ~ **de estacionamiento** car park, parking lot *Am*

play-back *m* <play-backs> playback; **cantar en** ~ to mime a song

play-boy *m* <play-boys> playboy

playera *f Guat, Méx* (*camiseta*) T-shirt

playeras *fpl* (*zapatillas*) gym shoes *pl*

playo, -a *adj CSur* shallow; **plato** ~ dinner plate

plaza *f* **1.** (*espacio*) square; (*de mercado*) marketplace; (*de toros*) bullring; ~ **de abastos** (central) food market; **fuimos a la** ~ **a comprar** we went to the market to do the shopping **2.** (*asiento*) seat; (*de garage, parking*) space **3.** (*empleo*) post **4.** (*en instituciones, viajes*) place

plazo *m* **1.** (*vencimiento*) period; ~ **de entrega** delivery date; ~ **de preaviso** notice period; **a corto/largo** ~ in the short/long term; **fuera del** ~ after the closing date; **en el** ~ **de un mes** within a month; **en el banco tengo dos millones a** ~ **fijo** I have two million in the bank in a fixed-term deposit; **¿cuándo vence el** ~ **para la presentación de solicitudes?** when is the deadline for submitting applications? **2.** (*cantidad*) instalment *Brit,* installment *Am;* **a** ~**s** by instalments

plazoleta *f diminutivo de* **plaza**

pleamar *f* high tide

plebe *f sin pl* **1.** HIST masses *pl* **2.** *pey* (*chusma*)

rabble
plebeyo, -a I. *adj* **1.** *t.* HIST plebeian **2.** (*sin linaje*) common **3.** (*inculto*) uneducated; (*grosero*) uncouth II. *m, f* **1.** *t.* HIST plebeian **2.** (*sin linaje*) commoner **3.** (*grosero*) lout
plebiscito *m* plebiscite
plegable *adj* (*papel*) foldable; (*mueble*) folding; **silla** ~ folding chair
plegar *irr como fregar* I. *vt* (*doblar*) to fold; (*muebles*) to fold away II. *vr:* ~**se** to yield
plegaria *f* prayer
pleitear *vi* JUR to bring a lawsuit, to sue
pleito *m* **1.** JUR lawsuit **2.** (*disputa*) dispute
plenario, -a *adj* plenary; **sesión plenaria** plenary session
plenipotenciario, -a *adj, m, f* plenipotentiary
plenitud *f* **1.** (*totalidad*) fullness; **sensación de** ~ sensation of fullness **2.** (*apogeo*) height; **en la** ~ **de sus facultades físicas** at the height of his/her physical powers
pleno *m* plenary session; **el ayuntamiento en** ~ **aprobó la propuesta** the local council approved the proposal
pleno, -a *adj* full; ~ **empleo** full employment; **en el** ~ **uso de sus facultades mentales** in full command of his/her faculties; **le robaron a plena luz del día** they robbed him in broad daylight; **en** ~ **verano** at the height of summer
pletórico, -a *adj* full; ~ **de salud** bursting with health
pleura *f* pleura
pleuresía *f* MED pleurisy
plexiglás® *m sin pl* Perspex® *Brit,* Plexiglass® *Am*
plica *f* **1.** sealed envelope **2.** MÚS note stem
pliego *m* **1.** (*hoja*) sheet **2.** (*documento*) document; ~ **de cargos** list of charges; ~ **de condiciones** specifications *pl* **3.** (*libro*) section
pliegue *m* *t.* GEO (*doblez*) fold
plinto *m* **1.** ARQUIT plinth **2.** DEP vaulting horse
plisar *vt* to pleat
plomada *f* (*albañilería*) plumb line; **echar la** ~ to drop the plumb line
plomazo *m* **1.** *inf* (*pesado*) drag **2.** (*perdigón*) shot
plomería *f* *Arg* (*fontanería*) plumber's
plomero *m* *Arg* (*técnico fontanero*) plumber
plomizo, -a *adj* **1.** (*color*) lead-coloured *Brit,* lead-colored *Am* **2.** (*material*) lead(en)
plomo *m* **1.** (*metal*) lead; **gasolina sin** ~ unleaded petrol *Brit,* unleaded gas *Am;* **caer a** ~ to fall heavily **2.** *inf* (*pesado*) **ser un** ~ to be a real drag **3.** (*plomada*) plumb line **4.** (*bala*) bullet **5.** *pl* ELEC fuse
pluma *f* **1.** (*ave*) feather; **cambiar la** ~ to moult *Brit,* to molt *Am* **2.** (*escribir*) pen; ~ **estilográfica** fountain pen **3.** (*escritor*) writer **4.** (*estilo*) (writing) style ►**vestirse de** ~**s ajenas** to dress in borrowed finery; **quedarse cacareando y sin** ~**s** to remain defiant in defeat

plumada *f* stroke of the pen
plumaje *m* **1.** (*ave*) plumage **2.** (*adorno*) plume
plumario, -a *m, f* *AmC, Méx, pey* (*periodista*) hack
plumazo *m* (*trazo*) stroke of the pen; **suprimieron de un** ~ **las subvenciones** they abolished the subsidies at a stroke
plúmbeo, -a *adj* heavy; *fig* tedious
plumear *vt* *AmC* (*escribir*) to write
plumero *m* **1.** (*para limpiar*) feather duster **2.** (*plumier: estuche*) pencil case; (*caja*) pencil box **3.** (*adorno*) plume ►**vérsele el** ~ **a alguien** to be obvious what sb is up to
plumier *m* (*estuche*) pencil case; (*caja*) pencil box
plumilla *f* nib
plumón *m* **1.** (*ave*) down **2.** (*cama*) feather bed
plural I. *adj* plural; **número** ~ plural II. *m* plural; ~ **mayestático** royal 'we'
pluralidad *f* plurality; **a** ~ **de votos** by majority vote
pluralizar <z→c> *vt* **1.** (*generalizar*) to generalize; **tú cuenta lo que te pasó a ti y no pluralices** say what happened to you, but don't assume you're speaking for the rest of us **2.** LING to form the plural
pluriempleo *m* *situation where various positions are filled by the same person*
plurifamiliar *adj* for several families
pluripartidismo *m* multi-party system
plus *m* **1.** (*gratificación*) bonus; **de** ~ extra; ~ **de peligrosidad** danger money; ~ **por trabajar en días festivos** bonus for working on public holidays **2.** (*ventaja*) advantage
pluscuamperfecto *m* LING pluperfect
plusmarquista *mf* record holder; **ser el** ~ **mundial de lanzamiento de jabalina** to hold the world record for javelin-throwing
plusvalía *f sin pl* ECON appreciation
plutonio *m* plutonium
pluvial *adj* rain
pluviosidad *f* rainfall
p.m. *abr de* **post meridiem** pm
P.M. *f abr de* **policía militar** MP
PN *m abr de* **peso neto** net weight
PNB *m abr de* **producto nacional bruto** GNP
PNN *m abr de* **producto nacional neto** NNP
PNV *m abr de* **Partido Nacionalista Vasco** *Basque Nationalist Party*
p.o. *abr de* **por orden** by order
población *f* **1.** *t.* BIO (*habitantes*) population; ~ **activa** ECON working population **2.** (*localidad: ciudad*) city; (*ciudad pequeña*) town; (*pueblo*) village
poblado *m* (*pueblo*) village; (*colonia*) settlement
poblado, -a *adj* **1.** (*habitado*) inhabited; (*con árboles*) wooded **2.** (*cejas*) bushy; (*barba*) thick
poblador(a) *m(f)* (*habitante*) inhabitant; (*colono*) settler

poblar <o→ue> I. *vi, vt* **1.** (*colonizar*) to colonize **2.** (*de plantas*) to plant; (*de peces*) to stock; **han poblado el monte de pinos** they have planted the hillside with pines **3.** (*habitar*) to inhabit; **distintas especies pueblan el fondo del mar** various species inhabit the sea bed II. *vr:* ~**se** to fill; **la costa se pobló rápidamente** the coast quickly filled with people
pobre I. *adj* **1.** (*no rico*) poor; ~ **de algo** poor in sth; **es una lengua ~ de expresiones** it is a language with few expressions **2.** (*desgraciado*) unfortunate **3.** (*humilde*) humble **4.** (*exclamaciones*) **¡~ de ti si dices mentiras!** you'll be sorry if you lie! II. *mf* poor person; (*mendigo*) beggar; **los pobres** the poor *pl*
pobremente *adv* poorly
pobreza *f* **1.** (*necesidad*) poverty **2.** (*pusilanimidad*) cowardliness
pochismo *m Méx* **1.** *inf* (*angloamericanismo*) anglicism introduced into Spanish **2.** *inf* (*característica de los pochos*) characteristic of Americanized Mexicans
pocho, -a I. *m, f Méx, pey* Americanized Mexican II. *adj* **1.** (*fruta*) overripe **2.** (*persona*) off-colour *Brit,* off-color *Am*
pochoclo *m Arg* popcorn
pocilga *f t. fig* pigsty
pócima *f,* **poción** *f* potion; *pey* (*brebaje*) brew; **la ~ mágica** the magic potion
poco I. *m* **1.** (*cantidad*) **un ~ de azúcar** a little sugar; **acepta el ~ de dinero que te puedo dar** accept what little money I can give you; **espera un ~** wait a little **2.** *pl* few; ~**s de los presentes lo sabían** few of those present knew it; **los ~s que vinieron...** the few who came ...; **es un envidioso como hay ~s** there are few people who are as jealous as him II. *adv* little; **escribir ~** to write little; **es ~ simpático** he is not very friendly; **nos da ~ más o menos lo mismo** it really doesn't make much difference to us; ~ **a ~** bit by bit, little by little; ~ **a ~ dejamos de creerle** we gradually stopped believing him; **a ~ de llegar...** shortly after arriving ...; ~ **después** shortly afterwards; **dentro de ~** soon; **desde hace ~** since recently; **hace ~** recently, not long ago; **a/con/por ~ que se esfuerce lo conseguirá** with a little bit of effort he/she will get it; **por ~ me estrello** I very nearly crashed; **tener en ~ a alguien** to have a low opinion of sb; **y por si fuera ~...** and as if that wasn't enough ...
poco, -a <poquísimo> *adj* little; ~**s** few; **aquí hay poca comida para dos personas** there's not much food here for two people; **hay pocas colecciones mejores que ésta** there are few collections better than this one; **tiene pocas probabilidades de aprobar** he has little chance of passing
podadera *f* secateurs *pl,* pruning shears *pl*
podar *vt* to prune
podenco *m* breed of Spanish hunting dog
poder I. *irr vi* to be able to; **puedo** I can;

puedes you can; **no ~ más de hambre** to be starving; **yo a ti te puedo** *inf* I'm stronger than you; **no ~ con el alma** to be completely exhausted; **no puedes cogerlo sin permiso** you can't take it without permission; **no podemos abandonarlo** we can't abandon him; **¡bien pod(r)ías habérmelo dicho!** you could have told me!; **bien puede haber aquí un millón de abejas** there could easily be a million bees here; **no puedo verlo todo el día sin hacer nada** I can't stand seeing him do nothing all day long; **no puedo con mi madre** I can't cope with my mother; **la sala se llenó a más no ~** the room filled to bursting point; **de ~ ser, no dudes que lo hará** if it is at all possible, have no doubt that he/she will do it; **no pude menos que preguntarle qué hacía por allí** I couldn't help asking him/her what he/she was doing there; **lo menos que puedes hacer es llamar si vas a llegar tarde** the least you can do is phone if you're going to be late; **no puede ser** it is impossible; **a ~ ser** if possible II. *irr vimpers* **puede (ser) que después vuelva** maybe he/she will come back afterwards, he/she may come back afterwards; **¡puede!** maybe!; **¿se puede?** may I (come in)? III. *m* **1.** *t.* POL (*autoridad*) power; ~ **absoluto** absolute power; ~ **ejecutivo** executive power; ~ **judicial** judicial power; ~ **legislativo** legislative power; **los ~es fácticos** the powers that be; **los ~es públicos** the public authorities; **la división de ~es** the separation of powers; **el partido en el ~** the party in power; **subir al ~** to achieve power; **los documentos están en ~ del juez** the documents are in the hands of the judge; **haré todo lo que está en mi ~** I will do everything in my power **2.** (*autorización*) authority; ~ **notarial** power of attorney; **por ~es** by proxy; ~ **de decisión** decision-making power **3.** (*fuerza*) strength; ~ **adquisitivo** ECON buying [*o* purchasing] power
poderío *m* **1.** (*autoridad*) power **2.** (*riqueza*) wealth **3.** (*fuerza*) strength
poderoso, -a *adj* **1.** (*influyente*) powerful **2.** (*rico*) wealthy **3.** (*eficaz*) effective
podio *m* podium
podólogo, -a *m, f* podiatrist, chiropodist
podredumbre *f* **1.** (*putrefacción*) decay **2.** (*depravación*) corruption
podrido, -a *adj* **1.** (*descompuesto*) *t. fig* rotten; **estar ~ de dinero** *inf,* **estar ~ en plata** *Arg, inf* to be filthy rich **2.** *Arg, inf* (*aburrido*) fed up
podrir *irr vt, vr v.* **pudrir**
poema *m* poem; ~ **épico** epic poem; ~ **en prosa** prose poem; **¡fue todo un ~!** (*gracioso*) it was really funny!; **estar hecho un ~** to be a real sight
poesía *f* **1.** (*género*) poetry **2.** (*poema*) poem; **libro de ~(s)** poetry book
poeta, -isa *m, f* poet *m(f),* poetess *f*
poética *f* poetics

poético, -a *adj t. fig* poetic; **arte poética** poetics; **licencia poética** poetic licence *Brit* [*o* license *Am*]

poetisa *f v.* **poeta**

póker *m sin pl* poker; **poner cara de** ~ to look poker-faced

polaco, -a I. *adj* Polish **II.** *m, f* (*persona*) Pole; (*idioma*) Polish

polaina *f* gaiter; (*pantalón*) leggings *pl*

polar *adj* polar; **Círculo Polar Ártico/Antártico** Arctic/Antarctic Circle; **la estrella** ~ Polaris, Pole Star

polaridad *f* polarity

polarización *f* polarization

polarizar <z→c> *vt* **1.** FÍS to polarize **2.** *fig* (*opinión*) to polarize; (*atención*) to focus; **el espectáculo polarizó la atención de los visitantes** the spectators were completely absorbed by the show

polca *f* MÚS polka

polea *f* pulley; (*roldana*) pulley wheel; **sistema de ~s** pulley system

polémica *f* controversy, polemic

polémico, -a *adj* polemical

polemizar <z→c> *vi* to argue; ~ **con alguien** to have an argument with sb

polen *m* pollen; **tengo alergia al** ~ I have hay fever

polera *f* **1.** *Chile* (*camiseta*) t-shirt **2.** *Arg* (*de cuello alto*) polo neck *Brit,* turtleneck *Am*

poli *f inf abr de* **policía** cops *pl*

poliamida *f* polyamide; (*textil*) nylon

policía[1] *f* police; **agente de** ~ police officer; **coche de** ~ police car; **comisaría de** ~ police station; **jefatura de** ~ police headquarters

policía[2] *mf* policeman *m,* policewoman *f;* **perro** ~ police dog

policiaco, -a *adj,* **policíaco, -a** *adj* police; **estado** ~ police state; **película/novela policíaca** detective film/novel

policial *adj v.* **policíaco**

policlínica *f,* **policlínico** *m* hospital

polideportivo *m* sports centre *Brit* [*o* center *Am*]

poliéster *m* polyester

polietileno *m* polythene *Brit,* polyethylene *Am*

polifacético, -a *adj* multi-faceted; (*persona*) many-sided

poligamia *f sin pl* polygamy

polígamo, -a *adj* polygamous

políglota I. *adj* polyglot **II.** *mf* polyglot

poligonal *adj* polygonal

polígono *m* **1.** MAT polygon **2.** (*terreno*) site; ~ **industrial** industrial estate [*o* park]

polilla *f* moth; **no tener** ~ **en la lengua** *inf* not to mince one's words

polimorfo, -a *adj* polymorphous

polinesio, -a *adj, m, f* Polynesian

polinización *f* pollination

polio *f inv* MED polio, poliomyelitis

pólipo *m* MED polyp

polisemia *f sin pl* LING polysemy

polisílabo, -a *adj* LING polysyllabic

politécnica *f* polytechnic, technical school

politécnico, -a *adj* polytechnic

política *f* politics; **Política Agraria Común** Common Agricultural Policy; ~ **interior/exterior** domestic/foreign policy; ~ **monetaria** monetary policy; ~ **pesquera** fishing policy

político, -a I. *adj* **1.** POL political; **ciencias políticas** political science; **economía política** political economy **2.** (*parentesco*) in-law; **hermano** ~ brother-in-law; **hermana política** sister-in-law **II.** *m, f* politician

politizar <z→c> *vt, vr* to become politicized

politólogo, -a *m, f* political scientist

póliza *f* **1.** JUR policy; **me he hecho una** ~ **de seguros** I have taken out an insurance policy **2.** (*sello*) stamp

polizón *mf* stowaway

polizonte *m pey* cop

polla *f* **1.** (*gallina*) hen; ~ **de agua** ZOOL moorhen **2.** *inf* (*chica*) chick **3.** *vulg* (*pene*) dick; **ni ~s en vinagre** don't come to me with bullshit; **¡y una ~ como una olla!** like hell! **4.** *AmL* (*carrera*) horse race

pollera *f* **1.** (*gallinero*) chicken coop **2.** *Arg* (*falda*) skirt

pollería *f* poultry shop

pollerudo I. *adj* CSur **1.** (*chismoso*) gossipy **2.** (*blando*) weak; **niño** ~ sissy; **hombre** ~ wimp **II.** *m* CSur, *pey* (*clérigo*) priest

pollina *f* PRico, *Ven* (*del pelo*) fringe *Brit,* bangs *pl Am*

pollino, -a *m, f* **1.** (*borrico*) (young) donkey **2.** *fig* (*tonto*) fool

pollito, -a *m, f* **1.** (*ave*) chick **2.** *fig* (*niño*) kid

pollo *m* **1.** GASTR chicken; ~ **asado** roast chicken **2.** (*cría*) young; (*de gallina*) chick; **sacar ~s** to breed chickens; **voló el** ~ *fig* the chance has gone **3.** (*joven*) kid; *inf* (*tío*) bloke *Brit;* **¿quién es ese ~?** who's that guy?

polluelo *m* chick

polo *m* **1.** GEO, FÍS, ASTR pole; ~ **norte/ártico/boreal** North Pole; ~ **sur/antártico/austral** South Pole; ~ **industrial** development region **2.** DEP polo **3.** (*camiseta*) polo neck **4.** (*helado*) ice lolly

pololear *vi AmS* (*coquetear*) to flirt

pololo, -a *m, f* **1.** *And* (*novio*) boyfriend *m;* (*novia*) girlfriend *f* **2.** *CSur* (*coqueto*) flirt

polonesa *f* MÚS polonaise

Polonia *f* Poland

poltrón, -ona *adj* lazy

poltrona *f* easy chair, recliner

polución *f* **1.** (*contaminación*) pollution; ~ **ambiental** environmental pollution **2.** (*semen*) emission

polvareda *f* dust cloud; **levantar una** ~ *fig* to cause an uproar

polvera *f* powder compact

polvo *m* **1.** (*suciedad*) dust; **quitar el** ~ to dust; **hacer** ~ (*algo*) to smash; (*a alguien*) to annihilate; **estoy hecho** ~ *inf* I'm exhausted;

hacer morder el ~ a alguien to humiliate sb; **sacudir a alguien el ~** *fig* to give sb a beating **2.** (*sustancia*) powder; **levadura en ~** powdered yeast **3.** *vulg* (*coito*) screw; **echar un ~** to screw **4.** *pl* (*cosmética*) powder

pólvora *f* gunpowder; **no haber inventado la ~** *inf* to be a bit dim

polvoriento, -a *adj* dusty

polvorín *m* powder magazine; **estamos sentados sobre un ~** *fig* we're sitting on a powder keg

polvorón *m crumbly shortbread, eaten at Christmas*

polvoso, -a *adj AmL* dusty

pomada *f* ointment; **~ contra mosquitos** mosquito repellent

pomelo *m* grapefruit

pómez *f* pumice

pompa *f* **1.** (*burbuja*) bubble **2.** (*esplendor*) pomp; (*ostentación*) display; **~s fúnebres** (*ceremonia*) funeral ceremony; (*funeraria*) funeral parlour *Brit* [*o* parlor *Am*]

pompis *m inv, inf* bottom, backside *Brit,* tush *Am*

pompo, -a *adj Col, Ecua* (*sin filo*) blunt

pomposidad *f* pomposity

pomposo, -a *adj* magnificent; (*grandilocuente*) high-flown; (*estilo*) pompous

pómulo *m* cheekbone

ponchada *f CSur, inf* (*cantidad*) stack; **una ~ de** a load of

ponche *m* punch

poncho *m* poncho

poncho, -a *adj AmL* lazy

ponderación *f* **1.** (*elogio*) eulogy **2.** (*el sopesar*) deliberation; **con ~** carefully **3.** (*en estadística*) weighting **4.** (*exageración*) exaggeration

ponderar *vt* **1.** (*sopesar*) to weigh up **2.** (*encomiar*) to praise

ponencia *f* (*conferencia*) paper; (*informe*) report

ponente *mf* (*en conferencia*) speaker; (*informador*) reporter

poner *irr* **I.** *vt* **1.** (*colocar*) to put; (*horizontalmente*) to lie; (*inyección*) to give; (*sellos, etiqueta*) to stick on; (*tirita*) to put on; (*huevos*) to lay; **pon el espejo mirando hacia mí** put the mirror facing towards me; **pon la ropa en el tendedero** hang the clothes on the line; **¿dónde habré puesto...?** where can I have put ...?; **lo pongo en tus manos** *fig* I leave it in your hands **2.** (*disponer*) to place; (*la mesa*) to lay, to set; **~ algo a disposición de alguien** to make sth available to sb **3.** (*encender*) to switch on; **pon el despertador para las cuatro** set the alarm for four o'clock; **~ en marcha** to start **4.** (*convertir*) to make; **~ de mal humor a alguien** to put sb in a bad mood; **la noticia me puso de buen humor** the news put me in a good mood; **~ colorado a alguien** to make sb blush; **el sol te pondrá moreno** the sun will give you a tan

5. (*suponer*) to assume; **pon que no viene** let's assume he doesn't come; **pongamos que resolvemos el problema en dos días...** let's assume we solve the problem in two days ...; **pongamos el/por caso que no llegue a tiempo** let's consider what happens if she doesn't arrive on time **6.** (*exponer*) **~ la ropa a secar al sol** to put the clothes out to dry in the sun; **~ la leche al fuego** to put the milk on the stove; **~ en peligro** to endanger **7.** (*contribuir*) to put in; (*juego*) to bet; **¿cuánto has puesto tú en el fondo común?** how much have you put into the kitty?; **pusimos todo de nuestra parte** we did all that we could **8.** (*una expresión*) to take on; **~ mala cara** to look angry **9.** (*tratar*) to treat; **~ de idiota** *pey* to treat sb like a fool **10.** (*denominar*) to give; **le pusieron por** [*o* **de**] **nombre Manolo** they called him Manolo; **¿qué nombre le van a ~?** what are they going to call him/her? **11.** (*espectáculo*) to put on; **~ en escena** to stage; **¿qué ponen hoy en el cine?** what's on at the cinema today? **12.** (*imponer*) to impose; **nos han puesto muchos deberes** they have given us a lot of homework; **~ una multa** to impose a fine; **~ condiciones** to impose conditions **13.** (*instalar*) to install *Brit,* to instal *Am* **14.** (*a trabajar*) **tendrá que ~ a mis hijos a trabajar** I will have to send my children out to work; **puse a mi hijo de aprendiz de panadero** I found my son a position as an apprentice baker **15.** (*añadir*) to add **16.** (*escribir*) to write; (*un telegrama*) to send; **~ entre comillas** to put in inverted commas; **~ la firma** to sign; **~ un anuncio** to place an advertisement; **~ por escrito la propuesta** to put the proposal in writing; **te pongo cuatro letras para decirte que...** this is just a short note to tell you that ... **17.** (*estar escrito*) to say **18.** (*vestido, zapato*) to put on; **le pusieron el collar al cuello** they put his collar on **19.** (*teléfono*) to put through; **me puse al habla con mi amigo** I got through to my friend **II.** *vr:* **~se 1.** (*vestido, zapato*) to put on; **ponte guapo** make yourself look nice; **~se de invierno** to dress warmly; **~se de luto** to wear mourning clothes; **~se de largo** to dress up **2.** (*astro*) to set; **el sol se pone por el oeste** the sun sets in the west **3.** (*mancharse*) **se pusieron perdidos de barro** they got mud all over themselves **4.** (*comenzar*) to begin; **por la tarde se puso a llover** in the evening it started to rain **5.** (*con adjetivo o adverbio*) to become; **se puso chulo y no nos dejó entrar** he became rude and wouldn't let us in; **ponte cómodo** make yourself comfortable

póney *m* pony

pongo *1. pres de* **poner**

poni *m* pony

poniente *m* **1.** (*oeste*) west **2.** (*viento*) west wind

pontevedrés, -esa **I.** *adj* of/from Pontevedra **II.** *m, f* native/inhabitant of Pontevedra

ponzoña *f* poison
ponzoñoso, -a *adj* poisonous; *fig* harmful
pop I. *adj inv* pop II. *m inv* pop (music)
popa *f* 1. (*barco*) stern; **viento en** ~ following wind; **a** ~ astern 2. *inf* (*trasero*) bum *Brit,* butt *Am*
popero, -a *m, f inf* pop music fan
popó *m infantil* pooh *Brit,* poop *Am*
popocho, -a *adj Col* 1. (*repleto*) stuffed 2. (*rico*) loaded *inf* 3. (*gordo*) podgy *Brit,* pudgy *Am, inf*
popoff *adj inv, Méx, inf* posh
popote *m Méx* (*paja*) straw
populacho *m* masses *pl*
popular *adj* 1. (*del pueblo*) folk; **aire** ~ folk song 2. (*conocido*) well-known; (*admirado*) popular
popularidad *f* popularity
popularizar <z→c> I. *vt* to popularize; (*extender*) to spread II. *vr:* ~**se** to become popular
populoso, -a *adj* populous
popurrí *m* potpourri
poquedad *f* 1. (*escasez*) scarcity 2. (*pusilanimidad*) timidity 3. (*insignificancia*) insignificance
póquer *m* poker
poquito *adv* a little; **bébelo** ~ **a poco** drink it a little bit at a time
por *prep* 1. (*lugar: a través de*) through; (*vía*) via; (*en*) in; ~ **aquí** near here; **limpia la botella** ~ **dentro/fuera** clean the inside/outside of the bottle; **pasé** ~ **Madrid hace poco** I passed through Madrid recently; **adelantar** ~ **la izquierda** to overtake on the left; **volar** ~ **encima de los Alpes** to fly over the Alps; **ese pueblo está** ~ **Castilla** that town is in Castile; **la cogió** ~ **la cintura** he grasped her waist 2. (*tiempo*) in; ~ **la(s) mañana(s)** in the morning; **mañana** ~ **la mañana** tomorrow morning; ~ **la tarde** in the evening; **ayer** ~ **la noche** last night; ~ **noviembre** in November; ~ **fin** finally 3. (*a cambio de*) for; (*en lugar de*) instead of; (*sustituyendo a alguien*) in place of; **cambié el libro** ~ **el álbum** I exchanged the book for the album 4. (*agente*) by; **una novela** ~ **Dickens** a novel by Dickens 5. MAT (*multiplicación*) by 6. (*reparto*) per; **toca a cuatro** ~ **cabeza** it comes out at four each; **el ocho** ~ **ciento** eight per cent 7. (*finalidad*) for 8. (*causa*) because of; (*en cuanto a*) regarding; **lo merece** ~ **los esfuerzos que ha hecho** he/she deserves it for all his/her effort; **lo hago** ~ **ti** I'm doing it for you; ~ **desesperación** out of desperation; ~ **consiguiente** consequently; ~ **eso,** ~ (**lo**) **tanto** therefore, because of that; ~ **lo que a eso se refiere** as far as that is concerned; ~ **mí que se vayan** as far as I'm concerned, they can go; **no te preocupes** ~ **hacer muchas fotocopias** don't bother making lots of photocopies 9. (*preferencia*) in favour *Brit,* in favor *Am;* **estoy** ~ **comprarlo** I think we should buy it; **estar loco** ~ **alguien** to be crazy about sb 10. (*dirección*)

voy (**a**) ~ **tabaco** I'm going to get some cigarettes 11. (*pendiente*) **este pantalón está** ~ **lavar** these trousers need to be washed 12. (*aunque*) however; ~ **muy cansado que esté no lo dejará a medias** however tired he is, he won't leave it unfinished 13. (*medio*) by means of; (*alguien*) through; **poner** ~ **escrito** to put in writing; **al** ~ **mayor** wholesale 14. (*interrogativo*) **¿**~ (**qué**)**?** why? 15. ~ **si acaso** just in case 16. (*casi*) ~ **poco** almost; **por** ~ **me ahogo** I nearly drowned
porcelana *f* porcelain; (*vajilla*) china
porcentaje *m* percentage; ~ **de derechos del autor** author's royalties
porcentual *adj* percentage
porche *m* 1. (*pórtico*) porch, verandah *Am* 2. (*cobertizo*) arcade
porcino, -a *adj* pig; **ganado** ~ pigs *pl*
porción *f* portion; GASTR serving
pordiosear *vi* to beg
pordiosero, -a *m, f* beggar
porfía *f* persistence; **a** ~ in competition
porfiador(a) I. *adj* obstinate II. *m(f)* obstinate person
porfiar <*1. pres:* porfío> *vi* 1. (*insistir*) ~ **en algo** to insist on sth 2. (*disputar*) to quarrel
pormenor *m* detail
pormenorizado, -a *adj* detailed
pormenorizar <z→c> *vt* to describe in detail
porno *adj inv, m inf* porn
pornografía *f* pornography
pornográfico, -a *adj* pornographic
poro *m* pore
porongo *m* 1. *CSur* (*calabaza para el mate*) calabash 2. *Perú* (*lechera*) milk can
pororó *m CSur* (*palomitas*) popcorn
poroso, -a *adj* porous
poroto *m Chile* bean; (*guiso*) bean stew
porque *conj* 1. (*causal*) because; **lo hizo** ~ **sí** he/she did it because he/she wanted to 2. +*subj* (*final*) so that; **recemos** ~ **llueva** let us pray that it rains
porqué *m* reason
porquería *f inf* 1. (*suciedad*) filth 2. (*acto*) disgusting act 3. (*comida*) pigswill 4. (*cacharro*) piece of junk 5. (*pequeñez*) trifle
porqueriza *f* pigsty
porra *f* 1. (*bastón*) truncheon 2. GASTR *a large stick of fried batter* 3. *inf* (*expresión*) **¡vete a la** ~**!** go to hell!; **¡**~(**s**)**!** damn!
porrazo *m* blow; **de golpe y** ~ all of a sudden; **de un** ~ in one go
porreta *f* **en** ~(**s**) *inf* stark naked
porrista *mf Méx* fan
porro *m* 1. *inf* (*canuto*) joint, spliff *Brit* 2. (*puerro*) leek 3. *inf* (*torpe*) fool
porrón *m bottle with a long spout*
porrudo, -a *adj Arg* big-headed
portaaviones *m inv* aircraft carrier
portada *f* 1. (*fachada*) front 2. TIPO title page; PREN cover
portador(a) *m(f)* 1. (*de gérmenes*) carrier

P

2. COM bearer
portaequipaje(s) *m* (*inv*) **1.** (*maletero*) boot *Brit*, trunk *Am* **2.** (*baca, en tren*) luggage rack; (*en bicicleta*) carrier
portafolios *m inv* briefcase
portal *m* **1.** (*zaguán*) hall **2.** *pl* (*soportales*) arcade **3.** REL ~ **de Belén** Nativity scene **4.** INFOR portal
portalámpara(s) *m* (*inv*) (*de bombilla*) socket; (*de lámpara*) lamp-holder
portaligas *m inv, AmL* (*liguero*) suspender belt, garter belt *Am*
portalón *m* **1.** ARQUIT large doorway **2.** NÁUT gangway
portamaletas *m inv* AUTO boot *Brit*, trunk *Am*
portaminas *m inv* propelling pencil
portamonedas *m inv* purse
portante *m* **tomar el ~** *inf* to clear off; **dar el ~ a alguien** *inf* to sack sb, to fire sb
portar I. *vt* (*perro*) to fetch **II.** *vr:* ~**se** to behave; ~**se bien con alguien** to treat sb well; **el niño se porta bien/mal** the child is well-/badly behaved; ~**se como un hombre** to act like a man; **nuestro equipo se ha portado** our team performed well
portátil *adj* portable; **máquina de escribir ~** portable typewriter; **ordenador ~** laptop
portavoz¹ *mf* (*persona*) spokesperson, spokesman *m*, spokeswoman *f*
portavoz² *m* **1.** (*periódico*) organ **2.** (*bocina*) megaphone
portazo *m* slam (*of the door*); **dar un ~** to slam the door; **despedirse con un ~** to slam one's door on the way out; **dar a alguien un ~ en las narices** *inf* to slam the door in sb's face
porte *m* **1.** (*transporte*) transport; ~ **aéreo** air freight; **gastos de ~** transport costs; **a ~ debido** carriage forward **2.** (*gastos de transporte*) transport costs *pl*, shipping **3.** (*correo*) postage; ~ **por expreso** express postage; ~ **de un paquete** parcel post; ~ **suplementario** additional postage charge **4.** (*de buque*) capacity; **buque de gran ~** large vessel **5.** (*aspecto*) appearance; **es un hombre de ~ distinguido** he has a distinguished air; **mostrar un ~ severo** to look strict
portear I. *vi* to slam the door **II.** *vt* to transport, to ship
portento *m* marvel; **niño ~** child prodigy; **ser un ~ de energía** to be full of energy
portentoso, -a *adj* marvellous *Brit*, marvelous *Am*
porteño, -a I. *adj* of/from Buenos Aires **II.** *m, f* native/inhabitant of Buenos Aires
portería *f* **1.** (*en un edificio de viviendas*) porter's lodge **2.** DEP goal
portero, -a *m, f* **1.** (*conserje*) caretaker; (*en un edificio de viviendas*) porter; ~ **automático** entryphone **2.** *Arg* (*administrador*) building manager **3.** DEP (*fútbol*) goalkeeper, goaltender
portezuelo *m Arg, Chile* (*paso de montaña*) pass

pórtico *m* (*porche*) porch; (*galería*) arcade
portilla *f* NÁUT porthole
portillo *m* **1.** (*abertura*) gap **2.** (*postigo*) wicket **3.** (*entre montañas*) narrow pass **4.** (*punto débil*) weak point
portorriqueño, -a *adj, m, f* Puerto Rican
portuario, -a I. *adj* port **II.** *m, f* docker
portugués, -esa *adj, m, f* Portuguese
porvenir *m* future; **lleno de ~** full of promise; **tener el ~ asegurado** to have a secure future; **un joven de ~** a young man with great prospects
pos I. *adv* **ir en ~ de algo/alguien** to pursue sth/sb; **van en ~ del éxito** they are striving for success **II.** *conj Méx, inf v.* **pues**
posada *f* **1.** (*parador, fonda*) inn; (*pensión*) guest house **2.** (*hospedaje*) lodging; **dar ~ a alguien** to give sb lodging; **hacer ~** to stop for the night; **pedir ~** to ask for shelter **3.** (*casa*) residence
posaderas *fpl inf* bottom, backside
posadero, -a *m, f* landlord *m*, landlady *f*
posar I. *vi* **1.** (*reposar*) to rest **2.** (*modelo*) to pose **II.** *vt* **1.** (*poner suavemente*) to place **2.** (*carga*) to set down **3.** (*mirada*) to rest **III.** *vr:* ~**se** to settle; **el sol se posaba en el mar** the sun set over the sea; **el gorrión se posó en la rama** the sparrow alighted on the branch
posdata *f* postscript
pose *f* (*postura*) pose
poseedor(a) *m(f)* owner; (*póliza, acciones*) holder
poseer *irr como* **leer** *vt* to possess, to have; ~ **una importante posición social** to occupy an important position in society; ~ **a alguien a la fuerza** to rape sb
poseído, -a I. *adj* possessed; ~ **de odio** full of hatred; **una chica poseída de su belleza** a girl obsessed by her own beauty **II.** *m, f* madman *m*, madwoman *f*; **gritar como un ~** to shout like one possessed
posesión *f* (*propiedad*) possession; **estoy en ~ de su atenta carta...** I have received your kind letter ...
posesionar I. *vt* ~ **a alguien de algo** to hand sth over to sb **II.** *vr:* ~**se** to take possession; ~**se de un nuevo cargo** to take up a new position
posesivo, -a *adj t.* LING possessive
poseso, -a I. *adj* possessed **II.** *m, f* madman *m*, madwoman *f*
posguerra *f* postwar period (*in Spain, usually used to refer to the period after the Spanish Civil War*)
posibilidad *f* **1.** (*lo posible*) possibility; **tener grandes ~es de éxito** to have a good chance of success **2.** (*aptitud, facultad*) capability; **tienes ~es de llegar a ser un buen actor** you have the ability to become a good actor; **esto está por encima de mis ~es** this is beyond my capabilities **3.** *pl* (*medios económicos*) means *pl;* **estás viviendo por encima de tus ~es** you are living beyond your means
posibilitar *vt* to make possible

posible I. *adj* possible; **hacer** ~ to make possible; **hacer lo** ~ **para que** +*subj* to do everything possible so that; **hacer todo lo** ~ to do everything one can; **hacer todo lo humanamente** ~ to do everything humanly possible; **es muy** ~ **que lleguen tarde** they may very well arrive late; **es** ~ **que** +*subj* it is possible that; **es muy** ~ **que** +*subj* it is very likely that; **¡no es** ~**!** I can't believe it!; **¿será** ~**?** surely not?; **si es** ~ if possible; **en lo** ~ as far as possible; **lo antes** ~ as soon as possible; **no lo veo** ~ I don't think it's possible II. *m pl* (*recursos*) means *pl*

posiblemente *adv* possibly

posición *f* t. MIL (*colocación, postura*) position; ~ **clave** vital position; ~ **del cuerpo** posture; ~ **del cursor** INFOR cursor position; **la** ~ **económica** the economic situation; ~ **de empleado** position of employment; **la** ~ **geográfica** the geographic location; **en buena** ~ in a good position; **de** ~ of high social standing; **mi** ~ **ante este asunto...** my opinion on this affair ...; **tomar** ~ to adopt a stance

positivo *m* FOTO print

positivo, -a *adj* 1. *t.* MAT, FÍS (*afirmativo, favorable*) positive 2. (*práctico*) practical; **un hombre** ~ a practical man

poso *m* 1. (*sedimento*) sediment; (*de café*) grounds *pl;* (*de vino*) lees *pl;* **hasta los** ~**s** *fig* to the very last drop 2. (*descanso*) rest

posponer *irr como poner vt* 1. (*postergar*) to relegate 2. (*aplazar*) to postpone

postal I. *adj* postal, mail *Am;* **una fotografía tamaño** ~ a postcard-sized photograph II. *f* postcard

poste *m t.* TEL (*pilar*) post; ELEC pylon; ~ **indicador** signpost; ~ **kilométrico** ≈ milestone ►**más serio que un** ~ *inf* deadly serious

postema *f Méx* (*pus*) pus

póster *m* poster

postergar <g→gu> *vt* 1. (*aplazar*) to postpone; ~ **la fecha** to put back the date 2. (*posponer injustamente*) to delay; ~ **el ascenso de alguien** to pass sb over for promotion

posteridad *f* 1. (*descendencia*) descendants *pl* 2. (*generaciones venideras*) future generations *pl* 3. (*futuro, fama póstuma*) posterity; **pasar a la** ~ to be remembered by posterity

posterior *adj* 1. (*de tiempo*) later; ~ **a** after 2. (*de lugar*) back; ~ **a alguien** behind sb; **la parte** ~ **de la cabeza** the back of the head; **en la parte** ~ **del coche está el maletero** the boot is at the back of the car

posterioridad *f* posteriority; **con** ~ **de fecha** at a later date; **con** ~ subsequently

posteriormente *adv* subsequently, later

postigo *m* 1. (*puerta falsa*) blind door 2. (*portillo*) wicket gate 3. (*contraventana*) shutter

postín *m* 1. (*lujo*) luxury; **de** ~ luxurious 2. (*presunción*) ostentation; **darse mucho** ~ to show off

postinear *vi* to show off

postinero, -a *adj inf* vain

postizo *m* hairpiece

postizo, -a *adj* artificial; **cuello** ~ detachable collar; **dentadura postiza** false teeth; **nombre** ~ false name; **ojo** ~ artificial eye; **pelo** ~ wig

postor(a) *m(f)* bidder; **mejor** ~ highest bidder

postración *f* 1. (*humillación*) humiliation 2. (*por enfermedad, aflicción*) prostration; ~ **nerviosa** nervous breakdown

postrado, -a *adj* 1. (*arrodillado*) prostrate 2. (*humillado*) humiliated 3. (*abatido*) prostrate; ~ **de dolor** (*dolor físico*) in great pain; (*pena*) beside oneself with grief; ~ **en cama** laid up in bed; **quedar** ~ **por una enfermedad** to be struck down by an illness 4. (*desanimado*) depressed

postrar I. *vt* 1. (*derribar*) to prostrate 2. (*humillar*) to humiliate 3. (*debilitar*) to weaken II. *vr:* ~**se** 1. (*arrodillarse*) to prostrate oneself 2. (*perder las fuerzas*) to become weak

postre *m* dessert; **a** (**la**) ~ *fig* in the end, when all is said and done; **llegar a los** ~**s** *fig* to arrive too late

postrero, -a *adj* last

postrimerías *fpl* 1. (*de persona*) final years *pl;* **estar en sus** ~ to be at the end of one's life 2. (*tiempo*) final stages *pl;* **en las** ~ **del siglo pasado** at the end of the last century

postulado *m* proposition

postulante, -a *m, f* 1. (*solicitante*) petitioner 2. REL postulant 3. (*colecta*) collector

postular *vt* 1. (*pedir*) to request; (*donativos*) to collect 2. (*solicitar*) ~ **algo** to petition for sth

póstumo, -a I. *adj* posthumous; **fama póstuma** posthumous fame II. *m, f* posthumous son *m,* posthumous daughter *f*

postura *f* 1. (*colocación*) position; (*del cuerpo*) posture 2. (*actitud*) attitude 3. (*subasta*) bid; ~ **mayor** highest bad; **hacer** ~ to bid 4. (*apuesta*) amount bet 5. (*convenio*) agreed price 6. (*conjunto de huevos*) clutch; (*poner huevos*) egg-laying 7. BOT sapling 8. (*puesta*) ~ **del sol** sunset

post-venta I. *adj* after-sales; **servicio** ~ after-sales service II. *f* warranty period

potable *adj* 1. (*bebible*) drinkable; **agua** ~ drinking water 2. *inf* (*aceptable*) acceptable; **Juan es una persona** ~ Juan is a nice guy

potaje *m* 1. GASTR (*sopa*) soup; (*guiso*) stew (*containing pulses and vegetables*) 2. (*legumbres secas*) pulses *pl Brit,* dried legumes *pl* (*beans, peas, lentils and chickpeas*) 3. (*brebaje*) brew 4. *inf* (*mezcla*) mixture

potar *vi, vt inf* (*vomitar*) to puke

potasio *m* potassium

pote *m* 1. (*de barro, metal, para cocinar*) pot; (*para plantas*) flowerpot 2. GASTR stew ►**darse** ~ to show off

potencia *f* 1. (*fuerza*) strength; (*capacidad*) capacity; ~ **de carga** capacity; ~ **explosiva** explosive power; ~ **generativa** generative power; ~ **imaginativa** imaginative power; ~

intelectual intellectual power; ~ **mágica** magic power; ~ **del motor** engine capacity; ~ **motriz** motive power; ~ **visual** visual acuity **2.**(*poder*) power; **gran** ~ great power **3.** INFOR ~ **de entrada/de salida** input/output capacity **4.** FILOS possibility; **en** ~ potential **5.** MAT power; **elevar a la cuarta** ~ to raise to the power of four

potencial I. *adj* **1.**(*que tiene potencia*) powerful **2.**(*posible*) potential **3.** LING **el modo** ~ the conditional tense II. *m* **1.**(*poder, capacidad*) power; ~ **financiero** financial muscle **2.** FÍS potential energy; ELEC potential difference **3.** LING conditional

potente *adj* **1.**(*poderoso*) powerful **2.**(*eficiente*) efficient **3.**(*sexualidad*) potent

potestad *f* authority; ~ **electoral** electoral authority; ~ **legislativa** legislative jurisdiction; ~ **reglamentaria** regulatory authority; **patria** ~ paternal authority

potingue *m pey* **1.** *inf* (*cosmético*) lotion; **darse ~s** to put on one's war paint **2.**(*bebida*) concoction

poto *m* **1.** *Perú* (*vaso*) clay bowl **2.** *And, inf* (*trasero*) bum *Brit,* butt *Am*

potranca *f* filly

potranco *m* colt

potrear I. *vt* **1.** *inf* (*incomodar*) to vex **2.** *AmL* (*domar*) to break **3.** *Guat, Perú* (*pegar*) to beat II. *vi* (*actuar como joven y no serlo*) to frisk about like a young colt

potro *m* **1.** ZOOL colt **2.** DEP vaulting horse **3.**(*de tortura*) rack; **tener a alguien en el** ~ *fig* to have sb on the rack **4.**(*de herrar*) shoeing frame **5.**(*lo que atormenta*) torment

poza *f* (*charca*) puddle

pozal *m* (*cubo*) well-bucket

pozo *m* **1.**(*manantial*) well; ~ **de garrucha** well (*from which water is drawn by a bucket*) **2.**(*hoyo profundo*) shaft; ~ **airón** ventilation shaft; ~ **de extracción** extraction shaft; ~ **de lobos** trap; ~ **negro** cesspool; ~ **petrolífero** oil well; ~ **de retrete** latrine; ~ **séptico** septic tank; **caer en un** ~ *fig* to fall into oblivion; **ser un** ~ **sin fondo** *fig* to be a bottomless pit; **ser un** ~ **de ciencia** *fig* to be a fount of knowledge **3.** *CSur* (*bache*) pothole

pozole *m Méx* GASTR (*guiso*) pozole (*stew of young maize, meat and chili*)

PP *m abr de* **Partido Popular** Popular Party (*Spanish conservative party*)

p.p. *abr de* **por poder** pp

práctica *f* **1.**(*experiencia*) experience; ~ **en la conducción** driving experience; **una** ~ **de muchos años** many years' experience; **adquirir** ~ to gain experience; **perder la** ~ to get out of practice; **tener** ~ **en algo** to have experience of sth **2.**(*ejercitación*) practice; ~ **profesional** professional practice **3.**(*cursillo*) practical course; ~ **preprofesional** vocational training **4.**(*realización*) practice; **en la** ~ in practice; **llevar a la** ~ to carry out; **poner en** ~ to put into practice; **poner en** ~ **una posi-**

bilidad to put an idea into practice **5.**(*costumbre*) practice; ~ **judicial** normal legal practice; **la** ~ **de los negocios** business norms **6.**(*modo*) manner; (*método*) method; **la** ~ **comercial** business methods ►**la** ~ **hace al maestro** *prov* practice makes perfect

practicable *adj* **1.**(*realizable*) feasible **2.**(*camino, calle*) passable **3.**(*puerta, ventana*) that opens

practicar <c→qu> *vi, vt* to practise *Brit,* to practice *Am;* ~ **deporte** to play sport, to do sports; **estudió medicina, pero no practica** he/she studied medicine, but he/she doesn't work as a doctor; ~ **el español** to practise Spanish; ~ **una operación** to perform an operation

práctico *m* NÁUT pilot; ~ **de puerto** harbour [*o* harbor *Am*] pilot

práctico, -a I. *adj* practical; (*experimentado*) experienced II. *m, f* practitioner

pradera *f* grassland, prairie; (*prado*) meadow

pradería *f* meadowlands *pl*

prado *m* grassy field; (*para ganado*) meadow; (*para pasear*) park

Praga *f* Prague

pragmático, -a I. *adj* pragmatic II. *m, f* pragmatist

prángana *f Méx, PRico* extreme poverty

preámbulo *m* introduction, preamble; **sin ~s** *fig* without further ado; **no andarse con ~s** not to beat about the bush; **¡déjese de ~s!** get to the point!

preaviso *m* forewarning

prebenda *f* **1.** REL prebend **2.** *inf* (*trabajo*) soft job

precalentar <e→ie> I. *vt* to preheat II. *vr:* ~**se** DEP to warm up

precario, -a *adj* **1.**(*de poca estabilidad*) precarious **2.** unsafe

precaución *f* precaution; **tomar precauciones** to take precautions

precaver I. *vt* (*prevenir*) to prevent; (*evitar*) to avoid II. *vr:* ~**se de algo/alguien** to take precautions against sth/sb; **hay que ~se de todas las eventualidades** you have to be prepared for all eventualities

precavido, -a *adj* cautious

precedencia *f* **1.**(*prioridad*) precedence; **dar** ~ **a alguien** to give precedence to sb **2.**(*superioridad*) superiority

precedente I. *adj* preceding II. *m* precedent; **sentar un** ~ to establish a precedent; **sin ~s** unprecedented

preceder *vt* **1.**(*anteceder*) to precede; **un banquete precedido de varios discursos** a banquet preceded by several speeches **2.**(*tener primacía*) ~ **a algo/alguien** to have priority over sth/sb; ~ **en categoría** to have a higher position

preceptista I. *adj* preceptive II. *mf* LIT theorist

preceptiva *f* precepts *pl*

preceptivo, -a *adj* compulsory

precepto *m* **1.**(*mandamiento*) order

2.(*norma*) precept; ~ **básico** basic principle; ~ **de conducta** rule of behaviour *Brit* [*o* behavior *Am*]; ~ **jurídico** law; ~ **de ley** legal precept
preceptor(a) *m(f)* tutor
preceptuar <*1. pres:* preceptúo> *vt* to establish
preces *fpl* **1.**(*oraciones*) prayers *pl* **2.**(*súplicas*) pleas *pl*
preciado, -a *adj* **1.**(*estimado*) prized **2.**(*jactancioso*) boastful; ~ **de sí mismo** boastful
preciarse *vr* ~ **de algo** to boast about sth
precintar *vt* to seal
precinto *m* (*sello*) seal; ~ **de aduana** customs seal
precio *m* price; ~ **abordable** reasonable price; ~ **alzado** fixed price; ~ **al consumidor** retail price; ~ **al contado** cash price; ~ **de conversión** conversion rate; ~ **de coste** cost price; ~ **al detalle** retail price; ~ **de fábrica** price exworks, factory price; ~ **irrisorio** bargain price; ~ **al por mayor** wholesale price; ~ **preferente** preferential price; ~ **de presentación** introductory price; ~ **recomendado** recommended price; ~ **de rescate** ransom; ~ **de tarifa** list price; ~ **de temporada** seasonal price; ~ **unitario** single price; ~ **de venta al público** retail price; **a buen** ~ for a good price; **a** ~ **controlado** at a controlled price; **a mitad de** ~ at half price; **a poco** ~ cheaply; **a** ~ **de oro** for a very high price; **poner el** ~ to set the price; **¡qué** ~ **tiene el libro?** how much does this book cost?; **de todos los** ~**s** at all prices; **no tener** ~ *fig* to be priceless; **al** ~ **de la salud** at the cost of one's health; **querer conseguir algo a cualquier** ~ to want sth at any price; **poner** ~ **a la cabeza de alguien** to put a price on sb's head
preciosidad *f* value; **este cuadro es una** ~ this picture is very valuable; *fig* this picture is delightful; **esta chica es una** ~ this girl is lovely
precioso, -a *adj* **1.**(*valioso*) valuable **2.**(*hermoso*) lovely
precipicio *m* precipice; **estar al borde del** ~ *fig* to be on the brink of disaster
precipitación *f* **1.**(*prisa*) haste; **con** ~ hastily **2.** METEO rainfall
precipitadamente *adv* hastily
precipitado, -a *adj* (*apresurado*) hasty; **ser** ~ **en el hablar** to talk too soon
precipitar I. *vt* **1.**(*arrojar*) to throw down; **lo** ~**on por la ventana** they threw him out of the window **2.**(*apresurar*) to hasten; (*acelerar*) to hurry **II.** *vr:* ~**se 1.**(*arrojarse*) to throw oneself down **2.**(*atacar*) ~**se sobre algo/alguien** to hurl oneself at sth/sb **3.**(*acontecimientos*) to happen very quickly; (*personas*) to act hastily; **¡no se precipite!** don't be hasty!
precisamente *adv* exactly; **¿tiene que ser** ~ **hoy?** does it have to be today, of all days?; ~ **por eso** for that very reason
precisar I. *vi* to be necessary **II.** *vt* **1.**(*determinar*) to specify; **hay algo que no consigo** ~

there's sth I can't put my finger on **2.**(*necesitar*) to need; **preciso tu ayuda** I need your help
precisión *f* **1.**(*exactitud*) precision; ~ **de funcionamiento** reliability; ~ **de tiro** accuracy; **instrumento de** ~ precision instrument; **hablar con** ~ to speak clearly **2.**(*determinación*) clarification; **hacer precisiones** to clarify matters **3.**(*necesidad*) need; **tener** ~ **de hacer algo** to need to do sth
preciso, -a *adj* **1.**(*necesario*) necessary; **es** ~ **que** +*subj* it is necessary to; **es** ~ **que nos veamos** we need to see each other; **si es** ~... if necessary ... **2.**(*exacto*) precise; **a la hora precisa** punctually
preclaro, -a *adj* illustrious; (*destacado*) outstanding
precocidad *f* **1.**(*del niño*) precociousness **2.**(*de tiempo*) earliness
precocinado, -a *adj* pre-cooked; **plato** ~ ready-cooked dish, convenience food
preconcebido, -a *adj* preconceived; **tener ideas preconcebidas** to have preconceived ideas
preconizable *adj* foreseeable
preconizar <z→c> *vt* to recommend
precordillera *f Arg* Andean foothills *pl*
precoz *adj* precocious; (*diagnóstico, cosecha*) early; **eyaculación** ~ premature ejaculation
precursor(a) I. *adj* preceding **II.** *m(f)* precursor
predecesor(a) *m(f)* **1.**(*en el cargo*) predecessor **2.**(*antepasados*) ancestor
predecir *irr como decir vt* to predict; (*tiempo*) to forecast
predestinado, -a *adj* predestined; **estar** ~ **al crimen** to be destined for a life of crime
predestinar *vt* to predestine
predeterminar *vt* to predetermine
prédica *f* (*sermon*) sermon; (*discurso*) speech
predicación *f* **1.**(*sermonear*) preaching **2.**(*sermón*) sermon
predicado *m* LING predicate
predicador(a) I. *adj* preaching **II.** *m(f)* preacher
predicar <c→qu> *vt* **1.**(*sermonear*) to preach; ~ **en desierto** to preach in the wilderness; ~ **con el ejemplo** to practise [*o* practice *Am*] what one preaches **2.**(*publicar*) to publish **3.**(*elogiar*) to praise **4.**(*amonestar*) to admonish ▶**no se puede** ~ **y andar en la procesión** *prov* you can't be in two places at once; **una cosa es** ~ **y otra dar trigo** *prov* actions speak louder than words
predicativo, -a *adj* LING predicative
predicción *f* prediction; ~ **económica** economic forecast
predilección *f* predilection
predilecto, -a *adj* favourite *Brit,* favorite *Am;* **hijo** ~ favourite [*o* favorite *Am*] son; **plato** ~ favourite [*o* favorite *Am*] dish
predio *m* **1.** JUR estate; ~ **familiar** family estate; ~ **grande** large estate **2.**(*finca*) piece of

land; ~ **familiar** family holding; ~ **pequeño** smallholding

predisponer *irr como poner* **I.** *vt* **1.** (*fijar por anticipado*) to agree beforehand; **predispongamos ya la fecha de nuestra próxima reunión** let's set the date of our next meeting now; **venía predispuesto a pelearse** he arrived in a mood for a quarrel **2.** (*influir*) to predispose; ~ **a alguien a favor/en contra de alguien** to bias sb in favour [*o* favor *Am*] of/against sb **3.** (*inclinar*) to make receptive; MED to predispose **II.** *vr* **1.** (*prepararse*) ~**se a algo** to prepare oneself for sth **2.** (*tomar partido*) to have a bias; ~**se a favor/en contra de alguien** to be biased in favour [*o* favor *Am*] of/against sb

predisposición *f t.* MED predisposition; (*tendencia*) tendency; ~ **al crimen** criminal predisposition; **tener ~ a engordar** to have a tendency to put on weight

predispuesto, -a I. *pp de* **predisponer II.** *adj* **1.** *ser* (*sensible*) predisposed; **ser ~ a coger los virus** to have a tendency to catch viruses **2.** *estar* (*prevenido*) prejudiced; **estar** (**mal**) ~ **contra alguien** to be prejudiced against sb

predominar *vi, vt* **1.** (*prevalecer*) to predominate; **aquí predomina la corrupción** corruption is very common here; **en este parque las palomas predominan en número sobre los gorriones** in this park there are more pigeons than sparrows **2.** (*sobresalir*) to stand out; ~ **en algo/sobre alguien** to stand out at sth/over sb

predominio *m* **1.** (*poder*) predominance **2.** (*preponderancia*) preponderance **3.** (*superioridad*) ~ **sobre alguien** superiority over sb

preeminencia *f* pre-eminence

preeminente *adj* pre-eminent

preescolar *adj* pre-school; **edad ~** pre-school age

preestreno *m* preview

preexistir *vi* to pre-exist

prefabricado, -a *adj* prefabricated; **casa prefabricada** prefabricated house

prefacio *m* (*libro*) preface; (*discurso*) introduction

preferencia *f* **1.** (*elección, trato*) preference; **mostrar ~ por alguien** to show a preference for sb **2.** (*predilección*) predilection; **sentir ~ por alguien** to be biased in favour of sb **3.** (*prioridad*) priority; ~ **de paso** right of way; **precio de ~** preferential price; **tener ~ ante alguien** to have priority over sb; **dar ~** to give preference; **de ~** preferably

preferentemente *adv* preferably

preferible *adj* preferable; **sería ~ que lo hicieras** it would be best if you did it

preferiblemente *adv* preferably

preferido, -a *adj* favourite *Brit,* favorite *Am*

preferir *irr como sentir vt* to prefer; **prefiero ir a pie** I prefer to walk; **prefiero que no**

venga I would rather he/she didn't come

prefijar *vt* **1.** (*determinar*) to decide (in advance), to prearrange **2.** LING to prefix

prefijo *m* **1.** LING prefix **2.** TEL (dialling) code *Brit,* area code *Am*

pregón *m* proclamation; **con ~ fig** with much ado; **sin ~ fig** without a lot of fuss

pregonar *vt* **1.** (*en público*) to proclaim; ~ **mercancías** to publicize goods **2.** (*lo que estaba oculto*) to make public; ~ **a los cuatro vientos** *inf* to proclaim for all to hear; ~ **a tambor batiente** to proclaim loudly **3.** (*alabar*) to praise publicly

pregonero, -a *m, f* **1.** (*público*) town crier **2.** *inf* (*chismoso*) gossip

pregunta *f* **1.** (*demanda*) question; ~ **capciosa** trick question; **hacer ~s capciosas a alguien** to try to catch sb out; **estrechar a ~s a alguien** to bombard sb with questions; **a tal ~ tal respuesta** ask a silly question, get a silly answer; **estar a la cuarta ~** *inf* to be broke **2.** (*de datos*) inquiry

preguntar I. *vt* to ask; ~ **a alguien la lección** to test sb; ~ **a un sospechoso** to question a suspect; ~ **por alguien** to ask after sb ▸ **quien pregunta no yerra** *prov* he who asks questions won't go far wrong **II.** *vr* ~**se si/cuándo/qué...** to wonder if/when/what ...

preguntón, -ona *adj* inquisitive, nosy *pej*

prehistórico, -a *adj* prehistoric

prejubilación *f* early retirement

prejuicio *m* prejudice

prejuzgar <g→gu> *vt* to prejudge

preliminar *adj* preliminary

preludio *m t.* MÚS prelude

premamá *adj inv* **vestido ~** maternity dress

prematuro, -a *adj* **1.** (*persona*) precocious **2.** (*antes de tiempo, apresurado*) premature; **detección prematura del cáncer** early detection of cancer; **nacimiento ~** premature birth

premeditación *f* premeditation; **con ~** premeditated

premeditadamente *adv* with premeditation

premeditado, -a *adj* premeditated

premeditar *vt* **1.** (*pensar*) to think about **2.** (*planear*) to plan; JUR to premeditate

premiación *f And* awarding (of prizes)

premiado, -a I. *adj* prizewinning **II.** *m, f* prizewinner; (*literatura, ciencias*) laureate

premiar *vt* **1.** (*recompensar*) to reward **2.** (*dar un premio*) to give [*o* award] a prize to

premier *m f* premier

premio *m* **1.** (*galardón*) prize; ~ **Nobel** (**de literatura**) Nobel prize (for/in literature); **conceder un ~** to award a prize **2.** (*recompensa*) reward; ~ **por hallazgo** finder's reward **3.** (*remuneración*) bonus; ~ **al ahorro** savings bonus; ~ **de antigüedad** long-service bonus **4.** (*lotería*) prize; **el ~ gordo** the jackpot **5.** (*ganador*) prizewinner; **García Márquez es ~ Nobel de literatura** García Márquez is a Nobel laureate in literature

premioso, -a *adj* **1.** (*ajustado*) tight **2.** (*molesto*) annoying **3.** (*estrecho*) narrow **4.** (*torpe*) slow **5.** (*estricto*) strict

premisa *f* **1.** (*condición*) premise **2.** (*indicio*) indication

premonición *f* (*presentimiento*) premonition

premunir I. *vt AmL* ~ **de algo** to provide with sth **II.** *vr AmL* ~**se de algo** to provide oneself with sth

premura *f* **1.** (*apuro*) pressure **2.** (*prisa*) haste **3.** (*falta*) lack

prenatal *adj* prenatal

prenda *f* **1.** (*fianza*) guarantee; **en** ~ as security; **en ~s** as evidence; **hacer** ~ to hold as security; **soltar** ~ to commit oneself; **no soltar** ~ *inf* not to say a word; **a mí no me duelen ~s** I don't mind admitting it **2.** (*pieza de ropa*) garment; **~s interiores** underwear; ~ **protectora** protective clothing **3.** (*cariño*) darling; **la** ~ **de mi corazón** my darling **4.** (*cualidades*) talent; **~s del espíritu** spiritual qualities; **un hombre de ~s** a talented man

prendar I. *vt* **1.** (*tomar como prenda*) to take as security **2.** (*ganar el afecto*) to captivate **II.** *vr* ~**se de alguien** *elev* to fall in love with sb

prendedor *m* (*broche*) brooch, pin; (*de corbata*) tiepin

prender I. *vi* (*planta, ideas*) to take root; (*medicamentos*) to take effect; **sus ideas prendieron fácilmente en la juventud** his ideas quickly took root among the young **II.** *vt* **1.** (*sujetar*) to hold down; (*con alfileres*) to pin; (*con cola*) to stick; (*en un gancho*) to hang; (*el pelo*) to tie back; ~ **un alfiler de corbata** to put a tiepin on **2.** (*detener*) to catch **3.** (*fuego*) **el coche prendió fuego** the car caught fire **4.** *AmL* (*encender*) to light; (*luz*) to turn on; ~ **un cigarrillo** to light a cigarette **III.** *vr* **1.** (*mujeres*) to dress up; **~se una flor en el ojal** to put a flower in one's buttonhole **2.** *PRico* (*emborracharse*) to get drunk

prendimiento *m* **1.** (*captura*) capture **2.** *Col, Ven* (*irritación*) irritation **3.** *CSur* (*estreñimiento*) constipation

prensa *f* **1.** (*máquina*) press; ~ **de uvas** wine press **2.** (*imprenta*) printer's, press; **dar a la** ~ to send to the printer's; **estar en** ~ to be at the printer's **3.** PREN press; ~ **amarilla** tabloids *pl;* ~ **especializada** specialist publications; **rueda de** ~ press conference; **libertad de** ~ freedom of the press; **secretario de** ~ press secretary; **Prensa y Relaciones Públicas** Public Relations; **tener buena/mala** ~ *fig* to get a good/bad press

prensar *vt* to press

prensil *adj* prehensile

preñada *adj* (*mujer*) pregnant

preñado, -a *adj* **1.** (*animal*) pregnant **2.** (*lleno*) full; **una nube preñada de agua** a cloud full of water; **una palabra preñada** a word loaded with meaning; ~ **de dificultades** full of difficulties; ~ **de emoción** full of emotion

preñar *vt* **1.** (*mujer*) to make pregnant **2.** (*animal*) to impregnate **3.** (*llenar*) to fill

preñez *f* (*de la mujer, del animal*) pregnancy

preocupación *f* **1.** (*desvelo*) worry; ~ **por algo/alguien** worry about sth/sb; **¡déjate de preocupaciones!** stop worrying!; **sin preocupaciones** unworried **2.** (*pesadumbre*) worry; **causar preocupaciones a alguien** to be a cause of concern for sb **3.** (*obsesión*) concern; **tu única** ~ **es el dinero** the only thing you care about is money **4.** (*prejuicio*) prejudice

preocupado, -a *adj* worried; ~ **por algo/alguien** worried about sth/sb; **mi padre anda bastante** ~ my father is quite worried; **tener el espíritu** ~ **por algo** to be worried about sth

preocupante *adj* worrying

preocupar I. *vt* **1.** (*inquietar*) to worry; **¿por qué preocupas tanto a tus padres?** why do you make your parents worry so much? **2.** (*prevenir*) to prejudice **II.** *vr* **1.** (*inquietarse*) ~**se por algo/alguien** to worry about sth/sb; **¡no se preocupe!** don't worry!; **¡no te preocupes tanto!** don't worry so much! **2.** (*encargarse*) to take care; **no se preocupa de arreglar el asunto** he/she doesn't do anything to solve the problem **3.** (*tener prejuicios*) to be biased

prepa *f Méx* (*preparatoria*) secondary school

preparación *f* **1.** (*de un asunto, de la comida, de materias primas*) preparation; ~ **de datos** INFOR data processing **2.** (*formación*) training; ~ **académica** education; ~ **especializada** specialist training; ~ **profesional** professional training; **sin** ~ untrained **3.** (*farmacéutica*) preparation

preparado *m* preparation; ~ **listo** ready-made medicine; **¡~s, listos, ya!** ready, steady, go!

preparado, -a *adj* (*listo*) ready; ~ (**para funcionar**) ready for use; **tener** ~ to have ready

preparar I. *vt* **1.** (*disponer: la comida, materias primas*) to prepare; **en esta escuela profesional te preparan bien** in this professional training school they give you a good training; **en inglés me prepara una profesora nativa** I am taught English by a teacher who is a native speaker; ~ **un buque para zarpar** to get a boat ready for a journey; ~ **el camino** to prepare the way; ~ **una casa para vivir en ella** to make a house ready for living in; ~ **un discurso** to write a speech; ~ **las maletas** to pack one's bags; **ya puedes** ~ **la maleta** *inf* it's time you were leaving; ~ **la tierra** to prepare the ground **2.** QUÍM, ANAT to prepare **3.** INFOR (*datos*) to process; (*programa*) to compile **II.** *vr* to get ready; **me preparaba a salir, cuando empezó a llover** I was getting ready to leave when it started raining; **se preparaba una tormenta** there's a storm brewing; **~se para cualquier eventualidad** to prepare oneself for any eventuality

preparativo *m* preparation

preparativo, -a *adj* preparatory
preparatoria *f Méx* college prep (*3-year pre-university course and the school where it is given*)
preparatorio, -a *adj* preparatory; **curso ~** introductory course; **trabajos ~s** preliminary work
prepo *Arg* **de ~** by force
preponderancia *f* preponderance
preponderante *adj* preponderant
preponderar *vi* to prevail
preposición *f* preposition
prepotente *adj* arrogant
prerrogativa *f* (*privilegio*) prerogative
presa *f* **1.** (*acción*) capture; **las llamas hicieron ~ en la casa** the house went up in flames; **ser ~ del terror** to be seized by terror **2.** (*objeto, de caza*) prey; **animal de ~** prey; **ave de ~** bird of prey; **hacer una ~** to make a kill **3.** (*dique*) dam **4.** (*colmillo*) fang **5.** (*uña*) talon **6.** (*acequia*) channel **7.** (*de comida*) piece of food **8.** DEP hold; **~ de brazo** (*judo*) arm hold
presagiar *vt* to betoken *form;* **estas nubes presagian tormenta** these clouds mean there will be a storm
presagio *m* **1.** (*señal*) warning sign **2.** (*presentimiento*) premonition
presbicia *f* MED long-sightedness
presbiterio *m* presbytery
presbítero *m* priest
prescindible *adj* dispensable
prescindir *vi* **1.** (*renunciar a*) **~ de algo/alguien** to do without sth/sb; **tenemos que ~ del coche** we will have to get rid of the car; **no podemos ~ de él** we can't do without him **2.** (*pasar por alto*) **~ de algo/alguien** to overlook sth/sb; **han prescindido de mi opinión** they have ignored my opinion **3.** (*no contar*) **~ de algo/alguien** to disregard sth/sb
prescribir *irr como escribir* **I.** *vi* (*plazo*) to expire **II.** *vt* (*indicar*) *t.* MED to prescribe; **prescrito por la ley** prescribed by law
prescripción *f* **1.** (*indicación*) indication **2.** MED prescription **3.** (*plazo*) expiry
presencia *f* **1.** (*asistencia*) presence; **sin la ~ del ministro** without the minister being present; **hacer acto de ~** to put in an appearance **2.** (*aspecto*) appearance; **buena ~** stylish appearance **3.** (*existencia*) **estamos en ~ del aeropuerto más grande de Europa** this is the largest airport in Europe; **la gente está asustada por la ~ de ladrones** people are scared by the presence of thieves; **la constante ~ de ese recuerdo no le dejaba dormir** the persistence of the memory did not allow him to sleep
presencial *adj* **testigo ~** eyewitness
presenciar *vt* **1.** (*ver*) to witness **2.** (*asistir*) to attend; **10.000 personas ~on el concierto** 10,000 people attended the concert
presentable *adj* presentable; **ponerse ~** to make oneself presentable

presentación *f* **1.** (*de una novela, una película*) launch(ing) **2.** (*de un número artístico*) presentation; TEAT show **3.** (*de instancia, dimisión*) submission; **el plazo de ~ de solicitudes finaliza hoy** the period for presenting requests ends today **4.** (*de argumentos, documento, propuesta*) presentation **5.** (*de personas*) introduction **6.** (*aspecto*) appearance **7.** AmL (*súplica*) petition
presentador(a) *m(f)* (*de programa*) presenter; (*de telediario*) newsreader
presentar **I.** *vt* **1.** (*mostrar*) to show **2.** (*ofrecer*) to offer; **el viaje presenta dificultades** the journey poses difficulties; **la ciudad presenta un aspecto de gala** the city is in festive mood; **este informe presenta los sucesos de una manera clara** this report sets out the events clearly **3.** TV, RADIO to present; TEAT to put on; (*presentador*) to introduce **4.** (*instancia, dimisión, trabajo*) to submit **5.** (*argumentos*) to put forward; (*pruebas, propuesta*) to submit **6.** (*pasaporte, documento*) to show **7.** (*persona*) to introduce; **te presento a mi marido** may I introduce you to my husband? **8.** (*candidato*) to propose **II.** *vr:* **~se 1.** (*comparecer*) to present oneself; (*aparecer*) to turn up **2.** (*para elecciones*) **~se a** to stand at *Brit,* to run for *Am* **3.** (*concurso*) to enter
presente[1] **I.** *adj* **1.** (*que está*) present; **¡~!** present!; **estar ~** to be present **2.** (*actual*) current **3.** (*este*) **la ~ edición** this edition; **la ~ tesina** this thesis **4.** (*a considerar*) **hay que tener ~ las circunstancias** one must consider the circumstances; **ten ~ lo que te ha dicho** bear in mind what I have told you **5.** (*escrito*) **por la ~ deseo comunicarle que...** (*en una carta*) I write in order to tell you that ... **II.** *mf* (*asistente*) **los/las ~s** those present
presente[2] *m* **1.** (*actualidad*) present; **hasta el ~** until now; **por el ~** for the moment **2.** LING present (tense) **3.** (*regalo*) present, gift
presentimiento *m* premonition; **tengo el ~ de que...** I have a feeling that ...
presentir *irr como sentir* *vt* to have a premonition of; **presiento que mañana lloverá** I have a feeling it's going to rain tomorrow
preservación *f* preservation
preservar **I.** *vt* to protect **II.** *vr* to protect oneself
preservativo *m* condom
presidencia *f* **1.** (*mandato*) presidency; **asumir la ~** to take over the presidency; **esta orden viene de la ~** this order comes from the president **2.** (*edificio*) presidental palace **3.** (*de organización, asamblea: conjunto*) board; (*individuo*) chairperson, president; **asumir la ~** to take the chair
presidencial *adj* **1.** POL presidential **2.** (*de asamblea*) presiding
presidente *mf* **1.** POL president; **~ del gobierno Aznar** Spanish Prime Minister, Aznar **2.** (*de asociación*) chairperson

presidiario, -a *m, f* convict

presidio *m* prison; **condenar a 20 años de ~** to sentence to 20 years in prison

presidir *vt* **1.** (*ocupar presidencia*) to be president of **2.** (*mandar*) to rule **3.** (*dominar*) to dominate

presilla *f* fastener

presión *f* pressure; **~ arterial** blood pressure; **~ competitiva** competition; **~ fiscal** tax burden; **~ social** social pressure; **grupo de ~** pressure group; **zona de altas presiones** METEO high pressure area; **cerrado a ~** pressurized; **¿a qué ~ llevas las ruedas?** what is your tyre [*o* tire *Am*] pressure?; **estar bajo ~** to be under pressure; **hacer ~ sobre alguien** to put pressure on sb; **no acepto presiones de nadie** I don't allow anyone to pressurize [*o* pressure *Am*] me

presionar *vt* **1.** (*apretar*) to press **2.** (*coaccionar*) to put pressure on

preso, -a *m, f* prisoner, (prison) inmate

prestación *f* **1.** (*de ayuda, servicio*) provision; **~ por desempleo** unemployment benefit; **prestaciones en especie** payment in kind; **~ de servicios** provision of services; **Prestación Social Sustitutoria** social service (*as an alternative to military service*) **2.** *pl* (*de coche*) features *pl*; **un coche con todas las últimas prestaciones** a car with all the latest features

prestado, -a *adj* borrowed; **voy de ~, el traje me lo han dejado** I'm wearing borrowed finery, sb lent me the suit; **vivir de ~ en casa de alguien** to live off sb else

prestamista *mf* moneylender; (*contra prenda*) pawnbroker; (*banco*) lending bank

préstamo *m* **1.** (*acción*) lending **2.** *t.* FIN (*lo prestado: para exposición*) loan; **~ hipotecario** mortgage; **~ a interés fijo** fixed-interest loan; **la duración de un ~** the period of a loan **3.** LING loan word

prestancia *f* **1.** (*distinción*) distinction **2.** (*excelencia*) excellence

prestar I. *vt* **1.** (*dejar*) to lend; **¿me prestas la bici, por favor?** can I borrow your bike?; **el banco me ha prestado el dinero** I have borrowed money from the bank **2.** (*dedicar*) **~ ayuda** to help; **~ servicios** to provide services; **~ colaboración** to cooperate; **~ apoyo** to support **3.** (*declaración*) to make; (*juramento*) to swear **4.** (*atención*) to pay; **~ silencio** to remain silent; **~ paciencia** to be patient; **~ oídos** to lend an ear **II.** *vi* (*dar de sí*) **los zapatos son pequeños pero ya ~án** the shoes are small but they will stretch; **este pantalón presta mucho** these trousers have stretched a lot; **esta cuerda no presta** this rope doesn't have any give **III.** *vr:* **~se 1.** (*ofrecerse*) to offer oneself; **se prestó a ayudarme en la mudanza** he/she offered to help me move house **2.** (*avenirse*) to accept **3.** (*dar motivo*) to give rise to; **tus palabras se prestan a confusión** your words lend themselves to misinterpretation

prestatario, -a *m, f* borrower

presteza *f* speed

prestidigitación *f* conjuring; **un número de ~** a conjuring trick

prestidigitador(a) *m(f)* conjurer

prestigio *m* prestige; **una cuestión de ~** a matter of honour *Brit* [*o* honor *Am*]; **hoy viene un conferenciante de ~** today's speaker is very famous

prestigioso, -a *adj* prestigious

presto *adv* **1.** (*rápidamente*) quickly **2.** (*al instante*) at once

presto, -a *adj* **1.** (*listo*) ready **2.** (*rápido*) quick

presumido, -a *adj* **1.** (*arrogante*) arrogant **2.** (*vanidoso*) vain

presumir I. *vi* **1.** (*vanagloriarse*) **~ de algo** to boast about sth **2.** **~ más que una mona** *inf* to be as vain as a peacock **II.** *vt* to presume

presunción *f* **1.** (*sospecha*) assumption **2.** (*petulancia*) arrogance **3.** (*vanidad*) vanity

presunto, -a *adj* **1.** (*supuesto*) presumed; **el ~ asesino** the alleged murderer **2.** (*equivocadamente*) so-called

presuntuoso, -a *adj* conceited

presuponer *irr como* poner *vt* **1.** (*suponer*) to presuppose **2.** (*calcular*) to suppose

presupuestar *vt* **1.** POL, ECON to budget (for) **2.** (*gastos*) to calculate; **~ los gastos en tres millones** to calculate the costs to be three million

presupuestario, -a *adj* budget(ary)

presupuesto *m* **1.** POL, ECON budget; **~ anual** annual budget; **Presupuesto General del Estado** National Budget; **la confección del ~** the drawing up of the budget **2.** (*cálculo*) estimate **3.** (*suposición*) assumption

presuroso, -a *adj* hurried; **iba ~ por la calle** he hurried down the street

pretender *vt* **1.** (*aspirar a*) to aspire to; **~ subir de categoría** to be seeking promotion **2.** (*pedir*) to expect; **¿qué pretendes que haga?** what do you want me to do?; **no puedes ~ que te traten con corrección si...** you can't expect them to treat you with respect if... **3.** (*tener intención*) to mean; **no pretendía molestar** I didn't mean to disturb you **4.** (*intentar*) to try to **5.** (*afirmar*) to affirm **6.** (*puesto*) to aspire to **7.** (*cortejar*) to woo

pretendiente *m* (*de trabajo*) applicant; (*de mujer*) suitor; (*a la corona*) pretender

pretensión *f* **1.** (*derecho*) claim; **~ económica** financial demand **2.** (*ambición*) ambition; (*aspiración*) aim; **es una persona con muchas pretensiones** he is very ambitious; **es una persona con pocas pretensiones** he is easily pleased; **tener muchas pretensiones laborales** to be ambitious at work; **tiene la ~ de que vaya con él** he wants me to go with him **3.** *pl* (*vanidad*) **tiene pretensiones de actor** he fancies himself as an actor **4.** (*solicitud*) application

pretérito *m* LING past

pretérito, -a *adj* past

pretextar *vt* to use as an excuse; **pretextó que estaba enfermo** he pretended that he was ill; **siempre pretexta algo** he always has some excuse

pretexto *m* pretext; **a ~ de…** on the pretext of …

pretil *m* 1.(*de puente*) parapet 2. *AmL* (*atrio*) forecourt

pretina *f* 1.(*cinta*) band 2.(*de calzoncillos*) waistband 3.(*de prenda*) elastic 4.(*cintura*) waist

prevalecer *irr como crecer vi* 1.(*imponerse*) to prevail; **la verdad prevaleció sobre la mentira** truth prevailed over lies 2.(*predominar*) to predominate; **en esta ciudad prevalecen los de derechas sobre los de izquierdas** in this city there are more right-wingers than left-wingers 3.(*triunfar*) to win 4.BOT to take root 5.(*prosperar*) to thrive

prevaleciente *adj* (*moda*) current; (*costumbre*) prevailing

prevaricación *f* 1.JUR perversion of the course of justice 2.(*del deber*) dereliction of duty

prevaricar <c→qu> *vi* 1.JUR to pervert the course of justice 2.(*faltar al deber*) to fail to do one's duty 3. *inf* (*desvariar*) to talk nonsense

prevención *f* 1.(*precaución*) precaution 2. *t.* MED (*acción*) prevention; **~ del cáncer** cancer prevention; **~ de accidentes** accident prevention; **~ de siniestros** crash prevention 3.(*prejuicio*) prejudice; **tener ~ contra alguien** to be prejudiced against sb

prevenido, -a *adj* 1. *estar* (*alerta*) **estar ~** to be prepared 2. *ser* (*previsor*) prudent ▶**hombre ~ vale por dos** *prov* forewarned is forearmed *prov*

prevenir *irr como venir* I. *vt* 1.(*protegerse de, evitar*) to prevent 2.(*advertir*) to warn 3.(*predisponer*) to prejudice; **~ a alguien a favor de alguien/en contra de alguien** to prejudice sb in sb's favour [*o* favor *Am*]/against sb 4.(*preparar*) to prepare; **~ las armas** to get ready for battle 5.(*proveer*) **~ de algo** to provide with sth ▶**más vale ~ que curar** *prov* prevention is better than cure, a stitch in time saves nine *prov* II. *vr:* **~se** 1.(*tomar precauciones*) to take precautions 2.(*contra alguien*) to protect oneself 3.(*proveerse*) **~se de algo** to provide oneself with sth 4.(*prepararse*) to get ready

preventivo, -a *adj* preventive, preventative; **medida preventiva** preventive measure; **prisión preventiva** remand

prever *irr como ver vt* to foresee; (*esperar*) to expect

previo *m* TV, CINE playback

previo, -a *adj* previous; (*sin*) **~ aviso** (without) prior warning; **previa presentación del D.N.I.** on presentation of identity documents; **~ pago de la matrícula** on payment of the matriculation fee; **tuve una entrevista previa con él** I had a preliminary interview with him

previsible *adj* 1.(*probable*) predictable 2.(*que se puede prever*) foreseeable; **dentro de un futuro ~** in the foreseeable future; **era ~ it** was to be expected

previsión *f* 1.(*de prever*) prediction; **esto supera todas las previsiones** this surpasses all the predictions 2.(*precaución*) precaution; **hay que tener ~ de futuro** one must plan for the future; **en ~ de…** as a precaution against … 3.(*cálculo*) forecast; **las previsiones económicas** the economic forecasts

previsor(a) *adj* 1.(*con visión*) far-sighted 2.(*precavido*) prudent

previsto, -a *adj* predicted; **el éxito estaba ~** the success had been expected; **todo lo necesario está ~** everything necessary has been prepared

prez *m o f* 1.(*honor*) honour *Brit,* honor *Am* 2.(*gloria*) glory

PRI *m abr de* **Partido Revolucionario Institucional** *Mexican ruling party from 1929 onwards*

prieto, -a *adj* 1.(*apretado*) tight 2.(*negro*) black; (*negruzco*) blackish 3.(*tacaño*) stingy, mean *Brit* 4.(*compacto*) compact

prima *f* 1.(*pariente*) (girl) cousin; **~ hermana/segunda** first/second cousin 2.FIN bonus; (*seguro*) insurance premium

primacía *f* 1. *t.* MIL, POL (*supremacía*) supremacy 2.(*prioridad*) priority

primada *f inf* piece of foolishness; **no hagas la ~ de comprarte este traje** don't be so stupid as to buy this suit; **me han hecho una ~** they've ripped me off

primar I. *vi* to be of great importance; **en esta escuela prima el orden** in this school the most important thing is good behaviour *Brit* [*o* behavior *Am*]; **aquí priman los enchufes sobre la capacidad personal** here contacts are more important than ability II. *vt* to reward

primario, -a *adj* 1.(*principal, primero*) primary; **corriente primaria** ELEC primary current; **enseñanza primaria** primary education; **necesidades primarias** basic necessities 2.(*persona*) primitive

primate *m* primate

primavera I. *adj* spring II. *f* 1.(*estación*) spring; **estar en la ~ de la vida** *fig* to be in the prime of life 2.BOT primrose 3. *pl* (*años*) years

primaveral *adj* spring(like)

primer *adj v.* **primero, -a**

primera *f* 1.AUTO first (gear); **ir en ~** to be in first (gear) 2.FERRO, AVIAT first class; **viajar en ~** to travel first class

primeriza *f* first-time mother

primerizo, -a *m, f* (*novato*) novice

primero *adv* 1.(*en primer lugar*) first; **~…, segundo…** first …, second …; **~ dice una cosa, luego dice otra** first he says one thing, then another 2.(*antes*) rather

primero, -a I. *adj* (*ante sustantivo masculino: primer*) first; **primera calidad** top quality; **primera edición** first edition; **el Primer Mi-**

nistro the Prime Minister; **primera representación** première (performance); **estado** ~ initial state; **a primera hora (de la mañana)** first thing (in the morning); **a ~s de mes** at the beginning of the month; **lo hice a la** ~ I did it at the first attempt; **de primera** first-rate; **de primera calidad** top quality; **ser/estar de primera** to be really good; **desde un primer momento** from the outset; **en primer lugar** in the first place; **ocupar una de las primeras posiciones** to occupy one of the top positions; **lo ~ es lo** ~ first things first; **para mí tú eres lo** ~ for me you are more important than anything else; **lo ~ es ahora la familia** the most important thing now is the family **II.** *m, f* first; **el ~ de la carrera** the winner of the race; **el ~ de la clase** the top of the class; **estar entre los ~s** to be among the leaders; **eres el ~ en llegar** you are the first to arrive

primicia *f* 1.(*lo primero*) first one 2. PREN, TV, RADIO scoop 3. *pl* (*frutos*) **las ~s** the first fruits

primitivo, -a *adj* primitive; **los habitantes ~s** the original inhabitants; **lotería primitiva** *Spanish state lottery;* **palabra primitiva** LING non-derived word

primo *m* 1.(*pariente*) (boy) cousin; ~ **hermano/segundo** first/second cousin 2. *inf* (*ingenuo*) mug; **he hecho el ~: he pagado 50 euros por esto** I've been taken for a ride: I paid 50 euros for this; **¡no seas ~!** don't be such a fool!

primo, -a *adj* 1. *elev* (*primero*) first; **materia prima** raw material 2.(*primoroso*) exquisite 3.(*excelente*) excellent 4. MAT **número ~** prime number

primogénito, -a *adj, m, f* first-born

primor *m* 1.(*habilidad*) skill 2.(*esmero*) care; **hacer algo con ~** to take great care in doing sth

primordial *adj* 1.(*más importante*) supreme; **este asunto es de interés ~** this affair is of fundamental concern 2.(*fundamental*) essential, fundamental; **para vivir en Gran Bretaña es ~ hablar inglés** if you are going to live in Great Britain it is essential that you speak English

primoroso, -a *adj* 1.(*hábil*) skilful *Brit,* skillful *Am* 2.(*con esmero*) careful; **es un bordado ~** it is a delicate piece of embroidery 3.(*excelente*) excellent; **labios ~s** beautiful lips

prímula *f* primrose

princesa *f v.* **príncipe, princesa**

principado *m* principality; **el Principado** Asturias; **el Principado de Andorra** the Principality of Andorra

principal¹ **I.** *adj* 1.(*más importante*) principal; **el problema ~** the main problem; **su carrera profesional era lo ~ para él** his career was his main priority 2.(*esencial*) essential **II.** *mf* (*de negocio: propietario*) owner; (*jefe*) boss

principal² *m* 1.(*piso*) first floor *Brit,* second

floor *Am* 2.(*edición*) first edition

principalmente *adv* mainly, principally; **él ha sido ~ el que ha hecho el trabajo** he is the one who did most of the work

príncipe *adj* **edición ~** first edition

príncipe, princesa *m, f* prince *m,* princess *f;* ~ **heredero** crown prince; **el Príncipe de Asturias** the Prince of Asturias (*title held by the heir to the Spanish throne);* ~ **azul** Prince Charming

principesco, -a *adj* princely

principiante *mf* beginner, novice

principio *m* 1.(*comienzo*) beginning; **al ~** at the beginning; **ya desde el ~** right from the beginning; **desde un ~** from the first; **a ~s de diciembre** at the beginning of December; **dar ~ a algo** to start sth 2.(*causa*) cause; (*origen*) origin; **el ~ de la discusión** the cause of the argument 3.(*de ética*) principle; **sin ~s** unprincipled; **hombre de ~s** a man of principle(s); **por ~** on principle 4. *t.* FÍS (*fundamento*) principle; **en ~** in principle 5. QUÍM element 6. *pl* (*de ciencia*) fundamentals *pl*

pringado, -a *m, f inf* (*primo*) chump, mug *Brit*

pringar <g→gu> **I.** *vt* 1.(*manchar*) ~ **de/con algo** to smear with sth 2.(*mojar*) to dip 3. *inf* (*herir*) to wound 4. *inf* (*desacreditar*) to run down **II.** *vi* 1. *pey, inf* (*en negocio*) to make a bit on the side 2. *inf* (*trabajar*) to slog one's guts out 3. *AmL* (*lloviznar*) to drizzle 4. *inf* (*morir*) to snuff it **III.** *vr:* **~se** 1.(*mancharse*) **~se de/con algo** to cover oneself with sth 2.(*en negocio*) to make a bit on the side; **se ha pringado en 200 marcos** *pey* he has raked off 200 marks

pringoso, -a *adj* 1.(*grasiento*) greasy 2.(*pegajoso*) sticky

pringue *m* 1.(*grasa*) grease 2.(*suciedad*) grime 3. *inf* (*jugada*) **¿que tienes que repetir el trabajo? ¡vaya ~ tío!** *inf* you've got to do the work again? what a drag!

prioridad *f* 1.(*anterioridad, urgencia*) priority; **de máxima ~** top priority; **dar ~ a un asunto** to give an affair priority 2. AUTO right of way

prioritario, -a *adj* priority; **este plan es ~** this plan has priority

prisa *f* hurry; **a toda ~** at full speed; **de ~** quickly; **de ~ y corriendo** (*con demasiada prisa*) in a rush; (*rápidamente*) quickly; **no corre ~** there's no hurry; **¡date ~!** hurry up!; **meter ~ a alguien** to hurry sb; **tengo ~** I'm in a hurry; **no tengas ~** take your time

prisión *f* 1.(*reclusión*) imprisonment; ~ **celular** confinement in cells; ~ **preventiva** remand 2.(*edificio*) prison; ~ **de alta seguridad** high-security prison; **estar en ~** to be in prison

prisionero, -a *m, f* prisoner; **hacer ~ a alguien** to take sb prisoner

prisma *m* 1.(*figura*) prism 2.(*perspectiva*)

angle
prismáticos *mpl* binoculars *pl*
privación *f* 1.(*desposesión*) deprivation; ~ **de libertad** JUR loss of liberty 2.(*carencia*) privation
privado *m* (*de rey*) royal favourite *Brit* [*o* favorite *Am*]; (*de ministro*) protégé
privado, -a *adj* 1.(*reunión, fiesta*) private; (*sesión*) closed 2.(*personal, confidencial*) private; **vida privada** private life; **en el trabajo es insoportable, pero en ~...** at work he is unbearable, but outside ...; **quisiera hablar en ~ contigo** I would like to speak to you in private 3.(*falto*) **~ de...** without ...; **~ de flexibilidad** (*cosa*) inelastic; (*persona*) inflexible; **~ de inteligencia** slow-witted; **~ de la libertad** deprived of one's freedom; **~ de medios** without means
privanza *f* (*de príncipe*) favour *Brit*, favor *Am*; (*de ministro*) protection
privar I. *vt* 1.(*desposeer*) to deprive; **~ a alguien del permiso de conducir** to take away sb's driving licence *Brit* [*o* driver's license *Am*]; **~ a alguien de libertad** to deprive sb of his freedom; **~ a alguien de un derecho** to deprive sb of a right; **~ a alguien de un cargo** to remove sb from a position 2.(*prohibir*) to forbid; **no me prives de visitarte** don't stop me from visiting you 3.(*gustar*) to delight; **está privado por esa chica** he's crazy about that girl II. *vi* 1.(*estar de moda*) to be fashionable 2.(*influir*) to have influence III. *vr* to deny oneself; **no se privan de nada** they don't want for anything
privativo, -a *adj* (*propio*) exclusive; **~ de alguien** exclusive to sb; **esta facultad es privativa del presidente** that power belongs exclusively to the president
privatización *f* privatization
privatizar <z→c> *vt* to privatize
privilegiado, -a I. *adj* privileged; (*memoria*) exceptional II. *m, f* privileged person
privilegiar *vt* to grant a privilege to
privilegio *m* privilege; **~ fiscal** tax concession
pro I. *m o f* 1.(*provecho*) advantage; **valorar los ~s y los contras** to weigh up the pros and cons; **en ~ de** in favour [*o* favor *Am*] of; **campaña en ~ de la erradicación de las pruebas nucleares** campaign for the banning of nuclear tests 2.(*de bien*) **un hombre de ~** an honest man II. *prep* for
proa *f* NÁUT bow; AVIAT nose; **poner la ~ en un asunto** to tackle an affair; **poner la ~ a alguien** to take a stand against sb
probabilidad *f* 1.(*verosimilitud*) probability; **con toda ~** in all likelihood 2.(*posibilidad*) prospect; **hay ~es de rescatar los rehenes** there is a good chance of rescuing the hostages
probable *adj* 1.(*verosímil*) probable; **un resultado ~** a likely result; **lo más ~ es que...** chances are that ...; **el ~ campeón** the likely winner 2.(*que se puede probar*) provable

probablemente *adv* probably
probado, -a *adj* (*cosa, cualidad, método*) proven; (*trabajador*) experienced
probador *m* fitting room
probar <o→ue> I. *vt* 1.(*demostrar*) to prove; **todavía no está probado que sea culpable** it still hasn't been proved that he is guilty 2.(*experimentar*) to try; (*aparato*) to test 3.(*a alguien*) to test 4.(*vestido*) to try on 5. GASTR to taste; **no he probado nunca una paella** I have never tried paella II. *vi* (*intentar*) to try
probatorio, -a *adj* evidential
probatura *f* *inf* go; TEAT, CINE rehearsal
probeta *f* (*tubo*) test tube; **~ graduada** graduated flask
probidad *f* probity
problema *m* (*cuestión, dificultad, ejercicio*) problem; **~s de adaptación** teething problems; **~ de liquidez** cash flow problem; **el planteamiento del ~** the way in which the problem is presented
problemática *f* problems *pl*, questions *pl*
problemático, -a *adj* problematic
probo, -a *adj* 1.(*honrado*) honest 2.(*íntegro*) upright
proboscide *f* proboscis
procacidad *f* 1.(*insolencia*) shamelessness 2.(*grosería*) obscenity
procaz *adj* 1.(*insolente*) shameless 2.(*grosero*) obscene
procedencia *f* 1.(*origen*) origin; **anunciar la ~ del tren** to announce where the train has come from 2. JUR legitimacy
procedente *adj* 1.(*oportuno*) appropriate 2.(*que viene de*) **~ de** from; **el tren ~ de Nueva York con destino a Chicago** the train from New York to Chicago 3. JUR fitting
proceder I. *m* 1.(*comportamiento*) behaviour *Brit*, behavior *Am* 2.(*actuación*) (course of) action II. *vi* 1.(*familia*) to descend; (*de un lugar*) to come; (*pasión*) to spring 2.(*actuar*) to act 3.(*ser oportuno*) to be appropriate; **no ~** to be inappropriate; **ahora procede guardar silencio** now we (etc.) should remain silent; **táchese lo que no proceda** delete as applicable 4.(*pasar a*) to proceed 5. JUR (*iniciar un proceso*) to begin proceedings; (*procesar*) to process; **no procede** it is not appropriate
procedimiento *m* 1.(*actuación*) procedure; **¿qué ~ se puede seguir aquí?** what procedure should be followed here? 2.(*método*) method 3. JUR proceedings *pl*
prócer I. *adj* illustrious II. *m* national hero
procesado, -a *m, f* JUR defendant; **el ~** the accused
procesador *m* processor, computer *Am*; **~ de textos** word processor
procesal *adj* (*costos, actuación*) legal; (*regla, derecho*) procedural
procesamiento *m* 1. JUR prosecution 2. INFOR processing; **~ en línea** on-line processing

procesar *vt* **1.** JUR to prosecute; **le procesan por violación** he is being prosecuted for rape **2.** TÉC to process

procesión *f* **1.** *t.* REL (*marcha*) procession **2.** (*hilera*) line; (*de personas*) procession **3.** inf (*preocupación*) **permaneció tranquilo aunque la ~ iba por dentro** he remained outwardly calm, but he was actually rather worried

proceso *m* **1.** (*método*) process; **~ de una enfermedad** development of an illness **2.** (*procedimiento*) procedure **3.** JUR (*causa*) trial **4.** (*intervalo*) course

proclama *f* **1.** (*matrimonial*) banns *pl* **2.** (*política*) proclamation

proclamación *f* proclamation

proclamar **I.** *vt* **1.** (*hacer público*) to announce; **~ la República** to proclaim a Republic **2.** (*aclamar*) to acclaim **3.** (*sentimiento*) to declare **4.** (*ganador*) to declare; **fue proclamado Premio Nobel** he was awarded the Nobel Prize **II.** *vr* **~se presidente** to proclaim oneself president; **~se ganador** to declare oneself the winner

proclive *adj* prone

procrear *vt* **1.** (*engendrar*) to procreate **2.** (*reproducirse*) to reproduce

proctólogo, -a *m, f* MED proctologist *m, f*

procura *f* **1.** JUR power of attorney **2.** *Méx* **en ~ de** in an attempt to

procurador(a) *m(f)* attorney; (*en negocios*) agent

procurar **I.** *vt* **1.** (*intentar*) to try; **procura hacerlo lo mejor que puedas** do it to the best of your abilities; **procura que no te vean más por aquí** make sure you're not seen around here any more; **procura que no te oigan** make sure they don't hear you **2.** (*proporcionar*) to obtain **II.** *vr* to secure (for oneself)

prodigalidad *f* **1.** (*despilfarro*) wastefulness **2.** (*abundancia*) profusion

prodigar <g→gu> **I.** *vt* **1.** (*malgastar*) to waste **2.** (*dar*) to lavish **II.** *vr* **se prodigó en toda clase de atenciones con nosotros** he attended to our every need; **se prodigó en elogios hacia él** he/she showered him with praise; **se prodiga tanto en las explicaciones que nadie la entiende** her explanations are so detailed that nobody understands her

prodigio *m* prodigy; **niño ~** child prodigy

prodigioso, -a *adj* **1.** (*sobrenatural*) miraculous **2.** (*extraordinario*) marvellous *Brit*, marvelous *Am*

pródigo, -a *adj* **1.** (*malgastador*) wasteful; **el hijo ~** the prodigal son **2.** (*generoso*) generous; **la pródiga naturaleza** bountiful nature

producción *f* **1.** *t.* TÉC, CINE production; **~ en cadena** assembly line production; **~ por encargo** manufacture to order; **~ en masa** mass production; **~ a medida** made-to-measure fabrication **2.** (*productos*) output **3.** JUR (*de pruebas, documentos*) presentation

producir *irr como traducir* **I.** *vt* **1.** *t.* TÉC, CINE to produce; (*energía*) to generate **2.** (*beneficios*) to generate; (*intereses*) to yield **3.** (*alegría, impresión*) to create; (*aburrimiento, miedo*) to produce; (*daño, tristeza*) to cause **4.** JUR (*pruebas, documentos*) to present **II.** *vr:* **~se 1.** (*fabricarse*) to be produced **2.** (*tener lugar*) to take place; **se produjo una crisis** a crisis occurred; **se ha producido una mejora** there has been an improvement **3.** (*ocurrir*) to occur; **cuando se produzca el caso...** as the case arises ...

productividad *f* (*de máquina, mina*) productivity; (*de negocio*) profitability; (*de tierra*) fertility

productivo, -a *adj* (*máquina, mina*) productive; (*negocio*) profitable; (*tierra*) fertile

producto *m* **1.** *t.* QUÍM, MAT (*objeto*) product; **~s básicos** commodities; **~s agrícolas** agricultural produce; **~ alimenticio** food item; **~s alimenticios** foodstuffs *pl*; **~ de belleza** beauty product; **~ estancado** product sold by state monopoly; **~ de línea blanca** no-name product; **~ de marca** brand-name product; **~s químicos** chemicals *pl*; **~s (semi)manufacturado** manufactured good; **~ terminado** finished product; **~ derivado** [*o* **secundario**] by-product **2.** (*de un negocio*) profit; (*de una venta*) proceeds *pl*; **Producto Interior Bruto** Gross Domestic Product; **Producto Nacional Bruto** Gross National Product

productor(a) **I.** *adj* producing **II.** *m(f)* producer

proemio *m* preface

proeza *f* exploit

profanar *vt* **1.** (*templo, cementerio*) to desecrate **2.** (*memoria, nombre*) to profane

profano, -a *adj* **1.** (*secular*) secular **2.** (*irreverente*) irreverent **3.** (*ignorante*) ignorant; **soy ~ en esta materia** I am not an expert in this subject

profecía *f* prophecy

proferir *irr como sentir* *vt* (*palabra, grito*) to utter; (*insulto*) to hurl; (*queja*) to express

profesar **I.** *vt* **1.** (*oficio*) to practise *Brit*, to practice *Am* **2.** (*admiración*) to declare **3.** (*religión, doctrina*) to profess **4.** ENS to teach **II.** *vi, vr:* **~se** to take one's vows

profesión *f* **1.** (*empleo*) profession; **la ~ más antigua del mundo** the world's oldest profession; **las profesiones liberales** the professions; **de ~** by profession **2.** (*de admiración*) declaration **3.** (*de religión, doctrina*) profession; **~ de fe** profession of one's faith ▶ **hacer ~ de algo** to boast about sth

profesional **I.** *adj* **1.** (*de la profesión, no aficionado*) professional; **deportista ~** professional sportsman, sportswoman; **ética ~** professional ethics; **secreto ~** trade secret **2.** (*académico*) academic **II.** *mf* **1.** (*experto, no aficionado*) professional **2.** (*académico*) academic

profesionista *mf Méx* professional
profesor(a) *m(f)* (*no universitario*) teacher; (*universitario*) lecturer *Brit*, professor *Am*; (*catedrático*) senior teacher; ~ **agregado** senior lecturer *Brit*, assistant professor *Am*; ~ **numerario** [*o* **titular**] full professor
profesorado *m* **1.** (*cargo no universitario*) teaching post; (*cargo universitario*) lectureship *Brit*, professorship *Am* **2.** (*conjunto*) teaching staff *Brit*, faculty *Am*
profeta, -isa *m, f* prophet *m(f)*, prophetess *f*; **nadie es ~ en su tierra** no one is a prophet in his own land
profetizar <z→c> *vt* to prophesy; *fig* (*adivinar*) to conjecture
profiláctico *m* condom
profiláctico, -a *adj* preventive, preventative
profilaxis *f inv* prophylaxis
prófugo *m* MIL deserter
prófugo, -a *m, f* JUR fugitive
profundamente *adv* profoundly; ~ **ofendido** deeply offended; ~ **sentido** heartfelt; **una persona ~ moral** a profoundly moral person
profundidad *f* depth; **analizar en ~** to analyse in depth; **tener mucha/poca ~** to be very deep/not very deep; **una cueva de cinco metros de ~** a cave five metres deep
profundizar <z→c> **I.** *vt* (*hoyo, zanja*) to make deeper; *fig* to study in depth **II.** *vi* ~ **en algo** to study [*o* to go into] sth in depth
profundo, -a *adj* (*hoyo, lago, voz*) deep; (*capa, estrato*) deep-lying; (*observación*) incisive; (*pena*) heartfelt; (*dificultad*) extreme; (*pensamiento, misterio*) profound; (*conocimiento*) thorough; **psicología profunda** deep psychology; **en lo más ~ de mi corazón** from the very bottom of my heart
profusión *f* profusion; ~ **de ideas** profusion of ideas; ~ **de trabajo** surplus of work; **con ~ de detalles** with a wealth of details; **hay gran ~ de noticias** there is a lot of news
profuso, -a *adj* profuse
progenie *f* **1.** (*casta*) lineage **2.** (*descendencia*) offspring, progeny
progenitor(a) *m(f)* **1.** (*antepasado*) for(e)bear **2.** (*mayor*) father *m*, mother *f*; **los ~es** the parents
programa *m* programme *Brit*, program *Am*; ~ **de las clases** (**de la Universidad**) (university) timetable; ~ **de estudios** study plan; ~ **de trabajo** work schedule; ~ **antivirus** INFOR antivirus program; ~ **aplicativo** INFOR application; ~ **contaminado** INFOR infected program; ~ **de demostración** INFOR trial software; ~ **de gráficas** INFOR graphics programme; ~ **de tratamiento de textos** INFOR word-processing package; ~ **utilitarios** INFOR utilities *pl*
programación *f* **1.** (*acción*) programming **2.** TV, RADIO programme *Brit*, program *Am*
programador(a) *m(f)* programmer
programar *vt* to plan; **la conferencia está**

programada para el domingo the talk is scheduled for Sunday; **¿qué tienes programado para esta tarde?** what have you got planned for this evening?
progre **I.** *adj inf* trendy; POL left-wing; **sus ideas son ~s** he/she is a lefty **II.** *mf* trendy liberal; POL lefty
progresar *vi* to make progress; (*enfermedad, ciencia*) to develop; ~ **profesionalmente** to progress [*o* get ahead] in one's career
progresión *f* **1.** (*avance*) progress **2.** MAT, MÚS progression
progresista **I.** *adj* progressive **II.** *mf* progressive person
progresivamente *adv* progressively; **recuperarse ~** to recover gradually
progresivo, -a *adj* t. FIN (*que progresa*) progressive; (*que aumenta*) increasing; **aspecto ~** LING continuous tense
progreso *m* progress
prohibición *f* prohibition
prohibido, -a *adj* ~ **fumar** no smoking; **fruto ~** forbidden fruit; **prohibida la entrada** no entry
prohibir *irr vt* to prohibit, to ban; **en los hospitales prohiben fumar** in hospitals smoking is not allowed
prohibitivo, -a *adj* prohibitive; **a precio ~** prohibitively expensive
prohijar *irr como airar vt t. fig* to adopt
prójimo *m* **1.** (*semejante*) fellow man; **amor al ~** love of one's neighbour *Brit* [*o* neighbor *Am*] **2.** *pey* (*sujeto*) specimen; **¡menudo ~ tenemos de vecino!** what a neighbour *Brit* [*o* neighbor *Am*] we've got!
prole *f* offspring *pl*; **padre con numerosa ~** father with several children
prolegómeno *m* (*a un escrito*) preface; (*al hablar*) introduction; **déjate de ~s y ve al grano** *inf* stop beating around the bush and get to the point
proletariado *m* proletariat
proletario, -a **I.** *adj* proletarian; **barrio ~** working-class area **II.** *m, f* proletarian
proliferación *f* **1.** (*en cantidad*) proliferation; **tratado de no ~ de armas nucleares** nuclear non-proliferation treaty **2.** *t.* MED (*incontrolada*) spread
proliferar *vi* **1.** (*en cantidad*) to proliferate **2.** (*epidemia, rumor*) to spread
prolífico, -a *adj* prolific
prolijo, -a *adj* **1.** (*extenso*) protracted **2.** (*esmerado*) detailed **3.** (*cargante*) long-winded
prólogo *m* (*de libro*) foreword; TEAT, DEP prelude
prolongación *f* extension; (*de decisión*) postponement
prolongado, -a *adj* prolonged; **un sobre ~** a long envelope
prolongar <g→gu> **I.** *vt* to extend; (*decisión*) to postpone; (*un estado*) to prolong **II.** *vr:* **~se** to continue; (*un estado*) to be pro-

longed; (*reunión*) to overrun; **la fiesta se prolongó hasta bien entrada la noche** the party carried on well into the night; **las negociaciones se están prolongando demasiado** the negotiations are dragging on for too long
promediar I. *vt* 1. (*repartir*) to divide in two 2. (*sacar promedio*) to average out II. *vi* 1. (*mediar*) to mediate 2. (*temporal*) **antes de ~ el año** before the year was halfway through; **promediaba el mes cuando...** the month was halfway through when ...
promedio *m* average; **veo la tele un ~ de dos horas al día** I watch an average of two hours' TV a day
promesa *f* promise; REL vow; **~ de matrimonio** promise of marriage; **el jefe me ha dado su ~ de que...** the boss has promised me that ...
prometedor(a) *adj* promising
prometer I. *vt* to promise; REL to vow; **te prometo que lo haré** I promise you I'll do it; **te prometo por mis muertos que...** I promise on my mother's grave that ...; **~ el oro y el moro** to promise the earth ►**lo prometido es deuda** *prov* a promise is a promise II. *vi* **este negocio promete** this business is promising III. *vr:* **~se** 1. (*novios*) to get engaged 2. (*esperar*) to hope; **prometérselas muy felices** to have high hopes
prometido, -a *m, f* fiancé *m*, fiancée *f*
prominencia *f* 1. (*abultamiento*) bulge 2. (*del terreno*) rise 3. MED swelling
prominente *adj* prominent
promiscuidad *f* 1. (*mezcla*) mixture 2. (*sexual*) promiscuity
promiscuo, -a *adj* 1. *pey* (*mezclado*) mixed 2. (*ambiguo*) ambiguous 3. (*sexualmente*) promiscuous
promoción *f* 1. (*de empresa, categoría, producto*) promotion 2. (*de licenciados*) year, graduating class; **ser de la misma ~** to have graduated in the same year
promocionar I. *vt* (*a empresa, de categoría, a producto*) to promote; **está promocionando su nueva película** she is promoting her new film II. *vi* DEP to be promoted
promontorio *m* 1. (*terreno*) promontory; (*colina*) hill 2. (*de papeles*) pile
promotor(a) *m(f)* 1. (*de altercado*) instigator 2. (*patrocinador*) sponsor; (*deportivo, artístico, de espectáculo*) promoter
promover <o→ue> *vt* 1. (*querella, escándalo*) to cause; (*proceso*) to advance ... 2. (*en el cargo*) to promote 3. (*aplausos*) to bring forth; (*altercado*) to instigate
promulgación *f* enactment; (*divulgación*) announcement
promulgar <g→gu> *vt* to enact; (*divulgar*) to announce
pronombre *m* LING pronoun
pronominal *adj* LING pronominal; **verbo ~** reflexive verb
pronosticar <c→qu> *vt* to forecast

pronóstico *m t.* ECON forecast; MED prognosis; DEP prediction; **lesiones de ~ reservado** injuries of unknown seriousness
prontitud *f* 1. (*celeridad*) speed; (*de ejecución*) promptness 2. (*de ingenio*) sharpness
pronto I. *adv* 1. (*rápido*) quickly 2. (*enseguida*) at once 3. (*temprano*) early ►**al ~** at first; **de ~** suddenly; **¡hasta ~!** see you!; **por de** [*o* **por lo**] **~** for the time being II. *conj* **tan ~ como** as soon as; **tan ~ como llegaron/lleguen** as soon as they arrived/arrive
pronto, -a *adj* 1. (*rápido*) quick; (*despierto*) sharp; **inteligencia pronta** lively intelligence 2. (*dispuesto*) ready; **estar ~** CSur to be ready
prontuario *m* 1. (*resumen*) summary 2. (*manual*) handbook
pronunciación *f* LING pronunciation
pronunciado, -a *adj* pronounced; (*pendiente, cuesta*) steep; **arrugas pronunciadas** deep lines; **acento ~** strong [*o* marked] accent; **una curva pronunciada** a sharp bend; **rasgos ~s** strong features
pronunciamiento *m* 1. (*alzamiento*) (pronouncement of a) military coup 2. JUR pronouncement; **~ judicial** legal judgement; **~ de sentencia** sentencing
pronunciar I. *vt* 1. (*articular*) to pronounce; **~ un brindis por alguien** to propose a toast in sb's honour *Brit* [*o* honor *Am*]; **~ un discurso** to make a speech; **~ unas palabras** to say a few words; **~ sentencia** to pass sentence 2. (*resaltar*) to emphasize II. *vr:* **~se** 1. (*levantarse*) to launch a military coup 2. (*apoyar*) to declare oneself 3. (*opinar*) **~se sobre algo** to state one's opinion on sth 4. (*acentuarse*) to become more pronounced
propagación *f* 1. (*multiplicación, reproducción*) propagation 2. (*extensión, transmisión*) spreading
propaganda *f* 1. (*publicidad, promoción*) publicity; **hacer ~** to advertise, to publicize 2. MIL, POL propaganda
propagar <g→gu> I. *vt* 1. (*multiplicar, reproducir*) to propagate 2. (*extender, divulgar*) to spread; **~ un rumor** to spread a rumour II. *vr:* **~se** 1. (*multiplicarse, reproducirse*) to propagate 2. (*extenderse, divulgarse, transmitirse*) to spread
propalar *vt, vr:* **~se** to spread
propano *m* propane
propasar I. *vt* to overstep II. *vr:* **~se** (*extralimitarse*) to go too far; (*excederse*) to overstep the mark; **~se con alguien** to take liberties with sb
propender *vi* **~ a algo** to tend towards sth; MED to be prone to sth
propensión *f* **~ a algo** tendency towards sth; MED predisposition to sth; **tener gran ~ a resfriarse** to catch colds very easily
propenso, -a *adj* (*a enfermedades*) susceptible; (*dispuesto*) inclined; **ser ~ a algo** to be prone to sth
propiamente *adv* (*realmente*) really; (*exacta-*

mente) exactly; ~ **dicho** strictly speaking
propiciar I. *vt* **1.** (*aplacar*) to placate **2.** (*favo-recer*) to favour *Brit*, to favour *Am*; (*posibili-tar*) to make possible; **el viento propició la extensión de las llamas** the wind helped the flames to spread II. *vr*: ~**se** (*conseguir*) to gain; **con sus palabras se propició el respeto de todos** with his/her words he/she won every-one's respect
propicio, -a *adj* **1.** (*favorable*) favourable *Brit*, favorable *Am*; **en el momento** ~ at the right moment **2.** (*dispuesto*) inclined; **mostrarse (poco)** ~ **para...** (not) to be prepared to ...
propiedad *f* **1.** (*pertenencia*) property; (*inmuebles*) property, estate; (*derechos*) right; ~ **exclusiva** exclusive ownership; ~ **horizon-tal** joint ownership (*in a block of flats*); ~ **industrial** patent rights; ~ **intelectual** intel-lectual property; ~ **inmobiliaria** real assets *Brit*, real estate *Am*; ~ **mobiliaria** movable property; ~ **rústica** farm property; **un piso de mi** ~ a flat *Brit* [*o* an apartment *Am*] which I own; **tener algo en** ~ to own sth; **ser** ~ **de al-guien** to be sb's property **2.** *t.* FÍS (*cualidad*) property **3.** (*corrección*) correctness; (*exacti-tud*) precision; **expresarse con** ~ to speak correctly
propietario, -a I. *adj* proprietary II. *m, f* owner; (*terrateniente*) landowner; (*casero*) landlord
propina *f* tipo; **dejar** ~ to leave a tip; **me dio dos libras de** ~ he/she gave me a two pound tip; **de** ~ *fig* for good measure
propinar *vt* (*golpes*) to give
propio, -a *adj* **1.** (*de uno mismo*) own; **con la propia mano** with one's own hand; **entregar en propia mano** to deliver personally; **en defensa propia** in self-defence *Brit*, in self-defense *Am*; **es tu propia culpa** it's your own fault; **lo he visto con mis** ~**s ojos** I have seen it with my own eyes; **tengo piso** ~ I own my flat *Brit* [*o* apartment *Am*] **2.** (*mismo*) same; **lo** ~ the same; **el** ~ **jefe** the boss himself; **al** ~ **tiempo** at the same time; **nombre** ~ LING proper noun **3.** (*característico*) characteristic; **los productos** ~**s del país** the products of the country; **eso (no) es** ~ **de ti** that is (not) like you **4.** (*apropiado*) proper
proponer *irr como poner* I. *vt* **1.** (*sugerir, presentar*) to propose; ~ **un brindis por al-guien** to propose a toast in sb's honour *Brit* [*o* honor *Am*] **2.** (*plantear*) to put forward; ~ **un acertijo** to ask a riddle; ~ **una cuestión** to set out a matter II. *vr* to propose; (*tener inten-ción*) to intend; **¿qué te propones?** what are you trying to do?
proporción *f* **1.** (*relación, porcentaje*) pro-portion; **no guardar** ~ **con algo** to be out of proportion with sth; **en una** ~ **de 8 a 1** in a ratio of 8 to 1 **2.** *pl* (*dimensión*) proportions *pl*; **un accidente de enormes proporciones** a major accident
proporcional *adj* proportional; **reparto** ~

proportional distribution; **sistema** ~ POL pro-portional representation
proporcionar *vt* **1.** (*facilitar*) to provide; (*conseguir, procurar*) to obtain; ~ **víveres a alguien** to provide sb with supplies **2.** (*oca-sionar*) to cause; ~ **disgustos a alguien** to upset sb **3.** (*dar proporción*) to proportion; (*adecuar*) to fit **4.** (*repartir*) to distribute **5.** (*crear*) to create **6.** (*producir*) to produce
proposición *f* **1.** (*propuesta*) proposal; ~ **de ley** bill; ~ **de matrimonio** marriage proposal **2.** (*solicitud*) request **3.** (*oferta*) offer **4.** LING (*oración*) sentence; (*parte*) clause
propósito I. *m* **1.** (*intención*) intention; (*plan*) plan; **buenos** ~**s** good intentions; **tener el** ~ **de...** to intend to ... **2.** (*objetivo*) objec-tive ►**fuera de** ~ irrelevant; **a** ~ (*adrede*) on purpose; (*adecuado*) suitable; (*por cierto*) by the way; **¡a** ~**!** **tu hermana viene mañana** talking of that, your sister is coming tomorrow II. *prep* **a** ~ **de** with regard to
propuesta *f* **1.** (*proposición*) proposal **2.** (*so-licitud*) request **3.** (*oferta*) offer **4.** (*recomenda-ción*) suggestion; **a** ~ **de alguien** on sb's suggestion; **formular una** ~ to draw up a pro-posal
propugnar *vt* **1.** (*defender*) to defend **2.** (*apoyar, promover*) to advocate
propulsar *vt* **1.** TÉC to propel **2.** (*fomentar*) to promote
propulsión *f* TÉC propulsion; ~ **a hélice** pro-peller power; ~ **por reacción** jet propulsion; ~ **total** AUTO four-wheel drive
prorrata *f* (*parte*) portion; (*cuota*) quota
prórroga *f* **1.** (*prolongación*) prolongation; ECON extension; ~ **de pago** extension of pay-ment deadline **2.** (*dilatoria, retraso*) delay; (*aplazamiento*) deferral; (*cambio de fecha*) postponement **3.** DEP extra time, overtime
prorrogación *f* extension
prorrogar <g→gu> *vt* **1.** (*prolongar*) to pro-long; ECON to extend **2.** (*dilatar, retrasar*) to delay **3.** *t.* JUR (*aplazar*) to defer; (*cambiar de fecha*) to postpone
prorrumpir *vi* **1.** (*salir*) to burst forth **2.** (*esta-llar*) to break out; ~ **en algo** to break out into sth
prosa *f* prose; **texto en** ~ piece of prose
prosaico, -a *adj* prosaic
prosapia *f* ancestry; **de mucha** ~ from an illustrious family
proscribir *irr como escribir* *vt* to ban
proscrito, -a I. *pp de* **proscribir** II. *m, f* exile
prosecución *f* **1.** (*continuación*) continu-ation **2.** *t.* JUR prosecution; (*de un fin*) pursuit; ~ **criminal** pursuit of a criminal
proseguir *irr como seguir* I. *vi* (*alguien*) to continue; (*mal tiempo*) to persist; ~ **con/en algo** to persist with sth II. *vt* **1.** (*continuar*) *t.* JUR to continue; ~ **diligencias** to continue pro-ceedings **2.** (*un fin*) to pursue
prosista *mf* prose writer
prospección *f* MIN prospecting; ~ **petro-**

lífera oil prospecting; ~ **de mercado** ECON market research

prospecto *m* (*folleto*) prospectus; (*de instrucciones*) instruction leaflet; (*informativo*) (information) leaflet; (*de un medicamento*) directions *pl* for use

prosperar *vi* 1.(*crecer*) to grow; (*florecer*) to thrive; (*tener éxito*) to prosper 2.(*imponerse*) to become established

prosperidad *f* (*bienestar*) prosperity; ~ **económica** economic prosperity

próspero, -a *adj* 1.(*feliz*) happy; **¡Próspero Año Nuevo!** Happy New Year! 2.(*floreciente*) thriving 3.(*rico, con éxito*) prosperous

próstata *f* prostate

prosternarse *vr* to prostrate oneself

prostíbulo *m* brothel

prostitución *f* prostitution; **ejercer la** ~ to be a prostitute

prostituir *irr como huir* I. *vt* to prostitute II. *vr:* ~**se** *t. fig* to prostitute oneself

prostituto, -a *m, f* male prostitute *m,* prostitute *f*

prosudo, -a *Chile, Ecua, Perú* I. *adj* affectedly formal II. *m, f* pompous person

protagonista I. *adj* **la actriz** ~ the leading actress; **el papel** ~ the leading role II. *mf* key participant; CINE, TEAT leading actor *m,* leading actress *f;* LIT main character

protagonizar <z→c> *vt* (*un papel*) to play; **un gran actor protagoniza esta película** a famous actor stars in this film

protección *f* 1.(*salvaguarda*) protection; ~ **acústica** sound-proofing; ~ **antiaérea** anti-aircraft defences *Brit* [*o* defenses *Am*]; ~ **contra incendios** fire protection; ~ **sanitaria** health cover; **crema de alta** ~ high-protection sun cream; **poner a alguien bajo** ~ to place sb under protection; **tomar a alguien bajo su** ~ to take sb into one's protection 2. *t.* POL (*mecenazgo, patrocinio*) patronage 3. MIL defence *Brit,* defense *Am*

protector *m* (*cosa que protege*) protector; (*en boxeo*) mouthguard; ~ **labial** lip salve; ~ **solar** sunscreen

protector(a) I. *adj* protective; **casco** ~ protective helmet; **sociedad** ~**a de animales** society for the prevention of cruelty to animals II. *m(f)* 1.(*persona*) protector 2. *t.* POL (*mecenas*) patron 3.(*patrocinador*) sponsor

protectorado *m* protectorate

proteger <g→j> I. *vt* 1. *t.* ECOL (*resguardar, asegurar*) to protect 2. *t.* POL (*como mecenas*) to act as a patron to II. *vr:* ~**se** to protect oneself; ~**se los ojos** to protect one's eyes

protegido, -a I. *adj* protected; ~ **contra escritura** INFOR write-protected; ~ **contra el uso indebido** protected against unauthorized use; ~ **por patente** protected by patent II. *m, f* protégé *m,* protégée *f*

proteína *f* protein

prótesis *f inv* prosthesis; ~ **auditiva** hearing aid

protesta *f* 1.(*queja*) protest 2. JUR objection 3.(*aseveración*) protestation

protestante *adj, mf* REL Protestant

protestar I. *vi* to protest II. *vt* 1.(*confesar*) to avow 2. JUR to raise an objection

protestón, -ona I. *adj inf* grumbling II. *m, f inf* grouch

protocolo *m* protocol; **de** ~ formal

protón *m* proton

prototipo *m* prototype

protuberancia *f* protuberance; (*bulto*) bulge

protuberante *adj* protuberant

provecho *m* 1.(*aprovechamiento*) use; (*ventaja*) advantage; (*producto*) yield; (*beneficio*) benefit; **para su propio** ~ for one's own use; **de** ~ useful; **nada de** ~ nothing of use; **en** ~ **de alguien** to sb's advantage; **sacar** ~ **de algo/alguien** to do benefit from sth/sb, to profit from sth/sb 2.(*progreso*) progress; (*mejora*) improvement 3.(*en comidas*) **¡buen** ~! enjoy your meal!, bon appétit!; **hacer** (**buen**) ~ to be beneficial

provechoso, -a *adj* beneficial; (*productivo*) productive; (*útil*) useful; (*ventajoso*) advantageous; (*saludable*) healthy

proveedor(a) I. *adj* supplying II. *m(f)* 1.(*suministrador*) supplier 2. INFOR provider

proveer *irr* I. *vi* to provide; ~ **a algo** to provide for sth; ~ **a las necesidades de alguien** to attend to sb's needs; **¡Dios** ~**á!** the Lord will provide! II. *vt* 1.(*abastecer, suministrar*) to supply; ~ **de algo** to furnish with sth; (*dotar*) to provide with sth 2.(*un puesto*) to fill; (*conceder*) to award 3. JUR ~ **sobre algo** to give an interim ruling on sth III. *vr:* ~**se** to supply oneself; ~**se de algo** to provide oneself with sth

proveniente *adj* **el tren** ~ **de Madrid** the train from Madrid

provenir *irr como venir vi* ~ **de** to come from, to stem from

proverbial *adj* proverbial

proverbio *m* proverb

providencia *f* 1.(*prevención, medida*) precaution 2. JUR ruling; (*disposición*) measure; ~ **ejecutoria** writ of execution 3. REL Providence

provincia *f* province; *AmS* (*estado*) state; **ciudad de** ~**s** provincial town

---

The 17 **Comunidades Autónomas** in Spain are subdivided into 52 **provincias**. Consequently, the **Comunidad de Castilla-León**, for example, consists of the following nine **provincias**: **Ávila, Burgos, León, Palencia, Salamanca, Segovia, Soria, Valladolid** and **Zamora**.

---

provincial I. *adj* provincial; **capital** ~ provincial capital; **delegación** ~ provincial authority II. *m* REL provincial

provincialismo *m* provincialism; *pey* parochialism

provinciano, -a I. *adj t. pey* provincial II. *m, f*

t. pey provincial

provisión *f* 1.(*reserva*) supply; **provisiones** provisions *pl* 2.(*suministro*) supply 3.(*cobertura*) cover; (*reserva*) reserve 4.(*comisión*) commission 5.(*medida*) provision 6.(*de un cargo*) filling 7. JUR provision

provisional *adj* provisional; **gobierno** ~ provisional government; **medida** ~ temporary measure

provisto, -a I. *pp de* **proveer** II. *adj* provided; ~ **al efecto** provided for the purpose

provocación *f* 1.(*ataque*) provocation; (*instigación*) instigation 2.(*causa*) cause; MED (*del parto*) induction, induced labour *Brit* [*o* labor *Am*]

provocador *m* stirrer

provocador(a) I. *adj* provocative II. *m(f)* POL agitator

provocar <c→qu> I. *vt* 1.(*incitar, irritar*) to provoke; (*excitar*) to arouse; (*instigar*) to instigate; POL to agitate; ¡no me provoques! don't provoke me! 2.(*causar*) *t.* MED to cause; (*artificialmente*) to induce; ~ **risa a alguien** to make sb laugh; ~ **lástima a alguien** to make sb feel sorry for one; ~ **un cambio** to bring about a change; ~ **una guerra** to start a war; ~ **una escena** to create a scene; ~ **un incendio** to start a fire II. *vi AmL* (*apetecer*) (no) **me provoca** I (don't) feel like it

provocativo, -a *adj* provocative

proxeneta *mf* (*de prostitutas*) pimp *m;* (*alcahuete*) procurer *m,* procuress *f*

próximamente *adv* soon

proximidad *f* 1.(*cercanía*) proximity; **en las** ~es in the vicinity 2.(*parentesco*) closeness

próximo, -a *adj* 1.(*cercano*) near, neighbouring *Brit,* neighboring *Am;* (*temporal*) close; **en fecha próxima** shortly, soon; **estar** ~ **a...** to be close to ... 2.(*siguiente*) next; **el** ~ **año** next year; **el** ~ **viernes** next Friday; **el** ~ **3 de octubre** on the 3rd of October this year; **la próxima vez** the next time; ¡hasta la próxima! see you soon!

proyección *f* 1. FÍS, ARQUIT, CINE, PSICO projection; (*sesión*) screening 2.(*lanzamiento*) throwing (forwards); (*impulso*) stimulation; ~ **de sombras** casting of shadows 3.(*influencia*) influence; (*orientación*) orientation; **una empresa de** ~ **internacional** a business with a global presence 4.(*proyecto*) planning

proyectable *adj* **asiento** ~ AVIAT ejector seat

proyectar I. *vt* 1. FÍS, FOTO, CINE to project 2.(*lanzar*) to throw 3.(*luz*) to shine; (*sombra*) to cast 4.(*planear, proponerse*) to plan 5. *t.* TÉC (*diseñar*) to design II. *vr:* ~**se** 1.(*luz*) to be shone; (*sombra*) to be cast 2. PSICO ~**se en algo** to project onto sth 3.(*orientarse*) to get one's bearings

proyectil *m* projectile; MIL missile; ~ **anticarro** anti-tank missile

proyecto *m* plan; (*proyección*) projection; (*borrador*) draft; (*propuesta*) proposal; ~ **de fin de carrera** UNIV final year project; (*en Le-*

tras) final year dissertation; ~ **de ley** bill; **en** ~ planned; **tener** ~s to have plans; **tener algo en** ~ to be planning sth

proyector *m* FOTO, CINE projector; ~ **de cine** film projector; **de diapositivas** slide projector; ~ **de cuerpos opacos** overhead projector; ~ **de luz** floodlight

prudencia *f* 1.(*precaución, previsión*) prudence; (*cautela*) caution 2.(*cordura*) wisdom; (*astucia*) good sense 3.(*moderación*) moderation

prudencial *adj* (*razonable*) reasonable; (*adecuado*) sufficient; (*previsor*) prudent; **una cantidad** ~ an adequate amount

prudenciarse *vr AmL* 1.(*ser prudente*) to be cautious 2.(*moderarse*) to be moderate 3.(*conservar la calma*) to remain calm

prudente *adj* 1.(*precavido, previsor*) prudent; (*cauteloso*) cautious 2.(*razonable*) reasonable 3.(*adecuado*) sufficient

prueba *f* 1. *t.* TÉC (*test*) test; (*experimento*) experiment; ~ **de alcoholemia** breathalyser® test; ~ **de aptitud** aptitude test; ~ **al azar** random trial; ~ **de azúcar en la sangre** blood sugar test; ~s **nucleares** nuclear tests; ~ **de paternidad** paternity test; **período de** ~ trial period; **poner a** ~ to try out; **someter a** ~ to test; **sufrir una dura** ~ to be put through a stern test; **a** ~ **de agua** waterproof; **a** ~ **de balas** bullet-proof; **a** ~ **de robo** theftproof; **a título de** ~ as a test; **a toda** ~ fully tested; *fig* cast-iron; ~ **de fuego** *fig* acid test 2.(*comprobación*) proof; (*de ropa*) trying on; ~ **de degustación** tasting; (*cata*) (wine)-tasting 3.(*examen*) exam; ~ **de acceso** entry exam 4. DEP (*competición*) event; ~ **clasificatoria/eliminatoria** qualifier/eliminator 5. TIPO proof; ~ **de imprenta** proof 6.(*testimonio*) piece of evidence; ~ **circunstancial** circumstantial evidence; ~ **documental** documentary evidence; **dar** ~s **de afecto** to show one's affection; **en** ~ **de nuestro reconocimiento** as a token of our gratitude; **presentar la** ~ to present the evidence; **ser** ~ **de algo** to be proof of sth; **tener** ~s **de que...** to have evidence that ...

prurito *m* MED 1.(*picor*) itch 2.(*afán*) urge

Prusia *f* Prussia

prusiano, -a *adj, m, f* Prussian

P.S. *abr de* **post scriptum** PS

(p)seudónimo *m* pseudonym

(p)sicoanálisis *m sin pl* psychoanalysis

(p)sicoanalista *mf* psychoanalyst

(p)sicodélico, -a *adj* psychedelic

(p)sicofármaco *m* psychotropic drug

(p)sicología *f sin pl* (*ciencia, vida anímica*) psychology; ~ **infantil** child psychology; ~ **evolutiva** developmental psychology

(p)sicológico, -a *adj* psychological; **terror** ~ psychological terror

(p)sicólogo, -a *m, f* psychologist; **es muy/poco** ~ *inf* he is very/not very perceptive

(p)sicópata *mf* psychopath; ~ **sexual** sexual

psychopath
(p)sicosis *f inv* psychosis; ~ **colectiva** collective psychosis
(p)sicosomático, -a *adj* psychosomatic
(p)sicoterapeuta *mf* psychotherapist
(p)sicoterapia *f* psychotherapy
(p)sique *f* psyche
(p)siquiatra *mf* psychiatrist
(p)siquiatría *f* psychiatry
(p)siquiátrico *m* (*hospital*) mental [*o* psychiatric] hospital
(p)siquiátrico, -a *adj* psychiatric
(p)síquico, -a *adj* psychic, mental; **problemas** ~**s** mental problemas
PSOE *m abr de* **Partido Socialista Obrero Español** *Spanish Socialist Party*
pta. *f* <pt(a)s.> *abr de* **peseta** peseta
púa *f* 1. (*espina*) spike; (*de planta*) thorn; (*de animal, pez*) spine, quill 2. (*del peine*) tooth; (*de tenedor*) prong 3. MÚS plectrum
pub <pubs> *m* bar, cocktail lounge
púber *adj* adolescent
pubertad *f* puberty
púbico, -a *adj* pubic; **zona púbica** pubic area
pubis *m inv* (*zona*) pubic area; (*hueso*) pubis
publicable *adj* publishable
publicación *f* 1. (*acción, edición*) publication; ~ **electrónica** e-publication; ~ **reciente** recent publication 2. *t.* JUR (*proclamación*) issue
publicar <c→qu> I. *vt* to publish; (*proclamar*) to make known; JUR to issue II. *vr:* ~**se** to be published
publicidad *f* 1. (*carácter público*) publicity; **dar** ~ to publicize; **este programa le ha dado mucha** ~ this programme [*o* program *Am*] has given him/her a lot of publicity 2. (*propaganda*) advertising; ~ **disimulada** subliminal advertising; ~ **sobreimpresa** press advertising; ~ **en TV** TV advertisements *pl;* **hacer** ~ **de algo** to advertise sth
publicista *mf* publicist
publicitario, -a *adj* advertising
público *m* 1. (*colectividad*) public; **en** ~ in public; **aparecer en** ~ to appear in public; **el gran** ~ the general public 2. (*asistente*) audience; **para todos los** ~**s** for all audiences; CINE U-certificate *Brit,* rated G *Am;* **abierto/cerrado al** ~ open/closed to the public; **hoy hay poco** ~ there aren't many people today
público, -a *adj* 1. (*no privado, estatal*) public; **deuda pública** national debt; **relaciones públicas** public relations; **el sector** ~ the public sector; **transporte** ~ public transport 2. (*común*) public; **de utilidad pública** of general use 3. (*conocido*) public; **escándalo** ~ public scandal; **hacer** ~ to make public; **hacerse** ~ to become known; **ser del dominio** ~ to be public domain
pucha *interj CSur* (*caramba*) ¡**la** ~! damn!
pucherazo *m* ~ **electoral** electoral fraud
puchero *m* 1. (*olla*) pot 2. GASTR stew 3. *inf* (*alimento*) grub; **ganarse el** ~ to earn a crust

4. *inf* (*gestos*) **hacer** ~**s** to pout
pucho *m AmL* (*resto*) leftover; (*colilla*) cigarette butt
pudibundo, -a *adj pey* prudish
púdico, -a *adj v.* **pudoroso**
pudiente *adj* (*poderoso*) powerful; (*rico*) well-off
pudin *m* pudding
pudor *m* 1. (*recato*) shyness; (*decencia*) decency; (*vergüenza*) shame 2. (*modestia*) modesty
pudoroso, -a *adj* 1. (*recatado*) shy; (*vergonzoso*) bashful; (*decente*) decent 2. (*modesto*) modest
pudridero *m* (*estercolero*) compost heap; (*muladar*) midden; (*de cadáveres*) temporary vault
pudrir *irr* I. *vt* 1. (*descomponer*) *t. fig* to rot 2. *inf* (*molestar*) to annoy II. *vr:* ~**se** 1. (*descomponerse*) *t. fig* to rot; ~**se en la cárcel** *inf* to rot in prison; ¡**ahí te pudras!** *vulg* go to hell! 2. *Arg, inf* (*aburrirse*) to get bored
pueblerino, -a I. *adj t. pey* small-town II. *m, f* villager; *pey* yokel
pueblo *m* 1. (*nación*) people; **el** ~ **bajo** the common people; **un hombre del** ~ a man of the people 2. (*aldea*) village; (*población*) (small) town; ~ **costero** seaside town; ~ **de mala muerte** *inf* dead-end town; ~ **joven** *AmL* shanty town; **de** ~ from a small town; *pey* small-town
puente *m* 1. NÁUT (*construcción, de las gafas*) bridge; ~ **levadizo** drawbridge; ~ **colgante** suspension bridge; ~ **aéreo** (*servicio*) shuttle; MIL airlift; ~ **dental** bridge; ~ **de mando** (compass) bridge; ~ **de maniobras** working deck; ~ **de paseo** promenade deck 2. ELEC bridge (circuit); **hacer un** ~ **a un coche** to hot-wire a car 3. (*fiesta*) long weekend (*a public holiday plus an additional day off*); **hacer/tener** ~ to take/have a long weekend
puenting *m sin pl* bungee jumping
puerco, -a I. *adj* 1. **estar** *inf* (*sucio*) filthy 2. **ser** (*indecente*) gross II. *m, f* 1. (*cerdo*) pig; (*macho*) hog; (*hembra*) sow; ~ **espín** porcupine 2. *inf* (*persona sucia u obscena*) pig 3. *inf* (*canalla*) swine
puericultor(a) *m(f)* MED paediatrician *Brit,* pediatrician *Am;* (*en la guardería*) nursery nurse
puericultura *f sin pl* (*general*) childcare, paediatrics *Brit,* pediatrics *Am*
pueril *adj* 1. (*infantil*) infant; **edad** ~ childhood 2. (*inmaduro*) childish
puerro *m* leek
puerta *f* 1. (*abertura*) door; (*portal*) doorway; (*portalón*) portal; (*acceso*) entry; ~ **de la calle** front door; ~ **corredera** sliding door; ~ **cortafuego** fire door; ~ **de servicio** service door; ~ **de socorro** emergency exit; ~ **giratoria** revolving door; **día de** ~**s abiertas** open day; **quinta** ~ AUTO rear door; **entrar por la** ~ **grande** to make a grand entrance; **escuchar**

P

detrás de la ~ to eavesdrop; **a la ~ de casa** at the front door; **a ~ abierta** *t.* JUR in public; **a ~ cerrada** *t.* JUR in private; **a las ~s de la muerte** at death's door; **enseñar la ~ a alguien** to show sb the door; **estar a las ~s** *fig* to be on the brink; **dar a alguien con la ~ en las narices** to slam the door in sb's face; **de ~s adentro** *fig* in private; **ir de ~ en ~** to go from door to door; **cerrar las ~s a alguien** *fig* to block sb's path; **poner a alguien en la ~ (de la calle)** to throw sb out; **eso es querer poner ~s al campo** *fig* that is like trying to turn back the waves; **por la ~ grande** *t. fig* in triumph; **tiene todas las ~s abiertas** *fig* he has a wealth of opportunities **2.** DEP goal; **disparo a ~** shot at goal **3.** INFOR gate

puerto *m* **1.** NÁUT harbour *Brit,* harbor *Am;* (*ciudad*) port; ~ **deportivo** marina; ~ **franco** free port; ~ **interior** river port; ~ **marítimo** seaport; ~ **de matrícula** home port; **tomar ~** to come into port **2.** (*de montaña*) pass **3.** INFOR port; ~ **para módem** modem port; ~ **de transmisión en paralelo/en serie** parallel/serial port **4.** (*refugio*) haven

Puerto Rico *m* Puerto Rico

Puerto Rico, a state associated with the USA since 1952, consists of a main island and several small islands situated in the Greater Antilles. The capital of Puerto Rico is **San Juan.** The official languages of the country are both Spanish and English.

puertorriqueño, -a *adj, m, f* Puerto Rican
pues **I.** *adv* **1.** (*entonces*) then; (*así que*) so; **Ana quiere conocerte – ~ que venga** Ana wants to meet you – well, she should come then; **he vuelto a suspender – ~ estudia más** I've failed again – well, you should study more; ~ **entonces, nada** well that's it, then **2.** (*ilativo*) so; ~ **bien** okay; **la consecuencia es, ~,** ... so the result is ...; **dejémoslo, ~** let's leave it, then **3.** (*causal*) **estudio inglés – ¡ah, ~ yo también!** I study English – ah, me too!; **yo soy de Salamanca – ~ yo, de Soria** I'm from Salamanca – I'm from Soria; **¿quién es? – ~ no sé** who is it? – I don't know **4.** (*expletivo*) well; **¿estuvisteis por fin en Toledo? – ~ no/sí** did you go to Toledo in the end? – no, I didn't/yes, I did; **¡~ esto no es nada!** this is nothing compared with what's to come!; **estoy muy cansado – ~ aún queda mucho camino** I'm very tired – well, there's still a long way to go; **¡qué caro! – ¿sí? ~ a mí me parece barato** how expensive! – do you think so? it seems cheap to me **5.** (*exclamativo*) **¡~ vaya lata!** what a pain!; **¡~ no faltaría más!** (*naturalmente*) but of course!; (*el colmo*) that's all we (etc.) need! **6.** (*interrogativo*) **no voy a salir – ¿~ cómo es eso?** I'm not going out – why not?; **¿~ qué quieres?** what do you want, then?; **¿y ~?** and?; **¿~ qué ha pasado?** so what happened?

7. (*atenuación*) well; **¿por qué no viniste a la fiesta? – ~ es que tenía mucho que hacer** why didn't you come to the party? – well, I was really busy; **¿nos vemos mañana? – ~ no sé todavía** shall we meet tomorrow? – well, I'm not sure yet **8.** (*insistencia*) ~ **así es** well that's how it is; ~ **claro** but of course; **¡vamos ~!** come on then!; **¡~ entonces!** for that very reason! **II.** *conj* ~ **no me queda otro remedio, venderé el coche** so I don't have any choice, I'll sell the car; **no voy de viaje, ~ no tengo dinero** I'm not going on holiday because I don't have any money; ~ **que** *elev* since

puesta *f* **1.** (*general*) putting; ~ **a cero** resetting; ~ **al día** updating; ~ **en escena** TEAT staging; ~ **en funcionamiento** activation; ~ **en hora** setting (*of time*); ~ **en libertad** release; ~ **en marcha** start button; AUTO starter; ~ **en práctica** putting into effect; ~ **a punto** final check; AUTO service **2.** (*de aves*) laying **3.** (*de sol*) setting; ~ **de sol** sunset **4.** (*en el juego*) bet

puestero, -a *m, f* stallholder; (*en el mercado*) market trader

puesto *m* **1.** (*lugar*) place; (*posición*) position; ~ **de información** information point; ~ **de observación** ASTR observation station; MED observation post; **ceder/mantener el ~** DEP to lose/keep one's place **2.** (*empleo*) job; (*cargo*) post; (*posición*) position **3.** (*tenderete*) stall; (*feria de muestras*) stand; (*chiringuito*) open-air bar; ~ **de periódicos** newspaper stand **4.** MIL post **5.** (*guardia*) post; ~ **de policía** police post; ~ **de socorro** first-aid station **6.** (*caza*) stand

puesto, -a **I.** *pp de* poner **II.** *adj* **1.** COM (*ex*) from; ~ **en fábrica** ex works **2.** *inf* (*arreglado*) **ir muy bien** ~ to be very smartly dressed; **tienen la casa muy bien puesta** they've done the house up very nicely; **tenerlos muy bien ~s** *vulg* to be a real man **3.** *inf* (*entendido*) **estar ~ en un tema** to be well-informed about a subject; ~ **al día** up to date **III.** *conj* ~ **que** given that

pufo *m inf* dirty trick; **meter un ~ a alguien** to pull a fast one on sb
pugna *f* (*lucha*) struggle; (*conflicto*) conflict
pugnar *vi* **1.** *t. fig* to fight **2.** (*esforzarse*) to strive; ~ **por algo/alguien** to struggle for sth/sb **3.** (*intentar*) ~ **por algo** to strive for sth
puja *f* **1.** (*esfuerzo*) effort **2.** (*en una subasta*) bid; ~ **mínima** minimum bid
pujante *adj* strong; *fig* vigorous
pujanza *f* (*fuerza*) strength; (*impulso*) drive; (*brío*) vigour *Brit,* vigor *Am*
pujar *vi* **1.** (*esforzarse*) to struggle; ~ **por** to strive for **2.** (*en una subasta*) to bid
pulcritud *f* **1.** (*aseo*) tidiness **2.** (*cuidado*) neatness; (*finura*) delicacy
pulcro, -a <pulquérrimo> *adj* **1.** (*aseado*) tidy **2.** (*cuidadoso*) neat; (*fino*) delicate

pulga *f* flea; INFOR bug; **tener ~s** to be restless; **tener malas ~s** *inf* to be bad-tempered; **buscar las ~s a alguien** *inf* to tease sb
pulgada *f* (*medida*) inch
pulgar I. *adj* **dedo ~** thumb II. *m* thumb
Pulgarcito *m* LIT Tom Thumb
pulgón *m* aphid
pulguiento, -a *adj AmL* (*pulgoso*) flea-ridden
pulido *m* polishing; (*con cera*) waxing
pulido, -a *adj* 1. (*brillante*) polished 2. (*fino*) refined; (*estilo*) polished
pulidor *m* TÉC polisher
pulidor(a) *adj* TÉC polishing
pulimentar *vt* to polish; (*alisar*) to smooth; (*esmerilar*) to smooth with emery
pulimento *m* 1. *v.* **pulido** 2. (*sustancia*) polish
pulir I. *vt* 1. (*abrillantar*) to polish; (*suavizar*) to smooth; (*esmerilar*) to smooth with emery; (*con cera*) to wax 2. (*perfeccionar, refinar*) to polish up II. *vr:* **~se** 1. (*refinarse*) to become more refined 2. *inf* (*derrochar*) to squander
pulla *f* jibe *Brit,* gibe *Am*
pullman *m AmL* (*coche cama*) sleeping car
pullover *m AmL* (*jersey*) pullover
pulmón *m* lung; **~ de acero** iron lung; **~ acuático** aqualung; **gritar a pleno ~** to shout at the top of one's voice [*o* lungs]; **enfermo de ~** lung patient; **padecer de los pulmones** to have bad lungs
pulmonar *adj* MED pulmonary
pulmonía *f* MED pneumonia
pulóver *m AmL v.* **pullover**
pulpa *f* 1. ANAT soft matter; **~ dental** dental pulp 2. (*de la fruta*) flesh; **~ de madera** wood pulp
pulpería *f AmL* local shop, general store

In Latin America a **pulpería** is a general store selling alcoholic drinks, where all kinds of items can be bought. **Pulperías** are very similar to the small **tiendas de pueblo** that are still frequently encountered in small villages in Spain.

pulpero, -a *m, f AmL* grocer
púlpito *m* pulpit
pulpo *m* 1. ZOOL octopus; **como un ~ en un garaje** *inf* completely out of place 2. (*sujeción*) bunjee strap
pulquería *f AmC, Méx* (*pulpería*) general store
pulquero, -a *m, f AmS, Méx* (*pulpero*) storekeeper
pulquérrimo, -a *adj superl de* **pulcro**
pulsación *f* 1. ANAT (*latido*) beat, throbbing 2. (*de una tecla*) striking; (*mecanografía*) key-stroke; **~ doble** INFOR strikeover
pulsador *m* 1. (*tecla*) key 2. (*botón*) button 3. (*conmutador*) switch
pulsar *vt* 1. (*oprimir*) to press; (*teclado*) to strike; **~ el timbre** to ring the bell 2. (*tomar el pulso*) to take the pulse of; **~ la opinión pú-**

blica to gauge [*o* gage *Am*] public opinion
pulsera *f* bracelet; **reloj de ~** wristwatch
pulso *m* 1. (*muñeca*) wrist; *fig* steadiness of hand; **a ~** (*sin apoyarse*) freehand; (*por su propio esfuerzo*) on one's own; **con ~** carefully; **tener buen ~** to have a steady hand; **tomar el ~ a alguien** to take sb's pulse 2. (*desafío*) **echar un ~ a alguien** to arm wrestle sb
pulular *vi* 1. (*bullir*) **los turistas pululaban por la plaza** the square was swarming with tourists 2. (*multiplicarse*) to abound 3. (*brotar*) to swarm
pulverizador *m* (*aparato*) sprayer; (*botella*) spray bottle; (*atomizador*) atomizing spray; (*spray*) spray can
pulverizar <z→c> I. *vt* 1. (*reducir a polvo*) to pulverize; (*rallar*) to grate; (*moler*) to grind 2. (*atomizar*) to atomize 3. *fig* (*aniquilar*) to pulverize; (*argumento*) to destroy II. *vr:* **~se** to be pulverized
pum *interj* bang; **ni ~** *inf* not a thing
puma *m* puma
pumita *f* MIN pumice stone
puna *f AmS* 1. (*altiplano*) Andean plateau 2. (*malestar*) altitude sickness
punción *f* MED puncture
pundonor *m* 1. (*honorabilidad*) dignity, sense of honour *Brit* [*o* honor *Am*] 2. (*honor*) honour *Brit,* honor *Am*
pundonoroso, -a *adj* (*honorable*) honourable *Brit,* honorable *Am*
punga *f Arg, inf,* **punguista** *m Arg, inf* (*carterista*) pickpocket
punible *adj* punishable
punición *f* punishment
punitivo, -a *adj* punitive
punki *adj, mf* punk
punta *f* 1. (*extremo*) end; (*de lengua, iceberg*) tip; (*de tierra*) headland; **hora(s) ~** rush hour; **de ~ a ~** from end to end; **lo tenía en la ~ de la lengua** it was on the tip of my tongue 2. (*pico*) point; **a ~ de navaja** at knifepoint; **a ~ de pistola** at gunpoint; **acabar en ~** to come to a point; **sacar ~** (*afilar*) to sharpen 3. (*un poco*) touch ▸**de ~ en** blanco all dressed up; **estar de ~ con alguien** to be annoyed with sb; **ponerse de ~ con alguien** to fall out with sb
puntada *f* (*costura*) stitch; (*pinchazo*) prick; *fig* hint
puntaje *m AmL v.* **puntuación**
puntal *m* 1. (*madero*) prop; *fig* (*apoyo*) mainstay 2. *AmL* (*refrigerio*) snack
puntapié *m* kick; **pegar un ~ a alguien** to kick sb; **tratar a alguien a ~s** *fig* to walk all over sb
puntear *vt* 1. (*marcar con puntos, motear*) to dot 2. (*dar puntadas*) to stitch 3. MÚS to pluck
puntería *f* 1. (*apuntar*) aim 2. (*destreza*) marksmanship; **tener buena/mala ~** to be a good/bad shot
puntero *m* (*vara*) pointer

puntero, -a I. *adj* 1. (*con puntería*) accurate 2. (*sobresaliente*) leading; **tecnología puntera** cutting-edge technology; **el equipo ~** DEP the top team II. *m, f* leader

puntiagudo, -a *adj* (sharp-)pointed

puntilla *f* 1. (*encaje*) lace (edging) 2. (*marcador*) marker 3. (*puñal*) dagger (*used in bullfighting*); **dar la ~ a alguien** *fig* to finish sb off 4. (*del pie*) **de ~s** on tiptoe; **andar de ~s** to walk on tiptoe; **ponerse de ~s** to stand on tiptoe

punto *m* 1. (*general*) point; **~ álgido** crucial moment; **~ de arranque** starting point; **~ cardinal** point of the compass; **~ cero** starting point; **~ clave** key point; **no hay ~ de comparación** there's no comparison; **~ de destino** destination; **~ de ebullición** boiling point; **~ de encuentro** meeting place; **~ esencial** main point; **~ fuerte** strong point; **~ de intersección** intersection; **~ máximo** high point; **~ muerto** AUTO neutral; **~ de referencia** reference point; **~ a tratar** item (on the agenda); **~ de venta** point of sale; **~ de vista** point of view; **dar el ~ a algo** to get sth just right; **ganar por ~s** to win on points; **al ~** (*en seguida*) at once; **hasta tal ~ que...** to such a degree that ...; **de todo ~** absolutely; **la una en ~** exactly one o'clock; **en ~** a with reference to; **hasta cierto ~** up to a point; **¿hasta qué ~?** how far?; **¡vamos por ~s!** let's take it step by step!; **a ~ de** on the point of; **está a ~ de llover** it's about to rain; **a ~ fijo** exactly; **¡~ en boca!** *inf* mum's the word!; **¡y ~!** *inf* and that's that!; **en su ~** *fig* just right 2. TIPO full stop; **~ y aparte** full stop, new paragraph; **~ y coma** semicolon; **~ final** full stop (*end of paragraph*); **poner ~ final a algo** *fig* to bring sth to an end; **~ y seguido** full stop (*no new paragraph*); **~s suspensivos** suspension points, dot, dot, dot *inf*; **dos ~s** colon; **poner los ~s sobre las íes** *fig* to dot the i's and cross the t's; **con ~s y comas** very precise 3. (*calceta, labor*) knitting; **~ de media** plain stitch; **chaqueta de ~** knitted jacket; **hacer ~** to knit 4. (*puntada*) stitch; **~ de sutura** MED stitch; **la herida necesitó diez ~s** the wound needed ten stitches 5. *pey* (*tipo*) bloke; **es un ~ filipino** he's a rogue 6. GASTR **a/en su ~** done; **batir a ~ de nieve** to beat until stiff 7. (*preparado*) **a ~** ready; **poner a ~** TÉC to fine-tune; (*ajustar*) to adjust; **tener a ~** to have ready 8. INFOR dot; **~ .com** dot.com

puntuación *f* 1. LING punctuation; **signo de ~** punctuation mark 2. (*calificación*) mark *Brit,* grade *Am;* DEP score; **sistema de ~** scoring system

puntual *adj* 1. (*concreto*) specific 2. (*exacto*) precise 3. (*sin retraso*) punctual

puntualidad *f* punctuality

puntualizar <z→c> *vt* (*especificar, precisar*) to specify; (*aclarar*) to clarify

puntuar <1. *pres:* puntúo> *vt* 1. (*un escrito*) to punctuate 2. (*conseguir puntos*) to score

3. (*calificar*) to mark *Brit,* to grade *Am;* DEP to score

punzada *f* (*dolor*) sharp pain; (*en los costados*) stitch

punzante *adj* 1. (*puntiagudo*) sharp 2. (*mordaz*) scathing

punzar <z→c> I. *vt* 1. (*pinchar*) to prick; (*agujerear*) to puncture 2. (*conciencia*) to prick II. *vi* (*doler*) to stab

punzó *adj CSur, Col* **rojo ~** bright red

punzón *m* punch; **para cuero** awl; (*sello*) stamp; (*cincel*) graver; (*taladro*) drilling bit; (*buril*) burin

puñado *m* handful; **a ~s** (*mucho*) by the handful; **un ~** *inf* (*mucho*) a lot

puñal *m* dagger; **poner a alguien el ~ al pecho** *fig* to hold a gun to sb's head

puñalada *f* stab; (*herida*) stab wound; *fig* blow; **coser a ~s** to stab repeatedly; **dar una ~ trapera a alguien** *fig* to stab sb in the back

puñeta *f vulg* 1. (*molestia*) **¡(qué) ~(s)!** hell!; **hacer la ~ a alguien** to screw things up for sb 2. (*bobada*) stupid thing; **¡déjate de ~s!** stop messing about!; **¿qué ~s estás diciendo?** what the hell are you on about?; **en la quinta ~** in the back of beyond 3. *AmL* (*masturbación*) wank *Brit,* jerk-off *Am* 4. *vulg* (*expresión de enfado*) **mandar a alguien a hacer ~s** to tell sb to go to hell; **¡vete a hacer ~s!** go to hell!

puñetazo *m* punch

puñetero, -a *adj inf* damn(ed); **el muy ~ no me ayudó** the bastard didn't help me

puño *m* 1. (*mano*) fist; **~ cerrado** clenched fist; **con el ~ en alto** with one's fist raised; **apretar los ~s** *fig* to struggle hard; **comerse los ~s** *fig* to be starving; **como un ~** (*huevo, mentira*) enormous; (*casa, habitación*) tiny; **verdades como ~s** fundamental truths; **de su ~ y letra** in his/her own hand; **meter a alguien en un ~** *fig* to intimidate sb; **tener a alguien en un ~** *fig* to have sb under one's thumb 2. (*puñado*) handful 3. (*mango*) handle; (*pomo*) hilt 4. (*de la ropa*) cuff; **~ vuelto** turned-up cuff

pupa *f* 1. (*ampolla*) blister; (*heridilla*) small wound; (*úlcera*) ulcer 2. *inf* (*dolor*) pain; **¡~!** ouch! 3. ZOOL pupa

pupila *f* pupil; **tener ~** *inf* to be sharp

pupilaje *m* (*tutela*) pupillage

pupilar *adj* pupillary

pupilo, -a *m, f* ward

pupitre *m* 1. (*escritorio*) desk 2. TÉC console; **~ de control** control panel

pupo *m Arg, Bol, Chile* navel

purasangre *adj, m* thoroughbred

puré *m* purée; **~ de patatas** mashed potatoes; **hacer ~** to purée; *fig* to beat to a pulp; **estar hecho ~** *fig* to be knackered

pureza *f* purity

purga *f* 1. (*medicamento*) purgative 2. (*eliminación*) purge

purgación *f* 1. MED purging 2. TÉC draining 3. *pl, inf* (*blenorragia*) gonorrhoea *Brit,* gonorrhea *Am*

purgante *adj, m* purgative

purgar <g→gu> I. *vt* **1.** *t. fig* to clean **2.** MED to purge **3.** (*evacuar*) to empty; (*aguas*) to drain **4.** (*expiar*) to expiate **5.** JUR to clear II. *vr:* ~**se 1.** *t. fig* to clean oneself **2.** MED to take a purge

purgativo, -a *adj* purgative

purgatorio *m* purgatory

purificador *m* purifier; ~ **de humos** smoke filter

purificador(a) *adj* **planta** ~**a** water treatment plant

purificar <c→qu> I. *vt t. fig* to purify II. *vr:* ~**se** to be purified; *fig* to purify oneself

Purísima *f* **la** ~ the Virgin (Mary)

purista *adj, mf* purist

puritano, -a I. *adj* puritanical II. *m, f* puritan

puro *m* cigar

puro, -a *adj* **1.** (*sin imperfecciones*) pure; (*auténtico*) authentic; **por pura cortesía** as a matter of courtesy; **pura lana** pure wool; **la pura verdad** the honest truth; **pura casualidad** sheer chance; **de** ~ **miedo** from sheer terror; **se cae de** ~ **bueno/tonto** he is unbelievably kind/stupid **2.** (*sin mezcla*) unadulterated **3.** (*íntegro*) whole

púrpura *adj, f* purple

purpúreo, -a *adj* purple

purrete, -a *m, f RíoPl, inf* (*chiquillo*) kid *inf*

purulento, -a *adj* purulent

pus *m sin pl* MED pus

pusilánime *adj* cowardly

pústula *f* MED pustule

puta *f vulg* whore; **casa de** ~**s** brothel; *fig* everyone for himself, to each his own; **ir de** ~**s** to go whoring; **hijo de** ~ son of a bitch; **pasarlas** ~**s** to go through hell

putada *f vulg* **¡qué** ~**!** what a bloody nuisance!; **hacer una** ~ **a alguien** to play a dirty trick on sb

putañear *vi inf* to go whoring

putativo, -a *adj* putative

puteada *f AmS, vulg* swearword; **dar** ~**s** to swear

putear I. *vi vulg* (*ir de putas*) to go whoring II. *vt vulg* (*fastidiar*) to annoy; **me putea tanta gilipollez** all this stupidity really pisses me off; **estoy puteado** I'm really pissed off; **¡te han puteado bien!** they've really messed you about!

puticlub *m inf* singles bar

puto, -a *adj vulg* bloody; **¡de puta madre!** bloody brilliant!; **¡qué puta suerte!** what bloody awful luck!; **el** ~ **coche no arranca** the damn car won't start; **ni puta idea** not a bloody clue; **las estoy pasando putas** I'm having a really shitty time

putrefacción *f* decay

putrefacto, -a *adj* rotten

pútrido, -a *adj* putrid

puya *f* **1.** (*punta*) point **2.** (*injuria*) jibe *Brit,* gibe *Am;* **echar una** ~ **a alguien** to make a gibe at sb

puzzle *m* (*rompecabezas*) jigsaw (puzzle); *fig* puzzle

PVP *m abr de* **Precio de Venta al Público** RRP

Q

Q, q *f* Q, q; ~ **de Quebec** Q for Queenie *Brit,* Q for Queen *Am*

qm *abr de* **quintal métrico** 100 kg

que I. *pron rel* **1.** (*con antecedente: personas, cosas*) that, which (*often omitted when referring to object*); **la pelota** ~ **está pinchada** the ball that is punctured; **la pelota** ~ **compraste** the ball you bought; **la historia de** ~ **te hablé** the story I told you about; **reacciones a las** ~ **estamos acostumbrados** reactions which we are accustomed to; **el proyecto en el** ~ **trabajo** the project that I am working on; **la empresa para la** ~ **trabajo** the company that I work for **2.** (*con antecedente: personas*) who, whom (*often omitted when referring to the object*); **la mujer que trabaja conmigo** the woman who works with me; **el rey al** ~ **sirvo** the king (whom) I serve **3.** (*sin antecedente*) **el/la/lo** ~**...** the one (that/who/which) ...; **los** ~ **hayan terminado** those who have finished; **el** ~ **quiera,** ~ **se marche** whoever wants to, can leave; **es de los** ~**...** he/she/it is the type that ...; **el** ~ **más y el** ~ **menos** every single one; **es todo lo** ~ **sé** that's all I know; **lo** ~ **haces** what you do; **no sabes lo difícil** ~ **es** you don't know how difficult it is **4.** (*con preposición*) **de lo** ~ **habláis** what you are talking about II. *conj* **1.** (*completivo*) that; **me pidió** ~ **le ayudara** he/she asked me to help him/her **2.** (*estilo indirecto*) that; **ha dicho** ~**...** he/she said that ... **3.** (*comparativo*) **más alto** ~ taller than; **lo mismo** ~ the same as **4.** (*porque*) because; **le ayudaré, seguro,** ~ **se lo he prometido** I'll help him/her, of course, because I promised **5.** (*para que*) **dio órdenes a los trabajadores** ~ **trabajaran más rápido** he/she ordered the workers to work faster **6.** (*sin que*) **no voy de vacaciones,** ~ **no me roben** I can't go on holiday without getting robbed **7.** (*de manera que*) **corre** ~ **vuela** he/she runs like the wind **8.** (*o, ya*) ~ **paguen,** ~ **no paguen, eso ya se verá** we'll see whether they pay or not **9.** (*y*) **lo hizo él,** ~ **no yo** he did it, not me **10.** (*frecuentativo*) **y él dale** ~ **dale con la guitarra** and he kept on playing and playing the guitar **11.** (*explicativo*) **hoy no vendré, es** ~ **estoy cansado** I'm not coming in today because I'm tired; **no es** ~ **no pueda, es** ~ **no quiero** it's not that I can't, it's that I don't want to; **¿es** ~ **no puedes venir?** can't you come then?

12. (*enfático*) ¡~ sí/no! I said "yes"/"no"!; sí ~ lo hice I did do it! **13.** (*de duda*) ¿~ no está en casa? are you saying he/she isn't at home? **14.** (*exclamativo*) ¡~ me canso! I'm getting tired!; ¡~ sea yo el que tenga que hacerlo! I would be the one who has to do it! **15.** (*con verbo*) hay ~ trabajar más you/we/they have to work harder; tener ~ hacer algo to have to do something; dar ~ hablar to set tongues wagging ►a la ~ llegue as soon as he/she arrives; a menos ~ +*subj* unless; antes ~ before; con tal (de) ~ +*subj* as long as; por mucho ~ tú digas... no matter what you say ...; yo ~ tú... if I were you ...

qué *adj, pron interrog* **1.** (*general*) what; (*cuál*) which; (*qué clase de*) what kind of; ¿por ~? why?; ¿en ~ piensas? what are you thinking about?; ¿para ~? what for?; ¿de ~ hablas? what are you talking about?; ¿a ~ esperas? what are you waiting for?; ¿~ día llega? what day is he/she arriving?; ¿~ cerveza tomas? what kind of beer do you drink?; ¿a ~ vienes? what are you here for?; ¿~ edad tienes? how old are you?; según ~ gente no la soporto some people I just can't stand **2.** (*exclamativo*) ¡~ alegría! how nice!; ¡~ gracia! how funny!; ¡~ suerte! what luck! **3.** (*cuán*) ¡~ magnífica vista! what a magnificent view!; ¡mira ~ contento está! look how happy he is! **4.** (*cuánto*) ¡~ de gente! what a lot of people! ►¿~ tal? how are you [*o* things]?; ¿~ tal si salimos a cenar? how about going out to dinner?; ¿y ~? so what?; ¿y a mí ~? and what about me?; ¿~? well?; ~, ¿vienes o no? well, are you coming, or not?

quebrada *f* **1.** (*paso*) ravine **2.** (*hendidura*) gap **3.** *AmL* (*arroyo*) stream

quebradizo, -a *adj* **1.** (*objeto*) brittle **2.** (*de salud*) sickly; (*persona mayor*) frail **3.** (*voz*) faltering

quebrado *m* MAT fraction

quebrado, -a *adj* **1.** (*empresa*) bankrupt **2.** (*herniado*) ruptured **3.** (*terreno*) rough **4.** (*rostro*) pale

quebrantado, -a *adj* **1.** (*salud*) tengo las espaldas quebrantadas my back is killing me; la operación me dejó muy ~ the operation left me very weak **2.** (*pared*) cracked

quebrantar I. *vt* **1.** (*romper*) to break; (*cascar*) to crack; (*machacar*) to crush; ~ la prisión to break out of prison **2.** (*ley, secreto*) to break; (*obligación*) to violate **3.** (*furia*) to diminish; (*autoridad*) to breach; (*salud*) to debilitate II. *vr:* ~se (*estado de salud*) to be ruined; (*fuerza*) to be weakened

quebranto *m* **1.** (*de romper*) breaking; (*de cascar*) cracking; (*de machacar*) crushing **2.** (*económico*) heavy loss **3.** (*moral*) breakdown; (*físico*) weakening **4.** (*pena*) suffering

quebrar <e→ie> I. *vt* **1.** (*romper*) to break **2.** (*interrumpir*) to interrupt **3.** (*el cuerpo*) to bend **4.** (*rostro*) to distort **5.** (*ley*) to break

6. (*suavizar*) to moderate II. *vi* **1.** (*con alguien*) to break up **2.** (*ceder*) to break down **3.** COM to go bankrupt **4.** (*intento*) to fail **5.** *Méx* (*darse por vencido*) to give in III. *vr:* ~se **1.** MED to rupture oneself **2.** (*la voz*) to go hoarse **3.** (*rostro*) to turn pale **4.** (*cuerpo*) to bend; ~se de dolor to double over [*o* up] with pain

quebrazón *m AmL* **1.** (*resultado*) breakage **2.** (*acción*) shattering

quechua I. *adj* Quechua II. *mf* Quechuan

> **Quechua** is the name given both to the original inhabitants of **Perú** as well as their language. **Quechua** is the second official language of **Perú**.

quedada *f* **1.** *inf* (*burla*) joke; lo de largarse en medio de la reunión fue sólo una ~ I was only fooling when I got up and left in the middle of the meeting **2.** *Méx, pey* (*solterona*) old maid

quedado, -a *adj Arg, Chile* slow

quedar I. *vi* **1.** (*permanecer*) to remain; los problemas quedan atrás the problems are a thing of the past; ¿cuánta gente queda? how many people are left?; ~ a deber algo to owe sth **2.** (*sobrar*) to be left; no nos queda otro remedio que... there's nothing left for us to do but ...; no queda pan there's no bread left; no queda ningún ejemplar de este libro there are no copies of this book left **3.** (*resultar*) todo quedó en una simple discusión it ended up in a mere argument; ~ acordado to be arranged; ~ cojo to go lame; ~ eliminado to be eliminated; ~ en ridículo to make a fool of oneself **4.** (*acordar*) ~ en algo to agree to sth; ¡en qué habéis quedado? what have you decided?; quedamos a las 10 we agreed to meet at 10; ¿quedamos a las 10? shall we meet at 10?; primero dices una cosa y luego otra, ¿en qué quedamos? first you say one thing and then another, make up your mind! **5.** (*estar situado*) to lie; queda por/hacia el norte it lies to the north; quedar lejos de aquí to be a long way from here **6.** (*faltar*) quedan aún 100 km para llegar a casa there are still 100 km left before we get home; aún queda mucho por hacer there's still a lot to do; por mí que no quede I'll do all that I can **7.** (*terminar*) to end; ... y ahí quedó el concierto ... the concert ended there **8.** (*en una subasta*) el cuadro queda por un millón de libras the painting goes for one million pounds **9.** (+ *por*) ~ por cobarde to come across as a coward; algo queda por ver sth remains to be seen **10.** (+ *bien/mal*) ~ bien/mal to come off well/badly **11.** (+ *como*) ~ como un señor to behave like a real gentleman; ~ como un idiota to look a fool II. *vr:* ~se **1.** (*permanecer*) to stay; ~se atrás to stay behind; ~se colgado (*ordenador*) to block; durante la tormenta nos quedamos a oscuras during the storm the lights went out; **cuando me lo dijo me quedé mudo** when he told me I was speechless **2.** (*resultar*) ~**se ciego** to go blind; ~**se viuda/viudo** to become a widow/widower; **al freír la carne se ha quedado en nada** when the meat was fried it shrunk to almost nothing **3.** (*conservar, adquirir*) **me quedo con el coche pequeño** I'll take the small car; **quédate con el libro** keep the book; ~**se sin nada** to be left with nothing; **entre el mar y la montaña me quedo con el mar** if I have to choose between the sea and the mountains, I'll take the sea **4.** (*burlarse*) ~**se con alguien** to make fun of sb

quehacer *m* chores *pl;* **los ~es de la casa** housework; **dar ~ a alguien** to assign work to sb

queja *f* complaint; **no tengo ~ de él** I have nothing against him

quejarse *vr* **1.** (*formular queja*) ~ **de algo** to complain about sth; **se queja del frío** he complains about the cold; **¿qué tal te va el negocio? – bien, gracias, no puedo quejarme** how's business? – fine, thanks, I can't complain **2.** (*gemir*) ~ **de algo** to moan about sth

quejica **I.** *adj* (*por dolor*) moaning; (*por manera de ser*) complaining; **¡no seas ~, hombre!** stop whining! **II.** *mf* complainer, bellyacher *inf;* (*criticón*) faultfinder

quejido *m* moan; (*constante*) lament; ~ **de dolor** cry of pain; **dar ~s** to groan

quejoso, -a *adj* complaining; **estar ~ de alguien** to be annoyed at sb

quejumbroso, -a *adj* (*voz*) whining; (*por dolor*) moaning

quelite *m Méx* greens *pl*

quelonio *m* chelonian

queltehue *m Chile* ZOOL teruteru

quema *f* **1.** (*acción*) burning; (*completa*) incineration **2.** (*incendio, fuego*) fire; **huir de la ~** *fig* to flee from danger

quemada *f* **1.** *Arg, Méx* (*acción que pone en ridículo*) embarrassment **2.** *Méx* (*quemadura*) burn

quemado, -a *adj* burnt; **este político está ~** *inf* this politician is finished; **estar ~ con alguien** *inf* to have had it with sb

quemadura *f* burn; ~ **de primer grado** first degree burn

quemar **I.** *vi* to burn; **cuidado, esta sopa quema** be careful, the soup is boiling hot **II.** *vt* **1.** (*comida, sol*) to burn; (*casa: completamente*) to burn down; ~ **un bosque** to set fire to a forest; **este chili quema la garganta/la lengua** this chilli burns my throat/tongue **2.** (*planta: calor*) to scorch; (*frío*) to damage by frost **3.** (*fortuna*) to squander **4.** (*fastidiar*) to mess up **5.** *AmC* (*denunciar*) ~ **a alguien** to inform against sb **III.** *vr:* ~**se 1.** (*arder*) to burn; **el bosque se quema** the forest is on fire; **me he quemado los cabellos** I've singed my hair **2.** (*herir*) to be hurt **3.** (*comida*) to burn; (*lige-*

ramente) to singe **4.** (*tener calor*) **me estoy quemando** I'm boiling **5.** (*por una pasión*) ~**se de amor** to burn with love **6.** (*acertar*) **¡que te quemas!** you're getting warm!

quemarropa **disparar a ~** to shoot at very close range; **hacer preguntas a ~** to ask point-blank

quemazón *f* **1.** (*quema*) burning **2.** (*calor*) intense heat **3.** (*ardor*) **siento una ~ en el estómago** I have a burning sensation in my stomach

quemo *m Arg* **¡que ~!** how embarrassing!

quemón *m Méx* dope smoker

quena *f* MÚS *reed flute used in Andean music*

quepi(s) *m* (*inv*) (*gorro militar*) kepi

quepo *1. pres de* **caber**

queque *m Chile, Perú, AmC* (*bollo*) cake

querella *f* **1.** JUR lawsuit; ~ **criminal** criminal action; **poner una ~ contra alguien** to sue sb **2.** (*discordia*) dispute

querellarse *vr* **1.** (*quejarse*) to complain; ~ **por algo** to complain about sth **2.** JUR to bring an action

querencia *f* (*aprecio*) attachment; (*cariño*) affection; (*afición*) liking; **tomar ~ a algo/alguien** to take a liking to sth/sb

querendón, -ona *adj AmL* loving, affectionate

querer *irr* **I.** *vt* **1.** (*desear*) to desire; (*más suave*) to want; **como tú quieras** as you like; **has ganado, ¿qué más quieres?** you win, what more do you want?; **hacer algo queriendo/sin ~** to do something on purpose/unintentionally; **quisiera tener 20 años menos** I wish I were 20 years younger; **eso es lo que quería decir** that's what I meant to say; **quiero que sepáis que...** I want you to know that ...; **y yo, ¡qué quieres que le haga!** what do you expect me to do?; **donde quiera que esté** wherever he/she/it may be; **¡por lo que más quieras, deja ese tema!** for God's sake, change the subject! **2.** (*amar*) to like; (*más fuerte*) to love; **te quiero con locura** I love you madly **3.** (*pedir*) to require **4.** (*requerir*) **estas plantas quieren mucha agua** these plants need a lot of water ▶ ~ **es poder** *prov* where there's a will, there's a way; **como quiera que sea** anyhow **II.** *v impers* **parece que quiere llover** it looks like rain **III.** *m* love

querido, -a **I.** *adj* dear **II.** *m, f* (*amante*) lover; (*como vocativo*) darling

queroseno *m* kerosene *Am*, paraffin *Brit*

quesadilla *f* GASTR **1.** (*pastel*) cheesecake **2.** (*pastelillo*) pastry **3.** *AmL* (*tortilla*) quesadilla (*folded tortilla filled with a spicy mixture and topped with cheese*)

quesera *f* (*plato*) cheese dish

queso *m* **1.** GASTR cheese; ~ **de bola** Edam cheese; ~ **rallado** grated cheese **2.** *inf* (*pie*) foot; **te huelen los ~s** your feet smell

quicio *m* (*de puerta, ventana*) hinge post ▶ **sacar las cosas de ~** to make a mountain out of a molehill; **estar** <u>fuera</u> **de** ~ to be in disorder; <u>sacar</u> **a alguien de** ~ to drive sb up the wall *inf;* **me saca de** ~ **verla llorar** it gets on my nerves to see her crying

quico *m inf* toasted corn snack

quid *m* crux; **ese es el** ~ **de la cuestión** that is the crux of the matter; **dar en el** ~ to hit the nail on the head

quiebra *f* 1. COM bankruptcy; **dar en** ~ to go bankrupt 2. (*hendidura*) fissure; (*rotura*) break 3. (*fracaso*) failure; (*pérdida*) loss, breakdown; **la** ~ **de los valores** the breakdown of values; **este asunto no tiene** ~ this can't go wrong

quiebro *m* 1. (*movimiento*) dodge; **Maradona le hizo un** ~ **al defensa** Maradona dribbled around the defender 2. (*gorgorito*) trill

quien *pron rel* 1. (*con antecedente*) who, that, whom (*often omitted when referring to object*); **el chico de** ~ **te hablé** that boy I told you about; **las chicas con** ~**es...** the girls with whom ... 2. (*sin antecedente*) that; **hay** ~ **dice que...** some people say that ...; **no hay** ~ **lo aguante** nobody can stand him; ~ **opine eso...** whoever thinks so ...; ~ **más,** ~ **menos, todos tenemos problemas** everybody has problems

quién *pron interrog* who; **¿**~ **es?** (*llama*) who is it?; **¿**~**es son tus padres?** who are your parents?; **¿a** ~ **has visto?** who did you see?; **¿a** ~ **se lo has dado?** who did you give it to?; **¿**~ **eres tú para decirme esto?** who do you think you are telling me this?; **¿por** ~ **me tomas?** what do you take me for?; **¡**~ **tuviera 20 años!** If only I were 20!

quienquiera <quienesquiera> *pron indef* whoever; ~ **que sea que pase** whoever it is, come in

quieto, -a *adj* 1. (*tranquilo*) calm; **no puede estar nunca** ~ (*niño*) he/she can never keep still 2. (*parado*) motionless; **quedarse** ~ to stand still

quietud *f* 1. (*calma*) calm 2. (*inmovilidad*) stillness

quijada *f* jaw(bone)

quilate *m* carat *Brit,* karat *Am;* **de muchos** ~**s** *t. fig* of great value

quilco *m Chile* (large) basket

quilla *f* NÁUT keel

quillango *m CSur* (*manta de pieles*) fur blanket

quillay *m Arg, Chile* BOT soapbark tree

quilo *m* 1. (*peso*) kilo(gramme) *Brit,* kilo(gram) *Am;* **sudar el** ~ *inf* to sweat blood 2. *inf* (*dinero*) million

quilombo *m* 1. *Chile* (*burdel*) whorehouse 2. *Ven* (*choza*) hut 3. *Arg* (*lío*) mess

quiltro *m Chile, pey* (*perro*) yapper, mutt *Am*

quimba *f* 1. *AmL* (*garbo*) grace 2. *AmL* (*sandalia*) sandal 3. *pl Col* (*conflicto*) difficulties *pl*

quimbo *m Cuba* knife, machete

quimera *f* (*ilusión*) chimera *form*

química *f* chemistry

químico, -a I. *adj* chemical; **productos** ~**s** chemicals *pl* II. *m, f* chemist

quimioterapia *f* chemotherapy

quimono *m* kimono

quina *f* cinchona bark; **ser más malo que la** ~ *inf* to taste terrible; **tragar** ~ *fig* to put up with a lot

quincalla *f* 1. (*objetos*) ironmongery *Brit,* hardware *Am* 2. (*adornos*) trinkets *pl*

quincallería *f* 1. (*tienda*) ironmonger's *Brit,* hardware store *Am* 2. (*objetos*) ironmongery *Brit,* hardware *Am* 3. (*adornos*) trinkets *pl*

quince I. *adj inv* fifteen; **dentro de** ~ **días** in a fortnight *Brit,* in fifteen days II. *m* fifteen; *v.t.* ocho

quincena *f* (*días*) fortnight *Brit,* fifteen days

quincenal *adj* fortnightly *Brit,* twice-monthly, bi-weekly; **revista** ~ fortnightly journal *Brit,* twice-monthly journal

quincuagésimo, -a *adj* fiftieth; *v.t.* octavo

quingos *m inv, AmL* zigzag

quiniela *f* 1. (*juego*) sports pools *pl;* **jugar a las** ~**s** to do the pools 2. (*boleto*) pools coupon 3. *CSur* (*lotería*) lottery

quinientos, -as *adj* five hundred; *v.t.* ochocientos

quinina *f* quinine

quino *m AmL* BOT cinchona tree

quinqué *m* oil lamp

quinqui *mf inf* delinquent

quinta *f* 1. (*casa*) country house 2. MIL call-up, draft *Am;* **entrar en** ~**s** to be called up, to be drafted *Am;* **ese es de mi** ~ he is my age

quintaesencia *f* quintessence *elev*

quintal *m* quintal; ~ **métrico** 100 kgs

quintar *vt* MIL to call up, to draft *Am*

quinteto *m* MÚS quintet

quintillizo, -a *m, f* quintuplet

Quintín *m* **se armó la de San** ~ *inf* all hell broke loose

quinto *m* conscript, draftee *Am*

quinto, -a *adj, m, f* fifth; *v.t.* octavo

quintuplicar <c→qu> *vt* to quintuple

quíntuplo, -a *adj* quintuple

quiosco *m* 1. (*de jardín*) gazebo 2. (*de periódicos*) news-stand

quipo(s) *m(pl),* **quipu(s)** *m(pl) AmL* HIST quipu (*ancient Peruvian system of coloured threads and knots for recording facts and events*)

quiquiriquí *m* (*onomatopeya*) cock-a-doodle-doo

quirófano *m* operating theatre *Brit,* operating room *Am;* **pasar por el** ~ to be operated on

quirquincho *m CSur* 1. ZOOL (*armadillo*) small armadillo 2. (*guitarra*) charango

quirúrgico, -a *adj* surgical

quisicosa *f inf* riddle, puzzle

quiso *3. pret de* querer

quisque *pron indef, inf,* **quisqui** *pron indef, vulg* **cada** ~ every man-Jack; **todo** ~ anyone and everyone; **se lo dijo a todo** ~ he told every Tom, Dick and Harry

quisquilla *f* 1.(*pequeñez*) trifle 2.ZOOL shrimp

quisquilloso, -a *adj* 1.(*susceptible*) touchy 2.(*meticuloso*) fussy

quiste *m* MED cyst

quitaesmalte *m* nail varnish remover

quitagusto *m* Ecua, Perú (*intruso*) intruder

quitaipón *m* de ~ detachable

quitamanchas *m inv* stain remover

quitamiedos *m inv* (*en carretera*) guardrail

quitanieves *f inv* snowplough *Brit*, snowplow *Am*

quitar I. *vt* 1.(*piel, funda*) to remove; (*sombrero, tapa, ropa*) to take off; (*botón*) to pull off; ~ **la mesa** to clear the table; **una capucha de quita y pon** a detachable hood 2.(*desposeer*) to take; (*robar*) to steal; **me lo has quitado de la boca** *fig* you took the words right out of my mouth; **el café me quita el sueño** coffee keeps me awake; **ese asunto me quita el sueño** that matter is keeping me awake at night 3.(*mancha*) to get out; (*obstáculo*) to remove; (*dolor*) to relieve; (*vida*) to take 4.(*de plan, horario, texto*) to leave out 5.(*regla*) to do away with 6.(*apartar*) to get out of the way; (*mueble*) to remove; **¡quita!** (*no me molestes*) don't bother me!; (*deja eso*) leave that alone!; (*déjate de tonterías*) stop it!; **el médico me ha quitado de fumar** the doctor has told me to quit smoking 7.MAT to subtract; **quitando dos** taking away two ►**ni ~ ni poner en algo** not to have any say in sth II. *vr:* ~**se** (*sombrero, gafas, ropa*) to take off; (*barba*) to shave off; ~**se la vida** to commit suicide; ~**se de la bebida** to give up drinking; ~**se de encima algo/a alguien** to get rid of sth/sb; **quítate de mi vista** get out of my sight; ~**se años** (**de encima**) to look years younger

quitasol *m* sunshade

Quito *m* Quito

quizá(s) *adv* perhaps, maybe; ~ **y sin** ~ without a doubt

R

R, r *f* R, r; ~ **de Ramón** R for Roger

rabadilla *f* ANAT coccyx

rabanito *m* radish

rábano *m* radish; ~ **picante** [*o* blanco] horseradish ►**tomar el** ~ **por las hojas** *inf* (*interpretación*) to get the wrong end of the stick; (*ejecución*) to get it back to front; **me importa un** ~ *inf* I couldn't care less; **¡y un** ~! no way!; **déjame tu coche** – **¡y un** ~! *inf* can I borrow your car? – no way!; **tu hermano es más listo que tú** – **¡y un** ~! *inf* your brother is brighter than you – you must be joking!

rabí <rabíes> *m* REL rabbi

rabia *f* 1.MED (*hidrofobia*) rabies *pl* 2.(*furia*) rage; **¡qué** ~! how infuriating! 3.(*enfado, manía*) **tener** ~ **a alguien** (*enfado*) to be furious with sb; (*manía*) not to be able to stand sb; **tomar** ~ **a alguien** (*enfado*) to become furious with sb; (*manía*) to take a dislike to sb; **me da** ~ **sólo pensarlo** just thinking about it makes me mad; **con** ~ angrily

rabiar *vi* 1.(*padecer rabia: animal*) to be rabid, to have rabies; (*persona*) to have rabies 2.(*enfadarse*) to be furious; **hacer** ~ **a alguien** to infuriate sb 3.(*sufrir*) to be in great pain; ~ **de...** to be dying of ... 4.(*ansiar, desear*) ~ **por...** to be dying to ... ►**está que rabia** *inf* (*picante*) it's incredibly hot; **a** ~ (*mucho*) incredibly

rabieta *f* tantrum; **coger una** ~ to throw a tantrum [*o* fit]

rabillo *m* **el** ~ **del ojo** the corner of the eye

rabimocho, -a *adj AmL* (*rabón*) short

rabino *m* rabbi

rabioso, -a *adj* 1.(*hidrofóbico*) rabid 2.(*furioso*) furious; (*desconsiderado*) inconsiderate 3.*inf* (*picante*) really hot 4.*fig* (*vehemente*) fervent; **un tema de rabiosa actualidad** a highly topical issue

rabo *m* 1.(*cola*) tail; **salir con el** ~ **entre las piernas** *inf* to go away with one's tail between one's legs; **aún queda el** ~ **por desollar** *inf* the worst is yet to come 2.(*extremo*) end 3.(*tallo*) stem 4.*vulg* (*pene*) cock

rabona *f CSur*, *inf* (*falta a la escuela*) truant; **hacer(se) la** ~ to play truant

racanear I. *vi inf* to be stingy II. *vt inf* ~ **algo a alguien** to be stingy with sth to sb; ~ **dinero a alguien** not to give sb enough money

rácano, -a *adj* 1.*inf* (*tacaño*) mean 2.*inf* (*gandul*) lazy

racha *f* 1.(*de aire*) gust of wind 2.(*fase*) series; **tener buena/mala** ~ to have a good/bad run; **a** [*o* por] ~**s** in fits and starts; **arrancar un coche a** ~**s, dar una** ~ **a un coche** to jump-start a car

racial *adj* (*étnico*) racial; **disturbios** ~**es** race riots

racimo *m* bunch; ~ **de uvas** bunch of grapes

raciocinio *m* 1.(*facultad, razón*) reason 2.(*proceso mental*) reasoning

ración *f* 1.(*tapa*) portion (*portion of food served as a large snack in a bar or restaurant*); **una** ~ **de patatas fritas** a portion of chips *Brit* [*o* French fries *Am*]; **una** ~ **de queso** a plate of cheese 2.en casa, helping, serving; (*en restaurante*) plate, portion 3.MIL ration ►**poner a alguien a media** ~ to put sb on half rations

racional *adj* rational; (*razonable*) reasonable

racionalización *f* ECON, PSICO rationalization

racionalizar <z→c> *vt* to rationalize

racionamiento *m* rationing

racionar *vt* 1.(*repartir*) to ration out 2.(*limitar*) to ration

racismo *m sin pl* racism

racista *adj*, *mf* racist

radar *m* ELEC radar; **por** ~ by radar
radiación *f* 1. Fís radiation; ~ **solar** solar radiation 2. RADIO, TV broadcasting
radiactividad *f* Fís radioactivity
radiactivo, -a *adj* radioactive
radiado, -a *adj* 1. (*forma*) radiate 2. RADIO broadcast
radiador *m* (*de casa, coche*) radiator
radial *adj* 1. (*forma*) radial; **músculo** ~ ANAT radial muscle 2. *AmL* RADIO radio
radiante *adj* (*brillante*) radiant; ~ **de alegría/ felicidad** radiant with joy/happiness; **estás** ~ **con ese vestido** you look wonderful in that dress; **está** ~ **con su nuevo trabajo** he/she is delighted with his/her new job
radiar I. *vi* 1. (*irradiar*) to radiate 2. RADIO to broadcast II. *vt* 1. (*irradiar*) to radiate 2. RADIO to broadcast; **un debate radiado** a radio debate 3. MED to treat with X-rays 4. *AmL* (*eliminar*) to delete
radical I. *adj* 1. BOT, MAT (*t. extremado*) radical 2. (*fundamental*) drastic II. *m* 1. LING root 2. MAT, QUÍM, PSICO radical 3. MAT (*signo*) radical (sign) III. *mf* POL radical; ~ **de derecha** extreme right-winger
radicalizar <z→c> I. *vt* to radicalize II. *vr:* ~**se** 1. (*extremar*) to become radical 2. (*agudizarse*) to intensify
radicar <c→qu> I. *vi* 1. *fig* (*arraigar*) to take root; **el problema radica en su comportamiento** the problem lies in his/her behaviour *Brit* [*o* behavior *Am*] 2. (*estar asentado*) to reside 3. (*basarse*) ~ **en algo** to be based on sth 4. (*consistir*) ~ **en algo** to consist of sth II. *vr:* ~**se** (*establecerse*) to settle
radicheta *f Arg, Urug* (*achicoria*) chicory
radio¹ *f* RADIO, TEL 1. (*radiodifusión*) radio; **hablar por la** ~ to talk by radio; **retransmitir por** ~ to send by radio 2. (*receptor*) radio; (*radiotelefonía*) radiophone; ~ **del coche** car radio; **dirigido por** ~ radio-controlled 3. (*emisora*) radio station; ~ **pirata** pirate radio ▶~ **macuto** *inf* the grapevine
radio² *m* 1. MAT, ANAT radius; **en un** ~ **de varios kilómetros** within a radius of several kilometres 2. (*en la rueda*) spoke 3. QUÍM radium 4. (*ámbito*) range; (*esfera*) field; ~ **de acción** operational range; *fig* sphere of influence; ~ **de alcance** reach; ~ **de atracción** field of attraction; ~ **visual** visual field of vision
radioactivo, -a *adj* radioactive
radioaficionado, -a *m, f* radio ham
radiocasete *m o f* radio cassette player
radiocomunicación *f* radio communication
radiodespertador *m* radio alarm (clock)
radiodifusión *f* broadcasting
radiodifusora *f AmL* radio transmitter
radioescucha *mf v.* **radioyente**
radiofonía *f* 1. (*radiodifusión*) broadcasting 2. (*radiotelefonía*) radio-telephony
radiofónico, -a *adj* RADIO, TEL radio; **guión** ~ radio guide; **programa** ~ (*programación*)

radio schedule; (*emisión*) radio programme *Brit* [*o* program *Am*]
radiografía *f* 1. (*técnica*) radiography 2. (*placa*) radiograph, X-ray photograph
radiografiar <*1. pres:* radiografío> *vt* 1. RADIO, TEL to radiograph 2. MED to X-ray
radiólogo, -a *m, f* MED radiologist
radiopatrulla *f* patrol car
radiotaxi *m* radiocab
radiotelegrafiar <*1. pres:* radiotelegrafío> *vt* to radiotelegraph
radioterapia *f* MED radiotherapy
radioyente *mf* RADIO listener; ~ **clandestino** illegal listener
RAE *f abr de* **Real Academia Española** Spanish Royal Academy (*organization which is responsible for setting linguistic standards for Spanish*)

Since its inception in 1714, the **Real Academia Española** (**RAE**) has made the standardization and purity of the Spanish language one of its objectives.

---

raedera *f* scraper
raedura *f* 1. (*rascado*) scrape 2. (*brizna*) scraping 3. MED graze
raer *irr vt* 1. (*raspar*) to scrape 2. MED to graze 3. (*desgastar*) to wear out; (*deslucir*) to spoil
ráfaga *f* 1. (*de aire*) gust 2. (*de lluvia*) squall 3. (*de luz, inspiración*) flash 4. (*de disparos*) burst
ragú <ragús> *m* ragout
raído, -a *adj* (*deslucido*) spoilt; (*gastado*) worn-out; (*rozado*) scratched
raigambre *f* 1. BOT (*raíces*) roots *pl* 2. *fig* (*tradición*) tradition; **sin** ~ rootless; **tener** ~ to have strong roots; **mi familia es de** ~ **conservadora** my family has always been conservative
raíl *m* FERRO rail
raíz *f* 1. ANAT, BOT *t. fig* root; **echar raíces** (*persona*) to put down roots; (*costumbre*) to take root; **como si hubiera echado raíces** *fig* well-established; **tener sus raíces en un lugar** *fig* to have one's roots in a place 2. (*causa*) cause; (*origen*) origin; **a** ~ **de** because of; **tener su** ~ **en algo** to be due to sth 3. MAT, LING root; ~ **cuadrada/cúbica** square/cube root; **extraer la** ~ to calculate the root ▶**de** ~ completely; **atajar de** ~ to nip in the bud; **arrancar de** ~ to destroy
raja *f* 1. (*grieta*) crack; (*hendedura*) split 2. (*abertura*) opening; (*separación*) gap 3. *vulg* (*vulva*) cunt 4. (*rodaja*) slice
rajada *f inf* 1. *Arg* (*fuga*) flight 2. *Méx* (*cobardía*) chickening out 3. *Col* (*examen*) fail
rajadiablo(s) *m* (*inv*), *Chile* young rogue
rajante *adj Arg* (*definitivo*) definitive
rajar I. *vi* 1. *inf* (*charlar*) to chatter 2. *AmL, pey* (*hablar mal*) ~ **de alguien** to slag sb off II. *vt* 1. (*cortar*) to cut; (*abrir*) to cut open; (*hender*) to split; (*quitar*) to cut off; (*partir*) to cut up;

(*en rajas*) to slice **2.** *inf* (*apuñalar*) to knife **III.** *vr:* ~**se 1.** (*abrirse*) to split open; (*agrietarse*) to crack **2.** *inf* (*echarse atrás*) to back out **3.** *inf* (*disculparse*) to apologize **4.** (*cortarse*) to cut oneself

rajatabla a ~ (*estrictamente*) strictly; (*exactamente*) to the letter; (*a toda costa*) at all costs

raje *m* *Arg* **1.** *inf* (*huída*) flight; **al** ~ in a rush **2.** *inf* (*el despedir*) sacking, firing; **dar el** ~ **a alguien** to get rid of sb

rajo *m* *AmC* (*desgarrón*) tear; (*rotura*) rip

rajón, -ona *adj* **1.** *AmC, Méx* (*fanfarrón*) bragging **2.** *AmC* (*ostentoso*) lavish **3.** *Cuba, Méx* (*cobarde*) chicken *inf* **4.** *Méx* (*poco fiable*) unreliable

ralea *f* *pey* sort; **son todos de la misma** ~ they're all as bad as each other

ralentí *m* *sin pl* **1.** AUTO timing; **al** ~ ticking over **2.** CINE slow motion; **al** ~ in slow motion

rallador *m* grater

ralladura *f* gratings *pl;* ~ **de queso** grated cheese

rallar *vt* (*fino*) to grate; (*menos fino*) to shred

rally(e) <rallys> *m* rally

ralo, -a *adj* **1.** (*escaso*) scarce; (*árboles*) sparse; (*cabello*) thin; (*tejido*) threadbare **2.** *CSur* (*insustancial*) flimsy

rama *f* **1.** BOT, MAT (*t. de árbol*) branch; ~ **florida** flowering branch; ~**s secas** brushwood **2.** (*ámbito*) branch; ECON (*t. sector*) sector **3.** (*derivación*) branch **4.** (*parentesco*) branch; **por la** ~ **materna/paterna** on the mother's/father's side ▸**andarse por las** ~**s** (*rodeos*) to beat about the bush; **irse por las** ~**s** (*desviarse*) to go off at *Brit* [*o* on *Am*] a tangent

ramada *f* *Chile* (*puesto de feria*) festival stand

ramaje *m* **1.** (*ramas*) branches **2.** (*follaje*) foliage

ramal *m* **1.** (*cabo*) strand **2.** (*ramificación*) branch; FERRO branch line

ramalazo *m* **1.** (*trallazo*) lash; (*marca*) weal; *fig* (*de dolor*) sharp pain **2.** *inf* (*parecido*) likeness; **tener un** ~ **a su padre** to look like one's father; **tener un** ~ **de loco** to be slightly mad

rambla *f* (*paseo*) boulevard

ramera *f* *pey* whore

ramificación *f* ramification; **ramificaciones** consequences *pl*

ramificarse <c→qu> *vr* to branch out

ramillete *m* bouquet

ramo *m* **1.** (*de flores*) bunch **2.** (*de árbol*) (small) branch **3.** (*ámbito*) area; ECON (*t. sector*) sector; ~ **de la construcción** construction sector; **del** ~ appropriate **4.** REL **Domingo de Ramos** Palm Sunday

rampa *f* (*inclinación*) ramp; (*en carretera*) access road *Brit*, ramp *Am;* **en** ~ sloping

rampla *f* *Chile* (*carrito de mano*) handtruck

ramplón, -ona *adj* **1.** (*basto*) coarse; (*chapucero*) shoddy **2.** (*vulgar*) vulgar; (*chabacano*) tasteless **3.** (*simplón*) dim

rana *f* frog; ~ **de San Antonio** jumping frog;

hombre ~ frogman; **el príncipe** ~ the frog prince ▸**cuando las** ~**s críen pelo** when pigs fly; **salir** ~ **a alguien** *inf* to be a disappointment to sb

ranchera *f* *AmL* **1.** (*canción*) typical popular Mexican song **2.** (*furgoneta*) estate car *Brit*, station wagon *Am*

ranchería *f* **1.** *Col* (*chabolas*) shantytown **2.** (*barraca*) bunkhouse

ranchero, -a *m, f* **1.** (*granjero*) rancher **2.** (*colono*) settler **3.** MIL cook

rancho *m* **1.** (*comida*) food; MIL mess; *pey* (*de mala calidad*) swill; **hacer el** ~ to cook **2.** (*granja*) ranch ▸**hacer** ~ **aparte** to go one's own way

ranciarse *vr* to go rancid

rancio, -a *adj* **1.** (*grasas*) rancid **2.** (*antiguo*) ancient; *pey* (*anticuado*) old-fashioned

rancotán *adv* *AmL* (*al contado*) in cash

rango *m* **1.** (*categoría, puesto*) rank; **de primer/segundo** ~ first/second-level; **según el** ~ according to rank; **de** (**alto**) ~ high-ranking; **de** ~ **abolengo** of ancient lineage **2.** (*ordenación*) order

rangoso, -a *adj* *AmC* **1.** (*generoso*) generous **2.** (*ostentoso*) ostentatious

ranúnculo *m* buttercup

ranura *f* groove; (*muesca*) notch; (*junta*) joint; (*fisura*) slot

rapacidad *f* rapacity

rapapolvo *m* *inf* dressing down; **echar un** ~ **a alguien** to give sb a dressing down

rapar *vt* **1.** ~**se el pelo** (*afeitar*) to shave one's head; (*cortar*) to have one's hair cut very short **2.** *inf* (*mangar*) to snatch

rapaz I. *adj* **1.** (*ávido*) greedy **2.** (*expoliador*) rapacious **II.** *f* bird of prey

rapaz(a) *m(f)* kid; (*muchacho*) boy, lad *Brit;* (*niña*) girl, lass *Brit*

rape *m* **1.** ZOOL (*pescado*) monkfish **2.** *inf* (*afeitado*) quick shave; **al** ~ (*pelo*) closely cropped

rapé *m* snuff; **polvos de** ~ snuff powder

rapear *vi* MÚS to rap

rapidez *f* speed; ~ **de reflejos** quick reflexes; **con** (**gran**) ~ (very) quickly

rápido *m* **1.** (*tren*) express **2.** *pl* (*de un río*) rapids *pl*

rápido, -a *adj* **1.** (*veloz*) fast **2.** (*breve*) quick **3.** (*corriente*) running

rapiña *f* robbery; (*saqueo*) pillage

rapiñar *vt* to steal; (*saquear*) to pillage

raposo, -a *m, f* **1.** (*zorro*) fox **2.** (*astuto*) sly fox

raptar *vt* to kidnap

rapto *m* **1.** (*secuestro*) kidnapping; ~ **de un niño** child abduction **2.** (*arrebato*) fit; **en un** ~ **de celos/generosidad** in a fit of jealousy/ generosity

raptor(a) *m(f)* kidnapper

raque *adj* *Ven* scrawny

raqueta *f* **1.** DEP (*pala*) bat **2.** DEP (*tenista*) racket **3.** (*para nieve*) snowshoe **4.** (*del croupier*) rake

raquítico, -a *adj* **1.** MED suffering from rickets **2.** *inf* (*enclenque*) sickly **3.** (*débil*) weak

raquitismo *m sin pl* MED rickets *pl*

raramente *adv* **1.** (*casi nunca*) rarely, seldom **2.** (*extrañamente*) strangely

rareza *f* **1.** (*cualidad*) rarity **2.** (*curiosidad*) strangeness **3.** (*peculiaridad*) peculiarity; (*manía*) eccentricity; **tener sus ~s** (*ser caprichoso*) to be a bit odd

rarífico, -a *adj Chile* implausible

raro, -a *adj* **1.** (*extraño, inesperado*) strange; ¡(qué) **cosa más rara!** how strange! **2.** (*inusual*) unusual; (*poco común*) rare; **rara vez** rarely; **raras personas** few people; **no es ~ que...** +*subj* it's not surprising that ... **3.** FÍS, QUÍM rarefied; **gases ~s** rarefied gases

ras *m* level; **a(l) ~ de** on a level with; **a ~ de agua** at water level; **a ~ de tierra** at ground level; **volar a ~ de suelo** to hedgehop; **al ~** level

rasante **I.** *adj* close **II.** *f* slope; **cambio de ~** brow of a hill

rasar **I.** *vt* **1.** (*igualar*) to level **2.** (*rozar*) to skim **3.** (*arrasar*) to raze **II.** *vr:* ~**se** (*cielo*) to clear

rasca *f* **1.** *inf* (*frío*) cold; ¡vaya ~ que hace! it's freezing! **2.** *AmL* (*mona*) drunkenness; **pegarse una ~** to get plastered

rascacielos *m inv* skyscraper

rascar <c→qu> **I.** *vt* **1.** (*con las uñas*) to scratch **2.** (*raspar*) to scrape **3.** *irón, inf* (*instrumento*) ~ **la guitarra** to bash away at the guitar; ~ **el violín** to scrape away on the violin **II.** *vr:* ~**se** **1.** (*con las uñas*) to scratch **2.** *AmS* (*achisparse*) to get tipsy

rascón, -ona *adj Méx* (*pendenciero*) troublemaker

rascuache *adj Méx: fam* **1.** (*miserable, pobre*) wretched **2.** (*de baja calidad*) cheap

rasgadura *f* tear, rip

rasgar <g→gu> **I.** *vt* **1.** (*romper por un lado*) to tear; (*en dos*) to tear in two; (*en pedazos*) to tear to pieces; (*abrir*) to tear open; **ojos rasgados** almond [*o* slanting] eyes **2.** (*cortar*) to cut **II.** *vr:* ~**se** **1.** (*desgarrarse*) to tear **2.** *AmL, vulg* (*diñarla*) to kick the bucket

rasgo *m* **1.** (*del rostro*) feature; (*del carácter*) trait **2.** (*acción*) deed; **un ~ de generosidad** a fit of generosity **3.** (*trazo*) stroke; **a grandes ~s** in outline, in general

rasgón *m* tear

rasguear **I.** *vi* (*en la escritura*) to write with a flourish **II.** *vt* MÚS to strum

rasguñar **I.** *vt* **1.** (*arañar*) to scratch; (*herir*) to wound; (*cortar*) to cut **2.** ARTE to sketch **II.** *vr:* ~**se** (*arañarse*) to scratch oneself; (*herirse*) to wound oneself; (*cortarse*) to cut oneself; ~**se con algo** (*excoriarse*) to graze oneself against sth

rasguño *m* (*arañazo*) scratch; (*rasponazo*) scrape; (*excoriación*) chafing; **sin un ~** *fig* unscathed

raso *m* satin

raso, -a *adj* **1.** (*liso*) smooth; (*llano*) flat **2.** (*cielo*) clear; **al ~** in the open air **3.** (*al borde*) level; **una cucharada rasa** a level spoonful

raspa *f* **1.** (*del pescado*) backbone **2.** (*del cereal*) stalk **3.** *AmL* (*ratero*) pickpocket; (*ramera*) prostitute **4.** *fig, inf* (*delgado*) beanstalk

raspada *f Méx, PRico* (*reprimenda*) scolding

raspado *m* **1.** TÉC scraping; (*limado*) filing **2.** MED dilatation and curettage, D and C

raspador *m* **1.** (*instrumento*) scraper; (*lima*) file; MED curette **2.** (*de fósforos*) friction strip

raspadura *f* **1.** (*raspado*) scratching; (*con espátula*) scraping **2.** (*brizna*) scraping

raspaje *m Arg* MED curettage

raspar **I.** *vi* (*ser rasposo*) to be rough; (*en sorteos*) to scratch **II.** *vt* **1.** (*rascar*) to scratch **2.** MED to scrape **3.** (*rozar*) to brush **4.** *AmL, inf* (*mangar*) to swipe **5.** *AmS, inf* (*abroncar*) to yell at **III.** *vr:* ~**se** to scratch oneself

raspón *m* **1.** (*arañazo*) scratch; (*excoriación*) chafing; (*rasguño*) scrape; (*de bala*) graze **2.** *Col* (*sombrero*) (large) straw hat

rasponazo *m* scratch

rasposo, -a *adj* rough

rasquetear *vt* **1.** *AmL* (*almohazar*) to groom **2.** *Arg* (*raer*) to scrape **3.** *AmS* (*caballo*) to curry

rasquiña *f AmL* (*comezón*) itch

rastra *f* (*rastrillo*) rake ►**a ~s** unwillingly; **ir a ~s** *inf* to drag along behind; **llevar a alguien a ~s** to drag sb along

rastrear **I.** *vt* **1.** (*seguir*) to track **2.** (*investigar*) ~ **algo** to make inquiries about sth **3.** (*llevar arrastrando*) to drag **4.** (*registrar*) to go through **5.** (*minas*) to sweep **II.** *vi* **1.** (*investigar*) to make inquiries **2.** (*rastrillar*) to rake

rastrero, -a *adj* **1.** (*por el suelo*) creeping; **planta rastrera** creeper **2.** *pey* (*servil*) cringing **3.** *pey* (*despreciable*) despicable; (*canallesco*) base

rastrillar *vt* to rake

rastrillo *m* **1.** (*herramienta*) rake **2.** (*mercadillo*) flea market

rastro *m* **1.** (*indicio, pista*) trace; **ni ~** not a trace; **sin dejar (ni) ~** without trace; **seguir el ~ a [o de] alguien** to follow sb's trail **2.** (*mercadillo*) flea market **3.** (*herramienta*) rake

rastrojo *m* (*de paja*) stubble

rasurar **I.** *vt* to shave **II.** *vr:* ~**se** to shave

rata¹ *f* ZOOL rat; ~ **de alcantarilla** sewer rat; **escabullirse como una ~** to run and hide ►~ **de biblioteca** bookworm; **más pobre que las ~s** as poor as a church mouse; **hacerse la ~** *AmL* to play truant

rata² *mf* **1.** *inf* (*rácano*) miser **2.** (*descuidero*) pickpocket

ratear **I.** *vi* (*gatear*) to crawl **II.** *vt* **1.** *inf* (*mangar*) to nick **2.** *inf* (*racanear*) ~ **algo** to be stingy with sth **3.** (*prorratear*) to share out

ratería *f* **1.** (*hurto*) theft **2.** (*racanería*) stinginess

ratero, -a *m, f* petty thief

raticida *m* rat poison

ratificación *f* 1.JUR, POL ratification 2.(*confirmación*) confirmation

ratificar <c→qu> I. *vt* 1.JUR, POL to ratify 2.(*confirmar*) to confirm II. *vr:* ~se 1.JUR, POL to be ratified 2.(*reafirmarse*) ~se en algo to reaffirm sth

rato *m* while; (*momento*) moment; **a** ~s from time to time; **a cada** ~ all the time; **al (poco)** ~ shortly after; **de** ~ **en** ~ from time to time; **en un** ~ **perdido** in a quiet moment; **todo el** ~ the whole time; **un buen** ~ for quite a time; **pasar un buen/mal** ~ to have a good/bad time; **hacer pasar un mal** ~ **a alguien** to give sb a rough [*o* hard] time; **pasar el** ~ to pass the time ▶ **¡hasta** otro ~! see you later!; **ser un** ~ tonto *inf* to be a bit stupid; **me** gusta **un** ~ *inf* I really like it; **aún** hay para ~ there's still plenty left to do; **tener para** ~ to have lots to do; **un** ~ (**largo**) *inf* a lot

ratón *m* mouse; ~ **de campo** fieldmouse; ~ (**electrónico**) INFOR mouse ▶ ~ **de** biblioteca bookworm

ratonera *f* 1.(*trampa*) mousetrap; *fig* trap; **estar en una** ~ *fig* to be caught in a trap; **caer en la** ~ *fig* to fall into the trap 2.(*agujero*) mousehole

ratonero *m* buzzard

raudal *m* torrent; ~ **de palabras** flood of words ▶ **a** ~es in floods; **por la ventana entra la luz a** ~es the light came flooding through the window

raudo, -a *adj* rapid

raya *f* 1.(*línea*) line; (*guión*) dash; **a** ~s (*papel*) lined; (*jersey*) striped; **tres en** ~ (*juego*) noughts and crosses *Brit,* tic(k)-tac(k)-toe *Am* 2.(*franja*) edge; (*cortafuegos*) firebreak 3.(*del pelo*) parting *Brit,* part *Am;* ~ **al lado/en medio** side/centre parting *Brit,* side/center part *Am;* **hacer la** ~ to comb one's hair into a parting *Brit,* to part one's hair *Am* 4.ZOOL ray, skate 5.(*doblez*) fold 6.(*cocaína*) line ▶ **pasar(se) de la** ~ to go too far; **tener a alguien a** ~ to keep sb in place [*o* under control]

rayado *m* 1.(*líneas*) lines 2.(*plumeado*) hatching 3.(*rayajo*) scrawl

rayano, -a *adj* ~ **en algo** bordering on sth

rayar I. *vi* 1.(*lindar*) ~ **con algo** to border on sth 2.(*asemejarse*) ~ **en algo** to come close to sth 3.(*amanecer*) to break; **está rayando el alba** dawn is breaking; **al** ~ **el día** at the break of day II. *vt* 1.(*marcar con rayas*) to line; (*plumear*) to hatch 2.(*tachar*) to cross out 3.(*arañar*) to scratch 4.(*grabar*) to engrave III. *vr:* ~se to get scratched

rayo *m* 1.(*de luz*) ray; ~ **de luna** shaft of moonlight 2.(*radiación*) ~s infrarrojos infrared rays; ~s X X-rays; ~ **láser** laser beam; **emitir** ~s to give out radiation 3.(*relámpago*) (bolt of)lightning; **ha caído un** ~ **en la torre** the tower was hit by lightning 4.(*infortunio*) (stroke of) bad luck 5.(*radio*) spoke ▶ ~s (y

centellas)! good heavens!; **echar** ~s **y** centellas to be furious; **¡mal** ~ **te parta!** *inf* go to hell!; **como** tocado **por el** ~ as if struck by lightning; **que me** parta **un** ~ **si no es verdad** *inf* I swear it on my mother's grave; **saber a** ~s to taste awful; **como un** ~ in a flash

raza *f* 1.(*casta*) race; (*estirpe*) strain; **de** ~ (*perro*) pedigree; (*caballo*) thoroughbred; **de** ~ **blanca/negra** white/black 2.(*temperamento*) character; **de (pura)** ~ true

razón I. *f* 1.(*discernimiento*) reason; (*entendimiento*) understanding; **puesto en** ~ reasonable; (**no**) **atender a razones** (not) to listen to reason; **privar de la** ~ **a alguien** to drive sb out of his/her mind 2.(*argumento*) argument; (*razonamiento*) reasoning; **ponerse a razones con alguien** to argue with sb; **venirse a razones con alguien** to reach an agreement with sb 3.(*motivo*) reason; (*justificación*) justification; ~ **de Estado** reasons *pl* of State; ~ **de ser** raison d'être; **de más para** +*infin,* ~ **de más para que** +*subj* more than enough reason to +*infin;* **la** ~ **por la que...** the reason why ...; **fuera de** ~ unreasonable; **por** ~ **de algo** due to sth; **por razones de seguridad** for security reasons; **por una u otra** ~ for one reason or another; **tener razones para...** +*infin* to have cause to ... 4.(*acierto*) right; **la** ~ **de la fuerza** the doctrine that might is right; **¡con (mucha)** ~! quite rightly!; **sin** ~ without justification; **cargarse de** ~ to be convinced that one is right; **dar la** ~ **a alguien** to agree with sb; **llevar la** ~ to be right; **tener (mucha)** ~ to be (absolutely) right; **en eso (no) tienes** ~ you are (not) right about that; **me asiste la** ~ most people would agree with me 5.(*información*) information; (*recado*) message; ~ **aquí** inquire here; **dar** ~ **de alguien** to give information about sb; **dar** ~ **de sí** to report; *fig* to give a good account of oneself; **mandar** ~ **a alguien de algo** to send sb a message about sb; **pedir** ~ **de alguien** to ask sb for information 6.MAT (*proporción*) ratio; **a** ~ **de tres por persona** at a rate of three per person; **a** ~ **del 10%** at 10%; **a** ~ **de 2 euros el kilo** at 2 euros per kilo 7.JUR ~ **social** trade name ▶ **entrar en** ~ to come to one's senses; **hacer perder la** ~ **a alguien** to make sb lose control; **meter a alguien en** ~ to make sb see sense; **perder la** ~ to take leave of one's senses II. *prep* **en** ~ **de** (*en cuanto a*) as far as; (*a causa de*) because of

razonable *adj* 1.(*sensato*) reasonable 2.(*justo*) fair; (*adecuado*) sufficient

razonamiento *m* 1.(*pensamientos, argumentación*) reasoning; (*reflexión*) reflection; **tus** ~s **no son convincentes** your argument is not convincing 2.(*conversación*) discussion

razonar I. *vi* 1.(*pensar, deducir, argumentar*) to reason 2.(*juzgar*) to judge 3.(*reflexionar*) to reflect 4.(*conversar*) to discuss; **es inútil tratar de** ~ **con él** there's no point trying to reason with him II. *vt* 1.(*exponer*) to show

2. (*fundamentar*) to establish

RDSI *f abr de* **Red Digital de Servicios Integrados** ISDN

re *m* MÚS (*de la escala diatónica*) D; (*de la solfa*) re; ~ **bemol** D flat; ~ **sostenido** D sharp

reabrir *irr como abrir vt t.* JUR to reopen

reacción *f* reaction; ~ **en cadena** chain reaction; ~ **excesiva** overreaction

reaccionar *vi* **1.** (*ante un estímulo*) ~ **a** [*o* ante] **algo** to react to sth **2.** (*responder*) ~ **a algo** to respond to sth **3.** (*repercutir*) ~ **en** [*o* sobre] **algo** to have repercussions on sth **4.** (*sobreponerse*) ~ **a algo** to overcome sth **5.** (*entrar en calor*) to get warm

reaccionario, -a *adj, m, f* reactionary

reacio, -a *adj* reluctant; **el pintor era** ~ **a mostrarse en público** the painter was reluctant to show his work; **es** ~ **a las fiestas** he/she is not very fond of parties

reactivar *vt* to reactivate; ECON to revive, to boost

reactivo *m* QUÍM reagent; (*indicador*) indicator; *fig* stimulant

reactor *m* **1.** (*motor*) jet engine **2.** (*avión*) jet **3.** FÍS reactor

readaptación *f* **1.** (*adaptación*) readaptation **2.** (*reintegración*) ~ **a algo** reintegration into sth; ~ **profesional** professional retraining

readaptar I. *vt* **1.** (*volver a adaptar*) to readapt **2.** (*reintegrar*) ~ **a algo** to reintegrate into sth **3.** (*profesión*) to retrain **II.** *vr:* ~**se 1.** (*adaptarse*) to readapt **2.** (*reintegrarse*) ~**se a algo** to reintegrate into sth

readmisión *f* readmission; (*de despedidos*) re-employment

readmitir *vt* to readmit; (*despedidos*) to re-employ

reafirmar I. *vt* **1.** (*apoyar*) to reaffirm **2.** (*poner firme*) to make firm; (*la piel*) to tone up **3.** (*insistir*) ~ **algo** to insist on sth **II.** *vr:* ~**se 1.** (*confirmarse*) to reaffirm **2.** (*insistir*) ~**se en algo** to insist on sth

reagrupar I. *vt* to regroup; (*redistribuir*) to redistribute **II.** *vr:* ~**se** to regroup

reajustar *vt* **1.** (*adaptar*) to readjust **2.** (*reestructurar*) to restructure **3.** (*reorganizar*) to reorganize **4.** TÉC, ECON to adjust

reajuste *m* **1.** (*adaptación*) readjustment **2.** (*reestructuración*) restructuring **3.** (*reorganización*) reorganization; , ~ **de gobierno** cabinet reshuffle **4.** TÉC, ECON adjustment; ~ **salarial** wage settlement

real I. *adj* **1.** (*verdadero*) real; **basado en hechos** ~**es** based on a true story; **no me da la** ~ **gana** *inf* I don't feel like it **2.** (*del rey*) royal; **Alteza** ~ Royal Highness; **palacio** ~ royal palace **3.** (*espléndido*) splendid **II.** *m* **1.** (*dinero*) real (*old coin worth quarter of a peseta*); **estar sin un** ~ *inf* to be pennniless **2.** (*de la feria*) fairground

realce *m* **1.** (*relieve*) relief **2.** (*esplendor*) splendour *Brit,* splendor *Am;* (*acento*) accent;

dar ~ to highlight

realengo, -a *adj* **1.** HIST Crown **2.** *AmL* (*sin amo*) ownerless; (*vagabundo*) stray

realeza *f* **1.** (*dignidad*) royalty **2.** (*grandeza*) magnificence; (*boato*) pomp

realidad *f* reality; (*verdad*) truth; ~ **virtual** virtual reality; **ajeno a la** ~ far removed from reality; **hacer** ~ to make come true; **hacerse** ~ to happen; (*cumplirse*) to come true; **en** ~ in fact

realismo *m sin pl* **1.** ARTE, LIT, CINE realism **2.** POL royalism

realista I. *adj* **1.** ARTE, LIT, CINE realistic **2.** POL royalist **II.** *mf* **1.** ARTE, LIT, FILOS, CINE realist **2.** POL royalist

realizable *adj* **1.** (*practicable*) practical; (*factible*) feasible **2.** ECON saleable; **bienes** ~**s** saleable goods

realización *f* **1.** (*ejecución*) execution **2.** (*materialización*) realization; (*cumplimiento*) fulfilment *Brit,* fulfillment *Am* **3.** (*organización*) organization **4.** ECON realization; ~ **de un pedido** fulfilment *Brit* [*o* fulfillment *Am*] of an order; ~ **de plusvalías** realization of capital gains **5.** CINE production

realizador(a) *m(f)* CINE, TV producer

realizar <z→c> **I.** *vt* **1.** (*efectuar*) to carry out; (*hacer*) to make **2.** (*hacer realidad*) to make real; (*sueños*) to fulfil *Brit,* to fulfill *Am* **3.** ECON to realize; (*ganancia, aportaciones*) to take **4.** CINE, TV to produce **5.** *AmL* (*notar*) to notice **II.** *vr:* ~**se 1.** (*desarrollarse*) to be carried out **2.** (*materializarse*) to happen; (*hacerse realidad*) to come true; (*cumplirse*) to be fulfilled

realmente *adv* (*en efecto, verdaderamente*) really; (*de hecho*) in fact

realquilar *vt* to sublet; **vivir en una vivienda realquilada** to live in a sublet property

realzar <z→c> *vt* **1.** (*labrar*) to emboss **2.** (*acentuar*) to bring out **3.** (*subrayar*) to highlight

reamargo, -a *adj AmL* very bitter

reamigo, -a *m, f AmL* very close friend; **son** ~**s del director** they are very close friends of the director

reanimación *f* **1.** revival **2.** MED resuscitation; (*posoperatorio*) reanimation; **unidad de** ~ intensive care unit

reanimar I. *vt* **1.** (*reavivar*) to revive **2.** (*reactivar*) to reactivate **3.** (*animar*) to liven up **4.** MED to resuscitate **II.** *vr:* ~**se 1.** (*recuperar el conocimiento*) to regain consciousness **2.** (*restablecerse*) to become re-established **3.** (*animarse*) to liven up

reanudar *vt* to resume

reaparición *f* reappearance; TEAT, CINE comeback

reapertura *f* reopening

reata *f* **1.** (*correa*) rope (*used to keep animals in file*); (*animales*) packtrain; **una** ~ **de mulos** a pack of mules **2.** *AmL* (*de flores*) border ▸**de** ~ (*sucesivamente*) one after the

other; (*en hilera*) in single file
reavivar *vt, vr:* ~**se** to revive
rebaba *f* (rough) edge; (*metales*) burr
rebaja *f* **1.** (*oferta*) sale; ~**s de verano** summer sales; **estar de** ~**s** to have a sale on **2.** (*descuento*) discount; (*reducción*) reduction
rebajar I. *vt* **1.** (*abaratar*) to reduce **2.** (*humillar*) to put down **3.** *t.* FOTO (*mitigar*) to soften; (*debilitar*) to weaken; (*disminuir*) to lessen **4.** (*una bebida*) to dilute **5.** (*dispensar*) to let off **6.** (*gastar*) to wear down II. *vr:* ~**se 1.** (*humillarse*) to be humiliated **2.** (*condescender*) to lower oneself **3.** (*dispensarse*) to be let off
rebanada *f* slice
rebanar *vt* **1.** (*hacer rebanadas*) to slice **2.** (*partir*) to cut up
rebañar *vt* **1.** (*apurar*) to finish off; ~ **el plato** to wipe the plate clean **2.** *pey* (*recoger*) to mop up
rebaño *m t. fig* herd
rebasar *vt* **1.** (*sobrepasar*) to exceed; MIL to overrun; ~ **el límite** *fig* to overstep the mark; **esto rebasa los límites de mi paciencia** this is trying my patience **2.** (*exceder*) ~ **en algo** to excel at sth
rebatir *vt* **1.** (*discutir*) to contest; (*refutar*) to refute; (*rechazar*) to reject **2.** (*repeler*) to repel **3.** (*batir*) to beat **4.** (*abatir*) to knock down
rebato *m* alarm; **tocar a** ~ to sound the alarm
rebeca *f* cardigan
rebeco *m* chamois
rebelarse *vr* to rebel; (*oponerse*) to be opposed
rebelde I. *adj* **1.** (*indócil*) unruly; (*levantisco*) restless **2.** (*insurrecto*) rebellious **3.** (*persistente*) persistent **4.** (*difícil*) troublesome **5.** JUR defaulting II. *mf* **1.** rebel **2.** JUR defaulter
rebeldía *f* **1.** (*cualidad*) rebelliousness **2.** (*oposición*) opposition **3.** *t.* MIL (*insubordinación*) insubordination **4.** JUR default; **declarar a alguien en** ~ to declare sb to be in default; **juzgar en** ~ to judge by default
rebelión *f* rebellion
rebenque *m* CSur riding crop
reblandecer *irr como crecer vt, vr:* ~**se** to soften
rebobinar *vt* (*retroceder*) to rewind
rebosante *adj* overflowing; ~ **de agua/alegría** brimming with water/hapiness; ~ **de salud** glowing with health
rebosar *vi* **1.** (*desbordar*) to overflow **2.** (*tener mucho*) ~ **de** to be brimming with; **le rebosa el dinero** he/she is rolling in money; **le rebosa la soberbia** he/she is very arrogant; **la gota que hizo** ~ **el vaso** the final straw, the straw which broke the camel's back **3.** (*estar lleno*) to be full to the brim; (*lleno*) **a** ~ full to the brim **4.** (*abundar*) to abound
rebotar I. *vi* **1.** (*botar*) to bounce; (*bala*) to

ricochet **2.** (*chocar*) ~ **en** [*o* contra] algo to bump into sth; **salir rebotado** to bounce back; *fig* to shoot off II. *vt* **1.** (*botar*) to bounce **2.** *inf* (*enfadar*) to anger III. *vr:* ~**se 1.** (*vino*) to turn **2.** *inf* (*enfadarse*) to get angry
rebote *m* (*bote*) bounce; DEP rebound; (*golpe*) blow; (*de bala*) ricochet; **de** ~ on the rebound **2.** *inf* (*enfado*) **coger un** ~ to have a fit
rebozar <z→c> I. *vt* **1.** GASTR (*con pan rallado*) to coat with breadcrumbs; (*con masa*) to coat with batter **2.** (*envolver*) to cover II. *vr:* ~**se** to cover one's face
rebozo *m* **1.** (*velo*) ≈ cloak **2.** (*pretexto*) pretext; **sin** ~ openly
rebujo *m* ball; (*trapos*) bundle; **hacer un** ~ **con la ropa** to gather clothes into a bundle
rebullir <3. *pret:* rebulló> *vi, vr:* ~**se** to stir; **sin** ~**se** very quietly
rebumbio *m Méx* (*alboroto*) commotion
rebuscado, -a *adj* pedantic; (*palabras*) obscure; (*estilo*) contrived
rebuscar <c→qu> I. *vi* to search thoroughly II. *vt* (*buscar*) to search for III. *vr* **rebuscárselas** CSur (*defenderse*) to get by
rebuznar *vi* (*burro*) to bray
rebuzno *m* bray
recabar *vt* **1.** (*obtener*) to manage to obtain **2.** (*pedir*) to ask for
recadero, -a *m, f* messenger
recado *m* **1.** (*mensaje*) message; **dar un** ~ **a alguien** to give a message to sb; **¿puedes darle el siguiente** ~**?** could you give him/her this message? **2.** (*encargo*) errand; **hacer** ~**s** to do errands
recaer *irr como caer vi* **1.** (*enfermedad*) to relapse **2.** (*delito*) to reoffend; ~ **en el mismo error una y otra vez** to repeat the same mistake again and again; ~ **en la bebida** to start drinking again **3.** (*culpa*) to fall; ~ **en alguien** (*herencia*) to fall to sb
recaída *f* relapse
recalar I. *vi* **1.** NÁUT to put in **2.** (*persona*) to appear II. *vt* to soak III. *vr:* ~**se** to get soaked
recalcar <c→qu> *vt* **1.** (*palabras*) to stress **2.** (*apretar*) to squeeze **3.** (*llenar*) to fill; ~ **la cuba con vino** to fill the barrel with wine
recalcificar *vt* MED to calcify
recalcitrante *adj* recalcitrant
recalentado *m Méx, inf* leftovers *pl*
recalentar <e→ie> I. *vt* **1.** (*comida*) to reheat **2.** (*aparato*) to overheat II. *vr:* ~**se** (*motor*) to overheat
recámara *f* **1.** (*para ropa*) dressing room **2.** (*arma*) chamber
recamarera *f Méx* chambermaid
recambiar *vt* **1.** (*sustituir*) to substitute **2.** (*intercambiar*) to exchange
recambio *m* (*repuesto*) spare (part); (*envase*) refill
recapacitar I. *vt* to consider II. *vi* to think

things over

recapitulación *f* summary, summing up

recapitular *vt* to summarize, to sum up

recargado, -a *adj* (*exagerado*) overelaborate; (*lenguaje*) overblown

recargar <g→gu> *vt* 1. (*pila*) to recharge 2. (*decorar*) to overdecorate; **el vestido recargado de lazos y botones no se vendió** nobody bought the dress which was dripping with laces and buttons 3. (*impuesto*) to increase 4. (*carga*) to overload; ~ **de trabajo** to overload with work

recargo *m* (*tasas*) increase; (*sobreprecio*) surcharge; **llamada sin** ~ freephone call *Brit,* tollfree call *Am*

recatado, -a *adj* 1. (*decoroso*) decent; (*modesto*) modest 2. (*cauto*) cautious

recato *m* 1. (*decoro*) decency 2. (*cautela*) caution; (*pudor*) modesty

recauchutar *vt* AUTO (*llanta*) to retread

recaudación *f* 1. (*cobro*) collection; (*cantidad*) takings *pl;* ~ **diaria** daily takings 2. (*de impuestos*) collection; (*cantidad*) receipts *pl*

recaudar *vt* (*impuestos, dinero*) to collect

recaudería *f Méx* (*especiería*) grocery store

recaudo *m* 1. (*ganancia*) collection 2. JUR (*seguridad*) surety 3. (*cuidado*) care; (*precaución*) precaution ►**estar a buen** ~ to be safe and sound; **poner algo a buen** ~ to put sth in safe keeping

recelar I. *vt* (*temer*) to fear II. *vi* to be suspicious; **recelo de mi secretaria** I don't trust my secretary

recelo *m* mistrust; **mirar algo con** ~ to be suspicious of sth

receloso, -a *adj* distrustful; **estar** ~ **de alguien** to be suspicious of sb; **ponerse** ~ to become suspicious; **poner** ~ **a alguien** to cause sb to be suspicious

recensión *f* PREN review

recepción *f* reception

recepcionista *mf* receptionist

receptáculo *m* (*cavidad*) receptacle

receptividad *f* receptiveness; MED susceptibility

receptivo, -a *adj* 1. (*sensible*) receptive 2. MED susceptible

receptor *m* (*radio, teléfono*) receiver; ~ **de televisión** TV set

receptor(a) *m(f)* recipient

recesión *f* ECON recession

receso *m AmL* (*vacaciones*) recess

receta *f* 1. GASTR recipe; **¿cuál es tu** ~ **para ser feliz?** *fig* what's your formula for happiness? 2. MED prescription; **con** ~ **médica** on prescription; **venta con** ~ available on prescription

recetar *vt* MED to prescribe

recetario *m* 1. GASTR cookery book *Brit,* cookbook 2. MED (*libro*) pharmacopoeia; (*talonario*) prescription pad; (*de un enfermo*) prescription record

rechazar <z→c> *vt* 1. (*no aceptar*) to reject 2. (*denegar, no tolerar*) to refuse; ~ **de plano las acusaciones** to flatly deny the accusations 3. (*ataque*) to repel, to push back

rechazo *m* rejection; (*denegación*) refusal

rechiflar I. *vt* to whistle at II. *vr:* ~**se de** to make fun of

rechinamiento *m* squeaking; ~ **de dientes** grinding of teeth

rechinar I. *vi* to squeak; (*puerta*) to creak II. *vt* ~ **los dientes** to grind one's teeth

rechistar I. *vi* to grumble; **sin** ~ without complaining

rechoncho, -a *adj inf* tubby

rechupete de ~ delicious

recibidor *m* 1. (*hotel, oficinas*) lobby 2. (*casa*) entry (hall) 3. (*persona*) recipient

recibimiento *m* 1. (*acogida*) welcome; **le dispensaron un** ~ **multitudinario** they gave him/her a tumultuous welcome 2. (*recibidor*) lobby

recibir I. *vt* 1. (*tomar*) to receive 2. (*personas*) to welcome 3. (*aceptar*) to accept II. *vi* (*médico*) to see patients; (*ministro*) to see people III. *vr* ~**se de algo** *AmL* to graduate as sth; (*médico, abogado*) to qualify as sth

recibo *m* 1. (*en tienda*) receipt; (*de la luz, del agua*) bill; ~ **de entrega** delivery note 2. (*de una carta*) receipt; **acusar** ~ to acknowledge receipt 3. (*recibidor*) lobby ►**si llaman, abre tú porque yo no estoy de** ~ if they call, can you go to the door? I don't want to see anybody; **ser de** ~ (*estar de moda*) to be in; (*ser apropiado*) to be acceptable

reciclaje *m* 1. (*de materiales*) recycling 2. ENS ~ **profesional** *fig* professional retraining; **curso de** ~ refresher course

reciclar *vt* 1. TÉC to recycle 2. (*formación*) to retrain

recién *adv* 1. (*acabado de*) recently; ~ **cocido/pintado** freshly cooked/painted; **los** ~ **casados** the newly weds; **el** ~ **nacido** the newborn baby 2. *AmL* (*en cuanto*) as soon as

reciente *adj* 1. (*nuevo*) new; (*fresco*) fresh 2. (*que acaba de suceder*) recent; **un libro de** ~ **publicación** a book which has recently been published

recientemente *adv* recently

recinto *m* enclosure; ~ **fortificado** fortified enclosure; ~ **universitario** university campus; ~ **ferial** fairgrounds *pl*

recio, -a I. *adj* 1. (*fuerte*) strong 2. (*rígido*) stiff; **en lo más** ~ **del invierno** in the depths of winter II. *adv* (*hablar*) loudly; (*llover*) heavily

recipiente *m* container; (*de vidrio, barro*) vessel

reciprocidad *f* reciprocity

recíproco, -a *adj* reciprocal; **...y a la recíproca ...** and vice versa

recital *m* MÚS concert, recital; LIT reading; *fig* exhibition

recitar *vt* to recite; ~ **maquinalmente el menú** to recite the menu from memory

reclamación *f* **1.**(*recurso*) protest; (*queja*) complaint **2.**(*exigencia*) claim; (*de deuda*) demand

reclamar **I.** *vi* **1.**(*protestar*) to protest **2.**(*quejarse*) ~ **por algo** to complain about sth **II.** *vt* (*pedir*) to claim; (*una deuda*) to demand; ~ **daños** to sue for damages; **nos reclaman el dinero que nos prestaron** they want us to repay the money which they lent us; **el terrorista es reclamado por la justicia sueca a Italia** the Swedish courts have asked Italy to hand over the terrorist; **España reclama Gibraltar** Spain claims sovereignty over Gibraltar

reclame *m Arg, Urug* advertisement

reclamo *m* **1.**(*caza, utensilio*) decoy; (*grito*) decoy call; **acudir al** ~ to answer the call **2.** COM advert(isement)

reclinable *adj* reclining; **asiento** ~ reclining chair

reclinar **I.** *vt* to lean; (*hacia atrás*) to lean back; **reclinó su cabeza contra** [*o* **sobre**] **mis hombros** he/she rested his/her head on my shoulders **II.** *vr:* ~**se** (*inclinarse*) to lean; (*apoyarse*) to rest

recluir *irr como huir* **I.** *vt* (*cárcel*) to imprison; (*hospital*) to confine **II.** *vr:* ~**se** to shut oneself away

reclusión *f* **1.** JUR imprisonment **2.**(*aislamiento*) seclusion

recluso, -a **I.** *adj* (*preso*) imprisoned; **la población reclusa vive en condiciones inhumanas** the prisoners live in inhuman conditions **II.** *m, f* prisoner

recluta *mf* (*voluntario*) recruit; (*obligado*) conscript, draftee *Am*

reclutamiento *m* recruiting

reclutar *vt* MIL to recruit; (*obligar*) to conscript, to draft *Am*

recobrar **I.** *vt* to recover; ~ **las fuerzas** to regain one's strength; ~ **las pérdidas** to make good one's losses; ~ **el sentido** to regain consciousness; ~ **la vista** to regain one's sight; ~ **las ganas de vivir** to recover one's enthusiasm for life **II.** *vr:* ~**se** to recover

recodo *m* (*río*) bend

recogedor *m* dustpan

recogepelotas *mf inv* DEP (*chico*) ballboy; (*chica*) ballgirl

recoger <g→j> **I.** *vt* **1.**(*buscar*) to collect; **te voy a** ~ **a la estación** I'll meet you at the station; **recogen las cartas a las ocho** they collect the post at eight o'clock *Brit,* they pick up the mail at eight *Am* **2.**(*coger*) to collect; (*ordenar*) to organize; (*guardar*) to keep; ~ **del suelo** to pick up from the floor; **¡es hora de** ~**!** let's call it a day! **3.**(*juntar*) to gather together **4.**(*cosecha*) to gather; ~ **el fruto de su trabajo** to reap the fruits of one's labour *Brit* [*o* labor *Am*] **5.**(*acoger*) to take in **6.**(*arremangar: vestido*) to lift up; (*pantalón*) to roll up

7.(*cabello*) to gather up **8.**(*enrollar: velas*) to take in; (*cortinas*) to roll up **II.** *vr:* ~**se** **1.**(*a casa*) to go home; (*a la cama*) to go to bed **2.** REL to withdraw

recogida *f* collection; ~ **de basuras** rubbish collection *Brit,* garbage collection *Am;* ~ **de beneficios** FIN profit taking; ~ **del correo** mail collection; ~ **de equipajes** AVIAT baggage reclaim *Brit,* baggage claim *Am*

recogido, -a *adj* **1.**(*acogedor*) welcoming **2.**(*retirado*) secluded

recolección *f* AGR harvest; (*periodo*) harvest time

recolectar *vt* **1.**(*cosas*) to gather **2.**(*frutos*) to harvest

recomendable *adj* recommendable

recomendación *f* recommendation; **con la ayuda de tu** ~ with the help of your recommendation; **por** ~ **de mi médico** on my doctor's advice; **al ser hijo del alcalde tiene muchas recomendaciones** being the mayor's son he has lots of contacts

recomendado, -a **I.** *adj* (*precio*) recommended; **precio de venta al público** ~ recommended retail price **II.** *m, f* person who has obtained a job by means of contacts

recomendar <e→ie> *vt* to advise; **nos recomendó no salir de casa** he/she advised us not to leave the house

recomenzar *irr como empezar vt* ~ **a** to begin again +*infin*

recompensa *f* reward; **ofrecer una** ~ **de 100 dólares por algo** to offer a reward of 100 dollars for sth; **¿es ésta la** ~ **a todos mis esfuerzos?** is this what I get for all my efforts?; **en** ~ as a reward

recompensar *vt* **1.**(*a alguien, un servicio*) ~ **por** [*o* **de**] **algo** to reward for sth **2.**(*de un daño*) to compensate; **fue recompensado por sus gastos** his/her expenses were paid

recomponer *irr como poner vt* (*reparar*) to repair, to put back together *inf;* (*reconstruir*) to rebuild

reconcentrar **I.** *vt* ~ **algo en algo** to concentrate sth on sth **II.** *vr* ~**se en algo** to concentrate on sth

reconciliación *f* reconciliation; **darse la mano en señal de** ~ to shake hands as a sign of reconciliation

reconciliar **I.** *vt* to reconcile **II.** *vr:* ~**se** to be reconciled

recóndito, -a *adj* hidden; **la casa está en lo más** ~ **del bosque** the house is hidden away in the depths of the forest; **en lo más** ~ **de mi corazón** in my heart of hearts

reconducir *vt* **1.**(*dirigir*) to reroute **2.** JUR to renew

reconfortar *vt* to comfort; (*consolar*) to console

reconocer *irr como crecer* **I.** *vt* **1.**(*identificar*) to recognize; ~ **a alguien por la voz** to recognize sb by his/her voice **2.**(*admitir*) to accept; (*un error*) to acknowledge; ~ **como hijo** to recognize as one's son **3.** (*examinar*) to check; MED to examine **4.** POL to recognize **5.** MIL to reconnoitre *Brit*, to reconnoiter *Am* **6.** (*advertir*) to warn; **reconociendo que...** in the knowledge that ... **II.** *vr:* ~**se 1.** (*declararse*) to admit; ~**se culpable** to admit one's guilt **2.** (*identificarse*) **no se reconoció a sí misma** she no longer knew who she was; **no me reconocí en la novela** I didn't recognize myself in the novel

reconocido, -a *adj* **1.** (*agradecido*) grateful **2.** (*aceptado*) recognized

reconocimiento *m* **1.** POL, JUR recognition; **el no ~ de Bosnia-Herzegovina** the non-recognition of Bosnia-Herzegovina; **~ de firma** authorization of signature **2.** (*exploración*) inspection; **~ médico** medical examination; **~ precoz** MED early diagnosis; **vuelo de ~** reconnaissance flight **3.** (*gratitud*) gratefulness; **en ~ de mi labor** in recognition of my work **4.** INFOR **~ de errores** error recognition

reconquista *f* reconquest

The **Reconquista** was ended after eight centuries of Moorish occupation by the reconquest of the Kingdom of **Granada**. For eight centuries, the sole objective of the Christian rulers had been to drive the Arabs out of the **Península Ibérica**. Those Moors and Jews who wished to remain in Spain had to convert to the Christian faith.

---

reconquistar *vt* to reconquer; *fig* to win back

reconstituir *irr como huir vt* **1.** (*restablecer*) to re-establish **2.** (*rehacer*) to reconstruct; **~ una escena histórica** to reconstruct a historical scene

reconstituyente *m* MED reconstituent

reconstrucción *f* **1.** (*país*) rebuilding **2.** JUR reconstruction

reconstruir *irr como huir vt* **1.** (*reedificar*) to rebuild **2.** (*componer*) to reconstruct; (*completar*) to complete

recontar <o→ue> *vt* **1.** (*contar*) to count; (*contar otra vez*) to recount **2.** (*cuento*) to retell

recontra *AmL, inf* **¡idiota! – ¡que te ~!** idiot! – the same to you!

recontrabueno, -a *adj AmL, inf* really good

recontracaro, -a *adj AmL, inf* really expensive

reconvenir *irr como venir vt* (*reprender*) **~ por algo** to reproach for sth

Recopa *f* DEP Cup Winners' Cup

recopilación *f* compilation

recopilar *vt* to compile

récord <récords> *m* record

recordar <o→ue> **I.** *vi, vt* **1.** (*acordarse*) to remember **2.** (*traer a la memoria, semejar*) to remind; **recuérdale a mamá que me traiga el libro** remind mum *Brit* [*o* mom *Am*] to bring me the book; **este paisaje me recuerda**

(a) **la Toscana** this landscape reminds me of Tuscany; **si mal no recuerdo** if I remember correctly **II.** *vi, vr:* ~**se** *Arg, Méx* (*despertarse*) to wake up **III.** *vr:* ~**se** (*acordarse*) to remember

recordatorio *m* **1.** (*comunión*) communion card; (*fallecimiento*) in memoriam card **2.** (*advertencia*) reminder

recorrer *vt* **1.** (*atravesar*) to cross; (*viajar por*) to travel around; **~ Europa en bicicleta** to travel around Europe by bicycle **2.** (*trayecto*) to travel; **recorrimos tres kilómetros a pie** we walked three kilometres *Brit* [*o* kilometers *Am*] **3.** (*registrar*) to check; (*terreno*) to search **4.** (*texto*) to skim; **~ con la vista** to look over

recortable *adj* cutout; **muñeca ~** cutout doll

recortado, -a *adj* (*hoja*) uneven; (*costa*) rugged; (*cortado*) cut out

recortar I. *vt* **1.** (*figuras*) to cut out; (*barba, uñas*) to trim; (*quitar*) to cut off **2.** (*disminuir*) to cut (down) **II.** *vr:* ~**se** to stand out; **el perfil de las montañas se recorta sobre el horizonte** the outline of the mountains stands out against the horizon

recorte *m* **1.** (*periódico*) cutting **2.** (*rebajamiento*) cut(back) **3.** *pl* (*cortaduras*) cuttings *pl*; **~s de papel/tela** scraps of paper/cloth

recostar <o→ue> **I.** *vt* **1.** (*apoyar*) to rest **2.** (*inclinar*) **~ contra/en algo** to lean against/on sth; **~ la espalda contra una columna** to lean one's back against a column **II.** *vr:* ~**se 1.** (*inclinarse*) ~**se contra/en algo** to lean against/on sth **2.** (*apoyarse*) to rest

recova *f* **1.** CSur (*arcadas*) arcade **2.** *And, Urug* (*mercado*) market

recoveco *m* **1.** (*escondrijo*) nook **2.** (*falta de claridad*) obscurity; **sin ~s** frankly; **persona con ~s** complicated person **3.** (*vuelta*) bend

recreación *f* **1.** (*reproducción*) reproduction **2.** (*diversión*) recreation

recrear I. *vt* **1.** (*reproducir*) to reproduce **2.** (*divertir*) to entertain **II.** *vr:* ~**se** to entertain oneself; **se recrea contemplando cuadros** he/she enjoys looking at pictures

recreativo, -a *adj* recreational; (**salón de juegos**) ~**s** amusement arcade

recreo *m* **1.** recreation; **de ~** recreational; **casa de ~** holiday home; **puerto de ~** marina **2.** (*en el colegio*) break, recess *Am*

recriminación *f* **1.** (*reproche*) reproach **2.** (*acusación*) recrimination

recriminar *vt* **1.** (*reprochar*) to reproach **2.** (*acusar*) to accuse

recrudecer *irr como crecer vi, vr:* ~**se** to worsen; (*conflicto*) to intensify

recrudecimiento *m* worsening; (*combate*) intensification

recta *f* straight; **entrar en la ~ final** *t.* DEP to enter the final straight

rectamente *adv* (*honradamente*) justly

rectangular *adj* rectangular

rectángulo *m* rectangle

rectángulo, -a *adj* rectangular

rectificación *f* (*corrección*) correction
rectificar <c→qu> *vt* **1.** (*corregir*) to correct **2.** (*carretera*) to straighten
rectilíneo, -a *adj* **1.** (*forma*) rectilinear **2.** (*persona*) rigid
rectitud *f* (*honradez*) uprightness
recto¹ *adv* straight; **siga todo** ~ go straight ahead [*o* on]
recto² *m* ANAT rectum
recto, -a *adj* **1.** *t.* MAT (*forma*) straight; **ángulo** ~ right angle; **línea recta** straight line **2.** (*honrado*) upright
rector(a) **I.** *adj* principal; (*responsable*) governing **II.** *m(f)* ENS, REL rector; (*universidad*) vice-chancellor *Brit*, president *Am*
rectorado *m* rectorship; (*lugar*) rectorate; (*cargo*) UNIV vice-chancellorship *Brit*, presidency *Am*
recua *f* train (*of pack animals*); **con él llegó toda su** ~ **de amigos** *inf* his band [*o* drove] of friends came along with him
recuadro *m* (*casilla*) box
recubierto *pp de* **recubrir**
recubrimiento *m* covering
recubrir *irr como* **abrir** *vt* to cover
recuento *m* count; **hacer el** ~ **de votos** to count the votes
recuerdo *m* **1.** (*evocación*) memory; **en** [*o* como] ~ **de nuestro encuentro** in memory of our meeting; **traer al** ~ to remind; **tener un buen** ~ **de algo** to have good memories of sth **2.** (*de un viaje*) souvenir **3.** *pl* (*saludos*) regards *pl*; **dales muchos** ~**s de mi parte** send them my regards; **María te manda muchos** ~**s** María sends you her regards
recular *vi* **1.** (*retroceder*) to go back; (*automóvil*) to reverse *Brit*, to back up *Am* **2.** *inf* (*ceder*) to give way
recuperación *f* **1.** (*recobrar*) recovery; MIL recapture; ~ **de datos** INFOR data retrieval **2.** ECON recovery; ~ **de las cotizaciones** share price recovery; **la** ~ **de los precios** rally of prices **3.** (*enfermo*) recovery **4.** (*papel, hierro*) recycling **5.** (*asignatura*) pass (*in a re-take exam*); **examen de** ~ re-sit (exam) **6.** (*rescate*) rescue
recuperar **I.** *vt* **1.** (*recobrar*) to recover; MIL to recapture **2.** (*tiempo*) to make up **3.** (*papel, hierro*) to recycle **4.** (*rescatar*) to rescue **5.** (*asignatura*) to pass (*a re-sit examination*); **mi hijo no recuperó la física en el examen de septiembre** my son failed his physics re-sit **II.** *vr*: ~**se** to recover
recurrir *vi* **1.** JUR to appeal **2.** (*acudir*) ~ **a** (*una persona*) to turn to; (*una institución*) to resort to; ~ **a la justicia** to turn to the law; ~ **a todos los medios** to resort to every measure available; **no tener a quien** ~ to have nobody to turn to; **si no me pagas** ~**é a un abogado** if you don't pay me I'm going to see a lawyer
recursivo, -a *adj Col* (*ocurrente*) resourceful
recurso *m* **1.** JUR appeal; ~ **de apelación** appeal; ~ **contencioso administrativo** action

against the administration; **interponer un** ~ **contra la sentencia** to lodge an appeal against the sentence **2.** (*remedio*) solution; (*expediente*) expedient; **no me queda otro** ~ **que...** I have no alternative but ...; **como último** ~ as a last resort **3.** *pl* (*bienes*) means *pl*; **familias sin** ~**s** families without means **4.** *pl* (*reservas*) resources *pl*; ~**s naturales** natural resources; **ser una persona de** ~**s** to be resourceful; **el país cuenta con abundantes** ~**s minerales** the country has rich mineral resources
recusar *vt* to reject; JUR to challenge
red *f* **1.** (*malla*) net; ~ **de arrastre** trawl net; **echar las** ~**es** to cast the nets **2.** (*sistema*) network; ~ **comercial** business [*o* sales] network; ~ **vial** road network; **han desarticulado una** ~ **de carteristas** they have broken up a gang of pickpockets **3.** ELEC mains *pl Brit*, power lines *pl*; **avería en la** ~ mains failure *Brit*, power failure ▶**caer en la** ~ to fall into the trap
redacción *f* **1.** ENS writing; **hacer una** ~ **sobre el mar** to write a composition on the sea **2.** PREN editing
redactar *vt* to write; (*documento*) to edit; (*testamento*) to draw up
redactor(a) *m(f)* writer; PREN editor
redada *f* **1.** (*de la policía*) roundup, raid **2.** (*pescado*) catch; *fig* haul
redecilla *f* (*pelo*) hairnet; (*equipaje*) luggage rack
rededor *m* **al** [*o* **en**] ~ around; **al** ~ **de la casa** around the house
redención *f* **1.** REL redemption **2.** (*cautivo*) freeing **3.** (*finca*) redemption (*by repaying a loan*)
redentor(a) *m(f)* redeemer
redicho, -a *adj inf* pretentious
redil *m* fold; **volver al** ~ *fig* to return to the fold
redimir *vt* **1.** REL to redeem **2.** (*esclavo*) to purchase the freedom of **3.** (*finca*) to redeem (*by repaying a loan*)
redistribución *f* redistribution
rédito *m* yield, revenue
reditar <3. *pres:* reditúa> *vt* to yield
redoblar **I.** *vt* **1.** (*aumentar*) to intensify **2.** (*clavo*) to clinch, to bend back **II.** *vi* (*tambor*) to play a roll on the drums; (*tormenta*) to intensify
redoble *m* drum roll
redomado, -a *adj* **1.** (*astuto*) sly **2.** (*total*) utter; **un tonto** ~ an utter fool
redomón *adj AmS* half-trained
redonda *f* **1.** (*dehesa*) pasture; **en tres kilómetros a la** ~ for three kilometres *Brit* [*o* kilometers *Am*] in all directions **2.** MÚS semibreve *Brit*, whole note *Am*
redondear *vt* to round off; ~ **por defecto/ por exceso** to round up/down
redondel *m* circle
redondela *f* **1.** *Arg, Chile* (*objeto circular*)

round object **2.** *Chile, inf* (*círculo*) circle
redondez *f* roundness ►**en toda la ~ de la Tierra** in the whole wide world
redondo, -a *adj t.* MAT (*circular*) round; (*redondeado*) rounded ►**un negocio ~** a great deal; **caer(se) ~** (*derrumbarse*) to fall flat; (*quedarse mudo*) to be struck dumb; **negarse en ~** to flatly deny
reducción *f* **1.** *t.* QUÍM, ECON (*disminución*) reduction; (*rebaja*) discount; (*de personal*) cut; **~ de la jornada laboral** reduction of the working day **2.** JUR remission **3.** FÍS, MAT reduction; **~ de quebrados** reduction of fractions **4.** MED setting
reducido, -a *adj* (*pequeño*) small; (*estrecho*) narrow; **tarifas reducidas** reduced rates
reducidor(a) *m(f) AmS* (*perista*) fence
reducir *irr como traducir* **I.** *vt* **1.** *t.* QUÍM (*disminuir*) to reduce; (*personal, gastos*) to cut; (*precios*) to lower **2.** (*foto, dibujo*) to reduce; **~ de escala** to scale down **3.** (*someter*) to subdue; **la policía redujo al agresor** the police overpowered the assailant **4.** (*convertir*) to reduce; **el fuego redujo la casa a cenizas** the fire reduced the house to ashes; **~/quedar reducido a escombros** to reduce/be reduced to rubble; **~ al absurdo algo** to make nonsense of sth **5.** (*limitar*) to reduce **6.** (*resumir*) to summarize; (*acortar*) to abbreviate **7.** MED to set **8.** MAT to reduce; **~ al común denominador** *t. fig* to reduce to the lowest common denominator **II.** *vi* AUTO to change down *Brit*, to shift into a lower gear *Am* **III.** *vr:* **~se** to come down
redundancia *f* redundancy
redundante *adj* redundant
redundar *vi* **eso redunda en beneficio nuestro** this works in our interest; **eso ~á en perjuicio vuestro** this will work against you
reedición *f* reissue; (*impresión*) reprint
reedificación *f* rebuilding
reedificar <c→qu> *vt* to rebuild
reeditar *vt* to republish; (*imprimir*) to reprint
reeducación *f* MED physiotherapy
reelección *f* re-election
reelegir *irr como elegir vt* to re-elect
reembolsar *vt* to repay, to reimburse
reembolso *m* (*devolución*) repayment; **enviar algo contra ~** to send sth cash on delivery
reemplazante *mf Méx* replacement
reemplazar <z→c> *vt* to replace; (*representar*) to substitute
reemplazo *m* **1.** (*sustitución*) replacement; DEP substitution **2.** (*tropas*) reserve; **ser del mismo ~** to have been called up together
reencarnación *f* reincarnation
reencauchar *vt Col, Perú* AUTO to retread
reencontrar <o→ue> **I.** *vt* to find again **II.** *vr:* **~se** to meet again
reencuentro *m* **1.** (*encuentro*) reunion **2.** (*choque*) collision **3.** MIL skirmish
reenganchar *vt* to re-enlist

reenviar <*1. pres:* reenvío> *vt* (*al remitente*) to return; (*a un nuevo destinatario*) to forward
reestreno *m* TEAT revival; TV rerun; CINE rehowing
reestructurar *vt* to restructure
refacción *f* snack
refaccionar *vt AmL* (*edificios*) to refurbish
refectorio *m* refectory
referencia *f* **1.** reference; **punto de ~** point of reference; **con ~ a** with reference to; **hacer una pequeña ~ a alguien** to make a slight reference to sb; **hacer una ~ a algo** to refer to sth **2.** *pl* (*informes*) report **3.** (*nota*) reference; **nuestra/su ~** (*en un escrito*) our/your ref. **4.** (*relato*) account
referéndum <referéndums> *m* POL (*popular*) referendum; (*sindical*) ballot
referente *adj* regarding; (**en lo**) **~ a su queja** with regard to your complaint
referí *m AmL* DEP referee
referir *irr como sentir* **I.** *vt* **1.** (*relatar*) to recount **2.** (*remitir*) to refer **II.** *vr:* **~se** to refer; **en** [*o por*] **lo que se refiere a nuestras relaciones** with regard to our relationship; **no me estaba refiriendo a Ud.** I was not referring to you
refilón mirar de ~ a alguien to look sideways at sb; **el sol da en mi ventana de ~** the sun comes slanting through my window
refinado, -a *adj* refined
refinamiento *m* refinement
refinanciar *vt* ECON to refinance
refinar **I.** *vt* to refine **II.** *vr:* **~se** to become refined
refinería *f* refinery
refino, -a *adj* extra fine
reflector *m* (*foco*) spotlight; DEP floodlight; MIL searchlight
reflector(a) *adj* reflective
reflejar **I.** *vi, vt* to reflect; **tus palabras reflejan miedo** your words show fear **II.** *vr:* **~se** to be reflected
reflejo *m* **1.** (*luz, imagen*) reflection; **las esmeraldas despiden unos preciosos ~s verdes** emeralds give off lovely green sparkles; **su comportamiento es un fiel ~ de su estado de ánimo** his/her behaviour *Brit* [*o* behavior *Am*] is an accurate reflection of how he/she is feeling **2.** MED, PSICO reflex; **para ello hay que ser rápido de ~s** you need fast reflexes for that
reflejo, -a *adj* reflective; **movimiento ~** reflex
reflexión *f* **1.** (*consideraciones*) reflection; **con ~** on reflection; **sin ~** without thinking **2.** (*rayos*) reflection
reflexionar *vi, vt* to reflect; **reflexiona bien antes de dar ese paso** think carefully before doing that
reflexivo, -a *adj* **1.** (*sensato*) thoughtful **2.** (*reflectante*) reflecting **3.** LING reflexive
refluir *irr como huir vi* to flow back; (*la marea*) to ebb

reflujo m 1. (*marea*) ebb 2. MED reflux; ~ **gástrico** gastric reflux

refocilarse vr pey ~ **con** [*o* en] **algo** to enjoy sth

reforma f 1. (*mejora, modificación*) reform; ~ **educativa** educational reform; ~ **monetaria** monetary reform; ~ **del sistema tributario** reform of the tax system 2. ARQUIT (*reestructuración*) rebuilding; (*renovación*) renovation; **hacer una** ~ **en el cuarto de baño** to have one's bathroom refurbished 3. REL **Reforma Protestante** Reformation 4. (*reparación*) repair

reformar I. vt 1. REL (*t. mejorar, modificar*) to reform; ~ **su conducta** to change one's ways 2. (*a alguien*) to reform 3. ARQUIT (*reestructurar*) to rebuild; (*renovar*) to renovate, to reform 4. (*rehacer*) to redo 5. (*deshacer*) to alter II. vr: ~**se** to mend one's ways; ~**se en el vestir** to dress better

reformatorio m reformatory; ~ **para delincuentes juveniles** borstal Brit

reformatorio, -a adj reforming

reformista I. adj reformist; **tendencias** ~**s** reformist tendencies; **ser** ~ to be a reformist II. mf reformist

reforzamiento m 1. (*de algo*) reinforcement; (*con vigas*) strengthening 2. (*de alguien*) encouragement

reforzar irr como forzar I. vt 1. (*fortalecer*) to reinforce; (*con vigas*) to strengthen 2. (*animar*) to encourage II. vr: ~**se** to be reinforced

refractar I. vt to refract II. vr: ~**se** to be refracted

refractario, -a adj 1. QUÍM, FÍS heat-resistant 2. (*rebelde*) recalcitrant; **ser** ~ **a algo** to be opposed to sth 3. (*inmune*) immune

refrán m saying, proverb; **como dice el** ~ as the saying goes

refranero m LING collection of proverbs/sayings

refregar irr como fregar I. vt 1. (*frotar*) to rub; ~ **con un cepillo** to scrub with a brush; ~ **la cacerola con un estropajo** to scrub the saucepan with a scouring pad 2. inf (*reprochar*) ~ **algo a alguien** (*por las narices*) to rub sb's nose in sth II. vr: ~**se** to rub; ~**se los ojos** to rub one's eyes; ~**se la manga contra la puerta recién pintada** to brush one's sleeve against the freshly painted door

refrenar I. vt to check II. vr: ~**se** to restrain oneself

refrendar vt 1. (*autorizar*) to approve 2. (*un pasaporte*) to stamp 3. (*aceptar*) to accept

refrescante adj refreshing

refrescar I. vt 1. (*algo, a alguien*) to refresh; **el baño me ha refrescado** the bath has revived me 2. (*cosas olvidadas*) to brush up; (*sentimiento*) to revive; ~ **la memoria** to refresh one's memory II. vi 1. (*aire, viento*) to cool down 2. (*dar fresco*) to refresh; **esta bebida refresca mucho** this drink is very refreshing 3. (*beber*) to have a refreshing drink

4. (*reponerse*) to refresh oneself III. vr: ~**se** 1. (*aire, viento, cosa*) to cool down; **el día se ha refrescado** the weather has become cooler 2. (*persona*) to cool down; (*beber*) to have a refreshing drink; **voy a ducharme para** ~**me** I'm going to have a shower to cool down; ~**se con una cerveza** to have a nice cool drink of beer 3. (*reponerse*) to freshen up 4. (*tomar el fresco*) to get some fresh air IV. vimpers **por la tarde refresca** in the evening it gets cooler

refresco m 1. (*bebida*) soft drink; (*gaseosa, naranjada*) fizzy drink 2. (*comidas y bebidas*) refreshment; (*refrigerio*) snack

refriega f 1. MIL skirmish 2. inf (*pelea*) scuffle; (*violenta*) brawl

refrigeración f 1. refrigeration; (*de una habitación*) air conditioning; ~ **por aire/agua** air/water-cooling 2. (*refrigerio*) refreshment, snack

refrigerador m 1. (*nevera*) refrigerator; (*cámara*) cool room; (*instalación*) cooling unit; (*líquido*) coolant, refrigerant 2. (*de un automóvil*) cooling system

refrigerador(a) adj cooling; **aparato** ~ (*para comestibles*) refrigerator; (*para habitaciones*) air-cooling unit

refrigeradora f Perú (*nevera*) refrigerator

refrigerar I. vt (*enfriar*) to refrigerate; (*una habitación*) to air-condition II. vr: ~**se** 1. (*enfriarse*) to cool down 2. (*reponer fuerzas*) to freshen up

refrigerio m snack

refuerzo m 1. (*reforzamiento*) reinforcement; (*viga*) strengthening; (*parche*) patch 2. (*ayuda*) support 3. pl MIL reinforcements pl

refugiado, -a m, f refugee; **el Alto Comisionado de las Naciones Unidas para los Refugiados** (**ACNUR**) United Nations High Commission for Refugees (UNHCR)

refugiarse vr (*en un lugar*) to take refuge; ~ **de algo** to flee from sth; ~ **en una mentira** to hide behind a lie; **se refugió en mis brazos** he/she sought shelter in my arms; **se refugió en la bebida** he/she turned to drink

refugio m 1. (*protección, consuelo, lugar*) ~ **de algo** refuge from sth 2. t. MIL (*construcción*) shelter; ~ (**montañero**) mountain shelter; ~ **nuclear** [*o* **atómico**] fallout shelter 3. (*persona*) protector 4. (*tráfico*) traffic island

refulgencia f brightness

refulgir <g→j> vi to shine

refundir I. vt 1. (*metal: fundir*) to recast 2. (*revisar*) to revise; (*obra*) to adapt 3. (*reunir*) to join 4. (*perder*) to lose II. vr: ~**se** 1. (*reunirse*) to be joined 2. AmC (*perderse*) to be lost

refunfuñar vi to grumble

refunfuñón, -ona I. adj grumpy II. m, f grouch

refutación f refutation

refutar vt to refute

regadera f 1. (*recipiente*) watering can 2. (*reguera*) irrigation channel ►**estar como**

una ~ *inf* to be as mad as a hatter

regaderazo *m Méx* shower

regadío *m* irrigation; **estos campos son de** ~ these fields are irrigated

regadío, -a *adj* 1. (*de riego*) irrigation 2. (*que se puede regar*) irrigable

regalado, -a *adj* 1. (*cómodo*) easy; **llevar una vida regalada** to lead a life of luxury 2. (*barato*) very cheap; **vender algo a precio** ~ to sell sth for a knock-down price; **a este precio el vestido es** ~ at this price they are practically giving the dress away 3. (*delicado*) delicate 4. (*deleitoso*) delightful; (*sabroso*) delicious

regalar I. *vt* 1. (*obsequiar*) to give; **en esta tienda regalan la fruta** *fig* in this shop the fruit is dirt-cheap; ~ **los oídos a alguien** to flatter sb 2. (*mimar*) to pamper 3. (*deleitar*) to delight 4. (*acariciar*) to stroke II. *vr:* ~**se** 1. (*llevar buena vida*) to live very well 2. (*proporcionarse*) to indulge oneself 3. (*deleitarse*) ~ **con algo** to delight in sth

regalía *f* 1. (*privilegio*) privilege; (*del Estado, la Corona*) prerogative 2. (*pago*) bonus 3. (*tasa*) royalties *pl*

regaliz *m* 1. (*golosina*) liquorice *Brit,* licorice *Am* 2. BOT liquorice plant

regalo *m* 1. (*obsequio*) present, gift; **a este precio el coche es un** ~ at this price the car is a steal; **una cesta de fruta de** ~ **en cada habitación** a complimentary basket of fruit in each room 2. (*gusto*) pleasure; **un** ~ **para la vista** a sight for sore eyes 3. (*comodidad*) luxury

regalón, -ona *adj inf* (*niño*) pampered

regañadientes a ~ reluctantly, grudgingly

regañar I. *vt inf* to scold II. *vi* 1. (*reñir*) to argue; (*dejar de tener trato*) to fall out; **ha regañado con su novio** (*reñir*) she has had a fight with her boyfriend; (*separarse*) she has split up with her boyfriend; **estoy regañado con mis vecinos** I have fallen out with my neighbours *Brit* [*o* neighbors *Am*] 2. (*refunfuñar*) to grumble

regañina *f* 1. (*reprensión*) telling off; **echar una** ~ **a alguien** to tell sb off, to give sb a telling off 2. (*riña*) quarrel; **tener una** ~ **por algo** to quarrel about sth

regañón, -ona I. *adj* grumpy II. *m, f* grouch

regar *irr como fregar vt* 1. (*con agua: una planta, el jardín*) to water; (*las calles*) to hose down; AGR to irrigate 2. (*con un líquido*) to wet; (*mojar*) to soak; (*con algo menudo*) to sprinkle; ~ **el suelo con arena** to sprinkle sand on the ground; ~ **la alfombra con pintura** to spatter the carpet with paint; ~ **algo con lágrimas** to bathe sth with tears 3. (*atravesar*) to cross

regata *f* DEP regatta

regate *m* dodge; (*con el balón*) dribble

regatear I. *vi* 1. (*mercadear*) to haggle 2. (*hacer regates*) to dodge; (*con el balón*) to dribble II. *vt* to haggle over

regateo *m sin pl* 1. (*negociar*) haggling 2. DEP dribbling

regazo *m* lap; *fig* warmth

regencia *f* 1. (*gobierno*) regency 2. (*dirección*) direction; (*de un negocio*) management

regeneración *f* regeneration

regenerar I. *vt* 1. ELEC (*algo*) to regenerate 2. (*a alguien*) to reform II. *vr:* ~**se** 1. (*renovarse*) to regenerate; (*cabello*) to grow back 2. (*reformarse*) to reform

regentar *vt* 1. (*dirigir*) to manage 2. (*ejercer*) to hold 3. POL to govern

regente *mf* 1. (*que gobierna*) regent 2. (*que dirige*) director; (*un negocio*) manager

régimen *m* <regímenes> 1. (*sistema*) system; (*reglamentos*) regulations *pl;* ~ **abierto** (*en una prisión*) open regime; ~ **legal de la seguridad social para jubilación e invalidez** social security system for retirement and invalidity; ~ **de patentes** patent regulation; ~ **penitenciario** prison system 2. POL government 3. (*dieta*) diet; ~ **de adelgazamiento** (slimming) diet; **estar a** ~ to be on a diet; **poner a alguien a** ~ to put sb on a diet 4. (*manera de vivir*) lifestyle; **llevar un** ~ **de austeridad** to have an austere lifestyle 5. LING government

regimiento *m* MIL regiment

regio, -a *adj* 1. (*real*) royal 2. (*magnífico*) magnificent

región *f* 1. (*territorio*) region 2. (*espacio*) area; (*del cuerpo*) region; ~ **abdominal** abdominal region

regional *adj* regional

regir *irr como elegir* I. *vt* 1. (*gobernar*) to govern; (*dirigir*) to direct 2. (*guiar*) to lead; (*ley*) to govern 3. LING to take II. *vi* 1. (*tener validez*) to apply 2. (*funcionar*) to work 3. *inf* (*estar cuerdo*) to be sane; **¡tú no riges!** you're out of your mind! III. *vr:* ~**se** to be guided

registrador(a) I. *adj* registering; **caja** ~**a** cash register II. *m(f)* 1. (*funcionario*) registrar; ~ **de la propiedad** property [*o* land] registrar 2. TÉC recorder; ~ **de sonidos** sound recorder

registrar I. *vt* 1. (*examinar*) to search 2. (*inscribir*) to record; (*una empresa, un patente*) to register 3. (*incluir*) to include 4. (*señalar*) to note; (*grabar*) to record ▶ **¡a mí que me registren!** I certainly didn't do it!, don't look at me! II. *vr:* ~**se** 1. (*inscribirse*) to register 2. (*observarse*) to be reported

registro *m* 1. (*inspección*) search; ~ **de la casa** house search 2. (*con un instrumento*) measurement; (*grabación*) recording 3. (*inscripción*) recording; (*inclusión*) inclusion; (*de una empresa, una patente*) registration 4. (*nota*) note; (*protocolo*) record; ~ **de entrada/de salida** note of arrival/departure; ~ **de inventario** inventory 5. (*libro*) register; ~ **de autores** list of authors; ~ **electoral** electoral register; ~ **de entradas/salidas** visitors' book; ~ **de la propiedad** land register 6. (*oficina, archivo*) registry; ~ **civil** registry

office; ~ **de la propiedad** land registry; ~ **de la propiedad industrial** industrial property registry **7.** (*abertura*) inspection hatch **8.** (*de un mecanismo*) regulator **9.** (*de un libro*) entry **10.** MÚS register; (*órgano*) stop; **tiene un** ~ **muy amplio** he/she has a very wide range ►**tocar todos los** ~**s** to pull out all the stops
regla *f* **1.** (*instrumento*) ruler; ~ **de cálculo** slide rule **2.** (*norma*) rule; ~**s de exportación** COM export regulations; **la** ~ **de oro** the golden rule; **por** ~ **general** as a general rule; **ser la** ~ to be the rule; **la** ~ **es que** +*subj* the rule is that **3.** MAT ~ **de tres** rule of three; **las cuatro** ~**s** addition, subtraction, multiplication and division **4.** (*moderación*) moderation; **beber con** ~ to drink in moderation **5.** (*menstruación*) period; **está con la** ~ she has her period ►**la excepción confirma la** ~ *prov* the exception confirms the rule *prov;* **por qué** ~ **de tres...** why on earth ...; **estar en** ~ to be in order; **poner en** ~ to put in order; **salir de la** ~ to go too far
reglamentación *f* **1.** (*acción*) regulation; *pey* regimentation **2.** (*reglas*) rules *pl*
reglamentar *vt* to regulate; *pey* to regiment
reglamentario, -a *adj* **1.** (*relativo al reglamento*) regulatory **2.** (*conforme al reglamento*) regulation
reglamento *m* rules *pl;* (*de una organización*) regulations *pl;* ~ (**de funcionarios**) civil service regulations; ~ (**interno**) rules *pl;* ~ **de tráfico** traffic regulations
reglar I. *vt* **1.** (*reglamentar*) to regulate **2.** (*con líneas*) to line II. *vr:* ~**se 1.** (*sujetarse*) to be regulated **2.** (*moderarse*) to limit oneself
regocijado, -a *adj* joyful
regocijar I. *vr:* ~**se 1.** (*alegrarse*) ~**se con algo** to delight in sth **2.** (*divertirse*) to amuse oneself II. *vt* to delight
regocijo *m* **1.** (*alegría*) delight; (*diversión*) pleasure; **esperar algo con** ~ to be really looking forward to sth **2.** (*júbilo*) rejoicing
regodearse *vr* **1.** ~ **con** [*o* **en**] **algo** (*gozar*) to enjoy sth; (*alegrarse*) to delight in sth; **se regodea viéndome sufrir** he/she takes pleasure in seeing me suffer **2.** *inf* (*chacotear*) to joke around
regodeo *m* **1.** (*placer*) pleasure **2.** *inf* (*chacoteo*) joking; (*burla*) mockery **3.** *inf* (*fiesta*) party
regodeón, -ona *adj Chile, Col, inf* hard to please, fussy
regoldar *vi inf* to burp
regordete, -a *adj* chubby, plump
regresar I. *vi* (*volver*) to return, to go back II. *vt Méx* (*devolver*) to give back III. *vr:* ~**se** *AmL* (*volver*) to return, to go back
regresión *f* **1.** (*retroceso*) regression **2.** (*declive*) decline
regresivo, -a *adj* regressive
regreso *m* (*vuelta*) return; (*viaje de*) ~ return journey; **estar de** ~ to have returned
reguero *m* **1.** (*chorro*) irrigation channel

2. (*señal*) trail ►**expandirse como un** ~ **de pólvora** to spread like wildfire
regulación *f* **1.** (*reglamentación*) regulation; ~ **administrativa** administrative regulations **2.** *t.* TÉC (*organización, ajustación*) adjustment; (*de un río*) channelling *Brit,* channeling *Am;* **de** ~ **automática** self-regulating; ~ **de la demanda** ECON management of demand
regulado, -a *adj* (*reglamentario*) regulatory
regulador *m* regulator; (*mecanismo*) control knob
regular I. *vt* **1.** *t.* TÉC (*organizar, ajustar*) to adjust **2.** (*reglamentar*) to regulate **3.** (*poner en orden*) to put in order II. *adj* **1.** (*conforme a una regla*) regular; **verbos** ~**es** regular verbs **2.** (*reglamentado, ordenado*) ordered **3.** (*estable*) stable **4.** (*uniforme*) regular **5.** (*mediano*) average; (*mediocre*) mediocre; (*nota*) satisfactory; **de tamaño** ~ normal size ►**tu comportamiento no me parece ni medio** ~ *inf* your behaviour *Brit* [*o* behavior *Am*] strikes me as most irregular; **por lo** ~ as a rule III. *adv* so-so
regularidad *f* **1.** (*conformidad, uniformidad*) regularity; **con** ~ regularly **2.** (*medianía*) averageness; (*mediocridad*) mediocrity **3.** (*puntualidad*) punctuality
regularizar <z→c> I. *vt* (*poner en orden*) to regularize; (*normalizar*) to standardize II. *vr:* ~**se** (*regularse*) to be regulated; (*normalizarse*) to become standardized
regularmente *adv* (*normalmente*) usually
regurgitar *vi, vt* to regurgitate
regusto *m* aftertaste; **el cuadro tiene un cierto** ~ **surrealista** the picture has a slightly surrealist feeling
rehabilitación *f* **1.** *t.* JUR, MED (*de alguien*) rehabilitation; (*restitución*) restitution **2.** (*de una cosa*) repair; (*de un edificio*) refurbishment
rehabilitar I. *vt* **1.** *t.* JUR, MED (*a alguien*) to rehabilitate; (*restituir*) to return **2.** (*una cosa*) to repair; (*un edificio*) to refurbish; ~ **la memoria** [*o* **la buena fama**] **de alguien** to restore sb's reputation II. *vr:* ~**se** to be rehabilitated
rehacer *irr como* **hacer** I. *vt* **1.** (*volver a hacer*) to redo; ~ **una carta** to rewrite a letter **2.** (*reconstruir*) to rebuild; (*reparar*) to repair; (*un edificio*) to refurbish; ~ **su vida con alguien** to rebuild one's life with sb II. *vr:* ~**se** (*recuperar las fuerzas*) to recover one's strength; (*la salud*) to regain one's health; (*la tranquilidad*) to regain one's peace of mind; ~**se de una desgracia** to recover from a misfortune
rehecho, -a I. *pp de* **rehacer** II. *adj* (*robusto*) thickset
rehén *m* **1.** (*persona*) hostage **2.** (*cosa*) pledge
rehogar <g→gu> *vt* to sauté
rehuir *irr como* **huir** *vt* **1.** (*eludir*) to avoid; ~ **a alguien** to avoid sb; ~ **una obligación** to shirk an obligation; **rehúye decir la verdad** he/she

avoids telling the truth **2.** (*rechazar*) to reject
rehusar *vt* to refuse; (*una reclamación*) to
reject; ¡**rehusado!** rejected!; **rehúsa verme**
he/she refuses to see me; ~ **una invitación** to
decline an invitation
reimpresión *f* reprint; ~ **pirata** pirate copy
reimprimir *irr como imprimir vt* to reprint
reina *f* **1.** *t.* ZOOL (*soberana, la mejor*) queen; ~
madre queen mother; **abeja** ~ queen bee
2. *inf* (*cariño*) darling
reinado *m t. fig* (*tiempo*) reign
reinar *vi* **1.** *t. fig* (*gobernar*) to reign **2.** (*dominar*) to prevail
reincidencia *f* relapse; JUR reoffending
reincidente **I.** *adj* reoffending **II.** *mf* (*delincuente*) reoffender
reincidir *vi* **1.** (*error*) ~ **en algo** to relapse
into sth; ~ **en un delito** to reoffend; ~
siempre en el mismo error to keep making
the same mistake **2.** MED to relapse
reincorporar **I.** *vt* ~ **a algo** to reincorporate
into sth; ~ **a alguien a un puesto** to restore sb
to a position; ~ **al servicio** to return to service
II. *vr*: ~**se** (*a un sitio*) to return; (*a una organización*) to rejoin; ~**se al trabajo** to return to
work
reineta *f* (*manzana*) pippin
reino *m* realm; (*de un monarca*) kingdom;
Reino Unido United Kingdom
reintegración *f* **1.** (*reincorporación*) reintegration; (*en un cargo*) reinstatement **2.** (*de
gastos*) reimbursement; ~ **de los daños** reimbursement for damages
reintegrar **I.** *vt* **1.** (*reincorporar*) to reintegrate; (*en un cargo*) to reinstate; ~ **a alguien a
su puesto de trabajo** to reinstate sb in his/
her job **2.** (*devolver*) to return; (*dinero*) to
repay; (*desembolsos*) to reimburse **II.** *vr*: ~**se**
1. (*reincorporarse*) to return; (*a una organización*) to rejoin; ~**se al trabajo** to return to
work **2.** (*recobrar*) to recover
reintegro *m* **1.** (*reintegración*) reintegration;
(*en un cargo*) reinstatement **2.** (*premio*) **me
tocó un** ~ I won back my stake **3.** (*pago*) reimbursement; (*de la cuenta*) withdrawal; (*devolución*) repayment
reír *irr* **I.** *vi* **1.** (*desternillarse*) to laugh;
echarse a ~ to burst out laughing; **no me
hagas** ~ *fig* don't make me laugh **2.** (*sonreír*)
to smile ▸**el que ríe último ríe mejor** *prov*
he who laughs last laughs longest [*o* best] *prov*
II. *vr*: ~**se 1.** (*desternillarse*) ~**se de algo** to
laugh at sth; ~**se a carcajadas** to laugh loudly;
~**se en las barbas de alguien** to laugh in sb's
face; ~**se hasta de su sombra** to laugh at the
slightest provocation; **me río de tu dinero** *fig*
I don't give a damn about your money; ~**se
para sus adentros** to chuckle; ~**se tontamente** to giggle **2.** (*sonreír*) to smile **3.** (*burlarse*) ~**se de algo** to laugh at sth **4.** *inf* (*romperse*) to come apart **III.** *vt* ~ **algo** to laugh at
sth

reiteración *f* repetition; JUR reoffending
reiteradamente *adv* repeatedly
reiterar **I.** *vt* to repeat; **te reitero las gracias** I
thank you once again; **reiteró su intención
de ayudarme** he/she repeated his/her intention of helping me **II.** *vr*: ~**se** to repeat; **se
reiteró en su decisión de dejar de fumar**
he/she reaffirmed his/her decision to stop
smoking
reivindicación *f* ~ **de algo** claim to sth
reivindicar <c→qu> *vt* **1.** (*pedir*) to claim;
(*exigir*) to demand **2.** (*recobrar*) to recover
3. (*una acción*) to claim; ~ **un atentado** to
claim responsibility for an attack
reja *f* **1.** (*barras*) grill; **estar entre** ~**s** *fig, inf* to
be behind bars **2.** (*del arado*) ploughshare *Brit*,
plowshare *Am* **3.** (*labor*) ploughing *Brit*, plowing *Am*
rejego *adj AmC, Méx* **1.** (*indomable*) wild;
(*alzado*) untamed **2.** (*intratable*) unmanageable; (*enojadizo*) cranky
rejilla *f* **1.** (*enrejado*) grating **2.** (*parrilla*) grill
3. (*brasero*) brazier **4.** (*tejido*) wickerwork
5. (*para equipaje*) luggage rack
rejo *m* **1.** (*punta*) spike **2.** *AmL* (*látigo*) whip
rejón *m* (*barra*) spike; TAUR lance
rejoneador(a) *m(f)* TAUR bullfighter on horseback
rejoneo *m* TAUR bullfighting on horseback
rejuntar **I.** *vt* to join **II.** *vr inf* **han decidido**
~**se** they've decided to live together
rejuvenecer *irr como crecer* **I.** *vt* **1.** (*hacer
más joven*) to rejuvenate; **este peinado te
rejuvenece** this haircut makes you look much
younger **2.** (*modernizar*) to modernize **II.** *vr*:
~**se** to be rejuvenated
relación *f* **1.** (*entre cosas, hechos*) relationship, relation; ~ **entre la causa y el efecto**
relationship between cause and effect; **hacer** ~
a algo to refer to sth; **con** ~ **a su petición**
with regard to your/his/her request **2.** (*entre
dos magnitudes*) relationship; ~ **calidad-pre-
cio** value for money; **los gastos no guardan** ~
con el presupuesto the expenses bear no
relation to the budget **3.** (*entre personas*) relationship; **relaciones públicas** public
relations; **tener relaciones con alguien** to be
in contact with sb; **tener muchas relaciones**
(*amigos*) to have lots of friends; (*influyentes*)
to have lots of contacts; **tienen buenas/
malas relaciones** they have a good/bad relationship **4.** *pl* (*noviazgo, amorío*) relationship;
han roto sus relaciones they have broken
up; **mantienen relaciones** they are going out
with each other; **mantener relaciones sexuales con alguien** to have a sexual relationship with sb **5.** (*relato*) account; (*informe*)
report; **hacer una** ~ **de algo** to report on sth;
hacer una ~ **detallada de algo** to make a
detailed report about sth **6.** (*lista*) list
relacional *adj* relational; **base de datos** ~
INFOR relational database
relacionar **I.** *vt* **1.** (*poner en relación*) to

relate **2.** (*relatar*) to report **II.** *vr:* ~se **1.** (*estar relacionado*) to be related **2.** (*iniciar relaciones*) to strike up a relationship; (*mantener relaciones*) to mix; ~se mucho (*tener amigos*) to have lots of friends; (*influyentes*) to have lots of contacts

relajación *f* **1.** (*distensión, distracción*) relaxation **2.** (*malas costumbres*) slackness **3.** (*debilitación*) weakening **4.** (*atenuación*) easing; ~ de la pena reduction of the sentence **5.** MED sprain; (*de la hernia*) hernia

relajado, -a *adj* **1.** (*sosegado*) relaxed **2.** (*débil*) loose **3.** (*vicioso*) dissolute

relajadura *f Méx* (*hernia*) rupture

relajar I. *vt* **1.** (*distender, distraer*) to relax **2.** (*suavizar*) to ease; (*la pena*) to reduce **II.** *vr:* ~se **1.** (*distenderse, descansar*) to relax **2.** (*debilitarse*) to weaken **3.** (*suavizarse*) to ease **4.** (*viciarse*) to become dissolute

relamer I. *vt* to lick **II.** *vr:* ~se **1.** (*los labios*) to lick one's lips **2.** (*gozar*) ~se con algo to relish sth; ~se con un manjar to eat a delicacy with great relish **3.** (*gloriarse*) ~se de algo to gloat over sth **4.** (*arreglarse*) to clean oneself up **5.** (*animal*) to lick its chops

relamido, -a *adj* **1.** (*arreglado*) prim and proper **2.** (*afectado*) affected

relámpago *m* flash of lightning; ser (veloz como) un ~ to be as fast as lightning

relampaguear I. *vi* to sparkle **II.** *v impers* relampagueaba there was lightning

relance *m* **1.** *Chile* (*piropo*) flirtatious compliment **2.** *Col* de ~ (*al contado*) in cash

relatar *vt* (*información*) to report; (*una historia*) to tell

relatividad *f sin pl* FÍS relativity

relativizar <z→c> *vt* to play down

relativo *m* LING (*pronombre*) relative pronoun; oración de ~ relative clause

relativo, -a *adj* **1.** (*referente*) relative; un artículo ~ a... an article about ... **2.** (*dependiente*) relative; pronombre ~ relative pronoun; ser ~ a algo to be relative to sth **3.** (*poco*) limited

relato *m* report; LIT story; ~ corto short story

relé *m* ELEC relay

relegar <g→gu> *vt* **1.** (*apartar*) to relegate; ser relegado al olvido to be consigned to oblivion; ~ algo a un plano secundario to push sth into the background **2.** (*desterrar*) to banish

relente *f* night dew; dormir al ~ to sleep out in the open

relevancia *f* importance, relevance

relevante *adj* **1.** (*importante*) important **2.** (*sobresaliente*) outstanding

relevar I. *vt* **1.** (*liberar*) to exempt; ~ a alguien de un juramento to release sb from an oath; ~ a alguien de sus deudas to release sb from his/her debts; ~ a alguien de sus culpas to exonerate sb from blame for his/her actions **2.** JUR (*destituir*) to remove; ~ a alguien de un cargo to relieve sb of his/her

post **3.** (*reemplazar*) to place; MIL to relieve; DEP to substitute **4.** (*acentuar*) to highlight **II.** *vr:* ~se to take turns

relevo *m* **1.** (*reemplazo*) change; tomar el ~ de alguien to take over from sb **2.** (*pl*) DEP (*competición*) relay; carrera de ~s relay race **3.** MIL change of the guard

relicario *m* **1.** (*para reliquias*) reliquary **2.** *AmL* (*medallón*) locket

relieve *m* **1.** ARTE, GEO relief; en bajo ~ in bas-relief **2.** (*renombre*) prominence ▶poner de ~ to emphasize; de ~ important

religión *f* **1.** (*creencia, doctrina*) religion; ~ reformada Protestantism; sin ~ godless **2.** (*virtud*) virtue **3.** (*orden*) entrar en ~ to take vows

religiosidad *f* **1.** (*observancia*) religiosity, religiousness **2.** (*piedad*) piety **3.** (*puntualidad*) punctuality; (*exactitud*) thoroughness

religioso, -a I. *adj* **1.** (*relativo a la religión*) religious **2.** (*pío*) pious **3.** (*puntual*) punctual; (*exacto*) thorough **II.** *m, f* member of a religious order, monk *m*, nun *f*

relinchar *vi* to neigh, to whinny

relincho *m* **1.** (*de un caballo*) neigh, whinny **2.** (*de alguien*) whoop

reliquia *f* **1.** *t.* REL relic; una ~ de familia a family heirloom **2.** (*antigüedad*) collector's item **3.** MED after-effect

rellano *m* (*de escalera*) landing

rellena *f Col, Méx* (*morcilla*) blood sausage

rellenar *vt* **1.** (*llenar*) ~ de [*o* con] algo to fill with sth; GASTR to stuff with sth; ~ los agujeros de yeso to fill in the holes with plaster **2.** (*por completo*) to fill up; (*demasiado*) to overfill **3.** (*volver a llenar*) to refill **4.** (*completar*) to fill out **5.** *inf* (*dar de comer*) to feed up *Brit*, to put on the feedbag *Am*

relleno *m* **1.** (*material*) filling; GASTR stuffing **2.** (*superfluidad*) padding; palabra de ~ filler

relleno, -a *adj* **1.** (*lleno*) full; (*demasiado*) stuffed full; GASTR stuffed **2.** *inf* (*gordo*) chubby

reloj *m* clock; (*de pulsera*) watch; ~ despertador alarm clock; ~ para fichar time clock; ~ de arena hourglass; ~ de sol sundial, ~ de caja [*o* de péndulo] grandfather clock; carrera contra ~ race against the clock; trabajar contra ~ to work against the clock; ser (como) un ~ (*mecanismo*) to go like clockwork; (*persona*) to be very punctual

relojear *vt Arg* **1.** (*tomar el tiempo*) to time **2.** *inf* (*controlar, espiar*) to keep tabs on; ~ a alguien de arriba abajo to look sb up and down

relojería *f* clockmaker's; (*de relojes de pulsera*) watchmaker's

relojero, -a *m, f* clockmaker; (*de relojes de pulsera*) watchmaker

reluciente *adj* shining; ~ de limpio shiny clean

relucir *irr como lucir* *vi* **1.** (*despedir, reflejar luz*) to shine **2.** (*sobresalir*) to stand out ▶sacar algo a ~ to bring sth up; salir a ~ to come up

reluctante *adj* reluctant

relumbrar *vi* 1. (*emitir, reflejar luz*) to shine 2. (*sobresalir*) to stand out

relumbrón *m* 1. (*destello*) flash 2. (*oropel*) flashiness ►**de** ~ flashy

remachado, -a *adj* 1. (*nariz*) flat 2. *Col* (*callado*) quiet

remachar I. *vt* 1. (*golpear*) to hammer 2. (*doblar*) to bend; (*aplastar*) to flatten 3. (*sujetar*) to rivet 4. (*subrayar*) to stress; ~ algo a alguien to stress sth to sb II. *vr:* ~se *Col* to remain silent

remanente I. *adj* remaining II. *m* remainder; COM surplus; (*contabilidad*) carry-over

remangar <g→gu> I. *vt* to roll up II. *vr:* ~se *t. fig* to roll up one's sleeves

remansarse *vr* (*corriente*) to be still

remanso *m* (*represa*) pool; (*agua muerta*) stagnant water ►~ de paz haven of peace

remar *vi* (*bogar*) to row

rematado, -a *adj* absolute; un tonto ~ an absolute idiot

rematar I. *vt* 1. (*concluir*) to finish (off); (*terminar de hacer*) to put the finishing touches to; nunca rematas lo que has empezado you never finish what you start 2. (*matar: animal*) to put out of its misery; (*persona*) to finish off 3. (*una costura*) to finish off 4. (*gastar*) to use up 5. DEP to shoot 6. (*en subasta*) to knock down 7. (*vender*) to sell off (cheap) II. *vi* 1. DEP to shoot 2. (*terminar*) to end; la torre remata en punta the tower ends in a point

remate *m* 1. (*conclusión*) conclusion; (*de un producto*) finishing touch; dar ~ a un edificio to put the finishing touches to a building 2. (*final, extremo*) end; poner ~ a un mueble to ornament a piece of furniture 3. (*matanza*) killing off, coup de grâce 4. (*adjudicación*) sale by auction 5. (*oferta*) highest bid 6. DEP shot 7. (*consumo*) consumption; dar ~ to use up 8. (*venta*) sale (*at a low price*) ►estar loco as a hatter; ser tonto de ~ to be completely stupid; para ~ to cap it all *Brit*, to top it all off *Am;* por ~ finally

remecer *irr como crecer vt, vr:* ~se *AmL* (*sacudir*) to shake

remedar *vt* (*imitar*) to imitate; (*parodiar*) to mimic

remediar *vt* 1. (*evitar*) to prevent; no me cae bien, no puedo ~lo I don't like him/her, I can't help it 2. (*acabar con*) to finish off; (*reparar*) to repair; (*compensar*) to make up for; llorando no remedias nada crying won't solve anything 3. (*corregir*) to correct 4. (*ayudar*) to help

remedio *m* 1. (*arreglo*) remedy; (*compensación*) compensation; (*corrección*) correction; no tener ~ to be a hopeless case; mi hermano no tiene ~ my brother is beyond help; tu problema/la crisis no tiene ~ there is no

solution to your problem/to the crisis; no llores, ya no tiene ~ don't cry, there's nothing that can be done now; eso tiene fácil ~ that is easy to fix; no hay ~ there's nothing we can do; no tenemos [*o* no hay] más ~ que... the only solution is ..., there is no choice but to ...; poner ~ a un mal to right a wrong; sin ~ (*inútil*) hopeless; (*sin falta*) inevitable; un idealista sin ~ an incurable idealist 2. (*ayuda*) help; buscar ~ en sus amigos to turn to one's friends for help; buscar ~ en la bebida to turn to drink 3. MED (*medio*) remedy; ~ naturalista natural remedy; ~ casero household [*o* home] remedy ►es peor el ~ que la enfermedad *prov* the remedy is worse than the disease; ¿qué ~? what choice is there?

remedo *m* 1. (*imitación*) imitation; (*mal hecha*) travesty 2. (*parodia*) parody

rememorar *vt* to remember

remendar <e→ie> *vt* (*reparar*) to mend; (*con parches*) to patch; (*zurcir*) to darn

remera *f* 1. ZOOL flight feather 2. *Arg* (*camiseta*) T-shirt

remero, -a *m, f* rower, oarsman

remesa *f* consignment, shipment; FIN remittance

remezón *m AmL* (*sacudida*) shake

remiendo *m* 1. (*reparación*) mending; (*con parches*) patching; (*zurcidura*) darning 2. (*corrección*) correction 3. (*extra*) addition 4. (*parche*) patch 5. (*mancha*) stain

remilgado, -a *adj* prim; (*quisquilloso*) fussy

remilgo *m* primness; (*quisquilloso*) fussiness; sin ~s without making a fuss; hacer ~s to make a fuss

reminiscencia *f* 1. (*en una obra*) influence; la ópera tiene ~s wagnerianas the opera shows Wagnerian influences 2. (*lo que sobrevive*) remainder 3. (*recuerdo*) reminiscence

remirar I. *vt* (*volver a mirar*) to look at again; (*mirar intensamente*) to scrutinize; por más que miro y remiro no encuentro tu libro however much I search I cannot find your book II. *vr:* ~se 1. (*poner cuidado*) ~se en algo to take great pains over sth 2. (*mirar*) to observe carefully

remisible *adj* (*deuda, pena*) which can be cancelled *Brit* [*o* canceled *Am*]; (*pecado*) remissible

remisión *f* 1. (*envío*) consignment 2. (*referencia*) reference 3. (*atenuación*) slackening 4. (*de una obligación*) excusal; (*de los pecados*) forgiveness; (*de una deuda*) cancellation *Brit*, cancelation *Am;* (*de una pena*) release; sin ~ without fail 5. MED remission

remiso, -a *adj* (*reacio*) reluctant; (*irresoluto*) hesitant; (*lento*) slow; mostrarse ~ a hacer algo to be reluctant to do sth

remite *m* sender's name and address

remitente *mf* sender

remitir I. *vt* 1. (*enviar*) to send; FIN to remit; ~ algo a alguien to send sth to sb 2. (*referirse*) to refer **3.** (*de una obligación*) to forgive; ~ **a alguien de una pena** to release sb from a punishment; ~ **a alguien de una deuda** to cancel sb's debt; ~ **a alguien de sus pecados** to forgive sb his/her sins **4.** (*aplazar*) to postpone; (*un juicio*) to adjourn **5.** (*confiar*) to entrust **6.** (*ceder*) to hand over **II.** *vi* (*calmarse*) to let up **III.** *vr:* ~**se 1.** (*referirse*) to refer **2.** (*calmarse*) to let up **3.** (*confiarse*) to trust; ~**se al juez** to abide by the ruling of the judge

remo *m* **1.** (*pala: con soporte*) oar; (*sin soporte*) paddle; **a**(**l**) ~ by rowing boat *Brit,* by rowboat *Am; fig* with difficulty **2.** DEP rowing ▶**a** ~ **y** <u>vela</u> *inf* speedily; <u>andar</u> **al** ~ *inf* to work like a slave; <u>tomar</u> **el** ~ *inf* to take the helm

remodelación *f* redesign, remodelling *Brit,* remodeling *Am;* ~ **del gabinete** cabinet reshuffle

remodelar *vt* to redesign, to remodel; (*gobierno*) to reshuffle

remojar I. *vt* **1.** (*mojar, sumergir*) to soak; (*empapar*) to drench; (*ablandar*) to soften; (*galleta*) to dip **2.** (*celebrar*) to drink to **II.** *vr:* ~**se** (*mojarse*) to get wet; (*bañarse*) to have a dip

remojo *m* **1.** (*empapamiento, sumersión*) soaking; (*baño*) dip; **poner en** ~ to leave to soak **2.** (*celebración*) toast

remojón *m* **1.** (*empapamiento, sumersión*) soaking; **darse un** ~ **en la piscina** to have a dip in the pool **2.** (*baño*) dip

remolacha *f* beet; (*roja*) beetroot; (*de azúcar*) (sugar) beet

remolcador *m* **1.** (*camión*) breakdown truck *Brit,* tow truck *Am* **2.** (*barco*) tug

remolcador(**a**) *adj* **grúa** ~**a** breakdown truck *Brit,* tow truck *Am*

remolcar <c→qu> *vt* **1.** (*un barco*) to tug; (*un vehículo averiado*) to tow **2.** (*convencer*) to rope in

remolienda *f Arg, Urug, inf* (*juerga*) binge

remolino *m* **1.** (*movimiento*) whirl; (*de agua*) whirlpool; ~ **de viento** whirlwind **2.** (*pelo*) cowlick **3.** (*gente*) throng **4.** (*confusión*) commotion **5.** *inf* (*persona*) whirlwind

remolón, -ona I. *adj* lazy **II.** *m, f* (*vago*) slacker; (*que evita algo*) shirker; **hacerse el** ~ (*vaguear*) to be lazy; **siempre se hace el** ~ **a la hora de fregar** he/she always tries to get out of doing the washing-up

remolonear *vi, vr:* ~**se 1.** (*vaguear*) to be lazy **2.** (*evitar*) to shirk

remolque *m* **1.** (*arrastre*) tow **2.** (*vehículo*) trailer **3.** (*cuerda*) towrope; **llevar a** ~ to tow ▶<u>hacer</u> algo **a** ~ to do sth reluctantly

remontar I. *vt* **1.** (*superar*) to overcome **2.** (*subir*) to go up; ~ **un río** (*navegar*) to go up a river; (*nadar*) to swim up a river **3.** (*elevar*) to fly; ~ **el vuelo** to soar **4.** (*la caza*) to beat **II.** *vr:* ~**se 1.** (*volar*) to climb; (*ave*) to soar **2.** (*gastos*) to amount **3.** (*pertenecer, retroceder*) to go back to; **la construcción de la**

iglesia se remonta al siglo pasado the construction of the church dates from the past century; **el discurso se remonta a los orígenes del automóvil** the speech goes back to the origins of the automobile

remorder <o→ue> **I.** *vt* **1.** (*atormentar*) to torment **2.** (*morder*) to bite again **II.** *vr:* ~**se** to suffer remorse

remordimiento *m* remorse; **tener** ~**s** (**de conciencia**) **por algo** to feel remorseful about sth; **el** ~ **no lo deja dormir** he can't sleep for remorse

remotamente *adv* **1.** (*vagamente*) vaguely **2.** (*lejos*) distantly; (*hace tiempo*) long ago ▶**ni** ~ not in the slightest, far from it

remoto, -a *adj* **1.** (*lejano*) remote; **en tiempos** ~**s** long ago **2.** (*improbable*) remote; **no existe ni la más remota posiblidad** there is not the slightest possibility; **no tener ni la más remota idea** to not have the slightest idea; **¡ni por lo más** ~**!** not on your life!

remover <o→ue> **I.** *vt* **1.** (*mover*) to remove **2.** (*agitar*) to shake; (*dar vueltas*) to stir; (*la ensalada*) to toss **3.** (*activar*) to stir up **II.** *vi* to investigate **III.** *vr:* ~**se 1.** (*moverse*) to roll about **2.** (*aguas*) to move about

remozar <z→c> *vt* to renovate

remunerable *adj* remunerable

remuneración *f* **1.** (*pago*) remuneration **2.** (*recompensa*) compensation **3.** (*rendimiento*) profit

remunerar *vt* **1.** (*pagar*) to remunerate; ~ **a alguien por un servicio** to pay sb for a service **2.** (*recompensar*) to compensate **3.** (*rendir*) to be profitable for

remunerativo, -a *adj* remunerative

renacer *irr como crecer vi* **1.** (*volver a nacer*) to be reborn **2.** (*regenerarse*) to revive; **sentirse** ~ to feel completely revived

renacimiento *m* **1.** ARTE, LIT renaissance **2.** *t.* FILOS, REL (*regeneración*) revival

renacuajo *m* tadpole

renacuajo, -a *m, f pey* shrimp

renal *adj* renal

Renania *f* Rhineland

rencilla *f* quarrel

rencor *m* ill feeling; **guardar** ~ **a alguien** to bear a grudge against sb

rencoroso, -a *adj* **1.** (*vengativo*) spiteful **2.** (*resentido*) resentful

rendición *f* **1.** (*capitulación, sumisión*) surrender **2.** (*entrega*) yield; ~ **de cuentas** balance **3.** (*utilidad*) usefulness **4.** (*fatiga*) exhaustion **5.** (*conquista*) conquest

rendidamente *adv* devotedly; **estar** ~ **enamorado de** to be besotted with

rendido, -a *adj* **1.** (*cansado*) exhausted **2.** (*sumiso*) submissive; **cayó** ~ **ante su belleza** he was enchanted by her beauty

rendija *f* crack

rendimiento *m* **1.** (*productividad*) yield; ECON (*máximo*) capacity; **a pleno** ~ at full capacity **2.** (*beneficio*) profit; **de gran** ~ very profitable **3.** (*cansancio*) exhaustion **4.** *pl* (*ingresos*) income **5.** (*humildad*) humility **6.** (*obsequiosidad*) servility

rendir *irr como pedir* **I.** *vt* **1.** (*rentar*) to yield; ~ **utilidad** to be useful; ~ **fruto** to bear fruit; **la inversión ha rendido mucho** the investment has been very profitable **2.** (*trabajar*) to produce; **estas máquinas rinden mucho** these machines are very productive **3.** (*tributar*) to attribute; ~ **las gracias a alguien** to thank sb; ~ **importancia a algo** to attribute importance to sth **4.** (*entregar*) to hand over; (*pruebas*) to bring; (*una confesión*) to make; ~ **cuentas** to settle the accounts; *fig* to account for one's actions; ~ **obsequios a alguien** to praise sb; ~ **las armas** to surrender one's arms **5.** (*vencer*) to defeat **6.** (*cansar*) to exhaust; **me rindió el sueño** I was overcome by tiredness **7.** (*substituir*) to replace **II.** *vr:* ~**se 1.** (*entregarse*) to surrender; ~**se al enemigo** to surrender to the enemy; ~**se a la evidencia de algo** to bow to the evidence of sth; ~**se a las razones de alguien** to yield to sb's arguments **2.** (*cansarse*) ~**se de cansancio** to give in to one's exhaustion

renegado, -a I. *adj* **1.** (*religión*) apostate **2.** *inf* (*carácter*) bad-tempered **II.** *m, f* **1.** (*religión*) apostate **2.** *inf* (*carácter*) grouch

renegar *irr como fregar* **I.** *vi* **1.** (*protestar*) ~ **de algo** to protest against sth **2.** (*renunciar*) to renounce; ~ **de la fe** to renounce one's faith; ~ **del partido** to renounce the party **II.** *vt* **1.** (*negar*) to deny **2.** (*detestar*) to detest

RENFE *f abr de* **Red Nacional de Ferrocarriles Españoles** *Spanish state railway company*

renglón *m* **1.** (*línea*) line; **poner cuatro renglones a alguien** to drop sb a line; **a ~ seguido** on the next line; *fig* straight away **2.** (*partida*) share

rengo, -a *adj CSur* (*cojo*) lame

renguear *vi CSur* (*cojear*) to limp

renguera *f CSur* limp

reno *m* reindeer

renombrado, -a *adj* (*célebre*) renowned

renombrar *vt* to name

renombre *m* renown; **una empresa de gran ~** a very well-known company; **una persona de ~** a famous person; **adquirir ~** to become renowned; **gozar de ~** to be renowned

renovación *f* renewal; (*de un edificio*) renovation

renovar <o→ue> *vt* to renew; (*una casa*) to renovate; (*un país*) to modernize; ~ **un pedido** to repeat a request; ~ **la pintura** to touch up the paintwork; ~ **la memoria** to refresh one's memory; ~ **un aviso** to repeat a warning

renquear *vi* to limp

renta *f* **1.** (*beneficio*) profit; (*ingresos*) income; ~ **per cápita** per capita income; ~**s públicas** national revenue **2.** (*pensión*) pension; ~ **por incapacidad laboral** invalidity benefit; ~ **vitalicia** life annuity; ~ **de viudez** widow's pension **3.** (*alquiler*) rent; **en ~** for rent; **tomar a ~ un negocio** to lease out a business

rentabilidad *f* profitability; ~ **competitiva** cost-effectiveness; **dar una ~ de...** to yield profits of ...

rentable *adj* profitable

rentar **I.** *vt* **1.** (*beneficio*) to yield **2.** *AmL* (*alquilar*) to rent **II.** *vi* to be profitable; ~ **bien** to yield a good profit

rentero, -a *m, f* **1.** (*arrendatario*) tenant farmer **2.** *Arg* (*contribuyente*) tax payer

rentista *mf* **1.** (*pensionista*) pensioner **2.** (*hacendista*) tax expert

renuencia *f* reluctance

renuente *adj* reluctant

renuevo *m* **1.** (*tallo*) shoot **2.** (*renovación*) renewal

renuncia *f* **1.** (*abandono*) ~ **a** [*o de*] **algo** resignation from sth; ~ **del cargo** resignation from the post; ~ **al contrato** withdrawal from the contract; **presentar su ~** to resign **2.** (*escrito*) waiver

renunciar *vi* **1.** (*desistir*) ~ **a** [*o de*] **algo** to renounce sth; ~ **al trono** to abdicate the throne; ~ **a un cargo** to resign from a post; ~ **a una herencia** to renounce an inheritance **2.** (*rechazar*) ~ **a algo** to reject sth

reñido, -a *adj* **1.** (*enojado*) angry; **estoy ~ con él** I have fallen out with him **2.** (*en oposición*) *fig* to be incompatible **3.** (*encarnizado*) bitter

reñir *irr como ceñir* **I.** *vi* to quarrel; **¿has reñido con tu novio?** have you had a row with your boyfriend? ►**dos no riñen si uno no quiere** it takes two to make a quarrel **II.** *vt* to scold

reo, -a I. *adj* accused **II.** *m, f* (*culpado*) defendant; (*autor*) culprit; ~ **de asesinato** murderer; ~ **habitual** persistent offender; ~ **preventivo** remand prisoner

reojo *m* **mirar de ~** (*con hostilidad*) to look askance at; (*con disimulo*) to look out of the corner of one's eye at

reorganización *f* reorganization; ~ **del gobierno** government reshuffle

reorganizar <z→c> *vt* to reorganize; (*gobierno*) to reshuffle

reorientación *f* reorientation; ~ **política** political realignment

repanchigarse <g→gu> *vr;* **repantigarse** <g→gu> *vr* to sprawl out

reparable *adj* (*arreglable*) repairable

reparación *f* **1.** (*arreglo*) repair **2.** (*indemnización, enmienda*) compensation; ~ **de perjuicios** damages *pl*

reparar **I.** *vt* **1.** (*arreglar*) to repair; ~ **el daño** to repair the damage **2.** (*indemnizar, enmendar*) to compensate **3.** (*recuperar*) ~ **fuerzas** to recover one's strength; **con la siesta reparo fuerzas** a nap refreshes me **II.** *vi* ~ **en** (*advertir*) to notice; (*considerar*) to consider;

sin ~ **en gastos** regardless of the cost; **no ~ en sacrificios/gastos** to spare no effort/ expense **III.** *vr:* **~se** to restrain oneself
reparo *m* **1.** (*arreglo*) repair **2.** (*inconveniente*) problem; **sin ~ alguno** without any difficulty; **me da ~ decírselo** I don't like to say it; **tener ~s para** to be reluctant [*o* hesitant] to **3.** (*objeción*) objection; **sin ~** without reservation; **no andar con ~s** to have no reservations; **poner ~s a algo** to raise objections to sth
repartición *f* **1.** *v.* **repartimiento 2.** *AmL* (*oficina*) office
repartidor(a) *m(f)* (*recadero*) delivery man, delivery woman *m, f;* **~ de periódicos** newspaper boy *m*, newspaper girl *f*
repartimiento *m* (*distribución*) distribution; (*división*) division
repartir I. *vt* to distribute; (*correos*) to deliver **II.** *vr:* **~se 1.** (*colocarse*) to place oneself **2.** (*dividir*) to divide up; **~se el mercado** to divide up the market
reparto *m* **1.** (*distribución*) distribution; (*división*) division; **~ de contribuciones** allotment of taxes; **~ domiciliario** home delivery; **~ de equipajes** baggage reclaim; **~ postal** mail delivery; **camión de ~** (*furgoneta*) delivery van; (*grande*) delivery lorry *Brit,* delivery truck *Am* **2.** (*relación*) division; **~ de poderes** ECON division of power
repasador *m Arg, Urug* (*paño de cocina*) dish cloth
repasar *vt* **1.** (*la ropa*) to mend **2.** (*un texto, la lección*) to revise; **segunda edición repasada y corregida** second edition, revised and amended **3.** (*la cuenta*) to check **4.** (*una carta*) to reread
repaso *m* **1.** (*revisión*) review **2.** (*inspección*) check
repatear *vt inf* **1.** (*molestar*) to annoy; **me repatean cosas así** things like that really get to me **2.** (*disgustar*) to dislike; **su mujer me repatea** I can't stand his wife
repatriar *vt* to repatriate
repe *m Ecua* GASTR *mashed cooked bananas with milk and cheese*
repecho *m* (steep) slope; **a ~** uphill
repeinar I. *vt* to comb carefully; *pey* to doll up **II.** *vr:* **~se** to comb one's hair carefully; *pey* to doll oneself up
repelente I. *adj* **1.** (*rechazador*) repellent; **~ al agua** water-repellent **2.** (*repugnante*) repulsive **3.** (*redicho*) affected **II.** *mf* (*sabelotodo*) know-all *Brit,* know-it-all *Am*
repeler *vt* **1.** (*rechazar*) to repel; **los imanes se repelen mutuamente** magnets repel one another **2.** (*repugnar*) to disgust
repelo *m* **1.** (*pelo*) hair which sticks up; **a ~** against the grain **2.** (*repugnancia*) repugnance
repelón *m* **dar repelones** to tug one's hair ▶**ser más viejo que el ~** to be as old as the hills; **a repelones** (*con dificultad*) with difficulty; (*con resistencia*) unwillingly; **de ~** with-

out stopping
repelús *m inf* sudden shiver; **las arañas me dan ~** spiders give me the creeps
repeluzno *m* (*escalofrío*) wave (of disgust)
repensar <e→ie> *vt* to reconsider
repente *m inf* (*movimiento*) start; (*ataque*) fit ▶**de ~** suddenly, all of a sudden; **de ~ se echó a llorar** suddenly he/she started to cry
repentino, -a *adj* sudden
repera *f* **¡eres la ~!** *inf* you really take the biscuit *Brit* [*o* cake *Am*]!
repercusión *f* **1.** (*efecto*) repercussion; **tener gran ~** (*éxito*) to meet with great success **2.** (*del choque*) reverberation
repercutir *vi* **1.** (*efecto*) **~ en algo** to have an effect on sth; **~ en la salud** to affect one's health **2.** (*del choque*) to rebound **3.** (*eco*) to reverberate
repertorio *m* **1.** (*lista*) list; **~ legislativo** legislative program **2.** *t.* TEAT repertoire, repertory
repesca *f inf* second chance; DEP play-off
repescar <c→qu> *vt inf* to give a second chance to
repetición *f* repetition; **~ de orden** repeat order; **fusil de ~** repeating rifle; **en caso de ~** in case of repetition
repetido, -a *adj* repeated; **repetidas veces** again and again; **tengo muchos sellos ~s** I have doubles of lots of my stamps
repetidor *m* TÉC repeater, booster
repetidor(a) I. *adj* repeating **II.** *m(f)* **1.** (*estudiante*) resit student *Brit,* repeating student **2.** (*profesor*) tutor (*who prepares students for resit examinations*)
repetir *irr como* **pedir I.** *vi* **1.** (*sabor*) to repeat; **los ajos repiten mucho** garlic comes back on you **2.** (*plato*) **~ de un plato de comida** to have second helpings of a dish **II.** *vt* (*reiterar, recitar*) to repeat; **~ curso** to stay down; **~ un pedido de mercancía** to reorder goods **III.** *vr:* **~se** to repeat oneself
repicar <c→qu> **I.** *vi* (*campanas*) to ring, to peal; (*castañuelas*) to click **II.** *vt* **1.** (*campanas*) to ring; (*instrumento*) to play **2.** (*despedazar*) to mince **III.** *vr:* **~se** to boast
repipi *adj* la-di-da; **niño ~** little know-all
repique *m* **1.** (*de las campanas*) peal **2.** *inf* (*riña*) squabble
repiquetear *vi, vt* to ring; (*castañuelas*) to click
repiqueteo *m* peal; (*castañuelas*) click
repisa *f* shelf; **~ de chimenea** mantelpiece; **~ de ventana** window ledge
replantear *vt* **1.** (*asunto*) to raise again; (*plan*) to revise; (*reconsiderar*) to rethink **2.** ARQUIT to lay out a ground plan of
replegar *irr como* **fregar I.** *vt* **1.** (*doblar*) to fold **2.** (*para atrás*) to fold back **II.** *vr:* **~se** MIL to fall back
repleto, -a *adj* **~ de algo** full of sth; (*demasiado*) crammed with sth; **tener una cartera repleta de billetes** to have a wallet full of notes *Brit* [*o* bills *Am*]; **el tren está ~** the train

R

is packed; **estoy ~** I'm full up; **está repleta de energía** she is full of energy

réplica f 1.(*respuesta*) reply; (*objeción*) rebuttal 2. ARTE replica

replicar <c→qu> I. *vt* to answer II. *vi* 1.(*replicar*) to reply 2.(*contradecir*) to contradict; **obedecer sin ~** to obey without argument

repliegue m 1.(*dobladura*) fold 2. MIL withdrawal

repoblación f (*de personas*) repopulation; (*de plantas*) replanting; **~ forestal** reafforestation *Brit*, reforestation *Am*

repoblar <o→ue> *vt* (*personas*) to repopulate; (*plantas*) to replant; (*árboles*) to reafforest *Brit*, to reforest *Am*

repollo m cabbage

repolludo, -a *adj fig* cabbage-headed; (*regordete*) chubby

reponer *irr como poner* I. *vt* 1.(*volver a poner*) to put back; (*teléfono*) to hang up; (*máquina*) to put back into service; (*en su cargo*) to reinstate 2.(*reemplazar*) to replace 3.(*completar*) to replenish 4.(*replicar*) to reply 5. CINE to rerelease; TEAT to revive; TV to rerun II. *vr:* ~se to recover

reportaje m report; PREN article; **~ gráfico** illustrated report; (*documental*) documentary

reportar I. *vt* 1.(*refrenar*) to check 2.(*proporcionar*) to bring 3. *AmL* (*informar*) to report II. *vr:* ~se to restrain oneself

reporte m 1.(*noticia*) news item 2. TIPO transfer

reportear *vt AmL* (*entrevistar*) to interview

reportero, -a m, f reporter; **~ gráfico** press photographer

reposabrazos m *inv* armrest

reposacabezas m *inv* headrest

reposado, -a *adj* peaceful; (*agua*) calm

reposapiés m *inv* footrest

reposar I. *vi* to rest; **aquí reposan los restos mortales de...** here lie the mortal remains of ... II. *vt* to settle; **~ la comida** to let one's food settle III. *vr:* ~se (*líquidos*) to settle; (*vino*) to lie

reposera f *AmL* (*tumbona*) deckchair

reposición f 1.(*de un objeto*) replacement; **~ de existencias** replenishment of stocks; **~ de maquinaria** replacement of machinery 2.(*del mercado, de una persona*) recovery 3.(*de una situación*) stabilization 4. TEAT revival; TV rerun; CINE rerelease

reposo m (*tranquilidad*) peace; (*descanso*) rest; **~ en cama** rest in bed, bed rest; **una máquina en ~** a machine at rest

repostada f *AmC* (*contestación*) rude reply

repostar *vt* 1.(*provisiones*) to stock up with 2.(*vehículo*) to refuel; (*combustible*) to fill up with

repostería f 1.(*pastelería*) cake [o pastry] shop 2.(*oficio*) pastrymaking 3.(*productos*) pastries pl

repostero, -a m, f pastrycook

reprender *vt* to reprimand; **~ algo a alguien** to scold [o to reprimand] sb for sth

reprensión f t. JUR reprimand

represa f 1.(*estancamiento*) pool 2.(*construcción*) dam

represalia f reprisal; **en ~ por...** in retaliation for ...

represar I. *vt* (*agua*) to hold back; (*río*) to dam; *fig* to contain II. *vr:* ~se (*agua*) to be held back; (*río*) to be dammed

representación f 1.(*substitución, delegación*) representation; **~ colectiva** collective representation; **~ exclusiva** exclusive representation; **~ mayoritaria** majority representation; **~ proporcional** POL proportional representation; **por [o en] ~ de** representing 2. TEAT performance 3.(*reproducción*) reproduction; (*ilustración*) illustration; **~ digital** digital display 4.(*idea*) idea 5.(*autoridad*) standing; **ser hombre de ~** to be a man of some standing

representante mf 1.(*delegado, suplente*) representative; **~ especial** special representative 2. TEAT, CINE agent, manager; (*actor*) actor, actress m, f 3. COM dealer, salesman m, saleswoman f

representar I. *vt* 1.(*sustituir*) to represent 2.(*actuar*) to act; (*una obra*) to perform; **~ el papel de amante** to play the role of lover 3.(*significar*) to mean 4.(*encarnar, personificar*) to embody; (*reproducir*) to reproduce; (*ilustrar*) to illustrate; **~ visualmente** INFOR to display visually 5.(*aparentar*) to seem; **representa ser más joven** he/she seems younger 6.(*evocar*) to evoke II. *vr:* ~se to imagine

representativo, -a *adj* representative; **gobierno ~** representative government

represión f (*contención*) suppression; (*limitación*) repression; **~ de crímenes** anti-crime measures

reprimenda f reprimand

reprimir I. *vt* to suppress II. *vr:* ~se 1.(*contenerse*) to control oneself; **~se de hablar** to refrain from speaking 2.(*cohibirse*) to be repressed

reprobable *adj* reprehensible

reprobación f 1.(*condenación*) condemnation 2.(*rechazamiento*) rejection

reprobar <o→ue> *vt* to condemn

réprobo, -a *adj, m, f* reprobate

reprochable *adj* reprehensible

reprochar *vt* to reproach

reproche m reproach; **en son de ~** in a reproachful tone; **hacer ~s a alguien por algo** to reproach sb for sth

reproducción f 1.(*procreación*) reproduction; **~ bovina** cattle breeding 2.(*repetición*) repetition; (*copia*) reproduction; **~ (de un libro)** copy (of a book); **~ de un discurso** repeat of a speech; (*documentos*) duplication 3.(*representación*) reproduction; **~ magnetofónica** tape recording; **~ radiofónica** radio reproduction

reproducir *irr como traducir* I. *vt* 1.(*pro-

crear) to reproduce **2.**(*repetir*) to repeat; (*copiar*) to reproduce; (*un libro*) to print; (*documento*) to duplicate **3.**(*representar*) to represent; (*imitar*) to imitate; (*contar*) to recount **II.** *vr:* ~**se** to reproduce

reproductor *m* (*aparato*) playback machine; ~ **de discos compactos** compact disc player; ~ **de video** video recorder

reproductor(a) I. *adj* reproductive **II.** *m(f)* (*animal*) breeder

reptar *vi* to crawl

reptil *m* reptile

república *f* republic; ~ **miembro** member republic; ~ **bananera** *pey* banana republic

republicano, -a *adj, m, f* republican

repudiar *vt* **1.**(*rechazar*) to reject **2.**(*parientes*) to disown

repudio *m* **1.**(*rechazo*) rejection **2.**(*de parientes*) repudiation

repuesto *m* **1.**(*pieza*) spare part; **rueda de** ~ spare tyre *Brit,* spare tire *Am* **2.**(*de alimentos*) supply

repuesto, -a *pp de* **reponer**

repugnancia *f* **1.**(*repulsión*) ~ **a algo** repugnance for sth **2.**(*asco*) ~ **a algo** disgust for sth; **tener** ~ **al pescado** to loathe fish **3.**(*resistencia*) reluctance; **hacer algo con** ~ to do sth reluctantly

repugnante *adj* disgusting

repugnar I. *vi* **1.**(*producir aversión*) to repel; (*asquear*) to disgust; **me repugna la carne grasosa** fatty meat makes me sick **2.**(*disgustar*) to disgust **II.** *vt* (*rehusar*) to refuse

repujar *vt* (*metal*) to work in relief; (*cuero*) to emboss

repulsa *f* (*rechazo*) rejection

repulsar *vt* (*persona*) to rebuff; (*deseo*) to reject

repulsión *f* (*aversión*) aversion; (*asco*) disgust

repulsivo, -a *adj* repulsive

repunte *m RíoPl* (*alza*) rise; **el** ~ **del dólar causó sensación hoy en la bolsa** the dollar's upturn caused a sensation in the stock market today

reputación *f* reputation; **mujer de mala** ~ woman of ill repute; **tener muy buena/mala** ~ to have a very good/bad reputation; **un local con mala** ~ a place with a bad reputation

reputar *vt* **1.**(*considerar*) ~ **a alguien de** [*o por*] **algo** to consider sb to be sth **2.**(*apreciar*) to respect

requebrar <e→ie> *vt* (*a una mujer*) to flatter

requemado, -a *adj* **1.**(*color*) brown; (*piel*) tanned **2.**(*persona*) angry

requemar I. *vt* **1.**(*asar bien*) to roast; (*demasiado*) to burn **2.**(*plantas*) to scorch **3.**(*doler*) ~ **la garganta/la lengua** to burn one's throat/tongue **II.** *vr:* ~**se 1.**(*quemarse*) to scorch **2.**(*enfadarse*) to become angry **3.**(*de un sentimiento*) ~**se de algo** to be consumed with sth

4.(*plantas*) to scorch

requenete *adj Ven* (*rechoncho*) tubby

requerimiento *m* **1.**(*requisitoria*) ~ **de algo** demand for sth; (*escrito*) writ for sth; ~ **de información** request for information; **a** ~ **de...** on the request of ...; **hacer el** ~ **para la publicación de las proclamas** to publish the (matrimonial) banns **2.**(*exigencia*) demand **3.**(*aviso*) warning

requerir *irr como sentir vt* **1.**(*necesitar*) to require; **esto requiere toda la atención** this calls for our fullest attention; **este asunto requiere mucho tiempo** this affair demands a lot of time **2.**(*amorosamente*) to woo; ~ **de amores** to woo **3.**(*intimar*) to urge; ~ **a alguien que...** +*subj* to urge sb to ...

requesón *m* cottage [*o* curd] cheese

requetebién *adv inf* really well

requetebueno, -a *adj AmL, inf* really good

requetecaro, -a *adj AmL, inf* really expensive

requiebro *m* (amorous) compliment

réquiem *m* MÚS requiem

requisa *f* **1.**(*inspección*) inspection **2.**(*confiscación*) confiscation; MIL requisition

requisar *vt* to confiscate; MIL to requisition

requisito *m* (*requerimiento*) requirement; (*condición*) condition; **ser** ~ **indispensable** to be absolutely essential; ~ **previo** prerequisite; **exigir ciertos** ~**s** to demand certain requirements; **cumplir con los** ~**s** to fulfil *Brit* [*o* fulfil *Am*] the requirements; **con todos los** ~**s** *fig, inf* with everything just as it should be

res *f* **1.**(*animal*) beast; ~**es de matadero** animals for slaughter; **carne de** ~ beef **2.** *AmL* (*vaca*) head of cattle

resabio *m* **1.**(*sabor*) unpleasant aftertaste **2.**(*costumbre*) bad habit

resaca *f* **1.**(*olas*) undertow, undercurrent **2.** *inf* (*malestar*) hangover

resalado, -a *adj* lively

resaltar I. *vi* **1.**(*sobresalir, distinguirse*) to stand out **2.**(*rebotar*) to bounce **II.** *vt* **hacer** ~ to highlight

resalte *m,* **resalto** *m* (*saliente*) projection, ledge

resanar *vt* to restore; (*con oro*) to repair the gilding of

resarcir <c→z> **I.** *vt* **1.**(*compensar*) ~ **de algo** to compensate for sth **2.**(*reparar*) to repay **II.** *vr* ~**se de algo** to make up for sth

resbalada *f AmL, inf* slip

resbaladilla *f Méx* slide

resbaladizo, -a *adj* slippery

resbalar *vi* to slide; (*sin querer*) to slip; (*coche*) to skid; **¡cuidado con no** ~**!** be careful not to slip!

resbalín *m Chile* slide

resbalón *m* slip; **dar un** ~ to slip

rescatar *vt* **1.**(*a un prisionero*) to rescue; (*con dinero*) to pay the ransom for **2.**(*a un náufrago*) to pick up **3.**(*un cadáver*) to recover **4.**(*algo perdido*) to recover **5.**(*una deuda*) to pay off **6.** (*tiempo*) to win back; **quisiera ~ mi juventud** I wish I could relive my youth **7.** ECON (*bonos*) to redeem **8.** *AmL* (*mercancías*) to peddle

rescate *m* **1.** (*de un prisionero*) rescue; (*con dinero*) ransoming **2.** (*de una prenda*) revival **3.** (*recuperación*) recovery; **con facultad de ~** redeemable **4.** (*dinero para rescatar*) ransom

rescindir *vt* (*la ley*) to repeal; (*un contrato*) to annul

rescisión *f* (*la ley*) repeal; (*un contrato*) annulment; **~ de una deuda** cancellation of a debt *Brit*, debt cancelation *Am*

rescoldo *m* **1.** (*borrajo*) embers *pl* **2.** (*sospecha*) lingering suspicion

resecar <c→qu> *vt* (*secar mucho*) to dry out; (*plantas*) to parch

reseco, -a *adj* **1.** (*muy seco*) very dry **2.** (*flaco*) skinny

resentido, -a *adj* **1.** *estar* (*ofendido*) resentful **2.** *estar* (*débil*) worn out **3.** *ser* (*rencoroso*) bitter

resentimiento *m* resentment

resentirse *irr como sentir vr* **1.** (*ofenderse*) **~ por** [*o* **de**] **algo** to feel resentful about sth **2.** (*sentir dolor*) **~ de** [*o* **con**] **algo** to suffer from sth; **~ del costado** to have a sore side; **todavía se resiente de las heridas del accidente** he/she is still suffering from the injuries he/she received in the accident **3.** (*debilitarse*) to be weakened; **los edificios se resintieron cuando abrieron el túnel** the buildings were weakened when they dug the tunnel

reseña *f* **1.** (*de un libro*) review **2.** (*de una persona*) description **3.** (*narración*) report **4.** MIL review

reseñar *vt* **1.** (*un libro*) to review **2.** (*una persona*) to describe **3.** (*resumir*) to summarize **4.** MIL to review

resero, -a *m, f CSur* (*arreador*) cowhand

reserva *f* **1.** (*previsión*) reservation; **~ de equipajes** *AmL* left luggage; **tener algo en ~** to hold sth in reserve **2.** FIN (*fondos*) reserves *pl* **3.** (*de plazas*) reservation; **hacer una ~** to reserve, to book **4.** (*biológica*) reserve **5.** MIL reserves *pl*; **pasar a la ~** to join the reserves **6.** (*discreción*) secrecy; **guardar la ~** to be discrete **7.** (*circunspección*) reservation; **~ mental** mental reservation; **sin la menor ~** unreservedly **8.** (*vino*) vintage **9.** (*lugar protegido*) reserve; (*para personas*) reservation; (*para animales*) wildlife reserve ►**a ~ de que** +*subj* unless

reservadamente *adv* in confidence

reservado *m* **1.** FERRO reserved compartment **2.** (*habitación*) reserved room

reservado, -a *adj* **1.** (*derecho*) reserved; **quedan ~s todos los derechos** all rights reserved **2.** (*callado*) reserved **3.** (*confidencial*) confidential; **fondos ~s** reptilian funds **4.** (*cauteloso*) cautious

reservar **I.** *vt* **1.** (*retener plaza*) to reserve; **~ un asiento** (*ocupar*) to occupy a seat; (*para un*

viaje) to save a seat **2.** (*guardar*) to put by **3.** (*ocultar*) to conceal **II.** *vr:* **~se** (*conservarse*) to save oneself

resfriado *m* MED cold

resfriar <3. *pres:* resfría> **I.** *vi* to cool **II.** *vt* to cool off **III.** *vr:* **~se 1.** (*enfriarse*) to get cold **2.** MED to catch a cold

resfrío *m AmL* cold

resguardar **I.** *vt* **1.** (*proteger*) **~ de algo** to protect from sth **2.** (*poner en seguridad*) to safeguard; **~ los derechos** to reserve the rights **II.** *vr* **~se de algo** to protect oneself from sth; **~se con un muro** to shelter behind a wall

resguardo *m* **1.** (*protección*) protection **2.** (*recibo*) receipt; (*vale*) voucher; **~ de almacén** warrant; **~ de entrega/de transferencia** proof of delivery/transfer

residencia *f* **1.** (*domicilio, estancia*) residence; **~ habitual** usual place of residence; **cambiar de ~** to change one's address **2.** (*casa lujosa*) residence; **~ real** royal residence; **~ señorial** palatial residence **3.** (*internado*) residence; (*colegio*) boarding school; **~ de ancianos** old people's home; **~ de huérfanos** children's home; **~ universitaria** hall of residence *Brit*, dormitory *Am* **4.** (*hostal*) small hotel

residencial **I.** *adj* residential **II.** *m* (*urbanización*) housing development

residente **I.** *adj* resident; **no ~** non-resident; **~ en el lugar** resident locally **II.** *mf* resident

residir *vi* **1.** (*habitar*) to reside **2.** (*radicar*) **~ en** to lie in

residual *adj* residual; **aguas ~es** sewage

residuo *m* **1.** (*resto*) residue; QUÍM residuum **2.** *pl* (*basura*) waste; (*géneros defectuosos*) leftovers *pl*; **~s de las fábricas** industrial waste; **~s radiactivos** radioactive waste; **~s tóxicos** toxic waste

resignación *f* resignation

resignar **I.** *vt* to resign from **II.** *vr:* **~se** to resign oneself; **~se con** [*o* **a**] **algo** to resign oneself to sth

resina *f* resin

resistencia *f* **1.** resistance; **~ a la autoridad** opposition to the authorities; **oponer ~** to offer resistance; **formar parte de la ~** to be part of the resistance; **la ~ francesa** the French Resistance **2.** (*aguante*) **~ física** stamina; **~ al choque** shock resistance; **~ al frío** resistance to the cold; **~ al pago** non-payment; **~ a la publicidad** publicity fatigue **3.** DEP **carrera de ~** endurance race **4.** ELEC resistor, resistance

resistente **I.** *adj* resistant; **~ al calor** heat-resistant; **~ a la intemperie** weatherproof; **~ a la lavadora** machine-washable; **~ a la luz** light-resistant; **~ a la rotura** shatterproof **II.** *mf* resistance fighter

resistir **I.** *vi, vt* **1.** (*oponer resistencia*) to resist; **~ a una tentación** to resist a temptation; **~ al enemigo** to resist the enemy; **resistió la enfermedad** he/she overcame the illness; **¡no resisto más!** I can't take any more! **2.** (*aguantar*) **no resisto la comida pesada** I can't cope handle heavy food; **no puedo** ~ **a esta persona** I can't stand this person **II.** *vr:* ~**se** to resist

resolana *f AmL* **1.** (*calor reflejado*) reflected sunlight **2.** (*lugar a pleno sol*) sunny windless spot **3.** (*resplandor*) sun glare

resollar *vi* **1.** (*aspirar*) to breathe heavily; ~ **comiendo** to slurp **2.** *inf* (*dar noticia de sí*) to show signs of life; **sin** ~ without a word; **beber algo sin** ~ to drink sth in one gulp; **trabajar horas y horas sin** ~ to work for hours without a break

resolución *f* **1.** (*firmeza*) resolve **2.** (*decisión*) decision; POL resolution; ~ **administrativa** administrative decision; ~ **arbitral** refereeing decision; ~ **judicial** adjudication; **tomar una** ~ to take [*o* reach] a decision **3.** (*solución*) solution

resoluto, -a *adj* resolute

resolver *irr como* volver **I.** *vt* **1.** (*acordar*) to agree **2.** (*solucionar*) to solve; (*dudas*) to resolve **3.** (*decidir*) to decide **4.** (*disolver*) to dissolve **II.** *vr:* ~**se** **1.** (*solucionarse*) to be solved **2.** (*decidirse*) to decide **3.** (*disolverse*) to dissolve

resonancia *f* resonance; **caja de** ~ soundbox; **de** ~ **universal** of great importance; **tener** ~ (*suceso*) to have an impact

resonante *adj* (*importante*) important; **con éxito** ~ with tremendous success; **una victoria** ~ a resounding victory

resonar <o→ue> *vi* to resound; **los gritos de angustia resuenan todavía en mis oídos** I can still hear the cries of anguish; ~ **fuera de las fronteras** *fig* to be heard beyond the borders

resoplar *vi* to huff and puff; ~ **de rabia** to snort angrily

resorte *m* **1.** (*muelle*) spring **2.** *fig* (*medio*) means *pl* ►**tocar todos los** ~**s** to pull out all the stops

resortera *f Méx* catapult *Brit,* slingshot *Am*

respaldar I. *vt* **1.** (*apoyar*) to support **2.** (*proteger*) to protect **3.** (*anotar*) to endorse **II.** *vr:* ~**se 1.** (*apoyarse*) to lean; (*hacia atrás*) to lean back; ~**se en el sillón** to sit back in one's chair **2.** (*ampararse*) to seek shelter **III.** *m* support

respaldo *m* **1.** (*respaldar*) support **2.** (*reverso*) back; **en el** ~ on the back **3.** (*apoyo*) support; (*protección*) protection

respectar *vi* (*verbo defectivo*) to regard; **por** [*o* **en**] **lo que respecta a él...** with regard to him ...

respectivamente *adv* respectively

respectivo, -a *adj* respective

respecto *m* (**con**) ~ **a** with regard to; **al** ~, **con** ~ **a eso** in that regard; **a este** ~ in this regard; **al** ~ **de** with regard to

respetabilidad *f* respectability

respetable *adj* **1.** (*digno de respeto*) respectable **2.** (*notable*) considerable

respetar *vt* **1.** (*honrar*) to respect; **hacerse** ~

to command respect **2.** (*considerar*) to consider **3.** (*cumplir*) to observe

respeto *m* (*veneración*) respect; ~ **a las leyes** respect for the law; ~ **de un plazo** compliance with a time limit; **falta de** ~ lack of respect; **tener mucho** ~ **a las tormentas** to be well aware of the dangers of storms; **¡mis** ~**s a su señora!** give your wife my regards! ►**campar por sus** ~**s** to do as one pleases; **faltar al** ~ **a alguien** to be disrespectful to(wards) sb; **ofrecer los** ~**s a alguien** to pay one's respects to sb; **de** ~ respectable; **una persona de** ~ a respectable person

respetuoso, -a *adj* respectful; **ser** ~ **con las leyes** to respect the law

respingar <g→gu> *vi* **1.** (*animal*) to buck, to balk **2.** (*falda*) to ride up **3.** (*refunfuñar*) to grumble

respingo *m* **1.** (*movimiento*) start; (*animal*) buck; **dar un** ~ to start, to jump **2.** (*refunfuño*) grumbling

respingón, -ona *adj* **1.** (*levantado*) turned-up; **nariz respingona** snub nose **2.** (*animal*) nervous

respiración *f* (*inhalación*) breathing; (*aliento*) breath; ~ **artificial** artificial respiration; ~ **boca a boca** mouth to mouth resuscitation; **dificultad de** ~ breathing difficulties; **cortar la** ~ to hold one's breath; **faltar a uno la** ~ to be breathless, to be short of breath

respirar *vi* to breathe; ~ **aliviado** to breathe easily; ~ **trabajosamente** to gasp for breath; **no me atrevo a** ~ **delante de él** I don't dare to open my mouth when he's around ►**¡déjame que respire!** leave me in peace! *Brit,* give me a break! *Am;* **ahora sé por dónde respira** now I know what makes him/her tick; **sin** ~ without stopping; **escuchar sin** ~ to listen with bated breath

respiratorio, -a *adj* respiratory; **vías respiratorias** air passages

respiro *m* **1.** (*respiración*) breathing **2.** (*pausa*) rest **3.** (*de alivio*) sign

resplandecer *irr como* crecer *vi* (*lucir, reflejar*) to shine; ~ **de alegría** to glow with happiness; ~ **por su inteligencia** to stand out for one's intelligence

resplandeciente *adj* shining; ~ **de limpio** shiny clean

resplandor *m* brightness

responder *vi* **1.** (*contestar*) to reply; **el perro responde al nombre de...** the dog answers to the name of ... **2.** (*contradecir*) to contradict **3.** (*corresponder*) to correspond; (*cumplir con*) to obey **4.** (*ser responsable*) ~ **por algo** to answer for sth **5.** (*garantizar*) ~ **de** [*o* **por**] **algo** to guarantee [*o* vouch for] sth; ~ **de una deuda** to guarantee a debt

respondón, -ona I. *adj* argumentative; (*niño*) cheeky *Brit,* sassy *Am* **II.** *m, f* argumentative person; (*niño*) cheeky child

responsabilidad *f* **1.** (*por un niño*) ~ **de** [*o* **por**] **alguien** responsibility for sb; ~ **propia**

personal responsibility; **exigir** ~ to demand that sb accept responsibility **2.** (*por un daño*) liability; ~ **civil** civililiy; ~ **del daño** liability for damages; **incurrir en** ~ to become liable; **no acepto la** ~ it has nothing to do with me
responsabilizar <z→c> **I.** *vt* ~ **de algo** to make responsible for sth **II.** *vr:* ~**se 1.** (*asumir la responsabilidad*) ~**se de algo** to accept the responsibility for sth **2.** (*garantizar*) ~**se de algo** to guarantee sth; JUR to accept liability for sth
responsable I. *adj* ~ **de algo** responsible for sth; **ser civilmente** ~ to be liable **II.** *mf* (*encargado*) person in charge; (*culpable*) culprit
respuesta *f* answer; ~ **negativa** negative reply; **en** ~ **a su carta del…** in reply to your letter of …; **dar la callada por** ~ to answer with silence; **por toda** ~ **se encogió de hombros** his/her only answer was a shrug of the shoulders
resquebrajadura *f* crack, chink
resquebrajar *vt, vr:* ~**se** to crack
resquemor *m* **1.** (*escozor*) sting **2.** (*resentimiento*) resentment, ill-feeling
resquicio *m* **1.** (*abertura*) crack **2.** (*ocasión*) opening; ~ **de esperanza** glimmer of hope
resta *f* MAT subtraction
restablecer *irr como crecer* **I.** *vt* to re-establish; (*democracia, paz*) to restore **II.** *vr:* ~**se** to recover
restablecimiento *m* **1.** (*recuperación*) re-establishment; (*de democracia, paz*) restoration **2.** (*cura*) recovery
restallar *vi* to crack; **hacer** ~ **el látigo** to crack the whip
restante I. *adj* remaining; **cantidad** ~ remainder **II.** *m* remainder
restañar *vt* (*la sangre*) to staunch *Brit,* to stanch *Am;* ~ **las heridas** *fig* to heal the wounds
restar I. *vi* to remain; **aún restan algunos días para finalizar el año** there are still a few days left until the end of the year **II.** *vt* to take away; ~ **energías a alguien** to drain sb's strength; **no** ~ **un ápice del mérito** not to detract in the slightest from the achievement; ~**se años** to seem much younger; ~ **importancia a algo** to play sth down; MAT to subtract
restauración *f* **1.** *t.* ARTE restoration; ~ **de la monarquía** restoration of the monarchy **2.** COM the restaurant business
restaurante *m* restaurant
restaurar *vt t.* ARTE to restore
restitución *f* **1.** (*devolución*) *t.* FIN return **2.** (*reposición*) replacement
restituir *irr como huir* **I.** *vt* **1.** (*devolver*) *t.* FIN to return **2.** (*restablecer*) to restore **II.** *vr:* ~**se** to go back
resto *m* (*lo que sobra*) rest; MAT remainder; ~**s de un buque** wreckage; **los** ~**s mortales** the mortal remains; **los** ~**s de la torre** the tower ruins; **lo recordaré el** ~ **de mis días** I will remember him for the rest of my life

restregar *irr como fregar* **I.** *vt* to rub; ~ **a alguien algo por las narices** *fig* to rub sb's nose in sth **II.** *vr:* ~**se** to rub; ~**se los ojos** to rub one's eyes
restregón *m* rub
restricción *f* (*limitación*) restriction; (*recorte*) cutback; ~ **de la natalidad** reduction of the birth rate; ~ **mental** evasiveness; **sin restricciones** freely
restrictivo, -a *adj* restrictive
restringir <g→j> *vt* to restrict
resucitar I. *vi* to resuscitate **II.** *vt* **1.** (*de la muerte*) to resuscitate **2.** (*un estilo, una moda*) to revive
resuello *m* breathing; **sin** ~ out of breath ►**meter a alguien el** ~ **en el** <u>cuerpo</u> to intimidate sb
resuelto, -a I. *pp de* **resolver II.** *adj* determined
resulta *f* result; **de** ~**s de algo** as a result of sth
resultado *m* result, outcome; ~ **del reconocimiento** (**médico**) results of the medical examination; **dar buen** ~ (*funcionar*) to work; (*no desgastarse*) to last; **dar mal** ~ (*no funcionar*) to fail; (*desgastarse*) to wear out fast; **tener por** ~ to lead to
resultar *vi* **1.** (*deducirse*) ~ **de algo** to result from sth **2.** (*surtir*) to be; ~ **muerto en un accidente** to be killed in an accident; ~ **en beneficio de alguien** to be to sb's benefit **3.** (*tener éxito*) to succeed, to work well **4.** (*comprobarse*) to turn out
resumen *m* **1.** (*sumario*) summary; **en** ~ in short **2.** (*extracto*) extract
resumidero *m AmL* **1.** (*alcantarilla*) drain **2.** (*pozo ciego*) cess pool
resumir I. *vt* to summarize **II.** *vr* ~**se en algo** to amount to sth
resurgimiento *m* resurgence; (*reaparición*)
resurgir <g→j> *vi* **1.** (*reaparecer*) to reappear **2.** (*renacer*) to be resurrected **3.** (*revivir*) to revive
resurrección *f* **1.** REL resurrection; **Pascua de Resurrección** Easter; **Domingo de Resurrección** Easter Sunday **2.** (*restablecimiento*) re-establishment
retablo *m* ARTE reredos, altarpiece
retacón, -ona *adj CSur* stubby
retaguardia *f* MIL rearguard ►**estar a la** ~ **de algo** to lag behind sth; **ir a la** ~ to bring up the rear; **quedarse en la** ~ to stay in the background; **a** [*o* **en**] ~ (*tarde*) late; **a** ~ **de** (*detrás de*) behind
retahíla *f* string; **soltar la** ~ to come out with a string of insults
retal *m* remnant
retama *f* broom
retar *vt* to challenge
retardar I. *vt* to delay **II.** *vr:* ~**se** to be late; **me he retardado** I was delayed
retardo *m* delay; **sufrir un** ~ to be delayed; **tener** ~ **con algo** to be late doing sth

retazo m 1.(*retal*) remnant 2.(*fragmento*) fragment; (*de conversación*) snippet

rete adj Méx (*muy*) very; **su hija es ~ alta** their daughter is very tall

retemblar <e→ie> vi to shake; **hacer ~ to shake**

retén m 1.MIL reserves pl; (*refuerzos*) reinforcements pl 2.(*reserva*) stock

retención f 1.(*custodia*) retention; (*deducción*) deduction; **~ fiscal** tax retention; **certificado de retenciones** certificate of tax retention 2.(*memorizar*) retention 3.(*moderación*) moderation 4.(*tráfico*) hold-up

retener irr como tener I. vt 1.(*conservar*) to retain; (*el pasaporte*) to withold; (*la respiración*) to hold 2.(*recordar*) to retain; (*detener*) to detain II. vr: **~se** to restrain oneself

retentiva f memory

reticencia f 1.(*indirecta*) insinuation; **andar con ~s** to drop hints 2.(*renuencia*) reluctance 3.(*reserva*) **~ ante** reticence towards

reticente adj 1.(*discurso*) insinuating 2.(*reacio*) reluctant

retículo m net

retina f ANAT retina; **desprendimiento de ~** detached retina

retintín m 1.(*tonillo*) sarcastic tone 2.(*son*) ringing

retirada f 1.(*abandono*) abandonment; MIL retreat 2.(*eliminación*) withdrawal 3.(*jubilación*) retirement

retirado, -a I. adj 1.(*lejos*) remote 2.(*jubilado*) retired II. m, f retired person

retirar I. vt 1.(*apartar*) to remove; (*tropas, dinero*) to withdraw 2.(*echar*) to remove; **~on de la sala a los manifestantes** they removed the demonstrators from the hall 3.(*recoger, quitar*) to take away 4.(*desdecirse*) to withdraw 5.(*negar*) to deny 6.(*jubilar*) to retire II. vr: **~se** 1.(*abandonar*) **~se de algo** to withdraw from sth 2. t. MIL (*retroceder*) to retreat 3.(*jubilarse*) to retire

retiro m 1.(*pensión*) pension 2.(*refugio*) retreat 3.(*retraimiento*) withdrawal

reto m challenge

retobado, -a adj 1. AmC, Méx, Ecua (*respondón*) insolent 2. AmC, Cuba, Ecua (*indómito*) wild 3. Arg, Méx, Urug (*enconado*) cheesed off Brit, inf, ticked off inf

retobar I. vt CSur (*forrar*) to cover with leather II. vi Méx (*rezogar*) to talk back

retocar <c→qu> vt 1.(*corregir*) FOTO to retouch, to touch up 2.(*perfeccionar*) to perfect

retoñar vi to sprout; fig to reappear

retoño m 1.(*vástago*) shoot 2.(*niño*) kid

retoque m 1.(*corrección*) alteration; FOTO retouch 2. FIN adjustment

retorcer irr como cocer I. vt 1.(*torcer*) to twist 2.(*enroscar*) to twine II. vr: **~se** 1.(*enroscarse*) to twist 2.(*de dolor*) to writhe

retorcido, -a adj 1.(*complicado*) **pensar de manera retorcida** to think in a very confused

way; **¡qué ~!** how complicated! 2.(*maligno*) twisted; **una mente retorcida** a warped mind 3.(*conceptuoso*) convoluted

retorcijón m stomach cramp

retorcimiento m 1.(*torcedura*) twist 2.(*vuelta*) turn 3.(*encorvadura*) curve

retórica f rhetoric

retórico, -a I. adj rhetorical II. m, f rhetorician

retornable adj **botella (no) ~** (non-)returnable bottle

retornar I. vi to return II. vt to give back

retorno m return

retorta f retort

retortijón m 1.(*ensortijamiento*) twist 2.(*dolor*) cramp; **tengo un ~ de estómago** I have a cramp in my stomach

retozar <z→c> vi 1.(*brincar*) to frolic 2.(*coquetear*) to flirt

retozón, -ona adj playful

retracción f 1. JUR retraction 2.(*retroceso, retiro*) withdrawal 3.(*impedimento*) obstacle 4. MED retraction

retractación f retraction

retractar I. vt (*desdecirse*) to take back; JUR to retract II. vr **~se de algo** to withdraw from sth

retráctil adj retractable; BIO retractile

retraer irr como traer I. vt 1.(*encoger*) to withdraw 2.(*traer*) to bring back 3.(*impedir*) to hinder 4. JUR to retract II. vr: **~se** 1.(*aislarse*) **~se a** [o **en**] **algo** to withdraw into sth 2.(*retirarse*) **~se de algo** to withdraw from sth 3.(*retroceder*) to retreat

retraído, -a adj (*reservado*) reserved; (*poco sociable*) withdrawn

retraimiento m reserve

retransmisión f broadcast; **~ deportiva** sports programme, sport(s) program; **~ por televisión** television broadcast; **~ en directo/diferido** live/pre-recorded broadcast

retransmitir vt to broadcast

retrasado, -a adj 1.(*atrasado*) backward; **~ en tecnología** technologically backward 2.(*anticuado*) old-fashioned 3.(*no actual*) out of date 4.(*subdesarrollado*) underdeveloped; **~ mental** mentally retarded

retrasar I. vt 1.(*demorar*) to delay 2.(*el reloj*) to put [o set] back II. vi 1.(*el reloj*) to be slow 2.(*no estar al día*) to be out of touch III. vr: **~se** to be late

retraso m 1.(*demora*) delay 2.(*del desarrollo*) underdevelopment 3.(*de la deuda*) arrears pl; **tener ~ en los pagos** to be in arrears

retratar vt 1.(*describir*) to depict, to portray 2.(*fotografiar*) to photograph 3.(*pintar*) to paint a portrait of

retratista mf (*dibujante*) portrait artist; (*fotógrafo*) portrait photographer

retrato m 1.(*representación*) t. FOTO portrait 2.(*descripción*) description ▶ **ser el vivo ~ de alguien** to be the spitting image of sb

retrato-robot <retratos-robot> m photo-

fit® picture
retreta *f* retreat
retrete *m* lavatory, toilet
retribución *f* reward; (*sueldo*) remuneration; **retribuciones dinerarias** money payment; **retribuciones en especie** payment in kind
retribuir *irr como huir vt* **1.**(*remunerar*) to remunerate **2.** *AmL* (*compensar*) to compensate
retro *adj inf* retro, old-fashioned looking
retroactividad *f* retroactivity
retroactivo, -a *adj* retroactive
retroalimentación *f* feedback
retroceder *vi* **1.**(*regresar*) to go back **2.**(*desistir*) to give up; (*echarse atrás*) to back down
retroceso *m* **1.**(*regresión*) reversal; ~ **en las negociaciones** setback in the negotiations **2.** MED relapse **3.**(*arma de fuego*) recoil, kick *inf*
retrógrado, -a *adj, m, f* reactionary
retropropulsión *f* AVIAT jet propulsion
retroproyector *m* overhead projector
retrospectivo, -a *adj* retrospective
retrovisor *m* AUTO rearview mirror; ~ **exterior** wing mirror, side mirror *Am;* **mirar por el espejo** ~ to look in the rearview mirror
retumbar *vi* to boom; (*resonar*) to resound
reuma *m o f,* **reúma** *m o f* MED rheumatism
reumático, -a *adj* rheumatic
reumatismo *m sin pl* MED rheumatism
reunificación *f* reunification
reunificar <c→qu> *vt* to reunify
reunión *f* **1.**(*encuentro, asamblea*) meeting; ~ **de los trabajadores** employees' meeting; ~ **de antiguos alumnos** class reunion; ~ **en la cumbre** summit meeting **2.**(*conferencia*) meeting; **estar en** ~ to be in a meeting; **celebrar una** ~ to hold a meeting **3.**(*el juntar*) collection **4.**(*grupo, invitados*) gathering
reunir *irr* **I.** *vt* **1.**(*congregar*) to assemble **2.**(*unir*) to gather **3.**(*juntar*) to reunite **4.**(*poseer*) to have; ~ **las cualidades necesarias** to have the necessary qualities **II.** *vr:* ~**se 1.**(*congregarse*) to meet; (*informal*) to get together **2.**(*unir*) to gather **3.**(*juntarse*) to reunite
reválida *f* **1.**(*confirmación*) confirmation **2.**(*examen*) final examination
revalidar **I.** *vt* to confirm **II.** *vr:* ~**se** to be recognized
revaloración *f* re-evaluation; FIN revaluation
revalorización *f* FIN appreciation
revalorizar <z→c> *vt* **1.** to re-evaluate **2.** FIN to appreciate; (*subir el valor*) to increase the value of
revaluación *f* **1.** re-evaluation **2.** FIN revaluation; (*elevamiento*) appreciation
revaluar <*1. pres:* revalúo> *vt* **1.** to re-evaluate **2.** FIN to revalue; (*subir el valor*) to increase the value of
revancha *f* **1.** revenge; **tomarse la** ~ **por algo** to get one's own back for sth; **tomarse la**

~ to take one's revenge **2.** DEP return match
revelación *f t.* REL revelation
revelado *m* FOTO developing
revelar *vt* **1.**(*dar a conocer*) to reveal, to disclose **2.** FOTO to develop
revellín *m Cuba* (*dificultad*) difficulty ►**echar** ~ to provoke anger
revender *vt* to resell
revenir *irr como venir vi, vr:* ~**se 1.**(*encoger*) to shrink **2.**(*agriarse*) to sour **3.**(*secarse*) to dry out
reventa *f* resale; (*entradas*) touting *Brit,* scalping *Am*
reventadero *m* **1.** *Col, Méx* (*hervidero*) bubbling spring **2.** *Chile* (*rompiente*) shoal
reventado, -a *adj* **1.** *inf* (*hecho polvo*) wiped out **2.** *Arg* (*sinuoso*) devious
reventar <e→ie> **I.** *vi* **1.**(*romperse*) to break; (*globo, neumático*) to burst; **lleno hasta** ~ full to bursting **2.** *vulg* (*morir*) to snuff it *Brit;* **¡que reviente!** I hope he/she drops dead! **II.** *vt* **1.**(*romper*) to break; (*globo, neumático*) to burst **2.** *inf* (*molestar*) to annoy **III.** *vr:* ~**se 1.**(*romperse*) to break; (*globo, neumático*) to burst **2.** *vulg* (*morirse*) to snuff it *Brit*
reventón *m* AUTO **tener un** ~ to have a flat tyre
reverberación *f* (*de la luz*) reflection; (*del sonido*) reverberation
reverberar *vi* (*luz*) to reflect; (*sonido*) to reverberate
reverbero *m* **1.** *v.* reverberación **2.** (*farol*) reflecting light; AUTO reflector **3.** *AmL* (*hornillo*) spirit stove
reverdecer *irr como crecer vi* **1.**(*verdear*) to become green **2.**(*vigorizar*) to revive
reverencia *f* **1.**(*veneración*) reverence; **Su Reverencia** Your Reverence **2.**(*inclinación*) bow
reverenciar *vt* to revere
reverendísimo, -a *adj* Most Reverend; **Su Reverendísimo** Your Most Reverend
reverendo, -a **I.** *adj* revered; REL Reverend **II.** *m, f* Reverend
reverente *adj* respectful
reversa *f Chile, Col, Méx* AUTO reverse
reversibilidad *f* reversibility
reversible *adj* reversible
reversión *f* reversion
reverso *m* other side ►**el** ~ **de la medalla** the other side of the coin
revertir *irr como sentir vi* to revert; **revirtió en su beneficio** it worked to his/her advantage
revés *m* **1.**(*reverso*) other side; **al** [*o del*] ~ back to front; (*con lo de arriba abajo*) upside down; **te has puesto el jersey del** ~ you have put your jumper on back to front; (*dentro para fuera*) inside out; **poner a alguien del** ~ (*confundir*) to confuse sb; (*poner a caldo*) to be blunt with sb **2.**(*golpe*) blow with the back of the hand **3.** DEP backhand **4.**(*infortunio*) set-

back; ~ **de fortuna** stroke of bad luck

revestimiento *m t.* ARQUIT ~ **de/con algo** covering with sth

revestir *irr como pedir* **I.** *vt* **1.** (*recubrir*) ~ **con** [*o* **de**] **algo** to cover with sth; ~ **de cinc** to coat with zinc **2.** (*tener*) ~ **importancia** to assume importance **II.** *vr:* ~**se** (*aparentar*) ~**se con** [*o* **de**] **algo** to arm oneself with sth

reviejo, -a *adj* very old

revirado, -a *adj* **1.** *Arg, Urug, inf* (*loco*) dotty *Brit, inf,* nutty *inf* **2.** BOT twisted

revire *m Arg, Urug, inf* crazy idea; **le dio uno de sus ~s** he/she had one of his/her crazy ideas

revisada *f AmL* (*revisión*) check, review

revisar *vt* to check; TÉC to inspect; (*textos, edición*) to revise

revisión *f* check; TÉC inspection; JUR, TIPO revision; MED checkup

revisor(a) *m(f)* **1.** (*controlador*) inspector; ~ **de cuentas** auditor **2.** FERRO ticket inspector

revista *f* **1.** PREN magazine; **las ~s del corazón** the gossip magazines; ~ **electrónica** e-zine; ~ **especializada** special interest magazine; ~ **ilustrada** illustrated magazine **2.** *t.* MIL (*inspección*) inspection; **pasar ~ a las tropas** to inspect the troops **3.** (*espectáculo*) revue, variety show

revistero *m* magazine rack

revival *m* revival

revivificar <c→qu> *vt* to revive

revivir **I.** *vi* to revive **II.** *vt* to revive; (*evocar*) to relive

revocación *f* (*anulación*) annulment

revocar <c→qu> **I.** *vt* **1.** (*anular*) to annul **2.** (*apartar*) to dismiss **3.** (*hacer retroceder*) to recall **4.** (*enlucir*) to plaster **II.** *vi* (*humo*) to blow back

revolcar *irr como volcar* **I.** *vt* **1.** (*derribar*) to knock over **2.** *inf* (*vencer*) to defeat **3.** *inf* (*suspender*) to fail **II.** *vr:* ~**se 1.** (*restregarse*) ~**se por algo** to roll around in sth **2.** (*obstinarse*) ~**se en algo** to insist on sth

revolcón *m* **dar un ~ a alguien** *fig* to wipe the floor with sb; **darse un ~** *inf* to have a roll in the hay *fig*

revolear *vt Méx, CSur* to whirl round

revolotear *vi* to flutter about

revoloteo *m* fluttering

revoltijo *m* **1.** (*embrollo*) jumble **2.** (*tripas*) tripe **3.** (*huevos*) scrambled eggs

revoltoso, -a I. *adj* **1.** (*travieso*) mischievous **2.** (*rebelde*) rebellious **3.** (*intrincado*) tangled **II.** *m, f* troublemaker

revoltura *f Méx* mixture

revolución *f* **1.** *t.* POL, ASTR (*cambio, rotación*) revolution; **número de revoluciones** number of revolutions **2.** (*inquietud*) disturbance

revolucionar *vt* **1.** (*amotinar*) to stir up **2.** (*transformar*) to revolutionize **3.** (*excitar*) to arouse interest in **4.** TÉC to increase the number of revolutions of

revolucionario, -a *adj, m, f* revolutionary

revoluta *f AmC v.* **revolución**

revolvedora *f Arg, Méx* (*de cemento*) cement mixer

revolver *irr como volver* **I.** *vt* **1.** (*mezclar*) to mix **2.** (*desordenar*) to mess up **3.** (*soliviantar*) to stir up **4.** (*investigar*) to investigate **5.** (*registrar*) to rummage through **II.** *vr:* ~**se 1.** (*moverse*) to toss and turn; **se me revuelve el estómago** it makes my stomach turn **2.** (*enfrentarse*) to turn **3.** (*el tiempo*) to break

revólver *m* revolver

revoque *m* **1.** (*acción*) plastering **2.** (*material*) plaster

revuelco *m* (*golpe*) blow

revuelo *m* **1.** (*turbación*) disturbance; **causar ~** to disturb **2.** (*segundo vuelo*) second flight ►**de ~** in passing

revuelta *f* **1.** (*tumulto*) disturbance **2.** (*rebelión*) revolt **3.** (*encorvadura*) bend; **carretera con muchas ~s** windy road **4.** (*cambio*) change

revuelto, -a I. *pp de* **revolver II.** *adj* **1.** (*agitado*) shaken **2.** (*desordenado*) chaotic **3.** (*tiempo*) unsettled **4.** (*irritado*) annoyed **5.** (*intrincado*) tangled **6.** (*huevos*) scrambled

revulsar *vt, vi Méx* (*vomitar*) to throw up

rey *m* king; **los Reyes** The King and Queen; **los Reyes Católicos** the Catholic Monarchs, Ferdinand and Isabella; **los Reyes Magos** the Magi, the Three Wise Men; **el día de Reyes** Epiphany, Twelfth Night ►**lo mismo me da ~ que roque** it's all the same to me; **no temer ~ ni roque** to fear nothing and nobody; **a ~ muerto ~ puesto** off with the old, on with the new

reyerta *f* quarrel, fight

reyezuelo *m* goldcrest

rezagado, -a *m, f* straggler

rezagar <g→gu> **I.** *vt* **1.** (*dejar atrás*) to leave behind **2.** (*suspender*) to postpone **II.** *vr:* ~**se** to fall behind

rezar <z→c> **I.** *vt* ~ **por alguien** to pray for sb; ~ **una oración** to say a prayer **II.** *vi* **1.** (*decir*) to pray **2.** (*corresponder*) ~ **con algo** to apply to sth

rezo *m* **1.** (*el rezar*) praying **2.** (*oración*) prayer

rezongar <g→gu> *vi* to grumble

rezongón, -ona I. *adj inf* grumpy **II.** *m, f inf* grouch

rezumar *vi* **1.** (*filtrarse*) ~ **por algo** to ooze from sth; **el sudor le rezumaba por la frente** sweat beaded his/her forehead **2.** (*rebosar*) ~ **algo** to ooze with sth

RFA *f v.* **República Federal de Alemania** FRG

ría *f* **1.** GEO ≈ estuary, sea loch *Scot* **2.** DEP water break

riachuelo *m* stream

riada *f* flood

ribazo *m* steep bank

ribera *f* **1.** (*orilla*) bank **2.** (*tierra*) riverside **3.** (*vega*) fertile plain

ribete *m* 1.(*galón*) trimming 2.(*adorno*) adornment; (*de una narración*) embellishment 3. *pl* (*indicios*) traces *pl*

ribetear *vt* to trim

ricamente *adv* 1.(*con abundancia*) richly 2.(*con placer*) splendidly

ricino *m* castor oil plant

rico, -a I. *adj* 1.(*acaudalado*) rich; **es muy ~** he/she is very rich 2.(*sabroso*) delicious; **la comida está muy rica** the food is delicious 3.(*abundante*) rich 4.(*fructífero*) fertile 5.(*excelente*) excellent 6.(*simpático*) lovely, cute II. *m, f* 1.(*rico*) rich person; **los ricos** the rich; **nuevo ~** nouveau riche 2. *inf*(*apelativo*) mate *Brit*

ricota *f* Arg GASTR ricotta cheese

ricura *f inf* **ser una ~** to be adorable; **¡anda, ~!** come on, darling!

ridiculez *f* 1.(*lo ridículo, nimiedad*) ridiculousness; **me pagan la ~ de tres dólares** I'm being paid the laughable sum of three dollars 2.(*tontería*) stupidity

ridiculizar <z→c> *vt* to ridicule

ridículo, -a *adj* 1.(*risorio*) ridiculous; **poner(se) en ~** to make a fool of (oneself) 2.(*tacaño*) stingy

riego *m* irrigation; **~ sanguíneo** blood flow

riel *m* 1. FERRO rail 2.(*para cortinas*) bar; **los ~es de la cortina** the curtain rod

rienda *f* 1.(*correa*) rein; **tener las ~s del poder** *fig* to hold the reins of power 2. *pl* (*gobierno*) reins *pl* ▶**a ~ suelta** *fig* wildly; **aflojar las ~s** to ease up; **dar ~ suelta a** to give free rein to; **llevar las ~s** to be in control; **tirar de la ~** to pressurize *Brit,* to pressure *Am*

riesgo *m* risk; **~ monetario** monetary risk; **a ~ de que... +***subj* at the risk of ...; **a ~ y ventura de...** at the risk of ...; **por cuenta y ~ propios** at one's own risk and expense; **asumir un ~** to assume a risk; **correr el ~ de...** to run the risk of ...; **estar asegurado a todo ~** AUTO to have comprehensive insurance *Brit,* to have full coverage insurance; **exponer a un ~** to expose to a risk; **exponerse a un ~** to run a risk; **~ profesional** occupational hazard

riesgoso, -a *adj AmL* 1.(*arriesgado*) risky 2.(*peligroso*) dangerous

rifa *f* 1.(*sorteo*) raffle 2.(*riña*) quarrel

rifar I. *vt* to raffle II. *vi* to quarrel

rifle *m* rifle

rigidez *f* 1.(*inflexibilidad*) rigidity 2.(*severidad*) strictness

rígido, -a *adj* 1.(*inflexible*) rigid 2.(*severo*) strict

rigor *m* 1.(*severidad*) strictness 2.(*exactitud*) rigorousness; **en ~** strictly speaking 3. METEO **~ del invierno** depths of winter; **~ del verano** height of summer ▶**de ~** de rigueur

riguroso, -a *adj* 1.(*severo*) strict 2.(*exacto*) rigorous 3. METEO harsh

rija *f* (*riña*) quarrel

rijoso, -a *adj* 1.(*lujurioso*) lustful; (*animal: macho*) in rut; (*hembra*) on heat 2.(*penden-*

ciero) quarrelsome

rima *f* LIT rhyme; **tener ~** to rhyme

rimar I. *vi* 1.(*versificar*) to write poetry 2.(*tener rima*) to rhyme II. *vt* to rhyme

rimbombante *adj* grandiloquent

rímel® *m* mascara

rin *m* 1. *Ven* (*llanta*) rim 2. *Perú* (*ficha telefónica*) telephone token

Rin *m* Rhine

rincón *m* 1.(*esquina*) corner 2.(*escondrijo, lugar tranquilo*) nook; **por todos los rincones** *fig* in every nook and cranny 3. *inf* (*habitación*) room

rinconera *f* corner cupboard

ringlera *f* row

rinitis *f* MED rhinitis; **~ alérgica** hay fever

rinoceronte *m* rhinoceros

riña *f* quarrel; **~ de gallos** cockfight

riñón *m* 1. ANAT kidney; **tener piedras en el ~** to have kidney stones 2. *pl* (*parte de la espalda*) lower back 3. *fig* (*centro*) heart ▶**tener el ~ bien cubierto** to be well off; **costar un ~** to cost an arm and a leg; **tener riñones** to have guts

riñonera *f* 1.(*faja*) cummerbund 2.(*cinturón con bolsa*) bum bag *Brit, inf,* fanny pack *Am, inf*

río *m* river; **~ abajo** downstream; **~ arriba** upstream ▶**tener un ~ de oro** to have a goldmine; **de perdidos al ~** in for a penny, in for a pound; **pescar en ~ revuelto** to fish in troubled waters; **cuando el ~ suena, algo lleva** *prov* where there's smoke, there's fire

riojano, -a I. *adj* of/from La Rioja II. *m, f* native/inhabitant of La Rioja

rioplatense I. *adj* of/from the River Plate region II. *mf* native/inabitant of the River Plate region

ripio *m* 1.(*cascajo*) rubble; **no valer un ~** (*sin valor*) to be completely worthless; (*feo*) to be really ugly 2.(*palabra inútil*) padding; **meter ~** to waffle; **no perder ~** not to miss a trick

riqueza *f* riches *pl*

risa *f* laughter; **digno de ~** laughable; **estar muerto de ~** to be laughing one's head off; **mondarse de ~** to split one's sides laughing; **llorar de ~** to laugh until one cries; **tener un ataque de ~** to have a fit of the giggles; **tomar algo a ~** to treat sth as a joke; **no quiero oír ~s a mis espaldas** I don't want any more laughing behind my back; **¡qué ~!** what a joke!; **no estoy para ~s** I'm in no mood for jokes

risco *m* crag

risotada *f* guffaw; **soltar una gran ~** to guffaw

ríspido, -a *adj AmL* (*rudo*) coarse

ristra *f* 1.(*trenza*) string; **una ~ de ajos/cebollas** a string of garlic/onions 2. *inf*(*sarta*) string; **una ~ de mentiras** a string of lies

risueño, -a *adj* 1.(*alegre*) smiling 2.(*placentero*) pleasant 3.(*próspero*) favourable *Brit,* favorable *Am*

rítmico, -a *adj* rhythmic

ritmo *m* rhythm

rito *m* (*costumbre*) ritual; REL rite

ritual *adj, m* ritual

rival *adj, m* rival

rivalidad *f* rivalry

rivalizar <z→c> *vi* ~ **por algo** to compete for sth

rizado, -a *adj* (*cabello*) curly

rizar <z→c> I. *vt* **1.** (*encrespar*) to curl **2.** (*plegar*) to crease II. *vr:* ~**se** to curl

rizo *m* **1.** (*mechón*) curl; **rizar el** ~ (*imponerse*) to win through; (*complicar*) to over-complicate things **2.** (*tela*) velvet; **tela de** ~ (*felpa*) terry towelling, terrycloth **3.** AVIAT loop; **rizar el** ~ to loop the loop; *fig* to split hairs

rizo, -a *adj* curly

rizoma *m* rhizome

RNE *f abr de* **Radio Nacional de España** Spanish national radio network

robar *vt* **1.** (*hurtar: algo*) to steal; (*a alguien*) to rob; (*a alguien con violencia*) to mug; **me** ~**on en París** I was robbed in Paris; **me robó la novia** *inf* he stole my girlfriend; **esto roba mucho tiempo** this takes up a lot of time **2.** (*un río*) to carry away **3.** (*estafar*) to cheat **4.** (*en juegos*) to draw

robellón *m* yellow boletus

roble *m* oak; **estar como un** ~ to be as fit as a fiddle

robo *m* **1.** (*hurto*) robbery; ~ **con homicidio** theft and murder; ~ **a mano armada** armed robbery; ~ **con allanamiento** breaking and entering **2.** (*presa*) loot **3.** (*estafa*) swindle; **ser un** ~ *fig* (*muy caro*) to be a rip-off; **¿20 libras? ¡qué** ~**!** twenty pounds? that's highway robbery!

robot <robots> *m* robot; ~ **de cocina** food processor

robustecer *irr como crecer* I. *vt* to strengthen II. *vr:* ~**se** to become strong

robusto, -a *adj* robust

roca *f* (*materia, peña*) rock; **ese hombre es una** ~ that man is as solid as a rock

rocalla *f* stone chippings *pl*

roce *m* **1.** (*fricción*) brush **2.** (*huella*) scrape **3.** (*contacto*) contact; **tener mucho** ~ **con alguien** to have a lot of contact with sb **4.** (*pelea*) scrape

rochar *vt* **1.** AGR to clear ground **2.** *Chile* (*sorprender*) to catch red-handed

rochela *f Col, PRico, Ven* hullabaloo

rociar <3. *pres:* rocía> I. *v imp ers* **ha rociado** dew has fallen II. *vt* **1.** (*regar*) to wash down **2.** (*esparcir*) to sprinkle

rocín *m* **1.** (*jamelgo*) nag; **ir de** ~ **a ruin** to go from bad to worse **2.** *inf* (*tosco*) lout

rocío *m* **1.** (*relente*) dew; **cae** ~ dew is forming **2.** (*lluvia*) drizzle **3.** (*rociada*) sprinkling

rock I. *adj* rock; **grupo de música** ~ rock group II. *m* MÚS rock

rockero, -a I. *adj* rock II. *m, f* (*fan*) rock fan;

(*músico*) rock musician

rocoso, -a *adj* rocky; **Montañas Rocosas** Rocky Mountains, Rockies

rocote *m*, **rocoto** *m Bol, Ecua, Perú* (*pimiento*) (large) green pepper

rodaballo *m* turbot

rodada *f* wheel track

rodado, -a *adj* **1.** (*fluido*) smooth; **venir** ~ (*sin dificultades*) to go smoothly; (*de perlas*) to come in very handy **2.** AUTO **tráfico** ~ vehicular traffic **3.** (*caballo*) dappled

rodaja *f* **1.** (*rueda*) small wheel **2.** (*trozo*) slice

rodaje *m* **1.** CINE shooting **2.** (*rodar*) rolling; **cuando tengamos más** ~ when we've got going **3.** (*impuesto*) road tax *Brit*, vehicle tax **4.** (*ruedas*) wheels *pl*

Ródano *m* Rhone

rodar <o→ue> I. *vi* **1.** (*dar vueltas, moverse sobre ruedas*) to roll; ~ **por el suelo** to roll across the floor **2.** (*girar sobre el eje*) to turn **3.** (*deslizarse*) to slide **4.** (*abundar*) to abound **5.** (*ir*) to wander; **he rodado de tienda en tienda** I've wandered from shop to shop ▶**echarlo todo a** ~ to spoil everything II. *vt* **1.** (*hacer dar vueltas*) to roll **2.** (*película*) to shoot **3.** (*coche*) to run in

rodear I. *vi* **1.** (*circunvalar*) to go round **2.** (*divagar*) to ramble II. *vt* **1.** (*cercar*) ~ **de algo** to surround with sth **2.** (*hacer dar vueltas*) to turn **3.** (*un tema*) to avoid III. *vr* ~**se de algo/alguien** to surround oneself with sth/sb

rodeo *m* **1.** (*desvío*) detour; **dar un** ~ to take a detour; **conseguir algo con** ~**s** to achieve sth in a roundabout manner **2.** (*evasiva*) evasion **3.** DEP rodeo ▶**andar(se) con** ~**s** to beat about the bush; **dejarse de** ~**s** stop beating about the bush; **sin** ~**s** without beating about the bush

rodilla *f* **1.** ANAT knee; **de** ~**s** on one's knees; **ponerse de** ~**s** to kneel **2.** (*paño*) cloth

rodillera *f* **1.** (*protección*) kneepad **2.** (*del pantalón*) knee patch; **para que no salgan** ~**s al pantalón** so that the trousers don't go baggy at the knees

rodillo *m* **1.** TÉC roller **2.** (*de cocina*) rolling pin

roedor *m* rodent

roer *irr vt* **1.** (*ratonar*) ~ **algo** to gnaw at sth; **los ratones royeron mi libro** the mice gnawed my book; ~**se las uñas** to bite one's nails **2.** (*concomer*) **las preocupaciones me roen el alma** I'm worrying my life away

rogar <o→ue> *vt* to request; (*con humildad*) to beg; JUR to plead; **rogamos nos contesten inmediatamente nuestra carta** we would be grateful if you could give us an immediate reply; **¡te ruego que me escuches!** I beg you to listen to me!; **le gusta hacerse de** ~ he/she likes playing hard to get

rojez *f* redness

rojizo, -a *adj* reddish

rojo, -a *adj* red; (*persona*) red-headed; ~ **chi-**

llón/subido bright/deep red; ~ **burdeos** maroon ▸ **al** ~ (**vivo**) red-hot; *fig* at fever pitch; **poner** ~ **a alguien** to make sb blush; **ponerse** ~ to go red

rol *m* **1.** (*papel*) role; **desempeñar un** ~ to play a role **2.** (*lista*) list; ~ **de pago** payroll

rollito *m* ~ **de primavera** GASTR spring roll, egg roll *Am*

rollizo, -a *adj* **1.** (*robusto*) plump **2.** (*cilíndrico*) round

rollo *m* **1.** *t.* FOTO (*de papel, alambre*) roll; **hacer un** ~ **de algo** to roll sth up **2.** *inf* (*cosa aburrida*) bore; **¡qué ~ de película!** what a boring film!; **soltar siempre el mismo** ~ to always come out with the same old stuff **3.** *inf* (*tipo de vida*) lifestyle; (*asunto*) affair; **montarse el** ~ to organize one's life; **ir a su** ~ to do as one likes; **tener mucho** ~ to be full of crap *inf*; **traerse un mal** ~ to be in a mess; **acaba con el ~, muchacho** get on with it, son; **corta el** ~ (*palabrería, mentiras*) cut the crap *inf*; **¿de qué va el ~?** what's it all about? **4.** (*del cuerpo*) roll (of fat) **5.** GASTR roll; **este niño está hecho un** ~ **de manteca** this child is a picture of health

Roma *f* Rome ▸ **revolver** ~ **con Santiago para conseguir algo** to move heaven and earth to achieve sth

romana *f* scales *pl*

romance I. *adj* LING Romance **II.** *m* **1.** *t.* LIT (*aventura*) romance; ~ **de ciego** popular ballad; **tiene un** ~ **con la vecina** he's having an affair with his neighbour *Brit* [*o* neighbor *Am*] **2.** HIST (*castellano*) Castilian; **hablar en** ~ *fig* to speak plainly

románico, -a *adj* Romanesque

romanista *mf* Romanist

romano, -a I. *adj* **1.** (*de Roma*) Roman **2.** REL Roman Catholic **3.** (*latín*) Latin **II.** *m*, *f* (*de Roma*) Roman

romanticismo *m sin pl* romanticism; (*movimiento*) Romanticism

romántico, -a *adj*, *m*, *f* romantic

romaza *f* sorrel

rombal *adj* rhombic

rombo *m* rhombus; **en forma de** ~ diamond-shaped

romería *f* **1.** (*peregrinaje*) pilgrimage **2.** (*fiesta*) festival **3.** (*muchedumbre*) throng

romerito *m Méx* vegetables *pl*

romero *m* rosemary

romero, -a *adj*, *m*, *f* pilgrim

romo, -a *adj* **1.** (*sin punta*) blunt **2.** (*de nariz pequeña*) snub-nosed **3.** (*tosco*) coarse

rompecabezas *m inv* (*juego*) brainteaser; (*acertijo*) riddle

rompehielos *m inv* NÁUT icebreaker

rompehuelgas *mf inv* strikebreaker

rompeolas *m inv* breakwater

romper I. *vi* **1.** (*las olas*) to break **2.** (*empezar bruscamente*) to burst; ~ **a llorar** to burst into tears **3.** (*el día*) to break; **al** ~ **el día** at the break of day **4.** (*separarse*) to break up **II.** *vt*

1. (*destrozar, quebrar*) to break; (*un cristal*) to shatter; (*un plato*) to smash; (*papel, tela*) to tear; (*los zapatos*) to wear out; (*un terreno*) to plough; ~ **algo a martillazos** to smash sth with a hammer; ~ **algo a golpes** to bash sth to pieces; ~ **algo doblando** to bend sth until it breaks; ~ **una ventana a pedradas** to break a window by throwing stones at it **2.** (*negociaciones, relaciones*) to break off; (*contrato, promesa*) to break; ~ **el silencio/el encanto** to break the silence/the spell; ~ **el hilo del discurso** to interrupt the speech; ~ (**las**) **filas** MIL to break ranks **3.** (*iniciar*) ~ **el fuego** to open fire; **los pájaros rompen vuelo** the birds take to flight ▸ **de rompe y rasga** determined; **una persona de rompe y rasga** a very determined person **III.** *vr:* ~**se 1.** (*hacerse pedazos*) to break **2.** (*fracturarse*) to break; ~**se la pierna** to break one's leg; ~**se la cabeza** *fig* to rack one's brains ▸ **¿qué tripa se te ha roto?** *inf* what are you so upset about?

rompiente *m* reef

rompimiento *m* (*rotura*) breaking; (*de negociaciones, relaciones*) breakdown

rompope *m AmC, Ecua, Méx* GASTR eggnog

ron *m* rum

roncar <c→qu> *vi* (*persona*) to snore; (*gamo*) to bellow; (*viento*) to howl; (*olas*) to roar; (*suelo*) to creak

roncear *vt Arg, Chile, Méx* to move by levering

roncha *f* **1.** (*hinchazón*) swilling; (*cardenal*) bruise; (*picadura*) sting **2.** (*loncha*) slice; **una** ~ **de chorizo** a slice of sausage

ronco, -a *adj* (*afónico*) voiceless; (*áspero*) hoarse

roncón, -ona *m*, *f Col, Ven* bragging

ronda *f* **1.** (*de vigilancia*) round; **hacer una** ~ **de inspección por la fábrica** to do an inspection tour of the factory **2.** (*de copas*) round; **pagar una** ~ to buy a round **3.** POL round (*of voting*) **4.** (*jóvenes*) group of serenaders; (*serenata*) serenade; **andar de** ~ (*tocar música*) to go serenading; (*buscar aventura*) to go courting **5.** (*avenida*) ring road *Brit*, beltway *Am*

rondalla *f* **1.** (*música*) street music **2.** (*conjunto musical*) street musicians

rondar I. *vi* **1.** (*vigilar*) to be on patrol **2.** (*andar paseando de noche*) to prowl about **II.** *vt* **1.** (*a las mujeres*) to court **2.** (*rodear*) to surround; **las mariposas nocturnas rondan la luz** moths are drawn to the light; **lo ronda a todas horas para conseguir el empleo** he/she pesters him night and day to try and get the job; **anda rondando los setenta años** he/she is about seventy years old

rondín *m* **1.** *Bol, Ecua, Perú* (*armónica*) harmonica **2.** *Bol, Chile* (*vigilante*) watchman

ronquera *f* hoarseness

ronquido *m* (*de una persona*) snore; (*del viento*) howl; (*del mar*) roar; (*de la sierra*) buzz; (*del suelo*) creak; (*del gamo*) bellow

ronronear *vi* (*gato*) to purr

ronzar <z→c> I. *vi* to crunch II. *vt* (*mascar*) to crunch

roña *f* 1.(*mugre*) filth 2.(*mezquindad*) meanness; (*tacañería*) stinginess 3.(*orín*) rust 4.(*sarna de carneros*) scab

roñería *f* 1.(*mezquindad*) meanness 2.(*tacañería*) stinginess

roñoso, -a *adj* 1.(*tacaño*) mean, tight 2.(*sucio*) filthy 3.(*sarnoso*) scabby 4.(*oxidado*) rusty

ropa *f* 1.(*géneros de tela*) ~ **blanca** white wash *pl,* whites *Brit;* ~ **de color** colored wash *pl,* coloureds *Brit;* ~ **delicada** delicates *pl;* ~ **interior** underwear; **cambiar la ~ de cama** to change the bedclothes 2.(*vestidos, traje*) clothes *pl;* ~**s hechas** ready-made clothes; **cambiar(se) la** ~ to change one's clothes; **estar en** ~**s menores** to be in one's underwear; **poner(se) la** ~ to get dressed; **ponerse** ~ **de abrigo** to put on warm clothing; **ligero de** ~ lightly dressed ▶**de buena** ~ of good family; **de poca** ~ insignificant; **a quema** ~ point-blank; **disparar a quema** ~ to shoot at close range; **¡cuidado que hay** ~ **tendida!** be careful what you say!; **no tocar la** ~ **a alguien** not to touch a hair of sb's head

ropaje *m* 1.(*ropas*) clothing 2.(*ropa elegante*) finery

ropero *m* 1.(*armario*) wardrobe 2.(*asociación benéfica*) charity which distributes clothing

roque *m* 1.(*ajedrez*) rook, castle 2.(*dormido*) **quedarse** ~ to fall fast asleep

roqueño, -a *adj* 1.(*rocoso*) rocky 2.(*duro*) rock hard

roquero, -a I. *adj* 1.(*de rocas*) rocky; **castillo** ~ mountain castle 2.MÚS rock II. *m, f* (*fan*) rock fan; (*músico*) rock musician

rosa I. *adj* pink II. *f* BOT rose; ~ **de azafrán** saffron crocus; **color de** ~ pink; **esencia de** ~**s** rose essence ▶**no hay** ~ **sin espinas** *prov* every rose has its thorn *prov;* ~ **náutica** compass rose

rosáceo, -a *adj* rosy

rosado, -a *adj* (*color*) pink; **vino** ~ rosé (wine)

rosal *m* rosebush

rosaleda *f* rose garden

rosario *m* 1.REL rosary; **rezar el** ~ to say the rosary 2.(*serie*) string; **un** ~ **de coches/de injurias** a string of cars/of insults ▶**acabar como el** ~ **de la aurora** to end in confusion; **tener el** ~ **al cuello y el diablo en el cuerpo** to be a complete hypocrite

rosbif <rosbifs> *m* roast beef

rosca *f* 1.TÉC thread; **el tornillo se pasó de** ~ the screw broke the thread 2.(*forma de espiral*) coil; **hecho una** ~ rolled up into a ball; **hacerse** ~ (*gato, serpiente*) to roll up into a ball 3.(*forma de anillo*) ring; (*bollo*) (ring--shaped) bread roll; (*torta*) sponge ring; ~ **de Reyes** *Méx* Christmas cake eaten on Epiphany ▶**no comerse una** ~ not to get off with anyone; **hacer la** ~ **a alguien** to suck up to sb;

pasarse de ~ to go too far; **tirarse una** ~ to fail

rosco *m* (ring-shaped) bread roll; ~ **de viento** *type of doughnut*

roscón *m* sponge ring; ~ **de Reyes** Christmas cake eaten on Epiphany

rosedal *m Arg, Urug* BOT rosebed

rosetón *m* ARQUIT rose window

rosquete *adj, m Perú, vulg* queer

rosquilla *f* doughnut ▶**venderse como** ~**s** to sell like hot cakes

rosticería *f Chile, Méx: shop that sells roast chicken, beef and other dishes*

rostro *m* 1.(*cara*) face 2.(*pico*) beak ▶**tener mucho** ~ to have a lot of nerve

rotación *f* rotation; ~ **de cultivos** AGR crop rotation; ~ **del capital** capital movement; ~ **de mercancías** stock turnover

rotativo *m* newspaper

rotativo, -a *adj* rotary; **impresión rotativa** TIPO rotary printing

rotatorio, -a *adj* rotating

rotería *f Chile* 1.(*acción*) inconsiderate act 2.(*plebe*) the masses, rabble *pej*

rotisería *f Arg: shop that sells roast chicken, beef and other dishes*

roto *m* (*desgarrón*) tear; (*agujero*) hole

roto, -a I. *pp de* romper II. *adj* 1.(*despedazado*) broken; **un vestido** ~ a torn dress; **un florero/un cristal** ~ a broken vase/glass 2.(*andrajoso*) wretched 3.(*licencioso*) debauched 4.(*destrozado*) destroyed

rotonda *f* AUTO roundabout *Brit,* traffic circle *Am*

rotoso, -a I. *adj AmL* tattered II. *m, f* wretch

rótula *f* 1.ANAT knee joint 2.TÉC ball-and--socket joint

rotulador *m* felt-tip pen

rotuladora *f* labelling *Brit* [*o* labeling *Am*] machine

rotular *vt* (*letreros*) to make; (*mercancías*) to label; CINE to subtitle

rótulo *m* sign; (*encabezamiento*) heading; (*etiqueta*) ticket; (*letrero*) sign; (*anuncio público*) notice; CINE subtitle; ~ **de población** town sign

rotundamente *adv* 1.(*sin rodeos*) directly 2.(*terminantemente*) emphatically; **negar** ~ to flatly deny

rotundo, -a *adj* 1.(*terminante*) emphatic; **un éxito** ~ a resounding success; **una negativa rotunda** a flat refusal 2.(*lleno y sonoro*) sonorous; **palabras rotundas** resounding words

rotura *f* (*acción*) breaking; (*parte quebrada*) break; ~ **de hueso** fracture; ~ **de ligamento** torn ligament

roturar *vt* AGR to plough *Brit,* to plow *Am*

rouge *m Arg, Chile* (*colorete*) blusher, rouge

roya *f* rust

roza *f,* **rozado** *m Arg* AGR cleared ground

rozadura *f* scratch; (*de la piel*) graze

rozamiento *m* 1.(*fricción*) rubbing 2.(*roce*) brush 3.(*desavenencias*) friction

rozar <z→c> I. *vi* to rub; **rozar (por) los cincuenta** *fig* to be pushing fifty II. *vt* **1.** *t. fig* (*tocar ligeramente*) to brush; ~ **la ridiculez** *fig* to border on the ridiculous **2.** (*frotar*) to rub **3.** AGR to clear; (*animales*) to graze III. *vr:* ~**se 1.** (*restregarse*) to rub **2.** (*relacionarse*) to rub shoulders

rte. *abr de* **remitente** sender

RTVE *f abr de* **Radio Televisión Española** Spanish state broadcasting corporation

rúa *f* street

ruana *f AmS* (*poncho*) poncho

rubéola *f sin pl* MED German measles

rubí *m* MIN ruby

rubicundo, -a *adj* **1.** (*pelo*) reddish **2.** (*rostro*) ruddy

rubio, -a I. *adj* fair; **tabaco** ~ Virginia tobacco II. *m, f* blond; (*mujer*) blonde

rublo *m* (*moneda*) rouble

rubor *m* **1.** (*color*) bright red; (*de vergüenza*) blush **2.** (*vergüenza*) shame; (*bochorno*) embarrassment; **lo confieso con el ~ de mi cara** my blushing face leaves me no choice but to confess; **el ~ le quema la cara** he has turned red with shame/embarrassment

ruborizado, -a *adj* blushing

ruborizar <z→c> I. *vt* to cause to blush II. *vr:* ~**se** to blush

ruboroso, -a *adj* **1.** (*vergonzoso*) ashamed; (*de bochorno*) embarrassed **2.** (*ruborizado*) blushing

rúbrica *f* **1.** (*firma*) signature; (*después del nombre*) flourish **2.** (*epígrafe*) heading

rubricar <c→qu> *vt* **1.** (*firmar*) to sign; (*ratificar*) to endorse **2.** (*sellar*) to seal

rubro *m AmL* **1.** (*título*) heading, title **2.** COM (*asiento, partida*) area

ruca *f Arg, Chile* (*choza*) shack

rucio, -a *adj* (*animales*) grey *Brit,* gray *Am;* **caballo** ~ grey

ruco, -a *adj AmC* old

rudeza *f* **1.** (*brusquedad*) rudeness **2.** (*tosquedad*) coarseness **3.** (*torpeza*) stupidity

rudimentario, -a *adj* rudimentary

rudo, -a *adj* **1.** (*material*) rough; (*sin trabajar*) raw **2.** (*persona tosca*) coarse; (*brusca*) rude; (*torpe*) clumsy; (*poco inteligente*) stupid **3.** (*penoso*) harsh

rueda *f* **1.** (*que gira*) wheel; (*de mueble*) castor; ~ **de aspas** wheel (*of windmill*); ~ **de paletas** paddle wheel; ~ **de repuesto** spare tyre; **vapor de** ~s paddle steamer; **hacer la** ~ DEP to do a cartwheel; **el pavo hace la** ~ the peacock spreads its tail; **hacer la** ~ **a una mujer** to court a woman **2.** (*de personas*) ring; ~ **de prensa** press conference; ~ **de identificación** (*sospechosos*) police line-up **3.** (*rodaja*) slice; **una** ~ **de salami** a slice of salami **4.** (*orden sucesivo*) ring ►**comulgar con** ~s **de molino** to be very gullible; **todo** **marcha** **sobre** ~s everything is going smoothly

ruedo *m* **1.** (*contorno*) ring **2.** (*borde*) edge; (*del vestido*) hem **3.** TAUR bullring **4.** (*estera*) (round) mat ►**echarse al** ~ to enter the fray

ruego *m* request ►~s **y preguntas** POL any other business; **no valen** ~s **ni súplicas** there is no point pleading

rufián *m* **1.** (*chulo*) pimp **2.** (*granuja*) scoundrel

rugby *m* DEP rugby

rugido *m* **1.** (*del león*) roar **2.** (*del viento*) howl **3.** (*de las tripas*) rumble

rugir <g→j> I. *vi* **1.** (*león*) to roar; (*viento*) to howl **2.** (*estómago*) to rumble, to growl; **sus tripas rugen** his/her stomach is rumbling **3.** (*persona*) **este hombre está que ruge** this man is beside himself with rage II. *vimpers* to become known; **rugía que...** it became known that ...

rugoso, -a *adj* **1.** (*arrugado*) wrinkled **2.** (*áspero*) rough **3.** (*ondulado*) wavy

ruibarbo *m* rhubarb

ruido *m* **1.** (*sonido*) *t.* ELEC noise; ~s **parásitos** interference, static **2.** (*estrépito*) noise; **nivel de** ~ noise level; ~ **de fondo** background noise ►**mucho** ~ **y pocas nueces** much ado about nothing; **hacer** ~ to cause a stir; **querer** ~ to be looking for trouble; **quitarse de** ~s to keep out of trouble

ruidoso, -a *adj* noisy; *fig* sensational; **una carcajada ruidosa** a loud guffaw

ruin *adj* **1.** (*malvado*) wicked; (*vil*) despicable **2.** (*tacaño*) mean

ruina *f* **1.** (*destrucción*) destruction; **este hombre está hecho una** ~ *fig* this man is a wreck **2.** ARQUIT ruin; **las** ~s **de un castillo** the ruins of a castle **3.** *pl* (*escombros*) ruins *pl;* **convertir una ciudad en** ~s to raze a city to the ground; **declarar una casa en** ~s to condemn a house **4.** (*perdición*) downfall; **causar la** ~ **de alguien** to cause sb's downfall; **estar en la** ~ to be bankrupt; **salvar a alguien de la** ~ to save sb from disaster

ruindad *f* **1.** (*maldad*) wickedness **2.** (*tacañería*) meanness

ruinoso, -a *adj* **1.** (*edificios*) dilapidated **2.** (*perjudicial*) disastrous; ECON ruinous

ruiseñor *m* nightingale

rulenco, -a *adj Chile* weak; (*raquítico*) stunted

rulero *m AmS* hair curler, roller

ruleta *f* (*juego*) roulette

ruletear *vi AmC, Méx* (*conducir un taxi*) to drive a taxi

ruletero, -a *m, f AmC, Méx* (*conductor*) taxi driver

rulo *m* **1.** (*del cabello*) curl **2.** (*rizador*) *t.* TÉC roller

rulota *f* (*caravana*) caravan *Brit,* trailer *Am*

ruma *f AmS* (*montón*) **una** ~ **de...** a pile of ...; ~s **de...** lots of ...

Rumania *f,* **Rumanía** *f* Romania

rumano, -a *adj, m, f* Romanian

rumba *f* MÚS rumba

rumbo *m* **1.** (*dirección*) direction; *t. fig* AVIAT, NÁUT course; **tomar** ~ **a un puerto** to head for a port; **con ~ a** bound [*o* headed] for; **dar otro ~ a la conversación** to change the topic of the conversation; **no tengo ~ fijo** I'm not going anywhere in particular; **la negociación está tomando un ~ favorable** the negotiation is taking a turn for the better; **tomar otro ~** POL to change course **2.** (*pompa*) lavishness; **de ~** lavish; **una fiesta con mucho ~** a spectacular party

rumboso, -a *adj* **1.** (*generoso*) generous **2.** (*pomposo*) lavish

rumiante *m* ruminant

rumiar *vt* **1.** (*vacas*) to ruminate **2.** *inf* (*cavilar*) to think over **3.** *inf* (*refunfuñar*) to grumble about

rumor *m* **1.** (*chisme*) rumour *Brit*, rumor *Am;* **a título de ~** as a rumour *Brit* [*o* rumor *Am*]; **poner un ~ en circulación** to spread a rumour *Brit*, to start a rumor (going) *Am;* **corren ~es de que...** it is rumoured that ... **2.** (*ruido*) murmur; (*del viento*) whistle; (*del bosque*) rustle; **~ de voces** buzz of conversation

rumorearse *vr* **se rumorea que...** it is rumoured *Brit* [*o* rumored *Am*] that ...

rumoroso, -a *adj* murmuring; (*viento*) whistling; (*bosque*) rustling

runa *f* rune

runcho *m Col* ZOOL opossum

rundún *m Arg* **1.** (*pájaro mosca*) tiny hummingbird **2.** (*juguete*) bull-roarer

runrún *m inf* **1.** (*ruido*) buzz; (*murmullo*) murmur **2.** (*chisme*) rumour *Brit*, rumor *Am*

rupestre *adj* rock; **pintura ~** cave painting

rupia *f* (*moneda*) rupee

ruptura *f* breaking; (*de relaciones*) breaking-off

rural I. *adj* rural; **vida ~** country life II. *m* **1.** *AmL, t. pey* (*rústico*) yokel **2.** *pl, Méx* (*policía*) rural police

Rusia *f* Russia

ruso, -a I. *adj* Russian; **ensaladilla rusa** Russian salad (*potato salad with carrots, eggs and tuna*); **filete ~** breaded hamburger steak II. *m, f* Russian

rústico, -a I. *adj* **1.** (*campestre*) rural; **finca rústica** farmhouse **2.** (*tosco*) rough; **en rústica** TIPO paperback II. *m, f* peasant; *pey* yokel

rustidera *f* roasting pan

ruta *f* **1.** (*camino*) route; **~ federal** *AmL* federal highway *Am;* **~ de itinerario** itinerary; **~ de vuelo** flight path **2.** (*conducta*) **tienes que cambiar de ~** you'll have to change your ways

rutina *f* **1.** (*costumbre*) routine; **~ cotidiana** daily routine **2.** INFOR routine

rutinario, -a *adj* routine; **un hombre ~** (*de costumbres*) a man of habit; (*aburrido*) an unimaginative man

S

S, s *f* S, s; **~ de Soria** S for Sugar

S. *abr de* San St

S.A. *f* **1.** *abr de* Sociedad Anónima plc **2.** *abr de* Su Alteza Your Highness

sábado *m* **1.** (*día*) Saturday; *v.t.* **lunes 2.** (*judaísmo*) sabbath

sabana *f* savanna(h)

sábana *f* sheet; **~ ajustable** fitted sheet; **~ encimera/bajera** top/bottom sheet; **se me han pegado las ~s** *inf* I've overslept

sabandija *f* **1.** (*insecto*) bug **2.** *pey* (*persona*) wretch; **¡qué ~s!** little wretches!

sabanear *vi AmL* to ride the plains

sabañón *m* chilblain; **comer como un ~** *inf* to eat like a horse

sabático, -a *adj* **1.** (*judaísmo*) sabbatical **2.** (*universidad*) **un año ~** a sabbatical year

sabelotodo *mf inv, inf* know-all *Brit*, know-it--all *Am*

saber *irr* I. *vt* **1.** (*estar informado*) to know; **¿se puede ~ si...?** could you tell me if ...?; **¿se puede ~ dónde/cómo/quién...?** can sb tell me where/how/who ...?; **sin ~lo yo** without my knowing; **se sabe que...** it is known that ...; **¡cualquiera sabe!** who knows?; **vete tú/vaya usted a ~** it's anyone's guess; **¡véte tu a ~ si es cierto!** your guess is as good as mine!; **(al menos) que yo sepa** as far as I know; **para que lo sepas** for your information; **¡pues no sé qué te diga!** I wouldn't be so sure!; **tener (un) no sé qué de raro** to have sth strange about one; **¡no sé ni por dónde ando!** *inf* I don't know whether I'm coming or going!; **¡y qué sé yo!** how should I know! **2.** (*tener habilidad*) **sabe (hablar) ruso** he/she can speak Russian; **no ~(se) la poesía** not to know the poem by heart **3.** (*conocer*) to know; **¿sabes mi nombre?** do you know my name?; **~ de algo** to know about sth; **~ mucho de literatura** to know a lot about literature **4.** (*noticia*) to find out; **lo supe por mi hermano** I heard about it from my brother; **lo supe por el periódico** I read it in the papers; **la prensa hizo ~ anoche la noticia** the papers gave out the news last night; **¡va a ~ quién soy yo!** he/she will find out who he/she is dealing with! ▶ **a ~** namely II. *vi* **1.** (*tener sabor*) **~ a algo** to taste of sth; **sabe mal** it tastes bad; **(me) supo a quemado** it tasted burnt; **sabe a traición** it sounds like treachery; **~ a gloria** to taste [*o* be] divine; **~ a cuerno quemado** to be fishy **2.** (*agradar*) **la conferencia me supo a poco** the conference was really good but it should have been longer; **me supo mal aquella respuesta** that reply upset me **3.** (*tener noticia*) to have news; **no sé nada de mi hermano** I have no news of my brother **4.** (*tener la habilidad*) **~ de algo** to know how to do sth; **él no sabe resolver ni los ejercicios**

más fáciles he can't do even the simplest exercises **III.** *vr* **sabérselas todas** *inf* she knows all the tricks **IV.** *m sin pl* knowledge ►**el ~ no ocupa** lugar *prov* you can't know too much
sabichoso, -a *adj Cuba, PRico* pedantic; (*sabiondo*) know-all *Brit,* know-it-all *Am*
sabido, -a *adj* **1.** (*conocido*) known; **es cosa sabida** it's well known; **dar por ~** to take for granted **2.** (*leído*) learned
sabiduría *f* **1.** (*conocimientos*) knowledge **2.** (*sensatez*) wisdom **3.** (*erudición*) learning
sabiendas a ~ knowingly; **lo hizo a ~ de que me molestaba** he/she did it knowing full well that it annoyed me
sabihondo, -a *m, f* know-all *Brit,* know-it-all *Am;* (*niño*) smart-aleck, smarty pants
sabio, -a I. *adj* wise **II.** *m, f* scholar ►**errar es de ~s** *prov* to err is human
sabiondo, -a *m, f v.* **sabihondo**
sablazo *m* **1.** (*golpe*) sable stroke; (*herida*) sable wound **2.** *inf* **dar a alguien un ~** to sponge off sb
sable *m* sabre *Brit,* saber *Am*
sablear *vi inf* to scrounge
sabor *m* taste; **tiene (un) ~ a naranja** it tastes of orange; **de ~ romántico** with a romantic flavour *Brit* [*o* flavor *Am*]; **dejar un mal ~ de boca** to leave a nasty taste in the mouth
saborear *vt* to savour *Brit,* to savor *Am;* (*triunfo*) to relish
sabotaje *m* sabotage
sabotear *vt* to sabotage
sabroso, -a *adj* **1.** (*sazonado*) tasty **2.** (*gracioso*) racy **3.** (*salado*) slightly salty
sabueso *m* **1.** ZOOL bloodhound **2.** *fig* sleuth
saca *f* **1.** (*saco*) sack; **~ de correos** mailbag **2.** (*extracción*) withdrawal **3.** (*exportación*) export **4.** (*copia*) authorized copy
sacabocados *m inv* TÉC punch; (*papel, billete*) hole [*o* ticket] punch
sacabuche *m* **1.** MÚS sackbut **2.** NÁUT hand pump **3.** *Méx* (*navaja*) pointed knife
sacacorchos *m inv* corkscrew
sacamanchas *m inv* stain remover
sacamuelas *mf inf* dentist
sacapuntas *m inv* pencil sharpener
sacar <c→qu> **I.** *vt* **1.** (*de un sitio*) to take out, to remove; (*agua, espada*) to draw; (*diente*) to pull (out); **~ a bailar** to invite to dance; **~ a alguien de la cama/de la cárcel** to get sb out of bed/of jail; **~ a pasear** to take out for a walk; **sácalo del garage** take it out of the garage; **saca las plantas al balcón** put the plants out on the balcony; **¿de dónde lo has sacado?** where did you get it from?; **recién sacado del horno** freshly baked; **¡te voy a ~ los ojos!** *fig* I'll teach you (to do that)! **2.** (*de una situación*) to get; (*adelante*) (*persona*) to look after; (*negocio*) to run; (*niño*) to bring up; **~ a alguien del atolladero** to get sb out of a jam; **~ a alguien de la pobreza** to rescue sb from poverty **3.** (*solucionar*) to solve **4.** (*reco-*

nocer) to recognize **5.** (*entrada*) to get **6.** (*obtener*) to obtain; (*premio, votos*) to get; **~ las consecuencias** to come to conclusions; **~ en claro (de)** to gather (from); **no ~ ni para vivir** not to make enough to live on; **~ a alguien 10 euros** to get 10 euros off sb **7.** MIN to extract **8.** (*parte del cuerpo*) to stick out **9.** *inf* (*foto*) to take; (*dibujo*) to do; **¡sácame una foto!** take a photo of me!; **el pintor te sacó muy bien** the painter got a good likeness of you **10.** (*mancha*) to remove **11.** (*producto*) to bring out; **~ a la venta** to put on sale [*o* the market]; (*libro*) to publish; **~ un apodo a alguien** to give sb a nickname **12.** (*mostrar*) to show; (*desenterrar*) to unearth; **~ en hombros** to carry out shoulder-high; **~ algo a relucir** to bring out the dirty linen **13.** (*ventaja*) **el ganador me sacó dos minutos** the winner was two minutes quicker than me; **mi hermana me saca tres años** my sister is three years older than I am **II.** *vi* (*tenis*) to serve; (*fútbol: portero*) to take a goal kick; (*fútbol: saque de banda*) to take a throw-in **III.** *vr* **se sacó una pestaña del ojo** he/she took an eyelash out of his/her eye
sacarina *f sin pl* saccharin
sacerdote *m* priest
sacho *m* **1.** (*para sachar*) weeder **2.** *Chile* (*ancla*) anchor
saciado, -a *adj* satiated
saciar I. *vt* (*hambre, curiosidad*) to satisfy; (*instintos sexuales*) to satiate; (*sed*) to quench **II.** *vr:* **~se** *t. fig* to satiate oneself; **me sacié de salchichas** I ate my fill of sausages
saciedad *f sin pl* satiation; **repetir hasta la ~** to repeat over and over
saco *m* **1.** (*bolsa*) bag; (*costal*) sack; **~ de trigo** sack of wheat; **~ de dormir** sleeping bag **2.** *AmL* (*prenda*) jacket **3.** (*saqueo*) sacking; **entrar a ~** to loot **4.** DEP (*boxeo*) punchball *Brit,* punching bag *Am* ►**en el mismo ~** in the same boat; **caer en ~ roto** to fall on deaf ears; **no echar algo en ~ roto** to take note of sth
sacón, -ona *m, f Méx, inf* (*miedica*) chicken
sacramento *m* sacrament; **el ~ de la Eucaristía** the Blessed Sacrament; **administrar a alguien los últimos ~s** to give sb the last rites; **con todos los ~s** *fig* without forgetting anything
sacrificar <c→qu> **I.** *vt* **1.** (*ofrecer*) to sacrifice; *t. fig* to give up **2.** (*animal*) to slaughter **II.** *vr:* **~se por algo/alguien** to sacrifice oneself for sth/sb
sacrificio *m* sacrifice; **el Santo Sacrificio** Holy Communion
sacrilegio *m* sacrilege
sacrílego, -a *adj* sacrilegious; **acción sacrílega** act of sacrilege
sacristán *m* sacristan ►**¡ése es un buen** ~! *inf* he's a right one!
sacristía *f* vestry, sacristy
sacro, -a *adj* **1.** (*sagrado*) sacred **2.** ANAT **hueso ~** sacrum

sacrosanto, -a *adj* most holy; *fig* sacrosanct
sacudida *f* shake; ~ **eléctrica** electric shock; ~ **sísmica** earthquake; **el coche pegaba ~s** the car was jolting; **dale una ~ a la alfombra** shake the carpet [*o* rug]
sacudir I. *vt* 1. (*agitar*) to shake; (*moscas*) to brush off; ~ **el rabo** to swish its tail; ~ **a alguien por los hombros** to shake sb by the shoulders; **un estremecimiento le sacudió todo el cuerpo** a shiver ran all through his/her body 2. (*pegar*) to belt II. *vr:* ~**se** to shake oneself; ~**se la duda** to dispel the doubt; ~**se el yugo** to shake off the yoke; ~**se a alguien de encima** *fig* to get rid of sb
sádico, -a I. *adj* sadistic II. *m, f* sadist
sadismo *m sin pl* sadism
sadomasoquismo *m sin pl* sadomasochism
sadomasoquista I. *adj* sadomasochistic II. *mf* sadomasochist
saeta *f* 1. (*flecha*) arrow 2. (*reloj*) hand; (*brújula*) magnetic needle 3. MÚS *pious song in flamenco style typically sung in the religious processions in Spain during Easter week*
safari *m* safari
sagacidad *f sin pl* astuteness
sagaz *adj* astute
Sagitario *m* Sagittarius
sagrado, -a <sacratísimo> *adj* sacred
sagrario *m* (*para las hostias*) tabernacle
sagú *m AmC* 1. (*planta*) arrowroot 2. (*harina*) sago starch
Sáhara *m* el ~ the Sahara
sahumar *vt* (*incienso*) to perfume; (*humo*) to smoke
sahumerio *m* smoking
sainete *m* 1. TEAT one-act farce 2. (*comida*) titbit
sajón, -ona *adj, m, f* Saxon
Sajonia *f* Saxony; **Baja** ~ Lower Saxony
sal *f* 1. (*condimento*) salt; ~ **común** table salt; **poner demasiada ~ a algo** to put too much salt in sth; ~ **marina** sea [*o* bay] salt; ~ **gorda** coarse [*o* rock] salt 2. *pl* (*perfume*) smelling salts *pl;* ~**es de baño** bath salts 3. (*gracia*) wit; (*encanto*) charm; **la ~ de la vida** the spice of life 4. *AmL* (*mala suerte*) bad luck ▶**tener poca ~ en la** <u>mollera</u> *inf* to be a bit dim
sala *f* 1. (*habitación*) room; (*grande*) hall; ~ **de espera** waiting room; ~ **de estar** living room; ~ **de fiestas** dance hall 2. JUR courtroom; **Sala de lo Civil/Penal** Civil/Criminal Court
salado, -a *adj* 1. (*comida*) salty 2. (*gracioso*) witty; (*encantador*) charming 3. *AmL* (*infortunado*) unfortunate
saladura *f* salting
salamanca *f* 1. *Arg* ZOOL flat-headed salamander 2. *CSur* (*cueva natural*) natural cave
salamandra *f* salamander; ~ **acuática** newt
salamanquesa *f* gecko; ~ **de agua** newt
salame *adj Arg, inf* (*tonto*) fool
salami *m* salami
salar *vt* 1. (*condimentar*) to add salt to; ~ **algo**

demasiado to put too much salt in sth 2. (*para conservar*) to salt 3. *AmL* (*echar a perder*) to spoil
salarial *adj* wage
salario *m* wages *pl;* ~ **en especie** payment in kind
salazón *m* 1. (*saladura*) salting 2. *pl* (*carne*) salted meat
salchicha *f* sausage; **perro** ~ *inf* sausage dog *Brit,* hotdog *Am*
salchichón *m* salami-type cured sausage
saldar *vt* 1. (*cuenta*) to pay; (*deuda*) to pay off; **todavía no hemos saldado nuestras diferencias** we still haven't settled our differences 2. (*mercancía*) to sell off
saldo *m* 1. (*diferencia*) balance; (*pago*) payment; ~ **acreedor** credit balance; ~ **de la cuenta** account balance 2. *pl* (*rebajas*) sales *pl*
salero *m* 1. (*objeto*) salt cellar *Brit,* salt shaker *Am* 2. (*gracia*) wit; (*encanto*) charm
saleroso, -a *adj inf* (*ingenioso*) witty; (*encantador*) charming
salida *f* 1. (*puerta*) way out; ~ **para coches** car exit; **a la ~ del teatro** coming out of the theatre *Brit* [*o* theater *Am*]; **callejón sin** ~ dead end; ~ **de emergencia** emergency exit 2. (*de un tren, avión*) departure; (*de un barco*) sailing 3. (*astr*) rising; ~ **del sol** sunrise 4. DEP start; **dar la** ~ to start the race 5. COM sale; (*partida*) consignment; **este producto no tiene** ~ there is no market for this product; ~ **de capital** capital outflow 6. *inf* (*ocurrencia*) witty remark; ~ **de tono** inappropriate remark; **¡menuda ~!** what a crazy idea! 7. (*pretexto*) pretext 8. (*solución*) way out; **en este asunto no hay** ~ there is no way out of this
salido, -a *adj inf* randy, horny; **más** ~ **que la punta de una plancha** randier than a rooster in the henhouse
salidor(a) *adj AmL* party-loving; **es muy** ~ he likes to go out a lot
saliente *adj* 1. (*excelente*) outstanding 2. (*ojos*) protruding 3. (*ministro*) outgoing
salina *f* 1. (*instalación*) salt works 2. (*mina*) salt mine
salinidad *f sin pl* salinity
salino, -a *adj* saline
salir *irr* I. *vi* 1. (*ir al exterior*) to go out; (*ir fuera*) to go away; ~ **a dar una vuelta** to go out for a stroll [*o* walk]; ~ **con alguien** *inf* to go out with sb; ~ **adelante** to make progress; ~ **mal con alguien** to fall out with sb 2. (*de viaje*) to leave; (*avión*) to depart; ~ **del cascarón** [*o* **del huevo**] to come out of the egg; **para** ~ **de dudas le pregunté directamente** to clear up any doubts I asked him/her directly; ~ **ileso** [*o* **bien librado**] to come out unscathed; ~ **ganando/perdiendo** to come out the better/the worse 3. (*flores, fuente*) to come out; (*sol*) to rise; ~ **a la luz** to come to light; ~ **en la tele** to be on TV 4. (*convertirse*) to turn into; **salió un buen artista** he became a good artist 5. (*parecerse*) ~ **a alguien** to look

like sb; **este niño ha salido a su padre** the boy takes after his father **6.** INFOR ~ **de un programa** to exit a program **7.** DEP to start **8.** (*costar*) to cost; **nos sale a 4 euros el metro** it costs us 4 euros per metre *Brit* [*o* meter *Am*] ► ~ **pitando** *inf* to beat it; **salga lo que salga** whatever happens **II.** *vr:* ~**se 1.** (*de un recipiente*) to spill; (*líquido*) to overflow; (*leche*) to boil over; (*vasija*) to leak; **el río se salió** (**de madre**) the river burst its banks **2.** (*de una organización*) ~**se de la Iglesia** to leave the Church ► ~**se con la suya** to get one's own way

salitre *m* saltpetre *Brit*, saltpeter *Am*

saliva *f* saliva; **gastar** ~ **en balde** *fig* to waste one's breath; **tragar** ~ *fig* to conceal one's feelings

salivadera *f Arg, Urug* (*escupidera*) spittoon

salmantino, -a I. *adj* of/from Salamanca **II.** *m, f* native/inhabitant of Salamanca

salmo *m* psalm; **cantar a alguien el** ~ *fig* to tell sb a few home truths

salmón I. *adj* salmon-pink **II.** *m* salmon

salmonete *m* red mullet

salmuera *f* brine

salobre *adj* salty; (*agua*) brackish

salón *m* **1.** (*de casa*) living-room **2.** (*local*) hall; ~ **de actos** assembly hall; ~ **de baile** dancehall **3.** (*feria*) show

salpicadera *f Méx* AUTO mudguard

salpicadero *m* AUTO dashboard

salpicadura *f* **1.** (*acción*) splashing **2.** (*mancha*) fleck, spatter

salpicar <c→qu> *vt* **1.** (*rociar*) to sprinkle; (*con pintura*) to splash; ~ **la mesa de flores** to decorate the table with flowers **2.** (*manchar*) to spatter **3.** (*con chistes*) to pepper

salpicón *m* **1.** GASTR ≈ salmagundi (*chopped seafood or meat with oil, vinegar and seasoning*) **2.** *Col, Ecua* (*bebida*) cold drink of fruit juice **3.** (*mancha*) spatter

---

In **Colombia** and **Ecuador** the **salpicón** is a cold fruit drink. In Spain, however, **salpicón** is a cold meat, fish or seafood dish.

---

salpimentar <e→ie> *vt* to season, to add salt and pepper; ~ **algo con algo** *fig* to liven sth up with sth

salsa *f* **1.** GASTR sauce; (*caldo*) gravy; ~ **mayonesa** mayonnaise; ~ **verde** parsley sauce; ~ **de tomate** (*de aderezo*) ketchup, catsup *Am;* (*para cocinar*) tomato sauce **2.** (*gracia*) humour *Brit,* humor *Am;* **este libro tiene mucha** ~ this book is very amusing; **esa es la** ~ **de la vida** she is the spice of life **3.** MÚS salsa ► **la** ~ **de San Bernardo** a healthy appetite; **estar en su propia** ~ to be in one's element

salsamentaría *f Col* COM delicatessen

salsera *f* gravy boat

saltado, -a *adj* **1.** (*desprendido*) missing

2. (*saltón*) protruding

saltador *m* (*comba*) skipping rope

saltador(a) I. *adj* jumping **II.** *m(f)* **1.** (*atleta*) jumper; ~ **de altura** high-jumper; ~ **de longitud** long-jumper; ~ **de pértiga** pole-vaulter **2.** (*saltimbanqui*) acrobat

saltamontes *m inv* grasshopper

saltaperico *m Cuba* BOT manyroot

saltar I. *vi* **1.** (*botar*) to jump; (*chispas*) to fly up; ~ **por los aires** to blow up; *fig* to get furious; ~ **de alegría** to jump for joy; ~ **a la cuerda** to skip; ~ **a la pata coja** to hop (on one leg); ~ **en pedazos** to break into pieces; **los jugadores** ~**on al terreno de juego** the players ran out onto the pitch [*o* the field *Am*] **2.** (*lanzarse*) to jump; ~ **al agua** to jump into the water; ~ **con paracaídas** to make a parachute jump **3.** (*explotar*) to explode; (*costura*) to burst; (*los plomos*) to blow **4.** (*picarse*) to explode **5.** (*irrumpir*) to come out **6.** (*trabajo*) to be promoted rapidly; (*ser destituido*) to be kicked out **7.** (*desprenderse*) to come off ► **estar a la que salta** to look out for an opportunity **II.** *vt* **1.** (*movimiento*) to jump (over) **2.** (*animal*) to cover **III.** *vr:* ~**se 1.** (*ley, norma*) to break **2.** (*línea, párrafo*) to miss out, to skip **3.** (*desprenderse*) to come off; **se me saltó un botón** one of my buttons came off; **se me** ~**on las lágrimas** my eyes filled with tears

saltarín, -ina I. *adj* **1.** (*inquieto*) restless **2.** (*inestable*) shaky **II.** *m, f* **1.** (*bailarín*) dancer **2.** (*zarandillo*) active person

salteador(a) *m(f)* holdup man *m,* holdup woman *f*

saltear *vt* **1.** (*asaltar*) to hold up **2.** GASTR to sauté **3.** (*interrumpir*) to do in fits and starts

saltimbanqui *m* acrobat

salto *m* **1.** (*bote*) jump; **de** [*o* en] **un** ~ with one jump; **apartarse de un** ~ to jump away; **dar un** ~ to jump; *fig* to jump with fright; **dar** ~**s de alegría** to jump for joy; **dar un** ~ **atrás** to jump backwards; **me pegó un** ~ **el corazón** my heart pounded; **moverse a** ~**s** to jump along **2.** DEP jump; ~ **de altura** high jump; ~ **de longitud** long jump; ~ **mortal** somersault; ~ **con pértiga** pole vault; ~ **del potro** vault; **a** ~**s** in leaps and bounds **3.** (*trabajo*) rapid promotion **4.** (*bata*) ~ **de cama** negligée **5.** INFOR ~ **de línea** line break; ~ **de página** page break **6.** (*omisión*) gap, omission ► ~ **de agua** waterfall; **a** ~ **de mata** *inf* (*repentinamente*) suddenly; (*superficialmente*) carelessly; **vivir a** ~ **de mata** *inf* to live from hand to mouth

saltón, -ona *adj* **1.** (*saltarín*) restless **2.** (*sobresaliente*) protruding; **ojos saltones** bulging eyes

salubre *adj* <salubérrimo> (*saludable*) healthy; (*curativo*) curative

salubridad *f sin pl* healthiness; *AmL* (*higiene*) hygiene

salud *f sin pl* (*estado físico*) health; ¡~! (*al estornudar*) bless you!; (*al brindar*) good health!; **beber a la** ~ **de...** to drink to the

health of ...; **rebosante de** ~ bursting with health; **¡~, dinero y amor!** *inf* cheers!; **curarse en** ~ *fig* to take precautions; **gastar** ~ to be in good health; **lo juro por la** ~ **de mis hijos** I swear on the Bible
saludable *adj* 1.(*sano*) healthy 2.(*provechoso*) beneficial
saludar *vt* 1.(*al encontrar*) to greet; (*con la mano*) to wave; MIL to salute; **le saluda atentamente su...** *form* yours faithfully ...; **he ido a** ~ **a mis padres** I went to visit my parents; **estos ya ni se saludan** they don't even speak to each other now 2.(*recibir*) to welcome 3.(*mandar saludos*) to send regards to
saludo *m* 1.(*palabras*) greeting; **con un cordial** ~ *form* yours sincerely; **¡dele ~s de mi parte!** give him/her my regards; **tu madre te manda ~s** your mother sends her love; **muchos ~s a tu hermano de mi parte** give my warmest regards to your brother 2.(*recibimiento*) welcome
salutación *f* greeting; (*recibimiento*) welcome; (*oración*) Hail Mary
salva *f* salvo; ~ **de aplausos** round of applause
salvación *f* rescue; REL salvation; **Ejército de Salvación** Salvation Army
salvado *m* bran
salvador(a) I. *adj* saving; REL salvational; (*curativo*) curative II. *m(f)* rescuer; REL saviour *Brit*, savior *Am*
Salvador *m* **El** ~ El Salvador

The Republic of **El Salvador** lies in the north-eastern part of Central America. The capital is **San Salvador**. The official language of the country is Spanish and the monetary unit of **El Salvador** is the **colón**. The country is the smallest and most densely populated in Central America.

---

salvadoreño, -a *adj, m, f* Salvadoran
salvaguardar *vt* to safeguard; (*derechos, intereses*) to protect
salvaguardia *f* 1.(*protección*) safeguard; (*de intereses*) safekeeping 2.(*salvoconducto*) safe-conduct
salvajada *f* savage deed, atrocity
salvaje I. *adj* (*planta, animal*) wild; (*persona*) uncivilized; (*acto*) savage; **huelga** ~ wildcat strike II. *mf* savage; (*persona ruda*) barbarian
salvajismo *m sin pl* 1.(*animal*) wild nature 2.(*gamberrismo*) vandalism 3.(*crueldad*) savagery
salvamanteles *m inv* table mat, place mat *Am*
salvamento *m* salvation; (*accidente, naufragio*) rescue
salvar I. *vt* & *t.* REL (*del peligro*) to save; ~ **del peligro** to save from danger 2.(*foso*) to jump across; (*distancia*) to cover; (*obstáculo*) to get round; (*problema*) to overcome; ~ **las apa-**

riencias to keep up appearances II. *vr:* ~**se** to save oneself; (*en sentido religioso*) to be saved; **¡sálvese quien pueda!** every man for himself!; ~**se por los pelos** to have a narrow escape
salvavidas *m inv* (*cinturón*) lifebelt; **bote** ~ lifeboat; **chaleco** ~ lifejacket
salvavidas *mf* lifeguard
salvedad *f* 1.(*excepción*) exception 2.(*condición*) reservation; **con la** ~ **de que...** with the proviso that ...
salvia *f* sage
salvilla *f Chile* cruet
salvo *prep* except; ~ **que** +*subj* unless; ~ **error u omisión** *form* errors and omissions excepted; ~ **aviso en contrario** *form* unless otherwise informed
salvo, -a *adj* safe; **poner a** ~ to put in a safe place; **sano y** ~ safe and sound
salvoconducto *m* safe-conduct
samba *f* samba
sambenito *m* **colgar un** ~ **a alguien** to give sb a bad name; (*culpar*) to put the blame on sb
sambumbia *f* 1.*Col* (*cosa desmoronada*) **volver algo** ~ to smash sth to pieces 2.*Cuba* GASTR *drink of cane syrup, water and peppers* 3.*Méx* GASTR pineapple cordial
san *adj* Saint
sanar I. *vi* ~ **de algo** to recover from sth II. *vt* to cure
sanatorio *m* sanatorium
sanción *f* 1.(*multa*) penalty; ECON sanction 2.(*ley*) passing 3.(*autorización*) endorsement
sancionable *adj* punishable
sancionar *vt* 1.(*castigar*) to punish; ECON (*aplicar sanciones*) to impose sanctions on 2.(*aprobar*) to authorize; JUR to ratify
sancochar *vt AmL* (*rehogar*) to parboil
sancocho *m* 1.*AmC, PRico, Ven* (*lío*) fuss 2.*And, Ven* parboiled meat
sandalia *f* sandal
sándalo *m* 1.(*árbol*) sandalwood tree 2.(*madera*) sandalwood
sandez *f* stupid action; **no decir más que sandeces** to say nothing but foolish things
sandía *f* watermelon
sandinista *adj, mf* Sandinista
sandunga *f inf* 1.(*gracia*) charm 2.*Col, Chile, PRico* celebration
sándwich *m* GASTR toasted sandwich; **día** ~ *Arg, inf*: day taken as vacation between two public holidays
saneado, -a *adj* (*renta, haber*) debt-free
saneamiento *m* 1.(*de un edificio*) repair; (*de un terreno*) drainage 2.(*de economía*) reform 3.JUR compensation
sanear *vt* 1.(*edificio*) to clean up; (*tierra*) to drain 2.(*economía*) to reform; ~ **un vicio** to break a bad habit 3.JUR to compensate
Sanfermines *mpl Pamplona bull-running festival*
sangrante *adj* bleeding; **un ejemplo** ~ *fig* a flagrant example

S

sangrar I. *vi* to bleed; **estar sangrando por la nariz** to have a nosebleed; **estar sangrando** *fig* to be very fresh **II.** *vt* **1.** MED to bleed **2.** (*dinero*) to bleed dry **3.** (*agua, resina*) to drain off **4.** TIPO to indent

sangre *f* **1.** (*líquido*) blood; **a ~ fría** in cold biood; **de ~ azul** blue-blooded; **animales de ~ caliente/fría** warm/cold-blooded animals; (**caballo de**) **pura ~** thoroughbred (horse); **chupar la ~** (**de las venas**) **a alguien** *inf* to bleed sb dry; **conservar la ~ fría** *fig* to keep one's cool; **dar** [*o* **donar**] **~** to give [*o* donate] blood; **dar la ~ de sus venas** *fig* to give everything one has; **hacer ~** (*en una pelea, lucha*) to draw blood; **aportar ~ nueva a algo** to inject new blood [*o* life] into sth; **llevar algo en la ~** to have sth in the blood; (*de familia*) to run in the family; **le hierve la ~** *fig* his/her blood boils; **la ~ se me heló en las venas** my blood ran cold; **se le subió la ~ a la cabeza** he/she saw red **2.** (*linaje*) lineage ▸**la letra con ~ entra** *prov* spare the rod and spoil the child; **no llegar la ~ al río** not to have disastrous results; **hacerse mala ~** to get bitter; **sudar ~** to go through hardships; **tener mala ~** to be bad-tempered; **la ~ tira** blood is thicker than water *prov*

sangría *f* **1.** MED bleeding; **una ~ de votos** a continuous loss of votes **2.** (*brazo*) inner angle of the elbow **3.** (*aguas*) irrigation channel **4.** TIPO indentation **5.** (*bebida*) sangria ▸**lo mismo son ~s que ventosas** that won't make any difference

---

Sangría is a punch made from red wine, water, sugar, lemon and orange. It is normally served in a **jarra de barro** (earthenware jug).

---

sangriento, -a *adj* bloody; (*injusticia*) cruel; **hecho ~** bloody event

sangriligero, -a *adj AmC* friendly, nice

sangripesado, -a *adj AmC* unpleasant, disagreeable

sangrón, -ona *adj Méx, inf* boring; **su novio es un ~, no lo soporto** her boyfriend is a bore, I can't stand him

sanguaraña *f* **1.** *Ecua, Perú* (*circunloquio*) evasion; **déjate de ~s** stop beating about the bush **2.** *Perú: popular Peruvian dance*

sanguijuela *f* **1.** ZOOL leech **2.** *pey* (*persona*) bloodsucker

sanguinario, -a *adj* (*persona, animal*) blood-thirsty; (*hecho*) cruel

sanguíneo, -a *adj* **1.** MED blood; **rojo ~** blood-red; **grupo ~** blood type [*o* group] **2.** (*temperamento*) sanguine

sanguinolento, -a *adj* bloody; (*color*) blood-red; (*ojos*) bloodshot

sanidad *f sin pl* health; **~** (**pública**) public health

sanitario *m* (*wáter*) toilet

sanitario, -a I. *adj* health; (*aparatos, medi-*

das) sanitary **II.** *m, f* health worker

sano, -a *adj* **1.** (*robusto, saludable*) healthy; **~ de juicio** of sound mind; **cortar por lo ~** to take extreme measures; **estar más ~ que una manzana** to be as sound as a bell; **salir ~ y salvo** to emerge safe and sound **2.** (*no roto*) intact **3.** (*sincero*) wholesome

santanderino, -a I. *adj* of/from Santander **II.** *m, f* native/inhabitant of Santander

santería *f AmL: shop selling religious items*

santero, -a I. *adj pey* (*beato*) pious; **ese es muy ~** he's very fond of the saints **II.** *m, f* **1.** *pey* (*beato*) Holy Joe **2.** (*guardián*) shrine keeper

Santiago *m* **~** (**de Chile**) Santiago

santiaguino, -a I. *adj* of/from Santiago (in Chile) **II.** *m, f* native/inhabitant of Santiago (in Chile)

santiamén *m* **en un ~** in a jiffy

santidad *f* holiness; **Su Santidad** His Holiness, the Pope

santificar <c→qu> *vt* **1.** (*consagrar*) to consecrate **2.** (*canonizar*) to sanctify **3.** (*respetar*) to glorify

santiguar <gu→gü> **I.** *vt* **1.** (*signarse*) to make the sign of the cross over **2.** *inf* (*maltratar*) to hit **II.** *vr:* **~se** to cross oneself

santo, -a I. *adj* sacred, holy; (*piadoso*) saintly; (*inviolable*) consecrated; **la Santa Sede** the Holy See; **el Santo Oficio** HIST the Inquisition; **campo ~** cemetery; **Jueves Santo** Maundy Thursday; **Semana Santa** Holy Week, Easter; **Viernes Santo** Good Friday; **¿qué haces en Semana Santa?** what are you doing over Easter?; **se pasó todo el ~ día haciendo...** he/she spent the whole blessed day doing ...; **¡y santas pascuas!** and that's that! **II.** *m, f* **1.** (*personaje*) saint; **día de Todos los Santos** All Saints' Day **2.** (*fiesta*) saint's day, name day; **el día de mi ~** my saint's day **3.** (*imagen*) (religious) illustration; **ver los ~s de un libro** to look at the pictures in a book ▸**hoy tengo el ~ de cara/espalda** I'm in/out of luck today; **se le fue el ~ al cielo** he/she forgot what he/she was going to say; **no ser ~ de la devoción de alguien** to not be particularly fond of sb; **alzarse con el ~ y la limosna** to clear off with everything; **ser mano de ~** to be good at everything; **~ y seña** password; **¡ésta se come los ~s!** *inf* she's very religious!; **desnudar a un ~ para vestir a otro** to rob Peter to pay Paul; **dormirse como un ~** (*bendito*) to sleep like a baby; **llegar y besar el ~** (*sin esfuerzo*) to pull it off at the first attempt; (*fácil*) like taking candy from a baby; **quedarse para vestir ~s** (*mujer*) to be left on the shelf, to remain an old maid; **no sé a ~ de qué me dijo eso** I don't know why on earth he/she told me that

santuario *m* **1.** (*templo*) shrine; (*capilla*) chapel **2.** (*refugio*) sanctuary, refuge **3.** *Col* (*tesoro*) buried treasure

santurrón, -ona I. *adj* sanctimonious; (*hipócrita*) hypocritical II. *m, f* sanctimonious individual; (*hipócrita*) hypocrite

saña *f* 1. (*ira*) anger 2. (*rencor*) viciousness; **lo hizo con toda la mala** ~ he/she did it with great cruelty

sapaneco, -a *adj Hond* chubby

sapiencia *f sin pl* 1. (*conocimientos*) wisdom 2. (*sensatez*) good sense

sapo *m* 1. ZOOL toad 2. (*persona*) nasty bit of work 3. *inf* (*bicho*) small animal ▶ **pisar el** ~ to have a lie-in, to sleep late

saponaria *f* soapwort

saque *m* DEP (*fútbol*) goal kick, throw-in; (*fútbol americano*) kick-off; (*tenis*) serve; ~ **de esquina** corner kick ▶ **tener buen** ~ to have a hearty appetite

saquear *vt* to loot

saqueo *m* looting

sarampión *m sin pl* MED measles

sarao *m* (*fiesta*) evening party; **¡menudo** ~ **se armó allí!** what a to-do that was!

sarape *m Méx* blanket

sarasa *m pey* lilac, pansy

sarazo, -a *adj Col, Cuba, Méx, Ven* (*Mais*) ripening

sarcasmo *m sin pl* sarcasm

sarcástico, -a *adj* sarcastic

sarcófago *m* sarcophagus; (*tumba*) tomb

sarcoma *m* MED sarcoma

sardana *f* MÚS *typical Catalan dance*

sardina *f* sardine; ~**s en aceite** sardines in oil; **entierro de la** ~ *festival to mark the beginning of Lent;* (**estar**) **como** ~**s en lata** to be packed like sardines

sardo, -a *adj, m, f* Sardinian

sardónico, -a *adj* sardonic

sargenta *f fig* bossy woman

sargento *m* sergeant

sargo *m* sea bream, sheepshead

sarmentoso, -a *adj* (*extremidades*) gnarled; (*plant*) climbing

sarmiento *m* (*tallo*) vine shoot

sarna *f sin pl* MED scabies; (*de los animales*) mange ▶ ~ **con gusto no pica(, pero mortifica**) *prov* if you like sth you'll do it whatever the cost; **ser más viejo que la** ~ *inf* to be as old as the hills

sarpullido *m* MED (*irritación*) rash

sarracina *f* quarrel

sarro *m* 1. MED (*de los dientes*) tartar; (*en la lengua*) fur 2. (*poso*) deposit

sarta *f* 1. (*hilo*) string 2. (*serie*) row; **una** ~ **de mentiras** a string [*o* pack] of lies

sartén *f* frying pan ▶ **saltar de la** ~ **y dar en las brasas** to jump from the frying pan into the fire; **tener la** ~ **por el mango** to have the whip [*o* upper] hand

sastre, -a *m, f* tailor; **traje** ~ tailor-made suit; **de eso, será lo que tase un** ~ *inf* that's more than doubtful

sastrería *f* tailor's shop; (*oficio*) tailoring

satánico, -a *adj* satanic

satélite *m* ASTR, TÉC satellite; (**país**) ~ satellite (state)

satén *m* satin

satinado, -a *adj* shiny, glossy; **papel** ~ shiny paper

sátira *f* LIT satire

satírico, -a I. *adj* satirical II. *m, f* satirist

satirizar <z→c> *vt* to satirize

sátiro *m* satyr; (*hombre lascivo*) lecher

satisfacción *f* 1. (*estado*) satisfaction; (*alegría*) happiness; **a mi entera** ~ to my complete satisfaction 2. (*pago*) settlement 3. REL fulfilment *Brit,* fulfillment *Am*

satisfacer *irr como hacer* I. *vt* 1. (*pagar*) to honour *Brit,* to honor *Am;* ~ **la penitencia por sus pecados** to do penitence for one's sins 2. (*deseo, curiosidad, hambre*) to satisfy; (*sed*) to quench; (*demanda*) to settle; ~ **todos los caprichos de sus hijos** to gratify all one's children's whims 3. (*requisitos*) to meet 4. (*agravio*) ~ **algo** to make amends for sth II. *vr:* ~**se** 1. (*contentarse*) to satisfy oneself 2. (*agravio*) to obtain redress

satisfactorio, -a *adj* (*solución*) satisfactory; **no ser** ~ to be unsatisfactory; **resulta** ~ **comprobar que...** it is pleasing to confirm that ...

satisfecho, -a I. *pp de* **satisfacer** II. *adj* (*contento*) contented; (*exigencias, deseo sexual*) satisfied; ~ **de sí mismo** self-satisfied; **estar** ~ (*harto*) to have had enough

saturación *f* saturation

saturar *vt* to saturate

sauce *m* willow; ~ **llorón** weeping willow

saúco *m* elder tree

saudí <saudíes>, **saudita** I. *adj* Saudi; **Arabia Saudí** Saudi Arabia II. *mf* Saudi

sauna *f* sauna

savia *f* 1. (*de árbol*) sap 2. (*energía*) vitality

saxofón *m,* **saxófono** *m* saxophone

saya *f* (*de mujer*) petticoat; (*falda*) skirt

sayo *m inf* smock ▶ **cortar a alguien un** ~ to speak ill of sb in his/her absence

sazón *f* 1. (*condimento*) flavour *Brit,* flavor *Am* 2. (*madurez*) ripeness; **estar en** ~ to be ripe ▶ **fuera de** ~ out of season; **a la** ~ at that time; **en** ~ opportunely

sazonado, -a *adj* 1. (*comida*) seasoned 2. (*fruta*) ripe 3. (*frase*) witty

sazonar *vt* 1. (*comida*) to season 2. (*madurar*) to ripen

se *pron pers* 1. *forma reflexiva: m sing* himself; *f sing* herself; *de cosa* itself; *pl* themselves; *de Ud.* yourself; *de Uds.* yourselves 2. *objeto indirecto: m sing* to him; *f sing* to her; *a una cosa* to it; *pl* to them; *a Ud., Uds.* to you; **mi hermana** ~ **lo prestó a su amiga** my sister lent it to her friend 3. (*oración impers*) you; ~ **aprende mucho en esta clase** you learn a lot in this class 4. (*oración pasiva*) ~ **confirmó la sentencia** the sentence was confirmed

sé 1. *pres de* **saber**

SE *abr de* **sudeste** SE

SEBC *abr de* **Sistema Europeo de Bancos**

Centrales European System of Central Banks
sebo *m* grease; (*vela*) tallow; **hacer** ~ *Arg, inf* to idle
seborrea *f* MED seborrhoea *Brit*, seborrhea *Am*
seboso, -a *adj* greasy
seca *f* **1.** (*sequía*) drought; *AmL* (*temporada*) dry season **2.** (*banco de arena*) dry sandbank
secadero *m* **1.** (*local*) drying shed **2.** (*recinto*) *place where fruit is placed to dry*
secado *m* drying
secador *m* hair dryer
secadora *f* tumble dryer, spin dryer
secano *m* **1.** (*tierra*) dry land; **cultivo de** ~ crop which can be grown in dry areas; **ése es de** ~ *inf* he's not one for drink **2.** (*isleta*) small sandy island
secante¹ I. *adj* drying; **línea** ~ secant; **papel** ~ blotting paper II. *m* **1.** (*pintura*) paint dryer **2.** (*papel*) blotting paper
secante² *f* MAT secant
secar <c→qu> I. *vt* **1.** (*deshumedecer*) to dry **2.** (*enjugar*) to wipe **3.** (*agostar*) to wither **4.** (*cicatrizar*) to heal II. *vr:* ~**se 1.** (*deshumedecer*) to dry up **2.** (*enjugar*) to wipe up **3.** (*desecarse*) to dry up; (*fuente*) to run dry; (*agostarse*) to wither away **4.** (*curarse*) to heal up **5.** (*enflaquecer*) to get thin **6.** (*insensibilizarse*) to become hardened **7.** (*estar sediento*) to be very thirsty; ~**se de sed** to have a raging thirst
sección *f* **1.** (*cortadura, perfil*) cross-section **2.** (*parte*) section **3.** (*departamento*) branch
seccionar *vt* to divide into sections
secesión *f* (*separación*) split; (*fracción de Estado*) secession
seco, -a *adj* **1.** (*sin agua*) dry; **golpe** ~ dull blow; **estar** ~ to be very thirsty; **limpiar en** ~ to dry clean **2.** (*desecado*) dried up; **frutos** ~**s** dried fruit and nuts **3.** (*río*) dried up **4.** (*marchito*) withered **5.** (*flaco*) skinny **6.** (*cicatriz*) healed **7.** (*tajante*) curt **8.** (*vino*) dry **9.** (*pasmado*) **dejar** ~ **a alguien** to dumbfound sb; (*matar*) to kill sb; **quedarse** ~ dumbfounded ►**a secas** on its own; **en** ~ suddenly; **frenar en** ~ to pull up sharply
secreción *f* **1.** (*sustancia*) secretion **2.** (*el segregar*) segregation
secretar *vt* to secrete
secretaría *f* **1.** (*oficina*) secretary's office **2.** (*cargo*) secretaryship **3.** *AmL* (*ministerio*) ministry **4.** (*organismo*) secretariat
secretariado *m* **1.** (*oficina*) secretary's office **2.** (*cargo*) secretaryship **3.** (*carrera*) profession of secretary **4.** (*organismo*) secretariat
secretario, -a *m, f* **1.** (*de oficina*) secretary **2.** *AmL* (*ministro*) minister
secretear *vi inf* to exchange secrets
secreter *m* (*mueble*) writing desk
secreto *m* **1.** (*misterio*) secret; ~ **profesional** trade secret; ~ **a voces** open secret; **en** ~ in secret; **mantener en** ~ to keep secret; **guardar un** ~ to keep a secret; ~ **de confesión** REL seal of confession **2.** (*reserva*) secrecy

3. (*lugar*) secret drawer
secreto, -a *adj* **1.** (*oculto*) secret **2.** (*callado*) secretive
secta *f* (*grupo*) sect
sectario, -a I. *adj* **1.** (*de secta*) sectarian **2.** (*fanático*) fanatical II. *m, f* **1.** (*de una secta*) member of a sect **2.** (*fanático*) fanatic
sector *m* **1.** *t.* MAT sector; ~ **económico** economic sector; ~ **hotelero** hotel [*o* hospitality] industry; ~ **de la informática** computing sector; ~ **de inicialización** INFOR initialization sector; ~ **multimedia** multimedia sector; ~ **servicios** service sector **2.** (*grupo*) group
secuaz *mf pey* henchman
secuela *f* consequence; ~ (**de una enfermedad**) after-effect (of an illness); **dejar** ~**s** to have after-effects
secuencia *f* **1.** (*serie*) *t.* CINE sequence; ~ **de caracteres** *t.* INFOR series of characters **2.** (*orden de las palabras*) word order
secuestrador(a) *m(f)* kidnapper
secuestrar *vt* **1.** (*raptar*) to kidnap **2.** (*embargar*) to confiscate
secuestro *m* **1.** (*rapto*) kidnapping **2.** (*bienes*) confiscation **3.** (*embargo*) seizure
secular *adj* secular; *fig* age-old
secundar *vt* to second
secundario, -a *adj* (*segundo*) secondary; (*cargo*) minor; **papel** ~ CINE, TEAT supporting role; **esto es** ~ that's of minor importance
sed *f* **1.** (*falta de agua*) thirst **2.** (*de plantas*) dryness; **tener** ~ to be thirsty **3.** (*afán*) ~ **de algo** longing for sth; ~ **de amor** hunger for love; ~ **de poder** thirst for power
seda *f* **1.** ZOOL bristle **2.** (*tela, hilo*) silk; **de** ~ **natural** of pure silk; **como una** ~ (*tacto*) as smooth as silk; (*persona*) sweet-tempered; (*sin tropiezos*) smoothly
sedal *m* (*fishing*) line
sedante I. *adj* (**de efecto**) ~ soothing II. *m* sedative
sedar *vt* to sedate
sedativo, -a *adj* sedative
sede *f* (*residencia*) seat; (*empresa*) headquarters *pl;* **la Santa Sede** the Holy See
sedentario, -a *adj* sedentary
sedente *adj* seated
sedición *f* sedition
sedicioso, -a I. *adj* seditious; **acto** ~ act of sedition II. *m, f* troublemaker
sediento, -a *adj* thirsty; ~ **de algo** thirsty for sth; ~ **de poder** eager for power
sedimentación *f* sedimentation
sedimentar I. *vt* (*sosegar*) to calm; (*sedimento*) to deposit II. *vr:* ~**se 1.** (*depositarse*) to settle **2.** (*sosegarse*) to calm down
sedimento *m* sediment, deposit
sedoso, -a *adj* silky, silken
seducción *f* **1.** (*persuasión*) seduction **2.** (*tentación*) fascination
seducir *irr como traducir vt* **1.** (*persuadir*) to seduce **2.** (*fascinar*) to charm
seductor(a) I. *adj* seductive; **artes** ~**as** wiles;

(*idea*) captivating; (*tentador*) tempting **II.** *m(f)* (*que seduce*) seducer; (*que encanta*) charmer

sefardí, sefardita I. *adj* Sephardic **II.** *mf* Sephardi, Sephardic Jew *m*, Sephardic Jewess *f*

A **sefardí** is the descendant of a Jewish person who originated from Spain or Portugal. The language is also called **sefardí** (or **ladino**). The **sefardíes** were driven out of the Iberian Peninsula at the end of the 15th century. They subsequently settled in North Africa and some European countries.

---

segador(a) I. *adj* reaping **II.** *m(f)* reaper
segadora *f* mower
segar *irr como fregar vt* **1.** (*cortar*) to reap; (*hierba*) to mow; ~ **algo en flor** *fig* to mow sth down **2.** (*frustrar*) to dash
seglar *adj* lay, secular
segmentar *vt* to divide into segments
segmento *m* (*parte*) segment; (*motor*) piston rings *pl*
segoviano, -a, segoviense I. *adj* of/from Segovia **II.** *m* native/inhabitant of Segovia
segregación *f* segregation
segregar <g→gu> *vt* to segregate
seguido, -a *adj* **1.** (*continuo*) consecutive; **un año** ~ a whole year **2.** (*en línea recta*) straight; **todo** ~ straight on
seguidor(a) *m(f)* follower, supporter; DEP fan
seguimiento *m* (*persecución*) chase; (*sucesión*) continuation; (*estudio*) follow-up
seguir *irr* **I.** *vt* **1.** (*suceder, ser adepto*) to follow **2.** (*perseguir*) to chase **3.** (*acompañar, cursar*) to follow; ~ **un curso de informática** to take a computing course **4.** (*continuar*) **adelante** to carry on; **¡que sigas bien!** I hope you keep well! **II.** *vi* **sigue por esta calle** follow this street **III.** *vr:* ~**se** to ensue
según I. *prep* according to; ~ **eso** according to that; ~ **la ley** in accordance with the law; ~ **tus propias palabras/tu sonrisa** judging by your own words/your smile **II.** *adv* **1.** (*como*) as; ~ **lo convenido** as we agreed **2.** (*mientras*) while; **podemos hablar** ~ **vamos andando** we can talk as we walk **3.** (*eventualidad*) ~ **(y como)** it depends; ~ **el trabajo iré o no** I'll go if work permits
segunda *f* AUTO second gear; FERRO second class ▶**con** ~**s** with veiled meaning
segundero *m* second hand
segundo *m* (*tiempo*) second
segundo, -a I. *adj* second; **primo** ~ second cousin; **segunda intención** implied second meaning; **vivir en el** ~ to live on the second floor **II.** *m, f* second (one); *v.t.* octavo
segundón, -ona *m, f* second son *m*, second daughter *f*
seguramente *adv* **1.** (*de modo seguro*) certainly **2.** (*probablemente*) probably
seguridad *f* **1.** (*protección*) security; **Seguri-**

dad Social ADMIN Social Security; **agente de** ~ security guard **2.** (*certeza*) certainty; **para mayor** ~ to be sure of it **3.** (*firmeza*) confidence; **habla con mucha** ~ he/she speaks with great self-confidence **4.** (*garantía*) surety **5.** (*confiabilidad*) trustworthiness
seguro I. *m* **1.** (*contrato*) insurance; ~ **médico** medical [*o* health] insurance; ~ **de protección jurídica** legal insurance; ~ **a riesgo parcial** AUTO third-party insurance; ~ **a todo riesgo** AUTO comprehensive insurance **2.** (*mecanismo*) safety device **II.** *adv* for sure; **a buen** [*o* **de**] ~ surely; **sobre** ~ on safe ground; **en** ~ in a safe place; **tener** ~ **algo** to have sth firmly fastened
seguro, -a *adj* **1.** (*exento de peligro*) safe **2.** (*firme*) secure **3.** (*sólido*) solid **4.** (*convencido*) certain; ~ **de sí mismo** confident; **¿estás** ~**?** are you sure?
seis *adj inv, m* six; *v.t.* ocho
seisavo, -a *adj* sixth; *v.t.* octavo
seiscientos, -as *adj* six hundred; *v.t.* ochocientos
seísmo *m* (*temblor*) tremor; (*terremoto*) earthquake
selección *f* selection; ~ **nacional** national team; ~ **natural** natural selection
seleccionador(a) *m(f)* DEP selector
seleccionar *vt* to select
selectividad *f* UNIV university entrance exam

The **selectividad** is a state school leaving exam, which all pupils must successfully sit after having completed the **bachillerato**, if they wish to enrol at a Spanish university.

---

selectivo, -a *adj* selective; **método** ~ selective criterion
selecto, -a *adj* select; (*ambiente*) exclusive
selector *m* selector; ~ **de cambio de marcha** gear lever [*o* stick]
self-service *m sin pl* self-service
sellado, -a *adj* (*timbrado*) stamped; (*precinto*) sealed
sellar *vt* **1.** (*timbrar*) to stamp **2.** (*dejar huella*) to leave a mark **3.** (*concluir*) to end **4.** (*precintar*) to seal; (*cerrar*) to close; ~ **los labios** to seal one's lips
sello *m* **1.** (*instrumento, marca*) stamp; ~ **de garantía** mark [*o* seal] of guarantee; ~ **oficial** official stamp **2.** (*correo*) (postage) stamp **3.** (*precinto*) seal; **cerrar con un** ~ to seal **4.** (*distintivo*) stamp, hallmark; **esta película lleva el** ~ **de su director** this film carries the stamp of its director **5.** (*anillo*) signet ring **6.** MED capsule
selva *f* (*bosque*) forest; (*tropical*) jungle; ~ **virgen** virgin forest
selvático, -a *adj* **1.** (*de la selva*) woodland; (*de jungla*) jungle **2.** (*salvaje*) wild
semáforo *m* **1.** (*de circulación*) traffic lights *pl* **2.** (*telégrafo*) signal

S

semana *f* week; **Semana Santa** Easter, Holy Week; **fin de** ~ weekend; **durante ~s (enteras)** for weeks (on end); **entre** ~ during the week

semanal *adj* weekly; **revista** ~ weekly magazine

semanario *m* weekly (magazine)

semanario, -a *adj* weekly

semántica *f sin pl* LING semantics

semblante *m* 1. (*cara*) face 2. (*expresión*) appearance; **tener un** ~ **alegre** to look cheerful; **componer el** ~ to regain one's composure

semblanza *f* 1. (*parecido*) similarity 2. (*bosquejo biográfico*) biographical sketch

sembrar <e→ie> *vt* 1. (*plantar*) to sow 2. (*esparcir*) to scatter; ~ **una calle de flores** to strew a street with flowers; ~ **para el futuro** to sow for the future; ~ **el terror** to spread terror ▶**quien mal siembra, mal coge** *prov* as you sow, so shall you reap

semejante I. *adj* 1. (*similar*) similar 2. (*tal*) such; ~ **persona** such a person II. *m* fellow man

semejanza *f* 1. (*similitud*) similarity; (*físico*) resemblance 2. MED mimosis

semejar I. *vi* to resemble II. *vr:* ~**se** to look alike; ~**se a alguien** to look like sb

semen *m* 1. (*espermatozoide*) semen 2. (*semilla*) seed

semental I. *adj* 1. AGR sowing 2. ZOOL breeding; **caballo** ~ stud II. *m* stud

sementar <e→ie> *vt* to sow

sementera *f* 1. (*siembra*) sowing 2. (*sembrado*) sown field 3. (*cosa sembrada*) crop 4. (*tiempo*) sowing season

semestral *adj* half-yearly

semestre *m* six-month period; UNIV semester

semiautomático, -a *adj* semi-automatic

semicírculo *m* semicircle **semiconductor** *m* semiconductor **semiconsciente** *adj* half-conscious **semidesnatado, -a** *adj* semi-skimmed **semidiós, -osa** *m, f* demigod **semidormido, -a** *adj* half-asleep

semifinal *f* semi-final; **pasar a la** ~ to get through to the semi-final

semifusa *f* MÚS hemidemisemiquaver

semilla *f* seed

semillero *m* 1. (*sementera*) seedbed 2. (*origen*) breeding ground

semilunar *adj* semicircular

seminal *adj* seminal

seminario *m* 1. ENS, REL seminary 2. (*sementera*) seedbed

seminuevo, -a *adj* almost new

semioscuridad *f* half-darkness

semiótica *f* LING semiotics

semiprecioso, -a *adj* **piedra semipreciosa** semi-precious stone **semirrecto, -a** *adj* **ángulo** ~ 45° angle

semiseco, -a *adj* medium-dry

semita I. *adj* Semitic II. *mf* Semite

semivocal *f* semivowel

sémola *f* semolina

sempiterno, -a *adj* everlasting

Sena *m* Seine

senado *m* senate

senador(a) *m(f)* senator

sencillamente *adv* simply

sencillez *f* 1. (*simplicidad*) simplicity 2. (*naturalidad*) naturalness 3. (*sinceridad*) sincerity 4. (*candidez*) straightforwardness

sencillo, -a *adj* 1. (*simple*) simple; (*fácil*) easy 2. (*natural*) natural; **gente sencilla** unaffected people 3. (*sincero*) straightforward 4. (*cándido*) ingenuous

senda *f,* **sendero** *m* 1. (*camino*) path; ~ **del jardín** garden path 2. (*método*) way

senderismo *m* hillwalking, hiking

sendos, -as *adj* each of two; **llegamos en** ~ **coches** we both arrived by car

senectud *f* old age

senegalés. -esa *adj, m, f* Senegalese

senil *adj* senile

senilidad *f* (*decrepitud*) senility

sénior I. *adj* senior II. *mf* senior

seno *m* 1. (*concavidad*) hollow; **un fregadero de dos ~s** a two-basin sink, a double sink 2. ANAT, MAT sinus; ~ **frontal** frontal sinus 3. (*matriz*) womb 4. (*pecho*) breast 5. (*de organización*) heart

sensación *f* 1. (*sentimiento*) feeling 2. (*novedad*) sensation 3. (*reacción*) **causar** ~ to cause a sensation

sensacional *adj* sensational

sensacionalismo *m sin pl* sensationalism

sensacionalista *adj* sensationalist; **prensa** ~ gutter [o tabloid] press

sensatez *f* good sense

sensato, -a *adj* sensible

sensibilidad *f* sensitivity

sensibilizar <z→c> *vt* to sensitize

sensible *adj* 1. (*sensitivo*) sensitive; (*impresionable*) impressionable; ~ **a los cambios de tiempo** sensitive to changes in the weather; ~ **a la luz** sensitive to light 2. (*perceptible*) noticeable

sensiblemente *adv* 1. (*perceptible*) perceptibly 2. (*evidente*) markedly

sensiblería *f* (over-)sentimentality, mawkishness

sensiblero, -a *adj* (over)sentimental

sensitiva *f* mimosa

sensitivo, -a *adj* 1. (*sensorial*) sensory; **tacto** ~ sense of touch 2. (*sensible*) sensitive 3. (*sensual*) sensual

sensor *m* sensor

sensorial *adj* sensory; **órgano** ~ sense organ

sensorio *m* sensorium

sensorio, -a *adj v.* **sensorial**

sensual *adj* sensual

sensualidad *f sin pl* sensuality

sentada *f* sit-in, sit-down protest; **hacer una** ~ to organize a sit-in; **hacer algo de una** ~ to do sth in one sitting

sentado, -a I. *pp de* **sentar** II. *adj* (*sensato*) sensible ▶**dar algo por** ~ to take sth for granted

sentador(a) *adj Arg, Chile* (*prenda de vestir*) becoming, well-fitting

sentar <e→ie> **I.** *vi* (*ropa*) to suit; ~ **bien/ mal a alguien** (*comida*) to agree/disagree with sb; ~ **como un tiro** to be as welcome as a hole in the head; **esa chaqueta me siente bien/mal** that jacket suits/doesn't suit me **II.** *vt* to sit; **estar sentado** to be sitting down; **estar bien sentado** *fig* to be well established **III.** *vr:* ~**se 1.** (*asentarse*) to sit down; **¡siéntese!** have a seat! **2.** (*establecerse*) to settle down **3.** (*estabilizarse*) to stabilize

sentencia *f* **1.** (*proverbio*) maxim **2.** JUR sentence; **dictar** ~ to pronounce sentence; ~ **de divorcio** decree of divorce

sentenciar *vt* **1.** (*decidir*) ~ **algo** to give one's opinion on [*o* about] sth **2.** (*condenar*) to sentence

sentido *m* **1.** (*facultad, significado*) sense; ~ **común** common sense; ~ **del deber** sense of duty; ~ **del humor** sense of humour *Brit* [*o* humor *Am*]; **doble** ~ (*significado*) double meaning; (*dirección*) two-way; **costar un** ~ to cost the earth; **estar con los cinco** ~**s en el asunto** to be totally absorbed in the subject; **estar sin** ~ to be unconscious; **perder el** ~ to lose consciousness; **sexto** ~ intuition, sixth sense **2.** (*dirección*) direction; **en el** ~ **de la flecha** in the direction of the arrow; **en el** ~ **de las agujas del reloj** clockwise; ~ **único** one-way **3.** (*significado*) meaning

sentido, -a *adj* **1.** (*conmovido*) deeply felt **2.** (*sensible*) sensitive; **ser muy** ~ to be easily hurt

sentimental *adj* sentimental

sentimentalismo *m* sentimentality

sentimiento *m* **1.** (*emoción*) feeling; **sin** ~**s** unfeeling **2.** (*pena*) sorrow; **le acompaño en el** ~ please accept my condolences

sentir *irr* **I.** *vt* **1.** (*percibir*) to feel; ~ **frío** to feel cold; **sin** ~ without noticing **2.** (*lamentar*) to be sorry for; **lo siento mucho** I am very sorry; **siento que** +*subj* I'm sorry that **II.** *vr:* ~**se 1.** (*estar*) to feel; ~**se bien/mal** to feel good/ bad **2.** (*padecer*) ~**se de algo** to suffer from sth **III.** *m* **1.** (*opinión*) opinion; ~ **popular** public opinion; **en mi** ~ in my view **2.** (*sentimiento*) feeling

seña *f* **1.** (*gesto*) sign; **hacer** ~**s** to make signs, to signal; **hablar por** ~**s** to use [*o* talk in] sign language **2.** (*particularidad*) distinguishing mark; **las** ~**s son mortales** the signs are unmistakable; **por más** ~**s** to be more specific **3.** *pl* (*dirección*) address

señal *f* **1.** (*particularidad*) distinguishing mark **2.** (*signo*) sign; ~ **de tráfico** road sign; **en** ~ **de** as a sign [*o* token] of; **dar** ~**es de vida** *fig* to show oneself **3.** (*teléfono*) tone; ~ **de comunicar** engaged tone *Brit,* busy signal *Am* **4.** (*huella*) mark; **ni** ~ no trace **5.** (*cicatriz*) scar **6.** (*adelanto*) deposit; **paga y** ~ first payment; **dejar una** ~ to leave a deposit

señalado, -a *adj* **1.** (*famoso*) distinguished **2.** (*importante*) special

señalar **I.** *vt* **1.** (*anunciar*) to announce **2.** (*marcar*) to mark **3.** (*estigmatizar*) to mark (for life) **4.** (*mostrar*) to show **5.** (*indicar*) to point out **6.** (*fijar*) to fix **II.** *vr* ~**se por algo** to distinguish oneself by sth

señalización *f* signposting

señalizar <z→c> *vt* to signpost

señero, -a *adj* **1.** (*único*) unequalled *Brit,* unequaled *Am;* (*importante*) outstanding **2.** (*solitario*) isolated

señor(a) **I.** *adj inf* **1.** (*noble*) lordly **2.** (*enorme*) huge **II.** *m(f)* **1.** (*dueño*) owner **2.** (*hombre*) (gentle)man; (*mujer*) wife; (*dama*) lady; ~**a de compañía** companion; **¡~as y ~es!** ladies and gentlemen! **3.** (*título*) Mister *m,* Mr *f;* **el** ~**/la** ~**a García** Mr/Mrs García; **los** ~**es García** the Garcías; **muy** ~ **mío:** Dear Sir; **¡no, ~!** not a bit of it!; **¡sí, ~!** it certainly is! **4.** REL **el Señor** Our Lord; **nuestra Señora** Our Lady; **descansar en el Señor** to rest in peace

señorear **I.** *vt* **1.** (*dominar*) to control **2.** (*sobresalir*) to soar above **II.** *vr:* ~**se** to seize control

señoría *f* rule; **Su Señoría** Your Lordship

señori(a)l *adj* lordly; **casa** ~ stately home

señorío *m* **1.** (*dominio*) rule **2.** (*territorio*) domain **3.** (*dignidad*) stateliness **4.** (*personas*) distinguished people *pl*

señorita *f* **1.** (*tratamiento*) Miss **2.** (*chica*) young lady

señorito *m* young gentleman

señuelo *m* decoy; *fig* lure

separación *f* **1.** (*desunión*) separation **2.** (*espacio*) distance

separado *adv* **por** ~ separately; **contar por** ~ to count one by one

separar **I.** *vt* **1.** (*desunir*) to separate; ~ **algo de algo** to separate sth from sth **2.** (*apartar*) to remove **3.** (*destituir*) to dismisss **II.** *vr:* ~**se** (*person*) to separate

separo *m Méx* (*celda*) cell

sepelio *m elev* religious funeral, Christian burial

sepia *f* cuttlefish; **de color** ~ sepia

septentrión *m elev* (*norte*) north; (*viento*) ~ north wind

septentrional *adj elev* northern

septicemia *f* MED blood poisoning, septicaemia *Brit,* septicemia *Am*

septiembre *m* September; *v.t.* **marzo**

séptimo, -a *adj, m, f* seventh; *v.t.* **octavo**

septuagésimo, -a *adj* seventieth; *v.t.* **octavo**

séptuplo, -a *adj* sevenfold

sepulcral *adj* sepulchral; **silencio** ~ deathly silence

sepulcro *m* **1.** (*tumba*) tomb; **es un** ~ *fig* he/ she can keep a secret **2.** (*relicario*) reliquary

sepultar **I.** *vt* **1.** *t. fig* (*inhumar*) to bury **2.** (*cubrir*) to conceal **II.** *vr:* ~**se** (*sumergir*) to hide away

S

sepultura *f* 1.(*sepelio*) burial 2.(*tumba*) grave; **dar ~ a alguien** to bury sb; **estar cavando su propia ~** to be digging one's own grave

sepulturero, -a *m, f* gravedigger

sequedad *f* 1.(*aridez*) dryness 2.(*descortesía*) bluntness; **con ~** curtly

sequía *f* drought

séquito *m* retinue

ser *irr* **I.** *aux* 1.(*construcción de la pasiva*) **las casas fueron vendidas** the houses were sold; **el triunfo fue celebrado** the triumph was celebrated 2.(*en frases pasivas*) **era de esperar** it was to be expected; **es de esperar que** +*subj* it is to be hoped that **II.** *vi* 1.(*absoluto, copulativo, existir, constituir*) to be; **cuatro y cuatro son ocho** four and four make eight; **éramos cuatro** there were four of us; **¿quién es?** (*puerta*) who is it?; (*teléfono*) who's calling?; **soy Pepe** (*a la puerta*) it's me, Pepe; (*al teléfono*) this is Pepe; **es de noche** it's night time; **son las cuatro** it's four o'clock; **el que fue director del teatro** the former theatre *Brit* [*o* theater *Am*] director 2.(*tener lugar*) **el examen es mañana** the exam is tomorrow; **el concierto es en el pabellón** the concert is in the pavillion; **eso fue en 2000** that was in 2000 3.(*costar*) **¿a cuánto es el pollo?** how much is the chicken?; **¿cuánto es todo?** how much is everything? 4.(*estar*) **el cine es en la otra calle** the cinema is in the next street 5.(*convertirse en*) **¿qué quieres ~ de mayor?** what do you want to be when you grow up?; **¿qué es de él?** what's he doing now?; **¿qué ha sido de ella?** whatever happened to her?; **llegó a ~ ministro** he became a minister 6.(*depender*) **todo es que se decida pronto** everything depends on a quick decision 7.(*con 'de': posesión*) **¿de quién es esto?** whose is this?; **el paquete es de él** the parcel belongs to him; **el anillo es de plata** the ring is made of silver; **el coche es de color azul** the car is blue; **~ de Escocia** to be from Scotland; **~ de 2 euros** to cost 2 euros; **es de 30 años** he/she is thirty years old; **lo que ha hecho es muy de ella** that's typical of her; **esta manera de hablar no es de un catedrático** that's no way for a lecturer to talk; **es de lo más guay** it's really great; **eres de lo que no hay** there's nobody like you; **es de un cobarde que no veas** he's a terrible coward 8.(*con 'para'*) **este estilo no es para ti** that's not your style; **¿para quién es el vino?** who is the wine for?; **la película no es para niños** it's not a film for children; **no es para ponerse así** there's no need to get so angry; **es como para no hablarte más** it's enough to never speak to you again 9.(*con 'que'*) **esto es que no lo has visto bien** you can't have seen it properly; **es que ahora no puedo** the thing is I can't at the moment; **si es que merece la pena** if it's worthwhile; **¡y es que tenía unas ganas de acabarlo!** I was longing to finish it! 10.(*oraciones enfáticas, interrogativas*) **¡esto es!** (*así se hace*) that's the way!; (*correcto*) that's right!; **¿pero qué es esto?** what's this then?; **¿cómo es eso?** how is that possible?; **¡como debe ~!** that's as it should be!; **¡no puede ~!** that can't be!; **¿no puede ~?** isn't that possible?; **¡eso es cantar!** that's what I call singing! 11.(*en futuro*) **¿~á capaz?** will he/she be up to it?; **¡~á capaz!** trust him/her!; **~á lo que sea** we can't change things now 12.(*en infinitivo*) **manera de ~** manner; **razón de ~** raison d'être; **a no ~ que** +*subj* unless; **todo puede ~** everything is possible; **quizá ganemos el campeonato – todo puede ~** we may yet win the championship – all is not over; **por lo que pueda ~** just in case 13.(*en indicativo, condicional*) **es más** what is more; **siendo así** that being so; **y eso es todo** and that's that; **~ más/menos que alguien** to be better/worse than sb; **es igual** (*no importa*) it doesn't matter; **yo soy de los que piensan que...** I'm one of those who think that ...; **de no haber sido por ti** if it hadn't been for you; **no es lo que tú piensas** it's not what you think; **con el carisma que tiene sería un buen líder** (*de un partido*) with his charisma he'd be a fine leader 14.(*en subjuntivo*) **si yo fuera tú** if I were you; **si no fuera por eso...** if it weren't for that ...; **si por mí fuera** if it were up to me; **me tratas como si fuera un niño** you treat me like a child; **sea lo que sea** whatever it is; **lo que sea ~á** whatever will be will be; **hazlo sea como sea** do it whatever; **sea quien sea** whoever it is; **dos reales, o sea, 50 céntimos** two reals, that is 50 cents; **el color que quieras, pero que no sea rojo** any colour *Brit* [*o* color *Am*] you like apart from red; **cómprame un chupa-chups o lo que sea** buy me a lollipop or sth; **por listo que sea...** however clever he is ...; **cualquiera que sea el día** whatever day it is **III.** *m* 1.(*criatura*) being; **~ vivo** living creature; **~ humano** human being 2.(*esencia*) essence 3. FILOS life

serba *f* service tree fruit

Serbia *f* Serbia

serbio, -a **I.** *adj* Serb, Serbian **II.** *m, f* Serb

serenar **I.** *vt* (*calmar*) to calm **II.** *vi, vr:* **~se** (*calmarse*) to calm down; (*tiempo*) to clear up

serenata *f* MÚS serenade

serenidad *f sin pl* 1.(*sosiego*) calmness 2.(*príncipe*) **Su Serenidad** His Serene Highness

sereno *m* 1.(*humedad*) night dew; **al ~** out in the open 2.(*vigilante*) night watchman

sereno, -a *adj* 1.(*sosegado*) calm 2.(*sin nubes*) clear

serial *m* RADIO, TV serial

serie *f* 1.(*sucesión*) series *inv;* **asesino en ~** serial killer; **~ televisiva** TV series *inv;* **fuera de ~** out of order; *fig* outstanding, special 2. *t.* MAT (*gran cantidad*) set; **fabricar en ~** to mass produce 3. DEP competition

seriedad *f sin pl* seriousness; **falta de ~** irresponsibility
serigrafía *f* TIPO serigraphy
serio, -a *adj* 1. (*grave*) serious 2. (*severo*) solemn 3. (*formal*) reliable 4. (*responsable*) trustworthy 5. (*sin burla*) serious; **esto va en ~** this is in earnest; **¿en ~?** are you serious?
sermón *m* sermon; **echar un ~ a alguien** to give sb a ticking off, to preach to sb
sermonear I. *vi* to sermonize II. *vt inf* to lecture
seropositivo, -a *adj* HIV-positive
serosidad *f* serosity
serpear *vi* to creep
serpenteante *adj* winding; **carretera ~** winding road
serpentear *vi* to creep; *fig* to wind
serpenteo *m* creeping
serpentina *f* (*de papel*) streamer
serpiente *f* snake; **~ de cascabel** rattlesnake; **~ de vidrio** slow worm; **~ de verano** *fig* made-up story
serrado, -a *adj* serrated
serraduras *fpl* sawdust
serranía *f* mountainous area
serrano, -a *adj* highland; **jamón ~** cured ham
serrar <e→ie> *vt* to saw
serrín *m* sawdust
serruchar *vt Arg, Chile, PRico* to saw
serrucho *m* (*sierra*) handsaw
servible *adj* serviceable
servicial *adj* obliging
servicio *m* 1. (*acción de servir*) service; **~ civil sustitutorio** community service; **~ a domicilio** home delivery; **~ de información telefónica** telephone answering service; **~ en línea** online service; **~ militar** military service; **~ postal express** express delivery service; **~ posventa** aftersales service; **estar de ~** to be on duty; **hacer el ~** to do military service; **hacer un ~ a alguien** to do sb a service; **hacer un flaco ~ a alguien** to do sb more harm than good 2. (*servidumbre*) (domestic) service; **entrada de ~** tradesman's entrance *Brit*, service entrance *Am* 3. (*culto*) service 4. (*cubierto*) set; **~ de té** tea set 5. (*retrete*) lavatory 6. DEP serve 7. MED sanitation
servidor *m* INFOR server
servidor(a) *m(f)* (*criado*) servant; **un ~** yours truly; **¿quién es el último? – ~** who is the last in the queue *Brit* [*o* line *Am*] ? – I am
servidumbre *f* 1. (*personal*) servants *pl* 2. (*esclavitud*) servitude 3. (*trabajo de siervo*) slave labour *Brit*, slave labor *Am* 4. (*sujeción*) compulsion 5. JUR obligation
servil I. *adj* servile II. *m* crawler
servilismo *m sin pl* servility
servilleta *f* napkin; **doblar la ~** *fig, inf* to kick the bucket
servilletero *m* napkin holder; (*aro*) napkin ring
servir *irr como pedir* I. *vi* 1. (*ser útil*) to be of use; **no sirve de nada** it's no use; **no sirve**

para nada it's useless [*o* no use at all] 2. (*ser soldado, criado*) to serve 3. (*ayudar*) to assist; **¿en qué puedo ~le?** can I help you?; **¡para ~le!** at your service! 4. (*atender a alguien*) to serve 5. DEP to serve 6. (*suministrar*) to supply 7. (*poner en el plato*) to serve; (*en el vaso*) to pour out II. *vr:* **~se** 1. (*utilizar*) to make use 2. (*dignarse*) **sírvase cerrar la ventana** please close the window
servoasistido, -a *adj* power-assisted **servodirección** *f* AUTO power steering
sésamo *m* 1. BOT sesame 2. TV **barrio ~** Sesame Street ▸ **¡ábrete, ~!** open sesame!
sesear *vi* to pronounce the Spanish 'c' and 'z' before 'e' and 'i' as 's'
sesenta *adj inv, m* sixty; *v.t.* ochenta
seseo *m* pronunciation of the Spanish 'c' and 'z' as 's' before 'e' and 'i'
sesera *f inf* 1. (*cerebro*) brainpan 2. (*cabeza*) brains *pl*; (*inteligencia*) intelligence
sesgar <g→gu> *vt* 1. (*cortar*) to cut down 2. (*torcer*) to slant 3. TÉC to bevel 4. (*estudio*) to bias
sesgo *m* 1. (*oblicuidad*) slant; **al ~** aslant 2. (*orientación*) direction 3. (*opinión, estudio*) bias
sesión *f* 1. (*reunión*) session; **~ a puerta cerrada** private session; **abrir/levantar la ~** to open/close [*o* adjourn] the meeting 2. (*representación*) show(ing); **~ de noche** night showing; **~ de tarde** matinée
seso *m* 1. ANAT brain 2. (*inteligencia*) brains *pl*; **beber(se) los ~s** *fig* to drive (oneself) mad; **calentarse los ~s** *inf* to rack one's brains 3. *pl* GASTR brains *pl* ▸ **tener sorbido el ~ a alguien** *inf* to have complete control over sb
sesudo, -a *adj* 1. (*inteligente*) brainy 2. (*sensato*) sensible
set *m* <sets> 1. DEP set 2. (*conjunto*) service
seta *f* mushroom; (*no comestible*) toadstool; **crecer como ~s** to mushroom
setecientos, -as *adj* seven hundred; *v.t.* ochocientos
setenta *adj inv, m* seventy; *v.t.* ochenta
setiembre *m v.* septiembre
seto *m* fence; **~ vivo** hedge
seudónimo *m* pseudonym; (*escritor*) pen name
Seúl *m* Seoul
severidad *f sin pl* severity; (*brusquedad*) roughness; (*rigurosidad*) strictness
severo, -a *adj* harsh; (*brusco*) rough; (*riguroso*) strict; (*austero*) austere; (*grave*) serious
Sevilla *f* Seville
sevillano, -a *adj, m, f* Sevillian
sexagésimo, -a *adj* sixtieth; *v.t.* octavo
sexismo *m* sexism, gender bias
sexista I. *adj* sexist II. *mf* sexist; (*machista*) male chauvinist
sexo *m* 1. (*individuos, actividad*) sex 2. (*órganos*) sex organs *pl*
sextante *m* sextant
sexteto *m* MÚS sextet

S

sexto, -a *adj, m, f* sixth; *v.t.* octavo
séxtuplo, -a I. *adj* sixfold II. *m, f* sextuplet
sexual *adj* sexual; **órganos ~es** sex organs
sexualidad *f sin pl* sexuality
shock *m* shock
short *m* shorts *pl*
si I. *conj* 1. (*condicional*) if; ~ **acaso** maybe; ~ **no** if not, otherwise; **por ~...** in case ...; **por ~ acaso** just in case 2. (*en preguntas indirectas*) whether, if; **¿y si ...?** what if ...? 3. (*en oraciones concesivas*) ~ **bien** although 4. (*comparación*) **como ~... +subj** as if ...; **el padre está más nervioso que ~ fuera él mismo a dar a luz** the father is as nervous as if he were going to give birth himself 5. (*en frases desiderativas*) **¡~ hiciera un poco más de calor!** if only it were a little warmer! 6. (*protesta, sorpresa*) but; **¡pero ~ ella se está riendo!** but she's laughing! 7. (*énfasis*) **fíjate ~ es tonto que...** he's so stupid that ... II. *m* MÚS B; **en Si bemol mayor** in B flat major
sí I. *adv* yes; **¡~, señor!** yes sir!; **¡~ que está buena la tarta!** the cake tastes really good!; **¡(claro) que ~!** of course!; **creo que ~** I think so; **¡eso ~ que no!** certainly not!; **por ~ o por no** in any case; **porque ~** (*es así*) because that's the way it is; (*lo digo yo*) because I say so; **volver en ~** to regain consciousness II. *pron pers*: *m sing* himself; *f sing* herself; *cosa, objeto* itself; **a ~ mismo** to himself; **de ~** in itself; **dar de ~** to be extensive; (*tela*) to give; **el tema da mucho de ~** it's a wide subject; **en** [*o* **de por**] ~ separately; **estar fuera de ~** to be beside oneself; **hablar entre ~** to talk among themselves; **por ~** in itself; **mirar por ~** to be selfish III. *m* consent; **dar el ~** to agree; (*casamiento*) to accept the proposal; **tener el ~ de la madre** to have the mother's consent; **no hay entre ellos ni un ~ ni un no** they get on extremely well
siamés, -esa *adj* Siamese; **gato ~** Siamese cat; **hermanos siameses** Siamese twins
sibarita I. *adj* sybaritic II. *mf* sybarite, pleasure seeker
Siberia *f* Siberia
siberiano, -a *adj, m, f* Siberian
sibilino, -a *adj* cryptic
sicalíptico, -a *adj* saucy
sicario *m* hired assassin [*o* gunman]
Sicilia *f* Sicily
siciliano, -a *adj, m, f* Sicilian
sicología *f v.* (**p**)**sicología**
sida, SIDA *m abr de* **síndrome de inmunodeficiencia adquirida** Aids, AIDS
siderurgia *f* iron and steel industry
siderúrgico, -a *adj* iron and steel
sidoso, -a I. *adj* Aids; **enfermo ~** Aids sufferer II. *m, f* Aids sufferer
sidra *f* cider
siega *f* 1. (*el segar*) reaping 2. (*tiempo*) harvest time 3. (*mieses*) cornfields *pl*
siembra *f* 1. (*el sembrar*) sowing 2. (*tiempo*) sowing time 3. (*terreno*) sown field

siempre *adv* always; **de ~** always; **a la hora de ~** at the usual time; **una amistad de ~** a lifelong friendship; **eso es así desde ~** that's always been so; **~ pasa lo mismo** the same thing always happens; **¡hasta ~!** see you!; **por ~** for ever; **por ~ jamás** for ever and ever; **~ que +subj** provided that, as long as
sien *f* ANAT temple
sierpe *f* 1. snake; **tener una lengua de ~** *fig* to have a sharp tongue 2. (*persona feroz*) fierce person; (*colérica*) bad-tempered person; (*fea*) ugly person
sierra *f* 1. (*herramienta*) saw; **~ continua** chainsaw; **~ mecánica** power saw 2. (*lugar*) sawmill 3. GEO mountain range; **~ de peñascos cortados** ridge
siervo, -a *m, f* 1. (*esclavo*) slave; **~ de la gleba** serf 2. (*servidor*) servant
siesta *f* 1. (*descanso*) siesta; **echar** [*o* **dormir**] **la ~** to have a nap 2. (*hora de calor*) hottest part of the day
siete I. *adj inv* seven II. *m* 1. (*número*) seven; *v.t.* ocho 2. *inf* (*rasgón*) rent 3. (*carpintería*) G-clamp 4. *AmS, Méx, vulg* (*ano*) arse *Brit*, ass *Am*
sietemesino, -a I. *adj* niño ~ baby born 2 months premature II. *m, f* 1. (*prematuro*) baby born 2 months premature 2. *inf* (*chico presumido*) little squirt
sífilis *f* syphilis
sifón *m* 1. TÉC (*tubo, tubería*) trap 2. (*botella*) siphon 3. (*soda*) soda, club soda *Am*
siga *f Chile* chase
sigilar *vt* 1. (*ocultar*) to conceal 2. (*sellar*) to stamp
sigilo *m* 1. (*discreción*) discretion; **~ profesional** client confidentiality 2. (*secreto*) stealth; **~ sacramental** secrecy of the confessional, seal of confession 3. (*sello*) stamp
sigla *f* 1. (*letra inicial*) initial 2. (*rótulo de siglas*) acronym; **~ de fabricante** manufacturer's mark
siglo *m* century; **Siglo de las Luces** Age of Enlightment; **el ~ XXI** the 21st century; **el Siglo de Oro** the Golden Age; **por los ~s de los ~s** for ever and ever; **hace un ~ que no te veo** I haven't seen you for ages; **retirarse del ~** to withdraw from the world
signar I. *vt* 1. (*marcar*) to put one's mark on 2. (*firmar*) to sign 3. REL to make the sign of the cross over II. *vr*: **~se** to cross oneself
signatario, -a I. *adj* signatory; **poder ~** JUR power of attorney II. *m, f* signatory
signatura *f* 1. (*firma*) *t.* TIPO signature 2. (*en biblioteca*) catalogue *Brit* [*o* catalog *Am*] number
significación *f* 1. (*importancia*) significance 2. (*sentido*) meaning
significado *m* meaning
significar <c→qu> I. *vt, vi* to mean; **¿qué significa eso?** what's the meaning of this? II. *vr* **~se por algo** to become known for sth
significativo, -a *adj* (*importante*) significant;

(*con significado*) meaningful

signo *m* **1.** *t.* LING, MAT (*señal*) sign; ~ **de enfermedad** sign of illness; ~ **de más/ menos** plus/minus sign; ~ **de la multiplicación** multiplication sign; ~ **de puntuación** punctuation mark **2.** (*escrito*) mark **3.** (*destino*) fate

siguiente I. *adj* following; **de la** ~ **manera** in the following way II. *mf* next; **¡el** ~**!** next please!

sílaba *f* syllable; ~ **aguda** stressed syllable; **de dos** ~**s** two-syllable

silba *f* hissing

silbar *vi, vt* **1.** (*persona*) to whistle; (*serpiente*) to hiss; (*sirena*) to blow; (*una flecha, bala*) to whizz **2.** (*abuchear*) to boo

silbatina *f AmS* hissing

silbato *m* whistle

silbido *m* whistle; (*serpiente*) hiss; (*sirena*) blast; (*viento*) whistling; ~ **de los oídos** ringing in the ears

silbo *m* **1.** (*silbido*) whistle **2.** (*voz, serpiente*) hiss; (*viento*) whistling

silenciador *m* silencer

silenciar *vt* **1.** (*suceso*) to hush up **2.** (*persona*) to silence

silencio *m* **1.** silence; **en** ~ in silence; **guardar** ~ to remain silent; **guardar** ~ **sobre algo** to keep silent about sth; **imponer** ~ to impose silence; **pasar algo en** ~ to pass over sth in silence; **romper el** ~ to break the silence; **entregar algo al** ~ *fig* to cast sth into oblivion; **¡**~**!** quiet! **2.** MÚS rest

silencioso, -a I. *adj* **1.** (*poco hablador*) quiet **2.** (*callado*) silent **3.** (*sin ruido*) soundless; (*motor*) noiseless II. *m, f* silencer

Silesia *f* Silesia

silesio, -a *adj, m, f* Silesian

silicio *m* silicon

silicona *f* silicone

silla *f* **1.** *t.* REL (*asiento*) chair; ~ **de manos** litter; ~ **de lona** deckchair; ~ **giratoria** swivel chair; ~ **plegable** folding chair; ~ **de ruedas** wheelchair **2.** (*montura*) saddle

sillín *m* saddle, seat *Am*

sillón *m* (*butaca*) armchair

silueta *f* silhouette; **cuidar la** ~ to look after one's figure; **la** ~ **de Nueva York** the New York skyline

silvestre *adj* wild

silvicultura *f* forestry

sima *f* GEO abyss

simbólico, -a *adj* symbolic

simbolismo *m* symbolism

simbolizar <z→c> *vt* to symbolize

símbolo *m* symbol; ~ **de prestigio** status symbol

simetría *f* symmetry

simétrico, -a *adj* symmetrical

simiente *f* seed

símil I. *adj* similar II. *m* simile

similar *adj* similar

similitud *f* similarity; (*física*) resemblance

simio *m* ape

simpatía *f* **1.** (*agrado*) liking; **sentir** ~ **por algo** to be attracted to sth; **tener** ~ **por alguien** to have a liking for sb **2.** (*carácter*) friendliness

simpático, -a *adj* friendly; **hacerse el** ~ to ingratiate oneself

simpatizante *mf* sympathizer

simpatizar <z→c> *vi* **1.** (*congeniar*) to get on *Brit*, to get along *Am* **2.** (*identificarse con*) to sympathize

simple <simplísimo *o* simplicísimo> I. *adj* **1.** (*sencillo*) simple **2.** (*fácil*) easy, straightforward **3.** (*mero*) pure; **a** ~ **vista** with the naked eye **4.** (*mentecato*) simple II. *m* **1.** (*persona*) simpleton **2.** (*tenis*) singles *inv*

simplemente *adv* simply

simpleza *f* **1.** (*bobería*) simpleness **2.** (*tontería*) silly thing **3.** (*insignificancia*) trifle

simplicidad *f sin pl* **1.** (*sencillez*) simplicity **2.** (*ingenuidad*) simpleness

simplicísimo, -a *adj superl de* **simple**

simplificar <c→qu> *vt* **1.** (*facilitar*) to simplify **2.** MAT to break down

simposio *m* symposium

simulación *f* simulation; (*fingir*) feigning

simulacro *m* **1.** (*apariencia*) simulacrum; ~ **de incendio** fire drill **2.** (*acción simulada*) sham

simulador *m* TÉC simulator; ~ **de vuelo** flight simulator

simulador(a) *m(f)* faker

simular *vt* to simulate

simultanear *vt* to do simultaneously

simultaneidad *f sin pl* simultaneity

simultáneo, -a *adj* simultaneous; **interpretación simultánea** simultaneous interpreting

sin *prep* without; ~ **dormir** without sleep; ~ **querer** unintentionally; ~ **más** nothing more; ~ **más ni más** without thinking about it, without further ado; **estar** ~ **algo** to be out of sth

sinagoga *f* REL synagogue

sincerarse *vr* (*exculparse*) ~ **ante alguien** to justify oneself to sb; (*abrirse*) to be completely honest with sb

sinceridad *f* sincerity; **con toda** ~ in all sincerity

sincero, -a *adj* sincere; **seré** ~ **contigo** I'll be honest with you

síncopa *f* MÚS syncopation

sincrónico, -a *adj* synchronous

sincronizador(a) *m(f)* synchro

sincronizar <z→c> *vt* to synchronize

sindical *adj* union

sindicalismo *m* **1.** (*movimiento*) trade unionism **2.** (*doctrina*) syndicalism

sindicalista I. *adj* (*sindical*) union II. *mf* (*miembro*) trade unionist

sindicar <c→qu> I. *vt* **1.** (*obreros*) to unionize **2.** (*delatar*) to betray **3.** (*poner bajo sospecha*) to place under suspicion II. *vr*: ~**se** to join a union

sindicato *m* trade union *Brit,* labor union *Am*
síndico *m* **1.** (*administrador de la quiebra*) official receiver **2.** (*representante*) trustee
síndrome *m* syndrome; ~ **de abstinencia** withdrawal symptoms; ~ **de Estocolmo** Stockholm syndrome
sinfín *m* huge number
sinfonía *f* symphony
sinfónico, -a *adj* symphonic; **orquesta sinfónica** symphony orchestra
Singapur *m* Singapore
singular **I.** *adj* **1.** (*único*) singular; **ejemplar** ~ unique example **2.** (*excepcional*) outstanding; **en** ~ in the singular; *fig* in particular **3.** (*extraño*) peculiar **II.** *m* LING singular; **¡habla en ~!** *fig* speak for yourself!
singularidad *f* **1.** (*unicidad*) singularity **2.** (*excepcionalidad*) exceptional nature **3.** (*distinción*) peculiarity
singularizar <z→c> **I.** *vt* (*particularizar*) to single out **II.** *vr:* ~**se** to stand out
singularmente *adv* especially
siniestro *m* (*accidente*) accident; (*catástrofe*) natural disaster; (*incendio*) fire
siniestro, -a *adj* *elev* **1.** (*maligno*) evil; **un personaje** ~ a sinister character **2.** (*funesto*) disastrous **3.** (*izquierdo*) left; **a diestra y siniestra** right and left
sinnúmero *m* huge number
sino **I.** *m* fate **II.** *conj* **1.** (*al contrario*) but **2.** (*solamente*) **no espero** ~ **que me creas** I only hope that you believe me **3.** (*excepto*) except
sinónimo *m* synonym
sinónimo, -a *adj* synonymous
sinopsis *f inv* **1.** (*resumen*) synopsis **2.** (*esquema*) diagram
sinóptico, -a *adj* **1.** (*resumido*) synoptic **2.** (*esquemático*) diagrammatic
sinrazón *f* injustice; (*absurdo*) unreasonableness
sinsabor *m* **1.** (*cosa desagradable*) unpleasantness **2.** (*disgusto*) sorrow
sinsentido *m* absurdity
sinsonte *m* *AmL* ZOOL mockingbird
sintáctico, -a *adj* syntactic
sintaxis *f inv* syntax
síntesis *f inv* synthesis; **en** ~ in a word
sintético, -a *adj* synthetic
sintetizador *m* MÚS synthesizer
sintetizar <z→c> *vt* **1.** QUÍM to synthesize **2.** (*resumir*) to summarize
síntoma *m* symptom
sintomático, -a *adj* symptomatic
sintomatología *f* symptomatology
sintonía *f* **1.** (*adecuación*) tuning **2.** (*señal sonora, melodía*) signature tune **3.** (*entendimiento*) **estar en** ~ (**con alguien**) to be on the same wavelength (as sb)
sintonizador *m* (*aparato*) tuner; (*botón, dial*) tuning knob
sintonizar <z→c> **I.** *vt* to tune in to; ~ **una emisora** to pick up a radio station **II.** *vi* to tune

in
sinuosidad *f* **1.** (*curvación*) sinuosity **2.** (*concavidad*) curve
sinuoso, -a *adj* **1.** (*curvado*) winding **2.** (*retorcido*) devious
sinvergüenza *pey* **I.** *adj* shameless **II.** *mf* rotter
sionismo *m* Zionism
síquico, -a *adj* *v.* (**p**)**síquico**
siquiera **I.** *adv* at least; **ni** ~ not even **II.** *conj* + *subj* even if
sirena *f* **1.** (*bocina*) siren **2.** (*mujer pez*) mermaid
sirga *f* towrope
Siria *f* Syria
sirio, -a *adj, m, f* Syrian
siroco *m* METEO sirocco
sirope *m* *AmC, Col* (*jarabe*) syrup
sirviente *mf* (*criado*) servant
sisa *f* **1.** (*corte*) armhole **2.** (*dinero*) petty theft
sisar *vt* **1.** (*cortar una sisa*) to take in **2.** (*hurtar*) to pilfer
sisear *vt* to hiss
siseo *m* hissing
sisirisco *m* *Méx* **1.** (*ano*) anus **2.** (*miedo*) fright
sísmico, -a *adj* seismic; **movimiento** ~ earth tremor
sismo *m* (*temblor*) tremor; (*terremoto*) earthquake
sismógrafo *m* seismograph
sistema *m* system; ~ **antibloqueo de frenos** AUTO antilocking brake system; ~ **de alarma** alarm system; **Sistema Europeo de Bancos Centrales** European System of Central Banks; ~ **inmunitario** immune system; **Sistema Monetario Europeo** European Monetary System; ~ **montañoso** mountain range; ~ **operativo** INFOR operating system; ~ **periódico** QUÍM periodic table; ~ **planetario** ASTR solar system; **por** ~ on principle
sistemático, -a *adj* systematic
sistematizar <z→c> *vt* to systematize
sitiar *vt* to besiege; *fig* to surround
sitio *m* **1.** (*lugar*) place; (*espacio*) room; ~ **de veraneo** holiday resort; **en cualquier** ~ anywhere; **en ningún** ~ nowhere; **en todos los** ~**s** everywhere; **guardar el** ~ **a alguien** to keep sb's place; **hacer** ~ to make room; **ocupar mucho** ~ to take up a lot of room; **poner a alguien en su** ~ *fig* to put sb in his/her place; **quedarse en su** ~ *fig* to be dead on the spot *Brit,* to drop dead *Am* **2.** MIL siege **3.** *Méx* ~ (**de taxis**) taxi stand
sito, -a *adj* ~ **en** situated in
situación *f* **1.** (*ubicación*) location **2.** (*estado*) situation; **estar en** ~ **desahogada** to be comfortably off
situado, -a *adj* situated; **estar** ~ to be financially secure; **estar bien** ~ (*trabajo*) to have a good job
situar <*1. pres:* sitúo> **I.** *vt* (*colocar*) to place; (*emplazar*) to locate **II.** *vr:* ~**se**

1. (*ponerse en un lugar*) to situate oneself **2.** (*abrirse paso*) to make one's way

siútico, -a *adj Chile, inf* **1.** (*de mal gusto*) vulgar **2.** (*de nuevo rico*) affected

S.M. *mf abr de* **Su Majestad** H.M.

SME *m abr de* **Sistema Monetario Europeo** EMS

smog *m sin pl* smog

s/n *abr de* **sin número** no number

so I. *interj* whoa! II. *prep* under; ~ **pena de...** on pain of ...; ~ **pretexto de que...** under the pretext of ... III. *m inf* ¡~ **imbécil!** you idiot!

SO *abr de* **sudoeste** SW

soba *f inf* **1.** (*a persona*) pawing, touching up *Brit*, feel-up *Am* **2.** (*de un objeto*) handling, fingering **3.** (*zurra*) hiding

sobaco *m* armpit

sobado *m* pawing

sobado, -a *adj* **1.** (*objetos*) worn **2.** (*papel*) dog-eared **3.** (*tema*) well worn

sobajar *vt* **1.** (*manosear con fuerza*) to paw **2.** *Méx* (*humillar*) to humiliate

sobandero *m Col* bonesetter

sobaquina *f* underarm odour *Brit* [*o* odor *Am*]

sobar I. *vt* **1.** *inf* (*a persona*) to paw, to touch up *Brit*, to feel up *Am* **2.** (*un objeto*) to handle, to finger **3.** (*ablandar*) to knead **4.** (*pegar*) to wallop **5.** (*molestar*) to pester II. *vi inf* (*dormir*) to sleep, to kip *Brit*

soberanamente *adv* (*extremadamente*) supremely; **divertirse** ~ to have a whale of a time

soberanía *f* sovereignty

soberano, -a I. *adj* **1.** POL sovereign **2.** (*excelente*) supreme **3.** *inf* (*enorme*) really big II. *m, f* (*monarca*) sovereign

soberbia *f* **1.** (*orgullo*) pride **2.** (*suntuosidad*) magnificence **3.** (*ira*) anger

soberbio, -a *adj* **1.** (*orgulloso*) proud **2.** (*suntuoso*) magnificent **3.** *inf* (*enorme*) really big

sobón, -ona *adj* **1.** (*impertinente*) over familiar **2.** *inf* (*vago*) lazy

sobornar *vt* to bribe

soborno *m* **1.** (*acción*) bribery **2.** (*dinero*) bribe; (*regalo*) gift (*given as a bribe*)

sobra *f* **1.** (*exceso*) surplus; **de** ~ (*en abundancia*) more than enough; (*inútilmente*) in the way; **saber algo de** ~ to know sth only too well **2.** *pl* (*desperdicios*) leftovers *pl*; (*restos*) remnants *pl*

sobradamente *adv* amply

sobrado I. *m* garret II. *adv* extremely

sobrado, -a *adj* **1.** (*demasiado*) more than enough; **estar** ~ **de algo** to have more than enough of sth **2.** (*atrevido*) bold **3.** (*rico*) wealthy

sobrador(a) *m(f) Arg, Urug* conceited person

sobrante I. *adj* **1.** (*que sobra*) spare; COM, FIN surplus **2.** (*de más*) excess II. *m* (*que sobra*) remainder; (*superávit*) surplus; (*saldo*) balance in hand

sobrar *vi* **1.** (*quedar*) to remain; **nos sobra**

bastante tiempo we have plenty of time **2.** (*abundar*) to be more than enough; **me sobran cinco kilos** I've got five kilos left over; (*perder peso*) I've got to lose five kilos; **aquí sobran las palabras** nothing more needs to be said **3.** (*estar de más*) to be superfluous; **creo que sobras aquí** I think you're in the way [*o* not needed] here

sobrasada *f* sausage spread, typical of the Balearic Islands

sobre I. *m* **1.** (*para una carta*) envelope; ~ **monedero** special delivery envelope; ~ **de ventanilla** window envelope; **un** ~ **de levadura** a packet of yeast **2.** *inf* (*cama*) bed; **irse al** ~ to go off to bed II. *prep* **1.** (*por encima de*) on; **deja el periódico** ~ **la mesa** leave the newspaper on the table; **marchar** ~ **la ciudad** to march on the town; **estar** ~ **alguien** to keep constant watch on sb **2.** (*cantidad aproximada*) **pesar** ~ **los cien kilos** to weigh about a hundred kilos **3.** (*aproximación temporal*) **llegar** ~ **las tres** to arrive at about three o'clock; **irse de vacaciones** ~ **el 20** to go on holiday on about the 20th **4.** (*tema, asunto*) about; ~ **ello** about it **5.** (*reiteración*) on top of; **le caía lágrima** ~ **lágrima** he/she shed tear after tear **6.** (*además de*) as well as **7.** (*superioridad*) **el boxeador triunfó** ~ **su adversario** the boxer triumphed over his opponent; **destacar** ~ **alguien por su estatura** to tower over sb **8.** (*porcentajes*) out of; **tres** ~ **cien** three out of a hundred **9.** FIN **un préstamo** ~ **una casa** a loan on a house; **préstame cien dólares** ~ **este anillo** lend me a hundred dollars on this ring

sobreabundancia *f* superabundance, over-abundance

sobreabundar *vi* to overabound, to be very abundant

sobrealimentación *f* overfeeding

sobrealimentar *vt* **1.** ELEC to supercharge **2.** (*animales*) to overfeed

sobrecama *f* bedspread

sobrecarga *f* excess; (*persona*) added burden; ELEC overload; COM surcharge

sobrecargar I. *vt* (*por peso*) to overload; (*por esfuerzo*) to overburden II. *vr:* ~**se** to overload oneself; ~**se de trabajo** to take on too much work

sobrecoger I. *vt* **1.** (*sorprender*) to take by surprise **2.** (*espantar*) to frighten II. *vr:* ~**se 1.** (*asustarse*) to be startled **2.** (*sorprenderse*) ~**se de algo** to be surprised by sth

sobrecubierta *f* outer cover; (*de libro*) jacket, dust cover

sobredicho, -a *adj* aforementioned, above-mentioned

sobredorar *vt* **1.** (*con oro*) to gild **2.** (*con palabras*) to gloss over

sobredosis *f inv* overdose

sobreentender <e→ie> I. *vt* **1.** (*adivinar*) to infer; **de todo ello sobreentendemos que...** we understand from all this that ...

2. (*presuponer*) to presuppose **II.** *vr:* ~**se** (*ser evidente*) to be obvious; **aquí queda sobreentendido que...** (*implicado*) it is implied here that ...
sobreestimar *vt* to overestimate
sobreexceder **I.** *vt* to surpass **II.** *vr:* ~**se** to lead a dissipated life
sobreexcitar **I.** *vt* (*órgano*) to overexcite **II.** *vr:* ~**se** to get overexcited
sobreexpuesto, -a *adj* **1.** FOTO overexposed **2.** (*arriba mencionado*) discussed above
sobrehilado *m* **1.** (*acción*) tacking *Brit*, basting *Am* **2.** (*puntada*) tacking stitch *Brit*, basting stitch *Am*
sobrehilar *vt* to tack *Brit*, to baste *Am*
sobrehumano, -a *adj* superhuman
sobrellevar *vt* **1.** (*aguantar*) to bear; ~ **mal** to take badly; ~ **bien** to take well **2.** (*peso*) ~ **algo a alguien** to help sb with sth
sobremanera *adv* exceedingly
sobremesa *f* **1.** (*mantel*) table cover **2.** (*postre*) dessert **3.** (*tras la comida*) **de** ~ after-dinner; INFOR desktop; **conversación de** ~ table talk; **programa de** ~ TV afternoon programme *Brit* [*o* program *Am*]; **estar de** ~ to be gathered after a meal
sobrenadar *vi* to float
sobrenatural *adj* **1.** (*fenómenos*) supernatural; **ciencias** ~**es** occult sciences; **la vida** ~ life after death **2.** (*extraordinario*) incredible
sobrenombre *m* **1.** (*calificativo*) epithet **2.** (*apodo*) nickname
sobrentender <e→ie> *vt, vr v.* **sobreentender**
sobreparto *m* confinement; **dolores de** ~ afterpains *pl;* **morir de** ~ to die in childbirth
sobrepasar *vt* **1.** (*en cantidad*) to surpass; (*límite*) to exceed; ~ **su ámbito de responsabilidades** to go beyond one's powers **2.** (*aventajar*) to pass; (*un récord, el mejor*) to beat **3.** (*adelantar*) to overtake
sobreponer *irr como poner* **I.** *vt* **1.** (*encima de algo*) to superimpose, to put on top; (*cubierta, funda*) cover; (*añadir*) to add **2.** (*en consideración, rango*) ~ **a algo/alguien** to place above sth/sb; (*anteponer*) to prefer to sth/sb; ~ **a alguien a todos los demás** to put sb before everyone else **II.** *vr:* ~**se 1.** (*calmarse*) to pull oneself together **2.** (*al enemigo, a una enfermedad*) to overcome; (*al miedo, a un susto*) to recover from
sobreprecio *m* surcharge
sobrepujar *vt* ~ **en algo** to outdo in sth
sobresaliente **I.** *adj* **1.** (*excelente*) outstanding **2.** ENS (*en títulos superiores*) first class; (*nota: nine or better on a scale of one to ten*) excellent **II.** *m* ENS (*nota*) distinction
sobresalir *irr como salir* *vi* **1.** *t.* ARQUIT (*por tamaño, estatura*) ~ **de algo** to stand out from sth **2.** (*distinguirse*) to stand out **3.** (*ser excelente*) ~ **en algo** to be outstanding at sth
sobresaltar **I.** *vi* to start **II.** *vt* to startle **III.** *vr* ~**se con** [*o* **de**] **algo** to be startled at sth

sobresalto *m* **1.** (*susto*) scare **2.** (*turbación*) sudden shock; **con** ~ shocked; **de** ~ suddenly
sobreseer *irr como leer* **I.** *vt* (*dejar*) to stop; (*aplazar*) to suspend; (*interrumpir*) to stay **II.** *vi* to desist; ~ **en los pagos** to interrupt payment
sobreseimiento *m* JUR stay of proceedings; (*aplazamiento*) discontinuance; (*renuncia*) dismissal
sobrestante *m* (*capataz*) foreman; ~ **de turno** foreman on duty
sobrestimar *vt* to overestimate
sobresueldo *m* extra pay [*o* wage]
sobretasa *f* (*suplemento*) surcharge; ~ **por retraso** surcharge for delayed payment
sobretodo *m* (*abrigo*) overcoat; (*mono*) overall
sobrevenir *irr como venir* *vi* (*epidemia*) to ensue; (*desgracia, guerra*) to happen unexpectedly; (*tormenta*) to break; **le sobrevino una sensación de gran tristeza** a feeling of deep sadness took [*o* came over] him/her
sobreviviente *mf* survivor
sobrevivir *vi* (*acontecimientos*) to survive; (*a alguien*) to outlive; **pero ella sigue sobreviviendo en mi recuerdo** but she lives on in my memory
sobrevolar <o→ue> *vt* to fly over
sobrexceder *vt, vr v.* **sobreexceder**
sobrexcitar *vt, vr v.* **sobreexcitar**
sobriedad *f sin pl* **1.** (*sin beber*) soberness **2.** (*moderación*) moderation **3.** (*prudencia*) restraint **4.** (*estilo*) plainness
sobrino, -a *m, f* nephew *m,* niece *f*
sobrinonieto, -a *m, f* great-nephew *m,* great-niece *f*
sobrio, -a *adj* **1.** (*no borracho*) sober **2.** (*moderado*) moderate **3.** (*prudente*) restrained; ~ **de palabras** of few words **4.** (*estilo*) plain
soca *f AmL* AGR ratoon
socaire *m* NÁUT lee; **al** ~ to leeward; **al** ~ **de** (*protección*) protected by; (*pretexto*) under the pretext that; **estar al** ~ (*vaguear*) to shirk
socaliña *f* (*astucia*) cunning
socar <c→qu> **I.** *vt AmC* to compress **II.** *vr:* ~**se** *AmC* to get drunk
socarrar **I.** *vt* to scorch; (*tela*) to singe **II.** *vr:* ~**se** to char
socarrón, -ona **I.** *adj* **1.** (*sarcástico*) ironic **2.** (*astuto*) crafty **II.** *m, f* **1.** (*pícaro*) rogue **2.** (*taimado*) sly devil
socavar *vt* to dig under; *fig* to undermine
socavón *m* **1.** MIN subsidence **2.** (*en el suelo*) hole
sociable *adj* **1.** (*tratable*) sociable; (*que no discute*) easy-going **2.** (*afable*) friendly
social *adj* **1.** (*relativo a la sociedad*) society; (*a la convivencia*) social **2.** (*por parte del estado*) **asistencia** ~ social work; **asistente** ~ social worker; **Estado Social** Welfare State **3.** JUR, ECON company, corporate; **razón** ~ company name
socialdemócrata **I.** *adj* social-democratic

II. *mf* social democrat
socialismo *m sin pl* socialism
socialista *adj, mf* socialist
socializar <z→c> *vt* to socialize
sociedad *f* **1.** (*población, humanidad*) society; ~ **del bienestar** welfare society [*o* state] **2.** (*trato*) company; **la ~ con la que tratas** the company you keep **3.** (*empresa*) company; ~ **anónima** corporation **4.** (*asociación*) association; ~ **protectora** (**de animales**) society for the prevention of cruelty to animals **5.** JUR ~ **conyugal** property held jointly by spouses **6.** (*mundo elegante*) society; **la buena** [*o* alta] ~ high society
socio, -a *m, f* **1.** (*de una asociación*) member **2.** (*en sociedad comercial*) partner; ~ **comercial** business partner **3.** *inf* (*compañero*) mate
socioeconómico, -a *adj* socioeconomic
sociología *f sin pl* sociology
sociólogo, -a *m, f* sociologist
sociopolítico, -a *adj* sociopolitical
socolar *vt* Col, Ecua, Hond, Nic to clear land
socollón *m* AmC, Cuba jolt
socorrer *vt* to help, to come to the aid of
socorrido, -a *adj* **1.** (*útil*) useful **2.** (*que ayuda*) helpful **3.** (*comprobado*) tried and tested **4.** (*común*) ordinary; (*trillado*) well worn
socorrismo *m* live-saving
socorrista *mf* (*de playas*) lifeguard; (*en piscinas*) pool attendant
socorro *m* **1.** (*ayuda*) help; (*salvamento*) rescue; **pedir ~** to ask for help; **puesto de ~** first--aid post; **señal de ~** distress signal, S.O.S. **2.** (*dinero*) money towards sth
socoyote *m* Méx (*benjamín*) youngest child
soda *f* (*bebida*) soda water
sódico, -a *adj* sodium
sodio *m* sodium
soez *adj* crude, coarse
sofá <sofás> *m* sofa
sofá-cama <sofás-cama> *m* sofa-bed
sofisticación *f* sophistication
sofisticado, -a *adj* **1.** (*afectado*) affected **2.** TÉC sophisticated
sofisticar <c→qu> *vt* **1.** (*refinar*) to over-refine **2.** (*falsificar*) to adulterate
sofocación *f* **1.** (*ahogo*) suffocation **2.** (*calor*) heat **3.** (*bochorno*) stifling atmosphere
sofocado, -a *adj* **estar ~** to be stifled
sofocante *adj* **1.** (*asfixiante*) stifling; (*ambiente, aire*) suffocating; **hace un calor ~** the heat is stifling **2.** (*avergonzante*) shameless
sofocar <c→qu> **I.** *vt* **1.** (*asfixiar*) to suffocate **2.** (*impedir que progrese*) to stifle; (*fuego*) to put out; (*revolución*) to crush; (*epidemia*) to stop **3.** (*avergonzar*) to embarrass **4.** (*enojar*) to upset **II.** *vr:* ~**se 1.** (*sonrojar*) to blush **2.** (*excitarse*) to get worked up; (*enojarse*) to get angry **3.** (*ahogarse*) to suffocate
sofoco *m* **1.** (*ahogo*) suffocation; (*después de un esfuerzo*) panting **2.** (*excitación*) shock

3. (*calor*) heat flush
sofocón *m inf* **1.** (*enojo*) annoyance **2.** (*excitación*) shock
sofreír *irr como* reír *vt* to fry lightly
soga *f* rope; (*para ahorcar*) noose; **dar ~ to** pay out rope; **dar ~ a alguien** (*mofarse*) to make fun of sb; (*llevar la corriente*) to humour sb Brit, to humor sb Am; **Pedro está con la ~ al cuello** *fig* Pedro has his back to the wall
sois 2. *pres pl de* ser
soja *f* soya Brit, soy Am; ~ **transgénica** GM soya; **semilla de ~** soya bean Brit, soybean Am
sojuzgar <g→gu> *vt* to subdue
sol *m* **1.** (*astro*) sun; (*luz*) sunlight; **al ~ puesto** at dusk; **de ~ a ~** from dawn to dusk; **día de ~** sunny day; **ponerse al ~** (*tumbarse*) to lie in the sun; (*sentarse*) to sit in the sun; **tomar el ~** to sunbathe; **hoy hace ~** it's sunny today **2.** (*bebida*) ~ **y sombra** brandy and anisette **3.** (*moneda*) sol **4.** *inf* (*alabanza*) **es un ~** he/she is an angel **5.** MÚS G; ~ **mayor** G major ▶**no dejar a alguien ni a ~ ni a sombra** not to leave sb alone; **arrimarse al ~ que más calienta** to know which side one's bread is buttered on
solamente *adv* **1.** (*únicamente*) only **2.** (*expresamente*) expressly
solana *f* **1.** (*en edificios*) suntrap; (*en montañas*) south-facing slope **2.** (*galería*) sun gallery
solano *m* east wind
solapa *f* **1.** (*chaqueta*) lapel **2.** (*libro*) flap
solapado, -a *adj* underhand Brit, underhanded Am
solapar **I.** *vi* to overlap **II.** *vt* **1.** (*cubrir*) to cover up **2.** (*chaqueta, vestido*) to put lapels on **3.** (*disimular*) to conceal
solar **I.** *adj* solar; **plexo ~** solar plexus **II.** *m* **1.** (*terreno*) plot; ~ **para edificaciones** building site **2.** (*casa*) family seat **3.** (*linaje*) line; **venir del ~ de...** to come from the ... family **4.** AmC (*patio*) yard **III.** <o→ue> *vt* **1.** (*pavimentar*) to tile **2.** (*calzado*) to sole
solariego, -a **I.** *adj* **1.** (*de linaje noble*) of noble birth **2.** (*propiedad*) manorial; **casa solariega** family seat **II.** *m, f* **1.** (*noble*) landowner **2.** (*propiedad*) estate
solaz *m* **1.** (*recreo*) recreation; (*esparcimiento*) relaxation **2.** (*consuelo*) solace
solazar <z→c> **I.** *vt* **1.** (*recrear*) to allow to relax **2.** (*entretener*) to amuse **3.** (*consolar*) to comfort **II.** *vr:* ~**se 1.** (*recrearse*) to relax **2.** (*divertirse*) to enjoy oneself; (*entretenerse*) to amuse oneself
soldada *f* (*salario*) salary; MIL service pay
soldado, -a *m, f* **1.** MIL soldier; ~ **de infantería** infantryman, foot soldier; ~ **de caballería** cavalryman; ~ **raso** private **2.** (*defensor*) defender
soldador *m* TÉC soldering iron [*o* gun]
soldador *mf* welder
soldadura *f* TÉC **1.** (*trabajo*) welding **2.** (*punto de unión*) soldered [*o* welded] joint **3.** (*material*) solder

soldar <o→ue> I. *vt* (*con metal fundido*) to weld; (*unir*) to join II. *vr:* ~se (*herida*) to heal; (*huesos*) to knit together

soleado, -a *adj* sunny

solear I. *vt* to put out in the sun; (*blanquear*) to bleach II. *vr:* ~se to bleach

soledad *f* (*estado*) solitude; (*sentimiento*) loneliness

solemne *adj* 1.(*ceremonioso*) solemn; **discurso** ~ formal speech 2.(*mentira*) monstruous; (*error*) monumental

solemnidad *f* 1.(*cualidad*) solemnity 2. REL (*festividad*) religious ceremony 3. *pl* (*formalidades*) formalities *pl*

solemnizar <z→c> *vt* to celebrate

soler <o→ue> *vi* ~ **hacer** to be in the habit of doing; **en España se suelen celebrar los santos** in Spain saints' days are usually celebrated; **suele ocurrir que...** it often occurs that ...; **solemos coger el tren** we usually catch the train; **solíamos coger el tren, pero ya no** we used to catch the train, but not any more

solera *f* 1.(*puntal*) support 2.(*del molino*) lower millstone 3.(*del vino*) *mature wine mixed with younger wine to give it flavour* 4.(*abolengo*) tradition; **con mucha** ~ with a lot of character

solfa *f* 1. MÚS (*signos*) musical notation; (*arte de solfear*) sol-fa; (*melodía*) music; **estar** (*escrito*) **en** ~ to be in musical notation 2. *inf* (*zurra*) hiding ▶**poner** algo **en** ~ (*ridiculizar*) to hold sth up to mockery; (*con arte y orden*) to put sth in order

solfear *vt* 1. MÚS to practise sol-fa *Brit*, to practice sol-fa *Am* 2.(*pegar*) to tan 3. *inf* (*reprender*) to tell off

solfeo *m* 1. MÚS (*acción*) solfeggio, singing of scales; (*fragmento*) sol-fa 2. *inf* (*zurra*) hiding

solicitación *f* 1.(*petición*) request 2.(*para un trabajo*) application

solicitante *mf* 1.(*de una petición*) petitioner; ~ **de asilo** asylum seeker 2.(*para un trabajo*) applicant

solicitar *vt* 1.(*pedir*) to ask for; (*gestionar*) to solicit; (*un trabajo*) to apply for; ~ **un médico** to call for a doctor 2.(*compañía, atención*) to seek; ~ **la mano de una mujer** to ask for a woman's hand in marriage; **te solicitan en todas partes** you're in great demand

solícito, -a *adj* (*diligente*) diligent; (*cuidadoso*) solicitous

solicitud *f* 1.(*diligencia*) diligence; (*cuidado*) solicitude 2.(*petición*) request; (*formal*) petition; ~ **de empleo** job application

solidaridad *f sin pl* solidarity; **por** ~ **con** out of solidarity with

solidario, -a *adj* shared; **hacerse** ~ **de alguien** to sympathize with sb

solidarizarse <z→c> *vr* to feel solidarity with; **me solidarizo con tu opinión** I share your view

solidez *f* solidity; (*estabilidad*) firmness

solidificación *f* FÍS solidification

solidificar <c→qu> I. *vt* to solidify; *fig* to harden II. *vr:* ~se to solidify

sólido *m* 1. FÍS solid 2.(*geometría*) solid shape

sólido, -a *adj t.* FÍS solid; (*colores*) fast; (*ingreso*) steady; (*precios*) stable; (*voz*) strong

soliloquio *m* monologue; TEAT soliloquy

solio *m* throne; ~ **pontificio** papacy

solista *mf* MÚS soloist

solitaria *f* ZOOL tapeworm

solitario *m* 1.(*diamante*) solitaire 2.(*cartas*) patience *Brit*, solitaire *Am*

solitario, -a I. *adj* 1.(*sin compañía*) alone; (*abandonado*) lonely; **en** ~ single-handed 2.(*lugar*) isolated II. *m, f* loner

soliviantar *vt* 1.(*incitar*) to stir up 2.(*enojar*) to anger 3.(*encandilar*) to arouse 4.(*inquietar*) to worry; **los celos le tienen soliviantado** he is consumed with jealousy

sollozar <z→c> *vi* to sob

sollozo *m* sob

solo *m* 1.*t.* MÚS (*baile*) solo 2.(*cartas*) patience *Brit*, solitaire *Am*

solo, -a *adj* 1.(*sin compañía*) alone; (*sin familia*) orphaned; (*solitario*) lonely; **a solas** alone; **por sí** ~ on one's own; **lo hace como ella sola** she does it as only she can 2.(*único*) only; **ni una sola vez** not once 3.(*sin añadir nada*) on its own; (*café*) black; (*alcohol*) straight, neat; **comer el pan** ~ to eat plain bread ▶**estar más** ~ **que la una** to be completely on one's own; **más vale** ~ **que mal acompañado** better to be alone than in bad company

sólo *adv* 1.(*únicamente*) only; ~ **que...** except that ...; **tan** ~ just; **aunque** ~ **sean 10 minutos de deporte al día** even if it's only 10 minutes sport a day 2.(*expresamente*) expressly

solomillo *m* sirloin

solsticio *m* solstice

soltar *irr* I. *vt* 1.(*dejar de sujetar*) to let go of; (*liberar*) to free; (*dejar caer*) to drop; **no** ~ **prenda** not to say a word about sth, to give nothing away; **¡suéltame!** let me go!, let go of me! 2.(*nudo*) to untie 3.(*expresión, grito*) to let out; (*tacos*) to come out with; ~ **una carcajada** to burst out laughing 4.(*golpe*) ~ **un golpe** to strike; ~ **una bofetada a alguien** to cuff [*o* slap] sb 5.(*puesto*) to give up 6.(*lágrimas*) to shed 7. AUTO (*embrague*) to let out; (*frenos*) to release; (*cinturón*) to undo 8.(*gases*) ~ **un pedo** *inf* to let out a fart 9. *inf* (*dinero*) to cough up; ~ **la mosca** to fork out II. *vr:* ~se 1.(*liberarse*) to escape; (*de unas ataduras*) to free oneself; ~se **de la mano** to let go of sb's hand 2.(*un nudo*) to come undone; (*un tiro*) to go off 3.(*al hablar*) to let oneself go; (*una palabra, expresión*) to let out; **se me soltó la lengua** I found my tongue 4.(*desenvoltura*) to become expert; ~se **a hacer algo** to become expert at sth 5.(*para independizarse*) to achieve independence

soltero, -a I. *adj* single II. *m, f* bachelor *m*, unmarried woman *f;* **apellido de soltera** maiden name; **de solteras solíamos salir mucho** we used to go out a lot before we all married

solterón *m* confirmed bachelor

solterona *f* old maid, spinster

soltura *f* 1.(*de una cuerda, del pelo*) looseness 2.(*de forma relajada*) ease; (*al hablar*) fluency

soluble *adj* 1.(*líquido*) soluble; ~ **en agua** water-soluble; **café** ~ instant coffee 2.(*problema*) solvable

solución *f* 1.(*líquido*) solution; ~ **anticongelante** antifreeze 2.(*de un problema*) solution; **este problema no tiene** ~ there's no solution to this problem; **no hay más** ~ there's nothing more to be done 3.(*interrupción*) ~ **de continuidad** break in continuity

solucionar *vt* to solve

solvencia *f* 1.FIN solvency 2.(*responsabilidad*) trustworthiness; ~ **moral** character; **de toda** ~ **moral** of excellent character

solventar *vt* 1.(*problema*) to resolve; (*asunto*) to settle; (*desavenencia*) to end 2.(*deuda, cuenta*) to pay

solvente I. *adj* 1.FIN solvent 2.(*sin deudas*) free of debts 3.(*reputación*) respectable II. *m* solvent

somatada *f* AmC blow

sombra *f* 1.(*proyección*) shadow; ~s chinescas shadow play; ~ **de ojos** (*producto cosmético*) eyeshadow; **se ha convertido en mi** ~ he/she follows me everywhere; **no es** ~ **de lo que era** he/she is a shadow of his/her former self 2.(*contrario de sol*) shade; **hacer** ~ to give shade; **hacer** ~ **a alguien** *fig* to put sb in the shade; **dar (una) buena** ~ to give good shade; **sentarse a la** ~ **de un árbol** to sit in the shade of a tree; **quita de ahí que me haces** ~ move over, you're blocking my light; **no ver más que** ~s **a su alrededor** to be pessimistic about everything; **no fiarse ni de su (propia)** ~ to be extremely suspicious 3. *pl* (*oscuridad*) darkness 4.(*clandestinidad*) **trabajar en la** ~ to work illegally 5.ARTE shading 6.(*cantidad mínima*) trace; **esto no tiene la más mínima** ~ **de verdad** there's not the slightest truth in this; **una** ~ **de tristeza** a trace of sadness; ~ **de duda** shadow of doubt 7.(*de un difunto*) ghost 8.(*defecto*) stain 9. *inf* (*cárcel*) **a la** ~ in the nick *Brit,* in the slammer *Am;* **poner a la** ~ to lock up ►**tener buena** ~ (*tener chiste*) to be witty; (*ser simpático*) to have charm; (*tener suerte*) to be lucky; **tener mala** ~ (*ser antipático*) to be a nasty bit of work; (*tener mala suerte*) to be unlucky; **¡vete por la** ~! watch how you go!; **ni por** ~ not in the least

sombreado *m* shading

sombrear *vt* 1.(*dar sombra*) to shade; (*a alguien*) to cast a shadow over; ~ **los ojos** to put eyeshadow on 2.ARTE to shade

sombrero *m* (*prenda*) hat; ~ **de copa** top hat; ~ **hongo** bowler (hat) *Brit,* derby *Am;* **quitarse el** ~ **ante algo** to take one's hat off to sth

sombrilla *f* parasol

sombrío, -a *adj* 1.(*en la sombra*) shady; (*oscuro*) dark 2.(*triste*) sad; (*pesimista*) gloomy

somero, -a *adj* 1.(*superficial*) superficial; (*vago*) imprecise 2.(*aguas*) shallow

someter I. *vt* 1.(*dominar*) to force to submit; (*subyugar*) to conquer; ~ **la voluntad** to subjugate one's will 2.(*proyecto, ideas, a un tratamiento*) to submit 3.(*encomendar*) **el asunto es sometido a los tribunales** the matter is referred to the courts 4.(*subordinar*) to subordinate; **todo está sometido a tu decisión** everything is subject to your decision II. *vr:* ~**se** 1.(*en una lucha*) to give in 2.(*a una acción, un tratamiento*) ~**se a algo** to undergo sth 3.(*a una decisión, opinión*) to bow; ~**se a las órdenes/la voluntad de alguien** to bow to sb's orders/will

somier <somieres> *m* bed base; (*de muelles*) bedsprings *pl;* (*de láminas*) slats *pl*

somnífero *m* sleeping pill

somnífero, -a *adj* sleep-inducing

somnolencia *f* (*sueño*) drowsiness

somnoliento, -a *adj* (*con sueño*) drowsy; (*al despertarse*) half asleep

somos *1. pres pl de* **ser**

son I. *m* 1.(*sonido*) sound 2.(*rumor, voz*) rumour *Brit,* rumor *Am;* **corre el** ~ **de que...** rumour *Brit* [*o* rumor *Am*] has it that ... 3.(*en actitud*) **venir en** ~ **de paz** to come in peace; **en** ~ **de broma** as a joke ►**bailar al** ~ **que tocan** to toe the line; **hacer algo a su** ~ to do sth one's own way; **¿a** ~ **de qué?, ¿a qué** ~? why?; **sin** ~ for no reason at all II. *3. pres pl de* **ser**

sonado, -a *adj* 1.(*corriente*) common; (*famoso*) famous; (*escandaloso*) scandalous; (*sensacional*) sensational 2. *inf* (*loco*) crazy 3.(*boxeador*) punch drunk [*o* happy]

sonajero *m* (baby's) rattle

sonambulismo *m sin pl* sleepwalking

sonámbulo, -a I. *adj* sleepwalking II. *m, f* sleepwalker

sonante *adj* **dinero contante y** ~ (hard) cash

sonar <o→ue> I. *vi* 1.(*timbre, teléfono, campana*) to ring; (*instrumento*) to be heard; **me suenan las tripas** my stomach is rumbling 2. *t.* LING, MÚS (*parecerse*) to sound; ~ **a algo** to sound like sth; ~ **a hueco** to sound hollow; **esto me suena** this sounds familiar; (*tal y*) **como suena** as I'm telling you; **lo que sea** ~**á** what will be, will be II. *vt* 1.(*instrumento*) to play 2.(*la nariz*) to blow; ~ **la nariz a un niño** to blow a child's nose III. *vr:* ~**se** to blow one's nose

sonata *f* sonata

sonda *f* 1.(*acción*) sounding 2.MED probe, catheter 3.NÁUT lead; ~ **acústica** echo-sounder

sondar *vt* 1. MED to probe 2. NÁUT to sound 3. MIN ~ **algo** to bore into sth 4. (*explorar*) to explore, to investigate

sondear *vt* 1. (*una persona*) to sound out 2. *v.* **sondar**

sondeo *m* 1. MED probing 2. MIN boring 3. NÁUT sounding 4. (*averiguación*) investigation; ~ **de mercado** ECON market survey; ~ **de la opinión pública** public opinion survey

soneto *m* LIT sonnet

songa-songa *AmC, Chile, Ecua* **a la** ~ underhand

songo, -a *adj Col, Méx* 1. (*tonto*) stupid 2. (*taimado*) sly

sonido *m* 1. (*ruido*) sound 2. *t.* MÚS (*manera de sonar*) tone 3. FÍS resonance 4. RADIO sound; ~ **estereofónico** stereo sound

sonoridad *f t.* MÚS (*características*) sonority; (*agradable*) sonorousness

sonorizar <z→c> *vt* 1. CINE to set to music, to record the soundtrack 2. LING to voice

sonoro, -a *adj* 1. (*que puede sonar*) resonant; (*acústico*) acoustic; (*bóveda*) echoing 2. (*fuerte*) loud; (*agradable*) sonorous; **una voz sonora/poco sonora** a rich/thin voice 3. LING voiced 4. FÍS resonant 5. CINE **banda sonora** soundtrack; **película sonora** talkie

sonreír *irr como* reír I. *vi, vr:* ~**se** (*reír levemente*) to smile; ~ **a alguien** to smile at sb; ~ **maliciosamente** to smile maliciously; ~ **de felicidad** to beam with happiness II. *vi* (*la vida, la suerte*) to smile; **le sonríe la fortuna** fortune smiles on him/her

sonrisa *f* (*leve*) smile; (*maliciosa*) smirk; ~ **de oreja a oreja** (broad) grin

sonrojar I. *vt* to make blush II. *vr:* ~**se** to blush

sonrojo *m* 1. (*acción*) blushing 2. (*rubor*) blush 3. (*causa*) naughty remark

sonrosar I. *vt* to make pink II. *vr:* ~**se** to turn pink

sonsacar <c→qu> *vt* 1. (*indagar*) ~ **a alguien** to find out from sb; (*secreto*) to worm [*o* wheedle] out from sb 2. (*empleado*) to pump for information

sonsear *vi CSur* (*tontear*) to behave stupidly

sonsera *f Arg* foolishness

sonso, -a *m, f CSur* (*tonto*) stupid

sonsonete *m* 1. (*golpecitos*) tapping; (*lluvia*) dripping 2. (*de mofa*) mocking tone 3. (*monotonía*) same old story

soñado, -a *adj* (*con que se sueña*) dreamt-of; **el hombre** ~ Mr Right

soñador(a) I. *adj* dreamy II. *m(f)* dreamer

soñar <o→ue> *vi, vt* to dream; ~ **con algo** to dream of sth; ~ **despierto** to daydream; ¡**ni** ~**lo!** no way!; **siempre he soñado con ser médico** I've always dreamt of being a doctor; **sueño con volver a verte** I dream of seeing you again; ¡**sueña** [*o* que sueñes] **con los angelitos!** sweet dreams!

soñoliento, -a *adj* drowsy

sopa *f* 1. (*caldo*) soup 2. *pl* (*pan*) ~**s de leche** bread and milk ▶**ése os da** ~**s con honda a todos vosotros** he's streets ahead of all of you; **poner a alguien como la** ~ **de Pascua** to give sb a ticking off; **comer la** [*o* andar a la] ~ **boba** to live off other people; **estar** ~ to be tight; **ver hasta en la** ~ to see everywhere; **como** [*o* hecho] **una** ~ (*mojado*) soaked to the skin

sopapo *m* 1. (*puñetazo*) punch 2. *inf* (*bofetada*) slap; **dar un** ~ **a alguien** to slap sb

sopera *f* soup tureen

sopero, -a I. *adj* soup; **ser muy** ~ to be very fond of soup II. *m, f* soup plate

sopesar *vt* to try the weight of; *fig* to weigh up

sopetón *m* punch; **de** ~ unexpectedly

soplar I. *vi* to blow ▶~ **y beber, no puede ser** *prov* you can't have your cake and eat it too; ¡**sopla!** well I'm blowed! II. *vt* 1. (*con la boca*) to blow on; (*apartar*) to blow away; (*velas*) to blow out; (*hinchar*) to blow up; (*fuego*) to blow on; **soplado a boca** (*vidrio*) hand-blown 2. (*en un examen*) to whisper; TEAT to prompt 3. *inf* (*delatar*) to inform [*o* squeal] on; (*entre alumnos*) to tell on 4. *inf* (*hurtar*) to nick *Brit,* to swipe; (*cobrar*) to sting for 5. (*golpe*) to deal 6. (*inspirar*) to inspire III. *vr:* ~**se** *inf* 1. (*comer*) to wolf down; (*beber*) to knock back 2. (*engreírse*) to get conceited

soplete *m* blow lamp *Brit,* blow torch; ~ **soldador** welding torch

soplillo *m* fan; **orejas de** ~ stick-out ears, Dumbo ears

soplo *m* 1. (*acción*) puff; **apagar las velas de un** ~ to blow out the candles with one puff 2. (*viento leve*) breeze; ~ **de viento** breath of wind 3. (*tiempo*) **como un** ~ like a flash 4. (*denuncia*) tip-off 5. (*sonido*) murmur; (*corazón*) heart murmur

soplón, -ona *m, f* 1. (*de la policía*) informer 2. TEAT prompter 3. (*entre alumnos*) talebearer *Brit,* tattletale *Am*

soponcio *m* 1. (*desmayo*) fainting fit 2. (*mareo*) dizzy spell

sopor *m* lethargy

soporífero *m* sleeping pill

soporífero, -a *adj* 1. (*que da sueño*) sleep-inducing 2. (*aburrido*) soporific, dull

soportable *adj* bearable

soportal *m* 1. (*entrada*) porch 2. *pl* (*arcos*) arcade

soportar *vt* 1. (*sostener*) to support 2. (*aguantar*) to stand

soporte *m* 1. *t. fig* (*apoyo*) support 2. (*pilar*) support pillar; (*de madera*) beam; ~ **para bicicletas** bike rack 3. INFOR ~ **físico** hardware; ~ **lógico** software

soprano¹ *m* MÚS (*voz*) soprano

soprano² *f* MÚS soprano

soquete *m AmL* (*calcetín*) (short) sock, anklet

sor *f* REL sister

sorber *vt* 1. (*con los labios*) to sip; (*por una pajita*) to suck; (*por la nariz*) to sniff; MED to

inhale; ~ **tabaco** to take snuff **2.**(*empaparse de*) to soak up **3.**(*escuchar*) to drink in
sorbete *m* GASTR sorbet *Brit*, sherbet *Am*
sorbo *m* (*cantidad, trago*) sip; **beber a ~s** to sip; **tomar de un** ~ to drink in one go; **échame otro** ~ give me another drop
sordera *f* **1.**(*privación*) deafness **2.**(*disminución*) loss of hearing
sordidez *f* sordidness
sórdido, -a *adj* sordid
sordina *f* MÚS (*instrumento de viento*) mute; (*piano*) damper
sordo, -a I. *adj* **1.**(*que no oye*) deaf; ~ **de un oído** deaf in one ear; **hacer oídos ~s** to turn a deaf ear; ~ **como una tapia** as deaf as a post, stone deaf; **quedarse** ~ to go deaf **2.**(*que oye mal*) hard of hearing **3.**(*algo que no hace ruido*) noiseless; **a sordas, a lo** ~ on the quiet **4.**(*de timbre oscuro*) dull; **un golpe** ~ a dull thud **5.**(*que no presta atención*) inattentive **6.**(*sentimiento, pasión*) repressed **7.** LING voiceless **II.** *m, f* deaf person; **los ~s** the deaf, deaf people; **hacerse el** ~ to pretend not to hear; **predicar a los ~s** to preach to the deaf; **no hay peor** ~ **que el que no quiere oír** *prov* there are none so deaf as those who will not hear
sordomudo, -a I. *adj* deaf and dumb **II.** *m, f* deaf mute
sorgo *m* sorghum
soriano, -a I. *adj* of/from Soria **II.** *m, f* native/inhabitant of Soria
sorna *f* **1.**(*al obrar*) slyness; **con** ~ slyly **2.**(*al hablar*) sarcasm; **con** ~ sarcastically
sorprendente *adj* **1.**(*inesperado*) unexpected; (*desarrollo, evolución*) surprising; (*asombroso*) amazing; **es** ~ **que** +*subj* it's surprising that **2.**(*que salta a la vista*) striking; **poseer una estatura** ~ to be surprisingly tall **3.**(*extraordinario*) incredible; **no es** ~ **que** +*subj* it's hardly surprising that
sorprender I. *vt* **1.**(*coger desprevenido*) to take by surprise; (*asombrar*) to startle, to amaze; (*extrañar*) to surprise; **no me** ~**ía que viniera** I wouldn't be surprised if he/she came; **durante un momento me quedé sorprendida** I was surprised for a moment **2.**(*descubrir algo*) to come across **3.**(*pillar*) to catch (in the act) **4.** MIL (*atacar*) to surprise **II.** *vr:* ~**se 1.**(*asombrarse*) ~**se de algo** to be amazed at sth **2.**(*extrañarse*) to be surprised
sorpresa *f* **1.**(*acción*) surprise; **coger a alguien de** [*o por*] ~ to take sb by surprise **2.**(*efecto*) suddenness; (*asombro*) amazement; (*extrañeza*) surprise
sorpresivo, -a *adj* **1.**(*inesperado*) surprising; (*asombroso*) amazing **2.**(*repentino*) sudden
sortear *vt* **1.**(*decidir*) to draw lots for; (*destino*) to toss up for; (*rifar*) to raffle **2.**(*esquivar*) to avoid
sorteo *m* **1.**(*decisión*) drawing of lots; (*rifa*) raffle; (*lotería*) draw **2.**(*esquivación*) avoidance

sortija *f* **1.**(*joya*) ring; (*con sello*) signet ring **2.**(*rizo*) curl
sortilegio *m* **1.**(*brujería*) sorcery **2.**(*vaticinio*) prediction; **hacer un** ~ **a alguien** (*vaticinar*) to tell sb's fortune; (*hechizar*) to cast a spell on sb
sosegado, -a *adj* **1.**(*apacible*) peaceful **2.**(*tranquilo*) calm
sosegar *irr como fregar* **I.** *vt* (*calmar*) to calm **II.** *vi, vr:* ~**se** (*descansar*) to rest **III.** *vr:* ~**se** (*calmarse*) to calm down
sosegate *m* *Arg, Urug* **dar** [*o* **pegar**] **un** ~ **a alguien** to give sb a telling-off
sosería *f* dullness; **esto es una** ~ this is boring
sosia *m* *elev* double
sosiego *m* calm; **hacer algo con** ~ to do sth calmly
soslayar *vt* **1.**(*objeto*) to put sideways **2.**(*evitar*) to avoid
soslayo, -a *adj* sideways; **mirar a alguien de** ~ to look at sb out of the corner of one's eye; **pasar de** ~ **por la casa de la abuela** to drop in at grandma's house; **pasar por un tema de** [*o al*] ~ to touch on a subject
soso, -a *adj* **1.**(*sin sal*) unsalted; (*sin sabor*) tasteless, insipid **2.**(*persona*) dull
sospecha *f* **1.**(*suposición*) supposition **2.**(*desconfianza*) mistrust **3.**(*de un crimen*) suspicion; (*contra alguien concreto*) accusation; **bajo** ~ **de asesinato** suspected of murder
sospechar I. *vt* **1.**(*creer posible*) to suppose; **¡ya lo sospechaba!** I thought as much! **2.**(*recelar*) to suspect **II.** *vi* to be suspicious
sospechoso, -a I. *adj* suspicious; **me resulta** ~ **que** +*subj* I find it suspicious that **II.** *m, f* suspect
sostén *m* **1.** *t. fig* (*apoyo*) support; **pilar de** ~ support pillar **2.**(*prenda*) bra **3.**(*de familia*) support; (*alimentos*) sustenance
sostener *irr como tener* **I.** *vt* **1.**(*sujetar*) to support **2.**(*aguantar*) to bear; (*por debajo*) to hold up **3.**(*afirmar*) to maintain; (*idea, teoría*) to stick to **4.**(*persona*) to support **5.**(*lucha, velocidad, posición*) to keep up; ~ **una larga conversación** to have a long conversation **II.** *vr:* ~**se 1.**(*sujetarse*) to hold oneself up **2.**(*aguantarse*) to keep going **3.**(*en pie*) to stand up **4.**(*económicamente*) **apenas me puedo** ~ I can hardly support myself **5.**(*en opinión*) ~**se en algo** to insist on sth
sostenido *m* MÚS sharp; **poner un** ~ to raise by a semitone
sostenido, -a *adj* **1.**(*esfuerzo*) sustained **2.** MÚS sharp; **fa** ~ F sharp
sostenimiento *m* **1.**(*acción*) support **2.**(*apoyo*) holding up **3.**(*manutención*) maintenance **4.**(*mantenimiento*) upkeep
sota *f* (*naipe*) jack
sotana *f* cassock, soutane
sótano *m* **1.**(*piso*) basement **2.**(*habitación*) cellar
sotavento *m* leeward

S

soterrar <e→ie> vt 1.(*enterrar*) to bury 2.(*esconder*) to hide away; (*sentimientos*) to conceal

sotreta *adj Arg, Bol, Urug* 1.(*caballo*) old and useless 2.(*holgazán*) idle; (*no fiable*) untrustworthy

soturno, -a *adj Ven* (*taciturno*) taciturn

soy *1. pres de* **ser**

spaguetti *mpl* spaghetti

sponsorizar <z→c> *vt* to sponsor

spot *m* <spots> TV commercial

spray *m* <sprays> spray

sprint *m* <sprints> sprint; **hacer un** ~ to sprint

sprintar *vt* DEP to sprint

squash *m sin pl* DEP squash

Sr. *abr de* señor Mr; (*en direcciones*) Esquire

Sra. *abr de* señora Mrs

S.R.C. *abr de* **se ruega contestación** R.S.V.P.

Srta. *f abr de* señorita Miss

Sta. *f abr de* santa St

stand *m* <stands> stand

standing *m* **de alto** ~ high-ranking; (*calidad*) **de luxe**, luxury

status *m inv* status

stick *m* DEP stick

Sto. *abr de* santo St.

stock *m* COM stock

stop *m* 1.(*acción*) stop 2.(*autobús*) bus stop 3.(*señal*) stop sign

su *adj* (*de él*) his; (*de ella*) her; (*de cosa, animal*) its; (*de ellos*) their; (*de Ud., Uds.*) your; (*de uno*) one's; ~ **familia** his/her/their family

suampo *m AmC* (*ciénaga*) swamp

suave *adj* 1.(*superficie, piel*) smooth; (*jersey, cabello, droga*) soft; (*viento, noche*) gentle; (*sopa, salsa*) mild 2.(*aterrizaje*) smooth; (*curva, subida*) gentle; (*temperatura, tabaco*) mild 3.(*carácter*) docile; (*maneras*) refined; (*palabras*) kind

suavidad *f sin pl* 1.(*de superficie, piel*) smoothness; (*de jersey, cabello*) softness; (*de viento, noche, temperatura*) gentleness; (*de sopa*) mildness 2.(*de aterrizaje*) smoothness; (*de caricia, subida*) gentleness 3.(*de carácter*) docility; (*de palabras*) kindness

suavizante I. *adj* **crema** ~ conditioner II. *m* 1.(*para la ropa*) fabric softener 2.(*para el cabello*) conditioner

suavizar <z→c> *vt* 1.(*hacer suave*) to smooth; (*pelo, piel*) to soften; (*superficie*) to smooth out; (*navaja*) to strop 2.(*expresión*) to soften; (*situación*) to relax, to ease 3.(*persona*) to mollify 4.(*recorrido, trabajo*) to make easy; (*velocidad*) to moderate

suba *f Arg* (*alza*) rise

subalimentación *f* undernourishment

subalimentado, -a *adj* undernourished

subalterno, -a I. *adj* secondary II. *m, f* (*empleado*) subordinate

subarrendar <e→ie> *vt* (*ceder: piso*) to sublet; (*finca*) to sublease

subarriendo *m* (*cesión: de piso*) subletting;

(*de finca*) sublease

subasta *f* 1.(*venta*) auction; ~ **forzada** forced auction; **sacar a** ~ **pública** to put up for auction 2.(*de contrato público*) tender

subastador(a) *m(f)* auctioneer

subastar *vt* 1.(*vender*) to auction 2.(*contrato público*) to put out to tender

subcampeón, -ona *m, f* runner-up; ~ **mundial** world number two

subconsciencia *f* subconscious

subconsciente *adj* subconscious

subcontinente *m* subcontinent

subcontratante *mf* subcontractor

subcontratar *vt, vi* to subcontract

subcultura *f* subculture

subcutáneo, -a *adj* subcutaneous

subdesarrollado, -a *adj* underdeveloped

subdirector(a) *m(f)* subdirector, assistant director [*o* manager]

súbdito, -a *m, f* 1.(*sometido*) vassal 2. POL (*de un rey*) subject; (*ciudadano*) citizen

subdividir *vt* to subdivide

subdivisión *f* subdivision

subempleo *m* underemployment

subestimar I. *vt* to underestimate; (*propiedad*) to undervalue II. *vr:* ~**se** to underestimate oneself

subida *f* 1.(*de una calle, un río*) rise 2.(*cuesta*) slope; **la calle hace** ~ the street is on a slope 3.(*de precios, temperaturas, costes*) increase 4.(*acción de subir*) ascent; (*en coche, teleférico*) climb 5. POL ~ **al poder** rise to power; ~ **al trono** ascent to the throne

subido, -a *adj* 1.(*color*) bright; (*olor*) strong; **rojo** ~ bright red 2. *inf* (*persona*) vain; (*tono*) proud 3.(*precio*) high

subinquilino, -a *m, f* subtenant

subir I. *vi* 1.(*ascender: calle, cuesta*) to go up; (*sol, pastel, globo, río*) to rise; ~ **a la cima** to climb to the peak; ~ **a primera** DEP to go up to the first division; **la marea ha subido** the tide has come in 2.(*andando*) to go up; **sube a por tus cosas** go up and get your things 3.(*aumentar*) ~ **en algo** to increase by sth; **la gasolina ha subido** petrol *Brit* [*o* gas *Am*] has gone up 4.(*montar: al coche*) to get in; (*al caballo, tren, a la bici*) to get on; ~ **a un árbol** to climb a tree II. *vt* 1.(*precio*) to raise; **hacer** ~ **los precios** to put up the prices 2.(*música*) to turn up; (*voz*) to raise 3.(*en coche*) to go up; (*montaña*) to climb 4.(*poner más alto: brazos*) to lift up; (*cortina, persiana*) to raise; (*cuello de abrigo*) to turn up; (*cabeza, pesas*) to lift; ~ **a un niño en brazos** to lift up a child 5.(*llevar*) to take up; ~ **al tercer piso** to go up to the third floor 6.(*pared*) to build III. *vr:* ~**se** (*al coche*) to get in; (*al tren, a la bici*) to get on; ~**se a un árbol/a una silla** to climb a tree/onto a chair; **se me ha subido el vino a la cabeza** the wine has gone to my head

súbito *adv* suddenly; **de** ~ (*repentinamente*) suddenly; (*inesperadamente*) unexpectedly

súbito, -a *adj* 1.(*repentino*) sudden; **muerte**

súbita MED sudden death; (*de bebés*) crib death **2.** (*inesperado*) unexpected **3.** (*carácter, genio*) irritable

subjefe, -a *m, f* assistant manager

subjetividad *f sin pl* subjectivity

subjetivizar <z→c> *vt* to subjectivize

subjetivo, -a *adj* subjective

subjuntivo *m* subjunctive

sublevación *f* uprising

sublevar I. *vt* **1.** (*amotinar*) to rouse to revolt **2.** (*irritar*) to upset **II.** *vr:* ~**se** to revolt

sublimación *f* **1.** (*de alguien*) praise **2.** PSICO, QUÍM sublimation

sublimar *vt* **1.** (*a alguien*) to praise **2.** PSICO, QUÍM to sublimate

sublime *adj* sublime

subliminal *adj* subliminal

submarinismo *m sin pl* scuba-diving, skin-diving; **hacer** ~ to go scuba-diving [*o* skin-diving]

submarinista *mf* scuba diver

submarino *m* submarine

submarino, -a *adj* submarine; (*vida*) underwater

subnormal I. *adj* subnormal **II.** *mf* (*persona*) subnormal person; **¡eres un** ~**!** *pey* you moron!

subordinación *f* subordination; (*obediencia*) obedience

subordinado, -a I. *adj* **1.** (*en el trabajo*) subordinate **2.** LING **oración subordinada** subordinate clause **II.** *m, f* (*en el trabajo*) subordinate

subordinar *vt* to subordinate

subproducto *m* by-product

subrayado *m* underlining

subrayar *vt* **1.** (*con raya*) to underline **2.** (*recalcar*) to emphasize

subrepticio, -a *adj* surreptitious

subrogante *adj Chile* (*interino*) substitute

subrogar <g→gu> *vt* **1.** (*a alguien: temporalmente*) to substitute; (*definitivamente*) to replace **2.** (*algo*) to replace

subsanar *vt* **1.** (*falta*) to make up for **2.** (*error*) to rectify; (*defecto*) to repair; (*mal*) to remedy **3.** (*dificultad*) to overcome

subscripción *f v.* **suscripción**

subsecretario, -a *m, f* **1.** POL undersecretary **2.** (*en oficina*) assistant

subseguir *irr como* seguir *vi, vr:* ~**se** **1.** (*seguir*) ~ **a alguien** to follow immediately behind sb **2.** (*deducirse*) ~ **de algo** to deduce from sth

subsidiar *vt* to subsidize

subsidiariedad *f* subsidiarity

subsidiario, -a *adj* **1.** (*de subsidio*) subsidiary; **órgano** ~ (*institución*) subsidiary company **2.** (*secundario*) complementary

subsidio *m* subsidy; ~ **de paro** [*o* de desempleo] unemployment benefit *Brit,* unemployment compensation *Am*

subsiguiente *adj* subsequent

subsistencia *f* **1.** (*hecho*) subsistence **2.** *pl*

(*alimentos*) sustenance **3.** (*material*) support

subsistente *adj* (*existente*) surviving

subsistir *vi* **1.** (*vivir*) to subsist **2.** (*perdurar*) to endure; (*creencia*) to exist; (*empresa*) to survive

substancia *f v.* **sustancia**

substantivo *adj, m v.* **sustantivo**

substitución *f v.* **sustitución**

substraer *irr como* traer *vt v.* **sustraer**

subsuelo *m* subsoil

subte *m Arg, inf* (*metro*) underground *Brit,* subway *Am*

subterfugio *m* (*evasiva*) subterfuge; (*pretexto*) pretext

subterráneo, -a *adj* underground, subterranean

subtitular *vt* CINE to subtitle; **película subtitulada en inglés** film with English subtitles

subtítulo *m t.* CINE subtitle

subtropical *adj* subtropical

suburbano, -a *adj* suburban; **línea suburbana** suburban line

suburbio *m* **1.** (*alrededores*) (poor) suburb; **vivir en los** ~**s de París** to live on the edge of Paris **2.** (*barrio*) slum area

subvención *f* grant; POL subsidy

subvencionar *vt* to aid; POL to subsidize; ADMIN to finance with a grant

subvenir *irr como* venir *vi* ~ **a las necesidades de alguien** to provide for sb's needs; ~ **a los gastos** to meet expenses

subversión *f* subversion

subversivo, -a *adj* subversive

subvertir *irr como* sentir *vt* **1.** (*sistema, gobierno*) to overthrow **2.** (*valor moral*) to undermine **3.** (*orden social*) to disrupt

subyacente *adj elev* **1.** (*capa*) underlying **2.** (*problema*) hidden

subyugar <g→gu> *vt* **1.** (*oprimir*) to subjugate **2.** (*sugestionar*) to dominate

succión *f* suction; **efecto de** ~ suction effect

succionar *vt* to suck; (*tierra, esponja*) to soak up

sucedáneo *m* substitute; (*imitación*) imitation

sucedáneo, -a *adj* substitute

suceder I. *vi* **1.** (*seguir*) to succeed **2.** (*ocurrir*) to happen; **¿qué sucede?** what's happening?; **por lo que pueda** ~ just in case; **suceda lo que suceda** whatever happens; **lo más que puede** ~ **es que** +*subj* the worst thing that can happen is; **sucede que...** the thing is that ... **3.** (*en cargo*) to follow on **II.** *vt* (*heredar*) to inherit; (*seguir*) to succeed; ~ **al rey** to succeed the king

sucedido *m* happening

sucesión *f* **1.** (*acción*) succession **2.** (*serie*) series *inv* **3.** (*cargo, trono*) succession **4.** (*herencia*) inheritance **5.** (*descendencia*) issue

sucesivo, -a *adj* following; **en lo** ~ henceforth; **hicimos el examen en dos días** ~**s** we did the exam on two consecutive days

suceso *m* **1.** (*hecho*) event; (*repentino*) inci-

S

dent **2.** (*transcurso*) outcome **3.** (*crimen*) crime; **página** [*o* **sección**] **de ~s** PREN accident and crime reports

sucesor(a) *m(f)* **1.** (*a un cargo*) successor **2.** (*heredero*) heir

sucesorio, **-a** *adj* succession; **comunidad sucesoria** inherited property

suche I. *adj Ven* (*agrio*) bitter **II.** *m Chile* **1.** (*subalterno*) assistant **2.** (*rufián*) pimp

suciedad *f* **1.** (*cualidad*) dirtiness **2.** (*porquería*) dirt **3.** (*jugada*) dirty act

sucinto, **-a** *adj* succinct

sucio *adv* jugar ~ to play dirty

sucio, **-a** *adj* dirty; (*jugada*) foul; **tengo los apuntes en ~** I've got the notes in rough; **hacer el trabajo ~** to do the dirty work

Sucre *m* Sucre

sucucho *m AmL* (*vivienda miserable*) hovel

suculento, **-a** *adj* **1.** (*sabroso*) tasty **2.** (*nutritivo*) nutritious **3.** (*jugoso*) juicy, succulent

sucumbir *vi* **1.** (*rendirse*) to succumb; JUR to lose; **Agassi sucumbió ante Pete Sampras** Agassi succumbed to Pete Sampras **2.** (*morir*) to die

sucursal *f* **1.** (*de empresa*) subsidiary; (*de banco, negocio*) branch **2.** (*negociado*) department

sucusumucu *adv Col, Cuba, PRico* **a lo ~** (*fingiéndose tonto*) playing dumb *inf*

sudaca *mf pey: pejorative term used to refer to a South American*

sudadera *f* sweatshirt

sudado, **-a** *adj* sweaty

Sudáfrica *f* South Africa

sudafricano, **-a** *adj, m, f* South African

Sudamérica *f* South America

sudamericano, **-a** *adj, m, f* South American

Sudán *m* Sudan

sudanés, **-esa** *adj, m, f* Sudanese

sudar I. *vi, vt* to sweat; **me sudan los pies** my feet are sweating; **estoy sudando a chorros** I'm dripping with sweat **II.** *vi inf* (*trabajar*) to sweat it out **III.** *vt* **1.** (*camisa*) to make sweaty **2.** (*conseguir*) **gano mucho pero lo sudo** I earn good money but I have to work for it ▶**me la suda** *vulg* I don't give a fuck

sudario *m* shroud

sudeste *m* south-east

sudoeste *m* south-west

sudor *m* (*de la piel*) sweat; **con el ~ de mi frente** with the sweat of my brow; **me costó ~es** *inf* I had to slog my guts out

sudoroso, **-a** *adj* sweaty

Suecia *f* Sweden

sueco, **-a I.** *adj* Swedish **II.** *m, f* Swede ▶**hacerse el ~** to pretend not to hear [*o* see]

suegro, **-a** *m, f* father-in-law *m*, mother-in-law *f*; **los ~s** the in-laws

suela *f* sole; **echar las medias ~s** to patch up; **tú no me llegas a la ~ del zapato** *fig* you can't hold a candle to me; **de siete ~s** out-and--out; **es un tonto de siete ~s** *inf* he's a total

idiot; **como la ~ de un zapato** tough as an old boot [*o* as shoe-leather]

suelazo *m Chile, Col, Ecua, Ven* hard fall

sueldo *m* pay; (*mensual*) salary; (*semanal*) wage; **~ base** basic salary; **~ fijo** regular wage; **un aumento de ~** a pay rise *Brit*, a pay raise *Am*; **¿qué ~ ganas?** how much do you earn?

suelo *m* **1.** (*de la tierra*) ground; **~ natal** native soil; **poner una maleta en el ~** to put a suitcase on the ground; **dar consigo en el ~** to hit the ground; **besar el ~** to kiss the ground; **está muy hondo, no toco (el) ~** it's very deep, I can't reach the bottom; **no toca con los pies en el ~ de contento** *fig* he's overjoyed **2.** (*de casa*) floor; **~ de tarima** wood flooring, floorboards *pl* **3.** (*terreno*) land; **~ edificable** building land **4.** (*de vasija*) bottom **5.** (*poso*) dregs *pl* **6.** DEP **ejercicios de ~** floor exercises ▶**no te dejes arrastrar por el ~** don't let them run you down; **estar por los ~s** (*deprimido*) to feel very down; (*de precio*) to be dirt cheap; **irse al ~** to fail; **poner algo/a alguien por el ~** to speak badly of sth/sb

suelto *m* **1.** (*dinero*) loose change **2.** (*artículo*) short item

suelto, **-a** *adj* **1.** (*desenganchado: tornillo, lana*) loose **2.** (*desatado: cordón, pelo, perro*) loose; (*broche*) unfastened; (*arroz*) fluffy; **dinero ~** ready money; **no dejar ni un cabo ~** to leave no loose ends; **un prisionero anda ~** a prisoner is on the loose; **voy ~ de vientre** *fig* I have diarrhoea *Brit* [*o* diarrhea *Am*] **3.** (*separado*) separate; **pieza suelta** individual piece **4.** (*vestido*) loose-fitting **5.** (*incontrolado*) **tener la lengua suelta** to have a ready tongue **6.** (*estilo*) free; (*lenguaje*) fluent; **dibujar con mano suelta** to draw free-hand **7.** (*no envasado*) loose **8.** *inf* (*no agarrotado*) free; **eso lo hago yo fácil y ~** I'll do that in a jiffy

sueño *m* **1.** (*acto de dormir*) sleep; **me cogió el ~** sleep overcame me; **descabezar** [*o* **echarse**] **un ~** to have a nap; **entre ~s** half asleep; **tener el ~ ligero/pesado** to be a light/heavy sleeper **2.** (*ganas de dormir*) sleepiness; **tener ~** to be sleepy; **entrar ~ a uno** to get sleepy [*o* drowsy]; **caerse de ~** to be falling asleep; **me quita el ~** it keeps me awake **3.** (*fantasía*) dream; **ni en** [*o* **por**] **~s** not even in your wildest dreams; **un coche que es un ~** a dream car; **los ~s, ~s son** dreams are dreams; **~ húmedo** wet dream

suero *m* **1.** (*de leche*) whey **2.** MED serum

suerte *f* **1.** (*fortuna*) luck; **¡(buena) ~!** good luck!; **estar de ~** to be in luck; **no estar de ~** to be out of luck; **tener buena/mala ~** to be lucky/unlucky; **traer/dar buena/mala ~** to bring/give good/bad luck; **por ~** fortunately; **probar ~** to try one's luck; **ser cuestión de ~** to be a matter of luck; **tener una ~ loca** to be amazingly lucky; **¡deséame ~!** wish me luck!; **la ~ está echada** the die is cast **2.** (*destino*) fate; **echar algo a ~(s)** to draw lots for sth; **¿quién sabe la ~ que te espera?** who knows what fate awaits you? **3.**(*casualidad*) chance **4.**(*manera*) way; **de ~ que...** in such a way that ...; **de esta ~** in this way **5.**(*tipo*) kind; **tratar con toda ~ de gente** to deal with all sorts of people **6.**(*condición*) state; **de tal ~ que** so that

suertero, -a I. *adj Ecua, Hond, Perú* lucky II. *m, f Perú* lottery ticket seller

suéter *m* sweater

suficiencia *f* **1.**(*lo bastante*) sufficiency **2.**(*presunción*) self-importance, smugness; **decir con aires de ~** to say with a superior air **3.**(*pedantería*) pedantry **4.**(*aptitud*) competence

suficiente I. *adj* **1.**(*bastante*) enough; **ser ~** to be sufficient; **~ que conozco eso yo** I know that well enough **2.**(*presumido*) self-important, smug **3.**(*pedante*) pedantic II. *m* ENS (*nota*) pass

sufijo *m* suffix

suflé *m* GASTR soufflé

sufragar <g→gu> I. *vt* **1.**(*ayudar*) to aid **2.**(*costear: gastos*) to meet; (*tasa*) to pay; (*beca*) to finance II. *vi AmL* (*votar*) **~ por alguien** to vote for sb

sufragio *m* **1.**(*voto*) vote **2.**(*derecho*) suffrage; **~ universal** universal suffrage **3.**(*sistema*) election **4.** REL suffrage

sufrible *adj* bearable

sufrido, -a *adj* **1.**(*persona*) patient, uncomplaining; **eres demasiado ~** you're too long-suffering **2.**(*color*) fast; **una tela sufrida** a hard-wearing material **3.**(*marido*) complaisant

sufrimiento *m* **1.**(*acción*) suffering **2.**(*moral*) tolerance; (*físico*) toughness

sufrir *vt* **1.**(*aguantar*) to bear; (*peso*) to support; (*a alguien*) to put up with **2.**(*padecer*) to suffer; **~ de celos** to suffer from jealousy; **~ de la espalda** to have back trouble; **~ persecuciones** to be persecuted; **~ quejas** to receive complaints; **~ las consecuencias** to suffer the consequences **3.**(*experimentar: cambio*) to undergo; (*examen*) to take; (*desengaño, accidente*) to have; (*pena*) to be stricken with; **~ una operación** to have an operation

sugerencia *f* **1.**(*propuesta*) suggestion **2.**(*recomendación*) recommendation **3.**(*inspiración*) inspiration

sugerir *irr como sentir vt* **1.**(*proponer*) to suggest **2.**(*insinuar*) to hint **3.**(*evocar*) to prompt **4.**(*inspirar*) to inspire

sugestión *f* **1.**(*de sugestionar*) hypnotic power **2.**(*propuesta*) suggestion **3.**(*inspiración*) inspiration

sugestionar I. *vt* (*influenciar*) to influence; (*dominar*) to dominate II. *vr:* **~se** to indulge in autosuggestion

sugestivo, -a *adj* **1.**(*que sugiere*) evocative **2.**(*que influencia*) thought-provoking **3.**(*plan*) attractive

suiche *m Méx* (*botón*) switch; (*de un coche*) ignition key

suicida I. *adj* suicidal II. *mf* **1.**(*muerto*) person

who has committed suicide **2.**(*loco*) suicidal person

suicidarse *vr* to commit suicide

suicidio *m* suicide; **intento de ~** suicide attempt

suite *f* suite; **~ nupcial** bridal suite

Suiza *f* Switzerland

suizo *m* GASTR sweet bun

suizo, -a I. *adj* Swiss; **chocolate ~** Swiss chocolate II. *m, f* Swiss

suje *m inf* bra

sujeción *f* **1.**(*dominio*) domination; (*sometimiento*) subjection; (*dependencia*) dependency **2.**(*agarre*) hold **3.**(*aseguramiento*) support **4.**(*a un convenio, una promesa*) binding

sujetador *m* **1.**(*sostén*) bra **2.**(*del bikini*) fastener

sujetapapeles *m inv* paperclip

sujetar I. *vt* **1.**(*agarrar*) **~ por algo** to seize by sth **2.**(*dominar*) to dominate **3.**(*someter*) to subject **4.**(*asegurar*) to support; (*pelo*) to hold in place; (*con clavos*) to nail down; (*con tornillos*) to screw down II. *vr:* **~se 1.**(*agarrarse*) to subject oneself **2.**(*a reglamento*) **~se a algo** to abide by sth

sujeto *m* **1.**(*tema*) subject **2.** *pey* (*individuo*) individual

sujeto, -a *adj* (*expuesto a*) subject; **~ a comprobación** subject to checking; **~ a la inflación** affected by inflation; **estar ~ a fluctuaciones** to be subject to fluctuation

sulfato *m* sulphate *Brit,* sulfate *Am*

sulfurar I. *vt* **1.**(*con azufre*) to sulphurate *Brit,* to sulfurate *Am* **2.**(*exasperar*) to infuriate II. *vr* **~se por algo/alguien** to get mad about sth/at sb

sulfúrico, -a *adj* sulphuric *Brit,* sulfuric *Am*

sulfuro *m* sulphide *Brit,* sulfide *Am*

sultán, -ana *m, f* sultan *m,* sultana *f*

suma *f* **1.** MAT (*acción*) adding (up); (*resultado*) total; **~ y sigue** (*cuenta*) carried forward; *fig* it's still going on; **en ~** in short **2.**(*cantidad*) sum **3.**(*esencia*) summary

sumamente *adv* extremely

sumar I. *vt* **1.** MAT to add (up) **2.**(*una obra*) to gather; (*hechos*) to summarize II. *vr:* **~se** (*a una manifestación, a una idea*) to join; (*a una discusión*) to participate in

sumario *m* **1.** JUR committal proceedings *pl* **2.**(*resumen*) summary

sumario, -a *adj* **1.**(*explicación*) concise **2.** JUR **juicio ~** summary trial

sumergible I. *adj* **1.**(*reloj*) waterproof **2.**(*submarino*) submersible II. *m* submarine

sumergir <g→j> I. *vt* to submerge II. *vr:* **~se** to submerge

sumidero *m* (*rejilla*) drain; (*de la calle*) sewer

sumiller *m* wine waiter

suministrador(a) *m(f)* supplier

suministrar *vt* **1.** *t.* COM (*datos, información*) to supply **2.**(*abastecer*) to stock **3.**(*facilitar*) to supply

suministro *m* **1.** *t.* COM (*de datos, infor*

mación) supply **2.**(abastecimiento) stock **3.** pl MIL supplies pl

sumir I. vt (hundir) to sink; ~ **en la miseria a alguien** to plunge sb into poverty **II.** vr: ~**se** to sink; ~**se en el trabajo** to become absorbed in one's work

sumisión f **1.**(acción) submission **2.**(carácter) submissiveness **3.**(obediencia) obedience

sumiso, -a adj **1.**(que se somete) submissive **2.**(que no rechista) uncomplaining

sumo, -a adj **1.**(más alto) high(est); ~ **sacerdote** high priest; **a lo ~** at most; **en grado ~** highly **2.**(mayor) great

sunco, -a I. adj Chile (de un brazo) one--armed; (de una mano) one-handed **II.** m, f Chile (de un brazo) one-armed person; (de una mano) one-handed person

sungo, -a adj Col (de raza negra) Black

suntuario, -a adj sumptuary

suntuosidad f **1.**(lujo) sumptuousness **2.**(opulencia) lavishness **3.**(aparatosidad) magnificence

suntuoso, -a adj **1.**(lujoso) sumptuous **2.**(opulento) lavish **3.**(aparatoso) magnificent

supeditar I. vt **1.**(subordinar) to subordinate **2.**(someter) to subdue **3.**(condicionar) to condition **II.** vr: ~**se** to submit

súper¹ I. adj inf super **II.** m supermarket

súper² f four-star petrol Brit, Premium (gas) Am

superable adj **1.**(récord) beatable **2.**(situación) surmountable

superabundancia f (en cantidad) superabundance; (en diversidad) great variety

superabundante adj superabundant; (negativo) excessive

superación f **1.**(de récord) improvement **2.**(de situación) surmounting

superar I. vt **1.**(sobrepasar: a alguien) to surpass; (límite) to exceed; (récord) to beat; ~ **todo lo que se había visto hasta ahora** to go beyond anything seen before **2.**(prueba) to pass **3.**(situación) to overcome **II.** vr: ~**se** to excel oneself

superávit m <superávit(s)> surplus

superchería f (engaño) fraud; (mentira) deceit

superdotado, -a adj extremely gifted

superferolítico, -a adj inf affected

superficial adj superficial; (detalle) minor; **herida ~** flesh wound

superficialidad f superficiality

superficie f **1.**(parte externa) surface; ~ **cultivable** arable area; **salir a la ~** (submarino) to surface; (minero) to come to the surface; fig to come to light **2.** MAT surface; (área) surface area **3.**(apariencia) external appearance

superfluo, -a adj superfluous; (gastos) unnecessary

superhombre m superman

superintendente mf supervisor; (de policía) superintendent

superior adj **1.**(más alto) higher; **el curso ~ de un río** the upper course of a river; **el piso ~ al mío** the flat Brit [o the apartment Am] above mine **2.**(en calidad) better; (en inteligencia, rango) superior **3.**(excelente) excellent; **mujer ~** superwoman

superior(a) m(f) superior

superioridad f superiority; ~ **sobre alguien** superiority over sb; **hablar con un tono de ~** to speak in a superior tone of voice

superlativo m LING superlative

superlativo, -a adj t. LING superlative

supermercado m supermarket

supermoderno, -a adj ultra-modern

supernumerario, -a I. adj **1.**(número) surplus **2.**(funcionario) supernumerary **II.** m, f supernumerary

superpetrolero m supertanker

superpoblación f overpopulation

superponer irr como poner vt **1.**(dos cosas) to superimpose; ~ **algo a algo** to superimpose sth on sth **2.**(dar prioridad) to give more importance to

superpotencia f superpower **superproducción** f **1.** COM overproduction **2.** CINE big--budget movie

supersónico, -a adj supersonic

superstición f superstition

supersticioso, -a adj superstitious

supervalorar vt to overvalue

superventas m inv bestseller; **lista de ~** MÚS charts pl

supervisar vt to supervise; (en un examen) to invigilate

supervisión f **1.**(vigilancia) supervision **2.**(en examen) invigilation

supervisor(a) m(f) supervisor; (funcionario) inspector

supervivencia f survival

superviviente I. adj surviving **II.** mf survivor

supino, -a adj **1.**(posición) supine **2.**(excesivo) **ignorancia supina** abject ignorance

suplantar vt **1.**(en el trabajo) to supplant **2.**(escrito) to forge

suplementario, -a adj supplementary; **tomo ~** additional volume

suplementero m Chile newspaper vendor

suplemento m **1.**(complemento) supplement **2.**(tomo) supplementary volume **3.**(de periódico) ~ **en color** colour supplement Brit, color supplement Am **4.**(precio) extra charge; (del tren) excess fare; (plus) bonus; ~ **por turnos** shift bonus

suplencia f substitution

suplente I. adj substitute; **maestro ~** supply teacher Brit, substitute teacher Am **II.** mf t. DEP substitute

supletorio m TEL extension

supletorio, -a adj supplementary; **cama supletoria** extra [o spare] bed

súplica f plea; (escrito) request; JUR petition

suplicar <c→qu> vt **1.**(rogar) to implore; ~

algo de rodillas to beg on one's knees for sth **2.** JUR ~ algo to appeal against sth
suplicio *m* **1.** (*tortura*) torture **2.** (*tormento*) torment; **el viaje fue un** ~ we had a terrible journey
suplir *vt* **1.** (*completar*) to make up for **2.** (*sustituir*) to substitute; ~ **el bolígrafo por un lápiz** to change the pen for a pencil **3.** (*en el trabajo*) to replace
supo *3. pret de* **saber**
suponer *irr como poner vt* **1.** (*dar por sentado*) to suppose; **vamos a** ~ **que...** let's suppose that ...; **se supone que...** it is assumed that ...; **suponiendo que...** supposing that ...; **supongamos que...** let us assume that ...; **dar algo por supuesto** to take sth for granted **2.** (*figurar*) to imagine; **supongo que vendrá Gema, no?** – supongo que sí I imagine Gema will come, won't she? – I suppose so; **no supongo que** +subj I don't imagine; **puedes** ~ **que...** you can imagine that ...; **¿estás suponiendo que...?** are you assuming that ...? **3.** (*atribuir*) le supongo unos 40 años I imagine him/her to be about 40; **no le suponía tan fuerte** I didn't realize he/she was so strong **4.** (*significar*) to mean; ~ un duro golpe para alguien to be a real blow for sb; **esto me supone 60 euros al mes** this amounts to 60 euros a month for me; **no** ~ **molestia alguna** to be no trouble
suposición *f* supposition; (*presunción*) assumption
supositorio *m* MED suppository
supremacía *f* **1.** (*superioridad*) supremacy **2.** (*prioridad*) priority
supremo, -a *adj* (*altísimo*) highest; *fig* supreme; **el instante** ~ the culminating moment; **el Tribunal Supremo** the Supreme Court
supresión *f* **1.** (*eliminación*) suppression; (*de fronteras*) elimination; (*de obstáculos*) removal; (*de una regla*) abolition **2.** (*omisión*) omission
suprimir *vt* **1.** (*poner fin*) to suppress; (*fronteras*) to eliminate; (*controles, obstáculos, amenaza*) to remove; (*regla*) to abolish **2.** (*omitir*) to omit **3.** (*silenciar*) to silence
supuesto *m* **1.** (*suposición*) assumption, supposition **2.** (*hipótesis*) hypothesis
supuesto, -a *adj* (*ladrón, asesino*) alleged; (*testigo, nombre*) assumed; (*causa*) supposed; **por** ~ of course; **dar algo por** ~ to take sth for granted; (*pretendido*) so-called; ~ **que** since, as
supurar *vi* MED to suppurate
sur *m* **1.** (*punto*) south; **el** ~ **de España** the south of Spain **2.** (*viento*) south wind
surafricano, -a *adj, m, f* South African
surazo *m Arg, Bol* (*viento*) strong southerly wind
surcar <c→qu> *vt* **1.** (*tierra*) to plough *Brit,* to plow *Am* **2.** elev (*mar*) ~ **el mar** to sail the seas

surco *m* **1.** (*en tierra*) furrow **2.** (*arruga*) wrinkle **3.** (*en disco*) groove
sureste *m* south-east
surf *m* DEP *sin pl* surfing; **hacer** ~ to windsurf
surfear *vi* to windsurf; INFOR to surf
surfista *mf* surfer; INFOR Internet surfer
surgir <g→j> *vi* **1.** (*agua*) to gush **2.** (*aparecer: dificultad, posibilidad*) to arise; (*pregunta*) to come up; (*persona*) to appear unexpectedly **3.** (*edificio*) to rise up
suroeste *m* south-west
surrealismo *m sin pl* ARTE surrealism
surrealista *adj, mf* surrealist
surtido *m* selection, assortment
surtido, -a *adj* **1.** (*mezclado*) mixed; **galletas surtidas** assorted biscuits **2.** (*variado*) varied **3.** (*bien provisto*) well-stocked
surtidor *m* **1.** (*lugar*) petrol [*o* filling] station *Brit,* gas station *Am* **2.** (*aparato*) petrol pump *Brit,* gas pump *Am* **3.** (*chorro*) jet; (*fuente*) fountain
surtir **I.** *vt* **1.** (*proveer*) ~ **de algo** to supply with sth **2.** (*tener*) ~ **efecto** (*palabras*) to have the desired effect; (*medicamento*) to work **II.** *vi* to spout **III.** *vr* ~**se de algo** to provide oneself with sth
suruco *m CSur, vulg* shit, crap
surumbo, -a *adj Guat, Hond* stunned
surupa *f Ven* (*cucaracha*) cockroach
susceptibilidad *f* (*sensibilidad*) *t.* MED susceptibility
susceptible *adj* **1.** (*cosa*) ~ **de mejora** capable of improvement; **materiales** ~**s de ser reutilizados** material which can be reused **2.** (*persona: sensible*) sensitive; (*irritable*) touchy
suscitar *vt* (*sospecha, discordia*) to cause; (*discusión*) to start; (*escándalo, comentarios*) to provoke; (*odio, conflicto*) to stir up; (*problema*) to raise; (*antipatías, curiosidad*) to arouse
suscribir *irr como escribir* **I.** *vt* **1.** (*escrito*) to sign **2.** (*opinión*) to endorse **3.** (*acciones*) to take out an option on **II.** *vr* ~**se a una revista** to subscribe to a magazine
suscripción *f* **1.** (*firma*) signature **2.** (*de acciones*) taking up **3.** (*a una revista*) subscription
suscri(p)tor(a) *m(f)* **1.** (*firmante*) signatory **2.** (*de acciones*) subscriber **3.** (*de una revista*) subscriber
susodicho, -a *adj* (*dicho arriba*) above-mentioned; (*dicho antes*) aforementioned
suspender *vt* **1.** (*tener en el aire*) ~ **de algo** to hang from sth **2.** (*trabajador, deportista*) to suspend **3.** (*en un examen*) to fail; **he suspendido matemáticas** I've failed maths *Brit,* I've flunked math *Am* **4.** (*interrumpir: sesión*) to adjourn; (*tratamiento*) to break off; (*embargo*) to lift; (*servicio*) to discontinue; ~ **las disputas** to end the dispute; **se ha suspendido la función de esta noche** tonight's show has been called off **5.** (*embelesar*) to astonish

suspense *m* suspense; **una película/novela de ~** a thriller

suspensión *f* **1.** (*acción de colgar*) suspension **2.** (*interrupción: de sesión*) adjournment; (*de tratamiento*) interruption; (*de disputas*) end; (*de producción*) break; (*de embargo*) lifting; **~ de armas** truce; **~ de la pena** annulment of the penalty; **~ de pagos** temporary receivership, suspension of payment

suspensivo, -a *adj* **puntos ~s** suspension points

suspenso *m* **1.** ENS fail; **sacar un ~** to fail, to flunk *Am* **2.** *AmL v.* **suspense**

suspenso, -a *adj* (*perplejo*) perplexed

suspensores *mpl AmL* (*tiradores*) braces *pl Brit*, suspenders *pl Am*

suspensorio *m* DEP athletic support, jockstrap

suspicacia *f* suspicion

suspicaz *adj* suspicious

suspirado, -a *adj* longed-for

suspirar *vi* **1.** (*dar suspiros*) to sigh **2.** (*anhelar*) **~ por algo** to long for sth

suspiro *m* (*de persona*) sigh; (*del viento*) breath

sustancia *f* **1.** (*materia, esencia*) substance; **~ activa** active ingredient; **~ gris** ANAT grey matter *Brit*, gray matter *Am*; **en ~** in essence; **este ensayo no tiene ~** this essay is lacking in substance **2.** (*de alimentos*) stock **3.** (*juicio*) **un fundamento sin ~** an unconvincing reason; **decir cosas sin ~** to say superficial things; **un comentario sin ~** a shallow commentary

sustancial *adj* **1.** (*esencial*) vital; (*fundamental*) essential **2.** (*comida*) substantial **3.** (*libro*) meaty

sustancioso, -a *adj* **1.** (*comida*) substantial **2.** (*libro*) meaty

sustantivo *m* noun

sustantivo, -a *adj* **1.** (*esencial*) vital; (*fundamental*) essential **2.** LING nominal

sustentáculo *m* sustenance

sustentar **I.** *vt* **1.** (*una cosa*) to hold up; (*columna*) to support **2.** (*esperanza*) to sustain **3.** (*familia*) to feed **II.** *vr:* **~se 1.** (*alimentarse*) to sustain oneself **2.** (*aguantarse*) **~se en algo** to rely on sth

sustento *m* **1.** (*mantenimiento*) maintenance **2.** (*apoyo*) support

sustitución *f* replacement; (*temporal*) substitution

sustituir *irr como huir vt t.* DEP to substitute; **~ a alguien** (*temporalmente*) to stand in for sb; (*definitivamente*) to replace sb

sustitutivo *m* substitute

sustitutivo, -a *adj* substitute

sustituto, -a *m, f* substitute, replacement

susto *m* scare; **poner cara de ~** to look scared; **darle un ~ a alguien** to give sb a fright; **pegarse** [*o* **llevarse**] **un ~** to get scared; **pegarle un ~ a alguien** to scare sb; **no ganar para ~s** to have one problem after another

sustraer *irr como traer* **I.** *vt* **1.** (*restar*) to sub-

tract **2.** (*robar*) to steal **3.** (*privar*) to remove **4.** (*separar*) to abduct **II.** *vr* **~se de algo** to get away from sth; **~se de los periodistas** to avoid the journalists

susurrar **I.** *vi* **1.** (*hablar bajo*) to whisper; (*no claro*) to mutter; **~ algo a alguien** to whisper sth to sb **2.** (*viento*) to murmur **II.** *vr:* **~se** to be rumoured *Brit*, to be rumored *Am* **III.** *vimpers* **se susurra que...** it is rumoured that ... *Brit*, it is rumored that ... *Am*

susurro *m* **1.** (*al hablar: bajo*) whisper; (*no claro*) mutter **2.** (*del viento*) murmur

sutil *adj* **1.** (*velo, hilo*) delicate; (*rebanada*) thin **2.** (*sabor*) subtle; (*aroma*) delicate **3.** (*diferencia, ironía*) fine; (*jugada, sistema*) refined **4.** (*persona*) sharp

sutileza *f*, **sutilidad** *f* **1.** (*de velo, hilo*) delicacy **2.** (*de sabor*) subtlety; (*de aroma*) delicacy **3.** (*de diferencia, ironía*) fineness; (*de jugada, sistema*) refinement **4.** (*de persona*) sharpness

sutilizar <z→c> *vt* **1.** (*hacer sutil*) to refine **2.** (*diferencia*) to quibble about; (*jugada*) to perfect **3.** (*discurrir*) to analyse *Brit*, to analyze *Am*

sutura *f* MED suture; **punto de ~** stitch

suturar *vt* to stitch

suyo, -a *adj, pron* (*de él*) his; (*de ella*) hers; (*de cosa, animal*) its; (*de ellos*) theirs; (*de Ud., Uds.*) yours; (*de uno*) one's; **este encendedor es ~** this lighter is his/hers; **siempre habla de los ~s** he/she is always talking about his/her family; **~ afectísimo** yours truly; **darle a alguien lo ~** to give sb what belongs to him/her; *fig* to give sb what he/she deserves; **ya ha hecho otra de las suyas** *inf* he/she has been up to his/her tricks again; **leer Hamlet tiene lo ~** (*es difícil*) reading Hamlet is not easy; (*es interesante*) reading Hamlet is rewarding; **el problema es ya de ~ difícil de resolver** (by its nature) the problem is hard to solve; **hacer suyas las quejas de los alumnos** to echo the pupils' complaints; **Albert es muy ~** Albert keeps to himself; **eso es muy ~** that's typical of him/her; **ir a lo ~** to go one's own way

swazilandés, -esa **I.** *adj* of/from Swaziland **II.** *m, f* native/inhabitant of Swaziland

Swazilandia *f* Swaziland

T

T, t *f* T, t; **~ de Tarragona** T for Tommy *Brit*, T for Tare *Am*

taba *f* **1.** ANAT anklebone; **menear las ~s** *inf* (*andar*) to get a move on; *fig* to shake a leg **2.** (*juego*) **jugar a las tabas** to play jacks

tabacal *m AmL* tobacco plantation

tabacalero, -a **I.** *adj* tobacco brown **II.** *m, f* tobacco grower

tabaco *m* 1.(*planta, producto*) tobacco; **de color** ~ tobacco; ~ **rubio** Virginia tobacco; ~ **de mascar** chewing tobacco 2.(*cigarrillo*) cigarettes *pl;* (*cigarro, puro*) cigar; ¿**tienes** ~? do you have any cigarettes?

tabalear I. *vt, vr:* ~**se** to rock to and fro II. *vi* to drum (with the fingers)

tabanco *m AmC* (*desván*) attic

tábano *m* 1.ZOOL horsefly 2.(*persona*) nuisance

tabaquera *f* tobacco pouch

tabardo *m* tabard

tabarra *f inf* nuisance; **dar la** ~ to pester, to bug

taberna *f* tavern, bar

tabernáculo *m* (*sagrario*) tabernacle

tabernario, -a *adj* 1.(*de la taberna*) tavern 2. *pey* coarse

tabernero, -a *m, f* (*dueño*) landlord; (*camarero*) barman, tavernkeeper *liter*

tabicar <c→qu> I. *vt* to partition II. *vr:* ~**se** to get stopped up

tabique *m* partition; ~ **nasal** nasal septum

tabla *f* 1.(*plancha*) board; ~ **de cocina** cutting board; ~ **de planchar** ironing board; **ser la única** ~ **de salvación** *fig* to be the last resort; ~ **de surf** surfboard; ~ **de windsurf** sailboard 2.(*de libro*) table of contents 3.(*lista*) list; (*cuadro*) table; **las Tablas de la Ley** the Tables of the Law; **decir la** ~ to recite the multiplication table 4.(*de vestido*) pleat 5.(*pintura*) panel 6.AGR (*para plantas*) garden patch; (*más grande*) plot 7. *pl* DEP draw, tie 8. *pl* TEAT stage 9. *pl* (*experiencia*) **un político con muchas** ~**s** an experienced politician ▸**a raja** ~ to the letter; **hacer** ~ **rasa de algo** to wipe the slate clean

tablada *f* 1.*CSur* (*lugar*) stockyard 2.*Par* (*matadero*) slaughterhouse

tablado *m* 1.(*suelo*) plank floor 2.(*entarimado*) wooden platform 3.(*del escenario*) stage

tablao *m* 1.(*escenario*) stage 2.(*sitio*) bar or place where a Flamenco show is performed

tablear *vt* 1.(*madero*) to cut into boards 2.(*tela*) to pleat 3.(*terreno*) to level 4.(*tierra*) to divide into plots

tablero *m* 1.(*de madera*) board; ~ **de anuncios** notice board *Brit,* bulletin board *Am* 2.(*pizarra*) blackboard 3.DEP ~ **de ajedrez** chess board; ~ **de damas** draught board *Brit,* checkers board *Am* 4.(*de mesa*) table top 5.AUTO dashboard 6.AVIAT ~ **de mandos** instrument panel 7.(*ábaco*) abacus

tableta *f* 1.(*de chocolate*) bar 2.MED tablet 3.(*papel*) (writing) pad, notepad

tabletear *vi* (*puerta*) to rattle; (*máquina*) to clack

tabloide *m AmL* tabloid

tablón *m* 1.(*de andamio*) plank; (*de anuncios*) notice board *Brit,* bulletin board *Am* 2. *inf* (*borrachera*) **coger** [*o* **agarrar**] **un** ~ to

get smashed 3.*AmL* (*para plantas*) patch; (*más grande*) plot

tabú *m* <tabúes> taboo

tabuco *m pey* hovel

tabulador *m* (*tecla*) tab

tabular *vt* (*listar*) to tabulate

tabular *m* stool

tacada *f* 1.(*golpe*) shot; **de una** ~ all in one go 2.(*carambolas*) break

tacañear *vi* to be stingy

tacañería *f* stinginess, miserliness

tacaño, -a I. *adj* stingy, mean *Brit* II. *m, f* miser, tightwad *Am, inf*

tacataca *m* baby-walker

tacha *f* 1.(*defecto*) blemish; **sin** ~ flawless; **es un joven sin** ~ he is an upright young man; **una reputación sin** ~ an untarnished reputation; **un diamante sin** ~ a flawless diamond 2.(*tachuela*) large tack

tachadura *f* 1.(*acción*) crossing out 2.(*tachón*) correction, erasure

tachar *vt* 1.(*rayar*) to cross out 2.(*atribuir*) ~ **de algo** to brand as sth 3.(*acusar*) to accuse; **le** ~**on de incompetencia** they accused him of being incompetent

tachero *m Arg, inf* (*taxista*) taxi driver

tacho *m* 1.*AmL* (*vasija*) metal basin 2.*AmL* (*hojalata*) tin 3.*AmL* (*cubo*) dustbin *Brit,* garbage can *Am* 4.*Arg, inf* (*taxi*) taxi ▸**irse al** ~ *Arg, inf* to collapse

tachón *m* 1.(*borrón*) crossing out 2.(*tachuela*) large stud

tachonado, -a *adj* ~ **de estrellas** star-studded

tachonar *vt* 1.(*clavetear*) to stud 2.(*adornar*) to dot

tachuela *f* (*clavo*) tack; (*ropa*) stud

tácito, -a *adj* tacit

taciturno, -a *adj* 1.(*callado*) taciturn 2.(*melancólico*) melancholy, glum

taco *m* 1.(*pedazo*) piece; ~**s de salida** DEP starting block 2.(*de arma*) wad 3.(*de billar*) cue 4.(*de bota*) stud; ~ **de rosca** screw-in stud 5.(*de papel*) pad; (*calendario*) tear-off desk, calendar; (*fajo*) wad 6.(*de jamón*) cube; (*bocado*) bite to eat 7.TÉC plug; (*para tornillo*) Rawlplug® 8. *inf* (*palabrota*) swearword, four-letter word; **decir** [*o* **soltar**] ~**s** to swear 9. *inf* (*lío*) mess; **estar hecho un** ~ to be all mixed up 10.*AmL* (*tacón*) heel 11. *pl inf* (*años*) years; **¡ya tengo mis 40** ~**s!** I'm already past 40!

tacómetro *m* TÉC tachometer

tacón *m* heel; ~ **de aguja** spike heel; **zapatos de** ~ **alto** high-heel(ed) shoes

taconear *vi* 1.(*suelo*) to tap one's heel 2.(*arrogantemente*) to strut

taconeo *m* heel clicking; (*andar*) noisy walking

táctica *f* tactic(s); **ir con** ~ to move strategically

táctico, -a I. *adj* tactical II. *m, f* tactician

táctil *adj* tactile

tacto *m* 1. (*sentido*) sense of touch; **al** ~ to the touch; **ser áspero al** ~ to feel rough 2. (*contacto*) touch 3. (*habilidad*) tact; **no tener** ~ to be tactless

tacuache *m Cuba, Méx* ZOOL (*Solenodon*) almique

tacuaco, -a *adj Chile* (*rechoncho*) chubby

tafetán *m* (*tela*) taffeta

tahona *f* (*panadería*) bakery

tahonero, -a *m, f* baker

tahúr *m* cardsharp; (*tramposo*) cheat

taifa *f geopolitical unit during Muslim domination of Spain*

tailandés, -esa *adj, m, f* Thai

Tailandia *f* Thailand

taimado, -a *adj* (*maligno*) sly, crafty

taita *m* 1. *CSur* expert 2. *Arg* (*matón*) bully, tough 3. *Ven* (*jefe de familia*) head of the family

Taiwán *m* Taiwan

taiwanés, -esa *adj, m, f* Taiwanese

tajada *f* 1. (*porción*) slice; **llevarse la mejor** ~ to take the lion's share; **sacar** ~ **de algo** to get something out of sth 2. *inf* (*ronquera*) **tener una** ~ to be hoarse 3. *inf* (*borrachera*) **anoche pilló una buena** ~ last night he/she got smashed 4. (*corte*) cut

tajamar *m* 1. (*espolón*) dike [*o* dyke] 2. (*de puente*) cutwater

tajante *adj* 1. (*respuesta*) categorical; (*actitud*) dogmatic; (*medidas*) unequivocal 2. (*absoluto*) in no uncertain terms 3. (*cortante*) sharp

tajar *vt* 1. (*cortar*) to cut; (*en lonchas*) to slice; (*trocear*) to chop 2. *AmL* (*afilar*) to sharpen

tajo *m* 1. (*corte*) cut; **darse un** ~ **en el dedo** to cut one's finger 2. GEO gorge 3. (*filo*) cutting edge 4. *inf* (*trabajo*) work; **ir al** ~ to go to work 5. (*de carnicero*) butcher's block; (*para decapitar*) executioner's block 6. (*mín*) face 7. (*taburete*) three-legged stool

tal I. *adj* 1. (*igual*) such; ~ **día hace un año** a day like this a year ago; **en** ~ **caso** in that case; **no digas** ~ **cosa** don't say any such thing; **no he dicho nunca** ~ **cosa** I never said anything of the kind 2. (*tanto*) so; **la distancia es** ~ **que...** it's so far away that ..., it's such a long way that ... 3. (*cierto*) certain; **un** ~ **Pérez... llamó...** somebody called Perez phoned ... **II.** *pron* 1. (*alguien*) ~ **habrá que piense así** there's bound to be sb who thinks so; **el** ~ **que** that fellow; ~ **o cual** someone or other; **¡ése es otro que** ~! he's another one! 2. (*cosa*) **no haré** ~ I won't do anything of the sort; **¡no hay** ~! there's no such thing!; **hablar de** ~ **y cual** to talk about one thing and another; **... y** ~ **y cual** (*enumeración*) and so on and so forth **III.** *adv* 1. (*así*) so 2. (*de la misma manera*) just; **es** ~ **cual lo buscaba** it's just what I was looking for; **son** ~ **para cual** they're two of a kind, they're made for each other; **estar** ~ **cual** to be just as it was; **lo dejé** ~ **cual** I left it just as I found it; ~ **y como** just as; ~ **y como**

suena just as I'm telling you 3. (*cómo*) **¿qué** ~ **(te va)?** how are things?; **¿qué** ~ **el viaje?** how was the trip?; **¿qué** ~ **te lo has pasado?** did you have a good time?; **¿qué** ~ **si tomamos una copa?** why don't we have sth to drink?; **¿qué** ~ **es tu nuevo jefe?** what's your new boss like?; ~ **y como están las cosas** the way things are now **IV.** *conj* **con** ~ **de** +*infin*, **con** ~ **de que** +*subj* (*mientras*) as long as; (*condición*) provided; ~ **vez** (*quizás*) perhaps, maybe

tala *f* 1. (*de árboles*) felling 2. (*destrucción*) destruction

taladradora *f* pneumatic drill

taladrar *vt* 1. (*con taladro*) to drill 2. (*oídos*) to pierce; **un ruido que taladra los oídos** an ear-splitting noise

taladro *m* drill; (*agujero*) (drill) hole

tálamo *m* 1. ANAT thalamus 2. *elev* (*lecho*) nuptial bed

talamoco, -a *adj Ecua* albino

talante *m* 1. (*modo*) disposition 2. (*humor*) mood; **de buen/mal** ~ good-/ill-tempered 3. (*gana*) **de buen** ~ willingly

talar I. *adj* **túnica** ~ full-length tunic **II.** *vt* 1. (*árboles*) to fell 2. (*destruir*) to lay waste

talco *m* 1. (*mineral*) talc 2. (*polvos*) talcum powder

talega *f* 1. (*bolsa*) bag 2. *inf* (*dinero*) dosh *Brit*, bread

talego *m* 1. (*talega*) sack 2. *inf* (*persona*) fat person 3. *inf* (*cárcel*) nick *Brit*, slammer *Am*

talento *m* (*capacidad*) talent; **de gran** ~ very talented; **tener** ~ **para los idiomas** to have a gift for languages

talentoso, -a *adj* talented

talero *m Arg, Chile, Urug* whip

Talgo *m abr de* **Tren Articulado Ligero Goicoechea Oriol** *high speed light articulated train of Spanish invention for intercity passenger transportation*

talismán *m* talisman, lucky charm

talla *f* 1. (*de diamante*) cutting 2. (*en madera*) carving; (*en piedra*) sculpting 3. (*estatura*) height; **ser de poca** ~ to be short; **no dar la** ~ MIL not to be qualified; *fig* not to be good enough 4. (*medidor*) measuring stick 5. (*de vestido*) size; **un abrigo de la** ~ **42** a size 42 coat 6. (*moral, intelectual*) stature

tallaje *m* sizes *pl*, sizing

tallar *vt* 1. (*diamante*) to cut 2. (*madera*) to carve; (*en piedra*) to sculpt 3. (*la estatura*) to measure the height of 4. (*en juego*) to deal

tallarín *m* noodle

talle *m* 1. (*cintura, del vestido*) waist 2. (*figura*) figure

taller *m* 1. TÉC workshop; ~ **artesanal** craft workshop; ~**es gráficos** printing works 2. (*seminario*) seminar 3. (*estudio*) studio 4. (*auto*) garage

tallo *m* 1. BOT stem, stalk 2. (*renuevo*) shoot, sprout

talludo, -a *adj* 1. BOT tall 2. (*mayor*) grown-up

3. (*espigado*) lanky

talón *m* **1.** (*del pie, zapato, calcetín*) heel; **pisar a alguien los talones** *inf* (*perseguir*) to be hot on sb's heels; (*emular*) to follow in sb's footsteps; **~ de Aquiles** Achilles' heel; *fig* weak point **2.** (*cheque*) cheque *Brit,* check *Am;* **hazme un ~ de 10.000 pts.** make me out a cheque for 10000 pesetas; **~ sin fondos** bad [*o* bounced] cheque **3.** (*resguardo*) voucher; (*recibo*) receipt

talonario *m* **1.** (*de cheques*) chequebook *Brit,* checkbook *Am* **2.** (*de recibos*) receipt book

talud *m* slope

tamal *m AmC, Méx* tamale (*dish made of cornmeal, meat or chicken, and chili wrapped in corn husks or banana leaves*)

tamalada *f Méx* GASTR tamale party

tamango *m CSur* (*calzado*) coarse leather shoe

tamaño *m* **1.** (*medida*) size; **de ~ natural** life size; **¿de qué ~ es?** what size is it?, how big is it?; **de gran~** large **2.** (*formato*) size; **en ~ grande** large size; **en ~ bolsillo** pocket size

tamaño, -a *adj* **1.** (*grande*) such a big, so big a **2.** (*pequeño*) such a small, so small a **3.** (*semejante*) such a; **tamaña tontería** such a stupid thing; **sólo a tí se te ocurre ~ disparate** only you would think of such an absurd idea

tamarindo *m* tamarind

tambache *m Méx, inf* bundle; **un ~ de ropa/ de hojas de papel** a pile of clothes/of papers; **hacer ~ a alguien** (*to play a dirty trick on sb*)

tambalear *vi, vr:* **~se** to stagger; *fig* to totter

tambarria *f Perú* (*fiesta*) party

tambembe *m Chile* (*trasero*) bottom, butt *inf*

tambero, -a **I.** *adj Arg* dairy; **vaca tambera** milking cow **II.** *m, f Arg* (*ganado manso*) tame livestock; (*vaca lechera*) milk cow

también *adv* also, as well, too; **yo lo ví ~** I also saw him, I saw him too [*o* as well]

tambocha *f Col, Ven* (*hormiga*) poisonous red-headed ant

tambor *m* **1.** (*cilindro, instrumento*) drum; **tocar el ~** to play the drum; **proclamar algo a ~ batiente** to proclaim sth triumphantly **2.** (*músico*) drummer **3.** ANAT eardrum

tamboril *m* MÚS small drum

tamborilear *vi* **1.** (*tocar*) to play the drum **2.** (*con dedos*) to drum, to tap

Támesis *m* **el ~** the Thames

tamiz *m* sieve, sifter; **pasar por el ~** to sift

tamizar <z→c> *vt* to sift, to sieve; *fig* to screen

tampoco *adv* not either, nor, neither; **ni puedo ni ~ quiero** I neither can nor do I want to; **~ me gusta éste** I don't like this one either; **si tú no lo haces yo ~** if you don't do it, neither will I

tampón *m* **1.** (*de tinta*) ink pad **2.** (*para la mujer*) tampon

tamuga *f* **1.** *AmC* (*fardo*) bundle; (*mochila*) knapsack **2.** *AmL* (*marihuana*) joint, reefer *inf*

tan *adv* so; **~... como...** as ... as ...; **~ es así**

que no he podido hacerlo so much so that I haven't been able to do it; **de ~ simpático me resulta insoportable** he/she is so nice I find him/her unbearable; **~ siquiera una vez** just once; **ni ~ siquiera** not even; **ni ~ siquiera han llamado** they haven't even called

tanate *m* **1.** *AmC, Méx* (*cesto*) pannier **2.** *AmC* (*fardo*) bundle **3.** *pl, Méx, vulg* (*testículos*) balls *pl* **4.** *pl, AmC* (*cachivaches*) gear, stuff

tanatorio *m* funeral parlour *Brit,* funeral parlor *Am*

tanda *f* **1.** (*turno*) shift, turn; **estar en la ~ de día** to be on the day shift; **¿me puedes guardar la ~?** will you keep my place for me? **2.** (*serie*) series *inv;* **por ~s** in batches; **en ~s de ocho** (*en filas*) in rows of eight; (*en grupos*) in groups of eight; **~ de palos** thrashing **3.** (*de trabajo, capa*) layer **4.** (*trabajo*) job, task

tándem *m* tandem

tanga *m* tanga, G-string

tangente *f* tangent; **salirse** [*o* **irse**] **por la ~** *fig* to go off on a tangent

Tánger *m* Tangier(s)

tangerino, -a *adj, m, f* Tangerine

tangible *adj* tangible; *fig* concrete

tango *m* MÚS tango

tanino *m* QUÍM tannin

tano, -a *adj, m, f Arg, Urug, inf* (*italiano*) Italian

tanque *m* **1.** MIL tank **2.** (*cisterna*) tanker **3.** (*vehículo*) road-tanker **4.** *inf* (*de cerveza*) large glass **5.** *vulg* (*gordo*) fatso **6.** *AmL* (*estanque*) pool

tanquear *vi Col* (*echar gasolina*) to get some petrol [*o* gas *Am*]

tantán *m* tom-tom

tantara(n)tán *m* **1.** (*onomatopeya*) rat-a-tat--tat **2.** (*golpe*) heavy punch, bang

tanteador *m* **1.** (*aparato*) scoreboard **2.** (*persona*) scorekeeper

tantear *vt* **1.** (*calcular: cantidad*) to calculate; (*tamaño, volumen*) to gauge, to weigh up; (*a ojo*) to size up; (*precio*) to estimate **2.** (*probar*) to try out; (*persona: sondear*) to sound out; **~ el terreno** *fig* to get the lay of the land **3.** (*dibujo*) to sketch **4.** DEP (*puntos*) to keep the score of; (*goles*) to score **5.** (*ir a tientas*) to grope; **tuvimos que bajar la escalera tanteando** we had to feel our way down the stairs

tanteo *m* **1.** (*cálculo: cantidad*) calculation; (*de tamaño, volumen*) weighing up; (*a ojo*) sizing up, gauging; (*de precio*) estimate; **al** [*o* **por**] **~** by trial and error **2.** (*sondeo*) sounding out **3.** DEP (*de puntos*) score; (*de goles*) scoring; **~ final** final score

tanto **I.** *m* **1.** (*cantidad*) certain amount; COM rate; **~ alzado** lump sum basis; **~ por ciento** percentage; **me pagan a ~ la hora** I'm paid so much the hour; **costar otro ~** to cost as much again; **un ~** a bit; **estar un ~ harto de algo** to be rather fed up with sth; **estoy un ~ sorprendido** I'm somewhat surprised **2.** (*punto*) point; (*gol*) goal; **un ~ a favor de algo** a point in sb's favour *Brit* [*o* favor *Am*]; **apuntarse un ~ a favor** to score a point ▶ **estar al ~ de algo** to be up to date on sth **II.** *adv* **1.** (*de tal modo*) so much, to such an extent; **no es para ~** there's no need to make such a fuss; **pensé que vendrías; ~ es así que no salí de casa** I thought you'd come; in fact, I was so sure, I stayed home **2.** (*en tal cantidad*) **no me das ni ~ así de pena** I don't feel the least bit sorry for you **3.** (*de duración*) so long; **tu respuesta tardó ~ que...** your answer took so long that ... **4.** (*comparativo*) **~ mejor/peor** so much the better/worse; **~ como** as much as; **eso era ~ como no decir nada** that was the same as not saying anything; **~ cuanto necesito para vivir** all I need to live on; **~ si llueve como si no...** whether it rains or not ... ▶ **¡ni ~ ni tan calvo!** neither one extreme nor the other!; **~...como...** both ... and ...; **~ él como su hermano juegan al baloncesto** both he and his brother play basketball; **en ~ (que +subj) (mientras)** as long as, provided; **entre ~** meanwhile, in the meantime; **por (lo) ~** therefore, so; **por lo ~ mejor callar** so best keep quiet

tanto, -a I. *adj* **1.** (*comparativo*) as much, as many; **no tengo ~ dinero como tú** I don't have as much money as you; **tenemos ~s días de vacación como ellos** we have as many vacation days as they do **2.** (*tal cantidad, ponderativo*) so much; **tantas posibilidades** so many possibilities; **¡hace ~ tiempo!** such a long time ago!; **¡hace ~ tiempo que no te veo!** I haven't seen you for so long!; **~ gusto en conocerle** a pleasure to meet you; **¿a qué se debe tanta risa?** what's so funny? **3.** *pl* (*número indefinido*) **en mil novecientos ochenta y ~s** in nineteen eighty-something; **uno de ~s** one of many; **a ~s de enero** on such and such a day of January; **tener 40 y ~s años** to be 40-odd years old; **a las tantas de la madrugada** *inf* in the wee hours of the morning; **quedarse despierto hasta las tantas** to stay up until all hours ▶ **~ tienes, ~ vales** *prov* a man's worth is the worth of his land **II.** *pron dem* **~s** as many; **coge ~s como quieras** take as many as you like; **no llego a ~** I won't go that far; **no me imaginaba que iba a llegar a ~** I never thought it would come to that; **jamás podré llegar a ~** I'll never be able to go so far

Tanzania *f* Tanzania
tanzano, -a *adj, m, f* Tanzanian
tañer <*3.pret:* tañó> **I.** *vt* **1.** (*instrumento*) to play **2.** (*campanas*) to ring **II.** *vi* to toll
tañido *m* sound
taoísmo *m* Taoism
taoísta *adj, mf* Taoist
tapa *f* **1.** (*cubierta*) lid; **~ de rosca** screw-top; **libro de ~s duras** hardback; **levantar** [*o* **saltar**] **a alguien la ~ de los sesos** *inf* to blow sb's brains out **2.** (*de zapato*) heelpiece

3. GASTR tapa; **una ~ de aceitunas** a small dish of olives **4.** (*carne*) **tapa de ternera** round of beef

---

> **Tapa** is the synonym for **pincho**, i.e. a snack or a bite to eat between meals. In **Andalucía**, however, a **tapa** consists exclusively of **embutido y/o jamón** (cured sausage and/or ham), which is served with wine or beer.

---

tapacubos *m inv* hubcap
tapada *f And, inf* save, stop
tapadera *f* **1.** (*de vasija*) lid **2.** (*negocio*) cover
tapadillo *m* **de ~** secretly
tapado *m Arg* (*abrigo*) coat
tapado, -a *adj AmL* (*animal*) all one colour *Brit* [*o* colored *Am*]
tapaporos *m inv* (*pintura*) sealer, primer
tapar I. *vt* **1.** (*cuerpo*) to cover; (*cazuela*) to put a lid on; (*en cama*) to cover up **2.** (*puerta*) to wall up; (*desagüe*) to obstruct; (*agujero*) to fill in; (*botella*) to put the cap on **3.** (*vista*) **¿te tapo?** am I blocking your view?; **la pared nos tapa el viento** the wall protects us from the wind **4.** (*ocultar*) to hide **II.** *vr:* **~se 1.** (*con ropa*) to wrap up; (*en cama*) to cover up; (*completamente*) to hide; (*con velo*) to shroud **2.** (*oídos, nariz*) to get blocked; **~se la cara/los ojos** to cover one's face/eyes
taparrabo(s) *m* (*inv*) **1.** (*de Tarzán*) loincloth **2.** (*bañador*) swimming trunks *pl*
tapayagua *f Hond* drizzle
tape *m* **1.** *Arg, Urug* (*aindiado*) Indian-looking person **2.** *Cuba, PRico* (*tapa*) lid **3.** *RíoPl* (*cinta de video*) tape
tapeo *m* **ir de ~** to go barhopping (*to go round the bars for beer or wine and tapas*)
tapete *m* table runner; **~ verde** card table; **estar sobre el ~** *fig* to be under consideration; **poner sobre el ~** *fig* to bring up
tapia *f* wall; (*de jardín*) garden wall; **estar más sordo que una ~** to be as deaf as a post
tapiar *vt* **1.** (*cerrar*) to wall up **2.** (*rodear*) to wall in
tapicería *f* **1.** (*tapices*) tapestries *pl*, wall-hangings *pl* **2.** (*tienda: de tapices*) tapestry shop; (*de muebles*) upholstery; (*taller*) upholsterer's **3.** (*arte*) tapestry-making **4.** (*tela*) upholstery material; **muebles de ~** upholstered furniture
tapicero, -a *m, f* **1.** (*de sillones*) upholsterer **2.** (*de paredes*) tapestry maker
tapisca *f AmC* AGR maize harvest *Brit*, corn harvest *Am*
tapiz *m* tapestry, wall-hanging; (*en el suelo*) rug
tapizar <*z→c*> *vt* (*muebles*) to upholster; (*acolchar*) to quilt
tapón *m* **1.** (*obturador*) stopper; (*cilindro, de fregadero*) drain plug; (*de corcho*) cork; (*de cuba*) bung; AUTO oil drain plug **2.** *inf* (*persona*) short stubby person **3.** MED tampon;

(*para el oído*) earplug **4.** (*cerumen*) wax in the ear **5.** (*de tráfico*) traffic jam

taponar *vt* **1.** (*cerrar*) to plug; (*con corcho*) to cork; (*de plástico*) to seal; (*cuba*) to bung; (*desagüe*) to clog **2.** (*herida*) to plug

tapujarse *vr inf* to muffle oneself up

tapujo *m* **1.** (*embozo*) muffler **2.** *inf* (*disimulo*) false pretext; **andar con ~s** (*obrar*) to behave deceitfully; **no andarse con ~s** (*hablar*) to speak plainly

taquear I. *vi AmL* **1.** *inf* (*jugar*) to shoot pool **2.** (*arma*) to ram **3.** (*llenar*) to stuff II. *vr:* **~se** *AmL* to tap one's heels

taquería *f* **1.** *Cuba* (*descaro*) cheek **2.** *Méx* (*tacos*) taco stand

taquicardia *f* MED tachycardia

taquigrafía *f* shorthand, stenography

taquigrafiar <*1. pres:* taquigrafío> *vt* to take down in shorthand

taquígrafo, -a *m, f* shorthand writer

taquilla *f* **1.** TEAT, CINE box office; DEP gate money; FERRO ticket window; (*de apuestas*) tote window; **éxito de ~** box-office hit **2.** (*recaudación*) receipts *pl,* takings *pl* **3.** (*armario*) locker; (*archivador*) filing cabinet

taquillero, -a I. *adj* **una artista ~** a crowd-puller; **una película taquillera** a box-office draw II. *m, f* **1.** FERRO ticket clerk, ticket seller **2.** TEAT, CINE ticket agent

taquimecanógrafo, -a *m, f* shorthand typist

tara *f* **1.** (*defecto*) defect **2.** COM (*peso*) tare

tarabilla *f* **1.** *inf* (*parlanchín*) chatter box; **hablar como una ~ descompuesta** to talk nine to the dozen *Brit,* to talk a blue streak *Am* **2.** (*palabra*) jabbering **3.** (*de ventana*) latch

taracea *f* marquetry, inlay

taracear *vt* to inlay

tarado, -a I. *adj* **1.** (*objeto*) defective, imperfect **2.** (*alocado*) crazy; (*imbécil*) stupid II. *m, f* (*loco*) nitwit

tarambana *mf inf* disaster

tarantín <tarantines> *m* **1.** *Ven* (*tenducha*) stall **2.** *pl, AmC, Cuba, PRico* (*cachivaches*) odds *pl* and ends

tarántula *f* tarantula

tarará *m v.* **tararí**

tararear *vt* to la-la-la, to croon; (*con labios cerrados*) to hum

tararí I. *adj* **estar ~** *inf* to be batty II. *m* (*de trompeta*) sound of trumpet

tarascón *m AmS* (*mordedura*) bite; (*herida*) bite wound

tardanza *f* delay; **perdona la ~ en escribirte** forgive me for taking so long to write

tardar *vi* to take time; **~ en llegar** to take a long time to arrive; FERRO to be late arriving; **~ en responder** to take a long time to answer; **~on tres semanas en contestar** it took them three weeks to answer; **~on mucho en arreglarlo** it took them a long time to fix it; **no tardo nada** I won't be long; **no ~é en volver** I'll be right back; **¡no tardes!** don't be gone

long!; **a más ~** at the latest; **sin ~** without taking long

tarde I. *f* **1.** (*primeras horas*) afternoon; **por la ~** in the afternoon; **¡buenas ~s!** good afternoon! **2.** (*últimas horas*) evening; **¡buenas ~s!** good evening!; (**todos**) **los viernes por la ~** Friday evenings II. *adv* late; **~ o temprano** sooner or later; **de ~ en ~** now and then, occasionally; **se me hace ~** it's getting late ►**más vale ~ que nunca** *prov* better late than never *prov*

tardío, -a *adj* **1.** (*atrasado*) late; **es un consejo ~** a belated piece of advice **2.** (*lento*) slow

tardo, -a *adj* slow; **~ de oído** hard of hearing

tardón, -ona I. *adj* **1.** (*lento*) slow **2.** (*tonto*) dense II. *m, f* **1.** (*lento*) slowcoach *Brit,* slowpoke *Am;* **es un ~** he/she's a slowcoach **2.** (*tardo*) dullard

tarea *f* **1.** (*faena*) task **2.** (*trabajo*) job; **~s de la casa** housework **3.** *pl* ENS homework; **¿has hecho tus ~s?** have you done your homework?

tareco *m Cuba, Ecua, Ven* **1.** (*herramienta*) tool of trade **2.** (*trasto*) old thing

tarifa *f* rate; (*transporte*) fare; **¿cuál es su ~?** how much does he/she charge?

tarima *f* platform

tarja *f* **1.** HIST (*escudo*) shield **2.** *AmL* (*tarjeta de visita*) visiting card ►**beber sobre ~** to drink on credit

tarjar *vt Chile* to cross out

tarjeta *f* **1.** card; **~ de crédito** credit card; **~ de embarque** AVIAT boarding pass; **~ postal** postcard; **~ de visita** visiting-card *Brit,* calling-card *Am* **2.** INFOR **~ de gráficos** graphics card; **~ de memoria** memory chip; **~ de sonido** sound card

tarjetero *m* card case

tarquín *m* mud, silt

tarraconense I. *adj* of/from Tarragona II. *mf* native/inhabitant of Tarragona

tarro *m* **1.** (*envase*) pot; (*de cristal*) jar; (*de metal*) tin, can **2.** *inf* (*cabeza*) head; **comer el ~ a alguien** to brainwash sb; **¿estás mal del ~?** are you off your head?; **comerse el ~** to think hard on sth

tarso *m* ANAT tarsus

tarta *f* cake; (*pastel*) pie

tartajear *vi* to stammer, to stutter

tartamudear *vi* to stammer, to stutter

tartamudo, -a I. *adj* stammering, stuttering II. *m, f* stammerer, stutterer

tartera *f* **1.** (*para tartas*) cake pan **2.** (*fiambrera*) lunchbox

tarugo *m* **1.** (*trozo*) chunk **2.** (*clavija*) wooden peg **3.** (*pan*) hunk of stale bread **4.** *inf* (*persona*) blockhead

tarumba *adj inf* confused; **estar ~** to be crazy; **volver a alguien ~** to drive sb mad [*o* crazy]

tasa *f* **1.** (*valoración*) valuation **2.** (*precio, derechos*) fee; (*de impuesto*) tax **3.** (*de joya*) appraisal **4.** (*porcentaje*) rate; **~ de desempleo** unemployment rate; **~ de interés** interest rate; ~ **impositiva** tax rate; ~ **de natalidad** birth rate

tasación *f* 1.(*de producto*) fixing of a price; (*de impuesto*) tax regulation 2.(*de joya*) appraisement

tasajear *vt AmL* 1.(*tajear*) to cut 2.(*carne*) to jerk

tasajo *m* 1.(*trozo*) piece of meat 2.(*salado*) jerked meat

tasar *vt* 1.(*precio*) to fix the price of; (*impuesto*) to tax 2.(*valorar*) to value; (*trabajo*) to regulate; ~ **en exceso** to overrate 3.(*tabaco, comida*) to ration; (*libertad*) to limit

tasca *f* (*taberna*) bar

tata¹ *f inf*(*niñera*) nanny

tata² *m AmL* (*papá*) daddy

tatarabuelo, -a *m, f* great-great-grandfather

tataranieto, -a *m, f* great-great-grandson

tate *interj* 1.(*cuidado*) watch out!, look out!, be careful! 2.(*despacito*) easy does it! 3.(*sorpresa*) good heavens! 4.(*comprensión*) so that's it!, I see!

tatuaje *m* tattoo

tatuar <*l. pres:* tatúo> *vt* to tattoo

tauca *f* 1.*Bol, Chile, Ecua* (*montón*) heap; **una** ~ **de papeles** a pile of papers 2.*Chile* (*talega grande*) large bag

taumaturgia *f* thaumaturgy, miracle-working

taumaturgo, -a *m, f* thaumaturge, miracle-worker

taurino, -a *adj* 1.(*del toro*) taurine 2.(*de la corrida*) bullfighting

Tauro *m* Taurus

tauromaquia *f sin pl* art of bullfighting

taxativo, -a *adj* restrictive; (*categórico*) precise; **de forma taxativa** in a categorical way

taxi *m* taxi, taxicab

taxímetro *m* taximeter

taxista *mf* taxi driver *Brit,* cabdriver *Am*

taza *f* 1.(*de café*) cup; **una** ~ **de café** (*con café*) a cup of coffee; (*para el café*) coffee cup 2.(*grande*) mug 3.(*del wáter*) toilet bowl 4.(*de fuente*) basin 5.(*medida*) cupful

tazón *m* (*taza grande*) large cup; (*cuenco*) bowl

te I.*f* **la letra** ~ the letter t II. *pron pers* (*objeto directo, indirecto*) you; **¡míra~!** look at yourself! III. *pron reflexivo* ~ **vistes** you get dressed; ~ **levantas** you get up; **no** ~ **hagas daño** don't hurt yourself; **¿~ has lavado los dientes?** have you brushed your teeth?

té *m* tea; **dar a alguien el** ~ *fig* to bore sb to tears

tea *f* 1.(*astillas*) firelighter; (*antorcha*) torch 2.*inf* (*borrachera*) **coger una** ~ to get plastered

teatral *adj* theatre; (*efecto, experiencia, autor*) stage; *fig* theatrical

teatralidad *f* drama, theatrics *pl; pey* staginess

teatro *m* 1.(*t. fig*) TEAT theatre *Brit,* theater *Am;* **obra de** ~ play; **el** ~ **de Calderón** Calderón's plays; **hacer** ~ to work in the theatre *Brit* [*o* theater *Am*]; *fig* to playact; (*exagerar*) exaggerate 2.(*escenario*) stage

tebeo *m* comic; **esto está más visto que el** ~ *inf* this is as old as the hills

teca *f* teak

techado *m* roof

techar *vt* to roof

techo *m* 1.(*de habitación*) ceiling 2.(*de casa*) roof; **vivir bajo el mismo** ~ to live under the same roof 3.(*tope*) maximum; (*de evolución*) peak

techumbre *f* 1.(*techo*) roof 2.(*estructura*) roofing; ~ **de paja** thatching

tecla *f* 1.(*de piano, ordenador*) key; ~ **de mayúsculas** shift key; ~ **de retroceso** backspace key; ~ **de intro** enter key; **tocar una** ~ (*piano, ordenador*) to press a key; **dar en la** ~ *inf* to hit the nail on the head; **hay que tocar muchas** ~**s para averiguar eso** a lot of strings will have to be pulled to find that out; **tocar demasiadas** ~**s** *fig* to do too many things at once 2.(*materia*) weak point; **tocar la** ~ **sensible** to touch a nerve

teclado *m* keyboard; **tocar los** ~**s en un grupo** to play the keyboards in a group

teclear *vi* 1.(*piano*) to play; (*ordenador*) to type 2.(*dedos*) to drum

técnica *f* 1.(*método*) technique 2.(*tecnología*) technology

técnicamente *adv* technically

tecnicismo *m* 1.(*término*) technical term 2.(*detalle*) technicality

técnico, -a I. *adj* 1.(*de la técnica*) technical 2.(*de especialidad*) technical; **término** ~ technical term II. *m, f* 1.TÉC technician; (*de lavadoras*) repairman, engineer 2.(*especialista*) expert, specialist 3.DEP trainer, coach

tecnicolor *m* Technicolor®

tecnócrata I. *adj* technocratic II. *mf* technocrat

tecnología *f* 1.TÉC, ECON technology; ~ **punta** leading-edge technology 2.(*técnica*) technique

tecnológico, -a *adj* 1.TÉC technological; (*desarrollo*) technological; **parque** ~ technology park 2.(*técnico*) technical

tecolote *m AmC, Méx* ZOOL (*búho*) owl

tedio *m* boredom

tedioso, -a *adj* tedious, wearisome

teína *f* QUÍM theine

teísmo *m* theism

teísta I. *adj* theistic II. *mf* theist

teja *f* 1.(*del tejado*) roof tile; **de color** ~ brownish-orange 2.(*sombrero*) shovel hat ► **pagar a toca** ~ to pay cash on the nail; **de** ~**s (para) abajo** in this world; **de** ~**s (para) arriba** in heaven

tejado *m* roof; **empezar la casa por el** ~ *fig* to put the cart before the horse; **la pelota sigue en el** ~ *fig* it is still in the air; **tirar piedras sobre su propio** ~ *fig* to foul one's own nest ► **quien tiene el** ~ **de** vidrio, **no tire**

piedras al de su vecino *prov* people who live in glass houses shouldn't throw stones *prov*
tejano, -a I. *adj* 1. (*de Tejas*) Texan 2. (*ropa*) denim; **pantalón** ~ jeans II. *m, f* Texan
tejanos *mpl* jeans
tejar I. *vt* to tile II. *m* tile works *pl*
tejaván *m AmL* 1. (*cobertizo*) shed 2. (*corredor*) corridor 3. (*alero*) eaves *pl* 4. (*casa*) rustic house with tiled roof
tejedor(a) *m(f)* 1. weaver 2. ZOOL water strider
tejemaneje *m inf* 1. (*actividad*) to-do; **traerse un** ~ **increíble con los papeles** to make such a fuss with the papers 2. (*intriga*) scheming; **se deben de traer algún** ~ they must be up to sth
tejer *vt* 1. (*tela*) to weave; (*tricotar*) to knit; ~ **y destejer** *fig* to blow hot and cold 2. (*cestos, trenzas*) to plait 3. ZOOL (*araña*) to spin 4. (*intrigas, plan*) to plot
tejido *m* 1. *t.* ANAT (*textura*) tissue 2. (*tela*) fabric; **los** ~s textiles *pl*
tejo *m* 1. (*disco*) disk; **tirar los** ~s **a alguien** *inf* to flirt with sb 2. BOT yew tree 3. (*juego*) hopscotch
tejón *m* badger
tejuelo *m* TIPO book label
tela *f* 1. (*tejido*) material, fabric; ~ **de araña** spider's web *Brit*, spiderweb *Am;* ~ **metálica** wire screen; ~ **de punto** knit; ~ **de saco** sackcloth, burlap; **lo cubrieron con una** ~ **blanca** they covered it with a white cloth 2. (*en leche*) film; **llegar a las** ~**s del corazón** *fig* to pull heartstrings 3. *inf* (*asunto*) matter; **hay** ~ **para rato** (*para discutir*) there's plenty to talk about; (*para trabajar*) there's a lot to be done; **este asunto trae** ~ it's a complicated matter; **este problema tiene** ~ this isn't an easy problem 4. (*lienzo*) canvas; **una** ~ **de Barceló** a painting by Barcelo 5. *inf* (*dinero*) dough ▶**poner algo en** ~ **de juicio** (*dudar*) to question sth; (*tener reparos*) to raise objections about sth
telar *m* (*máquina*) loom
telaraña *f* cobweb *Brit,* spiderweb *Am;* **mirar las** ~s *fig* to have one's head in the clouds; **tener** ~s **en los ojos** *fig* to be blind to what is going on
tele *f inf abr de* televisión TV, telly *Brit;* **ver la** ~ to watch TV
teleadicto, -a *adj inf* telly addict *Brit,* couch potato
telebanca *f* e-bank
telebanking *m sin pl* e-banking
telebasura *f* junk TV
telecabina *f* cable car
telecomedia *f* 1. (*serie*) sitcom, TV comedy show 2. (*película*) TV film
telecompra *f sin pl* teleshopping
telecomunicación *f* 1. (*sistema*) telecommunication; **ingeniero de Telecomunicaciones** telecommunications engineer 2. *pl* (*empresa*) telecommunications *pl*

teleconcurso *m* game show
teleconferencia *f* COM teleconference, video-phone conference
telecontrol *m* remote control
telediario *m* TV news; **el** ~ **de las 3** the 3 o'clock news
teledifusión *f* telecast
teledirigido, -a I. *adj* remote-controlled II. *m, f* (*juguete*) remote-controlled car
teledirigir <g→j> *vt* to operate by remote control
teléf. *abr de* teléfono tel.
teleférico *m* cable car
telefilm *m* TV film, made-for-TV movie *Am*
telefonazo *m inf* ring; **dar un** ~ **a alguien** to give sb a ring
telefonear I. *vt* 1. (*comunicar*) to telephone, to phone, to call 2. *inf* (*a alguien*) to ring II. *vi* to telephone
telefonía *f* telephony
Telefónica *f* national telephone company in *Spain*
telefónico, -a *adj* 1. (*de teléfono*) telephone; **cabina telefónica** phone box; **guía telefónica** telephone directory, phone book; **llamada telefónica** phonecall 2. (*de telefonía*) telephonic
telefonista *mf* telephone operator
teléfono *m* 1. (*sistema, aparato*) telephone; ~ **móvil** mobile phone, cellphone *Am;* ~ **público** public phone; ~ **rojo** *fig* hotline; ~ **de tarjeta** card phone; **por** ~ over the phone; **hablar por** ~ to talk on the phone; **llamar por** ~ to telephone 2. (*número*) phone number 3. *pl* (*compañía*) telephone company
telegrafía *f* telegraphy
telegrafiar <3. pret: telegrafió> *vt, vi* to telegraph
telegráfico, -a *adj* 1. (*por telégrafo*) telegraph 2. (*relativo a la telegrafía*) telegraphic
telégrafo *m* 1. (*aparato*) telegraph 2. *pl* (*administración*) post office
telegrama *m* telegram
teleimpresor *m* teleprinter
telele *m inf* fit; **como me digas que no, me da un** ~ if you say 'no', I'll have a fit
telemando *m* remote control; (*de la televisión*) remote control
telemarujeo *m pey:* women's TV programmes
telemática *f* telematics *pl*
telémetro *m* 1. FOTO rangefinder 2. TÉC telemeter
telenovela *f* TV soap opera
telenque I. *adj* 1. *Chile* (*temblón*) shaking; (*enfermizo*) sickly 2. *ElSal* (*torcido*) crooked II. *m Guat* (*cachivache*) junk
teleobjetivo *m* FOTO telephoto lens
telepatía *f sin pl* telepathy
telepático, -a *adj* telepathic
telequinesia *f* telekinesis
telera *f* 1. (*travesaño*) transom 2. (*de un arado, carro*) plough pin *Brit*, plow pin *Am*

3. (*de una prensa*) jaw
telescópico, -a *adj* telescopic
telescopio *m* telescope
telesilla *f* chair-lift
telespectador(a) *m(f)* TV viewer
telesquí *m* ski-lift
teletexto *m* teletext
teletienda *f* TV shop
teletipo *m* teletype®
teletrabajo *m* teleworking (from home)
televidente *mf v.* **telespectador**
televisar *vt* to televise, to broadcast; (*en directo*) to televise live
televisión *f* **1.** (*sistema, organización*) television; ~ **digital** digital television; ~ **de pago** pay-television **2.** *inf* (*televisor*) television, TV set; ~ **en color** colour TV *Brit,* color TV *Am*
televisivo, -a *adj* **1.** (*relativo a*) television **2.** (*apto para*) telegenic
televisor *m* television set
télex *m* telex
telón *m* curtain; **el** ~ **de acero** the iron curtain; ~ **de fondo** backdrop
tema *m t.* MÚS, LIT theme; **cada loco con su** ~ to each his own; **ése es el** ~ **de mi sermón** *fig* that's just what I'm always saying; **alejarse del** ~ to stray from the issue; ~**s de actualidad** current issues
temario *m* **1.** (*lista de temas*) programme *Brit,* program *Am* **2.** (*para un examen*) list of topics **3.** (*de una conferencia*) agenda
temática *f* subjects *pl*
temático, -a *adj* thematic
temblar <e→ie> *vi* to tremble; ~ **de miedo** to tremble with fear; ~ **por alguien** to fear for sb; **dejar temblando** (*comer*) to polish off; ~ **de frío** to shiver (with cold); ~ **de pensarlo** to shudder just to think of it; ~ **como un flan** to shake like a leaf; **me tiembla el ojo** my eye is twitching
tembleque *m inf* **1.** (*temblor*) shaking; **me dio un** ~ I got the shakes **2.** (*persona*) weakling
temblequear *vi inf* to shake
temblón *m* (*álamo*) ~ quaking aspen
temblón, -ona *adj inf* trembling
temblor *m* (*tembleque*) tremor; (*escalofrío*) shiver; ~ **de frío** shivers; ~ (**de tierra**) earthquake
tembloroso, -a *adj* shaky
temer I. *vt* **1.** (*sentir temor*) to fear **2.** (*sospechar*) to be afraid **II.** *vi* to be afraid; ~ **por alguien** to fear for sb **III.** *vr:* ~**se** to be afraid; **me temo que si/no** I'm afraid so/not
temerario, -a *adj* **1.** (*imprudente*) reckless **2.** (*sin fundamento*) rash
temeridad *f sin pl* **1.** (*imprudencia*) recklessness **2.** (*insensatez*) rashness
temeroso, -a *adj* **1.** (*medroso*) fearful; ~ **de Dios** God-fearing; ~ **de que...** +*subj* fearful that ... **2.** (*temible*) dreadful
temible *adj* fearsome
temor *m* **1.** (*miedo*) fear; **por** ~ **a lo que diga**

la gente for fear of what people will say **2.** (*sospecha*) suspicion
témpano *m* **1.** (*pedazo*) chunk; (*de hielo*) ice floe; **quedarse como un** ~ to be chilled to the bone; **tener las manos como un** ~ to have ice-cold hands; **él es como un** ~ *fig* he is as cold as stone **2.** (*tambor*) kettledrum; (*piel*) drumhead
temperamental *adj* **1.** (*del temperamento*) temperamental; **característica** ~ characteristic of one's nature **2.** (*persona*) spirited
temperamento *m* (*carácter, vivacidad*) temperament; **tener mucho** ~ to have a strong character
temperante I. *adj AmS* (*abstemio*) abstemious, teetotalling **II.** *mf AmS* teetotaller *Brit,* teetotaler *Am*
temperar I. *vt* to temper; MED to calm **II.** *vr:* ~**se** to warm up
temperatura *f* temperature; (*de una persona*) temperature; (*fiebre*) fever; **el niño tiene mucha** ~ the boy's running a very high temperature; **tengo algo de** ~ I have a slight fever
tempestad *f* (*tormenta*) storm; (*marejada*) gale; (*agitación*) turmoil; ~ **de aplausos** tumultuous applause; ~ **de injurias** storm of insults; ~ **de silbidos** outburst of whistling; **levantar** ~**es** to produce turmoil; **levantar una** ~ **de protestas** to raise a storm of protest; **una** ~ **en un vaso de agua** a storm in a teacup
tempestivo, -a *adj elev* timely, opportune
tempestuoso, -a *adj* tempestuous; (*ambiente*) stormy
templado, -a *adj* **1.** (*tibio*) lukewarm **2.** (*temperado*) tempered **3.** (*moderado*) moderate; **ser** ~ **en la bebida** to drink with moderation **4.** (*sereno*) composed **5.** (*valiente*) courageous **6.** *inf* (*bebido*) tipsy; **estar** ~ to be drunk **7.** MÚS tuned
templanza *f* **1.** (*moderación*) temperateness **2.** (*clima, temperatura*) mildness **3.** (*virtud*) temperance
templar I. *vt* **1.** (*moderar*) to moderate; (*suavizar*) to soften; (*calmar*) to calm down **2.** (*calentar*) to warm up **3.** (*entibiar*) to cool down **4.** MÚS (*afinar*) to tune; ~ **a alguien la gaita** *fig* to calm sb down **5.** (*apretar*) to tighten **6.** (*mezclar*) to blend **7.** (*acero*) to temper **II.** *vr:* ~**se 1.** (*moderarse*) to control oneself **2.** (*calentarse*) to get warm; (*enfriarse*) to cool off **3.** *AmL* (*enamorarse*) to fall in love **4.** *Col, Perú* (*emborracharse*) to get drunk
temple *m* **1.** (*valentía*) courage **2.** (*carácter*) disposition; (*humor*) mood; **estar de buen/mal** ~ to be in a good/bad mood **3.** (*temperatura*) temperature; (*tiempo*) weather **4.** (*del acero: proceso*) tempering; (*dureza*) hardness **5.** MÚS tuning **6.** ARTE tempera
templete *m* bandstand
templo *m* temple; (*iglesia*) church; **una verdad como un** ~ *inf* the naked truth

temporada _f_ (_tiempo_) season; (_época_) period; ~ **alta** high season; ~ **baja** low season; ~ **de caza/pesca** hunting/fishing season; **fruta de** ~ seasonal fruit; **están pasando por una** ~ **difícil** they're going through a difficult period; **llevo una** ~ **que salgo poco** I've been going out very little lately

temporal I. _adj_ 1. (_relativo al tiempo_) stormy 2. (_no permanente_) temporary, provisional; (_no eterno_) temporal; **contrato** ~ temporary contract 3. (_secular_) worldly 4. ANAT ~ temporal II. _m_ 1. (_tormenta_) storm; (_marejada_) stormy seas _pl;_ **capear el** ~ _fig_ to weather the storm 2. ANAT temporal bone

temporario, -a _adj AmL_ temporary

temporero, -a I. _adj_ seasonal; **trabajador** ~ seasonal worker II. _m, f_ seasonal worker, migrant worker; AGR seasonal worker

tempranero, -a I. _adj_ 1. (_anticipado_) premature; (_fruta_) early 2. (_madrugador_) **ser** ~ to be an early riser; **¡qué** ~ **estás hoy!** you're up early today! II. _m, f_ early riser, earlybird

temprano _adv_ 1. (_a primera hora_) early; ~ **por la mañana** early in the morning 2. (_antes_) early; **llegar** (**demasiado**) ~ to arrive (too) early

temprano, -a _adj_ early; **a edad temprana** at an early age

tenacidad _f sin pl_ 1. (_persona_) tenacity; (_porfía_) perseverance 2. (_material_) resilience 3. (_dolor_) persistence; (_mancha_) stubbornness

tenacillas _fpl_ tongs _pl;_ (_para rizar_) curling iron; (_para depilar_) tweezers _pl_

tenaz _adj_ 1. (_perserverante_) persevering; (_cabezota_) stubborn; **ser** ~ **en sus decisiones** to be firm in his/her decisions 2. (_resistente_) resistent 3. (_persistente_) persistent; (_niebla_) clinging

tenaza(s) _f(pl)_ pliers _pl_

tenca _f_ tench

tencha _f Guat_ (_cárcel_) jail

tendajo _m inf_ small tumble-down shop

tendajón _m Méx_ small shop

tendal _m_ (_toldo_) awning

tendear _vi Méx_ to windowshop

tendedero _m_ 1. (_lugar_) drying place 2. (_armazón_) clothes horse; (_cuerdas_) clothes line

tendencia _f_ 1. (_inclinación_) tendency; **tener** ~ **a** to have a tendency to 2. (_dirección_) trend; ~ **alcista** upward [_o_ bullish] trend; ~ **al alza/a la baja** upward/downward trend, bullish/bearish; **las últimas** ~**s de la moda** the latest fashion trends; (_aspiración_) ~ **a algo** drift toward sth; ~**s autonomistas** trend toward self-government

tendencioso, -a _adj pey_ tendentious

tender <e→ie> I. _vt_ 1. (_desdoblar, esparcir_) ~ **sobre algo** to spread over sth; ~ **la cama** _AmL_ to make the bed; ~ **la mesa** _AmL_ to lay the table 2. (_tumbar_) to lay; (_de golpe_) to throw down 3. (_colocar: ropa_) to hang out; (_cuerda_) to stretch; (_puente_) to build; (_línea, vía_) to lay 4. (_aproximar_) to hold out; ~ **la**

mano a alguien _fig_ to give sb a hand II. _vi_ 1. (_inclinarse, aspirar_) to tend; **tu cabello tiende a rojizo** your hair is slightly reddish; **tiendo a ser optimista** I tend to be optimistic 2. MAT to tend toward III. _vr:_ ~**se** 1. (_tumbarse_) to stretch out 2. (_abandonarse_) to let oneself go

tenderete _m_ COM stall, stand

tendero, -a _m, f_ 1. (_dueño_) shopkeeper _Brit,_ storekeeper _Am_ 2. (_dependiente_) shop assistant

tendido _m_ 1. (_de un cable_) laying 2. (_cables_) cables _pl,_ wiring 3. (_ropa_) washing _Brit,_ wash _Am_ 4. TAUR front rows of seats 5. _AmL_ (_de la cama_) bed linen

tendido, -a _adj_ (_galope_) at full gallop; **largo y** ~ long and hard

tendón _m_ ANAT tendon

tenebroso, -a _adj t. fig_ (_oscuro_) dark; (_tétrico_) gloomy

tenedor _m_ (_para comer_) fork

tenedor(a) _m(f)_ 1. (_propietario_) holder; ~ **de tierras** landowner 2. FIN ~ **de libros** bookkeeper

teneduría _f_ bookkeeping

tenencia _f_ JUR possession; ~ **ilícita de armas** illegal possession of arms

tener _irr_ I. _vt_ 1. (_poseer, disfrutar, sentir, padecer_) to have; ~ **los ojos azules** to have blue eyes; ~ **29 años** to be 29 years old; ~ **hambre/sed/calor/sueño** to be hungry/thirsty/hot/sleepy; ~ **poco de tonto** to be no fool; **no** ~ **nada de especial** to be nothing special; **¿(con que) ésas tenemos?** so that's the way it is?; ~**la tomada con alguien** _inf_ to have it in for sb; **no** ~**las todas consigo** not to be sure of something; **no** ~ **nada que perder** to have nothing to lose; **no** ~ **precio** to be priceless; ~ **cariño a alguien** to be fond of sb; ~ **la culpa de algo** to be to blame for sth; **¿tienes frío?** are you cold?; **le tengo lástima** I feel sorry for him/her; ~ **sueño** to be sleepy 2. (_considerar_) ~ **por algo** to consider sth; ~ **a alguien en menos/mucho** to think all the less/more of sb; **ten por seguro que...** rest assured that ...; **tengo para mí que...** I think that ... 3. (_guardar_) to keep 4. (_contener_) to have; **el frasco ya no tiene miel** there's no honey left in the jar 5. (_coger_) to take; **ten esto** take this 6. (_sujetar_) to hold; ~ **a alguien por el brazo** to hold sb by the arm 7. (_recibir_) to have; ~ **un niño** to have a baby 8. (_hacer sentir_) **me tienes preocupada** I'm worried about you; **me tienes loca** you're driving me mad! 9. (_cumplir_) ~ **su palabra** to keep one's word II. _vr:_ ~**se** 1. (_considerarse_) ~**se por algo** to consider oneself sth; ~**se en mucho** to think highly of oneself 2. (_sostenerse_) to stand; ~**se de pie** to stand; ~**se firme** to stand upright; _fig_ to stand firm; **estoy que no me tengo** I'm exhausted 3. (_dominarse_) to control oneself 4. (_atenerse_) to adhere III. _aux_ 1. (_con participio concordante_) ~ **pensado**

hacer algo to plan to do sth; **ya tengo com-prado todo** I've bought everything already; **~se algo callado** to keep quiet about sth; **ya me lo tenía pensado** I had already thought of that **2.**(*obligación, necesidad*) **~ que** to have to; **~ mucho que hacer** to have a lot to do; **¿qué tiene que ver esto conmigo?** what does this have to do with me?

Tenerife *m* Tenerife

tenia *f* tapeworm

tenida *f Chile* meeting; (*traje*) suit; (*uniforme*) uniform

teniente *m* MIL lieutenant; **~ coronel** lieutenant-colonel

tenis *m sin pl* tennis; **~ de mesa** table tennis

tenista *mf* tennis player

tenor *m* **1.** *t.* MÚS (*contenido*) tenor; **a este ~** at this rate; **a ~ de** according to **2.**(*constitución*) constitution

tenorio *m* Don Juan, womanizer

tensar *vt* (*músculo*) to tense; (*cuerda*) to tighten

tensión *f* **1.** FÍS tension **2.**(*estado: cosa*) stress; (*cuerda, piel*) tautness; (*nervios, músculos*) tension; (*impaciencia*) anxiety; **película de ~** thriller; **estar en ~** (*nervioso*) to be nervous; (*impaciente*) to be anxious **3.** MED **~ arterial** blood pressure **4.** ELEC voltage **5.** *pl* (*conflicto*) strained relations *pl*

tenso, -a *adj* (*cosa, situación*) tense; (*cuerda, piel*) taut; (*músculos, nervios*) tense; (*impaciente*) anxious

tentación *f* temptation; **me dan tentaciones de…** I'm tempted to …; **caer en la ~** to succumb [*o* give in] to the temptation

tentáculo *m* tentacle

tentador(a) I. *adj* tempting **II.** *m(f)* tempter *m*, temptress *f*

tentar <e→ie> *vt* **1.**(*palpar*) to feel; (*reconocer*) to probe **2.**(*atraer*) to tempt; (*seducir*) to entice; **no me tientes** don't tempt me

tentativa *f* attempt; **~ de robo** attempted robbery

tentempié *m inf* (*refrigerio*) bite to eat

tenue *adj* **1.**(*delgado*) fine; (*delicado*) delicate **2.**(*sutil*) subtle; (*débil*) weak; **luz ~** faint light **3.**(*sencillo*) simple

teñir *irr como ceñir* *vt, vr:* **~se** to dye; **~(se) de rojo** to dye red; **~se el cabello de negro** to dye one's hair black; **~ de tristeza** to tinge with sadness

teología *f* theology

teológico, -a *adj* theological

teólogo, -a I. *adj* theologic **II.** *m, f* theologian; (*estudiante*) divinity student

teorema *m* theorem

teoría *f* theory; **~ del caos** the chaos theory; **en ~** in theory

teórica *f* theoretics *pl*

teórico, -a I. *adj* theoretical **II.** *m, f* theorist, theoretician

teorizar <z→c> *vi, vt* to theorize

tepache *m Méx* GASTR tepache (*drink made of pulque, water, pineapple and cloves*)

tequesquite *m Méx* rock salt

tequiche *m Ven* GASTR dish made with toasted maize, coconut milk and butter

tequila *m* tequila

tequio *m AmC, Méx* **1.**(*molestia*) bother **2.**(*daño*) harm

tequioso, -a *adj AmC* **1.**(*travieso*) mischievous; (*niño*) trying **2.**(*molesto*) bothersome

TER *m abr de* **Tren Español Rápido** express train (*Spanish intercity high-speed train*)

terapeuta *mf* therapist

terapéutica *f* therapeutics *pl*

terapéutico, -a *adj* therapeutic(al)

terapia *f* therapy; **~ en** [*o* de] **grupo** group therapy

tercena *f Ecua* butcher's shop

tercer *adj v.* **tercero**

tercera *f* **1.** AUTO third gear **2.** MÚS third **3.** FERRO third-class

tercería *f* (*mediación*) mediation

tercermundista *adj* third-world, underdeveloped

Tercer Mundo *m sin pl* Third World

tercero I. *m* **1.** *t.* JUR third party **2.**(*alcahuete*) procurer **II.** *adv* third

tercero, -a I. *adj* (*delante de un sustantivo masculino: tercer*) third; **terceras personas** third parties; **en tercer lugar** thirdly; **ser ~** to be the odd man out; **viven en el ~** they live on the third floor; **tercera edad** senior citizens, retirement years ►**a la tercera va la vencida** *prov* third time lucky *prov* **II.** *m, f* third; *v.t.* **octavo**

terceto *m* LIT tercet, triplet; MÚS trio

tercia *f* REL tierce

terciar I. *vt* **1.**(*dividir*) to divide into three parts **2.**(*atravesar*) to place diagonally across **3.**(*la carga*) to balance **4.** *AmL* (*aguar*) to water down **II.** *vi* **1.**(*intervenir*) to intervene **2.**(*mediar*) to have a word **3.**(*participar*) to take part; **~ en un juego** to join in a game **III.** *vr, vimpers:* **~se 1.**(*ocurrir*) to arise; **si se tercia** should the occasion arise; **prepararse por lo que se pueda ~** to get ready for what may happen **2.**(*ponerse*) to make up the number

terciario *m* GEO Tertiary period

terciario, -a *adj t.* GEO Tertiary

tercio *m* (*parte*) third; *v.t.* **octavo** ►**hacer buen/mal ~ a alguien** to do sb a good/bad turn

terciopelo *m* velvet; **lazo de ~** velvet bow

terco, -a I. *adj* **1.**(*persona*) stubborn, obstinate **2.**(*niño*) unruly **3.**(*animal*) balky **4.**(*cosa*) tough **II.** *m, f* stubborn person

tereque *m Col, Dom, PRico, Ven* (*cachivache*) utensil

tergal® *m* type of synthetic fabric

tergiversar *vt* (*hechos*) to misrepresent; (*la verdad*) to distort; (*palabras*) to twist

termal *adj* thermal; **aguas ~es** hot springs

termas *fpl* (*baños*) hot baths *pl*; (*de los*

romanos) thermae

termes *m inv* termite

térmico, -a *adj* thermal, thermic; **central térmica** power station

terminación *f* 1.(*acción*) termination; (*de un proyecto*) completion; (*producción*) finish; (*de un plazo*) end 2.(*final*) end; (*borde*) end, edge

terminal[1] I. *adj* terminal; **parte ~** final part; **un enfermo ~** a terminally ill patient II. *m* INFOR terminal

terminal[2] *f* 1.(*estación*) terminal, terminus; FERRO station 2.(*de* (*aero*)*puerto*) terminal; **~ aérea** air terminal

terminante *adj* 1.(*claro*) clear 2.(*definitivo*) categorical

terminar I. *vt* 1.(*finalizar*) to finish; (*proyecto*) to complete; **¿cuándo terminas?** when will you be done? 2.(*producir*) to finish; **¿cuándo van a ~ el puerto?** when are they going to finish the port?; **estar bien terminado** to be well finished 3.(*consumir*) to finish up; (*beber*) to drink up; (*comer*) to eat up II. *vi* 1.(*tener fin*) to finish, to end; (*plazo, contrato*) to end; **~ bien/mal** to have a happy/unhappy ending; **~ en punta** to end in a point; **~ de construir** to finish building; **~ de hacer/coser/comer** to finish doing/sewing/eating; **cuando termines de comer...** when you finish eating ...; **¿cuándo termina la película?** what time does the film end?; **la escuela termina a las dos** school is out at 2 pm 2.(*acercarse al final*) to be ending; **ya termina la película** the film is almost over 3.(*poner fin*) to put an end to 4.(*destruir*) to do away; **el tabaco va a ~ contigo** tobacco is going to be the end of you! 5.(*separarse*) to break up 6.(*llegar a*) **~ por hacer algo** to end up doing sth; **terminaron peleándose** they wound up fighting 7.(*haber hecho*) **~ de hacer algo** to have just done sth III. *vr:* **~se** 1.(*aproximarse al final*) to be almost over 2.(*no haber más*) (for) there to be no more; **se me está terminando la paciencia** I'm running out of patience; **se terminaron las galletas** there aren't any more biscuits (left)

término *m* 1.(*fin*) end; **dar ~ a algo** to finish sth off; **llevar a ~** to carry out; **poner ~ a algo** to put an end to sth; **sin ~** endless; **me bajé en el ~** I got off at the terminus; **he llegado al ~ de mi paciencia** I've reached the end of my patience 2.(*plazo*) period; **en el ~ de quince días** within 15 days 3.(*linde*) boundary 4. ADMIN district; **~ municipal** township 5.(*vocablo*) word; (*especial*) term; **en buenos ~s** on good terms; **en otros ~s** in other words; **contestar en malos ~s** to answer rudely 6.(*parte*) term 7. *pl* (*de un contrato*) terms *pl,* conditions *pl* ►**estar en buenos/malos ~s** to be on good/bad terms; **separarse en buenos/malos ~s** to separate on good/bad terms; **en ~s generales** generally speaking; **~ medio** compromise; **en medios**

~s with vague half-answers; **en primer ~** first of all; **en último ~** as a last resort; **por ~ medio** on the average

terminología *f* terminology

terminológico, -a *adj* terminological; **diccionario ~** specialized dictionary

termita *f* termite

termo *m* thermos

termodinámica *f* thermodynamics *pl*

termómetro *m* thermometer; **~ clínico** clinical thermometer

termonuclear *adj* thermonuclear

termosifón *m* (*calentador*) boiler

termostato *m,* **termóstato** *m* thermostat, thermal switch

termotecnia *f* thermotechnics *pl,* heat engineering

terna *f* (*candidatos*) short list (*a list of three candidates for a job o position*)

ternario, -a *adj* ternary; (*de tres unidades*) three-part

terne I. *adj* 1. *inf* (*bravucón*) bullying 2. *inf* (*cabezota*) bullheaded 3.(*recio*) husky II. *m* *inf* (*bravucón*) bully

ternejo, -a *adj Ecua, Perú* (*persona*) lively

ternera *f* (*carne*) beef, veal

ternero, -a *m, f* calf

terneza *f v.* **ternura**

ternilla *f* gristle

terno *m* 1.(*conjunto*) set of three 2.(*traje*) three-piece suit 3.(*juramento*) swearword; **echar ~s** to curse

ternura *f* 1.(*cariño*) tenderness 2.(*dulzura*) sweetness 3.(*blandura, suavidad*) softness 4.(*delicadeza, sensibilidad*) gentleness 5. *Chile, Ecua, Guat* (*inmadurez*) greenness

terquedad *f* 1.(*testarudez*) stubbornness, obstinacy 2.(*porfía*) willfulness 3.(*de un niño*) unruliness 4.(*de un animal*) balkiness

terracota *f* terracotta

terrado *m* flat roof; (*terraza*) terrace

terral I. *adj* land II. *m* METEO land wind

Terranova *f* Newfoundland

terraplén *m* 1.(*montón*) mound; (*protección*) rampart 2.(*desnivel*) slope; **~ de un ferrocarril** railway embankment

terráqueo, -a I. *adj* terrestrial, terraqueous; **globo ~** globe II. *m, f* terraquean

terrario *m* terrarium

terrateniente *mf* landowner, landholder

terraza *f* 1.(*jardín*) terrace; (*balcón*) balcony; (*azotea*) flat roof 2.(*de una cafetería*) terrace (*area outside a bar or café where tables are placed to serve customers in good weather*)

terregal *m Méx* loose topsoil

terremoto *m* earthquake

terrenal *adj* worldly; **paraíso ~** earthly paradise

terreno *m* 1.(*suelo*) land; GEO terrain; **~ arcilloso** clayey ground 2.(*espacio*) lot; (*parcela*) plot of land; (*campo*) field; DEP playing field; **~ de fútbol** football pitch *Brit,* soccer field *Am;* **~ edificable** buildable land; **vehí-**

culo todo ~ all-terrain vehicle **3.** (*esfera*) sphere; ~ **desconocido** unfamiliar territory; **estar en su propio** ~ to be on one's own ground ▸**ceder** ~ to give up ground; **explorar el** ~ to see how the land lies; **ganar/perder** ~ to gain/lose ground; **minar el** ~ **a alguien** to undermine sb's plans; **preparar el** ~ **para algo** to pave the way for sth; **saber uno el** ~ **que pisa** to know what one's doing; **ser** ~ **abonado para...** to be ideal for ...; **sobre el** ~ on the spot

terreno, -a *adj* earthly

terrera *f* lark

terrestre **I.** *adj* **1.** (*de la Tierra*) terrestrial; **globo** ~ globe **2.** (*en la tierra*) earthly; **animal** ~ land animal; **transporte** ~ ground transport **3.** (*terrenal*) earthly **II.** *mf* terrestrial

terrible *adj* terrible; **hace un frío** ~ it's terribly cold; **tener un hambre** ~ to be terribly hungry

terrícola *mf* earthling, earth dweller

terrífico, -a *adj* terrifying

territorial *adj* territorial; **división** ~ territorial division

territorio *m* **1.** (*región*) territory; POL region/district; JUR district; ~ **jurisdiccional** jurisdictional territory; **en todo el** ~ **nacional** over the whole country, nationwide **2.** ZOOL territory

terrón *m* **1.** (*masa*) lump; ~ (**de azúcar**) lump; ~ (**de tierra**) clod; **azúcar de** ~ lump sugar **2.** (*pl*), *inf* (*campo*) land

terror *m* **1.** (*miedo*) terror; **película de** ~ horror film; **las arañas me dan** ~ I'm terrified of spiders; **me domina el** ~ I'm terrified **2.** (*que provoca miedo*) terror **3.** POL terror; **reino de** ~ reign of terror

terrorífico, -a *adj* terrifying

terrorismo *m sin pl* terrorism

terrorista **I.** *adj* terrorist; **organización** ~ terrorist organization **II.** *mf* terrorist

terroso, -a *adj* earthy; (*color*) earth-coloured *Brit,* earth-colored *Am*

terruño *m* **1.** (*trozo*) clod **2.** (*comarca*) region; (*patria*) native land **3.** (*terreno*) piece of land; AGR soil

terso, -a *adj* **1.** (*liso*) smooth; (*tirante*) taut **2.** (*limpio*) clean; (*transparente*) clear; (*brillante*) shiny **3.** (*sencillo*) easy; (*fluido*) flowing

tertulia *f* **1.** (*reunión*) gathering; **estar de** ~ to talk; **hacer** ~ to meet informally to talk; ~ **literaria** literary circle **2.** (*para jugar*) games room

tesina *f* project; UNIV (*trabajo*) minor thesis

tesis *f inv* **1.** (*proposición*) theory **2.** (*trabajo*) thesis; ~ **doctoral** doctorate [*o* doctoral] thesis

tesitura *f* **1.** (*disposición*) frame of mind **2.** MÚS range

tesón *m* tenacity; **trabajar con** ~ to work diligently

tesonero, -a *adj AmL* **1.** (*perseverante*) persevering **2.** (*tenaz*) tenacious

tesorería *f* **1.** (*cargo*) treasury **2.** *t.* FIN (*despacho*) treasurer's office

tesorero, -a *m, f* treasurer

tesoro *m* **1.** (*de gran valor*) treasure; **ser un** ~ **de una persona** to be a real treasure; **valer un** ~ to be worth a fortune **2.** (*fortuna*) fortune; ~ (**público**) Exchequer, Treasury **3.** (*cariño*) dear

test *m* test

testa *f* **1.** (*cabeza*) head; ~ **dura** hard head; ~ **de ferro** figurehead **2.** (*frente*) forehead **3.** *inf* (*sensatez*) brains *pl*

testaferro *m* man of straw

testamentario, -a **I.** *adj* testamentary **II.** *m, f* executor *m,* executrix *f*

testamento *m* will, testament; ~ **abierto** nuncupative will; **hacer** ~ to make one's will

testar *vi* to make a will

testarada *f* bump on the head; **darse una** ~ to bump one's head; **darse una** ~ **con alguien** *t. fig* to bump heads

testarudez *f* **1.** (*cualidad*) pigheadedness **2.** (*acción*) an act of stubbornness

testarudo, -a **I.** *adj* pigheaded **II.** *m, f* stubborn person

testera *f* **1.** (*de la cabeza*) forehead **2.** (*parte*) front part; (*fachada*) facade

testículo *m* ANAT testicle

testificar <c→qu> **I.** *vt* **1.** (*declarar*) to testify; (*testigo*) to witness **2.** (*afirmar: testigo*) to attest; (*documento*) to bear witness **3.** (*demostrar*) to give evidence **II.** *vi* to testify

testigo¹ *mf t.* JUR witness; ~ **de cargo/de descargo** witness for the prosecution/defence *Brit* [*o* defense *Am*]; ~ **de matrimonio** witness at sb's wedding; ~ **ocular** eyewitness; **fui** ~ **del accidente** I witnessed the accident; **examinar** ~**s** to examine witnesses; **poner a alguien por** ~ to cite sb as witness; **a Dios pongo por testigo** I swear to God

testigo² *m* **1.** (*prueba*) proof; **ser** ~ **de algo** to bear witness to sth **2.** DEP baton

testimonial *adj* **1.** (*que afirma*) attesting; **declaración** ~ testimony **2.** (*que prueba*) testificatory

testimoniar **I.** *vt* **1.** (*declarar*) to testify **2.** (*afirmar*) to attest **3.** (*dar muestra*) to show **4.** (*probar*) to be proof of **II.** *vi* to testify

testimonio *m* **1.** (*declaración*) testimony; **dar** ~ to testify; **no levantarás falso** ~ thou shalt not bear false witness **2.** (*afirmación*) affidavit **3.** (*muestra*) evidence **4.** (*prueba*) proof

testosterona *f* **1.** (*hormona*) testosterone **2.** *inf* (*violencia brutal*) **es una película con mucha** ~ it's a film with a lot of violence

testuz *m o f* **1.** (*frente*) forehead **2.** (*nuca*) nape

teta *f* **1.** *inf* (*pecho*) breast; **niño de** ~ *inf* babe-in-arms; **dar la** ~ to breast-feed; **quitar la** ~ to wean **2.** (*ubre*) udder **3.** (*pezón: mujer*) nipple; (*animal*) teat

tétano(s) *m* (*inv*) MED tetanus

tetera *f* **1.** (*para té*) teapot; (*para hervir*) kettle **2.** *AmL* (*tetilla*) nipple **3.** *AmL v.* **tetero**

tetero *m AmL* baby's bottle

tetilla *f* 1.(*biberón*) nipple 2.(*animal*) teat 3.(*queso*) cone-shaped cheese (*type of cheese made in Galicia*)

tetrabrik® *m* carton; **un ~ de leche/zumo** a carton of milk/juice

tétrico, -a *adj* dismal

tetuda *adj vulg* big-breasted

textil I. *adj* textile; **planta ~** textile mill II. *m* textile

texto *m* text; (*pasaje*) extract; (**libro de**) **~** textbook

textual *adj* 1.(*relativo al texto*) textual; (*escrito*) written 2.(*conforme al texto*) textual; (*literal*) word-for-word; (*exacto*) exact; **con las palabras ~es** with those exact words

textura *f* 1.(*tejido*) weave 2.(*estructura*) structure; GEO, QUÍM texture

tez *f* complexion; **de ~ morena** dark

ti *pron pers* a **~** (*objeto directo, indirecto*) you; **de ~** from you; **de ~ para mí** from you for me; **para ~** for you; **por ~** for you

tía *f* 1.(*pariente*) aunt; **~ abuela** great-aunt; ¡(**cuéntaselo a**) **tu ~!** *inf* tell that to the marines!; **no hay tu ~** *inf* nothing doing! 2. *inf* (*mujer*) woman; **ser una ~ buena** to be a good-looking woman; ¡**qué ~ más buena!** what a babe!; **vaya ~ más tonta** what a stupid woman!; **pero ~, ¿qué te pasa?** hey, girl, what's the matter with you?

tianguis *m inv, Méx* (*rastro indígena*) street market

tiarrón, -ona *m, f inf* big guy

tibetano, -a *adj, m, f* Tibetan

tibia *f* ANAT tibia, shinbone *inf*

tibiarse *vr AmC, Ven* (*irritarse*) to get cross

tibiera *f Ven* 1.(*molestia*) irritation 2.(*fastidio*) nuisance

tibieza *f* lukewarmness; (*apatía*) lack of enthusiasm; (*frialdad en el trato*) coolness

tibio, -a *adj* 1.(*temperatura*) lukewarm 2.(*carácter, sentimiento*) unenthusiastic 3. *AmL, inf* (*enfadado*) angry ▶**poner ~ a alguien** to lay in to sb; **ponerse ~ (de comida)** to stuff oneself

tibor *m* 1.(*vasija*) vase 2. *AmL* (*orinal*) chamber pot

tiburón *m* 1. ZOOL shark 2. FIN raider

tic *m* <tics> tic; (*manía*) habit

tico, -a *adj, m, f AmL, inf* (*costarricense*) Costa Rican

tictac I. *interj* tick-tock; **hacer ~** to tick II. *m sin pl* ticking

tiempo *m* 1.(*momento, duración, periodo*) time; **~ libre/de ocio** spare/leisure time; **al poco ~** shortly after; **~ de pago** payday; **los buenos ~s** the good old days; **a ~** in time; **a ~ parcial** part-time; **a su ~** in due course; **todo a su ~** all in good time; **cada cosa a su ~** there is a time for everything; **al (mismo) ~, a un ~** at the same time; **al ~ que...** while ...; **antes de ~** early; **llegar antes de ~** to arrive ahead of time; **andando el ~** in the course of time; **con ~** in good time; **llegué a la estación con** ~ I reached the station early; **hazlo con ~** don't leave it for the last minute; **de ~ en ~** from time to time; **desde hace mucho ~** for a long time; **durante cierto ~** for some time; **en estos ~s** nowadays; **en ~s de paz** in peacetime; **en ~s de Franco** in the Franco era; **en mis ~s** in my time [*o* day]; **en otros ~s** in the past; **el ~ pasa volando** time flies; **amanecerán ~s mejores** better days are coming; **dar ~ al ~** to give it time; **este problema ya viene de ~** this problem goes way back; **hace ~ que...** it's a long time since ...; **hace ~ que no voy al cine** I haven't been to the cinema for a long time; ¡**cuánto ~ sin verte!** long time no see!; **les faltó ~ para decirlo a todos** it didn't take them long to tell everyone; **hay ~** there's time; **matar el/hacer ~** to kill time; **mucho/demasiado ~** long/too long; **perder el ~** to waste time; **sin perder ~** losing no time; **si me da ~...** if I have enough time; **ya es ~ que +subj** it's about time; **tomarse ~** to take one's time 2.(*época*) time; (*estación*) season 3. METEO weather; **cerveza del ~** beer at room temperature; **~ de perros** filthy weather; **el ~ amenaza lluvia** it's threatening rain; **si el ~ no lo impide** weather permitting; **hoy hace mal ~** the weather is bad today 4. LING tense; **~ presente** present tense 5.(*edad*) age; ¿**cuánto ~ tiene el niño?** how old is the child? 6. DEP (*medio*) ~ half-time; ~ **muerto** time out 7. MÚS time, beat; (*parte*) movement; TÉC stroke; **motor de dos ~s** two-stroke engine ▶a(l) **mal ~ buena cara** *prov* you have to look on the bright side of things *prov;* **el ~ es oro** *prov* time is money *prov;* **el ~ no perdona** *prov* time and tide wait for no man *prov*

tienda *f* 1.(*establecimiento*) shop, store; **~ de comestibles** grocer's *Brit*, grocery store *Am;* **ir de ~s** to go shopping 2.(*alojamiento*) **~ (de campaña)** tent; **montar/desmontar una ~** to put up [*o* pitch]/take down a tent

tienta *f* 1. MED probe 2.(*astucia*) cleverness ▶**andar a ~s** to feel one's way

tiento *m* 1.(*acción*) touch; **a ~** gropingly 2.(*prueba*) try; **dar un ~ a la botella** *inf* to take a swig from the bottle 3.(*examen*) check; **dar un ~** to test; **dar un ~ al melón** to see if the melon is ripe 4.(*tacto*) tact; (*cautela*) caution; **con ~** carefully; (*cuidado*) care 5.(*de un ciego*) blindman's cane 6.(*tentáculo*) tentacle 7.(*pulso*) sureness of hand; **con ~** with a steady hand

tierno, -a I. *adj* 1.(*blando*) soft; (*pan, dulces*) fresh 2.(*suave, delicado, sensible*) tender; **a tierna edad** at a tender age; **desde mi más tierna edad...** since I was very young ...; **en mi más tierna niñez** in early childhood; ¡**qué ~!** how tender! 3.(*cariñoso*) affectionate 4. *Chile, Ecua, Guat* (*inmaduro*) green II. *m, f Guat, Nic* newborn or very young child

tierra *f* 1.(*materia, superficie, planeta*) earth; **~ vegetal** humus; **toma de ~** ELEC earth *Brit,* ground *Am;* **bajo** ~ MIN underground; **estar bajo** ~ to be buried; ~ **de nadie** no-man's-land; **~s altas/bajas** highlands/lowlands; **dar en** ~ to fall; **caer por** ~ *fig* to crumble; **echar** ~ **a algo** *fig* to cover sth up; **echar por** ~ to knock down; *fig* to ruin; **me falta** ~ *fig* I'm not sure; **¡trágame, ~!** *inf* I wish the ground would open up and swallow me!; **parece que se lo ha tragado la** ~ *inf* it is as if he had vanished off the face of the earth **2.** (*firme*) mainland; ~ **adentro** inland; **poner** ~ **por medio** to make oneself scarce; **tomar** ~ AVIAT to land, to touch down; NÁUT to land; **como no lleguemos pronto a la estación, nos vamos a quedar en** ~ if we don't get to the station soon, the train will leave without us **3.** (*región*) land; **Tierra Santa** Holy Land; ~ (**natal**) native land **4.** (*hacienda*) property; ~ **de labor** agricultural land; ~ **de pastos** grazing land; **poseer ~s** to own land; **aquí, como en toda la** ~ **de garbanzos...** *inf* here, like everywhere in the world

tierral *m AmL* (*polvareda*) cloud of dust

tieso *adv* firmly

tieso, -a *adj* **1.** (*rígido*) stiff; **dejar** ~ **a alguien** *inf* (*matar*) to bump sb off; (*sorprender*) to dumbfound; **quedarse** ~ (*de frío*) to be frozen stiff; (*miedo*) to be scared stiff; (*morirse*) to croak; (*dormirse*) to fall asleep **2.** (*erguido*) erect; (*orejas*) pricked up **3.** (*terco*) unbending; **tenérselas tiesas** to hold firm **4.** (*serio*) stiff **5.** (*engreído*) conceited; **no te pongas** ~ don't act so stuck up **6.** (*tirante*) taut **7.** (*valiente*) brave **8.** (*robusto*) robust; (*sano*) fit

tiesto *m* **1.** (*maceta*) flowerpot **2.** *Chile* (*vasija*) pot, bowl

tiesura *f* stiffness

tifoideo, -a *adj* typhoid; **fiebre tifoidea** typhoid fever

tifón *m* **1.** (*huracán*) typhoon **2.** (*tromba*) waterspout

tifus *m inv* MED typhus

tigre, -a *m, f AmL* ZOOL jaguar

tigre(sa) *m(f)* **1.** ZOOL tiger *m*, tigress *f;* **oler a** ~ *inf* to stink **2.** (*persona*) tiger

tijera *f* **1.** (*pl*) (*utensilio, con esta forma*) scissors *pl;* (*más grandes*) shears *pl;* **silla de** ~ folding chair; **echar** ~ **a algo** *inf* to start cutting sth **2.** (*persona*) gossip **3.** DEP scissor-kick

tijereta *f* earwig

tijeretada *f,* **tijeretazo** *m* snip

tijeretear I. *vt* to snip II. *vi* **1.** (*cortar*) to cut **2.** *inf* (*entrometerse*) to meddle

tila *f* **1.** (*tilo*) linden tree **2.** (*flor*) linden-blossom **3.** (*té*) linden-blossom tea

tildar *vt* **1.** (*con acento*) to put an accent on **2.** (*la ñ*) to put a tilde over **3.** (*a alguien*) ~ **de algo** to brand as sth **4.** (*tachar*) to cross out

tilde *f* **1.** (*acento*) accent **2.** (*de la ñ*) tilde **3.** (*tacha*) flaw **4.** (*cosa mínima*) jot

tiliches *mpl AmC, Méx* (*trastos*) junk

tilín *m sin pl* (*sonido*) tinkle; **¡~!** ting-a-ling! ▸ **hacer** ~ to appeal; **el pastel no me hace** ~ I

don't like the cake much

tilingo, -a *adj* **1.** *CSur, Méx* (*atolondrado*) silly **2.** *Arg* (*demente*) soft in the head

tilo *m* linden

timador(a) *m(f)* swindler

timar I. *vt* to con II. *vr:* ~**se** (*hacer guiños*) to make eyes at each other; (*tontear*) to flirt

timba *f inf* **1.** (*partida*) game **2.** (*lugar*) gambling den **3.** *AmL* (*barriga*) belly

timbal *m* **1.** MÚS small drum; (*grande*) kettledrum **2.** GASTR meat pie

timbrar *vt* (*pegar*) to put a stamp on; (*estampar*) to postmark

timbrazo *m* loud ring

timbre *m* **1.** (*aparato*) bell; (*de la puerta*) doorbell; **han tocado el** ~ somebody rang the bell **2.** *t.* MÚS (*sonido*) timbre **3.** (*sello que se pega*) stamp; (*que se estampa*) seal **4.** (*acción*) action to one's credit; ~ **de gloria** mark of honour *Brit,* mark of honor *Am;* **ser un** ~ **de gloria para alguien** to be a credit to sb

timidez *f* shyness

tímido, -a *adj* shy, timid

timo *m* **1.** (*fraude*) con; **dar un** ~ **de 5.000 ptas a alguien** to swindle sb out of 5000 pesetas **2.** (*glándula*) thymus

timón *m* rudder; **llevar el** ~ **de una empresa** *inf* to be at the helm of a business

timonel *mf* helmsman

timorato, -a *adj* **1.** (*tímido*) timid **2.** (*de Dios*) God-fearing; *pey* spineless

tímpano *m* **1.** ANAT (*membrana*) eardrum **2.** (*instrumento*) kettledrum

tina *f* vat; *AmL* (*bañera*) bathtub

tinaja *f* large earthenware jar

tincanque *m Chile, inf* flip

tincar <c→qu> *vt* **1.** *Chile* (*presentir*) to have a hunch **2.** *Arg, Chile* (*pelota*) to drive

tincazo *m Arg, Ecua, inf* flick

tinerfeño, -a I. *adj* of/from Tenerife II. *m, f* native/inhabitant of Tenerife

tinga *f Méx* (*alboroto*) uproar

tinglado *m* **1.** (*cobertizo*) shed **2.** *inf* (*lío*) tangle **3.** (*artimaña*) intrigue; **manejar el** ~ to pull the strings **4.** (*tablado*) platform

tingo *Méx* **del** ~ **al tango** from pillar to post

tiniebla *f* darkness

tino *m* **1.** (*puntería*) aim **2.** (*destreza*) skill **3.** (*moderación*) moderation; **a buen** ~ by guesswork; **sin** ~ recklessly; **estar a** ~ to be guessing; **sacar de** ~ **a alguien** to exasperate sb **4.** (*tina*) vat

tinoso, -a *adj Col, Ven* **1.** (*hábil*) skilful *Brit,* skillful *Am* **2.** (*sensato*) sensible

tinta *f* **1.** (*para escribir*) ink; ~ **china** Indian ink; ~ **de imprenta** printer's ink; **a dos ~s** in two colours *Brit* [*o* colors *Am*]; **cargar las ~s** to exaggerate; **saber algo de buena** ~ to know sth from a reliable source; **sudar** ~ to sweat blood; **sobre este asunto han corrido ríos de** ~ much has been written about this matter **2.** (*color*) hue; **medias ~s** half-tones;

fig half measures
tintar *vt* to dye
tinte *m* 1.(*teñidura*) dye 2.(*colorante*) colouring *Brit,* coloring *Am* 3.(*tintorería*) dry cleaner's 4.(*matiz*) tinge; (*apariencia*) touch; **un cierto ~ de escepticismo** a certain touch of scepticism *Brit* [*o* skepticism *Am*]; **tus palabras tenían un cierto ~ de ironía** his words were tinged with irony
tinterillo *m pey* 1.(*chupatintas*) penpusher 2.*AmL* (*picapleitos*) shyster lawyer
tintero *m* inkwell; **dejar(se) algo en el ~** *fig* to leave sth unsaid
tintín *m* clinking
tintin(e)ar *vi* to clink
tinto, -a *adj* (*rojo oscuro*) dark red; (*uvas*) red; **vino ~** red wine
tintorería *f* dry cleaner's
tintorro *m inf* cheap red wine, plonk *Brit*
tintura *f* 1.(*tinte*) tint 2.(*colorante*) dye 3.(*maquillaje*) rouge 4.*MED* tincture
tiña *f* 1.*MED* ringworm 2.*inf* (*miseria*) poverty
tiñoso, -a *adj* 1.*MED* scabby 2.*inf* (*mísero*) poor 3.(*tacaño*) stingy
tío *m* 1.(*pariente*) uncle; **~ abuelo** great--uncle; **mis ~s** my aunt and uncle; **tener un ~ en América** to have a rich friend or relative 2.*inf* (*hombre*) bloke *Brit,* guy; **¡oye ~!** hey, man!; **ser un ~ bueno** to be a good-looking guy
tiovivo *m* merry-go-round, carrousel *Am;* **dar más vueltas que un ~** *inf* to go all over the place
tipear *vi AmC, AmS* to type
tipejo *m pey* twerp
típico, -a *adj* typical; **plato ~** local or traditional dish
tipificar *vt* 1.(*normalizar*) to standardize 2.(*caracterizar*) to typify
tipismo *m* local colour *Brit,* local color *Am,* picturesqueness
tiple¹ *mf MÚS* (*persona*) soprano
tiple² *m MÚS* (*voz*) soprano
tipo *m* 1.(*modelo*) model 2.(*muestra*) sample; (*espécimen*) type; **un impreso/una carta ~** a standard form/letter 3.(*cuerpo*) build; **aguantar el ~** to hold out; **arriesgar el ~** *inf* to risk one's neck; **mover el ~** *inf* to get moving; **tener buen ~** to have a good figure; **él tiene buen ~** he's well-built 4.(*clase*) type, kind 5.*FIN* rate; **~ de cambio** exchange rate 6.*TIPO* type
tipo, -a *m, f* 1.*inf* guy *m,* woman *f* 2.*pey* character; **~ raro** weirdo; **no soporto esa tipa** I can't stand that bitch
tipografía *f* (*impresión*) printing; (*taller*) printing press
tipográfico, -a *adj* printing
tipógrafo, -a *m, f* printer
tiquear *vt* 1.*AmC, PRico, Col* (*chequear*) to check 2.*Chile* (*perforar*) to punch
tíquet *m* <tíquets> (*de viaje, de espectáculos*) ticket; (*de compra*) sales slip, receipt

tiquismiquis¹ *mf inv* (*remilgado*) fusspot
tiquismiquis² *mpl* 1.(*remilgo*) silly scruples *pl* 2.(*ñoñería*) finickiness
tira *f* 1.(*banda*) strip, band; **~ cómica** comic strip; **hacer ~s algo** to tear sth to shreds 2.*inf* (*mucho*) **esto me ha gustado la ~** I really liked this a lot
tirabuzón *m* 1.(*rizo*) ringlet, curl 2.(*sacacorchos*) corkscrew
tirachinas *m inv* catapult *Brit,* slingshot *Am*
tirada *f* 1.(*edición*) print run; **el periódico local tiene una ~ de 10.000 ejemplares** the local paper has a circulation of 10,000 copies; **de una ~** *fig* without stopping 2.(*distancia*) stretch
tiradero *m Méx* (*vertedero*) rubbish dump
tirado, -a I. *adj* 1. estar *inf* (*barato*) dirt cheap; **dejar ~ a alguien** (*decepcionar*) to let sb down; (*en situación difícil*) to leave in the lurch 2. ser *pey* (*descuidado*) slovenly 3. estar *inf* (*fácil*) very easy; **ese ejercicio está ~** that exercise is dead easy II. *m, f inf* nohoper
tirador *m* 1.(*agarradero*) handle, knob 2.(*cordón*) pull chain 3.(*tirachinas*) catapult *Brit,* slingshot *Am*
tirador(a) *m(f)* (*disparador*) shot, marksman
tiragomas *m inv* catapult *Brit,* slingshot *Am*
tiralevitas *mf inv* bootlicker
tiralíneas *m inv* ruling pen
tiranía *f* tyranny; **someterse a la ~ de la moda** to be a slave to fashion
tiránico, -a *adj* tyrannical
tiranizar <z→c> *vt* to tyrannize
tirano, -a I. *adj* tyrannic II. *m, f* tyrant, despot
tirante I. *adj* 1.(*tieso*) taut; **el pantalón me está ~** the trousers *Brit* [*o* pants *Am*] are tight on me 2.(*conflictivo*) tense; **estar ~ con alguien** to have strained relations with sb II. *m* 1.(*travesaño*) strut; **se me caen los ~s de este vestido** the straps on this dress keep slipping; **~s** (*elásticos*) braces *pl Brit,* suspenders *pl Am* 2.(*de caballería*) trace
tirantez *f* 1.(*tensión*) tension, strain 2.(*extensión*).stretch
tirar I. *vi* 1.(*arrastrar*) **~ de algo** to pull on sth; **tira y afloja** give and take; **a todo ~** at the most; **~ de la lengua a alguien** to draw sb out 2.(*atraer*) to attract; **no me tiran los libros** I'm not very interested in books 3.(*sacar*) **~ de algo** to pull out sth 4.(*chimenea*) to draw 5.(*colores*) **~ a rojo** to tend toward red 6.(*vestidos*) **esta camisa me tira de los hombros** this shirt is tight in the shoulders 7.(*querer lograr*) **~ para director** to be aiming at being director 8.(*parecerse*) to take after; **él tira a su padre** he takes after his father 9.(*torcer*) to turn; **aquí cada uno tira por su lado** here everyone takes his/her own turning 10.(*disparar*) to shoot; **~ al blanco** to target shoot ► **¿qué tal? – vamos tirando** *inf* how are you? – we're managing II. *vt* 1.(*lanzar*) to throw; **~ piedras a alguien** to throw stones at sb 2.(*malgastar*) to waste 3.(*de-*

sechar) to throw away **4.** (*disparar*) to shoot; (*bombas*) to drop; (*cohetes*) to launch **5.** (*derribar*) to knock down; (*árbol*) to fell; (*edificio*) to pull down **6.** (*trazar*) to draw **7.** (*imprimir*) to print **8.** (*extender*) to stretch **9.** FOTO to take **10.** (*derramar*) to spill **III.** *vr:* ~**se 1.** (*lanzarse*) to throw oneself **2.** (*echarse*) to lie down **3.** *inf* (*pasar*) to spend; ~**se una hora esperando** to spend an hour waiting **4.** (*acometer*) to throw oneself **5.** *vulg* (*copular*) ~**se a alguien** to lay sb

tirita *f* plaster *Brit,* Band Aid®

tiritar *vi* to shiver; **se me ha quedado la cuenta del banco tiritando** there isn't much left in my bank account

tiritón *m* shiver; **dar tiritones** to shiver

tiro *m* **1.** (*lanzamiento, disparo*) shot; ~ **a portería** shot at goal; ~ **al aire** warning shot; **barraca de** ~ **al blanco** shooting range; ~ **con arco** archery; **a** ~ in range; *fig* accessible; **a** ~ **limpio** guns blazing; **dar un** ~ to fire a shot; **estar a un** ~ **de piedra** to be a stone's throw away; **¡que le den un** ~**!** *inf* somebody shoot him!; **pegarse un** ~ to shoot oneself; **no van por ahí los** ~**s** *inf* that's not the way the wind is blowing; **me salió el** ~ **por la culata** *inf* it backfired on me **2.** (*munición*) round **3.** (*daño*) injury **4.** (*alcance*) range **5.** (*arrastre*) pull **6.** (*caballerías*) team **7.** (*arreos*) trace; **poner el** ~ **a los caballos** to harness the horses **8.** (*corriente de aire*) draught *Brit,* draft *Am* **9.** *inf* (*heroína*) heroin ▶**a** ~ **hecho** deliberately; **de** ~**s largos** all dressed up, dressed to kill; **sentar a alguien como un** ~ (*comida*) to disagree with sb; (*noticia*) to upset sb; **ni a** ~**s** not on a long shot

tiroides I. *adj inv* ANAT **glándula** ~ thyroid gland **II.** *m inv* MED thyroid

tirolés, -esa I. *adj* Tyrolese **II.** *m, f* Tyrolean

tirón *m* (*acción*) snatch; **de un** ~ (*bruscamente*) suddenly; (*de una vez*) without stopping, in one go *Brit;* **no lo sacan de aquí ni a (dos) tirones** not for a million years will they get him out of here

tironear *vt* to tug at

tirotear I. *vt* to shoot at **II.** *vr:* ~**se 1.** (*disparar*) to shoot at each other **2.** (*disputar*) to quarrel

tiroteo *m* shooting

tirria *f* *inf* dislike; **tener** ~ **a alguien** to have a grudge against sb

tisana *f* herbal tea

tísico, -a I. *adj* MED tubercular **II.** *m, f* consumptive person

tisis *f inv* MED tuberculosis

tisú *m* tissue

titán *m* Titan

titánico, -a *adj* titanic

titanio *m* QUÍM titanium

titeo *m* *Arg, Bol, Urug* **1.** (*burla*) mocking **2.** (*tomadura de pelo*) teasing; **tomar a alguien para el** ~ to make fun of sb

títere *m* **1.** *t. fig* (*muñeco*) puppet; **no dejar** ~

con cabeza to spare no one **2.** (*tipejo*) weakling **3.** *pl* (*espectáculo*) puppet show

titilar *vi* **1.** (*temblar*) to quiver **2.** (*centellear*) to twinkle

titipuchal *m* *Méx, inf* (*tropel*) throng

titiritero, -a *m, f* **1.** (*persona que maneja los títeres*) puppeteer **2.** (*acróbata*) acrobat

tito, -a *m, f* *inf* *diminutivo de* **tío**

titubear *vi* **1.** (*vacilar*) to waver; *fig* to hesitate **2.** (*balbucear*) to stutter

titubeo *m* **1.** (*vacilación*) tottering; *fig* hesitation; **deja a un lado tus** ~**s** put your doubts aside **2.** (*balbuceo*) stammering

titulación *f* (*denominación*) title; (*académica*) qualifications *pl*

titulado, -a I. *adj* titled **II.** *m, f* degree holder; ~ (**universitario**) university graduate

titular¹ I. *adj* **profesor** ~ full professor **II.** *mf* holder; ~ **de acciones** shareholder

titular² I. *m* headline; **aparecer en los** ~**es** to appear in the newspaper headlines; **ocupar los** ~**es** to be in all the newspapers **II.** *vt* (*poner título*) to title **III.** *vr:* ~**se** to be entitled; **el libro se titula…** the book is titled …

titularidad *f* ownership

título *m* **1.** (*rótulo, dignidad*) title; ~ **de crédito** credits **2.** (*diploma*) diploma; ~ **universitario** university degree **3.** (*motivo*) reason; **¿a** ~ **de qué hace Ud. eso?** why are you doing that?; **a justo** ~ rightly **4.** (*en calidad de*) **a** ~ **de** by way of; **a** ~ **de devolución** as a refund; **a** ~ **gratuito** for free; **a** ~ **de prueba** as a trial **5.** (*valor comercial*) bond **6.** ~ **de propiedad** (property) deeds *pl*

tiza *f* chalk

tizate *m* *Guat, Hond, Nic* chalk

tiznado, -a *adj* *AmC* drunk

tiznar I. *vt* **1.** (*ennegrecer*) to blacken **2.** (*desacreditar*) to sully **II.** *vr:* ~**se** (*entiznarse*) to get dirty

tizne *m o f* (*hollín*) soot

tiznón *m* smudge

tizón *m* **1.** (*palo*) partly-burned stick; **más negro que un** ~ as black as coal **2.** (*deshonra*) stain

tlachique *m* *Méx* GASTR unfermented pulque

tlacote *m* *Méx* MED **1.** (*absceso*) boil **2.** (*tumor*) tumour *Brit,* tumor *Am*

tlapalería *f* *Méx* (*ferretería*) ironmonger's *Brit,* hardware store *Am*

toalla *f* towel; ~ **de lavabo/baño** hand/bath towel; **arrojar la** ~ *fig* to throw in the towel

toallero *m* towel rail, towel rack *Am*

toallita *f* small towel, towelette; ~**s húmedas** wet wipes

toba *f* **1.** (*piedra*) tufa **2.** (*sarro*) tartar **3.** (*capa*) crust

tobera *f* nozzle

tobillera *f* ankle support

tobillo *m* ankle

tobo *m* *Ven* (*cubo*) bucket

tobogán *m* **1.** (*deslizadero*) slide **2.** (*pista*) chute **3.** (*trineo*) toboggan, sledge *Brit,* sled

Am
toca *f* headdress
tocadiscos *m inv* record player
tocado *m* **1.** (*peinado*) hairdo **2.** (*complemento*) headdress
tocado, -a *adj* **1.** (*perturbado*) slightly touched; **estar ~ (de la cabeza)** to be not all there **2.** (*lesionado*) injured **3.** (*medio podrido*) going bad **4.** (*cubierto en la cabeza*) **ir ~ de un sombrero** to be wearing a hat
tocador *m* **1.** (*mueble*) dressing table **2.** (*habitación*) ladies' dressing room; (*servicios*) ladies' room **3.** (*estuche*) vanity case
tocador(a) *m(f)* MÚS **~ de guitarra** guitarist
tocamiento *f* feeling, fondling
tocante *adj* **~ a** concerning
tocar <c→qu> I. *vt* **1.** (*contacto*) to touch, to feel; **tócame la frente (y dime si está caliente)** feel my forehead (and tell me if it's hot); **~ de cerca algo** *fig* to hit home; **~ fondo** to hit bottom; **¡no lo toques!** don't touch it! **2.** MÚS to play; (*campana*) to ring; (*tambor*) to beat; **~ la bocina** to blow the horn; **~ alarma** to sound the alarm; **~ a fuego** to sound the fire alarm; **~ a misa** to ring the bell for mass; **~ a muerto** to toll (a death knell); **el reloj tocó las tres** the clock struck three; **~ el timbre** to ring the doorbell; **~ a la puerta** to knock at the door **3.** (*modificar*) to change **4.** (*chocar*) to run into **5.** (*afectar*) to affect; **~ en el corazón** to touch one's heart **6.** (*peinar*) to comb II. *vi* **1.** (*corresponder*) **te toca a ti decidir** it's up to you to decide; **te toca jugar** it's your turn; **hoy me toca salir** today I have to go out **2.** (*obligación*) **me toca barrer el patio todas las mañanas** I have to sweep the courtyard every morning **3.** (*llegar el momento oportuno*) to be time; **toca ir a la compra** it's time to do the shopping **4.** (*caer en suerte*) to fall; **le tocó a él hacerlo** it fell to him to do it; **le tocó el premio gordo** he/she won the grand prize **5.** (*estar muy cerca*) to verge on **6.** (*ser parientes*) to be related III. *vr:* **~se 1.** (*estar en contacto*) to touch **2.** (*peinarse*) to do one's hair **3.** (*cubrirse la cabeza*) **~se con un sombrero** to wear a hat; **~se con un pañuelo** to cover one's head with a scarf ►**los extremos se tocan** *prov* extremes meet *prov*; **tocárselas** *inf* to beat it
tocateja **a ~** cash
tocayo, -a *m, f* namesake
tocho *m* **1.** (*hierro*) iron ingot **2.** *inf* (*libro*) thick book
tocho, -a *adj* **1.** (*tosco*) coarse **2.** (*necio*) foolish
tocineta *f Col v.* **tocino**
tocino *m* (*lardo*) pork fat; (*carne*) bacon; **confundir la velocidad con el ~** *inf* to mix up two completely different things
tocología *f sin pl* MED obstetrics *pl*
tocólogo, -a *m, f* MED obstetrician
tocón *m* stump
todavía *adv* **1.** (*aún*) still; **~ no** not yet; **es ~**

más caro que... it is even more expensive than ... **2.** (*sin embargo*) **pero ~** however
todo I. *pron indef* all; **~ lo que...**, **~ cuanto...** all ...; (o) **~ o nada** all or nothing; **~ lo más** at the most; **es ~ uno** it's all one and the same; **ante** [*o* **sobre**] **~** above all; **~ lo contrario** quite the contrary; **antes que ~** first of all; **después de ~** *inf* after all; **con ~** nevertheless; **en ~ y por ~** absolutely; **y ~** and all; **estar en ~** *inf* to be on the ball, not to miss a thing; **me invitaron a comer y ~** they even invited me to eat (and all); **para ~** all-purpose; **me es ~ uno** it's all the same to me II. *adv inf* all, completely III. *m sin pl* (*la totalidad*) the whole; **del ~** completely; **no del ~** not entirely; **jugarse el ~ por el ~** to risk all; **ser el ~** to be the chief
todo, -a *art indef* **1.** (*entero*) all; **toda la familia** the whole family; **toda España** all Spain; **en toda Europa** all over Europe; **a toda prisa**, **a ~ correr** as fast as possible **2.** (*cada*) every; **a toda costa** at all cost; **~ Dios** [*o* **quisqui**] *inf* absolutely everyone; **toda precaución es poca** there are never too many precautions taken **3.** *pl* all; **día de Todos los Santos** All Saints' Day; **a ~s los niños les gusta el chocolate** all children like chocolate; **~s los niños de la clase tomaron chocolate** all of the children in the class had chocolate; **~s y cada uno** each and every one; **a todas horas** at all hours; **en todas partes** everywhere; **de ~s modos** anyway **4.** (*intensificación*) **su cara es toda nariz** his face is all nose; **ser ~ nervios** to be a bundle of nerves
todopoderoso, -a *adj* almighty
todoterreno I. *adj inv* all-purpose, versatile II. *m* AUTO all-terrain vehicle; **ser un ~** *fig* to be a Jack-of-all-trades
toga *f* robe; (*romana*) toga
Togo *m* Togo
togolés, -esa *adj, m, f* Togolese
toldillo *m Col* mosquito net
toldo *m* **1.** (*marquesina*) marquee; (*en un balcón*) canopy; (*en una tienda*) awning *Brit*, sunshade *Am* **2.** (*de carro*) tarpaulin
tole *m* **1.** (*bulla*) hubbub; **se armó un ~ tremendo** there was a tremendous commotion **2.** (*rumor*) rumour *Brit*, rumor *Am* **3.** *inf* (*irse*) **tomar el ~** to beat it
toledano, -a I. *adj* Toledan; **noche toledana** *fig* sleepless night II. *m, f* Toledan
tolerancia *f* **1.** (*indulgencia*) tolerance **2.** (*resistencia*) tolerance
tolerante *adj* tolerant
tolerar *vt* **1.** (*soportar*) to bear, to tolerate; (*alimentos, medicinas*) to be able to take **2.** (*permitir*) **~ algo** to be lenient with sth, to allow sth; **una película tolerada para menores** a film suitable for children **3.** (*aceptar*) tolerate
tolete *m* **1.** *AmL* (*garrote*) bludgeon **2.** *Col, Cuba* (*trozo*) piece
tolvanera *f AmC, Méx* (*polvareda*) cloud of dust

toma *f* **1.** (*adquisición*) taking; ~ **de conciencia** awareness; ~ **de declaración** taking of evidence; ~ **de datos** INFOR data acquisition; ~ **de decisiones** decision making; ~ **de poder** takeover; ~ **de posesión** taking office; ~ **de rehenes** taking of hostages **2.** (*conquista*) capture; ~ **por asalto** to take by storm **3.** (*dosis*) dose **4.** TÉC inlet; ~ **de tierra** ground **5.** (*grabación*) take **6.** (*ingesta*) intake **7.** FOTO shot
tomacorriente *m* **1.** *AmL* (*colector*) collector **2.** *Arg, Perú* (*enchufe*) socket, plug
tomadura *f* taking; ~ **de pelo** (*burla*) joke; (*timo*) rip-off; (*engaño*) hoax
tomar I. *vi* to turn; ~ **por la derecha** to take a right **II.** *vt* **1.** (*coger, quitar, llevar*) to take; (*préstamo*) to borrow; (*aliento*) to catch; (*fuerzas*) to gather; ~ **las armas** to take up arms; ~ **una decisión** to make a decision; ~ **medidas** to take measures **2.** (*beber*) to have, to drink; ~ **café** to have coffee; **no tomes ese agua** don't drink that water **3.** (*to eat*) to have, to eat **4.** (*interpretar*) to take; ~ **a la ligera** to take lightly; ~ **algo a mal** to take offence at sth *Brit,* to take offense at sth *Am;* ~ **muy a pecho** to take to heart; ~ **a risa** to take as a joke; ~ **en serio** to take seriously; ~ **a alguien por ladrón** to take sb for a thief; **¿por quién me tomas?** what do you take me for? **5.** (*adquirir*) to take; ~ **conciencia de algo** to become aware of sth **6.** (*sentir*) to take; ~ **cariño/odio a alguien** to take a like/dislike to sb; ~ **confianza a alguien** to treat sb as a friend **7.** (*conquistar*) to take, to capture **8.** (*copiar*) to copy **9.** (*contratar*) to hire; ~ **un abogado** to hire a lawyer **10.** (*alquilar*) to rent **11.** (*adoptar*) adopt; ~ **una actitud de...** to adopt an attitude of ... **12.** (*hacerse cargo*) to take over; ~ **sobre sí** to take upon oneself **13.** (*filmar*) to shoot **14.** (*sobrevenir*) to come over **15.** (*transporte*) to take **16.** (*medir*) to take; **le ~ron la tensión** they measured [*o* took] his/her blood pressure **17.** *AmL* (*beber alcohol*) to drink; **no debes** ~ **ni fumar** you shouldn't drink or smoke; **~la** (*emborracharse*) to get drunk **18.** ZOOL (*copular*) to cover; **¡vete a** ~ **por culo!** *vulg* fuck off! ▶**¡toma** castaña**!** well, that will serve you right!; **~la** con **algo/alguien** to take it out on sth/sb; **¡toma!** well! **III.** *vr:* **~se 1.** (*coger*) to take; **~se libertades** to take liberties; **~se unas vacaciones** to take a vacation **2.** (*beber*) to drink, to have; **me he tomado un vaso de leche** I had a glass of milk **3.** (*comer*) to eat, to have **4.** (*ponerse la voz ronca*) **se me ha tomado la voz** I'm hoarse **5.** *AmL* (*emborracharse*) **tomársela** to get drunk **6.** *inf* (*expresión*) **¡tómate esa!** take that!
tomate *m* **1.** BOT tomato **2.** *inf* (*agujero*) hole **3.** *inf* (*situación poco clara*) **tener** ~ to be difficult ▶**ponerse** rojo **como un** ~ to turn as red as a beetroot
tomatera *f* tomato plant
tomavistas[1] *m inv* FOTO film camera *Brit,*

movie camera *Am*
tomavistas[2] *mf inv* FOTO (*operador*) camera(man)
tómbola *f* tombola, charity raffle
tomillo *m* thyme
tomo *m* (*volumen*) volume; **de cuatro ~s** in four volumes ▶**de** ~ **y** lomo out-and-out
tomografía *f* MED tomography; **tomografía axial computerizada** (**TAC**) computerized axial tomograph (CAT)
ton *inf* **sin** ~ **ni son** for no particular reason
tonada *f* **1.** (*canción*) song **2.** (*melodía*) tune, melody **3.** *AmL* (*tonillo*) accent
tonalidad *f* **1.** LING intonation **2.** MÚS tonality, tone; ~ **menor** minor key **3.** ARTE shade
tonel *m* **1.** (*barril*) barrel **2.** *inf* (*persona gorda*) fatso
tonelada *f* (*peso*) ton
tonelaje *m* tonnage
tonelero *m* cooper
tongo *m* DEP fixing; **hubo** ~ it was rigged
tónica *f* **1.** MÚS tonic, keynote **2.** (*bebida*) tonic water **3.** (*tono general*) general trend
tónico *m* **1.** MED tonic **2.** (*para el rostro*) toner; (*para el cabello*) hair tonic
tónico, -a *adj* **1.** LING stressed **2.** MÚS tonic; **nota tónica** keynote **3.** MED tonic
tonificar <c→qu> *vt* to tone up
tonillo *m* **1.** (*deje*) accent, lilt **2.** (*habla monótona*) monotonous tone **3.** (*retintín*) sarcastic tone
tonina *f* *Arg, Urug* ZOOL dolphin
tono *m* **1.** (*altura*) tone, pitch; ~ **agudo/grave** high/low pitch **2.** (*señal*) tone; ~ **de marcar** TEL dialling tone *Brit,* dialtone *Am* **3.** (*intensidad*) **bajar el** ~ to lower one's voice **4.** (*deje, estilo*) tone; **en** ~ **de reproche** reproachfully; **bajar el** ~ to tone down; **dar el** ~ to set the tone; **darse** ~ to put on airs; **fuera de** ~ out of place; **estar a** ~ **con algo** to be in tune with sth; **subirse de** ~ to become heated **5.** (*atmósfera*) tone **6.** (*maneras*) **el buen** ~ refinement; **de buen** ~ tasteful; **de mal** ~ vulgar **7.** MED tone **8.** MÚS (*modo*) key; **mayor/menor** ~ major/minor key; **~s y semitonos** whole tones and halftones
tontaina *mf inf* ninny
tontear *vi* **1.** (*bobear*) to fool around **2.** *inf* to flirt
tontera *f* foolishness
tontería *f* **1.** (*memez*) stupidity, foolishness **2.** (*nadería*) trifle
tonto, -a I. *adj* silly; **ser más** ~ **que Picio** *inf* to be as dumb as they come; **hacer algo a tontas y a locas** to do sth without thinking; **ponerse** ~ *inf* to get silly; **ser** ~ **del culo** *inf* to be a complete idiot; **ser** ~ **perdido** to be dead from the neck up **II.** *m, f* fool; **hacer el** ~ to clown around; **le gusta más que a un** ~ **un lápiz** he/she is crazy about it; **hacerse el** ~ to play dumb; **el** ~ **del pueblo** the village idiot

topacio *m* MIN topaz

topadora *f Arg, Méx, Urug* (*buldózer*) bull-dozer

topar I. *vi* 1. (*chocar*) ~ **con algo** to run into sth; ~ **contra algo** to bump against [*o* into] sth 2. (*hallar*) ~ **con alguien** to bump into sb 3. (*consistir*) to lie 4. *inf* (*salir bien*) to work 5. (*en el juego*) to take a bet II. *vt* 1. (*chocar*) to butt 2. (*hallar: algo*) to come across; (*a alguien*) to bump into III. *vr:* ~**se** 1. (*chocar*) ~**se con algo** to run into sth; ~**se contra algo** to bump against [*o* into] sth 2. (*hallar*) ~**se con alguien** to bump into sb

tope I. *adj* top, maximum; **fecha** ~ latest date, at the latest II. *m* 1. (*extremo*) end; **estar hasta el** ~ (*lleno*) to be jam-packed; (*harto*) to be fed up; **estoy a** ~ **de trabajo** I'm swamped with work 2. (*parachoques*) buffer; AUTO bumper 3. (*para impedir un movimiento*) check; (*puerta*) doorstop 4. (*obstáculo*) obstacle

topera *f* molehill

topetada *f* butt

topetar *vi, vt* to butt

topetazo *m* collision

topetear *vi, vt* to bump into

tópico *m* 1. (*lugar común*) commonplace 2. (*estereotipo*) cliché 3. MED **uso** ~ external application

tópico, -a *adj* 1. (*trivial*) trite 2. (*local*) local 3. MED for external application; **de uso** ~ for external use only

topinambur *m Arg, Bol* BOT Jerusalem artichoke

topless *m* **en** ~ topless

topo *m* 1. (*roedor, espía*) mole; **ver menos que un** ~ *inf* to be as blind as a bat; **ser un** ~ *inf* to be a bumbler 2. (*persona torpe*) clumsy clot 3. (*lunar*) polka dot

topocho, -a *adj Ven* plump

topografía *f* topography, surveying

topógrafo, -a *m, f* surveyor, topographer

topón *m* 1. *Chile, Col, Hond* (*topetazo*) butt 2. *Col* (*puñetazo*) punch

topónimo *m* place name

toposo, -a *adj Ven* 1. (*entrometido*) meddlesome 2. (*pedante*) pretentious

toque *m* 1. (*roce*) touch 2. (*golpe*) tap; **dar un** ~ **en la puerta** to tap on the door 3. (*sonido*) ~ **de campanas** ringing of bells; ~ **de queda** curfew; ~ **de tambor** drumbeat; ~ **de atención** warning note; **dáme un** ~ **más tarde** give me a ring later 4. (*advertencia*) warning 5. (*matiz*) touch; **el** ~ **femenino** a woman's touch 6. (*modificación*) touch up; **dar los últimos** ~**s a algo** to put the finishing touches to [*o* on *Am*] sth 7. (*pincelada*) dab 8. (*ensayo*) test; **piedra de** ~ touchstone 9. (*lo principal*) crux 10. (*aplicación medicinal*) painting of throat

toquetear *vt inf* to fiddle with, to finger

toquilla *f* (*pañuelo*) shawl

tora *f* REL Torah

torada *f* herd of bulls

tórax *m inv* thorax

torbellino *m* whirlwind; **ser un** ~ *inf* to be a bundle of energy

torcaz *adj* **paloma** ~ wood pigeon

torcedura *f* MED sprain

torcer *irr como cocer* I. *vi* to turn; ~ **a la izquierda** to turn left II. *vt* 1. (*encorvar*) to bend 2. (*dar vueltas, desviar*) to wind; ~ **el cuello a alguien** to wring sb's neck; ~ **las intenciones de alguien** to foil sb's plans; ~ **las manos** to wring one's hands; ~ **la vista** to squint 3. (*referente al gesto*) ~ **el gesto** to scowl III. *vr:* ~**se** 1. (*encorvarse*) to bend; **la madera se ha torcido con la humedad** the dampness has warped the wood 2. (*dislocarse*) to sprain; **me he torcido el pie** I've twisted my ankle 3. (*corromperse*) to go astray; (*fracasar*) to go wrong 4. (*agriarse*) to go sour

torcida *f* wick

torcido, -a *adj* 1. (*ladeado*) lopsided 2. (*encorvado*) crooked 3. (*artero*) devious

tordo *m* thrush

tordo, -a I. *adj* 1. (*color*) **yegua torda** dapple-grey mare *Brit*, dapple-gray mare *Am* 2. (*torpe*) dim II. *m, f* dapple-grey horse *Brit*, dapple-gray horse *Am*

torear I. *vi* (*lidiar*) to fight; (*toros*) to bullfight II. *vt* 1. (*lidiar*) to fight; (*toros*) to bullfight 2. (*evitar*) to dodge 3. (*engañar*) to string along 4. (*tomar el pelo*) to tease

toreo *m* 1. (*tauromaquia*) bullfighting 2. (*lidia*) fighting 3. (*burla*) covert mockery

torera *f* bolero (jacket)

torero, -a I. *adj* bullfighting; **valor** ~ outstanding figure in bullfighting II. *m, f* bullfighter, matador; **saltarse algo a la torera** *inf* to blatantly ignore sth; **tener más suerte que un** ~ *inf* to have the luck of the devil

toril *m* bullpen

tormenta *f* 1. *t. fig* (*temporal*) storm 2. (*agitación*) turmoil; **una** ~ **de celos** a fit of jealousy; ~ **de ideas** brainstorm; **una** ~ **en un vaso de agua** a storm in a teacup

tormento *m* 1. (*castigo*) torment; **potro de** ~ torture rack; **dar** ~ **a alguien** to torture sb 2. (*congoja*) anguish

tormentoso, -a *adj* stormy; (*situación*) turbulent

torna *f* 1. (*devolución*) restitution 2. (*regreso*) return ►**se han cambiado las** ~**s** the boot's *Brit* [*o* shoe's *Am*] on the other foot; **volver las** ~**s a alguien** to turn the tables on sb; **volverse las** ~**s** to turn the tables; **se han vuelto las** ~**s y ahora mando yo** the tables have turned and now I'm calling the tune

tornadizo, -a *adj* changeable

tornado *m* METEO tornado

tornar I. *vi* to return; ~ **en sí** to regain consciousness; ~ **a hacer algo** to do sth again II. *vt* 1. (*devolver*) to return 2. (*cambiar*) to make; ~ **triste** to make sad III. *vr:* ~**se** to turn;

~**se azul** to turn blue
tornasol m 1.(*girasol*) sunflower 2.(*reflejo*) iridescence 3.QUÍM litmus
torneado, -a *adj* shapely
tornear I. *vi* 1.(*dar vueltas*) to spin 2.(*en un torneo*) to joust 3.(*cavilar*) to ponder II. *vt* (*metal*) to work; (*madera*) to turn
torneo m tournament
tornero, -a m, f (*de metal*) machinist; (*de madera*) lathe operator
tornillo m 1.(*clavo con rosca*) screw; **apretar un** ~ to tighten a screw; **apretar los ~s a alguien** *fig* to put pressure on sb; **te falta un** ~ *inf* you have a screw loose; **beso de** ~ French kiss 2. *inf* (*deserción*) desertion 3.(*abrazadera*) clamp; ~ **de banco** vice *Brit,* vise *Am*
torniquete m 1.(*puerta*) turnstile 2.MED tourniquet
torniscón m *inf* 1.(*bofetón*) slap 2.(*pellizco*) pinch
torno m 1.(*máquina, para madera*) lathe; (*de alfarero*) potter's wheel; (*de banco*) vice *Brit,* vise *Am* 2.(*cabrestante*) winch 3.(*giro*) turn 4.(*freno*) brake 5.(*de un río*) bend in a river ▶**en** ~ **a** about; **en** ~ **a ese tema** with regard to this subject
toro m 1.(*animal*) bull; ~ **bravo** [o **de lidia**] *bull raised to fight in the bullring;* **coger el** ~ **por los cuernos** *fig* to take the bull by the horns; **fuerte como un** ~ strong as an ox; **¡otro** ~**!** *fig* change the subject! 2. *pl* (*toreo*) bullfighting; **ir a los ~s** to go to bullfights; **ver los ~s desde la barrera** *fig* to watch sth from the sidelines 3.(*hombre*) strong man
toronja f 1.(*naranja*) bitter orange 2.(*pomelo*) grapefruit
toronjil m lemon [o garden] balm
torpe *adj* 1.(*inhábil*) clumsy 2.(*pesado*) sluggish 3.(*obsceno*) lewd
torpedear *vt* to torpedo
torpedo m torpedo
torpeza f 1.(*pesadez*) heaviness 2.(*inhabilidad*) clumsiness 3.(*obscenidad*) baseness 4.(*tontería*) stupidity 5.(*error*) blunder
torrar *vt* to roast
torre f tower; ~ **de alta tensión** electricity plyon; ~ **de extracción** [o **de perforación**] derrick; ~ **de mando** control tower; ~ **del homenaje** donjon; ~ **de marfil** *fig* ivory tower; (*buque*) turret; (*campanario*) bell tower; (*ajedrez*) rook, castle
torrefacción f roasting
torrefacto, -a *adj* dark roasted
torreja f *AmL* GASTR ≈ French toast
torrencial *adj* **lluvia** ~ torrential rains
torrente m 1.(*corriente*) torrent 2.(*multitud*) flood
torrentoso, -a *adj AmL* (*lluvia*) torrential; (*caudal*) fast-flowing
torrero, -a m, f watchtower keeper; (*de un faro*) lighthouse keeper
torrezno m fried bacon

tórrido, -a *adj elev* torrid
torrija f ≈ French toast
torsión f (*desviación*) torsion; ~ **hacia la izquierda** twisting to the left
torso m torso; ARTE bust
torta f 1.(*tarta*) cake; *AmL* (*pastel*) pie 2. *inf* (*bofetada*) slap; (*golpe*) punch; **darse una** ~ to bang oneself 3. *inf* (*borrachera*) drunkenness ▶**ser ~s y** **pan pintado** *inf* to be child's play; **no saber ni** ~ *inf* not to know a thing
tortazo m *inf* 1.(*bofetada*) slap; **acabar a** ~ **limpio** *inf* to end up in a fight 2.(*choque*) crash; **darse un** ~ to come a cropper
tortícolis f *inv* MED torticollis, stiff neck
tortilla f (*de huevos*) ≈ omelette *Brit,* ≈ omelet *Am; AmL* (*de harina*) tortilla ▶**dar la vuelta a la** ~ to change things completely; **se ha vuelto la** ~ the tables have turned; **hacer** ~ **a alguien** to flatten sb

---

Tortilla is a type of Spanish omelette. A **tortilla de patatas** is an omelette with potatoes and onions, but there are also **tortillas** made from other ingredients, such as spinach, tuna, asparagus, etc. In Latin America, particularly in Mexico, a **tortilla** is a flat pancake prepared with maize and is one of the staple foods of this region.

---

tortillera m *vulg* dyke
tórtola f turtledove
tórtolo m 1.(*ave*) lovebird 2.(*hombre*) lover-boy 3. *pl* (*enamorados*) lovebirds *pl*
tortuga f turtle; **a paso de** ~ to walk at a snail's pace
tortuoso, -a *adj* 1.(*sinuoso*) winding 2.(*astuto*) tortuous
tortura f (*suplicio*) torture; **sufrir ~s** to be tortured
torturar *vt* to torture
torvo, -a *adj* fierce; (*mirada*) baleful
torzal m cord
tos f cough; ~ **ferina** whooping cough
tosco, -a *adj* rough, coarse
tosedera f *AmL* nagging cough
toser *vi* to cough; **no hay quien te tosa** *inf* nobody can compete with you
tostada f 1.(*para desayuno*) toast 2. *Méx:* fried tortilla ▶**olerse la** ~ *inf* to smell a rat
tostadero m roasting room
tostador m toaster
tostar <o→ue> I. *vt* 1.(*torrar*) to roast; (*pan*) to toast 2.(*curtir*) to brown II. *vr:* ~**se** to tan
tostón m 1.(*persona pesada*) drag; (*molestia*) nuisance 2.(*cochinillo*) roast suckling pig 3.(*de pan*) crouton
total I. *adj* total; **importe** ~ total amount; **en** ~ in all; **un cambio** ~ a complete change; **¡ha sido ~!** *inf* it was great! II. m MAT sum III. *adv* so, in the end
totalidad f *sin pl* totality, whole; **en su** ~ in its

entirety

totalitario, -a *adj* **1.**(*completo*) total **2.**(*dictatorial*) totalitarian

totalizar <z→c> *vt* to total

totalmente *adv* entirely, totally

totora *f* AmS BOT (*junco*) reed

toxicidad *f* toxicity

tóxico *m* toxic substance

tóxico, -a *adj* toxic

toxicomanía *f sin pl* drug addiction

toxicómano, -a I. *adj* addicted to drugs II. *m, f* drug addict, substance abuser

toxina *f* toxin

tozudo, -a I. *adj* obstinate II. *m, f* stubborn person

traba *f* **1.**(*trabamiento*) tie **2.**(*cuerda*) hobble **3.**(*obstáculo*) hindrance; **poner ~s a...** to put obstacles in the way of ... **4.** AmL, *inf* (*marihuana*) grass; (*efecto*) high

trabajado, -a *adj* **1.**(*cansado*) worn-out **2.**(*con esmero*) well-crafted

trabajador(a) I. *adj* hard-working II. *m(f)* worker

trabajar I. *vi* to work; ~ **de vendedora** to work as a saleswoman; **en edad de ~** of working age; ~ **como un condenado** to work like a slave; ~ **en balde** to work in vain; ~ **por horas** to be paid by the hour; ~ **por cuenta propia** to be self-employed; ~ **a tiempo completo/parcial** to work full-time/part-time II. *vt* **1.**(*tratar*) to work; (*caballo*) to train **2.**(*perfeccionar*) to work on; **tienes que ~ el acento** you have to work on your accent **3.**(*inquietar*) to disturb **4.**(*amasar*) to knead **5.**(*máquina*) to run, to operate III. *vr:* ~**se** to work

trabajo *m* (*acción*) work; (*puesto*) job; ~ **en cadena** assembly-line work; ~ **a destajo** piecework; ~ **estacional** seasonal work; ~**s manuales** handicrafts *pl*; ~**s forzados** hard labour *Brit,* hard labor *Am;* **con/sin ~** employed/unemployed; ~ **en equipo** team--work; ~ **perdido** wasted effort; **puesto de ~** post/job; ~ **de chinos** intricate laborious work; ~ **fijo** steady job; ~ **cualificado** skilled work; ~ **de campo** field work; ~ **negro** illegal work; ~ **eventual** temporary [*o* casual] work; ~ **intelectual** brainwork; **hacer un buen ~** to do a good job; **almuerzo de ~** working lunch; **tener ~ atrasado** to have a backlog; **¡buen ~!** well done!; **quedarse sin ~** to be let go; **mucha gente se quedó sin ~ cuando instalaron la nueva maquinaria** many people were made redundant when the new machinery was installed; **costar ~** to be difficult; **tomarse el ~ de hacer algo** to take the trouble to do sth; **ahorrarse el ~ de hacer algo** to spare oneself the trouble of doing sth

trabajoso, -a *adj* hard

trabalenguas *m inv* tongue twister

trabar I. *vt* **1.**(*juntar*) to join **2.**(*coger*) to seize **3.**(*atar*) to tie **4.**(*impedir*) to impede **5.**(*espesar*) to thicken **6.**(*comenzar*) to start;

(*contactos*) to strike up **7.**(*embargar bienes*) to put a lien on II. *vi* to take hold III. *vr:* ~**se** to get stuck; ~**se la lengua** to get tongue-tied

trabazón *f* **1.**(*enlace*) connection **2.**(*el espesar*) consistency

trabilla *f* belt loop; (*en la pernera*) foot strap

trabucar <c→qu> I. *vt* to jumble up II. *vr:* ~**se** (*al hablar*) to get tongue-tied; (*al escribir*) to get all mixed up

trácala *f* **1.** *Ecua* (*multitud*) mob **2.** *Méx, PRico* (*fullería*) fraud **3.** *Méx* (*persona tramposa*) trickster

tracalada *f* **1.** *AmC, AmS* (*multitud*) crowd, lot **2.** *Méx* (*fullería*) trickery

tracalero, -a *m, f Méx, PRico* cheat

tracción *f* **1.**(*tirar*) pulling **2.**(*accionar*) drive, traction; ~ **a cuatro ruedas** four-wheel drive; ~ **delantera/trasera** front/rear-wheel drive

tractor *m* tractor

tradición *f* tradition

tradicional *adj* traditional

traducción *f* translation; ~ **al/del inglés** translation into/from English; ~ **automática** machine [*o* automatic] translation; ~ **directa/inversa** translation from/into a foreign language; ~ **libre** free translation; ~ **simultánea** simultaneous translation

traducir *irr vt* to translate

traductor(a) I. *adj* translating II. *m(f)* translator; ~ **de bolsillo** pocket-size electronic translating device; ~ **jurado** sworn translator

traer *irr* I. *vt* **1.**(*llevar: a alguien*) to bring along; (*consigo*) to bring; (*vestido*) to wear; **tengo una carta para ti – trae** I have a letter for you – give it to me; **¿has traído la carta?** did you bring the letter?; **lo traigo en la cartera** I've got it in my briefcase; ~ **a alguien arrastra(n)do** to drag sb; **¿qué te trae por aquí?** what brings you here?; **el jefe me trae de aquí para allí todo el día** my boss has me running all day; **me la trae floja** *vulg* I don't give a damn; **me trae sin cuidado** I couldn't care less **2.**(*ir a por*) to fetch **3.**(*atraer*) to attract **4.**(*ocasionar*) to cause **5.**(*implicar*) involve **6.**(*más adjetivo*) ~ **convencido a alguien** to have sb convinced; ~ **preocupado a alguien** to have sb worried; ~ **de cabeza a alguien** *inf* to be driving sb mad; **esta mujer me trae perdido** this woman will be my ruin **7.**(*más sustantivo*) ~ **retraso** to be late; ~ **prisa** to be in a hurry; ~ **hambre** to be hungry; **traes cara de circunstancias** *inf* you look very serious **8.**(*razones, ejemplos*) to adduce **9.**(*más 'a'*) ~ **a colación** to bring up; ~ **a cuento** to mention; ~ **a alguien a razones** to get sb to listen to reason; ~ **a la memoria** to bring to mind II. *vr:* ~**se 1.**(*llevar a cabo*) ~**se algo entre manos** to be up to something **2.**(*vestirse*) ~**se bien** to dress well **3.**(*ser difícil, intenso*) **este examen se las trae** the exam is really tough; **hace un frío que se las trae** it's really cold

traficante *mf* dealer, trader; (*de drogas*) drug dealer; (*de personas, coches*) smuggler

traficar <c→qu> *vi* to deal; (*con drogas*) to traffic; (*con personas*) to smuggle

tráfico *m* 1.(*de vehículos*) traffic; ~ **por carretera** road traffic 2.COM trade; (*de drogas*) traffic; (*de personas, coches*) smuggling; ~ **de contrabando** smuggling; ~ **de blancas** white--slave traffic; ~ **de influencias** peddling of political favours *Brit* [*o* favors *Am*]

tragaderas *fpl* 1.(*faringe*) throat; **tener buenas** ~ *inf* to be a walking dustbin *Brit* [*o* garbage can *Am*]; *fig* to be ready to put up with a lot 2. *inf* (*credulidad*) **tener** ~ to be very gullible 3. *inf* (*tolerancia*) **tener buenas/ malas** ~ to be very tolerant/intolerant

tragaldabas *mf inv* glutton

tragaluz *m* (*grande*) skylight; (*pequeño*) transom

traganíqueles *f inv, Nic, inf* (*tragaperras*) slot machine

tragaperras *f inv* vending machine; (*de juego*) slot machine

tragar <g→gu> I.*vt, vr:* ~**se** (*comida, bebida, crítica*) to swallow; (*historia, mentira*) to fall for; **tuve que** ~**me el enfado** I had to hold back my anger; **ése se lo traga todo** *fig* he believes everything you tell him; **¡trágame tierra!** I wish the ground would open up and swallow me! II.*vt* 1.(*soportar*) **no** ~ **a alguien** to not be able to stand sb 2.(*consumir*) to down; (*absorber*) to soak up 3.(*aguantar*) **tuvimos que** ~ **toda la conferencia** we had to sit through the whole conference; ~ **saliva** to eat crow

tragedia *f* tragedy

trágico, -a I. *adj* tragic; **no te pongas** ~ don't get all melodramatic II. *m, f* TEAT, LIT tragedian *m*, tragedienne *f*

trago *m* 1.(*de bebida*) swig; **a** ~**s cortos** in sips; **a** ~**s largos** in long drinks; **de un** ~ in one gulp 2.(*bebida*) drink; **tomar un** ~ **de más** *inf* to have one drink too many 3.(*vicio*) bottle, drink 4.(*experiencia*) experience; **pasar un mal** ~ to have a bad time of it

tragón, -ona *m, f inf* glutton

traición *f* 1.(*acto desleal*) treachery, betrayal 2.JUR treason; **matar a** ~ to kill treacherously

traicionar *vt* to betray; (*adulterio*) to be unfaithful; **la memoria me traiciona** my memory fails me; **le traicionó su acento** his/her accent gave him/her away

traicionero, -a I. *adj* (*persona*) perfidious; (*acción*) traitorous; (*memoria*) unreliable; (*animal*) dangerous II. *m, f* traitor

traída *f* ~ **de aguas** water supply

traidor(a) I. *adj* traitorous; (*falso*) deceitful II. *m(f)* traitor

traigo *1. pres de* **traer**

traílla *f* 1.(*correa*) leash 2.(*dos perros*) team 3.AGR harrow

traje *m* 1.(*vestidura*) dress; ~ **de baño** bathing suit; ~ **de luces** bullfighter's costume

2.(*de hombre*) suit; ~ **de etiqueta** formal dress; ~ **hecho a la medida** custom-made suit; ~ **de confección** ready-to-wear suit 3.(*de mujer*) outfit; ~ **de noche** evening dress; ~ (**de**) **chaqueta** suit 4.(*popular*) regional costume 5.(*de época*) period costume

trajeado, -a *adj* **ir bien/mal** ~ to be well/ badly dressed

trajín *m* 1.(*de mercancías*) haulage 2.(*ajetreo*) rush; **el** ~ **de la ciudad** the hustle and bustle of the city; **había un gran** ~ there was a lot of commotion

trajinar I.*vt* to transport II.*vi* to rush about; **llevo todo el día trajinando** I've been on the go all day

trajinera *f Méx* (*canoa*) ≈ canoe (*small boat typical for canals that carries up to 15 people and is moved with the help of a long stick*)

tralla *f* 1.(*cuerda*) rope 2.(*látigo*) lash

trama *f* 1.(*de hilos*) weft 2.LIT plot 3.(*intriga*) scheme

tramar *vt* 1.(*traición*) to plot; (*intriga, plan*) to scheme; **¿qué estarán tramando?** what are they up to?; **aquí se está tramando algo** something's cooking here 2.(*tejidos*) to weave

tramitar *vt* 1.(*asunto*) to attend to; (*negocio*) to transact; **está tramitando el divorcio** he/ she has started divorce proceedings 2.(*expediente*) to process

trámite *m* 1.(*diligencias*) ~ **burocrático** administrative proceedings; **pasar por todos los** ~**s** to go through the whole procedure 2.(*formalidad*) formality; **estar en** ~**s de hacer algo** to be in the process of doing sth; **esto es puro** ~ this is just a formality; **¿has hecho los** ~**s para el pasaporte?** have you taken the necessary steps to obtain your passport?

tramo *m* 1.(*de camino*) stretch; FERRO section 2.(*de escalera*) flight

tramoya *f* 1.TEAT stage machinery 2.(*engaño*) scheme, scam

trampa *f* 1.(*para personas, animales*) trap; ~ **mortal** death trap; **caer en la** ~ (*animal*) to be caught in the snare; (*persona*) to fall into the trap; **poner una** ~ **a un alguien** to set a trap for an animal/for sb 2.(*trampilla*) trapdoor 3.(*del mostrador*) hinged section of a counter 4.(*engaño*) trick; (*en los juegos*) cheating; **hacer** ~ (*engañar*) to cheat; (*en el deporte*) fixing 5. *inf* (*deuda*) bad debt ▶ **sin** ~ **ni** cartón with no catches; **hecha la ley hecha la** ~ *prov* laws are made to be broken *prov*

trampear *vi* 1. *inf* (*estafar*) to swindle 2.(*de penuria*) to get by 3.(*ir tirando*) to manage

trampilla *f* 1.(*en habitación*) trapdoor 2.(*portezuela*) oven door 3.AUTO hatch

trampolín *m* (*de piscina*) diving board; (*de gimnasia*) trampoline; (*de esquí*) ski jump

tramposo, -a I. *adj* cheating II. *m, f* 1.(*estafador*) swindler 2.(*en los juegos*) cheat

tranca *f* 1.(*palo*) cudgel; (*de la puerta*) cross-bar 2. *inf* (*borrachera*) binge; **coger una ~** *inf* to get plastered ►**a ~s y barrancas** through fire and water

trance *m* 1.(*momento*) **pasar un ~** difícil to go through a difficult time 2.(*hipnótico*) trance 3.(*situación*) **estar en ~ de hacer algo** to be on the point of doing sth; **estar en ~ de muerte** to be at death's door ►**hacer algo a todo ~** to do sth at any cost

tranco *m* 1.(*paso*) stride; **andar a ~s** to stride; **subir una escalera a ~s** to go up the stairs two at a time 2.(*umbral*) threshold ►**a ~s** in a hurry

tranque *m Chile* (*embalse*) reservoir

tranqui *adj inf* **¡oye, ~!** hey, cool it!

tranquilamente *adv* calmly

tranquilidad *f* 1.(*calma, serenidad*) tranquility; (*del mar*) calm; **para mayor ~** to be on the safe side; **~ de conciencia** ease of mind; **trabajar con ~** to work calmly; **debo decirte para tu ~ que...** I must tell you, to put your mind at rest, that ... 2.(*autocontrol*) calmness 3.(*despreocupación*) lack of concern

tranquilizante *m* tranquillizer *Brit,* tranquilizer *Am*

tranquilizar <z→c> I. *vt* to calm down; (*con palabras*) to reassure II. *vr:* **-se** to calm down

tranquilla *f* 1.(*pasador*) bolt 2.(*para desorientar*) red herring

tranquillo *m* **coger el ~ a algo** to get the knack of sth

tranquilo, -a *adj* 1.(*no agitado, mar*) calm; **¡déjame ~!** leave me alone!; **mientras no te digan nada, tú ~** as long as they don't mention anything to you, don't worry 2.(*persona: serena*) serene; (*con autocontrol*) calm; (*despreocupada*) unconcerned; **tú ~, que no pasará nada** don't worry, everything will be all right

transa *f* 1. *AmL* (*espíritu de compromiso*) committedness 2. *Méx* (*engaño*) deceit 3. *RíoPl* (*transacción*) transaction; (*tráfico de droga*) drug dealing

transacción *f* 1. JUR settlement 2. POL agreement 3. COM deal 4. FIN transaction

transalpino, -a *adj* transalpine

transandino, -a *adj* trans-Andean

transar *vi AmL* (*transigir*) to compromise; **no pienso ~ en eso** I'm not giving in on that

transatlántico *m* ocean liner

transatlántico, -a *adj* transatlantic; **barco ~** ocean liner

transbordador *m* 1. NÁUT ferry 2. AVIAT shuttle

transbordar I. *vt* 1.(*por río*) to ferry across 2.(*mercancías*) to transfer; (*en grandes cantidades*) to transload; (*entre barcos*) to transship II. *vi* to change, to transfer

transbordo *m* 1.(*cambio*) change; **hay que hacer ~ en Barajas** you have to change [*o* transfer] planes at Barajas airport 2.(*mercancías*) transfer

transcendental *adj v.* **trascendental**

transcender <e→ie> *vi v.* **trascender**

transcribir *irr como escribir vt* 1.(*copiar*) to transcribe 2. *t.* MÚS (*transliterar*) to transpose

transcripción *f* (*acción*) transcription; (*resultado*) transcript

transcultural *adj* cross-cultural

transcurrir *vi* 1.(*el tiempo*) to elapse, to pass 2.(*acontecer*) to take place

transcurso *m* course; **en el ~ del día** during the course of the day

transeúnte I. *adj* transient; (*habitante*) temporary II. *mf* 1.(*peatón*) passer-by, pedestrian 2.(*habitante*) **los ~s** transients, temporary residents

transferencia *f* 1.(*traslado*) transfer 2. FIN transfer; **a través de una ~ bancaria** by bank draft 3.(*de propiedad*) transfer 4. PSICO transference

transferir *irr como sentir vt* 1.(*trasladar*) to transfer 2.(*posponer*) to postpone 3. FIN to make over 4.(*propiedad, derecho*) to transfer

transfigurar *vt* to transfigure

transformación *f* transformation; (*de costumbres*) change

transformador *m* ELEC transformer

transformar *vt* to transform; (*costumbres*) to change; **desde el accidente está transformado** he/she has changed completely since the accident

tránsfuga *mf* 1.(*fugitivo*) fugitive 2. MIL deserter 3. POL turncoat

transfundir *vt* (*líquido*) to transfuse

transfusión *f t.* MED transfusion

transgénico, -a *adj* genetically engineered

transgredir *irr como abolir vt* (*ley*) to violate, to break; (*orden*) to disobey

transgresión *f* (*ley*) transgression, violation; (*orden*) disobedience

transición *f* transition

transido, -a *adj elev* **~ de dolor** racked with pain; **~ de emoción** overcome with emotion; **~ de hambre** weak with hunger; **~ de miedo** panic-stricken

transigencia *f* 1.(*condescendencia*) obligingness 2.(*tolerancia*) tolerance 3. POL compromise

transigente *adj* 1.(*condescendiente*) broad-minded 2.(*tolerante*) tolerant 3. POL compromising

transigir <g→j> *vi* 1.(*ceder*) to yield 2.(*tolerar*) **~ con algo** to tolerate sth 3. JUR, POL to compromise; **~ sobre algo** to reach a settlement on sth

transistor *m* ELEC transistor

transitable *adj* (*en coche*) open to traffic; (*a pie*) passable

transitar *vi* **~ por algo** (*en coche*) to go along sth; (*por un túnel*) to go through sth; (*a pie*) to walk along sth; **una calle muy transitada** a very busy street; **nadie transitaba por la calle** there was no one on the streets

transitivo, -a *adj* LING transitive

tránsito *m* **1.** (*circulación*) traffic; **de mucho ~** very busy; **el ~ por esta calle es algo complicado** transit along this road is rather complicated **2.** (*de personas*) transit; COM transit

transitorio, -a *adj* **1.** (*temporal*) temporary; (*ley, periodo, disposición*) transitional **2.** (*pasajero*) fleeting, transitory

translúcido, -a *adj* translucent

transmigrar *vi* **1.** (*personas*) to migrate **2.** REL to transmigrate

transmisible *adj* transmissible

transmisión *f* **1.** (*de noticia*) broadcast; **~ en directo/diferida** live/pre-recorded transmission [*o* broadcast] **2.** TV, AUTO, INFOR transmission **3.** (*enfermedad*) transmission **4.** TÉC drive; (*mecanismo*) transmission; (*propulsión*) drive **5.** JUR transfer **6.** (*por herencia*) descent

transmisor *m* TÉC transmitter

transmisor(a) *adj* **estación ~a** transmitter, radio/TV station

transmitir *vt* **1.** (*noticia*) to broadcast **2.** TV, RADIO, TÉC to transmit **3.** (*enfermedad*) to give **4.** (*por herencia*) to pass on **5.** FÍS to transmit

transmutar *vt* to transmute

transparencia *f* **1.** (*calidad*) transparency **2.** (*de intención*) openness **3.** FOTO slide **4.** (*para un proyector*) overhead transparency

transparentar **I.** *vt* to reveal **II.** *vi, vr:* **~se** (*ser transparente*) to be transparent **III.** *vr:* **~se** (*dejarse ver, adivinar*) to show through

transparente **I.** *adj* **1.** (*material*) transparent **2.** (*intenciones*) clear **II.** *m* curtain, blind

transpiración *f* (*persona*) perspiration

transpirar *vi* (*persona*) to perspire

transponer *irr como poner* **I.** *vt* (*persona, cosa*) to move; (*trasplantar*) to transplant **II.** *vr:* **~se 1.** (*persona*) to move **2.** (*sol*) to go out of sight **3.** (*dormirse*) to doze off

transportar **I.** *vt* **1.** (*trasladar*) to transport; (*en brazos*) to carry; (*en un vehículo*) to take; **~ por barco** to ship **2.** MÚS to transpose **II.** *vr:* **~se** to be transported

transporte *m* **1.** COM transport; *t.* TÉC (*de personas*) carriage; **~ aéreo/marítimo** air/sea transport; **~ por carretera** road transport; **compañía de ~s** transport company **2.** (*vehículo*) **~s públicos** public transportation; **¿qué ~ utilizas para ir a la ciudad?** how do you get into town? **3.** *pl* (*conjunto*) carriage **4.** (*exaltación*) rapture **5.** MÚS transposition

transportista *mf* (*empresa, agente*) carrier, transporter

transpuesto, -a **I.** *pp de* transponer **II.** *adj* **quedarse ~** to doze off

transversal *adj* (*atravesado, perpendicular*) transverse, crosswise; **calle ~** cross street

transverso, -a *adj v.* **transversal**

transvestido *m* transvestite

tranvía *m* tram *Brit,* streetcar *Am*

trapa *m o f* **1.** (*de los pies*) stamping of feet **2.** (*vocerío*) uproar

trapacear *vi* to cheat

trapacería *f* racket

trapacero, -a *m, f* cheating

trapajoso, -a *adj* **1.** (*en el vestir*) shabby **2.** (*en el hablar*) **tener una lengua trapajosa** to speak thickly

trápala[1] *f* **1.** (*de gente*) hubbub **2.** (*de caballo*) clatter of hooves **3.** *inf* (*embuste*) scam

trápala[2] *m inf* jabbering

trápala[3] *mf* **1.** (*trapacero*) trickster **2.** (*parlanchín*) chatterbox

trapalear *vi* **1.** (*caballo*) to clatter **2.** (*hablar*) to chatter

trapatiesta *f inf* **1.** (*riña: verbal*) row; (*con puñetazos*) brawl **2.** (*jaleo*) ruckus

trapear *vt AmL* (*limpiar*) to mop

trapecio *m* **1.** (*de circo*) trapeze **2.** MAT trapezium *Brit,* trapezoid *Am* **3.** ANAT (*hueso*) trapezium; (*músculo*) trapezius

trapecista *mf* trapeze artist

trapero, -a *m, f* ragman

trapiche *m AmL* (*exprimidor de caña*) sugar mill

trapichear *vi* **1.** *inf* (*enredos*) to be mixed up in shady business; (*intrigar*) to scheme; (*artimaña*) to contrive; **~ en los negocios** to have crooked dealings **2.** (*comerciar*) to buy and sell small scale

trapicheo *m inf* **1.** (*enredo*) jiggery-pokery; (*negocio*) dealing **2.** (*intriga*) scheming; (*artimaña*) contriving; **ha habido ~s en las elecciones** there's been some tampering in the elections

trapío *m* **1.** (*de mujer*) gracefulness **2.** TAUR spirit and good looks

trapisonda *f* **1.** (*riña, alboroto*) squabble **2.** (*intriga*) schemery

trapo *m* **1.** (*tela*) rag **2.** (*para limpiar*) cleaning cloth; **~ de cocina** tea towel, dish towel *Am;* **pasar el ~ por algo** to wipe sth off **3.** *pl, inf* (*vestidos*) clothes *pl* **4.** NÁUT sails *pl;* **a todo ~** under full sail; *inf* (*a toda velocidad*) at top speed; **el coche iba a todo ~** *inf* the car was going at full speed; **poner la música a todo ~** *inf* to put music on full blast **5.** TEAT curtain ►**tener lengua de ~** to mumble; **tener manos de ~** to be a butterfingers; **estar hecho un ~** to be worn out; **sacar los ~s sucios a relucir** to wash one's dirty linen in public; **entrar al ~** to fall into the trap; **poner a alguien como un ~** to give sb a good telling off; **soltar el ~** (*reír*) to burst out laughing; (*llorar*) to burst into tears; **tratar a alguien como un ~** to treat sb like dirt

tráquea *f* ANAT trachea, windpipe *inf*

traquetear **I.** *vi* (*chapa, vajilla*) to clatter; (*motor, ametralladora*) to rattle; (*sillas, carro*) to jolt **II.** *vt* to shake

traqueteo *m* banging; (*chapa, vajilla*) clattering; (*ametralladora, motor*) rattling; (*de sillas, carro*) jolting

traquido *m* (*pistola*) report; (*madera*) crack

tras **I.** *prep* **1.** (*temporal*) after; **día ~ día** day after day **2.** (*espacial: detrás de*) behind;

(*orden*) after; **voy** ~ **tuyo** (*en la cola*) I'm behind you, I'm after you; (*en el coche*) behind; **ir** ~ **alguien** (*perseguir*) to go after sb **3.** (*con movimiento*) after; **ponerse uno** ~ **otro** to put one after the other **4.** (*además de*) besides; ~ **de ser de pésima calidad es caro** it's not just terrible quality but it's expensive too **II.** *m inf* bottom **III.** *interj* ¡~ ~! knock knock!

trasatlántico *m v.* **transatlántico**

trasatlántico, -a *adj v.* **transatlántico, -a**

trasbocar <c→qu> *vt AmC, AmS* to throw up

trasbordar *vt, vi v.* **transbordar**

trascendencia *f* (*importancia*) consequence; **no tener** ~ to be of little importance; **un incidente sin más** ~ an insignificant incident

trascendental *adj* **1.** (*importante*) important **2.** FILOS transcendental

trascender <e→ie> *vi* **1.** (*hecho, noticia*) to become known **2.** (*efecto, consecuencias*) ~ **a algo** to have a wide effect on sth **3.** (*ir más allá*) ~ **de algo** to go beyond sth **4.** (*olor*) to smell **5.** (*extenderse*) to spread; **el discurso transciende a fascismo** the speech reeks of fascism

trascurrir *vi v.* **transcurrir**

trasegar *irr como fregar vt* **1.** (*objetos: desordenar*) to turn upside down; (*cambiar*) to switch around **2.** (*líquidos*) to decant; (*de garrafa a botella*) to transfer **3.** (*alcohol*) to swill, to guzzle

trasera *f* back

trasero *m* **1.** (*animal*) hindquarters *pl* **2.** *inf* (*persona*) bottom, backside

trasero, -a *adj* back; **asiento** ~ back seat; **luz trasera** rear light; **parte trasera** rear; **propulsión trasera** rear-wheel drive; **rueda trasera** rear wheel

trasferir *irr como sentir vt v.* **transferir**

trasfigurar *vt* to transfigure

trasfondo *m* background

trasiego *m* **1.** (*de objetos: desorden*) clutter **2.** (*cambio*) shuffling **3.** (*de líquidos*) decanting; (*a botella*) transfer

traslación *f* (*de cosas*) transfer; (*de cuerpo*) moving; (*de tropa*) transfer

trasladar I. *vt* **1.** (*cosas*) to move; (*cuerpo*) to go; (*tropa, tienda*) to relocate; (*prisionero: a otra prisión*) to transfer; (*a otra comisaría*) to move **2.** (*funcionario*) to transfer **3.** (*fecha*) to postpone **4.** (*idea, obra*) ~ **al papel** to put on paper; ~ **a la pantalla** to make into a film **5.** (*orden, medida*) to notify **6.** (*escrito*) to copy **II.** *vr:* ~**se 1.** (*mudarse*) to move **2.** (*ir a*) to go to; ~**se en coche** to drive

traslado *m* **1.** (*de cosas, cuerpo*) movement; (*tropa*) relocation; (*prisionero: de prisión*) transfer; (*de comisaría*) move **2.** (*de funcionario*) transfer **3.** (*de fecha*) postponement **4.** (*mudanza*) removal **5.** (*copia*) copy **6.** (*de orden, medida*) notification

traslucir *irr como lucir* **I.** *vt* (*cara*) to reveal; **dejar** ~ **algo** (*alguien*) to hint at sth **II.** *vr:* ~**se 1.** (*ser translúcido*) to be translucent **2.** (*verse, notarse*) to show through **3.** (*hecho, intención*) to become evident

trasluz *m* diffused or reflected light; **mirar algo al** ~ to hold sth up to the light

trasmano no puedo cogerlo, me pilla a ~ I can't get it, it's out of my reach; **su casa cae tan a** ~ **que apenas lo visito** his house is so far out of the way that I seldom visit him

trasmigrar *vi v.* **transmigrar**

trasmitir *vt v.* **transmitir**

trasmutar *vt* to transmute

trasnochado, -a *adj* **1.** (*comida*) stale **2.** (*idea, plan*) outdated **3.** (*persona*) drawn

trasnochador(a) *m(f) fig* night owl

trasnochar I. *vi* **1.** (*no dormir*) to spend a sleepless night; (*ir de juerga*) to have a night out; (*trabajando*) to sleep on sth **2.** (*acostarse tarde*) to stay up late **3.** (*pernoctar*) to spend the night **II.** *vt* to sleep on

traspapelar I. *vt* to misplace, to mislay **II.** *vr:* ~**se** to get mislaid

trasparentar *vt, vr:* ~**se** *v.* **transparentar**

traspasar *vt* **1.** (*atravesar: arma, rayos*) to go through; (*penetrar, perforar*) to pierce; (*líquido*) to soak through; (*calle, río*) to cross **2.** (*pasar a*) to transfer; FIN to make over; **se traspasa tienda** shop for sale **3.** (*sentidos*) ~ **el corazón** to break sb's heart **4.** (*límite*) to go beyond; (*ley*) to break

traspaso *m* **1.** (*de piso, negocio, dinero*) transfer **2.** (*de límite*) exceeding; (*ley*) infringement **3.** (*de arma, rayos*) passage; (*de líquido*) soaking through; (*de calle, río*) crossing

traspatio *m AmL* backyard

traspié(s) *m* (*inv*) stumble; *fig* slip-up; **dar un** ~ (*tropezar*) to stumble; (*resbalar*) to slip; (*meter la pata*) to slip up; (*en sociedad*) to make a faux pas

trasplantar I. *vt* **1.** (*planta*) to transplant **2.** (*personas*) to transfer **3.** MED to transplant **II.** *vr:* ~**se** to migrate

trasplante *m* **1.** (*de plantas*) transplanting **2.** (*de persona*) transfer **3.** MED transplant

trasponer *irr como poner vt, vr:* ~**se** *v.* **transponer**

trasportar *vt, vr:* ~**se** *v.* **transportar**

trasquilar *vt* **1.** (*animal*) to shear **2.** (*persona*) to crop; **salir trasquilado** *fig, inf* to get fleeced **3.** *inf* (*cosa*) to cut down

trastabillar *vi* **1.** (*dar traspiés*) to stumble **2.** (*tambalear*) to stagger **3.** (*tartamudear*) to stutter

trastada *f* **1.** *inf* (*travesura*) prank; **hacer una** ~ **a alguien** to play a prank on sb **2.** (*mala pasada*) dirty trick

trastazo *m inf* bump; **pegarse un** ~ to come a cropper; **pegarse un** ~ **contra algo** to bang into sth

traste *m* **1.** (*de guitarra*) fret **2.** *AmL* (*trasto*) piece of junk ►**dar al** ~ **con algo** to spoil sth;

irse **al** ~ to fall through

trastear I. *vt* ~ **a alguien** *inf* to twist sb around one's little finger **II.** *vi* (*trastos*) to rummage through

trastero, -a *adj* **cuarto** ~ lumber room

trastienda *f* 1. (*de tienda*) back room 2. *inf* (*astucia*) **tener mucha** ~ to be very crafty; (*reserva*) to be a dark horse

trasto *m* 1. (*mueble*) piece of furniture; (*utensilio*) utensil; **tirarse los** ~**s a la cabeza** to have a knock down drag out fight 2. *pl* (*herramientas*) gear 3. *pl* (*para tirar*) junk 4. *inf*(*persona*) **mi hijo es un** ~ my son is a holy terror; **tratar como un** ~ to treat like a dog

trastornado, -a *adj* (*confundido*) confused; (*sicológicamente*) disturbed; (*loco*) mad, crazy

trastornar I. *vt* 1. (*cosa*) to disarrange; (*de arriba abajo*) to turn upside down 2. (*orden, plan, ideas*) disrupt; (*orden público*) to disturb 3. (*psicológicamente*) to traumatize; (*por amor*) to lose one's head over sb; **la muerte de su marido la trastornó** she was traumatized by her husband's death 4. (*encantar*) **me trastornan los coches** I'm crazy about cars **II.** *vr:* ~**se** 1. (*enloquecer*) to go mad 2. (*estropearse*) to fall through 3. (*turbarse*) to get upset

trastorno *m* 1. (*desorden*) disorder 2. (*del orden público*) disturbance; ~**s políticos** political upheaval; **ocasionar** ~**s** to disrupt 3. (*sicológicamente*) disorder 4. MED disorder; ~**s estomacales** stomach problems

trastrocar <c→qu> *vt* 1. (*el orden*) to invert 2. (*de sitio*) to switch around 3. (*el sentido*) to change 4. (*el estado*) to transform

trasunto *m* 1. (*escrito*) copy 2. (*imitación*) imitation; **ser un** ~ **de algo** (*reflectar*) to be a reflection of sth

trasvase *m* transfer; (*de río*) diversion

trasvasijar *vt* Chile (*trasvasar*) to pour from one container to another, to decant

trata *f* ~ **de blancas** white slave trade

tratable *adj* sociable

tratadista *mf* (treatise) writer, essayist

tratado *m* 1. *t.* POL treaty; ~ **de no agresión** non-aggression treaty; ~ **comercial** trade agreement 2. (*científico*) ~ **de algo** treatise on sth

tratamiento *m* 1. *t.* MED, QUÍM (*de asunto*) treatment 2. *t.* INFOR (*elaboración*) processing; ~ **de texto** word processing; ~ **de agua potable** drinking-water processing 3. (*de cortesía*) form of address; **el** ~ **de usted** the polite 'you' form; **¿qué** ~ **se le da a un cardenal?** what is the correct way to address a cardinal?

tratante *mf* dealer

tratar I. *vt* 1. (*manejar, portarse*) to deal with; **no es una persona fácil de** ~ he/she is not an easy person to deal with 2. MED, QUÍM to treat 3. *t.* INFOR (*elaborar, agua, minerales*) to process 4. (*dar tratamiento*) to address; ~ **de tú/usted** to adress sb in an informal/formal

manner using tú/usted; ~ **a alguien de loco** to treat sb as if he/she were mad 5. (*tema, asunto*) to discuss **II.** *vi* 1. (*libro, película*) ~ **de** [*o* **sobre**] **algo** to be about sth, to deal with sth 2. (*intentar*) to try; **trata de concentrarte** try to concentrate 3. (*con alguien*) to have contact with 4. COM to deal **III.** *vr:* ~**se** 1. (*tener trato*) to have to do; **no me trato con él** I don't have anything to do with him 2. (*ser cuestión de*) to be a question; **¿de qué se trata?** what's it about?; **tratándose de ti…** in your case …

tratativas *fpl* Arg, Par (*negociación*) negotiations *pl;* **siguen en** ~ they are still discussing terms

trato *m* 1. (*manejo, comportamiento*) treatment; **malos** ~**s** ill-treatment, abuse; **recibir un buen** ~ to be well-treated 2. (*contacto*) contact; ~ **carnal** sexual relations; **tener** ~ **de gentes** to have a way with people; **romper el** ~ **con alguien** to break off relations with sb; **no querer** ~**s con alguien** to want nothing to do with sb; **es una señora de un** ~ **exquisito** she is a lady of exquisite manners 3. (*pacto*) agreement; (*negocio*) deal; **cerrar un** ~ **con alguien** to close a deal with sb; **entrar en** ~**s con alguien** to open negotiations with sb; **¡~ hecho!** it's a deal!

trauma *m* trauma

traumático, -a *adj* traumatic

traumatismo *m* injury; ~ **cervical** whiplash injury; MED traumatism

traumatología *f* orthopedic surgery, orthopedics *pl*

través I. *m* 1. (*inclinación*) slant 2. (*contratiempo*) setback ▶ **dar al** ~ **con algo** to hit sth broadsides; (*arruinar*) to ruin sth; **mirar a alguien de** ~ to look at sb out of the corner of one's eye; **de** ~ crossways, crosswise **II.** *prep* ~ **de** (*de un lugar*) across; (*de la radio*) on; (*de una persona*) from, through

travesaño *m* 1. ARQUIT crosspiece 2. DEP crossbar 3. (*de una escalera*) rung

travesía *f* 1. (*por aire*) flight; (*por mar*) crossing 2. (*distancia*) distance 3. (*calle*) cross street

travesti *mf,* **travestí** *mf,* **travestido, -a** *m, f* transvestite

travesura *f* prank

traviesa *f* 1. FERRO sleeper 2. (*de poste*) crossbar

travieso, -a *adj* 1. (*de través*) across; **correr a campo traviesa** to run cross-country 2. (*niño*) mischievous, naughty; **Daniel el Travieso** Dennis the Menace 3. (*adulto*) dissolute

trayecto *m* (*trecho*) distance; (*ruta*) route; (*recorrido*) itinerary; **final de** ~ end of the line

trayectoria *f* 1. (*de cuerpo*) path; ~ **de la Luna** the moon's trajectory 2. (*profesional*) career

traza *f* 1. *t.* ARQUIT (*plan*) plan 2. (*habilidad*) ability; **tener** ~ **para escribir** to be good at writing; **tener** ~ **para hablar** to have a knack for speaking **3.** (*aspecto*) appearance; **por las ~s** from the look of things; **lleva todas las ~s de acabar mal** it clearly looks as though it isn't going to turn out well **4.** (*rastro*) trace

trazado *m* **1.** *t.* ARQUIT (*de plan*) design **2.** (*recorrido*) route; FERRO line **3.** (*dirección*) direction **4.** (*disposición*) layout

trazado, -a *adj* **bien ~** nice-looking; **mal ~** unattractive

trazar <z→c> *vt* **1.** (*líneas*) to trace; (*esquemáticamente*) to outline; (*dibujos*) to sketch **2.** *t.* ARQUIT (*plan*) to draw up **3.** (*describir*) to describe

trazo *m* **1.** (*de bolígrafo, lápiz*) mark; **dibujar al ~** to outline **2.** (*de escritura*) stroke **3.** (*dibujo*) sketch **4.** (*de la cara*) **de ~s suaves** with soft features

trébede(s) *f(pl)* trivet

trebejo *m* utensil; **~s de pesca** fishing gear

trébol *m* **1.** (*planta*) clover; (*hoja*) clover leaf; (*emblema nacional de Irlanda*) shamrock **2.** (*cartas*) clubs

trece **I.** *adj inv* thirteen; **seguir en sus ~** to stand firm; **en el siglo ~** in the thirteenth century; **martes y ~** ≈ Friday the thirteenth **II.** *m* thirteen; *v.t.* **ocho**

trecho *m* **1.** (*distancia*) distance, way **2.** (*tramo*) stretch **3.** (*tiempo*) period, spell **4.** (*trozo*) piece; **de ~ a** [*o* **en**] **~** every so often; **a ~s** at intervals; **hacer algo a ~s** to do sth in fits and starts

tregua *f* **1.** MIL truce **2.** (*descanso*) respite; **dar ~s** (*dolor*) to let up now and then; **la muela le daba ~s** his/her toothache would come and go; **sin ~** relentlessly

treinta *adj inv, m* thirty; *v.t.* **ochenta**

treintavo, -a *adj* thirtieth; *v.t.* **ochentavo**

treintena *f* **1.** (*treinta unidades*) **una ~** thirty; **una ~ de años** about thirty years; **aún están en la ~** they are still in their thirties **2.** (*parte*) thirtieth

tremebundo, -a *adj* terrible

tremendista *adj* alarmist; (*exagerado*) sensationalist

tremendo, -a *adj* **1.** (*temible*) frightful **2.** (*enorme*) tremendous **3.** (*niño*) full of mischief **4.** (*respetable*) imposing ▶**conseguir algo por la tremenda** to want to get sth by whatever means; **tomar las cosas a la tremenda** to make such a fuss over things

trementina *f* turpentine

tremolar *vi* to wave, to flutter

tremolina *f* **1.** (*del viento*) whistling **2.** (*bulla*) uproar

trémulo, -a *adj elev* tremulous; (*luz*) flickering

tren *m* **1.** FERRO train; **~ interurbano** intercity train; **~ de juguete** toy train; **~ rápido** express train; **~ de cercanías** suburban train; **~ de alta velocidad** high-speed train; **~ directo** through train; **coger el ~** to catch [*o* take] the train; **ir en ~** to go by train; **todas quieren subirse al ~** *fig* everyone wants to

get in on it, everyone wants to climb on the bandwagon; **perder el último ~** *fig* to miss the boat **2.** TÉC **~ de lavado** carwash **3.** (*lujo*) **~ de vida** lifestyle; **llevar un gran ~ de vida** to live in style **4.** (*ritmo*) **imponer un fuerte ~ en la carrera** to set a fast pace in the race **5.** *inf* (*muy bien*) **estar como un ~** (*persona*) to be very good-looking **6.** *inf* (*en abundancia*) **hay sangría como para parar un ~** there's plenty of sangria

trena *f inf* clink *Brit,* slammer *Am*

trenca *f* (*abrigo*) duffle coat

trenza *f* **1.** (*de pelo*) plait *Brit,* braid *Am* **2.** (*de cintas*) braid

trenzar <z→c> *vt* **1.** (*pelo*) to plait *Brit,* to braid *Am* **2.** (*fibras*) to plait

trepa[1] *f* (*astucia*) cunning

trepa[2] *m pey, inf* climber; **esta oficina esta llena de ~s luchando por llegar a la cima** this office is full of ambitious go-getters scrambling to reach the top

trepador(a) **I.** *adj* **planta ~a** climbing plant **II.** *m(f)* (*arribista*) social climber, go-getter

trepar **I.** *vi, vt* **1.** (*al árbol*) to climb **2.** (*planta*) to creep **II.** *vt* to climb

trepe *m* CRi (*regaño*) scolding; **echar un ~ a alguien por algo** to give sb a telling-off for sth

trepidar *vi* **1.** (*temblar*) to vibrate **2.** *AmL* (*vacilar*) to hesitate

treque *adj Ven* **1.** (*ingenioso*) witty **2.** (*chistoso*) funny

tres **I.** *adj inv* three; **esta traducción no me sale ni a la de ~** I just can't do this translation no matter how I try; **como ~ y dos son cinco** as sure as you are born; **de ~ al cuarto** two-bit; **~ en raya** (*juego*) noughts and crosses *Brit,* tic-tac-toe *Am* **II.** *m inv* three; *v.t.* **ocho**

trescientos, -as *adj* three hundred; *v.t.* **ochocientos**

tresillo *m* **1.** (*mueble*) three-piece living room suite **2.** MÚS triplet

treta *f* trick

tría *f* sorting

tríada *f* triad

triangular *adj* triangular

triángulo *m* **1.** (*figura*) triangle **2.** MÚS triangle **3.** (*sentimental*) **~ amoroso** eternal triangle

triar <*1. pres:* trío> *vt* to sort

triates *mpl Méx* (*trillizos*) triplets *pl*

tribu *f* tribe

tribulación *f* **1.** tribulation; (*pena*) grief **2.** (*sufrimiento*) suffering **3.** (*adversidad*) hardship

tribuna *f* **1.** (*en parlamento*) rostrum **2.** (*en desfile, estadio*) stand **3.** JUR **~ de jurados** jury box **4.** **~ de la prensa** press box

tribunal *m* **1.** JUR court; **Tribunal de Cuentas** National Audit Office; **Tribunal Europeo de Cuentas** European Court of Auditors; **Tribunal de Justicia Europeo** European Court of Justice; **llevar a los ~es** to take to court **2.** (*comisión*) **~ examinador** board of examiners

tributación f 1.(*acción*) payment 2.(*tributo*) taxation; ~ **por utilidades** income tax 3.(*sistema*) tax system

tributar vt 1.(*impuestos*) to pay 2.(*honor*) to render; (*respeto*) to show; ~ **un homenaje a alguien** to pay tribute to sb

tributario, -a adj tributary; (*imponible*) tax; **agencia tributaria** Inland Revenue

tributo m 1.(*impuesto*) tax 2.(*homenaje*) tribute; **pagar** ~ to pay tribute

triciclo m tricycle

tricolor adj tricolour *Brit*, tricolor *Am*

tricota f *AmL* (*chaqueta*) sweater

tricotar vt to knit

tridimensional adj three-dimensional

trienal adj 1.(*duración*) three-year 2.(*cada 3 años*) triennial

trifásico, -a adj three-phase

trifulca f *inf* rumpus

trigal m wheat field

trigésimo, -a adj thirtieth; v.t. octavo

trigo m 1.(*planta*) wheat 2.(*grano*) wheat; **no ser** ~ **limpio** *fig* not to be totally above board

trigueño, -a I. adj light brown; (*pelo*) dark blond; (*piel*) olive-skinned; *AmL* (*persona*) coloured *Brit*, colored *Am* II. m, f *AmL* coloured person

trilingüe adj trilingual

trilla f 1.(*acción*) threshing 2.(*época*) threshing season 3.*AmL*, *inf* (*paliza*) thrashing 4.(*trillo*) thresher

trillado, -a adj *inf* (*asunto*) over-worked

trilladora f threshing machine

trillar vt 1.(*grano*) to thresh 2.(*usar*) to overuse 3.*AmL*, *inf* (*golpear*) to beat

trillizo m triplet

trillo m 1.AGR (*máquina*) thresher 2.*AmC* (*senda*) narrow path

trillón m trillion

trimestral adj 1.(*duración*) three-month 2.(*cada tres meses*) three-monthly, quarterly

trimestre m 1.(*período*) three-month period 2.(*educación*) term *Brit*, semester *Am* 3.(*paga*) quarterly payment; (*alquiler*) quarter's rent

trinar vi 1.(*persona*) to sing; (*pájaro*) to warble 2.*inf* (*rabiar*) to fume; **está que trina** he/she is hopping mad 3.MÚS to trill

trinca f 1.(*tres*) threesome 2.*And*, *CSur* (*pandilla*) gang 3.*AmL*, *inf* (*embriaguez*) drunkenness 4.*CSur* (*canicas*) game of marbles

trincar <c→qu> I. vt 1.(*con cuerdas*) to tie up 2.(*detener*) to nab 3.(*romper*) to break up; (*papel*) to tear up 4.*inf* (*robar*) to steal 5.*inf* (*matar*) to bump off 6.*AmL* (*apretar*) to be too tight II. vr: ~**se** 1.*inf* (*emborracharse*) to get plastered 2.*vulg* (*copular*) to screw

trinchar vt (*carne*) to carve

trinchera f 1.MIL trench; **guerra de** ~**s** trench warfare 2.(*gabardina*) trench coat

trineo m sledge *Brit*, sled *Am*

trinidad f trinity; **la Santísima Trinidad** the Holy Trinity

trinitaria f 1.BOT (*pensamiento*) pansy 2.*Col*, *PRico*, *Ven* BOT bougainvillea

trino m 1.MÚS trill 2.(*pájaro*) warble

trinquete m 1.TÉC pawl 2.(*mástil*) foremast

trío m trio

tripa f 1.(*intestino*) intestine, gut; **quitar las** ~**s a un pez** to gut a fish 2. pl (*vísceras*) entrails pl, innards pl; (*comestibles*) tripe; **me suenan las** ~**s** my stomach's rumbling; **echar las** ~**s** *inf* (*vomitar*) to throw up; **hacer de** ~**s corazón** *inf* to pluck up courage, to grin and bear it; **¿qué** ~ **se te ha roto?** *inf* what's up with you?; **se me revuelven las** ~**s** it turns my stomach; **¡te voy a sacar las** ~**s!** *inf* I'm going to tear you to pieces!; **tener malas** ~**s** *inf* to be cruel 3.(*vientre*) tummy; **echar** ~ *inf* to get a paunch; **llenar(se) la** ~ *inf* to eat one's fill; **estar con** ~ (*embarazada*) to be in the family way; **dejar con** ~ *inf* to get sb pregnant 4. pl (*interior*) insides pl; (*de fruta*) core

tripi m *inf* dose of LSD

triple I. adj triple; (*de tres capas*) three-ply II. m (*cantidad*) triple; **ser el** ~ **de grande** to be three times as large

triplicado, -a adj triplicate; **por** ~ (*acta*) in triplicate

triplicar <c→qu> I. vt to triple, to treble II. vr: ~**se** to triple, to treble

trípode m FOTO tripod

tripón, -ona I. adj *inf* pot-bellied II. m, f 1.*Méx*, *inf* little boy or girl; **los tripones** the kids 2.*inf* (*persona gorda*) fatty

tríptico m (*documento*) three-page leaflet

triptongo m LING triphthong

tripudo, -a I. adj *inf* big-bellied II. m, f fatty

tripulación f (*avión, barco*) crew

tripulante m crew member

tripular vt 1.(*proveer de tripulación*) to man 2.(*conducir: coche*) to drive; (*avión, barco*) to pilot

tripulina f *Chile* hubbub, rumpus

triquiñuela f trick

triquitraque m 1.(*ruido*) clatter 2.(*tira*) string of firecrackers

tris m *inv* 1.(*ruido*) crack 2.(*porción pequeña*) bit 3.(*momento*) trice; **estar en un** ~ to be in a jiffy; **estar en un** ~ **de hacer algo** to be within an inch of doing sth; **por un** ~ by the skin of one's teeth

trisca f 1.(*crujido*) crunch 2.(*jaleo*) racket 3.*AmC* (*mofa*) surreptitious sneer

triscar <c→qu> I. vi 1.(*patalear*) to stamp 2.(*jugar*) to romp II. vt 1.(*mezclar*) to mingle 2.(*confundir*) to mix up 3.*AmC* (*mofar*) to make fun of

triste adj sad; (*mustio, pálido*) gloomy; (*descolorido*) dreary; (*paisaje*) dismal; (*flor*) withered; **un** ~ **sueldo** a sorry salary; **aún no he comido ni un** ~ **bocadillo** I haven't even had a measly sandwich yet; **aún no he ganado ni una** ~ **peseta** I've yet to earn a single peseta; **es** ~ **que no podamos ir** it's a pity that we can't go; **el caballero de la ~ figura** (**Don Quijote**) the knight of the sad countenance

tristeza *f* sadness, sorrow

tristón, -ona *adj* gloomy

tristura *f AmL* sadness

tritón *m* newt, triton

trituradora *f* TÉC crusher; (*de la cocina*) grinder; ~ **de carne** meat grinder; ~ **de forraje** forrage chopper; ~ **de papel** paper shredder; ~ **de basura** waste-disposal unit; ~ **de hielo** ice crusher

triturar *vt* 1.(*desmenuzar*) to chop; (*moler*) to grind; (*al masticar*) to chew 2.(*maltratar*) to beat to a pulp; (*destruir*) to pulverize 3.(*criticar*) to tear to pieces

triunfador(a) *m(f)* winner

triunfal *adj* triumphal, triumphant; **canto ~** song of triumph

triunfar *vi* 1.(*salir triunfador*) to triumph 2.(*ganar*) ~ **en algo** to win at sth; (*tener éxito*) to succeed; ~ **en la vida** to succeed in life 3.(*exultar*) ~ **de algo** to exult over sth 4.(*naipes*) to trump; (*jugar un triunfo*) to play a trump; **triunfan corazones** hearts are trumps

triunfo *m* 1.(*victoria*) triumph, victory; (*éxito*) success; **arco de ~** victory arch; **costar un ~** to be no easy task 2.(*naipe*) trump

trivial *adj* trivial

trivialidad *f* 1.(*cualidad*) triviality, pettiness 2.(*dicho*) trite remark

trivializar <z→c> *vt* 1.(*restar importancia*) to trivialize 2.(*simplificar*) to play down

triza *f* shred; **estar hecho ~s** to feel washed out; **hacer ~s** to tear into shreds; (*papel*) to shred; (*película*) to tear to pieces; **hacerse ~s** to smash to bits; (*jarrón*) to shatter; **hacer ~s a alguien** to tear sb apart

trocar *irr como volcar* I. *vt* 1.(*cambiar*) ~ **por algo** to exchange for sth, to barter for sth; (*palabras*) to interchange 2.(*dinero*) to change 3.(*confundir*) to confuse 4.(*vomitar*) to vomit 5. *CSur*(*vender*) to sell II. *vr:* ~**se** (*cambiar*) to change; (*transformarse*) to turn

trocear *vt* to cut up

trocha *f* 1.(*senda*) trail; (*atajo*) shortcut 2. *AmL* FERRO gauge

trochemoche a ~ (*sin orden*) helter-skelter; (*desparramado*) all over the place

trofeo *m* 1.(*señal*) trophy; ~ **de guerra** war trophy 2.(*victoria*) victory, triumph; (*éxito*) success

troglodita I. *adj* 1.(*cavernícola*) cave-dwelling 2. *inf*(*burdo*) brutish II. *m* 1.(*cavernícola*) troglodyte, cave-dweller 2. *inf*(*burdo*) lout

trola *f inf*(*mentira*) lie, whopper

trole *m* ELEC trolley pole

trolebús *m* trolley bus

trolero *m inf*(*mentiroso*) liar

tromba *f* METEO ~ (**de agua**) water spout; (*aguacero*) downpour; ~ (**terrestre**) whirlwind; **en ~** en masse

trombón *m* MÚS 1.(*instrumento*) trombone

2.(*músico*) trombonist

trombosis *f inv* MED thrombosis

trompa[1] *f* 1. ZOOL (*elefante*) trunk; (*insectos*) proboscis; ~ **de Falopio** Fallopian tube 2. *inf* (*nariz*) conk 3. *AmL, inf* (*labios*) lips *pl;* **¡cierra la ~!** shut your trap! 4. MÚS (*instrumento*) horn 5.(*peonza*) top 6. *inf* (*borrachera*) drunkenness; **coger una ~** to get smashed; **estar ~** to be drunk 7. METEO *v.* **tromba**

trompa[2] *mf* 1.(*músico*) horn player 2. *CSur, inf*(*patrón*) boss

trompada *f*, **trompazo** *m* (*porrazo*) bash; (*choque*) crash; (*puñetazo*) punch

trompear I. *vt AmL, inf* to punch II. *vr:* ~**se** *inf* 1.(*emborracharse*) to get plastered 2. *AmL* (*pelearse*) to fight

trompeta[1] *mf*(*músico*) trumpet player

trompeta[2] *f*(*instrumento*) trumpet

trompicar <c→qu> *vi* to stumble

trompicón *m* 1.(*tropezón*) stumble; **a trompicones** in fits and starts 2. *AmC* (*puñetazo*) punch

trompis *m inv, Arg, Urug* (*trompada*) punch; **agarrarse a ~** to start punching each other

trompiza *f AmS* fight

trompo *m* spinning top

trompudo, -a *adj AmL* thick-lipped

tronada *f* METEO thunderstorm

tronado, -a *adj* 1.(*desgastado*) worn 2. *inf* (*loco*) **estar ~** to be cracked; (*arruinado*) to be broke; *AmL* (*drogado*) to be high on drugs

tronar <o→ue> I. *vimpers* METEO to thunder II. *vi* 1.(*ruido*) to thunder; (*gritar*) to roar 2.(*oponerse*) to denounce violently, to thunder

troncal *adj* (*principal*) main; **asignaturas troncales** ENS core subjects

troncar *vt* to truncate

troncha *f Arg, Chile, Perú* (*lonja*) slice

tronchar I. *vt* 1.(*tronco*) to cut down; (*rama*) to snap 2.(*vida*) to cut short; (*esperanzas*) to shatter II. *vr:* ~**se** to split; ~**se de risa** *inf* to split one's sides laughing

troncho *m* 1. BOT stem; (*de hortaliza*) stalk 2. *CSur* (*trozo*) chunk

tronco *m* 1.(*árbol*) trunk; (*flor*) stem; (*hortaliza*) stalk; (*de un árbol talado*) stump; (*leño*) log; **dormir como un ~** *inf* to sleep like a log 2.(*cuerpo*) torso, trunk 3.(*de familia*) stock 4. *inf* (*amigo*) mate *Brit*, buddy; **tranqui ~** cool it, pal 5.(*conducto*) main line

tronera[1] *f* 1.(*ventana*) dormer; (*en el tejado*) small skylight 2. MIL crenel 3.(*billar*) pocket 4. *Méx* (*chimenea*) chimney

tronera[2] *mf* (*tarambana*) harebrained person

trono *m* 1.(*asiento*) throne; **ser leal al ~** to be loyal to the crown; **subir al ~** to come to the throne; **sucesor al ~** heir to the throne 2. *inf*(*inodoro*) loo *Brit,* John *Am*

tropa *f* 1.(*multitud*) crowd; *pey* (*grupo*) horde; **se presentaron Pepe y Clara y toda la ~** Pepe and Clara and the whole crew showed up; **en** ~ in disorganized groups **2.** MIL troop

tropear *vi Arg* (*conducir el ganado*) to herd

tropecientos, -as *adj inf* hundreds; **había ~ coches aparcados por todas partes** there were hundreds and hundreds of cars parked all over the place

tropel *m* **1.** (*mucha gente*) throng; **en** ~ in a mad rush; **salieron en** ~ **del estadio** they came pouring out of the stadium **2.** (*prisa*) rush **3.** (*desorden*) jumble

tropelía *f* **1.** (*abuso de autoridad*) abuse of authority; (*acto violento*) violent act **2.** (*prisa*) haste

tropero *m Arg* (*vaquero*) cowboy

tropezar *irr como empezar* **I.** *vi* **1.** (*con los pies*) to trip **2.** (*topar*) to come across **3.** (*cometer un error*) to make a mistake; (*moralmente*) to go astray **4.** (*reñir*) to quarrel **II.** *vr:* ~**se** (*encontrarse*) to run into

tropezón *m* **1.** (*acción*) stumble; **dar un** ~ to trip; **a tropezones** by fits and starts; *fig* falling and rising; **hablaba a tropezones** he/she spoke falteringly **2.** (*error*) mistake; (*desliz*) lapse **3.** (*persona*) run-in **4.** (*en sopas, legumbres*) small chunks of meat, vegetables or seafood

tropical *adj* tropical; **clima** ~ tropical climate; **fantasías** ~**es** exotic fantasies

trópico *m* tropic; ~ **de Cáncer** Tropic of Cancer; **pasar los** ~**s** *AmC, fig* to have a hard time

tropiezo *m* **1.** (*en el camino*) stumbling block; **dar un** ~ to trip **2.** (*error*) blunder; (*moralmente*) moral lapse **3.** (*revés*) setback **4.** (*desgracia*) misfortune; (*en el amor*) thwarting **5.** (*discusión*) quarrel

tropilla *f CSur* drove

troquel *m* die

trotamundos *mf inv* globetrotter

trotar *vi* **1.** (*caballos*) to trot; (*jinete*) to trot **2.** (*con prisas*) to hustle

trote *m* **1.** (*caballos*) trot; **ir al** ~ to trot **2.** (*con prisa*) bustle; **a(l)** ~ quickly **3.** (*ropa*) **para todo** ~ for everyday use; **ser de mucho** ~ to be very durable **4.** *inf* (*actividad*) **es demasiado viejo, ya no está para estos** ~**s** he's too old and is not up to that sort of thing any more

trova *f* (*verso*) verse; (*poema*) poem; (*canción*) ballad

trovador *m* troubadour

trozo *m* **1.** (*pedazo*) piece, bit; **a** ~**s** in pieces; **la pared se está cayendo a** ~**s** the wall is falling apart bit by bit **2.** LIT, MÚS excerpt, passage

trucaje *m* **1.** (*con trampa*) rigging **2.** CINE (*método*) trick photograply, special effects; FOTO touching up

trucar *vt* **1.** (*amañar*) to fix, to rig; FOTO to alter **2.** *inf* AUTO to soup up

trucha *f* **1.** (*pez*) trout; ~ **asalmonada** salmon trout **2.** *AmC* COM (*caseta*) stand

trucho, -a *adj Arg, Col* (*astuto*) crafty, rascally

truco *m* trick; **esto tiene** ~ there's a trick [*o* a catch] to this; **ése tiene muchos** ~**s** he's full of tricks ▶ **coger el** ~ **a algo** to get the hang of sth; **coger el** ~ **a alguien** to catch on to sb

truculento, -a *adj* **1.** (*cruel*) cruel **2.** (*terrible*) gruesome

trueno *m* **1.** (*ruido*) clap of thunder **2.** *inf* (*juerguista*) madcap; (*alborotador*) wild youth; **ir de** ~ to go on a spree

trueque *m* exchange; COM (*sin dinero*) barter; **a** ~ **de** in exchange for

trufa *f* **1.** *t.* BOT truffle **2.** (*mentira*) lie; (*embuste*) hoax; (*fanfarronada*) bluster **3.** (*bombón*) (chocolate) truffle

trufar **I.** *vi* (*mentir*) to lie; (*engañar*) to deceive; (*fanfarronear*) to bluster **II.** *vt* (*rellenar*) to stuff

truhán *m* (*estafador*) rogue; (*charlatán*) mountebank

trullo *m inf* (*prisión*) clink *Brit*, slammer *Am*

truncado, -a *adj* (*incompleto*) cut short, truncated

truncar <c→qu> *vt* **1.** (*cortar*) to truncate; (*la cabeza*) to cut off **2.** (*texto*) to abridge; (*significado*) to destroy; (*cita*) to mutilate **3.** (*desarrollo*) to stunt; (*esperanzas, ilusiones*) to shatter

trusa *f Méx, Perú* (*faja*) girdle

tu *art pos* your; ~ **padre/blusa/libro** your father/blouse/book; ~**s hermanos/hermanas** your brothers/sisters

tú *pron pers* you; **yo que** ~ if I were you; **tratar de** ~ to address in the familiar manner using 'tú'; **de** ~ **a** ~ on equal footing

tuba *f* tuba

tubérculo *m* **1.** BOT tuber **2.** *t.* MED (*bulto*) tubercle

tuberculosis *f inv* tuberculosis

tubería *f* **1.** (*tubo*) pipe **2.** (*conjunto*) pipes *pl*

tubo *m* **1.** (*para fluidos, gases*) tube; ~ **de chimenea** flue; ~ **digestivo** alimentary canal; ~ **de ensayo** test tube; ~ **de escape** exhaust pipe *Brit*, tailpipe *Am;* ~ **de respiración** breathing tube; **tienes que pasar por el** ~ *inf* you have to knuckle under; **fue como por un** ~ *inf* it was a cinch; **alucinar por un** ~ *inf* to really flip; **tenemos trabajo por un** ~ *inf* we have loads of work to do **2.** RADIO, TV tube **3.** (*recipiente*) tube; ~ **de pasta de dientes** tube of toothpaste **4.** *AmL* TEL (*auricular*) receiver **5.** *inf* (*metro*) tube *Brit*, metro

tubular *adj* tubular, tube-shaped

tucán *m* toucan

tuerca *f* nut; ~ **mariposa** wing nut

tuerto, -a **I.** *adj* **1.** (*de sólo un ojo*) one-eyed **2.** (*torcido*) crooked, twisted **II.** *m, f* injustice

tueste *m* toasting; (*café*) roasting

tuétano *m* **1.** (*médula*) marrow **2.** (*corazón, esencia*) core, heart; **hasta los** ~**s** through and through; **enamorado hasta los** ~**s** head over heels in love; **llegar al** ~ **de un asunto** to get to the crux of a matter; **calado hasta los** ~**s** soaked to the skin

tufarada *f* strong smell; ¡qué ~ a cerveza echaba! he/she reeked of beer!

tufillas *mf inf* irascible person

tufillo *m* ~ a algo slight smell of sth; este libro tiene un cierto ~ nostálgico *fig* this book has an air of nostalgia about it

tufo *m* 1. (*olor malo*) foul smell; (*de cuerpo*) body odour *Brit*, body odor *Am*; (*halitosis*) bad breath; (*a alcohol*) reek; (*a cerrado*) stuffy 2. (*vapor*) fume 3. (*rizo*) curl 4. *pl* (*vanidad*) airs *pl*; **tener** ~ *inf* to be conceited

tugurio *m* 1. (*chabola*) hovel; (*cuartucho*) small room 2. *pl* (*barrio*) slums *pl* 3. *pey* (*bar*) joint

tuición *f* JUR custody, protection; **bajo la** ~ **de** sponsored by

tul *m* tulle

tulipa *f* tulip-shaped lampshade

tulipán *m* tulip

tullido, -a I. *adj* (*persona*) disabled; *pey* crippled; (*brazo*) maimed II. *m, f* cripple

tullir <3. *pret:* tulló> *vt* 1. (*maltratar*) to maltreat 2. (*herir*) to injure; (*lisiar*) to cripple; **te voy a ~ a palos** I'm going to beat you to a pulp 3. (*paralizar*) to paralyze 4. (*agotar*) to wear out, to exhaust

tumba *f* 1. (*sepulcro*) grave, tomb; **ser** (**como**) **una** ~ (*callado*) to keep quiet; **soy una** ~ my lips are sealed; **llevar a alguien a la** ~ to carry sb off; **hablar a** ~ **abierta** to speak openly; **lanzarse a** ~ **abierta en algo** to go headlong into sth; **tu abuelo se revolvería en su** ~ your grandfather would turn in his grave; **cavar su propia** ~ to drive a nail into one's own coffin 2. (*voltereta*) somersault 3. *AmL* (*tala*) felling of trees; (*claro*) tree clearing

tumbar I. *vt* 1. (*tirar*) to knock down; (*pegando*) to flatten; **el campeón le tumbó en el tercer asalto** the champ knocked him out in the third round; *inf* (*matar*) to bump off; **estar tumbado** to be lying down 2. *inf* ENS (*suspender*) to fail, to flunk *Am* 3. *inf* (*perturbar, impresionar*) to bowl over 4. *AmL* (*árboles*) to fell; (*tierra*) to clear 5. *vulg* (*copular*) to screw II. *vr:* ~**se** 1. (*acostarse*) to lie down; ~**se en la cama** to lie down on the bed 2. (*desistir*) to give up 3. *inf* (*en el trabajo*) to ease up

tumbo *m* 1. (*caída*) fall, tumble 2. (*vaivén*) roll; **dar un** ~ to jolt; **ir por la vida dando ~s** to go through life moving from one hardship to another 3. (*voltereta*) somersault

tumbón, -ona I. *adj* 1. (*astuto*) cunning 2. (*vago*) lazy II. *m, f* 1. (*persona astuta*) sly person 2. (*vago*) idler, loafer

tumbona *f* deck chair

tumefacción *f* MED swelling

tumor *m* MED tumour *Brit*, tumor *Am*

tumulto *m* tumult; **un** ~ **de gente** a crowd of people

tuna *f* 1. MÚS tuna 2. (*vida picaresca*) **correr la** ~ to live it up

The **tuna** is a group of students who get together to sing and play music. Up until recently, only male students were admitted to **tunas**, but in the last few years new **tunas** have been formed for female students. In order to become a member of a **tuna**, certain initiation rites involving trials of courage have to be successfully completed.

tunante *mf v.* **tuno**

tunda *f* 1. (*paliza*) beating 2. (*esfuerzo*) exhausting effort; **darse una** ~ to wear oneself out 3. (*de paños*) clipping

tundir *vt* 1. (*pegar*) to thrash 2. (*paños*) to clip 3. (*hierba*) to mow, to cut

tunecino, -a *adj, m, f* Tunisian

túnel *m* tunnel; ~ **aerodinámico** wind tunnel; ~ **de lavado** car wash; **salir del** ~ *fig* to see the light at the end of the tunnel

Túnez *m* 1. (*país*) Tunisia 2. (*capital*) Tunis

túnica *f* 1. (*vestidura*) tunic, robe 2. (*membrana*) tunica

tuno, -a I. *adj* 1. (*astuto*) cunning 2. (*pícaro*) roguish II. *m, f* 1. (*truhán*) rogue 2. (*astuto*) crook 3. (*niño*) scamp 4. (*de la tuna*) member of a student 'tuna'

tuntún *m inf* **al** (**buen**) ~ any old way; **juzgar al buen** ~ to jump to conclusions

tupé *m* 1. (*cabello*) quiff *Brit*, pompadour *Am* 2. (*frescura*) cheek

tupí *mf AmL* (*aborígen del Brasil*) Tupi

tupido, -a I. *adj* 1. (*denso*) thick; **correr un** ~ **velo** to draw a veil over sth; *fig* to keep sth quiet 2. *AmL* (*obstruido*) blocked 3. *Méx* (*frecuente*) frequent 4. (*con tesón*) persistently II. *adv* (*a menudo*) often

tupir I. *vt* 1. (*apretar*) to pack tightly; (*tapar agujeros*) to fill in 2. (*obstruir*) to obstruct II. *vr:* ~**se** 1. (*comer mucho*) to gorge oneself; (*beber mucho*) to guzzle down 2. *AmL* (*obstruirse*) to get blocked up

turba *f* 1. (*materia*) peat 2. *v.* **turbamulta**

turbación *f* 1. (*disturbio*) disturbance 2. (*alarma*) concern 3. (*vergüenza*) embarrassment 4. (*confusión*) confusion

turbamulta *f* crowd; *pey* mob

turbante *m* turban

turbar I. *vt* 1. (*perturbar*) to disturb 2. (*alarmar*) to worry 3. (*avergonzar*) to embarrass 4. (*desconcertar*) to unsettle 5. (*agua*) to stir up II. *vr:* ~**se** 1. (*ser disturbado*) to be disturbed 2. (*alarmarse*) to get worried 3. (*avergonzarse*) to get embarrassed 4. (*desconcertarse*) to become confused 5. (*agua*) to get stirred up

turbina *f* turbine

turbio, -a *adj* (*líquido*) cloudy; (*asunto*) turbid, shady; (*sin transparencia, carácter*) opaque; (*negocio*) shady; (*vista*) blurry, unclear

turbión *m* 1. (*aguacero*) downpour; (*devastador*) hurricane 2. (*todo a la vez*) sweep; ~ **de**

balas hail of bullets
turbo *m t.* AUTO turbo
turborreactor *m* turbojet
turbulencia *f* 1.(*agua, aire*) turbulence 2.(*alboroto*) commotion; (*confusión*) turmoil 3.(*sin transparencia*) turbidness
turbulento, -a *adj* 1.(*agua, aire*) turbulent 2.(*alborotado*) stormy; (*confuso*) confused 3.(*rebelde*) disorderly 4.(*turbio*) cloudy
turco, -a I. *adj* Turkish II. *m, f* Turk; **cabeza de ~** *fig* scapegoat
turgencia *f* (*hinchazón*) swelling; (*firmeza*) turgidness
turgente *adj* 1.(*hinchado*) swollen 2.(*abultado*) protuberant; (*pechos*) firm
turismo *m* 1.(*viajar*) tourism; **~ verde** eco-tourism; **industria del ~** tourist trade; **oficina de ~** visitors' bureau; **hacer ~** to travel as a tourist 2. AUTO private car
turista *mf* tourist
turístico, -a *adj* tourist; **viaje ~** sightseeing trip
turnar *vi, vr:* **~se** to take turns
turno *m* 1.(*en la fábrica*) shift; **cambio de ~** shift change; **estar de ~** to be on duty; **trabajar por ~s** to work shifts; **~ de día/noche** day/night shift 2.(*orden*) turn; **a** [*o por*] **~s** by turns; **es tu ~** it's your turn; **pedir ~** to ask who is last in line; **aguardar su ~** to wait one's turn; **~ de preguntas** question and answer session; **hacer algo por ~s** to take turns doing sth; **de ~** current; **apareció con la novia de ~** he showed up with his latest girlfriend
turolense I. *adj* of/from Teruel II. *mf* native/inhabitant of Teruel
turón *m* polecat
turquesa¹ I. *adj* turquoise II. *m* (*color*) turquoise blue
turquesa² *f* MIN (*piedra*) turquoise
Turquía *f* Turkey
turrón *m* 1.(*dulce*) ≈ nougat 2.(*puesto*) cushy job; **comer del ~** *fig* to fill a government post

---

Like the British Christmas cake, **turrón** is a must in Spain at Christmas. The traditional **turrón** is either a soft or hard bar, rather like nougat, containing nuts or honey-coated almonds. The **turrón** is made particularly in **Levante**, and especially in **Jijona** and **Alicante**.

---

turulato, -a *adj inf* dazed, stunned; **dejar a alguien ~** to leave sb flabbergasted
tusar I. *vi Guat* (*murmurar*) to murmur II. *vt AmL* (*cortar mal el pelo*) to scalp *inf*
tuso, -a *adj* 1. *Col, PRico* (*pelón*) cropped, shorn 2. *Col, Ven* (*picado de viruelas*) pock-marked 3. *PRico* (*rabón*) tailless, bobtailed
tute *m* 1.(*juego*) Spanish card game 2. *inf* (*trabajo*) **darse un ~** to work one's fingers to the bone
tutear I. *vt* to address in the familiar manner

using 'tú' II. *vr:* **~se** to be on familiar terms
tutela *f* 1.(*cargo*) guardianship; **poner bajo ~** to place in ward 2.(*amparo*) protection; **estar bajo la ~ de alguien** to be under the protection of sb
tutelaje *m CSur, Guat, Méx* (*tutela*) guardianship, protection
tutelar I. *adj* 1. JUR tutelary; **juez ~** tutelary judge 2.(*protector*) protective, guardian II. *vt* 1.(*ejercer la tutela*) to have the charge of 2.(*proteger*) to protect, to guard 3.(*velar*) to supervise
tuteo *m* familiar use of 'tú'
tutilimundi *m* 1.(*mundonuevo*) cosmorama 2. *AmL, inf* everybody
tutiplén *adv inf* galore; **a ~** in abundance; **comer a ~** to eat like there's no tomorrow
tutor(a) *m(f)* 1. JUR guardian; **firma/consentimiento del padre o ~** signature/consent of parent or guardian 2.(*protector*) protector 3.(*profesor*) teacher 4. ENS, UNIV tutor
tutoría *f* 1. JUR guardianship, tutelage 2. UNIV tutorship; (*clase*) tutorial
tuyo, -a *pron pos* 1.(*propiedad*) **el perro es ~** the dog is yours; **la botella/la casa es tuya** the bottle/the house is yours; **¡ya es ~!** all yours! 2.(*tras artículo*) **el ~/la tuya/lo ~** yours; **mi coche está roto, vamos en el ~** my car isn't working, let's take yours; **no cojas mi lápiz, tienes el ~** don't take my pencil, you have your own; **los ~s** yours; (*parientes*) your family; **ésta es la tuya** *fig* this is your chance; **una de las tuyas** (*travesura*) one of your tricks 3.(*tras substantivo*) of yours; **una amiga tuya** a friend of yours; **una hermana tuya** one of your sisters; **es culpa tuya** it's your fault 4.(*tras impersonal 'lo'*) **lo ~** what is yours; **tú a lo ~** you mind your own business; **esto no es lo ~** this isn't your strong point
TVE *f abr de* **Televisión Española** *the Spanish state-owned television broadcasting company*
txacolí, txakolí *m type of white wine from the Basque country*

U

U, u *f* <úes> U, u; **~ de Uruguay** U for Uncle
U *abr de* **University** U., Univ.
u *conj* placed before words beginning with 'o' or 'ho' or; **diez u once** ten or eleven
ubérrimo, -a *adj* very fertile
ubicación *f* 1.(*lugar*) location; (*de una empresa*) site 2.(*situación*) situation 3.(*empleo*) position 4. *AmL* (*colocación*) placing
ubicar <c→qu> I. *vi* to be (situated) II. *vt AmL* (*situar*) to situate; (*guardar*) to place III. *vr:* **~se** to be (situated)
ubicuo, -a *adj* ubiquitous

ubre *f* udder

UC *f abr de* **Unión de Consumidores** *Consumers Association*

UCI *abr de* **Unidad de Cuidados Intesivos** ICU

Ucrania *f* Ukraine

ucrani(an)o, -a *adj, m, f* Ukrainian

Ud(s). *abr de* **usted(es)** you

UE *f abr de* **Unión Europea** EU

UEFA *f abr de* **Unión de Asociaciones Europeas de Fútbol** UEFA

UEME *abr de* **Unión Económica y Monetaria Europea** EEMU

UEO *f abr de* **Unión Europea Occidental** WEU

uf *interj* **1.** (*de asco, fastidio*) ugh **2.** (*de cansancio, alivio*) phew

ufanarse *vr* to boast; ~ **de algo** to brag about sth

ufanía *f* **1.** (*orgullo*) pride **2.** (*engreimiento*) conceit; (*arrogancia*) arrogance **3.** (*satisfacción*) complacency

ufano, -a *adj* **1.** (*orgulloso*) proud **2.** (*engreído*) conceited; (*arrogante*) arrogant **3.** (*satisfecho*) complacent; **va muy ~ con su nueva moto** he is very smug about his new motorbike **4.** (*planta*) lush, luxuriant

ufología *f sin pl* ufology

ugandés, -esa *adj, m, f* Ugandan

UGT *f abr de* **Unión General de Trabajadores** *socialist trade union, one of the two main TUs in Spain.*

ujier *m* **1.** (*de un tribunal*) usher **2.** (*de un palacio*) gatekeeper

úlcera *f* MED ulcer; (*pupa*) sore

ulcerar *vt, vr:* ~**se** to ulcerate, to fester

ulterior *adj* (*posterior*) later, subsequent; (*más*) further

ulteriormente *adv* later, subsequently

ultimación *f* completion, conclusion

últimamente *adv* **1.** (*recientemente, hace poco*) recently, lately **2.** (*por último*) lastly, finally

ultimar *vt* **1.** (*proyecto, obra*) to finish, to complete; (*acuerdo*) to conclude **2.** *AmL* (*matar*) to murder

ultimátum *m* <inv *o* ultimatos> ultimatum; **dar el ~ a alguien** to give sb an ultimatum

último, -a *adj* **1.** (*en orden*) last; **el ~ de cada mes** the last day of each month; **a ~s de mes** at the end of the month; **soy el ~ de la clase** I'm the worst student in the class; **fue el ~ en firmar** he was the last to sign; **siempre llega el ~** he/she is always the last to arrive; **por última vez** for the last time; **hacia la última parte la película mejora** the film gets better towards the end; **la última moda** the lastest fashion; **por ~** lastly, finally; **¿quién es el ~?** (*en una cola*) who is last in the queue? *Brit,* who's the last in line? *Am;* **unos estudian ciencias, otros letras; los ~s...** some study science, others Arts; the latter ... **2.** (*espacio*)

la última fila the last row; **en el ~ piso** on the top floor; **ocupar la última posición de la tabla** to be at the bottom of the chart; **el ~ rincón del mundo** *inf* the back of beyond *Brit,* the boondocks *pl Am* ▶ **estar en las últimas** (*muriéndose*) to be at death's door; (*arruinado*) to be on one's last legs; **ser lo ~** (*lo mejor*) to be great; (*lo peor*) to be the end

ultra I. *adj* extreme II. *mf* extreme right-winger, neo-fascist III. *adv* extremely

ultracongelado, -a *adj* deep-frozen

ultracongelar *vt* to deep-freeze

ultraconservador(a) *adj* ultraconservative

ultrafino, -a *adj* exceedingly fine

ultrajar *vt* **1.** (*insultar*) to insult; (*monumento*) to spoil; ~ **de palabra** to revile **2.** (*humillar*) to humiliate **3.** (*ajar*) to crumple

ultraje *m* abuse; **un ~ a la bandera** a dishonour *Brit* [*o* dishonor *Am*] to the flag

ultramar *m sin pl* foreign parts *pl;* **pasé mi infancia en ~** I spent my childhood in foreign parts [*o* overseas]; **han venido de ~** they have come from overseas **ultramarino, -a** *adj* overseas **ultramarinos** *mpl* **1.** (*tienda*) grocer's *Brit,* grocery store *Am* **2.** (*víveres*) groceries *pl* **ultramoderno, -a** *adj* extremely modern

ultranza 1. (*a muerte*) **el padre defendió el honor de su familia a ~** the father defended the honour of his family with his life; **luchar a ~** to fight to the death **2.** (*resueltamente*) **ser de izquierda a ~** to be an out-and-out left-winger; **ser un ecologista a ~** to be a radical ecologist

ultrarrápido, -a *adj* extra fast; **tren ~** a high-speed train **ultrasecreto, -a** *adj* top secret **ultrasensible** *adj* ultrasensitive **ultrasónico, -a** *adj* ultrasonic **ultrasonido** *m sin pl* ultrasound **ultratumba** *f* **la vida de ~** the next life **ultravioleta** *adj inv* ultraviolet; **rayos ~** ultraviolet rays

ulular *vi* **1.** (*animal, viento*) to howl; (*búho*) to hoot **2.** (*persona*) to shriek

umbilical *adj* umbilical

umbráculo *m* pergola

umbral *m* **1.** (*de puerta*) threshold; **atravesar los ~es de una casa** to set foot in a house **2.** (*principio*) beginning, outset **3.** ECON ~ **de rentabilidad** break even point

umbrío, -a *adj* shady

umbroso, -a *adj* shady

UME *f abr de* **Unión Monetaria Europea** EMU

un, una <unos, -as> I. *art indef* **1.** (*no determinado*) a; (*before a vowel or initial silent h*) an; **un perro** a dog; **una chica** a girl; **un elefante** an elephant; **¡tiene una jeta!** he/she's got a nerve! **2.** *pl* (*algunos*) some, a few **3.** *pl* (*aproximadamente*) approximately, about; **unos 30 euros** about 30 euros II. *adj v.* **uno, -a**

unánime *adj* (*opinión, decisión*) unanimous

unanimidad *f* (*de opinión, decisión*) unanimity; **aprobar algo por ~** to approve sth

U

unanimously
unción *f* anointing
uncir <c→z> *vt* to yoke
undécimo, -a *adj* eleventh; *v.t.* octavo
undulación *f* wave, ripple
undular *vi, vt* to wave
UNED *f abr de* **Universidad Nacional de Educación a Distancia** ≈ OU
ungir <g→j> *vt t.* REL to anoint
ungüento *m* 1. MED ointment 2. (*remedio*) salve
únicamente *adv* only, solely
unicameral *adj* single-chamber **unicelular** *adj* unicellular
unicidad *f* uniqueness
único, -a *adj* 1. (*solo*) only; **hijo** ~ only child; **heredero** ~ sole heir; **calle de dirección única** one-way street; **hoy hay plato** ~ today there is only one main course 2. (*extraordinario*) unique
unicornio *m* unicorn
unidad *f* 1. *t.* MIL, MAT unit; ~ **familiar** family unit; **Unidad de Cuidados Intensivos** intensive care unit; ~ **de medida** unit of measure; ~ **monetaria** currency unit 2. LIT unity 3. TÉC (*aparato*) unit; ~ **de control** control unit; ~ **externa de disco duro** INFOR external hard disc unit [*o* drive]; ~ **de visualización** visual display unit; ~ **periférica** peripheral (device); TV, RADIO mobile unit
unidimensional *adj* one-dimensional
unido, -a *adj* united; **estamos muy** ~s we are very close; **mantenerse** ~s to stay together
unifamiliar *adj* single-family; **una casa** ~ a detached house
unificación *f* 1. (*unión*) unification; **la** ~ **política** political unification 2. (*uniformización*) standardization
unificar <c→qu> *vt* 1. (*pueblos, esfuerzos*) to unite; ~ **posiciones** to unify positions 2. (*uniformar*) to standardize
uniformar *vt* 1. (*hacer unitario, impreso*) to standardize 2. (*vestir*) ~ **a alguien** to put sb into uniform; **ir uniformado** to be dressed in uniform
uniforme I. *adj* (*igual, de la misma forma*) uniform, same; (*movimiento*) steady II. *m* uniform; **vestir de** ~ to wear a uniform
uniformidad *f* 1. (*constancia*) regularity; (*movimiento*) steadiness 2. (*similaridad*) uniformity
uniformizar <z→c> *vt* to standardize; (*mezclar*) to blend
unigénito, -a *adj* only-begotten; **ser** ~ to be an only child
unilateral *adj* (*visión*) one-sided; POL unilateral
unión *f* 1. *t.* TÉC (*de dos elementos*) joint; **no hay muchos puntos de** ~ **entre nosotros** we haven't much in common 2. *t.* ECON, POL (*territorial*) union; **Unión Europea** European Union; ~ **monetaria** monetary union; **en** ~ **con** (together) with 3. (*matrimonio*) marriage

4. COM merger 5. (*armonía*) unity, closeness ►la ~ **hace la fuerza** *prov* united we stand
unipersonal *adj* 1. (*de una persona*) one-person; (*de un hombre*) one-man; (*de una mujer*) one-woman 2. (*individual*) single, individual 3. LING applying to a verb used only in the infinitive form or the 3rd person singular
unir I. *vt* 1. *t.* TÉC (*dos elementos*) to join 2. (*territorios, familia*) to unite; **nos une una gran amistad** there is a great bond of affection between us 3. (*ingredientes*) to mix 4. (*esfuerzos*) to combine II. *vr:* ~se (*territorios, dos personas*) to join together, to unite; ECON to merge; ~se **en matrimonio** to marry
unisex *adj* unisex; **moda** ~ unisex fashion; **peluquería** ~ unisex hairdresser's
unísono *m* MÚS unison; **protestaron al** ~ they unanimously protested; **trabajar al** ~ to work in harmony; **actuar al** ~ to act in complete agreement
unísono, -a *adj* 1. (*de un solo tono*) unisonal 2. (*de una sola voz*) in unison
unitario, -a *adj* unitary
universal *adj* 1. (*del universo*) universal; **receptor** ~ RADIO universal receiver 2. (*del mundo*) worldwide; **de renombre** ~ internationally known; **historia** ~ world history; **de fama** ~ world famous 3. (*general, amplio*) widespread; **regla** ~ general rule 4. TÉC (*máquina*) multi-purpose machine; **detergente** ~ all-purpose detergent
universalidad *f* (*de regla*) universality
universalizar <z→c> *vt* to make universal
universalmente *adv* 1. (*en todo el mundo*) universally; ~ **conocido** known all over the world 2. (*generalmente*) generally
universidad *f* university; **ir a la** ~ to be at university; **¿a qué** ~ **vas?** which university do you go to?
universitario, -a I. *adj* university; **estudiante** ~ university student; **profesor** ~ university teacher; **tener estudios** ~s to have studied at university II. *m, f* 1. (*estudiante*) university student 2. (*no licenciado*) undergraduate; (*licenciado*) graduate
universo *m* (*cosmos*) universe
unívoco, -a *adj* unanimous
uno *m* one
uno, -a I. *adj* 1. (*número*) one; **a la una** (*hora*) at one o'clock; **¡(a la) una, (a las) dos y (a las) tres!** ready, steady, go! *Brit,* ready, set, go!; **fila** ~ front row 2. (*único*) **sólo hay una calle** there's only one street ►**andar a una** to agree II. *pron indef* 1. (*alguno*) one, somebody; **cada** ~ each (one), every one; ~s **cuantos** some, a few; ~..., **el otro...** one ..., the other ...; ~ **de tantos** one of many; **aquí hay** ~ **que pregunta por ti** there's sb here asking for you; **una de dos, o... o...** the choice is simple, either ... or ....; **una que otra vez** once in a while; **de** ~ **en** ~ one by one, one at a time; **cantar a una** to sing all together; **luchar todos a una** to fight as one; **no acierto una** I

can't do anything right; **me ha dejado pero me he quedado el piso, lo ~ por lo otro** he left me but I've kept the flat, what you lose on the swings you gain on the roundabouts *Brit* **2.** *pl* (*algunos*) some **3.** (*indeterminado*) one, you

untar I. *vt* **1.** (*con mantequilla*) to spread **2.** (*mojar*) to dip **3.** (*con grasa*) to grease; (*con aceite*) to oil; (*el cuerpo*) to smear **4.** (*sobornar*) to bribe II. *vr* **1.** (*mancharse*) to smear; **~se de algo** to become smeared with sth **2.** (*crema*) **~se con/de algo** to rub sth in **3.** (*dinero*) to line one's pocket

unto *m* **1.** (*grasa*) grease **2.** MED ointment **3.** *Chile* (*betún*) shoe-polish

unt(u)oso, -a *adj* **1.** (*pegajoso*) sticky **2.** (*jabón*) slippery **3.** (*pingüe*) greasy

untura *f* **1.** MED ointment **2.** (*grasa*) grease

uña *f* **1.** (*de persona*) nail; **~ encarnada** ingrowing nail *Brit,* ingrown nail *Am;* (*de gato*) claw; **~s de los pies** toenails *pl;* **afilarse las ~s** *fig* to sharpen one's claws; **limarse las ~s** to file one's nails; **fue a la peluquería a hacerse las ~s** she went to the hairdresser's to have her nails done; **comerse las ~s** to bite one's nails; *fig* to become furious; **estar de ~s con alguien** *inf* to be at loggerheads with sb; **enseñar las ~s** (*mostrarse agresivo*) to show on's teeth; **para triunfar se dejó las ~s en el trabajo** *fig* to triumph at work he/she wore his/her fingers to the bone **2.** (*pezuña*) hoof **3.** (*del alacrán*) sting ▶**ser ~ y** carne to be inseparable; **defenderse con ~s y** dientes to fight tooth and nail to defend oneself; **ser** largo **de ~s** to be light-fingered

uñada *f* **1.** (*arañazo*) scratch **2.** (*señal*) nail mark

uñero *m* **1.** (*inflamación*) whitlow **2.** (*uña*) ingrowing nail *Brit,* ingrown nail *Am*

upa I. *interj inf* upsy-daisy [*o* upsadaisy]; **llevar a ~ un niño** to carry a child II. *adj Ecua, Perú* (*tonto*) idiot

upar *vt inf* to lift up

uperizado, -a *adj* **leche uperizada** UHT milk

Urales *mpl* Urals *pl*

uralita® *f* asbestos (cement)

uranio *m* uranium

urbanidad *f* urbanity, courtesy

urbanismo *m* (*planificación*) town planning

urbanístico, -a *adj* town-planning; **desarrollo ~** urban development; **plan ~** development plan

urbanización *f* **1.** (*acción*) urbanization **2.** (*de casas*) housing estate [*o* development]

urbanizar <z→c> I. *vt* to urbanize II. *vt, vr:* **~se** (*de personas*) to become civilized

urbano *m* traffic policeman

urbano, -a *adj* **1.** (*de la ciudad*) urban; **conferencia urbana** TEL local call; **un hombre ~** a city man; **planificación urbana** town [*o* city] planning **2.** (*cortés*) urbane, courteous

urbe *f* large city, metropolis

urdir *vt* (*conspiración*) to scheme; **~ intrigas** to plot a scheme

uréter *m* ANAT ureter

uretra *f* ANAT urethra

urgencia *f* **1.** (*cualidad*) urgency **2.** (*caso*) emergency; **llamada de ~** pressing/urgent call; **en caso de ~** if case of emergency; **tratar algo con la debida ~** to handle sth with due speed **3.** *pl* (*en hospital*) casualty room *Brit,* emergency room *Am;* **servicio de ~s** (*en ambulatorio*) emergency service

urgente *adj* urgent, pressing; (*carta, telegrama, pedido*) express; **un pedido ~** a rush order; **¿es ~?** is it urgent?

urgir <g→j> *vi* to be urgent, to be pressing

urinario *m* urinal, public lavatory

urinario, -a *adj* urinary; **aparato ~** MED urinary tract

urna *f* **1.** (*caja de cristal*) glass case **2.** (*para cenizas*) urn **3.** POL ballot box; **acudir a las ~s** to go and vote, to go to the polls

uro *m* aurochs *inv*

urogallo *m* capercaillie

urología *f* urology

urraca *f* **1.** ZOOL magpie **2.** (*cotorra*) chatterbox; **hablar más que una ~** to talk nineteen to the dozen *Brit,* to talk a blue streak *Am*

URSS *f abr de* **Unión de Repúblicas Socialistas Soviéticas** USSR

urticaria *f* MED hives *pl,* skin rash

Uruguay *m* Uruguay

> **Uruguay** (official title: **República Oriental del Uruguay**) lies in the southeastern part of South America. The capital and the most important city in Uruguay is **Montevideo**. The official language of the country is Spanish and the monetary unit is the **peso uruguayo**.

uruguayo, -a *adj, m, f* Uruguayan

usado, -a *adj* **1.** (*no nuevo*) secondhand; (*sello*) used **2.** (*gastado*) worn; (*expresión*) common, everyday

usanza *f* usage, custom

usar I. *vt* **1.** (*utilizar*) **~ algo** to use sth, to make use of sth; (*palabra*) to speak; (*libro*) to consult, to look up; (*ropa, gafas*) to wear; **~ la razón** to reason; **tuve que ~ (de) mis influencias** I had to use all my influence; **de ~ y tirar** disposable; **sin ~** brand new **2.** (*cargo*) to hold; (*oficio*) to discharge II. *vr* **1.** (*utilizar*) to use; **esta palabra ya no se usa** this word is no longer in use **2.** (*ropa*) top be in fashion; **los escotes ya no se usan** low necklines are out of fashion

usina *f AmL* (*de gas*) gasworks; (*de electricidad*) power plant

uso *m* **1.** (*utilización*) use; (*gramática*) usage; **~ ilegal** MED illegal use; **de ~ externo** MED for external application; **hacer ~ de algo** to make use of sth; **hacer ~ de la palabra** (*en parla-*

mento, senado) to take the floor, to speak; **una expresión de** ~ **corriente** an everyday expression; **tener muchos** ~**s** to have many uses; **en buen** ~ *inf* in good condition; **desde que tengo** ~ **de razón...** since I have been old enough to reason ...; **estar en pleno** ~ **de sus facultades** to be sound of mind **2.** (*moda*) fashion **3.** (*costumbre*) custom, usage; **métodos al** ~ methods; **al** ~ **francés** French style; **el dedal todavía está en** ~ the thimble is still used; **encalar las fachadas está fuera de** ~ whitewashing the outside of houses is no longer done

usted *pron* **1.** *sing* you; ~**es** you; **tratar de** ~ **a alguien** to address sb courteously; **gracias – a** ~ thank you – you're welcome **2.** *pl, AmL* (*vosotros*) you

usual *adj* **1.** (*de siempre*) usual **2.** (*común*) common **3.** (*tradicional*) customary

usuario, -a *m, f t.* INFOR user

usura *f* usury; **pagar con** ~ **un favor** to pay back a favour *Brit* [*o* favor *Am*] on unequal terms

usurario, -a *adj* usurious

usurero, -a *m, f* usurer

usurpador(a) I. *adj* usurping **II.** *m(f)* usurper

usurpar *vt* to usurp; (*derecho*) to encroach on sth

utensilio *m* utensil; (*herramienta*) tool; ~**s de pintor** painter's materials

uterino, -a *adj* ANAT, MED uterine; **furor** ~ nymphomania; **hermano** ~ a brother born of the same mother

útero *m* uterus, womb; **el cuello del** ~ the cervix

útil I. *adj* **1.** (*objeto*) useful, handy **2.** (*persona*) useful; **ser declarado** ~ MIL to be fit for military service **3.** (*ayuda*) helpful; **¿en qué puedo serle** ~**?** can I be of any help to you? **4.** (*inversión*) profitable **II.** *mpl* tools *pl*, implements *pl*

utilidad *f* **1.** *t.* INFOR (*de objeto*) utility; **ser de** ~ to be useful **2.** (*de persona*) usefulness **3.** (*de inversión*) profit

utilitario *m* **1.** (*calidad de útil*) utility **2.** (*coche*) small car

utilitario, -a *adj* (*edificio*) utilitarian; (*coche, tela*) utility; (*persona, punto de vista*) practical; **pensamiento** ~ utilitarian thinking

utilizable *adj* usable; (*terreno*) available; (*restos*) reusable

utilización *f* utilization; (*de un derecho*) application; (*de una persona*) employment

utilizar <z→c> **I.** *vt* to use; (*derecho, hospitalidad*) to avail oneself of sth; (*tiempo, a alguien*) to make use of sth **II.** *vr:* ~**se** to be used

utillaje *m* tackle

utopía *f* utopia

utópico, -a *adj* utopian

uva *f* grape; ~ **pasa** raisin ▶ **de** ~**s peras** *inf* once in a blue moon; **estar de mala** ~ *inf* to be in a bad mood; **tener mala** ~ *inf* to be bad--tempered

It is customary in Spain on New Year's Eve at exactly twelve seconds to midnight to eat one (white) **uva** (grape) for every **campanada** (chime of the bell), which can be heard on television at intervals of one second. This is supposed to bring good fortune for the coming year.

uve *f* v; ~ **doble** w

UVI *f abr de* **Unidad de Vigilancia Intensiva** ICU

úvula *f* ANAT uvula

Uzbekistán *m* Uzbekistan

uzbeko, -a *adj, m, f* Uzbek

V

V, v *f* V, v; ~ **de Valencia** V for Victor

vaca *f* **1.** ZOOL cow; ~ **marina** manatee; ~ **de San Antón** ladybird *Brit,* ladybug *Am;* **síndrome de las** ~**s locas** mad cow disease; ~**s gordas/flacas** *fig* prosperous/lean period; **ponerse como una** ~ to get as fat as a cow [*o* pig] **2.** (*carne*) beef **3.** (*cuero*) cowhide

vacaciones *fpl* holidays *pl Brit,* vacation *Am;* **estar de** ~ to be on holiday *Brit,* to be on vacation *Am;* **irse de** ~ **a Tenerife** to go on holiday to Tenerife; ~ **a la sombra** *inf* time served in jail

vacante I. *adj* vacant **II.** *f* vacancy; (*puesto*) unfilled post; **cubrir (las)** ~**s** to fill (the) vacancies

vaciado *m* **1.** (*molde*) cast **2.** (*ahuecamiento*) hollowing out **3.** (*de datos*) extraction of information **4.** INFOR dumping

vaciar <1. *pres:* **vacío**> *vt* **1.** (*dejar vacío*) to empty; (*con bomba de agua*) to pump out **2.** (*verter*) to pour **3.** (*hueco*) to hollow out **4.** (*escultura*) to cast **5.** (*afilar*) to sharpen **6.** (*información*) to extract **7.** *Col, inf* (*vituperar*) to give a dressing-down

vaciedad *f sin pl* **1.** (*vacío*) emptiness **2.** *fig* silliness

vacilación *f* hesitation; **sin vacilaciones** unhesitatingly

vacilada *f Méx, inf* (*borrachera*) binge, spree; (*chiste*) joke; (*chiste verde*) dirty joke; (*timo*) rip-off; **me dieron una** ~ they really ripped me off

vacilante *adj* **1.** (*persona*) hesitant **2.** (*estructura*) unsteady **3.** (*voz*) faltering

vacilar *vi* **1.** (*balancearse: objeto*) to sway; (*borracho*) to stagger; (*llama*) to flicker **2.** (*dudar*) to hesitate **3.** *inf* (*tomar el pelo*) ~ **a alguien** to have sb on, to pull sb's leg; **¡no me vaciles!** don't give me that!

vacío *m sin pl* **1.** (*espacio, ausencia*) emptiness; FÍS vacuum; (*hueco*) gap; (*abismo*) void;

~ **legal** gap in the law, legal void; ~ **de poder** political vacuum; **envasado al** ~ vacuum-packed; **hacer el** ~ FÍS to make a vacuum; **hacer el** ~ **a alguien** to give sb the cold shoulder; **la propuesta cayó en el** ~ the proposal fell flat **2.** ANAT side

vacío, -a adj **1.**(sin contenido, sin gente) empty; (hueco) hollow; **peso en** ~ unladen weight; **con las manos vacías** emptyhanded; **volver de** ~ fig to come back empty-handed **2.**(insustancial) insubstantial; (superficial) superficial

vacuidad f sin pl **1.**(vacío) emptiness **2.**(superficial) vacuity

vacuna f **1.**(substancia) vaccine; ~ **anticolérica** cholera vaccine **2.**(vacunación) vaccination; **poner una** ~ to vaccinate; ~ **antirrábica** rabies vaccination; **eso te servirá de** ~ fig that should teach you a lesson **3.**(de las vacas) cowpox

vacunación f vaccination; **cartilla de** ~ vaccination certificate

vacunar I. vt to vaccinate II. vr: ~**se** to get vaccinated; **se ha vacunado contra la gripe** he/she got vaccinated against flu

vacuno m cattle

vacuno, -a adj cow, bovine; (carne de) ~ beef; **ganado** ~ cattle

vacuo, -a adj vacuous

vade m satchel

vadeable adj **1.**(río) fordable **2.**(dificultad) surmountable

vadear vt **1.**(río) to ford **2.**(dificultad) to overcome **3.**(a pie) to wade across

vado m **1.**(río) ford **2.** AUTO ~ **permanente** no parking (garage entrance), keep clear ▶**tentar el** ~ to examine possible solutions

vagabundear vi **1.**(vagar) to wander **2.**(gandulear) to lay about **3.** pey to be a tramp [o bum]

vagabundo, -a I. adj wandering; (perro) stray; fig, pey vagrant II. m, f wanderer; fig tramp, bum

vagancia f sin pl laziness; JUR vagrancy

vagar I.<g→gu> vi **1.**(vagabundear) to wander **2.**(descansar) to be idle II. m leisure, free time

vagido m wail

vagina f ANAT vagina

vago, -a I. adj **1.**(perezoso) lazy **2.**(impreciso) vague **3.**(vagante) vagrant II. m, f **1.**(vagabundo) tramp **2.**(holgazán) layabout, lazybones; **hacer el** ~ to laze [o loaf] about

vagón m (de pasajeros) coach Brit, car Am; (de mercancías) goods wagon Brit, freight car Am; ~ **de cola** guard's van Brit, caboose Am; ~ **restaurante** dining car

vaguada f watercourse

vaguear vi **1.**(holgazanear) to laze about **2.**(vagar) to wander

vaguedad f **1.**(imprecisión) vagueness **2.**(palabras) vague remark

vaharada f **1.**(aliento) puff **2.**(olor) whiff

vahído m dizzy spell; **me dio un** ~ I felt dizzy

vaho m **1.**(vapor) vapour Brit, vapor Am **2.**(aliento) breath **3.** pl inhalation

vaina[1] f **1.**(de la espada) sheath **2.** BOT pod

vaina[2] m pey twit Brit, dork Am

vainica f CRi (judía verde) string bean

vainilla f vanilla; ~ **azucarada** vanilla sugar

vaivén m (balanceo) swaying; (sacudida) lurch; **los vaivenes de la vida** life's ups and downs

vajilla f crockery, dishes pl

vale m voucher; FIN promissory note; (pagaré) IOU inf

valedero, -a adj (válido) valid; (vigente) in force; **ser** ~ **por seis meses** to be valid for six months

valedor(a) m(f) (que protege) protector; (que favorece) patron

valedura f Méx (favor) favour Brit, favor Am; (protección) protection; (ayuda) help

valencia f QUÍM valency

valenciana f **1.** CSur (encaje) fine cotton lace **2.** Méx (del pantalón) turn-up Brit, cuff Am

valenciano, -a adj, m, f Valencian

valentía f **1.**(valor) bravery **2.**(hazaña) brave deed

valentón, -ona I. adj pey boastful II. m, f pey braggart

valer irr I. vt **1.**(costar) to cost **2.**(equivaler) to equal **3.**(producir) to earn **4.**(proteger) to protect ▶**valga la expresión** so to speak; **vale tanto oro como pesa** it/he/she is worth its/his/her weight in gold; **hacer** ~ **sus derechos** to assert one's rights; **vale más que te olvides de él** you'd best forget him; **¡vale ya!** that's enough!; **¡vale!** OK! II. vi **1.**(ropa) to be of use **2.**(tener validez) to be valid; **no vale** it's no good **3.**(funcionar) to be of use; **esta vez no te valdrán tus excusas** your excuses won't help you this time; **no sé para qué vale este trasto** I don't know what this piece of junk is for; **esta vez no hay peros que valgan** this time, no ifs, ands or buts! **4.**(tener mérito) to be worthy; **no** ~ **nada** to be worthless; ~ **poco** to be worth little **5.**(estar permitido) to be allowed; **¡eso no vale!** that's not allowed!, that's not fair! III. vr: ~**se 1.**(servirse) to make use; ~**se de los servicios de alguien** to avail oneself of sb's services **2.**(desenvolverse) to manage; **ya no puede** ~**se** he/she can't fend for him/herself any longer

valeriana f valerian

valeroso, -a adj brave

valía f sin pl worth

validar vt to validate

validez f sin pl validity; **dar** ~ **a algo** to validate sth; **tener** ~ to be valid; (ley) to be in force; **no tener** ~ to be invalid; (ley) to be inapplicable

válido, -a adj valid; **no ser** ~ to be invalid

valiente adj brave; **¡** ~ **amigo tienes!** irón a

fine friend you've got!

valija *f* case; (*del cartero*) mailbag; ~ **diplomática** diplomatic bag

valioso, -a *adj* valuable

valla *f* 1. (*tapia*) wall; (*barrera*) barrier; (*alambrada*) fence; (*defensa*) barricade 2. (*publicitaria*) hoarding *Brit,* billboard *Am* 3. DEP hurdle

vallado *m* fence

vallar *vt* to fence in; ~ **con un muro** to put a wall around

valle *m* valley; ~ **de lágrimas** vale of tears; **lirio del** ~ (*muguet*) lily-of-the-valley

vallunco, -a *adj AmC* 1. (*rústico*) rustic 2. (*campesino*) peasant

valona *f Méx* **hacer a alguien la** ~ *inf* to put in a good word for sb

valor *m* 1. (*valentía*) bravery; ~ **cívico** civil duty; **armarse de** ~ to pluck up courage 2. (*desvergüenza*) cheek 3. (*valía*) *t.* COM, MÚS value; (*cuantía*) amount; ~ **nutritivo/alimenticio** nutritional/food value; ~ **adquisitivo** purchasing power; ~ **nominal** face value; ~ **probatorio** JUR value as evidence 4. (*significado*) meaning; ~ **actual** current meaning 5. *pl* FIN securities *pl;* ~**es bursátiles** stock exchange securities; ~**es inmuebles** real estate 6. *pl* (*ética*) ~**es morales** moral principles; **escala de** ~**es** scale of values

valoración *f* valuation; (*del precio*) value; (*análisis*) assessment

valorar *vt* ~ **en algo** to value at sth; **valoro muchísimo tu generosidad** I greatly appreciate your generosity

valorizar <z→c> *vt v.* **valorar**

vals *m* MÚS waltz

valsar *vi* to waltz

valse *m AmL v.* **vals**

valuar <*1. pres:* valúo> *vt* ~ **en algo** to value at sth

valva *f* valve

válvula *f* ANAT, TÉC valve; ~ **de seguridad** safety valve

vampiresa *f* vamp, femme fatale

vampiro *m* vampire; *fig* bloodsucker

vanagloriarse *vr* to boast

vanaglorioso, -a *adj* boastful

vanamente *adv* vainly

vandalismo *m sin pl* vandalism

vándalo, -a I. *adj* HIST Vandal **II.** *m, f* HIST Vandal; *fig* vandal, hooligan

vanguardia *f* 1. MIL van 2. (*movimiento*) forefront; LIT avant-garde; **de** ~ ultra-modern

vanguardista I. *adj* ultra-modern **II.** *mf* ultra--modern individual; *fig* pioneer

vanidad *f* vanity

vanidoso, -a *adj* vain

vano *m* ARQUIT space

vano, -a *adj* 1. (*ineficaz*) vain, useless; **en** ~ in vain 2. (*infundado*) groundless; **es una vana ilusión** it's a mere illusion

vánova *f Arg* bedspread

vapor *m* (*vaho*) vapour *Brit,* vapor *Am;* (*de agua*) steam; (*barco de*) ~ steamer; **cocer al** ~ to steam

vaporizador *m* vaporizer; (*perfume*) atomizer

vaporizar <z→c> **I.** *vt* 1. (*evaporar*) to vaporize 2. (*perfume*) to spray **II.** *vr:* ~**se** to vaporize

vaporizo *m Méx, PRico* 1. (*vaho*) vapour *Brit,* vapor *Am;* (*para inhalar*) inhalation 2. (*calor*) sultry heat

vaporoso, -a *adj* 1. (*tela*) light, diaphanous *liter* 2. (*humeante*) steamy

vapulear *vt* 1. (*zurrar*) to beat; (*zarandear*) to shake 2. (*criticar*) to slate *Brit,* to slam *Am*

vapuleo *m* 1. (*paliza*) beating 2. (*crítica*) tongue-lashing

vaquería *f AmS* (*explotación*) cattle-rearing; (*lechería*) dairy

vaquero, -a I. *adj* cattle **II.** *m, f* cowherd; (*americano*) cowboy *m,* cowgirl *f*

vaquero(s) *m(pl)* jeans *pl*

vaqueta *f* cowhide

vaquetón, -ona *adj Méx* 1. *inf* (*lento*) sluggish 2. (*vago*) shiftless 3. (*descarado*) shameless

vaquilla *f,* **vaquillona** *f Arg, Chile, Nic, Perú* heifer

vara *f* 1. (*rama*) branch; (*palo*) stick; ~ **mágica** magic wand 2. (*medida*) ≈ yard (*approximately*) 3. ADMIN wand (of office); **tener alta** ~ to have authority [*o* influence]; **doblar la** ~ **de la justicia** to pervert the course of justice 4. TÉC (*bastón de mando*) rod 5. (*del trombón*) slide 6. TAUR pike

varadero *m* NÁUT dry dock

varado, -a *adj* (*anclado*) stranded

varal *m* long pole; (*de un carro*) shaft

varapalo *m* 1. (*rapapolvo*) dressing-down; **dar un** ~ **a alguien** to give sb a ticking off 2. (*golpe*) blow; (*paliza*) beating 3. (*palo*) stick

varar I. *vi* 1. (*encallar*) to run aground; *fig* to get bogged down 2. *AmL* (*coche*) to break down **II.** *vt* to beach

varear *vt* 1. (*fruta*) to knock down 2. (*lana*) to sell by the yard

varejón *m* 1. *AmS, Nic* (*verdasca*) switch 2. *Col* BOT type of yucca

variable I. *adj* variable; (*carácter*) changeable **II.** *f* MAT variable

variación *f* 1. MAT, MÚS variation 2. (*cambio*) change; (*oscilación*) oscillation

variado, -a *adj* (*no siempre igual*) varied; (*distinto*) mixed, assorted; (*colores*) variegated

variante *f* 1. (*variedad*) variety; (*versión*) version 2. (*diferencia*) variation 3. (*carretera*) bypass 4. LING variant

variar <*1. pres:* varío> **I.** *vi* 1. (*modificarse*) to vary 2. (*cambiar*) to change; ~ **de comida** to vary one's diet; ~ **de peinado** to change one's hairstyle; **y para** ~... and for a change ... **II.** *vt* 1. (*cambiar*) to change 2. (*dar variedad*) to vary

varicela *f sin pl* MED chickenpox

variedad *f* 1. (*clase*) variety 2. (*pluralidad*)

variation; **una gran ~ de ofertas** a wide range of offers **3.** *pl* (*espectáculo*) variety show; **teatro de ~es** music hall ►**en la ~ está el gusto** *prov* variety is the spice of life
vario, -a *adj pl* **1.** (*diferente*) several; **asuntos ~s** other business **2.** (*algunos*) some; **varias veces** several times
variopinto, -a *adj* **1.** (*diverso*) diverse **2.** (*color*) colourful *Brit,* colorful *Am*
variz *f* MED varicose vein
varón *m* **1.** (*hombre*) male; (*niño*) boy; **santo ~** *fig* extremely kind and patient man **2.** NÁUT rudder chain
varonil *adj* (*hombre*) manly, virile; **voz ~** deep voice; (*mujer*) mannish
Varsovia *f* Warsaw
vasallo, -a *m, f* HIST vassal
vasco, -a **I.** *adj* Basque; **País Vasco** Basque Country **II.** *m, f* Basque
Vascongadas *fpl* Basque Provinces *pl*
vascongado, -a *adj, m, f* Basque
vascuence *m* **1.** (*lengua*) Basque **2.** *inf* (*incomprensible*) Greek
vasectomía *f* MED vasectomy
vaselina® *f* Vaseline®
vasija *f* (*recipiente*) container
vaso *m* **1.** (*recipiente*) glass; **un ~ de agua** a glass of water; **~ de papel** paper cup **2.** ANAT vessel
vástago *m* **1.** BOT shoot **2.** *fig* (*hijo*) scion *liter;* **~s** offspring **3.** TÉC rod
vasto, -a *adj* vast; (*saber*) wide
vate *m* **1.** (*adivino*) seer **2.** *elev* (*poeta*) bard
váter *m* toilet
vaticano, -a *adj* Vatican
Vaticano *m* Vatican; **la Ciudad del ~** the Vatican City
vaticinador(a) *m(f)* prophet
vaticinar *vt* to predict, to prophesy
vaticinio *m* prediction, prophecy
vatio *m* watt; **una bombilla de 100 ~s a** 100-watt bulb
Vd. *pron pers abr de* **usted** you
vda. *abr de* **viuda** widow
Vds. *pron pers abr de* **ustedes** you
V.E. *abr de* **Vuestra Excelencia** Your Excellency
vecinal *adj* local; **camino ~** country road
vecindad *f* neighbourhood *Brit,* neighborhood *Am;* **chisme de ~** neighbours' gossip *Brit,* neighbors' gossip *Am*
vecindario *m* **1.** (*vecindad*) neighbourhood *Brit,* neighborhood *Am;* (*ciudadanos*) neighbours *pl Brit,* neighbors *pl Am;* (*comunidad*) local community **2.** (*padrón*) residence
vecino, -a **I.** *adj* **1.** (*cercano*) **~ de algo** near sth; **pueblo ~** next village **2.** (*parecido*) **~ a algo** similar to sth **II.** *m, f* **1.** (*que vive cerca*) neighbour *Brit,* neighbor *Am* **2.** (*habitante*) inhabitant; **José García, ~ de Villavieja** José García, a Villavieja resident ►**cada hijo de ~** *inf* anyone
vector *m* vector

veda *f* **1.** (*prohibición*) prohibition; **levantar la ~ de animales de caza** to open the hunting season **2.** (*temporada*) close season
vedado *m* reserve *Brit,* preserve *Am;* **~ de caza** game reserve *Brit,* game preserve *Am;* **cazar/pescar en ~** to poach
vedar *vt* to prohibit, to ban
vedette *f* (music hall) star
vedija *f* (*de lana*) tuft; (*de pelo*) mat
vega *f* **1.** (*de un río*) fertile plain **2.** *Cuba* (*tabacal*) tobacco plantation **3.** *Chile* (*terreno pantanoso*) marshland
vegetación *f* **1.** BOT vegetation **2.** *pl* ANAT adenoids *pl*
vegetal **I.** *adj* plant; **aceite ~** vegetable oil; **carbón ~** charcoal **II.** *m* vegetable
vegetar *vi* **1.** BOT to grow **2.** (*enfermo*) to be like a vegetable **3.** *pey* (*persona*) to vegetate
vegetariano, -a *adj, m, f* vegetarian
vehemencia *f sin pl* **1.** (*ímpetu*) impetuosity **2.** (*entusiasmo*) eagerness **3.** (*fervor*) vehemence
vehemente *adj* **1.** (*impetuoso*) impetuous **2.** (*ardiente*) passionate **3.** (*persona*) forceful
vehículo *m* **1.** (*transporte*) vehicle; **~ de motor** motor vehicle **2.** (*medio*) vehicle; MED carrier
veinte *adj inv* twenty; *v.t.* **ochenta**
veintena *f* (*unidades*) about twenty; **una ~ de personas** about twenty people
veintitantos *adj inv* twenty-odd
vejación *f,* **vejamen** *m* **1.** (*molestia*) annoyance **2.** (*humillación*) humiliation
vejar *vt* **1.** (*molestar*) to annoy **2.** (*humillar*) to humiliate
vejatorio, -a *adj* **1.** (*molesto*) annoying **2.** (*humillante*) humiliating
vejestorio, -a *m, f pey* old crock [*o* geezer]
vejete *m inf* old-timer
vejez *f sin pl* **1.** (*ancianidad*) old age; **pasar su ~ en Mallorca** to spend one's old age in Mallorca **2.** (*envejecimiento*) ageing *Brit,* aging *Am* ►**a la ~, viruelas** *prov* there's no fool like an old fool *prov*
vejiga *f* **1.** ANAT bladder **2.** (*ampolla*) blister
vela *f* **1.** NÁUT sail; **~ cuadra** squaresail; **~ mayor** mainsail; **alzar ~s** to raise the sails; *fig* to prepare to depart; **a toda ~** at full sail; *fig* energetically; **ser un aficionado a la ~** to be a sailing enthusiast; **recoger ~s** *fig* to back down **2.** (*luz*) candle; **se está acabando la ~** the candle is coming to an end; **derecho como una ~** *fig* straight as a ramrod ►**poner una ~ a San Miguel y otra al diablo** to have a foot in both camps; **¿a ti quién te ha dado ~ en este entierro?** who gave you any say in this matter?; **pasar la noche en ~** to have a sleepless night; **estar a dos ~s** to be broke
velación *f* wake, vigil
velada *f* evening gathering; LIT, MÚS, TEAT soirée
velador *m* **1.** (*mesita*) pedestal table **2.** (*candelero*) candlestick
veladora *f AmL* (*vela*) candlestick

velamen *m* NÁUT canvas
velar I. *vi* **1.** (*no dormir*) to stay awake; (*trabajar*) to work late **2.** (*cuidar*) ~ **por algo** to watch over sth; ~ **bien por sus intereses** to look after one's interests **II.** *vt* **1.** (*vigilar*) to keep watch over; ~ **al enfermo** to sit up with an ill person; ~ **a un muerto** to hold a wake **2.** (*ocultar*) to hide; (*tapar*) to veil **III.** *vr:* ~**se** (*ocultarse*) to hide; (*foto*) to blur
velatorio *m* wake, vigil
veleidad *f* (*inconstancia*) fickleness; (*capricho*) whim
veleidoso, -a *adj* (*inconstante*) fickle; (*caprichoso*) capricious
velero *m* NÁUT sailing ship
veleta[1] *f* (*para el viento*) weather vane, weathercock *Brit*
veleta[2] *mf* (*persona*) changeable person; **ser un** ~ to blow hot and cold
veliz *m* *Méx* (*de cuero*) valise; (*de metal*) case
vello *m* *sin pl* **1.** (*corporal*) (body) hair; ~ **de las axilas** hair under the armpits **2.** BOT, ZOOL down, fuzz
vellón *m* (*piel*) fleece
velloso, -a *adj* BOT, ZOOL downy; (*corporal*) hairy
velludo, -a *adj* hairy
velo *m* **1.** (*tela, prenda*) veil; **correr un** (**tupido**) ~ **sobre** *fig* to draw a veil over; **descorrer el** ~ **sobre** to reveal; **tomar el** ~ to take the veil **2.** ANAT ~ **del paladar** soft palate
velocidad *f* **1.** *t.* FÍS, INFOR speed; ~ **de crucero** cruising speed; ~ **de obturación** FOTO shutter speed; ~ **de transmisión de datos** INFOR data transfer rate; **exceso de** ~ speeding; **a gran** ~ at high speed; **a toda** ~ at full speed **2.** (*marcha*) gear; **cambio de** ~**es** gearchange
velocímetro *m* speedometer
velódromo *m* cycle track
velón *m* (*lámpara*) oil lamp
velorio *m* **1.** (*velatorio*) wake, vigil **2.** (*fiesta*) party
veloz *adj* swift; **raudo y** ~ in a flash
vena *f* **1.** ANAT vein; ~ **yugular** jugular vein **2.** BOT vein **3.** (*filón*) lode; ~ **de agua** underground stream **4.** (*inspiración*) talent **5.** *inf* (*disposición*) mood; **dar la** ~ **a alguien** to take it into one's head
venablo *m* javelin; **echar** ~**s** *fig* to explode in anger
venado *m* **1.** (*ciervo*) deer **2.** (*carne*) venison **3.** (*caza mayor*) big game
venal *adj* **1.** ANAT venous **2.** (*vendible*) saleable *Brit*, salable *Am* **3.** (*sobornable*) corrupt
venalidad *f* *sin pl* corruptness
vencedor(a) **I.** *adj* winning; **equipo** ~ winning team **II.** *m(f)* winner
vencejo *m* swift
vencer <c→z> **I.** *vi* **1.** (*ganar*) to win **2.** (*plazo*) to expire **II.** *vt* **1.** (*ganar*) to win; (*enemigos*) to defeat; **¡no te dejes** ~**!** don't let them beat you! **2.** (*obstáculo, sueño*) to over-

come; (*dificultad*) to get round; **me venció el sueño** sleep overcame me **3.** (*bajo peso*) to break ►**a la tercera va la vencida** *prov* third time lucky **III.** *vr:* ~**se** to collapse
vencimiento *m* COM expiry
venda *f* MED bandage; **tener una** ~ **en los ojos** to have a bandage over one's eyes; *fig* to be blinkered; **caérse a uno la** ~ **de los ojos** to see the truth
vendaje *m* bandaging
vendar *vt* to bandage
vendaval *m* (*viento*) strong wind; (*huracán*) hurricane
vendedor(a) *m(f)* seller; (*comerciante*) salesman *m*, saleswoman *f*; ~ **ambulante** hawker; ~ **a domicilio** door-to-door salesman
vender **I.** *vt* to sell **II.** *vr:* ~**se 1.** COM to sell, to be for sale; **se vende** for sale; ~**se al por menor/mayor** to sell (at) retail/wholesale; **se ha vendido todo** everything has been sold; ~**se muy caro** *fig* to play hard to get **2.** (*persona*) to give oneself away; **estar vendido** *inf* to be in a real fix
vendible *adj* saleable *Brit,* salable *Am*
vendimia *f* grape harvest
vendimiar *vi* to harvest grapes
Venecia *f* Venice
veneciano, -a *adj, m, f* Venetian
veneno *m* poison
venenoso, -a *adj* poisonous; **serpiente venenosa** poisonous snake
venera *f* **1.** (*concha*) scallop shell **2.** (*insignia*) scallop, *decoration worn by knights;* **no se te cae la** ~ *fig* it's not going to kill you
venerable *adj* venerable
veneración *f* *sin pl* (*adoración*) worship; (*respeto*) veneration
venerar *vt* **1.** (*adorar*) to worship **2.** (*respetar*) to venerate
venéreo, -a *adj* MED venereal
venero *m* **1.** (*manantial*) spring; *t. fig* source **2.** (*yacimiento*) lode
venezolano, -a *adj, m, f* Venezuelan
Venezuela *f* Venezuela

Venezuela (official title: **República de Venezuela**) borders both the Caribbean Sea and the Atlantic Ocean to the north, Guyana to the east, Brazil to the south and Colombia to the west. The capital is **Caracas**. Spanish is the official language of the country and the monetary unit is the **bolívar**.

---

vengador(a) **I.** *adj* (*que se venga*) avenging; (*propenso a*) vindictive **II.** *m(f)* avenger
venganza *f* vengeance; **deseo de** ~ thirst for vengeance
vengar <g→gu> **I.** *vt* to avenge; ~ **la muerte de alguien** to avenge sb's death **II.** *vr:* ~**se** to take revenge
vengativo, -a *adj* **1.** (*vengador*) avenging **2.** (*rencoroso*) vindictive, vengeful
venia *f* *sin pl, elev* permission

venial *adj* (*pecado*) venial
venida *f* **1.** (*llegada*) arrival; (*vuelta*) return **2.** (*de un río*) floodwater
venidero, -a *adj* future; **en años venideros** in years to come
venir *irr* **I.** *vi* **1.** (*trasladarse*) to come; (*llegar*) to arrive; **vengo (a) por la leche** I've come to fetch the milk **2.** (*ocurrir*) to happen; **vino la guerra** the war came **3.** (*proceder*) to come; **el dinero me viene de mi padre** I inherited the money from my father; **~ de una familia muy rica** to come from a very rich family **4.** (*idea, ganas*) to come; **me vinieron ganas de reír** I felt like laughing; **no sé por qué me vino eso a la memoria** I don't know why that came to my mind **5.** (*tiempo*) to come; (*seguir*) to follow; **el mes que viene** next month; **ya viene la primavera** spring is on its way **6.** (*figurar*) to appear; **no viene en la guía** it's not in the guide **7.** (*prenda*) to suit **8.** (*aproximadamente*) **vienen a ser unas 3000 pesetas para cada uno** it works out at about 3000 pesetas each **9.** *elev* (*servir para*) **aquel suceso vino a turbar nuestra tranquilidad** that event served to destroy our peace **10.** (*terminar por*) **vino a dar con sus huesos en la cárcel** *inf* he/she ended up in jail; **viene a querer decir que...** it amounts to saying that ... **11.** (*persistir*) to keep on; **ya te lo vengo advirtiendo hace mucho tiempo** I've been warning you for a long time ▶**el dinero me viene muy** <u>bien</u> the money comes in very handy; **¿te viene bien mañana después de comer?** would tomorrow after lunch suit you?; **el que venga** <u>detrás</u>**, que arree** every man for himself; **me viene** <u>mal</u> **darte la clase por la tarde** teaching you in the afternoon doesn't suit me; **es una familia venida a** <u>menos</u> that family has come down in the world; **a mí eso ni me** <u>va</u> **ni me viene** to me that's neither here nor there; **¿a qué viene ahora hacerme esos reproches?** why reproach me like that now? **II.** *vr:* **~se 1.** (*volver*) to come back **2.** (*hundirse*) **~se abajo** to collapse; *fig* to fail
venoso, -a *adj* venous
venta *f* **1.** COM sale; **~ callejera** street sale; **~ a domicilio** door-to-door sale; **~ al contado** cash sale; **~ al por menor/mayor** retail/wholesale; **~ por catálogo** mail order; **~ a plazos** hire purchase; **precio de ~ al público** retail price; **volumen de ~s** sales volume; **en ~** for sale; **precio a la** [*o* en] **~** to be for sale; **poner a la** [*o* en] **~** to put sth up for sale **2.** (*posada*) inn
ventaja *f t.* DEP advantage; **~ competitiva** competitive advantage; **sacar ~ de la debilidad del contrincante** to take advantage of the opponent's weakness; **tener ~ sobre alguien** to have an advantage over sb; **dar 300 metros de ~** to give 300 metres start *Brit,* to give 300 meters head start *Am*
ventajista **I.** *adj* unscrupulous **II.** *mf* un-

scrupulous individual
ventajoso, -a *adj* advantageous; (*negocio*) profitable
ventana *f* **1.** (*abertura*) window; **~ corrediza** sliding window; **~ de doble cristal** double-glazed window; **~ de guillotina** sash window **2.** ANAT **~ de la nariz** nostril ▶**echar la** <u>casa</u> **por la ~** to go to great expense
ventanal *m* large window
ventanilla *f* **1.** (*ventana*) small window; (*de coche*) side window; **sobre con ~** window envelope **2.** (*taquilla*) ticket office **3.** (*mostrador*) counter
ventear **I.** *vt* **1.** (*olfatear*) to sniff; *fig* to pry into **2.** (*airear*) to air **II.** *vi fig* to poke about **III.** *vimpers* **ventea** it's windy
ventilación *f* ventilation
ventilador *m* **1.** (*aparato*) fan **2.** (*conducto*) ventilator (shaft)
ventilar **I.** *vt* **1.** (*airear*) to ventilate **2.** (*resolver*) to clear up **II.** *vr:* **~se** (*persona*) to get some air
ventisca *f* blizzard
ventisquero *m* snowdrift
ventolera *f* **1.** (*viento*) gust of wind; **le ha dado la ~ de...** *fig* he/she has taken it into his/her head to ... **2.** (*juguete*) windmill
ventosa *f* **1.** (*objeto*) suction cup, sucker **2.** ZOOL sucker **3.** (*abertura*) vent
ventosear *vi* to break wind
ventosidad *f* fart
ventoso, -a *adj* windy; (*persona*) flatulent
ventral *adj* ventral
ventrículo *m* ANAT ventricle
ventrílocuo, -a *m, f* ventriloquist
ventrudo, -a *adj* pot-bellied
ventura *f* (good) fortune; **mala ~** ill luck; **a la (buena) ~** with no fixed plan; **echar la buena ~ a alguien** to tell sb's fortune; **por ~** fortunately; **probar ~** to try one's luck ▶**viene ~ a quien la** <u>procura</u> *prov* God helps those who help themselves
venturero, -a **I.** *adj* **1.** (*casual*) casual **2.** (*irregular*) irregular **II.** *m, f* wanderer
venturoso, -a *adj* fortunate
veo-veo *m* **jugar al ~** to play I-spy
ver *irr* **I.** *vi, vt* **1.** (*con los ojos*) to see; **no se ve ni torta** you can't see a thing; **véase la página dos** see page two; **¡que se vean los forzudos!** let's see what you're made of!; **lo nunca visto** something unheard of; **¡habráse visto!** did you ever!; **como vimos ayer en la conferencia** as we saw in the lecture yesterday; **no veas lo contenta que se puso** you should have seen how happy she was; **si no lo veo, no lo creo** if I hadn't seen it with my own eyes, I wouldn't have believed it; **a ~** let's see **2.** (*con la inteligencia*) to see, to understand; **a mi modo de ~** as I see it; **¿no ves que...?** don't you see that ...?; **quiero hacerte ~ esto** I want you to understand this; **veo bien que te cases** I approve of your getting married; **ya lo veo** I can see that; **bueno, ya ~emos** well,

we'll see **3.**(*observar*) to watch; (*documentos, información*) to examine **4.**(*visitar*) to see; (*encontrarse*) to meet; **es de ~** *inf* you can see that **5.**(*comprobar*) to check **6.**(*algo desagradable*) to see; **te veo venir** *fig* I know what you're up to; **veo que hoy me tocará a mí** I can see that it'll be my turn today; **~ás como al final te engaña** he/she will trick you in the end, you'll see **7.** JUR (*causa*) to hear **8.**(*relación*) **tener que ~ con alguien/algo** to have to do with sb/sth **9.**(*duda*) **eso está por ~** that remains to be seen; **estoy por ~ si me dan el crédito** I'll have to see if they give me credit; **habrá que ~ si eso es verdad** it remains to be seen whether that's true **10.**(*intentar*) **~é de hablarle** I'll try to speak to him/her ►**tengo un hambre/un sueño que no veo** I'm really tired/hungry; **no haberlas visto nunca más gordas** to never have been in such a spot; **si te he visto, no me acuerdo** out of sight, out of mind *prov;* **no veas la que se armó allí** there was a tremendous row; **¡hay que ~!** it just goes to show!; **hay que ~ lo tranquilo que es Pedro** Pedro is such a quiet fellow; **¡vamos a ~!** let's see!; **¡a ~, escuchadme todos!** come on, listen to me everybody!; **a ~,** **venga** come on, hurry up; **a ~ cómo lo hacemos** let's see how we can do this; **¡para que veas!** so there!; **luego ya ~emos** we'll see about that later; **~emos,...** let me see, ...; **veamos,...** let me see, ...; **¡~ás!** just you wait! **II.** *vr:* **~se 1.**(*encontrarse*) to meet **2.**(*estado*) to be; **~se apurado** to be in a jam; **se ve enfermo** he thinks he's ill; **~se negro** to be in a fix; **~se pobre** to feel poor **3.**(*imaginarse*) to imagine; **me lo estoy viendo de médico** I can just see him as a doctor **4.**(*parecer*) **se ve que no tienen tiempo** it seems they have no time **5.** *AmL* (*tener aspecto*) to look **III.** *m* **1.**(*aspecto*) appearance; **tener buen ~** to be good-looking **2.**(*opinión*) opinion; **a mi ~** in my view

vera *f* **1.**(*orilla*) bank; **~ de un río** river bank **2.**(*lado*) edge; **a la ~ de** beside

veracidad *f* truthfulness; (*de una declaración*) veracity

veraneante *mf* holidaymaker *Brit,* vacationer *Am*

veranear *vi* **~ en Ibiza** to spend the summer in Ibiza

veraneo *m* summer holiday *Brit,* summer vacation *Am;* **lugar de ~** holiday resort *Brit,* vacation spot *Am;* **estar de ~** to be on one's summer holiday

veraniego, -a *adj* summer

veranillo *m* **~ de San Miguel** [*o* **de San Juan** *AmL*] Indian summer

verano *m* summer

veras *fpl* **de ~** (*de verdad*) really; (*en serio*) in earnest; **esto va de ~** this is serious

veraz *adj* **1.**(*hechos*) true **2.**(*persona*) truthful

verbal *adj* **1.**(*del verbo*) verbal; **frase ~** verb

phrase **2.**(*oral*) oral

verbalizar <z→c> *vt* (*expresar*) to verbalize

verbena *f* **1.**(*fiesta*) street party **2.** BOT verbena

verbigracia *adv* for example

verbo *m* **1.**(*expresa acción*) verb; **~ auxiliar** auxiliary verb **2.**(*palabra*) curse

verborrea *f,* **verbosidad** *f* **1.**(*locuacidad*) verbosity; *pey* verbal diarrhoea **2.**(*palabras*) verbiage

verboso, -a *adj* verbose

verdad *f* truth; **una ~ a medias** a half truth; **a la ~** in truth; **bien es ~ que...** it is certainly true that ...; **bueno, a decir ~, ...** well, to tell you the truth, ...; **¡de ~!** really!; **¡es ~!** it's true!; **faltar a la ~** to be untruthful; **hay una parte de ~ en esto** there's some truth in this; **la ~ lisa y llana** the plain and simple truth; **pues la ~, no lo sé** I don't know, to tell you the truth; **si bien es ~ que...** although it's true that ...; **un héroe de ~** a real hero; **¿~?** isn't it?, aren't you?; **¿~ que no fuiste tú?** it wasn't you, was it?; **la ~ es que hace frío** it certainly is cold ►**~ de Perogrullo** truism; **~es como puños** self-evident truths; **decir cuatro ~es a alguien** to give sb a piece of one's mind; **la ~, toda la ~, y nada más que la ~** the truth, the whole truth, and nothing but the truth

verdaderamente *adv* truly

verdadero, -a *adj* **1.**(*cierto*) true **2.**(*real*) real **3.**(*persona*) truthful

verde I. *adj* **1.**(*color*) *t.* POL green; **~ oliva** olive-green **2.**(*fruta*) unripe, green; (*leña*) green **3.**(*chistes, canciones*) dirty **4.**(*personas*) randy; **viejo ~** *inf* dirty old man ►**estar ~ de envidia** to be green with envy; **poner ~ a alguien** to have a go at sb *Brit,* to badmouth sb *Am* **II.** *m* **1.**(*color*) green **2.**(*hierba*) green grass; (*pienso*) green fodder **3.**(*del árbol*) foliage **4.** *inf* (*billete*) thousand-peseta note **5.** *CSur* (*pasto*) pasture **6.** *CSur* (*mate*) maté **7.** *CSur* (*ensalada*) salad **8.** *AmC, Méx* (*campo*) countryside

verdear *vi* **1.**(*mostrarse verde*) to look green **2.**(*tirar a verde*) to be greenish **3.**(*ponerse verde*) to turn green **4.** *CSur* (*beber*) to drink maté

verdecer *irr como crecer vi* to turn green

verderón *m* greenfinch

verdín *m* **1.**(*del cobre*) verdigris **2.**(*verde*) fresh green **3.**(*musgo*) moss

verdor *m* **1.**(*verde*) greenness, verdure *form* **2.** BOT lushness **3.**(*juventud*) youth

verdoso, -a *adj* greenish

verdugo *m* **1.**(*de ejecuciones*) executioner **2.**(*tirano*) slave driver; (*atormentador*) tormentor **3.**(*tormento*) torment **4.**(*látigo*) lash **5.**(*hematoma*) weal **6.** BOT shoot **7.**(*gorro*) balaklava

verdugón *m* **1.**(*hematoma*) weal **2.** BOT shoot

verdulera *f pey* fishwife

verdulero, -a *m, f* greengrocer

verdura f 1. (hortalizas) vegetable, greens pl 2. (verdor) greenness 3. (obscenidad) smuttiness

verdusco, -a adj dark green

vereda f 1. (sendero) path 2. AmL (acera) pavement Brit, sidewalk Am ▸entrar en ~ to start to lead an orderly life; hacer entrar en ~ a alguien to make sb toe the line; ir por la ~ to do the right thing

veredicto m JUR verdict; ~ de culpabilidad/ inculpabilidad guilty/not guilty verdict

verga f 1. (vara) rod 2. vulg (pene) cock

vergajo m 1. (verga del toro) pizzle 2. vulg (pene) cock 3. (látigo) whip 4. And, vulg (canalla) bastard, son of a bitch

vergel m elev orchard

vergonzante adj 1. (acción) shameful 2. (persona) shamefaced

vergonzoso, -a adj 1. (persona) bashful; (tímido) shy 2. (acción) disgraceful

vergüenza f 1. (rubor) shame; se me cae la cara de ~ I feel so ashamed; me da ~... I'm ashamed to ...; ¿no te da ~? aren't you ashamed?; pasar ~ to feel embarrassed; ¡qué ~! shame on you!; tener poca ~ to have no shame, to be shameless; pasar ~ ajena to be embarrassed for sb else 2. (pundonor) shyness; perder la ~ to lose one's shyness 3. (persona, acción) timidity; (escándalo) disgrace; sacar a alguien a la ~ (pública) to disgrace sb publicly 4. (cortedad) modesty; (sexual) (sexual) shame; le da ~ al hablar he/she is embarrassed to speak 5. pl ANAT private parts pl

vericueto m rough terrain

verídico, -a adj 1. (verdadero) true 2. (muy probable) credible 3. (sincero) truthful

verificación f 1. (inspección) inspection 2. (prueba) testing 3. (realización) realization 4. (de una profecía) fulfilment Brit, fulfillment Am

verificar <c→qu> I. vt 1. (comprobar) to check 2. (controlar) to verify 3. (realizar) to carry out; (ceremonia) to perform II. vr: ~se 1. (acto solemne) to be held 2. (una profecía) to come true; (deseos) to be fulfilled; (temores) to be realized

verja f (rejas) grating; (cerca) grille; (puerta) iron gate

vermú m, **vermut** m <vermús> 1. (licor) vermouth 2. And, CSur TEAT early performance

vernáculo, -a adj vernacular; lengua vernácula vernacular

vero m sable

verónica f TAUR a type of pass with the cape

verosímil adj 1. (probable) likely 2. (creíble) credible

verosimilitud f likelihood

verraco m 1. (para procrear) boar 2. AmC, CSur (jabalí) wild boar

verraquera f inf 1. (llanto) crying spell 2. AmC, Col (borrachera) drunken bout

verruga f wart; fig defect

verrugoso, -a adj warty

versado, -a adj ~ en algo expert in sth

versal I. adj letra ~ capital letter II. f capital

versalita TIPO I. adj letra ~ small capital letter II. f small capital

versar vi 1. (tratar) ~ sobre algo to deal with sth; la conferencia ~á sobre las vacunas the lecture is about vaccines 2. (dar vueltas) to turn, to go round 3. AmC (escribir) to versify 4. AmC (charlar) to chat 5. Méx (bromear) to crack jokes

versátil adj 1. (persona) versatile 2. (que se dobla) flexible

versatilidad f 1. (inconstancia) changeableness 2. (flexibilidad) versatility

versículo m REL verse

versificar <c→qu> I. vt to put into verse II. vi to write verses

versión f 1. (interpretación) version; (descripción) account; ~ resumida abridged version 2. (traducción) translation 3. CINE ~ original in the original language

verso m 1. (palabras) line; en ~ in verse 2. (género) verse 3. (poema) poem

vértebra f ANAT vertebra

vertebrado m vertebrate

vertebral adj vertebral; columna ~ spinal column

vertedero m (escombrero) rubbish tip Brit, garbage dump Am

verter <e→ie> I. vt 1. (vaciar) to empty; (líquido) to pour; (sin querer) to spill; (basura) to dump; ~ el café en las tazas to pour the coffee into the cups 2. (traducir) to translate 3. (ideas, conceptos) to transfer II. vi to flow

vertical adj, f vertical

vértice m vertex

vertiente f 1. (declive) slope; (lado) side 2. (punto de vista) perspective 3. And, CSur, Méx (fuente) fountain

vertiginoso, -a adj 1. (que marea) giddy 2. (velocidad) excessive

vértigo m 1. (mareo) dizziness; (por las alturas) vertigo; causar ~(s) to cause dizziness; de ~ inf (jaleo) tremendous; (increíble) extraordinary; (fantástico) wonderful; (velocidad) giddy 2. (desmayo) fainting fit 3. (frenesí) frenzy; (locura) fit of madness

vesania f 1. (locura) rage 2. (ira) fury

vesícula f ANAT vesicle; (en la epidermis) blister; ~ biliar gall bladder

vespa® f motor scooter

vespasiana f Arg, Chile public toilet

vespertino, -a adj evening, crepuscular liter

vespino® m moped

vestíbulo m (de un piso) hall; (de un hotel) lobby; TEAT foyer; (atrio) atrium

vestido m 1. (prenda) item of clothing; (de mujer) dress 2. (ropa) clothing; ~ de etiqueta [o noche] evening [o formal] dress

vestidor m dressing room

vestidura f 1. elev (ropa) apparel 2. pl REL vestments pl ▸rasgarse las ~s to make a great show of being shocked

vestigio *m* 1.(*huella*) vestige 2.(*señal*) trace
vestimenta *f* clothing
vestir *irr como pedir* I. *vt* 1.(*cuerpo, persona*) to dress; ~ **de algo** to dress in sth; (*estatua*) to cover in sth; (*pared*) to hang with sth; (*adornar*) to adorn with sth; **estar vestido de pirata** (*disfrazado*) to be dressed as a pirate; ~ **a alguien con un abrigo** to dress sb in a coat 2.(*llevar*) to wear; (*ponerse*) to put on 3.(*confeccionar*) to make; **¿qué sastre le viste?** which tailor makes your clothes? 4.(*expresión*) ~ **el rostro de seriedad** to put on a serious expression ►**vísteme despacio que tengo** <u>prisa</u> *prov* make haste slowly II. *vi* to dress; ~ **de blanco** to dress in white; ~ **de uniforme** to wear a uniform; ~ **siempre muy bien** to always be very well-dressed; **de** ~ (*elegante*) formal; (*para una ocasión*) for special occasions; ~ **mucho** to be dressy ►**el** <u>mismo</u> **que viste y calza** the self-same III. *vr:* ~**se** 1.(*la ropa*) to get dressed; (*cubrirse*) to cover oneself; ~**se a la moda** to dress according to fashion; ~**se de azul** to dress in blue; **los árboles se visten de verde** the trees are coming out in leaf; **los campos se visten de blanco** the fields are turning white with snow; ~**se en Milán** (*comprar*) to buy one's clothes in Milan 2.(*estado de ánimo*) ~**se de cierta actitud** to adopt a certain attitude; ~**se de severidad** to adopt a severe tone
vestón *m Chile* (*chaqueta*) jacket
vestuario *m* 1.(*conjunto*) clothes *pl;* (*de una misma persona*) wardrobe 2.(*lugar*) TEAT dressing room; DEP changing room
veta *f* 1. MIN seam 2.(*en madera*) grain; (*en mármol*) vein
vetar *vt* to veto
vetarro, -a *adj Méx, inf* old; **ya estan muy ~s** they're getting on a bit
vetazo *m Ecua* whiplash
vetear *vt* 1.(*como la madera*) to grain 2.(*como el mármol*) to streak
veterano *m* MIL veteran
veterano, -a I. *adj* 1. MIL veteran 2.(*experimentado*) experienced II. *m, f* 1. MIL veteran 2.(*experto*) old hand
veterinaria *f sin pl* veterinary science
veterinario, -a *m, f* vet *inf,* veterinary surgeon *Brit,* veterinarian *Am*
veto *m* veto; **(inter)poner (su)** ~ **a algo** to veto sth
vetusto, -a *adj elev* 1.(*persona*) venerable 2.(*cosa*) very old; *pey* ancient
vez *f* 1.(*acto repetido*) time; **a la** ~ at the same time; **a veces** sometimes; **alguna que otra** ~ ocasionally; **cada** ~ **me gusta menos** I like him/it less and less; **cada** ~ **que...** each time that ...; **de una** ~ (*en un solo acto*) in one go; (*sin interrupción*) without a break; (*definitivamente*) once and for all; **de** ~ **en cuando** from time to time; **dilo otra** ~ say it again; **acabemos de una** ~ let's get it over with; **por primera** ~ for the first time; **aquella** ~ on that

occasion; **esta** ~ this time; **alguna** ~ sometimes; **muchas veces** many times; **¿cuántas veces ...?** how many times ...?, how often ...?; **repetidas veces** over and over again; **otra** ~ **será** it'll have to wait for another occasion; **pocas veces, rara** ~ seldom; **tal** ~ perhaps; **una y otra** ~ time and time again; **de una** ~ **por todas** once and for all; **una** ~ **que haya terminado, ...** once it is over, ...; **érase una ~...** once upon a time ... 2.(*con número*) time; **una** ~ once; **dos veces** twice; **una y mil veces** a thousand times; **3 veces 9** MAT 3 times 9; **dos veces más que** twice as much as; **por enésima** ~ for the umpteenth time 3.(*turno*) **cuando llegue mi ~...** when it's my turn ...; **él a su** ~ **no respondió** he didn't reply in his turn; **en** ~ **de** instead of; **hacer las veces de alguien** to take sb's place; **ceder la** ~ **en una cola** to give up one's place in a queue *Brit* [*o* line *Am*] ►**una** ~ **al** <u>año</u> **no hace daño** *prov* once won't do any harm
vía *f* 1.(*camino*) road; (*calle*) street; ~ **aérea** (*correos*) airmail; **Vía Láctea** Milky Way; ~ **pública** public thoroughfare; **por** ~ **aérea** by air; (*correos*) by air mail; **¡~ libre!** make way!; **la tradición está en ~s de recuperación** the tradition is being recovered 2.(*ruta*) via; **a Madrid** ~ **París** to Madrid via Paris 3.(*carril*) line; FERRO track; ~ **férrea** railway *Brit,* railroad *Am;* **por** ~ **férrea** by rail; ~ **muerta** siding; **de** ~ **estrecha** narrow gauge; *fig* narrow-minded; **de** ~ **única** single track 4. ANAT passage; ~**s digestivas** digestive tract; ~**s respiratorias** breathing passage; ~**s urinarias** urinary tract; **por** ~ **oral** by mouth 5.(*procedimiento*) proceedings *pl;* **por** ~ **judicial** by legal means 6. INFOR track
viable *adj* viable
vía crucis *m inv* Stations *pl* of the Cross; *fig* terrible ordeal
viada *f And* speed
viaducto *m* viaduct
viajante *mf* travelling salesman *Brit,* traveling salesman *Am;* COM commercial traveller *Brit,* commercial traveler *Am*
viajar *vi* to travel; ~ **por Italia** to travel round Italy; ~ **en avión** to travel by plane
viaje *m* 1.(*general*) travel; **estar de** ~ to be away (on a trip); **irse de** ~ to go on a trip; ~ **de negocios** business trip; ~ **de novios** honeymoon; ~ **organizado** package tour; ~ **de ida** outgoing trip; ~ **de ida y vuelta** return trip *Brit,* round trip *Am;* **cheque de** ~ traveller's cheque *Brit,* traveler's check *Am;* **¡buen ~!** bon voyage!, have a good trip! 2.(*carga*) load; (*recorrido*) trip; **un** ~ **de leña** a load of firewood; **hacer la mudanza en cinco ~s** to move house in five trips; **de un** ~ *AmC, fig* in one go 3. *inf* (*drogas*) trip
viajero, -a I. *adj* travelling *Brit,* traveling *Am;* ZOOL migratory; **ave viajera** migratory bird II. *m, f* traveller *Brit,* traveler *Am;* (*pasajero*) passenger; ~ **diario** commuter

vial I. *adj* (*caminos*) road; FERRO rail; **circulación** ~ road traffic; **fluidez** ~ traffic flow; **reglamento** ~ rules of the road **II.** *m* avenue

vianda *f* elev (*alimento*) provisions *pl;* (*comida*) food

viandante *mf* (*peatón*) pedestrian, passer-by

viaraza *f AmL* (*rapto de ira*) fit of rage; **me dio la** ~ I just felt like it

viático *m* **1.** REL viaticum **2.** (*subvención*) travel allowance

víbora *f* **1.** ZOOL viper **2.** *pey* (*persona*) snake; **lengua de** ~ *fig* venomous tongue; **nido de** ~**s** *fig* nest of vipers

viborear *vi* **1.** *AmL, inf* (*murmurar*) to backbite **2.** *CSur* (*serpentear*) to snake, to twist and turn

vibración *f* **1.** (*vaivén*) vibration **2.** (*sentimiento*) vibe *inf,* vibration; **ese tío me da buenas/malas vibraciones** that guy gives me good/bad vibes

vibrador *m* vibrator

vibrante *adj* **1.** (*sonoro*) resonant **2.** (*entusiasta*) vibrant; (*emoción*) quivering

vibrar I. *vi* **1.** (*oscilar*) to vibrate **2.** (*voz*) to quiver **II.** *vt* (*agitar*) to shake

vicario *m* vicar

vicedirector(a) *m(f)* COM deputy manager **2.** ENS deputy head teacher *Brit,* vice principal *Am*

vicenal *adj* **1.** (*que dura*) lasting 20 years **2.** (*que se repite*) occurring every 20 years

vicepresidente, -a *m, f* POL vice-president; (*en juntas*) vice-chairperson

vicerrector(a) *m(f)* UNIV vice-chancellor *Brit,* vice-president *Am*

vicetiple *f* chorus girl

viceversa *adv* vice versa

vichar *vt Arg, Urug* **1.** (*espiar*) to spy on **2.** (*ver*) to peep at **3.** (*buscar con la mirada*) to look around for

viciado, -a *adj* (*aire*) stuffy

viciar I. *vt* **1.** (*falsear*) to falsify; (*deformar*) to distort **2.** (*anular*) to invalidate **II.** *vr:* ~**se 1.** (*costumbres*) to deteriorate; (*persona*) to get a bad habit **2.** (*ser adicto*) ~**se con algo** to become addicted to sth; ~**se con la televisión** to get hooked on television **3.** (*deformarse*) to warp; (*romperse*) to break

vicio *m* **1.** (*mala costumbre*) bad habit; **el** ~ **de siempre** the same old bad habit; **hacer algo por** ~ to do sth for the hell of it; **tener el** ~ **de comerse las uñas** to have the bad habit of biting one's nails **2.** (*adicción*) vice; **no poder quitarse el** ~ **de fumar** to be unable to kick the smoking habit **3.** (*objeto*) defect **4.** JUR (*error*) flaw **5.** (*capricho*) whim; **quejarse de** ~ to complain out of sheer habit **6.** BOT **tener mucho** ~ to grow abundantly

vicioso, -a I. *adj* **1.** (*carácter*) dissolute **2.** (*que produce vicio*) habit-forming **3.** (*defecto*) defective **4.** (*consentido*) spoilt **5.** BOT luxuriant **II.** *m, f* **en lo que respecta a la bebida es un** ~ he drinks too much

vicisitud *f* **1.** (*acontecimiento*) important event; (*desgracia*) mishap **2.** (*cambio*) change **3.** *pl* (*alternancia*) ups *pl* and downs

víctima *f* victim; (*afectado*) person affected; **ser** ~ **de un fraude** to be the victim of fraud; **no hubo que lamentar** ~**s** fortunately there were no casualties; ~ **propiciatoria** scapegoat

victimar *vt AmL* **1.** (*herir*) to injure **2.** (*matar*) to kill

victimario, -a *m, f* **1.** (*el que daña*) victimizer **2.** *AmL* (*el que mata*) killer, murderer

victoria *f* victory; ~ **por puntos** victory on points; **cantar** ~ to count one's chickens

victorioso, -a *adj* victorious

vid *f* (*parra*) (grape)vine

vida *f* **1.** (*existencia, actividad*) life; ~ **íntima** private life; ~ **perra** dog's life; **amargar la** ~ **a alguien** to make sb's life miserable; (grape)**¿cómo te va la** ~**?** how's life treating you?; **complicarse la** ~ to make life difficult for oneself; **costo de la** ~ cost of living; **dar** ~ **a** TEAT, CINE to portray; (*animar*) to enliven; **dejarse la** ~ **en algo** to dedicate one's life to sth; **esperanza de** ~ life expectancy; **estar aún con** ~ to still be alive; **este material es de corta** ~ this material doesn't last; **hacer** ~ **marital** to live together; **llevar una** ~ **miserable** to lead a wretched existence; **me va la** ~ **en este asunto** this is a matter of life or death for me; **partir de esta** ~ to depart this life; **pasar a mejor** ~ to pass away; **pasarse la** ~ **haciendo algo** to spend one's life doing sth; **perder la** ~ to lose one's life; **¿qué es de tu** ~**?** what have you been up to lately?; **quitar la** ~ **a alguien** to take sb's life; **quitarse la** ~ to take one's own life; **salir con** ~ to survive; **tener siete** ~**s** to have the nine lives of a cat; **tren de** ~ lifestyle **2.** (*sustento*) livelihood; **buscarse la** ~ to get by on one's own **3.** (*biografía*) life; **de toda la** ~ all my life; **la** ~ **y milagros de alguien** sb's life story; **la otra** ~ afterlife **4.** (*placer*) pleasure; **este sol es** ~ this sun is a delight **5.** (*alegría*) joy **6.** (*cariño*) **¡mi** ~**!** my darling! **7.** (*prostituta*) **mujer de la** ~ prostitute; **hacer la** ~ *inf* to be on the game ▶**estar entre la** ~ **y la <u>muerte</u>** to be fighting for one's life; (*a punto de morir*) to be at death's door; **darse la <u>padre</u>** to live the life of Riley; **hacer por la** ~ *inf* to eat; **de por** ~ for life; **¡en** ~**!** not on your life!

videncia *f* clairvoyance

vidente *mf* (*que ve*) sighted person; (*que adivina*) clairvoyant

vídeo *m* **1.** (*aparato*) video (cassette) recorder, VCR *Am;* **cámara de** ~ video camera; **editar en** ~ to edit on video; **grabar en** ~ to record on video **2.** (*película*) video

videocámara *f* video camera

videocasete *m* videocassette

videoclip *m* music video

videoconferencia *f* INFOR video conference

videojuego *m* video game

videoteléfono *m* videophone

videotexto *m* teletext
vidorria *f* **1.** *Chile, RíoPl* (*vida fácil*) easy life **2.** *Col, PRico, Ven* (*vida dura*) dog's life
vidriado *m* **1.** (*barniz*) glaze **2.** (*loza*) (piece of) glazed pottery
vidriar I. *vt* (*loza*) to glaze **II.** *vr:* ~**se** (*hacerse transparente*) to become clear
vidriera *f* **1.** (*ventana*) stained-glass window; **puerta** ~ glazed door **2.** *AmL* (*escaparate*) shop window
vidriero, -a *m, f* glazier
vidrio *m* **1.** (*material*) glass; ~ **de color** coloured glass *Brit,* colored glass *Am;* **¡**~**!** (*frágil*) fragile – handle with care **2.** (*placa*) sheet of glass; (*de una ventana*) window pane **3.** (*objeto*) piece of glassware; (*productos*) glassware ►**pagar los** ~**s** **rotos** *inf* to carry the can *Brit,* to take the rap *Am*
vidrioso, -a *adj* **1.** (*como vidrio*) glassy; (*mirada*) glazed **2.** (*transparente*) like glass; **ojos** ~**s** glassy eyes **3.** (*frágil*) fragile **4.** (*superficie*) slippery **5.** (*persona*) easily discouraged **6.** (*asunto*) delicate
vidurria *f Arg, inf* (*vidorra*) life of leisure
viejales *m inv, inf* old boy *Brit,* old coot *Brit*
viejera *f PRico* **1.** (*vejez*) old age **2.** (*cosa inservible*) old piece of junk
viejo, -a I. *adj* old; (*usado*) used; (*gastado*) worn-out; **hacerse** ~ to grow [*o* get] old; **Noche Vieja** New year's Eve ►**tan** ~ **como Canalillo** *inf* as old as Moses **II.** *m, f* old man *m,* old woman *f;* **mi** ~ my old man; **mi vieja** my old lady; **mis** ~**s** *AmL* (*padres*) my folks, my parents
Viena *f* Vienna
vienés, -esa *adj, m, f* Viennese
viento *m* **1.** (*corriente*) wind; ~**s alisios** trade winds; ~ **ascendente** rising wind; ~ **de cola** tail wind; ~ **de frente** head wind; ~ **huracanado** hurricane; **instrumento de** ~ wind instrument; **hace** ~ it's windy; **como el** ~ like the wind; **corre un poquito de** ~ there's a slight breeze; **un pequeño soplo de** ~ a gentle breeze; **estar lleno de** ~ (*vacío*) to be full of (hot) air; (*vanidoso*) to be vain **2.** NÁUT (*rumbo*) course; (*dirección*) direction; **a los cuatro** ~**s** in all directions; **pregonar algo a los cuatro** ~**s** to shout sth from the rooftops **3.** *inf* (*irse*) **tomar** ~ to be off; **¡vete a tomar** ~**!** *inf* get lost! **4.** (*olor*) scent; (*olfato*) sense of smell; **me da el** ~ **que…** I have a feeling that … **5.** *AmC* MED flatulence ►**contra** ~ **y marea** against all odds, come hell or high water; **el negocio va** ~ **en popa** business is going well; **quien siembra** ~**s, recoge tempestades** *prov* sow the wind and reap the whirlwind *prov;* **echar a alguien con** ~ **fresco** to tell sb to get lost; **corren malos** ~**s para…** it's a bad time for …; **beber los** ~**s por algo** to crazy about sth
vientre *m* **1.** (*abdomen*) abdomen; **hacer de** ~ to have a bowel movement **2.** (*barriga*) belly; **danza del** ~ belly-dancing **3.** (*matriz*) womb

viernes *m inv* Friday; **Viernes Santo** Good Friday; *v.t.* **lunes** ►**la semana que no tenga** ~ when pigs fly
vietnamita *adj, mf* Vietnamese
viga *f* (*de madera*) beam; (*de metal*) girder
vigencia *f* validity; **estar en** ~ to be valid; **entrar en** ~ to come into effect; **perder** ~ to become invalid
vigente *adj* valid
vigésimo, -a *adj* twentieth; *v.t.* octavo
vigía[1] *f* watchtower
vigía[2] *mf* lookout
vigilancia *f* **1.** (*cuidado*) vigilance **2.** (*observación*) surveillance; (*servicio*) security service; **tener a alguien bajo** ~ to have sb under surveillance
vigilante I. *adj* (*despierto*) awake; (*en alerta*) alert **II.** *mf* **1.** (*guardián*) guard; (*de cárcel*) warder *Brit,* warden; (*en tienda*) night watchman; (*en museo*) attendant; ~ **nocturno** night watchman; ~ **de seguridad** security guard **2.** *CSur* (*policía*) policeman *m,* policewoman *f*
vigilar I. *vt* to guard; (*niños*) to watch **II.** *vi* ~ **por algo** to keep watch over sth
vigilia *f* **1.** (*no dormir*) wakefulness **2.** (*falta de sueño*) insomnia **3.** (*víspera*) vigil **4.** (*sin comer*) abstinence; (*comida*) meal without meat; **día de** ~ day of abstinence; **comer de** ~ to eat without meat **5.** (*en el trabajo*) late-night work
vigor *m* **1.** (*fuerza*) vigour *Brit,* vigor *Am;* (*energía*) energy; **con** ~ vigorously; **sin** ~ without vigour *Brit* [*o* vigor *Am*] **2.** (*vitalidad*) vitality; (*empuje*) drive **3.** (*vigencia*) validity; **entrar en** ~ to come into effect; **poner en** ~ to bring into effect
vigorizar <z→c> *vt* **1.** (*fortalecer*) to strengthen **2.** (*revitalizar*) to invigorate **3.** (*animar*) to encourage
vigoroso, -a *adj* **1.** (*fuerte*) vigorous; (*resistente*) tough **2.** (*animado*) lively; (*vital*) energetic **3.** (*protesta*) strong
viguería *f* (*de madera*) beams *pl;* (*de metal*) girderwork
vigués, -esa I. *adj* of/from Vigo **II.** *m, f* native/inhabitant of Vigo
vigueta *f* tie-beam
VIH *m sin pl abr de* **virus de inmunodeficiencia humana** HIV
vil *adj* (*malo*) vile; (*bajo*) base; (*infame*) despicable
vileza *f* **1.** (*cualidad*) vileness **2.** (*acción*) vile act
vilipendiar *vt* **1.** (*despreciar*) to revile; (*tratar*) to humiliate **2.** (*insultar*) to vilify
villa *f* **1.** HIST (*población*) town **2.** (*casa*) villa
Villadiego *m* **tomar las de** ~ *inf* to take to one's heels
villancico *m* (Christmas) carol
villanía *f* **1.** (*bajeza*) vile act **2.** (*expresión*) obscenity
villano, -a I. *adj* **1.** (*bajo*) villainous **2.** (*rús-*

tico) HIST peasant; (*expresión*) obscene **II.** *m, f* **1.** *pey* (*grosero*) rogue **2.** HIST villein; (*campesino*) peasant

villorrio *m pey, inf* one-horse town

vilo *adv* en ~ suspended; *fig* in suspense; **tener en** ~ to keep in suspense; **estar en** ~ to be up in the air

vinagre *m* **1.** (*condimento*) vinegar **2.** (*persona*) disagreeable person

vinagrera *f* **1.** (*recipiente*) vinegar bottle **2.** *pl* (*para la mesa*) cruet set **3.** *AmL* (*ardor*) indigestion

vinagreta *f* vinaigrette

vincha *f AmS* (*cinta*) hairband

vinchuca *f Arg, Chile, Par* ZOOL barbeiro, assassin bug

vinculación *f* link

vincular *vt* **1.** (*ligar*) to link; (*unir*) to join; ~ **a** [*o* **con**] **algo** to link to sth **2.** (*obligar*) to bind

vínculo *m* **1.** (*unión*) tie; **el** ~ **conyugal** the bond of matrimony; **~s familiares** family ties; **~s naturales** blood relations; **los ~s con el extranjero** links with foreign countries **2.** (*obligación*) bond

vindicación *f* **1.** (*venganza*) vengeance **2.** (*justificación*) vindication **3.** (*reivindicación*) claim

vindicar <c→qu> *vt* **1.** (*vengar*) to avenge **2.** (*justificar*) to vindicate **3.** (*reivindicar*) to claim

vinería *f And, CSur* (*vinatería*) wineshop

vinícola **I.** *adj* wine; (*cultivo*) wine-growing **II.** *mf* wine-grower

vinicultor(a) *m(f)* wine producer

vinicultura *f* wine production

vino *m* **1.** wine; ~ **rosado** rosé wine; ~ **tinto** red wine; ~ **caliente** hot punch; ~ **de mesa** table wine; ~ **de Jerez** sherry; ~ **generoso** full-bodied wine; ~ **de la casa** house wine; ~ **de Oporto** port; ~ **espumoso** [*o* **de aguja**] sparkling wine; ~ **peleón** cheap wine, plonk *Brit* **2.** (*recepción*) reception; ~ **de honor** reception ▶**echar agua al** ~ to tone things down; **tener buen** ~ to hold one's drink well; **tiene mal** ~ he/she can't hold his/her drink

viña *f* **1.** (*monte*) vineyard **2.** (*planta*) vine ▶**de todo hay en la** ~ **del Señor** *prov* it takes all sorts to make a world; **ser una** ~ to be useful; **tener una** ~ **con algo** to have a goldmine in sth

viñador(a) *m(f)* vineyard worker

viñatero, -a *m, f Arg, Perú* winegrower

viñedo *m* **1.** (*monte*) vineyard **2.** (*planta*) vine

viola *f* **1.** MÚS viola **2.** BOT violet

violáceo, -a *adj* purplish

violación *f* **1.** (*infracción*) violation; (*de una ley*) breaking; ~ **de contrato** breach of contract **2.** (*de una mujer*) rape **3.** (*invasión*) invasion

violado, -a *adj* (*color*) violet

violar *vt* **1.** (*mujer*) to rape **2.** (*ley, principio, sepultura*) to violate; (*contrato*) to break

violencia *f* **1.** (*condición*) violence; (*fuerza*) force; **no** ~ non-violence; **con** ~ by force; **sin** ~ peacefully **2.** (*acción*) violent action

violentar **I.** *vt* **1.** (*obligar*) to force; (*sexualmente*) to assault **2.** (*una casa*) to break into; (*un banco*) to rob **3.** (*principio*) to break **4.** (*al interpretar*) to distort **II.** *vr:* ~**se** (*obligarse*) to force oneself

violento, -a *adj* **1.** (*impetuoso*) impetuous; (*esfuerzo*) violent; (*discusión*) heated; (*temperamento*) fiery **2.** (*brutal*) aggressive; (*con violencia*) violent; **acto** ~ act of violence **3.** (*persona*) violent **4.** (*postura*) unnatural **5.** (*acto*) embarrassing; (*cohibido*) embarrassed; (*duro*) difficult; **me es muy** ~ **tener que aceptarlo** I'm embarrassed to have to accept it; **me resulta** ~ **decirle que no** I find it very hard to say no to him/her **6.** (*tergiversado*) distorted **7.** *AmL* (*de repente*) suddenly

violeta *adj, f* violet

violín *m* MÚS violin, fiddle *inf*

violinista *mf* violinist

violón *m* MÚS double bass ▶**tocar el** ~ to talk nonsense

violoncelista *mf* MÚS cellist

violonc(h)elo *m* MÚS cello

vip, VIP *m abr de* **Very Important Person** VIP; **sala** ~ VIP lounge

Viracocha *m And* **1.** (*dios inca*) Incan god of creation **2.** (*apelativo de conquistadores*) conquistador (*name applied to the Spanish conquistadors by the Incans*)

viraje *m* **1.** (*giro*) turn; (*curva*) bend; ~ **en horquilla** hairpin bend; **hacer** [*o* **dar**] **un** ~ to swerve **2.** (*cambio*) switch; (*de opinión*) shift; (*de dirección*) change **3.** NÁUT tack

virar **I.** *vi* **1.** (*girar*) to turn; (*curva*) to bend; ~ **en redondo** *t. fig* to retrace one's steps; **el coche viró a la izquierda** the car swerved to the left **2.** (*cambiar*) to switch, to change; (*de opinión*) to shift **3.** NÁUT to tack **II.** *vt* (*girar*) to turn

virgen **I.** *adj* virgin; *fig* pure; (*cinta*) blank; (*tierras*) virgin **II.** *f* REL **la Virgen** the Virgin; **la Santísima Virgen María** the Blessed Virgin Mary; **¡Santísima Virgen!** *inf* my goodness! ▶**ser de la Virgen del puño** *inf* to be tight-fisted; **aparecérsele a uno la Virgen** *inf* to hit the jackpot; **ser un viva la Virgen** *inf* to be happy-go-lucky

virginal *adj* (*inmaculado*) virginal; (*puro*) pure

virginidad *f sin pl* virginity

Virgo *m* Virgo

viril *adj* **1.** (*masculino*) virile; **edad** ~ adulthood **2.** (*enérgico*) vigorous

virilidad *f sin pl* **1.** (*masculinidad*) virility **2.** (*energía*) vigour *Brit*, vigor *Am* **3.** (*potencia*) strength **4.** (*edad*) adulthood

viringo, -a *adj Col* (*sin ropa*) naked; (*sin piel*) skinned; (*sin pelo*) hairless

virola *f* ferrule

virrey, -reina *m, f* viceroy *m*, vicereine *f*

virtual *adj* virtual

virtud f 1.(en las personas) virtue; **en ~ de** by virtue of 2.(poder) power; **tener la ~ de aliviar** to bring relief

virtuoso, -a adj 1.(con gran habilidad) virtuoso 2.(lleno de virtudes) virtuous

viruela f MED 1.(enfermedad) smallpox; ~ **loca** scarlet fever 2.(pústula) pustule; **picado de ~s** pockmarked; **señales de (la) ~** marks of smallpox

virulento, -a adj 1.MED virulent 2.(maligno) infected

virus m inv MED, INFOR virus

viruta f shaving; **un ~s irón** (carpintero) a carpenter; **echando ~s** inf very fast

vis f ~ **cómica** comic effect

visa m o f AmL, **visado** m visa; ~ **de entrada/de salida** entry/exit visa

visaje m (mueca) (funny) face; **hacer ~s** to make [o pull] faces

visar vt (pasaporte) to put a visa in

vísceras fpl entrails pl, viscera pl

viscosa f QUÍM viscose

viscosidad f 1.(consistencia) thickness 2.(mucosidad) viscosity

viscoso, -a adj 1.(espeso) thick 2.(glutinoso) viscous; (blando) soft

visera f 1.HIST, MIL visor 2.(de una gorra) peak

visibilidad f (cualidad) visibility

visible adj 1.(perceptible) visible 2.(obvio) clear 3.(persona) striking 4.inf (presentable) presentable

visillo m net curtain

visión f 1.(vista) sight, vision; **perder la ~ de un ojo** to lose the sight in one eye 2.(aparición) vision; **ver visiones** fig to be seeing things; **me quedé (como) viendo visiones** fig I was stunned 3.(punto de vista) view; ~ **de conjunto** overview; ~ **del mundo** view of the world 4.pey, inf (mamarracho) sight; **ir hecho una ~** to look a sight

visionario, -a I.adj 1.(con imaginación) visionary 2.(adivinatorio) prophetic 3.(soñador) idealistic, dreamy pej II.m, f 1.(con imaginación) vision 2.(adivinador) prophet 3.(soñador) idealist; pey dreamer

visita f 1.(visitante) visitor 2.(acción) visit; ~ **del médico** doctor's call; ~ **de médico** fig flying visit; ~ **guiada** guided tour; ~ **oficial** POL official visit; **estar de ~ en casa de alguien** to be staying with sb; **ir de ~** to go visiting; **rendir ~ a alguien** to pay sb a visit; **tener (a alguien de) ~** to have visitors

visitante I.adj visiting; **comisión ~** visiting commission II.mf visitor

visitar vt 1.(ir a ver) to visit 2.MED to call (on)

vislumbrar vt (ver) to make out, to distinguish

vislumbre f 1.(resplandor) glimmer 2.(idea) sign

viso m 1.(resplandor) glow; (irisación) sheen; **hacer ~s** to be irridescent 2.(aspecto) sign; **esto tiene ~s de no acabar nunca** this shows no sign of ever ending; **tiene ~s de**

llover it looks like rain

visón m mink

visor m 1.MIL sights pl; ~ **de luz infrarroja** infrared sights 2.FOTO (cámara) viewfinder; (para diapositivas) slide viewer

víspera f (noche anterior) night before, eve; (día anterior) day before; **en ~s de** just before; **estar en ~s de hacer algo** to be on the point of doing sth

vista f 1.(visión) sight, vision; **tener la ~ cansada** to have eye strain; (mirada) look; ~ **de lince** eyes like a hawk; **aguzar la ~** to keep one's eyes skinned Brit [o peeled Am]; **al alcance de la ~** within view; **fuera del alcance de la ~** out of sight; **a la ~** (al parecer) from what can be seen; (visible) visible; (previsible) in full view; **a la ~ de todos** in full view of everyone; **a la ~ está** anyone can see that; **alzar/bajar la ~** to look up/down; **apartar la ~** to look away; **no apartar la ~ de alguien** not to take one's eyes off sb; **no perder de ~ a alguien/algo** not to lose sight of sb/sth; **a primera ~** at first sight; **a simple ~** just by looking; fig superficially; **comerse a alguien con la ~** to devour sb with one's eyes; **con la ~ puesta en algo** with one's sights set on sth; **con ~s a...** with a view to ...; **corto de ~** short-sighted; **dejar vagar la ~** to let one's eyes wander; **dirigir la ~ a algo** to look towards sth; **a Paco no hay quien le eche la ~ encima** Paco's nowhere to be seen; **de ~** by sight; **en ~ de que...** in view of ...; **está a la ~ quién va a ganar** it's obvious who's going to win; **¡fuera de mi ~!** get out of my sight!; **¡hasta la ~!** see you!; **hasta donde alcanza la ~** as far as the eye can see; **se me nubló la ~** my eyes clouded over; **no perder de ~** not to lose sight of; **pagadero a la ~** COM due on demand; **perder de ~** to lose sight of; **quedar a la ~** to remain in sight; **saltar a la ~** to be patently obvious; **tener buena ~** to have good eyesight; **volver la ~ (atrás)** to look back 2.(panorama) view; ~ **panorámica** panoramic view; (mirador) viewpoint; **con ~s al mar** with sea views, overlooking the sea 3.(imagen, perspectiva) image; FOTO picture; ~ **aérea** aerial view; ARQUIT perspective; ~ **general** overall view 4.(aspecto) appearance; **tener buena ~** to look good 5.JUR hearing; ~ **oral** hearing ►~ **de pájaro** bird's-eye view; **ver algo a ~ de pájaro** to have a bird's-eye view of sth; **hacer la ~ gorda** to turn a blind eye; **tener ~** to be shrewd

vistazo m look; **de un ~** at a glance; **echar [o dar] un ~ a algo** to have a (quick) look at sth

visto, -a I.pp de ver II.adj 1.(poco original) common; **está muy ~** that's been seen before, that's old hat 2.(obvio) **está ~ que no puede ser de otra forma** it's clear that things can't be otherwise 3.JUR ~ **para sentencia** conclusion of the trial ►**nunca ~** unknown; (inaudito) unheard of; **el pastel desapareció ~ y no ~** the cake disappeared in a flash; **por**

lo ~ apparently **III.** *conj* ~ **que...** since ...

visto bueno *m* ADMIN, JUR approval; **dar el ~ a algo** to give sth the go-ahead

vistoso, -a *adj* (*atractivo*) colourful *Brit,* colorful *Am;* (*llamativo*) striking; (*hermoso*) attractive

visual I. *adj* visual; **campo ~** field of vision **II.** *f* line of sight

visualización *f* visualization; (*display*) *t.* INFOR visual display

visualizador *m* INFOR display (screen)

visualizar <z→c> *vt* **1.** (*representar*) to visualize **2.** *AmL* (*divisar*) to make out **3.** INFOR to display

vital *adj* **1.** *t.* MED vital; **constantes ~es** vital signs, basic functions; **fuerza ~** life force **2.** (*necesario*) essential **3.** (*vivaz*) lively

vitalicio, -a *adj* ADMIN, FIN life; **renta vitalicia** life pension; **seguro ~** life insurance

vitalidad *f sin pl* **1.** (*alegría de vivir*) vitality **2.** (*importancia*) vital importance

vitalizar <z→c> *vt* **1.** (*vivificar*) to revitalize **2.** (*fortalecer*) to strengthen

vitamina *f* vitamin; **pobre/rico en ~s** low/rich in vitamins

vitaminar *vt* to enrich with vitamins

vitícola *adj* vine growing

viticultor(a) *m(f)* vine grower

viticultura *f* viticulture

vítor *m* cheer, hurrah; **prorrumpir en ~es** to cheer

vitorear *vt* to cheer

vitoriano, -a I. *adj* of/from Vitoria **II.** *m, f* native/inhabitant of Vitoria

vítreo, -a *adj* **1.** (*de vidrio*) glass **2.** (*similar al vidrio*) vitreous; (*vidrioso*) glassy

vitrina *f* glass cabinet; *AmL* (*escaparate*) shop window

vituallas *fpl* MIL provisions *pl,* victuals *pl liter*

vituperable *adj* **1.** (*inmoral*) reproachable **2.** (*censurable*) reprehensible **3.** (*despreciable*) despicable

vituperación *f* **1.** (*reprobación*) condemnation **2.** (*censura*) censure **3.** (*injuria*) vituperation *liter*

vituperar *vt* **1.** (*reprobar*) to condemn **2.** (*censurar*) to censure **3.** (*injuriar*) ~ **a alguien** to vituperate against sb

vituperio *m* **1.** (*censura*) criticism **2.** (*injuria*) vituperation *liter*

viudedad *f* **1.** (*viudez*) widowhood **2.** (*pensión: de viuda*) widow's pension; (*de viudo*) widower's pension

viudez *f* widowhood

viudo, -a I. *adj* widowed; **quedarse ~** to be widowed **II.** *m, f* widower *m,* widow *f*

viva I. *interj* hurray!; **¡~ el rey!** long live the King!; **¡~n los novios!** three cheers for the bride and groom! **II.** *m* cheer; **dar ~s a alguien** to cheer sb; **recibir con ~s** to welcome with cheers

vivacidad *f sin pl* **1.** (*viveza*) vivacity **2.** (*energía*) vigour *Brit,* vigor *Am* **3.** (*agilidad*) liveli-

ness **4.** (*agudeza*) sharpness

vivales *m inv, inf* wide boy, punk *Am*

vivar I. *m* **1.** (*conejera*) warren **2.** (*criadero*) nursery, breeding place; (*de peces*) hatchery **II.** *vt AmL* (*vitorear*) to cheer

vivaracho, -a *adj* **1.** (*vivo*) vivacious **2.** (*despierto*) bright

vivaz *adj* **1.** BOT perennial **2.** (*vivaracho*) vivacious **3.** (*enérgico*) lively **4.** (*despierto*) bright

vivencia *f* experience

víveres *mpl* provisions *pl;* MIL supplies *pl*

vivero *m* **1.** (*de plantas*) nursery **2.** (*de peces*) hatchery; (*en un restaurante*) holding tank

viveza *f* **1.** (*celeridad*) swiftness; (*agilidad*) liveliness **2.** (*energía*) vigour *Brit,* vigor *Am* **3.** (*agudeza*) sharpness **4.** (*de colores*) brightness

vívido, -a *adj* vivid

vivienda *f* **1.** (*residencia*) residence; (*casa*) house; (*piso*) flat *Brit,* apartment *Am;* **sin ~** homeless; **el problema de la ~** the housing problem **2.** *AmL* (*modo de vida*) way of life

viviente *adj* living; **seres ~s** living beings; **ni alma ~** *fig* not a living soul; **todo bicho ~** every living creature

vivificar <c→qu> *vt* **1.** (*vitalizar*) to revitalize **2.** (*animar*) to invigorate

vivir I. *vi* **1.** (*estar vivo*) to be alive; **~ al día** to live from day to day; **~ a lo grande** to live it up; **~ como un rey** to live like a lord; **~ de rentas** to live off the rent; **¡~ para ver!** (*asombro*) who would believe it!, live and learn!; **no dejar ~ a alguien** not to leave sb alone; **no ~ de preocupación** to be worried to death; **¿quién vive?** MIL who goes there? **2.** (*habitar*) to live **3.** (*durar*) to last; (*perdurar*) to live on **II.** *vt* to live; **~ su (propia) vida** to live one's own life **III.** *m* life; (*modo de vida*) way of life; **gente de mal ~** (*vicio*) dissolute characters; (*delincuencia*) shady characters

vivo *m* **1.** (*borde*) edge, trim **2.** (*tira*) strip

vivo, -a *adj* **1.** (*viviente*) alive; **cal viva** quicklime; **ser ~** living being; **a fuego ~** GASTR on a high heat; **a lo ~** vividly; **al rojo ~** red-hot; **en ~** MÚS live; **estar ~** to be alive; **tener el ~ deseo de que** +*subj* to really hope that; **herir en lo más ~** to cut to the quick; **ser la viva imagen de alguien** to be the spitting image of sb; **~ o muerto** dead or alive **2.** (*vivaz*) lively **3.** (*enérgico*) vigorous; **de genio ~** quick-tempered **4.** (*color*) bright **5.** (*actual*) current; (*presente*) present; (*duradero*) lasting **6.** (*vívido*) vivid **7.** (*avispado*) sharp; *pey* crafty

vizcaíno, -a I. *adj* of/from Biscay **II.** *m, f* native/inhabitant of Biscay

Vizcaya *f* Biscay

V.O. *abr de* **versión original** original version

vocablo *m* word, term

vocabulario *m* **1.** (*léxico*) vocabulary; ~ **especializado** technical vocabulary; **tener un buen ~** to have a wide vocabulary **2.** (*lista*) vocabulary (list)

vocación *f* vocation; ~ **artística** artistic

vocation; **por** ~ from a sense of vocation; **sentir** ~ to feel an inclination; **tener** ~ to have a calling

vocal¹ I. *adj* MÚS vocal II. *f* LING vowel

vocal² *mf* **1.** (*de consejo, tribunal*) member **2.** (*portavoz*) spokesperson, spokesman *m,* spokeswoman *f*

vocalizar <z→c> *vt* to vocalize

voceador(a) I. *adj* shouting II. *m(f)* **1.** (*pregonero*) town crier **2.** *AmL* (*de periódicos*) news hawker

vocear I. *vi* to shout II. *vt* **1.** (*manifestar*) to express **2.** (*llamar*) to call **3.** (*pregonar*) to cry **4.** (*divulgar*) to spread **5.** (*aclamar*) to acclaim **6.** (*presumir*) ~ **algo** to boast of sth

vocerío *m* (*griterío*) clamour *Brit,* clamor *Am*

vocero, -a *m, f AmL* (*portavoz*) spokesperson, spokesman *m,* spokeswoman *f*

vociferar I. *vi* to yell II. *vt* **1.** (*gritar*) to shout **2.** *pey* (*proclamar*) to shout from the rooftops

vocinglero, -a *adj pey* loudmouthed; **ser** ~ to be a loudmouth

vodka *m o f* vodka

vol. *abr de* **volumen** vol.

volado, -a *adj* **1.** ARQUIT projecting **2.** *inf* (*loco*) crazy **3.** TIPO superior **4.** *AmL* (*ausente*) absent-minded; (*enamorado*) lovesick **5.** *CSur* ~ **de genio** *inf* quick-tempered **6.** (*inquieto*) uneasy

volador(a) *adj* flying

voladura *f* blowing-up

volandas *fpl* **en** ~ (*en el aire*) up in the air; (*deprisa*) in a rush; **llevar en** ~ to carry shoulder-high

volandero, -a *adj* **1.** (*volantón*) fledgling **2.** (*móvil*) loose **3.** *fig* (*inquieto*) fickle

volante I. *adj* (*móvil*) flying; **rueda** ~ band wheel; **platillo** ~ flying saucer II. *m* **1.** AUTO steering wheel; **ir al** ~ to be at the wheel; **ponerse al** ~ to take the wheel **2.** TÉC flywheel; (*manual*) handwheel **3.** (*del reloj*) balance wheel **4.** (*adorno*) flounce **5.** (*escrito*) leaflet **6.** MED referral note **7.** DEP shuttlecock **8.** *AmL* (*conductor*) racing driver; DEP winger

volantón *m* **1.** (*sedal*) fishing line **2.** *AmL* (*cometa*) kite **3.** *AmL* (*voltereta*) somersault; (*acrobacia*) acrobatics *pl*

volar <o→ue> I. *vi* **1.** (*en el aire*) to fly; **echar a** ~ to fly off; **el tiempo vuela** time flies; **las malas noticias vuelan** bad news travels fast, no news is good news **2.** (*desaparecer*) to disappear; **el dinero ha volado** the money has vanished **3.** (*apresurarse*) to dash; **¡voy volando!** I'm on my way!; ~ **a hacer algo** to rush off to do sth **4.** *inf* (*con drogas*) to be high II. *vt* **1.** (*hacer explotar*) to blow up **2.** (*enfadar*) to drive mad **3.** (*hacer volar*) to fly; (*ave*) to frighten off; **hacer** ~ **una cometa** to fly a kite **4.** TIPO to write in superscript III. *vr:* ~**se 1.** (*huir*) to run away **2.** (*desaparecer*) to vanish **3.** *AmL* (*enfadarse*) to get mad **4.** (*hacer novillos*) to bunk off (school) *Brit,* to play hooky *Am*

volatería *f* (*pájaros*) fowl *pl*

volátil I. *adj* **1.** (*volador*) flying **2.** QUÍM volatile **3.** (*inconstante*) unpredictable II. *m* poultry

volatilizar <z→c> *vt, vr:* ~**se** QUÍM to volatilize

volcán *m* **1.** GEO volcano; **un** ~ **activo/inactivo** an active/dormant volcano; **ser un** ~ **de pasión** *fig* to be afire with passion **2.** *AmL, fig* (*montón*) loads *pl*

volcánico, -a *adj* **1.** GEO volcanic **2.** (*ardiente*) fiery

volcar *irr* I. *vi* (*tumbarse*) to overturn; (*barco*) to capsize II. *vt* **1.** (*hacer caer*) to knock over; (*verter*) to spill **2.** (*dar la vuelta*) to turn over III. *vr:* ~**se 1.** (*darse la vuelta*) to overturn; (*caer*) to get knocked over; (*dar una voltereta*) to turn a somersault **2.** (*esforzarse*) to make an effort; ~**se en** [*o* **con**] **alguien** to be extremely kind to sb; ~**se en algo** to throw oneself into sth

volea *f v.* **voleo**

volear I. *vi, vt* (*dep*) to volley II. *vt* (*semillas*) scatter

voleibol *m* DEP volleyball

voleiplaya *m* DEP beach volleyball

voleo *m* DEP volley; **a** ~ on the volley; *fig* at random

volován *m* vol-au-vent

volquete *m* dumper [*o* tip] truck *Brit,* dump truck *Am*

voltaje *m* voltage

voltario, -a *adj Chile* **1.** (*gastador*) spendthrift; (*dadivoso*) generous **2.** (*obstinado*) self-willed

volteado *m Méx, inf* (*homosexual*) bender *Brit,* fag *Am*

voltear I. *vi* **1.** (*dar vueltas: persona*) to roll over; (*cosa*) to spin; (*campana*) to peal **2.** (*volcar*) to overturn **3.** *AmL* (*torcer*) to turn; (*girarse*) to turn around; ~ **a hacer algo** to do sth again **4.** *AmL* (*pasear*) to go for a walk II. *vt* **1.** (*invertir*) to turn over; (*volver del revés*) to turn the right way up **2.** (*hacer girar*) to spin; ~ **las campanas** to ring the bells **3.** *AmL* (*volcar*) to knock over; (*volver*) to turn; ~ **la espalda a alguien** to turn one's back on sb **4.** *AmL* (*lanzar al aire*) to throw into the air; (*el lazo*) to swing III. *vr:* ~**se 1.** (*dar vueltas*) to turn over **2.** (*cambiar de ideas*) to change one's ideas **3.** *AmL* (*volcar*) to overturn; (*darse la vuelta*) to turn around

voltereta *f* **1.** (*cabriola*) handspring; (*en el aire*) somersault; **dar una** ~ to do a handspring; (*en el aire*) to turn a somersault **2.** (*vuelco*) (sudden) change

voltio *m* volt

volubilidad *f* **1.** QUÍM instability **2.** (*inconstancia*) fickleness; (*imprevisibilidad*) changeableness

voluble *adj* **1.** QUÍM unstable **2.** (*inconstante*) fickle; (*imprevisible*) changeable **3.** BOT climbing

volumen *m* **1.** (*tamaño*) size; *t.* FÍS, MAT volume **2.** (*cantidad*) amount; (*del pelo*) body; ~

de ventas turnover; de gran ~ large, bulky 3. (*de sonido*) volume; a todo ~ (at) full volume; poner la música a todo ~ to put the music on full blast 4. (*tomo*) volume; en dos/varios volúmenes in two/several volumes

voluminoso, -a *adj* sizeable; (*poco manejable*) bulky; (*grueso*) thick; (*corpulento*) heavy

voluntad *f* 1. (*intención*) will; (*fuerza de voluntad*) will-power; ~ de vivir will to live; buena ~ goodwill; mala ~ evil intent; a ~ at one's discretion; con buena ~ with good intentions; con mucha/poca ~ willingly/unwillingly; contra su ~ against one's will; de última ~ as a last wish; hacer su santa ~ to do exactly as one pleases; poner ~ en algo to put one's heart into sth; por causas ajenas a nuestra ~ for reasons beyond our control; por propia ~ of one's own free will; quitar a alguien la ~ de algo to stop sb feeling like doing sth; tener mucha/poca ~ to have a lot of/not very much will-power; última ~ JUR last will 2. (*cariño*) affection; ganarse la ~ de alguien to win sb's affection

voluntariedad *f* 1. (*carácter voluntario*) voluntary nature; JUR intent 2. (*arbitrariedad*) arbitrary nature 3. (*fuerza de voluntad*) willingness; (*perseverancia*) persistence

voluntario, -a I. *adj* 1. (*libre*) voluntary 2. (*arbitrario*) arbitrary II. *m, f* volunteer; ofrecerse ~ para algo to volunteer for sth

voluntarioso, -a *adj* willing; (*perseverante*) persistent; (*caprichoso*) self-willed

voluptuosidad *f* voluptuousness

voluptuoso, -a *adj* voluptuous

volver *irr* I. *vi* 1. (*dar la vuelta*) to go back; ~ atrás to turn back 2. (*regresar*) to return; ~ a casa to go home; al ~ a casa me acosté when I got home I went to bed; al ~ compra el pan buy the bread on the way back; al ~ me llamó he/she called me when he/she got back; he vuelto por la autopista I came back on the motorway; ~ en sí to come round [*o* to]; ~ sobre sí to turn round; volviendo al tema to come back to the subject 3. (*repetir*) ~ a hacer algo to do sth again; he vuelto a cometer el mismo error I've made the same mistake again; he vuelto a casarme I've remarried II. *vt* 1. (*dar la vuelta*) to turn over; ~ la espalda a alguien *t. fig* to turn one's back on sb; ~ la vista a algo to look back at sth 2. (*poner del revés*) to turn inside out; (*manga*) to roll up 3. (*transformar*) to make; ~ furioso to make mad; ~ a su estado original to revert to its original state; ~ loco a alguien to drive sb crazy 4. (*devolver*) to return; ~ algo a su sitio to put sth back in its place; ~ a la vida to revive III. *vr:* ~se 1. (*darse la vuelta*) ~se a [*o* hacia] algo to turn around towards sth 2. (*dirigirse*) ~se a [*o* hacia] algo to turn towards sth; ~se contra alguien to turn against sb; ~se (para) atrás to retrace one's steps; *fig* to back out; no tengo dónde ~me

I've got no place to go 3. (*regresar*) to return 4. (*convertirse*) to become; (*ponerse*) to grow; ~se viejo to grow old; ~se rico to get rich

vomitar I. *vi* to vomit, to be sick *Brit;* es para ~ *vulg* it's enough to make you sick; este salchichón me da ganas de ~ this sausage makes me feel sick II. *vt* 1. (*comida*) to bring up; *fig* to spew out; (*insultos*) to hurl; (*sangre*) to cough up 2. *fig* (*desembuchar*) to spit out

vomitivo, -a *adj* 1. MED emetic 2. *inf* (*asqueroso*) revolting; ese es ~ that's disgusting

vómito *m* (*acción*) vomiting; (*lo vomitado*) vomit; ~ de sangre coughing up of blood; provocar ~s a alguien to make sb throw up *inf*

voracidad *f* voraciousness; (*avaricia*) greed

vorágine *f* 1. (*remolino*) whirlpool 2. (*confusión*) whirl, vortex

voraz *adj t. fig* voracious; (*hambriento*) ravenous; apetito ~ voracious appetite; (*avaro*) greedy

vórtice *m* (*de agua*) whirlpool; (*de viento*) whirlwind; (*de un ciclón*) eye

vos *pron pers* 1. AmL (*tú*) you; esto es para ~ this is for you; voy con ~ I'll go with you 2. HIST (*usted*) thou

> The term **vosear** means to address someone in a familiar way using '**vos**' instead of '**tú**'. This is very common practice in **Argentina** and other Spanish-speaking countries of Latin America.

vosotros, -as *pron pers, pl* you; ~ sois muy listos you are very clever; esto es para ~ this is for you

votación *f* vote; ~ a mano alzada vote by show of hands; someter algo a ~ to put sth to the vote

votar I. *vi* (*elegir*) to vote; ~ a [*o* por] alguien/algo to vote for sb/sth II. *vt* (*decidir*) ~ a alguien to vote for sb; ~ un presupuesto to approve a budget

voto *m* 1. POL (*opinión*) vote; (*acción*) voting; ~ afirmativo [*o* a favor] vote in favour *Brit,* vote in favor *Am;* ~ de castigo protest vote; ~ en blanco unmarked ballot (paper) (*as a protest*); ~ de censura vote of no confidence; ~ por correo postal vote *Brit,* mail vote *Am;* ~ negativo [*o* en contra] vote against; derecho a ~ right to vote; dar su ~ a algo to vote for sth; emitir su ~ to cast one's vote; tener (derecho a) ~ to have the (right to) vote 2. REL (*promesa*) vow; hacer ~s por +*infin,* hacer ~s por que +*subj t. fig* to vow to

voy 1. *pres de* ir

voz *f* 1. (*sonido, facultad, voto*) voice; ~ afeminada effeminate voice; ~ aguardentosa gravelly voice; ~ cantante melody line; ~ de mando voice of command; a dos/cuatro voces MÚS for two/four voices; aclarar la ~ to clear one's throat; ahuecar la ~ to deepen

one's voice; **levantar/bajar la** ~ to raise/ lower one's voice; **levantar la** ~ **a alguien** to raise one's voice to sb; **a media** ~ in a whisper; **de viva** ~ in person; **hablar en** ~ **alta/baja** to speak loudly/softly; **leer en** ~ **alta** to read aloud; **hacer oír su** ~ to make one's voice heard; **no tener ni** ~ **ni voto** to have no right to vote; *fig* to have no say in the matter; **se me quebró la** ~ I lost my voice; *fig* words failed me; **tener** ~ **en algo** to have a say in sth **2.** (*grito*) shouting; **voces** shouts; **a voces** in a loud voice; **a** ~ **en grito** at the top of one's voice; **dar una** ~ **a alguien** to give a shout to sb; **dar voces** to shout; **dar la** ~ **de alarma** to raise the alarm; **pegar** (**cuatro**) **voces** to shout; **pedir algo a voces** to cry out for sth **3.** (*sonido*) tone **4.** (*rumor*) rumour *Brit*, rumor *Am;* **corre la** ~ **de que…** rumour *Brit* [*o* rumor *Am*] has it that … **5.** (*vocablo*) word; ~ **técnica** technical term **6.** LING ~ **activa/ pasiva** active/passive voice ►**llevar la** ~ **cantante** to call the tune
vozarrón *m* booming voice
vudú *m* voodoo
vuelco *m* **1.** (*tumbo*) turning over; (*voltereta*) somersault **2.** (*cambio*) drastic change; **dar un** ~ to overturn; *fig* to change completely ►**me dio un** ~ **el corazón** my heart missed a beat
vuelo *m* **1.** (*en el aire*) flight; ~ **acrobático** acrobatic flight; ~ **en globo** balloon flight; ~ **sin motor** gliding; ~ **nacional/internacional** domestic/international flight; ~ **rasante** low- -level flight; ~ **regular** scheduled flight; **levantar** [*o* alzar] **el** ~ (*pájaro*) to fly off; (*avión*) to take off; **al** ~ in flight; *fig* quickly; **tomar** ~ to take flight; (*fig*) to leave **2.** (*de la ropa*) looseness; **falda de** ~ full skirt ►**oír el** ~ **de una mosca** to hear a pin drop; **de altos** ~s high-powered; **cogerlas al** ~ to be very quick on the uptake; **cortar los** ~s **a alguien** to clip sb's wings
vuelta *f* **1.** (*giro*) turn; **el camión dio una** ~ **de campana** the lorry *Brit* [*o* truck *Am*] turned over; **andar a** ~s **con algo** *inf* to be working on sth; **a la** ~ **de** (*lugar*) near; (*tiempo*) after; **a la** ~ **de la esquina** around the corner; **dar la** ~ (*rodear*) to go around; (*volver*) to turn back; (*poner cabeza abajo*) to put face down; (*llave*) to turn; **darse la** ~ to turn over; **dar media** ~ to turn around; **dar una** ~ to have a walk around; **dar** ~s **a algo** to turn sth over; **dar mil** ~s **a alguien** to run rings around sb; **no dar más** ~s **al tema** to stop worrying about sth; **la cabeza me da** ~s my head is spinning **2.** (*regreso*) return; (*viaje*) trip; ~ **atrás** return (trip); *fig* look back; CINE, LIT flashback; **a la** ~ **pasaremos por vuestra casa** we'll pass by your house on the way back; **a la** ~ **empezaré a trabajar** I'll start work when I get back; **de** ~ **a casa** back home; **estar de** ~ to be back; **la** ~ **al cole(gio)** back to school **3.** (*curva*) bend; **dar** ~s **y revueltas** to turn this way and that **4.** (*dinero*) change; **dar la** ~ to give change

5. (*cambio*) change; **la vida da muchas** ~s life has many ups and downs; **¡las** ~s **que da la vida!** how things change! **6.** DEP lap; ~ **ciclista** cycle race; **partida de** ~ return match **7.** POL round **8.** (*devolución*) refund **9.** (*reverso*) back **10.** (*de la ropa*) facing ►**a** ~ **de correo** by return of post; **esto no tiene** ~ **de hoja** (*está claro*) there's no doubt about it; (*no hay otra solución*) it's the only way; **poner a alguien de** ~ **y media** to tear sb off a strip *Brit*, to tell sb off *Am;* **estar de** ~ **de todo** to have seen it all before; **buscar las** ~s **a alguien** to try to catch sb out; **dar muchas** ~s **a algo** to think over sth again and again
vuelto *m AmL* (*cambio*) change; **dar el** ~ to give change
vuelto, -a *pp de* **volver**
vuestro, -a I. *adj* your; ~ **coche** your car; **vuestra hija** your daughter; ~s **libros** your books II. *pron pos* **1.** (*de vuestra propiedad*) yours; **¿es** ~**?** is this yours? **2.** (*tras artículo*) **el** ~ yours; **los** ~s yours; (*parientes*) your family; **mi radio no funciona, ¿me dejáis la vuestra?** my radio doesn't work, can I borrow yours? **3.** (*tras substantivo*) (of) yours; **un amigo** ~ a friend of yours; (**no**) **es culpa vuestra** it's not your fault ►**ésta es la vuestra** *inf* this is your chance
vulcanizadora *f Méx* vulcanizer
vulgar *adj* **1.** (*común*) common **2.** (*ordinario*) vulgar **3.** (*ramplón*) coarse
vulgaridad *f* **1.** (*normalidad*) ordinariness **2.** *pey* (*grosería*) vulgarity **3.** (*ramplonería*) coarseness
vulgarizar <z→c> I. *vt* **1.** (*simplificar*) to vulgarize **2.** (*popularizar*) to popularize II. *vr:* ~**se 1.** *pey* (*persona*) to become vulgar **2.** (*trivializarse*) to become trivial **3.** (*popularizarse*) to become popular
vulgo *m* **1.** (*mayoría*) public; *pey* (*masa*) masses *pl* **2.** (*pueblo, profanos*) ordinary [*o* common] people *pl*
vulnerabilidad *f* vulnerability; (*de la salud*) delicate nature; (*de máquinas*) poor quality
vulnerable *adj* vulnerable
vulneración *f* violation
vulnerar *vt* (*persona*) to hurt; (*derecho*) to violate
vulva *f* ANAT vulva

W

W, w *f* W, w; ~ **de Washington** W for William
walkie-talkie *m* walkie-talkie
walkman® *m* Walkman®
wampa *f Méx* (*ciénaga*) swamp
warrant <warrants> *m* FIN warrant
wáter *m* toilet
waterpolo *m* DEP water polo

watt *m* ELEC watt
W.C. *m abr de* **water-closet** toilet
web *m o f* INFOR web
wélter I. *adj AmL* DEP **peso** ~ welterweight II. *m AmL* DEP welterweight
whisky *m* whisky
windsurf *m* 1. DEP windsurfing 2. (*tabla*) windsurfer
windsurfing *m sin pl* windsurfing
wing *m AmL* 1. (*extremo delantero*) winger 2. (*extrema delantera*) wing
WWW *abr de* **World Wide Web** WWW

X

X, x *f* 1. (*letra*) X, x; ~ **de xilófono** X for Xmas *Brit,* X for X *Am;* **rayos** ~ X-rays *pl;* **en** (**forma de**) ~ X-shaped 2. MAT x; ~ **veces** x times 3. *fig* (*indeterminado*) x; **le presté x libras** I lent him/her x pounds 4. (*numeración romana*) ten
xenofobia *f* xenophobia
xenófobo, -a *adj* xenophobic
xerografía *f* xerography
xilófono *m* MÚS xylophone
xilografía *f* xylography
xirgo, -a *adj Méx* 1. (*desaseado*) untidy 2. (*hirsuto*) hairy
xocoyote *m Méx* (*benjamín*) youngest child

Y

Y, y *f* Y, y; ~ **de yema** Y for Yellow *Brit,* Y for Yoke *Am*
y *conj* and; **días** ~ **días** days and days; ¿~ **qué?** so what?; **me voy de vacaciones** – ¿~ **tu trabajo?** I'm going on holiday – what about your job?; ¿~ **tu marido**(, **qué tal?**) and how is your husband?; ¿~ **mi monedero?** – **en el coche** where's my purse? – it's in the car; ¿~ **este paquete?** – **de mis padres** whose is this packet? – it's my parents'; ~ **eso que...** despite that, ...; ¡~ **tanto!** you bet!, you can say that again!
ya I. *adv* 1. (*en el pasado*) already; ~ **es hora de que cambies** it's time you changed; ~ **en 1800** as early as 1800 2. (*pronto*) soon, right away; ¡~ **voy!** coming!; ~ **verás** you'll see 3. (*ahora*) now; ~ **falta poco para Navidades** Christmas is near now 4. (*negación*) ~ **no fumo** I don't smoke any more; ~ **no... sino...** not only ..., but ... 5. (*afirmación*) yes; ~, ~ all right, OK; *irón* oh, sure!; ¡ah ~! I get it now!; ¡anda ~! come off it!; ¡pues ~! right now! II. *conj* 1. (*porque*) ~ **que** since, as 2. (*apro-*

vechando que) ~ **que estás aquí...** now that you're here ...; ~ **que lo mencionas...** now that you mention it ... 3. (*o*) ~ **por...,** ~ **por...** either by ... or ... III. *interj* that's it!
yacaré *m Arg, Bol, Par, Urug* ZOOL alligator
yacer *irr vi elev* 1. (*estar echado*) to lie; **aquí yace el conde** here lies the count 2. (*acostarse*) to lie down 3. (*estar*) to be
yacija *f* 1. *pey* (*cama*) rough bed, pallet *liter;* (*de paja*) straw bed 2. (*sepultura*) grave
yacimiento *m* GEO, MIN deposit; (*capa*) layer
yagua *f* 1. *AmL* BOT royal palm 2. (*fibras*) royal palm fibre
yagual *m AmC* padded ring (*for carrying heavy loads on the head*)
yaguré *m AmL* ZOOL skunk
yak *m* yak
yámbico, -a *adj* LIT iambic
yambo *m* LIT iambus
yanqui I. *adj* Yankee II. *mf* Yank
yapa *f AmL* 1. (*a un precio*) bonus 2. (*objeto*) extra; **de** ~ as an addition
yapar *vt AmL* 1. (*el precio*) ~ **algo** to give sth as a bonus 2. (*un objeto*) ~ **algo** to add sth as an extra
yarda *f* (*medida*) yard
yate *m* yacht
yayo, -a *m, f inf* grandpa *m,* grandma *f*
yazco, yazgo 1. *pres de* **yacer**
ye *f* letter Y
yedra *f* ivy
yegua *f* 1. ZOOL mare 2. *AmC* (*colilla*) cigar stub

> The term **yeísmo** signifies the pronunciation of the 'll' as a 'y', e.g. '**gayo**' instead of '**gallo**'. The **yeísmo** is very widespread, particularly amongst city dwellers.

yelmo *m* helmet
yema *f* 1. (*de un huevo*) yolk 2. (*de un dedo*) fingertip 3. GASTR egg yolk 4. BOT young shoot 5. (*parte mejor*) best part; ~**s de espárrago** asparagus tips
Yemen *m* Yemen
yemení, yemenita I. *adj* of/from Yemen II. *mf* native/inhabitant of Yemen
yendo *gerundio de* **ir**
yerba *f* 1. (*planta*) grass; ~ **mate** *AmS* maté herb 2. (*césped*) lawn; (*pasto*) pasture; (*seco*) dry grass
yerbal *m RíoPl* maté plantation
yerbatal *m Arg* (*yerbal*) maté plantation
yerbatero, -a I. *adj AmL* maté II. *m, f AmS* 1. (*curandero*) folk healer 2. (*vendedor: de hierbas*) herbalist; (*de forraje*) person who sells fodder; (*de mate*) grower of maté
yerbear *vi AmL* to drink maté
yerbera *f RíoPl* maté container
yerbero, -a *m, f Méx* (*curandero*) herb doctor
yergo 1. *pres de* **erguir**
yermo *m* 1. (*terreno*) waste land 2. AGR uncultivated land

W
X
Y

yermo, -a *adj* **1.** (*inhabitado*) uninhabited **2.** AGR uncultivated; **dejar** ~ to leave unculti-vated

yerno *m* son-in-law

yernocracia *f inf* old-boy network

yero *m* vetch

yerra *f RíoPl* branding

yerro *m* **1.** (*equivocación*) confusion **2.** (*falta*) mistake

yérsey *m*, **yersí** *m AmC, AmS* jersey

yerto, -a *adj* stiff; **quedar** ~ (**de un susto**) to be scared stiff

yesca *f* tinder

yeso *m* **1.** (*material*) plaster; **dar de** ~ **una pared** to plaster a wall **2.** GEO gypsum

yesquero *m* tinder-box

yeta *f Arg, Urug* bad luck

yé-yé *adj inf* cool; **hoy vas muy** ~ you look very hip today

yira *f Arg, pey, inf* slut

yo I. *pron pers* I; ~ **que tú...** if I were you ...; **esto queda entre tú y** ~ this is between you and me; **¿quién lo hizo?** – ~ **no** who did it? – not me; **soy** ~, **Susan** it's me, Susan; ~ **mismo** myself II. *m t.* PSICO ego

yocalla *m Bol* **1.** (*niño callejero*) street urchin **2.** (*niño mestizo*) half-breed

yod *f* LING yod

yodado, -a *adj* iodized; **sal yodada** iodized salt

yodo *m* iodine

yoga *m* yoga

yogui *mf* yogi

yogur *m* **1.** GASTR yogurt; ~ **natural** plain yogurt; ~ **desnatado** low-fat yogurt **2.** *inf* (*genio*) **estar de mal** ~ to be like a bear with a sore head; **tener muy mal** ~ to be very hot-tempered

yolo *m Méx, inf* (*corazón*) darling; **¡~ mío!** my darling!

yonqui *mf inf* (*drogata*) junkie

yóquei *m*, **yoqui** *m* DEP jockey

yoyó *m* yoyo

yuca *f* yucca

yudo *m* judo

yugo *m* **1.** *t.* AGR (*dominio*) yoke; **someterse al** ~ to bow to the yoke **2.** (*de la campana*) bell cage

Yugoslavia *f* Yugoslavia

yugoslavo, -a I. *adj* Yugoslav(ian) II. *m, f* Yugoslav

yugular¹ *f* ANAT jugular vein

yugular² I. *vt* **1.** (*decapitar*) to decapitate **2.** (*detener*) to break off II. *adj* jugular

yunga *mf Bol, Chile, Ecua, Perú* valley native (*native or resident of the warm valleys on either side of the Andes*)

yungas *fpl Bol, Chile, Ecua, Perú* warm valleys *pl*

yunque *m t.* ANAT anvil

yunta *f* **1.** (*par*) yoke (of oxen), couple **2.** *pl, PRico, Urug, Ven* cufflinks *pl*

yuppy *mf* yuppy

yute *m* jute

yuxtaponer *irr como poner* I. *vt* (*a otra cosa*) to join; (*dos cosas*) to juxtapose II. *vr:* ~**se** join together

yuxtaposición *f* juxtaposition

yuxtapuesto, -a *adj* juxtaposed

yuyal *m CSur* weed-covered ground

yuyero, -a *m, f Arg, CSur* herbalist

yuyo *m* **1.** *CSur* (*yerbajo*) weed **2.** *pl, Col, Ecua* (*condimento*) seasoning **3.** *pl, Perú* (*verdura*) herbs *pl* **4.** *AmC* (*ampolla*) blister

Z

Z, z *f* Z, z; ~ **de Zaragoza** Z for Zebra

zabuir *vi PRico* (*zambullir*) to plunge

zacatal *m AmC, Méx* pasture

zacate *m AmL* (*paja*) hay

zafacoca *f* **1.** *AmC, AmS* (*pelea*) row, quarrel **2.** *Chile* (*alboroto*) commotion **3.** *Méx* (*reyerta*) brawl

zafacón *m PRico, RDom* (*cubo de la basura*) rubbish bin *Brit*, trash can *Am*

zafado, -a *adj Arg* (*descarado*) cheeky *Brit*, sassy *Am*

zafadura *f AmL* MED (*luxación*) dislocation

zafar I. *vt* NÁUT to free II. *vr:* ~**se** **1.** (*de una persona*) to get away; **el ladrón se zafó del policía** the thief gave the policeman the slip **2.** (*de un compromiso*) ~**se de** to get out of **3.** TÉC (*correa*) to come off **4.** *AmL* (*dislocarse*) to dislocate

zafarrancho *m* **1.** NÁUT clearing of the decks **2.** *inf* (*limpieza*) clearing up **3.** *inf* (*riña*) quarrel **4.** *inf* (*destrozo*) mess

zafio, -a *adj* **1.** (*grosero*) rude **2.** (*tosco*) rough, uncouth

zafiro *m* MIN sapphire

zafo *adv AmL* (*salvo*) except

zafo, -a *adj* **1.** NÁUT free **2.** (*indemne*) unhurt; **salir** ~ to escape unscathed

zafra *f* **1.** (*cosecha*) sugar harvest **2.** (*fabricación*) sugar production **3.** (*tiempo*) sugar season **4.** (*jarra*) oil jar

zaga *f* **1.** (*parte posterior*) rear; **ir a la** ~ **de alguien** to be behind sb; **el vicepresidente no le va a la** ~ **al presidente** the vicepresident is a match for the president **2.** DEP defence

zagal(a) *m(f)* (*muchacho*) boy, lad *Brit*; (*muchacha*) girl, lass *Brit*

zaguán *m* **1.** (*vestíbulo*) hall **2.** (*exterior*) entrance

zaguero *m* DEP (*en pelota*) deep ball; (*en fútbol*) defender

zaguero, -a *adj* rear

zahareño, -a *adj* wild

zaherir *irr como sentir* *vt* **1.** (*reprender*) to reprimand **2.** (*mortificar*) to humiliate

zahorí <zahoríes> *m* **1.** (*vidente*) seer

2.(*perspicaz*) very perceptive person **3.**(*buscar agua*) water diviner

zaino, -a *adj* **1.**(*persona*) treacherous; **mirar a lo ~** to look shifty **2.**(*res*) black; (*caballo*) chestnut

zaireño *adj, m, f* Zairean

zalamería *f* flattery

zalamero, -a I. *adj* flattering II. *m, f* flatterer

zalema *f* **1.**(*reverencia*) deep bow **2.**(*zalamería*) flattery

zamacuco, -a *m, f* (*zoquete*) dolt; (*astuto*) sly devil

zamarra *f* **1.**(*de pastor*) shepherd's waistcoat **2.**(*chaqueta*) sheepskin jacket **3.**(*piel*) sheepskin

zamarro *m* **1.**(*chaqueta*) sheepskin jacket **2.**(*piel*) sheepskin **3.**(*rústico*) yokel **4.**(*bribón*) sly individual **5.** *pl, AmL* (*pantalones*) breeches *pl*

Zambia *f* Zambia

zambiano, -a I. *adj* Zambian II. *m, f* Zambian

zambo, -a *adj* (*piernas*) knock-kneed, bow--legged

zambomba *f* MÚS *drum-like instrument played by rubbing a stick through the center of the drumskin*

zambombazo *m* *inf* **1.**(*porrazo*) blow **2.**(*explosión*) blast

zambra *f* **1.**(*bulla*) racket; (*riña*) quarrel **2.** HIST (*fiesta gitana*) gypsy festivity

zambucar <c→qu> *vt* *inf* to hide away

zambullir <3. *pret:* zambulló> I. *vt* to submerge II. *vr:* **~se 1.**(*en el agua*) to dive **2.**(*en un asunto*) **~se en algo** to plunge into sth **3.**(*ocultarse*) to hide; (*cubrirse*) to cover oneself

zambullón *m* *AmS* (*zambullida*) dip, dive

Zamora *f* Zamora ▸**~ no se ganó en una hora** *prov* Rome was not built in a day

zamorano, -a I. *adj* of/from Zamora II. *m, f* native/inhabitant of Zamora

zampabollos *mf inv, inf* greedyguts *Brit*

zampar I. *vt* **1.**(*comer*) to scoff *Brit,* to scarf down *Am* **2.**(*ocultar*) to whip out of sight **3.**(*tirar*) to dash (to the ground) II. *vr:* **~se 1.**(*comer*) to scoff **2.**(*en un lugar*) to crash **3.** *pey* (*invitarse*) to gatecrash

zampatortas *mf inv, inf* scoffer *Brit,* foodie

zampón, -ona I. *adj inf* greedy II. *m, f inf* glutton

zampoña *f* MÚS rustic flute

zamuro *m* *Ven* (*buitre*) turkey vulture

zanahoria[1] *f* BOT carrot

zanahoria[2] *m* *RíoPl* (*imbécil*) idiot

zanca *f* **1.**(*del ave*) shank **2.** *inf* (*del hombre*) long leg

zancada *f* stride; **dar ~s** to stride; **se recorrió la ciudad en dos ~s** he/she walked round the town in no time

zancadilla *f* **poner la ~ a alguien** to trip sb up; *fig* to ruin sb's chances

zancadillear *vt* **~ a alguien** to trip sb up; *fig* to ruin sb's chances

zanco *m* stilt

zancón, -ona *adj* **1.**(*zancudo*) long-legged **2.** *Col, Guat, Méx* (*demasiado corto*) too short; **el vestido le queda ~** the dress is too short on her

zancudo *m* *AmL* **1.**(*insecto*) mosquito **2.**(*ave*) wader

zancudo, -a *adj* long-legged

zanganear *vi* *inf* to idle

zángano *m* **1.**(*vago*) idler **2.** *t.* ZOOL drone **3.**(*torpe*) bore

zanja *f* **1.**(*excavación*) ditch **2.** *AmL* (*arroyada*) watercourse

zanjar *vt* **1.**(*abrir zanjas*) to dig ditches **2.**(*asunto*) to settle; (*disputa*) to end

zanjón *m* **1.**(*zanja*) gully, ditch **2.** *AmL* (*despeñadero*) gorge

zanquilargo, -a *adj* *inf* long-legged

zapa *f* **1.**(*pala*) hoe **2.** MIL sap; **labor de ~** *fig* scheming

zapallo *m* **1.** *AmL* (*calabaza*) pumpkin **2.** *Arg, Chile* (*chiripa*) fluke

zapar *vi* (*cavar*) to dig ditches

zapata *f* TÉC shoe; (*arandela*) washer; **~ de freno** brake shoe

zapatear I. *vt* (*golpear*) to kick II. *vi* **1.**(*bailando*) to tap dance **2.**(*velas*) to flap violently

zapatería *f* **1.**(*tienda*) shoeshop **2.**(*fábrica*) shoe factory **3.**(*taller*) cobbler's **4.**(*oficio*) shoemaking

zapatero *m* (*mueble*) shoe rack

zapatero, -a I. *adj* (*patatas*) hard II. *m, f* shoemaker ▸**~ a tus zapatos** *prov* cobbler, stick to your last *prov;* (*no meterse*) mind your own business

zapatilla *f* **1.**(*para casa*) slipper **2.**(*de deporte*) trainer, sneaker *Am;* **~s de clavos** spiked shoes; **~s de tenis** tennis shoes

zapato *m* shoe; **~ de salón** court shoe *Brit,* pump *Am;* **~s de tacón** high-heeled shoes; **un par de ~s** a pair of shoes ▸**tú no me llegas a la suela del ~** you can't hold a candle to me; **saber dónde aprieta el ~** to know which side one's bread is buttered on; **meter a alguien en un ~** to intimidate sb

zape *interj* **1.**(*animal*) shoo! **2.**(*peligro*) look out!

zapear *vt* **1.**(*espantar*) to scare away **2.** *inf* TV to channel-hop, to zap (channels)

zapotazo *m* *Méx, inf* thump

zapote *m* *AmC, Méx* BOT sapodilla

zapping *m* channel-hopping

zar, zarina *m, f* tsar *m,* tsarina *f*

zaragozano, -a I. *adj* of/from Zaragoza II. *m, f* native/inhabitant of Zaragoza

zaramullo *m* *Perú, Ven* silly thing

zarandajas *fpl* trifles *pl*

zarandear I. *vt* **1.**(*sacudir*) to shake hard **2.**(*ajetrear*) to keep busy **3.**(*cribar*) to sieve **4.** *AmL* (*ridiculizar*) to mock II. *vr:* **~se 1.**(*ajetrearse*) to busy oneself **2.**(*burlarse*) make fun

zarcillo *m* **1.**(*pendiente*) earring **2.** BOT tendril

zarco, -a adj light blue

zarina f v. **zar**

zarpa f 1.(del león) paw; inf (del hombre) huge hand, mitt; **echar la** ~ (animal) to claw; inf (persona) to grab 2.(barco) weighing anchor

zarpar vi NÁUT to set sail

zarrapastroso, -a adj inf dirty

zarza f bramble, blackberry bush

zarzal m bramble patch

zarzamora f blackberry

zarzo m Col loft ▶**ser caído del** ~ inf to be a sucker

zarzuela f 1.MÚS zarzuela (Spanish musical comedy or operetta) 2.GASTR dish made of fish and shellfish

zas interj 1.(de rapidez) whoosh! 2.(de golpe) bang!

zascandil m 1.(casquivano) scatterbrained 2.(entrometido) busybody

zascandilear vi 1.(tontear) to do foolish things 2.(entrometerse) to meddle

zenit m zenith

zepelín m zeppelin

zeta f zed

zigzag m <zigzagues o zigzags> zigzag

zigzaguear vi to zigzag

Zimbabue m Zimbabwe

zimbabuo, -a I. adj Zimbabwean II. m, f Zimbabwean

zinc m <cines o zines> zinc; **óxido de** ~ zinc oxide

zíngaro, -a m, f gipsy Brit, (Hungarian) gypsy Am

zíper m Méx (cremallera) zip fastener

zipizape m inf set-to

zócalo m 1.ARQUIT pedestal 2.(de pared) skirting board 3.Méx (plaza) (town) square

zodíaco m zodiac; **signos del** ~ signs of the Zodiac

zombi m 1.(muerto) zombie 2.(atontado) **estar** ~ to be like a zombie

zona f 1. t. POL, GEO, METEO (general) zone; (terreno) belt; (área) region; ~ **de ensanche** area to be built up; ~ **franca** (duty-)free zone; ~ **de influencia** area of influence; ~ **peatonal** pedestrian precinct; ~ **urbana** urban area; ~ **verde** green belt 2. DEP (baloncesto: área) area; (defensa) zone defender; (falta) zone fault

zoncera f AmL, **zoncería** f (tontería) foolishness

zonzo, -a adj 1.(aburrido) dull 2.AmL (tonto) stupid

zoo m zoo

zoología f sin pl zoology

zoológico, -a adj zoological; **parque** ~ zoo

zoólogo, -a m, f zoologist

zopenco, -a I. adj oafish II. m, f dolt

zopilote m Méx ZOOL turkey vulture

zopo, -a adj lame

zoquete m 1.(madera) block 2.(tonto) blockhead 3.Arg (calcetín) sock

zorra f 1.ZOOL vixen 2. inf (prostituta) whore; (insulto) bitch 3. inf (borrachera) drunkenness

zorrera f 1.(de zorros) earth 2.(habitación) smoky room 3.(modorra) drowsiness

zorrería f craftiness

zorrillo m AmL (mofeta) skunk

zorro m 1.ZOOL fox 2.(piel) foxskin 3. inf (astuto) crafty fellow ▶**hacerse el** ~ to act stupid; **estar hecho unos** ~**s** to be dead beat; **poner a alguien hecho unos** ~**s** to tire sb to death

zorzal m 1.ZOOL thrush 2.(listo) shrewd person 3.AmL (papanatas) simpleton

zote I. adj foolish II. mf fool

zozobra f anxiety

zozobrar I. vi 1.(barco) to capsize 2.(plan) to fail 3.(persona) to hesitate II. vt 1.(barco) to sink 2.(plan) to spoil

zueco m clog

zumba f 1.(cencerro) mule bell 2.(juguete) rattle 3.(burla) teasing 4.AmL (paliza) beating

zumbado, -a adj estar ~ inf to be barmy Brit, to be nuts

zumbador m ELEC buzzer

zumbar I. vi 1.(abejorro, máquina) to buzz; **salir zumbando** to rush [o zoom] off 2.(oídos) to hum II. vt 1.(golpe) to deal 2.AmL (arrojar) to throw; (expulsar) to chuck out 3.(guasear) to mock III. vr: ~**se** to make fun

zumbido m 1.(ruido) hum; ~ **de los oídos** ringing in the ears 2. inf (golpe) clout

zumbón, -ona m, f inf joker

zumo m 1.(de frutas) juice 2.fig (utilidad) profit; **sacar** ~ **de algo** to get benefit from sth

zuncho m ring

zupay m AmL (demonio) devil

zurcir <c→z> vt to mend; **¡que te zurzan!** inf to hell with you!

zurda f left hand; **hacer algo a** ~**s** to do sth with the left hand; fig to do sth the wrong way

zurdo, -a I. adj left-handed II. m, f left-handed person

zurra f 1.(de la piel) tanning 2.(paliza) hiding; **dar una** ~ **a alguien** to give sb a hiding

zurrapa f 1.(poso) dregs pl 2. inf (cosa) muck; (persona) weak and ugly person

zurraposo, -a adj full of dregs, muddy

zurrar vt 1.(pieles) to tan 2. inf (apalizar) to beat 3. inf (criticar) to knock

zurriagar <g→gu> vt to whip

zurriagazo m 1.(latigazo) lash 2.(desgracia) bad blow 3.(desdén) snub

zurriago m (látigo) whip

zurribanda f inf 1.(tunda) beating 2.(riña) fight

zurrumbanco, -a adj CRi, Méx half-drunk, light-headed

zurullo m inf 1.(grumo) lump 2.(excremento) turd

zutano, -a m, f fulano y ~ Tom, Dick and Harry; **fulano y** ~ **se han casado** what's-his-name and you-know-who have got married (when you can't remember sb's name)

Apéndice I

Supplement I

Correspondencia privada
Private correspondence

A la oficina de turismo: solicitud de folletos informativos

Sr. Silvinio Pérez
Pza. Padre Silverio, 35
09001 Burgos

Dirección General de Turismo de Tarragona
Rambla Nova, 46
43004 Tarragona

Burgos, a 13 de febrero de 2002

Distinguidos señores:

Me gustaría pasar las vacaciones con mi familia en agosto en la costa de Tarragona. Por este motivo les agradecería que fueran tan amables de enviarme prospectos de los lugares turísticos y de los hoteles de esta zona.

Sin otro particular y agradeciéndoles por adelantado su respuesta, les saluda atentamente,

Silvinio Pérez

Me gustaría pasar las vacaciones en…	*I wish to spend my holidays in …*
enviarme prospectos	*send me details*

Note: Spanish writers put both their name and address at the top left of the page, with the name and address of the other person below and to the left.

Tourist office: asking for information

65 Rogers Road,
Rickland
GN8 4BY

2 February 2002

England Tourist Board
New Park
Southbridge
Kent
XP1 7TU

Dear Sirs,

My family and I wish to spend our holidays in the South-East during July.

Could you kindly send me details of places of interest and hotels.

With thanks,

Yours faithfully,

John Roberts

¡Atención! En una carta inglesa el nombre no suele aparecer en el membrete. La dirección del remitente se pone arriba a la derecha, la dirección del destinatario a la izquierda.

Reservar una habitación de hotel

Distinguidos señores:

Les agradezco las molestias que se han tomado al enviarme folletos informativos sobre las condiciones de estancia en su hotel.

Les agradecería que reservaran para mi señora, para mí mismo y nuestros dos hijos dos habitaciones dobles con ducha, una con dos camas y la otra con una de matrimonio, en régimen de media pensión del 2 al 15 de julio.

Les agradezco por adelantado su confirmación.

Sin otro particular, les saluda atentamente,

José Otero

folletos informativos   *your leaflet giving details*
Les agradecería que reservaran…   *I would like to book …*

Booking a room in a hotel

Dear Sirs,

Thank you for your leaflet giving details about your hotel.

I would like to book two double rooms with bathroom at half-board from 2 to 15 July inclusive, one for my wife and myself with double bed, and one with twin beds for my two daughters.

I would be grateful if you could confirm this booking.

Yours faithfully,

Tim Smith

Pedir información sobre un apartamento para las vacaciones

Distinguidos señores:

La Oficina de Turismo me ha enviado la lista y la descripción de los chalets y apartamentos que se alquilan para las vacaciones en su ciudad y en los alrededores.

Me interesaría particularmente el apartamento amueblado que ustedes me recomiendan. Desearía alquilarlo por un período de un mes a partir del 1 de julio. Quisiera, no obstante, antes de tomar la decisión, que me dieran alguna información más.

¿Podrían precisarme si los gastos suplementarios (de gas, electricidad u otros) están incluidos en el precio de alquiler y cuál sería la cantidad del depósito a pagar? ¿Disponen las camas de sábanas y mantas? Y, por último, ¿se admiten animales?

Esperando su respuesta y sin otro particular, les saluda atentamente,

Juan Ibáñez

la lista y la descripción de los chalets y apartamentos	*a detailed list of holiday lettings*
apartamento amueblado	*furnished apartment*
por un período de un mes a partir del 1 de julio	*for one month from 1 July*
¿Podrían precisarme si…?	*Could you tell me if …*
el precio de alquiler	*the rent*
la cantidad del depósito	*the deposit*
¿Disponen las camas de sábanas y mantas?	*Is bedding provided?*

Information about a holiday apartment

Dear Sir,

The tourist office has sent me details of holiday lettings in and around your town and I am particularly interested in your furnished apartment. I would like to rent it for one month from 1 July. However I should be grateful for some further details before making a final decision.

Could you tell me if bills (gas, electricity and any taxes) are included in the rent? What deposit do you require? Is bedding provided? And finally, are pets welcome?

Yours faithfully,

John Roberts

Alquilar un apartamento para las vacaciones

Apreciados señores:

En primer lugar quisiera agradecerles su rápida respuesta.

Una vez obtenida la información adicional que han tenido la amabilidad de comunicarnos, les confirmo la decisión de alquilar el apartamento del 1 al 30 de julio, ambos incluidos.

Les adjunto un cheque de 200 euros en concepto de depósito. El resto del alquiler, es decir, 375 euros, les será entregado el día de nuestra llegada, el 1 de julio.

Sin otro particular, les saluda atentamente,

Silvia Gómez

P.S.: ¿Podrían precisarnos, por favor, dónde podemos recoger las llaves el día de nuestra llegada?

...que han tenido la amabilidad de comunicarnos	*... that you have kindly sent*
les confirmo la decisión de alquilar	*I confirm that we have decided to rent*
en concepto de depósito	*as a deposit*
El resto del alquiler les será entregado...	*We will pay the balance ...*
¿Podrían precisarnos, por favor, dónde...?	*Kindly let us know where ...*

Booking a holiday apartment

Dear Mr Hill,

Thank you for answering my letter so quickly.

I have read through the information and I can now confirm that we have decided to rent your apartment from 1 to 30 July inclusive.

I enclose a cheque for £150; and we will pay the balance of £700 on our arrival on 1 July.

Yours sincerely,

Steven Roberts

PS: Kindly let us know where to pick up the keys to the apartment on the day of our arrival.

553

Carta desde el lugar de vacaciones

Querido Mario, querida Inés:

Un gran saludo desde la isla de Cuba donde desde hace una semana disfrutamos del sol y de las playas a la sombra de un cocotero. Hemos degustado ya todas las especialidades culinarias de la isla. ¡Y qué decir del delicioso ron de aquí? En una palabra: unas vacaciones de ensueño, y eso que el hotel, aunque confortable, es bastante ruidoso. Espero que los dos estéis bien y que no sufráis demasiado con el frío invernal de la capital.

Un abrazo muy fuerte,

Juan y Christina

Familia Martínez
c/Ruiseñor 24

08034 Barcelona

Holiday postcard

Here we are in Barbados. There's plenty of sun, sand and palm trees. The beach suits me fine, but Peter keeps trying to tempt me off the beach to join him for some water-skiing. The hotel is good and the food is delicious, but the disco can be rather noisy if you want an early night! We have another week here before we head back home to a British winter. We hope that you're both well and we'll see you soon.

Love from

Maggie and Peter

Gemma and John Roberts
65 Rogers Road
Rickland
GN8 4BY

Felicitación de Navidad (registro informal)

Querido Pedro, querida María:
Muchas gracias por vuestra felicitación
de Navidad.
Igualmente queremos desearos una feliz
Navidad y un próspero Año Nuevo y que
el 2003 os traiga toda la felicidad del
mundo.
Hasta pronto, en Madrid o en Cambrid-
ge.
Besos,
Marga y David

Christmas Greetings (informal register)

Dear Julia and Robert,
Wishing you both a very Merry Christ-
mas and an excellent New Year, hoping
that it brings you all the joy and suc-
cess you wish for.
Hope to see you soon over here or back
home in the States.
Love from
Maddie and Neil

Felicitación de Navidad (registro formal)

Sr. D. Sergio López

Presidente de la Cámara de
Comercio regional

*Les deseo a usted y a su familia
una feliz Navidad y un próspero Año
Nuevo*

Atentamente,

Sergio Moreno

Christmas Greetings (formal register)

*A very Happy Christmas and good
wishes for the New Year*

from

Elaine Goodman

*Goodman and Hart
Solicitors
48 High Street
Rickland
GN8 4SK*

Felicitación de cumpleaños

> Querida Ángeles:
>
> 13 de diciembre: un año más... Pero qué importa eso, tú siempre serás joven.
>
> Te deseo de todo corazón un feliz cumpleaños.
>
> Si no fuera porque vivo tan lejos te habría llevado personalmente un pequeño regalo: Correos se encargará de ello. Espero que llegue a tiempo. Una cosa más: ¡que tengas un buen día!
>
> Un abrazo muy fuerte,
>
> Carmen

Te deseo de todo corazón un feliz cumpleaños.   *I wish you a very happy birthday.*

Birthday card

> Dear Simon,
>
> Happy Birthday! But I can't believe it's a year since the last one!
>
> It's far too long since we got together and it's a real shame that we won't be around for the celebrations. We hope you like our little present and that you'll have a good time on the day.
>
> Love from
>
> Sophie and Mike

Tarjeta de pésame

Los Srs. García

enterados de la cruel pérdida que han sufrido

quieren expresarles su más sincero pésame

su más sincero pésame — *our sincere condolences*

Condolences

We were deeply saddened to hear of your sad loss and wish to offer our sincere condolences

With our deepest sympathy,

James and Barbara Thornton

Invitación

> Queridos amigos:
>
> Hace un mes ya que nos hemos instalado en nuestra nueva casa de Orio, un pequeño y pintoresco pueblo del norte de España.
>
> Estaríamos encantados si os pudiéramos recibir el fin de semana de Carnaval. El sábado por la noche celebraremos el estreno de la casa con todos los amigos. Nos gustaría que estuvierais presentes.
>
> Os adjuntamos un plano para que podáis encontrar la casa.
>
> Esperando una respuesta afirmativa por vuestra parte os enviamos un cordial saludo,
>
> Belén y Ramón

celebramos el estreno de la casa	*we're throwing a house-warming party*
Os adjuntamos un plano	*We have enclosed a map*
Esperando una respuesta afirmativa…	*Hoping that you can make it …*

Invitation

> Dear Angela and Martin,
>
> It's just over a month since we moved into our new house at Bennington. We like it here in the north of England, and it's very picturesque.
>
> Would you be able to come and stay with us for the holiday weekend? We're throwing a house-warming party on Saturday night and would be very happy if you could be there.
>
> We have enclosed a map so that you don't get lost.
>
> Hoping that you can make it.
>
> With warm regards,
>
> Elizabeth and Paul

Aceptar una invitación

Queridos amigos:

Con gran placer queremos comunicaros que aceptamos vuestra amable invitación. Nos encantará poder volver a veros.

Llegaremos el viernes por la noche y nos quedaremos hasta el lunes por la mañana. Gracias por el plano.

Aprovechamos esta breve respuesta para felicitaros por vuestra nueva casa.

Saludos afectuosos,

Sinda y Miguel

Nos encantará poder volver a veros. *We're really looking forward to seeing you again.*

Accepting an invitation

Dear Elizabeth and Paul,

Of course we would be delighted to accept your kind invitation and we're really looking forward to seeing you again.

We should get there early on Friday evening we'll be off again on Monday morning. Thanks for the map.

Congratulations on your new home.

With warmest regards

Angela and Martin

Rechazar una invitación

Queridos amigos:

Vuestra amable invitación nos ha satisfecho mucho y os la agradecemos sinceramente. Desgraciadamente tenemos ya compromisos familiares que nos impedirán estar libres ese fin de semana. ¡Cuánto lo sentimos!

Nos hubiera encantado volver a veros; quizás se presente dentro de poco otra ocasión para podernos ver.

Os enviamos un afectuoso saludo,

Laura y Javier

Dear Elizabeth and Paul,

We were delighted to receive your kind invitation and would like to thank you very much.

We're terribly sorry but we already have family commitments that prevent us getting away on that weekend. Shame! It would have been great to get out into the country for a break.

We're terribly sorry we won't be seeing you, let's hope there'll be another chance to get together in the near future.

With our best wishes,

Angela and Martin

Agradecer a alguien su hospitalidad

Estimados señores:

Queremos por la presente agradecer sinceramente la acogida tan amable y calurosa que nos dispensaron.

No olvidaremos jamás los maravillosos momentos pasados en su compañía. Gracias a todas las excursiones que tuvieron la gentileza de organizarnos hemos podido descubrir su ciudad, su región y también otra manera de vivir.

Díganles a sus vecinos, los Sres. Alcántara, que guardamos un muy grato recuerdo de las partidas de mus que echamos con ellos.

Dándoles de nuevo las gracias por todo y esperando tener pronto el placer de enseñarles nuestro país cuando se presente la ocasión, les saludamos muy atentamente,

Susana y Roberto

la acogida tan amable y calurosa que nos dispensaron — *the warm welcome you gave us*

los maravillosos momentos pasados en su compañía — *the wonderful time we spent with you*

guardamos un muy grato recuerdo de… — *we won't forget …*

Dear Mr and Mrs Shaw,

We would like to say a big thank you for the warm welcome you gave us.

We had a wonderful time while we were with you. We have many happy memories of our outings in Exeter and its surroundings and I hope you'll enjoy the photographs we took.

Would you please thank all your friends, especially Bob and Sandra Carter from the tennis club, who did so much to make our stay enjoyable.

It was a holiday to remember and I hope it will not be too long before we are able to welcome you to our country.

Yours sincerely,

Eric and Mary

Anuncio de boda

D. Abelino Pérez y señora
y
D. Juan Carrascal y señora

tienen el placer de comunicarles la boda

de sus hijos,

Carmen y Javier.

El enlace tendrá lugar en la iglesia parroquial
el 11 de septiembre de 2002 a las 11 horas.

Se recibirá a los invitados tras la ceremonia religiosa
en la finca „Los Pinos" de Úbeda (Jaén)

Se agradecerá confirmación.

tras la ceremonia religiosa   *following the ceremony*
Se agracederá confirmación.   *R.S.V.P.*

Marriage announcement

Mr and Mrs Henry Grant

request the pleasure of your company at the marriage of their daughter
Christine to Mr Robin Davies

at St Anne's Church, Lewes on Saturday 17 June at 11 a.m.

and at the reception afterwards at

Hollyoak Manor, Kingston

R.S.V.P

Querida Isabel, querido Antonio:

He cogido la pluma más bonita que tengo para anunciaros una gran novedad: ¡María se casa! Pero seguramente ya lo habréis leído en la tarjeta que va incluida en esta carta.

Espero de todo corazón que nos complaceréis asistiendo a la boda. Estaríamos encantados de teneros entre nosotros ese día. Será una oportunidad para vernos de nuevo y celebrar la fiesta juntos. Contamos con vuestra presencia.

En cuanto al alojamiento, no os preocupéis, ¡todo está preparado!

Esperando veros pronto, os enviamos un saludo muy cordial.

Teresa y Manuel

Espero de todo corazón que nos complaceréis asistiendo a la boda.	*I really hope that you will be able to come to the wedding.*
Será una oportunidad para vernos de nuevo.	*It will be good to see each other again.*
Contamos con vuestra presencia.	*We are counting on you.*

Wedding invitation

Dear Helen and Mark,

I've got some news for you: Christine is getting married! You'll be getting the invitation card in the post soon.

We really hope that you can come to the wedding. We would be delighted to have you with us. It would be good to see each other again and celebrate together. We are counting on you.

Don't worry about where to stay, we'll take care of everything.

We hope to see you again soon,

With our very best wishes,

Lorna and Henry Grant

Aceptar la invitación a una boda

Querida Matilde, querido Juan:

Nos ha emocionado mucho recibir la amable invitación a la boda de vuestra hija María, invitación que aceptamos con sumo gusto. Estaremos encantados de poder felicitar personalmente a la joven pareja.

Os agradecemos sinceramente que hayáis pensado en nosotros y nos alegramos de poder volver a veros tras todos estos meses en los que no hemos dado señales de vida. Pero, como sabéis, nuestra profesión nos absorbe por completo y las semanas pasan volando.

Sin otro particular y esperando que vosotros y los vuestros gocéis de buena salud os saludamos hasta muy pronto.

Un abrazo,

Isabel y Antonio

P.S.: Quizás podríais sugerirnos un regalo de bodas que pudiera agradar a los recién casados. Gracias por adelantado.

...que aceptamos con mucho gusto — *... which we are delighted to accept*
tras todos estos meses — *after so many months*
nuestra profesión nos absorbe por completo — *our professional lives keep us so busy*
sugerir un regalo de bodas que pudiera agradar a los recién casados — *suggest a wedding gift that the newlyweds would like*

Dear Lorna and Henry

We were very so pleased to hear about Christine's wedding, and delighted to get your invitation. Of course we shall be coming and look forward to seeing the young couple and giving them our best wishes.

Things have been terribly busy at work over the past few months. Time passes too quickly and it's easy to lose touch with our friends, so it will be lovely to see you all again.

We hope that everyone is keeping well and we will see you soon.

With warmest regards,

Helen and Mark

P.S. Do you have any ideas for a wedding gift that Christine and Robin might like? We'd be very grateful for suggestions.

Agradecer un regalo de bodas

Queridos amigos:

¿Cómo os podemos agradecer el fantástico regalo que habéis tenido la gentileza de hacernos con motivo de nuestro enlace?

Nos ha encantado, de verdad, lo que habéis hecho y nos sentimos realmente agasajados.

Gracias de nuevo y sabed que siempre tendréis en nosotros a unos sinceros amigos.

Isabel y Diego

el fantástico regalo que habéis tenido la gentileza de hacernos	*the wonderful present that you gave us*
Nos ha encantado de verdad.	*It was really too much.*

Thanks for a wedding gift

Dear Helen and Mark

Thank you so much for the wonderful present that you gave us for our wedding.

We were very touched by your kindness. It was really too much.

Thank you once again.

With our love,

Christine and Robin

Agradecer un regalo de cumpleaños

Querida Antonia, querido Francisco:

Recibí vuestro regalo el mismo día de mi cumpleaños. Miles de gracias. Pero de verdad que es demasiado. Me habéis puesto casi en una situación embarazosa. Sabéis que no hay nada que me pueda satisfacer más y nunca dejáis pasar una ocasión para demostrar vuestro afecto que, como sabréis, es recíproco.

Una vez más, muchas gracias y hasta muy pronto. Un abrazo muy fuerte.

    Sonia

Miles de gracias.	*Thank you so much.*
Me habéis puesto casi en una situación embarazosa.	*I'm almost overwhelmed.*

Thanks for a birthday present

Dear Sophie and Mike,

You always remember my birthday – even though I'd rather forget about it now!

Thank you so much your present – really you shouldn't have. It made my day: you certainly know what I like! It will remind me of you, but don't think I really need any reminder. I could never forget good friends like you.

Thanks once again, and I hope it won't be too long before we see each other.

Love

Simon

Correspondencia comercial
Business correspondence

Carta de pedido

Pastelería RAMOS
Plaza de la Libertad, 21
34005 Zamora

Turrones, S.A.
c/Gijón, 13
46003 Valencia

Ref.: pedido n° 111

Zamora, a 18 de octubre de 2002

Estimados Sres.:

Hace quince días recibimos su envío de muestras, además de la lista correspondiente de precios. La relación precio-calidad de sus productos nos ha parecido sumamente interesante. De hecho creemos que también convencerá a nuestros clientes.

Por ello deseamos tomen nota del pedido que especificamos a continuación:

Cantidad/Unidades	Producto	Precio
30 cajas de 50 u.	Turrón duro	70 euros/caja
10 cajas de 50 u.	Turrón blando	70 euros/caja
10 cajas de 50 u.	Turrón Nata Nuez	80 euros/caja
10 cajas de 50 u.	Turrón Yema Tostada	80 euros/caja

Rogamos nos hagan llegar el envío antes del 1 de noviembre.

Como ya habíamos acordado por teléfono, el envío se efectuará a través de la empresa de transportes 'La Liebre', por supuesto con portes pagados. El pago, con una letra de cambio a 30 días.

En espera de sus prontas noticias, les saludamos muy atentamente,

Marcos Ruiz Pérez

(Encargado Pastelería RAMOS)

46, Ambrose Crescent
Silhurst
CW3 8DS

Hitchfield Electronics
Chingleford
QN4 6RT

10 March 2002

Dear Sir,

Re. Printer supplies

Further to our telephone conversation this morning, I would like to confirm my
order for the following items:

Type	Quantity
Printer cable, code HX398	1
Inkjet cartridges, black, code HW 546	2
Colour cartridge, code HW 756	1

Please debit my credit card, no. 1111 2222 3333 4444, expiry date 02/04

I understand that you deliver within three working days.

Yours faithfully,

Ronald Grieves

Acusar recibo de un pedido

Almacenes Guadalquivir
Ciudad Expo, bloque 22, bajo C
41927 Mairena del Aljarafe
(Sevilla)

Supermercados MERCAMIL
c/Torres Quevedo, 1, bajo
45004 Toledo

Sevilla, a 2 de julio de 2002

Distinguidos señores:

Ante todo, gracias por su pedido nº 32 del 15 del mes corriente que acabamos de recibir. Tengan la seguridad de que pondremos nuestro mayor esmero en llevarlo a cabo.

Aceptamos sus condiciones de entrega y de pago, a saber:

> Entrega: antes del 12 de mayo, portes pagados, por camión.
> Pago: 60 días fecha factura, sin descuento.

Condiciones particulares: les reconocemos, a partir de ahora, el derecho a rechazar los artículos que no les sean entregados antes del 12 de mayo.

Estando en todo momento a su disposición, aprovecho la oportunidad para saludarles atentamente,

Diego Blanco Novoa

(Gerente Almacenes GUADALQUIVIR)

Confirming receipt of an order

PWP Ceramics
15, Highbridge Road
Mingley
WP9 7SA
Tel.: 024 4825 3147

Hailingbury plc
11, Foghard Way
Hocksmore
TQ3 6BV

18 April 2002

Dear Sirs,

Thank you for your order number 32 dated 15 April.

This order will be dealt with and shipped as soon as possible

Our standard payment and delivery conditions apply, i.e.

Delivery: by 12 May, carriage paid, by courier service.
Payment: within 60 days of the billing date, without discount.

All goods should be inspected on delivery.

Yours faithfully,

A Black

Anne Black
Sales Department

Carta de reclamación

Manuel Gómez Marcos
c/Ruiseñor, 24–3 °C
08084 Barcelona

PRICAR, S.L.
Paseo Gaudí, 33
08080 Barcelona

Barcelona, a 11 de noviembre de 2002

Muy señores míos:

Hace dos días, es decir el sábado, día 9 de noviembre, adquirí en su establecimiento del Paseo Gaudí una antena parabólica de la casa 'Télix'. Cuál fue mi sorpresa cuando al llegar a mi domicilio y comenzar su instalación comprobé que faltaba el cable. Ruego me lo hagan llegar a la mayor brevedad a través de su servicio técnico.

Sin otro particular, atentamente,

Manuel Gómez Marcos

38, Swinburne Avenue
Hawdrey
MY7 9PL

20 April 2002

Dear Madam,

I have received the items ordered by letter dated 22 March.

However, further inspection has revealed a defect in the cooler unit, part reference PL-00274/B and this prevents its use in the manufacturing process.

I would therefore be grateful if you would supply a replacement unit a.s.a.p. Please advise us when you will be able to deliver and collect the defective item from us.

Yours faithfully,

C Benson

Charles Benson

Carta de solicitud de empleo

Carmen Bermúdez Díaz
c/Reyes Católicos, 42, 3° G
10002 Cáceres

IBERIA, L.A.E.
c/Henri Dunant, 2
28036 Madrid

Cáceres, a 28 de mayo de 2002

(Ref. 1324 Trip. Cab.)

Estimados señores:

Con fecha del 26 de mayo he leído su anuncio en el diario 'El País' en el que solicitan auxiliares de vuelo (tripulantes de cabina de pasajeros).

Entre mis aspiraciones profesionales siempre me atrajo un puesto como el que ofrecen en la presente convocatoria. De hecho creo reunir los requisitos que demandan.

En la actualidad tengo 24 años, domino tres idiomas y además cuento con otras aptitudes, adquiridas especialmente durante mi permanencia en la agencia de viajes HALCÓN.

En el currículum vitae que les adjunto describo con más detalle todos estos datos y otros que pudieran serles de interés.

Si ustedes lo estiman oportuno y creen ver en mí un posible candidato, estoy a su disposición para una entrevista personal.

Muy atentamente,

Carmen Bermúdez Díaz

Anexos: C.V., fotografía reciente

Sonia Gómez Ruiz
c/Santa Fé, 34–2 °C
08084 Barcelona

3 November 2002

Dear Sir or Madam,

Re: Application for post of Secretary/Personal Assistant

With reference to your advertisement in today's *Guardian*, I would like to apply for the position of Secretary/Personal Assistant to the Sales Manager.

I am currently looking for full-time work that will allow me to develop my organizational skills and to use my Spanish (mother tongue), English and German which I have been able to practise during several visits and training programmes abroad. My current position has enabled me to acquire sound computing skills.

I enclose my curriculum vitae.

Please do not hesitate to contact me to arrange a suitable time for an interview.

Yours faithfully,

Sonia Gómez

Carta de solicitud de empleo al azar

Laura Roberts
65 Rogers Road,
Rickland
GN8 4BY

Rickland, a 1 de mayo de 2002

Distinguido señor Director:

La reputación de su empresa va a la par con la calidad de sus productos y de su dinamismo. Me he enterado de que están a punto de adoptar una nueva política de marketing, área en la que tengo un particular interés.

En la empresa donde actualmente trabajo he organizado el departamento de publicidad que en tres años ha multiplicado su importancia por dos (ver currículum vitae adjunto).

Mi experiencia profesional, mis cualidades en concepto de rigor y de organización y también mi creatividad me hacen creer que reúno las condiciones para un puesto de trabajo en su equipo.

Si esta solicitud fuera de su interés estaría a su disposición para mantener en un próximo futuro un encuentro personal.

Esperando su respuesta, aprovecho la ocasión para saludarle afectuosamente,

Laura Roberts

Unsolicited application letter

Carmen Rodríguez Santos
c/Serafín, 53, 2°, 3ª
08014 Barcelona

1 September 2002

Dear Sir,

I have been following the performance of your company and have been particularly interested by press reports that you are currently overhauling your overseas marketing strategy.

Over the past three years I have been closely involved in the restructuring of our advertising department, which has led to an 80 % increase in public awareness of our brands at home, and a 50 % increase in overseas sales. You will find full details of my work and responsibilities in the enclosed CV.

I am proud of my achievements and I believe that my professionalism, creativity and discipline could be a major asset to your organization.

I hope that we will be able to meet and discuss this further.

Yours faithfully,

Carmen Rodríguez

Currículum vitae

I. DATOS PERSONALES

Apellidos	Iglesias Vieira
Nombre	Ana María
Dirección particular	c/Martínez Sueiro, 114, 1° M
	37004 Salamanca
	Tel. (988) 222225
Fecha de nacimiento	27.05.1970
Lugar de nacimiento	Celanova (Orense)
Estado civil	soltera
Nacionalidad	española

II. TITULACIÓN ACADÉMICA

Octubre 1989 – junio 1994   Licenciatura en Filología Inglesa,
Universidad de Salamanca

Octubre 1994 – junio 1997   Diplomatura en Ciencias Empresariales,
Universidad de Salamanca

III. FORMACIÓN PROFESIONAL

Octubre 1996 – junio 1997   Master en Comunidades Europeas y Derechos
Humanos, Universidad Pontificia de Salamanca

Octubre 1997 – enero 1998   Master en Marketing,
Universidad Politécnica de Alcalá de Henares

IV. EXPERIENCIA PROFESIONAL

Enero 1998 – diciembre 2000   Clases de inglés comercial en la Cámara de
Comercio de Salamanca

Agosto de 1999 – presente   Caja de Ahorros de Salamanca y Soria,
Responsable del Dpto. de Marketing

V. IDIOMAS

Excelente dominio del inglés y del portugués
Conocimientos de alemán, francés e italiano

VI. OTROS CONOCIMIENTOS

Conocimientos de informática a nivel de usuario

Ann Roberts
65 Rogers Road,
Rickland
GN8 4BY

Date of Birth: 02/07/1970
British
Single

EDUCATION & TRAINING

1991	BA – International Business
1990	Highfield Tertiary College (shorthand and typing)
1988	A Levels (English, Spanish, Maths, Economics)

PROFESSIONAL EXPERIENCE

Since October 1999 — Personal assistant to the Export Director of a software company.

Responsibilities: Follow-up of orders
Contacts with subsidiaries abroad
Canvassing foreign clients

April – August 1999 — Trainee at Publicat, press agency in Madrid, in the office of the director's secretary (learning computer page layout techniques)

October 1997 – March 1998 — Trainee at Sama in Salamanca, in Customer Relations, dealing with telephone enquiries in three languages

LANGUAGES

Trilingual: Spanish, English, German
6 months as a trainee for Sama in Spain

OTHER INTERESTS

Volunteer helper with a local disabled group
Sports: gymnastics, judo

Fórmulas útiles para la correspondencia

Useful expressions in letters

EL ENCABEZAMIENTO EN UNA CARTA – AT THE BEGINNING OF A LETTER

When you're writing ...	Escribes...
... to someone you know or to a friend Querida Sandra: Querido Pablo: ¡Hola Silvia!	...a un conocido o a un amigo Dear Mark, Dear Janet,
... to someone you know or to business contacts Estimada Srta. Hernández: Estimada Sra. Gómez: Estimado Sr. González:	...a alguien a quien conoces a nivel personal o profesional Dear Mrs Arnold, Dear Mr Arnold,
... to companies or organizations Muy señores míos: Estimados Sres:/Estimados señores:	...a una empresa o a una persona cuyo nombre desconoces Dear Sir or Madam, Dear Sirs,
... to someone whose title you know Distinguido/Estimado Dr. Pedro Santos: Distinguida/Estimada Catedrática D.ª Cristina Suárez:	...a una persona cuyo título o grado académico conoces Dear Sir, Dear Madam, Dear Doctor, *(dirigiéndose a un médico)*

LA DESPEDIDA EN UNA CARTA – ENDING A LETTER

Informally	Informal
Un abrazo muy fuerte, Un fuerte abrazo, Besos,	Love, (With) warmest regards,
Un cordial saludo, Un afectuoso saludo,	(With) kind regards, With best wishes,
Saludos ¡Hasta pronto!	Regards, Yours, Yours ever, Yours, with best wishes

Formal	Formal
Atentamente, Muy atentamente,	Yours sincerely, *(Si la carta comienza con "Dear Mr/Mrs ...")* Yours faithfully, *(Si la carta comienza con "Dear Sir/Madam")*

Very formal	Muy respetuoso
Sin otro particular, aprovechamos la oportunidad para saludarles muy atentamente/muy cordialmente.	Yours faithfully, (*a alguien cuyo nombre desconoces*)
Sin otro particular, le saludo atentamente.	Yours sincerely, *(Si la carta comienza con "Dear Mr/Mrs ...")*
Quedando en todo momento a su disposición, aprovecho la oportunidad para saludarles muy atentamente.	Yours faithfully, *(Si la carta comienza con "Dear Sir/Madam")*

Expresiones útiles

Useful phrases

La hora

Time

¿Qué hora es?	What time is it?
¿Me puede decir qué hora es, por favor?	Could you tell me the time please?
Es la una en punto.	It's one o'clock exactly.
Son casi…	It's nearly …
las tres.	three o'clock.
las tres y cinco.	five past three.
las tres y cuarto.	quarter past three.
las tres y veinticinco.	twenty-five minutes past three.
las tres y media.	half past three.
las cuatro menos veinticinco.	twenty-five minutes to four.
las cuatro menos cuarto.	quarter to four.
las doce del mediodía/de la noche.	twelve o'clock midday/midnight.
Son más de las cuatro./Son las cuatro pasadas.	It's already after four (o'clock).
Ven entre las cuatro y las cinco.	Come between four and half past (four).

Saludos, presentaciones, despedidas

Greetings, Introductions, Farewell

¡Buenos días!	Good morning!
¡Buenos días! *(until 2 pm)* ¡Buenas tardes! *(from 2 pm onwards)*	Hello!/Good day! (*Aus*)
¡Buenas tardes! *(until 9 pm)* ¡Buenas noches! *(from 9 pm onwards)*	Good evening!
¡Hola!	Hello!
Hola, ¿qué tal?	Hi!
Me llamo Chris.	My name is Chris.
¿Cómo está(n) usted(es)/estás? ¿Cómo le(s)/te va?	How are you?
¿Qué hay? ¿Qué tal? ¿Cómo te va?	How are you?
Bien, gracias, ¿y usted(es)/tú?	Fine, thanks! And you?
¡Adiós!	Goodbye!
¡Hasta luego!	Bye! See you later!
¡Hasta mañana!	Until tomorrow/Goodnight!
¡Que te lo pases/os lo paséis bien!	Enjoy yourself!/Have fun!
¡Buenas noches!	Goodnight!
Salude(n)/Saluda a la señora Gómez de mi parte.	Say hello to Ms Gómez for me.

Citas

Appointments

¿Le(s)/Te puedo invitar a comer?	May I invite you to a meal?
¿Tiene(n)/Tienes/Tenéis algo planeado para mañana?	Do you already have plans for tomorrow?
¿A qué hora quedamos?	When are we meeting?
¿Le(s)/Te/Os puedo pasar a recoger?	Can I pick you up?
Nos encontramos a las nueve delante del cine.	Let's meet in front of the cinema at nine o'clock.

Por favor y gracias

Please and Thank-You Expressions

Sí, gracias.	Yes, please.
No, gracias.	No, thanks.
¡Gracias!	Thank you!
¡Gracias, igualmente!	Thanks, same to you!
¿Me podría ayudar?	Can you help me please?
Gracias. De nada.	My pleasure!
Muchas gracias.	Many thanks!
No es nada.	It's not worth mentioning.

Pedir perdón, expresiones de lamento

Apologies, Regrets

¡Perdón!	Excuse me!
Debo disculparme.	I must apologise!
Lo siento mucho.	I am very sorry!
No era esa mi intención.	I did not mean it like that!
¡Qué lástima!	Pity!
¡Qué pena!	That is sad!

Felicitaciones en distintas ocasiones

Wishes and congratulations

¡Felicidades!	Congratulations!
¡Mucha suerte!	Good luck!
¡Que se mejore/te mejores pronto!	Get well soon!
¡Que pase(s)/paséis unas buenas vacaciones!	Have a great holiday!
¡Felices Pascuas!	Happy Easter!
¡Feliz Navidad y próspero Año Nuevo!	Merry Christmas and a Happy New Year!
¡Feliz cumpleaños!	Happy birthday!
Te deseo mucha suerte.	I'll keep my fingers crossed for you.

Preguntar por el camino, por la dirección

Asking Directions

Perdone, ¿cómo puedo ir a...?	Excuse me, how do I get to ...?
¿Me podría decir cómo puedo ir a...?	Can you tell me, how I get to the ...?
Todo recto hasta...	Straight ahead until ...
Cuando llegue al semáforo gire a la derecha.	Turn right at the traffic lights.
Siga las indicaciones.	Follow the signs.
No se puede perder.	You cannot miss it.
¿Qué autobús va a...?	Which bus goes to ...?
¿Es este el autobús que va a...?	Is this the right bus to ...?
¿Está muy lejos?	How far is it?
Por aquí no es.	You are at the wrong place.
Debe(n) volver hasta...	You need to go back to ...

En el restaurante

In a Restaurant

Quisiera reservar una mesa para cuatro personas.	I would like to reserve a table for four people.
Una mesa para dos, por favor.	A table for two, please.
¿Está libre esta mesa/este asiento?	Is this table/place free?
Tomaré...	I will take ...
¿Nos podría traer un poco más de pan?	Could we have some more bread please?
La cuenta, por favor.	I'd like to pay.
Todo junto.	All together please.
Cuentas separadas, por favor.	Seperate bills please.

De compras

Shopping

¿Dónde puedo encontrar...?	Where can I find ...?
Me podría recomendar una tienda de repostería/ de alimentación?	Can you recommend a delicatessen/food-store?
¿Le atienden?	Are you beeing served?
Gracias, solo quiero mirar.	Thanks, I'm just looking around.
¿Qué desea?	What would you like?
Póngame, por favor...	Could I please have ...
Quisiera...	I would like ...
¿Algo más?	Would you like anything else?
¿Aceptan tarjetas de crédito?	Do you accept credit cards?
¿Me lo puede envolver?	Could you wrap it up for me?

En el banco

	At the Bank
Quisiera cambiar 50 euros en dólares.	I would like to exchange 50 euros into dollars.
Quisiera cobrar este cheque de viaje.	I would like to cash this travellers cheque.
¿Cuál es importe máximo al que puedo extender el talón?	What is the maximum limit on the cheque?
Quisiera sacar 200 euros de mi cuenta.	I would like to withdraw 200 euros from my account.
¿Me enseña su carnet, por favor?	My I see your ID?
Firme, por favor.	Your signature please!

En Correos

	At the Post Office
¿Dónde está el buzón más cercano/la oficina de correos más cercana?	Where is the nearest postbox/postoffice?
¿Cuánto vale una carta para España?	How much is a letter to Spain?
Tres sellos de 1 euro, por favor	Three 1 euro stamps please.
Quisiera enviar un telegrama.	I would like to send a telegram.
Quisiera una tarjeta telefónica.	I would like a telephone card.
¿Puedo enviar desde aquí un fax a Londres?	Can I send a fax to London from here?

Llamar por teléfono

	Making a Phone Call
¿Dónde está la cabina de teléfonos más cerca?	Where is the nearest telephone box?
¿Cuál es el prefijo de España?	What's the international dialling code for Spain?
Quisiera hacer una llamada a cobro revertido.	I would like to make a reverse-charge call.
¿Sí?, ¿con quién hablo?	Hello, who's speaking?
Quisiera hablar con la señora Clear.	May I please speak to Ms Clear?
Le pongo.	Connecting now!
Espere, no cuelge.	Please hold the line.
Lo siento pero no está.	I am sorry, she is not here.
¿Quiere dejar un mensaje?	Would you like to leave a message?
Volveré a llamar más tarde.	I'll call again later.
Este abonado ha cambiado de número.	The number you have called has not been recognised.

A

A, a [eɪ] n 1. (letter) A, a f; ~ **for Andrew** Brit, ~ **for Abel** Am A de Antonio; **to get from** ~ **to B** ir de un lugar a otro; **from** ~ **to Z** de cabo a rabo 2. MUS (note) la m 3. SCHOOL ≈ sobresaliente m 4. Brit SCHOOL ~ **level** ≈ bachillerato m

a [ə, stressed: eɪ] indef art before consonant, **an** [ən, stressed: æn] before vowel 1. (in general) un, una; ~ **car** un coche; ~ **house** una casa; **in** ~ **day or two** en unos días 2. (not translated) **do you have** ~ **car?** ¿tienes coche?; **he is an Englishman** es inglés; **she is** ~ **teacher** es maestra; **a hundred days** cien días 3. (to express prices, rates) **£2** ~ **dozen** 2 libras la docena; **£6** ~ **week** 6 libras por semana 4. (before person's name) ~ **Mr Robinson** un tal Sr. Robinson

A n abbr of **answer** R

AA [ˌeɪˈeɪ] 1. abbr of **Alcoholics Anonymous** AA 2. Brit AUTO abbr of **Automobile Association** ≈ RACE m

AAA 1. Brit abbr of **Amateur Athletics Association** federación británica de atletismo aficionado 2. Am AUTO abbr of **American Automobile Association** ≈ RACE m

AB Am abbr of **Artium Baccalaureus** 1. (person) ldo., -a. m, f en Letras 2. (degree) licenciatura f en Letras

aback [əˈbæk] adv **to take sb** ~ coger a alguien de improviso; **to be taken** ~ (**by sth**) quedarse desconcertado (por algo)

abacus [ˈæbəkəs] n ábaco m

abandon [əˈbændən] I. vt 1. (vehicle, place, person) abandonar, dejar; **to** ~ **ship** evacuar el barco; **to** ~ **sb to his/her fate** abandonar a alguien a su suerte 2. (give up: plan) renunciar a; (game) suspender 3. (lose self-control) **to** ~ **oneself to sth** entregarse a algo II. n no pl abandono m; **with** (**wild**) ~ con desenfreno

abandoned [əˈbændənd] adj 1. (place, vehicle) abandonado, -a 2. (person) desamparado, -a

abashed [əˈbæʃt] adj avergonzado, -a; **to be** ~ **at sth** avergonzarse de algo

abate [əˈbeɪt] vi 1. (noise, anger) disminuir 2. (wind) amainar

abatement n no pl disminución f

abattoir [ˈæbətwɑːʳ, Am: -twɑːr] n matadero m

abbess [ˈæbes, Am: -əs] n REL abadesa f

abbey [ˈæbi] n abadía f

abbot [ˈæbət] n REL abad m

abbreviate [əˈbriːvɪeɪt] vt abreviar

abbreviation [əˌbriːvɪˈeɪʃən] n abreviatura f

ABC¹ [ˌeɪbiːˈsiː] n Am: pl 1. (alphabet) abecedario m 2. (rudiments) abecé m, nociones fpl básicas

ABC² [ˌeɪbiːˈsiː] n 1. Aus TV abbr of **Australian Broadcasting Corporation** compañía australiana de radiotelevisión 2. Am TV abbr of **American Broadcasting Company** compa-

ñía estadounidense de radiotelevisión

abdicate [ˈæbdɪkeɪt] I. vi abdicar II. vt (right) renunciar a; (throne) abdicar (de)

abdication [ˌæbdɪˈkeɪʃən] n no pl 1. (of right) renuncia f 2. (of throne) abdicación f

abdomen [ˈæbdəmən] n abdomen m

abdominal [æbˈdɒmɪnl, Am: -ˈdɑːmə-] adj abdominal

abduct [æbˈdʌkt] vt secuestrar, plagiar AmL

abduction [æbˈdʌkʃən] n secuestro m, plagio m AmL

aberration [ˌæbəˈreɪʃən] n aberración f

abet [əˈbet] <-tt-> vt instigar, incitar; **to aid and** ~ **sb** ser cómplice de alguien

abeyance [əˈbeɪəns] n no pl **to fall into** ~ caer en desuso

abhor [əbˈhɔːʳ, Am: æbˈhɔːr] <-rr-> vt aborrecer

abhorrence [əbˈhɒrəns, Am: æbˈhɔːr-] n no pl aborrecimiento m

abhorrent adj aborrecible

abide [əˈbaɪd] <-d o abode, -d o abode> vt soportar; **I can't** ~ **her** no la soporto
◆**abide by** vt 1. (rule, decision) atenerse a 2. (promise) cumplir

abiding adj duradero, -a

ability [əˈbɪləti, Am: -əti] <-ies> n 1. no pl (capability) capacidad f; **to the best of one's** ~ lo mejor que uno pueda 2. no pl (talent) aptitud f 3. pl (skills) dotes fpl

abject [ˈæbdʒekt] adj 1. (wretched) abyecto, -a 2. (absolute: poverty, failure) absoluto, -a

ablaze [əˈbleɪz] adj en llamas; fig resplandeciente

able [ˈeɪbl] adj 1. (capable: person) capaz; **to be** ~ **to do sth** (have ability, manage) poder hacer algo; (have knowledge) saber hacer algo 2. (piece of work) logrado, -a

able-bodied [ˌeɪblˈbɒdɪd, Am: -ˈbɑːdɪd] adj sano, -a y fuerte; ~ **seaman** marinero m de primera

ABM n abbr of **anti-ballistic missile** misil m antibalístico

abnormal [æbˈnɔːml, Am: -ˈnɔːr-] adj 1. (feature) anómalo, -a 2. (person) anormal

abnormality [ˌæbnəˈmælɪti, Am: -nɔːrˈmæləti] <-ies> n 1. (abnormal feature) anomalía f 2. no pl (unusualness) anormalidad f

aboard [əˈbɔːd, Am: əˈbɔːrd] I. adv a bordo; **all** ~! ¡pasajeros a bordo! II. prep a bordo de; **to go** ~ **a boat** subir a una barca; **to go** ~ **plane** embarcar en el avión, subir al avión

abode [əˈbəʊd, Am: əˈboʊd] I. pt, pp of **abide** II. n form domicilio m; **of no fixed** ~ sin domicilio fijo

abolish [əˈbɒlɪʃ, Am: -ɑːl-] vt abolir

abolition [əbəˈlɪʃən] n no pl abolición f

abominable [əˈbɒmɪnəbl, Am: əˈbɑːm-] adj abominable

abominate [əˈbɒmɪneɪt, Am: əˈbɑːm-] vt abominar (de)

abomination [əˌbɒmɪˈneɪʃən, Am:

ə'bɑ:m-] *n* **1.**(*abominable thing*) abominación *f* **2.**(*disgust*) aversión *f*
aboriginal [ˌæbəˈrɪdʒənl] **I.** *adj* aborigen **II.** *n* aborigen *mf*(de Australia)
Aborigine [ˌæbəˈrɪdʒɪni] *n* aborigen *mf*(de Australia)
abort [əˈbɔ:t, *Am:* əˈbɔrt] **I.** *vt* **1.**MED abortar **2.** *a.* INFOR abandonar **II.** *vi* **1.**MED abortar **2.**(*fail*) fracasar
abortion [əˈbɔ:ʃən, *Am:*əˈbɔr-] *n* MED aborto *m* (provocado); **to have an** ~ abortar, tener un aborto
abortive [əˈbɔ:tɪv, *Am:* əˈbɔːrt̬ɪv] *adj* malogrado, -a
abound [əˈbaʊnd] *vi* abundar
about [əˈbaʊt] **I.** *prep* **1.**(*on subject of*) sobre, acerca de; **a book** ~ **football** un libro sobre fútbol; **what is the film** ~? ¿de qué trata la película?; **to talk** ~ **cinema** hablar sobre cine; **while he is** ~ **it** *Brit, inf* mientras esté haciendo eso **2.**(*surrounding*) alrededor de; **the garden** ~ **the house** el jardín alrededor de la casa **3.**(*in and through*) por; **to go** ~ **a place** andar por un lugar **4.**(*characteristic of*) **that's what I like** ~ **him** eso es lo que me gusta de él **5.** *Brit* (*with*) **I have no money** ~ **me** no llevo dinero encima ►**how** ~ **that!** ¡vaya!; **what** ~ **it?** (*suggestion*) ¿quieres/queréis?; (*so what?*) ¿y qué?; **what** ~ **a drink?** ¿qué tal si tomamos algo? **II.** *adv* **1.**(*around*) **all** ~ por todas partes; **to leave things lying** ~ **somewhere** dejar cosas tiradas por un sitio; **to be the other way** ~ ser exactamente al revés; **is Paul** ~? ¿está Paul por ahí? **2.**(*approximately*) aproximadamente; ~ **my size** más o menos de mi tamaño; **round** ~ **5 km** cerca de 5 kilómetros; ~ **here** más o menos aquí; ~ **5 years ago** hace unos cinco años; ~ **twenty** unos veinte; **to be somewhere** ~ estar por aquí; **to have had just** ~ **enough of sth** estar harto de algo; **that's** ~ **it for today** eso es todo por hoy **3.**(*almost*) casi; **to be** (**just**) ~ **ready** estar casi listo **4.**(*willing to*) **not to be** ~ **to do sth** no estar dispuesto a hacer algo **5.**(*on the point of*) **to be** ~ **to do sth** estar a punto de hacer algo
about-face [əˈbaʊtfeɪs] *n Am, Aus,* **about--turn** [əˈbaʊttɜːn, *Am:* -tɜːrn] *n Aus, Brit* **1.**MIL media vuelta *f* **2.**(*opinion*) cambio *m* drástico de opinión; (*position*) cambio *m* drástico de postura
above [əˈbʌv] **I.** *prep* **1.**(*on the top of*) encima de **2.**(*over*) sobre; ~ **suspicion** por encima de toda sospecha **3.**(*greater than, superior to*) por encima de; ~ **3** más de 3; **those** ~ **the age of 70** los mayores de 70 años; **he is not** ~ **lying** es muy capaz de mentir; ~ **all** sobre todo; **to shout** ~ **the noise** tener que gritar porque hay ruido; **it's** ~ **me** no lo entiendo **4.**GEO (*upstream*) más arriba de; (*north of*) al norte de **II.** *adv* encima, arriba; **the floor** ~ la planta de arriba; **up** ~ **sth** por encima de algo; **up** ~ **in the sky** arriba en el

cielo; **from** ~ de las alturas; **see** ~ (*in text*) véase más arriba **III.** *adj* susodicho, -a **IV.** *n* **the** ~ **lo** antedicho
aboveboard *adj* legítimo, -a
above-mentioned *adj* anteriormente mencionado, -a
abrasion [əˈbreɪʒən] *n* MED abrasión *f*
abrasive [əˈbreɪsɪv] **I.** *adj* **1.**(*rough*) abrasivo, -a **2.**(*manner*) agresivo, -a **II.** *n* abrasivo *m*
abreast [əˈbrest] *adv* **1.**(*side by side*) **two/three** ~ en fila de a dos/tres **2.**(*up to date*) **to be/keep** ~ **of sth** estar/mantenerse al corriente de algo
abridge [əˈbrɪdʒ] *vt* abreviar; **an** ~**d version** una versión abreviada
abridgement *n,* **abridgment** [əˈbrɪdʒmənt] *n* **1.**(*version*) compendio *m* **2.** *no pl* (*action*) abreviación *f*
abroad [əˈbrɔːd, *Am:* əˈbrɑːd] *adv* **1.**(*in foreign country*) en el extranjero; **from** ~ del extranjero; **to be** ~ estar en el extranjero; **to go** ~ ir al extranjero; **at home and** ~ dentro y fuera del país **2.** *form* (*outside*) fuera; **the news quickly spread** ~ la noticia se divulgó rápidamente
abrupt [əˈbrʌpt] *adj* **1.**(*sudden*) repentino, -a; (*change*) brusco, -a; (*end*) inesperado, -a **2.**(*brusque*) brusco, -a **3.**(*steep*) abrupto, -a
ABS [ˌeɪbiːˈes] *n abbr of* **anti-lock braking system** ABS *m*
abscess [ˈæbses] *n* absceso *m*
abscond [əbˈskɒnd, *Am:* -ˈskɑːnd] *vi* fugarse; **to** ~ **with sb/sth** fugarse con alguien/algo
abseil [ˈæbseɪl] *vi Aus, Brit* hacer rappel
absence [ˈæbsəns] *n no pl* **1.**(*of person, thing*) ausencia *f*; **in the** ~ **of** en ausencia de; **on leave of** ~ MIL de permiso **2.**(*of money, information*) carencia *f*; **in the** ~ **of** a falta de ►~ **makes the** <u>heart</u> **grow fonder** *prov* la ausencia es al amor lo que el fuego al aire: que apaga al pequeño y aviva el grande *prov*
absent¹ [ˈæbsənt] *adj* **1.**(*not present*) ausente; ~ **without leave** MIL ausente sin permiso **2.**(*lacking*) que falta; **to be** ~ **in sth** no estar presente en algo **3.**(*distracted*) ausente, distraído, -a
absent² [əbˈsent] *vt form* **to** ~ **oneself** (**from sth**) ausentarse (de algo)
absentee [ˌæbsənˈtiː] *n* ausente *mf*
absenteeism *n no pl* absentismo *m*
absentee landlord *n* propietario, -a *m, f* absentista (*que apenas reside en su propiedad*) **absentee voting** *n Am* voto *m* por correo
absent-minded [ˌæbsəntˈmaɪndɪd] *adj* despistado, -a, volado, -a *AmL*
absolute [ˈæbsəluːt] **I.** *adj* **1.**(*total, not relative*) *a.* POL absoluto, -a; (*denial*) rotundo, -a; (*trust, power, confidence*) pleno, -a; (*disaster*) absoluto, -a, completo, -a **2.**CHEM puro, -a **II.** *n* **the** ~ PHILOS lo absoluto

absolutely adv 1. (comprehensively) absolutamente; ~! inf ¡claro que sí!; ~ **not!** ¡de ninguna manera! 2. (very) totalmente

absolution [ˌæbsə'luːʃən] n no pl REL absolución f

absolutism ['æbsəluːtɪzəm, Am: -səluːt̬-] n no pl POL absolutismo m

absolve [əb'zɒlv, Am: -'zɑːlv] vt absolver

absorb [əb'sɔːb, Am: -'sɔːrb] vt 1. (liquid) absorber; (shock) amortiguar 2. (understand) asimilar 3. (engross) ocupar; **to get ~ed in sth** estar completamente absorbido por algo; **to be ~ed in one's thoughts** estar abstraído [o absorto] en sus pensamientos

absorbent [əb'sɔːbənt, Am: -'sɔːrb-] adj absorbente

absorbing adj (book, story) absorvente, apasionante

absorption [əb'sɔːpʃən] n no pl 1. (of liquid) absorción f 2. (in book, story) concentración f 3. (in work) dedicación f absoluta

abstain [əb'steɪn] vi a. POL abstenerse; **to ~ from (doing) sth** abstenerse de (hacer) algo

abstemious [əb'stiːmɪəs] adj mesurado, -a, comedido, -a

abstention [əb'stenʃən] n no pl a. POL abstención f

abstinence ['æbstɪnəns] n no pl abstinencia f

abstract¹ ['æbstrækt] I. adj abstracto, -a; ~ **art/painting** arte abstracto/pintura abstracta II. n 1. (not concrete) abstracto m; **in the ~** en abstracto 2. (summary) extracto m

abstract² [əb'strækt] vt 1. a. CHEM extraer 2. (summarize) resumir 3. (steal) robar

abstracted [æb'stræktɪd] adj distraído, -a

abstraction [əb'strækʃən] n 1. (abstract concept) abstracción f 2. no pl (abstracted state) distracción f

abstruse [əb'struːs] adj abstruso, -a

absurd [əb'sɜːd, Am: -'sɜːrd] adj absurdo, -a

absurdity [əb'sɜːrdəti, Am: -'sɜːrdət̬i] <-ies> n 1. no pl (absurd state) absurdo m; (of idea, situation) ridiculez f 2. (absurd thing) disparate m, candinga f Chile

abundance [ə'bʌndəns] n no pl abundancia f

abundant [ə'bʌndənt] adj abundante

abuse¹ [ə'bjuːs] n 1. no pl (insults) insultos mpl, insultadas fpl AmL; **to hurl ~ at sb** lanzar improperios a alguien 2. no pl (mistreatment) maltrato m 3. no pl (misuse) abuso m; **sexual ~** abuso sexual 4. (infringement) infracción f; **~ of human rights** violación de los derechos humanos

abuse² [ə'bjuːz] vt 1. (insult) insultar 2. (mistreat) maltratar 3. (sexually) abusar de 4. (misuse) abusar de 5. (infringe) infringir

abusive [ə'bjuːsɪv] adj 1. (language) insultante, ofensivo, -a 2. (person) agresivo, -a

abut [ə'bʌt] <-tt-> I. vt lindar con II. vi **to ~ on** lindar con

abysmal [ə'bɪzməl] adj pésimo, -a

abyss [ə'bɪs] n a. fig abismo m

AC [ˌeɪ'siː] n abbr of **alternating current** CA f

a/c [ˌeɪ'siː] abbr of **account** c/, cta.

academic [ˌækə'demɪk] I. adj 1. UNIV académico, -a; SCHOOL escolar 2. (intellectual) erudito, -a 3. (theoretical) teórico, -a; (argument) especulativo 4. (irrelevant) irrelevante II. n académico, -a m, f

academy [ə'kædəmi] <-ies> n 1. (training school) academia f 2. Am, Scot (school) instituto m (de enseñanza secundaria) 3. CINE **the Academy Awards** los Óscars

ACAS ['eɪˌkæs] n Brit abbr of **Advisory, Conciliation and Arbitration Service** Instituto m de Mediación, Arbitraje y Conciliación

accede [æk'siːd] vi 1. (agree) **to ~ to sth** acceder a algo 2. (to a position) acceder a; **to ~ to the throne** subir al trono

accelerate [ək'seləreɪt] I. vi (car) acelerar; (growth) acelerarse II. vt acelerar

acceleration [əkˌselə'reɪʃən] n no pl aceleración f

accelerator [ək'seləreɪtə', Am: -eɪt̬ɚ] n 1. (in vehicle) acelerador m, chancleta f Ven, Col 2. a. PHYS acelerador m

accent¹ ['æksənt, Am: -sent] n 1. LING acento m 2. LIT, MUS énfasis m inv

accent² [æk'sent] vt 1. LIT, MUS acentuar 2. (emphasize) enfatizar

accentuate [ək'sentʃʊeɪt] vt acentuar

accept [ək'sept] I. vt 1. (take when offered) aceptar 2. (approve) aprobar 3. (believe) creer en 4. (acknowledge) reconocer 5. (include socially) acoger, dar acogida a II. vi aceptar

acceptable adj (behaviour, suggestion) aceptable; (explanation) admisible

acceptance [ək'septəns] n 1. no pl (of gift, help) aceptación f 2. (approval) aprobación f

accepted adj aceptado, -a; **the ~ procedure** el procedimiento habitual

access ['ækses] I. n no pl entrada f, aproches mpl AmL; a. INFOR acceso m; ~ **privileges** INFOR autorización de acceso; ~ **road** vía f de acceso; **Internet ~** INFOR acceso a Internet; **to gain ~ to sth** acceder a algo; **to have ~ to sth** tener acceso a algo; **easy/difficult of ~** asequible/inasequible II. vt INFOR entrar en, acceder a

accessibility [ækˌsesə'bɪləti, Am: -ət̬i] n no pl 1. accesibilidad f 2. fig carácter m accesible

accessible [ək'sesəbl] adj 1. (place, work of art) accesible 2. (person) tratable, accesible

accession [æk'seʃən] n no pl ascenso m

accessory [ək'sesəri] <-ies> n 1. (for outfit) complemento m, accesorio m 2. (for machine, toy) accesorio m 3. LAW cómplice mf

accident ['æksɪdənt] n accidente m; ~ **insurance** seguro m contra accidentes; **by ~** (accidentally) sin querer; (by chance) por casualidad; **more by ~ than by design** más por casualidad que por otra cosa; **~s will happen** son cosas que pasan

accidental [ˌæksɪ'dentəl, Am: -t̬əl] adj

1. (*unintentional*) casual, accidental; LAW (*death*) accidental **2.** (*discovery*) fortuito, -a

acclaim [ə'kleɪm] **I.** *vt* aclamar; **to ~ sb king** proclamar a alguien rey; **critically ~ed** elogiado por la crítica **II.** *n no pl* aclamación *f*

acclamation [ˌæklə'meɪʃən] *n no pl* aclamación *f*

acclimate ['æklɪmeɪt, *Am:* -lə-] *vt, vi Am s.* **acclimatize**

acclimation [ˌæklaɪ'meɪʃən] *n Am,* **acclimatization** [əˌklaɪmətaɪ'zeɪʃən, *Am:* -mətə'zeɪʃən] *n no pl* aclimatación *f*

acclimatize [ə'klaɪmətaɪz] **I.** *vi* aclimatarse **II.** *vt* aclimatar

accolade ['ækəleɪd] *n* elogio *m*

accommodate [ə'kɒmədeɪt, *Am:* -'kɑ:-] *vt* **1.** (*give place to stay*) alojar, hospedar; (*have room for*) albergar, alojar **2.** *form* (*adapt*) adaptar, acomodar; **to ~ oneself to sth** adaptarse a algo **3.** (*satisfy*) complacer

accommodating [ə'kɒmədeɪtɪŋ, *Am:* ə'kɑ:mədeɪʧɪŋ] *adj* servicial

accommodation [əˌkɒmə'deɪʃən, *Am:* -kɑ:-] *n* **1.** *no pl, Aus, Brit* (*place to stay*) alojamiento *m* **2.** *pl, Am* (*lodgings*) alojamiento *m* **3.** (*on vehicle, plane*) asientos *mpl* **4.** *form* (*compromise*) acuerdo *m*

accompaniment [ə'kʌmpənɪmənt] *n a.* MUS acompañamiento *m*

accompanist [ə'kʌmpənɪst] *n* MUS acompañante *mf*

accompany [ə'kʌmpəni] <-ie-> *vt a.* MUS (*go with*) acompañar; **to ~ sb on the violin** acompañar a alguien al violín

accomplice [ə'kʌmplɪs, *Am:* -'kɑ:m-] *n* cómplice *mf*

accomplish [ə'kʌmplɪʃ, *Am:* -'kɑ:m-] *vt* **1.** (*achieve*) efectuar **2.** (*finish*) concluir; **to ~ a task** realizar una tarea

accomplished [ə'kʌmplɪʃt, *Am:* -'kɑ:m-] *adj* consumado, -a

accomplishment *n* **1.** (*achievement*) logro *m* **2.** *no pl* (*completion*) conclusión *f*; **~ of a task** realización *f* de una tarea **3.** (*skill*) talento *m*

accord [ə'kɔ:d, *Am:* -'kɔ:rd] **I.** *n* **1.** (*treaty*) convenio *m* **2.** *no pl* (*agreement, harmony*) acuerdo *m*; **with one ~** de común acuerdo; **of one's own ~** espontáneamente; **to be in ~ with** estar de acuerdo con **II.** *vt form* conceder **III.** *vi* **to ~ with sth** concordar con algo

accordance [ə'kɔ:dəns, *Am:* -'kɔ:rd-] *prep* **in ~ with** de conformidad con, conforme a

accordingly *adv* **1.** (*appropriately*) como corresponde **2.** (*therefore*) por consiguiente

according to [ə'kɔ:dɪŋ tʊ, *Am:* ə'kɔ:rdɪŋ tə] *prep* **1.** (*as told by*) según; **~ her/what I read** según ella/lo que leí; **to go ~ plan** salir según lo previsto **2.** (*as basis*) con arreglo a; **~ the law** con arreglo a la ley; **~ the recipe** según la receta

accordion [ə'kɔ:dɪən, *Am:* -'kɔ:rd-] *n* acordeón *m*, filarmónica *f Méx*

accost [ə'kɒst, *Am:* -'kɑ:st] *vt form* abordar

account [ə'kaʊnt] **I.** *n* **1.** (*with bank*) cuenta *f* **2.** (*bill*) factura *f*; **to settle an ~** liquidar una cuenta **3.** *pl* (*financial records*) cuentas *fpl*; **to keep ~s** llevar las cuentas; **to keep an ~ of sth** llevar la cuenta de algo **4.** (*customer*) cliente *mf* **5.** (*description*) relato *m*; **an ~ of sth** un relato [*o* una relación] de algo; **to give an ~ of sth** informar sobre algo; **by all ~s** decir de todos; **by her own ~** según ella misma **6.** *no pl* (*consideration*) **to take sth into ~** tomar [*o* tener] algo en cuenta; **to take no ~ of sth** no tomar [*o* tener] en cuenta algo, no hacer caso de; **on ~ of sth** por causa de algo; **on no ~** de ninguna manera **7.** *no pl, form* (*importance*) **of little/no ~** de poca/ninguna importancia **8.** *no pl* (*responsibility*) responsabilidad *f*; **on one's own ~** por cuenta propia; **on sb's ~** a cuenta de alguien ▶ **to give a good ~ of oneself** lucirse; **to be called to ~ (for sth)** tener que rendir cuentas (de algo); **to settle ~s with sb** ajustar cuentas con alguien; **to turn sth to ~** sacar provecho de algo **II.** *vt form* considerar

◆**account for** *vt* **1.** (*explain*) explicar **2.** (*constitute*) representar

accountability [əˌkaʊntə'bɪlɪti, *Am:* -kaʊntə'bɪləţi] *n no pl* responsabilidad *f*

accountable [ə'kaʊntəbl, *Am:* -ţə-] *adj* responsable

accountancy [ə'kaʊntənsi, *Am:* -'kaʊntɲsi] *n no pl* contabilidad *f*

accountant [ə'kaʊntənt] *n* contable *mf*, contador(a) *m(f) And*

account(s) book *n* libro *m* de contabilidad [*o* de cuentas]

accredit [ə'kredɪt] *vt* **1.** (*recognize*) certificar **2.** POL acreditar **3.** (*credit*) atribuir

accrue [ə'kru:] *vi* **1.** **to ~ to sb** corresponder a alguien; **to ~ from** proceder de **2.** (*increase*) aumentar; (*interés*) acumularse

accumulate [ə'kju:mjʊleɪt] **I.** *vt* acumular **II.** *vi* acumularse

accumulation [əˌkju:mjʊ'leɪʃən] *n* **1.** *no pl* (*process*) acumulación *f* **2.** (*quantity*) cúmulo *m*, montón *m*

accumulator [ə'kju:mjʊleɪtə'] *n Aus, Brit* ELEC acumulador *m*

accuracy ['ækjərəsi, *Am:* -jəˈəsi] *n no pl* precisión *f*, exactitud *f*

accurate ['ækjərət, *Am:* -jəˈət] *adj* **1.** (*on target*) certero, -a **2.** (*correct*) preciso, -a, exacto, -a

accusation [ˌækju:'zeɪʃən] *n* acusación *f*

accusative [ə'kju:zətɪv, *Am:* -ţɪv] **I.** *n* acusativo *m* **II.** *adj* acusativo, -a

accusatory [ækju:'zeɪtəri, *Am:* ə'kju:zətɔ:ri] *adj form* acusador(a)

accuse [ə'kju:z] *vt* acusar; **she stands ~d of ...** se la acusa de...

accused [ə'kju:zd] *n* **the ~** el acusado, la acusada

accustom [ə'kʌstəm] *vt* acostumbrar

accustomed [ə'kʌstəmd] *adj* 1. (*used*) acostumbrado, -a; **to be ~ to doing sth** estar acostumbrado a hacer algo; **to grow ~ to doing sth** acostumbrarse a hacer algo 2. (*usual*) usual

AC/DC [ˌeɪsiː'diːsiː] *n* ELEC *abbr of* **alternating current/direct current** corriente *f* alterna/corriente *f* continua

ace [eɪs] I. *n* 1. (*playing card*) as *m* 2. *inf* (*expert*) as *m*, experto, -a *m*, *f* ►**to come within an ~ of doing sth** estar a punto de hacer algo II. *adj* 1. *inf* (*expert*) experto, -a 2. *inf* (*excellent*) genial; **~!** ¡genial!, ¡estupendo!

acetate ['æsɪteɪt] *n no pl* acetato *m*

acetic [ə'siːtɪk, *Am:* ə'siːt̬ɪk] *adj* acético, -a

acetylene [ə'setəliːn, *Am:* ə'set̬ə-] *n no pl* acetileno *m*

ache [eɪk] I. *n* dolor *m*; **~s and pains** dolores y achaques II. *vi* doler; **I am aching to see her again** me muero de ganas de volver a verla

achieve [ə'tʃiːv] *vt* (*aim, objective*) lograr; (*task*) llevar a cabo; (*victory*) conseguir; (*success*) alcanzar

achievement *n* 1. (*feat*) hazaña *f*; (*success*) éxito *m*, logro *m* 2. *no pl* (*achieving*) realización *f*

acid ['æsɪd] I. *n* 1. CHEM ácido *m* 2. *no pl, inf* (*LSD*) ácido *m* II. *adj* 1. CHEM ácido, -a 2. (*sarcastic*) mordaz

acid house *n* MUS música *f* acid

acidic [ə'sɪdɪk] *adj* ácido, -a

acidify [ə'sɪdɪfaɪ] <-ie-> I. *vt* acidificar II. *vi* acidificarse

acidity [ə'sɪdəti, *Am:* -ət̬i] *n no pl* 1. CHEM acidez *f* 2. *fig* mordacidad *f*

acid rain *n* lluvia *f* ácida **acid test** *n* prueba *f* de fuego

acknowledge [ək'nɒlɪdʒ, *Am:* -'nɑːlɪdʒ] *vt* 1. (*admit*) admitir; (*guilt*) confesar 2. (*recognize*) reconocer; (*letter*) acusar recibo de; (*favour*) agradecer

acknowledg(e)ment *n* 1. *no pl* (*admission*) admisión *f*; (*of guilt*) confesión *f* 2. *no pl* (*recognition*) reconocimiento *m* 3. (*reply*) acuse *m* de recibo 4. *pl* (*in book*) agradecimientos *mpl*

acne ['ækni] *n no pl* acné *m*

acorn ['eɪkɔːn, *Am:* -kɔrn] *n* bellota *f*

acoustic [ə'kuːstɪk] I. *adj* acústico, -a II. *npl* acústica *f*

acoustic coupler ['kʌplə^r] *n* acoplador *m* acústico **acoustic guitar** *n* guitarra *f* acústica **acoustic nerve** *n* ANAT nervio *m* auditivo

acquaint [ə'kweɪnt] *vt* 1. (*know*) **to be/become ~ed with sb** conocer a alguien 2. (*familiarize*) familiarizar; **to be ~ed with sth** estar al corriente de algo

acquaintance [ə'kweɪntəns] *n* 1. (*person*) conocido, -a *m*, *f* 2. *no pl* (*relationship*) relación *f*; **to make sb's ~** conocer a alguien 3. *no pl* (*knowledge*) conocimiento *m*

acquiesce [ˌækwɪ'es] *vi form* **to ~ in sth** estar conforme con algo

acquiescence [ˌækwɪ'esns] *n no pl, form* conformidad *f*, aquiescencia *f*

acquiescent [ˌækwɪ'esnt] *adj form* conforme, aquiescente

acquire [ə'kwaɪə^r, *Am:* -'kwaɪə-] *vt* adquirir

acquisition [ˌækwɪ'zɪʃən] *n* adquisición *f*

acquisitive [ə'kwɪzətɪv, *Am:* -ət̬ɪv] *adj* codicioso, -a

acquit [ə'kwɪt] <-tt-> *vt* 1. LAW absolver; **to ~ sb of a charge** absolver a alguien de una acusación 2. **to ~ oneself well/badly** salir bien/mal parado

acquittal [ə'kwɪtəl, *Am:* -'kwɪt̬-] *n no pl* absolución *f*

acre ['eɪkə^r, *Am:* 'eɪkə-] *n* acre *m*; **~s of space** *inf* un montón de espacio

acreage ['eɪkrədʒ] *n no pl* superficie (en acres) *f*

acrid ['ækrɪd] *adj* 1. (*smell, taste*) acre 2. *fig* áspero, -a

acrimonious [ˌækrɪ'məʊnɪəs, *Am:* -'moʊni-] *adj* (*remark*) mordaz; (*debate*) reñido, -a

acrimony ['ækrɪməni, *Am:* -moʊni] *n no pl, form* acrimonia *f*

acrobat ['ækrəbæt] *n* acróbata *mf*

acrobatic [ˌækrə'bætɪk, *Am:* -'bæt̬ɪk] *adj* acrobático, -a

acronym ['ækrəʊnɪm, *Am:* -rə-] *n* acrónimo *m*

across [ə'krɒs, *Am:* ə'krɑːs] I. *prep* 1. (*on other side of*) al otro lado de; **just ~ the street** justo al otro lado de la calle; **~ from sb/sth** enfrente de alguien/algo 2. (*from one side to other*) a través de; **to walk ~ the bridge** cruzar el puente andando; **the bridge ~ the river** el puente que cruza el río; **to go ~ the sea to France** ir a Francia cruzando el mar ►**~ the board** general, global II. *adv* de un lado a otro; **to run/swim ~** cruzar corriendo/a nado; **to be 2m ~** tener 2 m de ancho

act [ækt] I. *n* 1. (*action*) acto *m*; **~ of charity** obra *f* de caridad; **an ~ of God** LAW un caso de fuerza mayor; **the A~s of the Apostles** REL los Hechos de los Apóstoles; **to catch sb in the ~** coger a alguien con las manos en la masa 2. (*performance*) número *m*; **a hard ~ to follow** un número difícil de repetir 3. (*pretence*) fingimiento *m* 4. THEAT acto *m* 5. LAW ley *f* ►**to get one's ~ together** *inf* arreglárselas; **to get in on the ~** lograr tomar parte en el asunto II. *vi* 1. (*take action*) actuar; **to ~ for sb** representar a alguien 2. (*behave*) portarse 3. (*take effect*) dar resultados 4. THEAT actuar 5. (*pretend*) fingir III. *vt* THEAT representar; **to ~ the part of sb** hacer el papel de alguien; **to ~ the fool** hacer el tonto

◆**act on** *vt* obrar de acuerdo con

◆**act out** *vt* (*scene*) representar

◆**act up** *vi inf* 1. (*person*) hacer de las suyas 2. (*machine*) fallar, no funcionar

acting ['æktɪŋ] I. *adj* en funciones II. *n no pl*
THEAT arte *m* dramático

action ['ækʃən] *n* **1.** *no pl* (*activeness*) acción
f; **to be out of** ~ (*person*) estar inactivo;
(*machine*) no funcionar; **to put sth out of** ~
inutilizar algo; **to swing into** ~ ponerse en
marcha; **to take** ~ tomar medidas; **to take no**
~ no hacer nada **2.** *no pl* MIL acción *f;* **to see** ~
servir; **to go into** ~ entrar en combate; **killed
in** ~ muerto en acto de servicio **3.** (*mechanism*) mecanismo *m* **4.** (*motion*) movimiento
m **5.** LAW (*case*) demanda *f;* **civil** ~ demanda
civil; **to bring an** ~ **against sb** entablar una
demanda contra alguien **6.** *no pl, inf* (*exciting
events*) bullicio *m;* (*fun*) jarana *f* ► ~s **speak
louder than words** *prov* hechos son amores y
no buenas razones *prov,* obras son amores y no
buenas razones *prov*

action-packed *adj* de acción

action replay *n Brit* TV repetición *f*

activate ['æktɪveɪt] *vt a.* CHEM activar

active ['æktɪv] *adj* **1.** (*lively, not passive*)
activo, -a; **to be** ~ **in sth** participar en algo; **to
take an** ~ **part in sth** participar activamente
en algo **2.** (*energetic*) enérgico, -a

actively *adv* **1.** (*lively*) activamente **2.** (*energetically*) enérgicamente

activist ['æktɪvɪst] *n* POL activista *mf*

activity [æk'tɪvəti, *Am:* -ə̯ti] <-ies> *n* **1.** *no
pl* (*state*) actividad *f* **2.** *pl* (*pursuits*) actividades *fpl*

actor ['æktər, *Am:* -tə-] *n* actor *m*

actress ['æktrɪs] *n* actriz *f*

actual ['æktʃʊəl] *adj* **1.** (*real*) verdadero, -a;
in ~ **fact** en realidad **2.** (*precise*) exacto, -a;
what were her ~ **words?** ¿cuáles fueron sus
palabras exactas?

actually ['æktʃʊli] *adv* **1.** (*in fact*) en realidad
2. (*by the way*) ~ **I saw her yesterday** pues la
vi ayer

actuate ['æktʃʊeɪt] *vt* **1.** (*set going: mechanism*) accionar **2.** *form* (*motivate*) estimular

acumen ['ækjʊmən, *Am:* ə'kjuːmən] *n* perspicacia *f;* **business** ~ perspicacia para los negocios

acupuncture ['ækjʊpʌŋktʃər, *Am:* -tʃə-] *n
no pl* acupuntura *f*

acute [ə'kjuːt] I. *adj* **1.** (*serious*) agudo, -a;
(*anxiety*) extremo, -a; (*embarrassment*)
hondo, -a; (*difficulties*) grande; (*shortage*)
fuerte **2.** (*shrewd*) listo, -a **3.** MAT (*angle*)
agudo, -a II. *n* LING acento *m* agudo

acutely *adv* extremadamente; **to be** ~ **aware
of sth** ser plenamente consciente de algo

ad [æd] *n inf abbr of* **advertisement** anuncio
m

AD [ˌeɪ'diː] *abbr of* **anno Domini** d. (de) C.

adage ['ædɪdʒ] *n* refrán *m*

adagio [ə'dɑːdʒɪəʊ, *Am:* ə'dɑːdʒoʊ] I. *adv*
pausadamente II. *n* adagio *m*

Adam ['ædəm] *n* Adán *m* ► **not to** <u>know</u> **sb
from** ~ no conocer a alguien en absoluto

adamant ['ædəmənt] *adj* firme, categórico,
-a

Adam's apple *n* ANAT nuez *f,* bocado *m* de
Adán

adapt [ə'dæpt] I. *vt* adaptar; **to** ~ **oneself**
adaptarse II. *vi* adaptarse

adaptable *adj* adaptable

adaptation [ˌædæp'teɪʃən] *n* **1.** THEAT, MUS,
CINE, LIT adaptación *f,* versión *f* **2.** *no pl* (*act of
adapting*) adaptación *f*

adapter *n,* **adaptor** [ə'dæptər, *Am:*
ə'dæptə-] *n* ELEC adaptador *m;* (*for several
plugs*) ladrón *m*

add [æd] *vt* **1.** (*put with*) añadir, agregar *AmL*
2. (*say*) añadir, agregar **3.** MAT sumar

♦ **add up** I. *vi* sumar; **to** ~ **to ...** ascender
a...; **it doesn't** ~ **to much** *fig* no significa
mucho II. *vt* sumar

addendum [ə'dendəm] <-da> *n* adenda *f*

adder ['ædər, *Am:* 'ædə-] *n* víbora *f*

addict ['ædɪkt] *n* **1.** MED adicto, -a *m, f;* **drug**
~ drogadicto *m* **2.** *fig* partidario, -a *m, f;* **to be
a cinema** ~ ser un apasionado del cine

addicted [ə'dɪktɪd] *adj* adicto, -a; ~ **to drugs**
drogadicto, -a; **to be** ~ **to sth** ser adicto a algo;
fig ser muy aficionado a algo

addiction [ə'dɪkʃən] *n no pl* adicción *f;* **drug**
~ drogadicción *f*

addictive [ə'dɪktɪv] *adj* adictivo, -a

addition [ə'dɪʃən] *n* **1.** *no pl* MAT suma *f*
2. *no pl* (*act of adding*) adición *f;* **in** ~ además;
in ~ **to ...** además de... **3.** (*added thing*)
añadido *m,* añadidura *f;* **an** ~ **to the family**
uno más en la familia

additional [ə'dɪʃənl] *adj* adicional

additionally [ə'dɪʃənəli] *adv* por añadidura;
and ~ y además

additive ['ædɪtɪv, *Am:* -ə̯tɪv] *n* aditivo *m*

address [ə'dres, *Am:* 'ædres] I. *n* **1.** *a.* INFOR
dirección *f* **2.** (*speech*) discurso *m* **3.** (*title*)
form of ~ tratamiento *m* II. *vt* **1.** (*write
address on*) dirigir; **to be wrongly** ~**ed** llevar
la dirección equivocada **2.** (*speak to*) dirigirse a
3. (*use title*) **to** ~ **sb** (**as sth**) dar a alguien el
tratamiento (de algo) **4.** (*deal with*) abordar

addressee [ˌædre'siː] *n* destinatario, -a *m, f*

adenoids ['ædɪnɔɪdz, *Am:* 'ædnɔɪdz] *npl*
ANAT vegetaciones *fpl,* adenoides *fpl*

adept ['ædept, *Am:* ə'dept] *adj* experto, -a;
to be ~ **at sth** ser hábil para algo

adequacy ['ædɪkwəsi] *n no pl* **1.** (*being
enough*) suficiencia *f* **2.** (*being good enough*)
idoneidad *f*

adequate ['ædɪkwət] *adj* **1.** (*sufficient*) suficiente **2.** (*good enough*) adecuado, -a

adhere [əd'hɪər, *Am:* -'hɪr] *vi* **1.** *form* adherirse **2. to** ~ **to** (*rule*) observar; (*belief*) aferrarse a

adherence [əd'hɪərəns, *Am:* -'hɪrns] *n no pl*
(*to rule*) observancia *f;* (*to belief*) adhesión *f*

adherent [əd'hɪərənt] *n form* partidario, -a
m, f

adhesive [əd'hiːsɪv] I. *adj* adhesivo, -a II. *n
no pl* adhesivo *m*

ad hoc [ˌæd'hɒk, *Am:* -'hɑːk] *adj* ad hoc

adipose tissue ['ædɪpəʊs͵tɪʃuː, *Am:* -pəʊz͵tʃuː] *n* tejido *m* adiposo

adjacent [ə'dʒeɪsnt] *adj* contiguo, -a; MAT adyacente

adjectival [ˌædʒɪk'taɪvl] *adj* adjetivo, -a, adjetival

adjective ['ædʒɪktɪv] *n* adjetivo *m*

adjoin [ə'dʒɔɪn] I. *vt* lindar con II. *vi* colindar

adjoining *adj* colindante

adjourn [ə'dʒɜːn, *Am:* -'dʒɜːrn] I. *vt* aplazar, posponer II. *vi* 1. (*pause: meeting*) aplazarse 2. *form* (*go to*) **to ~ to another room** trasladarse a otra habitación

adjudicate [ə'dʒuːdɪkeɪt] I. *vt* juzgar II. *vi* actuar como árbitro

adjust [ə'dʒʌst] I. *vt* 1. a. TECH ajustar, regular 2. (*rearrange*) arreglar; **to ~ a seam** (*take it in*) meter el dobladillo; (*let it out*) sacar el dobladillo 3. (*change*) modificar 4. (*adapt*) adaptar II. *vi* adaptarse; **to ~ to sth** adaptarse a algo

adjustable *adj* ajustable

adjustable spanner *n* Aus, Brit llave *f* inglesa

adjustment *n* 1. (*mechanical*) ajuste *m* 2. (*mental*) adaptación *f*

adjutant ['ædʒʊtənt] *n* ayudante *mf*

ad-lib [ˌæd'lɪb] <-bb-> I. *adv* improvisando II. *vi, vt* improvisar

adman ['ædmæn] <-men> *n* ECON publicista *m*

admin ['ædmɪn] *abbr of* **administration** admón.

administer [əd'mɪnɪstə^r, *Am:* -stɚ] *vt* 1. a. POL (*manage: funds, estate*) administrar; **to ~ sth** estar al cargo de algo 2. (*dispense: punishment*) aplicar; (*medicine*) administrar; **to ~ aid** [*o* **relief**] **to sb** asistir a alguien; **to ~ first aid to sb** prestar primeros auxilios a alguien; **to ~ a severe blow to sb** dar un palo a alguien; **to ~ an oath** tomar juramento

administration [əd͵mɪnɪ'streɪʃən] *n* 1. *no pl* (*organization*) administración *f*; (*management*) gerencia *f*; **the ~** la dirección 2. *Am* (*time in power*) mandato *m* 3. POL gobierno *m* 4. *no pl* (*dispensing: of medicine*) administración *f*; **the ~ of an oath** la toma de un juramento

administrative [əd'mɪnɪstrətɪv] *adj* administrativo, -a

administrator [əd'mɪnɪstreɪtə^r, *Am:* -tɚ] *n* 1. (*of organization, institution*) administrador(a) *m(f)* 2. LAW albacea *mf*

admirable ['ædmərəbl] *adj* admirable

admiral ['ædmərəl] *n* almirante *m*

Admiralty ['ædmərəlti, *Am:* -t̬i] *n no pl*, Brit HIST Almirantazgo *m*

admiration [ˌædmə'reɪʃən] *n no pl* admiración *f*; **in ~** lleno de admiración

admire [əd'maɪə^r, *Am:* əd'maɪɚ] *vt* admirar; **to ~ sb for sth** admirar a alguien por algo; **to ~ sb from afar** embobarse con alguien desde lejos

admirer [əd'maɪərə^r, *Am:* -ɚ] *n* admirador(a) *m(f)*

admissible [əd'mɪsəbl] *adj* admisible

admission [əd'mɪʃən] *n* 1. *no pl* (*entry: to place, building*) entrada; (*to college, organization*) ingreso *m*, admisión *f* 2. (*entrance fee*) entrada *f* 3. (*acknowledgement*) confesión *f*; **by** [*o* **on**] **his own ~, ...** por confesión propia...

admit [əd'mɪt] <-tt-> I. *vt* 1. (*acknowledge: error*) reconocer; (*crime*) confesar; **to ~ that ...** reconocer que... 2. (*allow entrance to*) dejar entrar II. *vi* **to ~ to sth** confesarse culpable de algo

admittance [əd'mɪtns] *n no pl* entrada *f*; **to refuse sb ~** negar la entrada a alguien; **no ~** se prohíbe la entrada

admittedly [əd'mɪtɪdli, *Am:* -'mɪt̬ɪdli] *adv* **~, ...** es cierto que...

admonish [əd'mɒnɪʃ, *Am:* -'mɑːnɪʃ] *vt* amonestar

admonishment *n*, **admonition** [ˌædmə'nɪʃən] *n* amonestación *f*

ado [ə'duː] *n no pl* 1. (*commotion*) embrollo *m* 2. (*delay*) demora *f*; **without more** [*o* **further**] **~** sin más preámbulos ▸**much ~ about nothing** mucho ruido y pocas nueces

adolescence [ˌædə'lesns] *n no pl* adolescencia *f*

adolescent [ˌædə'lesnt] I. *adj* 1. (*relating to adolescence*) adolescente 2. (*immature*) inmaduro, -a II. *n* adolescente *mf*

adopt [ə'dɒpt, *Am:* -'dɑːpt] *vt* 1. (*child, strategy*) adoptar 2. (*candidate*) nombrar

adoption [ə'dɒpʃən, *Am:* -'dɑːp-] *n* 1. (*of child, strategy*) adopción *f* 2. (*of candidate*) nombramiento *m*

adorable [ə'dɔːrəbl] *adj* encantador(a); **just ~** irresistible

adoration [ˌædə'reɪʃən] *n no pl* adoración *f*; **the ~ of the Virgin Mary** REL el culto a la virgen María

adore [ə'dɔː^r, *Am:* -'dɔːr] *vt* 1. (*love strongly*) adorar 2. REL venerar

adoring [ə'dɔːrɪŋ] *adj* cariñoso, -a

adorn [ə'dɔːn, *Am:* -'dɔːrn] *vt form* adornar

adornment *n form* adorno *m*

adrenalin(e) [ə'drenəlɪn] *n no pl* adrenalina *f*

Adriatic [ˌeɪdri'ætɪk] *n* **the ~** (**Sea**) el (mar) Adriático

adrift [ə'drɪft] *adv* a la deriva; **to cut sth ~** cortar las amarras de algo; **to come** [*o* **go**] **~** Brit, *fig* fallar

adroit [ə'drɔɪt] *adj* mañoso, -a; (*mentally*) hábil; **to be ~ at sth** ser diestro en algo; **to be ~ at doing sth** ser habilidoso haciendo algo

adulation [ˌædjʊ'leɪʃən, *Am:* ˌædʒə-] *n no pl* adulación *f*

adult ['ædʌlt, *Am:* ə'dʌlt] I. *n* (*person*) adulto, -a *m, f*; (*animal*) animal *m* adulto II. *adj* 1. (*fully grown*) adulto, -a 2. (*mature*) maduro, -a; **let's try to be ~ about this problem** sea-

mos razonables con este problema **3.** (*explicit*) para adultos

adult education *n no pl* educación *f* para adultos

adulterate [ə'dʌltəreɪt, *Am:* -t̬əreɪt] *vt* adulterar

adulterer [ə'dʌltərə', *Am:* -t̬ə-ə-] *n* adúltero *m*

adulteress [ə'dʌltərɪs, *Am:* -t̬ə-] <-es> *n* adúltera *f*

adulterous [ə'dʌltərəs, *Am:* -t̬ə-] *adj* adúltero, -a

adultery [ə'dʌltəri, *Am:* -t̬ə-i] <-ies> *n no pl* adulterio *m;* **to commit** ~ cometer adulterio

adulthood ['ædʌlthʊd] *n* edad *f* adulta

advance [əd'vɑːns, *Am:* -'væːns] **I.** *vi* avanzar; **to** ~ **on sb/sth** avanzar hacia alguien/algo **II.** *vt* **1.** (*cause to move forward*) avanzar; (*interest, cause*) promover, fomentar **2.** (*pay in advance*) anticipar **III.** *n* **1.** (*forward movement*) avance *m*, progreso *m;* **in** ~ de antemano **2.** FIN anticipo *m* **3.** *pl* (*sexual flirtation*) insinuaciones *fpl;* **unwelcome** ~**s** molestias *fpl;* **to reject sb's** ~**s** rechazar las insinuaciones de alguien **IV.** *adj* avanzado, -a; **without** ~ **warning** sin previo aviso

advance booking *n* reserva *f* anticipada

advanced [əd'vɑːnst, *Am:* -'væːnst] *adj* (*country, pupil*) avanzado, -a; (*level*) superior

advancement [əd'vɑːnsmənt, *Am:* -'væːnsmənt] *n* **1.** (*improvement*) avance *m* **2.** *no pl* (*promotion*) fomento *m;* **an opportunity for** ~ una oportunidad para mejorar

advance notice *n no pl* aviso *m* (previo)

advance payment *n* anticipo *m*

advantage [əd'vɑːntɪdʒ, *Am:* -'væːnt̬ɪdʒ] *n* **a.** SPORTS ventaja *f;* ~ **Jackson** ventaja para Jackson; **to have an** ~ **over sb** tener ventaja sobre alguien; **to take** ~ **of sb/sth** aprovecharse de alguien/algo

advantageous [ˌædvən'teɪdʒəs, *Am:* -væn'-] *adj* ventajoso, -a

advent ['ædvənt] *n no pl* **1.** (*coming*) llegada *f* **2.** REL **Advent** Adviento *m*

adventure [əd'ventʃə', *Am:* -tʃə-] *n* aventura *f;* **to look for** ~ buscar el riesgo

adventurer *n* **1.** (*seeker of excitement*) aventurero, -a *m, f* **2.** (*opportunist*) aprovechado, -a *m, f*

adventurous [əd'ventʃərəs] *adj* (*person*) aventurero, -a; (*decision*) arriesgado, -a

adverb ['ædvɜːb, *Am:* -vɜːrb] *n* adverbio *m*

adverbial [æd'vɜːbɪəl, *Am:* -'vɜːr-] *adj* adverbial

adversary ['ædvəsəri, *Am:* -və-seri] <-ies> *n* adversario, -a *m, f*

adverse ['ædvɜːs, *Am:* -vɜːrs] *adj* (*decision, criticism, effect*) adverso, -a; (*conditions*) adverso, -a, desfavorable; (*reaction*) hostil

adversity [əd'vɜːsəti, *Am:* -'vɜːrsət̬i] <-ies> *n* adversidad *f;* **in** ~ en situaciones adversas

advert ['ædvɜːt, *Am:* -vɜːrt] *n s.* **advertisement**

advertise ['ædvətaɪz, *Am:* -və-] **I.** *vt* anunciar **II.** *vi* hacer publicidad

advertisement [əd'vɜːtɪsmənt, *Am:* ˌædvə'taɪzmənt] *n* COM anuncio *m*, aviso *m* *AmL;* **to be a good/bad** ~ **for sth** *fig* decir/no decir mucho en favor de algo; **job** ~ oferta *f* de empleo

advertiser ['ædvətaɪzə', *Am:* -və-taɪzə-] *n* anunciante *mf*

advertising ['ædvə-taɪzɪŋ, *Am:* -və-taɪzɪŋ] *n* publicidad *f*

advertising agency <-ies> *n* agencia *f* de publicidad **advertising campaign** *n* campaña *f* publicitaria

advice [əd'vaɪs] *n no pl* **1.** (*suggestion, opinion*) consejo *m;* **a piece of** ~ un consejo; **to ask for** ~ pedir consejo; **to ask sb for** ~ **on sth** pedir consejo a alguien sobre algo; **to give some good** ~ dar buenos consejos; **on sb's** ~ siguiendo el consejo de alguien **2.** COM aviso *m*

advisable [əd'vaɪzəbl] *adj* aconsejable; **it is (not)** ~ **(no)** es recomendable [*o* aconsejable]

advise [əd'vaɪz] **I.** *vt* aconsejar; (*specialist*) asesorar; **to** ~ **sb against sth** desaconsejar algo a alguien; **to** ~ **sb on sth** aconsejar a alguien sobre algo; **to** ~ **sb of sth** informar a alguien sobre algo **II.** *vi* dar un consejo; **to** ~ **against sth** desaconsejar algo; **to** ~ **on sth** asesorar en algo

adviser *n,* **advisor** [əd'vaɪzə', *Am:* -zə-] *n* asesor(a) *m(f)*

advisory [əd'vaɪzəri] *adj* consultivo, -a; **an** ~ **capacity** en calidad de asesor; ~ **committee** comité consultivo

advocate[1] ['ædvəkeɪt] *vt* recomendar; **to** ~ **doing sth** recomendar hacer algo

advocate[2] ['ædvəkət] *n* abogado, -a *m, f* defensor(a)

AEC *n Am abbr of* **Atomic Energy Commission** CEA *f*

Aegean [iː'dʒiːən] *n* **the** ~ **(Sea)** el (mar) Egeo

aegis ['iːdʒɪs] *n no pl* **under the** ~ **of ...** bajo los auspicios de...

aeon ['iːən, *Am:* -ɑːn] *n Brit* **1.** (*period of time*) eón *m* **2.** *fig* eternidad *f*

aerate ['eəreɪt, *Am:* 'ereɪt] *vt* **1.** (*expose to air*) airear **2.** (*drink*) oxigenar

aerial ['eərɪəl, *Am:* 'erɪ-] **I.** *adj* aéreo, -a; ~ **photography** fotografía *f* aérea **II.** *n* antena *f*

aerobatic [ˌeərəʊ'bætɪk, *Am:* ˌeroʊ'bæt̬-] *adj* de acrobacia aérea

aerobatics *npl* acrobacia *f* aérea

aerobics [eə'rəʊbɪks, *Am:* er'oʊ-] *n + sing/pl vb* aeróbic *m*, aerobic *m;* **to do** ~ hacer aeróbic

aerodrome ['eərədrəʊm, *Am:* 'erədroʊm] *n Brit* aeródromo *m*

aerodynamic [ˌeərəʊdaɪ'næmɪk, *Am:* ˌeroʊ-] *adj* aerodinámico, -a

aerodynamics *n + sing vb* aerodinámica *f*

aeronautic [ˌeərə'nɔːtɪk, *Am:* ˌerə'nɑːt̬ɪk] *adj* aeronáutico, -a

aeronautics [ˌeərəˈnɔːtɪks, Am: ˌerəˈnɑːtɪks] n + sing vb aeronáutica f

aeroplane [ˈeərəpleɪn, Am: ˈerə-] n Aus, Brit avión m

aerosol [ˈeərəsɒl, Am: ˈerəsɑːl] n aerosol m

aerospace industry [ˈeərəuspeɪs ˈɪndəstri, Am: ˈeroʊ-] n industria f aeroespacial

aesthetic [iːsˈθetɪk(l), Am: esˈθeṭ-] adj estético, -a

aesthetics [iːsˈθetɪks, Am: esˈθeṭ-] n + sing vb estética f

afar [əˈfɑːr, Am: -ˈfɑːr] adv form lejos; **from ~** desde lejos

affable [ˈæfəbl] adj afable

affair [əˈfeər, Am: -ˈfer] n 1. (matter) asunto m; **~s of state** asuntos de estado; **financial ~s** asuntos financieros; **to meddle in sb's ~s** meterse en los asuntos de alguien; **it's his own ~** eso es asunto suyo 2. (controversial situation) episodio m; (scandal) escándalo m 3. (sexual relationship) aventura f (amorosa); **to have an ~ (with sb)** tener una aventura (con alguien) 4. (event, occasion) acontecimiento m

affect [əˈfekt] vt 1. (have affect on) afectar; **to be ~ed by sth** (be moved) conmoverse por algo 2. (influence: decision) afectar a, influir en 3. (simulate) fingir

affectation [ˌæfekˈteɪʃən] n afectación f, amaneramiento m

affected [əˈfektɪd] adj (behaviour, accent) afectado, -a, amanerado, -a; (emotion) fingido, -a; (smile) falso, -a; (style) forzado, -a

affection [əˈfekʃən] n afecto m, cariño m; **to have a deep ~ for sb** tener mucho cariño a alguien

affectionate [əˈfekʃənət] adj afectuoso, -a, cariñoso, -a

affidavit [ˌæfɪˈdeɪvɪt] n declaración f jurada

affiliate [əˈfɪlɪeɪt] I. vt afiliar; **to be ~d to** [o **with**] **sb/sth** estar afiliado a alguien/algo II. n a. ECON filial f

affiliation [əˌfɪlɪˈeɪʃən] n afiliación f

affinity [əˈfɪnəti, Am: -əṭi] <-ies> n afinidad f

affirm [əˈfɜːm, Am: -ˈfɜːrm] vt afirmar

affirmation [ˌæfəˈmeɪʃən, Am: -ɚ-] n afirmación f

affirmative [əˈfɜːmətɪv, Am: -ˈfɜːrməṭɪv] I. adj afirmativo, -a II. n **to answer** [o **reply**] **in the ~** contestar afirmativamente, dar una respuesta afirmativa; **~ action** discriminación f positiva

affix¹ [əˈfɪks] vt (attach) poner; (stick on) pegar; (clip on) clavar

affix² [ˈæfɪks] n <-es> LING afijo m

afflict [əˈflɪkt] vt afligir; **to be ~ed with sth** padecer de algo

affliction [əˈflɪkʃən] n aflicción f

affluence [ˈæfluəns] n no pl riqueza f

affluent [ˈæfluənt] adj rico, -a; **an ~ way of life** una vida acomodada; **~ society** sociedad f opulenta

afford [əˈfɔːd, Am: -ˈfɔːrd] vt 1. (have money, time for) permitirse; **to be able to ~ sth** poder permitirse algo; **he can ill ~ it** a duras penas se lo puede permitir 2. (provide) proporcionar, dar; **to ~ protection** ofrecer protección

affordable [əˈfɔːdəbl, Am: -ˈfɔːr-] adj (price, purchase) asequible

afforestation [əˌfɒrɪˈsteɪʃən, Am: -ˌfɔːrə-] n no pl forestación f

affront [əˈfrʌnt] I. n afrenta f; **an ~ to sb's dignity** una afrenta [o ofensa] a la dignidad de alguien II. vt afrentar; **to be ~ed at** [o **by**] **sth** ofenderse por algo

Afghan [ˈæfgæn] I. n 1. (person) afgano, -a m, f 2. LING afgano m 3. (dog) galgo m afgano II. adj afgano, -a

Afghanistan [æfˈgænɪstæn, Am: -ə-] n Afganistán m

afield [əˈfiːld] adv **far ~** muy lejos; **further ~** más lejos

afloat [əˈfləʊt, Am: -ˈfloʊt] adj a flote; **to keep** [o **stay**] **~** a. fig mantenerse a flote

afoot [əˈfʊt] adj **there's sth ~** se está tramando algo

aforementioned [əˌfɔːˈmenʃnd, Am: -ˌfɔːr-,], **aforesaid** [əˌfɔːsed, Am: -ˌfɔːr-,] form I. adj (in text) anteriormente mencionado, -a; (in conversation) dicho, -a II. n inv **the ~** el mencionado/la mencionada; (of person mentioned in conversation) el susodicho/la susodicha

afraid [əˈfreɪd] adj 1. (scared) **to be ~** tener miedo; **to be ~ of doing** [o **to do**] **sth** tener miedo de hacer algo; **to be ~ of sb/sth** tener miedo a algo/alguien 2. (sorry) **I'm ~ so** lo siento, pero así es; **I'm ~ not** lo siento pero no; **I haven't got the time, I'm ~** me temo que no tengo tiempo

afresh [əˈfreʃ] adv de nuevo; **to start ~** empezar de nuevo

Africa [ˈæfrɪkə] n no pl África f

African [ˈæfrɪkən] I. n africano, -a m, f II. adj africano, -a

African-American [ˌæfrɪkənəˈmerɪkən] adj, n s. **Afro-American**

Afrikaans [ˌæfrɪˈkɑːns] n LING africaans m inv

Afro-American [ˌæfrəʊəˈmerɪkən, Am: -roʊ-] I. adj afroamericano, -a II. n afroamericano, -a m, f

Afro-Caribbean [ˌæfrəʊkærɪˈbiːən, Am: -roʊker-] I. adj afrocaribeño, -a II. n afrocaribeño, -a m, f

after [ˈɑːftər, Am: ˈæftɚ] I. prep 1. (at later time) después de; **~ two days** al cabo de dos días; (shortly) **~ breakfast** (poco) después de desayunar 2. (behind) detrás de; **to run ~ sb** correr detrás de alguien 3. (following) después de; **D comes ~ C** la D viene después [o detrás] de la C; **to have quarrel ~ quarrel** tener pelea tras pelea 4. (about) por; **to ask ~ sb** preguntar por alguien 5. (despite) **~ all** después de todo 6. (in the style of) **a drawing ~ Picasso** un dibujo al estilo de Picasso 7. (in *honour of*) **to name** sth/sb ~ sb llamar a algo/alguien a como alguien **II.** *adv* después; **soon** ~ poco después; **the day** ~ el día después **III.** *conj* después de que +*subj*; **he spoke** ~ **she went out** habló después de que ella se fuera; **I'll call him** (**straight**) ~ **I've taken a shower** le llamaré tan pronto (como) me haya duchado

aftercare ['ɑːftəkeəʳ, *Am:* 'æftəˌker] *n no pl* MED asistencia *f* postoperatoria

after-dinner *adj* de sobremesa

after-effects ['ɑːftərɪˌfektz, *Am:* 'æftə-] *npl* (*of drugs, treatment*) efectos *mpl* secundarios; (*of accident*) secuelas *fpl*

afterlife ['ɑːftəlaɪf, *Am:* 'æftə-] *n no pl* vida *f* más allá de la muerte; **the** ~ el más allá

aftermath ['ɑːftəmɑːθ, *Am:* 'æftəmæθ] *n no pl* secuelas *fpl*

afternoon [ˌɑːftə'nuːn, *Am:* ˌæftə-] **I.** *n* tarde *f;* **this** ~ esta tarde; **in the** ~ por la tarde; **all** ~ toda la tarde; **tomorrow/yesterday** ~ mañana/ayer por la tarde; **4 o'clock in the** ~ las 4 de la tarde; **good** ~**!** ¡buenas tardes! **II.** *adj* de la tarde; ~ **nap** siesta *f*

after-sales service [ˌɑːftə'seɪlz, *Am:* ˌæftə-'seɪlz] *n no pl* servicio *m* postventa

aftershave ['ɑːftəʃeɪv, *Am:* 'æftə-] *n* loción *f* para depués del afeitado

aftertaste ['ɑːftəteɪst, *Am:* 'æftə-] *n a. fig* regusto *m*

afterthought ['ɑːftəθɔːt, *Am:* 'æftəθɑːt] *n* idea *f* tardía

afterward *adv* *Am,* **afterwards** ['ɑːftəwədz, *Am:* 'æftəwədz] *adv* (*later*) más tarde; (*after something*) después; **shortly** ~ poco después

again [ə'gen] *adv* **1.** (*as a repetition*) otra vez; (*one more time*) de nuevo; **never** ~ nunca más; **once** ~ otra vez; **then** ~ por otra parte; **yet** ~ una vez más; ~ **and** ~ una y otra vez **2.** (*anew*) de nuevo

against [ə'genst] **I.** *prep* **1.** (*in opposition to*) (en) contra (de); **to be** ~ sth/sb estar en contra de algo/alguien; ~ **what he said** en contra de lo que dijo; ~ **my will** en contra de mi voluntad **2.** (*as protection from*) contra; **to protect oneself** ~ **rain** protegerse de la lluvia **3.** (*in contact with*) contra; **to lean** ~ **a tree** apoyarse en un árbol; **to run** ~ **a wall** estrellarse contra una pared **4.** (*in front of*) ~ **the light** a contraluz **5.** (*in competition with*) ~ **time/the clock** contra el tiempo/el reloj **6.** (*in comparison with*) **the dollar rose/fell** ~ **the euro** el dólar subió/bajó respecto al euro **7.** (*in exchange for*) **payment** ~ **invoice** pago *m* contra recibo **II.** *adv a.* POL en contra; **there were 10 votes** ~ hubo 10 votos en contra

agate ['ægət] *n* ágata *f*

age [eɪdʒ] **I.** *n* **1.** (*of person, object*) edad *f;* **old** ~ vejez *f;* **what is your age?** ¿qué edad tienes?; **when I was her** ~ cuando tenía su edad; **to be seven years of** ~ tener siete años;

to be under ~ ser menor de edad; **to improve with** ~ mejorar con los años [*o* la edad] **2.** (*era*) época *f;* **in this day and** ~ en estos tiempos **3.** (*long time*) siglos *mpl;* **I haven't seen you in** ~**s!** ¡hace siglos que no te veo! **II.** *vi* **1.** (*become older*) envejecer **2.** GASTR (*mature*) madurar **III.** *vt* **1.** (*make older*) envejecer **2.** GASTR (*mature*) madurar

age bracket *n s.* **age group**

aged¹ [eɪdʒd] *adj* (*with age of*) de…años de edad; **this game is for children** ~ **8 to 12** este juego es para niños de entre 8 y 12 años de edad

aged² ['eɪdʒɪd] **I.** *adj* (*old*) viejo, -a **II.** *n* **the** ~ los ancianos

age group *n* grupo *m* de edad

ageing ['eɪdʒɪŋ] **I.** *adj* envejecido, -a **II.** *n* envejecimiento *m;* **the** ~ **process** el proceso de envejecimiento

ageless ['eɪdʒlɪs] *adj* eterno, -a

age limit *n* límite *m* de edad

agency ['eɪdʒənsi] <-ies> *n* **1.** COM agencia *f;* **travel** ~ agencia de viajes **2.** ADMIN agencia *f,* organismo *m;* **government** ~ agencia [*o* organismo] gubernamental **3.** *no pl, form* **through the** ~ **of** por acción de

agenda [ə'dʒendə] *n* (*for meeting*) orden *m* del día; **to be at the top of the** ~ *fig* ser un asunto prioritario

agent ['eɪdʒənt] *n* agente *mf;* **secret** ~ agente secreto

agglomerate [ə'glɒmərət, *Am:* -'glɑː-] *n* aglomeración *f*

agglomeration [əˌglɒmə'reɪʃən, *Am:* -ˌglɑːmə-] *n* aglomeración *f*

aggravate ['ægrəveɪt] *vt* **1.** (*make worse*) agravar **2.** *inf* (*annoy*) fastidiar

aggravating *adj* (*annoying*) molesto, -a

aggravation [ˌægrə'veɪʃən] *n no pl, inf* fastidio *m*

aggregate ['ægrɪgɪt] **I.** *n* **1.** FIN, ECON conglomerado *m;* (*sum total*) suma *f* total; (*total value*) valor *f* total **2.** *no pl* MAT suma *f* **II.** *adj* FIN, ECON total **III.** *vt* FIN, ECON sumar

aggression [ə'greʃən] *n no pl* **1.** (*feelings*) agresividad *f* **2.** (*violence*) agresión *f;* **an act of** ~ una agresión

aggressive [ə'gresɪv] *adj* agresivo, -a

aggressor [ə'gresəʳ, *Am:* -ə-] *n* agresor(a) *m(f)*

aggrieved [ə'griːvd] *adj* ofendido, -a

aghast [ə'gɑːst, *Am:* -'gæst] *adj* horrorizado, -a; **to be** ~ **at sth** estar horrorizado por algo

agile ['ædʒaɪl, *Am:* 'ædʒl] *adj* ágil

agility [ə'dʒɪləti, *Am:* -ţi] *n no pl* agilidad *f*

aging *adj s.* **ageing**

agitate ['ædʒɪteɪt] **I.** *vt* **1.** (*make nervous*) inquietar; **to become** ~**d** inquietarse, ponerse inquieto **2.** (*shake*) agitar **II.** *vi* **to** ~ **for/against sth** hacer campaña en favor de/en contra de algo

agitation [ˌædʒɪ'teɪʃən] *n no pl a.* POL agitación *f*

agitator ['ædʒɪteɪtəʳ, *Am:* -ţə-] *n* agitador(a)

A

m(f), violentista *mf Chile*

AGM [ˌeɪdʒiːˈem] *n abbr of* **annual general meeting** junta *f* general anual

agnostic [ægˈnɒstɪk, *Am:* -ˈnɑːstɪk] I. *n* agnóstico, -a *m, f* II. *adj* agnóstico, -a

ago [əˈɡəʊ, *Am:* -ˈɡoʊ] *adv* a minute/a year ~ hace un minuto/un año; **a long time ~,** **long ~** hace mucho tiempo; **how long ~ was** **that?** ¿cuánto tiempo hace de eso?

agog [əˈɡɒɡ, *Am:* -ˈɡɑːɡ] *adj* **to watch/** **listen ~** mirar/escuchar con avidez

agonize [ˈæɡənaɪz] *vi* atormentarse; **to ~** **about whether to do sth** atormentarse respecto a hacer o no hacer algo; **an ~d cry** un grito de angustia

agonizing [ˈæɡənaɪzɪŋ] *adj* **1.** (*pain*) atroz; **to die an ~ death** tener una muerte espantosa **2.** (*delay, decision*) angustiante

agony [ˈæɡəni] <-ies> *n* agonía *f;* **to be in ~** sufrir fuertes dolores; **to prolong the ~** (of sth) prolongar la agonía (de algo)

agony aunt *n* PUBL consultora *f* sentimental

agree [əˈɡriː] I. *vi* **1.** (*hold same opinion*) estar de acuerdo; **to ~ on sth** (*be in agreement*) estar de acuerdo en algo; (*reach agreement*) acordar algo; **to ~ to do sth** (*reach agreement*) acordar hacer algo; (*consent*) acceder a hacer algo; **to ~ to a suggestion** aceptar una sugerencia; **we don't ~ on many** **things** no estamos de acuerdo en muchas cosas; **they can't ~** no pueden ponerse de acuerdo; **to ~ to differ** estar en desacuerdo amistoso **2.** (*be good for*) **to ~ with sb** sentar bien a alguien **3.** (*match up*) casar, concordar **4.** LING concordar II. *vt* **1.** (*concur*) acordar; **it is ~d that ...** se ha acordado que...; **at the ~d** **time** a la hora fijada **2.** *Brit* (*accept*) acceder a

agreeable *adj* **1.** *form* (*acceptable*) aceptable; **is that ~ to you?** ¿está de acuerdo? **2.** (*pleasant*) agradable; **he's quite an ~ guy** es un tipo muy agradable **3.** (*consenting*) **to be ~** (to sth) estar conforme (con algo)

agreement *n* **1.** *no pl* (*shared opinion*) acuerdo *m;* **to be in ~ with sb** estar de acuerdo con alguien; **to reach ~** llegar a un acuerdo **2.** (*contract, arrangement*) acuerdo *m;* **to break an ~** romper un acuerdo **3.** LING concordancia *f*

agribusiness [ˈæɡrɪˌbɪznɪs] *n no pl* industria *f* agropecuaria

agricultural [ˌæɡrɪˈkʌltʃərəl] *adj* agrícola; ~ **science** agronomía *f*

agriculture [ˈæɡrɪkʌltʃəʳ, *Am:* -tʃɚ] *n no pl* agricultura *f;* **subsistence ~** agricultura de subsistencia

agrotourism [æɡrəʊˈtʊərɪzəm, *Am:* æɡroʊˈtʊrɪ-] *n no pl* agroturismo

aground [əˈɡraʊnd] *adv* NAUT **to run ~** encallar; *fig* fracasar

ah [ɑː] *interj* ah

aha [ɑːˈhɑː] *interj* ajá

ahead [əˈhed] *adv* **1.** (*in front*) delante; **the** **road ~ was blocked** había atascos en la ca-

rretera delante de nosotros **2.** (*advanced position, forwards*) adelante; **to go ~** adelantarse; **to move ~ quickly** avanzar rápidamente; **to** **press ~ with the plan** tirar adelante con el plan **3.** (*in the future*) **to look ~** anticiparse; **to** **plan ~** hacer planes con antelación

ahead of *prep* **1.** (*in front of*) delante de; **to** **walk ~ sb** caminar delante de alguien; (*way*) **~ sb/sth** (muy) por delante de alguien/algo **2.** (*before*) antes de; **to decide/arrive ~ time** decidir/llegar antes de tiempo **3.** (*more advanced than*) **to be a minute ~ sb** llevar un minuto de ventaja sobre alguien; **to be ~** **one's time** anticiparse a su época **4.** (*informed about*) **to keep ~ sth** mantenerse al tanto de algo

ahem [əˈhəm] *interj* ejem

ahoy [əˈhɔɪ] *interj* **land/ship ~!** ¡tierra/barco a la vista!; **~ there!** ¡ah del barco!

AI [ˌeɪˈaɪ] *n no pl* **1.** INFOR *abbr of* **artificial intelligence** IA **2.** MED, BIO *abbr of* **artificial insemination** inseminación *f* artificial

aid [eɪd] I. *n* **1.** *no pl* (*assistance, support*) ayuda *f;* **to be in ~ of sb/sth** ser en beneficio de alguien/algo; **to come/go to the ~ of sb** ir en ayuda de alguien; **with the ~ of sb/sth** con (la) ayuda de alguien/algo **2.** *no pl* POL, ECON ayuda *f;* **emergency ~** ayuda de emergencia; **financial ~** asistencia *f* financiera **3.** (*device*) ayuda *f;* **hearing ~** audífono *m;* **slimming ~** producto de adelgazamiento ▶**what's all this in ~ of?** *Brit, inf* ¿a qué viene todo eso? II. *vt* ayudar; **to ~ and abet sb** ser cómplice de alguien

AID *n* **1.** *abbr of* **Agency for International** **Development** AID *f* **2.** *abbr of* **artificial insemination by donor** inseminación *f* artificial con donante

aid convoy *n* convoy *m* humanitario

aide [eɪd] *n* asistente *mf*

AIDS [eɪdz] *n no pl abbr of* **Acquired** **Immune Deficiency Syndrome** sida *m*

ail [eɪl] *form* I. *vi* estar enfermo, -a II. *vt* afligir; **what ~s you?** *a. iron* ¿qué te pasa?

aileron [ˈeɪlərɒn, *Am:* -rɑːn] *n* AVIAT alerón *m*

ailing [ˈeɪlɪŋ] *adj* **1.** (*person*) enfermo, -a **2.** (*company, economy*) debilitado, -a

ailment [ˈeɪlmənt] *n* dolencia *f*

aim [eɪm] I. *vi* **1.** (*point: weapon*) apuntar; **to** **~ at sb/sth** apuntar a alguien/algo **2.** (*plan to* *achieve*) **to ~ at** [*o* for] **sth** tener algo como objetivo; **to ~ to do sth** poner como objetivo hacer algo II. *vt* **1.** (*point a weapon*) apuntar; **to ~ sth at sb/sth** apuntar algo hacia alguien/algo **2.** (*direct at*) **to ~ sth at sb** dirigir algo hacia alguien **3.** *fig* **to be ~ed at doing sth** ir encaminado a hacer algo III. *n* **1.** *no pl* (*ability*) puntería *f;* **to take ~** apuntar **2.** (*goal*) objetivo *m,* meta *f;* **his ~ was to make fun of us** su objetivo era burlarse de nosotros; **sb's ~ in life** la meta de alguien en la vida; **with the ~ of** **doing sth** con el objetivo de hacer algo

aimless [ˈeɪmlɪs] *adj* sin objetivo(s)

ain't [eɪnt] *inf* 1. (*to be*) *s.* **am not**, **are not**, **is not** 2. (*to have*) *s.* **have not**, **has not**
air [eə^r, *Am:* er] I. *n* 1. *no pl* (*earth's atmosphere*) aire *m* 2. *no pl* (*space overhead, sky*) aire *m;* put your hands in the ~! ¡manos arriba!; to fire into the ~ disparar al aire; to be up in the ~ *fig* estar en el aire 3. *no pl* AVIAT by ~ por avión; to travel by ~ viajar en avión 4. *no pl* TV, RADIO, CINE to be on (the) ~ estar en antena [*o* en el aire]; to be taken off the ~ ser retirado de antena 5. *no pl* (*aura, quality*) aire *m;* he has a unbearable ~ of arrogance tiene un aire de arrogancia insoportable 6. MUS aire *m,* tonada *f* ►~s and graces *pej* melindres *mpl;* out of thin ~ de la nada; to disappear into thin ~ desaparecer como por arte de magia II. *adj* aéreo, -a III. *vt* 1. TV, RADIO emitir; the programme will be ~ed on Saturday el programa se emitirá el sábado 2. (*expose to air*) airear 3. (*publicize*) to ~ one's grievances ventilar sus quejas IV. *vi* 1. *Am* TV, RADIO airear, emitirse 2. (*be exposed to air*) ventilarse
air ambulance *n* avión *m* ambulancia **air bag** *n* airbag *m* **airbase** *n* base *f* aérea
airborne ['eəbɔːn, *Am:* 'erbɔːrn] *adj* 1. (*transported by aircraft*) aerotransportado, -a 2. (*in the air*) to be ~ volar; to get ~ (*plane*) despegar
air brake *n* freno *m* neumático **air bubble** *n* burbuja *f* de aire **air-conditioned** *adj* climatizado, -a **air conditioner** *n* acondicionador *m* de aire **air conditioning** *n no pl* aire *m* acondicionado, climatización *f;* to turn the ~ down/up bajar/subir el aire acondicionado **air-cooled** *adj* enfriado, -a por aire **air corridor** *n* corredor *m* aéreo
aircraft ['eəkrɑːft, *Am:* 'erkræft] *n* (*in general*) aeronave *f;* (*aeroplane*) avión *m* **aircraft carrier** *n* porta(a)viones *m inv* **aircraft industry** *n no pl* industria *f* aeronáutica
aircrew ['eəkruː, *Am:* 'er-] *n* + *sing/pl vb* tripulación *f* de vuelo **air cushion** *n* cojín *m* de aire **airfield** *n* aeródromo *m* **air filter** *n* filtro *m* de aire **air force** *n* fuerza *f* aérea **air freight** *n no pl* carga *f* aérea **air gun** *n* pistola *f* de aire comprimido **air hole** *n* respiradero *m*
airing cupboard ['eərɪŋ ˌkʌbəd, *Am:* 'erɪŋ ˌkʌbəd] *n* armario *m* (para orear la ropa)
airless ['eələs, *Am:* 'er-] *n* (*room*) mal ventilado, -a; (*day*) sin viento
air lift I. *n* puente *m* aéreo II. *vt* aerotransportar **airline** *n* línea *f* aérea, aerolínea *f AmL* **airliner** *n* avión *m* de pasajeros **airmail** *n no pl* correo *m* aéreo **airman** <-men> *n* 1. (*pilot*) aviador *m;* (*crew member*) tripulante *mf* 2. MIL soldado *m* de las fuerzas aéreas **airplane** *n Am* avión *m* **air pollutant** *n* agente *m* contaminante (del aire) **air pollution** *n* contaminación *f* atmosférica **airport** *n* aeropuerto *m* **air quality** *n* calidad *f* del

aire **air raid** *n* ataque *m* aéreo **airsick** *adj* mareado, -a; to get ~ marearse (en avión) **air space** *n no pl* espacio *m* aéreo **air stewardess** *n* azafata *f* **airstrip** *n* pista *f* de aterrizaje **air terminal** *n* terminal *f* aérea **air ticket** *n* billete *m* de avión
airtight ['eətaɪt, *Am:* 'er-] *adj* hermético, -a
air traffic *n no pl* tráfico *m* aéreo **air-traffic controller** *n* controlador(a) *m(f)* aéreo, -a **airway** ['eəweɪ, *Am:* 'er-] *n* 1. ANAT vía *f* respiratoria 2. (*path or route of aircraft*) vía *f* aérea **airworthy** ['eəˌwɜːði, *Am:* 'erˌwɜːr-] *adj* en condiciones para el vuelo
airy ['eəri, *Am:* 'er-] *adj* 1. ARCHIT espacioso, -a 2. (*light*) ligero, -a; with an ~ step con un paso grácil 3. (*lacking substance*) etéreo, -a
airy-fairy ['eərɪ'feəri, *Am:* 'erɪ'feri] *adj inf* fantasióso, -a
aisle [aɪl] *n* pasillo *m;* (*in church*) nave *f* lateral ►to have sb rolling in the ~s tener a alguien riéndose a carcajadas; to take sb down the ~ llevar al altar a alguien
ajar [ə'dʒɑː^r, *Am:* -'dʒɑːr] *adj* entreabierto, -a
a.k.a. *abbr of* also known as alias
akimbo [ə'kɪmbəʊ, *Am:* -boʊ] *adj* (with) arms ~ (con) los brazos en jarras
akin [ə'kɪn] *adj* ~ to parecido a
à la carte [æ lə 'kɑːt, *Am:* ɑː lə 'kɑːrt] *adj*, *adv* a la carta
alacrity [ə'lækrəti, *Am:* -t̬i] *n no pl* prontitud *f*
alarm [ə'lɑːm, *Am:* -'lɑːrm] I. *n* 1. *no pl* (*worry*) alarma *f;* to cause sb ~ alarmar a alguien 2. (*warning*) alarma *f;* fire ~ alarma contra incendios; burglar ~ dispositivo *m* antirrobo; a false ~ una falsa alarma; to give the ~ dar la (voz de) alarma; *a. fig* alertar 3. (*clock*) reloj *m* despertador II. *vt* alarmar; to be ~ed estar alarmado
alarm clock *n* reloj *m* despertador
alarming *adj* alarmante
alarmist [ə'lɑːmɪst, *Am:* -'lɑːr-] I. *adj* alarmista II. *n* alarmista *mf*
Albania [æl'beɪniə] *n* Albania *f*
Albanian I. *n* 1. (*person*) albanés, -esa *m, f* 2. LING albanés *m* II. *adj* albanés, -esa
albatross ['ælbətrɒs, *Am:* -trɑːs] *n* albatros *m*
albeit [ɔːl'biːɪt] *conj* aunque
albino [æl'biːnəʊ, *Am:* -'baɪnoʊ] I. *adj* albino, -a, ruaco, -a *Ven* II. *n* albino, -a *m, f*
album ['ælbəm] *n a.* MUS álbum *m;* the family ~ el álbum de la familia

---

Alcatraz es una antigua cárcel situada en la Isla de Alcatraz, que a su vez se encuentra en la bahía de San Francisco. Dado que la isla se erige sobre una base de cinco hectáreas de rocosos acantilados, la cárcel recibe el sobrenombre de 'La Roca'. Allí eran confinados presos considerados especialmente peligrosos.

alcohol ['ælkəhɒl, *Am:* -hɑːl] *n no pl* alcohol *m*

alcohol-free *adj* sin alcohol

alcoholic [ˌælkə'hɒlɪk, *Am:* -'hɑːlɪk] I. *n* alcohólico, -a *m, f* II. *adj* alcohólico, -a

alcoholism *n no pl* alcoholismo *m*

alcove ['ælkəʊv, *Am:* -koʊv] *n* nicho *m* (*para estantería o cama*)

alder ['ɔːldəʳ, *Am:* -dɚ] *n* aliso *m*

alderman ['ɔːldəmən, *Am:* -dɚ-] <-men> *n* POL 1. *Brit* HIST concejal(a) *m(f)* 2. *Am, Aus, Can* (*elected city government member*) regidor(a) *m(f)*

ale [eɪl] *n* cerveza *f*

alert [ə'lɜːt, *Am:* -'lɜːrt] I. *adj* despierto, -a; **to keep** ~ mantenerse alerta II. *n* 1. (*alarm*) alarma *f* 2. *no pl* (*period of watchfulness*) alerta *f*; **state of** ~ estado *m* de alerta; **to be on the** ~ estar alerta III. *vt* (*notify*) alertar

A-level ['eɪlevəl] *n Brit abbr of* **Advanced--level** ≈ bachillerato *m*

El **A-Level** es un tipo de examen final que realizan los alumnos al finalizar la enseñanza secundaria. La mayoría de los alumnos elige tres asignaturas de examen, pero también es posible examinarse de una sola asignatura. Aprobar los **A-Levels** le da al alumno la posibilidad de acceder a los estudios universitarios.

---

alga ['ælgə] *n* alga *f*

algal bloom ['ælgəlˌbluːm] *n* marea *f* de algas

algebra ['ældʒɪbrə] *n no pl* álgebra *f*

algebraic [ˌældʒɪ'breɪɪk] *adj* algebraico, -a

Algeria [æl'dʒɪərɪə, *Am:* -'dʒɪ-] *n* Argelia *f*

Algerian I. *n* argelino, -a *m, f* II. *adj* argelino, -a

Algiers [æl'dʒɪəz, *Am:* -'dʒɪrz] *n* Argel *m*

alias ['eɪlɪəs] I. *n* alias *m inv* II. *conj* alias

alibi ['ælɪbaɪ] *n* coartada *f*

alien ['eɪlɪən] I. *adj* 1. (*foreign*) extranjero, -a 2. (*strange*) extraño, -a; ~ **to sb** ajeno a alguien; **an** ~ **idea** una idea poco normal II. *n* 1. *form* (*foreigner*) extranjero, -a *m, f*; **illegal** ~ extranjero ilegal 2. (*extra-terrestrial creature*) extraterrestre *mf*

alienate ['eɪlɪəneɪt] *vt* 1. (*person*) distanciar; **to** ~ **sb from sb/sth** hacer que alguien se distancie de alguien/algo 2. LAW (*property*) enajenar

alienation [ˌeɪlɪə'neɪʃən] *n no pl* 1. (*of people*) distanciamiento *m* 2. LAW (*of property*) enajenación *f*

alight¹ [ə'laɪt] *adj* 1. (*on fire*) quemando; **to be** ~ estar ardiendo; **to set sth** ~ prender fuego a algo 2. *fig* (*with enthusiasm, joy*) resplandeciente; **to set sb's imagination** ~ despertar la imaginación a alguien

alight² [ə'laɪt] *vi form* 1. (*from vehicle*) apearse 2. (*on branch*) posarse

◆**alight on** *vi* **to** ~ **sth** dar con [*o* encontrar] algo

align [ə'laɪn] *vt* 1. (*two things*) poner en línea (recta); (*wheels*) alinear 2. *fig* **to** ~ **oneself with sb/sth** alinearse con alguien/algo

alignment *n no pl* alineación *f*; **to be out of** ~ no estar alineado

alike [ə'laɪk] I. *adj* 1. parecido, -a; **to look** ~ parecerse 2. **Clara and Clive** ~ ... (*both*) tanto Clara como Clive... II. *adv* (*similarly*) de un modo parecido; **to think** ~ pensar de forma parecida

alimony ['ælɪməni, *Am:* -moʊ-] *n no pl* pensión *f* alimenticia

aline [ə'laɪn] *vt s.* **align**

alive [ə'laɪv] *adj* 1. (*not dead*) vivo, -a; **to be** ~ estar vivo; **to be buried** ~ ser enterrado vivo; **to keep sb** ~ mantener a alguien con vida; **to keep hope** ~ mantener vivas las esperanzas 2. (*active*) activo, -a; **to make sth come** ~ dar vida a algo 3. (*aware*) **to be** ~ **to sth** ser consciente de algo

alkali ['ælkəlaɪ, *Am:* -kəlaɪ] I. <-s *o* -es> *n* álcali *m* II. *adj* alcalino, -a

alkaline ['ælkəlaɪn, *Am:* -kəlaɪn] *adj* alcalino, -a

all [ɔːl] I. *adj* todo, -a; ~ **the butter** toda la mantequilla; ~ **the wine** todo el vino; ~ **my sisters** todas mis hermanas; **with** ~ **possible speed** con la máxima velocidad posible II. *pron* 1. (*everybody*) todos, -as; ~ **aboard!** ¡todos a bordo!; ~ **but him** todos menos él; **he's got four daughters,** ~ **blue-eyed** tiene cuatro hijas, todas con ojos azules; **once and for** ~ de una vez por todas 2. (*everything*) todo; ~ **but** ... todo menos...; **most of** ~ sobre todo; **the best of** ~ **would be** ... lo mejor de todo sería...; **for** ~ **I know** que yo sepa; **for** ~ **he may think** a pesar de lo que pueda pensar 3. (*the whole quantity*) todo, -a; **they took/drank it** ~ se lo tomaron/bebieron todo; ~ **of France** toda Francia 4. (*the only thing*) todo, -a; ~ **I want is** ... lo único que quiero es...; **I am** ~ **the family she has** soy toda la familia que ella tiene 5. SPORTS **two** ~ dos a dos; **to draw two** ~ empatar a dos III. *adv* totalmente; ~ **round** completo; **not as stupid as** ~ **that** no del todo estúpido; **it's** ~ **the same** me da igual

Allah ['ælə] *n* Alá *m*

all-around *adj Am s.* **all-round**

allay ['əleɪ] *vt* (*fear*) calmar; (*doubt*) despejar

all clear [ˌɔːl'klɪəʳ, *Am:* -'klɪr] *n* cese *m* de alarma; **to give/hear the** ~ dar/oír el cese de alarma; **to give sth the** ~ *fig* dar la luz verde a algo

allegation [ˌælɪ'geɪʃən] *n* acusación *f*; **to make an** ~ **against sb** acusar a alguien

allege [ə'ledʒ] *vt* afirmar; **she is** ~**d to have stolen the money** se dice que ha robado el dinero; **it is** ~**d that** ... se dice que...

alleged [ə'ledʒd] *adj* supuesto, -a

allegedly [ə'ledʒɪdli] *adv* (*según*) se dice

allegiance [ə'liːdʒəns] *n no pl* lealtad *f;* **to pledge ~ to sb/sth** jurar lealtad a alguien/algo

allegoric(al) [ˌælɪ'gɒrɪk(əl), *Am:* -'gɔːr-] *adj* alegórico, -a

allegory ['ælɪɡəri, *Am:* -gɔːri] <-ies> *n* alegoría *f*

alleluia [ˌælɪ'luːjə] I. *interj* aleluya II. *n* aleluya *f*

allergen ['ælədʒən, *Am:* -ɚ-] *n* alergeno *m*, alérgeno *m*

allergenic [ælə'dʒenɪk, *Am:* -ɚ-] *adj* alergénico, -a

allergic [ə'lɜːdʒɪk, *Am:* -'lɜːr-] *adj* alérgico, -a; **~ reaction** reacción *f* alérgica

allergy ['ælədʒi, *Am:* -ɚ-] <-ies> *n* alergia *f;* **to trigger an ~** provocar una alergia

alleviate [ə'liːvɪeɪt] *vt* aliviar

alley ['æli] *n* 1.(*between buildings*) callejón *m;* **blind ~** callejón sin salida 2.(*in garden*) paseo *m*

alley cat *n* gato *m* callejero

All Fools' Day [ˌɔːl'fuːlzdeɪ] *n* ≈ Día *m* de los Santos Inocentes (*en Gran Bretaña el 1 de abril*)

alliance [ə'laɪəns] *n* alianza *f;* **to form an ~** formar una alianza; **to be in ~ with sth/sb** estar aliado con algo/alguien

allied ['ælaɪd] *adj* 1. *a.* MIL aliado, -a; **the Allied forces** las fuerzas aliadas 2.(*combined*) **~ with** [*o* **to**] **sth** unido a algo

alligator ['ælɪɡeɪtəʳ, *Am:* -t̬ɚ] *n* caimán *m*

all-in [ɔːl'ɪn] *adj* todo incluido; **~ rate** precio *m* con todo incluido

all-inclusive [ˌɔːlɪŋ'kluːsɪv, *Am:* -ɪn'-] *adj* todo incluido

all-in wrestling *n* lucha *f* libre

allocate ['æləkeɪt] *vt* 1.(*assign*) asignar 2.(*distribute*) repartir; **to ~ blame for sth to sb** echar las culpas a alguien de algo

allocation [ˌælə'keɪʃən] *n no pl* 1.(*assignment*) asignación *f* 2.(*act of distributing*) distribución *f*

allot [ə'lɒt, *Am:* -'lɑːt] <-tt-> *vt* asignar

allotment *n* 1.(*assignment*) asignación *f* 2.(*distribution*) distribución *f* 3.*Brit* (*plot of land*) ≈ huerto *m* particular (*en las afueras de la ciudad*)

all-out [ɔːl'aʊt] *adj* total; **to make an ~ effort** hacer un esfuerzo supremo; **~ attack** ataque *m* total

allow [ə'laʊ] *vt* 1.(*permit*) permitir; **to ~ access** permitir el acceso; **to ~ sb to do sth** dejar a alguien hacer algo; **~ me** *form* permíta(n)me; **will you ~ me?** ¿me permite(n)?; **please ~ me through** *form* déje(n)me pasar, por favor; **smoking is not ~ed** se prohíbe fumar 2.(*allocate*) asignar; **please ~ 7 days for delivery** entrega en un plazo máximo de 7 días 3.(*admit*) **to ~ that ...** reconocer que...

♦ **allow for** *vt* tener en cuenta

allowable *adj* 1.(*error*) permisible 2.(*expenses*) deducible

allowance [ə'laʊəns] *n* 1.(*permitted amount*) cantidad *f* permitida; **baggage ~** equipaje *m* no sujeto a tasas; **tax ~** desgravación *f* fiscal 2.*Am* (*money*) dinero *m* de bolsillo 3.(*preparation*) **to make ~(s) for sth** tener algo en cuenta 4.(*excuse*) **to make ~s for sb** ser indulgente con alguien; **to make ~s for sth** tolerar algo

alloy ['ælɔɪ] I. *n* aleación *f;* **~ wheels** llantas *fpl* de aleación II. *vt form* empañar

all-purpose [ɔːl'pɜːpəs, *Am:* -'pɜːr-] *adj* universal, multiuso

all right I. *adv* 1.(*o.k.*) bien; **that's ~** (*after thanks*) de nada; (*after excuse*) no pasa nada; **what do you think of the book? – it was ~ nothing special** ¿qué te parece el libro? – ah, pasable, nada del otro mundo; **she's a bit of ~!** *Brit, inf* ¡está buenísima!; **to be ~ with sb** comportarse bien con alguien 2.(*healthy*) bien; **to be ~** estar bien (de salud); (*safe*) estar sano y salvo; **to get home ~** llegar a casa sin ningún percance II. *interj* (*expressing agreement*) de acuerdo III. *adv* 1.(*well*) bien 2.(*certainly*) con (toda) seguridad 3.(*in answer*) vale

all-round [ɔːl'raʊnd] *adj* completo, -a; **~ talent** talento *m* para todo

all-rounder [ɔːl'raʊndəʳ, *Am:* -dɚ] *n Aus, Brit* persona *f* con talento en varias disciplinas; SPORTS deportista *mf* completo, -a (*que puede jugar en cualquier posición*)

All Saints' Day *n no pl* día *m* de Todos los Santos

All Souls' Day *n* día *m* de (los) Difuntos

all-time high [ɔːlˌtaɪm'haɪ] *n* máximo *m* histórico **all-time low** *n* mínimo *m* histórico

allude [ə'luːd] *vi* **to ~ to sth** aludir a algo

allure [ə'lʊəʳ, *Am:* -'lʊr] I. *n no pl* (*attractiveness*) atractivo *m;* (*charm*) encanto *m;* **sexual ~** atractivo sexual II. *vt* atraer

alluring [ə'lʊərɪŋ, *Am:* -'lʊrɪŋ] *adj* (*attractive*) atractivo, -a; (*enticing*) tentador(a)

allusion [ə'luːʒən] *n* alusión *f*

all-weather [ɔːl'weðəʳ] *adj* para todo tiempo

ally ['ælaɪ] I. <-ies> *n* 1.(*country*) aliado, -a *m, f* 2.(*supporter*) partidario, -a *m, f* II. <-ie-> *vt* **to ~ oneself with sb** POL aliarse con alguien

almanac ['ɔːlmənæk] *n* almanaque *m*

almighty [ɔːl'maɪti, *Am:* -t̬i] I. *adj inf* todopoderoso, -a II. *n* **the Almighty** el Todopoderoso

almond ['ɑːmənd] *n* 1.(*nut*) almendra *f* 2.(*tree*) almendro *m*

almost ['ɔːlməʊst, *Am:* -moʊst] *adv* casi; **~ half** casi la mitad; **we're ~ there** casi hemos llegado

alms [ɑːmz] *npl* limosna *f*

aloe vera [ˌæləʊ'vɪərə, *Am:* -oʊ'vɪrə] *n* áloe *m* vera

alone [ə'ləʊn, *Am:* -'loʊn] I. *adj* 1.(*without others*) solo, -a; **to do sth ~** hacer algo solo; **to**

go it ~ *inf* hacerlo por su cuenta; **to leave sb ~** dejar a alguien en paz; **to leave sth ~** dejar algo como está **2.** (*unique*) **to be ~ in doing sth** ser el único/los únicos en hacer algo; **Jane ~ can do that** Jane es la única que puede hacerlo ▶let ~ ... mucho menos... **II.** *adv* solamente, sólo

along [ə'lɒŋ, *Am:* -'lɑːŋ] **I.** *prep* por; **all ~** a lo largo de; **~ the road** por la carretera; **all ~ the river** a lo largo del río; **I lost it ~ the way** lo perdí por el camino; **it's ~ here** está por aquí **II.** *adv* **all ~** todo el tiempo; **to bring/take sb ~** traer/llevar a alguien; **to go ~** seguir adelante; **he will be ~ in an hour** llegará en una hora; **come ~!** ¡ven con nosotros!

alongside [ə,lɒŋ'saɪd, *Am:* ə'lɑːŋsaɪd] **I.** *prep* **1.** (*next to*) junto a; **to draw up ~ sb/sth** pararse al lado de alguien/algo; **~ each other** uno junto al otro; **to fight ~ sb** luchar al lado de alguien **2.** NAUT al costado de **II.** *adv* al lado; NAUT de costado

aloof [ə'luːf] *adj* distante; **to keep ~ from sth** mantenerse alejado de algo

aloud [ə'laʊd] *adv* en voz alta; **to think ~** pensar en voz alta

alpha ['ælfə] *n* **1.** (*Greek letter*) alfa *f* **2.** *Brit* (*student mark*) ≈ sobresaliente *m*

alphabet ['ælfəbet] *n* alfabeto *m*

alphabetical [,ælfə'betɪkl, *Am:* -'bet̮-] *adj* alfabético, -a; **in ~ order** en orden alfabético

alphanumeric [,ælfənjuː'merɪk, *Am:* -nuː-] *adj* alfanumérico, -a

alpha particle *n* partícula *f* alfa **alpha ray** *n* rayo *m* alfa

alpine ['ælpaɪn] **I.** *adj* alpino, -a **II.** *n* planta *f* alpestre

Alps [ælps] *npl* **the ~** los Alpes

already [ɔːl'redi] *adv* ya

alright [ɔl'raɪt] *adv* s. **all right**

Alsace [æl'sæs] *n* Alsacia *f*

Alsatian [æl'seɪʃən] **I.** *n* **1.** (*person*) alsaciano, -a *m, f* **2.** (*dog*) pastor *m* alemán **II.** *adj* alsaciano, -a

also ['ɔːlsəʊ, *Am:* 'ɔːlsoʊ] *adv* también

altar ['ɔːltə', *Am:* -t̮ə'] *n* altar *m*

altar boy *n* monaguillo *m*

alter ['ɔːltə', *Am:* -t̮ə'] **I.** *vt* **1.** (*change: text, plan*) cambiar; (*option*) cambiar de; (*paint*) retocar **2.** *Am* (*castrate*) castrar **II.** *vi* cambiarse

alterable ['ɔːltərəbl, *Am:* -t̮ə'əbl] *adj* modificable

alteration [,ɔːltə'reɪʃən, *Am:* -t̮ə-] *n* **1.** (*change*) modificación *f*; (*in house*) reforma *f* **2.** *no pl* (*act of changing*) modificación *f*

altercation [,ɔːltə'keɪʃən, *Am:* -t̮ə-] *n* altercado *m*

alternate¹ ['ɔːltəneɪt, *Am:* 'ɔːlt̮ə-] *vi, vt* alternar

alternate² [ɔːl'tɜːnət, *Am:* -'t̮ɜːr-] *adj* **1.** (*by turns*) alterno, -a; **on ~ days** en días alternos **2.** *Am* (*alternative*) alternativo, -a

alternating ['ɔːltəneɪtɪŋ, *Am:* -t̮ɪŋ] *adj*

alterno, -a

alternative [ɔːl'tɜːnətɪv, *Am:* -'tɜːrnət̮ɪv] **I.** *n* alternativa *f*; **to have no ~ but to do sth** no tener otra alternativa que hacer algo **II.** *adj* alternativo, -a

alternatively *adv* **1.** (*on the other hand*) si no **2.** (*as a substitute*) en lugar de esto

alternator ['ɔːltəneɪtə', *Am:* -tə'neɪt̮ə'] *n* alternador *m*

although [ɔːl'ðəʊ, *Am:* -'ðoʊ] *conj* aunque; **he is mean ~ he is rich** es tacaño a pesar de que es rico; **~ it's snowing ...** aunque está nevando...

altimeter ['æltɪmiːtə', *Am:* æl'tɪmət̮ə'] *n* altímetro *m*

altitude ['æltɪtjuːd, *Am:* -tətuːd] *n* altitud *f*

alto ['æltəʊ, *Am:* -toʊ] *n* **1.** (*woman*) contralto *f* **2.** (*man*) contralto *m*

altogether [,ɔːltə'geðə', *Am:* -ə'] **I.** *adv* **1.** (*completely*) totalmente; **not ~** no del todo **2.** (*in total*) en total **II.** *n* **in the ~** en cueros

alto saxophone *n* saxofón *m* alto

altruism ['æltruːɪzəm] *n no pl* altruismo *m*

altruist ['æltruːɪst] *n* altruista *mf*

altruistic [,æltruː'ɪstɪk] *adj* altruista

aluminium [,æljʊ'mɪnɪəm] *n no pl* aluminio *m*

aluminium foil *n* papel *m* de plata **aluminium oxide** *n* alúmina *f*

aluminum [ə'luːmɪnəm] *n Am s.* **aluminium**

always ['ɔːlweɪz] *adv* **1.** (*at all times*) siempre **2.** (*alternatively*) siempre, en todo caso

am [əm, *stressed:* æm] *vi* **1.** *pers sing of* **be**

a.m. [,eɪ'em] *abbr of* **ante meridiem** a.m.

amalgam [ə'mælgəm] *n* amalgama *f*

amalgamate [ə'mælgəmeɪt] **I.** *vt* **1.** (*metals*) amalgamar **2.** COM fusionar **II.** *vi* **1.** (*metals*) amalgamarse **2.** COM fusionarse

amalgamation [ə,mælgə'meɪʃən] *n no pl* **1.** (*process*) amalgamación *f* **2.** COM fusión *f*

amass [ə'mæs] *vt* (*money*) amasar; (*information*) acumular

amateur ['æmətə', *Am:* -tʃə'] **I.** *n* **1.** (*not professional*) aficionado, -a *m, f* **2.** (*lacking skill*) chapucero, -a *m, f* **II.** *adj* aficionado, -a; **~ sport** deporte *m* de aficionados

amateurish ['æmətərɪʃ, *Am:* ,æmə'tɜːrɪʃ] *adj* chapucero, -a

amaze [ə'meɪz] *vt* **1.** (*astound*) asombrar; **to be ~d that ...** quedar asombrado porque...; **to be ~d by sth** estar asombrado por algo **2.** (*surprise*) sorprender; **to be ~d by sth** estar sorprendido por algo

amazement *n no pl* asombro *m;* **to stare at sth in ~** quedarse boquiabierto mirando algo; **to my ~** para mi gran asombro

amazing *adj* asombroso, -a, sorpresivo, -a *AmL;* **truly ~** realmente increíble

Amazon ['æməzən, *Am:* -zɑːn] *n* **1.** (*female warrior*) amazona *f* **2.** (*river*) **the ~** el Amazonas

ambassador [æm'bæsədə^r, Am: -dəˑ] n embajador(a) m(f)

amber ['æmbə^r, Am: -bəˑ] I. n ámbar m II. adj ambarino, -a; **the traffic light is at ~** Brit el semáforo está en amarillo

ambidextrous [,æmbɪ'dekstrəs] adj ambidextro, -a

ambiguity [,æmbɪ'gjuːəti, Am: -bə'gjuːəʈi] <-ies> n ambigüedad f

ambiguous [æm'bɪgjʊəs] adj ambiguo, -a

ambition [æm'bɪʃən] n ambición f; **she lacks ~** no es nada ambiciosa

ambitious [æm'bɪʃəs] adj ambicioso, -a; **to be ~ for sb** tener grandes ambiciones para alguien; **to be ~ to do sth** tener la ambición de hacer algo

ambivalent [æm'bɪvələnt] adj ambivalente; **to feel ~ about** [o **towards**] **sth/sb** tener sentimientos encontrados hacia algo/alguien

amble ['æmbl] I. vi andar [o pasear] tranquilamente II. n no pl 1. (stroll) **to go for an ~** pasear sin prisas 2. (of horse) ambladura f

ambulance ['æmbjʊləns] n ambulancia f

ambush ['æmbʊʃ] I. vt **to ~ sb** tender una emboscada a alguien II. n <-es> emboscada f; **to lie in ~ for sb** aguardar emboscado a alguien

ameba [ə'miːbə] <-s o -bae> n Am s. amoeba

amebic adj Am s. amoebic

ameliorate [ə'miːlɪəreɪt] vt form mejorar

amelioration [ə,miːlɪə'reɪʃən] n no pl, form mejora f

amen [ɑː'men, Am: eɪ'men] interj amén; **~ to that!** ¡así es!

amenable [ə'miːnəbl] adj receptivo, -a; **to be ~ to sth** mostrarse receptivo a (aceptar) algo; **to be ~ to reason** estar dispuesto a entrar en razón

amend [ə'mend] vt (text, constitution) enmendar; (plan) modificar

amendment n (to text, constitution) enmienda f; (to plan) modificación f

amends npl **to make ~ for sth** reparar algo

amenities [ə'miːnətɪz, Am: -'menəʈɪz] npl comodidades fpl; (**public**) **~** instalaciones públicas

America [ə'merɪkə] n América f (del Norte); **the ~s** las Américas

American [ə'merɪkən] I. n 1. (person from USA) estadounidense mf, americano, -a m, f 2. (person from American continent) americano, -a m, f 3. LING inglés m americano II. adj americano, -a

American football n fútbol m americano

American Indian n amerindio, -a m, f

Americanism n americanismo m

Americanize vt americanizar

amethyst ['æmɪθɪst] I. n 1. (stone) amatista f 2. (colour) amatista m II. adj amatista

amiability [,eɪmiə'bɪləti, Am: -ʈi] n no pl amabilidad f

amiable ['eɪmiəbl] adj amable

amicable ['æmɪkəbl] adj amistoso, -a; **to reach an ~ settlement** llegar a un arreglo amistoso

amid(st) [ə'mɪd(st)] prep en medio de, entre

amino acid [ə'miːnəʊˈæsɪd, Am: -noʊ-] n aminoácido m

amiss [ə'mɪs] I. adj **there's something ~** algo va mal II. adv **to take sth ~** tomar algo a mal; **a little courtesy would not go ~** no vendría mal un poco de cortesía

ammeter ['æmɪtə^r, Am: -ʈəˑ] n amperímetro m

ammonia [ə'məʊnɪə, Am: -'moʊnjə] n no pl 1. (gas) amoniaco m, amoníaco m 2. (liquid) amoniaco m (líquido), amoníaco m (líquido)

ammunition [,æmjʊ'nɪʃən, Am: -jə-] n no pl 1. (for guns) municiones fpl 2. fig argumentos mpl

ammunition depot n, **ammunition dump** n depósito m de municiones

amnesia [æm'niːzɪə, Am: -ʒə] n no pl amnesia f

amnesty ['æmnəsti] <-ies> n amnistía f

amoeba [ə'miːbə] <-bas o -bae> n ameba f

amoebic [ə'miːbɪk] adj amébico, -a

amoebic dysentery n amebiasis f inv, disentería f amebiana

amok [ə'mɒk] adv de forma descontrolada; **to run ~** descontrolarse

among(st) [ə'mʌŋ(st)] prep entre; **~ friends** entre amigos; (**just**) **one ~ many** (sólo) uno entre muchos; **~ Scots** entre los escoceses; **to divide sth up ~ us** dividir algo entre nosotros; **~ the flowers/the pupils** entre las flores/los alumnos; **~ other things** entre otras cosas

amoral [,eɪ'mɒrəl, Am: -'mɔːr-] adj amoral

amorous ['æmərəs] adj amoroso, -a; **to make ~ advances to sb** insinuarse a alguien

amorphous [ə'mɔːfəs, Am: -'mɔːr-] adj amorfo, -a

amortization [ə,mɔːtɪ'zeɪʃən, Am: æm,ɔːrʈə-] n amortización f

amortize [ə'mɔːtaɪz, Am: æm'ɔːr-] vt amortizar

amount [ə'maʊnt] I. n 1. cantidad f; **any ~ of** grandes cantidades de; **any ~ of people** mucha gente; **a certain ~ of difficulty** alguna [o cierta] dificultad 2. (of money) suma f, importe m; **a check in the ~ of ...** Am un cheque por valor de...; **~ carried forward** traslado a cuenta nueva II. vi 1. (add up to) **to ~ to sth** ascender a algo; **that ~s to a refusal** eso viene a ser una negativa 2. (be successful) **to ~ to sth** llegar a algo; **he will never ~ to much** nunca llegará a nada

amp. abbr of **ampere** amp.

ampere ['æmpeə^r, Am: -pɪr] n amperio m

amphetamine [æm'fetəmiːn] n anfetamina f

amphibian [æm'fɪbɪən] I. adj anfibio, -a II. n 1. ZOOL anfibio m 2. AUTO vehículo m anfibio

amphibious [æm'fɪbɪəs] adj anfibio, -a

amphitheater *n Am,* **amphitheatre** ['æmpfɪˌθɪətəʳ, *Am:* -fəˌθiːəʈɚ] *n Aus, Brit* anfiteatro *m*

ample ['æmpl] *adj* 1. (*plentiful*) abundante 2. (*large*) amplio, -a 3. (*enough*) suficiente

amplification [ˌæmplɪfɪ'keɪʃən] *n no pl* 1. MUS amplificación *f* 2. (*increased detail*) ampliación *f;* **to say sth in ~ of sth** *form* decir algo como aclaración de algo

amplifier ['æmplɪfaɪəʳ, *Am:* -ɚ] *n* amplificador *m*

amplify ['æmplɪfaɪ] <-ie-> I. *vt* 1. MUS amplificar 2. (*enlarge upon: statement*) ampliar; (*idea*) desarrollar; (*remark*) aclarar II. *vi* **to ~ upon sth** extenderse sobre algo

amplitude ['æmplɪtjuːd, *Am:* -tuːd] *n no pl* amplitud *f*

ampoule *n Brit,* **ampule** ['æmpuːl] *n Am* MED ampolla *f*

amputate ['æmpjʊteɪt] *vt* amputar

amputation [ˌæmpjʊ'teɪʃən] *n* amputación *f*

amputee [ˌæmpjʊ'tiː] *n* mutilado, -a *m, f*

amuck [ə'mʌk] *adv s.* **amok**

amulet ['æmjʊlɪt] *n* amuleto *m,* cábula *f Arg, Par*

amuse [ə'mjuːz] *vt* 1. (*entertain*) entretener; **to ~ oneself** distraerse; **to keep sb ~d** entretener a alguien 2. (*cause laughter*) divertir, hacer gracia; **I'm not ~d** no me hace gracia

amusement [ə'mjuːzmənt] *n* 1. *no pl* (*entertainment*) entretenimiento *m,* entretención *f AmL;* **for one's own ~** para entretenerse 2. (*mirth*) diversión *f;* **(much) to my ~** con (gran) regocijo por mi parte; **he looked on in ~** miró divertido 3. (*laughter*) risa *f;* **to conceal one's ~** aguantarse la risa

amusement arcade *n Brit* sala *f* de juegos recreativos **amusement park** *n* parque *m* de atracciones

amusing *adj* divertido, -a, gracioso, -a

an [ən, *stressed:* æn] *indef art before vowel s.* **a**

anabolic steroid [ænə'bɒlik 'sterɔɪd] *n* esteroide *m* anabolizante

anachronism [ə'nækrənɪzəm] *n* anacronismo *m*

anachronistic [əˌnækrə'nɪstɪk] *adj* anacrónico, -a

anaconda [ˌænə'kɒndə, *Am:* -'kɑːn-] *n* anaconda *f*

anaemia [ə'niːmɪə] *n no pl* anemia *f*

anaemic [ə'niːmɪk] *adj* anémico, -a

anaesthesia [ˌænɪs'θiːzɪə] *n no pl* anestesia *f*

anaesthetic [ˌænɪs'θetɪk] I. *adj* anestésico, -a II. *n* anestésico *m;* **to be under ~** estar bajo los efectos de la anestesia; **to give sb an ~** anestesiar a alguien

anaesthetist [ˌænɪs'θetɪst] *n* anestesista *mf*

anaesthetize [ə'niːsθətaɪz] *vt* anestesiar

anagram ['ænəgræm] *n* anagrama *m*

anal ['eɪnəl] *adj* anal

analgesic [ˌænæl'dʒiːsɪk] I. *adj* analgésico, -a II. *n* analgésico *m*

analog ['ænəlɒg] *n Am s.* **analogue**

analogous [ə'næləgəs] *adj* análogo, -a; **to be ~ to sth** ser análogo a algo

analogue ['ænəlɒg] *n Brit* equivalente *m*

analogue computer *n* ordenador *m* analógico, computadora *f* analógica *AmL*

analogy [ə'nælədʒi] <-ies> *n* analogía *f;* **to draw an ~ between** establecer una analogía entre; **by ~ with sth** por analogía con algo

analyse ['ænəlaɪz] *vt Aus, Brit* analizar; PSYCH psicoanalizar

analysis [ə'næləsɪs] <-ses> *n* 1. (*examination*) análisis *m inv* 2. (*psychoanalysis*) psicoanálisis *m inv;* **to be in ~** *Am* seguir un tratamiento de psicoanálisis ► **in the final** [*o* **last**] **~** a fin de cuentas

analyst ['ænəlɪst] *n* 1. (*analyzer*) analista *mf;* **food ~** analista de alimentos; **financial ~** analista de inversiones 2. PSYCH psicoanalista *mf*

analytic(al) [ˌænə'lɪtɪk(əl), *Am:* -'lɪʈ-] *adj* analítico, -a

analyze ['ænəlaɪz] *vt Am s.* **analyse**

anarchic(al) [ə'nɑːkɪk(əl), *Am:* æn'ɑːr-] *adj* anárquico, -a

anarchism ['ænəkɪzəm, *Am:* -ɚ-] *n no pl* anarquismo *m*

anarchist ['ænəkɪst, *Am:* -ɚ-] I. *adj* anarquista II. *n* anarquista *mf*

anarchistic [ˌænə'kɪstɪk, *Am:* -ɚ-] *adj* anarquista

anarchy ['ænəki, *Am:* -ɚ-] *n no pl* anarquía *f*

anathema [ə'næθəmə] *n no pl* 1. REL anatema *m* 2. *fig* **the very idea was ~ to her** la sola idea le resultaba odiosa

anatomical [ˌænə'tɒmɪkl, *Am:* -'tɑː-] *adj* anatómico, -a

anatomy [ə'nætəmi, *Am:* -'næʈ-] <-ies> *n* 1. *no pl* BIO anatomía *f* 2. *iron* (*body*) anatomía *f,* cuerpo *m* 3. *no pl* (*analysis*) análisis *m inv*

ancestor ['ænsestəʳ, *Am:* -sestɚ] *n* 1. (*of person*) antepasado, -a *m, f* 2. (*of idea, organization*) precursor(a) *m(f)*

ancestral [æn'sestrəl] *adj* ancestral; **the ~ home** la casa solariega

ancestry ['ænsestri] <-ies> *n* ascendencia *f;* **she is of Polish ~** es de ascendencia polaca

anchor ['æŋkəʳ, *Am:* -kɚ] I. *n* 1. NAUT ancla *f,* sacho *m Chile;* **to be at ~** estar anclado; **to drop/weigh ~** echar/levar anclas 2. *fig* sostén *m* II. *vt* 1. NAUT anclar 2. (*rope, tent*) sujetar 3. RADIO, TV **to ~ a radio/TV programme** presentar un programa de radio/de televisión III. *vi* NAUT echar anclas

anchorage ['æŋkərɪdʒ] *n* 1. (*place*) fondeadero *m* 2. (*charge*) anclaje *m*

anchorman ['æŋkəmæn, *Am:* -kɚ-] <-men> *n* 1. RADIO, TV presentador *m* 2. *fig* hombre *m* clave

anchorwoman ['æŋkəˌwʊmən, *Am:* -kɚ-] <-men> *n* 1. RADIO, TV presentadora *f* 2. *fig* mujer *f* clave

anchovy ['æntʃəvi, Am: -tʃoʊ-] <-ies> n (fresh) boquerón m; (tinned, smoked) anchoa f

ancient ['eɪnʃənt] I. adj 1. a. HIST antiguo, -a; since ~ times desde tiempos remotos; in ~ days hace muchísimo tiempo; ~ history historia antigua; to be ~ history iron haber pasado a la historia 2. inf (very old) prehistórico, -a, del año de la pera; I feel pretty ~ me siento viejísimo II. n the ~s los antiguos

ancillary [æn'sɪləri, Am: 'ænsəleri] adj 1. (staff) auxiliar 2. (road) secundario, -a; to be ~ to sth estar subordinado a algo

and [ən, ənd, stressed: ænd] conj 1. (also) y; (before 'i' or 'hi') e; black ~ white blanco y negro; food ~ drink comida y bebida; parents ~ children padres e hijos 2. MAT y; 2 ~ 3 is 5 2 más 3 son 5; four hundred ~ twelve cuatrocientos doce 3. (then) she went ~ opened the window fue y abrió la ventana 4. (increase) more ~ more cada vez más; better ~ better cada vez mejor 5. (repetition) I tried ~ tried lo intenté una y otra vez [o repetidas veces] 6. (continuation) he cried ~ cried lloraba sin parar ►~ so on [o forth] etcétera

Andalusia [ˌændə'luːsiə, Am: -'luʒə] n Andalucía f

Andalusian I. adj andaluz(a) II. n 1. (person) andaluz(a) m(f) 2. LING andaluz m

Andean ['ændɪən] adj andino, -a

Andes ['ændiːz] npl Andes mpl

Andorra [æn'dɔːrə] n Andorra f

Andorran I. adj andorrano, -a II. n andorrano, -a m, f

androgynous [æn'drɒdʒənəs] adj andrógino, -a

android ['ændrɔɪd] n androide m

anecdotal [ˌænɪk'dəʊtəl, Am: -'doʊtəl] adj anecdótico, -a

anecdote ['ænɪkdəʊt, Am: -doʊt] n anécdota f

anemia [ə'niːmɪə] n Am s. **anaemia**

anemic [ə'niːmɪk] adj Am s. **anaemic**

anemone [ə'nemənɪ] n anémona f

anesthesia [ˌænɪs'θiːʒə] n Am s. **anaesthesia**

anesthetic [ˌænɪs'θetɪk] adj, n Am s. **anaesthetic**

anesthetist [ˌænɪs'θetɪst] n Am s. **anaesthetist**

anesthetize [ə'nesθətaɪz] vt Am s. **anaesthetize**

anew [ə'njuː, Am: -'nuː] adv de nuevo; to begin ~ volver a empezar (de nuevo)

angel ['eɪndʒl] n ángel m; ~ of death ángel exterminador; be an ~ and buy me these shoes sé bueno y cómprame estos zapatos; to be no ~ no ser ningún ángel

angelic [æn'dʒelɪk] adj angelical

anger ['æŋgəʳ, Am: -gɚ] I. n no pl enfado m, enojo m AmL; (stronger) ira f, cólera f; to speak in ~ hablar indignado II. vt enfadar,

enojar AmL

angina [æn'dʒaɪnə] n angina f; ~ pectoris angina de pecho

angle¹ ['æŋgl] I. n 1. a. MAT ángulo m; at an ~ of x degrees en ángulo de x grados; to be at an ~ (to sth) formar un ángulo (con algo); the picture was hanging at an ~ el cuadro estaba torcido; he wore his hat at an ~ llevaba el sombrero ladeado 2. (perspective) perspectiva f; to have a different ~ tener un modo diferente de enfocar la cuestión; what is the best news ~ for this story? ¿cuál es el mejor enfoque informativo para esta historia? 3. (opinion) punto m de vista; what's your ~ on this issue? ¿qué opina(s) sobre esta cuestión? 4. inf (scheme, ploy) she knows all the ~s se las sabe todas II. vt 1. (shot) ladear 2. (information) dirigir; this article is ~d towards teenagers este artículo se dirige a los adolescentes

angle² ['æŋgl] vi 1. (to fish) pescar (con caña) 2. fig to ~ for sth inf tratar de pescar algo

angler ['æŋgləʳ, Am: -glɚ] n pescador(a) m(f) de caña

Anglican ['æŋglɪkən] I. adj anglicano, -a II. n anglicano, -a m, f

Anglican Church n Iglesia f anglicana

Anglicanism ['æŋglɪkənɪzəm] n anglicanismo m

anglicise ['æŋglɪsaɪz] vt Aus, Brit s. **anglicize**

anglicism ['æŋglɪsɪzəm] n anglicismo m

anglicist ['æŋglɪsɪst] n anglicista mf

anglicize ['æŋglɪsaɪz] vt anglicanizar

angling ['æŋglɪŋ] n pesca f (con caña); to go ~ ir a pescar

Anglo-American [ˌæŋgləʊə'merɪkən, Am: -gloʊ] Am I. n angloamericano, -a m, f II. adj angloamericano, -a

anglophile [ˌæŋgləʊfaɪl, Am: -gloʊ] n anglófilo, -a m, f

anglophobe [ˌæŋgləʊ'fəʊb, Am: -glə-] n anglófobo, -a m, f

Anglo-Saxon [ˌæŋgləʊ'sæksən, Am: -gloʊ] I. adj anglosajón, -ona II. n 1. (person) anglosajón, -ona m, f 2. LING anglosajón m

Angola [æŋ'gəʊlə, Am: -'goʊ-] n Angola f

Angolan I. adj angoleño, -a II. n angoleño, -a m, f

angora [æŋ'gɔːrə, Am: -'gɔːrə] n no pl (fabric) angora f

angora cat n gato m de angora

angry ['æŋgri] adj 1. (person) enfadado, -a, enojado, -a AmL; (crowd) enfurecido, -a; (sky) tormentoso, -a; (sea) embravecido, -a; to make sb ~ enfadar [o enojar AmL] a alguien; to get ~ with sb enfadarse con alguien, enojarse con alguien AmL; to get ~ about sth enfadarse por algo, enojarse por algo AmL; to exchange ~ words intercambiar palabras llenas de ira 2. MED inflamado, -a

angst [æŋst] n no pl angustia f

anguish ['æŋgwɪʃ] n no pl angustia f; to be

in ~ (**at sth**) estar angustiado (por algo); **to cause sb** ~ angustiar a alguien

angular ['æŋgjʊlə', *Am:* -lə·] *adj* (*shape*) angular; (*face*) anguloso, -a

animal ['ænɪml] I. *n* 1. ZOOL animal *m;* ~ **fat** grasa *f* animal 2. *fig* (*person*) animal *m*, bestia *mf* II. *adj* (*instincts*) animal; (*desires*) carnal

animal husbandry *n no pl* cría *f* de animales **animal kingdom** *n no pl* reino *m* animal **animal rights** *npl* derechos *mpl* de los animales

animate ['ænɪmeɪt] I. *adj* animado, -a II. *vt* animar

animated *adj* animado, -a; **to become** ~ animarse

animated cartoon *n* dibujos *mpl* animados

animation [ˌænɪ'meɪʃən] *n no pl* animación *f;* **computer** ~ animación por ordenador [*o* computadora *AmL*]

animator ['ænɪmeɪtə', *Am:* -tə·] *n* animador(a) *m(f)*

animosity [ˌænɪ'mɒsəti, *Am:* -'mɑːsəţi] *n no pl* animosidad *f*

animus ['ænɪməs] *n* rencor *m*, animosidad *f*

anise ['ænɪs] *n no pl* (planta *f* de) anís *m*

aniseed ['ænɪsiːd] *n no pl* (semilla *f* de) anís *m*

ankle ['æŋkl] *n* tobillo *m*

anklebone ['æŋklbəʊn] *n* hueso *m* del tobillo

ankle-deep *adj* **to be** ~ **in sth** estar metido hasta los tobillos en algo

ankle sock *n Brit* calcetín *m* corto, soquete *m CSur*

anklet ['æŋklɪt] *n* 1. (*chain*) pulsera *f* tobillera 2. *Am* (*short sock*) calcetín *m* corto

annals ['ænlz] *npl* anales *mpl*

annex ['æneks] I. *vt* 1. (*territory*) anexionar 2. (*document*) adjuntar (como anexo); (*clause*) añadir II. *n* <-es> *Am s.* **annexe**

annexation [ˌænek'seɪʃən] *n no pl* anexión *f*

annexe ['æneks] *n Brit, Aus* 1. (*of building*) edificio *m* anexo 2. (*of document*) anexo *m*, apéndice *m*

annihilate [ə'naɪəleɪt] *vt a. fig* aniquilar

annihilation [əˌnaɪə'leɪʃən] *n a. fig* aniquilación *f*

anniversary [ˌænɪ'vɜːsəri, *Am:* -'vɜːr-] <-ies> *n* aniversario *m;* **wedding** ~ aniversario de bodas

annotate ['ænəteɪt] *vt* anotar; ~**d edition** edición *f* comentada

annotation [ˌænə'teɪʃən] *n* 1. *no pl* (*act of writing*) anotación *f* 2. (*note*) anotación *f*, nota *f*

annotator ['ænəteɪtə', *Am:* -ţə·] *n* anotador(a) *m(f)*

announce [ə'naʊns] *vt* anunciar; (*result*) comunicar

announcement *n* anuncio *m;* **official** ~ comunicado *m* oficial; **to make an** ~ **about sth** anunciar algo

announcer [ə'naʊnsə', *Am:* -sə·] *n* locutor(a) *m(f);* **sports** ~ comentarista *mf* depor-

tivo, -a

annoy [ə'nɔɪ] *vt* molestar, fastidiar, embromar *AmL*, enchilar *AmC;* **it** ~**s me to think that** ... me da rabia pensar que...; **to get** ~**ed with sb** enfadarse [*o* enojarse *AmL*] con alguien

annoyance [ə'nɔɪəns] *n* 1. (*irritation*) fastidio *m*, enojo *m AmL;* **much to my** ~, **she won** me fastidia que haya ganado 2. (*irritating thing*) molestia *f*, fastidio *m*

annoying *adj* (*noise, fact*) molesto, -a, chocante *AmL;* (*person*) pesado, -a; (*habit*) fastidioso, -a; **the** ~ **thing about it is that** ... lo que me da rabia es que... +*subj;* **how** ~! ¡qué fastidio!

annual ['ænjʊəl] I. *adj* anual II. *n* 1. (*book*) anuario *m* 2. BOT planta *f* anual

annual general meeting *n Brit* junta *f* general anual

annually ['ænjʊəli] *adv* anualmente

annuity [ə'njuːəti, *Am:* -'nuːəţi] <-ies> *n* renta *f* anual

annul [ə'nʌl] <-ll-> *vt* anular

annulment [ə'nʌlmənt] *n* anulación *f*

Annunciation [əˌnʌnsɪ'eɪʃən] *n* **the** ~ la Anunciación

anode ['ænəʊd, *Am:* -oʊd] *n* ánodo *m*

anodyne ['ænədaɪn, *Am:* -oʊ-] I. *adj* anodino, -a II. *n* MED analgésico *m*

anoint [ə'nɔɪnt] *vt* untar; (*oil*) ungir

anointing *n* unción *f*

anomalous [ə'nɒmələs, *Am:* -'nɑː-] *adj* anómalo, -a

anomaly [ə'nɒməli, *Am:* -'nɑː-] <-ies> *n* anomalía *f*

anonymity [ˌænə'nɪməti, *Am:* -ţi] *n no pl* anonimato *m*

anonymous [ə'nɒnɪməs, *Am:* -'nɑːnə-] *adj* anónimo, -a; ~ **letter** anónimo *m;* **to remain** ~ permanecer en el anonimato

anorak ['ænəræk] *n Brit* anorak *m*

anorexia [ˌænə'reksɪə] *n no pl* anorexia *f*

anorexia nervosa *n no pl* anorexia *f* nerviosa

anorexic [ˌænər'eksɪk] *adj* anoréxico, -a

another [ə'nʌðə', *Am:* -ə·] I. *pron* 1. (*one more*) otro, -a; **what with one thing and** ~, ... entre unas cosas y otras,... 2. (*mutual*) **one** ~ uno a otro; **they love one** ~ se quieren II. *adj* otro, -a; ~ **cake?** ¿otro pastel?; ~ **£30** otras 30 libras; **could he be** ~ **Mozart?** ¿podría ser otro Mozart?

answer ['ɑːnsə', *Am:* 'æːnsə·] I. *n* 1. (*reply*) respuesta *f*, contestación *f;* **to have an** ~ **for everything** tener respuesta para todo; **in** ~ **to your question** como respuesta a tu pregunta; **I called but there was no** ~ llamé pero no contestaron; **the short** ~ **is 'no'** en una palabra: no 2. (*solution*) solución *f* 3. LAW contestación *f* 4. (*equivalent*) **to be the French** ~ **to the Beatles** ser el equivalente francés de los Beatles II. *vt* 1. (*respond to*) contestar a; **to** ~ **the telephone** contestar al teléfono; **to** ~ **the door** abrir la puerta 2. (*fit, suit: description*)

responder a; (*need*) satisfacer; (*prayers*) escuchar III. *vi* contestar, responder
◆**answer back** *vi* contestar, replicar; **don't ~!** ¡no repliques!
◆**answer for** *vt* (*action, situation*) responder de; (*person*) responder por; **to have a lot to ~** tener mucha culpa
◆**answer to** *vt* **1.**(*obey*) obedecer a **2.**(*fit: description*) corresponder a **3.**(*be named*) **to ~ the name of Billy** responder al nombre de Billy
answerable ['ɑ:nsərəbl, *Am:* 'æn-] *adj* **1.**(*responsible*) **to be ~ for sth** ser responsable de algo **2.**(*accountable*) **to be ~ to sb** tener que rendir cuentas a alguien; **to be ~ to nobody** no tener que rendir cuentas a nadie
answering machine *n* contestador *m* automático **answering service** *n* servicio *m* de mensajes
ant [ænt] *n* hormiga *f* ►**to have ~s in one's pants** *inf* ser un polvorilla, ser un manojo de nervios
antagonism [æn'tægənɪzəm] *n* **1.**(*towards someone*) animadversión *f;* (*between people*) rivalidad *f* **2.** *pl* (*of ideas, systems*) antagonismo *m*
antagonistic [æn‚tægə'nɪstɪk] *adj* **1.**(*person, attitude*) antagónico, -a **2.** ANAT antagonista
antagonize [æn'tægənaɪz] *vt* enfadar, enojar *AmL*
Antarctic [æn'tɑ:ktɪk, *Am:* -'tɑ:rk-] I. *adj* antártico, -a II. *n* **the ~** el Antártico
Antarctica [æn'ɑ:ktɪkə] *n* la Antártida
Antarctic Circle *n* círculo *m* polar antártico **Antarctic Ocean** *n* Océano *m* Antártico **Antarctic Peninsula** *n* península *f* Antártica
ante ['ænti] *n* apuesta *f;* **to raise the ~** subir la apuesta
anteater ['ænt‚i:tər, *Am:* -tɚ] *n* oso *m* hormiguero
antecedent [‚æntɪ'si:dnt] I. *n* **1.**(*forerunner*) antecedente *m,* precedente *m* **2.** *pl* (*past history*) antecedentes *mpl* II. *adj form* antecedente, precedente
antechamber ['æntʃeɪmbər, *Am:* -tɪtʃeɪmbɚ] *n* antecámara *f*
antediluvian [‚æntɪdɪ'lu:vɪən, *Am:* -tɪdə-] *adj a. fig* antediluviano, -a
antelope ['æntɪləʊp, *Am:* -tloʊp] <-(s)> *n* antílope *m*
antenatal [‚æntɪ'neɪtəl, *Am:* -tɪ-] *adj* prenatal; **~ clinic** clínica *f* de asistencia prenatal
antenna [æn'tenə] <-nae *o* -s> *n* antena *f*
anterior [æn'tɪərɪər, *Am:* -'tɪrɪɚ] *adj* anterior
anteroom ['æntɪrʊm, *Am:* -tɪru:m] *n* antesala *f*
anthem ['ænθəm] *n* himno *m*
anthill ['ænthɪl] *n* hormiguero *m*
anthology [æn'θɒlədʒi, *Am:* -'θɑ:lə-] <-ies> *n* antología *f*
anthracite ['ænθrəsaɪt] *n no pl* antracita *f*

anthropoid ['ænθrəpɔɪd] I. *n* antropoide *mf* II. *adj* antropoide
anthropological [‚ænθrəpə'lɒdʒɪkl] *adj* antropológico, -a
anthropologist [‚ænθrəpə'lɒdʒɪst] *n* antropólogo, -a *m, f*
anthropology [‚ænθrə'pɒlədʒi, *Am:* -'pɑ:lə-] *n no pl* antropología *f*
anti ['ænti, *Am:* 'ænti] I. *adj* en contra; **to be ~** estar en contra II. *prep* en contra de
anti-abortion [‚ænti ə'bɔ:ʃən, *Am:* -tiə'bɔ:r-] *adj* antiabortista, contrario al aborto
anti-abortionist *n* antiabortista *mf*
anti-aircraft [‚ænti'eəkrɑ:ft, *Am:* -ti'erkræft] *adj* antiaéreo, -a
antibiotic [‚æntɪbaɪ'ɒtɪk, *Am:* -tɪbaɪ'ɑ:tɪk] I. *n* antibiótico *m* II. *adj* antibiótico, -a
antibody ['æntɪbɒdi, *Am:* -tɪbɑ:di] <-ies> *n* anticuerpo *m*
Antichrist ['æntɪkraɪst, *Am:* -tɪ-] *n* **the ~** el Anticristo
anticipate [æn'tɪsɪpeɪt, *Am:* -ə-] **1.**(*expect, foresee*) prever; **to ~ doing/being sth** tener previsto hacer/ser algo **2.**(*look forward to*) esperar (con ilusión) **3.**(*act in advance of*) anticiparse a; **to ~ one's inheritance** gastarse de antemano la herencia
anticipation [æn‚tɪsɪ'peɪʃən, *Am:* æn‚tɪsə-] *n no pl* **1.**(*foresight*) previsión *f;* **in ~ of** en previsión de **2.**(*funds*) anticipo *m* **3.**(*realization in advance*) **to thank sb in ~** dar las gracias a alguien de antemano **4.**(*excitement*) ilusión *f;* **to wait in ~** esperar con gran ilusión
anticipatory [æn‚tɪsɪ'peɪtəri, *Am:* æn'tɪsɪpətɔ:r-] *adj* previsor(a)
anticlerical [‚æntɪ'klerɪkl, *Am:* -tɪ-] *adj* anticlerical
anticlimactic [‚æntɪ'klaɪmæktɪk, *Am:* -tɪ-] *adj* decepcionante
anticlimax [‚æntɪ'klaɪmæks, *Am:* -tɪ-] <-es> *n* anticlímax *m inv;* (*disappointment*) decepción *f*
anti-clockwise [‚æntɪ'klɒkwaɪz, *Am:* -tɪ'klɑ:k-] *adv Aus, Brit* en sentido contrario a las agujas del reloj
anticoagulant [‚æntɪkəʊ'ægjʊlənt, *Am:* -tɪkoʊ'ægjə-] I. *n* anticoagulante *m* II. *adj* anticoagulante
anticorrosive [‚æntɪkə'rəʊsɪv] I. *adj* anticorrosivo, -a II. *n* anticorrosivo *m*
antics ['æntɪks, *Am:* -tɪks] *npl* **1.**(*foolish behaviour*) payasadas *fpl* **2.**(*tricks*) travesuras *fpl*
anticyclone [‚æntɪ'saɪkləʊn, *Am:* -tɪ'saɪkloʊn] *n* anticiclón *m*
antidazzle [‚æntɪ'dæzl] *adj* antideslumbrante
antidepressant [‚æntɪdɪ'presnt] I. *adj* antidepresivo, -a II. *n* antidepresivo *m*
antidote ['æntɪdəʊt, *Am:* -tɪdoʊt] *n* antídoto *m;* **an ~ to sth** un antídoto contra algo
antifreeze ['æntɪfri:z, *Am:* -tɪ-] *n no pl* anticongelante *m*

antigen ['æntɪdʒən, *Am:* -ṭɪ-] *n* antígeno *m*
Antigua and Barbuda [æn'tiːgə ən baː'bjuːdə] *n* Antigua y Barbuda
Antiguan [æn'tːgən] I. *adj* antigano, -a II. *n* antigano, -a *m, f*
anti-hero [æntɪ'hɪərəʊ, *Am:* ænṭɪ'hɪroʊ] <-es> *n* antihéroe *m*
antihistamine [ˌæntɪ'hɪstəˌmiːn, *Am:* -ṭɪ-] *n* antihistamínico *m*
anti-inflationary [ˌæntɪm'fleɪʃnri, *Am:* -ṭɪ-] *adj* antiinflacionista, antiinflacionario, -a
antiknock [ˌæntɪ'nɒk, *Am:* 'æn ṭɪ'naːk] *adj* antidetonante
Antilles [æn'tɪliːz] *npl* the ~ las Antillas
antilock braking system [æntɪ'lɒk 'breɪkɪŋ 'sɪstəm] *n* AUTO sistema *m* antibloqueo de frenos
antimatter ['æntɪmætəʳ, *Am:* -ṭɪmæṭəˑ] *n* no *pl* antimateria *f*
antimissile [ˌæntɪ'mɪsaɪl, *Am:* -ṭɪ'mɪsl] *adj* antimisil
antioxidant [ˌæntɪ'ɒksɪdənt, *Am:* -ṭɪ'aːk-] *n* antioxidante *m*
antipathy [æn'tɪpəθi] <-ies> *n* antipatía *f*
antiperspirant [ˌæntɪ'pɜːspərənt, *Am:* -ṭɪ'pɜːrspəˑ-] *n* antitranspirante *m*
antipodean [æn'tɪpə'diːən] I. *adj* de las antípodas; *iron* australiano, -a II. *n* habitante *mf* de las antípodas; *iron* australiano, -a *m, f*
antipodes [æn'tɪpədiːz] *npl* antípodas *fpl;* the Antipodes *Brit* Australia y Nueva Zelanda
antiquarian [ˌæntɪ'kweərɪən, *Am:* -ṭə'kwerɪ-] I. *n* (*dealer*) anticuario, -a *m, f;* (*collector*) coleccionista *mf* de antigüedades II. *adj* antiguo, -a
antiquarian bookseller *n* librero, -a *m, f* especializado, -a en libros antiguos **antiquarian bookshop** *n* librería *f* de libros antiguos
antiquary ['æntɪkwəri, *Am:* -ṭəkwər-] <-ies> *n s.* **antiquarian**
antiquated ['æntɪkweɪtɪd, *Am:* -ṭəkweɪṭɪd] *adj* anticuado, -a
antique [æn'tiːk] I. *n* (*object, piece of furniture*) antigüedad *f; pej, iron* antigualla *f* II. *adj* antiguo, -a; *pej* anticuado, -a
antique dealer *n* anticuario, -a *m, f* **antique shop** *n* tienda *f* de antigüedades, anticuario *m*
antiquity [æn'tɪkwəti, *Am:* -ṭi] <-ies> *n* 1. no *pl* (*ancient times*) antigüedad *f* 2. *pl* (*relics*) antigüedades *fpl*
anti-rust [ˌæntɪ'rʌst] *adj* antioxidante
anti-Semite [ˌæntɪ'siːmaɪt, *Am:* -ṭɪ'semaɪt] *n* antisemita *mf*
anti-Semitic [ˌæntɪsɪ'mɪtɪk, *Am:* -ṭɪsə'mɪṭ-] *adj* antisemita
anti-Semitism [ˌæntɪ'semɪtɪsm, *Am:* -ṭɪ'semə-] *n* no *pl* antisemitismo *m*
antiseptic [ˌæntɪ'septɪk, *Am:* -ṭə-] I. *n* antiséptico *m* II. *adj* 1. MED antiséptico, -a 2. *fig, pej* aséptico, -a
antisocial [ˌæntɪ'səʊʃl, *Am:* -ṭɪ'soʊ-] *adj*

antisocial
antistatic [ˌæntɪ'stætɪk, *Am:* -ṭɪ'stæṭ-] *adj* antiestático, -a
antitank [ˌæntɪ'tæŋk, *Am:* -ṭɪ-] *adj* antitanque
antithesis [æn'tɪθəsɪs] <-ses> *n* antítesis *f inv*
antithetic(al) [ˌæntɪ'θetɪk(əl), *Am:* -ṭə'θeṭ-] *adj* antitético, -a
antitoxin [ˌæntɪ'tɒksɪn, *Am:* -tɪ'taːk-] *n* antitoxina *f*
anti-virus [ˌæntɪ'vaɪrəs, *Am:* -ṭɪ-] *adj* antivirus *inv;* ~ **programme** (programa *m*) antivirus *m inv*
anti-war [ˌæntɪ'wɔːr, *Am:* -ṭɪ-] *adj* antibelicista
anti-wrinkle cream [ˌæntɪ'rɪŋklˌkriːm] *n* crema *f* antiarrugas
antler ['æntləʳ, *Am:* -ləˑ] *n* cuerno *m;* ~s cornamenta *f*
antonym ['æntənɪm, *Am:* -tnɪm] *n* antónimo *m*
Antwerp ['æntwɜːp] *n* Amberes *m*
anus ['eɪnəs] *n* ano *m*
anvil ['ænvɪl, *Am:* -vl] *n a.* ANAT yunque *m*
anxiety [æŋ'zaɪəti, *Am:* -ṭi] *n* 1. (*concern*) inquietud *f;* PSYCH ansiedad *f;* **a source of** ~ una fuente de preocupación 2. (*desire*) ansia *f;* ~ **to do sth** ansias de hacer algo; ~ **for sth** ansia de [*o por*] algo
anxiety attack *n* ataque *m* de ansiedad
anxious ['æŋkʃəs] *adj* 1. (*concerned*) preocupado, -a; (*look*) de inquietud; **to keep an** ~ **eye on sth** no quitar los ojos de encima a algo; **to be** ~ **about sth** estar preocupado por algo; **an** ~ **moment** un momento de preocupación 2. (*eager*) ansioso, -a, chingo, -a *Ven;* **to be** ~ **to do sth** estar ansioso por hacer algo; **to be** ~ **for sth** estar ansioso por algo
any ['eni] I. *adj* 1. (*some*) algún, alguna; ~ **books** algunos libros; **do they have** ~ **money?** ¿tienen dinero?; **do you want** ~ **more soup?** ¿quieres más sopa? 2. (*not important which*) cualquier; **come at** ~ **time** ven cuando quieras; **in** ~ **case** en cualquier caso 3. (*negative sense*) ningún, ninguna; **I haven't** ~ **money** no tengo dinero; **there aren't** ~ **cars** no hay ningún coche II. *adv* 1. (*not*) ~ **more** no más; **she does not come** ~ **more** ya no viene más 2. (*at all*) **does she feel** ~ **better?** ¿se siente algo mejor?; **it doesn't help him** ~ *inf* no le ayuda para nada III. *pron* 1. (*some*) alguno, alguna; ~ **of you** alguno de vosotros; ~ **but him would have gone** cualquier otro habría ido 2. (*negative sense*) ninguno, ninguna; **not** ~ ninguno; **he ate two cakes and I didn't eat** ~ él se comió dos pasteles y yo ninguno
anybody ['enɪbɒdi, *Am:* -baːdi] *pron indef* 1. (*someone*) alguien, alguno; **did you hear** ~? ¿has oído a alguien? 2. (*not important which*) cualquiera; ~ **but him** cualquiera menos él; ~ **else would have done it** cual-

quier otro lo hubiese hecho; ~ **will do** cualquiera sirve; **she's not just** ~ no es cualquiera **3.** (*no one*) nadie, ninguno; **I've not seen** ~ **like that** no he visto a nadie así; **more than** ~ más que nadie

anyhow ['enɪhaʊ] *adv* **1.** (*in any case*) de todas maneras, de todos modos **2.** (*well*) bueno; ~**, as I was saying** ... bueno, como iba diciendo... **3.** (*in a disorderly way*) de cualquier manera; **she dumped the tools into the box just** ~ metió las herramientas en la caja de cualquier manera

anyone ['enɪwʌn] *pron indef s.* **anybody**

anyplace ['enɪpleɪs] *adv Am s.* **anywhere**

anything ['enɪθɪŋ] *pron indef* **1.** (*something*) algo; ~ **else?** ¿algo más?; **is there** ~ **new?** ¿alguna novedad? **2.** (*each thing*) cualquier cosa; **they can choose** ~ **they like** pueden escoger cualquier cosa que quieran; **it is** ~ **but funny** es todo menos gracioso; ~ **and everything** cualquier cosa; **to be as fast as** ~ *inf* ser rapidísimo **3.** (*nothing*) nada; **hardly** ~ casi nada; **I didn't find** ~ **better** no encontré nada mejor; **I was afraid, if** ~ estaba asustado, si acaso; **for** ~ (**in the world**) por nada del mundo ▶~ **but!** ¡lo que sea menos eso!

anytime ['enɪtaɪm] *adv Am* = **any time**

anyway ['enɪweɪ] *adv,* **anyways** ['enɪweɪz] *adv Am, inf* **1.** (*in any case*) de todas maneras, de todos modos **2.** (*well*) bueno; ~**, as I was saying** ... bueno, como iba diciendo...

anywhere ['enɪweəʳ, *Am:* -wer] *adv* **1.** (*interrogative*) en alguna parte; **have you seen my glasses** ~**?** ¿has visto mis gafas en alguna parte?; **are we** ~ **near finishing yet?** *inf* ¿nos queda mucho para terminar? **2.** (*positive sense*) en cualquier parte [*o* sitio]; **I can sleep** ~ puedo dormir en cualquier sitio; ~ **else** en cualquier otro sitio; (*negative sense*) en ningún otro sitio; **to live miles from** ~ *inf* vivir en el quinto pino; **its value is** ~ **between £25 and £30** *inf* vale entre las 25 y las 30 libras **3.** (*negative sense*) en ninguna parte; **you won't see this** ~ no verás esto en ningún sitio; **he isn't** ~ **near as popular as he used to be** *inf* no es ni la mitad de popular de lo que era

El **A**nzac **D**ay (**A**ustralian and **N**ew **Z**ealand **A**rmed **C**orps) se celebra el 25 de abril y es un día de luto en Australia y Nueva Zelanda. Con misas y marchas fúnebres se conmemora el desembarco de las **Anzacs** en la península griega de Gallipoli que tuvo lugar el día 25 de abril de 1915, durante el transcurso de la I Guerra Mundial. Las **Anzacs** fueron derrotadas posteriormente. El significado simbólico de este acontecimiento radica en que los australianos lucharon por primera vez como ejército australiano fuera de sus fronteras.

a.o.b. *abbr of* **any other business** ruegos *mpl* y preguntas

aorta [eɪ'ɔːtə, *Am:* -'ɔːrtə] *n* aorta *f*

apace [ə'peɪs] *adv* aprisa

apart [ə'pɑːt, *Am:* -'pɑːrt] *adv* **1.** (*separated*) aparte; **to be 20 km** ~ estar a 20 km de distancia; **far** ~ lejos; **to live** ~ vivir separados; **to move** ~ apartarse **2.** (*aside*) **to be** ~ **from sth** estar apartado de algo; **to set** ~ apartar; **to stand** ~ mantenerse apartado **3.** (*into pieces*) **to come** ~ desprenderse; **to take sth** ~ desmontar algo **4.** (*separately*) **to consider each case** ~ considerar cada caso por separado **5.** (*except for*) **you and me** ~ excepto [*o* salvo] tú y yo; **joking** ~ bromas aparte

apart from *prep* **1.** (*except for*) excepto, salvo; ~ **that** excepto [*o* salvo] eso **2.** (*in addition to*) aparte de, además de **3.** (*separate from*) **to live** ~ **sb** vivir separado de alguien; **to live** ~ **each other** vivir separados el uno del otro

apartheid [ə'pɑːtheɪt, *Am:* -'pɑːrteɪt] *n no pl* apartheid *m*

apartment [ə'pɑːtmənt, *Am:* -'pɑːrt-] *n Am* apartamento *m*, piso *m*, departamento *m AmL;* **holiday** ~ apartamento *m*

apartment building *n Am,* **apartment house** *n Am* edificio *m* de apartamentos, bloque *m* de pisos, edificio *m* de departamentos *AmL*

apathetic [ˌæpə'θetɪk, *Am:* -'θeṯ-] *adj* apático, -a

apathy ['æpəθi] *n no pl* apatía *f;* ~ **about sth** apatía respecto a algo

ape [eɪp] **I.** *n* mono *m*, simio *m* ▶ **to go** ~ *inf* volverse loco **II.** *vt* imitar

aperitif [ə,perə'tiːf] *n* aperitivo *m*

aperture ['æpətʃəʳ, *Am:* -ətʃʊr] *n* **1.** (*crack*) rendija *f* **2.** PHOT abertura *f*

apex ['eɪpeks] <-es *o* apices> *pl n* **1.** (*top*) ápice *m* **2.** *fig* cumbre *f*, cima *f* **3.** MAT vértice *m*

aphid ['eɪfɪd] *n* áfido *m*, afídido *m*

aphorism ['æfərɪzəm, *Am:* -ɚ-] *n* aforismo *m*

aphrodisiac [ˌæfrə'dɪziæk] **I.** *n* afrodisíaco *m*, afrodisiaco *m* **II.** *adj* afrodisíaco, -a, afrodisiaco, -a

apiarist ['eɪpɪərɪst] *n* apicultor(a) *m(f)*

apiary ['eɪpɪəri, *Am:* -eri] <-ies> *n* colmenar *m*

apiculture ['eɪpɪkʌltʃəʳ, *Am:* -tʃɚ] *n* apicultura *f*

apiece [ə'piːs] *adv* cada uno; (*per person*) por persona; **they cost £5** ~ cuestan 5 libras cada uno

aplenty [ə'plenti] *adv* en abundancia; **there was beer** ~ había cerveza en abundancia

aplomb [ə'plɒm] *n* aplomo *m*

apocalypse [ə'pɒkəlɪps, *Am:* -'pɑːkə-] *n no pl* apocalipsis *m inv;* **the Apocalypse** REL el Apocalipsis

apocalyptic [əˌpɒkə'lɪptɪk, *Am:* -ˌpɑːkə-]

adj apocalíptico, -a

apogee ['æpədʒi:, *Am:* -ə-] *n no pl a.* ASTR apogeo *m*

apologetic [ə‚pɒlə'dʒetɪk, *Am:* -‚pɑ:lə'dʒeṭ-] *adj* (*tone, look, smile*) de disculpa; **to be ~ about sth** disculparse por algo

apologetically *adv* disculpándose, excusándose; **to say sth ~** decir algo disculpándose

apologize [ə'pɒlədʒaɪz, *Am:* -'pɑ:lə-] *vi* disculparse; **to ~ to sb for sth** pedir perdón a alguien por algo; **I do ~ if my voice is a little low** *form* pido disculpas si mi tono de voz es bajo

apology [ə'pɒlədʒi, *Am:* -'pɑ:lə-] <-ies> *n* disculpa *f*; **to make an ~** disculparse; **please accept my apologies** le ruego (que) me disculpe; **an ~ for a breakfast** una birria de desayuno

apoplectic [‚æpə'plektɪk] *adj* 1. MED apopléjico, -a, apoplético, -a 2. *fig* furioso, -a; **to be ~ with fury** estar hecho una furia

apoplectic stroke *n* apoplejía *f*

apostle [ə'pɒsl, *Am:* -'pɑ:sl] *n* apóstol *m*

apostolic [‚æpəs'tɒlɪk] *adj* apostólico, -a

apostrophe [ə'pɒstrəfi, *Am:* -'pɑ:strə-] *n* apóstrofo *m*

appal [ə'pɔ:l] <-ll-> *vt* horrorizar; **to be ~led at sth** estar horrorizado de [*o* por] algo

Appalachian Mountains [‚æpə'leɪʃən] *npl* Montes *mpl* Apalaches

appall [ə'pɔ:l] *vt Am s.* **appal**

appalling *adj* 1. (*shocking*) asombroso, -a 2. (*terrible*) horroroso, -a; **an ~ headache** un terrible dolor de cabeza; **~ luck** suerte pésima; **an ~ trip** un viaje espantoso

apparatus [‚æpə'reɪtəs, *Am:* -ə'ræṭ-] *n* 1. (*equipment*) equipo *m*; **climbing ~** equipo *m* de montañismo; **a piece of ~** un aparato 2. (*organization*) aparato *m*

apparel [ə'pærəl, *Am:* -'per-] *n no pl, form* indumentaria *f*; **sports ~** ropa *f* deportiva

apparent [ə'pærənt, *Am:* -'pernt] *adj* 1. (*clear*) evidente; **to become ~ that ...** hacerse evidente que...; **it is ~ to me that ...** me parece evidente que... +*subj* 2. (*seeming*) aparente; **for no ~ reason** sin motivo aparente

apparition [‚æpə'rɪʃən] *n* aparición *f*, espectro *m*, azoro *m AmC*

appeal [ə'pi:l] I. *vi* 1. (*attract*) atraer; **the idea doesn't ~ to me** no me atrae la idea 2. LAW apelar; **to ~ against sth** apelar contra algo 3. (*plead*) **to ~ to sb for sth** pedir algo a alguien; **to ~ for donations/help** solicitar donaciones/ayuda; **she ~ed for silence** rogó silencio II. *n* 1. (*attraction*) atractivo *m*; **to have ~** tener gancho *inf*; **to lose one's ~** perder su atractivo 2. LAW apelación *f*; **court of ~** tribunal *m* de apelación; **to lodge an ~ (against sth)** interponer una apelación (contra algo) 3. (*request*) petición *f*; **an ~ to sb for sth** una solicitud de algo a alguien; **to launch an ~ to do sth** hacer un llamamiento para hacer algo

appealing [ə'pi:lɪŋ] *adj* 1. (*attractive: smile*) atractivo, -a; (*idea*) tentador(a) 2. (*beseeching: eyes*) suplicante

appealingly *adv* 1. (*dress*) con estilo 2. (*look*) de manera suplicante; (*speak*) con tono suplicante

appear [ə'pɪə', *Am:* -'pɪr] *vi* 1. (*be seen*) aparecer 2. (*newspaper*) salir; (*book*) publicarse, aparecer; (*film*) estrenarse 3. LAW **to ~ in court/before a magistrate** comparecer ante un tribunal/ante un juez 4. (*seem*) **to ~ to be ... parecer ser...; it ~s to me that ...** me parece que...; **so it ~s** eso parece; **it would ~ that ...** parecería que...

appearance [ə'pɪərəns, *Am:* -'pɪrəns] *n* 1. (*instance of appearing*) aparición *f*; **to make an ~** aparecer 2. LAW comparecencia *f* 3. *no pl* (*looks*) aspecto *m* 4. *pl* (*outward signs*) apariencias *fpl*; **to [o from Am] all ~s** según parece; **to keep up ~s** guardar las apariencias 5. (*performance*) actuación *f*; **stage ~** aparición *f* en escena ►**~s can be deceptive** *prov* las apariencias engañan *prov*

appease [ə'pi:z] *vt form* 1. (*pacify: person*) apaciguar; POL contemporizar con 2. (*relieve: hunger, suspicion*) aplacar; (*pain*) mitigar

appeasement *n no pl* 1. (*conciliation*) apaciguamiento *m*; **policy of ~** POL política *f* de contemporización 2. (*relief: of anger*) aplacamiento *m*; (*of pain*) mitigación *f*

appellant [ə'pelənt] *n* apelante *mf*

appellation [‚æpə'leɪʃən] *n* título *m*; (*of wine*) denominación *f* de origen

append [ə'pend] *vt form* (*document, note*) adjuntar; (*signature*) añadir

appendage [ə'pendɪdʒ] *n* apéndice *m*, añadidura *f*

appendicitis [ə‚pendɪ'saɪtɪs] *n no pl* apendicitis *f inv*

appendix [ə'pendɪks] *n* 1. <-es> ANAT apéndice *m* 2. <-dices *o* -es> TYPO apéndice *m*

appertain [‚æpə'teɪn] *vi* **to ~ to** (*person*) relacionarse con; (*matter*) tener que ver con

appetite ['æpɪtaɪt, *Am:* -ə-] *n* 1. (*for food*) apetito *m*, antojo *m Méx*; **to have a healthy ~** tener buen apetito 2. *fig* afán *m*

appetite suppressant *n* inhibidor *m* del apetito

appetizer ['æpɪtaɪzə', *Am:* -ətaɪzɚ] *n* 1. (*snack*) aperitivo *m*, botana *f Méx*, pasabocas *m inv Col* 2. *Am* (*first course*) entrante *m*

appetizing ['æpɪtaɪzɪŋ, *Am:* -ə-] *adj* apetitoso, -a

applaud [ə'plɔ:d, *Am:* -'plɑ:d] I. *vi* aplaudir II. *vt a. fig* aplaudir

applause [ə'plɔ:z, *Am:* -'plɑ:z] *n no pl* aplauso *m*; **a round of ~ for the singer** un aplauso para el cantante; **loud ~** fuerte aplauso

apple ['æpl] *n* manzana *f* ►**a day keeps the doctor away** *prov* a diario una manzana es cosa sana; **to be the ~ of sb's eye** ser la niña de los ojos de alguien; **the Big Apple** *inf* Nueva York

applecart ['æplkɑːt, *Am:* -kɑːrt] *n* to upset the ~ desbaratar los planes

apple juice *n* zumo *m* de manzana **apple pie** *n* pastel *m* de manzana **apple sauce** *n* compota *f* de manzana **apple tart** *n* tarta *f* de manzana **apple tree** *n* manzano *m,* manzanero *m Ecua*

appliance [ə'plaɪəns] *n* aparato *m;* **electrical** ~ electrodoméstico *m*

applicability [ˌæplɪkə'bɪlɪti] *n* aplicabilidad *f*

applicable ['æplɪkəbl] *adj* aplicable; **delete where not** ~ táchese lo que no proceda; **those rules are not** ~ **any more** esas normas ya no están vigentes

applicant ['æplɪkənt] *n* (*for money, support*) solicitante *mf;* (*for job*) candidato, -a *m, f;* **an** ~ **for a job** un candidato a un puesto de trabajo

application [ˌæplɪ'keɪʃən] *n* 1.(*request*) solicitud *f;* **on** ~ mediante solicitud 2.(*coating*) aplicación *f* 3.(*use*) aplicación *f,* uso *m* 4.*no pl* (*perseverance*) diligencia *f* 5.INFOR aplicación *f*

application form *n* (hoja *f* de) solicitud *f*

applied [ə'plaɪd] *adj* aplicado, -a

appliqué [æ'pliːkeɪ, *Am:* ˌæplɪ'keɪ] *n* bordado *m* sobrepuesto

apply [ə'plaɪ] I. *vi* 1.(*request*) presentarse; to ~ to sb dirigirse a alguien; to ~ to sb for sth solicitar algo a alguien; to ~ for a job presentarse a [*o* solicitar] un puesto de trabajo; to ~ in writing dirigirse por escrito 2.(*be relevant*) to ~ to sb concernir a alguien II. *vt* 1.(*coat*) aplicar 2.(*use*) aplicar, usar; to ~ force hacer uso de la fuerza; to ~ pressure to sth ejercer presión sobre algo; to ~ sanctions aplicar sanciones; to ~ common sense usar el sentido común 3.*pl* (*persevere*) to ~ oneself to sth dedicarse a algo

appoint [ə'pɔɪnt] *vt* 1.(*select*) nombrar; to ~ sb as heir nombrar a alguien heredero 2.*form* (*designate*) to ~ a date fijar una fecha; at the ~ed time a la hora señalada

appointed *adj form* (*equipped*) equipado, -a

appointee [əpɔɪn'tiː] *n* persona *f* nombrada

appointment *n* 1.(*selection*) nombramiento *m* 2.(*meeting*) cita *f;* **dental** ~ cita *f* con el dentista; to have an ~ at the hairdresser's tener hora en la peluquería; to keep an ~ acudir a una cita; by ~ only sólo con cita previa 3. *pl* (*furniture*) mobiliario *m* ▶by ~ to the Queen proveedores de la reina

appointment book *n* libro *m* de visitas

apportion [ə'pɔːʃən] *vt* repartir

apposite ['æpəzɪt] *adj form* apropiado, -a; (*observation*) pertinente

apposition [ˌæpə'zɪʃən] *n* aposición *f*

appraisal [ə'preɪzl] *n* 1.(*evaluation*) evaluación *f;* (*of performance, evidence*) valoración *f;* (*of property*) tasación *f;* to carry out an ~ of sth efectuar una evaluación de algo 2.(*estimation*) estimación *f*

appraise [ə'preɪz] *vt* 1.(*evaluate*) evaluar; (*performance, evidence*) valorar; (*property*) tasar; to ~ sb's needs valorar las necesidades de alguien 2.(*estimate*) estimar

appreciable [ə'priːʃəbl] *adj* apreciable; (*change*) notorio, -a; (*progress*) considerable

appreciate [ə'priːʃɪeɪt] I. *vt* 1.(*value*) apreciar 2.(*understand*) comprender 3.(*be grateful for*) agradecer II. *vi* FIN (*price*) subir; (*property, shares*) revalorizarse

appreciation [əˌpriːʃɪ'eɪʃən] *n no pl* 1.(*gratitude*) agradecimiento *m* 2.(*understanding*) aprecio *m;* she has no ~ of my work no sabe apreciar mi trabajo 3.FIN (*of price*) subida *f;* (*of property, shares*) revalorización *f*

appreciative [ə'priːʃɪətɪv] *adj* agradecido, -a; an ~ audience un público que sabe apreciar

apprehend [ˌæprɪ'hend] *vt form* 1.(*arrest*) detener 2.(*comprehend*) entender; to ~ the importance of doing sth darse cuenta de la importancia de hacer algo 3.(*fear*) temer

apprehension [ˌæprɪ'henʃən] *n no pl* 1.*form* (*arrest*) detención *f* 2.*no pl, form* (*comprehension*) comprensión *f;* ~ of reality percepción *f* de la realidad 3.*no pl* (*fear*) aprensión *f;* ~ about sth temor *m* por algo

apprehensive [ˌæprɪ'hensɪv] *adj* aprensivo, -a, flatoso, -a *AmL;* to be ~ about sth estar preocupado por algo; to be ~ that temer que +*subj*

apprentice [ə'prentɪs, *Am:* -tɪs] I. *n* aprendiz(a) *m(f),* peón, -ona *m, f Méx* II. *vt* to ~ sb (to sb) colocar a alguien de aprendiz (de alguien)

apprenticeship [ə'prentɪʃɪp, *Am:* -təʃɪp] *n* aprendizaje *m*

approach [ə'prəʊtʃ, *Am:* -'proʊtʃ] I. *vt* 1.(*get close to*) acercarse a 2.(*ask*) dirigirse a; to ~ sb (about sth) dirigirse a alguien (para pedir algo) 3.(*deal with*) abordar II. *vi* acercarse III. *n* 1.(*coming*) aproximación *f;* at the ~ of winter al acercarse el invierno 2.(*access*) acceso *m* 3.(*proposition*) propuesta *f;* (*for help*) petición *f;* to make ~es to sb dirigirse a alguien 4.(*methodology*) enfoque *m*

approachable [ə'prəʊtʃəbl, *Am:* -'proʊ-] *adj* (*person, place*) accesible

approach road *n* (carretera *f* de) acceso *m,* aproches *mpl AmL*

approbation [ˌæprə'beɪʃən] *n no pl, form* aprobación *f*

appropriate¹ [ə'prəʊprɪət, *Am:* -'proʊ-] *adj* apropiado, -a, adecuado, -a; ~ to the occasion apropiado [*o* adecuado] para la ocasión

appropriate² [ə'prəʊprɪeɪt, *Am:* -'proʊ-] *vt form* 1.(*take*) apropiarse de 2.FIN asignar; to ~ funds (for sth) destinar fondos (a algo)

appropriation [əˌprəʊprɪ'eɪʃən, *Am:* -ˌproʊ-] *n* 1.(*taking*) apropiación *f* 2.FIN asignación *f*

approval [ə'pruːvl] *n no pl* aprobación *f;* **to meet with sb's** ~ obtener la aprobación de alguien; **to nod one's** ~ asentir con la cabeza; **on** ~ ECON a prueba

approve [ə'pruːv] I. *vi* estar de acuerdo; **to** ~ **of sth** estar de acuerdo con [*o* aprobar] algo; **she doesn't** ~ **of smoking** no le parece bien que se fume II. *vt* aprobar

approved *adj* **1.** (*agreed*) aprobado, -a **2.** (*authorized*) autorizado, -a; **an** ~ **qualification** un título homologado

approving [ə'pruːvɪŋ] *adj* de aprobación

approvingly [ə'pruːvɪŋli] *adv* con aprobación; **to smile** ~ sonreír en señal de aprobación

approx. [ə'prɒks, *Am:* -'prɑːk-] *n abbr of* **approximately** aprox.

approximate¹ [ə'prɒksɪmət, *Am:* -'prɑːk-] *adj* aproximado, -a

approximate² [ə'prɒksɪmeɪt, *Am:* -'prɑːk-] I. *vt form* aproximarse a II. *vi form* **to** ~ **to sth** aproximarse a algo

approximately [ə'prɒksɪmətli] *adv* aproximadamente

approximation [ə,prɒksɪ'meɪʃən, *Am:* -,prɑːk-] *n form* aproximación *f*

APR [,eɪpiː'ɑːʳ, *Am:* -'ɑːr] *n abbr of* **annual percentage rate** TAE *f*

apricot ['eɪprɪkɒt, *Am:* -kɑːt] I. *n* **1.** BOT albaricoque *m,* chabacano *m Méx,* damasco *m AmS* **2.** *no pl* (*colour*) (color *m*) albaricoque *m* II. *adj* (de color) albaricoque

apricot tree *n* albaricoquero *m,* chabacano *m Méx,* damasco *m AmS*

April ['eɪprəl] *n* abril *m;* **in** ~ en abril; **every** ~ todos los meses de abril; **the month of** ~ el mes de abril; **at the beginning/end of** ~ a principios/finales de abril; **on** ~ **the fourth** el cuatro de abril

April Fools' Day *n no pl* ≈ Día *m* de los Santos Inocentes (*en Gran Bretaña, el 1 de abril*)

a priori [,eɪpraɪ'ɔraɪ] *adv* a priori

apron ['eɪprən] *n* **1.** (*clothing*) delantal *m* **2.** AVIAT pista *f* de estacionamiento **3.** THEAT proscenio *m*

apron strings *n pl* cordeles *mpl* del delantal ▶to be <u>tied</u> to one's mother's ~ estar pegado a las faldas de la madre

apropos, a propos [,æprə'əʊ, *Am:* -'poʊ] I. *prep* ~ **of** a propósito de II. *adv* a propósito III. *adj* apropiado, -a

apse [æps] *n* ábside *m*

apt [æpt] *adj* **1.** (*appropriate*) apropiado, -a; (*comment*) oportuno, -a; (*description*) adecuado, -a **2.** (*clever*) inteligente **3.** (*likely*) **to be** ~ **to do sth** tener tendencia a hacer algo

APT *n abbr of* **advanced passenger train** tren de alta velocidad

aptitude ['æptɪtjuːd, *Am:* -tuːd] *n* aptitud *f*

aptitude test *n* prueba *f* de aptitud

aquaculture ['ækwə,kʌltʃəʳ, *Am:* 'ɑːkwə,kʌltʃəˈ] *n* acuicultura *f*

aqualung ['ækwəlʌŋ] escafandra *f* autónoma

aquamarine [,ækwəmə'riːn, *Am:* ,ɑːkwə-] I. *n* **1.** (*stone*) aguamarina *f* **2.** *no pl* (*colour*) color *m* verde mar II. *adj* de color verde mar

aquaplaning [,ækwə'pleɪnɪŋ, *Am:* ,ɑːkwə-] *n* **1.** SPORTS ≈ esquí *m* acuático **2.** AUTO aquaplaning *m*

Aquarian [əkwɛərɪən] *n* acuario *mf*

aquarium [ə'kweərɪəm, *Am:* -'kwerɪ-] <-s *o* -ria> *n* acuario *m,* acuárium *m*

Aquarius [ə'kweərɪəs, *Am:* -'kwerɪ-] *n* Acuario *m*

aquarobics [,ækwə'rɔbɪks] *npl* aeróbic *m* en el agua

aquatic [ə'kwætɪk, *Am:* -'kwæt̬-] *adj* acuático, -a

aqueduct ['ækwɪdʌkt] *n* acueducto *m*

aquifer ['ækwɪfəʳ] *n* acuífero *m*

aquiline ['ækwɪlaɪn, *Am:* -lən] *adj* aquilino, -a; ~ **nose** nariz *f* aguileña

Arab ['ærəb, *Am:* 'er-] I. *adj* árabe; **the (United)** ~ **Emirates** los Emiratos Árabes (Unidos) II. *n* árabe *mf*

arabesque [,ærə'besk, *Am:* ,er-] *n* arabesco *m*

Arabia [ə'reɪbɪə] *n* Arabia *f*

Arabian *adj* árabe, arábigo, -a

Arabic ['ærəbɪk, *Am:* 'er-] *n* LING árabe *m*

arable ['ærəbl, *Am:* 'er-] *adj* cultivable

arachnid [ə'ræknɪd] *n* arácnido *m*

arbiter ['ɑːbɪtəʳ, *Am:* 'ɑːrbɪt̬əˈ] *n* árbitro, -a *m, f*

arbitrage [,ɑːbɪtrɑːʒ] *n* arbitraje *m* (financiero)

arbitrariness ['ɑːbɪtrərɪnɪs] *n* arbitrariedad *f*

arbitrary ['ɑːbɪtrəri, *Am:* 'ɑːrbətreri] *adj* arbitrario, -a

arbitrate ['ɑːbɪtreɪt, *Am:* 'ɑːrbə-] I. *vt* arbitrar, mediar en; **to** ~ **an argument** mediar en una disputa II. *vi* arbitrar, mediar; **to** ~ **between ...** mediar entre...

arbitration [,ɑːbɪ'treɪʃən, *Am:* ,ɑːrbə-] *n no pl* arbitraje *m,* mediación *f;* **to go to** ~ recurrir al arbitraje

arbitrator ['ɑːbɪtreɪtəʳ, *Am:* 'ɑːrbə-] *n* árbitro, -a *m, f*

arbor ['ɑːbəˈ] *n Am, Aus s.* **arbour**

Con motivo del **Arbor Day** se plantan árboles en los EE.UU. En algunos estados es, incluso, un día festivo. La fecha exacta del **Arbor Day** varía en cada uno de los distintos estados, ya que la época apropiada para plantar árboles no es la misma en todos los sitios.

arboriculture ['ɑːbərɪ,kʌltʃəʳ, *Am:* 'ɑːrbəˈɪ,kʌltʃəˈ] *n* arboricultura *f*

arbour ['ɑːbəʳ] *n Aus, Brit* cenador *m*

arc [ɑːk, *Am:* ɑːrk] I. *n* arco *m* II. *vi* arquearse

arcade [ɑː'keɪd, *Am:* ɑːr-] *n* **1.** (*of shops*) galería *f* comercial **2.** (*around square*) soportales *mpl*

arch¹ [ɑːtʃ, *Am:* ɑːrtʃ] I. *n* arco *m* II. *vi* arquearse III. *vt* arquear; **to ~ one's eyebrows** arquear las cejas

arch² [ɑːtʃ, *Am:* ɑːrtʃ] <-er, -est> *adj* burlón, -ona

archaeological [ˌɑːkɪəˈlɒdʒɪkl, *Am:* ˌɑːrkɪəˈlɑːdʒɪ-] *adj* arqueológico, -a

archaeologist [ˌɑːkɪˈɒlədʒɪst, *Am:* ˌɑːrkɪˈɑːlə-] *n* arqueólogo, -a *m, f*

archaeology [ˌɑːkɪˈɒlədʒi, *Am:* ˌɑːrkɪˈɑːlə-] *n no pl* arqueología *f*

archaic [ɑːˈkeɪɪk, *Am:* ɑːr-] *adj* arcaico, -a

archangel [ˈɑːkeɪndʒl, *Am:* ˈɑːr-] *n* arcángel *m*

archbishop [ˌɑːtʃˈbɪʃəp, *Am:* ˌɑːrtʃ-] *n* arzobispo *m*

archdeacon [ˌɑːtʃˈdiːkən, *Am:* ˌɑːrtʃ-] *n* arcediano *m*

archdiocese [ˌɑːtʃˈdaɪəsɪs, *Am:* ˌɑːrtʃ-] *n* archidiócesis *f inv*

arch enemy <-ies> *n* archienemigo, -a *m, f*

archeological [ˌɑːrkɪəˈlɑːdʒɪkəl] *adj Am s.* **archaeological**

archeologist [ˌɑːrkiˈɑːlədʒɪst] *n Am s.* **archaeologist**

archeology [ˌɑːrkiˈɑːlədʒi] *n Am s.* **archaeology**

archer [ˈɑːtʃəʳ, *Am:* ˈɑːrtʃəʳ] *n* arquero, -a *m, f*

archery [ˈɑːtʃəri, *Am:* ˈɑːr-] *n no pl* tiro *m* con arco

archetype [ˈɑːkɪtaɪp, *Am:* ˈɑːr-] *n* arquetipo *m*

archipelago [ˌɑːkɪˈpeləgəʊ, *Am:* ˌɑːrkəˈpeləgoʊ] <-(e)s> *n* archipiélago *m*

architect [ˈɑːkɪtekt, *Am:* ˈɑːrkə-] *n* 1.(*of building*) arquitecto, -a *m, f* 2. *fig* artífice *mf*

architecture [ˈɑːkɪtektʃəʳ, *Am:* ˈɑːrkətektʃəʳ] *n no pl* arquitectura *f*

archive [ˈɑːkaɪv, *Am:* ˈɑːr-] *n a.* INFOR archivo *m*

archivist [ˈɑːkɪvɪst, *Am:* ˈɑːrkaɪ-] *n* archivero, -a *m, f*, archivista *mf Méx*

archway [ˈɑːtʃweɪ, *Am:* ˈɑːrtʃ-] *n* (*entrance*) arco *m;* (*passageway*) pasadizo *m* abovedado

arc lamp *n*, **arc light** *n* arco *m* voltaico

Arctic [ˈɑːktɪk, *Am:* ˈɑːrk-] *no pl* I. *n* **the ~** el Ártico II. *adj* 1. ártico, -a 2. (*extremely cold*) glacial

Arctic Circle *n* Círculo *m* Polar Ártico **Arctic Ocean** *n* Océano *m* Glacial Ártico

arc welding *n* soldadura *f* por arco

ardent [ˈɑːdnt, *Am:* ˈɑːr-] *adj* ferviente; (*desire, plea*) vehemente

ardor *n Am*, **ardour** [ˈɑːdəʳ, *Am:* ˈɑːrdəʳ] *n no pl, Brit* fervor *m*

arduous [ˈɑːdjʊəs, *Am:* ˈɑːrdʒu-] *adj* arduo, -a; (*task*) trabajoso, -a

are [əʳ, *stressed:* ɑːʳ, *Am:* əʳ, *stressed:* ɑːr] *vi s.* **be**

area [ˈeərɪə, *Am:* ˈerɪ-] *n* 1. *a.* MAT, SPORTS área *f*; **in the ~ of** alrededor de 2. (*field*) campo *m;* **~ of competence/knowledge** ámbito *m* de competencia(s)/conocimiento(s)

area code *n Am, Aus* prefijo *m*

arena [əˈriːnə] *n a. fig* arena *f*

Argentina [ˌɑːdʒənˈtiːnə, *Am:* ˌɑːr-] *n* Argentina *f*

Argentine [ˈɑːdʒəntaɪn, *Am:* ˈɑːrdʒən-], **Argentinian** [ˌɑːdʒənˈtɪnɪən, *Am:* ˌɑːr-] I. *adj* argentino, -a II. *n* argentino, -a *m, f*

arguable [ˈɑːgjuəbl, *Am:* ˈɑːrg-] *adj* discutible

arguably *adv* posiblemente

argue [ˈɑːgjuː, *Am:* ˈɑːrg-] I. *vi* 1. (*disagree*) discutir, alegar *AmL* 2. (*reason*) razonar; **to ~ against/for sth** abogar contra/a favor de algo II. *vt* 1. (*debate*) sostener; **to ~ that ...** sostener que... 2. (*persuade*) **to ~ sb into doing sth** persuadir a alguien de hacer algo; **to ~ sb out of doing sth** persuadir a alguien para que abandone la idea de hacer algo

argument [ˈɑːgjʊmənt, *Am:* ˈɑːrgjə-] *n* 1. (*disagreement*) discusión *f* 2. (*reasoning*) argumento *m;* **suppose for ~'s sake that ...** supongamos por caso que...

argumentative [ˌɑːgjʊˈmentətɪv, *Am:* ˌɑːrgjəˈmentətɪv] *adj* discutidor(a)

aria [ˈɑːrɪə] *n* MUS aria *f*

arid [ˈærɪd, *Am:* ˈer-] *adj* árido, -a

Aries [ˈeəriːz, *Am:* ˈeriːz] *n* Aries *m*

arise [əˈraɪz] <arose, arisen> *vi* 1. (*come about*) surgir; **to ~ from** surgir de; **should the need ~** si fuera necesario; **should doubt ~** en caso de presentarse la duda 2. *form* (*rise up*) alzarse

arisen [əˈrɪzn] *pp of* **arise**

aristocracy [ˌærɪˈstɒkrəsi, *Am:* ˌerəˈstɑːkrə-] <-ies> *n + sing/pl vb* aristocracia *f*

aristocrat [ˈærɪstəkræt, *Am:* əˈrɪs-] *n* aristócrata *mf*

aristocratic [ˌærɪstəˈkrætɪk, *Am:* eˌrɪstəˈkrætɪk] *adj* aristocrático, -a

arithmetic [əˈrɪθmətɪk, *Am:* ˌerɪθˈmetɪk] I. *n no pl* aritmética *f* II. *adj* aritmético, -a

arithmetical [ˌærɪθˈmetɪkl, *Am:* ˌerɪθˈmetɪkl] *adj* aritmético, -a

ark [ɑːk, *Am:* ɑːrk] *n no pl* arca *f;* **Noah's ark** el Arca de Noé

arm¹ [ɑːrm] *n* 1. ANAT, GEO brazo *m;* **to put one's ~s round sb** abrazar a alguien; **to hold sb in one's ~s** tener a alguien en brazos; **~ in ~** (agarrados) del brazo 2. (*sleeve*) manga *f* 3. (*division*) sección *f* ►**the** (**long**) **~ of the law** el brazo de la ley; **to cost an ~ and a leg** *inf* costar un ojo de la cara; **to keep sb at ~'s length** *fig* mantener a alguien a distancia

arm² [ɑːm, *Am:* ɑːrm] MIL I. *vt* 1. (*supply with weapons*) armar; **to ~ oneself against sth** armarse contra algo 2. (*prepare for detonation*) activar; (*rocket*) cebar II. *n* (*weapon*) arma *f;* **under ~s** en armas; **to lay down one's ~s** rendir las armas; **to present ~s** presentar armas; **to take up ~s** (**against sb/sth**) tomar las armas (contra alguien/algo) ►**to be up in ~s about ...** poner el grito en el cielo contra...

armaments ['ɑːməməntz, *Am:* 'ɑːr-] *npl* armamento *m*

armature ['ɑːmətʃʊəʳ, *Am:* 'ɑːrmətʃɚ] *n* 1. TECH, ZOOL, BOT armadura *f* 2. ELEC inducido *m*

armband ['ɑːmbænd, *Am:* 'ɑːrm-] *n* brazalete *m*

armchair [ˌɑːm'tʃeəʳ, *Am:* 'ɑːrmtʃer] *n* sillón *m*

armed [ɑːmd, *Am:* ɑːrmd] *adj* armado, -a

armed forces *npl* the ~ las fuerzas armadas

Armenia [ɑːˈmiːniə, *Am:* ɑːr-] *n* Armenia *f*

Armenian I. *n* 1. (*person*) armenio, -a *m, f* 2. LING armenio *m* II. *adj* armenio, -a

armful ['ɑːmfʊl, *Am:* 'ɑːrm-] *n* brazada *f*

armhole ['ɑːmhəʊl, *Am:* 'ɑːrmhoʊl] *n* sisa *f*

arming ['ɑːmɪŋ] *n* aprovisionamiento *m* de armas

armistice ['ɑːmɪstɪs, *Am:* 'ɑːrmə-] *n* armisticio *m*

armor ['ɑːməʳ, *Am:* 'ɑːrmɚ] *n Am s.* **armour**

armored ['ɑːməd, *Am:* 'ɑːrmɚd] *adj Am s.* **armoured**

armor-plated ['ɑːməˈpleɪtɪd] *adj Am s.* **armour-plated**

armour ['ɑːməʳ, *Am:* 'ɑːrmɚ] *n no pl, Brit* 1. (*protective covering*) blindaje *m* 2. *a.* MIL, ZOOL armadura *f* 3. (*tanks*) carros *mpl* blindados

armoured ['ɑːməd, *Am:* 'ɑːrmɚd] *adj Brit* (*car*) blindado, -a; (*train*) acorazado, -a

armour-plated ['ɑːməˈpleɪtɪd] *adj Brit* blindado, -a

armpit ['ɑːmpɪt, *Am:* 'ɑːrm-] *n* axila *f*

armrest ['ɑːmrest, *Am:* 'ɑːrm-] *n* descansabrazos *m inv*

arms control *n,* **arms limitation** *n* MIL control *m* de armamentos **arms race** *n* the ~ la carrera armamentista **arms reduction** *n* reducción *f* de armamentos

army ['ɑːmi, *Am:* 'ɑːr-] <-ies> *n* 1. MIL ejército *m;* **to join the** ~ alistarse 2. *fig* multitud *f*

aroma [əˈrəʊmə, *Am:* -ˈroʊ-] *n* aroma *m*

aromatherapy [əˌrəʊməˈθerəpi, *Am:* -ˌroʊ-] *n no pl* aromaterapia *f*

aromatic [ˌærəʊˈmætɪk, *Am:* ˌerəˈmæt̬-] *adj* aromático, -a

arose [əˈrəʊz, *Am:* əˈroʊz] *pt of* **arise**

around [əˈraʊnd] I. *prep* 1. (*surrounding*) alrededor de; **all** ~ **sth** por todas partes; **the earth goes** ~ **the sun** la tierra gira alrededor del sol; **to go** ~ **the corner** doblar la esquina 2. (*here and there within*) por; **to drive** ~ **France** viajar (en coche) por Francia; **to go** ~ **a museum** visitar un museo; **to go all** ~ **the world** viajar por el mundo; **to sit** ~ **the room** sentarse en la habitación 3. (*approximately*) más o menos, alrededor de; ~ **May 10** alrededor del 10 de mayo; **somewhere** ~ **here** en algún lugar por aquí II. *adv* 1. (*round about*) alrededor; **all** ~ en todas partes; **for 50 m** ~ en

un radio de 50 m; **for miles** ~ en millas a la redonda 2. (*aimlessly*) **to walk** ~ dar una vuelta; **to stand/hang** ~ estar/andar por ahí; **to have been** ~ haber visto mundo; (*be experienced*) tener mucha experiencia 3. (*near by*) por ahí; **is he** ~? ¿está por ahí?; **to be still** ~ seguir todavía ahí

arouse [əˈraʊz] *vt* 1. (*stir*) suscitar; (*anger*) provocar 2. (*sexually excite*) excitar

arr. *abbr of* **arrival** llegadas *fpl*

arrange [əˈreɪndʒ] I. *vt* 1. (*organize*) organizar; **to** ~ **a date** acordar una cita 2. (*put in order*) *a.* MUS arreglar II. *vi* disponer; **to** ~ **for sth** disponer algo; **to** ~ **to do sth** quedar en hacer algo

arrangement *n* 1. *pl* (*preparations*) preparativos *mpl;* **to make** ~**s** (**for sth**) hacer los preparativos (de algo) 2. (*agreement*) acuerdo *m;* **to come to an** ~ llegar a un acuerdo 3. (*method of organizing sth*) *a.* MUS arreglo *m*

array [əˈreɪ] I. *n* 1. (*display*) colección *f* 2. *form* (*clothes*) atavío *m* 3. MIL formación *f* II. *vt* 1. (*display*) colocar, exponer 2. *form* (*clothes*) ataviar 3. MIL desplegar

arrears [əˈrɪəz, *Am:* -ˈrɪrz] *npl* FIN atraso *m;* **to be in** ~ **on sth** estar atrasado en el pago de algo; **to pay in** ~ pagar con atraso

arrest [əˈrest] I. *vt* 1. LAW detener 2. *form* (*put a stop to*) detener 3. (*attract*) **to** ~ **sb's attention** captar la atención de alguien II. *n* detención *f;* **to be under** ~ estar detenido; **to put sb under** ~ detener a alguien

arresting *adj* llamativo, -a; (*account*) cautivante; (*performance*) impresionante

arrival [əˈraɪvl] *n* 1. (*at destination*) llegada *f;* **on his** ~ a su llegada 2. (*person*) persona *f* que llega; **new** ~ recién llegado *m*

arrive [əˈraɪv] *vi* 1. (*come*) llegar; **to** ~ **at a conclusion** llegar a una conclusión 2. *inf* (*establish one's reputation*) llegar a ser alguien 3. (*be born*) nacer

arriviste [ˌæriːˈviːst, *Am:* ˌer-] *n* arribista *mf*

arrogance ['ærəgəns, *Am:* 'er-] *n no pl* arrogancia *f*

arrogant ['ærəgənt, *Am:* 'er-] *adj* arrogante

arrow ['ærəʊ, *Am:* 'eroʊ] *n* flecha *f,* jara *f Guat, Méx*

arrowhead *n* punta *f* de flecha

arse [ɑːs, *Am:* ɑːrs] *n Aus, Brit, vulg* culo *m,* siete *m AmS, Méx* ▸**get your** ~ **in gear!** ¡espabílate!; **to make an** ~ **out of oneself** quedar como un gilipollas; **move your** ~! ¡muévete!; **to work one's** ~ **off** trabajar como un burro

arsenal ['ɑːsənl, *Am:* 'ɑːr-] *n* arsenal *m*

arsenic ['ɑːsnɪk, *Am:* 'ɑːr-] *n no pl* arsénico *m*

arson ['ɑːsn, *Am:* 'ɑːr-] *n* incendio *m* provocado

art [ɑːt, *Am:* ɑːrt] *n* arte *m*

art collection *n* colección *f* de arte **art critic** *n* crítico *m* de arte **art dealer** *n* marchante *mf* de arte

artefact [ˈɑːtɪfækt, *Am:* ˈɑːrṭə-] *n Brit* artefacto *m*

arterial [ɑːˈtɪərɪəl, *Am:* ɑːrˈtɪrɪ-] *adj* 1. ANAT arterial 2. AUTO, RAIL principal

arteriosclerosis [ɑːˌtɪərɪəʊskləˈrəʊsɪs, *Am:* ɑːrˌtɪriouskləˈrousəs] *n* arteriosclerosis *f inv*

artery [ˈɑːtəri, *Am:* ˈɑːrṭə] <-ies> *n* arteria *f*

artesian well [ɑːˈtiːzɪənˈwel, *Am:* ɑːrˈtiːʒənˈwel] *n* pozo *m* artesiano

artful [ˈɑːtfəl, *Am:* ˈɑːrt-] *adj* hábil, ingenioso, -a

art gallery *n* (*for public exhibitions*) museo *m* de arte; (*for sale of paintings*) galería *f* de arte

arthritic [ɑːˈθrɪtɪk, *Am:* ɑːrˈθrɪṭ-] *adj* artrítico, -a

arthritis [ɑːˈθraɪtɪs, *Am:* ɑːrˈθraɪṭəs] *n no pl* artritis *f inv*

artichoke [ˈɑːtɪtʃəʊk, *Am:* ˈɑːrṭətʃouk] *n* alcachofa *f*

article [ˈɑːtɪkl, *Am:* ˈɑːrṭɪ-] *n* 1. (*object*) artículo *m*, objeto *m*; ~ **of clothing** prenda *f* de vestir 2. *a.* LAW, LING, TYPO artículo *m*

articulate[1] [ɑːˈtɪkjʊlət, *Am:* ɑːrˈtɪkjə-] *adj* 1. (*person*) que se expresa con claridad; (*speech*) claro, -a 2. TECH articulado, -a

articulate[2] [ɑːˈtɪkjʊlaɪt, *Am:* ɑːrˈtɪkjə-] *vt form* 1. (*express*) expresar claramente; **to ~ an idea** articular una idea 2. (*pronounce*) articular

articulated lorry *n Brit* camión *m* articulado

articulation [ɑːˌtɪkjʊˈleɪʃən, *Am:* ɑːrˌtɪkjə-] *n no pl* (*of idea, feeling*) expresión *f*

artifact [ˈɑːtɪfækt, *Am:* ˈɑːrṭə-] *n Am* artefacto *m*

artifice [ˈɑːtɪfɪs, *Am:* ˈɑːrṭə-] *n form* artificio *m*

artificial [ˌɑːtɪˈfɪʃl, *Am:* ˌɑːrṭə-] *adj* artificial **artificial insemination** *n* inseminación *f* artificial **artificial intelligence** *n* inteligencia *f* artificial

artillery [ɑːˈtɪləri, *Am:* ɑːr-] *n no pl* artillería *f*

artilleryman [ɑːˈtɪlərɪmən, *Am:* ɑːrˈtɪlrɪmen] *n* artillero *m*

artisan [ˌɑːtɪˈzæn, *Am:* ˈɑːrṭəzn] *n* artesano, -a *m, f*

artist [ˈɑːtɪst, *Am:* ˈɑːrṭəst-] *n* artista *mf*

artiste [ɑːˈtiːst, *Am:* ɑːr-] *n* THEAT artista *mf*

artistic [ɑːˈtɪstɪk, *Am:* ɑːr-] *adj* artístico, -a

artistry [ˈɑːtɪstri, *Am:* ˈɑːrṭə-] *n no pl* arte *m* o *f*

artless [ˈɑːtlɪs, *Am:* ˈɑːrt-] *adj* 1. (*simple*) sencillo, -a 2. (*clumsy*) torpe

artwork [ˈɑːtwɜːk, *Am:* ˈɑːrtwɜːrk] *n no pl* material *m* gráfico, ilustraciones *fpl*

arty [ˈɑːti, *Am:* ˈɑːrṭi] <-ier, -iest> *adj inf* (*person*) pseudoartístico, -a; (*film*) pretencioso, -a

Aryan [ˈeərɪən, *Am:* ˈerɪ-] HIST I. *n* ario, -a *m, f* II. *adj* ario, -a

as [əz, *stressed:* æz] I. *prep* como; **dressed ~ a clown** vestido de payaso; **the king, ~ such**

el Rey, como tal; ~ **a baby, I was ...** de bebé, yo era...; **to use sth ~ a lever** utilizar algo como palanca II. *conj* 1. (*in comparison*) como; **the same name ~ sth/sb** el mismo nombre que algo/alguien; ~ **fast ~ sth/sb** tan rápido como algo/alguien; **to eat ~ much ~ sb** comer tanto como alguien; ~ **soon ~ possible** lo antes posible, tan pronto como sea posible 2. (*like*) (tal) como; ~ **it is** tal es como es; **I came ~ promised** vine, como (lo) prometí; **she was dressed ~ he was** llevaba la misma ropa que él; ~ **if it were true** como si fuese verdad 3. (*because*) como; ~ **he is here I'm going** como él está aquí, yo me voy 4. (*while*) mientras 5. (*although*) (~) **fine ~ the day is, ...** aunque el día está bien,...; **try ~ I would, I couldn't** por más que me esforzara, no podía ▶~ **far ~** (*to the extent that*) en la medida en que; (*concerning*) respecto a III. *adv* ~ **well** también; ~ **long as** mientras que +*subj*; ~ **much as** tanto como; ~ **soon as** en cuanto, tan pronto

a.s.a.p. [ˌeɪeseɪˈpiː] *abbr of* **as soon as possible** lo antes posible, tan pronto como sea posible

asbestos [æzˈbestɒs, *Am:* -təs] *n no pl* asbesto *m*

asbestosis [ˌæsbesˈtəʊsɪs, *Am:* -ˈtou-] *n pl* asbestosis *f inv*

ascend [əˈsend] I. *vt form* (*steps*) subir; (*mountain*) ascender; **to ~ the throne** subir al trono II. *vi* ascender; **in ~ing order** en orden ascendente

ascendancy [əˈsendənsi] *n no pl* ascendencia *f*; (*supremacy*) supremacía *f*

ascendant [əˈsendənt] I. *n no pl, form* 1. (*position of power*) **to be in the ~** estar en alza 2. ASTR ascendente *m* II. *adj* ascendente

ascendency [əˈsendənsi] *n s.* **ascendancy**

ascendent [əˈsendənt] *n, adj s.* **ascendant**

ascension [əˈsenʃən] *n* 1. (*going up*) ascensión *f* 2. REL **the Ascension** la Ascensión

Ascension Day *n no pl* día *m* de la Ascensión

ascent [əˈsent] *n* 1. *form* (*climb*) ascensión *f* 2. (*slope*) pendiente *f*

ascertain [ˌæsəˈteɪn, *Am:* -ɚ-] *vt form* 1. (*find out*) averiguar 2. (*make sure*) comprobar

ascetic [əˈsetɪk, *Am:* -ˈseṭ-] I. *n* asceta *mf* II. *adj* ascético, -a

asceticism [əˈsetɪsɪzəm, *Am:* -ˈseṭə-] *n no pl* ascetismo *m*

ASCII [ˈæskiː] *abbr of* **American Standard Code for Information Interchange** ASCII

Ascot es el nombre de una pequeña localidad en Berkshire en la que se encuentra un hipódromo construido en 1711 por expreso deseo de la Reina Anne. Con el nombre de

Royal Ascot se conocen unas jornadas hípicas, de cuatro días de duración, que se celebran con carácter anual durante el mes de Junio y a las que la reina suele acudir casi siempre.

ascribe [ə'skraɪb] *vt* **to** ~ **sth to sb** atribuir algo a alguien
ascription [ə'skrɪpʃən] *n* atribución *f*
asexual [ˌeɪ'sekʃʊəl, *Am:* -ʃʊəl] *adj* **1.** (*reproduction*) asexual **2.** (*person*) asexuado, -a
ash¹ [æʃ] *n no pl* (*powder*) ceniza *f*
ash² [æʃ] *n* **1.** (*tree*) fresno *m* **2.** *no pl* (*wood*) (madera *f* de) fresno *m*
ashamed [ə'ʃeɪmd] *adj* avergonzado, -a; **to feel** ~ estar avergonzado; **to be** ~ **of oneself** avergonzarse de uno mismo
ashcan ['æʃkæn] *n Am* cubo *m* de basura, bote *m* de basura *Méx*
ashore [ə'ʃɔːʳ] **I.** *adj* en tierra **II.** *adv* a tierra; **to go** ~ desembarcar; **to run** ~ encallar
ashtray ['æʃˌtreɪ] *n* cenicero *m*
Ash Wednesday *n* Miércoles *m* de Ceniza
Asia ['eɪʃə, *Am:* -ʒə] *n no pl* Asia *f*
Asia Minor *n* Asia *f* Menor
Asian ['eɪʃən, *Am:* -ʒən] **I.** *n* asiático, -a *m, f* **II.** *adj* asiático, -a
Asiatic [ˌeɪʃi'ætɪk] **I.** *adj* asiático, -a **II.** *n* asiático, -a *m, f*
aside [ə'saɪd] **I.** *n* **1.** (*in a speech*) digresión *f* **2.** (*in a conversation*) comentario *m* aparte **3.** THEAT aparte *m* **II.** *adv* a un lado; **to stand** ~ hacerse a un lado; **to leave sth** ~ dejar algo a un lado
aside from *prep* aparte de; **to turn** ~ **sb/sth** alejarse de alguien/algo
ask [ɑːsk, *Am:* æsk] **I.** *vt* **1.** (*request information*) preguntar; **to** ~ **sb sth** preguntar algo a alguien; **to** ~ (**sb**) **a question about sth** hacer (a alguien) una pregunta acerca de algo; **don't** ~ **me** ni me preguntes; **if you** ~ **me ...** en mi opinión... **2.** (*request*) pedir; **to** ~ **advice/a favour** pedir consejo/un favor **3.** (*invite*) invitar; **to** ~ **sb to do sth** invitar a alguien a hacer algo **4.** (*demand a price*) pedir; **to** ~ **100 euros for sth** pedir 100 euros por algo **5.** (*expect*) **to** ~ **too much of sb** pedir demasiado de alguien **II.** *vi* **1.** (*request information*) preguntar **2.** (*make a request*) pedir
◆**ask for** *vt* **1.** (*request*) pedir **2.** (*inquire about*) preguntar por **3.** (*deserve*) **to** ~ **trouble** buscar complicaciones
askance [ə'skæns] *adv* con recelo; **to look** ~ (**at sb/sth**) mirar con recelo (a alguien/algo)
askew [ə'skjuː] *adj* torcido, -a, ladeado, -a
asking ['ɑːskɪŋ, *Am:* 'æskɪŋ] *n no pl* petición *f*; **it's yours for the** ~ no tienes a pedir de boca
asleep [ə'sliːp] *adj* dormido, -a; **to be** ~ estar dormido; **to fall** ~ quedarse dormido
asparagus [ə'spærəgəs, *Am:* -'sper-] *n* **1.** (*vegetable*) espárrago *m* **2.** (*plant*) espa-

rraguera *f*
ASPCA [ˌeɪesˌpiːsiː'eɪ] *n abbr of* **American Society for Prevention of Cruelty to Animals** asociación americana protectora de los animales
aspect ['æspekt] *n* **1.** (*point of view*) punto *m* de vista **2.** (*feature*) faceta *f* **3.** (*direction*) orientación *f* **4.** (*appearance*) aspecto *m* **5.** *no pl* ASTR aspecto *m* **6.** LING aspecto *m*
aspen ['æspən] *n* álamo *m* temblón
asperity [æ'sperəti, *Am:* -əʈi] <-ies> *n form* aspereza *f*
aspersion [ə'spɜːʃən, *Am:* -'spɜːrʒən] *n form* calumnia *f*; **to cast** ~ **on sb** calumniar a alguien
asphalt ['æsfælt, *Am:* -faːlt] **I.** *n* asfalto *m*, asfaltado *m AmL* **II.** *vt* asfaltar
asphyxia [æs'fɪksɪə] *n no pl* asfixia *f*
asphyxiate [əs'fɪksɪeɪt] **I.** *vi form* asfixiarse **II.** *vt* asfixiar
asphyxiation [əsˌfɪksɪ'eɪʃən] *n no pl* asfixia *f*
aspirant [ə'spaɪərənt, *Am:* 'æspənt] *n form* aspirante *mf*; (*to job, position*) candidato, -a *m, f*
aspiration [ˌæspə'reɪʃən] *n* aspiración *f*
aspire [ə'spaɪəʳ, *Am:* -'spaɪ˞] *vi* **to** ~ **to sth** aspirar a algo
aspirin® ['æsprɪn] *n no pl* aspirina® *f*
aspiring [ə'spaɪərɪŋ, *Am:* -'spaɪ˞-] *adj* en ciernes
ass [æs] <-es> *n* **1.** (*donkey*) asno *m* **2.** *inf* (*stupid person*) burro, -a *m, f*; **to make an** ~ **of oneself** hacer el burro **3.** *Am, vulg* (*bottom*) culo *m*, siete *m AmS, Méx*
assail [ə'seɪl] *vt* **1.** (*attack*) atacar **2.** (*attack verbally*) insultar **3.** (*torment*) abrumar
assailant *n* asaltante *mf*, agresor(a) *m(f)*
assassin [ə'sæsɪn, *Am:* -ən] *n* asesino, -a *m, f*; **paid** ~ asesino a sueldo
assassinate [ə'sæsɪneɪt] *vt* asesinar
assassination [əˌsæsɪ'neɪʃən] *n no pl* asesinato *m*
assault [ə'sɔːlt] **I.** *n* **1.** (*attack*) ataque *m*, fajada *f Ant*; **to make an** ~ **on sth/sb** asaltar algo/a alguien **2.** (*attempted climb*) asalto *m* **II.** *vt* atacar
assault and battery *n* lesiones *fpl* **assault course** *n* pista *f* americana
assemble [ə'sembl] **I.** *vi* congregarse **II.** *vt* **1.** (*collect: people, things*) reunir **2.** (*put together*) armar
assembly [ə'sembli] <-ies> *n* **1.** (*meeting*) reunión *f* **2.** *no pl* TECH montaje *m*
assembly line *n* línea *f* de montaje
assent [ə'sent] **I.** *n no pl, form* consentimiento *m* **II.** *vi* **to** ~ **to sth** asentir a algo
assert [ə'sɜːt, *Am:* -'sɜːrt] *vt* afirmar; **to** ~ **oneself** imponerse
assertion [ə'sɜːʃən, *Am:* -'sɜːr-] *n* afirmación *f*
assertive [ə'sɜːtɪv, *Am:* -'sɜːrʈɪv] *adj* confiado, -a
assertiveness *n no pl* autoafirmación *f*

assess [ə'ses] *vt* **1.** (*evaluate*) evaluar **2.** (*tax*) calcular

assessment *n* **1.** (*calculation*) valoración *f* **2.** *no pl* (*evaluation*) evaluación *f* **3.** (*taxation*) cálculo *m* de los ingresos imponibles

assessor [ə'sesə', *Am:* -'sesə·] *n* **1.** (*evaluator*) evaluador(a) *m(f)* **2.** (*legal advisor*) asesor(a) *m(f)*; **legal** ~ asesor jurídico **3.** *Am* (*tax evaluator*) tasador(a) *m(f)*

asset ['æset] *n* **1.** (*benefit*) ventaja *f*; (*person*) persona *f* valiosa; **he is an** ~ **to the team** es una valiosa aportación al equipo **2.** *pl* FIN activo *m*; **liquid** ~s activos *mpl* líquidos

assiduous [ə'sɪdjʊəs, *Am:* -'sɪdʒu-] *adj* **1.** (*hardworking*) diligente **2.** (*keen*) asiduo, -a

assign [ə'saɪn] *vt* **1.** (*task, resources*) asignar, apropiar *AmL;* **to** ~ **sb to a position** destinar a alguien a un puesto; **to** ~ **sb to do sth** asignar a alguien la tarea de hacer algo; **to** ~ **the blame for sth to sb** atribuir la culpa de algo a alguien **2.** LAW ceder

assignment *n* **1.** (*task*) tarea *f*; **foreign** ~ cargo *m* en el extranjero; **diplomatic** ~ misión *f* diplomática; **to send sb on an** ~ mandar a alguien a una misión; **an** ~ **to do sth** un encargo de hacer algo **2.** *no pl* (*attribution*) asignación *f*

assimilate [ə'sɪm�əleɪt] **I.** *vt* asimilar **II.** *vi* asimilarse

assimilation [ə,sɪmə'leɪʃən] *n no pl* asimilación *f*

assist [ə'sɪst] **I.** *vt* ayudar; **to** ~ **sb with sth** ayudar a alguien con algo **II.** *vi* ayudar; **to** ~ **with sth** ayudar en algo

assistance [ə'sɪstəns] *n no pl* asistencia *f*; **to be of** ~ ser de ayuda; **can I be of any** ~? ¿puedo ayudar en algo?

assistant [ə'sɪstənt] *n* **1.** (*helper*) ayudante *mf*, suche *m Chile* **2.** INFOR asistente *m*

assistant manager *n* subdirector, -a *m, f*

assizes [ə'saɪzɪz] *npl Brit* LAW ≈ audiencia *f* provisional (*sesiones que solían celebrar los tribunales superiores en Gales e Inglaterra*)

associate¹ [ə'səʊʃiət, *Am:* -'souʃit] **I.** *n* asociado, -a *m, f*; **business** ~ socio, -a *m, f* **II.** *adj Am* UNIV adjunto, -a *m, f*

associate² [ə'səʊʃiət, *Am:* -'sou-] **I.** *vt* asociar; **to** ~ **oneself with sth** relacionarse con algo **II.** *vi* relacionarse

associate professor *n* profesor *m* adjunto, profesora *f* adjunta

association [ə,səʊsɪ'eɪʃən, *Am:* -,sou-] *n* **1.** (*organization*) asociación *f* **2.** *no pl* (*involvement*) colaboración *f* **3.** (*mental connection*) asociación *f*

assorted [ə'sɔːtɪd, *Am:* -'sɔːrṭɪd] *adj* (*mixed*) surtido, -a; (*goods*) variado, -a

assortment [ə'sɔːtmənt, *Am:* -'sɔːrt-] *n* surtido *m;* **a motley** ~ una mezcolanza; **a rich** ~ una rica variedad

assuage [ə'sweɪdʒ] *vt* (*pain*) aliviar; (*anger*) aplacar

assume [ə'sjuːm, *Am:* -'suːm] *vt* **1.** (*regard as true*) suponer, asumir *AmL;* **let's** ~ **that** ... supongamos que... **2.** (*adopt*) adoptar **3.** (*undertake*) asumir; (*power*) tomar

assumed [ə'sjuːmd, *Am:* -'suːmd] *adj* supuesto, -a; **under an** ~**d name** bajo un nombre falso

assumption [ə'sʌmpʃən] *n* **1.** (*supposition*) supuesto *m;* **on the** ~ **that** ... en el supuesto de que...; **to act on the** ~ **that** ... actuar suponiendo que... **2.** *no pl* (*hypothesis*) suposición *f* **3.** *no pl* (*taking over*) toma *f* **4.** REL **the Assumption** la Asunción

assurance [ə'ʃʊərəns, *Am:* 'ʃʊrns] *n* **1.** (*self-confidence*) seguridad *f*; **to have** ~ tener confianza **2.** (*promise*) garantía *f*; **to give an** ~ **of sth** dar garantías de algo **3.** *Brit* (*insurance*) seguro *m*

assure [ə'ʃʊə', *Am:* -'ʃʊr] *vt* **1.** (*guarantee*) asegurar **2.** (*promise*) garantizar; **to** ~ **sb of sth** asegurar algo a alguien **3.** *Brit* FIN asegurar

assured *adj* seguro, -a

assuredly [ə'ʃʊərɪdli, *Am:* -'ʃʊr-] *adv* **1.** (*confidently*) seguramente **2.** (*certainly*) ciertamente

asterisk ['æstərɪsk] *n* asterisco *m*

astern [ə'stɜːn, *Am:* -'stɜːrn] *adv* **1.** NAUT hacia popa; **to go** ~ ir atrás **2.** (*behind*) ~ **of** detrás de **3.** (*backwards*) hacia atrás

asteroid ['æstərɔɪd] *n* asteroide *m*

asthma ['æsmə, *Am:* 'æz-] *n no pl* asma *m*

asthma attack *n* ataque *m* de asma

asthmatic [æs'mætɪk, *Am:* æz'mæṭ-] **I.** *n* asmático, -a *m, f* **II.** *adj* asmático, -a

astonish [ə'stɒnɪʃ, *Am:* -'stɑːnɪʃ] *vt* asombrar; **to be** ~**ed** asombrarse

astonishing *adj* asombroso, -a

astonishment *n no pl* asombro *m;* **to her** ~ para gran sorpresa suya

astound [ə'staʊnd] *vt* asombrar; **to be** ~**ed** quedarse atónito

astounding *adj* asombroso, -a

astray [ə'streɪ] *adv* **to go** ~ (*letter*) extraviarse; (*person*) desencaminarse; **to lead sb** ~ llevar a alguien por mal camino

astride [ə'straɪd] **I.** *prep* a horcajadas [o a caballo] sobre **II.** *adv* a horcajadas

astringent [ə'strɪndʒənt] **I.** *n* astringente *m* **II.** *adj* **1.** MED astringente **2.** *fig* cáustico, -a

astrologer [ə'strɒlədʒə', *Am:* -'strɑːlədʒə·] *n* astrólogo, -a *m, f*

astrological [,æstrə'lɒdʒɪkl, *Am:* -'lɑːdʒɪkl] *adj* astrológico, -a

astrology [ə'strɒlədʒi, *Am:* -'strɑːlə-] *n no pl* astrología *f*

astronaut ['æstrənɔːt, *Am:* -nɑːt] *n* astronauta *mf*

astronomer [ə'strɒnəmə', *Am:* -'strɑːnəmə·] *n* astrónomo, -a *m, f*

astronomical [,æstrə'nɒmɪkl, *Am:* -'nɑːmɪkl] *adj a. fig* astronómico, -a

astronomy [ə'strɒnəmi, *Am:* -'strɑːnə-] *n no pl* astronomía *f*

Asturian [æs'tʊəriən, *Am:* ə'stʊri-] **I.** *adj*

asturiano, -a **II.** *n* (*person*) asturiano, -a *m, f*
astute [ə'stjuːt, *Am:* -'stuːt] *adj* astuto, -a
astuteness *n no pl* astucia *f*
asylum [ə'saɪləm] *n* **1.** (*protection*) asilo *m* **2.** (*institution*) asilo *m;* **mental** ~ manicomio *m*
asylum seeker *n* solicitante *mf* de asilo
asymmetrical [ˌeɪsɪ'metrɪkəl] *adj* asimétrico, -a
at¹ [ət] *prep* **1.** (*place*) en; ~ **the dentist's** en el dentista; ~ **home/school** en casa/la escuela; ~ **the table/office** en la mesa/oficina; ~ **the window** a la ventana **2.** (*time*) ~ **Easter** en Pascua; ~ **night** por la noche; ~ **once** en seguida; **all** ~ **once** de repente; ~ **present** en este momento; ~ **the time** en el momento; ~ **the same time** al mismo tiempo; ~ **three o'clock** a las tres; **while I am** ~ **it** mientras lo estoy haciendo **3.** (*towards*) **to laugh** ~ **sb** reírse de alguien; **to look/aim** ~ **sth/sb** mirar/apuntar a algo/alguien; **to point** ~ **sb** señalar a alguien; **to rush** ~ **sb/sth** abalanzarse sobre alguien/algo **4.** (*in reaction to*) ~ **sb's request** a petición de alguien; **to be astonished/annoyed** ~ **sth** estar asombrado/molesto por algo **5.** (*in amount of*) ~ **all** para nada; **to sell sth** ~ **£10 a kilo** vender algo a 10 libras el kilo; ~ **120 km/h** a 120 km/h **6.** (*in state of*) ~ **best/worst** en el mejor/peor de los casos; ~ **first** al principio; ~ **least** al menos; ~ **war/peace** en guerra/paz; ~ **20** a los 20 (años); **I feel** ~ **ease** me siento tranquilo; **to be** ~ **a loss** estar sin saber qué hacer; **to be** ~ **lunch** estar en el almuerzo; **a child** ~ **play** un niño jugando **7.** (*in ability to*) **to be good/bad** ~ **French** ser bueno/malo en francés; **to be** ~ **an advantage** estar en ventaja **8.** (*repeatedly do*) en; **to be mad** ~ **sb** estar enfadado con alguien; **to pull** ~ **sb's hair** tirar de los pelos a alguien; **to tug** ~ **the rope** tirar de la cuerda; **to be unhappy** ~ **sth** no estar feliz con algo; **to wear** ~ **sb's nerves** poner los nervios de punta a alguien ▶ ~ **all** en realidad; **did you know the film** ~ **all?** ¿conocías la película?; **not** ~ **all!** ¡para nada!, ¡en absoluto!; (*as answer to thanks*) ¡de nada!; **nobody** ~ **all** nadie en absoluto; **to hardly do sth** ~ **all** apenas hacer algo
at² [ɑːt, æt] (*in email address*) arroba *f*
atavistic [ˌætə'vɪstɪk, *Am:* ˌæt̬-] *adj* atávico, -a
ATC [ˌeɪtiː'siː] *n* *Brit abbr of* **Air Training Corps** *cuerpo militar de formación de aviadores*
ate [et, *Am:* eɪt] *pt of* **eat**
atheism ['eɪθɪɪzəm] *n no pl* ateísmo *m*
atheist ['eɪθɪɪst] **I.** *n* ateo, -a *m, f* **II.** *adj* ateísta
atheistic [ˌeɪθɪ'ɪstɪk] *adj* ateísta
Athens ['æθənz] *n* Atenas *f*
athlete ['æθliːt] *n* atleta *mf*
athletic [æθ'letɪk, *Am:* -'let̬-] *adj* atlético, -a
athletics [æθ'letɪks, *Am:* -'let̬-] *npl* atletismo

Atlantic [ət'læntɪk, *Am:* -t̬ɪk] **I.** *n no pl* the ~ (**Ocean**) el (Océano) Atlántico **II.** *adj* atlántico, -a
atlas ['ætləs] <-es> *n* atlas *m inv*
ATM [ˌeɪtiː'em] *n* *Am abbr of* **automated teller machine** cajero *m* automático
atmosphere ['ætməsfɪəʳ, *Am:* -fɪr] *n* **1.** *a.* PHYS atmósfera *f* **2.** *fig* ambiente *m*
atmospheric [ˌætməs'ferɪk] *adj* **1.** METEO atmosférico, -a **2.** *fig* evocador(a)
atoll ['ætɒl, *Am:* -aːl] *n* atolón *m*
atom ['ætəm, *Am:* 'æt̬-] *n a. fig* átomo *m*
atom bomb *n* bomba *f* atómica
atomic [ə'tɒmɪk, *Am:* -'tɑːmɪk] *adj* atómico, -a
atomic energy *n* energía *f* atómica
atomize ['ætəmaɪz, *Am:* 'æt̬-] *vt* atomizar; *fig* pulverizar
atomizer ['ætəmaɪzəʳ, *Am:* 'æt̬əmaɪzɚ] *n* atomizador *m*
atone for [ə'təʊn, *Am:* -'toʊn] *vi* (*sin*) expiar; (*mistake*) reparar
atonement *n no pl, form* expiación *f*
atrocious [ə'trəʊʃəs, *Am:* -'troʊ-] *adj* atroz
atrocity [ə'trɒsəti] <-ies> *n* atrocidad *f*
atrophy ['ætrəfi] <-ies> *vi* atrofiarse
at-sign *n* INFOR arroba *f*
attach [ə'tætʃ] **I.** *vt* **1.** (*fix*) fijar; (*label*) pegar; **to** ~ **sth to sth** fijar [*o* pegar] una cosa a otra **2.** (*connect*) ligar **3.** INFOR adjuntar **4.** (*join*) unir; **to** ~ **oneself to sb** unirse a alguien **5.** (*assign*) destinar; **to be ~ed to sth** estar destinado a algo **6.** (*associate*) vincular; **to** ~ **importance to sth** dar importancia a algo **II.** *vi form* acompañar; **no blame ~es to you** tú no tienes ninguna culpa
attaché [ə'tæʃeɪ, *Am:* ˌæt̬ə'ʃeɪ] *n* agregado, -a *m, f*
attaché case *n* cartera *f*, ataché *m*, portafolio *m AmL*
attachment [ə'tætʃmənt] *n* **1.** (*fondness*) apego *m;* **to form an** ~ **to sb** coger cariño a alguien **2.** *no pl* (*support*) adhesión *f* **3.** *no pl* (*union*) fijación *f* **4.** (*attached device*) accesorio *m* **5.** LAW incautación *f* **6.** INFOR attachment *m*, anexo *m*
attack [ə'tæk] **I.** *n* ataque *m;* **to be on the** ~ emprender una ofensiva; **to come under** ~ ser atacado **II.** *vt* **1.** (*use violence*) atacar, cachorrear *Col* **2.** (*tackle: problem*) afrontar **3.** (*eat greedily*) devorar **III.** *vi* atacar
attain [ə'teɪn] *vt form* alcanzar; (*independence*) lograr; **to** ~ **one's majority** LAW alcanzar la mayoría de edad
attainable *adj form* alcanzable
attainment *n* **1.** *form* logro *m* **2.** *pl* conocimientos *mpl*
attempt [ə'tempt] **I.** *n* **1.** (*try*) intento *m;* **to make an** ~ **at doing sth** intentar hacer algo **2.** (*attack*) atentado *m* **II.** *vt* intentar
attempted murder *n* intento *m* de asesinato

attend [ə'tend] I. *vt* **1.** (*be present at*) asistir a **2.** (*take care of*) atender II. *vi* **1.** (*be present*) asistir **2.** *form* (*listen carefully*) atender

attendance [ə'tendəns] *n* **1.** *no pl* (*presence*) asistencia *f;* **to be in** ~ estar presente **2.** (*people present*) concurrencia *f* **3.** (*care*) asistencia *f*

attendant [ə'tendənt] I. *n* **1.** (*servant*) encargado, -a *m, f* **2.** (*helper*) asistente, -a *m, f* II. *adj* relacionado, -a, asociado, -a

attention [ə'tenʃən] *n no pl* **1.** (*maintenance*) cuidado *m* **2.** (*care, notice*) atención *f;* **for the** ~ **of** *form* a la atención de; **to pay** ~ prestar atención; **to turn one's** ~**s to sth** dirigir la atención hacia algo **3.** *no pl* MIL **to stand at** ~ cuadrarse; ~! ¡firmes!

attention span *n* capacidad *f* de concentración

attentive [ə'tentɪv, *Am:* -t̬ɪv] *adj* atento, -a; **to be** ~ **to sb** ser atento con alguien; **to be** ~ **to sb's needs** preocuparse por las necesidades de alguien

attenuate [ə'tenjʊeɪt] *vt form* atenuar

attest [ə'test] I. *vt* **1.** (*demonstrate*) testimoniar **2.** (*authenticate*) atestiguar II. *vi* testimoniar

Att-Gen [ˌæt'dʒen] *n Am abbr of* **Attorney- -General** fiscal *mf* general del Estado

attic ['ætɪk, *Am:* 'æt̬-] *n* desván *m*, tabanco *m AmC*, entretecho *m CSur*

attire [ə'taɪə(r), *Am:* -taɪə-] *n* atavío *m*

attitude ['ætɪtjuːd, *Am:* 'æt̬ətuːd] *n* **1.** (*opinion*) actitud *f;* **a change of** ~ un cambio de actitud; **to have the** ~ **that ...** ser de la opinión de que...; **an** ~ **towards sb/sth** una actitud hacia alguien/algo **2.** (*position*) postura *f;* **to adopt an** ~ adoptar una postura **3.** ART posición *f*

attorney [ə'tɜːni, *Am:* -'tɜːr-] *n Am* abogado, -a *m, f;* **criminal** ~ abogado penalista; **legal** ~ apoderado *m* legal

attract [ə'trækt] *vt* atraer, jalar *AmL;* **to** ~ **attention/support** atraer la atención/conseguir el apoyo; **to** ~ **sb's notice** atraer la atención de alguien; **to be** ~**ed by sb/sth** sentirse atraído por alguien/algo

attraction [ə'trækʃən] *n* **1.** (*force, place of enjoyment*) atracción *f;* **tourist** ~ atracción turística **2.** *no pl* (*appeal*) atractivo *m;* **to feel an** ~ **to sb** sentirse atraído por alguien

attractive [ə'træktɪv] *adj* atractivo, -a

attribute¹ [ə'trɪbjuːt] *vt* **1.** (*ascribe*) atribuir; **to** ~ **the blame to sb** achacar la culpa a alguien; **to** ~ **importance to sth** dar importancia a algo **2.** (*give credit for*) **to** ~ **sth to sb** atribuir algo a alguien

attribute² ['ætrɪbjuːt] *n* atributo *m*

attributive [ə'trɪbjʊtɪv, *Am:* -jət̬ɪv] *adj* atributivo, -a

attrition [ə'trɪʃən] *n no pl* **1.** (*wearing down*) desgaste *m;* **war of** ~ guerra *f* de desgaste **2.** *Am, Aus* ECON reducción *f* **3.** REL atrición *f*

aubergine ['əʊbəʒiːn, *Am:* 'oʊbə-] *n Brit* berenjena *f*

auburn ['ɔːbən, *Am:* 'ɑːbə-n] *adj* castaño, -a

auction ['ɔːkʃən, *Am:* 'ɑːkʃən] I. *n* subasta *f;* **to hold an** ~ presidir una subasta; **to be sold at** [*o by Brit*] ~ ser vendido en [*o por*] subasta; **to put sth up for** ~ subastar algo II. *vt* **to** ~ **sth (off)** subastar algo

auctioneer [ˌɔːkʃə'nɪə(r), *Am:* ˌɑːkʃə'nɪr] *n* subastador(a) *m(f)*

audacious [ɔː'deɪʃəs, *Am:* ɑː-] *adj* **1.** (*bold*) audaz **2.** (*impudent*) descarado, -a

audacity [ɔː'dæsəti, *Am:* ɑː'dæsət̬i] *n no pl* **1.** (*boldness*) audacia *f* **2.** (*impudence*) descaro *m*

audible ['ɔːdəbl, *Am:* 'ɑː-] *adj* perceptible

audience ['ɔːdɪəns, *Am:* 'ɑː-] *n* **1.** (*spectators*) público *m;* TV, RADIO audiencia *f;* (*of book*) lectores *mpl* **2.** (*formal interview*) audiencia *f*

audio [ˌɔːdɪəʊ, *Am:* ˌɑːdɪoʊ] *adj inv* de sonido

audio cassette *n* casete *m o f*

audit¹ ['ɔːdɪt, *Am:* 'ɑː-] FIN I. *n* auditoría *f* contable II. *vt* auditar

audit² ['ɔːdɪt, *Am:* 'ɑː-] *vt* UNIV **to** ~ **a course** asistir de oyente a un curso

audition [ɔː'dɪʃən, *Am:* ɑː-] THEAT I. *n* audición *f* II. *vi* hacer una prueba III. *vt* **to** ~ **sb** hacer una prueba a alguien

auditor ['ɔːdɪtə(r), *Am:* 'ɑːdət̬ə-] *n* **1.** COM auditor(a) *m(f)* **2.** *Am* UNIV oyente *mf*

auditorium [ˌɔːdɪ'tɔːrɪəm, *Am:* ˌɑːdə-] <-s *o* auditoria> *n* auditorio *m*

augment [ɔːg'ment, *Am:* ɑːg-] *vt form* aumentar; **to** ~ **one's income** aumentar sus ingresos

augur ['ɔːgə(r), *Am:* 'ɑːgə-] I. *vi* **to** ~ **badly/ well** ser de mal/buen agüero II. *vt* augurar

august [ɔː'gʌst, *Am:* ɑː-] *adj form* augusto, -a

August ['ɔːgəst, *Am:* 'ɑː-] *n* agosto *m; s. a.* April

aunt [ɑːnt, *Am:* ænt] *n* tía *f*

au pair [ˌəʊ'peə(r), *Am:* oʊ'per] I. *n* au pair *f* II. *adj* ~ **girl** chica au pair

aura ['ɔːrə] *n* aura *f*

aural ['ɔːrəl] *adj* auditivo, -a

auricle ['ɔːrɪkl] *n* (*of heart*) aurícula *f*

auricular [ɔː'rɪkjʊlə(r), *Am:* -jələ-] *adj* **1.** (*relating to hearing*) auditivo, -a **2.** (*concerning the heart*) auricular

aurora [ɔː'rɔːrə] *n* aurora *f*

auspices ['ɔːspɪsɪz, *Am:* 'ɑː-] *n pl* auspicios *mpl;* **under the** ~ **of** bajo los auspicios de

auspicious [ɔː'spɪʃəs, *Am:* ɑː-] *adj form* propicio, -a

austere [ɔː'stɪə(r), *Am:* ɑː'stɪr] *adj* austero, -a

austerity [ɔː'sterəti, *Am:* ɑː'sterət̬i] <-ies> *n* austeridad *f;* ~ **programme** ECON programa *m* de austeridad

Australia [ɒ'streɪlɪə, *Am:* ɑː'streɪlʒə] *n* Australia *f*

El **Australia Day**, 26 de enero, conmemora la fundación del primer asentamiento británico en 1788 en Sydney Cove. Para los **Aborigines**, los primeros habitantes de Australia, es el día de la invasión de su país. Durante ese día tienen lugar distintos acontecimientos de tipo multicultural que suelen reunir a australianos de todas las procedencias.

Australian [ɒ'streɪlɪən, Am: ɑ:'streɪlʒən] I. n australiano, -a m, f II. adj australiano, -a
Austria ['ɒstrɪə, Am: 'ɑ:-] n Austria f
Austrian ['ɒstrɪən, Am: 'ɑ:-] I. n austriaco, -a m, f II. adj austriaco, -a
AUT n Brit abbr of Association of University Teachers asociación británica de profesores de universidad
authentic [ɔ:'θentɪk, Am: ɑ:'θenṭɪk] adj auténtico, -a; ~ **leather** cuero genuino; **an** ~ **Goya painting** un Goya auténtico
authenticate [ɔ:'θentɪkeɪt, Am: ɑ:'θenṭɪ-] vt autentificar
authentication [ɔ:ˌθentɪ'keɪʃən, Am: ɑ:ˌθenṭɪ-] n no pl autentificación f
authenticity [ˌɔ:θən'tɪsəti, Am: ˌɑ:θən'tɪsəṭi] n no pl autenticidad f
author ['ɔ:θəʳ, Am: 'ɑ:θɚ] I. n 1. (writer) autor m 2. fig creador(a) m(f) II. vt escribir
authoress ['ɔ:θərɪs, Am: 'ɑ:θɚ-] n autora f
authoritarian [ɔ:ˌθɒrɪ'teərɪən, Am: ə:ˌθɔ:rə'terɪ-] I. n autoritario, -a m, f II. adj autoritario, -a
authoritative [ɔ:'θɒrɪtətɪv, Am: ə:'θɔ:rəterṭɪv] adj 1. (assertive) autoritario, -a 2. (reliable) autorizado, -a
authority [ɔ:'θɒrəti, Am: ə:'θɔ:rəṭi] <-ies> n 1. no pl (right to control) autoridad f; **to be in** ~ tener autoridad 2. no pl (permission) autorización f 3. no pl (control) control m 4. (knowledge) **with** ~ con conocimiento de causa; **to be an** ~ **on sth** ser una autoridad en algo 5. (organization) autoridad f; **the authorities** las autoridades ▸**to have sth on good** ~ saber algo de buena tinta; **to have sth on sb's** ~ saber algo a través de alguien
authorization [ˌɔ:θəraɪ'zeɪʃən, Am: ˌɑ:θɚ-] n no pl autorización f; **to give one's** ~ **for sth** dar la autorización para hacer algo
authorize ['ɔ:θəraɪz, Am: 'ɑ:-] vt autorizar; **to** ~ **sb to do sth** autorizar a alguien para hacer algo
authorship ['ɔ:θəʃɪp, Am: 'ɑ:θɚ-] n no pl autoría f; **the article is of unknown** ~ el artículo es de autor desconocido
autistic [ɔ:'tɪstɪk] adj autista
auto ['ɔ:təʊ, Am: 'ɑ:ṭoʊ] n Am coche m, carro m AmL
autobiographical [ˌɔ:təbaɪə'græfɪkl, Am: ˌɑ:ṭə-] adj autobiográfico, -a
autobiography [ˌɔ:təbaɪ'ɒgrəfi, Am: ˌɑ:ṭəbaɪ'ɑ:grə-] n autobiografía f
autocracy [ɔ:'tɒkrəsi, Am: ɑ:'tɑ:krə-] n autocracia f
autocrat ['ɔ:təkræt, Am: 'ɑ:ṭə-] n autócrata mf
autocratic [ˌɔ:tə'krætik, Am: ˌɑ:ṭə'kræṭ-] adj autocrático, -a
autocue® ['ɔ:təˌkju:, Am: 'ɑ:ṭoʊ-] n Brit TV autocue® m
autograph ['ɔ:təgrɑ:f, Am: 'ɑ:ṭəgræf] I. n autógrafo m II. vt firmar
automate ['ɔ:təmeɪt, Am: 'ɑ:ṭə-] vt automatizar
automated ['ɔ:təmeɪtɪd, Am: 'ɑ:ṭəmeɪṭɪd] adj automatizado, -a
automated teller machine n cajero m automático
automatic [ˌɔ:tə'mætɪk, Am: ˌɑ:ṭə'mæṭ-] I. n 1. (machine) máquina f 2. (car) coche m automático 3. (pistol) pistola f automática; (rifle) metralleta f II. adj automático, -a
automatic pilot n piloto m automático
automation [ˌɔ:tə'meɪʃən, Am: ˌɑ:ṭə-] n no pl automatización f
automaton [ɔ:'tɒmətən, Am: ɑ:'tɑ:mə-] <automata> n a. fig autómata m
automobile ['ɔ:təməbi:l, Am: 'ɑ:ṭəmoʊ-] n Am automóvil m; ~ **accident/industry** accidente de coche/industria del automóvil
automotive [ˌɔ:tə'məʊtɪv, Am: ˌɑ:ṭə'moʊṭɪv] adj inv automovilístico, -a
autonomous [ɔ:'tɒnəməs, Am: ɑ:'tɑ:nə-] adj autónomo, -a; **to be** ~ **of sth** ser independiente de algo
autonomy [ɔ:'tɒnəmi, Am: ɑ:'tɑ:nə-] n pl autonomía f
autopsy ['ɔ:tɒpsi, Am: 'ɑ:tɑ:p-] <-ies> n autopsia f
autumn ['ɔ:təm, Am: 'ɑ:ṭəm] n otoño m; **in (the)** ~ en (el) otoño; ~ **colours** colores mpl otoñales
autumnal [ɔ:'tʌmnəl, Am: ɑ:-] adj otoñal
auxiliary [ɔ:g'zɪlɪəri, Am: ɑ:g'zɪljri] <-ies> I. n 1. HIST (soldier) soldado m auxiliar 2. (nurse) auxiliar mf 3. LING auxiliar m II. adj auxiliar; ~ **staff** personal m auxiliar
AV abbr of audiovisual audiovisual
av. abbr of average media f
Av. abbr of avenue Avda.
avail [ə'veɪl] I. n provecho m; **to no** ~ en vano II. vt **to** ~ **oneself of sth** aprovecharse de algo
available [ə'veɪləbl] adj 1. (obtainable) disponible; **to make sth** ~ **to sb** poner algo a la disposición [o al alcance] de alguien 2. (free) libre; **to be** ~ **to do sth** tener tiempo para hacer algo 3. (free for romantic involvement) **to be** ~ estar sin compromiso
avalanche ['ævəlɑ:nʃ, Am: -æntʃ] n 1. (of snow) alud m, avalancha f 2. fig torrente m
avant-garde [ˌævɒn'gɑ:d, Am: ˌævɑ:nt'gɑ:rd] I. n vanguardia f II. adj vanguardista, de vanguardia
avarice ['ævərɪs] n no pl, form avaricia f
avaricious [ˌævə'rɪʃəs] adj form ávaro, -a
Ave. n abbr of Avenue Avda.

avenge [ə'vendʒ] *vt* vengar; **to ~ oneself on sb** vengarse de alguien

avenue ['ævənjuː, *Am:* -nuː] *n* **1.** (*street*) avenida *f,* carrera *f AmL* **2.** (*possibility*) camino *m;* **to explore an ~** explorar una vía

average ['ævərɪdʒ] **I.** *n* MAT promedio *m,* media *f;* **above/below ~** por encima/por debajo de la media; **on ~** por término medio **II.** *adj* **1.** MAT medio, -a; **~ rainfall** precipitación media **2.** (*mediocre*) mediocre **III.** *vt* **1.** (*have mean value*) promediar **2.** (*calculate mean value of*) sacar la media de

averse [ə'vɜːs, *Am:* -'vɜːrs] *adj* **to be ~ to sth** ser contrario a algo; **I'm not ~ to the occasional glass of wine** no me opongo a tomar un vino de vez en cuando

aversion [ə'vɜːʃən, *Am:* -'vɜːrʒən] *n* **1.** (*dislike*) aversión *f;* **to have an ~ to sth/sb** sentir aversión hacia algo/alguien **2.** (*object of dislike*) fobia *f*

avert [ə'vɜːt, *Am:* -'vɜːrt] *vt* **1.** (*prevent*) prevenir **2.** (*turn away*) **to ~ one's eyes from sth** desviar la mirada de algo; **to ~ one's thoughts from sth** apartar sus pensamientos de algo

aviary ['eɪviəri, *Am:* -er-] *n* pajarera *f*

aviation [ˌeɪvi'eɪʃən] *n no pl* aviación *f*

aviation industry *n* industria *f* aeronáutica

avid ['ævɪd] *adj* ávido, -a

avidity [ə'vɪdəti, *Am:* -t̬i] *n no pl* avidez *f*

avocado [ˌævə'kɑːdəʊ, *Am:* -doʊ] <-s *o* -es> *n* aguacate *m,* abocado *m AmL,* ahuacatl *m Méx*

avoid [ə'vɔɪd] *vt* (*person, thing*) evitar; (*when moving*) esquivar; **to ~ doing sth** evitar hacer algo; **to ~ paying taxes** evadir impuestos

avoidable *adj* evitable

avoidance *n no pl* evasión *f;* **tax ~** evasión de impuestos

avow [ə'vaʊ] *vt form* **1.** (*admit*) admitir **2.** (*declare*) declarar

avowal [ə'vaʊəl] *n form* declaración *f*

avowedly [ə'vaʊɪdli] *adv* abiertamente

AWACS ['eɪwæks] *n abbr of* **airborne warning and control system** sistema *m* AWACS

await [ə'weɪt] *vt* aguardar; **eagerly ~ed** esperado con ansiedad

awake [ə'weɪk] <awoke, awoken *o* -d, awoken *Am*> **I.** *vi* despertarse; **to ~ to sth** *fig* darse cuenta de algo **II.** *vt* despertar **III.** *adj* **1.** (*not sleeping*) despierto, -a; **to stay ~** mantenerse despierto; **to keep sb awake** mantener a alguien despierto; **to lie ~** quedarse despierto **2.** *fig* alerta; **to be ~ to sth** estar alerta ante algo

awaken [ə'weɪkən] **I.** *vt form* despertar; **to ~ sb to sth** *fig* abrir los ojos a alguien sobre algo **II.** *vi fig* darse cuenta

awakening [ə'weɪknɪŋ] *n no pl* despertar *m;* **she's in for a rude ~** le espera una sorpresa desagradable

award [ə'wɔːd, *Am:* -'wɔːrd] **I.** *n* **1.** (*prize*) premio *m* **2.** (*reward*) recompensa *f* **3.** MIL condecoración *f* **II.** *vt* otorgar; **to ~ sth to sb** conferir algo a alguien; **to ~ damages** indemnizar por daños y perjuicios; **to ~ sb a grant** conceder a alguien una beca

aware [ə'weə^r, *Am:* -'wer] *adj* **1.** (*knowing*) **to be ~ that ...** saber que...; **as far as I'm ~ ...** por lo que yo sé...; **not that I'm ~ of** no, que yo sepa **2.** (*sense*) **to be ~ of sth** ser consciente de algo

awareness [ə'weənɪs, *Am:* -'wer-] *n no pl* conciencia *f*

awash [ə'wɒʃ, *Am:* -wɑːʃ] *adj* inundado, -a; **to be ~ with money** estar forrado de dinero

away [ə'weɪ] *adv* **1.** (*distant*) **10 km ~** a 10 km; **as far ~ as possible** lo más lejos posible; **to be miles ~** *fig* no prestar atención **2.** (*absent*) fuera; **to be ~ on holiday** estar de vacaciones **3.** (*in future time*) **to be only a week ~** no faltar más que una semana; **right ~!** ¡enseguida! **4.** (*continuously*) **to write ~** escribir sin cesar

away from *prep* **1.** (*at distance from*) **~ the town** lejos del pueblo; **~ each other** alejados el uno del otro; **to stay ~ sth/sb** mantenerse alejado de algo/alguien **2.** (*in other direction from*) **to go ~** sth alejarse de algo

away game *n* partido *m* fuera de casa

awe [ɔː, *Am:* ɑː] *n no pl* respeto *m;* **to hold sb in ~** tener un gran respeto por alguien; **to stand in ~ of sb** imponer alguien respeto a uno

awe-inspiring ['ɔːɪnspaɪərɪŋ, *Am:* 'ɑː-] *adj* imponente

awesome ['ɔːsəm, *Am:* 'ɑː-] *adj* **1.** (*impressive*) imponente **2.** (*fearsome*) temible **3.** (*daunting*) intimidatorio, -a **4.** *Am, inf* (*very good*) estupendo, -a

awestricken ['ɔːstrɪkən, *Am:* 'ɑː-] *adj,* **awestruck** ['ɔːstrʌk, *Am:* 'ɑː-] *adj* atemorizado, -a

awful ['ɔːfəl, *Am:* 'ɑː-] *adj* **1.** (*bad*) terrible **2.** (*as intensifier*) **an ~ lot** mucho

awfully ['ɔːfəli, *Am:* 'ɑː-] *adv* **1.** (*badly*) terriblemente **2.** (*very*) **~ clever/stupid** muy inteligente/tonto; **I'm ~ sorry** lo siento muchísimo; **not to be ~ good at sth** no ser muy bueno para algo

awhile [ə'hwaɪl] *adv* **to wait ~** esperar un rato

awkward ['ɔːkwəd, *Am:* 'ɑːkwə̃d] *adj* **1.** (*difficult*) difícil; **an ~ customer** *inf* un tipo difícil; **to make things ~ for sb** crear problemas a alguien **2.** (*embarrassed*) incómodo, -a; **an ~ silence** un silencio perturbador; **an ~ question** una pregunta delicada; **to feel ~** sentirse incómodo **3.** (*inconvenient*) **an ~ time** una hora inoportuna **4.** (*clumsy*) torpe **5.** *Brit* (*uncooperative*) terco, -a

awning ['ɔːnɪŋ, *Am:* 'ɑː-] *n* toldo *m*

awoke [ə'wəʊk, *Am:* -'woʊk] *pt of* **awake**

awoken [ə'wəʊkən, *Am:* -'woʊ-] *pp of* **awake**

AWOL ['eɪwɒl, *Am:* -wɑːl] MIL *abbr of* absent without (official) leave ausente sin permiso; **to go ~** *inf* desaparecer así como así

awry [ə'raɪ] *adj* **to go ~** salir mal

ax *n Am,* **axe** [æks] **I.** *n* hacha *f* ►**to get the ~** *inf* (*worker*) ser despedido; (*project*) ser anulado; **to have an ~ to grind** tener un interés personal **II.** <**axing**> *vt* recortar; **to ~ jobs** reducir los puestos de trabajo

axiom ['æksɪəm] *n form* axioma *m*

axis ['æksɪs] *n a.* MAT, POL eje *m*

axle ['æksl] *n* eje *m,* cardán *m AmC, Ven, Col;* **back/front ~** eje trasero/frontal

ayatollah [ˌaɪjə'tɔlə, *Am:* ˌaɪə'toʊlə-] *n* ayatolá *m*

aye [aɪ] **I.** *n* POL **the ~s** los votos a favor **II.** *interj Scot* sí

azalea [ə'zeɪlɪə, *Am:* -'zeɪljə] *n* azalea *f*

Azerbaijan [ˌæzəbaɪ'dʒaːn, *Am:* ˌaːzəˈ-] *n* Azerbaiyán *m*

Azerbaijani **I.** *adj* azerbaiyano, -a **II.** *n* azerbaiyano, -a *m, f*

Aztec ['æztɛk] **I.** *adj* azteca **II.** *n* azteca *mf*

azure ['æʒəʳ, *Am:* 'æʒɚ] **I.** *n* azul *m* celeste **II.** *adj* azul celeste

B

B, b [biː] *n* **1.** (*letter*) B, b *f;* **~ for Benjamin** *Brit,* **~ for Baker** *Am* B de Barcelona **2.** MUS si *m* **3.** SCHOOL notable *m*

b & b *n,* **B & B** [ˌbiːənd'biː] *n abbr of* bed and breakfast pensión *f* familiar

BA [ˌbiː'eɪ] *n* **1.** *abbr of* Bachelor of Arts Ldo., -a *m, f* (en Filosofía y Letras) **2.** *abbr of* British Airways BA *f*

baa [baː, *Am:* bæ] **I.** *n* balido *m* **II.** <-ed> *vi* balar

babble ['bæbl] **I.** *n no pl* **1.** (*of a baby*) balbuceo *m* **2.** (*of a stream*) murmullo *m* **II.** *vi* (*baby*) balbucear; (*adult*) parlotear

babe [beɪb] *n* **1.** *form* (*baby*) bebé *m inf;* **~ in arms** niño, -a *m, f* de pecho **2.** *Am, inf* (*term of address*) muñeca *f*

babel ['bæbl] *n no pl* babel *m of*

baboon [bə'buːn, *Am:* bæb'uːn] *n* babuino *m*

baby ['beɪbi] **I.** *n* **1.** (*child*) bebé *m;* **to expect/have a ~** esperar/tener un bebé **2.** (*youngest person*) benjamín *m* **3.** *inf* (*term of address*) nene, -a *m, f* ►**to throw out the ~ with the bathwater** tirar las frutas frescas con las pochas, actuar con exceso de celo **II.** *adj* **1.** (*person*) infantil **2.** (*tomato, carrot*) pequeño, -a **III.** *vt* mimar

baby carriage *n Am* coche *m* de bebé, carriola *f Méx* **baby food** *n no pl* comida *f* para bebés

babyhood ['beɪbɪhʊd] *n no pl* niñez *f*

babyish ['beɪbiɪʃ] *adj* infantil

babysitter ['beɪbɪˌsɪtəʳ, *Am:* -ˌsɪt̬ɚ] *n* canguro *mf,* nana *f Méx*

bachelor ['bætʃələʳ, *Am:* -lɚ] *n* **1.** (*man*) soltero *m* **2.** UNIV licenciado, -a *m, f;* **Bachelor of Arts** Licenciado, -a *m, f* en Filosofía y Letras; **Bachelor of Science** Licenciado, -a *m, f* en Ciencias

---

El **Bachelor's degree** es el título que obtienen los estudiantes después de haber cursado carreras universitarias de tres años (en algunos casos, de cuatro o cinco años). Este título recibe varios nombres según las disciplinas. Los títulos más importantes son: **BA (Bachelor of Arts)** en las disciplinas de humanidades, **BSc (Bachelor of Science)** en las disciplinas científicas, **BEd (Bachelor of Education)** en las disciplinas de tipo pedagógico, **LLB (Bachelor of Laws)** para los estudiantes de Derecho y **BMus** para los estudiantes de Musicología.

---

bacillus [bə'sɪləs] *n* <-li> bacilo *m*

back [bæk] **I.** *n* **1.** (*opposite of front*) parte *f* trasera; (*of a hand*) dorso *m;* (*of a chair*) respaldo *m;* (*reverse side*) revés *m;* (*of a piece of paper, envelope*) dorso *m;* **~ to front** al revés; **to know sth ~ to front** saberse algo al derecho y al revés **2.** (*end: of a book*) final *m* **3.** ANAT espalda *f;* (*of an animal*) lomo *m;* **to be on one's ~** estar boca arriba; **to break one's ~** *inf* deslomarse; **to do sth behind sb's ~** *a. fig* hacer algo a espaldas de alguien; **to turn one's ~ on sb** *a. fig* dar la espalda a alguien **4.** SPORTS defensa *mf* ►**to know sth like the ~ of one's hand** conocer algo al dedillo *inf;* **to make a rod for one's own ~** *Brit* cavarse la propia tumba; **to have one's ~ against the wall** estar entre la espada y la pared; **to break the ~ of sth** *Aus, Brit* hacer la peor parte de algo; **you scratch my ~ and I'll scratch yours** hoy por ti, mañana por mí; **to stab sb in the ~** dar a alguien una puñalada por la espalda **II.** *adj* **1.** (*rear*) trasero, -a **2.** MED dorsal **III.** *adv* **1.** **to be ~** estar de vuelta; **to come ~** volver; **to want sb ~** querer que alguien vuelva; **I want the money ~ (from them)** quiero que me devuelvan el dinero; **to bring ~ memories** traer viejos recuerdos a la memoria **2.** (*to the rear, behind*) detrás, atrás; **~ and forth** atrás y adelante; **to look ~** mirar hacia atrás; **to sit ~** recostarse **3.** (*in return*) de vuelta **4.** (*into the past*) atrás **IV.** *vt* apoyar

◆**back away** *vi* echarse atrás

◆**back down** *vi* retirar(se)

◆**back on to** *vt* **the building backs on to the garden** la parte trasera del edificio da al jardín

◆**back out of** *vt* salir de; *fig* retirarse de

◆**back up** *vt* **1.** (*reverse*) dar marcha atrás **2.** INFOR **to ~ data/files** hacer copias de seguridad de datos/archivos **3.** (*support*) respaldar

back-bencher [ˌbækˈbentʃəʳ, *Am:* -tʃɚ] *n*
Brit POL *diputado sin cargo específico ni en el
gobierno ni en la oposición*
backbiting [ˈbækˌbaɪtɪŋ, *Am:* -ṭɪŋ] *n no pl*
murmureo *m,* viboreo *m Méx*
backbone [ˈbækbəʊn, *Am:* -boʊn] *n*
1. (*spine*) columna *f* vertebral **2.** *fig* pilar *m*
3. *no pl* (*strength of character*) coraje *m*
backchat [ˈbæktʃæt] *n* réplicas *fpl*
backcloth [ˈbækˌklɒθ, *Am:* -klɑːθ] *n Brit, a.*
fig telón *m* de fondo
back door [ˌbækˈdɔːʳ] *n* puerta *f* trasera
backdrop [ˈbækdrɒp, *Am:* -drɑːp] *n a. fig*
telón *m* de fondo
backer [ˈbækəʳ, *Am:* -ɚ] *n* partidario, -a *m, f;*
financial ~ patrocinador *m* financiero
backfire [ˌbækˈfaɪəʳ, *Am:* -ˈfaɪɚ] *vi* **1.** (*go
wrong*) fallar; **his plans** ~**d** sus planes fracasa-
ron **2.** AUTO petardear, detonar *AmL*
backgammon [bækˈgæmən] *n no pl* back-
gamon *m*
background [ˈbækgraʊnd] *n* **1.** (*rear view*)
fondo *m;* **in the** ~ *fig* en segundo plano
2. (*education, family*) educación *f* **3.** (*training*)
formación *f;* **to have a** ~ **in mathematics**
tener una formación en matemáticas **4.** (*circumstances*) antecedentes *mpl*
background music *n* música *f* de fondo
backhand [ˈbækhænd] *n no pl* revés *m*
backhander [ˌbækˈhændəʳ, *Am:* -ɚ] *n inf*
soborno *m,* mordida *f Méx,* coima *f AmS*
backing [ˈbækɪŋ] *n no pl* **1.** (*support, aid*)
apoyo *m* **2.** FASHION refuerzo *m* **3.** MUS acompañamiento *m*
backlash [ˈbæklæʃ] *n* reacción *f*
backlog [ˈbæklɒg, *Am:* -lɑːg] *n* atraso *m*
back number *n* número *m* atrasado
backpack [ˈbækpæk] I. *n* mochila *f* II. *vi* viajar con mochila
backpacker *n* mochilero, -a *m, f*
back pay *n* atrasos *mpl* de sueldo
back seat *n* asiento *m* trasero
backside [ˈbæksaɪd] *n inf* trasero *m*
backslash [ˈbækslæʃ] *n* barra *f* inversa
  backspace (**key**) *n* tecla *f* de retroceso
backstage [bækˈsteɪdʒ] I. *adj* **1.** THEAT de
bastidores **2.** *fig* subrepticio, -a II. *adv* THEAT tras
bambalinas, entre bastidores
backstroke [ˈbækstrəʊk, *Am:* -stroʊk] *n no
pl* (estilo *m*) espalda *f,* nado *m* de dorso *AmL*
backtalk [ˈbæktɔːk] *n* réplicas *fpl*
backtrack [ˈbæktræk] *vi* **1.** retroceder **2.** *fig*
dar marcha atrás; **to** ~ **on one's statement**
retirar lo dicho
backup [ˈbækʌp] *n* **1.** INFOR copia *f* de seguridad **2.** (*support*) apoyo *m*
backward [ˈbækwəd, *Am:* -wɚd] I. *adj*
1. (*to the rear*) hacia atrás **2.** (*slow in learning*)
retrasado, -a **3.** (*underdeveloped*) atrasado, -a
II. *adv* hacia atrás
backwards [ˈbækwədz, *Am:* -wɚdz] *adv*
1. (*towards the back*) hacia atrás **2.** (*in reverse
order*) al revés **3.** (*from better to worse*) de

mal en peor **4.** (*into the past*) atrás en el
tiempo ► **to bend over** ~ (**to help sb**) hacer lo
imposible (por alguien); **to lean over** ~ **to do
sth** desvivirse por hacer algo
backwater [ˈbækˌwɔːtəʳ, *Am:* -ˌwɑːṭɚ] *n*
1. (*river*) remanso *m* **2.** *pej* lugar *m* atrasado
backwoods [ˈbækwʊdz] *npl* **the** ~ el
interior
backwoodsman [ˈbækwʊdzmən] *n*
<-men> *fig* patán *m*
back yard *n Brit* (*yard*) patio *m* trasero; *Am*
(*garden*) jardín *m* trasero
bacon [ˈbeɪkən] *n* beicon *m,* tocino *m AmL*
► **to bring home the** ~ *inf* ganar los garbanzos; **to save sb's** ~ salvar la vida a alguien
bacteria [bækˈtɪərɪə] *n pl of* **bacterium**
bacteriologist [bækˌtɪərɪˈɒlədʒɪst, *Am:*
-ˌtɪriˈɑːlə-] *n* bacteriólogo, -a *m, f*
bacterium [bækˈtɪərɪəm] *n* <-ria> bacteria
f
bad [bæd] <worse, worst> I. *adj* **1.** (*not
good*) malo, -a; **to have a** ~ **marriage** tener
un matrimonio difícil; **to feel** ~ sentirse mal;
to look ~ tener mal aspecto; **too** ~! ¡qué lástima!; ~ **dream** pesadilla *f;* (**to act**) **in** ~ **faith**
actuar de mala fe; ~ **habits** malas costumbres;
to use ~ **language** decir palabrotas; ~ **luck**
mala suerte, macacoa *f PRico;* **a** ~ **name** una
mala reputación; **in** ~ **taste** de mal gusto; **to
have a** ~ **temper** tener mal carácter; ~ **times**
tiempos *mpl* difíciles **2.** (*harmful*) dañino, -a;
to be ~ **for sth/sb** ser perjudicial para algo/al-
guien **3.** (*spoiled*) malo, -a; **to go** ~ echarse a
perder **4.** (*unhealthy*) enfermo, -a; **to have a** ~
heart/back estar mal del corazón/de la espalda **5.** (*serious: accident, mistake*) grave
6. (*severe: pain*) fuerte ► **to go from** ~ **to
worse** ir de mal en peor II. *adv inf* mal III. *n
no pl* **the** ~ lo malo; **to go to the** ~ echarse a
perder
badge [bædʒ] *n* insignia *f,* placa *f Méx*
badger [ˈbædʒəʳ, *Am:* -ɚ] I. *n* tejón *m* II. *vt*
importunar
badly [ˈbædli] <worse, worst> *adv*
1. (*poorly*) mal; **this house is** ~ **built** esta casa
está mal construida **2.** (*in a negative way*) mal;
to think ~ **of sb** pensar mal de alguien; **to
come out of sth** ~ salir mal parado de algo
3. (*very much*) desesperadamente; **to be** ~ **in
need of sth** necesitar algo desesperadamente;
he was ~ **defeated** fue derrotado estrepitosamente
badminton [ˈbædmɪntən] *n no pl* bádminton *m*
baffle [ˈbæfl] I. *vt* **1.** (*confuse*) desconcertar
2. (*hinder*) impedir II. *n* TECH deflector *m,* bafle
m Méx
baffling *adj* desconcertante
bag [bæg] I. *n* **1.** (*container*) bolsa *f,* busaca *f
Col, Ven;* (*handbag*) bolso *m;* (*sack*) saco *m;*
to pack one's ~**s** hacer las maletas; *fig* marcharse **2.** (*swollen skin*) **to have** ~**s under
one's eyes** tener ojeras **3.** *inf* (*grumpy*

woman) bruja *f* **4.** (*catch*) presa *f* ▶**to be a ~ of** bones *inf* estar en los huesos; **the whole ~ of** tricks *inf* todas las mañas; **a** mixed **~** un grupo heterogéneo; **~s of** *inf* un montón de; **to have ~s of** money/space/time *inf* tener montones de dinero/espacio/tiempo **II.** *vt* <-gg-> **1.** (*put in bag*) ensacar **2.** *inf* (*obtain*) obtener **3.** (*hunt*) cazar

bagel ['beɪgəl] *n* tipo de rosca de pan

baggage ['bægɪdʒ] *n no pl* **1.** (*luggage*) equipaje *m*; **excess ~** exceso *m* de equipaje **2.** (*army equipment*) bagaje *m* **3.** *pej* (*unpleasant woman*) bruja *f*

baggage allowance *n* límite *m* de equipaje **baggage car** *n Am, Aus* vagón *m* de equipaje, breque *m Ecua, Perú, RíoPl* **baggage check** *n Am* documentación *f* del equipaje **baggage claim** *n* recogida *f* del equipaje

baggy ['bægi] *adj* holgado, -a

bag lady *n inf* vagabunda *f*

bagpiper ['bægpaɪpəʳ, *Am:* -ɚ] *n* gaitero, -a *m, f*

bagpipes ['bægpaɪps] *npl* gaita *f*

Bahamas [bə'hɑːməz] *npl* the ~ las (Islas) Bahamas

Bahamian [bə'eɪmiən] **I.** *adj* de las Bahamas **II.** *n* habitante *mf* de las Bahamas

Bahrain [bɑː'reɪn] *n* Bahrein *m*

bail [beɪl] **I.** *n* fianza *f*; **on ~** bajo fianza; **to post ~ for sb** *Am* dar fianza por alguien **II.** *vi* achicar **III.** *vt* **1.** (*remove: water*) achicar **2.** (*guarantee*) afianzar

◆bail out *vt* **to bail sb out** sacar a alguien de apuros

bailiff ['beɪlɪf] *n* **1.** *Brit* (*landlord's agent*) administrador(a) *m(f)* **2.** *Am* (*court official*) alguacil *mf*

bait [beɪt] **I.** *n* **1.** (*for fish*) cebo *m* **2.** *fig* señuelo *m*; **to swallow the ~** *inf* morder el anzuelo **II.** *vt* **1.** (*put bait on*) cebar **2.** (*harass*) acosar

bake [beɪk] **I.** *vi* **1.** (*cook*) cocerse **2.** *inf* (*be hot*) achicharrarse **II.** *vt* **1.** (*cook*) hornear **2.** (*harden*) endurecer

baker ['beɪkəʳ, *Am:* -kɚ] *n* panadero, -a *m, f*

bakery ['beɪkəri] *n* panadería *f*

baking *adj* it's ~ **hot** hace un calor achicharrante

baking powder *n* levadura *f*

balance ['bælənts] **I.** *n* **1.** (*device*) balanza *f* **2.** *no pl, a. fig* equilibrio *m*; **to lose one's ~** perder el equilibrio **3.** (*state of equality*) equidad *f* **4.** (*amount in bank account*) saldo *m* **5.** (*difference between amount paid and owed*) balance *m* **II.** *vi* equilibrarse **III.** *vt* **1.** (*compare*) contrapesar; **to ~ sth against sth** comparar algo con algo **2.** (*keep in a position*) estabilizar **3.** (*achieve equilibrium*) equilibrar; **to ~ the books** hacer cuadrar los libros de cuentas

balanced *adj* equilibrado, -a

balance of trade *n* balanza *f* comercial **bal-**

ance sheet *n* balance *m*

balcony ['bælkəni] *n* balcón *m*

bald [bɔːld] *adj* **1.** (*lacking hair*) calvo, -a, pelón, -ona *Méx*; **to go ~** quedarse calvo **2.** (*plain*) escueto, -a

baldly ['bɔːldli] *adv* francamente

baldness ['bɔːldnɪs] *n no pl* calvicie *f*, pelada *f CSur*

bale [beɪl] **I.** *n* fardo *m* **II.** *vt* embalar

Balearic Islands *n* the ~ las Islas Baleares

Balearics [ˌbæli'ærɪks, *Am:* ˌbɑːli'-] *n* the ~ las Baleares

baleen whale [bə'liːn 'hweɪl] *n* misticeto *m*

baleful ['beɪlfʊl] *adj* siniestro, -a

balk [bɔːk] **I.** *n* viga *f* **II.** *vi* **to ~ at sth** resistirse a algo

Balkans ['bɔːlkəns] *n* the ~ los Balcanes

ball [bɔːl] *n* **1.** (*for golf, tennis*) pelota *f*; (*for football, basketball*) balón *m*, pelota *f*; **to play ~** jugar a la pelota; *fig* cooperar **2.** (*round form*) bola *f* **3.** (*dance*) baile *m* ▶**to** have **a ~** divertirse; **to get the ~** rolling poner las cosas en marcha

ballad ['bæləd] *n* balada *f*

balladeer [ˌbælə'dɪəʳ, *Am:* -'dɪr] *n* cantautor(a) *m(f)*

ballast ['bæləst] *n no pl* **1.** NAUT lastre *m* **2.** (*gravel*) balasto *m*

ball bearing *n* cojinete *m*

ballerina [ˌbælər'iːnə, *Am:* -ə'riː-] *n* bailarina *f*

ballet dancer ['bæleɪˌdɑːntsəʳ, *Am:* 'bæleɪˌdæːntsɚ] *n* bailarín, -ina *m, f*

ball game *n Am* partido *m* de béisbol ▶**that's a whole** new **~** eso es completamente distinto

ballistic [bə'lɪstɪk] *adj* balístico, -a ▶**to go ~** *inf* enfurecerse

balloon [bə'luːn] **I.** *n* globo *m* ▶**to go down like a** lead **~** fracasar estrepitosamente **II.** *vi* inflarse

balloonist *n* ascensionista *mf*, aeronauta *mf*

ballot ['bælət] **I.** *n* **1.** (*process*) votación *f* **2.** (*election*) sufragio *m* **3.** (*paper*) papeleta *f* **II.** *vi* invitar a votar **III.** *vt* consultar por votación

ballot box *n* urna *f* **ballot paper** *n* papeleta *f*

ball park *n* **1.** estadio *m* de béisbol **2.** *fig* **a ~ figure** una cifra aproximada **ball player** *n* jugador(a) *m(f)* de béisbol

ballpoint (**pen**) [ˌbɔːlpɔɪnt (pen)] *n* bolígrafo *m*, birome *m RíoPl*

ballroom ['bɔːlrʊm] *n* salón *m* de baile

ballroom dancing *n no pl* baile *m* de salón

balls-up ['bɔːlzʌp] *n Brit, vulg* lío *m*

balm [bɑːm] *n* **1.** (*ointment*) bálsamo *m* **2.** *fig* consuelo *m*

balmy ['bɑːmi] <-ier, -iest> *adj* (*weather*) templado, -a; (*breeze*) suave

Baltic ['bɔːltɪk] *n* the ~ (**Sea**) el (Mar) Báltico

balustrade [ˌbælə'streɪd, *Am:* 'bæl-] *n* balaustrada *f*, barandilla *f Méx*

bamboo [bæm'buː] *n no pl* bambú *m*

bamboozle [bæm'bu:zl] *vt inf* **1.** (*confuse*) enredar **2.** (*trick*) engatusar

ban [bæn] **I.** *n* prohibición *f;* **to put** [*o* **place**] **a ~ on sth** prohibir algo **II.** *vt* <-nn-> prohibir; **she was ~ned from driving** le prohibieron conducir

banal [bə'nɑːl] *adj* banal

banality [bə'næləti, *Am:* -ət̬i] *n* <-ies> banalidad *f*

banana [bə'nɑːnə, *Am:* -'nænə] *n* plátano *m,* banana *f AmL* ►**to go ~s** enfurecerse

banana republic *n pej* república *f* bananera

banana tree *n* platanero *m,* banano *m*

band¹ [bænd] *n* **1.** (*strip: of cloth, metal*) banda *f* **2.** (*stripe*) franja *f* **3.** (*ribbon*) cinta *f;* **head ~** cinta *f* de pelo; **waist ~** faja *f* **4.** (*range*) *a.* TEL banda *f* **5.** (*ring*) anillo *m;* **wedding ~** alianza *f*

band² [bænd] *n* **1.** MUS grupo *m;* **brass ~** charanga *f* **2.** (*of friends*) pandilla *f;* (*of robbers*) banda *f*

◆**band together** *vi* agruparse

bandage ['bændɪdʒ] **I.** *n* vendaje *m* **II.** *vt* vendar

band-aid ['bændeɪd] *n* tirita *f*

bandit ['bændɪt] *n* bandido, -a *m, f,* carrilano, -a *m, f Chile*

bandsman ['bændzmən] *n* <-men> músico *m* (de banda)

bandstand ['bændstænd] *n* quiosco *m* (de música)

bandwagon ['bændwægən] *n* **to jump on the ~** *fig* subirse al carro

bandwidth *n* INFOR ancho *m* de banda

bandy¹ ['bændi] <-ier, -iest> *adj* patizambo, -a

bandy² ['bændi] *vt* <-ies, -ied> (*insults, words*) intercambiar

◆**bandy about** *vt* **it was bandied about that ...** se rumoreaba que...

bang [bæŋ] **I.** *n* **1.** (*noise, blow*) golpe *m;* (*explosion*) detonación *f* **2.** *pl, Am* (*fringe*) flequillo *m,* pollina *f PRico, Ven* ►**to go** (**off**) **with a ~** *inf* tener éxito **II.** *adv* **1.** *inf* (*exactly*) directamente; **~ in the middle of the road** justo en medio de la carretera **2.** (*make noise*) **to go ~** estallar **III.** *interj* bang **IV.** *vi* (*make noise*) dar golpes; (*exploding noise*) estallar; (*slam*) cerrarse de golpe; **to ~ on sth** dar golpes en algo **V.** *vt* (*hit*) golpear; **to ~ one's head against/on sth** darse un golpe en la cabeza contra/en algo

◆**bang about** *vi inf* hacer ruido

banger ['bæŋə', *Am:* -ə·] *n* **1.** *Brit, inf* (*car*) coche *m,* cacharro *m* **2.** (*firework*) petardo *m* **3.** *Brit, inf* (*sausage*) salchicha *f*

Bangladesh [bæŋglə'deʃ] *n* Bangladesh *m*

Bangladeshi [bæŋglə'deʃi] **I.** *n* bangladesí *mf* **II.** *adj* bangladesí

bangle ['bæŋgl] *n* ajorca *f*

banish ['bænɪʃ] *vt a. fig* desterrar; **to ~ sth from one's mind** disipar algo de su mente

banishment *n no pl* destierro *m*

banister ['bænɪstə', *Am:* -əstə·] *n* pasamano *m*

banjo ['bændʒəʊ] *n* <-(oe)s> banjo *m*

bank¹ [bæŋk] **I.** *n* **1.** FIN banco *m;* (*in games*) banca *f;* **to break the ~** hacer saltar la banca **2.** (*storage place*) depósito *m;* **blood ~** banco *m* de sangre; **data ~** banco *m* de datos ►**to laugh all the way to the ~** *inf* ganar mucha pasta **II.** *vi* **to ~ with Barclays** tener una cuenta en el banco Barclays **III.** *vt* depositar

bank² [bæŋk] **I.** *n* (*edge: of river*) orilla *m* **II.** *vi* AVIAT ladearse

bank³ [bæŋk] *n* (*of earth*) terraplén *m;* (*of fog*) banco *m;* (*of cloud*) montón *m;* (*of switches*) batería *f*

◆**bank up I.** *vi* amontonarse **II.** *vt* amontonar

bank account *n* cuenta *f* bancaria **bank balance** *n* balance *m* bancario **bank book** *n* libreta *f* bancaria **bank charges** *n* gastos *mpl* bancarios **bank clerk** *n* empleado, -a *m, f* de banco

banker ['bæŋkə', *Am:* -kə·] *n* banquero, -a *m, f*

bank holiday *n Am, Brit* día *m* festivo

banking *n no pl* banca *f*

banking hall *n* sala *f* de ventanillas **banking hours** *npl* horario *m* bancario

bank manager *n* gerente *mf* de banco

banknote *n* billete *m* de banco **bank rate** *n* tipo *m* bancario **bank robber** *n* ladrón, -ona *m, f* de banco

bankrupt ['bæŋkrʌpt] **I.** *n* quebrado *m* **II.** *vt* llevar a la bancarrota **III.** *adj* **1.** (*bust*) insolvente; **to be ~** estar en quiebra; **to go ~** quebrar **2.** *fig* **to be morally ~** estar moralmente destrozado

bankruptcy ['bæŋkrəptsi] *n* <-ies> bancarrota *f*

bank statement *n* estado *m* de cuentas **bank transfer** *n* transferencia *f* bancaria

banner ['bænə', *Am:* -ə·] *n* **1.** (*flag*) bandera *f;* **under the ~ of ...** bajo la bandera de... **2.** (*placard*) pancarta **3.** (*in Internet*) anuncio *m*

banns [bænz] *npl* **to publish the ~** correr las amonestaciones

banquet ['bæŋkwɪt, *Am:* -kwət] **I.** *n* banquete *m* **II.** *vi* banquetear

bantam ['bæntəm, *Am:* -t̬əm] *n* gallina *f* de Bantam

banter ['bæntə', *Am:* -t̬ə·] **I.** *n* bromas *fpl* **II.** *vi* bromear

baptise [bæp'taɪz] *vt Aus, Brit s.* **baptize**

baptism ['bæptɪzəm] *n* bautismo *m;* **~ of fire** bautismo de fuego

baptismal ['bæptɪzməl] *adj* bautismal

baptismal font *n* pila *f* baptismal

Baptist ['bæptɪst] *n* bautista *mf;* **John the ~** Juan el Bautista; **the Baptist Church** la iglesia bautista

baptize [bæp'taɪz, *Am:* 'bæp-] *vt* bautizar; **I was ~d Clara** me bautizaron con el nombre de Clara

bar¹ [bɑːʳ, *Am:* bɑːr] I. *n* 1. (*of metal, wood*) barra *f;* (*of a cage, prison*) reja *f;* (*of chocolate*) tableta *f;* (*of gold*) lingote *m;* (*of soap*) pastilla *f;* **to be behind** ~**s** *inf* estar entre rejas 2. (*band of colour*) franja *f* 3. mus compás *m* 4. mil barra *f* 5. (*sandbank*) banco *m* de arena 6. (*restriction*) obstáculo *m* 7. (*place to drink*) bar *m;* (*counter*) barra *f,* mostrador *m* 8. infor barra *f;* **task/scroll/space** ~ barra de tareas/desplazamiento/espacio II. *vt* <-rr-> 1. (*fasten: door, window*) atrancar 2. (*obstruct*) obstruir; **to** ~ **sb's way/path** obstaculizar el camino/paso a alguien 3. (*prohibit*) prohibir; **to** ~ **sb from doing sth** prohibir a alguien hacer algo 4. (*exclude*) excluir

bar² [bɑːʳ, *Am:* bɑːr] *prep Brit* excepto; ~ **none** sin excepción

Bar [bɑːʳ, *Am:* bɑːr] *n* **the** ~ (*group of lawyers*) el Colegio de Abogados; (*profession*) el foro, la Barra *Méx*

barb [bɑːb, *Am:* bɑːrb] *n* 1. zool púa *f* 2. (*insult*) observación *f* aguda

Barbadian [bɑːˈbeɪdiən, *Am:* bɑːr-] I. *adj* de Barbados II. *n* habitante *mf* de Barbados

Barbados [bɑːˈbeɪdɒs, *Am:* bɑːrˈbeɪdoʊs] *n* Barbados *m*

barbarian [bɑːˈbeərɪən, *Am:* bɑːrˈberɪ-] *n* bárbaro, -a *m, f*

barbaric [bɑːˈbærɪk, *Am:* bɑːrˈber-] *adj* bárbaro, -a

barbarity [bɑːˈbærəti, *Am:* bɑːrˈberəti] *n* <-ies> crueldad *f*

barbarous [ˈbɑːbərəs, *Am:* bɑːr-] *adj* bárbaro, -a

barbecue [ˈbɑːbɪkjuː, *Am:* ˈbɑːr-] *n* 1. (*grill*) parrilla *f* 2. (*event*) barbacoa *f,* parrillada *f Col, Ven,* asado *m Chile*

barbed [bɑːbd, *Am:* bɑːrbd] *adj* 1. (*with barbs*) de púas 2. *fig* (*comment, criticism*) mordaz

barbed wire *n* alambre *m* de púas

barber [ˈbɑːbəʳ, *Am:* ˈbɑːrbəʳ] *n* barbero *m*

barbershop [ˈbɑːbəʃɒp, *Am:* ˈbɑːrbəʳʃɑːp] *n no pl* barbería *f*

barbiturate [bɑːˈbɪtjʊrɪt, *Am:* bɑːrˈbɪtʃrət] *n* barbitúrico *m*

bar chart *n* gráfico *m* de barras **bar code** *n* código *m* de barras

bard [bɑːd, *Am:* bɑːrd] *n* bardo *m;* **the Bard** Shakespeare

bare [beəʳ, *Am:* ber] I. *adj* 1. (*without any clothes*) desnudo, -a; (*uncovered*) descubierto, -a; **with one's** ~ **hands** con las propias manos; **to fight with one's** ~ **hands** luchar sin armas 2. (*empty*) vacío, -a; (*without plants, leaves*) desnudo, -a; **to be** ~ **of sth** estar desprovisto de algo 3. (*unadorned*) **to tell sb the** ~ **facts** [*o* **truth**] decir a alguien la pura verdad 4. (*little*) **the** ~ **minimum** lo mínimo; **the** ~ **necessities** las necesidades básicas II. *vt* desnudar; **to** ~ **one's head** decubrirse; **to** ~ **one's teeth** enseñar los dientes; **to** ~ **one's heart/soul to sb** abrir su corazón/alma a al-

guien

bareback [ˈbeəbæk, *Am:* ˈber-] *adv* a pelo

barefaced [ˈbeəfeɪst, *Am:* ˈber-] *adj* descarado, -a

barefoot [ˈbeəfʊt, *Am:* ˈber-] *adv,* **barefooted** [ˌbeəˈfʊtɪd, *Am:* ˌberˈfʊt-] *adv* descalzo, -a

barely [ˈbeəli, *Am:* ˈber-] *adv* 1. (*hardly*) apenas, agatas *Arg, Urug, Par* 2. (*scantily*) escasamente

barf [bɑːf, *Am:* bɑːrf] *vi Am, inf* vomitar

bargain [ˈbɑːgɪn, *Am:* ˈbɑːr-] I. *n* 1. (*agreement*) trato *m;* **to drive a hard** ~ saber regatear; **to strike a** ~ cerrar un trato 2. (*item*) ganga *f,* pichincha *f Arg, Bol, Par, Urug,* mamada *f AmC, Bol, Chile, Perú* ▶**into the** ~ por añadidura II. *vi* (*negotiate*) negociar; (*haggle*) regatear; **to** ~ **away sth** malvender algo

◆**bargain for** *vi,* **bargain on** *vi* contar con; **to get more than one bargained for** *fig* recibir más de lo que uno se esperaba

bargain basement *n* sección *f* de ofertas **bargain price** *n* precio *m* de oferta **bargain sale** *n* rebajas *fpl*

barge [bɑːdʒ, *Am:* bɑːrdʒ] I. *n* barcaza *f* II. *vt inf* empujar; **to** ~ **one's way through sth** abrirse paso por algo

◆**barge in** *vi* 1. (*intrude*) entrar sin pedir permiso 2. *fig* (*interrupt*) **sorry to** ~ disculpe si me entrometo

◆**barge into** *vi* **to** ~ **sb** chocar con alguien

◆**barge through** *vi* abrirse paso a empujones

baritone [ˈbærɪtəʊn, *Am:* ˈberətoʊn] I. *n* barítono *m* II. *adj* barítono, -a

bark¹ [bɑːk, *Am:* bɑːrk] I. *n* (*of a dog*) ladrido *m* ▶**his** ~ **is worse than his bite** perro ladrador poco mordedor *prov* II. *vi* ladrar; (*person*) gritar III. *vt* gritar

◆**bark out** *vt* gritar

bark² [bɑːk, *Am:* bɑːrk] *n no pl* (*of a tree*) corteza *f*

barkeeper [ˈbɑːkiːpəʳ, *Am:* ˈbɑːrkiːpəʳ] *n* (*owner*) tabernero, -a *m, f;* (*barperson*) camarero, -a *m, f*

barley [ˈbɑːli, *Am:* ˈbɑːr-] *n no pl* cebada *f*

barmaid [ˈbɑːmeɪd, *Am:* ˈbɑːr-] *n* camarera *f*

barman [ˈbɑːmən, *Am:* ˈbɑːr-] *n* <-men> camarero *m*

barmy [ˈbɑːmi, *Am:* ˈbɑːr-] *adj inf* chiflado, -a

barn [bɑːn, *Am:* bɑːrn] *n* granero *m*

barnacle [ˈbɑːnəkl, *Am:* ˈbɑːr-] *n* bálano *m*

barn yard *n* corral *m*

barometer [bəˈrɒmɪtəʳ, *Am:* -ˈrɑːmət̬əʳ] *n* barómetro *m*

baron [ˈbærən, *Am:* ˈber-] *n* 1. (*aristocrat*) barón *m* 2. *fig* magnate *m*

baroness [ˈbærənɪs, *Am:* ˈbernəs] *n* baronesa *f*

baronet [ˈbærənɪt, *Am:* ˈbernət] *n* baronet *m*

baronial [bəˈrəʊnɪəl, *Am:* -ˈroʊ-] *adj* baronial

baroque [bə'rɒk, Am: -'roʊk] adj a. fig barroco, -a

barrack ['bærək, Am: 'ber-] vt abuchear

barracks ['bærəks, Am: 'ber-] npl cuartel m

barrage ['bærɑːʒ, Am: bə'rɑːʒ] n 1. MIL cortina f de fuego 2. fig (of questions, complaints) aluvión m 3. Brit (barrier) barrera f

barrel ['bærəl, Am: 'ber-] I. n 1. (container) barril m, tonel m 2. (measure: of oil) barril m 3. (of a gun) cañón m ▶to be a ~ of fun ser divertido; to have sb over a ~ tener a alguien en un puño; to scrape (the bottom of) the ~ tener que recurrir a lo peor II. vi <Brit: -ll-, Am: -l-> inf correr III. vt <Brit: -ll-, Am: -l-> embarrilar

barrel organ n organillo m

barren ['bærən, Am: 'ber-] adj 1. (infertile) estéril; (landscape) árido, -a 2. (unproductive) improductivo, -a; ~ years años perdidos

barricade [ˌbærɪ'keɪd, Am: ˌberə-] I. n barricada f II. vt cerrar con barricadas; she ~d herself into her room se atrincheró en su habitación

barrier ['bærɪəʳ, Am: 'berɪɚ] n barrera f; language ~ barrera lingüística

barring ['bɑːrɪŋ] prep (except for) excepto; (if there are no) a menos que +subj; ~ accidents si Dios quiere; ~ complications a menos que se presenten complicaciones; ~ delays a menos que se produzcan retrasos

barrister ['bærɪstəʳ, Am: 'berɪstɚ] n Aus, Brit abogado, -a m, f

barrow ['bærəʊ, Am: 'beroʊ] n (wheelbarrow) carretilla f; (cart) carreta f

bartender ['bɑːtendəʳ, Am: 'bɑːrtendɚ] n camarero, -a m, f

barter ['bɑːtəʳ, Am: 'bɑːrtɚ] I. n no pl trueque m II. vi comerciar III. vt to ~ sth for sth trocar [o cambiar] algo por algo

basalt ['bæsɔːlt, Am: bə'sɔːlt] n no pl basalto m

base¹ [beɪs] I. n 1. (lower part) base f 2. (bottom) fondo m 3. (source of support) apoyo m 4. (basis) fundamento m 5. MIL base 6. (of a company) sede f ▶to be off ~ Am, inf estar equivocado; to touch ~ tocar fondo II. vt 1. (found) basar; to be ~d on basarse en 2. MIL estacionar 3. (stay) to be ~d in London (company) tener su sede en Londres; (person) trabajar en Londres; which hotel are you ~d at? ¿en qué hotel vives?

base² [beɪs] adj 1. (not honourable) vil 2. (not pure: metal) impuro, -a

baseball ['beɪsbɔːl] n béisbol m

base camp n campamento m base

Basel ['bɑːzl] n Basilea f

baseless ['beɪslɪs] adj sin fundamento; (accusation) infundado, -a

base rate ['beisreit] n Brit tipo m de interés base

bash [bæʃ] I. n 1. (blow) porrazo m 2. inf (party) fiesta f II. vt (hit hard: thing) golpear;

(person) pegar; to have a ~ at doing sth inf intentar hacer algo

◆**bash into** vi insep estrellarse contra

bashful ['bæʃfəl] adj tímido, -a

basic ['beɪsɪk] I. adj básico, -a; ~ idea idea f principal; ~ requirements requisitos mínimos; to have a ~ command of sth tener conocimientos básicos de algo II. npl the ~s lo básico

BASIC ['beɪsɪk] n INFOR abbr of Beginner's All-purpose Symbolic Instruction Code BASIC m

basically adv básicamente

basic vocabulary n vocabulario m básico

basic wage n salario m mínimo

basil ['bæzəl, Am: 'beɪzəl] n albahaca f

basilica [bə'zɪlɪkə, Am: -'sɪl-] n ARCHIT basílica f

basin ['beɪsn] n 1. (for cooking) cuenco m; (for washing hands) lavabo m 2. GEO cuenca f

basis ['beɪsɪs] n <bases> base f; on a weekly ~ semanalmente; to be the ~ for sth ser el fundamento de algo; on the ~ of sth sobre la base de algo

bask [bɑːsk, Am: bæsk] vi to ~ in the sun tomar el sol; to ~ in sb's favour gozar del favor de alguien

basket ['bɑːskɪt, Am: 'bæskət] n 1. (container) cesto m; (two handled) canasta f 2. (amount in basket) canastada f 3. SPORTS canasta f

basketball ['bɑːskɪtbɔːl, Am: 'bæskətbɔːl] n baloncesto m

basket case n inf to be a ~ ser un fracaso

basking shark n tiburón m peregrino

Basque [bæsk] I. adj vasco, -a; ~ Country País m Vasco II. n 1. vasco, -a m, f 2. no pl LING euskera m

bass¹ [beɪs] n 1. (voice) bajo m 2. (instrument: classical) contrabajo m; (electric) bajo m

bass² [bæs] n ZOOL lubina f

bass clef n clave f de fa

bass drum n bombo m

bassoon [bə'suːn] n fagot m

bastard ['bɑːstəd, Am: 'bæstɚd] n 1. (child) bastardo, -a m, f 2. vulg cabrón, -ona m, f

baste [beɪst] vt 1. GASTR pringar 2. Am, Aus (tack) hilvanar

bastion ['bæstɪən, Am: -tʃən] n a. fig baluarte m

bat¹ [bæt] n murciélago m ▶to have ~s in the belfry inf estar chiflado; to be as blind as a ~ no ver tres en un burro

bat² [bæt] vt to ~ one's eyelids pestañear; to ~ one's eyelids at sb guiñar un ojo a alguien; he/she didn't ~ an eyelid when ... fig permaneció indiferente cuando...

bat³ [bæt] n 1. (in baseball, cricket) bate m 2. (blow) golpe m ▶right off the ~ Am al instante; to do sth off one's own ~ Brit, inf hacer algo por su propia cuenta II. vt, vi <-tt-> SPORTS batear

batch [bætʃ] *n* <-es> tanda *f;* COM, INFOR lote *m;* (*of cakes*) hornada *f*

batch file *n* INFOR fichero *m* por lotes **batch processing** *n* INFOR procesamiento *m* por lotes

bated ['beɪtɪd, *Am:* 'bæt̬-] *adj* with ~ **breath** con ansiedad

bath [bɑːθ, *Am:* bæθ] **I.** *n* **1.** (*container*) bañera *f,* tina *f AmL,* bañadera *f Arg* **2.** (*action*) baño *m,* bañada *f Méx;* **to have** [*o* take] **a** ~ bañarse **II.** *vi* bañarse **III.** *vt* bañar

bathe [beɪð] **I.** *vi* bañarse **II.** *vt* (*wound, eyes*) lavar; (*person, animal*) bañar; **to be** ~**d in sweat/tears** estar bañado en sudor/lágrimas **III.** *n no pl* baño *m;* **to have a** ~ bañarse

bather ['beɪðəʳ, *Am:* -ðɚ] *n* bañista *mf*

bathing *n no pl* ~ **prohibited** prohibido bañarse

bathing cap *n* gorro *m* de baño **bathing costume** *n Aus, Brit,* **bathing suit** *n Am* bañador *m,* malla *f* (de baño) *RíoPl,* vestido *m* de baño *Col* **bathing trunks** *npl* bañador *m*

bathrobe ['bɑːθrəʊb] *n* albornoz *m*

bathroom ['bɑːθruːm] *n* **1.** (*room with bath*) (cuarto *m* de) baño *m* **2.** *Am, Aus* (*lavatory*) baño *m,* servicio *m*

bath towel *n* toalla *f* de baño

bathtub ['bɑːθtʌb, *Am:* 'bæθ-] *n* bañera *f,* tina *f AmL,* bañadera *f Arg*

baton ['bætən, *Am:* bə'tɑːn] *n* **1.** MUS batuta *f;* MIL bastón *m* **2.** (*of a policeman*) porra *f* **3.** SPORTS testigo *m;* ~ **change** relevo *m*

batsman ['bætsmən] <-men> *n* bateador *m*

battalion [bə'tæliən, *Am:* -jən] *n* batallón *m*

batten ['bætn] **I.** *n* **1.** ARCHIT (*for a door, wall*) listón *m;* (*for flooring*) tabla *f* **2.** NAUT (*for a sail*) sable *m;* (*for a hatch*) listón *m,* barra *f* de cierre **3.** THEAT guía *f* **II.** *vt* reforzar con listones **III.** *vi* **to** ~ **on sb** vivir a costa de alguien
♦**batten down** *vt* **to** ~ **the hatches** *fig* atarse los machos

batter ['bætəʳ, *Am:* 'bæt̬ɚ] **I.** *n* **1.** GASTR (*for fried food*) rebozado *m;* (*for a pancake, cake*) masa *f* **2.** *Am* SPORTS bateador(a) *m(f)* **II.** *vt* **1.** (*assault*) maltratar, pegar **2.** (*hit*) golpear; **to** ~ **the door in** [*o* down] derribar la puerta **3.** GASTR rebozar **III.** *vi* **to** ~ **at the door** aporrear la puerta; **the waves** ~**ed against the rocks** las olas azotaban las rocas

battered ['bætəd, *Am:* -ɚd] *adj* **1.** (*injured*) maltratado, -a **2.** (*damaged: hat, clothes*) estropeado, -a; (*reputation, image*) maltrecho, -a **3.** GASTR rebozado, -a

battering ['bætərɪŋ, *Am:* 'bæt̬-] *n* paliza *f;* **to give sb a** ~ dar una paliza a alguien

battering ram ['bætərɪŋræm, *Am:* 'bæt̬-] *n* HIST, MIL ariete *m*

battery ['bætəri, *Am:* 'bæt̬-] <-ies> *n* **1.** (*for a radio, torch*) pila *f;* (*for a car*) batería *f* **2.** (*large number*) serie *f;* **a** ~ **of questions** una sarta de preguntas **3.** MIL batería *f* **4.** LAW agresión *f*

battery charger *n* cargador *m* de pilas; AUTO cargador *m* de baterías

battery hen *n Aus, Brit* gallina *f* de criadero

battle ['bætl, *Am:* 'bæt̬-] **I.** *n* **1.** MIL batalla *f* **2.** (*struggle*) lucha *f* ▶**that's half the** ~ eso es la parte más difícil, con eso ya hay medio camino andado; **to fight a losing** ~ luchar por una causa perdida **II.** *vi* (*fight*) pelear; (*non-violently*) luchar **III.** *vt* combatir; **to** ~ **one's way to the top** abrirse paso hasta la cima

battleax *n Am,* **battleaxe** ['bætlæks, *Am:* 'bæt̬-] *n Aus, Brit* **1.** HIST hacha *f* de guerra **2.** *pej, inf* (*woman*) sargenta *f,* sisebuta *f RíoPl*

battle cry *n* grito *m* de guerra **battledress** *n no pl* traje *m* de campaña **battlefield** *n* campo *m* de batalla **battleground** *n* campo *m* de batalla

battlements ['bætlmənts, *Am:* 'bæt̬-] *npl* almenas *fpl*

battleship ['bætlʃɪp, *Am:* 'bæt̬-] *n* acorazado *m*

baud [bɔːd, *Am:* bɑːd] *n* INFOR baudio *m*

baud rate *n* INFOR velocidad *f* de transmisión

baulk [bɔːk, *Am:* bɑːk] *vi s.* **balk**

bauxite ['bɔːksaɪt, *Am:* 'bɑːk-] *n no pl* bauxita *f*

bawdy ['bɔːdi, *Am:* 'bɑː-] <-ier, -iest> *adj* (*scene*) subido, -a de tono; (*joke*) verde, colorado, -a *Méx*

bawl [bɔːl, *Am:* bɑːl] **I.** *vi* **1.** (*bellow*) vociferar; **to** ~ **at sb** gritar a alguien **2.** (*weep*) berrear **II.** *vt* gritar; **to** ~ **sb out** echar la bronca a alguien; **to** ~ **one's eyes out** desgañitarse

bay¹ [beɪ] *n* GEO bahía *f*

bay² [beɪ] *n* laurel *m*

bay³ [beɪ] *n* **1.** ARCHIT (*between columns*) intercolumnio *m;* (*in a church*) crujía *f;* (*of a factory*) nave *f;* (*in a house*) saliente *m* **2.** *Brit* (*marked-off space*) **parking** ~ plaza *f* de estacionamiento

bay⁴ [beɪ] *n* ZOOL caballo *m* zaino

bay⁵ [beɪ] **I.** *vi* aullar **II.** *n no pl* (*howling*) aullido *m* ▶**to be at** ~ estar acorralado; **to bring sth/sb to** ~ acorralar algo/a alguien; **to hold sth/sb at** ~ mantener algo/a alguien a raya

bay leaf *n* hoja *f* de laurel

Bay of Biscay *n* Golfo *m* de Vizcaya

bayonet ['beɪənɪt, *Am:* ˌbeɪə'net] **I.** *n* bayoneta *f* **II.** *vt* (*wound*) herir con una bayoneta; (*kill*) matar con una bayoneta

bay window *n* mirador *m*

bazaar [bə'zɑːʳ, *Am:* -'zɑːr] *n* **1.** bazar *m* **2.** (*event*) venta *f* benéfica, bazar *m Col*

BBC ['biːbiːˈsiː] *n abbr of* **British Broadcasting Corporation** BBC *f*

BC [ˌbiːˈsiː] **I.** *Can abbr of* **British-Columbia** Columbia *f* Británica **II.** *adv abbr of* **before Christ** a.C.

BCG [ˌbiːsiːˈdʒiː] *abbr of* **bacillus of Calmette and Guérin** vacuna *f* de la tuberculosis

be [biː] <was, been> **I.** *vi* **1.** + *n/adj* (*permanent state, quality, identity*) ser; **she's a cook** es cocinera; **she's Spanish** es española; **to** ~ **good** ser bueno; **to** ~ **able to do sth** ser capaz de hacer algo; **what do you want to ~ when you grow up?** ¿qué quieres ser de mayor?; **to ~ married/single** estar [*o* ser *CSur*] casado/soltero; **to ~ a widow** ser viuda **2.** + *adj* (*mental and physical states*) estar; **to ~ fat** estar gordo; **to ~ hungry** tener hambre; **to ~ happy** estar contento **3.** (*age*) tener; **I'm 21** tengo 21 años **4.** (*indicates sb's opinion*) **to ~ for/against sth** estar a favor/en contra de algo **5.** (*calculation, cost*) **two and two is four** dos y dos son cuatro; **these glasses are £2 each** estos vasos cuestan 2 libras cada uno; **how much is that?** ¿cuánto es? **6.** (*measurement*) medir; (*weight*) pesar; **to ~ 2 metres long** medir 2 metros de largo **7.** (*exist, live*) **there is/are …** hay…; **to let sth/sb ~** dejar en paz algo/a alguien; **I think, therefore I am** pienso, luego existo; **to ~ or not to ~** ser o no ser **8.** (*location, situation*) estar; **to ~ in Rome** estar en Roma; **to ~ in a bad situation** estar en una mala situación **9.** *pp* (*go, visit*) **I've never ~en to Mexico** nunca he estado en Méjico; **the plumber hasn't ~en yet** el fontanero todavía no ha venido **10.** (*take place*) ser, tener lugar; **the meeting is next Tuesday** la reunión es el próximo martes **11.** (*circumstances*) **to ~ on the pill** tomar la píldora; **to ~ on vacation** estar de vacaciones; **to ~ on a diet** estar a régimen **12.** (*in time expressions*) **don't ~ too long** no tardes mucho **13.** (*expresses possibility*) **can it ~ that …?** *form* ¿puede ser que… +*subj*?; **what are we to do?** ¿qué podemos hacer? ▶ **~ that as it may** sea como fuere; **so ~ it** así sea **II.** *impers vb* (*expressing physical conditions, circumstances*) **it's cloudy** está nublado; **it's sunny** hace sol; **it's two o'clock** son las dos; **it's ~en so long!** ¡cuánto tiempo!; **it's ten minutes by bus to the market** el mercado está a diez minutos en autobús; **it was Anne who drank it** fue Anne quien se lo bebió **III.** *aux vb* **1.** (*expresses continuation*) estar; **to ~ doing sth** estar haciendo algo; **don't sing while I'm reading** no cantes mientras estoy leyendo [*o* mientras leo]; **you're always complaining** siempre te estás quejando; **she's leaving tomorrow** se va mañana **2.** (*expresses passive*) ser; **to ~ discovered by sb** ser descubierto por alguien; **he was left speechless** lo dejaron sin palabras; **he was asked …** le preguntaron… **3.** (*expresses future*) **we are to visit Peru in the winter** vamos a ir a Perú en invierno **4.** (*expresses future in past*) **she was never to see her brother again** nunca más volvería a ver a su hermano **5.** (*expresses subjunctive possibility in conditionals*) **if he was to work harder, he'd get better grades** si trabajara más, tendría mejores notas; **were I to refuse, they'd ~ very annoyed** si me negara, se enfadarían mucho **6.** (*expresses obligation*) **you are to come here right now** tienes que venir aquí ahora mismo **7.** (*in question tags*) **she is tall, isn't she?** es alta, ¿no?

beach [biːtʃ] **I.** *n* playa *f* **II.** *vt* hacer embarrancar, varar

beach ball *n* balón *m* de playa

beachhead [ˈbiːtʃhed] *n* cabeza *f* de playa

beachwear [ˈbiːtʃweəʳ, *Am:* -wer] *n no pl* ropa *f* playera

beacon [ˈbiːkən] *n* **1.** (*signal*) baliza *f* **2.** (*lighthouse*) faro *m* **3.** (*fire*) almenara *f* **4.** *fig* (*guide*) luz *f*

bead [biːd] *n* **1.** (*ball: of glass*) abalorio *m*, cuenta *f;* (*of wood*) viruta *f* **2.** (*drop*) gota *f;* ~**s of sweat** gotas *fpl* de sudor **3.** *pl* rosario *m;* **to tell one's ~s** rezar el rosario **4.** (*on a gun*) punto *m* de mira; **to draw a ~ on sb/sth** apuntar a alguien/algo **5.** (*on a tyre*) talón *m*

beading *n* ARCHIT moldura *f*

beady [ˈbiːdi] <-ier, -iest> *adj* ~ **eyes** *ojos redondos, pequeños y brillantes;* **to cast a ~ eye on** [*o* over] **sth** mirar algo con lupa

beak [biːk] *n* **1.** ZOOL pico *m* **2.** *inf* (*nose*) napia *f*, naso *m* RíoPl **3.** Brit, *inf* (*magistrate*) juez *mf*

beaker [ˈbiːkəʳ, *Am:* -kəʳ] *n* **1.** (*cup*) jarra *f* **2.** CHEM vaso *m* de precipitados

be-all [ˈbiːˈɔːl] *n* **the ~** (**and end-all**) la única cosa que importa

beam [biːm] *n* **1.** (*ray*) rayo *m;* (*light*) haz *m* de luz; **full ~** luces *fpl* largas, luces *fpl* altas *Chile* **2.** ARCHIT viga *f* **3.** SPORTS barra *f* sueca ▶ **to be off** ~ *inf* estar equivocado **II.** *vt* transmitir; **to ~ a smile at sb** dedicar una sonrisa a alguien **III.** *vi* brillar; (*smile*) sonreír (abiertamente)

beaming *adj* **to be ~** estar radiante

bean [biːn] *n* **1.** (*seed*) semilla *f;* **coffee ~** grano *m* de café **2.** (*plant*) judía *f* **3.** (*vegetable: fresh*) judía *f* verde, ejote *m* Méx, chaucha *f* RíoPl, poroto *m* verde *Chile*, vainita *f* Ven; (*dried*) alubia *f;* **baked ~s** alubias *fpl* en salsa de tomate ▶ **to be full of** ~**s** *inf* estar lleno de vida; **old ~!** *inf* ¡viejo!; **to not have a ~** *inf* estar pelado; **to spill the ~s** *inf* descubrir el pastel, levantar la perdiz RíoPl

beanfeast [ˈbiːnfiːst] *n* Aus, Brit, *inf* fiestorro *m*, festichola *f* RíoPl, fiestoca *f* Chile **bean sprout** *n* brote *m* de soja

bear[1] [beəʳ, *Am:* ber] *n* **1.** ZOOL oso, -a *m, f;* **to be like a ~ with a sore head** *fig, inf* estar de mala leche **2.** FIN bajista *mf*

bear[2] [beəʳ, *Am:* ber] <bore, borne> **I.** *vt* **1.** (*carry*) llevar; **to ~ arms** *form* portar armas **2.** (*display*) **to ~ a resemblance to …** parecerse a … **3.** (*have, possess*) tener **4.** (*conduct*) **to ~ oneself** comportarse **5.** (*support: weight*) aguantar **6.** (*accept: cost*) correr con; (*responsibility*) cargar con **7.** (*endure: hardship, pain*) soportar; (*blame*) cargar con **8.** (*be fit for*) **what might have happened doesn't ~ thinking about** da miedo sólo de pensar lo que podía haber pasado; **he said something so awful that it doesn't ~ repeating** dijo algo tan horrible que no es como para repetirlo **9.** (*tolerate*) soportar, aguantar **10.** (*harbour*) to ~ **sb a grudge** tener [o guardar] rencor a alguien; **she ~s him no ill will** no le desea ningún mal **11.** (*keep*) **to ~ sth/sb in mind** tener algo/a alguien presente **12.** (*give birth to*) dar a luz a; **she bore him a daughter** tuvo una hija con él **13.** AGR, BOT (*fruit*) dar **14.** FIN, ECON (*interest*) devengar **15.** (*give*) **to ~ testimony** [o **witness**] **to sth** atestiguar algo **II.** *vi* (*tend*) **to ~ east** dirigirse al este; **to ~ left/right** torcer a la izquierda/a la derecha

◆**bear down on** *vt* avanzar hacia; **the train was bearing down on her** el tren se le venía encima

◆**bear off** *vt* llevarse

◆**bear on** *vt* **1.** (*be relevant to*) tener que ver con **2.** (*have affect on*) afectar a **3.** (*pressurize*) hacer presión sobre

◆**bear up** *vi* aguantar

◆**bear with** *vi* tener paciencia con

bearable ['beərəbl, *Am:* 'berə-] *adj* soportable

beard [bɪəd, *Am:* bɪrd] **I.** *n* **1.** (*hair*) barba *f;* **to shave off one's ~** afeitarse la barba **2.** ZOOL barbas *fpl* **II.** *vt* HIST desafiar

bearded *adj* barbudo, -a

beardless ['bɪədləs, *Am:* 'bɪrd-] *adj* lampiño, -a; **to be ~** ser imberbe

bearer ['beərər, *Am:* 'berə-] *n* portador(a) *m(f)*

bearing ['beərɪŋ, *Am:* 'berɪŋ] *n* **1.** NAUT rumbo *m;* **to get one's ~s** *a. fig* orientarse; **to lose one's ~s** *a. fig* desorientarse **2.** (*behaviour*) comportamiento *m* **3.** (*posture*) porte *m* **4.** TECH cojinete *m* **5.** ARCHIT soporte *m* ▶**to have some ~ on sth** tener que ver con algo

bearskin ['beəskɪn, *Am:* 'ber-] *n* **1.** (*bear fur*) piel *f* de oso **2.** (*military hat*) gorro *m* militar de piel de oso

beast [bi:st] *n* **1.** (*animal*) bestia *f;* **~ of burden** animal *m* de carga **2.** *inf* (*person*) animal *m;* **to be a ~ to sb** portarse como un animal con alguien **3.** *fig, inf* **a ~ of a day** un día asqueroso

beastly ['bi:stli] <-ier, -iest> *adj inf* horroroso, -a; **to be ~ to sb** portarse muy mal con alguien

beat [bi:t] <beat, beaten> **I.** *n* **1.** (*pulsation: of the heart*) latido *m;* (*of the pulse*) pulsación *f;* (*of a hammer*) martilleo *m* **2.** MUS (*stress*) tiempo *m;* (*stroke of the hand*) compás *m;* (*rhythm*) ritmo *m* **3.** *no pl* (*of a police officer*) ronda *f;* **to walk one's ~** hacer la ronda **II.** *adj inf* reventado, -a; **to be dead ~** *Brit* estar reventado [o molido] **III.** *vt* **1.** (*strike*) golpear; (*metal*) batir; (*carpet*) sacudir, festejar *Méx;* **to ~ sb black and blue** dar una paliza soberana a alguien; **to ~ a confession out of sb** hacer confesar a alguien a base de palos; **to ~ sb to death** matar a alguien a golpes **2.** (*wings*) batir **3.** GASTR batir **4.** (*cut through*) **to ~ a path through sth** abrirse paso en [o a través de] algo **5.** (*defeat*) derrotar, ganar; **Mary always ~s me at chess** Mary siempre

me gana al ajedrez **6.** (*surpass: record*) batir **7.** (*arrive before*) **she ~ me to the door** llegó antes que yo a la puerta **8.** (*be better than*) superar; **to ~ sb for sth** superar a alguien en algo; **taking the bus sure ~s walking there** *inf* es mucho mejor coger el autobús que ir caminando **9.** MUS (*drum*) tocar ▶**if you can't ~ them,** join **them** *prov* si no puedes con ellos, únete a ellos; **that ~s everything** *inf* ¡eso es el colmo!; **~ it!** *inf* ¡lárgate!, ¡mándate mudar! *RíoPl;* it **~s me how/why ...** no llego a comprender cómo/por qué... **IV.** *vi* **1.** (*pound: rain*) caer; (*sea*) batir; (*person*) golpear **2.** (*pulsate, vibrate: heart, pulse*) latir; (*wings*) batir; (*drum*) redoblar; (*hammer*) martillear

◆**beat about** *vi*, **beat around** *vi Am* **to ~ the bush** andarse con rodeos, firuletear *Arg, Urug*

◆**beat back** *vt* rechazar

◆**beat down I.** *vi* (*hail, rain*) caer con fuerza; (*sun*) picar **II.** *vt* **1.** (*haggle*) **to beat the price down** bajar el precio; **I managed to beat him down to 50 pence** conseguí que me lo dejara por 50 peniques **2.** (*flatten: door*) derribar

◆**beat off** *vt* rechazar

◆**beat up I.** *vt* dar una paliza a **II.** *vi Am* **to ~ on sb** dar una paliza a alguien

beaten ['bi:tn, *Am:* 'bi:tn̩] **I.** *pp of* beat **II.** *adj* **1.** (*metal*) batido, -a **2. to be off the ~ track** [o **path** *Am*] (*isolated*) estar aislado

beater ['bi:tər, *Am:* 'bi:tə-] *n* **1.** GASTR batidora *f;* (*for carpets*) sacudidor *m* **2.** (*in hunting*) batidor(a) *m(f)*

beatific [bɪə'tɪfɪk] *adj liter* beatífico, -a

beatification [bɪˌætɪfɪ'keɪʃən, *Am:* -ˌæṭə-] *n* beatificación *f*

beatify [bɪ'ætɪfaɪ, *Am:* -'æṭə-] *vt* beatificar

beating ['bi:tɪŋ, *Am:* 'bi:ṭɪŋ] *n* **1.** (*assault*) paliza *f,* cueriza *f AmL,* zumba *f AmL,* biaba *f Arg, Urug,* batida *f Perú, PRico,* fajada *f Arg;* **to give sb a ~** dar una paliza a alguien **2.** (*defeat*) derrota *f;* **to take a ~** recibir una paliza; **her time will take some ~** va a ser difícil superar su marca **3.** (*of the heart*) latido *m*

beautician [bju:'tɪʃən] *n* esteticista *mf*

beautiful ['bju:tɪfəl, *Am:* -ṭə-] *adj* hermoso, -a, precioso, -a; (*sight, weather*) estupendo, -a; **small is ~** lo bueno viene en frascos pequeños

beautify ['bju:tɪfaɪ, *Am:* -ṭə-] *vt* embellecer

beauty ['bju:ti, *Am:* -ṭi] <-ies> *n* **1.** *no pl* (*property*) belleza *f* **2.** (*beautiful woman*) belleza *f* **3.** *inf* (*specimen*) preciosidad *f,* maravilla *f* **4.** *inf* (*advantage*) **the ~ of ...** lo bueno de... ▶**~ is in the** eye **of the beholder** *prov* todo depende del color del cristal con que se mira; **~ is only** skin-deep *prov* la belleza está en el interior

beauty contest *n,* **beauty pageant** *n* concurso *m* de belleza **beauty parlour** *n,* **beauty salon** *n,* **beauty shop** *n Am* salón *m* de belleza **beauty spot** *n* **1.** (*location*)

lugar *m* pintoresco **2.** (*on the skin*) lunar *m*
beaver ['bi:vər, *Am:* -vəʳ] **I.** *n* **1.** ZOOL castor *m*
2. *no pl* (*fur*) piel *f* de castor **3.** *fig, inf* (*person*)
(**eager**) ~ persona *f* trabajadora **4.** *Am, vulg*
(*female genitals*) coño *m*, panocha *f Col, Méx,*
cola *f RíoPl* **II.** *vi inf* to ~ **away** trabajar como
una hormiguita
becalmed [bɪ'kɑ:md] *adj* to be ~ estar
inmóvil (a causa de la falta de viento)
became [bɪ'keɪm] *pt of* **become**
because [bɪ'kɒz, *Am:* -'kɑ:z] **I.** *conj* porque;
just ~ he smiles doesn't mean he is in love
inf sólo porque sonríe no significa que esté enamorado; ~ **I said that, I had to leave** como
dije eso, tuve que irme; **not ~ I am sad but ...**
no es porque esté triste, pero... **II.** *prep* ~ **of a**
causa de; ~ **of me** por mi culpa; ~ **of illness**
por enfermedad; ~ **of the fine weather**
debido al buen tiempo
beck [bek] *n* to be at sb's ~ **and call** estar
siempre a entera disposición de alguien
beckon ['bekən] **I.** *vt* llamar por señas; **to ~**
sb over hacer señas a alguien para que se acer-
que; **I ~ed her to follow** (**me**) le hice señas
para que me siguiera **II.** *vi* to ~ **to sb** hacer
señas a alguien; **I have to go because work**
~**s** me tengo que ir porque el trabajo me llama
become [bɪ'kʌm] <became, become>
I. *vi* (+ *adj*) volverse; (+ *n*) llegar a ser; **to ~**
angry enfadarse; **to ~ famous/old** hacerse
famoso/viejo; **to ~ sad/happy** ponerse triste/
feliz; **to ~ convinced that ...** convencerse de
que...; **to ~ interested in sth/sb** interesarse
por algo/alguien **II.** *vt* **1.** (*suit*) favorecer
2. (*befit*) ser apropiado para
becoming [bɪ'kʌmɪŋ] *adj* **1.** (*clothes, haircut*) favorecedor(a), sentador(a) *Arg, Chile*
2. (*behaviour*) apropiado, -a
bed [bed] **I.** *n* **1.** (*furniture*) cama *f;* **to get out**
of ~ levantarse de la cama; **to go to ~** acostarse; **to go to ~ with sb** acostarse con alguien; **to make the ~** hacer la cama; **to put**
sb to ~ acostar a alguien **2.** (*flower patch*) arriate *m,* cantero *m RíoPl* **3.** (*base*) base *f* **4.** (*bottom: of the sea*) fondo *m;* (*of a river*) lecho *m*
5. (*layer*) capa *f* ▶**a ~ of nails** un calvario; **a ~**
of roses un lecho de rosas; **to get out of** [*o* up
on *Am*] **the wrong side of the ~** levantarse
con el pie izquierdo; **you have made your ~**
and now you must lie in it quien mal cama
hace en ella se yace *prov;* **early to ~ and early**
to rise (**makes a man healthy, wealthy and**
wise) *prov* a quien madruga, Dios le ayuda
prov **II.** <-dd-> *vt* **1.** (*embed*) asentar **2.** *form*
(*have sex with*) acostarse con
◆**bed down** *vi* acostarse
BEd [bi:'ed] *abbr of* **Bachelor of Education**
Ldo., -a *m, f* en Magisterio
bed and breakfast *n* (*hotel*) pensión *f* familiar; (*service*) alojamiento *m* y desayuno
bedbug ['bedbʌg] *n* chinche *f*
bedclothes ['bedkləʊðz] *npl* ropa *f* de
cama, cobijas *fpl AmL*

bedding ['bedɪŋ] *n no pl* **1.** (*bed clothes*)
ropa *f* de cama **2.** (*for an animal*) cama *f*
bedecked [bɪ'dekt] *adj* to be ~ **with ...**
estar adornado con...
bedevil [bɪ'devəl] <*Brit:* -ll-, *Am:* -l-> *vt* to
be ~**ed with** [*o* by] **problems** estar plagado
de problemas
bedfellow ['bed,feləʊ, *Am:* -oʊ] *n* to make
strange ~**s** hacer una extraña pareja
bedlam ['bedləm] *n no pl* alboroto *m*
bedlinen ['bed,lɪnɪn, *Am:* -ən] *n* ropa *f* de
cama
Bedouin ['beduɪn] **I.** *adj* beduino, -a
II. <-(s)> *n* beduino, -a *m, f*
bedraggled [bɪ'drægld] *adj* **1.** (*wet*) empapado, -a **2.** (*dishevelled: person, appearance*)
desaliñado, -a; (*hair*) despeinado, -a
bedridden ['bed,rɪdn] *adj* postrado, -a en
cama
bedrock ['bedrɒk, *Am:* -rɑ:k] *n no pl* **1.** GEO
roca *f* firme **2.** *fig* cimientos *mpl,* base *f*
bedroom ['bedrʊm, *Am:* -ru:m] *n* dormitorio *m,* recámara *f Méx*
bedside ['bedsaɪd] *n no pl* cabecera *f*
bedside lamp *n* lámpara *f* de noche **bedside rug** *n* alfombrilla *f* de cama **bedside
table** *n* mesita *f* de noche, nochero *m Col,
Chile, Urug,* búro *m Méx*
bedsit ['bedsɪt] *n Brit,* **bed-sitting room**
n Brit habitación *f* de alquiler
bedsore ['bedsɔːʳ, *Am:* -sɔːr] *n* escara *f,*
úlcera *f* de decúbito
bedspread ['bedspred] *n* cubrecama *m,* colcha *f*
bedstead ['bedsted] *n* armazón *m o f* de
cama, catre *m CSur*
bedtime ['bedtaɪm] *n no pl* hora *f* de acostarse; **it's** (**way**) **past your** ~ hace rato que
deberías estar durmiendo
bee [bi:] *n* **1.** ZOOL abeja *f* **2.** *Am, Aus* (*group*)
círculo *m;* **sewing** ~ círculo de costura ▶**to
have a** ~ **in one's bonnet about sth** tener
algo metido entre ceja y ceja; **the** ~**s' knees**
Brit, inf el no va más; **to be a busy** ~ *iron* estar
muy atareado
beech [bi:tʃ] *n* haya *f*
beechnut ['bi:tʃnʌt] *n* hayuco *m*
beef [bi:f] *n no pl* **1.** GASTR carne *f* de ternera
[*o* de res *AmC, Méx*]; **minced** ~ carne de ternera picada; **roast** ~ rosbif *m* **2.** *inf* (*complaint*) queja *f* **II.** *vi inf* to ~ **about sth** quejarse de algo
beefburger ['bi:f,bɜːgəʳ, *Am:* -,bɜːrgəʳ] *n*
hamburguesa *f*
beefcake ['bi:fkeɪk] *n inf* machote *m,* cachas
m inv
beefeater ['bi:f,i:təʳ, *Am:* -ţəʳ] *n* alabardero
m de la Torre de Londres
beefsteak ['bi:fsteɪk] *n* bistec *m,* churrasco
m AmS, bife *m RíoPl*
beefy ['bi:fi] <-ier, -iest> *adj inf* fornido, -a,
cachas
beehive ['bi:haɪv] *n* colmena *f*

beekeeper ['biː,kiːpəʳ, *Am:* -pɚ] *n* apicultor(a) *m(f)*

beeline ['biːlaɪn] *n no pl, inf* to make a ~ for sth/sb ir derechito a algo/alguien

been [biːn, *Am:* bɪn] *pp of* be

beep [biːp] I. *n* pitido *m* II. *vi* pitar

beeper ['biːpəʳ, *Am:* -pɚ] *n* localizador *m*, busca *m inf*

beer [bɪəʳ, *Am:* bɪr] *n* cerveza *f*

beer garden *n* terraza *f* de verano **beer mat** *n* posavasos *m inv*

beery ['bɪəri, *Am:* 'bɪr-] *adj* de cerveza

beeswax ['biːzwæks] *n* cera *f* de abeja

beet [biːt] *n* 1.(*sugar beet*) remolacha *f* (azucarera) 2. *Am* (*beetroot*) remolacha *f*, betabel *f Méx*

beetle ['biːtl, *Am:* -t̬l] *n* escarabajo *m*
◆**beetle off** *vi inf* marcharse

beetroot ['biːtruːt] *n* remolacha *f*, betabel *f Méx;* to go [*o* turn] as red as a ~ ponerse rojo como un tomate **beet sugar** *n* azúcar *m* de remolacha

befit [bɪˈfɪt] <-tt-> *vt form* corresponder a; as ~s a princess como corresponde a una princesa

befitting *adj form* conveniente

before [bɪˈfɔːʳ, *Am:* -ˈfɔːr] I. *prep* 1.(*earlier*) antes de; to leave ~ sb salir antes que alguien; ~ doing sth antes de hacer algo; to wash one's hands ~ lunch lavarse las manos antes de la comida 2.(*in front of*) delante de; ~ my house delante de mi casa; to bow ~ sb inclinarse ante alguien; ~ our eyes ante nuestros ojos 3.(*preceding*) C comes ~ D la C va delante de la D; just ~ the bus stop justo antes de la parada del autobús 4.(*having priority*) antes que; ~ everything antes que nada; to put sth ~ sth else anteponer algo a algo 5.(*as future task*) to have sth ~ one tener algo ante sí II. *adv* 1.(*previously*) antes; I've seen it ~ lo he visto anteriormente; the day ~ el día anterior; two days ~ dos días antes; as ~ como antes 2.(*in front*) this word and the one ~ esta palabra y la anterior III. *conj* antes de que +*subj*; he spoke ~ she went out habló antes de que ella se fuera; he had a glass ~ he went se tomó una copa antes de irse; it was a week ~ he came pasó una semana antes de que llegara; he'd die ~ he'd tell the truth preferiría morir a decir la verdad

beforehand [bɪˈfɔːhænd, *Am:* -ˈfɔːr-] *adv* de antemano

befriend [bɪˈfrend] *vt* hacerse amigo de

beg [beg] <-gg-> I. *vt* (*request*) suplicar, rogar; to ~ sb to do sth suplicar a alguien que haga algo; to ~ sb's pardon pedir disculpas a alguien; I ~ your pardon! ¡disculpe!; I ~ to inform you that ... *form* tengo el gusto de comunicarle que... II. *vi* 1.(*seek charity*) pedir (limosna); to ~ on the streets mendigar por las calles; to ~ for sth pedir algo 2.(*request*) implorar; I ~ of you ¡te lo imploro!; to ~ for clemency implorar clemen-

cia; I ~ to differ *form* no estoy de acuerdo 3.(*sit up and request: dog*) pedir ▸there are jobs going ~ging *inf* hay trabajos a patadas

began [bɪˈgæn] *pt of* begin

beget [bɪˈget] <begot, begotten> *vt form* engendrar

beggar ['begəʳ, *Am:* -ɚ] I. *vt* to ~ belief parecer absolutamente inverosímil; to ~ description resultar indescriptible II. *n* 1.(*poor person*) mendigo, -a *m, f*, limosnero, -a *m, f AmL* 2.(*rascal*) pilluelo, -a *m, f* ▸~s can't be choosers *prov* a buen hambre no hay pan duro *prov*

begin [bɪˈgɪn] <began, begun> I. *vt* empezar, comenzar; to ~ a conversation entablar una conversación; to ~ doing sth empezar a hacer algo; to ~ work empezar a trabajar II. *vi* empezar, comenzar; the film ~s at eight la película comienza a las ocho; to ~ with ... al principio...; (*enumeration*) primero...; "well" he began ... "bueno", comenzó...

beginner [bɪˈgɪnəʳ, *Am:* -ɚ] *n* principiante *mf;* ~s' class curso *m* para principiantes; ~'s luck la suerte del principiante

beginning I. *n* 1.(*start*) principio *m*, comienzo *m*, empiezo *m Arg, Col, Ecua, Guat;* at [*o* in] the ~ al principio; from ~ to end de principio a fin 2.(*origin*) origen *m;* the ~s of humanity los albores de la humanidad II. *adj* inicial; ~ stage fase *f* inicial

begonia [bɪˈgəʊniə, *Am:* -ˈgoʊnjə] *n* begoña *f*

begot [bɪˈgɒt, *Am:* -ˈgɑːt] *pt, pp of* beget

begotten [bɪˈgɒtn, *Am:* -ˈgɑːt̬n] *pp of* beget

begrudge [bɪˈgrʌdʒ] *vt* 1.(*envy*) tener envidia a 2.(*resent*) to ~ doing sth hacer algo de mala gana

begun [bɪˈgʌn] *pp of* begin

behalf [bɪˈhɑːf, *Am:* -ˈhæf] *n no pl* on ~ of sb/sth (*for*) en beneficio de alguien/algo; (*from*) de parte de alguien/algo

behave [bɪˈheɪv] *vi* 1.(*act*) comportarse; (*in a proper manner*) conducirse; to ~ badly/well portarse mal/bien; ~! ¡pórtate bien! 2.(*function*) funcionar

behavior *n no pl, Am, Aus,* **behaviour** [bɪˈheɪvjəʳ, *Am:* -vjɚ] *n no pl, Aus, Brit* comportamiento *m;* to be on one's best ~ portarse lo mejor posible

behavioral *adj Am, Aus,* **behavioural** *adj Aus, Brit* de la conducta

behaviorism *n Am, Aus,* **behaviourism** [bɪˈheɪvjərɪzəm] *n no pl, Aus, Brit* conductismo *m*

behaviour pattern *n* patrón *m* de conducta

behead [bɪˈhed] *vt* decapitar

behind [bɪˈhaɪnd] I. *prep* 1.(*to the rear of*) detrás de; right ~ sb/sth justo detrás de alguien/algo; he walks ~ me camina detrás de mí; ~ the wheel al volante; a face ~ a mask un rostro detrás de una máscara 2.*fig* who is ~ that scheme? ¿quién está detrás de ese plan?; **there is somebody ~ this** hay alguien detrás de todo esto **3.** (*in support of*) **to be ~ sb/sth** (**all the way**) estar con alguien/algo (hasta el final) **4.** (*late for*) **~ time** retrasado; **to be ~ schedule** ir con retraso **5.** (*less advanced*) **to be ~ sb/the times** estar atrasado con respecto a alguien/la época **II.** *adv* **1.** (*at the back*) por detrás; **to fall ~** (*be slower*) quedarse atrás; (*in work, studies*) atrasarse; **to come from ~** venir desde atrás; **a blow from ~** un golpe por detrás; **to leave sb ~** dejar a alguien atrás; **to stay ~** quedarse atrás **2.** (*overdue*) **to be ~** retrasarse; **he is a long way ~** está muy retrasado; **to be ~** (**in sth**) estar atrasado (en algo) **III.** *n inf* trasero *m*; **to get off one's ~** mover el culo

behindhand [bɪ'haɪndhænd] *adv* atrasado, -a; **to be ~** estar atrasado

behold [bɪ'həʊld, *Am:* -'hoʊld] *vt* contemplar

beige [beɪʒ] *adj* beige

being ['biːɪŋ] **I.** *n* **1.** (*creature*) ser *m* **2.** (*life*) vida *f;* **to come into ~** nacer **3.** (*soul*) alma *f* **II.** *pres p of* **be III.** *adj after n* **for the time ~** por el momento

Belarus [belə'rʌs] *n* Bielorrusia *f*

belated [bɪ'leɪtɪd, *Am:* -t̬ɪd] *adj* tardío, -a

belch [beltʃ] **I.** *n* eructo *m* **II.** *vi* eructar **III.** *vt* vomitar; **to ~ clouds of smoke** arrojar nubes de humo

beleaguered [bɪ'liːgəʳd, *Am:* -gɚd] *adj* (*city*) asediado, -a; (*person, government*) acosado, -a

belfry ['belfri] *n* campanario *m*

Belgian ['beldʒən] **I.** *adj* belga **II.** *n* belga *mf*

Belgium ['beldʒəm] *n* Bélgica *f*

belie [bɪ'laɪ] *irr vt* **1.** (*disprove*) desmentir **2.** (*conceal*) ocultar

belief [bɪ'liːf] *n* **1.** REL creencia *f* **2.** (*conviction*) opinión *f;* **it is my firm ~ that ...** creo firmemente que...; **to the best of my ~** *Brit* que yo sepa; **to be beyond ~** ser increíble; **in the ~ that ...** con la convicción de que...

believable [bɪ'liːvəbl] *adj* creíble

believe [bɪ'liːv] **I.** *vt* creer; **~ you me!** ¡créeme!; **would you ~ it?** ¡no lo puedo creer!; **she couldn't ~ her eyes** no podía dar crédito a sus ojos; **I can't ~ how ...** me cuesta creer cómo...; **I'll ~ it when I see it!** ¡lo creeré cuando lo vea!; **~ it or not, ...** aunque parezca mentira... **II.** *vi* creer; **to ~ in sth** creer en algo; (*support*) ser partidario de algo

believer [bɪ'liːvəʳ, *Am:* -vɚ] *n* **1.** REL creyente *mf* **2.** (*supporter*) partidario, -a *m, f;* **to be a ~ in sth** ser partidario de algo

belittle [bɪ'lɪtl, *Am:* -'lɪt̬-] *vt* menospreciar

Belize [bə'liːz] *n* Belice *m*

Belizean [bə'liːzɪən] **I.** *adj* beliceño, -a **II.** *n* beliceño, -a *m, f*

bell [bel] *n* **1.** (*of a church*) campana *f;* (*handbell*) campanilla *f;* (*on a hat, cat*) cascabel *m;* (*of a bicycle, door*) timbre *m* **2.** (*signal*) campanada *f;* **to give sb a ~** *Brit, inf* llamar a alguien

(por teléfono) ►**as clear as a ~** más claro que el agua; **as sound as a ~** fuerte como un roble; **his name/face rings a ~** me suena su nombre/cara

belladonna [ˌbelə'dɒnə, *Am:* -'dɑːnə] *n no pl* belladona *f*

bellboy ['belbɔɪ] *n* botones *m inv*

bellicose ['belɪkəʊs, *Am:* -koʊs] *adj* belicoso, -a; **to be in a ~ mood** tener ganas de pelear

belligerent [bɪ'lɪdʒərənt] *adj* beligerante

bell jar *n* campana *f* de vidrio

bellow ['beləʊ, *Am:* -oʊ] **I.** *vt* gritar **II.** *vi* bramar **III.** *n* grito *m;* **to give a ~ of pain** lanzar un grito de dolor

bellows ['beləʊz, *Am:* -oʊz] *npl* fuelle *m;* **a pair of ~** un fuelle

bell push *n Brit* pulsador *m* de timbre

belly ['beli] <-ies> *n inf* barriga *f*, guata *f* *Chile* ►**to have fire in one's ~** tener mucho celo idealista; **to go** [*o* **turn** *Am*] **~ up** *inf* quebrar

bellyache *inf* **I.** *n* dolor *m* de barriga; **to have a ~** tener dolor(es) de barriga **II.** *vi* quejarse

belly button *n inf* ombligo *m* **belly dancer** *n* bailarina *f* de la danza del vientre **bellyflop** *n* panzazo *m*

belong [bɪ'lɒŋ, *Am:* -'lɑːŋ] *vi* **1.** (*be property of, be from*) **to ~ to sb/sth** pertenecer a alguien/algo **2.** (*be a member of*) **to ~ to** (*club*) ser socio de; (*party*) estar afiliado a **3.** (*have a place*) **where do these spoons ~?** ¿dónde pongo estas cucharas?; **this doesn't ~ here** esto no va aquí; **I feel I don't ~ here** no me encuentro a gusto aquí **4.** (*should be*) deber estar **5.** (*match*) **they ~ together** están hechos el uno para el otro

belongings *npl* pertenencias *fpl*

Belorussian [belə'rʌʃən] **I.** *adj* bielorruso, -a **II.** *n* **1.** (*person*) bielorruso, -a *m, f* **2.** *no pl* LING bielorruso *m*

beloved[1] [bɪ'lʌvɪd] *n no pl* amado, -a *m, f*

beloved[2] [bɪ'lʌvd] *adj* amado, -a; **her ~ husband** su amado marido; **to be ~ by sb** ser amado por alguien

below [bɪ'ləʊ, *Am:* -'loʊ] **I.** *prep* **1.** (*lower than, underneath*) debajo de, bajo; **~ the table/surface** debajo de la mesa/superficie; **~ us** debajo de nosotros; **~ sea level** por debajo del nivel del mar; **the sun sinks ~ the horizon** el sol se hunde bajo el horizonte; **to bend ~ sth** agacharse bajo algo **2.** GEO **London is ~ Oxford** Londres está debajo de Oxford; **the river ~ the town** el río abajo del pueblo **3.** (*less than*) **~ average** por debajo de la media; **~ freezing** bajo cero; **it's 4 degrees ~ zero** estamos a 4 grados bajo cero; **children ~ the age of twelve** menores de doce años **4.** (*inferior to*) **to be ~ sb in rank** tener un rango por debajo de alguien; **to work ~ sb** trabajar bajo (las órdenes de) alguien **5.** (*of a lower standard than*) **to be ~ sb** no ser digno de alguien; **to marry ~ oneself** casarse por debajo de sus expectativas **II.** *adv* abajo; **the family** ~ la familia de abajo; **from** ~ desde abajo; **see** ~ (*in a text*) ver más adelante

belt [belt] **I.** *n* **1.** FASHION cinturón *m;* **to fasten one's** ~ abrocharse el cinturón **2.** TECH correa *f* **3.** (*area*) zona *f* **4.** *inf* (*punch*) golpe *m* ▶**to tighten** one's ~ apretarse el cinturón; **to have some experience** under **one's** ~ tener algo de experiencia a sus espaldas **II.** *vt* **1.** (*secure with a belt*) ceñir **2.** *inf* (*hit*) zurrar **III.** *vi inf* correr a todo tren; **to** ~ **along** ir como una bala
◆**belt out** *vt inf* **to** ~ **a song** cantar una canción a pleno pulmón
◆**belt up** *vi* **1.** AUTO abrocharse el cinturón **2.** *inf* ~! ¡cierra el pico!

bemoan [bɪ'məʊn, *Am:* -'moʊn] *vt form* lamentar; **to** ~ **one's fate** quejarse de su destino

bemused [bɪ'mju:zd] *adj* desconcertado, -a; **a** ~ **look** una mirada de desconcierto

bench [bentʃ] *n* **1.** (*seat*) banco *m* **2.** SPORTS **the** ~ el banquillo **3.** LAW **the** ~ la judicatura; **to serve on the** ~ actuar como juez **4.** *pl, Brit* POL escaños *mpl* **5.** *Aus* (*worktop*) encimera *f*

benchmark ['bentʃmɑːk, *Am:* -mɑːrk] *n* punto *m* de referencia

bend [bend] <bent, bent> **I.** *n* **1.** (*of a river, road*) curva *f;* (*of a pipe*) codo *m;* **to take a** ~ tomar una curva **2.** *pl, inf* (*illness*) apoplejía *f* por descompresión ▶**to go/be** round **the** ~ *inf* volverse/estar loco **II.** *vi* **1.** (*move*) doblarse **2.** (*change direction*) hacer una curva **III.** *vt* **1.** (*move: arms, legs*) doblar; (*head*) inclinar **2.** (*change*) **to** ~ **sb to one's will** doblar a alguien a su voluntad **3.** (*interpret*) **to** ~ **the rules** interpretar las reglas a su manera
◆**bend back** *vt* doblar hacia atrás
◆**bend down** *vi* inclinarse
◆**bend over** *vi* inclinarse

bended ['bendɪd] *adj form* doblado, -a; **on** ~ **knee** de rodillas; **to go down on** ~ **knee** arrodillarse

beneath [bɪ'niːθ] **I.** *prep* **1.** (*lower than, underneath*) debajo de, bajo; ~ **the table/ surface** debajo de la mesa/superficie; ~ **us** debajo de nosotros; **the sun sinks** ~ **the horizon** el sol se hunde bajo el horizonte **2.** (*inferior to*) **to be** ~ **sb in rank** tener un rango por debajo de alguien **3.** (*lower standard than*) **to marry** ~ **one's self** casarse por debajo de sus expectativas; **to be** ~ **sb** no ser digno de alguien **II.** *adv* abajo

benediction [ˌbenɪ'dɪkʃən] *n form* bendición *f*

benefactor ['benɪfæktər] *n* benefactor *m*

benefactress ['benɪfæktrɪs] *n* benefactora *f*

beneficence [bɪ'nefɪsns] *n no pl* beneficencia *f*

beneficent [bɪ'nefɪsnt] *adj form* (*benign*) benéfico, -a; (*charitable*) caritativo, -a

beneficiary [ˌbenɪ'fɪʃəri] *n* <-ies> beneficiario, -a *m, f*

benefit ['benɪfɪt] **I.** *n* **1.** (*profit*) beneficio *m;*

to derive (**much**) ~ **from sth** sacar (mucho) provecho a algo; **I didn't derive much** ~ **from school** no aprendí gran cosa en la escuela; **for the** ~ **of sb** a beneficio de alguien; **to the** ~ **of sth/sb** para beneficio de algo/alguien **2.** (*welfare payment*) subsidio *m* **II.** <-t- *o* -tt-> *vi* **to** ~ **from sth** beneficiarse de algo **III.** <-t- *o* -tt-> *vt* beneficiar

Benelux ['benɪlʌks] *n* **the** ~ **countries** los países del Benelux

Bengali [beŋ'gɔːli] **I.** *adj* bengalí **II.** *n* bengalí *mf*

Benin [ben'iːn] *n* Benín *m*

Beninese [beni'niːz] **I.** *adj* de Benín **II.** *n* habitante *mf* de Benín

bent [bent] **I.** *pt, pp* of **bend II.** *n* **1.** (*aptitude*) inclinación *f;* **to have a** ~ **for sth** tener una inclinación por algo; **to follow one's** ~ obrar de acuerdo a sus inclinaciones **2.** (*preference*) afición *f* **III.** *adj* **1.** (*not straight*) torcido, -a **2.** (*determined*) **to be** ~ **on** (**doing**) **sth** estar empeñado en (hacer) algo **3.** *inf* (*corrupt*) corrupto, -a

benzene ['benziːn] *n no pl* benceno *m*

benzine ['benziːn] *n* bencina *f*

bequeath [bɪ'kwiːð] *vt* legar

bequest [bɪ'kwest] *n* legado *m*

berate [bɪ'reɪt] *vt form* regañar

bereave [bɪ'riːv] *vt* **he has recently been** ~**d of his son** acaba de perder a su hijo

bereaved *n* **the** ~ la familia del difunto

bereavement [bɪ'riːvmənt] *n* muerte *f* (de un familiar); **to suffer a** ~ sufrir la pérdida de un familiar

bereft [bɪ'reft] *adj form* **to be** ~ **of sth** estar privado de algo; **to feel** ~ sentirse desolado

beret ['bereɪ, *Am:* bə'reɪ] *n* boina *f*

Bermuda [bɜː'mjuːdə, *Am:* bəˈ-] *n* las Bermudas

Bermuda shorts [bɜː'mjuːdəʃɔːts, *Am:* bəˈ- ʃɔːrts] *n* bermudas *fpl*

Bern [bɜːn, *Am:* bɜːrn] *n* Berna *f*

berry ['beri] <-ies> *n* baya *f*

berserk [bə'sɜːk, *Am:* bəˈsɜːrk] *adj* **1.** (*frantic*) enloquecido, -a *inf* **2.** (*angry*) furioso, -a; **to go** ~ enfurecerse

berth [bɜːθ, *Am:* bɜːrθ] **I.** *n* **1.** (*on a ship*) camarote *m* **2.** (*on a train*) litera *f* **3.** (*in a harbour*) amarradero *m* **4.** *fig* **to give sb a wide** ~ evitar a alguien **II.** *vt, vi* NAUT atracar

beseech [bɪ'siːtʃ] <beseeched, besought> *vt form* **to** ~ **sb to do sth** suplicar a alguien que haga algo

beseeching *adj* suplicante

beset [bɪ'set] <beset, beset> *vt* acosar; **to be** ~ **by sth** estar acosado por algo; ~ **by worries** atormentado por las preocupaciones

beside [bɪ'saɪd] *prep* **1.** (*next to*) al lado de; **right** ~ **sb/sth** justo al lado de alguien/algo **2.** (*together with*) ~ **sb** junto a alguien **3.** (*in comparison to*) frente a **4.** (*overwhelmed*) **to be** ~ **oneself** estar fuera de sí **5.** (*irrelevant to*) **to be** ~ **the point** no venir al caso

besides [bɪˈsaɪdz] I. *prep* 1. (*in addition to*) además de 2. (*except for*) excepto II. *adv* 1. (*in addition*) además 2. (*else*) **nothing** ~ nada más

besiege [bɪˈsiːdʒ] *vt* 1. (*city*) sitiar 2. (*with questions, complaints*) acosar

besmirch [bɪˈsmɜːtʃ, *Am:* -ˈsmɜːrtʃ] *vt liter* manchar; **to** ~ **sb's good name** mancillar el buen nombre de alguien

besotted [bɪˈsɒtɪd, *Am:* ˈsɑːt̬ɪd] *adj* enamorado, -a; **to be** ~ **with sth** estar obsesionado con algo; **to be** ~ **with sb** estar chalado por alguien *inf*

besought [bɪˈsɔːt, *Am:* -ˈsɑːt] *pt, pp of* **beseech**

best [best] I. *adj superl of* **good** mejor; **the** ~ el/la mejor; **the** ~ **days of my life** los mejores días de mi vida; **the** ~ **part** (*the majority*) la mayor parte; **may the** ~ **man win** que gane el mejor; **with the** ~ **will** con la mejor voluntad II. *adv superl of* **well** mejor; **the** ~ lo mejor; **we'd** ~ **stay here** lo mejor es quedarse aquí; **as** ~ **you can** lo mejor que puedas; **do as you think** ~ haz lo que te parezca mejor III. *n no pl* 1. (*the finest*) **all the** ~! *inf* (*congratulation*) ¡felicidades!; (*end of letter*) un abrazo; **to be the** ~ **of friends** ser los mejores amigos; **to bring out the** ~ **in sb** sacar lo mejor de alguien; **to turn out for the** ~ ir para bien; **to wear one's Sunday** ~ llevar el traje de los domingos; **to the** ~ **of my knowledge** que yo sepa; **at** ~ como mucho, a lo mucho *Méx* 2. SPORTS récord *m* IV. *vt form* vencer

bestial [ˈbestɪəl, *Am:* -tʃl] *adj* bestial

bestiality [ˌbestɪˈæləti, *Am:* -tʃiˈæləti] *n no pl* 1. (*behaviour*) bestialidad *f* 2. LAW (*sexual*) zoofilia *f*

bestir [bɪˈstɜː, *Am:* -ˈstɜːr] <-rr-> *vt form* **to** ~ **oneself to do sth** avivarse para hacer algo

best man *n* padrino *m* de boda

bestow [bɪˈstəʊ, *Am:* -ˈstoʊ] *vt form* **to** ~ **sth on sb** otorgar algo a alguien; **to** ~ **a favour on sb** conceder un favor a alguien

bestowal [bɪˈstəʊəl, *Am:* -ˈstoʊ-] *n no pl, form* concesión *f*

bestseller [ˈbestseləʳ, *Am:* -əˑ] *n* éxito *m* de ventas

bet [bet] <bet *o* -ted, bet *o* -ted> I. *n* apuesta *f*; **it is a fair** [*o* **safe**] ~ **that ...** es casi seguro que... +*subj*; **to be the best** ~ ser la mejor opción; **to make a** ~ **with sb** hacer una apuesta con alguien; **to place a** ~ **on sth** apostar por algo ►**to hedge one's** ~**s** cubrirse contra un riesgo II. *vt* apostar; **I** ~ **you don't!** ¡a que no lo haces! III. *vi* apostar; **to** ~ **on sth** apostar por algo; **I wouldn't** ~ **on it** yo no estaría tan seguro ►**I'll** ~! ¡seguro!; **you** ~! *inf* ¡ya lo creo!

beta [ˈbiːtə, *Am:* ˈbeɪt̬ə] *n* beta *f*; ~ **version of a programme** INFOR versión *f* beta de un programa

betablocker [ˈbiːtəˈblɒkəʳ, *Am:* ˈbeɪt̬əˈblɑːkəˑ] *n* MED betabloqueador *m*,

betabloqueante *m*

beta testing *n* INFOR pruebas *fpl* beta **beta version** *n* INFOR versión *f* beta

betray [bɪˈtreɪ] *vt* 1. (*be disloyal to*) traicionar; **to** ~ **a promise** romper una promesa; **to** ~ **sb's trust** defraudar la confianza de alguien; **to be** ~**ed by sb** ser traicionado por alguien; **he** ~**ed his wife** engañó a su esposa 2. (*reveal*) delatar; **to** ~ **sth to sb** revelar algo a alguien; **to** ~ **one's ignorance** demostrar ignorancia

betrayal [bɪˈtreɪəl] *n* 1. (*disloyalty*) traición *f*; **an act of** ~ una traición 2. (*revelation*) revelación *f*

better¹ [ˈbetəʳ, *Am:* ˈbet̬əˑ] I. *adj comp of* **good** mejor; **to be** ~ MED estar mejor; ~ **than nothing** mejor que nada; **to appeal to sb's** ~ **nature** apelar a la bondad de alguien; ~ **luck next time** mejor suerte la próxima vez; **it's** ~ **that way** es mejor así II. *adv comp of* **well** mejor; **I like this** ~ me gusta más esto; **there is nothing I like** ~ **than ...** nada me gusta más que...; **It'll be** ~ **to tell her** más vale decírselo; **you had** ~ **go** mejor que te vayas; **to think** ~ **of sth** cambiar de opinión respecto a algo; **or** ~ **still ...** o mejor... III. *n no pl* 1. el/la mejor; **not to have seen** ~ no haber visto nada mejor; **to change for the** ~ cambiar para bien; **the sooner, the** ~ cuanto antes, mejor; **so much the** ~ tanto mejor 2. *pl* **my** ~**s** mis superiores ►**for** ~ **or** (**for**) **worse** para bien o para mal; **to get the** ~ **of sb** vencer a alguien IV. *vt* vencer; **to** ~ **oneself** prosperar; (*further one's knowledge*) superarse

better² *n*, **bettor** [ˈbetəʳ, *Am:* ˈbet̬əˑ] *n Am* apostador(a) *m(f)*

betterment [ˈbetəmənt] *n no pl* mejoramiento *m*

betting [ˈbetɪŋ] *n no pl* apuestas *fpl* ►**the** ~ **is that ...** lo más probable es que... +*subj*

betting office *n*, **betting shop** *n Brit* agencia *f* de apuestas

between [bɪˈtwiːn] I. *prep* entre; **to eat** ~ **meals** comer entre horas; ~ **now and tomorrow** entre hoy y mañana; ~ **the two of us** entre nosotros dos; **a misunderstanding** ~ **the couple** un malentendido entre la pareja; **nothing will come** ~ **them** nada se interpondrá entre ellos; **the 3 children have £10** ~ **them** entre los 3 niños tienen 3 libras; **the mule is a cross** ~ **a donkey and a horse** la mula es un cruce entre un burro y un caballo II. *adv* (*in*) ~ en medio de; (*time*) a mitad de

betwixt [bɪˈtwɪkst] *adv* **between and** ~ entre lo uno y lo otro

bevel [ˈbevl] I. <*Brit:* -ll-, *Am* -l-> *vt* biselar II. *n* bisel *m*

beverage [ˈbevərɪdʒ] *n form* bebida *f*; **alcoholic** ~ bebidas alcohólicas

bevy [ˈbevi] *n Brit* (*of birds*) bandada *f*; *inf* (*of people*) grupo *m*

bewail [bɪˈweɪl] *vt form* lamentar

beware [bɪˈweəʳ, *Am:* ˈwer] *vi* tener cuidado;

~! ¡ten cuidado!; ~ **of pickpockets!** ¡cuidado con los carteristas!

bewilder [bɪ'wɪldəʳ, *Am:* -dɚ] *vt* desconcertar

bewildered *adj* desconcertado, -a

bewildering *adj* desconcertante

bewilderment *n no pl* desconcierto *m,* azoro *m Méx, Perú, PRico*

bewitch [bɪ'wɪtʃ] *vt* 1. (*place magic charm on*) hechizar 2. (*fascinate*) fascinar

bewitching *adj* fascinante

beyond [bɪ'jɒnd, *Am:* -'ɑːnd] I. *prep* 1. (*on the other side of*) más allá de; ~ **the mountain** al otro lado de la montaña; **don't go** ~ **the line!** ¡no traspases la línea!; ~ **the wall** más allá del muro; **the regions** ~ **the sea** las regiones más allá del mar; **from** ~ **the grave** desde el más allá 2. (*after*) después de; (*more than*) más de; ~ **8:00** después de las 8:00; **to stay** ~ **a week** quedarse más de una semana; ~ **lunchtime** después del almuerzo 3. (*further than*) más allá de; **to see/go (way)** ~ **sth** ver/ir (mucho) más allá de algo; **it goes** ~ **a joke** va más allá de una broma; ~ **the reach of sb** fuera del alcance de alguien; ~ **belief/hope** más allá de cualquier creencia/esperanza; **he is** ~ **help** *a. iron* es un caso perdido; ~ **the shadow of a doubt** sin lugar a dudas; **to go** ~ **the point of no return** ir más allá de todo regreso 4. (*too difficult for*) **to be** ~ **sb** (*theory, idea*) ser demasiado difícil de entender para alguien; **that is** ~ **me** se me escapa; **this is** ~ **my abilities** esto sobrepasa mis capacidades 5. (*above*) por encima de; **to live** ~ **one's means** vivir por encima de sus posibilidades; **to value sth above and** ~ **all else** valorar algo por encima de todo 6. *with neg or interrog* (*except for*) fuera de, excepto II. *adv* 1. (*past*) **the house** ~ la casa de más allá 2. (*future*) **the next ten years and** ~ los próximos diez años y más allá III. *n* **the** ~ REL el más allá

biannual [ˌbaɪ'ænjʊəl] *adj* semestral

bias ['baɪəs] I. *n* 1. (*prejudice*) prejuicio *m;* **to have** ~**es against sb/sth** ser parcial contra alguien/algo 2. *no pl* (*one-sidedness*) parcialidad *f;* **without** ~ imparcial 3. (*tendency*) tendencia *f;* **to have a** ~ **towards sth** sentir inclinación por algo 4. *no pl* (*in sewing*) sesgo *m* II. <*Brit:* -ss-, *Am:* -s> *vt* influir; **to** ~ **sb towards/against sb** predisponer a alguien a favor de/en contra de alguien

biased *adj Am,* **biassed** *adj Brit* parcial; ~ **in sb's favour** predispuesto a favor de alguien; ~ **opinions** opiniones parciales

bib [bɪb] *n* babero *m*

Bible ['baɪbl] *n* **the** ~ la Biblia

biblical ['bɪblɪkl] *adj* bíblico, -a

bibliographer [ˌbɪblɪ'ɒgrəfəʳ, *Am:* -'ɑːgrəfɚ] *n* bibliógrafo, -a *m, f*

bibliographic(al) [ˌbɪblɪɒ'græfɪk(l)] *adj* bibliográfico, -a

bibliography [ˌbɪblɪ'ɒgrəfi, *Am:* -'ɑːgrə-]

<-ies> *n* bibliografía *f*

bibliophile ['bɪblɪəfaɪl] *n form* bibliófilo, -a *m, f*

bicarbonate [ˌbaɪ'kɑːbənət, *Am:* -'kɑːr-] *n no pl* bicarbonato *m*

bicarbonate of soda *n* bicarbonato *m* de soda

bicentenary [ˌbaɪsen'tiːnəri, *Am:* baɪ-'sentner-] <-ies> *n,* **bicentennial** *Am* I. *n* bicentenario *m* II. *adj* bicentenario, -a; ~ **celebration** celebración *f* del bicentenario

biceps ['baɪseps] *n inv* bíceps *m inv*

bicker ['bɪkəʳ, *Am:* -ɚ] *vi* reñir

bickering *n no pl* riñas *fpl*

bicycle ['baɪsɪkl] *n* bicicleta *f;* **to ride a** ~ montar en bicicleta; **by** ~ en bicicleta

bicycle lane *n* carril *m* de bicicletas

bid[1] [bɪd] <bid *o* bade, bid *o* bidden> *vt form* 1. (*greet*) **to** ~ **sb farewell** decir adiós a alguien; **to** ~ **sb good morning** desear buenos días a alguien; **to** ~ **sb welcome** dar la bienvenida a alguien 2. (*command*) ordenar 3. (*invite*) invitar

bid[2] [bɪd] I. *n* 1. (*offer*) oferta *f;* **hostile takeover** ~ COM oferta hostil de adquisición; **to make a** ~ **to do sth** concursar para hacer algo; **to make a** ~ **for sth** hacer una oferta sobre [*o* por] algo 2. (*attempt*) intento *m* II. <bid, bid> *vi* 1. (*at an auction*) pujar 2. COM hacer una oferta; **to** ~ **for a contract** concursar por un contrato III. <bid, bid> *vt* pujar

bidden ['bɪdn] *pp of* **bid**[1]

bidder ['bɪdəʳ, *Am:* -ɚ] *n* postor(a) *m(f);* **to the highest** ~ al mejor postor

bidding ['bɪdɪŋ] *n no pl* 1. FIN puja *f* 2. (*command*) orden *f;* **to do sb's** ~ cumplir las órdenes de alguien; **at sb's** ~ a las órdenes de alguien

bide [baɪd] *vt* **to** ~ **one's time** esperar el momento oportuno

bidet ['biːdeɪ, *Am:* bɪ'deɪ] *n* bidé *m*

biennial [baɪ'enɪəl] I. *adj a.* BOT bienal II. *n* planta *f* bienal

bier [bɪəʳ, *Am:* bɪr] *n* andas *fpl*

bifocal [baɪ'fəʊkl, *Am:* 'baɪˌfoʊ-] *adj* bifocal

bifocals [baɪ'fəʊklz, *Am:* 'baɪˌfoʊ-] *npl* gafas *fpl* bifocales, anteojos *mpl* bifocales *AmL*

big [bɪg] <-ger, -gest> *adj* 1. (*in size, amount*) grande; (*before singular nouns*) gran; **a** ~ **book** un libro grande; **a** ~ **budget film** una película de gran presupuesto; **a** ~ **house** una casa grande; ~ **letters** mayúsculas *fpl;* **to be a** ~ **spender** *inf* ser un derrochador; ~ **words** *inf* palabras *fpl* altisonantes; **the** ~**ger the better** cuanto más grande mejor 2. (*grown-up*) mayor; ~ **boy/girl** chico/chica mayor; ~ **sister/brother** hermana/hermano mayor 3. (*significant*) gran(de); **a** ~ **day** *inf* un día importante; **this group is** ~ **in Spain** este grupo es muy popular en España 4. (*on a large scale*) a gran escala ►**to make it** ~ *inf* triunfar a lo grande; **to think** ~ tener grandes aspiraciones

bigamist ['bɪgəmɪst] *n* bígamo, -a *m, f*
bigamy ['bɪgəmi] *n no pl* bigamia *f*
Big Apple *n* the ~ Nueva York *f*

El **Big Ben** era, originariamente, el sobrenombre de una gran campana, fundida en
1856, que se encontraba en la torre de las
Houses of Parliament. Sir Benjamin Hall,
entonces **Chief Commissioner of Works**,
es el que la bautizó con este nombre. Hoy en
día, por **Big Ben**, se conocen tanto la campana como la torre. Las campanadas con las
que el **Big Ben** da la hora se pueden oír en
los telediarios de algunas cadenas de radio y
televisión.

big business *n* el gran capital **Big Easy** *n*
the ~ Nueva Orleans *f* **big game** *n no pl*
caza *f* mayor
bigot ['bɪgət] *n* intolerante *mf;* REL fanático, -a
m, f
bigoted *adj* intolerante; REL fanático, -a
bigotry ['bɪgətri] *n no pl* fanatismo *m;* REL
intolerancia *f*
big shot *n inf* pez *m* gordo **big toe** *n* dedo
m gordo del pie **big top** *n* carpa *f* de circo
big wheel *n* noria *f* **bigwig** *n inf* pez *m*
gordo
bike [baɪk] *n inf* 1. (*bicycle*) bici *f;* **to get on a**
~ montar en una bici 2. (*motorcycle*) moto *f*
biker ['baɪkə', *Am:* -kə-] *n inf* motociclista *mf*
bikini [bɪ'ki:ni] *n* bikini *m*
bilateral [‚baɪ'lætərəl, *Am:* -'læt̬ə-l] *adj* bilateral
bilberry ['bɪlbəri, *Am:* -ber-] <-ies> *n* arándano *m*
bile [baɪl] *n* 1. *no pl* ANAT bilis *f* 2. *fig* mal
genio *m*
bilharzia [bɪl'hɑ:zɪə, *Am:* -'hɑ:rzɪ-] *n* MED
esquistosomiasis *f inv*
bilingual [baɪ'lɪŋgwəl] *adj* bilingüe
bilingual secretary *n* secretaria *f* bilingüe
bilious ['bɪliəs, *Am:* -jəs] *adj* 1. MED bilioso, -a
2. *fig* (*angry*) bilioso, -a; (*unpleasant*) asqueroso, -a
bill¹ [bɪl] I. *n* 1. (*invoice*) factura *f;* **phone** ~
factura del teléfono; **to foot the** ~ pagar la
cuenta; **the** ~**, please** la cuenta, por favor
2. *Am* (*banknote*) billete *m* 3. POL, LAW
proyecto *m* de ley; **to pass a** ~ aprobar un
proyecto de ley 4. (*poster, placard*) cartel *m*
► **to give sth/sb a clean** ~ **of** health dar a
algo/alguien el visto bueno; **to fit the** ~ convenir II. *vt* **to** ~ **sb** pasar la cuenta a alguien; **to** ~
sb for sth facturar algo a alguien
bill² [bɪl] I. *n* (*of a bird*) pico *m* II. *vi* **to** ~ **and**
coo *inf* estar como dos tortolitos
billboard ['bɪlbɔ:d, *Am:* -bɔ:rd] *n* valla *f*
publicitaria
billet ['bɪlɪt, *Am:* -ət] MIL I. *n* acantonamiento
m II. *vt* acantonar
billfold ['bɪlfəʊld, *Am:* -foʊld] *n Am* cartera
f

billiard ball *n* bola *f* de billar
billiards ['bɪliədz, *Am:* '-jə-dz] *n no pl* billar
m
billiard table *n* mesa *f* de billar
billing *n* **to be given top** ~ encabezar el reparto
billion ['bɪliən, *Am:* -jən] *n* mil millones *mpl*
billow ['bɪləʊ, *Am:* -oʊ] I. *vi* (*clothes, sails*)
hincharse II. *n* **a** ~ **of smoke** una nube de
humo
billowy *adj* (*waves, clouds*) ondulante; (*sail*)
ondeante
billposter ['bɪl‚pəʊstə', *Am:* -‚poʊstə-] *n,*
billsticker ['bɪlstɪkə', *Am:* -kə-] *n* cartelero
m
billy ['bɪli] <-ies> *n,* **billycan** *n Aus, Brit*
cacerola *f*
billy goat *n* macho *m* cabrío
bimbo ['bɪmbəʊ, *Am:* -boʊ] <-(e)s> *n pej,*
inf: mujer joven y guapa, pero tonta
bi-monthly [‚baɪ'mʌnθli] I. *adj* 1. (*twice a*
month) quincenal 2. (*every two months*)
bimestral II. *adv* 1. (*twice a month*) quincenalmente 2. (*once every two months*) bimestral-
mente
bin [bɪn] I. *n* 1. *Aus, Brit* (*for waste*) cubo *m*
de basura, basurero *m Méx;* **to consign sth**
to the ~ tirar algo a la basura; *fig* desechar
algo 2. (*for storage*) recipiente *m* II. *vt Brit*
tirar
binary ['baɪnəri] *adj* INFOR binario, -a
binary code *n* INFOR código *m* binario
bind [baɪnd] I. *n no pl, Brit, inf* apuro *m;* **to**
be in a ~ estar en un apuro II. <bound,
bound> *vi* unirse III. <bound, bound> *vt*
1. (*tie together*) atar; **to be bound hand and**
foot estar atado de pies y manos 2. (*unite*) **to** ~
(**together**) unir; **to be bound to sb** estar
ligado a alguien 3. (*commit*) vincular 4. (*sew*)
ribetear 5. (*book*) encuadernar 6. (*oblige*) **to** ~
sb to do sth obligar a alguien a hacer algo; **to**
~ **sb to a contract** comprometer a alguien
contractualmente
binder ['baɪndə', *Am:* -də-] *n* (*cover*) carpeta *f*
bindery ['baɪndəri] <-ies> *n* taller *m* de
encuadernación, encuadernadora *f Méx*
binding ['baɪndɪŋ] I. *n no pl* 1. TYPO encuadernación *f* 2. FASHION ribete *m* II. *adj* vinculante
bindweed ['baɪndwi:d] *n no pl* correhuela *f*
binge [bɪndʒ] *inf* I. *n* (*of drinking*) borrachera
f, vacilada *f Méx;* (*of eating*) comilona *f;* **to go**
on a ~ ir de farra, ir de parranda II. *vi* atibo-
rrarse
bingo ['bɪŋgəʊ, *Am:* -goʊ] I. *n no pl* bingo *m*
II. *interj inf* bingo
binoculars [bɪ'nɒkjʊləz, *Am:* -'nɑ:kjələ-z]
npl prismáticos *mpl*, binoculares *mpl AmL;* **a**
pair of ~ unos prismáticos
binomial [baɪ'nəʊmɪəl, *Am:* -'noʊ-] I. *n* MAT
binomio *m* II. *adj* MAT binomial
biochemical [‚baɪəʊ'kemɪkl, *Am:* -oʊ-] *adj*
bioquímico, -a

biochemist [ˌbaɪəʊ'kemɪst, *Am:* -oʊ-] *n* bioquímico, -a *m, f*

biochemistry [ˌbaɪəʊ'kemɪstri, *Am:* -oʊ-] *n no pl* bioquímica *f*

biodegradable [ˌbaɪəʊdɪ'greidəbl, *Am:* -oʊ-] *adj* biodegradable

biodegrade [ˌbaɪəʊdɪ'greid, *Am:* -oʊ-] *vi* biodegradarse

biodiversity [ˌbaɪəʊdaɪ'vɜːsəti, *Am:* -oʊdɪ'vɜːrsəti] *n no pl* biodiversidad *f*

bioengineering [ˌbaɪəʊendʒɪ'nɪərɪŋ, *Am:* -oʊendʒɪ'nɪrɪŋ] *n no pl* ingeniería *f* biológica

biofeedback [ˌbaɪəʊ'fiːdbæk, *Am:* -oʊ-] *n no pl* retroalimentación *f* biológica

biofuel ['baɪəʊˌfjuːl] *n* combustible *m* biológico

biogas ['baɪəʊˌgæs] *n no pl* biogás *m*

biographer [baɪ'ɒɡrəfəʳ, *Am:* -'ɑːɡrəfɚ] *n* biógrafo, -a *m, f*

biographical [ˌbaɪəʊ'ɡræfɪkəl] *adj* biográfico, -a

biography [baɪ'ɒɡrəfi, *Am:* -'ɑːɡrə-] <-ies> *n* biografía *f*

biological [ˌbaɪə'lɒdʒɪkəl, *Am:* -'lɑːdʒɪ-] *adj* biológico, -a; ~ **cycle/rhythm** ciclo/ritmo biológico

biological control *n* control *m* biológico
    biological indicator *n* indicador *m* biológico

biologist [baɪ'ɒlədʒɪst, *Am:* -'ɑːlə-] *n* biólogo, -a *m, f*

biology [baɪ'ɒlədʒi, *Am:* -'ɑːlə-] *n no pl* biología *f*

biomass [ˌbaɪəmæs] *n* BIO biomasa *f*

biopsy ['baɪɒpsi, *Am:* -ɑːp-] *n* MED biopsia *f*

biorhythm ['baɪərɪðəm, *Am:* -oʊ-] *n* biorritmo *m*

biosphere ['baɪəsfiːəʳ, *Am:* -sfir] *n no pl* biosfera *f*

biotechnology [ˌbaɪəʊtek'nɒlədʒi, *Am:* -oʊtek'nɑːlə-] *n no pl* biotecnología *f*

biotope ['baɪətəʊp, *Am:* -toʊp] *n* biótopo *m*

bipartisan [ˌbaɪpɑː'tɪ'zæn, *Am:* -'pɑːrtəzən] *adj* POL bipartidista

biped ['baɪped] *n* BIO bípedo *m*

biplane ['baɪpleɪn] *n* biplano *m*

bipolar [ˌbaɪ'pəʊləʳ, *Am:* -'poʊlɚ] *adj* ELEC, PHYS bipolar

birch [bɜːtʃ, *Am:* bɜːrtʃ] **I.** *n* **1.** (*tree*) abedul *m* **2.** *no pl* (*for punishment*) palo *m* **II.** *vt* castigar con el palo

bird [bɜːd, *Am:* bɜːrd] *n* **1.** ZOOL pájaro *m*; (*larger*) ave *f*; **a flock of ~s** una bandada de pájaros; **to feel as free as a ~** sentirse libre como un pájaro **2.** *inf* (*person*) **a strange** [*o* **queer**] ~ un bicho raro **3.** *Aus, Brit, inf* (*girl, woman*) chica *f*, chava *f Méx*, piba *f RíoPl* ▶ **~s of a feather flock together** *prov* Dios los cría y ellos se juntan *prov*; **a ~ in the hand is worth two in the bush** *prov* más vale pájaro en mano que ciento volando *prov*; **to kill two ~s with one stone** matar dos pájaros de un

tiro *fig*; **it's the early ~ that catches the worm** *prov* al que madruga, Dios le ayuda *prov*; **to give sb the ~** *inf* abuchear a alguien

birdcage *n* pajarera *f*

birdie ['bɜːdi, *Am:* 'bɜːr-] *n* **1.** *childspeak* pajarito *m*; **watch the ~** PHOT ¡mira el pajarito! **2.** (*in golf*) birdie *m*

Bird of Paradise *n* ave *f* del paraíso

birdseed ['bɜːdsiːd, *Am:* 'bɜːrd-] *n no pl* alpiste *m*

bird's-eye view [ˌbɜː'dzaɪ'vjuː, *Am:* ˌbɜːrdz-] *n no pl* vista *f* panorámica

bird table *n Brit* comedero *m* de aves **birdwatching** *n no pl* observación *f* de aves

biro® ['baɪərəʊ, *Am:* -roʊ] *n* bolígrafo *m*, birome *m RíoPl*

birth [bɜːθ, *Am:* bɜːrθ] *n* **1.** nacimiento *m*, paritorio *m Cuba, Ven;* MED parto *m*; **at ~** al nacer; **by ~** de nacimiento; **from ~** de nacimiento; **date/place of ~** fecha/lugar de nacimiento; **to give ~ to a child** dar a luz a un bebé **2.** *no pl* (*descent, beginning*) origen *m*; **to be of low/noble ~** ser de origen humilde/noble

birth certificate *n* certificado *m* de nacimiento **birth control** *n* control *m* de natalidad

birthday ['bɜːθdeɪ, *Am:* 'bɜːrθ-] *n* cumpleaños *m inv* **happy ~!** ¡feliz cumpleaños!

birthday cake *n* tarta *f* de cumpleaños, pastel *m* de cumpleaños *AmL* **birthday card** *n* tarjeta *f* de cumpleaños **birthday party** *n* fiesta *f* de cumpleaños **birthday present** *n* regalo *m* de cumpleaños **birthday suit** *n inf* **in one's ~** en cueros

birthmark ['bɜːθmɑːk, *Am:* 'bɜːrθmɑːrk] *n* marca *f* de nacimiento **birthplace** *n* lugar *m* de nacimiento **birth rate** *n* tasa *f* de natalidad; **falling/rising ~** natalidad decreciente/creciente **birthright** *n* derecho *m* de nacimiento; *fig* patrimonio *m*

Biscay ['bɪskeɪ] *n* Vizcaya *f*

biscuit ['bɪskɪt] *n* **1.** *Aus, Brit* galleta *f* **2.** *Am* (*soft cake*) bizcocho *m* ▶ **that (really) takes the ~!** *inf* ¡eso es el colmo!

Con la expresión **biscuits and gravy** se designa un desayuno típico de los EE.UU. procedente de los estados del sur. Los **biscuits** son una clase de panecillos planos servidos con **gravy** (un tipo de salsa de asado). En algunas zonas, este tipo de desayuno sólo se sirve en **truck stops** (locales frecuentados por camioneros).

---

bisect [baɪ'sekt, *Am:* 'baɪsekt] *vt* MAT bisecar

bisection [baɪ'sekʃən] *n* MAT bisección *f*

bisexual [ˌbaɪ'sekʃʊəl, *Am:* -ʃʊəl] **I.** *n* bisexual *m f* **II.** *adj* bisexual

bishop ['bɪʃəp] *n* **1.** REL obispo *m* **2.** (*chess piece*) alfil *m*

bishopric ['bɪʃəprɪk] *n* obispado *m*

bison ['baɪsən] *n* bisonte *m*

bit¹ [bɪt] *n* **1.** *inf* (*small piece*) trozo *m,* pedazo *m;* (*of glass*) fragmento *m;* **a ~ of paper** un trozo de papel; **little ~s** pedacitos *mpl;* **to smash sth to ~s** romper algo en pedazos **2.** (*some*) **a ~ of** un poco de; **a ~ of luck** un poco de suerte; **a ~ of news** una noticia; **a ~ of trouble** un problemilla **3.** (*part*) parte *f;* **the difficult ~ of sth** la parte difícil de algo; **~ by ~** poco a poco; **to do one's ~** *inf* hacer su parte **4.** *pl, inf* (*things*) **~s and pieces** cosas *fpl* **5.** *inf* (*short time*) momento *m;* **for a ~** por un momento; **hold on a ~** espera un momento **6.** (*somewhat*) **a ~** algo; **a ~ stupid** un poco tonto; **quite a ~** bastante; **not a ~** en absoluto

bit² [bɪt] *n* **1.** (*for horses*) bocado *m* **2.** (*for drill*) broca *f* ▶**to chafe** [*o* **champ**] **at the ~** impacientarse, comer ansias *Méx*

bit³ [bɪt] *n* INFOR bit *m*

bit⁴ [bɪt] *pt of* **bite**

bitch [bɪtʃ] **I.** *n* **1.** ZOOL perra *f* **2.** *inf* (*complaint*) queja *f;* **to have a good ~** quejarse **3.** *inf* (*woman*) zorra *f,* tusa *f AmL, Cuba;* **you ~!** ¡lagarta! **II.** *vi inf* quejarse; **to ~ about sb/sth** quejarse de alguien/algo

bitchy [ˈbɪtʃi] *adj* malicioso, -a

bite [baɪt] **I.** <bit, bitten> *vt* morder; (*insect*) picar; **to ~ one's nails/lips** morderse las uñas/los labios; **what's biting you?** *inf* ¿qué mosca te ha picado? **II.** <bit, bitten> *vi* **1.** (*dog, person*) morder; (*insect, fish*) picar **2.** (*have effect*) surtir efecto ▶**once bitten twice shy** *prov* al gato escaldado del agua fría huye *prov* **III.** *n* **1.** (*of a dog, person*) mordisco *m;* (*of an insect*) picadura *f;* **~ mark** marca *f* de mordedura; (*of an insect*) picadura *f;* **a dog's ~** una mordedura de un perro; **to give sb a ~** dar un mordisco a alguien; **to take a ~ of sth** tomar un bocado de algo **2.** (*mouthful*) bocado *m* **3.** *no pl, fig* (*sharpness*) mordacidad *f;* **to have** (**real**) **~** tener (verdadera) garra

biting [ˈbaɪtɪŋ, *Am:* -t̬ɪŋ] *adj* (*wind*) cortante; (*criticism*) mordaz

bitten [ˈbɪtn] *pp of* **bite**

bitter [ˈbɪtəʳ, *Am:* ˈbɪt̬əʳ] **I.** *adj* <-er, -est> **1.** (*acrid*) agrio, -a; (*fruit*) amargo, -a **2.** (*painful*) amargo, -a; **to be ~ about sth** estar amargado por algo; **to carry on to the ~ end** seguir hasta el final **3.** (*intense*) acérrimo, -a; (*dispute*) encarnizado, -a; (*disappointment*) agudo, -a; (*wind*) cortante **II.** *n Aus, Brit* (*beer*) cerveza *f* (amarga)

bitterly *adv* **1.** (*resentfully*) con rencor; **to weep ~** llorar a lágrima viva **2.** (*intensely*) intensamente; **to condemn sth ~** condenar algo firmemente

bitterness *n no pl* **1.** (*animosity*) amargura *f;* (*resentment*) resentimiento *m;* **~ towards sb** resentimiento contra alguien **2.** (*taste*) amargor *m*

bitumen [ˈbɪtjʊmən, *Am:* bɪˈtuːmən] *n no pl* betún *m*

bituminous [bɪˈtjuːmɪnəs, *Am:* -ˈtuː-] *adj* bituminoso, -a

bivalve [ˈbaivælv] *n* bivalvo *m*

bivouac [ˈbɪvʊæk, *Am:* -uæk] **I.** *n* vivaque *m,* vivac *m* **II.** <-k-> *vi* vivaquear

biweekly [ˌbaɪˈwiːkli] **I.** *adj* **1.** (*every two weeks*) quincenal **2.** (*twice a week*) bisemanal **II.** *adv* **1.** (*every two weeks*) quincenalmente **2.** (*twice a week*) bisemanalmente

bizarre [bɪˈzɑːʳ, *Am:* -ˈzɑːr] *adj* (*behaviour, person*) extraño, -a; (*clothes*) estrafalario, -a

blab [blæb] <-bb-> *vi inf* **1.** (*talk too much*) irse de la lengua **2.** *inf* (*inform*) cantar

black [blæk] **I.** *adj* **1.** (*colour*) negro, -a; **~ man** negro *m;* **~ woman** negra *f* **2.** *fig* (*extreme*) negro, -a; **~ despair** negra desesperación **3.** (*dark*) oscuro, -a **4.** (*very dirty*) mugriento, -a, mugroso, -a *Méx* ▶**to beat sb ~ and blue** *inf* moler a alguien a palos; **he is not as ~ as he is painted** no es tan malo como lo pintan **II.** *vt* **1.** (*make black*) ennegrecer; **to ~ one's face** pintarse la cara de negro; **to ~ sb's eye** poner a alguien el ojo morado [*o* a la funerala] **2.** *Brit* (*boycott*) boicotear **III.** *n* **1.** (*colour*) negro *m;* **in ~** de negro; **in ~ and white** CINE, PHOT en blanco y negro **2.** (*person*) negro, -a *m, f* **3.** FIN **in the ~** con saldo positivo

◆**black out I.** *vi* perder el conocimiento **II.** *vt* **1.** o(b)scurecer **2.** (*censure*) censurar

blackball [ˈblækbɔːl] *vt* (*vote*) votar en contra de; (*reject*) dar bola negra a

blackberry [ˈblækbəri, *Am:* -ˌber-] <-ies> *n* (*fruit*) zarzamora *f;* (*plant*) zarza *f*

blackbird [ˈblækbɜːd, *Am:* -bɜːrd] *n* mirlo *m*

blackboard [ˈblækbɔːd, *Am:* -bɔːrd] *n* pizarra *f*

black book *n* **to be in sb's ~(s)** figurar en la lista negra de alguien **black box** *n* AVIAT caja *f* negra

blackcurrant [ˌblækˈkʌrənt, *Am:* ˈblækˌkɜːr-] *n* casis *m inv,* grosella *f* negra

blacken [ˈblækən] **I.** *vt* **1.** (*make black*) ennegrecer **2.** (*slander*) desacreditar; **to ~ sb's name** manchar la reputación de alguien **II.** *vi* ennegrecerse

black eye *n* ojo *m* morado

blackguard [ˈblægɑːd, *Am:* -ɑːrd] *n* sinvergüenza *m*

blackhead [ˈblækhed] *n* barrillo *m,* espinilla *f* negro *m* **black hole** *n* agujero *m* negro **black ice** *n* hielo invisible en la carretera

blacking [ˈblækɪŋ] *n no pl* betún *m*

blackish [ˈblækɪʃ] *adj* negruzco, -a

blackjack [ˈblækˌdʒæk] *n* **1.** GAMES veintiuna *f* **2.** *Am* (*cosh*) (cachi)porra *f*

blackleg [ˈblækleg] *n Brit* esquirol(a) *m(f)*

blacklist [ˈblæklɪst] **I.** *vt* poner en la lista negra **II.** *n* lista *f* negra

blackmail [ˈblækmeɪl] **I.** *n* chantaje *m* **II.** *vt* chantajear; **to ~ sb into doing sth** chantajear a alguien para que haga algo

blackmailer [ˈblækmeɪləʳ, *Am:* -ɚ] *n* chantajista *mf*

black mark *n* punto *m* en contra **black market** *n* mercado *m* negro **black mar-**

keteer *n* estraperlista *mf*

blackness ['blæknɪs] *n no pl* (*colour*) negrura *f*; (*darkness*) oscuridad *f*

blackout ['blækaʊt] *n* **1.** (*faint*) desmayo *m*; **to have a ~** sufrir un desmayo **2.** (*censorship*) bloqueo *m*; **news ~** bloqueo informativo **3.** ELEC apagón *m*

black pudding *n Brit* morcilla *f*, moronga *f Méx* **Black Sea** *n* Mar *m* Negro **black sheep** *n a. fig* oveja *f* negra

blacksmith ['blæksmɪθ] *n* herrero *m*

bladder ['blædə', Am: -ə·] *n* ANAT vejiga *f*

blade [bleɪd] I. *n* (*of a tool, weapon*) hoja *f*; (*of an oar*) pala *f*; **~ of grass** brizna *f* de hierba II. *vi inf* patinar (en línea)

blah [blɑ:] *interj inf* ~**,** ~**,** (~) blabla

blame [bleɪm] I. *vt* culpar; **to ~ sb for sth, to ~ sth on sb** echar a alguien la culpa de algo; **to be to ~ for sth** tener la culpa de algo; **I don't ~ you** te comprendo II. *n no pl* culpa *f*; **to bear the ~** tener la culpa; **to lay the ~ for sth on sb** echar a alguien la culpa de algo; **to take the ~** declararse culpable

blameless ['bleɪmlɪs] *adj* libre de culpa; **~ life** vida *f* intachable

blameworthy ['bleɪmwɜ:ði, Am: -wɜ:r-] *adj form* censurable

blanch [blɑ:ntʃ, Am: blæntʃ] I. *vi* palidecer II. *vt* **1.** blanquear **2.** GASTR escaldar; **~ed almonds** almendras peladas

blancmange [blə'mɒnʒ, Am: 'mɑ:nʒ] *n no pl* flan de harina de maíz y leche

bland [blænd] *adj* **1.** (*mild*) suave **2.** (*insipid*) soso, -a

blandishments ['blændɪʃmənts] *npl* halagos *mpl*

blank [blæŋk] I. *adj* **1.** (*empty*) en blanco; **~ page/space** página *f* /espacio *m* en blanco; **~ tape** cinta *f* virgen; **to go ~** quedarse en blanco; **my mind went ~** me quedé con la mente en blanco; **the screen went ~** la pantalla se quedó negra **2.** (*unemotional: look*) sin expresión **3.** (*complete*) absoluto, -a; (*despair*) completo, -a; **to be met by a ~ refusal** encontrarse con un rechazo absoluto II. *n* **1.** (*space*) espacio *m* **2.** (*cartridge*) cartucho *m* de salvas ►**to draw a** (**complete**) **~** no encontrar nada

blanket ['blæŋkɪt] I. *n* **1.** (*cover*) manta *f*, frisa *f RDom*, cobija *f Méx*; *fig* cobertura *f* **2.** (*of snow*) capa *f* II. *vt* cubrir; **to ~ sth in sth** cubrir algo con algo III. *adj* general; LING (*term*) genérico, -a

blankly *adv* (*without expression*) inexpresivamente; (*without understanding*) sin comprender

blare [bleə', Am: bler] I. *vi* resonar II. *n no pl* estruendo *m*; (*of a trumpet*) trompetazo *m*

blaspheme [blæs'fi:m, Am: 'blæsfi:m] *vi* blasfemar

blasphemer [blæs'fi:mə', Am: 'blæsfi:mə·] *n* blasfemo, -a *m, f*

blasphemous ['blæsfəməs] *adj* blasfemo, -a

blasphemy ['blæsfəmi] *n no pl* blasfemia *f*

blast [blɑ:st, Am: blæst] I. *vt* **1.** (*with an explosive*) volar **2.** (*criticize*) criticar duramente II. *n* **1.** (*detonation*) explosión *f* **2.** (*gust of wind*) ráfaga *f* **3.** (*noise*) toque *m*; (*of a trumpet*) trompetazo *m*; **to blow a ~ on a trumpet** dar un trompetazo **4.** *Am, inf* (*party*) fiesta *f*, tambarria *f AmC, AmS*, guateque *m CRi* **5.** (**at**) **full ~** (*volume*) al máximo (de volúmen); (*speed*) a toda marcha III. *interj inf* maldición; **~ it!** ¡maldita sea!

blasted *adj inf* (*damned*) maldito, -a

blast furnace *n* alto horno *m*

blast-off ['blɑ:stɒf, Am: 'blæstɑ:f] *n* despegue *m*

blast wave *n* onda *f* expansiva

blatant ['bleɪtnt] *adj* descarado, -a

blaze [bleɪz] I. *vi* resplandecer, brillar; (*fire*) arder; **to ~ with anger** echar chispas II. *vt* **to ~ a trail** abrir camino III. *n* **1.** (*fire*) fuego *m*; (*flames*) llamarada *f* **2.** (*light, colour*) resplandor *m* **3.** (*display*) **a ~ of glory** un rayo de gloria; **a ~ of publicity** una campaña de publicidad a bombo y platillo; **~ of anger** arranque *m* de ira

◆**blaze away** *vi* **1.** (*burn*) arder **2.** (*shoot*) disparar rápidamente

◆**blaze up** *vi* encenderse vivamente

blazer ['bleɪzə', Am: -zə·] *n* chaqueta *f*; **school ~** chaqueta escolar

blazing ['bleɪzɪŋ] *adj* **1.** resplandeciente; (*heat*) abrasador(a); (*sunshine*) esplendoroso, -a; (*light*) brillante; (*fire*) vivo, -a **2.** (*argument*) violento, -a

bleach [bli:tʃ] I. *vt* blanquear II. *n* lejía *f*; (*for hair*) decolorante *m*

bleachers ['bli:tʃəz, Am: -tʃə·z] *n pl, Am* gradería *f*

bleak [bli:k] *adj* (*future*) sombrío, -a; (*weather*) gris; (*landscape*) desolador(a); (*smile*) triste

bleary ['blɪəri, Am: 'blɪri] *adj* <-ier, -iest> (*person*) cansado, -a; (*eyes*) lagañoso, -a

bleary-eyed [,blɪəri'aɪd, Am: 'blɪriaɪd] *adj* **to be ~** estar medio dormido

bleat [bli:t] I. *vi* **1.** (*sheep*) balar; (*calf*) mugir **2.** (*complain*) quejarse II. *n* **1.** (*of sheep*) balido *m* **2.** (*complaint*) quejido *m*

bled [bled] *pt, pp of* **bleed**

bleed [bli:d] <bled, bled> I. *vi* sangrar; **to ~ to death** morir desangrado; **my heart ~s** *iron* lo siento mucho II. *vt* **1.** hacer una sangría a; **to ~ sb dry** *inf* dejar seco a alguien **2.** TECH, AUTO purgar

bleeder ['bli:də', Am: -ə·] *n Brit, inf* cabrón *m*

bleeding I. *adj Brit, inf* puñetero, -a II. *n* **1.** MED sangría *f* **2.** TECH, AUTO purgamiento *m*

bleep [bli:p] I. *n* pitido *m* II. *vi* pitar III. *vt* llamar (con un localizador)

bleeper ['bli:pə', Am: -pə·] *n* localizador *m*, busca *m inf*

blemish ['blemɪʃ] I. *n a. fig* mancha *f*; **a reputation without ~** una reputación inta-

chable **II.** *vt a. fig* manchar
blemish-free *adj* sin defectos
blench [blentʃ] *vi* recular; **to ~ at a thought** retroceder ante un pensamiento
blend [blend] **I.** *n* mezcla *f* **II.** *vt* mezclar **III.** *vi* armonizar; **to ~ in** no desentonar
blender [blendə^r, *Am:* -də·] *n* licuadora *f*
bless [bles] *vt* bendecir ►**~ him/her!** ¡bendito sea!; **~ you!** (*on sneezing*) ¡Jesús!
blessed ['blesɪd] *adj* **1.** (*holy*) bendito, -a; (*ground*) santo, -a; **the Blessed Virgin** la Santísima Virgen; **~ are the meek ...** bienaventurados los humildes... **2.** *inf* dichoso, -a; **the whole ~ day** todo el santo día
blessing ['blesɪŋ] *n* **1.** (*benediction*) bendición *f*; **to give one's ~ to sth** dar su aprobación a algo **2.** (*benefit*) beneficio *m*; (*advantage*) ventaja *f* ►**it's a ~ in disguise** no hay mal que por bien no venga *prov*; **to count one's ~s** apreciar lo que uno tiene
blew [blu:] *pt of* **blow**
blight [blaɪt] **I.** *vt* AGR *a. fig* arruinar **II.** *n* **1.** AGR añublo *m* **2.** *fig* ruina *f*; **to cast a ~ on sth** arruinar algo
blighter ['blaɪtə^r, *Am:* -ʈə·] *n Brit, inf* canalla *m*
blimey ['blaɪmi] *interj Brit, inf* caray
blind [blaɪnd] **I.** *n* **1.** *pl* (*person*) **the ~** los ciegos **2.** (*window shade*) persiana *f* **3.** (*cover*) pantalla *f* **II.** *vt* **1.** ANAT, MED cegar **2.** (*dazzle*) deslumbrar **III.** *adj* **1.** (*unable to see*) ciego, -a; **to be ~ in one eye** ser tuerto; **to be ~ to sth** no ver algo **2.** (*without reason*) sin razón; (*acceptance, devotion*) apasionado, -a **3.** (*hidden: corner*) de poca visibilidad **4.** *Brit, inf* (*as intensifier*) **not to take a ~ bit of notice of sth** no conceder la más mínima importancia a algo **IV.** *adv* **to be ~ drunk** estar más borracho que una cuba; **to swear ~ that ...** jurar y perjurar que...
blind alley <-s> *n a. fig* callejón *m* sin salida
blinder ['blaɪndə^r, *Am:* -ə·] *n inf* SPORTS partido *m* excepcional
blindfold ['blaɪndfəʊld, *Am:* -foʊld] **I.** *n* venda *f* **II.** *vt* vendar los ojos a **III.** *adj* con los ojos vendados; **to be able to do sth ~** poder hacer algo con los ojos cerrados
blinding *adj* (*dazzling*) cegador(a)
blind man's buff *n no pl* gallina *f* ciega
blindness *n* ceguera *f*
blind spot *n* punto *m* ciego
blink [blɪŋk] **I.** *vt* parpadear; **to ~ one's eyes** parpadear **II.** *vi* pestañear; **to ~ back one's tears** contener las lágrimas; **she didn't even ~** ni se inmutó **III.** *n* parpadeo *m* ►**in the ~ of an eye** en un abrir y cerrar de ojos; **to be on the ~** *inf* estar averiado
blinker ['blɪŋkə^r, *Am:* -kə·] *n* anteojera *f*
blinkered *adj* estrecho, -a de miras
blinking *adj Brit, inf* maldito, -a
bliss [blɪs] *n no pl* dicha *f*; **marital ~** felicidad *f* conyugal
blissful ['blɪsfəl] *adj* **1.** (*happy*) bienaventu-

rado, -a **2.** (*enjoyable*) maravilloso, -a
blister ['blɪstə^r, *Am:* -tə·] **I.** *n* **1.** ANAT ampolla *f* **2.** (*bubble*) burbuja *f* **II.** *vt* ampollar **III.** *vi* ampollarse
blistering *adj* (*very hot*) abrasador(a)
blithering ['blɪðərɪŋ] *adj ~* **idiot!** ¡imbécil!
blitz [blɪts] **I.** *n no pl* bombardeo *m* aéreo; **the Blitz** el bombardeo alemán de Londres en 1940–41 **II.** *vt* bombardear desde el aire
blizzard ['blɪzəd] *n* ventisca *f*
bloated ['bləʊtɪd, *Am:* 'bloʊʈɪd] *adj* **1.** (*swollen*) hinchado, -a **2.** (*excessive*) excesivo, -a
blob [blɒb, *Am:* blɑ:b] *n* goterón *m*
bloc [blɒk] *n* POL bloque *m*
block [blɒk, *Am:* blɑ:k] **I.** *n* **1.** (*solid lump*) bloque *m*; (*of wood*) zoquete *m*; (*for executions*) tajo *m*; **to be sent to the ~** ser condenado a ser decapitado **2.** INFOR bloque *m* **3.** (*tall building*) edificio *m*; (*group of buildings*) manzana *f*, cuadra *f AmL*; **~ of flats** *Brit* bloque *m* de viviendas **4.** (*barrier*) barrera *f*; (*impediment*) obstrucción *f* **5.** (*child's toy*) cubo *m* **6.** SPORTS taco *m* de salida **II.** *vt* **1.** (*road, pipe*) bloquear; (*sb's progress*) obstaculizar **2.** INFOR **to ~ and copy** seleccionar y copiar
◆**block off** *vt* cortar
◆**block up** **I.** *vt* cerrar, tapar **II.** *vi* atascarse, atorozarse *AmC*; MED taparse
blockade [blɒ'keɪd, *Am:* blɑ:'keɪd] **I.** *n* bloqueo *m* **II.** *vt* bloquear; (*block off*) cortar
blockage ['blɒkɪdʒ, *Am:* 'blɑ:kɪdʒ] *n* obstrucción *f*
block capitals *n* letra *f* de imprenta
blockhouse ['blɒkhaʊs, *Am:* 'blɑ:k-] *n* bloccao *m*
bloke [bləʊk] *n Brit, inf* tío *m*
blond(e) [blɒnd, *Am:* blɑ:nd] **I.** *adj* (*hair*) rubio, -a, güero, -a *Méx, Guat, Ven* **II.** *n* rubio, -a *m, f*, güero, -a *Méx, Guat, Ven*
blood [blʌd] *n no pl* sangre *f*; **to be of the same ~** ser parientes ►**to have ~ on one's hands** tener las manos manchadas de sangre *fig*; **~ is thicker than water** la sangre siempre tira; **bad ~** mala sangre; **in cold ~** a sangre fría; **her ~ ran cold** se le heló la sangre; **it makes my ~ boil** hace que me hierva la sangre; **to make sb's ~ curdle** [*o* **freeze**] hacer que a alguien se le hiele la sangre; **to smell ~** oler la sangre; **to sweat ~** sudar tinta; **to be after sb's ~** tener un odio mortal a alguien
blood bank *n* banco *m* de sangre
bloodbath ['blʌdbɑ:θ, *Am:* -bæθ] *n* baño *m* de sangre
blood clot *n* coágulo *m* de sangre
bloodcurdling ['blʌd,kɜ:dlɪŋ, *Am:* -,kɜ:rdlɪŋ] *adj* espeluznante **blood donor** *n* donante *mf* de sangre **blood group** *n* grupo *m* sanguíneo
bloodhound ['blʌdhaʊnd] *n a. fig* sabueso *m*

bloodless ['blʌdlɪs] *adj* **1.** (*face, lips*) exangüe **2.** (*coup*) incruento, -a **3.** (*emotionless: film, style*) soso, -a

blood poisoning *n no pl* septicemia *f*

blood pressure *n no pl* tensión *f* arterial

blood relation *n,* **blood relative** *n* pariente, -a *m, f* consanguíneo, -a

bloodshed ['blʌdʃed] *n no pl* derramamiento *m* de sangre

bloodshot ['blʌdʃɒt, *Am:* -ʃɑːt] *adj* inyectado, -a de sangre; (*eyes*) rojo, -a **blood sport** *n* (*hunting*) deporte *m* cinegético

bloodstained ['blʌdsteɪnd] *adj* manchado, -a de sangre

bloodstock ['blʌdstɒk, *Am:* -stɑːk] *n no pl* caballos *mpl* de raza

bloodstream ['blʌdstriːm] *n* corriente *f* sanguínea

bloodsucker ['blʌdˌsʌkəʳ, *Am:* -ɚ] *n* sanguijuela *f*

blood sugar *n no pl* azúcar *m* de la sangre **blood test** *n* análisis *m inv* de sangre

bloodthirsty ['blʌdˌθɜːsti, *Am:* -ˌθɜːr-] *adj* sanguinario, -a

blood transfusion *n* transfusión *f* de sangre **blood type** *n* grupo *m* sanguineo **blood vessel** *n* vaso *m* sanguíneo

bloody ['blʌdi] <-ier, -iest> **I.** *adj* **1.** (*with blood*) ensangrentado, -a **2.** *Aus, Brit, inf* (*for emphasis*) puñetero, -a; (*what the*) ~ **hell!** ¡(qué) coño! **II.** *adv Aus, Brit, inf* **1.** (*very*) muy; **to be** ~ **useless** no servir para nada **2.** (*for emphasis*) **I don't** ~ **know** no tengo ni puñetera idea

bloody-minded [ˌblʌdi'maɪndɪd] *adj* terco, -a

bloom [bluːm] **I.** *n no pl, a. fig* flor *f;* **to come into** ~ florecer; **in the full** ~ **of youth** en la flor de la juventud **II.** *vi* **1.** (*produce flowers*) florecer **2.** (*peak*) prosperar

bloomer ['bluːməʳ, *Am:* -mɚ] *n Brit, inf* (*gaffe*) metedura *f* de pata; **to make a** ~ meter la pata

blooming¹ ['bluːmɪŋ] *adj* floreciente

blooming² *adj,* **bloomin'** ['bluːmɪŋ] *adj Brit, inf* puñetero, -a

blossom ['blɒsəm, *Am:* 'blɑːsəm] **I.** *n* flor *f;* **in** ~ en flor; **orange** ~ azahar *m* **II.** *vi* **1.** (*flower*) florecer **2.** (*mature*) madurar

blot [blɒt, *Am:* blɑːt] **I.** *n* **1.** (*mark*) borrón *m* **2.** (*on sb's reputation*) mancha *f* **II.** *vt* **1.** (*mark*) emborronar **2.** (*dry*) secar

blotch [blɒtʃ, *Am:* blɑːtʃ] *n* borrón *m;* (*on the skin*) mancha *f*

blotchy ['blɒtʃi, *Am:* 'blɑːtʃi] <-ier, -iest> *adj* lleno, -a de manchas

blotter ['blɒtəʳ, *Am:* 'blɑːtɚ] *n* hoja *f* de papel secante

blotting paper ['blɒtɪŋˌpeɪpəʳ, *Am:* 'blɑːtɪŋˌpeɪpɚ] *n no pl* papel *m* secante

blotto ['blɒtəʊ, *Am:* 'blɑːtou] *adj inf* **to be** ~ estar como una cuba

blouse [blaʊz] *n* blusa *f*

blow¹ [bləʊ, *Am:* bloʊ] *n* **1.** (*hit*) golpe *m,* zuque *m Col;* (*with the fist*) puñetazo *m;* **to come to** ~**s** llegar a las manos **2.** (*setback*) disgusto *m*

blow² [bləʊ, *Am:* bloʊ] **I.** <blew, blown> *vi* **1.** (*expel air*) soplar **2.** (*fuse*) fundirse **3.** (*tyre*) reventar **II.** *vt* **1.** (*instrument*) tocar **2.** (*clear*) **to** ~ **one's nose** sonarse la nariz **3.** (*burn through*) fundir; (*burst*) reventar **4.** *inf* (*spend*) despilfarrar ► ~ **it!** *inf* ¡al diablo!

◆**blow away** *vt* **1.** (*wind*) arrancar, llevar **2.** *inf* (*kill*) liquidar

◆**blow down I.** *vi* caerse **II.** *vt* derribar

◆**blow off** *vt* quitar soplando; (*wind*) llevarse

◆**blow out I.** *vt* apagar **II.** *vi* apagarse

◆**blow over** *vi* (*scandal*) pasar al olvido; (*argument, dispute*) calmarse

◆**blow up I.** *vi* (*storm, gale*) levantarse **II.** *vt* **1.** (*fill with air*) inflar **2.** PHOTO ampliar **3.** (*explode*) volar

blow-by-blow [ˌbləʊbaɪ'bləʊ, *Am:* ˌbloʊbaɪ'bloʊ] *adj* **a** ~ **account** una descripción con todo lujo de detalles

blow-dry ['bləʊˌdraɪ, *Am:* 'bloʊ-] *vt* secar con secador

blower ['bləʊəʳ, *Am:* 'bloʊɚ] *n Aus, Brit, inf* teléfono *m*

blowfly ['bləʊflaɪ, *Am:* 'bloʊ-] <-ies> *n* moscarda *f*

blowhole ['bləʊhəʊl, *Am:* 'bloʊhoʊl] *n* orificio *m* nasal

blowjob ['bləʊdʒɒb, *Am:* 'bloʊdʒɑːb] *n vulg* mamada *f*

blowlamp ['bləʊlæmp, *Am:* 'bloʊ-] *n* soplete *m*

blown [bləʊn, *Am:* 'bloʊn] *vt, vi pp of* **blow**

blowout ['bləʊaʊt, *Am:* 'bloʊ-] *n inf* **1.** *Brit* (*huge meal*) comilona *f* **2.** (*burst tyre*) reventón *m*

blowpipe ['bləʊpaɪp, *Am:* 'bloʊ-] *n* (*weapon*) cerbatana *f*

blowtorch ['bləʊtɔːtʃ, *Am:* 'bloʊtɔːrtʃ] *n* soplete *m*

blow-up ['bləʊʌp] *n* PHOTO ampliación *f*

blub [blʌb] <-bb-> *vi s.* **blubber¹**

blubber¹ ['blʌbəʳ, *Am:* -ɚ] *vi* lloriquear

blubber² ['blʌbəʳ, *Am:* -ɚ] *n* grasa *f* (de ballena)

bludgeon ['blʌdʒən] **I.** *n* porra *f,* tolete *m AmC, AmS* **II.** *vt* aporrear

blue [bluː] **I.** *adj* **1.** (*colour*) azul *m;* **light/dark** ~ azul claro/oscuro; **pale/deep** ~ azul pálido/intenso **2.** (*sad*) triste; **to feel** ~ sentirse triste **II.** *n* azul *m;* **sky** ~ azul cielo; **the door is painted** ~ la puerta está pintada de azul ►**out of the** ~ cuando menos se espera

bluebell ['bluːbel] *n* campánula *f* azul

blueberry ['bluːbəri, *Am:* -ˌber-] <-ies> *n* arándano *m*

bluebottle ['bluːˌbɒtl, *Am:* -ˌbɑːtl̩] *n* mosca *f* azul

blue chip *adj* puntero, -a **blue collar** *adj*

(*union, background*) obrero, -a; (*job*) manual
blueprint ['blu:prɪnt] *n* plano *m;* (*programme*) programa *m*
blues [blu:z] *npl* 1. melancolía *f* 2. MUS blues *m*
blue whale *n* ballena *f* azul
bluff¹ [blʌf] I. *vi* tirarse un farol II. *vt* engañar III. *n* farol *m,* bluff *m AmL;* **to call sb's ~** descubrir a alguien la farolada
bluff² [blʌf] *n* (*steep bank*) risco *m;* (*cliff*) acantilado *m*
bluff³ [blʌf] <-er, -est> *adj* campechano, -a
bluffer ['blʌfəʳ, *Am:* -ɚ] *n* farolero, -a *m, f*
bluish ['blu:ɪʃ] *adj* azulado, -a
blunder ['blʌndəʳ, *Am:* -dɚ] I. *n* error *m* garrafal, embarrada *f AmL* II. *vi* 1. (*make a mistake*) cometer un error garrafal 2. (*move clumsily*) **to ~ into sth** tropezar con algo
◆**blunder about** *vi* andar dando tropezones
blunt [blʌnt] I. *adj* 1. (*not sharp*) desafilado, -a, pompo, -a *Ecua, Col* 2. (*direct*) directo, -a II. *vt* despuntar; *fig* suavizar
bluntly *adv* sin rodeos; **to put it ~, ...** para decirlo sin rodeos,...
bluntness *n no pl* 1. (*of a blade*) falta *f* de filo 2. (*directness*) franqueza *f*
blur [blɜːʳ, *Am:* blɜːr] I. *vi* <-rr-> desdibujarse II. *vt* <-rr-> desdibujar; (*picture*) desenfocar III. *n no pl* (*shape*) contorno *m* borroso; (*memory*) vago recuerdo *m*
blurb [blɜːb, *Am:* blɜːrb] *n no pl, inf* propaganda *f* publicitaria
blurred [blɜːd, *Am:* blɜːrd] *adj* indistinto, -a; (*photograph, picture*) borroso, -a
blurt out [blɜːtˈaʊt, *Am:* blɜːrtˈaʊt] *vt* soltar
blush [blʌʃ] I. *vi* ruborizarse II. *n* rubor *m*
blusher ['blʌʃəʳ, *Am:* -ɚ] *n* colorete *m,* rouge *m Chile*
blushing *adj* ruboroso, -a
bluster ['blʌstəʳ, *Am:* -tɚ] I. *vi* 1. (*speak*) bravuconear 2. (*blow*) rugir II. *n no pl* bravuconería *f*
BMA *abbr of* **British Medical Association** *colegio de médicos británico*
BO [ˌbiːˈəʊ, *Am:* -ˈoʊ] *n abbr of* **body odour** olor *m* corporal
boa ['bəʊə, *Am:* 'boʊə] *n* boa *f*
boar [bɔːʳ, *Am:* bɔːr] *n* (*male pig*) cerdo *m* macho; (**wild**) ~ jabalí *m*
board [bɔːd, *Am:* bɔːrd] I. *n* 1. (*wood*) tabla *f* 2. (*blackboard*) pizarra *f;* (*notice board*) tablero *m* 3. GAMES tablero *m* 4. ADMIN consejo *m* de administración, junta *f;* ~ (**of directors**) junta directiva; **Board of Trade** *Am* Cámara *f* de Comercio 5. (*in a hotel*) **full ~** pensión *f* completa; **half ~** media pensión *f* 6. NAUT **on ~** a bordo ▸**to let sth go by the ~** dejar algo a un lado; **to sweep the ~** llevarse todos los premios; (*in gambling*) limpiar la mesa; **to take sth on** ~ adoptar algo; **to tread the ~s** THEAT salir a escena; **across the** ~ en general II. *vt* (*get on: ship*) subir a bordo de; (*bus, train*) subir a III. *vi* (*stay*) alojarse; (*in school*) estar

interno; **to ~ with sb** hospedarse en casa de alguien
◆**board up** *vt* entablar
boarder ['bɔːdəʳ, *Am:* 'bɔːrdɚ] *n* SCHOOL interno, -a *m, f*
board game *n* juego *m* de mesa
boarding card *n Brit* tarjeta *f* de embarque
boarding house *n* pensión *f*
boarding pass *n* tarjeta *f* de embarque
boarding school *n* internado *m*
board meeting *n* reunión *f* de la junta directiva **boardroom** *n* sala *f* de juntas
boardwalk ['bɔːdwɔːk, *Am:* 'bɔːrdwɔːk] *n Am: paseo marítimo entablado*
boast [bəʊst, *Am:* boʊst] I. *vi* alardear; **to ~ about/of sth** vanagloriarse sobre/de algo II. *vt* (*have*) tener; (*be proud of*) enorgullecerse de III. *n* alarde *m*
boastful ['bəʊstfəl, *Am:* 'boʊst-] *adj* fanfarrón, -ona, bocatero, -a *AmL*
boat [bəʊt, *Am:* boʊt] *n* barco *m;* (*small*) barca *f,* bote *m;* (*large*) buque *m;* **to go by ~** ir en barco ▸**to be in the same** ~ estar en la misma situación; **to burn one's ~s** (**behind one**) quemar las naves; **to miss the** ~ perder la oportunidad; **to push the** ~ **out** *Brit* tirar la casa por la ventana; **to rock the** ~ *inf* hacer olas
boat hook *n* bichero *m* **boat house** *n* cobertizo *m*
boating ['bəʊtɪŋ, *Am:* 'boʊt̬ɪŋ] *n no pl* **to go** ~ dar un paseo en barca
boatman ['bəʊtmən, *Am:* 'boʊt-] *n* barquero *m*
boat people *npl* refugiados *mpl* del mar
boat race *n* regata *f;* **the Boat Race** *Brit: carrera anual de remo entre Oxford y Cambridge*

La anual **Boat Race** (competición de remo) se celebra un sábado de marzo en el río **Thames** (Támesis). Ocho remeros de las universidades de Oxford y Cambridge compiten en dicha carrera. Es un acontecimiento nacional muy importante seguido por 460 millones de espectadores de todo el mundo.

boatswain ['bəʊsən, *Am:* 'boʊ-] *n* contramaestre *m*
boat train *n* tren *m* que enlaza con un barco
boat trip *n* viaje *m* en barco
bob¹ [bɒb, *Am:* baːb] *n* (*hairstyle*) pelo *m* a lo garçon
bob² [bɒb, *Am:* baːb] <-bb-> I. *vi* **to ~** (**up and down**) agitarse II. *n* meneo *m*
bob³ [bɒb, *Am:* baːb] *n Brit* (*shilling*) chelín *m*
bobbin ['bɒbɪn, *Am:* 'baːbɪn] *n* bobina *f*
bobble hat ['bɒblˌhæt, *Am:* 'baːbl-] *n* gorro *m* con pompón
bobby ['bɒbi, *Am:* 'baːbi] <-ies> *n Brit, inf* poli *mf*
bobsled ['bɒbsled, *Am:* 'baːb-] *n,*

bobsleigh ['bɒbsleɪ, Am: 'baːb-] n SPORTS bobsleigh m
bobtail ['bɒbteɪl, Am: 'baːb-] n 1.(docked tail) cola f cortada 2.(animal) animal m rabicorto
bode [bəʊd, Am: boʊd] I. vi to ~ well/ill ser una buena/mala señal II. vt presagiar
bodice ['bɒdɪs, Am: 'baːdɪs] n (of a dress) canesú m; (underwear) corpiño m
bodily ['bɒdəli] I. adj corpóreo, -a; (harm, injury) corporal; (functions, needs) fisiológico, -a II. adv (in person) en persona; (as a whole) en conjunto
body ['bɒdi, Am: 'baːdi] <-ies> n 1.a. ANAT, ASTR, CHEM cuerpo m 2.(person) a cheerful old ~ un tipo alegre 3. ADMIN, POL unidad f; (governing) organismo m; (group) grupo m; in a ~ en bloque 4.(amount) cantidad f; (of water) masa f 5. AUTO caja f, carrocería f 6.(dead corpse) cadáver m ▶to keep ~ and soul together sobrevivir; to throw oneself ~ and soul into sth entregarse a algo en cuerpo y alma; over my dead ~ ¡por encima de mi cadáver!; to sell one's ~ prostituirse
body bag n bolsa f para cadáveres
bodybuilding n no pl culturismo m
bodyguard ['bɒdigaːd, Am: 'baːdigaːrd] n guardaespaldas mf inv, espaldero m Ven
body language n no pl lenguaje m corporal **body lotion** n loción f corporal **body politic** n no pl POL estado m **body search** n cacheo m
bodysuit n body m
bodywork ['bɒdiwɜːk, Am: 'baːdiwɜːrk] n carrocería f
bog [bɒg, Am: baːg] n 1.(wet ground) ciénaga f, estero m Bol, Col, Ven; peat ~ turbera f 2. Aus, Brit, inf (toilet) retrete m
♦bog down <-gg-> vt to get bogged down in sth quedar atascado en algo; fig atrancarse en algo
bogey ['bəʊgi, Am: 'boʊ-] n 1.(unreasoned fear) coco m 2. inf (snot) moco m seco 3.(golf score) bogey m
boggle ['bɒgl, Am: 'baːgl] I. vi quedarse atónito II. vt to ~ the mind ser increíble
boggy ['bɒgi, Am: 'baːgi] <-ier, -iest> adj pantanoso, -a
bogie ['bəʊgi, Am: 'boʊgi] n Am s. **bogey**
bogus ['bəʊgəs, Am: 'boʊ-] adj (document) falso, -a; (argument) falaz; (person) presuntuoso, -a
bogy ['bəʊgi, Am: 'boʊ-] n s. **bogey**
bohemian [bəʊ'hiːmiən, Am: boʊ-] I. n bohemio, -a m, f II. adj bohemio, -a
boil [bɔɪl] I. vi, vt a. fig hervir; a (hard/soft) ~ed egg un huevo duro/pasado por agua II. n 1. no pl to bring sth to the ~ calentar algo hasta que hierva; to be on the ~ estar hirviendo; fig (person) estar furioso; to go off the ~ dejar de hervir 2. MED furúnculo m
♦boil away vi evaporarse
♦boil down I. vi reducirse por cocción II. vt

reducir
♦boil down to vt fig reducirse a
♦boil over vi 1. GASTR rebosar 2.(person) perder el control; (situation) estallar
♦boil up vt hervir
boiler ['bɔɪlə', Am: -lə-] n caldera f
boilerhouse n edificio m de la caldera **boiler room** n sala f de calderas **boiler suit** n Aus, Brit mono m
boiling adj 1.hirviendo 2.fig (day, weather) abrasador(a); (angry: person) enfadadísimo, -a; I am ~ (feeling hot) me estoy asando; it's ~ (hot) today hace un calor achicharrante
boiling point n punto m de ebullición; to reach ~ fig ponerse al rojo vivo
boisterous ['bɔɪstərəs] adj 1.(person, party) bullicioso, -a 2.(sea) enfurecido, -a
bold [bəʊld, Am: boʊld] <-er, -est> adj 1.(brave, audacious) audaz 2.(strong: colour) llamativo, -a 3. INFOR, TYPO ~ (type) negrita f; in ~ en negrita 4.(not shy) atrevido, -a; (cheeky) descarado, -a
boldness n audacia f
bole [bəʊl, Am: boʊl] n tronco m
bolero [bə'leərəʊ, Am: -'leroʊ] <-s> n 1.(short jacket) torera f 2. MUS bolero m
Bolivia [bə'lɪvɪə] n Bolivia f
Bolivian [bə'lɪvɪən] I. adj boliviano, -a II. n boliviano, -a m, f
bollard ['bɒlaːd, Am: 'baːlə-d] n Brit baliza f
bolster ['bəʊlstə', Am: 'boʊlstə-] I. n cabezal m II. vt 1.(support) reafirmar 2.(encourage) alentar 3.(increase) levantar
bolt [bəʊlt, Am: boʊlt] I. vi fugarse II. vt 1. GASTR engullir 2.(lock) echar el pestillo a 3.(fix) atornillar III. n 1.(on a door) pestillo m 2.(screw) tornillo m 3.(of lightning) rayo m 4.(roll: of cloth) rollo m 5.(arrow) flecha f ▶to make a ~ for it fugarse; a ~ from the blue un acontecimiento inesperado IV. adv ~ upright rígido, derecho
bolt hole n refugio m
bomb [bɒm, Am: baːm] I. n 1.(explosive) bomba f 2. Brit, inf to cost/be worth a ~ costar/valer un dineral ▶to go like a ~ Brit, inf (go well) marchar a las mil maravillas; (go very quickly) ir como un bólido; (be a success) ser un exitazo II. vt bombardear III. vi inf estrellarse
bombard [bɒm'baːd, Am: baːm'baːrd] vt bombardear; to ~ sb with questions acribillar a alguien a preguntas
bombardment [bɒm'baːdmənt, Am: baːm'baːrd-] n bombardeo m
bombast ['bɒmbæst, Am: 'baːm-] n no pl grandilocuencia f
bombastic [bɒm'bæstɪk, Am: baːm-] adj grandilocuente; (style) rimbombante
bomb crater n cráter m de bomba **bomb disposal unit** n brigada f de bombas
bombed [bɒmd] adj 1.bombardeado, -a 2. Am, inf (on drugs) colocado, -a
bomber ['bɒmə', Am: 'baːmə-] n 1. AVIAT

bombardero *m* **2.** (*terrorist*) terrorista *mf* (que coloca bombas)

bombing *n* **1.** MIL bombardeo *m* **2.** (*by terrorists*) atentado *m* (con bomba)

bombproof *adj* a prueba de bombas

bombshell ['bɒmʃel, *Am:* 'bɑːm-] *n* **1.** MIL obús *m* **2.** (*woman*) mujer *f* despampanante **3.** (*surprise*) bombazo *m inf*

bona fide [ˌbəʊnə'faɪdi, *Am:* ˌboʊ-] *adj* **1.** (*genuine*) genuino, -a; (*agreement, alibi*) auténtico, -a **2.** (*serious*) serio, -a

bonanza [bə'nænzə] **I.** *n a. fig* bonanza *f* **II.** *adj* próspero, -a

bond [bɒnd, *Am:* bɑːnd] **I.** *n* **1.** (*connection*) vínculo *m*; (*of friendship, love*) lazo *m*; **to break one's ~** romper sus cadenas *fig* **2.** (*obligation*) obligación *f* **3.** FIN bono *m*; **to place goods in ~** poner mercancías en el almacén aduanero **4.** LAW garantía *f*; *Am* (*bail*) fianza *f* **5.** *pl, liter* (*chains*) cadenas *fpl* **6.** (*joint*) junta *f* **II.** *vt* **1.** (*stick*) pegar **2.** (*unite emotionally*) **to ~** (*together*) vincular **3.** COM depositar bajo fianza **III.** *vi* adherirse

bondage ['bɒndɪdʒ, *Am:* 'bɑːn-] *n no pl* **1.** *liter* (*slavery*) esclavitud *f*; **to be in ~ to sb/sth** estar esclavo de alguien/algo **2.** (*for sexual pleasure*) bondage *m*

bonded *adj* **1.** COM en depósito aduanero **2.** FIN garantizado, -a por obligación escrita

bonded debt *n* FIN deuda *f* consolidada

bonded warehouse *n* COM almacén *m* aduanero

bondholder *n* FIN titular *mf* de bonos

bone [bəʊn, *Am:* boʊn] **I.** *n* ANAT hueso *m*; (*of a fish*) espina *f* ►~ **of contention** manzana *f* de la discordia; **to work one's fingers to the ~** trabajar como un esclavo; **close to the ~** fuera de tono; **to cut sth to the ~** reducir algo a lo esencial; **to feel sth in one's ~s** tener un presentimiento de algo; **to make no ~s about sth** no ocultar algo; **to have a ~ to pick with sb** *inf* tener que ajustar cuentas con alguien **II.** *adj* de hueso **III.** *vt* (*piece of meat*) deshuesar; (*fish*) quitar las espinas a

bonehead ['bəʊnhed, *Am:* 'boʊn-] *n inf* estúpido, -a *m, f*

bone idle *adj*, **bone lazy** *adj inf* vago, -a

bone marrow *n no pl* médula *f* ósea **bonemeal** *n no pl* harina *f* de huesos

boneshaker ['bəʊnʃeɪkəʳ, *Am:* 'boʊnʃeɪkɚ] *n inf* carraca *f*

bonfire ['bɒnfaɪəʳ, *Am:* 'bɑːnfaɪɚ] *n* hoguera *f*

bonkers ['bɒŋkəz, *Am:* 'bɑːŋkɚz] *adj inf* loco, -a; **to go ~** volverse loco

bonnet ['bɒnɪt, *Am:* 'bɑːnɪt] *n* **1.** (*hat*) sombrero *m*; (*baby's*) gorrito *m* **2.** *Aus, Brit* AUTO capote *m*

bonny ['bɒni, *Am:* 'bɑːni] *adj Scot* hermoso, -a

bonus ['bəʊnəs, *Am:* 'boʊ-] *n* **1.** (*money*) prima *f*, abono *m AmL*; (*for Christmas*) bonificación *f*; **productivity ~** plus *m* **2.** (*advan-*

tage) ventaja *f*

bony ['bəʊni, *Am:* 'boʊ-] *adj* <-ier, -iest> **1.** (*with prominent bones*) huesudo, -a; (*fish*) con muchas espinas **2.** (*like bones*) óseo, -a

boo [buː] **I.** *interj inf* bu **II.** *vi* abuchear, pifiar *Chile, Méx* III. *vt* abuchear; **he was ~ed off the stage** lo abuchearon hasta que abandonó el escenario

boob [buːb] **I.** *n* **1.** *inf* (*breast*) teta *f* **2.** *Brit, inf* (*blunder*) metedura *f* de pata **3.** *Am* (*fool*) bobo, -a *m, f* II. *vi Brit, inf* meter la pata

booby ['buːbi] *n* bobo, -a *m, f*

booby prize *n* premio *m* al peor **booby trap** *n* trampa *f*

book [bʊk] **I.** *n* **1.** libro *m*; **the Good Book** la Biblia **2.** (*of stamps*) taco *m*; (*of tickets*) talonario *m* **3.** (*register*) registro *m* **4.** COM, FIN **the ~s** las cuentas ►**to be in sb's bad ~s** estar en la lista negra de alguien; **to be a closed ~** (**to sb**) ser un misterio (para alguien); **to be in sb's good ~s** gozar de las simpatías de alguien; **to bring sb to ~** pedir cuentas a alguien; **to cook the ~s** *inf* amañar las cuentas; **to be able to read sb like a ~** conocer a alguien a fondo; **to suit sb's ~** convenir a alguien; **to throw the ~ at sb** castigar duramente a alguien, cantar las cuarenta a alguien; **in my ~** en mi opinión **II.** *vt* **1.** (*reserve*) reservar **2.** (*register*) fichar **III.** *vi* reservar

◆**book in I.** *vi* inscribirse **II.** *vt* **to book sb in** (*register*) registrar a alguien; (*make a reservation for*) reservar una habitación para alguien

◆**book up** *vt* **to be booked up** estar completo

bookable ['bʊkəbl] *adj* **~ in advance** que se puede reservar por adelantado

bookbinder ['bʊkˌbaɪndəʳ, *Am:* -dɚ] *n* encuadernador(a) *m(f)*

bookbinding *n no pl* encuadernación *f*

bookcase ['bʊkkeɪs] *n* estantería *f*

book club *n* club *m* de lectores

bookend ['bʊkend] *n* sujetalibros *m inv*

bookie ['bʊki] *n inf* corredor(a) *m(f)* de apuestas

booking ['bʊkɪŋ] *n* reserva *f*; **to make/cancel a ~** hacer/cancelar una reserva

booking clerk *n* taquillero, -a *m, f* **booking office** *n* **1.** (*theatre*) taquilla *f* **2.** (*station*) ventanilla *f* de venta de billetes

bookish ['bʊkɪʃ] *adj* libresco, -a; *pej* pedante

bookkeeper ['bʊkˌkiːpəʳ, *Am:* -pɚ] *n* contable *mf*

bookkeeping ['bʊk ˌkiːpɪŋ] *n no pl* contabilidad *f*

booklet ['bʊklɪt] *n* folleto *m*

bookmaker ['bʊkˌmeɪkəʳ, *Am:* -kɚ] *n* corredor(a) *m(f)* de apuestas

bookmark ['bʊkmɑːk, *Am:* -mɑːrk] *n a.* INFOR marcador *m*

bookplate ['bʊkpleɪt] *n* ex libris *m*

book review *n* crítica *f* de libros **book reviewer** *n* crítico, -a *m, f* de libros

bookseller ['bʊkˌseləʳ, *Am:* -ɚ] *n* (*person*)

librero, -a *m, f; (shop)* librería *f*
bookshelf ['bʊkʃelf] <-shelves> *n* estante *m*
bookshop ['bʊksɒp, *Am:* -ʃɑːp] *n* librería *f*
bookstall ['bʊkstɔːl, *Am:* -stɔːl] *n* quiosco *m*
bookstore ['bʊkstɔːr, *Am:* -stɔːr] *n Am* librería *f*
book token *n* vale *m* cancejable por libros
book trade *n no pl* comercio *m* de libros
bookworm ['bʊkwɜːm, *Am:* -wɜːrm] *n* ratón *m* de biblioteca
boom¹ [buːm] ECON I. *vi* estar en auge II. *n* boom *m* III. *adj* en alza; **a ~ time** un período de prosperidad; **a ~ town** una ciudad próspera
boom² [buːm] I. *n (sound)* estruendo *m* II. *vi* to ~ **(out)** tronar; *(voice)* resonar III. *vt* tronar
boom³ [buːm] *n* 1. *(floating barrier)* barrera *f* 2. NAUT botavara *f* 3. *(for a microphone)* jirafa *f*
boomerang ['buːməræŋ] I. *n* bumerán *m* II. *vi* **it ~ed on her/him** le salió el tiro por la culata *inf*
boon [buːn] *n no pl* beneficio *m;* **to be a ~ (to sb)** ser de gran ayuda (para alguien); **~ companion** *liter* amigo, -a *m, f* del alma
boor [bʊər, *Am:* bʊr] *n* grosero, -a *m, f*
boorish ['bɔːrɪʃ, *Am:* 'bʊrɪʃ] *adj* grosero, -a
boost [buːst] I. *n no pl* incentivo *m;* **to give a ~ to sth, to give sth a ~** estimular algo II. *vt* 1. *(increase)* aumentar, incrementar; *(morale)* reforzar; *(process)* estimular 2. *inf (promote)* promover; *(image, ego)* potenciar
booster [buːstər, *Am:* -stər] *n* 1. *(improvement)* mejora *f* 2. MED vacuna *f* de refuerzo
booster rocket *n* TECH cohete *m* propulsor
booster seat *n* AUTO booster *m*
boot [buːt] I. *n* 1. *(footwear)* bota *f;* **ankle ~** botín *m;* **wellington ~** bota *f* de goma 2. *inf (kick)* patada *f,* puntapié *m;* **to put the ~ in** *inf* emplear la violencia; *fig* obrar decisivamente 3. INFOR arranque *m,* inicialización *f;* **warm/cold ~** arranque en frío/en caliente 4. *Brit, Aus* AUTO maletero *m,* cajuela *f Méx,* baúl *m Arg* ▶**the ~'s on the other foot** se ha vuelto la tortilla; **to be too big for one's ~s** *inf* tener muchos humos; **to get the ~** *inf* ser despedido; **to give sb the ~** *inf* echar a alguien; **to lick sb's ~s** hacer la pelota a alguien; **to shake in one's ~s** *inf* temblar de miedo II. *vt inf* 1. *(kick)* dar un puntapié a 2. INFOR arrancar ▶**to ~** además, por si fuera poco
◆**boot out** *vt inf* poner de patitas en la calle
bootblack ['buːtblæk] *n* limpiabotas *mf inv*
bootee ['buːtiː, *Am:* -ţi] *n* patuco *m*
booth [buːð] *n* 1. *(cubicle)* cubículo *m;* *(telephone)* cabina *f;* *(polling)* casilla *f* 2. *(at a fair, market)* caseta *f*
bootlace ['buːtleɪs] *n* cordón *m*
bootleg ['buːtleg] <-gg-> *adj* 1. *(alcohol, cigarettes)* de contrabando 2. *(recording, software)* pirata
bootlicker ['buːtlɪkər] *n inf* lameculos *m inv,* olfa *mf Arg, Par, Urug*

bootmaker *n* fabricante *mf* de zapatos
booty ['buːti, *Am:* -ţi] *n* botín *m*
booze [buːz] I. *n inf* bebida *f;* **to go out on the ~** salir de juerga II. *vi inf* empinar el codo, chupar *AmL*
boozer ['buːzər, *Am:* -ər] *n inf* 1. *Brit (pub)* bar *m* 2. *(person)* borrachín, -ina *m, f*
boozy ['buːzi] <-ier, -iest> *adj inf* borrachín, -ina
border ['bɔːdər, *Am:* 'bɔːrdər] I. *n* 1. *(frontier)* frontera *f* 2. *(edge, boundary)* borde *m* 3. FASHION cenefa *f* 4. *(in a garden)* arriate *m* II. *adj* fronterizo, -a III. *vt* limitar con
◆**border on** *vi* 1. *(share border with)* limitar con 2. *fig* rayar en
bordering *adj* limítrofe
borderland ['bɔːdələænd, *Am:* 'bɔːrdər-] *n* zona *f* fronteriza
borderline ['bɔːdəlaɪn, *Am:* 'bɔːrdər-] I. *n no pl* frontera *f* II. *adj (candidate, case)* dudoso, -a
bore¹ [bɔːr, *Am:* bɔːr] I. *n* 1. *(thing)* aburrimiento *m;* *(task)* lata *f,* fastidio *m;* **what a ~!** ¡qué lata! 2. *(person)* pesado, -a *m, f* II. <bored> *vt* aburrir; **to ~ sb to death** *inf* aburrir a alguien como una ostra
bore² [bɔːr, *Am:* bɔːr] I. *n (of a pipe)* alma *f; (of a gun)* calibre *m* II. *vt* perforar; **to ~ a hole** abrir un agujero
bore³ [bɔːr, *Am:* bɔːr] *pp of* **bear**
bored *adj* aburrido, -a
boredom ['bɔːdəm, *Am:* 'bɔːr-] *n no pl* aburrimiento *m*
boric ['bɔːrɪk] *adj* bórico, -a; **~ acid** ácido bórico
boring ['bɔːrɪŋ] *adj* aburrido, -a, cansador(a) *Arg, Chile, Urug,* fome *Chile;* **to find sth ~** encontrar algo pesado
born [bɔːn, *Am:* bɔːrn] *adj* 1. *(brought into life)* nacido, -a; **to be ~** nacer; **where were you ~?** ¿dónde naciste?; **he was ~ in the year 1975** nació en el año 1975; **he was ~ blind** es ciego de nacimiento 2. *(ability)* nato, -a; *(quality, sympathy)* innato, -a ▶**I wasn't ~ yesterday** *inf* no nací ayer
born-again ['bɔːnəgen, *Am:* ˌbɔːrn-] *adj* renacido, -a; **~ Christian** cristiano convertido
borne [bɔːn, *Am:* bɔːrn] *pt of* **bear**
borough ['bʌrə, *Am:* 'bɜːroʊ] *n* municipio *m*
borrow ['bɒrəʊ, *Am:* 'bɑːroʊ] *vt* 1. *(be given temporarily)* tomar prestado; *(ask for)* pedir prestado; **may I ~ your bag?** ¿me prestas tu bolso? 2. LING tomar
borrower *n* prestatario, -a *m, f*
borrowing *n no pl* préstamo *m;* **public ~** oferta *f* pública
Bosnia ['bɒzniə, *Am:* 'bɑːz-] *n* Bosnia *f*
Bosnia-Herzegovina ['bɒzniəˌhɜːzəˈɡoʊvɪnə, *Am:* 'bɑːzniəˌhertsəɡoʊviːnə] *n* Bosnia *f* Herzegovina
Bosnian ['bɒznɪən, *Am:* 'bɑːz-] I. *adj* bosnio, -a II. *n* bosnio, -a *m, f*
bosom ['bʊzəm] *n no pl* 1. pecho *m* 2. *fig*

seno *m;* in the ~ of one's family en el seno de
su familia
bosom buddy *n* amigo *m* del alma
boss¹ [bɒs, *Am:* bɑːs] I. *n (person in charge)*
jefe, -a *m, f; (owner)* patrón, -ona *m, f;* to be
one's own ~ ser su propio jefe II. *vt inf* to ~ sb
about mandonear a alguien
boss² [bɒs, *Am:* bɑːs] *adj Am, inf* chulo, -a
bossy ['bɒsi, *Am:* 'bɑːsi] <-ier, -iest> *adj*
mandón, -ona
bossy boots *n inf* mandón, -ona *m, f*
bosun ['bəʊsən, *Am:* 'boʊ-] *n* contramaestre
m
botanical [bə'tænɪkəl] *adj* botánico, -a
botanist ['bɒtənɪst, *Am:* 'bɑːtnɪst] *n* botánico, -a *m, f*
botany ['bɒtəni, *Am:* 'bɑːtni] *n no pl* botánica *f*
botch [bɒtʃ, *Am:* bɑːtʃ] I. *n* chapuza *f;* to
make a ~ of sth hacer una chapuza de algo
II. *vt* to ~ sth (up) hacer una chapuza de algo
botch-up ['bɒtʃʌp, *Am:* 'bɑːtʃ-] *Aus, Brit s.*
botch I.
both [bəʊθ, *Am:* boʊθ] I. *adj, pron* los dos,
las dos, ambos, ambas; ~ of them ellos dos,
ellas dos; ~ of us nosotros dos, nosotras dos; ~
(the) brothers los dos hermanos; on ~ sides
en ambos lados II. *adv* ~ Mathilde and Sara
tanto Mathilde como Sara; to be ~ sad and
pleased estar a la vez triste y satisfecho
bother ['bɒðər, *Am:* 'bɑːðɚ] I. *n* molestia *f,*
friega *f AmL;* it is no ~ no es ninguna molestia;
not to want to be a ~ no querer molestar; it
is not worth the ~ no vale la pena; to get
into a spot of ~ *Brit, inf* meterse en un lío
II. *vi* molestarse; (not) to ~ to do sth (no)
molestarse en hacer algo; why ~? ¿para qué
molestarse? III. *vt* 1. *(annoy)* molestar
2. *(worry)* preocupar; he doesn't seem to be
~ed by ... no parece que le preocupa...; what
~s me is ... lo que me preocupa es...
bothersome ['bɒðəsəm, *Am:* 'bɑːðɚ-] *adj*
molesto, -a, tequioso, -a *AmC,* espeso, -a *Perú,*
Ven
Botswana [ˌbɒt'swɑːnə, *Am:* bɑːt-] *n* Bot-
suana *f*
Botswanan [ˌbɒt'swɑːnən] I. *adj* botsuano,
-a II. *n* botsuano, -a *m, f*
bottle ['bɒtl, *Am:* 'bɑːtl̩] I. *n* 1. *(container)*
botella *f; (of ink, perfume)* frasco *m; (baby's)*
biberón *m* 2. *no pl, inf (alcohol)* the ~ la
bebida; to hit the ~ empinar el codo 3. *no pl,*
Brit, inf (courage) agallas *fpl* II. *vt Brit* embotellar
bottle bank *n* contenedor *m* de recogida de
vidrio **bottle brush** *n* limpiabotellas *m inv*
bottled ['bɒtld, *Am:* 'bɑːtl̩d] *adj* embotellado, -a; *(beer, gas)* de botella
bottle-feeding ['bɒtlˌfiːdɪŋ] *n no pl* alimentación *f* con biberón **bottle-green** *adj* verde
botella
bottleneck ['bɒtlnek, *Am:* 'bɑːtl̩-] *n a. fig*
cuello *m* de botella

bottle opener *n* abrebotellas *m inv*
bottom ['bɒtəm, *Am:* 'bɑːt̬əm] I. *n no pl*
1. *(of sea, street, glass)* fondo *m; (of chair)*
asiento *m; (of stairs, page)* pie *m;* to touch ~
(reach bottom of water) llegar al fondo; *fig*
tocar fondo 2. *(lower part)* parte *f* inferior;
from top to ~ de arriba a abajo 3. *(buttocks)*
trasero *m* ►from the ~ of one's heart de
todo corazón; ~s up! ¡al centro y para adentro!; to get to the ~ of sth llegar al fondo de
algo; at ~ en el fondo; to be at the ~ of sth ser
el motivo de algo II. *adj (lower)* más bajo; the
~ half of society la clase media-baja; in ~
gear en primera; the ~ end of the table la
mitad inferior de la mesa
bottomless ['bɒtəmləs, *Am:* 'bɑːt̬əm-] *adj*
1. *(without limit)* sin fondo 2. *(very deep)*
infinito, -a; a ~ pit *fig* un pozo sin fondo; she
is a ~ pit tiene la solitaria
bottom line *n* the ~ *fig* lo fundamental
botulism ['bɒtjʊlɪzəm, *Am:* 'bɑːtʃə-] *n no*
pl botulismo *m*
bough [baʊ] *n liter* rama *f*
bought [bɔːt, *Am:* bɑːt] *vt pt of* buy
boulder ['bəʊldər, *Am:* 'boʊldɚ] *n* roca *f*
boulevard ['buːləvɑːd, *Am:* 'bʊləvɑːrd] *n*
bulevar *m*
bounce [baʊnts] I. *vi* 1. *(rebound)* (re)botar;
to ~ against sth botar contra algo; to ~ an
idea off sb pedir la opinión a alguien; to ~ sb
into doing sth presionar a alguien para hacer
algo 2. *(jump or spring up and down)* dar brincos 3. *inf* COM ser devuelto II. *vt* 1. *(cause to*
rebound) hacer (re)botar; to ~ a baby hacer el
caballito a un niño 2. *inf* COM to ~ a cheque
devolver un cheque III. *n* 1. *(rebound)*
(re)bote *m* 2. *no pl (spring)* bote *m* 3. *no pl*
(vitality) vitalidad *f; (energy)* energía *f* 4. *Am,*
inf to give sb the ~ poner a alguien de patitas
en la calle
◆**bounce back** *vi* recuperarse
bouncer ['baʊntsər, *Am:* -sɚ] *n inf* gorila *m*
bouncing *adj* robusto, -a
bouncy ['baʊntsi] *adj* 1. *(ball)* que rebota
2. *(lively)* animado, -a
bound¹ [baʊnd] I. *vi* 1. *(leap)* saltar
2. *(bounce: ball)* botar, rebotar *AmL* II. *n* salto
m; with one ~ de un salto
bound² [baʊnd] *vt* to be ~ed by sth estar
rodeado por algo
bound³ [baʊnd] *adj* to be ~ for ... ir rumbo
a...; where is this ship ~ for? ¿a dónde se
dirige este barco?
bound⁴ [baʊnd] I. *pt, pp of* bind II. *adj*
1. *(sure)* she's ~ to come seguro que viene;
it's ~ to be cheap seguro que es barato; it
was ~ to happen sooner or later tarde o
temprano tenía que suceder 2. *(obliged)* to be
~ to do sth estar obligado a hacer algo ►to be
~ and determined *Am* tener intenciones
firmes
boundary ['baʊndri] <-ies> *n* 1. a. *fig (line)*
límite *m;* to blur the boundaries *fig* desdibu-

jar los límites; **to transgress the boundaries of good taste** transgredir los límites del buen gusto **2.** (*border*) frontera *f;* **to cross a ~** cruzar una frontera; **to mark a ~** (**between two places**) establecer una frontera (entre dos lugares) **3.** SPORTS banda *f*

boundless ['baʊndlɪs] *adj* (*love, patience*) sin límites; (*energy*) ilimitado, -a, inagotable; (*universe*) infinito, -a

bounds [baʊndz] *n pl* límites *mpl;* **to know no ~** no conocer límites; **to be beyond the ~ of possibility** no ser posible; **to be outside the ~ of acceptable behaviour** estar lejos de ser un comportamiento aceptable; **this area is out of ~ to civilians** los civiles tienen prohibida la entrada en esta zona; **within ~** dentro de ciertos límites; **to be within the ~ of the law** estar dentro de los límites legales

bounty ['baʊnti, *Am:* -t̬i] <-ies> *n* **1.** (*reward*) recompensa *f* **2.** (*gift*) regalo *m* **3.** *no pl, liter* (*generosity*) munificencia *f*

bouquet [bʊ'keɪ, *Am:* boʊ-] *n* **1.** (*of flowers*) ramo *m* **2.** (*smell, aroma*) aroma *m;* (*of wine*) bouquet *m* **3.** (*compliment*) elogio *m*

bourbon ['bɜːbən, *Am:* 'bɜːr-] *n* bourbon *m*

bourgeois ['bɔːʒwɑː, *Am:* 'bʊrʒ-] *adj* burgués, -esa

bout [baʊt] *n* **1.** (*of illness*) ataque *m;* **~ of coughing** ataque *m* de tos; **~ of insanity** período *m* de locura; **drinking ~** borrachera *f* **2.** SPORTS (*in boxing, wrestling*) combate *m;* (*in fencing*) asalto *m*

boutique [buː'tiːk] *n* boutique *f*

bovine ['bəʊvaɪn, *Am:* 'boʊ-] *adj* **1.** (*of cows*) bovino, -a **2.** *fig* (*stupid*) tonto, -a

bovver boy ['bɒvəˌbɔɪ] *n inf* gamberro *m*

bow¹ [baʊ, *Am:* boʊ] *n* **1.** (*weapon*) a. MUS arco *m* **2.** (*slip-knot*) lazo *m,* moño *m AmL,* moña *f Urug,* rosa *f Chile* ▶**to have more than one <u>string</u> to one's ~** ser una persona de recursos

bow² [baʊ] *n* NAUT proa *f*

bow³ [baʊ] **I.** *vi* **1.** (*greet*) hacer una reverencia; *fig* ceder; **to ~ to sb** hacer una reverencia ante alguien **2.** (*yield*) **to ~ to sth** someterse a algo ▶**to ~ and <u>scrape</u>** hacer la pelota, hacer la barba *Méx* **II.** *vt* (*one's head*) inclinar, agachar; (*body*) doblegar **III.** *n* reverencia *f,* venia *f CSur, Col,* caravana *f Méx;* **to take a ~** recibir un aplauso

◆**bow out** *vi* retirarse

bowdlerise *vt Aus, Brit,* **bowdlerize** ['baʊdləraɪz, *Am:* 'boʊdləraɪz] *vt* expurgar

bowel ['baʊəl] *n* MED intestino *m* grueso; **to move one's ~s** hacer de vientre, mover el vientre *RíoPl*

bowel movement *n* evacuación *f* (intestinal)

bowl¹ [bəʊl, *Am:* boʊl] *n* **1.** (*dish*) bol *m;* (*for soup*) plato *m* hondo; (*of toilet*) taza *f;* (*for washing*) palangana *f;* (*of pipe*) cazoleta *f;* (*of fountain*) pila *f;* **fruit ~** frutero *m,* frutera *f*

CSur **2.** *Am* (*stadium*) estadio *m* **3.** (*hollow*) hondonada *f*

bowl² [bəʊl, *Am:* boʊl] SPORTS **I.** *vi* **1.** (*in cricket, bowling*) lanzar **2.** (*play bowls, go bowling*) jugar a los bolos **II.** *vt* lanzar **III.** *n* **1.** (*in bowls, bowling*) bola *f,* bocha *f* **2.** *pl* juego semejante a la petanca o las bochas que se juega sobre el césped

◆**bowl out** *vt* eliminar

◆**bowl over** *vt* **1.** (*knock over*) tumbar **2.** (*astonish*) dejar atónito; **to be bowled over** estar desconcertado

bow-legged [ˌbəʊ'legd, *Am:* boʊ-] *adj* (*person*) patizambo, -a, cascorvo, -a *Col;* (*table*) de patas arqueadas

bowler ['bəʊlə', *Am:* 'boʊlə-] *n* **1.** (*in cricket*) lanzador(a) *m(f)* **2.** (*at bowling, bowls*) jugador(a) *m(f)* **3.** (*hat*) bombín *m*

bowling *n no pl* **1.** (*game*) bolos *mpl* **2.** (*in cricket*) lanzamiento *m*

bowling alley *n* bolera *f* **bowling green** *n* pista donde se juega a los bolos

bowman ['bəʊmən, *Am:* 'boʊ-] *n* arquero *m*

bowstring ['bəʊstrɪŋ, *Am:* 'boʊ-] *n* MUS cuerda *f* del arco

bow tie *n* pajarita *f,* corbatín *m Col,* moñita *f Urug*

bow window *n* mirador *m*

box¹ [bɒks, *Am:* baːks] **I.** *vi* SPORTS boxear **II.** *vt* **1.** SPORTS boxear con [*o* contra] **2.** **to ~ sb's ears** dar un sopapo a alguien **III.** *n* sopapo *m;* **to give sb a ~ on the ears** dar un sopapo a alguien

box² [bɒks, *Am:* baːks] **I.** *n* **1.** (*container*) caja *f;* **cardboard ~** caja de cartón; **tool ~** caja de herramientas **2.** (*rectangular space*) casilla *f;* (*in soccer, baseball*) área *f;* (*at road junction*) parrilla *f;* (*penalty*) **~** (*in soccer*) área (de castigo); (*in ice hockey*) banquillo *m* **3.** (*small space*) agujero *m;* **their new house is just a ~** su nueva casa es un agujero **4.** THEAT palco *m;* (*booth*) cabina *f;* **sentry ~** garita *f;* **witness ~** estrado *m* **5.** *Aus, Brit* SPORTS (*protector*) protector *m,* concha *f Méx* **6.** *inf* (*television*) **the ~** la caja tonta **7.** *no pl* (*tree*) boj *m* **8.** INFOR **dialogue ~** cuadro *m* de diálogo **II.** *vt* poner en una caja

◆**box in** *vt* acorralar; **to ~ a car** cerrar el paso a un coche; **to feel boxed in** *fig* sentirse limitado

◆**box off** *vt* compartimentar

◆**box up** *vt* poner en una caja

boxer ['bɒksə', *Am:* 'baːksə-] *n* **1.** (*dog*) bóxer *mf* **2.** (*person*) boxeador(a) *m(f)*

boxer shorts *npl* calzoncillos *mpl*

boxing ['bɒksɪŋ, *Am:* 'baːksɪŋ] *n no pl* boxeo *m,* box *m AmL*

El **Boxing Day** se celebra el 26 de diciembre. El nombre de este día proviene de cuando los aprendices de un oficio, el día después de Navidad, recogían en **boxes** (cajas) las propinas que los clientes del taller de su maestro les daban. Antiguamente se denominaba **Christmas box** a la paga navideña que recibían los empleados.

boxing glove *n* guante *m* de boxeo **boxing match** *n* partido *m* de boxeo **boxing ring** *n* ring *m*

box number *n* (*at a newspaper*) (número *m* de) referencia *f*; (*at the post office*) apartado *m* de correos, apartado *m* postal *Méx*, casilla *f* postal *CSur* **box office** *n* taquilla *f*, boletería *f AmL*

boy [bɔɪ] I. *n* 1. (*child*) niño *m* 2. (*young man*) chico *m*, muchacho *m*, chamaco, -a *m*, *f Méx*, pibe *m Arg* 3. (*son*) hijo *m*, chico *m* 4. (*servant*) criado *m*, mozo *m* 5. (*boyfriend*) novio *m* ►**the old ~ network** el amiguismo; **the ~s in** blue *inf* la policía; **~s will be ~s** así son los chicos [*o* niños] II. *interj* (oh) ~! ¡vaya!

boycott ['bɔɪkɒt, *Am:* -kaːt] I. *vt* boicotear II. *n* boicot *m*

boyfriend ['bɔɪfrend] *n* novio *m*

boyhood ['bɔɪhʊd] *n no pl* niñez *f*

boyish ['bɔɪɪʃ] *adj* (*woman*) de chico; (*enthusiasm*) de niño

Boy Scout *n* boy scout *m*

Bq *abbr of* **becquerel** Bq

BR [ˌbiːˈɑr, *Am:* -ˈɑːr] *n abbr of* **British Rail** compañía ferroviaria británica

bra [brɑː] *n* sujetador *m*, brasier *m Col*, *Méx*, corpiño *m RíoPl*

brace [breɪs] I. *vt* 1. (*prepare*) **to ~ oneself for sth** prepararse para algo 2. (*support: wall*) reforzar II. *n* 1. (*for teeth*) aparato(s) *m(pl)* 2. (*for the back*) aparato *m* ortopédico 3. *pl*, *Aus*, *Brit* (*suspenders*) tirantes *mpl*, tiradores *mpl RíoPl* 4. *pl*, *Am* (*callipers*) corrector *m*

bracelet ['breɪslɪt] *n* pulsera *f*

bracken ['brækn] *n no pl* helechos *mpl*

bracket ['brækɪt] I. *n pl* TYPO (*round*) paréntesis *m inv*; **in ~s** entre paréntesis; **angled ~** corchete *m* agudo; **curly ~** llave *f*; **square ~** corchete *m* II. *n* 1. (*category*) categoría *f*; **age ~** grupo *m* etario; **income ~** nivel *m* de ingresos; **tax ~** banda *f* impositiva 2. (*for a shelf*) soporte *m* III. *vt* 1. TYPO poner entre paréntesis 2. (*include*) agrupar; **to ~ sb with sb else** equiparar a alguien con alguien

brackish ['brækɪʃ] *adj* salobre

brag [bræg] <-gg-> *inf* I. *vi* fanfarronear; **to ~ about sth** alardear de algo II. *vt* **to ~ that ...** hacer alarde [*o* jactarse] de que...

braid [breɪd] I. *n* 1. *no pl* FASHION galón *m* 2. *Am* (*plait*) trenza *f*, chongo *m Méx*, chapeca *f Arg* II. *vt*, *vi Am* (*plait*) trenzar

Braille [breɪl] *n no pl* braille *m*

brain [breɪn] I. *n* 1. (*organ*) cerebro *m* 2. *pl* (*substance*) sesos *mpl* 3. (*intelligence*) cerebro *m*; **to have ~s** ser inteligente 4. *inf* (*intelligent person*) cerebro *m*, lumbrera *f*; **the best ~s** los mejores cerebros ►**to beat one's ~s out** *inf* estrujarse el cerebro; **to blow sb's**

~s out *inf* levantar la tapa de los sesos a alguien; **to have sth on the ~** *inf* estar obsesionado con algo; **to pick sb's ~s** *inf* hacer preguntas a alguien; **to rack one's ~** devanarse los sesos II. *vt inf* romper la crisma a

brainchild ['breɪntʃaɪld] *n no pl* creación *f*

brain damage *n* lesión *f* cerebral **brain-dead** *adj* 1. MED clínicamente muerto, -a 2. *fig* subnormal **brain death** *n* muerte *f* clínica [*o* cerebral] **brain drain** *n no pl* fuga *f* de cerebros

brainless ['breɪnləs] *adj* estúpido, -a

brain scan *n* exploración *f* cerebral mediante escáner

brainstorm ['breɪnstɔːm, *Am:* -stɔːrm] I. *vi* hacer un brainstorming II. *vt* hacer un brainstorming sobre [*o* de] III. *n* 1. *Brit*, *inf* (*confusion*) **she had a ~** se le cruzaron los cables 2. *Am* (*great idea*) idea *f* brillante

brainstorming ['breɪnˌstɔːmɪŋ, *Am:* -ˌstɔːr-] *n no pl* brainstorming *m*

brains trust *n* grupo *m* de peritos

brain tumor *n Am*, **brain tumour** *n* tumor *m* cerebral

brainwash ['breɪnwɒʃ, *Am:* -waːʃ-] *vt* lavar el cerebro a

brainwashing ['breɪnwɒʃɪŋ, *Am:* -waːʃ-] *n no pl* lavado *m* de cerebro

brainwave ['breɪnweɪv] *n inf* idea *f* brillante, lamparazo *m Col*; **she had a ~** tuvo una idea genial, tuvo un lamparazo *Col*, se le prendió el foco *Méx*, se le prendió la lamparilla *RíoPl*

brainwork *n* trabajo *m* intelectual

brainy ['breɪni] <-ier, -iest> *adj* inteligente

braise [breɪz] *vt* estofar

brake [breɪk] I. *n* freno *m*; **to apply the ~s** frenar; **to put a ~ on sth** *fig* poner freno a algo II. *vi* frenar

brake block *n* pastilla *f* del freno **brake fluid** *n* AUTO líquido *m* de frenos **brake shoe** *n* AUTO zapata *f* del freno

braking *n no pl* frenado *m*

braking distance *n* distancia *f* de frenado

bramble ['bræmbl] *n* 1. (*bush*) zarza *f* 2. (*fruit*) zarzamora *f*

bran [bræn] *n no pl* salvado *m*

branch [brɑːntʃ, *Am:* bræntʃ] I. *n* 1. (*of a tree*) rama *f* 2. (*of a railway, river, road*) ramal *m* 3. (*office: of a company, bank, library*) sucursal *f*; (*of a union, government department*) delegación *f* 4. (*subdivision*) rama *f*; **the ~es of learning** las ramas del saber II. *vi* 1. (*tree*) echar ramas 2. (*river, road*) bifurcarse

◆**branch off** *vi* 1. (*start*) bifurcarse 2. (*digress*) **to ~ from a subject** salirse de un tema

◆**branch out** *vi* diversificarse; **to ~ on one's own** establecerse por su cuenta

branch line *n* ramal *m* **branch office** *n* sucursal *f*

brand [brænd] I. *n* 1. COM marca *f* 2. *fig* clase *f*; **do you like his ~ of humour?** ¿te gusta su

tipo de humor? **3.**(*mark*) hierro *m* **II.** *vt*
1.(*label*) **to** ~ **sth/sb** (**as**) **sth** tachar algo/a alguien de algo; **to** ~ **sb a liar** tildar a alguien de
mentiroso **2.**(*cattle, slave*) marcar con hierro
candente
brandish ['brændɪʃ] *vt* blandir
brand name ['brændneɪm] *n* marca *f*
brand-new [ˌbrænd'nju:] *adj inv* completamente nuevo, -a; ~ **baby** recién nacido *m*
brandy ['brændi] <-ies> *n* brandy *m;*
French ~ coñac *m*
brandy snap *n* barquillo dulce que a veces se
sirve relleno de nata
brash [bræʃ] *adj* **1.**(*cocky: attitude*) chulo, -a
2.(*gaudy: colours*) chillón, -ona
brass [brɑːs, *Am:* bræs] *n* **1.** *no pl* (*metal*)
latón *m* **2.**(*engraving: in a church*) placa *f*
conmemorativa (*de latón*) **3.** + *pl/sing vb* MUS
the ~ los metales
brass band *n* banda *f* de música, orfeón *m*
Chile **brass plate** *n* placa *f* conmemorativa
brass section *n* MUS **the** ~ los metales
brassware *n no pl* latonería *f*
brassy ['brɑːsi, *Am:* 'bræsi] <-ier, -iest> *adj*
1.(*of brass*) de latón; ~ **colour** color *m* dorado
2.(*voice*) estridente **3.**(*cocky*) ordinario, -a
brat [bræt] *n inf* mocoso, -a *m, f;* **he is a**
spoilt ~ es un niño mimado, es un sute *Col,*
Ven
bravado [brə'vɑːdəʊ, *Am:* -doʊ] *n no pl*
bravuconada *f*
brave [breɪv] **I.** *adj* valiente **II.** *vt* afrontar
bravery ['breɪvəri] *n no pl* valentía *f*
brawl [brɔːl, *Am:* brɑːl] **I.** *n* pelea *f,* bulla *f*
AmL **II.** *vi* pelearse
brawling *n no pl* alboroto *m*
brawn [brɔːn, *Am:* brɑːn] *n no pl* **1.**(*physical strength*) fuerza *f* muscular **2.** *Aus, Brit*
GASTR cabeza *f* de jabalí
brawny ['brɔːni, *Am:* brɑː-] <-ier, -iest> *adj*
musculoso, -a
bray [breɪ] **I.** *vi* rebuznar; ~**ing laugh** risa *f*
estridente **II.** *n* rebuzno *m*
brazen ['breɪzn] *adj* descarado, -a; ~ **lie**
mentira *f* descarada
◆**brazen out** *vt* **to brazen it out** defenderse
con argumentos descarados
brazier ['breɪziəʳ, *Am:* -ʒɚ] *n* brasero *m*
Brazil [brə'zɪl] *n* Brasil *m*
Brazilian [brə'zɪliən, *Am:* -jən] **I.** *n* brasileño, -a *m, f* **II.** *adj* brasileño, -a
Brazil nut *n* coquito *m* del Brasil
breach [briːtʃ] **I.** *n* **1.**(*infraction: of a regulation*) infracción *f,* violación *f;* (*of an agreement*) ruptura *f;* (*of confidence*) abuso *m;* (*of
a contract*) incumplimiento *m;* **to be in** ~ **of**
the law infringir la ley **2.**(*estrangement*) ruptura *f* **3.**(*opening*) brecha *f* **II.** *vt* **1.**(*break:
law*) infringir, violar; (*agreement*) romper;
(*contract*) incumplir; (*security*) poner en peligro **2.**(*infiltrate*) abrir una brecha en
breach of the peace *n no pl* alteración *f* del
orden público

bread [bred] *n* **1.** pan *m;* **a loaf of** ~ un pan
2. *inf* (*money*) pasta *f* ▶**to cast one's** ~ **upon**
the waters *form* hacer el bien sin mirar a
quien; **to want one's** ~ **buttered on both**
sides querer el oro y el moro, querer la chan-
cha y los cinco reales *RíoPl;* **to earn one's**
(**daily**) ~ *form* ganarse el pan (de cada día)
bread and butter *n no pl* sustento *m;* ~
issues asuntos *mpl* básicos
breadbasket *n* **1.**(*container*) panera *f*
2.(*region*) granero *m* **breadbin** *n* panera *f*
breadcrumb ['bredkrʌm] *n* **1.**(*small fragment*) miga *f* (de pan) **2.** *pl* GASTR pan *m* rallado
breadth ['bretθ] *n no pl* **1.** anchura *f;* **to be 5**
metres in ~ tener 5 metros de ancho **2.** *fig*
amplitud *f*
breadwinner ['bred,wɪnəʳ, *Am:* -ɚ] *n*
sostén *m*
break [breɪk] **I.** *n* **1.**(*crack, gap*) grieta *f*
2.(*escape*) fuga *f* **3.**(*interruption*) interrupción *f;* (*commercial*) pausa *f* **4.**(*rest period*)
descanso *m* **5.** *Brit* (*pause in school*) recreo *m*
6.(*vacation*) vacaciones *fpl* **7. the** ~ **of day** el
amanecer **8.**(*divergence*) ruptura *f* **9.**(*opportunity*) oportunidad *f* **10.** SPORTS saque *m* ▶**to**
make a clean ~ cortar por lo sano; **give me a**
~**!** ¡déjame en paz! **II.**<**broke, broken**> *vt*
1.(*shatter, damage, fracture*) romper; **to** ~ **sth**
into pieces hacer algo añicos; **to** ~ **the sonic**
[*o* **sound**] **barrier** AVIAT romper la barrera del
sonido **2.**(*interrupt: circuit*) cortar; (*silence*)
romper **3.**(*put an end to: deadlock, impasse*)
salir de; (*peace, silence*) romper; (*strike*)
poner fin a; (*give up: habit*) dejar; **to** ~ **sb of a**
habit quitar a alguien una costumbre **4.**(*in
tennis*) **to** ~ **sb's service** romper el servicio a
alguien **5.**(*violate: agreement*) incumplir;
(*date*) no acudir a; (*treaty*) violar **6.**(*decipher*)
descifrar **7.**(*make public*) revelar **8.**(*tell*)
decir; **to** ~ **the news to sb** dar la noticia a alguien; ~ **it to me gently!** *iron* ¡dímelo con
tacto! **9.**(*make change for*) cambiar; **to** ~ **a**
bill cambiar un billete **10.** MIL **to** ~ **formation**
romper filas **III.**<**broke, broken**> *vi*
1.(*shatter or separate*) romperse; **to** ~ **into**
pieces hacerse añicos **2.**(*interrupt*) **shall we**
~ (**off**) **for lunch?** ¿paramos para comer?
3.(*strike: wave*) romper **4.**(*change of voice*)
the boy's voice is ~**ing** la voz del niño está
cambiando **5.**(*under the strain*) **her voice**
broke (**with emotion**) se le entrecortó la voz
(de la emoción) **6.** METEO (*weather*) cambiar;
(*dawn, day*) romper, despuntar **7.**(*in pool,
snooker*) abrir el juego **8.**(*giving birth*) **her**
waters broke on the way to hospital rompió aguas en el camino al hospital ▶**to** ~ **even**
salir sin ganar ni perder; **to** ~ **free** liberarse; **to**
~ **loose** soltarse
◆**break away** *vi* (*piece, from friends*) desprenderse; (*boat*) soltarse; POL (*faction, region*)
escindirse
◆**break down I.** *vi* **1.**(*stop working*) dejar

de funcionar; (*car, machine*) averiarse **2.** (*marriage*) romperse; (*negotiation*) fracasar **3.** (*physically, psychologically*) derrumbarse **4.** (*decompose*) descomponerse **II.** *vt* **1.** (*door*) echar abajo **2.** (*opposition, resistance*) acabar con **3.** CHEM descomponer **4.** (*separate into parts: sentence*) separar, dividir; (*process*) dividir

◆**break forth** *vi* to ~ **into song** ponserse a cantar

◆**break in** **I.** *vi* **1.** (*enter: burglar*) entrar (para robar) **2.** (*butt in, interrupt*) interrumpir; to ~ **on sb** interrumpir a alguien **II.** *vt* **1.** (*make comfortable: shoes*) ablandar **2.** *Am* AUTO hacer el rodaje de **3.** (*tame*) domar

◆**break into** *vi* **1.** (*enter: car*) entrar (para robar) **2.** (*start doing*) to ~ **laughter/tears** echarse a reir/llorar; to ~ **song** ponerse a cantar **3.** (*get involved in: business*) introducirse en

◆**break off** **I.** *vt* **1.** (*detach*) partir **2.** (*end: relationship*) romper **II.** *vi* **1.** (*become detached*) desprenderse **2.** (*stop speaking*) callarse

◆**break out** *vi* **1.** (*escape*) escaparse; (*of a prison*) fugarse **2.** (*begin: war, storm, laughing*) estallar **3.** to ~ **in a sweat** empezar a sudar; **she broke out in a rash** le salió un sarpullido; **he broke out in spots** le salieron granos

◆**break through** **I.** *vi* penetrar; (*sun*) salir **II.** *vt* atravesar; to ~ **a crowd** abrirse paso entre una multitud

◆**break up** **I.** *vt* **1.** (*end: meeting, strike*) terminar; **break it up, you two!** *inf* ¡vosotros dos, basta ya! **2.** (*split up: coalition, union*) disolver; (*collection*) dividir; (*family*) separar; (*gang, monopoly, cartel*) desarticular **3.** *Am* (*make laugh*) to **break sb up** hacer reír a alguien **II.** *vi* **1.** (*end a relationship*) separarse **2.** (*come to an end: marriage*) fracasar; (*meeting*) terminar **3.** (*fall apart: coalition*) fracasar; (*ship*) irse a pique **4.** *Brit* SCHOOL terminar

breakable ['breɪkəbl] *adj* frágil

breakage ['breɪkɪdʒ] *n* roturas *fpl*; **all ~s must be paid for** el cliente debe pagar lo que se rompa

breakaway ['breɪkəweɪ] *adj* POL disidente

breakdown ['breɪkdaʊn] *n* **1.** (*collapse: of negotiations, relationship*) ruptura *f* **2.** TECH avería *f* **3.** (*division*) división *f* **4.** (*decomposition*) descomposición *f* **5.** PSYCH (**nervous**) ~ crisis *f inv* nerviosa

breakdown lorry *n Brit* grúa *f* **breakdown service** *n* servicio *m* de asistencia en carretera

breaker ['breɪkə', *Am:* -kə-] *n* **1.** (*wave*) gran ola *f* **2.** *inf* RADIO radioaficionado, -a *m, f*

breakfast ['brekfəst] **I.** *n* desayuno *m;* to **have** ~ desayunar **II.** *vi form* desayunar

breaking and entering *n* allanamiento *m* de morada **breaking point** *n* límite *m;* to **reach** ~ llegar al límite

breakneck ['breɪknek] *adj* vertiginoso, -a; **at** ~ **speed** a una velocidad vertiginosa

breakout ['breɪkaʊt] *n* fuga *f*

breakthrough ['breɪkθruː] *n* **1.** (*in science*) adelanto *m* **2.** MIL avance *m*

breakup ['breɪkʌp] *n* (*of marriage*) separación *f;* (*of group, empire*) disolución *f;* (*of talks*) fracaso *m;* (*of family, physical structure*) desintegración *f*

breakwater ['breɪkwɔːtə', *Am:* -ˌwɑːt̬ə-] *n* rompeolas *m inv,* molo *m Chile*

breast [brest] *n* **1.** ANAT pecho *m* **2.** GASTR pechuga *f*

breastbone ['brestbəʊn, *Am:* -boʊn] *n* **1.** ANAT esternón *m* **2.** GASTR hueso *m* de la pechuga

breast cancer *n no pl* cáncer *m* de mama **breastfeed** ['brestfiːd] *vt* amamantar

breast pocket *n* bolsillo *m* superior

breaststroke ['breststrəʊk, *Am:* -stroʊk] *n no pl* (estilo *m*) braza *f;* to do (**the**) ~ nadar a braza

breath [breθ] *n* aliento *m;* to **be out of** ~ estar sin aliento; to **be short of** ~ ahogarse; to **catch one's** ~ (*stop breathing*) quedarse sin respiración; (*return to normal breathing*) volver a respirar; to **draw** ~ respirar; to **hold one's** ~ *a. fig* contener la respiración; to **mutter sth under one's** ~ decir algo entre dientes; to **take a deep** ~ respirar hondo; to **go out for a** ~ **of fresh air** salir para que le dé a uno el aire; **there wasn't a** ~ **of air** no había ni un soplo de viento ►**in the same** ~ a continuación; to **take sb's** ~ **away** dejar a alguien sin habla

breathalyse *vt Aus, Brit,* **breathalyze** ['breθəlaɪz] *vt Am* hacer la prueba de la alcoholemia a

breathalyser® *n,* **breathalyzer**® *n* alcoholímetro *m*

breathe [briːð] **I.** *vi* respirar; to ~ **again** [*o* **easily**] respirar tranquilo; to ~ **through one's nose** respirar por la nariz; to ~ **a wine** ~ dejar respirar un vino **II.** *vt* **1.** (*exhale*) to ~ **alcohol** echar aliento a alcohol; to ~ **smoke on sb** echar el humo a alguien **2.** (*whisper*) musitar **3.** (*let out: sigh*) dejar escapar

breather ['briːðə', *Am:* -ðə-] *n* descanso *m,* respiro *m;* to **take a** ~ descansar

breathing *n no pl* respiración *f*

breathing apparatus *n* respirador *m* **breathing room** *n no pl,* **breathing space** *n no pl* respiro *m*

breathless ['breθlɪs] *adj* (*person*) sin aliento; (*words*) entrecortado, -a

breathtaking ['breθteɪkɪŋ] *adj* imponente, impresionante

breath test *n* prueba *f* de la alcoholemia

bred [bred] *pt, pp of* **breed**

breech [briːtʃ] *n* recámara *f*

breeches ['brɪtʃɪz] *npl* **1.** (*knee-length trousers*) pantalones *mpl* bombachos; **riding** ~ pantalones *mpl* de montar, zamarros *mpl*

Col, Ecua, Ven **2.** *inf* (*trousers*) pantalones *mpl*
breed [briːd] **I.** *vt* <bred, bred> **1.** criar **2.** (*disease, violence*) engendrar, generar **II.** *vi* <bred, bred> reproducirse; (*violence*) generarse **III.** *n* **1.** ZOOL raza *f*; BOT variedad *f* **2.** *inf* (*type of person*) tipo *m*; **a dying ~** una especie en vías de extinción
breeder ['briːdəʳ, *Am:* -dɚ] *n* (*of animals*) criador(a) *m(f)*; (*of plants*) cultivador(a) *m(f)*
breeding *n no pl* **1.** (*of animals*) cría *f* **2.** *fig* (*upbringing*) educación *f*
breeding ground *n fig* caldo *m* de cultivo
breeze [briːz] **I.** *n* **1.** (*wind*) brisa *f* **2.** *inf* (*easy task*) **to be a ~** ser pan comido, ser un bollo *RíoPl* **3.** *no pl* (*cinders*) cisco *m* de carbón y leña **II.** *vi Am* **to ~ into the room** entrar en la habitación como Pedro por su casa
breeze block [briːz blɒk] *n Brit* bloque *m* de cemento
breezy ['briːzi] <-ier, -iest> *adj* **1.** (*windy*) ventoso, -a; **it is ~** hace aire **2.** (*jovial*) alegre
breve [briːv] *n* MUS breve *f*
breviary ['briːvɪəri] <-ies> *n* breviario *m*
brevity ['brevəti, *Am:* -t̬i] *n no pl* **1.** (*shortness*) brevedad *f* **2.** (*conciseness*) concisión *f*
brew [bruː] **I.** *n* **1.** (*mixture*) brebaje *m* **2.** *Brit, inf* **to have a ~** tomar un té **II.** *vi* **1.** (*beer*) fermentar **2.** (*tea*) hacerse; **to let the tea ~** dejar reposar el té **3.** (*storm, trouble*) avecinarse; **there's something ~ing** se está cociendo algo **III.** *vt* (*beer*) elaborar; (*tea*) hacer
◆**brew up** *vi* **1.** *Brit, inf* (*make tea*) hacer un té **2.** (*develop: storm, trouble*) avecinarse
brewer ['bruːəʳ, *Am:* -ɚ] *n* cervecero, -a *m, f*
brewery ['bruːəri, *Am:* 'bruːɚi] <-ies> *n* **1.** (*company*) cervecería *f*, cervecera *f Méx* **2.** (*place*) fábrica *f* de cerveza
briar ['braɪəʳ, *Am:* 'braɪɚ] *n* brezo *m*
bribe [braɪb] **I.** *vt* sobornar; **to ~ sb into doing sth** sobornar a alguien para que haga algo **II.** *n* soborno *m*; **to take a ~** dejarse sobornar, aceptar un soborno
bribery ['braɪbəri] *n no pl* soborno *m*, coima *f Perú, CSur*; mordida *f Méx*
bric-a-brac ['brɪkəbræk] *n no pl* baratijas *fpl*
brick [brɪk] *n* **1.** (*block*) ladrillo *m* **2.** *inf* **~s and mortar** inmueble *m*; **to invest in ~s and mortar** invertir en bienes inmuebles ►**you can't make ~s without straw** *prov* sin paja no hay ladrillos
◆**brick in** *vt* tapiar
◆**brick up** *vt* tapiar
brickie ['brɪki] *n Aus, Brit, inf*, **bricklayer** ['brɪkˌleɪəʳ, *Am:* -ɚ] *n* albañil *mf*
brick wall *n* pared *f* (de ladrillos) ►**to be banging one's head against a ~** *inf* llevar todas las de perder
brickwork ['brɪkwɜːk, *Am:* -wɜːrk] *n no pl* enladrillado *m*
brickworks *n*, **brickyard** ['brɪkjɑːd, *Am:* -jɑːrd] *n* fábrica *f* de ladrillos
bridal ['braɪdəl] *adj* (*suite*) nupcial; (*shop*)

para novias; (*gown*) de novia
bride ['braɪd] *n* novia *f*
bridegroom ['braɪdgrʊm, *Am:* -gruːm] *n* novio *m*
bridesmaid ['braɪdzmeɪd] *n* dama *f* de honor
bridge [brɪdʒ] **I.** *n* **1.** *a.* ARCHIT, MED, MUS puente *m* **2.** ANAT caballete *m* **3.** NAUT puente *m* (de mando) **4.** *no pl* GAMES bridge *m* **II.** *vt* **1.** (*build a bridge over*) construir un puente sobre **2.** (*decrease the difference*) salvar
bridging loan ['brɪdʒɪŋˈləʊn, *Am:* -ˈloʊn] *n Aus, Brit* préstamo *m* puente, crédito *m* puente
bridle ['braɪdl] **I.** *n* brida *f* **II.** *vt* (*horse*) embridar **III.** *vi* **to ~ at sth** molestarse por algo
bridle path *n*, **bridleway** *n* camino *m* de herradura
brief [briːf] **I.** *adj* **1.** (*short*) corto, -a **2.** (*concise*) conciso, -a, sucinto, -a; **be ~!** ¡sé breve!; **in ~** en resumen **II.** *n* **1.** *Aus, Brit* (*instructions*) instrucciones *fpl* **2.** LAW escrito *m* **3.** *pl* (*underpants: man's*) calzoncillos *mpl*, slip *m*; (*woman's*) bragas *fpl* **III.** *vt* **1.** (*inform*) informar **2.** (*give instructions to*) dar instrucciones a
briefcase ['briːfkeɪs] *n* maletín *m*
briefing *n* **1.** (*instructions*) instrucciones *fpl* **2.** (*information session*) reunión *f* informativa
briefly *adv* **1.** (*for short time*) por poco tiempo **2.** (*concisely*) brevemente; **~, ...** en resumen,...
briefness *n no pl* brevedad *f*
brier ['braɪəʳ, *Am:* 'braɪɚ] *n* brezo *m*
brigade [brɪˈgeɪd] *n* MIL brigada *f*
brigadier [ˌbrɪgəˈdɪəʳ] *n Brit*, **brigadier general** [ˌbrɪgədɪrˈdʒenərəl] *n Am* MIL general *m* de brigada
bright [braɪt] **I.** *adj* **1.** (*light*) brillante, fuerte; (*room*) con mucha luz; (*star*) brillante; **a ~ day** un día soleado **2.** (*colour*) vivo, -a, fuerte; **to go ~ red** ponerse como un tomate **3.** (*intelligent: person*) inteligente; (*idea*) brillante **4.** (*cheerful, happy*) vivaracho, -a **5.** (*promising: future*) prometedor(a) ►**to look on the ~ side of sth** mirar [*o* ver] el lado bueno de algo; **to get up ~ and early** levantarse tempranito **II.** *n pl, Am* AUTO (luces *fpl*) largas *fpl*, (luces *fpl*) altas *fpl And*
◆**brighten** (**up**) ['braɪtən('ʌp)] **I.** *vt* **1.** (*make brighter*) iluminar **2.** (*become cheerful*) alegrar, animar **II.** *vi* **1.** (*become brighter*) hacerse más brillante; (*weather*) mejorar **2.** (*become cheerful*) animarse, alegrarse; (*eyes, face*) iluminarse **3.** (*become more promising*) mejorar
brightness *n no pl* **1.** brillo *m*; (*of sound*) claridad *f* **2.** (*cheerfulness*) alegría *f* **3.** (*cleverness*) inteligencia *f*
brill¹ ['brɪl] *adj Aus, Brit* genial
brill² ['brɪl] *n* rodaballo *m* menor
brilliance ['brɪlɪəns] *n no pl* **1.** (*cleverness*) brillantez *f* **2.** (*brightness*) resplandor *m*

brilliant ['brɪlɪənt, *Am:* -jənt] I. *adj* 1. (*shining: colour*) brillante; (*sunlight, smile*) radiante; (*water*) resplandeciente 2. (*clever*) brillante; (*idea*) genial 3. *Brit, inf* (*excellent*) fantástico, -a; ~ **success** gran éxito II. *interj Brit, inf* genial

brim [brɪm] I. *n* 1. (*of a hat*) ala *f* 2. (*of a vessel*) borde *m;* **to fill sth to the** ~ llenar algo hasta el borde II. *vi* <-mm-> **to** ~ **with happiness/energy** rebosar de felicidad/energía
◆**brim over** *vi a. fig* rebosar

brimful [ˌbrɪmˈfʊl] *adj* repleto, -a; (*of life, confidence*) rebosante

brine [braɪn] *n no pl* GASTR salmuera *f;* (*sea water*) agua *f* salada [*o* de mar]

bring [brɪŋ] <brought, brought> *vt* 1. (*come with, carry*) traer; ~ **her here!** ¡tráela aquí!; **to** ~ **sb in** hacer pasar a alguien; **to** ~ **sth in** entrar algo; **to** ~ **news** traer noticias 2. (*take*) llevar; **this subject** ~**s me to the second part** este tema me lleva a la segunda parte; **to** ~ **sth/sb with oneself** llevar algo/a alguien consigo 3. (*cause to come, cause to happen*) causar, traer; **to** ~ **poverty/ fame to a town** traer pobreza/fama a un pueblo; **to** ~ **sb luck** traer suerte a alguien 4. LAW interponer; **to** ~ **an action** (**against sb**) interponer una demanda (contra alguien); **to** ~ **a complaint against sb** formular un queja contra alguien 5. (*force*) **to** ~ **oneself to do sth** resignarse a hacer algo 6. FIN dar
◆**bring about** *vt* 1. (*cause to happen*) provocar 2. (*achieve*) lograr
◆**bring along** *vt* traer
◆**bring back** *vt* 1. (*reintroduce*) volver a introducir 2. (*call to mind*) recordar 3. (*return*) devolver
◆**bring down** *vt* 1. (*reduce: benefits, level*) reducir; (*temperature*) hacer bajar 2. (*fell: tree*) talar; (*person*) derribar; (*dictator, government*) derrocar 3. (*knock down*) tirar, echar abajo 4. (*make sad*) deprimir
◆**bring forth** *vt insep, form* procrear, dar a luz
◆**bring forward** *vt* 1. (*reschedule for an earlier date*) adelantar 2. (*present for discussion*) presentar 3. FIN (*carry over*) transferir
◆**bring in** *vt* 1. (*introduce*) introducir; (*bill*) presentar 2. (*call in*) llamar 3. FIN (*earn*) **to** ~ **a profit** reportar un beneficio 4. (*reap*) cosechar 5. LAW (*produce*) **to** ~ **a verdict of not guilty** pronunciar un veredicto de inocente
◆**bring off** *vt inf* lograr
◆**bring on** *vt* 1. (*cause to occur*) provocar; (*shame, dishonour, discredit*) causar, acarrear; **to bring sth on oneself** buscarse algo uno mismo 2. (*improve*) mejorar
◆**bring out** *vt* 1. COM introducir (en el mercado); (*book*) publicar 2. (*reveal*) **to** ~ **sth in sb** realzar algo de alguien 3. *Aus, Brit* (*encourage*) **to bring sb out** hacer que alguien pierda la timidez
◆**bring over** *vt* 1. (*person*) convertir, con-

vencer 2. (*take with*) traer
◆**bring round** *vt* 1. MED hacer volver en sí 2. (*persuade*) convencer
◆**bring to** *vt always sep* reanimar
◆**bring up** *vt* 1. (*child*) criar; **to bring sb up to be/to do sth** educar a alguien para que sea/haga algo 2. (*mention*) sacar 3. *inf* (*vomit*) vomitar ▶**to bring sb up short** dejar helado a alguien

brink [brɪŋk] *n no pl* borde *m;* **to drive sb to the** ~ **of sth** llevar a alguien al borde de algo; **to be on the** ~ **of bankruptcy/war** estar al borde de la bancarrota/la guerra

briny ['braɪni] I. <-ier, -iest> *adj liter* salobre II. *n iron* **the** ~ el mar

briquet(te) [brɪˈket] *n* briqueta *f*

brisk [brɪsk] *adj* 1. (*fast: pace*) rápido, -a; (*walk*) a paso ligero 2. (*refreshing: breeze*) fresco, -a 3. (*manner, voice*) enérgico, -a

briskness *n no pl* (*of pace*) brío *m;* (*of trading*) dinamismo *m;* (*of business*) eficiencia *f*

bristle ['brɪsl] I. *n* (*of an animal*) cerda *f;* (*on the face*) barba *f* II. *vi* 1. (*fur, hair*) erizarse, ponerse de punta 2. *fig* **to** ~ **with anger** enfurecerse

bristly ['brɪsli] <-ier, -iest> *adj* hirsuto, -a

Brit [brɪt] *n inf* británico, -a *m, f*

Britain ['brɪtən] *n* Gran Bretaña *f*

British ['brɪtɪʃ, *Am:* 'brɪt̬-] I. *adj* británico, -a; ~ **English** inglés *m* británico II. *n pl* **the** ~ los británicos

British Columbia *n* Columbia *f* Británica
British Isles *n* **the** ~ las Islas Británicas

Briton ['brɪtn] *n* británico, -a *m, f*

Brittany ['brɪtæni] *n* Bretaña *f*

brittle ['brɪtl, *Am:* 'brɪt̬-] *adj* 1. (*fragile*) quebradizo, -a 2. (*irritable*) susceptible

broach [brəʊtʃ, *Am:* broʊtʃ] I. *vt* (*mention*) mencionar II. *n Am* broche *m*

broad [brɔːd, *Am:* brɑːd] I. *adj* 1. (*wide*) ancho, -a 2. (*spacious*) amplio, -a 3. (*obvious*) **a** ~ **hint** una clara indirecta 4. (*general*) general 5. (*wide-ranging*) amplio, -a; ~ **interests** intereses diversos 6. (*liberal*) liberal; **a** ~ **mind** una mente abierta 7. (*strong: accent*) cerrado, -a II. *n Am, inf* tipa *f*

broad bean *n* haba *f*

broadcast ['brɔːdkɑːst, *Am:* 'brɑːdkæst] I. *n* RADIO programa *m* (de radio); TV programa *m* (de televisión); (*of a concert*) emisión *f* II. *vi,v* <broadcast *Am:* broadcasted, broadcast *Am:* broadcasted> transmitir, emitir III. *vt* <broadcast *Am:* broadcasted, broadcast *Am:* broadcasted> TV transmitir; RADIO emitir; (*rumour*) difundir

broadcaster *n* (*person*) locutor(a) *m(f);* (*station*) emisora *f*

broadcasting *n no pl* TV transmisión *f;* RADIO radiodifusión *f*

broadcasting station *n* emisora *f*

broaden ['brɔːdn, *Am:* 'brɑː-] I. *vi* (*interests*) ampliarse; (*valley*) ensancharse II. *vt* (*horizons*) ampliar; **to** ~ **the mind** abrir la mente

broadly ['brɔːdli] *adv* 1. (*generally*) en líneas generales 2. (*widely: smile*) de oreja a oreja

broad-minded [ˌbrɔːd'maɪndɪd, *Am:* ˌbrɑːd-] *adj* con mentalidad abierta

broadsheet ['brɔːdʃiːt, *Am:* ˌbrɑːd-] *n Aus, Brit:* periódico de formato grande

broadside ['brɔːdsaɪd, *Am:* ˌbrɑːd-] *n* 1. NAUT, MIL andanada *f* 2. (*verbal attack*) invectiva *f*, ataque *m* verbal

> **Broadway** es el nombre que recibe una larga calle de New York City. En esta calle se localiza el conocido barrio de **Broadway** famoso por su intensa actividad teatral. Prácticamente todas las piezas dramáticas americanas de importancia se representan allí. Aquellas que, bien por tratarse de producciones baratas, bien por ser de carácter experimental no se representan, reciben el nombre de **off-Broadway plays**

brocade [brə'keɪd, *Am:* broʊ-] *n no pl* brocado *m*

broccoli ['brɒkəli, *Am:* 'brɑːkl-] *n no pl* brócoli *m*, brécol *m*

brochure ['brəʊʃəʳ, *Am:* broʊ'ʃʊr] *n* folleto *m*

brogue¹ [brəʊg, *Am:* broʊg] *n* (*shoe*) zapato bajo y resistente, normalmente para hombre

brogue² [brəʊg, *Am:* broʊg] *n* LING acento *m* irlandés

broil [brɔɪl] *vt Am* asar a la parrilla

broiler ['brɔɪləʳ, *Am:* -lə-] *n* 1. (*chicken*) pollo *m* para asar, pollo *m* parrillero *RíoPl*, broiler *m* *Chile* 2. *Am* (*grill*) parrilla *f*, grill *m*

broke [brəʊk, *Am:* broʊk] I. *pt of* break II. *adj inf* pelado, -a, planchado, -a *Chile* ►**to go** ~ *inf* arruinarse; **to go for** ~ *inf* jugarse el todo por el todo

broken ['brəʊkən, *Am:* 'broʊ-] I. *pp of* break II. *adj* 1. (*damaged*) roto, -a; ~ **heart** corazón destrozado 2. LING **in** ~ **English** en un inglés incorrecto 3. (*interrupted*) interrumpido, -a

broken-down [ˌbrəʊkən'daʊn, *Am:* ˌbroʊ-] *adj* 1. TECH averiado, -a, en pana *Chile*, varado, -a *Col* 2. (*dilapidated: building*) ruinoso, -a

broken-hearted [ˌbrəʊkən'hɑːtɪd, *Am:* ˌbroʊkən'hɑrtɪd] *adj* destrozado, -a, deshecho, -a; **to die** ~ morir de pena

broker ['brəʊkəʳ, *Am:* 'broʊkə-] I. *n* 1. FIN corredor(a) *m(f)* de bolsa 2. (*of an agreement, marriage*) agente *mf* II. *vt* 1. FIN hacer corretaje de 2. (*agreement*) negociar

brokerage ['brəʊkərɪdʒ, *Am:* 'broʊ-] *n no pl* FIN 1. (*commission*) corretaje *m* 2. (*business*) agencia *f* de corredores de bolsa

brolly ['brɒli, *Am:* 'brɑːli] *n Aus, Brit, inf* paraguas *m inv*

bromide ['brəʊmaɪd, *Am:* 'broʊ-] *n* 1. CHEM bromuro *m* 2. (*platitude*) lugar *m* común,

tópico *m*

bromine ['brəʊmiːn, *Am:* 'broʊ-] *n no pl* bromo *m*

bronchi ['brɒŋkaɪ] *npl* bronquios *mpl*

bronchial ['brɒŋkɪəl, *Am:* 'brɑːŋ-] *adj* bronquial

bronchitis [brɒŋ'kaɪtɪs, *Am:* brɑːŋ'kaɪʧɪs] *n no pl* bronquitis *f*

bronze [brɒnz, *Am:* brɑːnz] I. *n* bronce *m* II. *adj* de bronce; (*hair*) dorado, -a; (*skin*) bronceado, -a

Bronze Age I. *n* **the** ~ la Edad de Bronce II. *adj* de la Edad de Bronce **bronze medal** *n* medalla *f* de bronce

brooch [brəʊʧ, *Am:* broʊʧ] *n* broche *m*

brood [bruːd] I. *n* 1. (*of mammals*) camada *f*; (*of birds*) nidada *f* 2. *iron* (*children*) prole *f* II. *vi* 1. (*reflect at length*) **to** ~ **over sth** dar vueltas a algo 2. (*hatch*) empollar

broody ['bruːdi] <-ier, -iest> *adj* 1. (*hen*) clueco, -a 2. (*motherly*) con sentimientos maternales 3. (*gloomy*) melancólico, -a

brook¹ [brʊk] *n* arroyo *m*

brook² [brʊk] *vt form* (*tolerate*) tolerar

broom [bruːm] *n* 1. (*brush*) escoba *f* 2. *no pl* BOT retama *f*, hiniesta *f* ►**a new** ~ **sweeps clean** *prov* escoba nueva barre bien *prov*

broomstick ['bruːmstɪk] *n* palo *m* de escoba

broth [brɒθ, *Am:* brɑː θ] *n no pl* caldo *m*

brothel ['brɒθl, *Am:* 'brɑːθl] *n* burdel *m*

brother ['brʌðəʳ, *Am:* -ə-] *n* 1. hermano *m* 2. *Am, inf* (*male friend*) colega *m*

brotherhood ['brʌðəhʊd, *Am:* '-ə--] *n + pl/ sing vb* 1. (*fellowship*) fraternidad *f* 2. (*organization*) hermandad *f* 3. REL cofradía *f*

brother-in-law ['brʌðərɪnlɔː, *Am:* -ə-lɑː] <brothers-in-law *Brit:* brother-in-laws> *n* cuñado *m*, concuño *m AmL*

brotherly ['brʌðəli, *Am:* -ə-li] *adj* fraternal

brought [brɔːt, *Am:* brɑːt] *pp, pt of* **bring**

brow [braʊ] *n* 1. *no pl, liter* (*forehead*) frente *f* 2. (*of a hill*) cima *f*

browbeat ['braʊbiːt] <browbeat, browbeaten> *vt* intimidar; **to** ~ **sb into doing sth** intimidar a alguien para que haga algo

brown [braʊn] I. *n* marrón *m* II. *adj* marrón; (*eyes, hair*) castaño, -a III. *vi* (*leaves*) amarillearse; (*person*) broncearse; GASTR dorarse IV. *vt* broncear; GASTR dorar

◆**brown off** *vt* **to be browned off** *inf* estar hasta las narices

brown bread *n* pan *m* integral

brownie ['braʊni] *n Am* bizcocho *m* de chocolate y nueces

brownish ['braʊnɪʃ] *adj* pardusco, -a

brown paper ['braʊn'peɪpəʳ, *Am:* -ə-] *n no pl* papel *m* de estraza **brown rice** *n no pl* arroz *m* integral

brownstone ['braʊnstəʊn, *Am:* -stoʊn] *n Am* 1. (*sandstone*) piedra *f* rojiza 2. (*house*) casa *f* de piedra rojiza

browse [braʊz] I. *vi* 1. (*skim*) **to** ~ **through**

sth echar un vistazo a algo; (*book, magazine*) hojear algo **2.** (*look around*) mirar **3.** (*graze*) pastar **II.** *n no pl* **1.** (*act of looking around*) **to go for a ~ around the shops** ir de tiendas **2.** (*act of skimming*) ojeada *f,* vistazo *m;* **to have a ~ through sth** echar una ojeada [*o* un vistazo] a algo; (*book, magazine*) hojear algo

browser [brauzə, *Am:* -ə·] *n* INFOR navegador *m*

bruise [bru:z] **I.** *n* morado *m,* moretón *m;* (*on fruit*) magulladura *f;* **to be covered in ~s** estar lleno de morados **II.** *vt* (*person*) contusionar; (*fruit*) magullar; *fig* (*hurt*) herir; **to ~ one's arm** hacerse morados [*o* un morado] en el brazo; **to ~ sb's feelings** herir los sentimientos de alguien **III.** *vi* (*fruit*) magullarse; **she ~s easily** le salen morados con mucha facilidad

bruiser ['bru:zə·, *Am:* -ə·] *n iron, inf* bestia *f*

brunch [brʌntʃ] *n* desayuno-almuerzo *m*

Brunei ['bru:naɪ] *n* Brunei *m*

brunette [bru:'net] *n* morena *f,* morocha *f CSur*

brunt [brʌnt] *n no pl* (*impact*) impacto *m;* **to bear the ~ of sth** aguantar lo más duro de algo

brush [brʌʃ] **I.** *n* **1.** (*for hair*) cepillo *m* **2.** (*broom*) escoba *f* **3.** (*for painting*) pincel *m;* (*bigger*) brocha *f* **4.** (*action*) cepilladura *f;* **to give one's teeth a brush** lavarse los dientes **5.** *no pl* (*stroke*) pincelada *f* **6.** (*encounter*) roce *m* **7.** *no pl, Am* (*brushwood*) maleza *f* **8.** (*fox's tail*) cola *f* **II.** *vt* **1.** (*clean: teeth, hair*) cepillar; (*floor*) barrer **2.** (*remove*) **to ~ sth off** quitar algo con un cepillo **3.** (*graze, touch lightly*) rozar

◆**brush against** *vt* rozar

◆**brush aside** *vt* **1.** (*push to one side*) apartar **2.** (*disregard*) hacer caso omiso de; (*criticism*) pasar por alto

◆**brush away** *vt* quitar

◆**brush off** *vt* (*person*) no hacer caso a; (*criticism*) pasar por alto

◆**brush up I.** *vt* dar un repaso a **II.** *vi* **to ~ on sth** dar un repaso a algo

brush-off ['brʌʃɒf, *Am:* -ɑ:f] *n inf* **to give sb the ~** dar calabazas a alguien; **to get the ~ from sb** recibir calabazas de alguien

brushwood ['brʌʃwʊd] *n no pl* maleza *f*

brusque [bru:sk, *Am:* brʌsk] *adj* brusco, -a

brusqueness *n no pl* brusquedad *f*

Brussels ['brʌsəlz] *n* Bruselas *f*

Brussels sprout *n* col *f* de Bruselas

brutal ['bru:təl, *Am:* -t̬əl] *adj* **1.** (*cruel, savage: attack*) brutal; (*words*) cruel **2.** (*harsh: honesty, truth*) crudo, -a

brutality [bru:'tæləti, *Am:* -ət̬i] *n* (*cruelty: of an attack*) brutalidad *f;* (*of words*) crueldad *f;* (*harshness*) crudeza *f*

brutalize ['bru:təlaɪz, *Am:* -t̬əl-] *vt* **1.** (*treat cruelly*) tratar con crueldad **2.** (*make brutal*) brutalizar

brute [bru:t] **I.** *n* **1.** (*brutal person*) bestia *f,* bruto, -a *m, f* **2.** (*animal*) bestia *f* **II.** *adj* ~ **force** fuerza *f* bruta

brutish ['bru:tɪʃ, *Am:* -t̬ɪʃ] *adj* **1.** (*cruel*) brutal, salvaje **2.** (*coarse*) bruto, -a **3.** (*like an animal*) animal

BSc [,bi:es'si:] *abbr of* **Bachelor of Science** Ldo., -a *m, f* (en Ciencias)

BSE [,bi:es'i:] *n abbr of* **bovine spongiform encephalopathy** encefalopatía *f* espongiforme bovina

BST [,bi:es'ti:] *abbr of* **British Summer Time** horario de verano británico, adelantado una hora respecto al meridiano 0

bubble ['bʌbl] **I.** *n* burbuja *f;* (*in cartoons*) bocadillo *m;* **to blow a ~** hacer una burbuja ▶**to burst sb's ~** desengañar a alguien; **the ~ has burst** se ha roto el encanto **II.** *vi* **1.** (*boil*) hervir **2.** (*make boiling sound*) borbotear

◆**bubble over with** *vi* **to ~ joy** no caber en sí de alegría

bubble bath *n* espuma *f* de baño **bubble gum** *n* chicle *m* **bubblejet** (**printer**) *n* INFOR impresora *f* de inyección de burbujas

bubbly ['bʌbli] **I.** *n inf* champán *m* **II.** *adj* **1.** (*full of bubbles*) burbujeante **2.** *fig* (*lively*) animado, -a

bubonic plague [bju:,bɒnɪk'pleɪg, *Am:* -,bɑ:nɪk'pleɪg] *n no pl* peste *f* bubónica

buccaneer [,bʌkə'nɪə·, *Am:* -'nɪr] *n* bucanero *m*

buck[1] [bʌk] <-(s)> **I.** *n* **1.** (*male: deer*) ciervo *m* (macho); (*rabbit*) conejo *m;* (*hare*) liebre *f* macho **2.** *liter* (*man*) galán *m* **II.** *vi* corcovear **III.** *vt* ir contra; **to ~ the trend** invertir la tendencia

buck[2] [bʌk] *n Am, Aus, inf* (*dollar*) dólar *m;* **to make a fast ~** hacer dinero fácil

buck[3] [bʌk] *n no pl, inf* **to pass the ~** escurrir el bulto; **the ~ stops here** *prov* yo soy el responsable

◆**buck up** *inf* **I.** *vi* **1.** (*cheer up*) levantar el ánimo; ~**!** ¡arriba ese ánimo! **2.** (*hurry up*) darse prisa **II.** *vt* **1.** (*cheer up*) **to buck sb up** levantar el ánimo a alguien **2. to ~ one's ideas** espabilarse

bucket ['bʌkɪt] *n* **1.** (*pail*) cubo *m* **2.** *pl, inf* (*a lot*) **to rain ~s** llover a cántaros; **to weep ~s** llorar a moco tendido ▶**to kick the ~** *inf* estirar la pata

bucketful ['bʌkɪtfʊl] <-s *o* bucketsful> *n* cubo *m* (lleno)

El **Buckingham Palace** es la residencia londinense de la familia real británica. El palacio dispone de unas 600 habitaciones y fue construido por John Nash por expreso deseo del rey George IV entre los años 1821-1830. El edificio fue inaugurado en 1837 con motivo de la subida al trono de la reina Victoria.

buckle ['bʌkl] **I.** *n* hebilla *f* **II.** *vt* **1.** (*fasten: belt, shoes*) abrochar **2.** (*bend*) torcer **III.** *vi*

1.(*fasten*) abrocharse **2.**(*bend*) torcerse; (*knees*) doblarse
buckshot [ˈbʌkʃɒt, *Am:* -ʃɑːt] *n no pl* perdigón *m*
buckskin [ˈbʌkskɪn] **I.** *n no pl* gamuza *f* **II.** *adj* de gamuza
buckwheat [ˈbʌkwiːt] *n no pl* alforfón *m*, trigo *m* sarraceno
bud [bʌd] **I.** *n* (*of leaf, branch*) brote *m;* (*of a flower*) capullo *m;* **to be in ~** tener brotes **II.** *vi* <-dd-> echar brotes
Buddhism [ˈbʊdɪzəm, *Am:* ˈbuːdɪ-] *n no pl* budismo *m*
Buddhist I. *n* budista *mf* **II.** *adj* budista
budding [ˈbʌdɪŋ] *adj* en ciernes
buddy [ˈbʌdi] *n Am, inf* colega *m*, cuate *m Méx*
budge [bʌdʒ] **I.** *vi* **1.**(*move*) moverse; **~ over!** ¡córrete un poquito! **2.**(*change opinion*) **to ~** (**from sth**) cambiar de opinión (en algo) **II.** *vt* **1.**(*move*) mover **2.**(*cause to change opinion*) hacer cambiar de opinión a
budgerigar [ˈbʌdʒərɪgɑːʳ, *Am:* -gɑːr] *n* periquito *m*
budget [ˈbʌdʒɪt] **I.** *n* presupuesto *m* **II.** *vt* presupuestar; (*wages, time*) administrar **III.** *vi* **to ~ for sth** presupuestar algo **IV.** *adj* (*travel, prices*) económico, -a
budgetary [ˈbʌdʒɪtəri] *adj* presupuestario, -a
budget deficit *n* déficit *m inv* presupuestario
budgie [ˈbʌdʒi] *n inf* periquito *m*
buff [bʌf] **I.** *n* **1.**(*leather*) gamuza *f* **2.** *inf* (*person*) entusiasta *mf;* **film ~** cinéfilo, -a *m, f* ►**in the ~** *inf* en cueros **II.** *adj* color de ante **III.** *vt* (*metal*) pulir; (*shoes*) sacar brillo a
buffalo [ˈbʌfələʊ, *Am:* -əloʊ] <-(es)> *n* búfalo *m*
buffer¹ [ˈbʌfəʳ, *Am:* -ə˞] **I.** *n* **1.**(*of a car*) parachoques *m inv;* (*of a train*) tope *m* **2.** INFOR memoria *f* intermedia **3.** CHEM regulador *m* **II.** *vt* proteger
buffer² [ˈbʌfəʳ, *Am:* -ə˞] *n Brit, inf* (*person*) **old ~** carca *m*
buffer zone *n* zona *f* de protección
buffet¹ [ˈbʊfeɪ, *Am:* bəˈfeɪ] *n* **1.**(*meal*) buffet *m* **2.**(*bar*) cafetería *f*
buffet² [ˈbʌfɪt] *vt* zarandear, sacudir
buffet car *n Brit* vagón *m* restaurante
buffet lunch *n* buffet *m*
buffoon [bəˈfuːn] *n* bufón, -ona *m, f;* **to play the ~** hacer el payaso, hacer payasadas
bug [bʌg] **I.** *n* **1.** ZOOL chinche *f;* (*any insect*) bicho *m* **2.** MED virus *m inv* **3.** INFOR error *m* **4.** TEL micrófono *m* oculto **5.** *no pl, inf* (*enthusiasm*) fiebre *f*, entusiasmo *m;* **she's caught the travel ~** le ha picado el gusanillo de viajar ►**to be** [*o feel*] **snug as a ~ in a rug** estar muy cómodo **II.** *vt* <-gg-> **1.**(*tap: telephone*) pinchar; (*conversation*) escuchar clandestinamente; (*room*) ocultar micrófonos en; **~ging operation** vigilancia secreta **2.** *inf* (*annoy*) fastidiar

bugbear [ˈbʌgbeəʳ, *Am:* -ber] *n* pesadilla *f*
bugger [ˈbʌgəʳ, *Am:* -ə˞] **I.** *n inf* (*person*) gilipollas *mf inv;* **poor ~** pobre desgraciado **II.** *interj Aus, Brit, vulg* (*damn*) mierda ►**~ it** ¡mierda! **III.** *vt vulg* cometer sodomía con
◆**bugger off** *vi vulg* **~!** ¡vete a la mierda!
◆**bugger up** *vt vulg* joder
buggery [ˈbʌgəri] *n no pl* sodomía *f*
buggy [ˈbʌgi] *n* **1.** *Brit* (*pushchair*) sillita *f* de paseo **2.** *Am* (*pram*) cochecito *m* (de niño) **3.**(*carriage*) calesa *f*
bugle [ˈbjuːgl] *n* clarín *m*
bugler [ˈbjuːgləʳ] *n* corneta *mf*
build [bɪld] **I.** *vt* <built, built> **1.**(*make: house*) construir; (*fire*) hacer; (*car*) fabricar **2.**(*establish: trust*) cimentar; (*relationship*) establecer **II.** *vi* <built, built> **1.**(*construct*) edificar **2.**(*increase*) aumentar **III.** *n* complexión *f*
◆**build in** *vt* incorporar
◆**build on** *vt* **to build sth on sth** agregar algo a algo
◆**build up I.** *vt* **1.**(*increase*) acrecentar **2.**(*accumulate*) acumular **3.**(*strengthen*) fortalecer **4.**(*develop*) desarrollar **5.**(*praise*) **to build sb up** poner a alguien por las nubes **II.** *vi* **1.**(*increase*) ir en aumento **2.**(*accumulate*) acumularse
builder [ˈbɪldəʳ, *Am:* -də˞] *n* (*company*) constructor(a) *m(f);* (*worker*) albañil *mf*
building *n* edificio *m*
building contractor *n* contratista *mf* (de obras) **building site** *n* obra *f* **building society** *n Aus, Brit* sociedad *f* de crédito hipotecario
build-up [ˈbɪldʌp] *n* **1.**(*accumulation*) acumulación *f;* (*of pressure*) aumento *m* **2.**(*publicity*) propaganda *f*
built [bɪlt] **I.** *pp, pt* of **build II.** *adj* **1.**(*house*) **well ~** bien construido **2.**(*person*) **slightly ~** menudo; **well ~** de complexión robusto
built-in [ˈbɪltˈɪn, *Am:* ˈbɪltɪn] *adj* **1.**(*cupboard*) empotrado, -a **2.**(*feature*) incorporado, -a **3.**(*advantage*) intrínseco, -a
built-up [ˈbɪltʌp] *adj* **1.**(*area*) edificado, -a **2.**(*heels, shoes*) con alza
bulb [bʌlb] *n* **1.** BOT bulbo *m;* **~ of garlic** cabeza *f* de ajo **2.**(*of a thermometer*) cubeta *f* **3.** ELEC bombilla *f*, bombillo *m* AmL
bulbous [ˈbʌlbəs] *adj* bulboso, -a; **~ nose** nariz *f* protuberante
Bulgaria [bʌlˈgeərɪə, *Am:* -ˈgerɪ-] *n* Bulgaria *f*
Bulgarian [bʌlˈgeərɪən, *Am:* -ˈgerɪ-] **I.** *adj* búlgaro, -a **II.** *n* **1.**(*person*) búlgaro, -a *m, f* **2.** *no pl* LING búlgaro *m*
bulge [bʌldʒ] **I.** *vi* sobresalir; **her eyes ~d in surprise** su sorpresa fue tal que los ojos se le salían de las órbitas; **to ~** (**with sth**) estar repleto (de algo) **II.** *n* **1.**(*swelling*) bulto *m* **2.**(*in a statistical trend*) alza *f*
bulging *adj* abultado, -a; (*bag, box*) repleto, -a; **~ eyes** ojos *mpl* saltones

bulimia [bʊlɪːmiə, *Am:* bjuː'-] *n no pl* MED bulimia *f*

bulk [bʌlk] I. *n* 1. *no pl* (*magnitude*) volumen *m* 2. *no pl* (*mass*) mole *f* 3. *no pl* (*quantity*) **in ~ a** granel; ECON al por mayor; **to ~ buy sth, to buy (sth) in ~** comprar (algo) en grandes cantidades; ECON comprar (algo) al por mayor 4. (*largest part*) **the ~ of** la mayor parte de II. *vi* **to ~ large** ser importante

bulk buying *n* ECON *no pl* compra *f* al por mayor

bulkhead ['bʌlkhed] *n* NAUT mamparo *m*

bulky ['bʌlki] <-ier, iest> *adj* (*large*) voluminoso, -a; (*heavy*) pesado, -a; (*person*) corpulento, -a

bull¹ [bʊl] *n* 1. (*male bovine*) toro *m* 2. (*male animal*) macho *m;* ~ **elephant** elefante *m;* ~ **whale** ballena *f* macho ▶**like a ~ in a china shop** como un elefante en una cacharrería; **to take the ~ by the horns** coger [*o* agarrar *AmL*] el toro por los cuernos; **to be like a red rag to a ~** to sb poner furioso a alguien

bull² [bʊl] *n* 1. *no pl* (*nonsense*) chorradas *fpl*, macanas *fpl RíoPl* 2. FIN alcista *m;* ~ **market** mercado *m* alcista 3. *Brit* SPORTS diana *f*

bulldog ['bʊldɒg, *Am:* -dɑːg] *n* bulldog *m*

bulldoze ['bʊldəʊz, *Am:* -doʊz] *vt* 1. ARCHIT demoler 2. *fig* **to ~ sth through** conseguir algo a la fuerza; **to ~ sb into doing sth** forzar a alguien a hacer algo

bulldozer ['bʊldəʊzər, *Am:* -doʊzɚ] *n* bulldozer *m*, topadora *f Arg, Méx, Urug*

bullet ['bʊlɪt] *n* MIL bala *f;* **to fire a ~** disparar una bala ▶**to bite the ~** *inf* apretar los dientes, hacer de tripas corazón

bulletin ['bʊlətɪn, *Am:* -əţɪn] *n* boletín *m;* (*news*) ~ TV, CINE boletín (informativo)

bulletin board *n Am a.* INFOR tablón *m* de anuncios

bulletproof ['bʊlɪtpruːf] *adj* a prueba de balas; ~ **glass** vidrio *m* antibalas

bulletproof vest *n* chaleco *m* antibalas

bullfight ['bʊlfaɪt] *n* corrida *f* de toros

bullfighter ['bʊlfaɪtər, *Am:* -ţɚ] *n* torero, -a *m, f*

bullfinch ['bʊlfɪntʃ] *n* pinzón *m*

bullion ['bʊlɪən, *Am:* -jən] *n no pl* **gold/silver ~** oro *m*/plata *f* en lingotes

bullock ['bʊlək] *n* buey *m*

bullring ['bʊlrɪŋ] *n* plaza *f* de toros

bull's-eye ['bʊlzaɪ] *n* blanco *f;* **to hit the ~** *a. fig* dar en el blanco

bullshit ['bʊlʃɪt] I. *n no pl, inf* gilipolleces *fpl;* **don't give me that ~!** ¡no me vengas con hostias! *vulg* II. *interj inf* y una mierda *vulg* III. <-tt-> *vi inf* decir gilipolleces

bully ['bʊli] I. <-ies> *n* (*person*) matón, -ona *m, f* II. <-ie-> *vt* intimidar; **to ~ sb into doing sth** intimidar a alguien a hacer algo III. *interj inf* ~ **for you!** ¡qué bien!; *iron* ¡bravo!

bully beef *n* carne *f* de vaca enlatada

bulrush ['bʊlrʌʃ] <-es> *n* anea *f*

bulwark ['bʊlwək, *Am:* -wɚk] *n* 1. baluarte *m* 2. NAUT macarrón *m*

bum [bʌm] I. *n* 1. *Am* (*lazy person*) vago, -a *m, f* 2. *Am* (*tramp*) vagabundo, -a *m, f* 3. *Aus, Brit, inf* (*bottom*) culo *m* ▶**to give sb the ~'s rush** *Am, inf* echar a alguien a patadas II. *adj inf* (*bad, useless*) malo, -a; **a ~ job** una porquería de trabajo III. <-mm-> *vt inf* **to ~ sth off sb** gorronear algo a alguien IV. *vi inf* 1. **to ~ about** [*o* around] vagabundear 2. **to ~ off sb** gorronear a alguien

bumble ['bʌmbl] *vi* andar a tropezones

bumblebee ['bʌmblbiː] *n* abejorro *m*

bumbling *adj* torpe

bumf [bʌmf] *n no pl, Aus, Brit, inf* 1. (*printed matter*) papeles *mpl* 2. (*paperwork*) papeleo *m*

bump [bʌmp] I. *n* 1. (*lump*) bulto *m;* (*on head*) chichón *m;* (*on road*) bache *m* 2. *inf* (*blow*) porrazo *m* 3. (*thud*) golpe *m* 4. (*collision*) topetazo *m* II. *vt* chocar contra; **to ~ one's head on/against sth** darse un golpe en la cabeza con/contra algo

◆**bump into** *vt insep* 1. (*collide with*) chocar contra 2. (*meet*) topar con

◆**bump off** *vt inf* **to bump sb off** cargarse a alguien

bumper ['bʌmpər, *Am:* -pɚ] I. *n Brit, Aus* AUTO parachoques *m inv*, paragolpes *m inv AmL*, defensa *f Méx;* **the traffic is ~ to ~** hay un atasco II. *adj* 1. (*crop*) abundante 2. (*edition*) especial

bumper car *n* auto *m* de choque, carrito *m* chocón *Méx, Ven*, carro *m* loco *Col* **bumper sticker** *n* pegatina *f*

bumph [bʌmpf] *n no pl s.* **bumf**

bumpkin ['bʌmpkɪn] *n inf* (**country**) ~ paleto, -a *m, f*

bumptious ['bʌmpʃəs] *adj* engreído, -a

bumpy ['bʌmpi] <-ier, iest> *adj* (*surface*) desigual; (*road*) lleno, -a de baches; (*journey*) zarandeado, -a

bun [bʌn] *n* 1. (*pastry*) bollo *m* 2. *Am* (*roll*) panecillo *m*, pancito *m CSur* 3. (*knot of hair*) moño *m*, chongo *m Méx*

bunch [bʌntʃ] <-es> I. *n* 1. (*of bananas, grapes*) racimo *m;* (*of carrots, radishes, keys*) manojo *m;* (*of flowers*) ramo *m* 2. (*group: of people*) grupo *m;* (*of friends*) pandilla *f* 3. *Am* (*a lot*) **a ~ of problems** un montón de problemas 4. *pl, Brit* (*hair style*) coletas *fpl* ▶**to be the best of the ~** ser lo mejor II. *vt* agrupar III. *vi* **to ~ (together)** amontonarse

bundle ['bʌndl] I. *n* (*of clothes*) fardo *m;* (*of money*) fajo *m;* (*of sticks*) haz *f* ▶**to be a ~ of joy** *inf* ser un cascabel; **to be a ~ of laughs** ser muy divertido; **to be a ~ of nerves** ser un manojo de nervios; **to go a ~ on sth** *Brit, inf* volverse loco por algo II. *vt* **to ~ sb into a car** meter a alguien a empujones en un coche

◆**bundle up** I. *vt* atar, liar II. *vi* (*dress warmly*) abrigarse

bung [bʌŋ] I. *n Brit* tapón *m* II. *vt* **1.** *Brit* (*close*) taponar **2.** *Aus, Brit, inf* (*throw*) tirar; (*put*) poner

bungalow ['bʌŋgələʊ, *Am:* -oʊ] *n* bungaló *m*, bóngalo *m AmL*

bungee jumping ['bʌndʒɪˌdʒʌmpɪŋ] *n no pl* puenting *m*

bungle ['bʌŋgl] *vt* chapucear

bungler *n* chapucero, -a *m, f*

bungling *adj* torpe

bunk [bʌŋk] *n* NAUT litera *f*; cucheta *f RíoPl*
► to **do** a ~ *Aus, Brit, inf* poner pies en polvorosa

◆ **bunk down** *vi inf* echarse a dormir

bunk bed *n* litera *f*

bunker ['bʌŋkəʳ, *Am:* -kɚ] *n* búnker *m*

bunkum ['bʌŋkəm] *n* chorradas *fpl*

bunny (**rabbit**) ['bʌni ('ræbɪt)] *n childspeak* conejito *m*

bunsen burner [ˌbʌntsən'bɜːnəʳ, *Am:* 'bʌntsɪnˌbɜːrnɚ] *n* mechero *m* Bunsen

bunting ['bʌntɪŋ, *Am:* -t̬ɪŋ] *n no pl* banderitas *fpl*

buoy [bɔɪ] *n* boya *f*

◆ **buoy up** *vt* **1.** (*cause to float*) mantener a flote **2.** *fig* (*cause to rise*) aumentar **3.** *fig* **to buoy sb up** animar a alguien

buoyancy ['bɔɪənsi, *Am:* -jən-] *n no pl* **1.** *a.* NAUT capacidad *f* para flotar **2.** (*cheerfulness*) optimismo *m*

buoyant ['bɔɪənt, *Am:* -jənt] *adj* **1.** (*able to float*) flotante **2.** (*cheerful*) optimista; **to be in a ~ mood** estar de buen humor **3.** FIN **a ~ currency** una moneda fuerte

burble ['bɜːbl, *Am:* 'bɜːr-] *vi* **1.** (*make burbling noise*) borbotar **2.** (*talk nonsense*) parlotear

burden ['bɜːdən, *Am:* 'bɜːr-] I. *n* **1.** (*load*) carga *f* **2.** *fig* carga *f*; (*responsibility*) responsabilidad *f*; **tax ~** ECON gravamen *m*; **the ~ of proof** LAW la carga de la prueba; **to be a ~ on** [*o* **to**] **sb** ser una carga para alguien II. *vt* **1.** (*load*) cargar **2.** *fig* estorbar; **I don't want to ~ you with my problems** no quiero preocuparte con mis problemas

burdensome ['bɜːdənsəm, *Am:* 'bɜːr-] *adj form* oneroso, -a

bureau ['bjʊərəʊ, *Am:* 'bjʊroʊ] <-x *Am, Aus:* -s> *n* **1.** *Am* (*government department*) departamento *m*; (*office*) agencia *f*; **employment ~** oficina *f* de empleo **2.** *Brit* (*desk*) escritorio *m* **3.** *Am* (*chest of drawers*) cómoda *f*

bureaucracy [bjʊə'rɒkrəsi, *Am:* bjʊ-'rɑːkrə-] *n* burocracia *f*

bureaucrat ['bjʊərəkræt, *Am:* 'bjʊrə-] *n* burócrata *mf*

bureaucratic [ˌbjʊərə'krætɪk, *Am:* ˌbjʊrə-'kræt̬-] *adj* burocrático, -a

burgeoning ['bɜːdʒənɪŋ, *Am:* 'bɜːr-] *adj* creciente

burger ['bɜːgəʳ, *Am:* 'bɜːrgɚ] *n inf abbr of* **hamburger** hamburguesa *f*

burglar ['bɜːgləʳ, *Am:* 'bɜːrglɚ] *n* ladrón, -ona *m, f*

burglar alarm *n* alarma *f* antirrobo

burglarize ['bɜːgləraɪz, *Am:* 'bɜːrglə-] *vt Am s.* **burgle**

burglary ['bɜːgləri, *Am:* 'bɜːr-] <-ies> *n* robo *m*

burgle ['bɜːgl, *Am:* 'bɜːr-] *vt* robar; **five houses have been ~d** han entrado a robar en cinco casas

burial ['berɪəl] *n* entierro *m*

burial ground *n* cementerio *m* **burial service** *n* funerales *mpl*

Burkinabe ['bɜːkiːneɪb] I. *adj* de Burkina Faso II. *n* habitante *mf* de Burkina Faso

Burkina Faso [bɜːˌkiːnə'fæsəʊ] *n* Burkina *f* Faso

burlesque [bɜː'lesk, *Am:* 'bɜːr-] I. *n* parodia *f* II. *adj* burlesco, -a

burly ['bɜːli, *Am:* 'bɜːr-] <-ier, -iest> *adj* (*person*) fornido, -a; (*arm, leg*) musculoso, -a

Burma ['bɜːmə, *Am:* 'bɜːr-] *n* Birmania *f*

burn[1] [bɜːn, *Am:* bɜːrn] *n Scot* (*stream*) arroyo *m*

burn[2] [bɜːn, *Am:* bɜːrn] I. <burnt *o* -ed, burnt *o* -ed> *vi* **1.** (*be in flames: house*) arder; (*coal, wood*) quemarse **2.** (*be hot*) arder; **his forehead was ~ing** la frente le ardía **3.** (*be switched on*) estar encendido, -a; **he left all the lights ~ing** dejó todas las luces encendidas **4.** (*long*) **to be ~ing to do sth** estar deseando hacer algo **5.** (*feel emotion strongly*) **to ~ with sth** arder de algo; **to ~ with desire** desear ardientemente **6.** (*be red*) **his face ~ed with anger/shame** se puso rojo de furia/vergüenza II. <burnt *o* -ed, burnt *o* -ed> *vt* (*paper, rubbish, food*) quemar; (*building*) incendiar; (*throat, tongue*) quemar, escaldar; **to be ~ed** (*by the sun*) quemarse; (*injured*) sufrir quemaduras; **to ~ calories/fat** quemar calorías/grasa; **this machine ~s electricity** esta máquina funciona con electricidad; **we ~ a lot of gas** consumimos mucho gas III. *n* quemadura *f*, quemada *f Méx*; **severe/minor ~s** quemaduras graves/leves

◆ **burn away** I. *vi* (*forest*) quemarse; (*candle*) consumirse II. *vt* quemar

◆ **burn down** I. *vt* incendiar II. *vi* (*house*) incendiarse; (*fire, candle*) apagarse

◆ **burn out** I. *vi* (*engine*) quemarse; (*fire, candle*) apagarse; (*light bulb*) fundirse II. *vt* **to burn oneself out** agotarse, quemarse

◆ **burn up** I. *vt inf* (*fuel*) consumir; (*calories*) quemar II. *vi* abrasarse; **you're burning up!** *inf* (*have fever*) ¡estás ardiendo!

burner ['bɜːnəʳ, *Am:* 'bɜːrnɚ] *n* fogón *m*; TECH quemador *m*

burning ['bɜːnɪŋ, *Am:* 'bɜːrnɪŋ] *adj* **1.** (*hot*) ardiente; (*sun*) abrasador; **to be ~ hot** estar ardiendo; **a ~ sensation** una quemazón **2.** (*issue, question*) candente; (*desire, hatred*) ardiente

La **Burns Night** tiene lugar el 25 de enero. En este día se conmemora el nacimiento del poeta escocés Robert Burns (1759-1796). A la celebración acuden entusiastas de la obra de Burns, no sólo de Escocia sino de todas las partes del mundo. En ese día se sirve una comida especial llamada **Burns Supper** que se compone de **haggis** (una especie de asado de carne picada hecha de vísceras especiadas de oveja, mezclado con avena y cebolla. Todo ello es cocido dentro de la tripa de la oveja y después dorado al horno), **neeps** (nabos) y **mashed tatties** (puré de patatas).

burnt [bɜːnt, *Am:* 'bɜːrnt] I. *pt, pp of* burn II. *adj* quemado, -a; **a ~ smell/taste** un olor/sabor a quemado

burp [bɜːp, *Am:* bɜːrp] I. *n* eructo *m;* **to let out a ~** soltar un eructo II. *vi* eructar III. *vt* **to ~ a baby** hacer eructar a un bebé

burr [bɜːʳ, *Am:* bɜːr] *n* 1. BOT abrojo *m* 2. (*noise*) zumbido *m* 3. LING sonido *m* gutural

burrow ['bʌrəʊ, *Am:* 'bɜːroʊ] I. *n* madriguera *f;* **rabbit ~** conejera *f* II. *vi* (*dig a hole*) excavar un agujero; (*a tunnel*) excavar un túnel; (*a home*) excavar una madriguera; **to ~ into sth** horadar algo; *fig* hurgar en algo III. *vt* excavar

bursar ['bɜːsəʳ, *Am:* 'bɜːrsɚ] *n* tesorero, -a *m, f*

bursary ['bɜːsəri, *Am:* 'bɜːr-] *n Brit* beca *f*

burst [bɜːst, *Am:* bɜːrst] I. *n* 1. (*explosion*) explosión *f* 2. MIL (*of fire*) ráfaga *f* 3. (*brief period*) **a ~ of laughter** una carcajada; **a ~ of applause** una salva de aplausos; **a ~ of anger** un arranque de cólera II. <burst *Am:* bursted, burst *Am:* bursted> *vi* 1. (*balloon, tyre*) reventar; (*storm*) desatarse; **to ~ into tears** romper a llorar 2. (*move suddenly*) **to ~ into a place** irrumpir en un lugar; **to ~ open** abrirse de golpe 3. *fig* **to be ~ing to do sth** morirse de ganas de hacer algo; **to be ~ing with health** rebosar de salud; **to be ~ing with curiosity** morirse de curiosidad III. <burst *Am:* bursted, burst *Am:* bursted> *vt* reventar; **to ~ its banks** (*river*) desbordarse

◆**burst forth** *vi* brotar

◆**burst in** *vi* entrar de sopetón

◆**burst out** *vi* 1. (*exclaim*) saltar 2. (*break out*) **to ~ laughing/crying** echarse a reír/llorar

Burundi [bʊ'rʊndi] *n* Burundi *m*

bury ['beri] <-ie-> *vt* 1. (*put underground*) enterrar 2. (*hide*) ocultar; **to ~ oneself in sth** enfrascarse en algo; **to be buried in thought** estar ensimismado; **to ~ one's head in one's hands** ocultar el rostro en las manos

bus [bʌs] I. <-es> *n* (*local*) autobús *m,* colectivo *m Arg, Ven,* guagua *f Cuba,* omnibús *m Perú, Urug;* **school ~** autobús escolar; **to**

catch/miss the ~ coger/perder el autobús; **to go by ~** ir en autobús ▸**to miss the ~** perder el (último) tren II. <-ss-> *vt* llevar en autobús III. <-ss-> *vi* ir en autobús

bus driver *n* conductor(a) *m(f)* de autobús

bush [bʊʃ] <-es> *n* 1. BOT arbusto *m;* **a ~ of hair** una mata de pelo 2. *no pl* (*land*) **the ~** el monte ▸**to beat about the ~** andarse con rodeos; **to beat the ~es for sth** *Am* buscar algo por todas partes

bushel ['bʊʃl] *n* fanega *f* (*en Gran Bretaña, esta medida equivale a 36,4 l; en Estados Unidos a 35,2 l.*) ▸**to hide one's light under a ~** ocultar sus talentos

bushman ['bʊʃmən] <-men> *n* bosquimano *m*

bushy ['bʊʃi] <-ier, -iest> *adj* (*hair*) tupido, -a; (*beard, moustache*) espeso, -a; (*eyebrows*) poblado, -a

busily *adv* afanosamente

business ['bɪznɪs] *n* 1. *no pl* (*trade, commerce*) negocios *mpl;* **to be away on ~** estar de viaje de negocios; **to do ~ with sb** hacer negocios con alguien; **to get down to ~** empezar a trabajar; **to go out of ~** cerrar; **to set up in ~** montar un negocio; **to set up in ~ as a lawyer** establecerse como abogado; **to work in ~** dedicarse a los negocios; **~ is booming** el negocio va muy bien; **once we get the computer installed, we'll be in ~** *inf* una vez que hayamos instalado el ordenador podremos empezar 2. <-es> (*sector*) industria *f;* **the frozen food ~** la industria de los congelados; **what line of ~ are you in?** ¿en qué ramo trabajas? 3. <-es> (*firm*) empresa *f;* **to start up/run a ~** poner/llevar un negocio 4. *no pl* (*matter*) asunto *m;* **an unfinished ~** un asunto pendiente; **it's none of your ~!** *inf* ¡no es asunto tuyo!; **mind your own ~!** *inf* ¡no te metas donde no te llaman!; **to have no ~ doing sth** no tener derecho a hacer algo; **I make it my ~ to do that** me encargo de hacer eso; **it's a time-consuming ~** requiere mucho tiempo ▸**~ before pleasure** *prov* antes es la obligación que el placer; **~ as usual** *prov* todo sigue igual; **to (not) be in the ~ of doing sth** (no) tener por costumbre hacer algo; **to mean ~** hablar en serio; **like nobody's ~** *inf* como loco

business address *n* dirección *f* comercial **business card** *n* tarjeta *f* comercial **business class** *n* clase *f* preferente **business expenses** *npl* gastos *mpl* comerciales **business hours** *n* horas *fpl* de oficina **business letter** *n* carta *f* comercial

businesslike ['bɪznɪslaɪk] *adj* 1. (*serious*) formal 2. (*efficient*) eficiente

businessman ['bɪznɪsmæn] <-men> *n* hombre *m* de negocios

business park *n* parque *m* de negocios **business trip** *n* viaje *m* de negocios **businesswoman** ['bɪznɪsˌwʊmən] <-women> *n* mujer *f* de negocios

busk [bʌsk] *vi Aus, Brit: tocar un instrumento en la calle*

busker ['bʌskəʳ, *Am:* -ɚ] *n Aus, Brit* músico, -a *m, f* ambulante

busload ['bʌsləʊd, *Am:* -loʊd] *n* ~s of tourists autobuses *mpl* llenos de turistas

bus service *n* servicio *m* de autobuses **bus station** *n* estación *f* de autobuses **bus stop** *n* parada *f* de autobús

bust¹ [bʌst] *n* busto *m*

bust² [bʌst] I. *adj inf* 1. (*broken*) destrozado, -a 2. (*bankrupt*) en bancarrota; **to go** ~ quebrar II. <*bust Am:* busted, bust *Am:* busted> *vt inf* 1. (*break*) destrozar 2. (*raid*) realizar una redada en

bustle ['bʌsl] I. *vi* **to** ~ **about** ir y venir; **to** ~ **with activity** rebosar de actividad II. *n* 1. *no pl* ajetreo *m*; **hustle and** ~ bullicio *m* 2. HIST (*dress part*) polisón *m*

bustling *adj* (*town, street*) animado, -a

bust-up ['bʌstʌp] *n Aus, Brit, inf* riña *f*; **to have a (big)** ~ **with sb** partir peras con alguien

busy¹ ['bɪzi] <-ier, -iest> *adj* 1. (*occupied*) atareado, -a; **to be** ~ **doing sth** estar muy ocupado haciendo algo; **to be** ~ **with sth** estar ocupado con algo; **to get** ~ empezar a trabajar 2. (*full of activity*) activo, -a; (*exhausting*) agotador(a); ~ **street** calle *f* concurrida; ~ **seaport** puerto *m* marítimo de gran actividad; **a** ~ **time** un tiempo de actividad frenética; **I've had a** ~ **day** he tenido un día ajetreado 3. *Am* TEL **to be** ~ estar comunicando

busy² ['bɪzi] <-ie-> *vt* **to** ~ **oneself with sth** ocuparse de algo

busybody ['bɪzi,bɒdi, *Am:* -,bɑ:di] <-ies> *n inf* entrometido, -a *m, f*; **to be a** ~ ser un metomentodo

but [bʌt] I. *prep* excepto; **all** ~ **one** todos excepto uno; **anything** ~ ... lo que sea menos...; **nothing** ~ ... nada más que...; **no one** ~ **he** nadie salvo él; ~ **for that I'd have had an accident** si no fuera por eso habría tenido un accidente; **there is nothing for it** ~ **to go in** no hay nada que hacer excepto entrar II. *conj* pero; **I'm not an Englishman** ~ **a Scot** no soy inglés sino escocés; **he has paper** ~ **no pen** tiene papel pero no una pluma; **it is not red** ~ **pink** no es rojo sino rosa III. *adv* sólo; **he is** ~ **a baby** no es más que un bebé; **I can** ~ **hope she wins** solamente puedo esperar que gane; **I can't help** ~ **cry** no puedo evitar llorar IV. *n* pero *m*; **there are no** ~s **about it!** ¡no hay peros que valgan!

butane ['bju:teɪn] *n no pl* butano *m*

butch [bʊtʃ] *adj* 1. (*man*) macho 2. (*woman*) marimacho

butcher ['bʊtʃəʳ, *Am:* -ɚ] I. *n* carnicero, -a *m, f* II. *vt* 1. (*slaughter*) matar 2. (*murder*) asesinar (brutalmente), masacrar 3. *fig* **to** ~ **a language** mutilar una lengua

butchery ['bʊtʃəri] *n no pl* 1. (*of an animal*) matanza *f* 2. (*killing*) carnicería *f*

butler ['bʌtləʳ, *Am:* -lɚ] *n* mayordomo *m*

butt [bʌt] I. *n* 1. (*of rifle*) culata *f* 2. (*of cigarette*) colilla *f* 3. (*blow: with the head*) cabezada *f* 4. (*target*) **to be the** ~ **of sth** ser el blanco de algo 5. (*container*) tonel *m* 6. *Am, inf* (*buttocks*) culo *m* II. *vt* (*with the horns*) topetar; (*with the head*) dar una cabezada contra

butter ['bʌtəʳ, *Am:* 'bʌtɚ] I. *n no pl* mantequilla *f* ►**he/she looks as if** ~ **wouldn't melt in his/her** mouth parece que no haya roto un plato en su vida II. *vt* untar con mantequilla

◆**butter up** *vt* dar jabón a, cepillar *AmL*

buttercup ['bʌtəkʌp, *Am:* 'bʌtɚ-] *n* ranúnculo *m*

butter dish *n* recipiente *m* para mantequilla

butterfingers ['bʌtə,fɪŋgəz, *Am:* 'bʌtɚ-,fɪŋgɚz] *n inv* manazas *mf inv*

butterfly ['bʌtəflaɪ, *Am:* 'bʌtɚ-] <-ies> *n* 1. ZOOL mariposa *f*; *fig* (*person*) persona *f* frívola 2. TECH calón *m* 3. *no pl* SPORTS mariposa *f* ►**to have butterflies in one's** stomach estar con los nervios a flor de piel

buttermilk ['bʌtəmɪlk, *Am:* 'bʌtɚ-] *n no pl* suero *m* de leche

buttery ['bʌtəri, *Am:* 'bʌt-] <-ier, -iest> *adj* de mantequilla

buttock ['bʌtək, *Am:* 'bʌt-] *n* nalga *f*

button ['bʌtən] I. *n* 1. botón *m*; **start** ~ botón de inicio; **right/left mouse** ~ botón derecho/izquierdo del ratón; **to push a** ~ apretar un botón; **at the push of a** ~ con sólo pulsar un botón ►**to be (as)** bright **as a** ~ ser más listo que el hambre; **to be** right **on the** ~ *Am* estar en lo cierto II. *vi* abrocharse III. *vt* abrochar ►**to** ~ **it** *Am, inf* no decir ni esta boca es mía

◆**button up** *vt* abrochar

buttonhole ['bʌtənhəʊl, *Am:* -hoʊl] I. *n* 1. FASHION ojal *m* 2. *Brit* (*flower*) flor que se lleva en el ojal II. *vt* obligar a escuchar

buttress ['bʌtrɪs] <-es> *n* ARCHIT contrafuerte *m*; *fig* apoyo *m*

buxom ['bʌksəm] *adj* pechugona

buy [baɪ] I. *n* compra *f*; **a good** ~ una ganga II. <bought, bought> *vt* 1. (*purchase*) comprar; **to** ~ **sth from** [*o* off] **sb** *inf* comprar algo a alguien; **to** ~ **sb's silence** comprar el silencio de alguien 2. *inf* (*believe*) creer; **did the teacher** ~ **your excuse?** ¿se tragó el profesor tu excusa?

◆**buy back** *vt* volver a comprar

◆**buy in** *vt always sep, Brit* aprovisionarse de

◆**buy off** *vt always sep* sobornar

◆**buy out** *vt* com comprar la parte de

◆**buy up** *vt insep* acaparar

buyer ['baɪəʳ, *Am:* -ɚ] *n* 1. (*purchaser*) comprador(a) *m(f)* 2. (*buying agent*) encargado, -a *m, f* de compras

buyout ['baɪaʊt] *n* FIN compra *f* (*de la totalidad de las acciones*); **management/worker** ~ compra de una empresa por los gerentes/empleados

buzz [bʌz] I. *vi* **1.** (*hum*) zumbar; (*bell*) sonar; my ears were ~ing me zumbaban los oídos; the village was ~ing with rumours el pueblo era un hervidero de rumores **2.** *Am, inf* (*be tipsy*) ir borracho II. *vt inf* TEL llamar III. *n* **1.** (*humming noise*) zumbido *m*; (*low noise*) rumor *m*; (*of a doorbell*) llamada *f*; **the ~ of conversation** el rumor de la conversación **2.** *no pl, inf* (*telephone call*) llamada *f*; **to give sb a ~** llamar a alguien **3.** *no pl, inf* (*feeling*) excitación *f*; (*of alcohol*) subidón *m*; **I get a ~ from** [*o* out of] **surfing** el surf me entusiasma; **sb gets a ~ from sth** algo excita a alguien; **I get a ~ from champagne** el champán se me sube a la cabeza
◆**buzz off** *vi inf* largarse
buzzard ['bʌzəd, *Am:* -əd] *n* **1.** *Brit* (*hawk*) ratonero *m* común **2.** *Am* (*turkey vulture*) gallinazo *m* común
buzzer ['bʌzəʳ, *Am:* -ə·] *n* timbre *m*
buzz word *n* palabra *f* de moda
by [baɪ] I. *prep* **1.** (*near*) cerca de; **close** [*o* **near**] **~ ...** cerca de...; **to be/lie/stand ~ ...** estar/yacer/permanecer cerca de...; **~ the sea** junto al mar **2.** (*at*) junto a; **to remain ~ sb for two days** quedarse junto a alguien durante dos días **3.** (*during*) **~ day/night** durante el día/la noche; **~ moonlight** a la luz de la luna **4.** (*at the latest time*) para; **~ tomorrow/midnight** para mañana/la medianoche; **~ then/now** para entonces/este momento **5.** (*cause*) por; **a novel ~ Joyce** una novela de Joyce; **to be killed ~ sth/sb** ser matado por algo/alguien; **surrounded ~ dogs** rodeado de perros **6.** (*through means of*) **~ rail/plane/tram** en tren/avión/tranvía; **made ~ hand** hecho a mano; **to hold sb ~ the arm** tomar a alguien por el brazo; **to go in ~ the door** entrar por la puerta; **~ doing sth** haciendo algo **7.** (*through*) **~ chance/mistake** por suerte/error **8.** (*under*) **to call sb/sth ~ their/it's name** llamar a alguien/algo por su nombre; **what does he mean ~ that?** ¿a qué se refiere con eso? **9.** (*alone*) **to be ~ oneself** estar solo; **to do sth ~ oneself** hacer algo solo **10.** (*as promise to*) **to swear ~ God/sth** jurar por Dios/algo **11.** (*in measurement, arithmetic*) **to buy ~ the kilo/dozen** comprar por kilo/docenas; **to divide ~ 6** dividir entre 6; **to increase ~ 10%** aumentar en un 10%; **to multiply ~ 4** multiplicar por 4; **paid ~ the hour/day** pagado por hora/día; **4 metres ~ 6** 4 metros por 6; **one ~ one** uno a uno **12.** (*from the perspective of*) **to judge ~ appearances** juzgar por las apariencias; **all right ~ me** *inf* por mí, de acuerdo II. *adv* **1.** (*near*) cerca; **to put/lay sth ~** poner/dejar algo a mano **2.** (*in a while*) **~ and ~** dentro de poco **3.** (*past*) **to go/pass ~** pasar ▶**~ and large** en general
bye [baɪ] *interj*, **bye-bye** [ˌbaɪ'baɪ] *interj inf* adiós
bye-law ['baɪlɔː] *n Brit s.* **by-law**

by-election ['baɪɪlekʃən] *n Brit* elección *f* parcial
bygone ['baɪgɒn, *Am:* -gɑːn] I. *adj inv* pasado, -a II. *n* **let ~s be ~s** lo pasado pasado está
by-law ['baɪlɔː, *Am:* -lɑː] *n* **1.** (*regional law*) reglamento *m* local **2.** (*organization's rule*) estatuto *m*

El **BYO-restaurant** (**B**ring **Y**our **O**wn) se encuentra en Australia. Es un tipo de restaurante que no tiene licencia para servir bebidas alcohólicas. Por ello, si los clientes desean consumir esta clase de bebidas, deben de traerlas ellos mismos.

by-pass ['baɪpɑːs, *Am:* -pæs] I. *n* **1.** AUTO carretera *f* de circunvalación **2.** ELEC desviación *f* **3.** MED by-pass *m* II. *vt* **1.** (*make a detour*) evitar **2.** *fig* (*act without permission of*) **to ~ sb** actuar sin el consentimiento de alguien **3.** *fig* (*avoid*) evitar
byplay ['baɪpleɪ] *n no pl* THEAT acción *f* de segundo plano
by-product ['baɪprɒdʌkt, *Am:* -prɑːdəkt] *n* subproducto *m*; *fig* derivado *m*
by-road ['baɪrəʊd, *Am:* -roʊd] *n* carretera *f* secundaria
bystander ['baɪstændəʳ, *Am:* -dɚ] *n* espectador(a) *m(f)*
byte [baɪt] *n* byte *m*
byway ['baɪweɪ] *n* camino *m* poco concurrido
byword ['baɪwɜːd, *Am:* -wɜːrd] *n* ejemplo *m;* **to be a ~ for sth** ser sinónimo de algo

C

C, c [siː] *n* **1.** (*letter*) C, c *f;* **~ for Charlie** C de Carmen **2.** MUS do *m* **3.** SCHOOL ≈ suficiente *m*
C *after n abbr of* **Celsius** C
c. **1.** *abbr of* **circa** (*by numbers*) aprox.; (*by dates*) hacia **2.** *abbr of* **cent** cent **3.** *abbr of* **century** s.
ca. *abbr of* **circa 1.** (*by numbers*) aprox. **2.** (*by dates*) hacia
CAA [ˌsiːeɪ'eɪ] *n abbr of* **Civil Aviation Authority** (autoridades *fpl* de) Aviación *f* Civil
cab [kæb] *n* **1.** (*vehicle's driver area*) cabina *f* **2.** *Am, Aus* (*taxi*) taxi *m;* **by ~** en taxi **3.** HIST (*horse-drawn vehicle*) carruaje *m*
CAB [ˌsiːeɪ'biː] *n* **1.** *abbr of* **Citizens' Advice Bureau** Oficina *f* de Atención al Ciudadano **2.** *Am abbr of* **Civil Aeronautics Board** Oficina *f* de Aviación Civil
cabaret ['kæbəreɪ, *Am:* ˌkæbə'reɪ] *n* cabaret *m*
cabbage ['kæbɪdʒ] *n* **1.** GASTR col *f* **2.** ZOOL **~ white** mariposa *f* de la col **3.** *Brit* (*person*)

vegetal *m*

cabbie *n*, **cabby** ['kæbi] *n*, **cabdriver** [kæb,draɪvəʳ, *Am:* -vəʳ] *n Am* taxista *mf*

cabin ['kæbɪn] *n* 1. (*in a vehicle*) cabina *f* 2. (*simple wooden house*) cabaña *f*

cabin class *n* AVIAT clase *f* de compartimento **cabin cruiser** *n* yate *m* de motor

cabinet ['kæbɪnɪt] *n* 1. (*storage place*) armario *m;* (*glass-fronted*) vitrina *f;* **filing** ~ archivador *m* 2. + *sing/pl vb* (*group of ministers*) gabinete *m*, consejo *m* de ministros

cabinet maker *n* ebanista *mf*

cable ['keɪbl] I. *n* 1. (*wire rope*) cable *m;* **coil of** ~ rollo *m* de cable 2. *no pl* TV televisión *f* por cable 3. HIST (*electrically transmitted message*) cablegrama *m;* **to send sth by** ~ cablegrafiar algo II. *vt* HIST cablegrafiar

cable car *n* teleférico *m* **cable network** *n* cableado *m* **cable railway** *n Am* funicular *m* **cable stitch** *n no pl* punto *m* trenzado **cable television** *n no pl*, **cable TV** *n no pl* televisión *f* por cable

caboodle [kə'buːdl] *n Am, inf* **the whole** (**kit and**) ~ toda la pesca

cab rank *n*, **cab stand** *n Am* (*taxi rank*) parada *f* de taxis

cabriolet ['kæbriəʊleɪ, *Am:* ,kæbriə'leɪ] *n* descapotable *m*

cacao [kə'kɑːəʊ, *Am:* -oʊ] *n no pl* cacao *m;* ~ (**bean**) (semilla *f* de) cacao *m*

cache [kæʃ] *n* 1. (*hiding place*) escondite *m;* (*secret stockpile*) alijo *m;* ~ **of weapons** alijo de armas 2. INFOR caché *m;* ~ **memory** memoria *f* caché

cachet ['kæʃeɪ, *Am:* kæʃ'eɪ] *n no pl* distinción *f*, prestigio *m*

cackle ['kækl] I. *vi* 1. (*hen*) cacarear 2. *fig* (*laugh*) reírse escandalosamente 3. (*talk*) cotorrear II. *n* 1. *no pl* (*of hen*) cacareo *m* 2. (*laugh*) risotada *f* ▸**cut the** ~**!** *Brit, Aus, iron* ¡corta el rollo!

cacophony [kæ'kɒfəni, *Am:* kə'kɑːfə-] *n no pl* (*loud discord*) cacofonía *f;* (*noise*) estrépito *m*

cactus ['kæktəs] <-es *o* cacti> *n* cactus *m inv*, ulala *f Bol*

CAD [kæd] *n abbr of* Computer-Aided Design DAO *m*, DAC *m AmL*

cadaver [kə'deɪvəʳ, *Am:* -'dævəʳ] *n* MED cadáver *m*

CAD/CAM ['kædkæm] *n abbr of* computer-aided design and manufacture CAD/CAM *m*

caddie, caddy ['kædi] <-ies> I. *n* caddie *mf*, caddy *mf* II. <caddied, caddied, caddying> *vi* **to** ~ **for sb** hacer de caddy de alguien

cadence ['keɪdns] *n* cadencia *f*

cadet [kə'det] *n a.* MIL cadete *mf*

cadge [kædʒ] I. *vt inf* **to** ~ **sth** (**off sb**) (*get by begging*) obtener algo (de alguien) mendigando; (*get for free*) gorronear algo (a alguien) II. *vi inf* (*get by begging*) obtener mendigando;

(*get something for free*) gorronear

cadger ['kædʒəʳ, *Am:* -əʳ] *n* gorrón, -ona *m, f*

cadmium ['kædmjəm] *n no pl* cadmio *m*

cadre ['kɑːdəʳ, *Am:* 'kædriː] *n* 1. (*elite trained group*) cuadro *m* 2. (*group member*) (miembro *mf* del) cuadro *m*

Caesar ['siːzəʳ, *Am:* -zəʳ] *n* César *m;* **Julius** ~ HIST Julio César

caesarean [si'zeəriən, *Am:* si'zeri] *n* ~ (**section**) cesárea *f*

caesium ['siːzjəm] *n no pl*, *Brit* cesio *m*

cafe, **café** ['kæfeɪ, *Am:* kæf'eɪ] *n* café *m*

cafeteria [,kæfɪ'tɪəriə, *Am:* -'tɪri-] *n* restaurante *m* autoservicio, self-service *m*

caffeine ['kæfiːn, *Am:* kæf'iːn] *n no pl* cafeína *f*

cage [keɪdʒ] I. *n* jaula *f* II. *vt* enjaular

cagey ['keɪdʒi] <-ier, -iest> *adj inf* reservado, -a; **to be** ~ **about sth** ocultar [*o* reservarse] información sobre algo

cahoots [kə'huːts] *npl inf* **to be in** ~ (**with sb**) estar compinchado (con alguien)

cairn [keən, *Am:* kern] *n* mojón *m* (de piedras)

Cairo ['keərəʊ, *Am:* 'keroʊ] *n* El Cairo

cajole [kə'dʒəʊl, *Am:* -'dʒoʊl] I. *vt* engatusar; **to** ~ **sb into/out of doing sth** engatusar a alguien para que haga/no haga algo II. *vi* engatusar, camelar *inf*

cake [keɪk] I. *n* 1. GASTR pastel *m;* (*small*) pasta *f;* **iced** ~ tarta *f* helada; **sponge** ~ bizcocho *m*, queque *m AmL* 2. (*of soap*) pastilla *f;* (*of chocolate*) barra *f* ▸**to sell like hot** ~**s** *inf* venderse como rosquillas; **to want to have one's** ~ **and eat it** quererlo todo II. *vt* (*cover with*) **his boots were** ~**d with mud** sus botas estaban cubiertas de barro III. *vi* (*dry*) endurecerse

cal. *n abbr of* **calorie** cal *f*

calamity [kə'læməti, *Am:* -əti] <-ies> *n* calamidad *f*

calciferous [kæl'sɪfərəs] *adj* calizo, -a

calcify ['kælsɪfaɪ] <-ie-> I. *vt* calcificar II. *vi* calcificarse

calcium ['kælsɪəm] *n no pl* calcio *m*

calculable ['kælkjʊləbl, *Am:* -kjə-] *adj* MAT, ECON calculable; **the total damage is** ~ **at £15,000** los daños totales se estiman en 15.000 libras

calculate ['kælkjʊleɪt, *Am:* -kjə-] I. *vt* calcular; **to** ~ **sth at …** calcular algo en… II. *vi* calcular

calculated *adj* calculado, -a; **to be** ~ **to do sth** estar pensado para hacer algo

calculating *adj* calculador(a)

calculation [,kælkjʊ'leɪʃən, *Am:* -kjə-] *n* 1. MAT cálculo *m; no pl* (*figures*) cómputo *m* 2. (*foreseeing*) cálculo *m* 3. *no pl* (*selfish planning*) premeditación *f*

calculator ['kælkjʊleɪtəʳ, *Am:* -kjəleɪtəʳ] *n* calculadora *f*

calculus ['kælkjʊləs, *Am:* -kjə-] *n no pl* cálculo *m*

calendar ['kælɪndəʳ, *Am:* -dɚ] I. *n* calendario *m*, exfoliador *m Chile, Méx* II. *adj* ~ **year** año *m* civil

calendar month <-es> *n* mes *m*

calf¹ [kɑːf, *Am:* kæf] <calves> *n* 1. (*young cow or bull*) ternero, -a *m, f;* **to be in** ~ estar preñada 2. *no pl* (*leather*) piel *f* de becerro ▸**to kill the fatted** ~ echar la casa por la ventana (para celebrar la llegada de alguien)

calf² [kɑːf, *Am:* kæf] <calves> *n* (*lower leg*) pantorrilla *f*

calf-love *n no pl* amor *m* de adolescente

caliber ['kæləbɚ] *n no pl, Am s.* **calibre**

calibrate ['kælɪbreɪt] *vt* calibrar

calibre ['kælɪbəʳ, *Am:* -əbɚ] *n* calibre *m;* **to be of (a) high** ~ ser de grueso calibre

calico ['kælɪkəʊ, *Am:* -koʊ] *n no pl* calicó *m*, percal *m*

California [ˌkælɪˈfɔːniə, *Am:* -əˈfɔrnjə] *n* California *f*

call [kɔːl] I. *n* 1. (*telephone*) llamada *f* 2. (*visit*) visita *f;* **to be on a** ~ estar haciendo una visita; **to be on** ~ estar de guardia; **to pay a** ~ **on sb** hacer una visita a alguien 3. (*shout*) grito *m;* **to give a** ~ pegar un grito 4. (*animal cry*) grito *m;* (*bird*) canto *m* 5. *a.* POL llamamiento *m;* **a** ~ **for help** una llamada de socorro 6. *no pl a.* ECON requerimiento *m;* **money on** ~ dinero *m* a la vista; **there is not much** ~ **for sth** no hay demasiada demanda de algo 7. *form* (*need*) **to have no** ~ **for sth** no tener ninguna necesidad de algo; **you had no** ~ **to say that** no tenías por qué decir eso ▸**to have a close** ~ salvarse por los pelos II. *vt* 1. (*name, address as*) llamar; **to** ~ **sb names** insultar a alguien; **what's that actor** ~**ed?** ¿cómo se llama ese actor?; **what's his new film** ~**ed?** ¿cómo se titula su nueva película?; **she's** ~**ed by her second name, Jane** la llaman por su segundo nombre, Jane 2. (*telephone*) llamar, telefonear *AmL;* **to** ~ **sb collect** *Am* llamar a alguien a cobro revertido 3. (*make noise to attract*) **to** ~ **sb's attention** llamar la atención de alguien; **I** ~**ed you to come to eat ten minutes ago** te he llamado para que vinieras a comer hace diez minutos 4. (*ask to come*) reclamar; **she was** ~**ed to a meeting in London** fue convocada para una reunión en Londres 5. (*ask for quiet*) **to** ~ **for order** pedir orden 6. (*reprimand*) amonestar; **to** ~ **sth to mind** (*recall*) acordarse de algo; (*remember*) recordar algo 7. (*regard as*) **to** ~ **sth one's own** poder decir que algo es de uno; **you** ~ **this a party?** ¿a eso llamas fiesta?; **I'm not** ~**ing you a liar** no digo que seas un mentiroso; **I don't know exactly how much you owe me, but let's** ~ **it £10** no sé cuánto me debes exactamente, ¿lo dejamos en 10 libras?; **he has very few ideas that he can genuinely** ~ **his own** tiene muy pocas ideas realmente propias 8. (*decide to have*) **to** ~ **a meeting** convocar una reunión; **to** ~ **a halt to sth** suspender algo; **to** ~ **a strike** declarar una

huelga III. *vi* 1. (*telephone*) llamar 2. (*drop by*) pasar 3. (*shout*) gritar

◆**call at** *vt insep* 1. (*place*) pasar por 2. (*port*) hacer escala en

◆**call away** *vt* **he was called away** tuvo que salir; **he was called away on business** tuvo que irse por negocios

◆**call back** I. *vt* 1. (*telephone*) volver a llamar 2. (*ask to return*) hacer volver 3. ECON requerir; **the company has called back a type of toy** la empresa ha pedido la devolución de un tipo de juguete II. *vi* (*phone again*) volver a llamar

◆**call down on** *vt* **he called curses down on his boss** puso verde a su jefe

◆**call for** *vi insep* 1. (*come to get*) pasar a recoger 2. (*ask*) pedir 3. (*demand, require*) exigir; (*require*) requerir; **this calls for a celebration** esto hay que celebrarlo

◆**call forth** *vi form* suscitar

◆**call in** *vt* 1. (*ask to come*) llamar 2. FIN **to** ~ **a loan** pedir la devolución de un préstamo

◆**call off** *vt* 1. (*cancel*) suspender 2. (*order back*) **he called off his dog** llamó a su perro

◆**call on** *vt insep* 1. (*appeal to*) **to** ~ **sb** (to do sth) apelar a alguien (para que haga algo); **to** ~ **a witness** citar a un testigo; **I now** ~ **everyone to raise a glass to our friend** *form* propongo un brindis por nuestro amigo 2. (*visit*) visitar

◆**call out** I. *vt* (*shout*) gritar II. *vi* 1. (*shout*) gritar 2. *fig* (*demand*) **to call out for sth** exigir algo

◆**call up** *vt* 1. *Am* (*telephone*) llamar 2. INFOR **to** ~ **sth** sacar algo en pantalla 3. (*order to join the military*) **to call sb up** llamar a alguien a filas 4. (*conjure up*) conjurar

call box <-es> *n* cabina *f* telefónica

caller ['kɔːləʳ, *Am:* -lɚ] *n* 1. (*person on the telephone*) persona *f* que llama por teléfono; **hold the line please,** ~ espere, por favor 2. (*visitor, guest*) visita *f;* **they don't get many** ~**s at the shop** no tienen muchos clientes en la tienda

call girl *n* prostituta *f*

calligraphy [kəˈlɪgrəfi] *n no pl* caligrafía *f*

call-in *n* RADIO, TV *programa con llamadas del público*

calling ['kɔːlɪŋ] *n form* vocación *f*

calling card *n Am* 1. (*telephone credit card*) tarjeta *f* telefónica 2. (*card with one's name*) tarjeta *f* de visita

callous ['kæləs] *adj* (*heartless*) cruel; (*insensitive*) insensible

call-sign ['kɔːlsaɪn] *n* distintivo *m* de llamada

call-up ['kɔːlʌp] *n* MIL llamamiento *m* a filas

callus ['kæləs] <-es> *n* MED callo *m*

calm [kɑːm] I. *adj* 1. (*not nervous*) tranquilo, -a; **to keep** ~ mantenerse tranquilo 2. (*peaceful*) pacífico, -a 3. (*not windy*) sin viento 4. (*not wavy*) sin olas II. *n* tranquilidad *f;* **the** ~ **before the storm** *fig* la calma que precede a la tormenta **III.** *vt* tranquilizar; **to** ~ **oneself** calmarse

calmness *n no pl* **1.** (*lack of agitation*) tranquilidad *f* **2.** (*of the sea*) calma *f*

caloric ['kælərɪk, *Am:* kə'lɔ:r-] *adj* calórico, -a

calorie ['kæləri] *n* caloría *f*

calorific [ˌkælər'ɪfək] *adj* calorífico, -a

calumny ['kæləmni] *n no pl, form* calumnia *f*

Calvary ['kælvəri] *n no pl* Calvario *m*

calve [kɑ:v, *Am:* kæv] *vi* parir

Calvinism ['kælvɪnɪzəm] *n no pl* REL calvinismo *m*

Calvinist ['kælvɪnɪst] REL **I.** *n* calvinista *mf* **II.** *adj* calvinista

CAM [kæm] *n abbr of* **computer assisted manufacture** FAO *f*

cam [kæm] *n* TECH leva *f*

camaraderie [ˌkæmə'rɑ:dəri, *Am:* -'rædər-] *n no pl* compañerismo *m*

camber ['kæmbər, *Am:* -bə-] *n* (*of road*) peralte *m*

Cambodia [kæm'bəʊdɪə, *Am:* -'boʊ-] *n* Camboya *f*

Cambodian [kæm'bəʊdɪən, *Am:* -'boʊ-] **I.** *adj* camboyano, -a **II.** *n* camboyano, -a *m, f*

camcorder ['kæmkɔːdər] *n* videocámara *f*

came [keɪm] *vi pt of* **come**

camel ['kæml] **I.** *n* **1.** ZOOL camello *m* **2.** (*colour*) beige *m* **II.** *adj* **1.** (*camel-hair*) de pelo de camello **2.** (*colour*) beige

camel-hair ['kæməlheər, *Am:* -her] *n no pl* pelo *m* de camello

cameo ['kæmɪəʊ, *Am:* -oʊ] *n* **1.** (*jewellery*) camafeo *m* **2.** CINE, TV aparición *f* breve, papel *m* corto

camera ['kæmərə] *n* **1.** PHOT máquina *f* fotográfica; CINE cámara *f;* **to be on** ~ estar en imagen **2.** LAW **in** ~ a puerta cerrada; *fig* en secreto

camera angle *n* ángulo *m* de cámara **cameraman** <-men> *n* cámara *m* **camera-ready copy** <-ies> *n* TYPO material *m* preparado para la cámara **camera shot** *n* CINE toma *f* **camera-shy** *adj* **to be** ~ no ser muy amigo de las fotografías **camerawoman** <-women> *n* cámara *f*

Cameroon [ˌkæmə'ru:n] *n* Camerún *m*

Cameroonian [ˌkæmə'ru:nɪən, *Am:* -'roʊ-] **I.** *adj* camerunés, -esa **II.** *n* camerunés, -esa *m, f*

camomile ['kæməmaɪl, *Am:* -mi:l] *n* camomila *f;* ~ **tea** manzanilla *f*

camouflage ['kæməˌflɑ:ʒ] **I.** *n no pl* camuflaje *m* **II.** *vt* camuflar; **to** ~ **oneself** camuflarse

camp[1] [kæmp] **I.** *n* **1.** (*encampment*) campamento *m;* **army** ~ campamento militar; **summer** ~ *Am* campamento de verano; **to break** ~ levantar el campamento; **to pitch** ~ acampar **2.** (*group*) bando *m;* **to go over to the other** ~ pasarse al otro bando; **to have a foot in both** ~s estar en ambos bandos, nadar entre dos aguas **II.** *vi* acampar; **to** ~ **out** acampar; **to go** ~**ing** ir de cámping, campear *AmL*

camp[2] [kæmp] **I.** *n no pl* (**high**) ~ amaneramiento *m* **II.** *adj* (*affected*) afectado, -a; (*effeminate*) amanerado, -a **III.** *vt* **to** ~ **it up** actuar con afectación

campaign [kæm'peɪn] **I.** *n* campaña *f;* ~ **trail** campaña *f* electoral **II.** *vi* hacer campaña; **to** ~ **for sth/sb** hacer campaña a favor de algo/alguien

campaigner [kæm'peɪnər, *Am:* -ə-] *n* **1.** (*election worker*) partidario, -a *m, f* **2.** (*person who campaigns*) defensor(a) *m(f);* **a** ~ **for sth** un luchador a favor de algo

camp bed *n Brit, Aus* cama *f* plegable **camp chair** *n Brit, Aus* silla *f* plegable

camper ['kæmpər, *Am:* -pə-] *n* **1.** (*person*) campista *mf* **2.** AUTO caravana *f*

campfire *n* fogata *f;* ~ **song** canción *f* de hoguera

camp follower *n* **1.** (*civilian worker*) trabajador(a) *m(f)* civil **2.** (*supporter*) simpatizante *mf*

camphor ['kæmfər, *Am:* -fə-] *n no pl* MED alcanfor *m*

camping ['kæmpɪŋ] *n no pl* cámping *m;* **to go** ~ ir de acampada

camping ground *n Aus,* **camping site** *n Brit* (terreno *m* de) cámping *m* **camping van** *n* autocaravana *f*

campsite ['kæmpsaɪt] *n* cámping *m; Am* (*for one tent*) parcela *f* de cámping **camp stool** *n Brit* silla *f* plegable

campus ['kæmpəs] <-es> *n* campus *m inv*

camshaft ['kæmʃɑ:ft, *Am:* -ʃæft] *n* TECH árbol *m* de levas

can[1] [kæn] **I.** *n* **1.** (*container*) lata *f;* (*of oil*) bidón *m* **2.** *Am, inf* (*prison*) trullo *m* **3.** *Am, inf* (*toilet*) trono *m* ►**a** ~ **of worms** un problema peliagudo; **to open (up) a** ~ **of worms** abrir la caja de los truenos; **to carry the** ~ *Brit, inf* pagar el pato **II.** <-nn-> *vt* **1.** (*put in cans*) enlatar **2.** *Am, inf* (*stop*) ~ **it!** ¡basta ya!

can[2] [kən] <could, could> *aux* **1.** (*be able to*) poder; **if I could** si pudiera; **I think she** ~ **help you** creo que ella te puede ayudar; **I could have kissed her** hubiera podido besarla **2.** *inf* (*be permitted to*) poder; **you can't go** no puedes ir; **could I look at it?** ¿podría verlo? **3.** (*know how to*) saber; ~ **you swim?** ¿sabes nadar?

Canada ['kænədə] *n* Canadá *m*

Canadian [kə'neɪdɪən] **I.** *n* canadiense *mf* **II.** *adj* canadiense

canal [kə'næl] *n* canal *m*

canalization [ˌkænəlaɪ'zeɪʃən, *Am:* -ɪ'-] *n no pl* canalización *f*

canalize ['kænəlaɪz] *vt* **1.** (*provide with canals*) *a. fig* encauzar **2.** (*convert into a canal*) canalizar

canary [kə'neəri, *Am:* -'neri] **I.** <-ies> *n* **1.** ZOOL canario *m* **2. to sing like a** ~ *Brit, inf* chivarse **II.** *adj* ~ **yellow** amarillo canario

Canary Islands *n* Islas *fpl* Canarias

canary seed *n* alpiste *m*

canasta [kə'næstə] *n* GAMES canasta *f*
cancel ['kænsl] <-ll-, *Am:* -l-> I. *vt* 1.(*reservation, meeting*) cancelar; (*party, concert*) suspender; (*result, licence*) anular; (*payment*) retirar 2. MAT **to ~ each other out** anularse mutuamente 3. INFOR cancelar II. *vi* (*reservation*) cancelar una reserva; (*meeting*) cancelar una reunión
cancellation [ˌkænsə'leɪʃən] *n* (*of reservation, meeting*) cancelación *f*; (*of party, concert*) suspensión *f*; (*of licence*) anulación *f*; (*of contract*) rescisión *f*
cancer ['kænsə', *Am:* -sə'] *n* MED *no pl* cáncer *m*, cangro *m Col, Guat;* ~ **specialist** oncólogo, -a *m, f;* ~ **cell** célula *f* cancerígena
Cancer ['kænsə', *Am:* -sə'] *n* Cáncer *m*
cancer check-up *n* MED control *m* oncológico **cancer clinic** *n* MED clínica *f* oncológica
cancerous ['kænsərəs] *adj* MED canceroso, -a
cancer research *n no pl* MED investigación *f* oncológica
candelabra [ˌkændəl'ɑːbrə] <-(s)> *n* candelabro *m*, candil *m AmL*
candid ['kændɪd] *adj* franco, -a; (*talks*) sincero, -a; (*picture*) natural
candidacy ['kændɪdəsi] *n no pl* candidatura *f*
candidate ['kændɪdət] *n* 1. POL (*competitor*) candidato, -a *m, f* 2.(*possible choice*) aspirante *mf*
candidature ['kændɪdətʃə', *Am:* -dədətʃʊr] *n no pl, Brit s.* **candidacy**
candid camera *n* cámara *f* indiscreta
candied ['kændɪd] *adj* confitado, -a
candle ['kændl] *n* 1.(*light*) vela *f* 2. BOT castaña *f* de Indias ►**to burn one's ~ at both ends** hacer de la noche día; **she can't hold a ~ to him** no le llega ni a la suela del zapato
candlelight ['kændllaɪt] *n no pl* luz *f* de una vela; **to do sth by ~** hacer algo a la luz de una vela
Candlemas ['kændlməs] *n no pl* REL Candelaria *f*
candle-power ['kændlpaʊə', *Am:* -paʊə'] *n no pl* bujía *f*
candlestick ['kændlstɪk] *n* candelero *m*
candlewick ['kændlwɪk] *n no pl* (*textile*) chenilla *f*
candor *n Am,* **candour** ['kændə', *Am:* -də'] *n no pl, Brit, Aus, form* franqueza *f*
candy ['kændi] I. <-ies> *n Am* (*sweets*) golosinas *fpl* II. *vt* escarchar
candy bar *n Am* tableta *f* de chocolate **candyfloss** *n no pl, Brit* algodón *m* de azúcar **candy store** *n Am* tienda *f* de golosinas
cane [keɪn] I. *n* 1. *no pl* (*dried plant stem*) caña *f* 2. *no pl* (*furniture*) mimbre *m* 3. (*stick*) bastón *m*; (*for punishment*) palmeta *f* II. *vt* dar palmetazos
cane chair *n* silla *f* de mimbre **cane sugar** *n no pl* azúcar *m* de caña
canine ['keɪnaɪn] I. *n* 1. ZOOL canino *m*

2.(*tooth*) colmillo *m* II. *adj* canino, -a
canister ['kænɪstə', *Am:* -əstə'] *n* (*metal*) lata *f;* (*plastic*) bote *m*
cannabis ['kænəbɪs] *n no pl* (*plant*) cannabis *f;* (*drug*) marihuana *f*
canned [kænd] *adj* 1.(*in metal containers*) enlatado, -a; (*fruit, vegetables*) en conserva; (*food, meat, beer*) de lata 2. MUS, TV ~ **music** música *f* enlatada; ~ **laughter** risas *fpl* grabadas 3. *inf* (*drunk*) mamado, -a; **to get** ~ acabar borracho como una cuba
cannery ['kænəri] <-ies> *n* fábrica *f* de conservas
cannibal ['kænɪbl] *n* caníbal *mf*
cannibalism ['kænɪbəlɪzəm] *n no pl* canibalismo *m*
cannibalize ['kænɪbəlaɪz] *vt* AUTO desguazar
canning ['kænɪŋ] *n no pl* enlatado *m;* ~ **factory** fábrica *f* de conservas
cannon ['kænən] I. *n* cañón *m* II. *vi* **to** ~ **into sb/sth** chocar contra alguien/algo
cannon ball *n* bala *f* de cañón **cannon fodder** *n no pl* carne *f* de cañón
cannot ['kænɒt, *Am:* -ɑːt] *aux =* **can not** *s.* **can²**
canny ['kæni] <-ier, -iest> *adj* (*clever*) astuto, -a
canoe [kə'nuː] *n* canoa *f; Brit* (*kayak*) piragua *f* ►**to paddle one's own ~** arreglárselas solo
canoeing *n no pl* piragüismo *m*
canoeist [kə'nuːɪst] *n* piragüista *mf*
canon ['kænən] *n* 1. REL, MUS canon *m* 2.(*person*) canónigo *m* 3. LIT obra *f* (literaria)
canonization [ˌkænənaɪ'zeɪʃən, *Am:* -nɪ'-] *n* canonización *f*
canonize ['kænənaɪz] *vt* canonizar
can opener ['kænˌəʊpənə', *Am:* -oʊpnə'] *n* abrelatas *m inv*
canopy ['kænəpi] <-ies> *n* 1.(*roof-like covering*) toldo *m* 2. AVIAT cubierta *f* transparente 3. ARCHIT baldaquín *m* 4. *form* (*sky*) bóveda *f* celeste
cant¹ [kænt] *n no pl* 1.(*insincere talk*) hipocresía *f* 2. LING jerga *f*
cant² [kænt] I. *n* inclinación *f* II. *vt* inclinar III. *vi* inclinarse, ladearse
can't [kɑːnt, *Am:* kænt] *=* **cannot**
cantankerous [kæn'tæŋkərəs] *adj* intratable
cantata [kæn'tɑːtə, *Am:* kən'tɑːt̬ə] *n* MUS cantata *f*
canteen¹ [kæn'tiːn] *n* (*cafetería*) cantina *f*
canteen² [kæn'tiːn] *n* 1.~ **of cutlery** juego de cubiertos 2. MIL (*drink container*) cantimplora *f*
canter ['kæntə', *Am:* -t̬ə'] I. *n* medio galope *m* II. *vi* ir a medio galope
cantilever ['kæntɪliːvə', *Am:* -t̬əliːvə'] *n* viga *f* voladiza; ~ **bridge** puente *m* voladizo
Cantonese [ˌkæntə'niːz] I. *adj* cantonés, -esa II. *n* 1.(*language*) cantonés *m* 2.(*person*) cantonés, -esa *m, f*
canvas ['kænvəs] <-es> *n* 1. *no pl* (*cloth*)

lona *f;* NAUT velamen *m;* **under** ~ (*in a tent*) en una tienda de campaña **2.** ART lienzo *m,* holán *m AmC*

canvass ['kænvəs] **I.** *vt* **1.** (*gather opinion*) sondear; **to** ~ **sth** hacer una encuesta de algo **2.** POL (*votes*) solicitar **II.** *vi* POL hacer campaña

canvasser ['kænvəsə^r, *Am:* -ə·] *n* POL persona que va de puerta en puerta solicitando votos para un determinado partido político

canvassing *n* POL solicitación *f* de votos

canyon ['kænjən] *n* cañón *m*

CAP [ˌsiːeɪ'piː] *n abbr of* **Common Agricultural Policy** PAC *f*

cap[1] [kæp] **I.** *n* **1.** (*without peak*) gorro *m* **2.** (*with peak*) gorra *f;* ~ **and gown** UNIV toga *f* y birrete **3.** (*cover*) tapón *m;* PHOT tapa *f;* **screw-on** ~ casquete *m* **4.** (*of tooth*) funda *f* **5.** (*limit*) tope *m;* **salary** ~ *Am* salario *m* máximo **6.** (*contraceptive*) diafragma *m* **7.** (*in toy gun*) fulminante *m* ►**to go** ~ **in hand** mendigar; **to put on one's thinking** ~ *inf* hacer uso de la materia gris; **if the** ~ **fits, wear it** *Brit, prov* el que se pica, ajos come *prov;* **to set one's** ~ **at sb** poner los ojos en alguien **II.** <-pp-> *vt* **1.** (*limit*) limitar **2.** SPORTS **he has been** ~**ped two times for Spain** ha integrado dos veces la selección española **3.** (*cover*) tapar; (*tooth*) enfundar **4.** (*outdo*) coronar; **to** ~ **it all** para colmo

cap[2] [kæp] *n abbr of* **capital** (**letter**) mayúscula *f*

capability [ˌkeɪpə'bɪləti, *Am:* -ţi] <-ies> *n* **1.** *no pl* (*ability*) capacidad *f;* (*power*) poder *m* **2.** (*skill*) aptitud *f*

capable ['keɪpəbl] *adj* **1.** (*competent*) competente **2.** (*able*) capaz; **to be** ~ **of doing sth** ser capaz de hacer algo

capacity [kə'pæsəti, *Am:* -ţi] <-ies> *n* **1.** *no pl* (*volume*) cabida *f,* capacidad *f;* **to be full to** ~ estar completamente lleno; **filled to** ~ completamente lleno **2.** *no pl* (*ability*) capacidad *f;* (*mental*) aptitud *f* **3.** (*amount*) capacidad *f;* **seating** ~ aforo *m* **4.** (*output*) rendimiento *m;* **to work at full** ~ trabajar a pleno rendimiento **5.** (*role*) calidad *f*

cape[1] [keɪp] *n* GEO cabo *m*

cape[2] [keɪp] *n* (*cloak*) capa *f*

caper[1] ['keɪpə^r, *Am:* -ə·] **I.** *n* **1.** (*joyful leaping movement*) cabriola *f;* **to cut** ~**s** hacer cabriolas **2.** (*dubious activity*) travesura *f* **II.** *vi* dar brincos

caper[2] ['keɪpə^r, *Am:* -pə·] *n* BOT alcaparra *f*

Cape Town ['keɪptaʊn] *n* Ciudad *f* del Cabo

Cape Verde ['keɪpvɜːd, *Am:* -vɜːrd] *n* Cabo *m* Verde

capillary [kə'pɪləri, *Am:* 'kæpələr-] <-ies> *n* vaso *m* capilar

capital ['kæpɪtl, *Am:* -əţl] **I.** *n* **1.** (*principal city*) capital *f* **2.** TYPO mayúscula *f;* **small** ~**s** versalitas *fpl* **3.** ARCHIT capitel *m* **4.** FIN capital *m;* **to make** ~ (**out**) **of sth** *fig* sacar partido de algo **II.** *adj* **1.** (*principal*) primordial; ~ **city** capital *f* **2.** TYPO (*letter*) mayúscula **3.** LAW capi-

tal; ~ **punishment** pena *f* capital [*o* de muerte] **4.** *Brit* (*very good*) estupendo, -a

capital assets *npl* FIN activo *m* fijo **capital crime** *n* LAW crimen *m* capital **capital gains tax** <-es> *n* impuesto *m* sobre la plusvalía **capital investment** *n* FIN inversión *f* de capital **capital investment company** <-ies> *n* sociedad *f* inversora

capitalism ['kæpɪtəlɪzəm, *Am:* 'kæpəţ-] *n* *no pl* capitalismo *m*

capitalist ['kæpɪtəlɪst, *Am:* 'kæpəţəl-] **I.** *n* capitalista *m/f* **II.** *adj* capitalista

capitalistic [ˌkæpɪtə'lɪstɪk, *Am:* -əţə'lɪs-] *adj* capitalista

capitalization [ˌkæpɪtəlaɪ'zeɪʃən, *Am:* ˌkæpəţlɪ-] *n* capitalización *f*

capitalize ['kæpɪtəlaɪz, *Am:* 'kæpəţəlaɪz] *vt* **1.** TYPO escribir en mayúsculas **2.** *a.* FIN capitalizar

capital letter ['kæpɪtl 'letə^r, *Am:* -əţl 'leţə·] *n* mayúscula *f;* **in** ~**s** con mayúsculas **capital punishment** *n* *no pl* pena *f* de muerte

capitulate [kə'pɪtʃʊleɪt, *Am:* -'pɪtʃə-] *vi* **1.** MIL **to** ~ **to sth/sb** capitular ante algo/alguien **2.** (*give way*) ceder

capitulation [kəˌpɪtʃʊ'leɪʃən, *Am:* -'pɪtʃə-] *n* capitulación *f;* ~ **to sb/sth** capitulación ante alguien/algo

cappuccino [ˌkæpʊ'tʃiːnəʊ, *Am:* ˌkæpə'tʃiːnoʊ] *n* capuchino *m*

caprice [kə'priːs] *n liter* capricho *m*

capricious [kə'prɪʃəs] *adj* caprichoso, -a

Capricorn ['kæprɪkɔːn, *Am:* -rəkɔːrn] *n* Capricornio *m*

Caps. *n abbr of* **capitals** mayúsculas *fpl*

capsize [kæp'saɪz, *Am:* 'kæpsaɪz] **I.** *vt* NAUT hacer zozobrar; *fig* volcar **II.** *vi* NAUT zozobrar; *fig* volcar

capstan ['kæpstən] *n* NAUT cabrestante *m*

capsule ['kæpsjuːl, *Am:* -sl] *n* cápsula *f*

captain ['kæptɪn] **I.** *n* capitán, -ana *m, f* **II.** *vt* capitanear

captaincy ['kæptɪnsi] *n* *no pl* capitanía *f*

caption ['kæpʃən] *n* **1.** TYPO, PUBL (*heading*) título *m;* (*for cartoon*) leyenda *f* **2.** CINE subtítulo *m*

captivate ['kæptɪveɪt, *Am:* -tə-] *vt* cautivar

captive ['kæptɪv] **I.** *n* cautivo, -a *m, f* **II.** *adj* cautivo, -a; **to hold sb** ~ tener prisionero a alguien

captivity [kæp'tɪvəti, *Am:* -ţi] *n* *no pl* cautiverio *m;* **to be in** ~ estar en cautividad

capture ['kæptʃə^r, *Am:* -tʃə·] **I.** *n* **1.** (*take prisoner*) prender **2.** (*take possession of*) capturar; (*city*) conquistar; (*ship*) apresar; (*votes*) conseguir **3.** (*gain*) captar; **to** ~ **the market** COM hacerse con el mercado **4.** ART captar; **to** ~ **sth on film** reproducir algo en una película **II.** *n* captura *f;* (*of city*) conquista *f;* (*of ship*) presa *f*

car [kɑː^r, *Am:* kɑːr] *n* **1.** AUTO coche *m,* carro *m AmL,* auto *m Arg, Chile, Urug* **2.** RAIL vagón *m* **3.** (*in airship, balloon*) barquilla *f*

car accessories npl accesorios mpl para el coche **car aerial** n antena f del coche

carafe ['kærəf] n garrafa f

caramel ['kærəmel, Am: 'kɑ:rml] I. n 1. no pl (burnt sugar) azúcar m quemado 2. (sweet) caramelo m II. adj de caramelo; ~ **cream** flan m

carat ['kærət, Am: 'ker-] <-(s)> n quilate m

caravan ['kærəvæn, Am: 'ker-] n 1. Brit (vehicle) caravana f; **gypsy** ~ carromato m de gitanos 2. (group of travellers) caravana f

caravansary [,kærə'vænsəri, Am: ,ker-] n, **caravanserai** [,kærə'vænsəraɪ, Am: ,ker-] n caravasar m

caraway ['kærəweɪ, Am: 'ker-] n no pl alcaravea f

caraway seed n carvi m

carbide ['kɑ:baɪd, Am: 'kɑ:r-] n carburo m

carbine ['kɑ:baɪn, Am: 'kɑ:rbi:n] n carabina f

car body ['kɑ:bɒdi, Am: 'kɑ:rbɑ:-] <-ies> n chasis m inv del automóvil

carbohydrate [,kɑ:rbəʊ'haɪdreɪt, Am: ,kɑ:rboʊ-] n hidrato m de carbono; ~ **content** contenido m de carbohidratos

carbolic [kɑ:'bɒlɪk, Am: kɑ:r'bɑ:lɪk] adj ~ **acid** ácido m fénico

car bomb ['kɑ:bɒm, Am: 'kɑ:rbɑ:m] n coche m bomba

carbon ['kɑ:bən, Am: 'kɑ:r-] I. n 1. no pl CHEM carbono m 2. (copy) copia f al carbón 3. (paper) papel m de calco II. adj de carbono **carbon copy** <-ies> n copia f en papel de calco **carbon-copy crime** n crimen m calcado **carbon dating** n no pl datación f por C-14 **carbon dioxide** n no pl dióxido m de carbono

carbonic [kɑ:'bɒnɪk, Am: kɑ:r'bɑ:nɪk] adj ~ **acid** ácido m carbónico

carbonize ['kɑ:bənaɪz, Am: 'kɑ:r-] I. vt carbonizar II. vi carbonizarse

carbon monoxide n no pl monóxido m de carbono **carbon paper** n no pl papel m de calco

car-boot sale ['kɑ:bu:t,seɪl] n Brit: venta de objetos expuestos en los maleteros de los coches

carbuncle ['kɑ:bʌŋkl, Am: 'kɑ:r-] n 1. MED furúnculo m 2. (gem) carbúnculo m

carburet ['kɑ:bjʊ,ret] vt mezclar con carbono

carburetor n Am, **carburettor** [,kɑ:bjə-'retə', Am: 'kɑ:rbəreɪt ̧ə'] n carburador m

carcass ['kɑ:kəs, Am: 'kɑ:r-] <-es> n 1. (of animal) cadáver m de animal 2. (of vehicle) armazón m 3. (of cooked chicken) huesos mpl

carcinogen ['kɑ:sɪnə,dʒen, Am: kɑ:r'sɪn-] n MED (agente m) carcinógeno m

carcinogenic [,kɑ:sɪnəʊ'dʒenɪk, Am: ,kɑ:r-sənoʊ'-] adj MED cancerígeno, -a

carcinoma [,kɑ:sɪ'nəʊmə, Am: kɑ:rsn'oʊ-] n MED carcinoma m

card¹ [kɑ:d, Am: kɑ:rd] I. n 1. no pl a. FIN, INFOR tarjeta f 2. (postcard) postal f 3. GAMES carta f, naipe m; **pack of** ~s baraja f; **to play** ~s jugar a las cartas 4. SPORTS (programme) programa m 5. (index ~) ficha f 6. (proof of identity) carnet m; **membership** ~ carnet de socio 7. Brit, inf **to give sb his/her** ~s echar a alguien; **to get one's** ~s ser despedido ►**to hold one's** ~s **close to one's** chest no soltar prenda; **to have a** ~ **up one's** sleeve tener un as en la manga; **to put one's** ~s **on the** table poner las cartas sobre la mesa; **to have** all **the** ~s controlar la situación; **to hold** all **the** ~s tener todas las de ganar; **to play one's** ~s right hacer una buena jugada II. vt Am, inf pedir la documentación

card² [kɑ:d, Am: kɑ:rd] n inf cómico, -a m, f, persona f chusca

card³ [kɑ:d, Am: kɑ:rd] I. n carda f II. vt cardar

cardboard ['kɑ:dbɔ:d, Am: 'kɑ:rdbɔ:rd] n no pl cartón m

cardiac ['kɑ:dɪæk, Am: 'kɑ:r-] adj MED cardíaco, -a; (disease) cardiovascular

cardigan ['kɑ:dɪgən, Am: 'kɑ:r-] n cárdigan m; (for women) rebeca f

cardinal ['kɑ:dɪnl, Am: 'kɑ:r-] I. n 1. REL, ZOOL cardenal m 2. (number) cardinal m II. adj (importance: rule) fundamental; (error) grave; (sin) capital

cardinal number n número m cardinal **cardinal points** npl puntos mpl cardinales

card index ['kɑ:d,ɪndeks, Am: 'kɑ:rd-] <-es> n fichero m

cardiogram ['kɑ:dɪəʊgræm, Am: 'kɑ:r-dioʊ-] n MED cardiograma m

car door ['kɑ:dɔ:ʳ, Am: 'kɑ:r] n puerta f del coche

cardphone ['kɑ:dfəʊn, Am: 'kɑ:rdfoʊn] n teléfono m de tarjeta **cardpunch** n Brit INFOR perforadora f de tarjetas **card reader** n lector m de tarjetas perforadas **card table** n tapete m verde

care [keəʳ, Am: ker] I. n 1. (attention) cuidado m; **to take** ~ **of** cuidar de; (object) guardar; (situation) encargarse de; **take** ~ (of yourself)! ¡cuídate!; **to do sth with** ~ hacer algo con cuidado; **that takes** ~ **of that!** ¡eso ya está!; **handle with** ~ frágil 2. (worry) preocupación f; **to not have a** ~ **in the world** no tener ninguna preocupación; **to be free from** ~ no tener problemas II. vi 1. (be concerned) preocuparse; **to** ~ **about sb/sth** preocuparse por alguien/algo; **as if I** ~d! ¿y a mí qué?; **for all I** ~ (as far as I'm concerned) por mí; **who** ~s? ¿qué más da? 2. (feel affection) importar 3. (want) **to** ~ **to do sth** estar dispuesto a hacer algo

CARE [keəʳ, Am: ker] n abbr of **Cooperative for American Relief Everywhere** cooperativa de auxilio estadounidense en cualquier parte del mundo

career [kə'rɪəʳ, Am: -'rɪr] I. n 1. (profession) profesión f 2. (working life) carrera f profesional II. *vi* ir a toda velocidad; **to ~ out of control** (*car*) perder el control

careerist [kəˈrɪərɪst, *Am:* -ˈrɪrɪst] I. *n* ambicioso, -a *m*, *f*, arribista *mf* II. *adj* ambicioso, -a

careers officer *n* consejero, -a *m*, *f* de orientación profesional

career woman <-women> *n* mujer *f* dedicada por completo a su profesión

carefree [ˈkeəfriː, *Am:* ˈker-] *adj* despreocupado, -a

careful [ˈkeəfəl, *Am:* ˈker-] *adj* 1. (*cautious*) cuidadoso, -a; (*driver*) prudente; **to be ~ of sth** tener cuidado con algo; **to be ~ to do sth** procurar hacer algo 2. (*painstaking, meticulous*) meticuloso, -a; (*worker*) esmerado, -a

carefulness *n no pl* 1. (*caution*) cuidado *m* 2. (*meticulousness*) meticulosidad *f*

careless [ˈkeəlɪs, *Am:* ˈker-] *adj* 1. (*lacking attention*) distraído, -a 2. (*unthinking*) irreflexivo, -a, despistado, -a 3. (*not painstaking*) descuidado, -a, imprudente 4. (*carefree*) despreocupado, -a

carelessness *n no pl* 1. (*lack of attention*) falta *f* de atención 2. (*lack of concern*) despreocupación *f*

carer *n persona que cuida a una persona anciana o enferma, sin recibir remuneración alguna*

caress [kəˈres] I. <-es> *n* caricia *f* II. *vi, vt* acariciar, barbear *AmC*

caretaker [ˈkeəˌteɪkəʳ, *Am:* ˈkerˌteɪkɚ] *n* 1. *Brit* (*janitor*) conserje *mf* 2. *Am* (*job*) portero, -a *m*, *f*

careworn [ˈkeəwɔːn, *Am:* ˈkerwɔːrn] *adj* agobiado, -a por las preocupaciones

car ferry <-ies> *n* NAUT transbordador *m*

cargo [ˈkɑːgəʊ, *Am:* ˈkɑːrgoʊ] <-(e)s> *n* 1. *no pl* (*goods*) carga *f* 2. (*load*) cargamento *m*

cargo aircraft *n* avión *m* de carga **cargo boat** *n* carguero *m* **cargo plane** *n* avión *m* de carga **cargo ship** *n* barco *m* de carga **cargo vessel** *n* carguero *m*

car hire [ˈkɑːˌhaɪəʳ, *Am:* ˈkɑːrˌhaɪr] *n no pl* alquiler *m* de coches

Caribbean [ˌkærɪˈbiːən, *Am:* ˌkerɪˈbiː-] I. *n* **the ~** el Caribe II. *adj* caribeño, -a, caribe *AmL*

caricature [ˈkærɪkətʊəʳ, *Am:* ˈkerəkətʊr] I. *n a.* ART caricatura *f* II. *vt* LIT caricaturizar

caricaturist [ˈkærɪkətʊərɪst, *Am:* ˈkærəkətʃʊrɪst] *n* ART caricaturista *mf*

caries [ˈkeəriːz, *Am:* ˈkeriːz] *n no pl* MED caries *f inv*

caring *adj* compasivo, -a

car insurance *n no pl* seguro *m* de vehículos

carjacking *n Am* robo *m* de coche

car license *n Brit* permiso *m* de circulación

carnage [ˈkɑːnɪdʒ, *Am:* ˈkɑːr-] *n no pl* matanza *f*

carnal [ˈkɑːnl, *Am:* ˈkɑːr-] *adj* carnal

carnation [kɑːˈneɪʃən, *Am:* kɑːr-] I. *n* 1. BOT clavel *m* 2. (*colour*) rosa *m* vivo II. *adj* rosa vivo

carnival [ˈkɑːnɪvl, *Am:* ˈkɑːrnə-] *n* carnaval *m*, chaya *f Arg, Chile*

carnivore [ˈkɑːnɪvɔːʳ, *Am:* ˈkɑːrnəvɔːr] *n* carnívoro, -a *m*, *f*

carnivorous [kɑːˈnɪvərəs, *Am:* kɑːr-] *adj* carnívoro, -a

carol [ˈkærəl, *Am:* ˈker-] *n* villancico *m*

carol singer *n* persona *f* que canta villancicos

carotene [ˈkærətiːn] *n no pl* BIO caroteno *m*

carousel [ˌkærəˈsel] *n* 1. (*merry-go-round*) tiovivo *m* 2. (*baggage return*) cinta *f* transportadora

car owner [ˈkɑːrəʊnəʳ, *Am:* -oʊnɚ] *n* propietario, -a *m*, *f* de un coche

carp¹ [kɑːp, *Am:* kɑːrp] *n* <-(s)> carpa *f*

carp² [kɑːp, *Am:* kɑːrp] *vi* criticar por criticar; **to ~ about sth/sb** quejarse de algo/alguien sin motivo

car park [ˈkɑːpɑːk, *Am:* ˈkɑːrpɑːrk] *n Brit, Aus* aparcamiento *m*, párking *m*

carpenter [ˈkɑːpəntəʳ, *Am:* ˈkɑːrpn̩t̬ɚ] *n* carpintero, -a *m*, *f*

carpentry [ˈkɑːpəntri, *Am:* ˈkɑːrpn-] *n no pl* carpintería *f*

carpet [ˈkɑːpɪt, *Am:* ˈkɑːrpət] I. *n* (*fitted*) moqueta *f*, alfombra *f AmL*; (*not fitted*) alfombra *f* ▶**to sweep sth under the ~** correr un velo sobre algo; **to be on the ~** *inf* tener una bronca II. *vt* 1. (*cover floor*) moquetar, alfombrar *AmL* 2. *inf* (*reprimand*) **to ~ sb** (**for sth**) echar un rapapolvo a alguien (por algo)

carpet-bag [ˈkɑːpɪtbæg, *Am:* ˈkɑːrpət-] *n* maletín o bolso de tejido de alfombra

carpetbagger [ˈkɑːpɪtˌbægəʳ, *Am:* ˈkɑːrpətˌbægɚ] *n Am: persona que intenta entrar en el mundo de la política lejos de su lugar de origen porque piensa que así tiene más posibilidades de triunfar*

carpeting [ˈkɑːpɪtɪŋ, *Am:* ˈkɑːrpət̬ɪŋ] *n no pl* alfombrado *m*

carpet sweeper *n* cepillo *m* mecánico para alfombras

car pool [ˈkɑːpuːl, *Am:* ˈkɑːr-] *n* grupo de personas que comparten el mismo coche para desplazarse al trabajo

carriage [ˈkærɪdʒ, *Am:* ˈker-] *n* 1. (*horse-drawn vehicle*) carruaje *m* 2. *Brit* (*train wagon*) vagón *m* 3. (*posture*) andares *mpl* 4. (*part of typewriter*) carro *m* 5. *no pl, Brit* (*transport costs*) porte *m*

carriage-return *n* TYPO retorno *m* del carro

carriageway [ˈkærɪdʒweɪ, *Am:* ˈker-] *n Brit* calzada *f*; **dual ~** autovía *f*

carrier [ˈkærɪəʳ] *n* 1. (*person who carries*) transportista *mf*; (*messenger*) mensajero, -a *m*, *f* 2. MIL (*vehicle*) vehículo *m* transportador; **aircraft ~** portaviones *m inv* 3. MED portador(a) *m(f)* 4. (*transport company*) empresa *f* de transportes 5. *Brit, inf* bolsa *f*

carrier bag *n Brit* bolsa *f*

carrion [ˈkærɪən, *Am:* ˈker-] *n no pl* carroña *f*

carrion crow *n* corneja *f*

carrot ['kærət, *Am:* 'ker-] *n* **1.** (*vegetable*) zanahoria *f* **2.** *inf* (*reward*) incentivo *m;* **the ~ and stick approach** la política de incentivos y amenazas

carroty ['kærəti, *Am:* 'kerəɾi] <-ier, -iest> *adj* color zanahoria

carry ['kæri, *Am:* 'ker-] <-ies, -ied> I. *vt* **1.** (*transport in hands or arms*) llevar; (*take*) traer **2.** (*transport*) transportar, acarrear **3.** (*have on one's person*) llevar encima **4.** MED (*transmit*) transmitir **5.** (*support*) soportar **6.** *Am* (*sell*) vender **7.** (*win: position*) conquistar; **to ~ conviction** ser convincente; **to ~ all before one** arrasar **8.** (*approve*) aprobar **9.** PUBL **to ~ an article** publicar un artículo **10.** (*develop*) **to ~ consequences** tener consecuencias; **to ~ an argument to its (logical) conclusion** desarrollar un argumento hacia su conclusión (lógica) **11.** (*be pregnant*) **to ~ a child** esperar un hijo ▶**to ~ sb** back **to sth** recordar algo a alguien II. *vi* **1.** (*be audible*) oírse **2.** (*fly*) volar

◆**carry along** *vt* llevar; (*water*) arrastrar

◆**carry away** *vt* **1.** (*remove*) arrastrar **2.** **to be carried away (by sth)** (*be overcome by*) dejarse llevar (por algo); (*be enchanted by*) entusiasmarse (con algo); **to get carried away** exaltarse

◆**carry forward** *vt* FIN transferir

◆**carry off** *vt* **1.** llevarse; (*win: prize*) ganar; **to ~ sth** hacerse con algo **2.** (*succeed*) **to carry sth off** salir airoso de algo

◆**carry on** I. *vt insep* continuar con; **~ the good work!** ¡sigue con el buen trabajo! II. *vi* **1.** (*continue*) seguir; **to ~ doing sth** continuar haciendo algo **2.** *inf* (*make a fuss*) montar un número

◆**carry out** *vt* (*repairs*) hacer; (*plan, attack*) llevar a cabo; (*job*) realizar; (*order*) cumplir

◆**carry over** I. *vt* **1.** (*bring forward*) pasar a cuenta nueva; FIN transferir **2.** (*postpone*) posponer II. *vi* **1.** **to ~ into sth** (*have an effect on*) influir en algo **2.** (*remain*) quedar

◆**carry through** *vt* **1.** (*support*) sostener **2.** (*complete successfully*) llevar a término

carry-all ['kæriɔ:l] *n Am* bolso *m* grande

carry-cot ['kærɪˌkɒt, *Am:* 'kerɪka:t] *n* cuna *f* portátil **carrying agent** *n* agente *mf* de carga **carrying capacity** <-ies> *n* capacidad *f* de carga **carrying-on** <carryings-on> *n inf* **1.** *no pl* (*dubious affair*) enredos *mpl* **2.** (*dubious activity*) líos *mpl* **carry-over** *n* **1.** FIN pérdida trasladada al ejercicio siguiente **2.** (*remnant*) remanente *m*

cart [ka:t, *Am:* ka:rt] I. *n* **1.** (*vehicle*) carreta *f*, carro *m* **2.** *Am* (*supermarket trolley*) carrito *m* ▶**to put the ~ before the** horse empezar la casa por el tejado II. *vt* (*transport*) acarrear; (*carry*) cargar

carte blanche [ˌka:t'blã:ntʃ, *Am:* ˌka:rt-'bla:nʃ] *n no pl* carta *f* blanca

cartel [ka:'tel, *Am:* ka:r-] *n* cartel *m*

carter ['ka:tə*r*, *Am:* 'ka:rtə*·*] *n* carretero *m*

carthorse ['ka:tˌhɔ:s, *Am:* 'ka:rthɔ:rs] *n* caballo *m* de tiro

cartilage ['ka:tɪlɪdʒ, *Am:* 'ka:rt̬lɪdʒ] *n no pl* cartílago *m*

cartload ['ka:tˌləʊd, *Am:* 'ka:rtloʊd] *n* carretada *f;* **~s of rubbish** montones *mpl* de basura

cartographer [ka:'tɒgrəfə*r*, *Am:* ka:r'ta:-grəfə*·*] *n* cartógrafo, -a *m, f*

cartography [ka:'tɒgrəfi, *Am:* ka:r'ta:grə-] *n no pl* cartografía *f*

carton ['ka:tn, *Am:* 'ka:r-] *n* (*box*) caja *f* de cartón; (*of juice, milk*) envase *m* de cartón

cartoon [ka:'tu:n, *Am:* ka:r-] *n* **1.** ART viñeta *f* **2.** CINE dibujos *mpl* animados

cartoonist *n* dibujante *mf*

cartridge ['ka:trɪdʒ, *Am:* 'ka:r-] *n* **1.** (*for ink, ammunition, cassette*) cartucho *m*, cachimba *f AmL* **2.** (*pick-up head*) cápsula *f*

cartridge case *n* cartucho *m* **cartridge paper** *n no pl* papel *m* de dibujo

cartwheel ['ka:twhi:l, *Am:* 'ka:rt-] I. *n* **1.** (*wheel*) rueda *f* de carro **2.** (*playing*) rueda *f;* **to do a ~** hacer la rueda II. *vi* hacer ruedas

carve [ka:v, *Am:* ka:rv] I. *vt* **1.** (*cut*) cortar; **to ~ (out) a name for oneself** *fig* hacerse un nombre **2.** (*stone, wood*) tallar **3.** (*cut meat*) trinchar II. *vi* cortar

carver ['ka:və*r*, *Am:* 'ka:rvə*·*] *n* **1.** ART escultor(a) *m(f)* **2.** *pl* GASTR trinchantes *mpl*

carvery ['ka:və*r*i, *Am:* 'ka:rvə*·*i] <-ies> *n* asador *m*

carving *n* ART **1.** *no pl* (*art of cutting*) arte *m* de esculpir **2.** (*ornamental figure*) escultura *f;* (*of wood*) talla *f*

carving knife <knives> *n* cuchillo *m* de trinchar

car wash <-es> *n* túnel *m* de lavado

cascade [kæ'skeɪd] I. *n* **1.** (*waterfall*) cascada *f* **2.** *liter* (*flowing mass*) torrente *m* II. *vi* **to ~ from sth** caer en cascada de algo

case[1] [keɪs] *n* **1.** *a.* MED caso *m;* **in any ~** en cualquier caso; **just in ~** por si acaso; **in ~ it rains** en caso de que llueva; **as the ~ stands** tal como está el caso **2.** LING caso *m* **3.** LAW caso *m;* **to close the ~** cerrar el caso; **to lose one's ~** perder el caso **4.** (*argument*) **to make out a ~ for sth** argumentar a favor de algo

case[2] [keɪs] *n* **1.** *Brit* (*suitcase*) maleta *f;* (*chest*) arcón *m*, veliz *m Méx* **2.** (*container*) caja *f;* (*for jewels, spectacles*) estuche *m;* (*for camera, musical instrument*) funda *f;* **glass ~** vitrina *f*

case book *n* diario *m;* MED registro *m* **case law** *n no pl* LAW jurisprudencia *f* **case study** <-ies> *n* monografía *f*

cash [kæʃ] I. *n no pl* dinero *m* en efectivo; **~ in advance** adelanto *m;* **to be strapped for ~** *inf* andar corto de dinero II. *vt* cobrar; (*cheque*) cambiar; **to ~ sth in** canjear algo; **to ~ in (one's chips)** *inf* (*die*) palmarla

◆**cash down** *vt*, **cash over** *vt Am, inf* pagar al contado

◆**cash in** I. *vt insep* canjear II. *vi* **to ~ on sth** sacar provecho de algo

cash-and-carry [ˌkæʃənd'kæri, *Am:* -ənd-'ker-] I.<-ies> *n* tienda *f* de venta al por mayor II. *adj* de venta al por mayor III. *adv* al por mayor

cash balance *n* saldo *m* de caja **cash box** <-es> *n* caja *f* del dinero **cash card** *n Brit* tarjeta *f* del cajero automático **cash crop** *n* cultivo *m* comercial **cash dispenser** *n Brit* cajero *m* automático

cashew ['kæʃuː] *n,* **cashew nut** *n* anacardo *m,* acajú *m Cuba, Méx, PRico, RDom*

cash flow ['kæʃˌfləʊ, *Am:* -ˌfloʊ] *n* FIN flujo *m* de caja

cashier[1] [kæ'ʃɪəʳ, *Am:* kæʃ'ɪr] *n* cajero, -a *m, f*

cashier[2] [kæ'ʃɪəʳ, *Am:* kæʃ'ɪr] *vt* MIL destituir

cash machine *n* cajero *m* automático

cashmere ['kæʃmɪə, *Am:* 'kæʒmɪr] *n* cachemir *m*

cash payment ['kæʃˌpeɪmənt] *n* pago *m* al contado **cashpoint** *n Brit* cajero *m* automático **cash register** *n* caja *f* registradora **cash sale** *n* venta *f* al contado

casing ['keɪsɪŋ] *n* cubierta *f;* (*of machine*) carcasa *f;* (*of cable*) tubo *m* de revestimiento

casino [kə'siːnəʊ, *Am:* -noʊ] *n* casino *m*

cask [kɑːsk, *Am:* kæsk] *n* tonel *m;* (*of wine*) barril *m*

casket ['kɑːskɪt, *Am:* 'kæskɪt] *n* **1.** (*box*) cofre *m;* (*for jewels*) joyero *m* **2.** *Am* (*coffin*) ataúd *m*

Caspian Sea ['kæspiən] *n* Mar *m* Caspio

casserole ['kæsərəʊl, *Am:* -əroʊl] I. *n* **1.** (*cooking vessel*) cazuela *f;* (*of iron*) cacerola *f* **2.** GASTR guiso *m* II. *vt* guisar (en una cazuela)

cassette [kə'set] *n* casete *m o f;* **video ~** videocasete *m*

cassette deck *n* platina *f* **cassette player** *n,* **cassette recorder** *n* casete *m*

cast [kɑːst, *Am:* kæst] I. *n* **1.** THEAT, CINE reparto *m;* **supporting ~** reparto secundario **2.** (*mould*) molde *m* **3.** MED escayola *f* **4.** (*of worm*) rastro *m* II.<cast, cast> *vt* **1.** (*throw*) lanzar; (*fishing line*) arrojar **2.** (*direct*) **to ~ doubt on sth** poner algo en duda; **to ~ a shadow on sth** ensombrecer algo; **to ~ light on sth** proyectar luz sobre algo; *fig* echar luz sobre algo; **to ~ an eye over sth** echar una ojeada a algo **3.** (*allocate roles*) asignar; **to ~ sb as sb/sth** dar a alguien el papel de alguien/algo; **to ~ sb in a role** elegir a alguien para un papel **4.** (*give*) dar; (*vote*) emitir **5.** (*make in a mould*) vaciar

◆**cast about** *vi,* **cast around** *vi* **to ~ for sth** ir a por algo

◆**cast aside** *vt,* **cast away** *vt* (*rid oneself of*) dejar de lado; (*free oneself of*) desechar

◆**cast down** *vt* **to be ~** estar deprimido

◆**cast off** I. *vt* **1.** (*stitch*) cerrar **2.** (*throw off*) desechar II. *vi* **1.** NAUT soltar amarras **2.** (*in knitting*) terminar

◆**cast on** I. *vt* (*in knitting: stitch*) echar II. *vi* (*in knitting*) montar los puntos

◆**cast out** *vt* arrojar; (*demons, ideas*) echar fuera de sí; (*person*) expulsar

◆**cast up** *vt* echar

castanets [kæstə'nets] *npl* castañuelas *fpl*

castaway ['kɑːstəweɪ, *Am:* 'kæstə-] *n* **1.** (*survivor from a ship*) náufrago, -a *m, f* **2.** (*discarded object*) trasto *m*

caste [kɑːst, *Am:* kæst] *n* (*social class*) casta *f;* **~ system** sistema *m* de castas

caster ['kɑːstəʳ, *Am:* 'kæstəʳ] *n* ruedecita *f*

castigate ['kæstɪgeɪt, *Am:* -tə-] *vt form* fustigar; **to ~ sb for sth** censurar a alguien por algo

castigation [ˌkæstɪ'geɪʃən, *Am:* -ə'-] *n no pl* censura *f;* (*rebuke*) reprobación *f*

casting ['kɑːstɪŋ, *Am:* 'kæstɪŋ] *n* **1.** (*forming in a mould*) vaciado *m* **2.** THEAT reparto *m* de papeles

casting vote *n* voto *m* de calidad

cast iron [ˌkɑː'staɪən] I. *n no pl* hierro *m* fundido II. *adj* **1.** (*made of cast iron*) de hierro fundido **2.** *fig* (*evidence*) irrefutable; (*alibi*) a toda prueba; (*promise*) firme

castle ['kɑːsl, *Am:* 'kæsl] I. *n* **1.** (*building*) castillo *m* **2.** (*chess piece*) torre *f* ▶**to build ~s in the air** construir castillos en el aire II. *vi* (*in chess*) enrocar

cast-off [ˌkɑː'stɒf, *Am:* 'kæstɑːf] I. *n* (*garment*) prenda *f* desechada [*o* vieja]; **~s** ropa *f* desechada [*o* vieja] II. *adj* (*clothes, shoes*) desechado, -a, viejo, -a

castor ['kɑːstəʳ, *Am:* 'kæstəʳ] *n* ruedecita *f*

castor oil *n no pl* aceite *m* de ricino **castor stand** *n Am* puesto *m* de los espolvoreadores **castor sugar** *n no pl, Brit* azúcar *m* blanco muy fino

castrate [kæ'streɪt] *vt* castrar, componer *AmL*

casual ['kæʒʊəl, *Am:* 'kæʒuː-] *adj* **1.** (*relaxed*) relajado, -a **2.** (*not permanent*) casual; (*sex*) ocasional **3.** (*not serious*) despreocupado, -a; (*glance*) al azar; (*remark*) a la ligera; (*meeting*) fortuito, -a **4.** (*not habitual*) de vez en cuando **5.** (*informal*) informal; (*clothes*) deportivo, -a

casual labour *n no pl,* **casual work** *n no pl* trabajo *m* temporal

casual labourer *n,* **casual worker** *n* trabajador(a) *m(f)* temporero, -a

casually *adv* de forma relajada

casualty ['kæʒʊəlti, *Am:* 'kæʒuː-] <-ies> *n* **1.** (*accident victim*) víctima *f;* (*injured person*) herido, -a *m, f;* MIL (*dead person*) baja *f* **2.** (*negative result*) pérdidas *fpl* **3.** *no pl* (*hospital department*) urgencias *fpl*

cat [kæt] *n* gato, -a *m, f* ▶**to let the ~ out of the bag** descubrir el pastel; **to not have a ~ in hell's chance** *inf* no tener la más mínima posibilidad; **to fight like ~ and dog** llevarse como (el) perro y (el) gato; **to rain ~s and dogs** llover a cántaros; **to put the ~ among the pigeons** armar un revuelo; **there's not**

enough room to swing a ~ no cabe ni un alfiler; **to look like something the** ~ **brought in** ir hecho un pordiosero
CAT [kæt] *n* 1. INFOR *abbr of* computer-assisted translation TAO *f* 2. MED *abbr of* computerized axial tomography TAC *m o f;* ~ **scan** (escáner *m*) TAC *m*
cataclysmic [ˌkætəˈklɪzmɪk, *Am:* ˌkæt̬əˈ-] *adj* desastroso, -a
catacombs [ˈkætəkuːmz, *Am:* ˈkæt̬əkoʊm] *npl* catacumbas *fpl*
Catalan [ˌkætəˈlæn, *Am:* ˈkæt̬əlæn] I. *adj* catalán, -ana II. *n* 1. (*habitant*) catalán, -ana *m, f* 2. (*language*) catalán *m*
catalog *Am,* **catalogue** [ˈkætəlɒg, *Am:* ˈkæt̬əlɑːg] *Brit* I. *n* catálogo *m;* (*repeated events*) serie *f;* **a** ~ **of mistakes** *fig* un error detrás de otro II. *vt* catalogar
Catalonia [ˌkætəˈləʊniə, *Am:* -ˈloʊ-] *n* Cataluña *f*
Catalonian [ˌkætəˈləʊniən, *Am:* -ˈloʊ-] *adj, n s.* **Catalan**
catalysis [kəˈtæləsɪs] *n no pl* catálisis *f inv*
catalyst [ˈkætəlɪst, *Am:* ˈkæt̬-] *n a. fig* catalizador *m*
catalytic [kætəˈlɪtɪk] *adj* catalítico, -a; ~ **converter** AUTO catalizador *m*
catamaran [ˌkætəməˈræn, *Am:* ˌkæt̬-] *n* catamarán *m*
catapult [ˈkætəpʌlt, *Am:* ˈkæt̬-] I. *n* tirachinas *m inv;* HIST catapulta *f* II. *vt* catapultar
cataract¹ [ˈkætərækt, *Am:* ˈkæt̬ərækt] *n* MED catarata *f*
cataract² [ˈkætərækt, *Am:* ˈkæt̬ərækt] *n* (*waterfall*) catarata *f*
catarrh [kəˈtɑːʳ, *Am:* kəˈtɑːr] *n no pl* catarro *m*
catastrophe [kəˈtæstrəfi] *n* catástrofe *f*
catastrophic [ˌkætəˈstrɒfɪk, *Am:* ˌkæt̬əˈstrɑːfɪk] *adj* catastrófico, -a
catcall [ˈkætkɔːl] *n* (*booing*) abucheo *m;* (*whistling*) silbido *m*
catch [kætʃ] <-es> I. *n* 1. *no pl* (*fish caught*) pesca *f* 2. (*fastening device*) pestillo *m;* (*on window*) cierre *m* 3. *inf* (*suitable partner*) **he's a good** ~ es un buen partido 4. (*trick*) trampa *f* II. <caught, caught> *vt* 1. (*hold moving object*) agarrar; (*person*) atrapar; **to** ~ **sb at a bad moment** pillar a alguien en un mal momento 2. (*entangle*) involucrar; **to get caught in sth** quedar atrapado en algo; **to get caught up in sth** quedar involucrado en algo; **to get caught on sth** engancharse a algo 3. (*collect*) acumular; (*liquid*) recoger 4. (*capture an expression*) percibir; (*hear*) oír 5. (*attract*) atraer 6. (*get*) coger, tomar *AmL;* **to** ~ **the bus** coger el bus 7. (*discover*) descubrir 8. (*notice*) darse cuenta de; (*by chance*) pillar por casualidad 9. (*discover by surprise*) **to** ~ **sb** (**doing sth**) sorprender [*o* pillar] a alguien (haciendo algo); **to** ~ **sb red handed** *fig* coger [*o* pillar] a alguien con las manos en la masa; **to** ~ **sb with their trousers down, to** ~ **sb**

napping *fig* coger [*o* pillar] a alguien desprevenido 10. MED (*become infected*) contagiarse de 11. (*start burning: fire*) prender
◆**catch at** *vi* tratar de coger
◆**catch on** *vi* 1. (*be popular*) ponerse de moda 2. *inf* (*understand*) entender
◆**catch out** *vt* 1. (*discover wrongdoing*) **to catch sb out** pescar [*o* sorprender] a alguien; **we were caught out by his reaction** su reacción nos cogió desprevenidos 2. (*ask trick questions*) pillar, engañar
◆**catch up** I. *vi* **to** ~ **with sb** alcanzar el nivel de alguien; **to** ~ **with sth** (*make up lost time*) ponerse al corriente de algo; (*equal the standard*) igualarse a algo II. *vt* **to catch sb up** *Brit, Aus* alcanzar a alguien
catchall [ˈkætʃɔːl] *adj* comodín
catcher [ˈkætʃəʳ, *Am:* -ɚ] *n* SPORTS receptor(a) *m(f)*
catching [ˈkætʃɪŋ] *adj a. fig, inf* contagioso, -a
catchment [ˈkætʃmənt] *n* captación *f*
catchphrase [ˈkætʃfreɪz] *n* eslogan *m*
catch question *n* pregunta *f* capciosa
catchup [ˈkætʃəp] *n* ketchup *m*
catchword [ˈkætʃwɜːd, *Am:* -ˌwɜːrd] *n* eslogan *m*
catchy [ˈkætʃi] <-ier, -iest> *adj* pegadizo, -a
catechism [ˈkætɪkɪzəm, *Am:* ˈkæt̬-] *n* 1. (*instruction*) catequesis *f inv* 2. (*book*) catecismo *m*
categorical [ˌkætɪˈgɒrɪkl, *Am:* ˌkæt̬əˈgɔːr-] *adj* (*denial, refusal*) categórico, -a
categorise *vt Brit, Aus,* **categorize** [ˈkætəgəraɪz, *Am:* ˈkæt̬əgəraɪz] *vt Am* clasificar
category [ˈkætəgəri, *Am:* ˈkæt̬əgɔːr-] <-ies> *n* categoría *f*
cater [ˈkeɪtəʳ, *Am:* -t̬ɚ] *vi* encargarse del servicio de comidas
caterer [ˈkeɪtərəʳ, *Am:* ˈkeɪt̬ɚɚ] *n* encargado, -a *m, f* del servicio de comidas
catering [ˈkeɪtərɪŋ] *n no pl* restauración *f;* (*service*) servicio *m* de comidas
caterpillar [ˈkætəpɪləʳ, *Am:* ˈkæt̬ɚpɪlɚ] *n* 1. ZOOL oruga *f* 2. (*on vehicle wheels*) rodado *m* de oruga 3. (*vehicle*) tractor *m* oruga
caterpillar tractor *n* tractor *m* oruga
caterwaul [ˈkætəwɔːl, *Am:* ˈkæt̬ɚ-] I. *n* aullido *m* II. *vi* aullar
catgut [ˈkætgʌt] *n no pl* cuerda *f* de tripa; MED catgut *m*
cathartic [kəˈθɑːtɪk, *Am:* kəˈθɑːrt̬ɪk] *adj* catártico, -a
cathedral [kəˈθiːdrəl] *n* catedral *f;* ~ **city** ciudad *f* episcopal
catherine wheel [ˈkæθərɪnˌhwiːl] *n* (*firework*) girándula *f*
catheter [ˈkæθɪtəʳ, *Am:* -ət̬ɚ] *n* MED catéter *m*
cathode [ˈkæθəʊd, *Am:* -oʊd] *n* ELEC cátodo *m*
cathode ray *n* rayo *m* catódico
Catholic [ˈkæθəlɪk] REL I. *n* católico, -a *m, f*

II. *adj* católico, -a
catholic [ˈkæθəlɪk] *adj* variado, -a
Catholicism [kəˈθɒləsɪzəm, *Am:* -ˈθɑ:lə-] *n no pl* catolicismo *m*
catkin [ˈkætkɪn] *n* amento *m*
cat litter *n no pl* arena *f* higiénica
catnap [ˈkætˌnæp] I. *n inf* siestecita *f;* **to have a ~** echar una cabezada II. <-pp-> *vi inf* echar una siestecita
cat's cradle [ˌkætsˈkreɪdl] *n* juego *m* de la cuna
cat's eye [ˈkætsaɪ] *n Brit, Aus* ojo *m* de gato
catsup [ˈkætsəp] *n Am* ketchup *m*
cattle [ˈkætl, *Am:* ˈkæt̬-] *npl* (*bovines*) ganado *m;* **beef ~** ganado vacuno; **dairy ~** vacas *fpl* lecheras
cattle-breeder *n* ganadero, -a *m, f* **cattle-breeding** *n no pl* ganadería *f* **cattle-car** *n Am* RAIL vagón *m* de ganado **cattle-thief** <-thieves> *n* ladrón, -ona *m, f* de ganado
catty [ˈkæti, *Am:* ˈkæt̬-] <-ier, -iest> *adj* (*hurtful*) malicioso, -a; (*remark*) intencionado, -a
cat-walk [ˈkætˌwɔ:k, *Am:* -wɑ:k] *n* **1.** THEAT puente *m* de trabajo **2.** *Brit* FASHION pasarela *f*
Caucasian [kɔ:ˈkeɪzɪən, *Am:* kɑ:ˈkeɪʒən] *form* I. *n* **1.** (*white*) blanco, -a *m, f* **2.** (*European*) caucásico, -a *m, f* **3.** (*languages*) caucásico *m* II. *adj* **1.** (*white*) blanco, -a **2.** (*European*) caucásico, -a **3.** (*of the Caucasus*) caucasiano, -a; (*language*) caucásico, -a
caucus [ˈkɔ:kəs, *Am:* ˈkɑ:-] I. *n* <-es> **1.** (*group*) comité *m* **2.** (*members*) camarilla *f* **3.** *Am* (*meeting*) reunión *f* del comité de un partido II. *vi* celebrar una reunión del comité del partido
caught [kɔ:t, *Am:* kɑ:t] *pt, pp of* **catch**
cauldron [ˈkɔ:ldrən, *Am:* ˈkɑ:l-] *n* caldero *m; fig* hervidero *m*
cauliflower [ˈkɒlɪflaʊəʳ, *Am:* ˈkɑ:lɪˌflaʊɚ] *n* coliflor *f*
caulk [kɔ:k, *Am:* kɑ:k] *vt* enmasillar; NAUT calafatear
causal [ˈkɔ:zl, *Am:* ˈkɑ:-] *adj a.* LING causal; (*relationship*) de causa-efecto
causality [kɔ:ˈzæləti, *Am:* kɑ:ˈzælət̬i] *n no pl, form* causalidad *f*
causative [ˈkɔ:zətɪv, *Am:* ˈkɑ:zət̬ɪv] *adj form* **1.** (*acting as a cause*) causante **2.** LING causativo, -a
cause [kɔ:z] I. *n* **1.** (*a reason for*) causa *f,* motivo *m;* **he is the ~ of all her woes** él es el causante de todas sus penas; **this is no ~ for ... esto no justifica... 2.** *no pl* (*objective*) causa *f* **3.** (*principle*) causa *f;* **to do sth in the ~ of sth** hacer algo en pro de algo **4.** LAW pleito *m* II. *vt* causar; (*an accident*) provocar; **to ~ sb/ sth to do sth** hacer que alguien/algo haga algo; **to ~ sb harm** ocasionar daños a alguien; **this medicine may ~ dizziness and nausea** este medicamento puede provocar mareos y náuseas
causeway [ˈkɔ:zˌweɪ, *Am:* ˈkɑ:z-] *n* **1.** (*road*

bridge) carretera *f* elevada **2.** (*pathway*) paso *m* elevado
caustic [ˈkɔ:stɪk, *Am:* ˈkɑ:-] *adj a. fig* cáustico, -a; (*lime*) vivo, -a; (*remark*) mordaz; (*tongue*) viperino, -a
cauterise *vt Brit, Aus,* **cauterize** [ˈkɔ:təraɪz, *Am:* ˈkɑ:t̬əraɪz] *vt a. fig* cauterizar
caution [ˈkɔ:ʃən, *Am:* ˈkɑ:-] I. *n no pl* **1.** (*carefulness*) cautela *f; ~* **is advised** se recomienda prudencia; **to throw ~ to the winds** jugársela; **to treat sth with ~** tratar algo con cuidado **2.** (*warning*) advertencia *f;* **a note of ~** un aviso; **~!** ¡cuidado! **3.** *Brit* LAW fianza *f;* **to let sb off with a ~** dejar a alguien en libertad bajo fianza II. *vt form* **1.** (*warn*) prevenir a; **to ~ sb to do sth** aconsejar a alguien que haga algo **2.** *Brit* (*reprimand*) amonestar a; **to ~ sb about sth** llamar la atención a alguien por algo
cautionary [ˈkɔ:ʃənəri, *Am:* ˈkɑ:ʃənɚ-] *adj* aleccionador(a); **a ~ tale** un cuento con moraleja
cautious [ˈkɔ:ʃəs, *Am:* ˈkɑ:-] *adj* cauto, -a; (*optimism*) moderado, -a; **to be ~ in sth** ser prudente en algo
cavalcade [ˌkævlˈkeɪd] *n* **1.** (*procession*) cabalgata *f* **2.** (*succession*) desfile *m;* (*of memories*) sucesión *f*
cavalier [ˌkævəlˈɪəʳ, *Am:* -əlɪr] I. *n* HIST caballero *m* II. *adj* arrogante; **a ~ attitude** una actitud desdeñosa
cavalry [ˈkævəlri] *n pl vb* MIL caballería *f*
cavalryman [ˈkævəlrimən] <-men> *n* **1.** HIST (*mounted*) caballero *m* **2.** MIL (*in armoured vehicles*) soldado *m* de caballería
cave[1] [keɪv] *n* **to keep ~** vigilar
cave[2] [keɪv] I. *n* (*natural*) cueva *f;* (*man-made*) caverna *f* II. *vi* **1.** (*hollow out*) cavar **2.** *Brit* SPORTS hacer espeleología
♦cave in *vi* ceder
caveat [ˈkæviæt] *n* **1.** (*warning*) advertencia *f* **2.** LAW anotación provisional para asegurar el cumplimiento de la resolución judicial
cavedweller *n* cavernícola *mf*
cave-in *n* derrumbamiento *m*
caveman [ˈkeɪvmæn] <-men> *n* **1.** (*prehistoric man*) hombre *m* de las cavernas **2.** *inf* (*socially underdeveloped*) bruto *m inf,* troglodita *m* **cave painting** *n* pintura *f* rupestre
caver [ˈkeɪvəʳ, *Am:* -ɚ] *n Brit, Aus* espeleólogo, -a *m, f*
cavern [ˈkævən, *Am:* -ɚn] *n* caverna *f*
cavernous [ˈkævənəs, *Am:* -ɚn-] *adj* cavernoso, -a; (*hole, room*) oscuro, -a; (*pit*) profundo, -a; (*eyes*) hundido, -a
caviar(e) [ˈkæviɑːʳ, *Am:* -ɑːr] *n no pl* caviar *m*
cavity [ˈkævɪti, *Am:* -t̬i] <-ies> *n* **1.** *a.* ANAT cavidad *f;* **nasal ~** fosa *f* nasal **2.** MED caries *f inv*
caw [kɔː, *Am:* kɑː] I. *n* graznido *m* II. *vi* graznar
cayenne [keɪˈen, *Am:* kaɪ-] *n,* **cayenne**

pepper *n no pl* (pimienta *f* de) cayena *f*
Cayman Islands ['keɪmən,aɪləndz] *n* Islas *fpl* Cayman
CB [,si:'bi:] *n no pl abbr of* Citizen's Band banda *f* ciudadana
CBI [,si:bi:'aɪ] *n Brit abbr of* Confederation of British Industry ≈ CEOE *f*
CBT *abbr of* Computer Based Training CBT
CBW *n abbr of* chemical and biological warfare guerra *f* bioquímica
cc [,si:'si:] *abbr of* cubic centimetres cc
CCTV [,si:si:ti:'vi:] *n abbr of* closed-circuit television circuito *m* cerrado de televisión
ccw. *adj, adv abbr of* counterclockwise en sentido contrario a las agujas del reloj
CD [,si:'di:] *n abbr of* compact disc CD *m*
CDI [,si:di:'aɪ] *n* INFOR *abbr of* compact disk interactive CDI *m*
CD-player *n abbr of* compact disc player reproductor *m* de CD
CD-R *n abbr of* Compact Disc Recordable CD-R *m*
CD-ROM [,si:di:'rɒm, *Am:* -'rɑːm] *n abbr of* compact disc read-only memory CD-ROM *m;* on ~ en CD-ROM
CD-ROM drive *n* unidad *f* de CD-ROM
CD-ROM player *n* lector *m* de CD-ROM
CD-ROM writer *n* grabador *m* de CD-ROM
CD-RW *n abbr of* Compact Disc Rewritable Unit CD-RW *m*
cease [si:s] *form* I. *n no pl* without ~ sin cesar II. *vi* cesar; to ~ from sth cesar de (hacer) algo III. *vt* suspender; it never ~s to amaze me nunca deja de sorprenderme; ~ firing! MIL ¡alto el fuego!
cease-fire [,si:s'faɪər, *Am:* -'faɪɚ] *n* MIL alto *m* el fuego, cese *m* del fuego *AmL*
ceaseless ['si:slɪs] *adj* incesante
cedar ['si:dər, *Am:* -dɚ] *n* 1. (*tree*) cedro *m* 2. *no pl* (*wood*) (madera *f* de) cedro *m*
cede [si:d] *vt form* ceder
ceiling ['si:lɪŋ] *n* 1. ARCHIT, AVIAT techo *m* 2. (*upper limit*) tope *m;* (*on prices*) límite *m;* to impose a ~ on sth poner un tope a algo 3. METEO cielo *m* (raso) ►to hit the ~ *inf* subirse por las paredes
celebrate ['selɪbreɪt] I. *vi* celebrar; let's ~! ¡vamos a celebrarlo! II. *vt* celebrar; (*anniversary of death*) conmemorar; they ~d him as a hero lo agasajaron como a un héroe
celebrated *adj* célebre
celebration [,selɪ'breɪʃən] *n* 1. (*party*) fiesta *f* 2. (*of an occasion*) celebración *f;* (*of an event*) conmemoración *f;* to throw a party in ~ of sth dar una fiesta para celebrar algo; this calls for a ~! ¡esto hay que celebrarlo!
celebratory [,selə'breɪtəri, *Am:* 'seləbrətɔːri] *adj* we went for a ~ dinner fuimos a cenar para celebrarlo
celebrity [sɪ'lebrəti, *Am:* sə'lebrəti] *n* 1. <-ies> (*person*) famoso, -a *m, f* 2. *no pl* (*fame*) celebridad *f*
celeriac [sə'leriæk] *n no pl* apio *m* nabo

celery ['seləri] *n no pl* apio *m*, panul *m* CSur
celestial [sɪ'lestrəl, *Am:* -tʃl] *adj a. fig* celestial
celestial body <-ies> *n* cuerpo *m* celeste
celibacy ['selɪbəsi] *n no pl* 1. *a.* REL celibato *m* 2. (*being single*) soltería *f*
celibate ['selɪbət] I. *n* célibe *mf* II. *adj* 1. *a.* REL (*refraining from sex*) célibe 2. (*unmarried*) soltero, -a
cell [sel] *n* 1. (*in prison*) celda *f*, separo *m* Méx 2. BIO, POL célula *f*; a single ~ animal un animal unicelular; grey ~s materia *f* gris *inf* 3. ELEC pila *f*
cellar ['selər, *Am:* -ɚ] *n* 1. (*basement*) sótano *m;* (*for wine*) bodega *f* 2. *Am* SPORTS último lugar *m*
cellist ['tʃelɪst] *n* MUS violoncelista *mf*
cell nucleus ['sel,nju:klɪəs, *Am:* -nu:-] <-clei *o* -es> *n* núcleo *m* celular
cello ['tʃeləʊ, *Am:* -oʊ] <-s *o* -li> *n* MUS violoncelo *m*
cellophane® ['seləfeɪn] *n* celofán *m*
cellular ['seljʊlər, *Am:* -lɚ] *adj* 1. BIO celular 2. (*porous*) poroso, -a
cellular phone *n*, **cellphone** ['selfəʊn, *Am:* -foʊn] *n* teléfono *m* móvil
cellulite ['seljəlaɪt] *n no pl* celulitis *f inv*
celluloid ['seljʊlɔɪd] I. *n no pl* celuloide *m* II. *adj* de celuloide
cellulose ['seljʊləʊs, *Am:* -loʊs] *n no pl* celulosa *f*
Celsius ['selsiəs] *adj* PHYS Celsius
Celt [kelt, selt] *n* HIST celta *mf*
Celtic ['keltik, 'seltik] I. *adj* céltico, -a; (*language*) celta II. *n* celta *m*
cement [sɪ'ment] I. *n no pl* 1. ARCHIT cemento *m* 2. (*glue*) cola *f* 3. MED empaste *m* 4. (*uniting idea*) aglutinante *m* II. *vt* 1. (*cover with cement*) revestir de cemento; to ~ over sth revestir algo de cemento 2. (*stabilize*) fortalecer; (*a friendship*) consolidar 3. MED empastar
cement mixer *n* hormigonera *f*
cemetery ['semətri, *Am:* -teri] <-ies> *n* cementerio *m*, panteón *m AmL*
censer ['sensər, *Am:* -sɚ] *n* REL incensario *m*
censor ['sensər, *Am:* -sɚ] I. *n* 1. (*official*) censor(a) *m(f)* 2. PSYCH censura *f* II. *vt* censurar
censorious [sen'sɔːriəs, *Am:* -'sɔːri-] *adj* censurador(a); (*comments*) de reprobación; to be ~ about [*o* of] sth/sb censurar algo/a alguien
censorship ['sensəʃɪp, *Am:* -sɚ-] *n no pl* censura *f*
censure ['sentʃər] *vt* censurar
census ['sensəs] <-es> *n* censo *m*
cent [sent] *n Am* centavo *m* ►to not have a red ~ *Am, inf* no tengo ni un céntimo; I don't care a ~ me importa un bledo
centenarian [,sentɪ'neərɪən, *Am:* -teri-] *n* centenario, -a *m, f*
centenary [sen'ti:nəri, *Am:* 'sentnər-]

I. <-ies> *n* centenario *m* **II.** *adj* (*once every century*) secular; ~ **year** año *m* del centenario
centennial [sen'tenɪəl] *n, adj Am s.* **centenary**
center ['sentə˞] *n, vt Am s.* **centre**
centerpiece ['sentə˞'piːs] *n Am s.* **centrepiece**
centigrade ['sentɪgreɪd, *Am:* -tə-] *adj* centígrado, -a
centigram(me) ['sentɪgræm, *Am:* -tə-] *n* centigramo *m*
centimeter *n Am,* **centimetre** ['sentɪ,-miːtə˞, *Am:* -tə,miːtə˞] *n Brit, Aus* centímetro *m*
centipede ['sentɪpiːd, *Am:* -tə-] *n* ciempiés *m inv*
central ['sentrəl] *adj* **1.** (*at the middle*) central; (*street*) céntrico, -a; **in** ~ **Madrid** en el centro de Madrid **2.** (*important: issue*) fundamental; **to be** ~ **to sth** ser vital para algo; **to be of** ~ **importance (to sb)** ser de una importancia primordial (para alguien); **the** ~ **character** el protagonista **3.** (*from a main point: bank, heating*) central; AUTO (*locking*) centralizado, -a; ~ **processing unit** INFOR unidad *f* central de procesamiento
Central African I. *adj* centroafricano, -a **II.** *n* centroafricano, -a *m, f*
Central African Republic *n* República *f* Centroafricana
Central Bank *n* Banco *m* Central
centralization [,sentrəlaɪ'zeɪʃən, *Am:* -lɪ'-] *n no pl* centralización *f*
centralize ['sentrəlaɪz] *vt* centralizar
centre ['sentə˞] *Brit* **I.** *n* **1.** (*focus*) *a.* PHYS, POL, SPORTS centro *m;* ~ **party** partido *m* de centro **2.** (*of population*) núcleo *m* **3.** (*building*) centro *m* **4.** SPORTS (*in football*) centro *m* **II.** *vt* **1.** *a.* SPORTS, TYPO centrar **2.** (*efforts*) concentrar
◆**centre around** *vi* girar en torno a; **his life centres around his family** su vida se centra en su familia
◆**centre on** *vi* concentrarse en
centrepiece ['sentəpiːs, *Am:* -tə˞-] *n Brit* eje *m;* **racial integration was the** ~ **of the party's proposals** la integración racial era el aspecto fundamental de las propuestas del partido
centrifugal [sen'trɪfjʊgl, *Am:* -jəgl] *adj* PHYS centrífugo, -a
centrifuge ['sentrɪfjuːdʒ, *Am:* -trə-] *n* MED, TECH centrifugadora *f*
centripetal [sen'trɪpɪtl, *Am:* -pəţl] *adj* PHYS centrípeto, -a
century ['sentʃəri] <-ies> *n* **1.** (*100 years*) siglo *m;* **the twentieth** ~ el siglo veinte; **a centuries-old custom** una costumbre secular **2.** SPORTS (*cricket*) cien carreras *fpl*
CEO [,siːiː'əʊ, *Am:* -'oʊ] *n abbr of* **chief executive officer** director(a) *m(f)* general
ceramic [sɪ'ræmɪk, *Am:* sə-] *adj* de cerámica
ceramics *n pl* cerámica *f*
cereal ['sɪərɪəl, *Am:* 'sɪrɪ-] **I.** *n* **1.** *no pl* (*culti-*

vated grass) cereal *m* **2.** (*breakfast food*) cereales *mpl* **II.** *adj* cereal
cerebellum [,serɪ'beləm, *Am:* ,serə-] <-s *o* -la> *n* cerebelo *m*
cerebral ['serɪbrəl, *Am:* ,serə-] *adj* cerebral; ~ **palsy** parálisis *f inv* cerebral
cerebrum ['serɪbrəm, *Am:* ,serə-] <-(bra)> *n* cerebro *m*
ceremonial [,serɪ'məʊnɪəl, *Am:* -ə'moʊ-] **I.** *n form* ceremonial *m* **II.** *adj* ceremonial; (*event*) solemne; (*uniform*) de gala
ceremonious [,serɪ'məʊnɪəs, *Am:* -ə'moʊ-] *adj* ceremonioso, -a
ceremony ['serɪməni, *Am:* -əmoʊ-] <-ies> *n* ceremonia *f;* **to stand on** ~ ser muy ceremonioso; **to go through the** ~ **of sth** *fig* cumplir con todas las formalidades de algo
cert [sɜːt, *Am:* sɜːrt] *n Brit, inf abbr of* **certainty that's a** (**dead**) ~ *inf* eso está claro
certain ['sɜːtn, *Am:* 'sɜːr-] **I.** *adj* **1.** (*sure*) seguro, -a; **it is quite** ~ (**that**) ... es muy probable que... +*subj;* **to be** ~ **about sb** confiar en alguien; **to be** ~ **about sth** estar convencido de algo; **to make** ~ **of sth** asegurarse de algo; **it is not yet** ~ ... todavía no se sabe con certeza...; **to feel** ~ (**that** ...) estar convencido (de que...); **to make** ~ (**that** ...) asegurarse (de que...); **please make** ~ **that he has answered** por favor, asegúrate de que ha respondido; **I don't know yet for** ~ todavía no lo sé a ciencia cierta; **one thing is** (**for**) ~ ... de lo que no cabe duda es...; **for** ~ con certeza **2.** (*undeniable*) cierto, -a; **it is** ~ **that** ... es cierto que...; **the disaster seemed** ~ el desastre parecía inevitable **3.** (*specified*) cierto, -a; **a** ~ **Steve Rukus** un tal Steve Rukus; **to a** ~ **extent** hasta cierto punto **II.** *pron* cierto, -a
certainly *adv* **1.** (*surely*) por supuesto; **she is a looker, isn't she?** es guapa, ¿verdad?; **she** ~ **had a friend called Mark** está claro que tenía un amigo que se llamaba Mark; **he is** ~ **strong** desde luego es fuerte **2.** (*gladly*) desde luego; ~**, Sir!** ¡por supuesto, señor!; ~ **not!** ¡desde luego que no!
certainty ['sɜːtənti, *Am:* 'sɜːr-] <-ies> *n* certeza *f;* **Joan is a** ~ **to win** está claro que Joan ganará; **with** ~ a ciencia cierta
certifiable [,sɜːtɪ'faɪəbl, *Am:* 'sɜːrtə-] *adj* **1.** (*declared*) certificable **2.** PSYCH (*mentally ill*) demente; **he is** ~**!** *inf* ¡está para que lo encierren!
certificate [sə'tɪfɪkət, *Am:* sə-] *n* **1.** (*document*) certificado *m;* (*of baptism, birth, death*) partida *f;* (*of ownership*) título *m* **2.** SCHOOL título *m*
certification [,sɜːtɪfɪ'keɪʃən, *Am:* ,sɜːrtə-] *n no pl* **1.** (*process*) certificación *f* **2.** (*document*) certificado *m*
certify ['sɜːtɪfaɪ, *Am:* -tə-] <-ie-> *vt* certificar; **certified copy** copia *f* legalizada; **this is to** ~ **that** ... *form* por la presente certifico que...; **he is certified to practise medicine**

está habilitado para ejercer la medicina; **to ~ sb (as)** mad declarar a alguien demente

certitude ['sɜ:tɪtjuːd, *Am:* 'sɜ:rt̬ətuːd] *n no pl* certidumbre *f*

cervical ['sɜ:vɪkl, sɜ:'vaɪkl, *Am:* 'sɜ:rvɪ-] *adj* **1.** (*neck*) cervical; **~ collar** collarín *m;* **~ vertebra** vértebra *f* cervical **2.** (*cervix*) del cuello del útero

cervix ['sɜ:vɪks, *Am:* 'sɜ:r-] <-es *o* -vices> *n* **1.** (*neck*) cerviz *f* **2.** (*womb*) cuello *m* del útero

cesarean [sɪ'zeərɪən, *Am:* sə'zeri-] *n* **a ~ section** una cesárea

cesium ['siːzɪəm] *n Am s.* **caesium**

cessation [se'seɪʃən] *n no pl, form* (*end*) cesación *f;* (*of hostilities*) cese *m*

cesspit ['sespɪt] *n,* **cesspool** ['sespuːl] *n* **1.** (*for excrements*) pozo *m* negro **2.** (*unpleasant area*) cloaca *f*

CET *n abbr of* **Central European Time** horario *m* de Centroeuropa

Ceylon [sɪ'lɒn, *Am:* -'lɑːn] *n no pl* **1.** HIST (*Sri Lanka*) Ceilán *m* **2.** (*Ceylon tea*) té *m* de Ceilán

Ceylonese [sɪlɒ'niːz, *Am:* ˌsiːlə'niːz] I. *n* ceilanés, -esa *m, f* II. *adj* HIST ceilanés, -esa

cf. *abbr of* **confer** cf.

CFC [ˌsiːef'siː] *n abbr of* **chlorofluorocarbon** clorofluorocarbono *m*

c/h *n abbr of* **central heating** calef. *f*

Chad [tschæd] *n no pl* Chad *m*

Chadian I. *adj* chadiano, -a II. *n* chadiano, -a *m, f*

chafe [tʃeɪf] I. *vi* **1.** (*sore*) rozar; (*worn*) desgastarse **2.** *fig* (*irritated*) irritarse; **to ~ at sth** enfadarse por algo; **to ~ to do sth** estar impaciente por algo II. *vt* **1.** (*rub sore*) irritar **2.** (*rub*) rozar; (*rub for warmth*) frotar **3.** *fig* enfadar

chafer ['tʃeɪfər, *Am:* -fɚ] *n* abejorro *m*

chaff¹ [tʃɑːf, *Am:* tʃæf] *n no pl* AGR **1.** (*husks*) granza *f* **2.** (*cut grass*) forraje *m* **3.** (*worthless material*) paja *f*

chaff² [tʃɑːf, *Am:* tʃæf] I. *n no pl* broma *f* II. *vt* tomar el pelo a

chaffinch ['tʃæfɪntʃ] <-es> *n* pinzón *m*

chagrin ['ʃæɡrɪn, *Am:* ʃə'ɡrɪn] I. *n no pl* irritación *f* II. *vt* irritar

chain [tʃeɪn] I. *n* **1.** cadena *f;* **~ gang** cuerda *f* de presos; **to be in ~s** estar encadenado **2.** (*restrictions*) cadenas *fpl* **3.** (*series*) cadena *f;* (*of mishaps*) sucesión *f* II. *vt* encadenar; **to ~ sth/sb (up) to sth** encadenar algo/a alguien a algo; **to be ~ed to a desk** *fig* estar encerrado en un despacho

chain letter *n* carta *f* en cadena (*que debe ser copiada y remitida a varias personas*) **chainmail** *n no pl* cota *f* de malla **chain reaction** *n* reacción *f* en cadena; **to set off a ~** provocar una reacción en cadena **chain saw** *n* motosierra *f* **chainsmoker** *n* fumador(a) *m(f)* empedernido, -a **chain store** *n* tienda *f* de una cadena

chair [tʃeər, *Am:* tʃer] I. *n* **1.** (*seat*) silla *f;* **take** [*o* **have**] **a ~ please** siéntese, por favor **2.** (*head*) presidente, -a *m, f;* **to be ~ of a department** ser jefe de un departamento; **to be in the ~** ocupar la presidencia **3.** (*position*) cargo *m* **4.** *Am* (*electric chair*) silla *f* eléctrica **5.** UNIV cátedra *f;* **to hold a ~ in sth** ocupar una cátedra de algo II. *vt* (*a meeting*) presidir

chair lift *n* telesilla *m*

chairman ['tʃeəmən, *Am:* 'tʃer-] <-men> *n* presidente *m*

chairmanship ['tʃeəmənʃɪp, *Am:* 'tʃer-] *n* presidencia *f*

chairperson ['tʃeəˌpɜːsən, *Am:* 'tʃerˌpɜːr-] *n* presidente, -a *m, f* **chairwoman** <-women> *n* presidenta *f*

chalet ['ʃæleɪ, *Am:* ʃæl'eɪ] *n* chalet *m*

chalk [tʃɔːk] I. *n no pl* **1.** GEO (*stone*) caliza *f* **2.** (*stick*) tiza *f,* gis *m Méx* ▶ **to be as different as ~ and cheese** ser (como) la noche y el día; **to be as alike as ~ and cheese** parecerse una cosa a otra como un huevo a una castaña; **not know ~ from cheese** no distinguir lo blanco de lo negro; **she is the most intelligent by a long ~** es la más inteligente con mucho; **not by a long ~** ni mucho menos II. *vt* (*write*) escribir con tiza; (*draw*) dibujar con tiza

♦**chalk out** *vt* marcar con tiza

♦**chalk up** *vt* **1.** (*write with chalk*) escribir con tiza **2.** (*make an achievement*) apuntar; (*a victory*) anotarse; **to ~ sth to sb** anotar algo en la cuenta de alguien; **never mind, chalk it up to experience** no importa, es una experiencia más

chalkboard ['tʃɔːkbɔːd, *Am:* -bɔːrd] *n* pizarra *f*

chalky ['tʃɔːki] <-ier, -iest> *adj* **1.** (*made of chalk*) cretáceo, -a; (*water*) calcáreo, -a **2.** (*dusty*) **to be all ~** estar lleno de tiza **3.** (*chalk-like*) terroso, -a **4.** (*pale*) apagado, -a

challenge ['tʃælɪndʒ] I. *n* **1.** (*a call to competition*) desafío *m;* **to be faced with a ~** enfrentarse a un reto; **to present sb (with) a ~** enfrentar a alguien con un reto; **to pose a ~ to sth** poner algo en tela de juicio **2.** *a.* MIL alto *m* **3.** LAW recusación *f* II. *vt* **1.** (*ask to compete*) desafiar; **to ~ sb to a duel** retar a alguien a duelo **2.** (*question*) cuestionar, poner en tela de juicio **3.** (*test*) poner a prueba; **that's a matter that ~s attention** es una cuestión que requiere atención **4.** *a.* MIL dar el alto; **I was ~d by the new security guard** me paró el nuevo guardia de seguridad **5.** LAW recusar

challenger ['tʃælɪndʒər, *Am:* -ɚ] *n* desafiador(a) *m(f);* (*for a title*) aspirante *mf*

challenging *adj* (*book, movie*) que hace pensar; (*look, smile*) desafiante; (*work*) estimulante

chamber ['tʃeɪmbər, *Am:* -bɚ] *n* **1.** (*room*) cámara *f;* **torture ~** sala *f* de torturas **2.** ANAT, POL cámara *f;* **~ of Deputies** cámara de los diputados; **Upper/Lower** ~ cámara alta/baja **3.** ECON ~ **of commerce** cámara de comercio **4.** pl LAW (barrister's office) bufete m; **the case will be heard in ~s** la vista será a puerta cerrada **5.** TECH (of a gun) recámara f; **combustion** ~ cámara de combustión

chamberlain ['tʃeɪmbəlɪn, Am: -bɚ-] n HIST chambelán m

chambermaid ['tʃeɪmbəmeɪd, Am: -bɚ-] n camarera f

chamber music n no pl música f de cámara

chamber pot n orinal m, escupidera f AmL, tibor m Cuba

chameleon [kə'miːlɪən] n a. fig camaleón m

chamois ['ʃæmwɑ, Am: 'ʃæmi] <- o chamoix> n inv gamuza f

champ [tʃæmp] I. n inf campeón, -ona m, f II. vi morder ▶**to ~ at the bit** estar impaciente III. vt morder

champagne [ʃæm'peɪn] I. n no pl champán m II. adj **1.** (colour) champán **2.** (expensive) **he has ~ tastes** tiene gustos caros

champion ['tʃæmpɪən] I. n **1.** SPORTS campeón, -ona m, f **2.** (supporter) defensor(a) m(f); **to be a ~ of sth** ser un paladín de algo II. vt defender; **to ~ a cause** abogar por una causa III. adj **1.** SPORTS campeón, -ona **2.** Brit, inf estupendo, -a IV. adv Brit, inf de primera

championship ['tʃæmpɪənʃɪp] n **1.** (competition) campeonato m **2.** no pl (supporting) defensa f

chance [tʃɑːns, Am: tʃæns] I. n **1.** no pl (random force) casualidad f; **a ~ encounter** un encuentro casual; **~ was against me** la suerte me fue contraria; **a game of ~** un juego de azar; **to leave nothing to ~** no dejar nada al azar; **by ~** por casualidad **2.** no pl (likelihood) probabilidad f; **there's not much of a ~ of my coming to the party** no es muy probable que vaya a la fiesta; **the ~s are that she's already gone** lo más probable es que ya se haya marchado; **to be in with a ~** tener posibilidades; **to do sth on the off ~ that …** hacer algo con la esperanza de que…; **to stand a ~ of doing sth** inf tener posibilidades de hacer algo; **not stand a ~ with sb** tenerlo muy difícil con alguien; **it's a long ~** es poco probable; **not a ~!** inf ¡ni en broma! **3.** (opportunity) oportunidad f; **the ~ of a lifetime** la oportunidad de la vida; **to give sb a ~ (to do sth)** dar a alguien una oportunidad (de hacer algo); **given half a ~ …** a la menor ocasión…; **to have the ~ (to do sth)** tener la ocasión (de hacer algo); **to jump at the ~** no dejar escapar la oportunidad; **to miss one's ~ (to do sth)** desperdiciar la ocasión (de hacer algo); **to not have a ~ in hell** no tener ninguna posibilidad; **you must take your ~s when they arise** cuando se presenta una oportunidad debes aprovecharla **4.** (hazard) riesgo m; **to run a ~** correr un riesgo; **to take a ~** arriesgarse II. vi **to ~ (up) on sth/sb** encontrarse algo/a alguien por casualidad; **they ~d to be in the restaurant**

just when I arrived justamente estaban en el restaurante cuando llegué III. vt arriesgar; **to ~ one's luck** probar suerte; **to ~ it, to ~ one's arm** arriesgarse

chancellor ['tʃɑːnsələ', Am: 'tʃæn-] n **1.** POL (head of state) canciller mf; **~ of the Exchequer** ministro, -a m, f de Hacienda; **Lord ~** presidente m de la Cámara de los Lores **2.** (head of a university) rector(a) m(f)

chancellory ['tʃɑːnsəlri, Am: 'tʃæn-] <-ies> n cancillería f

chancy ['tʃɑːnsi, Am: 'tʃæn-] <-ier, -iest> adj arriesgado, -a

chandelier [ʃændə'lɪə', Am: -'lɪr] n araña f

change ['tʃeɪndʒ] I. n **1.** (alteration) cambio m; **a ~ of clothes** una muda; **the ~ (of life)** inf la menopausia; **for a ~** para variar; **that would make a (nice) ~** no estaría mal hacer eso para variar; **to ring the ~s** fig hacer una cosa de todas las formas posibles **2.** no pl (coins) cambio m, sencillo m AmL, feria f Méx; **small ~** calderilla f inf; **five pounds in ~** cinco libras en monedas; **have you got ~ for [o of] a twenty-dollar bill?** ¿tienes cambio de 20 dólares?; **how much do you have in ~?** ¿cuánto dinero suelto llevas? **3.** no pl (money returned) cambio m, vuelto m AmL; **no ~ given** se ruega importe exacto **4.** no pl (exact amount) **to have the correct ~** tener el importe exacto **5.** (travel connection) transbordo m II. vi **1.** (alter) cambiar; **to ~ into sth** convertirse en algo; **the traffic light ~d back to red** el semáforo se puso en rojo **2.** (get off a train and board another) hacer transbordo **3.** (put on different clothes) cambiarse **4.** (change speed) cambiar de marcha III. vt **1.** (exchange) cambiar; **to ~ places with sb** fig ponerse en el lugar de alguien; **to ~ sth/sb into sth** convertir algo/a alguien en algo **2.** (give coins for bills) **to ~ a dollar/a pound** cambiar un dólar/una libra **3.** (get off a train and board another) **to ~ trains** cambiar de tren **4.** (alter speed) **to ~ gear(s)** cambiar de marcha

◆**change down** vi reducir (de marcha)

◆**change up** vi aumentar (de marcha)

changeable ['tʃeɪndʒəbl] adj cambiante; (weather) inestable

changeover ['tʃeɪndʒəʊvə', Am: -ˌoʊvɚ'] n **1.** (transition) cambio m **2.** (in a race) relevo m

changing ['tʃeɪndʒɪŋ] adj cambiante; **~ room** SPORTS vestuario m; (in a shop) probador m

channel ['tʃænl] I. n **1.** TV canal m **2.** (waterway) canal m; **The (English) Channel** el Canal de la Mancha; **irrigation ~** acequia f **3.** (means) conducto m; **distribution ~** canal de distribución; **through diplomatic ~s** por la vía diplomática II. <Brit: -ll-, Am: -l-> vt canalizar; fig encauzar

Channel Islands n Islas fpl Normandas

Channel Tunnel n no pl túnel m del Canal

de la Mancha

chant [tʃɑːnt, *Am:* tʃænt] **I.** *n* **1.** REL canto *m;* (*singing*) salmodia *f;* **gregorian** ~ canto gregoriano **2.** (*utterance*) consigna *f* **II.** *vi* **1.** REL (*intone*) salmodiar **2.** (*repeat*) gritar al unísono **III.** *vt* **1.** REL (*sing*) cantar; (*speak in a monotone*) salmodiar **2.** (*repeat*) repetir al unísono

chanterelle [ˌtʃæntəˈrel, *Am:* ˌtʃænt̬ə-] *n* mízcalo *m*

Chanukah [ˈhɑːnuːkɑː, *Am:* ˈhɑːnəkə] *n* REL Januká *m*

chaos [ˈkeɪɒs, *Am:* -ɑːs] *n no pl* caos *m inv*

Chaos Theory *n no pl* PHYS teoría *f* del caos

chaotic [keɪˈɒtɪk, *Am:* -ˈɑːt̬ɪk] *adj* caótico, -a

chap¹ [tʃæp] *n* (*fellow, friend*) tío *m*

chap² [tʃæp] <-pp-> **I.** *vi* agrietarse, pasparse *RíoPl* **II.** *vt* agrietar

chap. *n abbr of* chapter cap. *m*

chapel [ˈtʃæpl] *n* **1.** (*room*) capilla *f;* **funeral** ~ capilla ardiente **2.** *Brit* (*church*) templo *m* **3.** (*service*) servicio *m* religioso

chaperon(e) [ˈʃæpərəʊn, *Am:* -əroʊn] *n* carabina *f;* (*supervisor*) acompañante *f*

chaplain [ˈtʃæplɪn] *n* REL capellán *m*

chapter [ˈtʃæptəʳ, *Am:* -tɚ] *n* **1.** *a. fig* capítulo *m;* **to quote** ~ **and verse** citar textualmente **2.** *Am* (*local branch*) sección *f* **3.** *Brit, Aus, form* (*series of disasters*) **their trip was a** ~ **of accidents** sufrieron toda una serie de desgracias durante el viaje ▸**to give** ~ **and verse for sth** contar algo con pelos y señales

chapter-house *n* **1.** *Am* (*fraternity*) sala *f* capitular **2.** (*chapter*) sala *f* de reuniones

char [tʃɑːʳ, *Am:* tʃɑːr] <-rr-> **I.** *n* **1.** (*charwoman*) asistenta *f* **2.** (*charcoal*) carbón *m* de leña **II.** *vi* (*be burned black*) carbonizarse **III.** <-rr-> *vt* (*burn black*) carbonizar

character [ˈkærəktəʳ, *Am:* ˈkerəktɚ] *n* **1.** *no pl* (*qualities*) carácter *m;* **to be in/out of** ~ **with sb/sth** ser/no ser típico de alguien/algo **2.** (*moral integrity*) reputación *f;* ~ **reference** referencias *fpl;* **to be a bad** ~ tener mala reputación; **of dubious** ~ de dudosa reputación; **of irreprochable** ~ de reputación intachable **3.** (*unique person*) personaje *mf* **4.** (*representation*) personaje *m*, carácter *m* Col, Méx; **in the** ~ **of ...** en el papel de... **5.** TYPO carácter *m*

character actor *n* actor *m* de carácter

characteristic [ˌkærəktəˈrɪstɪk, *Am:* ˌker-] **I.** *n* característica *f* **II.** *adj* característico, -a; **with her** ~ **dignity** con la dignidad que le caracteriza

characteristically [ˌkærəktəˈrɪstɪkli, *Am:* ˌker-] *adv* característicamente

characterization [ˌkærəktəraɪˈzeɪʃən, *Am:* ˌkerəktɚˈrɪ-] *n* caracterización *f*

characterize [ˈkærəktəraɪz, *Am:* ˈkerək-] *vt* **1.** *a.* CINE, THEAT caracterizar **2.** (*outline*) describir; **to** ~ **sth/sb as sth** calificar algo/a alguien de algo

charade [ʃəˈrɑːd, *Am:* -ˈreɪd] *n* **1.** *pl* GAMES charada *f* **2.** (*pretence*) farsa *f*

charcoal [ˈtʃɑːkəʊl, *Am:* ˈtʃɑːrkoʊl] **I.** *n no*

pl **1.** (*fuel*) carbón *m* vegetal **2.** ART (*for drawing*) carboncillo *m*, carbonilla *f RíoPl;* **to draw in** ~ dibujar al carboncillo **II.** *adj* **1.** (*of charcoal*) ~ **drawing** dibujo *m* al carboncillo **2.** (*dark grey*) ~ **grey** gris marengo

charcoal-burner *n* quemador *m* de carbón

charge [tʃɑːdʒ, *Am:* tʃɑːrdʒ] **I.** *n* **1.** (*load*) carga *f* **2.** (*cost*) precio *m;* **overhead** ~s gastos *mpl* generales; **scale of** ~s tarifa *f* de precios; **travel** ~s gastos *mpl* de viaje; **at no extra** ~ sin cargo adicional; **free of** ~ gratis **3.** LAW (*accusation*) cargo *m;* **to bring** ~s **against sb** presentar cargos contra alguien **4.** (*attack: of a bull*) embestida *f;* MIL carga *f;* SPORTS ofensiva *f* **5.** *no pl* (*authority*) responsabilidad *f;* **in the** ~ **of sb** a cargo de alguien; **to be in** ~ **of sb/sth** tener algo/a alguien a su cargo; **who is in** ~ **here?** ¿quién es el responsable aquí? **6.** *no pl* ELEC carga *f* **II.** *vi* **1.** FIN cobrar **2.** (*attack*) **to** ~ **at sb/sth** arremeter contra alguien/algo; MIL cargar contra alguien/algo; ~! ¡al ataque! **3.** ELEC cargarse **III.** *vt* **1.** FIN (*ask a price*) cobrar; **to** ~ **sth to sb's account** cargar algo en la cuenta de alguien **2.** LAW (*accuse*) acusar; **she's been** ~**d with murder** se le acusa de asesinato; **the crimes with which he is** ~**d** los delitos que se le imputan *form* **3.** MIL cargar contra **4.** ELEC cargar

chargeable [ˈtʃɑːdʒəbl, *Am:* ˈtʃɑːr-] *adj* FIN ~ **to the customer** a cargo del cliente; **to be** ~ **to tax** estar sujeto a impuestos

charge account *n Am* cuenta *f* de crédito

charge card *n* tarjeta *f* de pago

charged *adj* cargado, -a

chargé d'affaires [ˌʃɑːʒeɪdæˈfeəʳ, *Am:* ˌʃɑːrʒeɪdəˈfer] <chargés d'affaires> *n* encargado, -a *m, f* de negocios

chariot [ˈtʃæriət] *n* HIST carro *m*

charisma [kəˈrɪzmə] *n no pl* carisma *m*

charitable [ˈtʃærɪtəbl, *Am:* ˈtʃer-] *adj* **1.** (*with money*) generoso, -a; (*with kindness*) bueno, -a **2.** (*concerning charity*) caritativo, -a; (*gifts, donation*) benéfico, -a; (*organisation*) de beneficencia

charity [ˈtʃærəti, *Am:* ˈtʃerət̬i] <-ies> *n* **1.** *no pl* (*generosity of spirit*) caridad *f* **2.** (*compassion*) compasión *f;* **to depend on** ~ depender de limosnas **3.** (*organization*) institución *f* benéfica

charity organisation *n* organización *f* benéfica

charity shop *n* tienda *f* de una organización benéfica

charlatan [ˈʃɑːlətən, *Am:* ˈʃɑːrlətən] *n* charlatán *m*

Charles [tʃɑːlz, *Am:* tʃɑːrlz] *n* Carlos *m;* ~ **the Fifth** (**of Spain**) Carlos V (de España)

Charlie [tʃɑːli, *Am:* tʃɑːrli] *n inf* Carlitos *m*

charm [tʃɑːm, *Am:* tʃɑːrm] **I.** *n* **1.** (*quality*) encanto *m;* **she used all her** ~**s** usó todos sus encantos **2.** (*bangle*) colgante *m* **3.** (*talisman*) amuleto *m*, payé *m CSur* **II.** *vt* cautivar; **to** ~ **sb into doing sth** embelesar a alguien para que haga algo ▶ **to ~ the** <u>pants</u> **off** (**of**) **sb** *inf* llevarse a alguien de calle

charmed *adj* afortunado, -a; **to lead a ~ existence** tener una vida afotunada

charmer ['tʃɑːmə^r, *Am:* 'tʃɑːrmɚ] *n* persona *f* encantadora

charming ['tʃɑːmɪŋ, *Am:* 'tʃɑːr-] *adj* encantador(a); **oh, that's just ~!** ¡es de lo más encantador!

charred *adj* carbonizado, -a

chart [tʃɑːt, *Am:* tʃɑːrt] **I.** *n* **1.** (*display of information*) tabla *f;* **weather ~** mapa *m* meteorológico **2.** *pl* MUS **the ~s** la lista de éxitos; **to top the ~s** llegar al número uno de la lista **II.** *vt* **1.** *a. fig* trazar; **the map ~s the course of the river** el mapa reproduce gráficamente el curso del río **2.** (*observe*) seguir atentamente

charter ['tʃɑːtə^r, *Am:* 'tʃɑːrt̬ɚ] **I.** *n* **1.** (*government statement*) estatutos *mpl* **2.** (*document stating aims*) carta *f* **3.** (*exclusive right*) privilegio *m* **4.** (*founding document*) escritura *f* de constitución **5.** *no pl* COM fletamiento *m* **6.** COM contrato *m* de fletamiento **II.** *vt* **1.** (*sign founding papers*) estatuir **2.** COM fletar

charter company <-ies> *n* compañía *f* de vuelos chárter

chartered ['tʃɑːtəd, *Am:* 'tʃɑːrt̬ɚd] *adj* **1.** COM fletado, -a **2.** *Brit, Aus* (*qualified*) jurado, -a

charterer ['tʃɑːtərə^r, *Am:* 'tʃɑːrt̬ɚɚ] *n* COM fletador *m*

charter flight *n* vuelo *m* chárter

chase [tʃeɪs] **I.** *n* **1.** (*pursual*) persecución *f;* **to give ~ to sb** salir en busca de alguien **2.** (*hunt*) *a. fig* caza *f* **II.** *vi* (*rollick about*) **they ~ed after her** fueron en busca de ella **III.** *vt* **1.** (*pursue: dreams*) perseguir; (*women*) andar detrás de **2.** (*scare away*) **to ~ away sth** ahuyentar algo **3.** *Brit, inf* (*follow up on*) **to ~ sb** (**up**) **to do sth** recordar a alguien que haga algo

chasm ['kæzəm] *n* **1.** (*deep cleft*) abismo *m* **2.** (*omission*) hueco *m* **3.** *fig* (*great discrepancy*) diferencias *fpl;* **to bridge a ~** salvar las diferencias

chassis ['ʃæsi] *n inv* chasis *m inv*

chaste [tʃeɪst] *adj form* casto, -a

chasten ['tʃeɪsn] *vt* **1.** (*admonish*) reprender **2.** (*punish*) castigar

chastise [tʃæ'staɪz, *Am:* 'tʃæstaɪz] *vt* reprender

chastity ['tʃæstəti, *Am:* -təţi] *n no pl* castidad *f;* **vow of ~** voto *m* de castidad

chat [tʃæt] **I.** *n* **1.** charla *f* **2.** *no pl* (*gossip*) parloteo *m* **II.** *vi* <-tt-> **1.** (*informally*) charlar, versar *AmC* **2.** (*animatedly*) **to ~ away** estar de cháchara **3.** (*idly*) hablar sin ton ni son

chateau ['ʃætəʊ, *Am:* ʃæt'oʊ] *n* casa *f* señorial

chat room *n* foro *m* de chat **chat show** *n* programa *m* de entrevistas

chatter ['tʃætə^r, *Am:* 'tʃæţɚ] **I.** *no pl* chá-

chara *f;* (*of birds*) cotorreo *m* **II.** *vi* **1.** (*converse superficially*) **to ~ about sth** charlar sobre algo; **they ~ed about everything and nothing** chacharearon de todo y de nada **2.** (*make clacking noises: machines*) tabletear; (*birds*) cotorrear; (*teeth*) castañear

chatty ['tʃæti, *Am:* 'tʃæţ-] <-ier, -iest> *adj inf* **1.** (*friendly person*) hablador(a) **2.** LIT (*informal*) informal; (*style*) llano, -a

chauffeur ['ʃəʊfə^r, *Am:* 'ʃɑːfɚ] **I.** *n* chófer *mf* **II.** *vt* **to ~ sb around** *a. fig* hacer de chófer de alguien

chauvinism ['ʃəʊvɪnɪzəm, *Am:* 'ʃoʊ-] *n no pl* chovinismo *m*

chauvinist *n* chovinista *mf*

chauvinistic [ˌʃəʊvɪ'nɪstɪk, *Am:* ˌʃoʊ-] *adj* chovinista

cheap [tʃiːp] *adj* **1.** (*inexpensive*) barato, -a; (*ticket*) económico, -a; **dirt ~** tirado, -a **2.** (*exploited*) **~ labour** mano *f* de obra barata **3.** (*worthless*) regalado, -a **4.** (*inexpensive but bad quality*) ordinario, -a **5.** (*miserly*) chapucero, -a **6.** (*sexually easy*) fácil ▶**~ and** <u>cheerful</u> *Brit, Aus, inf* bueno, bonito y barato; **~ and** <u>nasty</u> *inf* ordinario, -a; **on the ~** *inf* barato, -a; **to buy something on the ~** *inf* comprar algo por poco dinero

cheapen ['tʃiːpən] *vt* **1.** (*lower price of*) rebajar **2.** (*reduce morally*) degradar

cheap labour *n* mano *f* de obra barata

cheaply *adv* de forma barata

cheapness ['tʃiːpnɪs] *n no pl* **1.** (*low price*) baratura *f* **2.** (*vulgarity*) ordinariez *f*

cheapskate ['tʃiːpˌskeɪt] *inf* **I.** *n* tacaño, -a *m, f* **II.** *adj* tacaño, -a, agarrado, -a

cheat [tʃiːt] **I.** *n* **1.** (*dishonest person*) estafador(a) *m(f)* **2.** (*trick*) trampa *f* **II.** *vi* **to ~ at sth** hacer trampa en algo; **to ~ in a test** copiar en un examen **III.** *vt* engañar; **to ~ the taxman** timar a Hacienda

check [tʃek] **I.** *n* **1.** (*inspection*) control *m;* **security ~** control de seguridad; **to keep sth in ~** mantener algo bajo control **2.** MED chequeo *m* **3.** (*a look*) vistazo *m* **4.** (*search for information*) verificación *f;* **to run a ~** realizar una inspección **5.** *Am* (*deposit receipt*) resguardo *m* **6.** (*textile*) tela *f* de cuadros **7.** GAMES jaque *m;* **to be in ~** estar en jaque **8.** *Am* (*tick*) marca *f,* visto *m* **9.** *Am* cheque *m;* **open ~** cheque, al portador; **to make out a blank ~** hacer un cheque en blanco; *fig* dar carta blanca; **to pay by ~** pagar con cheque **10.** *Am, Scot* (*bill*) cuenta *f* **II.** *adj* a cuadros **III.** *vt* **1.** (*inspect for problems*) comprobar, chequear *AmL* **2.** (*prevent*) frenar **3.** (*temporarily deposit*) dejar en consigna; AVIAT facturar **4.** GAMES dar jaque a **5.** *Am* (*make a mark*) marcar **IV.** *vi* **1.** (*examine*) revisar **2.** (*ask*) consultar **3.** *Am* (*be in accordance with*) coincidir

◆**check in** *vi* **1.** (*at airport*) facturar **2.** (*at hotel*) registrarse

◆**check off** *vt* verificar (haciendo marcas)

◆**check out I.** *vi* **to ~ of a room** dejar libre

una habitación **II.** *vt Am* investigar
◆**check up on** *vt* controlar; (*person*) hacer averiguaciones sobre
checkbook ['tʃek‚bʊk] *n Am* talonario *m* de cheques
checked *adj* a cuadros
checkerboard ['tʃekə^r‚bɔːd, *Am:* -ə‚bɔːrd] *n Am* (*chessboard for draughts*) tablero *m* de ajedrez
checkered ['tʃekə^rd, *Am:* -ə·d] *adj Am*
1. (*patterned with squares*) a cuadros
2. (*inconsistent*) accidentado, -a; **to have a ~ past** tener un pasado con altibajos
checkers ['tʃekəz, *Am:* -ə·z] *n* + *sing vb*
GAMES damas *fpl*
check-in ['tʃekɪn] *n* facturación *f*
check-in counter *n,* **check-in desk** *n* mostrador *m* de facturación
checking account *n Am* cuenta *f* corriente
check-in time *n* hora *f* de facturación
checklist ['tʃeklɪst] *n* lista *f* **checkmate**
I. *n no pl* **1.** GAMES jaque *m* mate; **to be ~ en** jaque mate **2.** (*defeat*) fracaso *m* **II.** *vt*
1. GAMES dar jaque mate a **2.** (*win a victory over*) ganar
checkout ['tʃekaʊt] *n* caja *f*
checkout counter *n* caja *f*
checkpoint ['tʃekpɔɪnt] *n* punto *m* de control **check room** *n Am* **1.** (*for coats*) guardarropa *m* **2.** (*for luggage*) consigna *f*
checkup ['tʃekʌp] *n* comprobación *f;* MED chequeo *m* médico
cheddar ['tʃedə^r, *Am:* -ə·] *n no pl* queso *m* de cheddar
cheek [tʃiːk] *n* **1.** (*soft skin connecting jaws*) mejilla *f* **2.** *no pl* (*impertinence*) descaro *m,* empaque *m AmL;* **to have a ~** ser un caradura; **to have the ~ to do sth** tener la caradura de hacer algo ►**to go ~ by jowl** ir codo con codo; **to turn the other ~** poner la otra mejilla
cheekbone ['tʃiːkbəʊn, *Am:* -boʊn] *n* pómulo *m*
cheeky ['tʃiːki] <-ier, -iest> *adj* descarado, -a, fregado, -a *AmL;* **to be ~ to sb** ser descarado con alguien
cheep [tʃiːp] **I.** *n* (*of bird*) pío *m;* **to not get a ~ out of sb** no sacarle ni una palabra a alguien; **to not hear a ~ out of sb** no decir alguien esta boca es mía **II.** *vi* piar
cheer [tʃɪə^r, *Am:* tʃɪr] **I.** *n* **1.** (*exuberant shout*) ovación *f;* **three ~s for the champion!** ¡tres hurras por el campeón!; **to give a ~** vitorear **2.** *no pl* (*joy*) alegría *f;* **to be of good ~** estar animado **II.** *interj* **pl 1.** (*said when drinking*) salud **2.** *Brit* (*thanks*) gracias **III.** *vi* **to ~ for sb** animar a alguien
cheerful ['tʃɪəfʊl, *Am:* 'tʃɪr-] *adj* **1.** (*happy*) alegre; (*with a positive attitude*) jovial **2.** (*colour*) vivo, -a **3.** (*encouraging*) alentador(a)
cheerfulness *n no pl* alegría *f*
cheeriness *n no pl* **1.** (*happiness*) alegría *f* **2.** (*brightness*) jovialidad *f*
cheering I. *n no pl* aplausos *mpl* **II.** *adj* alenta-

dor(a)
cheerio [‚tʃɪərɪ'əʊ, *Am:* ‚tʃɪrɪ'oʊ] *interj Brit, inf* hasta luego, chao *AmL*
cheerleader ['tʃɪə‚liːdə^r, *Am:* 'tʃɪr‚liːdə·] *n Am* animadora *f*

Con el nombre de **cheerleaders** se designa en los EE.UU. a aquellas chicas jóvenes que animan a un equipo deportivo. Su labor consiste fundamentalmente en guiar las canciones y gritos de ánimo de los fans y entretener al público asistente con pequeñas coreografías en las que utilizan los característicos **pom-poms**. Su vestuario suele consistir en un vestido corto o falda y blusa además de calcetines y zapatos de cuero, todo ello en los colores de su equipo o colegio.

cheery ['tʃɪəri, *Am:* 'tʃɪr-] <-ier, -iest> *adj* alegre
cheese [tʃiːz] *n no pl* queso *m;* **hard ~** queso curado; **melted ~** queso fundido ►**hard ~** *inf* mala pata; **say ~!** ¡decid patata!
cheeseburger ['tʃiːz‚bɜːgə^r, *Am:* -‚bɜːrgə·] *n* hamburguesa *f* con queso
cheesecake ['tʃiːzkeɪk] *n* pastel *m* de queso
cheesecloth ['tʃiːzklɒθ, *Am:* -klɑːθ] <-es> *n no pl* estopilla *f*
cheesed off *adj Brit, Aus, inf* **to be ~ with sb** estar hasta la coronilla de alguien
cheeseparing ['tʃiːz‚peərɪŋ, *Am:* -‚perɪŋ] *n no pl* tacaño, -a *m, f*
cheesy ['tʃiːzi] <-ier, -iest> *adj* **1.** (*like cheese*) como queso **2.** *inf* (*cheap and shoddy*) chungo, -a
cheetah ['tʃiːtə, *Am:* -tə] *n* guepardo *m*
chef [ʃef] *n* jefe, -a *m, f* de cocina, chef *mf*
chemical ['kemɪkl] **I.** *n* (*atoms*) sustancia *f* química; (*additive*) aditivo *m* **II.** *adj* químico, -a
chemist ['kemɪst] *n* **1.** (*person*) químico, -a *m, f* **2.** *Brit, Aus* (*store*) farmacia *f;* (*person*) farmacéutico, -a *m, f*
chemistry ['kemɪstri] *n no pl* química *f*
chemotherapy [‚kiːmə'θerəpi, *Am:* ‚kiː-moʊ-] *n no pl* quimioterapia *f;* **to undergo ~** seguir un tratamiento de quimioterapia
cheque [tʃek] *n Brit, Aus s.* **check**
chequeaccount *n* cuenta *f* corriente
cheque book *n Brit, Aus* talonario *m* de cheques
chequered ['tʃekəd, *Am:* -ə·d] *adj Brit, Aus s.* **checkered**
cherish ['tʃerɪʃ] *vt* (*hold dear*) apreciar; (*remember fondly*) recordar
cheroot [ʃə'ruːt] *n* puro *m* (*cortado por ambos extremos*)
cherry ['tʃeri] <-ies> **I.** *n* **1.** (*fruit*) cereza *f* **2.** (*tree*) cerezo *m* **II.** *adj* (de) color rojo cereza
cherry-blossom *n* flor *f* de cerezo **cherry brandy** *n no pl* aguardiente *m* de cerezas
cherub ['tʃerəb] <-s *o* -im> *n* querubín *m*
chervil ['tʃɜːvɪl, *Am:* 'tʃɜːr-] *n no pl* perifollo *m*

chess [tʃes] *n no pl* ajedrez *m*
chessboard ['tʃesbɔːd, *Am:* -bɔːrd] *n* tablero *m* de ajedrez
chessman ['tʃesmæn] <-men> *n* pieza *f* de ajedrez
chest [tʃest] *n* **1.** (*human torso*) pecho *m;* ~ **pains** dolores *mpl* pectorales; **to fold one's arms across one's** ~ cruzarse de brazos **2.** (*breasts*) senos *mpl* **3.** (*trunk*) baúl *m*, petaca *f AmL;* **medicine** ~ botiquín *m* ▶**to get sth off one's** ~ desahogarse confesando algo
chestnut ['tʃesnʌt] I. *n* **1.** (*fruit*) castaña *f* **2.** (*joke*) chiste *m* viejo **3.** (*horse*) caballo *m* castaño ▶**to pull sb's** ~**s out of the fire** sacarle a alguien las castañas del fuego II. *adj* castaño, -a
chesty ['tʃesti] <-ier, -iest> *adj* pectoral; ~ **cough** tos *f* de pecho; **to get** ~ *Brit* coger un resfriado (de pecho)
chew [tʃuː] I. *n* **1.** (*bite*) bocado *m* **2.** (*candy*) mascada *f* II. *vt* masticar
chewing gum ['tʃuːɪŋɡʌm] *n no pl* chicle *m*
chewy ['tʃuːi] <-ier, -iest> *adj* masticable; (*meat*) duro, -a
chic [ʃiːk] I. *n* chic *m* II. *adj* chic, a la moda
chicane [ʃɪ'keɪn] *n* chicane *f*
chicanery [ʃɪ'keɪnəri] *n no pl* artimaña *f*
chick [tʃɪk] *n* **1.** (*baby chicken*) pollito, -a *m, f* **2.** (*young bird*) polluelo, -a *m, f* **3.** *inf* (*young woman*) tía *f*
chicken ['tʃɪkɪn] *n* **1.** (*farm bird*) pollo, -a *m, f* **2.** *no pl* (*meat*) carne *f* de pollo; **fried/roasted** ~ pollo frito/asado; **grilled** ~ pollo a la brasa **3.** *inf* (*person*) gallina *m*, rajado *m*, rajón, -ona *m, f Cuba, Méx* ▶**it's a** ~ **and egg situation** es como aquello de la gallina y el huevo; **to not be a** (**spring**) ~ ya no ser ningún crío
chicken broth *n no pl* sopa *f* de pollo
chicken farm *n* granja *f* de pollos
chickenfeed *n no pl* **1.** (*food*) pienso *m* **2.** (*small amount of money*) calderilla *f*
chicken-hearted *adj* cobarde **chicken-pox** *n no pl* varicela *f* **chicken-run** *n* gallinero *m*
chickpea ['tʃɪkpiː] *n* garbanzo *m*
chicory ['tʃɪkəri] *n no pl* **1.** ʙᴏᴛ endivia *f*, endibia *f* **2.** (*in coffee*) achicoria *f*, radicheta *f Arg, Urug*
chief [tʃiːf] I. *n* **1.** (*boss*) jefe, -a *m, f* **2.** (*of a tribe*) jerarca *m* II. *adj* **1.** (*top*) primero, -a **2.** (*major*) principal
chief clerk *n* encargado, -a *m, f* **chief editor** *n* editor(a) *m(f)* jefe **chief executive** *n*, **chief executive officer** *n Am* director(a) *m(f)* general **chief justice** *n* presidente, -a *m, f* del Tribunal Supremo
chiefly *adv* principalmente
chieftain ['tʃiːftən] *n* cacique *m*
chiffon ['ʃɪfɒn, *Am:* ʃɪ'fɑːn] *n no pl* chifón *m*, chiffon *m*
chilblain ['tʃɪlbleɪn] *n* sabañón *m*
child [tʃaɪld] <children> *pl n* **1.** (*person*

who's not fully grown) niño, -a *m, f;* **unborn** ~ feto *m* **2.** (*offspring*) hijo, -a *m, f;* **illegitimate** ~ hijo bastardo; **to be a** ~ **of the eighties** *fig* ser un producto de los (años) ochenta ▶**spare the** **rod** **and spoil the** ~ *prov* quien bien te quiere te hará llorar *prov*
child abuse ['tʃaɪldəbjuːs] *n no pl* abuso *m* (sexual) de los niños **childbearing** *n no pl* maternidad *f;* **women of** ~ **age** mujeres *fpl* en edad de tener hijos **child benefit** *n Brit* subvención *f* familiar por hijos **childbirth** *n no pl* parto *m*, parición *f AmL* **childcare** *n no pl* cuidado *m* de los niños **childhood** *n no pl* infancia *f*
childish ['tʃaɪldɪʃ] *adj pej* infantil, achiquillado, -a *Méx;* **don't be** ~! ¡no seas niño!
childless ['tʃaɪldlɪs] *adj* sin hijos
childlike ['tʃaɪldlaɪk] *adj* infantil
childminder ['tʃaɪld,maɪndə', *Am:* -dər] *n Brit* canguro *mf* **childproof** *adj* a prueba de niños; ~ **lock** cerradura *f* de seguridad para niños
children ['tʃɪldrən] *n pl of* **child**
child-resistant *adj form* a prueba de niños
child's play *n fig* juego *m* de niños
child support *n no pl* subsidio *m* de maternidad
Chile ['tʃɪli] *n* Chile *m*
Chilean ['tʃɪliən, *Am:* tʃɪ'liː-] I. *adj* chileno, -a II. *n* chileno, -a *m, f*
chili ['tʃɪli] <-es> *n Am s.* **chilli**
chill [tʃɪl] I. *n* **1.** (*coldness*) frío *m;* **to catch a** ~ resfriarse; **to take the** ~ **off of something** calentar algo un poco **2.** (*shiver*) escalofrío *m;* **to send a** ~ **down someone's spine** hacer entrar escalofríos a alguien II. *adj* (*cold*) frío, -a; (*frightening*) estremecedor(a) III. *vt* enfriar; **to be** ~**ed to the bone** estar como un témpano
chilli ['tʃɪli] <-es> *n* chile *m*, ají *m* (picante) *AmS, Ant*
chill(i)ness *n no pl* frío *m; fig* frialdad *f*
chilling *adj* terrorífico, -a
chilly ['tʃɪli] <-ier, -iest> *adj a. fig* frío, -a; **to feel** ~ tener frío
chime [tʃaɪm] I. *n* repique *m;* **wind** ~**s** carillón *m* II. *vi* repicar III. *vt* **to** ~ **eleven** dar las once
chimney ['tʃɪmni] *n* **1.** (*in a building*) chimenea *f*, tronera *f Méx* **2.** (*in rock*) cañón *m*
chimneypot *n* cañón *m* de la chimenea **chimneystack** *n Brit* fuste *m* de chimenea **chimneysweep** *n*, **chimneysweeper** *n a.* ʜɪsᴛ deshollinador(a) *m(f)*
chimpanzee [,tʃɪmpæn'ziː, *Am:* tʃɪm'pænziː] *n* chimpancé *m*
chin ['tʃɪn] *n* barbilla *f* ▶**to keep one's** ~ **up** no desanimarse
china ['tʃaɪnə] *n no pl* **1.** (*porcelain*) porcelana *f* **2.** (*crockery*) vajilla *f*
China ['tʃaɪnə] *n* China *f*
chinchilla [tʃɪn'tʃɪlə] *n* chinchilla *f*
Chinese [tʃaɪ'niːz] I. *adj* chino, -a II. *n*

1. (*person*) chino, -a *m, f* **2.** LING chino *m*
Chinese cabbage *n* col *f* china **Chinese lantern** *n* farolillo *m* **Chinese restaurant** *n* restaurante *m* chino
chink [tʃɪŋk] I. *n* **1.** (*thin opening*) hendidura *f;* **the ~ in sb's armour** *fig* el punto débil de alguien **2.** (*clinking noise*) tintineo *m* II. *vi* tintinear
chintz [tʃɪnts] *n no pl* chintz *m*
chip [tʃɪp] I. *n* **1.** (*flake*) pedazo *m;* (*stone*) lasca *f;* (*wood*) astilla *f* **2.** *pl, Brit* (*French fries*) patatas *fpl* fritas, papas *fpl* fritas *AmL; Am* (*crisp potato snack*) patatas *fpl* fritas (de churrería), papas *fpl* fritas (de churrería) *AmL* **3.** INFOR chip *m* **4.** (*money token for gambling*) ficha *f;* **bargaining ~** moneda *f* de cambio ► **he's a ~ off the old block** *inf* de tal palo tal astilla; **to have a ~ on one's shoulder** *inf* estar resentido; **when the ~s are down** *Brit, inf* a la hora de la verdad II. *vt* <-pp-> desportillar III. *vi* <-pp-> desportillarse
chip-basket *n Brit* envase *m* de patatas
chipmunk ['tʃɪpmʌŋk] *n* ardilla *f* listada
chip-pan *n Brit* freidora *f*
chipped ['tʃɪpt] *adj* desportillado, -a
chipping ['tʃɪpɪŋ] *n pl, Brit* gravilla *f*
chippy ['tʃɪpi] <-ies> *n* **1.** *Brit, inf* tienda *f* de comida rápida (*donde se venden fritos*) **2.** *Am, inf* (*prostitute*) fulana *f*
chiropodist [kɪ'rɒpədɪst, *Am:* kɪ'rɑːpə-] *n* podólogo, -a *m, f*
chiropody [kɪ'rɒpədi, *Am:* kɪ'rɑːpə-] *n no pl* podología *f*
chiropractic ['kaɪrəpræktɪk] *n no pl* quiropráctica *f*
chiropractor ['kaɪrəpræktə', *Am:* ˌkaɪroʊpræktə-] *n* quiropráctico, -a *m, f*
chirpy ['tʃɜːpi, *Am:* 'tʃɜːr-] <-ier, -iest> *adj* animado, -a
chirrup ['tʃɪrəp], **chirp** I. *n* gorjeo *m* II. *vi* gorjear III. *vt* decir alegremente
chisel ['tʃɪzl] I. *n* cincel *m* II. <-ll-, *Am* -l-> *vt* **1.** (*cut*) esculpir **2.** *Am, inf* (*get by trickery*) estafar
chit [tʃɪt] *n* **1.** (*note*) nota *f* **2.** (*voucher*) vale *m*
chit-chat ['tʃɪtˌtʃæt] I. *n no pl, inf* cháchara *f* II. *vi inf* **to ~ about sth** estar de palique sobre algo
chivalrous ['ʃɪvlrəs] *adj* caballeroso, -a
chivalry ['ʃɪvlri] *n no pl* **1.** (*gallant behavior*) caballerosidad *f* **2.** HIST caballería *f*
chives [tʃaɪvz] *npl* cebollinos *mpl*
chloride ['klɔːraɪd] *n no pl* cloruro *m*
chlorinate ['klɔːrɪneɪt] *vt* clorar
chlorine ['klɔːriːn] *n no pl* cloro *m*
chlorofluorocarbon ['klɔːrəˌfluːərəˌkɑː-bən, *Am:* ˌklɔːroʊˌflɔːroʊˌkɑːr-] *n* clorofluorocarbono *m*
chloroform ['klɒrəfɔːm, *Am:* 'klɔːrəfɔːrm] I. *n no pl* cloroformo *m* II. *vt* cloroformizar
chlorophyll ['klɒrəfɪl, *Am:* 'klɔːrə-] *n no pl* clorofila *f*

chlorous ['klɔːrəs] *adj* cloroso, -a
choc-ice ['tʃɒkˌaɪs, *Am:* 'tʃɑːk-] *n Brit* bombón *m* helado
chock [tʃɒk, *Am:* 'tʃɑːk] *n* cuña *f*
chock-a-block [ˌtʃɒkə'blɒk, *Am:* ˌtʃɑːkə-'blɑːk] *adj* **~ with people** abarrotado de gente **chock-full** *adj* **to be ~ of sth** estar abarrotado de algo; **~ of calories** cargado de calorías
chocolate ['tʃɒklət, *Am:* 'tʃɑːk-] *n* **1.** *no pl* (*sweet*) chocolate *m;* **dark ~** chocolate negro; **a bar of ~** una tableta de chocolate **2.** (*piece of chocolate candy*) bombón *m*
choice ['tʃɔɪs] I. *n* **1.** *no pl* (*possibility of selection*) elección *f;* **to make a ~** elegir; **to have no ~** no tener alternativa; **she didn't have much ~** no tenía muchas opciones **2.** *no pl* (*selection*) selección *f;* **a wide ~ of sth** un amplio surtido de algo **3.** (*selected person or thing*) preferencia *f* II. *adj* **1.** (*top quality*) selecto, -a **2.** *fig* (*bitingly angry*) furioso, -a
choir ['kwaɪə', *Am:* 'kwaɪə·] *n* coro *m*
choirmaster ['kwaɪəˌmɑːstə', *Am:* 'kwaɪə·-ˌmæstə·] *n* director(a) *m(f)* de coro **choir stalls** *npl* coro *m*
choke [tʃəʊk, *Am:* tʃoʊk] I. *vi* sofocarse; **to ~ to death** morir asfixiado II. *n* AUTO estárter *m* III. *vt* **1.** (*deprive of air*) estrangular **2.** (*block*) obstruir; **~d with leaves** atascado de hojas
♦**choke back** *vt* ahogar; **to ~ tears** contener las lágrimas
♦**choke down** *vt* ahogar
♦**choke off** *vt* cortar; **to choke sb off** *inf* echar un rapapolvo a alguien
♦**choke up** *vt* obstruir
choker ['tʃəʊkə', *Am:* 'tʃoʊkə·] *n* gargantilla *f*
cholera ['kɒlərə, *Am:* 'kɑːlə·-] *n no pl* cólera *m*
choleric ['kɒlərɪk, *Am:* 'kɑːlə·-] *adj* colérico, -a
cholesterol [kə'lestərɒl, *Am:* kə'lestərɑːl] *n no pl* colesterol *m*
cholesterol level *n no pl* nivel *m* de colesterol
choose [tʃuːz] <chose, chosen> I. *vt* elegir; (*prefer*) preferir, decidirse por II. *vi* elegir; **to have to ~ between** tener que elegir entre; **I cannot ~ but** no tengo más remedio que
choos(e)y ['tʃuːzi] <-ier, -iest> *adj inf* quisquilloso, -a
chop [tʃɒp, *Am:* tʃɑːp] I. *vt* <-pp-> cortar; (*wood*) partir; (*meat*) picar II. *vi* <-pp-> **to ~ and change** (*vacillate*) cambiar constantemente de opinión; (*switch jobs*) cambiar constantemente de trabajo III. *n* **1.** GASTR chuleta *f* **2.** (*blow*) golpe *m;* **to get the ~** *inf* ser despedido
♦**chop away** *vt* cortar
♦**chop down** *vt* talar
♦**chop off** I. *vt* tronchar II. *vi* (*wind*) cambiar repentinamente de dirección
chop-chop [ˌtʃɒp'tʃɒp, *Am:* ˌtʃɑːp'tʃɑːp]

interj inf ¡vamos, de prisa!

chopper ['tʃɒpəʳ, *Am:* 'tʃɑːpɚ] *n* **1.** (*tool*) hacha *f* **2.** *inf* AVIAT helicóptero *m*

chopping block *n* tajo *m* **chopping board** *n* tabla *f* de cortar

choppy ['tʃɒpi, *Am:* 'tʃɑːpi] <-ier, -iest> *adj* **1.** NAUT agitado, -a **2.** (*words, sentences*) entrecortado, -a

chopsticks ['tʃɒpstɪks, *Am:* 'tʃɑːp-] *npl* palillos *mpl* (para comer comida oriental)

chop suey [ˌtʃɒp'suːi, *Am:* ˌtʃɑːp-] *n* chop suey *m*

choral ['kɔːrəl] *adj* coral; ~ **society** coral *f*

chord ['kɔːd, *Am:* 'kɔːrd] *n* MUS acorde *m* ►to **strike** a ~ **(with sb)** tocar la fibra sensible (a alguien)

chore [tʃɔːʳ, *Am:* tʃɔːr] *n* **1.** (*routine job*) tarea *f;* **household** ~s quehaceres *mpl* domésticos **2.** (*tedious task*) lata *f*

choreograph ['kɒriəgrɑːf, *Am:* 'kɔːriəgræf] *vi, vt* coreografiar

choreographer [ˌkɒrɪ'ɒgrəfəʳ, *Am:* ˌkɔːrɪ-'ɑːgrəfɚ] *n* coreógrafo, -a *m, f*

choreography [ˌkɒrɪ'ɒgrəfi, *Am:* ˌkɔːrɪ'ɑː-grə-] *n no pl* coreografía *f*

chorister ['kɒrɪstəʳ, *Am:* 'kɔːrɪstɚ] *n* corista *mf*

chorus ['kɔːrəs, *Am:* 'kɔːrəs] **I.** <-es> *n* **1.** (*refrain*) estribillo *m;* **to join in the** ~ cantar el estribillo **2.** + *sing/pl vb* (*group of singers*) coral *f* **3.** + *sing/pl vb* (*supporting singers*) coro *m;* ~ **girl** corista *f;* **in** ~ a coro **II.** *vi, vt* corear

chose [tʃəʊz, *Am:* tʃoʊz] *pt of* **choose**

chosen ['tʃəʊzn, *Am:* 'tʃoʊ-] *pp of* **choose**

chow [tʃaʊ] *n inf* (*food*) manduca *f*, lata *f Col*, morfi *m CSur*

chow chow *n* chow-chow *mf*

chowder ['tʃaʊdəʳ, *Am:* -dɚ] *n no pl* sopa espesa o guiso de pescado o verduras

Christ [kraɪst] **I.** *n* Cristo *m* **II.** *interj inf* ¡Dios!, ¡Jesús!; **for** ~'s **sake** ¡por amor de Dios!

christen ['krɪsən] *vt* **1.** (*baptise*) bautizar **2.** (*give name to*) **they** ~ed **their second child Sara** a su segundo bebé le pusieron Sara **3.** (*use for first time*) estrenar

Christendom ['krɪsəndəm] *n no pl* HIST cristiandad *f*

christening ['krɪsənɪŋ] *n,* **christening ceremony** *n* bautismo *m*, bautizo *m*

Christian ['krɪstʃən] **I.** *n* cristiano, -a *m, f* **II.** *adj* **1.** (*of Christ's teachings*) cristiano, -a **2.** (*kind*) amable **3.** (*decent*) honrado, -a

Christian burial *n* cristiana sepultura *f*

Christianity [ˌkrɪstɪ'ænəti, *Am:* -tʃɪ'ænəˌti] *n no pl* cristianismo *m*

Christianize ['krɪstʃənaɪz] *vt* cristianizar

Christian name *n Brit* nombre *m* de pila

Christmas ['krɪstməs, *Am:* 'krɪs-] <-es *o* -ses> *n no pl* Navidad *f;* **at** ~ en Navidad; **Merry** [*o* **Happy**] ~! ¡Feliz Navidad!; **Father** ~ Papá *m* Noel, viejo *m* Pascuero *Chile*

En Gran Bretaña el envío de **Christmas cards** (postales de Navidad) comienza a principios del mes de diciembre. Esta costumbre surgió a mediados del siglo XIX. Otra de las tradiciones navideñas británicas consiste en colgar los **Christmas stockings** (unos grandes calcetines) o fundas de almohadas para que aparezcan llenas de regalos a la mañana siguiente. Este ritual navideño es llevado a cabo por los niños durante el **Christmas Eve** (día de Nochebuena) que es día laborable en Gran Bretaña. La comida tradicional del **Christmas Day** consiste en pavo acompañado de patatas salteadas y de postre **Christmas pudding** o **plum pudding** que es un pastel hecho al vapor con diversos tipos de pasas, entre otras, pasas sultanas y de Corinto. Los **Christmas crackers** (otro invento británico de mediados del siglo XIX) son unos pequeños cilindros de cartón muy decorados que contienen en su interior un pequeño regalo, un proverbio y una corona de papel. Este cilindro de cartón se abre durante la comida de Navidad tirando dos personas de él simultáneamente, una por por cada lado.

Christmas carol *n* villancico *m* **Christmas cracker** *n* sorpresa *f* de Navidad **Christmas Day** *n* día *m* de Navidad, día *m* de Pascua *Perú, Chile* **Christmas Eve** *n* Nochebuena *f* **Christmas pudding** *n* pudín *m* de Navidad (con frutas confitadas y coñac) **Christmas tree** *n* árbol *m* de Navidad

Christopher ['krɪstəfəʳ, *Am:* -fɚ] *n* Cristóbal *m;* ~ **Columbus** HIST Cristóbal Colón

chromatic [krəʊ'mætɪk, *Am:* kroʊ'mæt̬ɪk] *adj* cromático, -a

chrome [krəʊm, *Am:* kroʊm] *n no pl* cromo *m*

chrome-plated *adj* cromado, -a

chromosome ['krəʊməsəʊm, *Am:* 'kroʊ-məsoʊm] *n* cromosoma *m*

chronic ['krɒnɪk, *Am:* 'krɑːnɪk] *adj* **1.** (*lasting a long time*) crónico, -a **2.** (*habitual: liar*) empedernido, -a **3.** *Brit, Aus, inf* (*extremely bad*) malísimo, -a, terrible

chronicle ['krɒnɪkl, *Am:* 'krɑːnɪ-] **I.** *vt* registrar **II.** *n* crónica *f*

chronicler ['krɒnɪkləʳ, *Am:* 'krɑːnɪklɚ] *n* cronista *mf*

chronological [ˌkrɒnə'lɒdʒɪkl, *Am:* ˌkrɑː-nə'lɑːdʒɪ-] *adj* cronológico, -a; **in** ~ **order** en orden cronológico

chronology [krə'nɒlədʒi, *Am:* krə'nɑːlə-] *n no pl* cronología *f*

chrysalis ['krɪsəlɪs] <-es> *n* crisálida *f*

chrysanthemum [krɪ'sænθəməm] *n* crisantemo *m*

chubby ['tʃʌbi] <-ier, -iest> *adj* (*fingers, legs, face*) regordete, -a; (*child*) gordinflón,

-ona, rechoncho, -a, tacuaco, -a *Chile*

chuck [tʃʌk] I. *n* 1. (*playful touch*) palmadita *f* 2. (*device for holding tool*) portabrocas *m inv* 3. (*beef cut*) corte de carne vacuna del cuarto delantero II. *vt* 1. *inf* (*throw*) tirar 2. *inf* (*give up*) dejar; to ~ sb cortar con alguien 3. (*touch playfully*) to ~ sb under the chin tocarle la barbilla a alguien

◆**chuck away** *vt inf* 1. (*money*) derrochar, despilfarrar 2. (*old things*) tirar

◆**chuck out** *vt* 1. (*throw away*) tirar 2. (*force sb to leave*) echar, zumbar *AmL*

◆**chuck up** I. *vt* abandonar II. *vi inf* devolver, guacarear *Méx*

chucker-out [ˌtʃʌkərˈaʊt] <chuckers-out> *n Brit, inf* gorila *m* (de una discoteca)

chuckle [ˈtʃʌkl] I. *n* risita *f* II. *vi* reírse

chug [tʃʌg] I. <-gg-> *vi* resoplar II. *n* resoplido *m*

chum [tʃʌm] *n inf* amigo, -a *m, f*, colega *mf*, cuate *m Méx*

◆**chum around** <-mm-> *vi*, **chum up** <-mm-> *vi Brit, inf* to ~ with sb hacerse amigo de alguien

chummy [ˈtʃʌmi] <-ier, -iest> *adj inf* (*friendly*) simpático, -a; to get ~ with sb hacerse amigo de alguien

chump [tʃʌmp] *n Brit, inf* (*likeable fool*) tontorrón, -ona *m, f* ►to go off one's ~ *Brit, inf* volverse medio chiflado

chunk [tʃʌŋk] *n* 1. (*thick lump: of cheese, bread, meat*) pedazo *m*, trozo *m*, troncho *m CSur* 2. *inf* (*large part*) buena parte *f*

chunky [ˈtʃʌŋki] <-ier, -iest> *adj* (*clothes*) grueso, -a; (*person*) fornido, -a, macizo, -a

Chunnel [ˈtʃʌnl] *n inf* the ~ el Eurotúnel, el túnel del Canal de la Mancha

church [tʃɜːtʃ, *Am:* tʃɜːrtʃ] I. *n* iglesia *f*; to go to ~ ir a misa; to enter the ~ hacerse sacerdote; (*become a nun*) meterse a monja II. *adj* 1. (*of the organization: parade, fête*) religioso, -a 2. (*of a building*) de iglesia

churchgoer [ˈtʃɜːtʃˌgəʊəʳ, *Am:* ˈtʃɜːrtʃˌgoʊəʳ] *n* practicante *mf*

churchwarden [ˌtʃɜːtʃˈwɔːdn, *Am:* ˌtʃɜːrtʃˈwɔːr-] *n Brit* 1. REL coadjutor(a) *m(f)* 2. (*pipe*) pipa de arcilla de cañón largo

churchyard [ˌtʃɜːtʃˈjɑːd, *Am:* ˌtʃɜːrtʃˈjɑːrd] *n* cementerio *m*

churlish [ˈtʃɜːlɪʃ, *Am:* ˈtʃɜːr-] *adj* grosero, -a, maleducado, -a

churn [tʃɜːn, *Am:* tʃɜːrn] I. *n* 1. (*for milk*) lechera *f* 2. (*for butter*) mantequera *f* II. *vt* batir; *fig* agitar III. *vi* (*liquid*) arremolinarse; (*wheels*) girar rápidamente; my stomach was ~ing tenía un nudo en el estómago

chute [ʃuːt] *n* 1. (*sloping tube*) rampa *f*; rubbish ~ *Brit*, garbage ~ *Am* vertedero *m* de basuras 2. (*swimming pool slide*) tobogán *m* (de agua) 3. *inf* AVIAT paracaídas *m inv*

chutney [ˈtʃʌtni] *n* chutney *m* (*conserva agridulce que se come con carnes, queso, etc.*)

CIA [ˌsiːaɪˈeɪ] *n Am abbr of* Central Intelli-gence Agency CIA *f*

CID [ˌsiːaɪˈdiː] *n Brit abbr of* Criminal Investigation Department departamento *m* de Investigación Criminal

cider [ˈsaɪdəʳ, *Am:* -dəʳ] *n* 1. *Brit* (*alcoholic apple drink*) sidra *f* 2. *Am* (*unfermented apple juice*) sweet ~ zumo *m* de manzana

cigar [sɪˈgɑːʳ, *Am:* -gɑːr] *n* puro *m*

cigarbox <-es> *n*, **cigarcase** *n* cigarrera *f*

cigar-cutter *n* cortapuros *m inv*

cigarette [ˌsɪgəˈret] *n* cigarrillo *m*; to light a ~ encender un cigarrillo

cigarette case *n* pitillera *f* **cigarette end** *n* colilla *f* **cigarette holder** *n* boquilla *f* **cigarette paper** *n* papel *m* de fumar, mortaja *f AmL*

cigarillo [sɪgəˈrɪləʊ, *Am:* -oʊ] *n* purito *m*

cilantro [sɪˈlɑntrəʊ, *Am:* -roʊ] *n no pl* cilantro *m*

cinch [sɪntʃ] <-es> *n* it's a ~ *inf* está tirado [*o* chupado]

cinder [ˈsɪndəʳ, *Am:* -dəʳ] *n* 1. (*burnt residue*) carbonilla *f*, carboncillo *m* 2. *pl* (*ashes*) ceniza *f*; to burn sth to a ~ carbonizar algo

Cinderella [ˌsɪndəˈrelə] *n* Cenicienta *f*

cine-camera [ˈsɪniˌkæmərə] *n* filmadora *f*; (*professional*) cámara *f* cinematográfica

cine-film [ˈsɪnifɪlm] *n* película *f*

cinema [ˈsɪnəmə] *n* cine *m*, biógrafo *m Arg, Chile, Urug*

cinemagoer [ˈsɪnəməˌgəʊəʳ, *Am:* -goʊəʳ] *n* cinéfilo, -a *m, f*

cinematic [ˌsɪnəˈmætɪk, *Am:* -ˈmæt̬-] *adj* cinematográfico, -a

cine-projector [ˈsɪnɪprəˌdʒektəʳ, *Am:* -təʳ] *n* proyector *m* de cine

cinnamon [ˈsɪnəmən] *n no pl* canela *f*; a ~ stick un trozo de canela en rama

CIO *n Am abbr of* Congress of Industrial Organizations Congreso *m* de Organizaciones Industriales

cipher *n*, **cypher** [ˈsaɪfəʳ, *Am:* -fəʳ] *n* 1. (*code*) clave *f*; in ~ en clave 2. (*unimportant person*) cero *m* a la izquierda 3. *Am* (*zero*) cero *m*

cipher code *n no pl* clave *f*

circa [ˈsɜːkə, *Am:* ˈsɜːr-] *prep* hacia; ~ 1850 hacia (el año) 1850

circle [ˈsɜːkl, *Am:* ˈsɜːr-] I. *n* 1. *a.* MAT círculo *m*; to go round in ~s dar vueltas; to run round in ~s *fig* dar vueltas y más vueltas a algo; to have ~s under one's eyes tener ojeras 2. *no pl* THEAT anfiteatro *m* ►to come full ~ volver al punto de partida; to square the ~ intentar la cuadratura del círculo II. *vt* trazar un círculo alrededor de; (*move in a circle*) dar vueltas alrededor de, rodear III. *vi* dar vueltas; (*aircraft*) volar en círculos

circuit [ˈsɜːkɪt, *Am:* ˈsɜːr-] *n* 1. ELEC circuito *m* 2. SPORTS pista *f* 3. (*circular route*) vuelta *f* 4. (*district under circuit judge*) distrito *m*, territorio *m* jurisdiccional

circuit board *n* placa *f* base

circuit breaker 685 **Civil Service**

circuit breaker n cortacircuitos m inv
circuitous [sɜːˈkjuːɪtəs, Am: səˈkjuːəʒəs] adj (route) tortuoso, -a
circular [ˈsɜːkjʊləʳ, Am: ˈsɜːrkjələʳ] I. adj circular II. n circular f
circular letter n circular f **circular saw** n sierra f circular **circular tour** n, **circular trip** n circuito m
circulate [ˈsɜːkjʊleɪt, Am: ˈsɜːrkjə-] I. vt hacer circular, divulgar; (card) enviar una circular a II. vi circular
circulating library <-ies> n biblioteca f itinerante
circulation [ˌsɜːkjʊˈleɪʃən, Am: ˌsɜːr-] n no pl circulación f; to be out of ~ estar fuera de circulación
circulatory [ˌsɜːkjʊˈleɪtəri, Am: ˈsɜːrkjələtɔːri] adj circulatorio, -a
circumcise [ˈsɜːkəmsaɪz, Am: ˈsɜːr-] vt circuncidar
circumcision [ˌsɜːkəmˈsɪʒən, Am: ˌsɜːr-] n circuncisión f
circumference [səˈkʌmfərəns, Am: səˈ-] n 1. (circle's boundary line) circunferencia f 2. (perimeter) perímetro m
circumlocution [ˌsɜːkəmləˈkjuːʃən, Am: ˌsɜːr-] n form 1. no pl (expression) circunlocución f 2. (way of speaking) circunloquio m
circumnavigate [ˌsɜːkəmˈnævɪgeɪt, Am: ˌsɜːr-] vt form circunnavegar
circumnavigation [ˌsɜːkəmˌnævɪˈgeɪʃən, Am: ˌsɜːr-] n form circunnavegación f
circumscribe [ˈsɜːkəmskraɪb, Am: ˈsɜːr-] vt form circunscribir
circumscription [ˌsɜːkəmˈskrɪpʃən, Am: ˌsɜːr-] n no pl 1. circunscripción f 2. (on coin) grafila f
circumspect [ˈsɜːkəmspekt, Am: ˈsɜːr-] adj form circunspecto, -a
circumstance [ˈsɜːkəmstəns, Am: ˈsɜːrkəmstæns] n circunstancia f; in no ~s bajo ningún concepto, bajo ninguna circunstancia
circumstantial [ˌsɜːkəmˈstænʃl, Am: ˌsɜːr-] adj circunstancial
circumvent [ˌsɜːkəmˈvent, Am: ˌsɜːr-] vt form (regulations) burlar; (obstacle) sortear, salvar
circus [ˈsɜːkəs, Am: ˈsɜːr-] I. <-es> n circo m II. adj de circo
cirrhosis [sɪˈrəʊsɪs, Am: səˈroʊ-] n no pl cirrosis f inv
cirrus [ˈsɪrəs] n METEO cirro m, cirrus m inv
CIS [ˌsiːaɪˈes] n abbr of **Commonwealth of Independent States** CEI f
cissy [ˈsɪsi] inf I. <-ies> n marica m II. <-ier, -iest> adj mariquita
cistern [ˈsɪstən, Am: -tən] n cisterna f, jagüel m AmL
citadel [ˈsɪtədəl, Am: ˈsɪt-] n ciudadela f
citation [saɪˈteɪʃən] n 1. (written quotation) cita f 2. Am MIL mención f
cite [saɪt] vt form 1. (offer as proof) alegar 2. (quote) citar 3. Am MIL to be ~d recibir una

mención
citizen [ˈsɪtɪzn, Am: ˈsɪt̬-] n 1. (subject) ciudadano, -a m, f 2. (resident of town) habitante mf
Citizens' Band n s. CB banda f ciudadana
citizenship [ˈsɪtɪzənʃɪp, Am: ˈsɪt̬-] n no pl ciudadanía f
citric [ˈsɪtrɪk] adj cítrico, -a
citrus [ˈsɪtrəs] <citrus o citruses> I. n cítrico m II. adj cítrico, -a
city [ˈsɪti, Am: ˈsɪt̬-] <-ies> I. n ciudad f II. adj (scape) urbano, -a; (life) ciudadano, -a

Muchas **cities** (grandes ciudades) americanas son conocidas entre sus ciudadanos por sus sobrenombres. Así **New York** es conocida como **Gotham** o **The Big Apple**. **Los Angeles** como **The Big Orange** o como **The City of the Angels**. De la misma manera **Chicago** es conocida como **The Windy City**. La expresión **The City of Brotherly Love** se usa para referirse a **Philadelphia**. **Denver**, debido a su situación, es conocida como **The Mile-High City** y **Detroit**, a causa de su industria automovilística, como **Motor City**.

city father n mandatario m municipal **city hall** n Am ayuntamiento m
civic [ˈsɪvɪk] <inv> adj (authorities) civil; (education) cívico, -a
civies [ˈsɪviz] npl traje m de paisano
civil [ˈsɪvl] adj 1. civil 2. (courteous) cortés; to not have a ~ word to say for sb hablar mal de alguien
civil action n procedimiento m civil **civil court** n sala f de lo Civil **civil defence** n defensa f civil **civil disobedience** n resistencia f pasiva **civil engineer** n ingeniero, -a m, f de caminos
civilian [sɪˈvɪliən, Am: -jən] <inv> I. n civil mf II. adj (clothes) de paisano, -a; (population) civil
civility [sɪˈvɪləti, Am: -t̬i] <-ies> n 1. no pl (formality) urbanidad f 2. (formal remarks) cumplido m
civilization [ˌsɪvəlaɪˈzeɪʃən, Am: ˌsɪvəlɪ-] n civilización f
civilize [ˈsɪvəlaɪz] vt civilizar
civil law [ˈsɪvlˈlɔː, Am: -ˈlɑː] n derecho m civil **civil liberties** npl derechos mpl civiles **civil marriage** n matrimonio m civil **civil population** n población f civil **civil rights** npl derechos mpl civiles **civil servant** n funcionario, -a m, f **Civil Service** n Administración f Pública

En Gran Bretaña el **Civil Service** forma parte de la administración central del país. Dentro de él se encuentran el cuerpo diplomático, **Inland Revenue** (Hacienda), la Seguridad Social y los centros de enseñanza estatales. Los **civil servants** (funcionarios) son fijos y, dado que su puesto no es político, no se ven afectados por los cambios de gobierno.

civil war *n* guerra *f* civil

civvies ['sɪvɪz] *npl inf* in ~ de paisano

ckw. *adj, adv abbr of* clockwise en sentido de las agujas del reloj

clack [klæk] **I.** *vi* **1.** (*heels*) taconear; (*typewriter*) teclear **2.** (*talk rapidly*) parlotear **II.** *n* (*with heels*) taconeo *m*; (*continual rapid talk*) parloteo *m*

clad [klæd] *adj a. iron* vestido, -a

claim [kleɪm] **I.** *n* **1.** (*assertion*) afirmación *f* **2.** (*written demand*) demanda *f*; (*insurance*) reclamación *f*; **to put in a ~** (**for sth**) presentar una demanda (por algo) **3.** (*right*) derecho *m*; **to lay ~ to sth** reivindicar algo **II.** *vt* **1.** (*assert*) asegurar, afirmar; (*right, responsibility*) reivindicar **2.** (*declare ownership*) reclamar; (*reward, title*) reivindicar; (*diplomatic immunity*) solicitar **3.** (*require: time*) llevar, requerir **4.** (*demand in writing*) reclamar; **to ~ damages** reclamar daños y perjuicios **III.** *vi* **to ~ for sth** reclamar algo

claimant ['kleɪmənt] *n* solicitante *mf*; (*to a throne*) pretendiente, -a *m, f*

clairvoyance [ˌkleə'vɔɪənts, *Am:* ˌkler-] *n no pl* clarividencia *f*

clairvoyant [ˌkleə'vɔɪən, *Am:* ˌkler-] **I.** *n* clarividente *mf* **II.** *adj* extrasensorial; **to be ~** ser clarividente

clam [klæm] *n* almeja *f* ▶**to shut up** like a ~ quedarse como una tumba

◆**clam up** <-mm-> *vi* (*not say anything*) no abrir la boca

clamber ['klæmbə', *Am:* -bɚ] **I.** *vi* trepar **II.** *n* ascensión *f*

clam chowder ['klæmˌtʃaʊdə', *Am:* -dɚ] *n* sopa *f* de almejas

clammy ['klæmi] <-ier, -iest> *adj* (*feet*) sudoroso, -a; (*weather*) bochornoso, -a

clamor ['klæmɚ] *n Am s.* **clamour**

clamorous ['klæmərəs] *adj* **1.** (*vociferous*) vociferante **2.** (*loud, noisy*) ruidoso, -a

clamour ['klæmə', *Am:* -ɚ] *Brit* **I.** *vi* (*demand loudly*) pedir a gritos, clamar **II.** *n* clamor *m*

clamp [klæmp] **I.** *n* **1.** ARCHIT abrazadera *f*; **wheel ~** *Brit* cepo *m* **2.** TECH tornillo *m* de banco **II.** *vt* **1.** (*fasten together*) sujetar con abrazaderas **2.** (*impose forcefully*) imponer **3.** *Brit* (*immobilise a vehicle*) **to ~ a car** poner el cepo a un coche

◆**clamp down** *vi* **to ~ on sth** tomar medidas drásticas contra algo

clan [klæn] *n + sing/pl vb, Scot* clan *m*

clandestine [klæn'destɪn] *adj form* clandestino, -a

clang [klæŋ] **I.** *vi* (*bells*) repicar **II.** *vt* **to ~ sth shut** cerrar algo con estruendo **III.** *n* sonido *m* metálico fuerte; **the ~ of the bell** el repique-

teo de la campana

clanger ['klæŋə', *Am:* -ɚ] *n Brit, inf* metedura *f* de pata; **to drop a ~** meter la pata

clangor *n Am,* **clangour** ['klæŋə', *Am:* 'klæŋgɚ] *n no pl* sonido *m* metálico fuerte

clank [klæŋk] **I.** *vi* hacer ruido **II.** *vt* hacer sonar **III.** *n* ruido *m* metálico

clap [klæp] **I.** <-pp-> *vt* **1.** (*slap palms together*) **to ~ one's hands** (**together**) batir palmas, dar palmadas **2.** (*applaud*) aplaudir **3.** (*place quickly*) poner **II.** <-pp-> *vi* **1.** (*slap palms together*) dar palmadas **2.** (*applaud*) aplaudir **III.** *n* **1.** (*slap*) palmada *f* **2.** (*applause*) aplauso *m*; **to give sb a ~** aplaudir a alguien **3.** (*noise*) ruido *m*; **a ~ of thunder** un trueno

clapped-out [ˌklæpt'aʊt] *adj Brit, Aus, inf* (*machine, car*) destartalado, -a; (*person*) hecho, -a polvo, reventado, -a

clapper ['klæpə', *Am:* -ɚ] *n* badajo *m*; **like the ~s** como una bala

claptrap ['klæptræp] *n no pl, inf* tonterías *fpl*

claret ['klærət, *Am:* 'kler-] *n* **1.** (*wine*) burdeos *m inv* **2.** (*colour*) granate *m*

clarification [ˌklærɪfɪ'keɪʃən, *Am:* ˌkler-] *n no pl* aclaración *f*

clarify ['klærɪfaɪ, *Am:* 'kler-] <-ie-> *vt* **1.** (*make clearer*) aclarar **2.** (*explain*) explicar **3.** (*purify*) clarificar

clarinet [ˌklærɪ'net, *Am:* ˌkler-] *n* clarinete *m*

clarity ['klærəti, *Am:* 'klerəti] *n no pl* claridad *f*

clash [klæʃ] **I.** *vi* **1.** (*fight*) tener un enfrentamiento; (*argue*) discutir; **to ~ over sth** discutir sobre algo **2.** (*compete against*) enfrentarse **3.** (*contradict: views*) contradecirse **4.** (*not match: colours*) desentonar **5.** *Brit, Aus* (*coincide inconveniently*) coincidir **6.** (*make loud noise*) sonar fuerte **II.** *vt* **1.** (*strike*) golpear con estruendo **2.** (*produce sound*) tocar **III.** <-es> *n* **1.** (*hostile encounter*) enfrentamiento *m* **2.** (*contest*) contienda *f* **3.** (*conflict*) conflicto *m* **4.** (*incompatibility*) choque *m* **5.** *Brit, Aus* (*coincidence*) coincidencia *f* **6.** (*loud harsh noise*) estruendo *m*

clasp [klɑːsp, *Am:* klæsp] **I.** *n* **1.** (*firm grip: of hands*) apretón *m* **2.** (*fastening device*) broche *m*, cierre *m* **II.** *vt* **1.** (*grip*) agarrar, sujetar; **to ~ one's hands** darse un apretón de manos; **to ~ sb in one's arms** estrechar a alguien entre sus brazos **2.** (*fasten: belt*) apretar

clasp knife <-knives> *n* navaja *f*

class [klɑːs, *Am:* klæs] **I.** <-es> *n* **1.** clase *f* **2.** *Brit, Aus* (*type of degree*) **a first/second ~ honours degree** licenciatura *f* superior con sobresaliente/notable ▶**the ~ chattering ~es** *Brit, pej* los intelectualoides **II.** *adj* (*excellent*) de primera clase **III.** *vt* catalogar; **to ~ sb as sth** catalogar a alguien de algo; **to ~ sb among sth** considerar a alguien como algo

class-conscious ['klɑːsˌkɒntʃəs, *Am:* 'klæsˌkɑːntʃəs] *adj* con conciencia de clase; (*classist*) clasista

classic [ˈklæsɪk] I. adj 1. clásico, -a; (typical) típico, -a 2. inf (joke, story) genial II. n 1. (work) clásico m 2. (garment) prenda f clásica

classical [ˈklæsɪkl] adj clásico, -a

classicism [ˈklæsɪsɪzəm] n no pl clasicismo m

classicist [ˈklæsɪsɪst] n clasicista mf

classics [ˈklæsɪks] n 1. pl the ~ (great literature) los clásicos 2. + sing vb (Greek and Roman studies) clásicas fpl inf

classification [ˌklæsɪfɪˈkeɪʃən, Am: ˌklæsə-] n clasificación f

classified [ˈklæsɪfaɪd] <inv> adj clasificado, -a; (confidential) confidencial, secreto, -a

classify [ˈklæsɪfaɪ] <-ie-> vt clasificar; (designate as secret) clasificar como secreto

classless [ˈklɑːslɪs, Am: ˈklæs-] adj (society) sin clases

classmate n compañero, -a m, f de clase

classroom n clase f, aula f class struggle n, class war n lucha f de clases

classy [ˈklɑːsi, Am: ˈklæsi] <-ier, -iest> adj con estilo, con clase

clatter [ˈklætər, Am: ˈklæt̬ər] I. vi 1. (make rattling noise) hacer ruido 2. (walk noisily) chacolotear II. n estruendo m; (of hooves) chacoloteo m

clause [klɔːz, Am: klɑːz] n cláusula f; LING oración f

claustrophobia [ˌklɔːstrəˈfəʊbɪə, Am: ˌklɑːstrəˈfoʊ-] n claustrofobia f

claustrophobic adj claustrofóbico, -a

clavicle [ˈklævɪkl] n clavícula f

claw [klɔː, Am: klɑː] I. n garra f; (of sea creatures) pinza f; to show one's ~s fig sacar [o enseñar] las uñas II. vt arañar

clay [kleɪ] I. n no pl 1. arcilla f; fig, liter barro m 2. SPORTS tierra f batida II. adj de arcilla

clay pigeon n plato m de tiro

clean [kliːn] I. adj 1. (free of dirt) limpio, -a; (as) ~ as a new pin limpio como una patena 2. (free from bacteria) desinfectado, -a 3. (fair) honrado, -a 4. (morally acceptable) decente; (reputation) sin tacha; (driving licence) sin sanciones; ~ police record registro m de antecedentes penales limpio 5. (smooth: cut) limpio, -a; (design) elegante 6. (complete) to make a ~ break with sth romper por completo con algo 7. (blank: piece of paper) en blanco II. n limpieza f III. adv completamente; to ~ forget that ... olvidarse por completo de que... IV. vt limpiar V. vi hacer la limpieza; the coffee stain ~ed off easily la mancha de café salió fácilmente
◆**clean down** vt limpiar
◆**clean out** vt 1. (clean thoroughly) limpiar; (with water) lavar 2. (make penniless) dejar sin blanca a
◆**clean up** I. vt 1. (make clean) limpiar; (tidy up) ordenar; to ~ the city limpiar la ciudad; to clean oneself up asearse 2. (remove illegal) acabar con II. vi 1. (make clean) limpiar

2. Am, inf (make profit) hacer un buen negocio

clean-cut [ˌkliːnˈkʌt] adj (straight) preciso, -a; (features) perfilado, -a; (person) de buen parecer

cleaner [ˈkliːnər, Am: -nər] n 1. (person) asistente, -a m, f 2. no pl (substance) producto m de limpieza

cleaning [kliːnɪŋ] n no pl limpieza f

cleaning lady <-ies> n, **cleaning woman** <women> n mujer f de la limpieza

cleanliness [ˈklenlɪnɪs] n no pl aseo m

cleanly [ˈklenli] adv limpiamente

cleanse [klenz] vt 1. (make clean) limpiar 2. (make morally pure) purificar

cleanser [ˈklenzər, Am: -ər] n leche f limpiadora

clean-shaven [ˈkliːnˈʃeɪvn] adj bien afeitado, -a

cleansing cream n no pl leche f limpiadora

cleansing tissue n toallita f desmaquilladora

clean-up [ˈkliːnʌp] n limpieza f

clear [klɪər, Am: klɪr] I. n to be in the ~ estar fuera de peligro II. adv claramente; to get ~ of sth deshacerse de algo; to stand ~ (of sth) mantenerse a distancia (de algo) III. adj 1. (transparent) claro, -a; (air) transparente; (picture) nítido, -a; to make oneself ~ explicarse con claridad; as ~ as day más claro que el agua 2. (certain) evidente 3. (free from guilt: conscience) tranquilo, -a; to be ~ of debt estar libre de deudas 4. (complete) completo, -a; three ~ months tres meses enteros 5. (net) neto, -a IV. vt 1. (remove obstacles) limpiar; (empty) desocupar 2. (remove blockage) desatascar; to ~ the way abrir el camino 3. (remove doubts) aclarar; to ~ one's head despejar la cabeza 4. (acquit) absolver 5. (net) sacar beneficio de 6. (jump) saltar por encima de 7. (give official permission) autorizar V. vi (water) aclararse; (weather) despejarse
◆**clear away** I. vt quitar II. vi irse
◆**clear off** I. vi inf largarse, jalar Bol, PRico, Urug II. vt liquidar
◆**clear out** I. vt limpiar; (throw away) vaciar II. vi irse
◆**clear up** I. vt aclarar; (tidy) ordenar II. vi despejarse

clearance [ˈklɪərəns, Am: ˈklɪr-] n no pl 1. (act of clearing) despeje m 2. (space) espacio m libre 3. (permission) autorización f

clearance sale n liquidación f

clear-cut [ˈklɪəˈkʌt, Am: ˌklɪrˈkʌt] I. adj bien definido, -a; fig claro, -a II. vt cortar de forma neta **clear-headed** adj perspicaz

clearing [ˈklɪərɪŋ, Am: ˈklɪrɪŋ] n claro m

clearing bank n Brit banco m de compensación **clearing house** n Brit cámara f de compensación **clearing office** n Brit cámara f de compensación

clearly [ˈklɪəli, Am: ˈklɪr-] adv 1. (distinctly) claramente 2. (obviously) evidentemente;

(*undoubtedly*) sin duda

clearness ['klɪənɪs, *Am:* 'klɪr-] *n* claridad *f*

clear-sighted [ˌklɪə'saɪtɪd] *adj* clarividente

cleavage ['kli:vɪdʒ] *n* **1.** *no pl* (*in a dress*) escote *m* **2.** *form* (*division*) división *f*

cleave [kli:v] <-ed *Am:* clove, -ed *Am:* cloven> I. *vi liter* henderse II. *vt* partir

cleaver ['kli:və', *Am:* -və·] *n* cuchilla *f*

clef [klef] *n* clave *f*

cleft [kleft] I. <inv> *adj* dividido, -a; (*lip*) partido, -a II. *n* grieta *f*

clematis ['klemətɪs, *Am:* 'kleməţəs] *n inv* clemátide *f*

clemency ['klemənsi] *n no pl, form* clemencia *f*

clement ['klemənt] *adj* **1.** *form* (*mild*) benigno, -a **2.** *form* (*merciful*) clemente

clench [klentʃ] *vt* presionar; (*one's fist*) apretar

Cleopatra [ˌkliə'pætrə, *Am:* ˌklioʊpætrə] *n* Cleopatra *f*

clergy ['klɜ:dʒi, *Am:* 'klɜ:r-] *n* + *sing/pl vb* clero *m*

clergyman ['klɜ:dʒɪmən, *Am:* 'klɜ:r-] <-men> *n* sacerdote *m*; (*protestant*) pastor *m*

clergywoman ['klɜ:dʒɪˌwʊmən, *Am:* 'klɜ:r-] <-women> *n* pastora *f*

cleric ['klerɪk] *n* clérigo *m*

clerical ['klerɪkl] *adj* **1.** (*of the clergy*) clerical **2.** (*of offices*) de oficina; ~ **worker** oficinista *mf*

clerical error *n* error *m* administrativo

clerical staff *n* personal *m* de oficina

clerical work *n no pl* trabajo *m* de oficina

clerk [klɑ:k, *Am:* klɜ:rk] *n* **1.** (*in office*) oficinista *mf* **2.** *Am* (*in hotel*) recepcionista *mf*; (*in shop*) dependiente *mf*; **sales** ~ vendedor(a) *m(f)*

clever ['klevə', *Am:* -və·] *adj* **1.** (*intelligent*) inteligente **2.** (*skilful*) hábil; (*invention*) ingenioso, -a **3.** *pej* astuto, -a; **to be too** ~ **by half** pasarse de listo

clever clogs *n*, **clever dick** *n Brit* sabelotodo *mf*

cleverness *n no pl* **1.** (*intelligence*) inteligencia *f* **2.** (*skill*) habilidad *f*

cliché ['kli:ʃeɪ, *Am:* kli:'ʃeɪ] *n* **1.** cliché *m* **2.** (*platitude*) tópico *m*

click [klɪk] I. *n* clic *m*; (*of one's heels*) taconeo *m*; (*of one's tongue*) chasquido *m* II. *vi* **1.** (*make short, sharp sound*) chasquear **2.** INFOR hacer clic; **to** ~ **on a symbol** hacer clic en un símbolo **3.** (*become friendly*) congeniar; (*become popular*) tener éxito **4.** (*become clear*) caer en la cuenta III. *vt* **1.** (*make short, sharp sound: tongue*) chasquear; (*heels*) taconear **2.** (*press button on mouse*) pulsar

◆**click on** *vi* INFOR pulsar, hacer clic

client ['klaɪənt] *n* cliente *mf*

clientele [ˌkli:ɒn'tel, *Am:* ˌklaɪən-] *n* clientela *f*

cliff [klɪf] *n* precipicio *m*; (*on coast*) acantilado *m*

cliffhanger ['klɪfˌhæŋə', *Am:* -ə·] *n* situación *f* de suspense

climacteric [klaɪ'mæktərɪk, *Am:* -tə·-] *n form* climaterio *m*

climactic [ˌklaɪ'mæktɪk] *adj* culminante

climate ['klaɪmɪt] *n* **1.** (*weather*) clima *m* **2.** (*general conditions*) ambiente *m*; **the** ~ **of opinion** la opinión general

climatic [klaɪ'mætɪk] *adj* climático, -a

climatologist [ˌklaɪmə'tɒlədʒɪst, *Am:* -'tɑ:-lə-] *n* climatólogo, -a *m, f*

climatology [ˌklaɪmə'tɒlədʒi, *Am:* -'tɑ:lə-] *n no pl* climatología *f*

climax ['klaɪmæks] I. <-es> *n* clímax *m inv*; (*sexual*) orgasmo *m* II. *vi* llegar a un punto culminante; (*sexual*) llegar al orgasmo

climb [klaɪm] I. *n* subida *f*; (*to power*) ascenso *m* II. *vt* (*stairs*) subir; (*tree*) trepar a; (*mountain*) escalar III. *vi* subir; **to** ~ **to a height of ...** AVIAT ascender a una altura de...

◆**climb down** *vi* bajar; *fig* volverse atrás

climbdown ['klaɪmdaʊn] *n* vuelta *f* atrás

climber ['klaɪmə', *Am:* -mə·] *n* **1.** (*of mountains*) alpinista *mf*, andinista *mf AmL;* (*of rock faces*) escalador(a) *m(f)* **2.** (*plant*) enredadera *f* **3.** *inf* (*striver for higher status*) arribista *mf*

climbing ['klaɪmɪŋ] I. *n no pl* **1.** (*ascending mountains*) alpinismo *m*, andinismo *m AmL* **2.** (*ascending rock faces*) escalada *f* II. *adj* (*plant*) trepador(a); (*boots*) de montaña

climbing irons *npl* crampones *mpl*

clinch [klɪntʃ] I. <-es> *n* abrazo *m* II. *vt* **1.** (*settle decisively*) resolver; (*a deal*) cerrar **2.** *inf* (*embrace*) abrazar **3.** (*secure a nail*) remachar

clincher ['klɪntʃə', *Am:* -ə·] *n inf* argumento *m* decisivo

cling [klɪŋ] <clung, clung> *vi* **1.** (*embrace*) abrazarse **2.** (*hold*) agarrarse; *fig* aferrarse **3.** (*stick*) adherirse **4.** (*stay close*) pegarse **5.** (*follow closely*) no separarse de

clingfilm ['klɪŋfilm] *n no pl, Brit* papel *m* de plástico para envolver

clinging *adj* **1.** (*clothes*) ajustado, -a, ceñido, -a **2.** (*person*) pegajoso, -a

clingy ['klɪŋi] <-ier, -iest> *adj* pegajoso, -a

clinic ['klɪnɪk] *n* clínica *f*

clinical ['klɪnɪkl] *adj* **1.** clínico, -a **2.** (*emotionless*) frío, -a

clinician [klɪ'nɪʃən] *n* médico, -a *m, f* especializado, -a

clink [klɪŋk] I. *vt* hacer tintinear; (*glasses*) chocar II. *vi* tintinear III. *n no pl* **1.** tintineo *m*; (*of glasses*) choque *m* **2.** *inf* (*prison*) chirona *f*

clinker ['klɪŋkə', *Am:* -kə·] *n no pl* escoria *f*

clip[1] [klɪp] I. *n* **1.** (*fastener*) clip *m*; (*for paper*) sujetapapeles *m inv*, broche *m AmL;* (*for hair*) horquilla *f* **2.** (*gun part*) cargador *m* **3.** (*jewellery*) broche *m* II. <-pp-> *vt* sujetar

clip[2] [klɪp] <-pp-> I. *vt* **1.** (*cut*) recortar; (*hair, nails*) cortar; (*sheep*) esquilar; (*ticket*) picar **2.** (*reduce*) abreviar; (*words*) comerse **3.** (*attach*) sujetar **4.** (*hit*) dar una bofetada a

II. *n* **1.** (*trim*) recorte *m* **2.** (*extract*) fragmento *m* **3.** (*hit*) bofetada *f*

clipboard ['klɪpbɔːd, *Am:* -bɔːrd] *n* tablilla *f* con sujetapapeles

clipped *adj* cortado, -a

clipper ['klɪpəʳ, *Am:* -ɚ] *n* NAUT clíper *m*

clipping ['klɪpɪŋ] *n* recorte *m*

clique [kliːk] *n* pandilla *f*

cliquey ['kliːki] <cliquier, cliquiest> *adj*, **cliquish** ['kliːkɪʃ] *adj* exclusivista

clitoris ['klɪtərəs, *Am:* 'klɪt̬ɚəs] <-es> *n* clítoris *m inv*

cloak [kləʊk, *Am:* kloʊk] I. *n* **1.** *a. fig* capa *f* **2.** *no pl* (*covering*) manto *m;* **under the ~ of darkness** al amparo de la oscuridad II. *vt* encapotar; (*hide*) encubrir

cloakroom ['kləʊkrʊm, *Am:* 'kloʊkruːm] *n* **1.** (*for coats*) guardarropa *m* **2.** *Brit* (*toilet*) lavabo *m*

clobber ['klɒbəʳ, *Am:* 'klɑːbɚ] I. *vt inf* dar una paliza a II. *n no pl, Brit, Aus, inf* bártulos *mpl*

clock [klɒk, *Am:* klɑːk] I. *n* **1.** (*for time*) reloj *m;* **alarm ~** despertador *m;* **round the ~** las 24 horas; **to run against the ~** correr contra reloj **2.** (*speedometer*) velocímetro *m;* (*mileometer*) cuentakilómetros *m inv* II. *vt* **1.** (*take amount of time*) cronometrar **2.** (*measure time*) registrar; **this car can ~ 150mph** este coche alcanza una velocidad de 150 millas por hora **3.** *inf* (*hit*) dar un bofetón a

◆**clock in** *vi* **1.** (*record time*) fichar **2.** *inf* (*arrive*) llegar al trabajo

◆**clock out** *vi* **1.** (*record time*) fichar **2.** *inf* (*leave work*) salir del trabajo

◆**clock up** *vt insep* (*attain*) alcanzar; (*travel*) recorrer

clockface *n* esfera *f* del reloj **clock radio** *n* radiodespertador *m* **clock timer** *n* temporizador *m* **clock-watcher** *n inf: persona que mira el reloj ansiando salir del trabajo*

clockwise *adj*, *adv* en el sentido de las agujas del reloj

clockwork *n no pl* mecanismo *m* de relojería; **to go like ~** salir todo bien; **as regular as ~** como un reloj

clod [klɒd, *Am:* klɑːd] *n* **1.** (*earth*) terrón *m* **2.** (*person*) zopenco, -a *m, f*

clog [klɒg, *Am:* klɑːg] I. *n* zueco *m*, zueca *f* II. <-gg-> *vi* atascarse III. <-gg-> *vt* atascar

◆**clog up** *vt* atascar

clog-dance ['klɒgdɑːns] *n baile en el que se usan zuecos para seguir el ritmo de la música*

cloister ['klɔɪstəʳ, *Am:* -stɚ] *n pl* claustro *m*

clone [kləʊn, *Am:* kloʊn] I. *n* **1.** BIO clon *m* **2.** INFOR clónico *m* II. *vt* clonar

cloning ['kləʊnɪŋ, *Am:* 'kloʊn-] *n no pl* clonación *f*

close¹ [kləʊs, *Am:* kloʊs] I. *adj* **1.** (*near in location*) cercano, -a; **~ combat** combate *m* cuerpo a cuerpo **2.** (*intimate*) íntimo, -a; **~ relatives** parientes *mpl* cercanos **3.** (*almost even*) exacto, -a **4.** (*similar*) parecido, -a

5. (*unwilling to be frank*) reservado, -a **6.** (*airless*) sofocado, -a; (*stuffy*) cargado, -a II. *adv* **1.** (*near in location*) cerca; **to move ~** acercarse **2.** (*near in time*) casi

close² [kləʊz, *Am:* kloʊz] I. *n* **1.** *no pl* (*end*) fin *m;* (*finish*) final *m;* **to bring sth to a ~** terminar algo **2.** *Brit* (*cul-de-sac road*) callejón *m* sin salida II. *vt* **1.** (*shut*) cerrar; **to ~ ranks** cerrar filas **2.** (*end*) terminar; (*bring to an end*) concluir; **to ~ a deal** cerrar un trato III. *vi* **1.** (*shut*) cerrarse **2.** (*end*) terminarse

◆**close down** I. *vi* cerrarse (definitivamente) II. *vt* cerrar (definitivamente)

◆**close in** *vi* **1.** (*surround*) rodear **2.** (*get shorter*) acortarse

◆**close off** *vt* cerrar

◆**close up** I. *vi* **1.** (*people*) arrimarse **2.** (*wound*) cicatrizar II. *vt* cerrar del todo

closed *adj* cerrado, -a; **behind ~ doors** a puerta cerrada

closed-door *adj* a puerta cerrada **close-down** *n* cierre *m* **close-knit** *adj* unido, -a

closely ['kləʊsli, *Am:* 'kloʊs-] *adv* **1.** (*near*) de cerca **2.** (*intimately*) estrechamente **3.** (*carefully*) atentamente

closeness ['kləʊsnɪs, *Am:* 'kloʊs-] *n* **1.** *no pl* (*nearness*) proximidad *f* **2.** *no pl* (*intimacy*) intimidad *f* **3.** (*airlessness*) bochorno *m*

close season *n Am* veda *f*

closet ['klɒzɪt, *Am:* 'klɑːzɪt] I. *n Am* (*cupboard*) armario *m;* (*for clothes*) ropero *m;* (*for food*) alacena *f* ▶**to come out of the ~** declararse homosexual II. *adj* secreto, -a III. *vt* **to be ~ed with sb** estar reunido con alguien a puerta cerrada

close to I. *prep* **1.** (*near*) cerca de; **to be ~ the beginning/end of sth** estar cerca del comienzo/final de algo; **to live ~ the airport** vivir cerca del aeropuerto **2.** (*almost*) **~ tears/death** a punto de llorar/morir; **~ doing sth** cerca de hacer algo; **~ three metres** cerca de tres metros **3.** (*in friendship with*) **to be ~ sb** estar unido a alguien II. *adv* (*almost*) **~ finished/complete** casi terminado/completo

close-up ['kləʊsʌp, *Am:* 'kloʊs-] *n* CINE primer plano *m*

closing I. *adj* último, -a; (*speech*) de clausura II. *n no pl* **1.** (*ending*) conclusión *f;* (*act*) clausura *f* **2.** COM cierre *m*

closing date *n* fecha *f* límite **closing down** *n no pl* cierre *m* **closing-down sale** *n* liquidación *f* **closing price** *n* cotización *f* de cierre **closing time** *n Brit,* **closing hour** *n* hora *f* de cierre

closure ['kləʊʒəʳ, *Am:* 'kloʊʒɚ] *n* (*closing*) cierre *m;* (*end*) fin *m;* (*in Parliament*) clausura *f*

clot [klɒt, *Am:* klɑːt] I. *n* **1.** MED coágulo *m;* **~ of blood** coágulo *m* sanguíneo **2.** *Brit, inf* (*person*) bobo, -a *m, f* II. <-tt-> *vi* cuajar; (*blood*) coagular

cloth [klɒθ, *Am:* klɑːθ] I. *n* **1.** (*material*) tela *f;* (*for cleaning*) trapo *m* **2.** (*clergy*) clero *m;* **a**

man of the ~ un clérigo II. *adj* de tela
clothe [kləʊð, *Am:* kloʊð] *vt* vestir; *fig* revestir de
clothes [kləʊðz, *Am:* kloʊðz] *npl* vestidos *mpl;* (*collectively*) ropa *f* **clothes-hanger** *n* percha *f* **clothes horse** *n* tendedero *m* plegable **clothes line** *n* cuerda *f* para tender la ropa **clothes-moth** *n* polilla *f* **clothes peg** *n Brit,* **clothes pin** *n Am* pinza *f* (para la ropa)
clothing ['kləʊðɪŋ, *Am:* 'kloʊ-] *n no pl* ropa *f;* **article of** ~ prenda *f* de vestir
clothing industry <-ies> *n* industria *f* textil
cloud [klaʊd] I. *n* nube *f* ▶**every** ~ **has a silver** lining *prov* no hay mal que por bien no venga *prov;* **to be on** ~ **nine** estar en el séptimo cielo; **to be** under **a** ~ estar bajo sospecha II. *vt a. fig* anublar
◆**cloud over** *vi* 1. METEO nublarse 2. (*become gloomy*) ensombrecerse; (*face*) entristecerse 3. (*become misty: eyes*) empañarse
cloud bank *n* banco *m* de niebla **cloudburst** *n* chaparrón *m* **cloud-capped** *adj* envuelto, -a en nubes **cloud-chamber** *n* PHYS cámara *f* de niebla **cloud-cuckooland** *n* Babia *f;* **to live in** ~ estar en Babia
clouded ['klaʊdɪd] *adj* 1. (*cloudy*) nublado, -a 2. (*not transparent: liquid*) turbio, -a 3. (*confused: mind*) confuso, -a
cloudless ['klaʊdlɪs] *adj* despejado, -a
cloudy ['klaʊdi] <-ier, -iest> *adj* 1. (*overcast*) nublado, -a 2. (*not transparent: liquid*) turbio, -a
clout [klaʊt] I. *n* 1. *inf* (*hit*) tortazo *m* 2. *no pl* (*power*) influencia *f* ▶**ne'er cast a** ~ **till** May **is out** *prov* hasta el cuarenta de mayo no te quites el sayo *prov* II. *vt inf* dar un tortazo a
clove[1] [kləʊv, *Am:* kloʊv] *n* clavo *m;* (*of garlic*) diente *m*
clove[2] [kləʊv, *Am:* kloʊv] *pt of* **cleave**
cloven ['kləʊvn, *Am:* 'kloʊ-] I. *pp of* **cleave** II. *adj* hendido, -a
clover ['kləʊvəʳ, *Am:* 'kloʊvɚ] *n no pl* trébol *m* ▶**to** live in ~ vivir a cuerpo de rey
cloverleaf *n* <-leaves> hoja *f* de trébol
clown [klaʊn] I. *n* payaso, -a *m, f* II. *vi* **to** ~ **around** hacer el payaso
clownish ['klaʊnɪʃ] *adj* torpe; (*behaviour*) grosero, -a
cloying [klɔɪɪŋ] *adj* empalagoso, -a
cloyingly *adv* de manera empalagosa; ~ **sweet** empalagoso, -a
club [klʌb] I. *n* 1. (*group*) asociación *f* 2. (*team*) club *m* 3. SPORTS palo *m* de golf 4. (*weapon*) cachiporra *f* 5. (*playing card*) trébol *m;* (*in Spanish cards*) basto *m* 6. (*disco*) sala *f* de fiestas, club *m* II. <-bb-> *vt* aporrear
◆**club together** *vi* reunirse
clubbing *vi* **to go** ~ salir por la noche (a las discotecas)
club car *n Am* coche *m* salón **club foot**

<feet> *n* pie *m* zopo **club-house** *n* sede *f* de un club **club member** *n* socio, -a *m, f* de un club **club sandwich** <-es> *n Am* bocadillo *m* vegetal con pollo y bacon **club soda** *n Am* soda *f*
cluck [klʌk] *vi* cloquear; *fig* parlotear
clue [klu:] *n* 1. (*evidence*) indicio *m;* (*hint*) pista *f* 2. (*secret*) clave *f* 3. (*idea*) idea *f;* I **haven't a** ~ *inf* no tengo ni idea
◆**clue up** *vt Aus* **to clue sb up** (**on sth**) informar a alguien (de algo)
clueless ['klu:lɪs] *adj inf* despistado, -a
clump [klʌmp] I. *vt* **to** ~ **sth together** agrupar algo II. *vi* 1. (*group*) **to** ~ **together** agruparse 2. (*walk noisily*) caminar haciendo ruido III. *n* 1. (*thick group: of trees*) grupo *m;* (*of flowers*) macizo *m* 2. (*lump*) terrón *m*
clumsiness ['klʌmzɪnɪs] *n no pl* torpeza *f*
clumsy ['klʌmzi] <-ier, -iest> *adj* pesado, -a; (*bungling*) torpe
clung [klʌŋ] *pp, pt of* **cling**
clunk [klʌŋk] *n* sonido *m* metálico
cluster ['klʌstəʳ, *Am:* -tɚ] I. *n* (*of people*) grupo *m;* (*of fruits*) racimo *m* II. *vi* agruparse
cluster bomb *n* bomba *f* de dispersión
clutch [klʌtʃ] I. *vi* **to** ~ **at sth** agarrarse a algo II. *vt* agarrar III. *n* 1. AUTO embrague *m* 2. (*set: of eggs*) nidada *f* 3. (*control*) **to be in the ~s of sb/sth** estar en las garras de alguien/algo
clutch bag *n* bolso *m* de mano **clutch hitter** *n* bateador(a) *m(f)* clave
clutter ['klʌtəʳ, *Am:* 'klʌtɚ] I. *n no pl* desorden *m* II. *vt* desordenar
◆**clutter up** *vt* atestar
cluttered *adj* desordenado, -a; *fig* confuso, -a; **to be** ~ **with** estar atestado de
cm *inv abbr of* **centimetre** cm
c'mon *inf* = **come on**
CND [ˌsi:en'di:] *abbr of* **Campaign for Nuclear Disarmament** Campaña *f* pro Desarme Nuclear
CO [ˌsi:'əʊ, *Am:* -'oʊ] *abbr of* **Commanding Officer** oficial *m/f* al mando
Co [kəʊ, *Am:* koʊ] 1. *abbr of* **company** Cía. 2. *Am, Brit* GEO *abbr of* **county** condado *m* 3. CHEM *abbr of* **cobalt** Co
c/o *abbr of* **care of** a/c
coach [kəʊtʃ, *Am:* koʊtʃ] I. <-es> *n* 1. (*private bus*) autocar *m* 2. (*horse-drawn carriage*) coche *m* de caballos, diligencia *f* 3. (*railway carriage*) vagón *m* 4. (*teacher*) profesor(a) *m(f)* particular; SPORTS entrenador(a) *m(f)* II. *vt* **to** ~ **sb** (**in sth**) enseñar (algo) a alguien III. *vi* dar clases particulares
coachbuilder ['kəʊtʃbɪldəʳ] *n Brit* carrocero, -a *m, f*
coaching *n no pl* preparación *f*
coaching staff *n + sing/pl vb* personal *m* de entrenamiento
coachman ['kəʊtʃmən, *Am:* 'koʊtʃ-] <-men> *n* cochero *m*
coach station *n Brit* estación *f* de autocares
coachwork *n no pl, Brit* carrocería *f*

coagulate [kəʊ'ægjʊleɪt, *Am:* koʊ'ægjə-] **I.** *vi* (*blood*) coagularse; (*sauce*) ligarse **II.** *vt* (*blood*) coagular; (*sauce*) ligar

coagulation [kəʊ,ægjʊ'leɪʃən, *Am:* koʊ,ægjə-] *n no pl* coagulación *f*

coal [kəʊl, *Am:* koʊl] *n no pl* carbón *m;* **piece of ~** hulla *f* ►**to carry ~s to New-castle** echar agua en el mar

coal-bed *n* estrato *m* de carbón **coal black** *adj* negro, -a como el carbón **coal-box** <-es> *n* coquera *f* **coal bunker** *n* carbonera *f*

coalesce [kəʊə'les, *Am:* koʊə-] *vi form* (*to merge*) fundirse; (*to unit in coalition*) unirse

coalescence [kəʊə'lesnts, *Am:* koʊə-] *n no pl, form* (*merger*) fusión *f;* (*coalition*) unión *f*

coal face *n* frente *m* de arranque del carbón **coal field** *n* yacimiento *m* de carbón **coal-fired** *adj* que quema carbón

coalition [,kəʊə'lɪʃən, *Am:* ,koʊə-] *n* coalición *f*

coal mine *n* mina *f* de carbón **coal miner** *n* minero *m* de carbón **coal mining** *n no pl* explotación *f* hullera **coal scuttle** *n* cubo *m* para el carbón **coal tar** *n no pl* alquitrán *m* mineral

coarse [kɔːs, *Am:* kɔːrs] <-r, -st> *adj* **1.** (*rough*) basto, -a; (*sand*) grueso, -a; (*skin*) áspero, -a **2.** (*vulgar*) grosero, -a; (*joke*) verde

coarsely *adv* toscamente

coarsen ['kɔːsn, *Am:* 'kɔːr-] **I.** *vt* curtir **II.** *vi* curtirse

coarseness ['kɔːsnɪs, *Am:* 'kɔːrs-] *n no pl* **1.** (*roughness*) tosquedad *f* **2.** (*rudeness*) grosería *f*

coast [kəʊst, *Am:* koʊst] **I.** *n* costa *f* ►**the ~ is clear** *inf* no hay moros en la costa **II.** *vi* avanzar sin esfuerzo

coastal ['kəʊstl, *Am:* 'koʊ-] *adj* costero, -a, abajeño, -a *AmL;* **~ traffic** cabotaje *m*

coaster ['kəʊstəʳ, *Am:* 'koʊstə-] *n* **1.** (*boat*) barco *m* de cabotaje **2.** (*mat*) salvamanteles *m inv* **3.** (*dripmat*) posavasos *m inv*

coastguard ['kəʊstgaːd, *Am:* 'koʊstgaːrd] *n* guardacostas *mf inv* **coastline** *n no pl* litoral *m* **coast-to-coast** *adj* de costa a costa

coat [kəʊt, *Am:* koʊt] **I.** *n* **1.** (*overcoat*) abrigo *m,* tapado *m AmS;* (*jacket*) chaqueta *f* **2.** (*animal's skin*) pelaje *m* **3.** (*layer*) capa *f;* (*of paint*) mano *f;* (*of chocolate*) baño *m* ►**to cut one's ~ according to one's cloth** vivir según sus posibilidades **II.** *vt* **to ~ sth in sth** cubrir algo de algo

coated ['kəʊtɪd, *Am:* 'koʊt-] *adj* cubierto, -a; (*tongue*) saburral

coat-hanger *n* percha *f* **coat-hook** *n* colgador *m*

coati [kəʊ'ati] *n* coatí *m*

coating ['kəʊtɪŋ, *Am:* 'koʊt-] *n s.* **coat**

coat of arms <coats of arms> *n* escudo *m* de armas **coat peg** *n Brit* colgador *m* **coat-tails** *npl* faldones *mpl* (*de un frac, etc.*) ►**to ride on sb's ~** salir adelante gracias al favor de alguien

co-author [kəʊ'ɔːθəʳ, *Am:* koʊ'aːθə-] **I.** *n* coautor(a) *m(f)* **II.** *vt* escribir conjuntamente

coax [kəʊks, *Am:* koʊks] *vt* convencer; **to ~ sth out of sb** sonsacarle algo a alguien

coaxing I. *n no pl* persuasión *f* **II.** *adj* persuasivo, -a

coaxingly *adv* persuasivamente

cobalt ['kəʊbɔːlt, *Am:* 'koʊbɔːlt] *n no pl* cobalto *m*

cobalt blue *n* azul *m* cobalto

cobble¹ ['kɒbl, *Am:* 'kaːbl] **I.** *n* adoquín *m* **II.** *vt* adoquinar

cobble² ['kɒbl, *Am:* 'kaːbl] *vt* (*repair*) remendar

♦cobble together *vt* improvisar

cobbled *adj* ~ **streets** calles *fpl* adoquinadas

cobbler ['kɒbləʳ, *Am:* 'kaːblə-] *n* zapatero *m* remendón ►**the ~ should stick to his last** *prov* zapatero, a tus zapatos *prov*

cobblestone ['kɒblstəʊn, *Am:* 'kaːblstoʊn] *n* adoquín *m*

cobnut ['kɒbnʌt, *Am:* 'kaːb-] *n* avellana *f*

cobol *n,* **COBOL** ['kəʊbɒl, *Am:* 'koʊbɔːl] *n* INFOR *abbr of* **common business-oriented language** COBOL *m*

cobra ['kəʊbrə, *Am:* 'koʊbrə] *n* cobra *f*

cobweb ['kɒbweb, *Am:* 'kaːb-] *n* telaraña *f*

coca ['kəʊkə, *Am:* 'koʊ-] *n* coca *f*

Coca-Cola® [,kəʊkə'kəʊlə, *Am:* ,koʊkə-'koʊ-] *n* Coca-Cola® *f*

cocaine [kəʊ'keɪn, *Am:* koʊ-] *n no pl* cocaína *f*

coccyx ['kɒksɪks, *Am:* 'kaːk-] <-es *o* coccyges> *n* coxis *m inv*

cochineal [,kɒtʃɪ'niːl, *Am:* 'kaːtʃəniːl] *n no pl* cochinilla *f*

cochlea ['ɒkliə, *Am:* 'kaːk-] <-e *o* -s> *n* cóclea *f*

cock [kɒk, *Am:* kaːk] **I.** *n* **1.** (*male chicken*) gallo *m* **2.** *vulg* (*penis*) polla *f,* pichula *f Chile* **3.** *Brit, inf* (*form of address*) macho *m* **II.** *vt* **1.** (*turn*) ladear **2.** (*ready gun*) amartillar **III.** *adj* (*in ornitology*) macho

cockade [kɒ'keɪd, *Am:* kaː'keɪd] *n* escarapela *f*

cock-a-doodle-doo [,kɒkə,duːdl'duː, *Am:* ,kaːk-] *n childspeak* quiquiriquí *m* **cock-a-hoop** *adj Brit, inf* **to be ~** estar más contento que unas pascuas **cock-a-leekie** *n* caldo *m* de pollo y puerros **cock-and-bull story** <-ies> *n* cuento *m* chino

cockatoo [,kɒkə'tuː, *Am:* 'kaːkə-] <-(s)> *n* cacatúa *f*

cockchafer ['kɒktʃeɪfəʳ, *Am:* 'kaːktʃeɪfə-] *n* abejorro *m*

cockcrow ['kɒkkrəʊ, *Am:* 'kaːkkroʊ] *n* canto *m* del gallo; **at ~** al amanecer

cocked *adj* ~ **hat** sombrero *m* de tres picos

cocker ['kɒkəʳ, *Am:* 'kaːkə-] *n,* **cocker spaniel** *n* cócker *mf*

cockerel ['kɒkərəl, *Am:* 'kaːkə-] *n* gallo *m* joven

cockeyed ['kɒkaɪd, *Am:* 'kaːk-] *adj* **1.** *inf*

(*not straight*) torcido, -a **2.** (*ridiculous*) disparatado, -a

cock fight n pelea f de gallos

cockiness ['kɒkɪnɪs] n no pl presunción f

cockle ['kɒkl, Am: 'kɑ:kl] n berberecho m

cockney ['kɒkni, Am: 'kɑ:k-] n **1.** (*person*) londinense de un barrio de clase obrera **2.** (*dialect*) cockney m (*dialecto de un barrio del East End londinense*)

Cockney rhyming slang n jerga en la que se sustituyen palabras o frases por rimas

cockpit ['kɒkpɪt, Am: 'kɑ:k-] n **1.** (*pilot's area*) cabina f **2.** (*area of fighting*) campo m de batalla

cockroach ['kɒkrəʊtʃ, Am: 'kɑ:kroʊtʃ] <-es> n cucaracha f, surupa f Ven

cockscomb ['kɒkskəʊm, Am: 'kɑ:kskoʊm] n cresta f de gallo

cocksure [ˌkɒk'ʃʊəʳ, Am: ˌkɑ:k'ʃʊr] adj inf engreído, -a

cocktail ['kɒkteɪl, Am: 'kɑ:k-] n **1.** (*drink*) cóctel m, copetín m Arg **2.** inf (*mixture*) mezcla f

cocktail cabinet n mueble-bar m **cocktail dress** <-es> n vestido m de cóctel **cocktail lounge** n salón m de cóctel **cocktail stick** n palillo m de cóctel

cock-up ['kɒkʌp, Am: 'kɑ:k-] n inf lío m

cocky ['kɒki, Am: 'kɑ:ki] <-ier, -iest> adj inf engreído, -a

cocoa ['kəʊkəʊ, Am: 'koʊkoʊ] n no pl **1.** (*chocolate powder*) cacao m **2.** (*hot drink*) chocolate m

cocoa butter n manteca f de cacao

coconut ['kəʊkənʌt, Am: 'koʊ-] n coco m **coconut butter** n no pl manteca f de coco **coconut matting** n no pl estera f de (fibras de) coco **coconut milk** n no pl leche f de coco **coconut oil** n no pl aceite m de coco **coconut palm** n cocotero m **coconut shy** <-ies> n Brit (*game*) tiro m al coco

cocoon [kə'ku:n] **I.** n capullo m **II.** vt a. fig arropar

cod [kɒd, Am: kɑ:d] n inv bacalao m

COD [ˌsi:əʊ'di:, Am: -oʊ'-] abbr of **cash on delivery** pago m contra reembolso

coda ['kəʊdə, Am: 'koʊ-] n mus coda f

coddle ['kɒdl, Am: 'kɑ:dl] vt **1.** (*cook gently*) cocer a fuego lento **2.** (*treat tenderly*) mimar

code [kəʊd, Am: koʊd] **I.** n **1.** (*ciphered language*) clave f **2.** law código m **II.** vt cifrar

coded adj codificado, -a

codeine ['kəʊdi:n, Am: koʊ-] n no pl codeína f

code name n nombre m en clave **code-named** adj the mission is ~ 'Dolores' la misión tiene el nombre en clave de 'Dolores' **code number** n prefijo m en clave **code of conduct** n código m de conducta **code of practice** n código m deontológico

co-determination [ˌkəʊdɪtɜ:mɪ'neɪʃən, Am: ˌkoʊdɪtɜ:r-] n no pl codeterminación f

code word n palabra f en clave

codex ['kəʊdeks, Am: 'koʊ-] <codices> n códice m

codger ['kɒdʒəʳ] n iron vejete m

codices ['kəʊdɪsi:z, Am: 'koʊdəsi:z] n pl of **codex**

codicil ['kəʊdɪsɪl] n codicilo m

codify ['kəʊdɪfaɪ, Am: 'kɑ:-] <-ie-> vt codificar

codling ['kɒdlɪŋ, Am: 'kɑ:d-] n bacalao m pequeño

codling moth n gusano m de la manzana

cod-liver oil n aceite m de hígado de bacalao

codpiece ['kɒdpi:s, Am: 'kɑ:d-] n bragueta f

codswallop ['kɒdzˌwɒləp, Am: 'kɑ:zˌwɑ:-ləp] n no pl, Aus, Brit, inf tonterías fpl

co-ed ['kəʊed, Am: 'koʊed] **I.** adj inf mixto, -a **II.** n inf alumna f de un colegio mixto

co-education [ˌkəʊedʒʊ'keɪʃən, Am: ˌkoʊ-] n no pl educación f mixta

co-educational [ˌkəʊedʒʊ'keɪʃənəl, Am: ˌkoʊedʒə'-] adj mixto, -a

coefficient [ˌkəʊɪ'fɪʃnt, Am: ˌkoʊ-] n coeficiente m

coequal [ˌkəʊ'i:kwl, Am: ˌkoʊ-] **I.** n form igual m f **II.** adj form igual

coerce [kəʊ'ɜ:s, Am: koʊ'ɜ:rs] vt form coaccionar

coercion [kəʊ'ɜ:ʃən, Am: koʊ'ɜ:rʒən] n no pl coacción f

coercive [kəʊ'ɜ:sɪv, Am: koʊ'ɜ:r-] adj coactivo, -a

coeval [kəʊ'i:vl, Am: koʊ-] form **I.** n coetáneo, -a m, f **II.** adj coetáneo, -a

coexist [ˌkəʊɪg'zɪst, Am: ˌkoʊ-] vi coexistir

coexistence [ˌkəʊɪg'zɪstəns, Am: ˌkoʊ-] n no pl coexistencia f

coexistent [ˌkəʊɪg'zɪstənt, Am: ˌkoʊ-] adj coexistente

C of E [ˌsi:əv'i:] abbr of **Church of England** Iglesia f Anglicana

coffee ['kɒfi, Am: 'kɑ:fi] n café m

coffee bar n café m **coffee bean** n grano m de café

coffee break n pausa f para tomar café

coffee cake n Aus, Brit pastel m de café

coffee-coloured adj de color café

coffee cup n taza f de café **coffee-grinder** n molinillo m de café **coffee grounds** n pl poso m **coffee house** n café m **coffee klatch** <-es> n Am tertulia f **coffee machine** n máquina f de café, greca f AmL **coffee mill** n molinillo m de café **coffee morning** n Brit tertulia f para tomar el café por la mañana **coffeepot** n cafetera f **coffee shop** n cafetería f **coffee table** n mesa f baja **coffee-table book** n libro m de gran formato

coffer ['kɒfəʳ, Am: 'kɑ:fəʳ] n **1.** (*storage place*) cofre m **2.** pl (*money reserves*) fondos mpl

coffin ['kɒfɪn, Am: 'kɔ:fɪn] n Aus, Brit ataúd m

cog [kɒg, Am: kɑ:g] n tech diente m; (*wheel*)

rueda *f* dentada; **to be a ~ in a machine** ser una pieza más de una organización

cogency [ˈkəʊdʒəntsi, *Am:* ˈkoʊ-] *n no pl, form* fuerza *f*

cogent [ˈkəʊdʒənt, *Am:* ˈkoʊ-] *adj form* fuerte; (*argument*) convincente

cogently *adv form* convincentemente

cogitate [ˈkɒdʒɪteɪt, *Am:* ˈkɑːdʒə-] *vi* reflexionar

cogitation [ˌkɒdʒɪˈteɪʃən, *Am:* ˌkɑːdʒə-] *n* reflexión *f*

cognac [ˈkɒnjæk, *Am:* ˈkoʊnjæk] *n* coñac *m*

cognate [ˈkɒgneɪt, *Am:* ˈkɑːg-] *adj* afín

cognition [kɒgˈnɪʃən, *Am:* kɑːg-] *n form* **1.** (*thought*) percepción *f* **2.** (*mental processes*) cognición *f*

cognitive [ˈkɒgnɪtɪv, *Am:* ˈkɑːgnət̬ɪv] *adj* cognitivo, -a

cognitive psychology *n no pl* psicología *f* cognitiva **cognitive therapy** <-ies> *n* terapia *f* cognitiva

cognizance [ˈkɒgnɪznts, *Am:* ˈkɑːgnə-] *n no pl* LAW competencia *f;* **to take ~ of sth** tener algo en cuenta

cognizant [ˈkɒgnɪznt, *Am:* ˈkɑːgnə-] *adj* conocedor(a); LAW competente

cognomen [kɒgˈnəʊmən, *Am:* kɑːgˈnoʊ-] *n* **1.** (*nickname*) apodo *m* **2.** HIST apellido *m*

cognoscenti [ˌkɒnjəʊˈʃenti, *Am:* ˌkɑːgnəˈʃenti] *npl* expertos *mpl*

cogwheel [ˈkɒgwiːl, *Am:* ˈkɑːg-] *n* rueda *f* dentada

cohabit [kəʊˈhæbɪt, *Am:* koʊ-] *vi* cohabitar

cohabitant [kəʊˈhæbɪtænt, *Am:* koʊ-] *n* cohabitante *mf*

cohabitation [kəʊˌhæbɪˈteɪʃən, *Am:* koʊˌhæb-] *n no pl* cohabitación *f*

cohabitee [ˌkəʊhæbɪˈtiː, *Am:* ˌkoʊ-] *n form s.* **cohabitant**

cohere [kəʊˈhɪər, *Am:* koʊˈhɪr] *vi* ser coherente

coherence [kəʊˈhɪərəns, *Am:* koʊˈhɪr-] *n no pl* coherencia *f*

coherent [ˈkəʊˈhɪərənt, *Am:* ˈkoʊˈhɪr-] *adj* coherente

coherently *adv* coherentemente

cohesion [kəʊˈhiːʒən, *Am:* koʊ-] *n no pl* cohesión *f*

cohesive [kəʊˈhiːsɪv, *Am:* koʊ-] *adj* cohesivo, -a

cohesiveness *n no pl* cohesión *f*

cohort [ˈkəʊhɔːt, *Am:* ˈkoʊhɔːrt] *n* cohorte *f*

COI *n Brit abbr of* **Central Office of Information** oficina *f* central de información

coil [kɔɪl] **I.** *n* **1.** rollo *m* **2.** ELEC bobina *f* **3.** MED espiral *f* (intrauterina) **II.** *vi* enrollarse **III.** *vt* enrollar

coiled *adj* enrollado, -a

coin [kɔɪn] **I.** *n* moneda *f;* **to toss a ~** echar una moneda al aire **II.** *vt* acuñar ►**to ~ a phrase** ... como se suele decir...

coinage [ˈkɔɪnɪdʒ] *n* **1.** *no pl* (*system*) sistema *m* monetario **2.** (*act*) acuñación *f*

coin-box telephone *n* teléfono *m* público de monedas

coincide [ˌkəʊɪnˈsaɪd, *Am:* ˌkoʊ-] *vi* coincidir; (*agree*) estar de acuerdo

coincidence [kəʊˈɪnsɪdəns, *Am:* koʊ-] *n* coincidencia *f;* (*chance*) casualidad *f*

coincident [kəʊˈɪnsɪdənt, *Am:* koʊ-] *adj* coincidente

coincidental [kəʊˌɪnsɪˈdentəl, *Am:* koʊˌɪnsɪˈdentəl] *adj* coincidente

coincidentally *adv* por casualidad

coitus [ˈkəʊɪtəs, *Am:* ˈkoʊət̬əs] *n no pl, form* coito *m*

coitus interruptus *n* coitus *m inv* interruptus

coke [kəʊk, *Am:* koʊk] *n no pl* **1.** (*fuel*) coque *m* **2.** *inf* coca *f,* pichicata *f Arg*

Coke® [kəʊk, *Am:* koʊk] *n* Coca-Cola® *f*

col [kɒl, *Am:* kɑːl] *n abbr of* **column** columna *f*

Col *n abbr of* **colonel** coronel *m*

COL *n abbr of* **computer-oriented language** COL *m*

cola [ˈkəʊlə, *Am:* ˈkoʊ-] *n* Coca-Cola® *f*

colander [ˈkɒləndər, *Am:* ˈkʌləndər] *n* colador *m*

cold [kəʊld, *Am:* koʊld] **I.** *adj* frío, -a; **to be ~** tener frío; **to go ~** (*soup, coffee*) enfriarse; **to get ~** (*person*) tener frío; **it's bitterly ~** hace un frío que pela ►**to leave sb ~** dejar frío a alguien **II.** *n* **1.** METEO frío *m* **2.** MED resfriado *m;* **to catch a ~** acatarrarse; **to have a ~** estar acatarrado ►**to leave sb out in the ~** dejar a alguien al margen

cold bag *n Brit* nevera *f* portátil **cold-blooded** *adj* (*animal*) de sangre fría; (*person*) cruel **cold call** *n* estilo de venta que consiste en llamar a la puerta del potencial cliente o llamarle por teléfono **cold comfort** *n* poco consuelo *m* **cold cream** *n* crema *f* para el cutis **cold cuts** *npl* fiambres *mpl* **cold-eyed** *adj* hostil **cold frame** *n* vivero *m* de plantas **cold front** *n* frente *m* frío **cold-hearted** *adj* insensible

coldish [ˈkəʊldɪʃ, *Am:* ˈkoʊl-] *adj* fresquito, -a **coldness** [ˈkəʊldnɪs, *Am:* ˈkoʊld-] *n no pl* frialdad *f*

cold shower *n a. fig* ducha *f* fría **cold snap** *n* ola *f* de frío **cold sore** *n* MED boquera *f* **cold start** *n* AUTO, INFOR arranque *m* en frío **cold storage** *n no pl* conservación *f* en cámara frigorífica **cold store** *n* cámara *f* frigorífica **cold sweat** *n* sudor *m* frío **cold truth** *n* the ~ la cruda verdad **cold turkey** *n no pl, fam, Aus, inf* mono *m* **cold war** *n* guerra *f* fría **cold wave** *n* ola *f* de frío

coleslaw [ˈkəʊlslɔː, *Am:* ˈkoʊlslɑː] *n no pl* ensalada *f* de col con salsa

coley [ˈkəʊli, *Am:* ˈkoʊ-] <-(s)> *n* abadejo *m*

colic [ˈkɒlɪk, *Am:* ˈkɑːlɪk] *n no pl* cólico *m*

collaborate [kəˈlæbəreɪt] *vi* colaborar

collaboration [kəˌlæbəˈreɪʃən] *n* colaboración *f*

collaborationist [kə͵læbə'reɪʃnɪst] *adj* colaboracionista *mf*
collaborative [kə'æbərətɪv] *adj* de colaboración; (*effort*) común
collaborator [kə'læbəreɪtəʳ, *Am:* -t̬əʳ] *n* 1. colaborador(a) *m(f)* 2. *pej* colaboracionista *mf*
collage ['kɒlɑ:ʒ, *Am:* kəlɑ:ʒ] *n* collage *m*
collagen ['kɒlədʒən, *Am:* 'kɑ:lə-] *n* no *pl* colágeno *m*
collagen implant *n*, **collagen injection** *n* implante *m* de colágeno
collapse [kə'læps] I. *vi* 1. MED sufrir un colapso 2. (*fall down: buildings*) derrumbarse; (*people*) hundirse 3. (*fail*) fracasar II. *n* 1. MED colapso *m* 2. (*act of falling down*) derrumbamiento *m;* (*of people*) hundimiento *m* 3. (*failure*) fracaso *m*
collapsible [kə'læpsɪbl] *adj* plegable
collar ['kɒləʳ, *Am:* 'kɑ:ləʳ] I. *n* 1. FASHION cuello *m* 2. (*of a dog, cat*) collar *m; Brit* (*leash*) correa *f* ▶ **to get** (**all**) **hot under the** ~ acalorarse II. *vt inf* coger por el cuello; *fig* capturar
collar bone *n* clavícula *f*
collate [kə'leɪt] *vt* 1. (*analyze*) cotejar 2. (*arrange in order*) ordenar
collateral [kə'lætərəl, *Am:* -'læt̬-] I. *n* FIN garantía *f* subsidiaria II. *adj* colateral
collateral damage *n* daño *m* colateral **collateral loan** *n* FIN préstamo *m* pignoraticio
collaterally [kə'lætərəli, *Am:* -'læt̬-] *adv* colateralmente
colleague ['kɒli:g, *Am:* 'kɑ:li:g] *n* colega *mf*
collect [kə'lekt, *Am:* 'kɑ:l-] I. *vi* 1. (*gather*) reunirse 2. (*money: contributions*) hacer una colecta; (*money: payments due*) cobrar II. *n* REL colecta *f* III. *adj Am* TEL a cobro revertido IV. *vt* 1. (*gather*) reunir; (*money*) recaudar; (*stamps*) coleccionar 2. (*pick up*) recoger 3. *form* (*regain control*) **to ~ oneself** reponerse; **to ~ one's thoughts** poner en orden sus ideas
◆**collect up** *vt* recoger
collectable [kə'lektəbl] I. *adj* coleccionable II. *n* coleccionable *m*
collect call *n Am* llamada *f* a cobro revertido
collected [kə'lektɪd] *adj* sosegado, -a
collectible [kə'lektəbl] I. *adj* coleccionable II. *n* coleccionable *m*
collection [kə'lekʃən] *n* 1. (*money gathered*) recaudación *f;* REL colecta *f* 2. (*object collected*) colección *f* 3. (*large number*) montón *m* 4. (*act of getting*) recogida *f*
collective [kə'lektɪv] I. *adj* colectivo, -a II. *n* colectivo *m*
collective bargaining *n* negociación *f* colectiva **collective farm** *n* granja *f* colectiva
collectively *adv* colectivamente
collective noun *n* nombre *m* colectivo
collectivism [kə'lektɪvɪzm, *Am:* -tə-] *n* no *pl* colectivismo *m*

collector [kə'lektəʳ, *Am:* -ə-] *n* 1. (*one who gathers objects*) coleccionista *mf* 2. (*one who collects payments*) cobrador(a) *m(f)*
collector's item *n*, **collector's piece** *n* pieza *f* de coleccionista
colleen ['kɒli:n, *Am:* 'kɑli:n] *n Irish* muchacha *f*
college ['kɒlɪdʒ, *Am:* 'kɑ:lɪdʒ] *n* 1. (*school*) colegio *m* 2. (*university*) universidad *f*

El término **college** designa el tiempo necesario en la universidad para alcanzar el **bachelor's degree**, aproximadamente 4–5 años. Las universidades en las que los estudiantes sólo pueden obtener el **bachelor's degree** se llaman **colleges**, el mismo nombre reciben algunas escuelas profesionales. Las universidades, en sentido estricto, son aquellas que ofrecen también **higher degrees** (títulos superiores) como por ejemplo, **master's degrees** y **doctorates**. En los **junior colleges** se pueden cursar los dos primeros años de estudios universitarios o capacitarse para aprender una profesión técnica.

college graduate *n Am* licenciado, -a *m, f*
collegiate [kə'li:dʒɪət, *Am:* -dʒɪt] *adj* colegiado, -a; *Am* universitario, -a
collide [kə'laɪd] *vi* chocar
collie ['kɒli, *Am:* 'kɑ:li] *n* collie *m*
collier ['kɒlɪəʳ, *Am:* 'kɑ:ljəʳ] *n form* 1. MIN minero, -a *m, f* de carbón 2. (*ship*) barco *m* carbonero
colliery ['kɒlɪəri, *Am:* 'kɑ:ljə-] <-ies> *n* mina *f* de carbón
collision [kə'lɪʒən] *n* choque *m*
collocate ['kɒləʊkeɪt, *Am:* 'kɑ:lə-] I. *vi* LING **to ~ with sth** aparecer en combinación con algo II. *n* LING colocación *f*
collocation [͵kɒləʊkeɪʃən, *Am:* ͵kɑ:lə'-] *n* colocación *f*
colloquial [kə'ləʊkwɪəl, *Am:* -'loʊ-] *adj* familiar; (*language*) coloquial
colloquialism *n* expresión *f* coloquial
colloquy ['kɒləkwi, *Am:* 'kɑ:lə-] *n* coloquio *m*
collude [kə'lu:d] *vi form* confabularse
collusion [kə'lu:ʒən] *n* no *pl, form* confabulación *f*
collusive [kə'lu:sɪv] *adj form* colusorio, -a
collywobbles ['kɒli͵wɒblz, *Am:* 'kɑ:li͵wɑ:-] *npl iron* ruido *m* de tripas; (*nervousness*) nervios *mpl*
cologne [kə'ləʊn, *Am:* -loʊn] *n* no *pl, Am* (*perfume*) colonia *f*
Colombia [kə'lʌmbɪə] *n* Colombia *f*
Colombian [kə'lʌmbɪən] I. *adj* colombiano, -a II. *n* colombiano, -a *m, f*
colon ['kəʊlən, *Am:* 'koʊ-] *n* 1. ANAT colon *m* 2. LING dos puntos *mpl*
colon cancer *n* cáncer *m* de colon
colonel ['kɜ:nl, *Am:* 'kɜ:r-] *n* coronel *mf*

colonial [kəˈləʊniəl, *Am:* -ˈloʊ-] I. *adj* colonial II. *n* colono, -a *m, f*

colonialism [kəˈləʊniəlɪzəm, *Am:* -ˈloʊ-] *n no pl* colonialismo *m*

colonialist I. *n* colonialista *mf* II. *adj* colonialista

colonial mentality *n no pl* mentalidad *f* colonial

colonisation [ˈkɒlənaɪzeɪʃən, *Am:* ˈkɑːl-] *n Aus, Brit* colonización *f*

colonise [ˈkɒlənaɪz, *Am:* ˈkɑːlənaɪz] *vt Aus, Brit* colonizar

colonist [ˈkɒlənɪst, *Am:* ˈkɑːlə-] *n* 1. (*foreigner*) colonizador(a) *m(f)* 2. (*former inhabitant*) colono, -a *m, f*

colonization [ˌkɒlənaɪˈzeɪʃən, *Am:* ˌkɑːlənɪ-] *n no pl, Am* colonización *f*

colonize [ˈkɒlənaɪz, *Am:* ˈkɑːlə-] *vt* colonizar

colonizer [ˈkɒlənaɪzəʳ, *Am:* ˈkɑːlənaɪzɚ] *n* colonizador(a) *m(f)*

colony [ˈkɒləni, *Am:* ˈkɑːlə-] <-ies> *n a.* ZOOL colonia *f*

color [ˈkʌləʳ, *Am:* -ɚ] *n, adj, vi, vt Am s.* **colour**

Colorado beetle [ˌkɒləˈrɑːdəʊˈbiːtl̩, *Am:* ˌkɑːləˈrædoʊˈbiːt̬l̩] *n,* **Colorado potato beetle** *n* escarabajo *m* de la patata

coloration [ˌkʌləˈreɪʃən] *n no pl* coloración *f*

colored *adj Am s.* **coloured**

colorful *adj Am s.* **colourful**

coloring *n Am s.* **colouring**

colorless *adj Am s.* **colourless**

color line *n Am* barrera *f* racial

colossal [kəˈlɒsl̩, *Am:* -ˈlɑːsl̩] *adj* colosal

colossus [kəˈlɒsəs] *n* <-es *o* colossi> coloso *m*

colour [ˈkʌləʳ, *Am:* -ɚ] I. *n* 1. (*appearance*) color *m;* **primary ~** color primario; **what ~ is your dress?** ¿de qué color es tu vestido?; **to have ~ in one's cheeks** tener las mejillas sonrosadas 2. (*vigour*) colorido *m* 3. (*dye*) tinte *m* 4. *pl* SCHOOL, UNIV (*sports honour*) colores *mpl* del equipo 5. *pl* POL, MIL (*official flag*) bandera *f;* **to call to ~s** llamar a filas 6. (*character*) **to show one's true ~s** mostrar el verdadero rostro; **to see sb in their true ~s** ver a alguien tal como es II. *vt* 1. (*change colour of*) colorear, pintar; **to ~ a room blue** pintar una habitación de azul 2. (*dye*) teñir 3. (*distort*) alterar III. *vi* sonrojarse

colour bar *n Brit* barrera *f* racial

colour blind *adj* daltónico, -a

colour blindness *n no pl* daltonismo *m*

coloured *adj* coloreado, -a; (*pencil, people*) de color

colour-fast [ˈkʌləfɑːst, *Am:* -ɚfæst] *adj* no desteñible

colour filter *n* PHOT filtro *m* de color

colourful [ˈkʌləfəl, *Am:* -ɚ-] *adj* 1. (*full of colour: paintings, clothing*) lleno, -a de colorido 2. (*lively*) vivo, -a; (*countryside*) pintoresco, -a; **~ part of town** zona *f* animada de

la ciudad

colouring [ˈkʌlərɪŋ] *n no pl* 1. (*complexion*) color *m* 2. (*chemical*) colorante *m*

colourless [ˈkʌlələs, *Am:* -ɚ-] *adj Brit* 1. (*having no colour*) incoloro, -a 2. (*bland*) soso, -a; **a grey, ~ city** una ciudad gris, apagada

colour scheme *n* combinación *f* de colores

colour slide *n* diapositiva *f* de color

colour television *n* televisión *f* en color

cols *n abbr of* **columns** columnas *fpl*

colt [kəʊlt, *Am:* koʊlt] *n* potro *m*, potranco *m* AmL

Columbia [kəˈlʌmbiə] *n* **the District of ~** el distrito de Columbia

Columbus Day [kəˈlʌmbəsˌdeɪ] *n no pl, Am* día *m* de la Hispanidad, día *m* de la Raza AmL

Columbus Day es el día en el que se conmemora que Colón descubrió el Nuevo Mundo el 12 de octubre de 1492. Desde 1971 este día se celebra siempre el segundo lunes del mes de octubre.

---

column [ˈkɒləm, *Am:* ˈkɑːləm] *n a.* ARCHIT, ANAT, TYPO columna *f;* **spinal ~** columna vertebral; **to march in ~s** MIL, NAUT marchar en filas

columnist [ˈkɒləmnɪst, *Am:* ˈkɑːləm-] *n* columnista *mf*

coma [ˈkəʊmə, *Am:* ˈkoʊ-] *n* coma *m;* **to go into a ~** entrar en coma; **to wake up out of one's ~** salir del coma

comatose [ˈkəʊmətəʊs, *Am:* ˈkoʊmətoʊs] *adj* comatoso, -a; **~ state** estado *m* de coma

comb [kəʊm, *Am:* koʊm] I. *n* 1. (*hair device*) peine *m* 2. ZOOL cresta *f* de gallo II. *vt* 1. (*tidy with a comb*) **to ~ one's hair** peinarse el pelo 2. (*search thoroughly*) **to ~ an apartment for clues** rastrear un apartamento en busca de pruebas

♦comb out *vt* (*a knot, tangles, lice*) desenredar

combat [ˈkɒmbæt, *Am:* ˈkɑːm-] I. *n* 1. *no pl* (*wartime fighting*) combate *m;* **hand-to-hand ~** combate cuerpo a cuerpo 2. (*battle*) lucha *f* II. *vt* luchar contra; (*crime*) combatir; (*a desire*) resistirse a

combat aircraft *n* avión *m* de combate

combatant [ˈkɒmbətənt, *Am:* kəmˈbæt-] *n* combatiente *mf*

combative [ˈkɒmbətɪv, *Am:* kəmˈbæt̬ɪv] *adj* combativo, -a

combination [ˌkɒmbɪˈneɪʃən, *Am:* ˌkɑːmbə-] *n* 1. (*mixture*) combinación *f* 2. (*sequence of numbers*) combinación *f;* **in ~** (*together*) en combinación

combine [kəmˈbaɪn, *Am:* ˈkɑːmbaɪn] I. *vt* combinar; **to ~ family life with a career** compaginar la vida familiar con una carrera profesional; **to ~ ingredients** mezclar ingredientes; **to ~ forces against sb/sth** reunir fuerzas contra alguien/algo II. *vi* asociarse

combined [kəmˈbaɪnd, *Am:* ˈkɑːm-] *adj*

combinado, -a; (*efforts*) conjunto, -a

combine harvester *n* cosechadora *f*

combustible [kəm'bʌstəbl] *adj form*
1.(*highly flammable*) combustible **2.**(*easily angry*) excitable

combustion [kəm'bʌstʃən] *n no pl* combustión *f*

combustion chamber *n* cámara *f* de combustión

come [kʌm] <came, come, coming> *vi*
1.(*move towards*) venir; **to ~ towards sb** venir hacia alguien **2.**(*go*) venirse; **are you coming to the pub with us?** ¿te vienes al pub con nosotros? **3.**(*arrive*) llegar; **January ~s before February** enero precede a febrero; **the year to ~** el próximo año; **to ~ to an agreement** llegar a un acuerdo; **to ~ to a decision** llegar a una decisión; **to ~ home** volver a casa; **to ~ to sb's rescue** socorrer a alguien; **to ~ first/second/third** *Aus, Brit* ser primero/segundo/tercero **4.**(*happen*) pasar; **to ~ to pass** suceder, ocurrir; **~ what may** pase lo que pase; **how ~?** *inf* ¿cómo es?; **nothing came of it** todo quedó en nada **5.**(*behave like*) **to ~ the poor little innocent** hacerse el pobre niño inocente **6.**(*become*) hacerse, llegar a; **my dream has ~ true** mi sueño se ha hecho realidad; **I like it as it ~s** me gusta tal cual; **to ~ open** abrirse; **to ~ in red** haberlo en rojo **7.** *vulg*(*have an orgasm*) correrse, acabar *AmL* ►**~ again?** *inf* ¿cómo?; **to ~ clean** (**about sth**) ser sincero (acerca de algo); **everything ~s to him who waits** *prov* con paciencia y esperar se gana el cielo *prov;* **don't ~ it** (**with me**)! ¡(a mí) no me vengas con ésas!; **to have it coming** tenerlo merecido

◆**come about** *vi* suceder

◆**come across I.** *vt insep* encontrarse con, dar con; **to ~ a problem** topar con un problema **II.** *vi* **1.**(*be evident*) ser entendido **2.**(*create an impression*) dar una imagen

◆**come along** *vi* **1.**(*hurry*) darse prisa; **~!** ¡date prisa! **2.**(*go too*) venir también **3.**(*progressing*) progresar

◆**come apart** *vi* separarse

◆**come around** *vi s.* **come round**

◆**come at** *vt insep* **1.**(*attack*) atacar **2.**(*arrive*) llegar a

◆**come away** *vi* **1.**(*leave*) irse **2.**(*become detached*) separarse; **to ~ from sth** desprenderse de algo

◆**come back** *vi* **1.**(*return*) regresar **2.**(*be remembered*) volver (a la memoria) **3.**(*return to fashion*) volver **4.** SPORTS contraatacar

◆**come by I.** *vt insep* **1.** dar con; (*a problem*) topar con **2.**(*obtain by chance*) recibir **II.** *vi* pasar (por)

◆**come down** *vi* **1.**(*move down*) bajar; (*move down in rank: people*) descender **2.**(*drop: roof*) venirse abajo **3.**(*land*) aterrizar **4.**(*fall: rain, snow*) caer **5.**(*visit southern place*) viajar al sur **6.**(*become less: prices, cost, inflation*) reducirse; (*lower one's price*)

rebajarse

◆**come forward** *vi* **1.**(*advance*) avanzar **2.**(*offer assistance*) ofrecerse (voluntariamente); **to ~ to do sth** ofrecerse para hacer algo

◆**come from** *vt* ser de; (*a family*) descender de; **where do you ~?** ¿de dónde eres?; **to ~ a good family** ser de buena familia

◆**come in** *vi* **1.**(*enter*) entrar **2.**(*arrive*) llegar **3.**(*become fashionable*) ponerse de moda **4.**(*be useful*) servir **5.**(*be*) resultar **6.**(*participate in*) tomar parte en **7.** *Am* (*be positioned*) **to ~ first** situarse primero

◆**come into** *vt insep* **1.**(*enter*) entrar en; (*power*) tomar; **to ~ office** tomar posesión de un cargo; **to ~ fashion** ponerse de moda; **to ~ sb's life** entrar en la vida de alguien **2.**(*inherit*) heredar

◆**come off I.** *vi* **1.** *inf*(*succeed*) tener éxito **2.**(*end up*) terminar **3.**(*become detached*) desprenderse **4.**(*fall*) caerse **II.** *vt insep* **1.**(*fall*) **to ~ the bike** caerse de la bici **2.** *Am* (*complete*) terminar; **to ~ an injury** MED recuperarse de una herida ►**~ it!** *inf* ¡anda ya!

◆**come on I.** *vi* **1.**(*improve*) progresar **2.** THEAT, CINE (*actor, performer*) aparecer **3.**(*begin: film, programme*) empezar; **what time does the news ~?** ¿a qué hora dan las noticias? **4.**(*start gradually*) **I've got a headache coming on** me está cogiendo dolor de cabeza **II.** *vt insep* encontrar **III.** *interj* (*hurry*) ¡date prisa!, ¡ándale! *Méx;* (*encouragement*) ¡ánimo!, ¡órale! *Méx;* (*annoyance*) ¡venga ya!

◆**come out** *vi* **1.**(*express opinion*) **to ~ in favour of/against sth** pronunciarse a favor/en contra de algo **2.**(*end up*) **how did your painting ~?** ¿cómo quedó tu cuadro? **3.** + *n* **to ~ a mess** resultar un desastre **4.** + *adj* **to ~ wrong/right** salir mal/bien **5.**(*go out socially*) presentarse en sociedad **6.**(*become known*) darse a conocer; **to ~ that ...** revelarse que... **7.**(*reveal one's homosexuality*) declararse homosexual **8.** *Brit* (*strike*) declararse en huelga **9.**(*be removed*) salir, quitarse **10.**(*become available: stamp, book, magazine*) publicarse **11.**(*appear in sky: moon, stars, sun*) aparecer **12.**(*open: flowers*) florecer

◆**come over I.** *vi* **1.**(*come nearer*) acercarse **2.**(*visit sb's home*) visitar **3.** *Aus, Brit* (*feel*) sentir **II.** *vt* **to ~ sb** apoderarse de alguien

◆**come round** *vi* **1.**(*change one's mind*) cambiar de opinión; **to ~ to sb's point of view** adoptar el punto de vista de alguien **2.** MED volver en sí **3.**(*visit sb's home*) pasarse **4.**(*arrive: a holiday, letter*) llegar

◆**come through I.** *vi* **1.**(*show: one's nervousness, excitement, charm*) mostrar **2.** *Aus, Brit* (*arrive: results, visa, call*) llegar **3.**(*survive*) sobrevivir **II.** *vt insep* superar

◆**come to I.** *vt insep* **1.**(*reach*) llegar a; **to come down to sth** bajar a algo; **to come up**

to sth subir a algo; **to ~ rest** irse a dormir; **to ~ nothing** quedarse en nada **2.**(*amount to*) subir a **II.** *vi* MED volver en sí
◆**come under** *vt no pl* **1.**(*be listed under*) aparecer bajo **2.**(*be dealt with*) ser competencia de **3.**(*be subjected to*) **to ~ criticism** ser objeto de crítica
◆**come up** *vi* **1.**(*be mentioned*) mencionarse **2.**(*happen*) suceder
◆**come upon** *vt no pl* encontrarse con
comeback ['kʌmbæk] *n* **1.** vuelta *f;* SPORTS recuperación *f* **2.**(*retort*) réplica *f*
Comecon ['kɒmɪkɒn, *Am:* 'kɑ:mɪkɑ:n] *n abbr of* **Council for Mutual Economic Assistance** COMECON *m*
comedian [kə'mi:dɪən] *n* **1.**(*person telling jokes*) cómico, -a *m, f* **2.**(*funny person*) payaso, -a *m, f*
comedienne [kə,mi:di'ən] *n* **1.**(*female comedian*) cómica *f* **2.**(*funny female*) payasa *f*
comedown ['kʌmdaʊn] *n no pl, inf* **1.**(*anticlimax*) revés *m* **2.**(*decline in status*) humillación *f*
comedy ['kɒmədi, *Am:* 'kɑ:mə-] <-ies> *n* **1.** CINE, THEAT, LIT comedia *f* **2.**(*funny situation*) comicidad *f*
comeliness ['kʌmlɪnɪs] *n no pl* encanto *m*
comely ['kʌmli] <-ier, -iest> *adj* (*woman*) atractiva
come-on ['kʌmɒn, *Am:* -ɑ:n] *n Am, inf* **1.**(*expression of sexual interest*) invitación *f;* **to give sb the ~** tirar los tejos a alguien **2.**(*enticement*) reclamo *m*
comet ['kɒmɪt, *Am:* 'kɑ:mɪt] *n* cometa *m*
come-uppance [kʌm'ʌpənts] *n* merecido *m;* **he got his ~ in the end** al final se llevó su merecido
comfort ['kʌmfət, *Am:* -fɚt] **I.** *n* **1.**(*comfortable feeling*) comodidad *f* **2.**(*consolation*) consuelo *m;* **to be a ~ to sb** ser un consuelo para alguien **3.**(*pleasurable things in life*) bienestar *m;* **the ~s of life** las cosas agradables de la vida **II.** *vt* consolar
comfortable ['kʌmftəbl, *Am:* 'kʌmfɚt̬ə-] *adj* **1.**(*offering comfort*) cómodo, -a; **to make oneself ~** ponerse cómodo **2.**(*financially stable*) acomodado, -a; **~ life** vida *f* holgada **3.** SPORTS (*substantial*) fácil
comfortably ['kʌmftəbli, *Am:* 'kʌmfɚt̬ə-] *adv* **1.**(*in a comfortable manner: sit, lie*) cómodamente **2.**(*easily*) fácilmente **3.**(*in financially stable manner*) **to live ~** vivir de forma acomodada
comforter ['kʌmfətə', *Am:* -fɚt̬ɚ] *n Am* (*duvet*) edredón *m*
comforting ['kʌmfətɪŋ, *Am:* -fɚt̬ɪŋ] *adj* (*thought, words*) reconfortante
comfortless ['kʌmfətlɪs, *Am:* -fɚt-] *adj form* incómodo, -a
comfort station *n Am* (*public toilet*) servicios *mpl* públicos
comfy ['kʌmfi] <-ier, -iest> *adj inf* (*furniture, clothes*) cómodo, -a

comic ['kɒmɪk, *Am:* 'kɑ:mɪk] **I.** *n* **1.**(*cartoon magazine*) cómic *m* **2.**(*person*) cómico, -a *m, f* **II.** *adj* cómico, -a; **~ play** comedia *f*
comical ['kɒmɪkl, *Am:* 'kɑ:mɪ-] *adj* cómico, -a; (*idea*) divertido, -a
comic book *n Am* (*comic*) tebeo *m* **comic strip** *n* tira *f* cómica
coming ['kʌmɪŋ] **I.** *adj* **1.**(*next*) próximo, -a; **the ~ year** el año que viene **2.**(*approaching*) venidero, -a **II.** *n* llegada *f;* **~s and goings** idas y venidas
comma ['kɒmə, *Am:* 'kɑ:mə] *n* coma *f*
command [kə'mɑ:nd, *Am:* -'mænd] **I.** *vt* **1.**(*order*) **to ~ sb to do sth** ordenar a alguien que haga algo; **to ~ that** mandar que +*subj* **2.**(*have command over*) estar al mando de **3.**(*have at one's disposal*) disponer de **4.**(*overlook: view*) tener **5.**(*respect*) imponer; (*sympathy*) inspirar **II.** *n* **1.**(*order*) mandato *m;* **to obey a ~** acatar una orden; **to take ~ of** asumir el mando de; **to have ~ over a fleet** estar al mando de una flota; **at sb's ~** a la disposición de alguien; **under sb's ~** bajo las órdenes de alguien **2.**(*control*) mando *m;* **to be in ~ of sth** estar al mando de algo **3.** MIL comandancia *f* **4.** INFOR orden *f* **5.** *no pl* (*knowledge*) dominio *m* **6.** *no pl, form* (*view*) vista *f*
commandant [,kɒmən'dænt, *Am:* 'kɑ:-məndænt] *n* MIL comandante *mf*
commandeer [,kɒmən'dɪə', *Am:* ,kɑ:mən-'dɪr] *vt* apropriarse de
commander [kə'mɑ:ndə', *Am:* -'mændɚ] *n* **1.** MIL (*officer in charge*) comandante *mf* **2.** *Brit* MIL, NAUT (*naval officer*) capitán *m* de fragata
commanding [kə'mɑ:ndɪŋ, *Am:* -'mæn-] *adj* **1.**(*authoritative*) dominante; (*voice*) imponente **2.**(*dominant: position*) dominante **3.**(*considerable*) abrumador(a)
command key *n* INFOR tecla *f* de comando
commandment [kə'mɑ:ndmənt, *Am:* -'mænd-] *n liter* orden *f*
Commandment [kə'mɑ:ndmənt, *Am:* -'mænd-] *n* **the Ten ~s** REL los diez mandamientos
command module *n* AVIAT módulo *m* de maniobra y mando
commando [kə'mɑ:ndəʊ, *Am:* -'mændoʊ] <-s *o* -es> *n* MIL **1.**(*group of soldiers*) comando *m* **2.**(*member of commando*) miembro *mf* de un comando
command post *n* MIL puesto *m* de mando **command prompt** *n* INFOR línea *f* de comandos
commemorate [kə'meməreɪt] *vt* conmemorar
commemoration [kə,memə'reɪʃən] *n no pl* conmemoración *f;* **in ~ of ...** en conmemoración de...
commemorative [kə'memərətɪv, *Am:* -t̬ɪv] *adj* conmemorativo, -a
commence [kə'ments] *vi form* empezar; **to**

~ **speaking** comenzar un discurso
commencement [kə'mentsmənt] *n form*
1. (*beginning*) inicio *m* **2.** *Am* SCHOOL, UNIV ceremonia *f* de graduación
commend [kə'mend] *vt* **1.** (*praise*) elogiar; to ~ sth/sb (on sth) alabar algo/a alguien (por algo) **2.** (*entrust*) encomendar; to ~ sth to sb encomendar algo a alguien **3.** (*recommend*) recomendar
commendable [kə'mendəbl] *adj* recomendable; ~ **bravery** valor *m* loable
commendation [ˌkɒmen'deɪʃən, *Am:* ˌkaːmen-] *n* **1.** (*praise*) elogio *m* **2.** (*recommendation*) recomendación *f*
commendatory [kə'mendətəri, *Am:* -tɔːri] *adj* loable
commensurable [kə'menʃərəbl, *Am:* -sɚ-] *adj* conmensurable
commensurate [kə'menʃərət, *Am:* -sɚ-] *adj form* proporcionado, -a
comment ['kɒment, *Am:* 'kaːment] **I.** *n* comentario *m;* **no** ~ sin comentarios; to **make a** ~ hacer una observación **II.** *vi* comentar; to ~ **that** ... observar que...
commentary ['kɒməntəri, *Am:* 'kaːmənter-] <-ies> *n* comentario *m;* **colour** ~ reportaje *m* en color; **literary** ~ crítica *f* literaria
commentate ['kɒmənteɪt, *Am:* 'kaːmən-] *vi* TV, RADIO to ~ **on sth** hacer un reportaje sobre algo
commentator ['kɒmənteɪtəʳ, *Am:* 'kaːmənteɪtɚ] *n* TV, RADIO comentarista *mf*
commerce ['kɒmɜːs, *Am:* 'kaːmɜːrs] *n no pl* comercio *m*
commercial [kə'mɜːʃl, *Am:* -'mɜːr-] **I.** *adj* **1.** (*relating to commerce*) comercial **2.** RADIO, TV publicitario, -a **II.** *n* RADIO, TV anuncio *m,* comercial *m AmL*
commercialism [kə'mɜːʃəlɪzəm, *Am:* -'mɜːr-] *n no pl* comercialismo *m*
commercialization [kəˌmɜːʃəlaɪ'zeɪʃən] *n no pl, Am* comercialización *f*
commercialize [kə'mɜːʃəlaɪz, *Am:* -'mɜːr-] *vt Am* comercializar
commercialized *adj* comercializado, -a
commiserate [kə'mɪzəreɪt] *vi* mostrar conmiseración
commiseration [kəˌmɪzə'reɪʃən] *n* conmiseración *f;* ~s **for failing the exam** siento que suspendieras el examen
commission [kə'mɪʃən] **I.** *vt* **1.** (*order*) encargar **2.** MIL (*appoint*) to ~ **sb as sth** nombrar a alguien algo; ~**ed officer** oficial *mf* **II.** *n* **1.** (*order*) encargo *m* **2.** (*system of payment*) comisión *f;* to **be on** ~ estar a comisión **3.** (*investigative body*) comisión *f* **4.** MIL (*appointment*) nombramiento *m;* to **resign one's** ~ dimitir del cargo **5.** *no pl* LAW (*perpetration*) perpetración *f* **6.** NAUT, AVIAT **out of** ~ fuera de servicio
commissionaire [kəˌmɪʃə'neəʳ, *Am:* -'er] *n Brit* conserje *mf*

commissioned officer *n* oficial *m* en activo
commissioner [kə'mɪʃənəʳ, *Am:* -ɚ] *n* comisario, -a *m, f;* ~ **for oaths** notario, -a *m, f* público, -a
commit [kə'mɪt] <-tt-> *vt* **1.** (*carry out*) cometer; to ~ **suicide** suicidarse; to ~ **an error** incurrir en un error **2.** (*bind*) to ~ **oneself** (to sth) comprometerse (a algo); to ~ **soldiers to the defence of a region** enviar soldados a defender la región **3.** (*institutionalize*) to ~ sb **to prison** encarcelar a alguien; to ~ sb **to hospital** internar a alguien en un hospital **4.** (*entrust*) to ~ sth **to memory** memorizar algo; to ~ sth **to paper** poner algo por escrito
commitment [kə'mɪtmənt] *n* **1.** (*dedication*) dedicación *f* **2.** (*obligation*) obligación *f;* **family** ~s compromisos *mpl* familiares; to **make a** ~ hacer una promesa
committed *adj* comprometido, -a
committee [kə'mɪti, *Am:* -'mɪt̬-] *n* comité *m;* to **appoint a** ~ nombrar un comité; to **be** [*o* **sit**] **on a** ~ ser miembro de un comité
commode [kə'məʊd, *Am:* -'moʊd] *n* **1.** (*chest of drawers*) cómoda *f* **2.** (*toilet*) silla *f* con orinal
commodious [kə'məʊdɪəs, *Am:* -'moʊ-] *adj* amplio, -a, espacioso, -a
commodity [kə'mɒdəti, *Am:* -'maːdət̬i] <-ies> *n* **1.** (*product*) mercancía *f;* ~ **markets** mercados *mpl* de mercancías **2.** *pl* (*raw material*) materia *f* prima
commodore ['kɒmədɔːʳ, *Am:* 'kaːmədɔːr] *n* comodoro *m*
common ['kɒmən, *Am:* 'kaːmən] **I.** *adj* **1.** (*ordinary*) corriente; (*usual*) usual; (*widespread*) frecuente; **a** ~ **disease** una enfermedad común; to **be** ~ **knowledge** ser de dominio público; **a** ~ **name** un nombre común; **the** ~ **man** el hombre medio **2.** (*shared*) común; ~ **property** propiedad *f* comunal; **by** ~ **assent** por unanimidad; **for the** ~ **good** en beneficio de todos **3.** (*vulgar*) vulgar **II.** *n* **1.** (*land*) ejido *m* **2.** *Am* UNIV comedor *m*
common denominator *n* denominador *m* común
commoner ['kɒmənəʳ, *Am:* 'kaːmənɚ] *n* plebeyo, -a *m, f*
common ground *n no pl* puntos *mpl* en común; to **be on** ~ **with sb** coincidir con alguien **common land** *n* ejido *m* **common law** *n no pl* ≈ derecho *m* consuetudinario **common-law wife** <-wives> *n* mujer *f* en una pareja de hecho
commonly *adv* (*often*) frecuentemente; (*usually*) normalmente
common-or-garden [ˌkɒmənɔː'gaːdən, *Am:* ˌkaːmənɔːr'gaːr-] *adj* normal y corriente
commonplace ['kɒmənpleɪs, *Am:* 'kaːmən-] **I.** *adj* corriente; **it is** ~ **to see that** ... es frecuente ver que... **II.** *n* lugar *m* común
common room *n Brit* sala *f* de reuniones (de un colegio) **common sense** *n no pl* sentido

m común; **a ~ solution** una solución lógica
common stock *n Am* FIN acciones *fpl* ordinarias
Commonwealth ['kɒmənwelθ, *Am:* 'kɑːmən-] *n* **the ~** la Commonwealth

La **Commonwealth of Nations** (antiguamente la **British Commonwealth**) es una organización libre de estados independientes, que se ha ido desarrollando a partir del antiguo **British Empire**. Fue fundada oficialmente en 1931 a partir de los **Statute of Westminster**. En aquel momento, Canadá, Australia, Sudáfrica y Nueva Zelanda ya habían alcanzado la independencia y junto con el Reino Unido fueron los primeros miembros. La mayoría de los países que formaban el antiguo Imperio Británico al alcanzar la independencia han ido engrosando la lista de los países pertenecientes a dicha organización. Hoy en día esta organización trabaja en la línea de la colaboración económica y cultural. Los jefes de estado de los países integrantes de la **Commonwealth** se reúnen dos veces al año.

commotion [kə'məʊʃən, *Am:* -'moʊ-] *n* alboroto *m*
communal ['kɒmjʊnl, *Am:* kə'mjuː] *adj* comunal
commune [kə'mjuːn] *n* comuna *f*
communicable [kə'mjuːnɪkəbl] *adj* **1.** (*information*) comunicable **2.** MED transmisible
communicate [kə'mjuːnɪkeɪt] **I.** *vt* **1.** (*information*) comunicar **2.** MED transmitir **II.** *vi* **1.** (*give information*) comunicar(se); **I'm afraid we just don't ~** creo que simplemente no conectamos **2.** (*connect*) comunicar(se); **the bedroom ~s with the hall** el dormitorio comunica con el recibidor
communication [kəˌmjuːnɪ'keɪʃən] *n* **1.** *no pl* (*process*) comunicación *f* **2.** (*missive*) comunicación *f* **3.** *pl* (*means*) comunicaciones *fpl*
communicative [kə'mjuːnɪkətɪv, *Am:* -nəkeɪt̬ɪv] *adj* comunicativo, -a
communion [kə'mjuːnɪən, *Am:* -njən] *n no pl* comunión *f*; **to take ~** comulgar
communiqué [kə'mjuːnɪkeɪ, *Am:* kəˌmjuːnɪ'keɪ] *n* comunicado *m*
communism ['kɒmjʊnɪzəm, *Am:* 'kɑːmjə-] *n no pl* comunismo *m*
communist ['kɒmjʊnɪst, *Am:* 'kɑːmjə-] **I.** *n* comunista *mf* **II.** *adj* comunista
community [kə'mjuːnəti, *Am:* -nət̬i] <-ies> *n* **1.** (*of people*) comunidad *f*; **the local ~** el vecindario **2.** (*of animals, plants*) colonia *f* **3.** (*togetherness*) colectividad *f*
community centre *n* centro *m* social
community home *n* centro *m* de reeducación **community service** *n* trabajo *m* social **community singing** *n no pl* canto

m colectivo **community worker** *n* asistente *mf* social
commutable [kə'mjuːtəbl, *Am:* -t̬ə-] *adj* conmutable
commutation [ˌkɒmjuː'teɪʃən, *Am:* ˌkɑːmjə-] *n* conmutación *f*
commutation ticket *n Am* abono *m* de temporada
commute [kə'mjuːt] **I.** *vi* viajar (diariamente) al lugar de trabajo **II.** *n inf* viaje *m* (diario) al trabajo **III.** *vt* **1.** (*change, convert*) convertir **2.** FIN, LAW conmutar
commuter [kɒ'mjuːtə', *Am:* -t̬ɚ] *n persona que debe viajar diariamente para ir al trabajo*
commuter belt *n* barrios *mpl* periféricos **commuter train** *n* tren *m* de cercanías
Comoran ['kɒmərən, *Am:* 'kɑːm-] **I.** *adj* comorano, -a **II.** *n* comorano, -a *m, f*
Comoros ['kɒmərəʊz, *Am:* 'kɑːmərəʊz] *npl* **the ~** las Islas Comoras
compact¹ ['kɒmpækt, *Am:* 'kɑːm-] **I.** *adj* (*small*) compacto, -a; (*material*) apretado, -a **II.** *vt* condensar **III.** *n* **1.** *Am, Aus* AUTO utilitario *m* **2.** (*powder*) polvera *f*
compact² ['kɒmpækt, *Am:* 'kɑːm-] *n* acuerdo *m*
compact disc *n* compact *m*, disco *m* compacto
compact disc player *n* reproductor *m* de discos compactos
compactness [kəm'pæktnɪs, *Am:* kəm-] *n no pl* compresión *f*
companion [kəm'pænjən] *n* **1.** (*person, animal*) compañero, -a *m, f*; **travelling ~** compañero de viaje **2.** (*guidebook*) guía *f*
companionable [kəm'pænjənəbl] *adj* simpático, -a
companionship *n no pl* compañerismo *m*
companionway [kəm'pænjənweɪ] *n* NAUT escalerilla *f*
company ['kʌmpəni] <-ies> *n* **1.** (*firm, enterprise*) empresa *f*; **Duggan and Company** Duggan y Compañía; **~ union** *Am* sindicato *m* de empresa **2.** *no pl* (*companionship*) compañía *f*; **you are in good ~** estás en buena compañía; **to keep sb ~** hacer compañía a alguien; **he's been keeping bad ~** va con malas compañías; **Margaret stayed for a week as ~ for my mother** Margaret se quedó una semana para hacer compañía a mi madre **3.** (*group*) *a.* MIL compañía *f* ▶**two's ~** (**three's a crowd**) *prov* dos son compañía, tres son multitud
comparable ['kɒmpərəbl, *Am:* 'kɑːm-] *adj* comparable; **~ to** equiparable a
comparative [kəm'pærətɪv, *Am:* -'perət̬ɪv] **I.** *n* comparativo *m* **II.** *adj* comparativo, -a; **~ literature** literatura *f* comparada
comparatively *adv* (*by comparison*) comparativamente; (*relatively*) relativamente
compare [kəm'peə', *Am:* -'per] **I.** *vt* comparar; **to ~ sth/sb to** [*o* **with**] **sth/sb** comparar algo/a alguien con algo/alguien; **instant**

coffee can't be ~d with an expresso el café instantáneo no puede compararse con un expreso; **to ~ notes on sth** hacer un intercambio de impresiones sobre algo **II.** *vi* compararse; **to ~ favourably with sth** ser mejor que algo; **last year's weather just doesn't ~** el tiempo del año pasado no puede compararse

comparison [kəm'pærɪsn, *Am:* -'per-] *n* comparación *f*; **to make a ~** hacer una comparación; **by ~ with sb/sth** en comparación con alguien/algo; **there's no ~ between the two restaurants** no hay ni punto de comparación entre los dos restaurantes

compartment [kəm'pɑ:tmənt, *Am:* -'pɑ:rt-] *n* **1.** RAIL compartimiento *m* **2.** (*section*) departamento *m*

compass ['kʌmpəs] <-es> *n* **1.** *a.* NAUT brújula *f* **2.** *no pl, form* (*range*) alcance *m*; (*area*) ámbito *m*; **to be beyond the ~ of sb's knowledge** sobrepasar los límites de los conocimientos de alguien

compassion [kəm'pæʃən] *n no pl* compasión *f*

compassionate [kəm'pæʃənət] *adj* compasivo, -a

compatibility [kəm,pætə'bɪləti, *Am:* -,pætə'bɪlət̬i] *n no pl* compatibilidad *f*

compatible [kəm'pætəbl, *Am:* -'pæt̬-] *adj* **1.** *a.* MED, INFOR compatible **2.** (*consistent*) conciliable

compatriot [kəm'pætrɪət, *Am:* -'peɪtrɪ-] *n* **1.** (*countryman*) compatriota *mf* **2.** *Am* (*companion*) colega *mf*

compel [kəm'pel] <-ll-> *vt* **1.** (*force*) obligar; **the new circumstances ~led a change in policy** las nuevas circunstancias exigían un cambio de política **2.** (*produce*) imponer

compelling *adj* (*reason*) imponente; (*film*) convincente

compendium [kəm'pendɪəm] <-s *o* -dia> *n* compendio *m*

compensate ['kɒmpənseɪt, *Am:* 'kɑ:m-] **I.** *vt* (*make up for*) compensar; (*for loss, damage*) indemnizar **II.** *vi* **to ~ for sth** (*reward*) compensar algo

compensation [,kɒmpen'seɪʃən, *Am:* ,kɑ:m-] *n no pl* **1.** (*award*) compensación *f*; (*for loss, damage*) indemnización *f*; **to claim ~** reclamar una indemnización; **in ~ for sth** en compensación por algo **2.** (*recompense*) recompensa *f*; **in ~** como recompensa

compere ['kɒmpeər, *Am:* 'kɑ:mper] *Brit* **I.** *n* presentador(a) *m(f)* **II.** *vt* presentar

compete [kəm'pi:t] *vi* **1.** (*strive*) competir; **to ~ for sth** competir por algo; **the new shop will have a tough time competing with the two supermarkets** la nueva tienda lo tendrá difícil si quiere competir con los dos supermercados; **turn the music down – I'm not competing with that noise** baja la música – no pienso gritar para que me puedas oír **2.** (*take part*) participar; **to ~ in an event** participar en un acontecimiento

competence ['kɒmpɪtənts, *Am:* 'kɑ:m-] *n,* **competency** *n no pl* competencia *f*

competent ['kɒmpɪtənt, *Am:* 'kɑ:mpɪt̬ənt] *adj* competente; **to be ~ at sth** ser competente en algo

competition [,kɒmpə'tɪʃən, *Am:* ,kɑ:m-] *n* **1.** (*state of competing*) competencia *f* **2.** (*rivalry*) rivalidad *f* **3.** (*contest*) concurso *m*; **beauty ~** concurso de belleza; **to enter a ~** presentarse a un concurso

competitive [kəm'petətɪv, *Am:* -'pet̬ət̬ɪv] *adj* competitivo, -a; **~ spirit** espíritu *m* competitivo; **~ sports** deportes *mpl* de competición; **their prices are very ~** sus precios son muy competitivos

competitiveness [kəm'petətɪvnəs] *n no pl* competitividad *f*

competitor [kəm'petɪtər, *Am:* -'pet̬ət̬ər] *n* **1.** *a.* ECON competidor(a) *m(f)* **2.** SPORTS rival *mf*; (*participant*) participante *mf*

compilation [,kɒmpɪ'leɪʃən, *Am:* ,kɑ:m-pə-] *n* **1.** (*act of compiling*) compilación *f* **2.** (*collection*) recopilación *f*

compile [kəm'paɪl] *vt* **1.** *a.* INFOR compilar **2.** (*collect*) recopilar

compiler [,kɒm'paɪlər, *Am:* -ɚ] *n* **1.** (*person*) recopilador(a) *m(f)* **2.** *a.* INFOR compilador *m*

complacence [kəm'pleɪsənts] *n,* **complacency** *n no pl* complacencia *f* (excesiva)

complacent [kəm'pleɪsənt] *adj* satisfecho, -a de sí mismo, -a

complain [kəm'pleɪn] *vi* quejarse; **to ~ about** [*o* **of**] **sth** quejarse de algo

complainant [kəm'pleɪnənt] *n* LAW demandante *mf*

complaint [kəm'pleɪnt] *n* **1.** (*expression of displeasure*) queja *f*; **to have cause for ~** tener motivo de queja; **to make a ~ about sb/sth** quejarse de alguien/algo; **to lodge a ~** formular una queja **2.** LAW querella *f* **3.** (*illness*) enfermedad *f*

complaisance [kəm'pleɪzənts, *Am:* -sənts] *n no pl, form* complacencia *f*

complaisant [kəm'pleɪzənt, *Am:* -sənt] *adj form* complaciente

complement ['kɒmplɪmənt, *Am:* 'kɑ:m-] *vt* complementar

complementary [,kɒmplɪ'mentəri, *Am:* ,kɑ:mplə'men̬t̬ɚi] *adj* complementario, -a

complete [kəm'pli:t] **I.** *vt* **1.** (*add what is missing*) completar **2.** (*finish*) terminar; **to ~ doing sth** terminar de hacer algo **3.** (*fill out entirely*) rellenar **II.** *adj* completo, -a, entero, -a; **~ coverage** cobertura *f* total; **in ~ darkness** en la más absoluta oscuridad; **~ paralysis** parálisis *f inv* total; **he wore the whole rabbit, ~ with teeth** llevaba el conejo entero, con dientes y todo; **the man's a ~ fool!** ¡el hombre es un loco de remate!; **are we ~?** ¿estamos todos?

completely *adv* totalmente

completeness *n no pl* totalidad *f*

completion [kəm'pli:ʃən] *n no pl* finaliza-

ción *f;* **to be nearing** ~ estar a punto de terminarse; **you'll be paid on** ~ **of the project** cobrarás cuando se haya terminado el proyecto
complex ['kɒmpleks, *Am:* 'kɑ:m-] I. *adj* complejo, -a II.<-es> *n* **1.** PSYCH complejo *m;* **guilt/inferiority** ~ complejo de culpabilidad/inferioridad; **to have a** ~ **about sth** estar acomplejado por algo; **to give sb a** ~ acomplejar a alguien; **I've got a real** ~ **about spiders** tengo verdadera fobia a las arañas **2.** ARCHIT complejo
complexion [kəm'plekʃən] *n* **1.** (*skin*) cutis *m inv;* (*colour*) tez *f;* **a healthy** ~ un cutis sano **2.** (*character*) cariz *m;* (*of people*) aspecto *m;* **MPs of all ~s have mounted this campaign** diputados de todos los colores han organizado esta campaña; **that puts a different** ~ **on things** eso le da un cariz nuevo a las cosas
complexity [kəm'pleksəti, *Am:* -səṭi] *n no pl* complejidad *f*
compliance [kəm'plaɪənts] *n no pl* obediencia *f;* (*agreement*) conformidad *f;* **in** ~ **with the law** conforme a la ley; **to act in** ~ **with sth** actuar de acuerdo con algo
compliant [kəm'plaɪənt] *adj form* (*obedient*) obediente; (*overly obedient*) sumiso, -a
complicate ['kɒmplɪkeɪt, *Am:* 'kɑ:mplə-] *vt* complicar; (*make worse*) empeorar; **his breathing problem has been** ~**d by the flu** su problema respiratorio se ha visto agravado por una gripe
complicated *adj* complicado, -a
complication [ˌkɒmplɪ'keɪʃən, *Am:* ˌkɑ:mplə-] *n* complicación *f;* **if any** ~**s arise, let me know and I'll help** si surge alguna dificultad, avísame y te ayudaré
complicity [kəm'plɪsəti, *Am:* -əṭi] *n no pl* complicidad *f*
compliment ['kɒmplɪmənt, *Am:* 'kɑ:mplə-] I. *n* **1.** (*expression of approval*) cumplido *m;* (*flirt*) piropo *m;* **to pay sb a** ~ hacer un cumplido a alguien; **to repay a** ~ devolver un cumplido; **I take it as a** ~ **that ...** me halaga que... **2.** *pl* saludos *mpl;* **to present one's ~s** *form* presentar sus respetos; **to send ~s** enviar saludos; **with ~s** con un atento saludo ▶**to fish for ~s** buscar elogios II. *vt* **to** ~ **sb on sth** felicitar a alguien por algo
complimentary [ˌkɒmplɪ'mentəri, *Am:* ˌkɑ:mplə'menṭəi] *adj* **1.** (*praising*) positivo, -a; **to be** ~ **about sth** hablar en términos muy favorables de algo **2.** (*free*) gratuito, -a
compliments slip *n* tarjeta *f* comercial
comply [kəm'plaɪ] <-ie-> *vi* cumplir; **to refuse to** ~ negarse a obedecer; **to** ~ **with the law/the rules** acatar la ley/las normas
component [kəm'pəʊnənt, *Am:* -'poʊ-] *n* componente *m;* **key** ~ pieza *f* clave
component parts *npl* piezas *fpl*
compose [kəm'pəʊz, *Am:* -'poʊz] I. *vi* (*write music, poetry*) componer II. *vt* **1.** (*music, poetry*) componer **2.** (*write*) redactar **3.** (*make up*) **to be** ~**d of sth** constar de

algo; **the committee is** ~**d of experts** el comité está formado por expertos **4.** (*calm*) **to** ~ **oneself** calmarse; **she tried hard to** ~ **her features into a smile** se esforzó mucho para mostrar una sonrisa; **to** ~ **one's thoughts** ordenar sus pensamientos **5.** TYPO componer
composed [kəm'pəʊzd, *Am:* -'poʊzd] *adj* tranquilo, -a
composer [kəm'pəʊzəʳ, *Am:* -'poʊzə·] *n* compositor(a) *m(f)*
composite ['kɒmpəzɪt, *Am:* kəm'pɑ:-] *adj* compuesto, -a
composition [ˌkɒmpə'zɪʃən, *Am:* ˌkɑ:m-] *n* **1.** composición *f* **2.** LAW arreglo *m* **3.** *no pl* (*make-up: of a group*) formación *f*
compositor [kəm'pɒzɪtəʳ, *Am:* -'pɑ:zɪṭə·] *n* TYPO cajista *m, f*
compost ['kɒmpɒst, *Am:* 'kɑ:mpoʊst] I. *n no pl* abono *m* orgánico II. *vt* **1.** (*turn into fertilizer*) convertir en abono **2.** (*fertilize*) abonar
composure [kəm'pəʊʒəʳ, *Am:* -'poʊʒə·] *n no pl* compostura *f;* **to lose/regain one's** ~ perder/recobrar la compostura
compound ['kɒmpaʊnd, *Am:* 'kɑ:m-] I. *vt* **1.** (*make worse*) agravar **2.** (*mix*) combinar **3.** (*make up*) **to be** ~**ed of sth** constar de algo II. *n* **1.** (*combination*) mezcla *f* **2.** CHEM compuesto *m* **3.** (*enclosure*) recinto *m*
compound fracture *n* fractura *f* múltiple
compound interest *n* interés *m* compuesto
comprehend [ˌkɒmprɪ'hend, *Am:* ˌkɑ:m-] *vi, vt* comprender
comprehensible [ˌkɒmprɪ'hensəbl, *Am:* ˌkɑ:m-] *adj* comprensible
comprehension [ˌkɒmprɪ'henʃən, *Am:* ˌkɑ:m-] *n no pl* comprensión *f;* **beyond** ~ incomprensible; **he has no** ~ **of the size of the problem** no es consciente de la envergadura del problema
comprehensive [ˌkɒmprɪ'hensɪv, *Am:* ˌkɑ:mprə-] I. *adj* (*exhaustive*) exhaustivo, -a; (*global*) completo, -a; ~ **coverage** cobertura *f* global; ~ **list** lista *f* detallada II. *n Brit* SCHOOL escuela para niños mayores de once años en la que no hay separación de alumnos según su nivel de aptitud

La **comprehensive school** es una escuela integrada para chicos de edades comprendidas entre los 11-18 años. La **comprehensive school** es el resultado de la unificación de la **secondary modern school** y la **grammar school** (para alumnos que habían aprobado el **eleven-plus examination**), producida en los años 60 y 70.

compress [kəm'pres] I. *vt* **1.** a. INFOR comprimir **2.** (*make shorter*) condensar; **I had to** ~ **ten pages of notes into four paragraphs** tuve que resumir diez páginas de apuntes en cuatro párrafos II. <-es> *n* compresa *f*
compressed [kəm'prest] *adj* comprimido, -a

compression [kəm'preʃən] *n a.* INFOR compresión *f*

compressor [kəm'presəʳ, *Am:* -ɚ] *n* compresor *m*

comprise [kəm'praɪz] *vt* **1.**(*include*) comprender **2.**(*consist of*) constar de, componerse de

compromise ['kɒmprəmaɪz, *Am:* 'kɑːm-] **I.** *n* **1.**(*concession*) transigencia *f;* **to agree to a** ~ consentir en transigir; **to make a** ~ hacer una concesión **2.**(*agreement*) arreglo *m;* **to reach a** ~ llegar a un acuerdo **II.** *vi* transigir **III.** *vt* **1.**(*betray*) comprometer; **to** ~ **one's beliefs/principles** dejar de lado sus creencias/principios **2.**(*endanger*) poner en peligro; **to** ~ **one's reputation** poner en entredicho su reputación

compromising *adj* comprometido, -a

comptroller [kən'trəʊləʳ, *Am:* -'troʊlɚ] *n* interventor(a) *m(f)*, contralor(a) *m(f) AmL*

compulsion [kəm'pʌlʃən] *n no pl* obligación *f;* **to be under no** ~ **to do sth** no estar obligado a hacer algo; **he seems to have a constant** ~ **to eat** parece que tiene una obsesión constante por la comida

compulsive [kəm'pʌlsɪv] *adj* compulsivo, -a

compulsory [kəm'pʌlsəri] *adj* obligatorio, -a; ~ **purchase** expropiación *f;* ~ **by law** preceptivo por ley

compunction [kəm'pʌŋkʃən] *n no pl* remordimiento *m;* **to have no** ~ **about sth** no tener reparo en algo

computation [ˌkɒmpjʊ'teɪʃən, *Am:* ˌkɑːm-pjə-] *n* cómputo *m;* INFOR computación *f*

compute [kəm'pjuːt] *vt* computar

computer [kəm'pjuːtəʳ, *Am:* -ɚ] *n* ordenador *m*, computador(a) *m(f) AmL;* **to do sth by** ~ hacer algo con el ordenador

computer-aided *adj* asistido, -a por ordenador

computer centre *n* centro *m* de informática **computer game** *n* videojuego *m* **computer graphics** *n* + *sing/pl vb* gráficos *mpl* por ordenador [*o* computadora *AmL*]

computerization [kəmˌpjuːtəraɪˈzeɪʃən, *Am:* -ɪ-] *n no pl* **1.**(*computer storage*) computerización *f* **2.**(*equipping with computers*) instalación *f* de equipo informático

computerize [kəm'pjuːtəraɪz, *Am:* -tə-raɪz] **I.** *vt* **1.**(*store on computer*) informatizar, computerizar **2.**(*equip with computers*) instalar ordenadores [*o* computadoras *AmL*] en **II.** *vi* informatizarse

computer network *n* red *f* de ordenadores [*o* computadoras *AmL*] **computer programmer** *n* programador(a) *m(f)* **computer science** *n no pl* informática *f;* ~ **course** curso *m* de informática **computer scientist** *n* informático, -a *m, f* **computer search** <-es> *n* búsqueda *f* por ordenador [*o* computadora *AmL*] **computer virus** <-es> *n* virus *m inv* informático **computer workstation** *n* terminal *m* de trabajo

computing *n no pl* informática *f*

comrade ['kɒmreɪd, *Am:* 'kɑːmræd] *n* **1.**(*friend*) compañero, -a *m, f* **2.** POL camarada *mf*

comradeship ['kɒmreɪdʃɪp, *Am:* 'kɑːmræd-] *n no pl* camaradería *f;* **there's a great sense of** ~ **among the team** hay mucho compañerismo en el grupo

COMSAT ['kɒmsæt, *Am:* 'kɑːm-] *n Am abbr of* **communications satellite** COMSAT *m*

con[1] [kɒn, *Am:* kɑːn] <-nn-> *vt inf* engañar; **to** ~ **sb** (**into doing sth**) engañar a alguien (para que haga algo); **to** ~ **sb into believing that ...** hacer creer a alguien que...; **to** ~ **sb out of sth** estafar algo a alguien

con[2] [kɒn, *Am:* kɑːn] *n* contra *m;* **the pros and** ~**s of sth** los pros y los contras de algo

con artist [ˌkɒn'ɑːtɪst, *Am:* ˌkɑːn'ɑːrtəst] *n inf* estafador(a) *m(f)*

concatenation [kɒnˌkætɪ'neɪʃən, *Am:* kənˌkætə-] *n* concatenación *f*

concave ['kɒnkeɪv, *Am:* kɑːn-] *adj* cóncavo, -a

concavity [kən'kævɪti, *Am:* kɑːn'kævəti] <-ies> *n* concavidad *f*

conceal [kən'siːl] *vt* esconder; (*a surprise*) contener; (*the truth*) encubrir

concealment [kən'siːlmənt] *n no pl* (*of information, evidence*) encubrimiento *m;* (*of feelings*) disimulación *f;* **to watch sth from a place of** ~ ver algo desde un escondrijo

concede [kən'siːd] **I.** *vt* **1.**(*acknowledge*) conceder; (*defeat*) aceptar; **to** ~ **that ...** admitir que... **2.**(*surrender*) ceder; **to** ~ **sth to sb** otorgar algo a alguien **3.**(*permit*) acceder a **4.**(*allow to score*) **to** ~ **a goal** encajar un gol **II.** *vi* darse por vencido

conceit [kən'siːt] *n* **1.** *no pl* (*vanity*) vanidad *f;* **to be full of** ~ tener muchas presunciones **2.** *liter* (*elaborate comparison*) concepto *m*

conceited [kən'siːtɪd, *Am:* -t̮ɪd] *adj* vanidoso, -a; **without wishing to sound** ~ sin querer parecer presuntuoso

conceivable [kən'siːvəbl] *adj* concebible; **it's** ~ es verosímil

conceive [kən'siːv] **I.** *vt* **1.**(*imagine, become pregnant with*) concebir **2.**(*devise*) idear; (*arrange*) preparar **II.** *vi* **1.**(*think*) **to** ~ **of sb/sth** formarse un concepto de alguien/algo; **other people may influence how we** ~ **of ourselves** los demás pueden influir en el concepto que tenemos de nosotros mismos **2.**(*devise*) imaginar(se) **3.**(*become pregnant*) concebir

concentrate ['kɒnsəntreɪt, *Am:* 'kɑːn-] **I.** *vi* **1.**(*focus one's thoughts*) concentrarse; **to** ~ **on sth** concentrarse en algo **2.**(*gather*) reunirse **II.** *vt* **1.**(*focus*) concentrar; (*search*) centrar **2.**(*accumulate*) reunir; (*population*) concentrar **3.**(*not dilute*) concentrar **III.** *n* concentrado *m*

concentrated *adj a. fig* concentrado, -a; (*attack*) conciso, -a

concentration [ˌkɒnsn'treɪʃən, Am: ˌkɑːn-] n no pl **1.** concentración f; ~ **on sth** concentración en algo; **to lose (one's)** ~ perder la concentración **2.** (accumulation) acumulación f; (of troops) concentración f

concentration camp n campo m de concentración

concentric [kən'sentrɪk] adj concéntrico, -a

concept ['kɒnsept, Am: 'kɑːn-] n concepto m; **to grasp a** ~ coger una idea

conception [kən'sepʃən] n **1.** (notion) noción f; (idea) idea f; (creation) concepción f **2.** no pl BIO concepción f

conceptual [kən'septʃuəl] adj conceptual

conceptualise Aus, Brit, **conceptualize** [kən'septʃuəlaɪz] Am **I.** vi formarse un concepto **II.** vt conceptualizar

concern [kən'sɜːn, Am: -'sɜːrn] **I.** vt **1.** (apply to) referirse a; **to** ~ **oneself about sth** interesarse por algo; **there's no need for you to** ~ **yourself with this matter** no tienes porqué meterte en este asunto **2.** (affect) incumbir; **to whom it may** ~ a quien le corresponda **3.** (be about) tener que ver con; **to be** ~**ed with sth** ocuparse de algo; **as far as I'm** ~**ed** por lo que a mí respecta; **I'd like to thank everyone** ~**ed** me gustaría dar las gracias a todos los que han colaborado; **I'm not very good where money is** ~**ed** no soy muy bueno en cuestiones de dinero; **her job is something** ~**ed with computers** su trabajo tiene que ver con los ordenadores **4.** (worry) preocuparse; **to be** ~**ed about sth** estar preocupado por algo **II.** n **1.** (matter of interest) asunto m; **a major** ~ una grave preocupación; **it's no** ~ **of mine** eso no es de mi incumbencia; **what's happening? – that's none of your** ~ ¿qué ocurre? – no es asunto tuyo; **to be of** ~ **to sb** interesar a alguien **2.** (worry) preocupación f; **a matter of** ~ un asunto de interés; **the** ~ **for sth** la inquietud por algo; **his** ~ **to appear sophisticated amused her** sus esfuerzos para parecer sofisticado le hacían gracia **3.** (company) empresa f; **a going** ~ una empresa próspera

concerning prep acerca de

concert ['kɒnsət, Am: 'kɑːnsət] n **1.** (musical performance) concierto m; ~ **hall** sala f de conciertos; ~ **pianist** pianista mf; ~ **tour** gira f de conciertos **2. in** ~ (performing live) en concierto; form (all together) conjuntamente; **in** ~ **with sb** conjuntamente con alguien; **to act in** ~ actuar de común acuerdo

concerted [kən'sɜːtɪd] adj **1.** (joint) concertado, -a; (action) conjunto, -a; (exercise) acordado, -a **2.** (resolute) resuelto, -a; (effort) enérgico, -a

concert grand ['kɒnsət grænd, Am: 'kɑːnsət-] n piano m de cola

concertina [ˌkɒnsə'tiːnə, Am: ˌkɑːnsə-] **I.** n concertina f **II.** vi Aus, Brit colisionar en cadena **III.** vt Aus, Brit **it wasn't possible to** ~ **the three meetings into one afternoon** fue imposible concentrar las tres reuniones en una tarde

concertmaster [ˌkɒnsət'mæstəʳ, Am: ˌkɑːnsət'mæstəʳ] n Am concertino m

concerto [kən'tʃeətəʊ, Am: -'tʃertoʊ] <-s o -ti> n concierto m

concert pitch n MUS diapasón m ▶**to be at** ~ estar preparado

concession [kən'seʃən] n **1.** (tax compensation) desgravación f **2.** (compromise) concesión f; ~ **to sell goods** licencia f para vender productos

conciliate [kən'sɪlɪeɪt] **I.** vi conciliarse **II.** vt **1.** (placate) apaciguar **2.** (reconcile) conciliar

conciliation [kən,sɪlɪ'eɪʃən] n no pl, form conciliación f

conciliation board n equipo m de conciliación

conciliatory [kən'sɪlɪətəri, Am: -tɔːri] adj conciliador(a)

concise [kən'saɪs] adj conciso, -a

conciseness n no pl, **concision** [kən'sɪʒən] n no pl concisión f

conclave ['kɒnkleɪv, Am: 'kɑːn-] n form **1.** (private meeting) reunión f a puerta cerrada **2.** REL (gathering of cardinals) cónclave m

conclude [kən'kluːd] **I.** vi concluir **II.** vt **1.** (finish) finalizar; **to** ~ **by doing sth** terminar haciendo algo **2.** (decide) resolver; **we talked all night, but nothing was** ~**d** hablamos toda la noche, pero no llegamos a ninguna conclusión **3.** (infer) **to** ~ (**from sth**) **that ...** deducir (de algo) que... **4.** (ratify) pactar; (a contract) firmar; (a peace treaty) ratificar

concluding adj final; (chapter) último, -a

conclusion [kən'kluːʒən] n **1.** (end) conclusión f; (of a story) final m **2.** (decision) decisión f **3.** (inference) conclusión f; **to come to a** ~ llegar a una conclusión **4.** (ratification) ratificación f; (of a contract) firma f **5.** (lastly) **in** ~ en conclusión; **in** ~, **I should like to say that ...** para terminar, me gustaría decir que...

conclusive [kən'kluːsɪv] adj **1.** (convincing) concluyente; ~ **arguments** argumentos mpl irrefutables **2.** (decisive) decisivo, -a

concoct [kən'kɒkt, Am: -'kɑːkt] vt **1.** (create by mixing ingredients: a dish) preparar **2.** (devise) tramar; (a plan) maquinar **3.** (fabricate) inventar

concoction [kən'kɒkʃən, Am: -'kɑːk-] n (dish) mezcla f; (drink) brebaje m; **is this dish of your** ~, **Paul?** iron ¿este plato es invento tuyo, Paul?

concourse ['kɒnkɔːs, Am: 'kɑːnkɔːrs] n vestíbulo m

concrete ['kɒnkriːt, Am: 'kɑːn-] **I.** n no pl hormigón m **II.** adj de hormigón **III.** vt revestir de hormigón

concrete mixer n hormigonera f

concubine ['kɒnkjʊbaɪn, Am: 'kɑːŋ-] n HIST concubina f

concur [kən'kɜːʳ, Am: -'kɜːr] <-rr-> vi form **1.** (agree) coincidir; **to** ~ **with sb** (**in sth**) estar de acuerdo con alguien (en algo) **2.** (happen *simultaneously*) concurrir

concurrence [kən'kʌrəns] *n no pl, form*
1. (*agreement*) conformidad *f* **2.** (*simultaneous occurrence*) concurrencia *f*

concurrent [kən'kʌrənt] *adj* concurrente

concuss [kən'kʌs] *vt* **to be ~ed** tener una
conmoción cerebral

concussed *adj* que padece una conmoción
cerebral

concussion [kən'kʌʃən] *n no pl* conmoción
f cerebral; **to suffer** (**from**) ~ padecer una
conmoción cerebral

condemn [kən'dem] *vt* **1.** (*reprove*) condenar; **to ~ sb for sth** censurar a alguien por algo
2. (*sentence*) **to be ~ed to death** ser condenado a muerte **3.** (*pronounced unsafe: building*) declarar en ruina; (*food*) declarar no apto
para el consumo

condemnation [ˌkɒndem'neɪʃən, *Am:*
ˌkɑːn-] *n* **1.** (*reproof*) condena *f* **2.** (*reason to
reprove*) motivo *m* de crítica

condensation [ˌkɒnden'seɪʃən, *Am:*
ˌkɑːn-] *n no pl* **1.** (*process of changing to
liquid*) condensación *f* **2.** (*reducing in size*)
abreviación *f*

condense [kɒn'dens] **I.** *vt* **1.** (*shorten*) sintetizar **2.** (*concentrate*) **to ~ a liquid** condensar un líquido **3.** (*form droplets from*) **the air
was ~d into clouds** el aire formó nubes por
condensación **II.** *vi* condensarse

condenser [kɒn'densəʳ, *Am:* -səˈ] *n* condensador *m*

condescend [ˌkɒndɪ'send, *Am:* ˌkɑːn-] *vi* **to
~ to do sth** rebajarse [*o* condescender] a hacer
algo

condescending [ˌkɒndɪ'sendɪŋ, *Am:*
ˌkɑːn-] *adj* con aires de superioridad

condescension [ˌkɒndɪ'senʃən, *Am:* ˌkɑːn-]
n no pl aires *mpl* de superioridad

condiment ['kɒndɪmənt, *Am:* 'kɑːndə-] *n
form* condimento *m*; **~ set** aliño *m*

condition [kən'dɪʃən] **I.** *n* **1.** (*state*) condición *f*; **in perfect** ~ en perfecto estado; **in
peak** ~ en condiciones óptimas; **in a terrible
** ~ en un estado deplorable; **to be out of** ~ (*person*) estar en baja forma; (*thing*) estar en mal
estado; **to be in no** ~ **to do sth** no estar en
condiciones de hacer algo; **for a man of sixty-
-three,** Jim's in pretty good ~ para tener
sesenta y tres, Jim está en plena forma **2.** (*mental or physical state*) estado *m*; **heart** ~ afección *f* cardíaca **3.** (*circumstances*) ~**s** *pl* condiciones *fpl* **4.** (*stipulation*) condición *f*; **to
make a** ~ poner una condición; **on the** ~ **that**
con la condición de que +*subj*; **under the** ~**s
of sth** según los términos de algo **II.** *vt*
1. (*train*) preparar; (*influence*) condicionar
2. (*treat hair*) acondicionar

conditional [kən'dɪʃənl] **I.** *adj* (*provisory*)
condicional; ~ **on sth** condicionado a algo **II.** *n*
LING **the** ~ el condicional

conditionally [kən'dɪʃənəli] *adv* con reservas

conditioned [kən'dɪʃənd] *adj* (*trained*) preparado, -a; (*place, air*) acondicionado, -a;
(*reflex*) condicionado, -a

conditioner [kən'dɪʃənəʳ, *Am:* -əˈ] *n* **1.** (*for
hair*) acondicionador *m* **2.** (*for clothes*) suavizante *m*

conditioning *n no pl* condicionamiento *m*

condo [ˌkɒndəʊ, *Am:* ˌkɑːndoʊ] *n Am, inf s.*
condominium

condolence [kən'dəʊləns, *Am:* -'doʊ-] *n
no pl* ~**s** pésame *m*; **to offer one's ~s** (**to sb**)
form dar el pésame (a alguien)

condom ['kɒndəm, *Am:* 'kɑːn-] *n* condón *m*

condominium [ˌkɒndə'mɪnɪəm, *Am:*
ˌkɑːn-] *n* **1.** *Am* (*apartment building*) propiedad *f* horizontal, condominio *m AmL* **2.** *Am*
(*unit*) piso *m* **3.** POL condominio *m*

condone [kən'dəʊn, *Am:* -'doʊn] *vt*
1. (*approve*) aprobar **2.** (*forgive*) condonar

conducive [kən'djuːsɪv, *Am:* -'duː-] *adj*
propicio, -a; **to be** ~ **to sth** ser apropiado para
algo

conduct [kən'dʌkt, *Am:* 'kɑːn-] **I.** *vt* **1.** (*carry
out*) llevar a cabo **2.** (*direct*) dirigir; **to ~ a
business** conducir un negocio; **to ~ the religious service** dirigir el oficio religioso; (*guide*)
guiar **3.** (*behave*) **to ~ oneself** comportarse
4. ELEC, PHYS (*transmit*) conducir **II.** *vi* MUS llevar la batuta **III.** *n no pl* **1.** (*management*)
dirección *f* **2.** (*behaviour*) conducta *f*; **sb's ~
towards sb** el comportamiento de alguien
hacia alguien

conductive [kən'dʌktɪv] *adj* ELEC, PHYS con-
ductor(a)

conductor [kən'dʌktəʳ, *Am:* -təˈ] *n* **1.** (*director*) director(a) *m(f)* **2.** PHYS, ELEC conductor *m*
3. (*fare collector*) cobrador *m*; (*of train*) revi-
sor *m*

conductress [kən'dʌktrɪs] <-es> *n* cobra-
dora *f*; (*of train*) revisora *f*

conduit ['kɒndjuɪt, *Am:* 'kɑːnduɪt] *n* conducto *m*

cone [kəʊn, *Am:* koʊn] *n* **1. a.** MAT cono *m*
2. (*cornet for ice cream*) cucurucho *m*
3. (*fruit*) piña *f*

confection [kən'fekʃən] *n form* **1.** COM confección *f* **2.** GASTR dulce *m*; (*sweet*) golosina *f*

confectioner [kən'fekʃnəʳ, *Am:* -əˈ] *n* con-
fitero, -a *m, f*

confectionery [kən'fekʃənəri, *Am:* -eri] *n
no pl* confitería *f*

confederacy [kən'fedərəsi] <-ies> *n* **1.** +
pl/sing vb (*union*) confederación *f*; **the Confederacy** *Am* HIST la Confederación **2.** (*plot*)
complot *m*

confederate [kən'fedərət] **I.** *n* cómplice *mf*
II. *adj* POL, HIST confederado, -a

confederation [kənˌfedə'reɪʃən] *n* + *pl/
sing vb* POL confederación *f*

El **Confederation Day** o **Canada Day** es
la fiesta nacional de Canadá que se celebra
el día 1 de julio.

confer [kən'fɜ:ʳ, Am: -'fɜ:r] <-rr-> I. vi consultar II. vt otorgar

conference ['kɒnfərəns, Am: 'kɑːnfə-] n conferencia f; **to be in ~ (with sb)** estar reunido (con alguien)

confess [kən'fes] I. vi confesarse; **to ~ to a crime** confesarse de un crimen II. vt confesar; **I must ~ that I'm a little bit confused** tengo que admitir que estoy un poco confuso

confessedly adv con franqueza

confession [kən'feʃən] n 1. (admission) confesión f; **I have a ~ to make** tengo que hacer una confesión 2. (profession) profesión f; **~ of faith** profesión de fe

confessional [kən'feʃənl] n confesionario m

confessor [kən'fesəʳ, Am: -'fesəˈ] n confesor m

confetti [kən'feti, Am: -'feṭ-] n no pl confeti m; **to shower sb in ~** tirar confeti a alguien

confidant [ˌkɒnfɪ'dænt, Am: ˌkɑːnfə-] n confidente m

confidante [ˌkɒnfɪ'dænt, Am: ˌkɑːnfə-] n confidente f

confide [kən'faɪd] vt confiar; **to ~ (to sb) that ...** decir (a alguien) en confidencia que...

confidence ['kɒnfɪdəns, Am: 'kɑːnfə-] n 1. (trust) confianza f; **to have every ~ in sb** tener toda la confianza en alguien; **to place one's ~ in sb/sth** poner la confianza en alguien/algo; **to take sb into one's ~** confiar en alguien; **to win sb's ~** ganarse la confianza de alguien; **he certainly doesn't lack ~** desde luego no le falta confianza en sí mismo 2. no pl (secrecy) **~s** confidencia f

confident ['kɒnfɪdənt, Am: 'kɑːnfə-] adj 1. (sure) seguro, -a; **to be ~ about oneself** tener confianza en uno mismo; **to be ~ about sth** estar seguro de algo 2. (self-assured) confiado, -a

confidential [ˌkɒnfɪ'denʃl, Am: ˌkɑːnfə-] adj confidencial

confidentially [ˌkɒnfɪ'denʃəli, Am: ˌkɑːnfə-] adv confidencialmente

confiding [kən'faɪdɪŋ] adj confiado, -a

configuration [kən,fɪgə'reɪʃən, Am: kən-,fɪgjə'-] n a. INFOR configuración f

confine ['kɒnfaɪn, Am: 'kɑːn-] I. vt 1. (limit) **to ~ sth to sth** restringir algo a algo; **to be ~d to doing sth** limitarse a hacer algo 2. (imprison) confinar 3. (shut in: person) recluir; (animal) encerrar; **to be ~d to quarters** MIL estar retenido en los barracones II. n pl the **~s** los confines; **beyond the ~s of sth** más allá de los límites de algo

confined adj (prisoner) recluido, -a; (space) reducido, -a

confinement [kən'faɪnmənt] n no pl 1. (act of being confined) reclusión f; (state of being confined) confinamiento m; **his ~ to bed really annoyed him** le resultaba especialmente fastidioso tener que quedar en cama 2. (childbirth) parto m

confines n pl límites mpl

confirm [kən'fɜ:m, Am: -'fɜ:rm] I. vt 1. (verify) verificar 2. REL **to ~ sb's faith** confirmar la fe de alguien II. vi confirmarse

confirmation [ˌkɒnfə'meɪʃən, Am: ˌkɑːn-fəˈ-] n a. REL confirmación f

confirmed [kən'fɜ:md, Am: -'fɜ:rmd] adj 1. (established) firme 2. (chronic) **~ alcoholic** alcohólico m empedernido 3. (proved) confirmado, -a

confiscate ['kɒnfɪskeɪt, Am: 'kɑːnfə-] vt confiscar

conflict¹ ['kɒnflɪkt, Am: 'kɑːn-] n 1. (clash) conflicto m; **to come into ~ with sb** entrar en conflicto con alguien 2. (battle) discrepancia f

conflict² [kən'flɪkt] vi **to ~ with sb** chocar con alguien

conflicting [kən'flɪktɪŋ] adj opuesto, -a; (evidence) contradictorio, -a; (interest) encontrado, -a

confluence ['kɒnfluːəns, Am: 'kɑːn-] n confluencia f

conform [kən'fɔ:m, Am: -'fɔ:rm] vi conformarse; **to ~ to the law** ser conforme a la ley

conformist [kən'fɔ:mɪst, Am: -'fɔ:r-] I. n conformista mf II. adj conformista

conformity [kən'fɔ:mɪti, Am: -'fɔ:rməṭi] n no pl conformidad f; **in ~ with sth** conforme con algo

confound [kən'faʊnd] vt confundir

confounded adj inf maldito, -a

confront [kən'frʌnt] vt (a danger) enfrentarse a; (the enemy) plantar cara a

confrontation [ˌkɒnfrʌn'teɪʃən, Am: ˌkɑːn-frən-] n confrontación f

confrontational [ˌkɒnfrʌn'teɪʃnəl, Am: ˌkɑːnfrən-] adj contencioso, -a; (of opinions) polémico, -a

confuse [kən'fjuːz] vt 1. (perplex) desconcertar 2. (put into disarray) turbar 3. (mix up) confundir

confused [kən'fjuːzd] adj (perplexed) confundido, -a; (disordered) confuso, -a

confusing [kən'fjuːzɪŋ] adj confuso, -a

confusion [kən'fjuːʒən] n no pl 1. (perplexity) desconcierto m 2. (mix up) confusión f 3. (disorder) desorden m

congeal [kən'dʒiːl] vi (sauce) espesarse; (fat) cuajar; (blood) coagular(se)

congenial [kən'dʒiːnɪəl, Am: -njəl] adj placentero, -a; (people) agradable

congenital [kən'dʒenɪtəl, Am: -əṭəl] adj congénito, -a

congested [kən'dʒestɪd] adj 1. (overcrowded) congestionado, -a; (people) abarrotado, -a 2. MED (blocked) congestionado, -a

congestion [kən'dʒestʃən] n no pl (overcrowding) congestión f; (on roads, freeways) caravana f

conglomerate [kən'glɒmərət, Am: -'glɑː-məˈ-] n conglomerado m

conglomeration [kən,glɒmə'reɪʃən, Am: -,glɑː'mə-] n conglomeración f

Congo ['kɒŋgəʊ, Am: 'kɑːŋgoʊ] I. n the **~**

el Congo **II.** *adj* del Congo
Congolese [ˌkɒŋɡəʊˈliːz, *Am:* ˌkɑːŋɡə'-]
I. *adj* congoleño, -a **II.** *n* congoleño, -a *m, f*
congratulate [kənˈɡrætʃʊleɪt, *Am:* -ˈɡræ-
tʃə-] *vt* felicitar; **to ~ sb (on sth)** felicitar a alguien (por algo)
congratulation [kənˌɡrætʃʊˈleɪʃən, *Am:*
-ˌɡrætʃə-] *n* felicitación *f;* **~s!** ¡felicitaciones!;
a note of ~ una postal de felicitación
congregate [ˈkɒŋɡrɪɡeɪt, *Am:* ˈkɑːŋ-] *vi*
congregarse
congregation [ˌkɒŋɡrɪˈɡeɪʃən, *Am:* ˌkɑːŋ-]
n congregación *f*
congregational [ˌkɒŋɡrɪˈɡeɪʃənl, *Am:*
ˌkɑːŋ-] *adj* congregacionalista
congress [ˈkɒŋɡres, *Am:* ˈkɑːŋ-] *n* congreso
m
congressional [kənˈɡreʃənəl, *Am:* kən-]
adj Am congresista
congressman [ˈkɒŋɡresmən, *Am:* ˈkɑːŋ-]
n <-men> *Am* congresista *m* **congresswoman** *n* <-women> *Am* congresista *f*
congruence [ˈkɒŋɡrʊəns, *Am:* ˈkɑːŋ-] *n no
pl a.* MAT congruencia *f*
congruent [ˈkɒŋɡrʊənt, *Am:* ˈkɑːŋ-] *adj a.*
MAT congruente
conical [ˈkɒnɪkl, *Am:* ˈkɑːnɪ-] *adj* cónico, -a
conifer [ˈkɒnɪfəʳ, *Am:* ˈkɑːnəfəʳ] *n* conífera *f*
coniferous [kəˈnɪfərəs, *Am:* koʊ'-] *adj*
conífero, -a
conjectural [kənˈdʒektʃərəl] *adj* conjetural
conjecture [kənˈdʒektʃəʳ, *Am:* -tʃəʳ] **I.** *n*
conjetura *f* **II.** *vi* conjeturar
conjugal [ˈkɒndʒʊɡl, *Am:* ˈkɑːndʒə-] *adj
form* conyugal; **~ bed** lecho *m* conyugal
conjugate [ˈkɒndʒʊɡeɪt, *Am:* ˈkɑːndʒə-] *vt*
conjugar
conjugation [ˌkɒndʒʊˈɡeɪʃən, *Am:* ˌkɑːn-
dʒə-] *n* conjugación *f*
conjunction [kənˈdʒʌŋkʃən] *n a.* LING conjunción *f;* **in ~ with** conjuntamente con
conjunctivitis [kənˌdʒʌŋktɪˈvaɪtɪs, *Am:*
-təˈvaɪtɪs] *n* conjuntivitis *f inv*
conjure [ˈkʌndʒəʳ, *Am:* -dʒəʳ] **I.** *vi* hacer
magia **II.** *vt* conjurar; *fig* evocar
◆**conjure up** *vt* hacer aparecer; **to ~ an
image** evocar una imagen
conjurer [ˈkʌndʒəʳəʳ, *Am:* -dʒəʳ] *n* mago, -a
m, f
conjuring *n no pl* ilusionismo *m*
conjuring trick *n* truco *m* de magia
conjuror [ˈkʌndʒərəʳ, *Am:* -əʳ] *n* mago, -a
m, f
conk [kɒŋk, *Am:* kɑːŋk] **I.** *n Brit, Aus, iron*
narizota *f* **II.** *vt iron, inf* **to ~ one's head on
sth** darse un porrazo (en la cabeza) contra algo
◆**conk out** *vi inf* **1.** (*break down: machine,
vehicle*) averiarse **2.** (*become exhausted*)
quedarse hecho polvo
conker [ˈkɒŋkəʳ, *Am:* ˈkɑːŋkəʳ] *n Brit, childspeak* castaña *f* de Indias
con man [ˈkɒnˌmæn, *Am:* ˈkɑːn-] *n abbr of*
confidence man estafador *m*

connect [kəˈnekt] **I.** *vi* conectar(se); **to ~ to**
the Internet conectarse a internet **II.** *vt*
1. (*join*) conectar **2.** (*associate*) **to ~ sth/sb
with sth** asociar algo/a alguien con algo
3. (*join by telephone*) poner en contacto **4.** (*in
tourism*) enlazar
connected *adj* **1.** (*joined together*) conectado, -a **2.** (*having ties*) **to be ~d to sb** tener
relación con alguien
connecting *adj* comunicado, -a; **~ link**
enlace *m* de conexión
connection *n,* **connexion** [kəˈnekʃən] *n*
1. *a.* ELEC, INFOR conexión *f* **2.** (*relation*) relación *f*
connector *n* conector *m*
connivance [kəˈnaɪvənts] *n no pl* connivencia *f*
connive [kəˈnaɪv] *vi* **to ~ with sb** confabularse con alguien
connoisseur [ˌkɒnəˈsɜːʳ, *Am:* ˌkɑːnəˈsɜːr] *n*
entendido, -a *m, f;* **art/wine ~** experto, -a *m, f*
en arte/vino
connotation [ˌkɒnəˈteɪʃən, *Am:* ˌkɑːnə-] *n*
connotación *f*
conquer [ˈkɒŋkəʳ, *Am:* ˈkɑːŋkəʳ] *vt* **1.** *a.* HIST
conquistar **2.** (*a problem*) acabar con
conqueror [ˈkɒŋkərəʳ, *Am:* ˈkɑːŋkərəʳ] *n*
1. *a.* HIST conquistador(a) *m(f)* **2.** (*in a competition*) vencedor(a) *m(f)*
conquest [ˈkɒŋkwəst, *Am:* ˈkɑːn-] *n no pl,*
a. iron conquista *f*
conscience [ˈkɒnʃəns, *Am:* ˈkɑːn-] *n* conciencia *f;* **a clear ~** una conciencia limpia; **a
guilty ~** remordimientos *mpl* de conciencia;
to prey on sb's ~ *fig* pesar en la conciencia de
alguien; **to prick sb's ~** *fig* hacer sentir culpable a alguien; **in all** [*o* **good** *Am*] **~** en conciencia
conscientious [ˌkɒntʃiˈentʃəs, *Am:* ˌkɑːn-]
adj concienzudo, -a
conscientiousness *n no pl* escrupulosidad *f*
conscientious objector *n* objetor *m* de
conciencia
conscious [ˈkɒnʃəs, *Am:* ˈkɑːn-] *adj*
1. (*deliberate*) expreso, -a **2.** (*aware*) consciente; **fashion ~** preocupado por la moda; **to
be ~ of sth** ser consciente de algo; **to become
~ of sth** darse cuenta de algo
consciousness [ˈkɒnʃəsnɪs, *Am:* ˈkɑːn-] *n*
no pl **1.** MED (*state of being conscious*) conocimiento *m* **2.** (*awareness*) conciencia *f;* **politi-
cal/social ~** conciencia política/social; **to
raise one's ~** concienciarse
conscript [kənˈskrɪpt, *Am:* ˈkɑːn-] **I.** *n* MIL
recluta *mf* **II.** *adj* MIL reclutado, -a **III.** *vt* MIL
reclutar
conscription [kənˈskrɪpʃən] *n no pl* MIL servicio *m* militar, conscripción *f AmL*
consecrate [ˈkɒnsɪkreɪt, *Am:* ˈkɑːnsə-] *vt*
consagrar
consecration [ˌkɒnsɪˈkreɪʃən, *Am:* ˌkɑːn-
sə-] *n no pl* REL consagración *f*
consecutive [kənˈsekjʊtɪv, *Am:* -jət̬ɪv] *adj*

consecutivo, -a

consecutively *adv* consecutivamente

consensus [kən'sensəs] *n no pl* consenso *m*

consent [kən'sent] **I.** *n form* consentimiento *m;* **by common** ~ de común acuerdo **II.** *vi* (*agree*) **to** ~ **to do sth** consentir en hacer algo

consequence ['kɒntsɪkwənts, *Am:* 'kɑːnt-] *n* consecuencia *f;* **as a** ~ como consecuencia; **in** ~ por consiguiente; **nothing of** ~ nada importante

consequent ['kɒntsɪkwənt, *Am:* 'kɑːnt-] *adj,* **consequential** [ˌkɒntsɪ'kwentʃəl, *Am:* ˌkɑːnt-] *adj* consiguiente

consequently *adv* por consiguiente

conservation [ˌkɒntsə'veɪʃən, *Am:* ˌkɑːntsə-] *n* conservación *f;* ~ **environment** ~ preservación *f* del medio ambiente

conservationist [ˌkɒntsə'veɪʃənɪst, *Am:* ˌkɑːntsə-] *n* conservacionista *mf*

conservation technology <-ies> *n* tecnología *f* para la conservación del medio ambiente

conservatism [kən'sɜːvətɪzəm, *Am:* -'sɜːr-] *n no pl* conservadurismo *m*

conservative [kən'sɜːvətɪv, *Am:* -'sɜːrvə̣tɪv] *adj* **1.** *a.* POL (*opposed to change*) conservador(a) **2.** (*cautious*) cauteloso, -a; ~ **estimate** estimación *f* prudente

conservatoire [kən'sɜːvətwɑːʳ, *Am:* -'sɜːrvətwɑːr] *n,* **conservatory** [kən'sɜːvətri, *Am:* -'sɜːrvətɔːri] *n* conservatorio *m*

conserve [kən'sɜːv, *Am:* -sɜːrv] *vt* conservar; **to** ~ **energy** ahorrar energía; **to** ~ **strength** reservar energías

consider [kən'sɪdəʳ, *Am:* -ə-] *vt* **1.** (*contemplate*) considerar **2.** (*look attentively at*) examinar **3.** (*show regard for*) tener en cuenta **4.** (*regard as*) **to be** ~**ed to be the best** ser considerado el mejor; **to** ~ **that ...** creer que...

considerable [kən'sɪdərəbl] *adj* considerable

considerate [kən'sɪdərət] *adj* considerado, -a

consideration [kənˌsɪdə'reɪʃən] *n no pl* consideración *f;* **to take sth into** ~ tener algo en cuenta; **the project is under** ~ el proyecto se está estudiando; **for a small** ~ *iron* por una módica cantidad

considered [kən'sɪdəd, *Am:* -ə-d] *adj* considerado, -a; **highly** ~ muy bien considerado

considering [kən'sɪdərɪŋ] **I.** *prep* teniendo en cuenta; ~ **the weather** en vista del tiempo **II.** *adv* a pesar de todo **III.** *conj* ~ (**that**) ... ya que..., teniendo en cuenta que...

consignment [kən'saɪnmənt] *n* **1.** (*instance of consigning*) envío *m* **2.** ECON remesa *f;* **goods on** ~ mercancías *fpl* en consignación

consist [kən'sɪst] *vi* **to** ~ **of sth** consistir en algo

consistency [kən'sɪstəntsi] *n no pl* **1.** (*degree of firmness*) consistencia *f* **2.** (*being coherent*) coherencia *f*

consistent [kən'sɪstənt] *adj* **1.** (*keeping to*

same principles) consecuente; **to be** ~ **with sth** ser consecuente con algo **2.** (*not varying*) estable

consolation [ˌkɒnsə'leɪʃən, *Am:* ˌkɑːn-] *n no pl* consuelo *m;* **it was** ~ **to him to know that ...** le reconfortó saber que...; **if it's of any** ~ ... si te sirve de consuelo...

consolation prize *n* premio *m* de consolación

consolatory [kən'sɒlətəri, *Am:* -'sɑːlətɔːri] *adj* consolador(a); ~ **words** palabras *fpl* reconfortantes

console[1] ['kɒnsəʊl, *Am:* 'kɑːnsɔʊl] *vt* (*comfort*) consolar

console[2] [kən'səʊl, *Am:* -'sɔʊl] *n* (*switch panel*) consola *f*

consolidate [kən'sɒlɪdeɪt, *Am:* -'sɑːlə-] **I.** *vi* **1.** (*reinforce*) consolidarse **2.** (*unite*) fusionarse **II.** *vt* consolidar

consolidated *adj* consolidado, -a

consolidation [kənˌsɒlɪ'deɪʃən, *Am:* -ˌsɑː-lə-] *n no pl* **1.** (*becoming stronger*) fortalecimiento *m* **2.** ECON consolidación *f*

consommé [kən'sɒmeɪ, *Am:* ˌkɑːnsə'meɪ] *n no pl* consomé *m*

consonance ['kɒnsənəns, *Am:* 'kɑːn-] *n* MUS consonancia *f*

consonant ['kɒnsənənt, *Am:* 'kɑːn-] *n no pl* consonante *f*

consort [kən'sɔːt, *Am:* -'sɔːrt] **I.** *vi* **to** ~ **with sb** tratar con alguien **II.** *n* consorte *mf;* **prince** ~ príncipe *m* consorte

consortium [kən'sɔːtɪəm, *Am:* -'sɔːrt̬-] *n* <consortiums *o* consortia> consorcio *m;* ~ **of companies** grupo *m* de empresas

conspicuous [kən'spɪkjʊəs] *adj* conspicuo, -a; (*beauty*) destacable; (*figure*) llamativo, -a; **to be** ~ **by one's absence** *iron* brillar por su ausencia

conspicuous consumption *n* consumo *m* destinado a la ostentación

conspiracy [kən'spɪrəsi] <-ies> *n* conspiración *f;* **a** ~ **against sb** un complot contra alguien

conspirator [kən'spɪrətəʳ, *Am:* -t̬ə-] *n* conspirador(a) *m(f)*

conspire [kən'spaɪəʳ, *Am:* -'spaɪə-] *vi* conspirar; **to** ~ **to do sth** conspirar para hacer algo

constable ['kʌnstəbl, *Am:* 'kɑːn-] *n Brit* policía *mf*

constabulary [kən'stæbjʊləri, *Am:* -jələr-] *n Brit* cuerpo *m* de policía

constancy ['kɒnstəntsi, *Am:* 'kɑːn-] *n no pl, form* constancia *f*

constant ['kɒnstənt, *Am:* 'kɑːn-] **I.** *n* constante *f* **II.** *adj* **1.** (*continuous*) constante; (*noise*) continuo, -a; (*surveillance*) incesante **2.** (*unchanging*) inalterable; (*love*) fiel; (*friend*) leal; (*temperature*) constante **3.** (*frequent*) asiduo, -a; ~ **use** uso *m* frecuente; **to be in** ~ **trouble** meterse en problemas constantemente

constantly *adv* constantemente

constellation [ˌkɒnstəˈleɪʃən, *Am:* ˌkɑːn-] *n* constelación *f*
consternation [ˌkɒnstəˈneɪʃən, *Am:* ˌkɑːnstə-] *n no pl* consternación *f*
constipate [ˈkɒnstɪpeɪt, *Am:* ˈkɑːnstə-] *vt* MED estreñir
constipated *adj* estreñido, -a
constipation [ˌkɒnstɪˈpeɪʃən, *Am:* ˈkɑːnstə-] *n* MED estreñimiento *m*, prendimiento *m* *CSur*
constituency [kənˈstɪtjuəntsi, *Am:* -ˈstɪtʃu-] *n* **1.** (*electoral district*) distrito *m* electoral **2.** (*body of voters in this area*) electorado *m* **3.** (*seat*) escaño *m*
constituent [kənˈstɪtjuənt, *Am:* -ˈstɪtʃu-] **I.** *n* **1.** (*voter*) elector(a) *m(f)* **2.** CHEM, PHYS (*component*) constituyente *m* **II.** *adj* constituente
constitute [ˈkɒnstɪtjuːt, *Am:* ˈkɑːnstətuːt] *vt* constituir
constitution [ˌkɒnstɪˈtjuːʃən, *Am:* ˌkɑːnstəˈtuː-] *n* constitución *f*
constitutional [ˌkɒnstɪˈtjuːʃənl, *Am:* ˌkɑːnstəˈtuː-] **I.** *adj* constitucional; ~ **law** derecho político **II.** *n iron* paseo *m*
constrain [kənˈstreɪn] *vt* **1.** (*restrict*) constreñir **2.** LAW (*imprison*) encarcelar
constraint [kənˈstreɪnt] *n* **1.** *no pl* (*compulsion*) coacción *f*; **under** ~ bajo coacción **2.** (*limit*) restricción *f*; **to impose** ~**s on sb/sth** imponer limitaciones a alguien/algo
constrict [kənˈstrɪkt] *vt* constreñir
constriction [kənˈstrɪkʃən] *n* constricción *f*
constrictor *n* constrictor(a) *m(f)*
construct [kənˈstrʌkt] **I.** *n* construcción *f* **II.** *vt* construir
construction [kənˈstrʌkʃən] *n* **1.** *no pl* (*act of making or building*) construcción *f* **2.** (*building*) edificio *m* **3.** LING construcción *f* **4.** (*interpretation*) interpretación *f*; **to put a** ~ **on sth** interpretar algo
constructional [kənˈstrʌkʃnl] *adj* estructural
constructive [kənˈstrʌktɪv] *adj* constructivo, -a
constructor [kənˈstrʌktəʳ, *Am:* -tɚ] *n* constructor(a) *m(f)*
construe [kənˈstruː] *vt* interpretar
consul [ˈkɒnsl, *Am:* ˈkɑːn-] *n* cónsul *mf*
consular [ˈkɒnsjʊləʳ, *Am:* ˈkɑːn-] *adj* consular
consulate [ˈkɒnsjʊlət, *Am:* ˈkɑːn-] *n* consulado *m*
consulate general *n* consulado *m* general
consul general *n* cónsul *mf* general
consult [kənˈsʌlt] **I.** *vi* consultar **II.** *vt* **1.** (*seek information or advice*) consultar **2.** (*examine*) tener en cuenta; **to** ~ **one's feelings** considerar sus sentimientos
consultancy [kənˈsʌltəntsi] <-ies> *n* asesoría *f*
consultant [kənˈsʌltənt] *n* **1.** ECON asesor(a) *m(f)*; **management** ~ asesor de gestión; **tax** ~

asesor fiscal **2.** *Brit* MED especialista *mf*
consultation [ˌkɒnsʌlˈteɪʃən, *Am:* ˌkɑːn-] *n* consulta *f*
consultative [kənˈsʌltətɪv, *Am:* -t̬ət̬ɪv] *adj* consultivo, -a
consulting [kənˈsʌltɪŋ, *Am:* -t̬ɪŋ] *adj* ~ **engineer/lawyer** ingeniero *m* asesor/abogado *m* asesor
consume [kənˈsjuːm, *Am:* -ˈsuːm] *vt* consumir; **to be** ~**d by sth** estar consumido por algo; **to be** ~**d by anger** estar corroído por la ira; **to be** ~**d by envy** estar muerto de envidia; **to** ~ **all the money** gastar todo el dinero
consumer [kənˈsjuːməʳ, *Am:* -ˈsuːmɚ] *n* consumidor(a) *m(f)*; ~ **credit** crédito *m* al consumidor; ~ **demand** demanda *f* de consumo; ~ **society** sociedad *f* de consumo
consumerism [kənˈsjuːmərɪzəm, *Am:* -ˈsuːmɚ-] *n no pl* **1.** (*protection*) defensa *f* del consumidor **2.** *pej* (*exaggerated purchasing*) consumismo *m*
consummate [ˈkɒnsəmeɪt, *Am:* ˈkɑːn-] *adj* **form** consumado, -a; ~ **happiness** felicidad *f* completa; ~ **skill** suma habilidad *f*
consummation [ˌkɒnsəˈmeɪʃən, *Am:* ˌkɑːnsə-] *n no pl, form* consumación *f*
consumption [kənˈsʌmpʃən] *n no pl* **1.** consumo *m* **2.** HIST, MED tisis *f inv*
consumptive [kənˈsʌmptɪv] *adj* HIST, MED tísico, -a
contact [ˈkɒntækt, *Am:* ˈkɑːn-] **I.** *n* **1.** *no pl* (*state of communication*) contacto *m* **2.** (*connection*) relación *f*; **to have** ~**s** tener contactos **3.** (*act of touching*) *a.* ELEC contacto *m*; **physical** ~ contacto físico; **to come into** ~ **with sth** entrar en contacto con algo **II.** *vt* contactar con
contact-breaker *n* ELEC, TECH interruptor *m*
contact lens *n* lentilla *f* **contact man** *n* intermediario *m* **contact print** *n* contacto *m*
contagion [kənˈteɪdʒən] *n form* contagio *m*
contagious [kənˈteɪdʒəs] *adj a. fig* contagioso, -a
contain [kənˈteɪn] *vt* contener
container [kənˈteɪnəʳ, *Am:* -nɚ] *n* **1.** (*vessel*) recipiente *m*; **unbreakable** ~ envase *m* irrompible **2.** (*for transport*) contenedor *m*
containerize [kənˈteɪnəraɪz] *vt* poner en contenedores
container ship *n* buque *m* contenedor
containment [kənˈteɪnmənt] *n no pl* contención *f*
contaminate [kənˈtæmɪneɪt] *vt* contaminar
contamination [kənˌtæmɪˈneɪʃən] *n no pl* contaminación *f*
contemplate [ˈkɒntempleɪt, *Am:* ˈkɑːnt̬em-] *vt* **1.** (*gaze at*) contemplar **2.** (*consider*) reflexionar acerca de **3.** (*intend*) **to** ~ **doing sth** tener la intención de hacer algo; **to** ~ **suicide** pensar suicidarse
contemplation [ˌkɒntemˈpleɪʃən, *Am:* ˌkɑːnt̬em-] *n no pl* contemplación *f*

contemplative [kən'templətɪv, *Am:* -t̬ɪv] *adj* **1.** (*reflective*) contemplativo, -a **2.** (*meditative*) meditativo, -a

contemporary [kən'tempərəri, *Am:* -pərer-] **I.** *n* contemporáneo, -a *m, f* **II.** *adj* contemporáneo, -a

contempt [kən'tempt] *n no pl* desprecio *m;* **to be beneath** ~ ser despreciable; **to hold sth/sb in** ~ despreciar algo/a alguien

contemptible [kən'temptəbl] *adj* despreciable

contemptuous [kən'temptʃuəs] *adj* desdeñoso, -a; (*look*) de desprecio; **to be** ~ **of sb** menospreciar a alguien

contend [kən'tend] **I.** *vi* **1.** (*compete*) competir; **to** ~ **for sth** competir por algo **2.** (*struggle*) luchar, contender; **to** ~ **against sb/sth** contender contra alguien/algo; **to have sb/sth to** ~ **with** tener que enfrentarse a alguien/algo **II.** *vi* **to** ~ **that ...** afirmar que...

contender *n* aspirante *mf*

content[1] ['kɒntent, *Am:* 'kɑːn-] *n* contenido *m*

content[2] [kən'tent] **I.** *vi* (*satisfy*) contentarse; **to** ~ **oneself with sth** contentarse con algo **II.** *vt* satisfacer **III.** *adj* contento, -a; **to one's heart's** ~ a más no poder; **to be** ~ **with sth** estar satisfecho con algo; **to be** ~ **to do sth** estar contento de hacer algo

contented *adj* satisfecho, -a

contention [kən'tenʃən] *n no pl* **1.** (*disagreement*) controversia *f;* **teams in** ~ grupos *mpl* rivales **2.** (*opinion*) opinión *f* **3.** (*competition*) **to be in** ~ **for sth** competir por algo; **to be out of** ~ **for sth** no tener posibilidades de algo

contentious [kən'tenʃəs] *adj* conflictivo, -a

contentment [kən'tentmənt] *n no pl* satisfacción *f*

contents ['kɒntents, *Am:* 'kɑːntents] *n pl* contenido *m;* (*index*) índice *m*

contest [kən'test, *Am:* 'kɑːn-] **I.** *n* **1.** (*competition*) concurso *m;* **beauty** ~ certamen *m* de belleza; **sports** ~ competición *f* deportiva **2.** (*dispute*) controversia *f* **II.** *vt* **1.** (*challenge*) rebatir; (*claims, a will*) impugnar; (*a decision*) cuestionar **2.** (*compete for*) presentarse como candidato a

contestant [kən'testənt] *n* (*match*) contrincante *mf;* (*election*) candidato, -a *m, f;* (*contest*) concursante *mf*

context ['kɒntekst, *Am:* 'kɑːn-] *n* contexto *m*

contextual [kən'tekstjuəl, *Am:* kən'tekstʃu-] *adj form* contextual

contextualize [kən'tekstjuəlaɪz, *Am:* kən'tekstʃu-] *vt* contextualizar

continent[1] ['kɒntɪnənt, *Am:* 'kɑːntnənt] *n* **1.** (*landmass*) continente *m* **2.** *Brit* **the Continent** el continente europeo

continent[2] ['kɒntɪnənt, *Am:* 'kɑːntnənt] *adj a.* MED continente

continental [ˌkɒntɪ'nentl, *Am:* ˌkɑːntn̩'entl] **I.** *adj* **1.** (*relating to a continent*) continental; ~ **drift** movimiento *m* de los continentes; ~ **shelf** plataforma *f* continental **2.** *Brit* (*of mainland Europe*) de Europa continental **II.** *n* europeo, -a *m, f* continental

continental breakfast *n* desayuno de café o té con bollería y mermelada

contingency [kən'tɪndʒəntsi] <-ies> *n form* (*possibility*) contingencia *f;* (*event*) acontecimiento *m* fortuito

contingent [kən'tɪndʒənt] **I.** *n* **1.** (*part of a larger group*) representación *f* **2.** MIL contingente *m* **II.** *adj* **1.** (*liable to happen*) eventual **2.** (*dependent*) **to be** ~ **on sth** depender de algo **3.** (*incidental*) **risks** ~ **to a profession** riesgos derivados de una profesión

continual [kən'tɪnjuəl] *adj* continuo, -a

continually *adv* continuamente

continuation [kənˌtɪnju'eɪʃən] *n no pl* continuación *f*

continue [kən'tɪnjuː] **I.** *vi* **1.** (*persist*) continuar; **he** ~**d by saying that ...** prosiguió diciendo que...; **to** ~ **to do** [*o* **doing**] **sth** seguir haciendo algo **2.** (*remain unchanged*) seguir; **to** ~ **(on) one's way** seguir su camino; **to be** ~**d** continuará **II.** *vt* **1.** (*go on*) seguir con **2.** (*lengthen*) prolongar **3.** LAW aplazar

continued *adj* **to be** ~ continuará

continuity [ˌkɒntɪ'njuːəti, *Am:* ˌkɑːntən'uːəti] *n no pl* **1.** (*fact of continuing*) continuidad *f* **2.** RADIO, TV (*between two programs*) intervalo *m* hablado [*o* musical] **3.** CINE, TV (*scenario*) guión *m;* ~ **boy/girl** secretario, -a *m, f* de rodaje

continuous [kən'tɪnjuəs] *adj* continuo, -a

contort [kən'tɔːt, *Am:* -'tɔːrt] **I.** *vi* crisparse; **his face had** ~**ed with bitterness and the rabia** tenía el rostro desencajado por la amargura y la rabia **II.** *vt* torcer; **to** ~ **sb's words** deformar las palabras de alguien

contortion [kən'tɔːʃən, *Am:* -'tɔːr-] *n* contorsión *f;* **bodily** ~**s** contorsiones *fpl;* **a** ~ **of reality** una deformación de la realidad

contortionist [kən'tɔːʃənɪst, *Am:* -'tɔːr-] *n a. fig* contorsionista *mf*

contour ['kɒntʊər, *Am:* 'kɑːntʊr] **I.** *n* contorno *m;* (*face*) perfil *m* **II.** *vt* perfilar

contour line *n* GEO curva *f* de nivel **contour map** *n* GEO mapa *m* topográfico

contraband ['kɒntrəbænd, *Am:* 'kɑːn-] **I.** *n no pl* contrabando *m* **II.** *adj* de contrabando

contraception [ˌkɒntrə'sepʃən, *Am:* ˌkɑːn-] *n no pl* anticoncepción *f*

contraceptive [ˌkɒntrə'septɪv, *Am:* ˌkɑːn-] *n* anticonceptivo *m*

contract[1] [kən'trækt] **I.** *vi* contraerse **II.** *vt* **1.** (*make shorter*) contraer **2.** (*catch*) **to** ~ **smallpox/AIDS/a cold** contraer la viruela/el SIDA/un resfriado

contract[2] ['kɒntrækt, *Am:* 'kɑːn-] **I.** *n* contrato *m;* ~ **of employment** contrato laboral; **temporary** ~ contrato temporal; **to**

sign/enter into a ~ firmar/celebrar un contrato **II.** *vi* to ~ with sb celebrar un contrato con alguien **III.** *vt* contratar
◆**contract in** *vt* tomar parte en
◆**contract out** *vi Brit* to ~ of sth optar por no participar en algo
contraction [kənˈtrækʃən] *n* contracción *f*
contractor [kənˈtræktəʳ, *Am:* ˈkɑːntræktɚ] *n* contratista *mf*
contractual [kənˈtræktʃʊəl, *Am:* -tʃu-] *adj* contractual; ~ **conditions** condiciones *fpl* de contrato; ~ **terms** términos *mpl* del contrato; **to be under a** ~ **obligation to sb** tener un contrato con alguien
contradict [ˌkɒntrəˈdɪkt, *Am:* ˌkɑːn-] **I.** *vi* contradecirse **II.** *vt* contradecir; **to** ~ **oneself** contradecirse; **everything I say you want to** ~ quieres contradecir todo lo que digo; **don't** ~ **me!** ¡no me contradigas!
contradiction [ˌkɒntrəˈdɪkʃən, *Am:* ˌkɑːn-] *n* contradicción *f*; **a** ~ **in terms** un contrasentido
contradictory [ˌkɒntrəˈdɪktəri, *Am:* ˌkɑːn-] *adj* contradictorio, -a
contralto [kənˈtræltəʊ, *Am:* -ˈtrælt̬oʊ] *n no pl* MUS **1.** (*voice*) contralto *m* **2.** (*person*) contralto *mf*
contraption [kənˈtræpʃən] *n* artilugio *m*; **don't ask me how to use this** ~ no me preguntes cómo funciona este chisme
contrary [ˈkɒntrəri, *Am:* ˈkɑːntrɚ-] **I.** *n no pl* **the** ~ lo contrario; **on the** ~ al contrario; **quite the** ~! ¡todo lo contrario!; **to the** ~ en contra **II.** *adj* contrario, -a; **to be** ~ **to ...** ser contrario a...
contrary to *prep* al contrario de; ~ **what he says** al contrario de lo que dice; ~ **to all our expectations** contra todo pronóstico
contrast [kənˈtrɑːst, *Am:* -ˈtræst] **I.** *n* contraste *m*; **to be a** ~ **to sb/sth** contrastar con alguien/algo; **by** [*o* **in**] ~ por contraste; **in** ~ **to** [*o* **with**] **sb/sth** a diferencia de alguien/algo **II.** *vt* contrastar
contrast control *n* TV control *m* del contraste
contrasting *adj* contrastante
contravene [ˌkɒntrəˈviːn, *Am:* ˌkɑːn-] *vt* contravenir
contravention [ˌkɒntrəˈvenʃən, *Am:* ˌkɑːn-] *n* contravención *f*; **to act in** ~ **of the regulations** obrar en contravención de las normas
contribute [kənˈtrɪbjuːt] **I.** *vi* **1.** (*money, time*) contribuir; **to** ~ **towards sth** contribuir en algo; **to** ~ **to a fund** hacer aportaciones [*o* aportes *AmL*] a un fondo **2.** (*participate*) intervenir **3.** PUBL colaborar **II.** *vt* **1.** (*money*) contribuir; **to** ~ (**sth**) **to sth** contribuir (con algo) a algo; **to** ~ **sth towards ...** aportar algo a... **2.** (*article*) escribir; (*information*) aportar
contribution [ˌkɒntrɪˈbjuːʃən, *Am:* ˌkɑːn-] *n* **1.** (*something contributed*) contribución *f* **2.** (*money*) aportación *f*; **a** ~ **to social secur-**

ity **fund** una cotización a la Seguridad Social **3.** (*text or article for publication*) colaboración *f*; **a** ~ **for the autumn issue of a magazine** un artículo para el número de otoño de una revista
contributor [kənˈtrɪbjuːtəʳ, *Am:* -ˈtrɪbjət̬ɚ] *n* contribuyente *mf*
contributory [kənˈtrɪbjʊtəri, *Am:* -jətɔːri] *adj* contributivo, -a
contrite [ˈkɒntraɪt, *Am:* kən'-] *adj* contrito, -a; ~ **expression** expresión *f* de arrepentimiento
contrition [kənˈtrɪʃən] *n no pl* contrición *f*
contrivance [kənˈtraɪvəns] *n* **1.** (*act of contriving*) artimaña *f* **2.** (*device*) artilugio *m* **3.** (*inventive capacity*) ingenio *m*
contrive [kənˈtraɪv] *vt* **1.** (*plan*) ingeniar; (*a meeting*) arreglar; (*a plan*) idear **2.** (*manage*) **to** ~ **to do sth** ingeniárselas para hacer algo; **she** ~**d to make it happen** se las ingenió para que ocurriera
contrived *adj* artificial
control [kənˈtrəʊl, *Am:* -ˈtroʊl] **I.** *n* **1.** control *m*; **to bring sth under** ~ controlar algo; **to go out of** ~ descontrolarse; **to have the** ~ **over sb** tener el control sobre alguien; **to lose** ~ **over sth** perder el control de algo; **to lose** ~ **of oneself** perder el control de uno mismo **2.** (*leadership*) mando *m*; **to be in** ~ mandar; **to be under the** ~ **of sb** estar bajo el dominio de alguien **3.** AVIAT estación *f* de control **4.** *pl* TECH mandos *mpl*; **to be at the** ~**s** llevar los mandos **II.** *vt* <-ll-> **1.** (*have power over*) controlar; (*vehicle*) manejar **2.** (*restrain: anger*) dominar; (*temper, urge*) controlar **3.** (*stop: epidemic, disease*) controlar **4.** ECON, FIN controlar
control board *n* tablero *m* de mando **control centre** *n* centro *m* de control **control column** *n* palanca *f* de mando **control desk** *n* consola *f*
controllable *adj* controlable
controlled [kənˈtrəʊld, *Am:* -ˈtroʊld] *adj* controlado, -a
controller [kənˈtrəʊləʳ, *Am:* -ˈtroʊlɚ] *n* (*person in charge*) director(a) *m(f)*; FIN, ECON director(a) *m(f)* financiero, -a
control panel *n* tablero *m* de control **control point** *n* punto *m* de control **control tower** *n* torre *f* de control **control unit** *n* INFOR unidad *f* de control
controversial [ˌkɒntrəˈvɜːʃəl, *Am:* ˌkɑːntrəˈvɜːr-] *adj* polémico, -a
controversy [ˈkɒntrəvəsi, *Am:* ˈkɑːntrəvɜːr-] *n* <-ies> polémica *f*; **to be beyond** ~ ser incuestionable
contusion [kənˈtjuːʒən, *Am:* -ˈtuː-] *n* contusión *f*
conundrum [kəˈnʌndrəm] *n* acertijo *m*
conurbation [ˌkɒnɜːˈbeɪʃən, *Am:* ˌkɑːnɜːr-] *n* conurbación *f*
convalesce [ˌkɒnvəˈles, *Am:* ˌkɑːn-] *vi* convalecer; **to** ~ **from sth** convalecer [*o* recupe-

rarse] de algo

convalescence [ˌkɒnvə'lesns, *Am:* ˌkɑːn-] *n* convalecencia *f*

convalescent [ˌkɒnvə'lesnt, *Am:* ˌkɑːn-] **I.** *n* convaleciente *mf* **II.** *adj* convaleciente; **a long ~ period** un largo período de convalecencia

convection [kən'vekʃən] *n* convección *f*

convection oven *n* horno *m* de convección

convector [kən'vektəʳ, *Am:* -təʳ] *n*, **convector heater** *n* estufa *f* de convección

convene [kən'viːn] **I.** *vi form* reunirse **II.** *vt form* citar; (*meeting*) convocar

convener [kən'viːnəʳ, *Am:* -əʳ] *n Brit* convocador(a) *m(f)*

convenience [kən'viːnɪəns, *Am:* -'viːnjəns] *n no pl* **1.** conveniencia *f* **2.** (*practicality*) comodidad *f*; (*advantage*) ventaja *f*; **for ~'s sake** por comodidad; **at your ~** cuando le venga(n) bien **3.** (*toilet*) servicio *m*

convenience store *n Am:* tienda que abre temprano y cierra tarde

convenient [kən'viːnɪənt, *Am:* -'viːnjənt] *adj* **1.** (*handy*) útil **2.** (*suitable*) conveniente **3.** (*practical*) práctico, -a **4.** (*easily accessible*) bien situado, -a

convenor [kən'viːnəʳ, *Am:* -əʳ] *n* convocador(a) *m(f)*

convent ['kɒnvənt, *Am:* 'kɑːn-] *n* convento *m*

convention [kən'venʃən] *n* **1.** (*custom*) convención *f*; **~ dictates that** es costumbre que +*subj* **2.** (*general agreement*) convenio *m*; (*of human rights*) convención *f* **3.** (*large meeting*) congreso *m*

conventional [kən'ventʃənəl] *adj* convencional; (*wisdom*) ortodoxo, -a; (*medicine*) tradicional

conventionally *adv* de manera convencional

converge [kən'vɜːdʒ, *Am:* -'vɜːrdʒ] *vi a. fig* converger; (*persons*) reunirse

convergence [kən'vɜːdʒəns, *Am:* -'vɜːr-] *n* convergencia *f*

convergent [kən'vɜːdʒent, *Am:* -'vɜːr-] *adj* convergente

conversant [kən'vɜːsnt, *Am:* -'vɜːr-] *adj* versado, -a; **to be ~ with sth** ser versado en algo

conversation [ˌkɒnvə'seɪʃən, *Am:* ˌkɑːn-vəʳ-] *n* (*word exchange*) conversación *f*, plática *f AmL;* **to strike up a ~ with sb** entablar conversación con alguien

conversational [ˌkɒnvə'seɪʃənəl, *Am:* ˌkɑːnvəʳ-] *adj* familiar; (*tone*) coloquial; (*skills*) conversacional

conversationally *adv* en tono familiar

converse[1] [kən'vɜːs, *Am:* -'vɜːrs] *vi form* **to ~ with sb** conversar con alguien, platicar con alguien *AmL*

converse[2] ['kɒnvɜːs, *Am:* 'kɑːnvɜːrs] **I.** *n* **the ~** lo opuesto **II.** *adj form* inverso, -a

conversely *adv* a la inversa

conversion [kən'vɜːʃən, *Am:* -'vɜːrʒən] *n* conversión *f*

conversion rate *n* precio *m* de conversión

convert [kən'vɜːt, *Am:* -'vɜːrt] **I.** *n* converso, -a *m, f* **II.** *vi* convertirse **III.** *vt* convertir

converter [kən'vɜːtəʳ, *Am:* -'vɜːrt̬əʳ] *n* **1.** (*person*) convertidor(a) *m(f)* **2.** ELEC transformador *m* **3.** TECH convertidor *m*

convertible [kən'vɜːtəbl, *Am:* -'vɜːrt̬ə-] **I.** *n* AUTO descapotable *m* **II.** *adj a.* FIN, ECON convertible; **~ sofa** sofá-cama *m*, convertible *m AmL*

convex ['kɒnveks, *Am:* 'kɑːn-] *adj* convexo, -a

convey [kən'veɪ] *vt* **1.** (*transport*) transportar; (*electricity*) conducir **2.** (*communicate*) transmitir; **to ~ how ...** expresar cómo...; **to ~ sth to sb** dar a entender algo a alguien

conveyance [kən'veɪənts] *n* **1.** (*act of carrying*) transporte *m;* **these pipes are used for the ~ of water** estas tuberías sirven para conducir agua **2.** (*communication*) transmisión *f* **3.** (*vehicle*) vehículo *m;* **form of ~** medio *m* de transporte **4.** LAW traspaso *m;* (*document*) escritura *f* de traspaso

conveyancing *n no pl* LAW traspaso; (*document*) redacción *f* de una escritura de traspaso

conveyor [kən'veɪəʳ, *Am:* -əʳ] *n* transportador *m;* (*belt*) cinta *f* transportadora, banda *f* transportadora *Méx*

convict ['kɒnvɪkt, *Am:* 'kɑːn-] **I.** *n* presidiario, -a *m, f* **II.** *vt* condenar

conviction [kən'vɪkʃən] *n* **1.** LAW condena *f* **2.** (*firm belief*) convicción *f;* **to have a ~ about sth** estar convencido de algo

convince [kən'vɪnts] *vt* convencer; **I'm not ~d** no estoy convencido

convincing [kən'vɪntsɪŋ] *adj* convincente

convoluted *adj* enrevesado, -a

convoy ['kɒnvɔɪ, *Am:* 'kɑːn-] **I.** *n* convoy *m;* **in** [*o* **under**] **~** en caravana **II.** *vt* escoltar

convulse [kən'vʌls] **I.** *vi* tener convulsiones; **to ~ in laughter** desternillarse de risa; **to ~ in pain** retorcerse de dolor **II.** *vt* convulsionar; **to be ~d with anger** descomponerse de ira

convulsion [kən'vʌlʃən] *n* **1.** (*violent motion*) convulsión *f;* **she went into ~s** le dio un ataque convulsivo; (*uncontrolled laughter*) le dio un ataque de risa **2.** (*violent natural occurrence*) conmoción *f*

convulsive [kən'vʌlsɪv] *adj* convulsivo, -a

coo [kuː] **I.** *vi* arrullar **II.** *vt* susurrar

cook [kʊk] **I.** *n* cocinero, -a *m, f* ►**too many ~s spoil the broth** *prov* muchas manos en un plato hacen mucho garabato *prov* **II.** *vi* hacerse; **how long does this cake take to ~?** ¿cuánto tarda en cocerse este pastel? ►**what's ~ing?** *inf* ¿qué pasa? **III.** *vt* cocinar; (*meat*) asar; **to ~ lunch** hacer la comida

cookbook ['kʊkbʊk] *n* libro *m* de cocina

cooker ['kʊkəʳ, *Am:* -əʳ] *n* **1.** *Brit* (*stove*) cocina *f*, estufa *f Col, Méx* **2.** *Brit* (*cooking apple*) manzana *f* para cocinar

cookery ['kʊkəri] *n no pl* cocina *f*

cookery book n Brit libro m de recetas
cookie ['kʊki] n Am 1. (biscuit) galleta f 2. inf
(person) tipo m 3. INFOR cookie m ▶ that's the
way the ~ crumbles inf ¡así es la vida!
cooking ['kʊkɪŋ] n no pl to do the ~ hacer la
comida
cool [kuːl] I. adj 1. (slightly cold) fresco, -a;
(color) frío, -a 2. (calm) tranquilo, -a; keep ~
tómatelo con calma 3. inf (impudent) fresco,
-a; to be a ~ one ser un fresco 4. (unfriendly)
frío, -a 5. inf (fashionable) to be ~ estar en la
onda; that disco is very ~ esa discoteca está
muy de moda II. interj inf ¡genial! III. n no pl
1. (coolness) fresco m 2. (calm) calma f IV. vt
enfriar; just ~ it inf ¡calma! V. vi (become
colder) enfriarse; to ~ down [o off] (become
cooler) enfriarse; (become calmer) calmarse
cooler ['kuːləʳ, Am: -ləʳ] n 1. (box) refrigerador m 2. (drink) refresco m
coolheaded [ˌkuːl'hedɪd] adj sereno, -a
cooling ['kuːlɪŋ] adj refrescante; (breeze)
fresco, -a
cooling tower n torre f de refrigeración
coolly ['kuːli] adv 1. (calmly) con serenidad
2. (coldly) fríamente
coolness ['kuːlnɪs] n no pl 1. METEO frescor m
2. (unfriendliness) frialdad f
coop [kuːp] I. n gallinero m II. vt encerrar
♦**coop up** vt encerrar
co-op ['kəʊɒp, Am: 'kəʊɑːp] n abbr of cooperative cooperativa f
cooper ['kuːpəʳ, Am: -pəʳ] I. n tonelero, -a m,
f II. vi (make barrels) fabricar barriles; (repair
barrels) reparar barriles
cooperate [kəʊ'ɒpəreɪt, Am: kəʊ'ɑːpəreɪt]
vi cooperar; to ~ with sb colaborar con alguien
cooperation [kəʊˌɒpə'reɪʃən, Am: kəʊ-
ˌɑːpə-] n cooperación f
cooperative [kəʊ'ɒpərətɪv, Am: kəʊ'ɑː-
pəʳətɪv] I. n ECON cooperativa f; ~ society
sociedad f cooperativa II. adj cooperativo, -a
co-opt [kəʊ'ɒpt, Am: kəʊ'ɑːpt] vt 1. (make
sb a member) to ~ sb onto sth nombrar a alguien para algo 2. (absorb into larger unit) to
be ~ed into sth ser incorporado a algo
coordinate [ˌkəʊ'ɔːdɪneɪt, Am: ˌkəʊ'ɔːr-]
I. n coordenada f II. vi 1. (work together effectively) coordinar(se) 2. (match) combinar
III. vt coordinar IV. adj 1. (equal) igualitario, -a
2. (involving coordination) coordinado, -a
coordination [ˌkəʊˌɔːdɪ'neɪʃən, Am: ˌkəʊ-
ˌɔːrdə'neɪ-] n no pl coordinación f
coordinator n coordinador(a) m(f)
coot [kuːt] n 1. ZOOL fúlica f 2. inf (rather dim
person) bobo, -a m, f
cop [kɒp, Am: kɑːp] I. n 1. inf (police officer)
poli mf; to play ~s and robbers jugar a poli-
cías y ladrones 2. Brit, inf (poor quality) to not
be much ~ no valer gran cosa II. <-pp-> vt
1. (grab) coger; to ~ a (quick) look at sth
echar una ojeada a algo 2. Am LAW to ~ a plea
declararse culpable

co-partner ['kəʊ'pɑːtnəʳ, Am: 'kəʊˌpɑːrt-
nəʳ] n copartícipe mf
copartnership ['kəʊ'pɑːtnəʃɪp, Am: 'kəʊ-
ˌpɑːrtnəʳ-] n coparticipación f
cope [kəʊp, Am: koʊp] vi 1. (master a situation) aguantar 2. (deal with) poder con; (situation) enfrentarse; (problem) hacer frente;
(pain) soportar
Copenhagen [ˌkəʊpən'heɪgən, Am: 'koʊ-
pənˌheɪ-] n Copenhague m
copier ['kɒpɪəʳ, Am: 'kɑːpɪəʳ] n copiadora f
co-pilot ['kəʊ'paɪlət, Am: 'koʊˌpaɪ-] n copiloto mf
copious ['kəʊpɪəs, Am: 'koʊ-] adj copioso,
-a; (amount) abundante
copper ['kɒpəʳ, Am: 'kɑːpəʳ] I. n 1. no pl
(metal) cobre m 2. Brit, inf (police officer) poli
mf 3. pl, Brit, inf (coin) calderilla f II. adj (colour) cobrizo, -a
copper beech <-es> n haya f roja **copper-
-ore** n mineral m de cobre **copperplate**
I. n 1. no pl (handwriting) caligrafía f
2. (metal plaque) lámina f de cobre II. adj cali-
grafiado, -a **copper-smith** n calderero, -a m,
f
coppice ['kɒpɪs, Am: 'kɑːpɪs] I. n bosquecillo m II. vt talar
copulate ['kɒpjʊleɪt, Am: 'kɑːpjə-] vi copular
copulation [ˌkɒpjʊ'leɪʃən, Am: ˌkɑːpjə-] n
no pl cópula f
copy ['kɒpi, Am: 'kɑːpi] I. <-ies> n 1. (facsimile) copia f; (of a book) ejemplar m; ART imitación f; to be a carbon ~ of sb ser idéntico a
alguien; an exact ~ una reproducción exacta
2. INFOR copia f; hard ~ copia en el disco duro;
to make a ~ hacer una copia 3. (text to be
published) original m; (advertisement text)
texto m publicitario 4. (topics for articles)
tema m II. <-ie-> vt 1. a. INFOR, MUS copiar
2. (imitate) imitar III. vi SCHOOL copiar
copybook ['kɒpibʊk, Am: 'kɑːpi-] I. adj
1. (exemplary) modélico, -a 2. (unoriginal)
convencional II. n cuaderno m de escritura
▶ to blot one's ~ manchar su reputación
copycat I. n childspeak, inf copión, -ona m, f
II. adj ~ version imitación f; a ~ crime un
crimen inspirado en otro **copy desk** n Am
mesa f de redacción **copy editor** n correc-
tor(a) m(f) de originales
copying ink n no pl tinta f de copiar **copying paper** n papel m de calcar
copy-protection n INFOR protección f contra
escritura **copyright** n derechos mpl de
autor; to hold the ~ of sth tener los derechos
de autor de algo; protected under ~ protegido según los derechos de la propiedad
intelectual; ~ reserved reservado el derecho
de reproducción **copywriter** n escritor(a)
m(f) de textos publicitarios
coral ['kɒrəl, Am: 'kɔːr-] I. n no pl coral m;
made of ~ de coral II. adj (reddish colour)
coralino, -a

coral island _n_ isla _f_ coralina **coral reef** _n_ arrecife _m_ de coral

cord [kɔːd, _Am:_ kɔːrd] _n_ **1.** (_rope_) cuerda _f;_ piola _f AmS;_ ELEC cable _m;_ **spinal** ~ médula _f_ espinal; **umbilical** ~ cordón _m_ umbilical **2.** (_corduroy_) pana _f;_ **a** ~ **shirt** una camisa de pana

cordial ['kɔːdɪəl, _Am:_ 'kɔːrdʒəl] I. _adj_ **1.** (_friendly_) cordial; (_relations_) amistoso, -a **2.** _form_ (_strong_) de corazón II. _n no pl, Brit, Aus:_ bebida con sabor a fruta a la que se le añade agua

cordiality [ˌkɔːdɪˈæləti, _Am:_ ˌkɔːrdʒɪˈæləṭi] <-ies> _n form_ cordialidad _f_

cordless ['kɔːdləs, _Am:_ 'kɔːrd-] _adj_ inalámbrico, -a

cordon ['kɔːdn, _Am:_ 'kɔːr-] I. _n_ **1.** (_line_) cordón _m;_ **police** ~ cordón policial **2.** (_fruit tree_) enredadera _f_ II. _vt_ acordonar

cords _npl_ pantalón _m_ de pana

corduroy ['kɔːdərɔɪ, _Am:_ 'kɔːr-] _n no pl_ pana _f_

core [kɔːʳ, _Am:_ kɔːr] I. _n_ **1.** (_centre_) centro _m;_ **to the** ~ _fig_ hasta la médula; **to be rotten to the** ~ _fig_ estar podrido hasta la médula, estar completamente corrompido; **to be at the** ~ **of a problem** llegar al quid de la cuestión **2.** (_sample of strata_) muestra _f_ **3.** (_centre with seeds_) corazón _m_ **4.** PHYS núcleo _m_ **5.** ELEC eje _m_ II. _adj_ **the** ~ **issue** la cuestión principal III. _vt_ deshuesar

CORE [kɔːʳ, _Am:_ kɔːr] _n Am abbr of_ **Congress of Racial Equality** Congreso _m_ de la Igualdad Racial

core subject _n_ tema _m_ central

coriander [ˌkɒriˈændəʳ, _Am:_ 'kɔːriˈædə] _n_ cilantro _m_

cork [kɔːk, _Am:_ kɔːrk] I. _n_ **1.** _no pl_ corcho _m_ **2.** (_stopper_) tapón _m_ II. _vt_ **1.** (_put stopper in_) taponar **2.** (_blacken_) **to** ~ **one's face** taparse la cara **3.** (_spoiled wine_) **the wine is** ~**ed** el vino sabe a corcho

corkage ['kɔːkədʒ, _Am:_ 'kɔːr-] _n no pl,_ **cork charge** _n precio que algunos restaurantes hacen pagar por servir vino comprado en otro lugar_

corkscrew ['kɔːkskruː, _Am:_ 'kɔːrk-] I. _n_ sacacorchos _m inv_ II. _adj_ en espiral; ~ **curls** tirabuzones _mpl_

corn[1] [kɔːn, _Am:_ kɔːrn] _n no pl_ **1.** _Brit_ (_cereal_) cereal _m_ **2.** _Am_ (_maize_) maíz _m,_ choclo _m AmS,_ abatí _m Arg;_ ~ **on the cob** mazorca _f_ de maíz **3.** _Am, inf_ (_something trite_) sensiblería _f_

corn[2] [kɔːn, _Am:_ kɔːrn] _n_ MED callo _m_ ▶**to tread on sb's** ~**s** herir los sentimientos de alguien

corncob _n_ mazorca _f_ de maíz

cornea ['kɔːnɪə, _Am:_ 'kɔːr-] _n_ córnea _f_

corner ['kɔːnəʳ, _Am:_ 'kɔːrnə] I. _n_ **1.** (_junction of two roads_) esquina _f;_ **to cut a** ~ doblar una esquina; **to be round the** ~ estar a la vuelta de la esquina; **to turn the** ~ doblar la esquina; _fig_ salir de un apuro **2.** (_of a room_)

rincón _m;_ **to put sb in the** ~ _a._ SCHOOL arrinconar a alguien **3.** (_place_) **a distant** ~ **of the globe** un rincón remoto de la tierra; **the four** ~**s of the world** todas las partes del mundo **4.** (_manoevre in sport_) córner _m_ **5.** SPORTS (_assistants_) recogepelotas _m inv_ **6.** (_difficult position_) **to be in a tight** ~ estar en un aprieto; **to drive sb into a** (**tight**) ~ poner a alguien entre la espada y la pared **7.** (_domination_) **to have a** ~ **of the market** controlar una parte del mercado **8.** (_periphery_) **out of the** ~ **of one's eye** con el rabillo del ojo; **out of the** ~ **of sb's mouth** en la comisura de los labios ▶**to cut** ~**s** ahorrar esfuerzos II. _vt_ **1.** (_hinder escape_) acorralar; _iron_ abordar; **to get sb** ~**ed** _fig_ acorralar a alguien **2.** ECON **to** ~ **the market** acaparar el mercado III. _vi_ (_auto_) tomar una curva

cornered ['kɔːnəd, _Am:_ 'kɔːrnəd] _adj_ acorralado, -a

corner house _n_ casa _f_ que hace esquina **corner seat** _n_ asiento _m_ en la esquina **corner shop** _n_ tienda _f_ de la esquina **cornerstone** _n a. fig_ piedra _f_ angular

cornet ['kɔːnɪt, _Am:_ kɔːrˈnet] _n_ **1.** (_brass instrument_) corneta _f_ **2.** (_wafer cone_) cucurucho _m_

cornflakes ['kɔːnfleɪks, _Am:_ 'kɔːrn-] _npl_ copos _mpl_ de maíz; **a bowl of** ~ un tazón de cereales

cornflour ['kɔːnflaʊəʳ, _Am:_ 'kɔːrnflaʊə] _n no pl, Brit, Aus_ harina _f_ de maíz

cornflower ['kɔːnflaʊəʳ, _Am:_ 'kɔːrnflaʊə] I. _n_ aciano _m_ II. _adj_ ~ **blue** azul aciano

cornice ['kɔːnɪs, _Am:_ 'kɔːr-] _n_ ARCHIT cornisa _f_

corn-poppy <-ies> _n_ amapola _f_

Cornwall ['kɔːnwɔːl] _n_ Cornualles _m_

corny ['kɔːni, _Am:_ 'kɔːr-] <-ier, -iest> _adj_ **1.** _inf_ viejo, -a; (_joke_) gastado, -a **2.** (_emotive_) sensiblero, -a

corollary [kərˈɒləri, _Am:_ 'kɔːrələr-] <-ies> _n form_ corolario _m_

coronary ['kɒrənəri, _Am:_ 'kɔːrəner-] I. _n_ infarto _m_ de miocardio; **when he got the bill he nearly had a** ~ _iron_ cuando le dieron la cuenta casi le coge un infarto II. _adj_ coronario, -a

coronation [ˌkɒrəˈneɪʃən, _Am:_ ˌkɔːr-] I. _n_ coronación _f_ II. _adj_ de coronación

coroner ['kɒrənəʳ, _Am:_ 'kɔːrənə] _n funcionario encargado de investigar muertes no naturales_

Corp **1.** _Am abbr of_ **corporation** sociedad _f_ anónima **2.** MIL _abbr of_ **corporal** cabo _m_

corporal ['kɔːpərəl, _Am:_ 'kɔːr-] I. _n_ MIL cabo _mf_ II. _adj_ _form_ corporal; **a** ~ **oath** HIST juramento _m_ a la corona

corporate ['kɔːpərət, _Am:_ 'kɔːr-] _adj_ **1.** (_shared by group_) colectivo, -a **2.** (_of corporation_) corporativo, -a, empresarial; ~ **capital** capital _m_ social; ~ **law** derecho _m_ de sociedades; ~ **policy** política _f_ de cooperación

corporation [ˌkɔːpəˈreɪʃən, _Am:_ ˌkɔːrpə-] _n_

+ *sing/pl vb* **1.** (*business*) sociedad *f* anónima; **multinational** ~ empresa *f* multinacional, empresa transnacional *AmL;* **a public** ~ *Brit* una empresa pública **2.** (*local council*) ayuntamiento *m;* **municipal** ~ corporación *f* municipal

corporation tax <-es> *n* impuesto *m* de sociedades

corps [kɔːʳ, *Am:* kɔːr] *n* + *sing/pl vb* **1.** MIL (*unit*) cuerpo *m* **2.** (*group*) equipo *m*

corps de ballet [ˌkɔːdəˈbæleɪ, *Am:* ˌkɔːr-] *n* cuerpo *m* de baile

corpse [kɔːps, *Am:* kɔːrps] *n* cadáver *m*

corpus [ˈkɔːpəs, *Am:* ˈkɔːr-] <-pora *o* -es> *n* **1.** LIT (*collection*) colección *f* **2.** LING corpus *m inv* **3.** ECON capital *m*

Corpus Christi [ˌkɔːpəsˈkrɪsti, *Am:* ˌkɔːr-] *n* REL Corpus *m inv*

corpuscle [ˈkɔːpʌsl, *Am:* ˈkɔːr-] *n* corpúsculo *m*

corral [kəˈrɑːl, *Am:* -ˈræl] **I.** *n* caballeriza *f* **II.** <-ll-> *vt* estabular

correct [kəˈrekt] **I.** *vt* (*put right*) corregir; ~ **me if I'm wrong but ...** corrígeme si me equivoco, pero... **II.** *adj* correcto, -a; **that is** ~ *form* así es

correction [kəˈrekʃən] *n* **1.** corrección *f;* **subject to** ~ sujeto a enmienda **2.** *no pl* (*improvememt*) rectificación *f*

correction fluid *n* líquido *m* corrector

corrective [kəˈrektɪv] **I.** *adj* correctivo, -a **II.** *n* medida *f* correctiva

correctly [kəˈrektli] *adv* correctamente

correctness [kəˈrektnɪs] *n no pl* corrección *f*

correlate [ˈkɒrəleɪt, *Am:* ˈkɔːrə-] **I.** *vt* correlacionar **II.** *vi* (*relate*) poner en correlación; *fig* estar en relación

correlation [ˌkɒrəˈleɪʃən, *Am:* ˌkɔːrə-] *n* (*connection*) correlación *f;* (*relationship*) relación *f;* **there is a** ~ **between smoking and lung cancer** el tabaco y el cáncer de pulmón están relacionados entre sí

correspond [ˌkɒrɪˈspɒnd, *Am:* ˌkɔːrə-] *vi* **1.** (*be equal to*) corresponder a **2.** (*write*) cartearse

correspondence [ˌkɒrɪˈspɒndəns, *Am:* ˌkɔːrəˈspɑːn-] *n no pl* correspondencia *f;* **business** ~ correspondencia comercial; **to enter into** ~ **with sb** *form* cartearse con alguien

correspondent [ˌkɒrɪˈspɒndənt, *Am:* ˌkɔːrəˈspɑːn-] *n* **1.** (*writer of letters*) remitente *mf* **2.** (*journalist*) corresponsal *mf;* **special** ~ enviado, -a *m, f* especial

corresponding [ˌkɒrɪˈspɒndɪŋ, *Am:* ˌkɔːrə-] *adj* correspondiente

corridor [ˈkɒrɪdɔːʳ, *Am:* ˈkɔːrədəʳ] *n* **1.** (*passage*) pasillo *m* **2.** (*land*) corredor *m*

corrie [ˈkɒri, *Am:* ˈkɔːr-] *n* GEO circo *m*

corroborate [kəˈrɒbəreɪt, *Am:* -ˈrɑːbə-] *vt* corroborar

corroboration [kəˌrɒbəˈreɪʃən, *Am:* -ˌrɑː-bə-] *n* corroboración *f;* **in** ~ **of sth** de conformidad con algo

corroborative [kəˈrɒbərətɪv, *Am:* -ˈrɑːbəəʈɪv] *adj* corroborable

corrode [kəˈrəʊd, *Am:* -ˈroʊd] **I.** *vi* corroerse **II.** *vt* corroer; *fig* menoscabar

corrosion [kəˈrəʊʒən, *Am:* -ˈroʊ-] *n no pl* **1.** corrosión *f* **2.** *fig* (*deterioration*) deterioro *m*

corrosive [kəˈrəʊsɪv, *Am:* -ˈroʊ-] **I.** *adj* **1.** (*destructive*) corrosivo, -a **2.** *fig* (*harmful*) destructivo, -a; ~ **attack** *fig* ataque *m* con malicia **II.** *n* corrosivo *m*

corrugated [ˈkɒrəgeɪtɪd, *Am:* -ʈɪd] *adj* **1.** (*furrowed*) ondulado, -a **2.** (*rutted: road*) de curvas

corrupt [kəˈrʌpt] **I.** *vt* **1.** (*debase*) corromper **2.** (*influence by bribes*) sobornar **3.** (*document*) dañar **II.** *vi* corromper **III.** *adj* **1.** (*influenced by bribes*) corrupto, -a; ~ **practices** prácticas *fpl* corruptas **2.** (*document*) dañado, -a

corruption [kəˈrʌpʃən] *n no pl* **1.** (*debasement*) corrupción *f* **2.** (*bribery*) soborno *m*

corset [ˈkɔːsɪt, *Am:* ˈkɔːr-] *n* corsé *m*

Corsica [ˈkɔːsɪkə, *Am:* ˈkɔːr-] *n* Córcega *f*

Corsican [ˈkɔːsɪkən, *Am:* ˈkɔːr-] **I.** *adj* corso, -a **II.** *n* **1.** (*person*) corso, -a *m, f* **2.** LING corso *m*

cos [kɒs, *Am:* kɑːs] MAT *abbr of* **cosine** cos

cosec [ˈkəʊsek, *Am:* ˈkoʊ-] MAT *abbr of* **cosecant** cosec

cosignatory [ˌkəʊˈsɪgnətəri, *Am:* ˌkoʊˈsɪgnətɔːri] <-ies> *n* cosignatario, -a *m, f*

cosine [ˈkəʊsaɪn, *Am:* ˈkoʊ-] *n* coseno *m*

cosiness [ˈkəʊzɪnɪs, *Am:* ˈkoʊ-] *n no pl* comodidad *f*

cos lettuce [ˈkɒsˌletɪs, *Am:* ˈkɑːsˌleʈ-] *n Brit, Aus* lechuga *f*

cosmetic [kɒzˈmetɪk, *Am:* kɑːzˈmeʈ-] **I.** *n* cosmético *m;* ~**s** cosméticos *mpl* **II.** *adj* **1.** cosmético, -a; ~ **cream** crema *f* cosmética **2.** (*superficial*) superficial

cosmetician [ˌkɒzməˈtɪʃən] *n* esteticista *mf*

cosmic [ˈkɒzmɪk, *Am:* ˈkɑːz-] *adj fig* cósmico, -a; **of** ~ **proportions** de proporciones astronómicas

cosmology [kɒzˈmɒlədʒi, *Am:* kɑːzˈmɑː-lə-] *n* cosmología *f*

cosmonaut [ˈkɒzmənɔːt, *Am:* ˈkɑːzmə-nɑːt] *n* cosmonauta *mf*

cosmopolitan [ˌkɒzməˈpɒlɪtən, *Am:* ˌkɑːzməˈpɑːlɪ-] **I.** *adj* cosmopolita **II.** *n* cosmopolita *mf*

cosmos [ˈkɒzmɒs, *Am:* ˈkɑːzmoʊs] *n no pl* cosmos *m inv*

cost [kɒst, *Am:* kɑːst] **I.** *vt* **1.** <cost, cost> (*amount to*) valer; **to** ~ **a packet** *inf* costar un ojo de la cara **2.** <cost, cost> (*cause the loss of*) costar; **to** ~ **sb dear** salir caro a alguien **3.** <costed, costed> (*calculate price*) calcular el precio de **II.** *n* **1.** (*price*) precio *m;* **at no extra** ~ sin costes adicionales; **to cut the** ~ recortar costes; **to defray the** ~ **of sth** *form* costear algo **2.** *pl* (*expence*) costes *mpl;* LAW costas *fpl;* **to cut ~s** recortar costes **3.** *fig* (*sacrifice*) **to count the ~(s) (of sth)** (*consider effects*) valorar el riesgo (de algo); (*suffer*) padecer las consecuencias (de algo); (**only**) **at the ~ of doing sth** (sólo) a costa de hacer algo; **to one's ~** a expensas de uno; **at all ~(s)** a toda costa

co-star [ˌkəʊˈstɑː^r, *Am:* ˈkoʊstɑːr] **I.** *n* coprotagonista *mf* **II.** <-rr-> *vt* coprotagonizar **III.** <-rr-> *vi* **to ~ with sb** protagonizar con alguien

Costa Rica [ˌkɒstəˈriːkə, *Am:* ˌkoʊstə-] *n* Costa Rica *f*

Costa Rican [ˌkɒstəˈriːkən, *Am:* ˌkoʊstə-] **I.** *adj* costarricense **II.** *n* costarricense *mf*

costly [ˈkɒstli, *Am:* ˈkɑːst-] <-ier, -iest> *adj* costoso, -a; (*mistake*) caro, -a; **to prove ~** *a. fig* resultar muy caro

cost price [ˈkɒstˌpraɪs, *Am:* ˈkɑːst-] *n* **~ a** precio de coste

costume [ˈkɒstjuːm, *Am:* ˈkɑːstuːm] *n* **1.** (*national dress*) traje *m;* **to dress in ~** ir trajeado **2.** (*decorative dress*) disfraz *m*

cosy [ˈkəʊzi, *Am:* ˈkoʊ-] **I.** <-ier, -iest> *adj* **1.** (*comfortable*) cómodo, -a; (*place*) acogedor(a); (*chat*) agradable **2.** *pej* (*convenient*) de conveniencia **II.** <-ies> *n* tapadera *f*

cot [kɒt, *Am:* kɑːt] *n* **1.** (*baby's bed*) cuna *f* **2.** *Am* (*camp bed*) cama *f* plegable

cotangent [ˈkəʊˌtændʒənt, *Am:* ˌkoʊˈtæn-] *n* cotangente *f*

cot death *n* muerte *f* súbita infantil

cottage [ˈkɒtɪdʒ, *Am:* ˈkɑːt̬ɪdʒ] *n* country **~** casa *f* de campo; **thatched ~** casa *f* con techo de paja

cottage cheese *n no pl* requesón *m* **cottage industry** <-ies> *n* industria *f* familiar

cot(an) MAT *abbr of* **cotangent** cot

cotton [ˈkɒtn, *Am:* ˈkɑːtn] **I.** *n* **1.** (*plant*) algodón *m* **2.** *no pl* (*material*) algodón *m* **3.** *no pl* (*thread*) hilo *m* de coser **II.** *vi* **to ~ on (to sth)** caer en la cuenta (de algo)

cotton bud *n* bastoncillo *m* de algodón **cotton-grower** *n* cultivador(a) *m(f)* de algodón **cotton mill** *n* fábrica *f* de algodón **cottonseed** *n* semilla *f* de algodón **cotton wool** *n no pl* **1.** (*common use*) algodón *m* en rama **2.** *Am* MED algodón *m* hidrófilo ▶**to wrap sb in ~** criar a alguien entre algodones

couch [kaʊtʃ] <-es> **I.** *n* canapé *m;* **psychiatrist's ~** diván *m* **II.** *vt* expresar

couchette [kuːˈʃet] *n* litera *f*

couch potato <- -es> *n* teleadicto, -a *m, f*

cough [kɒf, *Am:* kɑːf] **I.** *n* tos *f;* **chesty ~** tos seca **II.** *vi* **1.** toser **2.** (*auto*) rugir **III.** *vt* **to ~ blood** escupir sangre

◆**cough up I.** *vi inf* apoquinar **II.** *vt inf* **1.** (*bring up: blood*) escupir; (*give back*) MED expectorar **2.** (*give back*) devolver **3.** *inf* (*pay*) apoquinar

cough drop *n* pastilla *f* para la tos **cough medicine** *n*, **cough mixture** *n no pl* medicina *f* para la tos

could [kʊd] *pt, pp* **can²**

council [ˈkaʊntsəl] *n* + *sing/pl vb* ADMIN city **~** ayuntamiento *m;* MIL consejo *m;* **local ~** consejo local; **the United Nations Security Council** el Consejo de Seguridad de las Naciones Unidas

council estate *n Brit* ≈ urbanización *f* de protección oficial **council flat** *n*, **council house** *n Brit* ≈ piso *m* de protección oficial **council housing** *n Brit* ≈ viviendas *fpl* de protección oficial

council(l)or [ˈkaʊntsələ^r, *Am:* -ɚ] *n* concejal(a) *m(f)*

Council of Economic and Finance Ministers *n* Consejo *m* de Ministros de Economía y Finanzas **Council of Europe** *n* Consejo *m* de Europa **Council of Ministers** *n* Consejo *m* de Ministros **Council of the European Union** *n* Consejo *m* de la Unión Europea

council tax <-es> *n Brit* impuesto *m* municipal

counsel [ˈkaʊntsəl] **I.** <*Brit* -ll-, *Am* -l-> *vt* (*advise*) aconsejar; **to ~ sb against sth** *form* prevenir a alguien de algo **II.** *n* **1.** *no pl, form* (*advice*) consejo *m;* **a ~ of perfection** un ideal imposible; **to take ~ from sb** aconsejarse por alguien **2.** (*lawyer*) abogado, -a *m, f;* ~ **for the defence** abogado defensor; ~ **for the prosecution** fiscal *mf* ▶**to keep one's own ~** guardar silencio

counsel(l)ing I. *n no pl* asesoramiento *m* **II.** *adj* de orientación

counsel(l)or [ˈkaʊntsələ^r, *Am:* -ɚ] *n* **1.** (*adviser*) asesor(a) *m(f);* **marriage guidance ~** consejero, -a *m, f* matrimonial **2.** *Am* (*lawyer*) abogado, -a *m, f*

count¹ [kaʊnt] *n* conde *m*

count² [kaʊnt] *n* **1.** (*totalling up*) total *m;* **final ~** suma *f* final **2.** (*measured amount*) recuento *m* **3.** (*act of counting*) cuenta *f;* **to keep ~ of sth** contar algo; **to lose ~ of sth** perder la cuenta de algo **4.** LAW acusación *f* **5.** (*opinion*) opinión *f;* **to be angry with sb on several ~s** estar enfadado con alguien por varios motivos ▶**to be out for the ~** estar durmiendo **II.** *vt* **1.** (*number*) contar; **to ~ one's change** contar el cambio; **to ~ heads** contar uno por uno **2.** (*consider*) considerar; **to ~ sth a success/failure** considerar algo un éxito/fracaso; **to ~ sb as a friend** tener a alguien como amigo **III.** *vi* **1.** (*number*) contar; **that's what ~s** eso es lo que importa; **this doesn't ~ for anything** esto no cuenta para nada **2.** (*be considered*) **to not ~** no tener ni voz ni voto

◆**count down** *vi* hacer la cuenta atrás

◆**count out** *vt always sep* **1.** (*money*) contar **2.** *inf* (*leave out*) **to count sb out** no contar con alguien

countable noun [ˌkaʊntəblˈnaʊn] *n* nombre *m* contable

count-down [ˈkaʊntdaʊn] *n* cuenta *f* atrás

countenance [ˈkaʊntɪnəns, *Am:* -t̬ənəns] **I.** *n no pl* **1.** *form* (*facial expression*) rostro *m;*

to be of noble ~ tener rasgos nobles
2. (*approval*) aprobación *f;* **to give ~ to sth**
dar el visto bueno a algo **3.** (*composure*) compostura *f;* **to keep one's ~** *form* guardar la
compostura **II.** *vt form* aprobar

counter ['kaʊntər, *Am:* -t̬ər] **I.** *n* **1.** (*service
point*) mostrador *m;* **over the ~** sin receta
médica; **under the ~** *fig* subrepticiamente
2. (*person who counts*) cajero, -a *m, f*
3. (*machine*) caja *f;* TECH contador *m* **4.** (*disc*)
ficha *f* **II.** *vt* contrarrestar **III.** *vi* **1.** (*oppose*)
oponerse **2.** (*react by scoring*) contraatacar
IV. *adv* en contra; **to act ~ to sth** actuar
contrariamente a algo; **to run ~ to sth** oponerse a algo

counteract [ˌkaʊntər'ækt, *Am:* -t̬ər-] *vt* contrarrestar; **to ~ the effects of sth** neutralizar
los efectos de algo; **~ inflation** combatir la
inflación

counteractive [ˌkaʊntər'æktɪv, *Am:* -t̬ər-]
adj **1.** (*working against*) que contrarresta
2. (*neutralizing*) neutralizador(a)

counterattack ['kaʊntərətæk, *Am:*
'kaʊntə-] **I.** *n* contraataque *m* **II.** *vt* contraatacar **III.** *vi* (*attack in return*) contraatacar

counterbalance ['kaʊntəbæləns, *Am:*
-t̬ər-] **I.** *n* contrapeso *m; fig* compensación *f*
II. *vt* (*balance out*) contrapesar; *fig* compensar

countercharge ['kaʊntətʃɑːdʒ, *Am:* -t̬ər-
tʃɑːrdʒ] **I.** *n* LAW reconvención *f* **II.** *vt* LAW
reconvenir

countercheck ['kaʊntətʃek] **I.** *n* **1.** (*restraint*) obstáculo *m;* **to put a ~ on sth** *fig*
poner trabas a algo **2.** (*second check*) segunda
comprobación *f* **II.** *vt* volver a comprobar

counterclockwise [ˌkaʊntə'klɒkwaɪz,
Am: -t̬ə 'klɑːkwaɪz] *adj Am* en sentido
opuesto a las agujas del reloj

counterespionage [ˌkaʊntər'espiənɑːʒ,
Am: -t̬ə-] *n no pl* contraespionaje *m*

counterespionage service *n* servicio *m*
de contraespionaje

counterfeit ['kaʊntəfɪt, *Am:* -t̬ə-] **I.** *adj* falsificado, -a; (*money*) falso, -a **II.** *vt* falsificar
III. *n* falsificación *f*

counterfoil ['kaʊntəfɔɪl, *Am:* -t̬ə-] *n Brit*
FIN talón *m*

counterintelligence [ˌkaʊntər ɪn'telɪdʒəns, *Am:* -t̬ə-] *n no pl* contraespionaje *m*

countermand [ˌkaʊntə'mɑːnd, *Am:* -t̬ə-
'mænd] *vt* contramandar; MIL contradecir

countermeasure ['kaʊntəmeʒər, *Am:*
-t̬ə-meʒə-] *n* medida *f* en contra

counterpart ['kaʊntəpɑːt, *Am:* -t̬əpɑːrt] *n*
contrapartida *f;* POL homólogo, -a *m, f*

counterpoint ['kaʊntəpɔɪnt, *Am:* -t̬ə-] *n*
MUS contrapunto *m*

counterpoise ['kaʊntəpɔɪz, *Am:* -t̬ə-]
form **I.** *n* contrapeso *m; fig* compensación *f*
II. *vt* contrapesar; *fig* compensar

counterproductive [ˌkaʊntəprə'dʌktɪv,
Am: -t̬ə-] *adj* contraproducente

counter-revolution [ˌkaʊntəˌrevə'luːʃən,

Am: -t̬ə-] *n* contrarrevolución *f*

countersign ['kaʊntəsaɪn, *Am:* -t̬ə-] *vt*
refrendar

countersink ['kaʊntəsɪŋk, *Am:* -t̬ə-] *irr vt*
avellanar

counter-terrorism [ˌkaʊntə'terərɪzəm,
Am: -t̬ə'terə-] *n no pl* acción *f* contra el terrorismo

countess ['kaʊntɪs, *Am:* -t̬ɪs] *n* condesa *f*

countless ['kaʊntlɪs] *adj* incontable

country ['kʌntri] **I.** *n* **1.** *no pl* (*rural area*)
campo *m* **2.** <-ies> (*political unit*) país *m;*
(*native land*) patria *f* **3.** (*area of land*) territorio *m* **4.** MUS country *m* **II.** *adj* **1.** (*rural*) del
campo; (*life, manners*) rural **2.** MUS (*music*)
country

country bumpkin *n Brit* pueblerino, -a *m, f*
country club *n* club *m* de campo **country
dance** *n Brit* danza *f* folclórica **country-
-folk** *n + pl vb* gente *f* de campo **country
house** *n* casa *f* solariega

countryman ['kʌntrɪmən] <-men> *n*
1. (*same nationality*) compatriota *m* **2.** (*from
rural area*) campesino *m*

country music *n* música *f* country

country road *n* camino *m* rural

countryside ['kʌntrɪsaɪd] *n no pl* campo *m,*
verde *m AmC, Méx*

countrywide ['kʌntrɪwaɪd] *adj* a escala
nacional

countrywoman ['kʌntrɪwʊmən] <-women> *n* **1.** (*same nationality*) compatriota *f*
2. (*from rural area*) campesina *f*

county ['kaʊnti, *Am:* -t̬i] **I.** <-ies> *n* condado *m* **II.** *adj* **to be ~** *Brit* ser pijo

county borough *n Brit* HIST municipio *m*
county council *n Brit* delegación *f* de
gobierno en un condado **county court** *n
Brit* juzgado *m* comarcal **county seat** *n Am,*
county town *n Brit* capital *f* del condado

coup [kuː] <coups> *n* golpe *m*

coup de grâce [ˌkuːdə'grɑːs] *n* golpe *m* de
gracia **coup d'état** <coups d'état> *n*
golpe *m* de Estado

coupé ['kuːpeɪ] *n* cupé *m*

couple ['kʌpl] **I.** *n* **1.** *no pl* (*a few*) par *m;* **the
first ~ of weeks** las primeras dos semanas
2. + *sing/pl vb* (*two people*) pareja *f;* (*married*) matrimonio *m* **II.** *vt* **1.** RAIL, AUTO enganchar **2.** (*connect*) conectar **3.** (*link*) unir **III.** *vi*
HIST aparearse

couplet ['kʌplɪt] *n* dístico *m;* (*rhyming*)
pareado *m*

coupling ['kʌplɪŋ] *n* **1.** RAIL, AUTO enganche
m **2.** (*linking*) combinación *f* **3.** (*sexual intercourse: of people*) apareamiento *m;* (*of animals*) cópula *f*

coupon ['kuːpɒn, *Am:* -pɑːn] *n* **1.** (*voucher*)
vale *m* **2.** (*return-slip of advert*) cupón *m*
3. *Brit* SPORTS boleto *m*

courage ['kʌrɪdʒ] *n* coraje *m;* **to show great
~** mostrar gran valor; **to take one's ~ in both
hands** hacer de tripas corazón

courageous [kəˈreɪdʒəs] *adj* (*person*) valiente; (*act*) valeroso, -a

courgette [kʊəˈʒet, *Am:* kʊr-] *n* calabacín *m*

courier [ˈkʊrɪəʳ, *Am:* ˈkʊrɪəʳ] **I.** *n* **1.** (*tour guide*) guía *mf* **2.** (*delivers post*) mensajero, -a *m, f* **II.** *adj* ~ **service** servicio *m* de mensajería

course [kɔ:s, *Am:* kɔ:rs] **I.** *n* **1.** (*direction*) recorrido *m*; (*of a river*) curso *m*; **to be off** ~ *a. fig* desviarse; **to set** ~ **for sth** poner rumbo hacia algo; **your best** ~ **would be ...** lo mejor que podrías hacer sería... **2.** (*development*) transcurso *m*; **in the** ~ **of time** con el tiempo **3.** (*treatment*) tratamiento *m* **4.** SPORTS (*area*) pista *f*; (*golf*) campo *m* **5.** (*part of meal*) plato *m* **6.** (*layer*) hilada *f* ▶**to let sth run its** ~ dejar que algo siga su curso; **to stay the** ~ aguantar hasta el final; **of** ~ claro; **of** ~ **not** desde luego que no **II.** *vi* correr

coursebook *n* libro *m* de texto **courseware** *n no pl* INFOR material *m* de enseñanza informatizado

court [kɔ:t, *Am:* kɔ:rt] **I.** *n* **1.** (*room for trials*) juzgado *m* **2.** (*judicial body*) tribunal *m* **3.** (*marked out area for playing*) cancha *f*; (*tennis*) pista *f* **4.** (*yard*) patio *m* **5.** (*road*) calle *f* **6.** *Brit* (*apartment buildings*) apartamentos *mpl* **7.** HIST (*sovereign*) corte *f* ▶**to hold** ~ recibir en audiencia; **to laugh sb out of** ~ reírse de alguien **II.** *vt* (*woman*) cortejar; (*danger*) exponerse a **III.** *vi* (*couple*) salir

courteous [ˈkɜ:tɪəs, *Am:* ˈkɜ:rtɪ-] *adj* cortés

courtesy [ˈkɜ:təsi, *Am:* ˈkɜ:rtə-] <-ies> *n* **1.** (*politeness*) gentileza *f*, cortesía *f* **2.** *no pl* (*decency*) decencia *f* **3.** (*permission*) (**by**) ~ **of** por gentileza de

courtesy bus *n* autobús *m* de cortesía **courtesy light** *n* AUTO luz *f* interior **courtesy title** *n* tratamiento *m* de cortesía

court hearing *n* vista *f* judicial

courthouse [ˈkɔ:thaʊs, *Am:* ˈkɔ:rt-] *n Am* juzgado *m*

courtier [ˈkɔ:tɪəʳ, *Am:* ˈkɔ:rtɪəʳ] *n* cortesano, -a *m, f*

court martial I. <court martials> *n* consejo *m* de guerra **II.** <-ll-, *Am:* -l-> *vt* someter a consejo de guerra **court of appeal** *n* tribunal *m* de apelación

Court of Auditors *n* Tribunal *m* de Cuentas **Court of Justice** *n* Tribunal *m* de Justicia **courtroom** [ˈkɔ:trʊm, *Am:* ˈkɔ:rtru:m] *n* sala *f* de tribunal **courtship** *n* noviazgo *m*; *a.* ZOOL cortejo *m* **courtyard** *n* patio *m*

cousin [ˈkʌzn] *n* primo, -a *m, f*

couture [ku:ˈtjʊəʳ, *Am:* ku:ˈtʊr] *n* FASHION costura *f*; **haute** ~ alta costura

cove [kəʊv, *Am:* koʊv] *n* cala *f*

covenant [ˈkʌvənənt, *Am:* -ænt] **I.** *n* **1.** (*agreement*) contrato *m* **2.** *Brit* (*donation*) donación *f* **II.** *vt* contratar

Coventry [ˈkɒvntri, *Am:* ˈkʌv-] *n* **to send sb to** ~ hacer el vacío a alguien

cover [ˈkʌvəʳ, *Am:* -əʳ] **I.** *n* **1.** (*top*) tapa *f*

2. (*outer sheet: of a book*) cubierta *f*; (*of a magazine*) portada *f* **3.** (*bedding*) cubrecama *m* **4.** (*envelope*) sobre *m* **5.** (*concealment*) abrigo *m*; **to break** ~ salir al descubierto **6.** (*shelter*) refugio *m* **7.** (*insurance*) cobertura *f* **8.** (*provision*) suplencia *f* **9.** (*at table*) cubierto *m* **II.** *vt* **1.** (*hide: eyes, ears*) tapar; (*head*) cubrir **2.** (*put over*) tapar; (*book*) forrar **3.** (*keep warm*) abrigar **4.** (*travel*) recorrer **5.** (*deal with*) contemplar **6.** (*include*) incluir **7.** (*report on*) informar acerca de **8.** (*insure*) asegurar **9.** (*give armed protection*) cubrir **10.** MUS (*song*) versionar **III.** *vi* sustituir

◆**cover over** *vt* cubrir

◆**cover up I.** *vt* (*protect*) cubrir **II.** *vi* **to** ~ **for sb** encubrir a alguien

coverage [ˈkʌvərɪdʒ] *n no pl* **1.** (*reporting*) cobertura *f* **2.** (*dealing with*) contemplación *f*

coveralls [ˈkʌvərɔ:lz] *npl* mono *m*

cover charge [ˈkʌvətʃɑ:dʒ, *Am:* -əʳtʃɑ:rdʒ] *n dinero extra que se paga en un restaurante o discoteca para cubrir algunos gastos de éstos*

covered *adj* **1.** (*roofed over*) cubierto, -a **2.** (*insured*) asegurado, -a

cover girl [ˈkʌvəgɜ:l, *Am:* -əʳgɜ:rl] *n* modelo *f* de portada

covering *n* capa *f*

covering letter *n* carta *f* adjunta

cover note [ˈkʌvənəʊt, *Am:* -əʳnoʊt] *n Am, Aus* (*covering note*) seguro *m* provisional

covers [ˈkʌvəz, *Am:* -əʳz] *n* mantas *fpl*

cover story <-ies> *n* noticia *f* de primera página

covert¹ [ˈkʌvət, *Am:* ˈkoʊvɜ:rt] *adj* encubierto, -a

covert² [ˈkʌvət, *Am:* ˈkʌvəʳt] *n* espesura *f*

cover-up [ˈkʌvərʌp, *Am:* -əʳ-] *n* encubrimiento *m*

covet [ˈkʌvɪt] *vt* desear

cow¹ [kaʊ] *n* **1.** (*female ox*) vaca *f* **2.** (*female mammal*) hembra *f* **3.** *Brit, pej* (*woman*) tía *f*; **stupid** ~! ¡imbécil! ▶**until the** ~**s come home** hasta que las ranas críen pelo

cow² [kaʊ] *vt* intimidar

coward [ˈkaʊəd, *Am:* ˈkaʊəʳd] *n* cobarde *mf*

cowardice [ˈkaʊədɪs, *Am:* ˈkaʊəʳ-] *n no pl* cobardía *f*

cowardly [ˈkaʊədli, *Am:* ˈkaʊəʳd-] *adj* **1.** (*fearful*) cobarde **2.** (*nasty*) mezquino, -a

cowboy [ˈkaʊbɔɪ] **I.** *n* **1.** (*cattle hand*) vaquero *m*, cowboy *m*, tropero *m Arg* **2.** *inf* (*dishonest tradesperson*) pirata *mf* **II.** *adj* vaquero, -a

cower [ˈkaʊəʳ, *Am:* ˈkaʊəʳ] *vi* encogerse de miedo

cowherd [ˈkaʊhɜ:d, *Am:* -hɜ:rd] *n* vaquero, -a *m, f* **cowhide I.** *n no pl* cuero *m* **II.** *adj* de cuero

cowl [kaʊl] *n* **1.** (*hood*) capucha *f* **2.** (*hood on chimney*) sombrerete *m* **3.** (*engine hood*) cubierta *f*

cowling *n* cubierta *f* de proa

cowman [ˈkaʊmən] <-men> *n* **1.** (*male*

cowherd) vaquero *m* **2.** *Aus* (*cattle farm manager*) ganadero *m*

co-worker [ˌkəʊˈwɜːkəʳ, *Am:* ˈkoʊˌwɜːrkəʳ] *n* colaborador(a) *m(f)*

cowshed [ˈkaʊʃed] *n* establo *m*

cowslip [ˈkaʊslɪp] *n* prímula *f*

cox [ˈkɒks, *Am:* ˈkɑːks] <-es> *n,* **coxswain** [ˈkɒksən, *Am:* ˈkɑːk-] *n form* timonel *mf*

coy [kɔɪ, *Am:* -ɚ] <-er, -est> *adj* **1.** (*secretive*) tímido, -a **2.** (*flirtatiously shy*) coqueto, -a

coyote [kɔɪˈəʊt, *Am:* kaɪˈoʊt̬i] *n* coyote *m*

cozy [ˈkəʊzi, *Am:* ˈkoʊ-] *adj Am s.* **cosy**

CP *n abbr of* Communist Party PC *m*

CPU [ˌsiːpiːˈjuː] *n* INFOR *abbr of* central processing unit CPU *f*

crab¹ [kræb] *n* **1.** (*sea animal*) cangrejo *m,* jaiba *f AmL* **2.** ASTR Cáncer *m*

crab² [kræb] <-bb-> *vi* rezongar

crab (**apple**) [ˈkræb(ˌæpl)] *n* **1.** (*fruit*) manzana *f* silvestre **2.** (*tree*) manzano *m* silvestre

crabbed [ˈkræbɪd] *adj* **1.** (*handwriting*) apretado, -a **2.** (*mood*) refunfuñón, -ona

crabby [ˈkræbi] <-ier, -iest> *adj inf* rezongón, -ona

crab louse *n* ladilla *f*

crack [kræk] I. *n* **1.** (*fissure*) grieta *f* **2.** (*sharp sound: of a rifle*) estallido *m;* (*of a breaking branch*) crujido *m;* (*of the whip*) chasquido *m* **3.** *inf* (*drug*) crack *m* **4.** (*joke*) chiste *m* **5.** *inf* (*attempt*) intento *m* ▶**the ~ of dawn** el amanecer; **to give sb a fair ~ of the whip** dar a alguien las mismas posibilidades II. *adj* de primera III. *vt* **1.** (*break*) romper **2.** (*open: an egg*) cascar; (*nuts*) partir; (*safe*) forzar; (*code*) descifrar **3.** (*resolve*) resolver **4.** (*hit*) pegar; (*knuckles*) hacer crujir; (*whip*) hacer chasquear; **to ~ a joke** contar un chiste IV. *vi* **1.** (*break*) romperse; (*paintwork*) agrietarse **2.** (*break down*) sufrir una crisis nerviosa **3.** (*make a sharp noise*) chasquear ▶**to get ~ing** poner manos a la obra

◆**crack down** *vi* **to ~ on sb/sth** tomar medidas enérgicas contra alguien/algo

◆**crack up** *vi* **1.** MED sufrir un colapso nervioso **2.** (*break down: car*) averiarse; (*business*) fallar

crackdown [ˈkrækdaʊn] *n* ofensiva *f*

cracked [krækt] *adj* **1.** (*having fissures*) rajado, -a; (*lips*) agrietado, -a **2.** (*crazy*) chiflado, -a

cracker [ˈkrækəʳ, *Am:* -ɚ] *n* **1.** (*dry biscuit*) galleta *f* **2.** *Brit* (*device*) sorpresa *f* **3.** INFOR cracker *mf* **4.** *inf* (*excellent thing*) fenómeno *m;* (*woman*) pimpollo *m*

crackers [ˈkrækəz, *Am:* -ɚz] *adj* lelo, -a; **to be ~** estar chiflado

crackle [ˈkrækl] I. *vi* (*of paper*) crujir; (*telephone line*) hacer ruido; (*burning logs*) crepitar II. *vt* hacer crujir III. *n* (*of paper*) crujido *m;* (*of a telephone line*) ruido *m;* (*of burning wood*) chisporroteo *m*

crackling [ˈkræklɪŋ] *n* **1.** (*sound: of a fire*) crujido *m;* (*of a radio*) ruido *m* **2.** (*pork skin*)

chicharrón *m*

crackpot [ˈkrækpɒt, *Am:* -pɑːt] I. *n inf* chiflado, -a *m, f* II. *adj inf* chalado, -a

crack-up [ˈkrækʌp] *n inf* **1.** (*mental breakdown*) colapso *m* **2.** (*car crash*) choque *m*

cradle [ˈkreɪdl] I. *n* **1.** (*baby's bed*) cuna *f;* **from the ~ to the grave** durante toda la vida **2.** (*framework*) andamio *m* II. *vt* acunar

craft [krɑːft, *Am:* kræft] I. *n* **1.** (*means of transport*) nave *f* **2.** *no pl* (*special skill*) arte *m* **3.** (*trade*) oficio *m* **4.** *no pl* (*ability*) destreza *f* II. *vt* construir

craftiness *n no pl* astucia *f*

craft shop *n* tienda *f* de artesanía

craftsman [ˈkrɑːftsmən, *Am:* ˈkræfts-] <-men> *n* artesano *m*

crafty [ˈkrɑːfti, *Am:* ˈkræf-] <-ier, -iest> *adj* astuto, -a

crag [kræg] *n* peñasco *m*

craggy [ˈkrægi] <-ier, -iest> *adj* escarpado, -a; (*features*) marcado, -a

cram [kræm] <-mm-> I. *vt* meter; **to ~ sth with** llenar algo de II. *vi* memorizar

cramfull [ˌkræmˈfʊl] *adj* atestado, -a

crammer [ˈkræməʳ, *Am:* -ɚ] *adj inf:* escuela o libro para aprender rápidamente

cramp [kræmp] I. *vt* poner obstáculos a; **to ~ sb's style** cortar las alas a alguien II. *n Brit, Aus* calambre *m*

cramped *adj* apretujado, -a

crampon [ˈkræmpɒn, *Am:* -pɑːn] *n* crampón *m*

cranberry [ˈkrænbəri, *Am:* -ˌber-] <-ies> *n* arándano *m*

crane [kreɪn] I. *n* **1.** (*vehicle for lifting*) grúa *f* **2.** ZOOL grulla *f* II. *vt* **to ~ one's neck** estirar el cuello III. *vi* **to ~ forward** inclinarse estirando el cuello

crane fly <-ies> *n* típula *f*

cranium [ˈkreɪnɪəm] <craniums *o* crania> *n* cráneo *m*

crank¹ [kræŋk] I. *n inf* maniático, -a *m, f* II. *adj* raro, -a

crank² [kræŋk] *n* cigüeñal *m*

crankcase [ˈkræŋkkeɪs] *n* cárter *m* (del cigüeñal)

crankshaft [ˈkræŋkʃɑːft, *Am:* -ʃæft] *n* eje *m* (del cigüeñal)

cranky [ˈkræŋki] <-ier, -iest> *adj Am, Aus, inf* maniático, -a

cranny [ˈkræni] <-ies> *n* ranura *f;* **in every nook and ~** en el último rincón

crap [kræp] I. <-pp-> *vi vulg* cagar II. *n vulg* **1.** (*excrement*) mierda *f* **2.** *no pl* (*nonsense*) estupidez *f* III. *adj* de mierda

crape [kreɪp] *n* crespón *m*

crappy [ˈkræpi] <-ier, -iest> *adj inf* malo, -a

crash [kræʃ] I. *n* <-es> **1.** (*accident*) accidente *m;* (*of a car*) choque *m* **2.** (*noise*) estrépito *m* **3.** COM crac *m* **4.** INFOR caída *f* (del sistema) II. *vi* **1.** (*have an accident*) chocar; (*plane*) estrellarse **2.** (*make loud noise*) retumbar **3.** (*break noisily*) derrumbarse **4.** COM colapsar **5.** INFOR colgarse **III.** *vt* **1.** (*damage in accident*) chocar **2.** (*make noise*) hacer ruido ►**to ~ a** <u>party</u> colarse en una fiesta

crash barrier *n Brit, Aus* barrera *f* de protección **crash course** *n* curso *m* intensivo

crash diet *n* dieta *f* intensiva **crash helmet** *n* casco *m* protector

crashing *adj* **to be a ~ bore** ser un verdadero muermo

crash-land [ˌkræʃˈlænd, *Am:* ˈkræʃlænd] *vi* aterrizar forzosamente

crash-landing *n* aterrizaje *m* forzoso **crash programme** *n* SCHOOL curso *m* intensivo

crass [kræs] *adj* **1.** (*gross*) flagrante **2.** (*coarse: comment*) grosero, -a

crate [kreɪt] **I.** *n* **1.** (*open box*) cajón *m* **2.** *inf* (*old car*) carraca *f* **II.** *vt* embalar en cajones

crater [ˈkreɪtəʳ, *Am:* -ţɚ] *n* cráter *m*

cravat [krəˈvæt] *n* fular *m*

crave [kreɪv] *vt* ansiar; (*attention*) reclamar

craving [ˈkreɪvɪŋ] *n* ansia *f*

crawl [krɔːl, *Am:* krɑːl] **I.** *vi* **1.** (*go on all fours*) gatear **2.** (*move slowly*) arrastrarse **3.** *inf* (*be obsequious*) **to ~** (**up**) **to sb** hacer la pelota a alguien **4.** *inf* (*become infested*) **to be ~ing with sth** estar plagado de algo **II.** *n no pl* **1.** (*go very slowly*) arrastramiento *m* **2.** (*style of swimming*) crol *m;* **to do the ~** nadar crol

crawler [ˈkrɔːləʳ, *Am:* ˈkrɑːlɚ] *n* **1.** TECH tractor *m* de oruga **2.** (*baby*) bebé *mf* **3.** *inf* (*flatterer*) adulador(a) *m(f)*

crawler lane *n Brit* carril *m* para vehículos lentos

crawlers [ˈkrɔːləz, *Am:* ˈkrɑːlɚz] *npl* pijama *m* de cuerpo entero para bebés

crayfish [ˈkreɪfɪʃ] *n inv* **1.** (*Astacus*) cangrejo *m* de río **2.** GASTR (*in sea*) langosta *f*

crayon [ˈkreɪən, *Am:* -ɑːn] **I.** *n* lápiz *m* de color **II.** *vt* colorear **III.** *vi* dibujar

craze [kreɪz] *n* manía *f*

crazed [kreɪzd] *adj* de loco, -a; (*expression*) enloquecido, -a

craziness *n no pl* locura *f*

crazy [ˈkreɪzi] <-ier, -iest> *adj* loco, -a, tarado, -a *AmL;* **to go ~** volverse loco

creak [kriːk] **I.** *vi* (*door*) chirriar; (*bones*) crujir **II.** *n* (*of door*) chirrido *m;* (*of bones*) crujido *m*

creaky [ˈkriːki] <-ier, -iest> *adj* **1.** (*squeaky*) chirriante **2.** (*badly made*) poco firme **3.** (*unsafe*) inestable

cream [kriːm] **I.** *n* **1.** *no pl* (*milk fat*) nata *f;* **single ~** *Brit* crema *f* de leche; **double ~** *Brit* nata *f* para montar **2.** (*cosmetic product*) crema *f* **3.** (*the best*) flor y nata *f* **II.** *adj* **1.** (*containing cream*) cremoso, -a **2.** (*off-white colour*) de color crema **III.** *vt* (*butter*) batir; (*milk*) desnatar; **to ~ coffee** añadir crema al café

cream cheese *n no pl* queso *m* para untar

cream-colo(u)red *adj* de color crema

creamery [ˈkriːməri] <-ies> *n* lechería *f*

creamy [ˈkriːmi] <-ier, -iest> *adj*

1. (*smooth*) cremoso, -a; (*skin*) hidratado, -a **2.** (*off-white*) de color hueso

crease [kriːs] **I.** *n* **1.** (*fold*) arruga *f;* (*hat*) pliegue *m* **2.** (*cricket*) línea *f* **II.** *vt* arrugar **III.** *vi* arrugarse

create [kriːˈeɪt] **I.** *vt* **1.** (*produce new*) crear **2.** (*produce skillfully*) posibilitar **3.** (*cause*) causar; (*impression*) provocar; (*sensation*) hacer; (*scandal*) motivar **4.** (*appoint*) nombrar **II.** *vi Brit, Aus, inf* armar jaleo

creation [kriːˈeɪʃən] *n* **1.** *no pl* (*making*) creación *f* **2.** (*product*) producción *f* **3.** FASHION modelo *m*

creative [kriːˈeɪtɪv, *Am:* -ţɪv] *adj* creativo, -a; (*imagination*) original

creator [kriːˈeɪtəʳ, *Am:* -ţɚ] *n* creador(a) *m(f)*

creature [ˈkriːtʃəʳ, *Am:* -tʃɚ] *n* **1.** (*being*) criatura *f* **2.** (*person being discussed*) individuo, -a *m, f;* **to be a ~ of habit** ser un animal de costumbres; **poor ~!** ¡pobrecito! **3.** (*pawn*) títere *m*

creature comforts *npl inf* bienestar *m* material

creche [kreɪʃ] *n Brit, Aus* guardería *f*

credence [ˈkriːdns] *no pl n form* crédito *m*

credentials [krɪˈdenʃlz] *npl* credenciales *fpl*

credibility [ˌkredrˈbɪləti, *Am:* -əˈbrɪləţi] *n no pl* credibilidad *f*

credible [ˈkredəbl] *adj* verosímil; (*witness*) creíble

credit [ˈkredɪt] **I.** *n* **1.** (*belief*) crédito *m;* **to give ~ to sth** dar crédito a algo **2.** (*honour*) honor *m;* (*recognition*) mérito *m;* **to be a ~ to sb** ser un orgullo [*o* honor] para alguien; **to sb's ~** en favor de alguien; **to take (the) ~ for sth** atribuirse el mérito de algo; **~ where ~'s due** el honor a quien le corresponda **3.** FIN crédito *m;* **to buy sth on ~** comprar algo a plazos; **to give sb ~** abrir crédito a alguien **4.** *no pl* COM haber *m;* **to be in ~** *Brit* tener saldo positivo **5.** *pl* CINE títulos *mpl* de crédito, créditos *mpl* **II.** *vt* **1.** (*believe*) creer **2.** FIN **to ~ sb with 2000 euros** abonar 2000 euros en cuenta a alguien **3.** (*attribute*) **he is ~ed with ...** se le atribuye...

creditable [ˈkredɪtəbl, *Am:* -ţə-] *adj* **1.** (*believable*) digno, -a de crédito **2.** (*commendable*) digno, -a de elogio

credit card *n* tarjeta *f* de crédito **credit facilities** *npl* facilidades *fpl* de pago **credit limit** *n* límite *m* de crédito **credit note** *n Aus, Brit* nota *f* de crédito

creditor [ˈkredɪtəʳ, *Am:* -ţɚ] *n* acreedor(a) *m(f)*

creditor bank *n* banco *m* acreedor

credit rating *n* clasificación *f* de solvencia

credits *npl* CINE créditos *mpl*

credit side *n* COM haber *m* **credit terms** *npl* condiciones *fpl* de un crédito

creditworthy [ˈkredɪtˌwɜːði, *Am:* -wɜːr-] *adj* solvente

credulity [krɪˈdjuːləti, *Am:* krəˈduːlə-] *n no*

pl credulidad *f*

credulous ['kredjʊləs, *Am:* 'kredjə-] *adj* crédulo, -a

creed [kri:d] *n* credo *m;* **the Creed** el Credo

creek [kri:k] *n* **1.** *Brit* (*narrow bay*) cala *f* **2.** *Am, Aus* (*stream*) riachuelo *m* ►**to be up the ~** (*without a paddle*) *inf* estar en un aprieto

creep [kri:p] I.<crept, crept> *vi* **1.** (*crawl*) arrastrarse; (*snake*) reptar; (*baby*) andar a gatas; (*plant*) trepar **2.** (*move imperceptibly*) deslizarse **3.** (*move slowly*) moverse lentamente II. *n* **1.** (*act of creeping*) deslizamiento *m* **2.** *inf* (*sycophant*) pelotillero, -a *m, f,* lambiscón, -ona *m, f Méx,* lambón, -ona *m, f Col* **3.** (*pervert*) pervertido, -a *m, f* ►**to give sb the ~s** *inf* poner a alguien la carne de gallina

◆**creep into** *vt insep* entrar sigilosamente en

◆**creep up** *vi* **to ~ on sb** acercarse sigilosamente a alguien

creeper ['kri:pəʳ, *Am:* -pəʳ] *n* **1.** (*rope*) trepador *m* **2.** BOT enredadera *f* **3.** ZOOL ave *f* trepadora **4.** *pl, Am* (*babywear*) pelele *m* **5.** *pl, Am* zapatillas *f pl* deportivas

creeping *adj* progresivo, -a

creepy ['kri:pi] <-ier, -iest> *adj inf* espeluznante

creepy crawlie *n a. childspeak* bicho *m*

cremate [krɪ'meɪt, *Am:* kri:'meɪt] *vt* incinerar

cremation [krɪ'meɪʃən] *n* incineración *f*

crematorium [ˌkreməˈtɔːriəm, *Am:* ˌkri:-məˈtɔːri-] <-s *o* -ria> *n* crematorio *m*

crematory ['kremətəri] I. *n Am* (*crematorium*) crematorio *m* II. *adj* crematorio, -a

crème de la crème [ˌkremdəlɑːˈkrem] *n* **the ~** la flor y nata

crepe [kreɪp] *n* crepé *f,* crêpe *f*

crept [krept] *pp, pt of* **creep**

crescendo [krɪˈʃendəʊ, *Am:* -doʊ] *n* crescendo *m*

crescent ['kresnt] I. *n* **1.** (*shape*) media luna *f* **2.** (*curved street*) calle en forma de media luna II. *adj* creciente

cress [kres] *n no pl* berro *m*

crest [krest] I. *n* **1.** (*peak*) cima *f;* (*of wave, bird*) cresta *f* **2.** (*helmet decoration*) cimera *f* **3.** ARCHIT caballete *m* II. *vt* coronar III. *vi* (*wave*) encresparse

crestfallen ['krestˌfɔːlən] *adj* cabizbajo, -a

Crete [kri:t] *n* Creta *f*

cretin ['kretɪn, *Am:* 'kri:tn] *n inf* cretino, -a *m, f*

crevasse [krɪˈvæs, *Am:* krəˈvæs] *n* grieta *f* en un glaciar

crevice ['krevɪs] *n a. fig* grieta *f*

crew¹ [kru:] I. *n* + *pl/sing vb* **1.** NAUT, AVIAT tripulación *f;* RAIL personal *m;* **ground/flight ~** personal de tierra/de vuelo; **two ~** dos miembros de la tripulación **2.** (*team*) equipo *m* **3.** *inf* (*gang*) banda *f* II. *vt* **to ~ a boat** formar parte de la tripulación de una embarcación III. *vi* **to ~ for sb** formar parte de la tripulación del

barco de alguien

crew² [kru:] *Brit pp, pt of* **crow²**

crew cut *n* corte *m* de pelo al rape

crewman <-men> *n* miembro *m* de la tripulación

crewmember *n* miembro *mf* de la tripulación

crib [krɪb] I. *n* **1.** *Am, Brit* (*baby's bed*) cuna *f* **2.** (*nativity scene*) belén *m* **3.** *inf* (*plagiarized work*) plagio *m* **4.** *inf* SCHOOL chuleta *f,* acordeón *m Méx,* machete *m RíoPl* II. <-bb-> *vt inf* **1.** (*plagiarize*) plagiar **2.** SCHOOL copiar; **to ~ sth from a book** copiar algo de un libro III. <-bb-> *vi inf* **1.** (*plagiarize*) plagiar **2.** SCHOOL copiar; **to ~ from sb** copiar de alguien

cribbage ['krɪbɪdʒ] *n* GAMES *especie de juego de naipes*

crick [krɪk] I. *n* (*in the neck*) tortícolis *f inv;* (*in the back*) lumbago *m;* **to have a ~ in one's neck/back** tener tortícolis/lumbago II. *vt* I **have ~ed my neck/back** me ha dado tortícolis/lumbago

cricket¹ ['krɪkɪt] *n no pl* SPORTS cricket *m* ►**that's not ~!** ¡eso no es jugar limpio!

cricket² ['krɪkɪt] *n* ZOOL grillo *m,* siripita *f Bol*

cricket bat *n* bate *m* de cricket

cricketer ['krɪkɪtəʳ, *Am:* -t̬əʳ] *n* jugador(a) *m(f)* de cricket

cricket field *n,* **cricket ground** *n,* **cricket pitch** <-es> *n* campo *m* de cricket

crier ['kraɪəʳ, *Am:* -əʳ] *n* pregonero, -a *m, f*

crikey ['kraɪki] *interj inf* ¡santo Dios!

crime [kraɪm] *n* **1.** LAW (*illegal act*) delito *m;* (*more serious*) crimen *m;* **~ against humanity** un crimen contra la humanidad; **~ of passion** crimen pasional; **to accuse sb of a ~** imputar un delito a alguien; **to commit a ~** cometer un delito; **the scene of the ~** la escena del crimen; **it would be a ~** *inf* sería un pecado **2.** (*criminal activity*) delincuencia *f;* **~ rate** índice *m* de criminalidad; **organized ~** crimen organizado

crime prevention *n no pl* prevención *f* de la delincuencia **crime-ridden** *adj* con un alto índice de criminalidad **crime wave** *n* ola *f* de delincuencia

criminal ['krɪmɪnl] I. *n* (*offender*) delincuente *mf;* (*more serious*) criminal *mf* II. *adj* **1.** (*illegal*) delictivo, -a; (*more serious*) criminal **2.** LAW penal; **~ court** juzgado *m* de lo penal; **~ lawyer** abogado, -a *m, f* penalista; **~ record** antecedentes *mpl* penales **3.** *fig* (*shameful*) vergonzoso, -a; **to be ~ to do sth** ser un crimen hacer algo

criminality [ˌkrɪmɪˈnæləti, *Am:* -əˈnæləti] *n no pl* criminalidad *f*

criminologist [krɪmɪˈnɒlədʒɪst, *Am:* -ˈnɑːlə-] *n* criminólogo, -a *m, f*

criminology [ˌkrɪmɪˈnɒlədʒi, *Am:* -ˈnɑːlə-] *n no pl* criminología *f*

crimp [krɪmp] *vt* **1.** (*press into folds, frill*) plisar **2.** (*make wavy*) ondular; (*make curly*) rizar

crimson ['krɪmzn] I. *n no pl* carmesí *m* II. *adj*

1. (*colour*) carmesí **2.** (*red-faced*) colorado, -a; **to blush** ~ ponerse como un tomate
cringe [krɪndʒ] *vi* **1.** *inf* (*shrink*) encogerse; **to** ~ **with embarrassment at sth** morirse de vergüenza por algo **2.** (*lower*) humillarse; **to** ~ **before sb** arrastrarse ante alguien
crinkle [ˈkrɪŋkl] **I.** *vt* (*wrinkle*) arrugar; (*wave*) ondular **II.** *vi* **to** ~ (**up**) (*wrinkle*) arrugarse; (*ripple*) ondularse **III.** *n* arruga *f;* (*in hair*) rizo *m*
crinkly [ˈkrɪŋkli] <-ier, -iest> *adj* **1.** (*wrinkled*) arrugado, -a **2.** (*wavy*) ondulado, -a; (*curly*) rizado, -a
cripple [ˈkrɪpl] **I.** *n* lisiado, -a *m, f* **II.** *vt* **1.** (*disable*) lisiar; (*machine, object*) inutilizar **2.** (*paralyse*) paralizar
crippling *adj fig* terrible
crisis [ˈkraɪsɪs] <crises> *n* crisis *f inv;* **a** ~ **over sth** una crisis provocada por algo; ~ **in** [*o* **of**] **confidence** crisis de confianza; **to go through a** ~ atravesar una crisis
crisis management *n no pl* gestión *f* de crisis
crisp [krɪsp] **I.** <-er, -est> *adj* **1.** (*snow, bacon*) crujiente **2.** (*apple, lettuce*) fresco, -a **3.** (*shirt, trousers*) recién planchado, -a; (*banknote*) nuevo, -a **4.** (*air*) vivificante **5.** (*sharp*) nítido, -a **6.** (*lively*) animado, -a **7.** (*quick and precise*) escueto, -a; (*manner*) seco, -a; (*style*) conciso, -a **II.** *n Brit pl* (*thin fried potatoes*) patatas *fpl* de churrero, papas *fpl* fritas *AmL* **III.** *vt* **1.** (*make crisp*) tostar ligeramente **2.** (*curl*) encrespar
crispbread [ˈkrɪsbred] *n* galleta crujiente de centeno
crispy [ˈkrɪspi] <-ier, -iest> *adj* crujiente
criss-cross [ˈkrɪskrɒs, *Am:* -krɑːs] **I.** *vt* entrecruzar **II.** *vi* entrecruzarse **III.** *adj* entrecruzado, -a **IV.** <-es> *n* **1.** entramado *m* **2.** *fig* enredo *m*
criterion [kraɪˈtɪəriən, *Am:* -ˈtɪri-] <-ria> *n* criterio *m*
critic [ˈkrɪtɪk, *Am:* ˈkrɪt̬-] *n* crítico, -a *m, f*
critical [ˈkrɪtɪkl, *Am:* ˈkrɪt̬-] *adj* **1.** (*disapproving*) crítico, -a; **to be** ~ **of sth/sb** criticar algo/a alguien; **to be highly** ~ **of sth** criticar duramente algo **2.** (*decisive*) fundamental; **to be** ~ **to sth** ser de vital importancia para algo; **to be in a** ~ **condition** *a.* MED estar en estado crítico
criticism [ˈkrɪtɪsɪzəm, *Am:* ˈkrɪt̬-] *n* crítica *f;* **to take** ~ admitir la crítica; **I have a few ~s of what you say** tengo algunas críticas que hacer respecto a eso que dices
criticize [ˈkrɪtɪsaɪz, *Am:* ˈkrɪt̬-] *vt, vi* criticar
critique [krɪˈtiːk] *n* crítica *f*
croak [krəʊk, *Am:* kroʊk] **I.** *vi* **1.** (*crow*) graznar; (*frog*) croar; (*person*) gruñir **2.** *inf* (*die*) estirar la pata **II.** *vt* decir con voz ronca **III.** *n* (*crow*) graznido *m;* (*frog*) croar *m;* (*person*) gruñido *m*
Croat [ˈkrəʊæt, *Am:* ˈkroʊ-] *n* croata *mf*
Croatia [krəʊˈeɪʃiə, *Am:* kroʊ-] *n* Croacia *f*
Croatian [krəʊˈeɪʃiən, *Am:* kroʊ-] **I.** *adj*

croata **II.** *n* croata *mf*
crochet [ˈkrəʊʃeɪ, *Am:* kroʊˈʃeɪ] **I.** *n no pl* ganchillo *m,* croché *m* **II.** *vi* hacer ganchillo **III.** *vt* hacer a ganchillo
crochet hook *n,* **crochet needle** *n* aguja *f* de ganchillo [*o* de croché]
crock [krɒk, *Am:* krɑːk] *n* **1.** (*clay container*) vasija *f* de barro **2.** *iron old* ~ (*person*) carcamal *m inf;* (*thing*) cacharro *m inf* **3.** *Am, inf* **a** ~ **of shit** (*nonsense*) una chorrada
crockery [ˈkrɒkəri, *Am:* ˈkrɑːkə-] *n no pl* vajilla *f*
crocodile [ˈkrɒkədaɪl, *Am:* ˈkrɑːkə-] <-(s)> *n* **1.** ZOOL cocodrilo *m* **2.** *Brit, inf* (*line of pupils*) fila *f* de a dos
crocodile tears *npl* lágrimas *fpl* de cocodrilo; **to shed** ~ llorar lágrimas de cocodrilo
crocus [ˈkrəʊkəs, *Am:* ˈkroʊ-] <-es> *n* azafrán *m*
croft [krɒft, *Am:* krɑːft] *n Scot* (*small farm*) granja *f* pequeña
crofter [ˈkrɒftəʳ, *Am:* ˈkrɑːft̬ə] *n Scot* propietario, -a *m, f* de una granja pequeña
croissant [ˈkrwaːsɒn, *Am:* kwaːˈsɑ-] *n* croissant *m,* cruasán *m*
crony [ˈkrəʊni, *Am:* ˈkroʊ-] <-ies> *n iron, inf* amigote *m*
crook [krʊk] **I.** *n* **1.** (*criminal*) delincuente *mf* **2.** *inf* (*rogue*) sinvergüenza *mf* **3.** (*of elbow*) pliegue *m;* (*of leg*) corva *f* **4.** (*curve*) recodo *m* **5.** (*staff: of shepherd*) cayado *m;* (*of bishop*) báculo *m* **II.** *adj Aus, inf* **1.** (*ill*) **to feel** ~ encontrarse mal **2.** (*angry*) **to go** ~ (**at sb**) ponerse furioso (con alguien) **3.** (*out of order*) estropeado, -a **4.** (*unsatisfactory*) malo, -a **III.** *vt* doblar; **to** ~ **one's finger at sb** hacer señas con el dedo a alguien
crooked [ˈkrʊkɪd] *adj* **1.** (*not straight: nose, legs*) torcido, -a; (*back*) encorvado, -a; (*path*) tortuoso, -a **2.** *inf* (*dishonest*) deshonesto, -a
croon [kruːn] **I.** *vt, vi* canturrear **II.** *n* canturreo *m*
crooner [ˈkruːnəʳ, *Am:* -ə] *n iron, inf* cantante *mf* melódico, -a
crop [krɒp, *Am:* krɑːp] **I.** *n* **1.** AGR (*plant*) cultivo *m;* (*harvest*) cosecha *f* **2.** (*group: of people*) montón *m;* (*of things*) sarta *f;* **a** ~ **of lies** una sarta de mentiras **3.** (*haircut*) corte *m* de pelo muy corto; **to wear one's hair in a** ~ llevar el pelo muy corto **4.** (*of bird*) buche *m* **5.** (*whip*) fusta *f* **II.** <-pp-> *vt* **1.** AGR cultivar **2.** (*cut*) recortar; (*tail*) cortar; (*hair*) cortar muy corto; (*plant*) podar **3.** (*graze*) pacer **III.** *vi* AGR darse; (*land*) rendir
◆**crop out** *vi* GEO aflorar
◆**crop up** *vi* surgir
cropper [ˈkrɒpəʳ, *Am:* ˈkrɑːpə] *n no pl* **1.** (*person*) agricultor(a) *m(f)* **2.** (*plant*) cultivo *m;* **to be a good/bad** ~ tener buen/mal rendimiento ▶**to come a** ~ *inf* (*have a bad accident*) darse un porrazo; (*fail miserably*) fracasar abiertamente; (*in an exam*) catear
crop rotation *n* rotación *f* de cultivos

croquet ['krəʊkeɪ, *Am:* kroʊ'keɪ] *n no pl* croquet *m*

cross [krɒs, *Am:* krɑːs] I. *vt* 1. (*go across: road, threshold*) cruzar; (*desert, river, sea*) atravesar 2. (*lie across*) **the bridge ~es the river** el puente cruza el río 3. (*place crosswise*) **to ~ one's legs** cruzar las piernas; **to ~ one's arms** cruzarse de brazos; **to ~ one's fingers** *a. fig* cruzar los dedos 4. BIO (*crossbreed*) cruzar 5. REL **to ~ oneself** hacerse la señal de la cruz 6. (*oppose*) contrariar 7. (*mark with a cross*) marcar con una cruz 8. (*draw a line across*) cruzar, rayar; **to ~ a cheque** *Aus, Brit* cruzar un cheque ▶**I'll ~ that bridge when I come to it** me ocuparé de ello cuando llegue el momento; **~ my heart and hope to die** que me muera si no es verdad; **to ~ one's mind** ocurrírsele a alguien; **to ~ swords with sb** habérselas con alguien II. *vi* 1. (*intersect*) cruzarse 2. (*go across*) cruzar III. *n* 1. *a.* REL cruz *f;* **the sign of the ~** la señal de la cruz; **to bear one's ~** cargar con su cruz; **Maltese ~** cruz de Malta 2. (*crossing: of streets, roads*) cruce *m* 3. BIO cruce *m*, cruza *f AmL* 4. (*mixture*) mezcla *f* IV. *adj* enfadado, -a; **to be ~ about sth** estar enfadado por algo; **to get ~ with sb** enfadarse con alguien

♦**cross off** *vt,* **cross out** *vt* tachar
♦**cross over** *vi, vt* cruzar

crossbar ['krɒsbɑː', *Am:* 'krɑːsbɑːr] *n* travesaño *m;* (*of goal*) larguero *m;* (*of bicycle*) barra *f* **crossbeam** *n* viga *f* transversal **cross-border** *adj* transfronterizo, -a **crossbow** *n* ballesta *f* **crossbreed** *n* BIO cruce *m*, cruza *f AmL* **cross-channel** *adj* ~ **ferry** (*across the English channel*) ferry *m* del canal de la Mancha **crosscheck** I. *n* comprobación *f* adicional II. *vt* volver a comprobar **cross-country** I. *adj* a campo traviesa; ~ **race** cross *m;* ~ **skiing** esquí *m* nórdico II. *adv* a campo traviesa III. *n* competición *f* a campo a través **cross-current** *n* contracorriente *f* **cross-examination** *n* LAW interrogatorio *m* cruzado **cross-examine** *vt* contrainterrogar **cross-eyed** *adj* bizco, -a **cross-fertilization** *n no pl* BIO fecundación *f* cruzada **crossfire** *n no pl* fuego *m* cruzado; **to be caught in the ~** *fig* estar entre dos fuegos **cross-grained** *adj* (*wood*) de fibras cruzadas

crossing ['krɒsɪŋ, *Am:* 'krɑːsɪŋ] *n* 1. (*place to cross*) paso *m;* **level ~** RAIL paso *m* a nivel; **border ~** paso fronterizo; **pedestrian ~** paso de peatones 2. (*crossroads*) cruce *m* 3. ARCHIT crucero *m* 4. (*journey*) paso *m;* (*across the sea*) travesía *f;* **the ~ of the Alps** el paso de los Alpes

cross-legged [ˌkrɒs'legd, *Am:* ˌkrɑːs'legəd] *adj* con las piernas cruzadas **crossover** *n* paso *m;* **a ~ of popular and classical music** una fusión de música popular y clásica **cross-purposes** *npl* **to be talking at ~** estar hablando de cosas distintas **cross-reference**

n remisión *f* **crossroads** *n inv* 1. cruce *m* 2. *fig* encrucijada *f;* **to be at a ~** estar en una encrucijada **cross-section** *n* 1. sección *f* transversal 2. *fig* muestra *f* representativa **crosstalk** *n no pl* 1. TEL cruce *m* de líneas; RADIO interferencia *f* 2. *Brit* (*repartee*) intercambio *m* de réplicas ocurrentes **crosswalk** *n Am* (*pedestrian crossing*) paso *m* de peatones **crossways** *adv* transversalmente **crosswind** *n* viento *m* de costado **crosswise** *adv* transversalmente **crossword** (**puzzle**) *n* crucigrama *m*

crotch [krɒtʃ, *Am:* krɑːtʃ] <-es> *n* entrepierna *f*

crotchet ['krɒtʃɪt, *Am:* 'krɑːtʃət] *n* MUS negra *f*

crotchety ['krɒtʃɪti, *Am:* 'krɑːtʃəti] *adj inf* (*bad-tempered*) malhumorado, -a

crouch [kraʊtʃ] I. *vi* **to ~ (down)** agacharse; **to be ~ing** estar en cuclillas II. *n* **to lower oneself into a ~** agacharse

croup [kruːp] *n no pl* 1. (*rump*) grupa *f* 2. MED crup *m*, garrotillo *m*

croupier ['kruːpɪeɪ, *Am:* -eɪ] *n* crupier *mf*

crow[1] [krəʊ, *Am:* kroʊ] *n* ZOOL cuervo *m* ▶**to eat ~** *Am, inf* tener que reconocer un error; **as the ~ flies** en línea recta

crow[2] [krəʊ, *Am:* kroʊ] <crowed *Brit:* crew, crowed *Brit:* crew> I. *n* 1. (*call of a cock*) cacareo *m* 2. (*cry of pleasure*) grito *m* de alegría; (*of baby*) gorjeo *m* II. *vi* 1. (*cock*) cacarear 2. (*cry out happily*) gritar de entusiasmo; (*baby*) gorjear 3. (*boast*) alardear; **to ~ over sth** jactarse de algo

crowbar ['krəʊbɑː', *Am:* 'kroʊbɑːr] *n* palanca *f*

crowd [kraʊd] I. *n + pl/sing vb* 1. (*throng*) multitud *f;* **there was quite a ~** había mucha gente 2. *inf* (*group*) grupo *m;* **the usual ~** los de siempre 3. *inf* (*large number*) montón *m;* **a ~ of things** un montón de cosas 4. (*common people*) **the ~** el vulgo 5. (*masses*) masas *fpl;* **to stand out from the ~** *fig* destacar(se); **to follow the ~** *fig* dejarse llevar por los demás 6. (*audience*) público *m*, espectadores *mpl* II. *vi* aglomerarse; **to ~ into a place** entrar en tropel en un sitio; **to ~ round sb/sth** apiñarse alrededor de alguien/algo III. *vt* 1. (*fill*) llenar; **to ~ the streets/a stadium** abarrotar las calles/un estadio 2. (*cram*) amontonar 3. *inf* (*pressure*) atosigar

♦**crowd out** *vt* 1. (*exclude*) excluir 2. (*fill*) **to be crowded out** estar lleno de gente

crowded *adj* lleno, -a; ~ **together** amontonados; **the bar was ~** había mucha gente en el bar; **the drawer is ~ with useless things** el cajón está atiborrado de cosas inservibles

crowd-puller *n* gran atracción *f*

crown [kraʊn] I. *n* 1. corona *f;* **the Crown** (*monarchy*) la Corona 2. (*top part: of hill, mountain*) cima *f;* (*of hat, tree*) copa *f;* (*of head*) coronilla *f;* (*of road*) centro *m;* (*of roof*) caballete *m* 3. ZOOL (*of bird*) cresta *f* 4. (*culmi-*

nation) culminación *f* **5.** (*of tooth*) funda *f* **II.** *vt* **1.** (*coronate*) coronar; **to ~ sb queen** coronar reina a alguien **2.** (*complete*) rematar; **the church is ~ed by a golden dome** una cúpula dorada corona la iglesia; **the prize ~ed his career** el premio fue la culminación de su carrera **3.** *inf* (*hit on head*) dar un golpe en la cabeza **4.** MED (*tooth*) poner una funda en ▸ **to ~ it all** *Aus, Brit* para rematarlo todo; (*misfortune*) para colmo de desgracias

crown cap *n* cápsula *f* **crown colony** <-ies> *n* colonia *f* de la Corona **crown cork** *n* cápsula *f*

crowning *adj* supremo, -a

crown jewels *n a. fig, iron* joyas *fpl* de la Corona **crown prince** *n* príncipe *m* heredero

crow's feet ['krəʊzfiːt, *Am:* 'kroʊz-] *npl* patas *fpl* de gallo **crow's nest** *n* NAUT torre *f* de vigía

CRT [ˌsiːɑːˈtiː, *Am:* -ɑːrˈ-] *n abbr of* **cathoderay tube** TRC *m*

crucial ['kruʃl] *adj* (*decisive*) decisivo, -a; (*moment*) crucial; **to be ~ to sth** ser decisivo para algo; **it is ~ that ...** es de vital importancia que... +*subj*

crucible ['kruːsɪbl] *n a. fig* crisol *m*

crucifix [ˌkruːsɪˈfɪks] <-es> *n* crucifijo *m*

crucifixion [ˌkruːsɪˈfɪkʃən] *n* crucifixión *f*

crucify ['kruːsɪfaɪ] <-ie-> *vt* **1.** (*execute*) crucificar **2.** *fig* martirizar; **if she ever finds out, she'll ~ me** si alguna vez lo descubre, me matará

cruddy ['krʌdi] <-ier, -iest> *adj inf* asqueroso, -a; **a ~ book** una porquería de libro

crude [kruːd] **I.** *adj* **1.** (*rudimentary*) rudimentario, -a; (*letter*) tosco, -a **2.** (*unrefined*) bruto, -a; (*oil*) crudo, -a **3.** (*unfinished, undeveloped*) mal acabado, -a **4.** (*vulgar*) basto, -a; (*manners*) grosero, -a **II.** *n* crudo *m*

cruel [krʊəl] <-(l)ler, -(l)lest> *adj* cruel; **to be ~ to sb** ser cruel con alguien ▸ **to be ~ to be kind** *prov* hacer sufrir a alguien por su bien

cruelty ['krʊəlti, *Am:* -ţi] <-ies> *n* crueldad *f*; **~ to sb** crueldad con alguien; **society for the prevention of ~ to animals** sociedad *f* protectora de los animales

cruise [kruːz] **I.** *n* crucero *m*; **~ ship** transatlántico *m*; **to go on a ~** hacer un crucero **II.** *vi* **1.** NAUT (*take a cruise*) hacer un crucero **2.** (*travel at constant speed*) ir a una velocidad de crucero; (*aeroplane*) volar a una velocidad constante **3.** *inf* (*police car*) patrullar **4.** *inf* (*drive around aimlessly*) dar una vuelta en coche **5.** *inf* (*look for casual sex*) buscar plan

cruise missile *n* MIL misil *m* de crucero

cruiser ['kruːzər, *Am:* -ər] *n* **1.** (*warship*) crucero *m* **2.** (*pleasure boat*) embarcación *f* de recreo **3.** (*squad car*) coche *m* patrulla

cruise ship *n* transatlántico *m*

cruising *adj* (*speed*) de crucero

crumb [krʌm] *n* **1.** (*of bread*) miga *f* **2.** (*small amount*) pizca *f*; **a small ~ of ...** un poco

de...; **a ~ of hope** algo de esperanza **3.** *inf* (*worthless person*) mequetrefe *mf*

crumble ['krʌmbl] **I.** *vt* **1.** (*bread, biscuit*) desmigajar **2.** (*stone, cheese*) desmenuzar **II.** *vi* (*cliff*) derrumbarse; (*plaster, stone*) desmenuzarse; (*empire*) desmoronarse; (*resistance, opposition*) venirse abajo **III.** *n Brit:* postre de fruta cubierto de una pasta desmenuzada de azúcar, mantequilla y harina

crumbly ['krʌmbli] <-ier, -iest> *adj* (*bread, cake*) que se desmigaja; (*cheese*) desmenuzable; (*house, wall*) desmoronadizo, -a

crummy ['krʌmi] <-ier, -iest> *adj inf* (*film, idea, car*) de pena; (*furniture, house*) cutre; (*place*) de mala muerte; **a ~ salary** un sueldo miserable

crumpet ['krʌmpɪt] *n* **1.** *Brit:* panecillo blando que se come tostado **2.** *Brit, inf* (*sexually attractive woman*) tía *f* buena

crumple ['krʌmpl] **I.** *vt* (*clothes, paper*) arrugar; (*metal*) abollar; **to ~ a piece of paper into a ball** hacer una pelota con un papel **II.** *vi* **1.** (*become dented: mudguard*) abollarse **2.** (*become wrinkled: fabric, face*) arrugarse **3.** (*collapse*) desplomarse

crunch [krʌntʃ] **I.** *vt* **1.** (*in the mouth*) masticar (haciendo ruido) **2.** (*grind*) hacer crujir **II.** *vi* crujir **III.** <-es> *n* **1.** (*crushing sound*) crujido *m* **2.** *no pl, inf* (*important moment*) momento *m* decisivo; **when it comes to the ~** *inf* a la hora de la verdad

crunchy ['krʌntʃi] <-ier, -iest> *adj* crujiente

crusade [kruːˈseɪd] *n* **1.** REL, HIST cruzada *f* **2.** *fig* campaña *f*; **a ~ for/against sth** una campaña a favor/en contra de algo **II.** *vi* **1.** HIST, REL participar en una cruzada **2.** *fig* hacer una campaña; **to ~ for sth** hacer una cruzada en pro de algo

crusader [kruːˈseɪdər, *Am:* -dər] *n* **1.** REL, HIST cruzado *m* **2.** *fig* defensor(a) *m(f)*; **a ~ against sth** un detractor de algo

crush [krʌʃ] **I.** *vt* **1.** (*compress*) aplastar; (*paper*) estrujar; (*dress*) arrugar; (*person*) apretujar; **to be ~ed to death** morir aplastado **2.** (*grind: garlic*) machacar; (*grapes, olives*) prensar; (*stone*) triturar; (*ice*) picar **3.** (*extract by pressing*) **to ~ the juice from an orange** exprimir una naranja **4.** (*shock severely*) abatir **5.** (*defeat, suppress*) aplastar; (*rebellion, revolution*) reprimir; (*opponent*) derrotar; (*one's hopes*) frustrar; (*rumour*) acallar **II.** *vi* **1.** (*clothes, paper*) arrugarse **2.** (*people*) apretujarse **III.** <-es> *n* **1.** *no pl* (*act of crushing*) aplastamiento *m* **2.** *no pl* (*throng*) muchedumbre *f*; **there was a great ~** había una gran aglomeración **3.** *inf* (*temporary infatuation*) enamoramiento *m*; **to have a ~ on sb** encapricharse de alguien **4.** *Brit* (*crushed ice drink*) **orange ~** naranjada *f*

♦ **crush up** *vt* triturar

crush barrier *n Brit* valla *f* de contención

crushing **I.** *n* aplastamiento *m* **II.** *adj* (*defeat*) aplastante; (*reply, argument*) contundente

crust [krʌst] I. *n* 1. GASTR, BOT corteza *f;* (*dry bread*) mendrugo *m;* ~ **of the Earth** GEO corteza terrestre 2. (*hard external layer*) capa *f;* **a ~ of ice/dirt** una capa de hielo/suciedad 3. ZOOL caparazón *m* 4. MED costra *f* 5. (*deposit from wine*) poso *m* II. *vi* formar una costra III. *vt* **to be ~ed with mud** tener una capa de barro

crustacean [krʌ'steɪʃən] *n* crustáceo *m*

crusty ['krʌsti] <-ier, -iest> *adj* 1. GASTR crujiente 2. (*grumpy, surly*) malhumorado, -a

crutch [krʌtʃ] <-es> *n* 1. MED muleta *f;* **to be on ~es** andar con muletas 2. *fig* (*source of support*) apoyo *m* 3. ANAT horcajadura *f*

crux [krʌks] *n no pl* punto *m* clave; **the ~ of sth** lo esencial de algo; **the ~ of the matter** el quid de la cuestión

cry [kraɪ] I. <-ie-> *vi* 1. (*weep*) llorar; **to ~ for joy** llorar de alegría 2. (*shout*) gritar; (*animal*) aullar; **to ~ for help** pedir ayuda a gritos II. <-ie-> *vt* 1. (*shed tears*) llorar 2. (*shout*) gritar 3. (*announce publicly*) pregonar ► **to ~ one's eyes out** llorar a lágrima viva; **to ~ foul at sth** mostrarse indignado por algo; **to ~ wolf** dar una falsa alarma III. *n* 1. *no pl* (*weeping*) llanto *m;* **to have a ~** llorar 2. (*shout*) grito *m;* **to give a ~** dar un grito; **a ~ for help** una llamada de socorro 3. (*slogan*) lema *m* 4. ZOOL aullido *m* ► **to be a far ~ from sth** tener poco que ver con algo, ser muy distinto de algo; **to be in full ~ after sth** perseguir algo

◆ **cry down** *vt* 1. (*decry*) despreciar 2. (*disparage*) desacreditar

◆ **cry for** *vt insep* pedir

◆ **cry off** *vi inf* echarse atrás; **to ~ a deal** romper un trato

◆ **cry out** I. *vi* gritar; **to ~ against sth** clamar contra algo; **to ~ for sth** pedir algo a gritos; **for crying out loud!** *inf* ¡por el amor de Dios! II. *vt* gritar

crying ['kraɪɪŋ] I. *n no pl* lloro *m* II. *adj* (*need*) apremiante; (*injustice*) que clama al cielo; **a ~ shame** *inf* una verdadera vergüenza

crypt [krɪpt] *n* cripta *f*

cryptic ['krɪptɪk] *adj* críptico, -a; (*comment, remark*) ambiguo, -a; (*smile*) enigmático, -a

crystal ['krɪstl] I. *n* cristal *m* II. *adj* 1. cristalino, -a 2. (*made of crystal*) de cristal

crystal ball *n* bola *f* de cristal **crystal clear** *adj* 1. (*transparent: water*) cristalino, -a; (*image*) nítido, -a 2. (*obvious*) obvio, -a; **it is ~ (that)** está más claro que el agua (que +*subj*)

crystalline ['krɪstəlaɪn] *adj* cristalino, -a

crystallization [ˌkrɪstəlaɪˈzeɪʃən, *Am:* -ɪˈ-] *n no pl* cristalización *f*

crystallize ['krɪstəlaɪz] I. *vi* cristalizarse II. *vt* 1. cristalizar; (*plan, thought*) materializar 2. GASTR escarchar

CSCE *n abbr of* **Conference on Security and Cooperation in Europe** CSCE *f*

CSE [ˌsiːesˈiː] *n Brit abbr of* **Certificate of Secondary Education** título de formación secundaria

ct. 1. *abbr of* **cent** centavo *m* 2. *abbr of* **carat** quilate *m*

CTC *n Brit abbr of* **city technology college** instituto de tecnología

cub [kʌb] *n* 1. ZOOL cachorro *m* 2. (*person*) novato, -a *m, f*

Cuba ['kjuːbə] *n* Cuba *f*

Cuban ['kjuːbən] I. *adj* cubano, -a II. *n* cubano, -a *m, f*

cubby-hole ['kʌbɪhəʊl, *Am:* -hoʊl] *n* cuchitril *m*

cube [kjuːb] I. *n* cubo *m;* (*of cheese*) dado *m;* (*of sugar*) terrón *m;* **ice ~** cubito *m* de hielo; **~ root** MAT raíz *f* cúbica II. *vt* 1. GASTR cortar en dados 2. MAT elevar al cubo; **2 ~d** 2 (elevado) al cubo

cubic ['kjuːbɪk] *adj* 1. (*cube-shaped*) cúbico, -a; **~ centimetre/metre** centímetro *m* cúbico/metro *m* cúbico 2. MAT de tercer grado; **~ equation** ecuación *f* de tercer grado

cubicle ['kjuːbɪkl] *n* 1. (*changing room*) probador *m* 2. (*sleeping compartment*) cubículo *m*

cuckoo ['kʊkuː, *Am:* 'kuːkuː] I. *n* cuco *m* II. *adj inf* chiflado, -a

cuckoo clock *n* reloj *m* de cuco

cucumber ['kjuːkʌmbər, *Am:* -bɚ] *n* pepino *m* ► **(as) cool as a ~** *inf* más fresco que una lechuga

cud [kʌd] *n no pl* **to chew the ~** *a. fig, inf* rumiar

cuddle ['kʌdl] I. *vt* abrazar II. *vi* abrazarse III. *n* abrazo *m;* **to give sb a ~** abrazar a alguien

cuddly <-ier, -iest> *adj* mimoso, -a; **~ toy** juguete *m* de peluche

cudgel ['kʌdʒəl] I. *n* 1. (*short thick stick*) garrote *m* 2. (*weapon*) porra *f* ► **to take up (the) ~s for sb/sth** *Aus, Brit* romper una lanza por alguien/algo II. <-ll-, *Am:* -l-> *vt* (*with a cudgel*) dar garrotazos a; (*with a weapon*) golpear

cue [kjuː] *n* 1. THEAT pie *m;* **to miss one's ~** no salir a escena en el momento debido 2. MUS entrada *f* 3. (*billiards*) taco *m;* **~ ball** bola *f* blanca ► **to take one's ~ from sb** seguir el ejemplo de alguien; (**right**) **on ~** en el momento justo

cuff [kʌf] I. *n* 1. (*end of sleeve*) puño *m* 2. *Am, Aus* (*turned-up trouser leg*) vuelta *f,* valenciana *f Méx* 3. (*slap*) cachete *m* 4. *pl, inf* (*handcuffs*) esposas *fpl* ► **off the ~** improvisado, -a II. *vt* 1. (*slap playfully*) dar un cachete a 2. *inf* (*handcuff*) esposar

cuff links *npl* gemelos *mpl,* mellizos *mpl AmL,* mancuernas *fpl AmC, Méx, Ven, Fili,* colleras *f Chile, Col*

cuisine [kwɪˈziːn] *n no pl* cocina *f*

cul-de-sac ['kʌldəsæk] <-s *o* culs-de-sac> *n a. fig* callejón *m* sin salida

culinary ['kʌlɪneri, *Am:* -əner-] *adj* culinario, -a

cull [kʌl] I. *vt* 1. ZOOL sacrificar (*de forma*

selectiva) **2.**(*choose*) seleccionar; **to ~ sth from sth** entresacar algo de algo **II.** *n* matanza *f* (selectiva)

culminate ['kʌlmɪneɪt] *vi* culminar; **to ~ in sth** culminar en algo

culmination [ˌkʌlmɪ'neɪʃən] *n no pl* culminación *f*

culottes [kju:'lɒts, *Am:* 'ku:lɑ:ts] *npl* falda *f* pantalón, pollera *f* pantalón *AmL;* **a pair of ~** una falda pantalón

culpable ['kʌlpəbl] *adj form* culpable; **to hold sb ~ for sth** considerar a alguien culpable de algo

culprit ['kʌlprɪt] *n* culpable *mf*

cult [kʌlt] *n* **1.**(*worship*) culto *m;* **fitness ~** culto al cuerpo **2.**(*sect*) secta *f*

cult figure *n* ídolo *m*

cultivate ['kʌltɪveɪt, *Am:* -t̬ə-] *vt a. fig* cultivar

cultivated *adj* **1.** AGR cultivado, -a **2.**(*person*) culto, -a

cultivation [ˌkʌltɪ'veɪʃən, *Am:* -t̬ə-] *n no pl* **1.** AGR cultivo *m;* **to be under ~** estar en cultivo **2.**(*of a person*) cultura *f*

cultivator ['kʌltɪveɪtər, *Am:* -t̬əveɪt̬ɚ] *n* AGR **1.**(*tool, machine*) cultivador *m* **2.**(*person*) cultivador(a) *m(f)*

cultural ['kʌltʃərəl] *adj* cultural

culture ['kʌltʃər, *Am:* -tʃɚ] **I.** *n* **1.**(*way of life*) cultura *f;* **enterprise ~** cultura de empresa **2.** *no pl* (*arts*) cultura *f* **3.** AGR cultivo *m* **II.** *vt* cultivar

cultured ['kʌltʃəd, *Am:* -tʃɚd] *adj* **1.** AGR cultivado, -a **2.**(*intellectual*) culto, -a; (*taste*) refinado, -a **3.** BIO de cultivo

culture vulture *n Brit* intelectualoide *mf*

cumbersome ['kʌmbəsəm, *Am:* -bɚ-] *adj,* **cumbrous** ['kʌmbrəs] *adj* **1.**(*unwieldly*) engorroso, -a; (*heavy*) pesado, -a; (*big*) voluminoso, -a **2.**(*awkward*) torpe

cumin ['kʌmɪn] *n no pl* comino *m*

cumulative ['kju:mjʊlətɪv, *Am:* -mjələt̬ɪv] *adj* **1.**(*increasing*) acumulativo, -a **2.**(*accumulated*) acumulado, -a

cumulus ['kjumjʊləs, *Am:* -mjə-] <-li> *n* cúmulo *m*

cunning ['kʌnɪŋ] **I.** *adj* **1.**(*ingenious: person*) astuto, -a; (*device, idea, plan*) ingenioso, -a **2.**(*sly*) taimado, -a **3.** *Am* (*cute, attractive*) lindo, -a, mono, -a **II.** *n no pl* astucia *f*

cunt [kʌnt] *n* **1.** *vulg* coño *m* **2.** *vulg* (*despicable person*) cabrón, -a *m, f*

cup [kʌp] **I.** *n* **1.**(*container*) taza *f;* **coffee/ tea ~** taza de café/té; **egg ~** huevera *f;* **a ~ of flour/chocolate** una taza de harina/chocolate **2.** SPORTS (*trophy*) copa *f;* **the World Cup** la copa del mundo **3.** BOT, REL cáliz *m* **4.**(*part of bra*) copa *f;* **a C ~** una copa de la talla C ►**he isn't my ~ of tea** *inf* no es santo de mi devoción; **it's not my ~ of tea** no es plato de mi gusto; **to be in one's ~s** estar borracho **II.** <-pp-> *vt* **to ~ one's hands** ahuecar las manos; **to ~ one's hands to one's mouth**

hacer bocina con las manos

cupboard ['kʌbəd, *Am:* -ɚd] *n* armario *m;* **built-in ~** armario empotrado; **kitchen ~** armario de cocina

cup final *n Brit* final *f* de la copa

cupful ['kʌpfʊl] <-s, *Am:* cupsful> *n* taza *f;* **a ~ of sugar** una taza de azúcar

cupola ['kju:pələ] *n* ARCHIT cúpula *f*

cuppa ['kʌpə] *n Brit, inf* (taza *f* de) té *m*

cup tie *n* SPORTS partido *m* de copa **cup winner** *n* SPORTS ganador(a) *m(f)* de la copa

cur [kɜ:r, *Am:* kɜ:r] *n* **1.**(*dog*) perro *m* callejero **2.**(*person*) canalla *m*

curable ['kjʊərəbl, *Am:* 'kjʊr-] *adj* curable

curate ['kjʊərət, *Am:* 'kjʊrət] *n* coadjutor *m*

curator [kjʊə'reɪtər, *Am:* 'kjʊreɪt̬ɚ] *n* director(a) *m(f)* (*de museo o galería*)

curb [kɜ:b, *Am:* kɜ:rb] **I.** *vt* (*anger, passion*) dominar; (*inflation, appetite*) controlar; (*expenditure*) frenar **II.** *n* **1.**(*control*) freno *m;* **to keep a ~ on sth** refrenar algo; **to put a ~ on sth** poner freno a algo **2.**(*obstacle*) estorbo *m* **3.** *Am* (*at roadside*) bordillo *m*

curb bit *n* freno *m* de las caballerías

curbstone ['kɜ:bstəʊn, *Am:* 'kɜ:rbstoʊn] *n Am* bordillo *m*

curd [kɜ:d, *Am:* kɜ:rd] *n* cuajada *f;* **~ cheese** requesón *m*

curdle [kɜ:dl, *Am:* kɜ:r-] **I.** *vi* cuajar(se); (*sauce*) cortarse **II.** *vt* cuajar; (*sauce*) cortar

cure ['kjʊər, *Am:* 'kjʊr] **I.** *vt* **1.** MED, GASTR curar **2.**(*problem*) remediar **3.**(*leather*) curtir **II.** *vi* curar; (*meat, fish*) curarse **III.** *n* **1.** MED, GASTR cura *f;* **to be past ~** no tener curación; *fig* no tener remedio **2.**(*return to health*) curación *f* **3.**(*solution*) remedio *m* **4.**(*of leather*) curtido *m*

cure-all ['kjʊərɔ:l, *Am:* 'kjʊrɑ:l] *n* curalotodo *m;* **a ~ for sth** una panacea para algo

curfew ['kɜ:fju:, *Am:* 'kɜ:r-] *n* (toque *m* de) queda *f*

curiosity [ˌkjʊərɪ'ɒsəti, *Am:* ˌkjʊrɪ'ɑ:səti] <-ies> *n* **1.** *no pl* (*desire to know*) curiosidad *f* **2.**(*strange thing*) curiosidad *f* ►**~ killed the cat** *prov* no seas tan curioso

curious ['kjʊərɪəs] *adj* curioso, -a; **to be ~ to see sth/sb** tener curiosidad por ver algo/a alguien; **to be ~ about sth** tener curiosidad por algo; **it is ~ that** es curioso que +*subj*

curl [kɜ:l, *Am:* kɜ:rl] **I.** *n* **1.**(*loop of hair*) rizo *m* **2.**(*sinuosity*) serpenteo *m* **3.**(*spiral*) espiral *f;* **~ of smoke** voluta *f* de humo **4.**(*of the lips*) mueca *f* de desprecio **II.** *vi* (*hair*) rizarse; (*paper*) ondularse; (*path*) serpentear; (*smoke*) hacer volutas **III.** *vt* (*hair*) rizar; **to ~ oneself up** acurrucarse ►**to ~ one's lip** hacer una mueca de desprecio

curler ['kɜ:lər, *Am:* 'kɜ:rlɚ] *n* rulo *m*

curlew ['kɜ:lju:, *Am:* 'kɜ:rlu:] *n* zarapito *m*

curling ['kɜ:lɪŋ, *Am:* 'kɜ:r-] *n no pl* **1.**(*of hair*) rizado *m* **2.** SPORTS curling *m*

curling iron *n,* **curling tongs** *npl* tenacillas *fpl* de rizar

curly ['kɜːli, Am: 'kɜːr-] <-ier, -iest> adj
(hair) rizado, -,a; (path) sinuoso, -a
currant ['kʌrənt, Am: 'kɜːr-] n **1.** (dried
grape) pasa f de Corinto **2.** (berry) grosella f
currency ['kʌrənsi, Am: 'kɜːr-] <-ies> n
1. FIN moneda f; **foreign** ~ divisas fpl; ~ **con**
version reforma f monetaria; ~ **market** mercado m de divisas; ~ **unit** unidad f monetaria
2. no pl (acceptance) difusión f; **to enjoy**
wide ~ tener una amplia difusión; **to gain** ~
extenderse
current ['kʌrənt, Am: 'kɜːr-] I. adj **1.** (present) actual; (year, month) en curso; **in** ~ **use**
en uso **2.** (latest) último, -a; **the** ~ **issue** (of
magazine) el último número; **the** ~ **craze** el
último grito **3.** (prevalent: use) generalizado,
-a; (practice) común **4.** (valid) vigente II. n
1. a. ELEC corriente f **2.** (tendency: of fashion)
tendencias fpl ► **to drift with the** ~ dejarse
llevar por la corriente; **to swim against the** ~
nadar contra corriente
current account n Brit cuenta f corriente
current affairs npl, **current events** npl
sucesos mpl de actualidad **current**
expenses npl gastos mpl corrientes
currently adv **1.** (at present) actualmente
2. (commonly) comúnmente
current opinion n opinión f generalizada
current rate n tipo m actual
curriculum vitae [kə,rɪkjələm'viːtaɪ] <-s o
curricula vitae> n currículum m (vitae)
curry[1] ['kʌri, Am: 'kɜːr-] I. <-ies> n curry m;
chicken ~ pollo m al curry; **vegetable** ~
curry de verduras II. vt preparar con curry
curry[2] ['kʌri, Am: 'kɜːr-] vt **1.** (groom: horse)
almohazar **2.** (leather) curtir ► **to** ~ **favour**
with sb buscar el favor de alguien
curse [kɜːs, Am: kɜːrs] I. vi **1.** (swear) soltar
palabrotas **2.** (blaspheme) blasfemar II. vt
1. (swear at) insultar **2.** (damn) maldecir; ~ **it!**
¡maldito sea! III. n **1.** (oath) palabrota f; **to let**
out a ~ soltar un taco **2.** (evil spell) maldición
f; **to put a** ~ **on sb** echar una maldición a alguien **3.** (affliction) **the** ~ **of racism** la lacra
del racismo; **to be the** ~ **of sb's life** ser la cruz
de alguien
cursed ['kɜːsɪd, Am: 'kɜːr-] adj maldito, -a
cursor ['kɜːsəʳ, Am: 'kɜːrsəʳ] n INFOR cursor m
cursory ['kɜːsəri, Am: 'kɜːr-] adj (glance,
reading) rápido, -a; (check, examination)
superficial; (remark) somero, -a
curt [kɜːt, Am: kɜːrt] adj **1.** (brief) conciso, -a
2. (laconic) lacónico, -a **3.** (rudely brief) seco,
-a; (refusal) tajante
curtail [kɜː'teɪl, Am: kə-] vt **1.** (limit, reduce:
right, freedom) restringir; (expenses) reducir
2. (shorten) abreviar
curtailment n **1.** (of spending) reducción f;
(of right, freedom) restricción f **2.** (cutting
short) acortamiento m
curtain ['kɜːtn, Am: 'kɜːrtn] I. n **1.** a. fig cortina f; **lace** ~ visillo m; **to draw the** ~**s** correr
las cortinas; **a** ~ **of rain** una cortina de lluvia

2. THEAT telón m; **to raise/lower the** ~ subir/
bajar el telón ► **it's** ~**s for you** estás acabado
II. vt poner cortinas en; **to** ~ **off** separar con
una cortina
curtain call n THEAT salida f a escena para
saludar; **to take a** ~ salir al escenario a saludar
curtain raiser n THEAT pieza f preliminar
curts(e)y ['kɜːtsi, Am: 'kɜːrt-] I. vi hacer una
reverencia II. n reverencia f; **to make a** ~ **to**
sb hacer una reverencia a alguien
curvature ['kɜːvətʃəʳ, Am: 'kɜːrvətʃəʳ] n no
pl curvatura f; MED desviación f
curve [kɜːv, Am: kɜːrv] I. n curva f II. vi estar
curvado; (path, road) hacer una curva; **to** ~
round to the left (path) torcer a mano
izquierda III. vt curvar
cushion ['kʊʃən] I. n **1.** cojín m **2.** TECH colchón m; **a** ~ **of air** un colchón de aire **3.** (in billiards) banda f II. vt **1.** (furnish with cushions)
poner cojines en **2.** (pad) almohadillar **3.** (ease
the effects of) amortiguar **4.** (protect) proteger
cushy ['kʊʃi] <-ier, -iest> adj inf fácil; **a** ~
job un chollo; **to be on to a** ~ **number** Brit
haber encontrado una ganga
cuss [kʌs] inf I. vi **1.** (swear) decir palabrotas
2. (curse) despotricar II. n **1.** (rude word) palabrota f **2.** (person) tipo, -a m, f
custard ['kʌstəd, Am: -təd] n no pl ≈ natillas
fpl
custodial [kʌs'təʊdiəl, Am: -'toʊ-] adj **1.** LAW
carcelario, -a **2.** (care) protectivo, -a
custodian [kʌs'təʊdɪən, Am: kʌs'toʊ-] n
1. (keeper, conservator) custodio, -a m, f; (of
morals, of a castle) guardián, -ana m, f **2.** Am
(of a building) portero, -a m, f **3.** (of a
museum) conservador(a) m(f)
custody ['kʌstədi] n no pl **1.** (care) cuidado m
2. (guardianship) custodia f; **to award** ~ **of sb**
to sb conceder a alguien la custodia de alguien
3. LAW (detention) detención f; **to take sb into**
~ detener a alguien
custom ['kʌstəm] n **1.** (tradition) costumbre
f; **an ancient** ~ una antigua tradición; **accord**
ing to ~ según la costumbre; **it is his** ~ **to do**
sth tiene por costumbre hacer algo **2.** LAW derecho m consuetudinario **3.** no pl (clientele)
clientela f **4.** pl (place) aduana f; (tax) aranceles mpl; **to get through** ~**s** pasar por la
aduana; **to pay** ~**s** (**on sth**) pagar derechos de
aduana (por algo)
customary ['kʌstəməri, Am: -mer-] adj
1. (traditional) tradicional; **it is** ~ **to** +infin es
costumbre +infin **2.** (usual) habitual
custom-built ['kʌstəm,bɪlt] adj (car) hecho,
-a de encargo
custom clothes npl Am ropa f hecha a la
medida
customer ['kʌstəməʳ, Am: -məʳ] n COM,
ECON **1.** (buyer, patron) cliente, -a m, f; **regular**
~ cliente habitual **2.** inf (person) tío, -a m, f
customer number n número m de cliente
customer services n pl atención f al

cliente

customise ['kʌstəmaɪz] *vt Aus, Brit* adaptar (según las necesidades del cliente); *a.* INFOR personalizar

customised *adj Aus, Brit* personalizado, -a

customize ['kʌstəmaɪz] *vt Am s.* **customise**

customized *adj Am s.* **customised**

custom-made ['kʌstəm'meɪd, *Am:* 'kʌstəm,meɪd] *adj* (*clothes*) hecho, -a a medida; (*car, furniture*) hecho, -a de encargo

customs barrier ['kʌstəmz'bærɪəʳ, *Am:* -'berɪəʳ] *n* barrera *f* arancelaria

customs clearance *n* trámites *mpl* de aduana **customs declaration** *n* declaración *f* de aduana **customs dues** *npl,* **customs duties** *npl* derechos *mpl* arancelarios; **to pay ~** pagar derechos de aduana **customs examination** *n* inspección *f* aduanera **custom(s) house** *n* aduana *f* **customs officer** *n,* **customs official** *n* oficial *mf* de aduana **customs union** *n* unión *f* aduanera

cut [kʌt] **I.** *n* **1.** (*incision*) *a.* FASHION corte *m;* **to make a ~** hacer un corte; **the ~ of a shirt** el corte de una camisa **2.** (*gash, wound*) herida *f,* cortada *f AmL;* **a deep ~** un corte profundo; **to get a ~** cortarse **3.** (*action: with a knife*) cuchillada *f;* (*with a whip*) latigazo *m* **4.** (*portion*) parte *f;* (*slice*) tajada *f;* **to take one's ~ of sth** *inf* sacar tajada de algo **5.** (*part*) trozo *m;* **cold ~s** fiambres *mpl* **6.** (*decrease*) reducción *f;* **a ~ in production** una disminución de la producción; **a ~ in staff** una reducción de plantilla; **wage/budget ~** recorte *m* salarial/presupuestario **7.** (*part taken out*) *a.* CINE trozo *m* omitido, corte *m;* **to make a ~ in a film** cortar una secuencia de una película **8.** GAMES **who's ~ is it?** ¿quién corta? **9.** *inf* (*absence*) ausencia *f* ▶**the ~ and thrust** la lucha; **to be a ~ above sb/sth** ser superior a alguien/algo **II.** *adj* cortado, -a; (*glass, diamond*) tallado, -a **III.** <cut, cut, -tt-> *vt* **1.** (*make an incision*) cortar; **to ~ oneself** cortarse; **to ~ sth open** abrir algo con un corte; **to ~ sth in half** partir algo por la mitad; **to ~ sth to pieces** trocear algo; **to have one's hair ~** cortarse el pelo; **to ~ the lawn** cortar el césped; **who's going to ~ the cards?** GAMES ¿quién corta? **2.** (*saw down: trees*) talar **3.** (*reap: corn*) segar **4.** (*cause moral pain*) herir **5.** (*decrease size, amount, length*) reducir; (*costs, budget*) recortar; (*prices*) rebajar; (*wages, workforce*) hacer recortes en; **to ~ sth (a bit) fine** calcular algo muy justo **6.** (*divide: benefits*) repartir **7.** (*hollow out*) **to ~ a hole** hacer un agujero **8.** shorten; (*speech*) acortar, CINE, TV editar **9.** (*shape precisely: diamond*) tallar **10.** *Am, inf* (*skip: school, class*) faltar a **11.** TECH (*turn off: motor, lights*) apagar **12.** MUS (*record, CD*) grabar **13.** (*cease*) dejar de; **~ all this noise!** ¡basta ya de hacer ruido! ▶**to ~ sb dead** negar el saludo a alguien **IV.** <cut, cut, -tt-> *vi* **1.** (*slice*) cortar(se); **this knife ~s well** este

cuchillo corta bien; **this cheese ~s easily** este queso se corta con facilidad **2.** GAMES cortar; **let's ~ to see who starts** vamos a cortar para ver quién sale **3.** CINE **~!** ¡corten! **4.** (*change direction suddenly*) **to ~ to the right** torcer a mano derecha **5.** (*morally wound: remark, words*) herir ▶**to ~ both ways** ser un arma de doble filo; **to ~ and run** salir pitando *inf*

◆**cut across** *vt insep* **1.** (*take short cut*) tomar un atajo a través de **2.** (*transcend*) trascender

◆**cut away** *vt* cortar

◆**cut back I.** *vt* **1.** (*trim down*) recortar; (*bushes, branches*) podar **2.** (*reduce: production*) reducir; **to ~ (on) sth** hacer recortes en algo; **to ~ (on) costs** recortar costes **II.** *vi* CINE **to ~ to ...** volver a..., retroceder a...

◆**cut down I.** *vt* **1.** (*tree*) talar **2.** (*reduce: production*) reducir; **to ~ expenses** recortar gastos **3.** (*destroy, kill*) destruir; **he was ~ in his prime** murió en la flor de la vida **4.** (*remodel, shorten: garment*) acortar **II.** *vi* **to ~ on sth** reducir el consumo de algo; **to ~ on smoking** fumar menos

◆**cut in I.** *vi* **1.** (*interrupt*) **to ~ (on sb)** interrumpir (a alguien); **to ~ on a conversation** interrumpir una conversación; **may I ~?** (*in dance*) ¿me permite? **2.** AUTO meterse delante; **to ~ on sb** meterse delante de alguien, cerrar el paso a alguien **II.** *vt* **1.** (*divide profits with*) **to cut sb in on sth** hacer partícipe a alguien en los beneficios de algo **2.** (*include when playing*) **to cut sb in on the game** dejar entrar a alguien en el juego

◆**cut into** *vt insep* **1.** (*start cutting: cake*) empezar a cortar **2.** (*interrupt*) interrumpir **3.** AUTO meterse delante de

◆**cut off** *vt* **1.** (*sever*) *a.* ELEC, TEL cortar **2.** (*amputate*) amputar **3.** (*stop talking*) interrumpir **4.** (*separate, isolate*) aislar; **to cut oneself off (from sb)** aislarse (de alguien); **to be ~ by the snow** estar incomunicado por la nieve

◆**cut out I.** *vt* **1.** (*slice out of*) cortar, recortar **2.** (*suppress: sugar, fatty food*) eliminar; **to cut a scene out of a film** suprimir una escena de una película; **to cut sb out of one's will** desheredar a alguien **3.** (*exclude*) **to cut sb out (of sth)** no contar con alguien (para algo); **you can cut me out!** *Brit* ¡no cuentes conmigo! **4.** *inf* (*stop*) dejar; **to ~ smoking** dejar de fumar; **~ all this nonsense** ¡déjate de tonterías!; **cut it out!** ¡basta ya! **II.** *vi* TECH (*engine*) pararse; (*machine*) apagarse

◆**cut short** *vt* acortar

◆**cut up I.** *vt* **1.** (*slice into pieces*) cortar en pedazos; (*meat*) trinchar **2.** (*hurt*) herir; **to be badly ~** tener heridas graves **3.** *Brit* (*cause to suffer*) **to be ~ (about sth)** estar sufriendo (por algo) **II.** *vi Am* (*misbehave*) hacer el tonto

cut-and-dried [ˌkʌtən'draɪd] *adj* **1.** (*fixed in advance*) decidido, -a de antemano **2.** (*not original*) preparado, -a de antemano; (*idea*) preconcebido, -a

cut-and-paste [ˌkʌtənd'peɪst] *adj a.* INFOR de cortar y pegar

cutback ['kʌtbæk] *n* 1.(*reduction*) reducción *f;* ~ **in expenditure** recorte *m* de los gastos 2. CINE flashback *m*

cute [kjuːt] *adj* 1.(*sweet: baby*) mono, -a *inf* 2.(*remark, idea*) ingenioso, -a

cut(e)y ['kjuːti, *Am:* -ți] <-ies> *n Am, inf s.* **cutie**

cuticle ['kjuːtɪkl, *Am:* -țə-] *n* cutícula *f*

cutie ['kjuːti, *Am:* -ți] *n,* **cutiepie** ['kjuː-tɪpaɪ, *Am:* -ți-] *n Am, inf* (*woman*) bombón *m;* (*child*) monada *f*

cutlass ['kʌtləs] <-es> *n* MIL alfanje *m*

cutlery ['kʌtləri] *n no pl* cubiertos *fpl*

cutlet ['kʌtlɪt] *n* chuleta *f*

cut-off ['kʌtɒf, *Am:* 'kʌțɑːf] *n* 1. TECH corte *m,* cierre *m;* ~ **date** fecha *f* límite; ~ **point** tope *m* 2. *Am* (*short cut*) atajo *m* **cut-out** *n* 1.(*design prepared for cutting*) recortable *m* 2. ELEC cortacircuitos *m inv* 3. TECH válvula *f* de escape **cut-price** *adj* a precio reducido **cut--rate** *adj* rebajado, -a **cut-sheet feed** *n* INFOR alimentación *f* por hojas sueltas

cutter ['kʌtəʳ, *Am:* 'kʌțɚ] *n* 1.(*tool which cuts*) cuchilla *f;* (*for metal*) cizalla *f;* (*for glass*) diamante *m* 2.(*person*) cortador(a) *m(f);* (*of precious stones*) tallista *mf* 3. NAUT cúter *m*

cut-throat ['kʌtθrəʊt, *Am:* -θroʊt] I. *n* 1.(*murderer*) asesino, -a *m, f* 2.(*razor*) navaja *f* barbera II. *adj* salvaje; (*competition*) feroz

cutting ['kʌtɪŋ, *Am:* 'kʌț-] I. *n* 1.(*act*) corte *m* 2.(*piece*) recorte *m;* (*of cloth*) retal *m* 3. BOT esqueje *m,* gajo *m Arg* 4.(*for road, railway*) zanja *f* 5. CINE montaje *m* II. *adj* (*blade*) cortante; *fig* (*remark, comment*) hiriente

cutting-edge *adj* puntero, -a

cuttlefish ['kʌtlfɪʃ, *Am:* 'kʌț-] *n inv* sepia *f*

CV [ˌsiː'viː] *n abbr of* **curriculum vitae** CV *m*

cwt. *abbr of* **hundredweight** *unidad de peso de 45.36 kg. en EE.UU. y de 50.80 kg. en el Reino Unido*

cyanide ['saɪənaɪd] *n no pl* cianuro *m*

cybercafé ['saɪbəˌkæfeɪ] *n* cibercafé *m*

cybercash ['saɪbəˌkæʃ] *no pl n* dinero *m* electrónico

cybernaut [ˌsaɪbə'nɔːt] *n* cibernauta *mf*

cybernetics [ˌsaɪbə'netɪks, *Am:* -bɚ'neț-] *n + sing vb* cibernética *f*

cybersex ['saɪbəseks, *Am:* -bɚ-] *n no pl* cibersexo *m* **cyberspace** *n no pl* ciberespacio *m*

cyclamen ['sɪkləmən, *Am:* 'saɪklə-] *n* ciclamen *m*

cycle¹ ['saɪkl] I. *n* bicicleta *f* II. *vi* ir en bicicleta

cycle² ['saɪkl] *n* 1.(*of life, seasons*) ciclo *m* 2. ASTR órbita *f*

cyclic ['saɪklɪk] *adj,* **cyclical** *adj* cíclico, -a

cycling *n no pl* SPORTS ciclismo *m;* ~ **shorts** pantalones *mpl* de ciclista

cyclist ['saɪklɪst] *n* SPORTS ciclista *mf*

cyclone ['saɪkləʊn, *Am:* -kloʊn] *n* METEO ciclón *m*

cygnet ['sɪgnɪt] *n* pollo *m* de cisne

cylinder ['sɪlɪndəʳ, *Am:* -dɚ] *n* 1. MAT, AUTO, TECH cilindro *m* 2.(*container: of gas*) bombona *f,* garrafa *f Arg, Urug;* (*of water*) tanque *m*

cylinder block *n* TECH bloque *m* de cilindros **cylinder capacity** *n no pl* TECH cilindrada *f* **cylinder head** *n* TECH culata *f*

cylindrical [sɪ'lɪndrɪkl] *adj* cilíndrico, -a

cymbal ['sɪmbl] *n* MUS platillo *m*

cynic ['sɪnɪk] I. *n* cínico, -a *m, f,* valemadrista *mf Méx* II. *adj* cínico, -a, valemadrista *Méx*

cynical ['sɪnɪkl] *adj* cínico, -a

cynicism ['sɪnɪsɪzəm] *n no pl* cinismo *m*

cypher ['saɪfəʳ, *Am:* -fɚ] *n s.* **cipher**

cypress ['saɪprəs] <-es> *n* ciprés *m*

Cypriot ['sɪprɪət] I. *adj* chipriota II. *n* chipriota *mf*

Cyprus ['saɪprəs] *n* GEO Chipre *m*

cyst [sɪst] *n* MED quiste *m*

cystitis [sɪs'taɪtɪs, *Am:* -țɪs] *n no pl* MED cistitis *f inv*

czar [zɑːʳ, *Am:* zɑːr] *n Am* zar *m*

czarina [zɑː'riːnə] *n Am* zarina *f*

Czech [tʃek] I. *n* 1.(*person*) checo, -a *m, f* 2.(*language*) checo *m* II. *adj* checo, -a

Czech Republic *n* República *f* Checa

D

D, d [diː] *n* 1.(*letter*) D, d *f;* ~ **for David** *Brit,* ~ **for dog** *Am* D de Dolores 2. MUS re *m*

d. 1. *abbr of* **day** d. 2. *abbr of* **diameter** d. 3. *abbr of* **died** murió

DA [ˌdiː'eɪ] *n Am abbr of* **District Attorney** fiscal *mf* del distrito

dab [dæb] I. <-bb-> *vt* tocar ligeramente; **he** ~**bed the stain from the dress** quitó la mancha frotando suavemente el vestido II. <-bb-> *vi* **to** ~ **at sth** dar ligeros toques a algo III. *n* 1.(*pat*) toque *m;* **to give sth a** ~ (**with sth**) dar a algo un toque (de algo) 2.(*tiny bit*) pizca *f;* (*of liquid*) gota *f;* **a** ~ **of paint** un toque de pintura IV. *adj* **he's a** ~ **hand at darts** es un hacha con los dardos

dabble ['dæbl] I. <-ling> *vi* 1.(*play in water*) chapotear 2.(*work*) **to** ~ **in sth** interesarse superficialmente por algo II. <-ling> *vt* salpicar; **to** ~ **sth** (**in sth**) mojar algo (en algo)

dad [dæd] *n inf* papá *m*

daddy ['dædi] *n childspeak, inf* papaíto *m,* tata *m AmL*

daddy-longlegs [ˌdædɪ'lɒŋlegz, *Am:* -'lɑːŋ] *n* 1. *Brit,* *inf* (*crane fly*) típula *f* 2. *Am* (*spider-like insect*) segador *m*

daemon ['diːmən] *n* demonio *m*

daffodil ['dæfədɪl] *n* narciso *m*

daft [dɑːft, *Am:* dæft] *adj Brit, inf* (*idiotic*)

tonto, -a; **to be ~ about sth/sb** estar loco por algo/alguien

dagger ['dægəʳ, *Am:* -ɚ] *n* (*small knife*) puñal *m* ►**to be at ~s** drawn odiarse a muerte; **to** look **~s at sb** fulminar a alguien con la mirada

dahlia ['deɪliə, *Am:* 'dæljə] *n* dalia *f*

El **Dáil** es la cámara baja del **Oireachtas**, parlamento de la **Irish Republic**. Tiene 166 diputados, elegidos democráticamente para un mandato de cinco años. La cámara alta, el **Seanad** (senado), consta de 60 senadores, de los cuales, 11 son nombrados por el **taoiseach** (primer ministro), 6 por las universidades irlandesas y otros 43 son nombrados de forma que todos los intereses profesionales, culturales y económicos estén representados.

---

daily ['deɪli] I. *adj* (*each day*) diario, -a; **~ dozen** ejercicios *mpl* matinales; **on a ~ basis** por días; **to earn one's ~ bread** *inf* ganarse el pan II. *adv* a diario; **twice ~** dos veces al día III. <-ies> *n* 1. PUBL diario *m* 2. *Brit, inf* (*cleaning person*) asistente, -a *m, f*

daintiness *n no pl* 1. (*delicacy*) delicadeza *f* 2. (*affectation*) remilgos *mpl*

dainty ['deɪnti, *Am:* -t̬i] <-ier, -iest> *adj* 1. (*delicate: flowers, painting*) delicado, -a; (*manners*) refinado, -a 2. (*delicious*) exquisito, -a 3. (*scrupulous*) escrupuloso, -a 4. (*affected*) remilgado, -a

dairy ['deəri, *Am:* 'deri] I. *n* 1. (*shop*) lechería *f* 2. *Am* (*farm*) vaquería *f*, tambo *m* Arg II. *adj* 1. (*made from milk*) lácteo, -a 2. (*producing milk*) lechero, -a; (*farm, herd*) de vacas; **~ industry** industria láctea

dairy cattle *npl* vacas *fpl* lecheras **dairyman** *n* lechero *m* **dairy produce** *n* productos *mpl* lácteos

dais ['deɪɪs] *n* ARCHIT tarima *f*

daisy ['deɪzi] <-ies> *n* margarita *f* ►**to fell as** fresh **as a ~** sentirse tan fresco como una rosa; **to** push up **(the) daisies** *inf* criar malvas

daisy wheel *n* margarita *f;* **~ printer** impresora *f* de margarita

dally ['dæli] <-ie-> *vi* 1. (*dawdle*) perder el tiempo; **to ~ about** entretenerse; **to ~ over sth** perder el tiempo haciendo algo 2. (*play*) jugar; **to ~ with sb/sth** coquetear con alguien/algo; **to ~ with an idea** dar vueltas a una idea

dam [dæm] I. *n* 1. (*barrier*) presa *f* 2. (*reservoir*) embalse *m* II. <-mm-> *vt* 1. (*river*) represar 2. (*emotions, feelings*) contener

damage ['dæmɪdʒ] I. *vt* 1. (*harm, hurt: building, objects*) dañar; (*environment, health, reputation*) perjudicar; **to be badly ~d** sufrir daños de consideración 2. (*spoil*) estropear II. *n no pl* 1. (*harm: to objects*) daño *m;* (*to pride, reputation*) perjuicio *m;* **to do ~ to sb/sth** hacer daño a alguien/algo; **to cause**

serious **~ to sb's reputation** perjudicar seriamente la reputación de alguien 2. *pl* LAW daños *mpl* y prejuicios ►**the ~ is** done el daño ya está hecho; **what's the ~?** *iron, inf* ¿cuánto le debo?

damage limitation *n no pl* POL *táctica para minimizar el impacto negativo de una decisión*

Damascus [də'mæskəs] *n* Damasco *m*

damask ['dæməsk] I. *n no pl* damasco *m* II. *adj* de damasco

dame [deɪm] *n* 1. *Brit* (*title of honor*) dama *f* (*título honorífico concedido a mujeres*) 2. *Am, inf* (*woman*) tía *f*, tipa *f* AmL 3. *Brit* THEAT *papel de anciana que representa un hombre*

damn [dæm] *inf* I. *interj* mierda II. *adj* 1. (*blasted*) maldito, -a 2. (*great*) **to be a ~ fool** ser tonto de remate; **to be a ~ shame** ser una verdadera lástima; **to be a ~ sight better** ser mucho mejor III. *vt* 1. (*curse, be irritated with*) maldecir; **~ him!** he's borrowed my bike without asking! ¡ese idiota se ha llevado mi bicicleta sin pedirme permiso! 2. REL condenar ►**well, I'll** be **~ed!** ¡mecachis!; **I'll** be **~ed if I know** que me cuelguen si lo sé IV. *adv* muy; **to be ~ lucky** tener una suerte increíble ►**~** all *Brit* absolutamente nada; **I know ~ all about it** no tengo ni idea de eso V. *n no pl* **I don't give a ~ what he says!** ¡me importa un comino lo que diga!

damnable ['dæmnəbl] *adj inf* deplorable

damnation [dæm'neɪʃən] I. *n no pl* condenación *f* II. *interj* maldición

damned I. *adj inf* 1. (*blasted*) maldito, -a 2. (*damnable*) detestable II. *npl* REL **the ~** los condenados

damning *adj* **~ evidence** prueba *f* irrecusable

damp [dæmp] I. *adj* húmedo, -a II. *n no pl, Brit, Aus* humedad *f* III. *vt* 1. (*wet slightly*) humedecer 2. *a. fig* PHYS, TECH amortiguar; MUS (*sound*) apagar 3. (*extinguish*) **to ~ (down)** (*flames, fire*) sofocar; (*enthusiasm*) enfriar; **to ~ down sb's spirits** desalentar a alguien

damp-course *n* ARCHIT membrana *f* aislante

dampen ['dæmpən] *vt* 1. (*make wet*) humedecer 2. (*lessen enthusiasm*) desanimar; **to ~ sb's enthusiasm** apagar el entusiasmo de alguien; **to ~ sb's expectations** frustrar las esperanzas de alguien 3. *a. fig* PHYS, TECH amortiguar; MUS (*sound*) apagar

damper ['dæmpəʳ, *Am:* -pɚ] *n inf* sordina *f;* **to put a ~ on things** aguar la fiesta *inf;* **to put a ~ on one's enthusiasm** apagar el entusiasmo de uno

dampness *n no pl* humedad *f*

dance [dɑːnts, *Am:* dænts] I. <-cing> *vi* 1. (*move around to music*) bailar; **to ~ to sth** bailar al compás de algo; **shall we ~?** ¿bailas?; **to go dancing** ir a bailar 2. (*move energetically*) saltar; **to ~ with joy** dar saltos de alegría 3. (*bob*) agitarse; **the daffodils were dancing in the breeze** los narcisos se mecían con la brisa ▶ to ~ **to sb's** <u>tune</u> estar a las órdenes de alguien *fig* II. <-cing> *vt* bailar; **to ~ the night away** bailar toda la noche ▶ to ~ **attendance on sb** desvivirse por alguien III. *n* baile *m;* **end-of-term** ~ baile de fin de curso; **to have a ~ with sb** bailar con alguien; **the band played a slow** ~ la orquesta tocaba una (canción) lenta

dance band *n* orquesta *f* de baile **dance music** *n no pl* música *f* de baile

dancer ['dɑːntsər, *Am:* 'dæntsɚ] *n* bailarín, -ina *m, f*

dancing *n no pl* baile *m*

dancing master *n* profesor, -a *m, f* de baile **dancing partner** *n* pareja *f* de baile **dancing shoes** *npl* zapatillas *fpl* de baile

dandelion ['dændɪlaɪən, *Am:* -də-] *n* diente *m* de león

dandruff ['dændrʌf, *Am:* -drəf] *n no pl* caspa *f*

dandy ['dændi] I. <-ies> *n* dandi *m* II. <-ier, -iest> *adj Am* estupendo, -a

Dane [deɪn] *n* danés, -esa *m, f*

danger ['deɪndʒər, *Am:* -dʒɚ] *n* 1. *no pl* (*peril*) peligro *m;* **to be in** ~ correr peligro; **there's no** ~ **of him knowing that** no hay peligro de que lo sepa; **a** ~ **to sth/sb** un peligro para algo/alguien; **to be out of** ~ estar fuera de peligro 2. (*perilous aspect*) riesgo *m;* **the ~s of sth** los peligros de algo

danger area *n* zona *f* peligrosa **danger money** *n Brit, Aus* plus *m* de peligrosidad

dangerous ['deɪndʒərəs] *adj* peligroso, -a, riesgoso, -a *AmL*

dangle ['dæŋgl] I. <-ling> *vi* colgar; **to ~ from** [*o* off] **sth** colgar de algo; **to ~ after sb** ir detrás de alguien II. <-ling> *vt* 1. (*cause to hang down*) hacer oscilar 2. (*tempt with*) **to ~ sth before sb** tentar a alguien con algo

Danish ['deɪnɪʃ] I. *adj* danés, -esa II. *n* 1. (*person*) danés, -esa *m, f* 2. LING danés *m*

dank [dæŋk] *adj* (*air, building*) húmedo, -a

Danube ['dænjuːb] *n* GEO Danubio *m*

dapper ['dæpər, *Am:* -ɚ] *adj* (*man*) atildado, -a; **a ~ appearance** un aspecto pulcro

dapple ['dæpl] *vt* motear

dare [deər, *Am:* der] I. <-ring> *vt* 1. (*risk doing*) **to ~ to do sth** atreverse a hacer algo; **not ~ to do sth** no atreverse a hacer algo; **I ~ not go there** no me atrevo a ir 2. (*face*) desafiar; **to ~ sb** (**to do sth**) retar a alguien (a hacer algo) ▶ <u>don't</u> **you ~!** ¡ni se te ocurra!; **I ~** <u>say</u> me lo imagino; **how** ~ **you speak to me like that?** ¿cómo se atreve a hablarme de esa forma? II. <-ring> *vi* atreverse; **just you ~!** ¡atrévete y verás! III. *n* desafío *m;* **to take a ~** aceptar un reto

dare-devil ['deə‚devəl, *Am:* 'der-] *inf* I. *n* atrevido, -a *m, f* II. *adj* temerario, -a

daring ['deərɪŋ, *Am:* 'derɪŋ] I. *adj* 1. (*courageous*) temerario, -a 2. (*provocative: dress*) atrevido, -a II. *n no pl* osadía *f*

dark [dɑːk, *Am:* dɑːrk] I. *adj* 1. (*without

light, black) oscuro, -a; ~ **blue** azul oscuro; ~ **chocolate** *Am, Aus* chocolate *m* sin leche 2. (*not pale: complexion, hair*) moreno, -a 3. (*tragic, depressing*) sombrío, -a; **a** ~ **chapter** un capítulo oscuro; **to have a** ~ **side** tener un lado oscuro; **to look on the** ~ **side of things** ver el lado malo de las cosas 4. (*bad, mean, evil*) tenebroso, -a 5. (*unknown, secret*) oculto, -a; **the** ~ **side of sth** la cara oculta de algo II. *n no pl* 1. (*darkness*) oscuridad *f;* **to be in the** ~ estar a oscuras; **to be afraid of the** ~ tener miedo de la oscuridad 2. **at** ~ al caer la noche; **to do sth before/after** ~ hacer algo antes/después de que anochezca ▶ **to** <u>keep</u> **sb in the** ~ **about sth** ocultar algo a alguien

Dark Ages *npl* HIST **the** ~ la Alta Edad Media; *fig* la prehistoria **Dark Continent** *n* GEO, HIST **the** ~ el Continente Negro

darken ['dɑːkən, *Am:* 'dɑːr-] I. *vi* oscurecerse; (*sky*) nublarse; *fig* ensombrecerse II. *vt* (*make darker*) oscurecer; *fig* ensombrecer

dark horse *n* SPORTS, POL 1. *Brit, Aus* (*unknown candidate*) competidor(a) *m(f)* desconocido 2. *Am* (*unexpected victor*) ganador(a) *m(f)* sorpresa

darkly *adv* 1. (*mysteriously*) misteriosamente 2. (*gloomily*) tristemente; **to look at sb** ~ mirar a alguien con aire sombrío

darkness *n no pl* 1. (*dark*) oscuridad *f;* **to plunge sth into** ~ sumir algo en la oscuridad 2. *fig* (*lack of knowledge*) tinieblas *fpl*

darkroom ['dɑːkrʊm, *Am:* 'dɑːrkruːm] *n* PHOT cámara *f* oscura

dark-skinned *adj* de piel oscura

darling ['dɑːlɪŋ, *Am:* 'dɑːr-] I. *n* 1. (*beloved person*) amor *m* 2. (*form of address*) cariño *mf* II. *adj* 1. (*beloved*) querido, -a; **my** ~ **John** mi querido John 2. (*cute*) mono, -a; **a** ~ **little room** una monada de habitación

darn[1] [dɑːn, *Am:* dɑːrn] I. *vt* zurcir II. *n* zurcido *m*

darn[2] [dɑːn, *Am:* dɑːrn] *vt inf* ~ **it!** ¡maldita sea!; **I'll be ~ed if I'll do it!** ¡no lo hago ni que me maten!

darning *n no pl* zurcido *m*

darning needle *n* aguja *f* de zurcir

dart [dɑːt, *Am:* dɑːrt] I. *n* 1. (*type of weapon*) dardo *m;* **to fire a** ~ **at sb/sth** disparar un dardo a alguien/algo 2. *pl* (*pub game*) dardos *mpl;* **to play ~s** jugar a los dardos; **a game of ~s** una partida de dardos 3. (*quick run*) movimiento *m* rápido; **to make a** ~ **for sb/sth** precipitarse hacia alguien/algo 4. FASHION pinza *f* II. *vi* **to** ~ (**for sth**) precipitarse (hacia algo); **to** ~ **away** salir disparado; ~**ed behind the sofa** corrí a esconderme detrás del sofá III. *vt* 1. (*send quickly: look*) lanzar 2. (*stick out quickly*) sacar; **the lizard** ~**ed out its tongue** la lagartija disparó la lengua

dartboard ['dɑːtbɔːd, *Am:* 'dɑːrtbɔːrd] *n* diana *f*

dash [dæʃ] I. <-es> *n* 1. (*rush*) carrera *f;* **to make a** ~ **for sth** precipitarse hacia; **to make a** ~

for it huir precipitadamente **2.** (*pinch*) poquito *m;* (*of salt*) pizca *f;* **a** ~ **of colour** una nota de color **3.** TYPO guión *m* **4.** (*flair*) brío *m* **5.** (*Morse*) raya *f* **II.** *vi* **1.** (*hurry*) precipitarse **2.** (*slam into*) **to** ~ **against sth** romperse contra algo **III.** *vt* **1.** (*shatter*) romper **2.** (*hopes*) defraudar

dashboard ['dæʃbɔːd, *Am:* -bɔːrd] *n* salpicadero *m*

dashing ['dæʃɪŋ] *adj* gallardo, -a

dastardly ['dæstədli, *Am:* 'dæstɚdli] *adj liter* (*crime, act*) ruin

DAT [dæt] *n abbr of* digital audio tape DAT *m*

data ['deɪtə, *Am:* 'deɪt̬ə] *npl + sing/pl vb a.* INFOR datos *mpl*

data bank *n* banco *m* de datos **database** *n* base *f* de datos **data file** *n* archivo *m* de datos **dataglove** *n* INFOR guante *m* de datos **data processing** *n no pl* procesamiento *m* de datos **data protection** *n no pl, Brit* protección *m* de datos

date¹ [deɪt] **I.** *n* **1.** (*calendar day*) fecha *f;* **expiry** ~, **expiration** ~ *Am* fecha *f* de vencimiento; **what** ~ **is it today?** ¿cuál es la fecha de hoy?; **to be out of** ~ FASHION estar pasado de moda; GASTR estar caducado **2.** (*appointment*) cita *f;* **to have a** ~ tener una cita; **to make a** ~ **with sb** quedar con alguien **3.** FIN plazo *f* **4.** *Am, inf* (*person*) novio, -a *m, f* **II.** *vt* **1.** (*recognize age of*) fechar; **to** ~ **sth at …** fechar algo en… **2.** (*give age to*) asignar una fecha a algo **3.** *Am, inf* (*have relationship with*) **to** ~ **sb** salir con alguien **III.** *vi* **1.** (*go back to*) **to** ~ **back to** remontarse a **2.** (*go out of fashion*) pasar de moda

date² [deɪt] *n* (*fruit*) dátil *m;* (*tree*) palmera *f* datilera

dated ['deɪtɪd, *Am:* -t̬ɪd] *adj* anticuado, -a

dateline ['deɪtlaɪn] *n* línea *f* de cambio de fecha

date-stamp ['deɪtstæmp] *n* fechador *m*

dative ['deɪtɪv, *Am:* -t̬ɪv] **I.** *n no pl* dativo; **to be in the** ~ estar en dativo **II.** *adj* dativo, -a

daub [dɔːb, *Am:* dɑːb] **I.** *vt* **1.** (*smear*) **to** ~ **sth with sth** manchar algo de algo **2.** (*paint unskilfully*) pintarrajear **II.** *n* **1.** (*smear*) mancha *f* **2.** (*painting*) pintarrajo *m*

daughter ['dɔːtəʳ, *Am:* 'dɑːt̬ɚ] *n* hija *f*

daughter-in-law ['dɔːtəʳɪnlɔː, *Am:* 'dɑː-t̬ɚɪnlɑː] <daughters-in-law> *n* nuera *f*

daunt [dɔːnt, *Am:* dɑːnt] *vt* **1.** (*intimidate*) intimidar; **nothing** ~**ed** *Brit* sin inmutarse **2.** (*discourage*) desalentar

daunting *adj* amedrentador(a)

dauntless ['dɔːntləs, *Am:* 'dɑːnt-] *adj* intrépido, -a

dawdle ['dɔːdl, *Am:* 'dɑː-] *vi* holgazanear

dawdler ['dɔːdləʳ, *Am:* 'dɑːdlɚ] *n* persona *f* lenta

dawn [dɔːn, *Am:* dɑːn] **I.** *n* **1.** *no pl* alba *m,* amanezca *f Méx;* **from** ~ **to dusk** de sol a sol; **at** ~ al alba **2.** *fig* (*beginning*) nacimiento *m*

II. *vi* amanecer; *fig* (*era*) nacer; **it** ~**ed on him that …** cayó en la cuenta de que…

day [deɪ] *n* **1.** día *m;* ~ **after** ~ día tras día; ~ **by** ~ día a día; **all** ~ (**long**) todo el día; **any** ~ **now** cualquier día de estos; **by** ~ de día; **by the** ~ diariamente; **for a few** ~**s** durante algunos días; **from that** ~ **on(wards)** desde ese día; **from this** ~ **forth** de aquí en adelante; **from one** ~ **to the next** de un día para otro; **one** ~ algún día; **two** ~**s ago** hace dos días; **the** ~ **before yesterday** anteayer; **the** ~ **after tomorrow** pasado mañana; **in the (good) old** ~**s** en los buenos tiempos; **the examination is ten** ~**s from now** el examen es dentro de diez días **2.** (*working period*) jornada *f;* **to take a** ~ **off** tomarse un día de descanso ▶ **in this** ~ **and age** en estos tiempos nuestros; **Day of** Judgement día *m* del Juicio Final; **to have seen better** ~**s** haber conocido tiempos mejores; **to call it a** ~ dejarlo para otro día; **to carry the** ~ salir victorioso; ~ **in** ~ **out** un día sí y otro también

daybreak ['deɪbreɪk] *n no pl* alba *m*

daycare ['deɪkeəʳ] *n* **1.** (*for children*) servicio *m* de guardería **2.** (*for old people*) atención *f* geriátrica de día

daydream ['deɪdriːm] **I.** *vi* soñar despierto **II.** *n* ensueño *m*

daylight ['deɪlaɪt] *n no pl* luz *f* del día; **in broad** ~ a plena luz del día ▶ **to scare the living** ~**s out of sb** *inf* dar un susto de muerte a alguien **day nursery** <-ies> *n* guardería *f* **day return** *n Brit* billete *m* de ida y vuelta **day shift** *n* turno *m* de día

daytime ['deɪtaɪm] *n* día *m;* **in the** ~ de día

day-to-day [ˌdeɪtə'deɪ, *Am:* -t̬ə-] *adj* cotidiano, -a **day trip** *n* excursión *f* (de un día)

daze [deɪz] **I.** *n no pl* aturdimiento *m;* **to be in a** ~ estar aturdido **II.** *vt* aturdir

dazed *adj* aturdido, -a

dazzle ['dæzl] **I.** *vt* deslumbrar **II.** *n no pl* deslumbramiento *m*

dazzled *adj* deslumbrado, -a

dB *n abbr of* decibel dB

DC [ˌdiː'siː] *n* **1.** *abbr of* direct current CC **2.** *abbr of* District Commissioner comisario, -a *m, f* de distrito **3.** *abbr of* District of Colombia DC *m*

DD [ˌdiː'diː] *n abbr of* Doctor of Divinity Dr. en Teología

D-Day ['diːdeɪ] *n* el día D

DDT [ˌdiːdiː'tiː] *n no pl abbr of* dichloro-diphenyl-trichloroethane DDT *m*

deacon ['diːkən] *n* diácono *m*

deaconess [ˌdiːkə'nes, *Am:* 'diːkənəs] *n* diaconisa *f*

dead [ded] **I.** *adj* **1.** (*no longer alive*) muerto, -a; **to be** ~ **on arrival** ingresar cadáver (en el hospital) **2.** (*inactive*) parado, -a; (*fire*) apagado, -a **3.** (*quiet, boring*) muerto, -a; (*town*) desierto, -a **4.** (*numb*) dormido, -a **5.** (*silence*) profundo, -a; **to be a** ~ **loss** ser un desastre total; **to come to a** ~ **stop** pararse en seco ▶ **as**

~ **as a doornail** muerto y bien muerto; **to be a ~ duck** ser un fracaso seguro; ~ **men tell no tales** *Am, prov* los muertos no hablan; **she wouldn't be seen ~ wearing that** *inf* por nada del mundo se pondría eso **II.** *n* the ~ los muertos ▸**in the ~ of night/winter** en plena noche/pleno invierno **III.** *adv* **1.** *inf* (*totally*) completamente; ~ **beat** completamente rendido; **to be ~ set against sth** estar completamente en contra de algo; **to be ~ set on sth** estar completamente decidido a algo **2.** (*directly*) justo; ~ **ahead** justo al frente

deadbeat [ˌded'biːt] *adj Am, inf* rendido, -a

dead centre *n* punto *m* muerto

deaden ['dedən] *vt* (*pain*) aliviar; (*noise*) amortiguar

dead-end [ˌded'end] **I.** *n* callejón *m* sin salida **II.** *adj* sin salida; ~ **job** trabajo *m* sin porvenir

dead heat *n* empate *m*

deadline ['dedlaɪn] *n* plazo *m* límite; **to meet/to miss the ~** cumplir/incumplir el plazo

deadlock ['dedlɒk, *Am:* -laːk] *n no pl* punto *m* muerto *inv;* **to reach ~** llegar a un punto muerto

deadly ['dedli] **I.** <-ier, -iest> *adj* **1.** (*capable of killing*) mortal **2.** *inf* (*very boring*) aburridísimo, -a **II.** <-ier, -iest> *adv* extremadamente; ~ **pale** blanco como la cera

deadpan ['dedpæn] *adj* inexpresivo, -a

Dead Sea *n* Mar *m* Muerto

deadwood ['dedwʊd] *n no pl* **1.** (*branch, tree*) madera *f* seca **2.** *inf* (*person*) persona *f* inútil; (*people*) gente *f* inútil; (*thing*) cosa *f* inútil

deaf [def] **I.** *adj* sordo, -a; ~ **in one ear** sordo de un oído; **to go ~** volverse sordo; **to be ~ to sth** hacer oídos sordos a algo **II.** *npl* the ~ los sordos

deaf aid *n* audífono *m*

deafen ['defən] *vt* ensordecer

deafening *adj* ensordecedor(a)

deaf-mute [ˌdef'mjuːt] *n* sordomudo, -a *m, f*

deafness *n no pl* sordera *f*

deal[1] [diːl] *n no pl* (*large amount*) cantidad *f;* **a great ~** una gran cantidad; **a great ~ of effort** mucho esfuerzo

deal[2] [diːl] <dealt, dealt> **I.** *n* **1.** COM negocio *m;* **a big ~** un negocio importante **2.** (*agreement*) pacto *m;* **to do a ~** (**with sb**) hacer un trato (con alguien) **3.** GAMES (*of cards*) reparto *m;* **it's your ~** te toca dar a ti ▸**big ~!** *iron, inf* ¡gran cosa!; **it's no big ~!** *inf* ¡no es para tanto! **II.** *vi* **1.** (*do business*) negociar; **to ~ with sb** hacer negocios con alguien; **to ~ in sth** comerciar con algo **2.** GAMES repartir **III.** *vt* **1.** GAMES (*cards*) repartir **2.** (*give*) dar; **to ~ sb a blow** propinar un golpe a alguien

◆**deal out** *vt* repartir

◆**deal with** *vt* **1.** (*take care of: problem*) ocuparse de; (*person*) tratar con **2.** (*be about: book*) tratar de **3.** (*punish*) castigar

dealer ['diːlə*r*, *Am:* -lə*r*] *n* **1.** COM negociante *mf;* **drug ~** traficante *mf* de drogas; **he's a ~ in antiquities** es un marchante de antiguedades **2.** GAMES (*in cards*) mano *mf*

dealership ['diːləʃɪp, *Am:* -lə*r*-] *n* COM concesión *f*

dealing ['diːlɪŋ] *n* **1.** COM comercio *m* **2.** *pl* FIN transacciones *fpl* **3.** *pl* (*relations*) relaciones *fpl;* **to have ~s with sb** tratar con alguien **4.** GAMES reparto *m*

dealt [delt] *pt, pp of* **deal**

dean [diːn] *n* **1.** UNIV decano, -a *m, f* **2.** REL deán *m*

dear [dɪə*r*, *Am:* dɪr] **I.** *adj* **1.** (*much loved*) querido, -a; **it is ~ to me** le tengo mucho cariño **2.** (*in letters*) estimado, -a; **Dear Sarah** Querida Sarah; **Dear Sir** Muy señor mío **3.** (*expensive*) caro, -a **II.** *adv* caro **III.** *interj inf* **oh ~!** ¡Dios mío! **IV.** *n* encanto *m;* **she is a ~** es encantadora

dearly *adv* **1.** mucho; **I love her ~** la quiero mucho **2.** *fig* caro; **he paid ~ for his success** su éxito le costó caro

dearness *n no pl* alto precio *m*

dearth [dɜːθ, *Am:* dɜːrθ] *n no pl* escasez *f;* **to suffer from a ~ of sth** sufrir la escasez de algo

deary *n,* **dearie** ['dɪəri, *Am:* 'dɪri] *n inf* querido, -a *m, f*

death [deθ] *n* muerte *f;* **frightened to ~** muerto de miedo; **to die a natural ~** morir de muerte natural; **to put sb to ~** matar a alguien; **to catch one's ~ of cold** coger una gripe de muerte ▸**to be at ~'s door** estar a las puertas de la muerte; **to be bored to ~ with sth** morirse de aburrimiento con algo; **to dice with ~** jugar con la muerte; **to laugh oneself to ~** morirse de la risa

deathbed ['deθbed] *n* lecho *m* de muerte

death-blow *n* golpe *m* mortal **death-certificate** *n* certificado *m* de defunción **death duties** *npl Brit, inf* impuesto *m* de sucesiones

deathly ['deθli] **I.** *adv* de muerte; ~ **pale** pálido como un muerto **II.** *adj* mortífero, -a

death penalty *n* pena *f* de muerte **death-rate** *n* tasa *f* de mortalidad **death row** *n Am* corredor *m* de la muerte **death sentence** *n* pena *f* de muerte **death squad** *n* escuadrón *m* de la muerte **death trap** *n* trampa *f* mortal

debacle [deɪ'baːkl, *Am:* dɪ-] *n* debacle *f*

debar [dɪ'baː*r*, *Am:* -'baːr] <-rr-> *vt* excluir; **to ~ sb from doing sth** privar a alguien de hacer algo

debase [dɪ'beɪs] *vt* (*reduce in quality or value*) degradar; ECON devaluar

debatable [dɪ'beɪtəbl, *Am:* dɪ'beɪtə-] *adj* discutible

debate [dɪ'beɪt] **I.** *n no pl* debate *m;* **a ~ over sth** un debate sobre algo **II.** *vt* debatir **III.** *vi* debatir; **to ~ about sth** debatir acerca de algo

debater [dɪ'beɪtə*r*, *Am:* -tə*r*] *n* polemista *mf*

debauch [dɪ'bɔːtʃ, *Am:* -'baːtʃ] **I.** *vt* corromper **II.** *n* orgía *f*

debauchery [dɪ'bɔːtʃəri, Am: 'bɑː-] n no pl vicio m

debenture [dɪ'bentʃəʳ, Am: -'bentʃə˞] n Brit FIN obligación f

debilitate [dɪ'bɪlɪteɪt] vt debilitar

debilitating adj debilitante

debility [dɪ'bɪləti, Am: dɪ'bɪləţi] n no pl debilidad f

debit ['debɪt] I. n débito m; **to be in ~** estar en números rojos II. vt **the bank ~ed the rent to my account** el banco cargó la renta a mi cuenta bancaria

debit card n tarjeta f de débito **debit column** n, **debit-side** n debe m

debonair [ˌdebə'neəʳ, Am: -'ner] adj form refinado, -a

debris ['deɪbriː, Am: də'briː] n no pl escombros mpl

debt [det] n deuda f; **to be in ~** tener deudas; **to pay off a ~** pagar una deuda; **to be out of ~** estar libre de deudas

debt-collector n cobrador(a) m(f) de deudas

debtor ['detəʳ, Am: 'deţə˞] n deudor(a) m(f)

debtor country n, **debtor nation** n país m deudor

debt servicing n no pl pago m de una deuda

debug [ˌdiː'bʌg] <-gg-> vt INFOR depurar

debunk [diː'bʌŋk] vt desacreditar

debut ['deɪbjuː, Am: -'-] I. n 1. (first public appearance) debut m; **to make one's ~** debutar 2. (introduction into society) presentación en sociedad II. vi debutar; **to ~ in/as sth** debutar en/como algo

debutante ['debjuːtɑːnt] n (young woman who is introduced into society) debutante f; **a ~'s ball** un baile de debutantes

decade ['dekeɪd] n década f

decadence ['dekədəns] n no pl decadencia f

decadent ['dekədənt] adj decadente

decaf ['diːkæf] adj, n inf abbr of **decaffeinated** descafeinado

decaffeinated [ˌdiː'kæfɪneɪtɪd] I. adj descafeinado, -a II. n inf descafeinado m

decamp [dɪ'kæmp] vi inf (leave secretly) fugarse, rajarse AmL; (run away) huir; (set off) irse

decant [dɪ'kænt] vt decantar

decanter [dɪ'kæntəʳ, Am: -ţə˞] n licorera f

decapitate [dɪ'kæpɪteɪt] vt decapitar

decapitation [dɪˌkæpɪ'teɪʃən] n no pl decapitación f

decathlete [dɪ'kæθliːt] n decatleta mf

decathlon [dɪ'kæθlən, Am: -lɑːn] n decatlón m

decay [dɪ'keɪ] I. n no pl (of food) descomposición f; (of building, intellect) deterioro m; (dental) caries f inv; (of civilization) decadencia f; **to be in an advanced state of ~** estar en avanzado estado de descomposición II. vi (food) pudrirse; (building, intellect) deteriorarse; (teeth) cariarse III. vt descomponer

decease [dɪ'siːs] n no pl fallecimiento m

deceased [dɪ'siːst] I. n difunto, -a m, f II. adj difunto, -a

deceit [dɪ'siːt] n engaño m, transa f Méx

deceitful [dɪ'siːtfəl] adj engañoso, -a

deceive [dɪ'siːv] vt engañar; **to ~ oneself** engañarse a sí mismo ▶**appearances ~** prov las apariencias engañan prov

deceiver [dɪ'siːvəʳ, Am: -ə˞] n impostor(a) m(f)

decelerate [diː'seləreɪt] I. vi desacelerarse; (vehicle, driver) aminorar la velocidad II. vt desacelerar

December [dɪ'sembəʳ, Am: -bə˞] n diciembre m; s. a. **April**

decency ['diːsəntsi] n 1. no pl (respectability) decencia f 2. pl (approved behaviour) buenas costumbres fpl

decent ['diːsənt] adj 1. (socially acceptable) decente; **are you ~?** iron ¿estás visible? 2. inf (kind) amable

decentralization [diːˌsentrəlaɪ'zeɪʃən, Am: -ɪ'-] n no pl descentralización f

decentralize [diː'sentrəlaɪz] vt descentralizar

decentralized adj descentralizado, -a

deception [dɪ'sepʃən] n engaño m; **to practise ~ on sb** engañar a alguien

deceptive [dɪ'septɪv] adj engañoso, -a

decibel ['desɪbel] n decibel(io) m

decide [dɪ'saɪd] I. vi decidirse; **to ~ on sth** decidirse [o optar] por algo II. vt decidir

decided [dɪ'saɪdɪd] adj (person, manner) decidido, -a; (improvement) indudable

deciduous [dɪ'sɪdjuəs, Am: -'sɪdʒʊ-] adj caducifolio, -a

decimal ['desɪml] I. n decimal m II. adj decimal

decimalize ['desɪməlaɪz] vt aplicar el sistema decimal a

decimate ['desɪmeɪt] vt diezmar

decipher [dɪ'saɪfəʳ, Am: -fə˞] vt descifrar

decision [dɪ'sɪʒən] n 1. (choice, resolution) decisión f; **to make a ~** tomar una decisión 2. LAW fallo m 3. no pl (resoluteness) resolución f

decision-making [dɪ'sɪʒənˌmeɪkɪŋ] n no pl **~ process** proceso m decisorio

decisive [dɪ'saɪsɪv] adj (factor) decisivo, -a; (manner) categórico, -a

deck [dek] I. n 1. (of ship) cubierta f; **to go below ~s** ir bajo cubierta 2. (of bus) piso m 3. Am (cards) baraja f 4. MUS, ELEC platina f ▶**to clear the ~s** prepararse para algo; **to hit the ~** inf caerse al suelo II. vt ~ **out** adornar; **to be ~ed (out) in one's best** ir de tiros largos

deckchair ['dektʃeəʳ, Am: -tʃer] n tumbona f, reposera f Arg

declaim [dɪ'kleɪm] vi, vt declamar

declamation [ˌdeklə'meɪʃən] n no pl declamación f

declamatory [dɪ'klæmətəri, Am: dɪ'klæmətɔːri] adj form declamatorio, -a

declaration [ˌdeklə'reɪʃən] n declaración f

declare [dɪ'kleəʳ, Am: dɪ'kler] I. vt declarar; to ~ war on sb declarar la guerra a alguien; to ~ goods declarar mercancías; to ~ oneself (to be) bankrupt declararse en bancarrota II. vi declararse

decline [dɪ'klaɪn] I. vi 1. (price) bajar; (power, influence) disminuir; (civilization) decaer; to ~ in value disminuir de valor 2. MED debilitarse 3. (refuse) rehusar II. n no pl 1. (of price, power, influence) disminución f; (of civilization) decadencia f; to be in ~ estar en declive 2. MED debilitación f III. vt 1. (refuse) rehusar 2. LING declinar

declutch [ˌdiː'klʌtʃ] vi desembragar

decode [ˌdiː'kəʊd, Am: -'koʊd] vi, vt descodificar

decoder n descodificador m

decolonization [ˌdiːˌkɒlɪnaɪ'zeɪʃən, Am: -ˌkɑːlənɪ'-] n no pl descolonización f

decompose [ˌdiːkəm'pəʊz, Am: -'poʊz] I. vi descomponerse II. vt descomponer

decomposition [ˌdiːkɒmpə'zɪʃən, Am: ˌdiːkɑːm-] n no pl descomposición f

decompress [ˌdiːkəm'pres] vt descomprimir

decompression [ˌdiːkəm'preʃən] n no pl descompresión f

decompression chamber n cámara f de descompresión

decontaminate [ˌdiːkən'tæmɪneɪt] vt descontaminar

decontamination [ˌdiːkənˌtæmɪ'neɪʃən] n no pl descontaminación f

decontrol [ˌdiːkən'trəʊl, Am: -'troʊl] <-ll-> vt liberalizar

decor ['deɪkɔːʳ, Am: 'deɪkɔːr] n decorado m

decorate ['dekəreɪt] I. vt 1. (adorn) decorar 2. (add new paint) pintar; (wallpaper) empapelar 3. (honour) condecorar II. vi 1. (add new paint) pintar 2. (wallpaper) empapelar

decoration [ˌdekə'reɪʃən] n 1. (ornament) adorno m 2. (act of decorating) decoración f 3. (medal) condecoración f

decorative ['dekərətɪv, Am: -t̬ɪv] adj decorativo, -a; just sit there and look ~ iron siéntate y estate calladito

decorator ['dekəreɪtəʳ, Am: -t̬ɚ] n Brit 1. (one who plans interior design) decorador(a) m(f) 2. (painter) pintor(a) m(f) 3. (paperhanger) empapelador(a) m(f)

decorous ['dekərəs, Am: -əs] adj form decoroso, -a

decorum [dɪ'kɔːrəm] n no pl, form decoro m

decoy ['diːkɔɪ] I. n a. fig señuelo m; to act as a ~ hacer de señuelo II. vt atraer con un señuelo

decrease [dɪ'kriːs, Am: 'diːkriːs] I. vi disminuir; (prices) bajar II. vt disminuir III. n disminución f

decree [dɪ'kriː] I. n 1. (command) decreto m; to issue a ~ promulgar un decreto 2. LAW sentencia f II. vt decretar

decree nisi [dɪ'kriː 'naɪsaɪ] n sentencia f provisional de divorcio

decrepit [dɪ'krepɪt] adj (in bad condition) deteriorado, -a; (house) destartalado, -a; (person) decrépito, -a

decrepitude [dɪ'krepɪtjuːd, Am: -tuːd] n no pl deterioro m; (of person) decrepitud f

decriminalize [ˌdiː'krɪmɪnəlaɪz] vt despenalizar

decry [dɪ'kraɪ] vt form censurar

dedicate ['dedɪkeɪt] vt 1. (devote) to ~ oneself to sth dedicarse a algo 2. (do in sb's honour) to ~ sth to sb dedicar algo a alguien 3. form (formally open) inaugurar; (a church) dedicar

dedicated adj dedicado, -a

dedication [ˌdedɪ'keɪʃən] n 1. (devotion) dedicación f 2. (inscription) dedicatoria f 3. (official opening) inauguración f; (of a church) dedicación f

deduce [dɪ'djuːs, Am: dɪ'duːs] vt (infer) deducir

deducible [dɪ'djuːsəbl, Am: dɪ'duː-] adj deducible

deduct [dɪ'dʌkt] vt deducir

deductable adj Aus, **deductible** adj deducible

deduction [dɪ'dʌkʃən] n deducción f; £1000 after ~s 1000 libras netas

deductive [dɪ'dʌktɪv] adj deductivo, -a

deed [diːd] n 1. (act) acto m; (remarkable feat) hazaña f; in word and ~ de palabra y obra 2. LAW escritura f

deed poll n to do sth by ~ hacer algo por escritura unilateral

deem [diːm] vt form considerar; he was ~ed to be of sound mind se juzgó que estaba en plenas facultades mentales

deep [diːp] I. adj 1. (not shallow) profundo, -a 2. (full) to take a ~ breath respirar hondo 3. (extending back) the wardrobe is 60 cm ~ el armario tiene 60 cm de fondo 4. (extreme: regret, disappointment) gran(de); in ~ mourning de luto riguroso; to be in ~ trouble estar metido en un buen lío inf 5. (absorbed by) to be in ~ thought estar absorto en sus pensamientos 6. inf (hard to understand) difícil de entender 7. (low in pitch) grave 8. (dark) oscuro, -a; ~ red rojo intenso II. adv 1. (far down) to dig ~ fig cavar hondo; ~ in the forest en lo más profundo del bosque 2. (extremely) mucho; to be ~ in debt estar cargado de deudas ▶to go ~ into sth ahondar en algo III. n liter the ~ el piélago; in the ~ of winter en lo más crudo del invierno

deepen ['diːpən] I. vt 1. (make deeper) hacer más profundo 2. (increase) aumentar; (knowledge) ampliar II. vi 1. (become deeper) hacerse más profundo 2. (increase) aumentar 3. (become lower in pitch) volverse grave 4. (color) intensificarse

deep-freeze n congelador m **deep-frozen** adj ultracongelado, -a **deep-fry** vt freir en aceite abundante

deeply *adv* profundamente; (*breathe*) hondo; **to be ~ interested in sth** sentir un profundo interés por algo

deepness *n* profundidad *f*

deep-rooted [ˌdiːpˈruːtɪd, *Am:* -t̬ɪd] *adj* **1.** (*well-established*) profundamente arraigado, -a **2.** BOT de raíces profundas **deep-sea animal** *n* animal *m* de las profundidades marinas **deep-seated** *adj* profundamente arraigado, -a; (*hatred*) de raíces profundas **deep space** *n* AVIAT espacio *m* interplanetario

deer [dɪəʳ, *Am:* dɪr] *n inv* ciervo *m*

deerstalker [ˈdɪəˌstɔːkəʳ, *Am:* ˈdɪrˌstɔːkɚ] *n* gorra *f* de cazador

deface [dɪˈfeɪs] *vt* (*damage the appearance of*) afear; (*a wall*) pintarrajear; (*a stamp*) matar

defamation [ˌdefəˈmeɪʃən] *n no pl* difamación *f*

defamatory [dɪˈfæmətəri, *Am:* -tɔːri] *adj* difamatorio, -a

defame [dɪˈfeɪm] *vt* difamar

default [dɪˈfɔːlt, *Am:* dɪˈfɑːlt] **I.** *vi* **1.** FIN no pagar; **to ~ on a payment** estar en mora en un pago **2.** LAW estar en rebeldía **3.** SPORTS no presentarse **II.** *n* **1.** omisión *f*; FIN mora *f* **2.** LAW **judgement by ~** sentencia *f* en rebeldía; **to win a case by ~** ganar un caso en rebeldía del adversario **3.** *no pl* (*pre-selected option*) **by ~** por defecto **4.** *form* (*absence*) **in ~ of any better alternative ...** a falta de una alternativa mejor...

default value *n* INFOR valor *m* por defecto

defeat [dɪˈfiːt] **I.** *vt* derrotar; (*hopes*) frustrar; (*a proposal*) rechazar **II.** *n* **1.** (*by an opponent*) derrota *f*; **to admit ~** darse por vencido **2.** (*of plans*) fracaso *m*

defeatism [dɪˈfiːtɪzəm, *Am:* dɪˈfiːt̬ɪ-] *n* derrotismo *m*

defeatist *adj* derrotista

defecate [ˈdefəkeɪt] *vi* MED defecar

defecation [ˌdefəˈkeɪʃən] *n no pl* MED defecación *f*

defect[1] [ˈdiːfekt] *n a.* TECH, MED defecto *m*

defect[2] [dɪˈfekt] *vi* POL (*from a country*) huir; (*from the army*) desertar

defection [dɪˈfekʃən] *n* defección *f*; MIL deserción *f*

defective [dɪˈfektɪv] *adj* defectuoso, -a; **mentally ~** deficiente *mf* mental

defence [dɪˈfents] *n Aus, Brit* **1.** defensa *f*; **to rush to sb's ~** acudir en defensa de alguien **2.** LAW **the ~** la defensa; **counsel for the ~** abogado(a) *m(f)* defensor(a) **3.** SPORTS **to play in** [*o* **on** *Am*] **~** jugar en la defensa **4.** MED **the body's ~s** las defensas del organismo **5.** PSYCH **~ mechanism** mecanismo *m* de defensa

defenceless [dɪˈfentsləs] *adj* indefenso, -a

defence minister *n* ministro, -a *m, f* de defensa

defend [dɪˈfend] **I.** *vt* **1.** (*protect*) defender; **to ~ oneself (from sb/sth)** defenderse (de al-

guien/algo) **2.** *a.* LAW defender **3.** SPORTS (*a title*) defender **II.** *vi* **1.** LAW **who is ~ing in that case?** ¿quién actúa por la defensa en esa causa? **2.** SPORTS **the team we were playing against ~ed badly** el equipo contrario no era bueno en la defensa

defendant [dɪˈfendənt] *n* LAW (*in a civil case*) demandado, -a *m, f*; (*in a criminal case*) acusado, -a *m, f*

defense [dɪˈfents] *n Am s.* **defence**

defensible [dɪˈfentsəbl] *adj* **1.** (*capable of being defended*) defendible **2.** (*justifiable*) justificable

defensive [dɪˈfentsɪv] **I.** *adj* (*intended for defence*) defensivo, -a; **she's rather ~ about her family background** se pone a la defensiva cuando se le habla de su situación familiar **II.** *n* **to be/go on the ~** estar/ponerse a la defensiva

defer [dɪˈfɜːʳ, *Am:* dɪˈfɜːr] <-rr-> *vt* aplazar

deference [ˈdefərənts] *n no pl* deferencia *f*

deferential [ˌdefəˈrentʃəl] *adj* respetuoso, -a

deferred payment *n* pago *m* aplazado

defiance [dɪˈfaɪənts] *n no pl* desafío *m*; **in ~ of sth** a despecho de algo

defiant [dɪˈfaɪənt] *adj* **1.** (*person*) rebelde **2.** (*attitude*) desafiante; **to be in a ~ mood** mostrar una actitud desafiante

deficiency [dɪˈfɪʃəntsi] *n* **1.** (*shortage*) escasez *f* **2.** COM déficit *m* **3.** MED deficiencia *f*

deficient [dɪˈfɪʃənt] *adj* deficiente; **to be ~ in sth** carecer de algo

deficit [ˈdefɪsɪt] *n* déficit *m*

defile [dɪˈfaɪl] **I.** *vt form* **1.** (*spoil*) corromper; (*reputation*) mancillar **2.** (*desecrate*) profanar **II.** *n* desfiladero *m*

define [dɪˈfaɪn] *vt* **1.** (*give definition of*) definir **2.** (*explain*) determinar; (*rights*) formular **3.** (*characterize*) caracterizar **4.** (*clearly show*) **the outline of the castle was clearly ~d against the sky** el contorno del castillo se recortaba claramente contra el cielo

definite [ˈdefɪnət] *adj* **1.** (*final*) definitivo, -a **2.** (*certain*) seguro, -a; (*date*) confirmado, -a; (*opinion*) claro, -a; **to be ~ about sth** ser categórico respecto a algo; **it's ~ that ...** no hay duda de que...

definite article *n* artículo *m* determinado

definitely *adv* definitivamente; **to ~ decide sth** decidir algo de forma definitiva

definition [ˌdefɪˈnɪʃən] *n* definición *f*; **to give ~ to sth** realzar algo; **her ideas lack ~** sus ideas no son muy claras

definitive [dɪˈfɪnətɪv, *Am:* -t̬ɪv] *adj* **1.** (*final*) definitivo, -a, rajante *Arg* **2.** (*best*) de mayor autoridad

deflate [dɪˈfleɪt] **I.** *vt* **1.** (*reduce*) reducir; (*hopes*) frustrar **2.** (*cause to lose confidence*) deprimir **3.** (*let air out of*) desinflar **4.** ECON, FIN provocar la deflación de **II.** *vi* desinflarse

deflation [dɪˈfleɪʃən] *n no pl* **1.** ECON, FIN deflación *f* **2.** (*act of deflating*) desinflamiento *m* **3.** (*reduction*) caída *f*

deflationary adj deflacionario, -a
deflect [dɪ'flekt] I. vt desviar II. vi (change direction of) to ~ off sth desviarse de algo
deflection [dɪ'flekʃən] n desviación f
defoliant [ˌdiː'fəʊliənt, Am: -'foʊ-] n defoliante m
defoliate [ˌdiː'fəʊlieɪt, Am: -'foʊ-] vt defoliar
deforest [ˌdiː'fɒrɪst, Am: -'fɔːr-] vt deforestar
deforestation [diːˌfɒrɪ'steɪʃən, Am: diːˌfɔːr-] n no pl deforestación f
deform [dɪ'fɔːm, Am: dɪ'fɔːrm] I. vt deformar; (person) desfigurar II. vi deformarse; (person) desfigurarse
deformation [ˌdiːfɔː'meɪʃən, Am: ˌdiːfɔːr-] n no pl deformación f; (of a person) desfiguración f
deformed adj deformado, -a
deformity [dɪ'fɔːməti, Am: dɪ'fɔːrməti] n deformidad f
defraud [dɪ'frɔːd, Am: dɪ'frɑːd] vt estafar; to ~ one's creditors defraudar a sus acreedores; to ~ sb (of sth) estafar (algo) a alguien
defray [dɪ'freɪ] vt form costear
defrost [ˌdiː'frɒst, Am: -'frɑːst] I. vt deshelar; (a fridge) descongelar; (the windscreen) desempañar II. vi deshelarse; (fridge, food) descongelarse
deft [deft] adj hábil; to be ~ at sth ser diestro en algo
defunct [dɪ'fʌŋkt] adj (dead) difunto, -a; (idea) caduco, -a; (institution) extinto, -a
defy [dɪ'faɪ] vt 1. (challenge) desafiar 2. (resist) resistirse a; it defies description es indescriptible 3. (disobey) desobedecer
deg. abbr of **degree** grado m
degenerate[1] [dɪ'dʒenəreɪt] vi (lose quality) degenerar; (health) deteriorarse; to ~ into sth degenerar en algo
degenerate[2] [dɪ'dʒenərət] I. adj degenerado, -a II. n degenerado, -a m, f
degeneration [dɪˌdʒenə'reɪʃən] n no pl degeneración f
degrade [dɪ'greɪd] I. vt 1. a. CHEM degradar; to ~ oneself rebajarse 2. (destroy: the environment) destruir II. vi ELEC distorsionarse
degree [dɪ'griː] n 1. MAT, METEO grado m; 5 ~s below zero 5 grados bajo cero; first/second ~ murder LAW homicidio en primer/segundo grado; first/second ~ burns MED quemaduras de primer/segundo grado 2. (amount) nivel m 3. (extent) I agree with you to some ~ estoy de acuerdo contigo hasta cierto punto; by ~s gradualmente; to the last ~ en grado sumo 4. UNIV título m; to have a ~ in sth ser licenciado en algo; she's got a physics ~ from Oxford es licenciada en física por la universidad de Oxford; to have a master's ~ in sth tener un máster en algo; to do a ~ in chemistry estudiar la carrera de química
degree course n carrera f (universitaria)
dehumanise vt Brit, Aus, **dehumanize** [ˌdiː'hjuːmənaɪz] vt deshumanizar
dehydrate [ˌdiːhaɪ'dreɪt] I. vt deshidratar

II. vi MED deshidratarse
dehydrated adj deshidratado, -a; (milk) en polvo; to become ~ deshidratarse
dehydration [ˌdiːhaɪ'dreɪʃən] n no pl MED deshidratación f
de-ice [ˌdiː'aɪs] vt deshelar
deign [deɪn] vi to ~ to do sth dignarse a hacer algo
deism ['deɪɪzəm, Am: 'diː-] n no pl deísmo m
deity ['deɪti, Am: 'diːəti] n deidad f
deject [dɪ'dʒekt] vt desanimar
dejected adj desanimado, -a
dejection [dɪ'dʒekʃən] n no pl desánimo m
delay [dɪ'leɪ] I. vt aplazar; to be ~ed retrasarse; to ~ doing sth posponer el momento de hacer algo II. vi tardar; to ~ in doing sth dejar algo para más tarde; don't ~! ¡no te entretengas! III. n tardanza f; without ~ sin dilación; a two-hour ~ un retraso de dos horas
delayed-action adj de efecto retardado; ~ bomb bomba de efecto retardado
delaying adj ~ tactics tácticas dilatorias
delectable [dɪ'lektəbl] adj (taste) delicioso, -a; (person) encantador, -a
delectation [ˌdiːlek'teɪʃən] n no pl delectación f; for the public's ~ para deleite del público
delegate[1] ['delɪgət] n delegado, -a m, f
delegate[2] ['delɪgeɪt] vt delegar
delegation [ˌdelɪ'geɪʃən] n delegación f
delete [dɪ'liːt] vt 1. borrar; please ~ as appropriate táchese lo que no corresponda 2. INFOR suprimir; (file) eliminar
deletion [dɪ'liːʃən] n 1. (act of erasing) eliminación f 2. (removal) supresión f
deli ['deli] n inf s. **delicatessen**
deliberate[1] [dɪ'lɪbərət] adj 1. (intentional) deliberado, -a 2. (cautious: decision) meditado, -a 3. (unhurried) lento, -a; (movement) pausado, -a
deliberate[2] [dɪ'lɪbəreɪt] I. vi to ~ on sth reflexionar sobre algo; to ~ on a case deliberar sobre una causa III. vt deliberar sobre
deliberately adv 1. (intentionally) adrede 2. (unhurriedly) pausadamente
deliberation [dɪˌlɪbə'reɪʃən] n 1. no pl (formal discussion) deliberación f 2. (consideration) reflexión f; after due ~ después de pensarlo bien 3. (unhurried manner) parsimonia f
delicacy ['delɪkəsi] n 1. no pl (tact) delicadeza f 2. (trickiness) the ~ of the situation lo delicado de la situación 3. (food) manjar m
delicate ['delɪkət] adj 1. (fragile) frágil 2. (tricky: situation) delicado, -a 3. (highly sensitive) muy sensible 4. (fine) primoroso, -a; (balance) delicado, -a 5. (easily injured) to be in ~ health estar delicado (de salud) 6. (soft) suave; (aroma) exquisito, -a
delicatessen [ˌdelɪkə'tesən] n delicatessen m
delicious [dɪ'lɪʃəs] adj delicioso, -a
delight [dɪ'laɪt] I. n placer m; to do sth with

~ hacer algo a gusto; **to take ~ in sth** disfrutar con algo; **the children squealed in ~** los niños gritaron de júbilo **II.** *vt* deleitar; **to be ~ed with sth** estar encantado con algo
◆**delight in** *vi* to ~ **doing sth** deleitarse haciendo algo

delighted *adj* encantado, -a

delightful [dɪˈlaɪtfəl] *adj* delicioso, -a; (*person*) encantador(a)

delimit [dɪˈlɪmɪt] *vt* delimitar

delineate [dɪˈlɪnieɪt] *vt* **1.** (*draw*) delinear **2.** (*describe: plan*) trazar; (*character*) perfilar

delinquency [dɪˈlɪŋkwəntsi] *n* delincuencia *f*

delinquent [dɪˈlɪŋkwənt] **I.** *n* LAW delincuente *mf* **II.** *adj* **1.** (*behaviour*) delictivo, -a **2.** *Am* (*debtor*) moroso, -a

delirious [dɪˈlɪriəs] *adj* **1.** MED **to be ~** delirar **2.** (*ecstatic*) **to be ~ with joy** estar delirante de alegría

deliriously *adv* **1.** (*in a delirious manner*) delirantemente; **she raves ~** desvaría en su delirio **2.** (*extremely*) locamente; **she was ~ happy** estaba loca de alegría *inf*

delirium [dɪˈlɪriəm] *n no pl* delirio *m*

deliver [dɪˈlɪvəʳ, *Am:* dɪˈlɪvɚ] **I.** *vt* **1.** (*hand over*) entregar; (*to addressee*) repartir a domicilio **2.** (*recite: lecture*) dar; (*speech, verdict*) pronunciar **3.** (*direct*) **to ~ a blow to sb's head** asestar a alguien un golpe en la cabeza; **he ~ed a sharp rebuke to his son** dirigió una severa reprimenda a su hijo **4.** SPORTS (*throw*) lanzar **5.** (*give birth to*) **to ~ a baby** asistir al parto de un niño; **to be ~ed of a baby** dar a luz a un niño **6.** (*save*) librar **7.** (*produce*) **to ~ a promise** cumplir una promesa; **to ~ the goods** cumplir lo prometido **II.** *vi* COM **we ~** se entrega a domicilio
◆**deliver of** *vr* **to deliver oneself of sth** expresar algo

deliverance [dɪˈlɪvərənts] *n no pl* liberación *f*

deliverer *n* libertador(a) *m(f)*

delivery [dɪˈlɪvəri] *n* **1.** (*act of distributing goods*) reparto *m;* **~ charges** gastos *mpl* de envío; **~ man** repartidor *m;* **~ woman** repartidora *f;* **to pay on ~** pagar contra reembolso; **to take ~ of sth** recibir algo **2.** (*manner of speaking*) pronunciación *f* **3.** SPORTS lanzamiento *m* **4.** (*birth*) parto *m*

delivery note *n* albarán *m* **delivery room** *n*, **delivery suite** *n*, **delivery unit** *n* sala *f* de partos **delivery service** *n* servicio *m* de reparto a domicilio **delivery van** *n* furgoneta *f* de reparto

delta [ˈdeltə, *Am:* -ţə] *n* GEO delta *m*

delta wing *n* AVIAT ala *f* delta

delude [dɪˈluːd] *vt* engañar; **to ~ sb into believing sth** hacer creer algo a alguien

deluge [ˈdeljuːdʒ] **I.** *n* **1.** (*downpour*) diluvio *m;* (*flood*) inundación *f* **2. a.** *fig* (*inundation*) avalancha *f;* (*of complaints*) aluvión *m* **II.** *vt* **a.** *fig* inundar; **to be ~d with tears** estar bañado

en lágrimas; **she is ~d with offers** le llueven las ofertas

delusion [dɪˈluːʒən] *n* **1.** (*wrong idea*) error *m;* **to labour under a ~** estar equivocado **2.** PSYCH alucinación *f;* **~s of grandeur** megalomanía *f* **3.** (*deceit*) engaño *m*

de luxe [dəˈlʌks, *Am:* dɪˈlʌks] *adj* de lujo

delve [delv] *vi* **1.** (*explore*) **to ~ into sth** ahondar en algo **2.** (*rummage*) hurgar

demagog [ˈdeməgɑːg] *n Am s.* **demagogue**

demagogic [ˌdeməˈgɒgɪk, *Am:* -ˈgɑːdʒɪk] *adj* demagógico, -a

demagogue [ˈdeməgɒg, *Am:* -gɑːg] *n* demagogo, -a *m, f*

demagoguery [ˌdeməˈgɒgəri, *Am:* -ˈgɑː-dʒɚ-] *n*, **demagogy** [ˈdeməgɒgi, *Am:* -gɑːdʒi] *n no pl* demagogia *f*

demand [dɪˈmɑːnd, *Am:* dɪˈmænd] **I.** *vt* **1.** (*ask for forcefully*) exigir; (*a right*) reclamar; **to ~ that...** exigir que... *+subj;* **she demanded to see the person in charge** insistió en ver a la persona responsable **2.** (*require*) requerir **II.** *n* **1.** (*insistent request*) exigencia *f;* **~ for independence** reivindicación *f* de independencia; **to make a ~ on sth** exigir algo; **to make a ~ that ...** hacer una petición de que... *+subj;* **to make heavy ~s on sb's time** ocupar gran parte del tiempo de alguien; **to meet a ~ for sth** satisfacer las exigencias de algo; **by popular ~** a petición del público **2.** *Brit* (*request for payment*) reclamación *f* de un pago **3.** COM demanda *f;* **to be in ~** (*object*) tener mucha demanda; (*person*) estar muy solicitado

demanding [dɪˈmɑːndɪŋ, *Am:* dɪˈmæn-] *adj* exigente

demand note *n Am* título *m* pagadero a la vista

demarcate [ˈdiːmɑːkeɪt, *Am:* diːˈmɑːr-] *vt* demarcar

demarcation [ˌdiːmɑːˈkeɪʃən, *Am:* -mɑːr-] *n* demarcación *f*

demarcation line *n* MIL, POL línea *f* de demarcación

demean [dɪˈmiːn] *vt* degradar; **to ~ oneself** rebajarse

demeaning *adj* degradante

demeanor *n Am, Aus,* **demeanour** [dɪˈmiːnəʳ, *Am:* dɪˈmiːnɚ] *n Brit, Aus no pl, form* (*behaviour*) conducta *f;* (*bearing*) porte *m*

demented [dɪˈmentɪd, *Am:* -ˈmenţɪd] *adj inf* **1.** (*insane*) demente **2.** *fig, inf* (*extremely worried*) histérico, -a; **to drive sb ~** volver loco a alguien

demerit [ˌdiːˈmerɪt, *Am:* dɪˈmer-] *n* **1.** (*fault*) desmerecimiento *m* **2.** *Am* SCHOOL punto *m* negativo

demesne [dɪˈmeɪn] *n* **1.** (*possession of property as one's own*) propiedad *f* **2.** (*domain*) esfera *f* de actividad

demigod [ˈdemigɒd, *Am:* -gɑːd] *n* semidiós

m

demilitarize [ˌdiːˈmɪlɪtəraɪz, *Am:* -ˌtəraɪz] *vt* desmilitarizar

demise [dɪˈmaɪz] *n no pl* 1. (*death*) deceso *m* 2. *fig* (*end*) desaparición *f; (of a company*) cierre *m*

demist [ˌdiːˈmɪst] *vt Brit* (*window*) desempañar

demister [ˌdiːˈmɪstə^r] *n Brit* AUTO dispositivo *m* anti-vaho

demobilize [ˌdiːˈməʊbəlaɪz, *Am:* -ˈməʊbəlaɪz] I. *vt* desmovilizar II. *vi* desmovilizarse

democracy [dɪˈmɒkrəsi, *Am:* dɪˈmɑː-] *n* democracia *f*

democrat [ˈdeməkræt] *n* demócrata *mf*

democratic [ˌdeməˈkrætɪk, *Am:* -ˈkræt̪-] *adj* democrático, -a

democratisation *n Brit, Aus,* **democratization** [dɪˌmɒkrətaɪˈzeɪʃən, *Am:* dɪˌmɑː-krət̪ɪˈ-] *n no pl* democratización *f*

democratize [dɪˈmɒkrətaɪz, *Am:* dɪˈmɑː-krə-] *vt Am* democratizar

demolish [dɪˈmɒlɪʃ, *Am:* dɪˈmɑːlɪʃ] *vt* (*a building*) demoler; (*a car*) destrozar; *fig* (*argument*) echar por tierra

demolition [ˌdeməˈlɪʃən] *n* (*of a building*) demolición *f; fig* destrucción *f*

demon [ˈdiːmən] *n* 1. (*evil spirit*) demonio *m* 2. (*naughty child*) diablillo *m* ►**to be a ~ at** sth *inf* ser un hacha haciendo algo; **to work like a ~** trabajar como una fiera; **to be a ~ for work,** to be a ~ **worker** *inf* ser una fiera para el trabajo

demoniac [dɪˈməʊniæk, *Am:* dɪˈmoʊ-] *adj,* **demonic** [dɪˈmɒnɪk, *Am:* dɪˈmɑːnɪk] *adj* 1. (*devilish*) demoníaco, -a 2. (*evil*) diabólico, -a

demonstrable [dɪˈmɒntstrəbl, *Am:* dɪˈmɑːnt-] *adj* demostrable

demonstrate [ˈdemənstreɪt] I. *vt* (*show clearly*) mostrar; (*prove*) demostrar; **to ~ that ...** demostrar que... II. *vi* POL manifestarse

demonstration [ˌdemənˈstreɪʃən] *n* 1. (*act of showing*) demostración *f;* **she gave him a kiss as a ~ of her affection** le dio un beso como muestra de su afecto 2. (*march*) manifestación *f;* **to hold a ~** manifestarse

demonstration model *n* modelo *m* de muestra

demonstrative [dɪˈmɒntstrətɪv, *Am:* dɪˈmɑːnstrət̪ɪv] *adj* 1. (*illustrative*) concluyente 2. (*expressing feelings*) efusivo, -a

demonstrator [ˈdemənstreɪtə^r, *Am:* -ˈt̬ə^r] *n* 1. (*person who demonstrates a product*) demostrador(a) *m(f)* 2. (*protester*) manifestante *mf*

demoralize [dɪˈmɒrəlaɪz, *Am:* -ˈmɔːr-] *vt Am* desmoralizar

demote [dɪˈməʊt, *Am:* -ˈmoʊt] *vt* bajar de categoría; MIL degradar

demure [dɪˈmjʊə^r, *Am:* -ˈmjʊr] *adj* 1. (*sedate*) recatado, -a 2. (*affectedly modest*) remilgado, -a

den [den] *n* 1. (*lair*) guarida *f* 2. *Am* (*small room*) estudio *m* 3. *iron* (*place for vice*) antro *m;* **a ~ of thieves** una guarida de ladrones

denationalize [ˌdiːˈnæʃənəlaɪz] *vt* privatizar

denial [dɪˈnaɪəl] *n* 1. (*act of refuting*) negación *f* 2. (*refusal*) negativa *f* 3. *no pl* (*of a right*) denegación *f* 4. (*rejection*) desmentido *m;* **to issue a ~ of sth** desmentir algo

denigrate [ˈdenɪgreɪt] *vt* denigrar

denim [ˈdenɪm] *n* 1. *no pl* (*cloth*) tela *f* vaquera 2. *pl, inf* (*clothes*) mono *m*

denim jacket *n* chaqueta *f* vaquera **denim shirt** *n* camisa *f* vaquera

denizen [ˈdenɪzən] *n liter* morador(a) *m(f)*

Denmark [ˈdenmɑːk, *Am:* ˈdenmɑːrk] *n* Dinamarca *f*

denomination [dɪˌnɒmɪˈneɪʃən, *Am:* -ˌnɑːmə-] *n* 1. (*religious group*) confesión *f* 2. (*unit of value*) denominación *f*

denominational [dɪˌnɒmɪˈneɪʃənl, *Am:* -ˌnɑːmə-] *adj* confesional

denominator [dɪˈnɒmɪneɪtə^r, *Am:* -ˈnɑː-məneɪtə·] *n* denominador *m*

denotation [ˌdiːnəʊˈteɪʃən, *Am:* -noʊˈ-] *n* denotación *f*

denote [dɪˈnəʊt, *Am:* -ˈnoʊt] *vt* 1. (*indicate*) denotar 2. (*show: displeasure*) mostrar

denouement [deɪˈnuːmɑ̃ːŋ] *n* desenlace *m*

denounce [dɪˈnaʊnts] *vt* 1. (*condemn*) censurar 2. (*give information against*) denunciar

dense [dents] *adj* 1. (*thick*) espeso, -a 2. (*closely packed*) denso, -a; (*compact*) compacto, -a; (*print*) apiñado, -a 3. (*complex*) difícil 4. *inf* (*stupid*) duro, -a de mollera

densely *adv* densamente

density [ˈdentsɪti, *Am:* -sət̪i] *n* 1. (*compactness*) densidad *f;* **to be high/low in ~** ser de alta/baja densidad 2. (*complexity*) impenetrabilidad *f*

dent [dent] I. *n* 1. (*mark*) abolladura *f* 2. (*adverse effect*) mella *f* II. *vt* 1. (*put a dent in*) abollar 2. (*have adverse effect on: confidence*) hacer mella en

dental [ˈdentəl] *adj* dental

dental practitioner *n,* **dental surgeon** *n,* **dentist** [ˈdentɪst, *Am:* -t̪ɪst] *n* dentista *mf*

dentistry [ˈdentɪstri, *Am:* -t̪ɪ-] *n no pl* odontología *f*

dentition [denˈtɪʃən] *n* dentición *f*

dentures [ˈdentʃəz, *Am:* ˈdentʃə·z] *npl* dentadura *f* postiza

denude [dɪˈnjuːd, *Am:* -ˈnuːd] *vt* (*surface*) denudar; **the sheep have denuded the field of grass** *fig* las ovejas han despojado el campo de hierba

denunciation [dɪˌnʌntsiˈeɪʃən] *n* 1. (*condemnation*) censura *f* 2. (*accusation*) denuncia *f*

deny [dɪˈnaɪ] *vt* 1. (*declare untrue*) negar; (*report*) desmentir; **to ~ having done sth** negar haber hecho algo; **she denies that she**

saw it niega haberlo visto **2.** (*refuse*) denegar; **to ~ sb a privilege** negar a alguien un privilegio; **you cannot ~ me my right to free speech** no me puedes privar de mi derecho a la libertad de expresión **3.** (*do without things*) **to ~ oneself sth** privarse de algo **4.** (*disown*) renegar de

deodorant [di'əʊdərənt, *Am:* -'oʊ-] *n* desodorante *m*

deodorise *vt Aus, Brit,* **deodorize** [di'əʊdəraɪz, *Am:* -'oʊdəraɪz] *vt Am* desodorizar

dep. *abbr of* department dpto.

depart [dɪ'pɑːt, *Am:* dɪ'pɑːrt] **I.** *vi* (*person*) partir; (*plane*) despegar; (*train*) salir; (*ship*) zarpar **II.** *vt* **to ~ this life** dejar de existir

◆**depart from** *vi* desviarse de

departed I. *adj* **1.** (*dead*) difunto, -a **2.** (*past: triumph*) pasado, -a **II.** *n pl* **the ~** los difuntos; **to mourn the ~** llorar por las almas

department [dɪ'pɑːtmənt, *Am:* dɪ'pɑːrt-] *n* **1.** (*division: of a university, company*) departamento *m;* (*of a shop*) sección *f* **2.** ADMIN, POL ministerio *m;* **~ of Health and Social Security** Ministerio *m* de Sanidad y Seguridad Social **3.** *inf* (*domain*) ramo *m*

departmental [ˌdiːpɑːt'mentəl, *Am:* -pɑːrt'menţəl] *adj* departamental

department store *n* grandes almacenes *mpl,* tienda *f* por departamentos *AmS*

departure [dɪ'pɑːtʃər, *Am:* dɪ'pɑːrtʃɚ] *n* **1.** (*act of leaving*) partida *f;* (*of vehicle*) salida *f;* (*of plane*) despegue *m;* **~ from politics** alejamiento *m* de la política; **to take one's ~** marcharse **2.** (*deviation*) desviación *f;* (*new undertaking*) nuevo rumbo *m;* **to be a new ~ for sb/sth** ser una novedad para alguien/algo

departure gate *n* puerta *f* de embarque **departure lounge** *n* AVIAT sala *f* de embarque **departure time** *n* AVIAT hora *f* de salida

depend [dɪ'pend] *vi* **1.** (*be determined by*) **to ~ on sth** depender de algo; **~ing on the weather...** según el tiempo que haga... **2.** (*rely on for aid*) **she depends on her father for money** depende del dinero de su padre **3.** (*trust*) **to ~ on sb/sth** confiar en alguien/algo

dependability [dɪˌpendə'bɪləti, *Am:* dɪˌpendə'bɪləţi] *n no pl* (*reliability*) seriedad *f*

dependable [dɪ'pendəbl] *adj* (*thing*) seguro, -a; (*person*) serio, -a

dependant [dɪ'pendənt] *n* familiar *m* dependiente

dependence [dɪ'pendənts] *n no pl* dependencia *f*

dependency *n* **1.** *no pl* (*overreliance*) dependencia *f* **2.** (*dependent state*) posesión *f;* **Puerto Rico is a U.S. ~** Puerto Rico es una posesión de EE.UU.

dependent [dɪ'pendənt] **I.** *adj* **1.** (*conditional*) **to be ~ on sth** depender de algo **2.** (*in need of*) dependiente; **to be ~ on sth** depender de algo; **to be ~ on drugs** ser drogadicto; **she has two ~ children** tiene dos niños

a su cargo **II.** *n Am s.* **dependant**

depict [dɪ'pɪkt] *vt* representar

depiction [dɪ'pɪkʃən] *n* representación *f*

depilatory [dɪ'pɪlətəri, *Am:* -tɔːri] **I.** *n* depilatorio *m* **II.** *adj* depilatorio, -a

depilatory cream *n* crema *f* depilatoria

deplete [dɪ'pliːt] *vt* reducir

depleted *adj* agotado, -a

depletion [dɪ'pliːʃən] *n* (*of resources*) agotamiento *m;* (*of money*) merma *f;* **~ of the ozone layer** reducción *f* de la capa de ozono

deplorable [dɪ'plɔːrəbl] *adj* deplorable

deplore [dɪ'plɔːʳ, *Am:* -'plɔːr] *vt* deplorar; **it is to be ~d** *Aus, Brit* es lamentable

deploy [dɪ'plɔɪ] *vt* (*resources*) desplegar; (*skills*) demostrar

deployment [dɪ'plɔɪmənt] *n no pl* despliegue *m*

depopulate [ˌdiː'pɒpjəleɪt, *Am:* -'pɑːpjə-] *vt* despoblar

deport [dɪ'pɔːt, *Am:* dɪ'pɔːrt] *vt* deportar

deportation [ˌdiːpɔː'teɪʃən, *Am:* -pɔːr'-] *n* deportación *f*

deportee [ˌdiːpɔː'tiː, *Am:* -pɔːr'-] *n* deportado, -a *m, f*

deportment [dɪ'pɔːtmənt, *Am:* dɪ'pɔːrt-] *n no pl* porte *m*

depose [dɪ'pəʊz, *Am:* dɪ'poʊz] *vt* destituir

deposit [dɪ'pɒzɪt, *Am:* dɪ'pɑːzɪt] **I.** *vt* **1.** (*leave*) depositar; (*eggs*) poner; (*luggage*) guardar en consigna; **the bus ~ed me in the middle of nowhere** el bus me dejó donde Cristo perdió el gorro **2.** FIN (*store, pay into account*) ingresar; **to ~ £1000** dejar 1000 libras en depósito **II.** *n* **1.** (*sediment*) sedimento *m* **2.** GEO yacimiento *m* **3.** (*payment made as pledge*) depósito *m;* **to make a ~** efectuar un depósito; **to leave a ~** dejar un depósito; **to leave sth as a ~** dejar algo en garantía; **on ~** en depósito

deposit account *n Brit* cuenta *f* de depósitos a plazo

deposition [ˌdepə'zɪʃən] *n* **1.** *no pl* (*removal from power*) destitución *f;* (*of a dictator*) derrocamiento *f* **2.** (*formal written statement*) declaración *f;* **to file a ~** dar testimonio

depositor [dɪ'pɒzɪtəʳ, *Am:* dɪ'pɑːzəţɚ] *n* cuentahabiente *mf*

depot ['depəʊ, *Am:* 'diːpoʊ] *n* **1.** (*storehouse*) almacén *m;* *Brit* (*for vehicles*) cochera *f* **2.** (*station*) estación *f*

deprave [dɪ'preɪv] *vt* pervertir

depraved *adj* depravado, -a

depravity [dɪ'prævəti, *Am:* dɪ'prævəţi] *n no pl* depravación *f*

deprecate ['deprəkeɪt] *vt* **1.** (*show disapproval of*) desaprobar **2.** (*belittle*) menospreciar

deprecating *adj* **1.** (*strongly disapproving*) de desaprobación **2.** (*belittling*) de menosprecio

deprecation [ˌdeprə'keɪʃən] *n no pl* **1.** (*disapproving*) desaprobación *f* **2.** (*belittling*)

deprecatory ['deprəkətəri, Am: 'deprəkə-tɔːri] adj s. **deprecating**

depreciate [dɪ'priːʃieɪt] I. vi depreciarse II. vt depreciar

depreciation [dɪ,priːʃi'eɪʃən] n no pl depreciación f

depredation [,deprə'deɪʃən] n estragos fpl

depress [dɪ'pres] vt 1.(sadden) deprimir; it ~es me that ... me deprime que... +subj 2.(reduce activity of) disminuir; (the economy) paralizar; (earnings) reducir; (prices) bajar 3.(press down) presionar; (a pedal) apretar

depressant I. n sedante m II. adj deprimente

depressed adj 1.(sad) deprimido, -a, apolismado, -a Méx, Ven; to feel ~ sentirse abatido 2.(impoverished: period) de depresión; (area) deprimido, -a; (economy) en crisis

depressing [dɪ'presɪŋ] adj deprimente

depression [dɪ'preʃən] n 1. a. METEO, FIN depresión f 2.(hollow) hoyo m

depressive [dɪ'presɪv] I. n depresivo, -a m, f II. adj depresivo, -a

deprivation [,deprɪ'veɪʃən] n privación f

deprive [dɪ'praɪv] vt (of dignity) despojar; (of sleep) quitar; to ~ sb of sth privar a alguien de algo

deprived adj desvalido, -a

depth [depθ] n 1. a. fig profundidad f; in the ~ of her heart en lo más hondo de su corazón; in the ~ of winter en pleno invierno 2.(intensity) intensidad f 3. no pl (low sound) gravedad f ▶to get out of one's ~ perder pie; to sink to a ~ degenerar mucho; in ~ en detalle

depth charge n carga f de profundidad

deputation [,depjə'teɪʃən] n + pl/sing vb delegación f

depute [dɪ'pjuːt] vt 1.(appoint) comisionar 2.(delegate) to ~ sth to sb delegar algo en alguien

deputise vi Aus, Brit, **deputize** ['depjətaɪz] vi to ~ for sb suplir a alguien

deputy ['depjəti, Am:-ṭi] n delegado, -a m, f; ~ manager subdirector(a) m(f)

derail [dɪ'reɪl] I. vt hacer descarrilar II. vi descarrilar

derailment [dɪ'reɪlmənt] n descarrilamiento m

derange [dɪ'reɪndʒ] vt perturbar

deranged adj trastornado, -a

derangement n no pl trastorno m mental

derby ['dɑːbi, Am:'dɜːr-] n 1. Brit derby (partido entre equipos locales) 2. Am (hat) hongo m

Derby ['dɑːbi, Am: 'dɑːrb-] n no pl (horse race) Derby m

deregulation [,dɪregjə'leɪʃən] n no pl deregulación f

derelict ['derəlɪkt] I. adj (building) abandonado, -a; (site) baldío, -a II. n (tramp) desposeído, -a m, f

dereliction [,derə'lɪkʃən] n 1. no pl (dilapidation) abandono m 2.(deliberate neglect) negligencia f

deride [dɪ'raɪd] vt burlarse de; to ~ sb for doing sth ridiculizar a alguien por hacer algo

derision [dɪ'rɪʒən] n no pl burla f; to meet sth with ~ hacer burla de algo

derisive [dɪ'raɪsɪv] adj burlón, -ona

derisory [dɪ'raɪsəri] adj (amount) irrisorio, -a

derivation [,derɪ'veɪʃən] n (origin) origen m; (process of evolving) derivación f

derivative [dɪ'rɪvətɪv, Am: dɪ'rɪvəṭɪv] I. adj pej poco original II. n derivado m

derive [dɪ'raɪv] I. vt (get from) to ~ sth from sth obtener algo de algo; I ~ a lot of pleasure from working with children disfruto mucho trabajando con niños II. vi (come from) to ~ from sth derivar de algo

dermatitis [,dɜːmə'taɪtɪs, Am: ,dɜːrmə-'taɪṭəs] n no pl dermatitis f

dermatologist n dermatólogo, -a m, f

dermatology [,dɜːmə'tɒlədʒi, Am: ,dɜːr-mə'tɑːlə-] n no pl dermatología f

derogate ['derəʊgeɪt, Am: 'derə-] vi (detract from) to ~ from sth atentar contra algo

derogation [,derəʊ'geɪʃən, Am: ,derə'-] n no pl 1.(lessening) menosprecio m 2.(abolition) abolición f

derogatory [dɪ'rɒgətəri, Am: dɪ'rɑːgətɔːri] adj desdeñoso, -a

derrick ['derɪk] n 1.(crane) grúa f 2.(framework) torre f de perforación

DES [,diːiː'es] n Brit abbr of **Department of Education and Science** MEC m

desalinate [,diː'sælɪneɪt] vt desalinizar

desalination [diː,sælɪ'neɪʃən] n no pl desalinización f

desalination plant n planta f desalinizadora

descale [,diː'skeɪl] vt desincrustar

descant ['deskænt, Am: 'deskænt] n MUS contrapunto m

descend [dɪ'send] I. vi 1.(go down) descender; (fall) caer 2.(lower oneself) to ~ to stealing rebajarse a robar 3. to ~ from sb/sth provenir de alguien/algo II. vt descender; (a ladder) bajar

descendant [dɪ'sendənt] n descendiente mf

descent [dɪ'sent] n 1.(landing approach) descenso m; (way down) bajada f 2.(decline) declive m 3. no pl (ancestry) origen m; of Irish ~ de ascendencia irlandesa

describe [dɪ'skraɪb] vt 1.(tell in words) describir; (an experience) relatar; to ~ sb as stupid calificar a alguien de tonto 2.(draw) trazar

description [dɪ'skrɪpʃən] n 1.(account) descripción f; to answer a ~ of sb/sth corresponder a una descripción de alguien/algo 2.(sort) clase f; of every ~ de todo tipo

descriptive [dɪ'skrɪptɪv] adj descriptivo, -a

desecrate ['desɪkreɪt] vt profanar

desecration [,desɪ'kreɪʃən] n no pl profanación *f*

desegregate [ˌdiːˈsegrɪgeɪt] *vt* desegregar

desegregation [ˌdiːˈsegrɪgeɪʃən, *Am:* diː-ˌsegrɪˈgeɪʃən] *n no pl* desegregación *f*

desensitize [ˌdiːˈsensɪtaɪz] *vt Am* a. MED insensibilizar

desert[1] [dɪˈzɜːt, *Am:* -ˈzɜːrt] I. *vi* MIL desertar II. *vt* **1.** MIL desertar de **2.** (*abandon*) abandonar; (*one's post*) retirarse de; **luck ~ed me** la suerte me abandonó; **to ~ sb** (**for sb else**) dejar a alguien (por otra persona)

desert[2] [ˈdezət, *Am:* -ət] *n* desierto *m;* **~ plant/animal** planta/animal del desierto

deserted *adj* **1.** (*place*) desierto, -a **2.** (*person*) abandonado, -a

deserter *n* MIL desertor(a) *m(f);* POL tránsfuga *mf*

desertification [dɪˌzɜːtɪfɪˈkeɪʃən, *Am:* dɪ-ˌzɜːrt̬ə-] *n no pl* desertificación *f*

desertion [dɪˈzɜːʃən, *Am:* dɪˈzɜːr-] *n* MIL deserción *f*; (*act of leaving*) abandono *m*

deserts [dɪˈzɜːts, *Am:* dɪˈzɜːrts] *npl* merecido *m;* **to get one's ~** tener su merecido

deserve [dɪˈzɜːv, *Am:* dɪˈzɜːrv] *vt* merecer; **what have I done to ~** (**all**) **this?** ¿qué he hecho para merecer (todo) esto?

deservedly *adv* merecidamente

deserving *adj* meritorio, -a; **to be ~ of sth** ser digno de algo

design [dɪˈzaɪn] I. *vt* **1.** (*plan*) **to ~ sth** (**for sb**) planear algo (para alguien) **2.** (*intend*) **to ~ sth for sb/sth** concebir algo para alguien/algo; **this dictionary is ~ed for advanced learners** este diccionario está dirigido a estudiantes de nivel avanzado; **these measures are ~ed to reduce criminality** estas medidas buscan reducir la criminalidad II. *vi* hacer diseños III. *n* **1.** (*plan*) diseño *m* **2.** (*sketch*) bosquejo *m* **3.** (*pattern*) dibujo *m* **4.** *no pl* (*intention*) propósito *m;* **to do sth by ~** hacer algo adrede **5.** *pl, inf* (*dishonest intentions*) malas intenciones *fpl;* **to have ~s on a championship** pretender un campeonato IV. *adj* de diseño

designate [ˈdezɪgneɪt] I. *vt* **1.** (*name for a duty*) nombrar; **to ~ sb to do sth** designar a alguien para hacer algo **2.** (*indicate*) señalar II. *adj* electo, -a; **the Governor ~** el gobernador electo

designation [ˌdezɪgˈneɪʃən] *n* **1.** (*appointment*) nombramiento *m* **2.** (*act of indicating*) señalamiento *m*

designedly *adv* a propósito

designer [dɪˈzaɪnəʳ, *Am:* dɪˈzaɪnɚ] I. *n* diseñador(a) *m(f)* II. *adj* de marca

designing I. *n* (*art*) diseño *m* II. *adj pej* intrigante

desirable [dɪˈzaɪərəbl, *Am:* dɪˈzaɪ-] *adj* **1.** (*necessary*) conveniente; **it is ~ that ...** sería deseable que... +*subj* **2.** (*sexually attractive*) deseable **3.** (*popular or fashionable: area, job*) codiciado, -a

desire [dɪˈzaɪəʳ, *Am:* dɪˈzaɪɚ] I. *vt* **1.** (*want*)

desear; **I ~ you to leave** le ruego que se vaya **2.** (*request*) **to ~ that ...** desear que... +*subj* **3.** (*be sexually attracted to*) **to ~ sb** desear a alguien II. *n* **1.** (*craving*) deseo *m* **2.** (*request*) petición *f* **3.** (*sensual appetite*) apetencia *f* sexual; **to be the object of sb's ~** ser el objeto de deseo de alguien

desired *adj* deseado, -a

desirous [dɪˈzaɪərəs, *Am:* dɪˈzaɪrəs] *adj* deseoso, -a; **to be ~ of sth** estar deseoso de algo

desist [dɪˈsɪst] *vi form* desistir

desk [desk] *n* **1.** (*table*) escritorio *m* **2.** (*counter*) mostrador *m* **3.** (*section of a newspaper*) sección *f*

desk lamp *n* lámpara *f* de escritorio

desktop [ˈdesktɒp, *Am:* -tɑːp] *n* INFOR ~ (*computer*) microordenador *m* de mesa

desktop publishing *n* autoedición *f*

desolate[1] [ˈdesələt] *adj* **1.** (*barren*) solitario, -a; (*landscape, prospect*) desierto, -a **2.** (*sad*) desolado, -a; **to feel ~** sentirse desconsolado

desolate[2] [ˈdesəleɪt] *vt* asolar

desolation [ˌdesəˈleɪʃən] *n no pl* **1.** (*barrenness*) desolación *f* **2.** (*sadness*) aflicción *f*

despair [dɪˈspeəʳ, *Am:* dɪˈsper] I. *n no pl* (*feeling of hopelessness*) desesperación *f*; **to be in ~ about sth** estar desesperado por algo; **to drive sb to ~** desesperar a alguien; **to the ~ of sb** para desesperanza de alguien ▶ **to be the ~ of sb** tener loco a alguien II. *vi* desesperarse; **to ~ of sb/sth** perder las esperanzas con alguien/algo

despairing *adj* desesperado, -a; (*glance*) de desesperación

despatch [dɪˈspætʃ] *n, vt s.* **dispatch**

desperado [ˌdespəˈrɑːdəʊ, *Am:* -doʊ] <-(e)s> *n* criminal *mf* peligroso, -a

desperate [ˈdespərət] *adj* **1.** (*risking all on a small chance*) temerario, -a; (*violent*) encarnizado, -a; (*measure, solution*) desesperado, -a **2.** (*serious*) grave; (*poverty*) extremo, -a; (*situation*) difícil; **to be in ~ straits** estar en grandes apuros **3.** (*great*) extremo, -a; **to be in a ~ hurry** estar muy apurado; **to be in ~ need of help** tener necesidad extrema de ayuda **4.** (*having great need or desire*) **to be ~ for sth** necesitar algo con suma urgencia; **I'm ~ for a drink!** *iron* ¡me muero por un trago!

desperation [ˌdespəˈreɪʃən] *n no pl* desesperación *f*; **in ~** a la desesperada; **to drive sb to ~** desesperar a alguien

despicable [dɪˈspɪkəbl] *adj* despreciable

despise [dɪˈspaɪz] *vt* despreciar; **to ~ sb for sth** menospreciar a alguien por algo

despite [dɪˈspaɪt] *prep* a pesar de

despoil [dɪˈspɔɪl] *vt* saquear

despondent [dɪˈspɒndənt, *Am:* -ˈspɑːn-] *adj* desalentado, -a; **to feel ~ about sth** sentirse desanimado por algo

despot [ˈdespɒt, *Am:* -pət] *n* déspota *mf*

despotic [dɪˈspɒtɪk, *Am:* desˈpɑːt̬ɪk] *adj* despótico, -a

despotism ['despətɪzəm] *n no pl* despotismo *m*

dessert [dɪ'zɜːt, *Am:* -'zɜːrt] *n* postre *m;* **there's apple pie for** ~ hay pastel de manzana de postre

dessertspoon [dɪ'zɜːt‚spuːn, *Am:* -'zɜːrt] *n* **1.**(*spoon for dessert*) cuchara *f* de postre **2.**(*dessertspoonful*) cucharadita *f*

destabilization [‚diː'steɪbəlaɪz'eɪʃən, *Am:* -bəlɪ'zeɪ-] *n no pl* desestabilización *f*

destabilize [‚diː'steɪbəlaɪz] *vt* desestabilizar

destination [‚destɪ'neɪʃən] *n* destino *m*

destiny ['destɪni] *n* destino *m;* **to be a victim of** ~ ser una víctima del destino; **to fight against** ~ luchar contra el destino; **to shape one's** ~ hacerse su propio destino

destitute ['destɪtjuːt, *Am:* -tuːt] I. *adj* necesitado, -a II. *n* **the** ~ *pl* los indigentes

destitution [‚destɪ'tjuːʃən, *Am:* -'tuː-] *n no pl* **1.**(*deprivation of office*) destitución *f* **2.**(*poverty*) miseria *f*

destroy [dɪ'strɔɪ] *vt* **1.**(*demolish*) destruir **2.**(*kill*) matar; (*animal*) sacrificar **3.**(*ruin*) arruinar

destroyer [dɪ'strɔɪəʳ, *Am:* dɪ'strɔɪɚ] *n* NAUT destructor *m*

destructible [dɪ'strʌktəbl] *adj* destructible

destruction [dɪ'strʌkʃən] *n no pl* destrucción *f;* **mass** ~ destrucción en masa; **to leave a trail of** ~ dejar una estela de destrucción

destructive [dɪ'strʌktɪv] *adj* destructivo, -a

destructiveness *n no pl* destructividad *f*

desulphurization [diː‚sʌlfəraɪ'zeɪʃən] *n no pl* desulfurización *f*

desultory ['desəltəri, *Am:* -tɔːri] *adj* (*disconnected*) inconexo, -a; (*lacking plan*) desordenado, -a

Det *n abbr of* **Detective** detective *mf*

detach [dɪ'tætʃ] *vt* separar

detachable *adj* separable

detached *adj* **1.**(*separated*) separado, -a; ~ **house** chalet *m* **2.**(*aloof*) indiferente **3.**(*impartial*) imparcial

detachment [dɪ'tætʃmənt] *n* **1.** *no pl* (*separation*) separación *f* **2.** *no pl* (*disinterest*) desinterés *m* **3.**(*group of soldiers*) destacamento *m*

detail ['diːteɪl, *Am:* dɪ'teɪl] I. *n* **1.**(*item of information*) detalle *m;* **in** ~ en detalle **2.**(*unimportant item*) minucia *f;* **gory** ~**s** *iron* intimidades *fpl;* **to go into** ~ entrar en detalles **3.**(*small feature*) elemento *m* **4.** MIL (*group*) destacamento *m* II. *vt* **1.**(*explain fully*) detallar **2.**(*tell, mention*) pormenorizar **3.**(*assign a duty to*) **to** ~ **sb to do sth** destacar a alguien para que haga algo

detailed *adj* detallado, -a; (*report, study*) pormenorizado, -a

detain [dɪ'teɪn] *vt* **1.**(*hold as prisoner*) detener **2.**(*delay*) entretener; (*keep waiting*) retener

detainee [‚diːteɪ'niː] *n* detenido, -a *m, f*

detect [dɪ'tekt] *vt* **1.**(*discover*) descubrir

2.(*note*) advertir; (*sense presence of*) percibir; (*a mine*) hallar

detectable [dɪ'tektəbl] *adj* (*able to be found*) averiguable; (*discernible*) perceptible

detection [dɪ'tekʃən] *n no pl* descubrimiento *m*

detective [dɪ'tektɪv] *n* detective *mf*

detective inspector *n* comisario, -a *m, f*

detective novel *n* novela *f* policíaca

detective story *n* novela *f* policíaca

detective superintendent *n* superintendente *mf* general

detector [dɪ'tektəʳ, *Am:* -tɚ] *n* detector *m*

detention [dɪ'tenʃən] *n* **1.**(*being held as a prisoner*) arresto *m* **2.**(*act*) detención *f* **3.**(*school punishment*) castigo *f*

detention centre *n* **1.**(*for youths*) correccional *m* **2.**(*for refugees*) campo *m* de refugiados

deter [dɪ'tɜːʳ, *Am:* -'tɜːr] <-rr-> *vt* disuadir

detergent [dɪ'tɜːdʒənt, *Am:* -'tɜːr] *n* detergente *m*

deteriorate [dɪ'tɪərɪəreɪt, *Am:* -'tɪri-] *vi* **1.**(*wear out*) deteriorarse **2.**(*become worse*) empeorar

deterioration [dɪ‚tɪərɪə'reɪʃən, *Am:* -'tɪri-] *n no pl* **1.**(*wearing out*) deterioro *m* **2.**(*worsening*) empeoramiento *m*

determinable [dɪ'tɜːmɪnəbl, *Am:* -'tɜːr-] *adj* determinable

determinant [dɪ'tɜːmɪnənt, *Am:* -'tɜːr-] I. *n* determinante *m* II. *adj* determinante

determinate [dɪ'tɜːmɪnət, *Am:* -'tɜːr-] *adj* **1.**(*limited*) definido, -a **2.**(*of specific scope*) determinado, -a

determination [dɪ‚tɜːmɪ'neɪʃən, *Am:* -‚tɜːr-] *n no pl* **1.**(*firmness of purpose*) resolución *f* **2.**(*decision*) determinación *f*

determine [dɪ'tɜːmɪn, *Am:* -'tɜːr-] I. *vi* **1.**(*decide*) **to** ~ **on sth** decidirse por algo **2.** LAW expirar II. *vt* **1.**(*decide*) decidir **2.**(*settle*) establecer **3.**(*find out*) fijar **4.**(*influence*) influir **5.** LAW (*terminate*) rescindir

determined [dɪ'tɜːmɪnd, *Am:* -'tɜːr-] *adj* decidido, -a; **to be** ~ **to do sth** estar resuelto a hacer algo

deterrence [dɪ'terəns] *n no pl* disuasión *f*

deterrent [dɪ'terənt] I. *n* (*obstacle*) freno *m;* **to act as a** ~ **to sb** disuadir a alguien II. *adj* disuasivo, -a

detest [dɪ'test] *vt* detestar

detestable [dɪ'testəbl] *adj* detestable

detestation [‚diːte'steɪʃən] *n no pl* aborrecimiento *m*

dethrone [‚diː'θrəun, *Am:* dɪ'θroun] *vt* destronar

detonate ['detəneɪt] I. *vi* detonar II. *vt* hacer detonar

detonation [‚detə'neɪʃən] *n* detonación *f*

detonator ['detəneɪtəʳ, *Am:* -ṭɚ] *n* detonador *m*

detour ['diːtʊəʳ, *Am:* 'diːtʊr] *n* desvío *m;* **to**

make a ~ desviarse

detoxify [dɪ'tɒksɪfaɪ, Am: di:'tɑ:k-] vt desintoxicar

detract [dɪ'trækt] vi 1.(devalue) **to ~ from** sth quitar mérito a algo 2.(take away) apartar

detractor [dɪ'træktəʳ, Am: -təʳ] n detractor(a) m(f)

detriment ['detrɪmənt] n no pl perjuicio m; **to the ~ of** sth en detrimento de algo; **without ~ to** sth sin perjuicio de algo

detrimental [ˌdetrɪ'mentəl, Am: -ʈl] adj nocivo, -a

detritus [dɪ'traɪtəs, Am: -ʈəs] n no pl 1.(small fragments) detrito m 2.(debris) escombros mpl

deuce [dju:s, Am: du:s] n no pl 1.(in cards) dos m 2.(in tennis) empate m

devaluate [ˌdi:'væljueɪt] vt s. **devalue**

devaluation [ˌdi:væljuˈeɪʃən] n devaluación f

devalue [ˌdi:'vælju:] vt devaluar

devastate ['devəsteɪt] vt devastar

devastating adj 1.(causing great destruction) desolador(a); (powerful) devastador(a) 2.(with great effect) abrumador(a); (beauty) arrollador(a); (charm) irresistible

devastation [ˌdevə'steɪʃən] n no pl devastación f

develop [dɪ'veləp] I. vi (grow) desarrollarse; (become more advanced) progresar; **to ~ into** sth transformarse en algo II. vt 1.(expand) desarrollar; (improve) ampliar 2.(create) crear 3.(begin to show) revelar; (catch) empezar a tener; (an illness) contraer 4.(build) construir; (build on) urbanizar 5.PHOT revelar 6.MUS elaborar

developed adj desarrollado, -a

developer [dɪ'veləpəʳ, Am: -pəʳ] n 1.(one who develops) promotor(a) m(f) inmobiliario, -a; (company) inmobiliaria f 2.PHOT revelador m

developing adj de desarrollo

development [dɪ'veləpmənt] n 1.(process) desarrollo m; (growth) crecimiento m 2.(growth stage) avance m; (of skills) evolución f 3.(progress) progreso m; (of products) explotación f 4.(event) acontecimiento m 5.(building of) construcción f; **housing ~** construcción de viviendas 6.(building on: of land) urbanización f 7.(industrialization) industrialización f 8.MUS (elaboration) elaboración f

deviant ['di:viənt] adj (behaviour) que se aparta de la norma, desviado, -a; (sexually) pervertido, -a

deviate ['di:vieɪt] vi apartarse; **to ~ from** sth desviarse de algo

deviation [ˌdi:vi'eɪʃən] n desviación f

deviationist [ˌdi:vi'eɪʃənɪst] n desviacionista mf

device [dɪ'vaɪs] n 1.(mechanism) dispositivo m; **sound ~** INFOR dispositivo m de sonido; **input/output ~** INFOR dispositivo m de

entrada/salida 2.(method) estrategia f; **literary/rhetorical ~** recurso m literario/retórico 3.(bomb) artefacto m; **nuclear ~** ingenio m nuclear ▶**to leave sb to their own ~s** abandonar a alguien a su suerte

devil ['devəl] n 1.(Satan) diablo m, mandinga m; **to be possessed by the Devil** estar poseído por el demonio 2.(evil spirit) espíritu m maligno 3.inf (wicked person) diablo m 4.(mischievous person) **to be a ~** ser malo; **go on, be a ~!** inf ¡venga, pórtate mal!; **lucky ~!** ¡qué suerte!; **the poor ~!** ¡pobre diablo! 5.(difficult thing) **to have the ~ of a job doing** sth costar Dios y ayuda hacer algo 6.(feisty energy) arrojo m 7.(machine) máquina f deshilachadora ▶**~ take the hindmost** camarón que se duerme se lo lleva la corriente prov; **between the ~ and the deep blue sea** entre la espada y la pared; **to sell one's soul to the ~** vender el alma al diablo; **better the ~ you know (than the devil you don't)** más vale malo conocido que bueno por conocer prov; **to go to the ~** irse al infierno; **there'll be the ~ to pay** se formará un lío de todos los diablos; **to play the ~ with** sth estropear algo; **speak of the ~** hablando del rey de Roma, por la puerta asoma; **how/who/what/where the ~ ...?** ¿cómo/quién/qué/dónde diablos...?; **like the ~** como el demonio

devilish ['devəlɪʃ] adj 1.(evil) diabólico, -a 2.(mischievous) malvado, -a 3.(extreme) muy difícil; (terrible) extremo, -a 4.(very clever) ingenioso, -a

devil-may-care [ˌdevəlmeɪ'keəʳ, Am: -'ker] adj irresponsable

devilment ['devəlmənt] n, **devilry** ['devəlri] n no pl diablura f

devious ['di:viəs] adj 1.(dishonest) insincero, -a 2.(winding) tortuoso, -a; (route) intrincado, -a

devise [dɪ'vaɪz] I. n legado m II. vt 1.(plan, think out) idear; (a plot) diseñar; (a scheme) trazar 2.(leave property via a will) legar

devoid [dɪ'vɔɪd] adj **to be ~ of** sth estar desprovisto de algo

devolution [ˌdi:və'lu:ʃən, Am: ˌdevə'lu:-] n no pl 1.POL (decentralisation of power) delegación f 2.(progression through stages) transferencia f 3.(transference of wealth) traspaso m

devolve [dɪ'vɒlv, Am: dɪ'vɑ:lv] I. vi recaer II. vt (transfer) transferir; (powers) delegar

devote [dɪ'vəʊt, Am: -'voʊt] vt dedicar; **to ~ oneself to** sth dedicarse a algo

devoted [dɪ'vəʊtɪd, Am: -'voʊʈɪd] adj dedicado, -a; (husband, mother) devoto, -a; **to be ~ to** sb/sth estar consagrado a alguien/algo

devotee [ˌdevə'ti:, Am: -ə'ti:] n 1.(supporter) partidario, -a m, f; (admirer) fanático, -a m, f; (advocate) devoto, -a m, f

devotion [dɪ'vəʊʃən, Am: dɪ'voʊ-] n no pl 1.(loyalty) lealtad f; (affection) afecto m;

devotional (*admiration*) fervor *m;* (*great attachment*) dedicación *f;* **to inspire** ~ inspirar devoción **2.** REL devoción *f* **3.** (*devoutness*) piedad *f*

devotional [dɪ'vəʊʃənəl, *Am:* dɪ'voʊ-] *adj* (*attitude*) devoto, -a; (*music, practices*) piadoso, -a

devour [dɪ'vaʊər, *Am:* dɪ'vaʊɚ] *vt* **1.** (*eat eagerly*) tragar **2.** (*engulf*) devorar **3.** (*consume quickly*) consumir **4.** (*feel strongly*) **to be ~ed by jealousy** estar consumido por los celos

devouring *adj* devorador(a)

devout [dɪ'vaʊt] *adj* **1.** REL devoto, -a **2.** (*compulsive*) fervoroso, -a

dew [dju:, *Am:* du:] *n no pl* rocío *m*

dewdrop ['dju:drɒp, *Am:* 'du:drɑ:p] *n* gota *f* de rocío

dewy ['dju:i, *Am:* 'du:-] *adj* cubierto, -a de rocío

dexterity [ˌdek'sterəti, *Am:* -əti] *n no pl* (*skilful handling*) agilidad *f*

dexterous ['dekstərəs] *adj* diestro, -a

dextrose ['dekstrəʊs, *Am:* -stroʊs] *n no pl* dextrosa *f*

dextrous ['dekstrəs] *adj s.* **dexterous**

diabetes [ˌdaɪə'bi:ti:z, *Am:* -təs] *n no pl* diabetes *f*

diabetic [ˌdaɪə'betɪk, *Am:* -'beţ-] **I.** *n* diabético, -a *m, f* **II.** *adj* (*who has diabetes*) diabético, -a

diabolic(al) [ˌdaɪə'bɒlɪk(əl), *Am:* -'bɑ:lɪk-] *adj* **1.** (*of Devil*) diabólico, -a **2.** (*evil*) malvado, -a **3.** *inf* (*very bad*) maligno, -a

diadem ['daɪədem] *n* (*crown*) diadema *f*

diagnose ['daɪəgnəʊz, *Am:* ˌdaɪəg'noʊs] **I.** *vi* hacer un diagnóstico **II.** *vt* diagnosticar

diagnosis [ˌdaɪəg'nəʊsɪs, *Am:* -'noʊ-] <-ses> *n* **1.** (*of a disease*) diagnóstico *m* **2.** (*science*) diagnosis *f inv*

diagnostic [ˌdaɪəg'nɒstɪk, *Am:* -'nɑ:stɪk] **I.** *n* diagnóstico *m* **II.** *adj* diagnóstico, -a

diagonal [daɪ'ægənl] **I.** *n* diagonal *f* **II.** *adj* diagonal

diagram ['daɪəgræm] **I.** *n* **1.** (*drawing*) diagrama *f;* (*plan*) esquema *f* **2.** (*chart*) gráfico *m* **3.** (*figure*) figura *f* **II.** <-mm-> *vt* diagramar

dial ['daɪəl] **I.** *n* **1.** (*clock face*) esfera *f* **2.** (*part of scale*) cuadrante *m* **3.** (*movable disc on a telephone*) disco *m* **4.** Brit, *inf* (*face*) cara *f* **II.** <Brit: -ll-, *Am:* -l-> *vi* marcar un número, discar *Arg, Perú, Urug* **III.** *vt* **1.** TEL marcar; **to ~ direct** hacer una llamada directa **2.** RADIO sintonizar

dialect ['daɪəlekt] *n* dialecto *m*

dialectal [ˌdaɪə'lektəl] *adj* dialectal

dialectical [ˌdaɪə'lektɪkəl] *adj* dialéctico, -a

dialling *n no pl* (*telephone*) marcación *f*, discado *m* Arg, Perú, Urug

dialog *n Am,* **dialogue** ['daɪəlɒg, *Am:* -lɑ:g] *n* **1.** (*conversation*) diálogo *m* **2.** POL interlocución *f;* **to engage in** ~ dialogar

dial-up service *n* INFOR servicio *m* de marcado

dialysis [daɪ'æləsɪs] *n no pl* diálisis *f*

diameter [daɪ'æmɪtər, *Am:* -əţɚ] *n* diámetro *m*

diametrically [ˌdaɪə'metrɪkəli] *adv* **1.** (*as a diameter*) diametralmente **2.** (*completely*) en su totalidad

diamond ['daɪəmənd] *n* **1.** (*precious stone*) diamante *m;* **the ace/king of ~s** GAMES el as/rey de diamantes **2.** (*rhombus*) rombo *m* **3.** (*tool for cutting glass*) cortavidrios *m inv* **4.** (*baseball field*) diamante *m;* (*infield*) cuadro *m* ►**a rough** ~ un diamante en bruto; ~ **cut** ~ Brit tal para cual

diamond cutter *n* diamantista *mf* **diamond wedding** *n* bodas *fpl* de diamante

diaper ['daɪəpər, *Am:* -pɚ] *n Am* pañal *m*

diaphanous [daɪ'æfənəs] *adj liter* diáfano, -a; (*cloth*) transparente

diaphragm ['daɪəfræm] *n* diafragma *m*

diarist ['daɪərɪst] *n* diarista *mf*

diarrhea *n,* **diarrhoea** [ˌdaɪə'rɪə, *Am:* -'ri:ə] *n no pl* diarrea *f*

diary ['daɪəri] *n* **1.** (*journal*) diario *m* **2.** (*planner*) agenda *f*

diatonic [ˌdaɪə'tɒnɪk, *Am:* -'tɑ:nɪk] *adj* MUS diatónico, -a

diatribe ['daɪətraɪb] *n* diatriba *f*

dice [daɪs] **I.** *npl* **1.** (*cubes with spots*) dados *mpl;* **to roll the** ~ echar los dados **2.** (*game with dice*) juego *m* de dados **3.** (*food in small cubes*) tacos *mpl* ►**no** ~ *Am, inf* de ninguna manera **II.** *vi* jugar a los dados **III.** *vt* cortar en tacos

dicey ['daɪsi] <-ier, -iest> *adj* Brit, Aus, *inf* peligroso, -a

dichotomy [daɪ'kɒtəmi, *Am:* -'kɑ:ţə-] *n* dicotomía *f*

dick [dɪk] *n* **1.** vulg (*penis*) polla *f*, pija *f* AmL, paloma *f* Méx, Ven, pajarito *m* RioPl **2.** vulg (*stupid person*) gilipollas *mf inv*

dickens ['dɪkɪnz] *npl inf* **what the** ~ **...?** ¿qué diablos...?

dicky ['dɪki] *n* Brit, *inf* **a ~ heart** una debilidad cardiaca

dictaphone® ['dɪktəfəʊn, *Am:* -foʊn] *n* dictáfono *m*

dictate¹ ['dɪkteɪt] *n* dictado *m*

dictate² [dɪk'teɪt, *Am:* 'dɪkteɪt] **I.** *vi* **1.** (*command*) mandar **2.** (*state sth exactly*) dictar; **to** ~ **to sb** dictar a alguien **II.** *vt* **1.** (*give orders*) ordenar **2.** (*make necessary*) influir; (*state exactly*) imponer

dictation [dɪk'teɪʃən] *n no pl* SCHOOL dictado *m*

dictator [dɪk'teɪtər, *Am:* 'dɪkteɪţɚ] *n* POL dictador(a) *m(f)*

dictatorial [ˌdɪktə'tɔːriəl] *adj* dictatorial

dictatorship [dɪk'teɪtəʃɪp, *Am:* -ţɚ-] *n* dictadura *f*

diction ['dɪkʃən] *n no pl* dicción *f*

dictionary ['dɪkʃənəri, *Am:* -eri] *n* diccionario *m*

did [dɪd] *pt of* **do**

didactic [dɪ'dæktɪk, *Am:* daɪ-] *adj* didáctico, -a

diddle ['dɪdl] *vt inf* timar; **to ~ sb out of sth** estafar algo a alguien

didn't [dɪdənt] = **did not** *s.* **do**

die¹ [daɪ] *n* 1. dado *m* 2. TECH molde *m* ▶ **as straight as a ~** más derecho que una vela; **the ~ is cast** la suerte está echada

die² [daɪ] <dying, died> *vi* 1. (*cease to live*) morir; **to ~ a violent/natural death** morir de muerte violenta/natural; **to ~ by one's own hand** suicidarse 2. (*end*) desaparecer; **the secret will ~ with her** se llevará el secreto a la tumba 3. (*stop functioning*) dejar de servir; **the engine just ~d** *Am* el motor se ha muerto 4. (*go out, fade away*) extinguirse ▶ **to ~ hard** persistir; **never say ~!** ¡nunca te rindas!; **to do or ~** vencer o morir; **to ~ to do sth** tener muchas ganas de hacer algo; **I'm dying for a cup of tea** me muero por una taza de té

◆ **die away** *vi* desaparecer; (*sobs, anger*) calmarse; (*enthusiasm*) decaer; (*wind*) amainar; (*sound*) apagarse

◆ **die back** *vi* secarse

◆ **die down** *vi* apagarse

◆ **die off** *vi* (*species*) extinguirse; (*customs*) desaparecer

◆ **die out** *vi* extinguirse

dieback ['daɪˌbæk] *n* muerte *f* de los bosques (*a causa de la polución del medio ambiente*)

diehard ['daɪhɑːd, *Am:* -hɑːrd] *n* intransigente *mf;* **a ~ conservative** un conservador recalcitrante

diesel ['diːzəl, *Am:* -səl] *n no pl* diesel *m*

diesel engine *n* motor *m* diesel **diesel oil** *n* aceite *m* diesel

diet¹ ['daɪət] I. *n* dieta *f;* **staple ~** dieta básica; **to be on a ~** estar a dieta; **to put sb on a ~** poner a alguien a dieta; **to go on a ~** seguir una dieta II. *vi* estar a dieta III. *vt* **to ~ sb** poner a alguien a dieta

diet² ['daɪət] *n* (*legislative body*) asamblea *f* legislativa

dietary ['daɪətəri, *Am:* 'daɪəter-] *adj* (*food*) dietético, -a; (*habit*) de alimentación

dietary fibre *n* fibra *f* dietética

dietetic [ˌdaɪə'tetɪk, *Am:* -'teṭ-] *adj* dietético, -a

dietetics *n no pl* dietética *f*

dietician *n,* **dietitian** [ˌdaɪə'tɪʃən] *n* dietista *mf*

differ ['dɪfər, *Am:* -ɚ] *vi* 1. (*be unlike*) ser diferente; **to ~ from sth** ser distinto de algo 2. (*disagree*) no estar de acuerdo; **to ~ about sth** (*persons*) discrepar en algo

difference ['dɪfərənts] *n* 1. (*state of being different*) diferencia *f* 2. (*distinction*) distinción *f;* **that makes all the ~** eso cambia todo; **to make a ~** importar; **to not make any ~** ser igual 3. (*new feature*) singularidad *f* 4. (*amount left*) **to pay the ~** pagar la diferencia 5. (*disagreement*) discrepancia *f;* **to put aside ~s** apartar las diferencias; **to settle ~s**

resolver diferencias; **to sink one's ~s** olvidar las diferencias

different ['dɪfərənt] *adj* 1. (*not the same*) diferente 2. (*distinct*) distinto, -a 3. (*unusual*) raro, -a; **to do something ~** romper la rutina ▶ **to be as ~ as chalk and cheese** *Brit, Aus,* **to be as ~ as night and day** *Am* ser la noche y el día

differential [ˌdɪfə'rentʃəl] I. *n* 1. *a.* MAT diferencial *m* 2. (*difference in pay*) **pay ~s** diferencia *f* de sueldo II. *adj* 1. (*different*) diferente 2. MAT diferencial

differentiate [ˌdɪfə'rentʃieɪt] I. *vi* distinguir II. *vt* **to ~ one wine from another** distinguir un vino de otro

differentiation [ˌdɪfərentʃi'eɪʃən] *n* diferenciación *f*

difficult ['dɪfɪkəlt] *adj* 1. (*not easy*) difícil; **she is said to be a very ~ person** dicen que es una persona muy difícil 2. (*troublesome*) duro, -a

difficulty ['dɪfɪkəlti, *Am:* -ṭi] <-ies> *n* 1. *no pl* (*being difficult*) dificultad *f;* **with ~** difícilmente 2. (*problem*) obstáculo *m;* **to be in difficulties** estar en apuros; **to be in difficulties with sb** tener problemas con alguien; **to encounter difficulties** encontrar dificultades; **to have ~ doing sth** tener problemas para hacer algo

diffident ['dɪfɪdənt] *adj* (*shy*) tímido, -a; (*modest*) modesto, -a

diffract [dɪ'frækt] *vt* difractar

diffuse¹ [dɪ'fjuːz] I. *vi* difundirse II. *vt* difundir

diffuse² [dɪ'fjuːs] *adj* 1. (*spread out*) dilatado, -a 2. (*imprecise*) difuso, -a 3. (*verbose*) verboso, -a

diffusion [dɪ'fjuːʒən] *n no pl* 1. (*process of diffusing*) difusión *f* 2. CHEM, PHYS dispersión *f*

dig [dɪg] I. *n* 1. (*excavation*) excavación *f* 2. (*poke*) empujón *m* 3. (*sarcastic remark*) pulla *f;* **to have ~s at sb** meterse con alguien II. <-gg-, dug, dug> *vi* 1. (*turn over ground*) escarbar; **to ~ deeper** ahondar 2. (*poke*) empujar III. *vt* 1. (*move ground*) cavar; (*a well, canal*) abrir 2. (*excavate*) excavar 3. (*stab, poke*) clavar; **to dig one's elbow into sb's ribs** dar un codazo en las costillas a alguien; **to dig one's spurs into a horse** hincar las espuelas en un caballo 4. *inf* (*like*) gustar ▶ **to ~ one's own grave** cavarse su propia tumba

◆ **dig in** I. *vi inf* (*start eating*) atacar II. *vt* 1. enterrar 2. (*dig trenches*) atrincherarse 3. (*establish oneself*) instalarse; (*settle in*) asentarse

◆ **dig into** I. *vi* clavar ▶ **to dig (deeper) into one's pockets** buscar en los bolsillos II. *vt always sep inf* atacar ▶ **to dig oneself into a hole** meterse en un problema

◆ **dig out** *vt* (*hole*) excavar; (*buried object*) extraer

◆ **dig up** *vt* 1. (*retrieve from ground*) desenterrar **2.**(*excavate*) remover **3.**(*find out*) descubrir

digest¹ ['daɪdʒest] *n* **1.**(*summary of laws*) digesto *m* **2.**(*summary of report*) resumen *m*

digest² [daɪ'dʒest] **I.** *vi* (*food*) digerirse; (*break down food*) digerir la comida **II.** *vt* **1.**(*break down: food*) digerir **2.**(*understand*) asimilar **3.**(*decompose*) descomponer **4.**(*classify*) clasificar

digestible [daɪ'dʒestəbl] *adj* digerible

digestion [daɪ'dʒestʃən] *n* digestión *f*

digestive [daɪ'dʒestɪv] *adj* digestivo, -a

digger ['dɪgər, *Am:* -ɚ] *n* **1.**(*machine for digging*) excavadora *f* **2.**(*person*) cavador(a) *m(f)*; *Aus* (*gold miner*) minero, -a *m, f* **3.** *Aus, inf*(*soldier*) australiano, -a *m, f*

digit ['dɪdʒɪt] *n* **1.**(*number from 0 to 9*) dígito *m* **2.**(*finger, toe*) dedo *m*

digital ['dɪdʒɪtl, *Am:* -t̬l] *adj* digital

digitalize ['dɪdʒɪtəlaɪz, *Am:* -t̬əlaɪz] *vt* digitalizar

digitize ['dɪdʒɪtaɪz] *vt* INFOR digitalizar

digitizer ['dɪdʒɪtaɪzər, *Am:* -ɚ] *n* INFOR digitalizador *m*

dignified ['dɪgnɪfaɪd] *adj* **1.**(*worthy of respect*) digno, -a **2.**(*solemn*) solemne

dignify ['dɪgnɪfaɪ] <-ie-> *vt* dignificar

dignitary ['dɪgnɪtəri, *Am:* -nəter-] <-ies> *n* dignatario, -a *m, f*

dignity ['dɪgnəti, *Am:* -t̬i] *n no pl* **1.**(*composed style*) decoro *m* **2.**(*state worthy of respect*) dignidad *f* **3.**(*respect*) respeto *m*; **to be beneath sb's** ~ no ser digno de alguien

digress [daɪ'gres] *vi* **1.**(*wander*) hacer una digresión **2.**(*deviate*) desviarse; **to** ~ **from sth** salirse de algo

digressive [daɪ'gresɪv] *adj* digresivo, -a

dike [daɪk] *n* dique *m*

dilapidated [dɪ'læpɪdeɪtɪd, *Am:* -t̬ɪd] *adj* (*house*) derruido, -a; (*car*) destartalado, -a

dilate [daɪ'leɪt, *Am:* 'daɪleɪt] **I.** *vi* dilatarse **II.** *vt* dilatar

dilation [daɪ'leɪʃən] *n no pl* dilatación *f*

dilatory ['dɪlətəri, *Am:* -tɔːri] *adj* **1.**(*slow*) lento, -a **2.** LAW dilatorio, -a

dilemma [dɪ'lemə, daɪ'lemə] *n* dilema *m*; **to be in a** ~ estar en un dilema; **to face a** ~ enfrentarse a un dilema

dilettante [ˌdɪlɪ'tænti, *Am:* -ə'tɑːnt] *n* <-s *o* -ti> diletante *mf*

diligence ['dɪlɪdʒəns] *n no pl* (*effort, care*) diligencia *f*

diligent ['dɪlɪdʒənt] *adj* (*careful*) concienzudo, -a; (*hard-working*) diligente; **he is** ~ **about his work** es diligente en su trabajo

dill [dɪl] *n no pl* eneldo *m*

dillydally ['dɪlɪdæli] *vi* **1.** *inf* (*dawdle*) perder el tiempo **2.** *inf*(*vacillate*) vacilar

dilute [daɪ'ljuːt, *Am:* -'luːt] **I.** *vt* diluir **II.** *vi* diluirse **III.** *adj* diluido, -a

dilution [daɪ'ljuːʃən, *Am:* -'luː-] *n no pl, a. fig* disolución *f*

dim [dɪm] **I.** <-mm-> *vi* (*colour*) apagarse

II. *vt* apagar **III.** <-mm-> *adj* **1.**(*not bright*) tenue **2.**(*unclear*) borroso, -a **3.**(*stupid*) lerdo, -a **4.**(*unfavourable*) sombrío, -a

dime [daɪm] *n* moneda *f* de diez centavos ▶ **a** ~ **a** **dozen** del montón

dimension [daɪ'mentʃən, *Am:* dɪ'mentʃən] **I.** *n* dimensión *f* **II.** *vt Am* dimensionar

dimensional [ˌdaɪ'mentʃənəl, *Am:* dɪ'mentʃən-] *adj* dimensional

diminish [dɪ'mɪnɪʃ] **I.** *vi* disminuir; **to** ~ (**greatly**) **in value** perder mucho valor **II.** *vt* **1.**(*make less*) disminuir **2.**(*damage sb's reputation*) rebajar

diminution [ˌdɪmɪ'njuːʃən, *Am:* -ə'nuː-] *n* disminución *f*

diminutive [dɪ'mɪnjʊtɪv, *Am:* -jət̬ɪv] **I.** *n* LING diminutivo *m* **II.** *adj* (*very small*) diminuto, -a

dimmer ['dɪmər, *Am:* -ɚ] *n*, **dimmer switch** *n* potenciómetro *m*

dimness *n no pl* penumbra *f*

dimple ['dɪmpl] **I.** *n* hoyuelo *m* **II.** *vt* formar hoyuelos en

din [dɪn] *n no pl* estrépito *m*

dine [daɪn] *vi* cenar

diner ['daɪnər, *Am:* -nɚ] *n* **1.**(*person*) comensal *mf* **2.** *Am* (*restaurant at the side of the road*) restaurante *m* de carretera

dinghy ['dɪŋgi, *Am:* 'dɪŋi] *n* <-ies> bote *m*

dingo ['dɪŋgəʊ, *Am:* -goʊ] *n* <-es> dingo *m*

dingy ['dɪndʒi] <-ier, -iest> *adj* deslustrado, -a

dining car *n no pl* (*car*) vagón *m* restaurante **dining room** *n* comedor *m*

dinky¹ ['dɪŋki] <-ies> *n abbr of* **double income no kids** pareja con dos sueldos y sin hijos

dinky² ['dɪŋki] *adj* **1.**(*dainty*) mono, -a **2.** *Am* (*insignificant*) pobre

dinner ['dɪnər, *Am:* -ɚ] *n* (*evening meal*) cena *f*; (*lunch*) almuerzo *m*; **to make** ~ hacer la cena

dinner jacket *n* esmoquin *m* **dinner party** *n* cena *f* **dinner service** *n*, **dinner set** *n* vajilla *f* **dinner table** *n* mesa *f* de comedor

dinnertime *n no pl* hora *f* de cenar

dinosaur ['daɪnəsɔːr, *Am:* -sɔːr] *n* **1.**(*extinct reptile*) dinosaurio *m* **2.** *fig* (*old-fashioned object*) antigualla *f*

dint [dɪnt] *n* **by** ~ **of sth** a fuerza de algo

diocese ['daɪəsɪs] *n* diócesis *f*

dioxide [daɪ'ɒksaɪd, *Am:* -'ɑːk-] *n no pl* dióxido *m*

dioxin [daɪ'ɒksɪn, *Am:* -'ɑːk-] *n* dioxina *f*

dip [dɪp] **I.** *n* **1.**(*instance of dipping*) baño *m* **2.**(*sudden drop*) caída *f*; (*of a road*) hondonada *f* **3.**(*liquid*) salsa *f* **4.**(*brief swim*) chapuzón *m* **5.**(*depression of horizon, ground*) depresión *f* **6.**(*angle made by magnetic field*) inclinación *f* **II.** *vi* **1.**(*drop down*) descender **2.**(*slope down*) inclinarse **3.**(*submerge and re-emerge*) zambullirse **III.** *vt* **1.**(*immerse*) sumergir; *a.* GASTR mojar **2.**(*put into*) meter

3.(*lower*) bajar **4.**(*dye*) teñir **5.**(*wash*) desinfectar

◆**dip into** I. *vt always sep* (*put*) meter II. *vi* (*look at casually*) hojear

Dip *abbr of* Diploma D

diphtheria [dɪf'θɪəriə, *Am:* -'θɪri-] *n* MED difteria *f*

diphthong ['dɪfθɒŋ, *Am:* -θɑːŋ] *n* LING diptongo *m*

diploma [dɪ'pləʊmə, *Am:* -'ploʊ-] *n* (*certificate*) diploma *m;* **a** ~ **in sth** un diploma de algo

diplomacy [dɪ'pləʊməsi, *Am:* -'ploʊ-] *n no pl* **1.**(*managing relationships between countries*) diplomacia *f* **2.**(*tact*) tacto *m*

diplomat ['dɪpləmæt] *n* **1.**(*of country*) diplomático, -a *m, f* **2.**(*tactful person*) persona *f* diplomática

diplomatic [ˌdɪplə'mætɪk, *Am:* -'mæt̬-] *adj* diplomático, -a

diplomatist [dɪ'pləʊmətɪst, *Am:* -'ploʊmətɪst] *n s.* **diplomat**

dipper ['dɪpər, *Am:* -ɚ] *n* mirlo *m* acuático

dipsomania [ˌdɪpsəʊ'meɪniə, *Am:* -sə'-] *n no pl* MED dipsomanía *f*

dipsomaniac [ˌdɪpsəʊ'meɪniæk, *Am:* -sə'-] *n* MED dipsómano, -a *m, f*

dipstick ['dɪpstɪk] *n* varilla *f* de medir

dip-switch ['dɪpswɪtʃ] *n* AUTO conmutador *m* de luces

dire ['daɪər, *Am:* 'daɪɚ] *adj* **1.**(*terrible*) horrendo, -a **2.**(*serious*) grave **3.**(*extreme*) extremo, -a

direct [dɪ'rekt] I. *vi* MUS dirigir II. *vt* **1.** dirigir; **to** ~ **sth at sb** dirigir algo a alguien **2.**(*command*) ordenar **3.**(*indicate*) **to** ~ **sb to a place** indicar a alguien el camino hacia un sitio III. *adj* **1.**(*straight*) directo, -a **2.**(*exact*) exacto, -a; **the** ~ **opposite of sth** exactamente lo contrario de algo IV. *adv* **1.**(*with no intermediary*) directamente **2.**(*by a direct way*) recto

direct action *n* acción *f* directa **direct current** *n no pl* corriente *f* continua **direct debit** *n* domiciliación *f* bancaria **direct dial** *n* marcación *f* directa, discado *m* directo *Arg, Perú, Urug*, marcado *m* automático *Méx* **direct hit** *n* impacto *m* en la diana

direction [dɪ'rekʃən] *n no pl* **1.**(*supervision*) dirección *f* **2.**(*movement*) **in the** ~ **of sth** en dirección a/hacia algo; **sense of** ~ sentido *m* de la orientación **3.** *pl* (*information*) instrucciones *fpl;* **can you give me directions?** ¿me puedes indicar el camino?

directional [dɪ'rekʃənəl] *adj* direccional

directive [dɪ'rektɪv] *n* directriz *f*, directiva *f* *AmL*

directly [dɪ'rektli] I. *adv* **1.**(*frankly*) directamente **2.**(*immediately*) inmediatamente; (*right after*) inmediatamente después **3.**(*shortly*) pronto **4.**(*exactly*) exactamente II. *conj* en cuanto

direct object *n* objeto *m* directo

director [dɪ'rektər, *Am:* dɪ'rektɚ] *n* **1.** ECON (*manager*) director(a) *m(f)* **2.**(*board member*) miembro *m* del consejo; **board of** ~**s** consejo *m* de administración

directorate [dɪ'rektərət] *n* **1.**(*responsible department*) directiva *f* **2.**(*board of directors*) junta *f* directiva

directorship [dɪ'rektəʃɪp, *Am:* dɪ'rektɚ-] *n* dirección *f*

directory [dɪ'rektəri] *n* **1.**(*book*) guía *f*, directorio *m Méx;* **to look up sth in a** ~ buscar algo en una guía **2.** INFOR directorio *m;* ~ **structure** estructura *f* de directorios

directory enquiries *n* Brit servicio *m* de información telefónica

dirt [dɜːt, *Am:* dɜːrt] *n no pl* **1.**(*unclean substance*) suciedad *f* **2.**(*earth, soil*) tierra *f* **3.**(*foul language*) obscenidad *f* **4.**(*scandal*) trapos *mpl* sucios *fig* **5.**(*excrement*) excremento *mpl* **6.**(*worthless thing*) porquería *f;* **to treat sb like** ~ tratar a alguien como basura

▶**to eat** ~ tragar quina

dirt cheap *adj inf* tirado, -a, botado, -a *Méx*

dirt road *n* Brit, Aus, **dirt track** *n* pista *f* de tierra, camino *m* de terracería *Méx*

dirty ['dɜːti, *Am:* 'dɜːrt̬i] I. *n* Brit, Aus **to do the** ~ **on sb** hacer una mala pasada a alguien II. *vt* ensuciar; **to** ~ **one's hands** ensuciarse las manos III.<-ier, -iest> *adj* **1.**(*unclean*) sucio, -a, chancho, -a *AmL* **2.**(*mean, nasty*) bajo, -a **3.**(*lewd*) obsceno, -a; (*joke*) verde; (*look*) lascivo, -a; ~ **old man** viejo verde **4.**(*unpleasant*) sucio, -a; **to do the** ~ **work** hacer el trabajo sucio IV. *adv* Brit suciamente; **to play** ~ jugar sucio

disability [ˌdɪsə'bɪləti, *Am:* -ət̬i] *n* **1.**(*incapacity*) discapacidad *f*, invalidez *f AmL* **2.** *no pl* (*condition of incapacity*) incapacidad *f*

disable [dɪ'seɪbl] *vt* **1.** incapacitar **2.** MED lisiar

disabled I. *npl* **the** ~ los discapacitados II. *adj* incapacitado, -a

disablement *n no pl* incapacitación *f;* MED minusvalía *f*

disabuse [ˌdɪsə'bjuːz] *vt* **to** ~ **sb of sth** desengañar a alguien de algo

disadvantage [ˌdɪsəd'vɑːntɪdʒ, *Am:* -'væntɪdʒ] I. *n* desventaja *f;* **to be at a** ~ estar en desventaja II. *vt* perjudicar

disadvantaged *adj* desfavorecido, -a

disadvantageous [ˌdɪsˌædvən'teɪdʒəs, *Am:* ˌdɪsˌædvæn'-] *adj* desventajoso, -a

disaffected [ˌdɪsə'fektɪd] *adj* **1.**(*disloyal*) desleal **2.**(*estranged*) desafecto, -a

disaffection [ˌdɪsə'fekʃən] *n no pl* desafección *f*

disagree [ˌdɪsə'griː] *vi* **1.**(*not agree*) discrepar; **to** ~ **on sth** no estar de acuerdo en algo **2.**(*differ*) diferir; **the answers** ~ las respuestas no concuerdan **3.**(*have bad effect*) sentar mal; **spicy food** ~**s with me** la comida picante me sienta mal

disagreeable [ˌdɪsə'griːəbl] *adj* desagradable

disagreement [ˌdɪsəˈgriːmənt] *n* no pl **1.** (*lack of agreement*) desacuerdo *m* **2.** (*argument*) discusión *f* **3.** (*discrepancy*) discrepancia *f*

disallow [ˌdɪsəˈlaʊ] *vt* (*not allow*) rechazar; *a.* LAW, SPORTS anular

disappear [ˌdɪsəˈpɪəʳ, *Am:* -ˈpɪr] *vi* desaparecer; **to ~ from sight** desaparecer de la vista; **to ~ without a trace** desaparecer sin dejar rastro; **to have all but ~ed** haber casi desaparecido

disappearance [ˌdɪsəˈpɪərənts, *Am:* -ˈpɪr-] *n* no pl desaparición *f*

disappoint [ˌdɪsəˈpɔɪnt] *vt* decepcionar, enchilar *AmC*

disappointed *adj* decepcionado, -a; **to be ~ in sb** estar decepcionado con alguien

disappointing *adj* decepcionante

disappointment [ˌdɪsəˈpɔɪntmənt] *n* decepción *f*

disapprobation [ˌdɪsæprəʊˈbeɪʃən, *Am:* ˌdɪsˌæprə-] *n* no pl desaprobación *f*

disapproval [ˌdɪsəˈpruːvəl] *n* no pl desaprobación *f*

disapprove [ˌdɪsəˈpruːv] *vi* desaprobar
◆**disapprove of** *vt* desaprobar

disarm [dɪsˈɑːm, *Am:* -ˈɑːrm] **I.** *vi* (*stop holding weapons*) deponer las armas **II.** *vt* **1.** (*take weapons away*) desarmar **2.** (*remove fuse*) desactivar **3.** (*placate*) apaciguar

disarmament [dɪsˈɑːməmənt, *Am:* -ˈɑːr-] *n* no pl desarme *m*

disarming [dɪsˈɑːmɪŋ, *Am:* -ˈɑːrmɪŋ] *adj* **1.** MIL que quita las defensas **2.** (*person*) encantador(a)

disarrange [ˌdɪsəˈreɪndʒ] *vt* desarreglar

disarray [ˌdɪsəˈreɪ] *n* no pl (*disorder*) desorden *m*; (*confusion*) confusión *f*

disaster [dɪˈzɑːstəʳ, *Am:* dɪˈzæstəʳ] *n* **1.** (*great misfortune*) desastre *m*; **~ area** zona *f* catastrófica **2.** (*failure*) fiasco *m*

disastrous [dɪˈzɑːstrəs, *Am:* dɪˈzæstrəs] *adj* **1.** (*causing disaster*) desastroso, -a **2.** (*very unsuccessful*) catastrófico, -a

disband [dɪsˈbænd] *vt* disolver

disbelief [ˌdɪsbɪˈliːf] *n* no pl incredulidad *f*

disbelieve [ˌdɪsbɪˈliːv] *vt* no creer

disbeliever *n* incrédulo, -a *m, f*

disburse [dɪsˈbɜːs, *Am:* -ˈbɜːrs] *vt* desembolsar

disbursement [dɪsˈbɜːsmənt, *Am:* -ˈbɜːrs-] *n* desembolso *m*

disc [dɪsk] *n* disco *m*

discard[1] [ˈdɪskɑːd, *Am:* -kɑːrd] *n* descarte *m*

discard[2] [dɪˈskɑːd, *Am:* -skɑːrd] *vt* **1.** (*get rid of*) desechar **2.** *a.* GAMES descartar

disc brake *n* freno *m* de disco

discern [dɪˈsɜːn, *Am:* dɪˈsɜːrn] *vt* **1.** (*perceive*) percibir; (*distinguish*) distinguir **2.** (*make out*) discernir

discernable *adj*, **discernible** [dɪˈsɜːnəbl, *Am:* dɪˈsɜːr-] *adj* (*with senses*) perceptible;

(*mentally*) discernible

discerning [dɪˈsɜːnɪŋ, *Am:* dɪˈsɜːr-] *adj* (*discriminating*) exigente; (*acute*) perspicaz

discernment [dɪˈsɜːnmənt, *Am:* dɪˈsɜːrn-] *n* no pl (*good judgement*) criterio *m;* (*clear perception*) discernimiento *m*

discharge[1] [ˈdɪstʃɑːdʒ, *Am:* ˈdɪstʃɑːrdʒ] *n* no pl **1.** (*release*) liberación *f* **2.** (*release papers*) alta *f* **3.** (*firing off*) disparo *m* **4.** (*emission*) emisión *f* **5.** (*of liquid*) secreción *f* **6.** (*debt payment*) liquidación *f* **7.** (*performing of a duty*) desempeño *m* **8.** (*energy release*) descarga *f*

discharge[2] [dɪsˈtʃɑːdʒ, *Am:* -ˈtʃɑːrdʒ] **I.** *vi* **1.** (*ship*) descargar **2.** (*produce liquid*) secretar; (*wound*) supurar **II.** *vt* **1.** LAW liberar **2.** MIL, ECON (*dismiss*) despedir **3.** (*let out*) emitir **4.** (*utter*) gritar **5.** (*perform*) **to ~ one's duty** cumplir con sus obligaciones **6.** (*pay: debt*) liquidar **7.** (*cancel*) cancelar **8.** (*release*) liberar **9.** (*unload*) descargar

disciple [dɪˈsaɪpl] *n* **1.** (*follower*) seguidor(a) *m(f)* **2.** *a.* REL (*pupil*) discípulo, -a *m, f*

disciplinary [ˌdɪsəˈplɪnəri, *Am:* ˈdɪsəplɪnɚ-] *adj* disciplinario, -a

discipline [ˈdɪsəplɪn] **I.** *n* **1.** no pl (*obedience*) disciplina *f* **2.** no pl (*self-punishment*) auto-castigo *m* **II.** *vt* **1.** (*punish*) castigar; **to ~ oneself to do sth** obligarse a hacer algo **2.** (*train*) disciplinar

disciplined *adj* disciplinado, -a

disc jockey *n* disc jockey *mf*, pinchadiscos *mf inv*

disclaim [dɪsˈkleɪm] *vt* **1.** (*deny*) negar **2.** (*give up right to*) renunciar a

disclaimer [dɪsˈkleɪməʳ, *Am:* -məˠ] *n* **1.** (*denial*) descargo *m* de responsabilidad **2.** (*repudiating a claim*) repudio *m*

disclose [dɪsˈkləʊz, *Am:* -ˈkloʊz] *vt* **1.** (*make public*) divulgar **2.** (*uncover*) desvelar

disclosure [dɪsˈkləʊʒəʳ, *Am:* -ˈkloʊʒɚ] *n* **1.** (*act of making public*) divulgación *f* **2.** (*revelation*) revelación *f*

disco [ˈdɪskəʊ, *Am:* -koʊ] *n* **1.** no pl (*music*) música *f* disco **2.** (*place*) discoteca *f*

discolor *Am, Aus*, **discolour** [dɪˈskʌləʳ, *Am:* -ˈskʌləˠ] **I.** *vi* desteñirse **II.** *vt* decolorar; **my blue shirt has ~d the curtains** mi camisa azul ha desteñido en las cortinas

discomfit [dɪˈskʌmfɪt] *vt* desconcertar

discomfiture [dɪˈskʌmfɪtʃəʳ, *Am:* -tʃɚ] *n* no pl (*uneasiness*) turbación *f;* (*confusion*) desconcierto *m*

discomfort [dɪˈskʌmfət, *Am:* -fɚt] *n* **1.** no pl (*uneasiness*) malestar *m;* **~ at sth** malestar respecto a algo **2.** (*inconvenience*) molestia *f*

disconcert [ˌdɪskənˈsɜːt, *Am:* -ˈsɜːrt] *vt* desconcertar

disconnect [ˌdɪskəˈnekt] *vt* **1.** (*phone*) desconectar **2.** (*customer*) cortar el suministro a **3.** (*unfasten*) separar

disconnected *adj* **1.** (*cut off*) desconectado, -a **2.** (*incoherent*) inconexo, -a

disconsolate [dɪ'skɒntsələt, *Am:* -skɑːnt-] *adj* desconsolado, -a

discontent [ˌdɪskən'tent] I. *n no pl* descontento *m* II. *adj* descontento, -a

discontented *adj* descontento, -a

discontentment *n no pl s.* **discontent**

discontinue [ˌdɪskən'tɪnjuː] I. *vi* desistir II. *vt* suspender

discontinuity [ˌdɪsˌkɒntɪ'njuːəti, *Am:* ˌdɪskɑːntən'uːəti] <-ies> *n* 1. (*lack of continuity*) discontinuidad *f* 2. (*gap*) laguna *f*

discontinuous [ˌdɪskən'tɪnjuəs] *adj* (*without continuity*) discontinuo, -a; (*broken*) interrumpido, -a

discord ['dɪskɔːd, *Am:* -kɔːrd] *n no pl* 1. (*disagreement*) discordia *f* 2. (*clashing noise*) discordancia *f* 3. (*lack of harmony*) disonancia *f*

discordant [dɪ'skɔːdənt, *Am:* -'skɔːr-] *adj* 1. (*disagreeing*) discordante 2. (*not in harmony*) disonante

discotheque ['dɪskətek] *n* discoteca *f*

discount¹ ['dɪskaʊnt] *n* descuento *m;* **at a ~** con descuento

discount² [dɪ'skaʊnt] *vt* 1. (*reduce selling price*) descontar 2. (*disregard*) no hacer caso de 3. (*leave out*) dejar de lado

discount store *n* tienda *f* de descuento

discourage [dɪ'skʌrɪdʒ, *Am:* -'skɜːr-] *vt* 1. (*dishearten*) desanimar 2. (*dissuade*) **to ~ sb from doing sth** disuadir a alguien de hacer algo 3. (*oppose*) desaprobar

discouragement [dɪ'skʌrɪdʒ, *Am:* -'skɜːr-] *n* 1. *no pl* (*feeling discouraged*) desaliento *m* 2. (*deterrent*) impedimento *m*

discouraging *adj* desalentador(a)

discourse¹ ['dɪskɔːs, *Am:* -kɔːrs] *n* discurso *m;* (*written*) tratado *m;* **a ~ about** [*o* **on**] **sth** un discurso sobre algo; (*written*) un tratado sobre algo

discourse² [dɪ'skɔːs, *Am:* -'skɔːrs] *vi* hablar; **to ~ upon sth** conversar sobre algo, platicar sobre algo *AmL*

discourteous [dɪs'kɜːtiəs, *Am:* -kɜːrʈi-] *adj* descortés

discourtesy [dɪs'kɜːtəsi, *Am:* -kɜːrʈə-] <-ies> *n* 1. *no pl* (*rudeness*) descortesía *f* 2. (*act of rudeness*) grosería *f*

discover [dɪ'skʌvəʳ, *Am:* -ɚ] *vt* 1. (*find out*) descubrir 2. (*find*) hallar

discoverer *n* descubridor(a) *m(f)*

discovery [dɪ'skʌvəri] <-ies> *n* descubrimiento *m*

Discovery Day *n no pl, Can* Día *m* del Descubrimiento (de América)

discredit [dɪ'skredɪt] I. *n no pl* 1. (*disrepute*) desprestigio *m* 2. (*disgrace*) vergüenza *f;* **she is a ~ to her school** es una vergüenza para su escuela 3. (*doubt*) duda *f* II. *vt* desacreditar

discreditable [dɪ'skredɪtəbl, *Am:* -ʈə-] *adj* deshonroso, -a

discreet [dɪ'skriːt] *adj* discreto, -a

discrepancy [dɪ'skrepəntsi] <-ies> *n* discrepancia *f*

discrete [dɪ'skriːt] *adj* separado, -a

discretion [dɪ'skreʃən] *n no pl* 1. (*discreet behaviour*) discreción *f;* **to leave sth to sb's ~** dejar algo a discreción de alguien 2. (*good judgment*) criterio *m* 3. LAW (*of court*) arbitrio *m*

discriminate [dɪ'skrɪmɪneɪt] I. *vi* 1. (*see a difference*) discernir 2. (*treat unfairly*) **to ~ against sb** discriminar a alguien II. *vt* distinguir

discriminating *adj* 1. (*able to discern*) discerniente 2. (*palate, taste*) exigente

discrimination [dɪˌskrɪmɪ'neɪʃən] *n no pl* 1. (*unfair treatment*) discriminación *f* 2. (*good judgement*) criterio *m* 3. (*ability to differentiate*) discernimiento *m*

discriminatory [dɪ'skrɪmɪnətəri, *Am:* -tɔːri] *adj* discriminatorio, -a

discursive [dɪ'skɜːsɪv, *Am:* -'skɜːr-] *adj* digresivo, -a

discus ['dɪskəs] *n* SPORTS disco *m*

discuss [dɪ'skʌs] *vt* 1. (*exchange ideas about*) discutir 2. (*consider*) tratar sobre

discussion [dɪ'skʌʃən] *n* discusión *f*, argumento *m AmL;* **~ group** grupo *m* de discusión

disdain [dɪs'deɪn] I. *n no pl* desdén *m* II. *vt* desdeñar; **to ~ to do sth** no dignarse a hacer algo; **powerful men ~ the weak** los poderosos desdeñan al débil

disdainful [dɪs'deɪnfəl] *adj* desdeñoso, -a

disease [dɪ'ziːz] *n a. fig* enfermedad *f;* **to catch a ~** contraer una enfermedad

diseased *adj a. fig* enfermo, -a

disembark [ˌdɪsɪm'bɑːk, *Am:* -'bɑːrk] *vi* desembarcar

disembarkation [ˌdɪsˌɪmbɑː'keɪʃən, *Am:* -bɑːrʹ-] *n* desembarque *m*

disembodied [ˌdɪsɪm'bɒdid, *Am:* -bɑːdid] *adj* incorpóreo, -a

disenchant [ˌdɪsɪn'tʃɑːnt, *Am:* -'tʃænt] *vt* desencantar

disenchanted *adj* desencantado, -a

disenfranchise [ˌdɪsɪn'fræntʃaɪz] *vt* 1. (*deprive of vote*) privar del voto 2. (*deprive of rights*) privar de derechos

disengage [ˌdɪsɪn'geɪdʒ] I. *vi* 1. (*become detached*) separarse 2. (*make a fencing move*) fintar II. *vt* 1. (*uncouple*) separar 2. (*detach*) desconectar; (*a clutch*) quitar 3. MIL retirar

disengagement [ˌdɪsɪn'geɪdʒmənt] *n no pl* desconexión *m*

disentangle [ˌdɪsɪn'tæŋgl] I. *vi* desenredarse II. *vt* 1. (*untangle*) desenredar 2. *fig* (*unravel*) desembrollar

disfavor *Am, Aus,* **disfavour** [ˌdɪs'feɪvəʳ, *Am:* -və-] I. *n no pl* desaprobación *f;* **to fall into ~** caer en desgracia II. *vt* desfavorecer

disfigure [dɪs'fɪgəʳ, *Am:* -jə-] *vt* desfigurar

disfigurement *n no pl* desfiguración *f*

disfranchise [dɪs'fræntʃaɪz] *s.* **disenfranchise**

disgorge [dɪs'gɔːdʒ, *Am:* -'gɔːrdʒ] *vt* arrojar; *fig* vomitar

disgrace [dɪs'greɪs] I. *n no pl* 1. (*loss of honour*) deshonra *f* 2. (*shameful thing or person*) vergüenza *f* II. *vt* deshonrar

disgraced *adj* deshonrado, -a

disgraceful [dɪs'greɪsfəl] *adj* vergonzoso, -a

disgruntled [dɪs'grʌntld, *Am:* - t̬ld] *adj* contrariado, -a; **to be ~ at sth** estar descontento de algo

disguise [dɪs'gaɪz] I. *n* disfraz *m*; **to be in ~** estar disfrazado II. *vt* 1. (*change appearance*) disfrazar; **to ~ oneself as sth** disfrazarse de algo 2. (*hide*) encubrir

disgust [dɪs'gʌst] I. *n no pl* 1. (*repugnance*) asco *m*; **to turn away from sth in ~** alejarse con repugnancia de algo 2. (*indignation*) indignación *f*; **~ at sth** indignación por algo II. *vt* 1. (*sicken*) dar asco, repugnar, chocar *AmL* 2. (*revolt*) indignar

disgusted *adj* 1. (*sickened*) asqueado, -a 2. (*indignant*) indignado, -a

disgusting [dɪs'gʌstɪŋ] *adj* 1. (*repulsive*) repugnante, chocante *AmL* 2. (*unacceptable*) indignante

dish [dɪʃ] I.<-es> *n* 1. (*for food*) plato *m*; **oven-proof ~** plato térmico; **to do the ~es** fregar los platos 2. (*equipment*) (antena *f*) parabólica *f* 3. *inf* (*sexually attractive person*) bombón *m* II. *vt inf* 1. (*serve*) servir 2. (*spoil*) arruinar

◆**dish out** *vt* 1. (*distribute too liberally*) repartir a diestro y siniestro 2. (*serve*) servir

◆**dish up** *vt inf* 1. (*serve*) servir 2. (*offer*) ofrecer

dish aerial *n Brit* (antena) parabólica *f*

disharmonious [ˌdɪshɑː'məʊniəs, *Am:* -hɑːrmoʊ-] *adj* discordante

disharmony [dɪs'hɑːməni, *Am:* -'hɑːr-] *n no pl* falta *f* de armonía

dishcloth ['dɪʃklɒθ, *Am:* -klɑːθ] *n* trapo *m* de cocina, repasador *m Arg, Urug*

dishearten [dɪs'hɑːtən, *Am:* -'hɑːr-] *vt* descorazonar

disheveled *adj Am,* **dishevelled** [dɪ-'ʃevəld] *adj* desaliñado, -a; **with ~ hair** despeinado

dishonest [dɪ'sɒnɪst, *Am:* -'sɑːnɪst] *adj* deshonesto, -a; **to be ~ about sth** ser falso acerca de algo

dishonesty [dɪ'sɒnɪsti, *Am:* -'sɑːnə-] *n no pl* 1. (*lack of honesty*) falta *f* de honestidad 2. (*dishonest act*) fraude *m*

dishonor [dɪ'sɑːnɚ] *n Am s.* **dishonour**

dishonorable [dɪ'sɑːnərəbl] *adj Am s.* **dishonourable**

dishonour [dɪ'sɒnər, *Am:* -'sɑːnɚ] I. *n no pl* deshonor *m*; **to bring ~ on sb** traer la deshonra a alguien II. *vt* 1. (*disgrace*) deshonrar 2. (*not keep*) incumplir

dishonourable [dɪ'sɒnərəbl, *Am:* -'sɑːnɚ-] *adj* deshonroso, -a

dishtowel ['dɪʃtaʊəl] *n Am* paño *m* de

cocina **dishwasher** *n* 1. (*machine*) lavavajillas *f inv*; **to run the ~** poner el lavaplatos *m* 2. (*person*) lavaplatos *mf* **dishwater** *n no pl* agua *f* de lavar platos

disillusion [ˌdɪsɪ'luːʒən] I. *vt* desilusionar II. *n no pl* desilusión *f*

disillusioned *adj* desilusionado, -a; **to be ~ with sth** estar desilusionado con algo; **to be ~ with sb** estar desilusionado de alguien

disillusionment *n no pl* desilusión

disinclination [ˌdɪsɪnklɪ'neɪʃən] *n no pl* renuencia *f*

disinclined [ˌdɪsɪn'klaɪnd] *adj* renuente; **to be ~ to do sth** tener pocas ganas de hacer algo

disinfect [ˌdɪsɪn'fekt] *vt* desinfectar

disinfectant [ˌdɪsɪn'fektənt] I. *n* desinfectante *m* II. *adj no pl* desinfectante

disinfection [ˌdɪsɪn'fekʃən] *n no pl* desinfección *f*

disingenuous [ˌdɪsɪn'dʒenjuəs] *adj* insincero, -a

disinherit [ˌdɪsɪn'herɪt] *vt* desheredar

disintegrate [dɪ'sɪntɪgreɪt, *Am:* -t̬ə-] I. *vi* desintegrarse II. *vt* desintegrar

disintegration [dɪˌsɪntɪ'greɪʃən, *Am:* -t̬ɚ'-] *n no pl* desintegración *f*

disinterested [dɪ'sɪntrəstɪd, *Am:* -'sɪntrɪstɪd] *adj* 1. (*impartial*) imparcial 2. (*uninterested*) desinteresado, -a

disjointed [dɪs'dʒɔɪntɪd, *Am:* -t̬ɪd] *adj* inconexo, -a

disk [dɪsk] *n* INFOR disco *m*; **hard ~** disco duro; **floppy ~** disquete *m*; **installation ~** disco de instalación; **start-up ~** disco de arranque; **high density ~** disquete de alta densidad; **compact laser ~** laserdisc *m*

disk drive *n* disquetera *f*

diskette [dɪs'kæt] *n* disquete *m*

dislike [dɪs'laɪk] I. *vt* tener aversión a II. *n no pl* aversión *f*; **to take a ~ to sb/sth** tomar aversión a alguien/algo

dislocate ['dɪsləkeɪt, *Am:* dɪ'sloʊ-] *vt* 1. (*put out of place*) desplazar 2. MED **he discolated his shoulder** se dislocó el hombro 3. *fig* (*disturb the working of*) trastornar

dislocation [ˌdɪslə'keɪʃən, *Am:* -loʊ'-] *n* 1. (*displacement*) desplazamiento *m* 2. MED dislocación *f* 3. *no pl, fig* (*disturbance*) trastorno *m*

dislodge [dɪ'slɒdʒ, *Am:* -'slɑːdʒ] *vt* desalojar

disloyal [dɪ'slɔɪəl] *adj* desleal; **to be ~ to sb/sth** ser desleal a alguien/algo

dismal ['dɪzməl] *adj* 1. (*depressing*) deprimente 2. *inf* (*awful*) terrible; (*truth*) triste

dismantle [dɪ'smæntl, *Am:* dɪ'smæntl̩] *vt* desmontar; (*system*) desmantelar

dismay [dɪ'smeɪ] I. *n no pl* consternación *f*; **to sb's (great) ~** para (gran) consternación de alguien II. *vt* consternar

dismayed *adj* consternado, -a

dismember [dɪ'smembər, *Am:* -bɚ] *vt a. fig* desmembrar

dismiss [dɪ'smɪs] *vt* 1. (*not consider*) descartar **2.** (*let go*) dejar ir **3.** (*from job*) despedir; **to be ~ed from one's job** ser despedido del trabajo **4.** LAW desestimar

dismissal [dɪ'smɪsəl] *n no pl* **1.** (*disregarding*) descarte *m* **2.** (*from job*) despido *m*

dismissive [dɪ'smɪsɪv] *adj* **she was dismissive about the idea** no daba crédito a la idea

dismount [dɪ'smaʊnt] *vi* desmontar(se)

disobedience [ˌdɪsəʊ'biːdiənts, *Am:* -ə'-] *n no pl* desobediencia *f*

disobedient [ˌdɪsəʊ'biːdiənt, *Am:* -ə'-] *adj* desobediente

disobey [ˌdɪsəʊ'beɪ, *Am:* -ə'-] *vi, vt* desobedecer

disoblige [ˌdɪsə'blaɪdʒ] *vt* disgustar

disobliging *adj* desatento, -a

disorder [dɪ'sɔːdəʳ, *Am:* -'sɔːrdəʳ] *n* **1.** *no pl* (*lack of order*) desorden *m*, desparramo *m* *CSur* **2.** (*sickness*) trastorno *m*

disordered *adj* desordenado, -a

disorderly [dɪ'sɔːdəli, *Am:* -'sɔːrdəʳ-] *adj* **1.** (*untidy*) desordenado, -a **2.** (*unruly*) escandaloso, -a; **~ conduct** alteración *f* del orden público

disorganized [dɪ'sɔːgənaɪzd, *Am:* dɪ'sɔːr-] *adj* desorganizado, -a

disorient [dɪ'sɔːriənt, *Am:* -ent] *vt Am*, **disorientate** [dɪ'sɔːriənteɪt] *vt* desorientar; **to get ~ed** desorientarse

disoriented *adj* desorientado, -a

disown [dɪ'saʊn, *Am:* dɪ'soʊn] *vt* repudiar

disparage [dɪ'spærɪdʒ, *Am:* -'sper-] *vt* menospreciar

disparagement *n no pl* menosprecio *m*

disparaging *adj* (*disdainful*) despreciativo, -a; (*remark*) desdeñoso, -a

disparate ['dɪspərət] *adj* dispar

disparity [dɪ'spærəti, *Am:* -'peraţi] *n* disparidad *f*

dispassionate [dɪ'spæʃənət] *adj* desapasionado, -a

dispatch [dɪ'spætʃ] **I.**<-es> *n* **1.** *no pl* (*sending*) despacho *m;* **I have just received the latest ~ of our war correspondent** acabo de recibir el último despacho de nuestro corresponsal de guerra **2.** (*something sent*) envío *m* **II.** *vt a. fig* despachar

dispel [dɪ'spel] <-ll-> *vt* (*fears, doubts*) disipar; (*a rumour*) desmentir

dispensable [dɪ'spensəbl] *adj* prescindible

dispensary [dɪ'spensəri] *n Brit* dispensario *m*

dispensation [ˌdɪspen'seɪʃən] *n* **1.** (*special permission*) dispensa *f* **2.** (*distributing*) administración *f*

dispense [dɪ'spens] *vt* **1.** (*give out*) repartir **2.** MED (*medicine*) administrar

♦**dispense with** *vi* prescindir de

dispenser [dɪ'spensəʳ, *Am:* -əʳ] *n* **1.** (*device*) máquina *f* expendedora; **cash ~** cajero *m* automático **2.** (*one who distributes*) distribuidor(a) *m(f)*

dispersal [dɪ'spɜːsl, *Am:* -'spɜːr-] *n no pl* (*dispersing*) dispersión *f*

disperse [dɪ'spɜːs, *Am:* -'spɜːrs] **I.** *vt* dispersar **II.** *vi* dispersarse

dispersion [dɪ'spɜːʃən, *Am:* -'spɜːrʒən] *n no pl* dispersión *f*

dispirited [dɪ'spɪrɪtɪd, *Am:* -ţɪd] *adj* desanimado, -a

displace [dɪs'pleɪs] *vt* **1.** (*eject*) desplazar **2.** (*take the place of*) reemplazar

displacement [dɪs'pleɪsmənt] *n no pl* desplazamiento *m*

display [dɪ'spleɪ] **I.** *vt* **1.** (*arrange for showing*) exhibir; **to ~ sth in a shop window** exhibir algo en un escaparate **2.** (*show*) demostrar **II.** *n* **1.** (*arrangement*) exposición *f;* **firework ~** *Am, Aus* exhibición *f* pirotécnica **2.** *no pl* (*demonstration*) demostración *f* **3.** INFOR pantalla *f;* **liquid crystal ~** pantalla de cristal líquido

display case *n* estuche *m* **display window** *n* escaparate *m*

displease [dɪ'spliːz] *vt* disgustar; **to be ~d by sth** estar disgustado con algo

displeasing *adj* desagradable

displeasure [dɪ'spleʒəʳ, *Am:* -əʳ] *n no pl* disgusto *m*

disposable [dɪ'spəʊzəbl, *Am:* -'spoʊ-] *adj* desechable

disposable income *n* renta *f* disponible

disposal [dɪ'spəʊzl, *Am:* dɪ'spoʊ-] *n* **1.** *no pl* (*getting rid of*) eliminación *f* **2.** *Am* (*grinding machine*) trituradora *f* ▶**to be at sb's ~** estar a disposición de alguien

dispose [dɪ'spəʊz, *Am:* -'spoʊz] **I.** *vt* **1.** (*place*) disponer **2.** (*incline*) predisponer **II.** *vi* **to ~ of sth** (*throw away*) desechar algo; (*get rid of*) deshacerse de algo

disposed *adj* **to be well ~ towards sb** estar bien dispuesto hacia alguien

disposition [ˌdɪspə'zɪʃən] *n* disposición *f;* **to have a happy ~** mostrar una buena disposición

dispossess [ˌdɪspə'zes] *vt* desposeer

disproportionate [ˌdɪsprə'pɔːʃənət, *Am:* -'pɔːr-] *adj* desproporcionado, -a

disprove [dɪ'spruːv] *vt* refutar

disputable [dɪ'spjuːtəbl, *Am:* dɪ'spjuːţə-] *adj* discutible

disputation [ˌdɪspjʊ'teɪʃən, *Am:* -pju:'-] *n* debate *m*

disputatious [ˌdɪspjʊ'teɪʃəs, *Am:* -pju:'-] *adj* disputador(a)

dispute [dɪ'spjuːt] **I.** *vt* **1.** (*argue*) discutir **2.** (*doubt*) poner en duda **II.** *vi* **to ~ (with sb) over sth** discutir (con alguien) sobre algo **III.** *n* discusión *f;* **a ~ over sth** una discusión sobre algo

disqualification [dɪˌskwɒlɪfɪ'keɪʃən, *Am:* dɪˌskwɑːlə-] *n* **1.** *no pl* SPORTS descalificación *f* **2.** (*incapacity*) incapacidad *f*

disqualify [dɪ'skwɒlɪfaɪ, *Am:* dɪ'skwɑːlə-] <-ie-> *vt* descalificar; **to ~ sb from an event**

descalificar a alguien de un evento

disquiet [dɪ'skwaɪət] **I.** *n no pl* inquietud *f;* ~ **over sth** inquietud acerca de algo **II.** *vt* inquietar

disquieting *adj* inquietante

disregard [ˌdɪsrɪ'gɑːd, *Am:* -rɪ'gɑːrd] **I.** *vt* desatender **II.** *n no pl* despreocupación *f*

disrepair [ˌdɪsrɪ'peəʳ, *Am:* -rɪ'per] *n no pl* deterioro *m;* **to be in a state of** ~ estar en mal estado

disreputable [dɪs'repjətəbl, *Am:* -jət̬ə-] *adj* de mala fama

disrepute [ˌdɪsrɪ'pjuːt] *n* desprestigio *m*

disrespect [ˌdɪsrɪ'spekt] *n no pl* falta *f* de respeto; **to show** ~ mostrar descortesía

disrespectful [ˌdɪsrɪ'spektfəl] *adj* descortés

disrupt [dɪs'rʌpt] *vt* (*interrupt*) interrumpir; (*disturb*) trastornar

disruption [dɪs'rʌpʃən] *n* (*interruption*) interrupción *f;* (*disturbance*) perturbación *f;* *fig* (*disorder*) desorganización *f*

disruptive [dɪs'rʌptɪv] *adj* que trastorna

dissatisfaction [dɪsˌsætɪs'fækʃən, *Am:* ˌdɪssæt̬əs'-] *n no pl* insatisfacción *f*

dissatisfied [dɪs'sætɪsfaɪd, *Am:* -'sæt̬əs-] *adj* insatisfecho, -a

dissect [dɪ'sekt] *vt* **1.** (*cut open*) diseccionar **2.** *fig* (*examine*) examinar

dissection [dɪ'sekʃən] *n* disección *f*

dissemble [dɪ'sembl] *vi, vt* disimular

disseminate [dɪ'semɪneɪt] *vt* diseminar

dissemination [dɪˌsemɪ'neɪʃən] *n no pl* diseminación *f*

dissension [dɪ'sentʃən] *n* disensión *f;* **to sow** ~ sembrar la discordia

dissent [dɪ'sent] **I.** *n no pl* disidencia *f* **II.** *vi* **1.** (*not agree with*) disentir; **to** ~ **from sth** disentir de algo **2.** (*reject a doctrine*) disidir

dissenter *n* disidente *mf*

dissertation [ˌdɪsə'teɪʃən, *Am:* -əˈ-] *n* **1.** (*long piece of writing*) disertación *f* **2.** UNIV tesis *f*

disservice [ˌdɪs'sɜːvɪs, *Am:* -'sɜːr-] *n no pl* perjuicio *m;* **to do sth/sb a** ~ perjudicar a algo/a alguien

dissident ['dɪsɪdənt] **I.** *n* disidente *mf* **II.** *adj* disidente

dissimilar [ˌdɪs'sɪmɪləʳ, *Am:* -lə-] *adj* diferente, disímbolo, -a *Méx;* **to be** ~ **to sb/sth** ser distinto de alguien/algo

dissimilarity [ˌdɪsˌsɪmɪ'lærəti, *Am:* -'lerət̬i] <-ies> *n* desemejanza *f*

dissimulation [ˌdɪsˌsɪmjə'leɪʃən] *n* disimulo *m*

dissipate ['dɪsɪpeɪt] **I.** *vi* **1.** (*disperse*) disiparse **2.** *fig* (*engage in frivolous pleasures*) llevar una vida disoluta **II.** *vt* disipar

dissipated *adj* disipado, -a

dissipation [ˌdɪsɪ'peɪʃən] *n* **1.** (*wasting frivolously*) desperdicio *m;* (*of money*) derroche *m* **2.** (*damaging indulgence in pleasure*) disipación *f*

dissociate [dɪ'səʊʃieɪt, *Am:* -'soʊ-] *vt* **to** ~

carbon from sth disociar el carbono de algo; **to** ~ **oneself from sb/sth** disociarse de alguien/algo

dissociation [dɪˌsəʊʃi'eɪʃən, *Am:* -ˌsoʊ-] *n no pl* disociación *f*

dissolute ['dɪsəluːt] *adj liter* disoluto, -a

dissolution [ˌdɪsə'luːʃən] *n no pl* disolución *f*

dissolve [dɪ'zɒlv, *Am:* -'zɑːlv] **I.** *vi* **1.** (*become part of a liquid*) disolverse **2.** *fig* (*collapse*) deshacerse; **to** ~ **into tears** deshacerse en lágrimas **3.** *fig* (*disappear*) desvanecerse **II.** *vt* disolver; **to** ~ **a society** disolver una sociedad

dissonance ['dɪsənənts] *n no pl* disonancia *f*

dissonant ['dɪsənənt] *adj* disonante; *fig* discordante

dissuade [dɪ'sweɪd] *vt* disuadir

distance ['dɪstənts] **I.** *n* **1.** (*space*) distancia *f;* **his house is within walking** ~ se puede ir andando a su casa; **to keep one's** ~ guardar las distancias **2.** (*space far away*) lejanía *f* **II.** *vt* **to** ~ **oneself from sb/sth** distanciarse de alguien/algo

distant ['dɪstənt] *adj* **1.** (*far away*) distante **2.** (*not closely related*) lejano, -a

distantly *adv* **1.** (*in the distance*) de lejos **2.** *fig* (*in an unfriendly manner*) distantemente

distaste [dɪ'steɪst] *n no pl* aversión *f*

distasteful [dɪ'steɪstfəl] *adj* desagradable

distemper [dɪ'stempəʳ, *Am:* -pə-] *n* **1.** (*animal disease*) moquillo *m* **2.** (*type of paint*) temple *m* **3.** (*bad temper*) malhumor *m*

distend [dɪ'stend] *vi* distenderse

distension [dɪ'stentʃən] *n no pl* distensión *f*

distil [dɪ'stɪl] <-ll-> *vt*, **distill** *vt Am, Aus* destilar

distillation [ˌdɪstɪ'leɪʃən] *n no pl* destilación *f*

distiller [dɪ'stɪləʳ, *Am:* dɪ'stɪlə-] *n* **1.** (*company*) destilería *f* **2.** (*person*) destilador(a) *m(f)*

distillery [dɪ'stɪləri] *n* destilería *f*

distinct [dɪ'stɪŋkt] *adj* **1.** (*separate*) distinto **2.** (*marked*) definido, -a **3.** (*noticeable*) nítido, -a

distinction [dɪ'stɪŋkʃən] *n* **1.** (*difference*) distinción *m* **2.** *no pl* (*eminence*) distinción *m;* **of great** ~ de gran renombre **3.** *Brit* (*excellent marks*) sobresaliente *m*

distinctive [dɪ'stɪŋktɪv] *adj* característico, -a

distinguish [dɪ'stɪŋgwɪʃ] **I.** *vi* distinguir **II.** *vt* **1.** (*tell apart*) distinguir **2.** (*be excellent in*) **to** ~ **oneself in sth** destacar en algo

distinguishable [dɪ'stɪŋgwɪʃəbl] *adj* distinguible

distinguished *adj* **1.** (*celebrated*) eminente **2.** (*stylish*) distinguido, -a

distort [dɪ'stɔːt, *Am:* -'stɔːrt] *vt* torcer; (*facts, the truth*) tergiversar

distortion [dɪ'stɔːʃən, *Am:* -'stɔːr-] *n* (*of the truth, facts*) distorsión *f;* (*of a face*) contorsión *f*

distract [dɪ'strækt] *vt* distraer

distracted *adj* distraído, -a

distraction [dɪ'strækʃən] *n* **1.** (*disturbing factor*) distracción *f* **2.** (*pastime*) entretenimiento *m* **3.** *no pl* (*confused agitation*) aturdimiento *m*

distraught [dɪ'strɔːt, *Am:* -'strɑːt] *adj* turbado, -a

distress [dɪ'stres] **I.** *n no pl* **1.** (*extreme pain*) aflicción *f* **2.** (*anguish*) congoja *f* **3.** (*state of danger*) apuro *m* **II.** *vt* afligir

distressed *adj* **1.** (*unhappy*) afligido, -a **2.** (*in difficulties*) apurado, -a

distressful [dɪ'stresfəl] *adj Am*, **distressing** *adj* **1.** (*causing great worry*) angustioso, -a **2.** (*painful*) doloroso, -a

distribute [dɪ'strɪbjuːt] *vt* **1.** (*share*) repartir **2.** (*spread over space*) distribuir; **to be widely ~d** estar ampliamente repartido

distribution [ˌdɪstrɪ'bjuːʃən] *n no pl* **1.** (*giving out*) reparto *m* **2.** (*spread*) distribución *f*

distribution area *n* ECON área *f* de distribución **distribution channel** *n* ECON canal *m* de distribución **distribution rights** *npl* derechos *mpl* de distribución

distributive [dɪ'strɪbjətɪv, *Am:* -jəṭɪv] *adj* distributivo, -a

distributor [dɪ'strɪbjətəʳ, *Am:* -ṭəʳ] *n* **1.** (*person*) distribuidor(a) *m(f)* **2.** (*device*) distribuidor *m*

district [dɪ'strɪkt] *n* **1.** (*defined area*) distrito *m*, intendencia *f CSur* **2.** (*region*) región *f*

district attorney *n Am* fiscal *m* de distrito **district council** *n Brit* ayuntamiento *m* de distrito **district court** *n Am* tribunal *m* federal

distrust [dɪ'strʌst] **I.** *vt* desconfiar de **II.** *n no pl* desconfianza *f*

distrustful [dɪ'strʌstfəl] *adj* desconfiado, -a

disturb [dɪ'stɜːb, *Am:* -'stɜːrb] *vt* **1.** (*bother*) molestar **2.** (*worry*) preocupar **3.** (*move around*) perturbar

disturbance [dɪ'stɜːbənts, *Am:* -'stɜːr-] *n* **1.** (*bother*) molestia *f* **2.** (*public incident*) disturbio *m*

disturbed *adj* **1.** (*restless*) inquieto, -a **2.** (*moved around*) perturbado, -a

disturbing *adj* **1.** (*annoying*) molesto, -a **2.** (*worrying*) preocupante

disunite [ˌdɪsjuː'naɪt] *vt* desunir

disunity [dɪ'sjuːnəti, *Am:* -ṭi] *n no pl* desunión *f*

disuse [dɪ'sjuːs] *n no pl* desuso *m*

disused [dɪ'sjuːzd] *adj* en desuso

ditch [dɪtʃ] **I.** <-es> *n* **1.** zanja *f*; (*road*) cuneta *f*; **irrigation ~** acequia *f* **2.** (*for defense*) foso *m* **II.** *vt* **1.** (*discard*) deshacerse de; (*car*) abandonar; (*idea*) descartar **2.** (*escape from*) zafarse de **3.** *inf* (*end a relationship*) cortar con **4.** (*land in water*) **to ~ a plane** hacer un amaraje forzoso **III.** *vi* abrir zanjas

dither ['dɪðəʳ, *Am:* -əʳ] **I.** *n no pl* **to be in a ~** estar hecho un flan **II.** *vi inf* **1.** (*be indecisive*) vacilar; **to ~ over whether to do sth** vacilar sobre si hacer algo **2.** (*behave nervously*) ponerse nervioso

ditto ['dɪtəʊ, *Am:* 'dɪṭoʊ] **I.** *n* (*mark indicating repetition*) comillas *fpl* **II.** *adv* (*so do I*) ídem; *Am* (*same for me*) lo mismo

ditty ['dɪti, *Am:* 'dɪṭ-] <-ies> *n* cancioncilla *f*

diurnal [daɪ'ɜːnəl, *Am:* -'ɜːr-] *adj* diurno, -a

divan [dɪ'væn] *n* diván *m*

dive [daɪv] **I.** *n* **1.** (*jump into water*) salto *m* de cabeza **2.** (*plunge*) inmersión *f* **3.** *a. fig* (*sudden decline*) descenso *m* en picado; **to take a ~** caer en picado **4.** *inf* (*undesirable establishment*) antro *m* **II.** *vi* <dived *o Am:* dove, dived *o Am:* dove> **1.** (*plunge into water*) zambullirse; **to ~ under sth** bucear por debajo de algo; **to ~ to a depth of ...** sumergirse a una profundidad de... **2.** (*jump head first into water*) tirarse de cabeza **3.** (*go sharply downwards*) bajar en picado **4.** (*move towards*) precipitarse; **to ~ for cover** buscar abrigo precipitadamente

diver ['daɪvəʳ, *Am:* -vəʳ] *n* **1.** (*person who dives*) buceador(a) *m(f)* **2.** (*person working under water*) buzo *m*

diverge [daɪ'vɜːdʒ, *Am:* -'vɜːrdʒ] *vi* divergir **to ~ from sth** apartarse de algo

divergence [daɪ'vɜːdʒəns, *Am:* dɪ'vɜːr-] *n no pl* divergencia *f*

divergent [daɪ'vɜːdʒənt, *Am:* dɪ'vɜːr-] *adj* **1.** (*differing*) divergente **2.** (*different*) distinto, -a

diverse [daɪ'vɜːs, *Am:* dɪ'vɜːrs] *adj* **1.** (*varied*) variado, -a **2.** (*not alike*) diverso, -a

diversification [daɪˌvɜːsɪfɪ'keɪʃən, *Am:* dɪˌvɜːr-] *n no pl* diversificación *f*

diversify [daɪ'vɜːsɪfaɪ, *Am:* dɪˌvɜːr-] <-ie-> **I.** *vi* diversificarse **II.** *vt* diversificar

diversion [daɪ'vɜːʃən, *Am:* dɪ'vɜːr-] *n* **1.** *no pl* (*changing of direction*) desviación *f*; (*of railway, river*) desvío *m* **2.** (*distraction*) entretenimiento *m* **3.** (*activity*) diversión *f*

diversity [daɪ'vɜːsəti, *Am:* dɪ'vɜːrsəṭi] *n no pl* diversidad *f*

divert [daɪ'vɜːt, *Am:* dɪ'vɜːrt] *vt* **1.** (*change direction*) desviar **2.** (*distract*) distraer **3.** (*amuse*) divertir

diverting [daɪ'vɜːtɪŋ, *Am:* dɪ'vɜːrṭɪŋ] *adj* divertido, -a

divest [daɪ'vest, *Am:* dɪ-] **I.** *vt* despojar de **II.** *vi* **1.** *Am* (*sell*) vender **2.** (*get rid of involvement in*) **to ~ from sth** renunciar a algo

◆**divest of** *vr fig* (*take from*) despojarse de

divide [dɪ'vaɪd] **I.** *n* **1.** (*gulf*) separación *f* **2.** *Am* (*watershed*) punto *m* de inflexión **II.** *vt* **1.** *a.* MAT dividir; **to ~ sth into three groups** dividir algo en tres grupos; **the party is ~d** *fig* el partido está dividido **2.** (*allot*) repartir **III.** *vi* **1.** (*split*) dividirse; **their paths ~d** sus caminos se separaron **2.** *Brit* (*vote for or against*) votar

► **~ and rule** divide y vencerás

◆**divide off** *vt always sep* dividir
◆**divide out, divide up** *vt always sep*
(re)partir
divided *adj* 1.(*undecided*) **to be ~ between
two options** encontrarse en un dilema entre
dos opciones 2.(*in disagreement*) dividido, -a
dividend ['dɪvɪdend] *n* MAT, FIN dividendo *m*
dividing line *n* línea *f* divisoria
divination [ˌdɪvɪ'neɪʃən] *n no pl* adivinación
f
divine [dɪ'vaɪn] I. *adj* 1.(*of or from God*)
divino, -a 2.(*wonderful*) sublime II. *vt* (*guess
correctly*) adivinar; (*the future*) predecir III. *vi*
hacer pronósticos
diviner *n* adivinador(a) *m(f)*; (*of future
events*) vidente *mf*
diving *n no pl* 1.(*jumping*) zambullida *f*
2.(*swimming*) buceo *m*
diving bell *n* campana *f* de buzo **diving
board** *n* trampolín *m* **diving-suit** *n* escafandra *f*
divining-rod [dɪ'vaɪnɪŋˌrɔd, *Am:* -'rɑːd] *n*
varilla *f* de zahorí
divinity [dɪ'vɪnəti, *Am:* -əti] <-ies> *n* 1.*no
pl* (*state*) divinidad *f* 2. *pl* (*god*) deidad *f* 3.*no
pl* (*study*) teología *f*
divisible [dɪ'vɪzəbl] *adj* divisible
division [dɪ'vɪʒən] *n* 1.*a.* MIL, MAT, SPORTS
división *f* 2.*no pl* (*splitting up*) repartimiento
m 3.(*disagreement*) discordia *f* 4.(*gulf*) separación *f* 5. *Brit* (*voting*) votación *f*
divisive [dɪ'vaɪsɪv] *adj* divisivo, -a
divorce [dɪ'vɔːs, *Am:* -'vɔːrs] I. *n* divorcio *m*;
fig separación *f* II. *vt* 1.(*break marriage*) **to
get ~d** (**from sb**) divorciarse (de alguien); **he
~d her for infidelity** se divorció de ella por
infidelidad 2.*fig* (*separate*) separar III. *vi*
divorciarse
divorced *adj* divorciado, -a
divorcee *n,* **divorcée** [dɪˌvɔː'siː, *Am:*
dɪˌvɔːr'seɪ] *n* divorciado, -a *m, f*
divulge [daɪ'vʌldʒ, *Am:* dɪ-] *vt* divulgar
DIY [ˌdiːaɪ'waɪ] *abbr of* **do-it-yourself** bricolaje *m*
dizziness *n no pl* (*feeling of spinning round*)
mareo *m;* (*because of height*) vértigo *m*
dizzy ['dɪzi] <-ier, -iest> *adj* 1.(*having a
spinning sensation*) mareado, -a 2.(*causing a
spinning sensation*) vertiginoso, -a 3.*inf*(*silly*)
tonto, -a
DJ [ˌdiː'dʒeɪ, *Am:* 'diːdʒeɪ] *n* 1.*abbr of*
dinner jacket chaqué *m* 2.*abbr of* **disc
jockey** DJ *m*
Djibouti [dʒɪ'buːti] *n* Yibuti *m*
Djiboutian [dʒɪ'buːtiən] I. *adj* de Yibuti II. *n*
habitante *mf* de Yibuti
DNA [ˌdiːen'eɪ] *n no pl abbr of* **deoxyribonu-
cleic acid** ADN *m*
do [duː] I. *n* 1. *Brit, inf* (*treatment of people*)
trato *m;* **a poor ~** un mal trato 2. *Brit, Aus, inf*
(*party*) fiesta *f* II. <does, did, done> *aux*
1.(*word to form questions*) **~ you own a
dog?** ¿tienes un perro? 2.(*word to form*

negatives) **Frida ~esn't like olives** a Frida no
le gustan las aceitunas 3.(*word to form
imperatives*) **~ your homework!** ¡haz los
deberes!; **~ come in!** ¡pero pasa, por favor!
4.(*word used for emphasis*) **~ go to the
party!** ¡ve a la fiesta!; **he ~es get on my
nerves** me saca de quicio, la verdad; **he did ~
it** sí que lo hizo 5.(*replaces a repeated verb*)
so ~ I yo también; **neither ~ I** yo tampoco;
she speaks more fluently than he ~es ella
habla con mayor fluidez que él 6.(*word
requesting affirmation*) ¿verdad?; **you ~n't
want to answer, ~ you?** no quieres contestar,
¿no? III. <does, did, done> *vt* 1.(*carry out*)
hacer; **to ~ nothing but ...** hacer sólo...; **to ~
one's best** emplearse a fondo; **to ~ justice**
hacer justicia; **to ~ everything possible** hacer
todo lo posible; **what on earth are you ~ing
(there)?** ¿que diablos haces (ahí)?; **what is to
be ~ne about that?** ¿qué se puede hacer al
respecto?; **~n't just stand there, ~ something!** ¡no te quedes ahí plantado, haz algo!
2.(*undertake*) realizar 3.(*place somewhere*)
poner 4.(*help*) **to ~ something for sb/sth**
hacer algo por alguien/algo 5.(*act*) actuar; **to
~ as others ~** hacer como hacen los demás
6.(*deal with*) encargarse de; **if you ~ the
washing up, I'll ~ the drying** si tú lavas los
platos yo los secaré 7.(*construct*) producir
8.(*learn*) estudiar 9.(*figure out*) resolver
10.(*finish*) terminar 11.(*put in order*) ordenar; (*clean*) limpiar; **to ~ one's nails** (*varnish*)
pintarse las uñas; (*cut*) cortarse las uñas; **to ~
one's shoes** limpiarse los zapatos; **to ~ one's
teeth** lavarse los dientes 12.(*make neat*)
arreglar 13.(*tour*) visitar 14.(*go at a speed of*)
to ~ Barcelona to Geneva in seven hours
cubrir el trayecto de Barcelona a Ginebra en
siete horas 15.(*be satisfactory*) **"I only have
beer – will that ~ you?"** "sólo tengo cerveza
– ¿te va bien?" 16.(*sell*) vender; (*offer*) servir
17.(*cook*) cocer; **to ~ sth for sb** cocinar algo
para alguien 18.(*cause*) **to ~ sb credit** decir
mucho a favor de alguien; **to ~ sb a good turn**
echar una mano a alguien; **to ~ sb good** sentar
bien a alguien 19. *Brit* (*offer good service*) **to
~ sb well** tratar bien a alguien 20.(*act*) desempeñar 21.*inf* (*burglarize*) allanar 22.*inf*
(*swindle*) estafar 23. *Brit, inf* (*make suffer*)
amargar 24.*inf*(*take drugs*) chutarse ▸**just ~
it!** ¡hazlo!; **what's ~ne is ~ne** a lo hecho,
pecho; **that ~es it** eso es el colmo IV. <does,
did, done> *vi* 1.(*finish with*) **to have ~ne
with sb/sth** haber terminado con algo/alguien 2.(*be satisfactory*) **this behaviour just
won't ~!** ¡no se puede tolerar este comportamiento! 3.(*function as*) **it'll ~ for a spoon**
servirá de cuchara 4.*inf*(*going on*) **to be ~ing**
suceder 5.(*manage*) salir adelante; **mother
and baby are ~ing well** la madre y el bebé se
encuentran bien; **many shops are ~ing well**
muchas tiendas van prosperando; **how are
you ~ing?** ¿qué tal estás?; **to ~ well for one-**

self darse una buena vida **6.** *Brit* (*clean house*) **to** ~ **for sb** trabajar como criada para alguien **7.** *Brit, Aus* (*treat*) **to** ~ **badly/well by sb** tratar bien/mal a alguien **8.** *Brit, inf* (*beat up*) **to** ~ **for sb** acabar con alguien **9.** *inf* (*serve prison time*) cumplir condena ►**that will** never ~ eso no sirve; ~ **unto** others **as you would have them** ~ **unto you** *prov* no quieras para los otros lo que no quieras para ti; ~ **as you would** be ~**ne by** *Brit, prov* trata a los demás como te gustaría que te trataran a ti; **that will** ~! ¡ya basta!

♦**do away with** *vi* **1.** (*dispose of*) suprimir **2.** *inf* (*kill*) **to** ~ **sb** liquidar a alguien

♦**do down** *vt* **1.** (*humiliate*) humillar **2.** (*cheat*) estafar

♦**do in** *vt always sep* **1.** (*murder*) **to do sb in** acabar con alguien **2.** *fig* (*make exhausted*) agotar

♦**do out** *vt always sep* **1.** *Brit, inf* (*tidy up*) arreglar **2.** (*adorn*) decorar **3.** (*cheat*) **to do sb out of sth** quitar una cosa a alguien por engaño

♦**do over** *vt always sep* **1.** *Am, inf* (*redo*) **to do sth over again** volver a hacer algo **2.** *Am, inf* (*redecorate*) redecorar **3.** (*burglarize*) robar **4.** *Brit, Aus, inf* (*beat up*) **to do sb over** dar una paliza a alguien

♦**do up** *vt* **1.** (*fasten: button*) abrochar; (*tie*) hacer el nudo; (*shoes*) atar; (*zip*) cerrar **2.** (*restore*) renovar; (*a house*) restaurar; (*one's hair*) arreglarse; **to do oneself up** acicalarse **3.** (*wrap*) envolver

♦**do with** *vi* **1.** (*be related to*) **to have to do with sth** (*book*) tratar de algo; (*person*) tener que ver con algo; **to not have anything to do with sb** no tener tratos con alguien **2.** *Brit, inf* (*need*) **I could do with a drink** me hace falta tomar algo; **I can't do with pop music** no soporto la música pop

♦**do without** *vi* apañarse sin

DOA [ˌdiːəʊ'eɪ] *abbr of* **dead on arrival** ingresó cadáver

docile ['dəʊsaɪl, *Am:* 'daːsəl] *adj* dócil

docility [dəʊ'sɪləti, *Am:* daː'sɪlət̬i] *n no pl* docilidad *f*

dock¹ [dɒk, *Am:* daːk] **I.** *n* **1.** (*wharf*) desembarcadero *m* **2.** (*enclosed part of port*) dársena *f*; **the car is in** ~ *Brit, Aus* el coche está en el taller **3.** *Am* (*pier*) dique *m* **II.** *vi* **1.** NAUT atracar **2.** (*spacecraft*) acoplarse **III.** *vt* NAUT atracar

dock² [dɒk, *Am:* daːk] *n no pl, Brit* **to be in the** ~ estar en el banquillo; *fig* estar en apuros

dock³ [dɒk, *Am:* daːk] *vt* **1.** (*take away*) deducir **2.** (*cut tail off*) descolar

dock⁴ [dɒk, *Am:* daːk] *n no pl* BOT romaza *f*

docker ['dɒkə^r, *Am:* 'daːkə] *n inf* estibador *m*

docket ['dɒkɪt, *Am:* 'daːkɪt] **I.** *n* **1.** *Brit, Aus* (*document*) cédula *f* **2.** *Am* LAW (*list of cases*) registro *m* de sumarios de causas **3.** *Am* (*business agenda*) agenda *f*; (*in a meeting*) orden *m* del día **II.** *vt* registrar

docking ['dɒkɪŋ, *Am:* 'daːk-] *n no pl* **1.** NAUT amarre *m* **2.** (*joining of spacecraft*) acoplamiento *m* **3.** (*cutting*) reducción *f*; (*of wages*) reajuste *m*

dockyard ['dɒkjaːd, *Am:* 'daːkjaːrd] *n* astillero *m*

doctor ['dɒktə^r, *Am:* 'daːktə] **I.** *n* **1.** (*physician*) médico, -a *m, f*; **to be at the** ~**'s** estar en la consulta; **to go to the** ~**'s** ir al médico; **this hot bath is just what the** ~ **ordered** *fig* este baño caliente es justo lo que necesitaba **2.** UNIV doctor(a) *m(f)* **II.** *vt* **1.** (*illegally alter*) falsear **2.** *Brit* (*add poison*) envenenar **3.** *Am* (*adulterate*) adulterar **4.** *Brit, Aus, inf* (*animal*) castrar

doctorate ['dɒktərət, *Am:* 'daːk-] *n* doctorado *m*

El **doctorate** o **doctor's degree** en una disciplina es el título académico más alto que se puede obtener en una universidad. En las universidades anglosajonas los doctorados reciben diversas denominaciones según las materias. El doctorado más común es el **PhD**, también llamado **Dphil (Doctor of Philosophy)**. Este título se concede tras la realización de una tesis doctoral en cualquier materia exceptuando Derecho y Medicina. Otros títulos de doctorado son: **Dmus (Doctor of Music)**, **MD (Doctor of Medicine)**, **LLD (Doctor of Laws)** y **DD (Doctor of Divinity**, Doctor en Teología). Las universidades también pueden conceder el título de doctor a aquellas personalidades de alto rango que han destacado por su contribución a la investigación científica, su trabajo o sus importantes publicaciones. Este tipo de doctorado se denomina doctorado Honoris Causa. A esta modalidad pertenecen el **Dlitt (Doctor of Letters)** o el **DSc (Doctor of Science)**.

doctrinaire [ˌdɒktrɪ'neə^r, *Am:* ˌdaːktrə'ner] *adj* doctrinario, -a

doctrine ['dɒktrɪn, *Am:* 'daːk-] *n* doctrina *f*; **military** ~ credo *m* militar

document ['dɒkjʊmənt, *Am:* 'daːkjə-] **I.** *n* documento *m* **II.** *vt* documentar

documentary [ˌdɒkjʊ'mentəri, *Am:* ˌdaːkjə'ment̬ə-] **I.** <-ies> *n* documental *m* **II.** *adj* documental

documentation [ˌdɒkjʊmen'teɪʃən, *Am:* ˌdaːkjə-] *n no pl* documentación *f*

docusoap *n* docudrama *m*

DOD *n Am abbr of* **Department of Defense** Departamento *m* de Defensa

doddery ['dɒdəri, *Am:* 'daːdə-] <-ier, -iest> *adj* chocho, -a

dodge [dɒdʒ, *Am:* daːdʒ] **I.** *vt* (*avoid by moving aside*) esquivar; (*a question*) eludir; **to** ~ **doing sth** escaquearse de hacer algo **II.** *vi* SPORTS regatear **III.** *n inf* truco *m*; **tax** ~ evasión *f* de impuestos

dodger ['dɒdʒə^r, *Am:* -ə] *n pej* granuja *mf*

dodgy ['dɒdʒi, *Am:* 'daːdʒi] <-ier, -iest>

adj Brit, Aus, inf **1.** (*of person*) tramposo, -a; **to sound** ~ sonar a timo **2.** (*of situation*) delicado, -a **3.** (*of weather*) variable

doe [dəʊ, *Am:* doʊ] *n* **1.** (*female deer*) cierva *f*, venada *f AmL* **2.** (*female rabbit*) coneja *f*

DoE *n Brit abbr of* **Department of the Environment** Departamento *m* de Medioambiente

doer ['duːəʳ, *Am:* -ɚ] *n* **1.** (*person acting*) hacedor(a) *m(f)* **2.** (*active person*) persona *f* dinámica

does [dʌz] *vt, vi, aux* **3.** *pers sing of* **do**

doeskin ['dəʊskɪn, *Am:* 'doʊ-] *n* ante *m*

doesn't ['dʌznt] = does not *s.* **do**

dog [dɒg, *Am:* dɑːg] **I.** *n* (*animal*) perro, -a *m, f*; **hunting** ~ perro de caza; **pet** ~ perro mascota; **the** (**dirty**) ~! *inf* ¡el muy canalla! ►**a** ~'**s breakfast** *inf* un revoltijo; **he hasn't a** ~'**s chance** *inf* no tiene la más remota posibilidad; **every** ~ **has its day** *prov* a cada uno le llega su momento de gloria; **to be done up like a** ~'**s dinner** estar hecho un adefesio; **to lead a** ~'**s life** llevar una vida de perros; **to be a** ~ **in the manger** ser como el perro del hortelano; **to give a** ~ **a bad name** *Brit, prov* por un perro que maté, mataperros me llamaron *prov;* **to go to the** ~**s** ir de capa caída; **to put on the** ~ darse pisto **II.** <-gg-> *vt* (*pursue*) seguir; *fig* acosar

dog biscuit *n* canil *m* **dog collar** *n* collar *m* de perro; *iron* alzacuello *m* **dog days** *n pl* canícula *f* **dog-eared** *adj* (*book*) **to be** ~ tener las puntas dobladas

dogged ['dɒgɪd, *Am:* 'dɑːgɪd] *adj* obstinado, -a

doggerel ['dɒgərəl, *Am:* 'dɑːgɚ-] *n no pl* poesía *f* barata

doghouse ['dɒghaʊs, *Am:* 'dɑːg-] *n Am* perrera *f*; **to be in the** ~ estar en desgracia

dogma ['dɒgmə, *Am:* 'dɑːg-] *n* dogma *m*

dogmatic [dɒg'mætɪk, *Am:* dɑːg'mæt̬-] *adj* dogmático, -a

dogmatism ['dɒgmətɪzəm, *Am:* 'dɑːg-] *n no pl* dogmatismo *m*

dogsbody ['dɒgzˌbɒdi, *Am:* 'dɑːgzˌbɑːdi] *n Brit, Aus, inf* burro *m* de carga

dog-tired [ˌdɒg'taɪəd, *Am:* ˌdɑːg'taɪɚd] *adj inf* hecho, -a polvo

doing ['duːɪŋ] *n no pl* actividad *f*; **to be** (**of**) **sb's** ~ ser asunto de alguien; **to take some** ~ requerir esfuerzo

doings ['duːɪŋz] *n pl* **1.** *Brit, inf* (*thing needed*) chisme *m* **2.** (*activities*) actividades *fpl*

do-it-yourself ['duːɪtjɔː'self, *Am:* ˌduːɪtjɚ'-] *n no pl* bricolaje *m*

doldrums ['dɒldrəmz, *Am:* 'doʊl-] *npl* GEO zona *f* de las calmas ecuatoriales; **to be in the** ~ (*person*) estar deprimido; (*business*) estar estancado

dole [dəʊl, *Am:* doʊl] *n* subsidio *m* de desempleo; **to be on the** ~ estar cobrando el paro

◆**dole out** *vt* (*money, food*) repartir

doleful ['dəʊlfəl, *Am:* 'doʊl-] *adj* (*person*) triste; (*expression*) compungido, -a; (*cry*) lastimero, -a

doll [dɒl, *Am:* dɑːl] *n* **1.** (*toy*) muñeco, -a *m, f*; ~'**s house** casa *f* de muñecas **2.** *Am, inf* (*term of address*) muñeca *f*

◆**doll up** *vt* emperifollar; **to** ~ **oneself up** ponerse de punta en blanco

dollar ['dɒləʳ, *Am:* 'dɑːlɚ] *n* dólar *m* ►**to feel/look like a million** ~**s** sentirse/verse a las mil maravillas

dollop ['dɒləp, *Am:* 'dɑːləp] *n* (*amount*) porción *f*; (*spoonful*) cucharada *f*

dolly ['dɒli, *Am:* 'dɑːli] <-ies> *n* **1.** *childspeak* (*doll*) muñequita *f* **2.** CINE travelín *m*

dolly bird *n Brit, inf* (*attractive girl*) barbie *f*

dolphin ['dɒlfɪn, *Am:* 'dɑːl-] *n* delfín *m*, bufeo *m Perú*

dolt [dəʊlt, *Am:* doʊlt] *n* imbécil *mf*

domain [dəʊ'meɪn, *Am:* doʊ-] *n* **1.** POL, INFOR dominio *m*; (*lands*) propiedad *f* **2.** (*sphere of activity*) ámbito *m*; **to be in the public** ~ ser de dominio público; **that is outside my** ~ eso está fuera de mi campo

dome [dəʊm, *Am:* doʊm] *n* **1.** (*rounded roof*) cúpula *f* **2.** (*rounded ceiling*) bóveda *f* **3.** *inf* (*bald head*) calva *f*

domestic [də'mestɪk] **I.** *adj* **1.** (*of the house*) doméstico, -a **2.** (*home-loving*) casero, -a **3.** *a.* ECON, FIN, POL (*produce, flight, news*) nacional; (*market, trade, policy*) interior; **gross** ~ **product** producto *m* interior bruto **II.** *n* doméstico *m*

domestic appliance *n* electrodoméstico *m*

domesticate [də'mestɪkeɪt] *vt* (*animal*) domesticar; (*plant*) aclimatar; (*person*) volver casero; **he is a very** ~**d man** es un hombre muy de su casa

domesticated *adj* domesticado, -a

domesticity [ˌdəʊmes'tɪsəti, *Am:* ˌdoʊmes'-] *n* domesticidad *f*

domestic science *n* economía *f* doméstica

domicile ['dɒmɪsaɪl, *Am:* 'dɑːmə-] **I.** *n* domicilio *m* **II.** *vt* domiciliar; **to be** ~**d in** residir en

dominance ['dɒmɪnənts, *Am:* 'dɑːmə-] *no pl n* **1.** (*rule*) dominación *f* **2.** MIL supremacía *f*

dominant ['dɒmɪnənt, *Am:* 'dɑːmə-] *adj* dominante

dominate ['dɒmɪneɪt, *Am:* 'dɑːmə-] *vi, vt* dominar

domination [ˌdɒmɪ'neɪʃən, *Am:* ˌdɑːmə-] *no pl n* dominación *f*

domineer [ˌdɒmɪ'nɪəʳ, *Am:* ˌdɑːmə'nɪr] *vi* dominar; **to** ~ **over sb** tiranizar a alguien

domineering *adj* dominante; **a** ~ **management style** una forma de dirigir muy tiránica

Dominica [ˌdɒmɪ'niːkə, *Am:* ˌdɑːmɪ'niː-] *n* Dominica *f*

Dominican [də'mɪnɪkən, *Am:* doʊ'mɪn-] **I.** *adj* (*from Dominican Republic*) dominicano, -a **II.** *n* **1.** (*nationality*) dominicano, -a *m, f* **2.** REL dominico, -a *m, f*

Dominican Republic *n* República *f* Dominicana

dominion [dəˈmɪnjən] *n* dominio *m;* **to have ~ over sb/sth** tener a alguien/algo bajo su dominio

domino [ˈdɒmɪnəʊ, *Am:* ˈdɑːmənoʊ] <-es> *n* 1. *pl* (*games*) dominó *m;* **to play ~es** jugar al dominó 2. (*piece*) ficha *f* de dominó

domino effect *n no pl* efecto *m* dominó

don [dɒn, *Am:* dɑːn] I. *n* UNIV profesor(a) *m(f)* II. *vt* (*of clothing*) ponerse

donate [dəʊˈneɪt, *Am:* ˈdoʊneɪt] *vt* donar

donation [dəʊˈneɪʃən, *Am:* doʊˈneɪ-] *n* 1. (*contribution*) donativo *m* 2. *no pl* (*act*) donación *f*

done [dʌn] *pp of* **do**

donkey [ˈdɒŋki, *Am:* ˈdɑːŋ-] *n a. fig* burro *m,* burra *f*

donkey jacket *n Brit* chaqueta *f* de obrero **donkey work** *no pl n inf* trabajo *m* pesado

donor [ˈdəʊnəʳ, *Am:* ˈdoʊnɚ] *n* donante *mf*

don't [dəʊnt, *Am:* doʊnt] = **do not** *s.* **do**

donut [ˈdəʊnʌt, *Am:* ˈdoʊ-] *n Am, Aus* donut *m*

doodle [ˈduːdl] I. *vi* garabatear II. *n* garabato *m*

doom [duːm] I. *n* 1. (*destiny*) suerte *f* 2. (*death*) muerte *f* II. *vt* condenar

doomed *adj* condenado, -a; **to be ~ to failure** estar condenado al fracaso; **~ to die** condenado a muerte

doomsday [ˈduːmzdeɪ] *no pl n* día *m* del juicio final

door [dɔːʳ, *Am:* dɔːr] *n* 1. puerta *f;* **main/back ~** puerta principal/trasera; **revolving/sliding ~** puerta giratoria/corredera; **to knock at** [*o* **on**] **the ~** llamar a la puerta; **there's someone at the ~** llaman a la puerta; **to answer the ~** abrir la puerta; **to see sb to the ~** acompañar a alguien hasta la puerta; **to live next ~** (**to sb**) vivir al lado (de alguien); **to show sb the ~** echar a alguien; **out of ~s** al aire libre; **behind closed ~s** a puerta cerrada; **to close the ~ on sb** cerrar la puerta a alguien; **to leave the ~ open to sb** dejar la puerta abierta a alguien; **~ to ~** puerta a puerta 2. (*doorway*) entrada *f* ▶**to slam the ~ in sb's** face dar a alguien con la puerta en las narices; **to never** darken **sb's ~s again** *liter* no volver a poner los pies en casa de alguien; **to** lay **sth at sb's ~** echar a alguien la culpa de algo

doorbell [ˈdɔːbel, *Am:* ˈdɔːr-] *n* timbre *m* **doorframe** *n* marco *m* de la puerta **doorkeeper** *n s.* **doorman doorknob** *n* pomo *m* de la puerta **doorman** <-men> *n* portero *m* **doormat** *n* felpudo *m* **doornail** *n inf* as **dead as a ~** muerto y bien muerto **doorplate** *n* placa *f* (*que se pone en la puerta de una casa*) **doorstep** *n* peldaño *m* (*de la puerta de entrada*) ▶**to be** right **on the ~** estar a la vuelta de la esquina

door-to-door [ˌdɔːtəˈdɔːʳ, *Am:* ˌdɔːrtˌəˈdɔːr] I. *adj* de puerta a puerta; **~ selling** venta *f* a

domicilio II. *adv* de puerta a puerta

doorway [ˈdɔːweɪ, *Am:* ˈdɔːr-] *n* entrada *f*

dope [dəʊp, *Am:* doʊp] I. *n* 1. *no pl, inf* (*drugs*) drogas *fpl;* (*marijuana*) marihuana *f* 2. SPORTS doping *m;* **~ test** control *m* antidoping 3. *inf* (*stupid person*) idiota *mf* 4. *no pl, inf* (*information*) información *f;* **to give sb the ~ on** [*o* about] **sth** pasar informes a alguien sobre algo II. *vt* (*drug*) drogar; SPORTS dopar

dope dealer *n*, **dope peddler** *n*, **dope pusher** *n inf* camello *mf*

dopey *adj*, **dopy** [ˈdəʊpi, *Am:* ˈdoʊ-] *adj* <-ier, -iest> 1. (*drowsy*) atontado, -a, abombado, -a *AmS* 2. (*stupid*) tonto, -a

dormant [ˈdɔːmənt, *Am:* ˈdɔːr-] *adj* (*volcano*) inactivo, -a; (*animal*) aletargado, -a; (*law*) inaplicado, -a; (*idea*) latente; **to lie ~** permanecer latente

dormer (**window**) *n* buhardilla *f*

dormitory [ˈdɔːmɪtəri, *Am:* ˈdɔːrmətɔːri] <-ies> *n* 1. dormitorio *m;* **~ town** ciudad *f* dormitorio 2. *Am* UNIV residencia *f* de estudiantes

Dormobile® [ˈdɔːməbiːl, *Am:* ˈdɔːr-] *n* autocaravana *f*

dormouse [ˈdɔːmaʊs, *Am:* ˈdɔːr-] <-mice> *n* lirón *m*

dorsal [ˈdɔːsəl, *Am:* ˈdɔːr-] *adj* dorsal

DOS [dɒs, *Am:* dɑːs] *n no pl abbr of* **disk operating system** DOS *m*

dosage [ˈdəʊsɪdʒ, *Am:* ˈdoʊ-] *n* dosis *f inv*

dose [dəʊs, *Am:* doʊs] I. *n a. fig* dosis *f inv;* **a ~ of bad news** una mala noticia; **a nasty ~ of flu** una gripe muy fuerte II. *vt* administrar una dosis a; **to ~ oneself with** medicarse con

doss [dɒs, *Am:* dɑːs] *vi Brit, Aus, inf* 1. (*sleep*) sobar, apolillar *RíoPl;* **to ~ down on the sofa** apañarse para dormir en el sofá 2. (*do nothing*) hacer el vago; **he's just ~ing** (**around**) sólo está haciendo el vago

dosser *n Brit, inf* 1. (*tramp*) vagabundo, -a *m, f* 2. (*lazy*) vago, -a *m, f*

dosshouse [ˈdɒshaʊs, *Am:* ˈdɑːs-] *n Brit, inf* albergue *m* de acogida

dossier [ˈdɒsieɪ, *Am:* ˈdɑːsieɪ] *n* expediente *m;* **to keep a ~ on sb/sth** llevar un expediente sobre alguien/algo

dot [dɒt, *Am:* dɑːt] I. *n* 1. punto *m;* **on the ~** en punto; **she arrived at half past three on the ~** llegó a las tres y media en punto 2. *pl* TYPO puntos *mpl* suspensivos II. <-tt-> *vt* 1. (*mark with a dot*) puntuar 2. (*put a dot on*) poner el punto en 3. (*scatter*) esparcir ▶**to ~ one's i's and** cross **one's t's** poner los puntos sobre las íes

dote on [ˌdəʊtˈɒn, *Am:* ˌdoʊtˈɑːn] *vt*, **dote upon** *vt* adorar

doting *adj* muy cariñoso, -a; **we saw photos of the ~ father with the baby** le vimos en unas fotos, hecho todo un padrazo con el bebé

dot-matrix printer [ˌdɒtmeɪtrɪksˈprɪntəʳ, *Am:* ˌdɑːtˈmeɪtrɪksprɪntɚ] *n* impresora *f* matricial

dotty ['dɒti, *Am:* 'dɑːt̬i] *adj* <-ier, -iest>
(*person*) chiflado, -a; (*idea*) descabellado, -a
double ['dʌbl] **I.** *adj* **1.** (*twice as much/
many*) doble; **a** ~ **door** una puerta de dos
hojas; **a** ~ **whisky** un whisky doble; **it is** ~
that es el doble de eso; **to have a** ~ **meaning**
tener un doble sentido; **to lead a** ~ **life** llevar
una doble vida **2.** (*composed of two*) **in** ~ **figures** más de diez; **the number of deaths has
now reached double figures** la cifra de
muertos ya ha pasado de diez; **a** ~ **'s'** dos eses;
his number is ~ **two five three five six** su
número es el dos dos cinco tres cinco seis
3. (*for two*) ~ **mattress** colchón *m* de matrimonio; ~ **room** habitación *f* doble **II.** *adv*
doble; **to see** ~ ver doble; **to fold sth** ~ doblar
algo por la mitad); ~ **four is eight** el doble de
cuatro es ocho; **he's** ~ **your age** te dobla la
edad; **to be bent** ~ estar encorvado **III.** *vt*
(*increase*) doblar; (*efforts*) redoblar; **we have
~d our profits** hemos duplicado los beneficios
IV. *vi* duplicarse; **to** ~ **for sb** CINE, THEAT doblar
a alguien **V.** *n* **1.** (*double quantity*) doble *m*
2. (*person*) doble *mf;* **sb's** ~ el/la doble de alguien **3.** *pl* SPORTS doble *m;* **to play ~s** jugar
una partida de dobles ►**at** [*o* **on**] **the** ~ *inf*
inmediatamente
◆**double back** *vi* (*person, animal*) volver
sobre sus pasos; (*path, river*) describir una
curva
◆**double up** *vi* **1.** (*bend over*) retorcerse; **to**
~ **with laughter** troncharse de risa; **to** ~ **with
pain** retorcerse de dolor **2.** (*share room*) compartir habitación
double-barrelled [ˌdʌblˈbærld, *Am:* -ˈber-]
adj **1.** (*shotgun*) de dos cañones **2.** *Am, Aus*
(*having two purposes*) de doble efecto **3.** *Brit*
(*surname*) compuesto, -a
double bass <-es> *n* contrabajo *m* **double
bed** *n* cama *f* de matrimonio
double-breasted [ˌdʌblˈbrestɪd] *adj* (*of
jacket*) cruzado, -a
double-check [ˌdʌblˈtʃek] *vt* comprobar dos
veces
double chin *n* papada *f*
double-click *vi* INFOR hacer doble clic; **to** ~
on the left mouse button hacer doble clic
con el botón izquierdo del ratón **double-
-cross I.** *vt* traicionar **II.** <-es> *n* traición *f*
double-crosser [ˌdʌblˈkrɒsəʳ, *Am:* -ˈkrɑː-
səʳ] *n* traidor(a) *m(f)* **double-dealer** *n*
embustero, -a *m, f* **double-dealing** *n*
engaño *m* **double-decker** *n* **1.** (*bus*) autobús *m* de dos pisos **2.** (*sandwich*) sandwich *m*
doble **double Dutch** *no pl n Brit, inf*
(*incomprehensible language*) chino *m fig;* **to
talk** ~ hablar en chino
double-edged [ˌdʌblˈedʒd] *adj a. fig* de
doble filo
double-entry bookkeeping *n* contabilidad *f* por partida doble **double feature** *n*
programa *m* doble
double-glaze [ˌdʌblˈgleɪz] *vt* to ~ a

window instalar doble aislamiento en
double-glazing [ˌdʌblˈgleɪzɪŋ] *no pl n*
doble acristalamiento *m*
double-jointed [ˌdʌblˈdʒɔɪntɪd, *Am:* -t̬ɪd]
adj con articulaciones dobles
double-park [ˌdʌblˈpɑːk, *Am:* -ˈpɑːrk] *vi, vt*
aparcar en doble fila
double-quick [ˌdʌblˈkwɪk] **I.** *adv* (*very
quickly*) a paso ligero; **to get home** ~ llegar a
casa en un momento **II.** *adj* (*step*) ligero, -a; **in**
~ **time** volando
doublespeak ['dʌblspiːk] *n no pl* palabras
fpl ambiguas
double standard *n* **to have ~s** no medir
con el mismo rasero **double take** *n* reacción
f retardada; **to do a** ~ tardar en reaccionar
double-talk *n no pl s.* **double-speak
double-think** *n no pl* aceptación *f* de principios contradictorios **double time** *no pl n*
1. COM, ECON paga *f* doble **2.** MIL paso *m* ligero
doubly ['dʌbli] *adv* doblemente; **to make** ~
sure that ... asegurarse bien de que... +*subj*
doubt [daʊt] *no pl* **I.** *n* duda *f;* **to be in** ~
whether to ... dudar si...; **without the
shadow of a** ~ sin sombra de duda; **no** ~ sin
duda; **without a** ~ sin duda alguna; **he will
no** ~ **come at Christmas** seguramente vendrá en Navidad; **there is no** ~ **about it** no
cabe la menor duda; **to have one's ~s about
sth** tener sus dudas respecto a algo; **the future
of the project is in** ~ no se sabe si el proyecto
seguirá adelante; **beyond all reasonable** ~
más allá de toda duda fundada; **to raise ~s
about sth** hacer dudar de algo; **to cast** ~ **on
sth** poner algo en tela de juicio **II.** *vt* **1.** (*be
unwilling to believe*) dudar de; **to** ~ **sb's word**
dudar de la palabra de alguien **2.** (*call into
question: capability, sincerity*) poner en duda
3. (*feel uncertain*) dudar; **to** ~ **that** dudar que
+*subj;* **to** ~ **if** [*o* **whether**] ... dudar si...; **I
very much** ~ **it** lo dudo mucho **III.** *vi* dudar
doubtful ['daʊtfəl] *adj* **1.** (*uncertain, undecided*) indeciso, -a; **to be** ~ **whether to** ...
dudar si...; **to be** ~ **about going** estar indeciso
respecto a si ir o no **2.** (*unlikely*) incierto, -a
3. (*questionable*) dudoso, -a
doubtless ['daʊtlɪs] *adv* sin duda
dough [dəʊ, *Am:* doʊ] *n* **1.** GASTR masa *f*
2. *Am, inf* (*money*) pasta *f,* plata *f AmS*
doughnut ['dəʊnʌt, *Am:* 'doʊ-] *n Brit* donut
m
doughy ['dəʊi, *Am:* 'doʊ-] *adj* pastoso, -a
dour [dʊəʳ, *Am:* dʊr] *adj* (*manner*) adusto, -a;
(*appearance*) austero, -a
douse [daʊs] *vt* **1.** (*throw liquid on*) mojar;
to ~ **sth in petrol** mojar algo con gasolina
2. (*extinguish: light, candle*) apagar
dove[1] [dʌv] *n* ZOOL paloma *f*
dove[2] [dəʊv, *Am:* doʊv] *Am pt of* **dive**
dovecot(e) ['dʌvkəʊt, *Am:* -kɑːt] *n* palomar
m
Dover ['dəʊvəʳ, *Am:* 'doʊvəʳ] *n* Dover *m*
dovetail ['dʌvteɪl] **I.** *n* TECH cola *f* de milano

II. *vi* encajar **III.** *vt* **1.** TECH ensamblar a cola de milano **2.** (*fit*) **to ~ into/with sth** encajar en/con algo

dowager ['daʊədʒəʳ, *Am:* -dʒɚ] *n* viuda *f* de un noble; **~ duchess** duquesa *f* viuda

dowdy ['daʊdi] *adj* <-ier, -iest> poco atractivo, -a; **to wear ~ clothes** vestir con poca gracia

dowel ['daʊəl] *n* TECH espiga *f*

down¹ [daʊn] *n* (*feathers*) plumón *m;* (*hairs*) pelusa *f;* (*on body*) vello *m;* (*on face*) bozo *m*

down² [daʊn] **I.** *adv* **1.** (*movement*) abajo; **to fall ~** caerse; **to lie ~** acostarse **2.** (*from another point*) **to go ~ to Brighton/the sea** bajar a Brighton/al mar; **~ South** hacia el sur **3.** (*less volume or intensity*) **to be ~** estar gastado; **the wind died ~** el viento se calmó; **the sun is ~** se ha puesto el sol; **the fire is burning ~** el fuego se está consumiendo; **the tyres are ~** los neumáticos están desinflados; **the price is ~** el precio ha bajado **4.** (*temporal*) **from 1900 ~ to the present** desde 1900 hasta el presente; **~ through the ages** a través de la historia **5.** (*in writing*) **to write/get sth ~** escribir/anotar algo ▶ **to be ~ on sb** tener manía a alguien; **~ with the dictator!** ¡abajo el dictador! **II.** *prep* **1.** (*lower*) **to go ~ the stairs** bajar las escaleras; **to run ~ the slope** correr cuesta abajo **2.** (*along*) **to go ~ the street** ir por la calle

down and out, down-and-out [,daʊnənd'aʊt] **I.** *adj* **to be ~** no tener donde caerse muerto **II.** *n* vagabundo, -a *m, f*

downcast ['daʊnkɑːst, *Am:* 'daʊnkæst] *adj* alicaído, -a

downfall ['daʊnfɔːl] *n* (*of government*) caída *f;* (*of organization, firm*) derrumbamiento *m;* (*of person*) perdición *f;* **that will be his ~** eso será su ruina

downgrade [,daʊn'greɪd] **I.** *vt* **1.** (*lower category of*) bajar de categoría **2.** (*disparage*) minimizar; **to ~ the importance of sth** minimizar la importancia de algo **II.** *n* bajada; **to be on the ~** *fig* ir cuesta abajo

downhearted [,daʊn'hɑːtɪd, *Am:* -'hɑːrtɪd] *adj* descorazonado, -a

downhill [,daʊn'hɪl] **I.** *adv* cuesta abajo; **to go ~** ir cuesta abajo; *fig* ir de mal en peor **II.** *adj* (*path*) cuesta abajo; **it's all ~ from now on** (*easy*) ya lo tenemos chupado *inf*

download [,daʊn'ləʊd, *Am:* 'daʊnloʊd] *vt* INFOR bajar

downmarket [,daʊn'mɑːkɪt, *Am:* 'daʊn,mɑːr-] **I.** *adj* (*neighbourhood, newspaper*) popular; (*shop, store*) barato, -a; (*programme*) de masas **II.** *adv* **to move ~** perder prestigio; (*intentionally*) dirigirse a un sector popular del público

down payment *n* entrada *f,* cuota *f* inicial *AmL;* **to make a ~ on sth** dar la entrada para comprar algo

downplay [,daʊn'pleɪ, *Am:* 'daʊnpleɪ] *vt* restar importancia a

downpour ['daʊnpɔːʳ, *Am:* -pɔːr] *n* chaparrón *m*

downright ['daʊnraɪt] **I.** *adj* (*refusal, disobedience*) completo, -a; (*lie*) abierto, -a; (*liar*) redomado, -a; (*fool*) de remate; **it is a ~ disgrace** es una auténtica vergüenza; **that's ~ stupid** eso es una solemne tontería **II.** *adv* completamente; **to be ~ difficult** ser dificilísimo; **to refuse ~** *Am* negarse rotundamente

downside ['daʊnsaɪd] *n no pl* inconveniente *m;* **on the ~, it is far from the village** tiene el inconveniente de que está lejos del pueblo

downsize [,daʊn'saɪz, *Am:* 'daʊnsaɪz] *vt* reducir

downsizing *n no pl* reducción *f*

Down's Syndrome ['daʊnz'sɪndrəʊm, *Am:* -,sɪndroʊm] *n no pl* síndrome *m* de Down

downstairs [,daʊn'steəz, *Am:* -'sterz] **I.** *adv* abajo; **to go ~** bajar; **to run ~** bajar corriendo (las escaleras) **II.** *adj* (del piso) de abajo **III.** *n no pl* planta *f* baja

downstream [,daʊn'striːm] *adv* río abajo; **it is another few miles ~ from here** eso está a unas millas más abajo de aquí; **to paddle downstream** remar río abajo

downtime ['daʊntaɪm] *n no pl* INFOR, TECH tiempo *m* improductivo

down-to-earth [,daʊntə'ɜːθ, *Am:* -'ɜːrθ] *adj* (*explanation*) realista; (*person*) práctico, -a

downtown ['daʊntaʊn, *Am:* ,daʊn'-] **I.** *n no pl, Am* centro *m* (de la ciudad) **II.** *adv Am* **to go ~** ir al centro; **to live ~** vivir en el centro **III.** *adj Am* (*situated in the central section*) céntrico, -a; (*related to the central section*) del centro de la ciudad; **~ Los Angeles** el centro de Los Ángeles

downtrodden ['daʊntrɒdn, *Am:* -trɑːdn] *adj* (*grass*) pisoteado, -a; (*person*) oprimido, -a

downturn ['daʊntɜːn, *Am:* -tɜːrn] *n* empeoramiento *m;* **a ~ in sth** un giro negativo en algo; **to take a ~** dar un bajón; **an economic ~** un empeoramiento de la situación económica

downward ['daʊnwəd, *Am:* -wəd] **I.** *adj* (*movement*) descendente; (*direction*) hacia abajo; (*path*) cuesta abajo; (*tendency, prices*) a la baja; **inflation is on a ~ trend** la inflación está disminuyendo **II.** *adv Am s.* **downwards**

downwards ['daʊnwədz, *Am:* -wɚdz] *adv* hacia abajo

downy ['daʊni] *adj* aterciopelado, -a

dowry ['daʊəri] <-ies> *n* dote *f*

dowse¹ [daʊs] *vi* buscar con una varilla de zahorí; **to ~ for water** buscar agua con una varilla de zahorí

dowse² [daʊs] *vt s.* **douse**

dowser [daʊs] *n* zahorí *mf*

dowsing *n no pl* búsqueda de agua o metales con una varilla de zahorí

dowsing rod *n* varilla *f* de zahorí

doyen ['dɔɪən] *n* decano *m*

doyenne ['dɔɪen] *n* decana *f*

doz. *abbr of* **dozen** docena *f*

doze [dəʊz, *Am:* doʊz] I. *vi* dormitar; **to ~ off** dormirse II. *n* cabezada *f;* **to have a ~** echar un sueño

dozen ['dʌzn] *n* 1. (*twelve*) docena *f;* **half a ~** media docena; **two ~ eggs** dos docenas de huevos 2. (*many*) **~s of times** montones de veces; **by the ~** por docenas ▶**it's six of one and half a ~ of the other** da lo mismo; **to talk nineteen to the ~** hablar por los codos

dozy ['dəʊzi, *Am:* 'doʊ-] *adj* <-ier, -iest> 1. (*drowsy, sleepy*) soñoliento, -a 2. *Brit, inf* (*stupid*) tonto, -a, abombado, -a *AmL*

DP 1. *abbr of* **data processing** PD *m* 2. *abbr of* **displaced person** desplazado, -a *m, f*

DPhil *n abbr of* **Doctor of Philosophy** doctor(a) *m(f)* en Filosofía

Dr *abbr of* **Doctor** Dr. *m*, Dra. *f*

drab [dræb] *adj* <drabber, drabbest> (*food*) soso, -a; (*colour*) apagado, -a; (*existence*) monótono, -a

drachma ['drækmə] *n* dracma *f*

draconian [drə'kəʊnɪən, *Am:* -'koʊ-] *adj* draconiano, -a

draft [drɑːft, *Am:* dræft] I. *n* 1. (*drawing*) boceto *m* 2. (*preliminary version*) borrador *m;* (*of novel, speech*) primera versión *f;* (*of contract*) minuta *f;* **~ bill** LAW anteproyecto *m* de ley 3. *no pl, Am* MIL reclutamiento *m* 4. *Brit* FIN, ECON letra *f* de cambio II. *vt* 1. (*prepare a preliminary version*) hacer un borrador de; (*novel*) redactar la primera versión de; (*plan*) trazar; (*contract*) redactar la minuta de 2. *Am* MIL llamar a filas

draft dodger *n Am* MIL prófugo *m*

draftee ['drɑːftiː, *Am:* 'dræf-] *n Am* MIL recluta *mf*

draftsman ['drɑːftsmən, *Am:* 'dræfts-] <-men> *n Am, Aus* TECH *s.* **draughtsman**

drafty ['dræfti] *adj Am s.* **draughty**

drag [dræg] <-gg-> I. *vt* 1. (*pull*) arrastrar; **to ~ oneself somewhere** arrastrarse hasta un sitio; **to ~ one's heels** arrastrar los pies; *fig* dar largas a un asunto; **to ~ sb's name through the mud** dejar a alguien por los suelos 2. (*in water*) dragar II. *vi* 1. (*trail along*) arrastrarse por el suelo 2. (*time*) pasar lentamente; (*meeting, conversation*) hacerse interminable 3. (*lag behind*) rezagarse III. *n* 1. (*device*) draga *f* 2. *no pl* PHYS resistencia *f* al avance; AVIAT resistencia *f* aerodinámica 3. *no pl* (*hindrance*) estorbo *m;* **to be a ~ on sb** ser una carga para alguien 4. *no pl, inf* (*boring experience*) lata *f;* **what a ~!** ¡qué rollo! 5. *no pl, inf* (*boring person*) pelmazo *m* 6. *no pl, inf* (*women's clothes*) disfraz *m* de mujer; **to be in ~** ir vestido de mujer 7. *inf* (*inhalation*) calada *f;* **to take a ~** dar una calada ▶**the main ~** *Am, Aus, inf* la calle principal

◆**drag along** *vt* arrastrar con dificultad

◆**drag away** *vt* arrancar

◆**drag behind** *vi* seguir con atraso

◆**drag down** *vt* 1. (*force to a lower level*) arrastrar hacia abajo 2. (*make depressed*) hundir; (*make weak*) debilitar

◆**drag in** *vt* (*person*) involucrar; (*subject*) traer por los pelos

◆**drag on** *vi* (*meeting, film*) hacerse interminable

◆**drag out** <-gg-> *vt* (*meeting, conversation*) alargar

◆**drag up** *vt* sacar a relucir

drag lift *n Brit* telearrastre *m*

dragon ['drægən] *n* 1. (*mythical creature*) dragón *m* 2. (*fierce woman*) arpía *f*

dragonfly ['drægənflaɪ] <-ies> *n* libélula *f*, alguacil *m* RíoPl

dragoon [drə'guːn] *n* MIL dragón *m*

drain [dreɪn] I. *vt* 1. AGR, MED drenar; (*pond*) vaciar; (*river*) desaguar; (*food*) escurrir; (*machine*) purgar 2. (*empty by drinking: glass, cup*) apurar; (*bottle*) acabar 3. (*exhaust, tire out: person*) dejar agotado; (*resources*) agotar; **to ~ sb's energies** consumir las energías de alguien; **war ~s the nation of its youth and its wealth** la guerra mina la juventud y la riqueza de una nación II. *vi* (*dishes*) escurrirse III. *n* 1. (*conduit*) canal *m* de desagüe 2. (*sewer*) alcantarilla *f*, resumidero *m* AmL; **the ~s** el alcantarillado 3. (*plughole*) desagüe *m;* **to throw sth down the ~** tirar algo por la borda; **to throw** [*o* **to pour**] **money down the ~** tirar el dinero por la ventana 4. (*constant outflow*) fuga *f;* **brain ~** fuga de cerebros; **to be a ~ on sb's resources** consumir los recursos de alguien ▶**to laugh like a ~** *Brit, inf* reírse a mandíbula batiente

◆**drain away** *vi* (*water*) irse; (*energy*) agotarse; (*tension*) disiparse

◆**drain off** *vt* (*liquid*) extraer

drainage ['dreɪnɪdʒ] *n no pl* 1. AGR, MED drenaje *m* 2. TECH desagüe *m;* **~ system** alcantarillado *m*

drainage basin *n* cuenca *f* hidrográfica

draining board ['dreɪnɪŋ'bɔːd, *Am:* -ˌbɔːrd] *n* escurridero *m*

drainpipe ['dreɪnpaɪp] *n* 1. (*pipe*) tubo *m* de desagüe 2. *pl* (*trousers*) pantalones *mpl* pitillo

drainpipe trousers *npl* pantalones *mpl* pitillo

drake [dreɪk] *n* pato (macho) *m*

dram [dræm] *n Scot* (*of whisky, liquor*) copita *f*

drama ['drɑːmə] *n* 1. LIT drama *m* 2. THEAT arte *m* dramático; **~ teacher** profesor(a) *m(f)* de arte dramático ▶**high ~** *inf* follón padre

drama school *n* escuela *f* de arte dramático

dramatic [drə'mætɪk, *Am:* -'mæt̬-] *adj* 1. THEAT dramático, -a; (*artist, production*) teatral 2. (*very noticeable: rise*) espectacular; (*effect, discovery*) notable

dramatics [drə'mætɪks, *Am:* -'mæt̬-] *npl* 1. + *sing vb* THEAT teatro *m;* **amateur ~** teatro amateur 2. *pej* (*behaviour*) teatralidad *f*

dramatis personae [ˌdræmətɪspɜ:'səʊ-naɪ, *Am:* ˌdrɑːməʈɪspə'soʊ-] *npl* THEAT personajes *mpl* (*de una obra de teatro*)

dramatist ['dræmətɪst, *Am:* 'drɑːməʈɪst] *n* THEAT dramaturgo, -a *m, f*

dramatization [ˌdræmətaɪ'zeɪʃən, *Am:* ˌdrɑːməʈɪ-] *n* dramatización *f*

dramatize ['dræmətaɪz, *Am:* 'drɑːmə-] *vt* 1. THEAT adaptar al teatro 2. (*exaggerate*) dramatizar

drank [dræŋk] *pt of* **drink**

drape [dreɪp] I. *vt* 1. (*hang*) cubrir; **to ~ sth (in a flag)** cubrir algo (con una bandera) 2. (*place*) colocar; **she ~d the scarf around her shoulders** se puso el chal sobre las espaldas; **to lie ~d over sth** estar tendido sobre algo II. *vi* colgar; **to ~ well** (*clothes*) tener caída III. *n* 1. *no pl* (*loose*) caída *f* 2. (*fold*) pliegue *m* 3. *pl, Am, Aus* (*curtains*) cortinas *fpl*

draper ['dreɪpə', *Am:* -pə'] *n Brit* pañero, -a *m, f*, mercero, -a *m, f AmL*

drapery ['dreɪpəri] <-ies> *n* 1. *no pl* (*hangings*) ropaje *m* 2. *no pl, Brit* (*cloths, fabrics*) pañería *f* 3. *pl, Am, Aus* (*curtains*) cortinas *fpl*

drastic ['dræstɪk] *adj* (*measure*) drástico, -a; (*change*) radical

drat [dræt] *interj* maldita sea

draught [drɑːft, *Am:* dræft] I. *n* 1. (*air current*) corriente *f* de aire; **to feel the ~** *fig* sufrir las consecuencias 2. (*drink*) trago *m*; **to take at one ~** apurar de un trago 3. MED dosis *f inv* 4. GASTR **on ~** de barril 5. NAUT calado *m* 6. *pl* GAMES damas *fpl* II. *adj* 1. (*beer*) de barril 2. (*horse*) de tiro

draught board *n* tablero *m* de damas

draughtsman ['drɑːftsmən, *Am:* 'dræfts-] <-men> *n* delineante *m*

draughty ['drɑːfti, *Am:* 'dræf-] *adj* <-ier, -iest> lleno, -a de corrientes de aire; **it's ~ here with the door open** hace corriente con la puerta abierta

draw [drɔː, *Am:* drɑː] I. <drew, drawn> *vt* 1. ART dibujar; (*line*) trazar; (*character*) perfilar; (*diagram*) representar; **to ~ sth to scale** reproducir algo a escala 2. (*pull, haul: cart, wagon*) arrastrar; **to ~ the curtains** correr las cortinas; **to ~ sb aside** llevarse a alguien aparte; **to ~ sb into (an) ambush** meter a alguien en una emboscada; **I was soon drawn into the argument** pronto me vi envuelto en la discusión 3. (*attract*) atraer; **to ~ applause** arrancar aplausos; **to be ~n toward(s) sb** sentirse atraído por alguien; **to ~ attention to** llamar la atención sobre; **to ~ criticism** suscitar críticas 4. (*elicit, evoke*) **to ~ sth (from sb/sth)** conseguir algo (de alguien/algo); **to ~ a confession from sb** sacar una confesión a alguien; **to ~ a reply** obtener una respuesta; **to ~ laughter** provocar risa 5. (*formulate, perceive*) **to ~ an analogy** establecer una analogía; **to ~ a conclusion** sacar una conclusión; **to ~ an inference** inferir 6. (*take out*) sacar; (*money*) retirar; **to ~ a card (from the deck)**

GAMES escoger una carta (de la baraja); **to ~ blood** *fig* hacer sangrar 7. (*obtain*) obtener; (*salary*) ganar; (*pension*) cobrar 8. (*lottery*) sortear 9. SPORTS, GAMES empatar 10. GASTR **to ~ a beer** poner una cerveza de barril 11. FIN, ECON (*write out a bill, cheque or draft*) **to ~ a cheque on sb** extender un cheque a cargo de alguien; **to ~ a bill on sb** girar una letra a cargo de alguien 12. NAUT **the boat ~s 1.5 metres** el barco tiene un calado de 1,5 metros 13. SPORTS **to ~ a bow** tensar un arco II. <drew, drawn> *vi* 1. ART dibujar 2. (*move, procede*) **to ~ ahead** adelantarse; **to ~ away** apartarse; **~ up here and he'll get into the car** para aquí y podrá subir en el coche; **to ~ level with sb/sth** *Brit* alcanzar a alguien/algo 3. (*approach*) acercarse; **to ~ to a close** finalizar; **to ~ to an end** concluir 4. (*draw lots*) echar a suertes 5. SPORTS, GAMES empatar III. *n* 1. (*attraction*) atracción *f* 2. SPORTS, GAMES empate *m* 3. (*drawing of lots*) sorteo *m* 4. (*act of drawing a gun*) **to be quick on the ~** ser rápido en sacar la pistola; *fig* pescarlas al vuelo

♦**draw apart** *vi* distanciarse

♦**draw aside** *vt always sep* (*person*) apartar; (*curtain*) correr

♦**draw away** I. *vi* 1. (*move off*) alejarse 2. (*move ahead*) **to ~ from sb** dejar atrás a alguien 3. (*move away*) apartarse II. *vt* apartar

♦**draw down** *vt* bajar; **to wear a hat drawn down over one's ears** llevar un gorro calado hasta las orejas

♦**draw in** I. *vi* 1. (*car, bus, train*) llegar 2. (*days*) acortarse II. *vt* 1. (*breath*) tomar 2. (*attract*) atraer

♦**draw off** *vt* (*boots*) quitarse; (*liquid*) vaciar

♦**draw on** I. *vt* 1. (*make use of*) usar; **to ~ sb's own resources** utilizar sus propios recursos; **to ~ the stocks** tirar de existencias 2. (*put on*) ponerse II. *vi* 1. (*continue: time, day*) seguir su curso 2. (*approach*) acercarse

♦**draw out** I. *vt* 1. (*prolong*) alargar 2. (*elicit*) sacar; **to be highly skilled at drawing out information** ser muy hábil para sonsacar información; **to ~ feelings and memories** hacer aflorar sentimientos y recuerdos; **to draw sb out (of himself)** hacer que alguien se desinhiba 3. FIN, ECON, COM retirar II. *vi* 1. (*car, bus, train*) salir 2. (*day*) hacerse más largo

♦**draw together** I. *vt* juntar II. *vi* acercarse

♦**draw up** I. *vt* 1. (*draft*) redactar; (*list*) hacer; (*guidelines, plan*) trazar; **to ~ a constitution** LAW redactar una constitución 2. (*pull toward one*) arrimar 3. (*raise*) levantar; **to draw oneself up** erguirse II. *vi* (*vehicle*) pararse

drawback ['drɔːbæk, *Am:* 'drɑː-] *n* desventaja *f* **drawbridge** *n* puente *m* levadizo

drawer ['drɔː', *Am:* 'drɔːr] *n* cajón *m*

drawing *n* ART dibujo *m*; **pencil ~** dibujo a lápiz

drawing board *n* tablero *m* de delineación;

back to the ~! ¡vuelta a empezar! **drawing pin** *n Brit, Aus* chincheta *f* **drawing room** *n* salón *m*

drawl [drɔːl, *Am:* drɑːl] I. *n* habla *f* lenta II. *vi* hablar arrastrando las vocales

drawn [drɔːn, *Am:* drɑːn] I. *pp of* **draw** II. *adj* 1. (*face*) demacrado, -a; **you look tired and** ~ se te ve cansado y ojeroso 2. GASTR derretido, -a

dread [dred] I. *vt* temer; I ~ **to think** … me da miedo pensar… II. *n no pl* terror *m;* **to fill sb with** ~ aterrorizar a alguien III. *adj liter* aterrador(a)

dreadful ['dredfəl] *adj* 1. (*terrible*) atroz; (*mistake*) terrible; (*atrocity*) espantoso, -a 2. (*of very bad quality*) fatal 3. (*very great*) horroroso, -a; **I feel** ~ **about it** me da mucha pena

dreadfully ['dredfəli] *adv* 1. (*in a terrible manner*) terriblemente 2. (*very poorly*) fatal 3. (*extremely*) enormemente

dream [driːm] I. *n* 1. sueño *m;* **a bad** ~ una pesadilla 2. (*daydream*) ensueño *m;* (*fantasy*) ilusión *f;* **to be in a** ~ estar en las nubes; **like a** ~ como un sueño; **he cooks like a** ~ cocina de maravilla; **to go like a** ~ ir como la seda; **a** ~ **come true** un sueño hecho realidad; **in your ~s!** ¡ni lo sueñes! II. <dreamt *o* dreamed, dreamt *o* dreamed> *vi* soñar; **to** ~ **of** (**doing**) **sth** soñar con (hacer) algo; ~ **on!** *inf* ¡ni de coña!; **I would not** ~ **of** (**doing**) **that** no se me pasaría por la cabeza hacer eso III. <dreamt *o* dreamed, dreamt *o* dreamed> *vt* soñar; **I never ~t that** … nunca se me había ocurrido que… +*condicional* IV. *adj* ideal; **his** ~ **house** la casa de sus sueños; **to be** (**living**) **in a** ~ **world** vivir en las nubes

♦**dream away** *vt* **to** ~ **the day** pasarse el día soñando

♦**dream up** *vt* idear

dreamer ['driːmər, *Am:* -mɚ] *n* soñador(a) *m(f);* *pej* iluso, -a *m, f*

dreamland *n inf* país *m* de los sueños

dreamless *adj* sin sueños

dreamlike *adj* de ensueño

dreamt [dremt] *pt, pp of* **dream**

dreamy ['driːmi] *adj* <-ier, -iest> 1. (*dreamlike*) de ensueño 2. (*daydreaming*) soñador(a) 3. *inf* (*wonderful*) maravilloso, -a

dreary ['drɪəri, *Am:* 'drɪr-] *adj* <-ier, -iest> (*life*) deprimente; (*place*) lóbrego, -a; (*weather*) gris

dredge[1] [dredʒ] I. *n* TECH red *f* de arrastre II. *vt* TECH dragar

dredge[2] [dredʒ] *vt* GASTR espolvorear

dredger[1] ['dredʒər, *Am:* -ɚ] *n* TECH draga *f*

dredger[2] ['dredʒər, *Am:* -ɚ] *n* GASTR espolvoreador *m*

dregs [dregz] *npl* 1. (*sediment*) poso *m* 2. (*undesirable part*) **the** ~ **of society** la escoria de la sociedad

drench [drentʃ] *vt* empapar; **to be ~ed with**

estar calado de

dress [dres] I. *n* <-es> vestido *m;* **strapless/ sleeveless** ~ vestido sin tirantes/sin mangas; **evening** ~ (*for woman*) vestido de noche; (*for man*) traje *m* de etiqueta II. *vi* vestirse; **to** ~ **in blue** vestir de azul; **to** ~ **smartly for sth** ponerse elegante para algo III. *vt* 1. (*put clothes on*) vestir 2. GASTR (*greens, salad*) aliñar 3. MED (*wound*) vendar 4. (*decorate*) adornar; (*hair*) peinar; **to** ~ **shop windows** decorar escaparates IV. *adj* de gala; **a** ~ **suit** traje *m* de gala

♦**dress down** I. *vi* vestir informal II. *vt Brit, inf* regañar

♦**dress up** I. *vi* ponerse elegante; **to** ~ **as** disfrazarse de II. *vt* 1. (*put on formal clothes*) poner elegante 2. (*disguise*) disfrazar; **to dress sb up as** disfrazar a alguien de 3. (*embellish*) adornar

dress circle *n* THEAT piso *m* principal **dress coat** *n* frac *m*

dresser ['dresər, *Am:* -ɚ] *n* 1. FASHION **to be a very stylish** ~ vestir con mucho estilo 2. THEAT encargado, -a *m, f* de vestuario 3. (*sideboard*) aparador *m; Am, Can* (*dressing table*) tocador *m*

dressing ['dresɪŋ] *n* 1. *no pl* FASHION el vestir *m* 2. GASTR aliño *m* 3. MED vendaje *m*

dressing-down *n Brit* reprimenda *f* **dressing gown** *n* (*garment worn inside the house*) bata *f;* (*towel*) albornoz *m* **dressing room** *n* vestidor *m;* THEAT camerino *m* **dressing table** *n* tocador *m*

dressmaker ['dres,meɪkər, *Am:* -kɚ] *n* modisto, -a *m, f*

dressmaking I. *n no pl* costura *f* II. *adj* ~ **course** curso *m* de corte y confección; ~ **and tailoring shop** sastrería *f*

dress rehearsal *n* ensayo *m* general **dress shirt** *n* camisa *f* de etiqueta **dress suit** *n* vestido *m* de gala **dress uniform** *n* uniforme *m* de gala

dressy ['dresi] *adj* <-ier, -iest> (*clothing*) elegante

drew [druː] *pt of* **draw**

dribble ['drɪbl] I. *vi* 1. (*person*) babear 2. (*water*) gotear 3. SPORTS regatear con; **to** ~ **past a defender** driblar a un defensa II. *vt* 1. (*water*) dejar caer gota a gota 2. SPORTS regatear con III. *n* 1. *no pl* (*saliva*) baba *f* 2. (*water*) chorrito *m* 3. SPORTS dribling *m*

driblet ['drɪblɪt] *n* trocito *m;* **in ~s** en pequeñas cantidades

dribs [drɪbz] *npl* **in** ~ **and drabs** poco a poco

dried [draɪd] I. *pt, pp of* **dry** II. *adj* seco, -a; ~ **meat** cecina *f;* ~ **milk** leche *f* en polvo

dried-up [,draɪd'ʌp] *adj,* **dried up** *adj* seco, -a

drier *adj,* **dryer** ['draɪər, *Am:* -ɚ] *adj comp of* **dry**

drift [drɪft] I. *vi* 1. (*on water*) dejarse llevar por la corriente; (*in air*) dejarse llevar por el viento; **to** ~ **out to sea** ir a la deriva 2. (*move* *aimlessly*) dejarse llevar **3.** (*progress aim-lessly*) vivir sin rumbo **4.** METEO (*sand, snow*) amontonarse **II.** *n* **1.** NAUT deriva *f* **2.** *fig* (*movement*) movimiento *m* **3.** (*trend*) tendencia *f* **4.** METEO montón *m;* **a sand** ~ un montón de arena **5.** (*sense*) significado *m;* **to catch sb's** ~ caer en la cuenta de lo que alguien quiere decir

◆**drift apart** *vi* (*people*) distanciarse (progresivamente)

◆**drift off** *vi* dormirse lentamente

drifter ['drɪftə^r, *Am:* -tɚ] *n* vagabundo, -a *m, f*

drift-ice *n no pl* hielo *m* flotante

drifting *adj* ~ **fog banks** bancos *mpl* de niebla empujados por la corriente

driftwood *n no pl* madera que flota en el mar arrastrada por la corriente

drill¹ [drɪl] **I.** *n* TECH taladro *m;* (*dentist's*) fresa *f;* ~ **bit** broca *f* **II.** *vt* TECH perforar; **to** ~ **a hole** hacer un agujero **III.** *vi* TECH perforar

drill² [drɪl] **I.** *n* MIL, SCHOOL ejercicios *fpl;* **to do spelling** ~**s** hacer ejercicios de ortografía ▶**to know** ~ *inf* saber lo que hay que hacer; **what's the** ~? *inf* ¿cómo se hace? **II.** *vt* **1.** SCHOOL instruir; **to** ~ **sth into sb** inculcar algo a alguien **2.** MIL enseñar la instrucción a **III.** *vi* **1.** (*go through exercise*) hacer ejercicios **2.** MIL hacer la instrucción **IV.** *adj* MIL de instrucción

drilling rig ['drɪlɪŋˌrɪg] *n* torre *f* de perforación

drink [drɪŋk] **I.** <drank, drunk> *vi* beber; **to** ~ **heavily** beber en exceso; **to** ~ **in moderation** beber con moderación; **to** ~ **to sb** brindar por alguien; **to** ~ **like a fish** beber como una esponja **II.** <drank, drunk> *vt* beber; **to** ~ **a toast** (**to sb/sth**) brindar (por alguien/algo); **to** ~ **sb under the table** tener mucho más aguante que alguien **III.** *n* bebida *f;* (*alcoholic beverage*) copa *f;* **to have a** ~ tomar algo; **to drive sb to** ~ llevar a alguien a la bebida; **the** ~ *inf* el agua

◆**drink in** *vt* beber; (*words*) estar pendiente de

drinkable ['drɪŋkəbl] *adj* potable

drinker *n* bebedor(a) *m(f)*

drinking *n no pl* (*act*) el beber *m;* (*drunkenness*) bebida *f;* **no** ~ **allowed in these premises** se prohíbe el consumo de bebidas alcohólicas

drinking fountain *n* fuente *f* de agua potable **drinking song** *n* canción *f* de taberna **drinking straw** *n* caña *f*

drinking water *no pl n* agua *f* potable **drinking-water supply** *n* abastecimiento *m* de agua potable

drip [drɪp] **I.** <-pp-> *vi* gotear **II.** <-pp-> *vt* dejar caer gota a gota **III.** *n* **1.** *no pl* (*act of dripping*) goteo *m* **2.** (*drop*) gota *f* **3.** MED gota a gota *m* **4.** *inf* (*person*) pánfilo, -a *m, f*

drip-dry [ˌdrɪp'draɪ] <-ie-> *adj* de lava y pon

dripping ['drɪpɪŋ] **I.** *adj* **1.** (*tap*) que gotea **2.** (*extremely wet*) chorreante **II.** *adv* **to be** ~ **wet** estar empapado **III.** *n* *Am: pl* pringue *m*

drive [draɪv] **I.** <drove, driven> *vt* **1.** AUTO conducir, manejar *AmL;* **to** ~ **sb home** llevar a alguien a casa (en coche); **to** ~ **a race car** (*operate*) pilotar un coche de carreras; **to** ~ **a sports car** tener un coche deportivo **2.** (*urge*) empujar; **to** ~ **sb to** (**do**) **sth** forzar a alguien a (hacer) algo **3.** (*cattle*) guiar **4.** (*render, make*) volver; **to** ~ **sb mad** sacar a alguien de quicio **5.** (*ball*) golpear; (*tunnel*) abrir; (*road*) construir; **to** ~ **a passage** abrir un camino **6.** TECH mover **II.** <drove, driven> *vi* AUTO **1.** (*steer*) conducir, manejar *AmL* **2.** (*travel*) ir en coche **3.** (*function*) funcionar **III.** *n* **1.** AUTO paseo *m;* (*journey*) viaje *m;* **to go for a** ~ ir a dar una vuelta en coche **2.** (*driveway*) entrada *f* **3.** *no pl* TECH transmisión *f;* **front-wheel** ~ tracción delantera; **all-wheel** ~ tracción a las cuatro ruedas **4.** *no pl* PSYCH impulso *m;* **to have** ~ ser emprendedor; **sex** ~ apetito *m* sexual **5.** (*campaign*) campaña *f;* **to be on an economy** ~ estar en una economía restrictiva; **a fund--raising** ~ campaña para recaudar fondos **6.** SPORTS golpe *m* fuerte **7.** INFOR unidad *f* de disco; **to insert a floppy disk into the disk** ~ insertar un disquete en la disquetera

◆**drive at** *vt inf* insinuar

◆**drive in I.** *vi* entrar (en coche) **II.** *vt* (*nail*) clavar

◆**drive off I.** *vt always sep* ahuyentar **II.** *vi* irse (en coche)

◆**drive out** *vt* expulsar

◆**drive up** *vi* **to** ~ (**somewhere**) acercarse (a algún sitio)

drive-in ['draɪvɪn] **I.** *adj Am, Aus* ~ **cinema** autocine *m* **II.** *n Am, Aus* (*drive-in restaurant*) *restaurante donde se sirve a los clientes en su propio coche;* (*drive-in cinema*) autocine *m*

drive-in bank *n Am, Aus* autobanco *m* **drive-in cinema** *n,* **drive-in movie** *n Am, Aus* autocine *m*

drivel ['drɪvəl] *n no pl* tonterías *fpl*

driven ['drɪvən] *pp of* **drive**

driver ['draɪvə^r, *Am:* -vɚ] *n* **1.** AUTO conductor(a) *m(f);* **truck** ~ camionero, -a *m, f;* **taxi** ~ taxista *mf;* ~**'s license** *Am* carné *m* de conducir, brevete *m Perú;* **to be in the** ~**'s seat** *fig* llevar las riendas de algo **2.** INFOR driver *m*

Las **Drive through bottle shops** son un tipo de tiendas que se pueden encontrar por toda Australia. Generalmente pertenecen a hoteles y por su aspecto se parecen a un garaje abierto o a un granero en el que se puede entrar con el coche. A este tipo de tiendas también se las conoce como **liquor barns**. En ellas, sin tener que apearse del vehículo, se puede comprar vino, cerveza y cualquier bebida alcohólica. El cliente es servido directamente en la ventanilla de su coche.

driveway ['draɪvweɪ] *n* camino de entrada *m*

driving I. *n* conducción *f*, manejo *m AmL* II. *adj* **1.** AUTO, TECH de conducir **2.** METEO (*rain*) torrencial **3.** (*powerful: ambition, force*) impulsor(a)

driving ban *n* retirada *f* del carné de conducir **driving force** *n no pl* fuerza *f* motriz **driving instructor** *n* profesor(a) *m(f)* de autoescuela **driving lessons** *npl* prácticas *fpl* de conducir **driving licence** *n Brit* carné *m* de conducir **driving pool** *n* flota *f* de automóviles **driving school** *n* autoescuela *f* **driving test** *n* examen *m* de conducir

drizzle ['drɪzl] I. *n no pl* METEO llovizna *f*, garúa *f AmL*, chipichipi *m Méx* II. *vi* METEO lloviznar, garuar *AmL*

drizzly ['drɪzli] *adj* it was a grey ~ afternoon la tarde era gris y lloviznaba

droll [drəʊl, *Am:* drəʊl] *adj* divertido, -a

dromedary ['drɒmədəri, *Am:* 'drɑːmədər-] <-ies> *n* dromedario *m*

drone [drəʊn, *Am:* drəʊn] I. *n no pl* **1.** ZOOL zángano *m* **2.** (*person*) vago, -a *m, f* **3.** (*tone*) zumbido *m* II. *vi* **1.** (*make a monotonous sound*) zumbar **2.** (*speak in a monotonous tone*) hablar con monotonía

drool [druːl] I. *vi* babear; **to ~ over sth/sb** *fig* caérse a uno la baba con algo/alguien II. *n no pl* baba *f*

droop [druːp] I. *vi* **1.** (*fall*) colgar **2.** (*flowers*) marchitarse **3.** (*person*) desanimarse; (*mood, spirits*) decaer II. *vt* inclinar

drop [drɒp, *Am:* drɑːp] I. *n* **1.** (*of liquid*) gota *f*; **~ by ~** gota a gota **2.** (*vertical distance*) declive *f*; **a sheer ~** un profundo precipicio **3.** (*decrease*) disminución *f*; (*of temperature*) descenso *m* **4.** (*fall*) caída *f*; (*distribution by aircraft*) lanzamiento *m*; **~ of medical supplies** aprovisionamiento *m* aéreo de suministros médicos **5.** *inf* (*of drink*) sorbo *m*; **just a ~** sólo un poco; **to have had a ~ too much** (to drink) llevar una copa de más; **to take a ~** tomar un trago **6.** (*sweet*) pastilla *f* **7.** (*secret collection point*) escondrijo *m* ▸ **at the ~ of a hat** en seguida; **it's a ~ in the** ocean es una gota de agua en el mar II. <-pp-> *vt* **1.** (*allow to fall*) dejar caer; **to ~ anchor** echar el ancla; **to ~ a bomb** lanzar una bomba; **to ~ ballast** soltar lastre **2.** (*lower*) bajar; **to ~ prices** reducir los precios; **to ~ one's voice** bajar la voz **3.** *inf* (*send*) enviar; **to ~ a letter into a mailbox** *Am* echar una carta al correo **4.** *inf* (*express*) soltar; **to ~ a hint** soltar una indirecta; **to ~ a word in sb's ear** decir una palabra al oído a alguien **5.** (*dismiss*) despedir **6.** (*abandon, give up*) renunciar a; **to ~ a demand** retirar una demanda; **to ~ sb** romper con alguien **7.** (*leave out*) omitir; **to ~ one's** aitches *Brit, Aus* no pronunciar las haches ▸ **to ~ a** brick, **to ~ a** clanger *Brit* meter la pata III. <-pp-> *vi* **1.** (*descend*) bajar **2.** (*go to*) **to ~ into a bar/a shop** pasarse por un bar/una tienda **3.** (*go lower: prices*) bajar **4.** *inf* (*become exhausted*) estar agotado, -a; **to ~**

with exhaustion caer rendido; **he is ready to ~** está que no se tiene; **to ~** (**down**) **dead** caerse muerto; **~ dead!** *inf* ¡muérete! ▸ **to** let it **~** dejarlo; **to** let it **~ that ...** dar a entender que...

◆ **drop across** *vt insep, inf* encontrarse con
◆ **drop behind** *vi* quedarse atrás; **to ~ in sth** rezagarse en algo
◆ **drop down** *vi* caer
◆ **drop in** I. *vi inf* entrar un momento; **to ~ on sb** ir a ver a alguien; (*unexpectedly*) visitar a alguien inesperadamente II. *vt* **to drop sb right in it** *inf* meter a alguien en problemas
◆ **drop off** I. *vt inf* (*passenger*) dejar II. *vi* **1.** (*decrease*) disminuir **2.** *inf* (*fall asleep*) quedarse dormido **3.** (*become separated*) desprenderse
◆ **drop out** *vi* **1.** (*person*) darse de baja; **to ~ of a course** darse de baja de un curso **2.** LING omitir

drop-down menu *n* INFOR menú *m* desplegable

drop kick *n* SPORTS botepronto *m*

droplet ['drɒlət, *Am:* 'drɑːp-] *n* gotita *f*

dropout ['drɒpaʊt, *Am:* 'drɑːp-] *n* **1.** (*person who lives in an unusual way*) automarginado, -a *m, f* **2.** UNIV, SCHOOL persona *f* que ha abandonado los estudios

dropper ['drɒpər, *Am:* 'drɑːpə] *n* cuentagotas *m inv*, gotero *m AmL*

droppings ['drɒpɪŋz, *Am:* 'drɑːpɪŋz] *npl* excremento *m*

drop shot *n* SPORTS dejada *f*

dross [drɒs, *Am:* drɑːs] *n no pl, Brit* escoria *f*

drought [draʊt] *n* sequía *f*

drove[1] [drəʊv, *Am:* drəʊv] I. *vt* modelar con cincel II. *n* **1.** (*chisel*) cincel *m* **2.** (*of animals*) rebaño *m* **3.** *pl, inf* (*large group of people*) multitud *f*; **in ~s** en tropel

drove[2] [drəʊv, *Am:* drəʊv] *pt of* **drive**

drover ['drəʊvər, *Am:* 'drəʊvə] *n* pastor(a) *m(f)*

drown [draʊn] I. *vt* **1.** (*cause to die*) ahogar; **to look like a ~ed rat** *inf* estar calado hasta los huesos **2.** (*engulf in water*) anegar **3.** (*make inaudible*) apagar ▸ **to ~ one's sorrows in** drink ahogar las penas en alcohol II. *vi* **1.** (*die through submersion*) ahogarse **2.** *inf* (*have too much*) **to be ~ing in work** estar hasta arriba de trabajo

drowning *n* ahogo *m*

drowse [draʊz] *vi* dormitar

drowsy ['draʊzi] <-ier, -iest> *adj* soñoliento, -a

drudge [drʌdʒ] I. *n* esclavo, -a *m, f* del trabajo II. *vi* trabajar como un esclavo

drudgery ['drʌdʒəri] *n no pl* trabajo *m* penoso

drug [drʌg] I. *n* **1.** MED fármaco *m* **2.** (*narcotic*) droga *f*; **to take ~s** tomar drogas II. <-gg-> *vt* drogar

drug abuse *n* toxicomanía *f* **drug addict** *n* toxicómano, -a *m, f* **drug addiction** *n* drogadicción f **drug dealer** n traficante mf de drogas **drug dependency** n drogodependencia f **drug manufacturer** n fabricante mf de drogas sintéticas **drug pusher** n inf camello mf **drug squad** n, **drugs squad** n Brit brigada f de estupefacientes

drugstore ['drʌgstɔːʳ, Am: -stɔːr] n Am farmacia f (donde suelen venderse otros artículos, además de productos farmacéuticos)

drug taking n consumo m de drogas **drug traffic** n tráfico m de drogas **drug trafficker** n narcotraficante mf **drug trafficking** n narcotráfico m

druid ['druːɪd] n druida m

drum [drʌm] I. n 1. MUS, TECH tambor m 2. pl (in a band) batería f 3. (for oil) bidón m 4. ANAT tímpano m II.<-mm-> vi (play percussion) tocar el tambor; (with fingers) tamborilear con los dedos; **to ~ on sth** tamborilear con los dedos sobre algo III. vt inf **to ~ sth into sb** meter a alguien algo en la cabeza

drumbeat ['drʌmbiːt] n redoble m

drum brake n freno m de tambor

drumhead ['drʌmhed] n parche m de tambor

drum major n tambor m mayor

drummer ['drʌməʳ, Am: -ɚ] n (in a band) tambor m; (in a group) batería f

drumstick ['drʌmstɪk] n 1. MUS palillo m 2. GASTR pierna f de pollo

drunk [drʌŋk] I. vt, vi pp of **drink** II. adj 1. (inebriated) borracho, -a, jumo, -a AmL, ido, -a AmC, bota Méx; **to be ~** estar borracho; **to get ~** emborracharse 2. fig (very much affected) **to be ~ with joy** estar ebrio de alegría III. n borracho, -a m, f

drunkard ['drʌŋkəd, Am: -kəd] n borracho, -a m, f

drunken ['drʌŋkən] adj borracho, -a; **a ~ brawl** una reyerta de borrachos; **~ driving** Am conducción f en estado de embriaguez

drunkenness ['drʌŋkənɪs] n no pl embriaguez f, bomba f AmL

dry [draɪ] I.<-ier o -er, -iest o -est> adj 1. (not wet) seco, -a; **to go ~** secarse; **~ red wine** vino tinto seco 2. (climate, soil) árido, -a 3. (bread) sin mantequilla 4. (without alcohol: state) prohibicionista 5. (uninteresting) aburrido, -a 6. (brief) lacónico, -a; **~ (sense of) humour** (sentido del) humor agudo ►**to bleed sb ~** sacar a alguien hasta el útimo céntimo; **to run ~** agotarse II.<-ie-> vt secar; (tears) enjugarse III.<-ie-> vi secarse; **to put sth out to ~** sacar algo para que se seque

◆**dry up** I. vi 1. (become dry) secarse 2. (dry the dishes) secar los platos 3. (stop talking) callarse; (on stage) quedarse en blanco 4. (run out) agotarse 5. inf (become silent) enmudecer II. vt secar

dryad ['draɪæd] n dríade f

dry cell n ELEC pila f seca

dry cell battery n batería f de pila seca

dry-clean [ˌdraɪˈkliːn] vt limpiar en seco

dry cleaner's n no pl tintorería f

dry cleaning n limpieza f en seco

dry dock n dique m seco

dryer ['draɪəʳ, Am: -ɚ] n 1. (for hair) secador m 2. (machine for drying clothes) secadora f

dry goods npl Am mercería f **dry ice** n nieve f carbóica **dry land** n (not sea) tierra f firme **dry measure** n medida f para áridos

dryness ['draɪnəs] n no pl, a. fig sequedad f

dry rot n putrefacción f de la madera **dry-shod** adj, adv a pie enjuto

drystone wall n Brit muro m seco

DS n abbr of **Detective Sergeant** comisario m

DSc abbr of **Doctor of Science** doctor(a) m(f) en Ciencias

DTP [ˌdiːtiːˈpiː] n abbr of **desktop publishing** DTP m

dual ['djuːəl, Am: 'duː-] adj inv doble; **~ ownership** ECON condominio m

dual carriageway n Brit autovía f, autocarril m Bol, Chile, Nic **dual-currency period** n período m de convivencia de dos monedas

dualism ['djʊəlɪzəm, Am: 'duː-] n no pl dualismo m

dub[1] [dʌb] <-bb-> vt 1. (confer knighthood) armar caballero 2. (give sb a nickname) apodar

dub[2] [dʌb] <-bb-> vt (film) doblar; **to be ~bed into English/French** estar doblado en inglés/francés

dubbing ['dʌbɪŋ] n doblaje m

dubious ['djuːbɪəs, Am: 'duː-] adj 1. (doubtful) dudoso, -a 2. (untrustworthy) sospechoso, -a

Dubliner ['dʌblɪnəʳ] n dublinés, -esa m, f

duchess ['dʌtʃɪs] n duquesa f

duchy ['dʌtʃi] n ducado m

duck[1] [dʌk] n Brit, inf cariño mf

duck[2] [dʌk] I. n 1. (bird) pato m 2. SPORTS cero m; **to be out for a ~** ser eliminado a cero ►**to take to sth like a ~ to water** inf sentirse como pez en el agua con/en algo II. vi 1. (dip head) agachar la cabeza 2. (go under water) chapuzarse 3. (hide) agacharse; **to ~ out of sth** escabullirse de algo III. vt 1. (lower suddenly) **to ~ one's head** agachar la cabeza; **to ~ one's head under water** sumergir la cabeza dentro del agua 2. (avoid) esquivar; fig eludir; **to ~ an issue** eludir un tema

duckboards ['dʌkbɔːdz, Am: -bɔːrdz] npl pasadera f

duckling ['dʌklɪŋ] n patito m

ducky ['dʌki] n inf cariño m

duct [dʌkt] n 1. (pipe) conducto m; **air ~** conducto del aire 2. ANAT canal m; **ear ~** canal auditivo

dud [dʌd] I. n 1. (person) persona f inútil 2. (bomb) bomba f que no estalla 3. (failure) fallo m II. adj 1. (useless, worthless) falso, -a 2. (forged) falsificado, -a; **~ cheque** cheque m sin fondos

dude [djuːd] n Am, inf (guy) individuo m; (smartly dressed) figurín m

due [djuː, Am: duː] I. adj 1. (payable)

pagadero, -a; (*owing*) debido, -a; ~ **date** fecha *f* de vencimiento; **the loan is now ~ for repayment** hay que devolver el préstamo; **to fall ~** vencer **2.** (*appropriate*) conveniente; **with (all) due respect** con el debido respeto; **in ~ course** a su debido tiempo **3.** *after n, Brit, Aus* (*appropriate, owing*) **to treat sb with the respect ~ to him/her** tratar a alguien con el respeto que se merece **4.** (*expected*) esperado, -a; **I'm ~ in Berlin this evening** esta noche me esperan en Berlín **5.** (*owing to, because of*) **~ to** debido a; **~ to circumstances beyond our control …** por circunstancias ajenas a nuestra voluntad… **II.** *n* **1.** (*fair treatment*) merecido *m;* **to give sb his/her ~** dar a alguien lo que se merece **2.** (*debts*) deuda *f; pl* (*obligations*) deberes *mpl;* **to pay one's ~s** (*meet obligations/duties*) cumplir con sus obligaciones/deberes; (*meet debts*) pagar las deudas **3.** *pl* (*regular payment*) cuota *f* **III.** *adv before adv* exactamente; **~ north/south** derecho hacia el norte/sur

duel ['djuːəl, *Am:* 'duː-] **I.** *n* duelo *m;* **to fight a ~** batirse en duelo **II.** *vi* <*Brit:* -ll-, *Am:* -l-> HIST batirse en duelo

duet [djuˈet, *Am:* du-] *n* dúo *m;* **to play a ~** interpretar un dueto

duffel bag ['dʌfəlˌbæg] *n* NAUT bolsa *f* de lona **duffel coat** *n* trenca *f*

duffer ['dʌfəʳ, *Am:* -ɚ] *n* zoquete *m*

dug[1] [dʌg] *pt, pp of* **dig**

dug[2] [dʌg] *n* (*of mammal*) teta *f;* (*of cow*) ubre *f*

dugout ['dʌgaʊt] *n* **1.** MIL refugio *m* subterráneo **2.** SPORTS banquillo *m* **3.** NAUT piragua *f* (*hecha de un tronco*)

duke [djuːk, *Am:* duːk] *n* duque *m*

dull [dʌl] **I.** *adj* **1.** (*boring*) aburrido, -a; (*life*) monótono, -a; **as ~ as ditchwater** más aburrido que un entierro de tercera **2.** (*not bright: surface*) deslustrado, -a; (*sky*) gris; (*weather*) desapacible; (*colour*) apagado, -a; (*light*) pálido, -a **3.** (*muffled, muted*) callado, -a; (*ache, thud*) sordo, -a **4.** *Am* (*blunt, unsharpened*) desafilado, -a **II.** *vt* **1.** (*alleviate*) aliviar **2.** (*desensitize*) insensibilizar

dullard ['dʌləd, *Am:* -ɚd] *n* zoquete *m*

dullness ['dʌlnɪs] *n no pl* **1.** (*lack of excitement*) insipidez *f* **2.** (*tediousness*) pesadez *f*

duly ['djuːli, *Am:* 'duː-] *adv* **1.** (*appropriately*) debidamente **2.** (*on time*) a su debido tiempo

dumb [dʌm] *adj* **1.** (*mute*) mudo, -a; **deaf and ~** sordomudo, -a; **to be struck ~** quedarse mudo de asombro **2.** *inf* (*stupid*) estúpido, -a; **to play ~** hacerse el tonto

dumbbell ['dʌmbel] *n* **1.** (*weight*) pesa *f* **2.** *Am, inf* (*person*) bobo, -a *m, f*

dumbfound [ˌdʌmˈfaʊnd, *Am:* 'dʌmfaʊnd] *vt* dejar mudo (de asombro)

dumbfounded *adj* mudo, -a de asombro

dumbshow ['dʌmʃəʊ, *Am:* -ʃoʊ] *n Brit, inf* pantomima *f;* **to use ~** emplear la mímica

dumbstricken ['dʌmˌstrɪkən] *adj,* **dumbstruck** ['dʌmstrʌk] *adj* mudo, -a (de asombro)

dumb waiter *n* montaplatos *m*

dumfound [ˌdʌmˈfaʊnd, *Am:* 'dʌmfaʊnd] *vt s.* **dumbfound**

dummy ['dʌmi] **I.** <-ies> *n* **1.** (*mannequin*) maniquí *m* **2.** (*duplicate*) imitación *f* **3.** *Brit, Aus* (*for baby*) chupete *m* **4.** (*fool*) tonto, -a **II.** *adj* (*duplicate*) copiado, -a; (*false*) falso, -a; **~ run** prueba *f;* (*tryout*) ensayo *m* **III.** *vi Am, inf* **to ~ up** callarse como un muerto

dump [dʌmp] **I.** *n* **1.** (*for waste*) vertedero *m*, botadero *m Ven* **2.** (*nasty place*) tugurio *m* **3.** MIL depósito *m;* **ammunition ~** almacén *m* de municiones **II.** *vt* **1.** (*drop carelessly*) verter; (*get rid of*) deshacerse de **2.** (*abandon*) abandonar **3.** *inf* (*end relationship with*) dejar **4.** INFOR volcar **III.** *vi Am, inf* **to ~ on sb** pagarla con alguien

dumper ['dʌmpəʳ, *Am:* -pɚ] *n* dúmper *m*

dumping *n* dúmping *m*

dumping ground *n* vertedero *m*

dumpling ['dʌmplɪŋ] *n* bolita de masa que puede estar rellena de carne o bien de fruta

dumpy ['dʌmpi] <-ier, -iest> *adj* regordete, -a

dun[1] [dʌn] *adj* pardo, -a

dun[2] [dʌn] **I.** <-nn-> *vt* **to ~ sb** apremiar a alguien para que pague lo que debe **II.** *n* petición *f* de reembolso

dunce [dʌns] *n* burro, -a *mf*

dune [djuːn, *Am:* duːn] *n* duna *f*

dung [dʌŋ] *n no pl* excrementos *mpl*, estiércol *m*

dungarees [ˌdʌŋgəˈriːz] *npl Brit* (*overall*) peto *m; Am* (*denim clothes*) mono *m*

dungeon ['dʌndʒən] *n* mazmorra *f*

dunghill ['dʌŋhɪl] *n* estercolero *m*

dunk [dʌŋk] *vt* mojar

duo ['djuːəʊ, *Am:* 'duːoʊ] *n* dúo *m;* **comedy ~** pareja cómica

duodenum [ˌdjuːəˈdiːnəm, *Am:* ˌduː-] <-na o -s> *n* duodeno *m*

dup. *n abbr of* **duplicate** dup.

dupe [djuːp, *Am:* duːp] **I.** *n* inocentón, -ona *m, f* **II.** *vt* **to be ~d** ser engañado

duplex ['djuːpleks, *Am:* 'duː-] **I.** *n* **1.** *Am* (*apartment*) dúplex **2.** *Aus* (*house*) casa *f* adosada **II.** *adj* doble

duplicate ['djuːplɪkət, *Am:* 'duː-] **I.** *vt* **1.** (*replicate*) duplicar; (*repeat*) repetir **2.** (*copy*) copiar; **to ~ a device** hacer una réplica de un dispositivo **II.** *adj inv* duplicado, -a; **~ key** duplicado *m* de una llave **III.** *n* duplicado *m*

duplicator ['djuːplɪkeɪtəʳ, *Am:* 'duːplɪkeɪtɚ] *n* multicopista *f*

duplicity [djuːˈplɪsəti, *Am:* duːˈplɪsəţi] *n no pl* duplicidad *f*

durability [ˌdjʊərəˈbɪləti, *Am:* ˌdʊrəˈbɪləţi] *n no pl* **1.** (*permanence, persistency*) durabilidad *f* **2.** (*life of a product*) duración *f*

durable ['djʊərəbl, *Am:* 'dʊrə-] *adj* **1.** (*hard-wearing*) resistente **2.** (*long-lasting*) duradero, -a

duration [djʊ'reɪʃən, *Am:* dʊ-] *n no pl* duración *f;* **a stay of two years'** ~ una estancia de dos años de duración; **for the** ~ hasta que se acabe

duress [djʊ'res, *Am:* dʊ-] *n no pl* coacción *f;* **under** ~ bajo coacción

during ['djʊərɪŋ, *Am:* 'dʊrɪŋ] *prep* durante; ~ **work/the week** durante el trabajo/la semana

dusk [dʌsk] *n no pl* crepúsculo *m;* **at** ~ al atardecer

dusky ['dʌski] <-ier, iest> *adj* **1.** (*dark*) oscuro, -a **2.** *a. pej* (*dark-skinned*) moreno, -a

dust [dʌst] **I.** *n no pl* polvo *m;* **coal** ~ cisco *m* ►**to** bite **the** ~ morder el polvo; **to wait till the** ~ **has** settled dejar que se aclare la atmósfera; **to** throw ~ **in the eyes of sb** engañar a alguien con falsas apariencias; **to** turn **to** ~ *liter* convertirse en polvo **II.** *vt* **1.** (*clean*) quitar el polvo a **2.** (*spread over*) salpicar; **to** ~ **sth with insecticide** espolvorear insecticida sobre la superficie de algo **III.** *vi* quitar el polvo

dustbin ['dʌstbɪn] *n Brit* cubo *m* de (la) basura **dustcart** *n Brit* camión *m* de la basura **dust-coat** *n* sobretodo *m* **dust cover** *n* **1.** (*for furniture*) guardapolvo *m* **2.** (*on book*) forro *m*

duster ['dʌstə*ʳ*, *Am:* -tə*ʳ*] *n* trapo *m*

dust jacket *n* (*of a book*) sobrecubierta *f* **dustman** <-men> *n Brit* basurero *m* **dustpan** *n* recogedor *m;* ~ **and brush** recogedor y escoba **dust storm** *n* vendaval *m* de polvo

dust-up ['dʌstʌp] *n inf* **1.** (*physical clash*) pelea *f* **2.** (*dispute*) enfrentamiento *m*

dusty ['dʌsti] <-ier, -iest> *adj* **1.** (*covered in dust*) polvoriento, -a **2.** (*of greyish colour*) ceniciento, -a; ~ **brown** marrón grisáceo

Dutch [dʌtʃ] **I.** *adj* holandés, -esa **II.** *n* **1.** *pl* (*people*) **the** ~ los holandeses **2.** LING holandés *m* ►**to** go ~ pagar a escote

Dutchman ['dʌtʃmən] <-men> *n* holandés *m* ►**if ... I'm a** ~ *Brit* que me maten si...

Dutchwoman ['dʌtʃˌwʊmən] <-women> *n* holandesa *f*

dutiable ['dju:tiəbl, *Am:* 'du:ʈi-] *adj* sujeto, -a a derechos de aduana

dutiful ['dju:tɪfəl, *Am:* 'du:ʈɪ-] *adj* obediente

duty ['dju:ti, *Am:* 'du:ʈi] <-ies> *n* **1.** (*moral*) deber *m;* (*obligation*) obligación *f;* **it's my** ~ es mi deber; **to do sth out of** ~ hacer algo por compromiso; **to do one's** ~ cumplir con su obligación **2.** (*task, function*) función *f* **3.** *no pl* (*work*) tarea *f;* **to do** ~ **for sb** sustituir a alguien; **to be suspended from** ~ ser suspendido del servicio; **to be on/off** ~ estar/no estar de servicio **4.** (*tax*) impuesto *m;* (*revenue on imports*) derechos *mpl* de aduana; **customs duties** arancel *m;* **to pay** ~ **on sth** pagar derechos de aduana por algo

duty call *n* visita *f* de cumplido

duty-free [ˌdju:ti'fri:, *Am:* ˌdu:ʈi-] **I.** *adj* libre de impuestos **II.** *n* bien *m* libre de impuestos

duty roster *n* lista *f* de guardias

duvet ['dju:veɪ, *Am:* du:'veɪ] *n Brit* edredón *m* nórdico

DVD *n inv* INFOR *abbr of* **Digital Versatile Disk** DVD *m*

DVLA *n Brit abbr of* **Driver and Vehicle Licensing Authority** ≈ DGT *f*

dwarf [dwɔ:f, *Am:* dwɔ:rf] **I.** <-s *o* -ves> *n* enano, -a *m, f* **II.** *vt* empequeñecer

dwell [dwel] <dwelt *o* -ed, dwelt *o* -ed> *vi* **1.** (*live*) morar **2.** (*give attention to*) **to** ~ **on sth** insistir en algo; **to** ~ **on a subject** explayarse en un tema

dweller *n* morador(a) *m(f)*

dwelling ['dwelɪŋ] *n* morada *f*

dwelling house *n* casa *f* particular

dwelt [dwelt] *pp, pt of* **dwell**

dwindle ['dwɪndl] *vi* menguar

dye [daɪ] **I.** *vt* teñir **II.** *n* tinte *m*

dyed-in-the-wool [ˌdaɪdɪnðə'wʊl] *adj* convencido, -a; ~ **opinions** opiniones *fpl* firmes

dye-works ['daɪwɜ:ks, *Am:* -wɜ:rks] *n* tintorería *f*

dying ['daɪɪŋ] *adj* **1.** (*approaching death*) moribundo, -a **2.** (*manifested before death: words*) último, -a

dyke¹ [daɪk] *n* **1.** *a. fig* dique *m* **2.** (*channel*) acequia *f*

dyke² [daɪk] *n inf* (*lesbian*) tortillera *f*

dynamic [daɪ'næmɪk] *adj* dinámico, -a

dynamics [daɪ'næmɪks] *n* **1.** PHYS dinámica *f;* (*development*) desarrollo *m* **2.** MUS (*alterations of volume*) crecimiento *m*

dynamite ['daɪnəmaɪt] **I.** *n no pl* dinamita *f* **II.** *vt* dinamitar

dynamo ['daɪnəməʊ, *Am:* -moʊ] <-s> *n* dinamo *f*

dynasty ['dɪnəsti, *Am:* 'daɪnə-] <-ies> *n* dinastía *f*

dysentery ['dɪsəntəri, *Am:* -teri] *n no pl* MED disentería *f*

dysfunctional [dɪs'fʌŋkʃənəl] *adj* disfuncional

dyslexia [dɪ'sleksiə] *n no pl* dislexia *f*

dyslexic [dɪ'sleksɪk] *adj* disléxico, -a

dyspepsia [dɪ'spepsiə] *n* MED dispepsia *f*

E

E, e [i:] *n* **1.** (*letter*) E, e *f;* ~ **for Edward** E de España **2.** MUS mi *m* **3.** SCHOOL ≈ insuficiente *m*

E *abbr of* **east** E *f*

each [i:tʃ] **I.** *adj* cada; ~ **one of you** cada uno de vosotros; ~ **and every house** cada casa sin excepción **II.** *pron* cada uno, cada una; ~ **of them could beat you** cada uno de ellos podría ganarte; **£70** ~ £70 cada uno; **he gave**

us £10 ~ nos dió a cada uno £10; **I'll take one kilo of** ~ tomaré un kilo de cada (uno)

each other *pron* uno a otro, una a la otra; **they are always arguing with** ~ siempre discuten entre ellos; **to help** ~ ayudarse mutuamente; **to be made for** ~ estar hechos el uno para el otro

eager ['iːgəʳ, *Am:*-gəʳ] *adj* ansioso, -a; **to be** ~ **for sth** ansiar algo; **to be** ~ **for revenge** tener sed de venganza; **to be** ~ **to start** estar ansioso por empezar

eager beaver *n inf* **he is an** ~ se esmera mucho en su trabajo

eagerness *n no pl* entusiasmo *m;* ~ **to please** deseo *m* de agradar

eagle ['iːgl] *n* águila *f*

eagle-eyed ['iːglaɪd] *adj* **to be** ~ tener ojos de lince

ear¹ [ɪəʳ, *Am:* ɪr] *n* ANAT oído *m;* (*outer part*) oreja *f;* ~**, nose and throat specialist** otorrinolaringólogo, -a *m, f;* **to have a good** ~ tener buen oído; **to have an** ~ **for music** tener buen oído para la música; **to smile from** ~ **to** ~ sonreír de oreja a oreja ▶**to be up to one's ~s in** <u>debt</u> *inf* estar endeudado hasta la camisa; **to have one's** ~ **to the** <u>ground</u> *inf* mantenerse al corriente; **to be** <u>all</u> ~**s** *inf* ser todo oídos; **to keep one's ~s** <u>open</u> *inf* abrir los oídos; **he'll be** <u>out</u> **on his** ~ *inf* lo van a poner de patitas en la calle; **his ~s must be** <u>burning</u> *inf* le deben de estar zumbando los oídos; **to turn a** <u>deaf</u> ~ **(to sth)** hacer oídos sordos (a algo); **to give sb a** <u>thick</u> ~ *inf* pegar una paliza a alguien; **to bend sb's** ~ *inf* fastidiar a alguien; **to** <u>close</u> **one's ~s to sth** hacer oídos sordos a algo; **sb's ~s are** <u>flapping</u> *inf* alguien tiene puesta la antena; **it** <u>goes</u> **in one** ~ **and out the other** *inf* por un oído le entra y por el otro le sale; **to** <u>have</u> **the** ~ **of sb** gozar de la confianza de alguien

ear² [ɪəʳ, *Am:* ɪr] *n* BOT espiga *f*

earache ['ɪəreɪk, *Am:* 'ɪr-] *n* dolor *m* de oído **eardrum** *n* tímpano *m* **ear infection** *n* infección *f* de oído

earl [ɜːl, *Am:* ɜːrl] *n* conde *m*

earlobe ['ɪələʊb] *n* lóbulo *m* de la oreja

early ['ɜːli, *Am:* 'ɜːr-] I.<-ier, -iest> *adj* **1.** (*ahead of time, near the beginning*) temprano, -a; **to be** ~ llegar temprano; ~ **retirement** jubilación *f* anticipada; **to take** ~ **retirement** jubilarse anticipadamente; **an** ~ **death** una muerte prematura; **the** ~ **hours** la madrugada; **in the** ~ **morning** de madrugada; **in the** ~ **afternoon** a primera hora de la tarde; **at an** ~ **age** a una edad temprana; **he is in his** ~ **twenties** tiene poco más de veinte años; **in the** ~ **15th century** a principios del siglo XV; ~ **education** primera enseñanza *f;* **to have an** ~ **night** acostarse temprano; **the** ~ **stages** las primeras etapas; **the** ~ **days/years of sth** los primeros tiempos de algo **2.** *form* (*prompt: reply*) rápido, -a; **at your earliest convenience** tan pronto como le sea posible **3.** (*first*)

primero, -a II. *adv* **1.** (*ahead of time*) temprano; **to get up** ~ madrugar; ~ **in the morning** por la mañana temprano; ~ **in the year** a principios de año; **to be half an hour** ~ llegar media hora antes **2.** (*soon*) pronto; **as** ~ **as possible** tan pronto como sea posible; **reply** ~ respondan cuanto antes; **book your tickets** ~ compren sus entradas con tiempo **3.** (*prematurely*) prematuramente; **to die** ~ morir joven

Early Church *n* **the** ~ la iglesia de los primeros cristianos

earmark ['ɪəmɑːk, *Am:* 'ɪrmɑːrk] I. *vt* **1.** (*animal*) marcar en la oreja; (*document*) marcar **2.** (*put aside*) reservar; (*funds*) destinar II. *n* marca *f* en la oreja; *fig* marca *f* distintiva

earmuffs ['ɪəmʌfs, *Am:* 'ɪr-] *npl* orejeras *fpl*

earn [ɜːn, *Am:* ɜːrn] I. *vt* **1.** (*be paid*) ganar; **to** ~ **one's daily bread** ganarse el pan; **to** ~ **a living** ganarse la vida **2.** (*bring in*) dar; (*interest*) devengar **3.** (*obtain*) **to** ~ **money from sth** obtener dinero de algo; **coffee exports** ~ **Brasil many millions of pounds** Brasil obtiene muchos millones de libras de la exportación de café **4.** (*deserve*) merecer, ganarse; **his decision ~ed him the confidence of his boss** su decisión le valió la confianza de su jefe II. *vi* trabajar

earned income *n* ingresos *mpl* en concepto de salario

earner *n* asalariado, -a *m, f*

earnest ['ɜːnɪst, *Am:* 'ɜːr-] I. *adj* **1.** (*serious*) serio, -a **2.** (*sincere*) sincero, -a; (*attempt*) concienzudo, -a; (*desire*) ferviente II. *n no pl* seriedad *f;* **in** ~ en serio; **school has now begun in** ~ ahora ha empezado de verdad el colegio; **to be in (deadly)** ~ hablar (completamente) en serio

earnestly *adv* **1.** (*speak*) seriamente **2.** (*desire*) de todo corazón

earning capacity *n Brit,* **earning power** *n Am* potencial *m* de ingresos

earnings ['ɜːnɪŋz, *Am:* 'ɜːr-] *npl* **1.** (*of a person*) ingresos *mpl* **2.** (*of a company*) beneficios *mpl,* utilidades *fpl AmL*

earnings-related *adj* proporcional al sueldo

earphones ['ɪəfəʊnz, *Am:* 'ɪrfoʊnz] *npl* auriculares *mpl*

earpiece ['ɪəpiːs, *Am:* 'ɪr-] *n* **1.** (*of a phone*) auricular *m* **2.** (*of glasses*) patilla *f*

earplug ['ɪəplʌg, *Am:* 'ɪr-] *n pl* tapón *m* para el oído

earring ['ɪərɪŋ, *Am:* 'ɪrɪŋ] *n* pendiente *m,* caravana *f CSur,* candonga *f Col;* **a pair of** ~**s** unos pendientes

earshot ['ɪəʃɒt, *Am:* 'ɪrʃɑːt] *n no pl* alcance *m* del oído; **in/out of** ~ al alcance/fuera del alcance del oído

earth [ɜːθ, *Am:* ɜːrθ] I. *n no pl* **1.** (*planeta*) tierra *f;* **on** ~ en el mundo; **you look like nothing (else) on** ~ estás espantoso **2.** (*animal's hole*) madriguera *f* **3.** ELEC toma *f* de tierra ▶**to bring sb back (down) to** ~ hacer bajar de las nubes a alguien; **to** <u>come back</u>

(**down**) **to** ~ bajar de las nubes; **to cost the** ~ costar un ojo de la cara; **to go to** ~ esconderse; **to promise the** ~ prometer el oro y el moro; **what/who/where/why on** ~ ...? *inf* ¿qué/ quién/dónde/por qué diablos...? **II.** *vt* conectar a tierra

earthbound ['ɜ:θbaʊnd, *Am:* 'ɜ:rθ-] *adj* **1.** terrestre **2.** *fig* prosaico, -a

earthenware ['ɜ:θnweə', *Am:* 'ɜ:rθnwer] **I.** *n* objetos *mpl* de barro **II.** *adj* de barro

earthiness ['ɜ:θɪnɪs] *n no pl* **1.** (*directness*) llaneza *f* **2.** (*coarseness*) grosería *f*

earthling ['ɜ:θlɪŋ, *Am:* 'ɜ:rθ-] *n* terrícola *mf*

earthly ['ɜ:θli, *Am:* 'ɜ:rθ-] *adj* **1.** (*concerning life on earth*) terreno, -a; (*existence, paradise*) terrenal; **her** ~ **belongings** form todo lo que posee en este mundo; ~ **remains** restos *mpl* mortales **2.** *inf* (*possible*) **to be of no** ~ **use** no servir absolutamente para nada ►**to not have an** ~ (**chance**) *Brit, inf* no tener ninguna posibilidad

earthquake ['ɜ:θkweɪk, *Am:* 'ɜ:rθ-] *n* **1.** terremoto *m*, temblor *m AmL* **2.** *fig* conmoción *f*

earth-shattering *adj* extraordinario, -a

earthwork *n* **1.** *pl* MIL terraplén *m* **2.** (*work*) trabajos *mpl* de preparación del terreno

earthworm *n* lombriz *f*

earthy ['ɜ:θi, *Am:* 'ɜ:r-] <-ier, -iest> *adj* **1.** (*with earth*) terroso, -a **2.** (*direct*) llano, -a **3.** (*vulgar*) grosero, -a

earwax ['ɪəwæks, *Am:* 'ɪr-] *n* cerumen *m*

earwig ['ɪəwɪg, *Am:* 'ɪr-] *n* tijereta *f*

ease [i:z] **I.** *n* **1.** (*without much effort*) facilidad *f*; **for** ~ **of access** para facilitar el acceso; **to do sth with** ~ hacer algo con facilidad **2.** (*comfort, uninhibitedness*) comodidad *f*; **to live a life of** ~ vivir con desahogo; **to feel at** (**one's**) ~ sentirse cómodo; **to be ill at** ~ estar molesto; **to be at** (**one's**) ~ estar a sus anchas; **to put sb at** (**his/her**) ~ hacer que alguien se relaje; (**stand**) **at** ~! MIL ¡descansen! **II.** *vt* **1.** (*relieve: pain*) aliviar; (*tension*) hacer disminuir; **to** ~ **one's conscience** descargarse la conciencia; **to** ~ **sb's mind** tranquilizar a alguien **2.** (*burden*) aligerar; (*screw*) aflojar **III.** *vi* (*pain*) aliviarse; (*tension, prices*) disminuir; (*wind*) amainar

◆**ease off** *vi*, **ease up** *vi* (*pain*) aliviarse; (*fever, sales*) bajar; (*tension*) disminuir; (*person*) relajarse; ~ **or you will have a nervous breakdown** si no te relajas tendrás una crisis nerviosa

easel ['i:zl] *n* caballete *m*

easily ['i:zəli] *adv* **1.** (*without difficulty*) fácilmente; **to be** ~ **impressed** ser fácil de impresionar; **to win** ~ ganar sin dificultades; **I get tired very** ~ me canso en seguida **2.** + *superl* (*clearly*) **to be** ~ **the best** ser con mucho el mejor **3.** (*probably*) perfectamente; **his guess could** ~ **be wrong** es fácil que se equivoque

easiness ['i:zɪnɪs] *n no pl* facilidad *f*

east [i:st] **I.** *n* este *m*; **to lie 5 km to the** ~ **of Bath** quedar a 5 km al este de Bath; **to go/**

drive to the ~ ir/conducir hacia el este; **further** ~ más hacia el este; **in the** ~ **of France** en el este de Francia; **Far East** Extremo *m* Oriente; **Middle East** Oriente *m* Medio **II.** *adj* del este; ~ **wind** viento *m* de Levante; ~ **coast** costa *f* del este; **East Indies** Indias *fpl* Orientales

eastbound ['i:stbaʊnd] *adj* que va en dirección este

Easter ['i:stə', *Am:* -stə·] *n* **1.** (*holiday*) Pascua *f* **2.** (*season*) Semana *f* Santa; **at** ~ en Semana Santa

---

At Easter (En Semana Santa) es costumbre en Gran Bretaña consumir dos tipos de dulce: los **hot cross buns**, por un lado, panecillos especiados que tienen una cruz en la parte de arriba hecha con la misma masa, y el **simnel cake**, por otro lado, un denso pastel de pasas, que se decora con mazapán. Durante estos días es costumbre que los niños jueguen a arrojar huevos cocidos cuesta abajo para ver cuál es el huevo que llega más lejos. Hoy en día con el término de **Easter egg** (huevo de Pascua) se denomina al huevo de chocolate relleno de dulces y golosinas que se suele regalar durante estos días.

Easter Day *n*, **Easter Sunday** *n* Domingo *m* de Pascua **Easter egg** *n* huevo *m* de Pascua **Easter holidays** *npl* vacaciones *fpl* de Semana Santa **Easter Island** *npl* Isla *f* de Pascua

easterly ['i:stəli, *Am:* -stə·-] **I.** *adj* (*wind*) del este; **in an** ~ **direction** en dirección este **II.** *adv* **1.** (*towards the east*) hacia el este **2.** (*from the east*) del este **III.** *n* viento *m* del este

Easter Monday *n* lunes *m* de Pascua

eastern ['i:stən, *Am:* -stə·n] *adj* del este, oriental

easterner ['i:stənə', *Am:* -tə·nə·] *n Am* habitante *mf* del nordeste de los Estados Unidos

easternmost ['i:stənməʊst, *Am:* -stə·n- moʊst] *adj* más oriental; **the** ~ **zone** la zona más oriental

East Germany [ˌi:st'dʒɜ:məni] *n* HIST Alemania *f* oriental

eastward ['i:stwəd, *Am:* -wə·d] **I.** *adj* **in an** ~ **direction** en dirección este **II.** *adv* hacia el este

eastwards ['i:stwədz, *Am:* -wə·dz] *adv* hacia el este

easy ['i:zi] <-ier, -iest> **I.** *adj* **1.** (*simple*) fácil; ~ **money** *inf* dinero *m* fácil; **the hotel is within** ~ **reach of the beach** el hotel está muy cerca de la playa; **to be far from** ~ no ser fácil en absoluto; ~ **to get on with** de trato fácil; **to take the** ~ **way out** optar por el camino más fácil; **to be as** ~ **as anything** *inf* estar tirado; **to be the easiest thing in the world** ser lo más fácil del mundo; **that's**

easier said than done *inf* es más fácil decirlo que hacerlo **2.** (*comfortable, carefree*) cómodo, -a; **I'm ~** *inf* me da lo mismo; **to feel ~ about sth** estar tranquilo por algo; **she won't be ~ in her mind until I call her** no se quedará tranquila hasta que la llame **3.** (*relaxed: manners*) natural; **at an ~ pace** sin prisa; **to be on ~ terms with sb** estar en confianza con alguien **4.** (*undemanding*) indulgente; **to be ~ on sb** ser poco severo con alguien **5.** (*pleasant*) **~ on the ear/eye** agradable al oído/a la vista **6.** FIN (*price, interest rate*) bajo, -a; **on ~ terms** con facilidades de pago; (*loan*) con condiciones favorables II. *adv* **1.** (*cautiously*) con cuidado; **~ does it** *inf* despacito y buena letra **2.** (*leniant*) **to go ~ on sb** *inf* no ser demasiado severo con alguien **3.** *inf* (*less actively*) **to take things ~** tomarse las cosas con calma; **take it ~!** ¡cálmate! ►**~ come, ~ go** *inf* tan fácil como viene, se va

easy-care *adj* que no necesita plancha **easy chair** *n* poltrona *f* **easy-going** *adj* (*person*) de trato fácil; (*attitude*) tolerante **easy-peasy** *adj* Brit, childspeak chupado, -a *inf*

eat [iːt] I. <ate, eaten> *vt* comer; **to ~ breakfast** tomar el desayuno; **to ~ lunch/supper** comer/cenar; **to ~ one's fill** comer bien; **to ~ in** comer en casa ►**what is ~ing him?** *inf* ¿qué mosca le ha picado? II. *vi* comer
♦**eat away** *vt* (*acid*) corroer; (*termites*) carcomer
♦**eat away at** *vt*, **eat into** *vt* corroer
♦**eat out** *vi* comer fuera
♦**eat up** *vt* comerse, terminar

eatable ['iːtəbl, *Am:* -ṭə-] *adj* comestible **eatables** ['iːtəblz, *Am:* -ṭə-] *npl* comestibles *mpl*

eat-by date ['iːtbaɪˌdeɪt] *n* fecha *f* de caducidad

eaten ['iːtn, *Am:* -ṭən] *pp of* **eat**

eater ['iːtəʳ, *Am:* -ṭəʳ] *n* **1.** (*person*) **to be a big ~** ser comilón; **to be a small eater** no ser de mucho comer **2.** Brit, *inf* (*apple*) manzana *f* de mesa

eatery ['iːtəri, *Am:* -ṭə-] *n inf* restaurante *m*

eating ['iːtɪŋ, *Am:* -ṭɪŋ] *n* comer *m*; **to be good ~** ser sabroso

eating apple *n* manzana *f* de mesa **eating disorder** *n* trastorno *m* alimenticio **eating habits** *npl* hábitos *mpl* alimenticios **eating house** *n* restaurante *m*

eau de Cologne [ˌəʊ də kəˈləʊn, *Am:* ˌoʊ də kəˈloʊn] *n* (agua *f* de) colonia *f*

eaves ['iːvz] *npl* ARCHIT alero *m*, tejaván *m* *AmL*

eavesdrop ['iːvzdrɒp, *Am:* -drɑːp] <-pp-> *vi* **to ~ on sth/sb** escuchar algo/a alguien a escondidas

eavesdropper ['iːvzdrɒpəʳ, *Am:* -drɑːpəʳ] *n* escuchón, -ona *m, f*

ebb [eb] I. *vi* **1.** (*tide*) bajar **2.** *fig* decaer II. *n* *no pl* **1.** (*tide*) reflujo *m*; **the tide is on the ~** la marea está bajando **2.** *fig* **the ~ and flow of**

sth los altibajos de algo; **to be at a low ~** estar en un punto bajo; (*person*) estar deprimido III. *adj* **~ tide** marea *f* menguante

ebony ['ebəni] *n* ébano *m*

ebullient [ɪ'bʌlɪənt, *Am:* -'bʊljənt] *adj* vivaz; **to be in an ~ mood** estar exaltado

EC [ˌiːˈsiː] *n abbr of* **European Community** CE *f*

e-car ['iːkɑːʳ, *Am:* -kɑːr] *n* automóvil *m* eléctrico

e-cash ['iːkæʃ] *n* dinero *m* electrónico

ECB [ˌiːsiːˈbiː] *n abbr of* **European Central Bank** BCE *m*

eccentric [ɪk'sentrɪk] I. *n* excéntrico, -a *m, f* II. *adj* excéntrico, -a

eccentricity [ˌeksen'trɪsəti, *Am:* -əṭi] *n* <-ies> excentricidad *f*

ecclesiastic [ɪˌkliːziˈæstɪk] I. *n form* eclesiástico *m* II. *adj form* eclesiástico, -a

ecclesiastical [ɪˌkliːziˈæstɪkl] *adj form* eclesiástico, -a

ECG [ˌiːsiːˈdʒiː] *n abbr of* **electrocardiogram** electrocardiograma *m*

echelon ['eʃəlɒn, *Am:* -lɑːn] *n* **1.** (*strata*) nivel *m*; (*of society*) capa *f*; **the highest ~s of** sth el más alto grado de algo **2.** MIL escalón *m*

echo ['ekəʊ, *Am:* -oʊ] I. <-es> *n* eco *m* ►**to cheer sb to the ~** ovacionar a alguien II. <-es, -ing, -ed> *vi* resonar III. <-es, -ing, -ed> *vt* **1.** (*reflect*) repetir; **the mountains ~ed (back) his voice** las montañas le devolvían el eco de su voz **2.** (*second*) hacerse eco de **3.** (*resemble*) parecerse a

echo chamber *n* cámara *f* de resonancia **echo sounder** *n* sonda *f* acústica

eclectic [ek'lektɪk] I. *n form* ecléctico, -a *m, f* II. *adj form* ecléctico

eclipse [ɪ'klɪps] I. *n* eclipse *m*; **solar/lunar ~** eclipse solar/de luna; **total/partial ~ of the sun** eclipse solar total/parcial; **to go into ~** entrar en eclipse; **to be in ~** *a. fig* estar eclipsado II. *vt* eclipsar

ECOFIN ['ekəʊfɪn] *n abbr of* **Economic and Finance Ministers Council** ECOFIN *m*

ecological [ˌiːkəˈlɒdʒɪkl, *Am:* -'lɑːdʒɪ-] *adj* ecológico, -a

ecologically [ˌɪkəˈlɒdʒɪkli, *Am:* -'lɑːdʒɪ-] *adv* ecológicamente; **~ friendly** ecológico, -a; **~ harmful** perjudicial para el medio ambiente

ecologist [iːˈkɒlədʒɪst, *Am:* -'kɑːlə-] *n* **1.** (*expert*) ecólogo, -a *m, f* **2.** POL ecologista *mf*

ecology [iːˈkɒlədʒi, *Am:* -'kɑːlə-] *n no pl* ecología *f*

ecology movement *n* movimiento *m* ecologista **ecology party** *n* partido *m* ecologista

e-commerce ['iːkɒmɜːs, *Am:* -kɑːmɜːrs] *n* comercio *m* electrónico

economic [ˌiːkəˈnɒmɪk, *Am:* -'nɑːmɪk] *adj* **1.** POL, ECON económico, -a **2.** (*profitable*) rentable

economical [ˌiːkəˈnɒmɪkl, *Am:* -'nɑːmɪ-] *adj* económico, -a ►**to be ~ with the truth**

iron decir verdades a medias

Economic and Monetary Unit *n* Unión *f* Económica y Monetaria

economics [ˌiːkəˈnɒmɪks, *Am:* -ˈnɑːmɪks] *npl* **1.** + *sing vb* (*discipline*) economía *f;* **School of Economics** Facultad *f* de Ciencias Económicas **2.** + *pl vb* (*matter*) aspecto *m* económico; **the ~ of the agreement** la rentabilidad del acuerdo

economist [ɪˈkɒnəmɪst, *Am:* -ˈkɑːnə-] *n* economista *mf*

economize [ɪˈkɒnəmaɪz, *Am:* -ˈkɑːnə-] *vi* ahorrar; **to ~ on sth** economizar en algo

economy [ɪˈkɒnəmi, *Am:* -ˈkɑːnə-] <-ies> *n* **1.** (*frugality*) ahorro *m;* **for the purposes of ~** por ahorro; **to make economies, to practise ~** ahorrar **2.** (*monetary assets*) economía *f;* **the state of the ~** la situación económica; **capitalist/market/planned ~** economía capitalista/de mercado/planificada

economy class *n* AVIAT clase *f* turista **economy drive** *n* campaña *f* para reducir gastos **economy size** *n* tamaño *m* familiar

ecosystem *n* ecosistema *m* **ecotourism** *n* ecoturismo *m* **eco-tourist** *n* ecoturista *mf* **ecowarrior** *n* ecologista *mf* militante

ecstasy [ˈekstəsi] <-ies> *n* éxtasis *m inv;* **to go into ecstasies** extasiarse

ecstatic [ɪkˈstætɪk, *Am:* ekˈstæt̬-] *adj* extático, -a; (*rapturous*) eufórico, -a; **to be ~ about sth** estar entusiasmado con algo

ECT [ˌiːsiːˈtiː] *n abbr of* **electroconvulsive therapy** terapia *f* de electroshock

ecu, ECU [ˈekjuː, *Am:* ˈeɪkuː] *n abbr of* **European Currency Unit** ecu *m,* ECU *m*

Ecuador [ˈekwədɔːʳ, *Am:* -dɔːr] *n* Ecuador *m*

Ecuadorian [ˌekwəˈdɔːrɪən] **I.** *n* ecuatoriano, -a *m, f* **II.** *adj* ecuatoriano, -a

ecumenical [ˌiːkjuːˈmenɪkl, *Am:* ˌekjʊˈ-] *adj* ecuménico, -a

eczema [ˈeksɪmə, *Am:* -sə-] *n no pl* eczema *m*

ed. 1. *abbr of* **editor** editor(a) *m(f)* **2.** *abbr of* **edition** ed. **3.** *abbr of* **edited** editado, -a

eddy [ˈedi] **I.** <-ie-> *vi* arremolinarse **II.** <-ies> *n* remolino *m*

Eden [ˈiːdn] *n no pl* Edén *m;* **the garden of ~** el jardín del Edén

edge [edʒ] **I.** *n sing* **1.** (*limit*) borde *m;* (*of a lake, pond*) orilla *f;* (*of a mountain*) cresta *f;* (*of a page*) margen *m;* (*of a table, coin*) canto *m;* **to bring sth to the ~ of disaster** llevar algo hasta el límite del desastre; **to take the ~ off one's appetite/hunger** calmar el apetito/hambre; **to take the ~ off an argument** restar fuerza a un argumento **2.** (*cutting part*) filo *m;* **to put an ~ on sth** afilar algo **3.** *no pl* (*anger*) **to be on ~** tener los nervios a flor de piel; **there's a definite ~ in her voice** hay un tono áspero en su voz **4.** SPORTS ventaja *f;* **to have the ~ over sb** tener ventaja sobre alguien ►**to be** (**balanced**) **on a** razor's ~

pender de un hilo; **to set sb's** teeth **on ~** poner nervioso a alguien; **to give sb the sharp ~ of one's** tongue echar una bronca a alguien **II.** *vt* **1.** (*border*) bordear **2.** (*in sewing*) ribetear **3.** (*move slowly*) **to ~ one's way through sth** ir abriéndose paso por algo; **she's edging her party towards extremism** está acercando su partido hacia el extremismo **III.** *vi* **to ~ closer to sth** ir acercándose a algo; **to ~ away from the danger** ir alejándose del peligro; **to ~ forward** ir avanzando

edgeways [ˈedʒweɪz] *adv,* **edgewise** *adv Am* de lado

edging [ˈedʒɪŋ] *n* borde *m;* (*of a ribbon*) ribete *m*

edgy [ˈedʒi] <-ier, -iest> *adj inf* nervioso

edible [ˈedɪbl] *adj* comestible

edict [ˈiːdɪkt] *n* **1.** HIST edicto *m* **2.** (*order*) mandato *m*

edification [ˌedɪfɪˈkeɪʃən] *n no pl, form* edificación *f*

edifice [ˈedɪfɪs] *n* **1.** *form* (*building*) edificio *m* **2.** *fig* (*of ideas*) estructura *f*

edify [ˈedɪfaɪ] <-ie-> *vt form* edificar

edifying *adj form* edificante

Edinburgh [ˈedɪnbrə, *Am:* -bʌrə] *n* Edimburgo *m*

Desde 1947 tiene lugar cada año en **Edinburgh**, la capital de Escocia, el **Edinburgh International Festival**. Se celebra en torno a mediados de agosto y dura tres semanas. En el marco de este festival tienen lugar numerosos espectáculos de tipo cultural: teatro, música, ópera y baile. Al mismo tiempo se celebran un **Film Festival**, un **Jazz Festival** y un **Book Festival**. Paralelamente al **Festival** oficial se ha ido desarrollando un **Festival Fringe** con alrededor de 1.000 espectáculos diferentes que se caracterizan por su vivacidad y su capacidad de innovación.

---

edit [ˈedɪt] *vt* **1.** (*correct*) corregir; (*articles*) editar **2.** (*newspaper*) dirigir **3.** CINE montar **4.** INFOR editar

♦**edit out** *vt* suprimir

edition [ɪˈdɪʃən] *n* edición *f;* (*set of books*) tirada *f;* **paperback ~** encuadernación *f* en rústica; **limited ~** edición limitada

editor [ˈedɪtəʳ, *Am:* -t̬əʳ] *n* **1.** (*of book*) editor(a) *m(f);* (*of article*) redactor(a) *m(f);* (*of a newspaper*) director(a) *m(f);* **chief ~** redactor(a) *m(f)* jefe; **sports ~** redactor(a) *m(f)* de deportes **2.** CINE montador(a) *m(f)* **3.** INFOR editor *m*

editorial [ˌedɪˈtɔːrɪəl, *Am:* -əˈ-] **I.** *n* editorial *m* **II.** *adj* editorial; **~ staff** redacción *f*

editor-in-chief [ˌedɪtəˈrɪnˈtʃiːf, *Am:* -t̬əʳ-] *n* redactor(a) *m(f)* jefe

EDP [ˌiːdiːˈpiː] *n abbr of* **electronic data processing** PED *m*

educate [ˈedʒʊkeɪt] *vt* **1.** (*bring up*) educar **2.** (*teach*) instruir; **to ~ the ear** educar el oído

3. (*inform*) concienciar; **to ~ sb in sth** concienciar a alguien de algo

educated ['edʒʊkeɪtɪd, *Am:* -t̬ɪd] *adj* culto, -a; **highly ~** cultivado, -a; **to be Oxford ~** haber estudiado en Oxford

education [,edʒʊ'keɪʃən] *n no pl* **1.** SCHOOL educación *f;* **primary/secondary ~** enseñanza *f* primaria/secundaria; **Ministry of Education** Ministerio *m* de Educación **2.** (*training*) formación *f;* **science/literary ~** formación científica/literaria **3.** (*teaching*) enseñanza *f;* (*study of teaching*) pedagogía *f* **4.** (*culture*) cultura *f*

educational [,edʒʊ'keɪʃənl] *adj* **1.** SCHOOL (*system*) educativo, -a; (*establishment*) docente; (*method*) pedagógico, -a; **for ~ purposes** con fines educativos **2.** (*instructive*) instructivo, -a **3.** (*raising awareness*) de concienciación

education(al)ist [,edʒʊ'keɪʃən(əl)ɪst] *n* pedagogo, -a *m, f*

educator ['edʒʊkeɪtər, *Am:* -t̬ər] *n Am* educador(a) *m(f)*

Edwardian [ed'wɔdiən, *Am:* -'wɔːr-] *adj* eduardiano, -a

EEC [,iːiː'siː] *n no pl* HIST *abbr of* **European Economic Community** CEE *f*

EEG [,iːiː'dʒiː] *n abbr of* **electroencephalogram** electroencefalograma *m*

eel [iːl] *n* anguila *f* ►**to be slippery as an ~** ser escurridizo

EEMU *n abbr of* **European Economic and Monetary Union** UEME *f*

eerie ['ɪəri, *Am:* 'ɪri] *adj,* **eery** <-ier, -iest> *adj* espeluznante

efface [ɪ'feɪs] *vt* **1.** *a.* *fig* borrar **2.** (*be humble*) **to ~ oneself** intentar pasar inadvertido

effect [ɪ'fekt] **I.** *n* **1.** (*consequence*) efecto *m;* **to have an ~ on sth** afectar a algo; **to have a disastrous ~ on** [*o* **upon**] **sth** tener consecuencias nefastas para algo; **to have no ~ on sb** no hacer ningún efecto a alguien **2.** (*result*) resultado *m;* **to be of little/no ~** dar poco/no dar resultado; **to take ~** surtir efecto; (*medicine, alcohol*) hacer efecto; **to the ~ that ...** con el propósito de...; **to no ~** en vano **3.** *no pl* LAW vigencia *f;* **to come into** [*o* **to take**] **~** entrar en vigor; **to remain/be in ~** permanecer/estar vigente **4.** (*gist*) **to the same ~** por el estilo; **he disapproved of our idea and wrote to us to that ~** no estaba de acuerdo con nuestra idea y nos escribió para manifestarlo **5.** (*impression*) impresión *f;* **the overall ~** la impresión general; **for ~** para llamar la atención **6.** *pl* (*belongings*) efectos *mpl;* **personal ~s** efectos personales ►**in ~** en efecto **II.** *vt* realizar; (*payment*) efectuar; (*cure*) lograr

effective [ɪ'fektɪv] *adj* **1.** (*giving result*) efectivo, -a; (*medicine*) eficaz; **he was an ~ speaker** tenía grandes dotes de orador **2.** (*real*) real; **~ control** control efectivo **3.** (*operative*) vigente; **to become ~** entrar en

vigor **4.** (*striking*) impresionante

effectively *adv* **1.** (*giving result*) eficazmente **2.** (*really*) realmente **3.** (*strikingly*) de manera impresionante

effectiveness *n no pl* **1.** (*efficiency*) efectividad *f;* (*of a plan*) eficacia *f* **2.** (*of a rule*) vigencia *f*

effectual [ɪ'fektʃʊəl, *Am:* -tʃu-] *adj* **1.** (*efficient*) efectivo, -a **2.** (*operative*) válido, -a

effectuate [ɪ'fektʃʊeɪt, *Am:* -tʃu-] *vt* efectuar

effeminacy [ɪ'femɪnəsi] *n no pl* afeminación *f,* afeminamiento *m*

effeminate [ɪ'femɪnət] **I.** *adj* afeminado, -a **II.** *n* afeminado *m*

effervesce [,efə'ves, *Am:* -ə˞'-] *vi* **1.** (*bubble*) burbujear **2.** *fig* (*person*) estar eufórico, -a

effervescence [,efə'vesns, *Am:* -ə˞'-] *n no pl* efervescencia *f*

effervescent [,efə'vesnt, *Am:* -ə˞'-] *adj* **1.** efervescente **2.** *fig* eufórico, -a

effete [ɪ'fiːt] *adj* **1.** (*enfeebled*) debilitado, -a **2.** (*decadent*) decadente **3.** (*effeminate*) amanerado, -a

efficacious [,efɪ'keɪʃəs] *adj form* eficaz; **an ~ medicine** un medicamento efectivo

efficacy ['efɪkəsi] *n no pl, form* eficacia *f*

efficiency [ɪ'fɪʃnsi] *n no pl* **1.** (*of a person*) eficiencia *f;* (*of a method*) eficacia *f* **2.** (*of a machine*) rendimiento *m*

efficient [ɪ'fɪʃnt] *adj* (*person*) eficiente; (*machine, system*) de buen rendimiento

effigy ['efɪdʒi] *n* efigie *f*

effluent ['eflʊənt] *n* **1.** efluente *m* **2.** (*liquid waste*) vertidos *mpl*

effort ['efət, *Am:* -ə˞t] *n* **1.** *a.* PHYS esfuerzo *m;* **to be worth the ~** valer la pena; **to make an ~ to do sth** esforzarse [*o* hacer un esfuerzo] para hacer algo; **to spare no ~** no escatimar esfuerzos; **without ~** sin esfuerzo **2.** (*attempt*) tentativa *f;* **please make an ~ to ...** por favor, intenten... **3.** (*work*) obra *f*

effortless ['efətləs, *Am:* -ə˞t-] *adj* fácil; **an ~ movement** un movimiento sin esfuerzo aparente; **an ~ grace** una gracia natural

effrontery [ɪ'frʌntəri, *Am:* e'frʌn-] *n no pl, form* descaro *m;* **to have the ~ to do sth** tener la desfachatez de hacer algo

effusion [ɪ'fjuːʒən] *n a. fig* efusión *f*

effusive [ɪ'fjuːsɪv] *adj form* efusivo, -a

EFL [,iːef'el] *n,* **Efl** *n abbr of* **English as a foreign language** inglés *m* como idioma extranjero

eft [eft] *n* tritón *m*

EFT *abbr of* **electronic funds transfer** servicio *m* de pagos electrónico

EFTA ['eftə] *n,* **Efta** *n abbr of* **European Free Trade Association** EFTA *f*

e.g. [,iː'dʒiː] *abbr of* **exempli gratia** (= **for example**) p.ej.

egalitarian [ɪ,gælɪ'teəriən, *Am:* -teri-] *adj* igualitario, -a

e-generation [iː,dʒenə'reɪʃən] *n* generación

f de internet

egg [eg] *n* huevo *m;* **fried/boiled** ~s huevos fritos/pasados por agua; **hard-boiled** ~ huevo duro; **scrambled** ~s huevos revueltos ►**to put all one's** ~s **in one** basket jugárselo todo a una carta; **they had** ~ **on their** faces *inf* quedaron en ridículo; **to be a bad** ~ *inf* ser un sinvergüenza

◆**egg on** *vt* incitar

egg cell *n* óvulo *m* **egg cup** *n,* **eggcup** *n* huevera *f* **egghead** *n inf* cerebro *m* **eggplant** *n Am, Aus* berenjena *f* **eggshell** *n* cáscara *f* de huevo **egg timer** *n* temporizador *m* para huevos **egg yolk** *n* yema *f* de huevo

ego ['egəʊ, *Am:* 'i:goʊ] *n* <-s> 1. PSYCH ego *m;* **to bolster sb's** ~ reforzar el ego de alguien 2. (*self-esteem*) amor *m* propio

egocentric [ˌegəʊ'sentrɪk, *Am:* ˌi:goʊ-] *adj* egocéntrico, -a

egoism ['egəʊɪzəm, *Am:* 'i:goʊ-] *n no pl* egoísmo *m*

egoist ['egəʊɪst, *Am:* 'i:goʊ-] *n* egoísta *mf*

egoistic(al) [ˌegəʊ'ɪstɪk(l), *Am:* ˌi:goʊ-] *adj* egoísta

egotism ['egəʊtɪzəm, *Am:* 'i:goʊ-] *n no pl* egotismo *m*

egotist ['egəʊtɪst, *Am:* 'i:goʊ-] *n* egotista *mf*

egotistic(al) [ˌegə'tɪstɪk(l), *Am:* ˌi:goʊ'-] *adj* 1. (*selfish*) egoísta 2. (*self-important*) egotista

ego trip ['egəʊtrɪp, *Am:* 'i:goʊ-] *n* **to be on an** ~ darse autobombo

egregious [ɪ'gri:dʒəs] *adj* escandaloso, -a

Egypt ['i:dʒɪpt] *n* Egipto *m*

Egyptian [ɪ'dʒɪpʃən] I. *n* egipcio, -a *m, f* II. *adj* egipcio, -a

eh [eɪ] *interj inf* (*asking for repetition*) ¿eh?; (*expressing surprise*) ¿qué?; (*inviting response*) ¿no?; **that's good,** ~? está bueno, ¿no?

eider ['aɪdəʳ, *Am:* -dəʳ] *n* eíder *m*

eiderdown ['aɪdədaʊn, *Am:* -dəʳ-] *n* edredón *m*

Eiffel tower [ˌaɪfl'taʊəʳ, *Am:* -'taʊəʳ] *n* **the** ~ la torre Eiffel

eight [eɪt] I. *adj* ocho *inv;* **there are** ~ **of us** somos ocho; ~ **and a quarter/half** ocho y cuarto/medio; ~ **o'clock** las ocho; **it's** ~ **o'clock** son las ocho; **it's half past** ~ son las ocho y media; **at** ~ **twenty/thirty** a las ocho y veinte/media II. *n* ocho *m* ►**to have had one** over **the** ~ *Brit, inf* llevar una copa de más

eighteen [ˌeɪ'ti:n] I. *adj* dieciocho II. *n* dieciocho *m; s. a.* eight

eighteenth [ˌeɪ'ti:nθ] I. *adj* decimoctavo, -a II. *n* 1. (*order*) decimoctavo, -a *m, f* 2. (*date*) ocho *m* 3. (*fraction*) dieciochoavo *m;* (*part*) decimoctava parte *f; s. a.* eighth

eighth [eɪtθ] I. *adj* octavo, -a; ~ **note** *Am* corchea *f* II. *n no pl* 1. (*order*) octavo, -a *m, f;* **to be** ~ **in a race** quedar de octavo en una carrera 2. (*date*) ocho *m;* **the** ~ el día ocho; **the** ~ **of December, December the** ~ el ocho de diciembre 3. (*fraction*) octavo *m;* (*part*) octava parte *f* III. *adv* (*in lists*) octavo

eight-hour day *n* jornada *f* de ocho horas

eightieth ['eɪtɪəθ, *Am:* -ˌt̬ɪəθ] I. *adj* octogésimo, -a II. *n no pl* (*order*) octogésimo, -a *m, f;* (*fraction*) octogésimo *m;* (*part*) octogésima parte *f; s. a.* eighth

eighty ['eɪti, *Am:* -ˌt̬i] I. *adj* ochenta *inv;* **he is** ~ (**years old**) tiene ochenta años; **a man of about** ~ **years of age** un hombre de alrededor de ochenta años II. *n* <-ies> 1. (*number*) ochenta *m;* **to do** ~ *inf* ir a 80 km por hora 2. (*age*) **a woman in her eighties** una mujer en sus ochenta 3. (*decade*) **the eighties** los (años) ochenta

Eire ['æərə, *Am:* 'erə] *n* Eire *m*

EIS [ˌi:aɪ'es] *n* 1. INFOR *abbr of* **executive information system** EIS *m* 2. SCHOOL *abbr of* **Education Insitute of Scotland** *sindicato de profesores*

either ['aɪðəʳ, *Am:* 'i:ðəʳ] I. *adj* 1. (*one of two*) **I'll do it** ~ **way** lo hará de una manera u otra; **I don't like** ~ **dress** no me gusta ninguno de los dos vestidos 2. (*each*) cada; **on** ~ **side of the river** a cada lado del río II. *pron* cualquiera (de los dos); **which one?** – ~ ¿cuál? – cualquiera III. *adv* tampoco; **if he doesn't go, I won't go** ~ si él no va, yo tampoco IV. *conj* ~ **... or ...** o... o...; ~ **buy it or rent it** cómpralo o alquílalo; **I can** ~ **stay or leave** puedo quedarme o irme

ejaculate [ɪ'dʒækjʊleɪt] *vt* 1. (*semen*) eyacular 2. (*blurt out*) exclamar

ejaculation [ɪˌdʒækjʊ'leɪʃən] *n* 1. (*of semen*) eyaculación *f* 2. (*sudden outburst*) exclamación *f*

eject [ɪ'dʒekt] I. *vt* echar, expulsar; (*liquid, gas*) expeler II. *vi* eyectarse

ejector seat [ɪ'dʒektəʳ si:t, *Am:* -t̬əʳ] *n* asiento *m* de eyección

eke out [i:k aʊt] *vt* (*money, food*) hacer durar; **to** ~ **one's salary** estirar su sueldo *inf;* **to** ~ **a living** ganarse la vida a duras penas

elaborate [ɪ'læbərət] I. *adj* (*complicated*) complicado, -a; (*very detailed: plan*) minucioso, -a; (*style*) trabajado, -a; (*excuse*) rebuscado, -a; (*meal*) de muchos platos II. *vt* elaborar; (*plan*) idear III. *vi* entrar en detalles; **to refuse to** ~ negarse a dar más detalles; **to** ~ **on an idea** explicar una idea con más detalles

elaboration [ɪˌlæbə'reɪʃən] <-(s)> *n* 1. (*of a theory*) elaboración *f;* (*of texts*) explicación *f;* **without any** ~s sin entrar en demasiados detalles 2. *no pl* (*complexity*) complicación *f*

elapse [ɪ'læps] *vi form* transcurrir

elastic [ɪ'læstɪk] I. *adj* elástico, -a II. *n* 1. (*material*) elástico *m* 2. (*garter*) liga *f*

elastic band *n Brit* gomita *f*

elasticity [ˌelæ'stɪsəti, *Am:* -t̬i] *n no pl, a. fig* elasticidad *f*

elate [ɪ'leɪt] *vt* regocijar; **to be** ~**d at sth** estar eufórico por algo

elated *adj* eufórico, -a

elation [ɪ'leɪʃən] n no pl regocijo m
Elba ['elbə] n Elba f
elbow ['elbəʊ, Am: -boʊ] I. n 1. (of people) codo m; (of animals) codillo m 2. (in a pipe) codo m; (in a road, river) recodo m ►out at the ~s (clothing) raído, -a; (person) desharrapado, -a; to be at one's ~ estar al alcance de la mano; to give sb the ~ deshacerse de alguien; to rub ~s with sb codearse con alguien II. vt dar un codazo a; to ~ one's way through the crowd abrirse paso a codazos entre la multitud
elbow grease n no pl, inf fuerza f; to put some ~ into sth poner empeño en algo
elbow room n no pl 1. (space) espacio m 2. (freedom) libertad f de acción
elder[1] ['eldər, Am: -dɚ] I. n 1. (older person) mayor mf; she is my ~ by three years es tres años mayor que yo 2. (senior person) anciano, -a m, f II. adj mayor; **Pliny the Elder** Plinio el Viejo; ~ **statesman/stateswoman** POL veterano, -a m, f de la política
elder[2] ['eldər, Am: -dɚ] n saúco m
elderberry ['eldəberi, Am: -dɚ-] <-ies> n 1. (berry) baya f del saúco 2. BOT saúco m
elderly ['eldəli, Am: -dɚ-] I. adj anciano, -a; an ~ **woman** una señora mayor II. n no pl the ~ los ancianos
eldest ['eldɪst] adj superl of old mayor; the ~ el/la mayor; her ~ (child) is nearly 14 su hijo mayor tiene casi 14 años
elect [ɪ'lekt] I. vt 1. (by vote) elegir 2. (not by vote) decidir; to ~ to resign optar por dimitir II. n no pl REL the ~ los elegidos III. adj the president ~ el presidente electo, la presidente electa
election [ɪ'lekʃən] n 1. (event) elecciones fpl; to call/hold an ~ convocar/celebrar elecciones; to stand for an ~ presentarse a las elecciones 2. no pl (action) elección f
election address n, **election speech** n discurso m electoral **election booth** n s. polling booth **election campaign** n campaña f electoral **election day** n, **Election Day** n Am jornada f electoral **election defeat** n derrota f electoral
electioneer [ɪˌlekʃə'nɪər, Am: -'nɪr] vi hacer campaña electoral
electioneering [ɪˌlekʃə'nɪərɪŋ, Am: -'nɪr-] n no pl campaña f electoral; pej promesas fpl electoralistas
election manifesto n manifiesto m electoral **election meeting** n mitin m electoral **election platform** n, **election programme** n programa m electoral **election poster** n cartel m de propaganda electoral **election results** npl, **election returns** npl resultados mpl electorales
elective [ɪ'lektɪv] I. adj 1. form (appointed by election) electivo, -a; (based on voting) electoral 2. (optional) optativo, -a 3. (selective) ~ **affinity** afinidad electiva II. n Am SCHOOL, UNIV optativa f
elector [ɪ'lektər, Am: -t̬ɚ] n 1. (voter) elec-

tor(a) m(f) 2. Am (member of electoral college) miembro mf de un colegio electoral
electoral [ɪ'lektərəl] adj electoral; ~ **college** colegio m electoral; ~ **register** [o **roll**] censo m electoral
electorate [ɪ'lektərət] n electorado m
electric [ɪ'lektrɪk] adj 1. ELEC eléctrico, -a; (fence) electrificado, -a; ~ **blanket** manta eléctrica; ~ **chair** silla eléctrica; ~ **cooker** cocina eléctrica; ~ **current** corriente eléctrica; ~ **fire** estufa eléctrica; ~ **light** luz eléctrica; ~ **shock** descarga eléctrica; ~ **windows** AUTO elevalunas eléctrico 2. fig electrizante; (atmosphere) cargado, -a de electricidad
electrical [ɪ'lektrɪkl] adj eléctrico, -a; ~ **tape** cinta f aislante; ~ **engineering** ingeniería f eléctrica, electrotecnia f
electrician [ɪˌlek'trɪʃən] n electricista mf
electricity [ɪˌlek'trɪsəti] n no pl electricidad f; **powered by** ~ eléctrico, -a; to run on ~ funcionar con electricidad
electricity board n Brit compañía f eléctrica
electrification [ɪˌlektrɪfɪ'keɪʃən] n no pl electrificación f
electrify [ɪ'lektrɪfaɪ] vt electrificar; fig electrizar
electroanalysis [ɪˌlektrəʊə'næləsɪs] n electroanálisis m
electrocardiogram [ɪˌlektrəʊ'kɑːdɪəʊgræm, Am: -troʊ'kɑːrdɪə-] n electrocardiograma m
electroconvulsive ['ɪˌlektrəʊkən'ʌlsɪv, Am: -troʊ-] adj ~ **therapy** electroterapia f
electrocute [ɪ'lektrəkjuːt] vt electrocutar
electrocution [ɪˌlektrə'kjuːʃən] n electrocución f
electrode [ɪ'lektrəʊd, Am: -troʊd] n electrodo m
electroencephalogram [ɪˌlektrəʊen'sefələgræm, Am: -troʊen'sefəloʊ-] n electroencefalograma m
electrolysis [ɪˌlek'trɒləsɪs, Am: -'trɑːlə-] n no pl electrólisis f
electromagnet [ɪ'lektrəʊ'mægnɪt, Am: -troʊ'-] n electroimán m
electromagnetic [ɪˌlektrəʊmæg'netɪk, Am: -troʊmæg'net̬-] adj electromagnético, -a
electron [ɪ'lektrɒn, Am: -trɑːn] n electrón m
electronic [ɪlek'trɒnɪk, Am: ɪˌlek'trɑːnɪk] adj electrónico, -a; ~ **data processing** procesamiento electrónico de datos; ~ **fund transfer** transferencia electrónica de fondos; ~ **mail** correo electrónico
electronics [ɪlek'trɒnɪks, Am: ɪˌlek'trɑːnɪks] n + sing vb electrónica f; the ~ **industry** la industria electrónica
electron microscope n microscopio m electrónico
electroplate [ɪ'lektrəʊpleɪt, Am: ɪ'lektroʊpleɪt] vt galvanizar
electroscope [ɪ'lektrəʊˌskəʊp, Am: -troʊˌskoʊp] n electroscopio m **electrotherapy** n electroterapia f

elegance ['elɪgəns, *Am:* '-ə-] *n no pl* elegancia *f*

elegant ['elɪgənt, *Am:* '-ə-] *adj* elegante

elegiac [ˌelɪ'dʒaɪək] I. *adj* elegíaco, -a II. *n pl* versos *mpl* elegíacos

elegy ['elədʒi] *n* elegía *f*

element ['elɪmənt, *Am:* '-ə-] *n* **1.** *a.* CHEM, MAT elemento *m;* **the four ~s** los cuatro elementos; **he's in his ~** está en su elemento **2.** (*factor*) factor *m;* **an ~ of luck** algo de suerte; **the ~ of surprise** el factor sorpresa; **there's an ~ of truth in what they say** hay algo de verdad en lo que dicen **3.** ELEC resistencia *f* **4.** *pl* (*rudiments*) rudimentos *mpl* **5.** *pl* METEO **the ~s** los elementos

elemental [ˌelɪ'mentl, *Am:* -ə'menṭl] *adj* elemental; (*forces*) de la naturaleza; (*feelings, needs*) primario, -a

elementary [ˌelɪ'mentəri, *Am:* -ə'menṭə-] *adj* elemental; (*course*) básico, -a; ~ **school** *Am* escuela *f* (de enseñanza) primaria

elephant ['elɪfənt] *n* elefante *m*

elephantiasis [ˌelɪfən'taɪəsɪs] *n* MED elefantiasis *f inv*

elephantine [ˌelɪ'fæntaɪn] *adj* **1.** (*huge*) colosal **2.** (*clumsy*) torpe

elevate ['elɪveɪt] *vt* **1.** (*raise*) elevar; (*prices*) aumentar; **to ~ the mind** ser edificante **2.** REL alzar **3.** (*in rank*) ascender

elevated ['elɪveɪtɪd, *Am:* -t̬ɪd] *adj* **1.** (*raised: part*) elevado, -a **2.** (*important*) alto, -a; (*position*) importante

elevation [ˌelɪ'veɪʃən] *n* **1.** (*rise*) elevación *f;* (*of person*) ascenso *m* **2.** (*height*) altura *f* **3.** GEO elevación *f* (del terreno) **4.** ARCHIT alzado *m*

elevator ['elɪveɪtə', *Am:* -t̬ə-] *n Am* (*for people*) ascensor *m,* elevador *m AmL;* (*for goods*) montacargas *m inv*

eleven [ɪ'levn] I. *adj* once II. *n* once *m; s. a.* **eight**

elevenses [ɪ'levnzɪz] *npl Brit, inf* **to have ~** tomar las once

eleventh [ɪ'levnθ] I. *adj* undécimo, -a II. *n no pl* **1.** (*order*) undécimo, -a *m, f* **2.** (*date*) once *m* **3.** (*fraction*) onceavo *m;* (*part*) onceava parte *f; s. a.* **eighth**

elf [elf] <elves> *n* (*folklore*) duende *m;* (*mythology*) elfo *m*

elicit [ɪ'lɪsɪt] *vt* **1.** (*obtain*) obtener **2.** (*provoke: criticism*) suscitar

eligibility [ˌelɪdʒə'bɪləti, *Am:* -t̬i] *n no pl* elegibilidad *f*

eligible ['elɪdʒəbl] *adj* **1.** elegible; ~ **to vote** con derecho a voto **2.** (*desirable*) deseable; **to be ~ for** [*o* **to**] **the job** reunir los requisitos necesarios para el puesto; **an ~ bachelor** un soltero codiciado; **an ~ young man/woman** un buen partido

eliminate [ɪ'lɪmɪneɪt] *vt* **1.** (*eradicate*) eliminar **2.** (*exclude from consideration*) descartar

elimination [ɪˌlɪmɪ'neɪʃən] *n no pl* eliminación *f;* **by a process of ~** por eliminación

elimination contest *n* prueba *f* eliminatoria

elite [eɪ'liːt] I. *n* élite *f* II. *adj* de élite

elitism [ei'liːtɪsm] *n no pl* elitismo *m*

elitist [ei'liːtɪst] *adj* elitista

elixir [ɪ'lɪksə', *Am:* -sə-] *n* elixir *m*

elk [elk] <-(s)> *n* (*European*) alce *m;* (*American*) uapití *m*

ellipse [ɪ'lɪps] *n* elipse *f*

elliptic(al) [ɪ'lɪptɪk(l)] *adj* elíptico, -a

elm [elm] *n* olmo *m*

elocution [ˌelə'kjuːʃən] *n no pl* dicción *f;* (*art*) elocución *f*

elongate ['iːlɒŋɡeɪt, *Am:* ɪ'lɑːŋ-] I. *vt* alargar II. *vi* alargarse

elongated *adj* alargado, -a

elope [ɪ'ləup, *Am:* -'loup] *vi* fugarse

elopement [ɪ'ləupmənt, *Am:* -'loup-] *n* fuga *f*

eloquent ['eləkwənt] *adj* elocuente

El Salvador [el'sælvə,dɔːr, *Am:* -dɔːr] *n* El Salvador

else [els] *adv* **1.** (*in addition*) más; **anyone/anything ~** cualquier otra persona/cosa; **anywhere ~** en cualquier otro lugar; **anyone ~?** ¿alquien más?; **anything ~?** ¿algo más?; **everybody ~** (todos) los demás; **I can't remember anything/anybody ~** no puedo recordar nada/a nadie más; **everything/all ~** todo lo demás; **someone/something ~** otra persona/cosa; **it's something ~!** ¡es algo fuera de serie!; **how ~?** ¿de qué otra forma?; **what/who ~?** ¿qué/quién más? **2.** (*otherwise*) **or ~** si no; **come here or ~!** ¡ven, o ya verás!; **shut up, or else!** ¡como no te calles!

elsewhere [ˌels'weə', *Am:* 'elswer] *adv* en otro sitio; **let's go ~!** ¡vamos a otra parte!

ELT [ˌiːel'tiː] *n abbr of* **English language teaching** enseñanza de inglés

elucidate [ɪ'luːsɪdeɪt] *form* I. *vt* dilucidar; (*mystery*) esclarecer II. *vi* **I don't understand, you'll have to ~** no lo entiendo, tendrás que aclarármelo

elude [ɪ'luːd] *vt* eludir; (*blow*) esquivar

elusive [ɪ'luːsɪv] *adj* **1.** (*evasive*) evasivo, -a; (*personality*) esquivo, -a; **memory** fugaz **2.** (*slippery*) escurridizo, -a **3.** (*difficult to obtain*) difícil de conseguir

elves [elvz] *n pl of* **elf**

emaciated [ɪ'meɪʃɪeɪtɪd, *Am:* -t̬ɪd] *adj form* demacrado, -a, jalado, -a *AmL*

e-mail ['iːmeɪl] *n abbr of* **electronic mail** e-mail *m*

e-mail address *n* dirección *f* de correo electrónico

emanate ['eməneɪt] I. *vi form* (*originate*) proceder; (*radiate*) emanar II. *vt* emanar

emancipate [ɪ'mænsɪpeɪt] *vt* emancipar

emancipated *adj* emancipado, -a; (*not constrained by tradition*) liberado, -a; (*ideas*) progresista

emancipation [ɪˌmænsɪ'peɪʃən] *n no pl* emancipación *f*

embalm [ɪm'bɑːm, *Am:* em-] *vt* embalsamar
embankment [ɪm'bæŋkmənt, *Am:* em-] *n* (*of a road*) terraplén *m;* (*by river*) dique *m*
embargo [ɪm'bɑːgəʊ, *Am:* em'bɑːrgoʊ] **I.**<-goes> *n* embargo *m;* **trade** ~ embargo comercial; **to be under** ~ estar sujeto a embargo; **to put** [*o* **lay**] **an** ~ **on a country** imponer un embargo sobre un país **II.** *vt* prohibir; LAW embargar
embark [ɪm'bɑːk, *Am:* em'bɑːrk] **I.** *vi* embarcar(se); **to** ~ **on** [*o* **upon**] **sth** emprender algo **II.** *vt* embarcar
embarkation [ˌembɑː'keɪʃən, *Am:* -bɑːr'-] *n* embarque *m*
embarrass [ɪm'bærəs, *Am:* em'ber-] *vt* **1.** (*make feel uncomfortable*) avergonzar **2.** (*disconcert*) desconcertar
embarrassed *adj* avergonzado, -a; (*silence*) violento, -a; **to be** ~ pasar vergüenza; **I felt** ~ **about saying that** me daba vergüenza decir eso; **to be financially** ~ tener problemas económicos
embarrassing *adj* embarazoso, -a
embarrassment [ɪm'bærəsmənt, *Am:* em'ber-] *n* **1.** (*shame*) vergüenza *f* **2.** (*trouble, nuisance*) molestia *f;* **to be an** ~ (**to sb**) ser un estorbo (para alguien)
embassy ['embəsi] <-ies> *n* embajada *f*
embed [ɪm'bed, *Am:* em-] <-dd-> *vt* **1.** (*fix*) hincar; (*in rock*) incrustar; (*in memory*) grabar **2.** LING insertar
embellish [ɪm'belɪʃ, *Am:* em-] *vt* adornar
embers ['embəʳz, *Am:* -bɚz] *npl* ascuas *fpl*
embezzle [ɪm'bezl] <-ing> *vt* desfalcar
embezzlement [ɪm'bezlmənt] *n no pl* desfalco *m;* ~ **of public funds** malversación *f* de fondos públicos
embezzler [ɪm'bezləʳ, *Am:* em'bezlɚ] *n* desfalcador(a) *m(f)*
embitter [ɪm'bɪtəʳ, *Am:* em'bɪt̬ɚ] *vt* amargar
emblem ['embləm] *n* emblema *m*
embodiment [ɪm'bɒdɪmənt, *Am:* em-'bɑːdɪ-] *n no pl* **1.** (*personification*) encarnación *f;* **the** ~ **of virtue** la virtud personificada **2.** (*inclusion*) incorporación *f*
embody [ɪm'bɒdi, *Am:* em'bɑːdɪ-] *vt* **1.** (*convey: theory, idea*) expresar **2.** (*personify*) personificar **3.** (*include*) incorporar
embolism ['embəlɪsm] *n* MED embolia *f*
emboss [ɪm'bɒs, *Am:* em'bɑːs] *vt* **1.** (*design, letters*) grabar en relieve **2.** (*leather, metal*) repujar; ~**ed writing paper** papel *m* de carta con membrete en relieve
embrace [ɪm'breɪs, *Am:* em-] **I.** *vt* **1.** (*hug*) abrazar **2.** (*accept: offer*) aceptar; (*ideas, religion*) incorporarse a **3.** (*include*) abarcar **II.** *vi* abrazarse **III.** *n* abrazo *m*
embrocation [ˌembrə'keɪʃən, *Am:* -broʊ'-] *n* cataplasma *f*
embroider [ɪm'brɔɪdəʳ, *Am:* em'brɔɪdɚ] **I.** *vi* bordar **II.** *vt* bordar; *fig* adornar
embroidery [ɪm'brɔɪdəri, *Am:* em-] *n*

1. bordado *m;* ~ **frame** bastidor *m* **2.** *no pl, fig* florituras *fpl*
embroil [ɪm'brɔɪl] *vt* embrollar
embryo ['embrɪəʊ, *Am:* -oʊ] *n* embrión *m*
embryonic [ˌembrɪ'ɒnɪk, *Am:* -'ɑːnɪk] *adj* embrionario, -a; *fig* en estado embrionario
emcee [ɛm'siː] *n Am* presentador(a) *m(f)*
emend [ɪ'mend] *vt form* enmendar
emerald ['emərəld] **I.** *n* esmeralda *f* **II.** *adj* de esmeraldas; (*colour*) esmeralda
emerge [ɪ'mɜːdʒ, *Am:* -'mɜːrdʒ] *vi* (*come out*) salir; (*secret*) revelarse; (*ideas*) surgir; **they** ~**d from the bushes** salieron de entre los arbustos; **new ideas** ~**d from the meeting** a partir de la reunión surgieron nuevas ideas
emergence [ɪ'mɜːdʒəns, *Am:* -'mɜːr-] *n no pl* salida *f;* (*of a secret*) revelación *f;* (*appearance*) aparición *f*
emergency [ɪ'mɜːdʒənsi, *Am:* -'mɜːr-] **I.**<-ies> *n* **1.** (*dangerous situation*) emergencia *f;* **in an** [*o* **in case of**] ~ en caso de emergencia; **to provide for emergencies** prevenirse contra cualquier eventualidad **2.** MED urgencia *f;* ~ **room** sala *f* de urgencias **3.** POL crisis *f inv;* **national** ~ crisis nacional; **to declare a state of** ~ declarar el estado de excepción **II.** *adj* (*exit*) de emergencia; (*services*) de urgencia; (*brake*) de seguridad; (*landing*) forzoso, -a; (*rations*) de reserva; ~ **cord** *Am* timbre de alarma; ~ **exit** salida de emergencia; ~ **landing** aterrizaje forzoso; ~ **service** servicio de urgencia
emergent [ɪ'mɜːdʒənt, *Am:* -'mɜːr-] *adj* emergente; (*democracy, nation*) joven
emerging *adj* emergente
emery ['eməri] *n no pl* esmeril *m*
emery board *n* lima *f* de esmeril **emery paper** *n* papel *m* de lija
emetic [ɪ'metɪk, *Am:* -'met̬-] **I.** *adj* emético, -a, vomitivo, -a **II.** *n* emético *m*, vomitivo *m*
EMI [ˌiːem'aɪ] *n s.* **European Monetary Institute** IME *m*
emigrant ['emɪgrənt] *n* emigrante *mf*
emigrate ['emɪgreɪt] *vi* emigrar
emigration [ˌemɪ'greɪʃən] *n* emigración *f*
eminence ['emɪnəns] *n no pl* eminencia *f;* **Your Eminence** REL Vuestra Eminencia
eminent ['emɪnənt] *adj* eminente
eminently *adv* sumamente
emissary ['emɪsəri, *Am:* -ser-] <-ies> *n* emisario, -a *m, f*
emission [mɪʃən] *n* emisión *f*
emit [ɪ'mɪt] <-tt-> *vt* (*radiation, light*) emitir; (*heat*) desprender; (*odour*) despedir; (*smoke*) echar; (*cry*) dar
emoluments [ɪ'mɒljʊməntz, *Am:* -'mɑːl-] *npl Brit, form* emolumentos *mpl*
emoticon *n* INFOR emoticón *m*
emotion [ɪ'məʊʃən, *Am:* -'moʊ-] *n* **1.** (*feeling*) sentimiento *m* **2.** (*affective state*) emoción *f*
emotional [ɪ'məʊʃənl, *Am:* -'moʊ-] *adj*

E

1. (*relating to the emotions*) emocional; (*involvement, link*) afectivo, -a **2.** (*moving*) conmovedor(a) **3.** (*governed by emotion*) emocionado, -a; **to get ~** emocionarse **4.** (*determined by emotion: decision*) impulsivo, -a

emotionless *adj* impasible

emotive [ɪˈməʊtɪv, *Am:* -ˈmoʊ̞tɪv] *adj* emotivo, -a

empathy [ˈempəθi] *n no pl* empatía *f*

emperor [ˈempərəʳ, *Am:* -ɚ-ɚ] *n* emperador *m*

emphasis [ˈemfəsɪs] <emphases> *n* **1.** LING acento *m* **2.** (*importance*) énfasis *m inv;* **to put** [*o* **lay**] **great ~ on punctuality** hacer especial hincapié en la puntualidad

emphasize [ˈemfəsaɪz] *vt* **1.** LING acentuar **2.** (*insist on*) poner énfasis en, enfatizar *AmL;* (*fact*) hacer hincapié en

emphatic [ɪmˈfætɪk, *Am:* emˈfæt̞-] *adj* (*forcibly expressive*) enfático, -a; (*strong*) enérgico, -a; (*assertion*) categórico, -a; (*refusal*) rotundo, -a; **to be ~ about sth** hacer hincapié en algo

emphatically *adv* (*expressively*) con énfasis; (*strongly*) enérgicamente; (*forcefully*) categóricamente

empire [ˈempaɪəʳ, *Am:* -paɪɚ] *n* imperio *m*

empirical [ɪmˈpɪrɪkl, *Am:* em-] *adj* empírico, -a

employ [ɪmˈplɔɪ, *Am:* em-] *vt* **1.** (*person*) emplear; **to ~ sb to do sth** contratar a alguien para hacer algo **2.** (*object*) utilizar

employee [ˌɪmplɔɪˈiː, *Am:* ˈem-] *n* empleado, -a *m, f*

employer [ɪmˈplɔɪəʳ, *Am:* emˈplɔɪɚ] *n* empresario, -a *m, f;* **~s' organization** organización *f* patronal

employment [ɪmˈplɔɪmənt, *Am:* ˈem-] *n no pl* **1.** (*of a person*) empleo *m;* **to be in ~** *Brit, form* tener trabajo **2.** (*of an object*) utilización *f*

employment agency *n* agencia *f* de empleo

emporium [ɪmˈpɔːrɪəm, *Am:* em-] <-s *o* emporia> *n* emporio *m*

empower [ɪmˈpaʊəʳ, *Am:* emˈpaʊɚ] *vt* **to ~ sb to do sth** (*give ability to*) capacitar a alguien para hacer algo; (*authorise*) autorizar a alguien a hacer algo

empowerment [ɪmˈpaʊəmənt, *Am:* emˈpaʊɚ-] *n no pl* autorización *f*

empress [ˈemprɪs] *n* emperatriz *f*

emptiness [ˈemptɪnɪs] *n no pl* vacío *m; fig* vacuidad *f*

empty [ˈempti] I. <-ier, -iest> *adj* **1.** (*with nothing inside*) vacío, -a; (*lorry, ship, train*) sin carga; (*house*) desocupado, -a **2.** (*useless*) inútil; (*words*) vano, -a; ▶ **phrase** frase vacía II. <-ie-> *vt* (*pour*) verter; (*deprive of contents*) vaciar III. <-ie-> *vi* vaciarse; (*river*) desembocar; **to ~ into the Nile** desembocar en el Nilo IV. <-ies> *n pl* envases *mpl* (vacíos)

◆**empty out** *vt* vaciar

empty-handed [ˌemptɪˈhændɪd] *adj* con las manos vacías **empty-headed** *adj* casquivano, -a **empty weight** *n* tara *f*

EMS [ˌiːemˈes] *n abbr of* **Economic and Monetary System** SME *m*

emu [ˈiːmjuː] *n* emú *m*

EMU [ˌiːemˈjuː] *n abbr of* **Economic and Monetary Union** UME *f*

emulate [ˈemjʊleɪt] *vt* emular

emulation [ˌemjʊˈleɪʃən] *n no pl* emulación *f;* **~ of sb** imitación *f* de alguien

emulsifier [ɪˈmʌlsɪfaɪəʳ, *Am:* -ɚ] *n* emulsionante *m*

emulsify [ɪˈmʌlsɪfaɪ] <-ie-> I. *vt* emulsionar II. *vi* emulsionarse

emulsion [ɪˈmʌlʃən] *n* **1.** *a.* PHOT emulsión *f* **2.** (*paint*) pintura *f* emulsionada

enable [ɪˈneɪbl] *vt* **1.** **to ~ sb to do sth** permitir a alguien que haga algo **2.** INFOR activar

enact [ɪˈnækt] *vt* **1.** (*carry out*) llevar a cabo **2.** THEAT representar **3.** (*law*) promulgar; **to ~ that ...** decretar que...

enactment *n* **1.** *no pl* (*carrying out*) puesta *f* en práctica; (*of legislation*) promulgación *f* **2.** THEAT representación *f*

enamel [ɪˈnæml] I. *n* esmalte *m* II. <-ll-, *Am:* -l-> *vt* esmaltar

enamored *adj Am,* **enamoured** [ɪˈnæməʳd, *Am:* -əᵊd] *adj Brit* **to be ~ of sb** estar enamorado de alguien; **to be ~ with sth** estar entusiasmado con algo

enc. *s.* **enc(l).**

encamp [ɪnˈkæmp, *Am:* en-] *vi Brit* acampar

encampment *n* campamento *m*

encapsulate [ɪnˈkæpsjəleɪt] *vt* encapsular; *fig* resumir

encase [ɪnˈkeɪs, *Am:* en-] *vt* encerrar

encephalitis [ˌensefəˈlaɪtɪs, *Am:* enˌsefəˈlaɪt̞ɪs] *n* encefalitis *f inv*

enchant [ɪnˈtʃɑːnt, *Am:* enˈtʃænt] *vt* **1.** (*charm*) encantar **2.** (*bewitch*) hechizar

enchanted *adj* (*charmed*) encantado, -a; (*bewitched*) hechizado, -a

enchanter *n* hechicero *m*

enchanting *adj* encantador(a)

enchantment *n* **1.** (*spell*) hechizo *m* **2.** (*charm*) encanto *m*

enchantress *n* (*witch*) hechicera *f;* (*alluring woman*) mujer *f* encantadora

encipher [ɪnˈsaɪfəʳ, *Am:* enˈsaɪfɚ] *vt* codificar

encircle [ɪnˈsɜːkl, *Am:* enˈsɜːr-] *vt* rodear; **to ~ the enemy** rodear al enemigo

encirclement *n* cerco *m;* MIL envolvimiento *m*

enc(l). *abbr of* **enclosure** recinto *m*

enclave [ˈenkleɪv] *n* enclave *m*

enclose [ɪnˈkləʊz, *Am:* enˈkloʊz] *vt* **1.** (*surround*) cercar; **to ~ sth in brackets** poner algo entre paréntesis; **to ~ the monument with a park** rodear el monumento con el parque **2.** (*include*) adjuntar, adosar *AmL*

enclosed [ɪnˈkləʊzd, *Am:* enˈkloʊzd] *adj*

1. (*confined*) cerrado, -a; (*garden*) vallado, -a; ~ **order** REL orden *f* de clausura **2.** (*included*) adjunto, -a

enclosure [ɪn'kləʊʒəʳ, *Am:* en'kloʊʒɚ] *n* **1.** (*enclosed area*) recinto *m;* (*for animals*) corral *m* **2.** (*action*) cercamiento *m* **3.** (*letter*) documento *m* adjunto

encode [ɪn'kəʊd, *Am:* en'koʊd] *vt a.* INFOR codificar; LING cifrar

encompass [ɪn'kʌmpəs, *Am:* en-] *vt* **1.** (*surround*) rodear **2.** (*include*) abarcar

encore ['ɒŋkɔːʳ, *Am:* 'ɑːnkɔːr] **I.** *n* repetición *f;* as [*o* for] an ~ como bis **II.** *interj* otra

encore marriage *n* segundo matrimonio *m*

encounter [ɪn'kaʊntəʳ, *Am:* en'kaʊntɚ] **I.** *vt* encontrar; **to** ~ **sb** encontrarse con alguien (por casualidad) **II.** *n* encuentro *m*

encourage [ɪn'kʌrɪdʒ, *Am:* en'kɜːr-] *vt* **1.** (*give confidence*) alentar; (*give hope*) dar ánimos a; **to** ~ **sb to do sth** animar a alguien a hacer algo **2.** (*support*) fomentar

encouragement [ɪn'kʌrɪdʒmənt, *Am:* en'kɜːr-] *n no pl* estímulo *m;* **to give** ~ **to sth** fomentar algo

encouraging *adj* alentador(a); **an** ~ **prospect** una perspectiva de futuro halagüeña

encroach [ɪn'krəʊtʃ, *Am:* en'kroʊtʃ] *vi* **to** ~ **on** [*o* **upon**] **sth** (*intrude*) invadir algo; *fig* usurpar algo

encroachment *n* **1.** (*intrusion*) invasión *f* **2.** *fig* usurpación *f;* **an** ~ **on human rights** una violación de los derechos humanos

encryption [ɪn'krɪpʃən] *n* INFOR codificación *f*

encumber [ɪn'kʌmbəʳ, *Am:* en'kʌmbɚ] *vt* **to be ~ed with sth** tener que cargar con algo; (*impede*) verse estorbado por algo

encyclop(a)edia [ɪn,saɪklə'piːdɪə, *Am:* en-] *n* enciclopedia *f*

encyclop(a)edic [ɪn,saɪklə'piːdɪk, *Am:* en-] *adj* enciclopédico, -a

end [end] **I.** *n* **1.** (*last, furthest point*) final *m* **2.** (*finish*) fin *m* **3.** (*extremities*) extremo *m* **4.** *pl* (*aims*) fin *m;* (*purpose*) intención *f;* **to achieve one's ~s** conseguir los propios objetivos; **for commercial ~s** con fines comerciales **5.** (*death*) muerte *f;* **he is nearing his** ~ está a punto de morir **6.** (*piece remaining*) resto *m* **7.** SPORTS lado *m* **8.** INFOR tecla *f* de fin ►**to reach the ~ of the** line [*o* road] llegar al final; **the ~ justifies the means** *prov* el fin justifica los medios *prov;* ~ **of** story punto y final; **you deserved to be punished,** ~ **of story** merecías ser castigado, y punto; **to be at the ~ of one's** tether [*o* rope *Am*] no poder más; **it's not the ~ of the** world no es el fin del mundo; **to come to a** bad [*o* sticky] ~ acabar mal; **to go off the** deep ~ *inf* subirse por las paredes; **this is** just **the** ~ esto (ya) es el colmo; **to** hold [*o* keep] **one's** ~ **up** defenderse bien; **to** make ~**s meet** llegar a fin de mes; **to** meet **one's** ~ encontrar la muerte; **to play both ~s against the** middle *Am* oponer

a dos contrincantes en beneficio propio; **to** put **an** ~ **to oneself** [*o* **it all**] acabar con su vida; **in the** ~ a fin de cuentas; **to** this ~ para ello **II.** *vt* **1.** (*finish*) acabar **2.** (*bring to a stop: reign, war*) poner fin a **III.** *vi* acabar; **to** ~ **in sth** terminar en algo

◆**end up** *vi* terminar; **to** ~ **in love with sb** acabar enamorándose de alguien; **to** ~ **a rich man** acabar siendo un hombre rico; **to** ~ **penniless** acabar sin dinero; **to** ~ **in prison** acabar en la cárcel; **to** ~ **doing sth** terminar haciendo algo

endanger [ɪn'deɪndʒəʳ, *Am:* en'deɪndʒɚ] *vt* poner en peligro; **an ~ed species** una especie en peligro de extinción

endear [ɪn'dɪəʳ, *Am:* en'dɪr] *vt* **to** ~ **oneself to sb** hacerse querer por alguien

endearing *adj* entrañable; **an** ~ **smile** una sonrisa agradable

endearment *n* ternura *f;* **terms of** ~ palabras *fpl* cariñosas; **to whisper ~s to each other** susurrarse tiernas palabras

endeavor *Am,* **endeavour** [ɪn'devəʳ, *Am:* en'devɚ] *Brit* **I.** *vi* **to** ~ **to do sth** esforzarse por hacer algo **II.** *n* esfuerzo *m;* **to make every** ~ **to do sth** hacer todo lo posible para conseguir algo

endemic [en'demɪk] *adj* endémico, -a

ending ['endɪŋ] *n* fin *m;* LING terminación *f*

endive ['endɪv, *Am:* 'endaɪv] *n Am* endibia *f*

endless ['endlɪs] *adj* interminable, inacabable

endorse [ɪn'dɔːs, *Am:* en'dɔːrs] *vt* **1.** (*declare approval for*) aprobar; (*product*) promocionar **2.** FIN endosar **3.** *Brit* LAW **to** ~ **a driving licence** dejar constancia de sanción en un permiso de conducir

endorsee [ɪn,dɔː'siː, *Am:* -dɔːr-] *n* endosatario, -a *m, f*

endorsement *n* **1.** (*support: of a plan*) aprobación *f;* (*recommendation*) recomendación *f* **2.** FIN endoso *m* **3.** *Brit* LAW nota *f* de sanción

endorser *n* endosante *mf*

endow [ɪn'daʊ, *Am:* en-] *vt* dotar; **to be ~ed with sth** estar dotado de algo

endowment *n* **1.** FIN dotación *f* **2.** (*talent*) talento *m* **3.** BIO **genetic** ~ dotación *f* genética

endpaper ['endpeɪpəʳ, *Am:* -pɚ] *n* guarda *f*

end product *n* producto *m* final **end result** *n* resultado *m* final

endurable [ɪn'djʊərəbl, *Am:* en'dʊrə-] *adj* soportable

endurance [ɪn'djʊərəns, *Am:* en'dʊrəns] *n no pl* resistencia *f*

endure [ɪn'djʊəʳ, *Am:* en'dʊr] **I.** *vt* **1.** (*tolerate*) soportar, aguantar **2.** (*suffer*) resisitir **II.** *vi form* durar

enduring *adj* duradero, -a

ENE *abbr of* **east-northeast** ENE

enema ['enɪmə, *Am:* -ə-] <-s *o* enemata> *n* enema *m*

enemy ['enəmi] **I.** *n* enemigo, -a *m, f* **II.** *adj* enemigo, -a

energetic [,enə'dʒetɪk, *Am:* -ɚ'dʒet̬-] *adj*

enérgico, -a; (*active*) activo, -a

energize ['enədʒaɪz, *Am:* -ə-] *vt* **1.** ELEC activar **2.** *fig* dar energía a

energy ['enədʒi, *Am:* -ə-] <-ies> *n* energía *f*; **to be full of** ~ estar lleno de energía; **to have the** ~ **to do sth** tener energías para hacer algo

energy crisis *n* asdl asldj asldj crisis *f inv* energética **energy resources** *npl* fuentes *fpl* energéticas [*o* de energía] **energy saving** *n* ahorro *m* de energía

enervate ['enəveɪt, *Am:* -ə-] *vt liter* enervar

enervating *adj liter* enervador(a)

enfeeble [ɪn'fi:bl, *Am:* en-] *vt form* debilitar

enforce [ɪn'fɔ:s, *Am:* en'fɔ:rs] *vt* aplicar; (*law*) hacer cumplir; (*regulation*) poner en vigor

enforceable *adj* ejecutable; (*law*) que se puede hacer cumplir

enforcement [ɪn'fɔ:smənt, *Am:* en'fɔ:rs-] *n no pl* (*of a law*) aplicación *f*; (*of a regulation*) ejecución *f*

enfranchise [ɪn'fræntʃaɪz, *Am:* en-] *vt form* conceder el derecho a voto a

engage [ɪn'geɪdʒ, *Am:* en-] **I.** *vt* **1.** *form* (*hold interest*) atraer; **to** ~ **sb's attention** llamar la atención de alguien **2.** (*put into use*) activar **3.** *Brit, form* (*employ*) contratar **4.** TECH (*cogs*) engranar; **to** ~ **the clutch** embragar **II.** *vi* **1.** MIL trabar batalla **2.** TECH engranar

engaged *adj* **1.** (*occupied*) ocupado, -a; **to be** ~ (*telephone*) estar comunicando **2.** (*to be married*) prometido, -a; **to get** ~ (**to sb**) comprometerse (con alguien)

engagement [ɪn'geɪdʒmənt, *Am:* en-] *n* **1.** (*appointment*) compromiso *m* **2.** MIL combate *m* **3.** (*marriage*) compromiso *m*

engagement book *n*, **engagement diary** *n* agenda *f* **engagement ring** *n* anillo *m* de compromiso

engaging *adj* atractivo, -a

engender [ɪn'dʒendə^r, *Am:* en'dʒendə-] *vt form* engendrar

engine ['endʒɪn] *n* **1.** (*motor*) motor *m*; **diesel/petrol** ~ motor diesel/gasolina; **jet** ~ motor a reacción **2.** *Brit* RAIL máquina *f*

engineer [ˌendʒɪ'nɪə^r, *Am:* -'nɪr] **I.** *n* **1.** (*with a degree*) ingeniero, -a *m, f*; **civil** ~ ingeniero de caminos **2.** (*technician*) técnico, -a *m, f* **3.** *Am* RAIL maquinista *mf* **II.** *vt* construir; *fig* maquinar

engineering [ˌendʒɪ'nɪərɪŋ, *Am:* -'nɪr-] *n no pl* ingeniería *f*; ~ **works** obras *fpl* de ingeniería

England ['ɪŋglənd] *n* Inglaterra *f*

English ['ɪŋglɪʃ] **I.** *n inv* **1.** (*language*) inglés *m* **2.** *pl* (*people*) **the** ~ los ingleses **II.** *adj* inglés, -esa; **an** ~ **film** una película inglesa; **an** ~ **class** una clase de inglés

English breakfast *n* desayuno *m* inglés **English Channel** *n* Canal *m* de la Mancha **Englishman** <-men> *n* inglés *m* **English-speaker** *n* persona *f* de habla inglesa **English-speaking** *adj* de habla inglesa **Englishwoman** <-women> *n* inglesa *f*

engrave [ɪn'greɪv, *Am:* en-] *vt* grabar; **to be** ~**d on the memory** estar grabado en la memoria

engraver [en'greɪvə-] *n* grabador(a) *m(f)*

engraving [ɪn'greɪvɪŋ, *Am:* en-] *n* grabado *m*

engross [ɪn'grəʊs, *Am:* en'groʊs] *vt* **1.** (*absorb the attention of*) absorber; **to be** ~**ed in sth** estar absorto en algo **2.** LAW copiar

engulf [ɪn'gʌlf, *Am:* en-] *vt* hundir

enhance [ɪn'hɑ:ns, *Am:* -'hæns] *vt* realzar; (*improve or intensify: chances*) aumentar; (*memory*) refrescar

enigma [ɪ'nɪgmə] *n* enigma *m*

enigmatic(al) [ˌenɪg'mætɪk(əl), *Am:* -'mæt̬-] *adj* enigmático, -a

enjoy [ɪn'dʒɔɪ, *Am:* en-] **I.** *vt* **1.** (*get pleasure from*) disfrutar de; **to** ~ **doing sth** disfrutar haciendo algo; ~ **yourselves!** ¡que lo paséis bien! **2.** (*have: health*) poseer; **to** ~ **sb's confidence** tener la confianza de alguien; **to** ~ **good health** gozar de buena salud **II.** *vi Am* pasarlo bien

enjoyable [ɪn'dʒɔɪəbl, *Am:* en-] *adj* agradable; (*film, book, play*) divertido, -a

enjoyment [ɪn'dʒɔɪmənt, *Am:* en-] *n no pl* disfrute *m*; **to get real** ~ **out of doing sth** disfrutar realmente haciendo algo

enlarge [ɪn'lɑ:dʒ, *Am:* en'lɑ:rdʒ] **I.** *vt* **1.** (*make bigger*) agrandar; (*expand*) extender; **to** ~ **one's vocabulary** ampliar su léxico **2.** PHOT ampliar **II.** *vi* extenderse

enlargement *n* aumento *m*; (*expanding*) extensión *f*; PHOT ampliación *f*

enlighten [ɪn'laɪtn, *Am:* en-] *vt* **1.** REL iluminar **2.** (*explain*) instruir; **to** ~ **the public of sth** informar al público de algo

enlightened *adj* (*person*) progresista; REL iluminado, -a; (*age*) ilustrado, -a

enlightenment [ɪn'laɪtnmənt, *Am:* en-] *n no pl* **1.** REL iluminación *f* **2.** PHILOS **the** (**Age of**) **Enlightenment** el Siglo de las Luces **3.** (*explanation*) aclaración *f*; **to give sb** ~ **on sth** hacer una aclaración a alguien sobre algo

enlist [ɪn'lɪst, *Am:* en-] **I.** *vi* MIL alistarse **II.** *vt* MIL alistar; (*support*) conseguir

enliven [ɪn'laɪvn, *Am:* en-] *vt* avivar; (*person*) animar

en masse [ˌɑ̃:m'mæs, *Am:* ɑ:n-] *adv* en masa

enmesh [ɪn'meʃ, *Am:* en-] *vt* coger en una red; **to be** ~**ed in sth** *a. fig* estar enredado en algo; **to get** ~**ed in sth** *a. fig* enredarse en algo

enmity ['enməti] <-ies> *n* enemistad *f*

ennoble [ɪ'nəʊbl, *Am:* e'noʊbl] *vt* ennoblecer

enormity [ɪ'nɔ:məti, *Am:* -'nɔ:rmət̬i] <-ies> *n* (*of damage*) magnitud *f*; (*of a task, mistake*) enormidad *f*; (*of a crime*) atrocidad *f*

enormous [ɪ'nɔ:məs, *Am:* -'nɔ:r-] *adj* enorme; ~ **difficulties** grandes dificultades *fpl*

enough [ɪ'nʌf] **I.** *adj* (*sufficient*) suficiente, bastante **II.** *adv* bastante; **to be experienced** ~ (**to do sth**) tener la suficiente experiencia (para hacer algo); **to have seen** ~ haber visto demasiado; **she was kind** [*o* **friendly**] ~ **to help me** tuvo la amabilidad de ayudarme; **bad ~, but his brother is worse** si él es malo, peor es su hermano; **oddly** [*o* **strangely**] ~ por extraño que parezca **III.** *interj* basta **IV.** *pron* bastante; **to have** ~ **to eat and drink** tener lo suficiente para comer y beber; **I know** ~ **about it** sé lo suficiente acerca de ello; **that should be** ~ eso debería ser suficiente; **more than** ~ más que suficiente; **it is** ~ **for me to know ...** me basta con saber...; **to have had** ~ (**of sb/sth**) estar harto (de alguien/algo); **as if that wasn't** ~ por si fuera poco; **that's** (**quite**) ~! ¡basta ya!; ~ **is** ~ basta y sobra

enquire [ɪnˈkwaɪərˌ *Am:* enˈkwaɪɚ] **I.** *vi* **1.** (*ask*) preguntar; **to** ~ **for sb** preguntar por alguien; **to** ~ **about sth** pedir información sobre algo; **to** ~ **after sb's health** preguntar por la salud de alguien **2.** (*investigate*) investigar; **to** ~ **into a matter** indagar en un asunto; **to** ~ **of sb whether ...** *form* preguntar a alguien si... **II.** *vt* preguntar; **to** ~ **the reason** preguntar por qué

enquiry [ɪnˈkwaɪəri, *Am:* enˈkwaɪri] <-ies> *n* **1.** (*question*) pregunta *f*; **to make an** ~ **into** sth indagar en algo **2.** (*investigation*) investigación *f*; **an** ~ **into sth** una investigación sobre algo; **to hold an** ~ llevar a cabo una investigación

enrage [ɪnˈreɪdʒ, *Am:* en-] *vt* enfurecer

enraged [ɪnˈreɪdʒd, *Am:* en-] *adj* enfurecido, -a

enrapture [ɪnˈræptʃəʳ, *Am:* enˈræptʃɚ] *vt* embelesar

enrich [ɪnˈrɪtʃ, *Am:* en-] *vt* enriquecer

enrol *Brit,* **enroll** [ɪnˈrəʊl, *Am:* enˈroʊl] *Am, Aus* **I.** *vi* inscribirse; **to** ~ **for/on a course** matricularse para/en un curso **II.** *vt* inscribir; (*on a course*) matricular

enrollment *n Am,* **enrolment** [ɪnˈrəʊlmənt, *Am:* enˈroʊl-] *n* inscripción *f*; (*on a course*) matriculación *f*

en route [ˌɒnˈruːt, *Am:* ˌɑːn-] *adv* en el camino

ensemble [ɒnˈsɒmbl, *Am:* ɑːnˈsɑːm-] *n* **1.** MUS, THEAT grupo *m* **2.** FASHION conjunto *m*

ensign [ˈensən] *n* MIL **1.** enseña *f* **2.** (*standard-bearer*) abanderado *m*

enslave [ɪnˈsleɪv, *Am:* en-] *vt* esclavizar; **to be** ~**d by sth** ser dominado por algo

ensnare [ɪnˈsneəʳ, *Am:* enˈsner] *vt liter* atrapar, coger en una trampa; **to be** ~**d in sth** estar atrapado en algo

ensue [ɪnˈsjuː, *Am:* enˈsuː] *vi form* seguirse; **to** ~ **from sth** resultar de algo

ensuing *adj* siguiente

en suite bathroom [ãːnswiːtˈbɑːθrʊm, *Am:* ˌɑːnswiːtˈbæθruːm] *n* baño *m* incorporado

ensure [ɪnˈʃʊəʳ, *Am:* enˈʃʊr] *vt* asegurar; (*guarantee*) garantizar

ENT *abbr of* **ear, nose and throat** otorrinola-

ringología *f*

entail [ɪnˈteɪl, *Am:* en-] *vt* **1.** (*involve*) acarrear; **to** ~ **some risk** entrañar algún riesgo **2.** (*necessitate*) **to** ~ **doing sth** implicar hacer algo

entangle [ɪnˈtæŋgl, *Am:* en-] *vt* enredar; **to** ~ **oneself** enredarse; **to get** ~**d in sth** quedar enredado en algo; *fig* verse envuelto en algo; **to get** ~**d with sb** meterse en un lío con alguien

entanglement *n* enredo *m;* (*situation*) embrollo *m;* **emotional** ~**s** aventuras *fpl* amorosas

enter [ˈentəʳ, *Am:* -t̬ɚ] **I.** *vt* **1.** (*go into*) entrar en; (*penetrate*) penetrar **2.** (*insert*) introducir; (*into a register*) inscribir **3.** (*join*) hacerse socio de; **to** ~ **school** ingresar en la escuela **4.** (*make known*) anotar; (*claim*) presentar; (*plea*) formular **II.** *vi* THEAT entrar

◆**enter into** *vi* (*form part of*) tomar parte en; **to** ~ **a marriage** contraer matrimonio; **to** ~ **conversation** entablar una conversación; **to** ~ **discussion** meterse en una discusión; **to** ~ **negotiations** iniciar negociaciones ►**to** ~ **the spirit of sth** tomar parte en algo con entusiasmo

◆**enter up** *vt* asentar; (*in accounts*) registrar

◆**enter upon** *vi* emprender

enter key *n* INFOR clave *f* de acceso

enterprise [ˈentəpraɪz, *Am:* -t̬ɚ-] *n* **1.** (*business firm*) empresa *f*; **to start an** ~ abrir un negocio **2.** (*initiative*) iniciativa *f*; **to show** ~ **in doing sth** mostrar un espíritu emprendedor para hacer algo

enterprise culture *n no pl* cultura *f* empresarial

enterprising *adj* emprendedor(a)

entertain [ˌentəˈteɪn, *Am:* -t̬ɚ-] **I.** *vt* **1.** (*amuse*) entretener **2.** (*guests*) recibir **3.** (*consider*) considerar; **to** ~ **doubts** abrigar dudas; **to** ~ **an idea/a plan** estudiar una idea/un proyecto **II.** *vi* (*invite guests*) recibir en casa

entertainer [ˌentəˈteɪnəʳ, *Am:* -t̬ɚˈteɪnɚ] *n* artista *mf*

entertaining *adj no pl* entretenido, -a; (*person*) divertido, -a

entertainment [ˌentəˈteɪnmənt, *Am:* -t̬ɚ-] *n* **1.** *no pl* (*amusement*) diversión *f*; **to provide some** ~ proporcionar entretenimiento **2.** (*show*) espectáculo *m*

enthral <-ll-> *vt,* **enthrall** [ɪnˈθrɔːl, *Am:* enˈθrɔːl] *vt Am* cautivar

enthrone [ɪnˈθrəʊn, *Am:* enˈθroʊn] *vt form* entronizar

enthuse [ɪnˈθjuːz, *Am:* enˈθuːz] **I.** <-sing> *vi* **to** ~ **about sth** entusiasmarse muchísimo con algo **II.** <-sing> *vt* **to** ~ **sb** (**with sth**) entusiasmar a alguien (con algo)

enthusiasm [ɪnˈθjuːzɪæzəm, *Am:* enˈθuː-] *n* entusiasmo *m;* ~ **for sth** entusiasmo por algo

enthusiast [ɪnˈθjuːzɪæst] *n* entusiasta *mf*

enthusiastic [ɪnˌθjuːzɪˈæstɪk, *Am:* enˌθuː-] *adj* entusiasta; **to be** ~ **about sth** estar entusiasmado con algo

entice [ɪn'taɪs, *Am:* en-] *vt* tentar; **to ~ sb to do sth** tentar a alguien a hacer algo; **to ~ sb away from sth** inducir con maña a alguien para que deje algo
enticement *n* tentación *f*
enticing *adj* tentador(a); *(smile)* atractivo, -a
entire [ɪn'taɪəʳ, *Am:* en'taɪɚ] *adj* 1. *(whole)* todo, -a; *(total)* total; **the ~ world** el mundo entero; **the ~ day** todo el día 2. *(complete)* entero, -a
entirely *adv* enteramente; **to be ~ sb's fault** ser toda la culpa de alguien; **to agree ~** estar completamente de acuerdo; **to disagree ~** estar del todo en desacuerdo
entirety [ɪn'taɪəʳəti, *Am:* en'taɪɾəʈi] *n* **in its ~** en su totalidad
entitle [ɪn'taɪtl, *Am:* en'taɪʈl] *vt* 1. *(give right)* autorizar; **to ~ sb to act** autorizar a alguien para actuar; **to ~ sb to a holiday** dar a alguien derecho a vacaciones 2. *(book)* titular
entitled *adj* 1. *(person)* autorizado, -a 2. *(book)* titulado, -a
entitlement [ɪn'taɪtlmənt, *Am:* en'taɪʈl-] *n* no *pl* autorización *f*; *(claim)* derecho *m*
entity ['entəti, *Am:* -ʈəʈi] <-ies> *n* *form* entidad *f*; **legal ~** persona *f* jurídica; **a single/ separate ~** un género único/separado
entomology [ˌentə'mɒlədʒi, *Am:* -ʈə-'mɑːlə-] *n* no *pl* entomología *f*
entourage ['ɒntʊraːʒ, *Am:* ˌaːntʊ'raːʒ] *n* séquito *m* form
entrails ['entreɪlz] npl entrañas *fpl*
entrance[1] ['entrəns] *n* 1. *(way in)* entrada *f*; *(door)* puerta *f*; **front ~** entrada *f* principal; **the ~ to sth** la entrada de algo; **to refuse ~** negar el acceso 2. THEAT entrada *f* en escena
entrance[2] [ɪn'traːns, *Am:* en'træns] *vt* encantar
entrance examination ['entrəns ɪgˌzæmɪ'neɪʃən] *n* examen *m* de ingreso **entrance fee** *n* cuota *f* de entrada [*o* de inscripción] **entrance form** *n* formulario *m* de inscripción **entrance hall** *n* vestíbulo *m* **entrance requirement** *n* requisito *m* de entrada
entrant ['entrənt] *n* participante *mf*
entreat [ɪn'triːt, *Am:* en-] *vt* **to ~ sb to do sth** suplicar a alguien que haga algo
entreaty [ɪn'triːti, *Am:* en'triːʈi] <-ies> *n* ruego *m*
entrench [ɪn'trentʃ, *Am:* en-] *vt passive* 1. **to become ~ed** *(idea)* arraigarse 2. **to ~ oneself** MIL atrincherarse
entrenched *adj* 1. *(idea)* arraigado, -a 2. MIL atrincherado, -a
entrepreneur [ˌɒntrəprə'nɜːʳ, *Am:* ˌaːntrəprə'nɜːr] *n* empresario, -a *m, f*
entrepreneurial spirit [ˌɒntrəprə'nɜːriəl 'spɪrɪt, *Am:* ˌaːn-] *n* no *pl* espíritu *m* empresarial
entrust [ɪn'trʌst, *Am:* en-] *vt* confiar; **to ~ sth to sb** confiar algo a alguien; **to ~ sth into sb's care** dejar algo al cuidado de alguien

entry ['entri] <-ies> *n* 1. *(act of entering)* entrada *f*; *(joining an organization)* ingreso *m* 2. *(entrance)* acceso *m*
entry fee *n* cuota *f* de entrada **entry form** *n* formulario *m* de inscripción **entry permit** *n* permiso *m* de entrada **entryphone** *n* Brit portero *m* automático **entry regulations** *n* normativa *f* de entrada **entry test** *n* prueba *f* de acceso
entwine [ɪn'twaɪn, *Am:* en-] *vt* *(weave)* entretejer; *(twist)* entrelazar; *(plants)* enredar; **to be ~d** *(together)* *fig* estar entrelazados
E-number ['iːnʌmbəʳ, *Am:* -bɚ] *n* número *m* E
enumerate [ɪ'njuːməreɪt, *Am:* -'nuː-] *vt* enumerar
enumeration [ɪˌnjuːmə'reɪʃən, *Am:* -ˌnuː-] *n* enumeración *f*
enunciate [ɪ'nʌnsɪeɪt] *vt* 1. *(sound)* pronunciar, articular 2. *(theory)* enunciar
envelop [ɪn'veləp, *Am:* en-] *vt* envolver
envelope ['envələʊp, *Am:* -loʊp] *n* sobre *m*, cierro *m* Chile
enviable ['envɪəbl] *adj* envidiable
envious ['envɪəs] *adj* envidioso, -a; **to be ~ of sb/sth** tener envidia de alguien/algo
environment [ɪn'vaɪərənmənt, *Am:* en'vaɪ-] *n* entorno *m*; **the ~** ECOL el medio ambiente; **home/professional ~** entorno familiar/profesional; **working ~** ambiente *m* de trabajo
environmental [ɪnˌvaɪərən'mentl, *Am:* enˌvaɪrən'menʈl] *adj* ambiental; ECOL medioambiental; **~ damage** daños *mpl* ecológicos; **~ impact** impacto *m* sobre el medio ambiente; **~ pollution** contaminación *f* ambiental; **~ stress** electrosmog *m*
environmentalist [ɪnˌvaɪərən'mentəlɪst, *Am:* enˌvaɪrən'menʈəl-] *n* ecologista *mf*
environmentally-friendly [ɪnˌvaɪərən-'mentəli'frendli, *Am:* enˌvaɪrən'menʈəl-] *adj* ecológico, -a
environs [ɪn'vaɪərənz, *Am:* en'vaɪ-] *npl* form alrededores *mpl*
envisage [ɪn'vɪzɪdʒ, *Am:* en-] *vt*, **envision** [ɪn'vɪʒən, *Am:* en-] *vt Am* 1. *(expect)* prever 2. *(imagine)* formarse una idea de; **to ~ that ...** prever [*o* calcular] que...
envoy ['envɔɪ, *Am:* 'aːn-] *n* enviado, -a *m, f*
envy ['envi] I. *n* no *pl* envidia *f*; **the car is the ~ of my brother** mi hermano me envidia el coche; **she feels ~ towards her sister** le tiene envidia a su hermana ►**to be green with ~** reconcomerse de envidia II. <-ie-> *vt* envidiar
enzyme ['enzaɪm] *n* enzima *f*
EOC *n* Brit abbr of **Equal Opportunities Commission** comisión para la igualdad de oportunidades
EOF *n* INFOR abbr of **end of file** fin *m* de archivo
EP [ˌiː'piː] *abbr of* **extended play** duración *m* ampliada

EPA [ˌiːpiːˈeɪ] *Am abbr of* Environmental Protection Agency Agencia *f* del Medio Ambiente

ephemeral [ɪˈfemərəl, *Am:* -ɚ-] *adj a.* BIO efímero, -a

epic [ˈepɪk] I. *n* epopeya *f* II. *adj* épico, -a; ~ poetry poesía épica; an ~ journey un viaje que es toda una epopeya

epicenter *n Am*, **epicentre** [ˈepɪsentəʳ, *Am:* -ţɚ] *n Brit, Aus* epicentro *m*

epicycle [ˈepɪsaɪkl, *Am:* ˈ-ə-] *n* MAT, ASTR epiciclo *m*

epidemic [ˌepɪˈdemɪk, *Am:* -ə'-] I. *n* epidemia *f* II. *adj* epidémico, -a; ~ proportions proporciones gigantescas

epidermis [ˌepɪˈdɜːmɪs, *Am:* -əˈdɜːr-] <-mes> *n* epidermis *f inv*

epigram [ˈepɪɡræm, *Am:* ˈ-ə-] *n* epigrama *m*

epilepsy [ˈepɪlepsi] *n no pl* epilepsia *f*

epileptic [ˌepɪˈleptɪk] I. *n* epiléptico, -a *m, f* II. *adj* epiléptico, -a; ~ fit ataque epiléptico

epilog *n Am*, **epilogue** [ˈepɪlɒɡ, *Am:* -əlɑːɡ] *n Brit* epílogo *m*

Epiphany [ɪˈpɪfəni] <-ies> *n* Epifanía *f*

episcopacy [ɪˈpɪskəpəsi] <-ies> *n* episcopado *m*

episcopal [ɪˈpɪskəpl] *adj* episcopal

Episcopalian [ɪˌpɪskəˈpeɪliən] I. *adj* episcopaliano, -a II. *n* episcopaliano, -a *m, f*

episode [ˈepɪsəʊd, *Am:* -əsoʊd] *n* episodio *m*

episodic [ˌepɪˈsɒdɪk, *Am:* -əˈsɑːdɪk] *adj* 1. (*occasional*) episódico, -a 2. LIT (*consisting of episodes*) por episodios [*o* capítulos]

epistle [ɪˈpɪsl] *n* epístola *f*

epistolary [ɪˈpɪstələri, *Am:* -eri] *adj* epistolar

epitaph [ˈepɪtɑːf, *Am:* -ətæf] *n* epitafio *m*

epithet [ˈepɪθet] *n* LING epíteto *m*

epitome [ɪˈpɪtəmi, *Am:* -ˈpɪţ-] *n* 1. (*embodiment*) personificación *f* 2. (*example*) arquetipo *m;* the ~ of poor taste el colmo del mal gusto

epitomise *vt Aus, Brit*, **epitomize** [ɪˈpɪtəmaɪz, *Am:* -ˈpɪţ-] *vt* personificar

epoch [ˈiːpɒk, *Am:* ˈepək] *n form* era *f;* historical ~ época *f* histórica

epoch-making [ˈiːpɒkˌmeɪkɪŋ, *Am:* ˈepək-] *adj* ~ discovery descubrimiento *m* que hace época

eponymous [ɪˈpɒnɪməs, *Am:* ɪˈpɑːnə-] *adj* epónimo, -a

equable [ˈekwəbl] *adj* (*temperament*) ecuánime; (*climate*) templado, -a; to have an ~ disposition ser de talante tranquilo

equal [ˈiːkwəl] I. *adj* 1. (*the same*) igual; (*treatment*) equitativo, -a; to have ~ reason to do sth tener las mismas razones para hacer algo; of ~ size de la misma medida; on ~ terms en igualdad de condiciones 2. (*able to do*) to be ~ to a task ser capaz de realizar una tarea II. *n* igual *mf;* it has no ~ no hay nada parecido III. <*Brit:* -ll-, *Am:* -l-> *vt* 1. *pl* MAT ser igual a 2. (*match*) igualar

equality [ɪˈkwɒləti, *Am:* -ˈkwɑːləţi] *n no pl* igualdad *f*

equalization [ˌiːkwəlaɪˈzeɪʃən, *Am:* -ɪˈ-] *n* nivelización *f*

equalize [ˈiːkwəlaɪz] I. *vt* nivelar II. *vi Aus, Brit* SPORTS empatar

equalizer [ˈiːkwəlaɪzəʳ, *Am:* -zɚ] *n Aus, Brit* SPORTS tanto *m* del empate; to score an ~ marcar el empate

equally [ˈiːkwəli] *adv* igualmente; to contribute ~ to sth contribuir por igual a algo; to divide sth ~ dividir algo equitativamente

equal opportunities *npl Brit*, **equal opportunity** *n Am* igualdad *f* de oportunidades **equal(s) sign** *n* MAT signo *m* de igual

equanimity [ˌekwəˈnɪməti, *Am:* -əţi] *n no pl* ecuanimidad *f;* to receive sth with ~ recibir algo serenamente

equate [ɪˈkweɪt] I. *vt* equiparar II. *vi* to ~ to sth ser equivalente [*o* igual] a algo

equation [ɪˈkweɪʒən] *n* ecuación *f*

equator [ɪˈkweɪtəʳ, *Am:* -tɚ] *n* ecuador *m*

equatorial [ˌekwəˈtɔːriəl] *adj* ecuatorial

Equatorial Guinea *n* Guinea *f* Ecuatorial

equestrian [ɪˈkwestriən] I. *adj* ecuestre; ~ events pruebas hípicas; ~ statue estatua *f* ecuestre II. *n* (*man*) jinete *m;* (*woman*) amazona *f*

equidistant [ˌiːkwɪˈdɪstənt] *adj* equidistante

equilateral [ˌiːkwɪˈlætərəl, *Am:* -ˈlæţ-] *adj* MAT equilátero, -a

equilibrium [ˌiːkwɪˈlɪbriəm] *n no pl* equilibrio *m*

equinoctial [ˌiːkwɪˈnɒkʃl, *Am:* -ˈnɑːk-] *adj* equinoccial

equinox [ˈiːkwɪnɒks, *Am:* -nɑːks] <-es> *n* equinoccio *m;* autumn ~ equinoccio de otoño

equip [ɪˈkwɪp] <-pp-> *vt* 1. (*fit out*) equipar; to ~ sb with sth proveer a alguien de algo 2. (*prepare*) preparar

equipment [ɪˈkwɪpmənt] *n no pl* equipo *m;* camping ~ accesorios *mpl* de cámping; office ~ material *m* de oficina

equitable [ˈekwɪtəbl, *Am:* -ţə-] *adj* equitativo, -a

equity [ˈekwəti, *Am:* -ţi] <-ies> *n no pl* 1. (*fairness*) equidad *f* 2. *pl, Brit* FIN acciones *fpl* ordinarias

eq(uiv). *abbr of* equivalent equivalente

equivalence [ɪˈkwɪvələns] *n no pl* equivalencia *f*

equivalent [ɪˈkwɪvələnt] I. *adj* equivalente; to be ~ to sth equivaler a algo II. *n* equivalente *m*

equivocal [ɪˈkwɪvəkl] *adj* equívoco, -a

equivocate [ɪˈkwɪvəkeɪt] *vi form* hablar de forma equívoca

equivocation [ɪˌkwɪvəˈkeɪʃən] *n no pl* ambigüedad *f*

ER [ˌiːˈɑːʳ, *Am:* -ˈɑːr] *n abbr of* Elizabeth Regina Reina *f* Isabel

era [ˈɪərə, *Am:* ˈɪrə] *n* era *f;* communist ~ era comunista; post-war ~ época *f* de la posguerra; **to usher in an** ~ marcar el cominezo de una era

eradicate [ɪ'rædɪkeɪt] *vt* erradicar

erase [ɪ'reɪz, *Am:* -'reɪs] *vt a.* INFOR borrar; **to ~ a deficit** eliminar un déficit

eraser [ɪ'reɪzəʳ, *Am:* -'reɪsəʳ] *n Am* goma *f* de borrar

erasure [ɪ'reɪʒəʳ, *Am:* -ʃəʳ] *n Am* borradura *f*

ere [eəʳ] **I.** *prep liter* antes de; **~ long** dentro de poco **II.** *conj liter* antes de que

erect [ɪ'rekt] **I.** *adj* erguido, -a; ANAT erecto, -a **II.** *vt* eregir; (*construct*) construir; (*put up*) levantar

erectile [ɪ'rektaɪl, *Am:* -təl] *adj* ANAT eréctil

erection [ɪ'rekʃən] *n* **1.** *no pl* ARCHIT construcción *f* **2.** ANAT erección *f*

erg [ɜ:g, *Am:* ɜ:rg] *n* PHYS ergio *m*

ergonomic [ˌɜ:gə'nɒmɪk, *Am:* ˌɜ:rgə-'nɑ:mɪk] *adj* ergonómico, -a

ergonomics *n* ergonomía *f*

ERM [ˌi:ɑ:r'em] *abbr of* **Exchange Rate Mechanism** SME *m*

ermine ['ɜ:mɪn, *Am:* 'ɜ:r-] *n* armiño *m*

erode [ɪ'rəʊd, *Am:* -'roʊd] **I.** *vt* erosionar **II.** *vi* erosionarse

erogenous [ɪ'rɒdʒənəs, *Am:* -'rɑ:dʒɪ-] *adj* erógeno, -a

erosion [ɪ'rəʊʒən, *Am:* -'roʊ-] *n no pl* erosión *f*

erotic [ɪ'rɒtɪk, *Am:* -'rɑ:t̬ɪk] *adj* erótico, -a

eroticism [ɪ'rɒtɪsɪzəm, *Am:* -'rɑ:t̬ə-] *n no pl* erotismo *m*

err [ɜ:ʳ, *Am:* ɜ:r] *vi* errar; **to ~ on the side of sth** pecar (por exceso) de algo; **to ~ on the side of caution** pecar de cauteloso ►**to ~ is human** *prov* errar es humano *prov*

errand ['erənd] *n* recado *m*; **to run an ~** (salir a) hacer un recado; **an ~ of mercy** *form* una misión de caridad

errand boy *n* chico *m* de los recados

errant ['erənt] *adj* **1.** *form* descarriado, -a **2.** *iron* (*unfaithful*) infiel

erratic [ɪ'rætɪk, *Am:* -'ræt̬-] *adj* **1.** GEO errático, -a **2.** MED (*pulse*) irregular

erratum [e'rɑ:təm, *Am:* -t̬əm] <-ta> *n form* errata *f*

erroneous [ɪ'rəʊnɪəs, *Am:* ə'roʊ-] *adj* erróneo, -a; ~ **assumption** suposición equivocada

error ['erəʳ, *Am:* -əʳ] *n* error *m*; **to do sth in ~** hacer algo por equivocación; **human ~** error humano ►**to see the ~ of one's ways** darse cuenta de lo mal que uno ha actuado; **to show sb the ~ of his/her ways** demostrar a alguien lo equivocado de su actuación

error message *n* INFOR mensaje *m* de error

error-prone *adj* propenso, -a a errores **error rate** *n* porcentaje *m* de errores

erudite ['eru:daɪt, *Am:* -jə-] *adj* erudito, -a

erudition [ˌeru:'dɪʃən, *Am:* -ju:'-] *n no pl* erudición *f*

erupt [ɪ'rʌpt] *vi* **1.** (*explode: volcano*) entrar en erupción; *fig* estallar **2.** MED salir

eruption [ɪ'rʌpʃən] *n* erupción *f*; *fig* estallido *m*

escalate ['eskəleɪt] **I.** *vi* (*increase*) aumentar; (*incidents*) intensificarse; **to ~ into sth** terminar en algo **II.** *vt* intensificar

escalation [ˌeskə'leɪʃən] *n* escalada *f*; **~ of tension** escalada de la tensión

escalator ['eskəleɪtəʳ, *Am:* -t̬əʳ] *n* escalera *f* mecánica

escalope ['eskələp, *Am:* ˌeskə'loʊp] *n* escalope *m*

escapade [ˌeskə'peɪd] *n* aventura *f*; (*mischievous*) travesura *f*

escape [ɪ'skeɪp] **I.** *vi* escaparse; (*person*) huir de; **to ~ from** escaparse de; **to ~ from a program** INFOR salir de un programa **II.** *vt* escapar a; (*avoid*) evitar; **to ~ sb('s attention)** pasar desapercibido a alguien; **nothing ~s his attention** no se le escapa ni una; **the word ~s me** se me ha ido la palabra (de la cabeza); **a cry ~d him** se le escapó un grito **III.** *n* **1.** (*act*) fuga *f*; **to have a narrow ~** salvarse por muy poco **2.** (*outflow*) escape *m* **3.** LAW **~ clause** cláusula *f* de excepción

escapee [ɪˌskeɪ'pi:] *n* fugitivo, -a *m, f*

escapism [ɪ'skeɪpɪzəm] *n no pl* escapismo *m*

escapist **I.** *n* escapista *mf* **II.** *adj* escapista; **~ literature** literatura *f* de evasión

escarpment [ɪ'skɑ:pmənt, *Am:* e'skɑ:rp-] *n* escarpa *f*

ESCB *n s.* European System of Central Banks SEBC *m*

eschew [ɪ'stʃu:, *Am:* es-] *vt form* evitar

escort ['eskɔ:t, *Am:* -kɔ:rt] **I.** *vt* acompañar; (*politician*) escoltar **II.** *n* **1.** (*companion*) acompañante *mf* **2.** (*paid companion*) señorito, -a *m, f* de compañía **3.** *no pl* (*guard*) escolta *f*

escutcheon [ɪ'skʌtʃən] *n* blasón *m* ►**a blot on sb's ~** una mancha en el honor de alguien

ESE *n abbr of* **east-southeast** ESE *m*

Eskimo ['eskɪməʊ, *Am:* -kəmoʊ] <-s> *n* **1.** (*person*) esquimal *mf* **2.** *no pl* LING esquimal *m*

ESL [ˌi:es'el] *n abbr of* **English as a second language** inglés *m* como segunda lengua

ESN [ˌi:es'en] *abbr of* **educationally subnormal** impedido, -a para aprender

esophagus [i:'sɒfəgəs, *Am:* ɪ'sɑ:fə-] *n Am* esófago *m*

esoteric [ˌesəʊ'terɪk, *Am:* ˌesə'-] *adj* esotérico, -a

ESP [ˌi:es'pi:] *n abbr of* **extrasensory perception** percepción *f* extrasensorial

esp. *abbr of* **especially** especialmente

espadrille ['espədrɪl] *n* alpargata *f*

especial [ɪ'speʃl] *adj* especial

especially [ɪ'speʃəli] *adv* **1.** (*particularly*) especialmente; **I bought this ~ for you** lo compré expresamente para ti **2.** (*in particular*) en particular

espionage ['espɪənɑ:ʒ] *n no pl* espionaje *m*;

industrial ~ espionaje industrial
esplanade [ˌesplə'neɪd, *Am:* 'esplənɑ:d] *n* paseo *m* marítimo
espousal [ɪ'spaʊzl] *n no pl, form* apoyo *m*
espouse [ɪ'spaʊz] *vt* apoyar
espresso [e'spresəʊ, *Am:* -oʊ] <-s> *n* café *m* exprés
Esq. *abbr of* Esquire Sr.
Esquire [ɪ'skwaɪəʳ, *Am:* 'eskwaɪɚ] *n Brit* (*special title*) Señor *m*
essay¹ ['eseɪ] *n* 1. LIT ensayo *m* 2. SCHOOL redacción *f;* **an ~ on sth** una redacción sobre algo
essay² [e'seɪ] *vt* 1. (*try*) intentar hacer 2. (*test*) probar
essayist *n* ensayista *mf*
essence ['esns] *n* 1. *no pl* esencia *f;* **time is of the ~ here** el tiempo es de vital importancia aquí 2. (*in food*) esencia *f,* extracto *m*
essential [ɪ'senʃl] I. *adj* esencial; (*difference*) fundamental; **to be ~ to sb/sth** ser esencial para alguien/algo II. *n pl* **the ~s** los elementos básicos [*o* esenciales]; **the bare ~s** lo justamente necesario
essentially [ɪ'senʃəli] *adv* esencialmente
est. 1. *abbr of* estimated est. 2. *abbr of* established fundado, -a
establish [ɪ'stæblɪʃ] I. *vt* 1. (*found*) fundar; (*commission, hospital*) crear; (*dictatorship*) instaurar 2. (*begin: relationship*) entablar 3. (*set: precedent*) sentar; (*priorities, norm*) establecer 4. (*secure*) asegurar; (*order*) imponer; **he ~ed his authority over the workers** afirmó su autoridad sobre los obreros; **to ~ a reputation as a pianist** hacerse un nombre como pianista 5. (*demonstrate*) **to ~ sb as sth** acreditar a alguien como algo 6. (*determine*) determinar, establecer; (*facts*) verificar; (*truth*) comprobar; **to ~ whether/where ...** determinar si/dónde...; **to ~ that ...** comprobar que... 7. ADMIN **to ~ residence** fijar la residencia II. *vi* establecerse
established [ɪ'stæblɪʃt] *adj* 1. (*founded*) fundado, -a 2. (*fact*) comprobado, -a; (*procedures*) establecido, -a
establishment [ɪ'stæblɪʃmənt] *n* 1. (*business*) empresa *f;* **family ~** empresa *f* familiar 2. (*organization*) establecimiento *m;* **educational ~** centro *m* educativo; **financial ~** institución *f* financiera; **the Establishment** POL la clase dirigente
estate [ɪ'steɪt] *n* 1. (*piece of land*) finca *f;* **country ~** finca *f,* hacienda *f AmL* 2. LAW patrimonio *m;* **housing ~** urbanización *f;* **industrial ~** polígono *m* industrial; **council ~** viviendas *fpl* de protección oficial 3. *Brit* (*car*) coche *m* familiar
estate agent *n Brit* agente *mf* de la propiedad inmobiliaria **estate car** *n Brit* coche *m* familiar **estate duty** <-ies> *n,* **estate tax** *n* impuesto *m* sobre sucesiones
esteem [ɪ'stiːm] I. *n no pl* estima *f;* **to fall/rise in sb's ~** perder/ganarse la estima de alguien; **to hold sb in high/low ~** tener a al-

guien en gran/poca estima II. *vt* 1. (*respect*) apreciar, valorar 2. (*consider*) considerar, estimar; **to ~ it an honour to do sth** considerar un honor (poder) hacer algo
esteemed *adj* apreciado, -a, valorado, -a; **highly ~** muy apreciado
esthetic [iːs'θetɪk] *adj* estético, -a
esthetics *n* estética *f*
estimable ['estɪməbl] *adj form* estimable
estimate ['estɪmeɪt, *Am:* -mɪt] I. *vt* calcular; **to ~ that ...** calcular que... II. *n* cálculo *m* (aproximado); **rough ~** *inf* cálculo aproximado; **at a rough ~** aproximadamente
estimated ['estɪmeɪtɪd, *Am:* -t̬ɪd] *adj* estimado, -a
estimation [ˌestɪ'meɪʃən] *n no pl* opinión *f;* **in my ~** a mi juicio
Estonia [es'təʊniə, *Am:* es'toʊ-] *n* Estonia *f*
Estonian [es'təʊniən, *Am:* es'toʊ-] I. *adj* estonio, -a II. *n* 1. (*person*) estonio, -a *m, f* 2. LING estonio *m*
estrange [ɪ'streɪndʒ] *vt* **to ~ sb from sb/ sth** distanciar a alguien de alguien/algo
estranged *adj* (*distance*) distanciado, -a; (*state*) separado, -a
estrangement [ɪ'streɪndʒmənt] *n* distanciamiento *m*
estrogen ['iːstrəʊdʒən, *Am:* 'estrədʒən] *Am s.* **oestrogen**
estuary ['estʃʊəri, *Am:* 'estʃuːeri] <-ies> *n* estuario *m*
ETA [ˌiːtiː'eɪ] *abbr of* estimated time of arrival hora *f* prevista de llegada
et al. [et'æl] *abbr of* et alii et al
etc. *abbr of* et cetera etc.
et cetera [ɪt'setərə, *Am:* -'set̬ɚ-] *adv* etcétera
etch [etʃ] *vt* 1. grabar (al agua fuerte) 2. *fig* **to be ~ed on sb's memory** estar grabado en la memoria de alguien
etcher *n* aguafuertista *mf*
etching *n* aguafuerte *m*
ETD *abbr of* estimated time of departure hora *f* prevista de salida
eternal [ɪ'tɜːnl, *Am:* -'tɜːr-] *adj* 1. (*lasting forever*) eterno, -a 2. (*constant*) constante, incesante ▶~ **triangle** *Brit* triángulo amoroso
eternally [ɪ'tɜːnəli, *Am:* -'tɜːr-] *adv* 1. (*forever*) eternamente 2. (*constantly*) constantemente, incesantemente
eternity [ɪ'tɜːnəti, *Am:* -'tɜːrnət̬i] *n no pl* eternidad *f;* **to seem like an ~** parecer una eternidad; **to wait an ~ for sb** esperar una eternidad a alguien
ether ['iːθəʳ, *Am:* -θɚ] *n no pl* éter *m*
ethereal [ɪ'θɪəriəl, *Am:* -'θɪrɪ-] *adj* etéreo, -a
ethic ['eθɪk] *n* **work ~** ética del trabajo *f*
ethical *adj* ético, -a
ethics *n* + *sing vb* ética *f*
Ethiopia [ˌiːθi'əʊpɪə, *Am:* -'oʊ-] *n no pl* Etiopía *f*
Ethiopian [ˌiːθi'əʊpɪən, *Am:* -'oʊ-] I. *n* etíope *mf* II. *adj* etíope

ethnic ['eθnɪk] *adj* étnico, -a; ~ **cleaning** limpieza étnica; ~ **costumes** trajes *mpl* tradicionales

ethnology [eθ'nɒlədʒi, *Am:* -'nɑ:lə-] *n no pl* etnología *f*

ethos ['i:θɒs, *Am:* -θɑ:s] *n no pl* espiritú *m;* **the working-class** ~ los valores de la clase trabajadora

ethyl alcohol ['eθɪl 'ælkəhɒl, *Am:* 'eθəl 'ælkəhɑ:l] *n* alcohol *m* etílico

etiquette ['etɪket, *Am:* 'eţɪkɪt] *n no pl* etiqueta *f;* **court** ~ etiqueta de palacio

etymological [ˌetɪmə'lɒdʒɪkl, *Am:* ˌeţɪmə'lɑ:dʒɪkl] *adj* etimológico, -a

etymology [ˌetɪ'mɒlədʒi, *Am:* ˌeţɪ'mɑ:lə-] *n no pl* etimología *f*

EU [ˌi:'ju:] *n abbr of* European Union UE *f*

eucalyptus [ˌju:kə'lɪptəs] <-es *o* -ti> *n* eucalipto *m*

eucalyptus oil *n no pl* bálsamo *m* de eucalipto

Eucharist ['ju:kərɪst] *n no pl* REL **the** ~ la Eucaristía

eulogize ['ju:lədʒaɪz] I. *vt form* elogiar II. *vi form* **to** ~ **over sth/sb** elogiar algo/a alguien

eulogy ['ju:lədʒi] <-ies> *n form* **1.** (*high praise*) elogio *m* **2.** LIT panegírico *m;* **to deliver a** ~ hacer un panegírico

eunuch ['ju:nək] *n* eunuco *m*

euphemism ['ju:fəmɪzəm] *n* eufemismo *m*

euphemistic [ˌju:fə'mɪstɪk] *adj* eufemístico, -a

euphony ['ju:fəni] *n no pl, form* eufonía *f*

euphoria [ju:'fɔ:rɪə] *n no pl* euforia *f*

euphoric [ju:'fɒrɪk, *Am:* -'fɔ:rɪk] *adj* eufórico, -a

EUR *n s.* Euro EUR *m*

Eurasia [juə'reɪʒə, *Am:* ju'-] *n no pl* Eurasia *f*

Eurasian [juə'reɪʒən, *Am:* ju'-] I. *adj* euroasiático, -a II. *n* euroasiático, -a *m, f*

Euratom [juə'rætəm, *Am:* ju'ræt-] *n abbr of* European Atomic Energy Community Euratom *f*

eurhythmics [ju:'rɪðmɪks, *Am:* ju'-] *n Brit,* **eurythmics** *n Am + sing vb* euritmia *f*

euro ['juərəu, *Am:* 'jurou] *n* euro *m*

euro cent *n* céntimo *m* de euro

Eurocheque ['juərətʃek, *Am:* 'jurou-] *n* eurocheque *m*

euro coins *npl* monedas *fpl* de euro

Eurocrat ['juərəukræt, *Am:* 'jurə-] *n* eurócrata *mf*

eurocurrency *n* eurodivisa *f* **Eurodollar** *n* eurodólar *m* **euro notes** *npl* billetes *mpl* de euro

Europe ['juərəp, *Am:* 'jurəp] *n no pl* Europa *f*

European [juərə'pɪən, *Am:* jurə-] I. *adj* europeo, -a II. *n* europeo, -a *m, f*

European Central Bank *n* Banco *m* Central Europeo **European Commission** *n* Comisión *f* Europea **European Community** *n* Comunidad *f* Europea **European Council** *n* Consejo *m* Europeo **European**

Court of Auditors *n* Tribunal *m* Europeo de Cuentas **European Court of Justice** *n* Tribunal *m* de Justicia Europeo **European Economic and Monetary Union** *n* Unión *f* Económica y Monetaria Europea **European Investment Bank** *n* Banco *m* Europeo de Inversiones **European Monetary Institute** *n* Instituto *m* Monetario Europeo **European Monetary System** *n* Sistema *m* Monetario Europeo **European Parliament** *n* Parlamento *m* Europeo **European Single Market** *n* Mercado *m* Único Europeo **European System of Central Banks** *n* Sistema *m* Europeo de Bancos Centrales **European Union** *n* Unión *f* Europea

euthanasia [ˌju:θə'neɪzɪə, *Am:* -ʒə] *n no pl* eutanasia *f*

evacuate [ɪ'vækjʊeɪt] *vt* (*people*) evacuar; (*building*) desocupar

evacuation [ɪˌvækjʊ'eɪʃən] *n* evacuación *f;* ~ **of the bowels** MED evacuación *f*

evacuee [ɪˌvækju:'i:] *n* evacuado, -a *m, f*

evade [ɪ'veɪd] *vt* (*responsibility, person*) eludir; (*police*) escaparse de; (*taxes*) evadir; **to** ~ **doing sth** evitar hacer algo

evaluate [ɪ'væljʊeɪt] *vt* (*value*) tasar; (*result*) evaluar; (*person*) examinar

evaluation [ɪˌvæljʊ'eɪʃən] *n* evaluación *f;* (*of an experience*) valoración *f;* (*of a book*) crítica *f*

evangelical [ˌi:væn'dʒelɪkl] I. *n* evangélico, -a *m, f* II. *adj* evangélico, -a

evangelist [ɪ'vændʒəlɪst] *n* evangelista *mf*

evangelize [ɪ'vændʒəlaɪz] I. *vt* evangelizar II. *vi* evangelizar

evaporate [ɪ'væpəreɪt] I. *vt* evaporar; ~**d milk** leche evaporada II. *vi* evaporarse; *fig* desaparecer

evaporation [ɪˌvæpə'reɪʃən] *n* evaporación *f*

evasion [ɪ'veɪʒən] *n* **1.** (*of tax, responsability*) evasión *f* **2.** (*avoidance*) evasiva *f*

evasive [ɪ'veɪsɪv] *adj* evasivo, -a

eve [i:v] *n no pl* víspera *f;* **on the** ~ **of** en vísperas de; **Christmas Eve** Nochebuena *f;* **New Year's Eve** Nochevieja *f*

Eve [i:v] *n* Eva *f*

even ['i:vn] I. *adv* **1.** (*indicates the unexpected*) incluso; **not** ~ ni siquiera **2.** (*despite*) ~ **if ...** aunque...; ~ **so ...** aun así...; ~ **though ...** aunque... **3.** (*used to intensify*) hasta **4.** + *superl* (*all the more*) aún; **it will be** ~ **colder** hará incluso más frío II. *adj* **1.** (*level*) llano, -a; (*surface*) liso, -a **2.** (*equalized*) igualado, -a; **the chances are about** ~ hay casi las mismas posibilidades; **to be on** ~ **terms** estar en las mismas condiciones; **to get** ~ **with sb** ajustar cuentas con alguien **3.** (*of same size, amount*) igual **4.** (*constant, regular*) uniforme; (*rate*) constante **5.** (*fair*) ecuánime **6.** MAT par III. *vt* **1.** (*make level*) nivelar; (*surface*) allanar **2.** (*equalize*) igualar

◆**even out** I. *vi* (*prices*) nivelarse II. *vt* igua-

lar
◆**even up** *vt* igualar
evening ['iːvnɪŋ] *n* (*early*) tarde *f;* (*late*) noche *f;* good ~! ¡buenas tardes/noches!; in the ~ por la tarde/noche; **that** ~ esa noche; **the previous** ~ la noche anterior; **every** Monday ~ cada lunes por la noche; **on Monday** ~ el lunes por la noche; **during the** ~ durante la noche; **one July** ~ una noche de julio; **8 o'clock in the** ~ las 8 de la noche; **at the end of the** ~ al final de la noche; **all** ~ toda la noche
evening class *n* clase *f* nocturna **evening dress** *n* traje *m* de noche; **to wear** ~ ir de etiqueta **evening edition** *n* edición *f* vespertina **evening gown** *n* traje *m* de noche **evening meal** *n* cena *f* **evening (news)paper** *n* periódico *m* de la tarde **evening performance** *n* función *f* de noche **evening prayer** *n* oración *f* de la tarde **evening service** *n* misa *f* vespertina **evening star** *n* estrella *f* vespertina
evenly ['iːvənli] *adv* **1.** (*calmly*) apaciblemente; **to state sth** ~ decir algo sin alterarse **2.** (*equally*) igualmente; **to divide sth** ~ dividir algo de forma equitativa
evenness ['iːvnnɪs] *n no pl* **1.** uniformidad *f* **2.** (*calmness*) serenidad *f*
evens *adj Brit* **the chances are** ~ las posibilidades son del cincuenta por ciento
event [ɪ'vent] *n* **1.** (*happening*) evento *m;* sporting ~ acontecimiento *m* deportivo; **to be swept along by the tide of** ~s dejarse llevar por los acontecimientos **2.** (*case*) caso *m;* **in any** ~, **at all** ~s *Brit* en cualquier caso; **in the** ~ (**that**) **it rains** en caso de que llueva; **in either** ~ en cualquier caso
even-tempered ['iːvən'tempəd] *adj* ecuánime
eventful [ɪ'ventfəl] *adj* accidentado, -a
eventual [ɪ'ventʃʊəl] *adj* final
eventuality [ɪˌventʃʊ'æləti, *Am:* -ṭi] <-ies> *n inv* eventualidad *f*
eventually [ɪ'ventʃʊəli] *adv* **1.** (*finally*) finalmente **2.** (*some day*) con el tiempo
ever ['evə', *Am:* -ə'] *adv* **1.** (*on any occasion*) alguna vez; **have you** ~ **been to Barcelona?** ¿has estado alguna vez en Barcelona?; **for the first time** ~ por primera vez; **the hottest day** ~ el día mas caliente; **better than** ~ mejor que nunca; **have you** ~ **seen such a thing!** ¡habráse visto semejante cosa!; **would you** ~ **dye your hair?** te teñirías el pelo? **2.** (*in negative statements*) nunca, jamás; **nobody has** ~ **heard of him** nadie ha oído nunca hablar de él; **never** ~ nunca jamás; **hardly** ~ casi nunca; **nothing** ~ **happens** nunca pasa nada; **don't you** ~ **do that again!** no se te ocurra volve **3.** (*always*) ~ **after** desde entonces; **as** ~ como siempre; ~ **since** ... desde que...; ~ **since** (*since then*) desde entonces **4.** *Brit, inf* (*very*) **I'm** ~ **so grateful** se lo agradezco profundamente; **your're** ~ **so kind!** ¡usted es

(*siempre*) tán amable!; **I am** ~ **so sorry** lo siento muchísimo; **it's** ~ **so hot** hace muchísimo calor; **thank you** ~ **so much** muchísimas gracias **5.** (*used to intensify*) **who** ~ **was that woman?** ¿quién demonios era esa mujer?; **all he** ~ **does is** +*infin* lo único que hace es +*infin;* **don't you** ~ **come here again!** ¡no se te ocurra volver a venir aquí!
everglade ['evəgleɪd, *Am:* -ə'-] *n Am:* tierra baja pantanosa cubierta de altas hierbas
evergreen ['evəgriːn, *Am:* -ə'-] **I.** *n* árbol *m* de hoja perenne **II.** *adj* de hoja perenne; *fig* imperecedero, -a
everlasting [ˌevə'lɑːstɪŋ, *Am:* -ə'læstɪŋ] *adj* **1.** (*undying*) imperecedero, -a; (*gratitude*) eterno, -a *f* **2.** (*incessant*) interminable
evermore [ˌevə'mɔː', *Am:* -ə'mɔːr] *adv liter* eternamente; **for** ~ por siempre jamás
every ['evri] *adj* **1.** (*each*) cada; ~ **time** cada vez; **her** ~ **wish** su más mínimo deseo; **not** ~ **book can be borrowed** no todo libro puede ser tomado en préstamo **2.** (*all*) todo, -a; ~ **one of them** todos y cada uno de ellos; **in** ~ **way** de todas las maneras **3.** (*repeated*) ~ **other week** en semanas alternas; ~ **now and then** [*o* **again**] de vez en cuando ►~ **little helps** *prov* cualquier ayuda es buena
everybody ['evriˌbɒdi, *Am:* -ˌbɑːdi] *pron indef, sing* todos, todo el mundo; ~ **but Paul** todos menos Paul; ~ **else** todos los demás; ~ **who agrees** todos los que están de acuerdo
everybody else *pron* todos los demás
everyday ['evrɪdeɪ] *adj* diario, -a; (*clothes*) de diario; (*event*) ordinario, -a; (*language*) corriente; (*life*) cotidiano, -a
everyone ['evrɪwʌn] *pron s.* **everybody**
everything ['evrɪθɪŋ] *pron indef, sing* todo; **is** ~ **all right?** ¿está todo bien?; ~ **they drink** todo lo que beben; **to be** ~ **to sb** serlo todo para alguien; **to do** ~ **necessary/one can** hacer todo lo necesario/lo posible; **time is** ~ el tiempo lo es todo; **wealth isn't** ~ la riqueza no lo es todo
everywhere ['evrɪweə', *Am:* -wer] *adv* en todas partes; ~ **else** en cualquier otro sitio; **to look** ~ **for sth** buscar algo por todas partes; **to travel** ~ viajar a todas partes
evict [ɪ'vɪkt] *vt* desahuciar
eviction [ɪ'vɪkʃən] *n* desahucio *m*
evidence ['evɪdəns] *n* **1.** *no pl* (*sign*) indicios *mpl* **2.** (*proof*) prueba *f* **3.** (*testimony*) testimonio *m;* **on the** ~ **of those present** según las declaraciones de los presentes; **to give** ~ (**on sth/against sb**) prestar declaración (sobre algo/contra alguien); **to turn Queen's** ~ *Brit* delatar a los cómplices; **to turn state's** ~ **against sb** *Am* delatar a alguien **4.** (*view*) evidencia *f;* **to be** (**much**) **in** ~ ser (muy) manifiesto
evident ['evɪdənt] *adj* evidente; **to be** ~ ser evidente; **to be** ~ **to sb** ser evidente para alguien; **to be** ~ **in sth** manifestarse en algo; **it is** ~ **that** ... está claro que...

evidently *adv* evidentemente
evil ['iːvl] I. *adj* malo, -a; **the ~ day** *iron* el día crítico; **~ eye** mal *m* de ojo; **~ spirit** espíritu maligno; **to have an ~ tongue** tener una lengua afilada II. *n* mal *m;* **social ~** lacra *f* social; **an aura of ~** un aura de maldad; **good and ~** el bien y el mal; **the lesser of two ~s** el menor de dos males
evil-doer [ˌiːvl'duːər, *Am:* -ɚ] *n* malhechor(a) *m(f)* **evil-minded** *adj* malintencionado, -a **evil-tempered** *adj* de muy mal genio; **to be ~** tener muy mal genio
evince [ɪ'vɪns] *vt form* dar señales de; **to ~ interest** mostrar interés
evocation [ˌevə'keɪʃən] *n form* evocación *f*
evocative [ɪ'vɒkətɪv, *Am:* -'vɑːkə̬tɪv] *adj* evocador(a); **an ~ image** una imagen sugerente; **to be ~ of sth** evocar algo
evoke [ɪ'vəʊk, *Am:* -'voʊk] *vt* evocar
evolution [ˌiːvə'luːʃən, *Am:* ˌevə-] *n no pl* evolución *f; fig* desarrollo *m*
evolve [ɪ'vɒlv, *Am:* -'vɑːlv] I. *vi* (*gradually develop*) desarrollarse; (*animals*) evolucionar; **to ~ into sth** convertirse en algo II. *vt* desarrollar; **to ~ new forms of life** crear nuevas formas de vida
ewe [juː] *n* oveja *f*
ewer ['juːər, *Am:* -ɚ] *n* aguamanil *m*
ex [eks] <-es> *n inf* ex *mf*
exacerbate [ɪg'zæsəbeɪt, *Am:* -ɚ-] *vt* exacerbar
exact [ɪg'zækt] I. *adj* exacto, -a; **to be ~ in one's reporting** ser muy preciso al informar; **the ~ opposite** justo el contrario II. *vt* exigir; **to ~ sth from sb** exigir algo a alguien
exacting *adj* exigente
exactitude [ɪg'zæktɪtjuːd, *Am:* -tətuːd] *n no pl* exactitud *f*
exactly [ɪg'zæktli] *adv* exactamente; **~ like ...** justo como...; **how/what/where ~ ...** cómo/qué/dónde exactamente...; **I don't ~ agree to that** no estoy del todo de acuerdo en eso; **not ~** no precisamente; **~!** ¡exacto!
exactness [ɪg'zæktnɪs] *n no pl* exactitud *f*
exaggerate [ɪg'zædʒəreɪt] *vi, vt* exagerar; **let's not ~!** ¡no exageremos!
exaggerated [ɪg'zædʒəreɪtɪd, *Am:* -t̬ɪd] *adj* exagerado, -a; **greatly ~** muy exagerado
exaggeration [ɪgˌzædʒə'reɪʃən] *n* exageración *f;* **it's no ~ to say that ...** no es exagerado decir que...
exalt [ɪg'zɔːlt] *vt* 1. (*praise*) exaltar; (*honour*) ensalzar; **to ~ sth as a virtue** elevar algo a la categoría de virtud 2. (*raise rank*) ascender
exaltation [ˌegzɔː'teɪʃən] *n no pl* exaltación *f*
exalted [ɪg'zɔːltɪd, *Am:* -t̬ɪd] *adj* 1. (*elevated*) elevado, -a; **~ rank** alto rango 2. (*jubilant*) exaltado, -a
exam [ɪg'zæm] *n* examen *m*
examination [ɪgˌzæmɪ'neɪʃən] *n* 1. (*exam*) examen *m* 2. (*investigation*) investigación *f;* **medical ~** reconocimiento *m* médico 3. LAW

interrogatorio *m*
examination paper *n* hoja *f* de examen **examination results** *n* resultados *m pl* del examen
examine [ɪg'zæmɪn] *vt* 1. (*test*) **to ~ sb** (**in sth**) examinar a alguien (de algo); **to be ~d** examinarse 2. (*study*) estudiar; **to ~ credentials** comprobar las credenciales; **to ~ the effects of sth** estudiar los efectos de algo 3. LAW interrogar 4. MED hacer un reconocimiento médico de
examinee [ɪgˌzæmɪ'niː] *n* examinando, -a *m, f*
examiner [ɪg'zæmɪnər, *Am:* -ɚ] *n* examinador(a) *m(f)*
examining board *n* junta *f* examinadora
example [ɪg'zɑːmpl, *Am:* ɪg'zæm-] *n* 1. (*sample, model*) ejemplo *m;* **for ~** por ejemplo; **to be a shining ~ of sth** ser un ejemplo magnífico de algo; **to follow sb's ~** seguir el ejemplo de alguien; **to give** (**sb**) **an ~** (**of sth**) dar (a alguien) un ejemplo (de algo); **to set a good ~** dar un buen ejemplo 2. (*copy*) ejemplar *m*
exasperate [ɪg'zɑːspəreɪt] *vt* exasperar; **he ~s me** me saca de quicio
exasperating [ɪg'zɑːspəreɪtɪŋ, *Am:* -t̬ɪŋ] *adj* irritante
exasperation [ɪgˌzɑːspə'reɪʃən] *n no pl* exasperación *f*
excavate ['ekskəveɪt] *vt* 1. (*expose*) desenterrar 2. (*hollow*) excavar
excavation [ˌekskə'veɪʃən] *n* excavación *f*
excavator ['ekskəveɪtər, *Am:* -t̬ɚ] *n Aus, Brit* excavadora *f*
exceed [ɪk'siːd] *vt* exceder; (*outshine*) sobrepasar
exceedingly *adv* excesivamente
excel [ɪk'sel] <-ll-> I. *vi* sobresalir; **to ~ at sth** destacar en algo II. *vt* **to ~ oneself** lucirse
excellence ['eksələns] *n no pl* excelencia *f*
Excellency ['eksələnsi] *n* Excelencia *f;* **His ~** Su Excelencia; (**Your**) **~** (Su/Vuestra) Excelencia
excellent ['eksələnt] *adj* excelente
except [ɪk'sept] I. *prep* **~** (**for**) excepto, salvo, zafo *AmL;* **to do nothing ~ wait** no hacer nada más que esperar II. *vt form* exceptuar; **to ~ sth/sb from sth** excluir algo/a alguien de algo
excepting *prep* excepto, salvo
exception [ɪk'sepʃən] *n* excepción *f;* **to be an ~** ser una excepción; **to make an ~** hacer una excepción; **with the ~ of ...** con excepción de...; **to take ~** (**to sth**) ofenderse (por algo); **I take great ~ to your last comment** me ha molestado mucho tu último comentario ▶**the ~ proves the rule** *prov* la excepción confirma la regla *prov*
exceptional [ɪk'sepʃənl] *adj* excepcional
exceptionally [ɪk'sepʃnəli] *adv* excepcionalmente; **to be ~ clever** ser especialmente listo
excerpt ['eksɜːpt, *Am:* -sɜːrpt] *n* extracto *m*

E

excess [ɪk'ses] <-es> *n* exceso *m;* **to eat to** ~ comer en exceso; **to carry sth to** ~ llevar algo al exceso; **in** ~ **of** superior a
excess amount *n* cantidad *f* excedente
excess baggage *n,* **excess luggage** *n* exceso *m* de equipaje **excess charge** *n* suplemento *m* **excess expenditure** *n* gastos *mpl* adicionales **excess fare** *n* suplemento *m*
excessive [ɪk'sesɪv] *adj* excesivo, -a; (*claim*) exagerado, -a; (*violence*) gratuito, -a
excess production *n* excedente *m* de producción **excess supply** *n* exceso *m* de oferta
exchange [ɪk'stʃeɪndʒ] I. *vt* 1. (*trade for the equivalent*) cambiar 2. (*interchange*) intercambiar; **to** ~ **blows** pegarse; **to** ~ **words** discutir II. *n* 1. (*interchange, trade*) intercambio *m;* **in** ~ **for sth** a cambio de algo; ~ **of (gun)fire** tiroteo *m* 2. FIN, ECON cambio *m;* **foreign** ~ divisas *fpl* 3. (*verbal interchange*) ~ **of threats** intercambio *m* de amenazas
exchangeable *adj* cambiable; (*goods*) canjeable; ~ **currency** divisa *f;* ~ **token** cupón *m* canjeable; **to be** ~ **for sth** ser intercambiable por algo
exchange broker *n,* **exchange dealer** *n* corredor(a) *m(f)* de bolsa **exchange conditions** *n* condiciones *fpl* de cambio **exchange control** *n* control *m* de divisas **exchange course mechanism** *n* ECON, FIN mecanismo *m* complementario de cambio **exchange market** *n* mercado *m* de divisas **exchange rate** *n* tipo *m* de cambio **exchange regulations** *npl* ECON, FIN normativa *f* cambiaria **exchange restrictions** *n* ECON, FIN control *m* de divisas **exchange stability** *n* ECON, FIN estabilidad *f* cambiaria **exchange student** *n* estudiante *mf* de intercambio **exchange teacher** *n* profesor(a) *m(f)* de intercambio **exchange value** *n* contravalor *m*
exchequer [ɪks'tʃekə', *Am:* -ɚ] *n no pl* erario *m;* **the Exchequer** Hacienda
excise[1] ['eksaɪz] *n no pl* FIN impuestos *mpl* interiores; ~ **on alcohol** impuestos especiales sobre el alcohol
excise[2] [ek'saɪz] *vt form* 1. quitar; (*tumour*) extraer 2. *fig* eliminar, suprimir
excitable [ɪk'saɪtəbl, *Am:* -t̬əbl] *adj* excitable
excite [ɪk'saɪt] *vt* 1. (*move*) emocionar; **to** ~ **an audience** entusiasmar al público; **to be** ~**d about an idea** estar entusiasmado ante una idea 2. (*stimulate*) estimular; **to** ~ **sb's curiosity** despertar la curiosidad de alguien
excited [ɪk'saɪtɪd, *Am:* -t̬ɪd] *adj* emocionado, -a
excitement [ɪk'saɪtmənt] *n* emoción *f;* **to be in a state of** ~ estar emocionado; **what** ~! ¡qué emoción!
exciting [ɪk'saɪtɪŋ, *Am:* -t̬ɪŋ] *adj* emocionante

excl. 1. *abbr of* **exluding** excepto, salvo 2. *abbr of* **exclusive** exclusive
exclaim [ɪk'skleɪm] *vi, vt* exclamar; **to** ~ **in delight** exclamar de placer
exclamation [ˌekskləˈmeɪʃən] *n* exclamación *f*
exclamation mark *n* signo *m* de exclamación
exclude [ɪk'sklu:d] *vt* 1. (*shut out*) expulsar; **to be** ~**d from school** ser expulsado de la escuela 2. (*leave out*) excluir; (*possibility*) descartar
excluding [ɪk'sklu:dɪŋ] *prep* excepto, salvo
exclusion [ɪk'sklu:ʒən] *n* exclusión *f;* **to the** ~ **of** con exclusión de
exclusive [ɪks'klu:sɪv] I. *adj* exclusivo, -a; ~ **interview** entrevista *f* en exclusiva; **in** ~ **circles** en círculos selectos; **to be** ~ **to sb** ser exclusivo de alguien; ~ **of** sin; **to be** ~ **of** not incluir II. *n* exclusiva *f* III. *adv* from 5 to 10 ~ del 5 al 10 exclusive
exclusively *adv* exclusivamente
excommunicate [ˌekskəˈmju:nɪkeɪt] *vt* excomulgar
excommunication [ˌekskəˌmju:nɪˈkeɪʃən] *n* excomunión *f*
excrement ['ekskrəmənt] *n no pl* excremento *m*
excrescence [ɪk'skresns] *n* 1. MED excrecencia *f* 2. *fig* (*ugly object*) adefesio *m*
excreta [ɪk'skri:tə, *Am:* -t̬ə] *n no pl, form* excrementos *mpl*
excrete [ɪk'skri:t] *vi, vt form* excretar
excretion [ɪk'skri:ʃən] *n form* excreción *f*
excruciating [ɪk'skru:ʃɪeɪtɪŋ, *Am:* -t̬ɪŋ] *adj* agudísimo, -a; (*pain*) atroz, insoportable
excursion [ɪk'skɜ:ʃən, *Am:* -'skɜ:rʒən] *n* excursión *f;* **to go on an** ~ ir de excursión
excursion ticket *n* billete *m* de excursión
excursion train *n* tren *m* de recreo
excusable [ɪk'skju:zəbl] *adj* perdonable
excuse [ɪk'skju:z] I. *vt* 1. (*justify: behaviour*) justificar; (*lateness*) disculpar; **to** ~ **sb for sth** excusar a alguien por algo 2. (*forgive*) perdonar; ~ **me!** ¡perdone! 3. (*allow not to attend*) **to** ~ **sb from sth** dispensar a alguien de algo 4. (*leave*) **after an hour she** ~**d herself** después de una hora se disculpó y se fue II. *n* 1. (*explanation*) excusa *f,* agarradera *f AmL* 2. (*pretext*) pretexto *m;* **poor** ~ mal pretexto; **to make** ~**s for sb** justificar a alguien
ex-directory [ˌeksdɪˈrektəri] *adj Aus, Brit* **to be** ~ no figurar en la guía
execrable ['eksɪkrəbl] *adj* execrable; (*meal*) abominable
execrate ['eksɪkreɪt] *vt form* execrar
execute ['eksɪkju:t] *vt* 1. (*carry out*) realizar; (*manoeuvre*) efectuar; (*plan*) llevar a cabo; (*order*) cumplir; **to** ~ **sb's will** otorgar el testamento de alguien 2. (*put to death*) ejecutar
execution [ˌeksɪˈkju:ʃən] *n* 1. *no pl* (*carrying out*) realización *f;* **to put a plan into** ~ llevar a cabo un plan 2. (*putting to death*) ejecución *f*

executioner [ˌeksɪ'kjuːʃnəʳ, Am: -ɚ] n verdugo m

executive [ɪg'zekjʊtɪv, Am: -t̬ɪv] I. n 1. (senior manager) ejecutivo, -a m, f 2. + sing/pl vb POL poder m ejecutivo; ECON órgano m ejecutivo II. adj ejecutivo, -a; ~ **branch** poder ejecutivo

executor [ɪg'zekjʊtəʳ, Am: -t̬ɚ] n albacea mf

exemplary [ɪg'zempləri] adj ejemplar

exemplification [ɪgˌzemplɪfɪ'keɪʃən, Am: -plə-] n ejemplificación f; (of an idea) ilustración f

exemplify [ɪg'zemplɪfaɪ] <-ie-> vt ejemplificar; (strategy) mostrar

exempt [ɪg'zempt] I. vt eximir II. adj exento, -a; to be ~ from sth estar exento de algo

exemption [ɪg'zempʃən] n no pl exención f

exercise ['eksəsaɪz, Am: -sɚ-] I. vt 1. (muscles) ejercitar; (dog) llevar de paseo; (horse) entrenar; to ~ one's muscles/memory ejercitar los músculos/la memoria 2. (apply: authority, control) ejercer; to ~ caution proceder con cautela; to ~ common sense hacer uso del sentido común; to ~ discretion actuar con discreción; to ~ self-discipline imponerse autodisciplina II. vi hacer ejercicio III. n 1. (physical training) ejercicio m; physical ~ gimnasia f; to do ~s hacer ejercicios 2. SCHOOL, UNIV ejercicio m; written ~s ejercicios mpl escritos 3. MIL maniobras fpl 4. no pl (action, achievement) acción f 5. no pl (use) uso m 6. pl, AM ceremonia f

exercise bike n bicicleta f de ejercicio **exercise book** n cuaderno m

exerciser ['eksəsaɪzəʳ, Am: -sɚsaɪzɚ] n máquina f de ejercicios

exercise studio n gimnasio m

exert [ɪg'zɜːt, Am: -'zɜːrt] vt ejercer; (apply) emplear; to ~ oneself esforzarse

exertion [ɪg'zɜːʃən, Am: -'zɜːr-] n 1. no pl (application) aplicación f 2. (physical effort) esfuerzo m

exfoliant [ɪks'fəʊlɪənt] n exfoliante m

exfoliating cream [eksˌfəʊlɪ'eɪtɪŋˌkriːm, Am: -ˌfoʊlɪ'eɪt̬ɪŋ-] n crema f exfoliante

exfoliation [eksˌfəʊlɪ'eɪʃən, Am: -ˌfoʊ-] n no pl exfoliación f

exhalation [ˌekshə'leɪʃən] n exhalación f

exhale [eks'heɪl] I. vt espirar; (gases, scents) despedir II. vi espirar

exhaust [ɪg'zɔːst, Am: -'zɑː-] I. vt a. fig agotar; to ~ oneself agotarse II. n 1. no pl AUTO (gas) gases mpl de escape 2. Aus, Brit (pipe) tubo m de escape

exhausted adj agotado, -a

exhaust fumes npl gases mpl de escape

exhausting adj agotador(a)

exhaustion [ɪg'zɔːstʃən, Am: -'zɑː-] n no pl agotamiento m; to suffer from ~ estar agotado

exhaustive [ɪg'zɔːstɪv, Am: -'zɑː-] adj exhaustivo, -a

exhaust pipe n tubo m de escape **exhaust system** n sistema m de escape

exhibit [ɪg'zɪbɪt] I. n 1. (display) objeto m expuesto 2. LAW documento m II. vt 1. (show) enseñar; (work) presentar 2. (display character traits) mostrar; (rudeness) manifestar

exhibition [ˌeksɪ'bɪʃən] n (display) exposición f; (performance) exhibición f ▶to make an ~ of oneself ponerse en ridículo

exhibitionism [ˌeksɪ'bɪʃnɪzəm] n no pl exhibicionismo m

exhibitionist [ˌeksɪ'bɪʃnɪst] n exhibicionista mf

exhibitor [ɪg'zɪbɪtəʳ, Am: -t̬ɚ] n expositor(a) m(f)

exhilarating [ɪg'zɪləreɪtɪŋ, Am: -t̬ɪŋ] adj estimulante; an ~ **walk** un paseo vivificante

exhilaration [ɪgˌzɪləreɪʃən] n no pl regocijo m; the ~ **of liberty/speed** la sensación estimulante de la libertad/velocidad; the ~ **of doing sth** la alegría de hacer algo

exhort [ɪg'zɔːt, Am: -'zɔːrt] vt form to ~ sb to do sth exhortar a alguien a hacer algo; she ~ed him to keep working le exhortó a que siguiera trabajando

exhortation [ˌeksɔː'teɪʃən, Am: ˌegzɔːr-] n no pl exhortación f

exhumation [ˌekshjuː'meɪʃən, Am: -] n no pl exhumación f

exhume [eks'hjuːm, Am: egz'uːm] vt exhumar

ex-husband n ex marido m

exigence ['eksɪdʒəns] n, **exigency** ['ekzɪdʒənsi] <-ies> n 1. no pl (extreme urgency) emergencia f 2. pl (urgent demands) exigencias fpl

exigent ['eksɪdʒənt] adj form 1. (urgent) apremiante; an ~ **issue** una cuestión urgente; an ~ **environmental problem** un problema medioambiental inaplazable 2. (demanding) exigente

exiguous [eg'zɪgjʊəs] adj form exiguo, -a

exile ['eksaɪl] I. n 1. no pl (banishment) exilio m; political ~ exilio político; to be in ~ estar en el exilio; to go into ~ exiliarse 2. (person) exiliado, -a m, f II. vt exili(a)r; to ~ sb to Siberia exiliar a alguien a Siberia

exist [ɪg'zɪst] vi 1. (be) existir 2. (live) vivir; to ~ on sth vivir de algo; to ~ without sth sobrevivir sin algo

existence [ɪg'zɪstəns] n 1. no pl (being) existencia f; to be in ~ existir; to come into ~ nacer 2. (life) vida f

existent [ɪg'zɪstent] adj existente; the only ~ **copy** la única copia que existe

existential [ˌegzɪ'stenʃl] adj existencial

existentialism [ˌegzɪ'stenʃəlɪzəm] n no pl existencialismo m

existing [ɪg'zɪstɪŋ] adj existente; the ~ **laws** la actual legislación

exit ['eksɪt] I. n salida f; (of road) desvío m; to make an ~ salir II. vt salir de III. vi 1. a. INFOR (leave) salir 2. THEAT hacer mutis

exit visa *n* visado *m* de salida

exodus ['eksədəs] *n* éxodo *m*

ex officio [ˌeks ə'fɪʃɪəʊ, *Am:* -oʊ] I. *adv* ADMIN oficialmente; **to act** ~ actuar de oficio II. *adj* ADMIN de oficio

exonerate [ɪg'zɒnəreɪt, *Am:* -'zɑ:nə-] *vt form* exonerar

exoneration [ɪgˌzɒnə'reɪʃən, *Am:* -ˌzɑ:nə-] *n no pl, form* exoneración *f*

exorbitance [ɪg'zɔ:bɪtəns, *Am:* -'zɔ:rbəʈəns] *n no pl* exorbitancia *f*

exorbitant [ɪg'zɔ:bɪtənt, *Am:* -'zɔ:rbəʈənt] *adj* exorbitante; (*demand*) excesivo, -a; (*price*) desorbitado, -a

exorcism ['eksɔ:sɪzəm, *Am:* -sɔ:r-] *n no pl* exorcismo *m*

exorcist ['eksɔ:sɪst, *Am:* -sɔ:r-] *n* exorcista *mf*

exorcize ['eksɔ:saɪz, *Am:* -sɔ:r-] *vt* exorcizar

exotic [ɪg'zɒtɪk, *Am:* -'zɑ:ʈɪk] *adj* exótico, -a

expand [ɪk'spænd] I. *vi* 1. (*increase*) expandirse; (*trade*) desarrollarse 2. (*spread*) extenderse 3. PHYS dilatarse II. *vt* 1. (*make larger*) ampliar; (*wings*) extender; (*trade*) desarrollar 2. PHYS dilatar 3. (*elaborate*) desarrollar

expandable [ɪk'spændəbl] *adj* expansible

expanse [ɪk'spæns] *n* 1. (*large area*) extensión *f* 2. (*expansion*) expansión *f*

expansion [ɪk'spænʃən] *n* 1. *no pl* (*spreading out*) expansión *f*; (*of a metal*) dilatación *f* 2. (*elaboration*) desarrollo *m*

expansionism [ɪk'spænʃənɪzəm] *n no pl* expansionismo *m*; **policy of** ~ política *f* expansionista

expansive [ɪk'spænsɪv] *adj* 1. (*sociable*) expansivo, -a 2. (*broad, vast*) amplio, -a 3. (*elaborated*) extenso, -a

expatriate [eks'pætrɪeɪt, *Am:* -'peɪ-] I. *n* expatriado, -a *m, f* II. *vt* expatriar

expect [ɪk'spekt] *vt* esperar; (*imagine*) imaginarse; **to** ~ **to do sth** esperar hacer algo; **to** ~ **sb to do sth** esperar que alguien haga algo; **you are** ~**ed to return books on time** debes devolver los libros puntualmente; **to** ~ **sth of sb** esperar algo de alguien; **to be** ~**ing** (**a baby**) esperar un bebé; **I** ~**ed as much** ya me lo esperaba; **I** ~**ed better of you than that** esperaba algo más de ti que eso; **I** ~ **you are hungry** supongo que estaréis hambrientos; **I** ~ **so** me lo imagino; **to** ~ **that** esperar que +*subj*

expectancy [ɪk'spektənsi] *n no pl* esperanza *f*; **life** ~ esperanza *f* de vida

expectant [ɪk'spektənt] *adj* expectante; (*look*) de esperanza; ~ **mother** futura madre

expectation [ˌekspek'teɪʃən] *n* 1. (*hope*) esperanza *f* 2. (*anticipation*) expectativa *f*; **in** ~ **of sth** en espera de algo

expectorate [ɪk'spektəreɪt] *vi form* expectorar

expedience *n,* **expediency** [ɪk'spi:dɪənsi] *n no pl* 1. (*advisability*) conveniencia *f*; **as a matter of** ~ **we will not be taking on any new staff this year** no nos conviene contratar a más personal este año 2. (*self-interest*) oportunismo *m*; **to operate on the basis of** ~ actuar por conveniencia

expedient [ɪk'spi:dɪənt] I. *adj* 1. (*advantageous*) conveniente; **it is** ~ **to do sth** es oportuno hacer algo *form* 2. (*necessary*) necesario, -a; (*measure*) oportuno, -a; **to be** ~ **that** ser conveniente que +*subj* II. *n* recurso *m*; **they took the** ~ **of asking advice** tomaron la precaución de informarse

expedite ['ekspɪdaɪt] *vt form* acelerar

expedition [ˌekspɪ'dɪʃən] *n* expedición *f*; **to be on an** ~ estar de expedición; **to go on an** ~ ir de expedición; **to go on a shopping** ~ *iron* ir de compras

expeditious [ˌekspɪ'dɪʃəs] *adj form* expeditivo, -a

expel [ɪk'spel] <-ll-> *vt* expeler, arrojar; (*person*) expulsar

expend [ɪk'spend] *vt form* dedicar; (*money*) gastar; **to** ~ **time on sth** dedicar tiempo a algo

expenditure [ɪk'spendɪtʃəʳ, *Am:* -tʃɚ] *n no pl* (*money*) gasto *m*; **public** ~ gasto público; **the** ~ **on cleaning** la cantidad dedicada a la limpieza

expense [ɪk'spens] *n* gasto(s) *m(pl)*; **all** ~(**s**) **paid** con todos los gastos pagados; **at great** ~ gastando mucho dinero; **at sb's** ~ *a. fig* a costa de alguien; **at the** ~ **of sth** *a. fig* a costa de algo; **to go to** ~ meterse en gastos; **to go to the** ~ **of** meterse en gastos para; **to spare no** ~ no reparar en gastos

expense account *n* cuenta *f* de gastos de representación

expensive [ɪk'spensɪv] *adj* caro, -a; **this was an** ~ **mistake for the ministry** este error le ha salido caro al ministerio

experience [ɪk'spɪərɪəns, *Am:* -'spɪrɪ-] I. *n* experiencia *f*; **to have** ~ **of translating** tener experiencia en traducir; **from** ~ por experiencia; **to know sth from** ~ saber algo por experiencia; **to learn by** ~ aprender a través de la experiencia II. *vt* experimentar; **to** ~ **happiness/pain** sentir alegría/dolor; **to** ~ **difficulty in passing an exam** tener dificultades para aprobar un examen; **to** ~ **a loss** sufrir una pérdida

experienced [ɪk'spɪərɪənst, *Am:* -'spɪrɪ-] *adj* experimentado, -a; **to be** ~ **at organising** tener experiencia en organización

experiment [ɪk'sperɪmənt] I. *n* experimento *m*; **as an** ~ como experimento; **by** ~ experimentando II. *vi* experimentar; **to** ~ **on a patient** hacer experimentos con un paciente; **to** ~ **with mice** hacer experimentos con ratones

experimental [ɪkˌsperɪ'mentl, *Am:* ek,sper-] *adj* experimental; ~ **psychology** psicología *f* experimental; **to be still at the** ~ **stage** estar todavía en fase experimental

experimentation [ɪkˌsperɪmen'teɪʃən] *n no pl* experimentación *f*

expert ['ekspɜ:t, *Am:* -spɜ:rt] I. *n* experto, -a

m, f; **gardening** ~ experto en jardinería; **to be an ~ at training athletes** ser un experto en el entrenamiento de atletas; **to be an ~ in** [*o* **on**] **computing** ser un experto en informática **II.** *adj* **1.** (*skilful*) experto, -a; **she's an ~ swimmer** es una experta nadadora **2.** LAW pericial; **~ report** informe *m* pericial
expert advice *n* **to seek ~** asesorarse con un experto
expertise [ˌekspɜːˈtiːz, *Am:* -spɜːr-] *n no pl* pericia *f;* (*knowledge*) conocimientos *mpl*
expert knowledge *n* conocimientos *mpl* de experto **expert opinion** *n* dictamen *m* pericial **expert system** *n* INFOR sistema *m* experto **expert witness** *n* perito, -a *m, f*
expiate [ˈekspɪeɪt] *vt form* expiar
expiation [ˌekspɪˈeɪʃən] *n form* expiación *f*
expiration [ˌekspɪˈreɪʃən, *Am:* -spə-] *n no pl* terminación *f;* COM vencimiento *f,* caducidad *f*
expire [ɪkˈspaɪəʳ, *Am:* -ˈspaɪɚ] **I.** *vi* **1.** (*terminate*) finalizar; (*contract, licence*) expirar; (*passport, food*) caducar **2.** (*die*) expirar **II.** *vt* espirar
expiry [ɪkˈspaɪəri, *Am:* -ˈspaɪ-] *n no pl s.* **expiration**
expiry date *n* vencimiento *m* de un plazo
explain [ɪkˈspleɪn] **I.** *vt* explicar; **to ~ a text to a pupil** explicar un texto a un alumno; **to ~ how/what/where/why ...** explicar cómo/qué/dónde/por qué...; **to ~ oneself** explicarse; **that ~s everything!** ¡eso lo aclara todo!; **to ~ away sth** justificar algo **II.** *vi* explicar
◆ **explain away** *vt* justificar
explanation [ˌekspləˈneɪʃən] *n* explicación *f;* **to give an ~ for an incident** dar una explicación de [*o* sobre] un incidente; **to offer no ~ for the delay** no dar explicaciones sobre el retraso; **by way of ~** como explicación
explanatory [ɪkˈsplænətri, *Am:* -ətɔːri] *adj* explicativo, -a
expletive [ɪkˈspliːtɪv, *Am:* ˈəkspləʧɪv] *n* palabrota *f;* **to let out a string of ~s** soltar una sarta de tacos
explicable [ekˈsplɪkəbl] *adj* explicable
explicate [ˈeksplɪkeɪt] *vt form* explicar
explicit [ɪkˈsplɪsɪt] *adj* explícito, -a; **~ directions** instrucciones explícitas; **~ film** película *f* no apta para menores; **he was very ~ about the plans** era muy categórico en cuanto a los planes
explode [ɪkˈspləʊd, *Am:* -ˈsploʊd] **I.** *vi* **1.** (*blow up*) explotar; (*bomb*) estallar; (*tyre*) reventar; **to ~ with anger** montar en cólera **2.** (*grow rapidly*) dispararse **II.** *vt* **1.** (*blow up: bomb*) hacer explotar; (*ball*) reventar **2.** (*discredit: rumours*) desmentir; (*theory*) refutar; (*myth*) destruir
exploit [ˈeksplɔɪt] **I.** *vt* explotar, pilotear *Chile* **II.** *n* hazaña *f*
exploitation [ˌeksplɔɪˈteɪʃən] *n no pl* explotación *f*
exploration [ˌekspləˈreɪʃən, *Am:* -splɔː-] *n*

1. *a.* MED exploración *f;* **voyage of ~** viaje *m* de exploración; **to make an ~ of sth** explorar algo **2.** (*examination*) estudio *m*
exploratory [ɪkˈsplɒrətəri, *Am:* -ˈsplɔːrətɔːri] *adj* (*voyage*) de exploración; (*test*) de sondeo; (*meeting*) preliminar
explore [ɪkˈsplɔːʳ, *Am:* -ˈsplɔːr] **I.** *vt* **1.** *a.* MED, INFOR explorar **2.** (*examine*) analizar; **to ~ sb's past** investigar sobre el pasado de alguien **II.** *vi* explorar
explorer [ɪkˈsplɔːrəʳ, *Am:* -ɚ] *n* explorador(a) *m(f)*
explosion [ɪkˈspləʊʒən, *Am:* -ˈsploʊ-] *n* explosión *f;* **gas ~** explosión de gas; **an ~ of applause** una gran ovación; **population ~** explosión demográfica; **there has been an ~ in demand for computers in the last few years** la demanda de ordenadores se ha disparado en los últimos años
explosive [ɪkˈspləʊsɪv, *Am:* -ˈsploʊ-] **I.** *adj* explosivo, -a; **~ device** artefacto explosivo; **an ~ situation** una situación delicada; **an ~ issue** un asunto espinoso; **to have an ~ temper** tener un genio muy vivo **II.** *n* explosivo *m*
exponent [ɪkˈspəʊnənt, *Am:* -ˈspoʊ-] *n* **1.** (*person*) exponente *mf;* **a leading ~ of neoclassicism** un máximo exponente del neoclasicismo **2.** MAT exponente *m*
export [ɪkˈspɔːt, *Am:* -ˈspɔːrt] **I.** *vt* exportar **II.** *n* **1.** (*product*) artículo *m* de exportación **2.** *no pl* (*selling*) exportación *f;* **~ duties** aranceles *mpl* de exportación
exportable [ɪkˈspɔːtəbl, *Am:* -ˈspɔːrʧə-] *adj* exportable
exportation [ˌekspɔːˈteɪʃən, *Am:* -spɔːr-] *n no pl* exportación *f*
export business *n* **1.** (*business which sells abroad*) negocio *m* de exportación **2.** *no pl* (*special branch*) exportación *f;* **to be in the ~** dedicarse a la exportación
exporter [ikˈspɔːtəʳ, *Am:* -ˈspɔːrʧɚ] *n* exportador(a) *m(f)*
export goods *npl* productos *mpl* de exportación **export licence** *n* licencia *f* de exportación **export marketing** *n no pl* marketing *m* de exportación **export regulations** *npl* normativa *f* de exportación **export surplus** *n no pl* excedente *m* de exportación **export trade** *n no pl* comercio *m* de exportación
expose [ɪkˈspəʊz, *Am:* -ˈspoʊz] *vt* **1.** (*uncover*) enseñar **2.** (*leave vulnerable to*) exponer; **to ~ sb to ridicule** poner a alguien en ridículo **3.** (*reveal: person*) descubrir; (*plot*) desvelar; (*secret*) sacar a la luz; **to ~ a business as a fraud** revelar un negocio como un fraude
exposed [ɪkˈspəʊzd, *Am:* -ˈspoʊzd] *adj* **1.** (*vulnerable*) expuesto, -a **2.** (*uncovered*) descubierto, -a **3.** (*unprotected*) desprotegido, -a
exposition [ˌekspəˈzɪʃən, *Am:* -pə-] *n* exposición *f*
expostulate [ɪkˈspɒstjʊleɪt, *Am:*

-'spɑːstʃə-] *vi form* protestar; **to ~ with the waiter about the bill** reconvenir al camarero sobre la factura

exposure [ɪk'spəʊʒəʳ, *Am:* -'spoʊʒɚ] *n* **1.** (*contact*) exposición *f;* **~ to the sun** exposición al sol; **~ to new ideas** contacto *m* con nuevas ideas **2.** *no pl* MED hipotermia *f;* **to die of ~** morir de frío **3.** *a.* PHOT revelación *f* **4.** (*revelation*) descubrimiento *m* **5.** *no pl* (*media coverage*) publicidad *f*

exposure meter *n* PHOT exposímetro *m*

expound [ɪk'spaʊnd] **I.** *vi form* hablar; **to ~ (at length) on** [*o* about] **sth** hablar (largo y tendido) sobre algo **II.** *vt form* exponer

express [ɪk'spres] **I.** *vt* **1.** (*convey: thoughts, feelings*) expresar; **to ~ oneself** expresarse; **to ~ oneself through music** expresarse a través de la música; **I would like to ~ my thanks for ...** querría expresar mi agradecimiento por... **2.** *inf* (*send quickly*) enviar por correo urgente; **to ~ sth to sb** enviar algo a alguien por correo urgente **3.** *form* (*squeeze out*) exprimir **II.** *adj* **1.** (*rapid*) rápido, -a; **by ~ delivery** por correo urgente; **~ train** tren expreso **2.** (*precise*) explícito, -a; **by ~ order** por orden expresa; **~ wish** deseo expreso **III.** *n* **1.** (*train*) expreso *m* **2.** *no pl* (*service*) **by ~** por correo urgente **IV.** *adv* **to send sth ~** enviar algo por correo urgente

expression [ɪk'spreʃən] *n* expresión *f;* (*of love, solidarity*) demostración *f;* **as an ~ of thanks** en señal de agradecimiento; **to give ~ to sth** expresar algo; **to find ~ in music** expresarse a través de la música

expressionism [ɪk'spreʃənɪzəm] *n* expresionismo *m*

expressionist [ɪk'spreʃənɪst] *n* expresionista *mf*

expressionless [ɪk'spreʃənlɪs] *adj* inexpresivo, -a

expressive [ɪk'spresɪv] *adj* expresivo, -a; **to be ~ of sadness** *form* denotar tristeza

expressly [ɪk'spresli] *adv* **1.** (*clearly*) claramente **2.** (*especially*) expresamente

expressway [ɪk'spresweɪ] *n Am, Aus* autopista *f*

ex-prisoner *n* ex prisionero, -a *m*

expropriate [eks'prəʊprɪeɪt, *Am:* -'proʊ-] *vt* expropiar

expropriation [eks'prəʊ prɪeɪʃən, *Am:* -'proʊ-] *n* expropiación *f*

expulsion [ɪk'spʌlʃən] *n* expulsión *f*

exquisite ['ekskwɪzɪt] *adj* **1.** (*delicate*) exquisito, -a; **an ~ piece of china** una delicada pieza de porcelana **2.** (*intense*) intenso, -a

ex-serviceman [ˌeks'sɜːvɪsmən, *Am:*-'sɜːr-] <-men> *n* excombatiente *m*

ext. TEL *abbr of* **extension** Ext.

extant [ek'stænt, *Am:* 'ekstənt] *adj form* (*todavía*) existente; **to be still ~** existir todavía

extemporaneous [ek,stempə'reɪnɪəs] *adj form* improvisado, -a

extempore [ek'stempəri] *form* **I.** *adj*

improvisado, -a **II.** *adv* improvisadamente; **to perform ~** improvisar; **to speak ~** improvisar un discurso

extemporise *vi Aus, Brit,* **extemporize** [ɪk'stempəraɪz] *vi form* improvisar

extend [ɪk'stend] **I.** *vi* extenderse; **to ~ beyond the river** extenderse más allá del río; **to ~ to a discussion** llegar a una discusión **II.** *vt* **1.** (*enlarge: house*) ampliar; (*street*) alargar **2.** (*prolong: deadline*) prorrogar; (*holiday*) prolongar **3.** (*offer*) ofrecer; **to ~ an invitation to sb** cursar una invitación a alguien; **to ~ one's hand as a greeting** tender la mano para saludar; **to ~ one's thanks to sb** dar las gracias a alguien; **to ~ a warm welcome to sb** dar una calurosa bienvenida a alguien **4.** FIN (*credit*) conceder

extended *adj* extenso, -a; **~ family** clan *m* familiar; **an ~ holiday** unas vacaciones prolongadas

extension [ɪk'stenʃən] *n* **1.** (*increase*) extensión *f;* (*of rights*) ampliación *f;* **by ~** por extensión **2.** (*of a deadline*) prórroga *f* **3.** (*appendage*) apéndice *m* **4.** TEL extensión *f,* supletorio *m AmL,* anexo *m Chile*

extension cable *n* ELEC extensión *f* **extension cord** *n Am s.* **extension lead extension ladder** *n* escalera *f* extensible **extension lead** *n* alargador *m,* alargue *m RíoPl*

extensive [ɪk'stensɪv] *adj* **1.** *a. fig* extenso, -a; (*knowledge*) exhaustivo, -a; (*experience*) amplio, -a **2.** (*large: repair*) importante; **~ damage** daños *mpl* de consideración **3.** AGR (*farming*) extensivo, -a

extensively *adv* intensamente

extent [ɪk'stent] *n no pl* **1.** (*size*) extensión *f;* **to its fullest ~** en toda su extensión **2.** (*degree*) alcance *m;* **to go to the ~ of striking sb** llegar al extremo de golpear a alguien; **to a great ~** en gran parte; **to the same ~ as ...** en la misma medida que...; **to some ~** hasta cierto punto; **to such an ~ that ...** hasta tal punto que...; **to that ~** hasta ese punto; **to what ~ ...?** ¿hasta qué punto...?

extenuate [ɪk'stenjʊeɪt] *vt form* atenuar

extenuating *adj form* atenuante

extenuation [ɪk,stenjʊ'eɪʃən] *n no pl, form* atenuación *f;* **in ~ of sth** como atenuante de algo

exterior [ɪk'stɪərɪəʳ, *Am:* -'stɪrɪɚ] **I.** *adj* exterior; **~ angle** MAT ángulo externo **II.** *n* **1.** (*outside surface*) exterior *m* **2.** (*outward appearance*) aspecto *m* **3.** CINE exteriores *mpl*

exterminate [ɪk'stɜːmɪneɪt, *Am:* -'stɜːr-] *vt* exterminar

extermination [ɪk,stɜːmɪ'neɪʃən, *Am:* -,stɜːr-] *n no pl* exterminio *m,* exterminación *f;* **~ of a plague** exterminación *f* de una plaga

external [ɪk'stɜːnl, *Am:* -'stɜːr-] **I.** *adj* **1.** (*exterior*) externo, -a; (*influence*) del exterior; (*wall*) exterior; **~ world** mundo *m* exterior; **to be ~ to the problem** ser ajeno al problema **2.** (*foreign*) exterior **3.** MED tópico, -a

II. *npl* las apariencias
externalize [ɪk'stɜ:nəlaɪz, *Am:* -'stɜ:r-] *vt* exteriorizar
external world *n no pl* mundo *m* exterior
exterritorial [ˌeksˌterɪ'tɔ:rɪəl] *adj* extraterritorial
extinct [ɪk'stɪŋkt] *adj* (*practice*) extinto, -a; (*volcano*) apagado, -a; **to become ~** extinguirse
extinction [ɪk'stɪŋkʃən] *n no pl* extinción *f*
extinguish [ɪk'stɪŋgwɪʃ] *vt* (*candle, cigar*) apagar; (*love, passion*) extinguir; (*life, memory*) apagar; (*debt*) amortizar
extinguisher [ɪk'stɪŋgwɪʃəʳ, *Am:* -ɚ] *n* extintor *m*
extirpate ['ekstəpeɪt, *Am:* -stɚ-] *vt form* extirpar; **to ~ an evil** erradicar un mal
extol <-ll-> *vt*, **extoll** [ɪk'stəʊl, *Am:* -'stoʊl] *vt Am* alabar; **to ~ the virtues of yoga** ensalzar las virtudes del yoga
extort [ɪk'stɔ:t, *Am:* -'stɔ:rt] *vt* extorsionar; (*confession*) arrancar
extortion [ɪk'stɔ:ʃən, *Am:* -'stɔ:r-] *n no pl* extorsión *f;* **that's sheer ~!** ¡esto es un robo!
extortionate [ɪk'stɔ:ʃənət, *Am:* -'stɔ:r-] *adj* excesivo, -a; **~ demands** peticiones desmesuradas; **~ prices** precios *mpl* exorbitantes
extra ['ekstrə] I. *adj* adicional; **to work an ~ two hours** trabajar dos horas más; **~ clothes** ropa *f* de repuesto; **it costs an ~ £2** cuesta dos libras más; **meals are ~** el precio no incluye las comidas II. *adv* (*more*) más; (*extraordinarily*) extraordinariamente; **they pay her ~ to work nights** le pagan más por trabajar por la noche; **I'll try ~ hard this time** esta vez voy a poner más empeño; **£10 ~** diez libras más; **to charge ~ for sth** cobrar algo aparte III. *n* 1. ECON suplemento *m;* AUTO extra *m* 2. CINE extra *mf*
extra charge *n* recargo *m*
extract [ɪk'strækt] I. *vt* 1. (*remove*) extraer 2. (*obtain: information*) sacar 3. MAT (*square root*) sacar II. *n* 1. (*concentrate*) extracto *m* 2. (*excerpt*) fragmento *m*
extraction [ɪk'strækʃən] *n* 1. (*removal*) extracción *f* 2. (*descent*) origen *m;* **he's of American ~** es de origen americano
extracurricular [ˌekstrəkə'rɪkjʊləʳ, *Am:* -jəlɚ] *adj* extraescolar
extradite ['ekstrədaɪt] *vt* extraditar
extradition [ekstrə'dɪʃən] *n no pl* extradición *f*
extramarital [ˌekstrə'mærɪtl, *Am:* -'merət̬l] *adj* extramatrimonial
extramural [ˌekstrə'mjʊərəl, *Am:* -'mjʊrəl] *adj Brit* (*course*) para estudiantes externos
extraneous [ɪk'streɪnɪəs] *adj* extraño, -a; **to be ~ to sth** no tener relación con algo
extranet ['ekstrənet] *n* INFOR extranet *f*
extraordinary [ɪk'strɔ:dənəri, *Am:* -'strɔ:rdənɚ-] *adj* 1. *a.* POL extraordinario, -a 2. (*astonishing*) asombroso, -a
extra pay ['ekstrəˌpeɪ] *n no pl* paga *f* extra

extrapolate [ek'stræpəleɪt] I. *vt form* extrapolar II. *vi form* **to ~ from sth** hacer una extrapolación de algo
extrasensory [ˌekstrə'sensəri] *adj* extrasensorial; **~ perception** percepción *f* extrasensorial
extraterrestrial ['ekstrətɪ'restrɪəl, *Am:* -tə'-] *adj* extraterrestre
extraterritorial [ˌekstrəˌterɪ'tɔ:rɪəl] *adj* extraterritorial
extra time ['ekstrətaɪm] *n no pl, Aus, Brit* SPORTS prórroga *f;* **to play ~** jugar la prórroga
extravagance [ɪk'strævəgəns] *n no pl* 1. (*wastefulness*) derroche *m* 2. (*luxury*) lujo *m* 3. (*elaborateness*) extravagancia *f*
extravagant [ɪk'strævəgənt] *adj* 1. (*wasteful*) despilfarrador(a) 2. (*luxurious*) lujoso, -a; **an ~ lifestyle** un tren de vida lujoso 3. (*exaggerated: praise*) excesivo, -a; **~ price** precio *m* exorbitante 4. (*elaborate*) extravagante
extravaganza [ɪkˌstrævə'gænzə] *n* (*spectacle*) **a film ~** una película espectacular
extreme [ɪk'stri:m] I. *adj* extremo, -a; **an ~ case** un caso excepcional; **with ~ caution** con sumo cuidado; **~ difficulties** grandes dificultades; **~ pain** dolor agudo; **in the ~ north** en la zona más septentrional; **~ sport** deporte de alto riesgo; **to be ~ in sth** ser extremista en algo II. *n* extremo *m;* **a man of ~s** un extremista; **at the ~** *fig* en el peor de los casos; **in the ~** sumamente; **to go from one ~ to the other** pasar de un extremo a otro; **to go to ~s** llegar a extremos
extremely *adv* extremadamente; **to be ~ sorry** estar muy arrepentido
extremism [ɪk'stri:mɪzəm] *n no pl* extremismo *m*
extremist [ɪk'stri:mɪst] I. *adj* extremista; **~ tendencies** tendencias extremistas II. *n* extremista *mf*
extremity [ɪk'streməti, *Am:* -ṭi] *n* 1. (*furthest point*) extremo *m;* **at the ~ of his endurance** al extremo de su resistencia 2. (*situation*) situación *f* extrema; **to be driven to the ~ of leaving the country** tener que llegar al extremo de abandonar el país 3. *pl* ANAT extremidades *fpl*
extricate ['ekstrɪkeɪt] *vt form* sacar; **to ~ oneself from sth** lograr salir de algo
extrovert ['ekstrəvɜ:t, *Am:* -vɜ:rt] I. *n* extrovertido, -a *m, f* II. *adj* extrovertido, -a
extrude [eks'tru:d] I. *vt* 1. TECH extruir 2. (*force out*) expulsar II. *vi* sobresalir
exuberance [ɪg'zju:bərəns, *Am:* -'zu:-] *n no pl* 1. (*abundance*) exuberancia *f* 2. (*liveliness*) exaltación *f*
exuberant [ɪg'zju:bərənt, *Am:* -'zu:-] *adj* 1. (*luxuriant*) exuberante 2. (*energetic*) desbordante; **young and ~** joven y lleno de energía
exude [ɪg'zju:d, *Am:* -'zu:d] I. *vt* 1. exudar; **to ~ pus** supurar 2. *fig* rezumar; **to ~ confidence** irradiar confianza II. *vi* exudar

exult [ɪgˈzʌlt] *vi form* regocijarse; **to ~ at** [*o* **in**] **the prize** regocijarse con [*o* de] [*o* en] el premio

exultant [ɪgˈzʌltənt] *adj form* regocijado, -a, exultante; **~ shout** grito *m* de júbilo

exultation [ˌegzʌlˈteɪʃən, *Am:* ˌeksʌlˈ-] *n no pl, form* regocijo *m,* exultación *f;* **~ at sth** regocijo *m* por algo

eye [aɪ] I. *n* 1. ANAT ojo *m;* **to blink one's ~s** parpadear; **to keep an ~ on sth/sb** *inf* echar un ojo a algo/alguien; **to roll one's ~s** poner los ojos en blanco; **to rub one's ~s** restregarse los ojos; **to set ~s on sb/sth** poner los ojos en alguien/algo; **visible to the naked ~** visible a simple vista; **her ~s flashed with anger** sus ojos echaban chispas; **his ~s (nearly) popped (out of his head)** (casi) se le salieron los ojos de las órbitas; **he couldn't take his ~s off the girl** *inf* no le quitaba ojo a la chica 2. BOT yema *f* ▶ **to have ~s in the back of one's head** *inf* tener ojos en la nuca; **to have ~s too big for one's stomach** *iron* llenar antes los ojos que la barriga; **an ~ for an ~, a tooth for a tooth** *prov* ojo por ojo y diente por diente; **to be up to one's ~s in work** *inf* estar muy agobiado con el trabajo; **to be all ~s** ser todo ojos; **to give sb a black ~** poner a alguien un ojo a la funerala; **to turn a blind ~ (to sth)** hacer la vista gorda (a algo); **as far as the ~ can see** hasta donde alcanza la vista; **to have a good ~ for sth** tener (buen) ojo para algo; **there's more to this than meets the ~** las apariencias engañan; **to be one in the ~ for sb** *Brit, inf* dejar a alguien con un palmo de narices; **to keep one's ~s open** mantener los ojos abiertos; **to do sth with one's ~s open** *inf* hacer algo sabiendo muy bien lo que se hace; **to keep one's ~s peeled for sth** *inf* estar ojo avizor; **to go around with one's ~s shut** *inf* andar siempre distraído; **to be able to do sth with one's ~s shut** *inf* poder hacer algo con los ojos cerrados; **(right) before** [*o* **under**] **my very ~s** delante de mis propios ojos; **to not believe one's ~s** no dar crédito a sus ojos; **to catch sb's ~** llamar la atención de alguien; **to give sb the ~** *inf,* **to make ~s at sb** *inf* echar miraditas a alguien; **to open sb's ~s** abrir los ojos a alguien; **to run one's ~ over sth** dar una ojeada a algo; **to (not) see ~ to ~ with sb** (no) estar de acuerdo con alguien; **in my ~s** en mi opinión II. <-ing> *vt* mirar; (*observe*) observar; **to ~ sb up and down** mirar a alguien de arriba abajo

eyeball [ˈaɪbɔːl] I. *n* globo *m* ocular ▶ **to meet ~ to ~ with sb** *inf* enfrentarse cara a cara con alguien II. *vt Am, inf* mirar de arriba abajo

eyebrow *n* ceja *f;* **bushy ~s** cejas pobladas; **to raise one's ~s at sth** asombrarse ante algo **eyebrow pencil** *n* lápiz *m* de cejas

eye-catching [ˈaɪˌkætʃɪŋ] *adj* llamativo, -a **eye contact** *n* contacto *m* ocular **eyedrops** *npl* gotas *f* para los ojos *pl* **eyeful** *n* **to be an** **~** *inf* estar de buen ver; **get an ~ of this!** *inf* ¡echa un vistazo a esto!; **I got an ~ of dust** me ha entrado polvo en el ojo **eyeglass** *n* 1. monóculo *m* 2. *pl Am* gafas *f* **eyelash** <-es> *n* pestaña *f;* **false ~es** pestañas *fpl* postizas **eyelet** *n* ojete *m* **eyelid** *n* párpado *m* **eyeliner** *n no pl* lápiz *m* de ojos **eye-opener** *n* revelación *f;* **it was a real ~ for me** me hizo abrir los ojos **eyepiece** *n* ocular *m* **eyeshadow** *n* sombra *f* de ojos **eyesight** *n no pl* vista *f;* **keen ~** vista aguda; **his ~ is failing** le está fallando la vista **eyesore** *n* **to be an ~** ofender a la vista **eyestrain** *n no pl* vista *f* cansada; **to cause ~** cansar la vista **eyetooth** <-teeth> *n* colmillo *m* ▶ **I'd give my eyeteeth for that** daría cualquier cosa por eso **eyewash** *n* 1. *no pl* MED colirio *m* 2. *no pl, inf* (*nonsense*) disparate *m;* **it's a lot of ~** eso es un cuento chino **eyewitness** <-es> *n* testigo *mf* ocular

eyrie [ˈaɪəri, *Am:* ˈeri] *n* aguilera *f*

e-zine [ˈiːziːn] *n* revista *f* electrónica

F

F, f [ef] *n* 1. (*letter*) F, f *f;* **~ for Frederick** *Brit,* **~ for Fox** *Am* F de Francia 2. MUS fa *m*

f 1. *abbr of* **folio** f 2. *abbr of* **feminine** f

F *abbr of* **Fahrenheit** F

FA [ˌefˈeɪ] *n Brit abbr of* **Football Association** federación inglesa de fútbol

fable [ˈfeɪbl] *n* 1. (*story*) fábula *f* 2. (*lie*) cuento *m*

fabled [ˈfeɪbld] *adj* legendario, -a

fabric [ˈfæbrɪk] *n* 1. *no pl* (*cloth, textile*) tejido *m;* **cotton ~** tela *f* de algodón; **woollen ~** género *m* de lana 2. *no pl* (*of building*) estructura *f;* **the ~ of society** el tejido social

fabricate [ˈfæbrɪkeɪt] *vt* 1. (*manufacture*) fabricar 2. *fig* (*invent*) **to ~ an excuse** inventar(se) una excusa 3. (*forge*) falsificar

fabulous [ˈfæbjʊləs, *Am:* -jə-] *adj* fabuloso, -a; **to look absolutely ~** estar estupendo; **a ~ bargain** una ganga increíble

facade [fəˈsɑːd] *n a. fig* fachada *f*

face [feɪs] I. *n* 1. *a.* ANAT cara *f;* **a happy/sad ~** una cara de felicidad/de tristeza; **a smiling ~** un rostro sonriente; **to dare (to) show one's ~** atreverse a dar la cara; **to have a puzzled expression on one's ~** tener un semblante preocupado; **to keep a smile on one's ~** no perder la sonrisa; **to keep a straight ~** mantenerse impávido; **to laugh in sb's ~** reírse en la cara de alguien; **to pull a ~ (at sb)** hacer una mueca (a alguien); **to tell sth to sb's ~** decir algo a la cara de alguien; **her ~ was a picture** *Brit* había que ver la cara que puso 2. (*front: of building*) fachada *f;* (*of coin*) cara *f;* (*of clock*) esfera *f,* carátula *f Méx;* (*of* _mountain_) pared _f_ **3.** (_respect, honour_) prestigio _m;_ **to lose** ~ desprestigiarse; **to save** ~ guardar las apariencias ►**to have a** ~ **like thunder** tener una cara de pocos amigos; **to put a brave** ~ **on sth** poner al mal tiempo buena cara; **to be brought** ~ **to** ~ **with sth** tener que enfrentarse a algo; **to make a long** ~ poner cara larga; **his** ~ **fell when he opened the letter** le mudó el semblante cuando abrió la carta; **if your** ~ **fits you will get the job** _Brit, inf_ si les caes bien conseguirás el trabajo; **to fly in the** ~ **of logic/reason** oponerse abiertamente a la lógica/razón; **on the** ~ **of it** a primera vista **II.** _vt_ **1.** (_turn towards_) mirar hacia; **to** ~ **the audience** volverse hacia el público; **please** ~ **me when I'm talking to you** por favor, mírame cuando te estoy hablando **2.** (_confront_) hacer frente a; **the two teams will** ~ **each other next week** los dos equipos se enfrentarán la próxima semana; **to** ~ **the facts** enfrentarse a los hechos; **to** ~ **one's fears/problems** afrontar los miedos/problemas de uno; **to be** ~**d with sth** verse frente a algo; **I can't** ~ **doing that** no me atrevo a hacer eso; **we are** ~**d by financial problems** estamos pasando por graves problemas financieros; **she can't** ~ **seeing him so soon after their breakup** no podría soportar verlo tan poco tiempo después de romper **3.** ARCHIT recubrir **4.** FASHION forrar ►**to** ~ **the music** _inf_ afrontar las consecuencias **III.** _vi_ **to** ~ **towards the street** dar a la calle; **about** ~! ¡media vuelta!

◆**face up to** _vi_ **to** ~ **sth** hacer frente a algo; **you must** ~ **the fact that ...** debes aceptar que...

facecloth [ˈfeɪsklɒθ, _Am:_ ˈfeɪsklɑ:θ] _n_ toallita _f_ **face cream** _n no pl_ crema _f_ facial **facelift** _n_ lifting _m_ **facepack** _n_ mascarilla _f_ **face powder** _n no pl_ polvos _mpl_ (para la cara)

facet [ˈfæsɪt] _n a. fig_ faceta _f_

facetious [fəˈsiːʃəs] _adj_ chistoso, -a, faceto, -a _Méx;_ **stop being so** ~ deja de hacerte el gracioso

face-to-face [ˌfeɪstəˈfeɪs, _Am:_ -ṭə-] _adv_ cara a cara; **to come** ~ **with sth/sb** encontrarse frente a frente con algo/alguien; **to discuss sth** ~ **with sb** discutir algo con alguien cara a cara

face value _n_ **1.** ECON valor _m_ nominal **2.** _fig_ **to take sth at** ~ creer algo a pie juntillas; **to take sb at** ~ fiarse de alguien

facial [ˈfeɪʃl] **I.** _adj_ facial **II.** _n_ mascarilla _f_ facial

facile [ˈfæsaɪl, _Am:_ -ɪl] _adj_ **1.** (_remark, argument_) simplista **2.** (_victory_) fácil

facilitate [fəˈsɪlɪteɪt] _vt_ facilitar

facilitator [fəˈsɪlɪteɪtər, _Am:_ -ṭɚ] _n_ promotor(a) _m(f)_

facility [fəˈsɪləti, _Am:_ -ṭi] _n_ <-ies> **1.** (_services_) servicio _m;_ **credit facilities** facilidades _fpl_ de pago; **transport facilities** medios _mpl_

de transporte **2.** (_ability, feature_) facilidad _f;_ ~ **for doing sth** facilidad para hacer algo **3.** (_building for a special purpose_) complejo _m;_ **research** ~ centro _m_ de investigación; **sports** ~ complejo _m_ deportivo

facing [ˈfeɪsɪŋ] _n_ **1.** ARCHIT revestimiento _m_ **2.** _no pl_ (_cloth strip_) vuelta _f_

facsimile [fækˈsɪməli] _n_ **1.** (_exact copy_) facsímil _m_ **2.** (_fax_) fax _m_

facsimile machine _n_ máquina _f_ de fax

fact [fækt] _n_ hecho _m;_ **the bare** ~**s** los hechos concretos; **to stick to the** ~**s** atenerse a los hechos ►~**s and figures** _inf_ información _f_ detallada; **a** ~ **of life** ley de vida; **the** ~**s of life** los detalles de la reproducción; **as a matter of** ~ ... de hecho...; **the** ~ **of the matter is that** ... la verdad es que...; **in** ~ de hecho

fact-finding [ˈfæktfaɪndɪŋ] _adj_ investigador(a); ~ **committee** comisión _f_ de investigación

faction [ˈfækʃən] _n_ POL facción _f_

factor [ˈfæktər, _Am:_ -tɚ] _n_ factor _m;_ **to be a contributing** ~ **in sth** contribuir a algo; **to be a crucial** ~ **in sth** ser de vital importancia para algo; **rhesus** ~ factor _m_ rhesus

factory [ˈfæktəri] <-ies> _n_ fábrica _f;_ **car** ~ fábrica de coches

factory farm _n_ granja _f_ industrial **factory worker** _n_ obrero, -a _m, f_ de fábrica

factotum [fækˈtəʊtəm, _Am:_ -ˈtoʊṭəm] _n form_ factótum _m_

factual [ˈfæktʃʊəl, _Am:_ -tʃuːəl] _adj_ basado, -a en hechos reales; **a** ~ **error** un error de hecho

faculty [ˈfæklti, _Am:_ -ṭi] <-ies> _n_ **1.** UNIV facultad _f_ **2.** _no pl, Am_ UNIV (_teachers_) cuerpo _m_ docente **3.** (_ability_) facultad _f;_ **to have a** ~ **for sth** tener facilidad para algo

fad [fæd] _n inf_ **1.** (_fashion_) moda _f;_ **a passing** ~ una moda pasajera **2.** (_obsession_) manía _f_

faddish [ˈfædɪʃ] _adj inf s._ **faddy**

faddy [ˈfædi] _adj inf_ maniático, -a, mañoso, -a _AmL_

fade [feɪd] **I.** _vi_ **1.** (_lose colour_) desteñirse **2.** (_lose intensity: light_) apagarse; (_sound_) debilitarse; (_smile_) borrarse; (_interest_) decaer; (_hope, optimism, memory_) desvanecerse; (_plant, beauty_) marchitarse; (_life_) apagarse **3.** (_disappear_) desaparecer; **to** ~ **from sight** perderse de vista; **to** ~ **from the scene** desaparecer del mapa **4.** CINE, TV fundirse **II.** _vt_ desteñir

◆**fade away** _vi_ (_hope, memory_) desvanecerse; (_sound, love, grief_) apagarse; (_beauty_) marchitarse; (_person_) consumirse

◆**fade in I.** _vi_ (_picture_) aparecer progresivamente; (_sound_) subir gradualmente **II.** _vt_ (_picture_) hacer aparecer progresivamente; (_sound_) subir gradualmente

◆**fade out** _vi_ (_picture_) desaparecer gradualmente; (_sound_) desvanecerse

faeces [ˈfiːsiːz] _npl form_ heces _fpl_

fag [fæg] **I.** _n inf_ **1.** (_cigarette_) pitillo _m_ **2.** _no pl, Brit, Aus_ (_bother_) fastidio _m;_ **to be a** ~ ser

una lata **3.** *Am, pej* (*homosexual*) marica *m*
II. <-gg-> *vt inf* fatigar; **I can't be ~ed** paso;
to be ~ed out estar rendido, -a
fag end *n* **1.** (*cigarette butt*) colilla *f* **2.** (*of
film, conversation*) final *m*
faggot ['fægət] *n* **1.** (*bundle of sticks*) haz *m*
de leña **2.** *Am, pej* (*homosexual*) marica *m*
3. *Brit* (*meatball*) albóndiga *f*
fagot ['fægət] *n Am s.* **faggot**
Fahrenheit ['færnhaɪt, *Am:* 'fern-] *n* Fahrenheit *m*
fail [feɪl] **I.** *vi* **1.** (*not succeed: person*) fracasar; (*attempt, plan, operation*) fallar; **if all
else ~s** como último recurso; **to ~ to do sth**
no conseguir hacer algo; **to never ~ to do sth**
siempre salirse con la suya; **to ~ to appreciate
sth** no saber apreciar algo; **to ~ in one's duty**
no cumplir con las obligaciones de uno; **I ~ to
see why that matters** no veo qué importancia tiene **2.** SCHOOL, UNIV (*in exam*) suspender,
ser reprobado *AmL* **3.** TECH, AUTO (*brakes, steering*) fallar; (*engine*) averiarse; (*eyesight, hearing, heart*) fallar **4. the light was ~ing** iba
oscureciendo **5.** FIN, COM (*go bankrupt*) quebrar **6.** AGR, BOT perderse **II.** *vt* **1.** (*not pass:
exam, pupil*) suspender **2.** (*not help*) **her
courage ~ed her** le abandonó el coraje; **his
nerve ~ed him** perdió el valor **III.** *n* SCHOOL,
UNIV suspenso *m*, reprobado *m AmL* ▸**without
~** (*definitely*) sin falta; (*always*) sin excepción
failing ['feɪlɪŋ] **I.** *adj* (*health*) débil; **in the ~
light** al anochecer **II.** *n* (*of mechanism*)
defecto *m*; (*of person*) debilidad *f* **III.** *prep* a
falta de
fail-safe ['feɪlseɪf] *adj* infalible
fail-safe device *n* mecanismo *m* de seguridad
failure ['feɪljə^r, *Am:* 'feɪljə-] *n* **1.** *no pl* (*lack of
success*) fracaso *m;* **crop ~** AGR pérdida *f* de la
cosecha; **to be doomed to ~** estar destinado
al fracaso; **the ~ to answer** el incumplimiento
de responder **2.** TECH, ELEC (*breakdown*) fallo *m*
3. COM quiebra *f*
faint [feɪnt] **I.** *adj* **1.** (*scent, odour, taste*) leve;
(*sound, murmur*) apenas perceptible; (*light,
glow*) ténue; (*line, outline, scratch*) apenas
visible; (*memory*) confuso, -a; (*smile*) ligero, -a
2. (*slight: resemblance, sign, suspicion*) vago,
-a; (*chance, hope, possibility*) ligero, -a; **not to
make the ~est attempt to do sth** no mostrar
la menor intención de hacer algo; **not to have
the ~est idea** *inf* no tener ni idea **3.** (*weak*) **to
be ~ with hunger** estar desfallecido por
hambre; **to feel ~** sentirse mareado **II.** *vi* desmayarse **III.** *n* desmayo *m;* **to fall down in a
faint** *Brit* caer desmayado
faint-hearted [,feɪnt'hɑːtɪd, *Am:* -'hɑːrtɪd]
adj (*person*) pusilánime
faintly *adv* (*barely perceptibly*) débilmente;
(*remember*) vagamente; (*slightly*) ligeramente
fair[1] [feə^r, *Am:* fer] **I.** *adj* **1.** (*just: society, trial,
wage*) justo, -a; (*price*) razonable; **a ~ share**
una parte equitativa; **~ enough** está bien; **it's**

only ~ that she should be told lo justo es
decírselo **2.** *inf* (*quite large: amount*) bastante;
it's a ~ size es bastante grande **3.** (*reasonably
good: chance, prospect*) bueno, -a **4.** (*not
bad*) aceptable **5.** (*light in colour: skin*) blanco,
-a, güero, -a *AmL;* (*hair*) rubio, -a **6.** METEO **~
weather** tiempo *m* agradable ▸**~ go** *Aus* sé
razonable; **by ~ means or foul** con métodos
ortodoxos o sin ellos; **it's ~ set** *Brit* la situación
es favorable; **~'s ~** *inf* lo justo es justo **II.** *adv* **to
play ~** jugar limpio ▸**~ and square** (*following
the rules*) con todas las de la ley; (*directly*) de
lleno
fair[2] [feə^r] *n* feria *f;* **trade ~** feria comercial
fair copy <-ies> *n* copia *f* en limpio **fair
game** *no pl n* caza *f* legal; *fig* objeto *m* legítimo
fairground ['feəgraʊnd, *Am:* 'fer-] *n* parque
m de atracciones
fair-haired [,feə'heəd, *Am:* ,fer'herd] *adj*
rubio, -a
fairly ['feəli, *Am:* 'fer-] *adv* **1.** (*quite*) bastante
2. (*justly*) con imparcialidad **3.** *liter* (*almost*)
prácticamente ▸**~ and squarely** *Brit, Aus* de
lleno
fair-minded [,feə'maɪndɪd, *Am:* ,fer-] *adj*
imparcial
fairness *n no pl* **1.** (*justice*) justicia *f;* **in (all)
~ ...** para ser justo... **2.** (*of skin*) blancura *f;* (*of
hair*) lo rubio
fair play *n no pl* juego *m* limpio
fairway ['feəweɪ, *Am:* 'fer-] *n* **1.** (*in golf*)
calle *f* **2.** NAUT canal *m* navegable
fairy ['feəri, *Am:* 'feri] <-ies> *n* **1.** (*creature*)
hada *f* **2.** *pej, inf* (*homosexual*) mariquita *m*
fairy-lights *npl* bombillas *fpl* de colores
fairytale *n* cuento *m* de hadas; *fig* cuento *m*
chino; **a ~ ending** un final feliz
faith [feɪθ] *n* fe *f;* **to have/lose ~ in sb/sth**
tener/perder la fe en alguien/algo; **to put
one's ~ in sb/sth** confiar en alguien/algo; **to
renounce one's ~** renunciar a sus creencias;
to keep the ~ mantener la fe
faithful ['feɪθfəl] **I.** *adj* fiel **II.** *n* **the ~** los
fieles
faithfully *adv* **1.** (*loyally: serve*) lealmente; **to
promise ~ to do sth** prometer sinceramente
hacer algo; **Yours ~** *Brit, Aus* (le saluda) atentamente **2.** (*exactly: copy, translate*) fielmente
faith healer *n* curandero, -a *m, f*
faithless ['feɪθləs] *adj* REL infiel; (*disloyal*)
desleal
fake [feɪk] **I.** *n* **1.** (*painting, jewel*) falsificación *f* **2.** (*person*) impostor(a) *m(f)* **II.** *adj* **~
fur** piel sintética; **~ jewel** joya falsa; **a ~ tan**
un bronceado artificial **III.** *vt* **1.** (*counterfeit*)
falsificar **2.** (*pretend to feel*) fingir **IV.** *vi* fingir
fakir ['feɪkɪə^r, *Am:* fɑː'kɪr] *n* faquir *m*
falcon ['fɔːlkən, *Am:* 'fæl-] *n* halcón *m*
Falkland Islands ['fɔːklæd,aɪləndz] *npl*
the ~ las (Islas) Malvinas
fall [fɔːl] <fell, fallen> **I.** *vi* **1.** (*drop down*)
caerse; (*rain, snow*) caer; (*tree*) venirse abajo;

THEAT (*curtain*) caer; **to ~ flat** (*joke*) no tener gracia; (*plan, suggestion*) no tener éxito; **to ~ down the stairs** caerse por las escaleras; **to ~ (down) dead** caer muerto; **to ~ flat on one's face** caerse de morros **2. to ~ to one's knees** arrodillarse **3.** (*land: bomb, missile*) caer **4.** (*accent, stress*) recaer **5.** (*decrease: prices*) bajar; (*demand*) descender; **to ~ sharply** caer de forma acusada **6.** (*temperature*) descender **7.** (*league table, charts*) bajar **8.** (*be defeated*) caer; **to ~ under sb's power** caer bajo el dominio de alguien; **the prize fell to him** le tocó el premio **9.** *liter* (*die in battle*) caer **10.** REL pecar **11.** (*occur*) **to ~ on a Monday** caer en lunes **12.** (*happen*) **night was ~ing** anochecía **13.** (*belong*) **to ~ into a category** pertenecer a una categoría **14.** (*hang down: hair, cloth*) colgar **15.** (*go down: cliff, ground, road*) descender **16.** + *adj* (*become*) **to ~ asleep** dormirse; **to ~ due** tocar (pagar); **to ~ foul of a law** infringir la ley; **to ~ foul of sb** tener desavenencias con alguien; **to ~ ill** caer enfermo; **to ~ vacant** quedar vacante **17.** (*enter a particular state*) **to ~ madly in love (with sb/sth)** enamorarse perdidamente (de alguien/algo) **II.** *n* **1.** (*drop from a height*) caída *f* **2.** (*decrease*) disminución *f*; **~ in temperature** descenso *m* de la temperatura **3.** (*defeat*) caída *f* **4.** *Am* (*autumn*) otoño *m* **5.** *pl* (*waterfall*) cascada *f*; **the Niagara Falls** las cataratas del Niágara **6.** *no pl* REL **the Fall** la Caída **III.** *adj Am* (*occuring in autumn*) en otoño; (*of autumn*) otoñal

◆**fall about** *vi Brit, Aus, inf* troncharse, partirse; **to ~ (laughing)** morirse de risa

◆**fall away** *vi* **1.** (*become detached: plaster, rock*) desprenderse **2.** (*slope downward*) caer en declive **3.** *Brit, Aus* (*decrease: attendance, support*) decaer; **to ~ sharply** irse a pique **4.** (*disappear: feeling*) desvanecerse

◆**fall back** *vi* **1.** (*move backwards: crowd*) quedarse atrás **2.** (*retreat: army*) replegarse **3.** SPORTS (*runner*) perder posiciones **4.** *Brit, Aus* (*decrease: production, prices*) reducirse

◆**fall back on** *vt*, **fall back upon** *vt* echar mano de

◆**fall behind** *vi* **1.** (*become slower*) quedarse atrás **2.** (*achieve less: team, country*) quedarse rezagado **3.** (*fail to do sth on time*) retrasarse **4.** SPORTS quedarse atrás

◆**fall down** *vi* **1.** (*person*) caerse; (*building*) derrumbarse; **to be falling down** estar viniéndose abajo **2.** (*be unsatisfactory: person, plan*) fallar; **to ~ on the job** *inf* no servir para el trabajo

◆**fall for** *vt* **to ~ sb** enamorarse de alguien; **to ~ a trick** caer en la trampa

◆**fall in** *vi* **1.** (*into water, hole*) caerse **2.** (*collapse: roof, ceiling*) venirse abajo **3.** MIL formar filas

◆**fall in with** *vt insep* **1.** (*agree to*) aceptar **2.** (*become friendly with*) **to ~ sb** juntarse con alguien

◆**fall off** *vi* **1.** (*become detached*) desprenderse **2.** (*decrease*) reducirse

◆**fall on** *vt insep* **1.** (*date*) caer en **2.** (*attack*) echarse encima de; **to ~ sb** (*cuts*) recaer sobre alguien **3.** *liter* (*embrace*) abrazar

◆**fall out** *vi* **1.** (*drop out: of container*) caer; (*teeth, hair*) caerse **2.** *inf* (*quarrel*) pelearse **3.** MIL romper filas

◆**fall over** **I.** *vi insep* caerse **II.** *vt* tropezarse con; **to fall over oneself to do sth** *inf* desvivirse por hacer algo

◆**fall through** *vi* fracasar

◆**fall to** *vt insep* **1.** (*be responsibility of*) tocar a **2.** (*fail*) **to ~ pieces** (*plan, relationship*) terminar en nada; (*person*) venirse abajo

◆**fall upon** *vt s.* **fall on**

fallacious [fəˈleɪʃəs] *adj form* falaz

fallacy [ˈfæləsi] <-ies> *n* falacia *f*

fallen [ˈfɔːlən] *adj* caído, -a; **~ arches** MED pies *mpl* planos; **a ~ dictator** un dictador derrocado; **a ~ woman** una mujer perdida

fall guy *n Am, inf* cabeza *f* de turco

fallible [ˈfæləbl] *adj* falible; **we are all ~** errar es humano

falling star *n* estrella *f* fugaz

fall-off [ˈfɔːlɒf, *Am:* -ɑːf] *n* COM baja *f*; (*lessening*) empeoramiento *m*

Fallopian tube [fəˈləʊpɪənˈtjuːb, *Am:* fəˈloʊpɪənˈtuːb] *n* trompa *f* de Falopio

fallout [ˈfɔːlaʊt] *n no pl* **1.** PHYS lluvia *f* radiactiva **2.** *fig* secuelas *fpl*

fallout shelter *n* refugio *m* antinuclear

fallow [ˈfæləʊ, *Am:* -oʊ] **I.** *adj* **1.** (*ground, field*) en barbecho **2.** (*period, time*) improductivo, -a **II.** *adv* **to lie ~** estar en barbecho

fallow deer [ˈfæləʊdɪəʳ, *Am:* -oʊdɪr] *n inv* gamo *m*

false [fɔːls] **I.** *adj* **1.** (*untrue: idea, information*) falso, -a; **a ~ dawn** una señal errónea; **~ economy** falso ahorro *m*; **~ move** movimiento *m* en falso; **to take a ~ step** dar un paso en falso; **a ~ pregnancy** MED, PSYCH embarazo *m* psicológico; **to give a ~ impression** dar una impresión equivocada; **to raise ~ hopes** levantar falsas esperanzas **2.** (*artificial: beard, eyelashes*) postizo, -a; **a ~ bottom** un doble fondo **3.** (*name, address, identity*) falso, -a; **to give ~ evidence in court** LAW dar falso testimonio en un juicio; **~ accounting** LAW, FIN falsificación *f* de la contabilidad; **under ~ colours** *liter* aparentando lo que no es; **under ~ pretences** con engaños **4.** (*insincere: smile, laugh, manner*) falso, -a; **to put on a ~ front** ser hipócrita; **~ modesty** falsa modestia *f* **5.** *liter* (*disloyal*) **a ~ friend** un amigo traicionero **II.** *adv* **to play sb ~** traicionar a alguien

false alarm *n* falsa alarma *f* **false friend** *n* LING falso amigo *m*

falsehood [ˈfɔːlshʊd] *n* **1.** *no pl* (*untruth*)

falsedad *f* **2.** (*lie*) mentira *f*

false imprisonment *n* detención *f* ilegal

falseness *n no pl* **1.** (*inaccuracy*) inexactitud *f* **2.** (*insincerity*) falsedad *f*

false start *n* SPORTS salida *f* nula **false teeth** *npl* dientes *mpl* postizos

falsetto [fɔːlˈsetəʊ, *Am:* fɔːlˈseˌtoʊ] I. *n* falsete *m;* ~ **voice** voz *f* de falsete II. *adv* to sing ~ cantar en falsete

falsification [ˌfɔːlsɪfɪˈkeɪʃən] *n no pl* falsificación *f;* ~ **of evidence** falseamiento *m* de las pruebas

falsify [ˈfɔːlsɪfaɪ] *vt* falsificar

falsity [ˈfɔːlsəti, *Am:* -ˌti] *n no pl* **1.** (*inaccuracy*) inexactitud *f* **2.** (*insincerity*) falsedad *f*

falter [ˈfɔːltər, *Am:* -ˌtə] *vi* (*person*) vacilar; (*conversation*) decaer; (*courage, negotiations*) tambalearse

faltering [ˈfɔːltərɪŋ, *Am:* -ˌtə-] *adj* (*voice, speech*) entrecortado, -a; (*steps*) indeciso, -a

fame [feɪm] *n no pl* fama *f;* **to rise to** ~ hacerse famoso

famed [feɪmd] *adj* famoso, -a

familiar [fəˈmɪliər, *Am:* -jə] *adj* **1.** (*well--known*) familiar; (*face*) conocido, -a **2.** (*acquainted*) familiarizado, -a **3.** (*friendly*) de familiaridad; ~ **form of address** LING forma *f* de trato informal; **to be on** ~ **terms** (**with sb**) tener un trato de confianza (con alguien)

familiarity [fəˌmɪliˈærəti, *Am:* -ˈerəˌti] *n no pl* **1.** (*intimacy*) familiaridad *f;* (*inappropriate friendliness*) confianza *f* excesiva **2.** (*knowledge*) conocimiento *m*

familiarize [fəˈmɪliəraɪz, *Am:* -jəraɪz] *vt* acostumbrar; **to** ~ **oneself with sth** familiarizarse con algo

family [ˈfæməli] <-ies> I. *n* familia *f;* **to be** ~ ser familia; **to be** (**like**) **one of the** ~ ser como uno más de la familia; **to run in the** ~ venir de familia; **to start a** ~ formar una familia II. *adj* familiar

family allowance *n Brit* subsidio *m* familiar

family doctor *n Brit* médico *m* de cabecera

family man *n* (*enjoying family life*) hombre *m* casero; (*with wife and family*) padre *m* de familia **family name** *n* apellido *m* **family planning** *n no pl* planificación *f* familiar

family tree *n* árbol *m* genealógico

famine [ˈfæmɪn] *n* hambruna *f*

famished [ˈfæmɪʃt] *adj inf* **to be** ~ estar muerto de hambre

famous [ˈfeɪməs] *adj* famoso, -a; **to become** ~ **for sth** hacerse célebre por algo

famously *adv* **to get on** ~ llevarse divinamente

fan¹ [fæn] I. *n* **1.** (*hand-held*) abanico *m* **2.** (*electrical*) ventilador *m* II. <-nn-> *vt* **1.** (*cool with fan*) abanicar; **to** ~ **oneself** abanicarse **2.** *fig* (*heighten: passion, interest*) avivar; **to** ~ **the flames** *fig* echar leña al fuego

fan² [fæn] *n* (*of person*) admirador(a) *m(f);* (*of team*) hincha *mf;* (*of music*) fan *mf*

fanatic [fəˈnætɪk, *Am:* -ˈnætɪk] *n* **1.** entu-

siasta *mf* **2.** *pej* fanático, -a *m, f*

fanatical *adj* fanático, -a; **to be** ~ **about sth** estar ciego por algo

fanaticism [fəˈnætɪsɪzəm, *Am:* -ˈnæt-] *n no pl* fanatismo *m*

fan belt *n* AUTO correa *f* del ventilador

fancied *adj* favorito, -a

fancier *n* **pigeon** ~ criador(a) *m(f)* de palomas

fanciful [ˈfænsɪfəl] *adj* **1.** (*idea, notion*) descabellado, -a **2.** (*design, style*) imaginativo, -a

fan club *n* club *m* de fans

fancy [ˈfænsi] I. <-ie-> *vt* **1.** *Brit* (*want, like*) **to** ~ **doing sth** tener ganas de hacer algo **2.** *Brit* (*be attracted to*) **he fancies you** le gustas; **to** ~ **oneself** ser un creído; **to** ~ **oneself as sth** dárselas de algo **3.** (*imagine*) **to** ~ (**that**) … imaginarse (que)…; ~ (**that**)! ¡lo que son las cosas!; …, I ~ *Brit* …,me parece; ~ **shouting at him!** ¡cómo se te (etc.) ocurre gritarle!; ~ **meeting here!** ¡qué casualidad encontrarnos aquí! II. *n* <-ies> **1.** *no pl* (*liking*) **to take a** ~ **to sth/sb** quedarse prendado de algo/alguien; **to take sb's** ~ dejar fascinado a alguien; **it tickled his** ~ le hizo gracia **2.** *no pl* (*imagination*) fantasía *f* **3.** (*whimsical idea*) capricho *m;* **whenever the** ~ **takes you** cuando se te antoje III. *adj* <-ier, -iest> **1.** (*elaborate: decoration, frills*) de adorno; **the speech was all** ~ **phrases** el discurso estaba lleno de florituras **2.** (*whimsical: ideas, notions*) extravagante **3.** *inf* (*expensive*) carísimo, -a; ~ **hotel** hotel *m* de lujo; ~ **prices** precios *mpl* exorbitantes

fancy dress *n no pl, Brit, Aus* disfraz *m*

fancy-free [ˌfænsiˈfriː] *adj* libre

fancy goods *npl* artículos *mpl* de regalo

fancy man *n* <-men> *n inf* amante *m*

fanfare [ˈfænfeər, *Am:* -fer] *n* fanfarria *f*

fang [fæŋ] *n* (*of dog, lion*) colmillo *m;* (*of snake*) diente *m*

fanlight [ˈfænlaɪt] *n* montante *m* (*de ventana*)

fan mail *n no pl* cartas *fpl* de admiradores

fanny [ˈfæni] *n* **1.** *Brit, vulg* coño *m* **2.** *Am, inf* culo *m*

fantasize [ˈfæntəsaɪz, *Am:* -ˌtə-] *vi* **to** ~ **about sth** fantasear sobre algo

fantastic [fænˈtæstɪk] *adj* **1.** (*excellent*) fantástico, -a **2.** (*unbelievable: coincidence*) increíble; (*notion, plan*) absurdo, -a

fantasy [ˈfæntəsi, *Am:* -ˌtə-] <-ies> *n* fantasía *f*

fanzine [ˈfænziːn] *n* fanzine *m*

FAO *n abbr of* Food and Agriculture Organization OAA *f*

FAQ *n* INFOR *abbr of* frequently asked questions FAQ *f*

far [faːr, *Am:* faːr] <farther, farthest *o* further, furthest> I. *adv* **1.** (*a long distance*) lejos; **how** ~ **is it from Boston to Maine?** ¿qué distancia hay entre Boston y Maine?; ~ **away** muy lejos; ~ **distant** *liter* muy lejos; ~ **from doing sth** lejos de hacer algo; ~ **from it**

todo lo contrario **2.** (*distant in time*) **as ~ back as I remember ...** hasta donde me alcanza la memoria...; **to be not ~ off sth** rondar algo; **so ~** hasta ahora **3.** (*in progress*) **to not get very ~ with sb/sth** no llegar muy lejos con alguien/algo; **he will go ~** llegará lejos; **to go too ~** ir demasiado lejos **4.** (*much*) **~ better** mucho mejor; **~ nicer** mucho más bonito; **to be the best by ~** ser el/la mejor con diferencia; **to be ~ too expensive** ser demasiado caro **5.** (*connecting adverbial phrase*) **as ~ as I know ...** que yo sepa...; **as ~ as you can** en (todo) lo que puedas; **as ~ as possible** en lo posible; **as ~ as I'm concerned ...** en lo que a mí se refiere...; **the essay is OK as ~ as it goes** la redacción es aceptable ▶**so ~ so good** hasta ahora todo va bien; **~ and wide** por todas partes **II.** *adj* **1.** (*distant*) lejano, -a; **in the ~ distance** a lo lejos; **a ~ country** *liter* un país lejano **2.** (*further away*) **the ~ bank of the river** el otro lado de la orilla; **the ~ left/right** (**of a party**) la extrema izquierda/derecha (de un partido)

faraway ['fɑːrəweɪ] *adj* **a ~ land** una tierra lejana; **to have a ~ expression** estar abstraído

farce [fɑːs, *Am:* fɑːrs] *n* **1.** THEAT farsa *f* **2.** *fig* follón *m*

farcical ['fɑːsɪkl, *Am:* 'fɑːr-] *adj* absurdo, -a

fare [feə^r, *Am:* fer] **I.** *n* **1.** (*for journey*) tarifa *f*; **single/return ~** billete sencillo/de ida y vuelta **2.** (*taxi passenger*) pasajero, -a *m*, *f* **3.** *no pl* GASTR comida *f*; **traditional British ~** comida tradicional británica **II.** *vi* **to ~ badly/well** salir mal/bien parado; **how did you ~ at the interview?** ¿qué tal te fue la entrevista?

Far East *n* **the ~** el Extremo Oriente

farewell [ˌfeə'wel, *Am:* ˌfer-] **I.** *interj form* adiós; **to bid ~ to sb/sth** despedirse de alguien/algo **II.** *n* despedida *f* **III.** *adj* de despedida

far-fetched [ˌfɑː'fetʃt, *Am:* ˌfɑːr-] *adj* inverosímil

far-flung [ˌfɑː'flʌŋ, *Am:* ˌfɑːr-] *adj liter* **1.** (*spread over wide area*) extenso, -a **2.** (*remote*) lejano, -a

farm [fɑːm, *Am:* fɑːrm] **I.** *n* (*small*) granja *f*, hacienda *f* AmL, chacra *f* CSur, Perú; (*large*) hacienda *f* **II.** *vt* cultivar **III.** *vi* cultivar la tierra ◆**farm out** *vt* **to ~ work** subcontratar; **to ~ children to sb** pedir a alguien que cuide de los niños

farmer ['fɑːmə^r, *Am:* 'fɑːrmə^r] *n* granjero, -a *m*, *f*, hacendado, -a *m*, *f*, chacarero, -a *m*, *f* CSur, Perú

farmhand *n* mozo *m* de labranza **farmhouse** *n* <-s> casa *f* de labranza **farmland** *n* terreno *m* agrícola **farmstead** *n Am:* edificios de una granja **farmyard** *n* corral *m*

far-off [ˌfɑː'ʰɒf, *Am:* ˌfɑːr'ɑːf] *adj* (*place, country*) lejano, -a; (*time*) remoto, -a

far-reaching [ˌfɑː'riːtʃɪŋ, *Am:* ˌfɑːr-] *adj* de grandes repercusiones

far-seeing [ˌfɑː'siːɪŋ, *Am:* ˌfɑːr-] *adj* (*deci-*

sion, policy) con visión de futuro; (*person*) previsor(a)

far-sighted [ˌfɑː'saɪtɪd, *Am:* ˌfɑːr'saɪtɪd] *adj Brit, Aus* (*decision, policy*) con visión de futuro; (*person*) previsor(a)

fart [fɑːt, *Am:* fɑːrt] *inf* **I.** *n* pedo *m*; **to do a ~** tirarse un pedo **II.** *vi* tirarse un pedo

farther ['fɑːðə^r, *Am:* 'fɑːrðə^r] **I.** *adv comp of* **far 1.** (*distance*) más allá; **~ away from ...** más lejos de...; **~ down/up** más abajo/arriba **2.** (*time*) **~ back in time** más atrás en el tiempo **3.** (*additional*) *s.* **further II.** *adj comp of* **far'** más lejano, -a

farthest ['fɑːðɪst, *Am:* 'fɑːr-] **I.** *adv superl of* **far** más lejos **II.** *adj superl of* **far** (*distance*) más lejano, -a; (*time*) más remoto, -a

farthing ['fɑːðɪŋ, *Am:* 'fɑːr-] *n* (*coin*) cuarto *m* de penique

fascia ['feɪʃə] *n* **1.** *Brit* (*dashboard*) tablero *m* de mandos **2.** (*board above shop window*) letrero *m* **3.** ARCHIT faja *f*

fascinate ['fæsɪneɪt, *Am:* -əneɪt] *vt* fascinar

fascinating ['fæsɪneɪtɪŋ, *Am:* -t̬ɪŋ] *adj* fascinante

fascination [ˌfæsɪ'neɪʃən, *Am:* -ə'-] *n no pl* fascinación *f*; **to listen in ~** escuchar fascinado

fascism *n*, **Fascism** ['fæʃɪzəm] *n no pl* fascismo *m*

fascist, Fascist ['fæʃɪst] **I.** *n* fascista *mf* **II.** *adj* fascista

fashion ['fæʃən] **I.** *n* **1.** (*popular style*) moda *f*; **to be in ~** estar de moda; **to be out of ~** estar pasado de moda; **to come into ~** ponerse de moda; **to be all the ~** estar muy de moda; **the latest ~** la última moda **2.** (*manner*) manera *f*; **in the usual ~** como de costumbre; **after a ~** si se le puede llamar así **II.** *vt form* dar forma a; (*create*) crear

fashionable ['fæʃənəbl] *adj* (*clothes, style*) moderno, -a; (*nightclub, restaurant*) de moda; (*person, set*) a la moda

fashion designer *n* diseñador(a) *m(f)* de moda **fashion parade** *n* desfile *m* de moda **fashion show** *n* desfile *m* de moda

fast¹ [fɑːst, *Am:* fæst] **I.**<-er, -est> *adj* **1.** rápido, -a; **the ~ lane** el carril de adelantamiento; **~ train** tren *m* expreso; **to be a ~ worker** trabajar rápido **2.** (*clock*) **to be ~** ir adelantado **3.** (*firmly fixed*) fijo, -a; **to make ~** NAUT amarrar firmemente; **to make sth ~** (**to sth**) fijar algo (a algo) **4.** (*immoral*) **~ woman** mujer *f* lanzada **II.** *adv* **1.** (*quickly*) rápidamente; **not so ~!** ¡no tan rápido! **2.** (*firmly*) firmemente; **to hold ~ to sth** agarrarse bien a algo; **to stand ~** mantenerse firme **3.** (*deeply*) profundamente; **to be ~ asleep** estar profundamente dormido

fast² [fɑːst, *Am:* fæst] **I.** *vi* ayunar **II.** *n* ayuno *m*

fasten ['fɑːsən, *Am:* 'fæsən] *vt* **1.** (*do up*) atar **2.** (*fix securely*) fijar **3. to ~ sth onto sth** atar firmemente algo a algo; **to ~ one's eyes on sth** fijar la mirada en algo; **to ~ sth**

together (*with paper clip*) unir algo; (*with string*) atar algo

♦**fasten down** *vt* sujetar

♦**fasten on** I. *vt* fijarse en; **to ~ an idea** aferrarse a una idea II. *vi* **to ~ to sb** pegarse a alguien

♦**fasten up** *vi*, *vt Brit*, *Aus* abrochar(se)

fastener ['faːsənər, *Am:* 'fæsənə·] *n* cierre *m*; **snap ~** cierre *m* automático; **zip ~** cremallera *f*

fast food *n no pl* comida *f* rápida

fast-forward [ˌfaːst'fɔːwəd, *Am:* ˌfæst'fɔːrwə·d] I. *vt* hacer avanzar rápidamente II. *vi* avanzar rápidamente III. *n no pl* botón *m* de avance

fastidious [fə'stɪdɪəs] *adj* escrupuloso, -a

fastness ['faːstnɪs, *Am:* 'fæst-] <-es> *n* 1. MIL fortaleza *f* 2. *liter* (*stronghold*) refugio *m*

fat [fæt] I. *adj* 1. gordo, -a; **to get ~** engordar 2. (*thick*) grueso, -a 3. (*large*) grande; **a ~ cheque** un cheque sustancioso ►**~ chance!** *inf* ¡para nada!, ¡ni soñarlo! II. *n* 1. *no pl* (*meat tissue*) carnes *fpl* 2. (*fatty substance*) grasa *f*; **vegetable ~** grasa vegetal ►**the ~ is in the fire** aquí se va a armar la gorda; **to live off the ~ of the land** vivir a cuerpo de rey; **to chew the ~ with sb** *inf* estar de palique [*o* de cháchara] con alguien

fatal ['feɪtəl, *Am:* -t̬əl] *adj* 1. (*causing death*) mortal 2. (*disastrous*) desastroso, -a 3. *liter* (*consequences*) funesto, -a

fatalism ['feɪtəlɪzəm, *Am:* -t̬əl-] *n no pl* fatalismo *m*

fatalist *n* fatalista *mf*

fatality [fə'tæləti, *Am:* -t̬i] <-ies> *n* fatalidad *f*

fatally *adv* 1. (*causing death*) mortalmente; **~ ill** enfermo de muerte 2. (*disastrously*) desastrosamente; **~ damaged** dañado de forma irreparable

fat cat *n inf* pez *m* gordo

fate [feɪt] *n no pl* (*destiny*) destino *m*; (*one's end*) suerte *f*; **to leave sb to his ~** dejar a alguien a su suerte; **to meet one's ~** hallar su destino; **to seal sb's ~** determinar el destino de alguien; **to share the same ~** compartir la misma suerte; **to tempt ~** tentar a la suerte; **a ~ worse than death** un destino peor que la muerte; **it must be ~** debe ser el destino

fated ['feɪtɪd, *Am:* -t̬ɪd] *adj* predestinado, -a; **to be ~ to do sth** estar predestinado a hacer algo; **it was ~ that ...** estaba escrito que...

fateful ['feɪtfəl] *adj* fatídico, -a

fat-free *adj* sin grasas

fathead ['fæthed] *n inf* imbécil *mf*

father ['faːðər, *Am:* -ðə·] I. *n* 1. (*parent*) padre *m*; **from ~ to son** de padre a hijo; **to be like a ~ to sb** ser como un padre para alguien; **on your ~'s side** por parte paterna 2. (*founder*) fundador *m* 3. *pl*, *liter* (*ancestors*) antepasados *mpl* ►**like ~, like son** de tal palo tal astilla II. *vt* (*child*) engendrar; (*idea*) crear

Father Christmas *n Brit* Papá *m* Noel

father figure *n* figura *f* paterna

fatherhood ['faːðəhʊd, *Am:* -ðə·-] *n no pl* paternidad *f*

father-in-law ['faːðərɪnlɔː, *Am:* -ðə·ɪnlaː] <fathers-in-law *o* father-in-laws> *n* suegro *m*

fatherland ['faːðəlænd, *Am:* -ðə·-] *n* patria *f*

fatherless ['faːðələs, *Am:* -ðə·-] *adj* huérfano, -a de padre

fatherly ['faːðəli, *Am:* -ðə·li] *adj* paternal

Father's Day *n no pl* Día *m* del Padre

fathom ['fæðəm] I. *n* NAUT braza *f* II. *vt* (*mystery*) desentrañar

fathomless *adj liter* 1. (*too deep to measure*) insondable 2. (*impossible to understand*) incomprensible

fatigue [fə'tiːg] I. *n* 1. *no pl* (*tiredness*) cansancio *m*, fatiga *f*; **to suffer from ~** estar cansado 2. TECH fatiga *f* 3. MIL faena *f*; (*uniform*) uniforme *m* de faena II. *vt* 1. *form* (*tire*) cansar 2. TECH (*weaken*) debilitar

fatigue dress *n*, **fatigues** *npl* MIL traje *m* de faena

fatten ['fætən] *vt* engordar

fattening *adj* que hace engordar

fatty ['fæti, *Am:* 'fæt̬-] I. *adj* 1. (*food*) graso, -a 2. (*tissue*) adiposo, -a II. <-ies> *n inf* gordinflón, -ona *m*, *f*

fatuous ['fætʃʊəs, *Am:* 'fætʃu-] *adj* fatuo, -a

faucet ['fɔːsɪt, *Am:* 'faː-] *n Am* grifo *m*, bitoque *m Méx*, *RíoPl*; **to turn a ~ on/off** abrir/cerrar el grifo

fault [fɔːlt] I. *n* 1. *no pl* (*responsibility*) culpa *f*; **it's not my ~** yo no tengo la culpa; **to be sb's ~ (that ...)** ser culpa de alguien (que ...); **to be at ~** tener la culpa; **to find ~ with sb** criticar a alguien 2. (*character weakness*) debilidad *f*; **to have its ~s** tener sus defectos; **to be generous to a ~** ser demasiado generoso 3. (*defect*) fallo *m*; **electrical/technical ~** fallo eléctrico/técnico 4. GEO falla *f* 5. SPORTS falta *f*; **double ~** doble falta; **foot ~** falta de pie; **to call a ~** pitar una falta II. *vt* encontrar defectos en

fault-finding ['fɔːltˌfaɪndɪŋ] I. *n no pl* 1. (*criticism*) crítica *f* 2. ELEC detección *f* de averías II. *adj* criticón, -ona

faultless ['fɔːltləs] *adj* impecable

faulty ['fɔːlti, *Am:* -t̬i] *adj* defectuoso, -a; **~ logic** lógica *f* imperfecta

faun [fɔːn, *Am:* faːn] *n* fauno *m*

fauna ['fɔːnə, *Am:* 'faː-] *n* fauna *f*

favor ['feɪvər, *Am:* -və·] *n*, *vt Am*, *Aus s.* **favour**

favorable ['feɪvərəbl] *adj Am*, *Aus s.* **favourable**

favored *adj Am*, *Aus s.* **favoured**

favorite ['feɪvərɪt] *adj*, *n Am*, *Aus s.* **favourite**

favoritism *n Am*, *Aus s.* **favouritism**

favour ['feɪvər, *Am:* -və·] *Brit*, *Aus* I. *n* 1. *no pl* (*approval*) favor *m*, aprobación *f*; **to be in ~**

of sb/sth estar a favor de alguien/algo; **to decide/vote in ~ of (doing)** sth decidir/votar a favor de (hacer) algo; **to come down in ~ of (doing) sth** ponerse a favor de (hacer) algo; **to be in ~** tener mucha aceptación; **to be in ~ with sb** tener el apoyo de alguien; **to be out of ~** no tener aceptación; **to reject sth in ~ of sth else** rechazar algo por otra cosa; **to find in ~ of sb** LAW fallar a favor de alguien; **to find ~ with sb** caer en gracia a alguien; **to gain** [o **win**] **sb's ~** ganarse la simpatía de alguien; **to show ~ to sb** *form* favorecer a alguien **2.** *no pl* (*advantage*) **to be in sb's ~** apoyar a alguien; **to have sth in one's ~** tener algo a favor; **to have the wind in one's ~** tener el viento a favor **3.** (*helpful act*) favor *m*, valedura *f Méx;* **to ask sb a ~** pedir un favor a alguien; **to do sb a ~** hacer un favor a alguien; **do me a ~!** *Brit, inf* ¡hazme el favor! **4.** *Am* (*small gift*) detalle *m* **II.** *vt* **1.** (*prefer*) preferir **2.** (*give advantage to*) favorecer **3.** (*show partiality towards*) mostrar parcialidad por **4.** *form* (*graciously give*) **to ~ sb with sth** dar algo a alguien

favourable [ˈfeɪvərəbl] *adj* **1.** (*approving*) favorable; **to make a ~ impression (on sb)** causar una impresión favorable (a alguien) **2.** (*advantageous*) ventajoso, -a; **~ to sth/sb** ventajoso para algo/alguien

favoured [ˈfeɪvəd, *Am:* -vɚd] *adj* predilecto, -a

favourite [ˈfeɪvərɪt] **I.** *adj* (*most liked*) favorito, -a; **~ son** *Am* POL hijo *m* predilecto **II.** *n* favorito, -a *m, f*

favouritism *n no pl* favoritismo *m*

fawn¹ [fɔːn, *Am:* fɑːn] **I.** *n* **1.** (*young deer*) cervato *m* **2.** (*colour*) beige *m* **II.** *adj* beige

fawn² [fɔːn, *Am:* fɑːn] *vi* **to ~ on sb** elogiar a alguien

fawning [ˈfɔːnɪŋ, *Am:* ˈfɑː-] *adj* adulador(a)

fax [fæks] **I.** *n no pl* fax *m;* **to send something by ~** enviar algo por fax **II.** *vt* mandar por fax; **to ~ sth through to sb** pasar algo por fax a alguien

fax machine *n* fax *m*

FBI [ˌefbiːˈaɪ] *n abbr of* **Federal Bureau of Investigation** FBI *m*

FCO [ˌefsiːˈəʊ, *Am:* -ˈoʊ] *n Brit* POL *abbr of* **Foreign and Commonwealth Office** *ministerio de asuntos exteriores y de la Commonwealth*

fear [fɪər, *Am:* fɪr] **I.** *n* miedo *m;* **to have a ~ of sth** tener miedo de algo; **~ of heights** miedo a las alturas; **for ~ of doing sth** por miedo a hacer algo; **for ~ that** por temor a; **to be in ~ of sth** temer algo; **to go in ~ of sth** temer por algo; **no ~!** *Brit, Aus, inf* ¡no temas!; **there's no ~ of death** no hay peligro de muerte; **to put the ~ of God into sb** dar un susto de muerte a alguien; **without ~ or favour** imparcialmente **II.** *vt* **1.** (*be afraid of*) tener miedo de; **to have nothing to ~** no tener nada que temer; **to ~ to do sth** tener

miedo de hacer algo **2.** *form* (*feel concern*) **to ~ (that ...)** temer (que ...) **III.** *vi liter* tener miedo; **to ~ for one's life** temer por la vida de uno; **never ~!** *iron* ¡no hay cuidado!

fearful [ˈfɪəfəl, *Am:* ˈfɪr-] *adj* **1.** (*anxious*) temeroso, -a; **~ of doing sth** temeroso de hacer algo **2.** (*terrible: pain, accident*) terrible **3.** *inf* (*very bad: noise, mess*) horrendo, -a

fearless [ˈfɪələs, *Am:* ˈfɪr-] *adj* intrépido, -a

fearsome [ˈfɪəsəm, *Am:* ˈfɪr-] *adj* temible

feasibility [ˌfiːzəˈbɪləti, *Am:* -ti] *n no pl* viabilidad *f*

feasibility study *n* estudio *m* de viabilidad

feasible [ˈfiːzəbl] *adj* **1.** (*plan*) factible **2.** (*story*) plausible

feast [fiːst] **I.** *n* **1.** (*meal*) banquete *m;* **a ~ for the eye** una fiesta para los ojos; **a ~ for the ear** un deleite para el oído **2.** REL festividad *f* **II.** *vi* **to ~ on sth** darse un banquete con algo **III.** *vt* preparar un banquete para ►**to ~ one's eyes on sth** regalarse la vista con algo

feat [fiːt] *n* hazaña *f;* **~ of agility** proeza *f* de agilidad; **~ of engineering** logro *m* de la ingeniería

feather [ˈfeðər, *Am:* -ɚ] **I.** *n* pluma *f;* **a ~ quilt** un edredón de plumas ►**to be a ~ in sb's cap** ser un triunfo para alguien; **as light as a ~** tan ligero como una pluma; **you could have knocked me down with a ~** *Brit, Aus, inf* casi me caigo de espaldas; **to rufle sb's ~s** buscar las cosquillas a alguien **II.** *vt* **to ~ one's own nest** barrer hacia dentro

featherbed [ˈfeðəbed, *Am:* -ɚ-] *vt* subvencionar (demasiado)

featherbrained [ˈfeðəbreɪnd, *Am:* -ɚ-] *adj* casquivano, -a

featherweight [ˈfeðəweɪt, *Am:* -ɚ-] *n* SPORTS peso *m* pluma

feathery [ˈfeðəri] *adj* (*clouds, leaves*) ligero, -a (como una pluma); (*feel, texture*) plumoso, -a

feature [ˈfiːtʃər, *Am:* -tʃɚ] **I.** *n* **1.** (*distinguishing attribute*) característica *f;* (*speciality*) peculiaridad *f;* **sb's/sth's best ~** lo mejor de alguien/algo; **a distinguishing ~** un rasgo distintivo; **a physical ~** un rasgo físico; **to make a ~ of sth** hacer de algo un rasgo distintivo **2.** *pl* (*facial attributes*) facciones *fpl;* **to have regular/strong ~s** tener las facciones normales/muy marcadas **3.** (*article*) reportaje *m* **4.** CINE largometraje *m* **II.** *vt* **1.** (*have as performer, star*) presentar; **a film featuring sb as ...** una película que presenta a alguien en el papel de... **2.** (*give special prominence to*) ofrecer (como atracción principal); **to ~ sth** (*article, report*) destacar algo; (*product*) ofrecer la prestación de algo **3.** (*include*) incluir **III.** *vi* **1.** (*appear*) constar; **to ~ in ...** constar en... **2.** (*be an actor in*) figurar; **to ~ in ...** figurar en...

feature film *n* largometraje *m*

featureless *adj* sin rasgos distintivos

feature story *n* reportaje *m*

febrile ['fiːbraɪl, *Am:* -brɪl] *adj liter* febril
February ['februəri, *Am:* -eri] *n* febrero *m; s. a.* April
feces ['fiːsiːz] *npl Am s.* **faeces**
feckless ['feklɪs] *adj form* irreflexivo, -a
Fed *abbr of* federal fed.
federal ['fedərəl] *adj* federal; ~ **republic** república *f* federal
federalism ['fedərəlɪzəm] *n no pl* federalismo *m*
federalist ['fedərəlɪst] *n* federalista *mf*
federate ['fedəreɪt] *vi, vt* federar(se)
federation [ˌfedə'reɪʃən] *n* federación *f*
fed up [ˌfed'ʌp] *adj inf* harto, -a; **to be ~ with sth/sb** estar harto de algo/alguien; **to be ~ to the back teeth with sb/sth** *Brit, Aus* estar hasta el gorro de alguien/algo
fee [fiː] *n* (*for doctor, lawyer*) honorarios *mpl;* (*membership*) cuota *f* de miembro; (*for school, university*) tasas *fpl* de matrícula; **to charge/receive a ~ for sth** cobrar/recibir unos honorarios por algo
feeble ['fiːbl] *adj* (*person, attempt*) débil; (*performance*) flojo, -a
feeble-minded [ˌfiːbl'maɪndɪd] *adj* lelo, -a
feebleness *n no pl* debilidad *f*
feed [fiːd] <fed> I. *vt* 1. (*give food to: person, animal*) alimentar; (*plant*) nutrir; (*baby*) amamantar; **to ~ the fire** avivar el fuego 2. (*provide food for: family, country*) dar de comer a 3. (*supply*) proporcionar; **to ~ the data from a scanner into the computer** introducir datos de un escáner al ordenador; **to ~ sb a line** THEAT apuntar a alguien II. *vi* alimentarse; (*baby*) amamantar III. *n* 1. *no pl* (*for farm animals*) pienso *m;* **cattle ~** pienso para ganado; **to be off its ~** no tener apetito 2. *inf* (*meal*) comida *f* 3. TECH tubo *m* de alimentación
◆**feed back** *vt* proporcionar
◆**feed in** *vt* alimentar; (*information*) introducir
◆**feed on** *vt insep, a. fig* alimentarse de
◆**feed up** *vt* (*person*) alimentar; (*animal*) cebar
feedback ['fiːdbæk] *n* 1. *no pl* (*information*) reacción *f;* **positive/negative ~** reacción *f* positiva/negativa 2. *no pl* ELEC realimentación *f*
feeder *n* 1. TECH alimentador *m* 2. (*river*) afluente *m; ~* **road** carretera *f* de acceso
feeding bottle *n* biberón *m*
feel [fiːl] <felt> I. *vi* 1. + *adj/n* (*sensation or emotion*) sentir; **to ~ well** sentirse bien; **to ~ hot/cold** tener calor/frío; **to ~ hungry/thirsty** tener hambre/sed; **to ~ certain/convinced** estar seguro/convencido; **to ~ as if ...** sentirse como si... + *subj;* **to ~ like a biscuit/a coffee** tener ganas de una galleta/un café; **to ~ like a walk** tener ganas de dar un paseo; **to ~ free to do sth** sentirse libre para hacer algo; **to ~ one's age** notar el peso de los años; **it ~s wonderful/awful** me parece maravilloso/fatal; **how do you ~ about him?** ¿qué opinas

de él?; **how would you ~ if ...?** ¿qué te parece si...? 2. + *adj* (*seem*) parecer 3. (*search*) **to ~ for sth** buscar algo; **to ~ (around) somewhere** buscar palpando por algún sitio II. *vt* 1. (*experience*) experimentar; **not to ~ a thing** no sentir nada; **to ~ the cold/heat** sentir frío/calor; **to ~ something/nothing for sb** sentir algo/no sentir nada por alguien; **to ~ it in one's bones (that ...)** sentir en la propia piel (que...) 2. (*think, believe*) **to ~ (that)** ... creer (que)...; **to ~ it appropriate/necessary to do sth** considerar adecuado/necesario hacer algo 3. (*touch*) tocar; (*pulse*) tomar III. *n* 1. *no pl* (*texture*) textura *f;* **the ~ of sth** el tacto de algo 2. *no pl* (*act of touching*) tacto *m;* **to have a ~ of sth** tocar algo 3. *no pl* (*character, atmosphere*) ambiente *m;* **a ~ of mystery** una atmósfera de misterio 4. *no pl* (*natural talent*) talento *m* natural; **to have a ~ for sth** tener talento natural para algo; **to get the ~ of sth** acostumbrarse a algo
◆**feel about** *vi* buscar palpando; **to ~ for sth** buscar algo a tientas
◆**feel for** *vt* **to ~ sb** sentirlo por alguien, compadecer a alguien
feeler ['fiːlə(ʳ), *Am:* -lə(ʳ)] *n* ZOOL antena *f* ▶**to put out ~s** tantear el terreno
feelgood ['fiːlgʊd] *adj* que hace sentir bien; **~ factor** sensación *f* de bienestar
feeling ['fiːlɪŋ] *n* 1. (*emotion*) sentimiento *m;* **mixed ~s** sentimientos entremezclados; **to hurt sb's ~s** herir los sentimientos de alguien 2. (*sensation*) sensación *f;* **a dizzy ~** una sensación de vértigo 3. (*impression*) impresión *f;* **to have the ~ (that)** ... tener la impresión (de que)... 4. (*opinion*) opinión *f;* **to have strong ~s about sth** tener firmes convicciones sobre algo 5. *no pl* (*strong emotion*) sentimiento *m;* **to say sth with ~** decir algo con emoción 6. *no pl* (*physical sensation*) sensibilidad *f;* **lose the ~ in one's leg** perder la sensibilidad de la pierna 7. (*natural talent*) **to have a ~ for sth** tener un talento innato para algo
feet [fiːt] *n pl of* **foot**
feign [feɪn] *vt liter* fingir; **to ~ madness** fingir estar loco
feigned ['feɪnd] *adj liter* fingido, -a
feint [feɪnt] I. *vi* hacer una finta; **to ~ left** fintar a la izquierda; **to ~ to do sth** simular la intención de hacer algo II. *n* SPORTS finta *f*
felicitous [fə'lɪsɪtəs, *Am:* -təs] *adj* feliz
felicity [fə'lɪsəti, *Am:* -t̬i] <-ies> *n no pl, liter* felicidad *f*
feline ['fiːlaɪn] I. *adj* 1. ZOOL felino, -a 2. (*cat-like*) de gato II. *n* felino *m*
fell¹ [fel] *pt of* **fall**
fell² [fel] *vt* 1. (*cut down*) cortar 2. (*knock down*) hundir
fell³ [fel] *n* (*mountain*) montaña *f*
fell⁴ [fel] *adj* HIST feroz ▶**at one ~ swoop** de un solo golpe
fellow ['feləʊ, *Am:* -oʊ] I. *n* 1. *inf* (*man*) tío

m; **an odd** ~ un tipo raro **2.** UNIV profesor(a) *m(f)* **3.** *form (colleague)* compañero, -a *m, f* **II.** *adj* ~ **student** compañero, -a *m, f* de clase
fellow being *n* prójimo *m* **fellow citizen** *n* conciudadano, -a *m, f* **fellow countryman** *n* compatriota *m* **fellow feeling** *n* compañerismo *m* **fellow member** *n* consocio *mf* **fellow passenger** *n* compañero, -a *m, f* de viaje
fellowship ['feləʊʃɪp, *Am:* -oʊ-] *n* **1.** *no pl (comradely feeling)* compañerismo *m* **2.** *(group)* asociación *f* **3.** UNIV **research** ~ beca *f* de investigación
fellow traveller *n* compañero, -a *m, f* de viaje **fellow worker** *n* compañero, -a *m, f* de trabajo
felon ['felən] *n* criminal *mf*
felonious [fɪ'ləʊnɪəs, *Am:* fə'loʊ-] *adj* criminal
felony ['feləni] <-ies> *n Am* crimen *m*
felt[1] [felt] *pt, pp of* **feel**
felt[2] [felt] **I.** *n no pl* fieltro *m* **II.** *adj* de fieltro
felt-tip (pen) [,felt'tɪp (pen)] *n* rotulador *m*
female ['fi:meɪl] **I.** *adj* femenino, -a; ZOOL, TECH hembra **II.** *n (woman)* mujer *f;* ZOOL hembra *f*
feminine ['femənɪn] **I.** *adj* femenino, -a **II.** *n* LING **the** ~ el femenino
femininity [,femə'nɪnəti, *Am:* -ţi] *n no pl* feminidad *f*
feminism ['femɪnɪzəm] *n no pl* feminismo *m*
feminist ['femɪnɪst] **I.** *n* feminista *mf* **II.** *adj* feminista
femur ['fi:mər, *Am:* -mə·] <-s *o* -mora> *n* fémur *m*
fen [fen] *n* pantano *m*
fence [fens] **I.** *n* **1.** *(barrier)* cerca *f* **2.** *inf (person)* perista *mf* ►**to** **mend** **one's** ~**s** mejorar su reputación; **to** **sit** **on the** ~ nadar entre dos aguas **II.** *vi* **1.** SPORTS esgrimir **2.** *form* **to** ~ **(with sb)** enfrentarse (a alguien) **III.** *vt (enclose)* cercar
fencer *n* esgrimidor(a) *m(f)*
fencing *n no pl* esgrima *f*
fend for ['fend,fɔ:r, *Am:* 'fend,fɔ:r] *vt* **to** ~ **oneself** arreglárselas
◆**fend off** *vt* apartar; **to** ~ **a question** esquivar una pregunta
fender ['fendər, *Am:* -də·] *n* **1.** *(around fireplace)* guardafuego *m* **2.** *Am* AUTO parachoques *m inv,* bómper *m AmL,* defensa *f Méx* **3.** NAUT defensa *f*
fennel ['fenl] *n no pl* hinojo *m*
ferment[1] [fə'ment, *Am:* fə·-] **I.** *vt* **1.** CHEM hacer fermentar **2.** *form (stir up)* agitar **II.** *vi* **1.** CHEM fermentar **2.** *form (develop)* desarrollarse
ferment[2] ['fɜːment, *Am:* 'fɜːr-] *n* **1.** *no pl, form (state of excitement)* agitación *f;* **to be in** ~ estar conmocionado **2.** *no pl (fermentation)* fermentación *f*
fermentation [,fɜːmen'teɪʃən, *Am:* ,fɜːr-] *n*

no pl fermentación *f*
fern [fɜːn, *Am:* fɜːrn] *n* helecho *m*
ferocious [fə'rəʊʃəs, *Am:* -'roʊ-] *adj (battle, criticism)* feroz; *(competition)* duro, -a; *(heat)* tremendo, -a; *(temper)* violento, -a
ferocity [fə'rɒsəti, *Am:* -'rɑːsəţi] *n no pl (of animal, person)* ferocidad *f;* *(of attack)* violencia *f;* *(of storm, wind)* intensidad *f*
ferret ['ferɪt] **I.** *n* hurón *m* **II.** *vi* **1.** *(search)* **to** ~ **around** [*o* **about**] **for sth** husmear en algo **2.** *(hunt with ferrets)* **to go** ~**ing** ir a cazar con hurones
Ferris wheel ['ferɪs,hwiːl] *n* noria *f*
ferrous ['ferəs] *adj* ferroso, -a
ferry ['feri] <-ies> **I.** *n (ship)* ferry *m;* *(smaller)* balsa *f;* **car** ~ ferry de coches **II.** *vt* **1.** *(in boat)* llevar en barca **2.** *inf (by car)* llevar en coche
ferry boat *n* ferry *m* **ferryman** <-men> *n* barquero *m*
fertile ['fɜːtaɪl, *Am:* 'fɜːrţl] *adj a. fig* fértil; **to be** ~ **ground for sth** *fig* ser terreno propicio para algo
fertility [fə'tɪləti, *Am:* fə·'tɪləţi] *n no pl* fertilidad *f*
fertilization [,fɜːtəlaɪ'zeɪʃən, *Am:* ,fɜːrţlɪ-] *n no pl* fertilización *f*
fertilize ['fɜːtəlaɪz, *Am:* 'fɜːrţə-] *vt* **1.** BIO fertilizar **2.** AGR abonar
fertilizer ['fɜːtəlaɪzər, *Am:* 'fɜːrţəl-] *n* fertilizante *m*
fervent ['fɜːvənt, *Am:* 'fɜːr-] *adj,* **fervid** ['fɜːvɪd, *Am:* 'fɜːr-] *adj form* ferviente
fervor *n Am,* **fervour** ['fɜːvər, *Am:* 'fɜːrvə·] *n Aus, Brit no pl* fervor *m*
fester ['festər, *Am:* -tə·] *vi (wound, quarrel)* enconarse
festival ['festɪvəl] *n* **1.** REL festividad *f* **2.** *(special event)* festival *m;* **a film/music** ~ una fiesta de cine/música
festive ['festɪv] *adj* festivo, -a; **to be in** ~ **mood** estar muy alegre
festivity [fe'stɪvəti, *Am:* -ţi] <-ies> *n* **1.** *pl (festive activities)* festejos *mpl* **2.** *(festival)* fiesta *f*
festoon [fe'stuːn] **I.** *n* guirnalda *f* **II.** *vt* adornar
fetal ['fiːtl, *Am:* -ţl] *adj Am s.* **foetal**
fetch [fetʃ] **I.** *vt* **1.** *(bring back)* traer; **to** ~ **the police** ir a por la policía; **to** ~ **sb sth (from somewhere)** traer algo a alguien (de algún sitio) **2.** *(be sold for)* venderse por **3.** *inf (blow)* **to** ~ **sb a blow** dar un golpe a alguien **II.** *vi* **to** ~ **and carry** ir de acá para allá; **to** ~ **and carry for sb** ser el esclavo de alguien
fetching ['fetʃɪŋ] *adj* atractivo, -a
fête [feɪt] **I.** *n Brit, Aus (fair)* fiesta *f* **II.** *vt* festejar
fetid ['fetɪd, *Am:* 'feţ-] *adj form* fétido, -a
fetish ['fetɪʃ, *Am:* 'feţ-] *n* fetiche *m;* **to make a** ~ **of sth** hacer que algo se convierta en una obsesión
fetishism ['fetɪʃɪzəm, *Am:* 'feţ-] *n no pl* feti-

chismo *m*

fetishist ['fetɪʃɪst, *Am:* 'feṭ-] *n* fetichista *mf*

fetter ['fetə', *Am:* 'feṭə'] *vt* **1.** (*chain up*) **to ~ sb** (**to sth**) encadenar a alguien (a algo); **to ~ a horse** atar a un caballo **2.** *liter* (*restrict freedom*) atar

fettle ['fetl, *Am:* 'feṭ-] *n no pl, inf* **to be in fine ~** estar lleno de vitalidad

fetus ['fi:təs, *Am:* -ṭəs] *n Am s.* **foetus**

feud [fju:d] **I.** *n* enemistad *f* (heredada); **a ~ between sb and sb** una enemistad de sangre entre alguien y alguien; **a ~ over sth** un odio de sangre por algo; **a family ~** una enemistad entre familias **II.** *vi* pelearse

feudal ['fju:dəl] *adj* HIST feudal

feudalism ['fju:dəlɪzəm] *n no pl* feudalismo *m*

fever ['fi:və', *Am:* -və'] *n* **1.** MED fiebre *f*; **to have** [*o* **run**] **a ~** tener fiebre **2.** (*excited state*) emoción *f*; **a ~ of excitement** un estado de emoción; **football ~** fiebre *f* de fútbol

feverish ['fi:vərɪʃ] *adj* **1.** MED con fiebre **2.** (*frantic*) febril

few [fju:] <-er, -est> **I.** *adj det* **1.** (*small number*) pocos, pocas; **there are ~ things that please him** hay pocas cosas que le agradan; **one of her ~ friends** uno de sus pocos amigos; **quite a ~ people** bastante gente; **not ~er than 100 people** no menos de 100 personas; **the takings are ~** las ganancias son pocas; **to be ~ and far between** ser poquísimos, ser contadísimos **2.** (*some*) algunos, algunas; **they left a ~ boxes** dejaron algunas cajas **II.** *pron* pocos, pocas; **a ~** unos pocos; **I'd like a ~ more** quisiera un poco más; **the ~ who have the book** los pocos que tienen el libro; **the happy/lucky ~** los pocos felices/afortunados

fewer ['fju:ə', *Am:* -ə'] *adj, pron* menos; **no ~ than** nada menos que

fewest ['fju:ɪst] *adj, pron* los menos, las menos

ff *abbr of* **the following** sigs.

fiancé [fɪ'ɒnseɪ, *Am:* ˌfi:ɑ:n'seɪ] *n* prometido *m*

fiancée [fɪ'ɒnseɪ, *Am:* ˌfi:ɑ:n'seɪ] *n* prometida *f*

fiasco [fɪ'æskəʊ, *Am:* -koʊ] <-cos *o* -coes> *n* fiasco *m*

fib [fɪb] <-bb-> *inf* **I.** *vi* decir mentirijillas; **to ~** (**to sb**) **about sth** decir mentirijillas (a alguien) sobre algo **II.** *n* mentirijilla *f*, pepa *f And;* **to tell a ~** (**about sth/sb**) decir una mentirijilla (sobre algo/alguien)

fibber ['fɪbə', *Am:* -ə'] *n* mentirosillo, -a *m, f*

fiber *n Am,* **fibre** ['faɪbə', *Am:* -bə'] *n* **1.** fibra *f* **2.** *fig* carácter *m*

fibreglass ['faɪbəglɑ:s, *Am:* -bə'glæs] *n* fibra *f* de vidrio

fibre optic cable *n* cable *m* de fibra óptica **fibre optics** *n* + *sing vb* transmisión *f* por fibra óptica

fibula ['fɪbjʊlə, *Am:* -jə-] <-s *o* -ae> *n* pe-

roné *m*

fickle ['fɪkl] *adj* inconstante

fiction ['fɪkʃən] *n* **1.** *no pl a.* LIT ficción *f*; **~ writer** escritor(a) *m(f)* de novelas de ficción **2.** (*false statement*) invención *f*

fictional ['fɪkʃənl] *adj* ficticio, -a

fictitious [fɪk'tɪʃəs] *adj* **1.** (*false, untrue*) falso, -a **2.** (*imaginary*) ficticio, -a; **~ character** personaje *m* de ficción

fiddle ['fɪdl] **I.** *vt Brit, inf* (*fraudulently change*) falsificar **II.** *vi* **1.** *inf* (*play the violin*) tocar el violín **2. to ~ with sth** (*fidget with*) juguetear con algo; (*try to repair*) intentar arreglar algo **III.** *n inf* **1.** *Brit* (*fraud*) trampa *f*; **to be on the ~** trapichear **2.** (*violin*) violín *m*; **to play the ~** tocar el violín **3.** *Brit* (*difficult task*) tarea *f* difícil; **it's a ~ to do it** resulta difícil hacerlo ▶**to be (as) fit as a ~** *inf* estar en plena forma; **to play second ~** desempeñar un papel secundario

fiddler ['fɪdlə', *Am:* -lə'] *n inf* **1.** (*violinist*) violinista *mf* **2.** *Brit* (*fraudster*) tramposo, -a *m, f*

fiddling ['fɪdlɪŋ] **I.** *adj* trivial; **~ restrictions** restricciones *fpl* insignificantes **II.** *n no pl* trampas *fpl*

fiddly ['fɪdli] <-ier, -iest> *adj inf* difícil

fidelity [fɪ'deləti, *Am:* -ṭi] *n no pl* fidelidad *f*

fidget ['fɪdʒɪt] **I.** *vi* agitarse (nerviosamente) **II.** *n* persona *f* inquieta; **to have the ~s** ponerse inquieto

fidgety ['fɪdʒɪti] *adj* inquieto, -a

fiefdom ['fi:fdəm] *n* feudo *m*

field [fi:ld] **I.** *n* **1.** *a.* ELEC, AGR, SPORTS campo *m*; (*meadow*) prado *m* **2.** + *sing/pl vb* (*contestants*) competidores *mpl;* **to lead the ~** ir en cabeza; **to play the ~** *fig* tantear el terreno **3.** (*sphere of activity*) esfera *f*; **to be outside sb's ~** estar fuera del ámbito de alguien; **it's not my ~** no es de mi competencia **4.** INFOR campo *m* **II.** *vt* **1.** (*return*) **to ~ the ball** recoger la pelota; **to ~ a question** sortear una pregunta **2.** (*candidate*) presentar

field day *n* **1.** MIL maniobras *fpl* **2.** SPORTS día *m* de competición ▶**to have a ~** divertirse muchísimo

fielder ['fi:ldə', *Am:* -də'] *n* SPORTS fildeador(a) *m(f)*

field event *n* SPORTS prueba *f* de atletismo **field glasses** *n* prismáticos *mpl* **field mouse** *n* ratón *m* de campo **field sports** *n* la caza y la pesca

fieldwork ['fi:ldwɜ:k, *Am:* -wɜ:rk] *n* trabajo *m* de campo

fieldworker *n* investigador(a) *m(f)* de campo

fiend [fi:nd] *n* **1.** (*brute*) demonio *m* **2.** *inf* (*enthusiast*) entusiasta *mf*; **a chess ~** un fanático del ajedrez

fiendish ['fi:ndɪʃ] *adj* **1.** (*cruel*) diabólico, -a **2.** *Brit* (*exceptional*) extraordinario, -a

fierce [fɪəs, *Am:* fɪrs] *adj* <-er, -est> **1.** (*animal*) salvaje **2.** (*love, jealousy*) ardiente; (*hate*) profundo, -a; (*competition, opposition*) intenso, -a; (*debate, discussion*) acalorado, -a; (*fighting*) encarnizado, -a; (*wind*) fuerte **3.** *Am, inf* (*hard*) difícil

fierceness ['fɪəsnɪs, *Am:* 'fɪrs-] *n no pl* **1.** (*wildness*) furia *f* **2.** (*of competition, opposition*) intensidad *f;* (*of emotions*) fogosidad *f* **3.** (*of wind*) ferocidad *f*

fiery ['faɪəri, *Am:* 'faɪri] <-ier, -iest> *adj* **1.** (*heat*) abrasador(a) **2.** (*passionate*) apasionado, -a **3.** (*intensely spiced*) muy picante

FIFA ['fi:fə] *n abbr of* **Federation of International Football Association** FIFA *f*

fife [faɪf] *n* pífano *m*

fifteen [ˌfɪf'ti:n] I. *adj* quince II. *n* quince *m; s. a.* **eight**

fifteenth I. *adj* decimoquinto, -a II. *n* **1.** (*order*) decimoquinto, -a *m, f* **2.** (*date*) quince *m* **3.** (*fraction*) quinceavo *m;* (*part*) decimaquinta parte *f; s. a.* **eighth**

fifth [fɪfθ] I. *adj* quinto, -a II. *n* **1.** (*order*) quinto, -a *m, f* **2.** (*date*) cinco *m* **3.** (*fraction*) quinto *m;* (*part*) quinta parte *f; s. a.* **eighth**

fiftieth ['fɪftiəθ] I. *adj* quincuagésimo, -a II. *n no pl* (*order*) quincuagésimo, -a *m, f;* (*fraction*) quincuagésimo *m;* (*part*) quincuagésima parte *f; s. a.* **eighth**

fifty ['fɪfti] I. *adj* cincuenta II. <-ies> *n* cincuenta *m; s. a.* **eighty**

fig [fɪg] *n* **1.** (*fruit*) higo *m* **2.** (*tree*) higuera *f* ▶**I** don't **give** [*o* **care**] **a** ~ **about it!** !me importa un comino!; **to be not worth a** ~ no valer nada

fig. I. *n abbr of* **figure** fig. II. *adj abbr of* **figurative** fig.

fight [faɪt] I. *n* **1.** (*physical*) pelea *f;* (*argument*) disputa *f;* **to put up a** ~ defenderse bien **2.** MIL combate *m* **3.** (*struggle*) lucha *f;* **the** ~ **against AIDS** la lucha contra el SIDA **4.** *no pl* (*spirit*) combatividad *f;* **to show some** ~ enseñar los dientes II. <fought, fought> *vi* **1.** (*exchange blows*) pelear; MIL combatir; **to** ~ **with each other** pelearse; **to** ~ **with sb** (*against*) luchar contra alguien; (*on same side*) luchar junto a alguien **2.** (*dispute*) discutir; **to** ~ **over sth** discutir por algo; **to** ~ **about sth** discutir sobre algo **3.** (*struggle to overcome*) luchar; **to** ~ **for/against sth** luchar por/contra algo III. *vt* **1.** (*exchange blows with, argue with*) pelearse con **2.** (*wage war, do battle*) luchar con; **to** ~ **a battle** librar una batalla; **to** ~ **a duel** batirse en duelo **3.** (*struggle to overcome*) combatir; **to** ~ **a case** LAW negar una acusación **4.** (*struggle to obtain*) **to** ~ **one's way through the crowd** hacerse paso entre la multitud; **to** ~ **one's way to the top** hacerse camino luchando hasta la cima

◆**fight back** I. *vi* (*counter-attack*) contraatacar; (*defend oneself*) defenderse II. *vt* **to** ~ **one's tears** contener las lágrimas

◆**fight off** *vt* (*repel*) rechazar; (*master, resist*) resistir; **to** ~ **the cold/depression** luchar por no sucumbir ante el frío/la depre-

sión

◆**fight on** *vi* seguir luchando

fighter ['faɪtər, *Am:* ʈər] *n* **1.** (*person*) luchador(a) *m(f)* **2.** AVIAT caza *m*

fighting ['faɪtɪŋ, *Am:* -ʈɪŋ] I. *n no pl* lucha *f;* (*battle*) combate *m* II. *adj* combativo, -a; ~ **spirit** espíritu *m* de lucha ▶**there's a** ~ **chance that ...** existen grandes posibilidades de que... +*subj*

figment ['fɪgmənt] *n* **a** ~ **of the imagination** un producto de la imaginación

figurative ['fɪgjərətɪv, *Am:* -jə-əʈɪv] *adj* **1.** LING figurado, -a **2.** ART figurativo, -a

figuratively *adv* en sentido figurado

figure ['fɪgər, *Am:* -jə-] I. *n* **1.** (*shape*) figura *f;* **mother** ~ figura materna; **a fine** ~ **of a man** un hombre de físico imponente; **to cut a fine** ~ causar buena impresión; **to cut a sorry** ~ parecer ridículo; **to keep one's** ~ guardar la línea **2.** ART estatua *f;* (*human being*) figura *f* **3.** (*digit*) dígito *m;* (*numeral*) cifra *f;* **column of** ~**s** columna *f* de números; **to have a head for** ~**s** ser bueno para los números; **to be good at** ~**s** saber de aritmética; **in round** ~**s** en cifras redondas; **single** ~**s** cifras de un sólo dígito; **double** ~**s** cifras de dos dígitos **4.** (*price*) precio *m;* **a high** ~ una gran suma de dinero **5.** (*diagram*) figura *f;* (*illustration*) ilustración *f* II. *vt* **1.** *Am* (*think*) figurarse; **to** ~ **that ...** figurarse que... **2.** (*in diagram*) representar **3.** (*calculate*) calcular III. *vi* (*feature*) figurar; **to** ~ **in sth** figurar en algo; **to** ~ **as sth/sb** figurar como algo/alguien; **that** ~**s** *Am* es natural

◆**figure out** *vt* (*comprehend*) entender; (*work out*) resolver; **to** ~ **why ...** explicarse por qué...

figurehead ['fɪgəhed, *Am:* -jə-] *n* **1.** NAUT mascarón *m* de proa **2.** *fig* testaferro *m*

figure skater *n* patinador(a) *m(f)* artístico, -a

figure skating *n* patinaje *m* artístico

Fiji ['fi:dʒi:] *n* **the** ~ **Islands** las Islas Fiji

Fijian ['fɪ'dʒi:ən] I. *adj* de Fiji II. *n* habitante *mf* de (las Islas) Fiji

filament ['fɪləmənt] *n* filamento *m*

filch [fɪltʃ] *vt inf* birlar

file¹ [faɪl] I. *n* **1.** (*folder*) carpeta *f* **2.** (*record*) expediente *m;* **to open a** ~ abrir un expediente; **to keep sth on** ~ guardar algo archivado **3.** INFOR fichero *m*, archivo *m* **4.** (*row*) fila *f;* **in single** ~ en fila india II. *vt* **1.** (*record*) archivar, failear *AmC, RíoPl* **2.** (*present: claim, complaint*) presentar; **to** ~ **a petition** interponer una demanda III. *vi* **1.** LAW **to** ~ **for bankruptcy** declararse en quiebra; **to** ~ **for divorce** presentar una demanda de divorcio **2.** (*move in line*) desfilar

◆**file away** *vt* archivar

file² [faɪl] I. *n* (*tool*) lima *f* II. *vt* limar; **to** ~ **one's nails** limarse las uñas III. *vi* ~ **down sth** limar algo; **to** ~ **through sth** partir algo con una lima

◆**file in** *vi* entrar en fila

◆**file out** *vi* salir en fila
file manager *n* administrador *m* de ficheros
file name *n* nombre *m* de fichero
filial ['fɪlɪəl] *adj form* filial
filibuster ['fɪlɪbʌstəʳ, *Am:* -təʳ] *vi* POL usar maniobras obstruccionistas
filigree ['fɪlɪgriː] *n no pl* filigrana *f*
filing ['faɪlɪŋ] *n* **1.** *no pl* (*archiving*) clasificación *f* **2.** LAW presentación *f* **3.** *pl* (*bits of metal*) limaduras *fpl*
filing cabinet *n* archivador *m*
Filipino [fɪlɪ'piːnəʊ, *Am:* -noʊ] I. *adj* filipino, -a II. *n* filipino, -a *m, f*
fill [fɪl] I. *vt* **1.** (*make full*) llenar; (*space*) ocupar; **to ~ a vacancy** cubrir una vacante; **to ~ a vacuum** llenar un vacío; **to ~ a need** satisfacer una necesidad; **to ~ a need in the market** satisfacer una demanda del mercado **2.** (*seal*) empastar, emplomar *AmL* **3.** GASTR rellenar **4.** (*fulfil: order, requirement*) cumplir II. *vi* llenarse III. *n* to drink/eat one's ~ hartarse de beber/comer; **to have one's ~ of sth** estar harto de algo
◆**fill in** I. *vt* **1.** (*seal opening*) llenar; **to ~ a hole** tapar un agujero **2.** (*document*) rellenar **3.** (*colour in*) colorear **4.** (*infor*) informar; **to fill sb in on the details** poner a alguien al corriente de los detalles **5.** (*time*) ocupar II. *vi* to ~ (**for sb**) hacer las veces (de alguien)
◆**fill out** I. *vt* (*document*) rellenar II. *vi* (*put on weight*) engordar
◆**fill up** I. *vt* llenar; (*completely*) colmar; **to fill oneself up** llenarse el estómago II. *vi* llenarse
filler ['fɪləʳ, *Am:* -əʳ] *n* **1.** (*sealing material*) masilla *f* **2.** TV relleno *m*
fillet ['fɪlɪt] I. *n* filete *m* II. *vt* cortar en filetes; **to ~ a fish** cortar un pescado en filetes
fillet steak *n* solomillo *m*
filling I. *n* **1.** (*substance*) relleno *m* **2.** (*in tooth*) empaste *m*, emplomadura *f AmL* II. *adj* sólido, -a; **to be ~** llenar el estómago
filling station *n* gasolinera *f*, bencinera *f Chile*, grifo *m Perú*
fillip ['fɪlɪp] *n* estímulo *m;* **to provide a ~ to sb** estimular a alguien; **to give sb a** (**big**) ~ dar un (gran) estímulo a alguien
film [fɪlm] I. *n* **1.** PHOT película *f;* **to make a ~** hacer una película; **to see** [*o* **watch**] **a ~** ver una película **2.** (*fine coating*) capa *f;* **a ~ of oil** una película de aceite II. *vt* filmar III. *vi* rodar
film buff *n* cinéfilo, -a *m, f* **film camera** *n* cámara *f* cinematográfica **film director** *n* director(a) *m(f)* de cine **film star** *n* estrella *f* de cine **film studio** *n* estudio *m* de cine
filter ['fɪltəʳ, *Am:* -t̬əʳ] I. *n* filtro *m;* **traffic ~** *Brit* semáforo *m* con flecha verde de giro II. *vt* filtrar III. *vi* filtrarse
◆**filter out** I. *vi* llegar a saberse II. *vt* quitar filtrando
◆**filter through** *vi* filtrarse
filter bed *n* lecho *m* de filtración **filter lane** *n* carril *m* de giro **filter paper** *n* papel *m* de

filtro **filter tip** *n* filtro *m*
filth [fɪlθ] *n no pl* **1.** (*dirt*) mugre *f;* (*excrement*) excrementos *mpl* **2.** (*obscenity*) obscenidad *f*
filthy ['fɪlθi] I. *adj* **1.** (*very dirty*) inmundo, -a; (*weather*) asqueroso, -a **2.** *inf* (*obscene*) obsceno, -a II. *adv inf* **to be ~ rich** estar forrado
filtration [fɪl'treɪʃən] *n no pl* filtración *f*
fin [fɪn] *n* aleta *f*
final ['faɪnl] I. *adj* **1.** (*last*) final; **~ instalment** último plazo *m* **2.** (*irrevocable*) definitivo, -a; **to have the ~ say** (**on sth**) tener la última palabra (sobre algo); **and that's ~** *inf* y sanseacabó II. *n* **1.** SPORTS final *f;* **to get** (**through**) **to the ~** llegar a la final **2.** *pl* UNIV examen *m* de fin de carrera; **to take one's ~s** hacer los exámenes de fin de carrera
finale [fɪ'nɑːli, *Am:* -'næli] *n* final *m;* **grand ~** gran escena final
finalist ['faɪnəlɪst] *n* finalista *mf*
finality [faɪ'næləti, *Am:* -t̬i] *n no pl* **1.** (*irreversibility*) finalidad *f* **2.** (*determination*) resolución *f*
finalize ['faɪnəlaɪz] *vt* ultimar
finally ['faɪnəli] *adv* **1.** (*at long last*) finalmente; (*expressing impatience*) por fin **2.** (*in conclusion*) en conclusión **3.** (*irrevocably*) definitivamente; (*decisively*) de forma decisiva
finance ['faɪnænts] *vt* financiar
finance company *n*, **finance house** *n* sociedad *f* financiera
finances ['faɪnæntsɪz] *npl* finanzas *fpl*
financial [faɪ'næntʃəl] *adj* financiero, -a; (*problem*) monetario, -a; **sb's ~ affairs** los asuntos financieros de alguien
financial adviser *n* asesor(a) *m(f)* financiero **financial year** *n* año *m* fiscal
financier [faɪ'næntsɪəʳ, *Am:* fɪ'næntsɪəʳ] *n* financiero, -a *m, f*, financista *mf AmL*
finch [fɪntʃ] *n* pinzón *m*
find [faɪnd] I.<found, found> *vt* **1.** (*lost object, person*) encontrar **2.** (*locate*) localizar, hallar; **to ~ support** encontrar apoyo; **to ~ happiness with sb** descubrir la felicidad con alguien; **to ~ oneself somewhere** encontrarse en algún sitio; **to be nowhere to be found** no encontrarse por ningún sitio; **to ~ no reason why ...** no hallar razón alguna por la que...; **to ~** (**the**) **time** sacar tiempo; **to ~ excuses** buscar pretextos; **to ~ the strength** (**to do sth**) hallar las fuerzas (para hacer algo); **to ~** (**enough**) **money** conseguir (suficiente) dinero **3.** (*experience*) sentir; **to ~ oneself alone** sentirse solo **4.** (*conclude*) **to ~ sb guilty/innocent** declarar a alguien culpable/inocente **5.** (*discover*) descubrir II. *n* hallazgo *m*
◆**find out** I. *vt* descubrir; (*dishonesty*) desenmascarar; **to ~ when/where/who ...** averiguar cuándo/dónde/quién... II. *vi* **to ~ about sth/sb** informarse sobre algo/alguien
finder ['faɪndəʳ, *Am:* -dəʳ] *n* (*of sth*

unknown) descubridor(a) *m(f);* (*of sth lost*) persona *f* que encuentra

finding ['faɪndɪŋ] *n* 1. LAW fallo *m* 2. (*recommendation*) recomendación *f* 3. (*discovery*) descubrimiento *m*

fine¹ [faɪn] I. *adj* 1. (*slender; light*) fino, -a; (*feature*) delicado, -a; (*nuance*) sutil 2. (*good*) bueno, -a; (*satisfactory*) satisfactorio, -a; ~ **weather** buen tiempo *m;* **to be ~ by sb** estar bien para alguien; **that's all very ~, but ...** está todo muy bien, pero... 3. (*excellent*) excelente; **the ~st wines in the world** los vinos más selectos del mundo; **to have a ~ time doing sth** pasarlo bien haciendo algo; ~ **words** *iron* palabras *fpl* valientes; **to appeal to sb's ~r feelings** apelar a los mejores sentimientos de alguien 4. (*deep*) profundo, -a II. *adv* 1. (*all right*) muy bien; **to feel ~** sentirse bien; **to work ~** funcionar bien 2. (*fine-grained*) fino, -a ▶**to cut it ~** dejar algo para el último momento

fine² [faɪn] I. *n* multa *f,* boleta *f AmS* II. *vt* multar

fine arts *n* bellas artes *fpl*

fineness *n no pl* (*lightness*) fineza *f;* (*delicacy, ornateness*) delicadeza *f*

finery ['faɪnəri] *n no pl* **in all one's ~** con las mejores galas

finesse [fɪ'nes] *n no pl* 1. (*elegance*) fineza *f* 2. (*skill*) habilidad *f*

fine-tooth comb [ˌfaɪntuːˈθ'kəʊm, *Am:* ˌfaɪntuːθˈkoʊm] *n* **to go through sth with a ~** revisar algo a fondo

finger ['fɪŋɡəʳ, *Am:* -ɡɚ] I. *n* dedo *m;* **little ~** dedo meñique ▶**to be able to be counted on the ~s of one hand** poderse contar con los dedos de una mano; **to have a ~ in every pie** meter baza en todo; **to have one's ~ on the pulse** estar al tanto de lo que pasa; **to put one's ~ on the spot** poner el dedo en la llaga; **to be all ~s and thumbs** *Brit, Aus* ser terriblemente desmañado; **to catch sb with their ~s in the till** pillar a alguien robando (en la empresa); **to get/have one's ~s burnt** pillarse los dedos *fig;* **to have sb wrapped round one's little ~** hacer que alguien baile al son que le tocan; **to get one's ~ out** *inf* espabilarse; **to keep one's ~s crossed** tener los dedos cruzados; **to lay a ~ on sb** poner la mano encima a alguien; **to not lift a ~** no mover ni un dedo II. *vt* 1. (*handle*) manosear 2. *inf* (*reveal*) delatar; **to ~ sb to the police** denunciar a alguien a la policía

fingering ['fɪŋɡərɪŋ] *n no pl* digitación *f*

fingermark ['fɪŋɡəmɑːk, *Am:* -ɡɚmɑːrk] *n* huella *f* (dactilar) **fingernail** *n* uña *f* **fingerprint** I. *n* huella *f* dactilar II. *vt* **to ~ sb** tomar las huellas dactilares a alguien **fingertip** *n* punta *f* del dedo; **to have sth at one's ~s** tener algo a mano; *fig* saber(se) algo al dedillo

finicky ['fɪnɪki] *adj* 1. (*person*) melindroso, -a 2. (*job*) delicado, -a

finish ['fɪnɪʃ] I. *n* 1. (*end*) final *m,* fin *m;* SPORTS meta *f;* **to be in at the ~** estar presente en la conclusión 2. (*sealing, varnishing: of fabric*) acabado *m;* (*of furniture*) pulido *m* II. *vi* terminar(se), acabar(se); **to ~ doing sth** terminar de hacer algo; **to ~ by saying that ...** concluir diciendo que... III. *vt* 1. (*bring to end*) terminar, acabar; **to ~ school** terminar los estudios; **to ~ a sentence** completar una oración 2. (*make final touches to*) acabar

◆**finish off** I. *vt* 1. (*end*) terminar, acabar 2. (*defeat*) acabar con 3. *Am, inf* (*murder*) liquidar II. *vi* concluir

◆**finish up** I. *vi* **to ~ at** ir a parar en II. *vt* (*food, drink*) terminar

◆**finish with** *vt* terminar con; **to ~ sb** romper con alguien; **to ~ politics** abandonar la política

finished *adj* 1. (*product*) terminado, -a, acabado, -a 2. *inf* (*tired*) hecho, -a polvo

finishing line *n,* **finishing post** *n* línea *f* de meta

finite ['faɪnaɪt] *adj a.* LING finito, -a

Finland ['fɪnlənd] *n* Finlandia *f*

Finn [fɪn] *n* finlandés, -esa *m, f*

Finnish ['fɪnɪʃ] I. *adj* finlandés, -esa II. *n* finlandés *m*

fiord [fɪ'ɔːd, *Am:* fjɔːrd] *n* fiordo *m*

fir [fɜːʳ, *Am:* fɜːr] *n* abeto *m*

fir cone *n Brit* piña *f*

fire ['faɪəʳ, *Am:* 'faɪɚ] I. *n* 1. (*flames*) fuego *m;* (*in fireplace*) lumbre *f;* (*accidental*) incendio *m;* **to set sth on ~** prender fuego a algo; **to catch ~** encenderse; **forest ~** incendio forestal 2. TECH calefacción *f;* (*stove*) hornillo *m* 3. MIL **to open ~ on sb** abrir fuego contra alguien; **to be under ~** MIL estar en la línea de fuego; *fig* ser criticado 4. (*passion*) pasión *f* ▶**there's no smoke without ~** *prov* cuando el río suena, agua lleva *prov;* **to go through ~ and water** afrontar todos los peligros; **to set the world on ~** hacerse famoso; **to hang ~** suspender operaciones; **to play with ~** jugar con fuego II. *vt* 1. (*set fire to*) encender; (*ceramics*) cocer 2. (*weapon*) disparar; **to ~ questions at sb** bombardear a alguien con preguntas 3. *inf* (*dismiss*) despedir, botar *AmL,* fletar *Arg* 4. (*inspire*) inspirar III. *vi* 1. (*with gun*) disparar; **to ~ at sb** disparar contra alguien 2. AUTO encenderse

◆**fire away** *vi inf* seguir adelante

◆**fire off** *vt* (*letter, reply*) despachar enseguida

fire alarm *n* alarma *f* contra incendios **firearm** *n* arma *f* de fuego **fireball** *n* bola *f* de fuego **firebrand** *n* 1. (*torch*) tea *f* 2. *fig* revoltoso, -a *m, f* **firebreak** *n* cortafuegos *m inv* **firebrick** *n* ladrillo *m* refractario **fire brigade** *n Brit* cuerpo de bomberos **firecracker** *n* petardo *m* **fire department** *n Am* cuerpo *m* de bomberos **fire-eater** *n* tragafuegos *mf inv* **fire engine** *n* bomba *m* de incendios **fire escape** *n* escalera *f* de incendios **fire exit** *n* salida *f* de incendios **fire extinguisher** *n* extintor *m* de incendios **firefighter** *n* bombero *mf* **firefly** *n* luciérnaga *f*, cocuyo *m AmL* **fireguard** *n* guardafuegos *m inv* **fire house** *n Am* parque *m* de bomberos **fire insurance** *n* seguro *m* contra incendios **fire irons** *npl* utensilios *mpl* de chimenea **fireman** <-men> *n* bombero *m* **fireplace** *n* chimenea *f*, hogar *m* **fireproof** [ˈfaɪəˈpruːf, *Am:* ˈfaɪə-] *adj* a prueba de incendios **fire-raiser** *n Brit* pirómano, -a *m, f* **fire-raising** *n Brit* piromanía *f* **fireside** *n* hogar *m* **fire station** *n* parque *m* de bomberos **fire wall** *n* muro *m* cortafuegos **firewater** *n* no *pl, inf* aguardiente *m* **firewoman** <-women> *n* mujer *f* bombero **firewood** *n* no *pl* leña *f* **firework** *n* 1. fuego *m* artificial 2. *pl, fig* explosión *f* (de cólera)

firing [ˈfaɪərɪŋ, *Am:* ˈfaɪə-] *n* 1. MIL disparo *m* 2. (*of ceramic*) cocción *f*

firing line *n* línea *f* de fuego **firing squad** *n* pelotón *m* de fusilamiento

firm¹ [fɜːm, *Am:* fɜːrm] I. *adj* 1. (*secure*) firme; (*strong*) fuerte; **a ~ offer** una oferta en firme 2. (*dense, solid*) duro, -a 3. (*resolute*) decidido, -a 4. (*strict*) estricto, -a II. *adv* firmemente; **to stand ~** mantenerse firme

firm² [fɜːm, *Am:* fɜːrm] *n* (*company*) empresa *f*; **~ of lawyers** bufete *m* de abogados

firmament [ˈfɜːməmənt, *Am:* ˈfɜːr-] *n* no *pl* firmamento *m*

firmness [ˈfɜːmnɪs, *Am:* ˈfɜːrm-] *n* no *pl* 1. (*hardness*) dureza *f* 2. (*strictness*) firmeza *f*

first [fɜːst, *Am:* fɜːrst] I. *adj* (*earliest*) primero, -a; **for the ~ time** por primera vez; **at ~ sight** a primera vista; **the ~ December** el primero de diciembre ▶**~ and foremost** ante todo II. *adv* primero; (*firstly*) en primer lugar; **~ of all** ante todo; **at ~** al principio; **to go head ~** meterse de cabeza ▶**~ come ~ served** *inf* por orden de llegada III. *n* 1. **the ~** el primero, la primera; **from the (very) ~** desde el principio 2. *Brit* UNIV *nota más alta que se puede obtener al final de los estudios universitarios*

first aid *n* primeros auxilios *mpl* **first aid box** *n* botiquín *m* de primeros auxilios **first-born** [ˈfɜːstbɔːn, *Am:* ˈfɜːrstbɔːrn] I. *adj* primogénito, -a II. *n* primogénito, -a *m, f* **first-class** I. *adj* de primera clase II. *adv* **to travel ~** viajar en primera **first cousin** *n* primo, -a *m, f* hermano **first floor** *n Aus, Brit* primer piso *m; Am* planta *f* baja **first-hand** [ˌfɜːstˈhænd, *Am:* ˌfɜːrst-] I. *adj* de primera mano II. *adv* directamente **first lady** *n Am* **the ~** la Primera Dama **firstly** [ˈfɜːstli, *Am:* ˈfɜːrst-] *adv* en primer lugar **first name** *n* nombre *m* (de pila) **first night** *n* noche *f* de estreno **first offender** *n* persona que comete un delito por primera vez **first person** *n* LING primera persona *f*

first-rate [ˌfɜːstˈreɪt, *Am:* ˌfɜːrst-] *adj* de primer orden **first strike** *n* primer golpe *m* **firth** [fɜːθ, *Am:* fɜːrθ] *n Scot* estuario *m* **fiscal** [ˈfɪskl] *adj* fiscal **fish** [fɪʃ] I. <-(es)> *n* 1. ZOOL pez *m* 2. no *pl* GASTR pescado *m;* **~ and chips** pescado frito con patatas fritas ▶**to be a big ~ in a small pond** ser un pez gordo (en un sitio pequeño); **there are plenty more ~ in the sea** hay mucho más donde elegir; (**like) a ~ out of water** como un pez fuera del agua; **to have bigger ~ to fry** tener cosas más importantes que hacer; **an odd ~** un tipo raro II. *vi* pescar; **to ~ for information** ir a la caza de información III. *vt* pescar

fishbone [ˈfɪʃbəʊn, *Am:* -boʊn] *n* espina *f* de pescado **fishcake** [ˈfɪʃkeɪk] *n* croqueta *f* de pescado **fisherman** [ˈfɪʃəmən, *Am:* -ə-] <-men> *n* pescador *m* **fishery** [ˈfɪʃəri] *n* pesquería *f* **fishfinger** *n* palito *m* de merluza **fish-hook** *n* anzuelo *m* **fishing** I. *n* no *pl* pesca *f* II. *adj* pesquero, -a **fishing grounds** *npl* zona *f* de pesca **fishing line** *n* sedal *m* **fishing rod** *n Brit, Aus* caña *f* de pescar **fishing tackle** *n* avío *m* de pesca **fishmonger** [ˈfɪʃmʌŋgəʳ, *Am:* -gə-] *n Brit* pescadero, -a *m, f* **fishpond** [ˈfɪʃpɒnd, *Am:* -pɑːnd] *n* estanque *m* para peces **fishy** [ˈfɪʃi] <-ier, -iest> *adj* 1. (*taste*) que sabe a pescado; (*smell*) que huele a pescado 2. *inf* (*dubious*) dudoso, -a ▶**to smell ~** oler a chamusquina

fissile [ˈfɪsaɪl, *Am:* -ɪl] *adj* físil **fission** [ˈfɪʃən] *n* no *pl* PHYS fisión *f;* BIO escisión *f* **fissure** [ˈfɪʃəʳ, *Am:* -ə-] *n* fisura *f* **fist** [fɪst] *n* puño *m;* **to clench one's ~s** cerrar los puños; **to shake one's ~ at sb** amenazar a alguien con el puño

fit¹ [fɪt] I. <-tt-> *adj* 1. (*apt, suitable*) apto, -a, apropiado, -a; (*competent*) capaz; **~ to eat** bueno para comer; **it's not ~ to eat** no se puede comer 2. (*ready*) listo, -a 3. SPORTS en forma 4. MED sano, -a ▶**to be ~ to be tied** *Am* estar fuera de sí II. <-tt-> *vt* 1. (*adapt*) ajustar; **to ~ the key in the lock** meter la llave en la cerradura 2. (*clothes*) sentar bien 3. (*facts*) corresponder con 4. TECH caber en, encajar en III. *vi* <-tt-> 1. (*be correct size*) ir bien 2. (*correspond*) corresponder IV. *n* no *pl* ajuste *m*
◆**fit in** I. *vi* 1. (*conform*) encajar 2. (*get on well*) llevarse bien II. *vt* tener tiempo para
◆**fit out** *vt* equipar
◆**fit together** *vi* encajar
◆**fit up** *vt* equipar

fit² [fɪt] *n* 1. MED ataque *m;* **coughing ~** acceso *m* de tos 2. *inf* (*outburst of rage*) arranque *m;* **they were in ~s of laughter** se morían de (la)

risa; **in ~s and starts** a empujones
fitful ['fɪtfəl] *adj* espasmódico, -a; (*breath*) entrecortado, -a; (*gusts*) intermitente; (*sleep*) irregular
fitment ['fɪtmənt] *n Brit* mueble *m*
fitness ['fɪtnɪs] *n no pl* **1.** (*competence, suitability*) conveniencia *f* **2.** (*good condition*) (buena) condición *f* física; (*health*) (buena) salud *f*
fitted ['fɪtɪd, *Am:* 'fɪt̮-] *adj* (*adapted, suitable*) idóneo, -a; (*tailor-made*) a medida; **~ kitchen** cocina *f* empotrada
fitter ['fɪtəʳ, *Am:* 'fɪt̮əʳ] *n* técnico, -a *m, f*
fitting ['fɪtɪŋ, *Am:* 'fɪt̮-] I. *n* **1.** *pl* (*fixtures*) accesorios *mpl* **2.** (*of clothes*) prueba *f* II. *adj* apropiado, -a
five [faɪv] I. *adj* cinco II. *n* cinco *m;* **gimme ~!** *Am, inf* ¡choca esos cinco!; *s. a.* **eight**
fivefold *adj* quíntuple
fiver ['faɪvəʳ, *Am:* -vəʳ] *n Brit, inf* billete *m* de 5 libras; *Am, inf* billete *m* de 5 dólares
fix [fɪks] I. *vt* **1.** (*fasten*) sujetar; **to ~ sth in one's mind** grabar algo en la memoria; **to ~ sb with one's eyes** fijar los ojos en alguien **2.** (*determine*) fijar; **to ~ a date** fijar una fecha **3.** (*arrange*) arreglar; **to ~ one's face** *inf* maquillarse **4.** (*repair*) arreglar **5.** *Am, inf* (*food*) preparar **6.** *inf* (*manipulate: election, result*) amañar **7.** *inf* (*take revenge on*) ajustar las cuentas con; **I'll ~ him** me las pagará **8.** PHYS, PHOT (*colour*) fijar II. *n* **1.** *inf* (*dilemma*) aprieto *m;* **to be in a ~** estar en un aprieto **2.** *inf* (*shot*) chute *m,* pichicata *f Arg* **3.** AVIAT, AUTO posición *f*
◆**fix on** *vt* **1.** (*choose*) escoger **2.** (*make definite*) fijar
◆**fix up** *vt* **1.** (*supply with*) **to fix sb up (with sth)** proveer a alguien (de algo) **2.** (*arrange*) organizar **3.** (*repair*) arreglar
◆**fix upon** *vt s.* **fix on**
fixation [fɪk'seɪʃən] *n* fijación *f*
fixed *adj* fijo, -a; **to be of no ~ abode** LAW no tener domicilio permanente
fixedly ['fɪksɪdli] *adv* fijamente
fixer *n inf* chanchullero, -a *m, f*
fixing bath *n* baño *m* fijador
fixity ['fɪksəti, *Am:* -ət̮i] *n no pl, form* fijeza *f*
fixture ['fɪkstʃəʳ, *Am:* -tʃəʳ] *n* **1.** (*furniture*) instalación *f* fija; **~s and fittings** muebles *mpl* y accesorios **2.** *Brit, Aus* SPORTS partido *m*
fizz [fɪz] I. *vi* burbujear II. *n no pl* **1.** (*bubble, frothiness*) efervescencia *f* **2.** *inf* (*champagne*) champán *m* **3.** *Am, Aus* (*sweet lemonade*) gaseosa *f*
fizzle ['fɪzl] *vi* chisporrotear
fizzy ['fɪzi] <-ier, -iest> *adj* (*bubbly*) efervescente; (*carbonated*) gaseoso, -a
fjord [fɪ'ɔːd, *Am:* fjɔːrd] *n* fiordo *m*
flabbergast ['flæbəgɑːst, *Am:* -əʳgæst] *vt inf* dejar sin habla
flabby ['flæbi] <-ier, -iest> *adj pej* **1.** (*body*) fofo, -a **2.** (*weak*) débil
flaccid ['flæksɪd] *adj* flácido, -a; *fig* flojo, -a

flag¹ [flæg] I. *n* **1.** (*national*) bandera *f;* (*pennant*) estandarte *m;* **to raise a ~** izar una bandera; **to fly the ~** *fig* hacer acto de presencia; **to keep the ~ flying** *fig* resistir **2.** (*marker*) señalizador *m* II. <-gg-> *vt* (*mark*) señalar; (*label computer data*) etiquetar III. <-gg-> *vi* flaquear
flag² [flæg] *n* (*stone*) losa *f*
flag day *n Brit: día de recaudación de fondos;* **Flag Day** *Am* Día *m* de la Bandera
flagellate ['flædʒəleɪt] *vt* flagelar
flagon ['flægən] *n* jarro *m*
flagpole ['flægpəʊl, *Am:* -poʊl] *n* asta *f*
flagrant ['fleɪgrənt] *adj* descarado, -a
flagship ['flægʃɪp] *n* buque *m* insignia
flagstaff ['flægstɑːf, *Am:* -stæf] *n s.* **flagpole**
flail [fleɪl] *vi* **to ~ (about)** agitarse
flair [fleəʳ, *Am:* fler] *n no pl* **1.** (*genius*) don *m* **2.** (*style*) estilo *m*
flak [flæk] *n* **1.** MIL fuego *m* antiaéreo **2.** (*criticism*) críticas *fpl*
flake [fleɪk] I. *vi* (*skin*) pelarse; (*paint*) desconcharse; (*wood*) astillarse; (*plaster*) descascararse II. *n* (*peeling*) hojuela *f;* (*shaving, sliver*) viruta *f;* (*of paint, wood*) lámina *f;* (*of plaster*) placa *f;* (*of skin*) escama *f;* (*of snow*) copo *m*
◆**flake out** *vi inf* caer rendido
flaky ['fleɪki] <-ier, -iest> *adj* **1.** (*skin*) escamoso, -a; (*paint*) de láminas **2.** *inf* (*strange*) chiflado, -a
flaky pastry *n* hojaldre *m*
flamboyant [flæm'bɔɪənt] *adj* (*manner, person*) exuberante; (*air, clothes*) vistoso, -a
flame [fleɪm] I. *n* **1.** llama *f;* **to be in ~s** arder en llamas; **to go up in ~s** ser presa de las llamas; **to burst into ~** estallar en llamas **2.** (*lover*) (*old*) ~ antiguo amor *m* II. *vi* (*blaze, burn*) llamear; (*glare*) brillar
flaming ['fleɪmɪŋ] *adj* **1.** (*burning*) en llamas **2.** *fig* (*quarrel*) acalorado, -a **3.** *Brit, inf* (*as intensifier*) condenado, -a
flamingo [flə'mɪŋgəʊ, *Am:* -goʊ] <-(e)s> *n* flamenco *m*
flammable ['flæməbl] *adj Am* inflamable
flan [flæn] *n* tarta *f* (de frutas)
Flanders ['flɑːndəz] *n* Flandes *m*
flange [flændʒ] *n* pestaña *f*
flank [flæŋk] I. *n* (*of person*) costado *m;* (*of animal*) ijada *f,* verija *f AmL;* (*of hill*) lado *m;* MIL flanco *m* II. *vt* flanquear
flannel ['flænl] I. *n* **1.** (*material*) franela *f* **2.** *Brit* (*facecloth*) toallita *f* **3.** *pl* (*trousers*) pantalones *mpl* de franela II. <-ll-> *vt Brit, Aus, inf* lisonjear III. <-ll-> *vi Brit, Aus, inf* hablar con rodeos
flap [flæp] I. <-pp-> *vt* (*wings*) batir; (*shake*) sacudir II. <-pp-> *vi* **1.** (*wings*) aletear; (*sails*) gualdrapear; (*flag*) ondear **2.** *inf* (*become nervous*) agitarse; **don't ~!** ¡con calma! III. *n* **1.** (*of cloth*) faldón *m;* (*of skin*) colgajo *m;* (*of pocket, envelope*) solapa *f;* (*of table*) hoja *f*

2. AVIAT flap *m* **3.** (*of wing*) aleteo *m* **4.** *inf*
(*panic*) **to get in a ~** ponerse nervioso
flapjack ['flæpdʒæk] *n* **1.** *Brit, Aus* galleta *f*
de avena **2.** *Am* (*pancake*) torta *f*, panqueque
m AmL
flare [fleəʳ, *Am:* fler] I. *n* **1.** (*blaze*) llamarada
f; (*of light*) resplandor *m* **2.** (*signal*) cohete *m*
de señales **3.** MIL bengala *f* **4.** (*of clothes*) vuelo
m II. *vi* **1.** (*blaze*) llamear; (*light*) resplandecer
2. (*trouble*) estallar **3.** (*skirt*) acampanarse
III. *vt* **to ~ one's nostrils** resoplar
flare-up ['fleəʳʌp, *Am:* 'fler-] *n* estallido *m fig*
flash [flæʃ] I. *vt* **1.** (*shine: light*) enfocar; **to ~
a light in sb's eyes** dirigir un rayo de luz a los
ojos de alguien **2.** (*show quickly*) mostrar (rápidamente); **to ~ sth on the screen** proyectar
algo en la pantalla muy rápidamente **3.** (*communicate*) transmitir; (*smile, look*) lanzar II. *vi*
1. (*lightning*) relampaguear; *fig* (*eyes*) brillar
2. *inf* (*expose genitals*) exhibirse **3.** (*move
swiftly*) **to ~ by** pasar como un rayo III. *n*
1. (*burst*) destello *m;* **~ of inspiration**
momento *m* de inspiración; **~ of light(ning)**
relámpago *m* **2.** PHOT flash *m* ▸ **a ~ in the pan**
flor de un día; **like a ~** como un relámpago; **in
a ~** en un instante IV. <-er, -est> *adj inf* llamativo, -a
♦ **flash back** *vi* volver atrás
flashback ['flæʃbæk] *n* CINE, LIT, THEAT escena
f retrospectiva, flashback *m*
flashbulb ['flæʃbʌlb] *n* bombilla *f* de flash
flasher ['flæʃəʳ, *Am:* -ɚ] *n Brit, inf* exhibicionista *m*
flashgun ['flæʃgʌn] *n* disparador *m* de flash
flashlight ['flæʃlaɪt] *n* linterna *f* eléctrica
flash point *n* **1.** CHEM punto *m* de inflamación
2. *fig* punto *m* crucial
flashy ['flæʃi] <-ier, -iest> *adj inf* ostentoso,
-a, llamativo, -a
flask [flɑːsk, *Am:* flæsk] *n* CHEM matraz *m;*
(*thermos*) termo *m;* **hip ~** petaca *f*
flat¹ [flæt] I. *adj* <-tt-> **1.** (*surface*) llano, -a,
plano, -a; **~ as a pancake** *inf* liso como la
palma de la mano **2.** (*unexciting*) deslustrado,
-a **3.** (*drink*) sin gas **4.** (*tyre*) desinflado, -a
5. *Aus, Brit* (*battery*) descargado, -a **6.** (*absolute: refusal, rejection*) categórico, -a; **and
that's ~** y no hay más de qué hablar **7.** COM
(*fixed*) fijo, -a **8.** MUS desafinado, -a II. <-tt->
adv **1.** (*level*) horizontalmente; **to lie ~ on
one's back** estar boca arriba **2.** *inf* (*absolutely*)
completamente ▸ **to be ~ broke** no tener ni
un centavo; **to fall ~** resultar un fracaso; **in
five minutes ~** *inf* en sólo cinco minutos III. *n*
1. (*level surface: of sword, knife*) plano *m;* **the
~ of the hand** la palma de la mano **2.** (*low
level ground*) llanura *f;* **salt ~s** salinas *fpl*
3. *Aus, Brit* (*tyre*) pinchazo *m* **4.** MUS bemol *m*
flat² [flæt] *n Aus, Brit* (*apartment*) piso *m*,
apartamento *m Ven, Col*, departamento *m*
Méx, CSur
flat feet *npl* pies *mpl* planos
flatfish ['flætfɪʃ] <-(es)> *n* pez *m* pleuro-

necto
flat-footed [,flæt'fʊtɪd, *Am:* -'fʊt-] *adj* de
pies planos
flatlet ['flætlɪt] *n Brit* piso *m* pequeño, apar-
tamentico *m Ven*
flatly *adv* (*deny, refuse*) rotundamente
flatmate ['flætmeɪt] *n Aus, Brit* compañero,
-a *m, f* de piso
flatness *n no pl* **1.** (*of surface*) llanura *f*
2. (*lack of excitement*) aburrimiento *m*
flatten ['flætn] *vt* **1.** (*make level*) allanar; **to ~
oneself against sth** pegarse contra algo **2.** MUS
bajar el tono
flatter ['flætəʳ, *Am:* 'flætɚ] *vt* **1.** (*gratify vanity*) adular **2.** (*make attractive*) favorecer **3.** (*be
proud of*) **to ~ oneself on sth** enorgullecerse
de algo
flatterer *n* adulador(a) *m(f)*
flattering *adj* **1.** (*clothes, portrait*) que favorece **2.** (*remark, description*) halagador(a)
flattery ['flætəri, *Am:* 'flæt-] *n no pl* adulación *f;* **~ will get you nowhere** adulando no
conseguirás tu propósito
flatulence ['flætjʊləns, *Am:* 'flætʃə-] *n no pl,
form* flatulencia *f*
flaunt [flɔːnt, *Am:* flɑːnt] *vt* hacer alarde de
flautist ['flɔːtɪst, *Am:* 'flɑːtɪst] *n* flautista *mf*
flavor ['fleɪvəʳ, *Am:* -vɚ] *Am* I. *n*, *vt* s. **flavour** II. *n* s. **flavouring**
flavour ['fleɪvəʳ, *Am:* -vɚ] *Brit, Aus* I. *n*
1. (*taste*) gusto *m;* (*ice cream, fizzy drink*)
sabor *m* **2.** *fig* sabor *m;* **a novel with a
romantic ~** una novela con sabor romántico
II. *vt* sazonar
flavouring ['fleɪvərɪŋ] *n Brit, Aus* condimento *m;* (*in industry*) aromatizante *m*
flaw [flɔː, *Am:* flɑː] I. *n* (*in machine*) defecto
m; (*in argument, character*) fallo *m;* (*in cloth*)
imperfección *f* II. *vt* dañar
flawless ['flɔːlɪs, *Am:* 'flɑː-] *adj* intachable; **~
performance** ejecución *f* perfecta
flax [flæks] *n no pl* lino *m*
flaxen ['flæksn] *adj liter* muy rubio, -a
flay [fleɪ] *vt* **1.** (*animal*) desollar **2.** *fig* despellejar
flea [fliː] *n* pulga *f* ▸ **to send sb away with a
~ in his/her ear** echar un buen rapapolvo a
alguien
fleabite ['fliːbaɪt] *n* picadura *f* de pulga
fleabitten *adj Brit, inf* miserable
flea market *n* rastrillo *m*
fleck [flek] I. *n* (*of colour*) mota *f;* (*of paint*)
salpicadura *f* II. *vt* salpicar
fled [fled] *pp of* **flee**
fledged [fledʒd] *adj* plumado, -a
fledgeling, fledgling ['fledʒlɪŋ] I. *n* (*young
bird*) volandero *m* II. *adj* (*inexperienced*)
inexperto, -a
flee [fliː] <fled> I. *vt* (*run away from*) huir de
II. *vi* (*run away*) escaparse; *liter* desaparecer
fleece [fliːs] I. *n* **1.** (*of sheep*) vellón *m*
2. (*clothing*) borreguillo *m* II. *vt* **1.** (*a sheep*)
esquilar **2.** *inf* (*cheat*) despojar

fleet¹ [fliːt] *n* **1.** NAUT flota *f;* **the British** ~ la armada británica **2.** (*of aeroplanes*) escuadrón *m;* **car** ~ parque *m* móvil
fleet² [fliːt] <-er, -est> *adj* veloz
fleeting ['fliːtɪŋ, *Am:* -t̬ɪŋ] *adj* (*encounter, romance*) pasajero, -a; (*glance, impression, smile*) efímero, -a; (*moment, opportunity, time*) breve; (*idea*) fugaz
Flemish ['flemɪʃ] *adj* flamenco, -a
flesh [fleʃ] *n no pl* (*body tissue*) carne *f;* (*pulp*) pulpa *f;* **to put** ~ **on an argument/idea** dar cuerpo a un argumento/idea ►**to be** (**only**) ~ **and blood** ser (sólo) de carne y hueso; **it made my** ~ **crawl** se me puso la piel de gallina; **in the** ~ en persona
flesh-coloured *adj Aus, Brit* de color carne
fleshpot ['fleʃpɒt, *Am:* -pɑːt] *n* antro *m* de placer
flesh wound *n* herida *f* superficial
fleshy ['fleʃi] <-ier, -iest> *adj* **1.** (*voluminous: person, limb*) gordo, -a; (*fruit*) carnoso, -a **2.** (*colour*) de carne
flew [fluː] *pp, pt of* **fly**
flex [fleks] **I.** *vt* flexionar ►**to** ~ **one's muscles** medir sus fuerzas **II.** *n* ELEC cable *m*
flexibility [ˌfleksə'bɪləti, *Am:* -t̬i] *n no pl* **1.** (*of material*) elasticidad *f* **2.** (*of person, approach*) flexibilidad *f*
flexible ['fleksəbl] *adj* **1.** (*pliable: material, tubing*) flexible **2.** (*arrangement, policy, schedule*) adaptable
flexitime ['fleksɪtaɪm] *n no pl* horario *m* flexible
flick [flɪk] **I.** *vt* (*with finger*) chasquear; **to** ~ **out one's tongue** lengüetear; **to** ~ **the light switch on/off** encender/apagar la luz; **to** ~ **channels** cambiar los canales **II.** *n* **1.** (*sudden movement, strike*) golpecito *m* **2.** **the** ~**s** *pl, inf* (*cinema*) el cine
flicker ['flɪkə', *Am:* -ə'] **I.** *vi* parpadear **II.** *n* parpadeo *m*
flick knife *n Aus, Brit* navaja *f* automática
flier ['flaɪə', *Am:* -ə'] *n* **1.** (*air traveller*) aviador(a) *m(f)* **2.** (*leaflet*) folleto *m*
flight [flaɪt] *n* **1.** (*act*) vuelo *m;* **the** ~ **of time** el paso del tiempo **2.** (*group: of birds*) bandada *f;* (*of aircraft*) escuadrilla *f* **3.** (*retreat*) escape *m;* ~ **of investment** fuga *f* de inversión; **to take** ~ darse a la fuga; **to put sb to** ~ poner a alguien en fuga **4.** (*series: of stairs*) tramo *m* ►**a** ~ **of** fancy una fantasía
flight attendant *n* auxiliar *mf* de vuelo
flight controller *n* controlador(a) *m(f)*
flight deck *n* **1.** (*cockpit*) cabina *f* de pilotaje **2.** (*on aircraft carrier*) cubierta *f* de aterrizaje **flight engineer** *n* mecánico *m* de vuelo
flightless *adj* incapaz de volar
flight number *n* número *m* de vuelo **flight path** *n* trayectoria *f* de vuelo
flighty ['flaɪti, *Am:* -t̬i] <-ier, -iest> *adj pej* (*woman*) frívolo, -a
flimsiness ['flɪmzɪnɪs] *n no pl* debilidad *f*

flimsy ['flɪmzi] <-ier, -iest> *adj* **1.** (*light: dress, blouse*) ligero, -a **2.** (*construction*) débil **3.** (*argument, excuse*) poco sólido, -a
flinch [flɪntʃ] *vi* (*in pain*) rechistar; **to** ~ **from doing sth** resistirse a hacer algo
fling [flɪŋ] <flung> **I.** *vt* (*throw*) lanzar; **to** ~ **oneself in front of a train** arrojarse al tren; **to** ~ **sb into prison** echar a alguien a la cárcel; **to** ~ **accusations at sb** lanzar acusaciones a alguien **II.** *n inf* **1.** (*short pleasant time*) rato *m* de juerga **2.** (*relationship*) aventura *f* (amorosa) **3.** (*try*) **to have a** ~ **at sth** intentar algo
◆**fling away** *vt* desechar
◆**fling off** *vt* **to** ~ **one's clothes** desvestirse con prisa
◆**fling on** *vt inf* **to** ~ **one's clothes** vestirse de prisa
◆**fling open** *vt* abrir de golpe
◆**fling out** *vt inf* (*throw out*) tirar
flint [flɪnt] *n* pedernal *m*
flip [flɪp] <-pp-> **I.** *vt* (*turn over quickly*) dar la vuelta a; **to** ~ **a coin** echar a cara o cruz **II.** *vi* **1.** (*turn quickly*) **to** ~ **over** dar una vuelta de campana **2.** *inf* (*go mad*) perder la chaveta **III.** *n* (*toss in the air*) ~ **of a coin** lanzamiento *m* de una moneda
flip chart *n* rotafolio *m*
flip-flop ['flɪpflɒp, *Am:* -flɑːp] *n* chancla *f*
flippancy ['flɪpəntsi] *n no pl* falta *f* de seriedad
flippant ['flɪpənt] *adj* poco serio, -a
flipper ['flɪpə', *Am:* -ə'] *n* aleta *f*
flipping *adj, adv Brit, inf* (*as intensifier*) maldito, -a
flip side *n* **1.** MUS (*of record*) cara *f* B **2.** (*of policy, situation*) **the** ~ la otra cara de la moneda
flirt [flɜːt, *Am:* flɜːrt] **I.** *n* (*woman*) coqueta *f;* (*man*) galanteador *m* **II.** *vi* **1.** (*be sexually attracted*) flirtear **2.** (*toy with*) **to** ~ **with sth** jugar con algo
flirtation [flɜː'teɪʃən, *Am:* flɜːr'-] *n* flirteo *m*
flirtatious [flɜː'teɪʃəs, *Am:* flɜːr'-] *adj* (*woman*) coqueta; (*man*) galanteador
flit [flɪt] <-tt-> **I.** *vi* **to** ~ (**about**) (*bats*) revolotear; (*bees*) volar; (*people*) moverse **II.** *n Brit, inf* **to do a** (**moonlight**) ~ huir a escondidas
float [fləʊt, *Am:* floʊt] **I.** *vi* **1.** (*in liquid, air*) flotar, boyar *AmL;* **to** ~ **to the surface** salir a la superficie **2.** (*move aimlessly*) moverse sin rumbo **3.** ECON fluctuar **II.** *vt* **1.** (*keep afloat*) poner a flote **2.** ECON, FIN **to** ~ **a business/company** lanzar una empresa/compañía a bolsa **3.** (*air*) **to** ~ **an idea/a plan** sugerir una idea/un plan **III.** *n* **1.** NAUT flotador *m;* (*for people*) salvavidas *m inv* **2.** (*vehicle*) carroza *f* **3.** *Aus, Brit* (*cash*) fondo *m*
◆**float about** *vi,* **float around** *vi inf* (*circulate*) circular; (*people*) moverse sin rumbo; (*rumour*) correr
◆**float off** *vi* irse a la deriva
floatation [fləʊ'teɪʃən, *Am:* floʊ-] *n s.* **flo-**

tation

floating ['fləʊtɪŋ, *Am:* 'floʊt̬ɪŋ] *adj* flotante

flock [flɒk, *Am:* flɑːk] I. *n* 1. (*group: of goats, sheep*) rebaño *m;* (*of birds*) bandada *f,* parvada *f AmL;* (*of people*) multitud *f* II. *vi* congregarse

floe [fləʊ, *Am:* floʊ] *n* témpano *m*

flog [flɒg, *Am:* flɑːg] <-gg-> *vt* 1. (*punish*) azotar; *fig* flagelar 2. *Brit, inf* (*sell*) vender ▶to ~ **sth to** death *inf* repetir algo hasta la saciedad

flogging *n* azotaina *f*

flood [flʌd] I. *vt* inundar; **the calls for tickets** ~ed **the switchboard** el aluvión de peticiones de entradas colapsó la centralita; **to** ~ **an engine** AUTO ahogar un motor II. *vi* METEO (*town*) inundarse; (*river*) desbordarse; **refugees have been** ~ing **in** un aluvión de refugiados ha estado llegando III. *n* 1. METEO inundación *f* 2. REL **the Flood** el Diluvio 3. (*outpouring*) torrente *m;* ~ **of tears** mar *m* de lágrimas; ~ **of products** productos *mpl* a raudales; ~ **of abuse** aluvión *m* de insultos; **to let out a** ~ **of abuse** soltar una retahíla de insultos; ~ **of complaints** lluvia *f* de quejas

floodgate ['flʌdgeɪt] *n fig* **to open the** ~**s to sth** abrir las puertas a algo

floodlight ['flʌdlaɪt] I. *n* foco *m* II. *vt irr* iluminar (con focos)

floor [flɔːʳ, *Am:* flɔːr] I. *n* 1. (*of room*) suelo *m;* **dance** ~ pista *f* de baile; **to take the** ~ (*in debate*) tomar la palabra; (*start dancing*) salir a bailar 2. (*level in building*) piso *m;* **sea** ~ fondo *m* del mar ▶to wipe **the** ~ **with sb** hacer trizas a alguien; **to go** through **the** ~ (*prices*) estar por los suelos II. *vt* (*knock down*) tumbar; **the question** ~ed **her** la pregunta la dejó sin respuesta

floorboard ['flɔːbɔːd, *Am:* 'flɔːrbɔːrd] *n* tabla *f* del suelo

flooring *n no pl* solado *m;* **wooden** ~ entablado *m*

floor lamp *n Am* lámpara *f* de pie **floor polish** *n* cera *f* para el suelo **floor show** *n* espectáculo *m* de cabaret **floor-walker** *n Am* vigilante *m*

flop [flɒp, *Am:* flɑːp] <-pp-> I. *vi* 1. (*fall*) dejarse caer 2. *inf* (*fail*) fracasar II. *n inf* (*failure*) fracaso *m*

floppy ['flɒpi, *Am:* 'flɑːpi] I. <-ier, -iest> *adj* (*ears*) caído, -a; (*hat*) flexible II. <-ies> *n* diskette *m*

floppy disk *n* diskette *m*

flora ['flɔːrə] *n no pl* flora *f;* ~ **and fauna** flora y fauna

floral ['flɔːrəl] *adj* floral

florid ['flɒrɪd, *Am:* 'flɔːr-] *adj* 1. (*style*) florido, -a; (*prose, rhetoric*) ornamentado, -a 2. *form* (*ruddy*) rojizo, -a

Florida ['flɒrɪdə, *Am:* 'flɔːr-] *n* Florida *f*

florist ['flɒrɪst, *Am:* 'flɔːr-] *n* florista *mf;* **the** ~'s la floristería

flotation [fləʊ'teɪʃən, *Am:* floʊ-] *n* ECON, FIN

salida *f* a Bolsa

flotilla [flə'tɪlə, *Am:* floʊ-] *n* MIL, NAUT flotilla *f*

flotsam ['flɒtsəm, *Am:* 'flɑːt-] *n no pl* restos *mpl* flotantes; ~ **and jetsam** desechos *mpl*

flounce¹ [flaʊnts] *vi* **to** ~ **about** moverse violentamente; **to** ~ **in/out** entrar/salir indignado

flounce² [flaʊnts] *n* (*decoration*) volante *m,* arandela *f Méx, Perú*

flounder¹ ['flaʊndəʳ, *Am:* -dɚ] *vi* 1. (*struggle*) sufrir 2. (*fail*) ir(se) a pique

flounder² ['flaʊndəʳ, *Am:* -dɚ] *n* (*flatfish*) platija *f*

flour ['flaʊəʳ, *Am:* -ɚ] I. *n no pl* harina *f* II. *vt* enharinar

flourish ['flʌrɪʃ, *Am:* 'flɝː-] I. *vi* florecer II. *n* **with a** ~ con un gesto ceremonioso

flourishing *adj* (*place*) esplendoroso, -a; (*business, market, trade*) próspero, -a

flour-mill *n* molino *m* de harina

floury ['flaʊəri] <-ier, -iest> *adj* harinoso, -a

flout [flaʊt] *vt* **to** ~ **a law/rule** incumplir una ley/regla; **to** ~ **tradition** no hacer caso de la tradición

flow [fləʊ, *Am:* floʊ] I. *vi* fluir, correr II. *n no pl* (*of water, ideas*) flujo *m;* (*of goods*) circulación *f;* ~ **of oil/water** chorro *m* de aceite/agua; ~ **of blood** derrame *m* de sangre ▶in full ~ en pleno discurso; **to go** against **the** ~ ir contra la corriente; **to go** with **the** ~ seguir la corriente

flowchart *n,* **flow diagram** *n* organigrama *m*

flower ['flaʊəʳ, *Am:* 'flaʊɚ] I. *n* 1. (*plant*) flor *f;* **to be in** ~ estar en flor 2. *liter* (*best*) **the** ~ la flor y nata II. *vi* florecer, florear *AmL; fig* desarrollarse

flower arrangement *n* arreglo *m* floral **flowerbed** *n* arriate *m* de flores **flower garden** *n* jardín *m* de flores **flower pot** *n* maceta *f*

flowery ['flaʊəri] <-ier, -iest> *adj* 1. (*material*) floreado, -a 2. (*style, language*) florido, -a

flowing *adj* (*hair, robes*) suelto, -a

flown [fləʊn, *Am:* floʊn] *pp of* **fly¹**

flu [fluː] *n no pl* gripe *f,* gripa *f Col*

fluctuate ['flʌktʃʊeɪt] *vi* fluctuar

fluctuation [ˌflʌktʃʊ'eɪʃən] *n* fluctuación *f*

flue [fluː] *n* cañón *m* de chimenea

fluency ['fluːəntsi] *n no pl* fluidez *f*

fluent ['fluːənt] *adj* (*style, movement*) con fluidez; **to speak** ~ **English** hablar inglés con soltura

fluff [flʌf] I. *n no pl* 1. (*furry piece*) lanilla *f;* (*dust*) pelusa *f* 2. *Am* (*trifle*) nimiedad *f* II. *vt inf* (*fail*) hacer mal

fluffy ['flʌfi] <-ier, -iest> *adj* (*furry: animal*) peludo, -a; (*toy*) de peluche; (*clothes*) lanudo, -a; GASTR (*light*) esponjoso, -a

fluid ['fluːɪd] I. *n* fluido *m* II. *adj* 1. (*liquid*) líquido, -a 2. (*situation*) inestable

fluid ounce *n* onza *f* fluida (*unidad de capacidad equivalente a 28,42 milímetros*)

flung [flʌŋ] *pp, pt of* **fling**

flunk [flʌŋk] *vt Am, inf* suspender

fluorescence [flʊəˈresns, *Am:* flɔ:-] *n no pl* fluorescencia *f*

fluorescent [flʊəˈresnt, *Am:* flɔ:-] *adj* fluorescente; ~ **tube** tubo *m* fluorescente

fluoride [ˈflʊəraɪd, *Am:* ˈflɔːraɪd] *n no pl* fluoruro *m*

fluorine [ˈflʊəriːn, *Am:* ˈflɔːriːn] *n no pl* flúor *m*

fluorocarbon [ˌflʊərəˈkɑːbən, *Am:* ˌflɔːrəˈkɑːr-] *n* fluorocarburo *m*

flurry [ˈflʌri, *Am:* ˈflɜːr-] <-ies> *n* agitación *f*; (*of snow*) ráfaga *f*; **a ~ of excitement** un frenesí; **a ~ of speculation** una ola de especulación

flush¹ [flʌʃ] I. *vi* (*blush*) ruborizarse II. *vt* **to ~ the toilet** tirar de la cadena III. *n* 1. *no pl* (*blush*) rubor *m*; ~ **of anger** sonrojo *m* de rabia 2. (*toilet*) cisterna *f*

flush² [flʌʃ] *adj* 1. (*level*) llano, -a 2. *inf* (*rich*) **to be ~ with money** andar bien de dinero

◆**flush out** *vt* hacer salir

flushed [flʌʃt] *adj* emocionado, -a; ~ **with anger** rojo de rabia; ~ **with joy** pletórico de alegría; ~ **with success** emocionado con el éxito

fluster [ˈflʌstər, *Am:* -tɚ] I. *vt* **to ~ sb** poner nervioso a alguien II. *n no pl* **to be in a ~** estar nervioso

flute [fluːt] *n MUS* flauta *f*

fluting *n* acanalado *m*

flutist [ˈfluːtɪst, *Am:* -t̬ɪst] *n Am s.* **flautist**

flutter [ˈflʌtər, *Am:* ˈflʌt̬ɚ] I. *n* 1. *no pl, Aus, Brit, inf* (*bet*) apuesta *f*; **to have a ~** apostar 2. (*sound*) revoloteo *m* 3. *fig* (*nervousness*) agitación *f*; **to put sb in a ~** poner nervioso a alguien; **to be all of a ~** ser un manojo de nervios II. *vi* 1. (*quiver*) temblar; **to make hearts ~** *fig* hacer palpitar los corazones 2. (*flap*) agitarse III. *vt* (*flap*) agitar; **to ~ one's wings** aletear; **to ~ one's eyelashes** pestañear

fluvial [ˈfluːvɪəl] *adj* fluvial

flux [flʌks] *n no pl* 1. (*change*) cambio *m* continuo; **to be in a state of ~** estar continuamente cambiando 2. *MED* flujo *m*

fly¹ [flaɪ] <flew, flown> I. *vi* 1. (*through air*) volar; (*travel by aircraft*) viajar en avión 2. (*move rapidly*) lanzarse; **to ~ at sb** precipitarse sobre alguien 3. (*leave*) salir corriendo ▶**to ~ high** *Am* volar muy alto II. *vt* 1. (*aircraft*) pilotar 2. (*make move through air*) hacer volar; **to ~ a flag** enarbolar una bandera; **to ~ a kite** hacer volar una cometa

fly² [flaɪ] *n* (*insect*) mosca *f* ▶**he wouldn't harm a ~** sería incapaz de matar una mosca; **to drop** (off) [*o* die] **like flies** *inf* caer como moscas; **a ~ in the** ointment la única pega

◆**fly away** *vi* irse volando

◆**fly in** *vi* **to ~ from somewhere** llegar (en avión) desde algún sitio

◆**fly off** *vi* irse volando

flyaway [ˈflaɪəweɪ] *adj* suelto, -a

fly-by-night [ˈflaɪbaɪnaɪt] *adj inf* nada serio, -a

flycatcher [ˈflaɪˌkætʃər, *Am:* -ɚ] *n* papamoscas *m*

flyer [ˈflaɪər, *Am:* -ɚ] *n* 1. (*air traveller*) aviador(a) *m(f)* 2. (*leaflet*) folleto *m*

flying [ˈflaɪɪŋ] *n no pl* el volar

flying boat *n* hidroavión *m* **flying fish** *n* pez *m* volador **flying fox** *n* panique *m* **flying saucer** *n* platillo *m* volante **flying squad** *n* brigada *f* móvil **flying start** *n* SPORTS salida *f* lanzada; **to get off to a ~** entrar con buen pie **flying time** *n* horas *fpl* de vuelo **flying visit** *n inf* visita *f* relámpago

flyleaf [ˈflaɪliːf] <flyleaves> *n* guarda *f*

flyover [ˈflaɪˌəʊvər, *Am:* -ˌoʊvɚ] *n* 1. *Brit* paso *m* elevado 2. *Am* desfile *m* aéreo

flypaper [ˈflaɪˌpeɪpər, *Am:* -pɚ] *n* papel *m* matamoscas

flypast [ˈflaɪpɑːst, *Am:* -pæst] *n MIL* desfile *m* aéreo

flysheet *n Brit* doble techo *m* (*de una tienda de campaña*)

fly-trap *n* atrapamoscas *m*

flyweight [ˈflaɪweɪt] *n SPORTS* peso *m* mosca

flywheel [ˈflaɪhwiːl] *n TECH* volante *m*

FM [ˌefˈem] PHYS *abbr of* **frequency modulation** FM

FO [ˌefˈəʊ, *Am:* -oʊ] *n Brit abbr of* **Foreign Office** Ministerio *m* de Asuntos Exteriores

foal [fəʊl, *Am:* foʊl] I. *n* potro, -a *m, f*; **to be in ~** estar preñada II. *vi* parir

foam [fəʊm, *Am:* foʊm] I. *n no pl* (*bubbles, foam rubber*) espuma *f*; **shaving ~** espuma de afeitar II. *vi* **to ~ with rage** echar espuma de (pura) rabia

foam bath *n* baño *m* de espuma **foam rubber** *n* goma espuma *f*

foamy [ˈfəʊmi, *Am:* ˈfoʊm-] <-ier, -iest> *adj* espumoso, -a

fob [fɒb, *Am:* fɑːb] *n* cadena *f* de reloj

focal [ˈfəʊkl, *Am:* ˈfoʊ-] *adj* focal; ~ **point** punto *m* central

focus [ˈfəʊkəs, *Am:* ˈfoʊ-] <-es *o* foci> I. *n* 1. foco *m*; **to be in/out of ~** estar enfocado/desenfocado 2. (*centre*) centro *m*; ~ **of interest** centro de interés; **the ~ of a programme** el enfoque de un programa; **to bring sth into ~** *fig* destacar algo II. <-s- *o* -ss-> *vi* enfocar; **to ~ on sth** (*concentrate*) concentrarse en algo III. *vt* enfocar; **to ~ one's attention on sth** centrar la atención en algo

fodder [ˈfɒdər, *Am:* ˈfɑːdɚ] *n no pl* 1. (*animal food*) forraje *m*; ~ **crop** cereal-pienso *m* 2. *fig, inf* pasto *m*

foe [fəʊ, *Am:* foʊ] *n* enemigo, -a *m, f*

foetal [ˈfiːtəl, *Am:* -t̬əl] *adj BIO* fetal

foetus [ˈfiːtəs, *Am:* -t̬əs] *n* feto *m*

fog [fɒg, *Am:* fɑːg] *n* niebla *f*; **to be in a ~** *fig* estar confundido

fog bank *n* banco *m* de niebla

fogbound ['fɒgbaʊnd, *Am:* 'fɑːg-] *adj* inmovilizado, -a por la niebla

fogey ['fəʊgi, *Am:* 'foʊ-] *n pej, inf* persona *f* chapada a la antigua; **old** ~ carroza *mf;* **young** ~ joven *mf* de ideas anticuadas

foggy ['fɒgi, *Am:* 'fɑːgi] <-ier, -iest> *adj* nebuloso, -a ▸ **to not have the foggiest** (idea) no tener la más remota idea

foghorn ['fɒghɔːn, *Am:* 'fɑːghɔːrn] *n* sirena *f* de niebla; **to have a voice like a** ~ tener una voz chillona

foglamp *n,* **foglight** *n* faro *m* antiniebla

fogy ['fɒgi, *Am:* 'fɑːgi] <-ies> *n inf s.* **fogey**

foible ['fɔɪbl] *n* debilidad *f*

foil[1] [fɔɪl] *n* 1. (*metal paper*) papel *m* de aluminio 2. (*sword*) florete *m* 3. *fig* **to act as a** ~ **to sth** servir de contraste con algo

foil[2] [fɔɪl] *vt* frustrar

foist (**up**)**on** [ˌfɔɪst(əˈp)ɒn, *Am:* ˌfɔɪst-(əˈp)ɑːn] *vt* **to foist sth** (**up**)**on sb** hacer que alguien se encargue de algo

fold[1] [fəʊld, *Am:* foʊld] I. *vt* 1. (*bend*) plegar; **to** ~ **sth back/down** plegar algo 2. (*wrap*) **to** ~ **sth** (**in sth**) envolver algo (en algo) II. *vi* 1. (*bend over*) doblarse 2. (*fail, go bankrupt*) fracasar III. *n* pliegue *m*

fold[2] [fəʊld, *Am:* foʊld] *n* (*sheep pen*) redil *m;* **to return to the** ~ *fig* volver al hogar

◆**fold up** *vt* doblar

folder ['fəʊldə', *Am:* 'foʊldə'] *n* a. INFOR carpeta *f,* fólder *m Col, Méx*

folding ['fəʊldɪŋ, *Am:* 'foʊld-] *adj* plegable; ~ **door** puerta *f* plegadiza; ~ **money** *Am* billetes *mpl* de banco

foliage ['fəʊlɪɪdʒ, *Am:* 'foʊ-] *n no pl* follaje *m*

folio ['fəʊliəʊ, *Am:* 'foʊlioʊ] *n* folio *m*

folk [fəʊk, *Am:* foʊk] *npl* pueblo *m;* **farming** ~ gente *f* de campo; **the old** ~ los viejos; **ordinary** ~ gente *f* corriente; (~ *memory*) memoria *f* colectiva; ~ **wisdom** sabiduría *f* popular

folk dance *n* baile *m* popular

folklore ['fəʊklɔː', *Am:* 'foʊklɔːr] *n no pl* folklore *m*

folk music *n* música *f* folk **folk song** *n* canción *f* popular

folksy ['fəʊksi, *Am:* 'foʊk-] <-ier, -iest> *adj* (*friendly*) amigable

folk tale *n* cuento *m* popular

foll. *abbr of* **followed, following** sig.

follow ['fɒləʊ, *Am:* 'fɑːloʊ] I. *vt* 1. (*take same route as*) seguir 2. (*happen next*) **to** ~ **sth** suceder a algo 3. **to** ~ **ancient traditions** seguir las antiguas tradiciones 4. (*understand*) **to** ~ **sb/sth** seguir a alguien/algo 5. (*have an interest in*) **to** ~ **sth** interesarse por algo II. *vi* 1. (*take same route as*) seguir 2. (*happen next*) suceder 3. (*result*) resultar; **to** ~ **from sth** ser consecuencia de algo

◆**follow on** *vi* seguir

◆**follow through** I. *vt* 1. (*study*) investigar 2. (*see through to end*) terminar II. *vi* SPORTS terminar

◆**follow up** *vt* 1. (*consider, investigate*) investigar 2. (*do next*) **to** ~ **sth by** [*o* **with**] ... hacer algo después de...

follower *n* seguidor(a) *m(f)*

following I. *n inv* 1. **I'd say the** ~ diría lo siguiente; **my idea was the** ~ mi idea era la siguiente 2. (*supporters: of idea*) partidarios, -as *m, f pl;* (*of doctrine*) seguidores, -as *m, f pl* II. *adj* 1. (*next*) siguiente; **the** ~ **ideas** las siguientes ideas 2. (*from behind*) ~ **wind** viento de cola [*o* de popa] III. *prep* después de; ~ **the dinner/your letter** después de la cena/tu carta

follow-up ['fɒləʊʌp, *Am:* 'fɑːloʊ-] *n* seguimiento *m*

folly ['fɒli, *Am:* 'fɑːli] *n* 1. (*foolishness*) locura *f;* **it's sheer** ~! ¡es una locura! 2. *Brit* ARCHIT capricho *m*

fond [fɒnd, *Am:* fɑːnd] <-er, -est> *adj* 1. (*with liking for*) **to be** ~ **of sb** tener cariño a alguien; **he is** ~ **of** ... le gusta... 2. (*loving*) cariñoso, -a; ~ **memories** tiernos recuerdos *mpl* 3. (*hope*) vano, -a

fondle ['fɒndl, *Am:* 'fɑːn-] <-ling> *vt* acariciar

fondness ['fɒndnɪs, *Am:* 'fɑːnd-] *n no pl* cariño *m;* **to have a** ~ **for sth** tener una afición por algo

font [fɒnt, *Am:* fɑːnt] *n* 1. (*receptacle*) pila *f* (bautismal) 2. TYPO fuente *f*

food [fuːd] *n* comida *f* ▸ **to give sb** ~ **for thought** dar a alguien algo en que pensar; **to be** off **one's** ~ estar desganado

food chain *n* cadena *f* alimentaria **food poisoning** *n no pl* envenenamiento *m* por alimentos **food processor** *n* procesador *m* de alimentos **foodstuff** *n* artículo *m* alimenticio

fool [fuːl] I. *n* idiota *mf;* **to be** ~ **enough to do sth** ser bastante idiota como para hacer algo; **to act the** ~ hacer el tonto; **to make a** ~ **of sb** poner a alguien en ridículo; **any** ~ cualquiera II. *vt* engañar; **you could have** ~**ed me!** *inf* ¡no me lo puedo creer! III. *vi* (*joke*) bromear IV. *adj Am, inf* (*silly*) tonto, -a

◆**fool about** *vi* hacer payasadas

foolhardy ['fuːlhɑːdi, *Am:* -hɑːr-] *adj* temerario, -a

foolish ['fuːlɪʃ] *adj* tonto, -a

foolproof ['fuːlpruːf] *adj* a toda prueba

foolscap ['fuːlskæp] *n no pl* papel *m* tamaño folio

foot [fʊt] I. <feet> *n* 1. (*of person*) pie *m;* (*of animal*) pata *f* 2. (*unit of measurement*) pie *m* (30,48 cm) 3. (*bottom or lowest part*) **at the** ~ **of one's bed** al pie de la cama; **at the** ~ **of the page** a pie de página ▸ **to get a** ~ **in the** door abrirse una brecha; **to have one** ~ **in the grave** estar con un pie en la tumba; **to have both feet on the** ground ser realista; **to set** ~ **on dry** land poner los pies en tierra firme; **to be** back **on one's feet** estar recuperado; **to have/get** cold **feet** estar/ponerse nervioso; **to catch sb on the <u>wrong</u>** ~ pillar a alguien desprevenido; **to <u>fall</u> on one's feet** caer de pie; **to <u>find</u> one's feet** acostumbrarse al ambiente; **to <u>put</u> one's ~ down** acelerar; **to <u>put</u> one's ~ in it** [*o* **in your mouth**] *Am* meter la pata; **to <u>set</u> ~ in sth** pisar algo; **I'll never set ~ in his house again** no volveré a pisar su casa; **to be <u>under</u> sb's feet** estar siempre pegado a alguien **II.** *vt inf* **to ~ the bill** pagar

footage ['fʊtɪdʒ, *Am:* 'fʊt̬-] *n no pl* CINE, TV secuencias *fpl*, imágenes *fpl*

foot-and-mouth disease [ˌfʊtənd'maʊθ-dɪˌziːz] *n* fiebre *f* aftosa

football ['fʊtbɔːl] *n no pl* **1.** *Brit* (*soccer*) fútbol *m* **2.** *Am* (*American football*) fútbol *m* americano **3.** (*ball*) balón *m*

football hooligan *n* hooligan *mf* **football player** *n* futbolista *mf* **football pools** *npl* quinielas *fpl*

foot board *n* AUTO estribo *m*

footbridge ['fʊtbrɪdʒ] *n* puente *m* peatonal

footer ['fʊtəʳ, *Am:* 'fʊt̬əʳ] *n* pie *m* de página

foothills ['fʊthɪlz] *n* estribaciones *fpl*

foothold ['fʊthəʊld, *Am:* -hoʊld] *n* asidero *m* para el pie; **to gain a ~** *fig* lograr establecerse

footing ['fʊtɪŋ, *Am:* 'fʊt̬-] *n no pl* **1. to lose one's ~** resbalar **2.** (*basis*) posición *f*; **on a war ~** en pie de guerra; **on an equal ~** en un mismo pie de igualdad

footlights ['fʊtlaɪts] *npl* candilejas *fpl*

footling ['fuːtlɪŋ] *adj* trivial

footloose ['fʊtluːs] *adj* libre ▶**to be ~ and <u>fancy-free</u>** estar soltero y sin compromiso

footman ['fʊtmən] <-men> *n* lacayo *m*

footnote ['fʊtnəʊt, *Am:* -noʊt] *n* nota *f* a pie de página

footpath ['fʊtpɑːθ, *Am:* -pæθ] *n* sendero *m*

footprint ['fʊtprɪnt] *n* huella *f*

footrest ['fʊtrest] *n* reposapiés *m inv*

footsie ['fʊtsi] *n no pl*, *inf* **to play ~ with sb** acariciar a alguien con el pie

footslog ['fʊtslɒg] <-gg-> *vi inf* andar hasta acabar rendido

footsore ['fʊtsɔːʳ, *Am:* -sɔːr] *adj liter* **to be ~** tener los pies cansados

footstep ['fʊtstep] *n* paso *m*

footstool ['fʊtstuːl] *n* reposapiés *m inv*

footwear ['fʊtweəʳ, *Am:* -wer] *n no pl* calzado *m*

footwork ['fʊtwɜːk, *Am:* -wɜːrk] *n no pl* juego *m* de piernas

for [fɔːʳ, *Am:* fɔːr] **I.** *prep* **1.** (*destined for*) para; **this is ~ you** esto es para ti; **a present ~ my mother** un regalo para mi madre **2.** (*to give to*) por; **to do sth ~ sb** hacer algo por alguien **3.** (*intention, purpose*) **~ sale/rent** en venta/alquiler; **sth ~ a headache** algo para el dolor de cabeza; **it's time ~ lunch** es hora del almuerzo; **it's time ~ sleep** es hora de dormir; **to invite sb ~ dinner** invitar a alguien para cenar; **to wait ~ sb** esperar a alguien; **to go ~ a walk** ir a dar un paseo; **fit ~ nothing** bueno

para nada; **what ~?** ¿para qué?; **what's that ~?** ¿para qué es eso?; **it's ~ cutting cheese** es para cortar queso; **~ this to be possible** para que esto sea posible; **to look ~ a way to do sth** buscar una manera de hacer algo **4.** (*to acquire*) **eager ~ power** ávido de poder; **to search ~ sth** buscar algo; **to ask/hope ~ news** pedir/esperar noticias; **to apply ~ a job** solicitar un trabajo; **to shout ~ help** gritar pidiendo ayuda **5.** (*towards*) **the train ~ Glasgow** el tren hacia Glasgow; **to make ~ home** dirigirse hacia casa; **to run ~ safety** correr a ponerse a salvo **6.** (*distance*) **to walk ~ 8 km** caminar durante 8 km **7.** (*time*) **~ now** por ahora; **~ a while/a time** por un rato/un momento; **to last ~ hours** durar horas y horas; **I'm going to be here ~ three weeks** voy a estar aquí durante tres semanas; **I haven't been there ~ three years** hace tres años que no estoy allí; **I have known her ~ three years** la conozco desde hace tres años **8.** (*on date of*) **to have sth finished ~ Sunday** acabar algo para el domingo; **to set the wedding ~ May 4** fijar la boda para el 4 de mayo **9.** (*in support of*) **is he ~ or against it?** ¿está a favor o en contra?; **to fight ~ sth** luchar por algo **10.** (*employed by*) **to work ~ a company** trabajar para una empresa **11.** (*the task of*) **it's ~ him to say/do ...** le toca a él decir/hacer... **12.** (*in substitution*) **the substitute ~ the teacher** el substituto del maestro; **say hello ~ me** dile hola de mi parte **13.** (*price*) **a cheque ~ £100** un cheque de £100; **I paid £10 ~ it** pagué £10 por ello **14.** (*concerning*) **as ~ me/that** en cuanto a mí/eso; **two are enough ~ me** dos son suficientes para mí; **sorry ~ doing that** perdón por hacer eso; **the best would be ~ me to go** lo mejor sería que me fuese **15.** (*in reference to*) **what's the Chinese ~ 'book'?** ¿cómo se dice 'libro' en chino? **16.** (*cause*) **excuse me ~ being late** discúlpame por llegar tarde; **as the reason ~ one's behaviour** como razón por su comportamiento; **~ lack of reasons** por falta de motivos **17.** (*because of*) **to do sth ~ love** hacer algo por amor; **~ fear of doing sth** por miedo a hacer algo; **to cry ~ joy** gritar de alegría; **he can't talk ~ laughing** no puede hablar de la risa **18.** (*despite*) **all that/her money** a pesar de todo eso/de su dinero; **~ all I know** por lo que yo sepa **19.** (*as*) **~ example** por ejemplo; **he ~ one** empezando por él ▶**she's ~ <u>it</u>!** ¡se la va a cargar!; **that's kids ~ <u>you</u>!** ¡así son los niños! **II.** *conj form* pues

forage ['fɒrɪdʒ, *Am:* 'fɔːr-] **I.** *vi* **to ~** (*about*) **for sth** buscar algo **II.** *n no pl* (*fodder*) forraje *m*

foray ['fɒreɪ, *Am:* 'fɔːr-] *n* (*raid*) correría *f*; **to make a ~** (*into sth*) hacer una incursión (en algo)

forbad(e) [fə'bæd, *Am:* fəʳ-] *pt of* **forbid**

forbear [fɔː'beəʳ, *Am:* fɔːr'ber] <forbore, forborne> *vi form* (*abstain, refrain*) contenerse; **to** ~ **from doing sth** abstenerse de hacer algo

forbearance [fɔːˈbeərəns, *Am:* fɔːrˈberəns] *n no pl, form* **1.** paciencia *f* **2.** (*self-control*) dominio *m* de sí mismo

forbid [fəˈbɪd, *Am:* fə-] <forbade, forbidden> *vt* prohibir; **to** ~ **sb from doing sth** prohibir a alguien hacer algo; **to** ~ **sb sth** *form* prohibir algo a alguien

forbidden [fəˈbɪdn, *Am:* fə-] *pp of* **forbid**

forbidding [fəˈbɪdɪŋ, *Am:* fə-] *adj* **1.** (*impressive*) imponente **2.** (*severe*) severo, -a

forbore [fɔːˈbɔːʳ, *Am:* fɔːrˈbɔːr] *pt of* **forbear**

forborne [fɔːˈbɔːn, *Am:* fɔːrˈbɔːrn] *pp of* **forbear**

force [fɔːs, *Am:* fɔːrs] **I.** *n* **1.** fuerza *f*; **by sheer** ~ **of numbers** por superioridad numérica; ~ **of gravity** PHYS fuerza de la gravedad; **to combine** ~s unir esfuerzos **2.** (*large numbers*) **in** ~ en grandes cantidades **3.** (*influence*) influencia *f*; **by** ~ **of circumstance** debido a las circunstancias; **by** ~ **of habit** por costumbre; **the** ~**s of nature** *liter* las fuerzas de la naturaleza **4.** (*validity*) validez *f*; **to come into** ~ entrar en vigor **5.** MIL **police** ~ cuerpo *m* de policía; **Air Force** Fuerzas Aéreas; **armed** ~**s** fuerzas *fpl* armadas **II.** *vt* **1.** (*use power*) forzar; **to** ~ **a door** forzar una puerta **2.** (*oblige to do*) obligar; **to** ~ **sb to do sth** obligar a alguien a hacer algo; **to** ~ **a smile** sonreír forzadamente; **to** ~ **words out of sb** hacer hablar a alguien **3.** (*cause to grow faster*) hacer madurar temprano

◆**force into** *vt* **to force sb into** (**doing**) **sth** forzar a alguien a (hacer) algo

◆**force off** *vt* quitar por la fuerza

◆**force on** *vt* **to force sth on sb** imponer algo a alguien

◆**force out** *vt* hacer salir

◆**force upon** *vt s.* **force on**

forced *adj* (*smile, friendliness*) forzado, -a; ~ **landing** aterrizaje *m* forzoso

force-feed [ˌfɔːsˈfiːd, *Am:* ˈfɔːrsfiːd] *vt* dar de comer a la fuerza

forceful [ˈfɔːsfəl, *Am:* ˈfɔːrs-] *adj* enérgico, -a

forceps [ˈfɔːseps, *Am:* ˈfɔːr-] *npl* MED fórceps *mpl*; **a pair of** ~ unos fórceps

forceps delivery *n* MED parto *m* con fórceps

forcible [ˈfɔːsəbl, *Am:* ˈfɔːr-] *adj* a la fuerza

forcibly *adv* a la fuerza

ford [fɔːd, *Am:* fɔːrd] **I.** *n* vado *m*, botadero *m* *Méx* **II.** *vt* vadear

fore [fɔːʳ, *Am:* fɔːr] **I.** *adj* anterior; ~ **and aft** de popa a proa **II.** *n no pl* **to be to the** ~ ir delante; **to come to the** ~ destacar

forearm¹ [ˈfɔːrɑːm, *Am:* -ɑːrm] *n* antebrazo *m*

forearm² [ˌfɔːrˈɑːm, *Am:* -ˈɑːrm] *vt liter* **to** ~ **oneself** (**against sth**) prevenirse (contra algo)

forebears [ˈfɔːbeəz, *Am:* ˈfɔːrberz] *npl form* antepasados *mpl*

forebode [fɔːˈbəʊd, *Am:* fɔːrˈboʊd] *vt liter*

presagiar

foreboding [fɔːˈbəʊdɪŋ, *Am:* fɔːrˈboʊ-] *n liter* presentimiento *m*; **to have a** ~ (**that**) ... tener una corazonada (de que)...

forecast [ˈfɔːkɑːst, *Am:* ˈfɔːrkæst] <forecast *o* forecasted> **I.** *n* predicción *f*; **weather** ~ previsión *f* meteorológica **II.** *vt* pronosticar

forecaster *n* ECON pronosticador(a) *m(f)*; **weather** ~ meteorólogo, -a *m, f*

forecastle [ˈfəʊksl, *Am:* ˈfoʊk-] *n* NAUT castillo *m* de proa

foreclose [fɔːˈkləʊz, *Am:* fɔːrˈkloʊz] **I.** *vt* **to** ~ **a possibility** descartar una posibilidad **II.** *vi* FIN extinguir; **to** ~ **on a loan** liquidar un préstamo

forecourt [ˈfɔːkɔːt, *Am:* ˈfɔːrkɔːrt] *n* explanada *f*

forefathers [ˈfɔːˌfɑːðəʳ, *Am:* ˈfɔːrˌfɑːðɚ] *npl liter* antepasados *mpl*

forefinger [ˈfɔːfɪŋɡəʳ, *Am:* ˈfɔːrfɪŋɡɚ] *n* índice *m*

forefront [ˈfɔːfrʌnt, *Am:* ˈfɔːr-] *n no pl* primer plano *m*; **to be at the** ~ **of sth** estar en la vanguardia de algo

forego [fɔːˈɡəʊ, *Am:* fɔːrˈɡoʊ] <forewent, foregone> *vt s.* **forgo**

foregoing [ˈfɔːɡəʊɪŋ, *Am:* ˈfɔːrɡoʊ-] **I.** *adj form* anterior **II.** *n no pl* **the** ~ *form* el anterior

foregone [ˈfɔːɡɒn, *Am:* fɔːrˈɡɑːn] *pp of* **forego**

foreground [ˈfɔːɡraʊnd, *Am:* ˈfɔːr-] **I.** *n no pl* **1.** ART **the** ~ el primer plano; **in the** ~ en primer término **2.** (*prominent position*) **to put oneself in the** ~ ponerse al frente **II.** *vt* destacar

forehand [ˈfɔːhænd, *Am:* ˈfɔːr-] *n* (*tennis shot*) derechazo *m*

forehead [ˈfɒrɪd, *Am:* ˈfɔːred] *n* frente *f*

foreign [ˈfɒrɪn, *Am:* ˈfɔːr-] *adj* **1.** (*from another country*) extranjero, -a; ~ **soil** *form* suelo *m* extranjero **2.** (*involving other countries*) exterior; ~ **relations** relaciones *fpl* exteriores; ~ **trade** comercio *m* exterior **3.** (*unknown*) extraño, -a; (*uncharacteristic*) impropio, -a; **to be** ~ **to sb** ser extraño para alguien; **to be** ~ **to one's nature** no ser propio de la naturaleza de alguien **4.** (*not belonging*) ajeno, -a; **a** ~ **body** un cuerpo extraño

foreign affairs *npl* asuntos *mpl* exteriores; **Ministry of Foreign Affairs** Ministerio *m* de Asuntos Exteriores **foreign correspondent** *n* corresponsal *mf* en el extranjero **foreign currency** *n* divisa *f*

foreign exchange *n no pl* **1.** (*system*) cambio *m* de divisas **2.** (*currency*) divisa *f*

foreign minister *n* ministro, -a *m, f* de Asuntos Exteriores, canciller *mf* *AmL* **Foreign Office** *n no pl, Brit* Ministerio *m* de Asuntos Exteriores **foreign policy** *n* política *f* exterior **Foreign Secretary** *n Brit* ministro, -a *m, f* de Asuntos Exteriores

foreknowledge [ˌfɔːˈnɒlɪdʒ, *Am:* ˌfɔːrˈnɑː-lɪdʒ] *n no pl* presciencia *f;* **to have ~ of sth** saber algo de antemano

foreman [ˈfɔːmən, *Am:* ˈfɔːr-] <-men> *n* **1.** (*in factory*) capataz *m* **2.** LAW (*head of jury*) presidente *m* (del jurado)

foremost [ˈfɔːməʊst, *Am:* ˈfɔːrmoʊst] *adj* **1.** (*most important*) principal; **to be ~ among ...** ser el más importante entre... **2.** (*furthest forward*) delantero, -a

forename [ˈfɔːneɪm, *Am:* ˈfɔːr-] *n form* nombre *m* (de pila)

forensic [fəˈrensɪk] *adj* forense; **~ medicine** medicina *f* forense

foreordain [ˌfɔːrɔːˈdeɪn, *Am:* -ɔːrˈ-] *vt form* predeterminar; **to be ~ed** (**to do sth**) estar predestinado (a hacer algo)

foreplay [ˈfɔːpleɪ, *Am:* ˈfɔːr-] *n no pl* juegos *mpl* eróticos preliminares

forerunner [ˈfɔːrʌnəʳ, *Am:* ˈfɔːrˌrʌnɚ] *n* precursor(a) *m(f)*

foresail [ˈfɔːseɪl, *Am:* ˈfɔːr-] *n* NAUT trinquete *m*

foresee [fɔːˈsiː, *Am:* fɔːr-] *irr vt* prever

foreseeable *adj* previsible; **in the ~ future** en el futuro inmediato

foreshadow [fɔːˈʃædəʊ, *Am:* fɔːrˈʃædoʊ] *vt* anunciar

foresight [ˈfɔːsaɪt, *Am:* ˈfɔːr-] *n* previsión *f;* **lack of ~** falta *f* de previsión

foreskin [ˈfɔːskɪn, *Am:* ˈfɔːr-] *n* prepucio *m*

forest [ˈfɒrɪst, *Am:* ˈfɔːr-] I. *n* (*wood*) bosque *m; (tropical)* selva *f* II. *adj* forestal

forestall [fɔːˈstɔːl, *Am:* fɔːr-] *vt* anticiparse a; **to ~ criticism** adelantarse a las críticas

forester [ˈfɒrɪstəʳ, *Am:* ˈfɔːr-] *n* guardabosques *mf*

forest fire *n* incendio *m* forestal **forest ranger** *n Am* guarda *mf* forestal

forestry [ˈfɒrɪstri, *Am:* ˈfɔːr-] *n no pl* silvicultura *f*

foretaste [ˈfɔːteɪst, *Am:* ˈfɔːr-] *n no pl* anticipo *m*

foretell [fɔːˈtel, *Am:* fɔːr-] <foretold> *vt* predecir

forever [fəˈrevəʳ, *Am:* fɔːrˈevɚ] *adv,* **for ever** *adv Brit* **1.** (*for all time*) para siempre **2.** *inf* (*continually*) continuamente; **to be ~ doing sth** estar haciendo algo sin cesar

forewarn [fɔːˈwɔːn, *Am:* fɔːrˈwɔːrn] *vt* prevenir ►**~ed is forearmed** *prov* hombre prevenido vale por dos

forewent [fɔːˈwent, *Am:* fɔːr-] *pp of* **forego**

foreword [ˈfɔːwɜːd, *Am:* ˈfɔːrwɜːrd] *n* prefacio *m*

forfeit [ˈfɔːfɪt, *Am:* ˈfɔːr-] I. *vt* **1.** (*lose*) perder **2.** (*renounce*) perder el derecho a II. *n* **1.** (*penalty*) multa *f;* **to pay a ~** pagar una multa **2.** *pl* (*game*) **to play ~s** jugar a las prendas **3.** *form* (*penalty*) pena *f* III. *adj* **her property was ~** sus bienes fueron confiscados

forfeiture [ˈfɔːfɪtʃəʳ, *Am:* ˈfɔːrfə-] *n no pl* pérdida *f*

forgather [fɔːˈgæðəʳ, *Am:* fɔːrˈgæðɚ] *vi form* reunirse

forgave [fəˈgeɪv, *Am:* fɚ-] *n pt of* **forgive**

forge [fɔːdʒ, *Am:* fɔːrdʒ] I. *vt* **1.** (*make illegal copy*) falsificar **2.** (*metal*) forjar **3.** *fig* **to ~ a bond** forjar un vínculo; **to ~ a career** forjarse un porvenir II. *vi* **to ~ into the lead** adelantarse mucho III. *n* **1.** (*furnace*) fragua *f* **2.** (*smithy*) herrería *f*
◆**forge ahead** *vi* **1.** (*make progress*) avanzar rápidamente **2.** (*move into lead*) ponerse en cabeza

forger [ˈfɔːdʒəʳ, *Am:* ˈfɔːrdʒɚ] *n* falsificador(a) *m(f)*

forgery [ˈfɔːdʒəri, *Am:* ˈfɔːr-] <-ies> *n* falsificación *f*

forget [fəˈget, *Am:* fɚ-] <forgot, forgotten> I. *vt* **1.** (*not remember*) olvidar; **to ~ to do sth** olvidarse de hacer algo; **to ~ (that) ...** olvidar (que)... **2.** (*leave behind*) **to ~ sth** dejarse algo; **to ~ one's keys** dejarse las llaves **3.** (*stop thinking about*) **to ~ sth/sb** dejar de pensar en algo/alguien; **to ~ one's quarrels** olvidar las rencillas; **to ~ one's dignity** dejar la dignidad de uno a un lado; **it's best forgotten** sería mejor olvidarlo **4.** (*give up*) **to ~ sth** dejar algo; **~ it** olvídalo **5. to ~ oneself** (*behave badly*) propasarse II. *vi* **1.** (*not remember*) olvidarse; **to ~ about sth/sb** olvidarse de algo/alguien; **to ~ about doing sth** olvidarse de hacer algo **2.** (*stop thinking about*) **to ~ about sth/sb** dejar de pensar en algo/alguien; **to ~ about a plan** abandonar un plan; **let's ~ about it!** ¡pelillos a la mar!

forgetful [fəˈgetfəl, *Am:* fɚ-] *adj* olvidadizo, -a

forget-me-not [fəˈgetmɪnɒt, *Am:* fɚˈgetmɪnɑːt] *n* nomeolvides *f inv*

forgive [fəˈgɪv, *Am:* fɚ-] <forgave, forgiven> I. *vt* **1.** (*pardon*) perdonar; **to ~ sb (for) sth** perdonar algo a alguien; **to ~ sb for doing sth** perdonar a alguien por hacer algo **2.** *form* (*pardon*) **~ me** discúlpeme; **~ my ignorance/language** disculpe mi ignorancia/ lenguaje; **~ me (for) mentioning it** perdone que lo mencione II. *vi* perdonar; **to ~ and forget** perdonar y olvidar

forgiven *pp of* **forgive**

forgiveness *n* perdón *m*

forgiving *adj* misericordioso, -a

forgo [fɔːˈgəʊ, *Am:* fɔːrˈgoʊ] *irr vt* privarse de

forgot [fəˈgɒt, *Am:* fɚˈgɑːt] *pt of* **forget**

forgotten [fəˈgɒtn, *Am:* fɚˈgɑːtn] I. *pp of* **forget** II. *adj* olvidado, -a

fork [fɔːk, *Am:* fɔːrk] I. *n* **1.** (*cutlery*) tenedor *m* **2.** (*tool*) horca *f* **3.** (*in road*) bifurcación *f* **4.** *pl* (*on bicycle*) horquilla *f* II. *vt* coger con tenedor, agarrar con tenedor *AmL* III. *vi* bifurcarse

forked *adj* bifurcado, -a

forked lightning *n* relámpago *m* en zigzag
fork-lift (**truck**) [ˌfɔːklɪft('trʌk), *Am:* ˌfɔːrk-lɪft('trʌk)] *n* carretilla *f* elevadora
forlorn [fə'lɔːn, *Am:* fɔːr'lɔːrn] *adj* (*person*) triste; (*place*) abandonado, -a; (*hope*) vano, -a
form [fɔːm, *Am:* fɔːrm] I. *n* 1. (*type, variety*) tipo *m*; ~ **of exercise** tipo de ejercicio; ~ **of government** sistema *m* de gobierno; ~ **of transport** medio *m* de transporte; ~ **of persuasion** medida *f* de persuasión; **a** ~ **of disease** un tipo de enfermedad; **in any** (**shape or**) ~ de cualquier modo; **in the** ~ **of sth** en forma de algo; **to take the** ~ **of sth** adoptar la forma de algo 2. (*outward shape*) forma *f*; (*of an object*) bulto *m*; **to take** ~ tomar forma; **in liquid/solid** ~ en estado líquido/sólido 3. LING (*of word*) forma *f*; **the singular** ~ la forma singular 4. (*document*) formulario *m*; **an application/entry** ~ un formulario de solicitud/admisión; **to fill in a** ~ rellenar un formulario 5. *no pl* SPORTS forma *f*; **to be in** ~ estar en forma; **to be out of** ~ estar en baja forma 6. *no pl* (*correct procedure*) **in due** ~ de la debida forma; **a matter of** ~ una cuestión de forma; **for** ~'**s sake** para salvar las apariencias; **to be bad** ~ ser de mal gusto 7. *Brit* (*class*) clase *f* 8. *Brit* (*bench*) banco *m* 9. (*mould*) molde *m* II. *vt* 1. (*make*) formar; **to** ~ **part of sth** formar parte de algo; **to** ~ **the basis of sth** constituir la base de algo; **to** ~ **a queue** formar una cola; **to** ~ **the impression** tener la impresión; **to** ~ **an opinion** formarse una opinión; **to** ~ **a habit** adquirir un hábito 2. (*mould*) moldear 3. (*set up*) establecer; **to** ~ **a committee/government** formar un comité/gobierno; **to** ~ **a relationship** iniciar una relación; **to** ~ **an alliance with sb** establecer una alianza con alguien III. *vi* formarse
formal ['fɔːməl, *Am:* 'fɔːr-] *adj* (*official, ceremonious*) formal; ~ **dress** traje *m* de etiqueta; ~ **procedures** procedimientos *mpl* oficiales; ~ **interest** interés *m* sólo de palabra
formaldehyde [fɔː'mældɪhaɪd, *Am:* fɔːr-] *n no pl* formaldehído *m*
formality [fɔː'mæləti, *Am:* -ţi] <-ies> *n* formalidad *f*; **to be merely a** ~ ser una pura formalidad
formalize ['fɔːməlaɪz, *Am:* 'fɔːr-] *vt* formalizar; **to** ~ **one's thoughts** dar forma a los pensamientos de uno
formally *adv* formalmente
format ['fɔːmæt, *Am:* 'fɔːr-] I. *n* formato *m* II. <-tt-> *vt* INFOR formatear
formation [fɔː'meɪʃən, *Am:* fɔːr-] *n* formación *f*; **rock** ~ formación *f* rocosa; **in battle** ~ en orden de batalla
formation flying *n no pl* vuelo *m* en formación
formative ['fɔːmətɪv, *Am:* 'fɔːrmətɪv] *adj* formativo, -a; **the** ~ **years** los años de formación
formatting *n* INFOR formateo *m*
former ['fɔːməʳ, *Am:* 'fɔːrmə-] *adj* 1. (*pre-*

vious) anterior; **in a** ~ **life** en una vida anterior 2. (*first of two*) primero, -a
formerly *adv* antes
form feed *n* INFOR avance *m* de página
formic acid [ˌfɔːmɪk'æsɪd, *Am:* ˌfɔːr-] *n* ácido *m* fórmico
formidable ['fɔːmɪdəbl, *Am:* 'fɔːrmə-] *adj* (*person*) extraordinario, -a; (*opponent, task*) difícil
formless ['fɔːmlɪs, *Am:* 'fɔːrm-] *adj* amorfo, -a
formula ['fɔːmjʊlə] <-s *o* -lae> *pl pl n* 1. MAT *a. fig* fórmula *f* 2. COM (*recipe for product*) receta *f*; **the** ~ **for success** la fórmula del éxito 3. (*form of words*) expresión *f* 4. *no pl, Am* (*milk*) leche *f* para lactantes
formulate ['fɔːmjʊleɪt, *Am:* 'fɔːr-] *vt* 1. (*draw up*) formular 2. (*express in words*) expresar
formulation [ˌfɔːmjʊ'leɪʃən, *Am:* 'fɔːr-] *n no pl* formulación *f*
fornicate ['fɔːnɪkeɪt, *Am:* 'fɔːr-] *vi* fornicar
forsake [fə'seɪk, *Am:* fɔːr-] <forsook, forsaken> *vt* (*abandon*) abandonar; (*give up*) renunciar a
forsaken [fə'seɪkən, *Am:* fɔːr-] I. *pp of* **forsake** II. *adj* abandonado, -a
forsook [fə'sʊk, *Am:* fɔːr-] *pt of* **forsake**
forswear [fɔː'sweəʳ, *Am:* fɔːr'swer] <forswore, forsworn> *vt liter* renunciar a
fort [fɔːt, *Am:* fɔːrt] *n* fortaleza *f*
forte[1] ['fɔːteɪ, *Am:* fɔːrt] *n no pl* (*strong point*) fuerte *m*
forte[2] ['fɔːteɪ, *Am:* fɔːrt-] *adv* MUS forte *m*
forth [fɔːθ, *Am:* fɔːrθ] *adv form* **to go** ~ irse; **back and** ~ de acá para allá; **from that day** ~ de ese día en adelante
forthcoming [ˌfɔːθ'kʌmɪŋ, *Am:* ˌfɔːrθ-] *adj* 1. (*happening soon*) venidero, -a; (*book*) de próxima aparición; (*film*) de próximo estreno 2. (*available*) **to be** ~ (**from sb**) venir (de alguien) 3. (*informative*) **to be** ~ (**about sth**) estar dispuesto a hablar (de algo)
forthright ['fɔːθraɪt, *Am:* 'fɔːrθ-] *adj* directo, -a
forthwith [ˌfɔːθ'wɪθ, *Am:* ˌfɔːrθ-] *adv form* en el acto
fortieth ['fɔːtɪəθ, *Am:* 'fɔːrţɪ-] I. *adj* cuadragésimo, -a II. *n* (*order*) cuadragésimo, -a *m, f*; (*fraction*) cuadragésimo *m*; (*part*) cuadragésima parte *f*; *s. a.* **eighth**
fortification [ˌfɔːtɪfɪ'keɪʃən, *Am:* ˌfɔːrţə-] *n no pl* fortificación *f*
fortify ['fɔːtɪfaɪ, *Am:* 'fɔːrţə-] <-ie-> *vt* 1. MIL fortificar 2. **to** ~ **oneself** (**with sth**) fortalecerse (con algo)
fortitude ['fɔːtɪtjuːd, *Am:* 'fɔːrţətuːd] *n no pl, form* fortaleza *f*
fortnight ['fɔːtnaɪt, *Am:* 'fɔːrt-] *n no pl, Brit, Aus* quince días *mpl*; (*business*) quincena *f*; **in a** ~'**s time** dentro de una quincena
fortnightly ['fɔːtnaɪtli, *Am:* 'fɔːrt-] I. *adj* quincenal II. *adv* cada quince días

fortress ['fɔːtrɪs, *Am:* 'fɔːr-] *n* fortaleza *f*
fortuitous [fɔː'tjuːɪtəs, *Am:* fɔːr'tuːɪətəs] *adj form* fortuito, -a
fortunate ['fɔːtʃənət, *Am:* 'fɔːr-] *adj* afortunado, -a; **to be ~ to do sth** tener la suerte de hacer algo; **to be ~ in sth** tener suerte en algo; **it is ~ for her that ...** tiene la suerte de que...
fortunately *adv* afortunadamente
fortune ['fɔːtʃuːn, *Am:* 'fɔːrtʃən] *n* **1.** (*money*) fortuna *f;* **a small ~** una pequeña fortuna; **to be worth a ~** valer una fortuna; **to cost a ~** costar un dineral; **to make a ~** hacer una fortuna **2.** *no pl, form* (*luck*) suerte *f;* **good/ill ~** buena/mala suerte; **to have the good ~ to do sth** tener la suerte de hacer algo; **to tell sb's ~** decir la buenaventura a alguien **3.** *no pl, liter* (*luck personified*) **~ smiled on him** la fortuna le sonrió **4.** *pl* (*fate*) peripecias *fpl*
fortune hunter *n* cazafortunas *mf* **fortune teller** *n* adivino, -a *m, f*
forty ['fɔːti, *Am:* 'fɔːrt̬i] I. *adj* cuarenta II. <-ies> *n* cuarenta *m; s. a.* **eighty**
forum ['fɔːrəm] *n* foro *m*
forward ['fɔːwəd, *Am:* 'fɔːrwəd] I. *adv* **1.** (*towards the front*) hacia adelante; **to lean ~** inclinarse hacia adelante; **a step ~** *fig* un paso hacia adelante **2.** *form* (*onwards in time*) en adelante; **from that day/time ~** de ese día/momento en adelante; **to put one's watch/the clock ~** adelantar el reloj II. *adj* **1.** (*towards the front*) hacia adelante; **~ movement** movimiento *m* hacia adelante; **~ gear** AUTO marcha *f* adelante **2.** (*in a position close to front*) en la parte delantera; **to be ~ of sth** estar en la parte de delante de algo **3.** (*near front of plane*) delantero, -a; (*ship*) de proa **4.** MIL (*close to enemy*) de avance **5.** (*relating to the future*) **~ buying** compra *f* a plazos; **~ look** mirada *f* hacia el futuro; **~ planning** planes *mpl* de futuro **6.** (*over-confident*) descarado, -a III. *n* SPORTS delantero, -a *m, f;* **centre ~** delantero centro IV. *vt* **1.** (*send*) remitir; **please ~** por favor, hacer seguir **2.** *form* (*help to progress*) promover
forwarding address *n* dirección *f* (*para enviar el correo*) **forwarding agent** *n* agente *mf* de tránsito
forward-looking *adj* con miras al futuro
forwardness *n no pl* precocidad *f*
forwards ['fɔːwədz, *Am:* 'fɔːrwədz] *adv s.* **forward**
forwent [fɔː'went, *Am:* fɔːr-] *pt of* **forgo**
fossil ['fɒsəl, *Am:* 'fɑːsəl] *n* **1.** GEO fósil *m* **2.** *inf* (*person*) carca *mf*
fossil fuel *n* combustible *m* fósil
fossilized ['fɒsəlaɪzd, *Am:* 'fɑːsə-] *adj* **1.** GEO fosilizado, -a **2.** *inf* (*outdated*) anticuado, -a
foster ['fɒstər, *Am:* 'fɑːstər] *vt* **1.** (*look after*) acoger **2.** (*encourage*) fomentar
foster brother *n* hermano *m* acogido **foster child** *n* hijo, -a *m, f* acogido, -a **foster father** *n* padre *m* de acogida **foster**

home *n* casa *f* de acogida **foster mother** *n* madre *f* de acogida **foster sister** *n* hermana *f* acogida
fought [fɔːt, *Am:* fɑːt] *pt, pp of* **fight**
foul [faʊl] I. *adj* (*disgusting: taste*) asqueroso, -a; (*air*) sucio, -a; (*smell*) fétido, -a; (*weather*) pésimo, -a; (*language*) ordinario, -a; (*mood, temper*) insoportable; **to be ~ to sb** ser insoportable con alguien II. *n* SPORTS falta *f,* penal *m* *AmL* III. *vt* **1.** (*pollute*) ensuciar; (*dog*) hacer sus necesidades en **2.** SPORTS **to ~ sb** cometer una falta contra alguien **3.** (*tangle*) liar
foul-mouthed [ˌfaʊl'maʊðd] *adj* malhablado, -a
foulness ['faʊlnəs] *n no pl* **1.** (*dirtiness*) suciedad *f* **2.** (*unpleasantness*) lo desagradable **3.** (*coarseness*) basteza *f*
foul play *n* SPORTS juego *m* sucio
found¹ [faʊnd] *pt, pp of* **find**
found² [faʊnd] *vt* **1.** (*establish*) fundar **2.** (*base*) basar; **to ~ a statement/a case on sth** basar una declaración/un caso en algo **3.** (*build*) **to be ~ed on sth** estar construido sobre algo
found³ [faʊnd] *vt* MIN fundir
foundation [faʊn'deɪʃən] *n* **1.** *pl* (*of building*) cimientos *mpl;* **to lay the ~(s)** (**of sth**) poner los cimientos (de algo); **to shake sth to its ~s** remover algo hasta los cimientos **2.** *fig* (*basis*) base *f;* **to lay the ~(s) of sth** establecer la(s)base(s) de algo **3.** *no pl* (*evidence*) fundamento *m;* **to have no ~** no tener fundamento alguno **4.** *no pl* (*establishment*) establecimiento *m* **5.** (*organization*) fundación *f* **6.** *no pl* (*make-up*) maquillaje *m* de base
foundation cream *n no pl* maquillaje *m* de base **foundation stone** *n* piedra *f* fundamental
founder¹ ['faʊndər, *Am:* -dər] *n* fundador(a) *m(f)*
founder² ['faʊndər, *Am:* -dər] *vi* **1.** (*sink*) hundirse **2.** *fig* (*fail*) fracasar; **to ~ on sth** fracasar en algo
Founding Fathers *npl* **the ~** *los fundadores de la nación americana*
foundry ['faʊndri] <-ries> *n* fundición *f,* fundidora *AmS*
fount [faʊnt] *n a. fig, form* fuente *f;* **to be the ~ of all knowledge/wisdom** ser la fuente del conocimiento/de la sabiduría
fountain ['faʊntɪn, *Am:* -tən] *n* fuente *f*
fountain pen *n* pluma *f* estilográfica
four [fɔːr, *Am:* fɔːr] I. *adj* cuatro II. *n* **1.** cuatro *m* **2.** (*group of four*) cuarteto *m* ►**to go on all ~s** andar a gatas; *s. a.* **eight**
four-by-four *n Am* AUTO cuatro por cuatro *m*
four-door car *n* coche *m* de cuatro puertas
fourfold ['fɔːfəʊld, *Am:* 'fɔːrfoʊld] I. *adj* cuádruple II. *adv* **to increase ~** aumentar en cuatro veces
four-footed [ˌfɔː'fʊtɪd, *Am:* ˌfɔːr'fʊt̬-] *adj* cuadrúpedo, -a
four-handed *adj* **1.** (*involving four people*)

de cuatro jugadores **2.** (*for two pianists*) para dos pianistas
four-leaf clover *n*, **four-leaved clover** *n* trébol *m* de cuatro hojas **four-letter word** *n* palabrota *f*
foursome ['fɔːsəm, *Am:* 'fɔːr-] *n* grupo *m* de cuatro personas; **to make up a** ~ hacer un grupo de cuatro
four-square [ˌfɔː'skweəʳ, *Am:* ˌfɔːr'swer] *adj* **1.** (*building*) firme **2.** (*person*) resoluto, -a; **to stand** ~ **behind sb** apoyar decididamente a alguien
fourteen [ˌfɔː'tiːn, *Am:* ˌfɔːr-] **I.** *adj* catorce **II.** *n* catorce *m; s. a.* **eight**
fourteenth I. *adj* decimocuarto, -a **II.** *n* **1.** (*order*) decimocuarto, -a *m, f* **2.** (*date*) quatorce *m* **3.** (*fraction*) catorceavo *m;* (*part*) catorceava parte *f; s. a.* **eighth**
fourth [fɔːθ, *Am:* fɔːrθ] **I.** *adj* cuarto, -a **II.** *n* **1.** (*order*) cuarto, -a *m, f* **2.** (*date*) ocho *m* **3.** (*fraction*) cuarto *m;* (*part*) cuarta parte *f* **4.** MUS cuarta *f; s. a.* **eighth**
fourth gear *n* AUTO cuarta marcha *f*
Fourth of July *n no pl, Am* Día *m* de la Independencia de Estados Unidos

---

El **Fourth of July** o **Independence Day** es el día de fiesta americano no confesional más importante. En este día se conmemora la **Declaration of Independence** (declaración de independencia), mediante la cual las colonias americanas se declaran independientes de Gran Bretaña. Esto ocurrió el 4 de julio de 1776. Esta festividad se celebra con meriendas campestres, fiestas familiares y partidos de baseball. Como broche de oro el día se cierra con unos vistosos fuegos artificiales.

---

four-wheel drive [ˌfɔː'hwiːl'draɪv, *Am:* ˌfɔːr-] *n* tracción *f* a cuatro ruedas
fowl [faʊl] <-(s)> *n* ave *f* de corral
fowlpest ['faʊlpest] *n no pl* enfermedad *f* de aves de corral
fox [fɒks, *Am:* faːks] **I.** *n* **1.** (*animal*) zorro *m* **2.** *no pl* (*fur*) piel *f* de zorro **3.** *inf* (*cunning person*) **an old** ~ un viejo zorro **4.** *Am, inf* (*sexy woman*) tía *f* buena **II.** *vt* **1.** (*mystify*) mistificar **2.** (*trick*) engañar
foxglove ['fɒksglʌv, *Am:* 'faːks-] *n* dedalera *f*
foxhunt ['fɒkshʌnt, *Am:* 'faːks-] *n* cacería *f* del zorro **fox terrier** *n* fox terrier *mf*
foxtrot ['fɒkstrɒt, *Am:* 'faːkstraːt] <-tt-> **I.** *n* foxtrot *m* **II.** *vi* bailar un foxtrot
foxy ['fɒksi, *Am:* 'faːk-] <-ier, -iest> *adj* **1.** (*crafty*) taimado, -a **2.** *Am, inf* (*sexy*) sexy
foyer ['fɔɪeɪ, *Am:* -ɚ] *n* **1.** (*entrance hall*) vestíbulo *m* **2.** *Am* (*hall of house*) recibidor *m*
fracas ['fræka:, *Am:* 'freɪkəs] <-(ses)> *n* gresca *f*
fractal ['fræktl] *n* MAT fractal *m*
fraction ['frækʃən] *n* fracción *f*
fractional ['frækʃənl] *adj* **1.** MAT fraccionario, -a **2.** (*difference*) mínimo, -a

fractious ['frækʃəs] *adj* díscolo, -a
fracture ['fræktʃəʳ, *Am:* -tʃɚ] **I.** *vt* **1.** MED fracturar; **to** ~ **one's leg** fracturarse la pierna **2.** (*break*) romper; **to** ~ **an agreement** romper un acuerdo **II.** *vi* fracturarse **III.** *n* MED fractura *f*
fragile ['frædʒaɪl, *Am:* -əl] *adj* delicado, -a; (*object, peace*) frágil; **to feel** ~ sentirse débil
fragility [frə'dʒɪləti, *Am:* -t̬i] *n no pl* fragilidad *f*
fragment ['frægmənt, *Am:* 'frægment] **I.** *n* fragmento *m;* **to smash sth (in)to** ~**s** hacer algo añicos **II.** *vi* **1.** (*break into pieces*) fragmentarse **2.** *fig* (*break up*) romperse **III.** *vt* **1.** (*break into pieces*) fragmentar **2.** *fig* (*break up*) romper
fragmentary ['frægməntri] *adj* fragmentario, -a
fragrance ['freɪgrəns] *n* fragancia *f*
fragrant ['freɪgrənt] *adj* fragante
frail [freɪl] *adj* (*person*) endeble; (*thing*) frágil
frailty ['freɪlti, *Am:* -t̬i] <-ies> *n* **1.** *no pl* (*weakness: of person*) flaqueza *f;* (*of thing*) fragilidad *f* **2.** (*moral flaw*) defecto *m* moral
frame [freɪm] **I.** *n* **1.** (*for door, picture*) a. INFOR marco *m* **2.** *pl* (*spectacles*) montura *f* **3.** (*supporting structure*) armazón *m o f* **4.** (*body*) cuerpo *m* **5.** CINE, TV fotograma *m* **II.** *vt* **1.** (*picture*) enmarcar **2.** (*act as a surround to*) servir de marco a **3.** (*put into words*) formular **4.** *inf* (*falsely incriminate*) incriminar dolosamente
frame-up ['freɪmʌp] *n inf* montaje *m* (*para inculpar a alguien*)
framework ['freɪmwɜːk, *Am:* -wɜːrk] *n* **1.** (*supporting structure*) armazón *m o f* **2.** *fig* (*set of rules, principles*) sistema *m*
franc [fræŋk] *n* franco *m*
France [fraːns, *Am:* fræns] *n* Francia *f*
franchise ['fræntʃaɪz] **I.** *n* franquicia *f* **II.** *vt* conceder en franquicia
Franciscan [fræn'sɪskən] **I.** *n* REL franciscano, -a *m, f* **II.** *adj* REL franciscano, -a
Franco- ['fræŋkəʊ, *Am:* -koʊ] *in compounds* franco-
frank [fræŋk] **I.** *adj* franco, -a; **to be** ~, ... sinceramente,... **II.** *vt* franquear
frankfurter ['fræŋkfɜːtəʳ, *Am:* -fɜːrt̬ɚ] *n* salchicha *f* de Frankfurt
frankincense ['fræŋkɪnsents] *n no pl* incienso *m*
franking machine *n* (máquina *f*) franqueadora
frankly *adv* sinceramente
frantic ['fræntɪk, *Am:* -t̬ɪk] *adj* (*hurry, activity*) frenético, -a; **to be** ~ **with rage** estar furioso; **to be** ~ **with worry** andar loco de inquietud; **to drive sb** ~ sacar a alguien de quicio
fraternal [frə'tɜːnl, *Am:* -'tɜːr-] *adj* **1.** (*brotherly*) fraternal **2.** *fig* (*friendly*) amical
fraternity [frə'tɜːnəti, *Am:* -'tɜːrnət̬i] <-ies> *n* **1.** *no pl* (*brotherly feeling*) fraterni-

dad *f* **2.**(*group of people*) cofradía *f* **3.** *Am*
UNIV club *m* de estudiantes
fraternize ['frætənaɪz, *Am:* '-ɚ-] *vi* fraternizar
fratricide ['frætrɪsaɪd, *Am:* -rə-] *n* (*crime*)
fratricidio *m*
fraud [frɔːd, *Am:* frɑːd] *n* **1.** *no pl a.* LAW
fraude *m* **2.**(*trick*) trampa *f* **3.**(*person*) impos-
tor(a) *m(f)*
fraudulence ['frɔːdjʊləns, *Am:* 'frɑːdʒə-] *n*
no pl **1.**(*financial dishonesty*) fraude *m* **2.**(*of
claim, behaviour*) fraudulencia *f*
fraudulent ['frɔːdjʊlənt, *Am:* 'frɑːdʒə-] *adj*
fraudulento, -a
fraught [frɔːt, *Am:* frɑːt] *adj* tenso, -a; **to be
~ with difficulties/problems** estar lleno de
dificultades/problemas
fray¹ [freɪ] *vi* (*rope, cloth*) deshilacharse;
tempers were beginning to ~ la gente
estaba perdiendo la paciencia
fray² [freɪ] *n* **the ~** la lucha; **to enter the ~**
pasar a la lucha
freak [friːk] I. *n* **1.**(*abnormal person, thing*)
monstruo *m;* **a ~ of nature** un fenómeno de la
naturaleza **2.**(*enthusiast*) fanático, -a *m, f*
II. *adj* anormal III. *vi s.* **freak out**
◆**freak out** I. *vi* flipar II. *vt* **to freak sb out**
alucinar a alguien
freckle ['frekl] *n pl* peca *f*
freckled ['frekld] *adj* pecoso, -a
free [friː] I.<-r, -est> *adj* **1.**(*not constrained:
person, country, elections*) libre; **to break ~**
(*of sth*) soltarse (de algo); **to break ~ of sb**
despegarse de alguien; **to go ~** salir en libertad;
to set sb ~ poner en libertad a alguien; **to be
~ to do sth** no tener reparos para hacer algo; **~
press** prensa *f* independiente **2.**(*not affected
by*) **to be ~ of sth** no estar afectado por algo;
to be ~ of a disease no estar afectado por una
enfermedad **3.**(*not attached*) **to get sth ~** liberar algo **4.**(*not busy*) **to be ~ to do sth** estar
libre para hacer algo; **to leave sb ~ to do sth**
dejar a alguien que haga algo **5.**(*not occupied*)
libre; **to leave sth ~** dejar algo libre **6.**(*costing
nothing*) gratis; **~ ticket** billete *m* gratis; **~ of
charge** gratis; **~ sample** muestra *f* gratuita; **~
on board** franco a bordo; **to be ~ of cus-
toms/tax** estar libre de aranceles/impuestos;
to be ~ to sb ser gratis para alguien **7.**(*generous*) **to be ~ with sth** dar algo en abundancia;
to make ~ with sth *pej* usar algo como si
fuera cosa propia **8.**(*translation, verse*) libre
▶**~ and easy** despreocupado II. *adv* gratis; **~
of charge** gratis; **for ~** *inf* gratis III. *vt*
1.(*release: person*) poner en libertad **2.**(*make
available*) permitir; **to ~ sb to do sth** dar libertad a alguien para que haga algo
freebie ['friːbiː] *n* obsequio *m*
freebooter ['friːbuːtər, *Am:* -t̬ɚ] *n* filibustero *m*
freedom ['friːdəm] *n* **1.**(*of person, country*)
libertad *f;* **to have the ~ to do sth** tener la libertad de hacer algo; **~ of action/movement**

libertad *f* de acción/movimiento; **~ of the
press** libertad *f* de prensa; **~ of speech/
thought** libertad *f* de expresión/pensamiento;
to have ~ from interference no sufrir intro-
misiones **2.**(*right*) derecho *m* **3.**(*room for
movement*) soltura *f* **4.**(*unrestricted use*) usufructo *m;* **to have the ~ of sb's house** tener el
usufructo de la casa de alguien
free enterprise *n no pl* libre empresa *f* **free
fall** *n no pl* caída *f* libre; **to go into ~** FIN caer
en picado
free-for-all ['friːfərˌɔːl, *Am:* 'friːfɚ·ɔːl] *n*
gresca *f*
freehold ['friːhəʊld, *Am:* -hoʊld] I. *n* plena
propiedad *f* II. *adj* de plena propiedad III. *adv*
en propiedad absoluta
freeholder *n* propietario, -a *m, f* absoluto, -a
free kick *n* SPORTS tiro *m* libre
freelance ['friːlɑːns, *Am:* 'friːlæns] I. *n* freelance *mf* II. *adj* autónomo, -a III. *adv* por
cuenta propia IV. *vi* trabajar por cuenta propia
freeload ['friːləʊd, *Am:* -loʊd] *vi Am, Aus,
pej* gorronear; **to ~ off sb** gorronear a alguien
freeloader *vi pej* gorrón, -ona *m, f*
freely *adv* **1.**(*unrestrictedly*) sin límite; **to be
~ available** poder obtenerse sin trabas
2.(*without obstruction*) libremente **3.**(*frankly*) francamente **4.**(*generously*) generosamente
freeman ['friːmən] <-men> *n* **1.** HIST (*not
slave*) hombre *m* libre **2.**(*honorary citizen*)
ciudadano *m* de honor
free market *n* libre mercado *m*
Freemason ['friːˌmeɪsən] *n* francmasón,
-ona *m, f*
Freephone [ˌfriːfəʊn, *Am:* -foʊn] *n Brit*
número *m* gratuito
free port *n* puerto *m* franco
free-range [ˌfriːˈreɪndʒ] *adj* de granja **free-
-range chicken** *n* pollo *m* de corral **free-
-range egg** *n* huevo *m* de granja
free speech *n no pl* libertad *f* de expresión
free-spoken [ˌfriːˈspəʊkən, *Am:* -ˈspoʊ-]
adj que habla sin reservas
free-standing [ˌfriːˈstændɪŋ] *adj* independiente
freestyle ['friːstaɪl] *n no pl* estilo *m* libre
freethinker [ˌfriːˈθɪŋkər, *Am:* -kɚ] *n* libre-
pensador(a) *m(f)*
freethinking *adj* librepensador(a)
free trade *n no pl* librecambio *m* **freeware**
n programa *m* de libre distribución **freeway**
n Am, Aus autopista *f*
freewheel [ˌfriːˈhwiːl, *Am:* 'friːhwiːl] *vi* ir en
punto muerto
free will *n no pl* libre albedrío *m*
freeze [friːz] <froze, frozen> I. *vi* **1.**(*liquid*)
helarse; (*food*) congelarse **2.**(*become totally
still*) quedarse completamente rígido, -a II. *vt*
(*liquid*) helar; (*food, prices*) congelar III. *n*
1. METEO ola *f* de frío **2.** ECON congelación *f*
◆**freeze up** *vi* helarse
freezer *n* congelador *m*, congeladora *f AmS*

freezing I. *adj* glacial; **it's** ~ hiela; **I'm** ~ estoy helado II. *n no pl* congelación *f*
freezing point *n* punto *m* de congelación
freight [freɪt] *no pl* I. *n* **1.** (*type of transportation*) flete *m* **2.** (*goods*) mercancías *fpl* **3.** (*charge*) porte *m* **4.** *Am* RAIL tren *m* de mercancías II. *adv* por flete III. *vt* fletar
freight car *n Am* RAIL vagón *m* de mercancías
freighter ['freɪtəʳ, *Am:* -t̬əʳ] *n* **1.** (*ship*) buque *m* de carga **2.** (*plane*) avión *m* de mercancías
freight train *n Am* tren *m* de mercancías
French [frentʃ] I. *adj* francés, -esa; ~ **speaker** francófono, -a *m, f* II. *n* **1.** (*person*) francés, -esa *m, f* **2.** (*language*) francés *m*
French bean *n Brit* judía *f* verde **French chalk** *n no pl* jabón *m* de sastre **French doors** *npl* puertaventana *f* **French dressing** *n no pl* vinagreta *f* **French fried potatoes** *npl*, **French fries** *npl* patatas *fpl* fritas **French horn** *n* trompa *f* de llaves **French letter** *n Brit, Aus, inf* (*condom*) condón *m* **Frenchman** <-men> *n* francés *m* **French windows** *npl Am s.* **French doors Frenchwoman** <-women> *n* francesa *f*
frenetic [frəˈnetɪk, *Am:* -ˈnet̬-] *adj* frenético, -a
frenzied *adj* frenético, -a
frenzy ['frenzi] *n no pl* frenesí *m*
frequency ['friːkwəntsi] <-cies> *n no pl* frecuencia *f*
frequency band *n* banda *f* de frecuencia **frequency modulation** *n* frecuencia *f* modulada
frequent[1] ['friːkwənt] *adj* frecuente, tupido, -a *Méx*
frequent[2] [frɪˈkwent] *vt* frecuentar
frequently ['friːkwəntli] *adv* con frecuencia
fresco ['freskəʊ, *Am:* -koʊ] <-s *o* -es> *n* fresco *m*
fresh [freʃ] *adj* **1.** (*not stale: air, water, food*) fresco, -a; (*bread*) recién hecho, -a **2.** (*new*) nuevo, -a; (*snow*) virgen; **to make a ~ start** volver a empezar; ~ **from the oven/the factory** recién salido del horno/de fábrica **3.** (*cool: breeze*) fresco, -a **4.** (*not tired*) como nuevo, -a **5.** *inf* (*disrespectful*) descarado, -a
freshen ['freʃən] I. *vt* refrescar II. *vi* (*wind*) soplar más recio
freshman ['freʃmən] <-men> *n* UNIV novato *m*, estudiante *m* de primer año

Con el nombre de **Freshman** se conoce en los EE.UU. a un alumno de la clase novena, con el de **Sophomore** a uno de la décima, con el de **Junior** al alumno de la decimoprimera clase y con el de **Senior** al de la decimosegunda. Estos términos se utilizan corrientemente para los alumnos de secundaria, aun incluso en el caso de aquellas **High Schools** en las que los alumnos sólo se incorporan a partir de la décima clase. Esta terminología es empleada también por los alumnos universitarios durante sus cuatro años de college.

freshness *n no pl* **1.** (*of air, water, food*) frescura *f* **2.** (*of ideas, approach*) novedad *f*
fresh water *n* agua *f* dulce
fret[1] [fret] I. <-tt-> *vi* inquietarse II. *n* **to be in a ~** estar muy inquieto
fret[2] [fret] *n* MUS traste *m*
fretful ['fretfəl] *adj* (*person, tone*) quejoso, -a
fretsaw ['fretsɔː, *Am:* -sɑː] *n* sierra *f* de calados
fretwork ['fretwɜːk, *Am:* -wɜːrk] *n no pl* calado *m*
friar ['fraɪəʳ, *Am:* -ɚ] *n* fraile *m*
fricative ['frɪkətɪv, *Am:* -t̬ɪv] LING I. *adj* fricativo, -a II. *n* fricativa *f*
friction ['frɪkʃən] *n no pl* **1.** (*rubbing*) fricción *f* **2.** *fig* (*disagreement*) desavenencia *f*
Friday ['fraɪdi] *n* viernes *m inv*; **on ~s** los viernes; **every ~** todos los viernes; **this** (**coming**) ~ este (próximo) viernes; **on ~ mornings** los viernes por la mañana; **on ~ night** el viernes por la noche; **last/next ~** el viernes pasado/que viene; **every other ~** un viernes sí y otro no; **on ~ we are going on holiday** el viernes nos vamos de vacaciones
fridge [frɪdʒ] *n* nevera *f*, refrigeradora *f AmS*
fried [fraɪd] *adj* frito, -a
fried chicken *n* pollo *m* frito **fried egg** *n* huevo *m* frito
friend [frend] *n* amigo, -a *m, f*; **to be ~s** ser amigos; **to make ~s** (**with sb**) hacerse amigo (de alguien); **a ~ of mine/his/hers/yours** un amigo mío/suyo/tuyo
friendless ['frendləs] *adj* sin amigos
friendly ['frendli] I. <-ier, -iest> *adj* **1.** (*person*) simpático, -a, entrador(a) *Arg*; (*house, environment*) acogedor(a); (*nation*) cordial; **to be on ~ terms with sb** estar a bien con alguien; **to be ~ towards sb** mostrarse amable con alguien; **to be ~ with sb** llevarse bien con alguien **2.** SPORTS (*not competitive*) amistoso, -a II. *n* SPORTS partido *m* amistoso
friendly society *n Brit* FIN sociedad *f* de socorro mutuo
friendship ['frendʃɪp] *n* amistad *f*
fries [fraɪz] *npl inf* patatas *fpl* fritas
frieze [friːz] *n* friso *m*
frigate ['frɪgət] *n* fragata *f*
fright [fraɪt] *n* **1.** (*feeling of fear*) terror *m;* **to take ~** (**at sth**) asustarse (por algo) **2.** *no pl* (*frightening experience*) susto *m*, jabón *m Arg, Méx, Prico;* **to get a ~** llevarse un susto; **to give sb a ~** dar un susto a alguien **3.** *inf* (*unattractive sight*) adefesio *m;* **to look a ~** tener un aspecto horrible
frighten ['fraɪtən] I. *vt* asustar II. *vi* asustarse
♦**frighten away** *vt* espantar
frightened *adj* asustado, -a
frightening *adj* aterrador(a)

frightful ['fraɪtfəl] adj espantoso, -a
frigid ['frɪdʒɪd] adj 1.(sexually) frígido, -a
2.(unfriendly) frío, -a 3.(very cold) glacial
frigidity [frɪ'dʒɪdəti, Am: -t̬i] n 1.(sexual)
frigidez f 2.(unfriendliness) frialdad f
frill [frɪl] n 1.(cloth) volante m 2. no ~s sin
excesos
frilly ['frɪli] adj (dress) de volantes; (style)
recargado, -a
fringe [frɪndʒ] I. n 1.(decorative edging) flecos mpl Brit, Aus (hair) flequillo m, pava f
AmC, And 3.(edge) margen m II. vt rodear
III. adj no pl secundario, -a
fringe benefits npl ECON beneficios mpl
complementarios **fringe group** n grupo m
marginal **fringe theatre** n no pl teatro m
experimental
frippery ['frɪpəri] <-ies> n pl perifollos mpl
frisk [frɪsk] I. vi juguetear II. vt cachear
frisky ['frɪski] <-ier, -iest> adj 1.(lively,
energetic) retozón, -ona; (horse) fogoso, -a
2. inf (sexually) juguetón, -ona
fritter[1] ['frɪtər, Am: 'frɪt̬ər] n buñuelo m, picarón m AmL
fritter[2] ['frɪtər, Am: 'frɪt̬ər] vt to ~ (away)
desperdiciar
frivolity [frɪ'vɒləti, Am: -'vɑːlət̬i] <-ties> n
frivolidad f
frivolous ['frɪvələs] adj frívolo, -a; (not serious) poco formal
frizzy ['frɪzi] adj (hair) encrespado, -a
fro [frəʊ, Am: froʊ] adv to and ~ de un lado a
otro
frock [frɒk, Am: frɑːk] n vestido m
frog[1] [frɒg, Am: frɑːg] n ZOOL rana f ►to
have a ~ in one's throat tener carraspera
frog[2] [frɒg, Am: frɑːg] n pej (French person)
gabacho, -a m, f
frogman ['frɒgmən, Am: 'frɑːg-] <-men>
n hombre-rana m
frogmarch ['frɒgmɑːtʃ, Am: 'frɑːgmɑːrtʃ]
vt llevar a la fuerza
frogspawn ['frɒgspɔːn, Am: 'frɑːgspɑːn] n
no pl huevos mpl de rana
frolic ['frɒlɪk, Am: 'frɑːlɪk] I. <-ck-> vi juguetear II. n jolgorio m
frolicsome ['frɒlɪksəm, Am: 'frɑːlɪk-] adj
juguetón, -ona
from [frɒm, Am: frɑːm] prep 1.(as starting
point) de; where is he ~? ¿de dónde es?; the
flight ~ London el vuelo procedente de
Londres; to fly ~ New York to Tokyo volar
de Nueva York a Tokio; to appear ~ among
the trees aparecer de entre los árboles; shirts
~ £5 camisas desde £5; ~ inside desde dentro; to drink ~ a cup/the bottle beber de una
taza/la botella 2.(temporal) ~ day to day día
tras día; ~ time to time de vez en cuando; ~
his childhood desde su infancia; ~ that date
on(wards) desde esa fecha 3.(at distance to)
100 metres ~ the river 100 metros del río; ~
far ~ doing sth lejos de hacer algo 4.(one to
another) to go ~ door to door ir de puerta en

puerta; to tell good ~ evil distinguir el bien
del mal 5.(originating in) a card ~ Paul/Cor-
sica una tarjeta de Paul/Córcega; ~ my point
of view en mi opinión 6.(in reference to) ~
what I heard según lo que he escuchado;
translated ~ the English traducido del inglés;
quotations ~ Joyce citas de Joyce; ~ 'War
and Peace' de 'Guerra y Paz'; to judge ~
appearances juzgar según las apariencias; different ~ the others diferente de los demás
7.(caused by) ~ experience por experiencia;
weak ~ hunger débil de [o por] hambre; to
die ~ thirst morir de sed 8.(removed) to
steal/take sth ~ sb robar/quitar algo a alguien; to prevent sb ~ doing sth evitar que
alguien haga algo; to keep sth ~ sb mantener
algo alejado de alguien; to shade ~ the sun
protegerse del sol; 4 (subtracted) ~ 7 equals
3 MAT 4 restado de 7 es igual a 3
front [frʌnt] I. n 1. no pl (forward-facing part)
frente f; (of building) fachada f 2.(outside
cover) cubierta f exterior; (first pages) principio m 3.(front area) parte f delantera; in ~
delante; in ~ of delante de 4. THEAT auditorio
m 5.(deceptive appearance) apariencias fpl;
he's/she's putting on a bold ~ la procesión
va por dentro 6. MIL frente m; on the
domestic/work ~ en el terreno doméstico/
laboral 7. POL frente m; a united ~ un frente
común 8. no pl (promenade) paseo m
marítimo 9. METEO frente m II. adj 1.(at the
front) delantero, -a 2.(first) primero, -a III. vt
1.(be head of) liderar 2. TV presentar IV. vi
estar enfrente de; the flat ~s north el piso da
al norte; to ~ for servir de fachada [o tapadera]
frontage ['frʌntɪdʒ, Am: -t̬ɪdʒ] n fachada f
frontal ['frʌntəl, Am: -t̬əl] adj ANAT, METEO
frontal; (attack) de frente
front bench n Brit POL los ministros del
gobierno o sus homólogos en la oposición
front door n puerta f principal **front-end**
n INFOR frontal m
frontier [frʌn'tɪər, Am: frʌn'tɪr] n 1.(border)
a. fig frontera f 2. Am (outlying areas) the ~
los límites
frontiersman <-men> n Am HIST hombre m
de la frontera **frontier station** n puesto m
fronterizo
frontispiece ['frʌntɪspiːs, Am: -t̬ɪs-] n
frontispicio m
front line n primera línea f **front page** n
primera página f **front-page** adj de primera
plana **front runner** n líder mf **front-
-wheel drive** n tracción f delantera
frost [frɒst, Am: frɑːst] I. n escarcha f; 12
degrees of ~ 12 grados bajo cero II. vt
1.(cover with frost) cubrir de escarcha 2. Am
(cover with icing) escarchar
frostbite ['frɒstbaɪt, Am: 'frɑːst-] n no pl
congelación f
frostbitten adj congelado, -a
frostbound adj helado, -a
frosted adj 1. Am (covered with icing) es-

carchado, -a **2.** (*opaque*) esmerilado, -a

frosting *n no pl, Am* (*icing*) azúcar *m* glaseado

frosty ['frɒsti, *Am:* 'frɑːsti] <-ier, -iest> *adj* **1.** (*with frost*) escarchado, -a **2.** (*unfriendly*) frío, -a

froth [frɒθ, *Am:* frɑːθ] **I.** *n no pl* **1.** (*bubbles*) espuma *f* **2.** *fig* banalidad *f* **II.** *vi* echar espuma **III.** *vt* espumar

frothy ['frɒθi, *Am:* 'frɑːθi] <-ier, -iest> *adj* espumoso, -a

frown [fraʊn] **I.** *vi* fruncir el ceño; **to ~ at sb/ sth** mirar con el ceño fruncido a alguien/algo **II.** *n* ceño *m* fruncido

frowsy *adj*, **frowzy** ['fraʊzi] <-ier, -iest> *adj inf* desaliñado, -a

froze [frəʊz, *Am:* frɒʊz] *pt of* **freeze**

frozen ['frəʊzn, *Am:* 'frɒʊzn] **I.** *pp of* **freeze** **II.** *adj* congelado, -a

frugal ['fruːgl] *adj* frugal

frugality [fruˈgæləti, *Am:* -t̬i] *n no pl* frugalidad *f*

fruit [fruːt] **I.** *n* **1.** *no pl* (*for eating*) fruta *f*; (*on tree, product*) fruto *m* **2.** (*results*) fruto *m* ▶ **to bear** ~ dar fruto; *fig* dar resultado **II.** *vi* dar fruto

fruitcake ['fruːtkeɪk] *n* **1.** *no pl* (*cake*) tarta *f* de frutas **2.** *Brit, Aus, inf* (*person*) chiflado, -a *m, f*

fruitful ['fruːtfəl] *adj* **1.** (*productive*) provechoso, -a; (*discussion*) productivo, -a **2.** *liter* (*fertile*) fructuoso, -a

fruition [fruːˈɪʃən] *n no pl* **to bring sth to ~** llevar algo a buen término; **to come to ~** realizarse

fruit knife *n* cuchillo *m* de la fruta

fruitless ['fruːtləs] *adj* infructuoso, -a

fruit salad *n no pl* macedonia *f*

fruity ['fruːti, *Am:* -t̬i] <-ier, -iest> *adj* **1.** afrutado, -a **2.** *inf* (*joke*) verde

frumpish ['frʌmpɪʃ] *adj pej* anticuado, -a

frustrate [frʌsˈtreɪt, *Am:* 'frʌstreɪt] <-ting> *vt* frustrar

frustrated *adj* frustrado, -a

frustrating *adj* frustrante

frustration [frʌsˈtreɪʃən] *n* frustración *f*

fry¹ [fraɪ] <-ie-> **I.** *vt* freír **II.** *vi* **1.** (*be cooked*) freírse **2.** *inf* (*get burnt*) quemarse

fry² [fraɪ] *n Am*, **fry-up** *n Brit* fritada *f*

frying pan *n* sartén *f*, paila *f AmL* ▶ **to jump out of the ~ into the fire** salir de Guatemala y meterse en Guatepeor

ft *abbr of* **foot, feet** pie

FT [ˌefˈtiː] INFOR *abbr of* **formula translation** TF

fuchsia ['fjuːʃə] **I.** *n* fucsia *m* **II.** *adj* fucsia

fuck [fʌk] *vulg* **I.** *vt* joder, coger *AmL*; ~ **you!** ¡jódete!; ~ **that idea** ¡a la mierda esa idea! **II.** *vi* joder, coger *AmL* **III.** *n no pl* polvo *m* **IV.** *interj* joder

◆ **fuck off** *vi* ~! ¡vete a la mierda!

fucker ['fʌkəʳ, *Am:* -ə·] *n vulg* gilipollas *mf inv*

fuddled ['fʌdld] *adj* **1.** (*confused*) aturdido, -a

2. (*drunk*) borracho, -a

fuddy-duddy ['fʌdiˌdʌdi] **I.** <-ies> *n pej, inf* persona *f* chapada a la antigua **II.** *adj pej, inf* chapado, -a a la antigua

fudge [fʌdʒ] **I.** *n* **1.** *no pl* (*sweet*) dulce *m* de azúcar **2.** (*compromise*) apaño *m* **II.** <-ging> *vt* (*issue*) esquivar **III.** <-ging> *vi* quedar indeciso, -a

fuel ['fjuːəl] **I.** *n no pl* combustible *m* **II.** < *Brit:* -ll-, *Am:* -l-> *vt* **1.** (*provide with fuel*) aprovisionar de combustible **2.** (*increase: tension, controversy*) avivar

fuel consumption *n no pl* AUTO consumo *m* de gasolina **fuel gauge** *n* indicador *m* del nivel de gasolina **fuel-injection engine** *n* motor *m* de inyección **fuel pump** *n* bomba *f* de combustible **fuel rod** *n* varilla *f* de combustible

fug [fʌg] *n no pl* aire *m* viciado

fuggy ['fʌgi] <-ier, -iest> *adj* cargado, -a

fugitive ['fjuːdʒɪtɪv, *Am:* -t̬ɪv] **I.** *n* fugitivo, -a *m, f* **II.** *adj* (*escaping*) fugitivo, -a

fugue [fjuːg] *n* MUS fuga *f*

fulfil <-ll-> *vt Brit*, **fulfill** [fʊlˈfɪl] *vt Am, Aus* (*ambition, task*) realizar; (*condition, requirement*) cumplir; (*need*) satisfacer; (*function, role*) desempeñar; **to ~ oneself** realizarse

fulfilment *n Brit*, **fulfillment** *n Am, Aus no pl* (*of condition, requirement*) cumplimiento *m*; (*of function, role*) desempeño *m*; (*satisfaction*) realización *f*

full [fʊl] **I.** <-er, -est> *adj* **1.** (*container, space*) lleno, -a; (*vehicle*) completo, -a **2.** (*total: support*) total; (*recovery*) completo, -a; (*member*) numerario, -a; **to be in ~ dress** estar de gala; **to be in ~ flow** estar en pleno discurso; **to be in ~ swing** estar en pleno apogeo **3.** (*maximum: marks*) máximo, -a; (*employment*) pleno, -a; **to be on ~ beam** (*car light*) tener puesta la larga; **at ~ speed** a toda velocidad; **at ~ stretch** al máximo **4.** (*busy and active*) ocupado, -a **5.** (*rounded*) redondo, -a **6.** (*wide*) amplio, -a; (*skirt*) holgado, -a **7.** (*wine*) con cuerpo **II.** *adv* **1.** (*completely*) completamente **2.** (*directly*) directamente **3.** (*very*) muy; **to know ~ well** (**that** ...) saber muy bien (que...) **III.** *n* **in ~** sin abreviar; **to the ~** al máximo

fullback ['fʊlbæk] *n* defensa *mf*

full-blooded [ˌfʊlˈblʌdɪd] *adj* **1.** (*wholehearted*) entusiasta **2.** (*animal*) de raza

full-blown [ˌfʊlˈbləʊn, *Am:* -ˈbloʊn] *adj* (*disaster, scandal*) auténtico, -a

full board *n* pensión *f* completa

full-bodied [ˌfʊlˈbɒdɪd, *Am:* -ˈbɑːdɪd] *adj* (*taste*) fuerte; (*wine*) con mucho cuerpo

full-cream milk *n* leche *f* entera

full-fledged [ˌfʊlˈfledʒd] *adj Am s.* **fully--fledged**

full-frontal **I.** *adj* desenfrenado, -a **II.** *n* desnudo *m* visto de frente **full-grown** *adj* crecido, -a **full-length** *adj* **1.** (*for entire body*) de cuerpo entero **2.** (*not short*) extenso,

-a **full moon** *n* luna *f* llena

fullness *n no pl* **1.** (*being full*) plenitud *f;* **in the ~ of time** a su debido tiempo **2.** (*roundedness*) redondez *f* **3.** (*richness*) riqueza *f*

full-page *adj* de página entera **full-scale** *adj* **1.** (*original size*) de tamaño natural **2.** (*all-out*) a gran escala **full stop** *Brit, Aus* **I.** *n* punto *m;* **to come to a ~** *fig* paralizarse **II.** *adv* y punto **full time** *n* SPORTS fin *m* del partido **full--time** *adj* de horario completo

fully ['fʊli] *adv* **1.** (*completely*) completamente **2.** (*in detail*) detalladamente **3.** (*at least*) al menos

fully-fledged [ˌfʊli'fledʒd] *adj Brit* (*bird*) plumado; (*person*) hecho, -a y derecho, -a

fulminate ['fʊlmɪneɪt] *vi* **to ~** (*against sth*) tronar (contra algo)

fulsome ['fʊlsəm] *adj pej* (*praise*) exagerado, -a; (*person, manner*) servil

fumble ['fʌmbl] **I.** *vi* **to ~ around for sth** buscar algo a tientas; **to ~ for words** titubear buscando las palabras **II.** *vt* SPORTS **to ~ the ball** dejar caer la pelota

fumbler ['fʌmblər, *Am:* -blɚ] *n* torpe *mf*

fume [fjuːm] *vi* **1.** (*be angry*) estar furioso, -a; **to ~ at sb** echar pestes de alguien **2.** (*emit fumes*) humear

fumigate ['fjuːmɪgeɪt] *vt* fumigar

fun [fʌn] **I.** *n no pl* diversión *f;* **it was good ~** fue muy agradable; **full of ~** pletórico de alegría; **to do sth for ~** hacer algo por placer; **to do sth in ~** hacer algo en broma; **to have (a lot of) ~** divertirse (mucho); **have ~ on your weekend!** ¡pásalo bien de fin de semana!; **have ~!** ¡diviértete!; **to have ~ at sb's expense** reírse a costa de alguien; **to get a lot of ~ out of** [*o* from] **sth** pasarlo bien con algo; **to make ~ of sb, to poke ~ at sb** reírse de alguien; **what ~!** ¡qué divertido! ▸ **~ and games** *pej* odisea *f;* **it's not all ~ and games** no todo el monte es orégano **II.** *adj Am, Aus* **1.** (*enjoyable*) agradable **2.** (*funny*) divertido, -a; **she's a real ~ person** *inf* es una persona divertidísima

function ['fʌŋkʃən] **I.** *n* **1.** *a.* MAT función *f;* **in my ~ as mayor, ...** como alcalde,... **2.** (*formal ceremony*) ceremonia *f;* (*formal social event*) acto *m* **II.** *vi* funcionar

functional ['fʌŋkʃənl] *adj* **1.** *a.* LING funcional **2.** (*operational, working*) práctico, -a

functionary ['fʌŋkʃənəri, *Am:* -eri] <-ies> *n* funcionario, -a *m, f*

function key *n* INFOR tecla *f* de función

fund [fʌnd] **I.** *n* fondo *m;* **to be short of ~s** ir mal de fondos; **to have a ~ of knowledge about sth** saber mucho de algo **II.** *vt* financiar

fundamental [ˌfʌndə'mentəl, *Am:* -t̬əl] **I.** *adj* fundamental; (*difference*) esencial; (*principles*) básico, -a; **to be of ~ importance** ser de vital importancia **II.** *n* **the ~s** los principios básicos

fundamentalism [ˌfʌndə'mentəlɪzəm, *Am:* -t̬əl-] *n no pl* fundamentalismo *m*

fundamentalist I. *n* integrista *mf* **II.** *adj* integrista

fundamentally *adv* **1.** (*basically*) fundamentalmente **2.** (*in the most important sense*) esencialmente

funding *n* (*act*) financiación *f;* (*resources*) fondos *mpl*

fundraising ['fʌndˌreɪzɪŋ] *n* recaudación *f* de fondos

funeral ['fjuːnərəl] *n* entierro *m;* **to attend a ~** asistir a un funeral ▸ **that's your/his ~** *inf* eso es tu/su problema

funeral director *n* director(a) *m(f)* de funeraria **funeral march** <-es> *n* márcha *f* fúnebre **funeral parlour** *n* funeraria *f* **funeral pyre** *n* pira *f*

funereal [fjuː'nɪəriəl, *Am:* -'nɪri-] *adj* fúnebre

funfair ['fʌnfeər, *Am:* -fer] *n Brit* **1.** (*amusement park*) parque *m* de atracciones **2.** (*fair*) feria *f*

fungicide ['fʌngɪsaɪd, *Am:* 'fʌndʒɪ-] *n* fungicida *m*

fungus ['fʌŋgəs] *n* (*wild mushroom*) hongo *m;* (*mould*) moho *m*

fun house *n Am* pasaje *m* del terror

funicular [fjuː'nɪkjələr, *Am:* -juːlə-] *n,* **funicular railway** *n* funicular *m*

funk [fʌŋk] *n no pl* **1.** *Am, Aus* (*depression*) abatimiento *m fig* **2.** *Brit, inf* (*fear*) **to be in a blue ~** estar paralizado por el miedo **3.** (*music*) funk *m*

funky ['fʌŋki] <-ier, -iest> *adj inf* **1.** (*cool*) genial **2.** (*music*) funky

fun-loving *adj* marchoso, -a

funnel ['fʌnəl] **I.** *n* **1.** (*implement*) embudo *m* **2.** NAUT chimenea *f* **II.** <*Brit:* -ll-, *Am:* -l-> *vt* canalizar

funnies ['fʌniz] *npl* **the ~** las tiras cómicas

funny ['fʌni] <-ier, -iest> *adj* **1.** (*amusing*) divertido, -a; **to see the ~ side of a situation** observar lo curioso de una situación **2.** (*odd, peculiar*) raro, -a; **to have a ~ feeling that ...** tener la extraña sensación de que...; **to have ~ ideas** tener ideas de bombero **3.** (*slightly ill*) **to feel ~** no encontrarse bien **4.** *Brit, inf* (*witty*) gracioso, -a; **to try to be ~** *inf* hacerse el gracioso

funny bone *n inf* hueso *m* de la alegría

fur [fɜːr, *Am:* fɜːr] **I.** *n* **1.** (*animal hair*) piel *f* **2.** *no pl* CHEM, MED sarro *m* **II.** <-rr-> *vi* **to ~ up** (*kettle, pipes*) cubrirse de sarro

fur coat *n* abrigo *m* de piel

furious ['fjʊəriəs, *Am:* 'fjʊri-] *adj* **1.** (*very angry*) furioso, -a, enchilado, -a *Méx,* caribe *Ant;* **to be ~ about sth** estar furioso por algo; **a ~ outburst** un acceso de furia **2.** (*intense, violent*) violento, -a; **at a ~ pace** a un ritmo vertiginoso

furl [fɜːl, *Am:* fɜːrl] *vt* (*flag, sail*) recoger

furlong ['fɜːlɒŋ, *Am:* 'fɜːrlɑːŋ] *n Brit: medida de longitud equivalente a 200 metros aproximadamente*

furlough ['fɜːləʊ, *Am:* 'fɜːrloʊ] *n* MIL permiso *m;* **to be on** ~ estar de permiso

furnace ['fɜːnɪs, *Am:* 'fɜːr-] *n a. fig* horno *m*

furnish ['fɜːnɪʃ, *Am:* 'fɜːr-] *vt* **1.** (*supply*) proporcionar; **to** ~ **sb with sth** suministrar algo a alguien; **to be** ~**ed with sth** estar provisto de algo **2.** (*provide furniture*) amueblar

furnished ['fɜːnɪʃt, *Am:* 'fɜːr-] *adj* amueblado, -a

furnishings ['fɜːnɪʃɪŋz, *Am:* 'fɜːr-] *npl* muebles *mpl*

furniture ['fɜːnɪtʃəʳ, *Am:* 'fɜːrnɪtʃɚ] *n no pl* mobiliario *m;* **piece of** ~ mueble *m*

furniture van *n* camión *m* de mudanzas

furore [fjʊəˈrɔːri, *Am:* 'fjʊrɔːr] *n* furor *m*

furrier ['fʌriəʳ, *Am:* 'fɜːriɚ] *n* peletero, -a *m, f*

furrow ['fʌrəʊ, *Am:* 'fɜːroʊ] **I.** *n* **1.** (*groove*) ranura *f* **2.** (*wrinkle*) arruga *f* **II.** *vt* arrugar; **to** ~ **one's brow** fruncir el ceño

furry ['fɜːri] <-ier, -iest> *adj* **1.** peludo, -a **2.** (*looking like fur*) peloso, -a; ~ **toy** peluche *m*

further ['fɜːðəʳ, *Am:* 'fɜːrðɚ] **I.** *adj comp of* **far 1.** (*greater distance*) más lejano; **nothing could be** ~ **from his mind** estará pensando en cualquier cosa menos en eso **2.** (*additional*) otro, -a; **if you have any** ~ **problems ...** si tienes más problemas...; **until** ~ **notice** hasta nuevo aviso **II.** *adv comp of* **far 1.** (*greater distance*) más lejos; **we didn't get much** ~ no llegamos mucho más allá; ~ **on** más adelante; ~ **and** ~ cada vez más lejos; **to go** ~ **with sth** hacer progresos con algo **2.** (*more*) más; **I have nothing** ~ **to say** no tengo (nada) más que decir ▸**to not go any** ~ no ir más allá; **this musn't go any** ~ esto debe quedar entre nosotros **III.** *vt* fomentar; **to** ~ **sb's interests** favorecer los intereses de alguien

furtherance ['fɜːðərəns, *Am:* 'fɜːr-] *n no pl, form* fomento *m*

furthermore [ˌfɜːðəˈmɔːʳ, *Am:* 'fɜːrðɚmɔːr] *adv* además

furthermost ['fɜːðəməʊst, *Am:* 'fɜːrðɚmoʊst] *adj* más lejano, -a

furthest ['fɜːðɪst, *Am:* 'fɜːr-] **I.** *adj* **1.** *superl of* **far 2.** (*greatest*) mayor; **prices have fallen/risen** ~ **in the south** los precios han bajado/subido más en el sur **3.** (*at the greatest distance*) más lejano, -a; **the** ~ **island from the mainland** la isla más apartada de tierra firme **II.** *adv* **1.** *superl of* **far 2.** (*greatest distance*) más lejos; **that's the** ~ **I can go** eso es lo más lejos que puedo ir

furtive ['fɜːtɪv, *Am:* 'fɜːrtɪv] *adj* furtivo, -a

furtiveness *n no pl* furtivismo *m*

fury ['fjʊəri, *Am:* 'fjʊri] *n no pl* furor *m;* **fit of** ~ ataque *m* de furia; **I've been working like** ~ he estado trabajando con frenesí

fuse [fjuːz] **I.** *n* **1.** ELEC fusible *m;* **the** ~ **has gone** *Brit, Aus* han saltado los plomos **2.** (*ignition device, detonator*) espoleta *f;* (*string*) mecha *f* ▸**to have a short** ~ tener mucho genio; **to light the** ~ encender la mecha **II.** *vi* **1.** ELEC fundirse **2.** (*join together*) fusionarse

III. *vt* **1.** ELEC fundir **2.** (*join*) fusionar

fuse box <-es> *n* caja *f* de fusibles

fuselage ['fjuːzəlɑːʒ, *Am:* -səlɑːʒ] *n* fuselaje *m*

fusion ['fjuːʒən] *n* **1.** (*joining together*) fusión *f* **2.** *no pl* PHYS fusión *f;* **nuclear** ~ fusión nuclear

fusion bomb *n* bomba *f* termonuclear

fusion reactor *n* reactor *m* nuclear

fuss [fʌs] **I.** *n* alboroto *m;* **it's a lot of** ~ **about nothing** mucho ruido y pocas nueces; **to make a** ~ armar un escándalo **II.** *vi* preocuparse; **to** ~ **over sth** preocuparse en exceso por algo **III.** *vt* molestar

fusspot ['fʌspɒt, *Am:* -pɑːt] *n inf* quisquilloso, -a *m, f*

fussy ['fʌsi] <-ier, -iest> *adj* **1.** (*over-particular*) puntilloso, -a; **I'm not** ~ *Brit, inf* no me importa **2.** (*quick to criticize*) quisquilloso, -a **3.** (*overdone, overdecorated*) recargado, -a

fusty ['fʌsti] <-ier, -iest> *adj pej* **1.** (*smelling damp and stale*) rancio, -a; (*room*) que huele a cerrado **2.** (*old-fashioned*) anticuado, -a

futile ['fjuːtaɪl, *Am:* -ʈəl] *adj* inútil; ~ **attempt** intento *m* en vano

futility [fjuːˈtɪləti, *Am:* -ʈi] *n no pl* inutilidad *f*

future ['fjuːtʃəʳ, *Am:* -tʃɚ] **I.** *n* **1.** *a.* LING futuro *m;* **to have plans for the** ~ tener planes de futuro; **in the** ~ **tense** en futuro; **the distant/near** ~ el futuro lejano/próximo; **what the** ~ **will bring** lo que depara el futuro **2.** (*prospects*) porvenir *m;* **she has a great** ~ **ahead of her** tiene un gran porvenir **II.** *adj* futuro, -a

future perfect *n* LING futuro *m* perfecto

futures market *n* mercado *m* de futuros

futuristic [ˌfjuːtʃəˈrɪstɪk] *adj* futurista

fuze [fjuːz] *Am* **I.** *n* (*ignition device, detonator*) espoleta *f;* (*string*) mecha *f* **II.** *vt* molestar

fuzz [fʌz] *n no pl* **1.** (*fluff*) pelusa *f* **2.** (*fluffy hair*) pelo *m* crespo **3.** (*short growing hair*) vello *m;* **peach** ~ *fig* piel *f* de melocotón **4.** *inf* (*police*) **the** ~ la pasma

fuzzy ['fʌzi] *adj* **1.** (*unclear*) borroso, -a **2.** (*hair*) (*short, soft*) velloso, -a; (*curly*) rizado, -a

f-word ['efˌwɜːd, *Am:* -wɜːrd] *n forma de evitar el uso de la palabra 'fuck'*

G

G, g [dʒiː] *n* G, g *f;* ~ **for George** G de Granada

g *abbr of* **gram** g.

gab [gæb] **I.** <-bb-> *vi inf* estar de palique **II.** *n* cháchara *f;* **to have the gift of the** ~ tener mucha labia

gabardine [ˌgæbəˈdiːn, *Am:* 'gæbədiːn] *n*

no pl gabardina *f*

gabble ['gæbl] I. *vi* (*talk inarticulately*) farfullar; (*talk quickly*) hablar atropelladamente II. *vt* (*utter too quickly*) decir atropelladamente; (*utter indistinctly*) pronunciar de modo ininteligible III. *n no pl* (*inarticulate speech*) farfulla *f*; (*quick speech*) habla *f* atropellada

gable ['geɪbl] *n* ARCHIT aguilón *m*; ~ **roof** tejado *m* de dos aguas

Gabon [gæ'bɒn, *Am:* -'boʊn] *n* Gabón *m*

Gabonese [ˌgæbɒn'iːz, *Am:* -'boʊn] I. *adj* de Gabón II. *n* habitante *mf* de Gabón

gad [gæd] <-dd-> *vi inf* **to** ~ **about** callejear

gadabout ['gædəbaʊt] *n* trotacalles *mf inv*

gadfly ['gædflaɪ] <-flies> *n* (*insect*) tábano *m*

gadget ['gædʒɪt] *n* artilugio *m*; ~**s** chismes *mpl*

gadgetry ['gædʒɪtri] *n no pl* chismes *mpl*

Gaelic ['geɪlɪk] I. *n* gaélico *m* II. *adj* gaélico, -a

gaff [gæf] *n* arpón *m* ►**to** blow **the** ~ *Brit, inf* descubrir el pastel

gaffe [gæf] *n* metedura *f* de pata; **to make a** ~ meter la pata

gaffer ['gæfər, *Am:* -ə] *n* 1. *Brit, inf* (*foreman*) capataz *m*; *fig* jefe *m* 2. (*head electrician on a film*) iluminista *mf* 3. *Brit, inf* (*old man*) viejo, -a *m, f*

gag [gæg] I. *n* 1. (*cloth*) mordaza *f* 2. (*joke*) chiste *m* 3. THEAT morcilla *f* II. <-gg-> *vt* amordazar; (*silence*) hacer callar III. <-gg-> *vi* (*to joke*) contar chistes; THEAT meter morcillas

gaga ['gɑːgɑː] *adj inf* chocho, -a; **to go** ~ chochear

gage [geɪdʒ] *n, vt Am s.* **gauge**

gagging order *n inf* bloqueo *m* informativo

gaggle ['gægl] *n a. iron* manada *f*

gaiety ['geɪəti, *Am:* -ţi] *n no pl* alegría *f*

gaily ['geɪli] *adv* alegremente

gain [geɪn] I. *n* 1. (*increase*) aumento *m*; ~ **in weight** aumento de peso 2. ECON, FIN (*profit*) beneficio *m*; **net** ~ beneficio neto 3. *fig* (*advantage*) ventaja *f* II. *vt* 1. (*obtain*) ganar 2. (*acquire*) adquirir 3. (*catch up*) alcanzar; **to** ~ **success** conseguir el éxito 4. (*increase: velocity*) adquirir; **to** ~ **weight** engordar ►**to** ~ **the upper** hand tomar ventaja III. *vi* (*increase*) aumentar; (*prices, numbers*) subir; (*clock, watch*) adelantarse; **once she went off the diet she started** ~**ing again** cuando dejó la dieta volvió a engordar

gainful ['geɪnfəl] *adj* lucrativo, -a

gait [geɪt] *n a.* SPORTS paso *m*

gaiter ['geɪtər, *Am:* -ţə] *n pl* polaina *f*

gala ['gɑːlə, *Am:* 'geɪ-] I. *n* 1. (*special public entertainment*) gala *f* 2. *Brit* (*sports competition*) competición *f* II. *adj* (*festive*) de gala; ~ **night** noche *f* de gala

galactic [gə'læktɪk] *adj* galáctico, -a

Galapagos Islands [gə'læpəgəs 'aɪlənd] *npl* Islas *fpl* Galápagos

galaxy ['gæləksi] <-ies> *n* 1. (*space*) galaxia *f* 2. *fig* constelación *f*

gale [geɪl] *n* tormenta *f*; **a** ~-**force wind** un vendaval; ~**s of laughter** carcajadas *fpl*

gale warning *n* aviso *m* de tormenta

Galicia [gə'lɪsiə] *n* Galicia *f*

Galician I. *adj* gallego, -a II. *n* gallego, -a *m, f*

gall [gɔːl] I. *n* 1. (*bile*) bilis *f inv* 2. (*impertinence*) impertinencia *f*; **to have the** ~ **to do sth** tener agallas para hacer algo; *pej* tener la cara de hacer algo II. *vt* mortificar

gall. *abbr of* **gallon** gal.

gallant ['gælənt] I. *adj* 1. (*chivalrous*) galante 2. (*brave*) valiente II. *n* HIST galán *m*

gallantry ['gæləntri] *n* 1. *no pl* (*chivalry*) cortesía *f* 2. *no pl* (*courage*) valentía *f* 3. <-tries> (*act of courtly politeness*) galanterías *fpl*

gall bladder *n* vesícula *f* biliar

galleon ['gælɪən] *n* galeón *m*

gallery ['gæləri] <-ries> *n* 1. (*for displaying art*) museo *m*; (*for paintings*) galería *f* 2. ARCHIT, THEAT tribuna *f*

galley ['gæli] *n* 1. NAUT, AVIAT (*kitchen*) cocina *f* 2. HIST (*ship*) galera *f*

galley-proof *n* galerada *f*

gallivant [ˌgælɪ'vænt, *Am:* -ə'-] *vi inf* **to** ~ **about** callejear

gallon ['gælən] *n* galón *m* (*Brit: 4,55 l, Am: 3,79 l*)

gallop ['gæləp] I. *vi* galopar II. *vt* (*cause to gallop*) hacer galopar III. *n* galope *m*; **to break into a** ~ echar a galopar; **at a** ~ *fig* al galope

gallows ['gæləʊz, *Am:* -oʊz] *npl* **the** ~ la horca; **to send sb to the** ~ mandar a alguien al patíbulo

gallstone ['gɔːlstəʊn, *Am:* -stoʊn] *n* cálculo *m* biliar

Gallup poll ['gæləp pəʊl, *Am:* -poʊl] *n* sondeo *m* de la opinión pública

galore [gə'lɔːr, *Am:* -'lɔːr] *adj* en cantidad

galoshes [gə'lɒʃɪz, *Am:* -'lɑːʃ-] *npl* chanclos *mpl*

galumph [gə'lʌmf] *vi inf* moverse torpemente

galvanize ['gælvənaɪz] *vt a. fig* galvanizar; **to** ~ **sb into sth** forzar a alguien a algo

Gambia ['gæmbɪə] *n no pl* Gambia *f*

Gambian I. *adj* gambiano, -a II. *n* gambiano, -a *m, f*

gambit ['gæmbɪt] *n* 1. (*chess move*) gambito *m* 2. (*tactic*) táctica *f*; **opening** ~ estrategia *f* inicial

gamble ['gæmbl] I. *n* jugada *f*; **business** ~ riesgo *m* comercial II. *vi* jugar; **to** ~ **on sth** confiar en algo; **to** ~ **on the stock market** jugar a la bolsa III. *vt* (*money*) jugar; (*one's life*) arriesgar; **to** ~ **one's fortune/future/money** jugarse la fortuna/el futuro/el dinero

gambler ['gæmblər, *Am:* -blə] *n* jugador(a) *m(f)*

gambling *n no pl* juego *m* **gambling den** *n* timba *f*

gambol ['gæmbl] <*Brit: -ll-, Am: -l-*> *vi liter* brincar

games¹ [geɪm] I. *n* 1. (*unit of sports*) juego *m* 2. (*unit of play*) partida *f*; **board** ~ juego de mesa; ~ **of chance** juego de azar; **a** ~ **of chess** una partida de ajedrez 3. SPORTS (*skill level*) **to be off one's** ~ *a. fig* estar en baja forma 4. (*tactic*) **the** ~ **is up** todo se acabó; **what's your** ~? ¿qué pretendes? 5. *pl, Brit* (*organized school sports*) educación *f* física; **the Olympic Games** los juegos olímpicos ▶ **to give the** ~ **away** descubrir las cartas; **two can play at that** ~ donde las dan las toman; **to beat sb at his/her own** ~ ganar a alguien a sus propias cartas; **to play the** ~ *Brit* jugar limpio; **to be on the** ~ *Brit, inf* hacer la calle II. *adj* 1. *inf* (*willing*) animoso, -a; **to be** ~ (*to do sth*) animarse (a hacer algo); **to be** ~ **for anything** no tener miedo a nada 2. *inf* (*lame*) lisiado, -a

game² [geɪm] *n no pl* (*in hunting*) caza *f*; **big** ~ caza mayor

game-cock ['geɪmkɒk, *Am:* -'kɑːk] *n* gallo *m* de pelea **gamekeeper** *n* guardabosque *mf* **game show** *n* concurso *m* de televisión

gaming ['geɪmɪŋ] *n no pl* juego *m*; ~ **house** casa *f* de juego

gaming table *n* tablero *m* de juego

gamma radiation *n no pl*, **gamma rays** *npl* rayos *mpl* gamma

gammon ['gæmən] *n no pl* jamón *m*

gammy ['gæmi] <*-ier, -iest*> *adj Brit, inf* lisiado, -a

gamut ['gæmət] *n* gama *f*

gander ['gændəʳ, *Am:* -dɚ] *n* 1. (*male goose*) ganso *m* 2. *inf* (*look*) **to take a** ~ echar una ojeada

gang [gæŋ] I. *n* 1. (*criminal group*) banda *f* 2. (*organized group*) cuadrilla *f*; (*of workers*) brigada *f*; **chain** ~ grupo *m* de presidiarios encadenados 3. *inf* (*group of friends*) pandilla *f*, barra *f AmL*, trinca *f And, CSur* II. *vi* to ~ **up on** unirse contra

ganger ['gæŋəʳ] *n Brit* capataz *mf*

gangling ['gæŋglɪŋ] *adj* larguirucho, -a

ganglion ['gæŋglɪən] <*-s o -glia*> *n* ANAT 1. (*group of nerves*) ganglio *m* 2. (*swelling*) protuberancia *f*

gangly ['gæŋgli] <*-ier, -iest*> *adj* desgarbado, -a

gangplank ['gæŋplæŋk] *n* plancha *f*

gangrene ['gæŋgriːn] *n no pl* gangrena *f*

gangrenous ['gæŋgrɪnəs, *Am:* -grə-] *adj* gangrenoso, -a

gangster ['gæŋstəʳ, *Am:* -stɚ] *n* gángster *m*

gang warfare *n no pl* guerra *f* entre bandas

gangway ['gæŋweɪ] I. *n* 1. NAUT (*gangplank*) pasarela *f*; (*ladder*) escalerilla *f* 2. *Brit* (*aisle*) pasillo *m* II. *interj inf* ¡abran paso!

gantry ['gæntri] <*-ies*> *n* caballete *m*; (*crane*) pórtico *m*; AVIAT torre *f* de lanzamiento

gaol [dʒeɪl] *n Brit s.* **jail**

gap [gæp] *n* 1. (*opening*) abertura *f*; (*empty space*) hueco *m*; (*in text*) laguna *f*; **to fill a** ~ llenar un espacio en blanco 2. (*break in time*) intervalo *m* 3. (*difference*) diferencia *f*; **age** ~ diferencia de edad

gape [geɪp] I. *vi* abrirse; (*person*) quedarse boquiabierto II. *n* (*look*) mirada *f* pasmada; (*yawn*) bostezo *m*

gaping *adj* (*hole*) enorme; (*person*) boquiabierto, -a

garage ['gæraːʒ, *Am:* gə'raːʒ] I. *n* 1. (*of house*) garaje *m* 2. *Brit, Aus* (*petrol station*) gasolinera *f* 3. (*for repair*) taller *m* II. *vt* **to** ~ **a car** guardar un coche en el garaje

garb [gɑːb, *Am:* gɑːrb] I. *n no pl* vestidura *f* II. *vt* **to be** ~**ed as** ir vestido de

garbage ['gɑːbɪdʒ, *Am:* 'gɑːr-] *n no pl, Am, Aus* basura *f*; **to take the** ~ **out** sacar la basura **garbage can** *n Am* (*dustbin*) cubo *m* de la basura, tacho *m AmL* **garbage chute** *n Am* (*rubbish chute*) vertedero *m* de basuras **garbage collector** *n Am* (*dustman*) basurero *m* **garbage disposal** *n*, **garbage disposer** *n Am* (*rubbish disposer*) triturador *m* de basuras **garbage dump** *n Am* (*rubbish dump*) vertedero *m* **garbage truck** *n Am, Aus* camión *m* de la basura

garble ['gɑːbl, *Am:* 'gɑːr-] *vt* 1. (*confuse*) confundir 2. (*distort*) distorsionar

garbled *adj* 1. (*confused*) confuso, -a 2. (*distorted*) distorsionado, -a

garden ['gɑːdn, *Am:* 'gɑːr-] I. *n* 1. jardín *m*; **vegetable** ~ huerto *m*; ~ **furniture** muebles *mpl* de jardín 2. *pl* (*ornamental grounds*) parque *m*; **botanical** ~ jardín *m* botánico II. *vi* (*flowers*) trabajar en el jardín; (*vegetables*) cultivar un huerto

garden centre *n* vivero *m* (de plantas)

garden city <*-ies*> *n* ciudad *f* jardín

gardener ['gɑːdnəʳ, *Am:* 'gɑːrdnɚ] *n* 1. (*of flowers*) jardinero, -a *m, f* 2. (*of vegetables*) hortelano, -a *m, f*

gardenia [gɑː'diːnɪə, *Am:* gɑːr-] *n* gardenia *f*

gardening ['gɑːdnɪŋ, *Am:* 'gɑːr-] *n no pl* (*of flowers*) jardinería *f*; (*of vegetables*) horticultura *f*

garden party <*-ies*> *n* fiesta *f* al aire libre

gargantuan [gɑː'gæntjʊən, *Am:* gɑːr-'gæntʃu-] *adj liter* colosal

gargle ['gɑːgl, *Am:* 'gɑːr-] I. *vi* hacer gárgaras II. *n* gárgaras *fpl*

gargoyle ['gɑːgɔɪl, *Am:* 'gɑːr-] *n* gárgola *f*

garish ['geərɪʃ, *Am:* 'ger-] *adj* chillón, -ona

garland ['gɑːlənd, *Am:* 'gɑːr-] I. *n* guirnalda *f* II. *vt* adornar con guirnaldas

garlic ['gɑːlɪk, *Am:* 'gɑːr-] *n no pl* ajo *m*; **clove of** ~ diente *m* de ajo; ~ **sauce** ajiaceite *m*

garlic press <*-es*> *n* triturador *m* de ajos

garment ['gɑːmənt, *Am:* 'gɑːr-] *n* prenda *f* de vestir

garnet ['gɑːnɪt, *Am:* 'gɑːr-] *n* granate *m*

garnish ['gɑːnɪʃ, *Am:* 'gɑːr-] I. *vt* adornar; GASTR aderezar II. <*-es*> *n* adorno *m*; GASTR aderezo *m*

garret ['gærət, *Am:* 'ger-] *n* ARCHIT buhardilla *f*; (*attic room*) desván *m*

garrison ['gærɪsn, *Am:* 'gerə-] I. *n* guarnición *f* II. *adj* de guarnición; ~ **town** ciudad *f* con guarnición III. *vt* (*troops*) poner en guarnición, acuartelar; (*place*) guarnecer

garrulous ['gærələs, *Am:* 'ger-] *adj* gárrulo, -a

garter ['gɑːtəʳ, *Am:* 'gɑːrtə] *n* liga *f*; **the Order of the Garter** *Brit* la orden de la Jarretera

garter stitch <-es> *n* punto *m* de media

gas [gæs] I. <-s(s)es> *n* 1. *a.* MED, CHEM gas *m*; **natural** ~ gas natural; **to cut off the** ~ cerrar el gas 2. *no pl, Am* (*fuel*) gasolina *f*; **leaded/unleaded** ~ gasolina con plomo/sin plomo; **to step on the** ~ acelerar II. <-ss-> *vt* asfixiar con gas III. <-ss-> *vi inf* charlar

gasbag ['gæsbæg] *n inf* loro *mf*

gas chamber *n* cámara *f* de gas **gas cooker** *n Brit* cocina *f* de gas

gaseous ['gæsɪəs] *adj* gaseoso, -a

gas field *n* yacimiento *m* de gas **gas fire** *n Brit* estufa *f* de gas **gas-fitter** *n Brit* técnico, -a *m, f* de la compañía del gas

gas gauge *n Am* (*petrol gauge*) medidor *m* del nivel de gasolina

gash [gæʃ] I. <-es> *n* (*deep cut*) raja *f*; (*wound*) cuchillada *f* II. *vt* rajar; (*wound*) acuchillar

gas heating *n* calefacción *f* de gas **gasholder** *n* gasómetro *m*

gasket ['gæskɪt] *n* junta *f*

gas lamp *n* lámpara *f* de gas **gas lighter** *n* mechero *m* de gas **gasman** <-men> *n Brit, inf* técnico *m* de la compañía del gas **gasmask** *n* máscara *f* antigás **gas meter** *n* contador *m* del gas

gasoline, gasolene ['gæsəliːn] *n Am* (*petrol*) gasolina *f*, nafta *f CSur* **gasoline tank** *n Am* depósito *m* de gasolina **gasometer** *n* gasómetro *m* **gas-oven** *n* horno *m* de gas

gasp [gɑːsp, *Am:* gæsp] I. *vi* 1. (*breathe*) jadear; **to** ~ **for air** hacer esfuerzos para respirar; **I ~ed in amazement** di un grito ahogado de asombro 2. (*speak*) hablar con voz entrecortada 2. *Brit, inf* **to be** ~ **for sth** morirse por algo II. *vt* **to** ~ **out sth** decir algo con voz entrecortada III. *n* jadeo *m*; **he gave a** ~ **of astonishment** dio un grito ahogado de asombro ▶ **to be at one's** <u>last</u> ~ estar en las últimas; **to do sth at the** <u>last</u> ~ hacer algo en el último momento

gas pedal *n* acelerador *m* **gas pipe** *n* tubería *f* de gas **gas pump** *n Am, Can* (*petrol pump*) surtidor *m* de gasolina **gas ring** *n Brit* hornillo *m* de gas **gas station** *n Am* (*petrol station*) gasolinera *f* **gas station operator** *n Am* (*petrol station operator*) empleado, -a *m, f* de una gasolinera **gas stove** *n* cocina *f* de gas

gassy ['gæsi] <-ier, -iest> *adj* 1. (*full of gas*)

gaseoso, -a 2. *inf* (*pointless, verbose*) rimbombante

gastric ['gæstrɪk] *adj* gástrico, -a

gastritis [gæ'straɪtɪs, *Am:* - t̬əs] *n no pl* gastritis *f inv*

gastroenteritis [ˌgæstrəʊˌentə'raɪtɪs, *Am:* -troʊˌentə'raɪt̬əs] *n no pl* gastroenteritis *f inv*

gastronomic [ˌgæstrə'nɒmɪk, *Am:* -'nɑːmɪk] *adj* gastronómico, -a

gastronomy [gæ'strɒnəmi, *Am:* -'strɑːnə-] *n no pl* gastronomía *f*

gastroscopy [ˌgæs'trəʊskɒpi] <-ies> *n* MED endoscopia *f*

gasworks ['gæswɜːks, *Am:* -wɜːrks] *n* + *sing vb* fábrica *f* de gas, usina *f AmL*

gate [geɪt] I. *n* 1. (*entrance barrier*) puerta *f*; RAIL barrera *f* 2. SPORTS entrada *f* 3. AVIAT puerta *f* de embarque 4. NAUT compuerta *f* II. *vt Brit* **to be ~d** SCHOOL estar castigado sin salir

gatecrash ['geɪtkræʃ] I. *vt* colarse en II. *vi* colarse

gatecrasher *n* intruso, -a *m, f*

gatehouse *n* casa *f* del guarda

gatekeeper *n* portero, -a *m, f*; RAIL guardabarrera *mf*

gate-legged table *n*, **gate-leg table** ['geɪtleg 'teɪbl] *n* mesa *f* plegable

gate money *n no pl, Brit, Aus* recaudación *f*

gatepost *n* poste *m* ▶ <u>between</u> you and me and the ~ entre tú y yo, que no salga de estas cuatro paredes

gateway *n* 1. (*entrance*) entrada *f* 2. (*means of access*) puerta *f*

gateway drug *n* primer droga *f* (*que lleva a una posterior adicción*)

gather ['gæðəʳ, *Am:* -ə] I. *vt* 1. (*collect together*) juntar; (*flowers*) recoger; (*information*) reunir; (*harvest*) cosechar 2. (*increase*) **to** ~ **speed** ganar velocidad 3. (*accumulate*) acumular; **to** ~ **one's strength** cobrar fuerzas 4. (*infer*) deducir; **to** ~ **that ...** sacar la conclusión de que... II. *vi* juntarse; (*people*) reunirse; (*things*) amontonarse; (*storm*) amenazar

gathering *n* reunión *f*

GATT [gæt] *n abbr of* **General Agreement on Tariffs and Trade** GATT *m*

gauche [gəʊʃ, *Am:* goʊʃ] *adj* torpe; (*shy*) poco seguro, -a de sí mismo, -a

gaudy[1] ['gɔːdi, *Am:* 'gɑː-] <-ier, -iest> *adj* llamativo, -a

gaudy[2] ['gɔːdi] <-ies> *n Brit* fanfarrón, -ona *m, f*

gauge [geɪdʒ] I. *n* 1. (*measure*) medida *f* 2. (*instrument*) indicador *m* 3. RAIL ancho *m* de vía 4. *fig* medidor *m*, indicador *m* II. *vt* 1. (*measure*) medir 2. (*assess*) determinar; **it's difficult to** ~ **what he will answer** resulta difícil determinar qué responderá

gaunt [gɔːnt, *Am:* gɑːnt] *adj* 1. (*very thin*) flaco, -a; (*too thin*) demacrado, -a 2. (*desolate*) lúgubre

gauntlet ['gɔːntlɪt, *Am:* 'gɑːnt-] *n* guante *m*;

HIST guantelete *m;* **to take up/throw down the ~** *fig* recoger/arrojar el guante ▶**to run the ~** MIL, HIST correr baquetas

gauze [gɔːz, *Am:* gɑːz] *n no pl a.* MED gasa *f*

gauzy ['gɔːzi, *Am:* 'gɑːz-] <-ier, -iest> *adj* diáfano, -a

gave [geɪv] *pt of* **give**

gavel ['gævl] I. *n* mazo *m* II.<*Brit:* -ll-, *Am:* -l-> *vt* golpear

gawk [gɔːk, *Am:* gɑːk] *vi inf* papar moscas; **to ~ at** mirar tontamente

gawky ['gɔːki, *Am:* 'gɑ:-] *adj* torpe; (*tall, awkward*) desgarbado, -a

gay [geɪ] I. *adj* 1. (*homosexual*) gay 2. (*cheerful*) alegre II. *n* gay *mf*

gaze [geɪz] I. *vi* mirar; **to ~ at sth** mirar algo fijamente II. *n* mirada *f* fija; **to be exposed to the public ~** estar expuesto para contemplación del público

gazelle [gə'zel] *n* gacela *f*

gazette [gə'zet] *n* gaceta *f*

gazetteer [ˌgæzə'tɪəʳ, *Am:* -'tɪr] *n* índice *m* geográfico

gazump [gə'zʌmp] *vt Brit, Aus, inf:* vender un inmueble a alguien que ofrece más dinero, sin tener en cuenta un acuerdo de venta anterior

GB [ˌdʒiː'biː] *n* 1. *no pl abbr of* **Great Britain** GB 2. INFOR *abbr of* **gigabyte** GB

GBH [ˌdʒiː'biː'eɪtʃ] *Brit abbr of* **grievous bodily harm** daño *m* personal grave

GCE [ˌdʒiː'siː'iː] *n Brit abbr of* **General Certificate of Education** GCE *m* (*título que permite el acceso a los estudios universitarios*)

GCHQ [ˌdʒiː'siː'eɪtʃ'kjuː] *n Brit abbr of* **Government Communications Headquarters** Centro *m* Gubernamental de Comunicaciones

GCSE [ˌdʒiː'siː'es'iː] *n Brit abbr of* **General Certificate of Secondary Education** GCSE *m* (*título de enseñanza secundaria que se consigue dos años antes que el GCE*)

Para obtener el **GCSE** (**General Certificate of Secondary Education**), antiguamente **O-level** (**Ordinary Level**), los alumnos ingleses, galeses y nordirlandeses de 16 años deben realizar un examen. Es posible examinarse de una única asignatura, pero la mayoría de los alumnos prefieren examinarse de siete u ocho. En Escocia este examen se conoce como **Standard Grade**.

Gdns *abbr of* **Gardens** Jardines *fpl*

GDP [ˌdʒiː'diː'piː] *n abbr of* **gross domestic product** PIB *m*

gear [gɪəʳ, *Am:* gɪr] *n* 1. TECH engranaje *m* 2. AUTO marcha *f* 3. *no pl* (*equipment*) equipo *m* 4. *no pl* (*clothes*) ropa *f*

gearbox ['gɪəbɒks, *Am:* 'gɪrbaːks] <-es> *n*, **gearcase** *n* caja *f* de cambios

gearing *n no pl* engranaje *m*

gear lever *n Brit, Aus,* **gearshift** ['gɪəʃɪft, *Am:* 'gɪr-] *n Am* palanca *f* de cambio

gearwheel *n* rueda *f* dentada

gee ['dʒiː] *interj Am, inf* caramba

geezer ['giːzəʳ, *Am:* -zəˠ] *n inf* tío *m;* **old ~** vejete *m*

geisha (**girl**) ['geɪʃə] *n* geisha *f*

gel [dʒel] *n* gel *m*

gelatin(e) ['dʒelətɪn] *n no pl* gelatina *f*

gelatinous [dʒɪ'lætɪnəs, *Am:* -ənəs] *adj* gelatinoso, -a

geld [geld] *vt* castrar

gelding ['geldɪŋ] *n* caballo *m* castrado

gem [dʒem] *n* 1. (*jewel*) piedra *f* preciosa 2. (*person*) joya *f fig*

Gemini ['dʒemɪni] *n* Géminis *mf*

gen [dʒen] *n no pl, Brit, inf* información *f;* **give sb the ~ on sth** poner a alguien al corriente de algo

◆**gen up** <-nn-> *vi Brit, inf* **to ~ on sth** informarse acerca de algo

gender ['dʒendəʳ, *Am:* -dəˠ] *n* 1. (*sexual identity*) sexo *m* 2. LING género *m*

gene [dʒiːn] *n* gen *m*

genealogical [ˌdʒiːnɪə'lɒdʒɪkl, *Am:* -'laːdʒɪ-] *adj* genealógico, -a

genealogist [ˌdʒiːnɪ'ælədʒɪst] *n* genealogista *mf*

genealogy [ˌdʒiːnɪ'ælədʒi] *n no pl* genealogía *f*

gene bank *n* banco *m* de genes

general ['dʒenrəl] I. *adj* general; **to be of ~ interest** ser de interés general; **as a ~ rule** por regla general; **to talk in ~ terms** hablar en términos generales II. *n* 1. MIL general *mf;* **~ lieutenant** teniente *mf* general 2. (*servant*) chica *f* para todo

general agency <-ies> *n* organismo *m* general **general agent** *n Brit* agente *mf* general **general anaesthetic** *n* anestesia *f* general **general assembly** <-ies> *n* asamblea *f* general **general delivery** *n no pl, Am, Can* (*poste restante*) lista *f* de correos **general director** *n* director(a) *m(f)* general **general editor** *n* editor(a) *m(f)* jefe **general election** *n* elecciones *fpl* generales **general endorsement** *n* aprobación *f* general **general headquarters** *n + sing vb* cuartel *m* general

generality [ˌdʒenə'ræləti, *Am:* -ţi] <-ies> *n* generalidad *f*

generalization [ˌdʒenərəlaiz'eɪʃən, *Am:* -ɪ'-] *n* generalización *f*

generalize ['dʒenərəlaɪz] *vi, vt* generalizar

generally ['dʒenrəli] *adv* 1. (*usually*) generalmente 2. (*mostly*) en general 3. (*widely, extensively*) por lo general; **~ speaking** hablando en términos generales

general management *n no pl* dirección *f* general **general manager** *n* director(a) *m(f)* general **general partnership** *n* sociedad *f* regular colectiva **General Post Office** *n* Administración *f* de Correos **general practitioner** *n Brit, Aus, Can* médico, -a *m, f* de cabecera **general staff** *n* *no pl* MIL estado *m* mayor **general store** *n* *Am* tienda *f* **general strike** *n* huelga *f* general **general view** *n* *no pl* opinión *f* general; **I do not subscribe to the ~ that ...** no estoy de acuerdo con la opinión general de que...

generate ['dʒenəreɪt] *vt* generar

generating station ['dʒenəreɪtɪŋ ˌsteɪʃən, *Am:* -tɪŋ ˌsteɪʃən] *n* central *f* generadora

generation [ˌdʒenə'reɪʃən] *n* generación *f;* **for ~s** durante generaciones

generative ['dʒenərətɪv, *Am:* -tɪv] *adj* generativo, -a

generator ['dʒenəreɪtə', *Am:* -tə] *n* a. ELEC generador *m*

generic [dʒɪ'nerɪk] I. *adj* genérico, -a II. *n* genérico *m*

generosity [ˌdʒenə'rɒsəti, *Am:* -'rɑːsəti] *n* *no pl* generosidad *f*

generous ['dʒenərəs] *adj* 1. (*magnanimous*) generoso, -a, rangoso, -a *AmS* 2. (*ample*) abundante 3. (*better than deserved*) espléndido, -a

genesis ['dʒenəsɪs] *n* *no pl* génesis *f inv*

gene therapy [ˌdʒiːn'θerəpi] *n* *no pl* terapia *f* génica

genetic [dʒɪ'netɪk, *Am:* -'net̬ɪk] *adj* genético, -a; **~ disease** enfermedad *f* genética

geneticist [dʒɪ'netɪsɪst, *Am:* -'net̬ə-] *n* genetista *mf*

genetics *n* + *sing vb* genética *f*

Geneva [dʒə'niːvə] *n* Ginebra *f*

genial ['dʒiːnɪəl] *adj* afable

geniality [ˌdʒiːnɪ'æləti, *Am:* -t̬i] *n* *no pl* afabilidad *f*

genie ['dʒiːni] <-nii *o* -ies> *n* genio *m*

genitalia [dʒenɪ'teɪlɪə] *npl*, **genitals** ['dʒenɪtəlz, *Am:* -ət̬əlz] *npl* genitales *mpl*

genitive ['dʒenətɪv, *Am:* -ət̬ɪv] I. *adj* genitivo, -a II. *n* genitivo *m*

genius ['dʒiːnɪəs] *n* <-ses> *no pl* genio *m*

genocide ['dʒenəsaɪd] *n* *no pl* genocidio *m*

genre ['ʒɑ̃ːnrə] *n* a. LIT género *m*

genre painting *n* pintura *f* de género

gent [dʒent] *n* *Brit, Aus, inf, iron* caballero *m;* **he is a true ~** es todo un caballero; **the ~s** el servicio de caballeros

genteel [dʒen'tiːl] *adj* distinguido, -a

gentian ['dʒenʃən] *n* genciana *f*

Gentile ['dʒentaɪl] I. *adj* gentil II. *n* gentil *mf*

gentle ['dʒentl] *adj* 1. (*kind*) amable; (*calm*) suave; **to be as ~ as a lamb** ser manso como un cordero 2. (*moderate*) moderado, -a 3. (*high-born*) **to be of ~ birth** ser de alcurnia; **~ reader** apreciado lector

gentlefolk ['dʒentlfəʊk, *Am:* -tlfoʊk] *npl* gente *f* de buena familia

gentleman ['dʒentlmən, *Am:* -tl-] <-men> *n* 1. (*man*) señor *m;* **ladies and ~** señoras y señores 2. (*well-behaved man*) caballero *m*

gentlemanly ['dʒentlmənli, *Am:* -tl-] *adj* caballeroso, -a

gentleness ['dʒentlnɪs] *n* *no pl* delicadeza *f*

gentlewoman ['dʒentlwʊmən, *Am:* -tl-] <-women> *n* dama *f*

gentry ['dʒentri] *n* *no pl, Brit* alta burguesía *f*

genuine ['dʒenjʊɪn] *adj* 1. (*not fake*) genuino, -a 2. (*real, sincere*) verdadero, -a

genus ['dʒiːnəs] <-nera> *n* BIO género *m*

geocentric [ˌdʒiːəʊ'sentrɪk, *Am:* -oʊ'-] *adj* geocéntrico, -a

geodesic [ˌdʒiːəʊ'desɪk, *Am:* -ə'-] *adj* geodésico, -a

geographer [dʒɪ'ɒɡrəfə', *Am:* -'ɑːɡrəfə] *n* geógrafo, -a *m, f*

geographic(al) [ˌdʒɪə'ɡræfɪk(l), *Am:* -ə'-] *adj* geográfico, -a

geography [dʒɪ'ɒɡrəfi, *Am:* -'ɑːɡrə-] *n* *no pl* geografía *f*

geological [ˌdʒɪəʊ'lɒdʒɪkəl, *Am:* -ə-'lɑːdʒɪk-] *adj* geológico, -a

geologist [dʒɪ'ɒlədʒɪst, *Am:* -'ɑːlə-] *n* geólogo, -a *m, f*

geology [dʒɪ'ɒlədʒi, *Am:* -'ɑːlə-] *n* *no pl* geología *f*

geometric(al) [ˌdʒɪə'metrɪk(l), *Am:* -ə'-] *adj* geométrico, -a

geometry [dʒɪ'ɒmətri, *Am:* -'ɑːmətri] *n* *no pl* geometría *f*

geophysical [ˌdʒɪə'fɪzɪkl, *Am:* -oʊ'-] *adj* geofísico, -a

geophysics [ˌdʒiːəʊ'fɪzɪks, *Am:* -oʊ'-] *n* + *sing vb* geofísica *f*

La **George Cross** y la **George Medal** son dos condecoraciones británicas introducidas en 1940 que reciben su nombre del Rey George VI. Con estas condecoraciones se distingue a aquellos civiles que han sobresalido por su valentía.

Georgia ['dʒɔːdʒə, *Am:* 'dʒɔːr-] *n* Georgia *f*

geothermal [ˌdʒiːəʊ'θɜːməl, *Am:* -oʊ'θɜːr-] *adj* geotérmico, -a

geranium [dʒə'reɪnɪəm] *n* geranio *m*, malvón *m Arg, Méx, Par, Urug*

geriatric [ˌdʒeri'ætrɪk] *adj* anciano, -a

geriatrician [ˌdʒerɪə'trɪʃən] *n* geriatra *mf*

geriatrics *n* + *sing vb* geriatría *f*

germ [dʒɜːm, *Am:* dʒɜːrm] *n* 1. (*causes disease*) microbio *m* 2. (*plant, principle*) germen *m*

German ['dʒɜːmən, *Am:* 'dʒɜːr-] I. *n* 1. (*person*) alemán, -ana *m, f* 2. (*language*) alemán *m* II. *adj* alemán, -ana

germane [dʒə'meɪn, *Am:* dʒə-] *adj form* relacionado, -a

Germanic [dʒə'mænɪk, *Am:* dʒə-] *adj* germánico, -a

German measles *n* + *sing vb* rubeola *f*

German shepherd (dog) *n* *Am* pastor *m* alemán

Germany ['dʒɜːməni, *Am:* 'dʒɜːr-] *n* Alemania *f*

germ-free *adj* esterilizado, -a

germicidal [ˌdʒɜːmɪ'saɪdəl, *Am:* ˌdʒɜːrmə'-]

adj germicida

germicide ['dʒɜːmɪsaɪd, *Am:* 'dʒɜːrmə-] *n* germicida *m*

germinal ['dʒɜːmɪnəl, *Am:* 'dʒɜːrmə-] *adj* germinal

germinate ['dʒɜːmɪneɪt, *Am:* 'dʒɜːrmə-] *vi, vt* germinar

germination [ˌdʒɜːmɪ'neɪʃən, *Am:* ˌdʒɜːrmə-] *n no pl* germinación *f*

germ warfare *n no pl* guerra *f* bacteriana

gerontologist [ˌdʒerɒn'tɒlədʒɪst, *Am:* ˌdʒern'tɑːlə-] *n* gerontólogo, -a *m, f*

gerontology [ˌdʒerɒn'tɒlədʒi, *Am:* ˌdʒern-'tɑːlə-] *n no pl* gerontología *f*

gerrymander ['dʒerɪmændər, *Am:* -dər] *vi* POL falsificar elecciones

gerund ['dʒerənd] *n* gerundio *m*

gestation [dʒe'steɪʃən] *n no pl* gestación *f*

gesticulate [dʒe'stɪkjʊleɪt, *Am:* -jə-] *vi form* gesticular

gesticulation [dʒeˌstɪkjʊ'leɪʃən, *Am:* -jə'-] *n form* gesticulación *f*

gesture ['dʒestʃər, *Am:* -tʃər] I. *n* 1. (*body movement*) gesto *m* 2. (*act*) muestra *f*; a ~ towards sb un detalle con alguien II. *vi* hacer un ademán III. *vt* indicar con un ademán

get [get] I. <got, got, *Am, Aus:* gotten> *vt inf* 1. (*obtain*) obtener; (*secure*) conseguir; (*gain*) ganar; (*buy*) comprar; (*find*) encontrar; (*take*) coger; to ~ the door *Am, inf* abrir la puerta; to ~ the telephone *Am, inf* coger el teléfono; to ~ a surprise llevarse una sorpresa; to ~ pleasure out of sth disfrutar con algo; to ~ the impression that ... tener la impresión de que...; to ~ a meal/drinks *Am, inf* comer/tomar algo 2. (*catch: plane, train*) coger 3. *inf* (*hear, understand*) comprender; (*message*) captar; (*picture*) entender; to ~ sth/sb wrong entender algo/a alguien mal 4. (*prepare: meal*) preparar 5. (*cause to be*) to ~ sth done hacer algo; to ~ sb to do sth hacer que alguien haga algo 6. *inf* (*irk*) fastidiar; (*make emotional*) afectar 7. *inf* (*start*) to ~ going poner en marcha; to ~ cracking poner manos a la obra II. *vi* 1. + *n/adj* (*become*) volverse; to ~ married casarse; to ~ upset enfadarse; to ~ used to sth acostumbrarse a algo; to ~ to be sth llegar a ser algo; to ~ to like sth coger afición a algo 2. (*have opportunity*) to ~ to do sth llegar a hacer algo; to ~ to see sb lograr ver a alguien 3. (*travel*) llegar; to ~ home llegar a casa

◆**get about** *vi* 1. desplazarse 2. (*travel*) viajar mucho

◆**get across** *vt* hacer pasar; to ~ a message to sb comunicar un mensaje a alguien

◆**get along** *vi* 1. (*good relationship*) llevarse bien 2. (*manage*) arreglárselas

◆**get around** I. *vt insep* (*avoid*) evitar II. *vi* 1. (*spread*) llegar a 2. (*travel*) viajar mucho

◆**get at** *vt insep, inf* 1. (*suggest*) apuntar a 2. *Aus, Brit* (*criticize*) meterse con 3. (*influence illegally*) sobornar 4. (*reach*) lle-

gar a

◆**get away** *vi* marcharse

◆**get back** I. *vt* recuperar II. *vi* volver

◆**get behind** I. *vi* quedarse atrás II. *vt insep* quedarse detrás de

◆**get by** *vi* (*manage*) arreglárselas

◆**get down** *vt always sep* 1. (*disturb*) deprimir 2. (*swallow*) tragar

◆**get in** I. *vt* 1. (*say*) decir 2. (*bring inside*) llevar dentro II. *vi* 1. (*become elected*) ser elegido 2. (*enter*) entrar 3. (*arrive*) llegar a casa

◆**get into** *vt insep* 1. (*become interested in*) interesarse por 2. (*involve*) meter; to get sb into trouble meter a alguien en problemas 3. (*enter*) entrar en

◆**get off** I. *vi* 1. (*start sleeping*) dormirse 2. (*avoid punishment*) librarse 3. (*depart*) marcharse II. *vt always sep* 1. (*help avoid punishment*) librarse de 2. (*remove from*) sacar 3. (*send*) enviar

◆**get on** *vi* 1. (*be friends*) llevarse bien 2. (*manage*) arreglárselas 3. (*get older*) envejecer 4. (*to get late*) time's getting on se está haciendo tarde

◆**get out** I. *vt* sacar II. *vi* salir

◆**get over** *vt insep* 1. (*recover from*) recuperarse de; (*illness*) reponerse de; (*difficulty*) superar 2. (*forget about*) to ~ sb/sth olvidarse de alguien/algo

◆**get round** *vt* 1. (*avoid*) evitar 2. *Brit* (*persuade*) persuadir

◆**get through** I. *vi* to ~ to sth/sb comunicarse con algo/alguien II. *vt* 1. (*make understood*) to get it through to sb that ... hacer que alguien entienda que... 2. (*survive*) pasar; (*exam*) aprobar

◆**get together** I. *vi* reunirse II. *vt* reunir

◆**get up** I. *vt* 1. (*organize*) organizar 2. *inf* (*dress*) ataviar 3. *always sep, Brit, inf* (*wake*) levantar 4. *insep* (*climb*) subir II. *vi* 1. (*get out of bed*) levantarse 2. (*rise*) subir

◆**get up to** *vt* llegar a

get-at-able [ˌget'ætəbl, *Am:* ˌɡet'æt-] *adj inf* accesible

getaway ['getəweɪ, *Am:* 'get-] *n inf* fuga *f*; to make a ~ fugarse

get-together ['gettə'geðər, *Am:* -ər] *n inf* reunión *f*

get-up ['getʌp, *Am:* 'get-] *n inf* atuendo *m*

geyser ['giːzər, *Am:* -zər] *n* 1. (*hot spring*) géiser *m* 2. *Brit* (*water heater*) calentador *m* de agua

Ghana ['gɑːnə] *n* Ghana *f*

Ghanaian [gɑː'neɪən, *Am:* -'niː-] I. *adj* ghanés, -esa II. *n* ghanés, -esa *m, f*

ghastly ['gɑːstli, *Am:* 'gæst-] <-ier, -iest> *adj inf* 1. (*frightful*) horroroso, -a 2. (*unpleasant*) desagradable 3. *liter* (*pallid*) ~ white/pale blanco, -a/pálido, -a (como la cera)

Ghent [gent] *n* Gante *m*

gherkin ['gɜːkɪn, *Am:* 'gɜːr-] *n* pepinillo *m*

ghetto ['getəʊ, *Am:* 'getoʊ] I. <-s *o* -es> *n*

gueto *m* **II.** *adj* (*life*) de [*o* en un] gueto; (*conditions*) de marginación

ghetto blaster *n inf* radio *f* portátil de gran frecuencia

ghost [gəʊst, *Am:* goʊst] **I.** *n a. fig* (*spirit*) fantasma *m*, espanto *m AmL*, azoro *m AmC*; **to believe in** ~**s** creer en fantasmas; **to be haunted by** ~**s** haber fantasmas; **the** ~ **of the past** los fantasmas del pasado ►**to give up the** ~ (*to die*) exhalar el último suspiro; (*to stop working*) dejar de funcionar **II.** *vt* escribir para otro; **his speech was** ~**ed** el discurso no lo escribió él **III.** *vi* hacer de negro

ghostly ['gəʊstli] <-ier, -iest> *adj* **1.** (*ghostlike*) fantasmal **2.** (*spooky*) escalofriante

ghost town *n* pueblo *m* fantasma **ghostwriter** *n* negro, -a *m, f* (*persona que escribe para otra*)

ghoul [guːl] *n* (*evil spirit*) espíritu *m* demoníaco

g.l. *n*, **G.I.** [ˌdʒiː'aɪ] *n inf* soldado *m* norteamericano (*especialmente en la II Guerra Mundial*)

GI *abbr of* **government issue** propiedad *f* del Estado

giant ['dʒaɪənt] **I.** *n* gigante *m;* **a political** ~ un coloso de la política **II.** *adj* gigantesco, -a

giantess ['dʒaɪəntes, *Am:* -təs] *n* **1.** (*female giant*) giganta *f* **2.** (*influential female*) colosa *f*

gibber ['dʒɪbəʳ, *Am:* -ɚ] *vi* farfullar; **to** ~ **with rage** hablar atropelladamente de rabia

gibberish ['dʒɪbərɪʃ] *n no pl* galimatías *m inv*

gibbet ['dʒɪbɪt] *n* horca *f*

gibbon ['gɪbən] *n* gibón *m*

gibe [dʒaɪb] **I.** *n* burla *f* **II.** *vi* **to** ~ **at sb/sth** burlarse de alguien/algo

giblets ['dʒɪblɪts] *npl* menudillos *mpl*

Gibraltar [dʒɪ'brɔːltəʳ, *Am:* -'brɑːltɚ] *n* Gibraltar *m*

giddy ['gɪdi] <-ier, -iest> *adj* mareado, -a

gift [gɪft] *n* **1.** (*present*) regalo *m;* **to bear** ~**s** traer [*o* llevar] regalos; **to be a** ~ **from the Gods** ser un regalo caído del cielo **2.** *inf* (*bargain*) **£100 for this bicycle? it's a** ~! ¿100 libras por esta bicicleta? ¡Está tirada! **3.** (*talent*) don *m;* **to have a** ~ **for languages** tener talento para los idiomas; **to have the** ~ **of the gab** *inf* tener mucha labia

gift certificate *n Am* vale *m* de [*o* por un] regalo

gifted *adj* **1.** (*talented*) de (gran) talento **2.** (*intellectually bright*) brillante; ~ **child** niño *m* superdotado

gift horse *n* **never look a** ~ **in the mouth** *prov* a caballo regalado, no le mires el dentado *prov* **gift shop** *n* tienda *f* de regalos **gift token** *n*, **gift voucher** *n* vale *m* de [*o* por un] regalo

gig[1] [gɪg] **I.** *n inf* (*musical performance*) concierto *m;* **to do a** ~ dar un concierto **II.** *vi* <-gg-> (*do a gig*) dar un concierto

gig[2] [gɪg] *n* calesín *m*

gigabyte ['gɪgəbaɪt] *n* gigabyte *m*

gigantic [dʒaɪ'gæntɪk, *Am:* -ţɪk] *adj* gigantesco, -a

giggle ['gɪgl] **I.** *vi* reír(se) tontamente **II.** *n* **1.** (*laugh*) risita *f;* **she got the** ~**s** le dio la risa tonta **2.** *no pl, Aus, Brit, inf* (*joke*) broma *f;* **to do sth for a** ~ hacer algo para reírse [*o* divertirse] un rato **3.** *pl* **the** ~**s, to get (a fit of) the** ~**s** tener un ataque de risa

gild [gɪld] *vt* **1.** (*cover with gold*) dorar **2.** (*light up*) iluminar ►**to** ~ **the lily** rizar el rizo

gilded *adj* dorado, -a

gill[1] [gɪl] *n* (*of a fish*) agalla *f* ►**to be green about the** ~**s** *iron* estar pálido como la cera; **to be packed to the** ~**s** estar a tope (de lleno); **to be stuffed to the** ~**s** estar a tope (de comida); **to the** ~**s** *inf* a tope

gill[2] [dʒɪl] *n* (*measure*) ≈ cuartillo *m*

gilt [gɪlt] **I.** *adj* dorado, -a **II.** *n no pl* dorado *m*

gilt-edged [ˌgɪlt'edʒd] *adj* (*securities, stocks*) de máxima garantía

gimcrack ['dʒɪmkræk] *adj* (*ideas*) de pacotilla; (*architecture*) de baja calidad

gimlet ['gɪmlɪt] *n* **1.** (*tool*) barrena *f* **2.** *Am* (*alcoholic drink*) cóctel *m* de zumo de lima y vodka o ginebra

gimlet-eyed *adj* penetrante; **to be** ~ tener una mirada penetrante

gimmick ['gɪmɪk] *n* **1.** (*commercial*) truco *m* (*para vender más*) **2.** (*attention-getter*) truco *m* efectista (*para atraer la atención*)

gimmicky ['gɪmɪki] *adj* efectista

gin[1] [dʒɪn] *n* ginebra *f;* ~ **and tonic** gin tonic *m*

gin[2] [dʒɪn] *n* **1.** (*trap*) trampa *f* **2.** AGR desmotadora *f* de algodón

ginger ['dʒɪndʒəʳ, *Am:* -dʒɚ] **I.** *n no pl* **1.** (*root spice*) jengibre *m* **2.** (*reddish-yellow*) rojo *m* anaranjado **3.** *s.* **ginger ale II.** *adj* rojizo, -a; (*hair*) pelirrojo, -a

ginger ale, **ginger beer** *n* ginger ale *m*, refresco *m* de jengibre

gingerbread ['dʒɪndʒəbred, *Am:* -dʒɚ] *n no pl* pan *m* de jengibre

ginger group *n Aus, Brit* POL grupo *m* de presión

ginger-haired *adj* pelirrojo, -a

gingerly ['dʒɪndʒəli, *Am:* -dʒɚli] *adv* con cautela

ginger nut *n Aus, Brit*, **ginger snap** *n Am* galleta *f* de jengibre

gingivitis [ˌdʒɪndʒɪ'vaɪtɪs, *Am:* -dʒə-'vaɪţəs] *n no pl* gingivitis *f inv*

ginseng ['dʒɪnseŋ] *n no pl* ginseng *m*

gipsy ['dʒɪpsi] *n s.* **gypsy**

giraffe [dʒɪ'rɑːf, *Am:* dʒɚ'ræf] *n* <-(s)> jirafa *f*

girder ['gɜːdəʳ, *Am:* 'gɜːrdɚ] *n* viga *f* (*de metal u hormigón*)

girdle ['gɜːdl, *Am:* 'gɜːr-] **I.** *n* **1.** *a. fig* (*belt*) cinturón *m* **2.** (*corset*) faja *f* **II.** *vt a. fig* (*surround*) rodear

girl [gɜːl, *Am:* gɜːrl] *n* **1.** (*child*) niña *f;* (*young* *woman*) joven *f*, piba *f Arg* **2.** (*daughter*) hija *f* **3.** the ~**s** *pl* (*at work*) las compañeras; (*friends*) las amigas

girl Friday *n* chica *f* para todo

girlfriend ['gɜːlfrend, *Am:* 'gɜːrl-] *n* **1.** (*of woman*) amiga *f* **2.** (*of man*) novia *f*, polola *f And*

girl guide *n Brit* guía *f*

girlhood ['gɜːlhʊd, *Am:* 'gɜːrl-] *n no pl* juventud *f*

girlie ['gɜːli, *Am:* 'gɜːr-] *adj* de destape

girlie magazine *n* revista *f* de chicas desnudas

girlish ['gɜːlɪʃ, *Am:* 'gɜːr-] *adj* de [*o* como una] niña

girl scout *n Am* exploradora *f*

giro ['dʒaɪrəʊ, *Am:* -roʊ] *n* **1.** *no pl* (*credit transfer system*) giro *m* bancario; **to transfer by** ~ enviar mediante giro (bancario) **2.** *Brit* (*social benefit cheque*) cheque *m* del subsidio (*que se recibe del Estado por desempleo o ayuda social*)

giro account *n* cuenta *f* de giros **giro system** *n* sistema *m* de giro bancario **giro transfer** *n* transferencia *f* bancaria

girth [gɜːθ, *Am:* gɜːrθ] *n* **1.** *no pl* (*circumference*) circunferencia *f* **2.** *no pl, iron* (*obesity*) obesidad *f* **3.** <-es> (*strap around horse*) cincha *f*

gist [dʒɪst] *n* the ~ lo esencial; **to give sb the** ~ (**of sth**) contar a alguien lo fundamental (sobre algo); **to get the** ~ **of sth** entender lo básico de algo

give [gɪv] **I.** *vt* <gave, given> **1.** (*offer*) dar, ofrecer; (*kiss, signal*) dar; (*a seat*) ceder; **to** ~ **sb an excuse for sth** dar una excusa a alguien para algo; **given the choice …** si pudiera elegir…; **to** ~ **sb something to eat/drink** dar a alguien algo de comer/beber; **to not** ~ **much for sth** *fig* no dar mucho por algo; **to** ~ **sb full life imprisonment** condenar a alguien a cadena perpetua; **don't** ~ **me that!** *inf* ¡venga ya, tú me la quieres dar con queso!; ~ **me a break!** ¡déjame en paz!; **I don't** ~ **a damn** *inf* me importa un bledo; **to** ~ **notice** avisar, hacer saber; **to** ~ **sb the creeps** producir a alguien escalofríos; **to** ~ (**it**) **one's all** [*o* best *Am*] dar todo de sí mismo; **to** ~ **anything for sth/to do sth** dar cualquier cosa por algo/por hacer algo; **to** ~ **one's life to sth** dedicar la vida de uno a algo; **to** ~ **sb what for** *inf* echar a alguien un rapapolvo **2.** (*lecture, performance*) dar; (*speech*) pronunciar; (*noise*) hacer; (*strange look*) echar; (*headache, trouble*) producir, dar; **to** ~ **sb a call** llamar a alguien (por teléfono); **to** ~ **sth a go** intentar algo; **to** ~ **sb to understand sth** *form* dar a entender algo a alguien **3.** (*organize*) dar, organizar **4.** (*pass on*) contagiar **II.** *vi* <gave, given> **1.** (*offer*) dar, ofrecer; **to** ~ **as good as one gets** devolver golpe por golpe; **to** ~ **of one's money** hacer una aportación (monetaria); **to** ~ **of one's best** dar todo de sí **2.** (*stretch*) esti-

rarse, dar de sí; **something will have to** ~ *fig* algo tendrá que cambiar **3.** **what** ~**s?** *Am, inf* ¿qué hay? ▶**it is better to** ~ **than to** <u>receive</u> *prov* es mejor dar que recibir *prov* **III.** *n* elasticidad *f*

◆**give away** *vt* **1.** (*reveal*) revelar; **to give the game away** tirar de la manta; **to give sb away** delatar a alguien **2.** (*offer for free*) regalar **3.** *form* (*bride*) entregar en matrimonio

◆**give back** *vt* devolver, regresar *Méx*

◆**give in I.** *vi* rendirse; **to** ~ to sth acceder (finalmente) a algo **II.** *vt* **1.** (*hand in*) entregar **2.** SPORTS **to give the ball in** *Brit* dar la pelota como buena

◆**give off** *vt* emitir; (*smell*) despedir; (*heat*) producir

◆**give out I.** *vi* **1.** (*run out*) acabar(se) **2.** (*machine*) estropearse; (*legs*) ceder **II.** *vt* **1.** (*distribute*) repartir **2.** (*announce*) anunciar **3.** (*produce*) producir; (*noise*) emitir **4.** SPORTS (*disallow*) **to give the ball out** *Brit* dar la pelota como mala

◆**give over** *vi Brit, inf* **1.** (*cease criticizing*) dejar de hacer; **he told me to** ~ me dijo que parara ya **2.** ~**!** ¡venga ya!

◆**give up I.** *vt* **1.** (*resign*) renunciar **2.** (*quit*) **to** ~ **doing sth** dejar de hacer algo; **to** ~ **smoking** dejar de fumar **3.** (*lose hope*) **to give sb up** (*patient*) desahuciar a alguien; (*missing person*) dar a alguien por desaparecido **4.** (*stop being friendly towards*) romper (la amistad); **to** ~ **one's friends** terminar (la amistad) con los amigos de uno **5.** (*hand over*) entregar; **to give oneself up** (**to the police**) entregarse (a la policía) **II.** *vi* **1.** (*quit*) dejar **2.** (*cease trying to guess*) rendirse

give-and-take [ˌgɪvənˈteɪk] *n* (*compromise*) toma *m* y daca

give-away ['gɪvəweɪ] **I.** *n* **1.** *no pl, inf* (*exposure*) prueba *f* (que delata algo) **2.** (*free gift*) regalo *m* **II.** *adj* **1.** (*very low*) ~ **price** precio *m* de saldo **2.** (*free*) gratis; ~ **newspaper** periódico *m* gratuito

given ['gɪvn] **I.** *n Am* dato *m* conocido; **to take sth as a** ~ dar algo por sentado **II.** *adj* **1.** (*arranged*) determinado, -a, acordado, -a; **in a** ~ **time** en un tiempo determinado **2.** **to be** ~ **to do sth** ser dado a hacer algo **III.** *pp of* **give** **IV.** *prep* ~ **that** dado que +*subj*, en el caso de que +*subj*; ~ **the chance I would go to Paris** si tuviese la oportunidad iría a París

given name *n Am, Scot* nombre *m* de pila

giver ['gɪvəʳ, *Am:* -ɚ] *n* donante *mf*

glacé ['glæseɪ, *Am:* glæs'eɪ] *adj*, **glacéed** *adj Am inv* glaseado, -a; ~ **fruit** fruta *f* confitada

glacial ['gleɪsiəl, *Am:* 'gleɪʃəl] *adj* GEO glacial; ~ **epoch/look** época *f*/mirada *f* glacial

glacier ['glæsiəʳ, *Am:* 'gleɪʃɚ] *n* glaciar *m*

glad [glæd] <gladder, gladdest> *adj* contento, -a; **to be** ~ **about sth** alegrarse de algo; **I'd be** ~ **to go with you** me encantaría ir contigo; **I'm** ~ **of your help** agradezco tu

ayuda
gladden ['glædn] *vt* alegrar
glade [gleɪd] *n* claro *m* (de un bosque)
gladiator ['glædɪeɪtə', *Am:* -t̬ə'] *n* gladiador
m
gladiolus [ˌglædɪ'əʊləs, *Am:* -'oʊ-] <-es *o*
-li> *n* gladiolo *m*
gladly ['glædli] *adv* con mucho gusto
gladness ['glædnɪs] *n no pl* alegría *f*
glad rags *n no pl, iron* **to put on one's ~**
ponerse las mejores galas
glamor ['glæmə', *Am:* -ə'] *n no pl, Am, Aus*
s. **glamour**
glamorise *vt,* **glamorize** ['glæməraɪz] *vt*
hacer más atractivo; **this film ~s violence**
esta película exalta la violencia
glamorous ['glæmərəs] *adj* glamoroso, -a,
atractivo, -a; (*traje*) con glamour, sofisticado, -a
glamour ['glæmə', *Am:* -ə'] *n no pl, Aus, Brit*
glamour *m*, encanto *m*, atractivo *m*
glamour boy *n* guapo *m*
glamour girl *n* guapa *f*
glance [glɑːns, *Am:* glæns] I. *n* mirada *f;* **to**
take a ~ at sth echar una mirada [*o* un vistazo]
a algo; **at first ~** a primera vista; **at a ~** de un
vistazo II. *vi* 1. (*look cursorily*) **to ~ up (from**
sth) levantar la mirada (de algo); **to ~ around**
sth mirar alrededor de algo; **to ~ over sth**
echar un vistazo a algo 2. (*shine*) brillar
◆**glance off** *vi* (chocar y) rebotar
gland [glænd] *n* glándula *f*
glandular ['glændjʊlə', *Am:* -dʒələ'] *adj*
glandular
glandular fever *n* mononucleosis *f inv* infecciosa
glare [gleə', *Am:* gler] I. *n* 1. (*mean look*)
mirada *f* (fulminadora); **to give sb a ~** fulminar a alguien con la mirada 2. *no pl* (*reflec-*
tion) resplandor *m;* **to give off ~** deslumbrar;
to be dazzled by the ~ of sth quedar deslumbrado por el resplandor de algo II. *vi* 1. (*look*)
fulminar con la mirada 2. (*shine*) resplandecer;
the sun ~s down on my eyes el sol me da
directamente a los ojos
glaring *adj* 1. (*which blinds*) deslumbrante
2. (*obvious*) que salta a la vista; **~ weakness**
debilidad *f* manifiesta; **~ injustice** injusticia *f*
que clama al cielo
glass [glɑːs, *Am:* glæs] <-es> *n* 1. *no pl*
(*material*) vidrio *m*, cristal *m;* **pane of ~** hoja *f*
de vidrio; **under ~** en invernadero 2. *no pl*
(*glassware*) cristalería *f* 3. (*for drinks*) vaso *m*
4. (*drink*) copa *f* 5. (*mirror*) espejo *m* 6. *pl*
gafas *fpl,* lentes *fpl AmL* 7. *pl* (*binoculars*) prismáticos *mpl*
glass-blower ['glɑːsˌbləʊə', *Am:*
'glæsˌbloʊə'] *n* soplador(a) *m(f)* **glass-**
cutter *n* cortador *m* de vidrio
glass fiber *n Am,* **glass fibre** *n Brit* fibra *f*
de vidrio
glassful ['glɑːsfʊl, *Am:* 'glæs-] *n* vaso *m; a ~*
of orange juice un vaso (lleno) de zumo de
naranja

glasshouse ['glɑːshaʊs, *Am:* 'glæs-] *n*
invernadero *m* **glassware** *n no pl* cristalería *f*
glassworks *npl* fábrica *f* de vidrio
glassy ['glɑːsi, *Am:* 'glæsi] <-ier, -iest> *adj*
1. *liter* (*as glass*) vítreo, -a 2. (*eyes*) vidrioso, -a
Glaswegian [glæz'wiːdʒən, *Am:* glæs-] *n*
habitante *mf* de Glasgow
glaucoma [glɔː'kəʊmə, *Am:* glɑː'koʊ-] *n*
glaucoma *m*
glaucous ['glɔːkəs, *Am:* 'glɑː-] *adj*
1. (*greenish-blue*) glauco, -a 2. BOT (*with*
bloom) cubierto, -a de una pelusilla verdosa
glaze [gleɪz] I. *n a.* GASTR glaseado *m;* (*paper*)
glaseado *m;* (*painting*) barniz *m;* (*pottery*)
vidriado *m* II. *vt* 1. (*paper*) glasear
2. (*window*) poner vidrios a
glazier ['gleɪziər] *n* vidriero, -a *m, f,* cristalero, -a *m, f*
gleam [gliːm] I. *n* reflejo *m*, destello *m; ~ of*
hope rayo *m* de esperanza II. *vi* brillar, relucir
glean [gliːn] *vt* **to ~ sth from sb** deducir algo
(de las palabras) de alguien
gleanings *npl* información *f* recogida
glee [gliː] *n no pl* júbilo *m;* **to do sth with ~**
hacer algo con gran alegría
gleeful ['gliːfəl] *adj* eufórico, -a
glen [glen] *n Scot* valle *m*
glib [glɪb] <glibber, glibbest> *adj* simplista
glide [glaɪd] I. *vi* 1. (*move smoothly*) deslizarse 2. AVIAT planear; **to take sb gliding** llevar
a alguien a volar con planeador II. *n* 1. (*sliding*
movement) deslizamiento *m* 2. AVIAT planeo
m; **with a ~** con un movimiento deslizante
glider ['glaɪdə', *Am:* -də'] *n* planeador *m*
glider pilot *n* piloto *mf* de planeador
gliding ['glaɪdɪŋ] *n no pl* vuelo *m* sin motor
gliding club *n* club *m* de vuelo sin motor
glimmer ['glɪmə', *Am:* -ə'] I. *vi* brillar tenuemente II. *n* (*light*) luz *f* tenue; *~ of* **hope**
atisbo *m* de esperanza
glimpse [glɪmps] I. *vt* (*signs*) vislumbrar
II. *n* **to catch a ~ of** vislumbrar; **to catch a ~**
of sb's life captar algo de la vida de alguien
glint [glɪnt] I. *vi* destellar; **to ~ with sth** brillar por causa de algo II. *n* destello *m*
glisten ['glɪsn] *vi* brillar, relucir
glitch [glɪtʃ] <-es> *n inf* fallo *m*
glitter ['glɪtə', *Am:* 'glɪt̬ə'] I. *vi* brillar, relucir
II. *n no pl* 1. (*sparkling*) brillo *m*, destello *m*
2. (*excitement*) esplendor *m* 3. (*shiny*
material) purpurina *f*
glittering *adj* 1. (*sparkling, impressive*) brillante 2. (*exciting*) esplendoroso, -a
glitz [glɪts] *n no pl* ostentosidad *f*
glitzy ['glɪtsi] <-ier, -iest> *adj* ostentoso, -a;
~ **car** cochazo *m* imponente
gloat [gləʊt, *Am:* gloʊt] I. *vi* disfrutar con
regocijo; **to ~ over sth** manifestar (gran) satisfacción por algo; **to ~ at sth** regodearse con
algo II. *n* regocijo *m*
global ['gləʊbl, *Am:* 'gloʊ-] *adj* 1. (*world-*
wide) a nivel mundial 2. (*complete*) global
global warming *n* calentamiento *m* de la

atmósfera terrestre

globe [gləʊb, Am: gloʊb] n 1.(map of world) globo m terráqueo 2.(object) globo m 3.Aus (light bulb) bombilla f

globetrotter ['gləʊb,trɒtəʳ, Am: 'gloʊb-,tra:ṭəʳ] n trotamundos mf inv

globule ['glɒbju:l, Am: 'glɑ:bju:l] n glóbulo m

gloom [glu:m] n no pl 1.(hopelessness) pesimismo m, melancolía f; ~ and doom profunda desesperación; ~ and despondency pesimismo y abatimiento 2.(darkness) oscuridad f

gloominess ['glu:mɪnəs] n no pl 1.(hopelessness) pesimismo m 2.(darkness) oscuridad f

gloomy ['glu:mi] <-ier, -iest> adj 1.(dismal) abatido, -a; (thoughts) melancólico, -a; to be ~ about sth ser pesimista respecto a algo; to turn ~ abatirse 2.(dark) oscuro, -a

glorification [ˌglɔ:rɪfɪ'keɪʃən, Am: ˌglɔ:rəfə'-] n no pl 1.(honouring, praising) alabanza f 2.(seem more splendid) glorificación f

glorify ['glɔ:rɪfaɪ, Am: ˌglɔ:rə-] <-ie-> vt 1.(make seem better) glorificar 2.(honour) alabar; to ~ God/Allah REL alabar a Dios/Alá

glorious ['glɔ:rɪəs] adj 1.(honourable, illustrious) glorioso, -a 2.(splendid: day, weather) espléndido, -a 3.iron (extreme) enorme; this bedroom is one ~ mess esta habitación es un completo desorden

glory ['glɔ:ri] I. n no pl 1.(honour) gloria f; to bathe in ~ bañarse de gloria; to cover oneself in ~ cubrirse de gloria; to deserve/get all the ~ for sth merecer/conseguir toda la gloria por algo 2.(splendour) esplendor m; in all her ~ en todo su esplendor 3.(state of delight) to be in one's ~ estar en la gloria 4.(adoration, praise) adoración f 5.REL (heaven) cielo m; to be in ~ estar en la gloria; to go to ~ inf ir al cielo ▶~ be! (thank God!) ¡gracias a Dios! II. <-ie-> vi vanagloriarse; to ~ in sth vanagloriarse de algo

glory-hole n inf leonera f

gloss¹ [glɒs, Am: glɑ:s] I. n no pl 1.(shine) brillo m, lustre m; high ~ mucho brillo m 2.(shiny substance) sustancia f abrillantadora 3.(shiny finish) acabado m brillante 4.(shiny paint) pintura f esmalte 5.(lip moisturizer) brillo m para labios ▶to take the ~ off sth desmejorar algo, quitar la gracia a algo II. adj de brillo

gloss² [glɒs, Am: glɑ:s] I.<-es> n glosa f II. vt glosar

◆**gloss over** vt pasar por alto

glossary ['glɒsəri, Am: 'glɑ:sər-] <-ies> n PUBL, LIT glosario m

gloss paint n no pl pintura f esmalte

glossy ['glɒsi, Am: 'glɑ:si] I.<-ier, -iest> adj 1.(shiny) brillante, lustroso, -a; (paper) satinado, -a; (magazine) elegante, de lujo 2.(superficially attractive) superficialmente

atractivo, -a II.<-ies> n 1. Am, Aus PHOT fotografía f brillante 2.PUBL revista f (impresa en papel satinado)

glottal stop ['glɒtl'stɒp, Am: 'glɑ:ṭəl'stɑ:p] n LING oclusión f glotal

glottis ['glɒtɪs, Am: 'glɑ:ṭəs] <-es> n ANAT, MED glotis f inv

glove [glʌv] I. n guante m; leather/wool ~s guantes mpl de piel/lana; a pair of ~s unos guantes; to put on/take off one's ~s ponerse/sacarse los guantes ▶to fit sb like a ~ venir a alguien como anillo al dedo, quedar a alguien como un guante II. vt Am 1.(dress in gloves) to ~ one's hands ponerse los guantes 2.(catch) atrapar

glove box n, **glove compartment** n AUTO guantera f

glover ['glʌvəʳ, Am: -əʳ] n guantero, -a m, f

glow [gləʊ, Am: gloʊ] I. n 1.(light) luz f 2.(warmth and redness) calor m 3.(good feeling) sensación f grata; ~ of happiness sensación f de felicidad; ~ of pride sentimiento m de orgullo; ~ of satisfaction sensación f de satisfacción II. vi 1.(illuminate) brillar 2.(be red and hot) arder 3.(look radiant) estar radiante

glower ['glaʊəʳ, Am: -əʳ] I. vi mirar con el ceño fruncido; to ~ at sb mirar con el ceño fruncido a alguien; large black rain clouds ~ in the sky fig LIT grandes nubes negras de lluvia amenazan en el cielo II. n mirada f furiosa

glowing adj ardiente; (report, praise) efusivo, -a

glow-lamp n, **glowlight** n lámpara f incandescente **glow-worm** n luciérnaga f, candelilla f CRi, Chile, Hond

glucose ['glu:kəʊs, Am: -koʊs] n no pl glucosa f; ~ syrup jarabe m de glucosa

glue [glu:] I. n no pl cola f, pegamento m; to fix sth with ~ fijar algo con cola; to sniff ~ esnifar pegamento II. vt encolar; to ~ sth together pegar algo; to ~ sth on encolar algo; to be ~d to sth fig estar pegado a algo; to keep one's eyes ~d to sth/sb fig mantener los ojos pegados a algo/alguien

glue-sniffing ['glu:ˌsnɪfɪŋ] n inhalación f de pegamento

glue stick n pegamento m

glum [glʌm] <glummer, glummest> adj 1.(morose, downcast) taciturno, -a; to be/feel ~ (about sth) ser/sentirse meláncolico (por algo) 2.(drab) monótono, -a

glut [glʌt] I. n ECON exceso m de oferta; a ~ of sth una superabundancia de algo II.<-tt-> vt ECON inundar

gluten ['glu:tən] n no pl gluten m

glutinous ['glu:tɪnəs, Am: -tnəs] adj glutinoso, -a

glutton [glʌtn] n 1.(overeater) glotón, -ona m, f 2.inf (enthusiast) entusiasta mf

gluttonous ['glʌtənəs] adj glotón, -ona, angurriento, -a AmL

gluttony ['glʌtəni] n no pl glotonería f

glycerin ['glɪsərɪn] *n Am,* **glycerine** ['glɪsəri:n] *n Brit, Aus,* **glycerol** ['glɪsərɒl, *Am:* -rɑ:l] *n no pl* glicerina *f*

glycol ['glaɪkɒl, *Am:* -kɑ:l] *n no pl* glicol *m*

GMT [ˌdʒi:em'ti:] *abbr of* Greenwich Mean Time hora *f* de Greenwich

gnarled [nɑ:ld, *Am:* nɑ:rld] *adj (knobby and twisted)* retorcido, -a; *(knotted)* nudoso, -a

gnash [næʃ] *vt* hacer rechinar; **to ~ one's teeth about sth** rechinar los dientes por algo

gnat [næt] *n* BIO mosquito *m,* jején *m AmS*

gnaw [nɔ:, *Am:* nɑ:] **I.** *vi* **1.** *(chew)* **to ~ at** [*o* on] sth roer algo **2.** *fig (deplete)* reducir; **to ~ away at sth** agotar algo **3.** *(bother)* molestar; **to ~ at sb** molestar a alguien **II.** *vt* **1.** *(chew)* roer **2.** *fig (pursue)* **to be ~ed by doubt/fear/guilt** ser asaltado por las dudas/el miedo/el sentimiento de culpa

◆**gnaw away** *vt* roer

gnawing I. *adj* persistente; *(pain)* punzante; *(doubt)* que atormenta **II.** *n no pl* roedura *f; (stomach)* retortijón *m*

gneiss [naɪs] *n no pl* GEO gneis *m*

gnome [nəʊm, *Am:* noʊm] *n* gnomo *m*

GNP [ˌdʒi:en'pi:] *no pl abbr of* Gross National Product PNB

gnu [nu:] <-(s)> *n* BIO ñu *m*

go [gəʊ, *Am:* goʊ] **I.**<went, gone> *vi* **1.** *(proceed)* ir; **to ~ (and) do sth** ir a hacer algo; **to ~ home** irse a casa **2.** *(travel)* viajar; **to ~ on a cruise** ir de crucero; **to ~ on holiday** irse de vacaciones; **to ~ on a trip** ir de viaje **3.** *(adopt position)* **when I ~ like this, my back hurts** cuando hago esto, me duele la espalda **4.** *(leave)* marcharse; **to have to ~** tener que irse; **when does the bus ~?** ¿a qué hora sale el autobús? **5.** *(do)* hacer; **to ~ biking** salir en bicicleta; **to ~ camping/fishing/shopping** ir de camping/pesca/compras; **to ~ jogging** hacer footing; **to ~ swimming** ir a nadar **6.** *(attend)* asistir; **to ~ to a concert** ir a un concierto; **to ~ to a movie** ir a ver una película; **to ~ to a party** ir a una fiesta **7.** + *adj or n (become)* volverse; **to ~ senile** volverse viejo; **to ~ bankrupt** caer en bancarrota; **to ~ public** hacerse público; **to ~ communist** volverse comunista; **to ~ adrift** fallar; *(be stolen)* ser robado; **to ~ bald** quedarse calvo; **to ~ haywire** volverse loco; **to ~ missing** *Aus, Brit* desaparecer; **to ~ to sleep** dormirse; **to ~ wrong** salir mal **8.** + *adj (exist)* **to ~ hungry/thirsty** pasar hambre/sed; **to ~ unmentioned/unsolved** no ser mencionado/no solucionarse; **to ~ unnoticed** pasar desapercibido; **as prices ~ ...** considerando los precios actuales... **9.** *(happen)* **to ~ badly/well** ir mal/bien; **to ~ from bad to worse** ir de mal en peor; **the way things are ~ing** tal como van las cosas **10.** *(pass)* pasar; **time seems to ~ faster as you get older** parece que pasa el tiempo más rápido a medida que envejeces **11.** *(begin)* empezar; **ready, steady, ~** preparados, listos, ya **12.** *(fail)* **to ~ downhill** ir

de capa caída **13.** *(belong)* pertenecer; **I'll put it where it ~es** lo pondré en su sitio **14.** *(fit)* quedar bien; **that old picture would ~ well on that wall** ese viejo cuadro quedaría bien en aquella pared; **two ~es into eight four times** MAT ocho entre dos da cuatro **15.** *(lead)* conducir; **this road ~es to Barcelona** esta carretera lleva a Barcelona **16.** *(extend)* extenderse; **those numbers ~ from 1 to 10** esos números van del 1 al 10 **17.** *(function)* funcionar; **to ~ slow** ir despacio; **to get sth to ~** hacer que algo funcione; **to keep a conversation ~ing** mantener una conversación **18.** *(be sold)* venderse; **the painting went for a lot more than was expected** el cuadro se vendió mucho más caro de lo esperado; **to ~ for £50** venderse por 50 libras; **to ~ like hot cakes** *fig* venderse como rosquillas **19.** *(contribute)* contribuir; **love and friendship ~ to make a lasting relationship** el amor y la amistad contribuyen a hacer duradera una relación **20.** *(sound)* sonar; **the ambulance had sirens ~ing** la ambulancia hacía sonar las sirenas **21.** *(be told)* **as the saying ~es** como dice el refrán; **the text ~es that ...** reza el texto que... **22.** GAMES tocar; **I ~ now** ahora me toca a mí **23.** *inf (use the toilet)* **do any of the kids have to ~?** ¿alguno de los niños tiene que ir al lavabo? **24.** *(express annoyance)* **~ jump in a lake!** *inf* ¡vete a freír espárragos! ▶**what he says ~es** lo que él dice va a misa; **anything ~es** cualquier cosa vale; **here ~!** ¡vamos a ver! **II.**<went, gone> *vt* **1.** *(travel)* **to ~ it some** *inf* ir a toda pastilla **2.** *inf (say)* decir; **ducks ~ 'quack'** los patos hacen 'cuac' **3.** *(bid)* apostar; **to ~ nap** *Brit* jugárselo todo **4.** *(make)* hacer; **to ~ it alone** hacerlo solo; **to ~ it** *inf* correrla; *(work)* darle duro **III.**<-es> *n* **1.** *(turn)* turno *m;* **I'll have a ~ at driving if you're tired** ahora conduciré yo si estás cansado; **it's my ~** me toca a mí **2.** *(attempt)* intento *m;* **all in one ~** todo de un tirón; **to have a ~ at sth** intentar algo; **to have a ~ at sb about sth** tomarla con alguien por algo **3.** *(a success)* éxito *m;* **to be no ~** ser imposible; **to make a ~ of sth** tener éxito en algo **4.** *(energy)* energía *f;* **she's full of ~ today** hoy está pletórica de energía **5.** *(activity)* actividad *f;* **to be on the ~** trajinar; **to keep sb on the ~** hacer que alguien siga trabajando **6.** *inf (business)* asunto *m;* **a rum ~** un asunto extraño **7.** MED caso *m* ▶**from the word ~** desde el principio **IV.** *adj* AVIAT listo, -a

◆**go about I.** *vt insep* **1.** *(proceed with)* ocuparse de; **to ~ one's business** ocuparse de sus asuntos **2.** *(perform a task)* llevar a cabo **II.** *vi* andar (de un sitio para otro)

◆**go abroad** *vi* **1.** *(rumour)* correr **2.** *(travel)* viajar al extranjero

◆**go after** *vt insep* **1.** *(follow)* seguir; **to ~ sb** ir detrás de alguien **2.** *(chase)* perseguir **3.** *(try to get)* intentar conseguir

◆**go against** *vt insep* **1.** *(contradict)*

contradecir 2.(*oppose*) ir en contra de, oponerse a 3.(*disobey*) desobedecer a

◆**go ahead** *vi* 1.(*begin*) empezar 2.(*go before*) ir adelante 3.(*proceed*) seguir adelante; ~! ¡sigue!; **all preparations have finished but they can't** ~ todos los preparativos están listos pero no pueden sacarlo adelante

◆**go along** *vi* 1.(*move onward*) ir hacia delante 2.(*proceed*) proceder a

◆**go around** *vi* 1.(*move around*) andar (de un lado para otro) 2.(*move in a curve*) girar 3.(*visit*) **to** ~ **to sb's** visitar a alguien; **to** ~ **and see sb** ir a ver a alguien 4.(*rotate*) rotar 5.(*be in circulation*) estar circulando; **it's going around that …** se dice que…

◆**go at** *vt insep* 1.(*attack*) acometer, lanzarse sobre 2.(*work hard*) **to** ~ **it** trabajar mucho

◆**go away** *vi* 1.(*travel*) viajar 2.(*leave*) marcharse 3.(*disappear*) desaparecer

◆**go back** *vi* 1.(*move backwards*) retroceder 2.(*return*) volver, regresarse *AmL* 3.(*date back*) remontarse

◆**go between** *vi* interponerse

◆**go beyond** *vt* 1.(*proceed past*) sobrepasar 2.(*exceed*) superar

◆**go by** *vi* 1.(*move past*) pasar (junto a) 2.(*pass*) transcurrir; **in days gone by** *form* en tiempos pasados; **to let sth** ~ no aprovechar algo 3.(*be guided by*) guiarse por

◆**go down** I. *vt insep* bajar, descender; **to** ~ **a mine** MIN bajar a una mina II. *vi* 1.(*set*) ponerse; (*ship*) hundirse; (*plane*) estrellarse; **to** ~ **on all fours** ponerse a gatas 2.(*collapse*) derrumbarse 3.(*decrease*) disminuir; FIN ir a la baja 4.(*decrease in quality*) empeorar; **to** ~ **in sb's estimation** bajar en la estima de alguien 5.(*decrease in size*) empequeñecer 6.(*break down*) estropearse 7.(*lose*) perder; **to** ~ **to sb/sth** ser derrotado por alguien/algo; SPORTS perder frente a alguien/algo; **to** ~ **without a fight** rendirse sin luchar 8.(*proceed*) proceder; *Brit* (*visit quickly*) hacer una visita rápida 9.(*travel southward*) ir hacia el sur 10.(*extend*) extenderse 11.(*be received*) ser recibido; **to** ~ **well/badly** (**with sb**) ser bien/mal recibido (por alguien) 12.(*be recorded*) quedar registrado; **to** ~ **in writing** quedar registrado por escrito 13.*Brit* UNIV acabar la universidad

◆**go far** *vi* 1.(*have success*) llegar lejos 2.(*contribute*) **to** ~ **towards sth** contribuir de forma significativa a algo; **not to** ~ no estirarse

◆**go for** *vt insep* 1.(*fetch*) ir a por, ir a buscar; **could you** ~ **oranges?** ¿puedes ir a buscar naranjas? 2.(*try to achieve*) intentar conseguir; (*try to grasp*) intentar alcanzar; ~ **it!** ¡a por ello! 3.(*choose*) elegir 4.(*attack*) atacar; **to** ~ **sb with sth** atacar a alguien con algo 5.(*sell for*) venderse por 6.*inf* (*like*) gustar; (*believe*) creer en

◆**go in** *vi* 1.(*enter*) entrar; (*go to work*) empezar a trabajar 2.(*belong in*) ir en; **those forks** ~ **the drawer** esos tenedores van en el

cajón 3.(*go behind a cloud*) esconderse 4.*inf* (*be understood*) ser entendido

◆**go into** *vt insep* 1.(*enter*) entrar en 2.(*fit into*) encajar en; **does two** ~ **six?** ¿seis es divisible por dos? 3.(*begin*) empezar; **to** ~ **a coma** MED entrar en coma; **to** ~ **a trance** entrar en trance; **to** ~ **action** pasar a la acción; **to** ~ **effect** entrar en vigor 4.(*begin*) **to** ~ **politics** dedicarse a la política; **to** ~ **production** empezar a producirse 5.(*examine and discuss*) examinar; **to** ~ **detail** entrar en detalles 6.(*be used in*) ser utilizado en 7.(*join*) unirse; **to** ~ **a group/an organization** unirse a un grupo/una organización 8.(*crash into*) dar de lleno contra

◆**go off** *vi* 1.(*leave*) irse; (*disappear*) desaparecer 2.(*spoil*) estropearse 3.(*ring*) dispararse 4.(*explode*) estallar 5.*Brit, Aus* (*decrease in quality*) perder calidad; (*diminish*) disminuir; GASTR (*rot*) pasarse 6.(*stop liking*) dejar de gustar 7.(*happen*) pasar; **to** ~ **badly/well** salir mal/bien 8.(*digress*) salirse; **to** ~ **the subject** salirse del tema 9.(*fall asleep*) quedarse dormido

◆**go on** I. *vi* 1.(*move on*) seguir su camino, seguir adelante 2.(*continue*) seguir; (*continue speaking*) seguir hablando 3.(*go further*) ir más allá; **to** ~ **ahead** seguir adelante 4.(*extend*) extenderse 5.(*pass*) pasar 6.(*happen*) suceder 7.(*start*) empezar; (*begin functioning*) empezar a funcionar; THEAT, MUS salir (a escena) II. *vt insep* basarse en III. *interj* (*as encouragement*) vamos; (*express disbelief*) anda ya

◆**go out** *vi* 1.(*leave*) salir; **to** ~ **to dinner** salir a cenar; **to** ~ **with sb** salir con alguien 2.(*stop working*) dejar de funcionar; (*light*) apagarse 3.RADIO, TV ser emitido 4.(*recede*) retirarse 5.(*become unfashionable*) pasar de moda

◆**go over** I. *vt insep* 1.(*examine*) examinar 2.(*cross*) atravesar; **to** ~ **a mountain** subir y bajar una montaña; **to** ~ **a border/river/street** cruzar una frontera/un río/una calle 3.(*exceed*) exceder; **to** ~ **a budget/limit** exceder un presupuesto/límite 4.(*attack*) atacar brutalmente II. *vi* **to** ~ **to** (*visit*) visitar a; (*change party*) pasarse a

◆**go through** *vt insep* 1.(*pass*) pasar por 2.(*experience*) experimentar; (*operation*) sufrir 3.(*practice, perform*) practicar; (*review, discuss*) repasar 4.(*be approved*) ser aprobado 5.(*use up*) gastar 6.(*look through*) examinar 7.(*wear through*) gastar

◆**go to** *vt insep* visitar; **to** ~ **the country** ir a elecciones generales; **to** ~ **court** acudir a los tribunales; **to** ~ **expense** gastar

◆**go together** *vi* 1.(*harmonize*) **to** ~ (**with sth**) armonizar (con algo) 2.(*go with*) ir juntos

◆**go under** *vi* 1.NAUT (*sink*) hundirse 2.(*move below*) ir por debajo de 3.(*fail*) fracasar; (*be defeated*) ser derrotado 4.(*be known by*) ser conocido como

◆**go up** *vi* **1.**(*move higher*) subir **2.**(*increase*) aumentar; FIN, ECON ascender **3.**(*approach*) **to ~ to sb/sth** acercarse a alguien/algo **4.**(*travel*) subir, viajar hacia el norte; **to ~ to London** ir a Londres **5.**(*be built*) ser construido **6.**(*burn up*) arder; **to ~ in flames** arder en llamas **7.** Brit UNIV (*begin*) entrar en la universidad; (*return*) volver a la universidad

◆**go with** *vt insep* **1.**(*accompany*) acompañar a **2.**(*harmonize*) armonizar con, hacer juego con **3.**(*agree with*) estar de acuerdo en; **to ~ sb on sth** coincidir con alguien en algo **4.**(*follow*) seguir **5.**(*date*) salir con

◆**go without** *vt insep* pasar sin, prescindir de

goad [gəʊd, *Am:* goʊd] **I.** *vt* **1.**(*spur*) incitar; (*curiosity*) despertar **2.**(*tease*) fastidiar **II.** *n* **1.**(*motivating factor*) estímulo *m* **2.** AGR aguijada *f*

go-ahead ['gəʊəhed, *Am:* 'goʊ-] **I.** *n no pl* (*permission*) luz *f* verde; **to give/receive the ~** dar/recibir luz verde **II.** *adj* Aus, Brit emprendedor(a)

goal [gəʊl, *Am:* goʊl] *n* **1.**(*aim*) objetivo *m*, meta *f*; **to achieve a ~** conseguir un objetivo; **to pursue a ~** perseguir un fin; **to set a ~** fijar un objetivo **2.** SPORTS (*scoring area*) portería *f*; **to keep ~** defender la portería; **to play in ~** Brit ser portero **3.** SPORTS (*point*) gol *m*; **to score a ~** marcar un gol; **a penalty ~** un gol de penalty

goalie ['gəʊli, *Am:* 'goʊ-] *n inf*, **goalkeeper** ['gəʊl‚ki:pəʳ, *Am:* 'goʊl‚ki:pɚ] *n* SPORTS portero, -a *m, f*

goal line *n* SPORTS línea *f* de la portería **goalpost** *n* SPORTS poste *m* de la portería ►**to move the ~s** *inf* cambiar las reglas del juego

goat [gəʊt, *Am:* goʊt] *n* **1.** ZOOL cabra *f*; **~'s milk** leche *f* de cabra; **~'s cheese** queso *m* de cabra; **mountain ~** cabra montesa; **to act the ~** Brit, *inf* hacer el imbécil **2.** *inf* (*man*) viejo *m* verde ►**to separate the sheep from the ~s** separar el grano de la paja; **to get sb's ~** sacar de quicio a alguien

goatee [gəʊ'ti:, *Am:* goʊ-] *n* perilla *f*

gobble ['gɒbl, *Am:* 'ga:bl] **I.** *vi* **1.** *inf* (*eat*) jalar **2.**(*make turkey noise*) gluglutear **II.** *vt inf* jalar **III.** *n* gluglú *m*

gobbledegook, **gobbledygook** ['gɒbldi‚gu:k, *Am:* 'ga:bl-] *n no pl, inf* galimatías *m; inv*

go-between ['gəʊbɪtwi:n, *Am:* 'goʊbə-] *n* medianero, -a *m, f*; **to act as a ~** hacer de intermediario

goblet ['gɒblɪt, *Am:* 'ga:blət] *n* cáliz *m*

goblin ['gɒblɪn, *Am:* 'ga:blɪn] *n* duende *m*

go-cart ['gəʊka:t, *Am:* 'goʊka:rt] *n Am* AUTO, SPORTS kart *m*

god [gɒd, *Am:* ga:d] *n* **1.** REL **God** Dios; **God bless** que Dios te/le... bendiga; **God forbid** no lo permita Dios; **God knows** quien sabe; **please God!** ¡Dios lo quiera!; **for God's sake!**

¡por el amor de Dios! **2.** REL **Greek/Roman ~s** dioses *mpl* griegos/romanos **3.**(*idolized person*) ídolo *m*

god-awful ['gɒd'ɔ:fəl, *Am:* ‚ga:d'ɑ:-] *adj inf* horrible **godchild** *n* ahijado, -a *m, f* **goddam(ned)** *adj inf* maldito, -a **goddaughter** *n* ahijada *f*

goddess ['gɒdɪs, *Am:* 'ga:dɪs] <-es> *n* **1.** REL diosa *f* **2.**(*idolized woman*) ídolo *m*

godfather ['gɒd‚fa:ðəʳ, *Am:* 'ga:d‚fa:ðɚ] *n* padrino *m* **god-fearing** *adj* temeroso, -a de Dios **god-forsaken** *adj* dejado, -a de la mano de Dios **godhead** *n*, **Godhead** ['gɒdhed, *Am:* 'ga:d-] *n no pl* divinidad *f*

godless ['gɒdlɪs, *Am:* 'ga:d-] *adj* **1.** REL impío, -a; (*without God*) sin Dios **2.**(*evil*) demoníaco, -a

godlike ['gɒdlaɪk, *Am:* 'ga:d-] *adj* divino, -a

godly ['gɒdli, *Am:* 'ga:d-] *adj* piadoso, -a; **to lead a ~ life** llevar una vida piadosa

godmother ['gɒd‚mʌðəʳ, *Am:* 'ga:d‚mʌðɚ] *n* madrina *f* **godparents** *npl* padrinos *mpl* **godsend** *n inf* cosa *f* llovida del cielo; **to be a ~ (to sb)** ser un regalo celestial (para alguien)

godson *n* ahijado *m*

goer ['gəʊəʳ, *Am:* 'goʊɚ] *n* **1.** *inf* (*party person*) juergista *mf*; (*promiscuous person*) calentón, -ona *m, f vulg* **2.** ECON proyecto *m* viable

goes [gəʊz, *Am:* goʊz] *3rd pers sing of* **go**

go-getter [‚gəʊ'getəʳ] *n* persona *f* emprendedora

go-getting [‚gəʊ'getɪŋ] *adj* emprendedor(a)

goggle ['gɒgl, *Am:* 'ga:gl] **I.** *vi inf* **to ~ at sb/sth** mirar con ojos desorbitados a alguien/algo **II.** *n pl* (*glasses*) gafas *fpl*; **safety ~s** gafas de protección; **ski/swim ~s** gafas de esquiar/natación

goggle-box ['gɒglbɒks, *Am:* 'ga:glba:ks] <-es> *n Brit, inf* caja *f* boba

goggle-eyed ['gɒglaɪd, *Am:* 'ga:gl-] *adj inf* con ojos desorbitados; (*person*) con [*o* de] ojos saltones

go-go dancer ['gəʊgəʊ'da:nsəʳ, *Am:* 'goʊgoʊ'dænsɚ] *n* gogó *mf*

go-go dancing *n no pl* baile *m* de gogós

going ['gəʊɪŋ, *Am:* 'goʊ-] **I.** *n* **1.**(*act of leaving*) ida *f*; (*departure*) salida *f* **2.**(*conditions*) **easy/rough ~** condiciones *fpl* favorables/adversas; **while the ~ is good** mientras las condiciones lo permitan **3.**(*progress*) progreso *m* ►**when the ~ gets tough** (**the tough get ~**) cuando las cosas se ponen feas (los fuertes entran en acción) **II.** *adj* **1.**(*available*) disponible **2.**(*in action*) en funcionamiento; **to get sth ~** poner algo en funcionamiento **3.**(*current*) actual **III.** *vi aux* **to be ~ to do sth** ir a hacer algo

going price *n* **1.**(*market price*) precio *m* de mercado **2.**(*current price*) precio *m* actual

goings-on [‚gəʊɪŋz'ɒn, *Am:* ‚goʊɪŋz'a:n] *npl* **1.**(*events*) sucesos *mpl* **2.**(*activities*) tejemanejes *mpl*

goiter n Am, **goitre** ['gɔɪtər, Am: -t̬ə·] n Brit, Aus no pl MED bocio m

go-kart ['gəʊkɑːt, Am: 'goʊkɑːrt] n Brit, Aus AUTO, SPORTS kart m

gold [gəʊld, Am: goʊld] I. n no pl 1. (metal) oro m; **to pan for ~** lavar oro; **to strike ~** encontrar oro; **to be dripping with ~** fig llevar puestas muchas joyas de oro 2. SPORTS medalla f de oro ▶**to be worth one's weight in ~** valer su peso en oro; **to be good as ~** portarse como un ángel; **all that glitters is not ~** prov no es oro todo lo que reluce prov II. adj de oro; **a ~ ring** un anillo de oro

gold brick I. n inf 1. (sham) estafa f 2. Am (person) gandul(a) m(f) II. vt estafar III. vi Am escurrir el bulto **gold bullion** n no pl oro m en lingotes **gold coin** n moneda f de oro **gold content** n no pl contenido m de oro **gold digger** n 1. (gold miner) buscador(a) m(f) de oro 2. (money-seeker) cazafortunas mf inv **gold dust** n no pl oro m en polvo; **to be like ~** fig ser muy cotizado

golden ['gəʊldən, Am: 'goʊl-] adj 1. de oro; **~ anniversary** bodas fpl de oro 2. (colour) dorado, -a; **~ brown** tostado, -a; (skin) bronceado, -a 3. (very good) excelente; **~ oldies** MUS melodías fpl de ayer; iron viejas cantinelas fpl

golden age n edad f de oro **golden goose** n gallina f de los huevos de oro **golden mean** n no pl justo medio m **golden triangle** n no pl **the ~** el Triángulo Dorado **golden wedding** n bodas fpl de oro

goldfinch ['gəʊldfɪntʃ, Am: 'goʊld-] <-es> n jilguero m **goldfish** n inv pez m de colores **gold foil** n no pl lámina f de oro **gold leaf** n no pl hoja f de oro **gold medal** n SPORTS medalla f de oro **goldmine** n 1. (mine) mina f de oro 2. FIN filón m **gold nugget** n pepita f de oro **gold plating** n no pl 1. (layer) baño m de oro 2. (production process) chapado m de oro **gold reserve** n reserva f de oro **goldsmith** n orfebre m **gold standard** n FIN patrón m oro

golf [gɒlf, Am: gɑːlf] I. n no pl golf m; **to play ~** jugar al golf; **crazy ~** minigolf m II. vi jugar al golf

golf ball n pelota f de golf **golf-ball typewriter** n máquina f de escribir a bola

golf club n 1. (stick) palo m de golf 2. (sports association) club m de golf **golf course** n campo m de golf

golfer ['gɒlfər, Am: 'gɑːlfə·] n golfista mf **golf links** npl campo m de golf

Goliath [gə'laɪəθ] n Goliat m; **a David and ~ battle** fig una batalla entre David y Goliat

golliwog n, **gollywog** ['gɒlɪwɒg, Am: 'gɑːlɪwɔːg] n Brit, Aus: muñeco negro de trapo; la expresión en inglés puede considerarse ofensiva

golly ['gɒli, Am: 'gɑːli] interj inf caramba; **by ~** ¡vaya!

goloshes [gə'lɒʃɪz, Am: -'lɑːʃ-] npl chanclos mpl; **rubber ~** chanclos de goma

gondola ['gɒndələ, Am: 'gɑːn-] n góndola f

gondolier [ˌgɒndə'lɪər, Am: ˌgɑːndə'lɪr] n gondolero, -a m, f

gone [gɒn, Am: gɑːn] I. pp of **go** II. prep Brit después de III. adj 1. (no longer there) ausente 2. (dead) muerto, -a 3. inf (pregnant) embarazada 4. inf (absorbed) ido, -a 5. inf (infatuated) **to be ~ on sb** estar loco, -a por alguien

goner ['gɒnər, Am: 'gɑːnə·] n **to be a ~** (bound to die) ser hombre muerto; (broken) estar para tirar

gong [gɒn, Am: gɑːn] n 1. (flat bell) gong m 2. Brit, Aus, inf (an award) medalla f; **to win a ~** (for sth) ganar una condecoración (por algo)

gonorrh(o)ea [ˌgɒnə'rɪə, Am: ˌgɑːnə'-] n no pl gonorrea f

goo [guː] n no pl 1. inf (substance) sustancia f viscosa 2. (sentimentality) sentimentalismo m

good [gʊd] I. <better, best> adj 1. (of high quality) bueno, -a; **~ buena vista**; **~ thinking!** ¡buena idea!; **to be a ~ catch** ser un buen partido; **to do a ~ job** hacer un buen trabajo; **to have the ~ sense to do sth** tener el sentido común para hacer algo; **to be in ~ shape** estar en buena forma; **to be/to be not ~ enough** ser/no ser lo suficientemente bueno 2. (skilled) capacitado, -a; **to be ~ at** [o in] **sth/doing sth** estar capacitado para algo/hacer algo; **to be ~ at sth** dársele bien algo; **to be ~ with one's hands** ser bueno con las manos 3. (pleasant) placentero, -a; **to have a ~ day/evening** tener un buen día/pasar una velada placentera; **to have a ~ time** pasar(se)lo bien 4. (appealing to senses) **to feel ~** sentirse bien; **to have ~ looks** ser guapo; **to look ~** tener buen aspecto; **to smell ~** oler bien 5. (favourable) **the ~ life** la buena vida; **~ luck** (**in sth**) buena suerte (en algo); **a ~ omen** un buen presagio; **~ times** buenos tiempos; **to be a ~ thing** [o **job** Brit] **that ...** ser bueno que... +subj; **to be too ~ to be true** ser demasiado bueno/sonar demasiado bien para ser verdad 6. (beneficial) beneficioso, -a; **a ~ habit** una buena costumbre; **to be ~ for sb/sth** ser bueno para alguien/algo; **to be ~ for business** ser bueno para el negocio 7. (useful) útil 8. (appropriate) adecuado, -a; (choice, decision) correcto, -a; **to be in a ~ position to do sth** estar en buena posición para hacer algo; **a ~ time to do sth** un buen momento para hacer algo 9. (kind) amable; **~ deeds/works** buenas obras 10. (moral) **the Good Book** la Biblia; **a ~ name/reputation** un buen nombre/una buena reputación; **to be ~ as one's word** cumplir su palabra 11. (well-behaved) de buenos modales; **a ~ loser** un buen perdedor; **to be on ~ behaviour** comportarse bien 12. (thorough) completo, -a; **a ~ beating** una paliza 13. (valid) válido, -a; (not forged) auténtico, -a; (useable) útil, provechoso, -a; **to**

make sth ~ (*pay for*) pagar por algo; (*do successfully*) cumplir algo; **to be ~ for nothing** ser completamente inútil **14.** (*substantial*) sustancial; **a ~ few/many** unos pocos/ muchos **15.** GASTR en su punto **16.** (*almost, virtually*) **it's as ~ as done** está prácticamente terminado; **to be as ~ as new** estar como nuevo **17.** (*said to emphasize*) **to be ~ and ready** estar listo **18.** (*said to express affection*) **the ~ old days** los buenos tiempos ▶**to give as ~ as one gets** devolver golpe por golpe **II.** *n no pl* **1.** (*moral force, not evil*) bien *m;* **to be no ~** ser inútil; **to be up to no ~** estar tramando algo **2.** (*profit, benefit*) beneficio *m;* **this soup will do you ~** esta sopa te sentará bien; **for one's own ~** en beneficio propio; **to do ~** hacer bien; **to do more harm than ~** hacer más daño que bien; **to be not much ~** no valer mucho **3.** *pl* (*moral people*) **the ~** la gente buena ▶**for ~** definitivamente **III.** *adv* **1.** *dial, inf* (*well*) bien **2.** (*thoroughly*) totalmente **IV.** *interj* **1.** (*to express approval*) bien **2.** (*to express surprise, shock*) **~ God!** ¡Dios mío!; **~ gracious!** ¡Dios mío!; **~ grief!** ¡madre mía! **3.** (*said as greeting*) **~ afternoon, ~ evening** buenas tardes; **~ morning** buenos días; **~ night** buenas noches **4.** *Brit* (*said to accept order*) **very ~** entendido

goodbye, goodby *Am* **I.** *interj* adiós **II.** *n* **1.** (*departing word*) adiós *m;* **to say ~** (**to sb**) decir adiós (a alguien); **to say ~** despedirse **2.** *inf* (*loss*) **to say ~ to sth** olvidarse definitivamente de algo; **to kiss sth ~** despedirse de algo

good-for-nothing ['gʊdfə‚nʌθɪŋ, *Am:* -fɚ‚-] **I.** *n* inútil *mf* **II.** *adj* inútil
Good Friday *n* Viernes *m* Santo
good-humoured, good-humored [‚gʊd-'hjuːməd, *Am:* -məˑd] *adj Am* afable
good-looking [‚gʊd'lʊkɪŋ] <better-looking, best-looking> *adj* guapo, -a
good looks *n no pl* buen parecer *m*
goodly ['gʊdli] <-ier, -iest> *adj* agradable
good-natured <better-natured, best-natured> *adj* **1.** (*pleasant*) afable **2.** (*inherently good*) bonachón, -ona
goodness ['gʊdnɪs] **I.** *n no pl* **1.** (*moral virtue*) bondad *f* **2.** (*kindness*) amabilidad *f* **3.** (*quality*) buena calidad *f* **4.** (*said for emphasis*) **~ knows** quién sabe; **for ~' sake** ¡por Dios!; **thank ~!** ¡gracias a Dios!; **to wish** [*o* to hope] **to ~** ojalá Dios quiera **II.** *interj* **~ gracious** (**me**)! ¡Dios mío!; (*surprise*) ¡Dios mío!; (*annoyance*) ¡vaya por Dios!
goods [gʊdz] *npl* **1.** (*freight*) mercancías *fpl;* **~ lorry** camión *m* de carga; **~ depot** depósito *m* de mercancías **2.** (*wares*) productos *mpl;* **manufactured ~** bienes *mpl* elaborados **3.** (*personal belongings*) pertenencias *fpl;* **~ and chattels** bienes *mpl* muebles **4.** (*desired things*) artículos *mpl* pedidos; **to deliver the ~** entregar la mercancía; *fig* dar la talla

good-sized [‚gʊd'saɪzd] <better-sized, best-sized> *adj* bastante grande
goods station *n* RAIL estación *f* de mercancías **goods traffic** *n no pl* tránsito *m* de mercancías **goods train** *n Brit* tren *m* de mercancías
good-tempered [‚gʊd'tempəd, *Am:* -pɚd] <better-tempered, best-tempered> *adj irr* afable
goodwill [‚gʊd'wɪl] *n no pl* buena voluntad *f;* **~ towards sb** buenas intenciones con alguien; **a gesture of ~** un gesto de buena voluntad
goody ['gʊdi] **I.** <-ies> *n* **1.** *childspeak* GASTR golosina *f* **2.** THEAT, CINE bueno, -a *m, f;* **the goodies** los buenos **II.** *interj childspeak* qué bien
gooey ['guːi] <gooier, gooiest> *adj* (*sticky*) pegajoso, -a; GASTR empalagoso, -a
goof [guːf] **I.** *vi inf* pifiarla **II.** *n inf* **1.** (*mistake*) error *m* **2.** (*silly person*) bobo, -a *m, f*
♦**goof up** *vt inf* fastidiar
goofy ['guːfi] <-ier, -iest> *adj Am, inf* bobo, -a
goolies ['guːliːz] *npl Brit, inf* cataplines *mpl*
goon [guːn] *n inf* **1.** (*stupid person*) imbécil *mf* **2.** *Am* gángster *m* a sueldo
goose [guːs] <geese> *n* ganso, -a *m, f* ▶**to kill the ~ that lays the golden eggs** matar la gallina de los huevos de oro; **to cook someone's ~** *inf* hacer la pascua a alguien; **to not say boo to a ~** *pej* no decir ni mu
gooseberry ['gʊzbəri, *Am:* 'guːsberi] <-ies> *n* grosella *f* espinosa ▶**to play ~** *Brit, inf* hacer de carabina **goose-flesh** *n no pl,* **goose-pimples** *npl* carne *f* de gallina **goose-pimply** *adj inf* **to go** [*o* get] (**all**) **~** ponerse a una la carne de gallina **goosestep** **I.** <-pp-> *vi* marchar a paso de oca **II.** *n no pl* paso *m* de oca
goos(e)y ['guːsi] <-ier, -iest> *adj Aus* s. **goose-pimply**
gore¹ [gɔːr, *Am:* gɔːr] *n* sangre *f* derramada
gore² [gɔːr, *Am:* gɔːr] *vt* cornear
gore³ [gɔːr, *Am:* gɔːr] *n* (*clothing*) godet *m*
gorge [gɔːdʒ, *Am:* gɔːrdʒ] **I.** *n* **1.** GEO cañón *m* **2.** ANAT garganta *f;* **my ~ rises** me da asco **3.** *inf* (*large feast*) banquete *m* **II.** *vi* engullir **III.** *vt* **~ oneself on sth** atracarse de algo
gorgeous ['gɔːdʒəs, *Am:* 'gɔːr-] **I.** *adj* **1.** (*beautiful*) precioso, -a **2.** (*pleasurable*) maravilloso, -a **II.** *n* **hello ~!** ¡hola ricura!
gorilla [gə'rɪlə] *n* gorila *m*
gormless ['gɔːmlɪs, *Am:* 'gɔːrm-] *adj Brit, inf* idiota
gorse [gɔːs, *Am:* gɔːrs] *n no pl* aulaga *f*
gory ['gɔːri] <-ier, -iest> *adj* sangriento, -a
gosh [gɒʃ, *Am:* gɑːʃ] *interj inf* dios mío
gosling ['gɒzlɪŋ, *Am:* 'gɑːz-] *n* ansarino *m*
go-slow [‚gəʊsləʊ, *Am:* 'gəʊsloʊ] *n Brit* huelga *f* de celo
gospel ['gɒspl, *Am:* 'gɑːs-] *n* **1.** REL evangelio *m;* **to spread/preach the ~** extender/predicar el evangelio; **~ singer** cantante *mf* de gos-

pel **2.** (*principle*) principio *m*

gossamer ['gɒsəmə', *Am:* 'gɑːsəmə·] **I.** *n* hilo *m* de telaraña **II.** *adj* sutil

gossip ['gɒsɪp, *Am:* 'gɑːsəp] **I.** *n* **1.** *no pl* (*rumour*) chismorreo *m;* **idle** ~ rumor *m* infundado; **the latest** ~ los últimos chismes; ~ **columnist** periodista *mf* de prensa rosa **2.** (*person*) chismoso, -a *m, f* **3.** (*conversation*) cotilleo *m;* **to have a** ~ **about sb** cotillear sobre alguien **II.** *vi* **1.** (*spread rumors*) chismorrear; **to** ~ **about sb** cotillear acerca de alguien **2.** (*chatter*) contar chismes

gossip column *n* columna *f* de cotilleo

gossipy ['gɒsɪpi, *Am:* 'gɑːsəp-] *adj* **1.** (*rumour-spreading*) chismoso, -a, lengún, -ona *AmL* **2.** (*containing gossip*) de cotilleo

got [gɒt, *Am:* gɑːt] *pt, Brit: pp of* **get**

Gothic ['gɒθɪk, *Am:* 'gɑːθɪk] **I.** *adj* **1.** ARCHIT, LIT gótico, -a; ~ **architecture** arquitectura *f* gótica **2.** (*of Goths*) godo, -a **3.** TYPO ~ **script** escritura *f* gótica **II.** *n no pl* **1.** LING gótico *m* **2.** TYPO letra *f* gótica

gotten ['gɒtən, *Am:* 'gɑːtən] *Am, Aus pp of* **get**

gouge [gaʊdʒ] **I.** *vt* **1.** (*pierce*) excavar; **to** ~ **a hole into sth** hacer un agujero en algo **2.** *Am, inf* (*overcharge*) cobrar de más **II.** *n* gubia *f*

goulash ['guːlæʃ, *Am:* -lɑːʃ] *n no pl* puchero *m* (húngaro)

gourd [gʊəd, *Am:* gɔːrd] *n* calabaza *f* (*para beber*)

gourmand ['gʊəmənd, *Am:* 'gʊrmɑːnd] *n* glotón, -ona *m, f*

gourmet ['gʊəmeɪ, *Am:* 'gʊr-] GASTR **I.** *n* gastrónomo, -a *m, f* **II.** *adj* de gastrónomo, -a

gout [gaʊt] *n no pl* gota *f*

Gov. *abbr of* **Governor** gobernador(a) *m(f)*

govern ['gʌvn, *Am:* -ə·n] **I.** *vt* **1.** POL, ADMIN (*country*) gobernar; (*organization*) dirigir **2.** LAW (*regulate*) regular; (*contract*) regir; **to** ~ **how/when/what ...** regular cómo/cuándo/qué... **3.** (*control*) controlar **4.** BIO **to be** ~**ed by sth** ser determinado por algo **5.** LING regir **II.** *vi* POL, ADMIN gobernar; **to be fit/unfit to** ~ tener/no tener las cualidades para gobernar

governess ['gʌvənɪs, *Am:* -ə·nəs] <-es> *n* institutriz *f,* gobernanta *f AmL*

governing *adj* directivo, -a

government ['gʌvənmənt, *Am:* -ə·n-] *n* **1.** (*ruling body*) gobierno *m,* administración *f Arg;* ~ **organization** organización *f* gubernamental; ~ **policy** política *f* estatal; ~ **bond/paper** FIN bono *m*/título *m* del Estado; ~ **securities** FIN valores *mpl* del Estado; **Government House** *Brit* residencia *f* del Gobernador **2.** (*administration*) administración *f;* **to form a** ~ formar gobierno **3.** *no pl* (*governing*) **to be in** ~ *Aus, Brit* estar en el gobierno

governmental [ˌgʌvən'mentəl, *Am:* -ə·n-'mentəl] *adj* gubernamental

governor ['gʌvənə', *Am:* -ə·nə·] *n* **1.** (*of area*) gobernador(a) *m(f)* **2.** *Brit* (*of organiz-*

ation) director(a) *m(f);* **the board of** ~**s** el consejo de dirección **3.** *Brit, inf* (*boss*) jefe *m;* (*father*) viejo *m* **4.** TECH regulador *m*

Govt. *abbr of* **Government** gobno.

gown [gaʊn] *n* **1.** (*evening dress*) traje *m;* **ball** ~ vestido *m* de baile **2.** MED bata *f;* **surgical** ~ bata de cirujano **3.** UNIV toga *f*

GP [ˌdʒiː'piː] *n Brit, Aus abbr of* **general practitioner** médico, -a *m, f* de cabecera

GPO [ˌdʒiː'piːˈəʊ, *Am:* -'oʊ] *n Brit* ADMIN *abbr of* **General Post Office** Administración *f* General de Correos

grab [græb] **I.** *n* **to make a** ~ **for sth** hacerse con algo; **to be up for** ~**s** *inf* estar libre **II.** <-bb-> *vt* **1.** (*snatch*) quitar; **to** ~ **sth (away) from sb** arrebatar algo a alguien; **to** ~ **sth out of sb's hands** quitar algo a alguien de las manos **2.** (*take hold of*) coger, hacerse con; **to** ~ **hold of sth** hacerse con algo **3.** (*arrest*) detener **4.** *inf* (*get, acquire*) conseguir; **to** ~ **some sleep** dormir un rato; **to** ~ **a chance** aprovechar una oportunidad; **to** ~ **sb's attention** captar la atención de alguien; **how does this** ~ **you?** *inf* ¿qué te parece esto? **III.** <-bb-> *vi* **1.** (*snatch*) arrebatar **2.** (*hold on*) asir

grace [greɪs] **I.** *n* **1.** *no pl* (*movement*) elegancia *f,* gracia *f* **2.** *no pl* (*elegant proportions*) elegancia *f* **3.** *no pl* REL gracia *f;* **divine** ~ gracia divina; **by the** ~ **of God** por la gracia de Dios; **to be in a state of** ~ estar en estado de buena esperanza; **the year of** ~ *form* el año de gracia **4.** (*favour*) favor *m;* **to be in/get into sb's good** ~**s** congraciarse con alguien; **to fall from** ~ caer en desgracia **5.** *no pl* (*politeness*) cortesía *f;* **to do sth with good/bad** ~ hacer algo de buen grado/a regañadientes; **to have the (good)** ~ **to do sth** tener la cortesía de hacer algo **6.** (*prayer*) bendición *f* (de la mesa); **to say** ~ bendecir la mesa **7.** (*leeway*) demora *f* **8.** (*Highness*) **Your/His/Her Grace** su Excelencia **9.** (*sister goddesses*) **the Graces** las Gracias **II.** *vt* **1.** (*honour*) honrar **2.** (*make beautiful*) embellecer

graceful ['greɪsfəl] *adj* **1.** (*moving*) grácil; ~ **movements** movimientos *mpl* garbosos **2.** (*elegant*) elegante **3.** (*polite*) educado, -a

graceless ['greɪslɪs] *adj* **1.** (*lacking smooth elegance*) desgarbado, -a **2.** (*impolite*) descortés

gracious ['greɪʃəs] **I.** *adj* **1.** (*warm and kind*) afable **2.** (*elegant*) elegante **3.** (*merciful*) clemente **II.** *interj* (*good*) ~ **(me)** ¡Dios mío!

gradation [grə'deɪʃən, *Am:* grəɪ'-] *n* gradación *f*

grade [greɪd] **I.** *n* **1.** (*rank*) rango *m* **2.** *Am* SCHOOL curso *m;* **to skip a** ~ perder un curso **3.** (*mark*) nota *f;* **good/bad** ~**s** buenas/malas notas **4.** (*level of quality*) clase *f,* calidad *f;* **high/low** ~ alta/baja calidad **5.** *Am* GEO pendiente *f;* **gentle/steep** ~ pendiente suave/pronunciada ▶**to be on the down** ~ ir cuesta abajo; **to be on the up** ~ prosperar; **to make**

the ~ dar la talla **II.** *vt* **1.** SCHOOL, UNIV (*evaluate*) evaluar; **to** ~ **up/down** subir/bajar la nota **2.** (*categorize*) clasificar

grade crossing *n Am* paso *m* a nivel

grade school *n Am* SCHOOL escuela *f* primaria

gradient ['greɪdɪənt] *n* GEO, AUTO pendiente *f*

grading ['greɪdɪŋ] *n* **1.** (*gradation*) gradación *f* **2.** (*classification*) clasificación *f*

El sistema de calificación que se utiliza en los EE.UU. recibe el nombre de **grading system**. Este sistema emplea las siguientes letras para expresar las distintas calificaciones: A, B, C, D, E y F. La letra E, sin embargo, no se suele utilizar. La A representa la máxima calificación, mientras que la F (**Fail**) significa suspenso. Las notas además pueden ir matizadas por un más o un menos. Quien obtiene una A+ es que ha tenido un rendimiento verdaderamente sobresaliente.

---

gradual ['grædʒʊəl] *adj* **1.** (*not sudden*) gradual **2.** (*not steep*) suave

gradually ['grædʒʊli] *adv* **1.** (*not steeply*) gradualmente **2.** (*not suddenly*) progresivamente, paulatinamente

graduate[1] ['grædʒʊət] *n* **1.** UNIV licenciado, -a *m, f*; **university** ~ licenciado *m* universitario **2.** *Am* SCHOOL graduado, -a *m, f* **3.** (*postgraduate*) pos(t)graduado, -a *m, f*; ~ **school** escuela *f* de pos(t)grado

graduate[2] ['grædʒʊeɪt] **I.** *vi* **1.** UNIV licenciarse; *Am* SCHOOL graduarse; **to** ~ **cum laude** graduarse cum laude **2.** (*move to a higher level*) subir de categoría; **to** ~ **to** ... ascender a... **3.** (*calibrate*) calibrar **II.** *vt Am* graduar

graduated *adj* graduado, -a

graduation [ˌgrædʒʊˈeɪʃən, *Am:* ˌgrædʒuˈ-] *n* **1.** SCHOOL, UNIV graduación *f*, egreso *m Arg, Chile* **2.** (*promotion*) ascenso *m* **3.** (*marks of calibration*) calibrado *m*

graffiti [grəˈfiːti, *Am:* - t̬i] *npl* graffiti *m*; **a** ~ **artist** un artista de graffiti

graft [grɑːft, *Am:* græft] **I.** *n* **1.** BOT, AGR, MED injerto *m*; **a skin** ~ un injerto de piel **2.** POL corrupción *f* **3.** *Brit, inf* (*work*) trabajo *m* duro **II.** *vt* **1.** BOT, AGR, MED injertar **2.** (*add on*) añadir **III.** *vi* **1.** POL trampear **2.** *Brit, inf* (*work hard*) currar mucho

grafter ['grɑːftər, *Am:* ˈgræftər] *n* **1.** BOT, AGR persona *f* que realiza injertos **2.** *Brit, inf* (*hard worker*) persona *f* que trabaja duro

Grail [greɪl] *n* **the Holy** ~ el Santo Grial

grain [greɪn] **I.** *n* **1.** (*smallest piece*) grano *m*; ~ **of sand/salt** grano de arena/sal **2.** *no pl* (*cereal*) cereal *m* **3.** (*direction of fibres*) fibra *f*; **wood** ~ hebra *f* de madera **4.** GASTR veta *f*; **meat** ~ veta de carne; **it goes against the** ~ (**for me**) *fig* se me hace cuesta arriba *inf* **5.** (*smallest quantity*) pizca *f*; **a** ~ **of hope** una pequeña esperanza; **a** ~ **of truth** una pizca de verdad ▶**to take sth with a** ~ **of salt** no creerse algo del todo **II.** *vt* **1.** (*granulate*)

granular **2.** (*remove hair from*) pelar

grain elevator *n* elevador *m* de granos

grain export *n* exportación *f* de grano

grain market *n* mercado *m* de cereales

grammar ['græmər, *Am:* -ər] *n no pl* gramática *f*

grammar book *n* libro *m* de gramática

grammarian [grəˈmeərɪən, *Am:* -ˈmerɪ-] *n* gramático, -a *m, f*

grammar school *n* **1.** *Am* (*elementary school*) colegio *m* **2.** *Brit* HIST (*upper level school*) colegio *m* de enseñanza secundaria al cual se accede por medio de un examen

---

Las antiguas **grammar schools** (que más o menos se corresponden con los institutos) fueron fundadas hace muchos siglos en Gran Bretaña para el estudio del latín. Hacia 1950 el alumno que quería acceder a esta escuela debía aprobar el **eleven-plus examination**. Pero sólo un 20% del alumnado aprobaba este examen. El resto continuaba su intinerario educativo en una **secondary modern school** (escuela secundaria de grado inferior). Estos dos tipos de escuela fueron reorganizados durante los años 60 y 70 como **comprehensive schools** (escuelas integradas).

---

grammatical [grəˈmætɪkl, *Am:* -ˈmæt̬ɪ-] *adj* gramatical

gram(me) [græm] *n* gramo *m*

gramophone ['græməfəʊn, *Am:* -foʊn] *n* gramófono *m*, vitrola *f AmL*

grampus ['græmpəs] <-es> *n* **1.** ZOOL orca *f* **2.** *Brit, inf* (*person*) abuelo *m*

gran [græn] *n inf abbr of* **grandmother** abuela *f*

granary ['grænəri] AGR **I.** <-ies> *n* **1.** (*silo*) granero *m* **2.** (*grain region*) región *f* de cereales **II.** *adj* granero, -a

granary bread *n no pl,* **granary loaf** <-loaves> *n Brit* pan *m* con granos enteros

grand [grænd] **I.** *adj* **1.** (*splendid*) magnífico, -a; **in** ~ **style** de estilo sublime; **a** ~ **opening** una gran apertura; **to make a** ~ **entrance** hacer una entrada triunfal; **the Grand Canyon** el Gran Cañón **2.** *inf* (*excellent*) sublime **3.** (*far-reaching*) importante; ~ **ambitions/ideas** grandes ambiciones/ideas **4.** (*large*) grande; **on a** ~ **scale** a gran escala **5.** (*overall*) **the** ~ **total** el importe total **6.** (*of upper class*) ~ **duke** gran duque *m* **II.** *n* **1.** *inv, inf* (*dollars*) mil dólares *mpl*; (*pounds*) mil libras *fpl* **2.** MUS piano *m* de cola

grandchild <-children> *n* nieto, -a *m, f*

grand(d)ad *n* **1.** *inf* (*grandfather*) abuelito *m* **2.** (*old man*) viejo *m* **granddaughter** *n* nieta *f*

grandee [grænˈdiː] *n* grande *m*, pez *m* gordo

grandeur ['grændʒər, *Am:* -dʒər] *n no pl* **1.** (*imposing splendor*) magnificencia *f* **2.** (*nobility*) nobleza *f*

grandfather n abuelo m
grandiloquent [græn'dıləkwənt] adj grandilocuente
grandiose ['grændıəʊs, Am: -oʊs] adj 1.(extremely grand) grandioso, -a 2.(excessively splendid) pomposo, -a
grand jury <- -ies> n Am LAW gran jurado m **grand larceny** n no pl hurto m mayor
grandly adv majestuosamente
grandma n inf abuelita f **grandmaster** n GAMES (chess pro) gran maestro m **grandmother** n abuela f ▶you can't teach your ~ to suck eggs ¡a mí me lo vas a decir!
grandpa n inf abuelito m **grandparents** npl abuelos mpl **grand piano** n piano m de cola **grandson** n nieto m **grandstand** n tribuna f; ~ **seat** asiento m de tribuna; ~ **ticket** entrada f de tribuna; **a ~ view** fig una vista que abarca todo el panorama **grand sum, grand total** n importe m total
grange [greɪndʒ] n Brit casa f solariega
granite ['grænɪt] n no pl granito m
grannie, granny ['græni] n inf abuelita f
grant [grɑ:nt, Am: grænt] I. n 1. UNIV beca f; **research** ~ subvención f a una investigación; **to be on a** ~ disfrutar de una beca; **to give sb a** ~ conceder una beca a alguien 2.(a government grant) subvención f 3.(from authority) concesión f; **federal** ~ ayuda f estatal; **maternity** ~ subsidio m por maternidad; **to apply for a** ~ solicitar una subvención 4. LAW cesión f II. vt 1.(allow) otorgar; **to ~ sb a permit/visa** conceder a alguien un permiso/visado 2.(transfer legally) ceder; (asylum) dar; **to ~ sb a pardon** conceder un indulto a alguien 3. form (consent to fulfil) **to ~ sb sth** conceder algo a alguien; **to ~ sb a favour** hacer un favor a alguien; **to ~ sb a request** acceder a la petición de alguien; **to ~ sb a wish** conceder un deseo a alguien 4.(admit to) reconocer, admitir; **~ed** de acuerdo; **~ed, it's not easy ...** de acuerdo, no es fácil...; **I ~ you, ...** estoy de acuerdo contigo,...; **to ~ that ...** estar de acuerdo en que... +subj ▶to **take sth for ~ed** dar algo por sentado; **to take sb for ~ed** no valorar a alguien como se merece
granular ['grænjʊləʳ, Am: -jələ·] adj granular
granulated ['grænjʊleɪtɪd, Am: -jəleɪ̣tɪd] adj 1.(in grains) granulado, -a; ~ **sugar** azúcar m cristalizado 2.(raised) rugoso, -a
granule ['grænju:l] n gránulo m; ~**s** granos mpl; **instant coffee** ~**s** granos de café instantáneo
grape [greɪp] n 1.(fruit) uva f; **a bunch of** ~**s** un racimo de uvas 2. iron (wine) **the** ~ el vino ▶it's just **sour** ~**s** es pura envidia
grapefruit ['greɪpfru:t] n inv pomelo m
grape juice n no pl mosto m
grapevine n vid f; (climbing plant) parra f ▶to **hear** sth on the ~ saber algo por los rumores que corren; **I heard it on the** ~ **that he is marrying** corren rumores de que se va a casar

graph¹ [grɑ:f, Am: græf] n gráfica f; (diagram) gráfico m; **temperature** ~ gráfico de temperaturas
graph² [grɑ:f, Am: græf] n LING grafía f
graphic ['græfɪk] adj gráfico, -a; **to describe sth in** ~ **detail** describir algo de forma gráfica; ~ **works** (of an artist) trabajos gráficos (de un artista)
graphic design n no pl diseño m gráfico
graphics n + sing vb 1.(drawings) artes fpl gráficas 2.(presentation) gráficos mpl 3. INFOR gráficos mpl; **computer** ~ gráficos de ordenador
graphics card n tarjeta f gráfica **graphics screen** n pantalla f gráfica
graphite ['græfaɪt] n grafito m
graphologist [græ'fɒlədʒɪst, Am: grə-'fɑ:lə-] n grafólogo, -a m, f
graphology [græ'fɒlədʒɪ, Am: grə'fɑ:lə-] n no pl grafología f
grapple ['græpl] vi **to** ~ **for/with sth** luchar a brazo partido por/con algo
grappling iron n, **grappling hook** n arpeo m
grasp [grɑ:sp, Am: græsp] I. n no pl 1.(grip) agarre m 2.(attainability) alcance m; **to be beyond sb's** ~ estar fuera del alcance de alguien 3.(understanding) comprensión f; (knowledge) conocimiento m ▶his **reach exceeds his** ~ alarga más el brazo que la manga II. vt 1.(take firm hold) agarrar; **to ~ sb by the arm/hand** coger a alguien del brazo/de la mano 2.(understand) entender III. vi 1.(try to hold) intentar coger 2. fig (take advantage) **to** ~ **at** sacar provecho de; **to** ~ **at the chance** aprovechar la oportunidad
grasping adj avaro, -a
grass [grɑ:s, Am: græs] I.<-es> n 1. hierba f; **wild** ~**es** hierbas silvestres 2. no pl (area of grass) prado m; (lawn) césped m; **to cut the** ~ cortar el césped; **to put a garden down to** ~ poner césped en un jardín 3. no pl (pasture) pasto m; **to be at** ~ pastar; **to put cattle out to** ~ sacar a pastar el ganado; **to put sb out to** ~ inf jubilar a alguien 4. no pl, inf (marijuana) hierba f inf, traba f AmL, inf 5. Brit, inf (an informer) soplón, -ona m, f ▶to **let the** ~ **grow under one's feet** perder el tiempo; **the** ~ **is** (always) **greener on the other side** (of **the fence**) prov (siempre) parece mejor lo de los demás II. vt cubrir de hierba III. vi Aus, Brit, inf dar el chivatazo; **to** ~ **on sb** (to sb) delatar a alguien (diciéndoselo a alguien)
grasshopper ['grɑ:shɒpəʳ, Am: 'græshɑ:pɚ] n saltamontes m inv, chapulín m AmC, Méx, saltagatos m inv AmC, Méx ▶to **be knee-high to a** ~ ser un renacuajo **grassland** n pastos mpl; (savannah) sabana f
grassroots I. npl (ordinary people) pueblo m; (of a party, organization) base f popular II. adj básico, -a; ~ **opinion** opinión f del pueblo; ~ **politics** política f que trata los problemas de la vida diaria **grass-snake** n cule-

bra f de collar **grass widow** n mujer cuyo marido está ausente **grass widower** n ≈ Rodríguez m inf (marido cuya mujer está ausente)

grassy ['grɑːsi, Am: 'græsi] <-ier, -iest> adj cubierto, -a de hierba, pastoso, -a AmL

grate¹ [greɪt] n 1. (grid in fireplace) rejilla f de la chimenea 2. (fireplace) chimenea f

grate² [greɪt] I. vi 1. (annoy: noise) rechinar; to ~ on sb molestar a alguien 2. (rub together) rozar; to ~ against each other rozar uno con otro II. vt GASTR rallar

grateful ['greɪtfəl] adj agradecido, -a; to be ~ (to sb) for sth agradecer algo (a alguien); I'd be most ~ if you ... form te agradecería mucho que... +subj

grater ['greɪtə', Am: -t̬ə'] n rallador m

gratification [ˌgrætɪfɪ'keɪʃən, Am: ˌgræt̬ə-] n gratificación f; (of a wish) satisfacción f; sexual ~ placer m sexual; with (some) ~ con (cierta) satisfacción

gratify ['grætɪfaɪ, Am: 'græt̬ə-] <-ie-> vt 1. (please) gratificar; to be gratified at sth estar complacido por algo 2. (satisfy) satisfacer

gratifying adj gratificante

grating ['greɪtɪŋ, Am: -t̬ɪŋ] I. n rejilla f II. adj 1. (scraping) que rasca; (squeaking) chirriante 2. (annoyingly harsh) áspero, -a; ~ voice voz f rasgada

gratis ['greɪtɪs, Am: 'græt̬əs] I. adj gratuito, -a II. adv gratis

gratitude ['grætɪtjuːd, Am: 'græt̬ətuːd] n no pl, form gratitud f; reconocimiento m; as a token of my ~ como muestra de mi gratitud

gratuitous [grə'tjuːɪtəs, Am: -'tuːətəs] adj 1. (free) gratuito, -a 2. (without justification) innecesario, -a

gratuity [grə'tjuːəti, Am: -'tuːət̬i] <-ies> n 1. form (tip) propina f 2. Brit MIL (monetary reward for service) pensión f militar 3. Am (bribe) illegal ~ soborno m

grave¹ [greɪv] n tumba f, sepultura f; mass ~ fosa f común; to go to one's ~ irse a la tumba; beyond the ~ más allá de la sepultura; from beyond the ~ desde el más allá

grave² [greɪv] adj 1. (seriously bad) grave; (serious) serio, -a; (be taken seriously) importante; (worrying) preocupante; a ~ mistake/risk un grave error/riesgo; ~ news noticias fpl alarmantes 2. (momentous) trascendental 3. (solemn) a ~ ceremony una ceremonia solemne; a ~ person/face una persona/cara seria

grave-digger ['greɪvˌdɪgə', Am: -ə'] n sepulturero, -a m, f

gravel ['grævəl] n 1. (small stones) gravilla f; GEO grava f; a ~ path un camino de grava 2. MED arenilla f

gravel-pit n gravera f **gravel-stone** n arenilla f

grave mound n túmulo m de una tumba **grave robber** n ladrón, -ona m, f de tumbas

gravestone n lápida f sepulcral **graveyard** n cementerio m

graving dock ['greɪvɪŋˌdɒk, Am: -dɑːk] n dique m seco [o de carena]

gravitate ['grævɪteɪt] vi gravitar; to ~ towards sth/sb tender hacia algo/alguien

gravitation [ˌgrævɪ'teɪʃən] n no pl 1. (movement) gravitación f; (tendency) tendencia f; the ~ of people to/towards the cities la emigración de la gente a/hacia las ciudades 2. (attracting force) atracción f

gravitational [ˌgrævɪ'teɪʃənl] adj gravitacional; ~ force fuerza f gravitatoria

gravity ['grævəti, Am: -t̬i] n no pl gravedad f; the law of ~ la ley de la gravedad

gravure [grə'vjʊə', Am: -'vjʊr] n fotograbado m

gravy ['greɪvi] n no pl 1. GASTR salsa hecha con el jugo de la carne 2. Am, inf (easy money) ganga f; the ~ train un chollo; to make some ~ conseguir un chollo

gravy boat n salsera f

gray [greɪ] adj Am s. **grey**

grayish ['greɪɪʃ] adj Am s. **greyish**

graze¹ [greɪz] I. n roce m II. vt rozar; the bullet just ~d his arm la bala sólo le rozó el brazo

graze² [greɪz] I. vi pastar II. vt apacentar

grease [griːs] n 1. (fat) grasa f 2. (lubricant) lubricante m II. vt engrasar; (in mechanics) lubricar

grease gun n pistola f de engrase **grease mark** n mancha f de grasa **greasepaint** n maquillaje m teatral **greaseproof paper** n papel m encerado **grease spot** n mancha f de grasa

greasy ['griːsi] <-ier, -iest> adj grasiento, -a

great [greɪt] I. n grande mf; the ~ and the good Brit los grandes y los buenos; Alexander the ~ Alejandro m Magno II. adj 1. (very big) enorme; a ~ amount una gran cantidad; a ~ deal of time/money muchísimo tiempo/dinero; a ~ joy/sadness una gran alegría/pena; a ~ many people muchísima gente; the ~ majority of people la gran mayoría (de la gente); it gives me ~ pleasure to announce ... form es un gran placer para mí anunciar...; it is with ~ sorrow that I tell you of ... lamento mucho comunicarles que... 2. (famous and important) famoso, -a; the ~est boxer el boxeador más destacado; ~ minds think that ... las mentes más prestigiosas creen que... 3. (wonderful) magnífico, -a; to be ~ at doing sth inf ser bueno en algo; she's ~ at playing tennis inf a ella se le da muy bien el tenis; to be a ~ one for doing sth encantar a uno hacer algo; it's ~ to be back home again es maravilloso estar de nuevo en casa; the ~ thing about sth/sb is (that) lo mejor de algo/alguien es (que); I had a ~ time with you lo he pasado fenomenal contigo; ~! ¡estupendo! 4. (very healthy) sano, -a; to feel not all that ~ no sentirse demasido bien 5. (for

emphasis) **you** ~ **idiot!** ¡pedazo de idiota!; **they're** ~ **friends** son muy amigos; ~ **big** muy grande **6.** (*good*) excelente; **Peter is a** ~ **organiser** Peter es un magnífico organizador
great-aunt *n* tía *f* abuela
Great Bear *n* Osa *f* Mayor **Great Britain** *n* Gran Bretaña *f*

Great Britain (Gran Bretaña) se compone del reino de Inglaterra, el de Escocia y el principado de Gales. (El rey Eduardo I de Inglaterra se anexionó Gales en 1282 y en 1301 nombró a su único hijo **Prince of Wales**. El rey Jacobo VI de Escocia heredó en 1603 la corona inglesa convirtiéndose en Jacobo I y en 1707 se unieron los parlamentos de ambos reinos). Estos países forman, junto con Irlanda del Norte, el **United Kingdom** (Reino Unido). El concepto geográfico de **British Isles** (Islas Británicas) incluye no sólo a la isla mayor que es Gran Bretaña, sino también a Irlanda, la Isla de Man, las Hébridas, Orkney, Shetland, las Islas Scilly y las **Channel Islands** (Islas del Canal de la Mancha).

---

greatcoat *n* sobretodo *m* **Great Depression** *n* Gran Depresión *f*
Greater London *n* la ciudad de Londres y su área metropolitana
great-grandchild *n* bisnieto, -a *m, f* **great-grandparents** *npl* bisabuelos *mpl* **great-great-grandparents** *npl* tatarabuelos *mpl*
Great Lakes *n* Grandes Lagos *mpl*
greatly ['greɪtli] *adv form* sumamente; **to improve** ~ mejorar mucho; **to** ~ **regret sth** lamentar algo muchísimo; **to be** ~ **impressed** estar muy impresionado
great-nephew *n* sobrino *m* nieto
greatness ['greɪtnɪs] *n no pl* grandeza *f*
great-niece *n* sobrina *f* nieta **great-uncle** *n* tío *m* abuelo
Grecian ['griːʃən] *adj* griego, -a
Greece [griːs] *n* Grecia *f*
greed [griːd] *n no pl* codicia *f*; (*for food*) gula *f*; (*for money*) avaricia *f*; ~ **for power** ansia *f* de poder
greediness ['griːdɪnɪs] *n no pl s.* **greed**
greedy ['griːdi] <-ier, -iest> *adj* (*wanting too much*) codicioso, -a; (*wanting food*) glotón, -ona; (*wanting money, things*) avaricioso, -a; ~ **for success/victory** ávido de éxito/victoria; ~ **-guts** *Aus, Brit, childspeak* comilón, -ona; **this plant's** ~ **for water** esta planta necesita agua
Greek [griːk] **I.** *n* **1.** (*person*) griego, -a *m, f* **2.** LING griego *m* **II.** *adj* griego, -a ▶**it's all** ~ **to me** eso me suena a chino
green [griːn] **I.** *n* **1.** (*colour*) verde *m* **2.** *pl* (*green vegetables*) verduras *fpl* **3.** ECOL, POL verde *mf* **4.** (*lawn*) césped *m* **5.** SPORTS pista *f*; **bowling** ~ pista de bolos **II.** *adj* **1.** *a.* ECOL, POL verde; **to turn** ~ (*traffic lights*) ponerse en verde **2.** (*unripe*) verde, tierno, -a *Chile, Ecua,*

Guat **3.** (*inexperienced*) novato, -a; (*naive*) ingenuo, -a **4.** (*covered with plants*) cubierto, -a de vegetación **5.** *fig* (*jealous*) ~ **with envy** muerto, -a de envidia ▶**to have** ~ **fingers** *Brit, Aus,* **to have** ~ **thumbs** *Am* tener habilidad para la jardinería
greenback *n Am, inf* billete *m* (de banco)
green belt *n* zona *f* verde (*zona en las afueras de las ciudades en la que no se permite construir*) **green card** *n* **1.** *Brit* AUTO carta *f* verde **2.** *Am* (*residence and work permit*) permiso *m* de residencia y de trabajo **green consumerism** *n* actitud consumista que respecta la protección del medioambiente
greenery ['griːnəri] *n no pl* vegetación *f*
green-eyed [ˌgriːn'aɪd, *Am:* 'griːnaɪd] *adj* **1.** (*with green eyes*) de ojos verdes **2.** *fig* (*jealous*) celoso, -a
greenfly <-ies> *n* pulgón *m*
greengage *n* ciruela *f* claudia; ~ **jam** mermelada *f* de ciruelas verdes; ~ **tree** ciruelo *m*
greengrocer [-ˌgrəʊsəʳ] *n Brit* verdulero, -a *m, f*; **at the** ~**'s** en la verdulería **greenhorn** *n Am* novato, -a *m, f* **greenhouse** *n* invernadero *m* **greenhouse effect** *n no pl* the ~ el efecto invernadero
greenish ['griːnɪʃ] *adj* verdoso, -a
green issue *n* cuestión *f* medioambiental
Greenland ['griːnlənd] *n* Groenlandia *f*
Greenlander ['griːnləndəʳ] *n* groenlandés, -esa *m, f*
greenness ['griːnnɪs] *n no pl* verdor *m*
green pepper [ˌgriːn'pepəʳ, *Am:* -ɚ] *n* pimiento *m* verde
green politics *n* + *sing vb* política *f* del medioambiente
Greenwich ['grɪnɪtʃ, *Am:* 'gren-] *n* Greenwich *m;* ~ **mean time** hora *f* de Greenwich

---

El **Royal Observatory** (observatorio astronómico) de **Greenwich** fue construido en 1675 para obtener datos exactos sobre la posición de las estrellas con vista a la creación de cartas de navegación. El **Greenwich meridian** (meridiano de Greenwich) no se fijó oficialmente como el grado cero de longitud con validez universal hasta 1884. Las 24 franjas horarias del planeta se fijan a partir de la hora local del meridiano que es conocida como **Greenwich Mean Time** o **Universal Time**.

---

greenwood ['griːnwʊd] *n* bosque *m* caducifolio
greeny <-ier, -iest> *adj* verdoso, -a
greet [griːt] *vt* **1.** (*welcome*) saludar; (*receive*) recibir; **to** ~ **each other** saludarse; **to** ~ **sb by shaking hands/with a smile** saludar a alguien con un apretón de manos/con una sonrisa **2.** (*react*) **to** ~ **sth** reaccionar ante algo; **to** ~ **sth with anger/applause**

recibir algo con enfado/un aplauso; **to ~ sth with delight** sentir gran placer ante algo **3.** *fig* (*make itself noticeable*) presentarse; **a scene of joy** ~**ed us** se mostró ante nosotros una escena de alegría

greeting *n* saludo *m;* (*receiving*) recepción *f*

gregarious [grɪˈgeərɪəs, *Am:* -ˈgerɪ-] *adj* **1.** (*liking company*) sociable **2.** ZOOL (*living in groups*) gregario, -a

Grenada [grəˈneɪdə] *n* Granada *f*

Grenadan I. *adj* granadino, -a II. *n* granadino, -a *m, f*

grenade [grɪˈneɪd] *n* granada *f;* **hand** ~ granada de mano

grenadier [ˌgrenəˈdɪəʳ, *Am:* -ˈdɪr] *n* **1.** HIST (*soldier*) granadero *m* **2.** (*member of regiment*) soldado *m* granadero; **the Grenadiers** *Brit* los Granaderos

grew [gruː] *pt of* **grow**

grey [greɪ] I. *n* *no pl* **1.** (*colour*) gris *m* **2.** (*regiment*) **the** (**Royal Scots**) **Greys** los Grises (Reales Escoceses) **3.** (*white horse*) rucio *m* II. *adj* **1.** (*coloured grey*) gris; ~ **weather** tiempo *m* gris **2.** (*grey-haired*) canoso, -a; **to go** ~ encanecer; **he has started to go** ~ empieza a tener canas **3.** (*white colour of horse*) rucio, -a **4.** (*pale*) pálido, -a **5.** *fig* (*sad*) triste

greybeard [ˈgreɪˌbɪəd, *Am:* -bɪrd] *n* anciano *m* **greyhound** *n* galgo *m*

greying *adj* con canas

greyish [ˈgreɪɪʃ] *adj* grisáceo, -a; (*hair*) entrecano, -a

grey matter *n* *inf* materia *f* gris

grid [grɪd] *n* parrilla *f;* SPORTS parrilla de salida

griddle [ˈgrɪdl] I. *n* GASTR plancha *f,* burén *m* Cuba II. *vt* **to** ~ **food** asar comida a la plancha

gridiron [ˈgrɪdaɪən, *Am:* -aɪɚn] *n* **1.** (*metal grid*) parrilla *f* **2.** *Am* (*American football field*) campo *m* de fútbol **3.** NAUT (*framework*) carenero *m* **4.** THEAT peine *m* **gridlock** *n* *no pl* paralización *f* del tráfico; *fig* inactividad *f* **grid square** *n* cuadrícula *f*

grief [griːf] *n* *no pl* (*extreme sadness*) aflicción *f;* (*individual mournful feelings*) pesar *m;* (*pain*) dolor *m;* **to cause** ~ *inf* dar pena; **to cause sb** ~ causar aflicción a alguien; **to give sb** (**a lot of**) ~ hacer sentir (muy) mal a alguien ►**to come to** ~ (*fail*) fracasar; (*have an accident*) sufrir un percance

grievance [ˈgriːvns] *n* **1.** (*complaint*) queja *f,* reivindicación *f;* **to harbour a** ~ **against sb** presentar una queja contra alguien **2.** (*sense of injustice*) injusticia *f*

grieve [griːv] I. *vi* sufrir; **to** ~ **for sth/sb** llorar por algo/alguien II. *vt* **1.** (*distress*) causar dolor; (*make sad*) afligir; **it** ~**s me to see your situation** me da pena ver tu situación **2.** (*annoy*) molestar; **it** ~**s me to see that you don't do anything to solve it** me molesta que no hagas nada para solucionarlo

grievous [ˈgriːvəs] *adj form* (*pain*) fuerte;

(*danger*) serio, -a; (*error*) craso, -a; (*injuries*) considerable; (*news*) lamentable; **a** ~ **crime** un crimen grave

grievous bodily harm *n* *no pl* graves daños *mpl* corporales

griffin [ˈgrɪfɪn] *n,* **griffon** [ˈgrɪfən] *n* grifo *m*

grill [grɪl] I. *n* **1.** (*part of cooker*) parrilla *f;* (*grid over fire*) parrilla *f,* grill *m* **2.** *Am* (*informal restaurant*) asador *m* II. *vt* (*cook*) asar a la parrilla

grille [grɪl] *n* rejilla *f;* (*of windows*) reja *f;* (*of doors*) verja *f*

grilling [ˈgrɪlɪŋ] *n* *inf* interrogatorio *m;* **to give sb a** (**good**) ~ interrogar a alguien (muy) intensamente

grim [grɪm] *adj* **1.** (*very serious*) severo, -a **2.** (*unpleasant*) desagradable; (*horrible*) horrible; ~ **outlook** mirada *f* inexorable; **to feel** ~ sentirse muy mal ►**to hang on like** ~ **death** (*dog*) no soltar la presa; (*person*) no cejar en el empeño

grimace [grɪˈmeɪs, *Am:* ˈgrɪməs] I. *n* (*facial expression*) mueca *f;* **to make a** ~ **of disgust/pain/hatred** hacer una mueca de disgusto/dolor/odio II. *vi* hacer muecas; **to** ~ **with pain** hacer muecas de dolor

grime [graɪm] I. *n* (*ingrained dirt*) mugre *f;* (*soot*) hollín *m* II. *vt* **to be** ~**d with soot** estar manchado de hollín

grimy [ˈgraɪmi] <-ier, -iest> *adj* mugriento, -a; (*sooty*) sucio, -a

grin [grɪn] I. *n* ancha sonrisa *f* II. *vi* (*smile widely*) sonreír de oreja a oreja; (*beam*) sonreír alegremente; **to** ~ **impishly at sb** dirigir una sonrisa traviesa a alguien ►**to** ~ **and bear it** poner al mal tiempo buena cara

grind [graɪnd] I. *n* *inf* **1.** (*tiring work*) trabajo *m* pesado; **to be a real** ~ ser un trabajo durísimo **2.** (*boring work*) rutina *f;* **the daily** ~ la rutina diaria II. <ground, ground> *vt* **1.** (*crush*) aplastar; (*mill*) moler; **to** ~ **sth** (**in**)**to flour/a powder** reducir algo a harina/polvo **2.** *Am, Aus* (*chop finely: meat*) picar **3.** (*press firmly and twist*) **to** ~ **a cigarette into an ashtray** apagar un cigarrillo en un cenicero **4.** (*sharpen*) afilar

♦**grind down** *vt* **1.** (*file*) pulir **2.** (*mill*) moler **3.** (*wear*) desgastar **4.** (*oppress*) oprimir; (*treat cruelly*) maltratar; **to grind sb down** destrozar a alguien

♦**grind out** *vt* (*produce continuously*) producir mecánicamente

grinder [ˈgraɪndəʳ, *Am:* -dɚ] *n* **1.** (*crushing machine*) molinillo *m;* **a hand/electric** ~ una picadora manual/eléctrica **2.** (*sharpener*) afiladora *f* **3.** (*person who sharpens things*) afilador(a) *m(f);* **knife/scissor** ~ afilador(a) *m(f)* de cuchillos/tijeras

grindstone [ˈgraɪndstəʊn, *Am:* -stoʊn] *n* muela *f,* piedra *f* de amolar ►**to keep one's nose to the** ~ *inf* trabajar como un enano

gringo [ˈgrɪŋgəʊ, *Am:* -goʊ] *n* gringo, -a *m, f*

grip [grɪp] **I.** *n* **1.** (*hold*) agarre *m;* *fig* control *m;* **to keep a firm ~ on the bag** agarrar fuertemente la bolsa; **to be in the ~ of sth** estar en poder de algo; **the economy is in the ~ of a crisis** la economía está atravesando una crisis **2.** (*way of holding*) asidero *m* **3.** (*bag*) maletín *m* ▸ **to get to ~s with sth** enfrentarse con algo; **to get a ~ on oneself** controlarse **II.** <-pp-> *vt* **1.** (*hold firmly*) agarrar **2.** (*overwhelm*) **to be ~ped by emotion** estar embargado por la emoción; **he was ~ped by fear** el miedo le invadió **3.** (*interest deeply*) absorber la atención de **III.** *vi* agarrarse

gripe [graɪp] **I.** *n* *inf* queja *f* **II.** *vi* *inf* quejarse

gripping ['grɪpɪŋ] *adj* **1.** (*exciting*) emocionante **2.** (*stabbing*) punzante

grisly ['grɪzli] <-ier, -iest> *adj* (*repellant*) espeluznante; *fig,* *inf* asqueroso, -a

grist [grɪst] *n* **it's all ~ to the mill** se puede sacar provecho de todo

gristle ['grɪsl] *n no pl* cartílago *m*

grit [grɪt] **I.** *n no pl* **1.** (*small stones*) arenilla *f* **2.** (*courage*) valor *m* **II.** <-tt-> *vt* **1.** **to ~ a road** echar grava a un camino **2.** (*press together*) **to ~ one's teeth** *a. fig* apretar los dientes

gritty ['grɪti, *Am:* 'grɪt̬i] <-ier, -iest> *adj* con arenilla; (*plucky*) valiente

grizzle ['grɪzl] *vi* *inf* **1.** (*cry continually: baby, small child*) gimotear **2.** (*complain*) quejarse

grizzled *adj* **1.** (*greying*) grisáceo, -a **2.** (*grey*) gris **3.** (*grey-haired*) de pelo canoso; **a ~ man** un hombre canoso

grizzly ['grɪzli] **I.** <-ier, -iest> *adj* gris **II.** <-ies> *n* oso *m* pardo americano

groan [grəʊn, *Am:* groʊn] **I.** *n* gemido *m* **II.** *vi* **1.** (*make a noise: people*) gemir; (*floorboards, hinges*) crujir; **to ~ in pain** gemir de dolor **2.** (*speak unhappily*) decir gimiendo; **to ~ inwardly** lamentarse para sus adentros **3.** *inf* (*complain*) quejarse; **to ~ about sth** quejarse de algo; **why are you moaning and ~ing about that?** ¿por qué te quejas de eso? **4.** (*bear a load*) llevar una carga a cuestas

grocer ['grəʊsər, *Am:* 'groʊsər] *n* **1.** (*shopkeeper*) tendero, -a *m, f* **2.** (*food shop*) tienda *f* de ultramarinos

grocery ['grəʊsəri, *Am:* 'groʊ-] **I.** *adj* de ultramarinos **II.** <-ies> *n* tienda *f* de ultramarinos

grog [grɒg, *Am:* grɑːg] *n* grog *m,* ponche *m*

groggy ['grɒgi, *Am:* 'grɑːgi] <-ier -iest> *adj* grogui

groin¹ [grɔɪn] *n* ingle *f;* (*male sex organs*) genitales *mpl*

groin² [grɔɪn] *n Am* arista *f*

groom [gruːm] **I.** *n* **1.** (*person caring for horses*) mozo *m* de cuadra **2.** (*bridegroom*) novio *m* **II.** *vt* **1.** (*clean: an animal*) cuidar; (*a horse*) almohazar **2.** (*prepare: a person*) preparar

groove [gruːv] *n* ranura *f;* MUS surco *m;* *fig* onda *f* ▸ **to be in a ~** estar metido en una rutina

groovy ['gruːvi] <-ier, -iest> *adj* *inf* guay

grope [grəʊp, *Am:* groʊp] **I.** *vi* ir a tientas; **to ~ for sth** buscar algo a tientas; **to ~ for the right words** buscar las palabras **II.** *vt* **1.** **to ~ one's way** ir a tientas **2.** *inf* (*touch sexually*) sobar

gropingly ['grəʊpɪŋli, *Am:* 'groʊp-] *adv* a tientas

gross¹ [grəʊs, *Am:* groʊs] <-sses> *n* gruesa *f;* **by the ~** en gruesas

gross² [grəʊs, *Am:* groʊs] **I.** *adj* **1.** LAW grave; (*neglect*) serio, -a; (*negligence*) grave **2.** (*very fat*) muy gordo, -a **3.** *Am* (*extremely offensive*) grosero, -a; (*revolting*) asqueroso, -a **4.** (*total*) total; (*without deductions*) bruto **II.** *vt* FIN (*earn before taxes*) ganar en bruto

gross cash flow *n* flujo *m* de caja bruto

gross domestic product *n* producto *m* interior bruto **gross income** *n* ingreso *m* bruto

grossly *adv* (*in a gross manner*) groseramente; (*extremely*) enormemente; **to be ~ unfair** ser totalmente injusto

gross national product *n* producto *m* nacional bruto **gross negligence** *n* imprudencia *f* temeraria **gross pay** *n* paga *f* íntegra **gross profit** *n* ganancia *f* bruta **gross tonnage** *n* tonelaje *m* bruto **gross weight** *n* peso *m* total

grotesque [grəʊˈtesk, *Am:* groʊ-] *n a.* ART, LIT grotesco, -a

grotto ['grɒtəʊ, *Am:* 'grɑːt̬oʊ] <-oes o -os> *n* gruta *f*

grotty ['grɒti, *Am:* 'grɑːt̬i] <-ier, -iest> *adj* *Brit, inf* chungo, -a

grouch [graʊtʃ] **I.** *n* **1.** (*grudge*) rencor *m;* (*complaint*) queja *f* **2.** (*grumpy person*) refunfuñón, -ona *m, f,* cascarrabias *mf inv* **II.** *vi* refunfuñar; **to ~ about sth/sb** quejarse de algo/alguien

grouchy ['graʊtʃi] <-ier, -iest> *adj* malhumorado, -a

ground¹ [graʊnd] **I.** *n* **1.** *no pl* (*the Earth's surface*) tierra *f;* **above/below ~** sobre el nivel del suelo/bajo tierra **2.** *no pl* (*soil*) suelo *m* **3.** (*area of land*) terreno *m;* **breeding ~** zona *f* de cría; **fishing ~s** pesquería *f;* **waste ~** tierra *f* baldía **4.** SPORTS campo *m* **5.** *no pl* (*bottom of the sea*) fondo *m* del mar; **to touch ~** (*ship*) varar **6.** *no pl* (*area of knowledge*) tema *m;* **to be on one's own ~** estar en su elemento; **to give ~** ceder terreno; **to stand one's ~** mantenerse firme **7.** (*reason*) motivo *m;* **to have ~s to do sth** tener motivos para hacer algo; **on the ~s that ...** porque... **II.** *vt* **1.** AVIAT no dejar despegar; **to be ~ed** no poder despegar **2.** (*unable to move*) **to be ~ed** estar encallado, -a **3.** *Am, Aus, fig, inf* no dejar salir

ground² [graʊnd] **I.** *vt pt of* **grind II.** *adj* (*cristal*) deslustrado, -a **III.** *n pl* sedimentos *mpl;* **coffee ~s** poso *m* de café

groundbreaking ['graʊndˌbreɪkɪŋ] *adj*

pionero, -a

ground control *n* control *m* de [*o* desde] tierra **ground crew** *n* + *sing/pl vb* personal *m* de tierra **ground floor** *n Brit* planta *f* baja; **on the ~** en la planta baja, en el primer piso *AmS;* **~ apartment** entresuelo *m* ▸ **to go in on the ~** empezar desde abajo **ground fog** *n* niebla *f* baja **ground frost** *n no pl* escarcha *f*

grounding ['graʊndɪŋ] *n no pl* rudimentos *mpl*, base *f*

groundkeeper *n* cuidador(a) *m(f)* del terreno de juego

groundless ['graʊndlɪs] *adj* infundado, -a

groundnut *n* cacahuete *m*, maní *m AmS*

ground personnel *n* + *pl vb* AVIAT personal *m* de tierra **ground rules** *npl* directrices *fpl* **groundsheet** *n* tela *f* impermeable **groundskeeper** *n Am s.* **groundkeeper groundsman** <-men> *n Brit, Aus* encargado *m* de campo **ground staff** *n* + *pl vb* **1.** (*maintenance at sports ground*) personal *m* de mantenimiento **2.** (*non-flying staff at airport*) personal *m* de tierra **ground-station** *n* RADIO, TV estación *f* terrena **groundswell** *n no pl* **1.** NAUT (*heavy sea*) mar *m o f* de fondo **2.** (*opinion*) sentimiento *m* acusado **ground--to-air missile** *n* misil *m* tierra-aire **ground water** *n no pl* aguas *fpl* subterráneas

groundwork ['graʊndwɜːk, *Am:* -wɜːrk] *n no pl* trabajo *m* preliminar; (*for further study*) trabajo *m* preparatorio; **to lay the ~ for sth** *fig* establecer las bases de algo

group [gruːp] **I.** *n* **1.** *a.* CHEM grupo *m;* ~ **photo** foto *f* de grupo; ~ **of trees** arboleda *f;* **in ~s** en grupos; **to get into ~s** hacer grupos **2.** (*specially assembled*) colectivo *m* **3.** (*business association*) agrupación *f* **4.** (*musicians*) conjunto *m* musical **II.** *vt* agrupar **III.** *vi* agruparse; **to ~ together round sb** agruparse en torno a alguien

group booking *n* reserva *f* para grupos **group captain** *n Brit* MIL jefe *m* de escuadrilla **group dynamics** *npl* dinámica *f* de grupo

groupie ['gruːpi] *n inf* groupie *mf*

grouping ['gruːpɪŋ] *n* agrupamiento *m*

group practice ['gruːpˌpræktɪs] *n* práctica *f* colectiva **group therapy** <-ies> *n* terapia *f* de grupo **group ticket** *n* AUTO billete *m* de grupo

grouse[1] [graʊs] *n* black ~ gallo *m* lira; red ~ urogallo *m* escocés

grouse[2] [graʊs] **I.** *n* **1.** (*complaint*) queja *f* **2.** (*complaining person*) cascarrabias *mf inv* **II.** *vi* quejarse; **to ~ at sb** quejarse de alguien

grove [grəʊv, *Am:* groʊv] *n* (*group of trees*) arboleda *f;* (*orchard*) plantación *f;* **olive ~** olivar *m;* **orange ~** naranjal *m*

grovel ['grɒvl, *Am:* 'grɑːvl] <*Brit:* -ll-, *Am:* -l-> *vi* **1.** (*behave obsequiously*) **to ~** (**before sb**) humillarse (ante alguien) **2.** (*crawl*) arrastrarse; **to ~ in the dust** *fig* morder el polvo

grow [grəʊ, *Am:* groʊ] <grew, grown> **I.** *vi* **1.** (*increase in size*) crecer; (*flourish*) florecer; **to ~ taller** crecer en estatura **2.** (*increase*) aumentar; **to ~ by 2 %** aumentar un 2 % **3.** (*develop*) desarrollarse **4.** (*become*) volverse; **to ~ old** hacerse viejo; **to ~ to like sth** llegar a querer algo **II.** *vt* **1.** (*cultivate*) cultivar **2.** (*let grow*) dejar crecer; **to ~ a beard** dejarse crecer la barba; **some animals ~ a thicker coat in winter** algunos animales desarrollan una piel más gruesa en invierno

♦**grow away from** *vt* irse alejando de

♦**grow into** *vt insep* llegar a ser; *fig* acostumbrarse a

♦**grow out of** *vt insep* **1.** (*become too big*) **she has grown out of her clothes** se le ha quedado la ropa pequeña **2.** (*habit*) perder

♦**grow up** *vi* **1.** (*become adult*) crecer; (*behave like an adult*) madurar; **when I grow up I'd like to ...** cuando sea mayor me gustaría... **2.** (*develop*) desarrollarse

grower ['grəʊə', *Am:* 'groʊ-] *n* **1.** (*gardener*) cultivador(a) *m(f)* **2.** (*plant*) **this plant is a good ~** esta planta crece rápido

growing ['grəʊɪŋ, *Am:* 'groʊ-] **I.** *n no pl* crecimiento *m* **II.** *adj* **1.** (*developing*) **a ~ boy/girl** un chico/una chica que está creciendo **2.** ECON que se expande **3.** (*increasing*) que aumenta

growing pains *npl* **1.** (*pains in the joints*) dolores *mpl* del crecimiento **2.** (*adolescent emotional problems*) problemas *mpl* de la adolescencia

growl [graʊl] **I.** *n* **1.** (*low throaty sound: of a dog*) gruñido *m;* (*of a person*) refunfuño *m* **2.** (*rumble*) ruido *m* sordo **II.** *vi* (*dog*) gruñir; (*person*) refunfuñar

grown [grəʊn, *Am:* groʊn] **I.** *adj* adulto, -a **II.** *pp of* **grow**

grown-up ['grəʊnʌp, *Am:* 'groʊn-] *n a. childspeak* adulto, -a *m, f*

growth [grəʊθ, *Am:* groʊθ] *n* **1.** *no pl* (*increase in size*) crecimiento *m* **2.** (*stage of growing*) madurez *f;* **to reach full ~** alcanzar su plenitud **3.** *no pl* (*increase*) aumento *m;* **rate of ~** tasa *f* de crecimiento **4.** (*development*) desarrollo *m* **5.** (*growing part of plant*) brote *m* **6.** (*whiskers*) crecimiento *m;* **to have a three days' ~ on one's chin** tener barba de tres días **7.** (*caused by disease*) bulto *m*

growth industries *n pl* sectores *mpl* en expansión **growth rate** *n* ECON tasa *f* de crecimiento **growth stock** *n* ECON acciones *fpl* con perspectivas de valorización

groyne [grɔɪn] *n* rompeolas *m inv*

grub [grʌb] **I.** *n* **1.** (*larva*) larva *f* **2.** *no pl, Brit, inf* GASTR rancho *m;* ~ **up!** ¡la comida está servida! **II.** <-bb-> *vi* cavar; **to ~ about** (**for sth**) remover la tierra (buscando algo) **III.** *vt* **to ~ up** arrancar

grubby ['grʌbi] <-ier, -iest> *adj inf* roñoso, -a

grudge [grʌdʒ] **I.** *n* rencor *m*, roña *f Cuba,*

Méx, PRico; **to have a ~ against sb** guardar rencor a alguien **II.** *vt* **to ~ sb sth** envidiar algo a alguien

grudging *adj* poco generoso, -a

grudgingly ['grʌdʒɪŋli] *adv* de mala gana

gruel ['gruːəl] *n no pl* gachas *fpl*

gruelling ['gruːəlɪŋ, *Am:* 'gruːlɪŋ] *adj* duro, -a, penoso, -a

gruesome ['gruːsəm] *adj* horripilante

gruff [grʌf] *adj* brusco, -a; **a ~ voice** una voz bronca

grumble ['grʌmbl] **I.** *n* (*complaint*) queja *f* **II.** *vi* (*person*) quejarse; (*stomach*) hacer ruido; **to ~ about sth/sb** quejarse de algo/alguien

grumpy ['grʌmpi] <-ier, -iest> *adj inf* (*bad tempered*) gruñón, -ona; (*annoyed*) cabreado, -a

grunt [grʌnt] **I.** *n* (*snort*) gruñido *m*; (*groan*) resoplido *m* **II.** *vi* **1.** (*snort*) gruñir **2.** (*groan*) resoplar

G-string ['dʒiːstrɪŋ] *n* **1.** (*musical instrument*) cuerda *f* para la nota Sol **2.** (*underwear*) tanga *m*

guarantee [ˌgærənˈtiː, *Am:* ˌger-] **I.** *n* **1.** (*a promise*) promesa *f*; **to give sb one's ~** hacer una promesa a alguien **2.** (*repair or replacement*) garantía *f* **3.** (*document*) certificado *m* de garantía **4.** (*certainty*) seguridad *f*; **there's no ~ that** no es seguro que +*subj* **5.** (*responsibility for debt*) aval *m* **6.** (*security*) prenda *f* **II.** *vt* **1.** (*promise*) prometer **2.** (*promise to correct faults*) ofrecer una garantía; **to be ~d for three years** tener una garantía de tres años **3.** (*make certain*) **to ~ that** asegurar que +*subj* **4.** (*another's debt*) avalar

guarantor [ˌgærənˈtɔːʳ, *Am:* 'gerənˈtɔːr] *n* garante *mf*

guaranty ['gærənti, *Am:* 'gerənt̮i] <-ies> *n* **1.** (*acceptance of debt*) garantía *f* **2.** (*thing offered as security*) prenda *f*

guard [gɑːd, *Am:* gɑːrd] **I.** *n* **1.** (*person*) guardia *mf*; **prison ~** *Am* carcelero, -a *m, f*; **security ~** guardia de seguridad; **to be on ~** estar de guardia; **to be on one's ~** (**against sth/sb**) estar en alerta (contra algo/alguien); **to be under ~** estar bajo guardia y custodia; **to drop one's ~** bajar la guardia; **to keep ~ over sth/sb** vigilar algo/a alguien; **to post ~s** designar las guardias **2.** SPORTS defensa *f* **3.** (*protective device*) resguardo *m* **4.** *Brit* (*railway official*) jefe, -a *m, f* de tren **5.** MIL **the Guards** la Guardia **II.** *vt* **1.** (*protect*) proteger; (*prevent from escaping*) vigilar **2.** (*keep secret*) guardar

◆**guard against** *vt always sep* (*protect from*) **to guard sth/sb against sth/sb** proteger algo/a alguien de algo/alguien

A las **Household Troops** de la monarquía británica pertenecen siete regimientos de los **Guards** (Guardia). Dos regimientos de **Household Cavalry** (caballería): los **Life**

Guards y los **Blues and Royals**. Y cinco regimientos de infantería: los **Grenadier Guards**, los **Coldstream Guards**, los **Scots Guards**, los **Irish Guards** y los **Welsh Guards**. La ceremonia del cambio de guardia tiene lugar cada dos días a las 11:30 en el **Buckingham Palace**.

guard dog *n* perro *m* guardián **guard duty** <-ies> *n* guardia *f*

guarded ['gɑːdɪd, *Am:* 'gɑːrd-] *adj* cauteloso, -a

guardhouse *n* cuartel *m* de la guardia

guardian ['gɑːdɪən, *Am:* 'gɑːr-] *n* **1.** (*responsible person*) guardián, -ana *m, f* **2.** (*protector*) protector(a) *m(f)*

guardian angel *n a. fig* ángel *m* de la guardia

guardianship *n no pl* **1.** (*being a guardian*) custodia *f* **2.** *form* (*care*) cuidado *m*; **to be in the ~ of sb** estar bajo la tutela de alguien

guardrail ['gɑːdreɪl, *Am:* 'gɑːrd-] *n* (*in bridge*) pretil *m*; (*in staircase*) barandilla *f*

guardroom *n* cuarto *m* de guardia

guardsman <-men> *n* guardia *m*

Guatemala [ˌgwɑːtɪˈmɑːlə, *Am:* -t̮əˈ-] *n* Guatemala *f*

Guatemala City *n* ciudad *f* de Guatemala

Guatemalan [ˌgwɑːtɪˈmɑːlən, *Am:* -t̮əˈ-] **I.** *adj* guatemalteco, -a **II.** *n* guatemalteco, -a *m, f*

guerilla [gəˈrɪlə] *n s.* **guerrilla**

Guernsey ['gɜːnzi, *Am:* 'ɛːrn-] *n* (**the island of**) ~ (la isla de) Guernesey *m*

guerrilla [gəˈrɪlə] *n* guerrilla *f*

guerrilla warfare *n* guerra *f* de guerrillas

guess [ges] **I.** *n* conjetura *f*; **a lucky ~** un acierto afortunado; **to have a ~,** **to take a ~** *Am* adivinar; **to make a wild ~** hacer una conjetura al azar; **at a ~** por decir algo; **your ~ is as good as mine!** ¡vaya Vd. a saber! ►**it's anybody's ~** ¿quién sabe? **II.** *vi* **1.** (*conjecture*) conjeturar; **to ~ right/wrong** adivinar/equivocarse; **~ what I'm doing now?** ¿adivinas qué estoy haciendo ahora?; **to ~ that ...** imaginar que...; **how did you ~?** ¿cómo lo has adivinado? **2.** *Am* (*believe, suppose*) suponer; (*suspect*) sospechar; **I ~ you're right** supongo que estás en lo cierto **III.** *vt* adivinar ►**to keep sb ~ing** tener a alguien en suspense; **~ what?** ¿sabes qué?

guessing game ['gesɪŋˌgeɪm] *n a. fig* adivinanza *f*

guesstimate *n,* **guestimate** ['gestɪmət] *n inf* estimación *f*

guesswork ['geswɜːk, *Am:* -wɜːrk] *n no pl* conjeturas *fpl*

guest [gest] **I.** *n* **1.** (*invited person*) invitado, -a *m, f*; **paying ~** (*person renting*) inquilino, -a *m, f*; (*lodger*) huésped *mf* **2.** (*hotel customer*) cliente *mf* ►**be my ~** *inf* ¡adelante! **II.** *vi a.* TV aparecer como invitado

guesthouse *n* casa *f* de huéspedes **guest-**

room _n_ habitación _f_ de invitados

guffaw [gə'fɔ:, _Am:_ -'fɑ:] **I.** _n_ carcajada _f_
II. _vi_ reírse a carcajadas

guidance ['gaɪdns] _n no pl_ (_help and advice_) consejo _m;_ (_direction_) orientación _f;_ ~ **system** _a._ MIL sistema _m_ de dirección

guide [gaɪd] **I.** _n_ **1.** (_person_) guía _mf;_ **tour/mountain** ~ guía turístico/de montaña **2.** (_book_) guía _f_ **3.** (_help_) orientación _f_ **4.** (_indication_) indicación _f_ **5.** (_girls' association_) **the Guides** las exploradoras **II.** _vt_ **1.** (_show_) guiar **2.** (_instruct_) orientar; **the manual will** ~ **you to ...** el manual te dará instrucciones para... **3.** (_steer, influence_) dirigir; **to be** ~**d by one's emotions** dejarse llevar por los sentimientos

guidebook _n_ guía _f_

guided ['gaɪdɪd] _adj_ **1.** (_led by a guide_) dirigido, -a; ~**ed tour** excursión _f_ con guía **2.** (_automatically steered_) teledirigido, -a; ~ **missile** MIL misil _m_ teledirigido

guide dog _n_ perro-guía _m_ **guideline** _n_ directriz _f;_ (_figure_) pauta _f_

guiding hand ['gaɪdɪŋ 'hænd] _n fig_ mano _f_ amiga **guiding principle** _n_ principio _m_ director

guild [gɪld] _n_ (_of merchants_) corporación _f;_ (_of craftsmen_) gremio _m;_ **Writers' Guild** asociación _f_ de escritores

guilder ['gɪldə', _Am:_ -dɚ] _n_ florín _m_ holandés

guile [gaɪl] _n no pl, form_ astucia _f_

guileful ['gaɪlfəl] _adj form_ astuto, -a

guileless ['gaɪllɪs] _adj_ inocente

guillotine ['gɪlətiːn] _n_ guillotina _f_

guilt [gɪlt] _n no pl_ **1.** (_shame for wrongdoing_) culpabilidad _f_ **2.** (_responsibility for crime_) culpa _f;_ **to admit one's** ~ confesarse culpable; **to establish sb's** ~ determinar la culpabilidad de alguien

guiltless ['gɪltləs] _adj_ inocente

guilt-ridden _adj_ atormentado, -a por un sentido de culpabilidad

guilty ['gɪlti, _Am:_ -ṭi] <-ier, -iest> _adj_ culpable; **to be** ~ **of a crime/murder** ser culpable de un delito/asesinato; **to have a** ~ **conscience** tener un sentimiento de culpabilidad; **to feel** ~ **about sth** sentirse culpable por algo; **to plead** ~ **to sth** declararse culpable de algo; **to prove sb** ~ demostrar la culpabilidad de alguien

guinea ['gɪni] _n Brit_ guinea _f_
Guinea ['gɪni] _n_ Guinea _f_

guinea fowl _n_ gallina _f_ de Guinea

Guinean I. _adj_ guineano, -a **II.** _n_ guineano, -a _m, f_

guinea pig _n_ conejillo _m_ de Indias, cuy _m_ _AmS_

guise [gaɪz] _n no pl_ **1.** (_style_) guisa _f_ **2.** (_appearance_) apariencia _f;_ **it's an old idea in new** ~ se trata de una antigua idea pero con un nuevo aspecto **3.** (_pretence_) pretensión _f;_ **under the** ~ **of sth** bajo el disfraz de algo

guitar [gɪ'tɑː', _Am:_ -'tɑːr] _n_ guitarra _f;_ **to play**

the ~ tocar la guitarra

guitarist [gɪ'tɑːrɪst] _n_ guitarrista _mf_

gulch [gʌltʃ] <-es> _n Am_ (_gully_) barranco _m_

gulf [gʌlf] _n_ **1.** (_area of sea_) golfo _m;_ **the Gulf of Mexico** el Golfo de Méjico; **the Gulf of Suez** el Golfo de Suez; **the (Persian) Gulf** el Golfo (Pérsico) **2.** (_chasm_) abismo _m_ **3.** (_difference of opinion_) diferencias _fpl;_ **to bridge a** ~ llenar un vacío

gull¹ [gʌl] _n_ gaviota _f_

gull² [gʌl] _vt_ **to** ~ **sb** estafar a alguien; **I was** ~**ed into believing that it was a great chance** me hicieron creer que era una gran oportunidad

gullet ['gʌlɪt] _n_ **1.** (_food pipe_) esófago _m_ **2.** (_throat_) garganta _f_

gullible ['gʌləbl] _adj_ crédulo, -a

gully ['gʌli] <-ies> _n_ (_narrow gorge_) barranco _m;_ (_channel_) hondonada _f_

gulp [gʌlp] **I.** _n_ trago _m;_ **a** ~ **of air** una bocanada de aire; **to take a** ~ **of milk/tea** beber un trago de leche/té; **in one** ~ de un trago **II.** _vt_ tragar; (_liquid_) beber; (_food_) engullir **III.** _vi_ **1.** (_swallow with emotion_) tragar saliva **2.** (_breath_) **to** ~ **for air** respirar hondo

gum¹ [gʌm] _n_ ANAT encía _f_

gum² [gʌm] **I.** _n_ **1.** _no pl_ (_soft sticky substance_) goma _f;_ BOT resina _f_ **2.** _no pl_ (_glue_) pegamento _m;_ (_on envelope flaps_) cola _f_ **3.** (_type of sweet_) gominola _f;_ **chewing** ~ chicle _m_ **II.** _vt_ pegar

◆ **gum up** _vt_ estropear ▶**to** ~ **the works** (_stop operation_) paralizar los trabajos; (_interfere_) estropearlo todo

gumboil ['gʌmbɔɪl] _n_ MED flemón _m_

gumdrop ['gʌmdrɒp, _Am:_ -drɑːp] _n_ pastilla _f_ de goma

gummy ['gʌmi] <-ier, -iest> _adj_ (_sticky_) pegajoso, -a; (_with glue on_) engomado, -a

gumption ['gʌmpʃən] _n no pl, inf_ **1.** (_courage_) valor _m;_ **to have the** ~ **to do sth** tener valor para hacer algo **2.** (_intelligence_) seso _m_

gumshield ['gʌmʃiːld] _n_ protector _m_ de dientes

gumshoe ['gʌmʃuː] _n_ **1.** (_overshoe_) chanclo _m_ **2.** _Am, inf_ (_detective_) detective _mf_

gumtree ['gʌmtriː] _n_ árbol _m_ de caucho, gomero _m AmL_ ▶**to be up a** ~ _inf_ estar en un aprieto

gun [gʌn] **I.** _n_ **1.** (_weapon_) arma _f_ de fuego; (_cannon_) cañón _m;_ (_pistol_) pistola _f;_ (_revolver_) revólver _m;_ (_rifle_) fusil _m;_ **to carry a** ~ llevar pistola **2.** SPORTS pistoletazo _m_ **3.** (_device_) pistola _f_ inyectora **4.** _Am_ (_person_) pistolero, -a _m, f;_ **a hired** ~ un pistolero a sueldo ▶**to jump the** ~ SPORTS salir antes de tiempo; **to stick to one's** ~**s** mantenerse en sus trece **II.** <-nn-> _vi_ (_vehicle_) acelerar a fondo

gun barrel _n_ cañón _m_ de un arma **gunboat** _n_ cañonera _f_ **gunfight** _n_ tiroteo _m_ **gunfire** _n no pl_ **1.** (_gunfight_) tiroteo _m;_ (_shots_) dis-

paros *mpl* **2.**(*cannonfire*) cañoneo *m* **gun-**
-licence *n* licencia *f* de armas **gunman**
<-men> *n* pistolero *m*
gunner ['gʌnəʳ, *Am:* -ɚ] *n* artillero *m*
gunpoint *n no pl* at ~ a punto de pistola **gun-**
powder *n no pl* pólvora *f* **gun-runner** *n*
traficante *mf* de armas **gun-running** *n no pl*
contrabando *m* de armas
gunshot ['gʌnʃɒt, *Am:* -ʃɑːt] *n* disparo *m*
gunshot wound *n* herida *f* de bala
gunslinger ['gʌn,slɪŋəʳ] *n* HIST pistolero, -a
m, f
gurgle ['gɜːgl, *Am:* 'gɜːr-] I. *n* (*happy noise*)
gorjeo *m;* (*noise of water*) borboteo *m* II. *vi*
1.(*baby*) gorjear; **to ~ with pleasure/with**
delight gorjear de felicidad/regocijo
2.(*water*) borbotear
guru ['gʊru, *Am:* 'guːruː] *n* gurú *mf*
gush [gʌʃ] I.<-es> *n* chorro *m; fig* efusión *f;*
a ~ of water un chorro de agua II. *vi* **1.**(*any*
liquid) chorrear **2.** *inf* (*praise excessively*) deshacerse en elogios III. *vt* derramar a borbo-
llones
gusher ['gʌʃəʳ, *Am:* -ɚ] *n* pozo *m* petrolífero
gushing *adj* excesivamente efusivo, -a;
(*enthusiastically*) efusivo, -a
gushy ['gʌʃi] <-ier, -iest> *adj* extremo, -a,
efusivo, -a
gusset ['gʌsɪt] *n* escudete *m*
gust [gʌst] I. *n* (*of wind*) ráfaga *f;* (*of rain*)
chaparrón *m* II. *vi* soplar
gusto ['gʌstəʊ, *Am:* -toʊ] *n no pl* entusiasmo
m
gusty ['gʌsti] <-ier -iest> *adj* borrascoso, -a
gut [gʌt] I. *n* **1.**(*intestine*) intestino *m;* **a ~**
feeling/reaction un instinto/una reacción
visceral **2.**(*string from animal intestine*)
tripa *f* **3.** *pl, inf* (*bowels*) entrañas *fpl* **4.** *pl*
(*courage*) valor *m;* (*strength of character*)
determinación *f;* **it takes ~s** se necesita
valor ►**to have sb's ~s for** garters *Brit,*
iron romper la cabeza a alguien; **to** bust **a ~**
inf echar los bofes II.<-tt-> *vt* **1.**(*remove*
the innards) destripar **2.**(*destroy by fire*) **to**
be ~ed estar destruido **3.**(*emotional suffer-*
ing) destrozar
gutless [gʌtlɪs] *adj inf* (*lacking courage*)
cobarde; (*lacking enthusiasm*) apático, -a
gutsy ['gʌtsi] <-ier, -iest> *adj* **1.**(*brave*) valiente; (*adventurous*) atrevido, -a **2.**(*powerful*)
vigoroso, -a
gutter ['gʌtəʳ, *Am:* 'gʌt̬ə] *n* (*drainage chan-*
nel: at the roadside) alcantarilla *f;* (*on the*
roof) canalón *m; fig* barrio *m* marginal
gutter journalism *n no pl* periodismo *m*
sensacionalista **gutter press** *n no pl, Brit*
prensa *f* amarilla
guttural ['gʌtərəl, *Am:* 'gʌt̬-] *adj a.* LING
gutural
guy [gaɪ] *n inf* **1.**(*man*) tío *m;* **hi ~s** *Am, Aus*
¿qué hay, colegas? **2.** *Brit* (*effigy of Guy*
Fawkes) nombre que se les da a unos muñe-
cos que se queman en hogueras la noche del 5

de noviembre en memoria de Guy Fawkes
3.(*rope to fix a tent, guy rope*) viento *m*
Guyana [gaɪ'ænə] *n* Guyana *f*
Guyanese [,gaɪə'niːz] I. *adj* guyanés, -esa
II. *n* guyanés, -esa *m, f*
guzzle ['gʌzl] I. *vt inf* (*eat*) jalar; (*drink*) tragar
II. *vi* zampar
gym [dʒɪm] *n inf* **1.** *no pl* (*gymnastics*) gimnasia *f* **2.**(*gymnasium*) gimnasio *m*
gymkhana [dʒɪm'kɑːnə] *n Brit* gincana *f;*
SPORTS carrera *f* de obstáculos
gymnasium [dʒɪm'neɪzɪəm] *n* gimnasio
m
gymnast ['dʒɪmnæst] *n* gimnasta *mf*
gymnastic [dʒɪm'næstɪk] *adj* gimnástico,
-a
gymnastics [dʒɪm'næstɪks] *npl* gimnasia *f*
gym shoes *n* zapatillas *fpl* de deporte
gynaecological *adj Brit,* **gynecological**
[,gaɪnəkə'lɒdʒɪkəl, *Am:* -'lɑːdʒɪ-] *adj Am,*
Aus ginecológico, -a
gynaecologist *n Brit,* **gynecologist** *n*
Am, Aus ginecólogo, -a *m, f*
gynaecology *n Brit,* **gynecology** [,gaɪnə-
'kɒlədʒi, *Am:* -'kɑːlə-] *n Am, Aus no pl* ginecología *f*
gyp [dʒɪp] *n Aus, Brit, inf* **1.**(*pain*) dolor *m*
2.(*ticking off*) bronca *f*
gypsum ['dʒɪpsəm] *n no pl* yeso *m*
gypsy ['dʒɪpsi] <-ies> I. *n* gitano, -a *m, f*
II. *adj* gitano, -a; ~ **encampment** campamento *m* de gitanos
gyrate [,dʒaɪ'reɪt] *vi* girar
gyration [,dʒaɪ'reɪʃən] *n* giro *m; fig* vuelco *m*
gyrocompass ['dʒaɪrəʊ'kɒmpəs, *Am:*
-roʊ,kʌm-] *n* brújula *f* giroscópica
gyroscope ['dʒaɪrəskəʊp, *Am:* -skoʊp] *n*
NAUT, AVIAT giroscopio *m*

H

H, h [eɪtʃ] *n* H, h *f;* ~ **for Harry** *Brit,* ~ **for**
How *Am* H de Huelva
ha [hɑː] *interj a. iron* ¡ajá!
habeas corpus [,heɪbɪəs'kɔːpəs, *Am:*
-'kɔːr-] *n no pl* LAW hábeas corpus *m;* **Habeas**
Corpus Act Ley *f* de Hábeas Corpus
haberdasher ['hæbədæʃəʳ, *Am:* -ɚdæʃɚ] *n*
1. *Brit* mercero, -a *m, f* **2.** *Am* camisero, -a *m, f*
haberdashery [,hæbə'dæʃəri, *Am:* 'hæbə-
dæʃɚ-] <-ies> *n* **1.** *no pl, Brit* (*wares*) artículos *mpl* de mercería **2.** *Brit* (*shop*) mercería *f*
3. *no pl, Am* (*clothing*) ropa *f* de caballero
4.(*shop*) camisería *f*
habit ['hæbɪt] *n* **1.**(*customary practice*)
hábito *m,* costumbre *f;* **to be in the ~ of**
doing sth tener por costumbre hacer algo; **by**
sheer force of ~ por pura costumbre; **to do**
sth out of ~ hacer algo por costumbre; **to get**

into the ~ (of doing sth) acostumbrarse (a hacer algo); **to get out of the ~ of doing sth** perder la costumbre de hacer algo; **a bad ~** una mala costumbre; **to break a ~** quitarse una costumbre; **don't make a ~ of it** no lo hagas por costumbre **2.** (*dress*) hábito *m;* **riding ~** traje *m* de montar **3.** (*addiction*) adicción *f;* **to have a heroin ~** ser adicto a la heroína

habitable ['hæbɪtəbl, *Am:* -t̬ə-] *adj* habitable

habitat ['hæbɪtæt, *Am:* '-ə-] *n* hábitat *m*

habitation [ˌhæbɪ'teɪʃən] *n* **1.** *no pl* (*occupancy*) **unfit for human ~** inhabitable **2.** (*dwelling*) morada *f* **3.** (*settlement*) asentamiento *m*

habitual [hə'bɪtʃuəl] *adj* **1.** (*usual*) habitual; **~ drug use** consumo frecuente de drogas **2.** (*describing person*) empedernido, -a

habituate [hə'bɪtʃueɪt] *vt* habituar; **to ~ oneself to do sth** habituarse a hacer algo

hack¹ [hæk] **I.** *vt* **1.** *Brit* (*football*) dar una patada a **2.** (*chop violently*) cortar a tajos; **to ~ to death** matar a cuchilladas; **to ~ sth to pieces** hacer algo trizas **3.** *Am, Aus, inf* (*cope with*) aguantar **II.** *vi* hacer tajos; **to ~ at sth** cortar algo a tajos **III.** *n* **1.** (*journalist*) periodista *mf* de pacotilla **2.** (*politician*) politicucho, -a *m, f* **3.** (*writer*) escritorzuelo, -a *m, f*

hack² [hæk] *vt* INFOR **to ~ (into) a system** introducirse ilegalmente en un sistema

hack³ [hæk] **I.** *vi* montar a caballo **II.** *n* **1.** (*rural horse-ride*) paseo *m* a caballo **2.** *Am, inf* (*taxi car*) taxi *m* **3.** (*driver*) taxista *mf*

hacker ['hækər, *Am:* -ə-] *n* INFOR hacker *mf*

hackles ['hæklz] *npl* (*on dogs' backs*) pelo *m* erizado; (*on birds' necks*) collar *m* ▶**to get one's ~ up** enfurecerse; **to make sb's ~ rise** poner furioso a alguien; **to raise ~** levantar ampollas

hackney ['hækni] *n,* **hackney carriage** *n* **1.** (*carriage*) coche *m* de alquiler **2.** (*taxi*) taxi *m*

hackneyed ['hæknɪd] *adj* (*argument, theme*) trillado, -a

hacksaw ['hæksɔ:, *Am:* -sɑ:] *n* sierra *f* para metales

had [həd, *stressed:* hæd] *pt, pp of* **have**

haddock ['hædək] *n* eglefino *m*

hadn't ['hædnt] = **had not** *s.* **have**

haematite ['hemətaɪt] *n* MIN hematites *f inv*

haemoglobin [ˌhi:mə'gləʊbɪn, *Am:* 'hi:-məgloʊ-] *n no pl, Brit, Aus* hemoglobina *f*

haemophilia [ˌhi:mə'fɪlɪə, *Am:* ˌhi:moʊ'-] *n no pl, Brit, Aus* hemofilia *f*

haemophiliac [ˌhi:məʊ'fɪlɪæk, *Am:* ˌhi:moʊ'-] *n Brit, Aus* hemofílico, -a *m, f*

haemorrhage ['hemərɪdʒ, *Am:* -ə-ɪdʒ] **I.** *n* hemorragia *f;* **brain ~** derrame *m* cerebral **II.** *vi Brit, Aus* tener una hemorragia

haemorrhoids ['hemərɔɪdz] *npl* hemorroides *fpl*

haft [hɑ:ft, *Am:* hæft] *n* (*of a knife*) mango

m; (*of a sword*) empuñadura *f*

hag [hæg] *n* (*ugly old woman*) bruja *f*

haggard ['hægəd, *Am:*-ə-d] *adj* macilento, -a

haggis ['hægɪs] *n no pl* plato escocés a base de vísceras de cordero

haggle ['hægl] *vi* regatear; **to ~ over sth** regatear el precio de algo

Hague [heɪg] *n* **the ~** la Haya

haha *interj,* **ha-ha** ['hɑ:hɑ:] *interj,* **ha ha** *interj iron* ¡ja, ja!

hail¹ [heɪl] **I.** *n no pl* METEO granizo *m;* (*of stones, insults*) lluvia *f* **II.** *vi* granizar; **to ~ down on sb/sth** *a. fig* llover sobre alguien/algo

hail² [heɪl] **I.** *vt* **1.** (*call*) llamar; **to ~ a taxi** parar un taxi **2.** (*acclaim*) aclamar **3.** (*welcome*) acoger; **she ~ed the news with joy** recibió la noticia con alegría **II.** *vi* **to ~ from** (*person*) ser de; (*thing*) proceder de

hail-fellow-well-met [ˌheɪlˌfeləʊˌwel'met, *Am:* ˌ-oʊˌ-] *n* (demasiado) campechano, -a

hair [heər, *Am:* her] *n* **1.** (*on the skin of an animal or a person*) pelo *m;* (*on human head*) cabello *m;* **to do one's ~** arreglarse el pelo (en una peluquería); **to have one's ~ cut** cortarse el pelo; **to wash one's ~** lavarse el pelo; **to wear one's ~ up/down** llevar el pelo recogido/suelto **2.** (*of body*) vello *m* **3.** (*on plant*) pelusa *f* ▶**that'll put ~s on your chest** *inf* eso te dejará como nuevo; **to make sb's ~s curl** *inf* poner los pelos de punta a alguien; **to get in sb's ~** poner a alguien nervioso; **to not harm a ~ on sb's head** no tocarle ni un pelo a alguien; **keep your ~ on!** *Brit, Aus, iron, inf* ¡no te sulfures!; **to split ~s** buscarle tres pies al gato; **to not turn a ~** no inmutarse

hairbrush ['heəbrʌʃ, *Am:* 'her-] <-es> *n* cepillo *m* (del pelo) **hair conditioner** *n* acondicionador *m* del cabello **hair curler** *n* tenacilla *f* de rizar **haircut** *n* corte *m* de pelo; **to get a ~** cortarse el pelo **hairdo** *n inf* peinado *m* **hairdresser** *n* peluquero, -a *m, f;* **the ~'s** la peluquería

hairdressing *n* **1.** *no pl* (*profession*) peluquería *f* **2.** (*action of styling hair*) peinado *m* **hairdressing salon** *n* (salón *m* de) peluquería *f*

hair drier *n,* **hair dryer** ['heəˌdraɪər, *Am:* 'herˌdraɪə-] *n* secador *m* (de pelo) **hairgrip** *n* horquilla *f*

hairless ['heəlɪs, *Am:* 'her-] *adj* (*head*) calvo, -a, pelado, -a *AmS;* (*body*) sin vello; (*face*) lampiño, -a; (*animal*) sin pelo

hairline ['heəlaɪn, *Am:* 'her-] *n* **1.** (*lower edge of the hair*) nacimiento *m* del pelo; **he has a receding ~** tiene entradas **2.** (*fine line*) línea *f* muy fina **hairline crack** *n,* **hairline fracture** *n* grieta *f* fina

hairnet ['heənet, *Am:* 'her-] *n* redecilla *f* **hairpiece** *n* postizo *m*

hairpin ['heəpɪn, *Am:* 'her-] *n* horquilla *f,* gancho *m AmL* **hairpin bend** *n Brit, Aus,* **hairpin curve** *n,* **hairpin turn** *n Am* curva *f* muy cerrada

hair-raising ['heə,reɪzɪŋ, *Am:* 'her-] *adj inf* espeluznante **hair remover** *n* depilatorio *m* **hair restorer** *n* tónico *m* capilar **hair slide** *n* pasador *m* **hair-splitting** I. *n no pl* sutilezas *fpl* II. *adj* (*argument, remark*) demasiado sutil; (*person*) quisquilloso, -a

hairspray ['heəspreɪ, *Am:* 'her-] *n* laca *f* (para el pelo) **hairstyle** *n* peinado *m*

hairy ['heəri, *Am:* 'heri] <-ier, -iest> *adj* 1. (*having much hair*) peludo, -a 2. *inf* (*frightening*) espeluznante

Haiti ['heɪti, *Am:* -t̬i] *n* Haití *m*

Haitian ['heɪʃən] I. *n* haitiano, -a *m, f* II. *adj* haitiano, -a

hake [heɪk] <-(s)> *n* merluza *f*

hale [heɪl] *adj* robusto, -a; ~ **and hearty** fuerte como un roble

half [hɑːf, *Am:* hæf] I. <halves> *n* 1. (*equal part*) mitad *f;* ~ **an apple** media manzana; **in** ~ por la mitad; ~ **and** ~ mitad y mitad; **to cut sth into halves** partir algo por la mitad; **a kilo and a** ~ un kilo y medio; **to go halves (on sth)** *inf* pagar (algo) a medias; **to go halves with sb** ir a medias con alguien; **to do things by halves** hacer las cosas a medias; **my other** ~ *fig* mi media naranja; **first/second** ~ SPORTS primer/segundo tiempo; **the first/second** ~ **of a century** la primera/segunda mitad de un siglo; **that was a game and a** ~! *fig* ¡menudo partido! 2. *Brit, inf* (*of beer*) media pinta *f* ►**to be too** <u>clever</u> **by** ~ pasarse de listo II. *adj* medio, -a; ~ **a pint** media pinta; ~ **an hour, a** ~ **hour** media hora; ~ **the country** medio país; **she's** ~ **the player she used to be** esta jugadora no es ni sombra de lo que era III. *adv* 1. (*almost*) casi; **to be** ~ **sure** estar casi seguro 2. (*partially*) a medias; ~ **asleep** medio dormido; ~ **cooked** medio crudo; ~ **done** a medio hacer; ~ **naked** medio desnudo; ~ **empty/full** medio vacío/lleno 3. (*by fifty percent*) ~ **as many/much** la mitad; ~ **as much again** la mitad más 4. *inf* (*most*) la mayor parte; ~ (**of**) **the time** la mayor parte del tiempo 5. (*thirty minutes after*) ~ **past three** las tres y media; (**at**) ~ **past nine** a las nueve y media; **at** ~ **past** *Brit, inf* a y media 6. *Brit, inf* (*intensifies negative statement*) **not** ~ no poco; **he wasn't** ~ **handsome** era guapísimo; **do you like it? – not** ~! ¿te gusta? – ¡no me gusta, me encanta! IV. *pron* la mitad; ~ **and** ~ mitad y mitad

halfback ['hɑːfbæk, *Am:* 'hæf-] *n* SPORTS medio *m* **half-baked** *adj* 1. (*food*) medio cocido, -a 2. *inf* (*plan*) sin sentido, estúpido, -a **half board** *n no pl* media pensión *f* **half-breed** *n,* **half-caste** *n* mestizo, -a **half-brother** *n* hermanastro *m* **half-crown** *n* HIST media corona *f* **half-dozen** *adj* media docena *f* **half-empty** *adj* medio vacío, -a **half-fare** *n* medio billete *m* **half-full** *adj* medio lleno, -a **half-hearted** *adj* poco entusiasta; **a** ~ **attempt** un intento desganado

half-mast *n* at ~ a media asta **half-moon** *n* media luna *f;* ~ **shaped** en forma de media luna **half note** *n Am* MUS blanca *f* **halfpence** *n inv,* **halfpenny** <-ies> *n* HIST medio penique *m* **half-price** *adj* at ~ a mitad de precio **half-sister** *n* hermanastra *f* **half-term** *n no pl, Brit* vacaciones *fpl* de mitad de trimestre **half-timbered** *adj* con entramado de madera **half-time** *n* 1. SPORTS descanso *m;* **at** ~ en el descanso 2. ECON media jornada *f;* **to be on** ~ trabajar media jornada **half-title** *n* 1. (*first printed page*) portadilla *f* 2. (*title*) titulillo *m* **half tone** *n* media tinta *f* **halfway** I. *adj* 1. (*midway*) medio, -a; ~ **point** punto medio; ~ **stage** etapa *f* intermedia 2. (*partial*) parcial II. *adv* 1. (*to or at half the distance*) a mitad de camino; **to be** ~ **between … and …** estar entre… y…; **to be** ~ **through sth** ir por la mitad de algo; ~ **through the year** a mediados de año; ~ **up** a media cuesta; **to meet sb** ~ *fig* llegar a un acuerdo con alguien 2. (*nearly, partly*) **to go** ~ **towards (doing) sth** hacer algo en parte; **the proposals only went** ~ **towards meeting their demands** las propuestas sólo satisfacían en parte sus exigencias **half-wit** *n* imbécil *mf* **half-yearly** I. *adj* semestral II. *adv* semestralmente

halibut ['hælɪbət] <-(s)> *n* halibut *m*

halitosis [ˌhælɪ'təʊsɪs, *Am:* -'toʊ-] *n no pl* halitosis *f inv*

hall [hɔːl] *n* 1. (*room by front door*) vestíbulo *m* 2. (*large public room*) sala *f;* (*in schools*) comedor *m;* ~ **concert** ~ sala *f* de conciertos; **town** ~, **city** ~ *Am* ayuntamiento *m* 3. UNIV colegio *m* mayor; ~ **of residence** residencia *f* universitaria 4. (*corridor*) pasillo *m* 5. (*country house*) casa *f* solariega

hallelujah [ˌhælɪ'luːjə] I. *interj* ¡aleluya! II. *n* aleluya *m*

hallmark ['hɔːlmɑːk, *Am:* -mɑːrk] I. *n* 1. *Brit* (*engraved identifying mark*) contraste *m* 2. (*identifying symbol*) distintivo *m;* **her** ~ su sello personal; **to bear all the** ~**s of …** *fig* tener todas las características de… II. *vt* contrastar

hallo [hə'ləʊ, *Am:* -'loʊ] <-s> *interj Brit* hola

hallow ['hæləʊ, *Am:* -oʊ] *vt* 1. (*sanctify*) santificar; (*consecrate*) consagrar; **to be** ~**ed** ser sagrado 2. (*venerate*) venerar

hallowed *adj* sagrado, -a

Halloween *n,* **Hallowe'en** [ˌhæləʊ'iːn, *Am:* ˌhæloʊ'-] *n* víspera *f* de Todos los Santos

La fiesta de **Hallowe'en** se celebra el día 31 de octubre, el día antes de **All Saints' Day**, también llamado **All Hallows** (Todos los Santos). Desde hace mucho tiempo en esta festividad cobran un protagonismo destacado los espíritus y las brujas. Los niños hacen **turnip lanterns**, (farolillos hechos con calabazas vaciadas) y en Escocia hacen **guising** (esto es, se disfrazan y van de casa en casa cantando o recitando poemas para que los dueños de la casa les den dinero]. En los EE.UU. los niños se difrazan al atardecer y van de puerta en puerta con un saco en la mano. Cuando el dueño de la casa abre la puerta los niños gritan: '**Trick or treat!**'; el inquilino elige entonces entre darles un **treat** (dulce) o sufrir un **trick** (susto). Hoy en día los sustos prácticamente han desaparecido, pues los niños sólo se acercan a aquellas casas en las que las luces de fuera están encendidas, lo cual funciona como señal de bienvenida.

hallucinate [həˈluːsɪneɪt] *vi a. fig* alucinar
hallucination [həˌluːsɪˈneɪʃən] *n no pl* alucinación *f*
hallucinogenic [həˌluːsɪnəˈdʒenɪk, *Am:* -noʊˈ-] *adj* alucinógeno, -a
halo [ˈheɪləʊ, *Am:* -loʊ] <-s *o* -es> *n* 1. *a. fig* ASTR halo *m* 2. *a. fig* REL aureola *f*
halogen [ˈhælədʒen, *Am:* ˈhæloʊ-] *n* halógeno *m*
halogen bulb *n* bombilla *f* halógena
halogen lamp *n* lámpara *f* halógena
halt [hɒlt, *Am:* hɔːlt] I. *n no pl* 1. (*standstill, stoppage*) parada *f;* **to bring sth/sb to a ~** detener algo/a alguien; **to call a ~ to sth** poner coto a algo; **to come to a ~** pararse 2. (*interruption*) interrupción *f* 3. RAIL apeadero *m* II. *vt* (*bring to a permanent stop*) parar; (*bring to a temporary stop*) interrumpir III. *vi* (*stop permanently*) parar; (*stop temporarily*) interrumpirse IV. *interj* ~! ¡alto!
halter [ˈhɔːltəʳ, *Am:* -tɚ] *n* 1. (*animals*) ronzal *m* 2. (*criminals*) soga *f*
halterneck [ˈhɒltənek, *Am:* -ˈhɔːltɚ-] *n* top *m* con tirante de cuello
halting *adj* (*speech, movement*) vacilante
halve [hɑːv, *Am:* hæv] I. *vt* 1. (*lessen*) reducir a la mitad; (*number*) dividir por dos 2. (*cut in two equal pieces*) partir por la mitad II. *vi* reducirse a la mitad
halyard [ˈhæljəd, *Am:* -jɚd] *n* NAUT driza *f*
ham [hæm] I. *n* 1. *no pl* (*cured*) jamón *m* (serrano); (*cooked*) jamón *m* (cocido); **a slice of ~** una loncha de jamón 2. (*actor*) histrión *m* 3. (*radio*) radioaficionado, -a *m, f* II. *vi* actuar con histrionismo III. *vt* ~ **up** interpretar con afectación; **to ~ it up** actuar histriónicamente
hamburger [ˈhæmbɜːgəʳ, *Am:* -bɜːrgɚ] *n* 1. (*take-away*) hamburguesa *f* 2. *no pl, Am* (*chopped beef*) carne *f* picada
ham-fisted [ˌhæmˈfɪstɪd, *Am:* ˈhæmfɪstɪd] *adj Brit, Aus,* **ham-handed** [ˌhæmˈhændɪd, *Am:* ˈhæmˌhændɪd] *adj Am* torpe
hamlet [ˈhæmlət] *n* aldea *f*
hammer [ˈhæməʳ, *Am:* -ɚ] I. *n* 1. (*tool*) martillo *m;* ~ **blow** *a. fig* martillazo *m;* **the ~ and sickle** POL, HIST la hoz y el martillo; **throwing the ~** SPORTS lanzamiento *m* de martillo; **to go under the ~** *a. fig* (*painting*) salir a subasta 2. (*part of modern gun*) percutor *m* ▶ **to go at**

it ~ **and tongs** *inf* (*do energetically*) echar el resto; (*fight*) luchar a brazo partido II. *vt* 1. (*hit with tool: metal*) martillear; (*nail*) clavar; **to ~ sth** (**into sth**) clavar algo (en algo); **to ~ sth into sb** *fig* meter algo en la cabeza a alguien 2. *inf* (*beat easily in sports*) dar una paliza 3. (*condemn: book, film*) machacar; **to ~ sb for sth** criticar duramente a alguien por algo 4. FIN, ECON declarar insolvente 5. *inf* (*become very drunk*) **to get ~ed** (**on sth**) emborracharse (de algo) III. *vi* 1. (*use a hammer*) martillear; **to ~ at sth** dar martillazos a algo 2. (*strike as with a hammer*) golpear; (*heart*) latir con fuerza; (*head*) estar a punto de estallar; **to ~ on sth** aporrear algo
◆**hammer in** *vt* clavar
◆**hammer out** *vt* 1. (*correct*) alisar a martillazos 2. (*find solution*) negociar; **to ~ a settlement** llegar a un arreglo
hammer drill *n* perforadora *f* de percusión
hammerhead *n* 1. (*head of a hammer*) cabeza *f* de martillo 2. ZOOL ~ **shark** pez *m* martillo
hammock [ˈhæmək] *n* hamaca *f*
hamper[1] [ˈhæmpəʳ, *Am:* -pɚ] *vt* (*hinder*) dificultar; **to ~ sb/sth** poner trabas a alguien/algo
hamper[2] [ˈhæmpəʳ, *Am:* -pɚ] *n* 1. (*picnic basket*) cesta *f* 2. *Am* (*for dirty linen*) cesto *m* de la ropa
hamster [ˈhæmstəʳ, *Am:* -stɚ] *n* hámster *m*
hamstring [ˈhæmstrɪŋ] I. *n* ANAT tendón *m* de la corva; ZOOL tendón *m* del corvejón II. *vt irr* 1. (*cut the hamstring*) desjarretar 2. (*render powerless: thing*) paralizar; (*person*) incapacitar; **to be hamstrung** estar atado de pies y manos
hand [hænd] I. *n* 1. ANAT mano *f;* **to be good with one's ~s** ser mañoso; **to deliver a letter by ~** entregar una carta en mano; **to do sth by ~** hacer algo a mano; **to keep one's ~s off** no tocar; **to shake ~s with sb** estrechar la mano a alguien; **to take sb by the ~** llevar a alguien de la mano; **to tie ~ and foot** *a. fig* atar de pies y manos; **sword in ~** espada en ristre; ~ **in ~** de la mano; **get your ~s off!** ¡no toques!; **~s up!** ¡manos arriba! 2. (*handy, within reach*) **at ~** muy cerca; **to ~ a mano; to keep sth close at ~** tener algo a mano; **to be at ~** acercarse; **in ~** (*available to use*) disponible; (*being arranged*) entre manos; **preparations are in ~** los preparativos están en marcha 3. (*what needs doing now*) **the problem in ~** el problema que nos ocupa; **to be on ~** (*object*) estar a mano; (*person*) estar ahí; **to get out of ~** (*things, situation*) irse de las manos; (*person*) descontrolarse 4. *pl* (*responsibility, authority, care*) **to be in good ~s** estar en buenas manos; **to fall into the ~s of sb** caer en manos de alguien; **to put sth into the ~s of sb** poner algo en manos de alguien; **at the ~s of sb** (*because of*) a manos de alguien 5. (*assistance*) **to give** (**sb**) **a ~** (**with sth**)

echar (a alguien) una mano (con algo); **to keep one's ~ in** no perder la práctica **6.** (*control*) **to have sth in ~** tener algo entre manos; **to have sth well in ~** tener algo bajo control; **to have a ~ in sth** intervenir en algo; **to take sb in ~** apretar las clavijas a alguien **7.** GAMES **to have a good/poor** ~ tener una buena/mala mano; **to show one's ~** *a. fig* enseñar las cartas; **a ~ of poker** una mano de póquer **8.** (*pointer on clock*) manecilla *f;* **the hour ~** la aguja de las horas; **the minute ~** el minutero; **the second ~** el segundero **9.** (*manual worker*) obrero, -a *m, f;* (*sailor*) marinero, -a *m, f;* **factory ~** operario, -a *m, f* **10.** (*skilful person*) old **~** veterano, -a *m, f;* **to be an old ~ at sth** tener mucha experiencia en algo **11.** (*applause*) aplauso *m;* **let's have a big ~ for ...** un gran aplauso para... **12.** (*measurement*) palmo *m* de alzada **13.** (*handwriting*) letra *f;* **in his own ~** de su puño y letra ▶**to make money ~ over fist** hacer dinero a espuertas; **to lose money ~ over fist** perder dinero rápidamente; **to be ~ in glove with sb** ser uña y carne con alguien; **to put one's ~ in one's pocket** contribuir con dinero; **to be able to turn one's ~ to anything** saber hacer cualquier cosa; **with a firm ~** con mano dura; **at first ~** de primera mano; **to have one's ~s full** estar muy ocupado; **with a heavy** [*o* an **iron**] **~** con mano dura; **to play a lone ~** actuar solo; **on the one ~ ... on the other** (~) **...** por un lado..., por otro (lado)...; **second ~** de segunda mano; **to have one's ~s tied** tener las manos atadas; **to ask for sb's ~ in marriage** *form* pedir la mano de alguien; **to have sb eat out of one's ~** meterse a alguien en el bolsillo; **to force sb's ~** forzar la mano a alguien; **to get one's ~s on sb** atrapar a alguien; **to lay one's ~s on sth** hacerse con algo; **to not soil one's ~s with sth** no mancharse las manos con algo; **to throw in one's ~** darse por vencido II. *vt* **1.** (*give*) dar; **will you ~ me my bag?** ¿puedes pasarme mi bolso? **2.** (*give credit to*) **you've got to ~ it to him** hay que reconocer que lo hace muy bien

◆**hand around** *vt* hacer circular

◆**hand back** *vt* devolver

◆**hand down** *vt* **1.** (*knowledge, tradition*) transmitir; (*objects*) pasar; **to hand sth down from one generation to another** transmitir algo de generación en generación **2.** *Am* LAW (*judgement*) pronunciar

◆**hand in** *vt* (*task, document*) entregar; **to ~ one's resignation** presentar la dimisión

◆**hand on** *vt* (*knowledge*) transmitir; (*object*) pasar; **to hand sth on to sb** pasar algo a alguien

◆**hand out** *vt* **1.** (*distribute*) repartir **2.** (*give: advice*) dar; (*punishment*) aplicar

◆**hand over** I. *vt* **1.** (*give, submit: money, prisoner*) entregar; (*cheque*) extender **2.** (*pass: power, authority*) transferir; (*property*) ceder **3.** TEL pasar; **to hand sb over to sb**

pasar a alguien con alguien II. *vi* **to ~ to sb** delegar en alguien; TV pasar la conexión a alguien

◆**hand round** *vt* hacer circular

handbag ['hændbæg] *n* bolso *m,* cartera *f AmL* **handball** *n no pl* SPORTS balonmano *m* **hand-barrow** *n Brit* carretilla *f* **handbill** *n* folleto *m* **handbook** *n* manual *m* **handbrake** *n Brit* AUTO freno *m* de mano **handcart** *n* carretilla *f* **handcuff** *vt* esposar **handcuffs** *npl* esposas *fpl;* **a pair of ~** unas esposas

handful ['hændfʊl] *n no pl* **1.** *a. fig* (*small amount*) puñado *m;* **a ~ of people** un puñado de personas **2.** (*person*) **to be a real ~** (*child*) ser un bicho; (*adult*) ser de armas tomar

hand grenade *n* granada *f* de mano **handgun** *n* pistola *f*

handicap ['hændɪkæp] I. *n* **1.** (*disability*) discapacidad *f;* **mental ~** discapacidad *f* mental; **physical ~** invalidez *f* **2.** (*disadvantage*) desventaja *f* **3.** SPORTS hándicap *m* II. <-pp-> *vt* perjudicar; **to be ~ped** estar en una situación de desventaja

handicapped I. *adj* **physically ~** minusválido, -a; **mentally ~** disminuido psíquico II. *n* **the ~** los minusválidos

handicraft ['hændɪkrɑːft, *Am:* -kræft] *n* **1.** (*art*) artesanía *f* **2.** SCHOOL trabajos *mpl* manuales

handiwork ['hændɪwɜːk, *Am:* -wɜːrk] *n no pl* **1.** (*work*) trabajo *m* artesanal **2.** (*product*) artesanía *f;* SCHOOL trabajos *mpl* manuales; **this must be Peter's ~** *iron* esto debe ser obra de Peter

handkerchief ['hæŋkətʃɪf, *Am:* -kɚtʃɪf] *n* pañuelo *m*

handle ['hændl] I. *n* **1.** (*of pot, basket, bag*) asa *f;* (*of drawer*) tirador *m;* (*of knife*) mango *m* **2.** (*knob*) pomo *m;* (*lever*) palanca *f* **3.** *inf* (*name*) título *m* ▶**to fly off the ~** *inf* perder los estribos II. *vt* **1.** (*touch*) tocar; **~ with care** frágil **2.** (*move, transport*) llevar **3.** (*machine, tool, weapon*) manejar; (*chemicals*) manipular; **to ~ a situation well** manejar bien una situación; **she ~s light expertly in her paintings** en sus cuadros maneja la luz con maestría; **I don't know how to ~ her** no sé cómo tratarla **4.** (*direct*) ocuparse de; (*case*) llevar; **I'll ~ this** yo me encargo de esto; **he ~s the márketing** es el responsable de marketing; **he doesn't know how to ~ other people** (*business*) no sabe dirigir; (*socially*) no tiene don de gentes **5.** (*control*) dominar; (*work, difficult situation*) poder con; **to ~ an increase in prices** hacer frente a un aumento de precios **6.** (*discuss, portray: subject*) tratar **7.** (*operate: car*) conducir, manejar *AmL;* (*boat*) dirigir **8.** *Brit* COM comerciar con III. *vi* + *adv/prep* responder; **to ~ poorly** no responder bien

handlebar moustache *n* bigote *m* afilado **handlebars** ['hændlbɑːz, *Am:* -bɑːrz] *npl* manillar *m*

handler *n* adiestrador(a) *m(f)*

handling *n no pl* **1.** (*management*) manejo *m;* (*of goods*) manipulación *f;* (*of subject*) tratamiento *m;* (*of person*) trato *m;* (*of car*) conducción, manejo *m AmL* **2.** COM porte *m*

hand luggage *n no pl* equipaje *m* de mano

handmade *adj* hecho, -a a mano

hand-me-down ['hændmɪdaʊn] *n* prenda *f* heredada

hand-operated *adj* manual

handout ['hændaʊt] *n* **1.** (*leaflet*) folleto *m* **2.** (*press release*) comunicado *m* de prensa **3.** (*written information*) apuntes *mpl* **4.** (*money*) limosna *f*

hand-picked [ˌhænd'pɪkt] *adj* cuidadosamente seleccionado, -a

handrail ['hændreɪl] *n* (*stairs*) pasamanos *m inv;* (*bridge*) barandilla *f* **hand saw** *n* serrucho *m* **handshake** *n* apretón *m* de manos

handsome ['hænsəm] *adj* **1.** (*man*) guapo; (*animal, thing*) bello, -a; **the most ~ man** el hombre más apuesto **2.** (*impressive*) magnífico, -a **3.** (*large*) considerable; (*price, salary*) elevado, -a; (*donation*) generoso, -a; **by a ~ margin** por un amplio margen **4.** (*gracious: gesture*) noble

hands-on [ˌhændz'ɒn, *Am:* -'ɑːn] *adj* **1.** (*instruction*) práctico, -a; **~ approach** enfoque práctico **2.** INFOR manual

handspring ['hændsprɪŋ] *n* salto *m* mortal; **backward ~** salto mortal hacia atrás **handstand** *n* pino *m;* **to do a ~** hacer el pino **hand-to-mouth** *adj* (*salary*) precario, -a; **to lead a ~ existence** tener lo justo para vivir **handwork** *n no pl* trabajo *m* hecho a mano **handwriting** *n no pl* letra *f*

handwritten [ˌhænd'rɪtn] *adj* manuscrito, -a

handy ['hændi] <-ier, -iest> *adj* **1.** (*user-friendly*) manejable; (*form, guide*) sencillo, -a **2.** (*conveniently available*) a mano; (*nearby*) cercano, -a; **to keep sth ~** tener algo a mano; **to be ~ for sth** quedar cerca de algo **3.** (*skilful*) hábil; **to be ~ with sth** ser mañoso para algo; **to be ~ about the house** ser un manitas **4.** (*convenient*) práctico, -a; (*useful*) útil; **to come in ~** venir bien; **to come in ~ for sb** venir muy bien a alguien

handyman ['hændɪmæn] <-men> *n* manitas *m inv*

hang [hæŋ] I. <hung, hung> *vi* **1.** (*be suspended*) colgar; (*picture*) estar colgado; **to ~ by/on/from sth** colgar de algo; **to ~ in a gallery** estar expuesto en una galería **2.** (*lean over or forward*) inclinarse **3.** (*float: smoke, fog*) flotar; (*bird*) planear; **to ~ above sb/sth** cernirse sobre alguien/algo; **to leave a question ~ing** dejar una pregunta en el aire **4.** (*be pending*) estar pendiente **5.** (*die*) morir en la horca **6.** (*fit, drape: clothes, fabrics*) caer; **to ~ well** tener buena caída ►**he can go ~** por mí como si se muere II. <hung, hung> *vt* **1.** (*attach*) colgar; (*washing*) tender; (*door*) colocar; **to ~ wallpaper** (**on a wall**) empapelar (una pared); **to ~ the curtains** colgar las cortinas; **the gal-**lery will ~ many of his paintings muchas de sus obras se expondrán en la galería **2.** (*decorate*) adornar **3.** (*head*) bajar **4.** (*execute*) ahorcar ►**I'll be ~ed if ...** que me ahorquen si...; ~ **it** (**all**) ¡caray! III. *n no pl* FASHION caída *f* ►**to get the ~ of sth** *inf* coger el truquillo a algo; **I don't give a ~** *Am, inf* me importa un bledo

◆**hang about, hang around** I. *vi* **1.** *inf* (*waste time*) perder el tiempo **2.** (*wait*) esperar **3.** (*idle*) no hacer nada; **there's a couple of kids hanging around on the street** dos niños andan vagabundeando por la calle II. *vt insep* rondar; **I had to ~ the bus station for an hour** tuve que estar una hora de plantón en la estación de autobuses; **to ~ a place** andar rondando por un sitio

◆**hang back** *vi* **1.** (*be reluctant to move forward*) quedarse atrás **2.** (*hesitate*) vacilar

◆**hang behind** *vi* rezagarse

◆**hang on** I. *vi* **1.** (*wait briefly*) esperar; **to keep sb hanging on** hacer esperar a alguien; **~!** *inf* ¡espera un momento!; **she's on the other phone, would you like to ~?** está hablando por la otra línea, ¿quiere esperar? **2.** (*hold on to*) **to ~ to sth** agarrarse a algo; **~ tight** agárrate fuerte **3.** (*persevere*) mantenerse firme; (*resist*) aguantar II. *vt insep* **1.** (*depend upon*) depender de **2.** (*give attention*) estar pendiente de; **to ~ sb's every word** estar pendiente de lo que dice alguien

◆**hang out** I. *vt* (*washing*) tender; (*tongue*) sacar; (*flag*) izar II. *vi* **1.** (*dangle*) colgar; **with his tongue hanging out** *a. fig* con la lengua fuera; **let it all ~!** *inf* ¡suéltate la melena! *fig* **2.** *inf* (*frequent*) andar; **where does he ~ these days?** ¿por dónde anda estos días? **3.** *inf* (*reside*) vivir

◆**hang over** *vt insep* estar suspendido sobre; *fig* cernirse sobre

◆**hang round** *vi, vt Brit s.* **hang around**

◆**hang together** *vi* **1.** (*make sense*) ser coherente **2.** (*remain associated*) permanecer unidos

◆**hang up** I. *vi* colgar; **to ~ on sb** colgar a alguien II. *vt* **1.** (*curtains, receiver*) colgar **2.** (*give up*) **to ~ one's football boots/boxing gloves** *fig* colgar las botas/los guantes **3.** *inf* (*delay*) causar un retraso a

hangar ['hæŋəʳ, *Am:* -ə] *n* hangar *m*

hangdog ['hæŋdɒg, *Am:* -dɑːg] *adj* **1.** (*defeated*) abatido, -a **2.** (*ashamed*) avergonzado, -a

hanger ['hæŋəʳ, *Am:* -ə] *n* (*clothes*) percha *f* **hanger-on** [ˌhæŋəʳ'ɒn, *Am:* -ə'ɑːn] <hangers-on> *n a. fig* lapa *f*

hang-glider ['hæŋglaɪdəʳ, *Am:* -də] *n* SPORTS ala *f* delta

hang-gliding ['hæŋglaɪdɪŋ] *n no pl* SPORTS vuelo *m* con ala delta

hanging ['hæŋɪŋ] I. *n* **1.** (*act of execution*) ejecución *f* (en la horca) **2.** *no pl* (*system of execution*) horca *f* **3.** *pl* (*curtains*) colgaduras *fpl* II. *adj* **1.** (*bridge*) colgante **2.** (*crime*) condenado, -a a la horca

hangman ['hæŋmən] <-men> *n* **1.**(*person*) verdugo *m* **2.** GAMES ahorcado *m* **hangnail** *n* padrastro *m* **hangout** *n inf* guarida *f;* **a favourite ~ of artists** un lugar frecuentado por artistas **hangover** *n* **1.**(*sickness*) resaca *f,* goma *f AmL* **2.**(*left-over*) vestigio *m* **hang-up** *n inf* complejo *m;* **to have a ~ about sth** estar acomplejado por algo

hank [hæŋk] *n* madeja *f*
♦**hanker after** *vt,* **hanker for** *vt* ansiar; **to ~ the past** sentir nostalgia del pasado

hankering *n* anhelo *m;* **to have a ~ for sth** ansiar algo

hankie *n,* **hanky** ['hæŋki] *n inf abbr of* **handkerchief** pañuelo *m*

hanky-panky [ˌhæŋki'pæŋki] *n no pl, inf* (*dishonest behaviour*) tejemanejes *mpl;* (*involving sex*) asunto *m*

hanukkah ['hɑːnəkə] *n* hanukah *m*

haphazard [hæp'hæzəd, *Am:* -ɚd] *adj* **1.**(*badly planned*) hecho, -a de cualquier manera **2.**(*random, arbitrary*) caprichoso, -a

hapless ['hæpləs] *adj* desafortunado, -a

happen ['hæpən] *vi* **1.**(*occur*) pasar; **if anything ~s to me ...** si me ocurre algo...; **these things ~ son** cosas que pasan; **whatever ~s** pase lo que pase; **what's ~ed to your hand?** ¿qué te ha pasado en la mano?; **something amazing ~ed to her that day** aquel día le sucedió una cosa asombrosa **2.**(*chance*) **I ~ed to be at home** dio la casualidad de que estaba en casa; **it ~ed** (**that**) ... resultó que...; **as it ~s ...** da la casualidad de que...; **how does it ~ that ...?** ¿cómo puede ser que...?; **he/it ~s to be my best friend** pues resulta que es mi mejor amigo

happening ['hæpənɪŋ] *n* **1.**(*events*) suceso *m* **2.**(*performance*) happening *m*

happily ['hæpɪli] *adv* **1.**(*contentedly*) felizmente; **they lived ~ ever after** fueron felices y comieron perdices **2.**(*willingly*) con mucho gusto **3.**(*fortunately*) afortunadamente

happiness ['hæpɪnɪs] *n no pl* felicidad *f;* **I wish you every ~** que seas muy feliz

happy ['hæpi] <-ier, -iest> *adj* **1.**(*feeling very good*) feliz; **to be ~ that ...** estar contento de que...; **to be ~ to know that ...** alegrarse de saber que...; **I'm so ~ for you** me alegro mucho por ti; **to be ~ to do sth** estar encantado de hacer algo; **I'll be ~ to see you tomorrow morning** les recibiré con mucho gusto mañana por la mañana; **~ birthday!** ¡feliz cumpleaños!; **many ~ returns** (**of the day**)! ¡que cumplas muchos más! **2.**(*satisfied*) contento, -a; **to be ~ about sb/sth** estar contento con alguien/algo; **to be ~ doing sth** estar contento de hacer algo; **are you ~ with the idea?** ¿te parece bien la idea? **3.**(*fortunate*) afortunado, -a; **a ~ coincidence** una feliz coincidencia **4.**(*suitable: phrase, behaviour*) acertado, -a; **a ~ thought** una feliz idea

happy-go-lucky [ˌhæpigəʊ'lʌki, *Am:*

-goʊ'-] *adj* despreocupado, -a

happy medium *n* justo medio *m*

harass ['hærəs, *Am:* hə'ræs] *vt* **1.**(*persistently annoy*) acosar; (*with cares*) abrumar; (*with troubles*) agobiar; **to ~ sb with questions** acosar a alguien a preguntas **2.**(*torment*) atormentar **3.**(*attack continually*) hostigar

harassed ['hærəst, *Am:* hə'ræst] *adj* agobiado, -a

harassment ['hærəsmənt, *Am:* hə'ræs-] *n no pl* **1.**(*pestering*) acoso *m;* **sexual ~** acoso sexual **2.**(*attack*) hostigamiento *m*

harbinger ['hɑːbɪndʒɚ, *Am:* 'hɑːrbɪndʒɚ] *n liter* (*person*) precursor(a) *m(f);* (*thing*) presagio *m;* **a ~ of doom** un mal presagio

harbor *Am, Aus,* **harbour** ['hɑːbɚ, *Am:* 'hɑːrbɚ] **I.** *n* **1.**(*port*) puerto *m;* **fishing ~** puerto pesquero **2.** *fig* (*shelter*) refugio *m* **II.** *vt* **1.**(*give shelter to*) dar cobijo a **2.**(*keep: feelings*) albergar; (*hopes*) abrigar; **to ~ suspicions** tener sospechas; **to ~ a grudge** (**against sb**) guardar rencor a alguien) **3.**(*keep in hiding*) esconder; (*criminal*) encubrir **4.**(*contain*) contener

hard [hɑːd, *Am:* hɑːrd] **I.** *adj* **1.**(*firm, rigid*) duro, -a; (*rule*) estricto, -a; (*fate*) cruel; **~ times** malos tiempos; **to have a ~ time** pasarlo mal; **to give sb a ~ time** hacérselo pasar mal a alguien; **the ~ left/right** POL la extrema izquierda/derecha; **~ luck!, ~ lines!** *Brit* ¡mala suerte! **2.**(*intense, concentrated*) **to take a** (**good**) **~ look at sth** analizar algo detenidamente; **a ~ fight** una lucha encarnizada; **to be a ~ worker** ser muy trabajador **3.**(*forceful*) fuerte **4.**(*difficult, complex*) difícil; **to be ~ work for sb to do sth** ser muy difícil para alguien hacer algo; **to be ~ to please** ser difícil de contentar; **to get ~** complicarse; **a ~ bargain** un trato poco ventajoso; **to learn the ~ way** *fig* aprender a base de errores [*o* palos] **5.**(*severe*) severo, -a **6.**(*hostile, unkind*) **a ~ heart** un corazón de piedra; **to be ~ on sb/sth** ser duro con alguien/algo; **to be** (**as**) **~ as nails** *fig* tener un corazón de piedra **7.**(*extremely cold*) riguroso, -a **8.**(*solid: evidence*) concluyente; (*fact*) innegable; **~ and fast information** información veraz **II.** *adv* **1.**(*forcefully*) fuerte; **to hit sb ~** pegar fuerte a alguien; **to press/pull ~** apretar/estirar con fuerza **2.**(*rigid*) **frozen ~** helado, -a **3.**(*energetically, vigorously*) mucho; **to fight ~** *fig* luchar con todas sus fuerzas; **to study/work ~** estudiar/trabajar mucho; **to try ~ to do sth** esforzarse en hacer algo; **to be ~ at it** trabajar con ahínco; **think ~** concéntrate; **to die ~** *fig* tardar en desaparecer **4.**(*intently*) detenidamente; **to look ~ at sth** estudiar algo con detenimiento **5.**(*closely*) **~ by** muy cerca; **~ upon** muy de cerca; **to be ~ up** no tener ni un céntimo **6.**(*heavy*) mucho; **it rained ~** llovió fuerte; **to take sth ~** tomarse algo muy mal; **I would be ~ pressed to choose one** me costaría mucho decidirme

por uno
hardback ['haːdbæk, Am: 'haːrd-] I. n libro m de tapa dura; **in ~** con tapa dura II. adj con tapa dura **hard-bitten** adj endurecido, -a **hardboard** n no pl chapa m de madera dura **hard-boiled** adj (egg) duro, -a; inf (person) endurecido, -a **hard cash** n no pl dinero m contante y sonante **hard copy** <-ies> n INFOR impresión f **hard core** n 1. (inner circle within group) núcleo m duro 2. Brit (road foundation mixture) balasto m 3. (pornography) pornografía f dura **hard court** n pista f (de tenis) dura **hard currency** <-ies> n moneda f fuerte **hard disk** n INFOR disco m duro **hard drink** n, **hard liquor** n bebida f fuerte **hard drinker** n gran bebedor(a) m(f) **hard drug** n droga f dura **hard-earned** adj (money) ganado, -a con el sudor de la frente; (rest, holiday) merecido, -a
harden ['haːdn, Am: 'haːr-] I. vt 1. (make more solid, firmer) endurecer; (steel) templar 2. (make tougher) curtir; **to ~ oneself to sth** acostumbrarse a algo; **to become ~ed** curtirse; **life has ~ed his personality** la vida lo ha endurecido; **to ~ one's heart** fig mostrarse inflexible 3. (opinions, feelings) afianzar; (character) confirmar II. vi 1. (become firmer: character) endurecerse 2. (become inured) **to ~ to sth** acostumbrarse a algo 3. (attitude) volverse inflexible 4. (become confirmed: idea) confirmarse; (feeling, intention) afianzarse
hard feelings [ˌhaːd'fiːlɪŋz, Am: ˌhaːrd-] npl resentimiento m; **no ~!** ¡olvidémoslo!
hard-fought adj reñido, -a **hard hat** n casco m **hard-headed** adj realista **hard-hearted** adj duro, -a de corazón **hard-hit** adj muy afectado, -a; **to be ~ by sth** ser azotado por algo **hard-hitting** adj impactante **hard labor** n Am, **hard labour** n Brit, Aus LAW trabajos mpl forzados **hard line** n no pl POL línea f dura **hardliner** n POL radical
hardly ['haːdli, Am: 'haːrd-] adv 1. (barely) apenas; **~ anything** casi nada; **~ ever** casi nunca; **she can ~ ...** apenas puede...; **she can ~ wait until tomorrow** tiene unas ganas locas de que llegue mañana 2. (certainly not) it's ~ my fault that it's raining ¿qué culpa tengo de que llueva?; **you can ~ expect him to do that** no puedes esperar que haga eso; **~!** ¡qué va! inf
hardness ['haːdnɪs, Am: 'haːrd-] n no pl 1. (solidity) dureza f; (unfeelingness) insensibilidad f; **~ of heart** dureza de corazón 2. (difficulty) dificultad f 3. (of winter) rigor m
hard-nosed [ˌhaːd'nəuzd, Am: ˌhaːrd-'nouzd] adj duro, -a **hard-pressed** n apurado, -a **hard sell** n venta f agresiva
hardship ['haːdʃɪp, Am: 'haːrd-] n (suffering) penas fpl; (adversity) adversidad f; (deprivation) penuria f; **to suffer great ~** pasar muchos apuros; **to live in ~** pasar privaciones
hard shoulder [ˌhaːd'ʃəuldər, Am: ˌhaːrd-

'ʃouldə-] n Brit arcén m, banquina f Arg, Urug
hardtop n AUTO coche m no descapotable
hardware n no pl 1. (household articles) ferretería f; **~ dealer** ferretero, -a m, f 2. (articles of metal) quincallería f 3. INFOR hardware m; **computer ~** soporte m físico del ordenador 4. MIL armamento m **hard-wearing** adj resistente **hardwood** n madera f noble **hard-working** adj trabajador(a)
hardy ['haːdi, Am: 'haːr-] <-ier, -iest> adj (person, animal) fuerte; (plant) resistente
hare [heər, Am: her] n liebre f ▸**to run with the ~ and hunt with the hounds** prov servir a Dios y al diablo; **to be (as) mad as a (March) ~** inf estar más loco que una cabra
harebrained ['heəbreɪnd, Am: 'her-] adj disparatado, -a **harelip** n MED labio m leporino
harem ['haːriːm, Am: 'herəm] n HIST harén m
hark [haːk, Am: haːrk] vi **~!** HIST ¡escucha!; **~ who's talking!** Brit, iron ¡mira quién habla!; **to ~ back to** fig evocar algo
harm [haːm, Am: haːrm] I. n no pl daño m; **to do ~ to sb/sth** hacer daño a alguien/algo; **to do more ~ than good** hacer más mal que bien; **(to put) out of ~'s way** (poner) a salvo; **to see no ~ in sth** no ver nada malo en algo; **I meant no ~** no pretendía hacer daño; **you will come to no ~** no te va a pasar nada; **there's no ~ in trying** no se pierde nada con intentarlo II. vt 1. (hurt, ruin) hacer daño; **it wouldn't ~ you to stay at home** iron no te morirás por quedarte en casa; (reputation) perjudicar 2. (spoil) estropear
harmful ['haːmfəl, Am: 'haːrm-] adj dañino, -a; (thing) nocivo, -a; **to be ~ to sth** ser perjudicial para algo
harmless ['haːmlɪs, Am: 'haːrm-] adj (animal, person) inofensivo, -a; (thing) inocuo, -a; (fun, joke) inocente
harmonic [haːˈmɒnɪk, Am: haːrˈmaːnɪk] adj armónico, -a
harmonica [haːˈmɒnɪkə, Am: haːrˈmaːnɪ-] n MUS armónica f, rondín m Bol, Ecua, Perú
harmonious [haːˈməunɪəs, Am: haːrˈmou-] adj armonioso, -a
harmonium [haːˈməunɪəm, Am: haːrˈmou-] n MUS armonio m
harmonization [ˌhaːmənɪˈzeɪʃən, Am: ˌhaːr-] n no pl armonización f
harmonize ['haːmənaɪz, Am: 'haːr-] I. vt armonizar II. vi **to ~ (with sb/algo)** armonizar (con alguien/algo)
harmony ['haːməni, Am: 'haːr-] <-ies> n armonía f; **in ~ (with sb/sth)** en armonía (con alguien/algo)
harness ['haːnɪs, Am: 'haːr-] I. n 1. (of animal) arnés m; (for children) correas fpl; **security ~** arnés de seguridad 2. (cooperation) **to work in ~** trabajar en equipo 3. (everyday life) **to get back in ~** fig volver a la rutina II. vt 1. (secure: horse) poner los arreos a; **to ~ a horse/donkey to a carriage**

enganchar un caballo/burro a un carro **2.** (*exploit: resources*) aprovechar

harp [hɑːp, *Am:* hɑːrp] I. *n* arpa *f* II. *vi* to ~ **on about sth** (*talk about*) insistir sobre algo; (*complain*) quejarse de algo

harpoon [hɑːˈpuːn, *Am:* hɑːrˈ-] I. *n* arpón *m* II. *vt* arponear

harpsichord [ˈhɑːpsɪkɔːd, *Am:* ˈhɑːrpsɪkɔːrd] *n* MUS clavicémbalo *m*

harrow [ˈhærəʊ, *Am:* ˈheroʊ] I. *n* grada *f* II. *vt* **1.** AGR gradar **2.** (*disturb*) atormentar

harrowing *adj* (*story, experience*) desgarrador(a); (*prospect*) angustioso, -a

harsh [hɑːʃ, *Am:* hɑːrʃ] *adj* **1.** (*severe: education, parents*) severo, -a; (*punishment*) duro, -a **2.** (*unfair: criticism*) cruel; (*words, reality*) duro, -a **3.** (*unfriendly*) desabrido, -a **4.** (*uncomfortable: light*) fuerte; (*climate, winter*) riguroso, -a; (*terrain*) desolado, -a; (*contrast*) violento, -a **5.** (*rough*) áspero, -a **6.** (*unaesthetic: colour*) chillón, -ona **7.** (*unpleasant to the ear: sound*) discordante; (*voice*) estridente

hart [hɑːt, *Am:* hɑːrt] *n* HIST ciervo *m*

harum-scarum [ˌheərəmˈskeərəm, *Am:* ˌherəmˈskerəm] I. *adv* alocadamente II. *adj* atolondrado, -a

harvest [ˈhɑːvɪst, *Am:* ˈhɑːr-] I. *n* (*of crops*) cosecha *f*; (*of grape*) vendimia *f*; (*of vegetables*) recolección *f*; **the apple** ~ la cosecha de la manzana; **a good** ~ **of potatoes** una buena cosecha de patatas II. *vt a. fig* cosechar; (*grape*) vendimiar; (*vegetables*) recolectar; **to** ~ **a field** hacer la cosecha en un campo III. *vi* cosechar

harvester *n* **1.** (*machine*) **combine** ~ cosechadora *f* **2.** (*person*) recolector(a) *m(f)*; (*of grain*) segador(a) *m(f)*; (*of grape*) vendimiador(a) *m(f)*

harvest festival *n* fiesta *f* de la cosecha **harvest moon** *n* luna *f* llena de otoño

has [həz, *stressed:* hæz] *3rd pers sing of* **have**

has-been [ˈhæzbiːn, *Am:* -bɪn] *n inf* vieja gloria *f*; **to be a** ~ ser alguien que ya ha pasado a la historia

hash¹ [hæʃ] I. *vt* GASTR picar II. *n* **1.** GASTR picadillo *m* **2.** *no pl, inf* lío *m*; **to make a** ~ **of sth** armarse un lío con algo
◆**hash up** *vt* volver a hacer

hash² [hæʃ] *n inf* chocolate *m*

hash browns *npl Am: patatas hervidas y después fritas*

hashish [ˈhæʃiːʃ] *n no pl* hachís *m inv*

hasn't [ˈhæznt] = **has not** *s.* **have**

hassle [ˈhæsl] I. *n no pl, inf* (*bother*) lío *m*; **to give sb** ~ fastidiar a alguien; **it's such a** ~ es un jaleo II. *vt inf* fastidiar; **to** ~ **sb to do sth** estar encima a alguien para que haga algo

hassock [ˈhæsək] *n* **1.** (*tuft of grass*) mata *f* de hierba **2.** (*in church*) cojín *m* (para arrodillarse)

haste [heɪst] *n no pl* prisa *f*; **to make** ~ apre-

surarse; **in** ~ de prisa ►**more** ~ **less** <u>speed</u> *prov* vísteme despacio, que tengo prisa *prov*

hasten [ˈheɪsn] I. *vt form* acelerar; **to** ~ **sb** dar prisa a alguien; **to** ~ **one's steps** apresurar el paso II. *vi* apresurarse; **to** ~ **to do sth** apresurarse a hacer algo

hasty [ˈheɪsti] <-ier, -iest> *adj* **1.** (*fast*) rápido, -a; **to beat a** ~ **retreat** *a. fig* retirarse a toda prisa **2.** (*rashly*) precipitado, -a; **to make** ~ **decisions** tomar decisiones irreflexivamente; **to leap to** ~ **conclusions** sacar conclusiones precipitadas; **to be** ~ **in doing sth** precipitarse en algo

hat [hæt] *n* sombrero *m*; **to pass round the** ~ pasar la gorra ►**I'll** <u>eat</u> **my** ~ **if ...** que me maten si...; **to** <u>keep</u> **sth under one's** ~ no decir ni una palabra sobre algo; **to** <u>talk</u> **through one's** ~ *inf* decir bobadas; <u>my</u> ~! ¡caracoles!

hatch¹ [hætʃ] I. *vi* salir del cascarón II. *vt* **1.** (*chick*) incubar, empollar **2.** (*devise in secret*) tramar; **to** ~ **a plan** urdir un plan

hatch² [hætʃ] <-es> *n* trampilla *f*; (*between kitchen and dining room*) ventanilla *f*; NAUT escotilla *f* ►**down the** ~! ¡salud!

hatch³ [hætʃ] *vt* sombrear

hatchback [ˈhætʃbæk] *n* AUTO coche *m* con puerta trasera

hatchet [ˈhætʃɪt] *n* hacha *f* (pequeña) ►**to** <u>bury</u> **the** ~ enterrar el hacha de guerra

hatchet-faced *adj inf* de cara chupada **hatchet man** *n inf* **1.** (*employee*) encargado de los trabajos sucios **2.** (*thug*) matón *m*

hatching [ˈhætʃɪŋ] *n no pl* salida *f* del huevo

hate [heɪt] I. *n* odio *m*; **to feel** ~ **for sb** odiar a alguien; **one of my pet** ~**s is ...** una de las cosas que más odio es... II. *vt* odiar; **to** ~ **sb's guts** *inf* odiar a alguien a muerte

hateful [ˈheɪtfəl] *adj* odioso, -a

hatpin [ˈhætpɪn] *n* alfiler *m* de sombrero

hatred [ˈheɪtrɪd] *n no pl* odio *m*; ~ **of sb/sth** odio a [*o* hacia] alguien/algo

hatstand [ˈhætstænd] *n* percha *f* para sombreros

hatter [ˈhætər, *Am:* ˈhæt̬ɚ] *n* **to be as mad as a** ~ estar como una cabra

hat-trick [ˈhættrɪk] *n* SPORTS tres goles marcados por un mismo jugador; **to score a** ~ marcar tres tantos

haughty [ˈhɔːti, *Am:* ˈhɑːt̬i] <-ier, iest> *adj* altivo, -a

haul [hɔːl, *Am:* hɑːl] I. *vt* **1.** (*pull with effort*) arrastrar; **to** ~ **up the sail** izar la vela; **to** ~ **a boat out of the water** sacar una barca del agua **2.** (*transport goods*) transportar II. *n* **1.** (*distance*) trayecto *m*; **long** ~ **flight** vuelo *m* intercontinental; **in** [*o* over] **the long** ~ *fig* a la larga **2.** (*quantity caught: of fish, shrimp*) redada *f*; (*of stolen goods*) botín *m* **3.** (*tug*) tirón *m*, jalón *m* CSur; **to give a** ~ dar un tirón
◆**haul down** *vt* (*flag, sail*) arriar
◆**haul off** *vi* NAUT cambiar de rumbo
◆**haul up** *vt inf* to haul sb up before sb

hacer que alguien dé explicaciones a alguien
haulage ['hɔ:lɪdʒ, *Am:* 'hɑ:-] *n no pl*
1. (*transportation*) transporte *m* **2.** (*costs*) gastos *mpl* de transporte
haulage business *n*, **haulage company**
n empresa *f* de transportes **haulage contractor** *n* transportista *mf* **haulage firm** *n*
s. **haulage company**
hauler ['hɔ:lər, *Am:* 'hɑ:lə-] *n Am*, **haulier**
['hɔ:liər, *Am:* 'hɑ:ljə-] *n Brit, Aus* (*business*)
empresa *f* de transportes; (*person*) transportista *mf*
haunch [hɔ:ntʃ, *Am:* hɑ:ntʃ] <-es> *n*
1. ANAT cadera *f*; **to sit on one's ~es** ponerse
de [*o* en] cuclillas **2.** (*of meat*) pierna *f*
haunt [hɔ:nt, *Am:* hɑ:nt] **I.** *vt* **1.** (*ghost*) rondar **2.** (*plague, bother*) perseguir; **to be ~ed**
by memories of an unhappy childhood
perseguir (a alguien) los recuerdos de una
infancia infeliz; **to be ~ed by sth** estar obsesionado por algo **3.** (*frequent*) frecuentar; **to ~**
a place rondar un lugar **II.** *n* lugar *m* preferido; **a student ~** un lugar frecuentado por
los estudiantes
haunted *adj* **1.** (*frequented by ghosts*) embrujado, -a **2.** (*troubled: look*) angustiado, -a, preocupado, -a
haunting *adj* **1.** (*disturbing*) **a ~ fear/memory** un miedo/recuerdo recurrente e inquietante **2.** (*memorable*) **to have a ~ beauty**
tener una belleza evocadora; **a ~ melody** una
melodía inolvidable
Havana [həˈvænə] *n* La Habana
have [həv, *stressed:* hæv] **I.** <has, had,
had> *vt* **1.** (*own*) tener, poseer; **she's got two**
brothers tiene dos hermanos; **~ you got a**
cold? – no, I've got a headache ¿estás resfriado? – no, me duele la cabeza; **to ~ sth to**
do tener algo que hacer **2.** (*engage in*) **to ~ a**
walk pasear; **to ~ a talk with sb** hablar con
alguien; **to ~ a bath/shower** bañarse/
ducharse; **to ~ a nap** echar una cabezadita; **to**
~ a game echar una partida **3.** (*eat*) **to ~**
lunch comer; **I ~n't had shrimp in ages!**
¡hace años que no como gambas!; **to ~ some**
coffee tomar un poco de café **4.** (*give birth to*)
to ~ a child tener un hijo **5.** (*receive*) tener,
recibir; **to ~ news of sb** tener [*o* recibir] noticias de alguien; **to ~ visitors** tener visita
6. (*prepare*) **to ~ dinner ready** tener la cena
preparada **7.** (*cause to occur*) **to not ~ sb/sth**
doing sth no dejar que alguien/algo haga algo;
I'll ~ Bob give you a ride home le pediré [*o*
diré] a Bob que te lleve a casa **8.** (*understand*) **I**
kept telling him you were French, but he
wouldn't ~ it le dije una y otra vez que eras
francesa, pero él no bajaba del burro ▸**to ~**
done **with it** acabar con el asunto; **to ~ it** in
for sb *inf* tenerla tomada con alguien; **to ~ it**
in **one to do sth** ser capaz de hacer algo; **I**
didn't think she had it in her! ¡no pensaba
que fuera capaz de eso!; **if she finds out**
about what you've done, you've ~ it! *inf* si

se entera de lo que has hecho, ¡estás listo!; **to ~**
had it with sb/sth *inf* haber tenido más que
suficiente de alguien/algo **II.**<has, had,
had> *aux* (*indicates perfect tense*) **he has**
never been to Scotland nunca ha estado en
Escocia; **we had been swimming** habíamos
estado nadando; **to ~ got to do sth** *Brit, Aus*
tener que hacer algo; **what time ~ we got to**
be there? ¿a qué hora tenemos que estar allí?;
do we ~ to finish this today? ¿tenemos que
acabar esto hoy?; **had I known you were**
coming, ... *form* si hubiera sabido que ibas a
venir,...
◆**have around** *vt always sep* (*gadget*) tener
a mano
◆**have back** *vt always sep* **can I have it**
back? ¿me lo devuelves?; **they solved their**
problems and she had him back resolvieron sus diferencias y ella le abrió las puertas de
casa de nuevo
◆**have in** *vt always sep* invitar; **they had**
some experts in llamaron a algunos expertos
◆**have off** *vt* **1.** *Brit, Aus, inf* (*have sexual*
intercourse) **to have it off with sb** hacerlo
con alguien **2.** (*remove: clothes*) quitar
◆**have on** *vt always sep* **1.** (*wear: clothes*)
llevar (puesto); **he didn't have any clothes**
on estaba desnudo **2.** (*carry*) **to have sth on**
oneself llevar algo encima; **have you got any**
money on you? ¿llevas dinero contigo?
3. *Brit, inf* (*fool*) **to have sb on** tomar el pelo a
alguien **4.** (*plan*) **have you got anything on**
this week? ¿tienes planes para esta semana?
◆**have out** *vt always sep* **1.** (*remove*) sacar
2. *inf* (*argue*) **to have it out with sb** tenerla
con alguien
◆**have over** *vt always sep* invitar
◆**have up** *vt always sep* **1.** (*invite*) invitar
2. *Brit, inf* (*take to court for a trial*) llevar a juicio
haven ['heɪvn] *n* refugio *m*
have-nots ['hævnɒts] *npl* **the ~** los pobres
haven't ['hævnt] = **have not** *s.* **have**
haves [hævz] *npl* **the ~ and the have-nots**
los ricos y los pobres
havoc ['hævək] *n no pl* estragos *mpl*; **the ~ of**
the fire/the storm los estragos del fuego/de
la tormenta; **to play ~ with sth** hacer estragos
de algo; **to wreak ~ on sth** desbaratar algo
Havre ['hɑ:vrə] *n* **Le ~** El Havre
haw [hɔ:, *Am:* hɑ:] **I.** *interj* (*to horse*) ¡ría!
II. *vi* **to** hem **and ~** *Am*, **to** hum **and ~** *Brit,*
Aus vacilar
Hawaii [həˈwaɪɪ:, *Am:* həˈwaː-] *n* Hawai *m*
Hawaiian [həˈwaɪjən, *Am:* həˈwaː-] **I.** *n*
1. (*person*) hawaiano, -a *m, f* **2.** LING hawaiano
m **II.** *adj* hawaiano, -a
hawk [hɔ:k, *Am:* hɑ:k] **I.** *n* halcón *m* **II.** *vt*
(*wares*) pregonar **III.** *vi* carraspear
hawker *n* vendedor(a) *m(f)* ambulante
hawk-eyed [ˌhɔ:kˈaɪd, *Am:* ˌhɑ:k-] *adj* **to be**
~ tener ojos de lince
hawk moth *n* esfinge *m*

hawser ['hɔːzəʳ, *Am:* 'hɑːzɚ] *n* NAUT guinda-leza *f*

hawthorn ['hɔːθɔːn, *Am:* 'hɑːθɔːrn] *n no pl* BOT espino *m*

hay [heɪ] *n no pl* heno *m* ▶ **to make ~ while the sun shines** aprovechar la oportunidad cuando se presenta; **to hit the ~** *inf* acostarse

haycock ['heɪkɒk, *Am:* -kɑːk, -] *n* montón *m* de heno **hay fever** *n no pl* fiebre *f* del heno **hayrick** *n,* **haystack** *n* almiar *m* **haywire** *adj inf* **to go/be ~** (*person*) volverse/estar loco; (*machine*) estropearse

hazard ['hæzəd, *Am:* -ɚd] I. *n* 1. (*danger*) peligro *m* 2. *no pl* (*risk*) riesgo *m;* **fire ~** peligro de incendio; **health ~** riesgo para la salud II. *vt* 1. aventurar; **to ~ a guess at sth** aventurar una respuesta a algo 2. (*risk*) arriesgar

hazardous ['hæzədəs, *Am:* -ɚ-] *adj* (*dangerous*) peligroso, -a; (*risky*) arriesgado, -a

hazard (warning) lights *npl* AUTO luces *fpl* de emergencia

haze [heɪz] I. *n* 1. (*mist*) neblina *f;* **~ of dust** nube *f* de polvo; **heat ~** calina *f* 2. (*mental*) aturdimiento *m* II. *vt Am* hacer novatadas a

hazel ['heɪzl] I. *adj* color avellana II. *n* BOT avellano *m*

hazelnut ['heɪzlnʌt] *n* BOT avellana *f*

hazy ['heɪzi] <-ier, -iest> *adj* 1. (*with bad visibility*) neblinoso, -a 2. (*confused, unclear*) vago, -a

h & c *abbr of* **hot and cold (water)** (agua *f*) caliente y fría

HDTV [ˌeɪtʃdiːtiːˈviː] *n* TV *abbr of* **high-definition television** televisión *f* de alta definición

he [hiː] I. *pron pers* 1. (*male person or animal*) él; **~'s** [*o* **~ is**] **my father** (él) es mi padre; **~'s gone away but ~'ll be back soon** se ha ido, pero volverá pronto; **here ~ comes** ahí viene 2. (*unspecified sex*) **if somebody comes, ~ will buy it** si alguien viene, lo comprará; **~ who ...** *form* aquél que... II. *n* (*of baby*) varón *m;* (*of animal*) macho *m*

head [hed] I. *n* 1. ANAT cabeza *f;* **to nod one's ~** asentir con la cabeza 2. *no pl* (*unit*) cabeza *f;* **a** [*o* **per**] **~** por cabeza; **a hundred ~ of cattle** cien cabezas de ganado; **to be a ~ taller than sb** sacar una cabeza a alguien 3. (*mind*) **to clear one's ~** aclararse las ideas; **to get sth/sb out of one's ~** sacarse algo/a alguien de la cabeza; **to have a good ~ for figures** tener cabeza para los números; **to need a clear ~ to do sth** necesitar tener la cabeza clara para hacer algo 4. *no pl* (*top: of queue*) cabeza *f;* (*of bed, table*) cabecera *f* 5. BOT cabeza *f;* **a ~ of lettuce** una lechuga 6. *no pl* (*letter top*) encabezamiento *m* 7. *pl* FIN (*coin face*) cara *f;* **~s or tails?** ¿cara o cruz? 8. (*beer foam*) espuma *f* 9. GEO (*of river*) nacimiento *m* 10. (*boss*) jefe, -a *m, f* 11. *Brit* (*headteacher*) director(a) *m(f)* de colegio 12. TECH (*device*) cabezal *m* 13. INFOR **read/write ~** cabeza *f* de lectura/escritura ▶ **to have one's ~ in the clouds** tener la cabeza llena de pájaros; **to be**

~ over heels in love estar locamente enamorado; **to fall ~ over heels in love with sb** enamorarse locamente de alguien; **to bury one's ~ in the sand** hacer como el avestruz; **to be ~ and shoulders above sb/sth** dar cien vueltas a alguien/algo; **to not be able to make ~ (n)or tail of sth** no entender ni jota de algo; **~s I win, tales you lose** o gano yo o gano yo; **to bang one's ~ against a brick wall** darse de cabeza contra la pared; **to keep one's ~ above water** mantenerse a flote; **keep one's ~ down** (*to avoid attention*) mantenerse al margen; (*to work hard*) no levantar la cabeza; **to hold one's ~ high** mantener la cabeza alta; **to be off one's ~** *inf* (*crazy*) estar mal de la cabeza; **to be out of one's ~** *inf* (*drunk*) estar pedo; (*stoned*) estar colocado; **to be soft in the ~** estar un poco tocado; **to have one's ~ screwed on (right)** tener la cabeza bien puesta; **to go straight to sb's ~** (*alcohol, wine*) subírse a la cabeza a alguien; **to bite sb's ~ off** echar una bronca a alguien; **to bring sth to a ~** llevar algo a un punto crítico; **to give sb his/her ~** dejar a alguien obrar a su antojo; **to laugh one's ~ off** desternillarse de risa; **~s will roll** van a rodar cabezas; **to scream one's ~ off** gritar a voz en grito II. *vt* 1. (*lead*) encabezar; (*a firm, organization*) dirigir; (*team*) capitanear 2. PUBL encabezar 3. SPORTS (*ball*) cabecear III. *vi* **to ~ (for) home** dirigirse hacia casa

◆**head back** *vi* volver, regresar

◆**head for** *vt insep* ir rumbo a; **to ~ the exit** dirigirse hacia la salida; **to ~ disaster** ir camino del desastre

◆**head off** I. *vt* cortar el paso a II. *vi* **to ~ towards** salir hacia

◆**head up** *vt* dirigir

headache ['hedeɪk] *n* dolor *m* de cabeza **headband** *n* cinta *f* de pelo **headbanger** *n inf* heavy *mf* **head cold** *n* resfriado *m* **head cook** *n* jefe, -a *m, f* de cocina **head-dress** <-es> *n* tocado *m*

header ['hedəʳ, *Am:* -ɚ] *n* 1. SPORTS cabezazo *m;* **to take a ~ into the water** tirarse de cabeza al agua 2. INFOR cabecera *f*

headfirst ['hedˈfɜːst, *Am:* -ˈfɜːrst] *adv* de cabeza; **to fall ~** caer de cabeza **headhunt** *vt* ECON cazar talentos **headhunter** *n* 1. (*warrior*) cazador *m* de cabezas 2. ECON cazatalentos *mf inv*

heading ['hedɪŋ] *n* (*of chapter*) encabezamiento *m;* (*letterhead*) membrete *m*

headland [ˌhedlænd] *n* cabo *m* **headless** *adj* sin cabeza **headlight** *n,* **headlamp** *n* faro *m* **headline** I. *n* titular *m* ▶ **to hit the ~s** salir en primera plana II. *vt* titular **headlong** *Am, Aus* I. *adv* precipitadamente; **to rush ~ into sth** hacer algo de forma precipitada II. *adj* precipitado, -a **headmaster** *n* director *m* de colegio **headmistress** <-es> *n* directora *f* de colegio **head office** *n* (oficina *f*) central *f* **head of state** <heads of state> *n* jefe, -a *m, f* de Estado **head-on I.** *adj* (*collision*) frontal **II.** *adv* frontalmente, de frente **headphones** *npl* auriculares *mpl* **headquarters** *n+ sing/pl vb* MIL cuartel *m* general; (*of company*) oficina *f* central; (*of party*) sede *f*; (*of the police*) jefatura *f* de policía **headrest** *n* reposacabezas *m inv* **head restraint** *n* apoyacabezas *m inv* **headroom** *n no pl* altura *f* **headscarf** <-scarves> *n* pañuelo *m* para la cabeza **headset** *n* auriculares *mpl* **headship** *n* **1.** ADMIN dirección *f* **2.** Brit SCHOOL dirección *f* de un colegio **headshrinker** *n inf* (*psychiatrist*) loquero, -a *m, f* **head start** *n* ventaja *f*; **to give sb a** ~ dar ventaja a alguien **headstone** *n* lápida *f* **headstrong** *adj* testarudo, -a **headteacher** *n* director(a) *m(f)* de un colegio **head waiter** *n* jefe *m* de comedor, maître *m* **headwaters** *npl* GEO cabecera *f* (de un río) **headway** *n no pl* progreso *m;* **to make** ~ hacer progresos **headwind** *n* viento *m* contrario [*o* en contra]; NAUT viento *f* de proa **headword** *n* encabezamiento *m*

heady ['hedi] <-ier, -iest> *adj* **1.** (*intoxicating*) embriagador(a) **2.** (*exciting*) emocionante **heal** [hi:l] **I.** *vt* (*wound*) curar; (*differences*) salvar **II.** *vi* (*wound, injury*) cicatrizar **health** [helθ] *n no pl* salud *f;* **to be in good/ bad** ~ estar bien/mal de salud; **to drink to sb's** ~ beber a la salud de alguien **healthcare** ['helθkeaᵇ, *Am:* -ker] *n no pl* asistencia *f* sanitaria [*o* médica] **health center** *n Am,* **health centre** *n Brit* centro *m* médico **health certificate** *n* certificado *m* médico **health club** *n* gimnasio *m* **health farm** *n* balneario *m* **health food** *n no pl* alimentos *mpl* naturales **health food shop** *n,* **health food store** *n* tienda *f* de productos naturales **health hazard** *n* riesgo *m* para la salud **health insurance** *n no pl* seguro *m* médico **health resort** *n Am* (*health farm*) balneario *m* **health service** *n Brit* servicio *m* sanitario **health visitor** *n Brit* MED *enfermera que hace visitas a domicilio para asesorar sobre el cuidado de los niños y de los ancianos* **healthy** ['helθi] <-ier, -iest> *adj* **1.** MED sano, -a **2.** (*strong*) próspero, -a; (*profit*) sustancial **3.** (*positive*) positivo, -a **heap** [hi:p] **I.** *n* (*pile*) pila *f*, montón *m;* **to collapse in a** ~ *fig* (*person*) caer desplomado; **a** (**whole**) ~ **of work** *inf* un montón de trabajo **II.** *vt* amontonar, apilar; **to** ~ **sth with sth** llenar algo de algo **hear** [hɪaᵇ, *Am:* hɪr] <heard, heard> **I.** *vt* **1.** (*perceive*) oír **2.** (*be told*) enterarse de; **to** ~ **that** ... enterarse de que..., oír que... **3.** (*listen*) escuchar; **Lord,** ~ **our prayers** REL escúchanos, Señor **II.** *vi* **1.** (*perceive*) oír; **to** ~ **very well** oír muy bien **2.** (*get news*) enterarse; **to** ~ **of** [*o* about] **sth** enterarse de algo ▶~, ~! ¡muy bien! **heard** [hɜ:d, *Am:* hɜ:rd] *pt, pp of* **hear**

hearing ['hɪarɪŋ, *Am:* 'hɪr-] *n* **1.** *no pl* (*sense*) oído *m* **2.** (*act*) audición *f* **3.** (*range*) **in sb's** ~ en presencia de alguien **4.** LAW vista *f* **hearing aid** *n* audífono *m* **hearsay** ['hɪaseɪ, *Am:* 'hɪr-] *n no pl* habladurías *fpl;* **by** ~ de oídas **hearse** [hɜ:s, *Am:* hɜ:rs] *n* coche *m* fúnebre **heart** [ha:t, *Am:* ha:rt] *n* **1.** ANAT corazón *m* **2.** (*seat of emotions*) **to break sb's** ~ partir el corazón a alguien; **to have a cold** ~ ser duro de corazón; **to have a change of** ~ cambiar de opinión; **to have a good** [*o* kind] ~ tener buen corazón; **to lose** ~ desanimarse; **to lose one's** ~ (**to sb/sth**) enamorarse (de alguien/algo); **to pour one's** ~ **out to sb** desahogarse con alguien; **to take** ~ animarse; **her** ~ **sank** se le cayó el alma a los pies **3.** *no pl* (*centre*) centro *m;* **to get to the** ~ **of the matter** llegar al fondo de la cuestión **4.** GASTR (*of lettuce*) cogollo *m;* **artichoke** ~**s** corazones *mpl* de alcachofa **5.** *pl* (*card suit*) corazones *mpl;* (*in Spanish pack*) copas *fpl* ▶**he had his** ~ **in his boots** Brit, *inf* tenía el ánimo por los suelos; **to one's** ~**'s** content hasta quedarse satisfecho; **to have a** ~ **of gold** tener un corazón de oro, ser todo corazón; **to have one's** ~ **in the right place** tener buen corazón; **to wear one's** ~ **on one's sleeve** ir con el corazón en la mano; **to have a** ~ **of stone** tener un corazón de piedra; **with all one's** ~ con toda su alma; **on your own** ~ be it por tu cuenta y riesgo; **she is a girl after my own** ~ es una chica de las que a mí me gustan; **to not have the** ~ **to do sth** no tener el valor para hacer algo; **by** ~ de memoria

heartache ['ha:teɪk, *Am:* 'ha:rt-] *n no pl* pena *f* **heart attack** *n* ataque *m* al corazón **heartbeat** *n* latido *m* (del corazón) **heartbreak** *n no pl* pena *f* **heartbreaking** *adj* desgarrador(a) **heartbroken** *adj* con el corazón partido **heartburn** *n no pl* acidez *f* de estómago **heart disease** *n no pl* enfermedad *f* coronaria **heartening** ['ha:tənɪŋ, *Am:* 'ha:rt-] *adj* alentador(a) **heart failure** *n no pl* colapso *m* cardíaco **heartfelt** ['ha:tfelt, *Am:* 'ha:rt-] *adj* sincero, -a; **my** ~ **condolences** mi más sentido pésame; ~ **relief** gran alivio **hearth** [ha:θ, *Am:* ha:rθ] *n* **1.** (*of fire place*) chimenea *f* **2.** *liter* (*home*) hogar *m;* **to leave** ~ **and home** abandonar el hogar **hearth rug** *n* alfombrilla *f* (de la chimenea) **heartily** *adv* con efusividad; **to dislike sth/sb** ~ detestar algo/a alguien; **to eat** ~ comer con ganas **heartland** ['ha:tlænd, *Am:* 'ha:rt-] *n* centro *m;* **the economic** ~ el corazón económico **heartless** ['ha:tləs, *Am:* 'ha:rt-] *adj* sin corazón **heart murmur** *n* soplo *m* cardíaco **heartrending** ['ha:t‚rendɪŋ, *Am:* 'ha:rt-] *adj* desgarrador(a)

H

heart-searching ['hɑːt̩ˌsɜːtʃɪŋ, *Am:* 'hɑːrt-] *n no pl* examen *m* de conciencia **heart-strings** *npl* to pull at sb's ~ *fig* tocar la fibra sensible a alguien **heart-throb** *n inf* ídolo *m* **heart-to-heart** I. *n* conversación *f* franca y abierta II. *adj* franco, -a y abierto, -a **heart transplant** *n* trasplante *m* de corazón

heartwarming ['hɑːt̩ˌwɔːmɪŋ, *Am:* 'hɑːrt-ˌwɔːr-] *adj* reconfortante

hearty ['hɑːti, *Am:* 'hɑːrt̩i] *adj* <-ier, -iest> **1.** (*enthusiastic*) entusiasta; ~ **congratulations** felicidades de todo corazón; ~ **welcome** bienvenida calurosa **2.** (*large, strong*) fuerte; ~ **appetite** buen apetito; **a** ~ **breakfast** un desayuno opíparo; **to have a** ~ **dislike for sth** tener manía a algo; **hale and** ~ sano y fuerte

heat [hiːt] I. *n no pl* **1.** (*warmth, high temperature*) calor; **in the** ~ **of the day** cuando más calor hace; **to cook sth on a high/low** ~ cocinar algo a fuego rápido/lento **2.** (*heating system*) calefacción *f*; **to turn down the** ~ bajar la calefacción **3.** (*emotional state*) acaloramiento *m*; **in the** ~ **of the argument** en el momento más acalorado de la discusión **4.** (*sports race*) eliminatoria *f* **5.** *no pl* ZOOL celo *m*; **to be on** ~ estar en celo ▶ **if you can't take the** ~**, get out of the kitchen** *prov* quien no aguante la presión, que no se meta en la olla *prov;* **to put the** ~ **on sb** presionar a alguien; **to take the** ~ **off sb** dar un respiro a alguien II. *vt* **1.** (*make hot*) calentar **2.** (*excite*) acalorar III. *vi* (*become hot*) calentarse; *fig* (*inflame*) acalorarse

◆**heat up** I. *vi* calentarse II. *vt* calentar

heated *adj* **1.** (*window*) térmico, -a; (*pool*) climatizado, -a; (*room*) caldeado, -a **2.** (*argument*) acalorado, -a

heatedly *adv* acaloradamente; **to** ~ **deny sth** negar algo con vehemencia

heater ['hiːtər, *Am:* -t̩ɚ] *n* calefactor *m;* **water** ~ calentador *m* de agua

heat exchanger *n* (inter)cambiador *m* térmico **heat gauge** *n* termostato *m*

heath [hiːθ] *n* brezal *m*

heathen ['hiːðən] I. *n* pagano, -a *m, f;* **the** ~ los infieles II. *adj* pagano, -a

heather ['heðər, *Am:* -ɚ] *n no pl* brezo *m*

heating *n no pl* calefacción *f*

heating engineer *n* técnico, -a *m, f* de la calefacción **heating system** *n* sistema *m* de calefacción

heat pump *n* bomba *f* de calor [*o* térmica] **heat rash** <-es> *n* sarpullido *m* **heat-resistant** *adj,* **heat-resisting** *adj* resistente al calor **heat-seeking** *adj* MIL termodirigido, -a **heat shield** *n* blindaje *m* térmico **heat stroke** *n* insolación *f* **heat treatment** *n* termotratamiento *m* **heatwave** *n* ola *f* de calor

heave [hiːv] I. *vi* **1.** (*pull*) tirar; (*push*) empujar **2.** (*move up and down*) subir y bajar; **to** ~ **into view** NAUT aparecer **3.** (*vomit*) tener bascas II. *vt* **1.** (*pull*) tirar; (*push*) empujar; **he** ~**d the door open** abrió la puerta de un empujón; **to** ~ **a sigh** (**of relief**) dar un suspiro (de alivio); **to** ~ **sth at sb** lanzar algo a alguien **2.** (*lift*) levantar III. *n* **1.** (*push*) empujón *m;* (*pull*) tirón *m* **2.** (*great effort*) gran esfuerzo *m*

◆**heave to** *vi* <hove to, hoved to> NAUT ponerse al pairo

◆**heave up** *vi* vomitar

heaven ['hevən] *n* cielo *m;* **to go to** ~ ir al cielo; **it's** ~ *fig, inf* es divino, es fantástico; **to be** ~ **on earth** *fig* (*place*) ser paradisíaco; **to be in** ~ *a. fig* estar en el cielo; **the** ~**s** (*sky*) el cielo ▶ **to move** ~ **and earth** remover Roma con Santiago, mover cielo y tierra; **what/where/when/who/why in** ~**'s name** …? ¿qué/dónde/cuándo/quién/por qué demonios…?; **for** ~**s sake** ¡por Dios!; **good** ~**s!** ¡santo cielo!; **to stink to high** ~ oler a perro muerto; ~ **only knows** sólo Dios lo sabe; **to be in seventh** ~ estar en el séptimo cielo; ~ **help us** que Dios nos ayude; **thank** ~**s** gracias a Dios

heavenly ['hevənli] *adj* <-ier, -iest> **1.** (*of heaven*) celestial; ~ **body** cuerpo *m* celeste **2.** (*wonderful*) divino, -a

heavens *npl liter* firmamento *m*

heaven-sent [ˌhevən'sent] *adj* caído, -a del cielo

heavy ['hevi] I. *adj* <-ier, -iest> **1.** (*weighing a lot*) pesado, -a; ~ **food** comida pesada **2.** (*difficult*) difícil; (*schedule*) apretado, -a; **the book was rather** ~ **going** la lectura del libro era bastante pesada **3.** (*strong*) fuerte; ~ **fall** *a.* ECON fuerte descenso **4.** (*not delicate, coarse*) poco delicado, -a; (*features*) basto, -a **5.** (*severe*) severo, -a; (*responsibility*) fuerte; (*sea*) grueso, -a; ~ **casualties** muchas bajas; **to be** ~ **on sb** ser duro con alguien **6.** (*abundant*) abundante; (*investment*) cuantioso, -a; ~ **frost/gale** fuertes heladas/chubascos; **to be** ~ **on sth** consumir mucho de algo; **to be** ~ **with sth** estar cargado de algo **7.** (*excessive*) ~ **drinker/smoker** bebedor/fumador empedernido; ~ **sleep** sueño profundo **8.** (*thick*) grueso, -a; (*beard*) denso, -a; (*sky*) encapotado, -a; (*shoe*) resistente II. *n* <-ies> *inf* matón *m*

heavy-duty [ˌhevi'djuːti, *Am:* -'duːt̩i] *adj* resistente; (*machine*) resistente; (*vehicle*) (muy) resistente **heavy-going** *adj* dificultoso, -a **heavy goods vehicle** *n* vehículo *m* pesado **heavy-handed** *adj* **1.** (*clumsy*) torpe **2.** (*harsh*) duro, -a **heavy-hearted** *adj* afligido, -a **heavy industry** *n no pl* industria *f* pesada **heavy metal** *n* **1.** (*lead, cadmium*) metal *m* pesado **2.** MUS heavy *m* (*metal*) **heavy water** *n* agua *f* pesada **heavyweight** I. *adj* **1.** SPORTS (de la categoría) de los pesos pesados **2.** (*cloth*) resistente **3.** (*important*) serio, -a e importante II. *n a. fig* peso pesado *m*

Hebrew ['hiːbruː] I. *n* **1.** (*person*) hebreo, -a *m, f* **2.** LING hebreo *m* II. *adj* hebreo, -a

Hebrides ['hebrɪdiːz] n the ~ las Hébridas
heck [hek] interj inf caramba; **where the ~
have you been?** ¿dónde demonios habéis
estado?; **what the ~!** ¿qué más da?
heckle ['hekl] vi, vt interrumpir con preguntas
[o comentarios]
heckler ['heklə', Am: -ɚ] n persona f que
interrumpe
hectare ['hekteə', Am: -ter] n hectárea f
hectic ['hektɪk] I. adj ajetreado, -a; ~ **fever**
fiebre hé(c)tica; ~ **pace** ritmo intenso II. n MED
hé(c)tico, -a m, f
hectoliter n Am, **hectolitre** ['hektəʊˌliːtə',
Am: -toʊˌliːʈɚ] n hectolitro m
he'd [hiːd] = he had, he would s. **have,
will**
hedge [hedʒ] I. n 1. (line of bushes) seto m
vivo 2. FIN (protection) cobertura f II. vi (avoid
action) dar rodeos; FIN cubrirse III. vt cercar
(con un seto vivo)
◆**hedge about** vt, **hedge around** vt
1. (surround with a hedge) cercar (con un seto
vivo) 2. (hinder, hamper) restringir
◆**hedge in** vt rodear; **to ~ an investment**
FIN cubrirse contra el riesgo de una inversión
hedgehog ['hedʒhɒg, Am: -haːg] n erizo m
hedgerow n seto m vivo
hedging ['hedʒɪŋ] n FIN cobertura f de riesgos
heebie-jeebies ['hiːbɪ'dʒiːbɪz] npl inf **to
give sb the ~** poner a alguien la carne de gallina
heed [hiːd] I. vt form hacer caso de; **to ~
advice** seguir los consejos II. n **to pay (no) ~
to sth, to take (no) ~ of sth** (no) prestar atención a algo
heedful ['hiːdfəl] adj **to be ~ of sb's advice**
prestar atención a los consejos de alguien
heedless ['hiːdlɪs] adj irresponsable; ~ **of sth**
sin hacer caso a algo; **to be ~ of the risk** no
preocuparse del riesgo
hee-haw ['hiːhɔː, Am: -haː] I. n rebuzno m
II. vi rebuznar
heel [hiːl] I. n 1. (of foot) talón m; **to be at
sb's ~s** pisar los talones a alguien 2. (of shoe)
tacón m, taco m AmL 3. (of the hand) base f
de la mano 4. (of loaf of bread) cuscurro m
5. inf (unfair person) canalla m ▶**to be down
at the ~** estar en mal estado; **to follow close
on the ~s of sth** seguir inmediatamente a
algo; **to be hard on sb's ~s** pisar los talones a
alguien; **under the ~ of sb/sth** sometido a al-
guien/algo; **to bring sb to ~** meter a alguien
en cintura; **to come to ~** acceder a obedecer;
to dig one's ~s in mantenerse en sus trece; **to
take to one's ~s** inf poner pies en polvorosa;
to turn on one's ~ dar media vuelta; **to walk
to ~** andar pegado a alguien II. interj (dogs)
ven aquí III. vt 1. (rugby kick) talonear 2. (football kick) pasar de tacón
heel bar n taller m de reparación de calzado
en el acto
hefty ['hefti] adj <-ier, -iest> (person) cor-

pulento, -a; (profit, amount) cuantioso, -a;
(book) gordo, -a; (price rise) alto, -a
heifer ['hefə', Am: -ɚ] n vaquilla f
height [haɪt] n 1. (of person) estatura f; (of
thing) altura f 2. pl (high places) alturas fpl;
to be afraid of ~s tener vértigo; **to attain
great ~s** fig alcanzar el punto (más) alto; **to
rise to giddy ~s** fig encumbrarse hasta el
puesto más alto; **to scale (new) ~s** fig alcanzar (nuevas) cotas 3. pl (hill) cerros mpl
4. (strongest point) cima f; **to be at the ~ of**
one's career estar en la cima de su carrera;
the ~ of fashion el último grito 5. (the greatest degree) cumbre; **the ~ of folly/stupidity**
el colmo de la locura/la estupidez; **the ~ of
kindness/patience** el súmmum de la ama-
bilidad/la paciencia
heighten ['haɪtn] I. vi aumentar II. vt
1. (elevate) elevar 2. (increase) aumentar; **to
~ the effect of sth** acentuar el efecto de algo
heinous ['heɪnəs] adj form atroz
heir [eə', Am: er] n heredero m; **to be (the) ~
to sth** ser el heredero de algo; ~ **apparent**
heredero forzoso; ~ **to the throne** heredero
del trono
heiress ['eərɪs, Am: 'erɪs] n heredera f
heirloom ['eəluːm, Am: 'er-] n reliquia f;
family ~ reliquia familiar
heist [haɪst] n inf robo m a mano armada
held [held] pt, pp of **hold**
helicopter ['helɪkɒptə', Am: -kɑːptɚ] n
helicóptero m
Heligoland ['helɪgəʊlænd, Am: -goʊ-] n
Hel(i)goland f
helipad ['helɪpæd] n plataforma f de aterrizaje de los helicópteros
heliport ['helɪpɔːt, Am: -pɔːrt] n helipuerto
m
helium ['hiːlɪəm] n no pl helio m
hell [hel] I. n no pl 1. (place of punishment)
infierno m; ~ **on earth** infierno en vida; **to be
(sheer) ~** ser un (auténtico) infierno; **to go to
~** ir al infierno; **to go through ~** pasar un calvario; **to make sb's life ~** inf hacer la vida
imposible a alguien 2. inf (as intensifier) **as
cold as ~** un frío de mil demonios; **as hot as ~**
un calor infernal; **as hard as ~** duro a más no
poder; **to hurt like ~** hacer un daño de mil
demonios; **to run like ~** correr (uno) que se
las pela; **a ~ of a decision** una decisión muy
importante; **a ~ of a noise** un ruido increíble
▶**the road to ~ is paved with good intentions** prov el camino que lleva al infierno está
lleno de buenas intenciones; **to go ~ for
leather** ir como alma que lleva el diablo;
come ~ or high water contra viento y marea;
to have been to ~ and back haber pasado un
calvario; **I'd see you in ~ first!** Brit ¡antes
muerto!; **all ~ broke loose** se armó la gorda;
to annoy the ~ out of sb inf molestar horrores a alguien; **to beat the ~ out of sb** dar a
alguien una paliza de padre y muy señor mío;
to catch ~ recibir una bronca; **to do sth for**

the ~ of it hacer algo porque sí; **to frighten the ~ out of sb** *inf* dar a alguien un susto de miedo; **to give sb ~ (for sth)** echar un rapapolvo a alguien (por algo); **go to ~!** *inf* (*leave me alone*) ¡déjame en paz!; (*stronger*) ¡vete a la mierda! *vulg;* **to hope to ~** *inf* esperar fervientemente; **to have ~ to pay** *inf* armarse la gorda; **like ~** *inf* y un cuerno; **what the ~** *inf* qué más da II. *interj* (*emphasis*) ¡demonios! ►~**'s bells!** ¡por Dios!; **what the ~ ...!** ¡qué diablos...!

he'll [hiːl] = he will *s.* **will**

hell-bent [,hel'bent, *Am:* '-,-] *adj* **to be ~ on (doing) sth** estar completamente decidido a (hacer) algo **hellfire** *n no pl* fuego *m* del infierno

hellish ['helɪʃ] *adj* infernal; (*experience*) horroroso, -a

hellishly *adv* endemoniadamente

hello [hə'ləʊ, *Am:* -'loʊ] I.<**hellos**> *n* hola *m;* **a big ~** un gran saludo II. *interj* **1.** (*greeting*) hola; **to say ~ to sb** saludar a alguien **2.** (*beginning of phone call*) diga, dígame, aló *AmC; AmS* **3.** (*to attract attention*) oiga **4.** (*surprise*) anda; ~,~ pero bueno

helm [helm] *n* timón *m;* **to be at the ~** llevar el timón; *fig* (*lead*) llevar el mando; **to take the ~** (*control*) tomar el mando; *fig* llevar las riendas

helmet ['helmɪt] *n* casco *m;* **crash ~** casco protector

helmsman ['helmzmən] *n* <-**men**> timonel *m*

help [help] I. *vi* **1.** (*assist*) ayudar **2.** (*make easier*) facilitar **3.** (*improve situation*) mejorar II. *vt* **1.** (*assist*) ayudar; **nothing can ~ him now** ya no se puede hacer nada por él; **can I ~ you?** (*in shop*) ¿en qué puedo servirle?; **to ~ sb with sth** ayudar a alguien con algo; **to ~ sb with his homework** ayudar a alguien a hacer sus deberes **2.** (*improve*) (ayudar a) mejorar; **this medicine will ~ your headache** esta medicina te aliviará el dolor de cabeza **3.** (*contribute to a condition*) contribuir [*o* ayudar] a **4.** (*prevent*) evitar; **it can't be ~ed** es así y no hay más remedio; **to not be able to ~ doing sth** no poder dejar de hacer algo; **I can't ~ it** no puedo remediarlo; **he can't ~ the way he is** él es así, ¿qué se le va hacer?; **to not be able to ~ but ...** no poder (por) menos de... **5.** (*take sth*) **to ~ oneself to sth** (*at table*) servirse algo III. *n* **1.** *no pl* (*assistance*) ayuda *f;* **to be a ~** ser una ayuda; **there'll be no ~ for it but to ...** no habrá más remedio que... **2.** (*servant*) mujer *f* de la limpieza; (*in a shop*) ayudante *mf* IV. *interj* ~! ¡socorro!; **so ~ me God** y que Dios me asista
♦**help out** *vt* ayudar

helper ['helpəʳ, *Am:* -ɚ] *n* ayudante *mf*

helpful ['helpfəl] *adj* **1.** (*willing to help*) servicial **2.** (*useful*) útil

helping ['helpɪŋ] I. *n* (*food*) ración *f,* porción *f AmL* II. *adj* **to give sb a ~ hand** echar una

mano a alguien

helpless ['helplɪs] *adj* indefenso, -a

helpline ['helplaɪn] *n* teléfono *m* de asistencia

helter-skelter [,heltə'skeltəʳ, *Am:* -ţɚ'skelţɚ] I. *adj* caótico, -a II. *adv* a la desbandada

hem [hem] I. *n* dobladillo *m,* basta *f AmL;* **to take the ~ up/down** meter/sacar el dobladillo II.<-**mm**-> *vt* hacer el dobladillo a III. *interj* ejem
♦**hem in** *vt* (*surround*) encerrar; (*constrain*) constreñir

he-man ['hiːmæn] <-**men**> *n inf* macho *m*

hemisphere ['hemɪsfɪəʳ, *Am:* -sfɪr] *n* hemisferio *m*

hemline ['hemlaɪn] *n* bajo(s) *m(pl)* (del vestido o la falda)

hemlock ['hemlɒk, *Am:* -lɑːk] *n no pl* cicuta *f*

hemp [hemp] *n no pl* cáñamo *m*

hen [hen] *n* **1.** (*female chicken*) gallina *f;* (*female bird*) hembra *f* **2.** *Scot, inf* (*woman*) guapa *f*

hence [hens] *adv* **1.** (*therefore*) de ahí **2.** *after n* (*from now*) dentro de; **two years ~** de aquí a dos años

henceforth [,hens'fɔːθ, *Am:* -'fɔːrθ] *adv,* **henceforward** [,hens'fɔːwəd, *Am:* -'fɔːrwɚd] *adv* de ahora en adelante

henchman ['hentʃmən] <-**men**> *n* secuaz *m*

hencoop ['henkuːp] *n,* **henhouse** ['henhaʊs] *n* gallinero *m*

henna ['henə] I. *n* gena *f,* jena *f* II. *vt* tintar con gena [*o* jena]

hen night *n,* **hen party** <-**ies**> *n* (*party*) fiesta *f* para mujeres; (*before wedding*) despedida *f* de soltera

henpecked ['henpekt] *adj* **a ~ husband** un calzonazos

hepatitis [,hepə'taɪtɪs, *Am:* -ţɪs] *n no pl* hepatitis *f inv*

heptathlon [hep'tæθlɒn, *Am:* -lɑːn] *n* heptatlón *m*

her [hɜːʳ, *Am:* hɜːr] I. *adj pos* su; ~ **dress/house** su vestido/casa; ~ **children** sus hijos II. *pron pers* **1.** (*she*) ella; **it's ~** es ella; **older than ~** mayor que ella; **if I were ~** si yo fuese ella **2.** *direct object* la; *indirect object* le; **look at ~** mírala; **I saw ~** la vi; **he told ~ that ...** le dijo que...; **he gave ~ the pencil** le dio el lápiz (a ella) **3.** *after prep* ella; **it's for/from ~** es para/de ella

herald ['herəld] I. *vt* presagiar; **to ~ a new era** anunciar una nueva era; **the much ~ed** el tan anunciado II. *n* **1.** (*sign*) presagio *m;* **to be a ~ of sth** ser una señal de algo **2.** HIST (*bringer of news*) heraldo *m*

heraldic [he'rældɪk, *Am:* hə-] *adj* heráldico, -a

heraldry ['herəldri] *n no pl* heráldica *f*

herb [hɜːb] *n* hierba *f*

herbaceous [hɜː'beɪʃəs, *Am:* hɚ'-] *adj* herbáceo, -a; ~ **border** arriate *m* de plantas diversas

herbalism ['hɜːbəlɪzəm, *Am:* 'hɜːr-] *n no pl* fitoterapia *f*

herbalist ['hɜːbəlɪst, *Am:* 'hɜːr-] *n* herbolario, -a *m*, *f*, yerbatero, -a *m*, *f AmS*

herbicide ['hɜːbɪsaɪd, *Am:* 'hɜːr-] *n* herbicida *m*

herbivorous [hɜː'bɪvərəs, *Am:* hɜːr-] *adj* herbívoro, -a

herculean [ˌhɜːkjʊ'liːən, *Am:* ˌhɜːrkjuː'-] *adj* hercúleo, -a; ~ **task** tarea *f* de romanos

Hercules ['hɛːkjəliːz, *Am:* 'hɜːrkjə-] *n* Hércules *m inv*

herd [hɜːd, *Am:* hɜːrd] **I.** *n* + *sing/pl vb* **1.** (*of animals*) manada *f*; (*of sheep*) rebaño *f*; (*of pigs*) piara *f* **2.** (*of people*) multitud *f*; **the common** ~ las masas; **to follow the** ~ seguir a la masa **II.** *vt* (*animals*) llevar en manada; (*sheep*) guardar **III.** *vi* ir en manada [*o* rebaño] ◆**herd together** *vt* (*animals*) reunir en una manada [*o* en un rebaño]

herd instinct *n* instinto *m* gregario

herdsman ['hɜːdzmən, *Am:* 'hɜːrdz-] *n* <-men> (*of cattle*) vaquero *m*; (*of sheep*) pastor *m*

here [hɪəʳ, *Am:* hɪr] *adv* **1.** (*in, at, to this place*) aquí; **over** ~ acá; **give it** ~ *inf* dámelo; ~ **and there** aquí y allá **2.** (*introduce*) **here is ...** aquí está... **3.** (*show arrival*) **they are** ~ ya han llegado **4.** (*next to*) **my colleague** ~ mi colega que está aquí **5.** (*now*) **where do we go from** ~? ¿dónde vamos ahora?; ~ **you are** (*giving sth*) aquí tienes; **the** ~ **and now** el presente; ~ **goes** *inf* allá voy; ~ **we go** ya estamos otra vez

hereabouts [ˌhɪərə'baʊts, *Am:* ˌhɪrə'bauts] *adv* por aquí

hereafter [hɪər'ɑːftəʳ, *Am:* hɪr'æftəʳ] **I.** *adv* en lo sucesivo **II.** *n* **the** ~ el más allá

hereby [hɪə'baɪ, *Am:* hɪr'baɪ] *adv form* por la presente

hereditary [hɪ'redɪtri, *Am:* hə'redɪtər-] *adj* hereditario, -a

heredity [hɪ'redəti, *Am:* hə'redɪ-] *n no pl* herencia *f*

herein [ˌhɪər'ɪn, *Am:* ˌhɪr-] *adv* en esto

hereof [hɪər'ɒv, *Am:* hɪr'ɑːv] *adv* de esto

heresy ['herəsi] <-ies> *n* herejía *f*

heretic ['herətɪk] *n* hereje *mf*

heretical [hɪ'retɪkl, *Am:* hə'reṯ-] *adj* herético, -a

hereupon [ˌhɪərə'pɒn, *Am:* ˌhɪrə'pɑːn] *adv form* en ese momento

herewith [ˌhɪə'wɪð, *Am:* ˌhɪr'-] *adv form* adjunto, -a

heritage ['herɪtɪdʒ, *Am:* -ṯɪdʒ] *n no pl* patrimonio *m*

hermaphrodite [hɜː'mæfrədaɪt, *Am:* hə-'mæfrou-] **I.** *n* hermafrodita *mf* **II.** *adj* hermafrodita

hermetic [hɜː'metɪk, *Am:* hə-'meṯ-] *adj* hermético, -a; ~ **seal** cierre hermético

hermit ['hɜːmɪt, *Am:* 'hɜːr-] *n* eremita *mf*

hermitage ['hɜːmɪtɪdʒ, *Am:* 'hɜːrmɪṯɪdʒ] *n* ermita *f*

hermit crab *n* cangrejo *m* ermitaño

hernia ['hɜːnɪə, *Am:* 'hɜːr-] *n* MED hernia *f*

hero ['hɪərəʊ, *Am:* 'hɪroʊ] <heroes> *n* **1.** (*brave man*) héroe *m* **2.** (*main character*) protagonista *m*; **the** ~ **of a film** el protagonista de una película **3.** (*idol*) ídolo *m* **4.** *Am* (*sandwich*) sándwich de carne fría, queso y lechuga

heroic [hɪ'rəʊɪk, *Am:* hɪ'roʊ-] *adj* **1.** (*brave, bold*) heroico, -a; ~ **attempt** intento heroico; ~ **deed** hazaña *f* **2.** (*epic*) heroico, -a; ~ **verse** verso heroico

heroics *n pl* **1.** (*language*) lenguaje *m* grandilocuente **2.** (*action*) acción *f* arriesgada

heroin ['herəʊɪn, *Am:* -oʊ-] *n no pl* heroína *f*

heroin addict *n* MED heroinómano, -a *m*, *f*

heroine ['herəʊɪn, *Am:* -oʊ-] *n* (*brave woman*) heroína *f*; (*of film*) protagonista *f*

heroism ['herəʊɪzəm, *Am:* -oʊ-] *n no pl* heroísmo *m*

heron ['herən] <-(s)> *n* garza *f* (real)

herpes ['hɜːpiːz] *n* herpes *m inv*

herring ['herɪŋ] <-(s)> *n* arenque *m*

herringbone ['herɪŋbəʊn, *Am:* -boʊn] FASHION **I.** *n no pl* espiga *f* **II.** *adj* de espiga

herring gull *n* gaviota *f* argéntea

hers [hɜːz, *Am:* hɜːrz] *pron pos* (el) suyo, (la) suya, (los) suyos, (las) suyas; **it's not my bag, it's** ~ no es mi bolsa, es la de ella; **this house is** ~ esta casa es suya; **this glass is** ~ este vaso es suyo; **a book of** ~ un libro suyo

herself [hɜː'self, *Am:* hə-] *pron* **1.** *reflexive* se; *after prep* sí (misma); **she lives by** ~ vive sola **2.** *emphatic* ella misma; **she hurt** ~ se hizo daño

hertz [hɜːts, *Am:* hɜːrts] *n inv* hercio *m*

he's [hiːz] **1.** = he is *s.* be **2.** = he has *s.* have

hesitant ['hezɪtənt] *adj* indeciso, -a; **to be** ~ **about doing sth** no estar decidido a hacer algo

hesitantly *adv* con indecisión

hesitate ['hezɪteɪt] *vi* vacilar, trepidar *AmL*; **to (not)** ~ **to do sth** (no) dudar en hacer algo

hesitation [ˌhezɪ'teɪʃən] *n* vacilación *f*; **without** ~ sin titubear; **to have no** ~ **in doing sth** no tener ninguna duda en hacer algo

hessian ['hesɪən, *Am:* 'heʃən] *n no pl, Brit* arpillera *f*

heterogeneous [ˌhetərə'dʒiːnɪəs, *Am:* ˌheṯərou'-] *adj* heterogéneo, -a

heterosexual [ˌhetərə'sekʃʊəl, *Am:* ˌheṯərou'-] **I.** *n* heterosexual *mf* **II.** *adj* heterosexual

het up [ˌhet'ʌp, *Am:* ˌheṯ-] *adj inf* alterado, -a

hew [hjuː] <hewed, hewed *o* hewn> **I.** *vt* **1.** (*cut away*) extraer **2.** (*cut into shape*) **to** ~ **stone/wood** tallar piedra/madera **II.** *vi* **to** ~ **to sth** *Am* atenerse a algo

hewn ['hjuːn] *pp of* **hew**

hex [heks] *n Am, Aus, inf* maleficio *m*; **to put a** ~ **on sb/sth** hacer un maleficio a alguien/

algo
hexagon ['heksəgən, *Am:* -gɑːn] *n* hexágono *m*
hexagonal [heks'ægənl] *adv* hexagonal
hexameter [heks'æmɪtəʳ, *Am:* -əţəʳ] *n* hexámetro *m*
hey [heɪ] *interj inf* eh, oye, órale *Méx*
heyday ['heɪdeɪ] *n* apogeo *m;* **in his/her/its** ~ en su apogeo
hey presto ['heɪ'prestəʊ, *Am:* -toʊ] *interj Brit, Aus, inf* sorpresa
HGV [ˌeɪtʃdʒiː'viː] *abbr of* **heavy goods vehicle** vehículo *m* pesado
hi [haɪ] *interj* hola
hiatus [haɪ'eɪtəs, *Am:* haɪ'eɪţəs] <-es> *n* **1.** LING hiato *m* **2.** (*pause*) pausa *f*
hibernate ['haɪbəneɪt, *Am:* -bəʳ-] *vi* hibernar
hibernation [ˌhaɪbəˈneɪʃən, *Am:* -bəʳ-] *n no pl* hibernación *f*
hibiscus [hɪ'bɪskəs] <-es> *n* BOT hibisco *m*
hiccup, hiccough ['hɪkʌp] I. *n* hipo *m;* **to have ~s** tener hipo II. *vi* <-p(p)-> tener hipo
hid [hɪd] *pt of* **hide²**
hidden ['hɪdn] I. *pp of* **hide²** II. *adj* (*person, thing*) escondido, -a; (*emotion, information*) oculto, -a; ~ **assets** ECON activos ocultos [*o* invisibles]; ~ **economy** economía sumergida
hide¹ [haɪd] *n* piel *f* ▸**to see neither ~ nor hair of sb** no verle el pelo a alguien
hide² [haɪd] <hid, hidden> I. *vi* esconderse, escorarse *Cuba, Hond* II. *vt* (*conceal: person, thing*) esconder; (*emotion, information*) ocultar; **to ~ one's face** taparse la cara III. *n Brit, Aus* observatorio *m* (*para ver animales salvajes*)
◆**hide away** *vt* esconder
◆**hide out** *vi,* **hide up** *vi* esconderse
hide-and-seek [ˌhaɪdn'siːk] *n* escondite *m;* **to play ~** jugar al escondite
hideaway ['haɪdəweɪ] *n inf* escondite *m*
hideous ['hɪdɪəs] *adj* **1.** (*very unpleasant, ugly*) espantoso, -a **2.** (*terrible*) terrible
hideout ['haɪdaʊt] *n* escondrijo *m;* **secret ~** guarida *f* secreta
hiding¹ ['haɪdɪŋ] *n a. fig* paliza *f;* **to get a real ~** (*defeat*) sufrir una fuerte derrota ▸**to be on a ~ to nothing** tener todas las de perder
hiding² ['haɪdɪŋ] *n no pl* **to be in ~** estar escondido; **to go into ~** ocultarse
hierarchic(al) [ˌhaɪə'rɑːkɪk(l), *Am:* ˌhaɪ-'rɑːr-] *adj* jerárquico, -a
hierarchy ['haɪərɑːki, *Am:* 'haɪrɑːr-] <-ies> *n* **1.** (*system*) jerarquía *f* **2.** (*upper levels of organization*) cúpula *f*
hieroglyph [ˌhaɪərəʊ'glɪf, *Am:* ˌhaɪroʊ'-] *n* jeroglífico *m*
hieroglyphics *npl* jeroglíficos *mpl*
hi-fi ['haɪfaɪ] I. *n abbr of* **high-fidelity** alta fidelidad *f* II. *adj abbr of* **high-fidelity** de alta fidelidad; ~ **equipment** equipo *m* de alta fidelidad
higgledy-piggledy [ˌhɪgldɪ'pɪgldi] *adj inf*

revuelto, -a
high [haɪ] I. *adj* **1.** (*elevated*) alto, -a; **one metre ~ and three metres wide** un metro de alto y tres metros de ancho; **knee/waist-~** hasta la rodilla/cintura; **to fly at ~ altitude** volar a gran altitud; ~ **cheekbones** pómulos elevados; **to do a ~ dive** lanzarse desde una altura considerable **2.** (*above average*) superior; **to have ~ hopes (for sb/sth)** tener grandes esperanzas (puestas en alguien/algo); **to have a ~ opinion of sb** estimar mucho a alguien; **to have ~ praise (for sb/sth)** elogiar mucho (a alguien/algo); **of the ~est calibre** de lo mejor; ~ **blood-pressure/fever** presión/fiebre alta; **a ~ calibre gun** un arma de gran calibre **3.** (*important, eminent*) elevado, -a; **of ~ rank** de alto rango; **to have sth on the ~est authority** *a. iron* saber algo de buena tinta; **to have friends in ~ places** tener amigos en las altas esferas; (*regarding job*) tener enchufe; **an order from on ~** una orden que viene de arriba; **to be ~ and mighty** ser un engreído **4.** (*under influence of drugs*) colocado, -a **5.** (*of high frequency, shrill: voice*) agudo, -a; **a ~ note** una nota alta **6.** FASHION **with a ~ neckline** con escote a (la) caja **7.** (*beginning to go bad: food*) pasado, -a ▸**to leave sb ~ and dry** dejar a alguien colgado II. *adv* **1.** (*at or to a great point or height*) a gran altura **2.** (*rough or strong*) con fuerza; **the sea runs ~** la mar está brava ▸**to search for sth ~ and low** buscar algo por todas partes III. *n* **1.** (*high*(*est*) *point*) punto *m* máximo; **an all-time ~** un récord de todos los tiempos; **to reach a ~** alcanzar un nivel récord **2.** *inf* (*trip*) **to be on a ~** estar colocado **3.** (*heaven*) **on ~** en el cielo
highball ['haɪbɔːl] *n Am* whisky *m* con soda
high beam *n Am* luces *fpl* largas **highboy** *n Am* cómoda *f* alta **highbrow** I. *adj* culto, -a II. *n* intelectual *mf* **highchair** *n* silla *f* alta **High Church** *n no pl* sector de la Iglesia anglicana de tendencia conservadora **high--class** *adj* de alta clase **high court** *n* tribunal *m* superior de justicia **high definition television** *n* televisión *f* de alta definición **high density** *adj a.* INFOR de alta densidad; ~ **disk** disco *m* de alta densidad
higher education *n no pl* enseñanza *f* superior

El **Higher Grade** es el nombre de un examen que hacen los alumnos escoceses que están en el quinto curso (un año después del **GCSE**). Los alumnos pueden elegir examinarse de una única asignatura, aunque lo normal es que ellos prefieran hacer aproximadamente cinco **Highers**.

higher-up ['haɪərʌp, *Am:* 'haɪəʳ-] *n inf* superior *m*
highfalutin [ˌhaɪfə'luːtɪn] *adj inf* presuntuoso, -a

high-fibre [ˌhaɪˈfaɪbəʳ] *adj* rico, -a en fibra **high fidelity** *n no pl* alta fidelidad *f* **high- -flier** *n* persona *f* de mucho talento **high- -flown** *adj* exagerado, -a; ~ **ideas** ideas *fpl* altisonantes **high frequency** *adj* de alta frecuencia **high-handed** *adj* arbitrario, -a; (*treatment*) despótico, -a **high-handed- ness** *n no pl* arbitrariedad *f* **high heels** *npl* tacones *mpl* altos **highjack** *vt s.* hijack **high jinks** *npl* jolgorio *m* **high jump** *n* salto *m* de altura ►he's <u>for</u> the ~ *inf* se la va a ganar

El **Highland dress** o **kilt** es el nombre que recibe el traje tradicional escocés. Procede del siglo XVI y en aquel entonces se componía de una única pieza. A partir del siglo XVII esta pieza única se convierte en dos distintas: el **kilt** (falda escocesa) y el **plaid** (capa de lana). De esta época procede también el **sporran** (una bolsa que cuelga del cinturón). Hasta el siglo XVIII no se diseñan los diferentes **tartans** (modelos de diseños escoceses) para cada familia o clan. Muchos hombres siguen poniéndose el **kilt** en acontecimientos especiales, como por ejemplo, una boda.

highlands *npl Scot* región *f* montañosa; **the Highlands** las Tierras Altas de Escocia **high- -level** *adj* de alto nivel **high life** *n* vida *f* de la alta sociedad; **to live the** ~ vivir la buena vida **highlight** I. *n* 1. (*most interesting part*) aspecto *m* interesante 2. *pl* (*bright tint in hair*) mechas *fpl* II. *vt* 1. (*draw attention to*) destacar; (*a problem*) señalar 2. (*mark*) subrayar **highlighter** *n* rotulador *m*
highly [ˈhaɪli] *adv* 1. (*very*) muy 2. (*very well*) **to speak** ~ **of someone** hablar muy bien de alguien; **to think** ~ **of someone** tener muy buen concepto de alguien
highly-educated *adj* de nivel cultural alto **highly-skilled** *adj* con grandes habilidades **highly-strung** *adj* muy excitable
High Mass [ˌhaɪˈmæs] *n* REL misa *f* mayor
highness [ˈhaɪnɪs] <-es> *n* 1. *no pl* (*level*) altura *f* 2. (*prince or princess*) His/Her/Your Highness Su Alteza **high-performance** *adj a.* AUTO de gran rendimiento **high- -pitched** *adj* 1. (*sloping steeply*) escarpado, -a; ~ **roof** tejado *m* de dos aguas 2. (*sound*) agudo, -a; **a** ~ **voice** una voz aflautada **high point** *n* **the** ~ (*most successful state*) el clímax; (*most enjoyable state*) el punto álgido **high-powered** *adj* 1. (*powerful*) de gran potencia 2. (*influential, important*) poderoso, -a 3. (*advanced*) avanzado, -a **high-press- ure** I. *n* METEO presión *f* alta; **a ridge of** ~ una zona de altas presiones II. *adj* enérgico, -a; ~ **sales techniques** ECON técnicas *f* de venta agresivas III. *vt* presionar **high priest** *n* REL sumo sacerdote *m* **high-profile** *adj* ilustre **high-protein** *adj* rico, -a en proteínas **high-**

-ranking *adj* de categoría **high-resolution** *n* INFOR alta resolución *f* **high-rise** *adj* elevado, -a **high-rise building** *n,* **high-rise flats** *npl* edificio *m* elevado **high-risk** *adj* de alto riesgo; (*investment*) arriesgado, -a **high school** *n Am* ≈ instituto *m;* **junior** ~ centro *m* de enseñanza secundaria

El término **high school** se utilizaba antiguamente en Gran Bretaña para designar una **grammar school** (escuela secundaria superior), pero hoy en día se emplea con el significado de **secondary school** (escuela secundaria inferior).

high seas *npl* alta mar *f* **high season** *n* temporada *f* alta; **at** ~ en temporada alta **high-security wing** *n* ala *m* de alta seguridad **high society** *n no pl* alta sociedad *f* **high-sounding** *adj* altisonante **high- -speed train** *n* tren *m* de alta velocidad **high-spirited** *adj* (*cheerful, lively*) animoso, -a; (*fiery: horse*) fogoso, -a **high spirits** *npl* buen humor *m* **high spot** *n inf* punto *m* culminante; **to be the** ~ **of sth** ser el punto álgido de algo **high street** *n Brit* calle *f* principal **high summer** *n* canícula *f* del verano **hightail** *vi Am, inf* darse el piro **high tea** *n Brit* merienda-cena *f* **high-tech** *adj* de alta tecnología **high technology** *n no pl* alta tecnología *f* **high-tension** *adj* de alta tensión **high tide** *n* 1. (*highest level of the tide*) marea *f* alta 2. *fig* (*highest or most successful point*) apogeo *m* **high treason** *n no pl* alta traición *f* **high-up** I. *adj* importante II. *n* alto cargo *m*
high water *n* marea *f* alta
high water mark *n* 1. (*mark showing water level*) línea *f* de pleamar 2. (*most successful point*) punto *m* culminante
highway [ˈhaɪweɪ] *n* carretera *f*
highway code *n* código *m* de la circulación **highwayman** <-men> *n* HIST salteador *m* de caminos **highway robbery** <-ies> *n* HIST asalto *m*
hijack [ˈhaɪdʒæk] I. *vt* 1. (*take over by force: plane*) secuestrar un avión 2. *fig* (*adopt as one's own*) **to** ~ **sb's ideas/plans** hacer propias las ideas/los planes de alguien II. *n* secuestro *m*
hijacker [ˈhaɪdʒækəʳ, *Am:* -ə-] *n* secuestrador(a) *m(f)* (aéreo)
hijacking [ˈhaɪdʒækɪŋ] *n no pl* secuestro *m* (aéreo)
hike [haɪk] I. *n* 1. (*long walk*) caminata *f;* **to go on a** ~ dar una caminata 2. *Am, inf* (*increase*) aumento *m* II. *vi* ir de excursión (a pie) III. *vt Am, inf* (*prices, taxes*) aumentar **hiker** [ˈhaɪkəʳ, *Am:* -ə-] *n* excursionista *mf*
hiking [ˈhaɪkɪŋ] *n no pl* excursionismo *m*
hilarious [hɪˈleərɪəs, *Am:* -ˈleɪr-] *adj* 1. (*very amusing*) divertidísimo, -a 2. (*boisterously merry*) alegre

hilarity [hɪˈlærəti, *Am:* -ˈlerəʈi] *n no pl* hilaridad *f*

hill [hɪl] *n* **1.** colina *f;* **the ~s** la sierra **2.** (*steep slope in road*) cuesta *f* **3.** (*small heap*) montoncito *m* ▶ **it ain't worth a ~ of** beans *Am, inf* no merece la pena; **as** old **as the ~s** tan viejo como el mundo; **to be** over **the ~** *inf* ser demasiado viejo

hillbilly [ˈhɪlbɪli] <-ies> *n Am* palurdo, -a *m, f*

hillock [ˈhɪlək] *n* montículo *m*

hillside [ˈhɪlsaɪd] *n* ladera *f*

hilltop [ˈhɪltɒp, *Am:* -taːp] I. *n* cumbre *f* II. *adj* de la cima

hill-walking [ˈhɪlwɔːkɪŋ] *n no pl* caminatas *fpl*

hilly [ˈhɪli] <-ier, -iest> *adj* montañoso, -a

hilt [hɪlt] *n* (*of a weapon*) empuñadura *f* ▶ (**up**) **to the ~** totalmente, hasta el cuello *inf;* **to be mortgaged up to the ~** estar completamente hipotecado; **to support sb to the ~** apoyar a alguien incondicionalmente

him [hɪm] *pron pers* **1.** (*he*) él; **it's ~** es él; **older than ~** mayor que él; **if I were ~** yo en su lugar **2.** *direct object* lo, le; *indirect object* le; **she gave ~ the pencil** le dio el lápiz (a él) **3.** *after prep* él; **it's for/from ~** es para/de él **4.** (*unspecified sex*) **if somebody comes, tell ~ that ...** si viene alguien, dile que...

Himalayas [ˌhɪməˈleɪəz] *npl* el Himalaya

himself [hɪmˈself] *pron* **1.** *reflexive* se; *after prep* sí (mismo); **for ~** para él (mismo); **he lives by ~** vive solo **2.** *emphatic* él mismo; **he hurt ~** se hizo daño

hind [haɪnd] I. *adj* trasero, -a II. <-(s)> *n* cierva *f*

hinder [ˈhɪndər, *Am:* -dəʳ] *vt* **1.** (*obstruct*) estorbar; **to ~ progress** frenar el progreso **2.** (*prevent*) **to ~ sb from doing sth** impedir a alguien hacer algo

Hindi [ˈhɪndiː] *n* hindi *m*

hind legs [ˌhaɪndˈlegz] *npl* patas *fpl* traseras ▶ **to talk the ~ off a** donkey *Brit, inf* hablar por los codos

hindmost [ˈhaɪndməʊst, *Am:* -moʊst] *adj* **1.** (*last*) último, -a **2.** (*rear*) trasero

hindquarters [ˌhaɪndˈkwɔːtəz, *Am:* ˈhaɪndˌkwɔːrʈəʳz] *npl* ZOOL cuartos *mpl* traseros

hindrance [ˈhɪndrəns] *n* **1.** (*obstruction*) estorbo *m* **2.** (*obstacle*) obstáculo *m;* **to allow sb to enter without ~** dejar que alguien entre sin poner obstáculos

hindsight [ˈhaɪndsaɪt] *n no pl* percepción *f* retrospectiva; **in ~** en retrospectiva; **with the benefit of ~** con la perspectiva del tiempo

Hindu [ˈhɪnduː] I. *n* hindú *mf* II. *adj* hindú

Hinduism [ˈhɪnduːɪzəm] *n no pl* REL hinduismo *m*

hinge [hɪndʒ] I. *n* bisagra *f* II. *vi* **to ~ on/upon sb/sth** depender de alguien/algo

hint [hɪnt] I. *n* **1.** (*trace*) indicio *m* **2.** (*allusion*) indirecta *f;* **to drop a ~** lanzar una indirecta **3.** (*practical tip*) consejo *m;* **a handy ~** una indicación útil **4.** (*slight amount*) pizca *f* II. *vt* **to ~ sth to sb** insinuar algo a alguien III. *vi* soltar indirectas; **to ~ at sth** hacer alusión a algo

hip [hɪp] I. *n* **1.** ANAT cadera *f;* **to stand with one's hands on** (**one's**) **~s** ponerse en jarras **2.** BOT escaramujo *m* II. *adj inf* (*fashionable*) moderno, -a

hipbone [ˈhɪp,bəʊn, *Am:* -boʊn] *n* hueso *m* de la cadera **hip flask** *n* petaca *m*

hippie [ˈhɪpi] *n* hippy *mf*

hippo [ˈhɪpəʊ, *Am:* -oʊ] *n inf abbr of* **hippopotamus** hipopótamo *m*

hippopotamus [ˌhɪpəˈpɒtəməs, *Am:* -ˈpaːʈə-] <-es *o* -mi> *n* hipopótamo *m*

hippy [ˈhɪpi] <-ies> *n* hippy *mf*

hire [ˈhaɪəʳ, *Am:* ˈhaɪr] I. *n no pl* alquiler *m;* **'for ~'** 'se alquila' *m* II. *vt* **1.** (*rent*) alquilar, fletar *AmL;* **to ~ sth by the hour/day/week** alquilar algo por horas/días/semanas **2.** (*employ*) contratar, conchabar *AmL;* **to ~ more staff** ampliar la plantilla
◆ **hire out** *vt* alquilar; **to ~ sth by the hour/day/week** alquilar algo por horas/días/semanas

hire purchase *n* compra *f* a plazos; **to buy something on ~** comprar algo a plazos **hire purchase agreement** *n* acuerdo *m* de compra a plazos

his [hɪz] I. *adj pos* su (de él); **~ car/house** su coche/casa; **~ children** sus hijos II. *pron pos* (el) suyo, (la) suya, (los) suyos, (las) suyas, de él; **it's not my bag, it's ~** no es mi bolsa, es la suya; **this house is ~** esta casa es suya; **this glass is ~** este vaso es suyo; **a book of ~** un libro suyo

Hispanic [hɪsˈpænɪk] I. *adj* hispánico, -a II. *n* hispano, -a *m, f*

hiss [hɪs] I. *vi* silbar; **to ~ at sb** silbar a alguien II. *vt* silbar III. *n* silbido *m*

histamine [ˈhɪstəmiːn] *n* MED histamina *f*

historian [hɪˈstɔːriən] *n* historiador(a) *m(f)*

historic [hɪˈstɒrɪk, *Am:* hɪˈstɔːrɪk] *adj* histórico, -a; **this is a ~ moment ...** es un momento clave...

historical *adj* histórico, -a

history [ˈhɪstəri] *n no pl* historia *f;* **a ~ book** un libro de historia; **sb's life ~** la vida de alguien; **to make ~** hacer época

histrionic [ˌhɪstrɪˈɒnɪk, *Am:* -ˈaːnɪk] *adj* histriónico, -a

hit [hɪt] I. *n* **1.** (*blow, stroke*) golpe *m* **2.** *inf* (*shot*) tiro *m* certero **3.** (*bomb*) impacto *m* **4.** SPORTS punto *m;* **to score a ~** marcar un tanto **5.** (*success*) éxito *m* II. <-tt-, hit, hit> *vt* **1.** (*strike*) golpear, pepenar *Méx;* **to ~ sb hard** *a. fig* pegar a alguien con fuerza **2.** (*crash into*) chocar contra; **to ~ a reef/a sandbank** dar contra un arrecife/banco de arena; **to ~ one's head on a shelf** dar con la cabeza contra un estante **3.** (*arrive at, reach target*) alcanzar **4.** (*wound*) herir; *inf* (*kill*) matar

5. (*affect*) afectar; **to ~ sb where it hurts** dar a alguien donde más le duele **6.** (*reach*) tocar; **to ~ rock bottom** *fig* tocar fondo **7.** (*encounter*) tropezar con; **to ~ a lot of resistance/a traffic jam** encontrar mucha resistencia/un atasco **8.** *inf* (*arrive in or at*) llegar a; **to ~ 200 kph** alcanzar los 200 km/h **III.** *vi* **1.** (*strike*) **to ~ against sth** chocar con algo; **to ~ at sb/sth** asestar un golpe a alguien/algo **2.** (*attack*) **to ~ at sth** atacar algo
◆**hit back** *vi* devolver el golpe; **to ~ at sb** defenderse de alguien
◆**hit off** *vt always sep* **to hit it off (with sb)** hacer buenas migas (con alguien)
◆**hit on** *vt* **1.** (*think of*) dar con **2.** *Am* (*show sexual interest*) ligar con
◆**hit out** *vi* lanzar un ataque; **to ~ at sb** asestar un golpe a alguien; *fig* tirar pullas a alguien
hit-and-run [ˌhɪtənˈrʌn] *adj* **~ accident** accidente de carretera en el que el conductor se da a la fuga; **~ attack** MIL ataque relámpago; **~ driver** conductor que se da a la fuga tras atropellar a alguien
hitch [hɪtʃ] **I.** <-es> *n* **1.** (*obstacle*) obstáculo *m;* **technical ~** problema *m* técnico; **to go off without a ~** salir a pedir de boca **2.** (*sudden pull*) tirón *m* **II.** *vt* **to ~ sth to sth** atar algo a algo; **to ~ an animal to sth** amarrar un animal a algo **2.** *inf* (*hitchhike*) **to ~ a lift** hacer dedo **III.** *vi inf* hacer dedo
◆**hitch up** *vt* **1.** (*fasten*) **to hitch sth up to sth** atar algo a algo; **to ~ an animal to sth** amarrar un animal a algo **2.** (*pull up quickly: clothes*) levantar
hitcher [ˈhɪtʃər] *n* autostopista *mf*
hitchhike [ˈhɪtʃhaɪk] *vi* hacer autostop, hacer colita *AmS*, pedir aventón *Méx*, pedir chance *Col*
hitchhiker [ˈhɪtʃhaɪkəʳ, *Am:* -ɚ] *n* autostopista *mf*
hitch-hiking *n no pl* autostop *m*
hi tech [ˌhaɪˈtek] *adj* de alta tecnología
hither [ˈhɪðəʳ, *Am:* -ɚ] *adv form* acá; **~ and thither** acá y allá
hitherto [ˌhɪðəˈtuː, *Am:* -ɚˈ-] *adv form* hasta ahora; **~ unpublished** no publicado por ahora; **to reveal ~ unsuspected talents** revelar talentos hasta el momento insospechados
hitman [ˈhɪtmæn] <-men> *n* pistolero *m*
hit-or-miss *adj* a la buena de Dios
hit parade *n* HIST (*top forty*) lista *f* de éxitos; **to be at the top of the ~** estar en lo más alto de la lista de éxitos
HIV [ˌeɪtʃaɪˈviː] *abbr of* **human immunodeficiency virus** VIH *m*
hive [haɪv] **I.** *n* **1.** (*beehouse*) colmena *f* **2.** + *sing/pl vb* (*swarm*) enjambre *m* **3.** (*busy place*) **to be a ~ of business** ser un punto neurálgico de negocios **II.** *vt* **to ~ sth off** (*separate*) separar algo; (*privatize*) privatizar algo
◆**hive off** *vi* separarse
hives [haɪvz] *n* MED urticaria *f*
hl *abbr of* **hectolitre** hl

HMG [ˌeɪtʃemˈdʒiː] *abbr of* **Her/His Majesty's Government** el Gobierno de S.M.
HMI [ˌeɪtʃemˈaɪ] *abbr of* **Her/His Majesty's Inspector (of schools)** Inspector(a) *m(f)* de S.M.
HMS [ˌeɪtʃemˈes] **1.** *abbr of* **Her/His Majesty's Service** el Servicio de S.M. **2.** *abbr of* **Her/His Majesty's Ship** Buque *m* de S.M.
HMSO [ˌeɪtʃemesˈəʊ, *Am:* -ˈoʊ] *abbr of* **Her/His Majesty's Stationery Office** imprenta *f* de S.M.
HNC [ˌeɪtʃenˈsiː] *abbr of* **Higher National Certificate** HNC *m* (*título nacional de enseñanza superior*)
HND [ˌeɪtʃenˈdiː] *abbr of* **Higher National Diploma** título *m* nacional de enseñanza superior
ho [həʊ, *Am:* hoʊ] *interj inf* (*expresses scorn, surprise*) oh; (*attracts attention*) oiga; **land ~!** NAUT ¡tierra a la vista!
HO [ˌeɪtʃˈəʊ, *Am:* -ˈoʊ] **1.** *abbr of* **head office** oficina *f* principal **2.** *abbr of* **Home Office** Ministerio *m* del Interior
hoard [hɔːd, *Am:* hɔːrd] **I.** *n* acumulación *f* **II.** *vt* acumular; (*food*) amontonar
hoarding [ˈhɔːdɪŋ, *Am:* ˈhɔːr-] *n* **1.** *Brit, Aus* (*advertising board*) valla *f* publicitaria **2.** (*temporary fence*) valla *f* de construcción
hoarfrost [ˌhɔːˈfrɒst, *Am:* ˌhɔːrˈfrɑːst] *n no pl* escarcha *f*
hoarse [hɔːs, *Am:* hɔːrs] *adj* ronco, -a
hoarseness *n no pl* MED ronquera *f;* (*quality*) ronquedad *f*
hoary [ˈhɔːri] <-ier, -iest> *adj* **1.** *liter* (*hair*) cano, -a **2.** *fig* (*old*) **~ old joke** chiste *m* viejo; **~ old excuse** excusa *f* de siempre
hoax [həʊks, *Am:* hoʊks] **I.** <-es> *n* (*fraud*) engaño *m;* (*joke*) broma *f* de mal gusto **II.** *vt* engañar
hoaxer *n* (*fraudster*) embaucador(a) *m(f);* (*joke*) gracioso, -a *m, f*
hob [hɒb, *Am:* hɑːb] *n Brit* hornillo *m*
hobble [ˈhɒbl, *Am:* ˈhɑːbl] **I.** *vi* cojear; **to ~ around** ir cojeando **II.** *vt* **1.** *liter* (*hinder*) obstaculizar **2.** (*tie legs: animal*) manear
hobby [ˈhɒbi, *Am:* ˈhɑːbi] <-ies> *n* hobby *m*
hobby-horse [ˈhɒbɪhɔːs, *Am:* ˈhɑːbɪhɔːrs] *n* **1.** (*toy*) caballito *m* **2.** (*topic*) tema *m* preferido (de conversación)
hobgoblin [ˌhɒbˈgɒblɪn, *Am:* ˈhɑːbˌgɑːb-] *n* duende *m*
hobnailed [ˈhɒbneɪld, *Am:* ˈhɑːb-] *adj* **~ed boots** botas con clavos
hobnob [ˈhɒbnɒb, *Am:* ˈhɑːbnɑːb] <-bb-> *vi inf* alternar; **to ~ with the rich and famous** codearse con los ricos y famosos
hobo [ˈhəʊbəʊ, *Am:* ˈhoʊboʊ] <-s *o* -es> *n Am, Aus* **1.** (*tramp*) vagabundo, -a *m, f* **2.** (*itinerant worker*) temporero, -a *m, f*
Hobson's choice [ˌhɒbsnzˈtʃɔɪs, *Am:* ˌhɑːb-] *n* opción *f* única
hock¹ [hɒk, *Am:* hɑːk] *n* (*wine*) vino *m* del Rin

hock² [hɒk, *Am:* hɑːk] *Am, inf* I. *n* to be in ~ (to sb) (*person*) estar endeudado (con alguien); to be in ~ (*object*) estar empeñado; my car is in ~ tengo el coche empeñado II. *vt* empeñar; to be ~ed up to the neck estar endeudado hasta las orejas

hock³ [hɒk, *Am:* hɑːk] *n* ANAT corvejón *m*

hockey ['hɒki, *Am:* 'hɑːki] *n no pl* hockey *m;* ice ~ hockey sobre hielo

hockey stick *n* SPORTS stick *m*

hocus-pocus [ˌhəʊkəs'pəʊkəs, *Am:* ˌhoʊkəs'poʊ-] *n no pl* camelo *m*

hodgepodge ['hɒdʒpɒdʒ, *Am:* 'hɑːdʒpɑːdʒ] *n* batiburrillo *m*

hoe [həʊ, *Am:* hoʊ] I. *n* azada *f* II. *vt* azadonar

hog [hɒg, *Am:* hɑːg] I. *n* 1. *Am* (*pig*) puerco *m*, chancho *m AmS* 2. *inf* (*person*) egoísta *mf* ►to live high on the ~ vivir como un rajá; to go (the) whole ~ no quedarse a medio camino II. <-gg-> *vt inf* (*keep for oneself*) acaparar; (*food*) devorar; to ~ sb/sth (all to oneself) acaparar a alguien/algo (para uno mismo)

Hogmanay ['hɒgmənei, *Am:* 'hɑːg-] *n Scot* Nochevieja *f*

hogshead ['hɒgzhed, *Am:* 'hɑːgz-] *n* 1. (*barrel*) pipa *f* 2. (*measurement*) medida de capacidad de aprox. 240 litros

hogwash ['hɒgwɒʃ, *Am:* 'hɑːgwɑːʃ] *n no pl, inf* monserga *f*

hoi polloi [ˌhɔɪpə'lɔɪ] *npl inf* the ~ las masas, el vulgo

hoist [hɔɪst] *vt* (*raise up*) alzar; (*flag*) enarbolar

hoity-toity [ˌhɔɪti'tɔɪti, *Am:* ˌhɔɪt̬i'tɔɪt̬i] *adj inf* repipi

hold [həʊld, *Am:* hoʊld] I. *n* 1. (*grasp, grip*) agarre *m;* to take ~ of sb/sth asirse de [*o* a] alguien/algo; to catch ~ of sb/sth agarrar a alguien/algo; to keep ~ of sth seguir agarrado a algo 2. (*thing to hold by*) asidero *m* 3. (*wrestling*) presa *f;* no ~s barred *fig* sin restricciones 4. (*control*) dominio *m;* to have a (strong/powerful) ~ over sb tener (mucha/gran) influencia sobre alguien 5. NAUT, AVIAT bodega *f* 6. (*delayed*) to be on ~ estar en espera; TEL estar a la espera; to put on ~ poner en espera 7. (*understand*) to get ~ of sth comprender algo; to have a ~ of sth tener idea de algo; to get ~ of the wrong idea hacerse una idea equivocada; I don't know where you got ~ of that idea no sé de dónde has sacado esa idea II. <held, held> *vt* 1. (*keep*) tener; (*grasp*) agarrar; to ~ a gun sostener un arma; to ~ hands agarrarse de la mano; to ~ sth in one's hand sostener algo en la mano; to ~ sb in one's arms estrechar a alguien entre los brazos; to ~ sb/sth (tight) sujetar a alguien/algo (con fuerza); to ~ the door open for sb aguantar la puerta a alguien 2. (*support*) soportar; to ~ one's head high mantener la cabeza alta 3. (*keep, retain*) mantener; to ~ sb's attention/interest mantener la aten-

ción/el interés de alguien; to ~ sb in custody LAW mantener a alguien a disposición policial; to ~ sb hostage retener a alguien como rehén; to ~ (on to) the lead seguir por delante 4. (*maintain*) to ~ oneself in readiness estar listo; to ~ oneself well mantenerse en forma 5. (*make keep to*) to ~ sb to his/her word hacer cumplir a alguien su palabra 6. (*control*) to ~ sth at the present/last year's level mantener algo al nivel actual/del año pasado; to ~ a note MUS sostener una nota 7. (*delay, stop*) detener; ~ it! ¡para!; to ~ one's breath contener la respiración; to ~ one's fire MIL detener el fuego; to ~ sb's phone calls TEL retener las llamadas de alguien 8. (*contain*) contener; it ~s many surprises conlleva muchas sorpresas; what the future ~s lo que depara el futuro 9. (*possess, own*) poseer; (*land, town*) ocupar; to ~ an account (with a bank) tener una cuenta (en un banco); to ~ the (absolute) majority contar con la mayoría (absoluta); to ~ a position (as sth) mantener un puesto (como algo); to ~ the fort MIL aguantar en su puesto; *fig* hacerse cargo de 10. (*make happen*) to ~ a conversation (with sb) mantener una conversación (con alguien); to ~ an election/a meeting/a news conference convocar elecciones/una reunión/una rueda de prensa; to ~ manoeuvres MIL estar de maniobras; to ~ talks dar charlas 11. (*believe*) creer; to be held in great respect ser muy respetado; to ~ sb responsible for sth considerar a alguien responsable de algo; to ~ sth in contempt despreciar algo 12. (*postpone*) to ~ sth in abeyance dejar algo pendiente III. *vi* 1. (*continue*) seguir; to ~ still pararse; to ~ true seguir siendo válido; ~ tight! ¡quieto! 2. (*stick*) pegarse 3. (*believe*) sostener

♦**hold against** *vt always sep* to hold sth against sb hacerse una mala idea de alguien por algo

♦**hold back** I. *vt* (*keep*) retener; to ~ information ocultar información; (*stop*) detener; (*impede development*) parar; to ~ tears contener las lágrimas ►there's no holding me (back) nada me retiene II. *vi* 1. (*be unforthcoming*) refrenarse 2. (*refrain*) to ~ from doing sth abstenerse de hacer algo

♦**hold down** *vt* sujetar; (*control, suppress*) oprimir; to ~ a job mantener un trabajo

♦**hold forth** *vi* to ~ (about sth) hablar largo y tendido (sobre algo)

♦**hold in** *vt* (*emotion*) contener

♦**hold off** I. *vt* (*enemy*) detener II. *vi* mantenerse a distancia

♦**hold on** *vi* 1. (*affix, attach*) agarrarse bien; to be held on by/with sth estar sujeto a/con algo 2. (*manage to keep going*) to ~ (tight) aguantar 3. (*wait*) esperar

♦**hold onto** *vt insep* 1. (*grasp*) agarrarse bien a 2. (*keep*) guardar

♦**hold out** I. *vt* extender; to ~ the hat *Brit*

pasar el sombrero II. *vi* 1. (*offer, chance*) ofrecer 2. (*manage to resist*) resistir; **to be unable to** ~ no poder aguantar; **to** ~ **for sth** resistir hasta conseguir algo 3. (*refuse to give sth*) **to** ~ **on sb** no acceder a los deseos de alguien

◆**hold over** *vt* 1. (*defer*) aplazar 2. *Am* (*extend*) alargar

◆**hold to** *vt insep* atenerse a

◆**hold together** I. *vi* mantenerse unidos; **to be held together with glue** mantenerse pegados II. *vt* mantener unidos

◆**hold under** *vt insep* someter

◆**hold up** I. *vt* 1. (*raise*) levantar; **to** ~ **one's hand** levantar la mano; **to be held up by** (**means of**)/**with sth** ser sostenido por (mediante)/con algo; **to hold up one's head high** *fig* mantener la cabeza alta 2. (*delay*) atrasar 3. (*rob with violence*) atracar 4. (*offer as example*) **to hold sb up as an example of sth** mostrar a alguien como ejemplo de algo II. *vi* (*weather*) seguir haciendo bueno; (*material*) durar

◆**hold with** *vt insep* estar de acuerdo con

holdall ['həʊldɔːl, *Am:* 'hoʊld-] *n Brit* bolsa *f* de viaje

holder ['həʊldə', *Am:* 'hoʊldə'] *n* 1. (*device*) soporte *m*; **cigarette** ~ boquilla *f* 2. (*person: of shares, of account*) titular *mf*; (*of title*) poseedor(a) *m(f)*; **world record** ~ plusmarquista *mf* mundial

holding *n* 1. *pl* (*tenure*) tenencia *f* 2. (*property*) propiedades *fpl* 3. ECON participación *f*; ~**s** valores *mpl* en cartera

holding company *n* holding *m*

hold-up ['həʊldʌp, *Am:* 'hoʊld-] *n* 1. (*robbery*) atraco *m* 2. (*delay*) retraso *m*

hole [həʊl, *Am:* hoʊl] I. *n* 1. (*hollow space*) agujero *m* 2. (*in golf*) hoyo *m* 3. (*of mouse*) ratonera *f*; (*of rabbit*) madriguera *f* 4. *inf* (*jam*) apuro *m*; **to be in a** ~ estar en un apuro [*o* aprieto]; **to be in the** ~ *Am* estar endeudado ▶**to be a round peg in a square** ~ estar fuera de lugar II. *vt* 1. (*perforate*) agujerear 2. (*in golf*) embocar

◆**hole up** *vi inf* esconderse

holiday ['hɒlədeɪ, *Am:* 'hɑːlə-] I. *n* 1. *Brit, Aus* (*vacation*) vacaciones *fpl*; **on** ~ de vacaciones; **to take a** ~ coger vacaciones 2. (*public day off*) día *m* festivo ▶**a busman's** ~ día de fiesta que uno pasa trabajando II. *vi* pasar las vacaciones; (*in summer*) veranear

holiday camp *n* campamento *f* de verano **holiday entitlement** *n* he has a ~ **of 30 days a year** le corresponden 30 días de vacaciones al año **holiday flat** *n* apartamento *m* de veraneo **holiday house** *n* casa *f* de veraneo **holidaymaker** *n* (*tourist*) turista *mf*; (*in summer*) veraneante *mf* **holiday resort** *n* centro *m* turístico

holiness ['həʊlɪnɪs, *Am:* 'hoʊ-] *n no pl* santidad *f*; **His/Your Holiness** Su Santidad

holism ['həʊlɪzəm, *Am:* 'hoʊ-] *n no pl* ho-

lismo *m*

holistic [həʊ'lɪstɪk, *Am:* hoʊ-] *adj* holístico, -a

Holland ['hɒlənd, *Am:* 'hɑːlənd] *n* Holanda *f*

holler ['hɒlə', *Am:* 'hɑːlə'] I. *vi Am, inf* gritar, chillar II. *n Am, inf* chillido *m*

hollow ['hɒləʊ, *Am:* 'hɑːloʊ] I. *adj* 1. (*empty*) hueco, -a 2. (*worthless, empty: promise*) vano, -a; (*victory*) vacío, -a; (*laughter*) falso, -a 3. (*sound*) sordo, -a II. *n* hueco *m*; *Am* (*valley*) hondonada *f* III. *vt* **to** ~ (**out**) (*coconut*) vaciar; (*tree trunk*) ahuecar IV. *adv* **to sound** ~ sonar a hueco ▶**to beat sb** ~ dar una paliza a alguien

holly ['hɒli, *Am:* 'hɑːli] *n no pl* BOT acebo *m*

hollyhock ['hɒlɪhɒk, *Am:* 'hɑːlɪhɑːk] *n* BOT malvarrosa *f*

holm oak ['həʊm,əʊk, *Am:* 'hoʊm,oʊk] *n* BOT encina *f*

holocaust ['hɒləkɔːst, *Am:* 'hɑːləkɑːst] *n* holocausto *m*

hologram ['hɒləgræm, *Am:* 'hɑːlə-] *n* holograma *m*

holster ['həʊlstə', *Am:* 'hoʊlstə'] *n* pistolera *f*, cañonera *f AmL*

holy ['həʊli, *Am:* 'hoʊ-] <-ier, -iest> *adj* 1. (*sacred*) santo, -a; (*water*) bendito, -a 2. *fig* **to be a** ~ **terror** ser el mismísimo demonio **Holy Communion** *n* Sagrada Comunión *f* **Holy Father** *n* Santo Padre *m* **Holy Scripture** *n* the ~ las Sagradas Escrituras **Holy See** *n* Santa Sede *f* **Holy Spirit** *n* Espíritu *m* Santo **Holy Week** *n* Semana *f* Santa

homage ['hɒmɪdʒ, *Am:* 'hɑːmɪdʒ] *n* homenaje *m*; **to pay** ~ **to sb** rendir homenaje a alguien

home [həʊm, *Am:* hoʊm] I. *n* 1. (*residence*) casa *f*; **at** ~ en casa; **to leave** ~ salir [*o* irse] de casa; **away from** ~ fuera de casa; **I live in London but my** ~ **is in Barcelona** vivo en Londres pero soy de Barcelona; **make yourself at** ~ ponte cómodo, estás en tu casa 2. (*family*) hogar *m* 3. (*institution*) asilo *m*; (*for old people*) residencia *f*; **children's** ~ orfanato *m* II. *adv* 1. (*one's place of residence*) **to be** ~ estar en casa; **to go**/**come** ~ ir/venir a casa; **to take work** ~ llevarse trabajo a casa 2. (*understanding*) **to bring sth** ~ **to sb** conseguir que alguien se dé cuenta de algo ▶**to be** ~ **and dry** *Brit*, **to be** ~ **and hosed** *Aus* tener la victoria asegurada; **this is nothing to write** ~ **about** esto no es nada del otro mundo III. *adj* 1. (*from own country*) nacional 2. (*from own area*) local; (*team*) de casa; (*game*) en casa; **the** ~ **ground** el campo de casa

◆**home in on** *vt insep, inf* 1. MIL apuntar 2. (*locate*) localizar y dirigirse hacia

home address *n* dirección *f* particular **home affairs** *npl Brit* POL asuntos *mpl* interiores **home-baked** *adj* casero, -a **homebanking** *n* telebanking *m* **home**

brew *n cerveza hecha en casa* **home-coming** *n regreso m (a casa)*

En los EE.UU. se utiliza el término **Home-coming** para referirse a una importante fiesta que tiene lugar en la High School y la universidad. Ese día el equipo de fútbol local juega en su propio campo. Se celebra una gran fiesta y se erige **homecoming queen** a la alumna más popular.

home computer *n ordenador m doméstico*
home cooking *n no pl cocina f casera*
Home Counties *n Brit: condados de los alrededores de Londres* **home economics** *n + sing vb economía f doméstica* **home-grown** *adj* 1.(*vegetables*) de cosecha propia 2.(*not foreign*) del país 3.(*local*) local **home help** *n asistente, -a m, f* (para las tareas domésticas) **homeland** *n* (*country of birth*) tierra *f* natal **homeless I.** *adj* sin hogar **II.** *n + pl vb* the ~ los sin techo **homelike** *adj* hogareño, -a **home loan** *n* hipoteca *f*
homely ['hǝumli, *Am:*'houm-] <-ier, -iest> *adj* 1.*Brit, Aus* (*plain*) casero, -a 2.*Am, Aus* (*ugly*) feo, -a
home-made [ˌhǝum'meɪd, *Am:* ˌhoum-] *adj* casero, -a **homemaker** *n Am* ama *f* de casa **home market** *n* mercado *m* nacional **Home Office** *n Brit* Ministerio *m* del Interior **homepage** *n* página *f* inicial, portal *m*
homeopath ['hǝumiǝupæθ, *Am:* 'hou-miou-] *n* homeópata *mf*
homeopathic [ˌhǝumiǝu'pæθɪk, *Am:*ˌhou-miou-] *adj* homeopático, -a
homeopathy [ˌhǝumi'ɒpǝθi, *Am:* ˌhou-mi'ɒpǝ-] *n no pl* homeopatía *f*
homeowner ['hǝum,ǝunǝ', *Am:* 'houm-,ounǝ'] *n* propietario, -a *m, f*
home plate *n Am* SPORTS base *f* del bateador
home rule *n* gobierno *m* autónomo **Home Secretary** <-ies> *n Brit* ministro, -a *m, f* del Interior
homesick ['hǝumsɪk, *Am:* 'houm-] *adj* nostálgico, -a; **to feel ~ (for)** tener morriña (de) **homesickness** *n no pl* morriña *f*
homespun ['hǝumspʌn, *Am:* 'houm-] *adj* de andar por casa; (*wisdom*) popular **homestead** *n Am, Aus* finca *f*
home straight *n,* **home stretch** <-es> *n* recta *f* final **home team** *n* equipo *m* local [o de casa] **home town** *n* ciudad *f* natal, pueblo *m* natal **home truth** *n* to tell sb a few ~s decir a alguien unas cuantas verdades **homeward** ['hǝumwǝd, *Am:* 'houmwǝ·d] **I.** *adv* de camino a casa **II.** *adj* (*journey*) de regreso **homewards** *adv s.* **homeward I.**
homework ['hǝumwɜ:k, *Am:* 'houmwɜ·rk] *n* SCHOOL deberes *mpl* **homeworker** *n* persona *f* que trabaja desde casa
homey ['hǝumi, *Am:*'hou-] <-ier, -iest> *adj* casero, -a

homicidal [ˌhɒmɪ'saɪdl, *Am:* ˌha:mǝ-] *adj Am, Aus* LAW homicida
homicide ['hɒmɪsaɪd, *Am:* 'ha:mǝ-] **I.** *n Am, Aus* 1.(*crime*) homicidio *m* 2.(*criminal*) homicida *mf* **II.** *adj* ~ **squad** *Am, Aus* homicidios *mpl*
homing ['hǝumɪŋ, *Am:*'hou-] *adj* (*instinct*) de volver al hogar; (*device*) buscador(a)
homing pigeon *n* paloma *f* mensajera
homogeneous *adj,* **homogenous** [ˌhɒmǝ'dʒi:niǝs, *Am:* ˌhoumou'dʒi:-] *adj* homogéneo, -a
homogenize [hǝ'mɒdʒǝnaɪz, *Am:* hǝ-'ma:dʒǝ-] *vt* homogeneizar
homograph ['hɒmǝgra:f, *Am:* 'ha:mǝ-græf] *n* homógrafo *m*
homonym ['hɒmǝnɪm, *Am:* 'ha:mǝ-] *n* homónimo *m*
homophobia [ˌhɒmǝ'fǝubiǝ, *Am:* ˌhoumǝ-'fou-] *n no pl* homofobia *f*
homophone ['hɒmǝfǝun, *Am:* 'ha:mǝ-foun] *n* homófono *m*
homosexual [ˌhɒmǝ'sekʃuǝl, *Am:* ˌhou-mou-] **I.** *adj* homosexual **II.** *n* homosexual *mf*
homosexuality [ˌhɒmǝsekʃu'ælǝti, *Am:* ˌhoumousekʃu'ælǝti] *n no pl* homosexualidad *f*
Hon. *abbr of* **Honorary** Hon.
Honduran [hɒn'djuǝrǝn, *Am:* ha:n'dur-] **I.** *adj* hondureño, -a **II.** *n* hondureño, -a *m, f*
Honduras [hɒn'djuǝrǝs, *Am:* ha:n'dur-] *n* Honduras *f*
hone [hǝun, *Am:* houn] *vt* (*sharpen*) afilar; *fig* (*refine*) afinar
honest ['ɒnɪst, *Am:* 'a:nɪst] *adj* 1.(*trustworthy*) honesto, -a 2.(*truthful*) sincero, -a; **to be ~ with oneself** ser sincero consigo mismo; ~ **(to God)** *inf* como Dios manda
honestly *adv* (*truthfully*) sinceramente; (*with honesty*) honradamente
honest-to-goodness ['ɒnɪstǝ'gudnɪs, *Am:* 'a:nɪst-] *adj* como Dios manda
honesty ['ɒnɪsti, *Am:* 'a:nɪ-] *n no pl* 1.(*trustworthiness*) honestidad *f* 2.(*sincerity*) sinceridad *f;* **in all ~** para ser sincero
honey ['hʌni] *n no pl* 1.GASTR miel *f* 2.*Am* (*sweet person*) encanto *m;* (*sweet thing*) preciosidad *f* 3.(*darling*) cariño *m* **honeybee** *n* abeja *f* **honeycomb I.** *n* panal *m* **II.** *adj* (*pattern*) de panal **honeydew (melon)** *n* melón *m* dulce **honeymoon I.** *n* luna *f* de miel **II.** *vi* pasar la luna de miel **honeysuckle** *n* BOT madreselva *f*
honk [hɒŋk, *Am:* ha:ŋk] **I.** *vi* 1.ZOOL graznar 2.AUTO tocar la bocina **II.** *n* 1.ZOOL graznido *m* 2.AUTO bocinazo *m*
honor ['ɑ:nǝ·] *n Am, Aus s.* **honour**
honorable ['ɑ:nǝrǝbl] *adj Am, Aus s.* **honourable**
honorary ['ɒnǝrǝri, *Am:* 'ɑ:nǝrer-] *adj* 1.(*conferred as an honour: title*) honorario, -a; (*president*) de honor 2.(*without pay*) no remunerado, -a

honors degree *n Am, Aus s.* **honours degree**

honour ['ɒnəʳ] I. *n Brit* **1.** (*respect*) honor *m;* **in ~ of sb/sth** en honor de alguien/algo; **to be** (**in**) **~ bound to ...** estar moralmente obligado a... **2.** LAW **Her/His/Your Honour** Su Señoría **3.** *pl* (*distinction*) honores *mpl;* **last ~s** honras *fpl* fúnebres; **to graduate with ~s** licenciarse con matrícula de honor II. *vt* **1.** (*fulfil: promise, contract*) cumplir (con) **2.** (*confer honour*) honrar; **to be ~ed** sentirse honrado

honourable ['ɒnərəbl] *adj Brit* **1.** (*worthy of respect: person*) honorable; (*agreement*) honroso, -a **2.** (*honest*) honrado, -a **3.** *Brit* POL **the Honourable member for ...** el Ilustre Señor Diputado de...

honours degree *n Brit* UNIV licenciatura *f* de matrícula de honor

hons *n abbr of* **honours** honores *mpl*

hood¹ [hʊd] *n* **1.** (*covering for head*) capucha *f* **2.** (*on machine*) cubierta *f;* (*on cooker*) campana *f* **3.** *Am* AUTO capó *m* **4.** *Brit* (*folding top*) capota *f*

hood² [hʊd] *n Am, inf* (*gangster*) matón, -ona *m, f*

hoodlum ['huːdləm] *n* matón, -ona *m, f*

hoodwink ['hʊdwɪŋk] *vt* engañar, emplumar *Guat, Cuba*

hoof [huːf, *Am:* hʊf] I. <hooves *o* hoofs> *n* casco *m,* pezuña *f;* **on the ~** (*cattle*) en pie II. *vt inf* **to ~ it** ir a pata

hoo-ha ['huːhɑː] *n no pl, inf* jaleo *m*

hook [hʊk] I. *n* (*device for holding*) gancho *m;* (*for clothes*) percha *f;* (*fish*) anzuelo *m;* **to leave the phone off the ~** dejar el teléfono descolgado ▸**by ~ or by crook** por las buenas o por las malas; **to fall for sth ~, line and sinker** tragárselo [*o* creérselo] todo; **to be off the ~** librarse; **to get one's ~ into sb** tener a alguien en las garras (de uno); **to sling one's ~** *Brit, inf* pirarse II. *vt* **1.** (*fasten*) enganchar **2.** (*fish*) pescar III. *vi* (*clothes*) abrocharse (con corchetes); (*parts*) engancharse

◆**hook on** I. *vi* conectarse II. *vt* enganchar

◆**hook up** I. *vt* **1.** (*hang: curtains*) poner **2.** (*link up*) enganchar; (*connect*) conectar II. *vi* **1.** (*connect*) conectarse **2.** (*clothes*) abrocharse

hooked [hʊkt] *adj* **1.** (*nose*) ganchudo, -a **2.** (*addicted*) enganchado, -a

hooker¹ ['hʊkəʳ, *Am:* -ɚ] *n Am, Aus, inf* prostituta *f*

hooker² ['hʊkəʳ, *Am:* -ɚ] *n* SPORTS talonador(a) *m(f)*

hooky ['hʊki] *n no pl, Am, Aus, inf* **to play ~** hacer novillos, capar clase *Col*

hooligan ['huːlɪɡən] *n* hooligan *mf*

hooliganism *n no pl* hooliganismo *m,* gamberrismo *m*

hoop [huːp] *n* aro *m* ▸**to put sb through the ~s** hacérselas pasar negras a alguien

hoopoe ['huːpuː] *n* abubilla *f*

hoot [huːt] I. *vi* (*owl*) ulular; (*with horn*) tocar la bocina; **to ~ with laughter** desternillarse de risa II. *vt* **to ~ sb** tocar la bocina [*o* pitar] a alguien III. *n* (*of owl*) ululato *m;* (*of horn*) bocinazo *m;* (*of train*) pitido *m;* **to give a ~ of laughter** soltar una carcajada; **to not give a ~** (*about sth*) importar algo un pito a alguien

◆**hoot down** *vt* abuchear

hooter ['huːtəʳ, *Am:* -t̬ɚ] *n* **1.** (*siren*) sirena *f* **2.** *inf* (*nose*) napia *f*

hoover® ['huːvəʳ, *Am:* -vɚ] I. *n Brit, Aus* aspirador *m* II. *vt* pasar el aspirador por III. *vi* pasar el aspirador

hop¹ [hɒp, *Am:* hɑːp] *n* BOT lúpulo *m*

hop² [hɒp, *Am:* hɑːp] <-pp-> I. *vi* saltar II. *vt Am, inf* (*bus*) subir a; **to ~ it** *Brit, inf* largarse III. *n* **1.** (*leap*) salto *m;* (*using only one leg*) salto *m* a la pata coja, brinco *m* de cojito *Méx* **2.** *inf* (*informal dance*) baile *m* **3.** (*short flight*) vuelo *m* corto ▸**to catch sb on the ~** *Brit, inf* pillar a alguien desprevenido

◆**hop about** *vi,* **hop around** *vi* saltar; **to ~ from one subject to another** saltar de un tema a otro

◆**hop in** *vt insep* pillar; **to ~ a taxi** *inf* pillar un taxi

◆**hop out** *vi* bajar (de un salto); **to ~ of bed** saltar de la cama

hope [həʊp, *Am:* hoʊp] I. *n* esperanza *f;* **to give up ~** perder la(s) esperanza(s); **to pin all one's ~s on sb/sth** poner todas las esperanzas en alguien/algo; **there is still ~** todavía hay esperanzas ▸**to not have a ~ in hell** no tener ni la más remota posibilidad II. *vi* (*wish*) esperar; **to ~ for the best** esperar que la suerte acompañe a uno

hopeful ['həʊpfəl, *Am:* 'hoʊp-] I. *adj* **1.** (*person*) esperanzado, -a; **to be ~** ser optimista **2.** (*promising*) esperanzador(a) II. *n pl* candidato, -a *m, f;* **young ~s** jóvenes aspirantes *mfpl*

hopefully *adv* **1.** (*in a hopeful manner*) con ilusión **2.** (*one hopes*) ~! ¡ojalá!; ~ **we'll be in Sweden at 6.00 PM** si todo sale bien estaremos en Suecia a las 6 de la tarde

hopeless ['həʊpləs, *Am:* 'hoʊp-] *adj* (*situation*) desesperado, -a; (*effort*) imposible; **to be ~** *inf* (*person*) ser inútil; (*service*) ser un desastre; **to be ~ at sth** ser negado para algo

hopelessly *adv* **1.** (*without hope*) sin esperanzas **2.** (*totally, completely*) ~ **lost** totalmente perdido

hopper ['hɒpəʳ, *Am:* 'hɑːpɚ] *n* tolva *f*

hopping mad ['hɒpɪŋ 'mæd, *Am:* 'hɑːp-] *adj inf* furioso, -a; **he is ~** está que trina

hopscotch ['hɒpskɒtʃ, *Am:* 'hɑːpskɑːtʃ] *n no pl* **to play ~** jugar a la rayuela

horde [hɔːd, *Am:* hɔːrd] *n* multitud *f*

horizon [həˈraɪzn] *n a. fig* horizonte *m*

horizontal [ˌhɒrɪˈzɒntl, *Am:* ˌhɔːrɪˈzɑːn-] I. *adj* horizontal II. *n no pl* horizontal *f*

hormone ['hɔːməʊn, *Am:* 'hɔːrmoʊn] *n* hormona *f*

horn [hɔːn, *Am:* hɔːrn] *n* **1.** ZOOL cuerno *m*

2. MUS trompa *f* **3.** AUTO bocina *f* **4.** *no pl* (*material*) cuerno *m* ►**to be on the ~s of a dilemma** estar entre la espada y la pared; **to draw in one's ~s** apretarse el cinturón; **to lock ~s (over sth)** tener un enfrentamiento (por algo)
◆**horn in** *vi Am* **to ~ on sth** entrometerse en algo
hornet ['hɔːnɪt, *Am:* 'hɔːr-] *n* avispón *m*
horn-rimmed ['hɔːnrɪmt, *Am:* 'hɔːrn-] *adj* (*glasses*) de concha
horny ['hɔːni, *Am:* 'hɔːr-] <-ier, -iest> *adj* **1.** (*made of horn*) córneo, -a **2.** *inf* (*lustful*) cachondo, -a **3.** *Am, inf* (*attractive*) macizo, -a
horoscope ['hɒrəskəʊp, *Am:* 'hɔːrəskoʊp] *n* horóscopo *m*
horrendous [hɒ'rendəs, *Am:* hɔː'ren-] *adj* **1.** (*crime*) horrendo, -a **2.** (*losses*) terrible
horrible ['hɒrəbl, *Am:* 'hɔːr-] *adj* horrible
horrid ['hɒrɪd, *Am:* 'hɔːr-] *adj* (*unpleasant*) horrible; (*unkind*) antipático, -a
horrific [hə'rɪfɪk, *Am:* hɔː'rɪf-] *adj* horroroso, -a
horrify ['hɒrɪfaɪ, *Am:* 'hɔːr-] <-ie-> *vt* horrorizar
horror ['hɒrər, *Am:* 'hɔːrɚ] *n* horror *m*, espantosidad *f* *AmC, Col, PRico;* ~ **film** película *f* de terror
horror-stricken ['hɒrəˌstrɪkən, *Am:* 'hɔːrɚ-] *adj*, **horror-struck** *adj* horrorizado, -a
hors d'œuvre [ɔː'dɜːv, *Am:* ɔːr'dɜːrv] <hors d'œuvre *o* hors d'oeuvres> *n* entremés *m*, entremeses *mpl*
horse [hɔːs, *Am:* hɔːrs] *n* **1.** ZOOL caballo *m*; **to ride a ~** montar a caballo **2.** SPORTS potro *m* ►**to change ~s (in) midstream** cambiar de parecer a mitad de camino; **to get sth straight from the ~'s mouth** saber algo de buena tinta; **don't look a gift ~ in the mouth** *prov* a caballo regalado, no le mires el dentado *prov;* **you can take a ~ to water but you can't make him drink** *prov* puedes darle un consejo a alguien, pero no puedes obligarlo a que lo siga; **to flog a dead ~** perder el tiempo (intentando algo), arar en el mar; **to be on one's high ~** *inf* tener muchos humos; **to eat like a ~** comer como una lima; **to hold one's ~s** *inf* parar el carro
◆**horse about** *vi*, **horse around** *vi* hacer el tonto
horseback ['hɔːsbæk, *Am:* 'hɔːrs-] **I.** *n* **on ~** a caballo **II.** *adj* ~ **riding** equitación *f* **horsebox** *n* remolque *m* para transportar caballos
horse chestnut *n* (*tree*) castaño *m* de Indias; (*fruit*) castaña *f* de Indias **horse-drawn** *adj* tirado, -a por caballos **horsefly** <-ies> *n* tábano *m* **horsehair** *n no pl* crin *f*
horseman ['hɔːsmən, *Am:* 'hɔːrs-] <-men> *n* jinete *m* **horsemanship** *n no pl* equitación *f*
horseplay ['hɔːspleɪ, *Am:* 'hɔːrs-] *n no pl* juguetecito(s) *m(pl)* **horsepower** *inv n no pl* caballo (*m* de vapor)

horse race *n* carrera *f* de caballos **horse racing** *n* carreras *fpl* de caballos **horseradish** *n* rábano *m* picante **horse riding** *n no pl* equitación *f* **horse sense** *n inf* sentido *m* común **horseshoe** *n* herradura *f* **horse-trading** *n no pl* tira *m* y afloja **horse van** *n Am s.* **horsebox**
horsewhip ['hɔːswɪp, *Am:* 'hɔːrs-] **I.** <-pp-> *vt* dar latigazos a **II.** *n* látigo *m*
horsewoman ['hɔːswʊmən, *Am:* 'hɔːrs-] <-women> *n* amazona *f*
hors(e)y ['hɔːsi, *Am:* 'hɔːr-] <-ier, -iest> *adj* **1.** (*interested in horses*) aficionado, -a a los caballos **2.** (*face*) de caballo
horticultural [ˌhɔːtɪ'kʌltʃərəl, *Am:* ˌhɔːrtə-'kʌltʃə-] *adj no pl* hortícola
horticulture ['hɔːtɪkʌltʃər, *Am:* 'hɔːrtə-kʌltʃɚ] *n no pl* horticultura *f*
hose [həʊz, *Am:* hoʊz] *n* manguera *f*
hosepipe ['həʊzpaɪp, *Am:* hoʊz-] *n Brit s.* **hose**
hosiery ['həʊziəri, *Am:* 'hoʊʒɚi] *n no pl* (*shop*) calcetería *f;* (*goods*) medias *fpl* y calcetines
hospice ['hɒspɪs, *Am:* 'hɑːspɪs] *n* **1.** (*house of shelter*) hospicio *m* **2.** (*hospital*) residencia *f* para enfermos terminales
hospitable [hɒ'spɪtəbl, *Am:* 'hɑːspɪtə-] *adj* hospitalario, -a
hospital ['hɒspɪtl, *Am:* 'hɑːspɪtl] *n* hospital *m*
hospitality [ˌhɒspɪ'tæləti, *Am:* ˌhɑːspɪ-'tæləti] **I.** *n no pl* hospitalidad *f* **II.** *adj* (*food, drinks*) de cortesía
hospitalization [ˌhɒspɪtəlaɪz'eɪʃən, *Am:* ˌhɑːspɪtəlɪ-] *n no pl* hospitalización *f*
hospitalize ['hɒspɪtəlaɪz, *Am:* 'hɑːspɪtəl-] *vt* hospitalizar
hospital ship *n* buque *m* hospital
host¹ [həʊst, *Am:* hoʊst] **I.** *n* **1.** (*person who receives guests*) anfitrión, -ona *m, f* **2.** (*presenter*) presentador(a) *m(f)* **3.** BIO huésped *m* **4.** INFOR servidor *m* **II.** *vt* **1.** (*party*) dar; (*event*) ser la sede de **2.** (*programme*) presentar
host² [həʊst, *Am:* hoʊst] *n* multitud *f;* **a whole ~ of reasons** muchas razones
Host [həʊst, *Am:* hoʊst] *n* REL Hostia *f*
hostage ['hɒstɪdʒ, *Am:* 'hɑːstɪdʒ] *n* rehén *mf;* **to take/hold sb ~** tomar/tener a alguien como rehén ►**to create a ~ to fortune** jugársela
host country <-ies> *n* país *m* anfitrión
hostel ['hɒstl, *Am:* 'hɑːstl] *n* **1.** (*cheap hotel*) hostal *m;* **student ~** residencia *f* de estudiantes; **youth ~** albergue *m* juvenil **2.** *Brit* (*for homeless*) casa *f* de acogida
hosteller ['hɒstələr, *Am:* 'hɑːstələ-] *n* alberguista *mf*
hostess ['həʊstɪs, *Am:* 'hoʊ-] <-es> *n* **1.** AVIAT azafata *f* **2.** (*woman who receives guests*) anfitriona *f* **3.** (*presenter*) presentadora *f*
hostile ['hɒstaɪl, *Am:* 'hɑːstl] *adj* hostil; ~

aircraft avión enemigo
hostility [hɒˈstɪləti, *Am:* haːˈstɪlət̬i] <-ies>
n hostilidad *f*
hot [hɒt, *Am:* haːt] *adj* **1.** (*very warm: food,
water*) caliente; (*day, weather*) caluroso, -a;
(*climate*) cálido, -a; **it's** ~ hace calor **2.** (*spicy*)
picante, bravo, -a *AmL* **3.** *inf* (*skilful*) hábil; **to
be** ~ **stuff at** (**doing**) **sth** ser un hacha en algo
4. *inf* (*demanding*) estricto, -a; **to be** ~ **on sth**
dar mucha importancia a algo **5.** (*dangerous*)
peligroso, -a; **to be too** ~ **to handle** *fig* ser
demasiado difícil de manejar **6.** *inf* (*sexually
attractive*) **to be** ~ estar bueno **7.** (*exciting:
music, party*) animado, -a; ~ **news** noticias
frescas ▸ **to be all** ~ **and** bothered estar sulfu-
rado
◆ **hot up** <-tt-> *vi* (*situation*) calentarse
hot air [ˌhɒtˈeəʳ, *Am:* ˌhaːˈteʳ] *n fig* palabras
fpl huecas; **to be** (**just**) **so much** ~ **air** ser sólo
palabrería **hot-air balloon** *n* globo *m* de
aire caliente
hotbed [ˈhɒtbed, *Am:* ˈhaːt-] *n fig* (*of vice,
disease, crime*) caldo *m* de cultivo **hot-
-blooded** *n* (*easy to anger*) irascible;
(*passionate*) apasionado, -a
hotchpotch [ˈhɒtʃpɒtʃ, *Am:* ˈhaːtʃpaːtʃ] *n
no pl* batiburrillo *m*
hot dog [ˌhɒtˈdɒg, *Am:* ˈhaːtdaːg] *n*
1. GASTR perrito *m* caliente, pancho *m* *Arg*
2. ZOOL perro *m* salchicha
hotel [həʊˈtel, *Am:* hoʊ-] *n* hotel *m*
hotel accommodation *n no pl* alojamiento
m **hotel bill** *n* factura *f* del hotel
hotelier [həʊˈteliɛɪ, *Am:* ˌhoʊtelˈjeɪ] *n*
(*owner*) hotelero, -a *m, f;* (*manager*) direc-
tor(a) *m(f)* del hotel
hotel industry *n no pl* industria *f* hotelera
hotel staff *n no pl* personal *m* del hotel
hotfoot [ˈhɒtfʊt, *Am:* ˈhaːt-] **I.** *adv* a toda
prisa **II.** *vt* **to** ~ **it somewhere** *inf* ir volando a
algún sitio **III.** *vi* ir volando
hothead [ˈhɒthed, *Am:* ˈhaːt-] *n* persona *f*
alocada **hotheaded** *adj* impulsivo, -a
hothouse [ˈhɒthaʊs, *Am:* ˈhaːt-] **I.** *n* invernadero *m* **II.** *adj* de invernadero **hotline** *n* TEL
línea *f* directa; **to set up a** ~ poner una línea
directa
hotly *adv* apasionadamente
hot metal *n* TYPO fundición *f* **hotplate** *n*
hornillo *m* **hot potato** <-oes> *n fig* patata *f*
caliente **hotrod** *n inf* AUTO coche *m* trucado
hot seat *n* **1.** (*difficult position*) **to be in
the** ~ estar en la línea de fuego **2.** (*electric
chair*) silla *f* eléctrica **hotshot** *n Am, Aus, inf*
hacha *f;* **to be a** (**real**) ~ **at sth** *fig* ser un as en
algo **hot spot** *n inf* **1.** (*popular place*) lugar
m concurrido **2.** (*nightclub*) club *m* nocturno
hot stuff *n* **1.** (*good*) **to be** ~ **at sth** ser un
as en algo **2.** (*sexy*) **to be** ~ estar bueno **hot-
-tempered** *adj* irascible **hot-water bottle**
n bolsa *f* de agua caliente
hound [haʊnd] **I.** *n* perro *m* de caza **II.** *vt*
perseguir

hour [ˈaʊəʳ, *Am:* ˈaʊr] *n* **1.** (*60 minutes*) hora
f; **to be paid by the** ~ cobrar por horas
2. (*time of day*) **at all** ~**s of the day and night**
noche y día; **ten minutes to the** ~ diez minutos para en punto; **till all** ~**s** hasta muy tarde;
out of ~**s, after** ~ *Am, Aus* fuera del horario
establecido **3.** (*time for an activity*) **lunch** ~
hora de comer; **at the agreed** ~ a la hora con-
venida; **opening** ~**s** horario *m* (comercial)
4. (*period of time*) momento *m; at any* ~ en
cualquier momento; **to spend long** ~**s doing
sth** pasarse mucho tiempo haciendo algo; **to
change from** ~ **to** ~ cambiar cada hora; **to
keep irregular/regular** ~**s** llevar un horario
variable/regular; **to work long** ~**s** trabajar
hasta muy tarde; ~ **after** ~ hora tras hora
hour hand *n* manecilla *f*
hourly *adv* (*every hour*) cada hora; (*pay*) por
horas
house [haʊs] **I.** *n* **1.** (*inhabitation*) casa *f;* **to
move** ~ mudarse; **to set one's** ~ **in order** *fig*
poner sus cosas en orden **2.** (*family*) familia *f;*
the House of Windsor la casa de Windsor
3. (*business*) empresa *f;* **it's on the** ~ invita la
casa **4.** *Brit, Aus* (*school group*) *grupo formado por niños en un colegio internado para
juegos y competiciones deportivas* **5.** (*legislative body*) cámara *f* **6.** (*audience*) público *m;*
'~ **full**' 'no quedan localidades'; **full** ~ (teatro
m) lleno *m; to bring the* ~ **down** *inf* ser todo
un éxito ▸ **to be as** save **as** ~**s** *Brit* ser comple-
tamente seguro **II.** *vt* **1.** (*give place to live*) alo-
jar **2.** (*contain*) albergar
house arrest *n no pl* arresto *m* domiciliario
houseboat *n* casa *f* flotante
housebreaker [ˈhaʊsˌbreɪkəʳ, *Am:* -kəʳ] *n*
ladrón, -ona *m, f* (que desvalija viviendas)
housebreaking *n no pl* allanamiento *m* de
morada con robo
housecoat [ˈhaʊskəʊt, *Am:* -koʊt] *n* bata *f*
housefly <-ies> *n* mosca *f* común
household [ˈhaʊshəʊld, *Am:* -hoʊld] **I.** *n*
hogar *m* **II.** *adj* doméstico, -a **householder**
n (*owner*) propietario, -a *m, f* de una casa;
(*head*) cabeza *m* de familia
house-hunt [ˈhaʊshʌnt] *vi inf* buscar casa
house husband *n* amo *m* de casa
housekeeper [ˈhaʊsˌkiːpəʳ, *Am:* -pəʳ] *n* ama
f de llaves **housekeeping** *n no pl* organización *f* doméstica **housekeeping money** *n
no pl* dinero *m* para los gastos de la casa
housemaid [ˈhaʊsmeɪd] *n* criada *f* **houseman** *n Brit* mayordomo *m* **house martin** *n*
avión *m* común **house physician** *n*
médico, -a *m, f* residente **houseplant** *n*
planta *f* de interior **houseproud** *adj Brit,
Aus* maniático, -a de la limpieza **houseroom**
n sitio *f* en una casa; **I wouldn't give it** ~ no
lo permitiría en casa **house rules** *npl* normas *fpl* de la casa **house surgeon** *n Brit*
cirujano, -a *m, f* residente **house-to-house**
adj puerta a puerta **housetrained** *adj Brit,
Aus* adiestrado, -a **house-warming** *n,*

house-warming party *n no pl* fiesta *f* de inauguración (de una nueva vivienda) **house-wife** <-wives> *n* ama *f* de casa, huarmi *f* *AmS* **housework** *n no pl* tareas *fpl* del hogar

housing ['haʊzɪŋ] *n* vivienda *f*

housing association *n* cooperativa *f* inmobiliaria **housing benefit** *n Brit* subsidio *m* para la vivienda **housing conditions** *npl* condiciones *fpl* de habitabilidad **housing development** *n Am* urbanización *f* **housing estate** *n Brit* urbanización *f*

hove [həʊv, *Am:* hoʊv] *vi pp of* **heave**

hovel ['hɒvl, *Am:* 'hʌv-] *n* tugurio *m*, sucucho *m AmL*

hover ['hɒvə', *Am:* 'hʌvɚ] *vi* 1. (*stay in air*) cernerse 2. (*be in an uncertain state*) estar vacilante 3. (*wait near*) rondar 4. (*hesitate*) dudar; **to ~ on the brink of accepting sth** estar casi a punto de aceptar algo

hovercraft ['hɒvəkrɑ:ft, *Am:* 'hʌvɚkræft] <-(s)> *n* aerodeslizador *m* **hoverport** *n* terminal *f* de aerodeslizadores

how [haʊ] I. *adv* 1. (*in this way*) como; (*in which way?*) cómo; ~ **do you mean?** ¿cómo dices?; ~ **do you mean you crashed the motorbike?** ¿cómo que te cargaste la moto? 2. (*in what condition?*) ~ **are you?** ¿qué tal?; ~ **do you do?** encantado de conocerle 3. (*for what reason?*) ~ **come ...?** *inf* ¿cómo es que...? 4. (*suggestion*) ~ **about ...?** ¿qué tal si... ?; ~ **about that!** ¡mira por dónde!; ~'s **that for an offer?** ¿trato hecho? 5. (*intensifier*) ~ **pretty she looked!** ¡qué guapa estaba!; **and ~!** ¡ni que lo digas! II. *n* modo *m*; **to know the ~(s) and why(s) of sth** saber el cómo y el porqué de algo

how-do-you-do [ˌhaʊdjʊ'du:, *Am:* 'haʊdəju:du:] *n inf* apuro *m*

however [haʊ'evə', *Am:* -ɚ] I. *adv* 1. (*no matter how*) por más que +*subj*; ~ **hard she tries ...** por mucho que lo intente... 2. (*in whichever way*) como; **do it ~ you like** hazlo como quieras II. *conj* (*nevertheless*) sin embargo

howl [haʊl] I. *vi* 1. (*person, animal*) aullar; (*wind*) silbar; **to ~ in** [*o* **with**] **pain** dar alaridos de dolor 2. (*cry*) chillar; (*child*) berrear 3. *inf* (*laugh*) morirse de risa II. *n* 1. (*person, animal*) aullido *m* 2. (*cry*) chillido *m*; (*of child*) berrido *m*; **to give a ~ of pain** soltar un alarido de dolor; ~s **of protest** gritos *mpl* de protesta

◆**howl down** *vt* hacer callar a gritos

howler ['haʊlə', *Am:* -lɚ] *n* error *m* garrafal; **to make a ~** meter la pata hasta el fondo

howling *adj* aullador(a)

hp [ˌeɪtʃ'pi:] *abbr of* **horsepower** CV

HP [ˌeɪtʃ'pi:] *n Brit, inf abbr of* **hire purchase** compra *f* a plazos

HQ [ˌeɪtʃ'kju:] *abbr of* **headquarters** sede *f* central

HRH [ˌeɪtʃɑ:'eɪtʃ, *Am:* -ɑ:r'-] *abbr of* **Her/His Royal Highness** S.A.R.

ht *abbr of* **height** a

HTML [ˌeɪtʃti:em'el] *n* INFOR *abbr of* **Hypertext Markup Language** HTML

http *n* INFOR *abbr of* **hypertext transfer protocol** http

hub [hʌb] *n* 1. (*of wheel*) cubo *m* 2. *fig* (*centre*) centro *m*

hubbub ['hʌbʌb] *n no pl* barullo *m*

hubcap ['hʌbkæp] *n* tapacubos *m inv*

huckleberry ['hʌklbəri, *Am:* -'ber-] <-ies> *n Am* BOT arándano *m*

huckster ['hʌkstə', *Am:* -stɚ] *n* 1. (*salesman*) charlatán, -ana *m, f* 2. *Am* (*writer*) publicista *mf* de pacotilla

huddle ['hʌdl] I. *vi* apiñarse II. *n* (*close group*) piña *f*; **to go into a ~** hacer grupo aparte

◆**huddle down** *vi* acurrucarse

◆**huddle together** *vi* amontonarse

◆**huddle up** *vi* acurrucarse

hue [hju:] *n no pl* 1. (*shade*) tonalidad *f*; **all ~s of ...** *fig* todo tipo de... 2. (*disapproval*) ~ **and cry** protesta *f*

huff [hʌf] I. *vi* **to ~ and puff** (*breathe loudly*) jadear; *inf* (*complain*) quejarse II. *vt* vociferar III. *n inf* enfado *m*; **to be in a ~** estar de morros; **to get into a ~** enfadarse; **to go off in a ~** irse ofendido

huffy ['hʌfi] <-ier, -iest> *adj* 1. (*offended*) ofendido, -a 2. (*touchy*) susceptible

hug [hʌg] I. <-gg-> *vt* 1. (*embrace*) abrazar 2. *fig* (*idea*) aferrarse a 3. (*not slide on*) **these tyres ~ the road** estos neumáticos se agarran a la carretera II. *n* abrazo *m*

huge [hju:dʒ] *adj* (*extremely big*) enorme; (*impressive*) imponente

hugely *adv* enormemente

hugeness *n no pl* enormidad *f*

hulk [hʌlk] *n* 1. (*old, large body*) carraca *f*; (*of ship*) casco *m* 2. (*mass*) mole *f*

hulking *adj* grandote, -a; ~ **great** *Brit* descomunal

hull[1] [hʌl] *n* NAUT casco *m*

hull[2] [hʌl] I. *n* (*shell*) cáscara *f*; (*of peas*) vaina *f*; (*of strawberry*) cabito *m* II. *vt* pelar

hullabaloo [ˌhʌləbə'lu:] *n* barullo *m*; **to make a ~** armar un follón

hullo [hə'ləʊ, *Am:* -'loʊ] *interj Brit s.* **hello**

hum [hʌm] <-mm-> I. *vi* 1. (*bee*) zumbar 2. (*sing*) tararear 3. (*be full of activity*) estar animado ►**to ~ and haw** *Brit, Aus* vacilar II. *vt* tararear III. *n* zumbido *m*; (*of traffic*) murmullo *m*

human ['hju:mən] *adj* humano, -a

humane [hju:'meɪn] *adj* humanitario, -a

humanism ['hju:mənɪzəm] *n no pl* humanismo *m*

humanistic [ˌhju:mə'nɪstɪk] *adj* humanista

humanitarian [hju:ˌmænɪ'teəriən, *Am:* hju:ˌmænə'teri-] I. *n* humanitario, -a *m, f* II. *adj* humanitario, -a; ~ **aid** ayuda humanitaria

humanities [hju:'mænətiz, *Am:* -ṭiz] *npl*

humanidades *fpl*
humanity [hjuːˈmænəti, *Am:* -ṭi] *n no pl* humanidad *f*
humanize [ˈhjuːmənaɪz] *vt* humanizar
humanly *adv* humanamente
human nature *n no pl* naturaleza *f* humana
  human race *n no pl* raza *f* humana **human resources** *npl* recursos *mpl* humanos
  human rights *npl* derechos *mpl* humanos
humble [ˈhʌmbl] I. *adj* humilde; **of ~ birth** de origen humilde; **in my ~ opinion, ...** en mi modesta opinión,... II. *vt* humillar; (*beat*) derrotar
humbleness *n* modestia *f*; (*humility*) humildad *f*
humbug [ˈhʌmbʌɡ] *n* 1. *no pl* HIST (*nonsense*) patrañas *fpl*; (*fraud*) engaño *m*; **~!** ¡paparruchas! 2. (*peppermint*) caramelo *m* de menta
humdrum [ˈhʌmdrʌm] *adj* (*dull*) aburrido, -a; (*lacking excitement*) rutinario, -a
humid [ˈhjuːmɪd] *adj* húmedo, -a
humidifier [hjuːmɪdɪfaɪəʳ] *n* humidificador *m*
humidify [hjuːˈmɪdɪfaɪ] *vt* humidificar
humidity [hjuːˈmɪdəti, *Am:* -ṭi] *n no pl* humedad *f*
humiliate [hjuːˈmɪlieɪt] *vt* 1. (*shame*) avergonzar, achunchar *AmC*; (*humble*) humillar 2. (*defeat*) derrotar
humiliating *adj* humillante
humiliation [hjuːˌmɪlɪˈeɪʃən] *n* humillación *f*
humility [hjuːˈmɪləti, *Am:* -ṭi] *n no pl* humildad *f*
hummingbird [ˈhʌmɪŋbɜːd, *Am:* -bɜːrd] *n* colibrí *m*, chupaflor *m AmC*
hummock [ˈhʌmək] *n liter* montículo *m*
humor [ˈhjuːməʳ, *Am:* -məʳ] *n Am, Aus s.* **humour**
humorist [ˈhjuːmərɪst] *n* 1. (*writer*) humorista *mf* 2. (*funny person*) cómico, -a *m, f*
humorous [ˈhjuːmərəs] *adj* (*speech*) humorístico, -a; (*situation*) divertido, -a; **~ story** historia graciosa
humour [ˈhjuːməʳ, *Am:* -məʳ] *n no pl* 1. (*capacity for amusement*) humor *m*; **sense of ~** sentido *m* del humor 2. *form* (*mood*) talante *m*; **in (a) good/bad ~** de buen/mal humor
humourless [ˈhjuːməʳlɪs, *Am:* -məʳ] *adj* sin sentido del humor; **a ~ smile** una sonrisa forzada
hump [hʌmp] I. *n* joroba *f*, petaca *f AmC* ▶to be <u>over</u> the ~ haber pasado lo más difícil; **to** <u>get</u> **the ~** cabrearse II. *vt* 1. *inf* (*lug, carry*) acarrear 2. *vulg* (*have sex*) follar, coger *AmL*
humpback [ˈhʌmpbæk] *n* joroba *f*
humpbacked [ˈhʌmpbækt] *adj* jorobado, -a; **~ bridge** ARCHIT puente peraltado
humph [hʌmpf, mm] *interj* ¡ja!
Hun [hʌn] *n* 1. HIST huno, -a *m, f* 2. *pej* (*German*) alemán, -ana *m, f*

hunch [hʌntʃ] I. <-es> *n* presentimiento *m*; **to have a ~ that ...** tener la corazonada de que...; **to act on a ~** actuar por intuición II. *vi* encorvarse III. *vt* curvar
hunchback [ˈhʌntʃbæk] *n* (*person*) jorobado, -a *m, f*
hundred [ˈhʌndrəd] <-(s)> I. *n* cien *m*; **~s of times** cientos de veces II. *adj* ciento; (*before a noun*) cien
hundredfold [ˈhʌndrədfəʊld, *Am:* -foʊld] *n* cien veces *fpl*
hundredth [ˈhʌndrədθ] I. *n* centésimo *m* II. *adj* centésimo, -a
hundredweight [ˈhʌndrədweɪt] <-(s)> *n* unidad de peso equivalente a 50,80 kg en Gran Bretaña y 45,36 en los EE.UU.
hung [hʌŋ] I. *pt, pp of* **hang** II. *adj* colgado, -a; **~ jury** LAW jurado que se disuelve porque no se llega a ningún acuerdo; **~ parliament** POL parlamento *m* sin mayoría absoluta
Hungarian [hʌŋˈɡeərɪən, *Am:* -ˈɡerɪ-] I. *adj* húngaro, -a II. *n* 1. (*person*) húngaro, -a *m, f* 2. LING húngaro *m*
Hungary [ˈhʌŋɡəri] *n* Hungría *f*
hunger [ˈhʌŋɡəʳ, *Am:* -ɡəʳ] I. *n no pl* 1. hambre *f*, filo *m AmC* 2. *fig* (*desire*) ansia *f*; **to have a ~ for sth** estar sediento de algo II. *vi* *fig* **to ~ after** [*o* **for**] ansiar
hungry [ˈhʌŋɡri] <-ier, -iest> *adj* 1. (*desiring food*) hambriento, -a; **to go ~** pasar hambre 2. *fig* (*wanting badly*) ansioso, -a; **to be ~ for sth** estar ávido de algo
hunk [hʌŋk] *n* 1. (*piece*) trozo *m* 2. *inf* (*man*) cachas *m inv*
hunky dory [ˌhʌŋkiˈdɔːri] *adj inf* guay
hunt [hʌnt] I. *vt* 1. (*chase to kill*) cazar 2. (*search for*) buscar II. *vi* 1. (*chase to kill*) cazar; **to go ~ing** ir de caza 2. (*search*) **to ~ for** buscar; **to ~ high and low for sth** buscar algo por todas partes III. *n* 1. (*chase*) cacería *f*; **to go on a ~** ir de caza 2. (*search*) búsqueda *f*
hunter *n* 1. (*person*) cazador(a) *m(f)* 2. (*dog*) perro *m* de caza 3. (*horse*) caballo *m* de caza
hunting *n no pl* caza *f*
hunting ground *n* coto *m* de caza **hunting licence** *n Brit, Aus,* **hunting license** *n Am* licencia *f* de caza **hunting-season** *n* temporada *f* de caza
huntress [ˈhʌntrɪs] *n* cazadora *f*
huntsman [ˈhʌntsmən] <-men> *n* cazador *m*
hurdle [ˈhɜːdl, *Am:* ˈhɜːr-] I. *n* 1. *a.* SPORTS (*fence*) valla *f* 2. (*obstacle*) obstáculo *m* II. *vi* SPORTS saltar vallas III. *vt* SPORTS saltar
hurdler *n* SPORTS vallista *mf*
hurdle-race *n* SPORTS carrera *f* de vallas
hurdy gurdy [ˈhɜːdiˌɡɜːdi, *Am:* ˌhɜːrdiˈɡɜːrdi] <-ies> *n* organillo *m*
hurl [hɜːl, *Am:* hɜːrl] *vt* 1. (*throw*) lanzar 2. *fig* (*utter: insults*) soltar
hurly-burly [ˈhɜːliˌbɜːli, *Am:* ˈhɜːrlɪbɜːr-] *n no pl* alboroto *m*
hurrah [həˈrɑː] *interj*, **hurray** [həˈreɪ] *interj*

hurra

hurricane ['hʌrɪkən, *Am:* 'hɜːrɪkeɪn] *n* huracán *m*

hurricane lamp *n* farol *m*

hurried ['hʌrɪd, *Am:* 'hɜːr-] *adj* apresurado, -a, apurado, -a *AmL*

hurry ['hʌri, *Am:* 'hɜːr-] <-ie-> I. *vi* darse prisa, apurarse *AmL* II. *vt* 1. (*rush*) meter prisas, apurar *AmL* 2. (*take quickly*) he was hurried to the hospital lo llevaron en seguida al hospital III. *n* prisa *f*, apuro *m AmL*; to leave in a ~ irse disparado; to do sth in a ~ hacer algo de prisa; what's (all) the ~? ¿a qué viene tanta prisa?

◆**hurry along** I. *vi* apresurarse II. *vt always sep* meter prisas

◆**hurry away, hurry off** I. *vi* marcharse de prisa II. *vt* (*person*) hacer marchar de prisa; (*object*) hacer llevar de prisa

◆**hurry on** *vi* continuar rápidamente

◆**hurry up** I. *vi* darse prisa II. *vt* meter prisa

hurt [hɜːt, *Am:* hɜːrt] I. <hurt, hurt> *vi* doler II. *vt* 1. (*wound*) herir 2. (*cause pain*) lastimar; it ~s me me duele 3. (*offend*) ofender 4. (*damage*) dañar III. *adj* (*in pain, injured*) dañado, -a; (*grieved, distressed*) dolido, -a IV. *n no pl* 1. (*pain*) dolor *m* 2. (*injury*) herida *f* 3. (*offence*) ofensa *f* 4. (*damage*) daño *m*

hurtful ['hɜːtfəl, *Am:* 'hɜːrt-] *adj* perjudicial

hurtle ['hɜːtl, *Am:* 'hɜːrt-] I. *vi* lanzarse; to ~ along ir como un rayo II. *vt* lanzar

husband ['hʌzbənd] I. *n* marido *m* II. *vt* economizar

husbandry ['hʌzbəndri] *n no pl* 1. (*care, management*) cuidado *m* 2. AGR agricultura *f*; animal ~ cría *f* de animales

hush [hʌʃ] I. *n no pl* silencio *m* II. *interj* ~! ¡chitón! III. *vi* callarse IV. *vt* (*make silent*) hacer callar; (*soothe*) acallar

◆**hush up** *vt* encubrir

hush-hush [ˌhʌʃ'hʌʃ] *adj inf* secreto, -a

hush money *n inf* unto *m* (*que se utiliza para comprar el silencio de alguien*)

husk [hʌsk] I. *n* (*outside covering*) cáscara *f*; *Am* (*of maize*) farfolla *f* II. *vt* descascarillar, destusar *AmC*, despancar *AmS*

husky¹ ['hʌski] <-ier, -iest> *adj* 1. (*low, rough: voice*) ronco, -a 2. *Am* (*big, strong*) fornido, -a

husky² ['hʌski] <-ies> *n* perro *m* esquimal

hussy ['hʌsi] *n* pendón *m*

hustings ['hʌstɪŋz] *npl* campaña *f* electoral

hustle ['hʌsl] I. *vt* 1. (*hurry*) dar prisa a; (*push*) empujar 2. (*achieve*) hacerse con II. *vi* 1. (*push for*) moverse *inf* 2. (*practice prostitution*) prostituirse III. *n* ajetreo *m*

hustler ['hʌslər, *Am:* -ə-] *n* 1. (*persuader*) camelador(a) *m(f)* 2. *Am* (*swindler*) estafador(a) *m(f)* 3. (*prostitute*) puto, -a *m, f*

hustling ['hʌslɪŋ] *n no pl* ajetreo *m*

hut [hʌt] *n* cabaña *f*

hutch [hʌtʃ] <-es> *n* (*box for animals*) jaula *f*; (*for rabbits*) conejera *f*

hyacinth ['haɪəsɪnθ] *n* BOT jacinto *m*

hyaena [haɪ'iːnə] *n* hiena *f*

hybrid ['haɪbrɪd] *n* híbrido, -a *m, f*

hydrangea [haɪ'dreɪndʒə] *n* BOT hortensia *f*

hydrant ['haɪdrənt] *n* boca *f* de riego

hydrate ['haɪdreɪt] *n* hidrato *m*

hydraulic [haɪ'drɒlɪk, *Am:* -'drɑːlɪk] *adj* hidráulico, -a

hydraulics [haɪ'drɒlɪks, *Am:* -'drɑːlɪks] *n* hidráulica *f*

hydrocarbon [ˌhaɪdrə'kɑːbən, *Am:* -drou-'kɑːr-] I. *n* hidrocarburo *m* II. *adj* de hidrocarburo

hydrochloric acid [ˌhaɪdrəuklɒrɪk'æsɪd, *Am:* -droukl ɔːrɪk'æsɪd] *n no pl* ácido *m* clorhídrico

hydroelectric [ˌhaɪdrəuɪ'lektrɪk, *Am:* -drou-] *adj* hidroeléctrico, -a

hydrofoil ['haɪdrəfɔɪl, *Am:* -drou-] *n* hidroala *m*

hydrogen ['haɪdrədʒən] *n no pl* hidrógeno *m*

hydrogen bomb *n* bomba *f* de hidrógeno

hydrophobia [ˌhaɪdrə'fəubɪə, *Am:* -drou-'fou-] *n no pl* hidrofobia *f*

hydroponics [ˌhaɪdrə'pɒnɪks, *Am:* -drou-'pɑːnɪks] *n + sing vb* hidroponía *f*

hyena [haɪ'iːnə] *n* hiena *f*

hygiene ['haɪdʒiːn] *n no pl* higiene *f*, salubridad *f AmL*

hygienic [haɪ'dʒiːnɪk, *Am:* ˌhaɪdʒi'enɪk] *adj* higiénico, -a

hygroscope ['haɪgrəskəup, *Am:* -grouskoup] *n* higroscopio *m*

hymn [hɪm] *n* himno *m*

hymnal ['hɪmnəl] *n*, **hymnbook** *n* himnario *m*

hype [haɪp] I. *n no pl* COM bombo publicitario II. *vt* dar bombo publicitario a

hyperactive [ˌhaɪpə'æktɪv, *Am:* -pə-'-] *adj* hiperactivo, -a

hyperbola [haɪ'pɜːbələ, *Am:* -'pɜːr-] *n* MAT hipérbola *f*

hyperbole [haɪ'pɜːbəli, *Am:* -'pɜːr-] *n no pl* LIT hipérbole *f*

hyperbolic [haɪpə'bɒlɪk, *Am:* -pə'bɑːlɪk] *adj* LIT hiperbólico, -a

hyperlink [ˌhaɪpə'lɪŋk] *n* INFOR hiperenlace *m*

hypermarket ['haɪpəmɑːkɪt, *Am:* -pə-mɑːr-] *n* hipermercado *m*

hypersensitive [ˌhaɪpə'sensətɪv, *Am:* -pə-'sensəṭɪv] *adj* hipersensible

hypertext ['haɪpətekst, *Am:* -pə-] *n no pl* INFOR hipertexto *m*

hyphen ['haɪfn] *n* guión *m*

hyphenate ['haɪfəneɪt] *vt* separar con guiones

hypnosis [hɪp'nəusɪs, *Am:* -'nou-] *n no pl* hipnosis *f inv*; to be under ~ estar hipnotizado

hypnotherapy [ˌhɪpnə'θerəpi, *Am:* -nou'-] *n no pl* hipnoterapia *f*

hypnotic [hɪp'nɒtɪk, *Am:* -'nɑːṭɪk] *adj* hip-

nótico, -a
hypnotist ['hɪpnətɪst] *n* hipnotizador(a) *m(f)*
hypnotize ['hɪpnətaɪz] *vt* hipnotizar
hypochondria [ˌhaɪpə'kɒndrɪə, *Am:* -pou-'kɑːn-] *n no pl* hipocondría *f*
hypochondriac [ˌhaɪpə'kɒn drɪæk, *Am:* -pou'kɑːn-] I. *n* hipocondríaco, -a *m, f* II. *adj* hipocondríaco, -a
hypocrisy [hɪ'pɒkrəsi, *Am:* -'pɑːkrə-] *n no pl* hipocresía *f*
hypocrite ['hɪpəkrɪt] *n* hipócrita *mf*
hypocritical [ˌhɪpə'krɪtɪkl, *Am:* -'krɪt̬-] *adj* hipócrita
hypodermic [ˌhaɪpə'dɜːmɪk, *Am:* -pou-'dɜːr-] *adj* hipodérmico, -a
hypotenuse [ˌhaɪ'pɒtənjuːz, *Am:* -'pɑː-tənuːs] *n* hipotenusa *f*
hypothermia [ˌhaɪpə'θɜːmɪə, *Am:* -pou-'θɜːr-] *n no pl* hipotermia *f*
hypothesis [haɪ'pɒθəsɪs, *Am:* -'pɑːθə-] *n* <-es> hipótesis *f inv*
hypothetical [ˌhaɪpə'θetɪkl, *Am:* -pou-'θet̬-] *adj* hipotético, -a
hysterectomy [ˌhɪstə'rektəmi] *n* MED histerectomía *f*
hysteria [hɪ'stɪərɪə, *Am:* -'sterɪ-] *n no pl* histeria *f*
hysteric [hɪ'sterɪk] I. *adj* histérico, -a II. *n* histérico, -a *m, f*
hysterical *adj* histérico, -a

I

I, i [aɪ] *n* I, i *f; ~* for Isaac *Brit, ~* for Item *Am* I de Italia
I [aɪ] *pron pers* (*1st person sing*) yo; *~*'m coming ya voy; *~*'ll do it (yo) lo haré; **am** *~* late? ¿llego tarde?; **she and** *~* ella y yo; **it was** *~* who did that fui yo quien lo hizo
IAEA *n abbr of* International Atomic Energy Agency OIEA *f*
IATA [aɪ'ɑːtə, *Am:* ˌaɪˌeɪˌtiː'eɪ] *n abbr of* International Air Transport Association IATA *f*
ibex ['aɪbeks] <-es> *n* íbice *m*, cabra *f* montesa
ibid. ['ɪbɪd] *adv abbr of* ibidem ibid.
IC [ˌaɪ'siː] *n abbr of* integrated circuit CI *m*
i/c *abbr of* in charge (of) a cargo de
ICBM [ˌaɪsiːbiː'em] *n abbr of* intercontinental ballistic missile ICBM *m*
ice [aɪs] I. *n* 1. *no pl* (*frozen water*) hielo *m* 2. *Brit* (*ice cream*) helado *m*, nieve *f AmC* ▶ to be skating on thin *~* andar sobre terreno peligroso; to break the *~ inf* romper el hielo; to cut no *~* (with sb) no tener importancia (para alguien); to put sth on *~* posponer algo II. *vt* 1. (*put in fridge*) enfriar 2. (*put icing on*) es-

carchar
♦**ice over** *vi* helarse
Ice Age *n* época *f* glacial **ice-axe** *n* piolet *m*
iceberg *n* iceberg *m;* the tip of the *~ fig* la punta del iceberg **icebound** *adj* bloqueado, -a por el hielo **ice-box** <-es> *n* 1. *Brit* (*freezer*) congelador *m* 2. *Am* (*fridge*) nevera *f*, refrigeradora *f AmL* **ice-breaker** *n* rompehielos *m inv* **ice cap** *n* casquete *m* de hielo **ice-cold** *adj* helado, -a
ice cream *n* helado *m*, nieve *f AmC*
ice-cream maker *n* heladero, -a *m, f* **ice--cream parlour** *n* heladería *f*
ice cube ['aɪskjuːb] *n* cubito *m* de hielo
iced [aɪst] *adj* 1. (*drink*) con hielo 2. (*covered with icing*) escarchado, -a
ice floe ['aɪsfləʊ, *Am:* -floʊ] *n* témpano *m* de hielo **ice hockey** *n no pl* hockey *m* sobre hielo
Iceland ['aɪslənd] *n* Islandia *f*
Icelander ['aɪsləndəʳ, *Am:* -dɚ] *n* islandés, -esa *m, f*
Icelandic [aɪs'lændɪk] I. *adj* islandés, -esa II. *n* islandés *m*
ice lolly [ˌaɪs'lɒli, *Am:* -'lɑːli] <-ies> *n Brit* polo *m*, paleta *f AmL* **ice pack** *n* bolsa *f* de hielo **ice rink** *n* pista *f* de patinaje **ice--skate** *vi* patinar sobre hielo **ice-skating** *n no pl* patinaje *m* sobre hielo
icicle ['aɪsɪkl] *n* carámbano *m*
icing ['aɪsɪŋ] *n* glaseado *m* ▶ to be the *~* on the cake ser la guinda del pastel
icing sugar *n no pl* azúcar *m* glas
icon ['aɪkɒn, *Am:* -kɑːn] *n* icono *m*
iconoclast [aɪ'kɒnəklæst, *Am:* -'kɑːnə-] *n* iconoclasta *mf*
iconoclastic [aɪˌkɒnə'klæstɪk, *Am:* -'kɑː-nə-] *adj* iconoclasta
ICU [ˌaɪsiː'juː] *n abbr of* intensive care unit UCI *f*
icy ['aɪsi] <-ier, -iest> *adj* 1. (*with ice*) helado, -a; (*very cold*) glacial 2. (*unfriendly*) frío, -a
ID [ˌaɪ'diː] *abbr of* identification identificación *f*
I'd [aɪd] 1. = I would *s.* would 2. = I had *s.* have
ID card [aɪ'diːˌkɑːd] *n s.* identity card carné *m* de identidad
IDDD *Am abbr of* international direct distance dial(ling) marcación *f* directa internacional
idea [aɪ'dɪə, *Am:* -'diːə] *n* 1. (*opinion*) idea *f* 2. (*conception*) concepto *m* 3. (*notion*) noción *f;* to get an *~* of sth hacerse una idea de algo
ideal [aɪ'dɪəl, *Am:* -'diː-] I. *adj* ideal II. *n* ideal *m*
idealise *vt Brit, Aus s.* idealize
idealism [aɪ'dɪəlɪzəm, *Am:* aɪ'diːə-] *n no pl* idealismo *m*
idealist [aɪ'dɪəlɪst, *Am:* -'diːə-] *n* idealista *mf*
idealistic [ˌaɪdɪə'lɪstɪk] *adj* idealista

idealize [aɪˈdɪəlaɪz, *Am:* -ˈdiːə-] *vt* idealizar
ideally [aɪˈdɪəli, *Am:* ˈdiːli] *adv* **1.** (*in an ideal way*) inmejorablemente **2.** ~, **we could catch the train** lo mejor sería coger el tren
identical [aɪˈdentɪkl, *Am:* -t̬ə-] *adj* idéntico, -a, individual *CSur*
identifiable [aɪˈdentɪˌfaɪəbl, *Am:* -ˌdent̬ə'-] *adj* identificable
identification [aɪˌdentɪfɪˈkeɪʃən, *Am:* -t̬ə-] *n no pl* identificación *f*
identification papers *npl* documentación *f*
identifier [aɪˈdentɪfaɪəʳ, *Am:* -t̬əfaɪɚ] *n* INFOR identificador *m*
identify [aɪˈdentɪfaɪ, *Am:* -t̬ə-] <-ie-> *vt* identificar
identikit® [aɪˈdentɪkɪt] *adj Brit, Aus* ~ **picture** retrato *m* robot
identity [aɪˈdentəti, *Am:* -t̬ət̬i] <-ies> *n* identidad *f*
identity card *n* carné *m* de identidad
ideological [ˌaɪdɪəˈlɒdʒɪkl, *Am:* -ˈlɑːdʒɪ-] *adj* ideológico, -a
ideologist [ˌaɪdɪˈɒlədʒɪst, *Am:* -ˈɑːlə-] *n* ideólogo, -a *m, f*
ideology [ˌaɪdɪˈɒlədʒi, *Am:* -ˈɑːlə-] <-ies> *n* ideología *f*
idiocy [ˈɪdɪəsi] <-ies> *n* idiotez *f*, imbecilidad *f*
idiom [ˈɪdɪəm] *n* LING **1.** (*phrase*) modismo *m* **2.** (*style of expression*) lenguaje *m*
idiomatic [ˌɪdɪəˈmætɪk, *Am:* -ˈmæt̬-] *adj* idiomático, -a
idiosyncrasy [ˌɪdɪəʊˈsɪŋkrəsi, *Am:* -oʊ-ˈsɪn-] <-ies> *n* idiosincrasia *f*
idiosyncratic [ˌɪdɪəʊsɪnˈkrætɪk, *Am:* -oʊ-sɪnˈkræt̬-] *adj* idiosincrático, -a
idiot [ˈɪdɪət] *n* idiota *mf*
idiotic [ˌɪdɪˈɒtɪk, *Am:* -ˈɑːt̬ɪk] *adj* tonto, -a
idle [ˈaɪdl] **I.** *adj* **1.** (*lazy*) holgazán, -ana **2.** (*with nothing to do*) desocupado, -a; (*machine*) parado, -a **3.** (*unfounded*) vano, -a; (*chatter*) insustancial; (*fear*) infundado, -a **4.** FIN de paro; (*capital*) improductivo, -a **II.** *vi* (*person*) haraganear; (*machine*) marchar al ralentí
idleness [ˈaɪdlnɪs] *n no pl* holgazanería *f*
idler [ˈaɪdləʳ, *Am:* -lɚ] *n* vago, -a *m, f*
idol [ˈaɪdl] *n* ídolo *m*
idolatrous [aɪˈdɒlətrəs, *Am:* -ˈdɑːlə-] *adj* REL idólatra
idolatry [aɪˈdɒlətri, *Am:* -ˈdɑːlə-] *n* idolatría *f*
idolise *vt Brit, Aus*, **idolize** [ˈaɪdəlaɪz] *vt Am* idolatrar
IDP **1.** *abbr of* integrated data processing IDP *m* **2.** *abbr of* International Driving Permit permiso *m* internacional de conducción
idyll [ˈɪdɪl, *Am:* ˈaɪdəl] *n* idilio *m*
idyllic [ɪˈdɪlɪk, *Am:* aɪ-] *adj* idílico, -a
i.e. [ˌaɪˈiː] *abbr of* id est i.e.
if [ɪf] **I.** *conj* **1.** (*supposing that*) si; ~ **it snows** si nieva; ~ **not** si no; **as** ~ **it were true** como si fuera verdad; ~ **they exist at all** si es que en

realidad existen; ~ **A is right, then B is wrong** si A es cierto, entonces B es falso; **I'll stay,** ~ **only for a day** me quedaré, aunque sea sólo un día **2.** (*every time that*) ~ **he needs me, I'll help him** si me necesita, le ayudaré **3.** (*whether*) **I wonder** ~ **he'll come** me pregunto si vendrá **4.** (*although*) aunque; **cold** ~ **sunny weather** clima soleado aunque frío **II.** *n* pero *m*; **no** ~**s and buts!** ¡no hay peros que valgan!
iffy [ˈɪfi] <-ier, -iest> *adj inf* dudoso, -a; (*person*) sospechoso, -a
igloo [ˈɪgluː] *n* iglú *m*
igneous [ˈɪgnɪəs] *adj* ígneo, -a
ignite [ɪgˈnaɪt] **I.** *vi* incendiarse **II.** *vt form* incendiar
ignition [ɪgˈnɪʃən] *n no pl* **1.** AUTO encendido *m;* **to switch the** ~ **on** dar al contacto **2.** *form* (*causing to burn*) ignición *f*
ignition coil *n* bobina *f* de encendido **ignition key** *n* llave *f* de contacto, suiche *m Méx* **ignition switch** <-es> *n* interruptor *m* de encendido
ignoble [ɪgˈnəʊbl, *Am:* -ˈnoʊ-] *adj liter* innoble
ignominious [ˌɪgnəˈmɪnɪəs] *adj liter* ignominioso, -a
ignominy [ˈɪgnəmɪni] *n no pl* ignominia *f*
ignoramus [ˌɪgnəˈreɪməs] *n* ignorante *mf*
ignorance [ˈɪgnərəns] *n no pl* ignorancia *f;* **to be left in** ~ **of sth** quedarse sin saber algo ►~ **is** <u>bliss</u> ojos que no ven corazón que no siente
ignorant [ˈɪgnərənt] *adj* ignorante; **to be** ~ **about sth** desconocer algo
ignore [ɪgˈnɔːʳ, *Am:* -ˈnɔːr] *vt* no hacer caso de, ignorar
iguana [ɪˈgwɑːnə] *n* iguana *f,* basilisco *m Méx*
ilk [ɪlk] *n no pl, liter* calaña *f*
ill [ɪl] **I.** *adj* **1.** (*sick*) enfermo, -a; **to fall** ~ caer enfermo **2.** (*bad*) malo, -a; (*harmful*) nocivo, -a; (*unfavourable*) perjudicial; **an** ~ **omen** un mal presagio **II.** *adv form* (*badly*) mal; **to bode** ~ ser de mal agüero; **to speak** ~ **of sb** hablar mal de alguien
I'll [aɪl] = I will *s.* will
ill-advised [ˌɪləd'vaɪzd] *adj* imprudente **ill at ease** *adj* incómodo, -a **ill-bred** *adj* mal educado, -a **ill-conceived** *adj* desacertado, -a
illegal [ɪˈliːgəl] *adj* ilegal
illegal immigrant *n* inmigrante *mf* ilegal
illegality [ˌɪlɪˈgæləti, *Am:* -t̬i] <-ies> *n* ilegalidad *f*
illegible [ɪˈledʒəbl] *adj* ilegible
illegitimate [ˌɪlɪˈdʒɪtɪmət, *Am:* -ˈdʒɪt̬ə-] *adj* ilegítimo, -a
ill-equipped [ˌɪlɪˈkwɪpt] *adj* mal equipado, -a **ill-fated** *adj* (*having bad luck*) desafortunado, -a; (*bringing bad luck*) gafe; **an** ~ **hour** una hora funesta **ill-favored** *adj Am*, **ill-favoured** *adj Brit* feo, -a, poco agraciado, -a

ill-fitting *adj* ~ **clothes** ropa *f* que no queda bien **ill-gotten** *adj* mal habido, -a

illiberal [ɪˈlɪbərəl] *adj form* **1.** (*repressive*) represivo, -a **2.** *Am* (*unaccepting of new ideas*) intolerante

illicit [ɪˈlɪsɪt] *adj* ilícito, -a

illimitable [ɪˈlɪmɪtəbl, *Am:* -t̬ə-] *adj* ilimitado, -a

ill-informed [ˈɪlɪnˌfɔːmd] *adj* **1.** (*wrongly informed*) mal informado, -a **2.** (*ignorant*) ignorante

illiteracy [ɪˈlɪtərəsi, *Am:* -ˈlɪt̬-] *n no pl* analfabetismo *m*

illiterate [ɪˈlɪtərət, *Am:* -ˈlɪt̬-] **I.** *adj* analfabeto, -a; *pej, fig* inculto, -a **II.** *n* analfabeto, -a *m, f*

ill-mannered [ˌɪlˈmænəd, *Am:* -ɚd] *adj* mal educado, -a **ill-natured** *adj* malicioso, -a

illness [ˈɪlnɪs] <-es> *n* enfermedad *f*

illogical [ɪˈlɒdʒɪkl, *Am:* -ˈlɑːdʒɪ-] *adj* ilógico, -a

illogicality [ɪˌlɒdʒɪˈkælɪti, *Am:* -ˌlɑːdʒɪˈkæləti] *n no pl* incongruencia *f*

ill-omened [ˌɪlˈəʊmend, *Am:* -ˈoʊ-] *adj* aciago, -a **ill-starred** *adj* desdichado, -a **ill-tempered** *adj* de mal genio **ill-timed** *adj* inoportuno, -a

ill-treat [ˌɪlˈtriːt] *vt* maltratar

ill-treatment [ˌɪlˈtriːtmənt] *n no pl* maltrato *m*

illuminate [ɪˈluːmɪneɪt, *Am:* -mə-] *vt* iluminar; *fig* aclarar

illuminating [ɪˈluːmɪneɪtɪŋ, *Am:* -t̬ɪŋ] *adj form* aclaratorio, -a

illumination [ɪˌluːmɪˈneɪʃən] *n* **1.** *no pl a.* ART iluminación *f* **2.** *pl, Brit* luces *fpl*

illus. *abbr of* ilustrated, illustration ilus.

illusion [ɪˈluːʒən, *Am:* -ˈluː-] *n* (*misleading appearance*) apariencia *f*; (*false impression*) ilusión *f*; **to have no ~s** (**about sth**) no tener esperanzas (en algo); **to be under the ~ that ...** estar equivocado creyendo que...

illusionist [ɪˈluːʒənɪst, *Am:* -ˈluː-] *n* ilusionista *mf*

illusive [ɪˈluːsɪv] *adj*, **illusory** [ɪˈluːsəri] *adj* ilusorio, -a

illustrate [ˈɪləstreɪt] *vt* ilustrar; *fig* ejemplificar

illustration [ˌɪləˈstreɪʃən] *n* **1.** (*drawing*) ilustración *f* **2.** (*example*) ejemplo *m;* **by way of** ~ a modo de ejemplo

illustrative [ˈɪləstrətɪv, *Am:* ɪˈlʌstrət̬ɪv] *adj form* ilustrativo, -a

illustrator [ˈɪləstreɪtər, *Am:* -t̬ɚ] *n* ilustrador(a) *m(f)*

illustrious [ɪˈlʌstrɪəs] *adj form* ilustre

ill will *n no pl* animadversión *f*

ILO *n abbr of* International Labour Organisation OIT *f*

ILS *n abbr of* instrument landing system ILS *m*

I'm [aɪm] = I am *s.* **am**

image [ˈɪmɪdʒ] *n* **1.** (*likeness*) imagen *f*; **to**

be the living ~ of sb ser el vivo retrato de alguien **2.** (*picture*) retrato *m* **3.** (*reputation*) reputación *f*

imagery [ˈɪmɪdʒəri] *n no pl* LIT imágenes *fpl*

imaginable [ɪˈmædʒɪnəbl] *adj* imaginable

imaginary [ɪˈmædʒɪnəri, *Am:* -əner-] *adj* imaginario, -a

imagination [ɪˌmædʒɪˈneɪʃən] *n* imaginación *f*; (*inventiveness*) inventiva *f*

imaginative [ɪˈmædʒɪnətɪv, *Am:* -t̬ɪv] *adj* imaginativo, -a

imagine [ɪˈmædʒɪn] *vt* **1.** (*form mental image*) imaginar **2.** (*suppose*) figurarse; ~ **that!** ¡figúratelo!

imaging *n no pl* INFOR tratamiento *m* de imágenes

imbalance [ˌɪmˈbæləns] *n* desequilibrio *m*

imbecile [ˈɪmbəsiːl, *Am:* -sɪl] *n* imbécil *mf*

imbecility [ˌɪmbəˈsɪləti, *Am:* -t̬i] *n no pl, form* imbecilidad *f*

imbibe [ɪmˈbaɪb] *vt* beber; *fig* empaparse de

imbroglio [ɪmˈbrəʊlɪəʊ, *Am:* -ˈbroʊlɪoʊ] *n liter* embrollo *m*

imbue [ɪmˈbjuː] *vt form* **1.** (*fill, inspire*) **to** ~ **sb with sth** imbuir a alguien de algo; **to be ~d with** estar empapado de **2.** (*soak*) empapar

IMF [ˌaɪemˈef] *n no pl abbr of* **International Monetary Fund** FMI *m*

imitate [ˈɪmɪteɪt] *vt* imitar; (*copy*) copiar

imitation [ˌɪmɪˈteɪʃən] **I.** *n* **1.** (*mimicry*) imitación *f*; **in** ~ **of sb/sth** a imitación de alguien/algo **2.** (*copy*) reproducción *f* **II.** *adj* de imitación; (*silk*) sintético, -a; ~ **jewels** bisutería *f*

imitative [ˈɪmɪtətɪv, *Am:* -teɪt̬ɪv] *adj* imitativo, -a

imitator [ˈɪmɪtətər, *Am:* -t̬ɚ] *n* imitador(a) *m(f)*

immaculate [ɪˈmækjʊlət] *adj* **1.** (*spotless, neat*) inmaculado, -a **2.** (*flawless*) impecable

immanence [ˈɪmənəns] *n no pl* PHILOS inmanencia *f*

immanent [ˈɪmənənt] *adj* inmanente

immaterial [ˌɪməˈtɪərɪəl, *Am:* -ˈtɪrɪ-] *adj* **1.** (*intangible*) inmaterial **2.** (*not important*) irrelevante

immature [ˌɪməˈtjʊər, *Am:* -ˈtʊr] *adj* inmaduro, -a; (*people, animals*) joven; (*fruit*) verde

immaturity [ˌɪməˈtjʊərəti, *Am:* -ˈtʊrət̬i] *n no pl* inmadurez *f*

immeasurable [ɪˈmeʒərəbl] *adj* **1.** (*boundless*) inconmensurable **2.** (*vast*) inmenso, -a; (*effect*) incalculable

immediacy [ɪˈmiːdɪəsi] *n no pl* inmediatez *f*; (*nearness*) proximidad *f*

immediate [ɪˈmiːdɪət, *Am:* -dɪt] *adj* inmediato, -a; **the ~ family** la familia directa; **in the ~ area** en las inmediaciones; **in the ~ future** en un futuro inmediato

immediately I. *adv* **1.** (*time*) inmediatamente; ~ **after ...** justo después de... **2.** (*place*) **my flat is the one ~ above yours** mi piso es el que se encuentra justo encima del tuyo **II.** *conj Brit* en cuanto; **call me** ~ **it is ready** llámame en cuanto esté preparado

immemorial [ˌɪməˈmɔːrɪəl, *Am:* -ˈmɔːrɪ-] *adj liter* inmemorial, inmemoriable

immense [ɪˈmens] *adj* inmenso, -a; (*importance*) extremo, -a

immensely *adv* enormemente

immensity [ɪˈmensəti, *Am:* -t̬i] *n* inmensidad *f*

immerse [ɪˈmɜːs, *Am:* -ˈmɜːrs] *vt* sumergir; **to be ~d in sth** *fig* estar absorto en algo; **to ~ oneself in sth** *fig* sumirse en algo

immersion [ɪˈmɜːʃən, *Am:* -ˈmɜːr-] *n no pl* 1. (*putting under water*) inmersión *f* 2. (*absorption*) sumersión *f*

immersion heater *n* calentador *m* de inmersión

immigrant [ˈɪmɪɡrənt] *n* inmigrante *mf*

immigrate [ˈɪmɪɡreɪt] *vi* inmigrar

immigration [ˌɪmɪˈɡreɪʃən] *n no pl* inmigración *f*

immigration country *n* país *m* receptor de inmigrantes

imminence [ˈɪmɪnəns] *n no pl* inminencia *f*

imminent [ˈɪmɪnənt] *adj* inminente *m*

immobile [ɪˈməʊbaɪl, *Am:* -ˈmoʊbl] *adj* 1. (*not moving*) inmóvil 2. (*rigid*) entumecido, -a

immobilise *vt Brit, Aus*, **immobilize** [ɪˈməʊbəlaɪz, *Am:* -ˈmoʊ-] *vt Am* inmovilizar

immobility [ˌɪməˈbɪləti, *Am:* -moʊˈbɪləti] *n no pl* inmovilidad *f*; (*being still*) entumecimiento *m*

immoderate [ɪˈmɒdərət, *Am:* -ˈmɑːdɚ-] *adj* excesivo, -a

immodest [ɪˈmɒdɪst, *Am:* -ˈmɑːdɪst] *adj* 1. (*conceited*) creído, -a 2. (*slightly indecent*) descarado, -a

immolate [ˈɪmələɪt] *vt form* inmolar

immoral [ɪˈmɒrəl, *Am:* -ˈmɔːr-] *adj* inmoral

immortal [ɪˈmɔːtl, *Am:* -ˈmɔːrt̬l] **I.** *adj* 1. (*undying*) inmortal 2. (*remembered forever*) imperecedero, -a **II.** *n* inmortal *mf*

immortalise *vt Brit, Aus*, **immortalize** [ɪˈmɔːtəlaɪz, *Am:* -ˈmɔːrt̬əl-] *vt Am* inmortalizar

immortality [ˌɪmɔːˈtæləti, *Am:* -ɔːrˈtæləti] *n no pl* inmortalidad *f*

immovable [ɪˈmuːvəbl] *adj* 1. (*not moveable*) inamovible 2. (*not changeable*) inalterable; (*belief*) inquebrantable

immune [ɪˈmjuːn] *adj* 1. MED inmune 2. POL, LAW exento, -a

immune system *n* sistema *m* inmunológico

immunise *vt Aus, Brit*, **immunize** [ˈɪmjənaɪz] *vt Am* inmunizar

immunity [ɪˈmjuːnəti, *Am:* -t̬i] *n no pl* 1. MED inmunidad *f* 2. (*lack of susceptibility*) insensibilidad *f* 3. LAW exención *f*; **diplomatic ~** inmunidad *f* diplomática

immunological [ˌɪmjʊnəʊˈlɒdʒɪkl, *Am:* -jənoʊˈlɑːdʒɪ-] *adj* inmunológico, -a

immunologist [ˌɪmjʊˈnɒlədʒɪst, *Am:* -ˈnɑː-]

lə-] *n* inmunólogo, -a *m, f*

immure [ɪˈmjʊər, *Am:* -ˈmjʊr] *vt liter* encerrar entre muros

immutable [ɪˈmjuːtəbl, *Am:* -t̬ə-] *adj* 1. (*unchangeable*) inmutable 2. (*ever-lasting*) imperecedero, -a 3. (*eternal*) eterno, -a

imp [ɪmp] *n* 1. (*small devil*) diablillo, -a *m, f* 2. (*mischievous child*) pillín, -ina *m, f*

impact [ˈɪmpækt] **I.** *n no pl* 1. (*striking contact*) choque *m*; (*force of striking contact*) impacto *m*; **on ~** por impacto 2. (*effect*) efecto *m* **II.** *vt Am, Aus* incidir en **III.** *vi Am, Aus* **to ~ on sb/sth** impactar en alguien/algo

impacted [ɪmˈpæktɪd] *adj* impactado, -a

impair [ɪmˈpeər, *Am:* -ˈper] *vt* 1. (*weaken*) debilitar 2. (*damage*) dañar; (*health*) perjudicar

impaired *adj* (*speech, vision, hearing*) dañado, -a; (*weakened*) debilitado, -a; (*health*) perjudicado, -a

impale [ɪmˈpeɪl] *vt* **to ~ sb/oneself on** atravesar a alguien/atravesarse en

impalpable [ɪmˈpælpəbl] *adj liter* impalpable; (*change*) imperceptible

impart [ɪmˈpɑːt, *Am:* -ˈpɑːrt] *vt form* impartir; (*bestow*) conferir; (*secret*) divulgar

impartial [ɪmˈpɑːʃl, *Am:* -ˈpɑːr-] *adj* imparcial

impartiality [ˌɪmˌpɑːʃɪˈæləti, *Am:* -ˌpɑːr-] *n no pl* imparcialidad *f*

impassable [ɪmˈpɑːsəbl, *Am:* -ˈpæsə-] *adj* intransitable; *fig* infranqueable

impasse [ˈæmpɑːs, *Am:* ˈɪmpæs] *n no pl, a. fig* callejón *m* sin salida

impassioned [ɪmˈpæʃnd] *adj form* apasionado, -a

impassive [ɪmˈpæsɪv] *adj* impasible

impatience [ɪmˈpeɪʃns] *n no pl* impaciencia *f*

impatient [ɪmˈpeɪʃnt] *adj* impaciente; **to be ~ to do sth** impacientarse por hacer algo

impeach [ɪmˈpiːtʃ] *vt* acusar, (someter a un proceso de incapacitación presidencial)

impeachment *n* acusación *f* (*proceso de incapacitación presidencial*)

impeccable [ɪmˈpekəbl] *adj* impecable; (*manners*) intachable

impecunious [ˌɪmpɪˈkjuːnɪəs] *adj form* sin dinero

impede [ɪmˈpiːd] *vt* impedir

impediment [ɪmˈpedɪmənt] *n* 1. (*hindrance*) impedimento *m* 2. MED defecto *m*

impel [ɪmˈpel] <-ll-> *vt* impeler

impend [ɪmˈpend] *vi* avecinarse

impending *adj* inminente

impenetrable [ɪmˈpenɪtrəbl] *adj* 1. impenetrable 2. (*incomprehensible*) incomprensible

impenitent [ɪmˈpenɪtənt, *Am:* -ətənt] *adj form* impenitente

imperative [ɪmˈperətɪv, *Am:* -t̬ɪv] **I.** *adj* 1. (*urgently essential*) imprescindible 2. LING imperativo, -a **II.** *n a.* LING imperativo *m*

imperceptible [ˌɪmpəˈseptəbl, *Am:* -pə-ˈseptə-] *adj* imperceptible

imperfect [ɪmˈpɜːfɪkt, *Am:* -ˈpɜːr-] I. *adj* imperfecto, -a; (*flawed*) defectuoso, -a II. *n no pl* LING (pretérito *m*) imperfecto *m*

imperfection [ˌɪmpəˈfekʃən, *Am:* -pəˈ-] *n* imperfección *f*

imperial [ɪmˈpɪəriəl, *Am:* -ˈpɪr-] *adj* imperial

imperialism [ɪmˈpɪəriəlɪzəm, *Am:* -ˈpɪrɪ-] *n no pl* imperialismo *m*

imperialist [ɪmˈpɪəriəlɪst, *Am:* -ˈpɪri-] I. *n* imperialista *mf* II. *adj* imperialista

imperil [ɪmˈperəl] <*Brit:* -ll-, *Am:* -l-> *vt form* poner en peligro

imperious [ɪmˈpɪəriəs, *Am:* -ˈpɪrɪ-] *adj* 1. (*bossy*) imperioso, -a 2. (*arrogant*) arrogante

imperishable [ɪmˈperɪʃəbl] *adj* imperecedero, -a

impermanent [ɪmˈpɜːmənənt, *Am:* -ˈpɜːr-] *adj* pasajero, -a

impermeable [ɪmˈpɜːmiəbl, *Am:* -ˈpɜːr-] *adj* impermeable

impersonal [ˌɪmˈpɜːsənl, *Am:* -ˈpɜːr-] *adj a.* LING impersonal

impersonate [ɪmˈpɜːsəneɪt, *Am:* -ˈpɜːr-] *vt* hacerse pasar por; (*imitate*) imitar

impersonator *n* imitador(a) *m(f)*

impertinent [ɪmˈpɜːtɪnənt, *Am:* -ˈpɜːrtn̩-] *adj* impertinente

imperturbable [ˌɪmpəˈtɜːbəbl, *Am:* -pəˈtɜːr-] *adj form* imperturbable

impervious [ɪmˈpɜːviəs, *Am:* -ˈpɜːr-] *adj* impermeable; (*not affected*) inmune

impetuous [ɪmˈpetʃuəs, *Am:* -ˈpetʃu-] *adj* impetuoso, -a; (*action*) precipitado, -a

impetus [ˈɪmpɪtəs, *Am:* -təs] *n no pl* 1. (*push*) impulso *m* 2. (*driving force*) ímpetu *m*

impiety [ɪmˈpaɪəti, *Am:* -ti] *n no pl* impiedad *f*

impinge [ɪmˈpɪndʒ] I. *vt form* afectar II. *vi* to ~ on sb/sth afectar a alguien/algo

impious [ˈɪmpiəs] *adj* impío, -a

impish [ˈɪmpɪʃ] *adj* 1. (*mischievous*) malicioso, -a 2. (*cheeky*) pillín, -ina; (*grin*) pícaro, -a

implacable [ɪmˈplækəbl] *adj form* implacable

implacably *adv form* implacablemente

implant [ɪmˈplɑːnt, *Am:* -ˈplænt] I. *n* implante *m* II. *vt* 1. (*add surgically*) implantar 2. (*put in the mind*) inculcar

implausible [ɪmˈplɔːzɪbl, *Am:* -ˈplɑː-] *adj* inverosímil

implement [ˈɪmplɪmənt] I. *n* (*tool*) instrumento *m;* (*small tool*) utensilio *m* II. *vt* implementar

implementation [ˌɪmplɪmenˈteɪʃən] *n no pl* (*of tools, devices*) puesta *f* en práctica; (*of measures, policies*) implementación *f*

implicate [ˈɪmplɪkeɪt] *vt* (*show sb's involvement*) implicar; (*involve*) involucrar

implication [ˌɪmplɪˈkeɪʃən] *n* 1. *no pl* (*hint-*

ing at) insinuación *f;* by ~ implícitamente 2. (*effect*) consecuencia *f* 3. (*showing of involvement*) implicación *f*

implicit [ɪmˈplɪsɪt] *adj* 1. (*suggested*) implícito, -a 2. (*total*) absoluto, -a; (*faith*) incondicional

implied [ɪmˈplaɪd] *adj* tácito, -a; (*criticism*) implícito, -a

implode [ɪmˈpləud, *Am:* -ˈploud] *vi* implosionar

implore [ɪmˈplɔːʳ, *Am:* -ˈplɔːr] *vt* implorar; to ~ sb to do sth suplicar a alguien que haga algo

imploring [ɪmˈplɔːrɪŋ, *Am:* -ˈplɔːr-] *adj* implorante; (*voice*) suplicante

implosion [ɪmˈpləuʒən, *Am:* -ˈplou-] *n* implosión *f*

imply [ɪmˈplaɪ] <-ie-> *vt* 1. (*suggest*) sugerir 2. *form* (*require*) implicar

impolite [ˌɪmpəˈlaɪt] *adj* descortés; (*rude*) grosero, -a

impoliteness *n no pl* descortesía *f*

impolitic [ɪmˈpɒlətɪk, *Am:* -ˈpɑːlə-] *adj form* imprudente

imponderable [ɪmˈpɒndərəbl, *Am:* -ˈpɑːn-] I. *adj* imponderable II. *n* imponderable *m*

import [ɪmˈpɔːt, *Am:* -ˈpɔːrt] I. *vt* 1. ECON, INFOR importar 2. *form* (*signify*) significar II. *n* 1. (*good*) producto *m* de importación 2. *form* (*significance*) importancia *f*

importance [ɪmˈpɔːtns, *Am:* -ˈpɔːr-] *n no pl* importancia *f*

important [ɪmˈpɔːtənt, *Am:* -ˈpɔːr-] *adj* importante

importantly *adv* significativamente

importation [ˌɪmpɔːˈteɪʃən, *Am:* -pɔːrˈ-] *n no pl* ECON importación *f*

import duty <-ies> *n* derecho *m* de aduana

importunate [ɪmˈpɔːtʃunət, *Am:* -ˈpɔːrtʃənɪt] *adj form* inoportuno, -a, molesto, -a

importune [ˌɪmpəˈtjuːn, *Am:* ˌɪmpɔːrˈtuːn] *vt form* importunar

impose [ɪmˈpəuz, *Am:* -ˈpouz] I. *vt* 1. (*implement*) imponer 2. (*force on*) obligar II. *vi* aprovecharse; to ~ on sb aprovecharse de alguien; I don't want to ~ no quiero molestar

imposing [ɪmˈpəuzɪŋ, *Am:* -ˈpou-] *adj* imponente

imposition [ˌɪmpəˈzɪʃən] *n* 1. *no pl* (*forcing, application*) imposición *f* 2. (*inconvenience*) molestia *f*

impossibility [ɪmˌpɒsəˈbɪləti, *Am:* -ˌpɑːsə-ˈbɪləti] *n no pl* imposibilidad *f*

impossible [ɪmˈpɒsəbl, *Am:* -ˈpɑːsə-] I. *adj* 1. (*not possible*) imposible 2. (*not resolveable*) irresoluble 3. (*difficult to deal with*) insoportable II. *n* the ~ lo imposible

impossibly *adv* extremadamente

imposter *n*, **impostor** [ɪmˈpɒstəʳ, *Am:* -ˈpɑːstɚ] *n* impostor(a) *m(f)*

imposture [ɪmˈpɒstʃəʳ, *Am:* -ˈpɑːstʃɚ] *n no pl* impostura *f*

impotence [ˈɪmpətəns, *Am:* -təns] *n no pl* impotencia *f*

impotent [ˈɪmpətənt, *Am:* -tənt] *adj* impotente

impound [ɪmˈpaʊnd] *vt* incautar

impoverish [ɪmˈpɒvərɪʃ, *Am:* -ˈpɑːvɚ-] *vt* 1.(*make poor*) empobrecer 2.(*deplete*) menguar

impoverished *adj* 1.(*made poor*) empobrecido, -a 2.(*depleted*) menguado, -a

impracticable [ɪmˈpræktɪkəbl] *adj* impracticable; (*person*) intratable

impractical [ɪmˈpræktɪkl] *adj* poco práctico, -a

imprecation [ˌɪmprɪˈkeɪʃən] *n form* imprecación *f*

imprecise [ˌɪmprɪˈsaɪs] *adj* impreciso, -a

impregnable [ɪmˈpregnəbl] *adj* 1.(*unable to be taken*) inexpugnable 2. Brit, Aus (*undefeatable*) imbatible

impregnate [ˈɪmpregneɪt, *Am:* ɪmˈpreg-] *vt* 1.(*make absorb*) impregnar 2. ZOOL fecundar

impresario [ˌɪmprɪˈsɑːriəʊ, *Am:* -prəˈsɑː-rioʊ] *n* empresario, -a *m, f*

impress [ɪmˈpres] I. *vt* 1.(*affect*) impresionar 2.(*stamp*) estampar; **to ~ sth on** [*o* **upon**] **sb** (*make realize*) inculcar algo a alguien; (*make remember*) recalcar algo a alguien II. *vi* impresionar

impression [ɪmˈpreʃən] *n* 1.(*general opinion*) impresión *f;* **to be of** [*o* **under**] **the ~ that ...** tener la impresión de que... 2.(*feeling*) sensación *f;* **to make an ~ on sb** causar impresión a alguien 3.(*imitation*) imitación *f* 4.(*imprint*) impresión *f; fig* huella *f*

impressionable [ɪmˈpreʃənəbl] *adj* impresionable

impressionism [ɪmˈpreʃnɪzəm] *n no pl* impresionismo *m*

impressionist [ɪmˈpreʃnɪst] I. *n* 1. ART impresionista *mf* 2.(*imitator*) imitador(a) *m(f)* II. *adj* impresionista

impressionistic [ɪmˌpreʃəˈnɪstɪk] *adj* impresionista

impressive [ɪmˈpresɪv] *adj* impresionante

imprint [ɪmˈprɪnt] I. *vt* 1.(*stamp*) estampar; (*paper*) imprimir; (*coins*) acuñar; (*leather*) grabar 2.(*in memory*) grabar 3. ZOOL marcar II. *n* 1.(*mark*) marca *f; fig* huella *f* 2. TYPO pie *m* de imprenta

imprison [ɪmˈprɪzən] *vt* encarcelar

imprisonment [ɪmˈprɪzənmənt] *n no pl* encarcelamiento *m;* **life ~** cadena *f* perpetua

improbability [ɪmˌprɒbəˈbɪləti, *Am:* ˌɪm-prɑːbəˈbɪləti] *n no pl* improbabilidad *f*

improbable [ɪmˈprɒbəbl, *Am:* -ˈprɑːbə-] *adj* improbable

impromptu [ɪmˈprɒmptjuː, *Am:* -ˈprɑːmp-tuː] *adj* de improviso

improper [ɪmˈprɒpəʳ, *Am:* -ˈprɑːpɚ] *adj* 1.(*incorrect*) incorrecto, -a; (*showing bad judgement*) injusto, -a 2.(*not socially decent*) indecoroso, -a; (*immoral*) indecente 3.(*dishonest*) deshonesto, -a

impropriety [ˌɪmprəˈpraɪəti, *Am:* -ti] <-ies> *n* 1.(*improper doings*) incongruencia *f;* (*language*) impropiedad *f* 2.*no pl* (*indecency*) indecoro *m*

improve [ɪmˈpruːv] I. *vt* mejorar II. *vi* 1. mejorar; (*progress*) hacer progresos 2.(*price*) subir

♦**improve on** *vi* superar

improvement [ɪmˈpruːvmənt] *n* 1.(*betterment*) mejora *f;* (*progress*) progreso *m* 2.*no pl* (*of illness*) mejoría *f* 3.(*increase in value*) revalorización *f*

improvident [ɪmˈprɒvɪdənt, *Am:* -ˈprɑːvə-] *adj form* 1.(*not planning*) improvisado, -a 2.(*imprudent*) imprudente

improvisation [ˌɪmprəvaɪˈzeɪʃən, *Am:* ɪmˌprɑːvɪˈ-] *n* improvisación *f*

improvise [ˈɪmprəvaɪz] *vi, vt* improvisar

imprudent [ɪmˈpruːdnt] *adj form* imprudente

impudence [ˈɪmpjʊdəns] *n no pl* descaro *m*

impudent [ˈɪmpjʊdənt] *adj* impertinente

impugn [ɪmˈpjuːn] *vt form* impugnar

impulse [ˈɪmpʌls] *n,* **impulsion** [ɪmˈpʌl-ʃən] *n* 1.*a.* ELEC, PHYS, BIO impulso *m;* **to do sth on** (**an**) **~** hacer algo por impulso 2.(*motive*) incentivo *m*

impulsive [ɪmˈpʌlsɪv] *adj* impulsivo, -a

impunity [ɪmˈpjuːnəti, *Am:* -ti] *n no pl* impunidad *f*

impure [ɪmˈpjʊəʳ, *Am:* -ˈpjʊr] *adj* impuro, -a

impurity [ɪmˈpjʊərəti, *Am:* -ˈpjʊrəti] <-ies> *n* impureza *f*

imputation [ˌɪmpjʊˈteɪʃən] *n form* imputación *f*

impute [ɪmˈpjuːt] *vt* imputar

in¹ [ɪn] I. *prep* 1.(*inside, into*) dentro de; **to be ~ bed** estar en la cama; **gun ~ hand** pistola en mano; **there is sth ~ the drawer** hay algo dentro del cajón; **to put sth ~ sb's hands** poner algo en las manos de alguien; **~ town/ jail** en la ciudad/cárcel; **~ the country/hospital** en el país/hospital; **~ France/Peru** en Francia/Perú 2.(*within*) **~ sb's face/the picture** en el rostro de alguien/la fotografía; **~ the snow/sun** en la nieve/el sol; **the best ~ France/the town** lo mejor de Francia/de la ciudad; **to find a friend ~ sb** encontrar un amigo en alguien 3.(*position of*) **~ the beginning/end** al principio/final; **right ~ the middle** justo en medio 4.(*during*) **~ the twenties** en los (años) veinte; **to be ~ one's thirties** estar en los treinta; **~ the reign of Caesar** en el reinado de César; **~ May/spring** en mayo/primavera; **~ the afternoon** por la tarde 5.(*at later time*) **~ a week/three hours** en una semana/tres horas; **~ (the) future** en el futuro 6.(*in less than*) **to do sth ~ 4 hours** hacer algo en 4 horas 7.(*for*) **he**

hasn't done that ~ **years/a week** no ha hecho eso desde hace años/una semana **8.** (*in situation, state of*) ~ **fashion** de moda; ~ **search of sth/sb** en busca de algo/alguien; ~ **this way** de esta manera; **when** ~ **doubt** en caso de duda; ~ **anger** enfurecido, alebrestado *Col, Ven;* ~ **fun** de broma, en chanza; ~ **earnest** sinceramente; **to be** ~ **a hurry** tener prisa; **to be** ~ **love (with sb)** estar enamorado (de alguien); ~ **alphabetical order** en orden alfabético; **written** ~ **black and white** *fig* claramente escrito; **dressed** ~ **red** vestido de rojo **9.** (*concerning*) **deaf** ~ **one ear** sordo de un oído; **to be interested** ~ **sth** estar interesado en algo; **to have faith** ~ **God** tener fe en Dios; **to have confidence** ~ **sb** tener confianza en alguien; **to have a say** ~ **the matter** tener algo que decir al respecto; **a change** ~ **attitude** un cambio de actitud; **a rise** ~ **prices** un aumento de los precios **10.** (*by*) ~ **saying sth** al decir algo; **to spend one's time** ~ **doing sth** dedicar el tiempo de uno a hacer algo **11.** (*taking the form of*) **to speak** ~ **French** hablar en francés; ~ **the form of a request** en forma de petición **12.** (*made of*) ~ **wood/stone** de madera/piedra **13.** (*sound of*) ~ **a whisper** en un murmullo; **to speak** ~ **a loud/low voice** hablar en voz alta/baja **14.** (*aspect of*) **2 metres** ~ **length/height** 2 metros de largo/alto; ~ **every respect** en todos los sentidos **15.** (*ratio*) **two** ~ **six** dos de cada seis; **to buy sth** ~ **twos** comprar algo de dos en dos; **10** ~ **number** 10 en número; ~ **part** en parte; ~ **tens** en grupos de diez **16.** (*substitution of*) ~ **your place** en tu lugar; ~ **lieu of sth** *form* en lugar de algo **17.** (*as conseqence of*) ~ **return** a cambio; ~ **reply** como respuesta ▶~ **all** con todo; **all** ~ **all** en resumen **II.** *adv* **1.** (*inside, into*) dentro, adentro; **to go** ~ entrar; **to put sth** ~ meter algo **2.** (*to a place*) **to be** ~ *inf* estar en casa; **to hand sth** ~ entregar algo **3.** (*popular*) **to be** ~ estar de moda **4.** SPORTS **to go** ~ **for sth** lanzarse a por algo **5.** (*up*) **the tide is coming** ~ la marea está entrando ▶**to be** ~ **for sth** *inf* estar a punto de recibir algo; **to be** ~ **on sth** estar enterado de algo **III.** *adj* de moda **IV.** *n* ~**s and outs** recovecos *mpl*

in² *abbr of* **inch** pulgada *f*

inability [ˌɪnəˈbɪləti, *Am:* -ţi] *n no pl* incapacidad *f*, ineptitud *f*

inaccessible [ˌɪnækˈsesəbl] *adj* inaccesible

inaccuracy [ɪnˈækjʊrəsi, *Am:* -jɚ-] <-ies> *n* **1.** (*fact*) error *m* **2.** *no pl* (*quality*) imprecisión *f*, inexactitud *f*

inaccurate [ɪnˈækjərət, *Am:* -jɚ-ət] *adj* **1.** (*inexact*) inexacto, -a **2.** (*wrong*) equivocado, -a

inaction [ɪnˈækʃən] *n no pl* inacción *f*

inactive [ɪnˈæktɪv] *adj* inactivo, -a

inactivity [ˌɪnækˈtɪvəti, *Am:* -ţi] *n no pl* inactividad *f*

inadequacy [ɪnˈædɪkwəsi] <-ies> *n*

1. (*insufficiency*) insuficiencia *f* **2.** *no pl* (*quality of being inadequate*) falta *f* de adecuación

inadequate [ɪnˈædɪkwət] *adj* inadecuado, -a; (*inept*) inepto, -a

inadmissible [ˌɪnədˈmɪsəbl] *adj* inadmisible

inadvertent [ˌɪnədˈvɜːtənt, *Am:* -ədˈvɜːr-] *adj* involuntario, -a

inadvisable [ˌɪnədˈvaɪzəbl] *adj* desaconsejable

inalienable [ɪnˈeɪlɪənəbl] *adj form* inalienable

inane [ɪˈneɪn] *adj* estúpido, -a

inanimate [ɪnˈænɪmət] *adj* inanimado, -a

inanity [ɪˈnænəti, *Am:* -ţi] <-ies> *n* necedad *f*

inapplicable [ɪnˈæplɪkəbl] *adj* inaplicable

inappropriate [ˌɪnəˈprəʊprɪət, *Am:* -ˈproʊ-] *adj* inapropiado, -a; (*not suitable*) inadecuado, -a

inapt [ɪnˈæpt] *adj* inadecuado, -a; (*not skilful*) inhábil, no capacitado, -a

inaptitude [ɪnˈæptɪtjuːd, *Am:* -tətuːd] *n no pl* inhabilidad *f*

inarticulate [ˌɪnɑːˈtɪkjʊlət, *Am:* -ɑːrˈ-] *adj* **1.** (*unable to express*) incapaz de expresarse **2.** (*unclear*) inarticulado, -a

inartistic [ˌɪnɑːˈtɪstɪk, *Am:* -ɑːrˈ-] *adj* poco artístico, -a

inasmuch as [ˌɪnəzˈmʌtʃ əz] *conj form* **1.** (*because*) ya que **2.** (*to the extent that*) en tanto que +*subj*

inattention [ˌɪnəˈtenʃən] *n no pl* inatención *f*

inattentive [ˌɪnəˈtentɪv, *Am:* -ţɪv] *adj* distraído, -a; **to be** ~ **to sb/sth** no prestar atención a alguien/algo

inaudible [ɪnˈɔːdəbl, *Am:* -ˈɑː-] *adj* inaudible

inaugural [ɪˈnɔːgjʊrəl, *Am:* -ˈnɑːg-] *adj* inaugural; (*speech*) de apertura

inaugurate [ɪˈnɔːgjʊreɪt, *Am:* -ˈnɑːg-] *vt* inaugurar

inauguration [ɪˌnɔːgjʊˈreɪʃən, *Am:* -ˌnɑːg-] *n* inauguración *f*

inauspicious [ˌɪnɔːˈspɪʃəs, *Am:* -ɑːˈspɪʃ-] *adj* poco propicio, -a

in-between *adj* intermedio, -a

inboard [ˈɪnbɔːd, *Am:* ˈɪnbɔːrd] *adj* interno, -a

inborn [ˌɪnˈbɔːn, *Am:* ˈɪnbɔːrn] *adj* innato, -a

in-box [ˈɪnbɒks, *Am:* -bɑːks] *n* INFOR buzón *m* de entrada

inbred [ˌɪnˈbred, *Am:* ˈɪnbred] *adj* **1.** (*too closely related*) endogámico, -a **2.** (*inherent*) innato, -a

inbreeding [ˌɪnˈbriːdɪŋ, *Am:* ˈɪnbriːdɪŋ] *n no pl* endogamia *f*

in-built [ˈɪnbɪlt] *adj* integrado, -a; *fig* inherente, innato, -a

Inc. [ɪŋk] *abbr of* **Incorporated** Inc.

incalculable [ɪnˈkælkjʊləbl] *adj* incalculable

incandescent [ˌɪnkænˈdesnt, *Am:* -ken-] *adj* incandescente

incantation [ˌɪnkænˈteɪʃən] n conjuro m, ensalmo m

incapability [ɪnˌkeɪpəˈbɪləti, Am: -t̬i] n no pl incapacidad f

incapable [ɪnˈkeɪpəbl] adj incapaz; **to be ~ of doing sth** no ser capaz de hacer algo

incapacitate [ˌɪnkəˈpæsɪteɪt] vt incapacitar

incapacity [ˌɪnkəˈpæsəti, Am: -t̬i] n no pl incapacidad f

incarcerate [ɪnˈkɑːsəreɪt, Am: -ˈkɑːr-] vt encarcelar

incarnate [ɪnˈkɑːneɪt, Am: -ˈkɑːr-] adj encarnado, -a; **the devil ~** el mismo diablo

incarnation [ˌɪnkɑːˈneɪʃən, Am: -kɑːrˈ-] n encarnación f; **to be the ~ of sth** ser la personificación de algo

incautious [ɪnˈkɔːʃəs, Am: -ˈkɑː-] adj form imprudente

incendiary [ɪnˈsendɪəri, Am: -eri] adj a. fig incendiario, -a

incense¹ [ˈɪnsents] n incienso m

incense² [ɪnˈsents] vt indignar

incensed adj indignado, -a

incentive [ɪnˈsentɪv, Am: -t̬ɪv] n incentivo m

incentive scheme n plan m de incentivos

inception [ɪnˈsepʃən] n no pl inicio m

incertitude [ɪnˈsɜːtɪtjuːd, Am: -ˈsɜːrt̬ɪtuːd] n incertidumbre f

incessant [ɪnˈsesnt] adj incesante

incest [ˈɪnsest] n no pl incesto m

incestuous [ɪnˈsestjuəs, Am: -tʃu-] adj a. fig incestuoso, -a

inch [ɪntʃ] I.<-es> n pulgada f; **she knows every ~ of Madrid** conoce cada centímetro de Madrid; **she's every ~ a lady** es una señora de pies a cabeza ▶**give someone an ~ and they'll take a mile** prov les das la mano y te cogen el brazo prov; **to do sth ~ by ~** hacer algo paso a paso II. vi moverse lentamente

◆**inch forward** vi avanzar lentamente

incidence [ˈɪntsɪdənts] n no pl incidencia f; **there is a higher ~ of left-handedness amongst girls than boys** existe un índice mayor de zurdos entre chicas que entre chicos

incident [ˈɪntsɪdənt] n incidente m; **an isolated ~** un episodio aislado

incidental [ˌɪntsɪˈdentəl, Am: -t̬əl] adj **1.** (related, of lesser importance) secundario, -a **2.** (occuring by chance) imprevisto, -a

incidentally adv por cierto, a propósito

incinerate [ɪnˈsɪnəreɪt] vt incinerar

incinerator [ɪnˈsɪnəreɪtəʳ, Am: -t̬ɚ] n incinerador m

incipient [ɪnˈsɪpɪənt] adj incipiente; **at an ~ stage** en una etapa naciente

incise vt Brit, Aus, **incize** [ɪnˈsaɪz] vt Am cortar; (in wood) grabar

incision [ɪnˈsɪʒən] n MED incisión f

incisive [ɪnˈsaɪsɪv] adj **1.** (clear) incisivo, -a; (penetrating) penetrante **2.** (keen, acute) agudo, -a; (mind) perspicaz

incisor [ɪnˈsaɪzəʳ, Am: -zɚ] n incisivo m

incite [ɪnˈsaɪt] vt instigar

incitement [ɪnˈsaɪtmənt] n no pl incitación f

incivility [ˌɪnsɪˈvɪləti, Am: -t̬i] n no pl, form descortesía f

inclement [ɪnˈklemənt] adj inclemente

inclination [ˌɪnklɪˈneɪʃən] n **1.** (tendency) propensión f; **to have an ~ to do sth** tener inclinación a hacer algo **2.** (slope) inclinación f

incline¹ [ˈɪnklaɪn] n inclinación f; (of hill, mountain) pendiente f

incline² [ɪnˈklaɪn] I. vi **1.** (tend) tender **2.** (lean) inclinarse II. vt **1.** (make sth tend) predisponer; **to ~ (sb) to do sth** influir (a alguien) para que haga algo **2.** (make lean) inclinar

inclined [ɪnˈklaɪnd] adj predispuesto, -a; **to be ~ to do sth** estar dispuesto a hacer algo

inclose [ɪnˈkləʊz, Am: -ˈkloʊz] vt encerrar

include [ɪnˈkluːd] vt incluir; (in a letter) adjuntar; **do you ~ that in the service?** ¿lo incluís en el servicio?

including [ɪnˈkluːdɪŋ] prep incluso; **(not) ~ tax** impuesto (no) incluido; **up to and ~ 6th June** hasta el 6 de junio inclusive

inclusion [ɪnˈkluːʒən] n no pl inclusión f

inclusive [ɪnˈkluːsɪv] adj incluido, -a; **all prices are ~ of Value Added Tax** todos los precios llevan incluido el Impuesto sobre el Valor Añadido

incognito [ˌɪnkɒgˈniːtəʊ, Am: ˌɪnkɑːgˈniːtoʊ] adv de incógnito, -a

incoherent [ˌɪnkəʊˈhɪərənt, Am: -koʊˈhɪrənt] adj incoherente

income [ˈɪŋkʌm, Am: ˈɪn-] n no pl ingresos mpl

income group n tramo m de renta **income support** n no pl, Brit subsidio m otorgado a personas de bajos ingresos **income tax** n no pl impuesto m sobre la renta; **graduated ~** impuesto m proporcional

incoming [ˈɪnˌkʌmɪŋ] adj entrante

incomings [ˈɪnˌkʌmɪŋz] npl ECON entradas fpl

incommensurate [ˌɪnkəˈmenʃərət, Am: -sɚ-] adj desproporcionado, -a; **to be ~ to** no guardar relación con

incommunicado [ˌɪnkəˌmjuːnɪˈkɑːdəʊ, Am: -doʊ] adj incomunicado, -a; **we wanted to invite you to the party, but you were ~** queríamos invitarte a la fiesta pero estabas ilocalizable

incomparable [ɪnˈkɒmprəbl, Am: -ˈkɑːm-] adj incomparable

incompatibility [ˌɪnkəmˌpætəˈbɪlti, Am: -ˌpæt̬əˈbɪləti] <-ies> n no pl incompatibilidad f; **~ with sth** falta de compatibilidad con algo; **Laura left the firm because of her ~ with her workmates** Laura dejó la empresa por falta de entendimiento con sus compañeros

incompatible [ˌɪnkəmˈpætəbl, Am: -ˈpæt̬-] adj incompatible

incompetence [ɪnˈkɒmpɪtənts, Am:

-'kɑːmpəʈənts] *n,* **incompetency** *n no pl* incompetencia *f*

incompetent [ɪn'kɒmpɪtənt, *Am:* -'kɑːm-pəʈənt] I. *adj* incompetente; **mentally** ~ deficiente mental; **she was mentally** ~ **when she wrote the will** no contaba con plenas facultades mentales cuando redactó el testamento II. *n* incompetente *mf*

incomplete [ˌɪnkəm'pliːt] *adj* incompleto, -a; (*not finished*) inacabado, -a

incomprehensible [ˌɪnˌkɒmprɪ'hensəbl, *Am:* ˌɪnkɑːm-] *adj* incomprensible

inconceivable [ˌɪnkən'siːvəbl] *adj* inconcebible

inconclusive [ˌɪnkən'kluːsɪv] *adj* 1.(*not convincing*) inconcluyente 2.(*without definite results*) no fructífero, -a

incongruous [ɪn'kɒŋgrʊəs, *Am:* -'kɑːŋ-] *adj* 1.(*unsuitable*) inapropiado, -a 2.(*strange*) fuera de lugar

inconsequent [ɪn'kɒnsɪkwənt, *Am:* -'kɑːn-] *adj form* intrascendente

inconsequential [ɪnˌkɒnsɪ'kwenʃl, *Am:* -'kɑːn-] *adj* 1.(*illogical*) inconsecuente 2.(*unimportant*) intrascendente

inconsiderable [ˌɪnkən'sɪdrəbl] *adj* **a not** ~ **amount** una suma nada desdeñable

inconsiderate [ˌɪnkən'sɪdərət] *adj* desconsiderado, -a; (*insensitive*) insensible

inconsistency [ˌɪnkən'sɪstəntsi] <-ies> *n* 1.(*lack of consistency*) falta *f* de coherencia 2.(*discrepancy*) contradicción *f*

inconsistent [ˌɪnkən'sɪstənt] *adj* 1.(*changeable*) incoherente 2.(*lacking agreement*) contradictorio, -a

inconsolable [ˌɪnkən'səʊləbl, *Am:* -'soʊ-] *adj* inconsolable

inconspicuous [ˌɪnkən'spɪkjʊəs] *adj* desapercibido, -a; **highly** ~ imperceptible; **to try to look** ~ tratar de pasar inadvertido

inconstant [ɪn'kɒnstənt, *Am:* -'kɑːn-] *adj* 1.(*changing*) inconstante; (*unpredictable*) imprevisible 2.(*unfaithful*) infiel

incontestable [ˌɪnkən'testəbl] *adj form* incontestable; **it is** ~ **that ...** es irrefutable que...

incontinent [ɪn'kɒntɪnənt, *Am:* -'kɑːntən-] *adj* MED incontinente

incontrovertible [ɪnˌkɒntrə'vɜːtəbl, *Am:* -ˌkɑːntrə'vɜːrʈə-] *adj* incontrovertible; **her logic is** ~ su lógica es indiscutible; ~ **proof** prueba *f* irrefutable; **it is** ~ **that ...** es incuestionable que...

inconvenience [ˌɪnkən'viːnɪəns] I. *n* inconveniencia *f* II. *vt* causar molestias

inconvenient [ˌɪnkən'viːnɪənt] *adj* inconveniente; (*time*) inoportuno, -a; **it's a very** ~ **place to hold the party** es un lugar muy poco adecuado para hacer la fiesta

incorporate [ɪn'kɔːpəreɪt, *Am:* -'kɔːr-] *vt* 1.(*integrate*) incorporar; (*work into*) integrar; (*add*) añadir 2.(*include*) incluir 3. *Am* LAW, ECON constituir; **to** ~ **a company** formar una empresa

incorporation [ɪnˌkɔːpə'reɪʃn, *Am:* -ˌkɔːr-] *n no pl* 1.(*integration*) incorporación *f;* (*working into*) integración *f* 2. LAW, ECON constitución *f*

incorporeal [ˌɪnkɔː'pɔːrɪəl, *Am:* -kɔːr'-] *adj form* incorpóreo, -a; **an** ~ **being** un ser impalpable

incorrect [ˌɪnkə'rekt] *adj* 1.(*wrong, untrue*) incorrecto, -a; (*diagnosis*) erróneo, -a; **it is** ~ **that ...** no es cierto que... 2.(*improper*) inapropiado, -a

incorrigible [ɪn'kɒrɪdʒəbl, *Am:* ɪn'kɔːrə-] *adj* incorregible

incorruptible [ˌɪnkə'rʌptəbl] *adj* 1.(*not able to be corrupted*) incorruptible; (*morally incorruptible*) íntegro, -a 2.(*not subject to decay*) inalterable

increase¹ ['ɪnkriːs] *n* (*raised amount*) incremento *m;* (*wilful*) subida *f;* (*be getting higher and higher*) crecimiento *m;* **to be on the** ~ ir en aumento

increase² [ɪn'kriːs] I. *vi* (*become more*) incrementar; (*grow*) crecer; **to** ~ **dramatically** aumentar espectacularmente; **to** ~ **ten-fold/threefold** multiplicarse por diez/tres II. *vt* (*make more*) incrementar; (*make stronger*) intensificar; (*make larger*) aumentar

increasing *adj* creciente

increasingly *adv* cada vez más

incredible [ɪn'kredɪbl] *adj* increíble

incredibly *adv* 1.(*in an incredible way*) increíblemente 2. ~, **nobody was hurt** parece increíble, pero no hubo heridos

incredulity [ˌɪnkrɪ'djuːləti, *Am:* -'duːləti] *n no pl* incredulidad *f;* (*bewilderment*) desconcierto *m*

incredulous [ɪn'kredjʊləs, *Am:* -'kredʒʊ-] *adj* incrédulo, -a

increment ['ɪŋkrəmənt] *n* incremento *m;* (*wilful*) subida *f;* **salary** ~ aumento *m* salarial

incremental [ˌɪŋkrə'məntəl, *Am:* ˌɪŋkrə'mənʈəl] *adj* ECON incremental

incriminate [ɪn'krɪmɪneɪt] *vt* incriminar; **to** ~ **oneself** autoinculparse

incriminating *adj* compremetedor(a)

incubate ['ɪnkjʊbeɪt] I. *vt* incubar II. *vi* incubarse

incubation [ˌɪnkjʊ'beɪʃən] *n no pl* incubación *f*

incubation period *n* período *m* de incubación

incubator ['ɪŋkjʊbeɪtə', *Am:* -ʈə'] *n* incubadora *f*

inculcate ['ɪnkʌlkeɪt] *vt* inculcar

incumbent [ɪŋ'kʌmbənt] I. *adj* **it is** ~ **on sb to do sth** incumbe a alguien hacer algo II. *n* titular *m*

incur [ɪn'kɜː', *Am:* -'kɜːr] <-rr-> *vt* 1. FIN, ECON (*debt*) contraer; (*costs*) incurrir en; (*losses*) sufrir 2.(*bring upon oneself*) acarrear; **to** ~ **the anger of sb** provocar el enfado de alguien

incurable [ɪn'kjʊərəbl, *Am:* -'kjʊrə-] *adj*

incurable; *fig* incorregible; **he is an ~ roman-tic** es un romántico empedernido

incursion [ɪnˈkɜːʃən, *Am:* -ˈkɜːr-] *n* **1.** MIL incursión *f* **2.** (*intrusion*) intrusión *f*

indebted [ɪnˈdetɪd, *Am:* -ˈdet̬-] *adj* **1.** (*obliged*) en deuda; **to be ~ to sb** (**for sth**) estar en deuda con alguien (por algo) **2.** (*having debt*) endeudado, -a

indebtedness *n no pl* **1.** (*state of obligation*) deuda *f* **2.** (*state of debt*) endeudamiento *m*

indecency [ɪnˈdiːsəntsi] *n no pl* **1.** (*impropriety*) indecencia *f* **2.** LAW abuso *m*

indecent [ɪnˈdiːsənt] *adj* indecente, indecoroso, -a

indecipherable [ˌɪndɪˈsaɪfrəbl] *adj* indescifrable

indecision [ˌɪndɪˈsɪʒən] *n no pl* indecisión *f*, irresolución *f*

indecisive [ˌɪndɪˈsaɪsɪv] *adj* **1.** (*unable to make decisions*) indeciso, -a **2.** (*not clear*) irresoluto, -a

indeclinable [ɪndɪˈklaɪnəbl] *adj* LING indeclinable

indecorous [ɪnˈdekərəs] *adj form* (*unsuitable*) indecoroso, -a; (*undignified*) indigno, -a

indeed [ɪnˈdiːd] I. *adv* **1.** (*really*) realmente; **this is good news ~!** ¡eso sí que es una buena noticia!; **many people here are very rich ~** mucha gente de aquí es verdaderamente rica **2.** (*expresses affirmation*) en efecto; **yes, he did ~** say that sí, en efecto dijo eso II. *interj* ya lo creo; **he's a lovely boy! ‒ ~!** es un chico encantador ‒ ¡ya lo creo!

indefatigable [ˌɪndɪˈfætɪgəbl, *Am:* -ˈfæt̬-] *adj form* infatigable

indefensible [ˌɪndɪˈfensəbl] *adj* insostenible; MIL indefendible

indefinable [ˌɪndɪˈfaɪnəbl] *adj* indefinible

indefinite [ɪnˈdefɪnət, *Am:* -ənət] *adj* indefinido, -a; **for an ~ period** por un tiempo indeterminado

indefinite article *n* LING artículo *m* indefinido

indefinitely *adv* indefinidamente

indelible [ɪnˈdeləbl] *adj* imborrable; (*colours, stains*) indeleble

indemnify [ɪnˈdemnɪfaɪ] <-ie-> *vt* **1.** (*insure against damage*) asegurar **2.** (*compensate for damage*) indemnizar

indemnity [ɪnˈdemnəti, *Am:* -t̬i] <-ies> *n form* **1.** *no pl* (*insurance for damage*) indemnidad *f* **2.** (*compensation*) indemnización *f* **3.** (*exemption*) inmunidad *f*

indent [ɪnˈdent] I. *vi* **1.** TYPO (*make a space*) sangrar **2.** *Brit, Aus* ECON encargar II. *vt* marcar; TYPO sangrar; **his footsteps ~ed the sand** sus pasos dejaron marcas en la arena III. *n* **1.** *Brit, Aus* ECON pedido *m* **2.** TYPO sangrado *m*

indentation [ˌɪndenˈteɪʃən] *n* **1.** TYPO sangría *f* **2.** (*notch*) hendidura *f*; (*cut*) mella *f*

independence [ˌɪndɪˈpendəns] *n no pl* independencia *f*

Independence Day *n Am* día *m* de la Independencia

independent [ˌɪndɪˈpendənt] I. *adj* independiente; **to be financially ~** ser económicamente independiente II. *n* POL diputado, -a *m, f* independiente

in-depth [ˈɪndepθ] *adj* exhaustivo, -a, a fondo

indescribable [ˌɪndɪˈskraɪbəbl] *adj* indescriptible

indestructible [ˌɪndɪˈstrʌktəbl] *adj* indestructible; **~ waste products** productos *mpl* no desechables

indeterminable [ˌɪndɪˈtɜːmɪnəbl, *Am:* -ˈtɜːr-] *adj* indeterminable

indeterminate [ˌɪndɪˈtɜːmɪnət, *Am:* -ˈtɜːr-] *adj* indeterminado, -a; **to take an ~ stance** adoptar una postura ecléctica

index [ˈɪndeks] I. *n* **1.** <-es> (*alphabetical list*) índice *m*; **card ~** fichero *m* de tarjetas **2.** <-ices *o* -es> ECON índice *m*; **the Dow Jones Index** el índice Dow Jones; **consumer price ~** índice de precios al consumo **3.** <-ices *o* -es> (*indication*) indicador *m* **4.** <-ices> MAT exponente *m* II. *vt* **1.** (*provide with a list*) poner índice a **2.** (*enter in a list*) indexar **3.** ECON **to ~ wages to inflation** equilibrar los sueldos a la inflación; **~ed pension** pensión *f* actualizada al coste de la vida

indexation [ˌɪndekˈseɪʃən] *n no pl* ECON indexación *f*

index card *n* ficha *f*

indexer [ˈɪndeksər, *Am:* -sər] *n* clasificador *m*

index finger *n* dedo *m* índice **index-linked** *adj Brit* ECON indexado, -a

India [ˈɪndɪə] *n no pl* la India *f*

Indian [ˈɪndɪən] I. *adj* **1.** (*of India*) indio, -a, hindú **2.** (*of America*) indio, -a, indígena II. *n* **1.** (*of India*) indio, -a *m, f* **2.** (*of America*) indígena *mf*

Indian club *n* SPORTS bolo *m* **Indian corn** *n no pl, Am* mazorca *f* **Indian file** *n* fila *f* india **Indian ink** *n no pl, Brit, Aus* tinta *f* china **Indian Ocean** *n no pl* Océano *m* Índico **Indian summer** *n* veranillo *m* de San Martín

India paper *n no pl* papel *m* biblia **India rubber** *n* **1.** *no pl* (*substance*) caucho *m* **2.** (*eraser*) goma *f*

indicate [ˈɪndɪkeɪt] I. *vt* indicar; **to ~ (to sb) that ...** señalar (a alguien) que... II. *vi Brit* AUTO poner el intermitente

indication [ˌɪndɪˈkeɪʃən] *n* **1.** (*evidence*) indicio *m*; **an ~ of willingness** una muestra de voluntad **2.** *a.* MED indicación *f*

indicative [ɪnˈdɪkətɪv, *Am:* -t̬ɪv] I. *adj* indicativo, -a II. *n* indicativo *m*

indicator [ˈɪndɪkeɪtər, *Am:* -t̬ər] *n* **1.** (*evidence*) indicador *m* **2.** *Brit* AUTO intermitente *m*

indices [ˈɪndɪsiːz] *n pl of* **index**

indict [ɪnˈdaɪt] *vt* **to ~ sb of sth** LAW acusar a alguien de algo

indictment [ɪnˈdaɪtmənt] *n* **1.** LAW acusación *f* **2.** *fig* crítica *f*

indie ['ɪndi] *adj inf* (*album, record company*) independiente

Indies ['ɪndiz] *npl* Indias *fpl;* **the West** ~ Las Antillas

indifference [ɪn'dɪfrəns] *n no pl* indiferencia *f*

indifferent [ɪn'dɪfrənt] *adj* **1.** (*not interested*) indiferente, valemadrista *inv Méx* **2.** (*neither good nor bad*) mediocre

indigenous [ɪn'dɪdʒɪnəs] *adj* indígena

indigestible [ˌɪndɪ'dʒəstəbl] *adj* **1.** (*food*) indigesto, -a **2.** *fig* indigerible

indigestion [ˌɪndɪ'dʒəstʃən] *n no pl* indigestión *f;* **to give oneself** ~ empacharse

indignant [ɪn'dɪgnənt] *adj* indignado, -a; **to become** ~ indignarse; **to be/feel** ~ **about sth** estar/sentirse indignado por algo

indignation [ˌɪndɪg'neɪʃən] *n no pl* indignación *f*

indignity [ɪn'dɪgnɪti, *Am:* -nət̬i] <-ies> *n* **1.** *no pl* (*humiliation*) indignidad *f* **2.** (*sth that humiliates*) afrenta *f*

indirect [ˌɪndɪ'rekt] *adj* indirecto, -a

indirect object *n* LING objeto *m* indirecto

indirect tax <-es> *n* contribución *f* indirecta

indiscernible [ˌɪndɪ'sɜːnəbl, *Am:* -'sɜːr-] *adj* indiscernible; (*not visible*) imperceptible; ~ **to the naked eye** imperceptible a simple vista

indiscipline [ɪn'dɪsɪplɪn] *n no pl, form* falta *f* de disciplina

indiscreet [ˌɪndɪ'skriːt] *adj* indiscreto, -a; (*tactless*) falto, -a de tacto

indiscretion [ˌɪndɪ'skreʃən] *n no pl* (*lack of discretion*) indiscreción *f;* (*lack of tactfulness*) falta *f* de tacto

indiscriminate [ˌɪndɪ'skrɪmɪnət] *adj* **1.** (*uncritical*) sin criterio **2.** (*random*) indiscriminado, -a

indispensable [ˌɪndɪ'spensəbl] *adj* indispensable

indisposed [ˌɪndɪ'spəʊzd, *Am:* -'spoʊzd] *adj* indispuesto, -a; **to be/feel** ~ **to do sth** estar/sentirse indispuesto para hacer algo

indisposition [ˌɪndɪspə'zɪʃən] *n form* **1.** (*illness*) indisposición *f* **2.** *no pl* (*disinclination*) reticencia *f*

indisputable [ˌɪndɪ'spjuːtəbl, *Am:* -t̬ə-] *adj* indiscutible; (*evidence*) incuestionable

indistinct [ˌɪndɪ'stɪŋkt] *adj* indistinto, -a; (*blurred*) borroso, -a

indistinguishable [ˌɪndɪ'stɪŋgwɪʃ əbl] *adj* indistinguible; (*not perceptible*) imperceptible

individual [ˌɪndɪ'vɪdʒuəl] **I.** *n* individuo, -a *m, f* **II.** *adj* individual; (*particular*) particular; **an** ~ **style** un estilo propio

individual case *n* caso *m* particular

individualise *vt Aus, Brit,* **individualize** [ˌɪndɪ'vɪdʒuəlaɪz] *vt Am* individualizar

individualism [ˌɪndɪ'vɪdʒuəlɪzəm] *n no pl* individualismo *m*

individualist *n* individualista *mf*

individualistic [ˌɪndɪˌvɪdʒuə'lɪstɪk] *adj* individualista

individuality [ˌɪndɪˌvɪdʒu'æləti, *Am:* -ˌvɪdʒu'æləti] *n no pl* individualidad *f*

individually *adv* individualmente

indivisible [ˌɪndɪ'vɪzəbl] *adj* indivisible

Indochina [ˌɪdəʊ'tʃaɪnə] *n* Indochina *f*

indoctrinate [ɪn'dɒktrɪneɪt, *Am:* -'dɑːk-] *vt* adoctrinar; **to** ~ **children in sth** adoctrinar a los niños en algo

indoctrination [ɪnˌdɒktrɪ'neɪʃən, *Am:* -ˌdɑːk-] *n no pl* adoctrinamiento *m*

indolent ['ɪndələnt] *adj* indolente

indomitable [ɪn'dɒmɪtəbl, *Am:* -'dɑːmə-t̬ə-] *adj* indómito, -a; **an** ~ **strength of character** una fuerza de carácter indomable

Indonesia [ˌɪndəʊ'niːziə, *Am:* -də'niːʒə] *n* Indonesia *f*

Indonesian **I.** *adj* indonesio, -a **II.** *n* indonesio, -a *m, f*

indoor ['ɪndɔːʳ, *Am:* ˌɪn'dɔːr] *adj* interior; (*pool*) cubierto, -a; (*clothes*) de casa; ~ **plant** planta *f* de interior

indoors [ˌɪn'dɔːz, *Am:* -'dɔːrz] *adv* dentro

indubitable [ɪn'djuːbɪtəbl, *Am:* -'duːbɪt̬ə-] *adj form* indudable

indubitably [ɪn'djuːbɪtəbli, *Am:* -'duːbɪt̬ə-] *adv form* indudablemente

induce [ɪn'djuːs, *Am:* -'duːs] *vt* **1.** (*persuade*) *a.* ELEC, PHYS inducir **2.** (*cause*) provocar

inducement [ɪn'djuːsmənt, *Am:* -'duːs-] *m* incentivo *m*

induct [ɪn'dʌkt] *vt* **1.** (*install*) instalar **2.** (*initiate*) iniciar **3.** (*recruit*) reclutar

induction [ɪn'dʌkʃən] *n* **1.** (*installation*) instalación *f;* (*into organization*) iniciación *f* **2.** (*initiation*) iniciación *f* **3.** *no pl* PHILOS, ELEC inducción *f*

induction coil *n* ELEC bobina *f* de inducción

induction course *n* curso *m* de iniciación

inductive [ɪn'dʌktɪv] *adj* inductivo, -a

indulge [ɪn'dʌldʒ] *vt* (*allow*) consentir; (*desire*) satisfacer; **to** ~ **oneself in ...** darse el lujo de..., permitirse...

indulgence [ɪn'dʌldʒəns] *n* **1.** (*treat*) placer *m;* (*satisfaction*) satisfacción *f;* ~ **in** abandono a **2.** (*tolerance*) tolerancia *f* **3.** REL indulgencia *f*

indulgent [ɪn'dʌldʒənt] *adj* **1.** (*lenient*) indulgente **2.** (*tolerant*) tolerante

industrial [ɪn'dʌstriəl] **I.** *adj* industrial; (*dispute*) laboral; **for** ~ **use** para uso industrial **II.** *npl* FIN acciones *fpl* industriales

industrial estate *n* polígono *m* industrial

industrialise *Brit, Aus,* **industrialize** [ɪn'dʌstriəlaɪz] **I.** *vi* industrializarse **II.** *vt* industrializar

industrialism [ɪn'dʌstriəlɪzəm] *n no pl* industrialismo *m*

industrialist *n* industrial *mf*

industrialization [ɪnˌdʌstriəlaɪ'zeɪʃən, *Am:* -lɪ'-] *n no pl* industrialización *f*

industrial park *n Am* polígono *m* industrial

Industrial Revolution *n* Revolución *f*

Industrial
industrious [ɪn'dʌstrɪəs] *adj* trabajador(a)
industry ['ɪndəstri] *n* **1.** *no pl* (*manufacturing production*) industria *f;* **heavy/light** ~ industria pesada/ligera **2.** <-ies> (*branch*) sector *m* **3.** *no pl* (*diligence*) laboriosidad *f*
inebriate [ɪ'niːbrɪeɪt] *vt form* embriagar
inedible [ɪn'edəbl] *adj* **1.** (*unsuitable as food*) no comestible **2.** (*extremely unpalatable*) incomible
ineducable [ɪn'edʒʊkəbl] *adj* ineducable
ineffable [ɪn'efəbl] *adj* inefable
ineffective [ˌɪnɪ'fektɪv] *adj* ineficaz
ineffectual [ˌɪnɪ'fektʃʊəl] *adj* ineficaz, inútil
inefficiency [ˌɪnɪ'fɪʃənsi] *n no pl* ineficiencia *f*
inefficient [ˌɪnɪ'fɪʃnt] *adj* ineficiente
inelegant [ˌɪn'elɪgənt] *adj* **1.** (*unattractive*) poco elegante **2.** (*unrefined*) tosco, -a; (*gesture, movement*) basto, -a
ineligible [ɪn'elɪdʒəbl] *adj* inelegible; to be ~ **for sth** no reunir los requisitos para algo; **to be** ~ **to do sth** no tener derecho a hacer algo
inept [ɪ'nept] *adj* (*unskilled*) inepto, -a; (*inappropriate*) inoportuno, -a; **to be** ~ **at sth** ser inepto para algo; **to be socially** ~ no tener don de gentes
inequality [ˌɪnɪ'kwɒləti, *Am:* -'kwɑːləti] <-ies> *n* desigualdad *f*
inequitable [ɪn'ekwɪtəbl, *Am:* -wətə-] *adj* injusto, -a
inequity [ɪn'ekwəti, *Am:* -ti] <-ies> *n* injusticia *f*
ineradicable [ˌɪnɪ'rædɪkəbl] *adj* inextirpable
inert [ɪ'nɜːt, *Am:* -'nɜːrt] *adj* **1.** (*not moving*) inerte; *fig* inmóvil **2.** CHEM inactivo, -a
inertia [ɪ'nɜːʃə, *Am:* ˌɪn'ɜːr-] *n no pl* inercia *f; fig* pereza *f*
inertia reel seat belt *n* cinturón *m* de seguridad retráctil
inescapable [ˌɪnɪ'skeɪpəbl] *adj* ineludible
inessential [ˌɪnɪ'senʃl] **I.** *adj* no esencial **II.** *n* cosa *f* no esencial
inestimable [ɪn'estɪməbl] *adj* inestimable; **to be of** ~ **value** ser de valor incalculable
inevitable [ɪn'evɪtəbl, *Am:* -tə-] **I.** *adj* inevitable; (*conclusion, consequence*) inexorable **II.** *n no pl* **the** ~ lo inevitable
inexact [ˌɪnɪg'zækt] *adj* inexacto, -a
inexcusable [ˌɪnɪk'skjuːzəbl] *adj* imperdonable
inexhaustible [ˌɪnɪg'zɔːstəbl, *Am:* -'zɔːstəbl] *adj* inagotable
inexorable [ˌɪn'eksərəbl] *adj form* inexorable
inexpedient [ˌɪnɪk'spiːdɪənt] *adj form* inapropiado, -a
inexpensive [ˌɪnɪk'spensɪv] *adj* económico, -a; **to be** ~ **to do sth** ser asequible hacer algo
inexperience [ˌɪnɪk'spɪərɪənts] *n no pl* falta *f* de experiencia
inexperienced [ˌɪnɪk'spɪərɪənst, *Am:*

-'spɪr-] *adj* inexperto, -a; **to be** ~ **with guns** no tener experiencia con armas
inexpert [ɪn'ekspɜːt, *Am:* -spɜːrt] *adj* inexperto, -a; (*unskilled*) inhábil
inexplicable [ˌɪnɪk'splɪkəbl, *Am:* ˌɪn'ək-] **I.** *adj* inexplicable **II.** *n no pl* **the** ~ lo inexplicable
inextricable [ˌɪnɪk'strɪkəbl] *adj* inextricable
infallible [ɪn'fæləbl] *adj* indefectible; (*incapable of being wrong*) infalible
infamous ['ɪnfəməs] *adj* **1.** (*shocking*) infame **2.** (*notorious*) de mala fama
infamy ['ɪnfəmi] *n* **1.** <-ies> (*shocking act*) infamia *f* **2.** *no pl* (*notoriety*) mala fama *f*
infancy ['ɪnfəntsi] *n no pl* infancia *f;* **from** ~ desde niño; **to be in its** ~ *fig* estar aún en pañales
infant ['ɪnfənt] *n* (*very young child*) bebé *m;* **a newborn** ~ un recién nacido
infanticide [ɪn'fæntɪsaɪd, *Am:* -tə-] *n no pl* infanticidio *m*
infantile ['ɪnfəntaɪl] *adj* infantil
infant mortality *n* mortalidad *f* infantil
infantry ['ɪnfəntri] *n + sing/pl vb* MIL infantería *f*
infantryman <-men> *n* MIL soldado *m* de infantería
infatuated [ɪn'fætʃʊeɪtɪd, *Am:* -ueɪtɪd] *adj* encaprichado, -a; **to become** ~ **with sb/sth** encapricharse por alguien/algo
infect [ɪn'fekt] *vt* infectar; *a. fig* (*person*) contagiar
infection [ɪn'fekʃən] *n* infección *f; fig* contagio *m;* **risk of** ~ riesgo *m* de contagio
infectious [ɪn'fekʃəs] *adj* infeccioso, -a; *a. fig* contagioso, -a
infelicitous [ˌɪnfɪ'lɪsɪtəs, *Am:* -ətəs] *adj* *iron* desafortunado, -a
infer [ɪn'fɜːˈ, *Am:* -'fɜːr] <-rr-> *vt* inferir
inference ['ɪnfərənts] *n form* **1.** (*conclusion*) conclusión *f;* **to draw the** ~ **that ...** sacar la conclusión de que... **2.** *no pl* (*process of inferring*) inferencia *f;* **by** ~ por inferencia
inferior [ɪn'fɪərɪəˈ, *Am:* -'fɪrɪəˈ] **I.** *adj* inferior **II.** *n* inferior *mf*
inferiority [ɪnˌfɪəri'ɒrəti, *Am:* -ˌfɪriˈɔːrəti] *n no pl* inferioridad *f*
inferiority complex <-es> *n* complejo *m* de inferioridad
infernal [ɪn'fɜːnəl, *Am:* -'fɜːr-] *adj* infernal
inferno [ɪn'fɜːnəʊ, *Am:* -'fɜːrnoʊ] *n* infierno *m;* **the building was an** ~ el edificio ardía en llamas
infertile [ɪn'fɜːtaɪl, *Am:* -'fɜːrtl̩] *adj* estéril
infertility [ˌɪnfə'tɪləti, *Am:* -fəˈtɪləti] *n no pl* esterilidad *f*
infest [ɪn'fest] *vt* infestar
infestation [ˌɪnfes'teɪʃən] *n* plaga *f,* infestación *f*
infidel ['ɪnfɪdəl, *Am:* -fədel] *n* infiel *mf*
infidelity [ˌɪnfɪ'deləti, *Am:* -fə'deləti] *n no pl* infidelidad *f*
infighting ['ɪnfaɪtɪŋ] *n no pl* lucha *f* interna

infiltrate ['ɪnfɪltreɪt, *Am:* ɪn'fɪl-] *vt* infiltrarse en

infiltration [ˌɪnfɪl'treɪʃən] *n no pl* infiltración *f*

infiltrator *n* infiltrado, -a *m, f*

infinite ['ɪnfɪnət, *Am:* -fənɪt] I. *adj* infinito, -a; **with ~ patience** con una paciencia infinita; **to take ~ care** poner sumo cuidado II. *n* **the Infinite** el infinito

infinitely *adv* infinitamente

infinitesimal [ˌɪnfɪnɪ'tesɪml] *adj form* infinitesimal

infinitive [ɪn'fɪnətɪv, *Am:* -ţɪv] LING I. *n* infinitivo *m* II. *adj* infinitivo, -a

infinity [ɪn'fɪnəti, *Am:* -ţi] <-ies> *n* **1.** *no pl* MAT infinito *m;* **to ~** al infinito **2.** (*huge amount*) infinidad *f*

infirm [ɪn'fɜːm, *Am:* -'fɜːrm] *adj* enfermizo, -a; (*weak*) débil

infirmary [ɪn'fɜːməri, *Am:* -'fɜːr-] <-ies> *n* **1.** (*hospital*) hospital *m* **2.** *Am* (*sick room*) enfermería *f*

infirmity [ɪn'fɜːməti, *Am:* -'fɜːrməţi] <-ies> *n* **1.** (*illness*) enfermedad *f* **2.** *no pl* (*weakness*) debilidad *f*

inflame [ɪn'fleɪm] *vt* **1.** *a.* MED inflamar **2.** (*stir up*) encender; **to ~ sb with passion** desatar la pasión de alguien

inflammable [ɪn'flæməbl] *adj* inflamable; (*situation*) explosivo, -a

inflammation [ˌɪnflə'meɪʃən] *n* MED inflamación *f*

inflammatory [ɪn'flæmətəri, *Am:* -tɔːr-] *adj* **1.** MED inflamatorio, -a **2.** (*speech*) incendiario, -a

inflatable [ɪn'fleɪtəbl, *Am:* -ţə-] I. *adj* hinchable II. *n* bote *m* hinchable

inflate [ɪn'fleɪt] I. *vt* **1.** (*fill with air*) hinchar, inflar **2.** (*exaggerate*) exagerar **3.** ECON (*prices*) aumentar excesivamente II. *vi* hincharse

inflated [ɪn'fleɪtɪd, *Am:* -ţɪd] *adj* **1.** (*filled with air*) hinchado, -a **2.** (*exaggerated*) exagerado, -a **3.** ECON (*price*) excesivo, -a

inflation [ɪn'fleɪʃən] *n no pl* inflación *f*

inflationary *adj* FIN inflacionario, -a

inflect [ɪn'flekt] *vt* (*verb*) conjugar; (*noun*) declinar; **to ~ one's voice** modular la voz de uno

inflection *n,* **inflexion** [ɪn'flekʃən] *n* inflexión *f*

inflexibility [ɪnˌfleksə'bɪləti, *Am:* -ţi] *n no pl* inflexibilidad *f;* (*rigidity*) rigidez *f*

inflexible [ɪn'fleksəbl] *adj* inflexible

inflict [ɪn'flɪkt] *vt* (*wound*) infligir; (*damage*) causar; (*punishment*) imponer

infliction [ɪn'flɪkʃən] *n no pl* imposición *f*

influence ['ɪnfluəns] I. *n* influencia *f;* **to exert one's ~** ejercer uno su influencia; **to bring one's ~ to bear on sb** ejercer presión sobre alguien; **to be under the ~** *fig* estar borracho; **to drive under the ~** *fig* conducir bajo los efectos del alcohol II. *vt* influir

influential [ˌɪnflu'enʃl] *adj* influyente

influenza [ˌɪnflu'enzə] *n no pl* gripe *f*

influx ['ɪnflʌks] *n no pl* influjo *m*

inform [ɪn'fɔːm, *Am:* -'fɔːrm] I. *vt* informar; **I'm happy to ~ you that ...** tengo el placer de comunicarle que...; **to be ~ed about sth** estar enterado de algo II. *vi* **to ~ against sb** delatar a alguien

informal [ɪn'fɔːml, *Am:* -'fɔːr-] *adj* informal; (*tone, manner*) familiar; (*person*) afable

informality [ˌɪnfɔː'mæləti, *Am:* -fɔːr'mæləti] *n no pl* **1.** (*lack of formality*) informalidad *f* **2.** (*lack of officiality*) falta *f* de ceremonia

informant [ɪn'fɔːmənt, *Am:* -'fɔːr-] *n* informante *mf;* **a reliable ~** una fuente fiable

information [ˌɪnfə'meɪʃən, *Am:* -fəˈ-] *n no pl* **1.** (*data*) información *f;* **a lot of/a little ~** mucha/poca información; **to ask for ~** pedir informes; **for further ~** para más información **2.** INFOR datos *mpl* **3.** (*knowledge*) conocimientos *mpl* **4.** (*enquiry desk*) punto *m* de información **5.** LAW denuncia *f*

information content *n no pl* INFOR contenido *m* de información **information management** *n no pl* gestión *f* de datos **information retrieval** *n no pl* INFOR recuperación *f* de información **information science** *n* ciencias *fpl* de la información **information storage** *n no pl* INFOR almacenaje *m* de información **information superhighway** *n* autopista *f* de la información **information technology** *n no pl* tecnologías *fpl* de la información

informative [ɪn'fɔːmətɪv, *Am:* -'fɔːrməţɪv] *adj* informativo, -a

informed *adj* informado, -a

informer [ɪn'fɔːmə^r, *Am:* -'fɔːrmə-] *n* denunciante *mf*

infotainment [ˌɪnfəʊ'teɪnmənt, *Am:* 'ɪnfoʊteɪn-] *n* infotainment *m*

infraction [ɪn'frækʃən] *n* infracción *f*

infra dig [ˌɪnfrə'dɪg] *adj Brit, iron, inf* deshonroso, -a

infrared ['ɪnfrəred] *adj* infrarrojo, -a

infrastructure ['ɪnfrəˌstrʌktʃə^r, *Am:* -tʃə-] *n* infraestructura *f*

infrequent [ɪn'friːkwənt] *adj* poco frecuente

infringe [ɪn'frɪndʒ] *vt* LAW infringir; **to ~ sb's right** vulnerar un derecho de alguien

infringement [ɪn'frɪndʒmənt] *n* LAW infracción *f;* (*of a rule*) violación *f,* vulneración *f;* **copyright ~** violación de los derechos de autor; **~ of a law** violación de una ley

infuriate [ɪn'fjʊərieɪt, *Am:* -'fjʊrɪ-] *vt* enfurecer

infuse [ɪn'fjuːz] *vt* **1.** (*fill*) infundir; **to ~ sb with courage** infundir ánimo a alguien **2.** (*tea, herbs*) hacer una infusión de

infusion [ɪn'fjuːʒən] *n a.* MED infusión *f;* ECON inyección *f*

ingenious [ɪn'dʒiːnɪəs, *Am:* -njəs] *adj* **1.** (*creatively inventive*) inventivo, -a; (*idea, method, plan*) ingenioso, -a **2.** (*innovative*) innovador(a)

ingenuity [ˌɪndʒɪ'njuːəti, *Am:* -ti] *n no pl* ingenuidad *f;* **to use one's** ~ utilizar el ingenio
ingenuous [ɪn'dʒenjuəs] *adj form* **1.** (*naive*) ingenuo, -a **2.** (*openly honest*) candoroso, -a
ingest [in'dʒest] *vt form* ingerir
inglenook ['ɪŋglnʊk] *n* ARCHIT rincón *m* de la chimenea
inglorious [ɪn'glɔːrɪəs, *Am:* -'glɔːrɪ-] *adj* ignominioso, -a; (*dishonourable*) deshonroso, -a
ingoing ['ɪngəʊɪŋ, *Am:* -goʊ-] *adj* entrante
ingot ['ɪŋgət] *n* barra *f;* (*of gold, silver*) lingote *m*
ingrained [ˌɪn'greɪnd] *adj* **1.** (*embedded: dirt*) incrustado, -a; **to be/become** ~ **in sth** estar/quedarse incrustado en algo **2.** (*deep--seated*) arraigado, -a
ingratiate [ɪn'greɪʃɪeɪt] *vr* **to** ~ **oneself** (**with sb**) congraciarse (con alguien)
ingratitude [ɪn'grætɪtjuːd, *Am:* -'græţə-tuːd] *n no pl* ingratitud *f*
ingredient [ɪn'griːdɪənt] *n* **1.** GASTR ingrediente *m* **2.** (*component*) *a.* MED componente *m*
in-group ['ɪngruːp] *n inf* grupo *m* exclusivista
ingrowing [ɪn'grəʊɪŋ, *Am:* 'ɪngroʊ-] *adj*, **ingrown** [ɪn'grəʊn, *Am:* 'ɪngroʊn] *adj* que crece hacia dentro (de la piel); ~ **toenail** uñero *f*
inhabit [ɪn'hæbɪt] *vt* habitar
inhabitable *adj* habitable
inhabitant [ɪn'hæbɪtənt] *n* habitante *mf*
inhale [ɪn'heɪl] **I.** *vt* aspirar; MED inhalar **II.** *vi* inhalar
inhaler [ɪn'heɪləʳ, *Am:* -ə-] *n* inhalador *m*
inharmonious [ˌɪnhɑː'məʊnɪəs, *Am:* -hɑːr-'moʊ-] *adj* **1.** (*not peaceful*) poco armonioso, -a **2.** MUS disonante **3.** (*not blending well*) discorde
inhere [ɪn'hɪəʳ, *Am:* -'hɪr] *vi form* **to** ~ **in sth/sb** ser inherente a algo/en alguien
inherent [ɪn'hɪərənt, *Am:* -'hɪr-] *adj* inherente; PHILOS intrínseco, -a; **to be** ~ **in sth** ser inherente a algo
inherit [ɪn'herɪt] **I.** *vt* heredar **II.** *vi* recibir una herencia
inheritable *adj* heredable
inheritance [ɪn'herɪtəns] *n* herencia *f; fig* legado *m;* **to come into an** ~ recibir una herencia
inhibit [ɪn'hɪbɪt] *vt* (*hinder*) impedir; (*impair*) inhibir; **to** ~ **sb from doing sth** impedir a alguien hacer algo
inhibition [ˌɪnɪ'bɪʃən] *n* inhibición *f*
inhospitable [ˌɪnhɒ'spɪtəbl, *Am:* ɪn'hɑːs-pɪţə-] *adj* inhospitalario, -a; (*attitude*) poco amistoso, -a; (*place*) inhóspito, -a
in-house ['ɪnhaʊs] COM **I.** *adj* interno, -a **II.** *adv* dentro de la empresa
inhuman [ɪn'hjuːmən] *adj* (*not human*) inhumano, -a
inhumane [ˌɪnhjuː'meɪn] *adj* (*cruel*) inhu-

mano, -a, cruel
inhumanity [ˌɪnhjuː'mænəti, *Am:* -ti] *n no pl* inhumanidad *f*
inimical [ɪ'nɪmɪkl] *adj form* **1.** (*hostile*) contrario, -a; **to be** ~ **to sth** ser contrario a algo **2.** (*harmful*) perjudicial
inimitable [ɪ'nɪmɪtəbl, *Am:* -ţə-] *adj* inimitable
iniquitous [ɪ'nɪkwɪtəs, *Am:* -ţəs] *adj* inicuo, -a
iniquity [ɪ'nɪkwəti, *Am:* -ti] <-ies> *n* **1.** *no pl* (*wickedness*) iniquidad *f;* (*sinfulness*) perversidad *f;* (*unfairness*) injusticia *f* **2.** *pl* (*act of wickedness*) iniquidades *fpl;* (*act of unfairness*) injusticias *fpl*
initial [ɪ'nɪʃəl] **I.** *n* inicial *f;* **one's** ~**s** las iniciales de uno **II.** *adj* inicial; (*first*) primero, -a; **in the** ~ **phases** en las primeras etapas **III.** <*Brit* -ll-, *Am* -l-> *vt* marcar con las iniciales
initialise *vt Aus, Brit,* **initialize** [ɪ'nɪʃəlaɪz] *vt Am* INFOR inicializar
initially [ɪ'nɪʃəli] *adv* en un principio
initiate [ɪ'nɪʃɪeɪt] **I.** *vt* **1.** (*start*) iniciar, dar comienzo a; (*proceedings*) entablar **2.** (*admit to group*) admitir (como miembro) **II.** *n* iniciado, -a *m, f*
initiation [ɪˌnɪʃɪ'eɪʃən] *n* **1.** *no pl* (*starting*) inicio *m* **2.** (*introducing*) iniciación *f;* (*as a member*) admisión *f*
initiative [ɪ'nɪʃətɪv, *Am:* -ţɪv] *n* iniciativa *f;* **to take the** ~ **in sth** tomar la iniciativa en algo; **to show** ~ demostrar iniciativa; **to use one's** ~ obrar por cuenta propia
inject [ɪn'dʒekt] *vt* **1.** *a.* MED inyectar **2.** (*introduce*) introducir; (*funds, money*) inyectar; (*invest*) invertir
injection [ɪn'dʒekʃən] *n* inyección *f*
injection moulding *n* moldura *f* por inyección
injudicious [ˌɪndʒuː'dɪʃəs] *adj* imprudente
injunction [ɪn'dʒʌŋkʃən] *n* mandato *m;* LAW auto *m* preventivo
injure ['ɪndʒəʳ, *Am:* -dʒə-] *vt* **1.** (*wound*) herir, victimar *AmL* **2.** (*damage*) estropear **3.** (*do wrong to*) perjudicar
injured *adj* **1.** (*wounded*) herido, -a, victimado, -a *AmL* **2.** (*damaged*) estropeado, -a **3.** (*wronged*) perjudicado, -a
injury ['ɪndʒəri] <-ies> *n* **1.** (*physical*) lesión *f,* herida *f;* **a knee/back** ~ una lesión de rodilla/espalda; **to receive an** ~ ser herido; **to do oneself an** ~ *Brit, Aus, iron* hacerse daño **2.** (*pschological*) daño *m*
injustice [ɪn'dʒʌstɪs] *n* injusticia *f;* **you do me an** ~ no eres justo conmigo
ink [ɪŋk] **I.** *n* tinta *f;* **to write in** ~ escribir con tinta **II.** *vt* TYPO entintar
ink bottle *n* bote *m* de tinta **ink-jet printer** *n* impresora *f* de chorro de tinta
inkling ['ɪŋklɪŋ] *n* **1.** (*suspicion*) sospecha *f;* **to have an** ~ **that ...** tener la sospecha de que... **2.** (*hint*) indicio *m*

ink-pad ['ɪŋkpæd, *Am:* -pɑːt] *n* almohadilla *f* **inkstain** *n* mancha *f* de tinta

inky ['ɪŋki] <-ier, -iest> *adj* **1.** (*stained*) manchado, -a de tinta **2.** (*black*) negro, -a como la tinta

inlaid [ˌɪn'leɪd, *Am:* 'ɪnleɪd] **I.** *vt pt, pp of* **inlay II.** *adj* taraceado, -a; ~ **work** taracea *f*

inland ['ɪnlənd] **I.** *adj* **1.** (*not coastal: sea, shipping*) interior; (*town, village*) del interior **2.** (*domestic*) nacional; ~ **flight** vuelo *m* nacional **II.** *adv* **1.** (*direction*) tierra adentro **2.** (*place*) hacia el interior

Inland Revenue *n Brit* Hacienda *f*

inland trade *n no pl, Brit* comercio *m* interior

in-laws ['ɪnlɔːz, *Am:* -lɑːz] *npl* suegros *mpl*

inlay [ˌɪn'leɪ] **I.** *n* **1.** *no pl* (*embedded pattern*) incrustación *f* **2.** MED empaste *m* **II.** <inlaid, inlaid> *vt* taracear

inlet ['ɪnlet] *n* **1.** GEO ensenada *f;* (*of sea*) cala *f* **2.** *Brit* TECH entrada *f;* (*pipe*) tubo *m* de admisión

in-line skate *n* patinaje *m* en línea

inmate ['ɪnmeɪt] *n* residente *mf;* (*prison*) preso, -a *m, f*

inn [ɪn] *n* posada *f*

innards ['ɪnədz, *Am:* -ədz] *npl inf* **1.** (*entrails*) tripas *fpl* **2.** TECH engranajes *mpl*

innate [ɪ'neɪt] *adj* innato, -a

inner ['ɪnəʳ, *Am:* -ə-] *adj* **1.** (*located in the interior*) interno, -a, interior; **in the ~ London area** en la zona céntrica de Londres **2.** (*deep*) íntimo, -a; (*secret*) secreto, -a; **one's ~ feelings** los sentimientos más íntimos de uno

inner city *n parte céntrica de la ciudad, habitada con frecuencia por gente pobre y marginada*

innermost ['ɪnəməʊst, *Am:* -ə-moʊst] *adj* más íntimo, -a; **in his/her ~ being** en lo más profundo de su ser

inner tube *n* cámara *f* de aire

inning ['ɪnɪŋ] *n Am* SPORTS (*baseball game*) inning *m*

innings ['ɪnɪŋz] *n + sing vb Brit* (*cricket*) turno *m* de entrada ▶**to have a good ~s** *Brit* tener una vida larga

innocence ['ɪnəsns] *n no pl* inocencia *f;* **to plead one's ~** declararse inocente; **in all ~** inocentemente

innocent ['ɪnəsnt] **I.** *adj* inocente; **to be ~ of sth** ser inocente de algo **II.** *n* inocente *mf;* **to be an ~** ser un inocente; **to come the ~** *inf* hacerse el inocente

innocuous [ɪ'nɒkjʊəs, *Am:* -'nɑːk-] *adj* inocuo, -a

innovate ['ɪnəveɪt] *vi* innovar; (*introduce changes*) introducir novedades

innovation [ˌɪnə'veɪʃən] *n* novedad *f,* innovación *f*

innovative ['ɪnəvətɪv, *Am:* -veɪ̯tɪv] *adj* (*model, product*) novedoso, -a; (*person*) innovador(a)

innovator *n* innovador(a) *m(f)*

innuendo [ˌɪnjuː'endəʊ, *Am:* -doʊ] <-(e)s>

n **1.** (*insinuation*) insinuación *f;* **to make an ~ (about sth)** hacer una insinuación (sobre algo) **2.** (*suggestive remark*) indirecta *f*

innumerable [ɪ'njuːmərəbl, *Am:* -'nuː-] *adj* innumerable

innumerate [ɪ'njuːmərət, *Am:* -'nuːmə-] *adj* **to be ~** ser incompetente en el cálculo

inoculate [ɪ'nɒkjʊleɪt, *Am:* -'nɑːkjə-] *vt* **to ~ sb (against sth)** inocular a alguien (contra algo)

inoculation [ɪˌnɒkjʊ'leɪʃən, *Am:* -ˌnɑːkjə-] *n* inoculación *f*

inoffensive [ˌɪnə'fensɪv] *adj* inofensivo, -a

inoperable [ˌɪn'ɒpərəbl, *Am:* -'ɑːpə-] *adj* inoperable

inoperative [ˌɪn'ɒpərətɪv, *Am:* -'ɑːpərəṯɪv] *adj* inoperante

inopportune [ˌɪn'ɒpətjuːn, *Am:* -ˌɑːpə-'tuːn] *adj* inoportuno, -a; (*inconvenient*) inconveniente

inordinate [ɪ'nɔːdɪnət, *Am:* -'nɔːr-] *adj* desmesurado, -a; **an ~ amount of sth** una cantidad excesiva de algo

inorganic [ˌɪnɔː'gænɪk, *Am:* -ɔːr'-] *adj* inorgánico, -a

in-patient ['ɪnpeɪʃnt] *n* paciente *mf* interno, -a

input ['ɪnpʊt] **I.** *n* **1.** (*contribution*) contribución *f,* aportación *f;* INFOR entrada *f;* **power ~** entrada (de potencia) **2.** *a.* FIN inversión *f* **II.** <-tt-> *vt* INFOR introducir; (*with a scanner*) entrar

input data *npl* INFOR datos *mpl* de entrada

input device *n* INFOR dispositivo *m* de entrada

inquest ['ɪnkwest] *n* **1.** LAW pesquisa *f* judicial; **to hold an ~ (into sth)** llevar a cabo una investigación (sobre algo) **2.** *fig* indagación *f;* **to hold an ~** realizar un análisis

inquire [ɪn'kwaɪəʳ, *Am:* -'kwaɪr] *Brit* **I.** *vi* **1.** (*ask*) preguntar; **to ~ for sb** preguntar por alguien; **to ~ about sth** pedir información sobre algo **2.** (*investigate*) investigar; **to ~ into a matter** indagar en un asunto **II.** *vt* preguntar; **to ~ the reason** preguntar por qué

inquiry [ɪn'kwaɪəri, *Am:* -'kwaɪri] *n Brit* **1.** (*question*) pregunta *f* **2.** (*investigation*) investigación *f*

inquisition [ˌɪnkwɪ'zɪʃən] *n* **1.** (*questioning*) investigación *f;* **to subject sb to an ~** someter a alguien a una investigación **2.** HIST **the Inquisition** la Inquisición

inquisitive [ɪn'kwɪzətɪv, *Am:* -ṯɪv] *adj* **1.** (*curious*) curioso, -a; (*look, face*) inquiridor(a); (*child*) preguntón, -ona; **to be ~ about sth/sb** sentir curiosidad sobre algo/alguien **2.** (*prying*) fisgón, -ona

inroad ['ɪnrəʊd, *Am:* -roʊd] *n* MIL incursión *f; fig* invasión *f;* **to make ~s into one's savings** mermar los ahorros de uno

inrush ['ɪnrʌʃ] <-es> *n* irrupción *f;* (*of people*) afluencia *f*

INS [ˌaɪen'es] *n abbr of* **International News**

Service servicio *m* internacional de noticias

insalubrious [ˌɪnsə'luːbrɪəs] *adj* (*unpleasant*) insalubre; (*unhealthy*) malsano, -a; (*dirty*) sucio, -a; **an ~ climate** un clima perjudicial para la salud

ins and outs *npl* pormenores *mpl*

insane [ɪn'seɪn] *adj* demente; *a. fig* (*crazy*) loco, -a; **to be/go ~** estar/volverse loco

insanitary [ɪn'sænɪtri, *Am:* -teri] *adj* antihigiénico, -a

insanity [ɪn'sænəti, *Am:* -t̬i] *n no pl* **1.** (*mental illness*) demencia *f* **2.** *a. fig* (*craziness*) locura *f*

insatiable [ɪn'seɪʃəbl] *adj* insaciable

inscribe [ɪn'skraɪb] *vt* inscribir; (*engrave*) grabar

inscription [ɪn'skrɪpʃən] *n* inscripción *f*; (*dedication*) dedicatoria *f*

inscrutable [ɪn'skruːtəbl, *Am:* -t̬ə-] *adj* (*look, smile*) enigmático, -a; (*person*) insondable

insect ['ɪnsekt] *n* insecto *m*; **~ bite** picadura *f* de insecto

insecticide [ɪn'sektɪsaɪd] *n* insecticida *m*

insecure [ˌɪnsɪ'kjʊəʳ, *Am:* -'kjʊr] *adj* inseguro, -a; (*future*) incierto, -a

insecurity [ˌɪnsɪ'kjʊərəti, *Am:* -'kjʊrət̬i] <-ies> *n* inseguridad *f*

inseminate [ɪn'semɪneɪt] *vt* inseminar

insemination [ɪnˌsemɪ'neɪʃən] *n no pl* inseminación *f*

insensible [ɪn'sensəbl] *adj form* **1.** (*unfeeling*) insensible; (*indifferent*) indiferente; **to be ~ to sth** ser indiferente a algo **2.** (*unaware*) inconsciente; **to be ~ of sth** no ser consciente de algo

insensitive [ɪn'sensətɪv, *Am:* -t̬ɪv] *adj* insensible; (*indifferent*) indiferente

inseparable [ɪn'seprəbl] *adj* inseparable, indisoluble

insert¹ ['ɪnsɜːt, *Am:* -sɜːrt] *n* **1.** (*page*) hoja *f* suelta **2.** (*piece*) material *m* insertado

insert² [ɪn'sɜːt, *Am:* -'sɜːrt] *vt* **1.** (*put into*) insertar; (*coins*) introducir **2.** (*add within a text*) intercalar; (*fill in*) añadir

insertion [ɪn'sɜːʃən, *Am:* -'sɜːr-] *n* **1.** *no pl* (*act of inserting*) inserción *f*; (*of coins*) introducción *f* **2.** (*thing inserted*) cosa *f* insertada **3.** (*in a newspaper*) publicación *f*

in-service ['ɪnsɜːvɪs, *Am:* -sɜːr-] *adj* en funcionamiento

inshore [ˌɪn'ʃɔːʳ, *Am:* -'ʃɔːr] I. *adj* cerca de la orilla; **~ waters** aguas *fpl* costeras II. *adv* hacia la costa

inside [ɪn'saɪd] I. *adj* **1.** (*internal*) interno, -a; **the ~ door** la puerta interior **2.** (*from within: information*) confidencial; **the robbery was an ~ job** el robo lo realizaron con ayuda de alguien de dentro **3.** AUTO **~ lane** carril *m* derecho; *Brit, Aus* carril *m* izquierdo **4.** (*inseam*) **~ leg** *Brit, Aus* entrepierna *f* II. *n* **1.** (*internal part or side*) interior *m*; **on the ~** por dentro; **to turn sth ~ out** volver algo del revés; **to**

turn the whole room **~ out** *fig* revolver toda la habitación; **to know a place ~ out** conocer muy bien un lugar; **to know the ~ of sth** conocer los entresijos de algo **2.** *pl, inf* (*entrails*) tripas *fpl* **3.** AUTO **to overtake on the ~** adelantar por la izquierda; *Brit, Aus* adelantar por la derecha III. *prep* **1.** (*within*) **~ (of)** dentro de; **to play ~ the house** jugar dentro de casa; **to go ~ the house** entrar en casa **2.** *inf* (*within time of*) **~ three days** en menos de tres días IV. *adv* **1.** (*within something*) dentro; **to go ~** entrar **2.** *inf* LAW en chirona, en el bote *Méx* **3.** (*internally*) internamente

insider [ɪn'saɪdəʳ, *Am:* 'ɪnˌsaɪdɚ] *n* persona *f* de la casa; (*with special knowledge*) persona *f* enterada

insidious [ɪn'sɪdɪəs] *adj* insidioso, -a; (*subversive*) subversivo, -a; **~ disease** enfermedad *f* maligna

insight ['ɪnsaɪt] *n* **1.** *no pl* (*capacity*) perspicacia *f* **2.** (*instance*) nueva percepción *f*; **to gain an ~ into sth/sb** entender mejor algo/a alguien; **the exhibition gave us an ~ into the 19th century** la exposición ha sido una revelación del siglo XIX

insignia [ɪn'sɪgnɪə] *n* insignia *f*

insignificance [ˌɪnsɪg'nɪfɪkəns] *n no pl* insignificancia *f*; **to fade into ~** hacerse insignificante

insignificant [ˌɪnsɪg'nɪfɪkənt] *adj* insignificante; (*trivial*) trivial

insincere [ˌɪnsɪn'sɪəʳ, *Am:* -'sɪr] *adj* poco sincero, -a

insinuate [ɪn'sɪnjueɪt] I. *vt* **1.** (*imply sth unpleasant*) insinuar **2.** (*manoeuvre*) introducir II. *vr* **to ~ oneself into** introducirse en

insinuation [ɪnˌsɪnjʊ'eɪʃən] *n* **1.** insinuación *f* **2.** (*hint*) indirecta *f*

insipid [ɪn'sɪpɪd] *adj* **1.** (*food, drink, entertainment*) insípido, -a **2.** (*person*) soso, -a

insist [ɪn'sɪst] I. *vi* insistir; **to ~ on doing sth** obstinarse en hacer algo; **if you ~** si insiste/si insistes II. *vt* **1.** (*state*) insistir **2.** (*demand*) exigir

insistence [ɪn'sɪstəns] *n no pl* insistencia *f*; **her ~ on ...** su insistencia en..; **to do sth at sb's ~** hacer algo por insistencia de alguien

insistent [ɪn'sɪstənt] *adj* insistente; **to be ~ (that) ...** insistir (en que)...

insofar as [ˌɪnsəʊ'fɑːr əz, *Am:* -soʊ'fɑːr əz] *adv form* en tanto que +*subj*

insole ['ɪnsəʊl, *Am:* -soʊl] *n* plantilla *f*

insolence ['ɪnsələns] *n no pl* insolencia *f*

insolent ['ɪnsələnt] *adj* insolente

insoluble [ɪn'sɒljʊbl, *Am:* -'sɑːljə-] *adj* insoluble

insolvency [ɪn'sɒlvəntsi, *Am:* -'sɑːl-] *n no pl* insolvencia *f*

insolvent [ɪn'sɒlvənt, *Am:* -'sɑːl-] I. *adj* insolvente II. *n* insolvente *mf*

insomnia [ɪn'sɒmnɪə, *Am:* -'sɑːm-] *n no pl* insomnio *m*; **to suffer from ~** padecer insomnio

insomniac [ɪn'sɒmnɪæk, *Am:* -'sɑːm-] *n* insomne *mf*

insomuch as [ˌɪnsəʊ'mʌtʃ, *Am:* -soʊ'-] *conj form* 1. (*because*) ya que 2. (*to the extent that*) en tanto que + *subj*

inspect [ɪn'spekt] *vt* 1. (*examine carefully*) inspeccionar 2. (*examine officially*) registrar; **to ~ the books** examinar los libros (de contabilidad) 3. MIL **to ~ the troops** pasar revista

inspection [ɪn'spekʃən] *n* inspección *f;* MIL revista *f*

inspector [ɪn'spektəʳ] *n* inspector(a) *m(f);* **school ~** inspector de enseñanza; **tax ~** inspector fiscal; **ticket ~** revisor(a) *m(f)*

inspiration [ˌɪnspə'reɪʃən] *n* 1. *a.* MED inspiración *f* 2. *no pl* (*source*) fuente *f* de inspiración; **to provide the ~ for sth** servir de inspiración para algo; **to lack ~** tener falta de inspiración

inspire [ɪn'spaɪəʳ, *Am:* -'spaɪr] *vt* 1. (*stimulate*) inspirar; **to ~ sb with hope** infundir esperanza a alguien 2. (*cause, lead to*) provocar

inspired *adj* inspirado, -a

instability [ˌɪnstə'bɪləti, *Am:* -ti] *n no pl* inestabilidad *f*

instal <-ll-> *Brit,* **install** [ɪn'stɔːl] I. *vt* 1. *a.* TECH, INFOR instalar 2. (*place*) colocar; **to ~ sb** colocar a alguien (en un cargo) II. *vr* **to ~ oneself** instalarse

installation [ˌɪnstə'leɪʃən] *n* instalación *f*

installment *n Am,* **instalment** [ɪn'stɔːlmənt] *n* 1. RADIO, TV entrega *f* 2. COM plazo *m;* **to pay (for sth) by ~s** pagar (algo) a plazos; **to be payable in monthly ~s** ser pagadero a plazos mensuales

instalment plan *n* compra *f* a plazos

instance ['ɪnstəns] I. *n* 1. (*case*) caso *m;* **in this ~** en este caso; **for ~** por ejemplo; **in the first ~** primero; **in the second ~** en segundo lugar 2. *form* (*request*) petición *f;* (*order*) pedido *m;* **to do sth at sb's ~** hacer algo a petición de alguien II. *vt* poner por caso

instant ['ɪnstənt] I. *n* instante *m,* momento *m;* **at the same ~** al mismo tiempo; **for an ~** por un momento; **in an ~** al instante; **to do sth this ~** hacer algo inmediatamente II. *adj* 1. (*immediate*) inmediato, -a 2. GASTR instantáneo, -a; **~ coffee** café *m* instantáneo; **~ soup** (*in bags*) sopa *f* de sobre; (*in tins*) sopa *f* en lata 3. *liter* (*urgent*) urgente

instantaneous [ˌɪnstən'teɪnɪəs] *adj* instantáneo, -a; (*effect, reaction*) inmediato, -a; (*spontaneous*) espontáneo, -a

instantaneously *adv* instantáneamente; (*spontaneously*) espontáneamente   ▾

instantly ['ɪnstəntli] *adv* al instante

instant replay *n* (*action replay*) repetición *f*

instead [ɪn'sted] I. *adv* en cambio, en lugar de eso II. *prep* **~ of** en vez de, en lugar de; **~ of him** en su lugar; **~ of doing sth** en lugar de hacer algo

instep ['ɪnstep] *n* 1. (*part of foot*) empeine *m*

2. (*part of shoe*) lengüeta *f*

instigate ['ɪnstɪɡeɪt] *vt* 1. (*initiate*) instigar 2. (*incite*) incitar

instigation [ˌɪnstɪ'ɡeɪʃən] *n no pl* instigación *f;* **to do sth at the ~ of sb** hacer algo a instigación de alguien

instil [ɪn'stɪl] <-ll-> *vt,* **instill** *vt Am* **to ~ sth (into sb)** infundir algo (a alguien); (*teach*) inculcar algo (a alguien)

instinct ['ɪnstɪŋkt] *n* instinto *m;* **to do sth by ~** hacer algo por instinto; **a business/political ~** instinto para los negocios/la política

instinctive [ɪn'stɪŋktɪv] *adj* instintivo, -a; (*innate*) innato, -a; (*without reflection*) irreflexivo, -a

institute ['ɪnstɪtjuːt, *Am:* -tuːt] I. *n* instituto *m;* (*of education*) escuela *f* II. *vt form* 1. (*establish: system, reform*) instituir 2. (*initiate: steps, measures*) iniciar; (*legal action*) emprender

institution [ˌɪnstɪ'tjuːʃən, *Am:* -'tuː-] *n* 1. (*act*) institución *f;* establecimiento *m* 2. (*society*) asociación *f* 3. (*home*) asilo *m* 4. *inf* (*person*) mito *m*

institutional [ˌɪnstɪ'tjuːʃənəl, *Am:* -'tuː-] *adj* institucional

institutionalise *vt Brit, Aus,* **institutionalize** [ˌɪnstɪ'tjuːʃənəlaɪz, *Am:* -'tuː-] *vt Am* institucionalizar; (*person*) ingresar

in-store [ˌɪn'stɔːʳ] *adj* en el establecimiento; **~ detective** detective *mf* del establecimiento

instruct [ɪn'strʌkt] *vt* 1. (*teach*) instruir 2. (*order*) ordenar; (*give instructions*) dar instrucciones; **to ~ sb (to do sth)** ordenar a alguien (hacer algo) 3. *Brit, Aus* LAW dar instrucciones

instruction [ɪn'strʌkʃən] *n* 1. *no pl* (*teaching*) instrucción *f;* **to give sb ~ in sth** enseñar algo a alguien 2. (*order*) orden *f;* **to give sb ~s** dar órdenes a alguien; **to act on ~s** actuar cumpliendo órdenes; **to carry out ~s** cumplir órdenes 3. *pl* (*information on method*) instrucciones *fpl*

instruction book *n* manual *m* de instrucciones **instruction leaflet** *n* folleto *m* de instrucciones **instruction manual** *n* manual *m* de instrucciones

instructive [ɪn'strʌktɪv] *adj* instructivo, -a

instructor [ɪn'strʌktəʳ, *Am:* -təʳ] *n* 1. (*teacher*) instructor(a) *m(f);* **driving ~** profesor(a) *m(f)* de autoescuela; **ski ~** profesor(a) *m(f)* de esquí 2. *Am* UNIV profesor(a) *m(f)*

instructress [ɪn'strʌktrɪs] *n* instructora *f*

instrument ['ɪnstrʊmənt, *Am:* -strə-] *n* 1. MUS instrumento *m* 2. (*tool*) herramienta *f* 3. LAW (*document*) documento *m*

instrumental [ˌɪnstrʊ'mentl, *Am:* -strə-'mentl] I. *adj* 1. MUS instrumental 2. (*greatly influencial*) **to be ~ to sth** contribuir materialmente a algo; **to be ~ in doing sth** jugar un papel clave en algo 3. (*relating to tools*)

herramental **II.** *n* MUS pieza *f* instrumental
instrumentation [ˌɪnstrʊmenˈteɪʃən, *Am:* -strə-] *n no pl* MUS instrumentación *f*
instrument board *n*, **instrument panel** *n* AUTO salpicadero *m;* AVIAT, NAUT cuadro *m* de mandos
insubordinate [ˌɪnsəˈbɔːdɪnət, *Am:* -ˈbɔːr-dənɪt] *adj* insubordinado, -a; ~ **behaviour** comportamiento *m* desobediente
insubstantial [ˌɪnsəbˈstænʃl] *adj* **1.** (*lacking substance*) insustancial **2.** (*lacking significance*) insignificante **3.** (*not real*) irreal
insufferable [ɪnˈsʌfrəbl] *adj* insufrible; (*person*) inaguantable; **to be** ~ ser inaguantable
insufficiency [ˌɪnsəˈfɪʃəntsi] <-ies> *n* insuficiencia *f*
insufficient [ˌɪnsəˈfɪʃənt] *adj* insuficiente
insular [ˈɪntsjələʳ, *Am:* -sələʳ] *adj* **1.** GEO insular **2.** (*person*) de miras estrechas
insularity [ˌɪntsjˈlærəti, *Am:* -səˈleɪrət̬i] *n no pl* **1.** GEO insularidad *f* **2.** (*of person*) estrechez *f* de miras
insulate [ˈɪntsjəleɪt, *Am:* -sə-] *vt* aislar; **to ~ sth (against sth)** aislar algo (de algo)
insulating [ˈɪnsjʊleɪtɪŋ, *Am:* -t̬ɪŋ] *adj* aislante; (*protective*) protector(a)
insulating tape *n Brit* cinta aislante [*o* aisladora]
insulation [ˌɪntsjəˈleɪʃən, *Am:* -sə'-] *n no pl* aislamiento *m*
insulin [ˈɪntsjʊlɪn, *Am:* -sə-] *n no pl* insulina *f*
insult [ˈɪnsʌlt] **I.** *vt* insultar **II.** *n* insulto *m*, insultada *f AmL* ▶**to add** ~ **to injury** ... y por si fuera poco...
insuperable [ɪnˈsjuːprəbl, *Am:* -ˈsuː-] *adj* insuperable
insupportable [ˌɪnsəˈpɔːtəbl, *Am:* -ˈpɔːr-t̬ə-] *adj form* insoportable
insurance [ɪnˈʃʊərəns, *Am:* -ˈʃʊrəns] *n no pl* **1.** (*financial protection*) seguro *m;* **life** ~ seguro de vida; **to have ~ (against sth)** tener un seguro (contra algo); **to take out ~ (against sth)** hacerse un seguro (contra algo) **2.** (*payment*) indemnización *f;* (*premium*) prima *f* de seguro **3.** (*measure*) medida *f* preventiva
insurance agent *n* agente *mf* de seguros **insurance broker** *n* corredor(a) *m(f)* de seguros **insurance company** <-ies> *n* compañía *f* de seguros **insurance cover** *n no pl* condiciones *fpl* que cubre el seguro **insurance policy** <-ies> *n* póliza *f* de seguros **insurance premium** *n* prima *f* de seguros
insure [ɪnˈʃʊəʳ, *Am:* -ˈʃʊr] *vt* asegurar
insured [ɪnˈʃʊəd, *Am:* -ˈʃʊrd] **I.** *adj* asegurado, -a **II.** *n* **the** ~ el asegurado, la asegurada
insurer [ɪnˈʃʊərəʳ, *Am:* -ˈʃʊrəʳ] *n* **1.** (*agent*) asegurador(a) *m(f)* **2.** (*company*) aseguradora *f*
insurmountable [ˌɪnsəˈmaʊntəbl, *Am:* -səʳˈmaʊnt̬ə-] *adj* insuperable
insurrection [ˌɪnsəˈrekʃən, *Am:* -səˈrek-] *n* insurrección *f;* **to crush the** ~ acabar con la

sublevación
intact [ɪnˈtækt] *adj* intacto, -a
intake [ˈɪnteɪk] *n* **1.** (*action of taking in*) toma *f;* (*of air, water*) entrada *f;* ~ **of breath** aspiración *f* **2.** (*amount taken in*) consumo *m;* **the recommended daily** ~ **of fibre** la cantidad diaria recomendada de fibra; **food** ~ ración *f* **3.** (*quantity of people*) número *m* de personas admitidas; **the college has increased its** ~ **of students** ha aumentado el número de estudiantes admitidos en la universidad **4.** MIL reemplazo *m* **5.** TECH (*mechanical aperture*) toma *f*
intangible [ɪnˈtændʒəbl] **I.** *adj* intangible; ~ **assets** activos *mpl* inmateriales **II.** *n* cosa *f* intangible
integer [ˈɪntɪdʒəʳ, *Am:* -dʒɚ] *n* MAT número *m* entero
integral [ˈɪntɪgrəl, *Am:* -t̬ə-] *adj* **1.** (*part of the whole*) integrante **2.** (*central, essential*) esencial; **to be** ~ **to sth/sb** ser de vital importancia para algo/alguien **3.** (*complete*) integral **4.** (*built into unit*) incorporado, -a; **the prison has no** ~ **sanitation** la cárcel no dispone de instalaciones de saneamiento **5.** MAT ~ **calculus** cálculo *m* integral
integrate [ˈɪntɪgreɪt, *Am:* -t̬ə-] **I.** *vt* (*cause to merge socially*) **to** ~ **sb/sth into sth** integrar a alguien/algo en algo; **to** ~ **oneself into sth** integrarse en algo; **to** ~ **learning with play** mezclar el aprendizaje y los juegos **II.** *vi* integrarse
integrated [ˈɪntɪgreɪtɪd, *Am:* -t̬ɪd] *adj* **1.** (*coordinating different elements*) integrado, -a **2.** (*with different ethnic groups*) ~ **school** escuela *f* no segregacionista
integration [ˌɪntɪˈgreɪʃən, *Am:* -t̬ə'-] *n no pl* **1.** *a.* MAT integración *f* **2.** (*unification, fusion*) unificación *f*
integrity [ɪnˈtegrəti, *Am:* -t̬i] *n no pl* **1.** (*incorruptibility, uprightness*) integridad *f;* **man of** ~ hombre *m* íntegro; **artistic/professional** ~ coherencia *f* artística/profesional **2.** *form* (*unity, wholeness*) totalidad *f*
intellect [ˈɪntəlekt, *Am:* -t̬ə-] *n no pl* **1.** (*faculty*) intelecto *m;* **a man/woman of** ~ un hombre/una mujer de gran inteligencia; **powers of** ~ capacidad *f* intelectual **2.** (*thinker, intellectual*) intelectual *mf*
intellectual [ˌɪntəˈlektʃʊəl, *Am:* -t̬ə-] **I.** *n* intelectual *mf* **II.** *adj* intelectual
intelligence [ɪnˈtelɪdʒəns] *n no pl* inteligencia *f;* ~ **agent** agente *mf* secreto, -a; **artificial** ~ inteligencia artificial; **the** ~ **community** los agentes de los servicios secretos; ~ **sources** fuentes *fpl* del servicio de inteligencia
intelligence quotient *n* coeficiente *m* de inteligencia **intelligence service** *n* MIL, POL servicio *m* de inteligencia **intelligence test** *n* test *m* de inteligencia
intelligent [ɪnˈtelɪdʒənt] *adj* inteligente
intelligentsia [ɪnˌtelɪˈdʒentsɪə] *n* **the** ~ la intelectualidad

intelligible [ɪn'telɪdʒəbl] *adj* inteligible; **this text is hardly** ~ este texto es muy difícil de entender

intend [ɪn'tend] *vt* 1.(*aim for, plan*) pretender; **to** ~ **doing sth** querer hacer algo; **to** ~ **to do sth** tener la intención de hacer algo; **I'm sure that remark was** ~**ed for me** estoy convencido de que el comentario iba dirigido a mí; **I** ~**ed no harm** no quería hacer daño 2.(*mean*) querer decir 3.(*earmark, destine*) **to be** ~**ed for sth** estar destinado a algo; **to be** ~**ed to do sth** estar destinado a hacer algo; **this film is not** ~**ed for children** esta película no es para niños

intended [ɪn'tendɪd] I. *adj* 1.(*planned, intentional*) intencional; (*sought*) deseado, -a 2.(*husband, wife*) futuro, -a II. *n inf* prometido, -a *m, f*

intense [ɪn'tents] *adj* 1.(*acute, concentrated, forceful*) intenso, -a; (*desire*) ardiente; (*feeling, hatred, friendship*) profundo, -a; (*interest*) sumo, -a; (*love*) apasionado, -a; (*pain, pressure, wind*) fuerte 2.(*demanding*) nervioso, -a

intensify [ɪn'tentsɪfaɪ] <-ie-> I. *vt* intensificar; (*joy, sadness*) aumentar; (*pain*) agudizar II. *vi* intensificarse; (*joy, sadness*) aumentar; (*pain*) agudizarse

intensity [ɪn'tentsəti, *Am:* -ţi] *n no pl* intensidad *f*

intensive [ɪn'tentsɪv] *adj* intensivo, -a **intensive care** *n* cuidados *mpl* intensivos

intent [ɪn'tent] I. *n* propósito *m*; **a declaration of** ~ una declaración de intenciones; **to all** ~**s and purposes** prácticamente; **with** ~ **to** con el objeto de; **with good/evil** ~ con buenas/malas intenciones II. *adj* 1.(*absorbed, concentrated, occupied*) abstraído, -a; (*look*) atento, -a; **to be** ~ **on sth** estar concentrado en algo 2.(*decided, set*) decidido, -a; **to be/ seem** ~ **on doing sth** estar/parecer resuelto a hacer algo

intention [ɪn'tentʃən] *n* intención *f*; **it is my** ~ **to …** tengo la intención de…; **to have no** ~ **of doing sth** no tener ninguna intención de hacer algo; **with the best of** ~**s** con la mejor intención

intentional [ɪn'tentʃənəl] *adj* intencional; (*insult*) deliberado, -a

interact [ˌɪntər'ækt, *Am:* ɪnţɚ'ækt] *vi* interaccionar

interaction [ˌɪntər'ækʃən, *Am:* -ţɚ'-] *n* interacción *f*; **non-verbal** ~ comunicación *f* no verbal

interactive [ˌɪntər'æktɪv, *Am:* -ţɚ'æk-] *adj* interactivo, -a

interactive TV [ˌɪntəræktɪvti:'vi:, *Am:* -ţɚ-] *n no pl* televisión *f* interactiva

interbreed [ˌɪntə'briːd, *Am:* -ţɚ'-] *irr* I. *vt* cruzar II. *vi* cruzarse

intercede [ˌɪntə'siːd, *Am:* -ţɚ'-] *vi* interceder; **to** ~ **for/on behalf of sb** interceder por/en nombre de alguien

intercept [ˌɪntə'sept, *Am:* -ţɚ'-] *vt* interceptar; MAT cortar; **to** ~ **sb** cerrar el paso a alguien

interception [ˌɪntə'sepʃən, *Am:* -ţɚ'-] *n* interceptación *f*; MAT intersección *f*

interceptor [ˌɪntə'septəʳ, *Am:* -ţɚ'septɚ] *n* MIL interceptador(a) *m(f)*

intercession [ˌɪntə'seʃən, *Am:* -ţɚ'-] *n* intercesión *f*; **through the** ~ **of sb/sth** gracias a la intercesión de alguien/algo; **the** ~ **of human rights organisations** la mediación de organizaciones pro derechos humanos

interchange [ˌɪntə'tʃeɪndʒ, *Am:* -ţɚ-] I. *n* 1.*form* intercambio *m*; ~ **of ideas** cambio *m* de impresiones 2.*Brit* (*of roads*) enlace *m* II. *vt* intercambiar; **to** ~ **letters** cartearse

interchangeable [ˌɪntə'tʃeɪndʒəbl, *Am:* -ţɚ-] *adj* intercambiable

intercity [ˌɪntə'sɪti] <-ies> *Brit* I. *n* tren *m* interurbano II. *adj* interurbano, -a

intercom ['ɪntəkɒm, *Am:* -ţɚkɑːm] *n* (*on a plane or ship*) intercomunicador *m*; (*on a building*) portero *m* automático; **through (an)** ~ por el interfono; **to speak over the** ~ hablar por el portero automático

intercommunicate [ˌɪntəkə'mjuːnɪkeɪt, *Am:* -ţɚ-] *vi* comunicarse

intercontinental [ˌɪntəˌkɒntɪ'nentl, *Am:* -ţɚˌkɑːntə'nenţl] *adj* intercontinental; ~ **flight** vuelo *m* intercontinental

intercourse ['ɪntəkɔːs, *Am:* -ţɚkɔːrs] *n no pl* 1.**sexual** ~ contacto *m* sexual; **to have sexual** ~ **with sb** tener relaciones sexuales con alguien 2.*form* **social** ~ trato *m* social; **commercial** ~ relaciones *fpl* comerciales

interdenominational [ˌɪntə dɪˌnɒmɪ'neɪʃnl, *Am:* -ţɚdɪˌnɑ:məˈ-] *adj* interconfesional

interdepartmental ['ɪntəˌdiːpɑ:t'mentl, *Am:* -ţɚˌdi:pɑ:rt'menţl] *adj* interdepartamental

interdependence [ˌɪntədɪ'pendəns, *Am:* -ţɚdi:'-] *n no pl* interdependencia *f*

interdependent [ˌɪntə dɪ'pendənt, *Am:* -ţɚdi:'-] *adj* interdependiente

interdict [ˌɪntə'dɪkt, *Am:* -ţɚ-] *n Scot* LAW interdicto *m*

interest ['ɪntrəst, *Am:* -trɪst] I. *n* 1.(*hobby*) interés *m*; **to take an** ~ **in sth** interesarse por algo 2.*no pl* (*curiosity*) **just out of** ~ *inf* por curiosidad; **to lose** ~ **in sb/sth** perder el interés por alguien/algo; **to take no further** ~ **in sth** dejar de interesarse por algo 3.*pl* (*profit, advantage*) beneficio *m*; **a conflict of** ~**s** un conflicto de intereses; **to look after the** ~**s of sb** velar por los intereses de alguien; **to pursue one's own** ~**s** perseguir los intereses de uno; **in the** ~ **of liberty** en pro de la libertad; **it's in your own** ~ **to do it** te conviene hacerlo por tu propio interés 4.*no pl* (*power to excite attentiveness*) interés *m*; **to be of** ~ **for sb** interesar a alguien; **this might be of** ~ **to you** esto puede interesarte; **this is of no** ~ **to me** eso no me interesa 5.*no pl* FIN interés *m*; ~ **rate** tipo *m* de interés; **at 5 %** ~ con un interés del 5 %; **to bear** ~ devengar interés; **to earn/ pay** ~ **on sth** percibir/pagar intereses por algo; **to pay back with** ~ pagar con intereses; *fig* pagar con creces **6.** (*legal right*) participación *f;* **to have an** ~ **in sth** tener una participación en algo; **to have a controlling** ~ **in a firm** tener una participación mayoritaria en una empresa; **business** ~**s** negocios *mpl;* **the chemicals** ~**s** la industria química; **vested** ~**s** intereses *mpl* creados **II.** *vt* interesar; **may I** ~ **you in this encyclopaedia?** ¿puedo mostrarle esta enciclopedia?

interested ['ɪntrəstɪd, *Am:* -trɪst-] *adj* interesado, -a; **to be** ~ **in sth/sb** estar interesado en algo/alguien; **I am** ~ **to know more about it** me interesaría saber más sobre eso; **the** ~ **parties** las partes interesadas

interest-free *adj* FIN sin intereses

interesting ['ɪntrəs'tɪŋ] *adj* interesante; **it is** ~ **to do sth** resulta interesante hacer algo

interface ['ɪntəfeɪs, *Am:* -t̬ə-] I. *n* **1.** (*point of contact*) punto *m* de contacto **2.** PHYS superficie *f* de contacto **3.** INFOR interfaz *f;* **user** ~ interfaz de usuario; **graphic/parallel/serial** ~ interfaz gráfica/en paralelo/en serie **II.** *vi* INFOR **to** ~ **with sth** funcionar conjuntamente con algo **III.** *vt* INFOR conectar

interfere [ˌɪntə'fɪəʳ, *Am:* -t̬ə'fɪr] *vi* **1.** (*become involved*) interferir; **to** ~ **between two people** entrometerse entre dos personas; **to** ~ **in sth** inmiscuirse en algo **2.** (*disturb*) molestar **3.** (*touch*) tocar; **someone has been interfering with my papers** alguien ha estado revolviendo mis papeles **4.** RADIO, TECH (*hamper signals*) producir interferencias **5.** *Brit* (*molest children*) **to** ~ **with** abusar de

interference [ˌɪntə'fɪərəns, *Am:* -t̬ə'fɪr-] *n no pl* **1.** intromisión *f* **2.** RADIO, TECH interferencia *f*

interim ['ɪntərɪm, *Am:* -t̬ə-] I. *n no pl* ínterin *m* II. *adj* provisional; (*payment*) a cuenta; ~ **dividend** FIN dividendo *m* a cuenta

interior [ɪn'tɪərɪəʳ, *Am:* -'tɪrɪə-] I. *adj* **1.** (*inner, inside, internal*) interno, -a; (*light*) interior; **the** ~ **market** el mercado interior **2.** (*central, inland, remote*) del interior **II.** *n* **1.** (*inside*) interior *m;* **the** ~ **of the country** el interior del país **2.** POL (*home affairs*) **the Ministry of the Interior** el Ministerio de Interior; **the U.S. Interior Department** el departamento de Interior de los Estados Unidos

interior decoration *n no pl* interiorismo *m*

interior designer *n* interiorista *mf*

interject [ˌɪntə'dʒekt, *Am:* -t̬ə-] *vt form* interponer; **to** ~ **a few remarks** hacer algunos comentarios

interjection [ˌɪntə'dʒekʃən, *Am:* -t̬ə-] *n* **1.** *form* (*verbal interruption*) exclamación *f;* ~**s from the audience** interrupciones *fpl* del público **2.** LING interjección *f*

interlace [ˌɪntə'leɪs, *Am:* -t̬ə-] I. *vt* entrelazar II. *vi* entrelazarse

inter-library loan [ˌɪntə'laɪbrərɪˌləʊn] *n*

préstamo *m* interbibliotecario

interlocutor [ˌɪntə'lɒkjʊtəʳ, *Am:* -t̬ə'laː-kjət̬ə·] *n form* interlocutor(a) *m(f)*

interloper ['ɪntələʊpəʳ, *Am:* -t̬ə·loupə·] *n* intruso, -a *m, f*

interlude ['ɪntəluːd, *Am:* -t̬əluːd] *n* **1.** (*interval*) intervalo *m* **2.** THEAT (*intermission*) entreacto *m;* (*short play*) entremés *m* **3.** MUS interludio *m*

intermarry [ˌɪntə'mæri, *Am:* 'ɪntə·ˌmer-] <-ie-> *vi* (*marry between groups*) casarse (personas de diferentes razas, grupos, clases, etc.); (*marry within family*) casarse (entre sí)

intermediary [ˌɪntə'miːdɪəri, *Am:* -t̬ə-'miːdɪr-] I. *adj* (*between persons*) intermediario, -a; (*intermediate*) intermedio, -a II. <-ies> *n* intermediario, -a *m, f*

intermediate [ˌɪntə'miːdɪət, *Am:* -t̬ə-] I. *adj* intermedio, -a; ~ **course** curso *m* de nivel intermedio; ~ **students** estudiantes *mpl* de ciclo medio; ~ **memory** INFOR memoria *f* intermedia II. *n* intermediario, -a *m, f*

intermezzo [ˌɪntə'metsəʊ, *Am:* -t̬ə'met-soʊ] <-s *o* -zi> *n* MUS intermezzo *m*

interminable [ɪn'tɜːmɪnəbl, *Am:* -'tɜːr-] *adj* interminable

intermission [ˌɪntə'mɪʃən, *Am:* -t̬ə-] *n* **1.** intermedio *m;* **without** ~ sin pausa **2.** CINE, THEAT descanso *m*

intermittent [ˌɪntə'mɪtnt, *Am:* -t̬ə-] *adj* intermitente; ~ **fever** fiebre *f* recurrente

intern¹ ['ɪntɜːn, *Am:* -tɜːrn] *n Am* estudiante *mf* en prácticas; **hospital** ~ médico *m* asistente; **she worked in the Washington Post as a summer** ~ durante el verano estuvo haciendo prácticas en el Washington Post

intern² [ɪn'tɜːn, *Am:* -'tɜːrn] I. *vt* recluir II. *vi* MED trabajar como interno, -a; SCHOOL hacer (las) prácticas

internal [ɪn'tɜːnl, *Am:* -'tɜːr-] *adj a.* MED interno, -a; (*trade*) interior; **Internal Revenue Service** *Am* Hacienda *f;* **for** ~ **use only** sólo para uso interno

international [ˌɪntə'næʃnəl, *Am:* -t̬ə-] I. *adj a.* LAW internacional; (*trade*) exterior II. *n* **1.** *Brit* SPORTS (*sb on national team*) internacional *mf;* (*sports match*) partido *m* internacional **2.** POL Internacional *f*

International Court of Justice *n* Tribunal *m* Internacional de Justicia **international date line** *n* línea *f* de (cambio de) fecha

internationalise *vt Aus, Brit,* **internationalize** [ˌɪntə'næʃənəlaɪz, *Am:* -t̬ə·-] *vt* internacionalizar

International Monetary Fund *n* Fondo *m* Monetario Internacional **International Olympic Committee** *n* Comité *m* Olímpico Internacional

internecine war [ɪntə'niːsaɪnˌwɔːʳ, *Am:* -t̬ə·'niːsɪn-] *n* guerra *f* de aniquilación recíproca

internee [ˌɪntɜː'niː, *Am:* -tɜːr-] *n* interno, -a

m, f

Internet ['ɪntənet, *Am:* -t̬ə-] *n* INFOR internet *f;* **to access the** ~ entrar en internet; **to do business over the** ~ hacer negocios a través de internet

Internet access *n* acceso *m* a internet

Internet-based learning *n no pl* aprendizaje *m* por Internet [*o* en línea] **Internet café** *n* ciber café *m* **Internet search engine** *n* motor *m* de búsqueda en la red **Internet user** *n* internauta *mf*

internist [ɪn't3ːnɪst, *Am:* -'t3ːr-] *n Am* internista *mf*

internment [ɪn't3ːnmənt, *Am:* -'t3ːrn-] *n no pl* internamiento *m*

internment camp *n* campo *m* de internamiento

interpellation [ɪn,t3ːpə'leɪʃən, *Am:* -,t3ːr-] *n* POL interpelación *f*

interphone ['ɪntəfəʊn] *n Am s.* **intercom**

interplanetary [,ɪntə'plænɪtəri, *Am:* -t̬ə-'plænət̬ər-] *adj* interplanetario, -a

interplay ['ɪntəpleɪ, *Am:* -t̬ə-] *n no pl* interacción *f*

Interpol ['ɪntəppl, *Am:* -t̬əpɑːl] *n abbr of* **International Criminal Police Commission** Interpol *f*

interpolate [ɪn't3ːpəleɪt, *Am:* -'t3ːr-] *vt* interpolar; **to** ~ **a text** introducir interpolaciones en un texto; **"that happened in Rome, not in Paris!" Sam** ~**d** *liter* "¡eso ocurrió en Roma, no en París!", puntualizó Sam

interpolation [ɪn,t3ːpə'leɪʃən, *Am:* -,t3ːr-] *n* interpolación *f*

interpret [ɪn't3ːprɪt, *Am:* -'t3ːrprət] I. *vt* 1. (*decode, construe*) interpretar 2. (*translate*) traducir II. *vi* interpretar; **to** ~ **from English into Spanish** interpretar del inglés al español

interpretation [ɪn,t3ːprɪ'teɪʃən, *Am:* -,t3ːrprə'-] *n* interpretación *f;* **to put an** ~ **on sth** interpretar algo; **the rules are open to** ~ las normas pueden interpretarse de varias formas

interpreter [ɪn't3ːprɪtə', *Am:* -'t3ːrprət̬ə-] *n* 1. MUS, THEAT, LING intérprete *mf* 2. INFOR intérprete *m*

interpreting [ɪn't3ːprɪtɪŋ, *Am:* -'t3ːrprət-] *n no pl* interpretación *f*

inter-rail ['ɪntəreɪl] *adj* inter-raíl; ~ **ticket** billete *m* inter-raíl

interrelate [,ɪntərɪ'leɪt, *Am:* -t̬ərɪ-] *vi* interrelacionarse; **to** ~ **with each other** relacionarse entre sí

interrogate [ɪn'terəgeɪt] *vt* interrogar

interrogation [ɪn,terə'geɪʃən] *n* 1. *a.* INFOR interrogación *f* 2. LAW interrogatorio *m;* **police** ~ interrogatorio policial; ~ **room** sala *f* de interrogatorios

interrogation mark *n,* **interrogation point** *n* interrogante *m*

interrogative [,ɪntə'rɒgətɪv, *Am:* -t̬ə'rɑː-gət̬ɪv] I. *n* LING (*word*) palabra *f* interrogativa; (*sentence*) oración *f* interrogativa II. *adj* 1. *liter* (*having questioning form*) interrogador(a) 2. LING interrogativo, -a

interrogator [ɪn'terəgeɪtə', *Am:* -t̬ə'rɑː-gət̬ɔːr] *n* interrogador(a) *m(f)*

interrogatory [,ɪntə'rɒgətəri, *Am:* -t̬ə'rɑː-gət̬ɔːr-] I. *adj* interrogador(a) II. <-ies> *n* interrogatorio *m*

interrupt [,ɪntə'rʌpt, *Am:* -t̬ə-] *vi, vt* interrumpir

interrupter [,ɪntə'rʌptə', *Am:* -t̬ə-'rʌptə-] *n* ELEC interruptor *m*

interruption [,ɪntə'rʌpʃən, *Am:* -t̬ə-] *n* interrupción *f;* **without** ~ sin interrupciones

intersect [,ɪntə'sekt] I. *vt* (*cross at a junction*) cruzar; (*lines*) cortar II. *vi* 1. (*cut, divide*) intersecarse *form;* (*cross at a junction*) cruzarse; ~**ing roads** carreteras *fpl* que se cruzan 2. MAT (*sets*) formar intersección

intersection [,ɪntə'sekʃən] *n* 1. (*crossing of lines*) intersección *f* 2. *Am, Aus* (*junction*) cruce *m*

intersperse [,ɪntə'sp3ːs, *Am:* -t̬ə-'sp3ːrs] *vt* intercalar; **to** ~ **sth with sth** intercalar algo en algo; **to** ~ **sth between sth** esparcir algo entre algo; **to** ~ **anecdotes throughout a speech** salpicar un discurso de anécdotas

interstate [,ɪntə'steɪt, *Am:* 'ɪntə-] *adj Am* interestatal

interstate highway *n* autopista *f* interestatal **interstate trade** *n* comercio *m* entre estados

interstellar [,ɪntə'stelə', *Am:* -t̬ə'stelə-] *adj form* interestelar

interstice [ɪn't3ːstɪs, *Am:* -'t3ːr-] *n form* intersticio *m*

intertwine [,ɪntə'twaɪn, *Am:* -t̬ə-] I. *vt* entrelazar II. *vi* (*flowers, hands*) entrelazarse; (*paths*) entrecruzarse

interurban [,ɪntə'3ːbən, *Am:* -t̬ə'3ːr-] *adj Am* interurbano, -a

interval ['ɪntəvl, *Am:* -t̬ə-] *n* 1. *a.* MUS intervalo *m;* **at** ~**s of five minutes** a intervalos de cinco minutos; **at five-centimetre** ~**s** con espacios de cinco centímetros; **at regular** ~**s** a intervalos regulares; **at** ~**s** de vez en cuando; **sunny** ~**s** METEO claros *mpl* 2. THEAT, MUS entreacto *m;* SPORTS descanso *m*

intervene [,ɪntə'viːn, *Am:* -t̬ə-] *vi* 1. (*involve oneself to help*) intervenir; **to** ~ **militarily/ personally** intervenir militarmente/personalmente; **to** ~ **on sb's behalf** interceder por alguien 2. (*meddle unhelpfully*) **to** ~ **in sth** mezclarse en algo 3. (*come to pass between*) sobrevenir; **six months** ~**d before the opening of the swimming-pool** transcurrieron seis meses antes de la inauguración de la piscina

intervening *adj* **in the** ~ **period** en el ínterin; **in the** ~ **days** en los días intermedios

intervention [,ɪntə'venʃən, *Am:* -t̬ə-] *n* intervención *f;* **military** ~ MIL intervención militar; ~ **price** ECON precio *m* de intervención

interventionist [ˌɪntəˈvenʃənɪst, *Am:* -t̬ɚˈ-] **I.** *n* POL, ECON intervencionista *mf* **II.** *adj* intervencionista

interview [ˈɪntəvjuː, *Am:* -t̬ɚ-] **I.** *n* **1.** *(formal conversation)* entrevista *f;* **telephone ~** encuesta *f* telefónica; **to have a job ~** tener una entrevista de trabajo; **to give an ~** conceder una entrevista **2.** *Brit* LAW interrogatorio *m* **II.** *vt* **1.** entrevistar; **to ~ sb on sth** encuestar a alguien sobre algo **2.** *Brit* LAW interrogar

interviewee [ˌɪntəvjuːˈiː, *Am:* -t̬ɚ-] *n* entrevistado, -a *m, f*

interviewer [ˈɪntəvjuːəʳ, *Am:* -t̬ɚvjuːɚ] *n* entrevistador(a) *m(f)*

interweave [ˌɪntəˈwiːv, *Am:* -t̬ɚ-] *irr* **I.** *vt* entretejer; **to be interwoven with sth** estar estrechamente unido a algo **II.** *vi* *(threads)* entretejerse; *(paths)* entrecruzarse

intestate [ɪnˈtesteɪt] *adj* intestado, -a

intestine [ɪnˈtestɪn] *n* intestino *m*

intimacy [ˈɪntɪməsi, *Am:* -t̬ə-] <-ies> *n* **1.** *no pl* *(familiarity)* intimidad *f;* **to be in terms of ~ with sb** tener intimidad con alguien **2.** *no pl* *(sexual relations)* relaciones *fpl* íntimas **3.** *pl* *(transactions)* gestos *mpl* de complicidad

intimate¹ [ˈɪntɪmət, *Am:* -t̬ə-] **I.** *adj* **1.** *(close, sexual)* íntimo, -a; **~ relationship** relaciones *fpl* íntimas; **to be on ~ terms with sb** tener intimidad con alguien; **to become ~ with sb** intimar con alguien; **to be ~ with sb** tener relaciones sexuales con alguien **2.** *(personal: style)* personal **3.** *(very detailed: knowledge)* profundo, -a; *(link)* estrecho, -a **II.** *n* amigo, -a *m, f* íntimo, -a

intimate² [ˈɪntɪmeɪt, *Am:* -t̬ə-] *vt form* insinuar; **to ~ to sb (that)** ... dar a entender a alguien (que)...

intimation [ˌɪntɪˈmeɪʃən, *Am:* -t̬ə-] *n form* *(hint)* insinuación *f;* *(sign)* indicación *f;* **~s** indicios *mpl*

intimidate [ɪnˈtɪmɪdeɪt] *vt* intimidar; **to ~ sb into doing sth** coaccionar a alguien para que haga algo

intimidating *adj* intimidante

intimidation [ɪnˌtɪmɪˈdeɪʃən] *n no pl* intimidación *f*

into [ˈɪntʊ, *Am:* -t̬ə] *prep* **1.** *(to the inside of)* en; *(towards)* hacia; **to walk ~ a place** entrar en un sitio; **to get ~ bed** meterse en la cama; **shall we walk ~ the garden?** ¿vamos a pasear al jardín? **the future** hacia el futuro **2.** *(indicating an extent in time or space)* **deep ~ the forest** en lo más profundo del bosque; **to work late ~ the evening** trabajar hasta tarde **3.** *(against)* contra; **to drive ~ a tree** chocar contra un árbol; **to bump ~ a friend** tropezar con un amigo **4.** *(to the state or condition of)* **to burst ~ tears** echarse a llorar; **to grow ~ a woman** convertirse en una mujer; **to translate from Spanish ~ English** traducir del español al inglés; **to turn sth ~ sth** convertir algo en algo **5.** *inf* *(interested in)*

she's really ~ her new job está entusiasmada con su nuevo trabajo; **I think they are ~ drugs** creo que andan metidos en drogas **6.** MAT **two ~ ten equals five** diez entre dos es igual a cinco; **two goes ~ five two and a half times** cinco dividido entre dos es igual a dos y medio

intolerable [ɪnˈtɒlərəbl, *Am:* -ˈtɑːlə-] *adj* intolerable

intolerance [ɪnˈtɒlərəns, *Am:* -ˈtɑːlə-] *n no pl* intolerancia *f*

intolerant [ɪnˈtɒlərənt, *Am:* -ˈtɑːlə-] *adj* intolerante; **to be ~ of different opinions** ser intolerante con las opiniones diferentes; **to be ~ of sb** ser intransigente con alguien; **to be ~ of alcohol** MED no tolerar el alcohol

intonation [ˌɪntəˈneɪʃən, *Am:* -toʊˈ-] *n* LING, MUS entonación *f*

intone [ɪnˈtəʊn, *Am:* -ˈtoʊn] *vt form* **1.** *(sing)* entonar **2.** *(say solemnly)* recitar

intoxicant [ɪnˈtɒksɪkənt, *Am:* -ˈtɑːk-] *n* MED *(alcohol)* bebida *f* alcohólica; *(drug)* estupefaciente *m*

intoxicate [ɪnˈtɒksɪkeɪt, *Am:* -ˈtɑːk-] **I.** *vt* **1.** *a. fig* *(induce inebriation)* embriagar **2.** MED intoxicar **II.** *vi* **1.** *a. fig* *(cause intoxication)* embriagar **2.** MED intoxicar

intoxicating [ɪnˈtɒksɪkeɪtɪŋ, *Am:* -ˈtɑːksɪkeɪt̬ɪŋ] *adj* **1.** *(exhilarating, stimulating)* embriagador(a) **2.** *(substance)* estupefaciente; *(causing drunkenness)* alcohólico, -a; **~ drink** bebida *f* alcohólica

intoxication [ɪnˌtɒksɪˈkeɪʃən, *Am:* -ˌtɑːksɪ-] *n no pl* **1.** *a. fig* *(drunkenness)* embriaguez *f;* **in a state of ~** en estado de embriaguez **2.** MED intoxicación *f*

intractable [ˌɪnˈtræktəbl] *adj form* **1.** *(temperament)* obstinado, -a; **an ~ pupil** un alumno incorregible **2.** *(problem)* insoluble; **an ~ situation** una situación difícil de resolver **3.** MED incurable

intracutaneous [ɪntrækjuːˈteɪnəs] *adj* intracutáneo, -a

intramural [ˌɪntrəˈmjʊərəl, *Am:* -ˈmjʊrəl] *adj* **1.** *(within a city or institution)* intramuros *inv* **2.** SCHOOL dentro de la escuela; UNIV dentro de la universidad; **~ contest** campeonato *m* de la escuela/universidad

Intranet [ˌɪntrəˈnet] *n* intranet *f*

intransigence [ɪnˈtrænsɪdʒəns, *Am:* -sə-] *n no pl, form* intransigencia *f*

intransigent [ɪnˈtrænsɪdʒənt, *Am:* -sə-] *adj form* intransigente

intransitive [ɪnˈtrænsətɪv, *Am:* -t̬ɪv] *adj* LING, MAT intransitivo, -a

intrauterine [ˌɪntrəˈjuːtəraɪn, *Am:* -t̬ɚɪn] *adj* MED intrauterino, -a

intravenous [ˌɪntrəˈviːnəs] *adj* MED intravenoso, -a; **~ feeding** alimentación *f* por vía intravenosa

in-tray [ˈɪntreɪ] *n* bandeja *f* de entrada

intrepid [ɪnˈtrepɪd] *adj* intrépido, -a

intricacy [ˈɪntrɪkəsi] <-ies> *n* complejidad *f*

intricate ['ɪntrɪkət] *adj* intrincado, -a; (*mechanism*) complejo, -a; (*problem*) complicado, -a
intrigue [ɪn'triːg] I. *vt* intrigar; **to be ~d by sth** estar intrigado con algo II. *vi* 1. (*plot*) intrigar 2. (*carry on a secret love affair*) tener una aventura III. *n* 1. (*complications of a plot, machinations*) intriga *f* 2. (*secret love affair*) aventura *f*
intriguing [ɪn'triːgɪŋ] *adj* 1. (*mysterious*) intrigante 2. (*fascinating*) fascinante; (*smile*) enigmático, -a
intrinsic [ɪn'trɪnsɪk] *adj* intrínseco, -a; **the ~ value of a coin** el valor real de una moneda; **this is ~ to ...** eso es esencial para...
introduce [ˌɪntrə'djuːs, *Am:* -'duːs] *vt* 1. (*acquaint*) presentar; **allow me to ~ myself** permítame que me presente; **may I ~ you to my husband?** ¿le presento a mi marido?; **they were ~d to each other** les presentaron 2. (*raise interest in subject*) **to ~ sb to sth** iniciar a alguien en algo 3. (*bring in*) introducir; (*question*) hacer; (*subject*) abordar; (*bill*) presentar; **to ~ a product into the market** lanzar un producto al mercado 4. (*insert*) introducir; **to ~ sb into a place** hacer entrar a alguien en un sitio 5. (*begin, present: book*) prologar; **the second movement is ~d by ...** el segundo movimiento está introducido por...; **the director will ~ the film personally** el director presentará personalmente la película
introduction [ˌɪntrə'dʌkʃən] *n* 1. (*making first acquaintance*) presentación *f*; **letter of ~** carta *f* de presentación; **to do the ~s** hacer las presentaciones 2. (*first contact with sth*) iniciación *f*; **my holidays served as an ~ to sailing** mis vacaciones fueron una primera toma de contacto con la navegación 3. (*establishment*) introducción *f*; (*of a bill*) presentación *f*; **~ into the market** lanzamiento *m* al mercado 4. (*insertion*) introducción *f* 5. (*preface*) prólogo *m*; MUS introducción *f*
introductory [ˌɪntrə'dʌktəri] *adj* 1. (*elementary, preparatory*) de introducción; (*course*) de iniciación 2. COM (*price*) de lanzamiento 3. (*beginning*) introductorio, -a; **~ chapter** introducción *f*; **~ remarks** aclaraciones *fpl* preliminares
introspection [ˌɪntrə'spekʃən, *Am:* -troʊ'-] *n no pl* introspección *f*
introspective [ˌɪntrə'spektɪv, *Am:* -troʊ'-] *adj* introspectivo, -a
introvert [ˌɪntrə'vɜːt, *Am:* -troʊ'vɜːrt] *n* introvertido, -a *m, f*
introverted *adj* introvertido, -a
intrude [ɪn'truːd] I. *vi* 1. (*meddle*) entrometerse; **to ~ into sth** inmiscuirse en algo; **to ~ upon sb's privacy** meterse en la vida privada de alguien 2. (*disturb*) estorbar; **to ~ on sb** importunar a alguien; **am I intruding?** ¿molesto? II. *vt* **to ~ sth on sb** importunar a alguien con algo
intruder [ɪn'truːdə', *Am:* -ə-] *n* intruso, -a *m,*
f
intrusion [ɪn'truːʒən] *n* 1. (*encroachment, infringement*) intrusión *f* 2. (*meddling*) intromisión *f*
intrusive [ɪn'truːsɪv] *adj* (*noise*) molesto, -a; (*question*) indiscreto, -a; (*person*) entrometido, -a
intuition [ˌɪntjuː'ɪʃən, *Am:* -tuː'-] *n no pl* intuición *f*; **to have an ~ (that) ...** tener la intuición (de que)...
intuitive [ɪn'tjuːɪtɪv] *adj* intuitivo, -a; **an ~ feeling** una intuición
inundate ['ɪnʌndeɪt, *Am:* -ən-] *vt a. fig* inundar; **to ~ sb with sth** inundar a alguien de algo; **to be ~d with presents** verse inundado de regalos; **to be ~d with letters** recibir un aluvión de cartas
inundation [ˌɪnʌn'deɪʃən, *Am:* -ən'-] *n no pl, a. fig* inundación *f*
inure [ɪ'njʊə', *Am:* -'njʊr] *vt form* (*become familiar with*) habituar; (*harden*) curtir, endurecer; **to ~ sb to sth** acostumbrar a alguien a algo; **to ~ oneself against sth** hacerse inmune a algo
invade [ɪn'veɪd] I. *vt* invadir; **to ~ the peace** perturbar la paz; **to ~ sb's privacy** invadir la intimidad de alguien; **to ~ sb's rights** usurpar los derechos de alguien II. *vi* invadir
invader [ɪn'veɪdə', *Am:* -ə-] *n* (*aggressive trespasser*) invasor(a) *m(f)*
invalid¹ ['ɪnvəlɪd] I. *n* (*incapacitated person*) inválido, -a *m, f*; (*sick person*) enfermo, -a *m, f* II. *adj* 1. (*disabled*) inválido, -a; **~ chair** silla *f* de ruedas 2. (*sick*) enfermo, -a; **~ diet** dieta *f* para enfermos III. *vt* 1. (*disable*) dejar inválido, -a; (*make sick*) poner enfermo, -a 2. **to ~ out** *Brit* dar de baja por invalidez; **to ~ sb home** *Brit* repatriar a alguien por invalidez
invalid² [ɪn'vælɪd] *adj* 1. LAW (*not legally binding*) nulo, -a; **legally ~** sin validez legal; **to become ~** caducar 2. (*unsound*) no válido, -a; **technically ~** técnicamente incorrecto
invalidate [ɪn'vælɪdeɪt] *vt* 1. (*argument, decision*) invalidar; (*results*) anular 2. LAW anular; **to ~ a judgement** revocar una sentencia
invalidism [ˌɪnvə'lɪdɪzəm] *n Am*, **invalidity** [ˌɪnvə'lɪdəti, *Am:* -ti] *n no pl* 1. (*convalescent state*) invalidez *f* 2. (*inadmissibility: of a contract*) nulidad *f*; (*of evidence*) invalidez *f*
invaluable [ɪn'væljʊəbl, *Am:* -juə-] *adj* inapreciable; (*help*) inestimable; **to be ~ to sb** tener un valor inapreciable para alguien
invariable [ɪn'veəriəbl, *Am:* -'veri-] *adj* (*form, custom*) invariable; (*smile, attitude*) eterno, -a
invariably *adv* invariablemente; **he would ~ be sitting at the bar** siempre se le veía sentado en la barra
invasion [ɪn'veɪʒən] *n* 1. MIL invasión *f*; **~ by enemy forces** invasión de las tropas enemigas 2. *no pl* (*interference*) violación *f*; **~ of privacy/of a right** violación de la intimidad/de

un derecho
invective [ɪn'vektɪv] *n no pl, form* invectiva
f; **a stream of** ~ un aluvión de invectivas
inveigle [ɪn'veɪgl] *vt* **to** ~ **sb into sth**
embaucar a alguien para algo
invent [ɪn'vent] *vt* inventar
invention [ɪn'venʃən] *n* **1.** (*gadget*) invención *f*, invento *m AmL* **2.** *no pl* (*creativity*)
inventiva *f* **3.** (*falsehood*) ficción *f*
inventive [ɪn'ventɪv, *Am:* -t̬ɪv] *adj* inventivo, -a
inventiveness [ɪn'ventɪvnɪs, *Am:* -t̬ɪv-] *n*
no pl inventiva *f*
inventor [ɪn'ventəʳ, *Am:* -t̬ɚ] *n* inventor(a)
m(f)
inventory ['ɪnvəntri, *Am:* -tɔːr-] <-ies> I. *n*
1. (*catalogue*) inventario *m;* **to draw up an** ~
levantar un inventario **2.** *Am* (*stock*) stock *m*
II. *vt* inventariar III. *adj* (*audit, level, number*)
de inventario
inverse [ɪn'vɜːs, *Am:* -'vɜːrs] I. *adj* inverso, -a
II. *n no pl* **the** ~ lo inverso; **the** ~ **of sth** lo
contrario de algo
inversion [ɪn'vɜːʃən, *Am:* -'vɜːrʒən] *n no pl*
inversión *f*
invert [ɪn'vɜːt, *Am:* -'vɜːrt] *vt* invertir;
(*reverse*) revertir
invertebrate [ɪn'vɜːtɪbrət, *Am:* -'vɜːrt̬ə-
brɪt] I. *n* invertebrado *m* II. *adj* invertebrado,
-a
invest [ɪn'vest] I. *vt* **1.** (*put in*) invertir; **to** ~
time and effort in sth invertir tiempo y
dinero en algo **2.** (*bestow attributes*) investir;
to ~ **sb with sth** investir a alguien de algo
II. *vi* invertir; **to** ~ **in sth** invertir en algo
investigate [ɪn'vestɪgeɪt] *vt* investigar
investigation [ɪnˌvestɪ'geɪʃən] *n* investigación *f*
investigative [ɪn'vestɪgətɪv, *Am:* -geɪt̬ɪv]
adj investigador(a); ~ **journalism** periodismo
m de investigación
investigator [ɪn'vestɪgeɪtəʳ, *Am:* -t̬ɚ] *n*
investigador(a) *m(f)*
investment [ɪn'vestmənt] I. *n* **a.** *fig* inversión *f*; **to be a good** ~ ser una buena inversión;
long-term ~**s** inversiones *fpl* a largo plazo
II. *adj* de inversión
investment fund *n* fondo *m* de inversiones
investment income *n no pl* ingresos *mpl*
procedentes de inversiones **investment
trust** *n* sociedad *f* de inversiones
investor [ɪn'vestəʳ, *Am:* -tɚ] *n* inversionista
mf
inveterate [ɪn'vetərət, *Am:* -'vet̬-] *adj*
inveterado, -a; (*smoker*) empedernido, -a;
(*liar*) incurable
invidious [ɪn'vɪdiəs] *adj* odioso, -a; (*unfair*)
injusto, -a; **to be in an** ~ **position** estar en una
posición poco envidiable
invigilate [ɪn'vɪdʒɪleɪt] *vt Brit, Aus* (*in
exam*) supervisar
invigorate [ɪn'vɪgəreɪt] *vt* vigorizar; (*stimulate*) estimular

invigorating [ɪn'vɪgəreɪtɪŋ, *Am:* -t̬ɪŋ] *adj*
vigorizante
invincible [ɪn'vɪnsəbl] *adj* invencible
invisible [ɪn'vɪzəbl] *adj* invisible; ~ **to sth**
invisible a algo
invitation [ˌɪnvɪ'teɪʃən] *n* invitación *f*; **an** ~
to sth una invitación a algo
invite[1] ['ɪnvaɪt] *n inf* invitación *f*
invite[2] [ɪn'vaɪt] *vt* **1.** (*request to attend*) invitar; **to** ~ **sb for/to sth** invitar a alguien para/a
algo **2.** (*request*) pedir; **to** ~ **offers** solicitar
ofertas; **they** ~**d readers to send in their
views** pidieron a los lectores sus opiniones; **to**
~ **questions** abrirse a preguntas **3.** (*provoke*)
buscarse; **to** ~ **trouble** buscar(se) problemas
inviting [ɪn'vaɪtɪŋ, *Am:* -t̬ɪŋ] *adj* **1.** (*attractive*) atractivo, -a, atrayente **2.** (*tempting*) ten-
tador(a)
in vitro [ɪn'viːtrəʊ, *Am:* -trəʊ] *adj, adv* in
vitro
in vitro fertilization *n no pl* fecundación *f*
in vitro
invocation [ˌɪnvə'keɪʃən] *n* invocación *f*
invoice ['ɪnvɔɪs] I. *vt* facturar II. *n* factura *f*;
~ **for sth** factura de algo
invoke [ɪn'vəʊk, *Am:* -'voʊk] *vt* invocar
involuntary [ɪn'vɒləntəri, *Am:* -'vɑːlənter-]
adj involuntario, -a
involve [ɪn'vɒlv, *Am:* -'vɑːlv] *vt* **1.** (*implicate*) implicar, involucrar; **to be** ~**d in sth**
estar metido [*o* envuelto] en algo; **to get** ~**d in
sth** meterse en algo; **to** ~ **sb in a quarrel** mezclar a alguien en una disputa **2.** (*entail*) comportar; **to** ~ **much expense** causar muchos
gastos
involved [ɪn'vɒlvd, *Am:* -'vɑːlvd] *adj*
1. (*implicated*) involucrado, -a **2.** (*complicated*) complicado, -a
involvement [ɪn'vɒlvmənt, *Am:* -'vɑːlv-] *n*
no pl implicación *f*
invulnerable [ɪn'vʌlnərəbl, *Am:* -nɚ-] *adj*
invulnerable; **to be** ~ **to sth** ser inmune a algo
inward ['ɪnwəd, *Am:* -wɚd] *adj* **1.** (*trade*)
interior; (*investment*) interno, -a **2.** (*inmost*)
interior; (*personal*) íntimo, -a
inwardly *adv* interiormente
inwardness *n no pl* interioridad *f*
inwards ['ɪnwədz, *Am:* -wɚdz] *adv* hacia
adentro, para dentro
I/O INFOR *abbr of* **input/output** E/S
IOC *n abbr of* **International Olympic Committee** COI *m*
iodine ['aɪədiːn, *Am:* -daɪn] *n no pl* yodo *m*
IOM *n abbr of* **Isle of Man** Isla *f* de Man
ion ['aɪən] *n* ión *m*
Ionic [aɪ'ɒnɪk, *Am:* -'ɑːnɪk] *adj* jónico, -a
iota [aɪ'əʊtə, *Am:* -'oʊt̬ə] *n no pl* **1.** (*letter*)
iota *f* **2.** *fig* ápice *m;* **there is not one** ~ **of
truth in that** no hay ni una pizca de verdad en
eso
IOU [ˌaɪəʊ'juː, *Am:* -oʊ'-] *n inf abbr of* **I owe
you** pagaré *m*
IOW *n abbr of* **Isle of Wight** Isla *f* de Wight

IPA [ˌaɪpiːˈeɪ] *n* 1. *abbr of* International Phonetic Association AFI *f* 2. *abbr of* International Phonetic Alphabet AFI *m*

IQ [ˌaɪˈkjuː] *n abbr of* intelligence quotient CI *m*

IRA [ˌaɪaːˈreɪ, *Am:* -aːrˈ-] *n no pl abbr of* Irish Republican Army IRA *m*

Iran [ɪˈrɑːn, *Am:* -ˈræn] *n* Irán *m*

Iranian [ɪˈreɪnjən] I. *n* iraní *mf* II. *adj* iraní

Iraq [ɪˈrɑːk] *n* Irak *m*

Iraqi [ɪˈrɑːki] I. *n* iraquí *mf* II. *adj* iraquí

irascible [ɪˈræsəbl] *adj* irascible

irate [aɪˈreɪt] *adj* airado, -a

IRBM *n abbr of* intermediate-range ballistic missile IRBM *m*

Ireland [ˈaɪələnd, *Am:* ˈaɪr-] *n* Irlanda *f*; Republic of ~ República *f* de Irlanda; Northern ~ Irlanda del Norte

iridescent [ˌɪrɪˈdesnt] *adj* iridiscente

iris [ˈaɪərɪs, *Am:* ˈaɪ-] <-es> *n* 1. BOT lirio *m* 2. ANAT iris *m*

Irish [ˈaɪərɪʃ, *Am:* ˈaɪ-] I. *adj* irlandés, -esa II. *n* 1. *pl* (*people*) the ~ los irlandeses 2. LING irlandés *m*; ~ Gaelic gaélico *m* irlandés

Irishman [ˈaɪərɪʃmən, *Am:* ˈaɪ-] <-men> *n* irlandés *m*

Irishwoman [ˈaɪərɪʃwʊmən, *Am:* ˈaɪ-] <-women> *n* irlandesa *f*

irk [ɜːk, *Am:* ɜːrk] *vt* fastidiar

irksome [ˈɜːksəm, *Am:* ˈɜːrk-] *adj* fastidioso, -a

iron [ˈaɪən, *Am:* ˈaɪɚn] I. *n* 1. *no pl* (*metal*) hierro *m*, fierro *m AmL* 2. (*for pressing clothes*) plancha *f*; steam ~ plancha de vapor 3. SPORTS (*golf club*) hierro *m* ▶to have many ~s in the fire tener muchos asuntos entre manos II. *vt* planchar; *fig* allanar III. *vi* planchar IV. *adj* de hierro; (*discipline*) férreo, -a

Iron Age I. *n* edad *f* de hierro II. *adj* de la edad de hierro **Iron Curtain** *n* HIST, POL Telón *m* de Acero

ironic(al) [aɪˈrɒnɪk(el), *Am:* aɪˈrɑːnɪk-] *adj* irónico, -a

ironing [ˈaɪənɪŋ, *Am:* ˈaɪɚn-] *n no pl* planchado *m*; to do the ~ planchar

ironing board *n* tabla *f* de planchar, burro *m* de planchar *Méx*

iron lung *n* pulmón *m* de acero

ironmonger *n Brit* ferretero *m*; ~'s *Brit* (*shop*) ferretería *f*

ironmongery *n no pl, Brit* (*goods*) objetos *mpl* de ferretería; (*shop*) ferretería *f*

iron ore *n no pl* mineral *m* de hierro **iron ration** *n* ración *f* de reserva

ironwork *n no pl* herraje *m*

ironworks *n inv* fundición *f*, herrería *f AmL*

irony [ˈaɪərəni, *Am:* ˈaɪ-] <-ies> *n* ironía *f*; ~ of fate ironía del destino

irradiate [ɪˈreɪdɪeɪt, *Am:* ɪrˈ-] *vt* irradiar

irrational [ɪˈræʃənəl] *adj* irracional

irrational number *n* MAT número *m* irracional

irreconcilable [ɪˌrekənˈsaɪləbl] *adj* (*posi-*tions) inconciliable; (*differences*) irreconciliable

irrecoverable [ˌɪrɪˈkʌvərəbl] *adj* irrecuperable

irredeemable [ˌɪrɪˈdiːməbl] *adj* irredimible

irrefutable [ˌɪrɪˈfjuːtəbl, *Am:* ɪˈrefjətə-] *adj* (*evidence*) irrefutable; (*argument, fact, logic*) irrebatible

irregular [ɪˈregjələr, *Am:* -lɚ] *adj* irregular; (*surface*) desigual; (*behaviour*) anómalo, -a; (*life*) desordenado, -a; ~ soldiers tropas *fpl* irregulares

irregularity [ɪˌregjəˈlærəti, *Am:* ɪˌregjəˈlerəti] <-ies> *n* irregularidad *f*; (*of surface*) desigualdad *f*; (*of behaviour*) anormalidad *f*

irrelevance [ɪˈreləvənts, *Am:* ɪrˈ-] *n*, **irrelevancy** <-ies> *n* irrelevancia *f*; to fade into ~ volverse irrelevante

irrelevant [ɪˈreləvənt, *Am:* ɪrˈ-] *adj* irrelevante; to be ~ to sth no ser relevante para algo

irremediable [ˌɪrɪˈmiːdɪəbl] *adj* irremediable; (*damage, loss*) irreparable

irreparable [ɪˈrepərəbl] *adj* irreparable

irreplaceable [ˌɪrɪˈpleɪsəbl] *adj* irreemplazable

irrepressible [ˌɪrɪˈpresəbl] *adj* irrefrenable, incontrolable

irreproachable [ˌɪrɪˈprəʊtʃəbl, *Am:* -ˈproʊ-] *adj* irreprochable; (*past*) intachable

irresistible [ˌɪrɪˈzɪstəbl] *adj* irresistible

irresolute [ɪˈrezəluːt] *adj* irresoluto, -a; (*reply*) indeciso, -a

irrespective [ˌɪrɪˈspektɪv] *prep* ~ of aparte de; ~ of whether he agrees or not con independencia de si está de acuerdo; ~ of sth/sb sin tener en cuenta algo/a alguien

irresponsible [ˌɪrɪˈspɒnsəbl, *Am:* -ˈspɑːn-] *adj* irresponsable

irretrievable [ˌɪrɪˈtriːvəbl] *adj* irrecuperable; (*mistake*) irreparable

irreverence [ɪˈrevərəns] *n no pl* irreverencia *f*

irreverent [ɪˈrevərənt] *adj* irreverente

irreversible [ˌɪrɪˈvɜːsəbl, *Am:* -ˈvɜːr-] *adj* irreversible; (*decision*) irrevocable

irrevocable [ɪˈrevəkəbl] *adj* irrevocable

irrigate [ˈɪrɪgeɪt] *vt* 1. AGR regar; to ~ land regar la tierra 2. MED irrigar

irrigation [ˌɪrɪˈgeɪʃən] I. *n no pl* 1. AGR riego *m* 2. MED irrigación *f* II. *adj* de riego; ~ canal acequia *f*

irrigation plant *n* planta *f* de riego

irritable [ˈɪrɪtəbl, *Am:* -t̬ə-] *adj* irritable

irritant [ˈɪrɪtənt, *Am:* -t̬ənt] *n* irritante *m*

irritate [ˈɪrɪteɪt] *vt* 1. (*aggravate*) irritar, molestar 2. MED irritar

irritated *adj* irritado, -a

irritating *adj* irritante

irritation [ˌɪrɪˈteɪʃən] *n* irritación *f*

is [ɪz] *vt, vi 3rd pers sing of* to be

ISBN [ˌaɪesbiːˈen] *n abbr of* International Standard Book Number ISBN *m*

ISD *n abbr of* international subscriber dial-

ling marcación *f* directa internacional
ISDN *n abbr of* **integrated services digital network** RDSI *f*
Islam [ɪzˈlɑːm] *n no pl* Islam *m*
Islamic [ɪzˈlæmɪk, *Am:* -ˈlɑː-] *adj* islámico, -a; ~ **law** ley islámica
island [ˈaɪlənd] *n* isla *f;* ~ **of calm** *fig* refugio *m* de paz
islander [ˈaɪləndəʳ, *Am:* -ɚ] *n* isleño, -a *m, f*
isle *n,* **Isle** [aɪl] *n* ínsula *f*
Isle of Man *n* Isla *f* de Man **Isle of Wight** *n* Isla *f* de Wight
islet [ˈaɪlɪt] *n liter* islote *m*
isn't [ˈɪznt] = **is not**
isobar [ˈaɪsəbɑːʳ, *Am:* -soʊbɑːr] *n* METEO isobara *f*
isolate [ˈaɪsəleɪt] *vt* aislar
isolated [ˈaɪsəleɪtɪd, *Am:* -t̬ɪd] *adj* **1.** (*outlying, disconnected*) aislado, -a **2.** (*lonely*) apartado, -a
isolation [ˌaɪsəˈleɪʃən] *n no pl* **1.** (*separation*) aislamiento *m* **2.** (*loneliness*) soledad *f*
isolation hospital *n* hospital *m* de enfermedades contagiosas
isolationism [ˌaɪsəˈleɪʃnɪzəm] *n no pl* aislacionismo *m*
isolation ward *n* sala *f* de aislamiento
isosceles triangle [aɪˈsɒsliːzˌtraɪæŋgl, *Am:* -ˈsɑːsl-] *n* MAT triángulo *m* isósceles
isotherm [ˈaɪsəθɜːm, *Am:* -soʊθɜːrm] *n* METEO, PHYS isotermo *m*
isotope [ˈaɪsətəʊp, *Am:* -toʊp] *n* PHYS, ELEC isótopo *m*
Israel [ˈɪzreɪl, *Am:* -riəl] *n* Israel *m*
Israeli [ɪzˈreɪli] I. *n* israelí *mf* II. *adj* israelí
Israelite [ˈɪzrɪəlaɪt] *n* israelita *mf*
issue [ˈɪʃuː] I. *n* **1.** (*problem, topic*) cuestión *f;* **family ~s** asuntos *mpl* familiares; **side ~** asunto *m* menor; **a burning ~** *fig* un asunto caliente; **the real ~s** las cuestiones de fondo; **the point at ~** el punto en cuestión; **to force an ~** forzar una decisión; **to make an ~ of sth** convertir algo en un problema; **at ~** a debate **2.** PUBL (*copy*) número *m;* **latest ~** último número **3.** FIN, ECON (*of shares, stamps*) emisión *f;* (*of cheques*) expedición *f* **4.** *form* (*offspring, children*) descendencia *f* II. *vt* emitir; (*passport*) expedir; (*patent*) conceder; (*newsletter*) publicar; (*ultimatum*) presentar; **to ~ a statement** hacer una declaración; **to ~ a call for sth** hacer un llamamiento para algo III. *vi* **to ~ from** (*born out of*) surgir de; (*come out of*) provenir de
isthmus [ˈɪsməs] <-es> *n* istmo *m*
it [ɪt] I. *pron dem* la, le, lo (*in many cases, 'it' is omitted when referring to information already known*); **who was ~?** ¿quién era?; **~'s in my bag** está en mi bolso; **~'s Paul who did that** fue Paul quien lo hizo; **~ was in London that ...** fue en Londres donde... II. *pron pers* **1.** él, ella, ello; *direct object:* lo, la; *indirect object:* le; **where is your pencil/card?** ~ **is on my desk** ¿en dónde está tu lápiz/tarjeta?

Está encima de mi escritorio; ~ **went off badly** aquello fue mal; **your card? I took ~** ¿tu tarjeta? La cogí yo; **~'s your cat, give ~ something to eat** es tu gato, dale algo de comer; **I'm afraid of ~** le tengo miedo; **I fell into ~** caí dentro **2.** (*time*) **what time is ~?** ¿qué hora es? **3.** (*weather*) **~'s cold** hace frío; **~'s snowing** está nevando **4.** (*distance*) **~'s 10 km to the town** hay 10 km hasta el pueblo **5.** (*empty subject*) ~ **seems that ...** parece que... **6.** (*passive subject*) ~ **is said/hoped that ...** se dice/espera que...
IT [ˌaɪˈtiː] *n no pl* INFOR *abbr of* **Information Technology** tecnología *f* de la información
ITA *n abbr of* **Independent Television Authority** ITA *f*
Italian [ɪˈtæljən] I. *adj* italiano, -a II. *n* **1.** (*person*) italiano, -a *m, f* **2.** LING italiano *m*
italic [ɪˈtælɪk] *adj* (*of Italy*) itálico, -a
italicise *vt Aus, Brit,* **italicize** [ɪˈtælɪsaɪz] *vt Am* poner en cursiva
italics [ɪˈtælɪks] *npl* cursiva *f;* **in ~** en cursiva
Italy [ˈɪtəli, *Am:* -ɪt̬-] *n* Italia *f*
itch [ɪtʃ] I. *vi* **1.** MED picar **2.** *fig, inf* **to ~ to do sth** morirse por hacer algo II. *n* **1.** MED comezón *f,* rasquiña *f Arg* **2.** *fig, inf* inmensas ganas *fpl*
itchy [ˈɪtʃi] <-ier, -iest> *adj* que escuece; **my arm feels ~** siento picazón en el brazo; **I've got an ~ feeling** tengo un sentimiento inquietante
item [ˈaɪtəm, *Am:* -t̬əm] *n* **1.** (*thing*) artículo *m,* objeto *m;* **luxury ~** artículo de lujo; **~ of clothing** prenda *f* de vestir **2.** (*topic*) asunto *m;* ~ **on the agenda** asunto a tratar; **~ by ~** punto por punto **3.** COM partida *f;* **~ of expenditure** partida de gasto **4.** PUBL noticia *f;* **news ~** noticia *f* **5.** *inf* (*couple*) pareja *f*
itemise *vt Brit, Aus,* **itemize** [ˈaɪtəmaɪz] *vt Am* detallar
itinerant [aɪˈtɪnərənt] I. *n* viajante *mf* II. *adj* itinerante; (*merchant*) ambulante
itinerary [aɪˈtɪnərəri, *Am:* -ərer-] <-ies> *n* itinerario *m*
it'll [ˈɪtl, *Am:* ˈɪt̬l] = **it will**
ITN [ˈaɪtiːˈen] *n Brit abbr of* **Independent Television News** ITN *f* (*sociedad por acciones creada y financiada por el conjunto de empresas de televisión que integran la cadena ITV*)
its [ɪts] *adj pos* su; **~ colour/weight** su color/peso; **~ mountains** sus montañas; **the cat hurt ~ head** el gato se lastimó la cabeza
it's [ɪts] **1.** = **it is 2.** = **it has**
itself [ɪtˈself] *pron reflexive* él mismo, ella misma, ello mismo; *direct, indirect object:* se; *after prep:* sí mismo, -a; **the place ~** el sitio en sí; **in ~** en sí
ITV [ˈaɪtiːˈviː] *n Brit abbr of* **Independent Television** ITV *f* (*cadena de televisión británica*)
IUD [ˌaɪjuːˈdiː] *n abbr of* **intrauterine device** DIU *m*

i.v. *abbr of* intravenous i.v.
I've [aɪv] = I have *s.* **have**
IVF [ˌaɪviːˈef] *n* MED *abbr of* in vitro fertilisation fecundación *f* in vitro
ivory ['aɪvəri] <-ies> *n* **1.** *no pl* marfil *m* **2.** *pl, inf* MUS teclas *fpl* (del piano); **to tickle the ivories** *fig* tocar el piano **3.** *pl, inf* ANAT dientes *mpl*
ivory carving *n* talla *f* en marfil **Ivory Coast** *n* Costa *f* de Marfil **ivory tower** *n* *fig* torre *f* de marfil **ivory trading** *n* *no pl* tráfico *m* de marfil
ivy ['aɪvi] <-ies> *n* hiedra *f*

J

J, j [dʒeɪ] *n, n* J, j *f;* ~ **for Jack** *Brit,* ~ **for Jig** *Am* J de Juan
J *n* PHYS *abbr of* joule julio *m*
jab [dʒæb] I. *n* **1.** (*with a pin*) pinchazo *m;* (*with the elbow*) codazo *m* **2.** (*in boxing*) (golpe *m*) corto *m* **3.** *Brit, Aus, inf* (*injection*) inyección *f* II. <-bb-> *vt* **to ~ a needle in sth** pinchar algo con una aguja; **to ~ a finger at sth** señalar algo con el dedo; **to ~ sb in the eye with sth** dar a alguien en el ojo con algo III. <-bb-> *vi* **to ~ at sb/sth** (**with sth**) dar a alguien/algo (con algo); **he ~bed at the paragraph with his pen** señaló el párrafo con su bolígrafo
jabber ['dʒæbəʳ, *Am:* -ɚ] *vi, vt* farfullar
jabbering *n* farfulla *f*
jack [dʒæk] *n* **1.** AUTO gato *m* **2.** (*in cards*) jota *f;* (*in a Spanish pack*) sota *f* **3.** (*in bowls*) boliche *m*
  ◆**jack in** *vt Brit, inf* dejar
  ◆**jack up** *vt* **1.** (*object*) levantar **2.** *inf* (*prices*) aumentar
Jack [dʒæk] *n* **every man ~** *inf* cada quisque; **before you could say ~ Robinson** en un abrir y cerrar de ojos, en un decir Jesús
jackal ['dʒækɔːl, *Am:* -əl] *n* **1.** ZOOL chacal *m* **2.** *pej, inf* (*person*) carroñero, -a *m, f*
jackass ['dʒækæs] *n* **1.** ZOOL asno *m* **2.** *pej, inf* (*idiot*) burro, -a *m, f*
jackboot ['dʒækbuːt] *n* bota *f* alta ►**under the ~** bajo el yugo
jackdaw ['dʒækdɔː, *Am:* -daː] *n* grajilla *f*
jacket ['dʒækɪt] *n* **1.** (*short coat*) chaqueta *f,* percha *f AmC,* chapona *f RíoPl,* cuácara *f Chile* **2.** (*of a book*) sobrecubierta *f;* (*of a record*) funda *f*
jacket potato *n* patata *f* asada (*con piel*)
jack-in-the-box ['dʒækɪndəbɒks, *Am:* -baːks] <-xes> *n* caja *f* de sorpresas
jackknife ['dʒæknaɪf] I. *n* **1.** (*knife*) navaja *f* **2.** (*dive*) salto *m* de carpa II. *vi* plegarse
jack-o'-lantern ['dʒækəʊˌlæntən, *Am:* -əˌlæntɚn] *n Am:* lámpara hecha con una calabaza ahuecada

jack plug *n Brit* enchufe *m* de clavija
jackpot ['dʒækpɒt, *Am:* -paːt] *n* (premio *m*) gordo *m* ►**she's hit the ~** *inf* le ha tocado el gordo
Jacuzzi® [dʒəˈkuːzi] *n* jacuzzi® *m*
jade [dʒeɪd] *no pl n* **1.** (*precious green stone*) jade *m* **2.** (*colour*) verde *m* jade
jaded ['dʒeɪdɪd] *adj* **to be ~ with sth** estar harto de algo
jagged ['dʒægɪd] *adj* irregular; (*coastline, rocks*) recortado, -a; (*cut, tear*) desigual
jaggy ['dʒægi] <-ier, -iest> *adj* irregular
jaguar ['dʒægjʊəʳ, *Am:* 'dʒægwɑːr] *n* jaguar *m*
jail [dʒeɪl] I. *n* cárcel *f,* prisión *f;* **to be in ~** (**for sth**) estar en la cárcel (por algo); **to put sb in ~** encarcelar a alguien II. *vt* encarcelar; **she was ~ed for life** la condenaron a cadena perpetua
jailbird ['dʒeɪlbɜːd, *Am:* -bɜːrd] *n inf* delincuente *mf* habitual **jailbreak** *n* fuga *f*
jailer *n,* **jailor** ['dʒeɪləʳ, *Am:* -lɚ] *n* carcelero, -a *m, f*
jalopy [dʒəˈlɒpi, *Am:* -ˈlɑːpi] *n inf* cacharro *m*
jam¹ [dʒæm] *n* GASTR mermelada *f* ►**~ tomorrow** promesas y más promesas
jam² [dʒæm] I. *n* **1.** *inf* (*awkward situation*) aprieto *m;* **to get into a ~** meterse en un lío **2.** *no pl* (*crowd*) gentío *m* **3.** AUTO atasco *m;* **paper ~** INFOR atasco de papel II. <-mm-> *vt* **1.** (*cause to become stuck*) atascar; (*door*) obstruir; **to ~ sth into sth** embutir algo en algo **2.** (*wheel*) trabar **3.** RADIO interferir III. <-mm-> *vi* **1.** (*become stuck*) atrancarse; (*brakes*) bloquearse; (*rifle*) encasquillarse **2.** (*play music*) tocar, improvisar
Jamaica [dʒəˈmeɪkə] *n* Jamaica *f*
Jamaican I. *adj* jamaicano, -a II. *n* jamaicano, -a *m, f*
jamb [dʒæm] *n* jamba *f*
jamboree [ˌdʒæmbəˈriː] *n* **1.** (*celebration*) juerga *f* **2.** (*scouts' meeting*) congreso *m* de exploradores
jam jar *n* bote *m* para mermelada
jammy ['dʒæmi] <-ier, -iest> *adj* **1.** (*covered with jam*) cubierto, -a de mermelada **2.** *Brit, inf* (*lucky*) afortunado, -a; **what a ~ goal!** ¡qué potra de gol! **3.** *Brit, inf* (*easy*) chupado
jam-packed [ˌdʒæmˈpækt] *adj inf* **to be ~** (**with sth**) estar repleto (de algo); **the streets were ~ with people** las calles estaban atestadas de gente
jam session *n inf* jam session *f*
jangle ['dʒæŋgl] I. *vt* (*coins, keys*) hacer tintinear II. *vi* tintinear; **to make sb's nerves ~** crispar los nervios a alguien III. *n no pl* sonido *m* metálico
janitor ['dʒænɪtəʳ, *Am:* -əţɚ] *n Am, Scot* conserje *mf*
January ['dʒænjuəri, *Am:* -jueri] <-ies> *n*

enero *m; s. a.* **April**

Jap [dʒæp] *abbr of* **Japanese I.** *n pej, inf* japo
m **II.** *adj pej, inf* japonés, -esa

japan [dʒə'pæn] *n no pl* laca *f* japonesa

Japan [dʒə'pæn] *n* Japón *m*

Japanese [ˌdʒæpə'niːz] **I.** *adj* japonés, -esa
II. *n* 1.(*person*) japonés, -esa *m, f* 2. *no pl* LING
japonés *m*

jar¹ [dʒɑːʳ, *Am:* dʒɑːr] *n* 1.(*container*) tarro
m 2. *inf* (*drink*) **to have a** ~ tomar una cerveza

jar² [dʒɑːʳ, *Am:* dʒɑːr] **I.** <-rr-> *vt* (*shake*)
sacudir **II.** <-rr-> *vi* 1.(*cause unpleasant feelings*) **to** ~ **on sb** crispar los nervios a alguien
2.(*make unpleasant sound*) chirriar 3.(*clash:
colours, design*) desentonar; **to ~ on the eye**
hacer daño a la vista **III.** *n* 1.(*shake*) sacudida
f 2.(*shock*) golpe *m*

jargon ['dʒɑːgən, *Am:* 'dʒɑːr-] *n no pl* jerga *f*

jasmine ['dʒæsmɪn] *n no pl* jazmín *m*

jaundice ['dʒɔːndɪs, *Am:* 'dʒɑː-] *n no pl*
MED ictericia *f*

jaundiced ['dʒɔːndɪst, *Am:* 'dʒɑːn-] *adj*
1. MED ictérico, -a 2.(*bitter*) negativo, -a; **to
look on sth with a** ~ **eye** ver algo con cierta
dosis de cinismo

jaunt [dʒɔːnt, *Am:* dʒɑːnt] *n* excursión *f;* **to
go on a** ~ salir de excursión

jaunty ['dʒɔːnti, *Am:* 'dʒɑːnt̬i] <-ier, -iest>
adj desenfadado, -a; ~ **step** paso *m* desenvuelto

Java ['dʒɑːvə] *n* Java *f*

javelin ['dʒævlɪn] *n* 1.(*spear*) jabalina *f* 2. *no
pl* (*competition*) lanzamiento *m* de jabalina

jaw [dʒɔː, *Am:* dʒɑː] **I.** *n* 1. ANAT mandíbula *f*
2. *pl* (*mouth*) boca *f; fig* fauces *fpl* 3. *pl* TECH
mordazas *fpl* ►**to have a** ~ *inf* mantener una
charla **II.** *vi inf* darle a la sinhueso; **to ~ away
to sb** cotorrear con alguien

jawbone ['dʒɔːbəʊn, *Am:* 'dʒɑː-] *n* maxilar
m

jawbreaker ['dʒɔːbreɪkə, *Am:* 'dʒɑː-] *n*
1. *Am, Aus* (*sweet*) caramelo *m* duro 2. *inf*
(*tongue twister*) trabalenguas *m inv*

jay [dʒeɪ] *n* arrendajo *m*

jaywalk ['dʒeɪwɔːk, *Am:* -wɑːk] *vi* cruzar la
calzada imprudentemente

jaywalker ['dʒeɪwɔːkəʳ, *Am:* -wɑːkɚ] *n*
peatón *m* imprudente

jaywalking *n no pl* cruce *m* de calzada
imprudente

jazz [dʒæz] *n no pl* jazz *m;* ~ **band/club**
grupo *m*/club *m* de jazz ►**and all that** ~ *inf* y
todo ese rollo

♦**jazz up** *vt inf* animar

jazzy ['dʒæzi] <-ier, -iest> *adj* 1. MUS de jazz
2. *inf* (*flashy*) llamativo, -a

JCB® [ˌdʒeɪsiː'biː] *n Brit:* máquina usada
para cavar y mover tierra

jealous ['dʒeləs] *adj* 1.(*envious*) envidioso,
-a; **to be** ~ **of sb** tener celos de alguien; **to
feel/be** ~ sentir/tener envidia 2.(*fiercely protective*) celoso, -a; **to be** ~ **of sth** ser celoso de

jealousy ['dʒeləsi] <-ies> *n* 1.(*possessive-
ness*) celos *mpl;* **to be consumed by** ~ estar
consumido por los celos 2. *no pl* (*envy*) envidia *f*

jeans [dʒiːnz] *npl* (pantalones *mpl*) vaqueros
mpl; **a pair of** ~ unos (pantalones) vaqueros

jeep [dʒiːp] *n* jeep *m*

jeer [dʒɪəʳ, *Am:* dʒɪr] **I.** *vt* abuchear **II.** *vi* mofarse; **to** ~ **at sb** burlarse de alguien **III.** *n* burla *f*

Jehovah [dʒɪ'həʊvə, *Am:* -'hoʊ-] *n no pl*
Jehová; ~**'s Witness** testigo *m* de Jehová

jell [dʒel] *vi s.* **gel**

jellied *adj* en gelatina; ~ **eels** anguilas *fpl* en
gelatina

jelly ['dʒeli] <-ies> *n* 1.(*soft transparent substance*) gelatina *f* 2. *Brit, Aus* (*dessert*) gelatina *f* (*con sabor a frutas*) 3.(*jam*) mermelada
f ►**my legs** turned **to** ~ *inf* se me pusieron las
piernas como un flan

jellybaby *n* caramelo *m* de goma (*en forma
de muñeco*) **jellybean** *n* caramelo *m* de
goma (*en forma de judía*) **jellyfish** <-es> *n*
medusa *f*

jemmy ['dʒemi] <-ies> *n Aus, Brit* palanqueta *f*

jeopardise *vt,* **jeopardize** ['dʒepədaɪz,
Am: '-ɚ-] *vt* poner en peligro

jeopardy ['dʒepədi, *Am:* '-ɚ-] *n no pl* peligro
m; **to put sth in** ~ poner algo en peligro

jerk [dʒɜːk, *Am:* dʒɜːrk] **I.** *n* 1.(*jolt*) sacudida
f; **with a** ~ con un sobresalto 2.(*movement*)
tirón *m;* **to give sth a** ~ tirar de algo 3. *pej, inf*
(*person*) estúpido, -a *m, f;* **to feel such a** ~
sentirse como un gilipollas **II.** *vi* sacudirse; **to** ~
to a halt detenerse con una sacudida **III.** *vt*
1.(*shake*) sacudir 2.(*pull*) tirar bruscamente
de

♦**jerk off** *vi vulg* hacerse una paja

jerkin ['dʒɜːkɪn, *Am:* 'dʒɜːr-] *n* chaleco *m*

jerky ['dʒɜːki, *Am:* 'dʒɜːr-] **I.** <-ier, -iest> *adj*
(*nervous*) nervioso, -a; (*uneven*) irregular;
(*sound, voice*) entrecortado, -a **II.** *n no pl, Am*
beef ~ cecina *f*

jerry-built ['dʒerɪbɪlt] *adj* mal construido, -a

jerrycan ['dʒerɪkæn] *n* bidón *m*

jersey ['dʒɜːzi, *Am:* 'dʒɜːr-] *n* 1.(*garment*)
jersey *m* 2.(*sports shirt*) camiseta *f* 3. *no pl*
(*cloth*) tejido *m* de punto 4.(*type of cow*) Jersey *f* (*raza de ganado vacuno*)

jest [dʒest] **I.** *n form* chanza *f;* **to say sth in** ~
decir algo en broma ►**many a true** word **is
spoken in** ~ *prov* bromeando, bromeando,
amargas verdades se van soltando *prov* **II.** *vi
form* bromear; **to** ~ **about sth** burlarse de algo

jester ['dʒestəʳ, *Am:* -tɚ] *n* HIST bufón *m*

jesting I. *n no pl* gracia *f* **II.** *adj* gracioso, -a

Jesuit ['dʒezjʊɪt] **I.** *n* jesuita *m* **II.** *adj* jesuita

Jesuitical [ˌdʒezjʊ'ɪtɪkl] *adj* jesuítico, -a

Jesus ['dʒiːzəs] **I.** Jesús **II.** *interj inf* ¡por
Dios!, ¡híjole! *AmL*

Jesus Christ *n* Jesucristo *m*

jet¹ [dʒet] I. *n* **1.** (*aircraft*) avión *m* a reacción, jet *m* **2.** (*stream*) chorro *m* **3.** (*nozzle*) surtidor *m* II.<-tt-> *vi* volar; **to ~ off** viajar en avión

jet² [dʒet] *n no pl* (*stone*) azabache *m*

jet-black *adj* negro azabache; **~ eyes/hair** ojos/pelo de azabache

jet engine *n* motor *m* a reacción **jet fighter** *n* caza *m* a reacción **jetfoil** *n* hidroala *f* a reacción **jet lag** *n no pl* desfase *m* horario, jet lag *m* **jet plane** *n* avión *m* a reacción **jet-propelled** *adj* a reacción **jet propulsion** *n no pl* propulsión *m* a chorro

jetsam ['dʒetsəm] *n no pl* s. **flotsam**

jet set *n inf* the ~ la jet-set

jettison ['dʒetɪsən, *Am:* 'dʒeʈə-] *vt* **1.** NAUT echar al mar **2.** (*get rid of: person*) deshacerse de; (*plan*) echar por la borda

jetty ['dʒeti, *Am:* 'dʒeʈ-] *n* embarcadero *m*

Jew [dʒuː] *n* judío, -a *m, f*

jewel ['dʒuːəl] *n* **1.** (*piece of jewellery*) a. *fig* joya *f*; (*precious stone*) piedra *f* preciosa **2.** (*watch part*) rubí *m*

jeweler *n Am*, **jeweller** ['dʒuːələʳ, *Am:* -lə˞] *n* joyero, -a *m, f*; **~'s** (**shop**) joyería *f*

jewellery *n*, **jewelry** ['dʒuːəlri] *n Am no pl* joyas *fpl*; **a piece of** ~ una joya

Jewess ['dʒuːes, *Am:* -ɪs] *n* judía *f*

Jewish ['dʒuːɪʃ] *adj* judío, -a

Jewry ['dʒuːri] *n no pl*, *form* los judíos

Jew's harp *n* birimbao *m*

jib¹ [dʒɪb] *n* (*sail*) foque *m*

jib² [dʒɪb] *n* (*of a crane*) brazo *m*

jib³ [dʒɪb] <-bb-> *vi* **to ~ at doing sth** resistirse a hacer algo

jibe [dʒaɪb] I. *n* burla *f*; **to make a ~** hacer una broma II. *vi* **to ~ at sth/sb** burlarse de algo/alguien

jiffy ['dʒɪfi] *n no pl*, *inf* **in a ~** en un santiamén

jig [dʒɪg] I.<-gg-> *vi* **1.** (*move around*) brincar **2.** (*dance a jig*) bailar la giga II. *n* **1.** (*dance*) giga *f* **2.** TECH (*device*) plantilla *f* de guía

jigger ['dʒɪgəʳ, *Am:* -ə˞] I. *n* medida *f* (*para bebidas alcohólicas*) II. *vt Am* (*rearrange*) reorganizar

jiggered ['dʒɪgəd, *Am:* -ə˞d] *adj* **1.** *Aus, Brit, inf* (*tired*) molido, -a **2.** *Brit, inf* (*broken*) roto, -a

jiggery-pokery [,dʒɪgəri'pəʊkəri, *Am:* -'poʊ-] *n no pl*, *inf* chanchullos *mpl*

jiggle ['dʒɪgl] I. *vt* mover; **to ~ sth about** menear algo II. *vi* moverse III. *n* meneo *m*

jigsaw ['dʒɪgsɔː, *Am:* -sɑː] *n* **1.** (*tool*) sierra *f* de vaivén **2.** (*puzzle*) puzzle *m*, rompecabezas *m inv*

jilt [dʒɪlt] *vt* dejar plantado

Jim Crow [,dʒɪm'krəʊ, *Am:* -'kroʊ] *n no pl*, *Am, pej* racista *mf*

jimjams ['dʒɪmdʒæmz] *npl* **1.** *Brit, inf* (*pyjamas*) pijama *m* **2.** *inf* (*shaking*) tembleque *m*

jimmy ['dʒɪmi] *n Am* palanqueta *f*

jingle ['dʒɪŋgl] I. *vt* hacer tintinear II. *vi* tintinear III. *n* **1.** *no pl* (*noise*) tintineo *m* **2.** (*in advertisments*) jingle *m*

jingoism ['dʒɪŋgəʊɪzəm, *Am:* -goʊ-] *n no pl*, *pej* patriotería *f*

jingoistic [,dʒɪŋgəʊ'ɪstɪk, *Am:* -goʊ'-] *adj* *pej* patriotero, -a

jinx [dʒɪŋks] I. *n no pl* gafe *f*; **there's a ~ on this computer** este ordenador está gafado; **to put a ~ on sb/sth** echar una maldición a alguien/algo II. *vt* gafar

jitterbug ['dʒɪtəbʌg, *Am:* 'dʒɪʈə˞-] I. *n* **1.** (*dance*) jitterbug *m* (*baile muy movido*) **2.** (*nervous person*) persona *f* nerviosa II.<-gg-> *vi* bailar el jitterbug

jitters ['dʒɪtəz, *Am:* 'dʒɪʈə˞z] *npl* **1.** *inf* (*nervousness*) nervios *mpl*; **he got the ~** le entró el canguelo **2.** (*shaking*) tembleque *m*

jittery ['dʒɪtəri, *Am:* 'dʒɪʈ-] <-ier, -iest> *adj* *inf* nervioso, -a; **he felt ~** le dió el tembleque; **he got ~** le entró el canguelo

jive [dʒaɪv] I. *n* swing *m* II. *vi* bailar el swing

job [dʒɒb, *Am:* dʒɑːb] *n* **1.** (*piece of work, employment*) trabajo *m*; **to make a good/bad ~ of sth** hacer algo bien/mal; **to apply for a ~** presentarse para un trabajo **2.** *no pl* (*duty*) deber *m*; **to do one's ~** cumplir con su deber; **it's not her job** no es asunto suyo **3.** *no pl* (*problem*) tarea *f* difícil; **it's quite a ~ doing that** resulta bastante difícil hacer eso; **I had a ~ doing it** me costó trabajo ►**it's a good ~ that ...** menos mal que...; **to be just the ~** *inf* venir como anillo al dedo; **to do a ~ on sb** *inf* hacer una putada a alguien *vulg*

job advertisement *n* anuncio *m* de trabajo **job analysis** *n* análisis *m inv* del puesto **job application** *n* demanda *f* de empleo

jobber ['dʒɒbəʳ, *Am:* 'dʒɑːbə˞] *n Am* (*wholesaler*) intermediario, -a *m, f*

job centre *n Brit* oficina *f* de empleo **job counsellor** *n* orientador(a) *m(f)* laboral **job creation** *n no pl* creación *f* de empleo **job cuts** *npl* recortes *mpl* laborales **job description** *n* descripción *f* del puesto **job interview** *n* entrevista *f* de trabajo

jobless ['dʒɒblɪs, *Am:* 'dʒɑːb-] I. *adj* desocupado, -a II. *npl* the ~ los parados *mpl*; ~ **figures** cifras *fpl* de paro

job lot *n* lote *m*

job market *n* mercado *m* de trabajo **job rating** *n* evaluación *f* del lugar de trabajo **job-seeker** *n* demandante *mf* de empleo **job sharing** *n no pl*, *Brit* jobsharing *m* **job title** *n* título *m* de un puesto de trabajo

Jock [dʒɒk, *Am:* dʒɑːk] *n Brit, inf* escocés *m*

jockey ['dʒɒki, *Am:* 'dʒɑːki] I. *n* jockey *mf* II. *vi* **to ~ for sth** competir por algo; **to ~ for position** disputarse un puesto

jocose [dʒəʊ'kəʊs, *Am:* dʒoʊ'koʊs] *adj* *form* jocoso, -a

jocular ['dʒɒkjʊləʳ, *Am:* 'dʒɑːkjələ˞] *adj* jocoso, -a

jocund ['dʒɒkənd, *Am:* 'dʒɑːkənd] *adj* jocundo, -a

jodhpurs ['dʒɒdpəz, *Am:* 'dʒɑːdpɚz] *npl* pantalones *mpl* de montar

Joe Bloggs [ˌdʒəʊ'blɒgz, *Am:* ˌdʒoʊ-'blɑːgz] *n Brit, inf* Perico *m* de los Palotes

jog [dʒɒg, *Am:* dʒɑːg] I. *n no pl* 1. (*run*) trote *m;* to go for a ~ hacer footing 2. (*knock*) golpe *m;* to give sth a ~ empujar algo ►to give sb's **memory** a ~ refrescar la memoria de alguien II. <-gg-> *vi* correr III. <-gg-> *vt* empujar; to ~ sb's **elbow** dar a alguien en el codo ►to ~ sb's **memory** refrescar la memoria de alguien ◆**jog along** *vi inf* ir tirando

jogger ['dʒɒgər, *Am:* 'dʒɑːgɚ] *n* persona *f* que hace footing

jogging ['dʒɒgɪŋ, *Am:* 'dʒɑːgɪŋ] *n no pl* footing *m;* to go (out) ~ hacer footing

joggle ['dʒɒgl, *Am:* 'dʒɑːgl] I. *vt* mover II. *n* meneo *m*

john [dʒɒn, *Am:* dʒɑːn] *n Am, Aus, inf* (*toilet*) váter *m*

John Bull *n no pl, inf* John Bull *m* (*personificación de todo lo inglés*)

johnnie *n,* **johnny** ['dʒɒni, *Am:* 'dʒɑːni] *n Brit, inf* (*condom*) goma *f*

join [dʒɔɪn] I. *vt* 1. (*connect*) juntar, unir; to ~ hands tomarse de la mano; to ~ sb (together) in marriage *form* unir a alguien en matrimonio 2. (*come together with sb*) reunirse [*o* juntarse] con; they'll ~ us after dinner vendrán después de cenar 3. (*become member of: club*) hacerse miembro de; (*society*) ingresar en; (*army*) alistarse en; to ~ the queue [*o* line *Am*] ponerse en la cola 4. (*begin to work with*) incorporarse a II. *vi* 1. (*unite*) unirse; to ~ with sb in doing sth sumarse a alguien para hacer algo 2. (*become member*) hacerse socio III. *n* unión *f,* juntura *f*

joiner ['dʒɔɪnər, *Am:* -nɚ] *n* carpintero, -a *m, f*

joinery ['dʒɔɪnəri] *n no pl* carpintería *f*

joint [dʒɔɪnt] I. *adj* conjunto, -a II. *n* 1. (*connection*) unión *f,* juntura *f* 2. ANAT articulación *f;* out of ~ dislocado; to come out of ~ dislocarse 3. TECH conexión 4. BOT nudo *m* 5. (*meat*) asado *m* 6. *inf* (*marihuana*) porro *m*

joint account *n* cuenta *f* conjunta **joint committee** *n* comisión *f* mixta **joint debtor** *n* codeudor(a) *m(f)*

jointed *adj* articulado, -a

joint effort *n* trabajo *m* de equipo

jointly *adv* conjuntamente

joint owner *n* copropietario, -a *m, f* **joint ownership** *n no pl* copropiedad *f* **joint property** *n* propiedad comunitaria *f*

joint stock *n* capital *m* social **joint-stock company** *n* sociedad *f* anónima

joint venture *n* empresa *f* conjunta

joist [dʒɔɪst] *n* viga *f*

joke [dʒəʊk, *Am:* dʒoʊk] I. *n* 1. (*amusing story*) chiste *m;* (*trick, remark*) broma *f;* to get a ~ captar una humorada; to get beyond a ~ pasarse de castaño oscuro *inf;* to make a ~ gastar una broma; to not be able to take a ~ no aceptar una broma; to do sth for a ~ hacer algo en broma; to play a ~ on sb gastar una broma a alguien 2. *inf* (*easy thing*) to be no ~ no ser cosa de broma 3. *no pl, inf* (*ridiculous thing or person*) ridiculez *f;* what a ~! ¡qué farsa! ►the ~ was on me me salió el tiro por la culata *inf* II. *vi* bromear; to ~ about sth hacer bromas sobre algo; you must be joking! ¿lo dices en serio?

joker ['dʒəʊkər, *Am:* 'dʒoʊkɚ] *n* 1. (*one who jokes*) bromista *mf* 2. *inf* (*annoying person*) idiota *m* 3. (*playing card*) comodín *m* ►to be the ~ in the pack ser la gran incógnita

joking I. *adj* jocoso, -a II. *n no pl* bromas *fpl*

jokingly *adv* en broma

jollification [ˌdʒɒlɪfɪ'keɪʃən, *Am:* ˌdʒɑːlə-] *n inf* 1. *no pl* (*merrymaking*) regocijo *m* 2. *pl* (*celebratory activities*) festividades *fpl*

jollity ['dʒɒləti, *Am:* 'dʒɑːləti] *n no pl* jovialidad *f*

jolly ['dʒɒli, *Am:* 'dʒɑːli] I. <-ier, -iest> *adj* 1. (*happy*) alegre 2. (*enjoyable*) agradable II. *adv Brit, inf* muy; ~ good estupendo 2. de verdad; you'll ~ °well have to! ¡no te queda más remedio! III. *vt* to ~ sb into doing sth convencer a alguien para que haga algo; to ~ sb along animar a alguien

jolt [dʒəʊlt, *Am:* dʒoʊlt] I. *n* 1. (*sudden jerk*) sacudida *f* 2. (*shock*) impresión *f* II. *vt* 1. (*jerk*) sacudir 2. (*shock*) sobresaltar III. *vi* dar una sacudida; (*vehicle*) traquetear

Jordan ['dʒɔːdn, *Am:* 'dʒɔːr-] *n* 1. (*country*) Jordania *f* 2. (*river*) Jordán *m*

Jordanian [dʒɔː'deɪniən, *Am:* dʒɔːr-] I. *adj* jordano, -a II. *n* jordano, -a *m, f*

josh [dʒɒʃ, *Am:* dʒɑːʃ] *vt, vi inf* tomar el pelo a

joss stick ['dʒɒsˌstɪk, *Am:* 'dʒɑːsˌstɪk] *n* pebete *m*

jostle ['dʒɒsl, *Am:* 'dʒɑːsl] I. *vt* empujar II. *vi* 1. (*push*) empujarse 2. (*compete*) to ~ for sth disputarse algo

jot [dʒɒt, *Am:* dʒɑːt] I. <-tt-> *vt* to ~ sth down apuntar algo II. *n no pl* there's not a ~ of truth in it eso no tiene ni pizca de verdad

jotter ['dʒɒtər, *Am:* 'dʒɑːtɚ] *n Aus, Brit* cuaderno *m*

jottings *npl* apuntes *mpl*

joule [dʒuːl] *n* PHYS julio *m*

journal ['dʒɜːnəl, *Am:* 'dʒɜːr-] *n* 1. (*periodical*) revista *f* especializada 2. (*diary*) diario *m*

journalism ['dʒɜːnlɪzəm, *Am:* 'dʒɜːr-] *n no pl* periodismo *m,* diarismo *m AmL*

journalist ['dʒɜːnlɪst, *Am:* 'dʒɜːr-] *n* periodista *mf*

journalistic [ˌdʒɜːnə'lɪstɪk, *Am:* ˌdʒɜːr-] *adj* periodístico, -a

journey ['dʒɜːni, *Am:* 'dʒɜːr-] I. *n* viaje *m* II. *vi liter* viajar

journeyman ['dʒɜːnɪmən, *Am:* 'dʒɜːr-] <-men> *n* trabajador *m* calificado

joust [dʒaʊst] I. *vi* justar II. *n* justa *f*

jovial ['dʒəʊviəl, *Am:* 'dʒoʊ-] *adj* jovial

joviality [ˌdʒəʊvi'æləti, *Am:* ˌdʒoʊvi'æləti]

n no pl jovialidad *f*

jowl ['dʒaʊl] *n* quijada *f*

joy [dʒɔɪ] *n* 1. (*gladness*) gozo *m;* **to jump for** ~ saltar de alegría 2. (*cause of joy*) placer *m* 3. *no pl, Brit, inf* (*success*) **did you have any** ~? ¿tuviste éxito?

joyful ['dʒɔɪfəl] *adj* feliz

joyless ['dʒɔɪləs] *adj* sin alegría; (*face*) triste

joyous ['dʒɔɪəs] *adj liter* de júbilo

joyride ['dʒɔɪraɪd] *n paseo en un coche robado*

joystick ['dʒɔɪstɪk] *n* 1. AVIAT palanca *f* de mando 2. INFOR joystick *m*

JP [,dʒeɪ'piː] *Brit abbr of* Justice of the Peace Juez *mf* de Paz

Jr *abbr of* Junior Jr.

jt *abbr of* joint adjunto, -a

jubilant ['dʒuːbɪlənt] *adj* jubiloso, -a; (*crowd*) exultante

jubilation [,dʒuːbɪ'leɪʃən] *n no pl* júbilo *m*

jubilee ['dʒuːbɪliː] *n* 1. (*anniversary*) aniversario *m* 2. REL jubileo *m*

Judaism ['dʒuːdeɪɪzəm] *n no pl* judaísmo *m*

judder ['dʒʌdə^r, *Am:* -ə^r] *Aus, Brit* I. *vi* trepidar II. *n no pl* sacudida *f*

judge [dʒʌdʒ] I. *n* 1. LAW juez *mf* 2. (*referee*) árbitro *m;* (*in a jury*) miembro *m* del jurado; **panel of** ~**s** jurado *m* II. *vi a.* LAW juzgar; (*give one's opinion*) opinar III. *vt* 1. *a.* LAW juzgar; (*question*) decidir; (*assess*) valorar; (*consider*) considerar; **to** ~ **that ...** opinar que... 2. (*as a referee*) arbitrar; (*in a jury*) actuar como miembro del jurado de la

judg(e)ment ['dʒʌdʒmənt] *n* 1. LAW fallo *m* 2. (*opinion*) opinión *f* 3. (*discernment*) criterio *m*

judg(e)mental [dʒʌdʒ'mentəl, *Am:* -ṭəl] *adj* sentencioso, -a

judicature ['dʒuːdɪkətʃə^r, *Am:* -tʃə^r] *n no pl* judicatura *f*

judicial [dʒuː'dɪʃl] *adj* judicial

judiciary [dʒuː'dɪʃəri, *Am:* -ier-] *n no pl, form* poder *m* judicial

judicious [dʒuː'dɪʃəs] *adj form* acertado, -a

judo ['dʒuːdəʊ, *Am:* -doʊ] *n no pl* judo *m*

jug [dʒʌg] *n* 1. *Aus, Brit* (*container*) jarra; (*small: for milk, cream*) jarrita *f* 2. *no pl, inf* (*prison*) cárcel *f;* **to be in the** ~ estar a la sombra

juggernaut ['dʒʌgənɔːt, *Am:* -ə^rnɑːt] *n* 1. AUTO camión *m* grande 2. (*overwhelming force*) monstruo *m*

juggle ['dʒʌgl] I. *vi a. fig* hacer juegos malabares II. *vt a. fig* hacer juegos malabares con

juggler *n* malabarista *mf*

jugular ['dʒʌgjələ^r, *Am:* -lə^r] *n* (vena *f*) yugular *f* ▶ **to go for the** ~ *inf* entrar a degüello

jugular vein *n* vena *f* yugular

juice [dʒuːs] *n* 1. *no pl* (*drink*) zumo *m* 2. (*of meat*) jugo *m* 3. *no pl, Am, inf* (*electricity*) corriente *f;* (*petrol*) combustible *m* ▶ **to stew in one's own** ~ cocerse en su propia salsa

juicy ['dʒuːsi] <-ier, -iest> *adj* 1. (*fruit,*

steak) jugoso, -a 2. *inf* (*profit*) sustancioso, -a; (*role*) suculento, -a 3. *inf* (*scandalous*) escabroso, -a; (*details*) picante

ju-jitsu [,dʒuː'dʒɪtsuː] *n no pl* jiujitsu *m*

jukebox ['dʒuːkbɒks, *Am:* -bɑːks] *n* máquina *f* de discos

julep ['dʒuːlɪp, *Am:* -ləp] *n* (*drink*) julepe *m;* **mint** ~ julepe de menta

July [dʒuː'laɪ] *n* julio *m; s. a.* **April**

jumble ['dʒʌmbl] I. *n no pl* 1. (*disorderly pile*) revoltijo *m* 2. *Brit* (*unwanted articles for sale*) cosas *fpl* usadas II. *vt* mezclar

jumble sale *n* bazar *m* benéfico

jumbo ['dʒʌmbəʊ, *Am:* -boʊ] I. *adj* gigante *m* II. *n inf* jumbo *m*

jump [dʒʌmp] I. *vi* 1. (*leap*) saltar; **to** ~ **up and down** pegar saltos; **to** ~ **up and down with frustration** *Aus, Brit* subirse por las paredes 2. (*skip*) brincar; **to** ~ **for joy** brincar de alegría 3. (*jerk*) sobresaltarse 4. (*increase suddenly*) subir de golpe ▶ **go** ~ **in the lake!** *inf* ¡vete a freír espárragos! II. *vt* 1. (*leap across or over*) saltar 2. (*attack*) atacar 3. (*disregard*) saltarse ▶ **to** ~ **a queue** colarse III. *n* 1. (*leap*) salto *m* 2. (*hurdle*) obstáculo *m*

◆ **jump about** *vi* dar saltos

◆ **jump at** *vt* (*opportunity*) no dejar escapar; (*offer*) aceptar con entusiasmo

◆ **jump down** *vi* bajar de un salto

◆ **jump in** *vi* entrar de prisa

◆ **jump on** *vt* (*criticise*) poner verde

◆ **jump out at** *vt* (*error, inconsistency*) saltar a la vista de

◆ **jump up** *vi* ponerse de pie de un salto

jumped-up [,dʒʌmpt'ʌp] *adj Brit, inf* presuntuoso, -a

jumper ['dʒʌmpə^r, *Am:* -pə^r] *n* 1. (*person, animal*) saltador(a) *m(f)* 2. *Aus, Brit* (*pullover*) suéter *m* 3. *Am* (*dress*) pichi *m*

jumping jack *n* (*toy*) títere *m*

jump jet *n* avión *m* de despegue vertical

jump lead *n Brit* cable *m* de arranque

jump-start *vt* hacer arrancar (*empujando o haciendo un puente*) **jump suit** *n* mono *m*

jumpy ['dʒʌmpi] <-ier, -iest> *adj inf* nervioso, -a

junction ['dʒʌŋkʃən] *n* (*road* ~) cruce *m;* (*motorway* ~) salida *f*

junction box *n* caja *f* de empalmes

juncture ['dʒʌŋktʃə^r, *Am:* -tʃə^r] *n no pl, form* coyuntura *f;* **at this** ~ en este momento

June [dʒuːn] *n* junio *m; s. a.* **April**

jungle ['dʒʌŋgl] *n* 1. (*forest*) selva *f* 2. *fig* (*tangled mass*) maraña *f;* (*of laws*) laberinto *m*

junior ['dʒuːniə^r, *Am:* '-njə^r] I. *adj* 1. (*younger*) más joven 2. SPORTS juvenil 3. (*lower in rank*) subalterno, -a; (*partner*) comanditario, -a II. *n* 1. (*younger person*) **which is the** ~? ¿quién es el más joven? 2. (*low-ranking person*) subalterno, -a *m, f* 3. *Brit* SCHOOL alumno, -a *m, f* de primaria 4. *Am* UNIV estudiante *mf* de tercer año

junior college *n Am:* colegio que com-

prende los dos primeros años universitarios
junior high school *n Am* instituto *m* de enseñanza media **junior school** *n Brit* escuela *f* primaria

juniper ['dʒuːnɪpəʳ, *Am:* -pɚ] *n* enebro *m*

junk¹ [dʒʌŋk] I. *n* **1.** *no pl* (*objects of no value*) trastos *mpl*, tiliches *mpl AmC, Méx* **2.** *Am, inf* (*drugs*) caballo *m* II. *vt inf* tirar a la basura

junk² [dʒʌŋk] *n* (*vessel*) junco *m*

junk food *n* comida *f* basura

junkie ['dʒʌŋki] *n inf* yonqui *mf*

junk room *n* trastero *m*, degredo *m Ven*
junk shop *n* tienda *f* de trastos viejos **junkyard** [-jɑːrd] *n* chatarrería *f*

junta ['dʒʌntə, *Am:* 'hʊntə] *n* gobierno *f* dictatorial; (**military**) ~ junta *f* militar

Jupiter ['dʒuːpɪtəʳ, *Am:* -t̬ɚ] *n* Júpiter *m*

juridical [dʒʊə'rɪdɪkəl, *Am:* dʒʊ'-] *adj* jurídico, -a

jurisdiction [ˌdʒʊərɪs'dɪkʃən, *Am:* ˌdʒʊrɪs-] *n no pl* jurisdicción *f*; **to have ~ in sth** tener competencia en algo

jurisprudence [ˌdʒʊərɪs'pruːdənts, *Am:* ˌdʒʊrɪs-] *n no pl* jurisprudencia *f*

jurist ['dʒʊərɪst, *Am:* 'dʒʊrɪst] *n* jurista *mf*

juror ['dʒʊərəʳ, *Am:* 'dʒʊrɚ] *n* miembro *mf* del jurado

jury ['dʒʊəri, *Am:* 'dʒʊri] *n* jurado *m*

juryman ['dʒʊərɪmən, *Am:* 'dʒʊri-] *n* miembro *m* del jurado

just [dʒʌst] I. *adv* **1.** (*very soon*) enseguida; **we're ~ about to leave** estamos a punto de salir **2.** (*now*) precisamente; **to be ~ doing sth** estar justamente haciendo algo **3.** (*very recently*) ~ **after 10 o'clock** justo después de las 10; **she's ~ turned 15** acaba de cumplir 15 años **4.** (*exactly, equally*) exactamente, justo; ~ **like that** exactamente así; ~ **as I expected** tal y como yo esperaba; ~ **now** ahora mismo; **not ~ yet** todavía no **5.** (*only*) solamente; ~ **a minute** espera un momento **6.** (*simply*) simplemente; ~ **in case it rains** por si llueve **7.** (*barely*) ~ (**about**), (**only**) ~ apenas; ~ **in time** justo a tiempo **8.** (*very*) muy; **you look ~ wonderful!** ¡estás maravillosa! **9.** ~ **about** (*nearly*) casi **10.** **it's ~ as well that ...** menos mal que... ▸~ **my luck!** ¡que mala suerte tengo!; **isn't it** ~? *inf* ¿verdad? II. *adj* (*fair*) justo, -a ▸**to get one's ~ deserts** llevarse su merecido

justice ['dʒʌstɪs] *n* **1.** justicia *f*; **to bring sb to** ~ llevar a uno ante al tribunal **2.** *Am* (*judge*) juez *mf*

justifiable [ˌdʒʌstɪ'faɪəbl, *Am:* ˌdʒʌstə'-] *adj* justificable

justification [ˌdʒʌstɪfɪ'keɪʃən, *Am:* -tə-] *n no pl* justificación *f*

justify ['dʒʌstɪfaɪ] *vt* justificar; **to ~ oneself** disculparse; **to ~ oneself to sb** dar explicaciones a alguien

justly ['dʒʌstli] *adv* justamente

jut [dʒʌt] <-tt-> *vi* **to ~ out** sobresalir

jute [dʒuːt] *n no pl* yute *m*

juvenile ['dʒuːvənaɪl, *Am:* -nl] *adj* **1.** *form* (*young*) juvenil **2.** *pej* (*childish*) infantil

juvenile court *n* tribunal *m* de menores
juvenile delinquency *n* delincuencia *f* juvenil

juxtapose [ˌdʒʌkstə'pəʊz, *Am:* 'dʒʌkstəpoʊz] *vt* yuxtaponer

juxtaposition [ˌdʒʌkstəpə'zɪʃən] *n no pl* yuxtaposición *f*

K

K, k [keɪ] *n* K, k *f*; ~ **for King** K de Kenia
K INFOR *abbr of* **kilobyte** K *m*

kajal (**eyeliner**) **pencil** [kə.jel('aɪlaɪnə)-ˌpentsəl] *n* delineador *m* de ojos

kale *n*, **kail** [keɪl] *n* col *f* rizada

kaleidoscope [kə'laɪdəskəʊp, *Am:* -skoʊp] *n* caleidoscopio *m*

kamikaze [ˌkæmɪ'kɑːzi, *Am:* ˌkɑːmə-] *adj* kamikaze *m*

kamikaze attack *n* ataque *m* kamikaze

Kampuchea [ˌkæmpʊ'tʃiːə, *Am:* -puː'-] *n* Kampuchea *f*

Kampuchean I. *adj* kampucheano, -a II. *n* kampucheano, -a *m*, *f*

kangaroo [ˌkæŋgə'ruː] <-(s)> *n* canguro *m*

kangaroo court *n* tribunal *m* desautorizado

kaolin ['keɪəlɪn] *n no pl* MIN caolín *m*

Kaposi's sarcoma [kæ'pəʊziz sɑː'kəʊmə, *Am:* kə'poʊziz sɑː'koʊ-] *n* MED sarcoma *m* de Kaposi

karaoke [kæri'əʊki, *Am:* 'kɑːr-] *n* karaoke *m*

karate [kə'rɑːti, *Am:* kæ'rɑːt̬i] *n no pl* kárate *m*

karate chop *n* golpe *m* de kárate

karma ['kɑːmə, *Am:* 'kɑːr-] *n no pl* karma *m*

kayak ['kaɪæk] *n* kayak *m*

kayaking *n no pl* **I love ~** me incanta ir en kayak

Kb, KB [ˌkeɪ'biː] INFOR *abbr of* **kilobyte** Kb

kbyte INFOR *abbr of* **kilobyte** kbyte

kc *abbr of* **kilocycle** kc

KC *n abbr of* **King's Counsel** abogado de la Corona

kebab [kə'bæb, *Am:* -'bɑːb] *n* kebab *m*

keel [kiːl] *n* NAUT quilla *f*

◆**keel over** *vi* volcarse; (*person*) desplomarse

keelhaul ['kiːlˌhɔːl, *Am:* -hɑːl] *vt fig, inf* echar un buen rapapolvo

keen [kiːn] I. *adj* **1.** (*intent, eager*) entusiasta; (*student*) aplicado, -a; **to be ~ to do sth** tener ganas de hacer algo; **to be ~ on sth** ser aficionado, -a a algo **2.** (*perceptive: intelligence*) agudo, -a; (*ear*) fino, -a; **to have ~ eyesight** tener muy buena vista; **to have a ~ sense of smell** tener un agudo sentido del olfato

3.(*extreme*) fuerte; **a ~ interest** un vivo interés; **to have a ~ appetite** tener buen apetito **4.** *liter* (*sharp*) afilado, -a; (*wind*) cortante **5.**(*shrill, piercing*) penetrante **II.** *n* lamento *m* fúnebre **III.** *vi* lamentar; **to ~ for sb** llorar la muerte de alguien

keep [ki:p] **I.** *n* **1.** *no pl* (*livelihood*) subsistencia *f*; **to earn one's ~** ganarse el sustento **2.** HIST (*castle tower*) torre *f* del homenaje ▸**for ~s** para siempre **II.**<kept, kept> *vt* **1.**(*have: shop*) tener; (*guesthouse*) dirigir; (*animals*) criar; *Am* (*children*) cuidar **2.**(*store: silence, secret*) guardar; **~ me a place** guárdame un sitio; **~ the change** quédese con el cambio **3.**(*maintain*) mantener; **to ~ sb under observation** tener a alguien en observación; **to ~ one's eyes fixed on sth/sb** no apartar los ojos de algo/alguien; **to ~ sb awake** no dejar dormir a alguien; **to ~ sth going** mantener algo a flote *fig* **4.**(*detain*) **to ~ sb waiting** hacer esperar a alguien; **to ~ sb in prison** tener a alguien en la cárcel; **he was kept in hospital** se quedó ingresado en el hospital; **what kept you?** ¿por qué tardaste? **5.**(*guard*) guardar; **to ~ one's temper** contener el genio **6.**(*fulfil*) cumplir; **to ~ an appointment** acudir a una cita; **to ~ one's word** cumplir su palabra **7.**(*record: diary*) escribir; (*accounts*) llevar **8.**(*person's expenses*) mantener; **to earn enough to ~ oneself** ganar lo bastante para mantenerse; **to ~ a mistress** mantener a una amante **9.**(*obey, respect*) obedecer; (*law*) observar **10.**(*remain involved*) **to ~ one's hand in** no perder la práctica ▸**to ~ one's balance** mantener el equilibrio; **to ~ time** marcar la hora **III.**<kept, kept> *vi* **1.** *a. fig* (*stay fresh*) conservarse **2.**(*stay*) mantenerse; **to ~ fit** mantenerse en forma; **to ~ silent** (**about sth**) guardar silencio (sobre algo); **to ~ to the left** circular por la izquierda; **~ quiet!** ¡cállate!; **~ still!** ¡estáte quieto! **3.**(*continue*) **to ~ going** (*person*) seguir tirando; (*machine*) seguir funcionando; **to ~ doing sth** seguir haciendo algo; **he ~s losing his keys** siempre está perdiendo sus llaves ▸**how are you ~ing?** *Brit* ¿cómo estás?

◆**keep ahead** *vi* seguir en cabeza; **to ~ of the others** seguir por delante de los demás

◆**keep at I.** *vi* perseverar; **to ~ work** seguir con el trabajo; **~ it!** ¡ánimo! **II.** *vt* **to keep sb at sth** tener a alguien haciendo algo

◆**keep away I.** *vi* mantenerse alejado, -a; **keep medicines away from children** mantenga los medicamentos fuera del alcance de los niños; **he can't ~ from it** no puede dejarlo; **~!** ¡no te acerques! **II.** *vt always sep* mantener alejado, -a

◆**keep back I.** *vi* (*stay away*) **to ~ from sth/sb** mantenerse alejado de algo/alguien **II.** *vt* **1.** to **~ one's tears** contener las lágrimas **2.**(*hide*) ocultar; **to keep the truth back from sb** ocultar la verdad a alguien **3.**(*retain* *sth*) **to keep sth back** quedarse con algo; (*slow down*) retrasar algo

◆**keep down** *vt* **1.** to **keep one's voice down** no levantar la voz; **to keep prices down** controlar los precios **2.**(*suppress*) **to keep sb down** oprimir a alguien **3.**(*not vomit*) retener

◆**keep from I.** *vt always sep* **1.**(*prevent*) impedir; **to keep sb from doing sth** impedir que alguien haga algo **2.**(*retain information*) **to keep sth from sb** ocultar algo a alguien **II.** *vi* evitar; **I couldn't ~ laughing** no me podía aguantar la risa

◆**keep in I.** *vt* (*person*) no dejar salir; (*emotions*) contener; **to keep a pupil in** retener a un alumno como castigo **II.** *vi* **to ~ line** comportarse bien; **to ~ with sb** tener buena relación con alguien

◆**keep off I.** *vi* (*stay off*) mantenerse alejado, -a; '**~**' 'prohibido el paso'; '**~ the grass**' 'prohibido pisar el césped'; **if the rain keeps off ...** si no llueve... **II.** *vt* mantener alejado, -a; **to keep the rain off sth/sb** resguardar algo/a alguien de la lluvia; **keep your hands off!** ¡no lo toques! **2.**(*avoid*) evitar; **to ~ a subject** *Brit* no mencionar un tema

◆**keep on I.** *vi* **1.**(*continue*) seguir; **to ~ doing sth** seguir haciendo algo **2.**(*pester*) **don't ~!** ¡no insistas!; **to ~ about sb/sth** no parar de hablar de alguien/algo; **to ~ at sb** estar siempre encima de alguien **II.** *vt always sep* **1.**(*not to dismiss*) no despedir **2.**(*not to get rid of*) no deshacerse

◆**keep out I.** *vi* no entrar; **~!** ¡prohibido el paso!; **to ~ of sth** no meterse en algo; **to ~ of trouble** no meterse en líos **II.** *vt* **to keep sth/sb out** (**of sth**) no dejar que entre algo/alguien (en algo); **to keep the rain/cold out** resguardar de la lluvia/del frío

◆**keep to I.** *vt always sep* (*remain private*) **to keep sth to oneself** guardarse algo para sí; **to keep oneself to oneself** ser poco sociable **II.** *vi* **1.**(*stay in*) **~ the right** seguir hacia la derecha; **to ~ one's bed** quedarse en cama **2.**(*respect*) **to ~ sth** ceñirse a algo; **to keep sb to his/her word** tomar la palabra a alguien

◆**keep together I.** *vt* mantener juntos, -as **II.** *vi* mantenerse unidos, -as; **please, ~** por favor, no se separen

◆**keep up I.** *vt* **1.**(*trousers*) sujetar; (*ceiling*) sostener; (*prices*) mantener alto, -a **2.**(*continue*) seguir; **to ~ the payments** estar al corriente de los pagos; **~ the good work!** ¡sigue así!; **keep it up!** ¡sigue! **3.**(*maintain*) **to ~ appearances** guardar las apariencias; **to ~ traditions** mantener las tradiciones **4.**(*stop sb sleeping*) tener en vela **II.** *vi* **1.**(*prices*) mantenerse estable; (*moral*) no decaer **2.**(*continue*) seguir; **the rain kept up all night** siguió lloviendo durante toda la noche **3.**(*to stay level with*) **to ~** (**with sb/sth**) seguir el ritmo (de alguien/algo); **wages are failing to ~ with inflation** los sueldos no aumentan a la par que

K

la inflación; **I cannot ~ with their conver-sations** no puedo seguir sus conversaciones; **to ~ with the Joneses** *fig* no ser menos que los demás **4.** (*maintain contact with*) **to ~ with sb** mantener el contacto con alguien **5.** (*remain informed*) **to ~ with sth** mantenerse al tanto de algo; **to ~ with the times** estar al día

keeper ['kiːpəʳ, *Am:* -pɚ] *n* (*in charge*) guarda *mf;* (*museum*) conservador(a) *m(f);* (*jail*) carcelero, -a *m, f*

keeping ['kiːpɪŋ] *n no pl* **1.** (*guarding*) cargo *m;* **to leave sth/sb in sb's ~** dejar algo/a alguien al cuidado de alguien; **to leave sth/sb in safe ~** dejar algo/a alguien en buenas manos **2.** **in ~ with sth** de acuerdo con algo; **to be out of ~ with sth** desentonar con algo

keepsake ['kiːpseɪk] *n* recuerdo *m*

keg [keg] *n* barril *m*

kelp [kelp] *n no pl* tipo de alga marrón usada en comidas

ken [ken] **I.** *n* **to be beyond sb's ~** ser desconocido para alguien **II.** <-nn-> *vt Scot* (*person*) conocer; (*thing*) saber

kennel ['kenl] *n* **1.** (*doghouse*) perrera *f* **2.** *pl* (*boarding*) residencia *f* canina; (*breeding*) criadero *m* de perros

Kenya ['kenjə] *n* Kenia *f*

Kenyan ['kenjən] **I.** *n* keniano, -a *m, f* **II.** *adj* keniano, -a

kept [kept] **I.** *pt, pp of* **keep II.** *adj* mantenido, -a; **a ~ woman** una amante; **a ~ man** un gigoló

kerb [kɜːb, *Am:* kɜːrb] *n Brit, Aus* bordillo *m*, cordón *m CSur*

kerchief ['kɜːtʃɪf, *Am:* 'kɜːrtʃɪf] *n* pañoleta *f*

kerfuffle [kə'fʌfl, *Am:* kɚ-] *n Brit, inf* jaleo *m*

kernel ['kɜːnl, *Am:* 'kɜːr-] *n* **1.** (*centre of fruit*) almendra *f* **2.** **maize ~** grano *m* de maíz **3.** (*essential part*) núcleo *m;* **a ~ of truth** una pizca de verdad

kerosene ['kerəsiːn] *n no pl, Am, Aus* queroseno *m*

kestrel ['kestrəl] *n* cernícalo *m*

ketch [ketʃ] <-es> *n* NAUT queche *m*

ketchup ['ketʃəp] *n no pl* ketchup *m*

kettle ['ketl, *Am:* 'keṭ-] *n* tetera *f*, pava *f AmL;* **to put the ~ on** poner agua a hervir ► **that's a different ~ of** fish eso es harina de otro costal; **to get into a pretty ~ of** fish meterse en un buen berenjenal *inf*

kettledrum ['ketldrʌm, *Am:* 'keṭ-] *n* MUS timbal *m*

key [kiː] **I.** *n* **1.** (*doors*) llave *f;* **master ~** llave maestra **2.** *a.* INFOR tecla *f;* **caps lock ~** tecla de bloqueo de mayúsculas; **to hit a ~** pulsar una tecla **3.** *no pl* (*essential point*) clave *f;* **the ~ to a mystery** la clave de un misterio; **a ~ factor/role** un factor/papel clave **4.** (*list*) clave *f;* (*map*) lista *f* de símbolos convencionales; (*exercises*) soluciones *fpl* **5.** MUS tono *m;* **change of ~** cambio *m* de tono; **in the ~ of C major** en (tono de) do mayor; **to go off ~**

desafinar ► **to hold the ~ to sth** tener la clave de algo **II.** *adj* clave **III.** *vt* **1.** (*type*) **to ~** (**in**) teclear **2.** (*make appropriate*) adaptar

◆ **key in** *vt* INFOR picar, teclear

◆ **key up** *vt* emocionar; **to be keyed up** estar emocionado, -a; **to be keyed up for sth** estar listo para algo

keyboard ['kiːbɔːd, *Am:* -bɔːrd] **I.** *n* teclado *m* **II.** *vi, vt* teclear

keyboarding *n no pl* introducción *f* desde teclado

keyboard instrument *n* instrumento *m* de teclado

keyhole ['kiːhəʊl, *Am:* -hoʊl] *n* ojo *m* de la cerradura **key money** *n no pl* adelanto *m;* **as ~** en concepto de adelanto

keynote ['kiːnəʊt, *Am:* -noʊt] *n* **1.** MUS nota *f* tónica **2.** (*central idea*) idea *f* fundamental; **to be the ~ of sth** ser la piedra angular de algo *fig*

keynoter *n* ponente *mf* del discurso central

keynote speech *n*, **keynote address** *n* discurso *m* central

keypad ['kiːpæd] *n* INFOR teclado *m* numérico

key ring *n* llavero *m* **keystone** *n* **1.** ARCHIT (*centre stone*) clave *f* **2.** (*crucial part*) piedra *f* angular **key stroke** *n* pulsación *f* (de una tecla) **key word** *n* palabra *f* clave

kg *abbr of* **kilogram** kg

khaki ['kaːki, *Am:* 'kæki] **I.** *n no pl* (*colour, cloth*) caqui *m;* **~s** pantalones *mpl* caqui **II.** *adj* caqui

kHz *n abbr of* **kilohertz** KHz *m*

KIA *adj abbr of* **killed in action** fallecido, -a en acto de servicio

kibbutz [kɪ'bʊts] *n* kibbutz *m*

kick [kɪk] **I.** *n* **1.** (*person*) patada *f;* (*horse*) coz *f;* (*in football*) tiro *m;* (*in swimming*) movimiento *m* de las piernas **2.** (*exciting feeling*) placer *m;* **to do sth for ~s** hacer algo para divertirse; **to get a ~ out of sth** encontrar placer en algo; **this drink has a ~ in it** esta bebida es fuerte **3.** (*craze*) **he is on an exercise ~ at the moment** ahora le ha dado por hacer ejercicio **4.** (*gun jerk*) culatazo *m* ► **to be a ~ in the** teeth ser como un jarro de agua fría **II.** *vt* **1.** dar una patada; **to ~ sth open** abrir algo de una patada; **to ~ a ball** chutar una pelota; **to ~ oneself** *fig* darse con la cabeza en la pared **2.** (*stop*) dejar; **to ~ a habit** dejar un vicio ► **to be ~ing one's** heels *Brit* estar de plantón; **to ~ sth into** touch posponer algo; **to ~ sb upstairs** ascender a alguien para librarse de él **III.** *vi* **1.** (*person*) dar patadas a; (*horse*) dar coces; SPORTS chutar **2.** (*gun*) dar culatazo **3.** (*complain*) protestar; **to ~ about sth** quejarse de algo; **to ~ against sth** oponerse a algo **4.** **to be alive and ~ing** *inf* estar vivito y coleando

◆ **kick about, kick around I.** *vi inf* (*hang about*) andar por ahí; (*thing*) andar rodando **II.** *vt* **1.** (*a ball*) dar patadas a **2.** (*treat badly*) maltratar

◆**kick against** vt insep protestar contra
◆**kick at** vt golpear
◆**kick away** vt apartar de un golpe
◆**kick back** I. vt (football) devolver II. vi inf 1. (recoil) retroceder; (gun) dar culatazo 2. (give a kickback) sobornar
◆**kick in** vt derribar a patadas; **to kick sb's teeth in** romper la cara a alguien
◆**kick off** I. vi (begin) empezar; (in football) hacer el saque de centro II. vt quitar de un puntapié
◆**kick out** I. vt **to kick sb out** poner a alguien de patitas en la calle inf; **he was kicked out of the party** lo echaron de la fiesta II. vi (person) dar patadas; (horse) dar coces
◆**kick over** vi **to ~ the traces** desmandarse
◆**kick up** vt **to ~ dust** a. fig levantar polvo; **to ~ a fuss/row** armar un escándalo ►**to ~ one's** heels echar una cana al aire
◆**kick upstairs** vt ascender
kickback ['kɪkbæk] n inf soborno m
kicker ['kɪkə', Am: -ə·] n 1. (person who kicks) pateador(a) m(f) 2. Am, fig **to be a ~** tener agallas 3. (surprise) **it was a real ~ for me** me dejó de piedra inf 4. (sth disadvantageous) pega f
kick-off ['kɪkɒf, Am: -ɑːf] n SPORTS saque m inicial **kick-starter** n AUTO pedal m de arranque
kid [kɪd] I. n 1. (child) niño, -a m, f, pipiolo, -a m, f; Am, Aus (young person) chico, -a m, f; **~ brother** Am hermano m pequeño; **as a ~ ...** de niño... 2. ZOOL cría f; (young goat) cabrito m 3. (goat leather) cabritilla f ►**to treat sb with ~** gloves tratar a alguien con guante blanco; **that's ~'s** stuff eso está tirado inf II. <-dd-> vi bromear; **are you ~ing?** ¿bromeas?; **just ~ding** es broma; **no ~ding!** ¡te lo juro! III. vt **to ~ sb (about sth)** tomar el pelo a alguien (con algo) IV. vr **to ~ oneself that ...** hacerse la ilusión de que...; **stop ~ding yourself!** ¡desengáñate!
kiddie n, **kiddy** ['kɪdi] n inf crío, -a m, f
kidnap ['kɪdnæp] I. <-pp-> vt secuestrar, plagiar AmL II. n secuestro m, plagio m AmL
kidnapper ['kɪdnæpə', Am: -ə·] n secuestrador(a) m(f)
kidnapping n secuestro m
kidney ['kɪdni] n riñón m; **~ disease** enfermedad f renal
kidney bean n judía f, poroto m CSur **kidney donor** n donante mf de riñón **kidney failure** n MED fracaso m renal **kidney machine** n MED riñón m artificial **kidney stone** n MED cálculo m renal
kidology [kɪ'dɒlədʒi] n inf decepción f
kill [kɪl] I. n no pl 1. (slaughter) matanza f 2. (hunting) pieza f ►**to be** in **at the ~** estar presente en el momento crucial; **to go in for the ~** entrar a matar II. vi matar; **thou shalt not ~** (Bible) no matarás ►**to be** dressed **to ~** ir despampanante III. vt 1. (cause to die) matar; **to ~ oneself** matarse; **to ~ oneself**

with laughter fig morirse de risa; **this will ~ you!** Am, fig ¡con esto te vas a morir de risa!; **not to ~ oneself trying** fig, inf no esforzarse mucho 2. (destroy) acabar con; **to ~ the flavour of sth** quitar el gusto a algo; **my feet are ~ing me!** ¡los pies me están matando!; **to ~ sb with kindness** abrumar a alguien con atenciones
◆**kill off** vt exterminar; (a disease) erradicar
killer ['kɪlə', Am: -ə·] n 1. (sb who kills) asesino, -a m, f; **to be a ~ (person)** ser un asesino; (disease) cobrar muchas víctimas; **the test was a real ~** fig, inf el test era matador 2. Am, Aus, inf (amusing, talented) **to be a ~** ser genial; **this joke is a ~** este chiste es para morirse de risa
killer disease n enfermedad f mortal **killer whale** n orca f
killing ['kɪlɪŋ] I. n (of a person) asesinato m; (of an animal) matanza f ►**to** make **a ~** inf hacer su agosto II. adj 1. (murderous) asesino, -a 2. (exhausting) matador(a) 3. (funny) para morirse de risa
killjoy ['kɪldʒɔɪ] n aguafiestas mf inv
kiln ['kɪln] n horno m
kilo ['kiːləʊ, Am: -oʊ] n kilo m
kilobyte ['kɪləʊbaɪt, Am: -oʊ-] n INFOR kilobyte m
kilocycle ['kɪləʊˌsaɪkl, Am: -oʊ-] n kilociclo m
kilogram n Am, **kilogramme** ['kɪləʊgræm, Am: -oʊ-] n kilogramo m
kilojoule ['kɪləʊdʒuːl, Am: -oʊ-] n kilojoule m
kilometre n Brit, Aus, **kilometer** [kɪ'lɒmɪtə', Am: kɪ'lɑːmət̬ə·] n Am kilómetro m
kilowatt ['kɪləʊwɒt, Am: -oʊwɑːt] n kilovatio m **kilowatt hour** n kilovatio-hora m
kilt [kɪlt] n falda f escocesa, pollera f escocesa CSur
kimono [kɪ'məʊnəʊ, Am: kə'mɔʊnə] n quimono m, kimono m
kin [kɪn] n no pl **next of ~** parientes mpl más cercanos
kind¹ [kaɪnd] adj amable; **to be ~ to sb** ser amable con alguien; **he was ~ enough to ...** tuvo la amabilidad de...; **would you be ~ enough/so ~ as to ...?** ¿me haría usted el favor de...?; **with ~ regards** (in a letter) muchos recuerdos
kind² [kaɪnd] I. n 1. (type) clase f; **sth of the ~** algo por el estilo; **he is not that ~ (of person)** no es de esa clase (de personas); **what ~ of ...?** ¿qué clase de...?; **all ~s of ...** todo tipo de...; **the first of its ~** el primero en su especie; **to hear/say nothing of the ~** no haber oído/dicho nada parecido; **they are two of a ~** son tal para cual 2. (sth similar to) especie f; **a ~ of soup** una especie de sopa 3. (sth equal to) **to do sth in ~** hacer algo de la misma manera; **he swore at me so I answered in ~** me insultó, así que le respondí de igual manera; **he repaid her betrayal in ~** pagó su

traición con la misma moneda **4.** (*limited*) **in a ~ of way** en cierta manera; **she has found happiness of a ~ with him** ha encontrado una cierta felicidad junto a él **5.** (*payment*) **to pay sb in ~** pagar a alguien en especias **II.** *adv inf* **I ~ of like it** me gusta en cierta manera; **he was ~ of sad** estaba como triste; **"do you like it?" – "~ of"** "¿te gusta?" – "no está mal"

kindergarten ['kɪndəgɑ:tn, *Am:* -dəˈgɑ:r-] *n* jardín *m* de infancia, jardín *m* infantil *Chile,* jardín *m* de infantes *RíoPl*

kind-hearted [ˌkaɪndˈhɑ:tɪd, *Am:* -ˈhɑ:rtɪd] *adj* bondadoso, -a; **he is very ~** tiene muy buen corazón

kindle ['kɪndl] **I.** *vt a. fig* encender; **to ~ sb's interest** despertar el interés de alguien; **to ~ sb's desire** provocar el deseo en alguien **II.** *vi a. fig* encenderse

kindling ['kɪndlɪŋ] *n no pl* **1.** (*firewood*) leña *f* **2.** *a. fig* (*act of lighting*) encendimiento *m*

kindly ['kaɪndli] **I.** <-ier, -iest> *adj* amable; (*person*) bondadoso, -a **II.** *adv* **1.** (*in a kind manner*) amablemente **2.** (*please*) **you are ~ requested to leave the building** se ruega abandonen el edificio; **~ put that book away!** ¡haz el favor de guardar ese libro! **3.** (*favourably*) **to take ~ to sth** aceptar algo de buen grado

kindness ['kaɪndnɪs] <-es> *n* **1.** *no pl* (*act of being kind*) amabilidad *f* **2.** (*kind act*) favor *m;* **to do sb a ~** hacer un favor a alguien

kindred ['kɪndrɪd] **I.** *n + pl vb* parientes *mpl* **II.** *adj* afín; **~ spirits** almas *fpl* gemelas

kinetic [kɪˈnetɪk, *Am:* -ˈneţ-] *adj* PHYS cinético, -a

kinfolk ['kɪnfəʊk, *Am:* -foʊk] *n + pl vb, Am* parientes *mpl*

king [kɪŋ] *n* **1.** *a.* GAMES rey *m;* **the ~ of beasts** el rey de la selva **2.** (*in draughts*) dama *f*

kingcup ['kɪŋkʌp] *n Brit* BOT botón *m* de oro

kingdom ['kɪŋdəm] *n* reino *m;* **animal/plant ~** reino animal/vegetal; **the ~ of God** REL el Reino de Dios ▶**to blow sth to ~ come** hacer saltar algo en pedazos; **(un)til ~ come** hasta el Día del Juicio Final

kingfisher ['kɪŋˌfɪʃəʳ, *Am:* -ɚ] *n* martín *m* pescador

kingly ['kɪŋli] *adj* regio, -a

kingpin ['kɪŋpɪn] *n* TECH pivote *m* central; **to be the ~** (*person*) ser el cerebro; (*thing*) ser la piedra angular

King's Bench *n Brit no pl* LAW Tribunal *m* Supremo

king-size ['kɪŋsaɪz] *adj* gigante; **~ cigarettes** cigarrillos *mpl* largos

kink [kɪŋk] *n* **1.** (*twist: in a pipe, rope*) retorcimiento *m;* (*in hair*) rizo *m* **2.** *Am, Aus* (*sore muscle*) tortícolis *f inv;* **to have a ~ in one's neck** tener tortícolis **3.** (*problem*) fallo *m;* **to iron out (a few) ~s** pulir algunos defectos **4.** (*strange habit*) manía *f*

kinky ['kɪŋki] <-ier, -iest> *adj* **1.** (*twisted*)

retorcido, -a **2.** (*with tight curls*) ensortijado, -a **3.** (*unusual*) raro, -a; (*involving unusual sexual acts*) pervertido, -a

kinsfolk ['kɪnzfəʊk, *Am:* -foʊk] *n* HIST + *pl vb* parientes *mpl* **kinship** *n no pl* (*family relationship*) parentesco *m;* (*similarity*) afinidad *f;* **to feel a ~ with sb** tener afinidad con alguien **kinsman** <-men> *n* HIST pariente *m* **kinswoman** <-women> *n* HIST parienta *f*

kiosk ['ki:ɒsk, *Am:* -ɑ:sk] *n* **1.** (*stand*) quiosco *m* **2.** *Brit, form* (*telephone box*) cabina *f* (telefónica)

kip [kɪp] *Brit, Aus, inf* **I.** *n no pl, inf* **to get some ~** echar una cabezada, apolillar un rato *RíoPl* **II.** <-pp-> *vi* dormir; **to ~ down** acostarse

kipper ['kɪpəʳ, *Am:* -ɚ] *n* arenque *m* ahumado

Kiribati [ˌkɪrəˈbæs, *Am:* ˈkɪrəbæs] *n* Kiribati *f*

kirk [kɜ:k, *Am:* kɜ:rk] *n Scot* iglesia *f;* **the Kirk** la Iglesia Presbiteriana de Escocia

kiss [kɪs] **I.** <-es> *n* beso *m;* **~ of life** respiración *f* boca a boca; **~ of death** *fig* beso de la muerte; **to blow sb a ~** lanzar un beso a alguien; **love and ~es** (*at the end of a letter*) muchos besos **II.** *vi* besarse **III.** *vt* besar; **to ~ sb goodnight/goodbye** dar un beso de buenas noches/despedida a alguien

kisser ['kɪsəʳ, *Am:* -ɚ] *n* **1.** (*person*) **he's a wonderful ~!** ¡besa muy bien! **2.** *vulg* (*mouth*) morro *m*

kiss-off ['kɪsɒf, *Am:* -ɑ:f] *n Am, inf* **to give the ~** dar calabazas **kiss-proof** *adj* indeleble

kit [kɪt] **I.** *n* **1.** (*set*) utensilios *mpl;* **first aid ~** botiquín *m* de primeros auxilios; **sewing ~** costurero *m;* **tool ~** caja *f* de herramientas **2.** (*parts to put together*) kit *m* **3.** *Brit* MIL, SPORTS (*uniform*) equipo *m* **II.** *vt Brit* **to ~ sb out/up** equipar a alguien

kitbag ['kɪtbæg] *n* macuto *m*

kitchen ['kɪtʃɪn] *n* cocina *f*

kitchenette [ˌkɪtʃɪˈnet] *n* cocina *f* pequeña **kitchen foil** *n* papel *m* de aluminio **kitchen garden** *n* huerto *m* **kitchen paper** *n no pl* papel *m* de cocina **kitchen range** *n Am,* **kitchen stove** *n* cocina *f* económica **kitchen sink** *n* fregadero *m,* lavaplatos *m inv And,* pileta *f RíoPl* ▶**to take everything but the ~** irse con la casa a cuestas **kitchen towel** *n Am* (*tea towel*) paño *m* de cocina **kitchen unit** *n* módulo *m* de cocina

kite [kaɪt] *n* **1.** ZOOL milano *m* **2.** FIN cheque *m* sin fondos **3.** (*toy*) cometa *f,* volantón *m AmL;* **to fly a ~** hacer volar una cometa; *fig* tantear el terreno ▶**go fly a ~!** *Am, inf* ¡vete a freír espárragos!

kite-mark ['kaɪtmɑ:k, *Am:* -mɑ:rk] *n Brit* marchamo *m*

kith [kɪθ] *n + pl vb* **~ and kin** familiares *mpl* y amigos

kitsch [kɪtʃ] **I.** *n no pl* kitsch *m inv* **II.** *adj* kitsch *inv*

kitten ['kɪtn] *n* gatito, -a *m, f* ▶**I nearly had**

~**s** casi me da un ataque

kittenish [ˈkɪtənɪʃ] *adj* coquetón, -ona

kitty [ˈkɪti, *Am:* ˈkɪt̬-] <-ies> *n* **1.** *childspeak* (*kitten or cat*) gatito, -a *m, f* **2.** (*money*) fondo *m*

kiwi [ˈkiːwiː] *n* **1.** ZOOL, BOT kiwi *m* **2.** *inf* (*New Zealander*) neozelandés, -esa *m, f*

kJ *abbr of* **kilojoule** kJ

KKK [ˌkeɪkeɪˈkeɪ] *n abbr of* **Ku Klux Klan** Ku Klux Klan *m*

klaxon [ˈklæksn] *n* sirena *f*, cláxon *m*

Kleenex® [ˈkliːneks] *n* kleenex® *m*

kleptomania [ˌkleptəˈmeɪnɪə, *Am:* -toʊˈ-] *n no pl* cleptomanía *f*

kleptomaniac [ˌkleptəˈmeɪnɪæk, *Am:* -toʊˈ-] *n* cleptómano, -a *m, f*

km *abbr of* **kilometre** km

km/h *abbr of* **kilometres per hour** km/h

knack [næk] *n no pl* habilidad *f*; **to have a ~ for sth** tener facilidad para algo; **to get the ~ of sth** coger el tranquillo a algo, tomar la mano a algo *AmL*

knacker [ˈnækəʳ, *Am:* -ə˞] *vt inf* hacer polvo

knackered [ˈnækəd, *Am:* -ə˞d] *adj Brit, Aus, inf* hecho, -a polvo

knapsack [ˈnæpsæk] *n Am* mochila *f*, tamuga *f AmC*

knead [niːd] *vt* **1.** GASTR amasar; (*clay*) modelar **2.** (*massage*) masajear

knee [niː] **I.** *n* rodilla *f*; **to be on one's ~s** *a. fig* estar de rodillas; **to get down on one's ~s** arrodillarse; **on your ~s!** ¡de rodillas! ▶**to bring sb to their ~s** derrotar a alguien **II.** *vt* **to ~ sb** dar un rodillazo a alguien

kneecap [ˈniːˌkæp] **I.** *n* rótula *f* **II.** <-pp-> *vt* disparar en la rodilla o en las piernas **knee-capping** *n* disparo *m* en la rodilla o en las piernas **knee-deep** *adj* **to be ~ in sth** estar metido hasta las rodillas en algo **knee-high** *adj* **to be ~** llegar hasta las rodillas

knee-jerk [ˈniːdʒɜːk, *Am:* -dʒɜːrk] *adj* previsible

kneel [niːl] <knelt *Am:* kneeled, knelt *Am:* kneeled> *vi* arrodillarse

knees-up [ˈniːzʌp] *n Brit, inf* fiesta *f*; **to have a ~** correr una juerga

knell [nel] *n* toque *m* de difuntos; **to sound the ~ for sth** *fig* anunciar el fin de algo

knelt [nelt] *pt of* **kneel**

knew [njuː, *Am:* nuː] *pt of* **know**

knickerbockers [ˈnɪkəbɒkəz, *Am:* -ə˞bɑː-kə˞z] *npl* pantalón *m* bombacho

knickers [ˈnɪkəz, *Am:* -ə˞z] *npl* **1.** *Brit* (*women's underwear*) bragas *fpl* **2.** *Am* (*knickerbockers*) bombachos *mpl* ▶**to get one's ~ in a twist** *Brit, Aus, inf* ponerse nervioso como un flan

knick-knack [ˈnɪknæk] *n inf* cachivache *m*

knife [naɪf] <knives> *n* **1.** cuchillo *m* **2.** (*dagger*) puñal *m*; **to wield a ~** blandir un puñal *elev* **3.** (*in a machine*) cuchilla *f* ▶**the ~s are out for him** *Brit, Aus, inf* se la tienen jurada; **to get one's ~ in(to)** sb ensañarse con

alguien; **to turn the ~ (in the wound)** poner el dedo en la llaga; **to be under the ~** MED estar en la mesa de operaciones

knife-edge *n* filo *m*; **to be (balanced) on a ~** *fig* pender de un hilo **knife sharpener** *n* afilador *m*

knifing [ˈnaɪfɪŋ] *n* pelea *f* con navajas

knight [naɪt] **I.** *n* **1.** (*man given honorable rank*) sir *m* **2.** HIST (*man of high social position*) caballero *m* **3.** (*chess figure*) caballo *m* ▶**~ in shining armour** príncipe *m* azul **II.** *vt* HIST armar caballero; (*give a honorable title*) conceder el título de sir

knight-errant [ˌnaɪtˈerənt] <knights-errant> *n* caballero *m* andante **knighthood** *n* título *m* de Sir; **to give sb a ~** conceder a alguien el título de sir

---

En Gran Bretaña, las personas que se han distinguido por sus méritos en favor de su país, son distinguidas con el honor de pasar a formar parte de la **knighthood** (nobleza) y reciben el título de **Sir** delante de su nombre, por ejemplo, **Sir John Smith**. La mujer de un **Sir** recibe el tratamiento de **Lady**, por ejemplo, **Lady Smith** (y se tiene que dirigir uno a ella de esta manera). Si se les quiere nombrar simultáneamente entonces se utilizaría la fórmula de **Sir John and Lady Smith**. A partir del año 1917 también una mujer puede ser distinguida por sus méritos. En ese caso recibe el título de **Dame**, por ejemplo, **Dame Mary Smith**.

---

knightly [ˈnaɪtli] *adj liter* caballeresco, -a

knit [nɪt] **I.** *vi* (*wool*) hacer punto; (*with a machine*) tejer **II.** *vt* (*wool*) tejer ▶**to ~ one's brows** fruncir el ceño

◆**knit together I.** *vi* **1.** (*combine or join*) unirse **2.** (*mend*) soldarse **II.** *vt* **1.** (*bones*) soldar **2.** *fig* (*join*) unir

knitter [ˈnɪtəʳ, *Am:* ˈnɪt̬ə˞] *n* **Paula is a wonderful ~** a Paula se le da muy bien hacer punto

knitting *n no pl* **1.** (*the product of knitting*) tejido *m* de punto **2.** (*material being knitted*) labor *f* de punto **3.** (*action of knitting*) **she likes ~** a ella le gusta hacer punto

knitting-needle *n* aguja *f* de hacer punto, aguja *f* de tejer *AmL* **knitting-yarn** *n no pl* lana *f* de tejer

knitwear [ˈnɪtweəʳ, *Am:* -wer] *n no pl* géneros *mpl* de punto

knob [nɒb, *Am:* nɑːb] *n* **1.** (*round handle: of a door*) pomo *m*; (*of switch*) botón *m*; (*of a drawer*) tirador *m* **2.** (*small amount*) pedazo *m*; (*of butter*) trocito *m* **3.** (*lump*) bulto *m* ▶**with (brass) ~s on** *Brit* hasta los tuétanos

knobbly [ˈnɒbli, *Am:* ˈnɑːbi] <-ier, -iest> *adj*, **knobby** [ˈnɒbi, *Am:* ˈnɑːbi] *adj Am* nudoso, -a; (*knees*) huesudo, -a

knock [nɒk, *Am:* nɑːk] **I.** *n* **1.** (*blow*) golpe *m* **2.** (*sound*) llamada *f*; **to give a ~ at the door** llamar a la puerta **3.** *fig, inf* crítica *f*; **to**

K

take a ~ aguantar un revés **II.** *vi* **1.**(*hit*) golpear; **to ~ on the window/at the door** llamar a la ventana/puerta **2.** TECH (*engine, pipes*) martillear **III.** *vt* **1.**(*hit*) golpear; **to ~ sb** dar un golpe a alguien; **to ~ a hole into the wall** abrir un agujero en la pared; **to ~ the bottom out of sth** *a. fig* desfondar algo **2.** *inf* (*criticize*) criticar

◆**knock about I.** *vi inf*andar vagando, vagabundear; **to ~ in town** andar por la ciudad **II.** *vt* (*person*) pegar; (*ball*) golpear

◆**knock around** *vi, vt s.* **knock about**

◆**knock back** *vt inf* **1.**(*drink quickly*) beber rápidamente; **to knock a beer back** beberse una cerveza de golpe **2.** *Brit, Aus* (*cost a lot*) costar **3.** *Brit, Aus, inf* (*reject advances*) dar calabazas **4.**(*surprise*) pasmar

◆**knock down** *vt* **1.**(*cause to fall*) derribar; (*with a car*) echar por tierra **2.**(*demolish*) demoler; **to ~ every argument** *fig* rebatir todos los argumentos **3.**(*reduce*) rebajar **4.**(*sell at auction*) adjudicar; **the picture was knocked down to Peter** se adjudicó el cuadro a Peter; **to knock sth down to sb for £100** dejar algo a alguien en 100 libras

◆**knock into** *vt* (*make understand*) inculcar; **to knock some sense into sb** hacer entrar en razón a alguien

◆**knock off I.** *vt* **1.**(*cause to fall off*) hacer caer; **to knock sb off his pedestal** *fig* hacer bajar a alguien de su pedestal **2.**(*reduce*) rebajar; **to knock £5 off the price** rebajar 5 libras el precio **3.** *inf* (*steal*) robar **4.** *inf* (*murder*) matar **5.**(*produce easily*) ejecutar prontamente; **to ~ some copies** hacer algunas copias **6.**(*stop*) **to knock it off** dejarlo; **knock it off!** ¡déjalo! **II.** *vi inf*terminar; **to ~ work at 3 p.m.** salir de trabajar a las 3 p.m.; **to ~ for lunch** salir para comer

◆**knock on** *vi* **to be knocking on 40** estar acercándose a los 40

◆**knock out** *vt* **1.**(*render unconscious*) dejar sin sentido; SPORTS dejar K.O.; (*cause to sleep*) hacer dormir; (*exhaust*) agotar **2.**(*remove*) quitar; (*contents in text*) suprimir **3.**(*eliminate*) eliminar; **to be knocked out of a competition** ser eliminado de una competición **4.**(*produce quickly*) hacer, producir **5.** *inf* (*astonish*) pasmar; **to knock sb out** dejar pasmado a alguien

◆**knock over** *vt* atropellar; (*objetos*) volcar

◆**knock together** *vt* construir deprisa; **to ~ something to eat** hacer algo rápido para comer

◆**knock up I.** *vt* **1.**(*make quickly*) construir deprisa **2.** *Brit, Aus, inf* (*awaken*) despertar **3.** *Am, inf* (*impregnate*) dejar encinta; **to get knocked up** quedarse embarazada **II.** *vi* SPORTS pelotear

knockabout ['nɒkəbaʊt, *Am:* 'nɑː k-] *adj* bullicioso, -a; (*comedy, humour*) cómico, -a

knockdown *adj* **1.**(*very cheap*) baratísimo, -a; **~ price** precio *m* de saldo; (*at auction*) pre-

cio *m* inicial **2.**(*violent: blow*) duro, -a; (*argument*) arrollador(a); (*fight*) violento, -a

knocker ['nɒkə', *Am:* 'nɑːkə] *n* (*on door*) aldaba *f*; *inf*(*person*) detractor(a) *m(f)*

knocking copy *n no pl* ECON contrapublicidad *f*

knocking-off time *n no pl* hora *f* de salir del trabajo

knock-kneed [ˌnɒk'niːd, *Am:* 'nɑːkniːd] *adj* patizambo, -a; *fig*débil **knock-on effect** *n* *Brit* efecto *m* dominó **knockout I.** *n* **1.** *Brit, Aus* (*competition*) eliminatoria *f* **2.** SPORTS (*boxing*) K.O. *m;* **to win sth by a ~** ganar algo por K.O. **3.** *inf* (*person*) persona *f* estupenda **II.** *adj* **1.** *Brit, Aus* (*competition*) eliminatorio, -a **2.**(*boxing*) **~ blow** golpe *m* duro; *fig* duro revés *m;* **to deal sb's hopes a ~ blow** acabar con las esperanzas de alguien **3.** *inf*(*attractive*) muy atractivo, -a **knock-up** *n* peloteo *m*

knoll [nəʊl, *Am:* noʊl] *n* montículo *m*

knot [nɒt, *Am:* nɑːt] **I.** *n* **i.**(*tied join*) *a.* NAUT nudo *m;* **to tie/untie a ~** hacer/deshacer un nudo **2.**(*bow*) lazo *m* **3.**(*chignon*) moño *m*, chongo *m Méx***4.**(*small group*) corrillo *m* ▶**to tie the ~** *inf*prometerse **II.**<-tt> *vt* anudar; **to ~ sth together** atar algo **III.**<-tt-> *vi* anudarse

knotty ['nɒti, *Am:* 'nɑː ti] <-ier, -iest> *adj* **1.**(*full of knots: lumber, wood*) nudoso, -a; (*hair*) enredado, -a **2.**(*difficult*) difícil

know [nəʊ, *Am:* noʊ] **I.**<knew, known> *vt* **1.**(*have information*) saber; **to ~ a bit of English** saber un poco de inglés; **she ~s all of their names** conoce los nombres de todos ellos; **to ~ how to do sth** saber hacer algo; **to ~ all there is to ~ about sth** saber todo lo que hay que saber sobre algo; **to ~ what one is talking about** saber de lo que uno habla; **to ~ sth (off) by heart** saber algo de memoria; **not to ~ the first thing about sth/sb** no saber nada de algo/alguien; **to ~ all the answers** tener todas las respuestas; **if you ~ what I mean** si sabes de qué hablo; **do you ~ what I mean?** ¿entiendes?; **to ~ that …** saber que…; **to want to ~ sth** querer saber algo; **do you ~ …?** ¿sabes…?; **you ~ what?** *inf* ¿sabes qué? **2.**(*be acquainted with*) conocer; **to ~ sb by sight/by name/personally** conocer a alguien de vista/por el nombre/personalmente; **(not) to ~ sb to speak to** (no) conocer a alguien como para entablar una conversación; **~ing sb, …** conociendo a alguien,…; **to get to ~ sb** llegar a conocer a alguien; **to get to ~ each other** llegar a conocerse (bien); **to have ~n sth** haber experimentado algo; **to ~ sth like the back of one's hand** *fig* conocer algo como la palma de la mano **3.**(*recognize*) conocer, reconocer; **to ~ sb/sth by sth** reconocer a alguien/algo por algo; **to ~ sb for sth** reconocer a alguien por algo **II.**<knew, known> *vi* **1.**(*be informed*) saber; **as far as I ~** por lo que sé; **to ~ better (than sb)** saber más (que alguien); **to ~ of** [*o* about] **sth** saber de algo, estar enterado de algo; **you** ~ (*you remember*) ya sabes; (*you understand*) entiendes; (**well**) **what do you** ~! *Am, iron* ¡no me digas!; **I** ~! (*I've got an idea!*) ¡lo tengo!; (*said to agree with sb*) ¡lo sé! **2.** (*be certain*) estar seguro; **there's no** ~**ing** no es seguro; **one never** ~**s** nunca se sabe **3.** *inf* (*understand*) entender **III.** *n no pl* **to be in the** ~ estar en el ajo; **to be in the** ~ **about sth** estar enterado de algo

know-all ['nəʊɔːl, *Am:* 'noʊ-] *n Brit, Aus, inf* sabelotodo *mf* **know-how** *n no pl* know--how *m;* **to have** ~ **about sth** tener el know--how de algo

knowing ['nəʊɪŋ, *Am:* 'noʊ-] **I.** *adj* astuto, -a; (*grins, look, smile*) de complicidad **II.** *n no pl* **there's no** ~ no hay forma de saberlo

knowingly *adv* **1.** (*meaningfully*) con conocimiento **2.** (*with full awareness*) a sabiendas

know-it-all ['nəʊɪtɔːl, *Am:* 'noʊɪt̬-] *n Am s.* **know-all**

knowledge ['nɒlɪdʒ, *Am:* 'nɑːlɪdʒ] *n no pl* **1.** (*body of learning*) conocimiento *m;* **to have** (**some**) ~ **of sth** tener (algún) conocimiento de algo; **to have a thorough** ~ **of sth** conocer algo a fondo **2.** (*acquired information*) saber *m;* **to have** (**no**) ~ **about sth/sb** (no) saber de algo/alguien; **to my** ~ que yo sepa; **to be common** ~ ser de dominio público **3.** (*awareness*) conocimiento *m;* **to bring sth to sb's** ~ poner a alguien en conocimiento de algo; **to do sth without sb's** ~ hacer algo sin que alguien lo sepa; **to deny all** ~ (**of sth**) negar cualquier conocimiento (de algo)

knowledgeable ['nɒlɪdʒəbl, *Am:* 'nɑːlɪ-] *adj* entendido, -a; **to be** ~ **about sth** ser un erudito en algo

known [nəʊn, *Am:* noʊn] **I.** *vt, vi pp of* **know II.** *adj* (*expert*) reconocido, -a; (*criminal*) conocido, -a; **no** ~ **reason** sin razón aparente; **to make sth** ~ dar a conocer algo; **to make oneself** ~ **to sb** darse a conocer a alguien

knuckle ['nʌkl] *n* nudillo *m* ▶ **to be near the** ~ *Brit, inf* rayar en la indecencia; **to rap sb's** ~**s** *inf* echar un rapapolvo a alguien

◆ **knuckle down** *vi* ponerse a hacer algo con ahinco; **to** ~ **to work** ponerse a trabajar concienzudamente

◆ **knuckle under** *vi* darse por vencido, -a

knuckle-duster ['nʌkldʌstər, *Am:* -t̬ər] *n* **1.** (*weapon*) puño *m* de hierro **2.** *inf* (*ring*) aro *m* de hierro

KO [ˌkeɪˈəʊ, *Am:* -ˈoʊ] *abbr of* **knockout** KO

koala [kəʊˈɑːlə, *Am:* koʊ-] *n,* **koala bear** *n* coala *m*

kooky ['kuːki] <-ier, -iest> *adj Am, inf* loco, -a

Koran [kəˈrɑːn, *Am:* -ˈræn] *n no pl* **the** ~ el Corán

Korea [kəˈrɪə] *n* Corea *f;* **North/South** ~ Corea del Norte/Sur

Korean [kəˈrɪən] **I.** *adj* coreano, -a **II.** *n*

1. (*person*) coreano, -a *m, f* **2.** LING coreano *m*

kosher ['kəʊʃər, *Am:* 'koʊʃər] *adj* autorizado, -a por la ley judía

kowtow [ˌkaʊˈtaʊ] *vi inf* saludar humildemente; **to** ~ **to sb** humillarse ante alguien

Kremlin ['kremlɪn] *n no pl* **the** ~ el Kremlin

krone ['krəʊnə] *n* corona *f*

kudos ['kjuːdɒs, *Am:* 'kuːdoʊz] *n no pl* gloria *f;* **to get** ~ **for sth** conseguir prestigio por algo

Ku Klux Klan ['kuːˈklʌksˈklæn] *n no pl* **the** ~ el Ku Klux Klan

kung fu [ˌkʊŋˈfuː] *n no pl* kung fu *m*

Kurd [kɜːd, *Am:* kɜːrd] *n* kurdo, -a *m, f*

Kurdish **I.** *adj* kurdo, -a **II.** *n* **1.** (*person*) kurdo, -a *m, f* **2.** LING kurdo *m*

Kurdistan [ˌkɜːdɪˈstɑːn, *Am:* ˌkɜːrdɪˈstæn] *n* Kurdistán *m*

Kuwait [kʊˈweɪt] *n* Kuwait *m*

Kuwaiti **I.** *adj* kuwaití **II.** *n* **1.** (*person*) kuwaití *mf* **2.** LING kuwaití *m*

kw *abbr of* **kilowatt** KW

kWh *abbr of* **kilowatt hour** kWh

KWIC [kwɪk] INFOR *abbr of* **key word in context** KWIC

KWOC INFOR *abbr of* **key word out of context** KWOC

L

L, l [el] *n* L, l *f;* ~ **for Lucy** *Brit,* ~ **for Love** *Am* L de Lisboa

l *abbr of* **litre** l.

L **1.** *Brit abbr of* **Learner** L **2.** *abbr of* **large** G

LA [ˌelˈeɪ] *n abbr of* **Los Angeles** Los Ángeles

lab [læb] *n abbr of* **laboratory** laboratorio *m*

lab coat *n* bata *f* de laboratorio

label ['leɪbəl] **I.** *n* **1.** (*on bottle, clothing*) etiqueta *f* **2.** (*brand name*) marca *f* **3.** (*description*) descripción *f* **II.** <-ll-, *Am:* -l-> *vt* **1.** (*affix label*) etiquetar **2.** (*categorize*) clasificar

labelling *n Brit,* **labeling** *n no pl, Am, Aus* etiquetado *m*

labor ['leɪbər] *Am, Aus s.* **labour**

laboratory [ləˈbɒrətəri, *Am:* 'læbrəˌtɔːri] <-ies> *n* laboratorio *m;* **to be still at the** ~ **stage** estar aún en fase experimental

laboratory assistant *n* auxiliar *mf* de laboratorio **laboratory test** *n* prueba *f* de laboratorio

laborer *n Am, Aus s.* **labourer**

laborious [ləˈbɔːrɪəs] *adj* **1.** (*task*) laborioso, -a **2.** (*style*) farragoso, -a

labour ['leɪbər, *Am:* -bər] **I.** *n* **1.** (*work*) trabajo *m;* **manual** ~ trabajo manual; **to be a** ~ **of love** ser una tarea muy grata **2.** *no pl* ECON (*workers*) mano *f* de obra; **skilled** ~ mano de obra cualificada **3.** *no pl* MED (*childbirth*) parto *m;* **to be in** ~ estar de parto **II.** *vi*

1. (*work*) trabajar; **to do ~ing work** trabajar de peón **2.** (*do sth with effort*) esforzarse; **to ~ on sth** esforzarse en algo **3.** (*move*) moverse penosamente **4.** (*act at a disadvantage*) **to ~ under a delusion** estar equivocado **III.** *vt* insistir en; **to ~ a point** insistir (demasiado) en un punto

labour camp *n* campo *m* de trabajo **labour costs** *npl* costes *mpl* de la mano de obra **Labour Day** *n no pl, Am* Día *m* del Trabajo **labour dispute** *n* conflicto *m* laboral **labourer** ['leɪbərə'] *n* peón *m* **Labour Exchange** *n Brit* HIST bolsa *f* de trabajo **labour force** *n* (*of country*) mano *f* de obra; (*of company*) plantilla *f* **labour-intensive** *adj* que requiere mucha mano de obra **labour market** *n* mercado *m* laboral **labour movement** *n* POL movimiento *m* obrero **labour pains** *npl* MED dolores *mpl* de parto **Labour Party** *n no pl, Brit, Aus* POL **the ~** el Partido Laborista **labour relations** *npl* relaciones *fpl* laborales **labour-saving** *adj* que ahorra trabajo **labour shortage** *n* escasez *f* de mano de obra **labour union** *Am* sindicato *m* **labour ward** *n* sala *f* de partos

Labrador (**retriever**) ['læbrədɔːr (rɪ'triːvə'), *Am:* -dɔːr (-ə')] *n* labrador *m*

laburnum [lə'bɜːnəm, *Am:* -'bɜːr-] *n* lluvia *f* de oro

labyrinth ['læbərɪnθ, *Am:* -ə'-] <-es> *n* laberinto *m*

lace [leɪs] **I.** *n* **1.** *no pl* (*cloth*) encaje *m;* (*edging*) puntilla *f* **2.** (*cord*) cordón *m;* **shoe ~s** cordones *mpl* de zapatos; **to do up one's ~s** atarse los cordones **II.** *vt* **1.** (*fasten*) atar **2.** (*add alcohol to*) echar licor a

◆**lace into** *vt* **to ~ sb** dar una paliza a alguien

◆**lace up** *vt* atar

lacerate ['læsəraɪt] *vt* lacerar

laceration [ˌlæsə'reɪʃən] *n* laceración *f*

lace-ups ['leɪsʌps] *npl* zapatos *mpl* con cordones

lachrymose ['lækrɪməʊs, *Am:* -moʊs] *adj liter* **1.** (*tending to cry easily*) llorón, -ona **2.** (*sad*) lacrimógeno, -a

lack [læk] **I.** *n no pl* falta *f;* **~ of funds** escasez *f* de fondos; **for ~ of ...** por falta de... **II.** *vt* carecer de; **she ~s talent/experience** le falta talento/experiencia; **to ~ the energy to do sth** no tener la fuerza para hacer algo

lackadaisical [ˌlækə'deɪzɪkl] *adj* apático, -a

lackey ['læki] *n a. fig* lacayo, -a *m, f*

lacking ['lækɪŋ] *adj* **he is ~ in talent/experience** le falta talento/experiencia

lackluster *adj Am,* **lacklustre** ['lækˌlʌstə', *Am:* -tə'] *adj Brit, Aus* **1.** (*not shiny*) deslustrado, -a **2.** (*dull*) gris

laconic [lə'kɒnɪk, *Am:* -'kɑːnɪk] *adj* lacónico, -a

lacquer ['lækə', *Am:* -ə'] **I.** *n* (*for wood, hair*) laca *f;* (*for nails*) esmalte *m* **II.** *vt* **1.** (*coat with varnish*) laquear **2.** (*spray hair*) echar laca a

lacrosse [lə'krɒs, *Am:* -'krɑːs] *n no pl* SPORTS lacrosse *m*

lad [læd] *n Brit, inf* (*boy*) chico *m;* **a young ~** un chico; **the ~s** los muchachos; **he's a bit of a ~** le gustan mucho las faldas

ladder ['lædə', *Am:* -ə'] **I.** *n* **1.** (*for climbing*) escalera *f* (de mano) **2.** (*hierarchy*) escala *f;* **to move up the ~** ascender de categoría; (*in company*) ascender en la empresa; **to climb the social ~** subir en la escala social **3.** *Brit, Aus* (*in stocking*) carrera *f* **II.** *vt* hacerse una carrera en **III.** *vi* **these tights ~ easily** a estas medias se les hacen carreras enseguida

laddie ['lædi] *n Scot, inf* muchacho *m*

laden ['leɪdn] *adj* cargado, -a; **to be ~ with ...** estar cargado de...

la-di-da [ˌlɑːdɪ'dɑː, *Am:* -diː-] *adj inf* repipi

lading ['leɪdɪŋ] *n* NAUT cargamento *m;* **bill of ~** conocimiento *m* de embarque

ladle ['leɪdl] **I.** *n* cucharón *m*, ramillón *m Col, Ven;* **soup ~** cucharón para la sopa **II.** *vt* **1.** (*soup*) servir (*con cucharón*) **2.** (*advice, sympathy*) repartir generosamente

lady ['leɪdi] <-ies> *n* señora *f;* (*aristocratic*) dama *f;* **young ~** señorita *f;* **the ~ of the house** la señora de la casa; **to be a real ~** ser toda una señora; **cleaning ~** mujer de la limpieza; **ladies and gentlemen!** ¡señoras y señores!

ladybird ['leɪdibɜːd, *Am:* -bɜːrd] *n Brit, Aus,* **ladybug** ['leɪdibʌg] *n Am* mariquita *f*

lady-in-waiting <-ies> *n* dama *f* de honor

ladykiller *n* casanova *m* **ladylike** *adj* femenino, -a **ladyship** *n form* **her/your ~** Su Señoría **lady's maid** *n* doncella *f*

LAFTA *n abbr of* **Latin American Free Trade Association** ALALC *f*

lag[1] [læg] **I.** *n* (*lapse*) lapso *m* **II.** <-gg-> *vi* rezagarse; **to ~ behind (sb/sth)** quedarse detrás (de alguien/algo)

lag[2] [læg] <-gg-> *vt* (*insulate*) revestir con aislantes

lag[3] [læg] *n Brit, inf* **old ~** presidiario *m*

lager ['lɑːgə', *Am:* -gə'] *n no pl* cerveza *f* rubia

lager lout *n Brit, inf* gamberro *m* de litrona

lagging ['lægɪŋ] *n* revestimiento *m*

lagoon [lə'guːn] *n* laguna *f*, cocha *f AmS*

laid [leɪd] *pt, pp of* **lay**[1]

laid-back [ˌleɪd'bæk] *adj inf* tranquilo, -a

lain [leɪn] *pp of* **lie**[2]

lair [leə', *Am:* ler] *n* **1.** (*of animal*) cubil *m* **2.** (*of criminal*) guarida *f*

laird [leəd, *Am:* lerd] *n Scot* terrateniente *m*

laissez-faire ['leɪseɪ'feə', *Am:* 'leser'fer] *n no pl* laissez-faire *m;* **~ attitude** actitud *f* permisiva

laity ['leɪəti] *n no pl* **the ~** el laicado

lake [leɪk] *n* lago *m*

lam [læm] **I.** *n Am, inf* **to be on the ~** ser fugitivo de la justicia **II.** <-mm-> *vt inf* pegar

lama ['lɑːmə] *n* REL lama *m*

lamb [læm] I. *n* 1. (*animal*) cordero *m* 2. *no pl* (*meat*) (carne *f* de) cordero *m* ▶ to go like a ~ to the <u>slaughter</u> ir como borrego al matadero II. *vi* parir

lambast(e) [læm'bæst, *Am:* -'beɪst] *vt* vapulear

lamb chop *n* chuleta *f* de cordero **lambskin** *n* (piel *f* de) cordero *m* **lambswool** *n no pl* lana *f* de cordero

lame [leɪm] *adj* 1. (*person, horse*) cojo, -a; to go ~ quedarse cojo 2. (*argument*) flojo, -a; (*excuse*) débil

lameness *n no pl* 1. (*of person, horse*) cojera *f* 2. (*of argument*) flojedad *f*; (*of excuse*) debilidad *f*

lament [lə'ment] I. *n* MUS, LIT elegía *f* II. *vt* lamentar; to ~ sb llorar a alguien III. *vi* to ~ over sth lamentarse de algo

lamentable ['læməntəbl, *Am:* lə'məntə-] *adj* lamentable

lamentation [ˌlæmen'teɪʃən, *Am:* -ən'-] *n* 1. (*regrets*) lamentos *mpl* 2. *no pl* (*mourning*) lamentación *f*

laminate¹ ['læmɪnət] *n* TECH laminado *m*

laminate² ['læmɪneɪt] *vt* (*glass, wood*) laminar; (*document*) plastificar

laminated ['læmɪneɪtɪd, *Am:* -t̬ɪd] *adj* (*glass, wood*) laminado, -a; (*document*) plastificado, -a

lamp [læmp] *n* lámpara *f*; **bedside** ~ lamparilla *f* de mesita de noche; **street** ~ farola *f*

lampoon [læm'puːn] I. *n* sátira *f* II. *vt* satirizar

lamppost ['læmppəʊst, *Am:* -poʊst] *n* farola *f*

lampshade ['læmpʃeɪd] *n* pantalla *f* (de lámpara)

LAN [læn] *n* INFOR *abbr of* local area network RAL *f*

lance [lɑːns, *Am:* læns] I. *n* MIL lanza *f* II. *vt* MED abrir con lanceta

lancet ['lɑːnsɪt, *Am:* 'lænsɪt] *n* MED lanceta *f*

land [lænd] I. *n* 1. *no pl* GEO, AGR tierra *f*; on ~ en tierra; to travel by ~ viajar por tierra; to work (on) the ~ trabajar (en) el campo; to have dry ~ under one's feet pisar tierra firme 2. (*area: for building*) terreno *m* 3. (*country*) país *m* ▶ to be in the ~ of the <u>living</u> *iron* estar despierto; to see how the ~ <u>lies</u> tantear el terreno II. *vi* 1. (*plane, bird*) aterrizar; to ~ on the moon alunizar; to come in to ~ aterrizar 2. (*arrive by boat*) llegar en barco 3. (*person, ball*) caer III. *vt* 1. (*bring onto land: aircraft*) hacer aterrizar; (*boat*) amarrar; to ~ a plane on water hacer aterrizar un avión en el agua 2. (*unload*) desembarcar 3. (*obtain*) conseguir; (*fish*) pescar; to ~ a job conseguir un trabajo 4. (*cause*) to ~ sb with a problem endosar un problema a alguien; to ~ sb in trouble meter a alguien en un lío

landed ['lændɪd] *adj* que posee tierras; a ~ family una familia hacendada; the ~ gentry los terratenientes

landfall ['lændfɔːl] *n* vista *f* de tierra; to make ~ avistar tierra

landfill site ['lændfɪl saɪt] *n* vertedero *m* de basuras

land forces *npl* MIL ejército *m* de tierra

landholder *n* terrateniente *mf*

landing ['lændɪŋ] *n* 1. (*on staircase*) rellano *m* 2. AVIAT aterrizaje *m*; to make a ~ realizar un aterrizaje 3. NAUT desembarco *m*

landing card *n* tarjeta *f* de desembarque **landing craft** *n* MIL lancha *f* de desembarco **landing field** *n* campo *m* de aterrizaje **landing gear** *n* AVIAT tren *m* de aterrizaje **landing net** *n* salabardo *m* **landing stage** *n* desembarcadero *m* **landing strip** *n* pista *f* de aterrizaje

landlady ['lændˌleɪdi] <-ies> *n* (*of house*) propietaria *f*; (*of pub, hotel*) dueña *f*; (*of boarding house*) patrona *f* **landless** *adj* sin tierras **landlocked** *adj* cercado, -a de tierra; a ~ country un país sin acceso al mar **landlord** *n* 1. (*of house*) propietario *m*; (*of pub, hotel*) dueño *m*; (*of boarding house*) patrón *m* 2. (*landowner*) terrateniente *m* **landlubber** *n inf* marinero *m* de agua dulce **landmark** *n* 1. (*object serving as a guide*) mojón *m*; (*point of recognition*) punto *m* destacado 2. (*monument*) monumento *m* histórico 3. (*event*) hito *m* **landmine** *n* mina *f* terrestre **land office** *n Am* HIST oficina *f* del catastro; to do a ~ business *Am, inf* hacer un buen negocio **landowner** *n* terrateniente *mf* **land reform** *n* reforma *f* agraria

landscape ['lændskeɪp] I. *n* 1. *no pl* (*scenery, painting*) paisaje *m*; urban ~ paisaje urbano 2. *fig* panorama *m*; the political ~ el panorama político 3. INFOR impresión *f* horizontal II. *vt* ajardinar

landscape architect *n*, **landscape gardener** *n* arquitecto, -a *m, f* de jardines **landscape architecture** *n*, **landscape gardening** *n no pl* arquitectura *f* de jardines **landscape painter** *n* paisajista *mf*

landslide ['lændslaɪd] *n* 1. GEO corrimiento *m* de tierras 2. POL victoria *f* arrolladora; to win by a ~ ganar por mayoría abrumadora **landslip** *n Brit* GEO corrimiento *m* de tierras **land tax** <-es> *n* contribución *f* territorial **landward** I. *adj* de la parte de la tierra; the ~ side el lado de la tierra II. *adv* hacia (la) tierra

lane [leɪn] *n* 1. (*narrow road: in country*) vereda *f*; (*in town*) callejón *m* 2. (*marked strip: on road*) carril *m*; SPORTS calle *f*; bus/cycle ~ carril de autobús/de bicicleta; to change ~s cambiar de carril 3. AVIAT vía *f* aérea; NAUT ruta *f* marítima

language ['læŋgwɪdʒ] *n* 1. *no pl* (*system of communication*) lenguaje *m*; bad ~ palabrotas *fpl*; formal/spoken/written ~ lengua formal/oral/escrita 2. (*of particular community*) idioma *m;* **native** ~ lengua *f* materna; **the English** ~ la lengua inglesa **3.**(*of specialist group*) lenguaje *m;* **computer programming** ~ lenguaje de programación (de ordenadores); **legal** ~ lenguaje jurídico ▶**to speak the same** ~ hablar el mismo idioma

language laboratory *n* laboratorio *m* de idiomas **language learning** *n* aprendizaje *m* de una lengua

languid ['læŋgwɪd] *adj liter* lánguido, -a

languish ['læŋgwɪʃ] *vi* languidecer; **he** ~**ed in bed for weeks** estuvo postrado en la cama durante semanas

languor ['læŋgəʳ, *Am:* -gɚ] *n no pl, liter* languidez *f*

languorous ['læŋgərəs, *Am:* -gɚ-] *adj liter* lánguido, -a

lank [læŋk] *adj* **1.**(*hair*) lacio, -a **2.**(*person*) larguirucho, -a

lanky ['læŋki] *adj* desgarbado, -a

lanolin ['lænəlɪn] *n* lanolina *f*

lantern ['læntən, *Am:* -ʈɚn] *n* linterna *f;* (*light*) farol *m*

lanyard ['lænjəd, *Am:* -jɚd] *n* **1.**(*short rope or cord*) cordel *m* **2.** NAUT acollador *m*

Laos [laʊs] *n* Laos *m*

lap¹ [læp] *n* falda *f* ▶**in the** ~ **of the gods** *Brit* en manos de Dios; **to live in the** ~ **of luxury** vivir a cuerpo de rey

lap² [læp] SPORTS **I.** *n* vuelta *f;* ~ **of honour** vuelta de honor **II.** <-pp-> *vt* sacar una vuelta de ventaja a

lap³ [læp] <-pp-> **I.** *vt* **1.**(*drink*) beber dando lengüetazos **2.**(*waves*) acariciar **II.** *vi* (*hit gently*) **to** ~ **against sth** chocar suavemente contra algo

♦**lap up** *vt* **1.**(*drink*) beber dando lengüetazos **2.** *fig, inf* aceptar entusiasmado; **he lapped up the praise** saboreaba las alabanzas

lapdog ['læp,dɒg, *Am:* -dɑːg] *n* perro *m* faldero

lapel [lə'pel] *n* solapa *f;* **to grab sb by the** ~**s** agarrar a alguien por las solapas

lapis lazuli [,læpɪs'læzjʊli, *Am:* -'læzə-] *n* **1.**(*blue gemstone*) lapislázuli *m* **2.**(*blue colour*) azul *m* de ultramar

Lapland ['læplænd] *n* Laponia *f*

Laplander ['læplændəʳ, *Am:* -ɚ] *n,* **Lapp** [læp] *n* lapón, -ona *m, f*

lapse [læps] **I.** *n* **1.** *no pl* (*period*) lapso *m* **2.**(*failure*) lapsus *m inv;* ~ **of judgement** desacierto *m;* ~ **of memory** lapsus de memoria **II.** *vi* **1.**(*deteriorate*) deteriorarse **2.**(*end*) terminar; (*contract*) vencer; (*subscription*) caducar **3.**(*revert to*) **to** ~ **into sth** reincidir en algo; **to** ~ **into one's native dialect** recurrir al dialecto nativo; **to** ~ **into silence** quedar(se) en silencio

lapsed [læpst] *adj* (*Catholic*) no practicante

laptop (**computer**) ['æptɒp, *Am:* -tɑːp] *n* (ordenador *m*) portátil *m*

lapwing ['læpwɪŋ] *n* avefría *f*

larceny ['lɑːsəni, *Am:* 'lɑːr-] <-ies> *n Am*

hurto *m*

larch [lɑːtʃ, *Am:* lɑːrtʃ] *n* alerce *m*

lard [lɑːd, *Am:* lɑːrd] **I.** *n no pl* manteca *f* de cerdo **II.** *vt* untar (con manteca de cerdo); **to** ~ **with sth** *fig* (*text*) salpicar de algo

larder ['lɑːdəʳ, *Am:* 'lɑːrdɚ] *n* (*room*) despensa *f;* (*cupboard*) alacena *f*

large [lɑːdʒ, *Am:* lɑːrdʒ] *adj* grande; **a** ~ **number of people** un gran número de gente; **a** ~ **family** una familia numerosa ▶**to be at** ~ andar suelto; **by and** ~ por lo general

largely ['lɑːdʒli, *Am:* 'lɑːrdʒ-] *adv* en gran parte

largeness *n no pl* (gran) tamaño *m*

large-scale [,lɑːdʒ'skeɪl, *Am:* ,lɑːrdʒ-] *adj* gran escala

largess *n Am,* **largesse** [lɑːˈdʒes, *Am:* lɑːr-] *n no pl* generosidad *f*

lariat ['lærɪət, *Am:* 'ler-] *n* lazo *m*

lark¹ [lɑːk, *Am:* lɑːrk] *n* (*bird*) alondra *f* ▶**to be up with the** ~ levantarse con las gallinas

lark² [lɑːk, *Am:* lɑːrk] **I.** *n* **1.** *Brit, inf* (*joke*) broma *f;* **for a** ~ de broma **2.** *Brit, inf* (*business*) asunto *m;* **don't get involved in that** ~**!** ¡no te metas en ese asunto [*o* negocio]!; **sod this for a** ~**!** ¡estoy hasta el gorro de eso! **II.** *vi Brit, inf* to ~ **about** hacer tonterías

larkspur ['lɑːkspɜːʳ, *Am:* 'lɑːrkspɜːr] *n* espuela *f* de caballero

larva ['lɑːvə] <-vae> *n* larva *f*

laryngitis [,lærɪn'dʒaɪtɪs, *Am:* ,lerɪn-'dʒaɪʈɪs] *n no pl* laringitis *f inv*

larynx ['lærɪŋks, *Am:* 'ler-] <-ynxes *o* -ynges> *n* laringe *f*

lasagne [lə'zænjə, *Am:* -'zɑːnjə] *n* lasaña *f*

lascivious [lə'sɪvɪəs] *adj* lascivo, -a

laser ['leɪzəʳ, *Am:* -zɚ] *n* láser *m*

laser beam *n* rayo *m* láser **laser printer** *n* impresora *f* láser **laser show** *n* espectáculo *m* con láser

lash¹ [læʃ] <-shes> *n* (*eyelash*) pestaña *f*

lash² [læʃ] **I.** <-shes> *n* **1.**(*whip*) látigo *m;* (*flexible part of a whip*) tralla *f* **2.**(*stroke of whip*) latigazo *m;* (*of tail*) coletazo *m* ▶**to feel the** ~ **of sb's tongue** ser fustigado **II.** *vt* **1.**(*whip*) azotar; (*rain*) golpear **2.**(*criticize*) fustigar

♦**lash about** *vi,* **lash around** *vi* golpear a diestro y siniestro

♦**lash down** *vt* atar firmemente

♦**lash out** *vi* **1.**(*attack*) **to** ~ **at sb** atacar a alguien; (*verbally*) arremeter contra alguien **2.** *inf* (*spend*) **to** ~ **on sth** gastarse mucho dinero en algo

lashing ['læʃɪŋ] *n* **1.** azotaina *f;* **to give sb a tongue** ~ echar un rapapolvo a alguien **2.** *Brit* ~**s of** montones *mpl* de

lass [læs] <-sses> *n,* **lassie** ['læsi] *n Scot, inf* (*girl*) chica *f*

lassitude ['læsɪtjuːd, *Am:* -tuːd] *n no pl, form* lasitud *f*

lasso [læ'suː, *Am:* 'læsoʊ] **I.** <-os *o* -oes> *n*

lazo *m* II. *vt* lazar
last¹ [lɑːst, *Am:* læst] *n* horma *f*
last² [lɑːst, *Am:* læst] I. *adj* 1. (*final: time, opportunity*) último, -a; **to have the ~ word** tener la última palabra; **to wait till the ~ minute** (**to do sth**) esperar hasta el último minuto (para hacer algo); **this will be the ~ time** esta será la última vez 2. (*most recent*) último, -a; **~ week** la semana pasada; **~ night** anoche II. *adv* 1. (*coming at the end*) por último; **~ but not least** por último, pero no por eso menos importante 2. (*most recently*) por última vez III. *n* **the ~ to do sth** el último en hacer algo; **the ~ but one** el penúltimo; **that was the ~ of the cake** era todo lo que quedaba de pastel ▸ **at** (**long**) **~** al fin; **to the ~** *form* hasta el final
last³ [lɑːst, *Am:* læst] I. *vi* durar II. *vt* **this coat has ~ed me five years** hace cinco años que tengo este abrigo
last-ditch [ˌlɑːstˈdɪtʃ, *Am:* ˌlæst-] *adj*, **last-gasp** [ˌlɑːstˈgɑːsp, *Am:* ˌlæstˈgæsp] *adj* desesperado, -a
lasting [ˈlɑːstɪŋ, *Am:* ˌlæst-] *adj* duradero, -a; **to his ~ shame** para su eterna vergüenza
lastly [ˈlɑːstli, *Am:* ˈlæst-] *adv* por último
last-minute [ˌlɑːstˈmɪnɪt, *Am:* ˌlæst-] *adj* de última hora
last name *n* apellido *m*
latch [lætʃ] <-tches> *n* pestillo *m;* **on the ~** cerrado con picaporte
♦ **latch on** *vi inf* 1. *Brit* (*understand*) darse cuenta; **to ~ to sth** captar algo 2. (*attach oneself*) **to ~ to sb/sth** agarrarse a alguien/algo
latchkey [ˈlætʃkiː] *n* llave *f* (de la casa)
late [leɪt] I. *adj* 1. (*after appointed time*) retrasado, -a; **you're ~!** ¡llegas tarde!; **the train was an hour ~** el tren llegó con una hora de retraso 2. (*occurring after the usual time*) tardío, -a; **~ developer** estudiante *mf* rezagado; **~ night TV show** programa *m* de televisión de noche; **in the ~ nineteenth-century** a finales del siglo XIX; **in ~ summer** a finales del verano 3. (*deceased*) fallecido, -a 4. (*recent*) reciente; **~ news** noticias *fpl* de última hora II. *adv* 1. (*after usual time*) tarde; **too little, too ~** demasiado poco y demasiado tarde; **to work ~** trabajar hasta (muy) tarde; **it's rather ~ in the day to do sth** es tarde para hacer algo 2. (*at advanced time*) **~ in the day** a última hora del día; **~ at night** muy entrada la noche; **he got his driver's licence ~ in life** se sacó el carnet de conducir de mayor 3. (*recently*) **as ~ as the 1980s** aún en los años ochenta; **of ~** últimamente ▸ **better ~ than never** *prov* más vale tarde que nunca *prov*
late-breaking *adj* de gran actualidad
latecomer [ˈleɪtˌkʌməʳ, *Am:* -ɚ] *n* persona o cosa que llega tarde
lately [ˈleɪtli] *adv* (*recently*) últimamente, ultimadamente *Méx;* **until ~** hasta hace poco
lateness [ˈleɪtnɪs] *n no pl* retraso *m*
late-night [ˈleɪtˌnaɪt] *adj* nocturno, -a

latent [ˈleɪtnt] *adj* latente
later [ˈleɪtəʳ] I. *adj comp of* **late** posterior; (*version*) más reciente II. *adv comp of* **late** más tarde; **no ~ than nine o'clock** no más tarde de las nueve; **~ on** después; **see you ~!** ¡hasta luego!
lateral [ˈlætərəl, *Am:* ˈlæt̬ərəl] *adj* lateral; **~ thinking** pensamiento *m* lateral (*manera de solucionar problemas utilizando más la imaginación que el pensamiento lógico*)
latest [ˈleɪtɪst] I. *adj superl of* **late** último, -a; **the ~ ...** el más reciente...; **his ~ movie** su última película; **at the ~** a más tardar II. *n* **the ~ las últimas noticias**; **have you heard the ~ about them?** ¿te has enterado de lo suyo?; **the ~ in art/physics** lo último en arte/física; **at the** (**very**) **~** a más tardar
latex [ˈleɪteks, *Am:* ˈlæt̬ɪ-] *n* látex *m*
lath [lɑːθ, *Am:* læθ] <-thes> *n* listón *m*
lathe [leɪð] *n* torno *m*
lathe operator *n* tornero, -a *m, f*
lather [ˈlɑːðəʳ, *Am:* ˈlæðɚ] I. *n no pl* 1. (*fine bubbles*) espuma *f* 2. (*sweat*) sudor *m*; **to be in a ~** *fig* estar histérico; **to get** (**oneself**) **into a ~** ponerse histérico II. *vi* hacer espuma III. *vt* enjabonar
Latin [ˈlætɪn, *Am:* -ən] I. *adj* latino, -a II. *n* 1. (*person*) latino, -a *m, f* 2. LING latín *m*
Latin America *n* América *f* Latina
Latin American I. *adj* latinoamericano, -a II. *n* (*person*) latinoamericano, -a *m, f*
Latino [ləˈtiːnəʊ, *Am:* -noʊ] *n* (*person*) latino, -a *m, f*
latish [ˈleɪtɪʃ, *Am:* -t̬ɪʃ] I. *adj* (*algo*) tardío, -a II. *adv* algo tarde
latitude [ˈlætɪtjuːd, *Am:* ˈlæt̬ətuːd] *n* 1. GEO latitud *f* 2. *form* (*freedom*) libertad *f*
latrine [ləˈtriːn] *n* letrina *f*
latter [ˈlætəʳ, *Am:* ˈlæt̬ɚ] *adj* 1. (*second of two*) **the ~** el último 2. (*near the end*) hacia el final; **in the ~ half of the year** en la segunda mitad del año
latterly *adv* últimamente
lattice [ˈlætɪs, *Am:* ˈlæt̬-] *n* (*framework*) enrejado *m;* (*window*) celosía *f;* **~ screen** pantalla *f* de retícula
Latvia [ˈlætvɪə] *n* Letonia *f*
Latvian [ˈlætvɪən] I. *adj* letón, -ona II. *n* 1. (*person*) letón, -ona *m, f* 2. LING letón *m*
laudable [ˈlɔːdəbl, *Am:* ˈlɑː-] *adj form* loable
laudanum [ˈlɔːdənəm, *Am:* ˈlɑː-] *n no pl* láudano *m*
laudatory [ˈlɔːdətəri, *Am:* ˈlɑːdətɔːr-] *adj form* laudatorio, -a
laugh [lɑːf] I. *n* 1. (*sound*) risa *f;* **to get a ~** hacer reír; **to do sth for a ~** hacer algo para divertirse 2. *inf* (*activity*) actividad *f* divertida; *Brit* (*person*) persona *f* divertida II. *vi* reír(se); **to ~ aloud** reírse a carcajadas; **to make sb ~** hacer reír a alguien; **to ~ at sb/sth** *a. fig* reírse de alguien/algo; **to ~ till one cries** llorar de la risa; **his threats make me ~** *inf* sus amenazas me hacen gracia ▸ **he who ~s last ~s longest**

prov quien ríe el último, ríe mejor *prov*
◆**laugh off** *vt* tomar a risa
laughable ['lɑːfəbl, *Am:* 'læfə-] *adj* de risa
laughing I. *n* risas *fpl* II. *adj* de risa; **this is no** ~ **matter** no es cosa de risa
laughing stock *n* hazmerreír *m*
laughter ['lɑːftər, *Am:* 'læftər] *n no pl* risa(s) *f(pl)*; **to roar with** ~ echarse a reír ► ~ **is the best medicine** *prov* quien canta, sus males espanta *prov*
launch [lɔːntʃ, *Am:* lɑːntʃ] I. <-ches> *n* 1. (*boat*) lancha *f* 2. (*act of setting in the water*) botadura *f* 3. (*act of sending forth: of missile*) lanzamiento *m* 4. (*introduction: of exhibition*) inauguración *f*; (*of book*) presentación *f* II. *vt* 1. (*set in the water*) botar 2. (*send forth: missile*) lanzar 3. (*introduce: book*) presentar 4. (*start: investigation*) emprender; (*exhibition*) inaugurar 5. **to** ~ **oneself at sb** lanzarse sobre alguien
◆**launch into** *vt* emprender
◆**launch out** *vi Brit* lanzarse
launching ['lɔːntʃɪŋ, *Am:* 'lɑːntʃ-] *n* 1. (*act of setting in the water*) botadura *f* 2. (*act of sending forth: of missile*) lanzamiento *m* 3. (*beginning: of exhibition, campaign*) inauguración *f* 4. (*introduction: of book*) presentación *f*
launching pad *n*, **launch pad** *n* rampa *f* de lanzamiento
launder ['lɔːndər, *Am:* 'lɑːndər] *vt* 1. *form* (*wash*) lavar y planchar 2. *fig* (*money*) blanquear, lavar *AmL*
launderette [lɔːn'dret, *Am:* lɑːndə'ret] *n Brit* lavandería *f* (automática)
laundry ['lɔːndri, *Am:* 'lɑːn-] *n* 1. *no pl* (*dirty clothes*) ropa *f* sucia; **to do the** ~ hacer la colada 2. *no pl* (*washed clothes*) ropa *f* lavada 3. <-ies> (*place*) lavandería *f*
laundry basket *n* cesto *m* de la ropa sucia
laundry service *n* servicio *m* de lavandería
laureate ['lɒrɪət, *Am:* 'lɔːriːt] *n* Nobel ~ premio *mf* Nobel; **Poet Laureate** poeta *m* laureado (*en Gran Bretaña, poeta elegido por la reina para escribir poemas en ocasiones especiales*)
laurel ['lɒrəl, *Am:* 'lɔːr-] *n* laurel *m* ►**to rest on one's** ~**s** dormirse en los laureles
lava ['lɑːvə] *n* lava *f*
lavatory ['lævətri, *Am:* -tɔːri] <-ies> *n* lavabo *m*, lavatorio *m AmL*; **public** ~ lavabo público; **to go to the** ~ ir al baño
lavatory seat *n* taza *f* del váter
lavender ['lævəndər, *Am:* -dər] I. *n* lavanda *f* II. *adj* (de) lavanda
lavish ['lævɪʃ] I. *adj* (*banquet*) opíparo, -a; (*party*) espléndido, -a; (*reception*) fastuoso, -a; (*praise*) abundante II. *vt* **to** ~ **sth on sb** prodigar algo a alguien
law [lɔː, *Am:* lɑː] *n* 1. a. PHYS ley *f*; **the** ~ **of supply and demand** la ley de la oferta y la demanda; **the** ~ **of averages** (lo que dicen)

las estadísticas; **the** ~**s governing the exportation of paintings** las leyes que regulan la exportación de cuadros; **his word is** ~ lo que dice él va a misa; **the first** ~ **of sth** el principio básico de algo 2. (*legal system*) derecho *m*; (*body of laws*) ley *f*; ~ **and order** la ley y el orden; **to be against the** ~ ser ilegal; **to take the** ~ **into one's own hands** tomarse la justicia por su mano 3. (*the police*) policía *f* 4. (*court*) **to go to** ~ recurrir a los tribunales ►**the** ~ **of the jungle** la ley de la selva; **to be a** ~ **unto oneself** dictar sus propias leyes
law-abiding ['lɔːə'baɪdɪŋ, *Am:* 'lɑː-] *adj* observante de la ley **law breaker** *n* transgresor(a) *m(f)* de la ley **law court** *n* tribunal *m* de justicia **law enforcement** *n no pl, Am* aplicación *f* de la ley
lawful ['lɔːfəl, *Am:* 'lɑː-] *adj form* 1. (*legal*) legal; (*demands*) legítimo, -a; ~ **owner** propietario, -a *m*, *f* en derecho 2. (*law-abiding*) observante de la ley
lawgiver ['lɔːˌgɪvər, *Am:* 'lɑːˌgɪvər] *n* legislador(a) *m(f)*
lawless ['lɔːlɪs, *Am:* 'lɑː-] *adj* sin leyes; (*country*) anárquico, -a
lawmaker ['lɔːˌmeɪkər, *Am:* 'lɑːˌmeɪkər] *n* legislador(a) *m(f)*
lawn [lɔːn, *Am:* lɑːn] *n* (*grass*) césped *m*, pasto *m AmL*
lawnmower *n* cortacésped *m* **lawn tennis** *n* tenis *m* sobre hierba
law school *n Am* facultad *f* de derecho **law student** *n* estudiante *mf* de derecho **lawsuit** *n* proceso *m*; **to bring a** ~ **against sb** presentar una demanda contra alguien
lawyer ['lɔːjər, *Am:* 'lɑːjər] *n* abogado, -a *m*, *f*
lax [læks] *adj* 1. (*lacking care*) descuidado, -a; ~ **security** seguridad *f* poco rigurosa; **to be** ~ **in doing sth** hacer algo de manera negligente 2. (*lenient*) indulgente; (*rules*) poco severo, -a
laxative ['læksətɪv, *Am:* -t̬ɪv] I. *n* laxante *m* II. *adj* laxante
laxity ['læksəti, *Am:* -t̬i] *n*, **laxness** *n no pl* descuido *m*
lay[1] [leɪ] I. *n* 1. (*situation*) situación *f*; **the** ~ **of the land** la configuración del terreno; *fig* la situación actual 2. *vulg* **to be a good** ~ tener buen polvo II. <laid, laid> *vt* 1. (*place*) poner; **to** ~ **sth on/over sth** poner algo en/encima de algo; **to** ~ **sth flat** derribar algo; **to lay stress on sth** poner énfasis en algo; **to lay the blame on sb** echar la culpa a alguien 2. (*install*) colocar; (*cable*) tender; (*carpet*) poner, extender; (*pipes*) instalar; **to** ~ **the foundations for sth** *a. fig* echar los cimientos de algo 3. (*prepare*) preparar; **to** ~ **the table** *Brit* poner la mesa 4. (*egg*) poner 5. *vulg* (*have sex with*) follar 6. (*bet*) apostar; **to** ~ **an amount on sth** apostar una cantidad en algo 7. (*state*) presentar; **to** ~ **one's case before sb/sth** presentar su caso ante alguien/algo; **to**

~ **a charge against sb** formular una acusación contra alguien; **to ~ claim to sth** reclamar algo **III.**<laid, laid> *vi* poner huevos

◆**lay about** *vt* **to ~ sb** emprenderla a golpes con alguien

◆**lay aside** *vt*, **lay away** *vt* **1.** (*put away*) guardar; **to ~ one's differences** dejar de lado las diferencias **2.** (*save: food*) guardar; (*money*) ahorrar

◆**lay back** *vt* reposar

◆**lay before** *vt* **to lay sth before sb** poner algo frente a alguien; **to lay one's case before sb** presentar su caso ante alguien

◆**lay by** *vt* reservar

◆**lay down** *vt* **1.** (*put down*) poner a un lado; (*arms*) deponer; (*life*) sacrificar **2.** (*establish*) estipular; (*law*) dictar; **it is laid down that ...** está estipulado que...

◆**lay in** *vt* proveerse de

◆**lay into** *vt* **1.** *inf* (*assault*) atacar **2.** (*criticize*) arremeter contra **3.** (*eat*) lanzarse sobre

◆**lay off I.** *vt* despedir (temporalmente) **II.** *vi* dejar; **to ~ sb** dejar en paz a alguien; **to ~ smoking** dejar de fumar

◆**lay on** *vt* **1.** (*instal*) instalar **2.** (*provide: food, drink*) proveer de

◆**lay open** *vt* **1.** (*uncover*) descubrir **2.** (*expose*) exponer; **to lay oneself open** exponerse

◆**lay out** *vt* **1.** (*organize*) organizar **2.** (*spread out*) extender **3.** (*prepare for burial*) amortajar **4.** *inf* (*render unconscious*) dejar fuera de combate **5.** *inf* (*money*) gastar **6.** *Am* (*explain*) presentar

◆**lay to** *vi* llevar a puerto seguro

◆**lay up** *vt* **1.** (*store*) guardar; (*money*) ahorrar **2.** (*ship*) desarmar; (*car*) dejar en el garaje **3.** (*in bed*) **to be laid up** guardar cama

lay² [leɪ] *adj* **1.** (*not professional*) lego, -a; **in ~ terms** en términos profanos **2.** (*not of the clergy*) laico, -a

lay³ [leɪ] *pt of* **lie²**

layabout ['leɪəˌbaʊt] *n inf* vago, -a *m, f*

lay-by ['leɪbaɪ] *n* **1.** *Brit* (*stopping place*) apartadero *m* **2.** *no pl, Aus* **to buy/put on ~** comprar a plazos

layer¹ ['leɪəʳ, *Am:* -ɚ] **I.** *n* **1.** capa *f*; **ozone ~** capa de ozono **2.** (*level*) estrato *m* **II.** *vt* acodar

layer² ['leɪəʳ, *Am:* -ɚ] *n* (*hen*) gallina *f* ponedora

layered *adj* en capas

layette [leɪ'et] *n* canastilla *f*

layman ['leɪmən] <-men> *n* lego *m*

lay-off ['leɪɒf, *Am:* -ɑːf] *n* despido *m* (*por falta de trabajo*)

layout ['leɪaʊt] *n* **1.** (*of letter, magazine*) diseño *m*; (*of town*) trazado *m* **2.** TYPO maquetación *f*

layover ['leɪəʊvəʳ, *Am:* -oʊvɚ] *n Am* (*on journey*) parada *f*; AVIAT escala *f*

laywoman ['leɪwʊmən] <-women> *n* lega *f*

laze [leɪz] <-zing> *vi* holgazanear

laziness ['leɪzɪnɪs] *n no pl* holgazanería *f*

lazy ['leɪzi] <-ier, -iest> *adj* (*person*) vago, -a; (*day*) perezoso, -a

lb *abbr of* **pound** libra *f* (= 0,45 kg)

LCD [ˌelsiːˈdiː] *n abbr of* **liquid crystal display** pantalla *f* de cristal líquido

lead¹ [liːd] **I.** *n* **1.** *no pl* (*front position*) delantera *f*; **to be in the ~** estar a la cabeza; **to hold the ~** llevar la delantera; **to lose one's ~** perder la delantera; **to move into the ~** ponerse a la cabeza; **to take** (*over*) **the lead** tomar la delantera **2.** (*example*) ejemplo *m*; (*guiding*) iniciativa *f*; **to follow sb's ~** seguir el ejemplo de alguien; **to give a ~** dar una indicación **3.** THEAT papel *m* principal; **to play the ~** representar el papel principal **4.** (*clue*) pista *f*; **to get a ~ on sth** recibir una pista acerca de algo **5.** (*connecting wire*) cable *m*, conductor *m* **6.** *Brit, Aus* (*for dog*) correa *f* **II.**<led, led> *vt* **1.** (*be in charge of*) dirigir; (*discussion, inquiry*) conducir, llevar; **to ~ the way** ir primero; *fig* mostrar el camino **3.** (*induce*) inducir; **to ~ sb to do sth** llevar a alguien a hacer algo; **to ~ sb to believe that ...** hacer creer a alguien que... **4.** COM, SPORTS (*be ahead of*) encabezar; **to ~ the field** *fig* ir a la cabeza **5.** (*live a particular way: life*) llevar; **to ~ a life of luxury** llevar una vida de lujos; **to ~ a quiet/hectic life** llevar una vida tranquila/ajetreada ►**to ~ sb by the nose** *inf* manejar a alguien fácilmente; **to ~ sb up the garden path** *inf* embaucar a alguien **III.**<led, led> *vi* **1.** (*be in charge*) dirigir **2.** (*guide followers*) guiar **3.** (*conduct*) llevar; **to ~ to/into sth** *a. fig* conducir a/hacia algo **4.** (*be ahead*) liderar; **to ~ by 2 metres** tener una ventaja de 2 metros

◆**lead along** *vt* llevar (de la mano)

◆**lead aside** *vt* llevar a un lado

◆**lead astray** *vt* llevar por mal camino

◆**lead away** *vt* llevar; **he was led away by the police** fue arrestado por la policía

◆**lead back** *vt* hacer volver

◆**lead off I.** *vt* (*person*) llevar afuera; (*room*) comunicar con **II.** *vi* empezar

◆**lead on** *vt* (*trick, fool*) engañar; (*encourage*) incitar a; **she doesn't want to lead him on** no quiere darle falsas expectativas

◆**lead to** *vt* llevar a

◆**lead up to** *vi* **1.** (*cause*) conducir a **2.** (*slowly introduce*) preparar **3.** (*precede*) preceder a

lead² [led] *n* **1.** *no pl* (*metal*) plomo *m* **2.** NAUT sonda *f* **3.** (*in pencil*) mina *f*

leaded ['ledəd] **I.** *adj* emplomado, -a; **fuel** gasolina *f* con plomo **II.** *n no pl* gasolina *f* con plomo

leaden ['ledn] *adj* **1.** (*dark*) plomizo, -a **2.** (*heavy*) pesado, -a; **~ limbs** pies *mpl* de plomo

leader ['liːdəʳ, *Am:* -dɚ] *n* **1.** (*of group*) líder *mf* **2.** (*guide*) guía *mf* **3.** *Brit* MUS (*first violin*) primer violín *m* **4.** *Am* MUS (*conductor*) direc-

tor(a) *m(f)* **5.** *Brit* (*in newspaper*) editorial
m
leadership ['liːdəʃɪp, *Am:* -dɚ-] *n no pl*
1. (*ability*) liderazgo *m;* ~ **qualities** dotes *fpl*
de mando **2.** (*leaders*) dirección *f* **3.** (*function*)
mando *m;* **to be under sb's** ~ estar bajo el
mando de alguien
lead-free ['ledfriː] *adj* sin plomo
lead guitar *n* **to play** ~ ser el guitarrista principal
leading[1] ['ledɪŋ] *n no pl, Brit* emplomado *m*
leading[2] ['liːdɪŋ] *n no pl* mando *m*
leading article *n Brit* editorial *m* **leading-**
-edge *adj* puntero, -a; ~ **technology** tecnología *f* punta **leading lady** *n* actriz *f* principal
leading light *n inf* to be a ~ in sth ser una
figura de referencia en algo **leading man** *n*
actor *m* principal **leading question** *n* pregunta *f* capciosa
lead pencil *n* lápiz *m* de mina **lead poi-**
soning *n* saturnismo *m*
lead singer *n* cantante *mf* principal **lead**
story *n* PUBL artículo *m* principal **lead time**
n tiempo *m* de entrega
lead up *n* tiempo *m* preparatorio
leaf [liːf] <leaves> *n* **1.** (*of plant*) hoja *f*
2. *no pl* (*foliage*) follaje *m;* **to be in** [*o* **come**
into] ~ echar hojas **3.** (*piece of paper*) hoja *f;* ~
of paper hoja de papel **4.** (*of table*) tablero *m*
►**to take a** ~ **from sb's** book seguir el ejemplo de alguien; **to** shake **like a** ~ temblar
como una pluma; **to** turn over **a new** ~ hacer
borrón y cuenta nueva
♦**leaf through** *vt* hojear
leafless ['liːfləs] *adj* deshojado, -a
leaflet ['liːflɪt] *n* folleto *m*
leafy ['liːfi] <-ier, -iest> *adj* frondoso, -a; **a** ~
suburb una zona residencial con muchos
árboles
league [liːg] *n* **1. a.** SPORTS liga *f;* **football** ~
liga de fútbol; **the** ~ **championship** el campeonato de liga; **to be/to be not in the same**
~ **as sb/sth** *fig* estar/no estar a la altura de al-
guien/algo; **to be out of sb's** ~ no tener comparación con alguien **2.** (*measurement*) legua *f*
►**to be** in ~ **with sb** estar confabulado con alguien
leak [liːk] **I.** *n* (*of gas, water*) fuga *f;* (*of*
information) filtración *f;* (*in roof*) gotera *f*
II. *vi* **1.** (*let escape*) tener una fuga; (*tyre*)
perder aire; (*hose, bucket*) perder agua; (*pen*)
perder tinta; (*tap*) gotear; **to** ~ **everywhere**
chorrear por todos lados **2.** (*information*) filtrarse **III.** *vt* **1.** (*let escape*) derramar; **to** ~
water perder agua **2.** (*information*) filtrar
leakage ['liːkɪdʒ] *n* **1.** (*leak*) fuga *f* **2.** *no pl*
(*of information*) filtración *f*
leaky ['liːki] <-ier, -iest> *adj* que tiene fugas
lean[1] [liːn] **I.** <leant *Am:* leaned, leant *Am:*
leaned> *vi* inclinarse; **to** ~ **against sth**
apoyarse en algo **II.** <leant *Am:* leaned,
leant *Am:* leaned> *vt* apoyar; **to** ~ **sth**
against sth apoyar algo contra algo

lean[2] [liːn] *adj* **1.** (*thin*) flaco, -a; (*meat*)
magro, -a; (*face*) enjuto, -a **2.** (*efficient: com-*
pany) eficiente
♦**lean back** *vi* reclinar(se)
♦**lean forward** *vi* inclinar(se) hacia adelante
♦**lean on** *vt* **1.** (*rely on*) apoyarse en **2.** *inf*
(*pressurize*) ejercer presión sobre
♦**lean out** *vi* asomarse
♦**lean over** **I.** *vt* inclinarse sobre **II.** *vi* inclinarse
leaning ['liːnɪŋ] *n* inclinación *f;* **political** ~s
tendencias *fpl* políticas
leant [lent] *pt, pp of* **lean**[1]
lean-to ['liːntuː] *n* **1.** (*building extension*)
anexo *m* **2.** *Am, Aus* (*shack*) cobertizo *m*
leap [liːp] **I.** <leapt *Am:* leaped, leapt *Am:*
leaped> *vi* saltar; **to** ~ **forward** saltar hacia
adelante; **to** ~ **to do sth** abalanzarse a hacer
algo; **to** ~ **with joy** saltar de alegría; **to** ~ **to**
sb's defence saltar en defensa de alguien; **his**
heart ~t le dio un vuelco el corazón; **to** ~ **to**
mind venir a la mente **II.** <leapt *Am:*
leaped, leapt *Am:* leaped> *vt* saltar **III.** *n*
salto *m;* **to take a** ~ dar un salto ►**by** ~**s and**
bounds a pasos de gigante; **a** ~ **in the** dark
un salto en el vacío
♦**leap at** *vt* **1.** (*jump*) saltar hacia **2.** (*accept*)
no dejar pasar; **to** ~ **the chance to do sth** no
dejar escapar la oportunidad de hacer algo
♦**leap out** *vi* saltar
♦**leap up** *vi* **1.** (*jump up*) ponerse en pie de
un salto; **to** ~ **to do sth** apresurarse a hacer
algo **2.** (*rise quickly*) subir de pronto
leapfrog [ˌliːpfrɒg, *Am:* -fraːg] **I.** *n no pl*
potro *m*, pídola *f;* **to play a game of** ~ jugar a
saltar al potro, jugar a la pídola, saltar el burro
Méx **II.** <-gg-> *vt* pasar por encima de
leapt [lept] *vt, vi pt, pp of* **leap**
leap year *n* año *m* bisiesto
learn [lɜːn, *Am:* lɜːrn] **I.** <learnt *Am:*
learned, learnt *Am:* learned> *vt* aprender;
to ~ **to do sth** aprender a hacer algo; **to** ~ **that**
enterarse de que **II.** <learnt *Am:* learned,
learnt *Am:* learned> *vi* aprender; **to** ~ **from**
one's mistakes aprender de los propios
errores
learned ['lɜːnɪd, *Am:* 'lɜːr-] *adj* erudito, -a
learner ['lɜːnə[r], *Am:* 'lɜːrnɚ] *n* aprendiz *mf;*
to be a quick ~ aprender rápido
learning ['lɜːnɪŋ, *Am:* 'lɜːr-] *n no pl*
1. (*acquisition of knowledge*) aprendizaje *m*
2. (*extensive knowledge*) saber *m*
learning disability *n* <-ies> dificultad *f* de
aprendizaje
learnt [lɜːnt, *Am:* lɜːrnt] *pt, pp of* **learn**
lease [liːs] **I.** *vt* alquilar **II.** *n* (*act*) arrendamiento *m;* (*contract*) contrato *m* de arrendamiento; **to take on** ~ tomar en arriendo
leasehold ['liːshəʊld, *Am:* -hoʊld] COM, FIN,
ECON **I.** *n* contrato *m* de arrendamiento; **to**
hold a ~ tener un contrato de arrendamiento;
to have sth on ~ tener algo bajo un contrato

de arrendamiento II. *adj* **1.** (*kept by lease*) en arrendamiento **2.** (*dealing with leases*) de arrendamiento

leaseholder ['liːʃəʊldəʳ, *Am:* -hoʊldəʳ] *n* arrendatario, -a *m, f*

leash [liːʃ] *n Am* correa *f* ►**to keep sb on a tight** ~ atar corto a alguien

leasing ['liːsɪŋ] *n no pl* FIN arrendamiento *m* (con opción de compra)

leasing company *n* empresa *f* de arrendamiento

least [liːst] I. *adj* mínimo, -a; (*age*) menor II. *adv* menos; **the** ~ **possible** lo menos posible; **she** ~ **of all** ella menos que nadie III. *n* lo menos; **at** (**the**) ~ por lo menos, al menos; **not in the** ~! ¡en absoluto!; **to say the** ~ para no decir más

leather ['leðəʳ] *n no pl* cuero *m*

leathering *n* cobertura *f* de cuero

leatherneck ['leðənek] *n Am, inf* soldado *m* de infantería (*de la marina estadounidense*)

leathery ['leðəri] *adj* (*skin*) curtido, -a; (*meat*) correoso, -a

leave¹ [liːv] I. <left, left> *vt* **1.** (*depart from*) salir de; (*school, unversity*) abandonar; (*work*) dejar; **to** ~ **home** irse de casa **2.** (*not take away with*) dejar; (*forget*) olvidar(se); **to** ~ **sth to sb** dejar algo a alguien; **to** ~ **sth at home** dejar(se) algo en casa; **to** ~ **a note/message** (**for sb**) dejar una nota/un mensaje (para alguien); **to** ~ **stains** dejar manchas **3.** (*put in a situation*) **to** ~ **sb alone** dejar en paz a alguien; **to be left homeless** quedarse sin hogar; **to** ~ **sth open** dejar algo abierto ►**to** ~ **a lot to be desired** dejar mucho que desear; **to** ~ **it at that** dejarlo II. <left, left> *vi* marcharse, despabilarse *AmL* III. *n* partida *f*; **to take** (**one's**) ~ (**of sb**) despedirse (de alguien) ►**to take** (**complete**) ~ **of one's senses** perder (completamente) la cabeza

◆**leave behind** *vt* **1.** (*not take along*) dejar **2.** (*forget*) olvidar **3.** (*progress beyond*) dejar atrás

◆**leave off** I. *vt* **1.** (*give up*) dejar de **2.** (*omit*) omitir II. *vi* acabar

◆**leave on** *vt* dejar(se) puesto; (*light*) dejar encendido

◆**leave out** *vt* **1.** (*omit*) omitir **2.** (*exclude*) excluir

◆**leave over** *vt* dejar; **there's nothing left over** no queda nada

leave² [liːv] *n* permiso *m;* **to have/get sb's** ~ (**to do sth**) tener/obtener el permiso de alguien (para hacer algo); **with/without sb's** ~ con/sin el permiso de alguien; **to go/be on** ~ MIL salir/estar de permiso; **sick** ~ baja *f* por enfermedad

leaven ['levn] I. *n* levadura *f* II. *vt* (a)leudar; *fig* impregnar; **to** ~**a speech with jokes** aligerar un discurso con bromas

leaves [liːvz] *n pl of* **leaf**

leave-taking ['liːvˌteɪkɪŋ] *n* despedida *f*

leaving ['liːvɪŋ] *n* **1.** *no pl* (*departure*) partida *f* **2.** *pl* (*remaining things*) restos *mpl* **3.** *pl* (*leftovers*) sobras *fpl*

leaving party *n* fiesta *f* de despedida

Lebanese [ˌlebə'niːz] I. *adj* libanés, -esa II. *n* libanés, -esa *m, f*

Lebanon ['lebənən, *Am:* -nɑːn] *n* (**the**) ~ el Líbano

lecher ['letʃəʳ, *Am:* -ɚ] *n* sátiro *m*

lecherous ['letʃərəs] *adj* lascivo, -a

lechery ['letʃəri] *n no pl* lascivia *f*, lujuria *f*

lectern ['lektən, *Am:* -tɚn] *n* atril *m;* REL facistol *m*

lecture ['lektʃəʳ, *Am:* -tʃɚ] I. *n a.* UNIV conferencia *f;* **a** ~ **on sth** una conferencia acerca de algo; **to give sb a** ~ *fig* sermonear a alguien II. *vi* (*give a lecture*) dar una conferencia; (*teach*) dar clases III. *vt* **1.** (*give a lecture*) dar una conferencia a; (*teach*) dar clases a **2.** *fig* (*reprove*) sermonear

lecture notes *npl* apuntes *mpl* de clase

lecturer ['lektʃərəʳ, *Am:* -ɚ] *n* **1.** (*person giving lecture*) conferenciante *mf* **2.** UNIV profesor(a) *m(f)* universitario, -a

lecture room *n* UNIV sala *f* de conferencias

lecture theatre *n* aula *f* magna **lecture tour** *n* gira *f* de conferencias

led [led] *pt, pp of* **lead¹**

LED [ˌeliː'diː] *n abbr of* **light-emitting diode** diodo *m* electroluminiscente

ledge [ledʒ] *n* (*shelf*) repisa *f;* (*on building*) cornisa *f;* (*on cliff*) saliente *m;* **window** ~ alféizar *m*

ledger ['ledʒəʳ, *Am:* -ɚ] *n* COM libro *m* mayor

lee [liː] *n* sotavento *m*

leech [liːtʃ] <-es> *n* sanguijuela *f*, saguaipé *m Arg* ►**to stick to sb like a** ~ pegarse a alguien como una lapa

leek [liːk] *n* puerro *m*

leer [lɪəʳ, *Am:* lɪr] I. *vi* mirar lascivamente II. *n* mirada *f* lasciva

leeward ['liːwəd, *Am:* -wɚd] METEO I. *adj* de sotavento II. *adv* a sotavento

leeway ['liːweɪ] *n no pl* flexibilidad *f*

left¹ [left] *pt, pp of* **leave¹**

left² [left] I. *n* **1.** *no pl* (*direction, sight*) izquierda *f;* **the** ~ la izquierda; **to turn to the** ~ girar a la izquierda; **on/to the** ~ en/a la izquierda; **on her** ~ a su izquierda **2.** *no pl* POL izquierda *f;* **on the** ~ de izquierda(s) II. *adj* izquierdo, -a III. *adv* a [*o* hacia] la izquierda; **to turn** ~ girar hacia la izquierda

left hand *n* izquierda *f;* **on the** ~ a la izquierda

left-hand [ˌleft'hænd] *adj* a la izquierda; ~ **side** lado *m* izquierdo; ~ **bend** curva *f* a la izquierda; ~ **drive** conducción *f* por la izquierda **left-handed** *adj* zurdo, -a; ~ **scissors** tijeras *fpl* para zurdos **left-hander** *n* **1.** (*left-handed*) zurdo, -a *m, f* **2.** SPORTS izquierdazo *m*

leftist ['leftɪst] POL I. *adj* izquierdista II. *n* izquierdista *mf*

left-luggage office *n Brit* consigna *f*, consignación *f AmC*

leftovers ['left‚əʊvəz, *Am:* -‚oʊvə‚z] *npl*
1. (*food*) sobras *fpl* 2. (*remaining things*)
restos *mpl*

left wing *n* POL izquierda *f*

left-wing [‚left'wɪŋ] *adj* POL de izquierda

left-winger *n* POL izquierdista *mf*

leg [leg] I. *n* 1. (*of person*) pierna *f*; (*of animal, furniture*) pata *f* 2. (*of trousers*) pernera *f*
3. GASTR (*of lamb, pork*) pierna *f*; (*of chicken*)
muslo *m* 4. (*segment*) etapa *f* ►to be on
one's **last** ~s estar para el arrastre; to give sb
a ~ **up** *inf* echar una mano a alguien; **break** a
~! ¡mucha suerte!; to **pull** sb's ~ *inf* tomar el
pelo a alguien; to **shake** a ~ *inf* apresurarse
II. *vt* <-gg-> *inf* to ~ **it** (*go by foot*) ir a pie;
(*run fast*) echar a correr

legacy ['legəsi] <-ies> *n* legado *m*; (*inheritance*) herencia *f*

legal ['liːgl] *adj* 1. (*in accordance with the
law*) legal 2. (*concerning the law*) jurídico, -a
legal advice *n* consejo *m* jurídico **legal aid**
n derecho a tener un abogado de oficio **legal
fee** *n* honorarios *mpl* de los abogados

legalisation *n s.* **legalization**

legalise *vt Brit, Aus s.* **legalize**

legality [liːˈgæləti, *Am:* -ṭi] *n no pl* legalidad
f

legalization [‚liːgəlaɪˈzeɪʃən, *Am:* -ɪ'-] *n no
pl* legalización *f*

legalize ['liːgəlaɪz] *vt* legalizar

legally ['liːgəli] *adv* legalmente

legal profession *n* abogacía *f* **legal system** *n* sistema *m* judicial

legate ['legɪt] *n* legado *m*

legation [lɪˈgeɪʃən] *n* legación *f*

legend ['ledʒənd] *n* leyenda *f*; ~ **has it that
...** dice la leyenda que...; **he was a ~ in his
own lifetime** era una leyenda viva

legendary ['ledʒəndri, *Am:* -der-] *adj* legendario, -a; to be ~ **for sth** ser legendario por
algo

legerdemain [‚ledʒədəˈmeɪn, *Am:* -ə‚də'-]
n no pl juego *m* de manos

leggings ['legɪŋz] *npl* mallas *fpl*

leggy ['legi] <-ier, -iest> *adj* patilargo, -a

legible ['ledʒəbl] *adj* legible

legion ['liːdʒən] I. *n* 1. HIST legión *f* 2. (*many*)
multitud *f* II. *adj form* **the difficulties are** ~
las dificultades son innumerables

legionary ['liːdʒənəri, *Am:* -eri] I. *adj* legionario, -a II. *n* <-ies> HIST legionario, -a *m, f*

legionnaire [‚liːdʒəˈneəʳ, *Am:* -'ner] *n*
legionario *m*

Legionnaire's disease [‚liːdʒəˈneəʳz
dɪˈziːz] *n* MED enfermedad *f* del legionario

legislate ['ledʒɪsleɪt] *vi* legislar

legislation [‚ledʒɪsˈleɪʃən] *n no pl* legislación *f*

legislative ['ledʒɪslətɪv, *Am:* -sleɪṭɪv] *adj*
legislativo, -a

legislator ['ledʒɪsleɪtəʳ, *Am:* -ṭə·] *n* legisla-
dor(a) *m(f)*

legislature ['ledʒɪsleɪtʃəʳ, *Am:* -sleɪtʃə·] *n*
cuerpo *m* legislativo

legitimacy [lɪˈdʒɪtɪməsi, *Am:* ləˈdʒɪṭə-] *n
no pl* legitimidad *f*

legitimate¹ [lɪˈdʒɪtɪmət, *Am:* ləˈdʒɪṭə-] *adj*
1. (*legal*) legal; **a ~ government** un gobierno
legítimo 2. (*reasonable*) válido, -a 3. (*born in
wedlock*) legítimo, -a

legitimate² [lɪˈdʒɪtɪmeɪt, *Am:* ləˈdʒɪṭ-] *vt*
legitimar

legitimise *vt Brit, Aus,* **legitimize** [lɪˈdʒɪt-
əmaɪz, *Am:* ləˈdʒɪṭə-] *vt* 1. (*make legal*)
legitimar 2. (*justify*) justificar

legless ['legləs] *adj* 1. (*without legs*) sin piernas 2. *Brit, inf* (*drunk*) borracho, -a, rascado, -a
Col, Ven, untado, -a *RíoPl*

legroom ['legrʊm, *Am:* -ruːm] *n no pl* espacio *m* para las piernas

legume ['legjuːm] *n* legumbre *f*

leguminous [lɪˈgjuːmɪnəs, *Am:* ləˈgjuː-] *adj*
leguminoso, -a

leisure ['leʒəʳ, *Am:* 'liːʒə·] *n no pl* ocio *m* ►at
one's ~ cuando quiera uno; **call me at your** ~
llámame cuando tengas tiempo

leisure activities *n* actividades *fpl* recreati-
vas **leisure centre** *n* centro *m* recreativo

leisured *adj* (*comfortable*) acomodado, -a

leisure hours *n* horas *fpl* libres

leisurely I. *adj* pausado, -a II. *adv* pausadamente

leisure time *n no pl* tiempo *m* libre **leisure
wear** *n* ropa *f* deportiva

lemming ['lemɪŋ] *n* lemming *m*; **like ~s** de
una manera suicida

lemon ['lemən] *n* 1. (*fruit*) limón *m*; **a slice
of** ~ una rodaja de limón 2. *no pl* (*colour*) amarillo *m* limón 3. *Brit, Aus, inf* (*foolish person*)
estúpido, -a *m, f,* gafo, -a *m, f Ven* ►to
squeeze sb like a ~ *inf* exprimir a alguien
como a un limón

lemonade [‚leməˈneɪd] *n* 1. (*still*) limonada
f 2. *Brit* (*fizzy*) gaseosa *f*

lemon juice *n* zumo *m* de limón **lemon
peel** *n* corteza *f* de limón **lemon squash**
<- -shes> *n Brit, Aus* refresco *m* de limón
lemon tea *n* té *m* con limón

lend [lend] <lent, lent> I. *vt* 1. (*give temporarily*) prestar; to ~ **money to sb** prestar dinero
a alguien 2. (*impart, grant*) dar; to ~ **colour to
sth** dar color a algo; to ~ **support to a view**
apoyar una opinión ►to ~ **an ear** prestar atención; to ~ **an ear to sb** prestar oído a alguien;
to ~ a **hand to sb** echar una mano a alguien;
to ~ **one's name to sth** ofrecer su nombre
para algo; to ~ **wings to sb/sth** dar alas a al-
guien/algo; to ~ **oneself to sth** prestarse uno
a algo II. *vi* prestar dinero

lender ['lendəʳ, *Am:* -də·] *n* FIN prestamista

lending ['lendɪŋ] *n* préstamo *m*

lending library *n* biblioteca *f* pública

length [leŋθ] *n* 1. *no pl* (*measurement*)
longitud *f*; **it's 3 metres in** ~ tiene 3 metros de

largo; (**along**) **the** ~ **of sth** a lo largo de algo **2.** (*piece: of pipe, string*) trozo *m* **3.** (*of swimming pool*) largo *m* **4.** *no pl* (*duration*) duración *f*; (**for**) **any** ~ **of time** (por) cualquier lapso de tiempo; **at** ~ al fin, finalmente; **to speak at** ~ hablar largamente; **at great** ~ detalladamente ▶**the** ~ **and breadth of** a lo largo y ancho de; **to go to great** ~**s to do sth** dar el máximo para hacer algo

lengthen [ˈleŋθən] I. *vt* **1.** (*in time*) prolongar **2.** (*physically*) alargar II. *vi* **1.** (*in time*) prolongarse **2.** (*physically*) alargarse

lengthways [ˈleŋθweɪz] *adv, adj*, **lengthwise** [ˈleŋθwaɪz] *adv, adj* a lo largo

lengthy [ˈleŋθi] <-ier, -iest> *adj* prolongado, -a; ~ **wait** (*speech*) prolijo, -a; **a** ~ **wait** una larga espera

lenience [ˈliːniənts] *n*, **leniency** *n no pl* indulgencia *f*

lenient [ˈliːniənt] *adj* (*judge*) indulgente; (*punishment*) poco severo, -a

lens [lenz] <-ses> *n* **1.** (*of glasses*) lente *m o f*; (*of camera*) objetivo *m*; ~**es of glasses** cristales *mpl* de las gafas; (**contact**) ~**es** lentes *fpl* de contacto; **zoom** ~ lente de acercamiento **2.** ANAT cristalino *m*

lent [lent] *pt, pp of* **lend**

Lent [lent] *n no pl* Cuaresma *f*

lentil [ˈlentl, *Am:* -t̬l] *n* lenteja *f*

Leo [ˈliːəʊ, *Am:* -oʊ] *n* Leo *m*

leonine [ˈlɪənaɪn] *adj form* leonino, -a

leopard [ˈlepəd, *Am:* -əd] *n* leopardo *m* ▶**a** ~ **can't change its spots** *prov* el árbol que nace torcido jamás sus ramas endereza *prov*, el que nace barrigón ni que lo fajen chiquito *Ven, prov*

leotard [ˈliːətɑːd, *Am:* -tɑːrd] *n* malla *f*

leper [ˈlepəʳ, *Am:* -əʳ] *n* **1.** (*leprosy sufferer*) leproso, -a *m, f* **2.** (*disliked person*) marginado, -a *m, f*

leprosy [ˈleprəsi] *n no pl* lepra *f*

leprous [ˈleprəs] *adj* leproso, -a

lesbian [ˈlezbɪən] I. *n* lesbiana *f* II. *adj* lesbiano, -a

lesbianism *n* lesbianismo *m*

lesion [ˈliːʒən] *n* lesión *f*

Lesotho [ləˈsuːtuː, *Am:* ləˈsoʊtoʊ] *n* Lesoto *m*

less [les] *comp of* **little** I. *adj* (*in degree, size*) menor; (*in quantity*) menos; **sth of** ~ **value** algo de menor valor; ~ **wine/nuts** menos vino/nueces II. *adv* menos; **to drink** ~ beber menos; **to see sb** ~ ver menos a alguien; ~ **than** 10 menos de [*o* que] 10; **to grow** [*o* **become**] ~ disminuir; **not him, much** [*o* **still**] ~ **her** él no, y mucho menos ella III. *pron* menos; ~ **than** ... menos que...; ~ **and** ~ cada vez menos; **to have** ~ **than** ... tener menos que...; **to cost** ~ **than** ... costar menos que...; **the** ~ **you eat, the** ~ **you get fat** mientras menos comas, menos gordo estarás IV. *prep* menos; **a month,** ~ **two days** un mes menos dos días

lessen [ˈlesn] I. *vi* (*danger*) reducirse; (*fever*) bajar; (*pain*) aliviarse II. *vt* (*diminish*) disminuir; (*risk*) reducir; (*pain*) aliviar

lesser [ˈlesəʳ, *Am:* -əʳ] *adj comp of* **less** menor; **to a** ~ **extent** en menor grado

lesson [ˈlesn] *n* **1.** SCHOOL clase *f*; ~**s** lecciones *fpl* **2.** *fig* lección *f*; **to draw a** ~ (**from sth**) aprender una lección (de algo); **to learn one's** ~ aprenderse la lección; **to teach sb a** ~ dar a alguien una lección

lest [lest] *conj liter* **1.** (*for fear that*) no sea que +*subj*; **I didn't do it** ~ **he should come** no lo hice por si venía **2.** (*if*) en caso de que +*subj*

let¹ [let] *n* SPORTS let *m* ▶**without** ~ **or hindrance** LAW sin estorbo ni obstáculo

let² [let] I. *n Brit* alquiler *m* II.<**let, let**> *vt* **1.** (*allow*) dejar; **to** ~ **sb do sth** dejar a alguien hacer algo; **to** ~ **sb know sth** hacer saber algo a alguien; **to** ~ **sth pass** pasar algo por alto; **to** ~ **sb alone** dejar a alguien en paz; ~ **him be!** ¡déjalo en paz! **2.** (*in suggestions*) ~**'s go!** ¡vámonos!; ~**'s say ... digamos...;** ~ **us pray** ¡oremos! **3.** (*filler while thinking*) ~**'s see** veamos; ~ **me think** déjame pensar **4.** MAT ~ **x be y** supongamos que x sea igual a y ▶~ **alone ...** (y) menos aún...; **to** ~ **sb have it** decir cuatro verdades a alguien; **to** ~ **sth lie** dejar algo como está; **to** ~ **fly** montar en cólera; **to** ~ **rip** (*become angry*) montar en cólera; (*drive fast*) correr

◆**let by** *vt* dejar pasar

◆**let down** *vt* **1.** (*disappoint*) decepcionar **2.** (*lower*) bajar; (*hair*) soltar; **to let one's hair down** *a. fig* soltarse el pelo **3.** FASHION alargar **4.** *Brit, Aus* (*deflate*) desinflar

◆**let in** *vt* (*person*) dejar entrar; (*light*) dejar pasar ▶**to let oneself in for sth** meterse en algo; **to let sb in on sth** revelar un secreto a alguien

◆**let off** *vt* **1.** (*forgive*) perdonar; **to let sb off with a fine** poner sólo una multa a alguien **2.** (*fire: gun*) disparar; (*bomb, firework*) hacer explotar

◆**let on** *vi inf* (*divulge*) **to** ~ **about sth** revelar algo; **to not** ~ **about sth** callarse algo

◆**let out** I. *vi Am* (*end*) culminar II. *vt* **1.** (*release*) dejar salir; (*prisoner*) poner en libertad; (*laugh*) soltar; **to** ~ **a scream** pegar un grito **2.** FASHION ensanchar **3.** (*reveal: secret*) revelar **4.** (*rent*) alquilar

◆**let up** *vi* **1.** (*become weaker, stop*) debilitarse; (*rain*) amainar; (*cold*) suavizarse; (*fog*) desvanecerse **2.** (*relent*) aflojar; **to** ~ **on sb** ser menos duro con alguien; **to** ~ **on the accelerator** soltar el acelerador

lethal [ˈliːθl] *adj* letal; (*poison*) mortífero, -a; (*weapon*) mortal; **this brandy's** ~! *inf* ¡este brandy es mortal!

lethargic [lɪˈθɑːdʒɪk, *Am:* lɪˈθɑːr-] *adj* **1.** (*lacking energy*) letárgico, -a **2.** (*drowsy*) somnoliento, -a

lethargy [ˈleθədʒi, *Am:* -əʳ-] *n no pl* **1.** (*lack of*

energy) letargo *m* **2.** (*drowsiness*) sopor *m*
letter ['letər, *Am:* 'leţə·] *n* **1.** (*message*) carta
f **2.** (*symbol*) letra *f* ►to stick to the ~ of the
<u>law</u> aplicar la ley en sentido estricto; <u>to</u> the ~
al pie de la letra
letter bomb *n* carta *f* bomba **letterbox** *n*
Brit, Aus buzón *m* de correos **letterhead** *n*
(*at top of letter*) membrete *m;* (*paper*) papel *m*
membreteado
lettering ['letərɪŋ] *n no pl* caracteres *mpl*
letterpress *n* TYPO prensa *f* de copiar
lettuce ['letɪs, *Am:* 'leţ-] *n* lechuga *f*
leucocyte *n*, **leukocyte** ['luːkəʊsaɪt, *Am:*
'luːkoʊ-] *n* MED leucocito *m*
leukaemia *n*, **leukemia** [luː'kiːmiə] *n Am*
leucemia *f*
level ['levəl] **I.** *adj* **1.** (*horizontal*) horizontal;
(*flat*) plano, -a; (*spoonful*) raso, -a **2.** (*having
same height*) **to be ~ with sth** estar a la
misma altura que algo **3.** *Brit, Aus* (*in same
position*) **to be ~ with sb/sth** estar a la par de
alguien/algo **4.** (*of same amount*) igual
5. (*calm*) sereno, -a; (*look*) sincero, -a; (*tone*)
tranquilo, -a; (*voice*) mesurado, -a; **to keep a
~ head** no perder la cabeza **6.** (*uniform*) uniforme ►to do one's ~ <u>best</u> *inf* hacer todo lo
posible **II.** *adv* a nivel **III.** *n* **1.** (*position,
amount*) nivel *m* **2.** (*height*) altura *f; above
sea ~* sobre el nivel del mar; **at ground ~** a ras
de tierra **3.** *no pl* (*position in hierarchy*) categoría *f; at a higher ~* en una categoría
superior; **at the (very) highest ~** en el nivel
más alto; **to be on a ~ with sb/sth** estar a la
misma altura que alguien/algo; **to find one's
(own) ~** *inf* encontrar su sitio en la sociedad
4. (*quality of performance*) nivel *m;* **intermediate ~ students** estudiantes *mfpl* de nivel
intermedio **5.** (*meaning*) **on another ~** en
otro sentido; **on a serious ~** en un plano serio
►to <u>be</u> on the ~ (*business, person*) ser serio
IV. <*Brit:* -ll-, *Am:* -l-> *vt* **1.** (*smoothen,
flatten*) nivelar **2.** (*demolish completely*) derribar **3.** (*point*) **to ~ sth at sb** apuntar con
algo a alguien
◆**level down** *vt* nivelar (por abajo)
◆**level off** *vi*, **level out** *vi* (*aircraft*) nivelarse; (*inflation*) equilibrarse
◆**level up** *vt* igualar
◆**level with** *vt inf* sincerarse con
level crossing *n Brit, Aus* paso *m* a nivel
level-headed *adj* sensato, -a **level peg-
ging** *n Brit, Aus* **to be (on) ~** estar en igualdad de condiciones
lever ['liːvər, *Am:* 'levə·] **I.** *n* palanca *f;* **brake
~** *Brit* freno *m* de mano **II.** *vt* apalancar, palanquear *AmL;* **to ~ sth open** abrir algo con palanca
leverage ['liːvərɪdʒ, *Am:* 'levə·-] *n no pl*
1. (*using lever*) apalancamiento *m* **2.** *fig*
influencia *f*
leveret ['levərɪt] *n* lebrato *m*
leviathan [lɪ'vaɪəθən] *n* **1.** *liter* (*machine,
organization*) gigante *mf* **2.** REL leviatán *m*

levitate ['levɪteɪt] **I.** *vt* mantener en el aire
por levitación **II.** *vi* mantenerse en el aire por
levitación
levity ['levəti, *Am:* -ţi] *n no pl* ligereza *f*
levy ['levi] **I.** <-ies> *n* tasa *f* **II.** <-ie-> *vt*
imponer; **to ~ a tax on sth** gravar algo con un
impuesto
lewd [ljuːd, *Am:* luːd] *adj* (*person*) lascivo, -a;
(*gesture, remark*) obsceno, -a
lewdness *n no pl* (*behaviour*) lascivia *f;* (*of
gesture, remark*) obscenidad *f*
lexical ['leksɪkl] *adj* léxico, -a
lexicographer [ˌleksɪ'kɒgrəfər, *Am:* -kɑː-
'grəfə·] *n* lexicógrafo, -a *m, f*
lexicography [ˌleksɪ'kɒgrəfi, *Am:* -kɑː'grə-]
n no pl lexicografía *f*
lexicology [ˌleksɪ'kɒlədʒi, *Am:* -'kɑːlə-] *n
no pl* lexicología *f*
lexicon ['leksɪkən, *Am:* -kɑːn] *n* **1.** (*vocabulary: of person, subject*) vocabulario *m;* (*of language*) léxico *m*, lexicón *m* **2.** (*dictionary*) diccionario *m*
lexis ['leksɪs] *n no pl* LING vocabulario *m*
LF *abbr of* **low frequency** BF
liability [ˌlaɪə'bɪləti, *Am:* -ţi] *n* **1.** *no pl* FIN,
LAW responsabilidad *f;* **to accept ~ for sth**
hacerse responsable de algo; **limited ~ company** compañía *f* de responsabilidad limitada
2. *inf* **he's a ~!** ¡es un estorbo!
liable ['laɪəbl] *adj* **1.** (*prone*) propenso, -a; **to
be ~ to do sth** ser propenso a hacer algo
2. LAW responsable; **to be ~ for sth** ser responsable de algo
liaise [lɪ'eɪz] *vi* **to ~ with sb/sth** servir de
enlace con alguien/algo
liaison [li'eɪzn, *Am:* 'liːəzɑːn] *n* **1.** *no pl* a.
LING (*contact*) enlace *m;* (*coordination*) coordinación *f* **2.** *Am* (*sb who connects groups*)
enlace *mf* **3.** (*sexual affair*) aventura *f*
liaison officer *n* oficial *mf* de enlace
liana *n*, **liane** [li'ɑːnə] *n* liana *f*
liar ['laɪər, *Am:* -ə·] *n* mentiroso, -a *m, f*
lib [lɪb] *n no pl, inf abbr of* **liberation** liberación *f*
libel ['laɪbl] **I.** *n* LAW libelo *m;* PUBL difamación
f; **to sue sb for ~** demandar a alguien por difamación **II.** <*Brit:* -ll-, *Am:* -l-> *vt* LAW, PUBL difamar
libellous *adj*, **libelous** ['laɪbələs] *adj Am*
LAW, PUBL difamatorio, -a
liberal ['lɪbərəl] **I.** *adj* **1.** (*tolerant*) a. POL liberal **2.** (*generous*) generoso, -a **3.** (*plentiful*)
copioso, -a **4.** (*not strict: interpretation*)
amplio, -a **II.** *n* liberal *mf*
liberal arts *n Am* humanidades *fpl*
liberalisation *n Brit, Aus s.* **liberalization**
liberalise *vt Brit, Aus s.* **liberalize**
liberalism ['lɪbərəlɪzəm] *n no pl* liberalismo
m
liberality [ˌlɪbə'ræləti, *Am:* -ţi] *n no pl*
1. (*tolerance*) liberalidad *f* **2.** (*generosity*) generosidad *f*
liberalization [ˌlɪbərəlaɪ'zeɪʃən, *Am:* -ɪ'-] *n*

liberalización *f*
liberalize ['lɪbərəlaɪz] *vt* liberalizar
liberate ['lɪbəreɪt] *vt* **1.**(*free*) liberar; (*slaves*) manumitir; **to ~ oneself from sth/sb** librarse de algo/alguien **2.***fig, iron, inf* (*steal*) robar
liberation [ˌlɪbərˈeɪʃən] *n no pl* liberación *f*
liberation organization *n* organización *f* para la liberación
liberator ['lɪbəreɪtəʳ, *Am:* - t̬ə-] *n* liberador(a) *m(f)*
Liberia [laɪˈbɪəriə] *n* Liberia *f*
Liberian I. *adj* liberiano, -a II. *n* liberiano, -a *m, f*
libertine ['lɪbəti:n, *Am:* -ɚ-] *n* libertino, -a *m, f*
liberty ['lɪbəti, *Am:* -ɚt̬i] *n no pl, form* **1.**(*freedom*) libertad *f;* **to be at ~** estar en libertad; **to be at ~ to do sth** tener el derecho de hacer algo; **to take the ~ of doing sth** tomarse la libertad de hacer algo; **to take liberties with sb** tomarse libertades con alguien; **what a ~!** ¡qué falta de respeto! **2.***form* (*right*) derechos *mpl*
libidinous [lɪˈbɪdɪnəs, *Am:* lə-ˈbɪdnəs] *adj form* libidinoso, -a
libido [lɪˈbi:dəʊ, *Am:* -doʊ] *n* libido *f*
Libra ['li:brə] *n* Libra *m*
Libran ['li:brən] I. *n* Libra *mf* II. *adj* de Libra
librarian [laɪˈbreəriən, *Am:* -ˈbrer-] *n* bibliotecario, -a *m, f*
library ['laɪbrəri, *Am:* -brer-] *n* <-ies> **1.**(*place*) biblioteca *f;* **film ~** filmoteca *f;* **newspaper ~** hemeroteca *f* **2.**(*collection*) archivo *m*
libretto [lɪˈbretəʊ, *Am:* -ˈbret̬oʊ] *n* libreto *m*
Libya ['lɪbɪə] *n* Libia *f*
Libyan ['lɪbɪən] I. *adj* libio, -a II. *n* libio, -a *m, f*
lice [laɪs] *npl s.* **louse**
licence ['laɪsənts] *n* **1.**(*document*) licencia *f,* permiso *m;* **driving ~, driver's ~** *Am* carnet *m* de conducir; **gun ~** permiso *m* de armas; **under ~** con licencia **2.** *no pl, form* (*freedom*) libertad *f;* **artistic ~** libertad artística; **to have ~ to do sth** tener libertad para hacer algo
licence number *n* AUTO número *m* de matrícula **licence plate** *n* AUTO matrícula *f*
license ['laɪsənts] I. *vt* autorizar II. *n Am s.* licence
licensed *adj* autorizado, -a; **a ~ restaurant** un restaurante con licencia de licores; **to be ~ to do sth** tener la autorización para hacer algo
licensee [ˌlaɪsənt'si:] *n form* concesionario, -a *m, f*
license fee *n Brit* TV impuesto *m* por el uso de un televisor
licensing ['laɪsəntsɪŋ] I. *n* autorización *f* II. *adj* **~ hours** horas *durante las cuales está permitida la venta y el consumo de alcohol*
licensing laws *n Brit* leyes *fpl* de control de licores

licentious [laɪˈsenʃəs] *adj form* licencioso, -a
lichen ['laɪkən] *n* liquen *m*
lick [lɪk] I. *n* **1.**(*with tongue*) lamedura *f* **2.**(*light coating*) **a ~ of paint** una mano de pintura **3.** MUS frase *f* ►**a (cat's) ~ and a promise** *Brit, inf* un lavoteo, un baño de vaquero *Ven* II. *vt* **1.**(*with tongue*) lamer **2.**(*lightly touch*) rozar **3.** *Am, inf* (*defeat*) derrotar **4.** *inf* (*beat*) dar una paliza a
licking *n* **1.** *inf* (*physical beating*) paliza *f* **2.** SPORTS derrota *f*
licorice ['lɪkərɪs, *Am:* -ɚɪʃ] *n no pl, Am* regaliz *f*
lid [lɪd] *n* **1.**(*for container*) tapa *f,* tape *m Cuba, PRico* **2.**(*eyelid*) párpado *m* ►**to keep the ~ on sth** ocultar algo; **to put the ~ on sth** *Brit, Aus* rematar algo; **that puts the ~ on it** *Am* se acabó
lie¹ [laɪ] I. <-y-> *vi* mentir; **to ~ about sth** mentir sobre algo II. <-y-> *vt* **to ~ oneself out of sth** salvarse de algo por una mentira III. *n* mentira *f,* guayaba *f AmL,* boleto *m Arg;* **to be an outright ~** ser de una falsedad total; **to give the ~ to sth** desmentir algo; **to live a ~** vivir en la mentira; **don't tell me ~s!** ¡no me mientas!, ¡no me caigas a cuentos! *Col, Ven*
lie² [laɪ] I. <-lay, lain> *vi* **1.**(*be lying down: person*) estar tumbado; **to ~ in bed** estar acostado en la cama; **to ~ on the ground** estar tumbado en el suelo; **to ~ awake** estar despierto; **to ~ still** quedarse inmóvil **2.**(*be positioned*) hallarse; **to ~ off the coast** (*boat*) hallarse lejos de la costa; **to ~ on the route to ...** encontrarse en la ruta de...; **to ~ to the east of ...** quedar al este de...; **to ~ in ruins** estar en ruinas; **to ~ in wait** estar a la espera; **to ~ fallow** AGR, BOT estar en barbecho **3.** *form* (*be buried*) estar enterrado, -a **4. to ~ with sb/sth** (*be responsibility of*) corresponder a alguien/ algo; (*be the reason for sth*) ser culpa de alguien/algo **5.** SPORTS ubicarse II. *n no pl, Brit, Aus* posición *f* ►**the ~ of the land** el estado de las cosas
◆**lie about** *vi* **1.**(*be somewhere*) estar por ahí **2.**(*be lazy*) holgazanear
◆**lie back** *vi* recostarse
◆**lie down** *vi* (*act*) acostarse; (*state*) estar acostado ►**to take sth lying down** aceptar algo sin protestar
◆**lie in** *vi inf* quedarse en cama
◆**lie over** *vi Am* quedar aplazado
◆**lie to** *vi* NAUT estar a la capa
◆**lie up** *vi Brit* esconderse, enconcharse *Ven, Perú*
lie detector *n* detector *m* de mentiras
lieu [lu:] *n no pl, form* **in ~ of** en lugar de
Lieut *n abbr of* **Lieutenant 1.** MIL teniente *mf* **2.**(*assistant*) lugarteniente *mf*
lieutenant [lefˈtenənt, *Am:* lu:-] *n* **1.** MIL teniente *mf* **2.**(*assistant*) lugarteniente *mf*
life [laɪf] <lives> *n* **1.** vida *f; ~* **after death** vida después de la muerte; **intelligent ~** vida inteligente; **plant ~** vida vegetal; **private ~**

vida privada; **a sign of** ~ una señal de vida; **to be full of** ~ estar lleno de vida; **to draw sth/ sb from** ~ ART copiar algo/a alguien del natural; **to lose one's** ~ perder la vida; **to take sb's** ~ matar a alguien; **to take one's (own)** ~ quitarse la vida, suicidarse **2.** *no pl* (*existence*) existencia *f;* **to want sth out of** ~ querer algo de la vida; **to be sb's (whole)** ~ ser la vida (entera) de alguien **3.** *no pl* (*duration*) vida *f* (útil), duración *f* **4.** *inf* (*prison sentence*) cadena *f* perpetua; **to get** ~ ser condenado a cadena perpetua ▶**a** ~ **and** death **struggle** una lucha a vida o muerte; **to be a matter of** ~ **and** death ser un asunto de vida o muerte; **to take one's** ~ **in one's** hands *inf* jugarse la vida; **to risk** ~ **and** limb (**to do sth**) jugarse la vida (para hacer una cosa); **to lay one's** ~ **on the** line poner la vida en peligro; **to be the** ~ **and** soul **of the party** *Brit* ser el alma de la fiesta; **to do sth for dear** ~ hacer algo desesperadamente; **to live the good** ~ darse la buena vida; **it's a hard** ~! *iron, inf* ¡qué le vamos a hacer!; **as large as** ~ en carne y hueso; **to breathe (new)** ~ **into sth** infundir (nueva) vida a algo; **to bring sth to** ~ animar algo; **to come to** ~ volver a la vida; **to frighten the** ~ **out of sb** dar un susto de muerte a alguien; **to give one's** ~ **for sb/sth** dar la vida por alguien/algo; **to make a new** ~ empezar una nueva vida; **for** ~ de por vida; **I'm not able for the** ~ **of me to ...** *inf* por mucho que lo intente no puedo...; **not on your** ~! *inf* ¡ni hablar!; **that's** ~! ¡así es la vida!; **this is the** ~ (**for me**)! ¡esto sí es vida!

life annuity <-ies> *n* pensión *f* vitalicia **life assurance** *n no pl, Brit* seguro *m* de vida **lifebelt** *n* salvavidas *m inv* **lifeboat** *n* bote *m* salvavidas **life buoy** *n* salvavidas *m inv* **life cycle** *n* ciclo *m* vital **life expectancy** <-ies> *n* esperanza *f* de vida **life form** *n* forma *f* de vida **lifeguard** *n* socorrista *mf,* salvavidas *mf inv AmL* **life imprisonment** *n no pl* cadena *f* perpetua **life insurance** *n no pl* seguro *m* de vida **life jacket** *n* chaleco *m* salvavidas

lifeless [ˈlaɪfləs] *adj* **1.** (*dead*) sin vida **2.** *fig* flojo, -a

lifelike [ˈlaɪflaɪk] *adj* natural

lifeline *n* **1.** NAUT cuerda *f* salvavidas **2.** *fig* cordón *m* umbilical; **to throw sb a** ~ dar una oportunidad a alguien

lifelong [ˌlaɪfˈlɒŋ, *Am:* ˌlaɪfˈlɑːŋ] *adj* de toda la vida

life peer *n Brit: miembro vitalicio de la Cámara de los Lores* **life preserver** *n Am* salvavidas *m inv*

lifer [ˈlaɪfəʳ, *Am:* -fəʳ] *n inf* condenado, -a *m, f* a cadena perpetua

life raft *n* bote *m* salvavidas **lifesaver** *n* socorrista *mf* **life sentence** *n* condena *f* a cadena perpetua **life-size** *adj*, **life-sized** *adj* de tamaño natural **lifespan** *n* (*of animals*) tiempo *m* de vida; (*of people*) longevi-

dad *f;* **the average** ~ el promedio de vida; (*of machines*) la vida útil **lifestyle** *n* estilo *m* de vida **life-support system** *n* sistema *m* de respiración artificial **life-threatening** *adj* mortífero, -a **lifetime** *n no pl* **1.** (*of person*) vida *f;* **in my** ~ durante mi vida; **the chance of a** ~ (**for sb**) la oportunidad de su vida; **to happen once in a** ~ suceder una vez en la vida; **to see sth during one's** ~ ver algo en vida; ~ **guarantee** garantía *f* de por vida **2.** (*eternity*) eternidad *f;* **to seem like a** ~ parecer toda una vida **life work** *n no pl* trabajo *m* de toda la vida

lift [lɪft] **I.** *n* **1.** (*upward motion*) elevación *f;* **to give sth a** ~ levantar algo **2.** *no pl* AVIAT fuerza *f* de ascensión **3.** *no pl, fig* (*positive feeling*) ánimos *mpl;* **to give sb a** ~ levantar la moral a alguien **4.** (*hoisting device*) montacargas *m inv* **5.** *Brit* (*elevator*) ascensor *m,* elevador *m AmL;* **to take the** ~ tomar el ascensor **6.** (*car ride*) viaje *m* en coche (*gratuito*), aventón *m Méx;* **to give sb a** ~ llevar (en coche) a alguien; **to hitch a** ~ hacer dedo **II.** *vi* levantarse **III.** *vt* **1.** (*move upwards*) levantar; (*slightly*) alzar; **to** ~ **potatoes** recoger patatas; **to** ~ **fingerprints from sth** sacar las huellas digitales de algo; **to** ~ **one's eyes** alzar los ojos; **to** ~ **one's head** levantar la cabeza; **to** ~ **one's voice** levantar la voz; **to** ~ **one's voice to sb** (*yell at*) levantar la voz a alguien; (*argue with*) discutir con alguien **2.** (*encourage*) animar; **to** ~ **sb's spirits** levantar los ánimos de alguien **3.** (*move by air*) transportar (en avión) **4.** (*stop*) suprimir; **to** ~ **restrictions** levantar las restricciones **5.** *inf* (*steal*) mangar; (*plagiarize*) plagiar; **to** ~ **a tune** copiar una melodía

◆**lift down** *vt Brit, Aus* bajar con cuidado

◆**lift off** *vi* AVIAT despegar

◆**lift up** *vt* alzar; **to** ~ **one's head** levantar la cabeza; **to** ~ **one's voice** alzar la voz

lift-off [ˈlɪftɒf, *Am:* -ɑːf] *n* AVIAT, TECH despegue *m*

ligament [ˈlɪgəmənt] *n* ligamento *m*

ligature [ˈlɪgətʃəʳ, *Am:* -tʃəʳ] *n* **1.** (*cord*) *a.* MED ligadura *f* **2.** MUS, TYPO ligado *m*

light [laɪt] **I.** *n* **1.** *no pl* (*energy, brightness*) luz *f;* **by the** ~ **of the moon** a la luz de la luna **2.** *no pl* (*daytime*) luz *f* (de día); **first** ~ primera luz del día **3.** (*source of brightness*) luz *f;* (*lamp*) lámpara *f;* **the** ~**s went down** se apagaron las luces; **to put a** ~ **off/on** apagar/ encender una luz **4.** *pl* (*traffic light*) semáforo *m* **5.** *no pl* (*clarification, insight*) comprensión *f;* **to cast** [*o* **shed**] ~ **on sth** arrojar luz sobre algo **6.** *no pl* (*perspective*) perspectiva *f;* **to see things in a new** ~ ver las cosas desde otra perspectiva **7.** *no pl* (*joy, inspiration*) sol *m;* **you are the** ~ **of my life** *fig* eres mi sol **8.** *no pl* (*flame*) fuego *m;* **to catch** ~ incendiarse; **to set** ~ **to sth** prender fuego a algo; **do you have a** ~? ¿tienes fuego? **9.** *pl* (*person's abilities*) conocimientos *mpl;* **to do sth according to one's** ~**s** hacer algo como Dios le da a entender a uno ▶to see the ~ at the end of the <u>tunnel</u> cobrar nuevas esperanza; **to go out** like a ~ *inf* (*fall deep asleep quickly*) quedarse dormido enseguida; (*faint suddenly*) perder el conocimiento; **to bring sth to ~** sacar algo a la luz; **to** <u>come</u> **to ~** salir a la luz **II.** *adj* **1.** (*not heavy*) ligero, -a; **a ~ touch** un pequeño toque **2.** (*not dark: colour*) claro, -a; (*skin*) blanco, -a; (*room*) luminoso, -a **3.** (*not serious*) ligero, -a; **~ opera** opereta *f* **4.** (*not intense: breeze, rain*) leve; **to be a ~ sleeper** tener el sueño ligero; **to be ~ on sth** carecer de algo **5.** GASTR frugal; **a ~ meal** una comida ligera **III.** *adv* ligeramente ▶to <u>get off</u> ~ salir bien parado; **to** <u>make</u> **~ of sth** no dar importancia a algo **IV.** *vt* <lit *Am:* lighted, lit *Am:* lighted> **1.** (*illuminate*) iluminar; **to ~ the way** mostrar el camino **2.** (*start burning*) encender, prender *AmL;* **to ~ a cigarette** encender un cigarrillo **V.** *vi* <lit *Am:* lighted, lit *Am:* lighted> (*catch fire*) encenderse

◆**light up I.** *vt* alumbrar, iluminar **II.** *vi* **1.** (*become bright*) iluminarse **2.** (*become animated*) animarse; **his face lights up** se le ilumina la cara **3.** (*start smoking*) encender un cigarrillo

◆**light upon** *vi* caer en la cuenta de; (*suddenly see*) dar con

light bulb ['laɪtbʌlb] *n* bombilla *f*, foco *m* *AmL*

lighten ['laɪtən] **I.** *vi* **1.** (*become brighter*) clarear **2.** (*become less heavy*) aligerarse; (*mood*) alegrarse **II.** *vt* **1.** (*make less heavy*) aligerar; **to ~ sb's burden** aligerar la carga a alguien **2.** (*bleach, make paler*) aclarar

◆**lighten up** *vi Am, Aus* relajarse

lighter ['laɪtə', *Am:* -tə·] *n* mechero *m*, encendedor *m AmL*

light-fingered [,laɪt'fɪŋgəd, *Am:* -gə·d] *adj* con las manos largas **light-footed** *adj* ligero, -a de pies **light-headed** *adj* **1.** (*faint*) mareado, -a **2.** (*excited*) delirante **light-hearted** *adj* (*carefree*) despreocupado, -a; (*happy*) alegre; **a ~ look at sth** una mirada alegre a algo **lighthouse** *n* faro *m*

lighting ['laɪtɪŋ, *Am:* -t̬ɪŋ] *n* iluminación *f*

lightly ['laɪtli] *adv* ligeramente; (*to rest, touch*) levemente; **to sleep ~** dormir ligeramente; **to take sth ~** tomar algo a la ligera; **to get off ~** salir bien parado

light meter *n* fotómetro *m;* PHOT exposímetro *m*

lightness ['laɪtnɪs] *n no pl* **1.** (*of thing, touch*) ligereza *f* **2.** (*brightness*) claridad *f*

lightning ['laɪtnɪŋ] *n no pl* relámpago *m;* **a ray of ~** un relámpago; **thunder and ~** rayos y centellas ▶<u>quick</u> **as ~** como el relámpago

lightning attack *n* ataque *m* relámpago **lightning conductor** *n Brit,* **lightning rod** *n Am* pararrayos *m inv* **lightning strike** *n Brit, Aus* huelga *f* convocada sin previo aviso

light pen *n* lápiz *m* óptico

lightship *n* buque-faro *m* **lightweight I.** *adj* (*clothing, material*) ligero, -a **II.** *n* **1.** SPORTS peso *m* ligero **2.** (*unimpressive person*) persona *f* de poco peso

light year *n* año *m* luz; **to be ~s away** *inf* estar a años luz de distancia

lignite ['lɪgnaɪt] *n* lignito *m*

likable ['laɪkəbl] *adj Am, Aus s.* **likeable**

like¹ [laɪk] **I.** *vt* **1.** (*find good*) **I ~ it** (esto) me gusta; **she ~s apples** le gustan las manzanas; **I ~ swimming** me gusta nadar; **I ~ her** (ella) me cae bien; **he ~s classical music** le gusta la música clásica; **I like it when/how ...** me gusta cuando/cómo...; **well, how do you ~ that?** (*expressing surprise*) ¿quién lo diría? **2.** (*desire, wish*) querer; **I would ~ to go to ...** me gustaría ir a...; **would you ~ a cup of tea?** ¿quieres un té?; **I should ~ a little bit more time** quisiera tener un poquito más de tiempo; **I should like to know ...** quisiera saber...; **I would ~ a steak** querría un filete **II.** *n pl* gustos *mpl;* **sb's ~s and dislikes** las preferencias de alguien

like² [laɪk] **I.** *adj* semejante; **to be of ~ mind** pensar de la misma manera **II.** *prep* **to be ~ sb/sth** ser como alguien/algo; **what was it ~?** ¿cómo fue?; **what does it look ~?** ¿cómo es?; **to work ~ crazy** *inf* trabajar como un burro; **there is nothing ~ ...** no hay nada que se parezca a... ▶**~ anything** a más no poder **III.** *conj inf* como si *+subj;* **he speaks ~ he was drunk** habla como si estuviera borracho; **he doesn't do it ~ I do** él no lo hace como yo

likeable ['laɪkəbl] *adj* simpático, -a

likelihood ['laɪklɪhʊd] *n no pl* probabilidad *f;* **in all ~** con toda probabilidad; **there is every/little ~ that ...** hay muchas/pocas probabilidades de que... *+subj*

likely ['laɪkli] **I.** <-ier, -iest> *adj* probable; **it is ~ (that ...)** es probable (que... *+subj*); **to be quite/very ~** ser bastante/muy probable; **to be a ~ story** *iron* ser un cuento chino, ser puro cuento *AmL;* **not ~!** *inf* ¡ni *inf!* **II.** *adv* probablemente; **as ~ as not** a lo mejor; **most/very ~** bastante/muy probablemente

like-minded [,laɪk'maɪndɪd, *Am:* '-,-] *adj* del mismo parecer

liken ['laɪkən] *vt* comparar; **to ~ sb to sb** comparar alguien con alguien

likeness ['laɪknɪs] <-es> *n* **1.** (*similarity*) semejanza *f;* **a family ~** un aire de familia; **to bear a ~ to sb** tener parecido con alguien **2.** (*painting*) retrato *m*

likewise ['laɪkwaɪz] *adv* de la misma forma, asimismo; **to do ~** hacer lo mismo

liking ['laɪkɪŋ] *n no pl* afición *f;* (*for particular person*) simpatía *f;* **to develop a ~ for sb** tomar cariño a alguien; **to be to sb's ~** *form* ser del agrado de alguien; **it's too sweet for my ~** es demasiado dulce para mi gusto

lilac ['laɪlək] **I.** *n* **1.** (*bush*) lila *f* **2.** *no pl* (*colour*) lila *m* **II.** *adj* lila

lilo® ['laɪləʊ, *Am:* -loʊ] *n Brit* colchoneta *f*

inflable

lilt [lɪlt] *n no pl* cadencia *f*

lily ['lɪli] <-ies> *n* lirio *m;* **water** ~ nenúfar *m*

lily-livered ['lɪlɪˌlɪvəd, *Am:* -əd] *adj liter* cobarde

lily pad *n* hoja *f* de nenúfar

limb [lɪm] *n* **1.** BOT rama *f* **2.** ANAT miembro *m* ▶**to be/go out on a** ~ **(to do sth)** estar/ ponerse en una situación arriesgada (para hacer algo); **to tear sb** ~ **from** ~ despedazar a alguien

limber ['lɪmbəʳ, *Am:* -bə-] *adj* (*person*) ágil; (*material*) flexible
◆**limber up** *vi* hacer ejercicios de precalentamiento

limbo ['lɪmbəʊ, *Am:* -boʊ] *n no pl* **1.** *a. fig* limbo *m;* **to be in** ~ estar en el limbo **2.** (*dance*) limbo *m;* **to do the** ~ bailar el limbo

lime[1] [laɪm] I. *n* **1.** (*fruit*) lima *f* **2.** (*tree*) limero *m* **3.** *no pl* (*juice*) zumo *m* de lima **4.** (*colour*) verde *m* lima II. *adj* de color verde lima

lime[2] [laɪm] I. *n no pl* CHEM cal *f* II. *vt* abonar con cal

lime[3] [laɪm] *n* (*linden tree*) tilo *m*

limelight ['laɪmlaɪt] *n no pl* foco *m* proyector; **to be in the** ~ estar en el candelero; **to hog the** ~ chupar cámara; **to steal the** ~ acaparar la atención del público

limerick ['lɪmərɪk, *Am:* -ə-] *n* quintilla *f* humorística

limestone ['laɪmstəʊn, *Am:* -stoʊn] *n no pl* caliza *f*

limit ['lɪmɪt] I. *n* límite *m;* (*speed*) ~ AUTO límite *m* de velocidad; **to put a** ~ **on sth** poner un límite a algo; **to overstep the** ~ pasarse del límite; **to know one's** ~s conocer los propios límites; **to know no** ~s no tener límites; **within** ~s dentro de ciertos límites; **to be off** ~s **(to sb)** *Am* quedar prohibido el acceso (a alguien); **it's the** ~! ¡es el colmo! II. *vt* limitar; **to** ~ **oneself to sth** limitarse a algo

limitation [ˌlɪmɪ'teɪʃən] *n* **1.** *no pl* (*lessening*) restricción *f;* (*of pollution, weapons*) limitación *f* **2.** *pl* limitaciones *fpl;* **she knows her** ~s ella sabe sus limitaciones **3.** LAW prescripción *f*

limited ['lɪmɪtɪd, *Am:* -t̬ɪd] *adj* limitado, -a; **to be** ~ **to sth** estar limitado a algo

limited company *n* sociedad *f* (de responsabilidad) limitada

limitless ['lɪmɪtlɪs] *adj* ilimitado, -a

limousine ['lɪməziːn] *n* limusina *f*

limp[1] [lɪmp] I. *vi* cojear II. *n no pl* cojera *f;* **to walk with a** ~ cojear

limp[2] [lɪmp] *adj* **1.** (*floppy*) flojo, -a; (*lettuce*) mustio, -a; **to have a** ~ **handshake** dar la mano de forma poco enérgica **2.** (*effort*) débil; (*excuse*) poco convincente

limpet ['lɪmpɪt] *n* lapa *f*

limpid ['lɪmpɪd] *adj liter* límpido, -a; (*air*) diáfano, -a; (*eyes*) claro, -a

limy ['laɪmi] *adj* calizo, -a

linchpin ['lɪntʃpɪn] *n* **1.** TECH pezonera *f* **2.** *fig* eje *m*

linden ['lɪndən] *n Am* BOT tilo *m*

line[1] [laɪn] <-ning> *vt* revestir; (*clothes*) forrar

line[2] [laɪn] I. *n* **1.** (*mark*) *a.* MAT línea *f;* **dividing** ~ línea divisoria; **to be in a** ~ estar en línea; **to form a** ~ formar una línea **2.** *Am* (*queue*) fila *f*, cola *f AmL;* **to get in** ~ ponerse en fila; **to stand in** ~ hacer cola **3.** (*chronological succession*) linaje *m;* **a** (**long**) ~ **of disasters/kings** una (larga) sucesión de desastres/reyes **4.** (*cord*) cuerda *f;* **clothes** ~ cuerda para colgar la ropa **5.** TEL línea *f;* ~**s will be open from** … las líneas estarán abiertas a partir de…; **to be/stay on the** ~ estar/seguir al habla; **hold the** ~! ¡no cuelgue! **6.** INFOR **on** ~ en línea; **off** ~ desconectado **7.** (*defence*) frente *m;* **front** ~ línea del frente; **to be the last** ~ **of defence** *fig* ser la última línea de defensa; **to be behind enemy** ~s estar detrás de las líneas enemigas **8.** (*set of tracks*) vía *f;* (*specific train route*) línea *f;* **the end of the** ~ el final de la línea; **to be at** [*o* **to reach**] **the end of the** ~ *fig* tocar fondo **9.** (*transport company*) línea *f;* **rail/shipping** ~ línea de transporte ferroviario/marítimo **10.** (*of text*) línea *f*, renglón *m;* **to drop sb a** ~ *inf* escribir a alguien **11.** MUS melodía *f* **12.** (*comment*) comentario *m;* **to come up with a** ~ **about sb/sth** salir con un comentario acerca de alguien/algo **13.** (*position, attitude*) línea *f;* ~ **of reasoning** razonamiento *m;* **to be divided along ethnic** ~s estar dividido según criterios étnicos; **the official** ~ (**on sth**) la línea oficial (acerca de algo); **to take a** ~ **on sth** tomar posición sobre algo **14.** (*field, pursuit, interest*) especialidad *f;* **what** ~ **are you in?** ¿a qué se dedica? **15.** (*product type*) línea *f;* FASHION línea *f* de moda; **to come out with a new** ~ *Am* sacar una nueva línea **16.** *inf* (*of cocaine*) raya *f;* **to do a** ~ **of cocaine, to do** ~s esnifar una raya ▶**somewhere** along the ~ en algún momento; **right down the** ~ *Am* hasta el último momento; **to cross the** ~ salirse de la raya; **to get a** ~ **on sb** obtener información acerca de alguien; **to give sb a** ~ **on sb** dar a alguien información sobre alguien; **to be in** ~ **for sth** tener muchas posibilidades de ascender; **to be in** ~ **with sb/sth** estar de acuerdo con alguien/algo; **to be out of** ~ estar fuera de lugar; **to be out of** ~ **with sb/sth** no estar de acuerdo con alguien/algo II. <-ning> *vt* **to** ~ **the streets** ocupar las calles; **to** ~ **the route** alinearse a lo largo de la ruta
◆**line up** I. *vt* alinear II. *vi* **1.** (*stand in row*) alinearse **2.** *Am* (*wait one behind another*) ponerse en fila, hacer cola **3.** (*oppose*) **to** ~ **against sb/sth** alinearse en contra de alguien/algo

lineage ['lɪnɪɪdʒ] *n* linaje *m*

lineal ['lɪnɪəl] *adj* en línea directa

linear [ˈlɪnɪəʳ, *Am:* -ɚ] *adj* lineal
linear equation *n* ecuación *f* lineal
linen [ˈlɪnɪn] *n no pl* lino *m;* **bed** ~ sábanas *fpl;* **table** ~ mantelería *f* ▸**to wash one's dirty** ~ **in** public sacar los trapos sucios a relucir
linen basket *n* cesto *m* de la ropa sucia
liner [ˈlaɪnəʳ, *Am:* -nɚ] *n* 1. (*lining*) forro *m;* **dustbin** ~ bolsa *f* de la basura 2. (*ship*) transatlántico *m*
linesman [ˈlaɪnzmən] <-men> *n* SPORTS juez *mf* de línea
lineup [ˈlaɪnʌp] *n* 1. SPORTS (*team*) alineación *f; Am* (*of baseball players*) orden *m* de los bateadores 2. (*identity parade*) rueda *f* de identificación
linger [ˈlɪŋgəʳ, *Am:* -gɚ] *vi* entretenerse; (*film*) hacerse largo; **to** ~ **in the memory** perdurar en la memoria; **to** ~ **on** permanecer, perdurar; **to** ~ **on sb/sth** entretenerse con alguien/algo; **to** ~ **over sth** tomarse tiempo para (hacer) algo
lingerie [ˈlænʒəri:, *Am:* ˌlɑːnʒəˈreɪ] *n no pl* lencería *f*
lingering [ˈlɪŋgərɪŋ] *adj* prolongado, -a; (*doubt*) persistente
lingo [ˈlɪŋgəʊ, *Am:* -goʊ] <-goes> *n inf* 1. (*foreign language*) idioma *m* (extranjero) 2. (*jargon*) jerga *f*
linguist [ˈlɪŋgwɪst] *n* lingüista *mf*
linguistic [lɪŋˈgwɪstɪk] *adj* lingüístico, -a
linguistics [lɪŋˈgwɪstɪks] *n* lingüística *f*
liniment [ˈlɪnɪmənt] *n no pl* linimento *m*
lining [ˈlaɪnɪŋ] *n* 1. (*of boiler, pipes*) revestimiento *m;* (*of coat, jacket*) forro *m* 2. ANAT pared *f*
link [lɪŋk] I. *n* 1. (*in chain*) eslabón *m* 2. (*connection*) conexión *f;* **rail** ~ enlace *m* ferroviario 3. INFOR vínculo *m*, enlace *m* II. *vt* 1. (*connect*) conectar; **to** ~ **hands** darse la mano 2. (*associate*) relacionar; **to be** ~**ed** (**together**) estar relacionado
linkman [ˈlɪŋkmæn] <-men> *n Brit* TV, RADIO locutor *m*
links [lɪŋks] *n* 1. (*golf course*) campo *m* de golf 2. *Scot* (*dunes*) dunas *fpl*
link-up [ˈlɪŋkʌp] *n* conexión *f;* (*of spacecraft*) acoplamiento *m;* **satellite** ~ conexión vía satélite
linkwoman [ˈlɪŋkˌwʊmən] <-women> *n Brit* TV, RADIO locutora *f*
linnet [ˈlɪnɪt] *n* pardillo *m*
linoleum [lɪˈnəʊlɪəm, *Am:* -ˈnoʊ-] *n*, **lino** [ˈlaɪnəʊ, *Am:* -noʊ] *n no pl* linóleo *m*
linotype® [ˈlaɪnəʊtaɪp] *n* linotipia *f*
linseed [ˈlɪnsiːd] *n no pl* linaza *f*
linseed oil *n no pl* aceite *m* de linaza
lint [lɪnt] *n no pl, Brit* pelusa *f*
lintel [ˈlɪntl, *Am:* -t̬l] *n* dintel *m*
lion [ˈlaɪən] *n* león *m* ▸**the** ~**'s** share la parte del león
lioness [laɪəˈnes] <-sses> *n* leona *f*
lion-hearted [ˈlaɪənˈhɑːtɪd, *Am:* -ɑn-

ˌhɑːrt̬ɪd] *adj* valiente
lionize [ˈlaɪənaɪz] *vt* tratar como a un personaje importante
lip [lɪp] *n* 1. ANAT labio *m;* **the question on everyone's** ~**s** la pregunta que se hace todo el mundo; **my** ~**s are sealed** soy una tumba 2. (*rim: of cup, bowl*) borde *m;* (*of jug*) pico *m* 3. *no pl, inf* (*impudence*) insolencia *f*
lip gloss *n no pl* brillo *m* de labios
liposuction [ˈlaɪpəʊˌsʌkʃən, *Am:* ˈlɪpoʊ-] *n* liposucción *f*
lip-read I. *vi* leer los labios II. *vt* leer los labios a
lip salve *n no pl* crema *f* de cacao
lip service *n no pl* jarabe *m* de pico; **to pay** ~ **to sth** apoyar algo sólo de boquilla
lipstick *n* barra *f* de labios
liquefy [ˈlɪkwəfaɪ] <-ie-> I. *vt* licuar II. *vi* licuarse
liqueur [lɪˈkjʊəʳ, *Am:* -ˈkɜːr] *n* licor *m*
liquid [ˈlɪkwɪd] I. *n* líquido *m* II. *adj* líquido, -a
liquidate [ˈlɪkwɪdeɪt] *vt a. fig* liquidar
liquidation [ˌlɪkwɪˈdeɪʃən] *n* liquidación *f;* **to go into** ~ ECON entrar en liquidación
liquidise [ˈlɪkwɪdaɪz] *vt Brit, Aus s.* **liquidize**
liquidiser [ˈlɪkwɪdaɪzəʳ] *n Brit, Aus s.* **liquidizer**
liquidity [lɪˈkwɪdəti, *Am:* -t̬i] *n no pl* liquidez *f*
liquidize [ˈlɪkwɪdaɪz] *vt* licuar
liquidizer [ˈlɪkwɪdaɪzəʳ, *Am:* -zɚ] *n* licuadora *f*
liquor [ˈlɪkəʳ, *Am:* -ɚ] *n no pl* licor *m*
liquorice [ˈlɪkərɪs, *Am:* -ɚ-] *n no pl* regaliz *m*
Lisbon [ˈlɪzbən] *n* Lisboa *f*
lisp [lɪsp] I. *n no pl* ceceo *m* II. *vi* cecear III. *vt* pronunciar ceceando
lissom(e) [ˈlɪsəm] *adj liter* grácil
list¹ [lɪst] I. *n* lista *f;* ~ **price** precio *m* según catálogo; **shopping** ~ lista de la compra; **to make a** ~ (**of sth**) hacer un listado (de algo) II. *vt* 1. (*make a list*) listar 2. (*enumerate*) enumerar
list² [lɪst] NAUT I. *vi* escorar II. *n* escora *f*
listen [ˈlɪsən] I. *n inf* **to have a** ~ (**to sth**) *inf* escuchar (algo) II. *vi* 1. (*hear*) escuchar; **to** ~ **to sth/sb** escuchar algo/a alguien; **to** ~ **to reason** atender a razones 2. (*pay attention*) estar atento; **to** ~ (**out**) **for sth** estar atento para oír algo
◆**listen in** *vi Brit* escuchar (a escondidas); **to** ~ **on sth** escuchar algo (a escondidas)
listener [ˈlɪsnəʳ, *Am:* -ɚ] *n* oyente *mf*
listeria [lɪˈstɪərɪə, *Am:* -ˈstɪrɪ-] *npl* listeria *f*
listing [ˈlɪstɪŋ] *n* 1. (*list*) lista *f*, listado *m* 2. (*entry in list*) entrada *f* 3. *pl, Brit* (*list of shows, films*) guía *f* de espectáculos
listless [ˈlɪstlɪs] *adj* 1. (*lacking energy: person*) apagado, -a; (*economy*) débil 2. (*lacking enthusiasm*) apático, -a; (*performance*) deslucido, -a

lit [lɪt] *pt, pp of* **light**

litany ['lɪtəni] <-ies> *n* letanía *f*

litchi ['laɪtʃiː, *Am:* 'liː-] *n* lichi *m*

liter ['liːtər, *Am:* -t̬ər] *n Am* litro *m*

literacy ['lɪtərəsi, *Am:* 'lɪt̬ə-] *n no pl* alfabetización *f;* ~ **rate** índice *m* de alfabetización

literal ['lɪtərəl, *Am:* 'lɪt̬ə-] *adj* literal; **to take sth in the** ~ **sense of the word** tomar algo al pie de la letra

literally ['lɪtərəli, *Am:* 'lɪt̬ə-] *adv* literalmente; **to take sth/sb** ~ tomar algo/a alguien al pie de la letra; **quite** ~ literalmente

literary ['lɪtərəri, *Am:* 'lɪt̬ərer-] *adj* literario, -a

literary criticism *n* crítica *f* literaria

literate ['lɪtərət, *Am:* 'lɪt̬ə-] *adj* 1. (*able to read and write*) que sabe leer y escribir; **to be** ~ saber leer y escribir 2. (*well-educated*) culto, -a

literature ['lɪtrətʃər, *Am:* 'lɪt̬ə·ətʃ·] *n no pl* 1. (*novels, poems*) literatura *f;* **nineteenth-century** ~ literatura del siglo XIX 2. (*promotional material*) material *m* informativo

lithe [laɪð] *adj* ágil

lithium ['lɪθiəm] *n no pl* litio *m*

lithograph ['lɪθəgrɑːf, *Am:* -græf] I. *n* litografía *f* II. *vi* litografiar

lithography [lɪˈθɒgrəfi, *Am:* -ˈθɑːgrə-] *n no pl* litografía *f*

Lithuania [ˌlɪθjʊˈeɪnɪə, *Am:* ˌlɪθuː-] *n* Lituania *f*

Lithuanian I. *n* 1. (*person*) lituano, -a *m, f* 2. LING lituano *m* II. *adj* lituano, -a

litigant ['lɪtɪgənt, *Am:* 'lɪt̬-] *n* litigante *mf*

litigate ['lɪtɪgeɪt, *Am:* 'lɪt̬-] *vi* litigar

litigation [ˌlɪtɪˈgeɪʃən, *Am:* ˌlɪt̬-] *n no pl* litigio *m*

litigious [lɪˈtɪdʒəs] *adj* pleiteador(a)

litmus ['lɪtməs] *n no pl* tornasol *m*

litmus paper *n no pl* papel *m* de tornasol **litmus test** *no pl n* prueba *m* de tornasol; *fig* prueba *f* de fuego

litre ['liːtər, *Am:* -t̬ər] *n* litro *m*

litter ['lɪtər, *Am:* 'lɪt̬ər] I. *n* 1. *no pl* (*refuse*) basura *f* 2. ZOOL camada *f* 3. *no pl* (*bedding for animals*) lecho *m* de paja 4. MED camilla *f* II. *vt* 1. (*make untidy*) ensuciar (tirando basura) 2. (*scatter*) esparcir; **the floor was ~ed with clothes** el suelo estaba cubierto de ropa

litter bug *n Am, Aus,* **litter lout** *n Brit:* persona *que tira basura en un lugar público* **litter tray** *n* bandeja *f* para la arena del gato

little ['lɪtl] I. *adj* 1. (*size, age*) pequeño, -a; **a** ~ **old man/woman** un viejecito/una viejecita; **the** ~ **ones** *inf* los niños 2. (*amount*) poco, -a; **a** ~ **something** alguna cosita; **a** ~ **bit (of sth)** un poco (de algo); **a** ~ **something** algo (de comida o de bebida); ~ **hope** pocas esperanzas; ~ **by** ~ poco a poco 3. (*distance*) corto, -a; **a** ~ **way** un camino corto 4. (*duration*) breve; **for a** ~ **while** durante un ratito; **to have a** ~ **word with sb** cruzar algunas palabras con alguien II. *n* poco *m;* **a** ~ un poco; **to know** ~

saber poco; **we see** ~ **of him** lo vemos poco; **to have** ~ **to say** tener poco que decir III. *adv* poco; ~ **less than** ... poco menos que...; ~ **more than an hour** poco más de una hora; **to make** ~ **of sth** sacar poco en claro de algo

liturgical [lɪˈtɜːdʒɪkl, *Am:* -ˈtɜːr-] *adj* litúrgico, -a

liturgy ['lɪtədʒi, *Am:* 'lɪt̬ə·-] <-ies> *n* REL liturgia *f*

live¹ [laɪv] I. *adj* 1. (*living*) vivo, -a 2. RADIO, TV en directo; THEAT en vivo 3. ELEC que lleva corriente; (*wire*) conectado, -a; **to be a (real)** ~ **wire** *fig* rebosar energía 4. (*cartridge*) cargado, -a; (*bomb*) con carga explosiva II. *adv* RADIO, TV en directo; THEAT en vivo

live² [lɪv] I. *vi* vivir; **to** ~ **above one's means** vivir por encima de las posibilidades de uno; ~ **in sb's memory** perdurar en la memoria de alguien; **long** ~ **the king!** ¡viva el rey!; **to** ~ **off sth/sb** vivir de algo/alguien; **to** ~ **on sth** (*eat*) alimentarse de algo ▶**to** ~ **and let** ~ vivir y dejar vivir II. *vt* vivir; **to** ~ **a happy life** llevar una vida feliz

◆**live down** *vt* lograr superar

◆**live in** *vi* vivir en el lugar donde uno trabaja

◆**live on** *vi* vivir; (*tradition*) seguir vivo

◆**live out** *vt* vivir; (*dreams*) realizar

◆**live through** *vt* (*experience*) vivir

◆**live together** *vi* vivir juntos

◆**live up** *vt* **to live it up** vivir a lo grande

◆**live up to** *vt* vivir conforme a; **to** ~ **expectations** estar a la altura de lo esperado

livelihood ['laɪvlɪhʊd] *n* sustento *m;* **to earn one's** ~ ganarse la vida

liveliness ['laɪvlɪnɪs] *n no pl* viveza *f*

lively ['laɪvli] *adj* (*person, conversation*) animado, -a; (*imagination, interest*) vivo, -a

liven up ['laɪvən ʌp] I. *vi* animarse II. *vt* animar

liver ['lɪvər, *Am:* -ər] *n* hígado *m*

liver complaint *n no pl* afección *f* hepática

liverish ['lɪvərɪʃ] *adj* 1. (*ill*) enfermo, -a del hígado 2. (*peevish*) malhumorado, -a

liver sausage *n,* **liverwurst** ['lɪvəwɜːst, *Am:* -ərwɜːrst] *n no pl, Am, Aus* (embutido *m* de) paté *m* de hígado

livery ['lɪvəri] *n no pl* 1. FASHION librea *f* 2. *Brit* (*company colours*) colores *mpl* distintivos (*de una empresa*)

livestock ['laɪvstɒk, *Am:* -stɑːk] *n no pl* ganado *m*

livid ['lɪvɪd] *adj* 1. (*discoloured*) lívido, -a 2. (*furious*) furioso, -a

living ['lɪvɪŋ] I. *n* 1. *no pl* (*livelihood*) vida *f;* **to work for one's** ~ trabajar para ganarse la vida; **to make a** ~ ganarse la vida 2. *no pl* (*way of life*) (modo *m* de) vida *f* 3. *pl* (*people*) **the** ~ los vivos II. *adj* vivo, -a; (*creature*) viviente; **to be the** ~ **image of sb/sth** ser el vivo retrato de alguien/algo

living conditions *npl* condiciones *fpl* de vida **living quarters** *npl* alojamiento *m* **living room** *n* cuarto *m* de estar, living *m AmL*

living space *no pl n a. fig* espacio *m* vital
living wage *no pl n* salario *m* digno
lizard ['lɪzəd, *Am:* -ə·d] *n* lagarto *m;* (*small*)
lagartija *f*
llama ['lɑːmə] *n* llama *f*
load [ləʊd, *Am:* loʊd] I. *n* 1. ELEC *a. fig* carga *f*
2. (*amount of work*) cantidad *f* (de trabajo); **a**
heavy/light ~ mucho/poco trabajo 3. *inf*
(*lots*) montón *m;* ~**s** [o **a** ~] **of ...** un montón
de... ►**to get a** ~ **of sth** *inf* fijarse en algo II. *vt*
a. AUTO, PHOT, INFOR cargar III. *vi* cargarse
◆**load down** *vt* recargar; *fig* agobiar
◆**load up** I. *vt* cargar II. *vi* cargarse
loaded ['ləʊdɪd, *Am:* 'loʊd-] *adj* 1. (*filled*)
cargado, -a 2. (*unfair: question*) tendencioso,
-a; ~ **dice** dados *mpl* cargados 3. *Brit, inf* (*rich*)
forrado, -a 4. *Am, inf* (*drunk*) mamado, -a
loadstone ['ləʊdstəʊn, *Am:* 'loʊdstoʊn] *n*
piedra *f* imán
loaf[1] [ləʊf, *Am:* loʊf] <loaves> *n* pan *m;* **a** ~
of bread un pan ►**half a** ~ **is better than no**
bread *prov* algo es algo; **use your** ~! *Brit* ¡usa
la cabeza!
loaf[2] [ləʊf, *Am:* loʊf] *vi* gandulear; **to** ~
about hacer el holgazán
loafer ['ləʊfər, *Am:* 'loʊfə·] *n* 1. (*lazy person*)
holgazán, -ana *m, f* 2. *Am* (*shoe*) mocasín *m*
loam [ləʊm, *Am:* loʊm] *n no pl* marga *f*
loan [ləʊn, *Am:* loʊn] I. *vt* prestar II. *n* préstamo *m,* avío *m AmS*
loanword ['ləʊnwɜːd, *Am:* 'loʊnwɜːrd] *n*
LING préstamo *m*
loath [ləʊθ, *Am:* loʊθ] *adj form* reacio, -a; **to**
be ~ **to do sth** resistirse a hacer algo
loathe [ləʊð, *Am:* loʊð] *vt* (*thing*) detestar;
(*person*) odiar
loathing *n no pl* odio *m;* **to have a** ~ **for sb**
odiar a alguien; **to have a** ~ **for sth** tener aversión a algo
loathsome ['ləʊðsəm, *Am:* 'loʊð-] *adj*
(*thing*) asqueroso, -a; (*person*) odioso, -a
loaves [ləʊvz, *Am:* loʊvz] *n pl of* **loaf**[1]
lob [lɒb, *Am:* lɑːb] I. <-bb-> *vt* lanzar; SPORTS
hacer un globo a II. *n* SPORTS lob *m*
lobby ['lɒbi, *Am:* 'lɑːbi] I. <-ies> *n* 1. ARCHIT
vestíbulo *m* 2. POL grupo *m* de presión
II. <-ie-> *vi* to ~ **to have sth done** hacer presión para que se haga algo; **to** ~ **against/for**
sth presionar en contra de/en pro de algo
III. <-ie-> *vt* presionar
lobbyist ['lɒbiɪst, *Am:* 'lɑːbi-] *n* miembro *m*
de un grupo de presión
lobe [ləʊb, *Am:* loʊb] *n* lóbulo *m*
lobster ['lɒbstər, *Am:* 'lɑːbstə·] *n* (*spiny*) langosta *f;* (*with claws*) bogavante *m*
lobster pot *n* nasa *f*
local ['ləʊkəl, *Am:* 'loʊ-] I. *adj* local; (*people*)
del lugar; (*official, police*) municipal; TEL
urbano, -a; ~ **colour** color *m* local II. *n*
1. (*inhabitant*) lugareño, -a *m, f* 2. *Am* (*bus*)
coche *m* de línea; (*train*) tren *m* de cercanías
3. *Brit* (*pub*) taberna *f* (*del barrio, pueblo,*
etc.)

local anaesthetic *n* anestesia *f* local **local**
authority *n* municipio *m,* ayuntamiento *m*
local call *n* llamada *f* local
locale [ləʊˈkɑːl, *Am:* loʊˈkæl] *n* escenario *m*
local elections *npl* elecciones *fpl* municipales **local government** *n* administración
f municipal
locality [ləʊˈkæləti, *Am:* loʊˈkælət̬i] <-ies>
n localidad *f*
localization [ˌləʊkəlaɪˈzeɪʃən, *Am:* ˌloʊ-
kəlɪ'-] *n no pl* localización *f*
localize ['ləʊkəlaɪz, *Am:* 'loʊ-] *vt* localizar
local paper *n* periódico *m* local **local time**
no pl n hora *f* local **local train** *n* tren *m* de
cercanías
locate [ləʊˈkeɪt, *Am:* 'loʊ-] *vt* 1. (*find*) localizar 2. (*situate*) situar; **to be** ~**d near sth**
estar situado cerca de algo
location [ləʊˈkeɪʃən, *Am:* loʊˈ-] *n* 1. (*place*)
posición *f* 2. (*act of locating*) localización *f*
3. CINE exteriores *mpl;* **to film sth on** ~ rodar
algo en exteriores
loc. cit. [ˌlɒkˈsɪt, *Am:* ˌlɑːkˈsɪt] *abbr of* **loco**
citato loc. cit.
loch [lɒk, *Am:* lɑːk] *n Scot* 1. (*lake*) lago *m*
2. (*inlet*) brazo *m* de mar
lock[1] [lɒk, *Am:* lɑːk] *n* (*of hair*) mechón *m*
lock[2] [lɒk, *Am:* lɑːk] I. *n* 1. (*fastening device*)
cerradura *f,* chapa *f Arg, Méx* 2. (*on canal*)
esclusa *f* 3. (*in wrestling*) llave *f* 4. *Aus, Brit*
AUTO tope *m* ►~, **stock and barrel** completamente, por completo; **to be under** ~ **and key**
estar cerrado bajo llave II. *vt* 1. (*fasten with*
lock) cerrar con llave; (*confine safely: thing*)
guardar bajo llave; (*person*) encerrar; **to be**
~**ed** (*be held fast*) estar sujeto 2. (*make*
immovable) bloquear; **be** ~**ed** estar bloqueado; **to be** ~**ed in(to) discussions** enredarse en discusiones III. *vi* cerrarse con llave
◆**lock away** *vt* (*jewels, document*) guardar
bajo llave; (*person*) encerrar
◆**lock in** *vt* encerrar
◆**lock on** *vi,* **lock onto** *vi* MIL localizar y
seguir
◆**lock out** *vt* impedir la entrada a; **to lock**
oneself out dejarse las llaves dentro
◆**lock up** *vt* (*jewels, document*) guardar
bajo llave; (*person*) encerrar
locker ['lɒkər, *Am:* 'lɑːkə·] *n* (*at railway*
station) consigna *f* automática; (*at school*)
taquilla *f*
locket ['lɒkɪt, *Am:* 'lɑːkɪt] *n* guardapelo *m*
lockjaw ['lɒkdʒɔː, *Am:* 'lɑːkdʒɑː] *n no pl*
trismo *m*
lockout ['lɒkaʊt, *Am:* 'lɑːk-] *n* cierre *m*
patronal
locksmith ['lɒksmɪθ, *Am:* 'lɑːk-] *n* cerrajero,
-a *m, f*
lockup ['lɒkʌp, *Am:* 'lɑːk-] *n inf* 1. (*cell*) calabozo *m* 2. (*storage space*) garaje *m*
locomotion [ˌləʊkəˈməʊʃən, *Am:* ˌloʊkə-
'moʊ-] *n no pl* locomoción *f*
locomotive [ˌləʊkəˈməʊtɪv, *Am:* ˌloʊkə-

'moʊt̬ɪv] I. n locomotora f II. adj locomotor(a); (force) locomotriz

locum ['ləʊkəm, Am: 'loʊ-] n Aus, Brit interino, -a m, f

locus ['ləʊkəs, Am: 'loʊ-] <-ci> n 1. (exact place) lugar m 2. MAT lugar m geométrico 3. BIO locus m

locust ['ləʊkəst, Am: 'loʊ-] n langosta f, chapulín m Méx

locution [lə'kju:ʃən, Am: loʊ'-] n locución f

lode [ləʊd, Am: loʊd] n MIN filón m

lodestar ['ləʊdstɑːʳ, Am: 'loʊdstɑːr] n estrella f polar

lodestone ['ləʊdstəʊn, Am: 'loʊdstoʊn] n piedra f imán

lodge [lɒdʒ, Am: lɑːdʒ] I. vi 1. (stay in rented room) alojarse 2. (become fixed) quedarse clavado, -a II. vt 1. (accommodate) alojar 2. (place) colocar 3. (insert) meter 4. Brit (deposit) depositar 5. (bring forward officially: appeal) interponer; (objection, protest) presentar III. n 1. (for hunters) refugio m 2. Brit (at entrance to building) portería f; porter's ~ casa f del guarda 3. (of freemasons) logia f 4. (of beaver) madriguera f

lodger ['lɒdʒəʳ, Am: 'lɑːdʒɚ] n inquilino, -a m, f; to take in ~s alquilar habitaciones

lodging ['lɒdʒɪŋ, Am: 'lɑːdʒɪŋ] n 1. no pl (accomodation) alojamiento m; board and ~ pensión f completa 2. pl, Brit (room to rent) habitación f de alquiler

lodging house n pensión f

loft [lɒft, Am: lɑːft] I. n 1. (space under roof) buhardilla f; hay ~ pajar m 2. (upstairs living space) loft m II. vt (ball) lanzar por lo alto

lofty ['lɒfti, Am: 'lɑːf-] <-ier, -iest> adj 1. liter (tall) altísimo, -a 2. (noble: aims, ideals) noble 3. (haughty) altivo, -a

log¹ [lɒg, Am: lɑːg] I. n 1. (tree trunk) tronco m 2. (firewood) leño m ▸to sleep like a ~ dormir como un tronco II. <-gg-> vt talar III. <-gg-> vi talar árboles

log² [lɒg, Am: lɑːg] inf abbr of **logarithm** log.

log³ [lɒg, Am: lɑːg] I. n registro m; ship's ~ cuaderno m de bitácora II. vt 1. (record) registrar 2. (achieve, attain) alcanzar

◆**log in** vi INFOR entrar en el sistema

◆**log off** vi INFOR salir del sistema

◆**log on** vi s. **log in**

◆**log out** vi s. **log off**

loganberry ['ləʊgənberi, Am: 'loʊ-] <-ies> n frambuesa f de Logan

logarithm ['lɒgərɪðəm, Am: 'lɑːgɚ-] n logaritmo m

logarithmic [ˌlɒgə'rɪðmɪk, Am: ˌlɑːgɚ'rɪθ-] adj logarítmico, -a

log book ['lɒgbʊk, Am: 'lɑːgbʊk] n NAUT diario m de navegación; AVIAT diario m de vuelo

log cabin n cabaña f de troncos **log fire** n fuego m de leña

logger ['lɒgəʳ, Am: 'lɑːgɚ] n leñador(a) m(f)

loggerheads ['lɒgəhedz, Am: 'lɑːgɚ-] npl to be at ~ (with sb/over sth) estar en desa-

cuerdo (con alguien/sobre algo)

logic ['lɒdʒɪk, Am: 'lɑːdʒɪk] n no pl lógica f

logical ['lɒdʒɪkl, Am: 'lɑːdʒɪk-] adj lógico, -a

login [lɒgɪn, Am: lɑːg-] n INFOR inicio m de sesión

logistics [lə'dʒɪstɪks, Am: loʊ'-] n logística f

logjam n atolladero m

logo ['lɒgəʊ, Am: 'loʊgoʊ] n logotipo m

logoff [lɒgɒf, Am: lɑːgɑːf] n INFOR fin m de sesión

logon n s. **login**

logrolling ['lɒgrəʊlɪŋ, Am: 'lɑːgroʊlɪŋ] n no pl, Am amiguismo m

loin [lɔɪn] I. n 1. pl (body area) bajo vientre m 2. pl, liter the fruit of his ~s su hijo/hija 3. GASTR lomo m II. adj de lomo

loincloth ['lɔɪnklɒθ, Am: '-klɑːθ] n taparrabos m inv

loiter ['lɔɪtəʳ, Am: -t̬ɚ] vi 1. (linger) entretenerse 2. a. LAW merodear

loiterer ['lɔɪtərəʳ, Am: 'lɔɪt̬ɚɚ] n 1. inf holgazán, -ana m, f 2. LAW merodeador(a) m(f)

loll [lɒl, Am: lɑːl] vi colgar; to ~ about holgazanear

lollipop ['lɒlipɒp, Am: 'lɑːlipɑːp] n chupachups® m inv

lollipop lady, lollipop man n Brit, inf: persona que detiene el tráfico para permitir que los escolares crucen la calle

lollop ['lɒləp, Am: 'lɑːləp] vi moverse torpemente

lolly ['lɒli, Am: 'lɑːli] <-ies> n 1. Aus, Brit (lollipop) chupachups® m inv; ice ~ polo m, palito m (helado) RíoPl, chupete m (helado) Chile 2. no pl, Brit, inf (money) pasta f

London ['lʌndən] n Londres m

Londoner I. adj londinense II. n londinense mf

lone [ləʊn, Am: loʊn] adj solitario, -a

loneliness ['ləʊnlɪnɪs, Am: 'loʊn-] n no pl soledad f

lonely ['ləʊnli, Am: 'loʊn-] <-ier, -iest> adj (person) solo, -a; (life) solitario, -a; (place) aislado, -a

loner ['ləʊnəʳ, Am: 'loʊnɚ] n solitario, -a m, f

lonesome ['ləʊnsəm, Am: 'loʊn-] adj (person) solo, -a; (place) aislado, -a

long¹ [lɒŋ, Am: lɑːŋ] I. adj (distance, time, shape) largo, -a; to have a ~ way to go tener mucho camino por recorrer; it's a ~ while since ... hace mucho tiempo desde que...; ~ time no see! inf ¡cuánto tiempo (sin verte)! II. adv 1. (a long time) mucho (tiempo); ~ after/before mucho después/antes; ~ ago hace mucho (tiempo); to take ~ (to do sth) tardar mucho (en hacer algo); to be not ~ in doing sth form no tardar en hacer algo; ~ live the king! ¡viva el rey! 2. (for the whole duration) all day ~ todo el día; as ~ as I live mientras viva 3. in comparisons as ~ as mientras +subj; to no ~er do sth ya no hacer algo ▸so ~ inf ¡hasta luego!; so ~ as mientras III. n mucho tiempo m ▸the ~ and the short of it is that ... en resumidas cuentas...

long² [lɒŋ, *Am:* lɑːŋ-] *vi* to ~ **for sb** echar de menos a alguien; **to ~ for sth** estar deseando algo; **to ~ to do sth** anhelar hacer algo

long. *abbr of* longitude long.

longboat *n* bote *m*

long-distance [ˌlɒŋˈdɪstənts, *Am:* ˌlɑːŋ-] **I.** *adj* (*bus, flight*) de largo recorrido; (*race, runner*) de fondo; (*negotiations, relationship*) a distancia; ~ **call** conferencia *f* **II.** *adv* **to phone** ~ hacer una llamada interurbana

longevity [lɒnˈdʒevəti, *Am:* lɑːnˈdʒevəti] *n no pl* longevidad *f*

long-haired [ˌlɒŋˈheəd] *adj* (*person*) melenudo, -a; (*animal*) de pelo largo **longhand** *n no pl* escritura *f* normal (*donde las palabras tienen todas sus letras*) **long-haul** *adj* AVIAT de larga distancia

longing [ˈlɒŋɪŋ, *Am:* ˈlɑːŋɪŋ] **I.** *n* **1.** (*nostalgia*) nostalgia *f;* **to feel a ~ for sb** echar de menos a alguien **2.** (*strong desire*) vivo deseo *m;* **to have a ~ to do sth** anhelar hacer algo **II.** *adj* anhelante

longish [ˈlɒŋɡɪʃ, *Am:* ˈlɑːŋ-] *adj inf* tirando a largo, -a

longitude [ˈlɒŋɡɪtjuːd, *Am:* ˈlɑːndʒətuːd] *n* longitud *f*

longitudinal [ˌlɒŋɡɪˈtjuːdɪnl, *Am:* ˌlɑːndʒə-ˈtuː-] *adj* longitudinal

long johns [ˈlɒndʒɒnz, *Am:* ˈlɑːndʒɑːnz] *npl inf* calzoncillos *mpl* largos **long jump** *n no pl* salto *m* de longitud, salto *m* largo *AmL* **long-life milk** *n* leche *f* uperizada **long--lived** *adj* **1.** (*person*) longevo, -a **2.** (*feud*) que viene de lejos **long-lost** *adj* perdido, -a hace mucho tiempo **long-range** *adj* (*missile*) de largo alcance; (*aircraft*) transcontinental; (*policy*) a largo plazo **longship** *n* barco *m* vikingo **long shot** *n* **to be a ~** ser una posibilidad muy remota **long-sighted** *adj* **1.** (*having long sight*) hipermétrope **2.** *Am* (*having foresight*) previsor(a) **long-standing** *adj* antiguo, -a **long-suffering** *adj* sufrido, -a **long-term** *adj* (*care*) prolongado, -a; (*loan, memory, strategy*) a largo plazo **long wave** *n* onda *f* larga **long-wave** *adj* de onda larga **longways** *adv,* **longwise** *adv* a lo largo **long-winded** *adj* prolijo, -a

loo [luː] *n Aus, Brit, inf* váter *m*

loofa(h) [ˈluːfə] *n* esponja *f* vegetal

look [lʊk] **I.** *n* **1.** (*act of looking: at person, thing*) mirada *f;* (*examination: of book, face*) ojeada *f;* **to take** [*o* **to have**] **a ~ at sth** echar un vistazo a algo; **to have a ~ for sth/sb** buscar algo/a alguien **2.** (*appearance*) aspecto *m;* **good ~** guapura *f;* **to have the ~ of sb/sth** parecerse a alguien/algo; **by the ~ of things** según parece **3.** (*style*) look *m* **II.** *vi* **1.** (*use sight*) mirar; **to ~ at sth/sb** mirar algo/a alguien; **to ~ at a book** echar una ojeada a un libro; **to ~ out (of) the window** mirar por la ventana; **oh, ~!** ¡mira!; **~ here** ¡oye tú! **2.** (*search*) buscar; **to ~ for sth/sb** buscar

algo/a alguien **3.** (*appear, seem*) parecer; **to ~ like sb/sth** parecerse a alguien/algo; **to ~ bad/good** tener mala/buena cara; **to ~ tired** parecer cansado; **to ~ as if ...** parecer como si... +*subj;* ~ **alive!** ¡espabila! ▶ ~ **before you leap** *prov* antes de que te cases, mira lo que haces *prov* **III.** *vt* **1.** (*examine*) mirar; **to ~ the other way** *fig* hacer la vista gorda **2.** (*seem*) parecer; **to ~ one's age** aparentar su edad; **to ~ the part** THEAT encajar muy bien en el papel **3.** (*face*) mirar a; **to ~ north** mirar al norte

◆**look about** *vi* mirar alrededor

◆**look after** *vi* **1.** (*tend, care for*) cuidar **2.** (*take responsibility for*) encargarse de

◆**look ahead** *vi* mirar hacia adelante; **looking ahead to ...** de cara a...

◆**look around** *vi s.* **look round**

◆**look away** *vi* apartar la mirada

◆**look back** *vi* **1.** (*look behind oneself*) mirar (hacia) atrás **2.** (*remember*) recordar

◆**look down** *vi* **1.** (*from above*) mirar hacia abajo; (*lower eyes*) bajar la vista **2.** (*feel superior*) **to ~ on sth/sb** menospreciar algo/a alguien

◆**look for** *vt* **1.** (*seek*) buscar **2.** (*expect*) esperar

◆**look forward** *vi* **to ~ to sth** tener muchas ganas de algo; **I ~ to hearing from you** espero tener pronto noticias suyas

◆**look in** *vi Brit, Aus* **to ~ on sb** ir a ver a alguien; **to ~ at the office** pasar por la oficina

◆**look into** *vi* investigar

◆**look on** *vi,* **look upon** *vi* **1.** (*watch*) mirar **2.** (*view*) ver

◆**look onto** *vi* dar a

◆**look out I.** *vt Brit* **to look sth out** buscar algo **II.** *vi* **1.** (*face a particular direction*) **to ~ on** (*window*) dar a **2.** (*watch out*) tener cuidado; **to ~ for** tener cuidado con; (*look for*) buscar

◆**look over** *vt* (*report*) revisar; (*house*) inspeccionar

◆**look round I.** *vi* **1.** (*look behind oneself*) girarse **2.** (*look in all directions*) mirar alrededor **3.** (*search*) **to ~ for** buscar **II.** *vt* (*inspect*) inspeccionar

◆**look through** *vt* **1.** (*look*) mirar por **2.** (*examine*) revisar **3.** (*peruse*) **to ~ sth** echar un vistazo a algo

◆**look to** *vi* **1.** (*attend to*) mirar por **2.** (*depend on*) depender de **3.** (*count on*) contar con

◆**look up I.** *vt* **1.** (*consult*) buscar **2.** (*visit*) ir a ver **II.** *vi* **1.** (*raise one's eyes upward*) mirar hacia arriba; **to ~ to sb** *fig* tener a alguien de [*o* como] ejemplo **2.** (*improve*) mejorar

lookalike [ˈlʊkəˌlaɪk] *n* (*person*) doble *mf;* (*thing*) imitación *f*

looker [ˈlʊkə, *Am:* -ɚ] *n inf* **to be a (real) ~** ser muy guapa

look-in [ˈlʊkɪn] *n Aus, Brit, inf* oportunidad *f;* **I didn't get a ~** no tuve ni la más mínima oportunidad

looking glass <-es> *n form* espejo *m*
lookout ['lʊk‚aʊt] *n* **1.**(*observation post*) puesto *m* de observación **2.**(*person*) centinela *mf;* **to be on the** ~ estar alerta **3.** *Brit* (*prospect*) panorama *m* **4.**(*concern*) asunto *m;* **that's his/your** ~ eso es asunto suyo/tuyo
look-over ['lʊkəʊvəʳ] *n* vistazo *m;* **to give sth a** ~ echar un vistazo a algo
loom¹ [luːm] *n* telar *m*
loom² [luːm] *vi* **1.**(*come into view*) surgir **2.**(*threaten*) amenazar; **to** ~ **large** cobrar mucha importancia
loony ['luːni] **I.**<-ier, -iest> *adj inf* (*person*) chiflado, -a; (*idea*) disparatado, -a **II.**<-ies> *n inf* loco, -a *m, f,* chiflado, -a *m, f*
loop [luːp] **I.** *n* **1.**(*bend*) curva *f;* (*of string*) lazada *f;* (*of river*) meandro *m* **2.** ELEC circuito *m* cerrado **3.** INFOR bucle *m* **4.**(*contraceptive coil*) espiral *f* ► **to throw sb for a** ~ *Am, inf* dejar a alguien de piedra **II.** *vi* serpentear **III.** *vt* atar con un lazo; **to** ~ **sth around ...** pasar algo alrededor de... ►**to** ~ **the** ~ AVIAT rizar el rizo
loophole ['luːphəʊl, *Am:*-hoʊl] *n fig* escapatoria *f;* **legal** ~ laguna legal
loose [luːs] **I.** *adj* **1.**(*not tight: clothing*) holgado, -a; (*knot, rope, screw*) flojo, -a; (*skin*) flácido, -a **2.**(*not confined*) suelto, -a; ~ **change** dinero *m* suelto, sencillo *m AmS* **3.**(*not exact: instructions*) poco preciso, -a; (*translation*) libre **4.**(*not strict or controlled: discipline*) relajado, -a; ~ **tongue** lengua *f* desatada **5.**(*sexually immoral*) disoluto, -a **II.** *n* **to be on the** ~ estar en libertad **III.** *vt* soltar
loose-leaf folder *n* carpeta *f* de anillas
loosely ['luːsli] *adv* **1.**(*not tightly*) sin apretar **2.**(*not exactly: translate*) libremente; (*speak*) en términos generales **3.**(*not strictly: organized*) de forma flexible
loosen ['luːsn] **I.** *vt* (*belt*) aflojar; (*tongue*) desatar **II.** *vi* aflojarse
loot [luːt] **I.** *n no pl* **1.**(*plunder*) botín *m* **2.** *inf* (*money*) pasta *f,* lana *f AmL* **II.** *vt, vi* saquear
looting *n no pl* saqueo *m*
lop [lɒp, *Am:* lɑːp] *vt s.* **lop off**
♦**lop off** <-pp-> *vt* **1.**(*branch*) podar; (*limb*) amputar **2.**(*pages*) eliminar
lope [ləʊp, *Am:* loʊp] *vi* (*person or animal*) andar con paso largo
lopsided [‚lɒp'saɪdɪd, *Am:* ‚lɑːp-] *adj* **1.**(*leaning to one side*) torcido, -a, chueco, -a *AmL* **2.**(*biased*) parcial
loquacious [lə'kweɪʃəs, *Am:* loʊ'-] *adj* locuaz
lord [lɔːd, *Am:* lɔːrd] *n* **1.** *Brit* (*British peer*) lord *m* **2.**(*aristocrat*) señor *m*
Lord Chancellor *n Brit* Lord *m* Canciller (*presidente de la Cámara de los Lores y máxima autoridad judicial*)
lordly ['lɔːdli, *Am:* 'lɔːrd-] <-ier, -iest> *adj* **1.**(*suitable to a lord*) señorial **2.**(*arrogant*) arrogante

Lord Mayor *n Brit* alcalde *m*
lordship ['lɔːdʃɪp, *Am:* 'lɔːrd-] *n no pl, form* **His Lordship** *Brit* Su Señoría
lore [lɔːʳ, *Am:* lɔːr] *n no pl* sabiduría *f*
lorry ['lɒri, *Am:* 'lɔːr-] <-ies> *n Brit* camión *m*
lorry driver *n Brit* camionero(a) *m(f)*
lose [luːz] <lost, lost> **I.** *vt* perder; **to get lost** (*person*) perderse; (*object*) extraviarse **II.** *vi* perder
loser ['luːzəʳ, *Am:* -zɚ] *n* perdedor(a) *m(f)*
losing ['luːzɪŋ] *adj* perdedor(a)
loss [lɒs, *Am:* lɑːs] <-es> *n* pérdida *f;* **to be at a** ~ no saber cómo reaccionar; **to be at a** ~ **for words** no encontrar palabras con que expresarse
loss leader *n* artículo *m* de gancho **loss--making** *adj* deficitario, -a
lost [lɒst, *Am:* lɑːst] **I.** *pt, pp of* **lose II.** *adj* **1.** perdido, -a; **to get** ~ perderse; **to give sth/ sb up for** ~ dar algo/a alguien por perdido; **to be** ~ **in a book** estar enfrascado en la lectura de un libro **2.**(*preoccupied*) perplejo, -a
lost property *n no pl* objetos *mpl* perdidos
lost property office *n Brit, Aus* oficina *f* de objetos perdidos
lot [lɒt, *Am:* lɑːt] *n* **1.**(*destiny*) destino *m;* (*fate*) suerte *f* **2.** *Brit* (*large quantity*) **a** ~ **of, lots of** mucho(s); **a** ~ **of wine** mucho vino; ~**s of houses** muchas casas; **I like it a** ~ me gusta mucho; **the whole** ~ todo **3.**(*plot of land*) terreno *m* **4.**(*in auction*) lote *m*
loth [ləʊθ, *Am:* loʊθ] *adj s.* **loath**
lotion ['ləʊʃən, *Am:* 'loʊ-] *n no pl* loción *f*
lottery ['lɒtəri, *Am:* 'lɑːtɚ-] <-ies> *n* lotería *f,* quiniela *f CSur*
lottery number *n* número *m* de lotería
lotus ['ləʊtəs, *Am:* 'loʊtəs] <-es> *n* loto *m*
lotus position *n no pl* posición *f* del loto
loud [laʊd] **I.** *adj* **1.**(*voice*) alto, -a; (*shout*) fuerte **2.**(*colour*) chillón, -ona **3.**(*noisy*) ruidoso, -a **4.**(*vigorous: complaint*) enérgico, -a **II.** *adv* alto; **to laugh out** ~ reír a carcajadas
loudhailer [‚laʊd'heɪləʳ, *Am:* -lɚ] *n Brit, Aus* megáfono *m*
loudmouth ['laʊdmaʊθ] *n inf* escandaloso, -a *m, f*
loudness *n no pl* **1.**(*volume*) volumen *m;* (*of explosion*) estruendo *m* **2.**(*of colour*) lo chillón
loudspeaker [‚laʊd'spiːkəʳ, *Am:* ‚laʊd-'spiːkɚ] *n* altavoz *m*
Louisiana [lu‚iːzi'ænə] *n* Luisiana *f*
lounge [laʊndʒ] **I.** *n* salón *m* **II.** *vi* **1.**(*recline*) repanchigarse **2.**(*be idle*) hacer el vago
♦**lounge about** *vt,* **lounge around** *vt* holgazanear
lounge bar *n Brit* bar *m* **lounge chair** *n* tumbona *f,* reposera *f RíoPl* **lounge lizard** *n hombre que frecuenta bares, salones de hoteles, etc., en busca de mujeres* **lounge suit** *n Brit* traje *m* (de calle)
louse [laʊs] *n* **1.**<lice> (*insect*) piojo *m*

2. <-es> *inf* (*person*) canalla *mf*

♦**louse up** *vt inf* echar a perder

lousy ['laʊzi] <-ier, -iest> *adj inf* **1.** (*infested with lice*) piojoso, -a **2.** (*of poor quality*) pésimo, -a; **to feel** ~ estar fatal **3.** (*contemptible*) asqueroso, -a ►**to be** ~ **with money** estar podrido de dinero

lout [laʊt] *n* patán *m*, jallán *m AmC*

loutish ['laʊtɪʃ, *Am:* -t̬ɪʃ] *adj* patán

louver *n Am,* **louvre** ['luːvəʳ, *Am:* -vɚ] *n* persiana *f* de listones

louvred door *n* puerta *f* de persiana

lovable ['lʌvəbl] *adj* adorable

lovage ['lʌvɪdʒ] *n no pl* ligustro *m*

love [lʌv] **I.** *vt* querer, amar; **I** ~ **swimming, I** ~ **to swim** me encanta nadar ►~ **me,** ~ **my dog** *prov* quien quiere a Beltrán, quiere a su can *prov* **II.** *n* **1.** *no pl* (*affection*) amor *m;* **to be in** ~ (**with sb**) estar enamorado (de alguien); **to fall in** ~ (**with sb**) enamorarse (de alguien); **to make** ~ **to sb** hacer el amor con alguien **2.** *no pl, Brit, inf* (*darling*) cariño *m* **3.** *no pl* (*in tennis*) cero *m;* ~ **game** juego en el que quien recibe no ha marcado ningún punto ►**not for** ~ (**n**)**or money** por nada del mundo; **there is no** ~ **lost between the two** no se pueden ver **III.** *vi* querer, amar

love affair *n* aventura *f,* romance *m* **love-bird** *n* periquito *m; fig* tortolito *m*

love-hate relationship *n* relación *f* de amor y odio

loveless [lʌvlɪs] *adj* sin amor

love letter *n* carta *f* de amor **love life** *n inf* vida *f* amorosa [*o* sentimental]

loveliness ['lʌvlɪnɪs] *n no pl* (*of scenery*) belleza *f;* (*of person*) encanto *m*

lovely ['lʌvli] <-ier, -iest> *adj* (*house, present*) bonito, -a; (*weather*) precioso, -a; (*person*) encantador(a); **to have a** ~ **time** pasarlo estupendamente

love-making ['lʌvˌmeɪkɪŋ] *n no pl* relaciones *fpl* sexuales

lover ['lʌvəʳ, *Am:* -ɚ] *n* amante *mf*

lovesick ['lʌvsɪk] *adj* locamente enamorado, -a, volado, -a *AmL*

love song *n* canción *f* de amor **love story** *n* historia *f* de amor

lovey [lʌvi] *n no pl, Brit, inf* cariño *m*

loving ['lʌvɪŋ] *adj* cariñoso, -a

low[1] [ləʊ, *Am:* loʊ] **I.** *adj* **1.** (*not high, not loud*) bajo, -a; **to be** ~ (**on sth**) tener poco (de algo); **to cook sth on a** ~ **heat** hacer algo a fuego lento; **stocks are running** ~ las existencias están casi agotadas; **the batteries are running** ~ las baterías se están acabando **2.** (*poor: opinion, quality*) malo, -a; (*self-esteem*) bajo, -a; (*visibility*) poco, -a; **a** ~ **trick** una mala jugada **II.** *adv* bajo, -a; **to feel** ~ estar deprimido **III.** *n* **1.** METEO depresión *f* **2.** (*minimum*) mínimo *m*

low[2] [ləʊ, *Am:* loʊ] **I.** *vi* mugir **II.** *n* mugido *m*

low-alcohol *adj* bajo, -a en alcohol **lowborn** *adj* de casa pobre **lowbrow** *adj* poco intelec-

tual **low-calorie** *adj* bajo, -a en calorías **low-cost** *adj* económico, -a **low-cut** *adj* escotado, -a **low demand** *n* baja demanda *f* **lowdown I.** *adj inf* bajo, -a; **a** ~ **trick** una mala jugada **II.** *n inf* **to give sb the** ~ **on sth** poner a alguien al tanto de algo

lower[1] ['ləʊəʳ, *Am:* 'loʊɚ] **I.** *vt* bajar; (*flag, sails*) arriar; (*lifeboat*) echar al agua; **to** ~ **one's eyes** bajar la vista; **to** ~ **oneself to do sth** rebajarse a hacer algo **II.** *vi* bajar **III.** *adj* inferior

lower[2] [laʊəʳ, *Am:* laʊr] *vi* **1.** (*person*) fruncir el ceño **2.** (*sky*) encapotarse

lower-case [ˌləʊəˈkeɪs, *Am:* ˌloʊɚ-] *adj* minúsculo, -a

Lower House *n* the ~ la Cámara Baja

low-fat *adj* bajo, -a en calorías; (*milk*) desnatado, -a **low-key** *adj* (*affair*) discreto, -a; (*debate, discussion*) mesurado, -a **lowland** *npl* tierras *fpl* bajas, bajío *m AmL* **low-level** *adj* **1.** (*discussion*) a bajo nivel **2.** (*bridge*) de poca altura **3.** (*radiation*) de baja intensidad

lowly ['ləʊli, *Am:* 'loʊ-] <-ier, -iest> *adj* humilde **low-minded** *adj* vulgar

lowness *n no pl* **1.** (*state of being low*) lo bajo **2.** MUS gravedad *f* **3.** (*baseness*) bajeza *f*, vileza *f* **4.** (*humbleness*) humildad *f*

low-pitched *adj* (*voice*) grave **low pressure** *n* baja presión *f* **low profile** *n* to keep a ~ tratar de pasar desapercibido **low season** *n* temporada *f* baja **low-spirited** *adj* deprimido, -a **low-tech** *adj* de baja tecnología **low tide, low water** *n* marea *f* baja

loyal ['lɔɪəl] *adj* leal; **to remain** ~ (**to sb/sth**) permanecer fiel (a alguien/algo)

loyalist ['lɔɪəlɪst] *n* partidario, -a *m, f* del régimen; **Loyalist** *Brit* unionista *mf*

loyalty ['lɔɪəlti, *Am:* -t̬i] <-ies> *n* lealtad *f*

lozenge ['lɒzɪndʒ, *Am:* 'laːzəndʒ] *n* pastilla *f*

LP [ˌelˈpiː] *n abbr of* **long-playing record** LP *m*

LPG *n abbr of* **liquid petroleum gas** GLP *m*

LSD [ˌelesˈdiː] *n abbr of* **lysergic acid diethylamide** LSD *f*

Ltd ['lɪmɪtɪd, *Am:* -ət̬ɪd] *abbr of* **Limited** SA

lubricant ['luːbrɪkənt] *n no pl* lubricante *m*

lubricate ['luːbrɪkeɪt] *vt* lubricar

lubrication [ˌluːbrɪˈkeɪʃən] *n no pl* lubricación *f*

lubricator ['luːbrɪˌkeɪtə, *Am:* -t̬ɚ] *n* lubricador *m*

lucerne [luːˈsɜːn, *Am:* -ˈsɜːrn] *n* alfalfa *f*

lucid ['luːsɪd] *adj* **1.** (*rational*) lúcido, -a **2.** (*easily understood*) claro, -a

luck [lʌk] *n no pl* suerte *f;* **good/bad** ~ buena/mala suerte; **a stroke of** ~ un golpe de suerte; **to bring sb** ~ traer suerte a alguien; **to wish sb** (**good**) ~ desear a alguien (buena) suerte; **with** (**any**) ~ con un poco de suerte; **with no** ~ sin éxito; **as** ~ **would have it** ... quiso la suerte que... +*subj;* **to be down on one's** ~ *Brit* estar de mala racha **2. to be the** ~ **of the** °**draw** ser cuestión de suerte; **no** °**such**

~! *inf* ¡qué va!; **to press one's** ~ tentar la suerte

luckless ['lʌkləs] *adj* desafortunado, -a

lucky ['lʌki] <-ier, -iest> *adj* afortunado, -a; **to be** ~ **in love** tener suerte en el amor; **to be** ~ **in that** tener la suerte de que +*subj;* **to make a** ~ **guess** acertar por pura casualidad; ~ **day** día *m* de suerte; ~ **number** número *m* de la suerte

lucrative ['lu:krətɪv, *Am:* -ṭɪv] *adj* lucrativo, -a

lucre ['lu:kəʳ, *Am:* -kɚ] *n no pl* lucro *m;* (*filthy*) ~ *iron* (cochino) dinero *m*

ludicrous ['lu:dɪkrəs] *adj* absurdo, -a

ludo ['lu:dəʊ, *Am:* -doʊ] *n Brit* parchís *m inv*

lug [lʌg] I. *vt* <-gg-> *inf* arrastrar II. *n Aus, Brit* oreja *f*

luggage ['lʌgɪdʒ] *n no pl* equipaje *m*

luggage rack *n Brit* baca *f* **luggage van** *n Aus, Brit* furgón *m* de equipajes

lugger ['lʌgəʳ, *Am:* -ɚ] *n* NAUT lugre *m*

lughole *n Brit, inf* oreja *f*

lugubrious [ləˈguːbrɪəs] *adj* lúgubre

lukewarm [ˌluːkˈwɔːm, *Am:* -ˈwɔːrm] *adj* **1.** (*liquid*) tibio, -a **2.** (*unenthusiastic*) poco entusiasta

lull [lʌl] I. *vt* calmar; **to** ~ **sb to sleep** dormir a alguien; **to** ~ **sb into believing that ...** hacer creer a alguien que... II. *n* **1.** (*temporary stillness*) período *m* de calma **2.** (*in conversation*) pausa *f* **3.** (*in fighting*) tregua *f*

lullaby ['lʌləbaɪ] <-ies> *n* nana *f*

lumbago [lʌmˈbeɪgəʊ, *Am:* -goʊ] *n no pl* lumbago *m*

lumbar ['lʌmbəʳ, *Am:* -bɑːr] *adj* ANAT lumbar

lumbar puncture *n* MED punción *f* lumbar

lumber¹ ['lʌmbəʳ, *Am:* -bɚ] *vi* moverse pesadamente

lumber² ['lʌmbəʳ, *Am:* -bɚ] I. *vt Aus, Brit, inf* **to** ~ **sb with sth** endilgar algo a alguien II. *n no pl* **1.** *Am, Aus* madera *f* **2.** (*junk*) trastos *mpl* III. *vi* aserrar **lumberjack** *n* leñador *m*

lumberjacket *n* chaquetón *m* de leñador **lumber room** *n* trastero *m* **lumber trade** *n Am* industria *f* maderera **lumberyard** *n* almacén *m* de maderas

luminary ['lu:mɪnəri, *Am:* 'lu:mənər-] <-ies> *n fig* lumbrera *f*

luminosity [ˌluːmɪˈnɒsəti, *Am:* ˌluː-məˈnɑːsəṭi] *n no pl* luminosidad *f*

luminous ['luːmɪnəs, *Am:* 'luːmə-] *adj* luminoso, -a

lump [lʌmp] I. *n* **1.** (*solid mass*) masa *f;* (*of coal*) trozo *m;* (*of sugar*) terrón *m;* ~ **sum** cantidad *f* única **2.** (*swelling: in breast, on head*) bulto *m* **3.** *inf* (*person*) zoquete *mf* ▶**to have a** ~ **in one's throat** tener un nudo en la garganta II. *vt* **1.** (*combine*) agrupar **2.** (*endure*) aguantar; **if you don't like it,** (**you can**) ~ **it** si no te gusta, te aguantas

lump payment *n* pago *m* único **lump sugar** *n* azúcar *m* en terrones

lumpy ['lʌmpi] <-ier, -iest> *adj* (*custard,*

sauce) grumoso, -a; (*surface*) desigual

lunacy ['luːnəsi, *Am:* 'luː-] *n no pl* locura *f*

lunar ['luːnəʳ, *Am:* 'luːnɚ] *adj* lunar

lunatic ['luːnətɪk] I. *n* loco, -a *m, f* II. *adj* lunático, -a

lunatic asylum *n inf* manicomio *m*

lunch [lʌntʃ] I. *n* comida *f;* **to have** ~ comer ▶**to be out to** ~ estar en Babia II. *vi* comer

lunch break *n* descanso *m* para comer

luncheon ['lʌntʃən] *n form* comida *f*

luncheon meat *n* fiambre de cerdo en conserva **luncheon voucher** *n Brit* vale *m* de comida

lunch hour *n* hora *f* de comer **lunchtime** I. *n* hora *f* de comer II. *adj* (*concert*) de mediodía

lung [lʌŋ] *n* pulmón *m* ▶**to shout at the top of one's** ~**s** gritar a voz en grito

lung cancer *n* cáncer *m* de pulmón

lunge [lʌndʒ] I. *vi* **to** ~ **at sb** arremeter contra alguien II. *n* arremetida *f*

lupin(e) ['luːpɪn] *Am* lupino *m*, altramuz *m*

lurch [lɜːtʃ, *Am:* lɜːrtʃ] I. *vi* (*people*) tambalearse; (*car, train*) dar sacudidas II. <-es> *n* sacudida *f* ▶**to leave sb in the** ~ *inf* dejar a alguien colgado

lure [lʊəʳ, *Am:* lʊr] I. *n* **1.** (*attraction*) atractivo *m* **2.** (*bait*) cebo *m;* (*decoy*) señuelo *m* II. *vt* atraer; **to** ~ **sb into a trap** hacer que alguien caiga en una trampa

lurid ['lʊərɪd, *Am:* 'lʊrɪd] *adj* **1.** (*details*) escabroso, -a; (*language*) morboso, -a **2.** (*extremely bright*) chillón, -ona

lurk [lɜːk, *Am:* lɜːrk] *vi* esconderse

luscious ['lʌʃəs] *adj* **1.** (*fruit*) jugoso, -a **2.** *inf* (*girl, curves*) voluptuoso, -a; (*lips*) carnoso, -a

lush [lʌʃ] I. *adj* **1.** (*vegetation*) exuberante **2.** (*luxurious*) opulento, -a II. *n* <-shes> *Am, inf* borracho, -a *m, f*

lust [lʌst] *n* **1.** (*sexual desire*) lujuria *f* **2.** (*strong desire*) anhelo *m;* ~ **for sth** ansia de algo; ~ **for life** ansias de vivir

luster ['lʌstəʳ] *n no pl, Am s.* **lustre**

lustful ['lʌstfəl] *adj* lujurioso, -a

lustre ['lʌstə, *Am:* -tɚ] *n Aus, Brit* lustre *m*

lusty ['lʌsti] <-ier, -iest> *adj* (*person*) sano, -a; (*voice*) potente

lute [luːt] *n* laúd *m*

Lutheran ['luːθərən] I. *adj* luterano, -a II. *n* luterano, -a *m, f*

Luxembourg ['lʌksəmbɜːg, *Am:* -bɜːrg] *n* Luxemburgo *m*

Luxembourger *n* luxemburgués, -esa *m, f*

luxuriant [lʌgˈʒʊərɪənt, *Am:* -ˈʒʊrɪ-] *adj* (*hair*) abundante; (*vegetation*) exuberante

luxuriate [lʌgˈʒʊərɪeɪt, *Am:* -ˈʒʊrɪ-] *vi* **1.** (*person*) deleitarse; **to** ~ **in sth** disfrutar con algo **2.** (*plant*) crecer de manera exuberante

luxurious [lʌgˈʒʊərɪəs, *Am:* -ˈʒʊrɪ-] *adj* lujoso, -a

luxury ['lʌkʃəri, *Am:* -ʃɚ-] <-ies> *n* lujo *m;* ~ **flat** piso *m* de lujo

LW *n abbr of* **long wave** OL *f*

lychee ['laɪtʃiː, *Am:* 'liːtʃiː] *n* lichi *m*
Lycra® ['laɪkrə] *n* licra® *f*
lye [laɪ] *n* lejía *f*
lying ['laɪɪŋ] I. *n* mentiras *fpl* II. *adj* mentiroso, -a
lymph [lɪmpf] *n no pl* linfa *f*
lymphatic [lɪm'fætɪk, *Am:* -'fæt̬-] *adj* linfático, -a
lymph gland *n*, **lymph node** *n* ganglio *m* linfático
lynch [lɪntʃ] *vt* linchar
lynx [lɪŋks] <-(es)> *n* lince *m*
lynx-eyed [ˌlɪŋks'aɪd] *adj* con ojos de lince
lyre ['laɪə^r, *Am:* 'laɪr] *n* lira *f*
lyric ['lɪrɪk] I. *adj* lírico, -a II. *n* 1. (*poem*) poema *m* lírico 2. *pl* (*words for song*) letra *f*
lyrical ['lɪrɪkl] *adj* lírico, -a; **to get ~ about sth** *fig* entusiasmarse por algo
lyricism ['lɪrɪˌsɪzəm] *n no pl* LIT, MUS lirismo *m*
lyricist ['lɪrɪsɪst] *n* letrista *mf*

M

M, m [em] *n* M, m *f*; **~ for Mary** *Brit*, **~ for Mike** *Am* M de María
m 1. *abbr of* **metre** m 2. *abbr of* **mile** milla *f* 3. *abbr of* **million** millón *m* 4. *abbr of* **minutes** min. 5. *abbr of* **married** casado, -a
M *n* 1. *abbr of* **male** H 2. *abbr of* **medium** M
ma [mɑː] *n inf* mamá *f*
MA [ˌem'eɪ] *n abbr of* **Master of Arts** máster *m* (*de Humanidades o de Filosofía y Letras*); **Louie Sanders, MA** Louie Sanders, licenciado con máster
ma'am [mæm] = **madam** (*form of address*) señora *f*; (*when addressing royalty*) Majestad *f*
mac¹ [mæk] *n Brit, inf* (*coat*) impermeable *m*
mac² [mæk] *n Am, inf* (*form of address*) amigo
Mac [mæk] *n* INFOR *abbr of* **Macintosh** Mac *m*, Mac *f AmL*
macabre [mə'kɑːbrə] *adj* macabro, -a
macadam [mə'kædəm] *n* macadán *m*
macaroni [ˌmækə'rəʊni, *Am:* -ə'roʊ-] *n* macarrones *mpl*
macaroni cheese *n* macarrones *mpl* con queso
mace¹ [meɪs] *n* (*club*) maza *f*
mace² [meɪs] *n* (*spice*) macis *f*
Mace® [meɪs] *n no pl* gas *m* lacrimógeno (*en spray*)
Macedonia [ˌmæsɪ'dəʊniə, *Am:* -ə'doʊni-] *n* Macedonia *f*
Macedonian I. *adj* macedonio, -a II. *n* 1. (*person*) macedonio, -a *m, f* 2. LING macedonio *m*
Mach [mɑːk] *n no pl* PHYS Mach *m*
machete [mə'ʃeti, *Am:* -'ʃet̬-] *n* machete *m*

machine [mə'ʃiːn] I. *n* 1. (*mechanical device*) máquina *f* 2. (*system*) aparato *m* II. *vt* 1. (*metal*) trabajar a máquina 2. (*sewing*) coser a máquina
machine gun *n* ametralladora *f* **machine language** *n* INFOR lenguaje *m* máquina
machine-made *adj* hecho, -a a máquina
machine-readable *adj* INFOR legible por máquina
machinery [mə'ʃiːnəri] *n no pl* 1. *a. fig* (*machines*) maquinaria *f* 2. (*mechanism*) mecanismo *m*
machine tool *n* máquina *f* herramienta
machinist [mə'ʃiːnɪst] *n* maquinista *mf*
macho ['mætʃəʊ, *Am:* 'mɑːtʃoʊ] I. *n* machista *m* II. *adj* machista
mackerel ['mækrəl] <-(s)> *n* caballa *f*
mackintosh ['mækɪntɒʃ, *Am:* -tɑːʃ] <-es> *n Brit* impermeable *m*
macro ['mækrəʊ, *Am:* -roʊ] *n* INFOR macro *f*
macrobiotic [ˌmækrəʊbaɪ'ɒtɪk, *Am:* -roʊbaɪ'ɑːt̬ɪk] *adj* macrobiótico, -a
macrocosm ['mækrəʊkɒzəm, *Am:* -roʊkɑːzəm] *n* macrocosmos *m inv*
macroeconomics [ˌmækrəʊiːkə'nɒmɪks, *Am:* -roʊˌekə'nɑːmɪks] *n* macroeconomía *f*
mad [mæd] *adj Brit, inf* 1. (*insane: person*) loco, -a; (*idea*) disparatado, -a; **to go ~** volverse loco; **to drive sb ~** volver loco a alguien 2. *inf* (*enthusiastic*) **to be ~ about sb** estar loco por alguien; **she's ~ about chocolate** le encanta el chocolate 3. (*frantic*) frenético, -a
Madagascar [ˌmædə'gæskə^r, *Am:* -kɚ] *n* Madagascar *m*
madam ['mædəm] *n no pl* señora *f*
madden ['mædən] *vt* enfurecer
maddening *adj* exasperante
made [meɪd] *pp, pt of* **make**
made-to-measure [ˌmeɪdtə'meʒə^r, *Am:* -ɚ] *adj* (hecho, -a) a medida
made-up ['meɪdʌp] *adj* 1. (*wearing make-up*) maquillado, -a 2. (*invented*) inventado, -a
madhouse ['mædhaʊs] *n inf* manicomio *m*
madly ['mædli] *adv* 1. (*frantically*) frenéticamente 2. (*intensely*) terriblemente
madman ['mædmən] <-men> *n* loco *m*
madness ['mædnɪs] *n no pl* locura *f*, loquera *f AmL*
madwoman ['mædˌwʊmən] <-women> *n* loca *f*
maelstrom ['meɪlstrəm] *n a. fig* vorágine *f*
maestro ['maɪstrəʊ, *Am:* -stroʊ] *n* maestro *m*
MAFF *n Brit abbr of* **Ministry of Agricultural, Fisheries and Food** *ministerio de agricultura, pesca y alimentación*
Mafia ['mæfiə, *Am:* 'mɑː-] *n* mafia *f*
mag [mæg] *n inf abbr of* **magazine** revista *f*
magazine [ˌmægə'ziːn, *Am:* 'mægəziːn] *n* 1. (*periodical publication*) revista *f* 2. MIL (*of gun*) recámara *f* 3. MIL (*store*) polvorín *m*
maggot ['mægət] *n* gusano *m*

Magi ['meɪdʒaɪ] *npl* the ~ los Reyes Magos

magic ['mædʒɪk] I. *n no pl* magia *f;* **as if by ~** como por arte de magia II. *adj* mágico, -a

magical *adj* 1.(*power*) mágico, -a 2.(*extraordinary, wonderful*) fabuloso, -a

magically *adv* por arte de magia

magic carpet *n* alfombra *f* mágica

magician [məˈdʒɪʃən] *n* mago, -a *m, f*

magisterial [ˌmædʒɪˈstɪərɪəl, *Am:* -ˈstɪrɪ-] *adj form* 1.(*having complete authority*) magistral 2.(*imperious: tone, way*) autoritario, -a

magistrate ['mædʒɪstreɪt] *n Brit: juez que se ocupa de los delitos menores*

magnanimity [ˌmægnəˈnɪməti, *Am:* -t̬i] *n no pl, form* magnanimidad *f*

magnanimous [mægˈnænɪməs, *Am:* -əməs] *adj form* magnánimo, -a

magnate ['mægneɪt] *n* magnate *m*

magnesia [mægˈniːʃə, *Am:* -ʒə] *n no pl* magnesia *f*

magnesium [mægˈniːzɪəm] *n no pl* magnesio *m*

magnet ['mægnɪt] *n* imán *m;* **to act as a ~ for sth** *fig* atraer como un imán a algo

magnetic [mægˈnetɪk, *Am:* -ˈnet̬-] *adj* 1.(*force*) magnético, -a 2.(*personality*) atrayente

magnetic field *n* campo *m* magnético **magnetic pole** *n* polo *m* magnético

magnetise ['mægnətaɪz] *vi Brit, Aus s.* **magnetize**

magnetism ['mægnətɪzəm, *Am:* -t̬ɪ-] *n no pl* magnetismo *m*

magnetize ['mægnətaɪz] *vt* magnetizar; **to ~ sb** cautivar a alguien

magneto [mægˈniːtəʊ, *Am:* mægˈniːt̬oʊ] *n* TECH, AUTO magneto *f*

magnification [ˌmægnɪfɪˈkeɪʃən] *n no pl* (*lens*) aumento *m;* (*photograph*) ampliación *f*

magnificence [mægˈnɪfɪsəns] *n no pl* magnificencia *f*

magnificent [mægˈnɪfɪsnt] *adj* magnífico, -a

magnify ['mægnɪfaɪ] <-ie-> *vt* 1.(*make larger*) ampliar; (*voice*) amplificar 2.(*make worse: problem*) exagerar

magnifying glass *n* lupa *f*

magnitude ['mægnɪtjuːd, *Am:* -tuːd] *n no pl* 1.(*importance*) magnitud *f* 2.(*large size*) envergadura *f*

magnolia [mægˈnəʊlɪə, *Am:* -ˈnoʊljə] *n* magnolia *f*

magnum opus [ˌmægnəmˈəʊpəs, *Am:* -ˈoʊpəs] *n no pl, form* obra *f* maestra

magpie ['mægpaɪ] *n* (*bird*) urraca *f*

maharaja [ˌmɑːhəˈrɑːdʒə] *n* HIST maharajá *m*

mahogany [məˈhɒgəni, *Am:* -ˈhɑːgən-] I. *n no pl* caoba *f* II. *adj* de caoba

maid [meɪd] *n* 1.(*female servant*) criada *f*, mucama *f AmL;* (*in hotel*) camarera *f* 2. *liter* (*girl, young woman*) doncella *f*

maiden ['meɪdən] I. *n liter* doncella *f* II. *adj* 1.(*unmarried*) soltera 2.(*first: flight*) primero, -a; (*speech*) inaugural

maidenhair fern [ˌmeɪdənheəˈrfɜːn, *Am:* -herˈfɜːrn] *n* cabellos *mpl* de Venus

maiden name *n* apellido *m* de soltera

maiden speech *n* discurso *m* inaugural

mail¹ [meɪl] I. *n no pl a.* INFOR correo *m;* **electronic ~** INFOR correo electrónico; **incoming/outgoing ~** INFOR correo entrante/saliente; **to send sth through the ~** mandar [*o* enviar] algo por correo II. *vt* mandar [*o* enviar] por correo

mail² [meɪl] *n no pl* (*armour*) malla *f*

mailbag ['meɪlbæg] *n* saca *f* de correos

mailbox *n* 1. *Am* (*postbox*) buzón *m* 2. INFOR (*electronic*) ~ buzón *m* electrónico

mailing list *n* lista *f* de direcciones (*a las que se envía publicidad o información*)

mailman *n Am* (*postman*) cartero *m* **mail order** *n* venta *f* por correo **mailshot** *n Brit* mailing *m*

maim [meɪm] *vt* lisiar

main [meɪn] I. *adj* (*problem, reason, street*) principal; ~ **cable** cable *m* principal II. *n* 1. TECH (*pipe*) cañería *f* principal 2.(*cable*) cable *m* principal 3. *pl, Brit* ELEC, TECH red *f* de suministro ▶**in the** ~ en general

mainframe ['meɪnfreɪm] *n* INFOR ordenador *m* central, computadora *f* central *AmL*

mainland ['meɪnlənd] I. *n no pl* continente *m* II. *adj* ~ **China** China continental; ~ **Spain** España peninsular

mainline ['meɪnlaɪn] *vi, vt inf* chutar(se)

mainly ['meɪnli] *adv* principalmente

main office *n* oficina *f* central **main road** *n* carretera *f* general **mainsail** *n* vela *f* mayor **mainspring** *n* motivo *m* principal **mainstay** *n* pilar *m* **mainstream** I. *n no pl* corriente *f* dominante II. *adj* 1.(*ideology*) dominante 2.(*film, novel*) comercial

maintain [meɪnˈteɪn] *vt* 1.(*preserve, provide for*) mantener 2.(*claim*) sostener

maintenance ['meɪntənəns] *n no pl* 1.(*keeping, preservation*) mantenimiento *m* 2.(*alimony*) pensión *f* alimenticia

maisonette [ˌmeɪzəˈnet] *n Brit* dúplex *m*

maize [meɪz] *n no pl* maíz *m*, milpa *f AmL*, capi *m AmS*

Maj. *abbr of* **Major** comandante *mf*

majestic [məˈdʒestɪk] *adj* majestuoso, -a

majesty ['mædʒəsti] <-ies> *n no pl* majestuosidad *f;* **Her/His/Your Majesty** Su Majestad

major ['meɪdʒər, *Am:* -dʒɚ] I. *adj* 1.(*important, significant*) muy importante, fundamental; **a ~ problem** un gran problema 2.(*serious: illness*) grave 3. MUS mayor; **in C ~** en do mayor II. *n* 1. MIL comandante *mf* 2. *Am, Aus* UNIV especialidad *f*

Majorca [məˈjɔːkə, *Am:* -jɔːr-] *n* Mallorca *f*

Majorcan I. *adj* mallorquín, -ina II. *n* mallorquín, -ina *m, f*

major-general [ˌmeɪdʒəˈdʒenərəl, *Am:* -dʒɚ] *n* general *m* de división

majority [məˈdʒɒrəti, *Am:* -ˈdʒɔːrət̬i]

<-ies> *n* **1.**(*greater part/number*) mayoría *f;* **a narrow/large** ~ POL un margen estrecho/ amplio **2.** *no pl* (*full legal age*) mayoría *f* de edad; **to reach one's** ~ llegar a la mayoría de edad

make [meɪk] **I.** *vt* <made, made> **1.**(*produce: coffee, soup, supper*) hacer; (*product*) fabricar; (*clothes*) confeccionar; (*record*) grabar; (*film*) rodar; **to make sth out of sth** hacer algo con algo; **to** ~ **time** hacer tiempo **2.**(*cause: trouble*) causar; **to** ~ **noise/a scene** hacer ruido/una escena; **to** ~ **oneself look ridiculous** ponerse en ridículo; **to** ~ **a wonderful combination** ser una combinación fabulosa **3.**(*cause to be*) **to** ~ **sb sad** poner triste a alguien; **to** ~ **sb happy** hacer feliz a alguien; **to** ~ **oneself heard** hacerse oír; **to** ~ **oneself understood** hacerse entender; **to** ~ **sth easy** hacer que algo sea fácil; **to** ~ **something of oneself** llegar a ser algo **4.**(*perform, carry out*) **to** ~ **a call** hacer una llamada; **to** ~ **a decision** tomar una decision; **to** ~ **a reservation** hacer [*o* efectuar] una reserva **5.**(*force*) obligar; **to** ~ **sb do sth** hacer que alguien haga algo **6.**(*amount to, total*) ser; **two plus two** ~**s four** dos y dos son cuatro **7.**(*calculate*) **how much do you** ~ **the total?** ¿cuánto te da? **8.**(*earn, get*) **to** ~ **friends** hacer amigos; **to** ~ **money** hacer [*o* ganar] dinero; **to** ~ **profits/losses** tener beneficios/ pérdidas; **to** ~ **a living** ganarse la vida **9.** *inf* (*get to, reach*) **to** ~ **it to somewhere** llegar a un sitio; **to** ~ **it** alcanzar el éxito **10.**(*make perfect*) **that made my day!** ¡eso me alegró el día! ►**to** ~ **or break** sth ser el éxito o la ruina de algo; **to** ~ **do** (**with sth**) arreglárselas (con algo) **II.** *vi* (*amount to, total*) **today's earthquake** ~**s five since the beginning of the year** el terremoto de hoy es el quinto de este año ►**to** ~ **as if to do** sth fingir hacer algo **III.** *n* (*brand*) marca *f* ►**to** **be** **on the** ~ *inf* (*for money, power*) intentar sacar tajada; (*sexually*) intentar ligar

◆**make away with** *vt* **1.**(*kill*) **to** ~ **sb** acabar con alguien **2.**(*steal*) **to** ~ **sth** llevarse algo

◆**make for** *vt insep* **1.**(*head for*) dirigirse a **2.**(*help to promote*) **to** ~ **sth** contribuir a algo

◆**make of** *vt* **what do you** ~ **this book?** ¿qué te parece este libro?

◆**make off** *vi inf* largarse

◆**make out I.** *vi* **1.** *inf* (*succeed, cope: person*) arreglárselas **2.** *vulg* (*have sex*) **to** ~ **with sb** tirarse a alguien **II.** *vt* **1.** *inf* (*pretend*) **he made himself out to be rich** se hizo pasar por rico **2.**(*claim*) **to** ~ **that …** dar a entender que… **3.**(*discern: writing, numbers*) distinguir; (*in the distance*) divisar, visualizar *AmL* **4.**(*write out*) **to** ~ **a cheque** extender un cheque

◆**make over** *vt* **1.** LAW (*transfer: ownership*) transmitir **2.** *Am* (*alter, convert*) **to make sth over into sth** convertir algo en algo

◆**make up I.** *vt* **1.**(*invent*) inventar **2.**(*pre-*

pare) preparar; (*page*) componer **3.**(*produce*) producir **4.**(*compensate*) **to** ~ **for sth** compensar algo; **to** ~ **sth by sth** compensar algo con algo **5.** *Brit* (*complete*) **to** ~ **the numbers** hacer cuentas **6.**(*constitute*) constituir **7.**(*decide*) **to** ~ **one's mind** decidirse **II.** *vi* reconciliarse

◆**make up to** *vt* **1.to make it up to sb** compensar a alguien **2.** *Brit, Aus, inf* (*flatter*) tratar de ganarse el favor de

make-believe ['meɪkbɪˌliːv] **I.** *n no pl* (*pretence*) fingimiento *m;* **a world of** ~ un mundo de fantasía [*o* de ensueño] **II.** *adj* imaginario, -a; (*weapon*) de mentira; **a** ~ **world** un mundo de fantasía

maker ['meɪkə', *Am:* -kə] *n* **1.**(*manufacturer*) fabricante *mf* **2.**(*God*) **to meet one's Maker** entregar el alma a Dios

makeshift ['meɪkʃɪft] *adj* provisional

make-up ['meɪkʌp] *n no pl* **1.**(*structure*) estructura *f* **2.**(*character*) carácter *m* **3.**(*cosmetics*) maquillaje *m;* **to put on** ~ maquillarse; **to wear** ~ llevar maquillaje

make-up artist *n* maquillador(a) *m(f)*

making ['meɪkɪŋ] *n* **1.** *no pl* (*production*) producción *m;* (*of clothes*) confección *f;* (*of meals*) preparación *f* **2.** *pl* (*essential qualities*) **to have the** ~**s of sth** tener madera de algo ►**to** **be** **the** ~ **of sb** ser decisivo para alguien

maladjusted [ˌmælə'dʒʌstɪd] *adj* PSYCH inadaptado, -a

maladministration ['mælədˌmɪnɪ'streɪʃən] *n no pl, form* mala administración *f*

maladroit ['mælədrɔɪt] *adj form* torpe

Malagasy [ˌmælə'gæsi] **I.** *adj* malgache **II.** *n a.* LING malgache *m*

malaise [mæ'leɪz] *n no pl* malestar *m*

malapropism ['mæləprɒpɪzəm, *Am:* -prɑːpɪ-] *n* LING equivocación *f* de palabras

malaria [mə'leərɪə, *Am:* -'lerɪ-] *n no pl* malaria *f*

Malawi [mə'lɑːwi] *n* Malaui *m*

Malawian I. *adj* malauiano, -a **II.** *n* malauiano, -a *m, f*

Malaysia [mə'leɪzɪə, *Am:* -ʒə] *n* Malaisia *f*

Malaysian [mə'leɪzɪən, *Am:* -ʒən] **I.** *adj* malaisio, -a **II.** *n* malaisio, -a *m, f*

malcontent ['mælkəntənt] *n form* descontento, -a *m, f*

Maldives ['mɔldiːvz, *Am:* 'mældaɪvz] *npl* Maldivas *fpl*

male [meɪl] **I.** *adj* (*person, hormone*) masculino, -a; (*animal*) macho; ~ **chauvinism** machismo *m* **II.** *n* (*person*) varón *m;* (*animal*) macho *m*

malediction [ˌmælɪ'dɪkʃən, *Am:* -ə'-] *n* maldición *f*

malevolent [mə'levələnt] *adj liter* (*malicious*) malévolo, -a; (*deity, powers*) maligno, -a

malformation [ˌmælfɔː'meɪʃən] *n* MED deformación *f*

malfunction [ˌmæl'fʌŋkʃən] **I.** *vi* **1.**(*not*

work properly) funcionar mal **2.**(*stop functioning*) fallar **II.** *n* **1.**(*defective functioning*) mal funcionamiento *m* **2.**(*sudden stop*) fallo *m*

Mali ['mɑːli] *n* Mali *m*

Malian **I.** *adj* malinés, -esa **II.** *n* malinés, -esa *m*, *f*

malice ['mælɪs] *n no pl* malicia *f*; **with ~ aforethought** con premeditación

malicious [mə'lɪʃəs] *adj* malicioso, -a

malign [mə'laɪn] **I.** *adj form* maligno, -a **II.** *vt* calumniar

malignancy [mə'lɪgnənsi] <-ies> *n a.* MED malignidad *f*

malignant [mə'lɪgnənt] *adj* maligno, -a

malinger [mə'lɪŋgər, *Am:* -gɚ] *vi* fingir estar enfermo

malingerer [mə'lɪŋgərər, *Am:* -ɚɚ] *n* persona que finge estar enferma

mall [mɔːl] *n Am* centro *m* comercial

mallard ['mælɑːd, *Am:* -ɚd] <-(s)> *n* ánade *m* real

malleable ['mæliəbl] *adj* (*material*) maleable; (*person*) dócil

mallet ['mælɪt] *n* mazo *m*

mallow ['mæləʊ, *Am:* -oʊ] *n* malva *f*

malnutrition [ˌmælnjuː'trɪʃən, *Am:* -nuː'-] *n no pl* desnutrición *f*

malodorous [ˌmæl'əʊdərəs, *Am:* -'oʊ-] *adj form* maloliente

malpractice [ˌmæl'præktɪs] *n* mala práctica *f*; **medical ~** negligencia *f* médica

malt [mɔːlt] *n no pl* malta *f* **II.** *vt* maltear

Malta ['mɔːltə, *Am:* -t̬ə] *n* Malta *f*; *s. a.* **Republic of Malta**

Maltese [ˌmɔːl'tiːz] **I.** *adj* maltés, -esa; **~ cross** cruz *f* de Malta **II.** *n* maltés, -esa *m*, *f*

maltreat [ˌmæl'triːt] *vt form* maltratar

maltreatment *n no pl* malos tratos *mpl*

mamma [mə'mɑː] *n* mamá *f*

mammal ['mæməl] *n* mamífero *m*

mammary gland ['mæmərɪˌglænd] *n* glándula *f* mamaria

mammography [mæ'mɒgrəfi, *Am:* mə'mɑːgrə-] <-ies> *n* mamografía *f*

mammoth ['mæməθ] **I.** *adj* gigantesco, -a **II.** *n* mamut *m*

man [mæn] **I.** *n* <men> **1.**(*male human*) hombre *m* **2.**(*the human race*) ser *m* humano **3.**(*in games*) ficha *f* ▶**to talk (as) ~ to ~** hablar de hombre a hombre; **as one ~** unánimemente **II.** *vt* <-nn-> (*operate*) encargarse de; (*ship*) tripular; **to ~ a factory** contratar personal para una fábrica; **some volunteers ~ the phones** algunos voluntarios cogen el teléfono

manacle ['mænəkl] **I.** *n pl* esposas *fpl* **II.** *vt* esposar

manage ['mænɪdʒ] **I.** *vt* **1.**(*accomplish*) lograr; **to ~ to do sth** conseguir hacer algo **2.** *Brit* (*fit into one's schedule*) **to not ~ the time** no tener tiempo **3.** *a.* ECON (*control, be in charge of*) dirigir; (*money, time*) administrar

II. *vi* **to ~ on sth** arreglárselas con algo

manageable ['mænɪdʒəbl] *adj* (*vehicle*) manejable; (*person, animal*) dócil; (*amount*) razonable

management ['mænɪdʒmənt] *n* **1.** *no pl* (*direction*) manejo *m* **2.** *no pl a.* ECON dirección *f*; **to study ~** estudiar administración de empresas

management buy-out *n* compra *f* de acciones de una empresa por los gerentes **management consultant** *n* consultor(a) *m(f)* gerencial **management negotiator** *n* intermediario, -a *m*, *f* **management studies** *npl* estudios *mpl* de administración de empresas **management team** *n* equipo *m* directivo

manager ['mænɪdʒər, *Am:* -dʒɚ] *n* **1.** COM (*administrator*) administrador(a) *m(f)*; (*of business unit*) gerente *mf* **2.** (*of performer, artist*) representante *mf* artístico, -a

manageress [ˌmænɪdʒə'res, *Am:* 'mæn-] *n* (*woman in charge of a shop*) encargada *f*

managerial [ˌmænə'dʒɪərɪəl, *Am:* -'dʒɪri-] *adj* (*relating to a manager*) gerencial; (*directorial*) directivo, -a; **~ position** posición directiva; **~ skills** dotes *fpl* de mando

managing director *n Brit* director(a) *m(f)* general

Mancunian [mæn'kjuːnɪən, *Am:* mæn-] *n* habitante *mf* de Manchester

mandarin ['mændərɪn, *Am:* -dɚ-] *n* mandarín *m*

Mandarin ['mændərɪn, *Am:* -dɚ-] *n no pl* LING mandarín *m*

mandarin (orange) ['mændərɪn, *Am:* 'mændɚɪn] *n* mandarina *f*

mandate ['mændeɪt] **I.** *n* **1.** *a.* POL mandato *m* **2.**(*territory*) territorio *m* bajo mandato **II.** *vt* aprobar oficialmente

mandatory ['mændətri, *Am:* -tɔːri] *adj form* obligatorio, -a; **to make sth ~** imponer algo

mandible ['mændɪbl] *n* mandíbula *f*

mandolin(e) ['mændəlɪn] *n* MUS mandolina *f*, bandolina *f AmL*

mandrake ['mændreɪk] *n* mandrágora *f*

mandrill ['mændrɪl] *n* mandril *m*

mane [meɪn] *n* (*of horse*) crin *f*; (*of person, lion*) melena *f*

man-eater ['mæniːtər, *Am:* -t̬ɚ] *n inf* devorador(a) *m(f)* de hombres

maneuver [mə'nuːvər, *Am:* -vɚ] *n, vi, vt Am s.* **manoeuvre**

maneuverability [məˌnuːvərə'bɪləti, *Am:* -ət̬i] *n Am s.* **manoeuvrability**

maneuverable [mə'nuːvərəbl] *adj Am s.* **manoeuvrable**

manfully ['mænfʊli] *adv* valientemente

manganese ['mæŋgəniːz] *n no pl* manganeso *m*

mange [meɪndʒ] *n no pl* sarna *f*, zarate *f Hond*

mangel ['mæŋgl] *n*, **mangel-wurzel** *n* remolacha *f* forrajera

manger ['meɪndʒəʳ, *Am:* -dʒɚ] *n* pesebre *m*
mangetout [mɑ̃:ʒ'tu:] *n Brit* tirabeque *m*
mangle¹ ['mæŋgl] *vt* (*body, text*) mutilar
mangle² ['mæŋgl] *n* 1. *Brit* (*for wet clothes*) exprimidor *m* 2. *Am* (*iron*) planchadora *f* mecánica
mango ['mæŋgəʊ, *Am:* -goʊ] *n* <-(e)s> mango *m*
mangrove ['mæŋgrəʊv, *Am:* 'mæŋgroʊv] *n* mangle *m*
mangy ['meɪndʒi] <-ier, -iest> *adj* 1. (*animal*) sarnoso, -a 2. *inf* (*carpet, coat*) raído, -a
manhandle ['mænhændl] *vt* 1. (*treat roughly: person*) maltratar 2. (*move by hand: heavy object*) empujar
manhole ['mænhəʊl, *Am:* -hoʊl] *n* pozo *m* de visita, boca *f* de visita *Ven*
manhole cover *n* tapa *f* de registro
manhood ['mænhʊd] *n no pl* 1. (*adulthood*) edad *f* adulta 2. (*masculinity*) masculinidad *f*
man-hour ['mænaʊəʳ] *n* ECON hora-hombre *f*
manhunt ['mænhʌnt] *n* persecución *f*
mania ['meɪnɪə] *n* (*obsession*) obsesión *f*; PSYCH manía *f*
maniac ['meɪnɪæk] *n* maníaco, -a *m, f*; **football** ~ fanático del fútbol
maniacal [mə'naɪəkl] *adj inf* maníaco, -a
manic ['mænɪk] *adj* maníaco, -a
manic depression *n* manía *f* depresiva
manic depressive *adj* maníaco, -a depresivo, -a **manic psychosis** *n* PSYCH psicosis *f inv* maníaca
manicure ['mænɪkjʊəʳ, *Am:* -kjʊr] I. *n* manicura *f* II. *vt* **to** ~ **one's nails** hacerse la manicura
manicure set *n* estuche *m* de manicura
manicurist ['mænɪkjʊərɪst, *Am:* -kjʊr-] *n* manicuro, -a *m, f*, manicurista *mf AmL*
manifest ['mænɪfest] I. *adj form* manifiesto, -a; **to make sth** ~ poner algo de manifiesto II. *vt form* declarar; **to** ~ **symptoms of sth** manifestar síntomas de algo
manifestation [ˌmænɪfe'steɪʃən] *n form* manifestación *f*
manifestly ['mænɪfestli] *adv form* evidentemente
manifesto [ˌmænɪ'festəʊ, *Am:* -toʊ] <-stos *o* -stoes> *n* manifiesto *m*
manifold ['mænɪfəʊld, *Am:* -foʊld] I. *adj liter* múltiple II. *n* TECH, AUTO colector *m*; **exhaust** ~ colector de gases
manikin ['mænɪkɪn] *n* 1. (*model*) maniquí *m* 2. (*dwarf*) enano, -a *m, f*
manil(l)a envelope [mə'nɪlə 'envələʊp, *Am:* -loʊp] *n* sobre *m* manila **manil(l)a paper** *n no pl* papel *m* manila
manioc ['mænɪɒk, *Am:* -ɑ:k] *n* 1. (*cassava*) yuca *f* 2. (*flour*) tapioca *f*
manipulate [mə'nɪpjʊleɪt, *Am:* -jə-] *vt* manipular
manipulation [məˌnɪpjʊ'leɪʃən, *Am:* -jə'-] *n* manipulación *f*
manipulative [məˌnɪpjʊ'letɪv, *Am:* -jə'-] *adj*

manipulador(a)
manipulator [mə'nɪpjʊleɪtəʳ, *Am:* -jəleɪtɚ] *n* manipulador(a) *m(f)*
mankind [ˌmæn'kaɪnd] *n no pl* humanidad *f*
manky [ˌmæŋki] <-ier, -iest> *adj Brit, inf* (*clothes*) sobado, -a; (*sofa, carpet*) sucio, -a
manliness ['mænlɪnəs] *n no pl* hombría *f*
manly ['mænli] <-ier, -iest> *adj* varonil
man-made ['mænmeɪd] *adj* (*lake*) artificial; (*fibre*) sintético, -a
manna ['mænə] *n no pl* maná *m*
manned [mænd] *adj* AVIAT tripulado, -a
mannequin ['mænɪkɪn] *n* 1. (*dummy*) maniquí *m* 2. (*person*) modelo *mf*
manner ['mænəʳ, *Am:* -ɚ] *n no pl* 1. (*way, fashion*) manera *f*; **in the** ~ **of sb** al estilo de alguien; **in a** ~ **of speaking** por así decirlo 2. (*behaviour*) ~**s** modales *mpl*; **to teach sb** ~**s** enseñar a alguien a comportarse; **it's bad** ~**s to ...** es de mala educación... 3. *form* (*kind, type*) clase *f*; **what** ~ **of man is he?** ¿qué tipo de hombre es?; **all** ~ **of ...** toda clase de... ►**as if to the** ~ **born** como si hubiera nacido para ello; **not by any** ~ **of means** *Brit* de ningún modo
mannered *adj* amanerado, -a
mannerism ['mænərɪzəm] *n* amaneramiento *m*
mannikin ['mænɪkɪn] *n s.* **manikin**
mannish ['mænɪʃ] *adj* hombruno, -a
manoeuvrability [mə'nu:vrəbɪləti] *n no pl, Brit, Aus* maniobrabilidad *f*
manoeuvrable [mə'nu:vrəbl] *adj Brit, Aus* maniobrable
manoeuvre [mə'nu:vəʳ, *Am:* -vɚ] *Brit, Aus* I. *n a.* MIL maniobra *f*; **army** ~**s** maniobras militares II. *vt* hacer maniobrar; **to** ~ **sb into doing sth** embaucar a alguien para que haga algo III. *vi* maniobrar
manometer [mə'nemɪtəʳ, *Am:* mə'nɑ:mətɚ] *n* manómetro *m*
manor ['mænəʳ, *Am:* -ɚ] *n* 1. (*house*) casa *f* solariega 2. HIST (*territory*) feudo *m*
manpower ['mænpaʊəʳ, *Am:* -ɚ] *n no pl* mano de obra *f*
manqué ['mɑ̃ŋkeɪ] *adj form* frustrado, -a; **a writer** ~ un escritor frustrado
manse [mæns] *n Scot:* casa de un pastor protestante
manservant ['mænsɜ:vənt, *Am:* -sɜːr-] *n* criado *m*
mansion ['mænʃən] *n* mansión *f*
man-sized *adj* muy grande
manslaughter ['mænslɔ:təʳ, *Am:* -slɑ:t̬ɚ] *n no pl* homicidio *m* involuntario
mantelpiece ['mæntlpi:s] *n* repisa *f* de la chimenea
mantis ['mæntɪs] *n* mantis *f* religiosa
mantle ['mæntl] *n* 1. *liter* (*cloak, layer*) manto *m*; **a** ~ **of snow** un manto de nieve 2. (*of gas lamp*) camisa *f*
man-to-man *adj* franco, -a
mantra ['mæntrə] *n* mantra *m*

M

manual ['mænjʊəl] I. *adj* manual; ~ **dexterity** habilidad manual II. *n* manual *m;* **instructions** ~ manual de instrucciones

manual labour *n* trabajo *m* manual

manually ['mænjʊəli] *adv* manualmente, con las manos

manual transmission *n* AUTO transmisión *f* manual **manual work** *n* trabajo *m* manual **manual worker** *n* trabajador(a) *m(f)*

manufacture [ˌmænjʊ'fæktʃəʳ, *Am:* -tʃəʳ] I. *vt* 1. *(produce)* fabricar; ~**d goods** artículos manufacturados 2. *(invent)* inventar; **to** ~ **an excuse/a story** inventar una excusa/un cuento II. *n* 1. *no pl (production)* manufactura *f* 2. *(product)* producto *m* manufacturado

manufacturer [ˌmænjʊ'fækʃərəʳ, *Am:* -əʳ] *n* fabricante *mf;* ~**'s label** etiqueta *f* de fábrica; **to send sth back to the** ~ devolver algo a la fábrica

manufacturing [ˌmænjʊ'fækʃərɪŋ, *Am:* -jə'-] *adj (region, firm)* industrial; ~ **industry** industria *f* manufacturera

manure [mə'njʊəʳ, *Am:* -'nʊr] *n no pl* abono *m*

manuscript ['mænjʊskrɪpt] *n* manuscrito *m*

many ['meni] <more, most> I. *adj* muchos, muchas; ~ **flowers** muchas flores; ~ **books** muchos libros; **how** ~ **bottles?** ¿cuántas botellas?; **too/so** ~ **people** demasiada/tanta gente; **one too** ~ uno de más; ~ **times** muchas veces; **as** ~ **as** ... tantos como... II. *pron* muchos, muchas; ~ **are here** hay muchos; ~ **think that** ... muchos piensan que...; **so** ~ tantos/tantas; **too** ~ demasiados/demasiadas III. *n* **the** ~ la mayoría; **a good** ~ un gran número

many-sided [ˌmenɪ'saɪdɪd] *adj* polifacético, -a

Maoism ['maʊɪzm] *n no pl* maoísmo *m*

Maoist ['maʊɪzt] I. *n* maoísta *mf* II. *adj* maoísta

Maori ['maʊri] I. *n* maorí *mf* II. *adj* maorí

map [mæp] I. *n* 1. *(of region, stars)* mapa *m;* *(of town)* plano *m;* ~ **of the world** mapamundi *m;* **road** ~ mapa de carreteras 2. *(simple diagram)* plano *m* ►**to blow** [*o* **wipe**] **sth off the** ~ borrar algo del mapa; **to put a town on the** ~ dar a conocer a un pueblo II. <-pp-> *vt* trazar un mapa de

◆**map out** *vt* planear, proyectar; **to** ~ **a route** planear una ruta; **to** ~ **a course/a plan/a strategy** proyectar un curso/un plan/una estrategia; **his future is all mapped out for him** tiene la vida planificada

maple ['meɪpl] *n* 1. *(tree)* arce *m* 2. *no pl (wood)* madera *f* de arce

maple leaf *n* hoja *f* de arce **maple sugar** *n no pl* azúcar *m* de arce **maple syrup** *n no pl* jarabe *m* de arce

map maker *n* cartógrafo, -a *m, f* **map making** *n* cartografía *f*

mar [maːʳ, *Am:* maːr] <-rr-> *vt (ruin)* echar a perder; *(enjoyment, day)* aguar

Mar *n abbr of* March marzo *m*

maraschino cherry [ˌmærə'ʃiːnəʊ-, *Am:* ˌmerə'ʃiːnoʊ-] *n* guinda *f* confitada

marathon ['mærəθən, *Am:* 'merəθɑːn] *n a. fig* maratón *m*

marathon runner *n* maratonista *mf*

maraud [mə'rɔːd, *Am:* -'rɑːd] *vi* merodear

marauder *n* merodeador(a) *m(f)*

marauding *adj* merodeador(a)

marble ['maːbl, *Am:* 'maːr-] *n* 1. *no pl (stone)* mármol *m;* ~ **table** mesa *f* de mármol 2. *(glass ball)* canica *f*, bolita *f CSur;* metra *f Ven;* **to play** ~**s** jugar a las canicas ►**to lose one's** ~**s** *inf* perder la cabeza

marble cake *n pastel de molde con chocolate*

marbled *adj* veteado, -a; **to be** ~ **with sth** estar veteado con algo

march [maːtʃ, *Am:* maːrtʃ] I. <-es> *n a.* MIL marcha *f;* **funeral** ~ marcha fúnebre; **a 20 km** ~ una marcha de 20 km; **to be on the** ~ estar en marcha; **to be within a day's** ~ estar a un día de camino II. *vi a.* MIL marchar; *(parade)* desfilar; **to** ~ **into a country** invadir un país III. *vt (compel to walk)* **to** ~ **sb off** hacer marchar a alguien

March [maːtʃ, *Am:* maːrtʃ] *n* marzo *m; s. a.* April

marching orders ['maːtʃɪŋˌɔːdəz, *Am:* 'maːrtʃɪŋˌɔːrdəz] *n Brit, inf* **to get one's** ~ ser despedido; **to give sb his** ~ despedir a alguien (del trabajo)

Mardi Gras [ˌmaːdi'graː, *Am:* 'maːrdiˌgraː] *n* martes *m* de carnaval

---

Mardi Gras es el equivalente americano del Carnaval. Esta fiesta la trajeron los colonizadores franceses de New Orleans (en lo que posteriormente será el estado de Louisiana). Aunque la mayoría de las personas piensan en New Orleans cuando escuchan la expresión **Mardi Gras**, lo cierto es que también se celebra en otros lugares como Biloxi/Mississippi y Mobile/Alabama. En New Orleans los **krewes** (agrupaciones de carnaval) celebran muchas fiestas y bailes durante estos días y el martes de carnaval salen en cabalgata.

---

mare ['meəʳ] *n* yegua *f*

mare's nest *n* hallazgo *m* ilusorio

margarine [ˌmaːdʒə'riːn, *Am:* 'maːrdʒəʳɪn] *n no pl* margarina *f*

marge [maːdʒ, *Am:* maːrdʒ] *n Brit, inf abbr of* margarine margarina *f*

margin ['maːdʒɪn, *Am:* 'maːr-] *n a.* TYPO margen *m;* **profit** ~ margen de ganancia; **narrow** [*o* **tight**] ~ margen reducido; ~ **of error** margen de error

marginal ['maːdʒɪnl, *Am:* 'maːr-] *adj* marginal; **to be of** ~ **interest** ser de interés secundario; **marginal land** tierra *f* marginal; ~ **constituency** *Brit, Aus* POL *circunscripción electoral* *de escasa mayoría*

marginalise *vt Brit, Aus,* **marginalize** ['mɑːdʒɪnəlaɪz, *Am:* 'mɑːr-] *vt* marginar

marigold ['mærɪɡəʊld, *Am:* 'merɪɡoʊld] *n* caléndula *f*

marihuana *n,* **marijuana** [ˌmærɪ'wɑːnə, *Am:* ˌmerɪ'-] *n no pl* marihuana *f*

marina [mə'riːnə] *n* puerto *m* deportivo

marinade [ˌmærɪ'neɪd, *Am:* ˌmer-] *n* escabeche *m*

marinate ['mærɪneɪt, *Am:* 'mer-] *vt* marinar

marine [mə'riːn] **I.** *adj* (*life*) marino, -a; (*insurance*) marítimo, -a; (*engineer*) naval **II.** *n* infante *m* de marina

marine biologist *n* biólogo, -a *m, f* marino, -a **Marine Corps** *n* Infantería *f* de Marina (EE.UU.)

mariner ['mærɪnəʳ, *Am:* 'merɪnɚ] *n liter* marinero, -a *m, f*

marionette [ˌmærɪə'net, *Am:* ˌmer-] *n* marioneta *f*

marital ['mærɪtəl, *Am:* 'merɪt̬əl] *adj* marital; ~ **bliss** felicidad *f* marital; ~ **problems** problemas *mpl* conyugales

marital status *n form* estado *m* civil

maritime ['mærɪtaɪm, *Am:* 'mer-] *adj form* marítimo, -a

maritime law *n* código *m* marítimo

marjoram ['mɑːdʒərəm, *Am:* 'mɑːrdʒɚəm] *n no pl* mejorana *f*

mark¹ [mɑːk, *Am:* mɑːrk] **I.** *n* **1.** (*spot, stain*) mancha *f;* (*scratch*) marca *f;* (*trace*) huella *f;* **to leave one's** ~ dejar sus huellas en algo/alguien **2.** (*written sign*) raya *f* **3.** SCHOOL nota *f;* **to get full** ~**s** *Brit, Aus* obtener las máximas calificaciones **4.** *no pl* (*required standard*) norma *f;* **to be up to the** ~ ser satisfactorio; **to not feel up to the** ~ no sentirse a la altura de las circunstancias **5.** (*target*) blanco *m;* **to hit the** ~ dar en el blanco **6.** (*starting line*) línea *f* de partida; **on your** ~**s, get set, go!** ¡preparados, listos, ya! **7.** LING signo *m;* **punctuation** ~ signo de puntuación ▶**there are no** ~**s for guessing that** no hace falta ser un genio para adivinar eso; **to be quick/slow off the** ~ ser rápido/lento de reflejos **II.** *vt* **1.** (*make a spot, stain*) manchar **2.** (*make written sign, indicate*) marcar; **I've** ~**ed the route on the map** he señalado la ruta en el mapa; **the bottle was** ~**ed 'poison'** la botella llevaba la etiqueta 'veneno' **3.** (*characterize*) distinguir; **to** ~ **sb as sth** distinguir a alguien como algo **4.** (*commemorate*) conmemorar; **to** ~ **the beginning/end of sth** conmemorar el principio/final de algo; **to** ~ **the 10th anniversary** celebrar el 10º aniversario **5.** SCHOOL puntuar **6.** SPORTS (*opponent*) marcar

◆**mark down** *vt* **1.** (*reduce: prices*) reducir **2.** *Brit* SCHOOL **to mark sb down** bajar las calificaciones de alguien **3.** (*jot down*) apuntar **4.** *fig* (*assess*) **to mark sb down as sth** catalogar a alguien como algo

◆**mark off** *vt* **1.** (*divide land from adjacent areas*) demarcar **2.** (*cross off*) tachar

◆**mark out** *vt* **1.** (*distinguish*) distinguir **2.** *Brit* (*indicate boundary*) trazar

◆**mark up** *vt* aumentar

mark² [mɑːk, *Am:* mɑːrk] *n* FIN marco *m*

marked [mɑːkt, *Am:* mɑːrkt] *adj* **1.** (*improvement, difference*) marcado, -a; (*contrast*) acusado, -a **2.** (*with distinguishing marks*) marcado, -a **3.** (*liable to be attacked*) **to be a** ~ **man/woman** estar en el punto de mira

markedly ['mɑːkədli, *Am:* 'mɑːrk-] *adv* notablemente

marker ['mɑːkəʳ, *Am:* 'mɑːrkɚ] *n* **1.** (*sign, symbol*) señal *f* **2.** SCHOOL, UNIV corrector(a) *m(f)* **3.** (*pen*) rotulador *m,* marcador *m Arg*

market ['mɑːkɪt, *Am:* 'mɑːr-] **I.** *n* mercado *m,* recova *f And, Urug;* **the coffee** ~ el mercado del café; **housing** ~ mercado inmobiliario; **job** ~ mercado de trabajo; **stock** ~ bolsa *f* de valores; **to put sth on the** ~ poner algo a la venta; **on the** ~ a la venta **II.** *vt* comercializar

marketable *adj* comercial; ~ **commodities** productos *mpl* comerciales

market day *n Brit* día *f* de mercado **market forces** *npl* fuerzas *fpl* del mercado **market garden** *n Brit, Aus* huerto *m* **market gardener** *n Brit, Aus* hortelano, -a *m, f*

marketing *n no pl* **1.** (*discipline*) marketing *m* **2.** (*commercialization*) comercialización *f*

marketing department *n* departamento *m* de marketing **marketing strategy** *n* estrategia *f* de mercado

market leader *n* líder *mf* del mercado **marketplace** *n* **1.** ECON mercado *m* **2.** (*square*) plaza *f* (del mercado) **market price** *n* precio *m* de mercado **market research** *n no pl* estudio *m* de mercado **market researcher** *n* investigador(a) *m(f)* de mercado **market town** *n Brit* población *f* con mercado **market trader** *n* comerciante *mf*

marking *n* (*identification*) señal *f;* (*on animal*) pinta *f*

marking ink *n no pl* tinta *f* indeleble

marksman ['mɑːksmən, *Am:* 'mɑːrks-] <-men> *n* tirador *m*

marksmanship ['mɑːksmənʃɪp, *Am:* 'mɑːrks-] *n no pl* puntería *f*

markswoman ['mɑːkswʊmən, *Am:* 'mɑːrks-] <-women> *n* tiradora *f*

mark-up ['mɑːkʌp, *Am:* 'mɑːrk-] *n* margen *m* de ganancia

marmalade ['mɑːməleɪd, *Am:* 'mɑːr-] *n no pl* mermelada *f* (*de cítricos*)

marmalade cat *n Brit:* gato con vetas de color naranja, amarillo y marrón

marmoset ['mɑːməzet, *Am:* 'mɑːrmə-] *n* tití *m*

maroon¹ [mə'ruːn] **I.** *n no pl* granate *m* **II.** *adj* granate

maroon² [mə'ruːn] *vt* abandonar

marquee [mɑː'kiː, *Am:* mɑːr-] *n* **1.** *Brit, Aus*

(*tent*) carpa *f* **2.** *Am* (*rooflike structure*) marquesina *f*

marriage ['mærɪdʒ, *Am:* 'mer-] *n* **1.** (*wedding*) boda *f* **2.** (*relationship, state*) matrimonio *m;* **arranged** ~ matrimonio arreglado; **related by** ~ emparentado por matrimonio; **he is a relative by** ~ es pariente político **3.** *fig* (*of organisations*) unión *f*

marriageable *adj* casadero, -a

marriage broker *n* casamentero, -a *m, f*
marriage bureau *n Brit* agencia *f* matrimonial **marriage certificate** *n* acta *f* matrimonial **marriage contract** *n* contrato *m* matrimonial **marriage counselling** *n Am, Aus* orientación *f* matrimonial

marriage guidance *n Brit* orientación *f* matrimonial **marriage guidance counsellor** *n Brit* consejero,-a *m, f* matrimonial **marriage guidance office** *n Brit* agencia *f* de orientación matrimonial

marriage licence *n* licencia *f* matrimonial **marriage of convenience** *n* matrimonio *m* de conveniencia **marriage vow** *n* voto *m* matrimonial

married *adj* (*person*) casado, -a; ~ **couple** matrimonio *m;* ~ **life** vida *f* conyugal; **to be** ~ **to sth** *fig* estar atado a algo

married name *n* apellido *m* de casada

marrow[1] ['mærəʊ, *Am:* 'meroʊ] *n Brit, Aus* (*vegetable*) calabacín *m*

marrow[2] ['mærəʊ, *Am:* 'meroʊ] *n* MED médula *f;* **to the** ~ *fig* hasta los tuétanos

marrow bone *n* hueso *m* medular

marrowfat pea [,mærəʊfæt'pi:, *Am:* 'meroʊ-] *n* guisante *m* de semilla grande

marry ['mæri, *Am:* 'mer-] <-ie-> **I.** *vt* **1.** (*become husband or wife*) **to** ~ **sb** casarse con alguien; **to get married** (**to sb**) casarse (con alguien) **2.** (*priest*) casar **II.** *vi* casarse; **to** ~ **above/beneath oneself** casarse con alguien de clase superior/inferior; **to** ~ **into a wealthy family** emparentar con una familia rica

Mars [mɑːz, *Am:* mɑːrz] *n no pl* Marte *m*

Marseilles [,mɑː'seɪ, *Am:* ,mɑːr] *n* Marsella *f*

marsh [mɑːʃ, *Am:* mɑːrʃ] <-es> *n* ciénaga *f*

marshal ['mɑːʃl, *Am:* 'mɑːr-] **I.** <*Brit:* -ll-, *Am:* -l-> *vt* ordenar **II.** *n* **1.** (*at public event*) maestro *m* de ceremonias **2.** *Am* LAW alguacil *mf* **3.** MIL mariscal *m;* **field** ~ mariscal de campo **4.** *Am* (*police or fire officer*) comisario *m*

marsh gas *n* metano *m*

marshland ['mɑːʃlænd, *Am:* 'mɑːrʃ-] *n* pantanal *m*

marshmallow ['mɑːʃmæləʊ, *Am:* 'mɑːrʃ-] *n* **1.** (*sweet*) dulce *m* de malvavisco, carlotina *f Ven* **2.** (*plant*) malvavisco *m* **3.** *Am, fig* (*weak person*) blando, -a *m, f*

marshy ['mɑːʃi, *Am:* 'mɑːr-] <-ier, -iest> *adj* pantanoso, -a

marsupial [mɑː'suːpɪəl, *Am:* mɑːr'-] **I.** *n* marsupial *m* **II.** *adj* marsupial

marten ['mɑːtɪn, *Am:* 'mɑːrtn] *n* marta *f*

martial ['mɑːʃəl, *Am:* 'mɑːr-] *adj* marcial

martial arts *n* SPORTS artes *mpl* marciales **martial law** *n* ley *f* marcial; **to impose** ~ **on a country** imponer la ley marcial en un país

Martian ['mɑːʃən, *Am:* 'mɑːr-] **I.** *adj* marciano, -a **II.** *n* marciano, -a *m, f*

martin ['mɑːtɪn, *Am:* 'mɑːrtn] *n* avión *m*

martinet [,mɑːtɪ'net, *Am:* ,mɑːrtə'-] *n form* rigorista *mf*

Martinique [,mɑːtɪ'niːk, *Am:* ,mɑːrtən'iːk] *n* Martinica *f*

martyr ['mɑːtəʳ, *Am:* 'mɑːrtɚ] **I.** *n* mártir *mf;* **to be a** ~ **to arthritis** *fig* estar martirizado por la artritis **II.** *vt* martirizar; ~**ed saint** santo *m* mártir

martyrdom ['mɑːtədəm, *Am:* 'mɑːrtɚ-] *n no pl* martirio *m;* **to suffer** ~ sufrir pena de martirio

marvel ['mɑːvl, *Am:* 'mɑːr-] **I.** *n* maravilla *f;* **it's a** ~ **to me how ...** me maravilla cómo... **II.** <*Brit:* -ll-, *Am:* -l-> *vi* **to** ~ **that ...** maravillarse de que... +*subj;* **to** ~ **at sb/sth** maravillarse de alguien/algo

marvellous *adj* *Brit,* **marvelous** ['mɑːvələs, *Am:* 'mɑːr-] *adj Am* maravilloso, -a; **to feel** ~ sentirse espléndido

Marxism ['mɑːksɪzm, *Am:* 'mɑːrk-] *n no pl* marxismo *m*

Marxist ['mɑːksɪst, *Am:* 'mɑːrk-] **I.** *n* marxista *mf* **II.** *adj* marxista

marzipan ['mɑːzɪpæn, *Am:* 'mɑːr-] *n no pl* mazapán *m*

masc. *adj abbr of* **masculine**

mascara [mæ'skɑːrə, *Am:* -'skerə] *n no pl* rímel *m*

mascot ['mæskət, *Am:* -kɑːt] *n* mascota *f*

masculine ['mæskjəlɪn] *adj a.* LING masculino, -a

masculinity [,mæskjə'lɪnəti, *Am:* ,mæskjə-'lɪnəti] *n* masculinidad *f*

mash [mæʃ] **I.** *n no pl* **1.** *Brit, inf* (*mashed potato*) puré *m* de patata **2.** AGR (*animal feed*) afrecho *m* **II.** *vt* machacar; **to** ~ **potatoes** hacer puré de patatas

◆mash up *vt* **1.** GASTR triturar **2.** *Am* (*damage*) despachurrar

mask [mɑːsk, *Am:* mæsk] **I.** *n a. fig* máscara *f;* (*only covering eyes*) antifaz *m;* **oxygen** ~ máscara de oxígeno **II.** *vt* enmascarar; **to** ~ **sth with sth** encubrir algo con algo; **to** ~ **the statistics** ocultar las estadísticas

◆mask out *vt* PHOT, TYPO ocultar

masked *adj* enmascarado, -a

masked ball *n* baile *m* de máscaras

masking tape *n no pl* cinta *f* adhesiva protectora

masochism ['mæsəkɪzəm] *n no pl* masoquismo *m*

masochist ['mæsəkɪst] *n* masoquista *mf*

masochistic ['mæsəkɪstik] *adj* masoquista

mason ['meɪsn] *n* **1.** (*stone-cutter*) cantero

m **2.** *Am* (*bricklayer*) albañil *m* **3.** (*freemason*) masón, -ona *m, f*

masonic [məˈsɒnɪk, *Am:* -ˈsɑːnɪk] *adj* masónico, -a

masonic lodge *n* logia *f* masónica
masonic order *n* sociedad *f* de los Masones

masonry [ˈmeɪsnri] *n no pl* **1.** (*occupation*) albañilería *f* **2.** (*stonework*) mampostería *f* **3.** (*freemasonry*) masonería *f*

masquerade [ˌmɑːskəˈreɪd] I. *n* mascarada *f* II. *vi* to ~ as sth hacerse pasar por algo

mass [mæs] I. *n no pl* **1.** *a.* PHYS masa *f* **2.** (*formless substance*) bulto *m* **3.** (*large quantity*) montón *m;* **to be a ~ of contradictions** estar lleno de contradicciones; **the ~ of the people** la muchedumbre; **the ~ of the population** la mayoría de la población II. *vi* (*gather*) juntarse; (*troops*) concentrarse

Mass [mæs] *n* misa *f;* **to attend ~** ir a misa; **to celebrate a ~** oficiar una misa

massacre [ˈmæsəkəʳ, *Am:* -kɚ] I. *n* **1.** (*killing*) masacre *f* **2.** *fig* (*defeat*) aniquilamiento *m* II. *vt* **1.** (*kill*) masacrar **2.** *fig* (*defeat*) aniquilar

massage [ˈmæsɑːdʒ, *Am:* məˈ-] I. *n* masaje *m;* **water ~** hidromasaje *m;* **to give sb a ~** dar a alguien un masaje II. *vt* **1.** dar masajes a **2.** *fig* manipular

massage parlor *n Am,* **massage parlour** *n Brit* salón *m* de relax

masseur [mæˈsɜːʳ, *Am:* -ˈsɜːr] *n* masajista *m*
masseuse [mæˈsɜːz] *n* masajista *f*
mass grave *n* fosa *f* común
massif [ˈmæsɪv] *n* GEO macizo *m*
massive [ˈmæsɪv] *adj* masivo, -a, enorme; **~ amounts of money** grandes cantidades de dinero

mass market *n* mercado *m* de masas **mass-market** *adj* de alto consumo **mass media** *n* **the ~** los medios de comunicación de masas **mass meeting** *n* mitin *m* **mass murder** *n* asesino *m* múltiple **mass murderer** *n* asesino, -a *m, f* múltiple **mass-produce** *vt* fabricar en serie **mass production** *n* fabricación *f* en serie **mass tourism** *n no pl* turismo *m* de masas **mass unemployment** *n no pl* paro *m* masivo

mast [mɑːst, *Am:* mæst] *n* **1.** NAUT mástil *m* **2.** (*flag pole*) asta *m;* **at half ~** a media asta **3.** RADIO, TV antena *f*

mastectomy [ˌmæsˈtektəmi] <-ies> *n* mastectomía *f*

master [ˈmɑːstəʳ, *Am:* ˈmæstɚ] I. *n* **1.** (*of house*) señor *m;* (*of slave*) amo *m;* (*of dog*) dueño *m;* **the young ~** el señorito **2.** (*one who excels*) maestro *m;* **~ craftsman** maestro *m;* **to be a ~ of sth** ser experto en algo **3.** (*instructor*) instructor *m;* **dancing/singing ~** instructor de baile/canto; **fencing ~** maestro de esgrima **4.** *Brit* (*schoolteacher*) profesor *m* **5.** (*master copy*) original *m* ▶**to be one's** <u>own</u> **~** no depender de nadie II. *vt* **1.** (*cope with*) vencer; **to ~ one's fear of flying** superar el miedo a volar **2.** (*become proficient at*) dominar

master bedroom *n* dormitorio *m* principal **master class** <-es> *n* clase *f* magistral **master copy** <-ies> *n* original *m*

masterful [ˈmɑːstəfəl, *Am:* ˈmæstɚ-] *adj* **1.** (*authoritative*) autoritario, -a **2.** (*skilful*) magistral

master key *n* llave *f* maestra

masterly [ˈmɑːstəli, *Am:* ˈmæstɚ-] *adj* magistral

mastermind [ˈmɑːstəmaɪnd, *Am:* ˈmæstɚ-] I. *n* cerebro *m* II. *vt* (*activity*) planear; (*crime*) ser el cerebro de

Master of Arts *n* licenciado, -a *m, f* con máster (*en Humanidades o en Filosofía y Letras*) **Master of Ceremonies** *n* maestro *m* de ceremonias

masterpiece *n* obra *f* maestra **master plan** *n* plan *m* maestro **master race** *n* raza *f* superior

Master's *n,* **Master's degree** *n* máster *m*

En Gran Bretaña se llama **Master's degree** al grado académico que se obtiene al finalizar una carrera tras la defensa de una tesina (**dissertation**). El **Master's degree** recibe distintos nombres según las disciplinas: **MA (Master of Arts), MSc (Master of Science), Mlitt (Master of Letters)** y **Mphil (Master of Philosophy)**. Sin embargo en Escocia con la expresión **MA** se designa un primer grado académico.

---

masterstroke *n* toque *m* magistral **master switch** <-es> *n* interruptor *m* principal **masterwork** *n s.* **masterpiece**

mastery [ˈmɑːstəri, *Am:* ˈmæstɚ-] *n no pl* (*skill*) maestría *f;* (*sway*) dominio *m*

masticate [ˈmæstɪkeɪt] *vt* masticar

mastication [ˌmæstɪˈkeɪʃən] *n no pl* masticación *m*

mastiff [ˈmæstɪf] *n* mastín *m*

mastitis [mæˈstaɪtɪs, *Am:* -t̬ɪs] *n no pl* mastitis *f*

masturbate [ˈmæstəbeɪt, *Am:* -t̬ə-] I. *vi* masturbarse II. *vt* masturbar

masturbation [ˌmæstəˈbeɪʃən, *Am:* -t̬ə'-] *n no pl* masturbación *f*, pascuala *f Méx*

mat [mæt] *n* **1.** (*on floor*) estera *f;* (*decorative*) tapiz *m;* **bath ~** alfombra *f* de baño **2.** (*on table*) salvamanteles *m inv* **3.** SPORTS (*in gymnastics*) colchoneta *f* **4.** (*thick layer of grass, hair*) maraña *f* ▶**to be** <u>on</u> **the ~** estar en apuros

matador [ˈmætədɔːʳ] *n* matador *m*

match¹ [mætʃ] <-es> *n* (*for making fire*) cerilla *f*, fósforo *m*, cerillo *m Méx;* **box of ~es** caja de fósforos

match² [mætʃ] I. *n* **1.** (*competitor*) contrincante *mf;* **to be a good ~ for sb** poder competir con alguien; **to be no ~ for sb** no poder competir con alguien; **to meet one's ~** encon-

trar la horma de su zapato **2.** SPORTS partido *m*
3. (*similarity*) **to be a good** ~ combinar bien
4. (*in marriage*) **to make a good** ~ casarse
bien **II.** *vi* (*harmonize: design, colour*) armonizar, pegar; (*description*) coincidir **III.** *vt*
1. (*have same colour*) hacer juego con
2. (*equal*) igualar
♦**match against** *vt always sep* enfrentar
♦**match up I.** *vi* **1.** (*make sense*) concordar
2. (*align*) alinear **3. to** ~ **to sth** estar a la altura
de algo **II.** *vt* (*put together*) emparejar
matchbox ['mætʃbɒks, *Am:* -baːks] <-es>
n caja *f* de cerillas, cerillero *m AmL*
matching ['mætʃɪŋ] *adj* que hace juego
matchless ['mætʃlɪs] *adv* incomparable
matchmaker ['mætʃmeɪkəʳ, *Am:* -kəʳ] *n*
casamentero, -a *m, f*
match point *n* SPORTS bola *f* de partido
matchstick ['mætʃˌstɪk] *n* cerilla *f*, fósforo
m, cerillo *m Méx*
matchstick figure *n*, **matchstick man**
n monigote *m*
matchwood ['mætʃwʊd] *n no pl* astillas *fpl*;
to be smashed to ~ hacerse añicos
mate¹ [meɪt] **I.** *n* **1.** (*spouse*) cónyuge *mf*
2. ZOOL (*male*) macho *m*; (*female*) hembra *f*
3. *Brit, Aus* (*friend*) amigo, -a *m, f* **4.** *Brit, Aus,*
inf (*form of address*) compadre *m* **5.** (*assistant*) ayudante *mf* **6.** *fig* (*one of a pair*) compañero, -a *m, f* **7.** NAUT oficial *m* de abordo;
first/second ~ primer/segundo oficial **II.** *vi*
aparearse **III.** *vt* aparear
mate² [meɪt] **I.** *n* GAMES mate *m* **II.** *vt* dar
jaque mate a
material [məˈtɪərɪəl, *Am:* -ˈtɪri-] **I.** *n*
1. PHILOS, PHYS materia *f* **2.** (*physical substance*)
material *m*; **raw** ~ materia *f* prima **3.** *no pl*
(*information*) **publicity** ~ material *m* publicitario **4.** *no pl* (*cloth*) tela *f* **5.** (*textile*) tejido *m*
6. *pl* (*equipment*) materiales *mpl*; **writing**
~(**s**) útiles *mpl* de escritura **II.** *adj* **1.** (*physical*)
material; ~ **damage** daño material **2.** (*important*) importante; **to be** ~ **to sth** ser importante
para algo
materialise [məˈtɪərɪəlaɪz] *vi Brit, Aus s.*
materialize
materialism [məˈtɪərɪəlɪzəm, *Am:* -ˈtɪri-] *n*
no pl materialismo *m*
materialist *n* materialista *mf*
materialistic [məˌtɪərɪəˈlɪstɪk, *Am:* -ˌtɪri-]
adj materialista
materialize [məˈtɪərɪəlaɪz, *Am:* -ˈtɪri-] *vi*
1. (*take physical form*) materializarse **2.** (*hope,*
idea) realizarse **3.** (*appear*) aparecer
material witness <-es> *n Brit* testigo *mf*
presencial
maternal [məˈtɜːnl, *Am:* -ˈtɜːr-] *adj* **1.** (*feeling*) maternal **2.** (*relative*) materno, -a
maternity [məˈtɜːnəti, *Am:* -ˈtɜːrnəti] *n no*
pl maternidad *f*
maternity clothes *npl* ropa *f* premamá
maternity dress <-es> *n* vestido *m*
premamá **maternity hospital** *n* materni-

dad *f* **maternity leave** *n* baja *f* por maternidad **maternity ward** *n* sala *f* de maternidad
matey ['meɪti, *Am:* -t̬i] <-ier, -iest> *adj Brit,*
Aus, inf amistoso, -a; **to get** ~ **with sb** hacerse
amigo de alguien
math [mæθ] *n Am, inf abbr of* **mathematics**
mates *fpl*
mathematical [ˌmæθəˈmætɪkl, *Am:*
-ˈmæt̬-] *adj* matemático, -a
mathematician [ˌmæθəməˈtɪʃən] *n* matemático, -a *m, f*
mathematics [ˌmæθəˈmætɪks, *Am:*
-ˈmæt̬-] *n* matemáticas *fpl*
maths [mæθs] *n Brit, Aus, inf abbr of* **mathematics** mates *fpl*
matinée ['mætɪneɪ, *Am:* -əneɪ] *n* CINE
primera sesión *f*; THEAT función *f* de tarde
mating *n* apareamiento *m*
mating season *n* época *f* de celo
matriarchy ['meɪtrɪɑːki, *Am:* -ɑːrk-] *n no pl*
matriarcado *m*
matrices ['meɪtrɪsiːz] *n pl of* **matrix**
matriculate [məˈtrɪkjʊleɪt, *Am:* -jə-] **I.** *vi*
matricularse **II.** *vt* matricular
matriculation [məˌtrɪkjʊˈleɪʃən, *Am:* -jə-]
n matrícula *f*
matrimonial [ˌmætrɪˈməʊnɪəl, *Am:*
-rəˈmoʊ-] *adj form* matrimonial
matrimony ['mætrɪməni, *Am:* -rəmoʊ-] *n*
no pl matrimonio *m*
matrix ['meɪtrɪks] <-ices> *n a.* MAT matriz *f*
matrix printer *n* INFOR impresora *f* de matriz
de punto
matron ['meɪtrən] *n* **1.** (*middle-aged*
woman) matrona *f* **2.** (*nurse*) enfermera *f* jefe
3. *Brit* SCHOOL ama *f* de llaves **4.** *Am* (*prison*
guard) carcelera *f*
matronly ['meɪtrənli] *adj iron* de matrona; **a**
~ **figure** una persona madura y corpulenta
matt *adj*, **matte** [mæt] *adj Am* mate
matted *adj* enmarañado, -a
matter ['mætəʳ, *Am:* 'mæt̬əʳ] **I.** *n* **1.** (*subject*)
materia *f*; (*question, affair*) asunto *m*; **that's**
another ~ **altogether** eso es harina de otro
costal *fig*; **that's no laughing** ~ no es cosa de
risa; **to do sth as a** ~ **of course** hacer algo
como parte del procedimiento habitual; **the** ~
in hand el asunto del que se trata; **it's a** ~ **of**
life or death es un asunto de vida o muerte;
money ~**s** asuntos financieros; **a** ~ **of opinion**
una cuestión de opinión; **the truth of the** ~ **is**
la verdad de las cosas; **personal** ~ asunto privado **2.** *pl* (*situation*) situación *f*; **now** ~**s are**
really bad ahora han empeorado las circunstancias; **to help** ~**s** mejorar las cosas; **to make**
~**s worse** por si eso fuera poco **3.** (*wrong*)
problema *m*; **what's the** ~ **with you?** ¿qué te
pasa?; **what's the** ~ **with asking for a pay**
rise? ¿qué problema hay en pedir un aumento
del sueldo? **4.** (*material*) material *m*; **advertising** ~ material publicitario **5.** (*amount*) **a** ~ **of**
... cosa de...; **in a** ~ **of seconds** en cuestión

de segundos **6.** *no pl* (*substance*) materia *f* **II.** *vi* importar; **it really ~s to me** me importa mucho; **no ~ what they say** no importa lo que digan, digan lo que digan; **it doesn't ~ if ...** no importa si...; **it ~s that ...** importa que... +*subj*; **what ~s now is that ...** lo que importa ahora es que...

matter-of-fact [ˌmætəˈʳəvˈfækt, *Am:* ˌmæt̬ɚ-] *adj* **1.** (*practical*) práctico, -a **2.** (*emotionless*) prosaico, -a

matter-of-factly *adv* **1.** (*practically*) prácticamente **2.** (*emotionlessly*) prosaicamente

matting [ˈmætɪŋ, *Am:* ˈmæt̬-] *n no pl* **1.** (*floor covering*) estera *f* **2.** (*tangling*) enmarañamiento *m*

mattress [ˈmætrɪs] *n* colchón *m*

mature [məˈtjʊəʳ, *Am:* -ˈtʊr] **I.** *adj* **1.** (*person, attitude*) maduro, -a; (*animal*) adulto, -a; **to be ~ beyond one's years** ser muy maduro para su edad; **after ~ reflection** después de una larga reflexión **2.** (*fruit*) maduro, -a; (*wine*) añejo, -a; (*cheese*) curado, -a **3.** FIN vencido, -a **II.** *vi* **1.** *a.* *fig* madurar **2.** FIN vencer **III.** *vt* **1.** (*cheese, ham*) curar; (*wine*) añejar **2.** (*person*) hacer madurar

maturity [məˈtjʊərəti, *Am:* -ˈtʊrət̬i] *n* <-ies> **1.** *no pl* (*of person, attitude*) madurez *f*; **to come to ~** llegar a la madurez **2.** FIN vencimiento *m*; **to reach ~** tener vencimiento

maudlin [ˈmɔːdlɪn, *Am:* ˈmɑːd-] *adj* **1.** (*sentimental*) sensiblero, -a **2.** (*tearful*) llorón, -ona

maul [mɔːl, *Am:* mɑːl] *vt* **1.** (*wound*) herir **2.** (*criticize*) vapulear

---

Maundy Thursday es el nombre que recibe el Jueves Santo dentro de la **Holy Week** (Semana Santa). Ese día el monarca reparte a unas cuantas personas pobres previamente escogidas el **Maundy money**. El número de personas a las que se dispensa esta limosna está en relación con la edad del monarca. Cada una de estas personas recibe además un set de monedas de plata acuñadas especialmente para la ocasión.

Mauritania [ˌmɒrɪˈteɪniə, *Am:* ˌmɔːrɪˈ-] *n* Mauritania *f*

Mauritanian **I.** *n* mauritano, -a *m, f* **II.** *adj* mauritano, -a

Mauritian **I.** *n* mauriciano, -a *m, f* **II.** *adj* mauriciano, -a

Mauritius [məˈrɪʃəs, *Am:* mɔːˈrɪʃiəs] *n* Mauricio *m*

mausoleum [ˌmɔːsəˈliːəm, *Am:* ˌmɑː-] *n* mausoleo *m*

mauve [məʊv, *Am:* moʊv] *adj* malva

maverick [ˈmævərɪk, *Am:* ˈmævɚ-] *n* **1.** *Am* ZOOL res *f* sin marcar **2.** (*person*) inconformista *mf*

mawkish [ˈmɔːkɪʃ, *Am:* ˈmɑː-] *adj* (*sentimental*) empalagoso, -a *fig*

max. *inf abbr of* **maximum** máx.

maxim [ˈmæksɪm] *n* máxima *f*

maximal [ˈmæksɪməl] *adj form* máximo, -a

maximise *vt Brit, Aus,* **maximize** [ˈmæksɪmaɪz] *vt* maximizar

maximum [ˈmæksɪməm] **I.** *n* máximo *m*; **to do sth to the ~** hacer algo al máximo; **to reach a ~** llegar al máximo **II.** *adj* máximo, -a; **this car has a ~ speed of 160 km/h** este coche alcanza una velocidad máxima de 160 km/h

maximum security prison *n* prisión *f* de máxima seguridad

may¹ [meɪ] <might, might> *aux* **1.** *form* (*be allowed*) poder; **~ I come in?** ¿puedo pasar?; **~ I ask you a question?** ¿puedo hacerte una pregunta?; **what time will we arrive? – you ~ well ask!** ¿a qué hora llegaremos? – ¡eso quisiera saber yo! **2.** (*possibility*) ser posible; **it ~ rain** puede que llueva; **that's as ~ be, be that as it ~** en cualquier caso **3.** (*hope, wish*) **~ she rest in peace** que en paz descanse

may² [meɪ] *n* (*bush*) espino *m*; (*flower*) flor *f* de espino

May [meɪ] *n* mayo; *s. a.* **April**

maybe [ˈmeɪbiː] **I.** *adv* **1.** (*perhaps*) quizás **2.** (*approximately*) probablemente; **~ as many as two hundred people** unas doscientas personas **II.** *n* quizás *m*; **a definite ~** un quizás definitivo

mayday [ˈmeɪdeɪ] *n* S.O.S. *m*

May Day *n* Primero *m* de mayo

El **May Day** (1 de mayo) se celebra en algunas partes de Gran Bretaña con el **morris dancing**. En algunos patios de colegios y pueblos se levanta un **maypole** (árbol de mayo) que es adornado con cintas de colores. Cada persona baila cogida a una de esas cintas unos detrás de otros, formándose así un bonito dibujo en torno al árbol.

---

mayfly [ˈmeɪflaɪ] *n* <-ies> cachipolla *f*

mayhem [ˈmeɪhem] *n no pl* caos *m inv*; **it was ~** era un caos total

mayo [ˈmeɪəʊ, *Am:* -oʊ] *n Am, inf abbr of* **mayonnaise** mayonesa *f*

mayonnaise [ˌmeɪəˈneɪz] *n* mayonesa *f*

mayor [meəʳ, *Am:* meɪɚ] *n* alcalde *m*

mayoress [meəˈres, *Am:* ˈmeɪɚɪs] <-es> *n* alcaldesa *f*

maypole [ˈmeɪpəʊl, *Am:* -poʊl] *n* mayo *m* (*palo*)

may've *inf* = **may have** *s.* **may**

maze [meɪz] *n* laberinto *m*

MB [ˌemˈbiː] *abbr of* **megabyte** MB

MBA [ˌembiːˈeɪ] *n abbr of* **Master of Business Administration** máster *m* en administración de empresas

MC [ˌemˈsiː] *n* **1.** *abbr of* **Master of Ceremonies** maestro, -a *m, f* de ceremonias **2.** *abbr of* **Member of Congress** diputado, -a *m, f* del Congreso (de los Estados Unidos)

MD [,em'di:] *n* **1.** *abbr of* **managing director** director(a) *m(f)* gerente **2.** *abbr of* **Doctor of Medicine** Dr. *m*, Dra. *f*

me [mi:] *pron* **1.** me; **look at ~** mírame; **she saw ~** me vió; **he told ~ that ...** me dijo que...; **he gave ~ the pencil** me dió el lápiz **2.** (*after verb 'to be'*) yo; **it's ~** soy yo; **she is older than ~** ella es mayor que yo **3.** (*after prep*) mí; **is this for ~?** ¿es para mí esto?

meadow ['medəʊ, *Am:* -oʊ] *n* pradera *f*

meager *adj Am,* **meagre** ['mi:gəʳ, *Am:* -gɚ] *adj* escaso, -a

meal¹ [mi:l] *n* comida *f;* **a heavy/light ~** una comida pesada/liviana; **to go out for a ~** comer/cenar fuera; **~s on wheels** *Brit:* distribución de comida a domicilio para gente necesitada o imposibilitada ▸**to make a ~ of sth** hacer una montaña de algo

meal² [mi:l] *n* (*flour*) harina *f*

meal ticket *n* **1.** *Am, Aus* (*luncheon voucher*) vale *m* de comida **2.** *fig* (*means of living*) fuente *f* de ingresos; **he's her latest ~** es el que la mantiene últimamente

mealtime ['mi:ltaɪm] *n* hora *f* de comer

mealy ['mi:li] *adj* <-ier, -iest> harinoso, -a

mealy-mouthed [,mi:li'maʊðd, *Am:* 'mi:li-maʊðd] *adj* camandulero, -a; **he's too ~** anda con demasiados rodeos

mean¹ [mi:n] *adj* **1.** (*miserly*) tacaño, -a, amarrado, -a *Arg, Par, PRico, Urug;* **to be ~ with sth** ser mezquino con algo **2.** (*unkind*) vil; **to be ~ to sb** tratar mal a alguien; **to have a ~ streak** tener muy mala uva **3.** (*bad*) malo, -a; **he's no ~ cook** *inf* es un excelente cocinero **4.** (*humble*) pobre **5.** *inf* (*excellent*) excelente

mean² [mi:n] <meant, meant> *vt* **1.** (*signify: word, event*) significar; **does that name ~ anything to you?** ¿te suena ese nombre? **2.** (*express, indicate: person*) querer decir; **what do you ~?** ¿a qué te refieres?; **what do you ~, it was my fault?** ¿quieres decir que fue mi culpa?; **I ~ what I say** pienso lo que digo **3.** (*intend for particular purpose*) destinar; **to be meant for sth** estar destinado a algo; **to be meant for each other** estar hechos el uno para el otro **4.** (*intend*) pretender; **to ~ to do sth** tener la intención de hacer algo; **what do you ~ by arriving so late?** ¿qué te propones al llegar tan tarde?; **to ~ mischief** proponerse alguna travesura; **to ~ well** tener buenas intenciones; **I ~ to say ...** quiero decir...

meander [mɪ'ændəʳ, *Am:* -dɚ] **I.** *n* meandro *m* **II.** *vi* **1.** (*flow*) serpentear **2.** *fig* (*wander*) vagar; (*digress*) divagar

meandering [mɪ'ændərɪŋ] *adj* **1.** (*river*) sinuoso, -a **2.** (*explanation*) confuso, -a

meanie [mi:ni] *n inf* **1.** (*miserly person*) avaro, -a *m, f* **2.** (*nasty person*) malo, -a *m, f*

meaning ['mi:nɪŋ] *n* significado *m;* **to give sth a whole new ~** dar a algo un significado completamente nuevo; **what is the ~ of this?**

¿qué significa esto?; **if you take my ~** *Brit* si entiendes lo que digo, ya me entiendes; **the full ~ of sth** el sentido completo de algo; **to have ~ for sb** tener significado para alguien

meaningful ['mi:nɪŋfəl] *adj* **1.** (*difference, change*) significativo, -a **2.** (*look, smile*) expresivo, -a

meaningless ['mi:nɪŋləs] *adj* sin sentido

meanness ['mi:nnɪs] *n no pl* **1.** (*lack of generosity*) mezquindad *f* **2.** (*unkindness*) bajeza *f*

means [mi:nz] *n* **1.** (*instrument, method*) medio *m;* **~ of communication/transport** medio de comunicación/transporte **2.** *pl* (*resources*) medios *mpl;* **~ of support** medios de subsistencia; **ways and ~** medios y arbitrios; **by ~ of sth** por medio de algo; **to try by all (possible) ~ to do sth** intentar hacer algo por todos los medios; **to use all ~ at one's disposal** usar todos los medios a su alcance **3.** *pl* (*income*) recursos *mpl;* **a person of ~** una persona acaudalada; **private ~** fondos *mpl* privados; **to be without ~** *form* estar sin recursos; **to live beyond one's ~** vivir por encima de sus posibilidades ▸**by all ~!** ¡por supuesto!; **by no ~** de ninguna manera

means test *n* FIN investigación *f* de los recursos económicos

meant [ment] *pt, pp of* **mean**

meantime ['mi:ntaɪm] **I.** *adv* mientras tanto **II.** *n* **in the ~** mientras tanto

meanwhile ['mi:nwaɪl] *adv* mientras tanto

meany ['mi:ni] *n inf s.* **meanie**

measles ['mi:zlz] *n* sarampión *m*

measly ['mi:zli] *adj* <-ier, -iest> miserable

measurable ['meʒərəbl] *adj* **1.** (*quantifiable*) medible **2.** (*perceptible*) apreciable

measure ['meʒəʳ, *Am:* -ɚ] **I.** *n* **1.** (*size*) medida *f;* **to get the ~ of sb** tomar la medida a alguien **2.** (*measuring instrument*) metro *m;* (*ruler*) regla *f* **3.** (*proof*) medición *f* **4.** (*degree, amount*) grado *m;* **there was some ~ of truth in what he said** hubo algo de cierto en lo que él dijo; **in some ~** hasta cierto punto **5.** *pl* (*action*) medidas *fpl;* **to take ~s to do sth** tomar medidas para hacer algo **6.** LIT metro *m* **7.** MUS compás *m* ▸**for good ~** por añadidura; **beyond ~** excesivamente **II.** *vt* medir; **to ~ sth in centimetres/weeks** calcular algo en centímetros/semanas **III.** *vi* medir; **the box ~s 10cm by 10cm by 12cm** la caja mide 10 cm por 10 cm por 12 cm

◆**measure out** *vt* **1.** (*weigh*) pesar **2.** (*measure length*) medir

◆**measure up** *vi* dar la talla; **to measure up to sth** estar a la altura de algo

measured *adj* (*voice, tone*) comedido, -a; (*response*) moderado, -a

measurement ['meʒəmənt, *Am:* 'meʒɚ-] *n* **1.** *no pl* (*act of measuring*) medición *f* **2.** (*size*) medida *f;* **to take sb's ~s** tomar a alguien las medidas

measuring cup *n Am, Aus* vaso *m* medidor
measuring jug *n Brit* jarra *f* graduada
measuring spoon *n* cuchara *f* medidora
meat [mi:t] *n no pl* **1.** carne *f* **2.** *no pl, fig* (*subject matter*) sustancia *f* ►**to be ~ and drink to sb** ser pan comido para alguien; **one man's ~ is another man's poison** *prov* lo que a uno cura a otro mata *prov*
meat-and-potatoes [ˌmiːtəndpəˈteɪtəʊz, *Am:* -pəˈteɪt̮oʊz] *n Am, inf* lo básico **meatball** *n* albóndiga *f* **meat cleaver** *n* cuchilla *f* de carnicero **meat grinder** *n Am* picadora *f* de carne **meat hook** *n* gancho *m* de carnicería **meat loaf** *n* pastel *m* de carne **meat pie** *n* empanada *f* de carne **meat products** *npl* productos *mpl* cárnicos
mecca *n,* **Mecca** [ˈmekə] *n* **1.** REL La Meca **2.** *fig* meca *f*
mechanic [mɪˈkænɪk] *n* mecánico, -a *m, f*
mechanical *adj* **1.** (*relating to machines*) mecánico, -a **2.** (*without thinking*) maquinal
mechanical engineer *n* ingeniero, -a *m, f* mecánico, -a **mechanical engineering** *n no pl* ingeniería *f* mecánica **mechanical pencil** *n Am* portaminas *mpl*
mechanics [mɪˈkænɪks] *npl* **1.** AUTO, TECH mecánica *f* **2.** *inf* (*how things are organized*) mecanismo *m*
mechanise [ˈmekənaɪz] *vt Brit, Aus s.* **mechanize**
mechanism [ˈmekənɪzəm] *n* mecanismo *m*
mechanize [ˈmekənaɪz] *vt* mecanizar
Med [med] *n inf abbr of* **Mediterranean the ~** el Mar Mediterráneo
med. *adj abbr of* **medium** mediano, -a
medal [ˈmedl] *n* medalla *f*
medallion [mɪˈdælɪən, *Am:* məˈdæljən] *n* medallón *m*
medal(l)ist [ˈmedəlɪst] *n* medallista *mf*
meddle [ˈmedl] *vi* **to ~ in sth** meterse en algo
meddlesome [ˈmedlsəm] *adj* entrometido, -a, metiche *Méx*, toposo, -a *Ven*
media [ˈmiːdiə] *n* **1.** *pl of* **medium 2. the ~** los medios; **the mass ~** los medios de comunicación de masas; **a ~ event** un acontecimiento mediático
mediaeval [ˌmediˈiːvəl] *adj s.* **medieval**
median [ˈmiːdiən] *adj* mediano, -a
median strip *n Am, Aus* AUTO raya *f* divisoria
media studies *n* ≈ estudios *mpl* de comunicación audiovisual
mediate [ˈmiːdɪeɪt] **I.** *vi* mediar; **to ~ between two groups** mediar entre dos grupos; **to ~ in sth** mediar en algo **II.** *vt* **to ~ a settlement** hacer de intermediario en un acuerdo
mediation [ˌmiːdɪˈeɪʃən] *n no pl* mediación *f*
mediator [ˈmiːdɪeɪtə^r, *Am:* -t̮ɚ] *n* mediador(a) *m(f)*
medic [ˈmedɪk] *n* **1.** *inf* (*doctor*) médico, -a *m, f* **2.** (*student*) estudiante *mf* de medicina
Medicaid [ˈmedɪkeɪd] *n no pl, Am:* programa de asistencia sanitaria gratuita para personas con pocos ingresos
medical [ˈmedɪkəl] **I.** *adj* médico, -a **II.** *n inf* reconocimiento *m* médico
medical certificate *n* certificado *m* médico **medical examination** *n* reconocimiento *m* médico **medical history** *n* historial *m* clínico
medicament [mɪˈdɪkəmənt] *n* medicamento *m*
Medicare [ˈmedɪkeə^r, *Am:* -ker] *n Am:* programa de asistencia sanitaria para personas mayores de 65 años
medicate [ˈmedɪkeɪt] *vt* (*treat medically*) medicar
medicated *adj* (*soap, shampoo*) medicinal
medication [ˌmedɪˈkeɪʃən] <-(s)> *n* medicamento *m*
medicinal [məˈdɪsɪnəl] *adj* medicinal
medicine [ˈmedsən, *Am:* ˈmedɪsən] *n* **1.** (*substance*) medicamento *m;* **to take (one's) ~** tomarse su medicina **2.** *no pl* (*medical knowledge*) medicina *f* **3.** (*remedy*) remedio *m* ►**to give sb a taste of his own ~** pagar a alguien con su misma moneda; **to take one's ~** sufrir las consecuencias
medicine ball *n* balón *m* medicinal **medicine chest** *n* botiquín *m* **medicine man** *n* <-men> hechicero *m*
medieval [ˌmedɪˈiːvl, *Am:* ˌmiːdɪ-] *adj* medieval
mediocre [ˌmiːdɪˈəʊkə^r, *Am:* -ˈoʊkɚ] *adj* mediocre
mediocrity [ˌmiːdɪˈɒkrəti, *Am:* -ˈɑːkrət̮i] *n no pl* **1.** (*person*) mediocre *mf* **2.** (*quality*) mediocridad *f*
meditate [ˈmedɪteɪt] **I.** *vi* **1.** (*engage in contemplation*) meditar **2.** (*think deeply*) reflexionar; **to ~ on sth** reflexionar sobre algo **II.** *vt* (*plan: revenge*) planear
meditation [ˌmedɪˈteɪʃən] *n no pl* meditación *f*
Mediterranean [ˌmedɪtəˈreɪnɪən] **I.** *n* Mediterráneo *m* **II.** *adj* mediterráneo, -a
Mediterranean Sea *n* mar *m* Mediterráneo
medium [ˈmiːdiəm] **I.** *adj* mediano, -a **II.** *n* **1.** <media *o* -s> (*method*) medio *m;* **through the ~ of** por medio de **2.** *no pl* (*spiritualist*) médium *mf*
medium-dry *adj* semi seco, -a **medium-rare** *adj* GASTR poco hecho, -a **medium-sized** *adj* mediano, -a **medium-term** *adj* a medio plazo **medium wave** *n Brit* RADIO onda *f* media
medley [ˈmedli] *n* **1.** (*mixture*) mezcla *f* **2.** MUS popurrí *m*
meek [miːk] *adj* manso, -a
meet [miːt] <met, met> **I.** *vt* **1.** (*encounter*) encontrarse con; (*intentionally*) reunirse con; (*for first time*) conocer a; **to arrange to ~ sb** quedar con alguien **2.** (*wait for: at station, airport*) ir a buscar a alguien **3.** (*confront: oppo-*

nent) enfrentarse con; (*problem*) tropezar con
4. (*fulfil*) reunir; (*cost*) correr con; (*demand*)
atender; (*obligation*) cumplir **II.** *vi*
1. (*encounter*) encontrarse; (*intentionally*)
reunirse; (*for first time*) conocerse; **to arrange
to ~** quedar **2.** (*join: lines*) unirse; (*rivers*) confluir **3.** SPORTS enfrentarse **III.** *n* **1.** (*sporting
event*) encuentro *m* **2.** Brit (*fox hunt*) cacería *f*
♦ **meet with** *vt insep* reunirse con; **to ~ an
accident** sufrir un accidente; **to ~ success**
tener éxito; **to meet force with force** combatir la fuerza con la fuerza
meeting ['miːtɪŋ, *Am:* - t̬ɪŋ] *n* **1.** (*gathering*)
reunión *f*; **to call a ~** convocar una reunión
2. POL mitin *m* **3.** (*casual*) *a.* SPORTS encuentro
m
meeting point *n* punto *m* de encuentro
megabyte ['megəbaɪt] *n* INFOR megabyte *m*
megahertz ['megəhɜːts, *Am:* -hɜːrts] *n* ELEC
megahercio *m*
megalomania [ˌmegələ'meɪnɪə, *Am:* -ouʼ-]
n megalomanía *f*
megalomaniac [ˌmegələ'meɪnɪæk, *Am:*
-ouʼ-] *n* megalómano, -a *m, f*
megaphone ['megəfəun, *Am:* -foun] *n*
megáfono *m*
megastore ['megəstɔːʳ, *Am:* -stɔːr] *n* gran
almacén *m*
megawatt ['megəwɒt, *Am:* -waːt] *n* megavatio *m*
melancholia [ˌmelən'kəulɪə, *Am:* -'kou-] *n*
no pl melancolía *f*
melancholic [ˌmelən'kɒlɪk, *Am:* -'kaːlɪk]
adj melancólico, -a
melancholy ['melənkɒli, *Am:* -kaːli] **I.** *n no
pl* melancolía *f* **II.** *adj* melancólico, -a

La **Melbourne Cup** (Copa), es una de las
competiciones hípicas más populares entre los
australianos. Siempre tiene lugar el primer
martes del mes de noviembre. Las apuestas alcanzan varios millones de dólares. Ese día
todo el país se pone sus mejores galas y a
mediodía se sirve pollo con champán.

melee ['meleɪ, *Am:* 'meɪleɪ] *n* **1.** (*fight*) riña
f **2.** (*crowd*) enjambre *m*
mellow ['meləu, *Am:* -lou] **I.** *adj* <-er, -est>
1. (*light: voice*) suave; (*flavour*) dulce
2. (*mature: wine*) añejo, -a **3.** (*relaxed*) tranquilo, -a **II.** *vi* (*person, fruit*) madurar; (*voice,
colour*) suavizarse **III.** *vt* **1.** (*wine*) añejar
2. (*make less severe*) suavizar
melodic [mə'lɒdɪk, *Am:* mə'laːdɪk] *adj* melódico, -a
melodious [mɪ'ləudɪəs, *Am:* mə'lou-] *adj*
melodioso, -a
melodrama ['melədraːmə, *Am:* -ou-] *n*
melodrama *m*
melodramatic [ˌmelədrə'mætɪk, *Am:*
-oudrə'mæt̬-] *adj* melodramático, -a
melody ['melədi] <-ies> *n* melodía *f*
melon ['melən] *n* melón *m*; (*watermelon*)

sandía *f*
melt [melt] **I.** *vt* (*metal*) fundir; (*ice, chocolate*) derretir **II.** *vi* **1.** (*metal*) fundirse; (*ice,
chocolate*) derretirse **2.** *fig* enternecerse
meltdown ['meltdaun] *n* fusión *f*
melting point *n* punto *m* de fusión **melting pot** *n a. fig* crisol *m*
member ['membəʳ, *Am:* -bɚ] *n* miembro
mf; (*of society, club*) socio, -a *m, f*
member of parliament *n* POL diputado, -a
m, f
membership *n* **1.** (*state of belonging*) calidad *f* de miembro; (*to society, club*) calidad *f*
de socio; **to apply for ~ of a club** solicitar
ingreso en un club; **~ dues** cuotas *fpl* de socio
2. (*number of members*) número *m* de miembros
membership card *n* carnet *m*
membrane ['membreɪn] *n* membrana *f*
memento [mɪ'mentəu, *Am:* mə'mentou]
<-s *o* -es> *n* recuerdo *m*
memo ['meməu, *Am:* -ou] *n abbr of* **memorandum** **1.** (*message*) memorándum *m*
2. (*note*) nota *f*
memoir ['memwaːʳ, *Am:* -waːr] *n* **1.** (*record
of events*) memoria *f* **2.** *pl* (*autobiography*)
memorias *fpl*
memo pad *n* bloc *m* de notas
memorabilia [ˌmemərə'bɪlɪə] *npl* recuerdos
mpl
memorable ['memərəbl] *adj* memorable
memorandum [ˌmemə'rændəm] <-s *o*
-anda> *n form* **1.** (*message*) memorándum *m*
2. (*note*) nota *f*
memorial [mə'mɔːrɪəl] *n* monumento *m*
conmemorativo
Memorial Day *n no pl, Am, Can* Día *m* de
los Caídos
memorize ['meməraɪz] *vt* memorizar
memory ['meməri] <-ies> *n* **1.** (*ability to
remember*) memoria *f*; **to recite sth from ~**
recitar algo de memoria; **if my ~ serves me
correctly** si la memoria no me falla **2.** (*remembered event*) recuerdo *m*; **to bring back
memories** evocar recuerdos **3.** INFOR memoria
f; **internal/external/core ~** memoria
interna/externa/del núcleo; **cache ~** memoria (intermedia) del caché; **read only ~**
memoria sólo de lectura; **random access ~**
memoria de acceso directo
memory bank *n* INFOR banco *m* de memoria
memory capacity <-ies> *n* INFOR capacidad *f* de memoria **memory chip** *n* INFOR
chip *m* de memoria **memory dump** *n* INFOR
vaciado *m* de la memoria **memory expansion card** *n* INFOR tarjeta *f* de expansión de
memoria **memory management** *n no pl*
INFOR administración *f* de memoria **memory
protection** *n no pl* INFOR protección *f* de
memoria
men [men] *n pl of* **man**
menace ['menəs] **I.** *n* **1.** (*threat*) amenaza *f*
2. (*child*) demonio *m*, peligro *m* **II.** *vt* amena-

zar

menacing *adj* amenazador(a)

menacingly *adv* de modo amenazador

mend [mend] I. *n* 1. (*repair*) reparación *f* 2. (*patch*) remiendo *m* 3. *inf* to be on the ~ ir mejorando II. *vt* 1. (*repair*) reparar 2. (*darn: socks*) zurcir III. *vi* (*improve*) mejorar; (*broken bone*) soldarse

mendacious [men'deɪʃəs] *adj* falso, -a

mendacity [men'dæsəti, *Am:* - t̬i] *n no pl* falsedad *f*

mending ['mendɪŋ] *n no pl* 1. (*repair*) reparación *f* 2. (*darning*) zurcido *m* 3. (*clothes*) ropa *f* por remendar

menial ['mi:nɪəl] *adj* de baja categoría

meningitis [ˌmenɪn'dʒaɪtɪs, *Am:* -t̬ɪs] *n no pl* meningitis *f*

menopause ['menəpɔːz, *Am:* -pɑːz] *n no pl* menopausia *f*

men's room ['menzˌruːm] *n Am* lavabo *m* de hombres

menstrual ['menstruəl, *Am:* -strəl] *adj* menstrual

menstruate ['menstrueɪt, *Am:* -stru-] *vi* menstruar

menstruation [ˌmenstru'eɪʃən, *Am:* -stru'-] *n no pl* menstruación *f*

mental ['mentəl, *Am:* -t̬əl] *adj* 1. (*of the mind*) mental 2. *Brit, inf* (*crazy*) chiflado, -a

mental arithmetic *n no pl* cálculo *m* mental

mental hospital *n* hospital *m* psiquiátrico

mental illness *n* <-es> enfermedad *f* mental

mentality [men'tæləti, *Am:* -t̬i] <-ies> *n* mentalidad *f*

mentally *adv* mentalmente; ~ **disturbed** trastornado, -a

mentally handicapped *adj* to be ~ tener una minusvalía psíquica

menthol ['menθɒl, *Am:* -θɔːl] *n no pl* mentol *m*

mention ['menʃən] I. *n* mención *f;* to receive a (**special**) ~ obtener una mención (especial); to make ~ of sth mencionar algo II. *vt* mencionar; **don't ~ it!** ¡no hay de qué!; not to ~ ... sin contar...

mentor ['mentɔːʳ, *Am:* -tɚ] *n* mentor(a) *m(f)*

menu ['menjuː] *n* 1. (*list of dishes*) carta *f;* (*fixed meal*) menú *m* 2. INFOR menú *m;* context/pull-down ~ menú contextual/desplegable

menu-bar *n* barra *f* de menús **menu-driven** *adj* INFOR guiado, -a por menús

MEP [ˌemiː'piː] *n abbr of* Member of the European Parliament eurodiputado, -a *m, f*

mercenary ['mɜːsɪnəri, *Am:* 'mɜːrsənɚ-] I. *n* <-ies> mercenario, -a *m, f* II. *adj* mercenario, -a

merchandise ['mɜːtʃəndaɪz, *Am:* 'mɜːr-] *n no pl* mercancía *f*

merchant ['mɜːtʃənt, *Am:* 'mɜːr-] *n* comerciante *mf*

merchant bank *n* banco *m* mercantil **merchantman** <-men> *n* buque *m* mercante **merchant navy** *n no pl* marina *f* mercante **merchant ship** *n* mercante *m*

merciful ['mɜːsɪfəl, *Am:* 'mɜːr-] *adj* misericordioso, -a

merciless ['mɜːsɪlɪs, *Am:* 'mɜːr-] *adj* despiadado, -a

mercurial [mɜː'kjʊərɪəl, *Am:* mɜːr'kjʊrɪ-] *adj* 1. CHEM mercurial 2. (*changeable*) voluble; (*weather*) cambiante 3. (*lively*) vivo, -a

mercury ['mɜːkjʊri, *Am:* 'mɜːrkjɚi] *n no pl* mercurio *m*

Mercury ['mɜːkjʊri, *Am:* 'mɜːrkjɚi] *n no pl* Mercurio *m*

mercy ['mɜːsi, *Am:* 'mɜːr-] *n no pl* 1. (*compassion*) compasión *f;* to have ~ on sb tener compasión de alguien 2. (*forgiveness*) misericordia *f;* to be at the ~ of sb estar a merced de alguien; to throw oneself upon sb's ~ abandonarse a la merced de uno; to plead for ~ pedir clemencia

mere [mɪəʳ, *Am:* mɪr] *adj* mero, -a; a ~ **detail** un simple detalle

merely ['mɪəli, *Am:* 'mɪr-] *adv* solamente

merge [mɜːdʒ, *Am:* mɜːrdʒ] I. *vi* unirse; ECON, POL fusionarse; to ~ **into** sth fundirse con algo II. *vt* unir; ECON, POL, INFOR fusionar

merger ['mɜːdʒəʳ, *Am:* 'mɜːrdʒɚ] *n* ECON fusión *f*

meridian [mə'rɪdɪən] *n* meridiano *m*

meringue [mə'ræŋ] *n* merengue *m*, espumilla *f Ecua, Guat, Hond*

merit ['merɪt] I. *n* 1. (*virtue*) cualidad *f* 2. (*advantage*) ventaja *f* 3. *pl* (*commendable quality or act*) mérito *m* II. *vt* merecer

meritocracy [ˌmerɪ'tɒkrəsi, *Am:* -ə'tɑːkrə-] <-ies> *n* meritocracia *f*

mermaid ['mɜːmeɪd, *Am:* 'mɜːr-] *n* sirena *f*

merriment ['merɪmənt] *n no pl* 1. (*laughter and joy*) regocijo *m* 2. (*amusement*) alegría *f*

merry ['meri] <-ier, -iest> *adj* 1. (*happy*) alegre 2. *Brit, inf* (*slightly drunk*) achispado, -a

merry-go-round [ˌmerigəʊˌraʊnd, *Am:* -goʊ-] *n* tiovivo *m*

mesh [meʃ] I. *n no pl* malla *f;* wire ~ red *f* de alambrado II. *vi* engranar III. *vt* hacer engranar

mesmeric [mez'merɪk] *adj* hipnótico, -a

mesmerism ['mezmərɪzəm] *n no pl* hipnosis *f inv*

mesmerize ['mezməraɪz] *vt* hipnotizar

mess [mes] <-es> *n* 1. *no pl* (*confusion*) confusión *f;* (*disorganized state*) desorden *m;* to be in a ~ (*things*) estar revuelto; (*person*) estar hecho un lío; to make a ~ of sth echar a perder algo; (*things*) desordenar algo 2. *no pl* (*trouble*) lío *m*, merengue *m Arg* 3. (*dirt*) suciedad *f* 4. *no pl, inf* (*animal excrement*) caca *f* 5. *Brit* MIL (*dining hall*) comedor *m*

◆**mess about** I. *vi* hacer el tonto II. *vt always sep* tratar mal

◆**mess up** *vt inf* 1. (*make untidy*) desordenar 2. (*dirty*) ensuciar 3. (*botch up*) desarre-

M

glar
◆**mess with** vi inf to ~ sb meterse con alguien; to ~ sth interferir con algo
message ['mesɪdʒ] n mensaje m; **error** ~ INFOR mensaje m de error
messenger ['mesɪndʒəʳ, Am: -dʒɚ] n mensajero, -a m, f
messenger boy n recadero m
messiah [mə'saɪə] n mesías m inv
mess-up ['mesʌp] n inf follón m
messy ['mesi] <-ier, -iest> adj 1. (untidy) desordenado, -a 2. (dirty) sucio, -a 3. (unpleasant) desagradable; ~ **business** asunto m turbio
met [met] vi, vt pt of **meet**
met. abbr of **meteorological** meteor.
metabolic [ˌmetə'bɒlɪk, Am: ˌmeṭə'baːlɪk] adj metabólico, -a
metabolism [mɪ'tæbəlɪzəm] n metabolismo m
metal ['metl, Am: 'meṭ-] I. n 1. (element) metal m 2. Brit (road) grava f 3. pl, Brit RAIL rieles mpl II. adj metálico, -a III. vt (road) engravar
metallic [mɪ'tælɪk, Am: mə'-] adj metálico, -a
metallurgy [mət'ælədʒi, Am: 'meṭəlɜ:r-] n no pl metalurgia f
metalwork ['metəlwɜːk, Am: 'meṭəlwɜːrk] n no pl metalistería f **metalworker** n metalista mf
metamorphosis [ˌmetə'mɔːfəsɪs, Am: ˌmeṭə'mɔːrfə-] <-es> n metamorfosis f inv
metaphor ['metəfəʳ, Am: 'meṭəfɔːr] n metáfora f
metaphorical [ˌmetə'fɒrɪkl, Am: ˌmeṭə-'fɔːr-] adj metafórico, -a
metaphysical [ˌmetə'fɪzɪkl, Am: ˌmeṭ-] adj metafísico, -a
metaphysics [ˌmetə'fɪzɪks, Am: ˌmeṭ-] n metafísica f
metastasis [mɪ'tæstəsɪs, Am: mə'-] <-ses> n metástasis f inv
mete [ˌmiːt] vt to ~ **out** (punishment) imponer
meteor ['miːtiəʳ, Am: -ṭiə] n meteoro m
meteoric [ˌmiːti'ɒrɪk, Am: -ṭi'ɔːr-] adj a. fig meteórico, -a
meteorite ['miːtiəraɪt, Am: -ṭi-] n meteorito m
meteorological [ˌmiːtiərə'lɒdʒɪkəl, Am: -ṭiɚə'laːdʒɪ-] adj meteorológico, -a
meteorologist [ˌmiːtiə'rɒlədʒɪst, Am: -ṭiə'raːl-] n meteorólogo, -a m, f
meteorology [ˌmiːtiə'rɒlədʒi, Am: -ɚ'raːlə-] n no pl meteorología f
meter[1] ['miːtəʳ, Am: -ṭɚ] n contador m, medidor m AmL; (**parking**) ~ parquímetro m; (**taxi**) ~ taxímetro m
meter[2] ['miːtəʳ, Am: -ṭɚ] n Am s. **metre**
methane ['miːθeɪn, Am: 'meθeɪn] n metano m
method ['meθəd] n método m; **there's** ~ **in**

his **madness** no está tan loco como parece
methodical [mɪ'θɒdɪkl, Am: mə'θɑːdɪk-] adj metódico, -a
Methodism ['meθədɪzəm] n metodismo m
Methodist I. n metodista mf II. adj metodista
methodology [ˌmeθə'dɒlədʒi, Am: -'dɑːlə-] n metodología f
Methuselah [mɪ'θjuːzələ, Am: mə'θuː-] n Matusalén ►**as** <u>old</u> **as** ~ más viejo que Matusalén
methyl alcohol ['meθɪl'ælkəhɒl, Am: -aɪl'ælkəhɑːl] n metanol m **methylated spirits** n no pl, Aus, Brit alcohol m desnaturalizado
meticulous [mɪ'tɪkjʊləs] adj meticuloso, -a, niquitoso, -a Arg
metre ['miːtəʳ, Am: -ṭɚ] n Brit, Aus metro m
metric ['metrɪk] adj métrico, -a
metrical ['metrɪkl] adj métrico, -a
metro ['metrəʊ, Am: -roʊ] n RAIL metro m
metronome ['metrənəʊm, Am: -noʊm] n metrónomo m
metropolis [mə'trɒpəlɪs, Am: -'trɑːpəl-] <-es> n metrópoli f
metropolitan [ˌmetrə'pɒlɪtən, Am: -'pɑːlə-] adj metropolitano, -a
mettle ['metl, Am: 'meṭ-] n no pl, form temple m; **to show one's** ~ demostrar su brío; **to be on one's** ~ mostrar todo lo que uno vale
mew [mjuː] I. n maullido m II. vi maullar
Mexican ['meksɪkən] I. n mexicano, -a m, f II. adj mexicano, -a
Mexico ['meksɪkəʊ, Am: -koʊ] n no pl México m; **New** ~ Nuevo México
Mexico City n Ciudad f de México
Mg abbr of **magnesium** Mg
MHR n Am abbr of **Member of the House of Representatives** diputado, -a m, f del Congreso (de los Estados Unidos)
Mhz abbr of **megahertz** MHz
miaow [mi:'aʊ] I. n miau m II. vi maullar
mica ['maɪkə] n no pl mica f
mice [maɪs] n pl of **mouse**
Michaelmas ['mɪklməs] n día m de San Miguel
mickey ['mɪki] n Aus, Brit, inf **to take the** ~ **out of sb** tomar el pelo a alguien
Mickey Mouse [ˌmɪki'maʊs] n ratoncito m Mickey, ratón m Miguelito Méx
MICR n INFOR abbr of **magnetic-ink character recognition** reconocimiento m de caracteres en tinta magnética
microbe ['maɪkrəʊb, Am: -kroʊb] n microbio m
microbiology [ˌmaɪkrəʊbaɪ'ɒlədʒi, Am: -kroʊbaɪ'ɑːlə-] n no pl microbiología f
microchip ['maɪkrəʊtʃɪp, Am: -kroʊ-] n microchip m
microclimate ['maɪkrəʊˌklaɪmɪt, Am: -kroʊ-] n microclima m
microcomputer ['maɪkrəʊkəmˌpjuːtəʳ, Am: -kroʊkəmˌpjuːṭɚ] n microordenador m, microcomputadora f AmL

microcosm ['maɪkrəʊkɒzəm, *Am:* -krou-kɑ:zəm] *n* microcosmos *m inv*

microelectronics [ˌmaɪkrəʊˌɪlek'trɒnɪks, *Am:* -krouˌɪlek'trɑ:nɪks] *n no pl* microelectrónica *f*

microfiche ['maɪkrəʊfi:ʃ, *Am:* -krou-] *n* microficha *f*

microfilm ['maɪkrəʊfɪlm, *Am:* -krou-] *n* microfilm *m*

micrometer [maɪ'krɒmɪtəʳ, *Am:* -'krɑ:-mətəʳ] *n* micrómetro *m*

Micronesia [ˌmaɪkrəʊ'ni:ziə, *Am:* -krou-'niʒə] *n* Micronesia *f*

microorganism [ˌmaɪkrəʊ'ɔ:gənɪzəm, *Am:* -krou'ɔ:r-] *n* microorganismo *m*

microphone ['maɪkrəfəʊn, *Am:* -foun] *n* micrófono *m;* **to speak into a ~** hablar por micrófono

microprocessor [ˌmaɪkrə'prəʊsesəʳ, *Am:* -krouˌprɑ:sesəʳ] *n* microprocesador *m*

microscope ['maɪkrəskəʊp, *Am:* -skoup] *n* microscopio *m*

microscopic [ˌmaɪkrə'skɒpɪk, *Am:* -'skɑ:pɪk] *adj* microscópico, -a

microwave ['maɪkrəʊweɪv, *Am:* -krou-] I. *n* 1. (*wave*) microonda *f* 2. (*oven*) microondas *m inv* II. *vt* poner en el microondas

microwave oven *n* microondas *m inv*

mid [mɪd] *prep* en medio de

midday [ˌmɪd'deɪ] I. *n no pl* mediodía *m;* **at ~** a mediodía; **~ meal** almuerzo *m,* comida *f* II. *adj* de mediodía

middle [mɪdl] I. *n* 1. (*centre*) medio *m;* **in the ~ of** sth en medio de algo; **in the ~ of the night** en plena noche; **to be in the ~ of doing** sth estar ocupado haciendo algo; **(in) the ~ of nowhere** donde da la vuelta el viento; **in the ~ of the square** en el centro de la plaza 2. *inf* (*waist*) cintura *f* II. *adj* 1. (*equidistant*) central 2. (*medium*) medio, -a

middle age *n* mediana edad *f* **middle-aged** *adj* de mediana edad **Middle Ages** *npl* Edad *f* Media

middlebrow ['mɪdlbraʊ] *adj* (*literature, music*) de nivel cultural medio

middle class *n* clase *f* media

middle-class *adj* de la clase media

middle ear *n* oído *m* medio

Middle East *n* Oriente *m* Medio

middleman ['mɪdlmæn] <-men> *n* intermediario *m*

middle name *n* segundo nombre *m*

middle-of-the-road *adj* moderado, -a

middleweight ['mɪdlweɪt] *n* SPORTS peso *m* medio

middling ['mɪdlɪŋ] I. *adj inf* 1. (*average*) mediano, -a 2. (*not very good*) regular II. *adv* regular

Mideast *n* Oriente *m* Medio

midge [mɪdʒ] *n* mosca pequeña de picadura muy irritante

midget ['mɪdʒɪt] I. *adj* en miniatura II. *n* enano, -a *m, f*

mid-life crisis [ˌmɪd'laɪf 'kraɪsɪs] *n* crisis *f inv* de los cuarenta

midnight ['mɪdnaɪt] I. *n no pl* medianoche *f* II. *adj* de medianoche

midpoint ['mɪdpɔɪnt] *n a.* MAT punto *m* medio

midriff ['mɪdrɪf] *n* ANAT diafragma *m*

midshipman ['mɪdʃɪpmən] <-men> *n Brit* guardia *m* marina

midships ['mɪdʃɪps] *adv* en medio del navío

midst [mɪdst] *n no pl* **in the ~ of** en medio de

midsummer [ˌmɪd'sʌməʳ, *Am:* -ə·] *n no pl* pleno verano *m*

Midsummer('s) Day *n* día *m* de San Juan

midterm [ˌmɪd'tɜ:m, *Am:* -'tɜ:rm] *adj* UNIV (*exam*) de mitad del trimestre

midway [ˌmɪd'weɪ] I. *adv* a mitad del camino II. *n Am* avenida *f* central

midweek [ˌmɪd'wi:k] *adv* a mediados de semana

midwife ['mɪdwaɪf] <-wives> *n* comadrona *f*

midwifery ['mɪdwɪfri, *Am:* ˌmɪd'wɪfə·-] *n no pl* partería *f*

midwinter [ˌmɪd'wɪntəʳ, *Am:* -t̬əʳ] *n no pl* pleno invierno *m*

might¹ [maɪt] *pt of* **may** **it ~ be that ...** podría ser que... +*subj;* **how old ~ she be?** ¿qué edad tendrá?; **~ I open the window?** ¿podría abrir la ventana?

might² [maɪt] *n no pl* 1. (*authority*) poder *m* 2. (*strength*) fuerza *f;* **military ~** poderío *m* militar; **with all one's ~** con todas sus fuerzas ►**with ~ and main** a más no poder

mightily ['maɪtɪli, *Am:* 'maɪt̬ɪ-] *adv liter* fuertemente

mighty ['maɪti, *Am:* 'maɪt̬i] I. <-ier, -iest> *adj* 1. (*powerful*) fuerte 2. (*great*) enorme II. *adv Am, inf* enormemente

migraine ['mi:greɪn, *Am:* 'maɪ-] <-(s)> *n* migraña *f*

migrant ['maɪgrənt] I. *n* 1. (*person*) emigrante *mf* 2. ZOOL ave *f* migratoria II. *adj* migratorio, -a

migrant worker *n* trabajador(a) *m(f)* emigrante

migrate [maɪ'greɪt, *Am:* '--] *vi* emigrar

migration [maɪ'greɪʃən] <-(s)> *n* emigración *f*

migratory ['maɪgrətri, *Am:* -tɔ:r-] *adj* migratorio, -a

mike [maɪk] *n inf abbr of* **microphone** micro *m*

mild [maɪld] I. <-er, -est> *adj* 1. (*not severe*) apacible; (*criticism*) moderado, -a; (*penalty*) leve 2. (*not strong tasting*) suave 3. METEO templado, -a 4. MED (*not serious*) benigno, -a II. *n no pl, Brit* cerveza *f* suave

mildew ['mɪldju:, *Am:* -du:] *n no pl* moho *m*

mildly ['maɪldli] *adv* 1. (*gently*) suavemente; **to punish sb ~** castigar a alguien de forma poco severa 2. (*slightly*) ligeramente ►**to put**

M

it ~, **that's** putting it ~ por no decir algo peor
mildness ['maɪldnɪs] *n no pl* **1.** (*placidity*)
apacibilidad *f* **2.** (*softness*) suavidad *f*
mile [maɪl] *n* milla *f* (*1,61 km*); **to walk for
~s** andar kilómetros y kilométros; **to be ~s
away** *fig* estar fuera de onda ►**to smell sth a
~ off** ver algo a la legua; **to stick** [*o* stand] **out
a ~** verse a la legua
mileage ['maɪlɪdʒ] *n no pl* AUTO kilometraje
m
mileometer [maɪ'lɒmɪtər, *Am:* -'lɑ:məţər]
n Aus, Brit cuentamillas *m inv*
milepost ['maɪlpəʊst] *n* mojón *m*
milestone ['maɪlstəʊn, *Am:* -stoʊn] *n*
1. (*marker*) mojón *m* **2.** *fig* hito *m*
militant ['mɪlɪtənt] **I.** *adj* militante **II.** *n* militante *mf*
militarism ['mɪlɪtərɪzəm, *Am:* -təˠ-] *n no pl*
militarismo *m*
militarist ['mɪlɪtərɪst, *Am:* -təˠ-] *n* militarista
mf
militaristic [ˌmɪlɪtə'rɪstɪk] *adj* militarista
militarize ['mɪlɪtəraɪz] *vt* militarizar
military ['mɪlɪtri, *Am:* -ter-] **I.** *n* **the ~** los
militares **II.** *adj* militar
military academy *n Am* academia *f* militar
military police *n* policía *f* militar **military
service** *n* servicio *m* militar
militia [mɪ'lɪʃə] *n* milicia *f*
milk [mɪlk] **I.** *n no pl* leche *f* ►**the ~ of
human kindness** la compasión personificada;
there's no use crying over spilt ~ a lo hecho
pecho **II.** *vt* **1.** ordeñar **2.** *fig* **to ~ sb dry** chupar la sangre a alguien
milk bar *n* cafetería *f* **milk chocolate** *n*
chocolate *m* con leche **milk float** *n Brit*
carro *m* de la leche
milking machine ['mɪlkɪŋməʃiːn] *n* orde-
ñador *m* automático
milkmaid *n* lechera *f* **milkman** <-men> *n*
lechero *m* **milkshake** *n* batido *m* de leche,
malteada *f Méx* **milksop** *n* marica *m* **milk
tooth** *n* diente *m* de leche
milky ['mɪlki] <-ier, -iest> *adj* **1.** (*colour,
skin*) lechoso, -a **2.** (*tea, coffee*) con mucha
leche
Milky Way *n no pl* **the ~** la Vía Láctea
mill [mɪl] **I.** *n* **1.** (*machine: for grain*) molino
m; (*for coffee*) molinillo *m* **2.** (*factory*) fábrica
f (de tejidos) ►**to go through the ~** pasarlas
moradas; **to** put sb through **the ~** someter a
alguien a duras pruebas **II.** *vt* **1.** (*grain, coffee*)
moler **2.** (*metal*) fresar
millennium [mɪ'lenɪəm] <-s *o* -ennia> *n*
milenio *m*
miller ['mɪləˠ, *Am:* -əˠ] *n* molinero, -a *m, f*
millet ['mɪlət] *n no pl* mijo *m*
millibar ['mɪlɪbɑː, *Am:* -bɑːr] *n* milibar *m*
milligram(me) ['mɪlɪɡræm] *n* miligramo *m*
millilitre *n Am,* **milliliter** ['mɪlɪˌliːtəˠ, *Am:*
-ţəˠ] *n* mililitro *m*
millimetre *n Am,* **millimeter** ['mɪlɪˌmiːtəˠ,
Am: -ţəˠ] *n* milímetro *m*

milliner ['mɪlɪnəˠ, *Am:* -nəˠ] *n* sombrerera *f*
millinery ['mɪlɪnəri, *Am:* -ner-] *n* sombrere-
ría *f*
million ['mɪlɪən, *Am:* -jən] <-(s)> *n* millón
m; **two ~ people** dos millones de personas; **a
~ times** *inf* una infinidad de veces; **to be one
in a ~** ser único
millionaire [ˌmɪlɪə'neəˠ, *Am:* -'ner] *n* millonario, -a *m, f*
millipede ['mɪlɪpiːd] *n* milpiés *m inv*
millpond *n* represa *f* de molino ►**as** still **as a
~** como una balsa de aceite **millstone** *n* piedra *f* de molino ►**to be a ~ round sb's** neck
ser una cruz para alguien **mill wheel** *n*
rueda *f* de molino
milt [mɪlt] *n* lecha *f*
mime [maɪm] **I.** *n* THEAT pantomima *f* **II.** *vi*
actuar de mimo **III.** *vt* imitar
mime artist *n* mimo *mf*
mimic ['mɪmɪk] **I.** *vt* <-ck-> imitar **II.** *n* imi-
tador(a) *m(f)*
mimicry ['mɪmɪkri] *n no pl* **1.** (*art*) mímica *f*;
(*imitation*) imitación *f* **2.** BIO mimetismo *m*
mimosa [mɪ'məʊzə, *Am:* -'moʊsə] *n* mimosa *f*
min. 1. *abbr of* **minute** min. **2.** *abbr of* **minimum** mín.
minaret [ˌmɪnə'ret] *n* alminar *m*
mince [mɪns] **I.** *vt* picar **II.** *vi* andar con pasos
muy cortos **III.** *n no pl, Aus, Brit* carne *f* picada
mincemeat *n no pl Brit* (*meat*) carne *f*
picada; (*fruit*) picadillo *m* de fruta ►**to** make
~ of sb *inf* hacer picadillo a alguien **mince
pie** *n* pastel *m* de frutas picadas
mincer ['mɪnsəˠ, *Am:* -əˠ] *n* picadora *f* de
carne
mincing ['mɪnsɪŋ] *adj* remilgado, -a, afectado, -a
mind [maɪnd] **I.** *n* **1.** (*brain*) mente *f*; **to be
in one's right ~** estar en sus cabales; **to be
out of one's ~** estar fuera de juicio
2. (*thought*) pensamiento *m*; **to have sth in ~**
tener algo presente; **to bring sth to ~** recordar
algo **3.** (*intention*) intención *f*; **to change
one's ~** cambiar de parecer; **to have sth in ~**
tener pensado algo; **to have half a ~ to ...**
estar casi por...; **to know one's own ~** saber
lo que uno quiere; **to make up one's ~** decidirse; **to set one's ~ on sth** desear algo con
vehemencia; **to set one's ~ to sth** estar
resuelto a algo; **to set one's ~ at ease** tranquilizarse **4.** (*consciousness*) conciencia *f*; **her
mother is on her ~** está preocupada por su
madre; **this will take your ~ off it** esto te dis-
traerá **5.** (*opinion*) opinión *f*; **to be of the
same ~** ser de la misma opinión; **to give sb a
piece of one's ~** cantar las cuarenta a alguien;
to be in two ~s dudar entre dos cosas, estar
en un dilema ►**in my ~'s** eye en mi imaginación; **it's a question of ~ over** matter es
una cuestión que requiere fuerza de voluntad;
to have a ~ like a sewer tener una mente
cochambrosa **II.** *vt* **1.** (*be careful of*) tener cui-

dado con; ~ **what you're doing!** ¡cuidado lo que haces!; ~ **the step!** ¡cuidado con la escalera! **2.**(*bother*) sentirse molesto por; **I don't ~ the cold** el frío no me molesta; **do you ~ my smoking?** ¿te molesta si fumo?; **would you ~ opening the window?** ¿haces el favor de abrir la ventana?; **I wouldn't ~ a beer** no vendría mal una cerveza **3.**(*look after*) estar al cuidado de; **don't ~ me** no te preocupes por mí ►**to ~ one's p's and q's** tener sumo cuidado en lo que uno dice **III.** *vi* **never ~!** ¡no importa!; **I don't ~** me es igual; **if you don't ~, I prefer ...** si no te importa, prefiero...; **would you ~ if ...** ¿le importa si...?

mind-bending ['maɪndbendɪŋ] *adj* increíble **mind-blowing** *adj inf* alucinante

minded *adj* dispuesto, -a; **to be ~ to** estar dispuesto a

minder ['maɪndə^r, *Am:* -də$^.$] *n* guardaespaldas *mf inv*

mindful ['maɪndfəl] *adj form* cuidadoso, -a; **to be ~ of sth** tener presente algo

mindless ['maɪndlɪs] *adj* **1.**(*job*) mecánico, -a **2.**(*violence*) gratuito, -a **3.**(*heedless*) descuidado, -a

mind reader *n* adivinador(a) *m(f)* de pensamientos

mine[1] [maɪn] *pron pos* (el) mío, (la) mía, (los) míos, (las) mías; **it's not his bag, it's ~** no es su bolsa, es la mía; **this glass is ~** este vaso es mío; **these are his shoes and those are ~** estos zapatos son suyos y estos (son) míos

mine[2] [maɪn] **I.** *n* MIN, MIL mina *f*; **a ~ of information** *fig* una fuente abundante de información **II.** *vt* **1.** MIN extraer **2.** MIL sembrar minas en

mine detector *n* detector *m* de minas

minefield ['maɪnfiːld] *n* **1.**campo *m* de minas **2.***fig* terreno *m* minado

miner ['maɪnə^r, *Am:* -nə$^.$] *n* minero, -a *m, f*

mineral ['mɪnərəl] **I.** *n* mineral *m* **II.** *adj* mineral

mineralogical [ˌmɪnərə'lɒdʒɪkl, *Am:* -'lɑːdʒɪ-] *adj* mineralógico, -a

mineralogist [ˌmɪnə'rælədʒɪst, *Am:* -'rɑːlə-] *n* mineralogista *mf*

mineralogy [ˌmɪnə'rælədʒi, *Am:* -'rɑːlə-] *n no pl* mineralogía *f*

mineral water *n* agua *f* mineral

minesweeper ['maɪnˌswiːpə^r, *Am:* -pə$^.$] *n inf* dragaminas *m inv*

mingle ['mɪŋgl] **I.** *vt* mezclar; **to be ~d with sth** confundirse con algo **II.** *vi* mezclarse; **to ~ with the guests** mezclarse con los invitados

miniature ['mɪnɪtʃə^r, *Am:* -ɪətʃə$^.$] **I.** *adj* de miniatura **II.** *n* miniatura *f*

miniature camera *n* cámara *f* de bolsillo **miniature railway** *n* ferrocarril *m* miniatura

minibus ['mɪnɪbʌs] *n* microbús *m*

minicab ['mɪnɪkæb] *n Brit* taxi *m*

minim ['mɪnɪm] *n Aus, Brit* MUS corchera *f*

minimal ['mɪnɪml] *adj* mínimo, -a

minimize ['mɪnɪmaɪz] *vt* minimizar; *fig* menospreciar

minimum ['mɪnɪməm] **I.**<-s *o* minima> *n* mínimo *m;* **to reduce sth to a ~** reducir algo al mínimo **II.** *adj* mínimo, -a; **~ requirements** requisitos *mpl* básicos

mining ['maɪnɪŋ] *n no pl* minería *f*

mining engineer *n* ingeniero, -a *m, f* de minas

minion ['mɪnjən] *n* secuaz *mf*

miniskirt ['mɪnɪskɜːt, *Am:* -skɜːrt] *n* minifalda *f*

minister ['mɪnɪstə^r, *Am:* stə$^.$] *n* **1.** POL ministro, -a *m, f* **2.** REL pastor *m*

ministerial [ˌmɪnɪ'stɪəriəl, *Am:* -'stɪri-] *adj* ministerial

ministrations [ˌmɪnɪ'streɪʃən] *n pl, liter* atenciones *fpl*

ministry ['mɪnɪstri] <-ies> *n* **1.** POL ministerio *m* **2.** REL sacerdocio *m;* **to enter the ~** (*Catholic*) hacerse sacerdote; (*Protestant*) hacerse pastor

mink [mɪŋk] *n no pl* visón *m*

minor ['maɪnə^r, *Am:* -nə$^.$] **I.** *adj* (*not great*) pequeño, -a; (*role*) secundario, -a; (*detail*) sin importancia; **~ offence** delito *m* de menor cuantía; **B ~** MUS si *m* menor **II.** *n* **1.**(*person*) menor *mf* de edad **2.** *Am* UNIV asignatura *f* secundaria

Minorca [mɪ'nɔːka, *Am:* -'nɔːr-] *n* Menorca *f*

Minorcan **I.** *adj* menorquín **II.** *n* menorquín, -ina *m, f*

minority [maɪ'nɒrəti, *Am:* -'nɔːrəti] **I.**<-ies> *n* minoría *f;* **to be a ~ of one** ser el único que piensa así; **in a ~ of cases** en muy raros casos **II.** *adj* minoritario, -a; **~ sport** deporte de minorías

minstrel ['mɪnstrəl] *n* HIST juglar *m*

mint[1] [mɪnt] *n* **1.** *no pl* (*herb*) hierbabuena *f* **2.**(*sweet*) caramelo *m* de menta

mint[2] [mɪnt] **I.** *n* (*coin factory*) casa *f* de la moneda; **to make a ~** *inf* ganar un montón de dinero **II.** *vt* acuñar; **to ~ a word** *fig* acuñar una palabra **III.** *adj* (*coin*) de reciente acuñación; (*stamp*) nuevo, -a; **in ~ condition** en perfecto estado

mint tea *n* té *m* de menta

minuet [ˌmɪnju'et] *n* minué *m*

minus ['maɪnəs] **I.** *prep* **1.** *a.* MAT menos; **5 ~ 2 equals 3** 5 menos 2 igual a 3; **~ ten Celsius** diez grados bajo cero **2.** *inf*(*without*) sin **II.** *adj* MAT menos; (*number*) negativo, -a; **to be in ~ figures** estar en números rojos **III.** *n* signo *m* de menos

minuscule ['mɪnəskjuːl, *Am:* -ɪ-] *adj* minúsculo, -a

minute[1] ['mɪnɪt] *n* **1.**(*sixty seconds*) minuto *m* **2.**(*moment*) momento *m;* **any ~** de un momento a otro; **at the last ~** a última hora; **in a ~** ahora mismo; **this very ~** ahora mismo; **to the ~** puntual; **wait a ~** espera un segundo **3.** *pl* (*of meeting*) acta(s) *f(pl)*

minute[2] [maɪ'njuːt, *Am:* -'nuːt] *adj* diminuto, -a

minute hand *n* minutero *m*

minutely *adv* minuciosamente

minutiae [mar'nju:ʃiː, *Am:* mr'nuː-] *npl* minucias *fpl*

minx [mɪŋks] *n iron* descarada *f inf*

miracle ['mɪrəkl] *n* milagro *m;* **by a ~** por milagro

miracle play *n* HIST, THEAT auto *m* sacramental

miraculous [mɪ'rækjʊləs, *Am:* -jə-] *adj* milagroso, -a

mirage ['mɪrɑːʒ] *n* espejismo *m*

mire ['maɪəʳ, *Am:* maɪr] I. *n* 1. (*swamp*) fango *m* 2. *fig* berenjenal *m* II. *vt* **to become ~d in sth** quedar atascado en algo

mirror ['mɪrəʳ, *Am:* -ə-] I. *n* espejo *m* II. *vt* reflejar

mirror image *n* contraimagen *f*

mirth [mɜːθ, *Am:* mɜːrθ] *n no pl* regocijo *m*

mirthful ['mɜːθfəl, *Am:* 'mɜːrθ-] *adj* alegre

mirthless ['mɜːθləs, *Am:* 'mɜːrθ-] *adj* 1. (*joyless*) triste 2. (*unhappy*) infeliz

misadventure [mɪsəd'ventʃəʳ, *Am:* -tʃɚ] *n* desgracia *f;* **death by ~** muerte *f* accidental

misalliance [mɪsə'laɪəns] *n* 1. (*alliance*) alianza *f* inconveniente 2. (*marriage*) matrimonio *m* desigual

misanthrope ['mɪsnθrəʊp, *Am:* -θroʊp] *n* misántropo, -a *m, f*

misanthropic [mɪsn'θrɒpɪk, *Am:* -ən-'θrɑːpɪk] *adj* misantrópico, -a

misanthropy [mɪs'ænθrəpi] *n no pl* misantropía *f*

misapply [mɪsə'plaɪ] <-ie-> *vt* **to ~ sth** hacer un uso indebido de algo

misapprehend [mɪsæprɪ'hend] *vt* comprender mal

misapprehension [mɪsæprɪ'henʃən] *n* mala interpretación *f;* **to be under a ~** estar equivocado

misappropriate [mɪsə'prəʊprɪeɪt, *Am:* -'proʊ-] *vt* FIN malversar

misappropriation [mɪsəprəʊprɪ'eɪʃən, *Am:* -proʊ-] *n no pl* FIN malversación *f*

misbehave [mɪsbɪ'heɪv] *vi* portarse mal

misbehavior *n Am, Aus,* **misbehaviour** [mɪsbɪ'heɪvjəʳ, *Am:* -vjɚ] *n no pl* mala conducta *f*

misc. *adj abbr of* **miscellaneous** diverso, -a

miscalculate [mɪs'kælkjʊleɪt, *Am:* -kjə-] *vt, vi* calcular mal

miscalculation [mɪskælkjʊ'leɪʃən, *Am:* -kjə'-] *n* error *m* de cálculo

miscarriage [mɪs'kærɪdʒ, *Am:* 'mɪskɚ-] *n* aborto *m* (espontáneo)

miscarry [mɪs'kæri, *Am:* 'mɪskɚ-] <-ied, -ying> *vi* 1. MED abortar 2. *fig* fracasar

miscellaneous [mɪsə'leɪnɪəs] *adj* diverso, -a; **~ expenses** gastos *mpl* varios

miscellany [mɪ'seləni, *Am:* 'mɪsəleɪ-] <-ies> *n* miscelánea *f*

mischance [mɪs'tʃɑːns, *Am:* 'tʃæns] *n* (*bad luck*) mala suerte *f;* (*unlucky event*) infortunio

m; **by some ~** por desgracia

mischief ['mɪstʃɪf] *n* 1. (*naughtiness*) travesura *f;* **to keep sb out of ~** impedir a alguien hacer travesuras 2. **to get (oneself) into ~** meterse en problemas; **to make ~ for sb** amargar la vida a alguien 3. (*wickedness*) malicia *f*

mischievous ['mɪstʃɪvəs, *Am:* -tʃə-] *adj* 1. (*naughty*) travieso, -a 2. (*malicious*) malicioso, -a; **~ rumours** rumores *mpl* malintencionados

misconceive [mɪskən'siːv] *vt form* malinterpretar

misconceived *adj* mal concebido, -a

misconception [mɪskən'sepʃən] *n* idea *f* equivocada; **a popular ~** un error común

misconduct [mɪskən'dʌkt, *Am:* -'kɑːn-] I. *n no pl* 1. (*misbehaviour*) mala conducta *f* 2. (*mismanage*) mala gestión *f* II. *vt* 1. (*behave badly*) **to ~ oneself** conducirse mal 2. (*organize badly*) gestionar mal

misconstruction [mɪskən'strʌkʃən] *n form* mala interpretación *f*

misconstrue [mɪskən'struː] *vt* malinterpretar

misdeed [mɪs'diːd] *n form* fechoría *f*

misdemeanor *n Am,* **misdemeanour** [mɪsdɪ'miːnəʳ, *Am:* -nɚ] *n Brit* 1. LAW falta *f* 2. (*bad behaviour*) mala conducta *f*

misdirect [mɪsdɪ'rekt, *Am:* -də'-] *vt* 1. (*letter*) mandar a una dirección equivocada; (*person*) dar indicaciones equivocadas 2. LAW instruir mal

miser ['maɪzəʳ, *Am:* -zɚ] *n* avaro, -a *m, f*

miserable ['mɪzrəbl] *adj* 1. (*unhappy*) triste; **to make life ~ for sb** hacer insoportable la vida a alguien 2. (*poor*) mísero, -a; **a ~ amount** una miseria 3. (*unpleasant*) lamentable

miserably *adv* 1. (*unhappily*) tristemente 2. (*completely*) **to fail ~** fallar del todo

miserly *adj* avaricioso, -a

misery ['mɪzəri] *n* 1. (*unhappiness*) infelicidad *f* 2. *no pl* (*suffering*) sufrimiento *m;* **to make sb's life a ~** amargar la vida a alguien 3. (*extreme poverty*) miseria *f,* lipidia *f AmC*

misfire [mɪs'faɪəʳ, *Am:* -'faɪɚ] *vi* 1. (*weapon*) encasquillarse 2. *fig* (*joke*) no tener éxito 3. (*engine*) fallar

misfit ['mɪsfɪt] *n* inadaptado, -a *m, f*

misfortune [mɪs'fɔːtʃuːn, *Am:* -'fɔːrtʃən] *n no pl* infortunio *m;* **to suffer ~** sufrir una desgracia

misgiving [mɪs'gɪvɪŋ] *n* recelo *m;* **to express ~s** recelar; **to be filled with ~** estar lleno de dudas

misgovern [mɪs'gʌvən, *Am:* -ɚn] *vt* (*country*) gobernar mal; (*business*) gestionar mal

misgovernment *n no pl* (*of country*) mal gobierno *m;* (*of company*) mala gestión *f*

misguided [mɪs'gaɪdɪd] *adj* desencaminado, -a; **~ idea** desacierto *m*

mishandle [ˌmɪs'hændl] *vt* **1.** (*handle without care*) manejar mal **2.** (*maltreat*) maltratar **3.** (*deal badly with*) llevar mal

mishap ['mɪshæp] *n form* percance *m;* **he had a ~** *iron* tuvo un percance; **a series of ~s** una serie de contratiempos

mishear [ˌmɪs'hɪəʳ, *Am:* -'hɪr] *vt irr* oír mal

mishmash ['mɪʃmæʃ] *n* revoltijo *m;* **a ~ of sth** una mezcolanza de algo

misinform [ˌmɪsɪn'fɔːm, *Am:* -'fɔːrm] *vt* informar mal, desinformar *Méx*

misinterpret [ˌmɪsɪn'tɜːprɪt, *Am:* -'tɜːr-] *vt* interpretar mal, malinterpretar *Méx*

misinterpretation [ˌmɪsɪntɜːprɪ'teɪʃən, *Am:* -tɜːr-] *n* interpretación *f* errónea

misjudge [ˌmɪs'dʒʌdʒ] *vt* juzgar mal

misjudgement [mɪs'dʒʌdʒmənt] *n* mal cálculo *m*

mislay [ˌmɪs'leɪ] *vt irr, form* extraviar

mislead [ˌmɪs'liːd] *vt irr* **1.** (*deceive*) engañar; **to ~ sb about sth** engañar a alguien acerca de algo; **to ~ sb into doing sth** engañar a alguien para que haga algo **2.** (*lead into error*) hacer caer en un error; **to let oneself be misled** dejarse engañar **3.** (*corrupt*) corromper

misleading *adj* engañoso, -a

mismanage [ˌmɪs'mænɪdʒ] *vt* administrar mal; **to ~ a business** gestionar mal una empresa

mismanagement *n* mala gestión *f*

misname [ˌmɪs'neɪm] *vt* **to ~ sth** dar un nombre equivocado a algo

misnomer [ˌmɪs'nəʊməʳ, *Am:* -'noʊməˮ] *n* nombre *m* equivocado

misogynist [mɪ'sɒdʒɪnɪst, *Am:* -'sɑːdʒən-] **I.** *n* misógino *m* **II.** *adj* misógino, -a

misplace [ˌmɪs'pleɪs] *vt* **1.** (*lose*) extraviar **2.** *fig* (*confidence*) dar indebidamente

misprint ['mɪsˌprɪnt] *n* errata *f*

mispronounce [ˌmɪsprə'naʊns] *vt* pronunciar mal

mispronunciation [ˌmɪsprəˌnʌnsɪ'eɪʃən] *n* mala pronunciación *f*

misread [ˌmɪs'riːd] *vt irr* **1.** (*read badly*) leer mal **2.** (*interpret badly*) interpretar mal, malinterpretar *Méx*

misrepresent [ˌmɪsˌreprɪ'zent] *vt* tergiversar

misrepresentation [ˌmɪsˌreprɪzen'teɪʃən] *n* tergiversación *f*

miss¹ [mɪs] *n* (*form of adress*) señorita *f;* **Miss Spain** Miss España

miss² [mɪs] **I.** <-es> *n* fallo *m;* **to give sth a ~** *Brit, Aus, inf* pasar de algo **II.** *vi* fallar **III.** *vt* **1.** (*not hit*) fallar **2.** (*not catch*) perder; **to ~ the bus/train** perder el bus/tren; **to ~ a deadline** no cumplir con una fecha límite **3.** (*avoid*) evitar **4.** (*not notice*) no fijarse en; **to ~ sb** no encontrar a alguien; **you didn't ~ much** no te has perdido nada; **you can't ~ it** no te lo puedes perder **5.** (*not hear*) no oír **6.** (*overlook*) saltarse; **to ~ a meeting** faltar a una reunión **7.** (*not take advantage*) dejar

pasar; **to ~ an opportunity** perder una oportunidad **8.** (*regret absence*) echar de menos **9.** (*notice loss*) echar en falta

◆**miss out I.** *vt* **1.** (*omit*) omitir **2.** (*overlook*) saltarse **II.** *vi* **to ~ on sth** perderse algo

misshapen [ˌmɪs'ʃeɪpən] *adj* (*malformed*) deformado, -a

missile ['mɪsaɪl, *Am:* 'mɪsəl] *n* (*rocket*) misil *m;* (*projectile*) proyectil *m*

missile base *n* base *f* de misiles **missile defence system** *n* sistema *m* defensivo de misiles **missile launcher** *n* lanzamisiles *m inv*

missing ['mɪsɪŋ] *adj* **1.** (*lost: person*) desaparecido, -a; (*thing or object*) perdido, -a; **~ in combat** desaparecido en combate; **to report sth ~** dar parte de la pérdida de algo **2.** (*absent*) ausente

missing link *n* eslabón *m* perdido **missing person** *n* desaparecido, -a *m, f*

mission ['mɪʃən] *n* **1.** *a.* REL (*task*) misión *f;* **peace ~** misión de paz; **rescue ~** operación *f* de rescate; **his ~ in life** su misión en la vida; **~ accomplished** misión cumplida **2.** (*space project*) misión *f* espacial **3.** (*trade centre*) misión *f* comercial **4.** POL delegación *f*

missionary ['mɪʃənəri, *Am:* -əner-] **I.** <-ies> *n* misionero, -a *m, f* **II.** *adj* misionero, -a

missionary position *n iron* postura *f* del misionero

mission control *n* centro *m* de control

missis ['mɪsɪz] *n inf s.* **missus**

misspell [ˌmɪs'spel] *vt irr* escribir mal

misspelling *n* falta *f* de ortografía

misspent [ˌmɪs'spent] *adj* desperdiciado, -a; **a ~ youth** una juventud malgastada

misstate [ˌmɪs'steɪt] *vt* sostener erróneamente

missus ['mɪsɪz] *n inf* (*wife*) parienta *f*

mist [mɪst] *n* **1.** (*light fog*) neblina *f;* **to be shrouded in ~** estar cubierto por la neblina **2.** *Brit* (*condensation*) vaho *m*

◆**mist up** *vi* empañarse

mistakable [mɪ'steɪkəbl] *adj* confundible

mistake [mɪ'steɪk] **I.** *n* error *m;* **typing ~** errata *f;* **to learn from one's ~s** aprender de los propios errores; **to make a ~** cometer un error; **make no ~ about it** no te equivoques; **to repeat past ~s** repetir los errores del pasado; **there must be some ~** tiene que haber un error; **by ~** por error **II.** *vt irr* confundir

mistaken [mɪ'steɪkən] **I.** *pp of* **mistake II.** *adj* (*belief*) equivocado, -a; (*identity*) confundido, -a; **to be** (**very much**) **~** estar (muy) equivocado; **unless I'm very much ~ ...** si no me equivoco...

Mister ['mɪstəʳ, *Am:* -təˮ] *n* señor *m*

mistime [ˌmɪs'taɪm] *vt* hacer algo a destiempo

mistletoe ['mɪsltəʊ, *Am:* -toʊ] *n* muérdago *m*

M

mistook [mɪ'stʊk] *pt of* **mistake**

mistranslate [ˌmɪstrænz'leɪt, *Am:* -'trænzleɪt] *vt* traducir mal

mistreat [ˌmɪs'triːt] *vt* maltratar

mistress ['mɪstrɪs] *n* 1. (*sexual partner*) amante *f* 2. (*woman in charge*) ama *f*; the ~ of the house la dueña de la casa 3. *Brit* SCHOOL maestra *f* 4. (*owner*) dueña *f*

mistrial [ˌmɪs'traɪəl, *Am:* 'mɪs,-] *n* juicio *m* invalidado

mistrust [ˌmɪs'trʌst] I. *n no pl* desconfianza *f*; to have a ~ of sb/sth recelar de alguien/algo II. *vt* to ~ sb/sth recelar de alguien/algo

mistrustful [ˌmɪs'trʌstfəl] *adj* receloso, -a; to be ~ of sb/sth recelar de alguien/algo

misty ['mɪsti] <-ier, -iest> *adj* 1. (*foggy*) neblinoso, -a; (*window, glasses*) empañado, -a 2. *fig* borroso, -a

misunderstand [ˌmɪsˌʌndə'stænd, *Am:* -dəʳ-] *vt irr* entender mal

misunderstanding *n* 1. (*failure to understand*) malentendido *m;* there must be some ~ debe haber un malentendido 2. (*disagreement*) desacuerdo *m*

misuse¹ [ˌmɪs'juːs] *n* 1. (*wrong use*) mal uso *m* 2. (*excessive consumption*) abuso *m*

misuse² [ˌmɪs'juːz] *vt* 1. (*handle wrongly*) manejar mal 2. (*consume to excess*) abusar de

mite [maɪt] *n* 1. (*insect*) ácaro *m* 2. *Brit, inf* (*child*) chiquillo, -a *m, f* 3. (*small amount*) pizca *f*

miter ['maɪtəʳ] *n Am s.* **mitre**

mitigate ['mɪtɪgeɪt, *Am:* -'mɪt̬-] *vt form* mitigar

mitigation [ˌmɪtɪ'geɪʃən, *Am:* ˌmɪt̬-] *n no pl* atenuación *f*; in ~ como atenuante

mitre ['maɪtəʳ, *Am:* -t̬əʳ] *n* mitra *f*

mitten ['mɪtn] *n* manopla *f*

mix [mɪks] I. *n* mezcla *f*; a ~ of people una mezcla de gente II. *vi* 1. (*combine*) mezclarse 2. (*socially*) to ~ with sb frecuentar a alguien; to ~ well llevarse bien III. *vt* 1. GASTR mezclar; (*dough*) amasar; (*cocktail*) preparar 2. (*combine*) combinar; to ~ business with pleasure combinar el placer con los negocios; religion and politics don't ~ la religión y la política no hacen buena combinación

♦**mix in** I. *vi* convivir II. *vt* to mix sth in with sth mezclar algo con algo

♦**mix up** *vt* 1. (*confuse*) confundir 2. (*put in wrong order*) revolver 3. GASTR mezclar ▶to mix it up <u>with</u> sb *Am, inf* pelearse con alguien

♦**mix up in** *vt* to be mixed up in sth estar involucrado en algo

♦**mix up with** *vt* to mix up sth with sth mezclar algo con algo; to be mixed up with sth estar involucrado en algo

♦**mix with** I. *vt always sep* confundir ▶to mix <u>it</u> with sb *Brit, inf* meterse con alguien II. *vi* (*associate with*) to ~ sb mezclarse con alguien

mixed *adj* 1. (*containing various elements*) mezclado, -a; (*team*) mixto, -a; ~ **marriage** matrimonio mixto; **person of** ~ **race** mestizo, -a *m, f* 2. (*contradictory*) contradictorio, -a; ~ **feelings** sentimientos contradictorios; **to be a** ~ **blessing** tener ventajas e inconvenientes

mixed doubles *npl* SPORTS dobles *mpl* mixtos

mixed economy *n* economía *f* mixta

mixed farming *n* agricultura *f* mixta

mixed grill *n* parrillada *f*

mixer ['mɪksəʳ, *Am:* -səʳ] *n* 1. (*machine*) batidora *f* 2. (*friendly person*) persona *f* sociable; **to be a good** ~ tener don de gentes 3. (*drink*) *bebida que se mezcla con alcohol en cócteles y combinados*

mixer faucet *n,* **mixer tap** *n Am* llave *f* mezcladora

mixture ['mɪkstʃəʳ, *Am:* -tʃəʳ] *n* mezcla *f*

mix-up ['mɪksʌp] *n* confusión *f*

Mk *n abbr of* **mark** 1. FIN marco *m* 2. AUTO modelo *m*

ml *n abbr of* **millilitre** ml

MLR *n abbr of* **minimum lending rate** tipo *m* de interés bancario

mm *abbr of* **millimetre** mm

mnemonic [nɪ'mɒnɪk, *Am:* nɪ'mɑːnɪk] *adj* mnemotécnico, -a

mo¹ [moʊ] *n Am abbr of* **month** mes *m*

mo² [məʊ, *Am:* moʊ] *inf abbr of* **moment** momento *m*

MO *n* 1. *abbr of* **modus operandi** procedimiento *m* 2. *abbr of* **Medical Office** médico *mf* militar 3. *abbr of* **money order** giro *m*

moan [məʊn, *Am:* moʊn] I. *n* 1. (*sound*) gemido *m* 2. (*complaint*) quejido *m* II. *vi* 1. (*make a sound*) gemir; **to** ~ **with pain** gemir de dolor 2. (*complain*) lamentarse; **to** ~ **about sth** lamentarse de algo; **to** ~ **that ...** lamentarse de que... +*subj*

moat [məʊt, *Am:* moʊt] *n* foso *m*

mob [mɒb, *Am:* mɑːb] I. *n* + *sing/pl vb* 1. (*crowd*) muchedumbre *f*; **angry** ~ turba *f*; ~ **law** la ley de la calle 2. *inf* **the Mob** la mafia 3. *Brit, inf* (*gang*) pandilla *f*; **iron** ~ banda *f* 4. *Aus* (*herd*) rebaño *m* II. <-bb-> *vt* acosar; **he was** ~**bed by his fans** sus fans se aglomeraron en torno a él

mobile [ˈməʊbaɪl, *Am:* ˈmoʊbəl] I. *n a.* TEL móvil *m* II. *adj* 1. (*able to move*) móvil; (*shop, canteen*) ambulante; **to be** ~ *inf* tener coche 2. (*movable*) movible

mobile home *n* caravana *f* **mobile phone** *n Brit* móvil *m*

mobilisation [ˌməʊbɪlaɪ'zeɪʃən] *n Brit, Aus s.* **mobilization**

mobilise *vt Brit, Aus s.* **mobilize**

mobility [məʊ'bɪləti, *Am:* moʊ'bɪlət̬i] *n no pl* movilidad *f*; **social** ~ *Brit* movilidad social

mobilization [ˌməʊbɪlaɪ'zeɪʃən, *Am:* -bəlɪ'-] *n a.* MIL movilización *f*

mobilize [ˈməʊbɪlaɪz, *Am:* -bə-] *vt* movilizar

moccasin [ˈmɒkəsɪn, *Am:* ˈmɑːkəsən] *n* mocasín *m*

mocha ['mɒkə, *Am:* 'moʊkə] *n no pl* moca *f;*
~ **ice cream** helado *m* de moca
mock [mɒk, *Am:* mɑːk] **I.** *adj* **1.** (*imitation*)
artificial; ~ **baroque** que imita el estilo barroco; ~ **leather** polipiel *f* **2.** (*practice*) ~
exam examen *m* de prueba **3.** (*fake*) ficticio,
-a; ~ **battle** simulacro *m* de batalla; ~ **façade**
fachada falsa; ~ **horror** horror fingido **II.** *vi*
burlarse; **to** ~ **at sb** burlarse de alguien **III.** *vt*
1. (*ridicule*) mofarse de **2.** (*imitate*) remedar
mocker ['mɒkə', *Am:* 'mɑːkə] *n* **to put the**
~**s on sth** frustrar algo
mockery ['mɒkəri, *Am:* 'mɑːkə-] *n* **1.** (*ridicule*) mofa *f* **2.** (*subject of derision*) hazmerreír *mf;* **to make a** ~ **of sth** ridiculizar a al-
guien/algo **3.** (*ridiculous imitation*) parodia *f*
mocking *n* burla *f*
mockingbird ['mɒkɪŋˌbɜːd, *Am:* 'mɑːkɪŋ-
ˌbɜːrd] *n* sinsonte *m*, cenzontle *m Méx*
mock-up ['mɒkʌp, *Am:* 'mɑːk-] *n* réplica *f*
MOD *n Brit s.* **Ministry of Defence** Ministerio
m de Defensa
modal ['məʊdəl, *Am:* 'moʊ-] *adj* modal
modal verb *n* verbo *m* modal
mode ['məʊd, *Am:* 'moʊd] *n* **1.** *a.* LING,
PHILOS (*style*) modo *m;* ~ **of life** modo de vida;
~ **of operation** forma *f* de operar; ~ **of transport** medio *m* de transporte **2.** *no pl, form*
(*fashion*) moda *f;* **to be all the** ~ estar a la
moda; **in** ~ a la moda
model ['mɒdəl, *Am:* 'mɑːdəl] **I.** *n* (*version,
example*) *a.* ART modelo *m;* (*of car, house*)
maqueta *f;* **to be the very** ~ **of sth** ser la viva
imagen de algo **II.** *adj* modélico, -a; **a** ~ **student** un alumno modelo **III.** <-ll-> *vt* **1.** (*make
figure, representation*) modelar; **to** ~ **sth in
clay** modelar algo en barro **2.** (*show clothes*)
desfilar **3. to** ~ **oneself on sb** tomar a alguien
como modelo
model maker *n* maquetista *mf*
modem ['məʊdem, *Am:* 'moʊdəm] *n* INFOR
módem *m*
moderate¹ ['mɒdərət, *Am:* 'mɑːdə-] **I.** *n*
POL moderado, -a *m, f* **II.** *adj* **1.** (*neither large
nor small*) mediano, -a **2.** *a.* POL (*not extreme:
speed*) moderado, -a; (*increase, means*) mesurado, -a; (*price*) módico, -a
moderate² ['mɒdəreɪt, *Am:* 'mɑːdər-] **I.** *vt*
moderar; **to** ~ **a discussion** moderar un
debate; **to** ~ **an examination** presidir un
examen **II.** *vi* **1.** (*become less extreme*) moderarse **2.** (*act as moderator*) moderar
moderation [ˌmɒdə'reɪʃən, *Am:* ˌmɑːdə-] *n
no pl* moderación *f;* **to drink in** ~ beber con
moderación
moderator ['mɒdəreɪtə', *Am:* 'mɑːdəˌeɪtə']
n form **1.** (*mediator*) mediador(a) *m(f)* **2.** *Am*
(*of discussion*) moderador(a) *m(f)* **3.** *Brit* (*of
exam*) supervisor(a) *m(f)*
modern ['mɒdən, *Am:* 'mɑːdə-n] *adj* moderno, -a
modernization [ˌmɒdənaɪ'zeɪʃən, *Am:*

ˌmɑːdənɪ-] *n* modernización *f*
modernize ['mɒdənaɪz, *Am:* 'mɑːdə-] *vt*
modernizar
modest ['mɒdɪst, *Am:* 'mɑːdɪst] *adj* **1.** (*not
boastful*) modesto, -a; **to be** ~ **about sth** ser
modesto en algo **2.** (*moderate*) moderado, -a; **a**
~ **wage** un sueldo modesto
modesty ['mɒdɪsti, *Am:* 'mɑːdɪst-] *n no pl*
modestia *f*
modicum ['mɒdɪkəm, *Am:* 'mɑːdɪ-] *n no pl*
pizca *f*, pisca *f Méx;* **a** ~ **of truth** una pizca de
verdad
modifiable ['mɒdɪfaɪəbl, *Am:* 'mɑːdɪ-] *adj*
modificable
modification [ˌmɒdɪfɪ'keɪʃən, *Am:*
ˌmɑːdɪ-] *n* modificación *f*
modifier ['mɒdɪfaɪə', *Am:* 'mɑːdɪfaɪə'] *n*
LING modificador *m*
modify ['mɒdɪfaɪ, *Am:* 'mɑːdɪ-] <-ie-> *vt*
a. LING modificar
modish ['məʊdɪʃ, *Am:* 'moʊ-] *adj* de moda
modular ['mɒdjʊlə', *Am:* 'mɑːdʒələ'] *adj*
modular; (*construction, degree*) por módu-
los
modulate ['mɒdjʊleɪt, *Am:* 'mɑːdʒə-] *vt a.*
ELEC, RADIO, TV modular
modulation [ˌmɒdjʊ'leɪʃən, *Am:*
ˌmɑːdʒə'-] *n* modulación *f*
module ['mɒdjuːl, *Am:* 'mɑːdʒuːl] *n*
módulo *m*
mohair ['məʊheə', *Am:* 'moʊher] *n* mohair
m
moist [mɔɪst] *adj* húmedo, -a
moisten ['mɔɪsn] **I.** *vt* humedecer **II.** *vi*
humedecerse
moisture ['mɔɪstʃə', *Am:* -tʃə'] *n* humedad *f*
moisturise ['mɔɪstʃəraɪz] *vt Brit, Aus s.*
moisturize
moisturiser *n Aus, Brit s.* **moisturizer**
moisturize ['mɔɪstʃəraɪz] *vt* hidratar
moisturizer *n* hidratante *m*
moisturizing cream *n* crema *f* hidratante
moisturizing lotion *n* loción *f* hidratant-
e
molar¹ ['məʊlə', *Am:* 'moʊlə'] *n* muela *f*
molar² ['məʊlə', *Am:* 'moʊlə'] *adj* CHEM
molar
molasses [məʊ'læsɪz, *Am:* moʊ-] *n* melaza
f
mold [məʊld, *Am:* moʊld] *n, vi Am s.*
mould²
Moldavia [mɒl'deɪviə, *Am:* mɑːl-] *n s.*
Moldova
Moldavian I. *adj* moldavo, -a **II.** *n* **1.** (*person*)
moldavo, -a *m, f* **2.** LING moldavo *m*
molder ['moʊldə'] *vi Am s.* **moulder**
molding *n Am s.* **moulding**
Moldova [mɒl'dəʊvə, *Am:* mɑːl'doʊ-] *n*
Moldavia *f*
Moldovan I. *adj* moldavo, -a **II.** *n* moldavo, -a
m, f
moldy ['moʊldi] *adj Am s.* **mouldy**
mole¹ [məʊl, *Am:* moʊl] *n* ZOOL topo *m*

mole² [məʊl, *Am:* moʊl] *n* ANAT lunar *m*
mole³ [məʊl, *Am:* moʊl] *n inf* (*spy*) espía *mf*
molecular [mə'lekjʊləʳ, *Am:* -jələ-] *adj* molecular
molecule ['mɒlɪkjuːl, *Am:* 'mɑːlɪ-] *n* molécula *f*
molehill ['məʊlhɪl, *Am:* 'moʊl-] *n* topera *f*
molest [mə'lest] *vt* **1.** (*pester*) importunar **2.** (*sexually*) abusar (sexualmente) de
moll [mɒl, *Am:* mɑːl] *n inf* amiga *f* de un gángster
mollify ['mɒlɪfaɪ, *Am:* 'mɑːlə-] <-ie-> *vt* **1.** (*pacify*) apaciguar **2.** (*reduce effect*) aplacar
mollusc *n*, **mollusk** ['mɒləsk, *Am:* 'mɑːləsk] *n* molusco *m*
mollycoddle ['mɒlɪkɒdl, *Am:* 'mɑːlɪkɑːdl] *vt inf* mimar, apapachar *Méx*
Molotov cocktail [ˌmɒlətɒf 'kɒkteɪl, ˌmɑːlətɔːf 'kɑːk-] *n* cóctel *m* Molotov
molt [məʊlt, *Am:* moʊlt] *n, vt, vi Am s.* **moult**
molten ['məʊltən, *Am:* 'moʊl-] *adj* fundido, -a
mom [mɒm, *Am:* mɑːm] *n Am, inf* mamá *f*
moment ['məʊmənt, *Am:* 'moʊ-] *n* momento *m*; **at the** ~ por el momento; **at any** ~ en cualquier momento; **at the last** ~ en el último momento; **in a** ~ enseguida; **not for a** ~ ni por un momento; **the** ~ **that ...** en cuanto... +*subj*; **the** ~ **of truth** la hora de la verdad; **at the (precise)** ~ **when ...** en el (preciso) momento en que...; **to choose one's** ~ escoger el momento; **to leave sth till the last** ~ dejar algo hasta el último momento
momentarily ['məʊməntrəli, *Am:* ˌmoʊmən'ter-] *adv* **1.** (*very briefly*) momentáneamente **2.** *Am* (*very soon*) en un momento
momentary ['məʊməntri, *Am:* 'moʊmənter-] *adj* momentáneo, -a
momentous [mə'mentəs, *Am:* moʊ'mentəs] *adj* (*fact*) trascendental; (*day*) memorable
momentum [mə'mentəm, *Am:* moʊ'mentəm] *n no pl* PHYS momento *m*; *fig* impulso *m*; **to gather** ~ tomar velocidad
momma ['mɒmə, *Am:* 'mɑːmə] *n*, **mommy** ['mˌaⓞˌmi, *Am:* 'mɑːmi] *n Am, inf* mamá *f*
Monaco ['ɒnəkəʊ, *Am:* 'mɑːnəkoʊ] *n* Mónaco *m*
monarch ['mɒnək, *Am:* 'mɑːnə-k] *n* monarca *mf*
monarchic(al) [mə'nɑːkɪk(l), *Am:* -'nɑːr-] *adj* monárquico, -a
monarchism ['mɒnəkɪzəm, *Am:* 'mɑːnə-] *n* monarquismo *m*
monarchist ['mɒnəkɪst, *Am:* 'mɑːnə-] *n* monarquista *mf*
monarchy ['mɒnəki, *Am:* 'mɑːnə-] <-ies> *n* monarquía *f*
monastery ['mɒnəstri, *Am:* 'mɑːnəster-]

<-ies> *n* monasterio *m*
monastic [mə'næstɪk] *adj* **1.** REL monástico, -a **2.** (*ascetic*) monacal
Monday ['mʌndi] *n* lunes *m inv*; **Easter** [*o* **Whit**] ~ lunes de Pascua; *s. a.* **Friday**
monetary ['mʌnɪtəri, *Am:* 'mɑːnəteri] *adj* monetario, -a
monetary fund *n* fondo *m* monetario **monetary policy** *n* política *f* monetaria **Monetary Union** *n* Unión *f* Monetaria
money ['mʌni] *n no pl* dinero *m*; **to be short of** ~ ir escaso de dinero; **to change** ~ cambiar dinero; **to make** ~ hacer dinero; **to raise** ~ recolectar fondos; **to throw** ~ **at sth** malgastar dinero en algo ▶ ~ **is the root of all** evil *prov* el dinero es la fuente de todos los males *prov*; **put your** ~ **where your** mouth **is** predica con el ejemplo; ~ **doesn't grow on** trees *prov* el dinero no cae del cielo *prov*; **to be** made **of** ~ nadar en la abundancia; **he has** ~ **to** burn le sobra el dinero; **to** marry ~ casarse con alguien rico; ~ talks *prov* poderoso caballero es don Dinero *prov*; **to be** in **the** ~ estar forrado; **for** my ~ en mi opinión
moneybags ['mʌnibægz] *npl inf* ricachón, -ona *m, f* **moneybox** *n* <-es> *Brit* hucha *f* **money-changer** *n* cambista *mf*
moneyed *adj form* adinerado, -a
money-maker *n* mina *f* de dinero *fig* **money-making** I. *adj* muy lucrativo, -a II. *n* ganancia *f* **money market** *n* mercado *m* monetario **money order** *n Am, Aus* giro *m* postal **money-spinner** *n* filón *m fig*
mongol ['mɒngl, *Am:* 'mɑːŋgəl] *adj* mongólico, -a
Mongol ['mɒngl, *Am:* 'mɑːŋgəl] I. *adj* mongol(a) II. *n* **1.** (*person*) mongol(a) *m(f)* **2.** LING mongol *m*
Mongolia [mɒŋ'gəʊlɪə, *Am:* mɑːŋ'goʊ-] *n* Mongolia *f*
Mongolian [mɒŋ'gəʊlɪən, *Am:* mɑːŋ'goʊ-] I. *adj* mongol(a) II. *n* **1.** (*person*) mongol(a) *m(f)* **2.** LING mongol *m*
mongolism ['mɒngəlɪzəm, *Am:* 'mɑːŋ] *n* mongolismo *m*
mongrel ['mʌŋgrəl, *Am:* 'mɑːŋ-] I. *n* perro *m* cruzado; *pej* chucho *m* II. *adj* mestizo, -a
monitor ['mɒnɪtəʳ, *Am:* 'mɑːnɪtə-] I. *n* **1.** INFOR monitor *m*; **15-inch** ~ monitor de 15 pulgadas **2.** (*person*) supervisor(a) *m(f)* II. *vt* controlar; **to** ~ **sth closely** seguir algo de muy cerca
monk [mʌŋk] *n* monje *m*
monkey ['mʌŋki] I. *n* mono, -a *m, f* ▶**to** make **a** ~ **out of sb** dejar a alguien en ridículo II. *vt Am* imitar
◆**monkey about** *vi inf* hacer el indio
monkey business *n* **1.** (*improper conduct*) tejemaneje *m* **2.** (*mischief*) travesura *f* **monkey nut** *n Brit* cacahuete *m*, maní *m AmL* **monkey wrench** *n* <-es> *Am* llave *f* inglesa

mono ['mɒnəʊ, *Am:* 'mɑːnoʊ] I. *n no pl* monofonía *f* II. *adj* mono

monochrome ['mɒnəʊkrəʊm, *Am:* 'mɑːnoʊkroʊm] *adj* monocromo, -a

monocle ['mɒnəkl, *Am:* 'mɑːnə-] *n* monóculo *m*

monogamous [mə'nɒɡəməs, *Am:* mə'nɑːɡə-] *adj* monógamo, -a

monogamy [mə'nɒɡəmi, *Am:* mə'nɑːɡə-] *n no pl* monogamia *f*

monogram ['mɒnəɡræm, *Am:* 'mɑːnə-] *n* monograma *m*

monolingual [ˌmɒnəʊ'lɪŋɡwəl, *Am:* ˌmɑːnə-] *adj* monolingüe

monolith ['mɒnəlɪθ, *Am:* 'mɑːnə-] *n* monolito *m*

monolithic [ˌmɒnə'lɪθɪk, *Am:* ˌmɑːnə-] *adj* monolítico, -a

monologue ['mɒnəlɒɡ, *Am:* 'mɑːnəlɑːɡ] *n* monólogo *m*

monopolize [mə'nɒpəlaɪz, *Am:* -'nɑːpəlaɪz] *vt* monopolizar

monopoly [mə'nɒpəli, *Am:* -'nɑːpəl-] <-ies> *n* monopolio *m*

monorail ['mɒnəʊreɪl, *Am:* 'mɑːnə-] *n* monorraíl *m*

monosyllabic [ˌmɒnəsɪ'læbɪk, *Am:* ˌmɑːnə-] *adj* monosilábico, -a

monotone ['mɒnətəʊn, *Am:* 'mɑːnətoʊn] *n no pl* tono *m* monocorde

monotonous [mə'nɒtənəs, *Am:* -'nɑːtən-] *adj* monótono, -a

monotony [mə'nɒtəni, *Am:* -'nɑːtən-] *n no pl* monotonía *f*

monotype® ['mɒnətaɪp, *Am:* 'mɑːnoʊ-] *n* monotipo *m*

monoxide [mɒ'nɒksaɪd, *Am:* mə'nɑːk-] *n* monóxido *m*

monsoon [mɒn'suːn, *Am:* mɑːn-] *n* monzón *m;* ~**s** lluvias *fpl* monzónicas

monster ['mɒnstər, *Am:* 'mɑːnstər] I. *n* monstruo *m* II. *adj inf* enorme

monstrosity [mɒn'strɒsəti, *Am:* mɑːn'strɑːsəti] <-ies> *n* monstruosidad *f*

monstrous ['mɒnstrəs, *Am:* 'mɑːn-] *adj* 1. (*awful*) monstruoso, -a 2. (*very big*) enorme 3. (*outrageous*) escandaloso, -a

montage [mɒn'tɑːʒ, *Am:* 'mɑːntɑːʒ] *n* montaje *m*

month [mʌnθ] *n* mes *m* ▶not in a ~ of Sundays ni por casualidad

monthly ['mʌnθli] I. *adj* mensual II. *adv* mensualmente III. *n* publicación *f* mensual

monument ['mɒnjʊmənt, *Am:* 'mɑːnjə-] *n* monumento *m*

monumental [ˌmɒnjʊ'mentl, *Am:* ˌmɑːnjə'mentl̩] *adj* (*very big*) monumental; (*error*) garrafal

moo [muː] I. <-s> *n* mugido *m* II. *vi* mugir

mood¹ [muːd] *n* humor *m;* in a good/bad ~ de buen/mal humor; the public ~ el ánimo general; to be in a talkative ~ estar dispuesto a hablar; to not be in the ~ to do sth no tener ganas de hacer algo; as the ~ takes her según le da la vena

mood² [muːd] *n Am* LING modo *m*

moodiness ['muːdɪnəs] *n no pl* mal humor *m*

moody ['muːdi] <-ier, -iest> *adj* 1. (*changeable*) voluble 2. (*bad-tempered*) malhumorado, -a

moon [muːn] *n no pl* luna *f;* full/new ~ luna llena/nueva ▶once in a blue ~ de Pascua a Ramos; to be over the ~ estar como un niño con zapatos nuevos

◆**moon about** *vi*, **moon around** *vi* vagar

moonbeam ['muːnbiːm] *n* rayo *m* de luna

moonboots *npl* botas *fpl* de après-ski

mooncalf <-ves> *n* imbécil *mf* **moonlight** I. *n no pl* luz *f* de la luna II. *vi inf* estar pluriempleado **moonlit** *adj* iluminado, -a por la luna **moonshine** *n no pl* 1. (*moonlight*) claro *m* de luna 2. *Am, inf* (*alcoholic drink*) bebida alcohólica destilada ilegalmente 3. *inf* (*nonsense*) pamplinas *fpl* **moonstone** *n* labradorita *f*

moony ['muːni] <-ier, -iest> *adj* soñador(a)

moor¹ [mɔːr, *Am:* mʊr] *n* (*area*) páramo *m*

moor² [mɔːr, *Am:* mʊr] *vt* NAUT amarrar

moorhen ['mɔːhen, *Am:* 'mʊr-] *n* polla *f* de agua

mooring ['mʊərɪŋ, *Am:* 'mʊrɪŋ] *n* amarra *f*

moose [muːs] *n* alce *m* americano

moot [muːt] I. *vt* it has been ~ed that ... se ha sugerido que... II. *adj* discutible

mop [mɒp, *Am:* mɑːp] I. *n* fregona *f;* a ~ of hair una mata de pelo II. <-pp-> *vt* fregar

mope [məʊp, *Am:* moʊp] *vi* estar deprimido

◆**mope about** *vi*, **mope around** *vi* andar deprimido

moped ['məʊped, *Am:* 'moʊ-] *n* ciclomotor *m*

moraine [mɒ'reɪn, *Am:* mə'-] *n* morena *f*

moral ['mɒrəl, *Am:* 'mɔːr-] I. *adj* moral; to give sb ~ support dar apoyo moral a alguien II. *n* 1. (*message*) moraleja *f* 2. *pl* (*standards*) moralidad *f*

morale [mə'rɑːl, *Am:* -'ræl] *n no pl* moral *f*

moralist ['mɒrəlɪst, *Am:* 'mɔːr-] *n* moralista *mf*

morality [mə'ræləti, *Am:* mɔː'ræləti] <-ies> *n* moralidad *f*

moralize ['mɒrəlaɪz, *Am:* 'mɔːr-] *vi* moralizar

morass [mə'ræs] *n* 1. (*boggy area*) cenagal *m* 2. *fig* (*complicated situation*) laberinto *m*

moratorium [ˌmɒrə'tɔːrɪəm, *Am:* ˌmɔːr-] <-s *o* -ria> *n form* moratoria *f*

morbid ['mɔːbɪd, *Am:* 'mɔːr-] *adj* 1. MED mórbido, -a 2. (*person, interest*) morboso, -a

morbidity [mɔː'bɪdəti, *Am:* mɔːr'bɪdəti] *n no pl* morbosidad *f*

more [mɔːr, *Am:* mɔːr] *comp of* **much, many** I. *adj* más; ~ wine/grapes más vino/

uvas; **a few ~ grapes** unas pocas uvas más; **no ~ wine at all** nada más de vino; **some ~ wine** un poco más de vino II. *adv* más; **~ beautiful than me** más bello que yo; **to drink (a bit/ much) ~** beber (un poco/mucho) más; **once ~** una vez más; **never ~** nunca más; **to see ~ of sb** volver a ver a alguien; **~ than 10** más de 10 III. *pron* más; **~ and ~** más y más; **to have ~ than sb** tener más que alguien; **to cost ~ than sth** costar más que algo; **the ~ you eat, the ~ you get fat** cuanto más comes, más gordo te pones; **what ~ does he want?** ¿qué más quiere?; **many do it but ~ don't** muchos lo hacen, pero la mayoría no ▶**all the ~** tanto más

morello [mə'reləʊ, *Am:* -oʊ] *n* guinda *f*

moreover [mɔː'rəʊvəʳ, *Am:* -'roʊvəˈ] *adv form* además

morgue [mɔːg, *Am:* mɔːrg] *n* depósito *m* de cadáveres, afanaduaría *f Méx*

moribund ['mɒrɪbʌnd, *Am:* 'mɔːr-] *adj form* moribundo, -a

Mormon ['mɔːmən, *Am:* 'mɔːr-] I. *n* mormón, -ona *m, f* II. *adj* mormónico, -a

morning ['mɔːnɪŋ, *Am:* 'mɔːr-] *n* mañana *f*; **good ~!** ¡buenos días!; **in the ~** por la mañana; **that ~** esa mañana; **the ~ after** la mañana después; **every ~** cada mañana; **every Monday ~** cada lunes por la mañana; **to come in the ~** venir por la mañana; **one July ~** una mañana de julio; **early in the ~** muy por la mañana; **6 o'clock in the ~** las 6 de la mañana; **from ~ till night** de la mañana a la noche

morning-after pill [ˌmɔːnɪŋ'ɑːftəˌpɪl, *Am:* ˌmɔːrnɪŋ'æftəˌpɪl] *n* píldora *f* del día después **morning coat** *n* chaqué *m* **morning paper** *n* diario *m* **Morning Prayer** *n* maitines *mpl* **morning sickness** *n* náuseas *fpl* matutinas **morning star** *n* lucero *m* del alba

Moroccan [mə'rɒkən, *Am:* -'rɑːkən] I. *n* marroquí *mf* II. *adj* marroquí

Morocco [mə'rɒkəʊ, *Am:* -'rɑːkoʊ] *n* Marruecos *m*

morocco leather *n* tafilete *m*

moron ['mɔːrɒn, *Am:* 'mɔːrɑːn] *n inf* imbécil *mf*

moronic [mə'rɒnɪk, *Am:* mɔː'rɑːnɪk] *adj inf* imbécil

morose [mə'rəʊs, *Am:* -'roʊs] *adj* (*person, mood*) taciturno, -a; (*expression*) sombrío, -a

morpheme ['mɔːfiːm, *Am:* 'mɔːr-] *n* LING morfema *m*

morphia ['mɔːfiə, *Am:* 'mɔːr-] *n*, **morphine** ['mɔːfiːn, *Am:* 'mɔːr-] *n* morfina *f*

morphological [ˌmɔːfə'lɒdʒɪkl, *Am:* ˌmɔːrfə'lɑːdʒɪ-] *adj* morfológico, -a

morphology [mɔː'fɒlədʒi, *Am:* mɔːr'fɑːlə-] *n* morfología *f*

El **Morris dancing** existe desde hace mucho tiempo, pero sus orígenes son desconocidos.

El nombre procede de 'Moorish' (árabe). Este baile cobra su principal significado en el **May Day** (1 de mayo) y en **Whitsuntide** (Pentecostés). Los **Morris dancers** son, la mayoría de las veces, grupos de hombres vestidos de blanco; algunos llevan campanillas en las pantorrillas y cada uno de ellos porta un bastón, un pañuelo o una corona en la mano. El baile está lleno de movimiento; los bailarines brincan, dan saltos y golpean el suelo con los pies.

Morse (code) [mɔːs, *Am:* mɔːrs-] *n no pl* morse *m*

morsel ['mɔːsl, *Am:* 'mɔːr-] *n* (*of food*) bocado *m*; (*of hope*) brizna *f*

mortal ['mɔːtl, *Am:* 'mɔːrt̪l] I. *adj* mortal; **~ danger** peligro *m* de muerte; **to be in ~ fear** estar aterrado II. *n liter* mortal *mf*

mortality [mɔː'tæləti, *Am:* mɔːr'tælət̪i] *n no pl, form* mortalidad *f*

mortar ['mɔːtəʳ, *Am:* 'mɔːrt̪əˈ] *n a.* MIL, TECH mortero *m*

mortarboard ['mɔːtəʳbɔːd, *Am:* 'mɔːrt̪ə-bɔːrd] *n* birrete *m*, capelo *m* Cuba, PRico, Ven

mortgage ['mɔːgɪdʒ, *Am:* 'mɔːr-] I. *n* hipoteca *f* II. *vt* hipotecar

mortice ['mɔːtɪs, *Am:* 'mɔːrt̪ɪs] *n s.* **mortise**

mortician [mɔː'tɪʃən, *Am:* mɔːr-] *n Am* director(a) *m(f)* de funeraria

mortification [ˌmɔːtɪfɪ'keɪʃən, *Am:* ˌmɔːrt̪ə-] *n no pl* 1. (*embarrassment*) humillación *f* 2. REL mortificación *f*

mortify ['mɔːtɪfaɪ, *Am:* 'mɔːrt̪ə-] *vt* <-ie-> mortificar

mortise ['mɔːtɪs, *Am:* 'mɔːrt̪ɪs] I. *n* entalladura *f* II. *vt* ensamblar

mortise lock *n* cerradura *f* embutida

mortuary ['mɔːtʃəri, *Am:* 'mɔːrtʃuer-] *n* 1. *Brit* (*morgue*) depósito *m* de cadáveres 2. *Am* (*funeral parlour*) tanatorio *m*

mosaic [məʊ'zeɪɪk, *Am:* moʊ-] *n* mosaico *m*

Moscow ['mɒskəʊ, *Am:* 'mɑːkaʊ] *n* Moscú *m*

Moses ['məʊzɪz, *Am:* 'moʊ-] *n* Moisés *m*

Moslem ['mɒzləm, *Am:* 'mɑːzlem] I. *adj* musulmán, -ana II. *n* musulmán, -ana *m, f*

mosque [mɒsk, *Am:* mɑːsk] *n* mezquita *f*

mosquito [mə'skiːtəʊ, *Am:* -t̪oʊ] <-(e)s> *n* mosquito *m*, zancudo *m AmL*

mosquito net *n* mosquitera *f*

moss [mɒs, *Am:* mɑːs] <-es> *n* musgo *m*

mossy ['mɒsi, *Am:* 'mɑːsi] <-ier, -iest> *adj* musgoso, -a

most [məʊst, *Am:* moʊst] *superl of* **many, much** I. *adj* la mayoría de; **~ people** la mayoría de la gente; **to have the ~ grapes/wine** tener más uvas/vino que nadie; **for the ~ part** en su mayor parte II. *adv* más; **the ~ beautiful** la más bella, el más bello; **a ~ beautiful even-**

ing una tarde de lo más bella; **what I want** ~ lo que más quiero; ~ **of all** más que nada; ~ **likely** my probablemente **III.** *pron* la mayoría; **at the** (**very**) ~ a lo sumo; ~ **of them/of the time** la mayor parte de ellos/del tiempo; **to make the** ~ **of sth/of oneself** sacar el máximo partido de algo/de sí mismo; **the** ~ **you can have is ...** lo máximo que puedes tener es...

mostly ['məʊstli, *Am:* 'moʊst-] *adv* **1.** (*usually*) en general **2.** (*nearly all*) casi todo **3.** (*in the majority*) principalmente

MOT [ˌeməʊ'tiː, *Am:* -oʊ'-] *n abbr of* **Ministry of Transport** Ministerio *m* de Transportes

motel [məʊ'tel, *Am:* moʊ-] *n* motel *m*, hotel-garaje *m AmL*

moth [mɒθ, *Am:* mɑːθ] *n* polilla *f*

mothball ['mɒθbɔːl, *Am:* mɑːθbɑːl] **I.** *n* bola *f* de naftalina **II.** *vt* (*idea, plan*) aparcar *fig*

moth-eaten ['mɒθˌiːtn, *Am:* 'mɑːθ-] *adj* apolillado, -a

mother ['mʌðəʳ, *Am:* -ɚ] **I.** *n* madre *f* **II.** *vt* mimar

mother country *n* madre patria *f* **motherhood** *n no pl* maternidad *f* **mother-in-law** *n* suegra *f*

motherly ['mʌðəli, *Am:* -ɚli] *adj* maternal

mother-of-pearl *n* nácar *m* **Mother's Day** *n no pl* día *m* de la madre **mother tongue** *n* lengua *f* materna

motif [məʊ'tiːf, *Am:* moʊ-] *n* ART motivo *m*

motion ['məʊʃən, *Am:* 'moʊ-] **I.** *n* **1.** (*movement*) movimiento *m*; **in slow** ~ a cámara lenta; **to put sth in** ~ poner algo en marcha **2.** *Brit, Aus* MED deposición *f* **3.** (*proposal*) moción *f* **II.** *vt* indicar con un gesto; **to** ~ **sb to do sth** indicar a alguien que haga algo **III.** *vi* hacer señas

motionless *adj* inmóvil

motion picture *n Am* película *f*

motivate ['məʊtɪveɪt, *Am:* 'moʊt̬ə-] *vt* **1.** (*cause*) motivar **2.** (*arouse interest of*) animar

motivation [ˌməʊtɪ'veɪʃən, *Am:* ˌmoʊt̬ə'-] *n* **1.** (*reason*) motivo *m* **2.** *no pl* (*ambition, drive*) motivación *f*

motive ['məʊtɪv, *Am:* 'moʊt̬ɪv] **I.** *n* motivo *m* **II.** *adj* PHYS, TECH motriz

motley ['mɒtli, *Am:* 'mɑːt-] <-ier, -iest> *adj pej* variopinto, -a

motor ['məʊtəʳ, *Am:* 'moʊt̬ɚ] **I.** *n* **1.** *a. fig* motor *m* **2.** *Brit, inf* (*car*) automóvil *m*, carro *m AmL* **II.** *adj a.* PHYS motor, motriz **III.** *vi* **1.** (*drive*) ir en coche **2.** (*go quickly*) ir rápido

motorbike *n inf* moto *f* **motorboat** *n* lancha *f* motora **motor car** *n Brit* automóvil *m* **motorcycle** *n form* motocicleta *f* **motorcycling** *n* motociclismo *m* **motorcyclist** *n* motociclista *mf* **motor-driven** *adj* motorizado, -a

motoring **I.** *adj Brit* automovilístico, -a **II.** *n* automovilismo *m*

motoring school *n* autoescuela *f*

motorist ['məʊtərɪst, *Am:* 'moʊt̬ɚ-] *n* conductor(a) *m(f)*

motorize ['məʊtəraɪz, *Am:* 'moʊt̬ə-] *vt* motorizar

motor racing *n Brit* automovilismo *m* **motor scooter** *n* scooter *f* **motor vehicle** *n form* automóvil *m* **motorway** *n Brit* autopista *f*

mottled ['mɒtld, *Am:* 'mɑːt̬ld] *adj* (*leaf, marble*) jaspeado, -a; (*skin*) manchado, -a

motto ['mɒtəʊ, *Am:* 'mɑːt̬oʊ] <-(e)s> *n* lema *m*

mould[1] [məʊld, *Am:* moʊld] *n no pl, Brit* BOT moho *m*

mould[2] [məʊld, *Am:* moʊld] *Brit* **I.** *n* (*for metal, clay, jelly*) molde *m* ►**to be cast in the same** ~ estar cortado por el mismo patrón **II.** *vt* moldear

moulder ['məʊldəʳ, *Am:* 'moʊldɚ] *vi Brit* echarse a perder; *fig* desmoronarse

moulding ['məʊldɪŋ, *Am:* 'moʊld-] *n Brit* ARCHIT moldura *f*

mouldy ['məʊldi, *Am:* 'moʊl-] <-ier, -iest> *adj Brit* **1.** GASTR (*food*) mohoso, -a **2.** *inf* (*shabby*) gastado, -a

moult [məʊlt, *Am:* moʊlt] *vt Brit* ZOOL mudar

mound [maʊnd] *n* **1.** (*elevation*) montículo *m* **2.** (*heap*) montón *m*

mount [maʊnt] **I.** *n* **1.** (*horse*) montura *f* **2.** (*frame*) marco *m* **II.** *vt* **1.** (*get on: horse*) montar; **to** ~ **a ladder** subirse a una escalera; **to** ~ **the throne** *form* ascender al trono **2.** (*organize*) organizar; **to** ~ **guard** montar guardia **3.** (*fix for display*) fijar **III.** *vi* montarse

mountain ['maʊntɪn, *Am:* -t̬ən] *n* **1.** GEO montaña *f* **2.** *inf* (*amount*) montón *m* ►**to make a** ~ **out of a** <u>molehill</u> ahogarse en un vaso de agua, hacer de la camisa un trapo *Col, Ven;* **to** <u>move</u> ~**s** mover cielo y tierra

mountain chain *n* GEO cordillera *f*

mountaineer [ˌmaʊntɪ'nɪəʳ, *Am:* -tən'ɪr] *n* montañista *mf*

mountaineering *n no pl* montañismo *m*

mountainous ['maʊntɪnəs, *Am:* -tnəs] *adj* **1.** GEO montañoso, -a **2.** (*large and high*) gigantesco, -a

mountain range *n* GEO sierra *f*

mounted ['maʊntɪd, *Am:* -t̬ɪd] *adj* montado, -a; ~ **police** policía *f* montada

mounting *n* (*of machine*) base *f*; (*in frame*) montaje *m*

mourn [mɔːn, *Am:* mɔːrn] **I.** *vi* lamentarse; **to** ~ **for sb** llorar la muerte de alguien **II.** *vt* llorar la muerte de

mourner ['mɔːnəʳ, *Am:* 'mɔːrnɚ] *n* doliente *mf*

mournful ['mɔːnfəl, *Am:* 'mɔːrn-] *adj* **1.** (*grieving*) afligido, -a **2.** (*gloomy*) triste

mourning ['mɔːnɪŋ, *Am:* 'mɔːrn-] *n no pl* luto *m*; **to be in** ~ estar de luto

mouse [maʊs] <mice> *n* ZOOL, INFOR ratón *m* ►**to be as poor as a** <u>church</u> ~ ser más pobre que las ratas

M

mousehole *n* ratonera *f* **mousemat** *n Brit,*
mousepad *n Am* INFOR alfombrilla *f* del ratón
mousetrap *n* ratonera *f*
mousse [muːs] *n* mousse *f*
moustache [məˈstɑːʃ, *Am:* ˈmʌstæʃ] *n*
bigote *m*
mousy [ˈmaʊsi] *adj* **1.** (*shy*) apocado, -a; **she
is very ~** es muy poquita cosa **2.** (*brown*)
pardo, -a
mouth[1] [maʊθ] *n* **1.** (*of person, animal*)
boca *f;* **to shut one's ~** *inf* callarse **2.** (*opening*) abertura *f;* (*of bottle, jar, well*) boca *f;* (*of
cave*) entrada *f;* (*of river*) desembocadura *f*
▸**to be born with a silver spoon in one's ~**
nacer con un pan debajo del brazo; **it made
her ~ water** se le hizo la boca agua con eso; **to
be all ~** ser un bocazas; **to be down in the ~**
estar deprimido; **to shoot off one's ~ about
sth** *Am, inf* hablar más de la cuenta sobre algo
mouth[2] [maʊð] *vt* **1.** (*form words silently*)
articular **2.** (*say insincerely*) soltar; **to ~ an
excuse** soltar la excusa de rigor
mouthful [ˈmaʊθfʊl] *n* (*of food*) bocado *m;*
(*of drink*) sorbo *m*
mouth organ *n* armónica *f* **mouthpiece** *n*
1. TEL micrófono *m* **2.** (*of pipe, instrument*)
boquilla *f* **3.** (*person*) portavoz *mf* **mouth-
-to-mouth resuscitation** *n* resucitación *f*
boca a boca **mouthwash** *n* enjuague *m*
bucal **mouthwatering** *adj* apetitoso, -a
movable [ˈmuːvəbl] *adj* móvil
move [muːv] I. *n* **1.** (*movement*) movimiento
m; **to be on the ~** (*travelling*) estar de viaje;
(*very busy*) no parar; **to get a ~ on** darse prisa
2. (*change of abode*) mudanza *f;* (*change of
job*) traslado *m* **3.** GAMES jugada *f;* **it's your ~** te
toca a ti **4.** (*action*) paso *m;* **to make the first
~** dar el primer paso II. *vi* **1.** (*change position*)
moverse; (*advance fast*) avanzar; (*make progress*) hacer progresos **2.** (*in games*) jugar
3. (*change abode*) mudarse; (*change job*)
cambiar de trabajo ▸**~ it!** *inf* ¡apúrate! III. *vt*
1. (*change position*) mover; (*make sb change
their mind*) hacer cambiar de idea; (*reschedule*) cambiar la fecha de **2.** (*cause emotions*)
conmover; **to be ~d by sth** estar afectado por
algo **3.** (*propose*) proponer
◆**move about** I. *vi* **1.** (*go around*) ir de un
lado a otro **2.** (*travel*) desplazarse **3.** (*change
abode*) mudarse; (*change job*) cambiar de trabajo II. *vt* (*furniture*) cambiar de sitio
◆**move along** I. *vt* hacer circular II. *vi* circular
◆**move away** I. *vi* mudarse de casa II. *vt*
apartar
◆**move back** I. *vi* retirarse II. *vt* colocar más
atrás
◆**move down** *vi, vt* bajar
◆**move forward** I. *vi* avanzar II. *vt* mover
hacia adelante; (*date*) adelantar
◆**move in** I. *vi* **1.** (*move into abode*) instalarse **2.** (*intervene*) intervenir **3.** (*advance to
attack*) avanzar; **to ~ on enemy territory**

invadir territorio enemigo II. *vt* instalar
◆**move off** *vi* marcharse
◆**move on** I. *vi* **1.** (*continue to move*) seguir
adelante; **to ~ to another subject** pasar a otro
tema **2.** (*make progress*) progresar **3.** (*go forward*) avanzar II. *vt* (*disperse*) dispersar
◆**move out** *vi* **1.** (*stop inhabiting*) dejar la
casa **2.** (*cease involvement*) **to ~ (of sth)** retirarse (de algo)
◆**move over** I. *vi* **1.** (*make room*) dejar sitio;
(*on seat*) correrse hacia un lado **2.** (*switch*) **to
~ towards sth** cambiar a algo II. *vt* mover a
un lado
◆**move up** I. *vi* **1.** (*make room*) hacer sitio;
(*on seat*) correrse hacia un lado **2.** (*increase*)
subir **3.** SCHOOL pasar a la clase superior II. *vt*
1. (*person, thing*) subir **2.** SCHOOL pasar a la
clase superior
movement [ˈmuːvmənt] *n* **1.** *a.* MUS (*act*)
movimiento *m* **2.** *no pl* FIN, COM actividad *f*
3. *no pl* (*tendency*) tendencia *f*
movie [ˈmuːvi] *n Am, Aus* película *f;* **the ~s** el
cine
movie camera *n* cámara *f* cinematográfica
moviegoer *n* aficionado, -a *m, f* al cine
movie star *n* estrella *f* de cine **movie theater** *n* cine *m*
moving [ˈmuːvɪŋ] I. *adj* **1.** (*that moves*)
móvil; **~ stairs** escaleras mecánicas **2.** (*motivating*) motor, motriz; **the ~ force** la fuerza
motriz **3.** (*causing emotion*) conmovedor(a)
II. *n no pl* mudanza *f*
mow [məʊ, *Am:* moʊ] <mowed, mown *o*
mowed> *vt* (*grass*) cortar; (*hay*) segar
mower [ˈməʊəʳ, *Am:* ˈmoʊɚ] *n* (*for lawn*)
cortacésped *m*
mown [məʊn, *Am:* moʊn] *pp of* **mow**
MP [ˌemˈpiː] *n* **1.** *Brit abbr of* **Member of Parliament** diputado, -a *m, f* **2.** *abbr of* **Military
Police** Policía *f* Militar
mpg *n abbr of* **miles per gallon** millas *fpl* por
galón
mph [ˌempiːˈeɪtʃ] *abbr of* **miles per hour** m/
h
Mr [ˈmɪstəʳ, *Am:* -tɚ] *n abbr of* **Mister** Sr.
Mrs [ˈmɪsɪz] *n abbr of* **Mistress** Sra.
ms [ˌemˈes] *abbr of* **manuscript** ms
Ms [mɪz] *n abbr of* **Miss** *forma de tratamiento
que se aplica tanto a mujeres solteras como
casadas*
MS [ˌemˈes] *abbr of* **multiple sclerosis** esclerosis *f inv* múltiple
MSc [ˌemesˈsiː] *abbr of* **Master of Science**
máster *m* (*de Ciencias*)*;* **Louie Sanders, MSc**
Louie Sanders, licenciado con máster
MSG *abbr of* **monosodium glutamate** gluta-
mato *m* monosódico
Mt *abbr of* **Mount** mte.
much [mʌtʃ] <more, most> I. *adj* mucho,
mucha; **too ~ wine** demasiado vino; **how ~
milk?** ¿cuánta leche?; **too/so ~ water** dema-
siada/tanta agua; **as ~ as** tanto como; **three
times as ~** tres veces más II. *adv* mucho; **~**

better mucho mejor; **thank you very ~** muchas gracias; **to be ~ surprised** estar muy sorprendido; **~ to my astonishment** para gran sorpresa mía; **not him, ~ less her** él no, y mucho menos ella III. *pron* mucho; **~ of the day** la mayor parte del día; **I don't think ~ of** it no le doy mucha importancia; **to make ~ of** **sb/sth** dar importancia a alguien/algo

muchness ['mʌtʃnəs] *n no pl, inf* **to be** **much of a ~** ser más o menos lo mismo

muck [mʌk] *n no pl, Brit, inf* **1.** (*dirt*) suciedad *f* **2.** (*manure*) estiércol *m* **3. to make a ~** **of sth** echar a perder algo **4.** *pej* (*bad food*) basura *f*

◆muck about I. *vi inf* **1.** (*waste time*) perder el tiempo **2.** (*handle*) **to ~ with sth** manosear algo II. *vt always sep* tratar mal

◆muck out *vt* limpiar

◆muck up *vt Brit, inf* estropear

muckheap *n* estercolero, -a *m, f*

muckraker ['mʌkreɪkəʳ, *Am:* -ɚ] *n* revelador(a) *m(f)* de escándalos

muck-up ['mʌkʌp] *n inf* lío *m* grande

mucky ['mʌki] <-ier, -iest> *adj* **1.** (*dirty*) sucio, -a **2.** (*pornographic*) porno

mucous ['mju:kəs] *n* MED mucosa *f*

mucus ['mju:kəs] *n* MED moco *m*

mud [mʌd] *n no pl* **1.** (*wet earth*) barro *m*; **to** **wallow in ~** revolcarse en el fango **2.** (*insult*) **to hurl ~ at sb** calumniar a alguien ▶**to drag** **sb's** <u>name</u> **through the ~** ensuciar el nombre de alguien

muddle ['mʌdl] I. *n no pl* desorden *m*, desparpajo *m AmL*; **to get in a ~** liarse II. *vt* **1.** (*mix up*) desordenar **2.** (*confuse*) confundir III. *vi* **to ~ along** ir tirando

muddle-headed ['mʌdl,hedɪd] *adj* atontado, -a

muddy ['mʌdi] I. *vt* **1.** (*make dirty*) manchar de barro **2.** (*confuse*) confundir II. <-ier, -iest> *adj* (*dirty*) lleno, -a de barro; (*water*) turbio, -a; (*ground*) fangoso, -a

mudguard ['mʌdgɑːd, *Am:* -gɑːrd] *n* guardabarros *m inv*, salpicadera *f Méx* **mud-** **pack** *n* mascarilla *f* de barro **mudslinging** *n inf* calumnia *f*

muff [mʌf] I. *n* FASHION manguito *m* II. *vt* (*opportunity*) echar a perder

muffin ['mʌfɪn] *n* **1.** *Am:* especie de magdalena **2.** *Brit* ≈ mollete *m*

muffle ['mʌfl] *vt* amortiguar

◆muffle up I. *vi* abrigarse II. *vt* abrigar

muffler ['mʌfləʳ, *Am:* -lɚ] *n Am* **1.** AUTO silenciador *m* **2.** (*scarf*) bufanda *f*

mufti ['mʌfti] *n no pl* **in ~** vestido de paisano

mug [mʌg] I. *n* **1.** (*for tea, coffee*) tazón *m*; (*for beer*) jarra *m* **2.** *Brit, inf* (*fool*) bobo, -a *m,* *f* **3.** *pej* (*face*) jeta *f*, escracho *m RíoPl* II. <-gg-> *vt* atracar

mugger ['mʌgəʳ, *Am:* -ɚ] *n* atracador(a) *m(f)*

mugging ['mʌgɪŋ] *n* atraco *m*

muggins ['mʌgɪnz] *n no pl, Brit* tonto, -a *m,* *f,* gafo, -a *m, f Ven*

muggy ['mʌgi] <-ier, -iest> *adj* bochornoso, -a

mugwump ['mʌgwʌmp] *n Am* POL independiente *mf*

mulberry ['mʌlbri, *Am:* -ber-] *n* **1.** (*fruit*) mora *f* **2.** (*tree*) morera *f*

mule [mju:l] *n* (*animal*) mulo, -a *m, f* ▶**as** <u>stubborn</u> **as a ~** terco como una mula

mull [mʌl] *vt* **to ~ sth over** meditar algo

mulled wine [mʌld waɪn] *n* vino tinto caliente aromatizado con especias

mullion ['mʌlɪən, *Am:* -jən] *n* ARCHIT parteluz *m*

multicolo(u)red [ˌmʌltɪ'kʌləd, *Am:* ˌmʌlti-'kʌlɚd] *adj* multicolor

multicultural [ˌmʌltɪ'kʌltʃərəl, *Am:* -t̬ɪ-] *adj* multicultural

multifarious [ˌmʌltɪ'feərɪəs, *Am:* -tə'ferɪ-] *adj form* diverso, -a

multifunctional [ˌmʌltɪ'fʌŋkʃənəl] *adj* multifuncional

multilateral [ˌmʌltɪ'lætərəl, *Am:* -t̬ɪ'læt̬-] *adj* POL multilateral

multilingual [ˌmʌltɪ'lɪŋgwəl, *Am:* -t̬ɪ-] *adj* plurilingüe

multimedia [ˌmʌltɪmi:dɪə, *Am:* -t̬ɪ-] *adj* multimedia *inv*

multimillionaire [ˌmʌltɪmɪljə'neəʳ, *Am:* -t̬ɪmɪljə'ner] *n* multimillonario, -a *m, f*

multinational [ˌmʌltɪ'næʃnəl, *Am:* -t̬ɪ-] I. *n* multinacional *f* II. *adj* multinacional

multiple ['mʌltɪpl, *Am:* -t̬ə-] *adj* múltiple

multiplex ['mʌltɪpleks, *Am:* -t̬ə-] *n* multicines *mpl*

multiplication [ˌmʌltɪplɪ'keɪʃən, *Am:* -t̬ə-] *n* multiplicación *f*

multiplicity [ˌmʌltɪ'plɪsəti, *Am:* -t̬ə-'plɪsət̬i] *n no pl, form* multiplicidad *f*

multiplier ['mʌltɪplaɪəʳ, *Am:* -t̬əplaɪɚ] *n* MAT multiplicador *m*

multiply ['mʌltɪplaɪ, *Am:* -t̬ə-] <-ie-> I. *vt* multiplicar II. *vi* multiplicarse

multipurpose [ˌmʌltɪ'pɜ:pəs, *Am:* -t̬ɪ'pɜ:r-] *adj* multiuso

multiracial [ˌmʌltɪ'reɪʃl, *Am:* -t̬ɪ-] *adj* multirracial

multistage [ˌmʌltɪ'steɪdʒ, *Am:* -t̬ɪ-] *adj* de varios escalones

multistor(e)y [ˌmʌltɪ'stɔ:ri, *Am:* -t̬ɪ-] *adj* de varios pisos [*o* plantas]

multitasking [ˌmʌltɪ'tɑ:skɪŋ, *Am:* -t̬ɪ-] *n* INFOR multitarea *f*

multitude ['mʌltɪtju:d, *Am:* -t̬ətu:d] *n* **1.** (*of things, problems*) multitud *f* **2.** (*crowd*) muchedumbre *f*; **the ~s** *liter* las masas

multitudinous [ˌmʌltɪ'tju:dɪnəs, *Am:* -t̬ə'tu:dn̩-] *adj* multitudinario, -a

multi-user system *n* INFOR sistema *m* multiusuario

mum[1] [mʌm] *n Brit, inf* mamá *f*

mum[2] [mʌm] *adj* **to keep ~** *inf* guardar silencio

mumble ['mʌmbl] *vi* hablar entre dientes

M

mumbo jumbo [ˌmʌmbəʊˈdʒʌmbəʊ, Am: -boʊˈdʒʌmboʊ] n no pl, inf galimatías m

mummify [ˈmʌmɪfaɪ, Am: -ə-] <-ie-> vt momificar

mummy¹ [ˈmʌmi] <-ies> n Brit, inf (mother) mami f, mamita f AmL

mummy² [ˈmʌmi] <-ies> n (preserved corpse) momia f

mumps [mʌmps] n MED paperas fpl; **he's got the** ~ tiene paperas

munch [mʌntʃ] vi, vt ronzar

mundane [mʌnˈdeɪn] adj prosaico, -a

municipal [mjuːˈnɪsɪpl, Am: -əpl] adj municipal

municipality [mjuːˌnɪsɪˈpæləti, Am: -əˈpæləti] n <-ies> (city, town) municipio m, comuna f AmL; (local government) municipalidad f

munitions [mjuːˈnɪʃənz] npl municiones fpl

mural [ˈmjʊərəl, Am: ˈmjʊrəl] n mural m

murder [ˈmɜːdəʳ, Am: ˈmɜːrdəʳ] I. n (killing) asesinato m; LAW homicidio m; **to commit** ~ cometer un asesinato; **this job is** ~ fig este trabajo es matador; **he gets away with** ~ fig se le consiente cualquier cosa ▶**to scream blue** ~ poner el grito en el cielo II. vt (kill) asesinar, ultimar AmL; fig (music, play) destrozar

murderer [ˈmɜːdərəʳ, Am: ˈmɜːrdərəʳ] n (killer) asesino, -a m, f; LAW homicida mf, victimario, -a m, f AmL

murderess [ˈmɜːdərɪs, Am: ˈmɜːrdərəs] n (killer) asesina f; LAW homicida f

murderous [ˈmɜːdərəs, Am: ˈmɜːr-] adj 1. (instinct, look) asesino, -a; (plan) criminal 2. (very taxing: heat) insufrible

murky [ˈmɜːki, Am: ˈmɜːr-] <-ier, -iest> adj (water, past) turbio, -a; (night) nublado, -a

murmur [ˈmɜːməʳ, Am: ˈmɜːrməʳ] I. vi, vt murmurar II. n murmullo m

muscle [ˈmʌsl] n 1. ANAT músculo m 2. fig poder m

♦**muscle in** vi **to** ~ (**on sth**) entrometerse (de algo)

muscle-bound [ˈmʌslˌbaʊnd] adj demasiado musculoso, -a

muscleman [ˈmʌslmæn] <-men> n forzudo m

muscular [ˈmʌskjʊləʳ, Am: -kjələʳ] adj 1. (pain, contraction) muscular 2. (arms, legs) musculoso, -a

muse [mjuːz] I. vi **to** ~ (**on sth**) cavilar [o reflexionar] (sobre algo) II. n musa f

museum [mjuːˈzɪəm] n museo m; ~ **piece** pieza f de museo

mush [mʌʃ] n no pl 1. inf (food) papilla f 2. (film, book) cursilada f

mushroom [ˈmʌʃrʊm, Am: -ruːm] I. n (wild) seta f, callampa f Col, Chile, Perú; (button mushroom) champiñón m II. vi (prices, population) dispararse; (town) crecer de la noche a la mañana

mushy [ˈmʌʃi] adj <-ier, -iest> 1. (soft: food) blando, -a 2. (film, book) sensiblero, -a

music [ˈmjuːzɪk] n 1. (art) música f; **it was** ~ **to her ears** le sonó a música celestial 2. (notes) partitura f; **to read** ~ leer música

musical [ˈmjuːzɪkəl] I. adj musical II. n musical m

music box n caja f de música **music hall** n music hall m

musician [mjuːˈzɪʃən] n músico, -a m, f

music stand n atril m

musk [mʌsk] n no pl almizcle m

musket [ˈmʌskɪt] n mosquete m

musketeer [ˌmʌskɪˈtɪəʳ, Am: -kəˈtɪr] n mosquetero m

muskrat [ˈmʌskræt] n almizclera f, rata f almizclada

Muslim [ˈmʊzlɪm, Am: ˈmʌzləm] I. adj musulmán, -ana II. n musulmán, -ana m, f

muslin [ˈmʌzlɪn] n muselina f

muss [mʌs] vt Am desordenar

mussel [ˈmʌsl] n mejillón m

must [mʌst] I. aux 1. (obligation) deber; ~ **you leave so soon?** ¿tienes que irte tan pronto?; **you** ~**n't do that** no debes hacer eso 2. (probability) deber de; **I** ~ **have lost it** debo de haberlo perdido; **you** ~ **be hungry** supongo que tendrás hambre; **you** ~ **be joking!** ¡estarás bromeando! II. n cosa f imprescindible; **this book is a** ~ este es un libro de lectura obligada

mustache [ˈmʌstæʃ] n Am bigote m

mustang [ˈmʌstæŋ] n mustang m

mustard [ˈmʌstəd, Am: -təd] n no pl mostaza f

muster [ˈmʌstəʳ, Am: -təʳ] I. vt 1. (gather) reunir; **to** ~ **the courage to do sth** armarse de valor para hacer algo 2. MIL alistar II. vi congregarse III. n **to pass** ~ ser aceptable

mustn't [ˈmʌsnt] must not **must**

musty [ˈmʌsti] <-ier, -iest> adj (room) que huele a humedad; (book) que huele a rancio [o a viejo]

mutant [ˈmjuːtənt] I. adj mutante II. n mutante mf

mutation [mjuːˈteɪʃən] n mutación f

mute [mjuːt] I. n 1. (person) mudo, -a m, f 2. MUS sordina f II. vt MUS poner sordina a III. adj mudo, -a; **to remain** ~ permanecer mudo

muted adj apagado, -a

mutilate [ˈmjuːtɪleɪt, Am: -təl-] vt mutilar

mutilation [ˌmjuːtɪˈleɪʃən, Am: -ˈtl-] n mutilación f

mutineer [ˌmjuːtɪˈnɪəʳ, Am: -tnˈɪr] n amotinador(a) m(f)

mutinous [ˈmjuːtɪnəs, Am: -ˈtn-] adj amotinado, -a

mutiny [ˈmjuːtɪni] I. n <-ies> no pl motín m II. vi <-ie-> amotinarse

mutter [ˈmʌtəʳ, Am: ˈmʌtəʳ] I. vi 1. (talk) murmurar 2. (complain) refunfuñar; **to** ~ **about sth** refunfuñar por algo II. vt 1. (say) murmurar 2. (complain) farfullar

mutton [ˈmʌtən] n no pl carne f de oveja

▶she's ~ **dressed as** <u>lamb</u> es un vejestorio disfrazado de jovencita

muttonchops *n pl,* **muttonchop whiskers** *n pl* patillas *fpl* de boca de hacha

mutual ['mjuːtʃuəl] *adj* (*understanding*) mutuo, -a; (*friend, interest*) común

mutual fund *n Am* fondo *m* de inversión mobiliaria

mutually *adv* mutuamente; **it was ~ agreed** se decidió de común acuerdo

muzak® ['mjuːzæk] *n* musical

muzzle ['mʌzl] **I.** *n* **1.** (*of horse, dog*) hocico *m* **2.** (*for dog*) bozal *m* **3.** (*of gun*) boca *f* **II.** *vt* **1.** (*dog*) poner un bozal a **2.** *fig* (*person, newspaper*) amordazar

muzzy ['mʌzi] <-ier, -iest> *adj* **1.** (*weather*) borroso, -a **2.** (*unable to think clearly*) atontado, -a

MW *abbr of* **medium wave** OM

my [maɪ] **I.** *adj pos* mi; **~ dog/house** mi perro/casa; **~ children** mis hijos; **this car is ~ own** este coche es mío; **I hurt ~ foot/head** me he hecho daño en el pie/la cabeza **II.** *interj* madre mía

myopia [maɪˈəʊpɪə, *Am:* -ˈoʊ-] *n* miopía *f*

myopic [maɪˈɒpɪk, *Am:* -ˈɑːpɪk] *adj form* **1.** (*shortsighted*) miope **2.** *fig* corto, -a de miras

myriad ['mɪrɪəd] *n* miríada *f*

myrrh [mɜːʳ, *Am:* mɜːr] *n* mirra *f*

myrtle ['mɜːtl, *Am:* 'mɜːrt̬l] *n* mirto *m*

myself [maɪˈself] *pron reflexive* **1.** (*direct, indirect object*) me; **I hurt ~** me hice daño; **I deceived ~** me engañé a mí mismo; **when I express/exert ~** cuando me expreso/ esfuerzo; **I bought ~ a bag** me compré una bolsa **2.** *emphatic* yo (mismo, misma); **my brother and ~** mi hermano y yo; **I'll do it ~** lo haré yo mismo; **I did it (all) by ~** lo hice (todo) yo solo **3.** *after prep* mi (mismo, misma); **I said to ~** me dije (a mí mismo); **I am ashamed at ~** estoy avergonzado de mí mismo; **I live by ~** vivo solo

mysterious [mɪˈstɪərɪəs, *Am:* -ˈstɪrɪ-] *adj* misterioso, -a

mystery ['mɪstəri] <-ies> *n* misterio *m*

mystic ['mɪstɪk] **I.** *n* místico, -a *m, f* **II.** *adj* místico, -a

mystical ['mɪstɪkl] *adj* místico, -a

mysticism ['mɪstɪsɪzəm] *n no pl* misticismo *m*

mystification [ˌmɪstɪfɪˈkeɪʃən] *n* **1.** (*mystery*) misterio *m* **2.** (*confusion*) confusión *f,* perplejidad *f*

mystify ['mɪstɪfaɪ] *vt* <-ie-> desconcertar

mystique [mɪsˈtiːk] *n* mística *f*

myth [mɪθ] *n* mito *m*

mythical ['mɪθɪkl] *adj* **1.** (*legendary*) mítico, -a **2.** (*supposed*) supuesto, -a

mythological [ˌmɪθəˈlɒdʒɪkl, *Am:* -ˈlɑːdʒɪk-] *adj* mitológico, -a

mythology [mɪˈθɒlədʒi, *Am:* -ˈθɑːlə-] *n* <-ies> mitología *f*

N

N, n [en] *n* N, n *f;* **~ for Nelly** *Brit,* **~ for Nan** *Am* N de Navarra

n *abbr of* **noun** n *m*

N *abbr of* **north** N *m*

Naafi ['næfi] *n abbr of* **Navy, Army and Air Force Institutes** **1.** (*shop*) tienda *f* de las Fuerzas armadas británicas **2.** (*canteen*) cantina *f* de las Fuerzas armadas británias

nab [næb] <-bb-> *vt inf* (*person*) coger, pescar; (*thing*) coger

nadir ['neɪdɪəʳ, *Am:* -dəʳ] *n* nadir *m*

naff [næf] *adj Brit, inf* hortera

nag[1] [næg] *n* (*horse*) jamelgo *m*

nag[2] [næg] **I.** <-gg-> *vi* regañar; **to ~ at sb** dar la lata a alguien **II.** <-gg-> *vt* regañar, dar la lata a **III.** *n inf* regañón, -ona *m, f,* criticón, -ona *m, f*

nagging ['nægɪŋ] **I.** *n no pl* quejas *fpl* **II.** *adj* **1.** (*criticizing*) criticón, -ona **2.** (*pain, ache*) persistente

nail [neɪl] **I.** *n* **1.** (*tool*) clavo *m* **2.** ANAT uña *f* ▶**to hit the ~ on the** <u>head</u> dar en el clavo; **to pay on the ~** pagar a toca teja **II.** *vt* **1.** (*fasten*) clavar **2.** *inf* (*catch: police*) coger; (*lie*) poner al descubierto ▶**to ~ one's** <u>colours</u> **to the mast** mantenerse firme **nail-biting** *adj fig* angustioso, -a **nail brush** <-es> *n* cepillo *m* de uñas **nail clippers** *npl* cortaúñas *m inv* **nail enamel remover** *n Am* quitaesmalte *m* **nail file** *n* lima *f* **nail polish** *n no pl, Am* quitaesmalte *m* **nail scissors** *npl* tijeras *fpl* para uñas **nail varnish** *n no pl* esmalte *m* de uñas

naive, naïve [naɪˈiːv, *Am:* naːˈiː-] *adj* ingenuo, -a

naivety [naɪˈiːvəteɪ, *Am:* ˌnaːiːvˈteɪ], **naïveté** [naɪˈiːvəti, *Am:* naːˈiːvəti] *n no pl* ingenuidad *f*

naked ['neɪkɪd] *adj* **1.** (*unclothed*) desnudo, -a, encuerado, -a *Cuba, Méx* **2.** (*uncovered: blade*) desenvainado, -a; (*aggression*) manifiesto, -a; (*ambition*) puro, -a; **to the ~ eye** a simple vista

nakedness *n no pl* desnudez *f*

NALGO ['nælgəʊ, *Am:* -goʊ] *n Brit abbr of* **National and Local Government Officers Association** *sindicato británico de funcionarios*

namby-pamby [ˌnæmbɪˈpæmbi] *adj inf* (*person*) ñoño, -a, remilgado, -a; (*poem*) ñoño, -a

name [neɪm] **I.** *n* **1.** nombre *m;* (*surname*) apellido *m;* **by ~** de nombre; **to know sb by ~** conocer a alguien de oídas; **to go by the ~ of ... form** hacerse llamar...; **in ~ only** sólo de nombre; **under the ~ of ...** bajo el seudónimo de...; **in God's ~** en nombre de Dios; **in the ~ of freedom and justice** en nombre de la libertad y de la justicia; **to call sb ~s** llamar a alguien de todo; **in all but ~** en la práctica

2. (*reputation*) fama *f*; **to give sb/sth a good ~** dar buena fama a alguien/algo; **his ~ is mud** *fig* es persona non grata; **to make a ~ for oneself** hacerse un nombre ▶**the ~ of the game** lo fundamental; **not to have a penny to one's ~** no tener ni un duro, no tener donde caerse muerto **II.** *vt* **1.** (*call*) poner nombre a, bautizar **2.** (*list*) nombrar **3.** (*choose*) **to ~ the time and the place** fijar la hora y el lugar

name-day *n* santo *m*

name-dropping ['neɪmdrɒpɪŋ, *Am:* -drɑːp-] *n* no pl práctica de mencionar gente importante para impresionar

nameless ['neɪmlɪs] *adj* indescriptible; (*author*) anónimo, -a

namely ['neɪmli] *adv* a saber

nameplate ['neɪmpleɪt] *n* placa *f* con el nombre

namesake ['neɪmseɪk] *n* tocayo, -a *m, f*

Namibia [næ'mɪbɪə, *Am:* nə'-] *n* Namibia *f*

Namibian [næ'mɪbɪən, *Am:* nə'-] **I.** *adj* namibio, -a **II.** *n* namibio, -a *m, f*

nan [nɑːn] *n Brit, childspeak, inf* abuela *f*

nanny ['næni] <-ies> *n* niñera *f*, nurse *f AmL*

nanny goat ['nænɪɡəʊt, *Am:* -ɡoʊt] *n* cabra *f*

nanosecond ['nɑːnəʊ'sekənd, *Am:* -oʊ,-] *n* nanosegundo *m*

nap¹ [næp] **I.** *n* cabezadita *f*; (*after lunch*) siesta *f*; **to have a ~** echarse un sueñecito [*o* una siesta] **II.** <-pp-> *vi* hacer una cabezadita

nap² [næp] *n* pelo *m*

napalm ['neɪpɑːm] *n no pl* napalm *m*

nape [neɪp] *n* nuca *f*, cogote *m*

napkin ['næpkɪn] *n* servilleta *f*

nappy ['næpi] <-ies> *n* pañal *m*

narcissism ['nɑːsɪsɪzəm, *Am:* 'nɑːrsəsɪ-] *n no pl* narcisismo *m*

narcissus [nɑː'sɪsəs, *Am:* nɑːr'-] <-es *o* narcissi> *n* narciso *m*

narcosis [nɑː'kəʊsɪs, *Am:* nɑːr'koʊ-] *n no pl* narcosis *f inv*

narcotic [nɑː'kɒtɪk, *Am:* nɑːr'kɑːt̬-] **I.** *n* narcótico *m* **II.** *adj* narcótico, -a

nark [nɑːk, *Am:* nɑːrk] **I.** *vt* cabrear **II.** *n inf* soplón, -ona *m, f*

narrate [nə'reɪt, *Am:* 'nereɪt] *vt* **1.** (*tale, story*) narrar, relatar **2.** TV hacer de comentarista de

narration [nə'reɪʃən, *Am:* ner'eɪʃən] *n no pl* (*tale*) narración *f*; TV comentario *m*

narrative ['nærətɪv, *Am:* 'nerət̬ɪv] *n no pl* narración *f*, relato *m*

narrator [nə'reɪtər, *Am:* 'nereɪt̬ər] *n* narrador(a) *m(f)*; TV comentarista *mf*

narrow ['nærəʊ, *Am:* 'neroʊ] **I.** <-er, -est> *adj* **1.** (*thin*) estrecho, -a **2.** (*limited*) limitado, -a **3.** (*small: margin*) escaso, -a, reducido, -a **II.** *vi* **1.** estrecharse; (*gap*) reducirse **2.** (*field*) limitarse, restringirse **III.** *vt* **1.** (*reduce width of*) estrechar; (*gap*) reducir **2.** (*restrict: field*) limitar, restringir

narrow boat *n* NAUT barcaza *f*

narrow-gauge *n* vía *f* estrecha

narrowly *adv* **1.** (*barely*) por poco, por un escaso margen **2.** (*meticulously*) meticulosamente

narrow-minded [,nærəʊ'maɪndɪd, *Am:* ,neroʊ'-] *adj* de mentalidad cerrada; (*opinions, views*) cerrado, -a

NASA ['næsə] *n Am abbr of* **National Aeronautics and Space Administration** NASA *f*

nasal ['neɪzl] *adj* nasal; (*voice*) gangoso, -a

nascent ['næsənt] *adj* naciente

nastiness ['nɑːstɪnəs, *Am:* 'næstɪ-] *n no pl* **1.** (*wickedness*) maldad *f* **2.** (*of accident*) gravedad *f*; (*of taste*) lo asqueroso; (*odour*) peste *f* **3.** (*dirtiness*) suciedad *f*

nasturtium [nə'stɜːʃəm, *Am:* -'stɜːr-] *n* BOT capuchina *f*

nasty ['nɑːsti, *Am:* 'næsti] <-ier, -iest> *adj* **1.** (*bad*) malo, -a; (*smell, taste*) asqueroso, -a, repugnante; (*surprise*) desagradable **2.** (*dangerous*) peligroso, -a **3.** (*serious*) serio, -a

natal ['neɪtl, *Am:* -t̬l] *adj* natal

natality [nə'tælɪti] *n no pl* natalidad *f*

nation ['neɪʃən] *n* **1.** (*country, state*) nación *f*, país *m*; **to serve the ~** servir a la nación **2.** (*people living in a state*) **the Jewish ~** la nación judía

national ['næʃənəl] **I.** *adj* nacional; **at the ~ level** a nivel nacional **II.** *n* ciudadano, -a *m, f*; **foreign ~** extranjero, -a *m, f*

national anthem *n* himno *m* nacional

national assembly <-ies> *n* asamblea *f* nacional **national bank** *n* banco *m* nacional

national costume *n* traje *m* nacional

national currency <-ies> *n* moneda *f* nacional **national debt** *n* deuda *f* nacional

---

El **national emblem** (emblema nacional) de Inglaterra es la **Tudor rose**, una rosa blanca y plana de la casa real de York sobre la rosa roja de la casa de Lancaster. El emblema nacional de Irlanda es la **shamrock**, una especie de trébol, que fue utilizado, al parecer, por el patrón de Irlanda, St. Patrick, para ilustrar el misterio de la Santísima Trinidad. El **thistle** (cardo) de Escocia fue elegido por el rey Jaime III en el siglo XV como símbolo nacional. El **dragon** de Gales fue utilizado desde hace mucho tiempo como emblema en las banderas de guerra. Los galos tienen también al **leek** (puerro) como símbolo, el cual, según Shakespeare, fue llevado en la batalla de Poitiers contra los franceses en 1356. la **daffodil** (campana pascual) es un sustituto del siglo XX más bonito.

National Front *n Brit* POL Frente *m* Nacional **national grid** *n Brit, Aus* red *f* eléctrica nacional **National Guard** *n Am* Guardia *f* Nacional **National Health (Service)** *n Brit* (servicio *m* de) asistencia *f* sanitaria de la Seguridad Social **national holiday** *n* fiesta *f* nacional **national income** *n no pl* renta *f*

nacional **National Insurance** n no pl, Brit
Seguridad f Social
nationalisation [ˌnæʃənəlaɪˈzeɪʃən, Am:
-ɪˈ-] n Brit, Aus s. **nationalization**
nationalise [ˈnæʃənəlaɪz] vt Brit, Aus s.
nationalize
nationalism [ˈnæʃnəlɪzəm] n no pl nacionalismo m
nationalist [ˈnæʃnəlɪst] I. adj nacionalista
II. n nacionalista mf
nationalistic [ˌnæʃnəˈlɪstɪk] adj nacionalista
nationality [ˌnæʃəˈnæləti] <-ies> n nacionalidad f; **to adopt British/Spanish** ~ adoptar
la nacionalidad británica/española
nationalization [ˌnæʃənəlaɪˈzeɪʃən, Am:
-ɪˈ-] n nacionalización f
nationalize [ˈnæʃənəlaɪz] vt nacionalizar
national park n, **National Park** n parque
m nacional **national product** n producto
m interior **national security** n no pl
seguridad f nacional **national service** n no
pl 1. Brit, Aus (military service) servicio m
militar; **to do** ~ hacer la mili 2. Am (youth
community service) prestación f social sustitutoria (del servicio militar) **national socialism** n no pl nacionalsocialismo m **national
unity** n no pl unidad f nacional
nation state n estado m nacional
nationwide [ˌneɪʃənˈwaɪd] I. adv nacional-
mente II. adj nacional
native [ˈneɪtɪv, Am: -t̬ɪv] I. adj 1. (indigenous) indígena; **to be** ~ **to Ireland** (plant, animal) ser originario de Irlanda 2. (of place of
origin) nativo, -a, natural; ~ **country** patria f
3. (indigenous, aboriginal, primitive) nativo,
-a, indígena 4. (original) nativo, -a; (innate)
innato, -a; (language) materno, -a II. n
(indigenous inhabitant) nativo, -a m, f, natural
mf; **a** ~ **of Monaco** un nativo de Mónaco; **to
speak English like a** ~ hablar el inglés como
un nativo
native American I. n indígena mf americano, -a II. adj indígena **native-born** adj
nativo, -a; **is he a** ~ **person or did he move
there?** ¿es natural de allí o viene de fuera?; ~
citizen of New York natural de Nueva York
native speaker n hablante mf nativo, -a
nativity [nəˈtɪvəti, Am: -t̬i] <-ies> n natividad f; **the Nativity** la Navidad
nativity play n auto m de Navidad
NATO [ˈneɪtəʊ, Am: -t̬oʊ] n abbr of **North
Atlantic Treaty Organisation** OTAN f
natter [ˈnætəʳ, Am: ˈnæt̬ɚ] inf I. vi inf charlar; **to** ~ **away** parlotear II. n charla f; **to have
a** ~ (**with sb**) tener una charla (con alguien)
natural [ˈnætʃərəl, Am: -ɚ-əl] I. adj 1. (not
artificial, inherent) natural; ~ **causes** causas
fpl naturales; **to die from** ~ **causes** morir de
causas naturales; ~ **disaster** desastre m natural; **to be a** ~ **blonde** ser rubio natural; ~
father padre m natural 2. (usual, to be
expected) normal; **I'm sure there's a** ~
explanation for it estoy seguro de que tiene

una explicación normal II. n 1. inf **to be a** ~
for sth tener un talento innato para algo 2. MUS
nota f natural
natural childbirth n no pl parto m natural
natural gas n no pl gas m natural **natural
history** n no pl historia f natural; ~ **museum**
museo m de Historia Natural
naturalisation [ˌnætʃərəlaɪˈzeɪʃən, Am:
-ɚəlɪˈ-] n no pl, Brit, Aus s. **naturalization**
naturalise [ˈnætʃərəlaɪz, Am: -ɚəl-] vt Brit,
Aus s. **naturalize**
naturalised adj Brit, Aus s. **naturalized**
naturalism [ˈnætʃərəlɪzəm, Am: -ɚəl-] n no
pl naturalismo m
naturalist I. n naturalista mf II. adj naturalista
naturalistic [ˌnætʃərəlˈɪstɪk, Am: -ɚəl-] adj
naturalista
naturalization [ˌnætʃərəlaɪˈzeɪʃən, Am:
-ɚəlɪˈ-] n no pl naturalización f
naturalize [ˈnætʃərəlaɪz, Am: -ɚəl-] vt Am
naturalizar
naturalized adj naturalizado, -a; ~ **citizen**
ciudadano, -a m, f naturalizado, -a
natural language n lenguaje m natural
naturally adv naturalmente
natural resources npl recursos mpl naturales; **to be rich/poor in** ~ ser rico/pobre en
recursos naturales **natural science** n,
natural sciences npl ciencias fpl naturales
natural selection n no pl selección f natural **natural wastage** n no pl, Brit desechos
mpl naturales
nature [ˈneɪtʃəʳ, Am: -tʃɚ] n 1. no pl (the
environment, natural forces) naturaleza f; **to
get back to** ~ volver a la naturaleza; **to let** ~
take its course dejar que la naturaleza siga su
curso 2. (essential or innate qualities) naturaleza f; **things of this** ~ cosas de esta índole; **in
the** ~ **of things** en la naturaleza de las cosas;
to be in sb's ~ estar en la naturaleza de alguien ▶**second** ~ hábito muy arraigado en
una persona
nature conservancy n no pl conservación f
natural **nature lover** n amante mf de la
naturaleza **nature reserve** n reserva f natural **nature study** n no pl historia f natural
nature trail n ruta f ecológica **nature
worship** n no pl culto m a la naturaleza
naturism [ˈneɪtʃərɪzəm] n no pl naturismo
m
naturist [ˈneɪtʃərɪst] n form naturista mf
naughty [ˈnɔːti, Am: ˈnɑːt̬i] <-ier, -iest> adj
1. (badly behaved: children) desobediente, travieso, -a 2. iron (adults) pícaro, -a 3. iron, inf
(sexually stimulating) picante; ~ **films** películas fpl porno
nausea [ˈnɔːsɪə, Am: ˈnɑːzɪə] n no pl
1. náusea f; **feeling of** ~ sensación f de
náusea; **to suffer from** ~ tener náuseas 2. fig
repugnancia f
nauseate [ˈnɔːsɪeɪt, Am: ˈnɑːzɪ-] vt form
asquear; **to be** ~**d by sth** tener náuseas por
algo

nauseating ['nɔːsıeıtıŋ, *Am:* 'nɑːzı-] *adj* repugnante, nauseabundo, -a

nauseous ['nɔːsıəs, *Am:*'nɑːʃəs] *adj* nauseabundo, -a; **she is** ~ tiene náuseas

nautical ['nɔːtıkəl, *Am:* 'nɑːtˌı-] *adj* náutico, -a; ~ **chart** carta *f* náutica

nautical mile *n* milla *f* marina

naval ['neıvəl] *adj* naval; ~ **commander** comandante *mf* naval; ~ **battle/engagement/force** batalla *f*/combate *m*/fuerza *f* naval

naval academy <-ies> *n* academia *f* naval **naval base** *n* base *f* naval **naval power** *n* potencia *f* naval **naval warfare** *n* no pl guerra *f* naval

nave [neıv] *n* nave *f*

navel ['neıvl] *n* ombligo *m* ►**to contemplate one's** ~ rascarse el ombligo

navigable ['nævıgəbl] *adj* navegable; ~ **waters** aguas *fpl* navegables

navigate ['nævıgeıt] I. *vt* 1. (*steer*) llevar; AUTO guiar 2. (*sail*) navegar por; **to** ~ **the ocean/a river** navegar por el océano/un río 3. (*traverse*) atravesar 4. INFOR **to** ~ **the Internet** navegar por la red, surfear II. *vi* NAUT, AVIAT navegar; AUTO guiar, hacer de copiloto

navigation [ˌnævı'geıʃən] *n no pl* navegación *f*

navigational [ˌnævı'geıʃnəl] *adj* de navegación; ~ **error** error *m* de navegación

navigator ['nævıgeıtəʳ, *Am:* -t̬ə-] *n* navegante *mf*; AUTO copiloto *mf*

navvy ['nævi] <-ies> *n Brit, inf* peón *m*

navy ['neıvi] I. <-ies> *n* (*country's military fleet and servicemen*) **the Navy** la Marina; **to be in the Navy** estar en la Marina; **to serve in the** ~ servir en la Marina II. *adj* (*dark blue*) azul marino

nay [neı] I. *adv form* no II. *n Am* (*negative vote*) voto *m* en contra

Nazi ['nɑːtsi] *n* nazi *mf*

Naziism *n no pl,* **Nazism** ['nɑːtsızəm] *n no pl* nazismo *m*

NB [ˌen'biː] *abbr of* nota bene N.B.

NCC ['ensi:'si:] *n Brit abbr of* Nature Conservancy Council ≈ ICONA *m*

NCO [ˌensi:'əʊ, *Am:* -'oʊ] *n abbr of* non commissioned officer suboficial *mf*

NE [ˌen'i:] *abbr of* northeast NE *m*

neap tide ['ni:p̩taıd] *n* marea *f* muerta

near [nıəʳ, *Am:* nır] I. *adj* 1. (*spatial*) cercano, -a 2. (*temporal*) próximo, -a; **in the** ~ **future** en un futuro próximo 3. (*dear*) **a** ~ **and dear friend** un amigo íntimo 4. (*similar: portrait*) parecido, -a; **the** ~**est thing to sth** lo más parecido a algo 5. (*almost true*) **to have a** ~ **accident** tener por poco un accidente; **that was a** ~ **miss** [*o* **thing**] faltó poco II. *adv* 1. (*spatial or temporal*) cerca; **to be** ~ estar cerca; **to come** ~ aproximarse, acercarse; **to live quite** ~ vivir bastante cerca; ~ **at hand** a mano; **to come** ~**er to sb/sth** acercarse más a alguien/algo 2. (*almost*) ~ **to tears** a punto de

llorar; **as** ~ **as I can guess** que yo sepa III. *prep* 1. (*in proximity to*) ~ (**to**) cerca de; ~ (**to**) **the house** cerca de la casa; ~ **the end of the film** hacia el final de la película 2. (*almost*) **it's** ~ **midnight** es casi medianoche; **it's nowhere** ~ **enough** no basta ni con mucho 3. (*about ready to*) **to be** ~ **to doing sth** estar a punto de hacer algo 4. (*like*) **the copy is** ~ **to the original** la copia es parecida al original IV. *vt* acercarse a; **it is** ~**ing completion** está casi terminado; **he is** ~**ing his goal** está alcanzando su meta

nearby ['nıəbaı, *Am:* ˌnır'-] I. *adj* cercano, -a II. *adv* cerca; **is it** ~? está cerca?

Near East *n* Oriente *m* Próximo

nearly ['nıəli, *Am:* nır-] *adv* casi; ~ **certain** casi seguro; **to be not** ~ **as bad** no estar tan mal; **to be** ~ **there** estar casi ahí; **to very** ~ **do sth** estar a punto de hacer algo; **to be** ~ **sth** estar cerca de algo; **that wall is** ~ **three metres high** esa pared tiene casi tres metros; **she's** ~ **as tall as her father** ella es casi tan alta como su padre

nearside ['nıəsaıd, *Am:* ˌnır'-] *Brit, Aus* I. *n* lado *m* cercano al arcén II. *adj* **the** ~ **lane** el lado derecho; *Brit* el lado izquierdo

near-sighted [ˌnıə'saıtıd, *Am:* ˌnır'saıtˌıd] *adj a. fig* miope

nearsightedness [ˌnıə'saıtıdnıs, *Am:* ˌnır-'saıtˌıd-] *n no pl, a. fig* miopía *f*

neat [ni:t] *adj* 1. (*orderly, well-ordered*) cuidado, -a, ordenado, -a; ~ **appearance/beard** apariencia *f*/barba *f* cuidada; **to be** ~ **in one's habits** ser de hábitos ordenados; ~ **and tidy** ordenado 2. (*deft*) cuidadoso, -a; ~ **answer** respuesta *f* exacta 3. (*undiluted, pure*) puro, -a; **I'll have a** ~ **gin please** tomaré un gin solo 4. *Am, Aus, inf* (*fine, good, excellent*) guay *inf;* **a** ~ **guy** un tipo guay

neaten ['ni:tən] *vt* ordenar; **to** ~ **sth up** poner orden en algo

neatly *adv* 1. (*with care*) cuidadosamente 2. (*in orderly fashion*) de forma ordenada 3. (*deftly*) con estilo

neatness ['ni:tnəs] *n no pl* pulcritud *f,* limpieza *f*

nebula ['nebjələ] <-lae *o* -las> *n* ASTR nebulosa *f*

nebulae *n pl of* **nebula**

nebular *adj* nebular

nebulous ['nebjʊləs] *adj* nebuloso, -a; ~ **promise** promesa *f* vaga

necessaries ['nesəsəriz] *npl* **the** ~ lo necesario

necessarily ['nesəsərəli] *adv* necesariamente; **not** ~ no necesariamente

necessary ['nesəsəri, *Am:* -ser-] I. *adj* necesario, -a; **to make the** ~ **arrangements** hacer los preparativos necesarios; **a** ~ **evil** un mal necesario; **strictly** ~ estrictamente necesario; **to be** ~ ser necesario; **that won't be** ~ no será necesario; **was it really** ~ **for you to say that?** ¿era necesario que dijeras eso?; **to do**

what is ~ hacer lo que es necesario; **if** ~ cuando sea necesario **II.** *n* **the** ~ lo necesario
necessitate [nɪ'sesɪteɪt, *Am:* nə'-] *vt form* necesitar; **to** ~ **doing sth** necesitar hacer algo
necessity [nɪ'sesəti, *Am:* nə'sesəṭi] <-ies> *n no pl* (*need*) necesidad *f*; **in case of** ~ en caso de necesidad; **when the** ~ **arises** cuando surja la necesidad; ~ **of doing sth** necesidad de hacer algo; ~ **for sb to do sth** necesidad de que alguien haga algo; **there's no** ~ **to pay in advance** no hay necesidad de pagar por adelantado; **by** ~ por necesidad; **bare** ~ primera necesidad ►~ **is the mother of** <u>invention</u> *prov* no hay mejor maestra que el hambre *prov*
neck [nek] **I.** *n* **1.** (*part of body connecting head and shoulders*) cuello *m;* (*nape*) cogote *m;* **to fling one's arms round sb's** ~ abrazar a alguien por el cuello **2.** FASHION cuello *m;* **round** ~ cuello redondo **3.** (*long thin object part*) cuello *m;* ~ **of the bottle/vase/violin** cuello de la botella/del jarrón/del violín ►**to be up to one's** ~ **in sth** *inf* estar (metido) hasta el cuello en algo; **to be** <u>breathing down</u> **sb's** ~ estar encima de alguien **II.** *vi Am, inf* besuquearse
neckband ['nekbænd] *n* collar *m*
neckerchief ['nekətʃɪf] <neckerchieves> *n* pañuelo *m* atado al cuello
necklace ['neklɪs] *n* collar *m*
necklet ['neklɪt] *n* collar *m;* (*small one*) gargantilla *f*
neckline ['neklaɪn] *n* escote *m* **necktie** *n* corbata *f*
nectar ['nektəʳ, *Am:* -təʳ] *n* néctar *m*
nectarine ['nektərɪn, *Am:* ˌnektə'riːn] *n* nectarina *f*
née [neɪ] *adj* de soltera
need [niːd] **I.** *n no pl* necesidad *f;* **in** ~ necesitado, -a; **basic** ~s necesidades básicas; ~ **for sb/sth** necesidad de alguien/algo; **to be in** ~ **of sth** necesitar (de) algo; **to have no** ~ **of sth** no necesitar (de) algo; **as the** ~ **arises** según se sienta la necesidad; **if** ~(**s**) **be** si es necesario; **no** ~ **to be sth** ninguna necesidad de ser algo; **there's no** ~ **to shout so loud** no hace falta gritar tan alto; **in sb's hour of** ~ (*emergency, crisis*) en un momento de necesidad **II.** *vt* **1.** (*require*) necesitar; **to** ~ **sb to do sth** necesitar que alguien haga algo **2.** (*ought to have*) **to** ~ necesitar; **not to** ~ **sth** no necesitar (de) algo; **to** ~ (**doing**) **sth** necesitar (hacer) algo; **I** ~ **it like** (**I** ~) **a hole in the head** *iron* me hace tanta falta como un agujero en la cabeza **3.** (*must, have*) **to** ~ **to do sth** tener que hacer algo; ~ **we/I/you?** ¿nos/me/te hace falta?; **there was no** ~ **to do sth** no había necesidad de hacer algo **4.** (*should*) **you** ~**n't laugh! – you'll be next** ¡no deberías reír! – tú serás el siguiente; **I** ~ **hardly say ...** no hace falta decir que...
needed *adj* necesario, -a
needle ['niːdl] **I.** *n* aguja *f;* **hypodermic needle** jeringa *f;* **knitting** ~ aguja de tejer; ~

and thread aguja e hilo; **to thread a** ~ enhebrar una aguja ►**a** ~ **in a** <u>haystack</u> una aguja en un pajar; **to look for a** ~ **in a haystack** buscar una aguja en un pajar **II.** *vt* pinchar, provocar
needle match *n* partido *m* importantísimo
needless ['niːdlɪs] *adj* innecesario, -a; ~ **to say ...** no hace falta decir...; ~ **to say, I didn't reply** ni que decir tiene que no respondí
needlework ['niːdlwɜːk, *Am:* -wɜːrk] *n no pl* labor *f* de aguja
needn't ['niːdənt] = need not *s.* **need**
needs [niːdz] *adv* necesariamente; ~ **must** si hace falta; **must** ~ *form* por necesidad
needy ['niːdi] **I.** <-ier, -iest> *adj* necesitado, -a **II.** *npl* **the** ~ los necesitados
nefarious [nɪ'feərɪəs, *Am:* nə'ferɪ-] *adj pej, form* nefario, -a
negate [nɪ'geɪt] *vt* negar
negation [nɪ'geɪʃən] *n no pl* negación *f*
negative ['negətɪv, *Am:* -ṭɪv] **I.** *adj* **1.** (*not positive*) negativo, -a; ~ **answer** respuesta *f* negativa; ~ **clause/form** cláusula *f* negativa; **to be** ~ **about sth/sb** ser negativo respecto a algo/alguien **2.** *a.* MED negativo, -a; ~ **pole** polo *m* negativo; ~ **number** número *m* negativo **II.** *n* **1.** (*rejection*) negativa *f* **2.** (*making use of negation*) negación *f* **3.** PHOT negativo *m* **III.** *vt* negar
negatively *adv* negativamente
negativity [ˌnegə'tɪvəti, *Am:* -əṭi] *n no pl* negatividad
neglect [nɪ'glekt] **I.** *vt* desatender; **to** ~ **one's duties** descuidar los propios deberes; **to** ~ **to do sth** descuidar hacer algo; **I'd** ~**ed to write to him** me olvidé de escribirle **II.** *n no pl* negligencia *f;* (*poor state, unrepaired state*) deterioro *m;* **to be in a state of** ~ estar en un estado de deterioro; **to fall in a state of** ~ deteriorarse
neglected *adj* descuidado, -a; (*undervalued, underappreciated*) desvalorado, -a; ~ **child** niño, -a *m, f* abandonado, -a
neglectful [nɪ'glektfəl] *adj* negligente; ~ **parents** padres *mpl* negligentes; **to be** ~ **of sth/sb** ser negligente respecto a algo/alguien
negligee *n,* **negligée** ['neglɪʒeɪ, *Am:* ˌneglə'ʒeɪ] *n* salto *m* de cama
negligence ['neglɪdʒənts] *n no pl* **1.** (*lack of care, inattention, indifference*) negligencia *f;* (*neglect*) descuido *m,* deterioro **2.** LAW negligencia *f;* **gross** ~ negligencia grave
negligible ['neglɪdʒəbl] *adj* insignificante
negotiable [nɪ'gəʊʃiəbl, *Am:* -'goʊ-] *adj* negociable; ~ **securities** FIN títulos *mpl* negociables; **not** ~ no negociable
negotiate [nɪ'gəʊʃieɪt, *Am:* -'goʊ-] **I.** *vt* **1.** (*discuss*) negociar; **to** ~ **a loan/treaty** negociar un préstamo/tratado **2.** (*convert into money*) **to** ~ **a cheque** cobrar un cheque; **to** ~ **securities** negociar títulos **II.** *vi* negociar; **to** ~ **on sth** negociar algo; **to** ~ **with sb** negociar con alguien

negotiating committee n comité m de negociación

negotiating table n fig mesa f de negociaciones

negotiation [nɪˌgəʊʃiˈeɪʃən, Am: -ˌgoʊ-] n negociación f; ~ **for sth** negociación de algo

negotiator [nɪˈgəʊʃieɪtər, Am: -ˈgoʊʃieɪt̬ə] n negociador(a) m(f)

Negress [ˈniːgres, Am: -grɪs] n negra f

negro <-es> n, **Negro** [ˈniːgrəʊ, Am: -groʊ] n negro m

negroid [niːgrɔɪd] adj negroide; ~ **hair** pelo m negroide

neigh [neɪ] I. n relincho m II. vi relinchar

neighbor [ˈneɪbə] n Am s. **neighbour**

neighborhood [ˈneɪbəhʊd] n Am s. **neighbourhood**

neighboring [ˈneɪbərɪŋ] adj Am s. **neighbouring**

neighborliness n no pl, Am s. **neighbourliness**

neighborly [ˈneɪbəli] adj Am s. **neighbourly**

neighbour [ˈneɪbər, Am: -bə] I. n vecino, -a m, f; (fellow-citizen) prójimo, -a m, f ▶**love your ~ as you love yourself** ama a tu prójimo como a ti mismo II. vi **to ~ on sth** lindar con algo

neighbourhood [ˈneɪbəhʊd, Am: -bə-] n 1. (smallish localized community) vecindario m; (people) vecinos mpl; **a closed/friendly ~** un vecindario cerrado/amigable; **the whole ~ is talking about it** todo el vecindario habla de ello; **in the ~** en el vecindario 2. (vicinity) alrededores mpl, cercanías fpl; **I wouldn't like to live in the ~ of the airport** no me gustaría vivir en los alrededores del aeropuerto 3. **in the ~ of** alrededor de; **we're hoping to get something in the ~ of £70,000 for the house** esperamos obtener alrededor de 70.000 libras por la casa

neighbourhood watch n vigilancia f vecinal

neighbouring [ˈneɪbərɪŋ] adj (nearby) cercano, -a; (bordering) adyacente; ~ **house** casa f adyacente; ~ **country** país m vecino

neighbourliness n no pl convivencia f; **an act of ~** un acto de convivencia; **good ~** buena vecindad

neighbourly [ˈneɪbəli, Am: -bəli] adj amable

neither [ˈnaɪðər, Am: ˈniːðə] I. pron ninguno, -a; **which one? – ~ (of them)** ¿cuál? – ninguno (de los dos) II. adv ni; ~ **... nor ...** ni... ni...; **he is ~ wounded nor dead** no está ni herido ni muerto III. conj tampoco; **if he won't eat, ~ will I** si él no come, yo tampoco IV. adj ningún, -una; **in ~ case** en ningún caso; ~ **book is good** ninguno de los dos libros es bueno

nemesis [ˈneməsɪs] <-ses> n a. fig justo castigo m

neoclassical [ˌniːəʊˈklæsɪkəl, Am: -oʊˈ-]

adj neoclásico, -a

neocolonialist [ˌniːəʊkəˈləʊniəlɪst, Am: -oʊkəˈloʊ-] adj neocolonialista

neolithic [ˌniːəʊˈlɪθɪk, Am: -oʊˈ-] adj neolítico, -a; ~ **Period** período m neolítico

neologism [niːˈɒlədʒɪzəm, Am: -ˈɑːlə-] n form neologismo m

neon [ˈniːɒn, Am: -ɑːn] n no pl neón m

neo-nazi [ˌniːəʊˈnɑːtsi] I. n neonazi mf II. adj neonazi

neon lamp n, **neon light** n luz f de neón

neon sign n letrero m de neón

nephew [ˈnevjuː, Am: ˈnef-] n sobrino m

nephritis [nɪˈfraɪtɪs, Am: -t̬əs] n no pl MED nefritis f inv

nepotism [ˈnepətɪzəm] n no pl nepotismo m

Neptune [ˈneptjuːn] n Neptuno m

nerd [nɜːd, Am: nɜːrd] n Am lerdo, -a m, f

nerdy <-ier, -iest> adj Am, inf lerdo, -a

nerve [nɜːv, Am: nɜːrv] I. n 1. (fibre) nervio m 2. (high nervousness) ~**s** nerviosismo m; **to be in a state of ~s** estar nervioso; **to be a bundle of ~s** fig ser un puñado de nervios; **to calm one's ~s** calmarse; **to get on sb's ~s** inf crispar los nervios a alguien 3. no pl (courage, bravery) valor m; **to hold/lose one's ~** mantener/perder el valor 4. (apprehension) ~**s** ansiedad f 5. (temerity) temeridad f; **to have the ~ to do sth** inf tener el morro de hacer algo; **of all the ~!** inf ¡qué morro! ▶ ~**s of iron** nervios mpl de acero; **to expose** [o **to hit**] **a (raw)** ~ tocar un tema sensible II. vt envalentonarse; **to ~ oneself (up) to do sth** Brit animarse a hacer algo

nerve cell n célula f nerviosa **nerve center** n Am, **nerve centre** n Aus, Brit 1. (group of closely connected nerve cells) centro m nervioso 2. fig (centre of control) centro m neurálgico **nerve gas** <-es> n gas m nervioso

nerveless [ˈnɜːvlɪs, Am: ˈnɜːrv-] adj 1. (calm) imperturbable 2. (lacking courage) cobarde

nerve-racking [ˈnɜːvræækɪŋ, Am: ˈnɜːrv-] adj perturbador(a)

nervous [ˈnɜːvəs, Am: ˈnɜːr-] adj (jumpy) nervioso, -a; (edgy) ansioso, -a; **of a ~ disposition** de disposición nerviosa; **to be ~ in sb's presence** estar nervioso en presencia de alguien; **you look a ~ wreck!** ¡pareces un manojo de nervios!; **to make sb ~** poner nervioso a alguien; **to be ~ about sth** estar nervioso por algo

nervous breakdown n ataque m de nervios; **to have a ~** sufrir un ataque de nervios **nervously** adv nerviosamente

nervousness n no pl (nervous condition or state) nerviosismo m; (fearfulness) ansiedad f; ~ **about sth** nerviosismo por algo

nervous system n sistema m nervioso

nervy [ˈnɜːvi, Am: ˈnɜːr-] <-ier, -iest> adj 1. Am (rude) descarado, -a 2. Am (courageous) atrevido, -a 3. Brit (nervous) nervioso, -a; (apprehensive) aprensivo, -a

nest [nest] I. *n* **1.** (*animal's home*) nido *m*; (*of hen*) nidal *m* **2.** (*cosy domicile*) nido *m*; **to leave the ~** dejar el nido **3.** *pej* (*den*) guarida *f* **4.** (*location that swarms with sth bad*) cueva *f*, nido *m* **5.** (*set, cluster, assemblage*) juego *m* II. *vi* anidar

nest box <-es> *n Am* nido *m* **nest egg** *n* **1.** (*egg in a nest*) nidal *m* **2.** (*money saved*) ahorros *mpl*

nesting *adj* **1.** (*of sets fitting together*) que encaja **2.** (*concerning nests*) **~ time** tiempo *m* de anidar

nesting box <-es> *n* nido *m*

nestle ['nesl] I. *vt* arrimar, apoyar; **to ~ sth on sth** apoyar algo contra algo II. *vi* **1.** (*snuggle up*) acomodarse; **to ~ up to sb** arrimarse a alguien **2.** (*be in sheltered position*) cobijarse

nestling ['nestlɪŋ] *n* pajarito *m*

net¹ [net] I. *n* **1.** (*material with spaces*) malla *f*; (*fine netted fabric*) tul *m*; **mosquito ~** mosquitera *f* **2.** (*device for trapping fish*) red *f*; **to haul in a ~** pescar con redes; **to fall** [*o* **slip**] **through the ~** *fig* zafarse de las redes de alguien **3.** SPORTS red *f* **4.** (*final profit*) beneficio *m* neto; (*final amount*) importe *m* neto II. <-tt-> *vt* (*catch: fish*) pescar; (*criminals*) capturar

net² [net] I. *adj* **1.** ECON neto, -a; **~ assets** activo *m* neto; **~ income** [*o* **earnings**] beneficio *m* neto **2.** (*excluding package: of a weight*) neto, -a; **~ tonnage** tonelaje *m* neto; **~ weight** peso *m* neto II. *vt* **to ~ to ~ sth** ganar algo en neto

Net [net] *n* INFOR **the ~** la red; **~ surfer** navegador(a) *m(f)* de la red

netball ['netbɔ:l] *n no pl, Brit*: juego semejante al baloncesto y practicado mayoritariamente por mujeres **Net Book Agreement** *n* ≈ acuerdo sobre el precio neto de los libros **net curtain** *n* visillo(s) *m(pl)*

nether ['neθəʳ] *adj iron, liter* de abajo, inferior; **~ regions** *a. fig* infierno *m*

Netherlands ['neðələndz, *Am*: -ələndz] *n* **the ~** los Países Bajos, Holanda

netiquette ['netɪket] *n no pl* INFOR etiqueta *f* de la red

Netspeak ['netspi:k] *adj* INFOR lenguaje *m* de internet [*o* de la red]

nett [net] *adj, vt s.* **net¹** II., **net²**

netting ['netɪŋ, *Am*: 'neṭɪŋ] *n no pl* **1.** (*net*) malla *f*; **you should get some ~ for those windows** deberías comprar un visillo para esas ventanas **2.** SPORTS red *f*

nettle ['netl, *Am*: 'neṭ-] I. *n* ortiga *f* ►**to grasp the ~** *Aus, Brit* coger el toro por los cuernos II. *vt* provocar, irritar; **to be ~d by sth** estar irritado por algo

nettle rash <-es> *n* urticaria *f*

net weight *n* peso *m* neto

network ['netwɜ:k, *Am*: -wɜ:rk] I. *n* **1.** INFOR, TEL red *f*; **cable ~** cableado *m*; **computer ~** red informática; **telephone ~** red telefónica **2.** TV cadena *f* II. *vt* **1.** (*link together*) poner en contacto, conectar **2.** (*broadcast*) emitir en red

III. *vi* interconectar

networking *n* INFOR interconexión *f*

neural ['njʊərəl, *Am*: 'nʊrəl] *adj* neural, del sistema nervioso

neuralgia [njʊə'rældʒə, *Am*: nʊ'-] *n no pl* neuralgia *f*

neuralgic [nju:'rældʒɪk, *Am*: nʊ'-] *adj* neurálgico, -a

neural network *n* INFOR red *f* nerviosa

neurasthenia [ˌnjʊərəs'θi:nɪə, *Am*: ˌnʊræs'-] *n no pl* neurastenia *f*

neuritis [njʊə'raɪtɪs, *Am*: nʊ'raɪṭəs] *n no pl* MED neuritis *f inv*

neurological [ˌnjʊərə'lɒdʒɪkəl, *Am*: ˌnʊrə'lɑ-] *adj* neurológico, -a; **~ disorder** trastorno *m* neurológico

neurologist [njʊə'rɒlədʒɪst, *Am*: nʊ'rɑ:lə-] *n* neurólogo, -a *m, f*

neurology [njʊə'rɒlədʒi, *Am*: nʊ'rɑ:lə-] *n no pl* neurología *f*

neuron ['njʊərɒn, *Am*: 'nʊrɑ:n] *n*, **neurone** ['njʊərəʊn, *Am*: 'nʊrəʊn] *n* neurona *f*

neuroscience [ˌnjʊə'rəʊsaɪənts, *Am*: ˌnʊrəʊ'saɪ-] *n no pl* neurología *f*

neurosis [njʊə'rəʊsɪs, *Am*: nʊ'rəʊ-] <-es> *n* neurosis *f inv*

neurosurgeon [ˌnjʊə's3:dʒən, *Am*: ˌnʊrəʊ's3:r-] *n* neurocirujano, -a *m, f*

neurosurgery [ˌnjʊə's3:dʒəri, *Am*: ˌnʊrəʊ's3:r-] *n no pl* neurocirujía *f*

neurotic [njʊə'rɒtɪk, *Am*: nʊ'rɑ:ṭɪk] I. *n* neurótico, -a *m, f* II. *adj* neurótico, -a

neurotransmitter [ˌnjʊərəʊtrænz'mɪtəʳ, *Am*: ˌnʊrəʊtræns'mɪtəˣ] *n* MED neurotransmisor *m*

neuter ['nju:təʳ, *Am*: 'nu:ṭəˣ] I. *adj* neutro, -a; **~ noun** LING sustantivo *m* neutro II. *vt* **1.** (*castrate: males*) castrar **2.** (*sterilize: females*) esterilizar **3.** (*neutralise*) neutralizar

neutral ['nju:trəl, *Am*: 'nu:-] I. *adj* **1.** (*uninvolved*) neutral; **~ country** POL país *m* neutral; **to remain ~** mantenerse al margen **2.** *a.* CHEM, ELEC neutro, -a **3.** (*unemotional*) objetivo, -a II. *n* **1.** (*non-combatant in war*) territorio *m* neutral **2.** (*part of gears system*) punto *m* muerto; **in ~** en punto muerto

neutralisation [ˌnju:trəlaɪ'zeɪʃən, *Am*: ˌnu:trəlɪ'-] *n Brit, Aus s.* **neutralization**

neutralise ['nju:trəlaɪz, *Am*: 'nu:-] *vt Brit, Aus s.* **neutralize**

neutrality [nju:'træləti, *Am*: nu:'træləṭi] *n no pl* neutralidad *f*

neutralization [ˌnju:trəlaɪ'zeɪʃən, *Am*: ˌnu:trəlɪ'-] *n no pl* neutralización *f*

neutralize ['nju:trəlaɪz, *Am*: 'nu:-] *vt* neutralizar; **the bomb was ~d by the specialists** los especialistas desactivaron la bomba

neutron ['nju:tron, *Am*: 'nu:trɑ:n] *n* neutrón *m*

neutron bomb *n* bomba *f* de neutrones

never ['nevəʳ, *Am*: -ə‍ˣ] *adv* **1.** (*at no time, on no occasion*) nunca, jamás; **I ~ forget a face** nunca olvido una cara **2.** (*under no circum-*

stances) jamás; ~ **again!** ¡nunca jamás!; ~ **fear!** ¡no te preocupes!; **well I ~ (did)** ¡no me digas!, ¿de veras?; **it's ~ too late to do sth** nunca es demasiado tarde para hacer algo; ~ **before** nunca antes; ~ **before had I had so much money** jamás había tenido tanto dinero; **as ~ before** como nunca; ~ **ever** nunca jamás; **he's ~ 61, he looks much younger** no aparenta 61, parece mucho más joven; ~ **mind** no importa, tanto da; ~ **say die** *fig* nunca tires la toalla

never-ending [ˌnevər'endɪŋ, *Am:* 'nevɚ-] *adj* interminable **never-failing** *adj* infalible **nevermore** *adv* nunca más **never-never** *n Brit, inf* compra *f* a plazos; **on the ~** a plazos **never-never land** *n fig, inf* paraíso *m* de irás y no volverás

nevertheless [ˌnevəðə'les, *Am:* ˌnevɚ-] *adv* sin embargo, con todo, no obstante

new [njuː, *Am:* nuː] **I.** *adj* **1.** (*latest, recent*) nuevo, -a, reciente; (*word*) de nuevo cuño; ~ **technology** tecnología *f* punta; **to be the ~est fad** [*o* **craze**] *inf* ser la última moda **2.** (*changed*) nuevo, -a; ~ **boy/girl** *Brit* SCHOOL novato, -a *m, f* **3.** (*inexperienced*) nuevo, -a, novato, -a; **to be a ~ one on sb** ser nuevo para alguien; **she's ~ to the job** es nueva en el trabajo **4.** (*in new condition*) nuevo, -a; **brand ~** completamente nuevo **5.** (*fresh*) fresco, -a; ~ **blood** *fig* sangre *f* fresca; **to feel like a ~ man/woman** sentirse un hombre nuevo/una mujer nueva **6.** (*freshly found or made public*) fresco, -a, reciente **II.** *n no pl* **the ~** lo nuevo **New Age** *n* **1.** (*movement*) New Age *m* **2.** (*music*) new age *f* **New Ager** *n* seguidor(a) *m(f)* del New Age **New Age Traveller** *n Brit* viajero(a) *m(f)* de la nueva era **newbie** *n* INFOR novato, -a *m, f* (en la red) **newborn** **I.** *adj* reciente; ~ **democracy/science** democracia *f* reciente/ciencia *f* reciente; ~ **baby** recién nacido, -a *m, f* **II.** *n* **the ~** los recién nacidos **New Brunswick** *n* Nueva Brunswick *f* **New Caledonia** *n* Nueva Caledonia *f* **newcomer** *n* **1.** (*person who has just arrived*) recién llegado, -a *m, f* **2.** (*stranger*) nuevo, -a *m, f* **3.** (*beginner, recent starter*) principiante *mf*, novato, -a *m, f*; **I'm a ~ to Chester** soy nuevo en Chester

newel ['njuːəl, *Am:* 'nuː-] *n* **1.** (*of a circular staircase*) espigón *m* **2.** (*supporting banister*) poste *m*

New England *n* Nueva Inglaterra *f* **newfangled** *adj* novedoso, -a **new-fashioned** *adj* moderno, -a, a la última (moda)

new-found [ˌnjuː'faʊnd, *Am:* ˌnuː-] *adj* recién descubierto; **a ~ friend** un amigo nuevo **New Foundland¹** ['njuːfəndlənd, *Am:* 'nuːfəndlənd] *n* Terranova *f*

New Foundland² [njuːˈfaʊndlənd, *Am:* 'nuːfəndlənd], **New Foundland dog** *n* ZOOL perro *m* de Terranova

newish ['njuːɪʃ, *Am:* 'nuː-] *adj inf* bastante nuevo, -a

new-laid [ˌnjuːˈleɪd, *Am:* 'nuː-] *adj* ~ **eggs** huevos *mpl* recién puestos

newly ['njuːli, *Am:* 'nuː-] *adv* **1.** (*recently*) recientemente; ~ **married** recién casados **2.** (*freshly*) recién; ~ **painted** recién pintado **3.** (*done differently than before*) nuevamente, de nuevo

newly-wed ['njuːlɪwed, *Am:* 'nuː-] **I.** *npl* recién casados *mpl* **II.** *adj* recién casado, -a

New Man <-men> *n Brit* hombre *m* moderno **new moon** *n* luna *f* nueva **New Orleans** *n* Nueva Orleans *f* **new potatoes** *npl* patatas *fpl* tiernas **New Right** *n* Nueva Derecha *f* (*movimiento político reaccionario a la nueva izquierda*)

news [njuːz, *Am:* nuːz] *n* + *sing vb* **1.** (*fresh information*) noticias *fpl*; **the ~ media** los medios de comunicación; **bad/good ~** buenas/malas noticias; **he's bad ~ for the company** es pájaro de mal agüero para la empresa; **to break the ~ to sb** dar la noticia a alguien; **when the ~ broke** cuando se supo la noticia; **really! that's ~ to me** ¿de veras? no lo sabía **2.** (*broadcast*) noticias *fpl*, informativo *m;* **to be ~** ser noticia ▶**no ~ is good ~** *prov* si no hay noticias, buena señal

news agency <-ies> *n* agencia *f* de noticias **newsagent** *n Brit, Aus* **1.** (*shop*) quiosco *m* **2.** (*person*) vendedor(a) *m(f)* de periódicos **news-boy** *n* **1.** (*seller*) vendedor(a) *m(f)* de periódicos **2.** (*sb delivering papers*) repartidor(a) *m(f)* de periódicos **newscast** *n Am* informativo *m* **newscaster** *n Am* locutor(a) *m(f)* de un informativo **news conference** *n* rueda *f* de prensa **news dealer** *n Am* vendedor(a) *m(f)* de periódicos **newsflash** <-es> *n* ≈ noticia *f* de última hora, flash *m* informativo **newsgroup** *n* INFOR grupo *m* de discusión, grupo *m* de noticias **newshound** *n fig, inf* cazanoticias *mf inv* **news item** *n* noticia *f* **newsletter** *n* nota *f* de prensa **newsmonger** *n* **1.** (*sb gathering news*) chismoso, -a *m, f* **2.** (*a gossip*) cotilleo *m* **newspaper** *n* periódico *m;* ~ **clipping** recorte *m* de periódico **newspeak** *n no pl, pej* lenguaje *m* de los políticos **newsprint** *n no pl* papel *m* de periódico **newsreader** *n Brit, Aus* locutor(a) *m(f)* de un informativo **newsreel** *n* noticiario *m* documental **news release** *n Am* noticiario *m* **news report** *n* informativo *m* **newsroom** *n* sala *f* de redacción **newsstand** *n* quiosco *m* **newsvendor** *n* vendedor(a) *m(f)* de periódicos **newsworthy** *adj* de interés periodístico

newsy ['njuːzi, *Am:* 'nuː-] <-ier, -iest> *adj* lleno, -a de noticias; **a ~ letter** una carta cargada de noticias

newt [njuːt, *Am:* nuːt] *n* tritón *m*

New Testament *n* REL Nuevo Testamento *m* **new town** *n Brit: ciudad creada para redistribuir la población* **new wave** *n fig* **1.** (*movement*) new wave *f* **2.** (*fresh outbreak*) nueva ola *f;* **a ~ of redundancies/violence**

una nueva ola de despidos/violencia **new world order** *n*, **New World Order** *n* nuevo orden *m* mundial **New Year** *n* 1. año *m* nuevo; **Happy ~** feliz año nuevo; **to celebrate ~** celebrar el año nuevo 2. (*opening weeks of year*) principios *mpl* de año **New Year's** *n no pl, Am, inf* (*New Year's Day*) día *f* de año nuevo; (*New Year's Eve*) nochevieja *f* **New Year's Day** *n no pl* día *m* de año nuevo **New Year's Eve** *n no pl* nochevieja *f* **New York** I. *n* Nueva York *f* II. *adj* neoyorquino, -a **New Yorker** *n* neoyorquino, -a *m*, *f* **New Zealand** I. *n* Nueva Zelanda *f* II. *adj* neozelandés, -esa **New Zealander** *n* neozelandés, -esa *m, f*

next [nekst] I. *adj* 1. (*nearest in location*) siguiente 2. (*following in time*) próximo, -a, que viene; **the ~ day** el día siguiente; **~ month** el mes que viene; **the ~ thing** el siguiente paso; (**the**) **~ time** la próxima vez 3. (*following in order*) siguiente; **to be ~** ser el siguiente; **to be** (**the**) **~ to do sth** ser el próximo en hacer algo; **the ~ sth but one** la siguiente cosa después de ésta; **~ to sth/sb** cerca de algo/alguien II. *adv* 1. (*afterwards, subsequently*) después, luego; **when are you ~ going to London?** ¿cuándo vuelves a ir a Londres? 2. (*almost as much*) **~ to** después de; **cheese is my favourite food and ~ to cheese I like chocolate best** el queso es mi comida preferida y después está el chocolate 3. (*again, once more*) de nuevo; **when I saw him ~** he had transformed cuando volví a verlo estaba desconocido 4. (*almost*) casi; **~ to impossible** casi imposible; **~ to nothing** casi nada 5. (*second*) **the ~ best thing** lo segundo mejor III. *prep* 1. (*beside*) **~ to** junto a; **~ to the skin** junto a la piel; **my room is ~ to yours** mi habitación está junto a la tuya 2. (*almost*) casi; **to cost ~ to nothing** no valer casi nada 3. (*second to*) **~ to last** penúltimo; **~ to Bach, I like Mozart best** después de Bach, Mozart es el que me gusta más

next door [ˌneks'dɔːr, *Am:* ˌnekst'dɔːr] I. *adv* al lado; **we live ~ to the airport** vivimos al lado del aeropuerto II. *adj* de al lado; **to be/feel ~ to sth** *Brit, fig* estar/sentirse cerca de algo **next-door neighbo(u)r** *n* vecino, -a *m, f* de al lado **next of kin** *n no pl* pariente *mf* cercano, -a

nexus ['neksəs] *n inv* nexo *m*

NF [ˌen'ef] *Brit abbr of* **National Front** FN *m*

NHS [ˌenəɪtʃ'es] *Brit abbr of* **National Health Service** servicio *m* de asistencia sanitaria de la Seguridad Social

Niagara Falls [naɪˌægərə'fɔːlz] *n* **the ~** las cataratas del Niágara

nib [nɪb] *n* punta *f*; (*of a pen*) plumilla *f*

nibble ['nɪbl] I. *n* 1. (*a small bite/peck*) mordisco *m*, bocado *m;* **to take a ~** (**at sth**) dar un mordisco (a algo) 2. (*expression of interest*) muestra *f* de interés 3. *Brit, inf* **~s** tentempié *m* II. *vt* 1. (*bite*) mordisquear; (*rat*) roer

2. (*pick at*) picar III. *vi* 1. *a. fig* picar 2. (*purchase little quantities of*) **to ~ at sth** comprar poca cantidad de algo 3. (*show interest in*) **to ~ at sth** mostrar interés por algo 4. (*deplete slowly*) **to ~ away at sth** desgastar algo

Nicaragua [ˌnɪkə'rægjʊə, *Am:* -ə'rɑːgwə] *n* Nicaragua *f*

Nicaraguan I. *n* nicaragüense *mf* II. *adj* nicaragüense

nice [naɪs] I. *adj* 1. (*pleasant, agreeable*) bueno, -a; **~ one!**, **~ work!** *inf* ¡bien hecho!; **~ weather** buen tiempo *m;* **~ work** *inf* buen trabajo *m;* **far ~er** mucho más bonito; **it is ~ to do sth** es agradable hacer algo 2. (*amiable*) simpático, -a; (*kind*) amable; **to be ~ to sb** ser amable con alguien; **it is/was ~ of sb to do sth** es/fue un detalle por parte de alguien hacer algo; **~ boys** chicos majos 3. *iron, inf* (*unpleasant*) **that's a ~ thing to say to your brother** vaya cosas de decir a tu hermano 4. (*subtle*) sutil, delicado, -a; (*fine*) fino, -a II. *adv* bien

nice-looking *adj* atractivo, -a

nicely ['naɪsli] *adv* 1. (*well, satisfactorily*) bien; **to do very ~** quedar muy bonito 2. (*having success*) espléndidamente 3. (*in healthy state*) **the princess and the baby were both doing ~** la princesa y el bebé gozaban de buena salud 4. (*pleasantly, politely*) amablemente

nicety ['naɪsəti, *Am:* -ʈi] <-ies> *n* 1. *no pl* (*subtle distinction*) sutileza *f* 2. (*precision*) precisión *f;* **~ of an argument** pormenores *mpl* de una discusión 3. (*precise differentiations*) **niceties** matices *mpl;* (*in negative sense*) nimiedades *fpl*

niche [niːʃ, *Am:* nɪtʃ] *n* 1. (*alcove*) nicho *m* 2. (*desired job*) buen puesto *m;* (*suitable position*) buena posición *f* 3. (*place suiting a particular group*) refugio *m*

niche market *n* ECON mercado *m* alternativo (especializado)

nick [nɪk] I. *n* 1. (*chip in surface*) mella *f* 2. *no pl, Brit, inf* (*prison*) **the ~** el trullo 3. *no pl, Brit, Aus, inf* (*specified state*) **in excellent ~** en perfecto estado *m* ► **in the ~ of time** por los pelos II. *vt* 1. (*chip*) mellar; (*cut*) cortar 2. *Brit, Aus, inf* (*steal*) mangar, chingar *Méx*, pispear *Arg* 3. *Brit, inf* **to ~ sb** (*arrest*) trincar a alguien; (*catch*) echar el guante a alguien 4. *Am, inf* (*trick*) engañar

nickel ['nɪkl] *n* 1. *no pl* CHEM níquel *m* 2. *Am* (*coin*) moneda *f* de cinco centavos

nickel-plated *adj* niquelado, -a

nick-nack ['nɪknæk] *n s.* **knick-knack**

nickname ['nɪkneɪm] I. *n* apodo *m* II. *vt* apodar

Nicosia [ˌnɪkəʊ'siːə] *n* Nicosia *f*

nicotine ['nɪkətiːn] *n no pl* nicotina *f*

nicotine patch <-es> *n* parche *m* de nicotina

niece [niːs] *n* sobrina *f*

niff [nɪf] *n Brit, inf* tufo *m*

niffy [nɪfi] <-ier, -iest> *adj Brit, inf* apestoso, -a

nifty ['nɪfti] <-ier, -iest> *adj inf* (*stylish, smart*) elegante; (*skilful*) diestro, -a

Niger ['naɪdʒəʳ, *Am:* -dʒɚ] *n* Níger *m*

Nigeria [naɪ'dʒɪərɪə, *Am:* -'dʒɪri-] *n* Nigeria *f*

Nigerian I. *adj* nigeriano, -a II. *n* nigeriano, -a *m, f*

niggardly ['nɪgədlɪ, *Am:* -ɚd-] *adj* (*stingy*) tacaño, -a; (*meagre*) miserable

nigger ['nɪgəʳ, *Am:* -ɚ] *n pej* negraco, -a *m, f*

niggle ['nɪgl] I. *vi* fastidiar; **to ~ at sth** preocuparse por algo II. *vt* 1. (*nag pettily*) reparar en minucias 2. (*irritate*) enfurecer, irritar III. *n* 1. (*doubt*) duda *f* 2. (*complaint*) queja *f*

niggling ['nɪglɪŋ] *adj* 1. (*irritating, troubling*) molesto, -a 2. (*needing very precise work*) meticuloso, -a

nigh [naɪ] *adj liter* inminente

night [naɪt] *n* noche *f*; **good ~!** ¡buenas noches!; **last ~** anoche; **10 (o'clock) at ~** las 10 de la noche; **the ~ before** la noche anterior; **open at ~** abierto por la noche; **~ and day** día y noche; **during the ~** durante la noche; **during Tuesday ~** durante la noche del martes; **far into the ~** a altas horas de la noche; **at dead of ~** a mitad de la noche; **wedding ~** noche de bodas; **the Arabian Nights** las mil y una noches; **Twelfth Night** víspera *f* de Reyes; **to work ~s** trabajar de noche

nightbird [naɪtbɜːd, *Am:* naɪtbɜːrd] *n* pájaro *m* nocturno; (*person*) trasnochador(a) *m(f)* **night blindness** *n no pl* ceguera *f* nocturna **nightcap** *n* 1. (*cap*) gorro *m* de dormir 2. (*drink*) bebida *f* (*que se toma antes de acostarse*) **nightclothes** *npl* ropa *f* de dormir **nightclub** *n* club *m* (nocturno) **nightdress** <-es> *n* camisón *m* **nightfall** *n no pl* atardecer *m* **nightgown** *n Am* camisón *m* **nightie** *n inf* camisón *m* **nightingale** *n* ruiseñor *m* **night life** *n no pl* vida *f* nocturna **nightlight** *n* lamparilla *f* **nightlong** *liter* I. *adv* durante toda la noche II. *adj* de toda la noche

nightly ['naɪtlɪ] I. *adv* cada noche II. *adj* 1. (*done or happening each night*) de todas las noches 2. (*nocturnal*) de noche

nightmare ['naɪtmeəʳ, *Am:* -mer] *n* pesadilla *f*

nightmarish ['naɪtmeərɪʃ, *Am:* -mer-] *adj* 1. (*like a horrible dream*) espeluznante 2. (*very distressing*) inquietante

night-night ['naɪt,naɪt] *interj inf* buenas noches **night-nurse** *n* enfermera *f* de noche **night owl** *n* lechuza *f*; *fig* noctámbulo, -a *m, f* **night-porter** *n* portero *m* nocturno **nights** *adv* por la noche, de noche **night safe** *n Brit* caja *f* fuerte **night school** *n* escuela *f* nocturna **night shift** *n* turno *m* de noche **nightshirt** *n* camisa *f* de dormir **nightspot** *n inf* club *m* (nocturno) **night stand** *n* mesilla *f* de noche **night stick** *n Am* porra *f* **night table** *n Am* mesilla *f* de

noche **night-time** *n no pl* noche *f* **night-watch** <-es> *n* vigilancia *f* nocturna **night watchman** *n* vigilante *m* nocturno, nochero *m CSur* **nightwear** *n no pl* ropa *f* de dormir

nihilism ['naɪɪlɪzəm, *Am:* 'naɪə-] *n no pl* nihilismo *m*

nihilist ['naɪɪlɪst, *Am:* 'naɪə-] *n* nihilista *mf*

nihilistic [ˌnaɪɪ'lɪstɪk, *Am:* 'naɪə-] *adj* nihilista

Nikkei [nɪ'keɪ, *Am:* 'niːkeɪ] *n*, **Nikkei Index** *n no pl* FIN índice *m* Nikkei

nil [nɪl] *n no pl* 1. (*nothing, nought*) nada *f* 2. *Brit* (*no score*) cero *m*

Nile [naɪl] *n* **the ~** el Nilo

nimble ['nɪmbl] *adj* (*agile*) ágil; (*quick and light in movement*) diestro, -a; (*quick-thinking*) listo, -a; **~ mind** mente *f* despierta

nimbus ['nɪmbəs] *n no pl* nimbo *m*

NIMBY, nimby ['nɪmbɪ] *n abbr of* **not in my back yard** persona que se opone a que en la zona donde vive se realice cualquier destrozo urbanístico o medioambiental

nincompoop ['nɪŋkəmpuːp, *Am:* 'nɪn-] *inf* zoquete *mf*

nine [naɪn] I. *adj* nueve *inv* ▸ **a ~ days' wonder** la flor de un día; **~ times out of ten** casi siempre II. *n* nueve *m* ▸ **to be done (up) to the ~s** *inf* ir de punta en blanco; *s. a.* **eight**

ninepins ['naɪnpɪnz] *npl Brit* bolos *mpl*; **to be going down like ~** caer como moscas

nineteen [ˌnaɪn'tiːn] I. *adj* diecinueve II. *n* diecinueve *m*; *s. a.* **eight**

nineteenth I. *adj* decimonoveno, -a II. *n* 1. (*order*) decimonoveno, -a *m, f* 2. (*date*) diecinueve 3. (*fraction*) diecinueveavo *m*; (*part*) diecinueveava parte *f*; *s. a.* **eighth**

nineteenth hole *n inf* (*golf club bar*) bar *m*

nineties *npl* **the ~** los noventa

ninetieth ['naɪntɪəθ, *Am:* -t̬ɪ-] I. *adj* nonagésimo, -a II. *n no pl* (*order*) nonagésimo, -a *m, f*; (*fraction*) noventavo *m*; (*part*) noventava parte *f*; *s. a.* **eighth**

nine-to-five I. *adv* de nueve a cinco, en horario de oficina II. *adj* de nueve a cinco; **~ schedule** horario *m* de nueve a cinco

ninety ['naɪntɪ, *Am:* -t̬ɪ] I. *adj* noventa II. <-ies> *n* noventa *m*; *s. a.* **eighty**

ninja ['nɪndʒə] *n* ninja *mf*

ninjutsu *n no pl* ninjutsu *m*

ninny ['nɪnɪ] <-ies> *n inf* bobo, -a *m, f*

ninth [naɪnθ] I. *adj* noveno, -a II. *n no pl* 1. (*order*) noveno, -a *m, f* 2. (*date*) nueve *m* 3. (*fraction*) noveno *m*; (*part*) novena parte *f*; *s. a.* **eighth**

nip¹ [nɪp] I. <-pp-> *vt* 1. (*bite sharply, bite*) morder; (*insects*) picar 2. (*pinch, squeeze*) pellizcar 3. (*cut*) cortar ▸ **to ~ sth in the bud** *fig* cortar algo de raíz II. <-pp-> *vi* 1. (*bite*) morder; (*insects*) picar 2. *Brit, Aus, inf* (*hurry*) apresurarse; **to ~ along** correr; **I ~ped round to Bill's to borrow some sugar** me dejé caer por casa de Bill para pedirle un poco de azúcar III. *n* 1. (*pinch, tight squeeze*) pellizco *m*;

(*bite*) mordisco *m;* (*of insects*) picadura *f*
2. (*sharp cold, chill*) helada *f*
nip² [nɪp] *n Brit, inf* chupito *m*
nipper ['nɪpəʳ, *Am:* -ɚ] *n Brit, inf* chiquillo, -a
m, f
nipple ['nɪpl] *n* ANAT pezón *m;* (*teat*) tetilla *f,*
tetera *f AmL*
nippy ['nɪpi] <-ier, -iest> *adj* **1.** *Brit, Aus, inf*
(*quick*) rápido, -a; (*nimble*) ágil **2.** *inf* (*cold*)
helado, -a
nirvana ['nɪə'vɑnə, *Am:* nɪr-] *n no pl* nirvana
m; fig perfección *f*
Nissen hut ['nɪsnhʌt] *n* barraca *f* prefabricada (*hecha de metal y cemento*)
nit [nɪt] *n* **1.** *Brit, Aus, pej, inf* (*stupid person*)
imbécil *mf* **2.** ZOOL liendre *f*
niter ['naɪtəʳ, *Am:* - t̬əʳ] *n Am* nitro *m*
nitpick ['nɪtpɪk] *vi* criticar
nitpicker ['nɪtpɪkəʳ, *Am:* -ɚ] *n* (*quibbler*)
quisquilloso, -a *m, f;* (*petty fault-finder*) criticón, -ona *m, f*
nitpicking ['nɪtpɪkɪŋ] **I.** *adj inf* criticón,
-ona; ~ **criticism** crítica *f* mordaz **II.** *n no pl,*
inf crítica *f*
nitrate ['naɪtreɪt] *n* nitrato *m*
nitre ['naɪtəʳ, *Am:* -t̬əʳ] *n* nitro *m*
nitric ['naɪtrɪk] *adj* nítrico, -a
nitric acid *n no pl* ácido *m* nítrico
nitrite ['naɪtraɪt] *n* nitrito *m*
nitrogen ['naɪtrədʒən] *n no pl* nitrógeno *m*
nitroglycerin(e) [ˌnaɪtrəʊ'glɪsəriːn, *Am:*
-troʊ'-] *n no pl* nitroglicerina *f*
nitrous ['naɪtrəs] *adj* nitroso, -a; ~ **acid** ácido
m nitroso
nitty-gritty [ˌnɪti'grɪti, *Am:* ˌnɪt̬i'grɪt̬-] *n no*
pl, inf the ~ lo esencial; **to get down to the** ~
ir al grano
nitwit ['nɪtwɪt] *n inf* idiota *mf*
nix *Am* **I.** *vt inf* rehusar **II.** *adv inf* ¡ni hablar!
III. *n no pl, inf* nada *f*
NLP [ˌenel'piː] *n abbr of* **Neuro-Linguistic**
Programming programación *f* neurolingüís-
tica
NNE *abbr of* **north-northeast** NNE *m*
NNW *abbr of* **north-northwest** NNO *m*
no [nəʊ, *Am:* noʊ] **I.** *adv* **1.** (*not to any*
degree) no; ~ **parking** prohibido estacionar; ~
way de ninguna manera; ~ **can do** *inf* no lo
puedo hacer; ~ **less than sth/sb** nada menos
que algo/alguien **2.** (*equivalent to a negative*
sentence) no; (*emphasises previous state-*
ment's falsity) en absoluto **II.** *n* <-(e)s>, *n*
(*denial, refusal*) no *m;* **to not take** ~ **for an**
answer no admitir un no por respuesta **III.** *in-*
terj (*word used to deny*) no; (*emphasises dis-*
tress) qué me dices
no, No. *abbr of* **number** núm., nº
Noah's ark [ˌnəʊəz'ɑːk, *Am:* ˌnoʊəz'ɑːrk] *n*
arca *f* de Noé
nob [nɒb, *Am:* nɑːb] *n Brit, iron, inf* pez *m*
gordo
nobble ['nɒbl] *vt Brit, Aus, inf* **1.** (*tamper*
with) **to** ~ **sth** entrometerse en algo **2.** (*suc-*

cessfully bribe) sobornar; (*spoil*) estropear
3. (*deliberately grab sb's attention*) **to** ~ **sb** llamar la atención de alguien
Nobel prize [ˌnəʊbel'praɪz, *Am:* ˌnoʊbel-
'praɪz] *n* premio *m* Nobel
Nobel prize winner *n* ganador(a) *m(f)* del
premio Nobel
nobility [nəʊ'bɪləti, *Am:* noʊ'bɪlət̬i] *n no pl*
1. + *sing/pl vb* (*aristocracy*) nobleza *f;* **the** ~ la
aristocracia **2.** (*nobleness of character*) generosidad *f;* (*selflessness*) altruismo *m*
noble ['nəʊbl, *Am:* 'noʊ-] **I.** *adj* **1.** (*of aristo-*
cratic or birth) noble **2.** (*honourable: person*)
noble; (*action*) generoso, -a; (*ideas*) grande; ~
act acto *m* noble **3.** (*splendid*) majestuoso, -a
4. (*excellent*) magnífico, -a; (*horse*) noble **II.** *n*
noble *mf*
nobleman ['nəʊblmən, *Am:* 'noʊ-]
<-men> *n* aristócrata *m* **noble-minded** *adj*
honesto, -a **noblewoman** <-women> *n*
aristócrata *f*
nobly ['nəʊbli, *Am:* 'noʊ-] *adv* noblemente
nobody ['nəʊbədi, *Am:* 'noʊbɑːdi] **I.** *pron*
indef, sing nadie; ~ **speaks** nadie habla; **we**
saw ~ (**else**) no vimos a nadie (más); **he told**
~ no se lo dijo a nadie **II.** *n inf* don nadie *m;*
those people are nobodies esa gente son un
cero a la izquierda
nocturnal [nɒk'tɜːnəl, *Am:* nɑːk'tɜːr-] *adj*
form nocturno, -a
nocturnally *adv* por la noche
nod [nɒd, *Am:* nɑːd] **I.** *n* cabezada *f,* inclinación *f* de cabeza ►**a** ~'s **as good as a wink to**
a blind horse *prov, inf* a buen entendedor
pocas palabras bastan *prov;* **on the** ~ *Brit, inf*
sin ser discutido **II.** <-dd-> *vt* **to** ~ **one's**
head asentir con la cabeza; **to** ~ **one's head**
to do sth dar el visto bueno para hacer algo; **to**
~ **one's head at sth** indicar algo con la
cabeza; **to** ~ **a farewell to sb** saludar a alguien
con una inclinación de cabeza **III.** <-dd-> *vi*
1. (*incline head in agreement*) asentir con la
cabeza; **to** ~ **to sb** saludar a alguien con una
inclinación de cabeza; **to** ~ **at sth** indicar algo
con la cabeza **2.** *inf* (*start sleeping, drift off*)
dar cabezadas
◆**nod off** *vi* dormirse
nodding ['nɒdɪŋ, *Am:* 'nɑːdɪŋ] *adj* ~
acquaintance conocimiento *f* superficial; **to**
have only a ~ **acquaintance with sth**
conocer algo sólo por encima
node [nəʊd, *Am:* noʊd] *n* **1.** ANAT (*tissue*)
ganglio *m* **2.** BOT (*on a stem*) nódulo *m* **3.** INFOR
nodo *m*
nodule ['nɒdjuːl, *Am:* 'nɑːdjuːl] *n* **a.** ANAT,
BOT nódulo *m*
no-fault ['noʊfɔːlt] *adj Am* (*insurance*) con
indemnización garantizada
noggin ['nɒgɪn, *Am:* 'nɑːgɪn] *n* **1.** (*small*
measure) vaso *m* pequeño **2.** *Am, Scot, inf*
(*head, mind*) coco *m*
no-go area [nəʊgəʊ'eərə, *Am:* noʊgoʊ-
'eri-] *n* MIL zona *f* prohibida

no-hoper [ˌnəʊˈhəʊpəʳ, *Am:* ˌnoʊˈhoʊpɚ] *n Brit, Aus, inf* caso *m* perdido

nohow [ˈnəʊhaʊ, *Am:* ˈnoʊ-] *adv Am* de ninguna manera

noise [nɔɪz] I. *n* 1. (*sound*) ruido *m;* **to make a ~** hacer ruido 2. *no pl* (*loud, unpleasant sounds*) estruendo *m* 3. *no pl* ELEC interferencia *f* ▶**to** make **a ~ about sth** *inf* quejarse mucho de algo; **to** make **(the right) ~s** (*to go along with*) seguir la corriente; (*be polite*) ser muy cortés II. *adj* de ruido, ruidoso, -a

noise barrier *n* barrera *f* del sonido

noiseless [ˈnɔɪzləs] *adj* silencioso, -a

noise pollution *n no pl* contaminación *f* acústica **noise prevention** *n no pl* prevención *f* del ruido

noisome [ˈnɔɪsəm] *adj form* asqueroso, -a; (*offensive*) fétido, -a

noisy [ˈnɔɪzi] <-ier, -iest> *adj* 1. ruidoso, -a; (*very loud, unpleasant*) estrepitoso, -a; (*protest*) escandaloso, -a; **to be ~** ser ruidoso 2. (*full of loud, unpleasant noise*) bullicioso, -a 3. ELEC (*signal*) acústico, -a 4. *fig* (*clothes*) llamativo, -a

no-jump [ˌnəʊˈdʒʌmp] *n* SPORTS salto *m* nulo

nomad [ˈnəʊmæd, *Am:* ˈnoʊ-] *n* nómada *mf*

nomadic [nəʊˈmædɪk, *Am:* noʊ-] *adj* nómada

no-man's-land [ˈnəʊmænzlænd, *Am:* ˈnoʊ-] *n no pl* tierra *f* de nadie

nomenclature [nəˈmenklətʃəʳ, *Am:* ˈnoʊmenkleɪtʃɚ] *n* nomenclatura *f*

nominal [ˈnɒmɪnl, *Am:* ˈnaːmə-] *adj* 1. (*in name*) nominal 2. (*small*) pequeño, -a

nominally [ˈnɒmɪnəli, *Am:* ˈnaːmə-] *adv* nominalmente

nominate [ˈnɒmɪneɪt, *Am:* ˈnaːmə-] *vt* 1. (*propose*) proponer; (*for an award*) nominar 2. (*appoint*) nombrar

nomination [ˌnɒmɪˈneɪʃən, *Am:* ˌnaːmə-] *n* 1. (*proposal*) propuesta *f* 2. (*appointment*) nombramiento *m;* (*for an award*) nominación *f* 3. *no pl* (*action of proposing*) proposición *f*

nominative [ˈnɒmɪnətɪv, *Am:* ˈnaːmənətɪv] I. *n* nominativo *m* II. *adj* nominativo, -a

nominee [ˌnɒmɪˈniː, *Am:* ˌnaːmə-] *n* candidato, -a *m, f;* (*for an award*) nominado, -a *m, f*

non-acceptance [ˌnɒnəkˈseptənts, *Am:* ˌnaːnək'-] *n no pl* 1. (*failure to accept*) rechazo *m* 2. FIN no aceptación *f*

nonagenarian [ˌnɒnədʒɪˈneərɪən, *Am:* ˌnaːnədʒəˈneri-] I. *n* nonagenario, -a *m, f* II. *adj* nonagenario, -a

non-aggression [ˌnɒnəˈgreʃən, *Am:* ˌnaːnə'-] *n no pl* no agresión *f*

non-aggression pact, **non-aggression treaty** <-ies> *n* pacto *m* de no agresión

non-alcoholic [ˌnɒnælkəˈhɒlɪk, *Am:* ˌnaːnælkəˈlɪk] *adj* sin alcohol

non-aligned [ˌnɒnəˈlaɪnd, *Am:* ˌnaːnə-] *adj* no alineado, -a

non-alignment [ˌnɒnəˈlaɪnmənt, *Am:* ˌnaːnə-] *n no pl* no alineamiento *m*

non-appearance [ˌnɒnəˈpɪərənts, *Am:* ˌnaːnəˈpɪrənts] *n no pl* LAW incomparecencia *f*

non-attendance [ˌnɒnəˈtendənts, *Am:* ˌnaːnə'-] *n no pl* ausencia *f*

non-belligerent [ˌnɒnbəˈlɪdʒərənt, *Am:* ˌnaːn-] *adj* no beligerante

nonce word [ˈnɒnswɜːd, *Am:* ˈnaːnswɜːrd] *n* palabra *f* creada para una ocasión especial

nonchalant [ˈnɒnʃələnt, *Am:* ˌnaːnʃəˈlaːnt] *adj* despreocupado, -a; **to appear ~** mostrarse indiferente; **to be ~ about sth** estar indiferente ante algo

non-com [ˈnɒnkɒm, *Am:* ˈnaːnkaːm] *adj inf abbr of* **non-commissioned officer** suboficial *mf*

non-combatant [ˌnɒnˈkɒmbətənt, *Am:* ˌnaːnkəmˈbætənt] *n* MIL no combatiente *mf*

non-combustible [ˌnɒnkəmˈbʌstəbl, *Am:* ˌnaːn-] *adj* incombustible

non-commissioned officer [ˌnɒnkə-mɪʃəndˈɒfɪsəʳ, *Am:* ˌnaːnkəmɪʃəndˈɑːfɪsɚ] *n* MIL suboficial *mf*

non-committal [ˌnɒnkəˈmɪtəl, *Am:* ˌnaːn-kəˈmɪt̬-] *adj* evasivo, -a

non-compliance [ˌnɒnkəmˈplaɪənts, *Am:* ˌnaːn-] *n no pl* incumplimiento *m*

non compos mentis [ˌnɒnˌkɒmpəsˈmen-tɪs, *Am:* ˌnaːnˌkaːmpoʊsˈmentɪs] *adj* LAW sin plenas facultades mentales

nonconformist [ˌnɒnkənˈfɔːmɪst, *Am:* ˌnaːnkənˈfɔːr-] I. *adj* inconformista II. *n* inconformista *mf*

nonconformity [ˌnɒnkənˈfɔːməti, *Am:* ˌnaːnkənˈfɔːrmət̬i] *n no pl* inconformidad *f*

non-contributory [ˌnɒnkənˈtrɪbjʊtri, *Am:* ˌnaːnkənˈtrɪbjuːtɔːr-] *adj* sin contribución; **~ pension scheme** plan *m* de pensiones no contributivo

non-cooperation [ˌnɒnkəʊˌɒpəˈreɪʃən, *Am:* ˌnaːnkoʊˌɑːpəˈreɪ-] *n no pl* no cooperación *f*

non-deposit bottle [ˌnɒndɪˈpɒzɪtˌbɒtl] *n* envase *m* no retornable

nondescript [ˈnɒndɪskrɪpt, *Am:* ˈnaːndɪ-] *adj* sin nada de particular; (*person*) anodino, -a; (*colour*) indefinido, -a

non-durables [ˌnɒnˈdjʊərəblz] *npl* productos *mpl* deshechables

none [nʌn] I. *pron* 1. (*nobody*) nadie, ninguno, -a; **~ of them** ninguno de ellos; **~ but he saw it** solo lo vio él; **~ of you helped me** ninguno de vosotros me ayudó 2. (*not any*) ninguno, -a; **~ of my letters arrived** ninguna de mis cartas llegó 3. (*not any*) nada; **nuts/ wine? I've ~ (at all)** ¿frutos secos/vino? no tengo nada; **~ of your speeches!** ¡nada de sermones!; **~ of that!** ¡déjate de eso! II. *adv* 1. (*not*) **~ the less** sin embargo; **to be ~ the wiser** seguir sin entender nada 2. (*not very*) **it's ~ too soon** ya era hora; **it's ~ too warm** no hace demasiado calor

nonentity [nɒˈnentəti, *Am:* naːˈnent̬ət̬i] <-ies> *n* 1. (*person*) cero *m* a la izquierda

2. *no pl* (*insignificance*) insignificancia *f*
non-essential [ˌnɒnɪˈsentʃəl, *Am:* nɑːnɪ-]
I. *adj* secundario, -a II. *n* cosa *f* no esencial
non-event [ˌnɒnɪˈvent, *Am:* ˌnɑːnɪˈvent] *n*
inf fiasco *m*
non-existence *n no pl* inexistencia *f*
non-existent [ˌnɒnɪgˈzɪstənt, *Am:* ˌnɑːnɪg-
ˈzɪs-] *adj* inexistente
non-fiction [ˌnɒnˈfɪkʃən, *Am:* ˌnɑːn-] *n no
pl* no ficción *f*
non-flammable [ˌnɒnˈflæməbl, *Am:*
ˌnɑːn-] *adj* no inflamable
non-infectious [ˌnɒnɪnfekʃəs, *Am:* ˌnɑːn-]
adj no infeccioso, -a
non-iron [ˌnɒnˈaɪən, *Am:* ˌnɑːnˈaɪən] *adj*
que no necesita plancha
non-member country [ˌnɒnˈmembə
ˈkʌntri, *Am:* ˌnɑːnˈmembə ˈkʌntri] <-ies> *n*
POL país *m* no miembro
non-negotiable [ˌnɒnɪˈgəʊʃiəbl, *Am:*
ˌnɑːnɪˈgoʊ-] *adj* LAW, FIN no negociable
non-pareil [ˈnɒnpərəl, *Am:* ˌnɑːnpəˈrel]
I. *adj* *liter* sin par II. *n* *liter* cosa *f* sin par
nonplus [ˌnɒnˈplʌs, *Am:* ˌnɑːn-] <-ss-> *vt*
dejar perplejo; **to be ~sed** quedarse sorprendido
non-polluting [ˌnɒnpəˈluːtɪŋ, *Am:* ˌnɑːn-]
adj no contaminante
non-productive [ˌnɒnprəˈdʌktɪv, *Am:*
ˌnɑːn-] *adj* improductivo, -a
nonprofit, non-profit-making [ˌnɒnˈprɒ-
fɪtˌmeɪkɪŋ, *Am:* ˌnɑːnˈprɑːfɪt-] *adj Am* no
lucrativo, -a
non-proliferation [ˌnɒnprəˌlɪfəˈreɪʃən,
Am: ˌnɑːn-] I. *n no pl* POL no proliferación *f*
II. *adj* POL de no proliferación
non-proliferation treaty <-ies> *n* POL tratado *m* de no proliferación
non-refundable [ˌnɒnrɪˈfʌndəbl, *Am:*
ˌnɑːn-] *adj* no reembolsable; **~ down payment** pago *m* a fondo perdido
non-resident [ˌnɒnˈrezɪdənt, *Am:* ˌnɑːn-]
I. *adj* no residente II. *n* transeúnte *mf*
non-returnable [ˌnɒnrɪˈtɜːnəbl, *Am:* ˌnɑːn-
rɪˈtɜːr-] *adj* no retornable
non-scheduled [ˌnɒnˈʃedjuːld, *Am:* ˌnɑːn-
ˈskedʒuːld] *adj* no programado, -a
nonsense [ˈnɒnsənts, *Am:* ˈnɑːnsents] I. *n
no pl* tonterías *fpl;* **to make** (**a**) **~ of sth** *Brit,
Aus* ridiculizar algo; **to talk ~** *inf* decir tonterías II. *adj* **1.** LIT (*invented for amusement*) disparatado, -a **2.** (*without meaning*) absurdo, -a
III. *interj* tonterías
nonsensical [ˌnɒnˈsentsɪkl, *Am:* ˌnɑːn-] *adj*
absurdo, -a
non-shrink [ˌnɒnˈʃrɪŋk, *Am:* ˌnɑːn-] *adj* que
no encoje
non-skid [ˌnɒnˈskɪd, *Am:* ˌnɑːn-] *adj* antideslizante
non-smoker [ˌnɒnˈsməʊkə, *Am:* ˌnɑːn-
ˈsmoʊkə] *n* persona *f* que no fuma
non-smoking *adj* no fumador(a)
non-starter [ˌnɒnˈstɑːtə, *Am:* ˌnɑːn-

ˈstɑːrtə] *n inf* **that proposal is a ~** esa propuesta es imposible
non-stick [ˌnɒnˈstɪk, *Am:* ˌnɑːn-] *adj* antiad-
herente
non-stop [ˌnɒnˈstɒp, *Am:* ˌnɑːnˈstɑːp] I. *adj*
1. (*without stopping, direct*) sin parar; (*flight*)
directo, -a **2.** (*uninterrupted*) incesante II. *adv*
sin pausa
non-swimmer [ˌnɒnˈswɪmə, *Am:* ˌnɑːn-
ˈswɪmə] *n* no nadador(a) *m(f)*
non-taxable [ˌnɒnˈtæksəble] *adj* no impositivo, -a
non-toxic [ˌnɒnˈtɒksɪk] *adj* no tóxico, -a
non-verbal [ˌnɒnˈvɜːbl, *Am:* ˌnɑːnˈvɜːr-] *adj*
no verbal
non-violent [ˌnɒnˈvaɪələnt, *Am:* ˌnɑːn-] *adj*
pacífico, -a
non-voting [ˌnɒnˈvəʊtɪŋ] *adj* sin derecho a
voto
noodle[1] [ˈnuːdl] I. *n* fideo *m* II. *adj* de fideos
noodle[2] [ˈnuːdl] *n Am, inf* **1.** (*head*) cabeza *f*
2. (*person*) bobo, -a *m, f*
noodle[3] [ˈnuːdl] *vi Am, inf* MUS tocar
nook [nʊk] *n liter* rincón *m;* **~s and crannies**
todos los rincones
noon [nuːn] *n no pl* mediodía *m;* **at ~** a mediodía; **about ~** alrededor de mediodía
no one [ˈnəʊwʌn, *Am:* ˈnoʊ-] *pron s.* **nobody**
noose [nuːs] *n* **1.** (*loop of rope*) soga *f*
2. (*loop of rope for trapping*) lazo *m* **3.** *fig*
(*problem*) aprieto *m* ►**to have a ~ around
one's neck** tener la soga al cuello
nope [nəʊp, *Am:* noʊp] *adv inf* no
nor [nɔː, *Am:* nɔːr] *conj* **1.** (*and also not*)
tampoco; **~** (**do**) **I** ni yo tampoco **2.** (*not
either*) ni
Nordic [ˈnɔːdɪk, *Am:* ˈnɔːr-] *adj* nórdico, -a
norm [nɔːm, *Am:* nɔːrm] *n* norma *f*
normal [ˈnɔːml, *Am:* ˈnɔːr-] *adj* **1.** (*not out of
the ordinary*) normal **2.** (*usual*) corriente; **as
(is) ~** como es normal
normalcy [ˈnɔːməlsi, *Am:* ˈnɔːr-] *Am*, **nor-
mality** [nɔːˈmæləti, *Am:* nɔːrˈmæləti] *n
Brit no pl* normalidad *f*
normalize [ˈnɔːməlaɪz, *Am:* ˈnɔːr-] *a.* INFOR
I. *vt* normalizar II. *vi* normalizar
normally [ˈnɔːməli, *Am:* ˈnɔːr-] *adv* normalmente
Normandy [ˈnɔːməndi, *Am:* ˈnɔːr-] *n* Nor-
mandía *f*
north [nɔːθ, *Am:* nɔːrθ] I. *n* **1.** (*cardinal
point*) norte *m;* **to lie 5 km to the ~ of sth**
quedar a 5 km al norte de algo; **to go/drive to
the ~** ir/viajar hacia el norte; **further ~** más al
norte **2.** GEO Norte *m;* **in the ~ of France** en el
norte de Francia; **the Far North** el extremo
Norte II. *adj* del norte, septentrional; **~ wind**
viento *m* del norte; **~ coast** costa *f* norte; **the
North Sea** El Mar del Norte; **North Star**
Estrella *f* Polar; **the North Pole** el Polo Norte
North Africa *n* África *f* del Norte **North
African** I. *n* norteafricano, -a *m, f* II. *adj* nor-

teafricano, -a

North America *n* América *f* del Norte

North American I. *n* norteamericano, -a *m*, *f* II. *adj* norteamericano, -a

North Carolina *n* Carolina *f* del Norte

North Dakota *n* Dakota *f* del Norte

northeast [ˌnɔːˈθiːst, *Am:* ˌnɔːrˈθ-] I. *n* nordeste *m* II. *adj* del nordeste

northeastern [ˌnɔːˈθiːstən, *Am:* ˌnɔːrˈθ-ˈiːstɚn] *adj* nororiental

northerly [ˈnɔːðəli, *Am:* ˈnɔːrðɚli] *adj* del norte; ~ **direction** dirección *f* norte

northern [ˈnɔːðən, *Am:* ˈnɔːrðɚn] *adj* del norte, norteño, -a, nortino, -a *Chile, Perú;* ~ **hemisphere** hemisferio *m* norte; **the** ~ **part of the country** la parte norte del país; ~ **lights** aurora *f* boreal

northerner [ˈnɔːðənər, *Am:* ˈnɔːrðɚnɚ] *n* norteño, -a *m, f*

Northern Marianas *n* Marianas *fpl* del Norte **northernmost** *adj* más septentrional **Northern Territory** *n* territorio *m* norte

North Pole [ˈnɔːθpəʊl, *Am:* ˈnɔːrθpoʊl] *n* the ~ el polo norte **North Sea** I. *n* Mar *m* del Norte II. *adj* del Mar del Norte **North-south divide** *n* ECON división *f* Norte-Sur

northward [ˈnɔːθwəd, *Am:* ˈnɔːrθwɚd] *adv* hacia el norte

northwest [ˌnɔːˈθˈwest, *Am:* ˌnɔːrˈθ-] I. *n* noroeste *m;* **to the** ~ **(of)** al noroeste (de) II. *adj* del noroeste; ~ **England** el noroeste de Inglaterra III. *adv* en dirección noroeste

northwesterly [ˌnɔːˈθˈwestəli, *Am:* ˌnɔːrˈθ-ˈwestɚli] *adj* en dirección noroeste; (*from the northwest*) del noroeste; ~ **part** parte *f* noroeste

Northwest Territories *n pl* territorios *mpl* del noroeste

Norway [ˈnɔːweɪ, *Am:* ˈnɔːr-] *n* Noruega *f*

Norwegian [nɔːˈwiːdʒən, *Am:* nɔːrˈ-] I. *adj* noruego, -a II. *n* 1.(*person*) noruego, -a *m, f* 2. LING noruego *m*

nose [nəʊz, *Am:* noʊz] I. *n* 1.(*smelling organ*) nariz *f;* **to blow one's** ~ sonarse la nariz 2. AVIAT (*front*) morro *m* 3.(*smell of wine*) bouquet *m* ▶**with one's** ~ **in the air** mirando por encima del hombro; **to put one's** ~ **to the** grindstone *inf* trabajar duro; **to put sb's** ~ **out of** joint *inf* tocar las narices a alguien; **to keep one's** ~ **clean** *inf* no meterse en líos; **to** follow **one's** ~ *inf* (*trust instincts*) guiarse por su olfato; (*go straight ahead*) seguir adelante; **to** get up **sb's** ~ *Brit, Aus, inf* poner de los nervios a alguien; **to** have **a (good)** ~ **for sth** tener buen olfato para algo; **to** have **one's** ~ **in sth** meter las narices en algo; **to** keep **one's** ~ **out of sth** *inf* no meterse en algo; **to** poke **one's** ~ **into sth** *inf* entrometerse en algo; **to** rub **sb's** ~ **in it** restregar algo a alguien por las narices; **to** thumb **one's** ~ **at sb** hacer un palmo de narices a alguien; **(from)** under **sb's (very)** ~ *inf*, right **out from under sb's** ~ *Am, inf* delante de las narices de

alguien II. *vi* fisgonear III. *vt* **to** ~ **one's way in/out/up** entrar/salir/pasar lentamente; **to** ~ **(its way) through sth** avanzar con precaución a través de algo

◆**nose about, nose around** *vi inf* fisgonear

◆**nose out** I. *vt* descubrir II. *vi* apartarse

nosebag [ˈnəʊzbæg, *Am:* ˈnoʊz-] *n* morral *m* **nosebleed** *n* hemorragia *f* nasal **nose-cone** *n* AVIAT cabeza *f* **nosedive** I. *n* 1.AVIAT descenso *m* en picado 2. FIN caída *f* en picado II. *vi* 1.AVIAT descender en picado 2. FIN caer en picado **nosegay** *n* ramillete *m* de flores **nose job** *n inf* operación *f* de cirugía plástica de la nariz **nose-wheel** *n* rueda *f* delantera de aterrizaje

nosey [ˈnəʊzi, *Am:* ˈnoʊ-] <-ier, -iest> *adj* fisgón, -ona; **to be** ~ ser curioso

nosh [nɒʃ, *Am:* nɑːʃ] I. *n no pl, Brit, Aus, inf* comida *f* II. *vi Brit, Aus, inf* papear

nosh-up [ˈnɒʃʌp, *Am:* ˈnɑːʃ-] *n Brit, Aus, inf* atracón *m*

nostalgia [nɒˈstældʒə, *Am:* nɑːˈ-] *n no pl* nostalgia *f*

nostalgic [nɒˈstældʒɪk, *Am:* nɑːˈ-] *adj* nostálgico, -a

no-strike agreement [ˌnəʊstraɪkəˈgriːmənt] *n* acuerdo *m* de no convocar huelgas

nostril [ˈnɒstrəl, *Am:* ˈnɑːstrəl] *n* ventana *f* de la nariz

nosy [ˈnəʊzi, *Am:* ˈnoʊ-] <-ier, -iest> *adj s.* **nosey**

nosy parker [ˈnəʊziˈpɑːkər, *Am:* ˈnoʊzi-ˈpɑːrkɚ] *n inf* fisgón, -ona *m, f*

not [nɒt, *Am:* nɑːt] *adv* no; **it's a woman,** ~ **a man** es una mujer, no un hombre; **he's asked me** ~ **to do it** me ha pedido que no lo haga; ~ **all the children like singing** no les gusta cantar a todos los niños; ~ **me!** ¡yo no!; **why** ~**?** ¿por qué no?; **he is** ~ **ugly** no es feo; **or** ~ o no; ~ **at all** (*nothing*) en absoluto; (*no need to thank*) de nada; ~ **only ... but also** ... no sólo... sino también; ~ **just** [*o* **simply**] no sólo; ~ **much** no demasiado

notable [ˈnəʊtəbl, *Am:* ˈnoʊtə-] I. *adj* 1.(*remarkable*) notable 2.(*eminent*) eminente II. *n* persona *f* importante

notably [ˈnəʊtəbli, *Am:* ˈnoʊtə-] *adv* notablemente

notary [ˈnəʊtəri, *Am:* ˈnoʊtɚ-] <-ies> *n* ~ **(public)** notario, -a *m, f*

notation [nəʊˈteɪʃən, *Am:* noʊ-] *n* MAT, MUS notación *f*

notch [nɒtʃ, *Am:* nɑːtʃ] <-es> I. *vt* 1.(*cut*) hacer una muesca 2. *inf* (*achieve*) conseguir II. *n* 1.(*cut*) muesca *f;* (*hole*) agujero *m* 2.(*degree*) punto *m* 3. *Am* (*narrow valley*) valle *m*

note [nəʊt, *Am:* noʊt] I. *n* 1.(*annotation*) nota *f;* **to take** ~ tomar nota 2. LIT apunte *m* 3. MUS nota *f;* (*sound*) tono *m;* **to strike the right** ~ *fig* dar con el tono apropiado 4. *Brit, Aus* (*piece of paper money*) billete *m*

5. (*importance*) of ~ *form* notable; **nothing of** ~ nada importante **II.** *vt form* anotar; (*mention*) observar; **to** ~ (**that**) ... hacer notar (que)...

notebook ['nəʊtbʊk, *Am:* 'noʊt-] *n* cuaderno *m*

noted ['nəʊtɪd, *Am:* 'noʊt̬ɪd] *adj* célebre; **to be** ~ **for** sth ser conocido por algo

notepad ['nəʊtpæd, *Am:* 'noʊt-] *n* bloc *m*

notepaper ['nəʊtˌpeɪpəʳ, *Am:* 'noʊtˌpeɪpə·] *n no pl* papel *m* de carta

noteworthy ['nəʊtˌwɜːði, *Am:* 'noʊtˌwɜːr-] *adj form* de interés; **nothing/something** ~ nada/algo digno de atención

nothing ['nʌθɪŋ] **I.** *pron indef, sing* **1.** (*no objects*) nada; ~ **happens** no pasa nada; **we saw** ~ (**else/more**) no vimos nada (más); ~ **new** nada nuevo; **next to** ~ casi nada **2.** (*not anything*) ~ **came of it** no salió nada (de allí); ~ **doing!** *inf* ¡para nada!; **fit for** ~ bueno para nada; **to make** ~ **of it** no darle importancia; **there is** ~ **to laugh at** no tiene nada de gracioso **3.** (*not important*) **that's** ~! ¡no es nada!; **time is** ~ **to me** el tiempo no es importante para mí **4.** (*only*) ~ **but** tan sólo; **she is** ~ **if not patient** es paciente por encima de todo; ~ **much** no gran cosa **II.** *adv* ~ **less than** ni más ni menos que; ~ **daunted, I went on** sin flaquear, seguí adelante **III.** *n* **1.** nada *f* **2.** MAT, SPORTS cero *m;* **three to** ~ *Am* tres a cero **3.** (*person*) don nadie *m*

nothingness ['nʌθɪŋnɪs] *n no pl* (*emptiness*) vacío *m;* (*worthlessness*) nada *f*

no-throw [ˌnəʊˈθrəʊ] *n* SPORTS lanzamiento *m* nulo

notice ['nəʊtɪs, *Am:* 'noʊt̬ɪs] **I.** *vt* **1.** (*see*) ver; (*perceive*) fijarse en; **to** ~ (**that**) ... darse cuenta de (que)... **2.** (*recognize*) reconocer **II.** *vi* percatarse **III.** *n* **1.** *no pl* (*attention*) interés *m;* **to take** ~ **of** sb/sth prestar atención a alguien/algo; **to come to** sb's ~ (**that** ...) llegar al conocimiento de alguien (que...); **to escape one's** ~ no percatarse de algo; **to escape** sb's ~ **that** ... pasarle a alguien por alto que... **2.** (*display*) letrero *m;* (*in a newspaper, magazine*) anuncio *m* **3.** *no pl* (*warning*) aviso *m;* **to give** sb ~ (**of** sth) avisar a alguien (de algo); **at short** ~ a corto plazo; **at a moment's** ~ al momento; **until further** ~ hasta nuevo aviso **4.** *no pl* LAW preaviso *m;* **to give** (**in**) **one's** ~ presentar la dimisión; **to give** sb **his** ~ despedir a alguien

noticeable ['nəʊtɪsəbl, *Am:* 'noʊt̬ɪ-] *adj* evidente; (*difference*) notable

notice board *n Aus, Brit* tablón *m* de anuncios

notifiable ['nəʊtɪfaɪəbl, *Am:* 'noʊt̬ə-] *adj* (*disease*) que hay que notificar

notification [ˌnəʊtɪfɪˈkeɪʃən, *Am:* ˌnoʊt̬ə-] *n* notificación *f*

notify ['nəʊtɪfaɪ, *Am:* 'noʊt̬ə-] <-ie-> *vt* informar; **to** ~ sb **of** sth notificar algo a alguien

notion ['nəʊʃən, *Am:* 'noʊ-] *n* **1.** (*idea*) noción *f;* **to have some** ~ **of** sth tener algunas nociones de algo; **to have no** ~ **of** sth no tener ni idea de algo **2.** (*silly idea*) burrada *f;* **to have a** ~ **to do** sth tener la intención de hacer algo

notional ['nəʊʃənl, *Am:* 'noʊ-] *adj form* teórico, -a

notoriety [ˌnəʊtəˈraɪəti, *Am:* ˌnoʊt̬əˈraɪət̬i] *n no pl* mala fama *f*

notorious [nəʊˈtɔːriəs, *Am:* noʊˈtɔːri-] *adj* de mala reputación; (*thief*) bien conocido, -a; **she's a** ~ **liar** tiene fama de mentirosa; **to be** ~ **for** sth tener mala fama por algo

notwithstanding [ˌnɒtwɪθˈstændɪŋ, *Am:* ˌnɑːt-] *form* **I.** *prep* a pesar de **II.** *adv* no obstante

nougat ['nuːgɑː, *Am:* 'nuːgət] *n no pl* ≈ turrón *m*

nought [nɔːt, *Am:* nɑːt] *n* **1.** *Brit* nada *f* **2.** MAT cero *m*

noun [naʊn] **I.** *n* nombre *m;* LING sustantivo *m* **II.** *adj* nominal

nourish ['nʌrɪʃ, *Am:* 'nɜːr-] *vt* **1.** (*provide with food*) alimentar; **to** ~ **oneself on** sth alimentarse de algo **2.** *fig, form* (*cherish*) fomentar

nourishing ['nʌrɪʃɪŋ, *Am:* 'nɜːr-] *adj* nutritivo, -a; (*rich*) rico, -a

nourishment *n no pl* **1.** (*food*) alimento *m* **2.** (*providing with food*) nutrición *f*

nous [naʊs, *Am:* nuːs] *n no pl, Aus, Brit, inf* cacumen *m*

Nova Scotia [ˌnəʊvəˈskəʊʃə, *Am:* ˌnoʊvəˈskoʊ-] *n* Nueva Escocia *f*

novel[1] ['nɒvl, *Am:* 'nɑːvl] *n* novela *f*

novel[2] ['nɒvl, *Am:* 'nɑːvl] *adj* nuevo, -a

novelette [ˌnɒvəˈlet, *Am:* ˌnɑːvə-] *n* novela *f* rosa

novelist ['nɒvəlɪst, *Am:* 'nɑːvə-] *n* novelista *mf*

novelty ['nɒvəlti, *Am:* 'nɑːvlt̬i] **I.** <-ies> *n* **1.** *no pl* (*newness*) novedad *f* **2.** (*innovation*) innovación *f* **3.** (*cheap trinket*) baratija *f* **II.** *adj* **1.** (*new*) nuevo, -a **2.** (*cheap*) barato, -a

November [nəʊˈvembəʳ, *Am:* noʊˈvembə·] *n* noviembre *m; s. a.* **April**

novice ['nɒvɪs, *Am:* 'nɑːvɪs] *n* novato, -a *m, f;* REL novicio, -a *m, f*

now [naʊ] **I.** *adv* **1.** (*at the present time*) ahora; **just** ~ ahora mismo **2.** (*currently*) actualmente **3.** (*then*) entonces; **any time** ~ en cualquier momento; (**every**) ~ **and then** de vez en cuando **4.** (*give emphasis*) ~, **where did I put her book?** ¿se puede saber dónde he puesto su libro?; ~ **we're talking!** ahora sí que estamos hablando...; ~ **then** ¡vamos a ver! ►(**it's**) ~ **or never** (es) ahora o nunca **II.** *n* (*present*) presente *m;* **before** ~ antes; **by** ~ ahora ya; **for** ~ por ahora; **as from** ~ a partir de ahora **III.** *conj* ~ (**that**) ... ahora que...

nowadays ['naʊədeɪz] *adv* hoy en día

nowhere ['nəʊweəʳ, *Am:* 'noʊwer] *adv* en ninguna parte; **to appear from** ~ aparecer de la nada; **to be going** ~ *a. fig* no llevar a ninguna parte

nowt [naʊt] *pron Brit* (*nothing*) nada ▶**there's** ~ **so queer as** <u>folk</u> *prov* hay de todo en la viña del Señor *prov*

noxious ['nɒkʃəs, *Am:* 'nɑ:k-] *adj form* nocivo, -a; (*very unpleasant*) desagradable

nozzle ['nɒzl, *Am:* 'nɑ:zl] *n* tobera *f;* (*of a petrol pump*) inyector *m;* (*of a gun*) boquilla *f*

NT **1.** *abbr of* **New Testament** Nuevo Testamento *m* **2.** *abbr of* **National Trust** *instituto del gobierno británico para la conservación del patrimonio histórico-artístico*

nuance ['nju:ɑːns, *Am:* 'nuː-] *n* matiz *m*

nub [nʌb] *n* **1.** (*point*) quid *m* **2.** (*piece*) trozo *m*

nubile ['njuːbaɪl, *Am:* 'nuːbɪl] *adj* núbil

nuclear ['njuːkliə', *Am:* 'nuːkliə'] *adj* nuclear

nuclear medicine *n no pl* medicina *f* nuclear **nuclear nonproliferation treaty** <-ies> *n* POL, MIL tratado *m* de no proliferación de armas nucleares **nuclear power station** *n* central *f* nuclear **nuclear reactor** *n* reactor *m* nuclear

nucleic acid [njuː'kleɪɪd'æsɪd, *Am:* nuː-'kliː-] *n* ácido *m* nucleico

nucleus ['njuːkliəs, *Am:* 'nuː-] <-ei *o* -es> *n* núcleo *m*

nude [njuːd, *Am:* nuːd] **I.** *adj* desnudo, -a **II.** *n* **1.** ART, PHOT desnudo *m* **2.** (*naked*) **in the** ~ desnudo

nudge [nʌdʒ] **I.** *vt* dar un codazo a; *fig* empujar; **to** ~ **sb into doing sth** empujar a alguien a hacer algo **II.** *vi* codear **III.** *n* **1.** (*push*) codazo *m* **2.** (*encouragement*) valor *m*

nudism ['njuːdɪzəm, *Am:* 'nuː-] *n no pl* nudismo *m*

nudist ['njuːdɪst, *Am:* 'nuː-] **I.** *n* nudista *mf* **II.** *adj* nudista

nudist beach *n* playa *f* nudista **nudist camp** *n* campamento *m* de nudistas

nudity ['njuːdəti, *Am:* 'nuːdəṭi] *n no pl* desnudez *f*

nugatory ['njuːgətəri, *Am:* 'nuːgətɔːr-] *adj form* insignificante

nugget ['nʌgɪt] *n* MIN pepita *f*

nuisance ['njuːsns, *Am:* 'nuː-] *n* **1.** molestia *f*, camote *m AmL;* **to make a** ~ **of oneself** dar la lata **2.** LAW perjuicio *m*

nuke [nuːk, njuːk] *vt inf* **1.** MIL bombardear con armas atómicas **2.** *Am, Aus, inf* (*cook*) cocinar en el microondas

null [nʌl] *adj* nulo, -a; ~ **and void** sin efecto

nullification [ˌnʌlɪfɪ'keɪʃən] *n* anulación *f*

nullify ['nʌlɪfaɪ] <-ie-> *vt* anular

nullity ['nʌləti, *Am:* -ṭi] *n no pl* nulidad *f*

numb [nʌm] **I.** *adj* entumecido, -a; **to go** ~ entumecerse **II.** *vt* entumecer; (*desensitize*) insensibilizar

number ['nʌmbə', *Am:* -bə] **I.** *n* **1.** MAT número *m;* (*symbol*) cifra *f;* **house** ~ número de casa; **telephone** ~ número de teléfono **2.** (*amount*) cantidad *f;* (a) **small/large** ~(s)

(**of children**) (una) pequeña/gran cantidad (de niños); **for a** ~ **of reasons** por una serie de razones; **to be 3 in** ~ ser 3; **to be few in** ~ ser pocos **3.** PUBL, MUS, THEAT número *m* ▶~ **one** uno *m* mismo; **to look after** ~ **one** cuidar de sí mismo; **to be** (**the**) ~ **one** ser el mejor; **to have sb's** ~ tener calado a alguien; **to be beyond** ~ ser tantos que no se pueden contar **II.** *vt* **1.** (*assign a number to*) poner número a; **to** ~ **sth from ... to ...** numerar algo del... al... **2.** (*count*) contar **3.** (*amount to*) sumar; **each group** ~**s 10 members** cada grupo tiene 10 miembros

El **Number 10 Downing Street** es la residencia oficial del **prime minister** (primer ministro). La casa data del siglo XVII y fue construida por Sir George Downing, político, especulador inmobiliario y espía. El primer ministro vive en el piso más alto y en el resto del edificio se encuentran las oficinas y las salas de reuniones del gabinete de gobierno. El **Chancellor of the Exchequer** (ministro de Hacienda) vive en la casa de al lado, en el **Number 11**. En la misma calle se encuentran además otras dependencias del gobierno.

numbering *n no pl* numeración *f*

numberless *adj* innumerable

number plate *n Brit* matrícula *f*

numbness ['nʌmnɪs] *n no pl* **1.** (*on part of body*) entumecimiento *m* **2.** (*lack of feeling*) insensibilidad *f*

numeracy ['njuːmərəsi, *Am:* 'nuː-] *n no pl* competencia *f* con los números

numeral ['njuːmərəl, *Am:* 'nuː-] *n* número *m*

numerate ['njuːmərət, *Am:* 'nuː-] *adj* MAT competente en matemáticas

numeration [ˌnjuːmə'reɪʃən, *Am:* ˌnuː-] *n no pl, form* numeración *f*

numerical [njuː'merɪkl, *Am:* nuː-] *adj* numérico, -a; **in** ~ **order** por orden numérico

numeric keypad [ˌnjuːmerɪk'kiːpæd, *Am:* nuː-] *n* INFOR teclado *m* numérico

numerous ['njuːmərəs, *Am:* 'nuː-] *adj* numeroso, -a

numismatics [ˌnjuːmɪz'mætɪks, *Am:* ˌnuː-mɪz'mæt-] *n + sing vb* numismática *f*

numskull ['nʌmskʌl] *n* idiota *mf*

nun [nʌn] *n* monja *f*

nuncio ['nʌnsɪəʊ, *Am:* -oʊ] *n* REL nuncio *m*

nunnery ['nʌnəri] <-ies> *n* convento *m* de monjas

nuptial ['nʌpʃl] *adj* nupcial

nurse [nɜːs, *Am:* nɜːrs] **I.** *n* **1.** MED enfermero, -a *m, f* **2.** (*nanny*) niñera *f;* (*wet-nurse*) nodriza *f* **II.** *vt* **1.** (*care for*) cuidar **2.** (*nurture*) nutrir **3.** (*harbour*) abrigar **4.** (*hold carefully*) sostener con cuidado **5.** (*breast-feed*) amamantar **III.** *vi* dar de mamar

nursery ['nɜːsəri, *Am:* 'nɜːr-] **I.** <-ies> *n* **1.** (*school*) guardería *f* **2.** (*bedroom*) cuarto *m*

O

de los niños **3.** BOT vivero *m* **II.** *adj* ~ **education** educación *f* preescolar
nursery rhyme *n* canción *f* infantil **nursery school** *n* parvulario *m* **nursery slopes** *npl Brit* SPORTS pistas *fpl* para principiantes
nursing I. *n no pl* enfermería *f* **II.** *adj* de enfermería
nursing home *n* asilo *m* de ancianos
nurture ['nɜːtʃəʳ, *Am:* 'nɜːrtʃɚ] **I.** *vt* alimentar; (*a plant*) cuidar **II.** *n no pl* nutrición *f*
nut [nʌt] *n* **1.** BOT nuez *f* **2.** TECH tuerca *f* **3.** *inf* (*madman*) chiflado, -a *m, f;* (*enthusiast*) entusiasta *mf* **4.** *inf* (*person's head*) coco *m;* **to be off one's** ~ estar grillado ►**the ~s and bolts of sth** los aspectos prácticos de algo; **a hard ~ to crack** (*situation*) una situación difícil de llevar; (*person*) un hueso duro de roer
nutcracker ['nʌtˌkrækəʳ, *Am:* -ɚ] *n* cascanueces *m inv* **nuthatch** <-es> *n* trepador *m* **nuthouse** <-s> *n inf* manicomio *m* **nutmeg** *n no pl* nuez *f* moscada
nutrient ['njuːtriənt, *Am:* 'nuː-] **I.** *n* nutriente *m* **II.** *adj* nutritivo, -a
nutrition [njuː'trɪʃən, *Am:* nuː-] **I.** *n no pl* nutrición *f* **II.** *adj* nutricional
nutritionist [njuː'trɪʃənɪst, *Am:* nuː-] *n* nutricionista *mf*
nutritious [njuː'trɪʃəs, *Am:* nuː-] *adj,* **nutritive** ['njuːtrətɪv, *Am:* 'nuːtrəʈɪv] *adj* nutritivo, -a
nuts [nʌts] **I.** *npl Am, vulg* cojones *mpl* **II.** *adj* **to be** ~ estar chiflado; **to go** ~ volverse loco; **to be** ~ **about sb** estar loco por alguien; **to be** ~ **about sth** pirrarse por algo
nutshell ['nʌtʃel] *n no pl* cáscara *f* de nuez ►**to put sth in a** ~ decir algo con gran concisión; **in a** ~ en resumidas cuentas
nutty ['nʌti, *Am:* 'nʌʈ-] <-ier, -iest> *adj* **1.** (*cake*) con nueces; (*ice cream*) de nueces; (*taste*) a nueces **2.** *inf* (*crazy*) loco, -a, revirado, -a *Arg, Urug;* **to be (as)** ~ **as a fruitcake** estar más loco que una cabra
nuzzle ['nʌzl] **I.** *vt* acariciar con el hocico **II.** *vi* acurrucarse; **to** ~ **closer** arrimarse; **to** ~ **(up) against sb/sth** apretarse contra alguien/algo
NW [ˌen'dʌbljuː] *abbr of* **northwest** NO *m*
NY [ˌen'waɪ] *abbr of* **New York** Nueva York *f*
nylon ['naɪlɒn, *Am:* -lɑːn] **I.** *n no pl* nailon *m* **II.** *adj* de nailon
nymph [nɪmf] *n* ninfa *f*
nymphomania [ˌnɪmfə'meɪnɪə, *Am:* -foʊ'-] *n no pl* ninfomanía *f*
nymphomaniac [ˌnɪmfə'meɪnɪæk, *Am:* -foʊ'-] *n* ninfómana *f*
NZ [ˌen'zed, *Am:* -'ziː] *abbr of* **New Zealand** Nueva Zelanda *f*

O, o [əʊ] *n* **1.** (*letter*) O, o *f;* ~ **for Oliver** *Brit,* O **for Oboe** *Am* O de Oviedo **2.** (*zero*) cero *m*
oaf [əʊf, *Am:* oʊf] *n inf* (*uncultured*) patán *m;* (*clumsy*) zoquete *mf*
oafish ['əʊfɪʃ, *Am:* 'oʊ-] *adj inf* (*uncultured*) zafio, -a; (*clumsy*) lerdo, -a
oak [əʊk, *Am:* oʊk] *n* (*tree, wood*) roble *m* ►**mighty ~s from little acorns grow** *prov* los grandes logros nacen de pequeñas cosas *prov*
OAP [ˌəʊeɪ'piː, *Am:* ˌoʊ-] *n abbr of* **old-age pensioner** pensionista *mf*
oar [ɔːʳ, *Am:* ɔːr] *n* remo *m* ►**to stick one's** ~ **in** *inf* meter cuchara
oarsman ['ɔːzmən, *Am:* 'ɔːrz-] <-men> *n* remero *m*
oarswoman ['ɔːzwʊmən, *Am:* 'ɔːrz-] <-women> *n* remera *f*
OAS [ˌəʊeɪ'es, *Am:* ˌoʊ-] *n abbr of* **Organization of American States** OEA *f*
oasis [əʊ'eɪsɪs, *Am:* oʊ-] <-es> *n* oasis *m inv*
oatcake ['əʊtkeɪk, *Am:* 'oʊt-] *n* torta *f* de avena
oath [əʊθ, *Am:* oʊθ] *n* juramento *m;* **to take the** ~ prestar juramento; **under** [*o* **upon**] ~ *Brit* bajo juramento; ~ **of allegiance** juramento de lealtad
oatmeal ['əʊtmiːl, *Am:* 'oʊt-] *n no pl* harina *f* de avena
oats [əʊts, *Am:* oʊts] *n pl* avena *f* ►**to sow one's wild** ~ *Am, inf* andar de picos pardos *inf;* **to feel one's** ~ *Am, inf* sentirse en plena forma; **to get one's** ~ *inf* mojar (con regularidad); **to be off one's** ~ estar desganado
OAU [ˌəʊeɪjuː, *Am:* ˌoʊ-] *n abbr of* **Organization of African Unity** OUA *f*
obduracy ['ɒbdjʊərəsi, *Am:* 'ɑːbdʊr-] *n no pl* obstinación *f*
obdurate ['ɒbdjʊərət, *Am:* 'ɑːbdʊrɪt] *adj form* obstinado, -a
obedience [ə'biːdɪəns, *Am:* oʊ'-] *n no pl* obediencia *f;* **in** ~ **to** conforme a
obedient [ə'biːdɪənt, *Am:* oʊ'-] *adj* obediente; **to be** ~ **to sb/sth** obedecer a alguien/algo
obelisk ['ɒbəlɪsk, *Am:* 'ɑːbəl-] *n* obelisco *m*
obese [əʊ'biːs, *Am:* oʊ'-] *adj* obeso, -a
obesity [əʊ'biːsəti, *Am:* oʊ'biːsəʈi] *n no pl* obesidad *f*
obey [əʊ'beɪ, *Am:* oʊ'-] *vt* (*person*) obedecer; (*instincts, advice*) hacer caso a; (*order, the law*) cumplir
obituary [əʊ'bɪtjʊəri, *Am:* oʊ'bɪtʃueri] <-ies> *n,* **obituary notice** *n* necrología *f,* obituario *m AmL*
object¹ ['ɒbdʒɪkt, *Am:* 'ɑːb-] *n* **1.** (*unspecified thing*) objeto *m* **2.** (*purpose, goal*) propósito *m,* objetivo *m;* **the** ~ **of the exercise is ...** el objeto del ejercicio es... **3.** (*obstacle*) **money is no** ~ el dinero no importa **4.** LING complemento *m*

O

object² [əbˈdʒekt] I. *vi* oponerse II. *vt* objetar; **to ~ that ...** objetar que...

objection [əbˈdʒekʃən] *n* objeción *f;* **to raise ~s** poner reparos; **to raise ~s to sth** protestar contra algo; **there is no ~** no hay inconveniente

objectionable [əbˈdʒekʃənəbl] *adj form* desagradable; (*person*) molesto, -a; (*conduct*) reprensible

objective [əbˈdʒektɪv] I. *n* objetivo *m* II. *adj* objetivo, -a

objectivity [ˌɒbdʒɪkˈtɪvəti, *Am:* ˌɑːbdʒekˈtɪvəti] *n no pl* objetividad *f*

object lesson *n* lección *f* práctica

objector *n* objetor(a) *m(f)*

obligate [ˈɒblɪgeɪt, *Am:* ˈɑːblɪ-] *vt* obligar; **to ~ sb to do sth** obligar a alguien a hacer algo

obligation [ˌɒblɪˈgeɪʃən, *Am:* ˌɑːbləˈ-] *n no pl* obligación *f;* **to be under an ~ to do sth** tener la obligación de hacer algo; **to have an ~ to sb** deber favores a alguien

obligatory [əˈblɪgətəri, *Am:* -tɔːri] *adj* obligatorio, -a

oblige [əˈblaɪdʒ] I. *vt* 1. (*force*) obligar 2. (*perform service for*) hacer un favor a; **to ~ sb with sth** hacer a alguien el favor de algo II. *vi* **to be happy to ~** estar encantado de ayudar

obliging [əˈblaɪdʒɪŋ] *adj* servicial, comedido, -a *AmL*

oblique [əˈbliːk, *Am:* oʊˈ-] I. *adj* 1. (*indirect*) indirecto, -a 2. (*slanting*) oblicuo, -a II. *n* barra *f* oblicua

obliterate [əˈblɪtəreɪt, *Am:* -ˈblɪt-] *vt* eliminar; (*writing*) borrar; (*town*) arrasar

obliteration [əˌblɪtəˈreɪʃən, *Am:* -ˌblɪt̬-] *n no pl* eliminación *f;* (*of writing*) borradura *f;* (*of town*) destrucción *f*

oblivion [əˈblɪvɪən] *n no pl* olvido *m;* **to fall into ~** caer en el olvido

oblivious [əˈblɪvɪəs] *adj* inconsciente; **~ of sth** inconsciente de algo

oblong [ˈɒblɒŋ, *Am:* ˈɑːblɑːŋ] I. *n* rectángulo *m*, oblongo *m* II. *adj* rectangular, oblongo, -a

obnoxious [əbˈnɒkʃəs, *Am:* -ˈnɑːk-] *adj* detestable

oboe [ˈəʊbəʊ, *Am:* ˈoʊboʊ] *n* oboe *m*

oboist [ˈəʊbəʊɪst, *Am:* ˈoʊboʊɪst] *n* oboe *mf*

obscene [əbˈsiːn] *adj* 1. (*indecent*) obsceno, -a, bascoso, -a *Col, Ecua* 2. (*scandalous*) escandaloso, -a

obscenity [əbˈsenəti, *Am:* -t̬i] <-ies> *n* obscenidad *f*, indecencia *f*, bascosidad *f Col, Ecua*

obscure [əbˈskjʊəʳ, *Am:* -ˈskjʊr] I. *adj* oscuro, -a II. *vt* 1. (*make difficult to see*) oscurecer 2. (*make difficult to understand*) complicar 3. (*hide*) ocultar

obscurity [əbˈskjʊərəti, *Am:* -ˈskjʊrət̬i] *n no pl* oscuridad *f*

obsequious [əbˈsiːkwɪəs] *adj* servil

observable [əbˈzɜːvəbl, *Am:* -ˈzɜːr-] *adj* observable

observance [əbˈzɜːvəns, *Am:* -ˈzɜːr-] *n* 1. *no pl* (*of laws, rules*) observancia *f;* (*of customs*) cumplimiento *m* 2. REL (*practice*) práctica *f*

observant [əbˈzɜːvənt, *Am:* -ˈzɜːr-] *adj* 1. (*quick to notice things*) observador(a) 2. (*respectful: of rules, laws*) respetuoso, -a; (*of one's duty*) cumplidor(a)

observation [ˌɒbzəˈveɪʃən, *Am:* ˌɑːbzɚˈ-] *n* 1. (*act of seeing*) observación *f;* LAW vigilancia *f;* **to keep sth/sb under ~** vigilar algo/a alguien; **under ~** MED en observación; **to escape ~** pasar inadvertido 2. (*remark*) comentario *m*, observación *f;* **to make an ~ (about sb/sth)** hacer una observación (sobre alguien/algo)

observation car *n Am* RAIL vagón *m* mirador

observation post *n* MIL puesto *m* de observación **observation tower** *n* atalaya *f*

observatory [əbˈzɜːvətri, *Am:* -ˈzɜːrvətɔːr-] *n* observatorio *m*

observe [əbˈzɜːv, *Am:* -ˈzɜːrv] I. *vt* 1. (*watch closely*) observar; (*notice*) fijarse en; **to ~ sb doing sth** ver a alguien haciendo algo 2. (*remark*) comentar 3. (*obey: rules*) observar; (*silence, religious holiday*) guardar; **to ~ a minute of silence** guardar un minuto de silencio; **to ~ Passover** celebrar la Pascua II. *vi* 1. (*watch*) observar 2. (*remark*) **to ~ (up)on sth** hacer una observación sobre algo

observer [əbˈzɜːvəʳ, *Am:* -ˈzɜːrvɚ] *n* observador(a) *m(f)*

obsess [əbˈses] *vt* obsesionar; **to be ~ed by sb/sth** obsesionarse por alguien/algo; **he is ~ed with being the best** está obsesionado con ser el mejor

obsession [əbˈseʃən] *n* obsesión *f;* **to have an ~ with sb/sth** estar obsesionado con alguien/algo

obsessive [əbˈsesɪv] *adj* 1. (*person, jealousy*) obsesivo, -a; **to be ~ about sth** estar obsesionado con algo; **to become ~ (about sth)** empezar a obsesionarse (con algo) 2. (*game*) obsesionante

obsolescence [ˌɒbsəˈlesənts, *Am:* ˌɑːb-] *n no pl* obsolescencia *f*

obsolescent [ˌɒbsəˈlesnt, *Am:* ˌɑːb-] *adj* que está quedando obsoleto, -a

obsolete [ˈɒbsəliːt, *Am:* ˌɑːb-] *adj* (*method, design*) obsoleto, -a; (*word, spelling*) caído, -a en desuso

obstacle [ˈɒbstəkl, *Am:* ˈɑːbstə-] *n* obstáculo *m;* **an insurmountable ~** un obstáculo insalvable; **to overcome an ~** superar un obstáculo; **to put ~s in the way of sb/sth** poner dificultades a alguien/algo; **to be an ~ to sth** ser un obstáculo para algo

obstacle race *n* carrera *f* de obstáculos

obstetrician [ˌɒbstəˈtrɪʃən, *Am:* ɑːbstə-ˈtrɪʃ-] *n* MED obstetra *mf*

obstetrics [ɒbˈstetrɪks, *Am:* əbˈ-] I. *npl* MED obstetricia *f* II. *adj* MED obstétrico, -a

obstinacy ['ɒbstɪnəsi, *Am:* 'ɑːbstə-] *n no pl* obstinación *f*

obstinate ['ɒbstɪnət, *Am:* 'ɑːbstə-] *adj* **1.** (*person, attitude*) obstinado, -a; **to be ~ about sth** ser terco en algo; **an ~ refusal** una negativa rotunda **2.** (*disease*) rebelde; (*problem*) persistente

obstreperous [əb'strepərəs] *adj form* **1.** (*unruly*) rebelde **2.** (*noisy*) ruidoso, -a

obstruct [əb'strʌkt] *vt* **1.** (*block*) obstruir; (*traffic*) bloquear; (*view*) tapar **2.** (*hinder*) dificultar; (*passage*) impedir; (*progress*) obstaculizar; **to ~ the traffic** obstruir el tráfico

obstruction [əb'strʌkʃən] *n* **1.** (*action*) a. MED, POL obstrucción *f* **2.** (*impediment*) obstáculo *m;* **an ~ to sth** un obstáculo para algo; **to cause an ~** causar un estorbo; AUTO obstruir el paso

obstructive [əb'strʌktɪv] *adj* (*tactic, attitude*) obstruccionista; (*person*) que pone obstáculos; **don't be so ~** no pongas tantos impedimentos

obtain [əb'teɪn] **I.** *vt* obtener; **to ~ sth from sb/sth** obtener algo de alguien/algo; **to ~ sth for sb** conseguir algo a alguien **II.** *vi form* prevalecer

obtainable [əb'teɪnəbl] *adj* que se puede conseguir; **it is not ~ in this country** no se puede adquirir en este país

obtrude [əb'truːd] **I.** *vt form* (*force*) imponer; **to ~ one's opinion(s) (up)on sb** imponer a alguien las propias opiniones **II.** *vi form* **to ~ upon sth** entrometerse en algo

obtrusive [əb'truːsɪv] *adj form* (*question, presence*) inoportuno, -a; (*noise*) molesto, -a; (*smell*) penetrante; (*colour, design*) (demasiado) llamativo, -a

obtuse [əb'tjuːs, *Am:* ɑːb'tuːs] *adj* obtuso, -a

obviate ['ɒbvɪeɪt, *Am:* 'ɑːb-] *vt* (*necessity, difficulty*) obviar; (*danger*) evitar

obvious ['ɒbvɪəs, *Am:* 'ɑːb-] *adj* obvio, -a; **a sign of ~ displeasure** un signo de evidente disgusto; **for ~ reasons** por razones obvias; **it is ~ what/where ...** está claro qué/dónde...; **it is ~ to me that ...** me doy perfecta cuenta de que...; **to make sth ~ to sb** hacer algo patente a alguien; **the ~ thing to do** lo que hay que hacer

obviously *adv* obviamente, claramente; **~, ...** como es lógico,...

occasion [ə'keɪʒən] **I.** *n* **1.** (*particular time*) ocasión *f;* **as ~ requires** si la ocasión lo requiere; **on ~** de vez en cuando; **on one ~** en una ocasión; **on several ~s** en varias ocasiones **2.** (*event*) acontecimiento *m;* **on the ~ of ...** con motivo de...; **to dress to suit the ~** vestirse para la ocasión; **to rise to the ~** estar a la altura de las circunstancias **3.** (*reason*) motivo *m;* **to give ~ to sth** dar lugar a algo **4.** (*opportunity*) oportunidad *f;* **should the ~ arise** si se presenta la ocasión; **to have ~ to do sth** tener ocasión de hacer algo; **to take an ~** aprovechar una oportunidad **II.** *vt* ocasionar

occasional [ə'keɪʒənəl] *adj* ocasional; **to pay very ~ visits to sb** visitar rara vez a alguien; **I have the ~ cigarette** fumo un cigarrillo de vez en cuando

occasionally *adv* ocasionalmente, de vez en cuando

occasional table *n* mesa *f* auxiliar

Occident ['ɒksɪdənt, *Am:* 'ɑːksə-] *n no pl* **the ~** Occidente

occidental [ˌɒksɪ'dentəl, *Am:* ˌɑːksə'dentəl] *adj* occidental

occult [ɒ'kʌlt, *Am:* ə'-] **I.** *adj* oculto, -a **II.** *n no pl* **the ~** las ciencias ocultas

occultism ['ɒkʌltɪzəm, *Am:* ə'kʌl-] *n no pl* ocultismo *m*

occupancy ['ɒkjəpəntsi, *Am:* 'ɑːkjə-] *n no pl* (*of building*) ocupación *f;* (*of post*) tenencia *f*

occupancy rate *n* tasa *f* de ocupación

occupant ['ɒkjəpənt, *Am:* 'ɑːkjə-] *n form* **1.** (*of building, vehicle*) ocupante *mf;* (*tenant*) inquilino, -a *m, f* **2.** (*of post*) titular *mf*

occupation [ˌɒkjə'peɪʃən, *Am:* 'ɑːkjə'-] *n* **1.** *a.* MIL ocupación *f;* **to take up ~ of a house** tomar posesión de una vivienda; **~ army** ejército *m* de ocupación **2.** (*profession*) profesión *f* **3.** (*pastime*) pasatiempo *m;* **what's your favourite ~?** ¿a qué prefieres dedicar tu tiempo libre?

occupational [ˌɒkjʊ'peɪʃənəl, *Am:* ˌɑːkjə'-] *adj* profesional

occupational disease *n* enfermedad *f* profesional **occupational hazard** *n* riesgo *m* laboral **occupational pension scheme** *n* plan *m* de pensiones **occupational therapy** *n* terapia *f* ocupacional

occupier ['ɒkjʊpaɪər, *Am:* 'ɑːkjəpaɪə] *n* (*of territory, building*) ocupante *mf;* (*tenant*) inquilino, -a *m, f*

occupy ['ɒkjʊpaɪ, *Am:* 'ɑːkjuː-] <-ie-> *vt* **1.** (*room, position*) *a.* MIL ocupar; **to ~ space** ocupar espacio; **the bathroom's occupied** el lavabo está ocupado; **~ing forces** fuerzas *fpl* de ocupación **2.** (*engage*) **to be occupied with sth** estar ocupado con algo; **to keep sb occupied** mantener a alguien ocupado; **to keep one's mind occupied** mantener la mente ocupada; **to ~ oneself** entretenerse; **the whole process occupied a week** todo el proceso llevó una semana **3.** (*hold*) **to ~ a post** ocupar un cargo **4.** (*dwell in*) **the house hasn't been occupied for a long time** nadie ha vivido en la casa durante mucho tiempo **5.** (*employ*) dar trabajo

occur [ə'kɜːr, *Am:* -'kɜːr] <-rr-> *vi* **1.** (*happen*) ocurrir; (*change, problem*) producirse; **don't let it ~ again!** ¡que no vuelva a suceder!; **if any of these symptoms ~ consult your doctor** si se presenta alguno de estos síntomas consulte a su médico; **to ~ every two years** tener lugar cada dos años **2.** (*exist*) encontrarse; **the disease does not ~ in this area** la enfermedad no se da en esta zona

3. (*come into mind*) **to** ~ **to sb** ocurrírse a alguien; **it** ~**d to me that ...** se me ocurrió que...; **did it ever** ~ **to you that ...?** ¿no se te ha ocurrido nunca que...?

occurrence [əˈkʌrəns, *Am:* -ˈkɜːr-] *n* **1.** (*event*) acontecimiento *m;* **an unexpected** ~ un suceso inesperado; **to be an everyday** ~ ser cosa de todos los días; **to be of frequent/rare** ~ ser/no ser frecuente **2.** (*case*) caso *m* **3.** *no pl* (*incidence: of disease*) incidencia *f*

ocean [ˈəʊʃən, *Am:* ˈoʊ-] *n* océano *m* ▸~**s of ...** un montón de... *inf*

oceangoing [ˈəʊʃənˌgəʊɪŋ, *Am:* ˈoʊʃn-ˌgoʊ-] *adj* transatlántico, -a

Oceania [ˌəʊʃiˈeɪniə, *Am:* ˌoʊ-] *n* Oceanía *f*

oceanic [ˌəʊʃiˈænɪk, *Am:* ˌoʊʃiˈ-] *adj* oceánico, -a

ocean liner *n* NAUT transatlántico *m*

oceanography [ˌəʊʃəˈnɒgrəfi, *Am:* ˌoʊʃə-ˈnɑːgrə-] *n no pl* oceanografía *f*

ocelot [ˈəʊsɪlɒt, *Am:* ˈɑːsələːt] *n* ocelote *m*, manigordo *m CRi*

ocher *Am,* **ochre** [ˈəʊkər, *Am:* ˈoʊkər] **I.** *n no pl* ocre *m* **II.** *adj* ocre

o'clock [əˈklɒk, *Am:* -ˈklɑːk] *adv* **it's one** ~ es la una; **it's two/seven** ~ son las dos/las siete

OCR [ˌəʊsiːˈɑːr, *Am:* ˌoʊ-] *n no pl abbr of* **optical character recognition** ROC *m*

octagon [ˈɒktəgən, *Am:* ˈɑktəgɑːn] *n* octógono *m*, octágono *m*

octagonal [ɒkˈtægənəl, *Am:* ɑːk-] *adj* octogonal, octagonal

octane [ˈɒkteɪn, *Am:* ˈɑːk-] *n* octano *m*

octave [ˈɒktɪv, *Am:* ˈɑːk-] *n* LIT, MUS octava *f*

octet [ɒkˈtet, *Am:* ɑːk-] *n* MUS octeto *m*

October [ɒkˈtəʊbər, *Am:* ɑːkˈtoʊbər] *n* octubre *m;* s. a. **April**

octogenarian [ˌɒktədʒɪˈneərɪən, *Am:* ˌɑːktoʊdʒɪˈneɪ-] **I.** *adj* octogenario, -a **II.** *n* octogenario, -a *m, f*

octopus [ˈɒktəpəs, *Am:* ˈɑːk-] <-es *o* -pi> *n* pulpo *m*

oculist [ˈɒkjʊlɪst, *Am:* ˈɑːkjə-] *n* oculista *mf*

OD [ˌəʊˈdiː, *Am:* ˌoʊ-] **I.** *n abbr of* **overdose** sobredosis *f inv* **II.** *vi* **to** ~ **on sth** tomar una sobredosis de algo; *fig* abusar de algo

odd [ɒd, *Am:* ɑːd] *adj* **1.** (*strange*) extraño, -a; **an** ~ **person/thing** una persona/cosa rara; **how** (**very**) ~! ¡qué raro!; **it is** ~ **that ...** es raro que +*subj;* **to look** ~ tener un aspecto extraño **2.** (*not even: number*) impar **3.** (*approximately*) **30** ~ **people** 30 y pico personas; **he is about 50** ~ tiene unos 50 y tantos años **4.** (*occasional*) ocasional; **at** ~ **times** algunas veces; **she does the** ~ **teaching job** da alguna que otra clase **5.** (*unmatched: glove, sock*) suelto, -a **6.** (*left over*) sobrante; **I've got a few** ~ **hours** tengo algunas horas libres; **to be the** ~ **one out** quedar excluido

oddball [ˈɒdbɔːl, *Am:* ˈɑːd-] **I.** *n inf* bicho *m* raro **II.** *adj inf* (*sense of humour*) raro, -a; (*idea*) descabellado, -a

oddity [ˈɒdəti, *Am:* ˈɑːdəti] <-ies> *n* (*per-*

son) excéntrico, -a *m, f;* (*thing*) cosa *f* rara; (*characteristic*) rareza *f*

odd-job man [ˌɒdˈdʒɒbmæn, *Am:* ˈɑːd-dʒɑːb-] *n* hombre *m* que hace pequeñas reparaciones

oddly *adv* **1.** (*in a strange manner*) de forma extraña **2.** (*curiously*) curiosamente; ~ **enough** por extraño que parezca

oddments [ˈɒdmənts, *Am:* ˈɑːd-] *npl* restos *mpl*

odds [ɒdz, *Am:* ɑːdz] *npl* **1.** (*probability*) probabilidades *fpl;* **the** ~ **against/on sth** las probabilidades en contra/a favor de algo; **to shorten/lengthen the** ~ disminuir/aumentar las posibilidades; **the** ~ **are against us** tenemos todo en contra; **the** ~ **are in his favour** tiene todas las de ganar; **the** ~ **are that ...** lo más seguro es que +*subj* **2.** *Aus, Brit, inf* (*difference*) **it makes no** ~ (**to me**) (me) da igual; **what's the** ~**?** ¿qué más da? ▸~ **and ends** [*o* **sods**] *Aus, Brit, inf* (*bits*) cosas *fpl* sueltas; (*of fabric*) retales *mpl;* (*of food*) sobras *fpl;* **to pay over the** ~ *Aus, Brit, inf* pagar más de la cuenta; **against all** (**the**) ~ a pesar de las circunstancias adversas; **to be at** ~ **with sb** estar en desacuerdo con alguien

odds-on [ˌɒdzˈɒn, *Am:* ˌɑːdzˈɑːn] *adj* seguro, -a; **it's** ~ **that ...** lo más probable es que +*subj;* **the** ~ **favourite to win the race** el gran favorito de la carrera

ode [əʊd, *Am:* oʊd] *n* oda *f*

odious [ˈəʊdɪəs, *Am:* ˈoʊ-] *adj* odioso, -a

odometer [ɒˈdɒmɪtər, *Am:* oʊˈdɑːmətər] *n Am* cuentaquilómetros *m inv*

odor *n Am, Aus,* **odour** [ˈəʊdər, *Am:* ˈoʊdər] *n Brit* (*smell*) olor *m;* (*fragance*) aroma *m;* **to be in good/bad** ~ **with sb** *fig* estar a bien/mal con alguien

odorless *adj Am, Aus,* **odourless** *adj form* inodoro, -a

odyssey [ˈɒdɪsi, *Am:* ˈɑːdɪ-] *n* odisea *f*

OECD [ˌəʊiːsiːˈdiː, *Am:* ˌoʊ-] *n abbr of* **Organization for Economic Cooperation and Development** OCDE *f*

oecumenical [iːkjʊˈmenɪkl, *Am:* ekjə'-] *adj* ecuménico, -a

oesophagus [iːˈsɒfəgəs, *Am:* ɪˈsɑːfə-] <-agi *o* -guses> *n* esófago *m*

oestrogen [ˈiːstrəʊdʒən, *Am:* ˈestrə-] *n no pl* estrógeno *m*

of [əv, *stressed:* ɒv] *prep* **1.** de **2.** (*belonging to*) de; **the works** ~ **Joyce** las obras de Joyce; **a friend** ~ **mine/theirs** un amigo mío/de ellos **3.** (*done by*) de; **it's kind** ~ **him** es amable de su parte **4.** (*representing*) de; **a drawing** ~ **Paul** un dibujo de Paul **5.** (*without*) **a tree bare** ~ **leaves** un árbol sin hojas; **free** ~ **charge** sin cargo; **free** ~ **tax** libre de impuestos; **to cure sb** ~ **a disease** curar a alguien de una enfermedad **6.** (*with*) **a man** ~ **courage** un hombre de valor; **a man** ~ **no importance** un hombre sin importancia; **a city** ~ **wide avenues** una ciudad con amplias avenidas **7.**(*away from*) **to be north ~ Lon-don** estar al norte de Londres **8.**(*temporal*) **the 4th ~ May** el 4 de mayo; **in May ~ 2003** en mayo del 2003 **9.** *Am* (*to*) **it is ten/a quarter ~ two** son las dos menos diez/cuarto **10.**(*consisting of*) de; **a ring ~ gold** un anillo de oro; **to smell/to taste ~ cheese** oler/ saber a queso; **to consist ~ six parts** constar de seis partes **11.**(*characteristic*) **with the patience ~ a saint** con la paciencia de un santo; **this idiot ~ a plumber** este idiota del fontanero; **doctor ~ medicine** doctor en medicina **12.**(*concerning*) **his love ~ jazz** su amor por el jazz; **to know sth ~ sb's past** saber algo del pasado de alguien; **to approve ~ sb's idea** estar de acuerdo con la idea de al-guien; **what has become ~ him?** ¿qué ha sido de él?; **what I think ~ him** lo que pienso de él **13.**(*cause*) **because ~ sth/sb** a causa de algo/alguien; **to die ~ grief** morir de pena; **it happened ~ itself** sucedió de por sí **14.**(*a portion of*) **there's a lot ~ it** hay mucho de eso; **one ~ the best** uno de los mejores; **the best ~ friends** los mejores amigos; **many ~ them came** muchos de ellos vinieron; **there are five ~ them** hay cinco de ellos; **he knows the five ~ them** los conoce a los cinco; **two ~ the five** dos de los cinco; **he ~ all people knows that** él debería saberlo mejor que nadie; **today ~ all days** hoy precisamente **15.**(*to amount of*) **80 years ~ age** 80 años de edad

off [ɒf, *Am:* ɑːf] **I.** *prep* **1.**(*close to*) **to be one metre ~ sth/sb** estar a un metro de algo/alguien **2.**(*away from*) **the mill is ~ the road** el molino está algo apartado de la ca-rretera; **to take sth ~ the shelf** coger algo del estante; **keep ~ the grass** mantenerse fuera del césped; **to sing ~ key** cantar fuera de tono; **get ~ me!** *Am, inf* ¡déjame! **3.**(*down from*) **to fall/jump ~ a ladder** caer/saltar de una esca-lera; **to get ~ the train** bajarse del tren **4.**(*from*) **to eat ~ a plate** comer de un plato; **to cut a piece ~ the cheese** cortar un pedazo del queso; **to take 10 euros ~ the price** reba-jar 10 euros del precio **5.** *inf*(*stop liking*) **to go ~ sb/sth** pasar de alguien/algo; **to be ~ smoking/drugs** pasar de fumar/las drogas **6.**(*as source of*) **to run ~ batteries** alimen-tarse de baterías **II.** *adv* **1.**(*not on*) **to switch/ turn sth ~** apagar algo; **it's ~ between them** *fig* lo han dejado **2.**(*away*) **the town is 8 km ~** el pueblo está a 8 km de distancia; **not far ~** faltar poco; **some way ~** a cierta distancia; **to go/run ~** irse/salir corriendo; **~ with him** fuera con él; **it's time I was ~** ya debería haber salido; **to be ~** SPORTS estar fuera de juego **3.**(*removed*) **there is a button ~** le falta un botón; **the lid is ~** la tapa está fuera; **with one's coat ~** con el abrigo quitado; **~ with that hat!** ¡quítate el sombrero! **4.**(*free from work*) **to get ~ at 4:00** salir (del trabajo) a las 4:00; **to get a day ~** tener un día libre **5.**(*com-*

pletely) **to kill ~** exterminar; **to pay sth ~** aca-bar de pagar **6.** COM **5% ~** 5% de descuento **7.**(*bad: food*) **to go ~** pasarse **8.**(*until gone*) **to walk ~ the dinner** caminar para bajar la comida; **to sleep ~ the wine** dormirse para bajar el vino **9.**(*separating*) **to fence sth ~** cercar algo ▶**straight** [*o* **right**] **~** enseguida; **~ and on, on and ~** de cuando en cuando; **it rained ~ and on** llovió intermitentemente **III.** *adj* **1.**(*not on: light*) apagado, -a; (*tap*) ce-rrado, -a; (*water*) cortado, -a; (*engagement*) suspendido, -a **2.**(*bad: milk*) cortado, -a; (*food*) malo, -a **3.**(*free from work*) **to be ~ at 5:00** salir del trabajo a las 5:00; **I'm ~ on Mondays** los lunes libro **4.** *Aus, Brit* (*provided for*) **to be well ~** tener dinero; **to be badly ~** andar mal de dinero; **to be badly ~ for sugar** andar escaso de azúcar **5.**(*sold out*) **veal is ~ now** ya no queda ternera **6.** *Am, inf* **to go ~ on sb** echar la bronca a alguien **IV.** *n no pl, Brit* salida *f* **V.** *vt Am, inf* **to ~ sb** cargarse a alguien

offal ['ɒfəl, *Am:* 'ɑːfəl] *n no pl* (*of animal*) despojos *mpl,* achura *f AmS*

offbeat [,ɒf'biːt, *Am:* ,ɑːf-] *adj* poco conven-cional

off-center *adj Am,* **off-centre** *adj Brit* **1.**(*diverging from the centre*) descentrado, -a **2.**(*unconventional*) poco convencional

off-chance ['ɒftʃɑːnts, *Am:* 'ɑːftʃænts] *n* **on the ~** por si acaso

off-color *adj Am, Aus,* **off-colour** [,ɒf'kʌ-lər, *Am:* ,ɑːf'kʌlər] *adj Brit* **1.**(*unwell*) indis-puesto, -a; **to feel ~** encontrarse mal; **to look ~** tener mala cara **2.**(*somewhat obscene: joke*) subido, -a de tono

off day *n* **to have an ~** tener un mal día

off-duty *adj* fuera de servicio

offence [ə'fents] *n* **1.**(*crime*) delito *m;* **minor ~** infracción *f;* **second ~** reincidencia *f;* **traffic ~** infracción de tráfico **2.**(*affront*) aten-tado *m;* **an ~ against sth** un atentado contra algo; **it is an ~ to the eye** *fig* hace daño a la vista **3.** *no pl* (*upset feeling*) ofensa *f;* **to cause ~ (to sb)** ofender (a alguien); **to take ~ (at sth)** ofenderse (por algo); **no ~ (intended)** *inf* sin ánimo de ofender **4.** REL pecado *m* **5.** *Am* SPORTS ofensiva *f*

offend [ə'fend] **I.** *vi* **1.**(*cause displeasure*) ofender **2.**(*violate*) **to ~ against sth** atentar contra algo; **his remarks ~ against common sense** sus comentarios atentan contra el sentido común **3.** LAW infringir la ley; (*commit a crime*) cometer un delito; **to ~ against a rule** infringir una norma **II.** *vt* **1.**(*upset sb's feelings*) ofender; **to be ~ed at sth** ofenderse por algo; **to be easily ~ed** ser muy suscep-tible; **she was ~ed that she had not been invited** se ofendió por no haber sido invitada **2.**(*affect disagreeably*) **to ~ the eye** hacer daño a la vista; **to ~ good taste** atentar contra el buen gusto

offender [ə'fendər, *Am:* -ər] *n* infractor(a) *m(f);* (*guilty of crime*) delincuente *mf;* **first ~**

delincuente sin antecedentes; **previous** [o **repeat**] ~ reincidente *mf;* **young** ~ delincuente juvenil

offense [ə'fens] *n Am s.* **offence**

offensive [ə'fensɪv] **I.** *adj* **1.** (*remark, joke*) ofensivo, -a; (*language, word*) grosero, -a; (*tone*) desagradable; **to be** ~ **to sb** insultar a alguien **2.** (*disagreeable: smell*) repugnante **II.** *n* MIL ofensiva *f;* **to go on the** ~ pasar a la ofensiva; **to launch an** ~ (**against sth**) lanzar una ofensiva (contra algo); **to take the** ~ tomar la ofensiva

offensive weapon *n* MIL arma *f* ofensiva

offer ['ɒfə', *Am:* 'ɑ:fə-] **I.** *vt* **1.** (*proffer: help, advice, money*) ofrecer; (*chance*) brindar; **to** ~ **sb sth** ofrecer algo a alguien; **to** ~ **an apology** pedir disculpas; **to** ~ **congratulations to sb** felicitar a alguien; **can I** ~ **you a drink?** ¿quiere tomar algo?; **to** ~ **a good price for sth** ofrecer un buen precio por algo; **to** ~ **information/advice** dar información/consejo; **to** ~ **a reward** ofrecer una recompensa; **to** ~ **an explanation** dar una explicación; **to** ~ **shelter** dar cobijo; **to have much to** ~ tener mucho que ofrecer; **to** ~ **oneself for a post** presentarse para un puesto **2.** (*give: gift*) dar **3.** (*volunteer*) **to** ~ **to do sth** ofrecerse para hacer algo **4.** (*propose: plan*) proponer; (*excuse*) presentar; (*opinion*) expresar; **to** ~ **a suggestion** hacer una sugerencia **5.** (*show*) **to** ~ **resistance** oponer resistencia **II.** *vi* (*present itself: opportunity*) presentarse **III.** *n* (*proposal*) propuesta *f;* (*of help*) ofrecimiento *m;* (*of job*) oferta *f;* **an** ~ **of marriage** una proposición de matrimonio; **to make sb an** ~ **they can't refuse** hacer a alguien una oferta muy tentadora; **that's my last** ~ es mi última oferta; **to make** [o **put in**] **an** ~ **of £1000 for sth** ofrecer 1000 libras por algo; **to be on** ~ *Aus, Brit* estar de oferta

offering ['ɒfərɪŋ, *Am:* 'ɑ:fə-] *n* **1.** (*thing given*) ofrecimiento *m;* **as an** ~ **of thanks** en señal de agradecimiento **2.** (*contribution*) donativo *m* **3.** REL (*sacrifice*) ofrenda *f*

offhand [ˌɒf'hænd, *Am:* ˌɑ:f-] **I.** *adj* **1.** (*uninterested*) brusco, -a; **an** ~ **reply** una respuesta desabrida; **to be** ~ **with sb** ser brusco con alguien **2.** (*without previous thought*) improvisado, -a **II.** *adv* de improviso; **to judge sb/sth** ~ juzgar algo/a alguien a la ligera

office ['ɒfɪs, *Am:* 'ɑ:fɪs] *n* **1.** (*of company*) oficina *f;* (*room in house*) despacho *m,* archivo *m Col;* **they've got** ~**s in Paris and Madrid** tienen oficinas en París y Madrid; **to stay at the** ~ quedarse en la oficina; **architect's** ~ estudio *m* (de arquitecto); **doctor's** ~ consultorio *m;* **lawyer's** ~ bufete *m* (de abogado) **2.** *Brit* POL **the Foreign Office** *el Ministerio de Relaciones Exteriores de Gran Bretaña;* **the Home Office** *el Ministerio del Interior británico* **3.** POL (*authoritative position*) cargo *m;* **to hold** ~ ocupar un cargo; **to be in** ~ (*person*) estar en funciones; (*party*) estar en el poder; **to**

be out of ~ haber dejado el cargo; **to take** ~ entrar en funciones **4.** *pl* (*assistance*) mediación *f;* **through the** ~**s of** gracias a la mediación de **5.** REL oficio *m*

office automation *n* INFOR ofimática *f*

office block *n Aus, Brit* bloque *m* de oficinas **office boy** *n* auxiliar *mf* de oficina

office building *n Am s.* **office block**

office equipment *n* material *m* de oficina

office hours *npl* horas *fpl* de oficina; **to do sth out(side) of** ~ hacer algo fuera de las horas de oficina

officer ['ɒfɪsə', *Am:* 'ɑ:fɪsə-] *n* **1.** MIL oficial *mf;* **naval** ~ oficial de marina **2.** (*policeman*) policía *mf;* **police** ~ agente *mf* de policía **3.** (*in organization*) directivo, -a *m, f;* (*in political party*) dirigente *mf* **4.** (*official*) funcionario, -a *m, f*

office staff *n no pl* personal *m* de oficina

office supplies *npl* artículos *mpl* de oficina

office worker *n* oficinista *mf*

official [ə'fɪʃl] **I.** *n* **1.** POL oficial *mf* **2.** (*civil servant*) funcionario, -a *m, f* **II.** *adj* oficial

officialdom [ə'fɪʃldəm] *n no pl, pej* burocracia *f*

officialese [ə,fɪʃə'li:z] *n no pl, Am* jerga *f* burocrática

officially [ə'fɪʃəli] *adv* oficialmente

officiate [ə'fɪʃreɪt] *vi form* oficiar; **to** ~ **at a ceremony** oficiar (en) una ceremonia

officious [ə'fɪʃəs] *adj pej* oficioso, -a

offing ['ɒfɪŋ, *Am:* 'ɑ:fɪŋ] *n no pl* **to be in the** ~ NAUT estar a la vista; *fig* estar en perspectiva; **good news is in the** ~ pronto habrá buenas noticias

off key MUS **I.** *adv* desafinadamente; **to play/sing** ~ desafinar **II.** *adj* desafinado, -a

off-licence ['ɒf,laɪsənts, *Am:* ,ɑ:f'laɪ-] *n Brit* ≈ tienda *f* de licores

off-limits *adj* fuera de los límites (permitidos)

off-line [,ɒf'laɪn, *Am:* ,ɑ:f-] *adj* INFOR desconectado, -a, fuera de línea

offload [,ɒf'ləʊd, *Am:* 'ɑ:floʊd] *vt* **1.** (*unload*) descargar **2.** (*get rid of*) **to** ~ **sth** deshacerse de algo; **to** ~ **sth onto sb** endosar algo a alguien; **to** ~ **work onto sb** descargar trabajo en alguien

off-peak [,ɒf'pi:k, *Am:* ,ɑ:f-] *adj* (*fare, rate*) fuera de las horas punta; (*phone call*) de tarifa reducida

off-piste [,ɒf'pi:st, *Am:* ,ɑ:f-] *adj* SPORTS fuera de pista

off-putting [,ɒf'pʊtɪŋ, *Am:* 'ɑ:f,pʊt̮-] *adj* **1.** (*smell, manner, appearance*) desagradable; (*person*) antipático, -a **2.** (*experience*) desalentador(a)

off-sales ['ɒfseɪlz] *n Brit* ≈ tienda *f* de licores

off-season ['ɒf,si:zən, *Am:* 'ɑ:f-] **I.** *n* temporada *f* baja **II.** *adj* de temporada baja

offset ['ɒfset, *Am:* 'ɑ:f-] **I.** *n* **1.** TYPO offset *m* **2.** BOT vástago *m* **3.** (*compensation*) compensación *f* **II.** <offset, offset> *vt* **1.** (*compensate*) compensar **2.** TYPO imprimir en offset

offshore [ˌɒfˈʃɔːˈ, *Am:* ˌɑːfˈʃɔːr] I. *adj* 1. (*from the shore: breeze, wind*) terral 2. (*at sea*) a poca distancia de la costa; ~ **fishing** pesca de bajura; ~ **oilfield** yacimiento *m* petrolífero marítimo II. *adv* mar adentro; **to anchor** ~ anclar a cierta distancia de la costa

offside [ˌɒfˈsaɪd, *Am:* ˌɑːfˈ-] I. *n* 1. SPORTS fuera de juego *m* 2. AUTO lado *m* del conductor; **the** ~ **door** la puerta del conductor II. *adv* SPORTS fuera de juego

offspring [ˈɒfsprɪŋ, *Am:* ˈɑːf-] *n inv* 1. (*animal young*) cría *f* 2. *pl* (*children*) prole *f*

offstage [ˌɒfˈsteɪdʒ, *Am:* ˌɑːf-] I. *adj* de entre bastidores II. *adv* entre bastidores

off-street parking [ˌɒfstriːˈtˈpɑːkɪŋ, *Am:* ˌɑːfstriːtˈpɑːrkɪŋ] *n* aparcamiento *m* fuera de la vía pública, estacionamiento *m* fuera de la vía pública *AmL*

off-the-cuff [ˌɒfðəˈkʌf, *Am:* ˌɑːf-] I. *adj* espontáneo, -a II. *adv* espontáneamente

off-the-job training *n no pl* formación *f* profesional en un centro especializado

off-the-peg [ˌɒfðəˈpeg, *Am:* ˌɑːf-] *adj Brit*, **off-the-rack** [ˌɒfðəˈræk, *Am:* ˌɑːf-] *adj Am* prêt à porter

off-white [ˌɒfˈhwaɪt, *Am:* ˌɑːf-] *adj* de color hueso

often [ˈɒfən, *Am:* ˈɑːfən] *adv* a menudo; **we** ~ **go there** solemos ir allí; **as** ~ **as** siempre que; **as** ~ **as not** la mitad de las veces; **every so** ~ alguna que otra vez; **how** ~? ¿cuántas veces?; **it's not** ~ **that ...** no es frecuente que +*subj;* **more** ~ **than not** la mayoría de las veces

ogle [ˈəʊgl, *Am:* ˈoʊ-] *vt* **to** ~ **sb** comerse a alguien con los ojos

ogre [ˈəʊgəˈ, *Am:* ˈoʊgəˈ] *n* ogro *m*

ogress [ˈəʊgres, *Am:* ˈoʊ-] *n* ogresa *f*

oh [əʊ, *Am:* oʊ] *interj* 1. (*expressing surprise, disappointment, pleasure*) oh; ~ **dear!** ¡Dios mío!; ~ **no!** ¡ay, no!; ~ **well** bueno; ~ **yes?** ¿ah, sí? 2. (*by the way*) ah

OHMS [ˌəʊeɪtʃemˈes, *Am:* ˌoʊ-] *abbr of* **On Her/His Majesty's Service** al servicio de Su Majestad

oil [ɔɪl] I. *n* 1. (*lubricant*) aceite *m;* **sunflower** ~ aceite de girasol 2. *no pl* (*petroleum*) petróleo *m;* **to strike** ~ encontrar petróleo; *fig* encontrar una mina de oro 3. (*grease*) grasa *f* 4. *pl* (*oil-based paint*) óleo *m;* **to paint in** ~**s** pintar al óleo ▶**to burn the** <u>midnight</u> ~ quemarse las pestañas; **to pour** ~ **on** <u>troubled</u> <u>waters</u> calmar los ánimos, poner paz II. *vt* engrasar

oil-based paint *n* pintura *f* al óleo **oilcan** *n* aceitera *f* **oil change** *n* AUTO cambio *m* de aceite **oilcloth** *n* hule *m* **oil company** *n* empresa *f* petroquímica **oil consumption** *n no pl* consumo *m* de petróleo **oil crisis** *n* crisis *f inv* del petróleo **oil-exporting** *adj* exportador(a) de petróleo **oilfield** *n* yacimiento *m* petrolífero **oil-fired** *adj* alimentado, -a a petróleo; ~ **heating system** calefac-

ción *f* a petróleo

oiliness [ˈɔɪlɪnɪs] *n no pl* 1. (*greasiness: of food*) lo aceitoso; (*of material, skin*) lo grasiento 2. *fig* lo empalagoso

oil lamp *n* quinqué *m* **oil level** *n* TECH nivel *m* de aceite **oil painting** *n* óleo *m* ▶**to be no** ~ *Aus, Brit, iron* no ser ninguna belleza **oil pipeline** *n* oleoducto *m*

oil-producing *adj* productor(a) de petróleo **oil-producing country** *n* país *m* productor de petróleo

oil production *n no pl* producción *f* de petróleo **oilrig** *n* plataforma *f* petrolífera **oil sheik** *n* magnate *m* del petróleo **oilskin** *n* 1. (*cloth*) hule *m* 2. *pl* (*clothing*) impermeable *m* **oil slick** *n* marea *f* negra **oil tanker** *n* NAUT petrolero *m* **oil well** *n* pozo *m* de petróleo

oily [ˈɔɪli] <-ier, -iest> *adj* 1. (*oil-like*) oleoso, -a 2. (*greasy: hands*) grasiento, -a; (*food*) aceitoso, -a; (*skin, hair*) graso, -a 3. (*manner*) empalagoso, -a

ointment [ˈɔɪntmənt] *n* MED pomada *f*

OK, okay [ˌəʊˈkeɪ, *Am:* ˌoʊ-] *inf* I. *adj* 1. (*acceptable*) **is it** ~ **with you if ...?** ¿te importa si...?; **it's** ~ **with me** por mí no hay problema; **to be** ~ **for money/work** tener suficiente dinero/trabajo 2. (*not bad*) **to be** ~ no estar mal; **her voice is** ~, **but it's nothing special** no tiene mala voz, pero tampoco es nada del otro mundo II. *interj* vale *inf*, okey *AmL, inf*, órale *Méx* III. <OKed, okayed> *vt* **to** ~ **sth** dar el visto bueno a algo IV. *n* visto bueno *m;* **to give the** ~ dar el visto bueno V. *adv* bastante bien

okra [ˈəʊkrə, *Am:* ˈoʊ-] *n no pl* quingombó *m*

old [əʊld, *Am:* oʊld] I. *adj* 1. (*not young*) viejo, -a; ~ **people** la gente mayor; **to be** ~ **to be doing sth** ser ya muy mayor para hacer algo; **to grow** ~**er** envejecer 2. (*not new*) viejo, -a; (*food*) pasado, -a; (*wine*) añejo, -a; (*furniture, house*) antiguo, -a 3. (*denoting an age*) **how** ~ **are you?** ¿cuántos años tienes?; **he's five years** ~ tiene cinco años; **she's three years** ~**er than me** me lleva tres años; **to be** ~ **enough to do sth** tener edad suficiente para hacer algo 4. (*former: job*) antiguo, -a; ~ **boyfriend** ex-novio *m;* ~ **English** inglés *m* antiguo 5. (*long known*) de siempre; ~ **friend** viejo amigo; **the same** ~ **faces** las mismas caras de siempre 6. *inf* (*expression of affection*) **I heard poor** ~ **Frank's lost his job** me oído que el pobre Frank se ha quedado sin trabajo II. *n* 1. (*elderly people*) **the** ~ los viejos, los ancianos *AmL;* **young and** ~ grandes y chicos 2. *liter* (*past*) **of** ~ antiguamente; **to know sb of** ~ conocer a alguien desde hace tiempo

old age *n* vejez *f;* **to reach** ~ llegar a viejo

old age pensioner *n* pensionista *mf* **old boy** *n* 1. *Brit, inf* (*old man*) abuelo *m* 2. *Aus, Brit* (*pupil*) antiguo alumno *m*

old-fashioned [ˌəʊldˈfæʃənd, *Am:* ˌoʊld-]

adj *pej* **1.**(*not modern: clothes*) pasado, -a de moda; (*views*) anticuado, -a; **to be** ~ estar chapado a la antigua **2.**(*traditional*) tradicional; **it has an** ~ **charm** tiene el encanto de lo antiguo

old girl *n* **1.** *Brit, inf* (*old woman*) viejecita *f* **2.** *Aus, Brit* (*pupil*) antigua alumna *f*

oldish ['əʊldɪʃ, *Am:* 'oʊl-] *adj* algo viejo, -a

old lady *n inf* **my** ~ (*mother*) mi vieja; (*wife*) mi parienta **old man** *n inf* **my** ~ (*father*) mi viejo; (*husband*) mi marido **old master** *n* ART **1.**(*artist*) gran maestro *m* de la pintura clásica **2.**(*painting*) obra *f* maestra de la pintura clásica **old people's home** *n* residencia *f* de ancianos **old school** I. *adj* de la vieja escuela II. *n fig* vieja escuela *f* **old stager** *n* veterano, -a *m, f*

old-style [ˌəʊld'staɪl, *Am:* ˌoʊld-] *adj* a la antigua

Old Testament *n* Antiguo Testamento *m*

old-timer [ˌəʊld'taɪməʳ, *Am:* 'oʊldˌtaɪmə˞] *n inf* **1.**(*old man*) viejo, -a *m, f* **2.**(*long-time worker, resident*) veterano, -a *m, f*

old wives' tale [ˌəʊld'waɪvzˌteɪl, *Am:* ˌoʊld-] *n* cuento *m* de viejas

oleander [ˌəʊli'ændəʳ, *Am:* ˌoʊli'ændə˞] *n* adelfa *f*

olfactory [ɒl'fæktəri, *Am:* ɑːl-] *adj* olfativo, -a

olive ['ɒlɪv, *Am:* 'ɑːlɪv] *n* **1.**(*fruit*) oliva *f*, aceituna *f* **2.**(*tree*) olivo *m* **3.**(*colour*) aceituna *m*

olive branch *n* rama *f* de olivo ▶**to hold out the** ~ **to sb** tender a alguien la mano en son de paz **olive grove** *n* olivar *m* **olive oil** *n* aceite *m* de oliva

Olympiad [ə'lɪmpiæd, *Am:* oʊ'-] *n* SPORTS olimpiada *f*

Olympian [ə'lɪmpiən, *Am:* oʊ'-] *adj* olímpico, -a

Olympic [ə'lɪmpɪk, *Am:* oʊ'-] *adj* olímpico, -a; **the Olympic Games** SPORTS los Juegos Olímpicos

Oman [əʊ'mɑːn, *Am:* oʊ'-] *n* Omán *m*

Omani [əʊ'mɑːni, *Am:* oʊ'-] I. *adj* omaní II. *n* omaní *mf*

ombudsman ['ɒmbʊdzmən, *Am:* 'ɑːm-bədz-] <-men> *n* POL defensor(a) *m(f)* del pueblo

omelet(te) ['ɒmlɪt, *Am:* 'ɑːmlət] *n* tortilla *f*

omen ['əʊmen, *Am:* 'oʊ-] *n* indicio *m*, augurio *m*; **to be a good/bad** ~ **for sth** ser un buen/mal augurio para algo

ominous ['ɒmɪnəs, *Am:* 'ɑːmə-] *adj* (*news*) ominoso, -a; (*implications*) funesto, -a; (*silence*) inquietante

omission [ə'mɪʃən, *Am:* oʊ'-] *n* omisión *f*

omit [ə'mɪt, *Am:* oʊ'-] <-tt-> *vt* (*person, information*) omitir; (*paragraph, passage*) suprimir; **to** ~ **any reference to sb/sth** evitar toda referencia a alguien/algo; **to** ~ **to do sth** (*neglect*) dejar de hacer algo; (*forget*) olvidarse de hacer algo

omnibus ['ɒmnɪbəs, *Am:* 'ɑːm-] I.<-es> *n* **1.**(*bus*) ómnibus *m* **2.**(*anthology*) antología *f* ▶**the man on the** Clapham ~ *Brit* el ciudadano de a pie II. *adj* ~ **edition** antología *f*

omnipotence [ɒm'nɪpətəns, *Am:* ɑːm'nɪ-pətəns] *n no pl* omnipotencia *f*

omnipotent [ɒm'nɪpətənt, *Am:* ɑːm'nɪ-pətənt] *adj* omnipotente

omnipresent [ˌɒmnɪ'preznt, *Am:* ˌɑːm-] *adj form* omnipresente

omniscient [ɒm'nɪʃnt, *Am:* ɑːm-] *adj form* omnisciente

omnivorous [ɒm'nɪvərəs, *Am:* ɑːm-] *adj* omnívoro, -a; **to be an** ~ **reader** *fig* ser un lector insaciable

on [ɒn, *Am:* ɑːn] I. *prep* **1.**(*place*) sobre, en; ~ **the table** sobre la mesa; ~ **the wall** en la pared; **to put sth** ~ **sb's shoulder/finger** poner algo sobre el hombro/en el dedo de alguien; **to be** ~ **the plane** estar en el avión; **to hang** ~ **a branch** colgar de una rama; **to have sth** ~ **one's mind** *fig* tener algo en mente **2.**(*by means of*) **to go** ~ **the train** ir en tren; **to go** ~ **foot** ir a pie; **to keep a dog** ~ **a leash** tener a un perro cogido por la correa **3.**(*source of*) con; **to run** ~ **gas** funcionar con gasolina; **to live** ~ **£2,000 a month** vivir con 2,000 libras al mes **4.** MED **to be** ~ **drugs/cortisone** tomar drogas/cortisona **5.**(*spatial*) ~ **the right/left** a la derecha/izquierda; ~ **the corner/back of sth** en la esquina/la parte posterior de algo; **a house** ~ **the river** una casa junto al río **6.**(*temporal*) ~ **Sunday** el domingo; ~ **Sundays** los domingos; ~ **the evening of May the 4th** el cuatro de mayo por la tarde; **at 2:00** ~ **the dot** a las 2:00 en punto **7.**(*at time of*) **to leave** ~ **time** salir a tiempo; ~ **her arrival** a su llegada; ~ **arriving there** al llegar allí; **to finish** ~ **schedule** acabar puntualmente **8.**(*about*) sobre; **a lecture** ~ **Joyce** una conferencia sobre Joyce; **to compliment sb** ~ **sth** felicitar a alguien por algo; **to be there** ~ **business** estar ahí por negocios **9.**(*through medium of*) ~ **TV/video/CD** en TV/vídeo/CD; **to speak** ~ **the radio/the phone** hablar en la radio/por teléfono; **to work** ~ **a computer** trabajar con un ordenador; **to play** ~ **the flute** tocar la flauta **10.**(*with basis in*) ~ **the principle that** en el supuesto de que; **to do sth** ~ **purpose** hacer algo a propósito **11.**(*in state of*) ~ **sale** en venta; **to set sth** ~ **fire** prender fuego a algo; **to go** ~ **holiday/a trip** ir de vacaciones/de viaje; ~ **the whole** en general **12.**(*involved in*) **to be** ~ **the committee** estar en el comité; **to work** ~ **a project** trabajar en un proyecto; **to be** ~ **page 10** estar en la página 10; **two** ~ **each side** dos en cada lado **13.**(*because of*) ~ **account of sth/sb** a causa de algo/alguien; **to depend** ~ **sb/sth** depender de alguien/algo **14.**(*against*) **to turn** ~ **sb** volverse contra alguien; **an attack** ~ **sb** un ataque contra alguien; **to cheat** ~ **sb** hacer trampa [*o* engañar] a alguien **15.** (*paid by*) **to buy sth ~ credit** comprar algo a crédito; **this is ~ me** *inf* esto corre por mi cuenta **16.** *Aus, Brit* SPORTS **to be ~ 10 points** tener 10 puntos **II.** *adv* **1.** (*covering one's body*) **to put a hat ~** ponerse un sombrero; **to have sth ~** llevar algo (puesto); **to try ~ sth** probarse algo **2.** (*connected to sth*) **make sure the top's ~ properly** asegúrate de que esté bien tapado; **to screw ~** enroscar **3.** (*aboard*) **to get ~ a train** subir a un tren; **to get ~ a horse** montar en un caballo; **to be ~ (a horse)** estar montado (en un caballo) **4.** (*not stopping*) **to keep ~ doing sth** seguir haciendo algo; **to get ~ with sth** ponerse a hacer algo **5.** (*in forward direction*) hacia adelante; **to move ~** avanzar; **to urge sb ~** *fig* animar a alguien; **from that day ~** desde aquel día; **later ~** más tarde; **and so ~** y así sucesivamente **6.** (*in operation*) **to turn ~** encender; (*tap*) abrir; **to put the kettle ~** poner agua a calentar **7.** (*performing*) en escena; **to go ~** salir a escena ►**I don't know what he's ~ about** *Aus, Brit* no sé qué está diciendo; **~ and off** de vez en cuando; **well ~ in the night** muy entrada la noche; **to be ~ at sb** (**about sth**) estar encima a alguien (con algo); **~ and ~** sin parar **III.** *adj* **1.** (*functioning: light*) encendido, -a; (*tap*) abierto, -a; (*brake*) puesto, -a; **to leave the light ~** dejar la luz encendida **2.** (*scheduled*) **what's ~ at the cinema this week?** ¿qué dan en el cine esta semana?; **the show will be ~ in Barcelona very soon** el espectáculo estará muy pronto en Barcelona; **have you got anything ~ tomorrow?** ¿tienes algún plan para mañana? **3.** THEAT (*performing*) **to be ~** estar en escena; *Am* (*performing well*) hacerlo muy bien **4.** (*job*) **to be ~ duty** estar de servicio; (*doctor*) estar de guardia **5.** (*good: day*) bueno, -a **6.** (*acceptable*) **that's not ~!** ¡no hay derecho!; **you're ~!** ¡de acuerdo!

once [wʌnts] **I.** *adv* **1.** (*one time*) una vez; **~ a week** una vez por semana; **~ in a lifetime** una vez en la vida; (**every**) **~ in a while** de vez en cuando; **~ again** de nuevo; **~ and for all** de una vez por todas; **just for ~** sólo una vez; **~ more** (*one more time*) otra vez; (*again, as before*) una vez más; **~ or twice** una o dos veces; **at ~** (*simultaneously*) al mismo tiempo; (*immediately*) en seguida **2.** *liter* (*at one time past*) hace tiempo; **~ upon a time there was ... ** *liter* érase una vez... **II.** *conj* una vez que +*subj*; **but ~ I'd arrived, ...** pero una vez que llegué... ►**all at ~** todos a la vez; **at ~ en seguida

once-over ['wʌnts,əʊvə', *Am:* 'wʌnts,oʊvə'] *n inf* **1.** (*examination*) ojeada *f*; **to give sth a ~** dar un vistazo a algo **2.** (*cleaning*) repaso *m*

oncoming ['ɒnkʌmɪŋ, *Am:* 'ɑːn-] *adj* que se aproxima; (*traffic, vehicle*) que viene en dirección contraria

one [wʌn] **I.** *n* (*number*) uno *m* ►**to land sb**

a alguien; (**all**) **in ~** todo en uno; **as ~** *form* a la vez; **in ~** de una sola pieza **II.** *adj* **1.** *numeral* un, uno, -a; **~ hundred** cien; **it's ~ o'clock** es la una; **as ~ man** todos a una; **~ man out of** [*o* **in**] **two** uno de cada dos hombres **2.** *indef* un, uno, -a; **we'll meet ~ day** nos veremos un día de estos; **~ winter night** una noche de invierno **3.** (*sole*) único, -a; **her ~ and only hope** su única esperanza **4.** (*single*) mismo, -a, único, -a; **all files on the ~ disk** todos los archivos en un único disco **III.** *pron pers* **1.** *impers, no pl* **what ~ can do** lo que uno puede hacer; **to wash ~'s face** lavarse la cara **2.** (*person*) **no ~** nadie; **every ~** cada uno; **the little ~s** los pequeños; **the ~ who ...** el que...; **I for ~** al menos yo **3.** (*particular thing or person*) **any ~** cualquiera; **this ~** éste; **which ~?** ¿cuál (de ellos)?; **the ~ on the table** el que está en la mesa; **the thinner ~** el más delgado

one-armed [,wʌn'ɑːmd, *Am:* -'ɑːrmd] *adj* manco, -a, sunco, -a *Chile*

one-armed bandit *n Am, Aus* máquina *f* tragaperras, máquina *f* tragamonedas *AmL*

one-eyed [,wʌn'aɪd] *adj* tuerto, -a **one-handed I.** *adv* con una sola mano **II.** *adj* manco, -a **one-horse** *adj* **1.** (*using one horse*) de un caballo **2.** (*second-rate*) de poca monta; **a ~ town** un pueblucho **one-legged** *adj* cojo, -a

one-liner [,wʌn'laɪnə', *Am:* -nə'] *n* frase *f* ingeniosa

one-man [,wʌn'mæn] *adj* **1.** (*consisting of one person*) de un solo hombre; **~ band** hombre *m* orquesta **2.** (*designed for one person*) individual

one-night stand [,wʌnnaɪt'stænd] *n* **1.** MUS, THEAT función *f* única **2.** *inf* (*relationship*) ligue *m* de una noche

one-off [,wʌn'ɒf, *Am:* 'wʌnɑːf] **I.** *n Aus, Brit* **to be a ~** ser un fuera de serie **II.** *adj* excepcional; **~ payment** pago *m* extraordinario

one-piece (swimsuit) ['wʌnpiːs] *n* bañador *m*

onerous ['ɒnərəs, *Am:* 'ɑːnə-] *adj* oneroso, -a

oneself [wʌn'self] *pron reflexive* **1.** se; *emphatic* sí (mismo, misma); **to deceive ~** engañarse a sí mismo; **to express ~** expresarse **2.** (*same person*) uno mismo

one-sided [,wʌn'saɪdɪd] *adj* (*contest*) desigual; (*decision*) unilateral; (*view, account*) parcial

one-time ['wʌntaɪm] *adj* **1.** antiguo, -a; **~ president** ex-presidente *mf* **2.** (*happening only once*) único, -a

one-track mind [,wʌntræk'maɪnd] *n* **to have a ~** no pensar más que en una cosa

one-upmanship [,wʌn'ʌpmənʃɪp] *n no pl, inf:* arte de estar por encima de los demás

one-way street [,wʌnweɪ'striːt] *n* calle *f* de sentido único **one-way ticket** *n* billete *m* sencillo

ongoing ['ɒŋgəʊɪŋ, *Am:* 'ɑːŋgoʊ-] *adj* en curso; ~ **state of affairs** situación que sigue en curso

onion ['ʌnɪən] *n* cebolla *f* ▶**to** <u>know</u> **one's** ~**s** *inf* conocer muy bien su oficio

on-line INFOR I. *adj* en línea; ~ **data service** servicio *m* de datos en línea; ~ **information service** servicio *m* de información en línea; ~ **shop** comercio *m* en línea II. *adv* en línea

onlooker ['ɒnlʊkəʳ, *Am:* 'ɑːnlʊkə-] *n* espectador(a) *m(f)*; **there were many** ~**s at the accident site** había muchos curiosos en el lugar del accidente

only ['əʊnli, *Am:* 'oʊn-] I. *adj* único, -a; **the** ~ **glass he had** el único vaso que tenía; **the** ~ **way of doing sth** la única manera de hacer algo; **I'm not the** ~ **one** no soy el único; **the** ~ **thing is ...** la única cosa es... II. *adv* sólo, nomás *AmL*; **not** ~ **... but** no solamente...sino; **I can** ~ **say ...** sólo puedo decir...; **he has** ~ **two** sólo tiene dos; ~ **Paul can do it** sólo Paul puede hacerlo; **I've** ~ **just eaten** acabo de comer ahora III. *conj inf* sólo que

o.n.o. [,əʊen'əʊ, *Am:* ,oʊ-] *adv Aus, Brit abbr of* **or nearest offer** negociable

onrush ['ɒnrʌʃ, *Am:* 'ɑːn-] <-es> *n* **1.**(*of waves*) embate *m* **2.**(*of people*) avalancha *f fig*

onset ['ɒnset, *Am:* 'ɑːn-] *n no pl* comienzo *m*; (*of winter*) llegada *f*; (*of illness*) aparición *f*

onshore ['ɒnʃɔːʳ, *Am:* 'ɑːnʃɔːr] I. *adj* (*wind*) del mar II. *adv* tierra adentro

onside [,ɒn'saɪt] SPORTS I. *adj* **to be** ~ (*player*) estar en posición correcta II. *adv* en posición correcta

onslaught ['ɒnslɔːt, *Am:* 'ɑːnslɑːt] *n* ataque *m* violento; *fig* crítica *f* violenta

on-the-job training *n* formación *f* en el puesto de trabajo

onto ['ɒntuː, *Am:* 'ɑːntuː] *prep*, **on to** *prep* **1.**(*in direction of*) sobre; **to put sth** ~ **the chair** poner algo sobre la silla; **to step** ~ **the road** pisar la calzada; **to come** ~ **a subject** llegar a un tema **2.**(*connected to*) **to hold** ~ **sb's arm** aferrarse al brazo de alguien; **to be** ~ **sb** ver a alguien su juego

onus ['əʊnəs, *Am:* 'oʊ-] *n* responsabilidad *f*

onward ['ɒnwəd, *Am:* 'ɑːnwəd] I. *adj* hacia adelante; **the** ~ **march of time** el avance inexorable del tiempo II. *adv* hacia adelante; **from today** ~ de hoy en adelante

onyx ['ɒnɪks, *Am:* 'ɑːnɪks] *n no pl* GEO ónice *f*, ónix *f*

oodles ['uːdlz] *npl inf* montones *mpl*; ~ **of money** cantidad *f* de dinero

oomph [ʊmf] *n no pl, inf* **1.**(*energy, vitality*) brío *m*; **to have a lot of** ~ estar lleno de vida **2.**(*sex appeal*) atractivo *m*

ooze [uːz] I. *vi* **1.**(*seep out*) exudar; **to** ~ **from sth** rezumar(se) de algo; **to** ~ **with sth** rezumar algo; **to** ~ **away** acabarse **2.** *fig* (*be full of*) rebosar de; **to** ~ **with confidence**

irradiar seguridad II. *vt* rezumar; **to** ~ **pus** supurar; **to** ~ **charisma** irradiar simpatía III. *n no pl* cieno *m*

opacity [əʊ'pæsəti, *Am:* oʊ'pæsəṭi] *n no pl* **1.**(*non-transparency*) opacidad *f* **2.**(*incomprehensibility*) oscuridad *f*

opal ['əʊpl, *Am:* 'oʊ-] *n* GEO ópalo *m*

opalescent [,əʊpə'lesnt, *Am:* ,oʊ-] *adj* opalescente

opaque [əʊ'peɪk, *Am:* oʊ-] *adj* **1.**(*not transparent*) opaco, -a **2.**(*unintelligible*) oscuro, -a

OPEC ['əʊpek, *Am:* 'oʊ-] *n abbr of* **Organization of Petroleum Exporting Countries** OPEP *f*

open ['əʊpən, *Am:* 'oʊ-] I. *adj* **1.**(*not closed*) abierto, -a; **wide** ~ completamente abierto; **to push sth** ~ abrir algo de un empujón **2.**(*undecided*) sin concretar; **to keep one's options** ~ dejar abiertas todas las alternativas **3.**(*not secret, public: scandal*) público, -a; (*hostility*) abierto, -a, manifiesto, -a; **to be an** ~ **book** *fig* ser un libro abierto; **an** ~ **secret** una cosa sabida **4.**(*unfolded: map*) desplegado, -a **5.**(*frank: person*) abierto, -a; **to welcome sb with** ~ **arms** recibir a alguien con los brazos abiertos **6.**(*accessible to all*) abierto, -a; (*discussion*) abierto, -a al público; (*session*) a puertas abiertas; (*trial*) público, -a **7.**(*willing to listen to new ideas*) abierto, -a de mente; **to have an** ~ **mind** tener una actitud abierta **8.**(*still available: job*) vacante **9.** LING (*vowel*) abierto, -a II. *n* **1.** *no pl* (*outdoors, outside*) (**out**) **in the** ~ al aire libre **2.**(*not secret*) **to get sth** (**out**) **in the** ~ sacar algo a la luz III. *vi* **1.**(*door, window, box*) abrirse **2.**(*shop*) abrir **3.**(*start*) comenzar, empezar IV. *vt* **1.**(*door, box, shop*) abrir; **to** ~ **the door to sth** *fig* abrir la puerta a algo; **to** ~ **sb's eyes** *fig* abrir los ojos a alguien; **to** ~ **fire** (**on sb**) disparar (a alguien) **2.**(*reveal feelings*) **to** ~ **one's heart to sb** abrir el corazón a alguien **3.**(*inaugurate*) inaugurar

◆**open onto** *vi* dar a

◆**open out** I. *vi* **1.**(*become wider*) ensancharse **2.**(*unfold*) abrirse II. *vt* abrir; (*map*) desplegar

◆**open up** I. *vi* **1.**(*shop*) abrir **2.**(*shoot*) abrir fuego II. *vt* abrir

open-air [,əʊpən'eəʳ, *Am:* ,oʊpən'er] *adj* al aire libre; ~ **swimming pool** piscina *f* descubierta

open-cast mining ['əʊpənkɑːst 'maɪnɪŋ, *Am:* 'oʊpənkæst 'maɪnɪŋ] *n* minería *f* a cielo abierto

open cheque *n* cheque *m* al portador **open credit** *n* crédito *m* abierto

open-ended [,əʊpn'endɪd, *Am:* ,oʊ-] *adj* (*contract*) de duración indefinida; (*question*) abierto, -a

opener ['əʊpənəʳ, *Am:* 'oʊpənə-] *n* abridor *m*, destapador *m AmL*; **bottle** ~ abrebotellas *m inv*; **can** ~ abrelatas *m inv*

open-eyed [,əʊpən'aɪd, *Am:* ,oʊ-] *adj* con

los ojos abiertos

open-heart surgery [ˌəʊpənhɑːt'sɜːdʒəri, *Am:* ˌoʊpənhɑːrt'sɜːr-] *n* cirugía *f* a corazón abierto

opening ['əʊpnɪŋ, *Am:* 'oʊp-] *n* **1.** (*gap, hole*) abertura *f*; (*in forest*) claro *m* **2.** (*job opportunity*) vacante *f* **3.** (*beginning*) apertura *f*; (*of book, film*) comienzo *m* **4.** (*ceremony*) inauguración *f*; (*new play, film*) estreno *m*

opening balance *n* FIN saldo *m* de apertura **opening bid** *n* oferta *f* inicial **opening hours** *npl* horario *m* comercial **opening night** *n* THEAT noche *f* del estreno **opening time** *n* hora *f* de apertura

openly ['əʊpənli, *Am:* 'oʊ-] *adv* **1.** (*frankly*) honestamente **2.** (*publicly*) abiertamente

open market *n* mercado *m* abierto

open-minded [ˌəʊpən'maɪndɪd, *Am:* ˌoʊpən'maɪn-] *adj* (*accessible to new ideas*) de actitud abierta; (*unprejudiced*) sin prejuicios **open-mouthed** *adj* boquiabierto, -a

openness ['əʊpənnəs, *Am:* 'oʊ-] *n no pl* franqueza *f*

open-plan [ˌəʊpən'plæn, *Am:* ˌoʊpən-] *adj* de planta abierta

open prison *n Brit* cárcel *f* en régimen abierto **open ticket** *n* billete *m* abierto **Open University** *n Brit* universidad *f* a distancia, universidad *f* abierta *Méx*

opera ['ɒprə, *Am:* 'ɑːpr-] *n* ópera *f*

operable ['ɒpərəbl, *Am:* 'ɑːpər-] *adj* **1.** (*workable: plan*) factible **2.** MED operable

opera glasses *n* gemelos *mpl* de teatro **opera house** *n* ópera *f*

operate ['ɒpəreɪt, *Am:* 'ɑːpər-] **I.** *vi* **1.** (*work, run*) funcionar **2.** (*have or produce an effect*) actuar, surtir efecto **3.** (*perform surgery*) operar; **to ~ on sb** operar a alguien **4.** (*do or be in business*) operar **II.** *vt* **1.** (*work*) manejar **2.** (*run, manage*) llevar, tener

operating ['ɒpəreɪtɪŋ, *Am:* 'ɑːpəreɪt̬-] *adj* **1.** ECON (*profit, costs*) de explotación **2.** TECH (*speed*) de funcionamiento **3.** MED de operaciones; **~ room, ~ theatre** [*o* **theater** *Am*] quirófano *m*

operation [ˌɒpə'reɪʃən, *Am:* ˌɑːpə-] *n* **1.** *no pl* (*way of working*) funcionamiento *m;* **to come into ~** (*machines*) entrar en funcionamiento **2.** *a.* MED, MIL, MAT operación *f;* **rescue ~** operación de rescate **3.** (*financial transaction*) operación *f* comercial

operational [ˌɒpə'reɪʃənl, *Am:* ˌɑːpə-] *adj* **1.** (*relating to operations*) operativo, -a; **~ commander** MIL jefe *mf* de operaciones **2.** (*working*) **to be ~** estar en funcionamiento

operative ['ɒpərətɪv, *Am:* 'ɑːpərət̬ɪv] **I.** *n* **1.** (*worker*) operario, -a *m, f* **2.** (*detective*) agente *mf* **II.** *adj* **1.** (*rules*) en vigor **2.** MED quirúrgico, -a

operator ['ɒpəreɪtə^r, *Am:* 'ɑːpəreɪt̬ə^r] *n* **1.** (*person*) operador(a) *m(f)*; TEL telefonista *mf;* **machine ~** maquinista *mf;* **he's a smooth** ~ *inf* sabe conseguir lo que quiere **2.** (*company*) empresa *f*

operetta [ˌɒpə'retə, *Am:* ˌɑːpə'ret̬-] *n* opereta *f*

ophthalmic [ɒf'θælmɪk, *Am:* ɑːf-] *adj* (*clinic*) oftalmológico, -a, de oftalmología; (*surgeon*) oftalmólogo, -a; (*vein*) oftálmico, -a

ophthalmic optician *n* oculista *mf*

ophthalmologist [ˌɒpθə'mɒlədʒɪst, *Am:* ˌɑːfθæl'mɑːlə-] *n* oftalmólogo, -a *m, f*

opiate ['əʊpiət, *Am:* 'oʊpiɪt] *n* opiáceo *m*

opinion [ə'pɪnjən] *n* opinión *f*

opinionated [ə'pɪnjəneɪtɪd, *Am:* -t̬ɪd] *adj pej* dogmático, -a

opinion poll *n* encuesta *f* de opinión

opium ['əʊpiəm, *Am:* 'oʊ-] *n no pl* opio *m*

opium den *n* fumadero *m* de opio

opossum [ə'pɒsəm, *Am:* -'pɑːsəm] *n* zarigüeya *f*, zorro *m Méx*

opponent [ə'pəʊnənt, *Am:* -'poʊ-] *n* **1.** POL opositor(a) *m(f)* **2.** SPORTS contrincante *mf*, rival *mf*

opportune ['ɒpətjuːn, *Am:* ˌɑːpə'tuːn] *adj* oportuno, -a

opportunism [ˌɒpə'tjuːhɪzəm, *Am:* ˌɑːpə-'tuː-] *n no pl* oportunismo *m*

opportunist [ˌɒpə'tjuːnɪst, *Am:* ˌɑːpə'tuː-] **I.** *n* oportunista *mf* **II.** *adj* oportunista

opportunity [ˌɒpə'tjuːnəti, *Am:* ˌɑːpə'tuː-nət̬i] <-ies> *n* oportunidad *f;* **~ to do** [*o* **of doing**] **sth** oportunidad de hacer algo; **at the earliest ~** lo antes posible

oppose [ə'pəʊz, *Am:* -'poʊz] *vt* **1.** (*be against*) oponerse a, estar en contra de **2.** (*resist*) combatir **3.** (*be on other team, play against*) enfrentarse a

opposed *adj* opuesto, -a; **to be ~ to sth** oponerse a algo, estar en contra de algo

opposing *adj* (*opinion*) opuesto, -a, contrario, -a; (*team*) contrario, -a

opposite ['ɒpəzɪt, *Am:* 'ɑːpə-] **I.** *n* contrario *m;* **quite the ~!** ¡todo lo contrario! **►~s attract** los extremos se atraen **II.** *adj* **1.** (*absolutely different*) contrario, -a; **the ~ sex** el sexo opuesto **2.** (*facing*) de enfrente; **~ to/ from sth** enfrente a/de algo; **his ~ number** su homólogo **III.** *adv* (*facing*) enfrente; **he lives ~** vive enfrente **IV.** *adj* enfrente de, frente a; **~ to sth** enfrente de algo; **~ me** frente a mí; **to sit ~** (*one another*) estar sentados uno frente al otro

opposition [ˌɒpə'zɪʃən, *Am:* ˌɑːpə-] *n no pl* **1.** POL oposición *f* **2.** (*contrast*) contraposición *f;* **in ~ to sth** en contraposición a algo **3.** (*opponent*) adversario, -a *m, f;* ECON competencia *f*

oppress [ə'pres] *vt* oprimir

oppression [ə'preʃən] *n no pl* **1.** (*submission*) opresión *f* **2.** (*feeling*) agobio *m*

oppressive [ə'presɪv] *adj* **1.** (*harsh: regime, measures*) opresivo, -a **2.** (*burdensome*) agobiante; (*heat*) sofocante

oppressor [ə'presə^r, *Am:* -ə^r] *n* opresor(a) *m(f)*

opt [ɒpt, *Am:* ɑːpt] *vi* optar; **to ~ to do sth** optar por hacer algo; **to ~ for sth** optar por algo

◆**opt in** *vi* **to ~ (to sth)** apuntarse (a algo)

◆**opt out** *vi* **to ~ (of sth)** borrarse (de algo)

optic ['ɒptɪk, *Am:* 'ɑːp-] **I.** *n inf* ojo *m* **II.** *adj* óptico, -a

optical ['ɒptɪkl, *Am:* 'ɑːp-] *adj* óptico, -a

optician [ɒp'tɪʃən, *Am:* ɑːp-] *n* MED óptico, -a *m, f*

optics ['ɒptɪks, *Am:* 'ɑːp-] *n* óptica *f*

optimal ['ɒptɪml, *Am:* 'ɑːp-] *adj* óptimo, -a

optimism ['ɒptɪmɪzəm, *Am:* 'ɑːptə-] *n no pl* optimismo *m*

optimist ['ɒptɪmɪst, *Am:* 'ɑːptə-] *n* optimista *mf*

optimistic [ˌɒptɪ'mɪstɪk, *Am:* ˌɑːptə-] *adj* optimista

optimize ['ɒptɪmaɪz, *Am:* 'ɑːptə-] *vt* optimizar

optimum ['ɒptɪməm, *Am:* 'ɑːptə-] **I.** *n* <-ma> **the ~** lo ideal **II.** *adj* óptimo, -a

option ['ɒpʃən, *Am:* 'ɑːp-] *n* **1.** (*choice*) *a.* ECON opción *f;* **to have no ~ but to do sth** no tener más remedio que hacer algo; **call ~** opción de compra **2.** (*possibility*) posibilidad *f*

optional ['ɒpʃənl, *Am:* 'ɑːp-] *adj* opcional; (*subject*) optativo, -a

opulence ['ɒpjʊləns, *Am:* 'ɑːpjə-] *n no pl* opulencia *f*

opulent ['ɒpjʊlənt, *Am:* 'ɑːpjə-] *adj* opulento, -a

or [ɔːʳ, *Am:* ɔːr] *conj* o; (*before o, ho*) u; (*between numbers*) ó; **seven ~ eight** siete u ocho; **6 ~ 7** 6 ó 7; **either ... ~ ...** o... o...; **to ask whether ~ not sb is coming** preguntar si alguien viene o no; **I can't read ~ write** no sé leer ni escribir

oracle ['ɒrəkl, *Am:* 'ɔːr-] *n* oráculo *m*

oracular [ə'rækjʊləʳ, *Am:* ɔː'rækjuːləʳ] *adj* del oráculo

oral ['ɔːrəl] *adj* **1.** (*tradition, exam, statement*) oral **2.** (*medication*) por vía oral; (*contraceptive, sex*) oral

orange ['ɒrɪndʒ, *Am:* 'ɔːrɪndʒ] **I.** *n* naranja *f;* **~ drink** naranjada *f* **II.** *adj* naranja

orangeade [ˌɒrɪndʒ'eɪd, *Am:* ˌɔːrɪndʒ'-] *n Am* naranjada *f*

orange grove *n* naranjal *m* **orange juice** *n* zumo *m* de naranja

orange peel *n* piel *f* de naranja **orange tree** *n* naranjo *m*

orang-outan(g) *n,* **orang-utan** [ɔːˌræŋ-uːˈtæn, *Am:* ɔːˈræŋətæn] *n* orangután *m*

oration [ɔː'reɪʃən] *n* discurso *m;* **funeral ~** oración *f* fúnebre

orator ['ɒrətəʳ, *Am:* 'ɔːrətəʳ] *n* orador(a) *m(f)*

oratorical [ˌɒrə'tɒrɪkl, *Am:* ˌɔːrə'tɔːr-] *adj* oratorio, -a

oratorio [ˌɒrə'tɔːrɪəʊ, *Am:* ˌɔːrə'tɔːrɪoʊ] *n* MUS oratorio *m*

orb [ɔːb, *Am:* ɔːrb] *n liter* esfera *f*

orbit ['ɔːbɪt, *Am:* 'ɔːr-] **I.** *n* **1.** ASTR órbita *f;* **to go into ~** entrar en órbita **2.** (*range of action, field*) campo *m* de influencia **II.** *vi* orbitar **III.** *vt* orbitar alrededor de

orbital ['ɔːbɪtl, *Am:* 'ɔːrbɪtl̩] *adj* orbital; **~ path** camino *m* de circunvalación

orchard ['ɔːtʃəd, *Am:* 'ɔːrtʃəd] *n* huerto *m;* **cherry ~** cerezal *m*

orchestra ['ɔːkɪstrə, *Am:* 'ɔːrkɪstrə] *n* orquesta *f*

orchestral [ɔː'kestrəl, *Am:* ɔːr'-] *adj* orquestal

orchestra pit *n* foso *m* orquestal **orchestra stalls** *n Brit* platea *f*

orchestrate ['ɔːkɪstreɪt, *Am:* 'ɔːr-] *vt* **1.** MUS orquestar **2.** *fig* (*arrange*) organizar

orchestration [ˌɔːkɪ'streɪʃən, *Am:* ˌɔːr-] *n* **1.** MUS orquestación *f* **2.** *fig* (*arrangement*) organización *f*

orchid ['ɔːkɪd, *Am:* 'ɔːr-] *n* orquídea *f*

ordain [ɔː'deɪn, *Am:* ɔːr'-] *vt* **1.** REL ordenar; **to ~ sb as a priest** ordenar sacerdote a alguien **2.** (*decree, order*) **to ~ that ...** decretar que +*subj*

ordeal [ɔː'diːl, *Am:* ɔːr'-] *n* calvario *m*

order ['ɔːdəʳ, *Am:* 'ɔːrdəʳ] **I.** *n* **1.** *no pl* (*sequence*) orden *m;* **to put sth in ~** poner en orden algo; **to leave sth in ~** dejar ordenado algo; **in alphabetical ~** en orden alfabético **2.** (*instruction*) *a.* LAW, REL orden *f;* **to give/ receive an ~** dar/recibir una orden; **by ~ of sb** por orden de alguien **3.** (*working condition, satisfactory arrangement*) orden *m;* **to keep ~** mantener el orden; **a new world ~** un nuevo orden mundial; **the car is in perfect working ~** el coche funciona perfectamente bien; **to be out of ~** no funcionar; (*toilet*) estar fuera de servicio; **are your immigration papers in ~?** ¿tienes los papeles de inmigración en regla? **4.** (*appropriate behavior*) **out of ~** improcedente **5.** (*purpose*) **in ~** (not) to para (no); **in ~ for, in ~ that** para que +*subj* **6.** *Brit* (*social class, rank, kind*) clase *f* **7.** (*request to supply goods or service*) pedido *m;* **made to ~** hecho por encargo **8.** (*architectural style*) orden *m;* **Doric ~** orden dórico **II.** *vi* pedir; **are you ready to ~?** ¿ya han decidido qué van a tomar [*o* pedir]? **III.** *vt* **1.** (*command*) **to ~ sb to do sth** ordenar a alguien que haga algo; **to ~ sb out** echar a alguien **2.** (*request goods or service*) pedir **3.** (*arrange*) ordenar, poner en orden; **to ~ one's thoughts** ordenar los pensamientos de uno **4.** (*arrange according to procedure*) organizar

order book *n* libro *m* de pedidos **order form** *n* hoja *f* de pedidos

orderly ['ɔːdəli, *Am:* 'ɔːrdəli] <-ies> **I.** *n* **1.** (*hospital attendant*) celador(a) *m(f)* **2.** MIL ordenanza *mf* **II.** *adj* **1.** (*tidy*) ordenado, -a **2.** (*well-behaved*) disciplinado, -a

ordinal ['ɔːdɪnəl, *Am:* 'ɔːrdənəl] *n,* **ordinal number** *n* ordinal *m*

ordinance ['ɔːdənənts, *Am:* 'ɔːrdən-] *n*

ordenanza *f*

ordinary [ˈɔːdənəri, *Am:* ˈɔːrdənər-] I. *n no pl* out of the ~ fuera de lo común; **nothing out of the** ~ nada excepcional II. *adj* normal, corriente; **in the** ~ **way** ... normalmente...

ordinary seaman <-men> *n* marinero *m* de segunda clase **ordinary share** *n* acción *f* ordinaria

ordnance [ˈɔːdnənts, *Am:* ˈɔːrd-] *n* artillería *f*

ordure [ˈɔːdjʊəʳ, *Am:* ˈɔːrdʒɚ] *n no pl* inmundicia *f*

ore [ɔːʳ, *Am:* ɔːr] *n* mena *f*; iron/copper ~ mineral *m* de hierro/cobre

oregano [ˌɒrɪˈɡɑːnəʊ, *Am:* ɔːˈreɡənoʊ] *n no pl* orégano *m*

organ [ˈɔːɡən, *Am:* ˈɔːr-] *n* órgano *m*

organ donor *n* donante *mf* de órganos **organ grinder** *n* organillero, -a *m, f*

organic [ɔːˈɡænɪk, *Am:* ɔːrˈ-] *adj* **1.** (*disease, substance, compound*) orgánico, -a **2.** (*produce, farming method*) biológico, -a **3.** (*fundamental: part*) inherente **4.** (*systematic: change*) sistemático, -a

organisation *n s.* **organization**

organism [ˈɔːɡənɪzəm, *Am:* ˈɔːr-] *n* organismo *m*

organist [ˈɔːɡənɪst, *Am:* ˈɔːr-] *n* organista *mf*

organization [ˌɔːɡənaɪˈzeɪʃən, *Am:* ˌɔːrɡənɪˈ-] *n* organización *f*

organizational [ˌɔːɡənaɪˈzeɪʃənəl, *Am:* ˌɔːrɡənɪˈ-] *adj* organizativo, -a

organization chart *n* ECON organigrama *m* **Organization for Economic Cooperation and Development** *n* Organización *f* para la Cooperación y el Desarrollo Económico **Organization of African Unity** *n no pl* Organización *f* para la Unidad Africana **Organization of Petroleum Exporting Countries** *n* Organización *f* de Países Exportadores de Petróleo

organize [ˈɔːɡənaɪz, *Am:* ˈɔːr-] I. *vt* organizar II. *vi* organizarse; (*form trade union*) sindicarse

organized *adj* **1.** (*systemized*) ordenado, -a **2.** (*arranged, brought together in a trade union*) organizado, -a

organizer *n* **1.** (*person*) organizador(a) *m(f)* **2.** INFOR agenda *f* electrónica

orgasm [ˈɔːɡæzəm, *Am:* ˈɔːr-] I. *n* orgasmo *m* II. *vi* tener un orgasmo

orgasmic [ɔːˈɡæsmɪk, *Am:* ɔːrˈ-] *adj* orgásmico, -a

orgy [ˈɔːdʒi, *Am:* ˈɔːr-] <-ies> *n* orgía *f*

orient [ˈɔːriənt] *vt Am* to ~ **oneself** orientarse

Orient [ˈɔːriənt] *n* the ~ el Oriente

oriental [ˌɔːriˈentəl] *adj* oriental

orientate [ˈɔːriənteɪt, *Am:* ˈɔːrien-] *vr* to ~ **oneself** orientarse

orientation [ˌɔːriənˈteɪʃən, *Am:* ˌɔːrien-] *n* orientación *f*

orienteering [ˌɔːriənˈtɪərɪŋ, *Am:* ˌɔːrienˈtɪr-] *n no pl* orientación *f*

orifice [ˈɒrɪfɪs, *Am:* ˈɔːrə-] *n form* orificio *m*

origin [ˈɒrɪdʒɪn, *Am:* ˈɔːrədʒɪn] *n* origen *m*

original [əˈrɪdʒənəl, *Am:* əˈrɪdʒɪ-] I. *n* original *m* II. *adj* original, originario, -a; ~ **sin** pecado *m* original

originality [əˌrɪdʒənˈæləti, *Am:* əˌrɪdʒɪˈnæləti] *n no pl* originalidad *f*

originally [əˈrɪdʒənəli, *Am:* əˈrɪdʒɪ-] *adv* **1.** (*initially*) originariamente **2.** (*unusually*) con originalidad

originate [əˈrɪdʒəneɪt, *Am:* əˈrɪdʒɪ-] I. *vi* originarse II. *vt* crear

Orkney Islands [ˈɔːkniˌaɪləndz, *Am:* ˈɔːrk-] *n* the ~ las Órcadas

Orleans [ˈɔːliənz, *Am:* ˈɔːrliənz] *n* Orleáns *m*

ornament[1] [ˈɔːnəmənt, *Am:* ˈɔːr-] *n* adorno *m*

ornament[2] [ɔːnəˈmənt, *Am:* ɔːr-] *vt* adornar

ornamental [ˌɔːnəˈmentl, *Am:* ˌɔːrnəˈmentl] *adj* ornamental, decorativo, -a

ornamentation [ˌɔːnəmenˈteɪʃən, *Am:* ˌɔːr-] *n no pl, form* ornamentación *f*, decoración *f*

ornate [ɔːˈneɪt, *Am:* ɔːrˈ-] *adj* **1.** (*elaborately decorated*) ornamentado, -a **2.** (*language, style*) florido, -a

ornithologist [ˌɔːnɪˈθɒlədʒɪst, *Am:* ˌɔːrnəˈθɑːlə-] *n* ornitólogo, -a *m, f*

ornithology [ˌɔːnɪˈθɒlədʒi, *Am:* ˌɔːrnəˈθɑːlə-] *n no pl* ornitología *f*

orphan [ˈɔːfn, *Am:* ˈɔːr-] I. *n* huérfano, -a *m, f*, guacho, -a *m, f Arg, Chi* II. *vt* to be ~ed quedar huérfano

orphanage [ˈɔːfnɪdʒ, *Am:* ˈɔːr-] *n* orfanato *m*, orfelinato *m*

orthodontist [ˌɔːθəʊˈdɒntɪst, *Am:* ˌɔːrθoʊˈdɑːntɪst] *n* ortodoncista *mf*

orthodox [ˈɔːθədɒks, *Am:* ˈɔːrθədɑːks] *adj* ortodoxo, -a

orthodoxy [ˈɔːθədɒksi, *Am:* ˈɔːrθədɑːk-] <-ies> *n* ortodoxia *f*

orthogonal [ɔːˈθɒɡənl, *Am:* ɔːrˈθɑːɡən-] *adj* MAT ortogonal

orthographic(al) [ˌɔːθəˈɡræfɪk(l), *Am:* ˌɔːrθoʊˈ-] *adj* ortográfico, -a

orthography [ɔːˈθɒɡrəfi, *Am:* -ˈθɑːɡrə-] *n no pl* ortografía *f*

orthopaedic [ˌɔːθəˈpiːdɪk, *Am:* ˌɔːrθoʊˈ-] *adj Brit* ortopédico, -a; ~ **surgery** ortopedia *f*

orthopaedics [ˌɔːθəˈpiːdɪks, *Am:* ˌɔːrθoʊˈ-] *npl Brit* ortopedia *f*

orthopaedist [ˌɔːθəˈpiːdɪst, *Am:* ˌɔːrθoʊˈ-] *n Brit* ortopedista *mf*

orthopedic [ˌɔːθəˈpiːdɪk, *Am:* ˌɔːrθoʊˈ-] *adj Am s.* **orthopaedic**

orthopedics [ˌɔːθəˈpiːdɪks, *Am:* ˌɔːrθoʊˈ-] *npl Am s.* **orthopaedics**

orthopedist [ˌɔːθəˈpiːdɪst, *Am:* ˌɔːrθoʊˈ-] *n Am s.* **orthopaedist**

OS [ˌəʊˈes, *Am:* ˌoʊ-] **1.** *abbr of* ordinary seaman marinero *m* **2.** *abbr of* Ordnance Sur-

O

vey servicio *m* oficial de topografía y cartografía

oscillate ['ɒsɪleɪt, *Am:* 'ɑːsleɪt] *vi a.* PHYS oscilar; (*prices*) fluctuar; **to ~ between hope and despair** moverse entre la esperanza y la resignación

oscillation [ˌɒsɪ'leɪʃən, *Am:* ˌɑːsl'eɪ-] *n a.* PHYS oscilación *f*; (*of prices*) fluctuación *f*

oscilloscope [ə'sɪləskəʊp, *Am:* -skoʊp] *n* osciloscopio *m*

osier ['əʊziə', *Am:* 'oʊʒɚ] *n* **1.**(*tree*) mimbrera *f* **2.**(*branch*) mimbre *m*

osmosis [ɒz'məʊsɪs, *Am:* ɑːz'moʊ-] *n* ósmosis *f inv*

osprey ['ɒsprɪ, *Am:* 'ɑːspri] *n* águila *f* pescadora

ossify ['ɒsɪfaɪ, *Am:* 'ɑːsə-] <-ie-> **I.** *vi* **1.**(*turn into bone*) osificarse **2.** *fig* (*become rigid*) anquilosarse **II.** *vt* **1.**(*turn into bone*) osificar **2.** *fig* (*cause to be rigid*) anquilosar

ostensible [ɒ'stensəbl, *Am:* ɑː'sten-] *adj* aparente, pretendido, -a

ostentation [ˌɒsten'teɪʃən, *Am:* ˌɑːstən'-] *n no pl, pej* ostentación *f*

ostentatious [ˌɒsten'teɪʃəs, *Am:* ˌɑːstən'-] *adj pej* ostentoso, -a

osteoarthritis [ˌɒstɪəʊə'θraɪtɪs, *Am:* ˌɑːstɪoʊɑːr'θraɪtɪs] *n no pl* osteoartritis *f*

osteopath ['ɒstɪəʊpɑːθ, *Am:* 'ɑːstɪoʊpæθ] *n* MED osteópata *mf*

osteoporosis [ˌɒstɪəʊpə'rəʊsɪs, *Am:* ˌɑːstɪoʊpə'roʊ-] *n no pl* osteoporosis *f*

ostracism ['ɒstrəsɪzəm, *Am:* 'ɑːstrə-] *n no pl* ostracismo *m*

ostracize ['ɒstrəsaɪz, *Am:* 'ɑːstrə-] *vt* hacer el vacío a, aislar

ostrich ['ɒstrɪtʃ, *Am:* 'ɑːstrɪtʃ] *n* avestruz *f*

OT *abbr of* **Old Testament** A. T.

other ['ʌðə', *Am:* -ɚ] **I.** *adj* **1.**(*different*) otro, -a; **some ~ way of doing sth** alguna otra forma de hacer algo **2.**(*remaining*) **the ~ one** el otro; **the ~ three** los otros tres; **any ~ questions?** ¿alguna otra pregunta? **3.**(*being vague*) **some ~ time** en algún otro momento; **the ~ day** el otro día; **every ~ day** un día sí y otro no **II.** *pron* **1.**(*people*) **the ~s** los otros; **no ~ than he** *form* nadie excepto él **2.**(*different ones*) **each ~** uno a(l) otro, mutuamente; **some eat, ~s drink** algunos comen, otros beben; **there might be ~s** puede haber otros **3.** *sing* (*either/or*) **to choose one or the ~** escoger uno u otro; **not to have one without the ~** no tener uno sin el otro **4.**(*being vague*) **someone or ~** alguien **III.** *adv* de otra manera; **somehow or ~** de una manera u otra

otherwise ['ʌðəwaɪz, *Am:* '-ɚ-] **I.** *adj form* distinto, -a **II.** *adv* **1.**(*differently: behave, act*) de otro modo **2.**(*in other ways*) ~, ... por lo demás,... **III.** *conj* si no

OTT [ˌəʊtiː'tiː, *Am:* ˌoʊ-] *Brit abbr of* **over the top** exagerado, -a

otter ['ɒtə', *Am:* 'ɑːt̬ɚ] *n* nutria *f*

OU [ˌəʊ'juː, *Am:* ˌoʊ-] *n Brit abbr of* **Open University** ≈ UNED *f*

ouch [aʊtʃ] *interj* ay

ought [ɔːt, *Am:* ɑːt] *aux* **1.**(*have as duty*) deber; **you ~ to do it** deberías [*o* tendrías que] hacerlo **2.**(*be likely*) tener que; **he ~ to be here** tendría que [*o* debería] estar aquí; **they ~ to win** merecerían ganar **3.**(*probability*) **she ~ to have arrived by now** debe haber llegado ya

ounce [aʊns] *n* **1.**(*weight*) onza *f* (*28,4 g*) **2.**(*of decency, sense*) pizca *f*

our ['aʊə', *Am:* 'aʊɚ] *adj pos* nuestro, -a; ~ **house** nuestra casa; ~ **children** nuestros hijos

ours ['aʊəz, *Am:* 'aʊɚz] *pron pos* el nuestro, la nuestro; **it's not their bag, it's ~** no es su bolsa, es nuestra; **this house is ~** esta casa es nuestra; **a book of ~** un libro nuestro; ~ **is bigger** el nuestro es mayor

ourselves [aʊə'selvz, *Am:* aʊɚ-] *pron reflexive* **1.** nos; *emphatic* nosotros mismos, nosotras mismas; **we hurt ~** nos lastimamos **2.** *after prep* nosotros, -as (mismos, mismas)

oust [aʊst] *vt* (*rival*) desbancar; (*president*) derrocar

out [aʊt] **I.** *vt* **1.**(*eject*) echar **2.**(*reveal homosexuality*) revelar la homosexualidad de **II.** *adj* **1.**(*absent: person*) fuera **2.**(*released: book, news*) publicado, -a **3.** BOT (*flower*) en flor **4.**(*visible*) **the sun/the moon is ~** ha salido el sol/la luna **5.**(*finished*) **before the week is ~** antes de que acabe la semana **6.**(*not functioning: fire, light*) apagado, -a; (*workers*) en huelga **7.** SPORTS (*not playing*) fuera; *a. fig* eliminado, -a; ~ **for the count** fuera de combate **8.**(*not possible*) **it is ~** está descartado, eso es imposible **9.**(*unfashionable*) pasado, -a de moda **III.** *adv* **1.**(*not inside*) fuera, afuera; **to go ~** salir fuera; **get ~!** ¡fuera! **2.**(*outside*) afuera; **keep ~!** ¡no entrar!; **to eat ~** comer fuera **3.**(*remove*) **to cross ~ words** tachar palabras; **to get a stain ~** sacar una mancha; **to put ~ a fire** apagar un fuego **4.**(*available*) **the best one ~** el mejor disponible **5.**(*away*) **to be ~** (*person*) no estar; **to go ~ to India** salir para la India; **to be ~ at sea** estar mar adentro; **the tide is going ~** la marea está bajando **6.**(*wrong*) **to be ~ in one's calculations** estar equivocado en los cálculos **7.**(*unconscious*) **to pass ~** perder el conocimiento; **to be ~ cold** estar fuera de combate ▶**to be ~ and about** (*on the road*) estar en camino; (*healthy*) estar repuesto; ~ **with it!** ¡desembucha! **IV.** *prep* **1.**(*towards outside*) ~ **of** fuera de; **to go ~ of the room** salir de la habitación; **to go ~ of the door** salir por la puerta; **to jump ~ of bed** saltar de la cama; **to take sth ~ of a box** sacar algo de una caja; **to look/lean ~ of the window** mirar por/apoyarse en la ventana **2.**(*outside from*) ~ **of sight/of reach** fuera de la vista/del alcance; **to drink ~ of a glass** beber de un vaso; **to be ~ of it** estar en otra honda **3.**(*away from*) **to be ~ of town/the country** estar fuera de la ciudad/del país; **to get** ~ **of the rain** salir de la lluvia; ~ **of the way!** ¡fuera del camino! **4.**(*without*) **to be** ~ **of money/work** estar sin dinero/trabajo; ~ **of breath** sin aliento; ~ **of order** averiado, -a **5.**(*not included in*) **to get** ~ **of the habit of doing sth** quitarse el hábito de hacer algo; **his dog is** ~ **of control** su perro está fuera de control **6.**(*from*) **made** ~ **of wood/a blanket** hecho de madera/una manta; **to copy sth** ~ **of a file** copiar algo de un archivo; **to get sth** ~ **of sb** sacar algo a alguien; **to read** ~ **of a novel** leer en una novela; **in 3 cases** ~ **of 10** en 3 de cada 10 casos **7.**(*because of*) **to do sth** ~ **of politeness** hacer algo por cortesía

out-and-out [ˌaʊtəndˈaʊt] *adj* (*liar*, *idiot*) consumado, -a, redomado, -a; (*lie*) como una casa; (*disaster*) total, absoluto, -a

outback [ˈaʊtbæk] *n no pl* **the** ~ el interior (*zona despoblada de Australia*)

outbid [ˌaʊtˈbɪd] *vt irr* **to** ~ **sb** (**for sth**) pujar más que alguien (por algo)

outboard [ˈaʊtbɔːd, *Am:* -bɔːrd] *n*, **outboard motor** *n* fueraborda *m*

outbreak [ˈaʊtbreɪk] *n* (*of flu*, *violence*) brote *m*; (*of war*) estallido *m*

outbuilding [ˈaʊtbɪldɪŋ] *n* dependencia *f*

outburst [ˈaʊtbɜːst, *Am:* -bɜːrst] *n* arrebato *m*

outcast [ˈaʊtkɑːst, *Am:* -kæst] **I.** *n* paria *mf*; **social** ~ marginado, -a *m, f* de la sociedad **II.** *adj* marginado, -a

outclass [ˌaʊtˈklɑːs, *Am:* -ˈklæs] *vt* superar, aventajar

outcome [ˈaʊtkʌm] *n* **1.**(*result*) resultado *m* **2.**(*consequence*) consecuencia *f*

outcrop [ˈaʊtkrɒp, *Am:* -krɑːp] **I.** *n* afloramiento *m* **II.** *vi* aflorar

outcry [ˈaʊtkraɪ] <-ies> *n* gran protesta *f*

outdated [aʊtˈdeɪtɪd, *Am:* -ţɪd] *adj* anticuado, -a, pasado, -a de moda

outdistance [aʊtˈdɪstəns] *vt* dejar atrás

outdo [aʊtˈduː] *vt irr* superar, mejorar; **to** ~ **sb in sth** superar a alguien en algo; **to** ~ **one-self** mejorarse

outdoor [ˈaʊtdɔːʳ, *Am:* ˌaʊtˈdɔːr] *adj* al aire libre; (*clothes*) de calle; (*plants*) de exterior

outdoors [ˌaʊtˈdɔːz, *Am:* ˌaʊtˈdɔːrz] *n* **the great** ~ el aire libre

outer [ˈaʊtəʳ, *Am:* -ţəʳ] *adj* exterior; ~ **ear** oído *m* externo

Outer Hebrides [ˈaʊtəʳ ˈhebrɪdiːz, *Am:* -ţəʳ-] *n* Hébridas *fpl* Exteriores

outermost [ˈaʊtəməʊst, *Am:* -ţəʳməst] *n* más exterior

outfield [ˈaʊtfiːld] *n no pl* (*in cricket, baseball*) parte *f* exterior del campo

outfit [ˈaʊtfɪt] *n* **1.**(*set of clothes*) conjunto *m* **2.**(*team, organization*) equipo *m*; **research** ~ unidad *f* de investigación

outfitter [ˈaʊtfɪtəʳ, *Am:* -fɪţəʳ] *n* **sports** ~**s** tienda *f* de artículos de deporte

outflow [ˈaʊtfləʊ, *Am:* -floʊ] *n* (*of liquid*)

desagüe *m*; (*of capital*) fuga *f*

outgoing [ˈaʊtɡəʊɪŋ, *Am:* ˈaʊtɡoʊ-] **I.** *adj* **1.**(*sociable, extrovert*) sociable, extrovertido, -a **2.**(*retiring: President*) saliente **3.**(*ship*) que sale; ~ **call** llamada *f* al exterior **II.** *n* ~**s** COM salidas *fpl*

outgrow [ˌaʊtˈɡrəʊ, *Am:* -ˈɡroʊ] *vt irr* **1.**(*habit*) pasar de la edad de; **to** ~ **an illness** superar una enfermedad con la edad; **she's** ~**n her trousers** se le han quedado pequeños los pantalones **2.**(*become bigger than*) crecer más que

outgrowth [ˈaʊtɡrəʊθ, *Am:* -ɡroʊθ] *n* **1.** BOT brote *m* **2.**(*result*) resultado *m*

outhouse [ˈaʊthaʊs] *n* **1.** *Brit* (*building*) dependencia *f* **2.** *Am* (*toilet*) retrete *m* exterior

outing [ˈaʊtɪŋ, *Am:* -ţɪŋ] *n* excursión *f*; **to go on an** ~ ir de excursión

outlandish [aʊtˈlændɪʃ] *adj* (*clothes*) estrafalario, -a, extravagante; (*idea*) descabellado, -a

outlast [ˌaʊtˈlɑːst, *Am:* -ˈlæst] *vt* **to** ~ **sth** durar más que algo; **to** ~ **sb** sobrevivir a alguien

outlaw [ˈaʊtlɔː, *Am:* -lɑː] **I.** *n* forajido, -a *m, f* **II.** *vt* (*product, practice*) prohibir; (*person*) proscribir

outlay [ˈaʊtleɪ] *n* desembolso *m*

outlet [ˈaʊtlet] *n* **1.**(*exit*) salida *f* **2.**(*means of expression*) válvula *f* de escape **3.** ECON punto *m* de venta; **retail** ~ tienda *f* al por menor **4.** ELEC toma *f* de corriente

outline [ˈaʊtlaɪn] **I.** *n* **1.**(*draft*) esbozo *m* **2.**(*shape*) perfil *m* **3.**(*general description*) resumen *m* **II.** *vt* **1.**(*draw outer line of*) perfilar **2.**(*describe*) dar una idea general de; (*summarise*) resumir

outlive [ˌaʊtˈlɪv] *vt* sobrevivir a

outlook [ˈaʊtlʊk] *n* **1.**(*prospects*) perspectivas *fpl* **2.**(*attitude*) punto *m* de vista **3.**(*view*) vista *f*

outlying [ˈaʊtˌlaɪɪŋ] *adj* distante, alejado, -a

outmaneuver *vt Am*, **outmanoeuvre** [ˌaʊtməˈnuːvəʳ, *Am:* -vɚ] *vt Brit, Aus* (*person*) mostrarse más hábil que; (*car*) ser más maniobrable que

outmoded [ˌaʊtˈməʊdɪd, *Am:* -ˈmoʊ-] *adj pej* anticuado, -a, pasado, -a de moda

outmost [ˈaʊtməʊst, *Am:* -moʊst] *adj* más remoto, -a

outnumber [ˌaʊtˈnʌmbəʳ, *Am:* -bɚ] *vt* superar en número a

out-of-court settlement *n* arreglo *m* extrajudicial

out-of-date [ˌaʊtəvˈdeɪt, *Am:* ˌaʊţ-] *adj* (*clothes*) anticuado, -a, pasado, -a de moda; (*ticket*) caducado, -a; (*person*) desfasado, -a

out-of-the-way [ˌaʊtəvðəˈweɪ, *Am:* ˌaʊ-ţəvðə-] *adj* apartado, -a

outpatient [ˈaʊtˌpeɪʃənt] *n* paciente *mf* externo, -a

outplay [ˌaʊtˈpleɪ] *vt* jugar mejor que

outpost [ˈaʊtpəʊst, *Am:* -poʊst] *n* **1.** MIL puesto *m* de avanzada **2.** *fig* reducto *m*

O

outpouring [ˈaʊtˌpɔːrɪŋ] *n* desahogo *m;* ~ **of grief** lamento *m* de dolor

output [ˈaʊtpʊt] *n no pl* ECON producción *f;* (*of machine*) rendimiento *m*

output device *n* INFOR dispositivo *m* de salida

outrage [ˈaʊtreɪdʒ] I. *n* 1.(*atrocity*) atrocidad *f;* (*terrorist act*) atentado *m* 2.(*scandal*) escándalo *m;* **to express** ~ (**at sth**) mostrar indignación (ante algo); **to feel a strong sense of** ~ **at sth** sentirse ultrajado por algo II. *vt* (*offend*) ultrajar

outrageous [aʊtˈreɪdʒəs] *adj* 1.(*cruel, violent*) atroz 2.(*shocking: behaviour*) escandaloso, -a; (*clothes*) extravagante, estrafalario, -a; (*person*) atrevido, -a

outré [ˈuːtreɪ, *Am:* uːˈtreɪ] *adj form* extravagante, estrafalario, -a

outrigger [ˈaʊtrɪgəʳ, *Am:* -ɚ] *n* 1.(*stabilizer*) balancín *m* 2.(*boat*) canoa *f* con balancines

outright [ˈaʊtraɪt] I. *adj* (*disaster, defeat*) total; (*winner*) indiscutido, -a; (*hostility*) declarado, -a II. *adv* 1.(*defeat, ignore*) totalmente; (*win*) absolutamente 2.(*declare, ask*) descaradamente

outrun [ˌaʊtˈrʌn] *vt irr* **to** ~ **sb** dejar atrás a alguien

outset [ˈaʊtset] *n no pl* principio *m;* **from the** ~ de entrada

outshine [ˌaʊtˈʃaɪn] *vt irr* eclipsar

outside [ˌaʊtˈsaɪd] I. *adj* 1.(*external*) externo, -a, exterior; (*world*) exterior; (*influence, help*) externo, -a; **the** ~ **door** la puerta exterior; ~ **influences** influencias *fpl* exteriores 2.(*not likely*) **an** ~ **chance that ...** una posibilidad remota de que +*subj* 3.(*highest*) extremo, -a II. *n* 1.(*external part or side*) exterior *m;* **judging from the** ~ a juzgar por el aspecto exterior 2.(*at most*) **at the** ~ a lo más III. *prep* 1.(*not within*) fuera de; **from** ~ **sth** desde fuera de algo; **to play** ~ jugar fuera; **to go** ~ **the house** salir de casa 2.(*next to*) **to wait** ~ **the door** esperar en la puerta 3.(*not during*) ~ **business hours** fuera de horas de oficina 4.(*besides*) además de IV. *adv* 1.(*outdoors*) fuera, afuera; **to go** ~ salir afuera; **to live an hour** ~ **Quito** vivir a una hora de Quito 2.(*beyond*) **to be** ~ **the perimeter** estar afuera del perímetro

outside broadcast *n* transmisión *f* de exteriores **outside lane** *n* AUTO carril *m* de adelantamiento **outside left** *n* extremo *m* izquierdo **outside line** *n* línea *f* exterior

outsider [ˌaʊtˈsaɪdəʳ, *Am:* -dɚ] *n* 1.(*person not from a group*) persona *f* de fuera 2.(*in race, competition*) **to be an** ~ ser un desconocido

outside right *n* extremo *m* derecho

outsize [ˌaʊtˈsaɪz] *adj* muy grande

outskirts [ˈaʊtskɜːts, *Am:* -skɜːrts] *npl* afueras *fpl*

outsourcing [ˈaʊtˌsɔːsɪŋ, *Am:* -ˌsɔːrs-] *n no pl* externalización *f*

outspoken [ˌaʊtˈspəʊkən, *Am:* -ˈspoʊ-] *adj* directo, -a; **to be** ~ no tener pelos en la lengua

outstanding [ˌaʊtˈstændɪŋ] *adj* 1.(*excellent*) destacado, -a 2. FIN (*account*) por pagar; (*debt*) pendiente (de pago) 3.(*unsolved*) por resolver

outstay [ˌaʊtˈsteɪ] *vt* **to** ~ **one's welcome** abusar de la hospitalidad

outstretched [ˌaʊtˈstretʃt] *adj* extendido, -a

outstrip [ˌaʊtˈstrɪp] *vt irr* 1.(*go faster than*) aventajar 2.(*be greater than, exceed*) sobrepasar

out-tray [ˈaʊtˌtreɪ] *n* bandeja *f* de salida

outvote [ˌaʊtˈvəʊt, *Am:* -ˈvoʊt] *vt* vencer en unas elecciones; **to be** ~**d** perder en las elecciones

outward [ˈaʊtwəd, *Am:* -wɚd] I. *n no pl* exterior *m* II. *adj* 1.(*exterior: appearance*) exterior; (*sign*) externo, -a 2.(*voyage*) de ida 3.(*superficial: similarity, difference*) aparente III. *adv* hacia afuera, hacia el exterior

outwardly [ˈaʊtwədli, *Am:* -wɚd-] *adv* aparentemente

outwards [ˈaʊtwədz, *Am:* -wɚdz] *adv* hacia afuera, hacia el exterior

outweigh [ˌaʊtˈweɪ] *vt* 1.(*weight*) pesar más que 2.(*in importance or influence*) tener más peso que

outwit [ˌaʊtˈwɪt] <-tt-> *vt* burlar

outwork [ˌaʊtˈwɜːk, *Am:* ˈaʊtwɜːrk] *n no pl* 1. MIL defensa *f* (fuera de los límites de la fortificación principal) 2. ECON trabajo *m* a domicilio

outworker [ˈaʊtwɜːkəʳ, *Am:* -wɜːrkɚ] *n* trabajador(a) *m(f)* a domicilio

oval [ˈəʊvəl, *Am:* ˈoʊ-] I. *n* óvalo *m* II. *adj* ovalado, -a, oval

Oval Office *n* **the** ~ el despacho oval

ovary [ˈəʊvəri, *Am:* ˈoʊ-] <-ies> *n* ovario *m*

ovation [əʊˈveɪʃən, *Am:* oʊ-] *n* ovación *f;* **to get an** ~ ser ovacionado

oven [ˈʌvən] *n* horno *m*

oven gloves *npl* guantes *mpl* para el horno **ovenproof** [ˈʌvənpruːf] *adj* refractario, -a **oven-ready** [ˌʌvənˈredi] *adj* listo, -a para hornear

over [ˈəʊvəʳ, *Am:* ˈoʊvɚ] I. *prep* 1.(*above*) encima de, por encima de; **to hang the picture** ~ **the desk** colgar el cuadro encima del escritorio; **the bridge** ~ **the motorway** el puente sobre la autopista; **to fly** ~ **the sea** volar sobre el mar; **they'll be a long time** ~ **it** estarán mucho tiempo en ello 2.(*on*) **to hit sb** ~ **the head** golpear a alguien en la cabeza; **to drive** ~ **sth** arrollar algo; **to spread a cloth** ~ **the table** extender un mantel sobre la mesa 3.(*across*) **to go** ~ **the bridge** cruzar el puente; **the house** ~ **the road** la casa de enfrente; **to come from** ~ **the Rhine** venir de la otra orilla del Rin; **it rained all** ~ **England** llovió por toda Inglaterra; **famous all** ~ **the world** famoso en todo el mundo 4.(*behind*) **to look** ~ **sb's shoulder** mirar por encima del hombro de alguien; ~ **the dune** detrás de la duna **5.** (*during*) durante; ~ **the winter** durante el invierno; ~ **time** con el tiempo; ~ **a two year period** durante un período de dos años; **to stay ~ the weekend** quedarse a pasar el fin de semana **6.** (*more than*) **to speak for ~ an hour** hablar durante una hora; ~ **150** más de 150; **children ~ 14** niños de más de 14 (años); ~ **and above that** además de eso **7.** (*through*) **I heard it ~ the radio** lo oí por la radio; **to hear sth ~ the noise** escuchar algo a pesar del ruido; **what came ~ him?** ¿qué le picó? *inf* **8.** (*in superiority to*) **to rule ~ the Romans** gobernar sobre los romanos; **to have command ~ sth** tener mando sobre algo; **to have an advantage ~ sb** tener ventaja sobre alguien **9.** (*about*) ~ **sth** acerca de algo; **to puzzle ~ a problem** romperse la cabeza sobre un problema **10.** (*for checking*) **to go ~ a text** revisar un texto; **to watch ~ a child** cuidar a un niño **11.** (*past*) **to be ~ the worst** haber pasado lo peor **12.** MAT **4 ~ 12 equals a third** 4 entre 12 es igual a un tercio **II.** *adv* **1.** (*moving above: go, jump*) por encima; **to fly ~ the city** volar sobre la ciudad **2.** (*at a distance*) **to move sth ~** apartar algo; ~ **here** acá; ~ **there** allá; ~ **the road** cruzando la calle **3.** (*moving across*) **to come ~ here** venir para acá; **to go ~ there** ir para allá; **he has gone ~ to France** se ha ido a Francia; **he swam ~ to me** nadó hacia mí; **he went ~ to the enemy** *fig* se cambió al bando enemigo **4.** (*on a visit*) **come ~ tonight** pásate por aquí esta noche **5.** (*changing hands*) **to pass/hand sth ~** pasar/dar algo **6.** (*downwards*) **to fall ~** caerse; **to knock sth ~** tirar algo **7.** (*another way up*) **to turn the page/the pancake ~** voltear la página/el pastel **8.** (*in exchange*) **to change ~** intercambiar; **to change ~ (from sth) to sth else** cambiar (de algo) a otra cosa **9.** (*completely*) **that's her all ~** eso es muy (típico) de ella; **to look for sb all ~** buscar a alguien por todos lados; **to turn sth ~ and ~** dar vueltas y vueltas a algo; **to think sth ~** pensar algo (detalladamente) **10.** (*again*) **to count them ~ again** contarlos otra vez; **I repeated it ~ and ~** lo repetí una y otra vez; **to do sth all ~** *Am* hacer algo desde el principio **11.** (*more*) **children of 14 and ~** niños de 14 años en adelante; **7 into 30 goes 4 and 2 ~** 30 entre 7 son 4 y nos quedan 2 **12.** (*sb's turn*) **it's ~ to him** es su turno; ~ RADIO, AVIAT cambio; ~ **and out** cambio y corto **III.** *adj* **1.** (*finished*) acabado, -a; **it's all ~** se acabó; **the snow is ~** se acabó la nieve **2.** (*remaining*) restante; **there are three left ~** quedan tres

overabundant [ˌəʊvərəˈbʌndənt, *Am:* ˌoʊvɚ-] *adj* superabundante

overact [ˌəʊvərˈækt, *Am:* ˌoʊvɚˈ-] *vi* THEAT sobreactuar

overall[1] [ˌəʊvərˈɔːl, *Am:* ˌoʊ-] *n* **1.** (*protective clothing*) bata *f* **2.** *pl* (*one-piece protective suit*) mono *m*; **a pair of ~s** un peto

overall[2] [ˈəʊvərɔːl, *Am:* ˈoʊ-] **I.** *adj* **1.** (*general*) global **2.** (*above all others*) total; ~ **winner** ganador *m* absoluto **II.** *adv* en conjunto

overanxious [ˌəʊvərˈæŋkʃəs, *Am:* ˌoʊvɚˈ-] *adj* demasiado preocupado, -a

overawe [ˌəʊvərˈɔː, *Am:* ˌoʊvɚˈɑː] *vt* intimidar; **to be ~d** sentirse sobrecogido

overbalance [ˌəʊvəˈbæləns, *Am:* ˌoʊvɚˈ-] *vi* perder el equilibrio

overbearing [ˌəʊvəˈbeərɪŋ, *Am:* ˌoʊvɚˈber-] *adj pej* despótico, -a

overblown [ˌəʊvəˈbləʊn, *Am:* ˌoʊvɚˈbloʊn] *adj* ampuloso, -a

overboard [ˈəʊvəbɔːd, *Am:* ˈoʊvɚbɔːrd] *adv* al agua; **to fall ~** caer al agua; **man ~!** ¡hombre al agua!; **to go ~** *inf* exagerar; **to go ~ for sth** *inf* entusiasmarse locamente por algo

overbook [ˌəʊvəˈbʊk, *Am:* ˌoʊvɚˈ-] *vt* sobrereservar

overbooking *n* AVIAT sobrecontratación *f*

overburden [ˌəʊvəˈbɜːdən, *Am:* ˌoʊvɚˈbɜːr-] *vt* sobrecargar

overcapacity <-ies> *n* sobrecapacidad *f*

overcast [ˌəʊvəˈkɑːst, *Am:* ˈoʊvɚkæst] *adj* nublado, -a

over-cautious [ˌəʊvəˈkɔːʃəs, *Am:* ˌoʊvɚˈkɑː-] *adj* demasiado cauto, -a

overcharge [ˌəʊvəˈtʃɑːdʒ, *Am:* ˌoʊvɚˈtʃɑːrdʒ] **I.** *vt* **to ~ sb** cobrar de más a alguien **II.** *vi* cobrar de más

overcoat [ˈəʊvəkəʊt, *Am:* ˈoʊvɚkoʊt] *n* abrigo *m*

overcome [ˌəʊvəˈkʌm, *Am:* ˌoʊvɚˈ-] *irr* **I.** *vt* **1.** (*defeat*) vencer **2.** (*cope with*) superar; (*difficulty*) salvar; **to ~ temptation** no sucumbir a la tentación **II.** *vi irr* vencer

overconfident [ˌəʊvəˈkɒnfɪdənt, *Am:* ˌoʊvɚˈkɑːnfə-] *adj* demasiado seguro, -a de sí mismo, -a

overcooked [ˌəʊvəˈkʊkt, *Am:* ˌoʊvɚˈ-] *adj* recocido, -a

overcrowded [ˌəʊvəˈkraʊdɪd, *Am:* ˌoʊvɚˈ-] *adj* abarrotado, -a

overdeveloped [ˌəʊvədɪˈveləpt, *Am:* ˌoʊvɚ-] *adj* superdesarrollado, -a; PHOT sobrerrevelado, -a

overdo [ˌəʊvəˈduː, *Am:* ˌoʊvɚˈ-] *vt* **1. to ~ things** pasarse; (*work too hard*) trabajar demasiado **2.** *inf* (*exaggerate*) exagerar **3.** (*cook too long*) cocer demasiado

overdone [ˌəʊvəˈdʌn, *Am:* ˌoʊvɚˈ-] *adj* **1.** (*overexaggerated*) exagerado, -a **2.** (*overcooked*) demasiado hecho, -a

overdose [ˈəʊvədəʊs, *Am:* ˈoʊvɚdoʊs] **I.** *n* sobredosis *f inv* **II.** *vi* **to ~ on sth** tomar una sobredosis de algo

overdraft [ˈəʊvədrɑːft, *Am:* ˈoʊvɚdræft] *n* FIN descubierto *m*; **to have an ~** tener un saldo deudor

overdraft facility *n* FIN crédito *m* al descubierto

overdraw [ˌəʊvəˈdrɔː, *Am:* ˌoʊvɚˈdrɑː] *irr* *vi, vt* girar en descubierto

O

overdress [ˌəʊvəˈdres, *Am:* ˌoʊvɚˈ-] *vi* vestirse con demasiada elegancia

overdrive [ˈəʊvədraɪv, *Am:* ˈoʊvɚ-] *n no pl, fig* to go into ~ ir a toda marcha

overdue [ˌəʊvəˈdjuː, *Am:* ˌoʊvɚˈduː] *adj* **1.** (*late*) atrasado, -a; **to be** ~ llevar retraso **2.** FIN (*account*) por pagar; (*debt*) pendiente (de pago)

overeat [ˌəʊvərˈiːt, *Am:* ˌoʊvɚˈ-] *irr vi* comer demasiado

overemphasize [ˌəʊvərˈemfəsaɪz, *Am:* ˌoʊvɚˈ-] *vt* sobreenfatizar

overestimate¹ [ˌəʊvərˈestɪmət, *Am:* ˌoʊvɚˈestɪmɪt] *n* sobreestimación *f*

overestimate² [ˌəʊvərˈestɪmeɪt, *Am:* ˌoʊvɚˈestə-] *vt* sobreestimar

overexcited [ˌəʊvərɪkˈsaɪtɪd, *Am:* ˌoʊvɚɪkˈsaɪt̬ɪd] *adj* sobreexcitado, -a

overexert [ˌəʊvəɪgˈzɜːt, *Am:* ˌoʊvɚɪgˈzɜːrt] *vt* to ~ oneself hacer un esfuerzo excesivo

overexpose [ˌəʊvərɪkˈspəʊz, *Am:* ˌoʊvɚɪkˈspoʊz] *vt* PHOT sobreexponer

overexposure [ˌəʊvərɪkˈspəʊʒəʳ, *Am:* ˌoʊvɚɪkˈspoʊʒɚ] *n no pl* **1.** PHOT sobreexposición *f* **2.** *fig* aparición *f* excesiva en los medios de comunicación

overextend [ˌəʊvərɪkˈstend] *vt* to ~ oneself contraer demasiadas obligaciones financieras

overflow [ˌəʊvəˈfləʊ, *Am:* ˌoʊvɚˈfloʊ] **I.** *n* **1.** (*excess: of liquid*) exceso *m* de líquido; (*of people*) exceso *m* **2.** (*outlet*) rebosadero *m* **II.** *vi* rebosar; (*river*) desbordarse

overfly [ˌəʊvɜˈflaɪ, *Am:* ˌoʊvɚˈ-] <-ie-> *irr vt* sobrevolar

overgrown [ˌəʊvəˈgrəʊn, *Am:* ˌoʊvɚˈgroʊn] *adj* (*garden*) abandonado, -a; **to be** ~ **with** estar cubierto de algo

overhang [ˌəʊvəˈhæŋ, *Am:* ˌoʊvɚˈ-] *irr* **I.** *n* (*cliff*) saliente *m;* ARCHIT alero *m* **II.** *vt* to ~ **sth** sobresalir por encima de algo

overhaul [ˌəʊvəˈhɔːl, *Am:* ˌoʊvɚˈhɑːl] **I.** *n* puesta *f* a punto, revisión *f* **II.** *vt* **1.** (*machine*) poner a punto; (*policy, system*) revisar **2.** (*overtake*) superar

overhead [ˌəʊvəˈhed, *Am:* ˌoʊvɚˈ-] **I.** *n Am* gastos *mpl* generales **II.** *adj* de arriba, encima de la cabeza; ~ **cable** cable *m* aéreo; ~ **light** luz *f* de techo **III.** *adv* en lo alto, por encima de la cabeza

overheads [ˌəʊvəˈheds, *Am:* ˌoʊvɚˈ-] *npl Brit, Aus s.* **overhead**

overhear [ˌəʊvəˈhɪəʳ, *Am:* ˌoʊvɚˈhɪr] *irr vt* oír por casualidad

overheat [ˌəʊvəˈhiːt, *Am:* ˌoʊvɚˈ-] **I.** *vt* sobrecalentar **II.** *vi* recalentarse

overindulge [ˌəʊvərɪnˈdʌldʒ, *Am:* ˌoʊvɚ-] **I.** *vt* consentir **II.** *vi* to ~ **in sth** abusar de algo

overjoyed [ˌəʊvəˈdʒɔɪd, *Am:* ˌoʊvɚˈ-] *adj* encantado, -a

overkill [ˈəʊvəkɪl, *Am:* ˈoʊvɚ-] *n* **1.** MIL sobrecapacidad *f* de exterminación **2.** *fig* exceso *m* de medios

overland [ˈəʊvəlænd, *Am:* ˈoʊvɚ-] **I.** *adj* terrestre; ~ **vehicle** vehículo *m* todoterreno; **by** ~ **mail** por vía terrestre **II.** *adv* por tierra

overlap¹ [ˈəʊvəlæp, *Am:* ˈoʊvɚ-] *n* (*between tiles, planks*) superposición *f;* *fig* (*between knowledge, authority*) coincidencia *f* parcial

overlap² [ˌəʊvəˈlæp, *Am:* ˌoʊvɚˈ-] <-pp-> **I.** *vi* (*between tiles, planks*) superponerse; *fig* (*between knowledge, authority*) coincidir en parte **II.** *vt* solapar

overleaf [ˌəʊvəˈliːf, *Am:* ˈoʊvɚliːf] *adv* al dorso

overload¹ [ˈəʊvələʊd, *Am:* ˈoʊvɚloʊd] *n* **1.** ELEC sobrecarga *f* **2.** (*of work*) exceso *m*

overload² [ˌəʊvəˈləʊd, *Am:* ˌoʊvɚˈloʊd] *vt* ELEC sobrecargar; **to be** ~**ed with sth** *fig* estar agobiado de algo

over-long [ˌəʊvəˈlɒŋ, *Am:* ˌoʊvɚˈlɑːŋ] *adj* demasiado largo, -a

overlook [ˌəʊvəˈlʊk, *Am:* ˌoʊvɚˈ-] **I.** *n Am* vista *f* **II.** *vt* **1.** (*look out onto*) tener vistas a **2.** (*not notice*) pasar por alto; (*deliberately*) no hacer caso de **3.** (*forget*) olvidar

overly [ˈəʊvəli, *Am:* ˈoʊvɚli] *adv* demasiado

overmanning [ˌəʊvəˈmænɪŋ, *Am:* ˌoʊvɚˈ-] *n* exceso *m* de personal

overmuch [ˌəʊvəˈmʌtʃ, *Am:* ˌoʊvɚˈ-] **I.** *adj* excesivo, -a **II.** *adv* en exceso

overnight [ˌəʊvəˈnaɪt, *Am:* ˌoʊvɚˈ-] **I.** *adj* de noche; ~ **bag** bolsa *f* de fin de semana; ~ **stay** estancia *f* de una noche **II.** *adv* durante la noche; **to stay** ~ pasar la noche

overpass [ˈəʊvəpɑːs, *Am:* ˈoʊvɚpæs] *n Am* paso *m* elevado

overpay [ˌəʊvəˈpeɪ, *Am:* ˌoʊvɚˈ-] *irr vt* pagar de más

overpopulated [ˌəʊvəˈpɒpjʊleɪtɪd, *Am:* ˌoʊvɚˈpɑːpjəleɪt̬ɪd] *adj* superpoblado, -a

overpopulation [ˌəʊvəˌpɒpjʊˈleɪʃən, *Am:* ˌoʊvɚˌpɑːpjə-] *n no pl* superpoblación *f*

overpower [ˌəʊvəˈpaʊəʳ, *Am:* ˌoʊvɚˈpaʊɚ] *vt* dominar

overpowering [ˌəʊvəˈpaʊərɪŋ, *Am:* ˌoʊvɚˈpaʊɚ-] *adj* (*person, attack*) abrumador(a); (*taste, smell*) muy fuerte

overproduce [ˌəʊvəprəˈdjuːs, *Am:* ˌoʊvɚproʊˈduːs] **I.** *vi* sobreproducir **II.** *vt* producir en exceso

overrate [ˌəʊvəˈreɪt, *Am:* ˌoʊvɚˈ-] *vt* sobrevalorar

overreach [ˌəʊvəˈriːtʃ, *Am:* ˌoʊvɚˈ-] *vt* to ~ oneself extralimitarse

overreact [ˌəʊvəriˈækt, *Am:* ˌoʊvɚriˈ-] *vi* reaccionar de forma exagerada

overreaction [ˌəʊvəriˈækʃən, *Am:* ˌoʊvɚriˈ-] *n* reacción *f* exagerada

override [ˌəʊvəˈraɪd, *Am:* ˌoʊvɚˈ-] **I.** *n* anulación *f* de automatismo **II.** *vt* **1.** (*not accept*) anular **2.** (*interrupt*) cancelar

overriding [ˌəʊvəˈraɪdɪŋ, *Am:* ˌoʊvɚˈ-] *adj* primordial

overrule [ˌəʊvəˈruːl, *Am:* ˌoʊvɚˈ-] *vt* anular; **to** ~ **an objection** LAW rechazar una objeción

overrun [ˌəʊvəˈrʌn, *Am:* ˌoʊvəʴˈ-] I. *n* sobrecoste *m* II. *vt irr* 1. (*invade*) invadir; **to be ~ with sth** estar plagado de algo 2. (*budget*) exceder III. *vi irr* prolongarse más de lo previsto; **to ~ on costs** excederse en los costes

overseas [ˌəʊvəˈsiːz, *Am:* ˌoʊvəʴˈ-] I. *adj* extranjero, -a; (*trade*) exterior II. *adv* **to go/travel ~** ir/viajar al extranjero

oversee [ˌəʊvəˈsiː, *Am:* ˌoʊvəʴˈ-] *irr vt* supervisar

overseer [ˈəʊvəsɪəʴ, *Am:* ˈoʊvəʴˌsiːəʴ] *n* supervisor(a) *m(f)*

oversell [ˌəʊvəˈsel, *Am:* -vəʴˈ-] *irr vt Am* insistir demasiado en

overshadow [ˌəʊvəˈʃædəʊ, *Am:* ˌoʊvəʴˈʃædoʊ] *vt* 1. (*cast shadow over*) ensombrecer 2. (*make insignificant*) eclipsar

overshoe [ˈəʊvəʃuː, *Am:* ˈoʊvəʴ-] *n* chanclo *m*

overshoot [ˌəʊvəˈʃuːt, *Am:* ˌoʊvəʴˈ-] *irr vt* pasar de, ir más allá de; AVIAT aterrizar más allá de ▶**to ~ the mark** pasarse de la raya

oversight [ˈəʊvəsaɪt, *Am:* ˈoʊvəʴ-] *n* 1. (*omission*) descuido *m;* **by an ~** por equivocación 2. (*supervision*) supervisión *f*

oversimplify [ˌəʊvəˈsɪmplɪfaɪ, *Am:* ˌoʊvəʴˈsɪmplə-] <-ie-> *vt* simplificar excesivamente

oversize [ˌəʊvəˈsaɪz, *Am:* ˌoʊvəʴ-] *adj*, **oversized** *adj* 1. (*too big*) demasiado grande 2. *Am* (*clothes*) de talla grande

oversleep [ˌəʊvəˈsliːp, *Am:* ˌoʊvəʴˈ-] *irr vi* quedarse dormido

overspend [ˌəʊvəˈspend, *Am:* ˌoʊvəʴˈ-] I. *vi* gastar demasiado II. *vt* **to ~ one's allowance** gastar más de la cuenta

overspill [ˈəʊvəspɪl, *Am:* ˈoʊvəʴ-] *n* excedente *m* de población; **~ town** ciudad *f* dormitorio

overstaffed [ˌəʊvəˈstɑːft, *Am:* ˌoʊvəʴˈstæft] *adj* con exceso de personal

overstate [ˌəʊvəˈsteɪt, *Am:* ˌoʊvəʴˈ-] *vt* exagerar

overstay [ˌəʊvəˈsteɪ, *Am:* ˌoʊvəʴˈ-] *vt* **to ~ one's welcome** quedarse más de lo conveniente, abusar de la hospitalidad

overstep [ˌəʊvəˈstep, *Am:* ˌoʊvəʴˈ-] *irr vt* sobrepasar ▶**to ~ the mark** pasarse de la raya

oversubscribed [ˌəʊvəsəbˈskraɪbd, *Am:* ˌoʊvəʴ-] *adj* FIN **the offer was ~** la demanda fue superior a la oferta

oversupply [ˌəʊvəsəˈplaɪ, *Am:* ˌoʊvəʴ-] *n* excedente *m*

overt [ˈəʊvɜːt, *Am:* ˈoʊvɜːrt] *adj* (*criticism*) abierto, -a; (*hostility*) declarado, -a

overtake [ˌəʊvəˈteɪk, *Am:* ˌoʊvəʴ-] *irr* I. *vt* 1. AUTO adelantar; **events have ~n us** los acontecimientos se nos han adelantado 2. (*in contest*) superar II. *vi* adelantar

overtax [ˌəʊvəˈtæks, *Am:* ˌoʊvəʴˈ-] *vt* 1. FIN gravar en exceso (con impuestos) 2. *fig* poner a prueba

over-the-counter [ˌəʊvəðəˈkaʊntəʴ, *Am:* ˌoʊvəʴðəˈkaʊnt̬əʴ] *adj* sin receta

overthrow [ˌəʊvəˈθrəʊ, *Am:* ˌoʊvəʴˈθroʊ] I. *n* derrocamiento *m* II. *vt irr* derrocar

overtime [ˈəʊvətaɪm, *Am:* ˈoʊvəʴ-] *n* 1. (*work*) horas *fpl* extra 2. *Am* SPORTS prórroga *f*

overtired [ˌəʊvəˈtaɪəd, *Am:* ˌoʊvəʴˈtaɪəʴd] *adj* rendido, -a

overtone [ˈəʊvətəʊn, *Am:* ˈoʊvəʴtoʊn] *n* 1. (*implication*) trasfondo *m* 2. MUS armónico *m*

overture [ˈəʊvətjʊəʴ, *Am:* ˈoʊvəʴtʃəʴ] *n* 1. MUS obertura *f* 2. (*show of friendliness*) acercamiento *m;* **to make ~s towards sb** intentar acercarse a alguien

overturn [ˌəʊvəˈtɜːn, *Am:* ˌoʊvəʴˈtɜːrn] I. *vi* volcar, voltearse *AmL* II. *vt* volcar; POL derrumbar

overvalue [ˌəʊvəˈvæljuː, *Am:* ˌoʊvəʴˈ-] *vt* sobrevalorar

overview [ˈəʊvəvjuː, *Am:* ˈoʊvəʴ-] *n* perspectiva *f* general

overweening [ˌəʊvəˈwiːnɪŋ, *Am:* ˌoʊvəʴˈ-] *adj* arrogante

overweight [ˌəʊvəˈweɪt, *Am:* ˌoʊvəʴˈ-] *adj* demasiado pesado, -a; **to be ~** pesar demasiado; **to be ~ by a few kilos** tener un sobrepeso de unos quilos

overwhelm [ˌəʊvəˈwelm, *Am:* ˌoʊvəʴˈ-] *vt* 1. (*overcome by force*) abrumar, sobrecoger; **to be ~ed by sth** estar agobiado por algo 2. (*swamp*) inundar

overwhelming [ˌəʊvəˈwelmɪŋ, *Am:* ˌoʊvəʴˈ-] *adj* abrumador(a); **~ grief** dolor inconsolable; **to feel an ~ need to do sth** sentir una necesidad irresistible de hacer algo

overwork [ˌəʊvəˈwɜːk, *Am:* ˌoʊvəʴˈwɜːrk] I. *n no pl* agotamiento *m* II. *vi* trabajar demasiado III. *vt* hacer trabajar demasiado

overwrought [ˌəʊvəˈrɔːt, *Am:* ˌoʊvəʴˈrɑːt] *adj* 1. (*person*) alterado, -a 2. (*style*) recargado, -a

oviduct [ˈəʊvɪdʌkt] *n* oviducto *m*

oviparous [əʊˈvɪpərəs, *Am:* oʊˈ-] *adj* ovíparo, -a

ovulate [ˈɒvjəleɪt, *Am:* ˈɑːvjuː-] *vi* ovular

ovulation [ˌɒvjəˈleɪʃən, *Am:* ˌɑːvjuːˈ-] *n no pl* ovulación *f*

ovum [ˈəʊvəm, *Am:* ˈoʊ-] <ova> *n* óvulo *m*

owe [əʊ, *Am:* oʊ] I. *vt* deber II. *vi* tener deudas

owing [ˈəʊɪŋ, *Am:* ˈoʊ-] *adj* por pagar

owing to *prep* debido a

owl [aʊl] *n* búho *m*, tecolote *m AmC, Méx;* **barn ~** lechuza *f;* **little ~** mochuelo *m*

owlish [ˈaʊlɪʃ] *adj* sabiondo, -a

own [əʊn, *Am:* oʊn] I. *adj* propio, -a; **to see sth with one's ~ eyes** ver algo con los propios ojos ▶**to be one's own man/person/woman** ser el jefe de uno mismo; **in one's ~ right** por derecho propio; **to do one's ~ thing** ir a su aire; **in one's ~ time** en su tiempo libre; **to hold one's ~** mantenerse firme II. *vt* poseer ▶**as if one ~ed the place** como Pedro por su

o

casa **III.** *vt* **to ~ ...** confesar que...
◆**own up** *vi* confesar; **to ~ up to sth** confesar algo
owner ['əʊnəʳ, *Am:* 'oʊnə-] *n* propietario, -a *m, f;* **to be the ~ of sth** ser el dueño de algo
ownerless ['əʊnələs, *Am:* 'oʊnə-] *adj* sin dueño
owner-occupied *adj* ocupado, -a por el dueño
owner-occupier [,əʊnəʳ'ɒkjəpaɪəʳ, *Am:* ,oʊnə-'ɑ:kju:paɪə] *n* ocupante *mf* propietario, -a
ownership ['əʊnəʃɪp, *Am:* 'oʊnə-] *n no pl* posesión *f;* **to claim ~** reclamar la propiedad; **to be under private/public ~** ser de propiedad privada/pública
own goal *n* autogol *m*
own label goods *npl* productos *mpl* con la etiqueta del establecimiento
ox [ɒks, *Am:* ɑ:ks] <-en> *n* buey *m*
Oxbridge ['ɒksbrɪdʒ, *Am:* 'ɑ:ks-] *n* las universidades de Oxford y Cambridge
ox cart *n* carro *m* de bueyes
OXFAM ['ɒksfæm, *Am:* 'ɑ:ks-] *n Brit abbr of* **Oxford Committee for Famine Relief** *organización benéfica contra el hambre*
oxidation [,ɒksɪ'deɪʃən, *Am:* ,ɑ:ksɪ-] *n* oxidación *f*
oxide ['ɒksaɪd, *Am:* 'ɑ:k-] *n* óxido *m*
oxidize ['ɒksɪdaɪz, *Am:* 'ɑ:k-] **I.** *vi* oxidarse **II.** *vt* oxidar
oxtail ['ɒksteɪl, *Am:* 'ɑ:ks-] *n* rabo *m* de buey
oxtail soup *n* sopa *f* de rabo de buey
oxyacetylene [,ɒksiə'setəli:n, *Am:* ,ɑ:ksiə'setəli:n] *n no pl* oxiacetileno *m*
oxygen ['ɒksɪdʒən, *Am:* 'ɑ:ksɪ-] *n no pl* oxígeno *m*
oxygen cylinder *n* bombona *f* de oxígeno
  oxygen mask *n* máscara *f* de oxígeno
  oxygen tent *n* cámara *f* de oxígeno
oxymoron [,ɒksɪ'mɔ:rɒn, *Am:* ,ɑ:ksɪ'mɔ:-rɑ:n] *n* oxímoron *m*
oyster ['ɔɪstəʳ, *Am:* -stə-] *n* ostra *f*
oyster bank *n,* **oyster bed** *n* banco *m* de ostras
oystercatcher ['ɔɪstəˌkætʃəʳ, *Am:* -stə-ˌkætʃə-] *n* ostrero, -a *m, f*
oz *n abbr of* **ounce** onza *f* (28,4 g)
ozone ['əʊzəʊn, *Am:* 'oʊzoʊn] *n no pl* ozono *m*
ozone layer *n* capa *f* de ozono

P

P, p [pi:] <-'s> *n* P, p *f;* **~ for Peter** P de París ►**to** <u>mind</u> **one's ~s and Qs** cuidarse de no meter la pata
p **1.** *abbr of* **page** pág. *f* **2.** *abbr of* **penny** penique *m*

pa [pɑː] *n inf* papá *m*
PA [,pi:'eɪ] *n* **1.** *abbr of* **personal assistant** ayudante *mf* personal **2.** *abbr of* **public address system** sistema *m* de megafonía **3.** *Am abbr of* **Pennsylvania** Pensilvania *f*
p.a. [,pi:'eɪ] *abbr of* **per annum** por año
pace [peɪs] **I.** *n* **1.** *no pl* (*speed*) velocidad *f;* **to force the ~** forzar el paso; **to quicken one's ~** acelerar el paso; **to set the ~** marcar el ritmo; **to keep ~ with sb** llevar el mismo paso que alguien; **to keep ~ with sth** avanzar al mismo ritmo que algo; **to keep up/to stand the ~** llevar/mantener el ritmo **2.** (*step*) paso *m* ►**to** <u>put</u> **sb through his/her ~s** poner a alguien a prueba; **to spot sth at 20 ~s** reconocer algo a la milla **II.** <pacing> *vt* **1.** (*walk and down*) pasearse por **2.** (*measure in strides*) medir a pasos **3.** SPORTS (*set a speed*) marcar el paso para; **to ~ oneself** controlarse el tiempo **III.** <pacing> *vi* **to ~ up and down** pasearse de un lado para otro
pacemaker ['peɪsˌmeɪkəʳ, *Am:* -kə-] *n* **1.** SPORTS liebre *f* **2.** MED marcapasos *m inv*
pace-setter ['peɪsˌsetəʳ, *Am:* -ˌseṯə-] *n* SPORTS liebre *f*
pachyderm ['pækɪdɜ:m, *Am:* -ədɜ:rm] *n* paquidermo *m*
pacific [pə'sɪfɪk] *adj* pacífico, -a
Pacific [pə'sɪfɪk] **I.** *n* **the ~** el Pacífico; **the ~ Ocean** el Océano Pacífico **II.** *adj* del Pacífico
pacification [,pæsɪfɪ'keɪʃən, *Am:* -əfɪ'-] *n no pl* pacificación *f*
pacifier ['pæsɪfaɪəʳ, *Am:* -əfaɪə-] *n* **1.** (*person*) pacificador(a) *m(f)* **2.** *Am* (*baby's dummy*) chupete *m*
pacifism ['pæsɪfɪzəm, *Am:* 'pæsə-] *n no pl* pacifismo *m*
pacifist ['pæsɪfɪst, *Am:* 'pæsə-] **I.** *n* pacifista *mf* **II.** *adj* pacifista
pacify ['pæsɪfaɪ, *Am:* 'pæsə-] <-ie-> *vt* **1.** (*establish peace*) pacificar **2.** (*calm*) calmar
pack [pæk] **I.** *n* **1.** (*bundle*) fardo *m;* (*rucksack*) mochila *f;* (*packet*) paquete *m;* **ice ~** bolsa *f* de hielo **2.** (*group*) grupo *m;* (*of wolves, hounds*) manada *f* **II.** *vi* (*prepare luggage*) hacer las maletas ►**to send sb ~ing** largar a alguien con viento fresco **III.** *vt* **1.** (*fill: box, train*) llenar; **~ed with information** repleto de información **2.** (*wrap*) envasar; (*put in packages*) empaquetar; **to ~ one's suitcase** hacer la maleta **3.** (*compress*) comprimir
◆**pack away** *vt* **1.** (*put back in place*) guardar **2.** *inf* (*eat*) engullir
◆**pack in I.** *vt* **1.** (*put in*) meter **2.** *inf* (*stop*) dejar; **pack it in!** ¡déjalo! **3.** (*attract audience*) captar **II.** *vi* apiñar
◆**pack off** *vt inf* **to pack sb off** deshacerse de alguien
◆**pack up I.** *vt* **1.** (*put away*) guardar **2.** *inf* (*finish*) terminar **II.** *vi inf* **1.** (*stop work*) dejar de trabajar **2.** *Brit* (*stop functioning*) averiarse
package ['pækɪdʒ] **I.** *n* paquete *m;* **software ~** paquete de software **II.** *vt* **1.** (*pack*)

empaquetar **2.** *fig* echar

package deal *n* acuerdo *m* global con concesiones mutuas **package holiday** *n Brit* viaje *m* organizado **package store** *n Am* licorería *f* **package tour** *n s.* **package holiday**

packaging *n no pl* **1.** (*wrapping*) embalaje *m* **2.** (*action*) envasado *m*

packer ['pækəʳ, *Am:* -ə·] *n* empaquetador(a) *m(f)*, embalador(a) *m(f)*

packet ['pækɪt] *n* **1.** (*parcel*) paquete *m;* (*of biscuits*) caja *f;* (*of cigarettes*) cajetilla *f* **2.** *inf* (*money*) dineral *m*

packing *n no pl* (*action, material*) embalaje *m;* **to do one's** ~ hacer las maletas

packing case *n Brit, Aus* caja *f* de embalaje **packing routine** *n* INFOR rutina *f* de empaquetado

pact [pækt] *n* pacto *m*

pad¹ [pæd] I. *n* **1.** (*cushion*) almohadilla *f;* **knee** ~ rodillera *f;* **mouse** ~ INFOR alfombrilla *f* del ratón; **shin** ~ espinillera *f;* **shoulder** ~ hombrera *f* **2.** (*of blank*) bloc *m* **3.** (*of animal's foot*) almohadilla *f* (de la pata) **4.** AVIAT plataforma *f* **5.** *inf* (*house, flat*) choza *f* **6.** (*water-lily leaf*) hoja *f* de nenúfar II. <-dd-> *vt* acolchar

pad² [pæd] <-dd-> *vi* andar silenciosamente
♦**pad out** *vt* meter paja en; **to** ~ **a speech/ text** inflar un discurso/texto con paja

padded *adj* acolchado, -a; ~ **cell** celda *f* de aislamiento

padding *n no pl, a. fig* relleno *m*

paddle ['pædl] I. *n* **1.** (*type of oar*) canalete *m* **2.** (*act of paddling*) chapoteo *m;* **to go for a** ~ ir a mojarse los pies II. *vt* **1.** (*row*) impulsar con canalete **2.** *Am, inf* (*spank*) zurrar III. *vi* **1.** (*row*) remar con canalete **2.** (*walk, swim*) chapotear

paddle boat *n* vapor *m* de paletas **paddle steamer** *n* vapor *m* de ruedas

paddling pool *n Brit, Aus* estanque *m* para chapotear

paddock ['pædək] *n* **1.** (*enclosed field*) corral *m;* (*at racecourse*) parque *m* **2.** *Aus* (*open field*) prado *m*

paddy¹ ['pædi] <-ies> *n Brit* rabieta *f;* **to get in(to) a** ~ coger una rabieta

paddy² ['pædi] *n,* **paddy field** *n* arrozal *m*

Paddy ['pædi] <-ies> *n pej, inf* irlandés, -esa *m, f*

paddy wagon *n Am, Aus, inf* coche *m* celular

padlock ['pædlɒk, *Am:* -lɑːk] I. *n* candado *m* II. *vt* cerrar con candado

paediatric [ˌpiːdɪˈætrɪk] *adj Brit* pediátrico, -a

paediatrician [ˌpiːdɪəˈtrɪʃən] *n Brit* MED pediatra *mf*

paediatrics [ˌpiːdɪˈætrɪks] *n no pl* pediatría *f*

paedophile ['piːdəʊfaɪl] *n* pederasta *m,* pedófilo *m*

pagan ['peɪgən] I. *n* pagano, -a *m, f* II. *adj*

pagano, -a

paganism ['peɪgənɪzəm] *n no pl* paganismo *m*

page¹ [peɪdʒ] *n* (*in book, newspaper*) a. INFOR página *f;* (*single sheet of paper*) hoja *f;* **front** ~ primera plana *f;* **web** ~ página web

page² [peɪdʒ] I. *n* **1.** (*knight's attendant*) paje *m* **2.** (*hotel worker*) botones *m inv* II. *vt* (*over loudspeaker*) llamar por el altavoz; (*by pager*) buscar llamando por el localizador

pageant ['pædʒənt] *n* (*show, ceremony*) festividades *fpl;* **beauty** ~ concurso *m* de belleza

pageantry ['pædʒəntri] *n no pl* pompa *f*

pageboy ['peɪdʒbɔɪ] *n* **1.** (*in hotel*) botones *m inv* **2.** (*at wedding*) paje *m* **3.** (*hairstyle*) peinado *m* de paje

page layout *n* disposición *f* de página **page proof** *n* prueba *f* de plana

pager ['peɪdʒəʳ, *Am:* -dʒə·] *n* localizador *m*

pagination [ˌpædʒɪˈneɪʃən, *Am:* -ənˈeɪʃən] *n no pl* INFOR, TYPO paginación *f*

pagoda [pəˈgəʊdə, *Am:* -ˈgoʊ-] *n* pagoda *f*

paid [peɪd] I. *pt, pp of* **pay** II. *adj* pagado, -a; ~ **holiday** vacaciones *fpl* remuneradas

paid-up *adj* (*member*) que ha pagado una cuota

pail [peɪl] *n Am* cubo *m*

pain [peɪn] I. *n* **1.** (*physical suffering*) dolor *m;* **to be in** ~ estar sufriendo; **I have a** ~ **in my foot** me duele el pie **2.** *pl* (*great care*) cuidados *mpl;* **to be at** ~s **to do sth** esmerarse en hacer algo; **to spare no** ~s no escatimar esfuerzos ▸**to be a** ~ **in the** backside ser un plomo; **to be a** ~ **in the** neck *inf* ser un coñazo; **on** [*o* under] ~ **of sth** so pena de algo II. *vt* doler; **it** ~s **me ...** me da lástima (que)...

pain barrier *n* umbral *m* de protección

pained *adj* afligido, -a; **a** ~ **expression** una cara de disgusto

painful ['peɪnfəl] *adj* **1.** (*causing physical pain*) doloroso, -a **2.** (*emotionally upsetting*) angustioso, -a **3.** (*embarrassing*) desagradable

painfully *adv* **1.** (*with pain*) dolorosamente **2.** (*shy, obvious*) totalmente

painkiller ['peɪnˌkɪləʳ, *Am:* 'peɪnˌkɪlə·] *n* analgésico *m*

painless ['peɪnləs] *adj* **1.** (*not painful*) indoloro, -a **2.** *fig* (*easy*) fácil

painstaking ['peɪnzˌteɪkɪŋ] *adj* (*research*) laborioso, -a; (*search*) exhaustivo, -a; (*effort*) grande

paint [peɪnt] I. *n no pl* pintura *f* II. *vi* pintar III. *vt* **1.** (*room, picture*) pintar; **to** ~ **a picture of sth** *fig* describir algo **2.** (*apply make-up*) **to** ~ **oneself** maquillarse

paint box *n* caja *f* de pinturas

paintbrush ['peɪntbrʌʃ] <-es> *n* (*for pictures*) pincel *m;* (*for walls*) brocha *f*

painted ['peɪntɪd, *Am:* -t̬ɪd] *adj* pintado, -a

painter¹ ['peɪntəʳ, *Am:* -t̬ə·] *n* **1.** (*artist*) pintor(a) *m(f)* **2.** (*decorator*) pintor(a) *m(f)* (de brocha gorda)

painter² ['peɪntəʳ, *Am:* -t̬ə·] *n* NAUT (*rope*)

amarra *f*

painting *n* **1.**(*painted picture*) cuadro *m*
2. *no pl* (*art*) pintura *f;* **19th century French**
~ pintura francesa del siglo XIX
paint pot *n* bote *m* de pintura **paint roller**
n rodillo *m* **paint stripper** *n* quitapintura *m*
paintwork *n no pl* pintura *f*
pair [peə^r, *Am:* per] *n* **1.**(*two matching*
items) par *m;* **a ~ of gloves/socks** un par de
guantes/calcetines; **a ~ of glasses** unas gafas;
a ~ of scissors unas tijeras; **a ~ of trousers**
un pantalón; **a ~ of tweezers** unas pinzas
2.(*group of two people, animals*) pareja *f;* **in**
~s de dos en dos; **a carriage and ~** un landó
con dos caballos
◆**pair off** I. *vi* aparearse II. *vt* **to pair sb off**
(with sb) emparejar a alguien (con alguien)
pairing *n no pl* apareamiento *m*
pajamas [pə'dʒɑ:məz] *npl Am* pijama *m;* **in**
(one's) ~ en pijama; **a pair of ~** un pijama
Pakistan [ˌpɑ:kɪ'stɑ:n, *Am:* 'pækɪstæn] *n*
Paquistán *m*
Pakistani [ˌpɑ:kɪ'stɑ:ni] I. *n* paquistaní *mf*
II. *adj* paquistaní
pal [pæl] *n inf* **1.**(*friend*) amigo, -a *m, f*
2.(*form of address*) camarada *mf*
◆**pal up** *vi Brit, Aus* hacerse amigos; **to ~**
with sb hacerse amigo de alguien
palace ['pælɪs, *Am:* -əs] *n* palacio *m*
palaeography [ˌpælɪ'ɒgrəfi, *Am:* ˌpeɪlɪ-
'ɑ:grə-] *n no pl* paleografía *f*
palaeolithic [ˌpælɪəʊ'lɪθɪk, *Am:* ˌpeɪlɪoʊ'-]
I. *adj* paleolítico, -a II. *n* **the Palaeolithic** el
Paleolítico
palaeontologist [ˌpælɪɒn'tɒlədʒɪst, *Am:*
ˌpeɪlɪɑ:n'tɑ:lə-] *n* paleontólogo, -a *m, f*
palaeontology [ˌpælɪɒn'tɒlədʒi, *Am:* ˌpeɪ-
lɪɑ:n'tɑ:lə-] *n no pl* paleontología *m*
palatable ['pælətəbl, *Am:* -əʈə-] *adj*
1.(*food*) sabroso, -a **2.**(*suggestion*) aceptable
palate ['pælət] *n* paladar *m;* **to have a deli-**
cate ~ *fig* tener un paladar delicado
palatial [pə'leɪʃl] *adj* suntuoso, -a
palaver [pə'lɑ:və^r, *Am:* -'lævə-] *n inf* lío *m;*
what a ~! ¡menudo follón!
pale¹ [peɪl] I. *adj* **1.**(*lacking colour*) pálido,
-a; **to look ~** tener mal color **2.**(*not dark*)
claro, -a II. *vi* palidecer; **to ~ in comparison**
with sth perder en comparación con algo; **to ~**
into insignificance verse insignificante
pale² [peɪl] *n* (*fence post*) estaca *f* ▶**to be**
beyond the ~ ser inaceptable
paleness ['peɪlnɪs] *n no pl* palidez *f*
Palestine ['pælɪstaɪn, *Am:* -ə-] *n* Palestina *f*
Palestinian [ˌpælə'stɪnɪən] I. *n* palestino, -a
m, f II. *adj* palestino, -a
palette ['pælɪt] *n* ART paleta *f*
palisade [ˌpælɪ'seɪd, *Am:* -ə'-] *n* **1.**(*fence*)
empalizada *f* **2.** *pl, Am* (*cliffs*) acantilados *mpl*
pall¹ [pɔ:l] *vi* perder su interés
pall² [pɔ:l] *n* **1.**(*cloth*) paño *m* mortuorio; **a ~**
of smoke una capa de humo **2.** *Am* (*coffin*)
féretro *m*

pallbearer ['pɔ:lˌbeərə^r, *Am:* -ˌberə-] *n* por-
tador(a) *m(f)* del féretro
pallet ['pælɪt] *n* **1.**(*wooden structure*) paleta
f **2.**(*bed*) jergón *m*
palliative ['pælɪətɪv, *Am:* -ʈɪv] I. *n* paliativo
m II. *adj* paliativo, -a
pallid ['pælɪd] *adj* **1.**(*very pale*) pálido, -a
2.(*lacking verve*) flojo, -a
pallor ['pælə^r, *Am:* -ə-] *n* palidez *f*
pally ['pæli] <-ier, -iest> *adj inf* afable; **to be**
~ with sb ser muy amigo de alguien
palm¹ [pɑ:m] I. *n* (*of hand*) palma *f;* **to read**
sb's ~ leer la mano a alguien ▶**to have sb in**
the ~ of one's hand tener a alguien en la
palma de la mano; **to have sb eating out of**
the ~ of one's hand tener a alguien a su disposición II. *vt* **1.**(*hide*) escamotear **2.**(*steal*)
robar
palm² [pɑ:m] *n* (*tree*) palmera *f*
◆**palm off** *vt* **to palm sth off on sb** encajar
algo a alguien; **to palm sb off with sth** apartar
a alguien con algo
palmist ['pɑ:mɪst] *n* quiromántico, -a *m, f*
palm leaf <leaves> *n* hoja *f* de palmera
Palm Sunday *n* Domingo *m* de Ramos
palpable ['pælpəbl] *adj* palpable
palpitate ['pælpɪteɪt, *Am:* -pə-] *vi* palpitar
palpitations [ˌpælpi'teɪʃnz, *Am:* -pə'-] *npl*
MED palpitaciones *fpl;* **to have ~** tener vahídos
palsy ['pɔ:lzi] *n* MED parálisis *f;* **cerebral ~**
parálisis *f* cerebral
paltry ['pɔ:ltri] <-ier, -iest> *adj* insignificante; (*wage*) miserable
pampas ['pæmpəs, *Am:* -pəz] *n* + *sing/pl vb*
pampa *f*
pamper ['pæmpə^r, *Am:* -pə-] *vt* mimar; **to ~**
oneself mimarse
pamphlet ['pæmflɪt] *n* (*leaflet*) folleto *m;* POL
panfleto *m*
pan¹ [pæn] I. *n* **1.**(*cooking container*)
cazuela *f;* **frying ~** sartén *f* **2.**(*of scales*) platillo *m* **3.**(*of lavatory*) taza *f;* **to go down the**
~ *fig* irse al traste II. *vt Am* (*gold*) separar en la
gamella
pan² [pæn] *vi* CINE panoramizar
pan³ [pæn] *vt inf* dar un palo a; **to ~ a book/**
a film dejar por los suelos un libro/una
película
◆**pan out** *vi* (*develop*) resultar; **to ~ well**
salir bien
panacea [ˌpænə'sɪə] *n* panacea *f*
panache [pə'næʃ] *n no pl* brío *m*
Panama [ˌpænə'mɑ:, *Am:* 'pænəmɑ:] *n*
Panamá *m*
Panama Canal *n* Canal *m* de Panamá
Panama City *n* Ciudad *f* de Panamá
Panamanian [ˌpænə'meɪnɪən] I. *adj* panameño, -a II. *n* panameño, -a *m, f*
Pan-American ['pænə'merɪkən] *adj* pana-
mericano, -a
pancake ['pænkeɪk] *n* crep *m*, panqueque *m*
AmL
Pancake Day *n Brit, inf* martes *m inv* de car-

naval
pancreas ['pæŋkriəs] *n* páncreas *m inv*
pancreatic [ˌpæŋkri'ætɪk, *Am:* ˌpæŋkri'æt̬-] *adj* pancreático, -a
panda ['pændə] *n* panda *m;* **red** ~ panda rojo
panda car *n Brit* coche *m* patrulla
pandemonium [ˌpændə'məʊniəm, *Am:* -də'moʊ-] *n* **1.** (*confusion*) pandemonio *m* **2.** (*noise*) alboroto *m*
pander to ['pædə' tʊ, *Am:* -ə· tə] *vt* consentir
p and p [ˌpiːən'piː] *n abbr of* **postage and packing** correo *m* y embalaje *m*
pane [peɪn] *n* cristal *m;* **window** ~ hoja *f* de cristal de una ventana
panel ['pænəl] **I.** *n* **1.** (*wooden*) tabla *f;* (*metal*) placa *f* **2.** FASHION paño *m* **3.** PUBL tabla *f* **4.** (*team*) panel *m;* (*in exam*) tribunal *m* **5.** (*instrument board*) panel *m;* **control** ~ panel de control; **instrument** ~ AUTO, AVIAT cuadro *m* de mandos **II.** *vt* poner paneles a
panel beater *n* AUTO chapista *mf* **panel discussion** *n* mesa *f* redonda **panel game** *n* TV concurso *m* por equipos
paneling *n no pl* paneles *mpl*
panelist ['pænəlɪst] *n* (*in discussion*) miembro *mf* de una mesa redonda; (*of quiz team*) miembro *mf* de un equipo (de un concurso)
panelling *n s.* **paneling**
panellist ['pænəlɪst] *n s.* **panelist**
pang [pæŋ] *n* punzada *f;* ~**s of remorse** remordimientos *mpl;* ~**s of guilt** sentimiento *m* de culpabilidad
panhandle ['pænhændl] **I.** *n* GEO *faja angosta de territorio de un estado que entra en el de otro* **II.** *vi* mendigar **III.** *vt* **to** ~ **money** pedir dinero
panhandler ['pænhændlə', *Am:* -lə·] *n inf* pordiosero, -a *m, f*
panic ['pænɪk] **I.** *n* pánico *m;* **to get into a** ~ ponerse nervioso; **to be in a** ~ estar nervioso **II.** <-ck-> *vi* ponerse nervioso
panicky ['pænɪki] <-ier, iest> *adj* (*person*) inquieto, -a; (*feeling*) de pánico
panic-stricken ['pænɪkˌstrɪkən] *adj* preso, -a de pánico
pannier ['pæniə', *Am:* -jə·] *n* **1.** (*for bicycle*) cesto *m* **2.** (*for horse*) alforja *f*
panorama [ˌpænə'rɑːmə, *Am:* -'ræmə] *n* panorama *m*
panoramic [ˌpænə'ræmɪk] *adj* panorámico, -a; ~ **view** vista *f* panorámica
panpipes ['pænpaɪps] *npl* zampoña *f*
pan scourer *n Brit* estropajo *m*
pansy ['pænzi] <-ies> *n* **1.** (*flower*) pensamiento *m* **2.** *pej* (*homosexual*) marica *m*
pant [pænt] **I.** *vi* jadear; **to be** ~**ing for** [*o* **after**] **sth** suspirar de [*o* por] algo **II.** *vt* decir jadeando
pantheism ['pænθiɪzəm] *n no pl* panteísmo *m*
pantheistic [ˌpænθi'ɪstɪk] *adj* panteístico, -a
pantheon ['pæθiən, *Am:* -ɑːn] *n* panteón *m*

panther ['pænθə', *Am:* -θə·] *n* **1.** (*black leopard*) pantera *f* **2.** *Am* (*puma*) puma *m*
panties ['pæntɪz, *Am:* -t̬ɪz] *npl* bragas *fpl*
panto ['pæntəʊ, *Am:* -toʊ] *n Brit, inf abbr of* **pantomime** *s.* **pantomime**
pantomime ['pæntəmaɪm, *Am:* -t̬ə-] *n* **1.** *no pl* (*mime*) pantomima *f* **2.** *Brit* (*play*) comedia musical navideña basada en cuentos de hadas **3.** *fig* (*farse*) farsa *f*
pantry ['pæntri] <-ies> *n* despensa *f*
pants [pænts] *npl* **1.** *Brit* (*underpants*) calzoncillos *mpl* **2.** *Am* (*trousers*) pantalones *mpl*
▶**to be caught with one's** ~ **down** *inf* ser cogido con las manos en la masa
pant(s) suit *n Am* traje *m* pantalón (de mujer)
panty-girdle *n* faja *f* pantalón **pantyhose** *npl Am, Aus* medias *fpl* **panty liner** *n* punta *f* del calzón
pap [pæp] *n no pl* **1.** (*food*) papilla *f* **2.** *inf* (*worthless entertainment*) chorrada *f*
papa [pə'pɑː] *n Am, form* papá *m*
papacy ['peɪpəsi] *n no pl* **1.** (*papal office*) pontificado *m* **2.** (*tenure of pope*) papado *m*
papal ['peɪpl] *adj* papal
paparazzo [pæpr'ætsəʊ, *Am:* paːpaˈrɑː-tsoʊ] <paparazzi> *n* paparazzo *m*
papaya [pə'paɪə] *n* papaya *f*, lechosa *f Col, PRico, Ven*
paper ['peɪpə', *Am:* -pə·] **I.** *n* **1.** *no pl* (*for writing*) papel *m;* **a sheet of** ~ una hoja de papel; **to put sth down on** ~ poner algo por escrito; **on** ~ sobre papel **2.** (*newspaper*) periódico *m* **3.** (*wallpaper*) papel *m* para empapelar **4.** (*official document*) documentación *f;* ~**s** papeles *mpl* **5.** *no pl, Brit* (*exam*) examen *m* **6.** (*academic discourse*) conferencia *f;* **to give a** ~ dar un discurso **II.** *vt* **to** ~ **the walls** empapelar las paredes
◆**paper over** *vt fig* disimular
paperback ['peɪpəbæk, *Am:* -pə·-] *n* libro *m* de bolsillo; **in** ~ en rústica
paperback edition *n* edición *f* de bolsillo **paper bag** *n* bolsa *f* de papel **paper boy** *n* repartidor *m* de periódicos **paper chase** *n* **1.** (*race*) carrera por el campo en la que los participantes deben seguir los papelitos que otros han dejado **2.** (*bureaucracy*) papeleo *m* **paper clip** *n* sujetapapeles *m inv*, clip *m* **paper cup** *n* vaso *m* de papel **paper cutter** *n* guillotina *f* **paper doll** *n* muñeca *f* de papel **paper girl** *n* repartidora *f* de periódicos **paper knife** <knives> *n Brit* abrecartas *m inv* **paper mill** *n* fábrica *f* de papel **paper money** *n no pl* papel *m* moneda **paper napkin** *n* servilleta *f* de papel **paper profit** *n* beneficio *m* ficticio **paper round** *n Brit* ruta *f* del repartidor de periódicos **paper route** *n Am s.* **paper round** **paper'thin** *adj* fino, -a como el papel **paper tiger** *n pej* he's only a ~ no es tan bravo el león como lo pintan **paper tissue** *n* pañuelo *m* de papel **paper towel** *n* toallita *f* de papel **paper trail** *n* rastro *m* de documentos **paperweight** *n*

pisapapeles *m inv* **paperwork** *n no pl* trabajo *m* administrativo, papeleo *m inf*

papery ['peɪpəri] *adj* de papel

papier-mâché [ˌpæpɪeɪ'mæʃeɪ, *Am:* ˌpeɪpə'məʃeɪ] *n no pl* cartón *m* piedra

papist ['peɪpɪst] I. *n pej* papista *mf* II. *adj pej* papista

papoose [pə'puːs, *Am:* pæp'uːs] *n* mochila *f* portabebés

pappy[1] ['pæpi] <-ier, -iest> *adj* 1. (*stodgy*) como papilla 2. *pej, inf* (*of poor quality*) mediocre

pappy[2] ['pæpi] *n Am* papá *m*

paprika ['pæprɪkə, *Am:* pæp'riː-] *n no pl* pimentón *m* dulce

Pap smear *n,* **Pap test** *n Am, Aus* MED Papanicolau *m*

Papua New Guinea [ˌpæpuənju:'gɪni, *Am:* ˌpæpjuənu:'gɪni] *n* Papua-Nueva Guinea *f*

papyrus [pə'paɪərəs, *Am:* -'paɪrəs] <-es *o* -ri> *n* papiro *m*

par [pɑːˤ, *Am:* pɑːr] *n no pl* 1. (*standard*) **to be on a ~ with sb** estar al mismo nivel que alguien; **below ~** por debajo de la media; **to feel below ~** no sentirse del todo bien; **not to be up to ~** no llegar a la media 2. SPORTS (*golfing term*) par *m* 3. FIN valor *m* nominal; **at/above/below ~** a/sobre/bajo la par ▸**to be ~ for the course** *inf* ser lo que uno se esperaba

par. *abbr of* **paragraph** párrafo *m*

para ['pærə, *Am:* 'perə] *n* 1. *Brit, inf* MIL *abbr of* **paratrooper** paracaidista *m* 2. (*text*) *abbr of* **paragraph** párrafo *m*

parable ['pærəbl, *Am:* 'per-] *n* parábola *f*

parabola [pə'ræbələ] *n* parábola *f*

parabolic [ˌpærə'bɒlɪk, *Am:* ˌperə'bɑːlɪk] *adj* parabólico, -a

paracetamol® [ˌpærə'siːtəmɒl, *Am:* perə'siːtəmɑːl] *n no pl* paracetamol *m*

parachute ['pærəʃuːt, *Am:* 'per-] I. *n* paracaídas *m inv; ~* **pack** equipo *m* de paracaídas II. *vi* lanzarse en paracaídas III. *vt* lanzar en paracaídas

parachute jump *n* salto *m* en paracaídas

parachuting *n no pl* paracaidismo *m*

parachutist ['pærəʃuːtɪst, *Am:* 'perəʃuːtɪst] *n* paracaidista *mf*

parade [pə'reɪd] I. *n* 1. (*procession*) *a.* MIL desfile *m;* (*inspection*) revista *f* de tropas 2. *fig* (*series*) retahíla *f* II. *vi* 1. (*walk in procession*) *a.* MIL desfilar 2. (*show off*) **to ~ about** jactarse; **to ~ up and down in one's best clothes** pasearse de un lado a otro con sus mejores ropas III. *vt* 1. (*exhibit*) lucir 2. *fig* (*show off*) ostentar; **to ~ one's knowledge** hacer alarde de erudición

parade ground *n* MIL plaza *f* de armas

paradigm ['pærədaɪm, *Am:* 'per-] *n* paradigma *m*

paradigmatic [ˌpærədɪg'mætɪk, *Am:* ˌperədɪg'mæt̬-] *adj* paradigmático, -a

paradigm shift *n* cambio *m* de paradigma

paradise ['pærədaɪs, *Am:* 'per-] *n* paraíso *m*

paradisiac(al) [ˌpærə'dɪsɪæk(l), *Am:* ˌperə'-] *adj* paradisíaco, -a

paradox ['pærədɒks, *Am:* 'perədɑːks] <-es> *n* paradoja *f*

paradoxical [ˌpærə'dɒksɪkəl, *Am:* ˌperə'dɑːk-] *adj* paradójico, -a

paradoxically *adv* paradójicamente

paraffin ['pærəfɪn, *Am:* 'per-] *n no pl* 1. *Brit* (*fuel*) queroseno *m* 2. (*wax*) parafina *f*

paraffin heater *n Brit* estufa *f* de queroseno

paraffin lamp *n Brit* quinqué *m* de petróleo

paraffin wax *n no pl* parafina *f*

paragliding ['pærəˌglaɪdɪŋ, *Am:* 'per-] *n no pl* parapente *m*

paragon ['pærəgən, *Am:* 'perəgɑːn] *n* arquetipo *m;* **a ~ of democracy** un modelo de democracia; **a ~ of virtue** *iron* un ejemplo de virtud

paragraph ['pærəgrɑːf, *Am:* 'perəgræf] *n* 1. LING párrafo *m* 2. PUBL (*short article*) breve *m*

Paraguay ['pærəgwaɪ, *Am:* 'perəgweɪ] *n* Paraguay *m*

Paraguayan [ˌpærə'gwaɪən, *Am:* ˌperə'gweɪ-] I. *adj* paraguayo, -a II. *n* paraguayo, -a *m, f*

parakeet ['pærəkiːt, *Am:* 'per-] *n* periquito *m*

parallel ['pærəlel, *Am:* 'per-] I. *adj* 1. MAT paralelo, -a; *~* **to sth** paralelo a algo; *~* **experiments** experimentos *mpl* paralelos 2. ELEC **in ~** en paralelo II. *n* 1. MAT paralela *f* 2. GEO paralelo *m* 3. (*similarity*) similitud *f* 4. **to draw a ~** (*make a comparison*) establecer un paralelismo; **to have no ~** no tener igual; **without ~** sin igual III. *vt* ser paralelo a

parallel bars *npl* SPORTS barras *fpl* paralelas

parallel line *n* línea *f* paralela

paralyse ['pærəlaɪz, *Am:* 'per-] *vt Brit, Aus s.* **paralyze**

paralysed *adj Brit, Aus s.* **paralyzed**

paralysis [pə'ræləsɪs] <-ses> *n* parálisis *f inv*

paralytic [ˌpærə'lɪtɪk, *Am:* ˌperə'lɪt̬-] I. *adj* 1. MED paralítico, -a 2. *inf* (*drunk*) **to be ~** estar como una cuba II. *n* paralítico, -a *m, f*

paralyze ['pærəlaɪz, *Am:* 'per-] *vt* 1. (*render immobile, powerless*) paralizar 2. (*stupefy*) dejar estupefacto, -a; **to be ~d with fear** estar paralizado de miedo

paralyzed *adj* 1. (*incapable of movement*) paralizado, -a 2. *fig* (*incapable of doing anything*) inmovilizado, -a

paramedic [ˌpærə'medɪk, *Am:* ˌper-] *n* paramédico, -a *m, f*

parameter [pə'ræmɪtəˤ, *Am:* -ət̬əˤ] *n* parámetro *m*

paramilitary [ˌpærə'mɪlɪtri, *Am:* ˌperə'mɪlət̬er-] I. *adj* paramilitar II. *n* paramilitar *mf*

paramount ['pærəmaʊnt, *Am:* 'per-] *adj form* supremo, -a; **of ~ importance** de extrema importancia

paranoia [ˌpærə'nɔɪə, *Am:* ˌper-] *n* paranoia

f

paranoiac [ˌpærəˈnɔɪæk, *Am:* ˌper-] **I.** *adj* paranoico, -a **II.** *n* paranoico, -a *m, f*

paranoid [ˈpærənɔɪd, *Am:* ˈperənɔɪd] *adj* **1.** PSYCH paranoico, -a **2.** (*very worried*) **to be ~ about sth** estar obsesionado por algo

paranoid schizophrenia *n* esquizofrenia *f* paranoide

paranormal [pærəˈnɔːməl, *Am:* ˈperə-ˈnɔːr-] **I.** *adj* paranormal; **~ powers** poderes *mpl* paranormales **II.** *n no pl* **the ~** lo paranormal

parapet [ˈpærəpɪt, *Am:* ˈperəpet] *n* parapeto *m*

paraphernalia [ˌpærəfəˈneɪlɪə, *Am:* ˌperə-fəˈneɪljə] *npl* parafernalia *f*

paraphrase [ˈpærəfreɪz, *Am:* ˈper-] **I.** *vt* **1.** (*reformulate*) parafrasear **2.** (*humourously imitate*) parodiar **II.** *n* (*reformulation*) paráfrasis *f inv;* **she gave us a quick ~ of what had been said** nos hizo un rápido resumen de lo que se había dicho

paraplegia [ˌpærəˈpliːdʒə, *Am:* ˌper-] *n no pl* paraplejía *f*

paraplegic [ˌpærəˈpliːdʒɪk, *Am:* ˌper-] **I.** *adj* parapléjico, -a **II.** *n* parapléjico, -a *m, f*

parapsychology [ˌpærəsaɪˈkɒlədʒi, *Am:* ˌperəsaɪˈkɑːlə-] *n no pl* parapsicología *f*

parasite [ˈpærəsaɪt, *Am:* ˈper-] *n a. fig* parásito *m*

parasitic [ˌpærəˈsɪtɪk, *Am:* ˌperəˈsɪt-] *adj a. fig* parásito, -a; **~ disease** enfermedad *f* parasitaria

parasol [ˈpærəsɒl, *Am:* ˈperəsɔːl] *n* sombrilla *f*

parathyroid (**gland**) [ˌpærəˈθaɪərɔɪd (glænd), *Am:* ˌperəˈθaɪ-] *n* paratiroides *f inv*

paratrooper [ˈpærətruːpəʳ, *Am:* ˈperə-truːpɚ] *n* paracaidista *mf*

paratroops [ˈpærətruːps, *Am:* ˈper-] *npl* paracaidistas *mpl*

paratyphoid [ˌpærəˈtaɪfɔɪd, *Am:* ˌper-] *n* MED paratifoidea *f*

parboil [ˈpɑːbɔɪl, *Am:* ˈpɑːr-] *vt* sancochar

parcel [ˈpɑːsəl, *Am:* ˈpɑːr-] **I.** *n* (*packet*) paquete *m;* (*of land*) terreno *m* **II.**<*Brit:* -ll-, *Am:* -l-> *vt* dividir; (*land*) parcelar
  ◆**parcel out** *vt* repartir en porciones; (*land*) parcelar
  ◆**parcel up** *vt* empaquetar

parcel bomb *n Brit* paquete-bomba *m* **parcel office** *n* oficina *f* de paquetes postales **parcel post** *n* servicio *m* de paquetes postales

parch [pɑːtʃ, *Am:* pɑːrtʃ] *vt* agostar

parched *adj* **1.** (*dried-out*) seco, -a; **to be ~ with heat** estar agostado por el calor **2.** *fig, inf* (*very thirsty*) **to be ~** estar muerto de sed

parchment [ˈpɑːtʃmənt, *Am:* ˈpɑːrtʃ-] *n* pergamino *m*

pardon [ˈpɑːdn, *Am:* ˈpɑːr-] **I.** *vt* (*forgive*) disculpar; (*prisoner*) indultar; **to ~** (**sb**) **sth** perdonar algo (a alguien); **to ~ sb for sth** per-

donar a alguien por algo; **~ me interrupting** siento interrumpir; **if you'll ~ the expression** si me permite la expresión; (**I beg your**) **~?** (*said to request repetition*) ¿cómo dice?; **~ me!** (*expressing indignation*) ¡usted perdone!; **~ me for breathing!** ¡no hace falta que te pongas así! **II.** *n* indulto *m*

pardonable [ˈpɑːdnəbl, *Am:* ˈpɑːr-] *adj* perdonable

pare [peəʳ, *Am:* per] *vt* **1.** (*fruit*) mondar **2.** (*fingernails*) **to ~ one's nails** cortarse las uñas **3.** *fig* (*costs*) recortar
  ◆**pare down** *vt* reducir; **to pare sth down to the minimum** reducir algo al mínimo
  ◆**pare off** *vt* pelar

parent [ˈpeərənt, *Am:* ˈperənt] *n* (*father*) padre *m;* (*mother*) madre *f;* **~s** padres *mpl*

parentage [ˈpeərəntɪdʒ, *Am:* ˈperənt̬ɪdʒ] *n no pl* familia *f*

parental [pəˈrentəl] *adj* de los padres

parental authority *n* patria *f* potestad **parental consent** *n* consentimiento *m* de los padres

parent company <-ies> *n* sociedad *f* matriz

parenthesis [pəˈrentθəsɪs] <-ses> *n* **1.** TYPO paréntesis *m inv;* **in parentheses** en paréntesis **2.** (*remark*) inciso *m*

parenthetical [ˌpærənˈθetɪkəl, *Am:* ˌpe-rənˈθet̬-] *adj form* parentético, -a; **~ remark** nota *f* explicativa

parenthetically *adv* a modo explicativo

parenthood [ˈpeərənthʊd, *Am:* ˈperənt-] *n no pl* (*of man*) paternidad *f;* (*of woman*) maternidad *f*

parenting [ˈpeərəntɪŋ, *Am:* ˈper-] *n no pl* cuidado *m* de los hijos; **~ skills** habilidades *fpl* en el cuidado de los hijos

parentless [ˈpeərəntlɪs, *Am:* ˈperənt-] *adj* huérfano, -a

Parents and Citizens *n Aus,* **Parent-Teacher Association** *n Brit, Am, Can* asociación *f* de padres y maestros

pariah [pəˈraɪə] *n* paria *mf*

paring [ˈpeərɪŋ, *Am:* ˈperɪŋ] *n* mondadura *f* **paring knife** <knives> *n* cuchillo *m* de mondar

Paris [ˈpærɪs, *Am:* ˈper-] *n* París *m*

parish [ˈpærɪʃ, *Am:* ˈper-] <-es> *n* **1.** REL parroquia *f* **2.** *Brit* POL distrito *m*

parish church <-es> *n* iglesia *f* parroquial **parish clerk** *n* sacristán *m* **parish council** *n* consejo *m* parroquial

parishioner [pəˈrɪʃənəʳ, *Am:* -ɚ] *n* feligrés, -esa *m, f*

parish priest *n* párroco *m* **parish-pump politics** *n Brit* parroquialismo *m* **parish register** *n* registro *m* parroquial

Parisian [pəˈrɪziən, *Am:* -ˈriʒ-] *n* parisino, -a *m, f*

parity [ˈpærəti, *Am:* ˈperət̬i] <-ies> *n* **1.** (*equality*) igualdad *f* **2.** FIN paridad *f*

park [pɑːk, *Am:* pɑːrk] **I.** *n* parque *m;* (*sur-*

P

rounding country house) jardines *mpl* **II.** *vt*
1. (*leave vehicle*) aparcar, estacionar *AmL;* to
~ **a satellite** AVIAT estacionar un satélite **2.** *pej,*
fig to ~ **oneself somewhere** arrellanarse en
algún sitio; **he ~ed himself in front of the**
TV se arrepanchingó delante del televisor
III. *vi* aparcar, estacionar *AmL*
parka ['pɑːkə, *Am:* 'pɑːr-] *n* parka *f*
park bench *n* banco *m* de un parque
parked *adj* aparcado, -a, estacionado, -a *AmL*
parking *n no pl* aparcamiento *m*, estacionamiento *m AmL*
parking area *n* zona *f* de estacionamiento
parking attendant *n* guarda *mf* del parking **parking bay** *n* zona *f* de aparcamiento
parking brake *n Am* freno *m* de mano
parking disc *n* disco *m* de estacionamiento
parking fine *n* multa *f* de estacionamiento
parking garage *n* parking *m* **parking**
lights *n Am, Aus* luces *fpl* de estacionamiento **parking lot** *n Am* aparcamiento
m **parking meter** *n* parquímetro *m* **park-**
ing offence *n* infracción *f* de estacionamiento **parking offender** *n* infractor(a)
m(f) que paga la multa de estacionamiento
parking permit *n* permiso *m* de aparcamiento **parking place** *n,* **parking space**
n aparcamiento *m*, estacionamiento *m AmL*
parking ticket *n* multa *f* por aparcamiento
indebido
Parkinson's disease ['pɑːkɪnsənzdɪˌziːz,
Am: 'pɑːr-] *n no pl* enfermedad *f* de Parkinson
Parkinson's law *n no pl, iron* ley *f* de Parkinson
park keeper *n Brit* guardabosque *mf*, guarda
mf forestal
parkland ['pɑːklænd, *Am:* 'pɑːrk-] *n no pl*
zona *f* verde
parkway ['pɑːkweɪ, *Am:* 'pɑːrk-] *n Am, Aus*
avenida *f* ajardinada
parky ['pɑːki, *Am:* 'pɑːr-] <-ier, -iest> *adj*
Brit, inf (*weather*) glacial
Parl. *abbr of* **Parliament** parlamento *m*
parlance ['pɑːlənts, *Am:* 'pɑːr-] *n no pl,*
form lenguaje *m;* in **common** ~ en lenguaje
corriente; **as it is known in common** ~ como
se conoce popularmente; **in medical** ~ en
jerga médica
parley ['pɑːli, *Am:* 'pɑːrleɪ] **I.** *n* parlamento
m **II.** *vi* parlamentar
parliament ['pɑːləmənt, *Am:* 'pɑːrlə-] *n*
(*institution*) parlamento *m;* (*time period*)
legislatura *f*

Las dos **Houses of Parliament** se encuentran en el **Palace of Westminster** de
Londres. La cámara baja, elegida por el pueblo, y de la que proceden la mayoría de los
ministros, se llama **House of Commons**.
Sus diputados reciben el nombre de
members of parliament o **MPs**. La cámara alta, **House of Lords**, sólo puede apro-

bar determinadas leyes. Los diputados, **peers**
of the realm, se pueden dividir en tres grupos. Los que tienen un escaño en la cámara
alta por razón de su trabajo, bien por ser
jueces, los **law lords**, o bien por ser obispos
de la iglesia anglicana, la **Church of Eng-**
land. En segundo lugar los que tienen un escaño vitalicio, los **life peers**, y en tercer lugar
los que han heredado el escaño junto con su
título nobiliario. Un comité de jueces de la
House of Lords constituye el máximo tribunal de justicia del Reino Unido.

parliamentarian [ˌpɑːləmən'teəriən, *Am:*
ˌpɑːrləmən'teri-] *n* (*MP*) diputado, -a *m, f*
parliamentary [ˌpɑːlə'mentəri, *Am:* ˌpɑːr-
lə'mentə-] *adj* parlamentario, -a
parliamentary candidate *n* candidato, -a
m, f parlamentario, -a **parliamentary**
chamber *n* cámara *f* de los diputados **par-**
liamentary debate *n* debate *m* parlamentario **parliamentary democracy** <-ies>
n democracia *f* parlamentaria **parliamen-**
tary election *n* elecciones *fpl* parlamenta-
rias **parliamentary government** *n* gobierno *m* parlamentario
parlor *n Am,* **parlour** ['pɑːlə', *Am:* 'pɑːrlə]
n Brit **1.** (*shop*) **beauty** ~ salón *m* de belleza;
ice-cream ~ heladería *f;* **pizza** ~ pizzería *f*
2. (*room in house*) salón *m*
parlour car *n Am* RAIL coche-salón *m*
parlour game *n* juego *m* de salón
parlourmaid *n* HIST camarera *f*
parlous ['pɑːləs, *Am:* 'pɑːr-] *adj* alarmante;
to be in a ~ **state** estar en un estado deplorable
Parmesan (**cheese**) ['pɑːmɪˌzæn (tʃiːz),
Am: 'pɑːrməzaːn (tʃiːz)] *n no pl* queso *m*
parmesano
parochial [pə'rəʊkiəl, *Am:* -'roʊ-] *adj* **1.** REL
parroquial **2.** (*narrow-minded*) de miras estrechas
parochialism *n no pl, pej* provincialismo *m*
parochial school *n Am* escuela *f* religiosa
parodist ['pærədɪst, *Am:* 'per-] *n* parodista
mf
parody ['pærədi, *Am:* 'per-] **I.** <-ies> *n*
1. (*humourous imitation*) parodia *f* **2.** *pej*
(*travesty*) burda imitación *f* **II.** <-ie-> *vt* parodiar
parole [pə'rəʊl, *Am:* -'roʊl] **I.** *n no pl* LAW libertad *f* condicional; **to be out on** ~ estar en
libertad condicional **II.** *vt* **to be** ~**d** ser puesto
en libertad condicional
paroxysm ['pærəksɪzəm, *Am:* 'per-] *n* paroxismo *m;* ~ **of joy** exaltación *f* de júbilo; ~
of rage paroxismo de rabia
parquet ['pɑːkeɪ, *Am:* pɑːr'keɪ] *n no pl* parqué *m;* ~ **floor** suelo *m* de parqué
parricide ['pærɪsaɪd, *Am:* 'perə-] *n form*
1. *no pl* (*murder*) parricidio *m* **2.** (*murderer*)
parricida *mf*

parrot ['pærət, *Am:* 'per-] I. *n* loro *m*, papagayo *m* ►to be <u>sick</u> as a ~ *Brit, iron* estar muerto de rabia II. *vt pej* repetir como un loro
parrot-fashion *adv* to repeat sth ~ repetir algo como un loro
parry ['pæri, *Am:* 'per-] <-ie-> *vt* 1. (*blow*) desviar 2. (*question*) eludir
parse [pɑːz, *Am:* pɑːrs] *vt* to ~ a sentence analizar una frase sintácticamente
Parsee *adj*, **Parsi** [pɑːˈsiː, *Am:* ˈpɑːrsiː] *adj* parsi
parsimonious [ˌpɑːsɪˈməʊniəs, *Am:* ˌpɑːr-sə'moʊ-] *adj form* parco, -a; to be ~ with the truth decir medias verdades
parsimoniously *adv pej, form* escasamente
parsimoniousness *n*, **parsimony** ['pɑː-sɪməni, *Am:* ˈpɑːrsəmoʊ-] *n no pl, pej, form* tacañería *f*
parsley ['pɑːsli, *Am:* ˈpɑːr-] *n no pl* perejil *m*
parsnip ['pɑːsnɪp, *Am:* ˈpɑːr-] *n* chirivía *f*
parson ['pɑːsən, *Am:* ˈpɑːr-] *n* cura *m*; (*protestant*) pastor *m*
parsonage ['pɑːsənɪdʒ, *Am:* ˈpɑːr-] *n* rectoría *f*
parson's nose *n* rabadilla *f*
part [pɑːt, *Am:* pɑːrt] I. *n* 1. (*not the whole*) parte *f*; the film was good in ~s la película tenía trozos buenos; ~ of the body parte del cuerpo; ~ of the family parte de la familia; the easy/hard ~ lo fácil/lo difícil; essential/important/integral ~ parte esencial/importante/integrante; in ~ en parte; in large ~ en gran parte; for the most ~ en la mayor parte 2. (*component*) componente *m*; spare ~s piezas *fpl* sueltas 3. (*area, region*) zona *f*; in these ~s *inf* en estas zonas 4. (*measure*) parte *f*; mix one ~ of the medicine with three ~s of water mezclar una parte de la medicina con tres partes de agua 5. (*role, involvement*) papel *m*; to want no ~ in sth no querer tener nada que ver en algo; to do one's ~ cumplir con su obligación 6. (*episode in media serial*) capítulo *m* 7. (*character in film*) papel *m*; to play the ~ of the King desempeñar el papel del rey 8. *Am* (*parting of hair*) raya *f* 9. (*score of particular musician*) parte *f* ►to be ~ and <u>parcel</u> of sth ser parte esencial de algo; for <u>my</u> ~ por mi parte; to <u>take</u> sb's ~ tomar partido por alguien; <u>on</u> sb's ~ de parte de alguien; it was a mistake on Julia's ~ fue un error por parte de Julia II. *adv* parcialmente; to be ~ African ser en parte africano III. *vt* 1. (*detach, split*) separar; to ~ sb from sb/sth separar a alguien de alguien/algo; to ~ company tomar direcciones distintas 2. (*divide*) partir, dividir; to ~ sth in two partir algo en dos; to ~ sb's hair hacer la raya a alguien IV. *vi* 1. (*separate*) separarse 2. (*say goodbye*) despedirse 3. (*curtains*) correr; to ~ from sb *form* separarse de alguien; to ~ with one's cash *inf* desprenderse de su dinero
partake [pɑːˈteɪk, *Am:* pɑːr-] *vi irr* 1. *form* to ~ in sth tomar parte en algo 2. *iron* to ~ of sth

(*eat*) comer algo; (*drink*) beber algo
parted *adj* 1. (*slightly opened*) ~ lips labios *mpl* entreabiertos 2. (*unwillingly separated*) to be ~ from sb estar separado de alguien
part exchange *n Brit* parte *f* del pago; to accept/give sth in ~ aceptar/dar algo como parte del importe
parthenogenesis [ˌpɑːθənəʊˈdʒenɪsɪs, *Am:* ˌpɑːrθənoʊˈdʒenə-] *n no pl* partenogénesis *f*
partial ['pɑːʃəl, *Am:* ˈpɑːr-] *adj* 1. (*incomplete*) parcial; ~ recovery recuperación *f* parcial 2. (*biased*) parcial 3. (*fond*) she is ~ to ... tiene debilidad por...
partial eclipse *n* eclipse *m* parcial
partiality [ˌpɑːʃiˈæləti, *Am:* ˌpɑːrʃiˈæləti] *n no pl* 1. (*bias*) parcialidad *f* 2. (*liking*) afición *f*
partially *adv* 1. (*partly*) parcialmente, en parte; ~ cooked medio hecho 2. (*with bias*) con parcialidad
partially sighted *adj* casi ciego, -a
participant [pɑːˈtɪsɪpənt, *Am:* pɑːrˈtɪsə-] *n* participante *mf*; (*in contest*) concursante *mf*
participate [pɑːˈtɪsɪpeɪt, *Am:* pɑːrˈtɪsə-] *vi* participar; (*in contest*) concursar
participation [pɑːˌtɪsɪˈpeɪʃən, *Am:* pɑːrˌtɪsə'-] *n no pl* participación *f*
participator [pɑːˈtɪsɪpeɪtər, *Am:* pɑːrˈtɪsəpeɪtə-] *n* participante *mf*
participatory [pɑːˈtɪsɪpətəri, *Am:* pɑːrˈtɪsəpətoːr-] *adj* participativo, -a
participatory democracy <-ies> *n* democracia *f* participativa
participle ['pɑːtɪsɪpl, *Am:* ˈpɑːrtɪsɪ-] *n* participio *m*
particle ['pɑːtɪkl, *Am:* ˈpɑːrtə-] *n* PHYS, LING partícula *f*
particle accelerator *n* acelerador *m* de partículas **particle physics** *n* física *f* de partículas
particular [pəˈtɪkjələr, *Am:* pə-ˈtɪkjələ-] I. *adj* 1. (*special*) particular, especial; (*specific*) concreto, -a, específico, -a; to be of ~ concern to sb ser de particular interés para alguien; no ~ reason ninguna razón en concreto; in ~ en especial; nothing in ~ nada en particular 2. (*fussy, meticulous*) quisquilloso, -a; (*demanding*) exigente; he is very ~ about his appearance es muy maniático con su imagen II. *n* detalle *m*; the ~ las especificidades
particularity [pətɪkjəˈlærəti, *Am:* pə-ˈtɪkjə-lə-] *n form* particularidad *f*
particularize [pəˈtɪkjʊləraɪz, *Am:* pə-ˈ] *vt* especificar
particularly [pəˈtɪkjʊləli, *Am:* pə-ˈtɪkjələ-] *adv* especialmente, particularmente; I didn't ~ want to go but I had to de hecho no tenía muchas ganas de ir, pero no tuve más remedio
parting ['pɑːtɪŋ, *Am:* ˈpɑːrtɪŋ] I. *n* 1. (*separation*) separación *f* 2. (*saying goodbye*) despedida *f* 3. *Brit, Aus* (*in hair*) raya *f*; centre/side ~ raya en medio/a un lado II. *adj* de des-

pedida; ~ **words** palabras *fpl* de despedida
parting shot *n* última palabra *f* (antes de irse)
partisan [ˌpɑːtɪˈzæn, *Am:* ˈpɑːrt̬ɪzən] I. *adj* partidista; ~ **spirit** partidismo *m* II. *n* 1. (*supporter*) partidario, -a *m, f* 2. MIL partisano, -a *m, f*
partisanship *n no pl* partidismo *m*
partition [pɑːˈtɪʃən, *Am:* pɑːrˈ-] I. *n* 1. (*wall*) tabique *m* 2. *no pl* (*of country*) división *f* 3. INFOR partición *f* II. *vt* 1. (*room*) dividir con un tabique; **to ~ sth off** tabicar algo 2. (*country*) dividir
partly [ˈpɑːtli, *Am:* ˈpɑːrt-] *adv* en parte, en cierto modo
partner [ˈpɑːtnəʳ, *Am:* ˈpɑːrtnɚ] I. *n* 1. COM socio, -a *m, f* 2. (*accomplice*) ~ **in crime** cómplice *mf* 3. (*in relationship*) pareja *f* 4. (*in tennis, dancing*) pareja *f* II. *vt* **to ~ sb** asociarse con alguien; **to be ~ed by sb** ir acompañado de alguien
partnership [ˈpɑːtnəʃɪp, *Am:* ˈpɑːrtnɚ-] *n* 1. (*association*) asociación *f* 2. COM sociedad *f* (comanditaria); (*of lawyers*) bufete *m;* **to go into ~ with sb** asociarse con alguien
partnership agreement *n* contrato *m* de sociedad
part of speech *n* LING parte *f* de oración
part owner *n* copropietario, -a *m, f* **part ownership** *n* copropiedad *f* **part payment** *n* pago *m* parcial
partridge [ˈpɑːtrɪdʒ, *Am:* ˈpɑːr-] *n* perdiz *f*
part song *n* canción *f* a voces
part-time [ˌpɑːtˈtaɪm, *Am:* ˌpɑːrt-] I. *adj* a tiempo parcial; ~ **worker** trabajador(a) *m(f)* a tiempo parcial II. *adv* **to work** ~ trabajar a tiempo parcial **part-time job** *n* empleo *m* a tiempo parcial
part-timer *n* (*worker*) empleado, -a *m, f* a tiempo parcial; (*student*) estudiante *mf* a tiempo parcial
part-time staff *n no pl* personal *m* a tiempo parcial **part-time student** *n* estudiante *mf* a tiempo parcial
party [ˈpɑːti, *Am:* ˈpɑːrt̬i] I. *n* <-ies> 1. (*social gathering*) fiesta *f;* **to have a ~** hacer una fiesta 2. + *sing/pl vb* POL partido *m;* **opposition/ruling ~** partido en la oposición/ en el poder 3. + *sing/pl vb* (*group*) grupo *m;* **coach ~** grupo en autocar; **school ~** grupo de escolares 4. *a.* LAW parte *f;* **the guilty ~** la parte inculpada; **to be a ~ to sth** ser partícipe en algo; **to be ~ to an arrangement** ser parte implicada en un acuerdo; **to be a ~ to a crime** ser cómplice de un delito 5. *Am, inf* (*person*) individuo *m* II. <-ie-> *vi* ir de fiesta
party conference *n Brit* congreso *m* del partido **party congress** *n Am* congreso *m* del partido **party headquarters** *n* sede *f* del partido **party leader** *n* líder *mf* del partido **party line** *n* 1. TEL línea *f* de varios abonados 2. POL política *f* del partido; **to follow the ~** seguir la política del partido **party politics**

npl política *f* de partidos **party popper** *n Brit* aguafiestas *mf inv*
parvenu [ˈpɑːvənjuː, *Am:* ˈpɑːrvənuː] *n pej, form* advenedizo, -a *m, f*
pass [pɑːs, *Am:* pæs] I. <-es> *n* 1. (*mountain road*) paso *m;* **mountain ~** puerto *m* de montaña 2. (*in rugby, soccer*) pase *m* 3. *no pl* (*sexual advances*) **to make a ~** (**at sb**) insinuarse (a alguien) 4. *Brit* (*in exam*) aprobado *m* 5. (*authorisation*) pase *m;* (*for festival, concert*) entrada *f* 6. (*public transport*) abono *m* 7. *Am* UNIV, SCHOOL (*permit to leave class*) permiso *m* ▶**to come to a** <u>pretty</u> **~** llegar a una situación crítica; **things have come to a pretty ~** las cosas se han puesto feas II. *vt* 1. (*go past*) pasar; (*cross*) cruzar 2. (*exceed*) sobrepasar; **to ~ a limit** sobrepasar un límite; **to ~ all belief** ser increíble 3. (*hand to*) **to ~ sth to sb** pasar algo a alguien 4. (*in rugby, soccer*) pasar 5. (*exam*) aprobar 6. (*avoid boredom*) **to ~ the time** pasar el rato 7. POL (*officially approve*) aprobar; **to ~ sb fit** dar a alguien de alta 8. (*utter, pronounce*) pronunciar; **to ~ a comment** hacer un comentario; **to ~ sentence** LAW dictar sentencia 9. MED excretar; **to ~ urine** orinar III. *vi* 1. (*move by*) pasar; **we often ~ed on the stairs** a menudo nos cruzábamos en la escalera; **to ~ unnoticed** pasar desapercibido 2. (*come to an end*) desaparecer; **it'll soon ~** se olvidará pronto 3. (*in rugby, soccer*) pasar la pelota 4. (*in exam*) aprobar 5. (*elapse: time*) transcurrir 6. (*not know answer*) pasar; **~!** ¡paso!
◆**pass away** *vi* (*die*) fallecer
◆**pass by** I. *vi* 1. (*elapse*) pasar 2. (*go past*) pasar de largo II. *vt* pasar algo por alto
◆**pass down** *vt* (*knowledge, beliefs*) transmitir; (*clothes, possessions*) pasar a
◆**pass off** I. *vt* (*treat as unimportant*) disimular II. *vi* 1. (*take place successfully*) tener lugar 2. (*fade away, wear off*) desaparecer
◆**pass on** I. *vi* 1. (*continue moving*) seguir su camino; **to ~ to a different topic** pasar a un tema diferente 2. (*die*) fallecer II. *vt* 1. BIO (*transmit*) contagiar 2. (*information, advice*) pasar 3. (*refer*) **to pass sb on to sb** poner a alguien con alguien
◆**pass out** I. *vi* 1. (*faint*) perder el conocimiento 2. *Brit, Aus* (*graduate from military college*) graduarse II. *vt Am* (*distribute, hand out*) repartir
◆**pass over** *vt* pasar por alto
◆**pass through** *vt* pasar por
◆**pass up** *vt* desperdiciar
passable [ˈpɑːsəbl, *Am:* ˈpæsə-] *adj* 1. (*unobstructed*) transitable 2. (*average, fair*) aceptable
passage [ˈpæsɪdʒ] *n* 1. (*corridor*) pasillo *m;* (*path*) pasadizo *m* 2. LIT, MUS pasaje *m* 3. (*onward journey*) viaje *m* 4. (*sea voyage*) travesía *f;* **bird of ~** ave *f* de paso; **to work one's ~** pagarse el pasaje trabajando a bordo 5. **with the ~ of time** con el transcurso del

tiempo

passageway ['pæsɪdʒweɪ] *n* pasillo *m*

passbook ['pɑːsbʊk, *Am:* 'pæs-] *n* libreta *f* de ahorros

passenger ['pæsəndʒə', *Am:* -əndʒɚ] *n* pasajero, -a *m, f*

passenger list *n* lista *f* de pasajeros

passer-by [,pɑːsə'baɪ, *Am:* ,pæsɚ'-] <passers-by> *n* transeúnte *mf*

passing I. *adj* 1. (*going past*) que pasa 2. (*brief: fad, infatuation*) pasajero, -a; (*glance*) rápido, -a; (*remark*) de pasada; ~ **fancy** capricho *m* II. *n no pl* (*death*) fallecimiento *m* ►**in** ~ al pasar

passing out *n Brit, Aus* MIL, UNIV graduación *f*

passing-out ceremony *n*, **passing-out parade** *n Brit, Aus* MIL, UNIV ceremonia *f* de graduación

passing place *n* apartadero *m*

passion ['pæʃən] *n* (*emotion*) pasión *f*; (*anger*) cólera *f*; **crime of** ~ crimen *m* pasional

passionate ['pæʃənət, *Am:* -ənɪt] *adj* (*emotional*) apasionado, -a; (*angry*) colérico, -a

passionflower ['pæʃən,flaʊə', *Am:* -,flaʊɚ] *n* pasionaria *f*

passion fruit *n* fruta *f* de la pasión

passionless ['pæʃənləs] *adj pej* sin pasión

passion play *n* drama *m* de La Pasión

Passion Week *n* Semana *f* Santa

passive ['pæsɪv] I. *n no pl* LING voz *f* pasiva II. *adj* pasivo, -a

passiveness *n*, **passivity** [pæs'ɪvəti, *Am:* pæs'ɪvəʈi] *n no pl* pasividad *f*

passkey ['pɑːskiː, *Am:* 'pæs-] *n* llave *f* maestra

pass mark *n Brit, Aus* nota *f* mínima para aprobar

Passover ['pɑːsəʊvə', *Am:* 'pæs,oʊvɚ] *n no pl* Pascua *f* judía

passport ['pɑːspɔːt, *Am:* 'pæspɔːrt] *n* pasaporte *m*

passport control *n*, **passport inspection** *n* control *m* de pasaportes **passport holder** *n* titular *mf* del pasaporte

password ['pɑːswɜːd, *Am:* 'pæswɜːrd] *n* INFOR contraseña *f*

past [pɑːst, *Am:* pæst] I. *n* pasado *m*; **to be a thing of the** ~ ser una cosa del pasado; **sb with a** ~ alguien con historia; **simple** ~ pasado *m* (simple); **to write in the** ~ escribir en pasado II. *adj* pasado, -a; **the** ~ **week** la última semana; **in times** ~ en otros tiempos; **that's** ~ **history** eso pertenece a la historia III. *prep* 1. (*temporal*) después de; **ten/ quarter/half** ~ **two** dos y diez/cuarto/ media; **it's** ~ **2** son las 2 pasadas 2. (*spatial*) después de 3. (*after*) **I'm** ~ **that** *iron* yo he superado eso 4. (*beyond*) **to be** ~ **thirty** pasar de los treinta; ~ **belief** increíble; ~ **description** indescriptible; **I'm** ~ **caring** ya no me trae sin cuidado IV. *adv* por delante; **to go/run/ march** ~ (**sb**) ir/correr/pasar por delante (de alguien)

pasta ['pæstə, *Am:* 'pɑːstə] *n no pl* pasta *f*

past continuous *n* pretérito *m* continuo

paste [peɪst] I. *n no pl* 1. (*glue*) engrudo *m*, pegamento *m* 2. (*sticky mixture*) pasta *f*; **meat/fish** ~ paté *m* de carne/pescado; **tomato** ~ concentrado *m* de tomate II. *vt* 1. *a.* INFOR (*stick*) pegar 2. *inf* (*beat*) dar una paliza a

pasteboard ['peɪstbɔːd, *Am:* -bɔːrd] *n no pl* cartón *m*

pastel ['pæstəl, *Am:* pæ'stel] I. *n* 1. ART (*drawing material*) pastel *m*; (*type of drawing*) pintura *f* al pastel 2. (*colour*) tono *m* pastel II. *adj* pastel

paste-up ['peɪstʌp] *n* maqueta *f*

pasteurization [,pæstʃəraɪ'zeɪʃən, *Am:* ,pæstʃɚ'-] *n no pl* pasteurización *f*

pasteurize ['pæstʃəraɪz] *vt* pasteurizar

pastime ['pɑːstaɪm, *Am:* 'pæs-] *n* pasatiempo *m*

pastor ['pɑːstə', *Am:* 'pæstɚ] *n* pastor *m*

pastoral ['pɑːstərəl, *Am:* 'pæs-] *adj* 1. REL pastoral 2. LIT, ART pastoril; ~ **scene** escena *f* bucólica

past participle *n* participio *m* pasado **past perfect** *n* pretérito *m* perfecto

pastry ['peɪstri] <-ies> *n* 1. *no pl* (*dough*) masa *f*; ~ **brush** pincel *m* de repostería 2. (*cake*) pastel *m*

pastry chef *n*, **pastry cook** *n* pastelero, -a *m, f*

past tense *n* tiempo *m* pasado

pasture ['pɑːstʃə', *Am:* 'pæstʃɚ] I. *n* 1. AGR pasto *m* 2. *fig* **new** ~**s** nuevos horizontes *mpl*; **to go to** ~**s new** pasar a mejor vida; **to put sb out to** ~ *inf* jubilar a alguien II. *vt* apacentar III. *vi* pacer

pasture land *n* prado *m*

pasty¹ ['pæsti] <-ies> *n* empanada *f*; **Cornish** ~ empanada de patata, cebolla y carne

pasty² ['peɪsti] <-ier, -iest> *adj* (*texture*) pastoso, -a; (*complexion*) pálido, -a

pat¹ [pæt] I. <-tt-> *vt* (*touch softly*) dar palmaditas a; **to** ~ **sb on the back** *fig* felicitar a alguien II. *n* 1. (*tap*) palmadita *f* 2. (*of butter*) porción *f*

pat² [pæt] *pej* I. *adj* (*answer*) fácil II. *adv* off ~ *Brit, Aus*, **down** ~ *Am* de memoria

patch [pætʃ] I. *n* 1. (*of land*) parcela *f* de tierra; (*of fog*) zona *f*; **vegetable** ~ huerto *m* 2. *Brit, inf* (*phase*) fase *f* 3. (*of salesman, criminal*) territorio *m* 4. (*piece of cloth*) parche *m*; (*for mending clothes*) remiendo *m*; (*knee*) rodillera *f*; (*elbow*) codera *f* ►**to be not a** ~ **on sb/sth** *Brit, Aus, inf* no tener ni punto de comparación con alguien/algo II. *vt* (*mend: hole, clothes*) remendar

♦**patch up** *vt* 1. (*mend*) hacer un arreglo provisional a 2. *fig* (*friendship*) arreglar; **to patch things up** hacer las paces

patchwork ['pætʃwɜːk, *Am:* -wɜːrk] I. *n no pl* 1. (*needlework*) patchwork *m* 2. *fig* (*mix*) mosaico *m* II. *adj* (*sewed from patches*) de retales; **a** ~ **quilt** un edredón de retazos

patchy ['pætʃi] <-ier, -iest> *adj* (*perform-ance, novel*) desigual; (*weather*) variable; (*results*) irregular

pâté ['pæteɪ, *Am:* pɑːˈteɪ] *n* paté *m*

patella [pəˈtelə] <-e> *n* rótula *f*

patent ['peɪtənt, *Am:* 'pætənt] I. *n* LAW pa-tente *f;* **to take out a ~ on sth** patentar algo II. *adj* 1. LAW patentado, -a 2. *form* (*uncon-cealed*) evidente 3. (*handbag, jacket*) de charol III. *vt* LAW patentar

patented ['peɪtəntɪd, *Am:* 'pætənṭɪd] *adj* LAW patentado, -a

patentee [ˌpeɪtənˈtiː, *Am:* ˌpætənˈtiː] *n* titu-lar *mf* de una patente

patent leather *n* charol *m*

patent medicine *n* específico *m* **patent office** *n* oficina *f* de patentes

paternal [pəˈtɜːnəl, *Am:* -ˈtɜːr-] *adj* paternal; **~ grandfather** abuelo paterno; **~ grand-mother** abuela paterna

paternalism [pəˈtɜːnəlɪzəm, *Am:* -ˈtɜːr-] *n no pl* paternalismo *m*

paternalistic [pəˌtɜːnəlˈɪstɪk, *Am:* -ˌtɜːr-] *adj pej* paternalista

paternity [pəˈtɜːnəti, *Am:* -ˈtɜːrnəṭi] *n no pl, form* paternidad *f*

paternity leave *n* permiso *m* de paternidad **paternity suit** *n* litigio *m* por paternidad

path [pɑːθ, *Am:* pæθ] *n* 1. (*footway, trail*) camino *m;* **to clear a ~** abrir un sendero; **to follow a ~** seguir una senda 2. (*way*) trayecto *m;* (*of bullet*) trayectoria *f;* **to cross sb's ~** tropezar con alguien 3. INFOR ruta *f*, localiza-ción *f*

pathetic [pəˈθetɪk, *Am:* -ˈθeṭ-] *adj* 1. (*arous-ing sympathy*) conmovedor(a); **a ~ sight** una escena lastimosa 2. *pej* (*arousing scorn*) patético, -a; **a ~ performance** una pésima actuación

pathfinder ['pɑːθfaɪndəʳ, *Am:* 'pæθˌfaɪn-dəʳ] *n* explorador(a) *m(f);* **to be a ~** ser un pionero

pathological [ˌpæθəˈlɒdʒɪkl, *Am:* -ˈlɑː-dʒɪk-] *adj inf* patológico, -a

pathologist [pəˈθɒlədʒɪst, *Am:* -ˈθɑːlə-] *n* patólogo, -a *m, f*

pathology [pəˈθɒlədʒi, *Am:* -ˈθɑːlə-] *n no pl* MED patología *f*

pathos ['peɪθɒs, *Am:* -θɑːs] *n* patetismo *m*

pathway ['pɑːθweɪ, *Am:* 'pæθ-] *n* camino *m*, sendero *m*

patience ['peɪʃns] *n no pl* 1. paciencia *f;* **to have the ~ of a saint** tener más paciencia que un santo 2. *Brit, Aus* GAMES solitario *m;* **to play ~** hacer solitarios

patient ['peɪʃnt] I. *adj* paciente; **to be ~ with sb** tener paciencia con alguien; **just be ~!** ¡ten paciencia! II. *n* MED paciente *mf*

patina ['pætɪnə, *Am:* -ənə] *n no pl* pátina *f*

patio ['pætiəʊ, *Am:* 'pæṭioʊ] <-s> *n* 1. (*paved area*) área pavimentada contigua a una casa; **~ door** puerta *f* que da al patio 2. (*courtyard*) patio *m*

patriarch ['peɪtriɑːk, *Am:* -ɑːrk] *n* patriarca *m*

patriarchal [ˌpeɪtriˈɑːkl, *Am:* -ˈɑːr-] *adj* patriarcal

patriarchy ['peɪtriɑːki, *Am:* -ɑːrki] <-ies> *n* patriarcado *m*

patrician [pəˈtrɪʃən] I. *n* patricio *mf* II. *adj* patricio, -a

patricide ['pætrɪsaɪd, *Am:* 'pætrə-] *n* (*per-son*) parricida *mf;* (*crime*) parricidio *m*

patriot ['pætrɪət, 'peɪtrɪət, *Am:* 'peɪ-] *n* patriota *mf*

patriotic [ˌpætrɪˈɒtɪk, ˌpeɪtrɪˈɒtɪk, *Am:* ˌpeɪ-trɪˈɑːtɪk] *adj* patriótico, -a

patriotism ['pætrɪətɪzəm, 'peɪtrɪətɪzəm, *Am:* 'peɪtrɪ-] *n no pl* patriotismo *m*

patrol [pəˈtrəʊl, *Am:* -ˈtroʊl] I. <-ll-> *vi* pa-trullar II. <-ll-> *vt* patrullar por III. *n* patrulla *f;* **to be on ~** patrullar

patrol car *n* coche *m* patrulla **patrol duty** *n* servicio *m* de patrulla **patrolman** *n* 1. *Am* policía *m* 2. *Brit* mecánico *m* del servicio de ayuda en carretera **patrol wagon** *n Am* coche *m* celular

patron ['peɪtrən] *n* 1. (*benefactor*) patrocina-dor(a) *m(f);* (*arts*) mecenas *mf* 2. REL patron(a) *m(f)*

patronage ['pætrənɪdʒ, *Am:* 'peɪtrən-] *n no pl* 1. (*support*) patrocinio *m;* ART mecenazgo *m* 2. ECON clientela *f*

patroness ['peɪtrənɪs] *n* 1. (*benefactor*) pa-trocinadora *f;* ART mecenas *f* 2. REL patrona *f*

patronize ['pætrənaɪz, *Am:* 'peɪtrən-] *vt* 1. *form* (*be customer*) ser cliente de 2. (*treat condescendingly*) tratar con condescendencia

patronizing ['pætrənaɪzɪŋ, *Am:* 'peɪtrən-] *adj* condescendiente

---

Inglaterra, Irlanda, Escocia y Gales tienen cada una sus propios **patron saints** (santos patrones). La festividad de **St George** de Inglaterra se celebra el 23 de abril; **St Pa-trick** de Irlanda el 17 de marzo; **St Andrew** de Escocia el 30 de noviembre y **St David** de Gales el 1 de marzo.

---

patter ['pætəʳ, *Am:* 'pæṭəʳ] I. *n no pl* 1. (*clever talk*) labia *f* 2. (*tapping: of rain*) gol-peteo *m;* (*of feet*) pasitos *mpl* II. *vi* (*make sound*) golpetear; (*walk lightly*) corretear; **to ~ about** andar con pasos ligeros

patter merchant *n inf* charlatán, -ana *m, f*

pattern ['pætən, *Am:* 'pæṭəʳn] I. *n* 1. (*model*) modelo *m* 2. ART (*design, motif*) diseño *m;* **floral ~** motivo *m* floral 3. FASHION (*paper guide*) patrón *m;* ECON (*sample*) mues-tra *f* II. *vt* (*emulate, follow, imitate*) seguir el modelo

pattern book *n* muestrario *m*

patterned *adj* estampado, -a

paunch [pɔːntʃ, *Am:* pɑːntʃ] *n* panza *f*

paunchy <-ier, -iest> *adj* panzudo, -a

pauper ['pɔːpəʳ, *Am:* 'pɑːpəʳ] *n* indigente

mf; ~**'s grave** fosa *f* común

pause [pɔːz, *Am:* pɑːz] **I.** *n* pausa *f* ▸**to give sb ~ for** thought *form* dar que pensar a alguien **II.** *vi* hacer una pausa

pave [peɪv] *vt* pavimentar; **to ~ the way for sth** *fig* preparar el terreno para algo

pavement ['peɪvmənt] *n* **1.** *Brit* (*beside road*) acera *f,* vereda *f AmL,* banqueta *f Guat, Méx* **2.** *Am, Aus* (*highway covering*) calzada *f*

pavement artist *n* artista *mf* de la calle

pavilion [pə'vɪljən] *n* pabellón *m*

paving *n no pl* **1.** (*space*) pavimento *m* **2.** (*material*) losas *fpl*

paving stone *n Brit* losa *f*

paw [pɔː, *Am:* pɑː] **I.** *n* pata *f;* (*of cat*) garra *f;* (*of lion*) zarpa *f; iron, inf* (*of person*) manaza *f* **II.** *vt* tocar con la pata; **to ~ sb** *pej* manosear a alguien **III.** *vi* **to ~ at sth** tocar algo con la pata

pawn[1] [pɔːn, *Am:* pɑːn] *n* GAMES peón *m; fig* títere *m*

pawn[2] [pɔːn, *Am:* pɑːn] **I.** *vt* empeñar **II.** *n* **to be in ~** estar en prenda

pawnbroker ['pɔːnˌbrəʊkəʳ, *Am:* 'pɑːnˌbrəʊkəʳ] *n* prestamista *mf* (sobre prenda), agenciero, -a *m, f Chile;* **the ~'s** la casa de empeños

pawnbroking *n* empeño *m*

pawn shop *n,* **pawnbroker's shop** *n* casa *f* de empeños

pay [peɪ] **I.** *n* paga *f;* **to be in the ~ of sb** estar a sueldo de alguien **II.**<paid, paid> *vt* **1.** (*redeem with money*) pagar; **to ~ cash** pagar al contado; **to ~ one's debts** liquidar las deudas de uno **2.** (*be worthwhile for*) ser provechoso, -a **3.** (*give, render*) **to ~ attention** (**to sth**) prestar atención (a algo); **to ~ a call** (**on sb**), **to ~ (sb) a call** hacer una visita (a alguien); **to ~ sb a compliment** hacer un cumplido a alguien; **to ~ homage to sb** rendir homenaje a alguien; **to ~ respects to sb** presentar los respetos a alguien **III.**<paid, paid> *vi* **1.** (*settle, recompense*) pagar **2.** (*benefit*) ser provechoso, -a

◆**pay back** *vt* devolver; **I'll pay you back!** ¡me las vas a pagar!; **to pay sb back in the same coin** pagar a alguien con la misma moneda

◆**pay in** *vt* ingresar

◆**pay off I.** *vt* **1.** (*debt*) liquidar **2.** *inf* (*bribe*) sobornar **II.** *vi fig* merecer la pena

◆**pay out I.** *vt* **1.** (*money*) desembolsar **2.** SPORTS **to ~ the rope** dar cuerda **II.** *vi* pagar

◆**pay over** *vt Brit* entregar

◆**pay up** *vi* pagar (lo que se debe)

payable ['peɪəbl] *adj* pagadero, -a; **to make a cheque ~ to sb** extender un cheque a favor de alguien

Pay As You Earn *n no pl, Brit:* sistema de recaudación de impuestos por medio de retenciones sobre el salario

pay award *n* adjudicación *f* de aumento de salario

payback clause ['peɪbæk 'klɔːz] *n* cláusula

f de restitución **payback period** *n* período *m* de restitución

paycheck *n Am,* **paycheque** ['peɪtʃek] *n Brit* cheque *m* de salario **pay claim** *n Brit, Aus* reivindicación *f* salarial **payday** *n no pl* día *m* de pago **pay deal** *n* acuerdo *m* salarial **pay desk** *n* caja *f* **pay differential** *n* diferencia *f* de salarios

PAYE [ˌpiːeɪwaɪ'iː] *n no pl, Brit abbr of* **Pay As You Earn**

payee [peɪ'iː] *n* beneficiario, -a *m, f*

payer ['peɪəʳ, *Am:* -ɚ] *n* pagador(a) *m(f);* **bad ~** moroso, -a *m, f*

pay freeze *n* congelación *f* salarial **pay hike** *n Am* aumento *m* de sueldo

paying *adj* rentable

payload ['peɪləʊd, *Am:* -loʊd] *n* **1.** AVIAT carga *f* útil **2.** MIL carga *f* explosiva

paymaster ['peɪmɑːstəʳ, *Am:* -mæstɚ] *n* pagador(a) *m(f)*

payment ['peɪmənt] *n* **1.** (*sum of cash*) pago *m;* **to make a down ~** pagar en efectivo **2.** (*installment*) plazo *m;* (*reward*) recompensa *f*

pay negotiations *npl* negociaciones *fpl* salariales

payoff ['peɪɒf, *Am:* -ɑːf] *n* **1.** (*payment*) pago *m* **2.** *inf* (*bribe*) soborno *m,* coima *f CSur,* mordida *f Méx;* **to make a ~ to sb** sobornar a alguien **3.** *inf* (*positive result*) beneficios *mpl;* (*on bet*) ganancias *fpl* **4.** *Am, inf* (*climax*) clímax *m* **5.** (*debt payment*) liquidación *f*

pay-office *n* caja *f*

payout *n* FIN desembolso *m*

pay packet *n Brit, Aus* sobre *m* de paga **pay--per-view** (**television**) *n no pl* televisión *f* de pago **payphone** *n* teléfono *m* público **pay raise** *n Am,* **pay rise** *n Brit, Aus* aumento *m* de sueldo **payroll** *n* nómina *f;* **~ tax** impuesto *m* sobre salarios **pay round** *n* serie *f* de negociaciones salariales **pay settlement** *n* acuerdo *m* salarial **payslip** *n* nómina *f* **pay station** *n Am* teléfono *m* público **pay talks** *npl* negociaciones *fpl* salariales **pay TV** *n* televisión *f* de pago; **to subscribe to ~** abonarse a la televisión de pago

PBS [ˌpiːbiː'es] *n no pl, Am abbr of* **Public Broadcasting System** *organismo americano de producción audiovisual*

PC [ˌpiː'siː] **I.** *n* **1.** *abbr of* **personal computer** PC *m* **2.** *Brit abbr of* **Police Constable** agente *mf* de policía **II.** *adj abbr of* **politically correct** políticamente correcto, -a

p.c. *abbr of* **per cent** p.c.

PE [ˌpiː'iː] *abbr of* **physical education** educación *f* física

pea [piː] *n* guisante *m,* arveja *f Col, Chile* ▸**to be like two ~s in a** pod ser como dos gotas de agua

peace [piːs] *n no pl* **1.** (*absence of war*) paz *f* **2.** (*social order*) orden *m* público; **to keep the ~** mantener el orden; **to make ~** hacer las paces; **to make one's ~ with sb** hacer las paces con alguien **3.** (*tranquillity*) tranquilidad *f*; **~ of mind** tranquilidad de ánimo; **to be at ~ about one's situation** estar satisfecho de la propia situación; **~ and quiet** paz y tranquilidad; **to be at ~** estar en paz; **to give sb no ~** no dejar a alguien en paz; **to leave sb in ~** dejar a alguien en paz **4.** REL **~ be with you** que la paz sea con vosotros; (**may he) rest in ~** que en paz descanse ▶**to be at ~ with the** world estar satisfecho de la vida; **to** hold **one's ~** guardar silencio; **speak now or forever** hold **your ~** que hable ahora o que calle para siempre

peaceable [ˈpiːsəbl] *adj* pacífico, -a

peace activist *n* pacifista *mf* **peace conference** *n* conferencia *f* de paz **peace enforcement** *n* imposición *f* de la paz

peaceful [ˈpiːsfəl] *adj* **1.** (*calm, quiet: animal*) manso, -a; (*place, person*) tranquilo, -a **2.** (*non-violent*) pacífico, -a

peace initiative *n* iniciativa *f* de paz

peacekeeping [ˈpiːsˌkiːpɪŋ] *n no pl* mantenimiento *m* de la paz

peacekeeping forces *npl* fuerzas *fpl* de paz

peace-loving *adj* amante de la paz

peacemaker [ˈpiːsˌmeɪkəʳ, *Am:* -kɚ] *n* (*between countries*) pacificador(a) *m(f)*; (*between friends*) conciliador(a) *m(f)*

peacemaking [ˈpiːsˌmeɪkɪŋ] **I.** *n* (*between countries*) pacificación *f*; (*between friends*) conciliación *f* **II.** *adj* (*between countries*) de pacificación; (*between friends*) de conciliación

peace march <-es> *n* marcha *f* por la paz **peace movement** *n* movimiento *m* pacifista **peace negotiations** *npl* negociaciones *fpl* de paz **peace offer** *n* oferta *f* de paz **peace offering** *n* prenda *f* de paz **peace pipe** *n* pipa *f* de la paz **peace settlement** *n* acuerdo *m* de paz **peace sign** *n* señal *f* de paz **peacetime** **I.** *n no pl* tiempo *m* de paz **II.** *adj* de tiempo de paz **peace treaty** <-ies> *n* tratado *m* de paz

peach [piːtʃ] **I.** <-es> *n* **1.** (*fruit*) melocotón *m*, durazno *m Arg, Chile*; **~ orchard** melocotonar *m* **2.** (*tree*) melocotonero *m*, duraznero *m Arg, Chile* **3.** *fig, inf* (*nice person*) monada *f*; **a ~ of a day** un día encantador **II.** *adj* de color melocotón

peach tree *n* melocotonero *m*, duraznero *m Arg, Chile*

peacock [ˈpiːkɒk, *Am:* -kɑːk] *n* **1.** ZOOL pavo *m* real **2.** (*vain person*) engreído, -a *m, f* ▶**as** proud **as a ~** orgulloso como un pavo real; **to** strut **like a ~** pavonearse

pea green **I.** *n* verde *m* claro **II.** *adj* verde claro

peahen [ˈpiːhen] *n* pava *f* real

peak [piːk] **I.** *n* **1.** (*mountain top*) cima *f*; **beat the egg whites until they are stiff enough to form firm ~s** bata las claras de huevo a punto de nieve **2.** (*highest point, summit*) punto *m* máximo; **to be at the ~ of one's**

career/power estar en la cúspide de su carrera/poder **3.** *Brit* (*of cap*) visera *f* **II.** *vi* (*career*) alcanzar el apogeo; (*athlete*) alcanzar el mejor rendimiento; (*skill*) alcanzar el nivel más alto; (*figures, rates, production*) alcanzar el máximo **III.** *adj* máximo, -a

peak capacity <-ies> *n* capacidad *f* óptima **peak demand** *n* demanda *f* máxima

peaked *adj Am* (*tired or sick*) enfermizo, -a; (*pale*) pálido, -a

peaked hat *n* gorra *f* con visera

peak hours *npl* horas *fpl* punta **peak level** *n no pl* nivel *m* máximo **peak load** *n* **1.** (*full capacity*) capacidad *f* máxima **2.** ELEC carga *f* máxima **peak period** *n* período *m* de máxima actividad **peak power** *no pl n* rendimiento *m* máximo **peak season** *n* temporada *f* alta **peak speed** *n* velocidad *f* máxima

peaky [ˈpiːki] <-ier, -iest> *adj Brit* paliducho, -a

peal [piːl] **I.** *n* **1.** (*of bell*) repique *m*; (*thunder*) trueno *m*; **a ~ of laughter** una carcajada **2.** (*set*) **~ of bells** carillón *m* **II.** *vi* (*thunderstorm*) tronar; (*bell*) repiquetear ◆**peal out** *vi* resonar; (*thunder*) tronar

peanut [ˈpiːnʌt] *n* **1.** (*nut*) cacahuete *m*, maní *m AmL*, cacahuate *m Méx* **2.** *inf* (*very little*) **to pay ~s** pagar una miseria

peanut butter *n no pl* mantequilla *f* de cacahuete

pear [peəʳ, *Am:* per] *n* **1.** (*fruit*) pera *f* **2.** (*tree*) peral *m*

pearl [pɜːl, *Am:* pɜːrl] *n* **1.** perla *f*; **to wear ~s** llevar perlas; **a string of ~s** un collar de perlas **2.** *fig* (*a drop*) gota *f*; **~ of dew** gota de rocío; **~s of sweat** gotas de sudor **3.** *fig* (*a fine example*) joya *f*; **a ~ of a ...** una joya de... ▶**to cast one's ~s before the** swine *prov* echarles margaritas a los cerdos *prov*

pearl barley *n no pl* cebada *f* perlada **pearl button** *n* botón *m* de perla **pearl diver** *n*, **pearl fisher** *n* pescador(a) *m(f)* de perlas **pearl-fishing** **I.** *n no pl* pesca *f* de perlas **II.** *adj* de pesca de perlas

pearly [ˈpɜːli, *Am:* ˈpɜːr-] <-ier, -iest> *adj* perlino, -a

pear tree *n* peral *m*

peasant [ˈpezənt] **I.** *n* **1.** (*small farmer*) campesino, -a *m, f* **2.** *pej, inf* (*uncouth person*) paleto, -a *m, f* **II.** *adj* campesino, -a, rural

peasantry [ˈpezəntri] *n no pl* campesinado *m*

pea-souper [ˌpiːˈsuːpəʳ, *Am:* ˈpiːˌsuːpɚ] *n* **1.** *Brit, fig, inf* (*fog*) niebla *f* espesa **2.** *Can, pej* (*French Canadian*) canadiense *mf* de habla francesa

peat [piːt] *n no pl* turba *f*

peat bog *n* turbera *f*

pebble [ˈpebl] *n* guijarro *m*

pebbly [ˈpebli] <-ier- iest> *adj* guijarroso, -a

pecan [pɪˈkæn, *Am:* pɪˈkɑːn] *n* pacana *f*

peccadillo [ˌpekəˈdɪləʊ, *Am:* -oʊ] <-(oe)s>

n desliz *m*

peck [pek] I. *n* 1.(*of bird*) picotazo *m* 2.(*quick kiss*) besito *m* II. *vt* 1.(*bird*) picar, picotear 2.(*kiss quickly*) besar III. *vi* 1.picar; **eat properly, don't ~!** ¡come bien, no picotees! 2.(*nag*) **to ~ at sb** fastidiar a alguien

pecker ['pekə', *Am:*-ə'] *n vulg* (*penis*) polla *f*, verga *f AmL*, pija *f Arg*, *Urug* ▶**to keep one's ~ up** *Brit, inf* no desanimarse

pecking order *n* orden *m* de picoteo de las gallinas; *fig* jerarquía *f*

peckish ['pekɪʃ] *adj* 1. *Brit, Aus* hambriento, -a 2. *Am* (*irritable*) irritable

pectin ['pektɪn] *n no pl* pectina *f*

pectoral ['pektərəl] *adj* pectoral

peculiar [pɪ'kju:lɪə', *Am:* -'kju:ljə'] *adj* 1.(*strange*) extraño, -a, raro, -a 2.(*sick, nauseous*) **to feel a little ~** no sentirse del todo bien; **to have a ~ feeling** tener malestar 3.(*belonging to*) propio, -a; **to be ~ to sb** ser propio de alguien

peculiarity [pɪˌkju:lɪ'ærəti, *Am:* -'erəti] <-ies> *n* 1.(*strangeness*) singularidad *f* 2.(*strange habit*) rareza *f* 3.(*idiosyncrasy*) peculiaridad *f*

peculiarly [pɪ'kju:lɪəli, *Am:* -'kju:ljə-] *adv* 1.(*strangely*) de forma rara 2.(*especially*) particularmente 3.(*belonging to*) típicamente

pecuniary [pɪ'kju:nɪəri, *Am:* -eri] *adj form* 1.(*motives*) pecuniario, -a 2.(*problems*) financiero, -a

pedagogic [ˌpedə'gɒdʒɪk, *Am:* -'gɑ:-] *adj* pedagógico, -a

pedagogue ['pedəgɒg, *Am:* -gɑ:g] *n* pedagogo, -a *m, f*

pedagogy ['pedəgɒdʒi, *Am:* -gɑ:dʒi] *n no pl* pedagogía *f*

pedal ['pedəl] I. *n* pedal *m* II.<*Brit:* -ll-, *Am:* -l-> *vt* **to ~ a bicycle** impulsar una bicicleta pedaleando III.<*Brit:* -ll-, *Am:* -l-> *vi* pedalear

pedal bin *n* cubo *m* de la basura (con pedal)

pedal boat *n*, **pedalo** ['pedələʊ, *Am:* -oʊ] *n* patín *m* a pedal

pedant ['pedənt] *n pej* pedante *mf*

pedantic [pɪ'dæntɪk, *Am:* pəd'æn-] *adj pej* pedante

pedantry ['pedəntri] <-ies> *n pej* pedantería *f*

peddle ['pedl] *vt pej* 1.(*sell*) vender (de puerta en puerta); **to ~ drugs** traficar con drogas 2.(*idea, lies*) difundir

peddler ['pedlə', *Am:* 'pedlə'] *n Am s.* **pedlar**

pederast ['pedəræst] *n* pederasta *m*

pederasty ['pedəræsti] *n no pl* pederastia *f*

pedestal ['pedɪstəl] *n* pedestal *m* ▶**to knock sb off their ~** bajar los humos a alguien; **to put sb on a ~** poner a alguien en un pedestal

pedestrian [pɪ'destrɪən, *Am:* pə'-] I. *n* peatón, -ona *m, f* II. *adj* 1.(*for walkers*) de peatones 2. *form* (*uninteresting*) pedestre

pedestrianise *vt Aus, Brit*, **pedestrianize**

[pɪ'destrɪənaɪz, *Am:* pə'-] *vt* convertir en zona peatonal

pedestrian mall *n Am, Aus*, **pedestrian precinct** *n Brit* zona *f* peatonal

pediatric [ˌpi:di'ætrɪk] *adj Am s.* **paediatric**

pediatrician [ˌpi:diə'trɪʃən] *n Am s.* **paediatrician**

pedicure ['pedɪkjʊə', *Am:* -kjʊr] *n* pedicura *f*

pedicurist ['pedɪkjʊərɪst] *n* pedicuro, -a *m, f*

pedigree ['pedɪgri:] I. *n* 1.(*genealogy: of animal*) pedigrí *m*; (*of person*) genealogía *f* 2.(*background*) expediente *m* II. *adj* (*animal*) de raza

pedlar ['pedlə', *Am:* -lə'] *n Brit, Aus* 1.(*travelling salesperson*) vendedor(a) *m(f)* ambulante 2.(*drug dealer*) traficante *mf* de drogas

pedometer [pɪ'dɒmɪtə', *Am:* pɪ'dɑ:mətə'] *n* podómetro *m*

pedophile ['pi:dəʊfaɪl] *n Am s.* **paedophile**

pee [pi:] *inf* I. *n no pl* pis *m*; **to have a ~** hacer pis II. *vi* hacer pis; **to ~ in one's pants** mearse encima III. *vt* **to ~ oneself** mearse encima

peek [pi:k] I. *n* mirada *f* rápida; **to have a ~ at sth** echar una mirada furtiva a algo II. *vi* mirar furtivamente; **to ~ at sth** echar una mirada furtiva a algo

♦**peek out** *vi* asomar; (*person*) asomarse

peel [pi:l] I. *n* (*skin*) piel *f*; (*of fruit*) cáscara *f*; (*peladuras*) mondas *fpl* II. *vt* (*fruit*) pelar; (*paper*) despegar; (*bark*) descortezar; (*skin*) levantar III. *vi* (*person*) pelarse; (*paint*) desconcharse; (*layer of paper*) despegarse; (*bark*) descortezarse

♦**peel off** I. *vt* (*paper*) despegar; (*paint*) quitar; (*bark*) descortezar; (*clothes*) quitarse II. *vi* 1.(*come off: paper*) despegarse; (*paint*) desconcharse; (*skin*) pelarse 2.(*veer away: car, motorbike*) desviarse

peeler ['pi:lə', *Am:* -lə'] *n* pelapatatas *m inv*

peelings ['pi:lɪŋz] *npl* (*of fruit*) peladuras *fpl*

peep[1] [pi:p] I. *n* (*sound: of bird*) pío *m*; (*of car horn*) pitido *m*; **not to give a ~** no decir ni pío II. *vi* piar

peep[2] [pi:p] I. *n* (*furtive look*) vistazo *m*; **to have a ~ at sth** echar una ojeada a algo II. *vi* 1.(*look quickly*) mirar rápidamente, vichar *Arg*; **to ~ at sth** echar un vistazo a algo; **to ~ through sth** atisbar a través de algo 2.(*appear, come partly out*) asomar III. *vt* asomar

♦**peep out** *vi* asomar

peephole ['pi:phəʊl, *Am:* -hoʊl] *n* mirilla *f*

peeping tom *n* mirón, -ona *m, f*

peepshow ['pi:pʃəʊ, *Am:* -ʃoʊ] *n* espectáculo *m* de striptease que funciona con monedas

peer[1] [pɪə', *Am:* pɪr] *vi* **to ~ at sth** escudriñar algo; **to ~ into the distance** fijar la mirada en la distancia; **to ~ over one's glasses** atisbar por encima de sus gafas

peer² [pɪəʳ, *Am:* pɪr] *n* **1.** (*equal*) igual *mf*, par *mf*; **to have no ~s** no tener par **2.** LAW **to be tried by a jury of one's ~s** ser juzgado por los iguales de uno **3.** *Brit* (*lord*) noble *mf*

peerage ['pɪərɪdʒ, *Am:* 'pɪrɪdʒ] *n* **1.** *no pl, Brit* (*aristocracy*) nobleza *f* **2.** (*title*) **to be given a ~** recibir un título nobiliario **3.** (*book*) guía *f* nobiliaria

peeress ['pɪəres, *Am:* 'pɪrɪs] <-es> *n Brit* paresa *f*

peerless ['pɪəlɪs, *Am:* 'pɪr-] *adj form* sin par, incomparable

peeve [pi:v] *vt inf* fastidiar

peeved [pi:vd] *adj inf* mosqueado, -a; **to be ~ at sb for sth** estar mosqueado con alguien por algo

peevish ['pi:vɪʃ] *adj* malhumorado, -a

peewit ['pi:wɪt] *n* avefría *f*

peg [peg] **I.** *n* **1.** (*for coat*) colgador *m* **2.** (*in furniture, for tent*) estaquilla *f*; (*in mountaineering, on guitar*) clavija *f*; **clothes ~** pinza *f* de tender la ropa, broche *m* de tender la ropa *Arg*; **to buy clothes off the ~** comprarse ropa de confección ► **to take sb** down **a ~ or two** bajar los humos a alguien; **to feel like a** square **~ in a round hole** sentirse fuera de lugar; **to** use **sth as a ~ to hang sth on** usar algo de apoyo para algo **II.** <-gg-> *vt* **1.** (*hold down with pegs*) enclavijar **2.** ECON fijar; **to ~ prices** congelar precios **3.** (*link*) **to ~ sth to sth** vincular algo a algo **4.** *Am* (*throw*) lanzar **5.** *fig* (*guess correctly*) acertar

♦**peg away** *vi inf* darle duro; **to ~ at sth** persistir en algo

♦**peg out I.** *vt* **1.** (*hang out*) tender; **to ~ clothes** tender la ropa **2.** (*mark*) señalar con estacas **II.** *vi Aus, Brit* **1.** *fig, inf* (*die*) palmarla **2.** (*stop working: car, machine*) quedarse, tronarse *Méx*

peg-leg *n inf* pata *f* de palo

pejorative [pɪ'dʒɒrətɪv, *Am:* -'dʒɔːrətɪv] *form* **I.** *adj* despectivo, -a **II.** *n* palabra *f* despectiva

Pekinese [ˌpi:kɪ'ni:z, *Am:* -kə'ni:z] **I.** *n* **1.** (*person*) pequinés, -esa *m*, *f* **2.** (*dog*) pequinés *m* **II.** *adj* pequinés, -esa

pelican ['pelɪkən] *n* pelícano *m*

pellet ['pelɪt] *n* (*small, hard ball*) bolita *f*; (*animal excrement*) cagadita *f inf*; (*gunshot*) perdigón *m*

pellet gun *n* pistola *f* de perdigones

pell-mell [ˌpel'mel] *adv* (*hurriedly*) atropelladamente; (*confusedly*) desordenadamente

pelt¹ [pelt] *n* (*animal skin*) pellejo *m*; (*fur*) piel *f*

pelt² [pelt] **I.** *n* **at** full **~ a todo correr II.** *vt* (*throw*) lanzar; **to ~ sb with stones** tirar piedras a alguien **III.** *vi* **1.** *impers* (*rain heavily*) llover a cántaros **2.** (*run, hurry*) apresurarse; **to ~ after sb** salir disparado tras alguien

pelvic ['pelvɪk] *adj* pélvico, -a

pelvis ['pelvɪs] <-es> *n* pelvis *f inv*

pen¹ [pen] **I.** *n* (*fountain pen*) pluma *f* estilográfica, pluma *f* fuente *AmL*; (*ballpoint*) bolígrafo *m*, birome *f Arg*, pluma *f* atómica *Méx*, lápiz *m* de pasta *Chile*; **felt-tip ~** rotulador *m*; **to put ~ to paper** ponerse a escribir ► **the ~ is mightier than the** sword *prov* más puede la pluma que la espada *prov* **II.** <-nn-> *vt* escribir

pen² [pen] *n* **1.** (*enclosure*) corral *m*; **pig ~** pocilga *f* **2.** *Am, inf* (*jail*) talego *m*, tanque *m Méx*

♦**pen in** <-nn-> *vt* (*enclose*) cercar

penal ['pi:nəl] *adj* penal

penal code *n* código *m* penal **penal institution** *n* penitenciaría *f*

penalise *vt Brit, Aus*, **penalize** ['pi:nəlaɪz] *vt Am* penalizar

penal offense *n Am* delito *m* penal

penalty ['penəlti, *Am:* -ti] <-ies> *n* **1.** LAW pena *f*; **death ~** pena de muerte; **to pay a ~ for sth** ser penalizado por algo **2.** (*punishment*) castigo *m* **3.** SPORTS castigo *m*; (*in football*) penalti *m*

penalty area *n* SPORTS área *f* de penalti **penalty box** <-es> *n* (*in ice hockey*) banquillo *m* **penalty clause** *n* cláusula *f* penal **penalty kick** *n* SPORTS tiro *m* de penalti; **to award a ~** señalar un penalti

penance ['penəns] *n no pl* REL penitencia *f*; **to do ~ for sth** hacer penitencia por algo

pence [pens] *n pl of* **penny**

penchant ['pɑːnʃɑːn, *Am:* 'pentʃənt] *n* (*liking*) inclinación *f*; **to have a ~ for sth** tener inclinación por algo

pencil ['pentsəl] **I.** *n* lápiz *m*; **coloured ~** lápiz de color; **a ~ of light** un haz de luz **II.** <*Brit:* -ll-, *Am:* -l-> *vt* dibujar a lápiz

♦**pencil in** *vt* apuntar (de forma provisional)

pencil beam *n* viga *f* delgada **pencil box** <-es> *n* estuche *m* (para lápices), cartuchera *f Arg*, alcancía *f Urug* **pencil case** *n* estuche *m* (para lápices), chuspa *f Col*, cartuchera *f Arg* **pencil sharpener** *n* sacapuntas *m inv*, tajalápiz *m Col* **pencil skirt** *n* falda *f* de tubo

pendant ['pendənt] **I.** *n* (*hanging*) colgante *m* **II.** *adj* colgante

pendant lamp *n* lámpara *f* de techo

pendent ['pendənt] *adj* LAW pendiente

pending ['pendɪŋ] **I.** *adj* pendiente; **~ deal** negocio *m* pendiente; **~ law suit** litigio *m* pendiente **II.** *prep* hasta; **~ further instructions** hasta nuevo aviso

pendulous ['pendjələs, *Am:* -dʒələs] *adj form* colgante

pendulum ['pendjələm, *Am:* -dʒələm] *n* péndulo *m*

penetrate ['penɪtreɪt] *vt* **1.** (*move into or through*) penetrar; **to ~ a market** introducirse en un mercado **2.** (*spread through, permeate*) impregnar, calar en **3.** *fig* (*see through*) entender

penetrating *adj* (*voice, gaze, insight*) penetrante; (*rain*) que cala; (*heat, cold*) agudo, -a

penetration [ˌpenɪ'treɪʃən] *n* **a.** *fig* penetración *f*

pen friend *n Aus, Brit* amigo, -a *m, f* por correspondencia

penguin ['peŋgwɪn] *n* pingüino *m*

penholder ['pen,həʊldə*ʳ*, *Am:* -,hoʊldə*ʳ*] *n* (*rack*) portalápices *m inv*

penicillin [,penɪ'sɪlɪn] *n no pl* penicilina *f*

peninsula [pə'nɪnsjʊlə, *Am:* -sələ] *n* península *f*

peninsular [pə'nɪnsjʊlə*ʳ*, *Am:* -sələ*ʳ*] *adj* peninsular

Peninsular War *n* the ~ la Guerra de la Independencia

penis ['piːnɪs] <-nises *o* -nes> *n* pene *m*

penitence ['penɪtəns] *n no pl* REL penitencia *f*; to perform ~ hacer penitencia

penitent ['penɪtənt] REL I. *n* penitente *mf* II. *adj* penitente

penitential [,penɪ'tentʃəl] *adj* penitencial

penitentiary [,penɪ'tentʃəri] *n Am* prisión *f* penitenciaria

penknife ['pennaɪf] <-knives> *n* navaja *f*

pen name *n* seudónimo *m*

pennant ['penənt] *n* banderín *m*; NAUT gallardete *m*

penniless ['penɪlɪs] *adj* to be ~ no tener un duro; to leave sb ~ dejar a alguien en la miseria

pennon ['penən] *n* pendón *m*; (*on lance*) banderola *f*

Pennsylvania [pensɪl'veɪnɪə] *n* Pensilvania *f*

penny ['peni] *n* 1. *Brit* penique *m* 2. *Am* centavo *m* ▶ a ~ for your thoughts ¿en qué piensas?; to earn/cost a pretty ~ ganar/costar un dineral; to earn a quick ~ ganar dinero fácil; two [*o* ten] a ~ está regalado; they're ten a ~ los hay a patadas; the ~ (has) dropped! por fin cayó en cuenta, por fin le cayó el veinte *Méx*; a ~ saved is a ~ gained *prov* muchos pocos hacen un montón *prov*

penny-pinching ['peni,pɪntʃɪŋ] I. *n no pl* tacañería *f* II. *adj* tacaño, -a

penny whistle *n* flautín *m*

penny-wise *adj* to be ~ and pound-foolish gastar a manos llenas y hacer economías en nimiedades

pen pal *n* amigo, -a *m, f* por correspondencia

pen pusher *n Aus, Brit, pej, inf* chupatintas *mf inv*, suche *mf Chile*

pension[1] ['pentʃən] I. *n* FIN pensión *f*; to draw a ~ cobrar una pensión II. *vt* to ~ sb off jubilar a alguien

pension[2] ['pãnsjɔ̃ːn, *Am:* pãn'sjɔ̃ʊŋ] *n* (*boarding house*) pensión *f*

pensionable ['pentʃənəbl, *Am:* -ʃən-] *adj Brit* de jubilación; of ~ age de edad de jubilación

pensioner ['pentʃənə*ʳ*, *Am:* -ʃənə*ʳ*] *n Brit* pensionista *mf*

pension fund *n* fondo *m* de pensiones **pension plan** *n* plan *m* de pensiones **pension reserves** *npl* reservas *fpl* para pensiones

pension scheme *n Aus, Brit* plan *m* de pensiones

pensive ['pentsɪv] *adj* pensativo, -a; to be in a ~ mood estar meditabundo, -a

pentagon ['pentəgən, *Am:* -ˌgɑːn] *n* pentágono *m*

pentameter [pen'tæmɪtə*ʳ*, *Am:* -ət̬ə*ʳ*] *n* LIT pentámetro *m*

pentathlete [pen'tæθliːt] *n* pentatleta *mf*

pentathlon [pen'tæθlən, *Am:* -lɑːn] *n* pentatlón *m*

Pentecost ['pentəkɒst, *Am:* -ˌt̬ɪkɑːst] *n no pl* REL Pentecostés *m*

penthouse ['penthaʊs] *n* (*flat*) ático *m* de lujo

pent-up [,pent'ʌp] *adj* 1. (*emotion*) contenido, -a, reprimido, -a 2. (*energy*) acumulado, -a

penultimate [pen'ʌltɪmət, *Am:* pɪ'nʌlt̬ə-] *form* I. *n* the ~ el penúltimo, la penúltima II. *adj* penúltimo, -a

penurious [pɪ'njʊərɪəs, *Am:* pə'nʊrɪ-] *adj form* miserable, paupérrimo, -a

penury ['penjʊəri, *Am:* -jʊri] *n no pl, form* penuria *f*, miseria *f*

peony ['piːəni] <-ies> *n* peonía *f*

people ['piːpl] I. *n* 1. *pl* (*plural of person*) gente *f*; city ~ gente de ciudad; country ~ gente de campo; the beautiful ~ la gente guapa, la gente linda *AmL*; the rich ~ la gente rica *f*. *no pl* (*nation, ethnic group*) pueblo *m*; ~'s democracy democracia *f* popular; ~'s republic república *f* popular; the chosen ~ REL el pueblo elegido 3. (*ordinary citizens*) ciudadanos, -as *m, f pl*; ~'s park parque *m* público II. *vt* ~d by poblado de

pep [pep] I. *n no pl, inf* empuje *m*; to be full of ~ estar lleno de vitalidad II. <-pp-> *vt* animar, levantar el ánimo

pepper ['pepə*ʳ*, *Am:* -ə*ʳ*] I. *n* 1. *no pl* (*spice*) pimienta *f*; black/white ~ pimienta negra/blanca 2. (*vegetable*) pimiento *m* II. *vt* 1. (*add pepper*) poner pimienta a 2. to ~ sb with bullets acribillar a alguien a balas; to be ~ed with sth (*speech, comments*) estar acribillado de algo; to be ~ed with mistakes estar lleno de errores

pepper-and-salt *adj* (*hair*) entrecano, -a

pepper box <-es> *n Am* pimentero *m*

peppercorn ['pepəkɔːn, *Am:* -ə*ʳ*kɔːrn] *n* grano *m* de pimienta

peppercorn rent *n no pl, Aus, Brit* alquiler *m* nominal

pepper mill *n* molinillo *m* de pimienta

peppermint ['pepəmɪnt, *Am:* -ə*ʳ*-] *n* 1. *no pl* (*mint plant*) menta *f* 2. (*sweet*) caramelo *m* de menta

peppermint tea *n* té *m* de menta

pepper pot *n Aus, Brit*, **pepper shaker** *n Am* pimentero *m*

peppery ['pepəri] *adj* 1. GASTR picante 2. *fig* (*irritable*) cascarrabias *inv*

pep pill *n inf* estimulante *m* **pep talk** *n inf*

P

to give sb a ~ dar ánimos a alguien
peptic ['peptɪk] *adj* péptico, -a
peptic ulcer *n* úlcera *f* péptica
per [pɜːˈ, *Am:* pɜːr] *prep* **1.** (*for a*) por; £5 ~ **kilo/hour** £5 por kilo/hora **2.** (*in a*) por, a; 100 km ~ **hour** 100 km por hora; ~ **cent** por ciento **3.** *form* (*as stated in*) (**as**) ~ **account** según consta; **as** ~ **usual** como siempre
perambulator [pəˈræmbjʊleɪtəˈ, *Am:* -t̬əˈ] *n form* cochecito *m*, carriola *f Méx*
per annum *adv form* al año, por año **per capita** *form* **I.** *adv* per cápita **II.** *adj* ~ **consumption** consumo *m* per cápita; ~ **income** ingresos *mpl* per cápita
perceivable [pəˈsiːvəbl, *Am:* pəˈ-] *adj* perceptible
perceive [pəˈsiːv, *Am:* pəˈ-] *vt* **1.** (*see*) ver; (*sense*) percibir, notar; **to** ~ **that ...** percibir que... **2.** (*view, regard*) considerar; **how do the Spanish** ~ **the British?** ¿qué piensan los españoles de los británicos? **3.** (*understand*) comprender
percent *n Am*, **per cent** [pəˈsent, *Am:* pəˈ-] *n Brit* porcentaje *m*; **25** ~ 25 por ciento; **what** ~ **...** ¿qué porcentaje...?
percentage [pəˈsentɪdʒ, *Am:* pəˈsent̬ɪdʒ] *n* **1.** (*proportion*) porcentaje *m*; **what** ~ **...?** ¿qué porcentaje...?; **to get a** ~ **of sth** recibir un tanto por ciento de algo **2.** *Am, Aus* (*advantage*) tajada *f inf* ▶**to play the** ~**s** sopesar las posibilidades
percentage point *n* punto *m* porcentual
perceptible [pəˈseptəbl, *Am:* pəˈ-] *adj* perceptible
perception [pəˈsepʃən, *Am:* pəˈ-] *n* **1.** percepción *f* **2.** (*idea*) idea *f* **3.** (*insight*) perspicacia *f*, agudeza *f*
perceptive [pəˈseptɪv, *Am:* pəˈ-] *adj* perspicaz, agudo, -a
perch[1] [pɜːtʃ, *Am:* pɜːrtʃ] **I.**<-es> *n* **1.** (*rod for birds*) percha *f* **2.** (*high location or position*) posición *f* privilegiada ▶**to come off one's** ~ bajarse del burro; **to knock sb off his** ~ bajar los humos a alguien **II.** *vi* (*person*) sentarse; (*bird*) posarse
perch[2] [pɜːtʃ, *Am:* pɜːrtʃ] *n* perca *f*
percolate ['pɜːkəleɪt, *Am:* 'pɜːr-] **I.** *vt* filtrar, colar; (*coffee*) preparar **II.** *vi* **1.** (*filter through*) filtrarse **2.** *fig* (*spread*) difundirse
percolator ['pɜːkə leɪtəˈ, *Am:* 'pɜːrkəleɪt̬əˈ] *n* cafetera *f* eléctrica
percussion [pəˈkʌʃən, *Am:* pəˈ-] **I.** *n no pl* MUS percusión *f*; **to play** ~ ser percusionista **II.** *adj* MUS de percusión
percussionist *n* MUS percusionista *mf*
perdition [pəˈdɪʃən, *Am:* pəˈ-] *n no pl* **1.** *liter* (*hell*) perdición *f* **2.** *fig* (*state of ruin*) desastre *m*
peregrine ['perɪɡrɪn] *n* peregrino, -a *m, f*
peregrine falcon *n* halcón *m* peregrino
peremptorily *adv* en tono perentorio, imperiosamente
peremptory [pəˈremptəri] *adj* **1.** (*person*) autoritario, -a; (*order, tone*) perentorio, -a, imperioso, -a **2.** LAW perentorio, -a
perennial [pəˈreniəl, *Am:* pəˈren-] **I.** *n* planta *f* perenne **II.** *adj* **1.** BOT perenne **2.** (*constant*) constante
perfect[1] ['pɜːfɪkt, *Am:* 'pɜːr-] **I.** *adj* perfecto, -a; (*calm*) total; (*opportunity*) ideal; (*silence*) absoluto, -a; **in** ~ **condition** en estado perfecto; **the** ~ **crime** el crimen perfecto; **a** ~ **gentleman** todo un señor; **a** ~ **idiot** un tonto de remate; **to be a** ~ **stranger** ser completamente desconocido; **to have the** ~ **right to do sth** tener todo el derecho a hacer algo; **to be far from** ~ estar (muy) lejos de ser perfecto; **to be a** ~ **match for sth** casarse a la perfección con algo; **to be a** ~ **match for sb** ser la pareja perfecta para alguien **II.** *n no pl* LING perfecto *m*
perfect[2] [pəˈfekt, *Am:* pɜːr-] *vt* perfeccionar
perfectible [pəˈfektəbəl, *Am:* pəˈ-] *adj* perfectible
perfection [pəˈfekʃən, *Am:* pəˈ-] *n no pl* perfección *f*; **to do sth to** ~ hacer algo a la perfección
perfectionist *n* perfeccionista *mf*
perfectly *adv* perfectamente; ~ **clear** completamente claro; ~ **happy** absolutamente contento; **to be** ~ **honest, ...** para serte sincero,...; **to be** ~ **right** tener toda la razón
perfidious [pəˈfɪdiəs, *Am:* pəˈ-] *adj liter* pérfido, -a; ~ **attack** ataque *m* a traición
perforate ['pɜːfəreɪt, *Am:* 'pɜːr-] *vt* perforar; (*ticket*) picar
perforated *adj* perforado, -a; **to have a** ~ **eardrum** tener una perforación de tímpano
perforation [ˌpɜːfəˈreɪʃən, *Am:* ˌpɜːrfəˈreɪ-] *n* perforación *f*
perform [pəˈfɔːm, *Am:* pəˈfɔːrm] **I.** *vt* **1.** MUS, THEAT, TV interpretar **2.** (*do, accomplish*) realizar; **to** ~ **one's duty/a function** cumplir con su deber/una función; **to** ~ **miracles/wonders** hacer milagros/maravillas; **to** ~ **a task** llevar a cabo una tarea; **to** ~ **a trick** realizar un truco **3.** INFOR ejecutar **4.** MED, SPORTS practicar **II.** *vi* **1.** THEAT actuar; MUS tocar **2.** (*operate*) funcionar
performance [pəˈfɔːməns, *Am:* pəˈfɔːr-] *n* **1.** (*of play*) representación *f*; (*by individual actor*) actuación *f*; **to give a** ~ hacer una representación; **to put on a** ~ **of a play** poner en escena una representación de una obra **2.** SPORTS actuación *f*; **high/low** ~ AUTO alto/bajo rendimiento *m* **3.** *inf* (*fuss*) lío *m*; **to make a** ~ **about sth** *Brit, fig* montar un jaleo por algo
performance level *n* **1.** (*degree of success*) nivel *m* de rendimiento **2.** ECON (*output*) rendimiento *m*; **a high/low** ~ un alto/bajo rendimiento **performance report** *n* informe *m* de rendimiento
performer [pəˈfɔːməˈ, *Am:* pəˈfɔːrməˈ] *n* **1.** THEAT artista *mf* **2.** (*achiever*) **star** ~ (*in a show*) estrella *f*; (*at work*) empleado, -a *m, f* modelo; **bad** ~ (*at school*) mal(a) estudiante

mf; (*at work*) mal(a) trabajador(a) *m(f)*

perfume ['pɜːfjuːm, *Am:* 'pɜːr-] **I.** *n* **1.** *no pl*
(*scented liquid*) perfume *m;* ~ **maker** perfu-
mista *mf;* **to put on** ~ ponerse perfume **2.** (*fra-*
grance) fragancia *f* **II.** *vt* perfumar

perfunctory [pə'fʌŋktəri, *Am:* pəˈ-] *adj*
(*inspection*) superficial; (*reading*) por encima;
(*mention*) de pasada; (*greeting, smile*) forzado, -a; (*examination*) rutinario, -a

pergola ['pɜːgələ, *Am:* 'pɜːr-] *n* pérgola *f*

perhaps [pə'hæps, *Am:* pəˈ-] *adv* quizá(s),
tal vez

peril ['perəl] *n form* peligro *m;* **to be in** ~
correr peligro; **at one's** ~ por su cuenta y
riesgo; **at** [*o* **in**] ~ **of sth** en peligro por algo;
the ~**s of sth** el peligro de algo

perilous ['perələs] *adj form* peligroso, -a

perimeter [pə'rɪmɪtə', *Am:* pə'rɪmət̬ə'] *n*
perímetro *m*

perimeter fence *n* cercado *m*

period ['pɪəriəd, *Am:* 'pɪri-] **I.** *n* **1.** *a.* GEO
período *m;* **in/over a** ~ **of sth** en/durante un
período de algo **2.** ECON plazo *m;* **a fixed** ~ un
plazo fijo; ~ **of grace** plazo *m* de gracia
3. SCHOOL (*lesson*) hora *f* **4.** (*distinct stage*)
época *f* **5.** (*menstruation*) período *m,* regla *f;*
to have one's ~ tener la regla **6.** *Am* LING
punto *m* final **II.** *interj Am* ¡y punto! *inf*

period furniture *n no pl* mobiliario *m* de
época

periodic [ˌpɪəri'ɒdɪk, *Am:* ˌpɪri'ɑːdɪk] *adj*
periódico, -a

periodical [ˌpɪəri'ɒdɪkl, *Am:* ˌpɪri'ɑːdɪ-] **I.** *n*
(*general*) revista *f;* (*specific*) boletín *m* **II.** *adj*
periódico, -a

periodic table *n* tabla *f* de elementos

peripheral [pə'rɪfərəl] **I.** *adj* **1.** (*importance,*
role) secundario, -a **2.** *a.* ANAT, INFOR periférico,
-a **II.** *n* INFOR periférico *m*

periphery [pə'rɪfəri] <-ies> *n* periferia *f;* (*of*
society) margen *m*

periscope ['perɪskəup, *Am:* -skoup] *n* periscopio *m*

perish ['perɪʃ] *vi* **1.** *liter* (*die*) perecer; ~ **the**
thought! ¡Dios nos libre! **2.** *Aus, Brit* (*deterio-*
rate: rubber, leather) deteriorarse; (*veg-*
etables) estropearse

perishable ['perɪʃəbl] *adj* perecedero, -a

perisher *n Brit, inf* pillo, -a *m, f*

perishing *adj* **1.** (*as intensifier*) dichoso, -a; I
forgot my ~ keys me olvidé las dichosas
llaves **2.** *Aus, Brit, inf* (*extremely cold*) it's ~!
¡hace un frío que pela!; **I'm** ~ estoy muerto de
frío

peritonitis [ˌperɪtə'naɪtɪs, *Am:* -tou'naɪt̬ɪs]
n no pl MED peritonitis *f inv*

perjure ['pɜːdʒə', *Am:* 'pɜːrdʒəˈ] *vt* to ~ oneself perjurar(se)

perjurer ['pɜːdʒərə', *Am:* 'pɜːrdʒəˈəˈ] *n* per-
juro, -a *m, f*

perjury ['pɜːdʒəri, *Am:* 'pɜːr-] *n* perjurio *m*

perk [pɜːk, *Am:* pɜːrk] *n* (*advantage*) ventaja *f*

◆**perk up** **I.** *vi* **1.** (*cheer up*) alegrarse; **to** ~

at sth alegrarse por algo **2.** (*improve*) mejorar
II. *vt* **1.** (*cheer up*) alegrar; (*make more lively*)
animar **2.** (*raise*) **to** ~ **one's ears** aguzar las
orejas

perky ['pɜːki, *Am:* 'pɜːr-] <-ier, -iest> *adj*
alegre

perm[1] [pɜːm, *Am:* pɜːrm] *n* **1.** *inf abbr of*
permanent wave permanente *f,* permanente
m Méx **2.** *Brit, inf abbr of* **permutation** combinación *f*

perm[2] [pɜːm, *Am:* pɜːrm] *vt* to ~ one's hair,
to have one's hair ~ed hacerse la permanente

permafrost ['pɜːməfrɒst, *Am:* 'pɜːrmə-
frɑːst] *n no pl* permafrost *m*

permanence ['pɜːmənənts, *Am:* 'pɜːr-] *n,*
permanency *n no pl* permanencia *f*

permanent ['pɜːmənənt, *Am:* 'pɜːr-] *adj*
(*job*) fijo, -a; (*damage*) irreparable; (*exhibition,*
situation, position) permanente; (*ink*) indeleble; (*relationship*) estable; (*tooth*) definitivo,
-a

permanent wave *n* permanente *f,* permanente *m Méx*

permanganate [pə'mæŋɡəneɪt, *Am:* pəˈ-]
n permanganato *m*

permeable ['pɜːmɪəbl, *Am:* 'pɜːr-] *adj* permeable

permeate ['pɜːmɪeɪt, *Am:* 'pɜːr-] **I.** *vt* (*liquid,*
smoke, smell) impregnar **II.** *vi* to ~ into/
through sth penetrar en/a través de algo

permissible [pə'mɪsəbl, *Am:* pəˈ-] *adj* (*per-*
mitted) permisible; (*acceptable*) tolerable

permission [pə'mɪʃən, *Am:* pəˈ-] *n no pl*
permiso *m*

permissive [pə'mɪsɪv, *Am:* pəˈ-] *adj pej* permisivo, -a

permissiveness *n no pl* permisividad *f*

permit[1] ['pɜːmɪt, *Am:* 'pɜːr-] *n* permiso *m*
(por escrito); **residence** ~ permiso de residencia; **to hold a** ~ tener un permiso

permit[2] [pə'mɪt, *Am:* pəˈ-] <-tt-> **I.** *vt* permitir; **I will not** ~ **you to go there** no te permito que vayas allí; **to** ~ **oneself sth** permitirse algo **II.** *vi* weather ~ing si hace buen
tiempo, si el tiempo no lo impide; **if time** ~s si
hay tiempo; **the law** ~s **of no other interpre-**
tation *form* la ley no acepta otra interpretación

permitted [pə'mɪtɪd, *Am:* pəˈ'mɪt̬-] *adj* permitido, -a

permutation [ˌpɜːmju'teɪʃən, *Am:* ˌpɜːr-] *n*
form **1.** MAT permutación *f* **2.** *Brit* SPORTS combinación *f*

pernicious [pə'nɪʃəs, *Am:* pəˈ-] *adj* **1.** *form*
(*harmful*) perjudicial **2.** MED pernicioso, -a

pernicious anaemia *n Brit,* **pernicious**
anemia *n Am* anemia *f* perniciosa

pernickety [pə'nɪkəti, *Am:* pəˈ'nɪkəti]
Brit, pej **1.** (*exacting*) puntilloso, -a; **to be** ~
about sth ser puntilloso con algo **2.** (*difficult*)
que requiere minuciosidad

peroxide [pə'rɒksaɪd, *Am:* -'rɑːk-] **I.** *n no pl*
peróxido *m;* **hydrogen** ~ agua *f* oxigenada

II. *vt* oxigenar
peroxide blonde *n* rubia *f* teñida
perpendicular [ˌpɜːpənˈdɪkjʊləʳ, *Am:* ˌpɜːr-pənˈdɪkjuːləˑ] I. *adj* perpendicular II. *n* perpendicular *f*
perpetrate [ˈpɜːpɪtreɪt, *Am:* ˈpɜːrpə-] *vt* *form* (*crime*) perpetrar, cometer; (*error*) cometer
perpetration [ˌpɜːpɪˈtreɪʃən, *Am:* ˌpɜːrpəˈ-] *n form* perpetración *f*
perpetrator [ˈpɜːpɪtreɪtəʳ, *Am:* ˈpɜːrpətreɪ-t̬əˑ] *n form* autor(a) *m(f)*, de un delito
perpetual [pəˈpetʃʊəl, *Am:* pəˈpetʃu-] *adj* 1. (*lasting forever*) perpetuo, -a 2. (*repeated*) continuo, -a
perpetuate [pəˈpetʃʊeɪt, *Am:* pəˈpetʃu-] *vt* perpetuar
perpetuity [ˌpɜːpɪˈtjuːəti, *Am:* ˌpɜːrpəˈtuː-əti] *n no pl, form* perpetuidad *f*; **for** [*o* **in**] ~ LAW a perpetuidad
perplex [pəˈpleks, *Am:* pəˈ-] *vt* desconcertar
perplexed [pəˈplekst, *Am:* pəˈ-] *adj* perplejo, -a
perplexity [pəˈpleksəti, *Am:* pəˈpleksəti] <-ies> *n* perplejidad *f*; **to look at sth in** ~ mirar algo con perplejidad
perquisite [ˈpɜːkwɪzɪt, *Am:* ˈpɜːr-] *n Brit, form* (beneficio *m*) extra *m*
persecute [ˈpɜːsɪkjuːt, *Am:* ˈpɜːrsɪ-] *vt* 1. *a.* POL perseguir 2. (*harass*) molestar
persecution [ˌpɜːsɪˈkjuːʃən, *Am:* ˌpɜːrsɪˈ-] *n* persecución *f*
persecution complex *n no pl* manía *f* persecutoria
persecutor *n* perseguidor(a) *m(f)*
perseverance [ˌpɜːsɪˈvɪərəns, *Am:* ˌpɜːrsə-ˈvɪr-] *n no pl* perseverancia *f*
persevere [ˌpɜːsɪˈvɪəʳ, *Am:* ˌpɜːrsəˈvɪr] *vi* perseverar
persevering *adj* perseverante
Persia [ˈpɜːʃə, *Am:* ˈpɜːrʒə] *n no pl* Persia *f*
Persian I. *adj* persa II. *n* 1. (*person*) persa *mf* 2. LING persa *m*
persist [pəˈsɪst, *Am:* pəˈ-] *vi* 1. (*continue: cold, heat, rain*) continuar; (*habit, belief, doubts*) persistir 2. (*person*) insistir
persistence [pəˈsɪstəns, *Am:* pəˈ-] *n no pl* 1. (*of cold, belief*) persistencia *f* 2. (*of person*) insistencia *f*
persistent [pəˈsɪstənt, *Am:* pəˈ-] *adj* 1. (*cold, belief*) persistente 2. (*person*) insistente
persistent offender *n* reincidente *mf*
person [ˈpɜːsən, *Am:* ˈpɜːr-] <people *o form* -s> *n* 1. (*human*) persona *f*; **about** [*o* **on**] **one's** ~ encima; **as a** ~ como persona; **per** ~ por persona 2. LING persona *f*; **first/second** ~ primera/segunda persona
persona [pəˈsəʊnə, *Am:* pəˈsoʊ-] *n form* 1. (*image*) imagen *f* 2. (*character*) personaje *m*
personable [ˈpɜːsənəbl, *Am:* ˈpɜːr-] *adj* agradable
personage [ˈpɜːsənɪdʒ, *Am:* ˈpɜːr-] *n iron,*

form personaje *m*
personal [ˈpɜːsənəl, *Am:* ˈpɜːr-] *adj* 1. (*property*) privado, -a; (*data, belongings, account*) personal 2. (*direct, done in person*) en persona 3. (*private: letter*) personal; (*question*) indiscreto, -a; (*matter*) privado, -a, personal; (*life*) privado, -a 4. (*offensive: comment, remark*) ofensivo, -a; **to get** ~ llevar las cosas al plano personal; **it's nothing** ~ no es nada personal 5. (*bodily, physical: appearance*) personal; (*hygiene*) íntimo, -a 6. (*human*) ~ **quality** calidad *f* humana
personal assistant *n* ayudante *mf* personal
personal computer *n* ordenador *m* personal, computadora *f* personal *AmL*
personality [ˌpɜːsənˈæləti, *Am:* ˌpɜːr-] *n* <-ies> 1. (*character*) personalidad *f* 2. (*famous person*) personalidad *f*, figura *f*
personally *adv* personalmente; **to take sth** ~ ofenderse con [*o* por] algo
personal pronoun *n* pronombre *m* personal
personalty [ˈpɜːsənəlti, *Am:* ˈpɜːrsənəlti] <-ies> *n* bienes *mpl* muebles
personification [pəˌsɒnɪfɪˈkeɪʃən, *Am:* pəˌsɑːnɪ-] *n* personificación *f*; **he is the** ~ **of kindness** es la amabilidad personificada
personify [pəˈsɒnɪfaɪ, *Am:* pəˈsɑːnɪ-] *vt* personificar
personnel [ˌpɜːsənˈel, *Am:* ˌpɜːr-] *n* 1. *pl* (*staff, employees*) personal *m* 2. *no pl* (*department*) departamento *m* de personal
personnel department *n* departamento *m* de personal **personnel director** *n* director(a) *m(f)* de personal **personnel manager** *n* jefe, -a *m, f* de personal
perspective [pəˈspektɪv, *Am:* pəˈ-] *n* perspectiva *f*; **you have to keep things in** ~ no tienes que perder de vista la verdadera dimensión de las cosas; **to put a different** ~ **on things** cambiar el cariz de las cosas
perspicacious [ˌpɜːspɪˈkeɪʃəs, *Am:* ˌpɜːr-] *adj form* perspicaz
perspicacity [ˌpɜːspɪˈkæsəti, *Am:* ˌpɜːr-spɪˈkæsəti] *n no pl, form* perspicacia *f*
perspicuity [ˌpɜːspɪˈkjuːəti, *Am:* ˌpɜːrspɪ-ˈkjuːəti] *n no pl, form* perspicuidad *f*
perspicuous [pəˈspɪkjʊəs, *Am:* pəˈ-] *adj form* perspicuo, -a
perspiration [ˌpɜːspəˈreɪʃən, *Am:* ˌpɜːr-] *n no pl* transpiración *f*; **beads of** ~ gotas *fpl* de sudor
perspire [pəˈspaɪəʳ, *Am:* pəˈspaɪəˑ] *vi* transpirar
persuade [pəˈsweɪd, *Am:* pəˈ-] *vt* convencer; **to** ~ **sb into sth** convencer a alguien de algo; **to** ~ **sb out of sth** disuadir a alguien de algo; **to** ~ **sb to do sth** convencer a alguien de que haga algo; **to** ~ **sb that …** convencer a alguien de que…
persuasion [pəˈsweɪʒən, *Am:* pəˈ-] *n* 1. (*act*) persuasión *f* 2. (*conviction*) creencia *f*
persuasive [pəˈsweɪsɪv, *Am:* pəˈ-] *adj* (*person, manner*) persuasivo, -a; (*argument*) con-

vincente

pert [pɜːt, *Am:* pɜːrt] *adj* **1.** (*nose, buttocks, breasts*) respingón, -ona **2.** (*reply*) descarado, -a **3.** (*hat*) garboso, -a

pertain [pəˈteɪn, *Am:* pəˈ-] *vi form* **to** ~ **to sth** concernir algo

pertinent [ˈpɜːtɪnənt, *Am:* ˈpɜːrtnənt] *adj form* pertinente; **to be** ~ **to sth** guardar relación con algo

perturb [pəˈtɜːb, *Am:* pəˈtɜːrb] *vt form* perturbar

perturbation [ˌpɜːtəˈbeɪʃən, *Am:* ˌpɜːrtəˈ-] *n form* perturbación *f*

Peru [pəˈruː] *n* Perú *m*

perusal [pəˈruːzl] *n no pl, form* lectura *f*; **he sent a copy of the report for their** ~ envió una copia del informe para que lo examinaran

peruse [pəˈruːz] *vt form* (*read*) leer detenidamente; (*examine*) examinar

Peruvian [pəˈruːvɪən] **I.** *adj* peruano, -a **II.** *n* peruano, -a *m, f*

pervade [pəˈveɪd, *Am:* pəˈ-] *vt form* (*attitude, idea*) dominar; (*smell, smoke*) invadir

pervasive [pəˈveɪsɪv, *Am:* pəˈ-] *adj form* (*attitude, idea*) dominante; (*influence*) omnipresente; (*smell*) penetrante

perverse [pəˈvɜːs, *Am:* pəˈvɜːrs] *adj* **1.** (*stubborn*) obstinado, -a **2.** (*unreasonable, deviant, corrupt*) perverso, -a **3.** (*contrary*) contradictorio, -a

perverseness *n no pl, pej* **1.** (*stubbornness*) obstinación *f* **2.** (*unreasonableness, deviancy*) perversidad *f* **3.** (*contrariness*) contradicción *f*

perversion [pəˈvɜːʃən, *Am:* pəˈvɜːrʒən] *n* **1.** (*sexual deviance*) perversión *f* **2.** (*corruption*) ~ **of justice** deformación *f* de la justicia; ~ **of the truth** distorsión *f* de la verdad

perversity [pəˈvɜːsəti, *Am:* pəˈvɜːrsəti] <-ies> *n* **1.** (*stubbornness*) obstinación *f* **2.** (*unreasonableness, wickedness*) perversidad *f*

pervert¹ [ˈpɜːvɜːt, *Am:* ˈpɜːrvɜːrt] *n* (*sexual deviant*) pervertido, -a *m, f*

pervert² [pəˈvɜːt, *Am:* pəˈvɜːrt] *vt* pervertir; **to** ~ **the truth** distorsionar la verdad

perverted *adj* (*person, practice*) pervertido, -a

peseta [pəˈseɪtə] *n* peseta *f*

peso [ˈpeɪsəʊ, *Am:* -soʊ] *n* peso *m*

pessary [ˈpesəri] <-ies> *n* **1.** (*device*) pesario *m* **2.** (*vaginal suppository*) supositorio *m* vaginal

pessimism [ˈpesɪmɪzəm, *Am:* ˈpesə-] *n no pl* pesimismo *m*

pessimist *n* pesimista *mf*

pessimistic [ˌpesɪˈmɪstɪk, *Am:* ˌpesəˈ-] *adj* pesimista; **to be** ~ **about sth** ser pesimista con respecto a algo

pest [pest] *n* **1.** (*destructive insect, animal*) plaga *f* **2.** *inf* (*annoying person*) pesado, -a *m, f*

pest control *n* (*of insects*) fumigación *f*; (*of rats*) desratización *f*

pester [ˈpestəʳ, *Am:* -əˈ-] *vt* molestar

pesticide [ˈpestɪsaɪd, *Am:* ˈpestə-] *n* pesticida *m*

pestiferous [peˈstɪfərəs] *adj* pestilente

pestilent [ˈpestɪlənt, *Am:* ˈpestlənt] *adj*, **pestilential** [ˌpestɪˈlentʃəl, *Am:* ˌpestəˈ-] *adj* **1.** (*deadly*) mortal **2.** (*troublesome*) pesado, -a

pestle [ˈpesl] *n* mano *f* de mortero

pet¹ [pet] **I.** *n* **1.** (*house animal*) animal *m* doméstico **2.** *pej* (*favourite person*) mimado, -a *m, f*; **he's the teacher's** ~ es el mimado del profesor **3.** *inf* (*nice or thoughtful person*) encanto *m* **4.** *Aus, Brit, inf* (*term of endearment*) cariño *m* **II.** *adj* **1.** (*cat, dog, snake*) doméstico, -a **2.** (*favourite: project, theory*) favorito, -a

pet² [pet] <-tt-> **I.** *vi* acariciarse **II.** *vt* **1.** (*caress*) acariciar **2.** (*pamper*) mimar

petal [ˈpetl, *Am:* ˈpetl] *n* **1.** BOT pétalo *m* **2.** *Brit, inf* (*term of endearment*) cariño *m*

petard [peˈtɑːd, *Am:* pɪˈtɑːrd] *n* **he was hoist with his own** ~ *prov* le salió el tiro por la culata

peter [ˈpiːtəʳ, *Am:* -təˈ-] *vi* **to** ~ **away** [*o* **out**] (*trail, track, path*) desaparecer; (*conversation, interest*) decaer

Peter [ˈpiːtəʳ, *Am:* -təˈ-] **to rob** ~ **to pay Paul** *prov* desnudar a un santo para vestir a otro *prov*

petite [pəˈtiːt] *adj* menudo, -a

petition [prˈtɪʃən, *Am:* pəˈ-] **I.** *n* **1.** POL petición *f* **2.** LAW demanda *f* **II.** *vi* **1.** POL **to** ~ **for sth** elevar una petición solicitando algo **2.** LAW **to** ~ **for divorce** presentar una demanda de divorcio **III.** *vt* POL elevar una petición a, peticionar *AmL*

petitioner *n* **1.** POL peticionario, -a *m, f* **2.** LAW demandante *mf*

pet name *n* apodo *m*, sobrenombre *m*

petrel [ˈpetrəl] *n* petrel *m*

Petri dish [ˈpetriˌdɪʃ, *Am:* ˈpiːtriˌdɪʃ] *n* plato *m* de Petri

petrifaction [ˌpetrɪˈfækʃən] *n*, **petrification** [ˌpetrɪfɪˈkeɪʃən] *n* **1.** GEO petrificación *f* **2.** (*terror*) terror *m*

petrified *adj* **1.** GEO petrificado, -a **2.** (*terrified*) aterrorizado, -a

petrify [ˈpetrɪfaɪ] <-ies> **I.** *vi* GEO petrificarse **II.** *vt* **1.** GEO petrificar **2.** (*terrify*) aterrorizar

petrochemical [ˌpetrəʊˈkemɪkəl, *Am:* -roʊˈ-] **I.** *n* producto *m* petroquímico **II.** *adj* petroquímico, -a

petrodollar [ˈpetrəʊˌdɒləʳ, *Am:* -roʊˌdɑːləˈ-] *n* petrodólar *m*

petrol [ˈpetrəl] *n no pl, Aus, Brit* gasolina *f*, nafta *f RíoPl*, bencina *f Chile*; **unleaded** ~ gasolina sin plomo

petrol can *n Aus, Brit* bidón *m* de gasolina

petrol consumption *n no pl, Aus, Brit* consumo *m* de gasolina

petroleum [prˈtrəʊlɪəm, *Am:* pəˈtroʊ-] *n* petróleo *m*, canfín *m AmC*

petrol gauge *n Aus, Brit* indicador *m* (del nivel) de la gasolina **petrol pipe** *n Aus, Brit* oleoducto *m* **petrol pump** *n Aus, Brit* **1.** (*at garage*) surtidor *m* de gasolina **2.** (*in engine*) bomba *f* de gasolina **petrol station** *n Aus, Brit* gasolinera *f,* bomba *f And, Ven,* estación *f* de nafta *RíoPl,* bencinera *f Chile,* grifo *m Perú* **petrol tank** *n Aus, Brit* depósito *m* de gasolina

pet shop *n* ≈ pajarería *f*

petticoat ['petɪkəʊt, *Am:* 'petɪkoʊt] *n* enagua *f,* combinación *f,* fondo *m Méx*

pettifogging ['petɪfɒgɪŋ, *Am:* 'petɪfɑ:gɪŋ] *adj pej* (*person*) puntilloso, -a; (*paper work*) farragoso, -a; (*details*) insignificante

pettiness ['petɪnəs, *Am:* 'pet-] *n no pl* **1.** (*triviality, insignificance*) nimiedad *f* **2.** (*small-mindedness*) mezquindad *f*

petting ['petɪŋ, *Am:* 'pet-] *n* **1.** (*stroking*) caricias *fpl* **2.** (*sexual fondling and touching*) manoseo *m*

petty ['peti, *Am:* 'pet-] <-ier, -iest> *adj* **1.** *pej* (*detail, amount*) trivial, insignificante; (*person, attitude*) mezquino, -a **2.** LAW menor

petty larceny *n* LAW hurto *m* de cosas de poco valor **petty officer** *n* NAUT suboficial *mf* de marina

petulant ['petjələnt, *Am:* 'petʃə-] *adj* enfurruñado, -a

petunia [pɪ'tjuːniə, *Am:* pə'tuːnjə] *n* petunia *f*

pew [pjuː] *n* banco *m* (de iglesia) ▶**take a ~ iron** ¡siéntate!

pewter ['pjuːtər, *Am:* -tə-] *n no pl* peltre *m*

PG *n abbr of* **parental guidance** película para menores acompañados

pg *Am abbr of* **page** pág. *f*

PGCE *n Brit abbr of* **Postgraduate Certificate in Education** diploma de postgrado de pedagogía

pH [ˌpiː'eɪtʃ] pH

phalanx ['fælæŋks, *Am:* 'feɪlæŋks] <-es *o* phalanges> *n form* falange *f*

phallic ['fælɪk] *adj* fálico, -a

phallus ['fæləs] <-es *o* phalli> *n* falo *m*

phantasmal [fæn'tæzməl] *adj liter* **1.** (*imaginary, unreal*) ilusorio, -a **2.** (*ghost-like*) fantasmal

phantom ['fæntəm, *Am:* -təm] I. *n* fantasma *m* II. *adj* **1.** *iron* (*ghostly*) fantasmal **2.** (*imaginary*) ilusorio, -a

pharaoh ['feərəʊ, *Am:* 'feroʊ] *n* faraón *m*

pharisaic(al) [ˌfærɪ'seɪɪk(əl), *Am:* ˌferɪ'-] *adj* farisaico, -a

Pharisee ['færɪsiː, *Am:* 'ferɪ-] *n* fariseo, -a *m, f*

pharmaceutic [ˌfɑːmə'sjuːtɪk, *Am:* ˌfɑːr-mə'suːtɪ-] *adj* farmacéutico, -a

pharmaceutical I. *adj* farmacéutico, -a II. *n pl* fármacos *mpl*

pharmaceutics *n no pl* farmacia *f*

pharmaceutics industry *n no pl* industria *f* farmacéutica

pharmacist ['fɑːməsɪst, *Am:* 'fɑːr-] *n* farmacéutico, -a *m, f,* farmaceuta *mf Col, Ven*

pharmacology [ˌfɑːmə'kɒlədʒi, *Am:* ˌfɑːr-

məˈkɑːlə-] *n no pl* farmacología *f*

pharmacopoeia [ˌfɑːməkə'piːə, *Am:* ˌfɑːr-mə'koʊ-] *n* farmacopea *f*

pharmacy ['fɑːməsi, *Am:* 'fɑːr-] <-ies> *n* farmacia *f*

pharyngitis [ˌfærɪn'dʒaɪtɪs, *Am:* ˌferɪn-'dʒaɪtɪs] *n no pl* faringitis *f*

pharynx ['færɪŋks] <pharynges> *n* faringe *f*

phase [feɪz] I. *n* (*stage*) fase *f;* (*period*) etapa *f;* **to go through a ~** pasar por una etapa; **to be in ~** estar sincronizado; **to be out of ~** estar desfasado II. *vt* **1.** (*do in stages*) realizar por etapas **2.** (*coordinate*) sincronizar

◆**phase in** *vt* introducir paulatinamente

◆**phase out** *vt* (*service*) retirar progresivamente; (*product*) dejar de producir paulatinamente

PhD [ˌpiː'eɪtʃ'diː] *n abbr of* **Doctor of Philosophy** **1.** (*award*) doctorado *m* **2.** (*person*) Dr. *m,* Dra. *f*

pheasant ['fezənt] <-(s)> *n* faisán *m*

phenomena *n pl of* **phenomenon**

phenomenal *adj* (*success, achievement*) espectacular; (*strength*) increíble

phenomenon [fɪ'nɒmɪnən, *Am:* fə'nɑːmə-nɑːn] <phenomena *o* -s> *n* fenómeno *m*

phew [fjuː] *interj inf* ¡uf!

phial ['faɪəl] *n Brit* ampolla *f*

philander [fɪ'lændər, *Am:* -də-] *vi pej* ir detrás de las mujeres

philanderer *n pej* mujeriego *m*

philanthropic [ˌfɪlən'θrɒpɪk, *Am:* -æn-'θrɑːpɪk-] *adj* filantrópico, -a

philanthropist [fɪ'lænθrəpɪst, *Am:* fə'-] *n* filántropo, -a *m, f*

philanthropy [fɪ'lænθrəpi, *Am:* fə'-] *n no pl* filantropía *f*

philatelic [fɪlə'telɪk] *adj* filatélico, -a

philatelist [fɪ'lætəlɪst, *Am:* -'læt-] *n* filatelista *mf*

philately [fɪ'lætəli, *Am:* -'læt-] *n no pl* filatelia *f*

philharmonic [ˌfɪlɑː'mɒnɪk, *Am:* ˌfɪlhɑːr-'mɑːnɪk] *adj* filarmónico, -a

Philippines ['fɪlɪpiːnz, *Am:* 'fɪlə-] *npl* the ~ las Filipinas

philistine ['fɪlɪstaɪn, *Am:* -stiːn] *pej* I. *n* ignorante *mf* II. *adj* ignorante

philological [ˌfɪlə'lɒdʒɪkl, *Am:* -'lɑːdʒɪk-] *adj* filológico, -a

philologist [fɪ'lɒlədʒɪst, *Am:* fɪ'lɑːlə-] *n* filólogo, -a *m, f*

philology [fɪ'lɒlədʒi, *Am:* fɪ'lɑːlə-] *n no pl* filología *f*

philosopher [fɪ'lɒsəfər, *Am:* -'lɑːsəfə-] *n* filósofo, -a *m, f*

philosophic(al) [ˌfɪlə'sɒfɪk(əl), *Am:* -ə'sɑː-fɪk-] *adj* filosófico, -a

philosophize [fɪ'lɒsəfaɪz, *Am:* -'lɑːsə-] *vi* filosofar

philosophy [fɪ'lɒsəfi, *Am:* -'lɑːsə-] *n no pl* filosofía *f*

philter n Am, **philtre** ['fɪltə', Am: -t̬ə'] n Brit filtro m

phlebitis [flɪ'baɪtɪs, Am: fli:'baɪt̬ɪs] n MED flebitis f inv

phlegm [flem] n no pl flema f

phlegmatic [fleg'mætɪk, Am: -'mæt̬-] adj flemático, -a

phobia ['fəʊbiə, Am: 'foʊ-] n PSYCH fobia f

phoenix ['fi:nɪks] n fénix m

phone [fəʊn, Am: foʊn] I. n teléfono m; to hang up [o put down] the ~ colgar el teléfono; to pick up the ~ coger el teléfono; by ~ por teléfono; to be on the ~ Brit estar hablando por teléfono II. vt telefonear, llamar (por teléfono) III. vi telefonear, llamar (por teléfono)

◆**phone back** vt volver a telefonear, volver a llamar (por teléfono)

◆**phone in** I. vi telefonear, llamar (por teléfono); to ~ sick telefonear para dar parte de enfermo II. vt telefonear, llamar por teléfono

◆**phone round** vi hacer llamadas

◆**phone up** vt telefonear, llamar (por teléfono)

phone book n guía f telefónica, directorio m Col, Méx **phone booth** <-es> n cabina f telefónica **phone box** <-es> n Brit cabina f telefónica **phone call** n Brit llamada f (telefónica) **phonecard** n tarjeta f telefónica

phone-in n programa de radio o televisión en el que el público participa por teléfono

phoneme ['fəʊni:m, Am: 'foʊ-] n LING fonema m

phone number n número m de teléfono

phonetic [fə'netɪk, Am: foʊ'net̬-] adj fonético, -a; the International Phonetic Alphabet el Alfabeto Fonético Internacional; ~ transcription transcripción f fonética

phonetician [,fəʊnɪ'tɪʃən, Am: ,foʊnə'-] n fonetista mf

phonetics [fə'netɪks, Am: foʊ'net̬-] n fonética f

phoney ['fəʊni, Am: 'foʊ-] I.<-ier, -iest> adj inf (person, address) falso, -a; (documents) falsificado, -a ▶to be as ~ as a two-dollar bill Am ser más falso que un duro sevillano, ser más falso que un billete de tres pesos Méx II. n (person) farsante mf

phonic ['fɒnɪk, Am: 'fɑ:nɪk] adj LING fónico, -a

phonology [fə'nɒlədʒi, Am: -'nɑ:lə-] n no pl fonología f

phony ['fəʊni, Am: 'foʊ-] adj Am s. **phoney**

phooey ['fu:i] interj iron, inf ¡bobadas!

phosphate ['fɒsfeɪt, Am: 'fɑ:s-] n fosfato m

phosphorescence [,fɒsfə'resns, Am: ,fɑ:s-] n no pl fosforescencia f

phosphorescent [,fɒsfə'resənt, Am: ,fɑ:sfə'res-] adj fosforescente

phosphoric [fɒs'fɒrɪk, Am: fɑ:s'fɔ:r-] adj, **phosphorous** ['fɒsfərəs, Am: 'fɑ:s-] adj fosfórico, -a

phosphorus ['fɒsfərəs, Am: 'fɑ:s-] n no pl fósforo m

photo ['fəʊtəʊ, Am: 'foʊt̬oʊ] <-s> n inf abbr of **photograph** foto f

photo call n rueda f fotográfica

photocell ['fəʊtəʊsel, Am: 'foʊt̬oʊ-] n célula f fotoeléctrica

photocopier ['fəʊtəʊ,kɒpiə', Am: ,foʊt̬oʊ-'kɑ:piə'] n fotocopiadora f

photocopy ['fəʊtəʊ,kɒpi, Am: 'foʊt̬oʊ-,kɑ:pi] I.<-ies> n fotocopia f; to make a ~ of sth hacer una fotocopia de algo II. vt fotocopiar

photocopying bureau n fotocopistería f

photoelectric [,fəʊtəʊɪ'lektrɪk, Am: ,foʊt̬oʊ-] adj fotoeléctrico, -a; ~ cell célula f fotoeléctrica

photo finish n SPORTS resultado m comprobado por fotocontrol

photoflash ['fəʊtəʊ,flæʃ] n flash m

photogenic [,fəʊtəʊ'dʒenɪk, Am: ,foʊt̬oʊ'-] adj fotogénico, -a

photograph ['fəʊtəgrɑ:f, Am: 'foʊt̬oʊ-græf] I. n fotografía f; aerial ~ fotografía aérea; colour/black-and-white ~ fotografía en color/blanco y negro; to take a ~ of sb sacar una fotografía de alguien II. vt fotografiar III. vi to ~ well ser fotogénico

photograph album n álbum m de fotos

photographer [fə'tɒgrəfə', Am: -'tɑ:grəfə'] n fotógrafo, -a m, f; amateur ~ fotógrafo aficionado; ~'s model modelo mf fotográfico, -a

photographic [,fəʊtə'græfɪk, Am: ,foʊt̬ə'-] adj fotográfico, -a

photography [fə'tɒgrəfi, Am: -'tɑ:grə-] n no pl fotografía f

photojournalism [,fəʊtəʊ'dʒɜːnlɪzəm, Am: ,foʊt̬oʊ'dʒɜ:r-] n no pl fotoperiodismo m

photometer [fəʊ'tɒmɪtə'] n fotómetro m

photomontage ['fəʊtəʊmɒn'tɑːʒ, Am: ,foʊt̬oʊmɑ:n'-] n fotomontaje m

photon ['fəʊtɒn, Am: 'foʊtɑ:n] n fotón m

photo opportunity n oportunidad f fotográfica

photo reporter n reportero, -a m, f fotográfico, -a

photosensitive [,fəʊtəʊ'sensɪtɪv, Am: ,foʊt̬oʊ'sensə-] adj fotosensible

photosetting ['fəʊtəʊ,setɪŋ] n ART fotocomposición f

photostat ['fəʊtəstæt, Am: 'foʊt̬oʊ-] <-tt-> vt fotostatar

photosynthesis [,fəʊtəʊ'sɪntθɪsɪs, Am: ,foʊt̬oʊ'-] n no pl fotosíntesis f

phrasal verb [,freɪzəl'vɜːb, Am: ,freɪzəl-'vɜːrb] n LING verbo m con partícula

phrase [freɪz] I. n frase f; (idiomatic expression) expresión f; verb/noun phrase sintagma verbal/nominal; to have a good turn of ~ ser muy elocuente II. vt to ~ sth well/badly expresar algo bien/mal

phrasebook ['freɪzbʊk] n libro m de frases

phraseology [,freɪzi'ɒlədʒi, Am: -'ɑ:lə-] n no pl fraseología f

P

phrenetic [frə'netɪk, *Am:* frɪ'net̪-] *adj s.*
frenetic

phut [fʌt] *interj* to go ~ *Brit, Aus, inf* estropearse

pH-value [ˌpiː'eɪtʃ'væljuː] *n* valor *m* del pH

physical ['fɪzɪkəl] **I.** *adj* físico, -a; ~ **attraction** atracción *f* física; **to be in a weak ~ condition** estar en bajas condiciones físicas; **to have a ~ disability** sufrir una discapacidad física; ~ **exercise** ejercicio *m* físico **II.** *n* MED reconocimiento *m* médico

physical education *n* educación *f* física

physically *adv* (*attractive*) físicamente; (*dangerous*) desde el punto de vista físico

physician [fɪ'zɪʃən] *n Am* médico, -a *m, f*

physicist ['fɪzɪsɪst] *n* físico, -a *m, f*; (*student*) estudiante *mf* de física

physics ['fɪzɪks] **I.** *n no pl* física *f* **II.** *adj* físico, -a

physio ['fɪziəʊ, *Am:* -oʊ] *n* **1.** *abbr of* **physiotherapist** fisioterapeuta *mf* **2.** *no pl abbr of* **physiotherapy** fisioterapia *f*

physiognomy [ˌfɪzi'ɒnəmi, *Am:* -'ɑːgnə-] *n no pl* fisonomía *f*

physiological [ˌfɪziə'lɒdʒɪkəl, *Am:* -'lɑːdʒɪk-] *adj* fisiológico, -a

physiologist *n* fisiólogo, -a *m, f*; (*student*) estudiante *mf* de fisiología

physiology [ˌfɪzi'ɒlədʒi, *Am:* -'ɑːlə-] *n no pl* fisiología *f*

physiotherapist *n* fisioterapeuta *mf*

physiotherapy [ˌfɪziəʊ'θerəpi, *Am:* -oʊ'-] *n no pl* fisioterapia *f*

physique [fɪ'ziːk] *n* físico *m*

pianist ['pɪənɪst, *Am:* 'piːnɪst] *n* pianista *mf*

piano ['pjɑːnəʊ, *Am:* pi'ænoʊ] <-s> *n* piano *m*; **to play the ~** tocar el piano

piazza [pɪ'ætsə, *Am:* -'ɑːt-] *n* plaza *f*

picaresque [ˌpɪkə'resk, *Am:* -ə·'-] *adj* LIT picaresco, -a

piccaninny [ˌpɪkə'nɪni, *Am:* 'pɪk-] <-ies> *n pej* (*child*) negrito, -a *m, f*

piccolo ['pɪkələʊ, *Am:* -loʊ] <-s> *n* flautín *m*

pick [pɪk] **I.** *vt* **1.** (*select*) elegir; **to ~ sb for sth** elegir a alguien para algo; **to ~ sth at random** elegir algo al azar; **to ~ a fine time to do sth** *iron* escoger un buen momento para hacer algo; **to ~ one's way** moverse con cuidado **2.** (*harvest: fruit, vegetables*) recoger **3.** (*touch*) tocar; **to ~ one's nose** hurgarse la nariz; **to ~ one's teeth** limpiarse los dientes con un mondador; **to ~ holes in sth** *fig* encontrar fallos a algo **4.** MUS (*guitar*) tocar **5.** (*steal*) robar; **to ~ a lock** forzar una cerradura; **to ~ sb's pocket** robar algo del bolsillo de alguien; **to ~ sb's brain** *fig* aprovecharse de los conocimientos de alguien **II.** *vi* **to ~ and choose** tardar en escoger **III.** *n* **1.** (*selection*) elección *f*; (*of people*) selección *f*; **to take one's ~** elegir; **to have one's ~** poder elegir; **the ~ of the bunch** el mejor del grupo **2.** (*pickaxe*) pico *m*; **with ~s and shovels** con

pico y pala

◆**pick at** *vt insep* **1.** (*toy with: food*) picotear **2.** (*handle*) manosear; (*scratch*) rascar **3.** (*bother*) **to ~ sb/sth** fastidiar a alguien/algo

◆**pick off** *vt* **1.** (*shoot*) abatir (a tiros) **2.** *fig* (*take the best*) escoger lo mejor **3.** (*pull off*) separar; **to pick an apple off the tree** coger una manzana del árbol

◆**pick on** *vt insep* **1.** (*victimize*) meterse con **2.** (*select*) **to ~ sb for sth** escoger a alguien para algo

◆**pick out** *vt* **1.** (*choose*) elegir **2.** (*recognize*) distinguir

◆**pick over** *vt* ir revolviendo y examinando

◆**pick up I.** *vt* **1.** (*lift*) levantar; **to ~ the phone** coger el teléfono; **to pick oneself up** ponerse de pie; **to pick oneself up off the floor** levantarse del suelo; **to ~ the pieces** *fig* empezar de nuevo **2.** (*get*) conseguir; (*conversation*) captar; **to ~ a bargain** conseguir una ganga; **to ~ an illness** contagiarse con una enfermedad; **to ~ speed** coger velocidad; **to ~ the bill** *inf* pagar la cuenta **3.** (*collect*) recoger; **to pick sb up** recoger a alguien **4.** (*buy*) adquirir **5.** (*detect: noise*) detectar **6.** (*learn*) aprender **7.** (*sexually*) **to pick sb up** ligarse a alguien **8.** *Brit, Aus, inf* (*halt*) detener; (*arrest*) arrestar **9.** (*reprimand*) reprender; **to pick sb up on sth** reprender a alguien por algo **10.** *inf* (*earn*) ganar **II.** *vi* **1.** (*improve*) mejorar; (*numbers*) ir a mejor; MED reponerse **2.** (*continue*) continuar; **to ~ where one left off** reanudar donde uno lo dejó

pickaback ['pɪkəbæk] *n inf s.* **piggyback**

pickax *n Am,* **pickaxe** ['pɪkæks] *n Brit, Aus* pico *m*

picker *n* recolector(a) *m(f)*

picket ['pɪkɪt] **I.** *n* **1.** (*striker*) a. MIL piquete *m* **2.** (*stake*) estaca *f* **II.** *vt* (*in strike*) formar piquete en

picket fence *n* valla *f* **picket line** *n* piquete *m*; **to be on the ~** participar en un piquete; **to cross the ~** no hacer caso de un piquete

picking *n* selección *f*

picking list *n Am* COM inventario *m* de ganancias

pickings ['pɪkɪŋz] *npl* sobras *fpl*

pickle ['pɪkl] **I.** *n* encurtido *m; Am* (*cucumber*) pepinillo *m* en vinagre al eneldo ▶**to be in a** (**pretty**) **~** *inf* estar en un (buen) berenjenal **II.** *vt* (*vegetables*) conservar en vinagre; (*fish*) conservar en escabeche

pickled *adj* **1.** (*vegetables*) encurtido, -a; (*fish*) en escabeche **2.** *fig, inf* (*drunk*) borracho, -a; **to get ~** emborracharse

picklock ['pɪklɒk, *Am:* -lɑːk] *n* **1.** (*burglar*) ladrón, -ona *m, f* **2.** (*instrument*) ganzúa *f*

pick-me-up ['pɪkmiʌp] *n* tónico *m*; (*drink*) bebida *f* estimulante

pickpocket ['pɪkpɒkɪt, *Am:* -ˌpɑːkɪt] *n* carterista *mf*, bolsista *mf Am C, Méx*

pick-up ['pɪkʌp] *n* **1.** (*part of record player*) brazo *m* del tocadiscos **2.** *inf* (*collection*) recogida *f* **3.** (*vehicle*) camioneta *f* con plataforma

pick-up point *n* punto *m* de recogida

picky ['pɪki] <-ier, -iest> *adj pej, inf* criticón, -ona; **to be a ~ eater** ser caprichoso para comer

picnic ['pɪknɪk] **I.** *n* picnic *m;* **to take a ~** hacer un picnic; **to go on a ~** ir de picnic; **to seem like a ~** parecer agradable; **to be no ~** *fig* no ser nada agradable **II.** <-ck-> *vi* ir de merienda al campo

picnicker *n* excursionista *mf*

picnic lunch *n* picnic *m* **picnic site** *n* lugar *m* para hacer picnics

pictogram ['pɪktəgræm] *n* pictograma *m*

pictorial [pɪk'tɔːriəl] *adj* (*form, method*) pictórico, -a; (*book, brochure*) ilustrado, -a

picture ['pɪktʃəʳ, *Am:* -tʃɚ] **I.** *n* **1.** (*image*) imagen *f;* (*painting*) pintura *f;* (*drawing*) ilustración *f;* **to draw a ~** hacer un dibujo; **to paint a ~** pintar un cuadro; **as pretty as a ~** como de postal **2.** (*photo*) fotografía *f;* **to take a ~** sacar una fotografía; **satellite ~** fotografía por satélite; **wedding ~** fotografía de boda **3.** (*film*) película *f;* **to make a ~** hacer una película; **to go to the ~s** ir al cine **4.** (*mental image*) imagen *f* **5.** *fig* (*depiction*) representación *f;* **to paint a ~ of sth** representar algo ►**a ~ is worth a thousand words** *prov* una imagen vale más que mil palabras; **to paint a very** <u>black</u> ~ pintar un panorama muy negro; **to** <u>be</u> **in the ~** estar al corriente; **to** <u>get</u> **the ~** entender; **to** <u>keep</u> **sb in the ~ (about sth)** mantener a alguien al tanto (de algo); **to** <u>put</u> **sb in the ~** poner a alguien en antecedentes **II.** *vt* imaginarse; (*depict*) representar; **to ~ oneself … imaginarse…**

picture book *n* libro *m* ilustrado **picture frame** *n* marco *m* (para cuadro) **picture gallery** *n* galería *f* de arte **picture-goer** *n* cinéfilo, -a *m, f* **picture library** *n* pinacoteca *f* **picture postcard** *n* tarjeta *f* postal **picture puzzle** *n* rompecabezas *m inv*

picturesque [ˌpɪktʃə'resk] *adj* **1.** (*scenic*) pintoresco, -a **2.** *iron* (*language*) vívido, -a

picture tube *n* tubo *m* de imagen **picture window** *n* ventanal *m*

piddle ['pɪdl] *inf* **I.** *n* orina *f* **II.** *interj* ¡mierda! **III.** *vi* mear

piddling ['pɪdlɪŋ] *adj pej, inf* de poca monta; **the ~ sum of £5** la insignificante suma de 5 libras

pidgin ['pɪdʒɪn] *n* **1.** LING *versión simplificada de una lengua* **2.** *inf* **to speak ~ English/French** chapurrear algo de inglés/francés

pie [paɪ] *n* tarta *f,* pay *m AmS* ►**it's ~ in the** <u>sky</u> es como prometer la luna; **(as)** <u>easy</u> **as ~** más fácil imposible; **to eat** <u>humble</u> ~ tragarse las palabras

piebald ['paɪbɔːld] *adj* pío, -a

piece [piːs] *n* **1.** (*bit: of wood, metal, food*) trozo *m;* (*of text*) sección *f;* (*of land*) terreno *m;* (*of broken glass*) fragmento *m;* **a ~ of paper** (*scrap*) un trozo de papel; (*sheet*) una hoja; **in one ~** en una sola pieza; **in ~s** en pedazos; **to break sth to/in ~** hacer algo pedazos; **to tear sth into ~s** desgarrar algo; **(all) in one ~** (todo) de una pieza; **~ by ~** pieza por pieza; **to come to ~s** (*shatter*) hacerse añicos; (*made to be disassembled*) ser desmontable; **to take sth to ~s** *Brit* desmontar algo; **to go (all) to ~s** (*trauma*) sufrir un ataque de nervios; (*collapse, break*) venirse abajo **2.** (*item, one of set*) unidad *f;* **~ of luggage** bulto *m;* **~ of clothing** prenda *f* de vestir; **~ of equipment** aparato *m* **3.** (*game*) pieza *f* **4.** (*scrap*) **a ~ of advice** un consejo; **~ of evidence** prueba *f;* **a ~ of information** una información; **a ~ of news** una noticia **5.** ART, MUS pieza *f;* PUBL anuncio *m;* **~ of theatre** obra *f* de teatro; **a ~ of writing** un texto **6.** (*coin*) moneda *f;* **a 50p ~** una moneda de 50 peniques ►**to get a ~ of the** <u>action</u> *Am* (*profits*) obtener una parte del beneficio; (*get excitement*) pasarlo bien; **to be a ~ of** <u>cake</u> *inf* ser pan comido; **to want a ~ of the** <u>cake</u> querer parte del pastel; **to give sb a ~ of one's** <u>mind</u> *inf* decir cuatro verdades a alguien; **to** <u>say</u> **one's ~** decir lo que uno quiere decir

◆**piece together** *vt* (*reconstruct*) reconstruir; **to ~ evidence** atar cabos

piecemeal ['piːsmiːl] **I.** *adv* poco a poco **II.** *adj* que va poco a poco

piece number *n* número *m* de pieza **piece price** *n* precio *m* por unidad **piece rate** *n* precio *m* por unidad

piecework ['piːswɜːk, *Am:* -wɜːrk] *n no pl* trabajo *m* a destajo; **to do ~** trabajar a destajo

piece-worker *n* destajista *mf*

pied [paɪd] *adj* pío, -a

pie-eyed [ˌpaɪ'aɪd] *adj inf* (*drunk*) **to be ~** estar como una cuba

pier [pɪəʳ, *Am:* pɪr] *n* **1.** (*jetty*) muelle *m,* malecón *m* **2.** ARCHIT (*pillar*) columna *f;* (*bridge support*) pila *f*

pierce [pɪəs, *Am:* pɪrs] **I.** *vt* (*perforate*) perforar; **to ~ a hole in sth** agujerear algo; **to have one's ears ~d** agujerearse las orejas **II.** *vi* (*drill*) **to ~ into sth** penetrar en algo; **to ~ through sth** atravesar algo

piercing I. *adj* **1.** (*wind*) cortante; **it's ~ cold!** ¡hace un frío que pela! **2.** (*eyes, gaze, look*) penetrante; (*question, reply, wit*) punzante; (*sarcasm*) agudo, -a **3.** (*cry*) desgarrador(a) **II.** *n* piercing *m*

piety ['paɪəti, *Am:* -ti] *n no pl* piedad *f*

piffle ['pɪfl] *n no pl, inf* disparates *mpl*

piffling ['pɪflɪŋ] *adj inf* insignificante

pig [pɪg] **I.** *n* **1.** ZOOL cerdo *m* **2.** *pej, inf* (*person*) cochino, -a *m, f;* **to be a ~** *Brit* ser un cerdo; **to be a ~ to sb** portarse mal con alguien ►**to make a ~'s** <u>ear</u> **of sth** *Brit, inf* hacer algo fatal; **to buy a ~ in a** <u>poke</u> cerrar un trato a ciegas; **to sell a ~ in a** <u>poke</u> dar gato por liebre; **~s might** <u>fly</u> *inf* ¡y un jamón!; **to** <u>make</u> **a ~ of oneself** ponerse como un cerdo II. *vt* **to ~ oneself on sth** comer demasiado de algo

◆**pig out** *vi inf* ponerse morado

pigeon ['pɪdʒən] *n* paloma *f;* **it's not my ~** eso no me corresponde

pigeon fancier *n Brit, Aus* colombófilo, -a *m, f*

pigeonhole ['pɪdʒənhəʊl, *Am:* -hoʊl] I. *n* casilla *f;* **to put sb in a ~** encasillar a alguien II. *vt* **to ~ sb** encasillar a alguien; **to ~ sb as sth** poner la etiqueta de algo a alguien

pigeon-toed ['pɪdʒəntəʊd, *Am:* -toʊd] *adj* **to be ~** tener los pies torcidos hacia dentro

piggery ['pɪgəri] <-ies> *n* **1.** AGR pocilga *f* **2.** (*gluttony*) glotonería *f*

piggish ['pɪgɪʃ] *adj pej* puerco, -a

piggy ['pɪgi] I. *adj* <-ier, -iest> *inf* **1.** (*pig-like*) con apariencia de cerdo; **~ eyes** ojos *mpl* pequeños **2.** (*greedy*) glotón, -ona II. <-ies> *n childspeak* cerdito *m*

piggyback ['pɪgibæk] *n* **to give a child a ~** llevar a un niño a caballito

piggy bank *n* hucha *f, en forma de cerdito*

pigheaded [ˌpɪg'hedɪd] *adj* testarudo, -a

pig iron *n* hierro *m* bruto

piglet ['pɪglət, *Am:* -lɪt] *n* cochinillo *m*

pigment ['pɪgmənt] *n* pigmento *m*

pigmentation [ˌpɪgmen'teɪʃən] *n no pl* pigmentación *f*

pigmy ['pɪgmi] I. <-ies> *n* **1.** (*short person*) pigmeo, -a *m, f* **2.** (*unimportant person*) enano, -a *m, f* II. *adj* ZOOL enano, -a

pigskin ['pɪgskɪn] *n* **1.** (*leather*) piel *f* de cerdo **2.** *Am, inf* (*American football ball*) pelota *f* de fútbol americano

pigsty ['pɪgstaɪ] *n a. fig, pej* pocilga *f*

pigswill ['pɪgswɪl] *n no pl* bazofia *f*

pigtail ['pɪgteɪl] *n* (*single*) coleta *f;* (*one of two plaits*) trenza *f;* **to have one's hair in ~s** llevar el pelo trenzado

pike¹ [paɪk] *n* (*fish*) lucio *m*

pike² [paɪk] *n* (*weapon*) pica *f*

pike³ [paɪk] *n Am* autopista *f*

pikestaff ['paɪkstɑːf, *Am:* -stæf] *n no pl* **as plain as a ~** *Brit* claro como la luz del día

pilaster [pɪ'læstəʳ, *Am:* -tə·] *n* pilastra *f*

pilchard ['pɪltʃəd, *Am:* -tʃə·d] *n* sardina *f*

pile [paɪl] I. *n* **1.** (*heap*) montón *m;* **to have ~s of sth** *inf* tener montones de algo; **to make a ~** *fig, inf* hacer fortuna **2.** (*stack*) pila *f* **3.** ELEC pila *f* **4.** ARCHIT pila *f* **5.** (*of carpet*) pelo *m* II. *vt* amontonar; **to ~ sth high** apilar algo

◆**pile in** *vi* ~! ¡todos dentro, que nos vamos!

◆**pile on** *vt* **1.** (*enter*) entrar desordenadamente **2.** (*heap*) amontonar; **to pile sth on sth** amontonar algo encima de algo **3. to pile it on** *inf* exagerar; **to ~ the agony** *Brit, inf* aumentar el dolor

◆**pile up** I. *vi* **1.** (*accumulate*) acumularse **2.** (*form a pile*) apilarse II. *vt* amontonar

pile-driver ['paɪlˌdraɪvəʳ, *Am:* -və·] *n* martinete *m*

piles *npl inf* almorranas *fpl*

pile-up ['paɪlʌp] *n* accidente *m* múltiple

pilfer ['pɪlfəʳ, *Am:* -fə·] *vt* ratear

pilfering *n* hurtos *mpl*

pilgrim ['pɪlgrɪm] *n* peregrino, -a *m, f*

pilgrimage ['pɪlgrɪmɪdʒ] *n* peregrinación *f;* **to make a ~** hacer una peregrinación

pill [pɪl] *n* pastilla *f,* píldora *f;* **the ~** (*contraception*) la píldora; **to be on the ~** estar tomando la píldora ►**to be a** <u>bitter</u> **~ to swallow** ser un trago amargo; **to** <u>pop</u> **~s** drogarse con pastillas; **to** <u>sweeten</u> [*o* sugar] **the ~** dorar la píldora

pillage ['pɪlɪdʒ] I. *vt form* saquear II. *vi* realizar un saqueo III. *n no pl, form* saqueo *m*

pillar ['pɪləʳ, *Am:* -ə·] *n* **1.** ARCHIT pilar *m,* columna *f;* **a ~ of flame/smoke** una columna de fuego/humo **2.** *fig* (*of support*) sostén *m;* **to be a ~ of strength** ser firme como una roca ►**to chase sb from ~ to** <u>post</u> acosar a alguien

pillar box *n Brit* buzón *m*

pillbox ['pɪlbɒks, *Am:* -bɑːks] *n* **1.** (*for tablets*) pastillero *m* **2.** MIL fortín *m*

pillion ['pɪliən, *Am:* 'pɪljən] *Brit, Aus* I. *n* (*motorbike*) asiento *m* de atrás II. *adv* **to ride/sit ~** montarse/sentarse en el asiento de atrás

pillory ['pɪləri] I. <-ie-> *vt* **to ~ sb/sth** poner en ridículo a alguien/algo II. *n* picota *f*

pillow ['pɪləʊ, *Am:* -oʊ] *n* **1.** (*for bed*) almohada *f* **2.** *Am* (*cushion*) cojín *m*

pillowcase ['pɪləʊkeɪs, *Am:* -oʊ-] *n,* **pillow cover** *n,* **pillowslip** *n* funda *f* de almohada

pilot ['paɪlət] I. *n* **1.** AVIAT piloto *mf* **2.** NAUT práctico *mf* **3.** TV programa *m* piloto **4.** TECH (*light*) piloto *m* II. *vt* **1.** (*plane*) pilotar **2.** (*boat*) guiar **3.** COM (*product*) desarrollar; **to ~ a bill** encargarse de un proyecto de ley

pilot boat *n* bote *m* del práctico **pilot fish** *n* pez *m* piloto **pilot instructor** *n* instructor(a) *m(f)* de vuelo

pilotless *adj* sin piloto

pilot light *n* piloto *m* **pilot plant** *n* planta *f* piloto **pilot program** *n Am,* **pilot scheme** *n Brit, Aus* programa *m* piloto **pilot's licence** *n* licencia *f* de vuelo **pilot study** *n* estudio *m* piloto **pilot survey** *n* estudio *m* experimental **pilot test** *n* prueba *f* piloto

pimento [pɪ'mentəʊ, *Am:* -toʊ] <-s> *n* pimiento *m*

pimp [pɪmp] I. *n* chulo *m* II. *vi* hacer de chulo

pimple ['pɪmpl] *n* grano *m*

pimply ['pɪmpli] <-ier, -iest> *adj* lleno, -a de granos

pin [pɪn] I. *n* **1.** (*needle*) alfiler *m;* MIL (*on grenade*) arandela *f;* **tie ~** alfiler *m* de corbata **2.** *Am* (*brooch*) prendedor *m* **3.** *pl, iron* patas *fpl* ►**to have ~s and** <u>needles</u> sentir un hormigueo; **as bright as a** <u>new</u> **~** brillante como una patena; **you could have heard a ~ <u>drop</u>** se podía oír hasta el vuelo de una mosca **II.** <-nn-> *vt* (*attach using pin*) **to ~ sth on** prender algo con un alfiler; **to ~ back one's ears** *fig* escuchar atentamente

◆**pin down** *vt* **1.** (*define*) precisar **2.** (*locate*) concretar **3.** (*pressure to decide*) presionar **4.** (*restrict movement*) inmovilizar

◆**pin together** *vt* unir; **to pin papers together** grapar papeles

◆**pin up** *vt* (*attach using pins*) recoger con alfileres; (*picture on wall*) fijar con chinchetas; **to ~ one's hair** recogerse el pelo con horquillas

PIN [pɪn] *n abbr of* **personal identification number** PIN *m* (*número de identificación personal*)

pinafore ['pɪnəfɔːʳ, *Am:* -fɔːr] *n* **1.** (*apron*) delantal *m* **2.** *Brit, Aus* pichi *m*

pinafore dress *n* pichi *m*

pinball ['pɪnbɔːl] *n* **to play ~** jugar al flíper

pinball machine *n* flíper *m*

pincers ['pɪntsəz, *Am:* -sɚz] *npl* **1.** ZOOL pinzas *fpl* **2.** (*tool*) tenazas *fpl*

pinch [pɪntʃ] **I.** *vt* **1.** (*nip, tweak*) pellizcar; **to ~ oneself** *fig* pellizcarse para ver si no se está soñando **2.** (*be too tight*) apretar; **the shoes ~ my feet** los zapatos me aprietan **3.** *inf* (*steal*) birlar **II.** *vi* **1.** (*squeeze with fingers*) estrujar **2.** (*boots, shoes, slippers*) apretar **III.** *n* **1.** (*nip*) pellizco *m;* **to give sb a ~** dar un pellizco a alguien; **at a ~, in a ~** *Am* si realmente es necesario; **to feel the ~** pasar apuros **2.** (*small quantity*) pizca *f* ▶**to take sth with a ~ of <u>salt</u>** tomar algo con cierto escepticismo

pinched ['pɪntʃt] *adj* demacrado, -a

pincushion ['pɪnˌkʊʃən] *n* acerico *m*

pine[1] [paɪn] *n* (*tree, wood*) pino *m*

pine[2] [paɪn] *vi* **to ~** (**away**) languidecer; **to ~ for sb** suspirar por alguien

◆**pine away** *vi* languidecer

pineal ['pɪniəl] *adj* pineal

pineal body *n,* **pineal gland** *n* glándula *f* pineal

pineapple ['paɪnæpl] *n* piña *f;* **tinned ~s** piña *f* en almíbar

pine cone *n* piña *f*

pine grove *n* pinar *m* **pine needle** *n* aguja *f* de pino **pine wood** *n no pl* madera *f* de pino

ping [pɪŋ] **I.** *n* (*sound: of bell*) tintín *m;* (*of glass, metal*) sonido *m* metálico **II.** *vi* tintinear; (*click*) hacer clic

ping-pong ['pɪŋˌpɒŋ, *Am:* -ˌpɑːŋ] *n no pl, inf* ping-pong *m*

pinhead ['pɪnhed] *n* **1.** (*part of pin*) cabeza *f* de alfiler **2.** *pej, inf* (*simpleton*) cabeza *f* de chorlito

pinion[1] ['pɪnjən] *vt* inmovilizar; **she was ~ed against the wall** estaba contra la pared sin poderse mover

pinion[2] ['pɪnjən] *n* TECH piñón *m*

pink [pɪŋk] **I.** *n* **1.** (*colour*) rosa *m* **2.** BOT cla-

velina *f* ▶**to be in the ~** rebosar de salud **II.** *adj* rosado, -a; **to turn ~ with pleasure/ embarrassment** ponerse colorado de placer/ vergüenza

pinkie ['pɪŋki] *n Am, Aus, inf* dedo *m* meñique

pinking shears *npl* tijeras *fpl* dentadas

pinko ['pɪŋkəʊ, *Am:* -koʊ] <-s *o* -es> *n pej* POL rojo, -a *m, f*

pinnacle ['pɪnəkl] *n* **1.** *pl* (*of mountain*) pico *m* **2.** ARCHIT (*tower*) pináculo *m* **3.** *no pl, fig* cúspide *f*

pinpoint ['pɪnpɔɪnt] **I.** *vt* (*location, reason*) indicar con toda precisión; **to ~ the cause of sth** señalar la causa de algo **II.** *adj* exacto, -a; **~ accuracy** gran precisión *f*

pinprick ['pɪnprɪk] *n pl* pinchazo *m*

pinstripe ['pɪnstraɪp] **I.** *adj* de raya diplomática **II.** *n no pl* (*stripe*) raya *f* fina; (*suit*) traje *m* de raya diplomática

pint [paɪnt] *n* pinta *f* (*Aus, Brit* = 0,57 l, *Am* = 0,47 l); **a ~ of beer/milk** una pinta de cerveza/leche

pinta ['paɪntə, *Am:* -ţə] *n Brit, inf* pinta *f* (de leche)

pint-size(d) ['paɪntsaɪz(d)] *adj inf* pequeño, -a

pin-up ['pɪnʌp] *n* **1.** (*poster*) póster *m* (*de una celebridad*) **2.** (*man*) chico *m* de póster; (*girl*) pin-up *f*

pioneer [ˌpaɪə'nɪəʳ, *Am:* -'nɪr] **I.** *n* pionero, -a *m, f* **II.** *vt* hacer los preparativos para

pioneering *adj* innovador(a)

pious ['paɪəs] *adj* **1.** REL piadoso, -a **2.** *iron* piadoso, -a; **~ intentions** intenciones *fpl* piadosas; **~ hope** *Brit* esperanza *f* piadosa

pip[1] [pɪp] *n* BOT pepita *f*

pip[2] [pɪp] *n pl, Brit* (*sound*) pitido *m*

pip[3] [pɪp] <-pp-> *vt Brit, inf* vencer; **to ~ sb at the post** ganar a alguien en el último momento

pipe [paɪp] **I.** *n* **1.** TECH (*tube*) tubo *m;* (*smaller*) caño *m;* (*for gas, water*) cañería *f* **2.** (*for smoking*) pipa *f,* cachimba *f AmL;* **to light one's ~** encenderse la pipa; **put that in your ~ and smoke it** *iron* ¡chúpate eso! **3.** MUS (*wind instrument*) caramillo *m;* (*in organ*) cañón *m;* **~s** gaita *f* **II.** *vt* **1.** (*transport*) transportar por tuberías **2.** (*speak shrilly, chirping*) decir con voz estridente **III.** *vi* trinar; (*very loudly*) hablar muy alto

◆**pipe down** *vi inf* (*be quiet*) callarse; (*become quieter*) calmarse

◆**pipe up** *vi* decir inesperadamente

pipe cleaner *n* limpiapipas *m inv*

pipe dream *n* sueño *m* imposible

pipe-fitter *n* fontanero, -a *m, f*

pipeline ['paɪplaɪn] *n* tubería *f;* **to be in the ~** *fig* estar tramitándose

piper ['paɪpəʳ, *Am:* -pɚ] *n* gaitero, -a *m, f* ▶**he who pays the ~ calls the <u>tune</u>** *prov* quien paga, manda

piping ['paɪpɪŋ] *n no pl* **1.** FASHION ribete *m*

2. (*pipes*) tubería *f*

piping hot *adv* bien caliente

pipsqueak ['pɪpskwiːk] *n pej, inf* fantoche *m*

piquant ['piːkənt] *adj* **1.** (*food*) picante **2.** (*intriguing*) intrigante

pique [piːk] **I.** *n no pl* resentimiento *m;* **to do sth in a fit of** ~ hacer algo motivado por el rencor **II.** *vt* **1.** (*annoy*) ofender **2.** (*arouse*) **to** ~ **sb's curiosity/interest** despertar la curiosidad/el interés de alguien

piracy ['paɪərəsi, *Am:* 'paɪrə-] *n no pl* NAUT, COM piratería *f;* **software** ~ piratería *f* de software

pirate ['paɪərət, *Am:* 'paɪrət] **I.** *n* pirata *m* **II.** *adj* pirata; ~ **copy** copia *f* pirata; ~ **video** vídeo *m* pirata **III.** *vt* piratear

pirouette [ˌpɪrʊ'et, *Am:* -u'et] **I.** *n* pirueta *f* **II.** *vi* piruetear

Pisces ['paɪsiːz] *n* Piscis *m*

piss [pɪs] *vulg* **I.** *n no pl* meada *f;* **to have a** ~ mear; **to need a** ~ tener ganas de mear ►**to take the** ~ (**out of sb**) *Brit* cachondearse (de alguien) **II.** *vi* **1.** (*urinate*) mear **2.** *Brit, Aus* (*rain*) llover; **it's** ~**ing with rain** estar lloviendo a cántaros **III.** *vt* **to** ~ **oneself laughing** mearse de risa

◆**piss about, piss around** *Brit, Aus* **I.** *vi inf* **1.** (*act silly*) hacer el burro **2.** (*waste time*) perder el tiempo **II.** *vt inf* **to piss sb about** [*o* **around**] (*waste time*) hacer perder el tiempo a alguien

pissed [pɪst] *adj inf* **to be** ~ **1.** *Brit, Aus* (*drunk*) estar borracho **2.** *Am* (*angry*) estar de mala leche

piss-up ['pɪsʌp] *n Brit, Aus, inf* juerga *f* de borrachera

pistachio [pɪ'staːʃiəʊ, *Am:* -'stæʃioʊ] <-s> *n* pistacho *m,* pistache *m Méx*

pistil ['pɪstɪl] *n* pistilo *m*

pistol ['pɪstəl] *n* pistola *f;* **to hold a** ~ **to sb's head** *fig* poner a alguien entre la espada y la pared

pistol shot *n* pistoletazo *m*

piston ['pɪstən] *n* TECH pistón *m*

piston engine *n* motor *m* de pistón **piston ring** *n* aro *m* de pistón

pit¹ [pɪt] **I.** *n* **1.** (*in ground*) hoyo *m;* (*on metal*) muesca *f;* (*on face*) marca *f;* **in the** ~ **of the stomach** en la boca del estómago **2.** (*mine*) mina *f;* **to go down the** ~ bajar a las minas; **to work in the** ~**s** trabajar en las minas **3. the** ~**s** *pl, fig, inf* lo peor **4.** *inf* (*untidy place*) lobera *f* **5.** THEAT (*seating area*) patio *m* de asientos; (*orchestral area*) platea *f* **6. the** ~**s** *pl* SPORTS los boxes **II.** <-tt-> *vt* **to be** ~**ted** (**with sth**) tener marcas (formadas por algo)

pit² [pɪt] <-tt-> *Am* **I.** *n* (*of fruit*) hueso *m* **II.** *vt* GASTR deshuesar

pit-a-pat [ˌpɪtə'pæt, *Am:* 'pɪɾəpæt] **I.** *adv* **his heart went** ~ su corazón empezó a palpitar a gran velocidad **II.** *n* (*of feet*) paso *m* ligero; (*of heart*) latido *m*

pitch¹ [pɪtʃ] **I.** *n* **1.** *Brit, Aus* (*playing field*) campo *m;* **football/rugby** ~ campo de fútbol/rugby **2.** *Brit* (*place for camping*) terreno *m* para acampar **3.** *Am* (*baseball*) lanzamiento *m* **4.** MUS, LING tono *m* **5.** (*volume*) volumen *m;* **to be at fever** ~ estar muy emocionado **6.** (*spiel*) rollo *m;* **sales** ~ labia *f* para vender; **to make a** ~ soltar un rollo **7.** (*slope*) grado *m* de inclinación; **low/steep** ~ pendiente *f* suave/pronunciada **II.** *vt* **1.** (*throw*) lanzar; **to** ~ **sb into a situation** mandar a alguien en una situación; **to be** ~**ed** (**headlong**) **into despair** estar sumido en la desesperación **2.** SPORTS (*throw*) tirar **3.** (*fix level of sound*) **this tune is** ~**ed** (**too**) **high/low** esta afinación es (demasiado) alta/baja **4.** (*aim at*) **to** ~ **sth at sb** diseñar algo para alguien **III.** *vi* **1.** (*thrust*) tirar **2.** *Am* SPORTS (*throw baseball*) lanzar **3.** (*slope*) inclinarse

◆**pitch in** *vi inf* contribuir

◆**pitch into** *vt* **1.** (*attack verbally*) arremeter contra **2.** (*begin enthusiastically*) emprender enérgicamente

◆**pitch out** *vt* tirar

pitch² [pɪtʃ] *n no pl* (*bitumen*) brea *f*

pitch-black [ˌpɪtʃ'blæk] *adj* (*extremely dark*) negro, -a como la boca de un lobo; (*very black*) muy negro, -a

pitched battle *n* batalla *f* campal

pitched roof *n* tejado *m* a dos aguas

pitcher¹ ['pɪtʃəʳ, *Am:* -ɚ] *n* (*large jug*) cántaro *m;* (*smaller*) jarra *f*

pitcher² ['pɪtʃəʳ, *Am:* -ɚ] *n* SPORTS (*baseball*) lanzador(a) *m(f)*

pitchfork ['pɪtʃfɔːk, *Am:* -fɔːrk] *n* (*for hay*) horca *f*

pitch pine *n* pino *m* tea

piteous ['pɪtiəs, *Am:* 'pɪɾ-] *adj* patético, -a; **a** ~ **sight** una escena patética

pitfall ['pɪtfɔːl] *n pl* escollo *m*

pith [pɪθ] *n no pl* **1.** BOT (*part of plants*) médula *f* **2.** *fig* (*main point*) meollo *m;* (*substance of speech*) esencia *f*

pithead ['pɪtˌhed] **I.** *n no pl* bocamina *f* **II.** *adj* de la bocamina

pith helmet *n* salacot *m*

pithy ['pɪθi] <-ier, -iest> *adj* (*succinct, concise*) sucinto, -a

pitiable ['pɪtiəbl, *Am:* 'pɪɾ-] *adj form* s. **pitiful**

pitiful ['pɪtifəl, *Am:* 'pɪɾ-] *adj* **1.** (*terrible*) lamentable; ~ **conditions** condiciones *fpl* lamentables; **a** ~ **sight** una escena patética **2.** (*unsatisfactory*) insatisfactorio, -a; ~ **excuse** excusa *f* pobre

pitiless ['pɪtiləs, *Am:* 'pɪɾ-] *adj* despiadado, -a

piton ['piːtɒn, *Am:* -taːn] *n* SPORTS pitón *m*

pitta (**bread**) ['pɪtəˌbred, *Am:* 'pɪɾ-] *n no pl* pan *m* de pitta

pittance ['pɪtənts] *n no pl* miseria *f,* pavada *f CSur;* **to live on a** ~ vivir de una renta miserable

pituitary (**gland**) [pɪ'tjuːɪtəri, *Am:* -'tuː-]

əter-] *n* glándula *f* pituitaria

pity ['pɪtɪ, *Am:* 'pɪt̬-] I. *n no pl* 1. (*compassion*) compasión *f;* in ~ por piedad; **to feel ~ for sb** compadecerse de alguien; **to take ~ on sb** apiadarse de alguien; **for ~'s sake** ¡por piedad! 2. (*shame*) **to be a ~** ser una pena; (**it's a**) ~ (es una) lástima; **the ~ of it is that …** lo lamentable es que…; **more's the ~!** ¡desgraciadamente!; **what a ~!** ¡qué pena! II. <-ies, -ied> *vt* compadecerse de

pitying *adj* compasivo, -a

pivot ['pɪvət] I. *n* 1. TECH eje *m* 2. (*focal point*) punto *m* central; **to be the ~ of sth** ser el eje de algo; (*person*) ser el centro de algo II. *vi* **to ~ round** girar; **to ~ around sth** *a. fig* girar en torno a algo; **to ~ through 90 degrees** dar un giro de 90 grados

pivotal ['pɪvətəl, *Am:* -t̬əl] *adj* fundamental

pixel ['pɪksəl] *n* INFOR pixel *m*

pixie *n,* **pixy** ['pɪksi] <-ies> *n* LIT duende *m*

pizza ['piːtsə] *n* pizza *f*

placard ['plækɑːd, *Am:* -ɑːrd] *n* pancarta *f*

placate [plə'keɪt, *Am:* 'pleɪkeɪt] *vt* 1. (*soothe*) aplacar 2. (*appease*) apaciguar

placatory [plə'keɪtəri, *Am:* 'pleɪkət̬ɔːr-] *adj form* 1. (*calming*) apaciguador(a) 2. (*appeasing, conciliatory*) conciliador(a)

place [pleɪs] I. *n* 1. (*location, area*) lugar *m;* ~ **of birth** lugar de nacimiento; ~**s of interest** lugares de interés; ~ **of refuge** refugio *m;* **people in high ~s** gente *f* bien situada; **to be in ~** estar en su sitio; *fig* estar listo; **to do sth in ~** *Am* hacer algo en el acto; **if I were in your ~, …** yo en tu lugar…; **in ~ of sb/sth** en vez de alguien/algo; **not to be the ~ to do sth** no ser el lugar apropiado para hacer algo; **this is no ~ to bring up your children** éste no es un lugar apropiado para criar a tus hijos; **it is not your ~ to say that** no eres quien para decir eso 2. *inf* (*house*) casa *f;* **at my ~** en mi casa 3. (*building*) edificio *m* 4. (*commercial location*) local *m* 5. (*position*) posición *f;* **to lose one's ~** (*book*) perder la página; **to take first/second ~** quedar en primer/segundo lugar; **in the first ~** primero; **in the second ~** segundo; **a ~ among the best directors** un lugar entre los mejores directores 6. (*seat*) sitio *m;* (*in theatre*) localidad *f;* **is this ~ taken?** ¿está libre este sitio?; **to change ~s with sb** cambiar el sitio con alguien; **to save sb a ~** guardar un sitio a alguien; **to lay** [*o* **set**] **a ~ at the table** poner un cubierto en la mesa 7. (*in organization*) plaza *f;* **she has got a ~ at university** ha obtenido una plaza en la universidad 8. MAT **decimal ~** decimal *m* ►**a ~ in the sun** una situación ventajosa; **to fall into ~** encajar; **to go ~s** *inf* (*become successful*) llegar lejos; **to know one's ~** – saber cuál es el lugar de uno; **to put sb in his ~** poner a alguien en su sitio; **all over the ~** por todas partes; **any ~** *Am, inf* en/a cualquier sitio; **every ~** *Am, inf* en todas partes; **some ~** *Am, inf* (a) algún sitio; **to feel out of ~** sentirse fuera de lugar; **a ~ for everything and everything in its ~** un sitio para cada cosa y cada cosa en su sitio; **no ~** *Am, inf* en ningún sitio II. *vt* 1. (*position, put*) colocar; **to ~ sth somewhere** colocar algo en un sitio; **to ~ an advertisement in the newspaper** poner un anuncio en el periódico; **to ~ a comma/a full stop** poner una coma/un punto; **to ~ sth on the agenda** apuntar algo en la agenda; **we are well ~d to see the match** estamos en un buen sitio para ver el partido; **how are you ~d for money?** ¿cuál es tu situación económica? 2. (*impose*) imponer; **to ~ an embargo on sth** prohibir algo; **to ~ a limit on sth** poner un límite a algo 3. (*ascribe*) poner; **to ~ the blame on sb** echar la culpa a alguien; **to ~ one's hopes on sb/sth** poner sus esperanzas en alguien/algo; **to ~ importance on sb/sth** conceder importancia a alguien/algo; **to ~ the emphasis on sth** hacer énfasis en algo; **to ~ one's faith in sb** depositar su confianza en alguien 4. (*arrange for*) hacer; **to ~ an order for sth** hacer un pedido de algo; **to ~ a bet** hacer una apuesta; **to ~ sth at sb's disposal** poner algo a disposición de alguien 5. (*appoint to a position*) **to ~ sb in charge** (**of sth**) poner a alguien a cargo (de algo); **to ~ sb under surveillance** poner a alguien bajo vigilancia; **to ~ sth under the control of sb** poner algo bajo el control de alguien; **to ~ sb in jeopardy** poner a alguien en peligro; **to ~ sb under pressure** someter a alguien a presión; **to ~ sb on (the) alert** alertar a alguien; **to ~ sth above sth** poner algo por encima de algo; **to be ~d first/second** SPORTS quedar en primer/segundo lugar 6. (*employ*) colocar 7. (*identify*) reconocer; **I can't ~ him** su cara me suena, pero no la puedo situar III. *vi Brit* SPORTS clasificarse

placebo [plə'siːbəʊ, *Am:* -boʊ] <-s> *n a. fig* placebo *m*

place card *n* tarjeta *f* (indicadora del puesto que se ocupa)

place kick *n* SPORTS tiro *m* libre **place mat** *n* salvamanteles *m inv*

placement ['pleɪsmənt] *n* colocación *f*

place name *n* topónimo *m*

placenta [plə'sentə, *Am:* -t̬ə] <-s *o* -ae> *n* MED placenta *f*

placid ['plæsɪd] *adj* plácido, -a

plagiarism ['pleɪdʒərɪzəm, *Am:* -dʒɚ-] *n no pl* plagio *m*

plagiarist ['pleɪdʒərɪst, *Am:* -dʒɚ-] *n* plagiario, -a *m, f*

plagiarize ['pleɪdʒəraɪz] I. *vt* plagiar; **to ~ sth from sth** plagiar algo de algo II. *vi* hacer un plagio; **to ~ from sth** hacer un plagio de algo

plague [pleɪg] I. *n* peste *f;* (*infestation of insects*) plaga *f;* (*source of annoyance*) pesadez *f;* **the ~** (*bubonic plague*) la peste; **to avoid sb like the ~** huir de alguien como de la peste II. *vt* fastidiar; **to ~ sb for sth** acosar a alguien por algo

plaice [pleɪs] *inv n* platija *f*

plaid [plæd] I. *n no pl, Am* tela *f* a cuadros II. *adj* de tartán; ~ **skirt** falda *f* escocesa

plain [pleɪn] I. *adj* 1. sencillo, -a; (*one colour*) de un solo color; (*without additions*) sin aditivos; ~ **yoghurt** yogur *m* natural 2. (*uncompli-cated*) fácil; **the ~ folks** el pueblo llano; ~ **and simple** liso y llano 3. (*clear, obvious*) evidente; **it is ~ that ...** es evidente que...; **to be ~ enough** estar lo suficientemente claro; **to make sth ~** dejar algo claro; **to make oneself ~ (to sb)** hacerse entender (a alguien); **to be ~ with sb** ser franco con alguien; **to be as ~ as the nose on your face** estar más claro que el agua 4. (*mere, pure*) puro, -a; **the ~ truth** la pura realidad 5. (*not pretty*) sin atractivo; **a ~ girl** una chica más bien fea II. *adv inf* (*down-right*) y punto; ~ **awful** horrible III. *n* 1. GEO llanura *f*; **the ~s** *pl* las llanuras; **the great Plains** la grandes llanuras (norteamericanas) 2. (*knitting stitch*) punto *m* de media

plain clothes LAW I. *n* ropa *f* de calle; **in ~** en traje de calle; (*of policeman*) ropa *f* de paisano II. *adj* (*policeman*) de paisano

plainly ['pleɪnli] *adv* 1. (*simply*) simplemente 2. (*clearly*) claramente; (*obviously*) evidente-mente; **to be ~ visible** ser muy visible 3. (*undeniably*) sin duda

plainness ['pleɪnnəs] *n no pl* 1. (*simplicity*) sencillez *f* 2. (*obviousness*) evidencia *f* 3. (*unattractiveness*) falta *f* de atractivo

plain sailing *n fig* **to be ~** ser cosa de coser y cantar

plain-spoken [ˌpleɪn'spəʊkən, *Am:* -'spoʊ-] *adj* franco, -a

plaintiff ['pleɪntɪf, *Am:* -t̬ɪf] *n* demandante *mf*

plaintive ['pleɪntɪv, *Am:* -t̬ɪv] *adj* lastimero, -a

plait [plæt] I. *n* trenza *f* II. *vt* trenzar III. *vi* hacer trenzas

plan [plæn] I. *n* 1. (*scheme, programme*) plano *m;* **to draw up a ~** elaborar un plan; **to go according to ~** ir de acuerdo con lo previsto; **to change ~s** cambiar de planes; **to have ~s** tener planes; **to make ~s for sth** hacer planes para algo 2. FIN, ECON (*insurance scheme*) seguro *m;* **healthcare ~** seguro *m* médico; **savings ~** plan *m* de ahorro 3. (*dia-gram*) plano *m;* **street ~** plano *m* de calles II. <-nn-> *vt* 1. (*work out in detail*) planificar; (*prepare*) preparar; ~**ned economy** economía *f* planificada; **to ~ sth for sb** preparar algo para alguien 2. (*intend*) proponerse; **to ~ to do sth** proponerse hacer algo III. *vi* hacer proyectos; **to ~ carefully** hacer proyectos de-tallados

plane¹ [pleɪn] I. *n* 1. (*level surface*) nivel *m;* MAT plano *m* 2. (*level of thought*) nivel *m* (intelectual) II. *vi* planear III. *adj* plano, -a; MAT llano, -a; ~ **angle** ángulo *m* plano

plane² [pleɪn] *n* (*airplane*) avión *m;* **by ~** en avión

plane³ [pleɪn] I. *n* cepillo *m* II. *vt* cepillar

plane⁴ [pleɪn] *n* (*tree*) plátano *m*

plane crash *n* accidente *m* de aviación

planet ['plænɪt] *n* planeta *m;* ~ **Earth** la Tierra; ~ **Jupiter/Venus** el planeta Júpiter/ Venus; **to be on a different ~** *fig* estar en otro mundo

planetarium [ˌplænɪ'teərɪəm, *Am:* -'teri-] <-s *o* -ria> *n* planetario *m*

planetary ['plænɪtəri, *Am:* -teri] *adj* plane-tario, -a; ~ **motion** movimiento *m* planetario

plane tree *n* plátano *m*

plank [plæŋk] *n* 1. (*long board*) tabla *f;* NAUT tablazón *m* 2. (*of policy, ideology*) puntal *m*

planking *n no pl* tablas *fpl*

plankton ['plæŋktən] *n no pl* plancton *m*

planner *n* planificador(a) *m(f);* **city ~** urba-nista *mf*

planning *n no pl* planificación *f;* **city ~** planifi-cación urbanística; **environmental ~** proyec-tos *mpl* medioambientales; **at the ~ stage** en la etapa de planificación

planning board *n* comisión *f* planificadora

planning permission *n* permiso *m* de construcción

plant [plɑːnt, *Am:* plænt] I. *n* 1. BOT planta *f* 2. (*factory*) fábrica *f* 3. *no pl* (*machinery*) maquinaria *f* 4. *no pl* (*misleading evidence*) **the drugs were a ~** la policía había colocado las drogas para inculparlo II. *vt* 1. AGR (*put in earth*) plantar; **to ~ sth with sth** sembrar algo de algo 2. (*put*) colocar; **to ~ oneself some-where** *inf* meterse en algún sitio; **to ~ a bomb** poner una bomba; **to ~ a secret agent** introducir a un agente secreto 3. *inf* (*to incriminate*) **to ~ evidence on sb** colocar pruebas para incriminar a alguien III. *adj* ve-getal; **the ~ kingdom** el reino vegetal; ~ **life** vida *f* vegetal

plantain ['plæntɪn] *n* (*fruit, tree*) plátano *m*

plantation [plæn'teɪʃən] *n* plantación *f;* (*of trees*) arboleda *f*

planter ['plɑːntəʳ, *Am:* 'plænt̬ɚ] *n* 1. (*owner of plantation*) hacendado, -a *m, f* 2. (*plant holder*) maceta *f*

plaque [plɑːk, plæk, *Am:* plæk] *n* 1. (*building*) placa *f;* **memorial ~** placa conme-morativa 2. *no pl* MED sarro *m*

plash [plæʃ] I. *n* (*splash*) salpicadura *f;* (*noise*) chapoteo *m* II. *vi* **to ~ about** (*play*) chapotear

plasm ['plæzm] *n* molde *m*

plasma ['plæzmə] *n no pl* plasma *m*

plaster ['plɑːstəʳ, *Am:* 'plæstɚ] I. *n* 1. *no pl* (*used in building*) a. MED yeso *m* 2. *Brit* (*stick-ing plaster*) tirita *f* II. *vt* 1. (*wall, ceiling*) enye-sar 2. *inf* (*put all over*) llenar

plasterboard ['plɑːstəbɔːd, *Am:* 'plæstɚ-bɔːrd] *n no pl* cartón *m* de yeso (y fieltro)

plaster cast *n* 1. MED escayola *f* 2. ART vaciado *m*

plastered *adj inf* (*drunk*) borracho, -a; **to get**

~ emborracharse
plasterer *n* yesero, -a *m, f*
plastic ['plæstɪk] I. *n* 1. (*material*) plástico *m* 2. ~s *pl* (*manufacturing sector*) sector *m* de los plásticos II. *adj* 1. (*made from plastic*) de plástico 2. *pej* (*artifical*) artificial 3. ART (*malleable*) ~ arts artes *fpl* plásticas 4. *fig* (*impressionable*) influenciable
plastic bag *n* bolsa *f* de plástico **plastic bomb** *n* bomba *f* de goma **plastic bullet** *n* bala *f* de goma **plastic explosive** *n* explosivo *m* plástico
Plasticine® ['plæstɪsiːn] *n no pl* plastilina *f*
plasticity [plæ'stɪsəti, *Am:* -t̬i] *n no pl* plasticidad *f*
plastic money *n no pl* dinero *m* plástico
plastics industry *n* sector *m* de los plásticos
plastic surgery *n* cirugía *f* plástica
plate [pleɪt] I. *n* 1. (*dinner plate*) plato *m* 2. (*panel, sheet*) lámina *f;* **steel** ~ lámina de acero 3. AUTO **number** ~ *Brit,* **license** ~ *Am,* **licence** ~ *Can* placa *f* 4. TYPO lámina *f* 5. *no pl* (*layer of metal*) capa *f;* **gold** ~ capa de oro 6. (*silver cutlery*) vajilla *f* de plata 7. (*picture in book*) ilustración *f* ►to have a lot on one's ~ tener muchos asuntos entre manos; to give sth to sb on a ~ servir algo a alguien en bandeja II. *vt* to ~ sth with gold/silver chapar algo con oro/plata
plateau ['plætəʊ, *Am:* plæt'oʊ] <*Brit:* -x, *Am, Aus:* -s> *n* meseta *f*
plated *adj* (*coated in metal*) chapeado, -a; (*jewellery*) chapado, -a
plateful ['pleɪtfʊl] *n* plato *m*
plate glass *n* luna *f*
platelet ['pleɪlət] *n* plaqueta *f*
plate rack *n* portaplatos *m inv* **plate- -warmer** *n* calentador *m* de platos
platform ['plætfɔːm, *Am:* -fɔːrm] *n* 1. *a.* INFOR plataforma *f* 2. *Brit, Aus* RAIL andén *m;* **railway** ~ andén de estación de trenes 3. (*stage*) escenario *m* 4. *Brit* (*at meeting*) tribuna *f* 5. (*political programme*) programa *m* electoral 6. *pl* (*shoes*) zapatos *mpl* de plataforma
platform shoes *npl* zapatos *mpl* de plataforma
plating *n* (*covering of metal*) enchapado *m;* **gold/silver** ~ chapado *m* de oro/de plata
platinum ['plætɪnəm, *Am:* 'plætnəm] *n no pl* platino *m*
platitude ['plætɪtjuːd, *Am:* 'plæt̬ətuːd] *n pej* perogrullada *f*
platonic [plə'tɒnɪk, *Am:* -'tɑːnɪk] *adj* platónico, -a; ~ **love** amor *m* platónico
platoon [plə'tuːn] *n* MIL pelotón *m*
platter ['plætər, *Am:* 'plæt̬ə'] *n* 1. (*large dish*) fuente *f* 2. (*food*) plato *m* fuerte
platypus ['plætɪpəs, *Am:* 'plæt̬ɪ-] <-es> *n* ornitorrinco *m*
plausibility [ˌplɔːzə'bɪlɪti, *Am:* ˌplɑːzə'bɪləti] *n no pl* plausibilidad *f*
plausible ['plɔːzəbl, *Am:* 'plɑː-] *adj* plausible

play [pleɪ] I. *n* 1. *no pl* (*recreation*) juego *m;* **to be at** ~ estar en juego; **to do sth in** ~ hacer algo en broma; **it's only in** ~ sólo es broma 2. *no pl* SPORTS juego *m;* **to be in/out of** ~ estar dentro/fuera de juego 3. SPORTS (*move*) jugada *f;* **foul** ~ juego sucio; **to make a bad/ good** ~ hacer una mala/buena jugada 4. THEAT obra *f* de teatro; **one-act** ~ obra de un acto; **radio** ~ emisión *f* dramática 5. *no pl* (*free movement*) juego *m;* **to allow** [*o* **give**] **sth full** ~ dar rienda suelta a algo 6. *no pl* (*interaction*) juego *m;* **to bring sth into** ~ poner algo en juego; **to come into** ~ entrar en juego ►**to make a** ~ **for sth** intentar conseguir algo II. *vi* 1. *a.* SPORTS jugar; **to** ~ **for a team** jugar en un equipo; **to** ~ **fair/rough** jugar limpio/sucio 2. (*perform*) actuar 3. MUS tocar III. *vt* 1. (*participate in game, sport*) jugar; **to** ~ **bridge/ football** jugar al bridge/al fútbol; **to** ~ **a card** jugar una carta 2. (*participate in sport*) jugar a; **to** ~ **football** jugar al fútbol; **to** ~ **a match/a round** jugar un partido/una ronda 3. (*perform a role*) interpretar, hacer el papel de; **to** ~ **the clown** [*o* **fool**] hacer el payaso; **to** ~ **to a full house** llenar un teatro 4. MUS tocar; **to** ~ **the piano** tocar el piano 5. (*operate an audio or video device*) poner; **do you have to play the music so loud?** ¿es necesario que pongas el equipo de música tan alto?; **to** ~ **a CD/video** poner un compact disc/un vídeo 6. (*perpetrate: joke*) gastar
♦**play about** *vi* jugar
♦**play along** *vi* **to** ~ **with sb** seguir la corriente a alguien
♦**play around** *vi* 1. (*play*) jugar 2. *pej* (*commit adultery*) **to** ~ **with sb** tener un lío con alguien 3. (*experiment*) **to** ~ **with sth** ensayar algo de varias maneras 4. *pej* (*tamper*) **to** ~ **with sth** manosear algo
♦**play at** *vt* 1. (*pretend*) **to** ~ (**being**) **sth** jugar a (ser) algo 2. (*do for amusement*) **to** ~ (**being**) **sth** hacer como que (se es) algo; **she is playing at being a student** hace como que estudia 3. *pej* (*do*) **what are you playing at?** ¿a qué viene esto?
♦**play back** *vt* poner
♦**play down** *vt* quitar importancia a
♦**play off** I. *vi* jugar un partido de desempate II. *vt* **to play sb off against sb** oponer a dos personas
♦**play on** I. *vt* 1. (*exploit*) **to** ~ **sb's feelings/weakness** aprovecharse de los sentimientos/la debilidad de alguien 2. (*phrase, word*) jugar con II. *vi* (*keep playing*) SPORTS, GAMES seguir jugando; MUS seguir tocando
♦**play out** *vt* representar; **to** ~ **one's fantasies** convertir sus fantasías en realidad
♦**play through** *vt* tocar
♦**play up** I. *vt* 1. (*exaggerate: problem, difficulty*) exagerar 2. *Brit* (*cause trouble*) fastidiar II. *vi* 1. *Aus, Brit* (*malfunction*) no marchar bien; (*hurt*) doler 2. *Brit* (*cause annoyance*) dar guerra

◆**play upon** vt 1.(exploit) to ~ sb's feelings/weakness aprovecharse de los sentimientos/la debilidad de alguien 2.(phrase, word) jugar con

◆**play with** vt 1.a. fig (play) jugar 2.(manipulate nervously) juguetear; to ~ one's food jugar con la comida 3.(consider, toy with) to ~ an idea dar vueltas a una idea

playable ['pleɪəbl] adj (pitch) que se puede jugar

play-act ['pleɪækt] vi 1.THEAT actuar 2.fig hacer teatro

playback ['pleɪbæk] n (of tape) reproducción f

playbill n THEAT 1.(poster) cartel m 2.Am (program) programa m

playboy ['pleɪbɔɪ] n playboy m

player ['pleɪəʳ, Am: -ə-] n 1.SPORTS jugador(a) m(f); **card** ~ jugador(a) m(f) de cartas; **football** ~ futbolista mf; **tennis** ~ tenista mf 2.MUS instrumentista mf; **cello** ~ violoncelista mf; **flute** ~ flautista mf; **oboe** ~ oboísta mf 3.THEAT actor m, actriz f 4.(playback machine) cassette ~ casete m; **CD** ~ compact disc m; **record** ~ tocadiscos m inv

playfellow ['pleɪˌfeləʊ, Am: -oʊ] n compañero, -a m, f de juego

playful ['pleɪfəl] adj 1.(full of fun) juguetón, -ona; **the children were in a ~ mood** los niños tenían ganas de jugar 2.(comment, tone) de guasa; **he's only being ~** sólo está bromeando

playground ['pleɪgraʊnd] n 1.(of school) patio m; (in park) campo m de recreo 2.fig (resort) lugar m de recreo

playgroup ['pleɪgru:p] n guardería f

playhouse ['pleɪhaʊs] n 1.(theatre) teatro m 2.(miniature house) casa f de muñecas

playing card n carta f, naipe m **playing field** n campo m de deportes

playmate ['pleɪmeɪt] n compañero, -a m, f de juego

play-off ['pleɪɒf, Am: -ɑ:f] n desempate m; ~ **match** partido m de desempate

playpen ['pleɪpen] n parque m

playroom ['pleɪrʊm, Am: -ru:m] n cuarto m de jugar

playschool ['pleɪsku:l] n Brit jardín m de infancia

playsuit ['pleɪsu:t] n (for baby) pelele m

plaything ['pleɪθɪŋ] n a. fig juguete m

playtime ['pleɪtaɪm] n no pl SCHOOL recreo m

playwright ['pleɪraɪt] n dramaturgo, -a m, f

plaza ['plɑ:zə] n 1.(open square) plaza f 2.(shopping centre) (shopping) ~ centro m comercial

plc [ˌpi:el'si:] n Brit abbr of public limited company S.A. f

plea [pli:] n 1.(appeal) petición f, súplica f; to make a ~ for help/mercy pedir ayuda/clemencia; a ~ that ... una petición de que... 2.LAW alegato m; to enter a ~ of guilty/not guilty declararse culpable/inocente 3.form (excuse) pretexto m

plea bargaining n Am: acuerdo táctico entre fiscal y defensa para agilizar los trámites judiciales

plead [pli:d] <pleaded Am: pled, pleaded Am: pled> I. vi 1.(implore, beg) implorar, suplicar; to ~ for forgiveness/justice suplicar perdón/justicia; to ~ with sb (to do sth) suplicar (hacer algo) a alguien 2.LAW to ~ guilty/innocent (to a charge) declararse culpable/inocente (de un cargo) II. vt 1.LAW to ~ sb's case defender el caso de alguien; to ~ insanity alegar enajenación mental 2.(claim as pretext) pretextar; to ~ ignorance of sth pretextar su ignorancia en algo 3.(argue for) to ~ sb's cause defender la causa de alguien; to ~ one's suit form pedir la mano de alguien

pleading ['pli:dɪŋ] I. n 1.(entreaty, appeal) súplicas fpl 2.LAW alegato m II. adj (look, tone) suplicante

pleasant ['plezənt] adj 1.(pleasing) agradable; **it is my ~ duty to inform you that ...** me complace comunicarle que...; **what a ~ surprise!** ¡qué agradable sorpresa!; **have a ~ journey!** ¡buen viaje!; ~ **weather** buen tiempo 2.(friendly) amable; **to make oneself ~ (to sb)** procurar ser amable (con alguien); **to be ~ (to sb)** ser amable (con alguien)

pleasantry ['plezəntri] <-ies> n 1.(joke) broma f 2.pl (remarks) cumplidos mpl; **an exchange of pleasantries** un intercambio de cumplidos

please [pli:z] I. vt 1.(make happy) gustar; **to be hard to ~** ser difícil de contentar; **she's notoriously hard to ~** es muy difícil complacerla 2.inf (do as one wishes) ~ **yourself** haz lo que te parezca II. vi 1.(be agreeable) eager **to ~** deseoso de agradar 2.(think fit, wish) **to do as one ~s** hacer lo que uno quiera; **you can do as you ~** como usted quiera; **to do whatever one ~s** hacer todo lo que se quiera III. interj por favor; **if you ~** form con su permiso; **more potatoes?** ~ ¿más patatas? Sí, por favor

pleased adj 1.(satisfied, contented) satisfecho, -a; **to be ~ about sth** estar contento de algo; **to be ~ that ...** estar contento de que +subj; **to be ~ with oneself** estar satisfecho de uno mismo 2.(happy, glad) contento, -a; **I'm ~ to report that ...** me complace informarle de que...; **I'm very ~ to meet you** encantado de conocerle 3.(willing) **to be ~ to do sth** estar encantado de hacer algo ►**to be as ~ as Punch (about sth)** estar más contento que unas Pascuas (con algo)

pleasing adj agradable; ~ **news** buenas noticias fpl

pleasurable ['pleʒərəbl] adj grato, -a; **a ~ sensation** una agradable sensación

pleasure ['pleʒəʳ, Am: -ə-] n 1.no pl (feeling of enjoyment) placer m; **it was such a ~ to meet you** ha sido un placer conocerle; **to take ~ in sth/in doing sth** disfrutar de algo/

haciendo algo; **with ~** con mucho gusto
2. (*source of enjoyment*) placer *m;* **the ~s and pains of camping** los pros y los contras de la acampada **3.** *form* (*will, desire*) **what is your ~, Madame?** ¿en qué puedo servirle, señora?
pleasure boat *n* embarcación *f* de recreo
pleasure principle *n no pl* PSYCH principio *m* del placer **pleasure trip** *n* viaje *m* de recreo
pleat [pli:t] *n* pliegue *m*
pleb [pleb] *n Brit, inf abbr of* **plebian** plebeyo, -a *m, f*
plebeian [plɪ'bi:ən] **I.** *adj form* plebeyo, -a **II.** *n* HIST plebeyo, -a *m, f*
plebiscite ['plebɪsɪt, *Am:* -əsaɪt] *n* plebiscito *m;* **to hold a ~** (**on sth**) someter (algo) a plebiscito
pled [pled] *Am, Scot pt, pp of* **plead**
pledge [pledʒ] **I.** *n* **1.** (*solemn promise*) promesa *f* solemne; **to fulfil a ~** cumplir un compromiso; **to make a ~ that ...** prometer solemnemente que... **2.** (*symbolic sign of a promise*) **as a ~ of sth** en señal de algo; **a ~ of good faith** una garantía de buena fe **3.** (*promised charitable donation*) donativo *m* prometido **4.** (*pawned item*) prenda *f* **II.** *vt* **1.** (*promise*) prometer; **to ~ loyalty** jurar lealtad; **to ~ to do sth** prometer hacer algo; **to ~ that ...** prometer que...; **we've ~d ourselves to fight for justice** nos hemos comprometido a luchar por la justicia; **I've been ~d to secrecy** he jurado guardar el secreto **2.** (*give as security*) **to ~ money** dar dinero como garantía
plenary ['pli:nəri] *adj* plenario, -a
plenary meeting *n* reunión *f* plenaria **plenary powers** *n* plenos poderes *mpl* **plenary session** *n* sesión *f* plenaria
plenipotentiary [ˌplenɪpə'tenʃəri, *Am:* -pou'tenʃieri] **I.** <-ries> *n* ADMIN, POL plenipotenciario, -a *m, f* **II.** *adj* ADMIN, POL plenipotenciario, -a; **~ power** plenipotencia *f*
plentiful ['plentɪf(ʊ)l, *Am:* -ṭɪ-] *adj* abundante; **strawberries are ~ in the summer** en verano hay abundancia de fresas
plenty ['plenti, *Am:* -ṭi] **I.** *n no pl* **1.** (*abundance*) abundancia *f;* **land of ~** tierra *f* de abundancia; **food in ~** comida *f* en abundancia **2.** (*a lot*) **~ of money/time** dinero/tiempo de sobra **II.** *adv* suficientemente; **~ more** mucho más; **there's ~ more beer in the fridge** hay mucha más cerveza en la nevera
plenum ['pli:nəm] *n* pleno *m*
plethora ['pleθərə, *Am:* 'pleθəɚ] *n* plétora *f*
pleurisy ['plʊərəsi, *Am:* 'plʊrə-] *n no pl* MED pleuresía *f*
plexus ['pleksəs] <-(es)> *n* plexo *m;* **solar ~** plexo solar
pliable ['plaɪəbl] *adj* **1.** (*supple*) flexible **2.** *fig* (*easily influenced*) dócil
pliers ['plaɪəz, *Am:* 'plaɪəɚz] *npl* alicates *mpl;* **a pair of ~** unos alicates
plight [plaɪt] **I.** *n* apuro *m;* **to be in a dread-**

ful **~** estar en una terrible situación **II.** *vt form* **to ~ one's troth** prometerse
plimsoll ['plɪmpsəl] *n Brit* zapatilla *f* de deporte
Plimsoll line *n* NAUT línea *f* de máxima carga
PLO [ˌpi:el'əʊ, *Am:* -'oʊ] *n abbr of* **Palestine Liberation Organization** OLP *f*
plod [plɒd, *Am:* plɑːd] **I.** *n* paso *m* lento **II.** <-dd-> *vi* **1.** (*walk heavily*) andar con paso pesado; **to ~ through the mud** andar con dificultad sobre el barro **2.** (*do without enthusiasm*) **to ~ through one's work** trabajar sin ganas; **to ~ through a book** leer un libro lentamente
♦**plod away** *vi* (*continue working*) ir tirando
♦**plod on** *vi* (*continue walking*) caminar penosamente
plodder ['plɒdə^r, *Am:* 'plɑːdɚ] *n* (*worker*) trabajador(a) *m(f)* más voluntarioso, -a que eficiente; (*student*) empollón, -ona *m, f inf*
plonk¹ [plɒŋk, *Am:* plʌŋk] *n Brit, Aus, inf* vino *m* peleón
plonk² [plɒŋk, *Am:* plʌŋk] **I.** *n inf* (*sound*) ruido *m* sordo **II.** *vt inf* (*set down heavily*) dejar caer pesadamente; **she ~ed the books on the table** dejó caer los libros sobre la mesa
♦**plonk down** *vt inf* dejar caer pesadamente; **to plonk oneself down on a chair** dejarse caer pesadamente en una silla
plop [plɒp, *Am:* plɑːp] **I.** *n* plaf *m;* **to fall with a ~** caerse haciendo plaf **II.** <-pp-> *vi* (*fall*) caerse haciendo plaf
plot [plɒt, *Am:* plɑːt] **I.** *n* **1.** (*conspiracy, secret plan*) conspiración *f;* **to foil a ~** hacer fracasar una conspiración; **to hatch a ~** tramar una intriga **2.** (*story line*) argumento *m* **3.** (*small piece of land*) terreno *m;* **a ~ of land** un terreno; **building ~** solar *m* ▶**the ~ thickens** *iron* el asunto se complica **II.** <-tt-> *vt* **1.** (*conspire*) tramar **2.** (*create*) **to ~ a story line** idear un argumento **3.** (*graph, line*) trazar; (*mark on map*) señalar; **to ~ a course** planear una ruta **III.** <-tt-> *vi* **to ~ against sb** conspirar contra alguien; **to ~ to do sth** planear hacer algo
♦**plot out** *vt* trazar
plotter ['plɒtə^r, *Am:* 'plɑːṭɚ] *n* **1.** (*person*) conspirador(a) *m(f)* **2.** INFOR plotter *m*, tabla *f* trazadora
plough [plaʊ] **I.** *n* arado *m* ▶**to put one's hand to the ~** ponerse manos a la obra **II.** *vt* **1.** AGR arar **2.** (*move through*) **to ~ one's way through sth** abrirse paso por algo; (*work through*) hacer algo sin ganas **3.** (*invest*) **to ~ money into a project** invertir mucho dinero en un proyecto **III.** *vi* **1.** AGR arar **2.** **to ~ through sth** (*move through*) abrirse paso por algo; (*work through*) terminar algo a duras penas
♦**plough back** *vt* **to plough sth back** (**into sth**) reinvertir algo (en algo); **to plough profits back** reinvertir los beneficios

P

◆**plough into** vt insep chocar contra

◆**plough up** vt (fields, land) roturar

Plough [plaʊ] n no pl **the ~** ASTR el Carro

plow [plaʊ] n Am s. **plough**

ploy [plɔɪ] n **1.** (activity) actividad f **2.** (tactics) táctica f

PLP n Brit POL abbr of **Parliamentary Labour Party** los diputados del Partido Laborista

pluck [plʌk] **I.** n **1.** (sharp pull) tirón m **2.** (courage) valor m; **to have a lot of ~** tener agallas; **it takes a lot of ~** hace falta mucho valor **II.** vt **1.** (remove quickly) arrancar **2.** (remove hair or feathers) **to ~ a chicken** desplumar un pollo; **to ~ one's eyebrows** depilarse las cejas **3.** MUS puntear **III.** vi **to ~ at sb's sleeve** tirar a alguien de la manga

◆**pluck out** vt arrancar

◆**pluck up** vt **to ~ one's courage** armarse de valor; **to ~ the courage to do sth** armarse de valor para hacer algo

plucky [ˈplʌki] <-ier, -iest> adj valiente

plug [plʌg] **I.** n **1.** ELEC (connector) enchufe m; (socket) toma f de corriente **2.** (stopper) tapón m **3.** inf (publicity) **to give sth a ~** dar publicidad a algo **4.** (spark plug) bujía f **5.** (chunk) **~ of tobacco** tableta f de tabaco de mascar **II.** <-gg-> vt **1.** (connect) conectar; ELEC enchufar **2.** (stop up, close) **to ~ a hole** tapar un agujero; **to ~ a leak** taponar un escape **3.** (publicize) anunciar **4.** Am, inf (shoot) pegar un tiro a

◆**plug away** vi **to ~ (at sth)** perseverar (en algo)

◆**plug in I.** vt conectar; ELEC enchufar **II.** vi conectar; ELEC enchufar

◆**plug up** vt tapar

plughole [ˈplʌghəʊl, Am: -hoʊl] n desagüe m ▶**to go down the ~** irse al garete

plug-in n INFOR plug-in m, enchufe m

plum [plʌm] **I.** n **1.** (fruit) ciruela f; (tree) ciruelo m **2.** (opportunity) chollo m **3.** (colour) color m ciruela **II.** adj **1.** (colour) de color ciruela **2.** (exceptionally good) inmejorable; **a ~ job** un trabajo fantástico

plumage [ˈpluːmɪdʒ] n no pl plumaje m

plumb [plʌm] **I.** vt a. fig sondar; **to ~ the depth** sondar la profundidad; **to ~ the depths** fig estar muy deprimido; **to ~ the mystery of the universe** plantearse los misterios del universo **II.** adv **1.** inf (exactly) exactamente; **he hit me ~ on the nose** me dio de lleno en la nariz **2.** Am, inf (completely) completamente **III.** n plomada f; **to be out of ~** no estar a plomo

◆**plumb in** vt **to plumb sth in** instalar algo

plumber [ˈplʌmər, Am: -ər] n fontanero, -a m, f, plomero, -a m, f AmL, gasfitero, -a m, f Chile, Perú

plumbing [ˈplʌmɪŋ] **I.** n no pl fontanería f **II.** adj **~ contractor** fontanero, -a m, f, gasfitero, -a m, f Chile, Perú; **~ fixture** instalación f sanitaria; **~ work** obra f de fontanería

plume [pluːm] **I.** n **1.** (feather) pluma f

2. (cloud: of smoke, gas) nube f ▶**to be dressed in borrowed ~s** liter atribuirse honores que no se merecen **II.** vt **to ~ oneself on sth** vanagloriarse de algo

plummet [ˈplʌmɪt] vi caer en picado

plummy [ˈplʌmi] <-ier, -iest> adj (voice, tone) pijo, -a inf, popoff Méx

plump [plʌmp] adj (person) rollizo, -a; (animal) gordo, -a

◆**plump down** inf **I.** vt dejar caer **II.** vi dejarse caer

◆**plump for** vt inf optar por

◆**plump up** vt **1.** (pillow) sacudir **2.** (chicken) cebar

plumpness [ˈplʌmpnəs] n no pl gordura f

plum pudding n Brit budín m de pasas

plum tree n Brit ciruelo m

plunder [ˈplʌndər, Am: -də] **I.** n no pl **1.** (stolen goods) botín m **2.** (act of plundering) saqueo m **II.** vt **1.** (steal) robar **2.** (loot) saquear **III.** vi robar

plunderer [ˈplʌndərər, Am: -dəə] n saqueador(a) m(f)

plunge [plʌndʒ] **I.** n **1.** (sharp decline) caída f **2.** (dive) zambullida f de cabeza ▶**to take the ~** dar el paso decisivo; (get married) casarse **II.** vi **1.** (fall suddenly) precipitarse; **to ~ to one's death** tener una caída mortal **2.** (leap, enter) **we ~d into the sea** nos zambullimos en el mar; **he ~d into the forest** se precipitó hacia el bosque **3.** (begin abruptly) **to ~ into sth** emprender algo **III.** vt hundir; **to ~ a knife into sth** clavar un cuchillo en algo; **we've ~d ourselves into debt** nos hemos metido en deudas

◆**plunge in** vi lanzarse

plunger [ˈplʌndʒər, Am: -dʒə] n (of syringe) émbolo m; (for drain, sink) desatascador m

plunk [plʌŋk] n Am s. **plonk²**

pluperfect [ˈpluːˌpɜːfɪkt, Am: -ˌpɜːr-] n LING pluscuamperfecto m

plural [ˈplʊərəl, Am: ˈplʊrəl] **I.** n plural m; **in the ~** en plural; **second person ~** segunda persona del plural **II.** adj **1.** a. LING plural **2.** (multiple) múltiple

pluralism [ˈplʊərəlɪzəm, Am: ˈplʊrəl-] n no pl PHILOS pluralismo m

pluralistic [ˌplʊərəlˈɪstɪk, Am: ˌplʊrəl-] adj pluralista

plurality [plʊəˈræləti, Am: plʊˈræləti] <-ies> n **1.** no pl (variety) pluralidad f; **~ of opinions** diversidad f de opiniones **2.** (largest single share of votes) mayoría f de votos; **to have a ~** ganar por mayoría

plus [plʌs] **I.** prep más; **5 ~ 2 equals 7** 5 más 2 igual a 7 **II.** conj además **III.** <-es> n **1.** (mathematical symbol) signo m más **2.** (advantage) punto m a favor **IV.** adj **1.** (above zero) positivo, -a; **~ 8** más 8; **~ two degrees** dos grados positivos **2.** (more than) algo más de; **200 ~** más de 200 **3.** (positive or advantageous) **the ~ side (of sth)** el lado positivo (de algo)

plus fours *npl* pantalones *mpl* de golf
plush [plʌʃ] I. *adj* 1. (*luxurious*) lujoso, -a, elegante 2. (*made of plush*) de felpa II. <-es> *n* felpa *f*
plus sign *n* signo *m* más
Pluto ['plu:təʊ, *Am:* -ţoʊ] *n* Plutón *m*
plutocracy [plu:'tɒkrəsi, *Am:* -'tɑ:krə-] <-ies> *n no pl* plutocracia *f*
plutocrat ['plu:təkræt, *Am:* -ţə-] *n* plutócrata *mf*
plutocratic [ˌplu:tə'krætɪk, *Am:* -toʊ'kræţ-] *adj* plutocrático, -a
plutonium [plu:'təʊniəm, *Am:* -'toʊ-] *n no pl* plutonio *m*
ply¹ [plaɪ] *n no pl* 1. (*thickness: of cloth, wood*) capa *f* 2. (*strand of rope*) two-~ rope cuerda *f* de dos cabos
ply² [plaɪ] <-ie-> I. *vt* 1. to ~ one's trade ejercer su profesión 2. to ~ sb with questions acosar a alguien con preguntas; to ~ sb with wine no parar de servir vino a alguien 3. (*sell*) to ~ drugs traficar con drogas; to ~ one's wares vender su mercancía 4. (*travel: ship*) navegar por; to ~ a route hacer un trayecto II. *vi* 1. *Brit* to ~ for business ofrecer sus servicios 2. (*travel*) to ~ between Paris and Lyon hacer regularmente el trayecto entre París y Lyon
plywood ['plaɪwʊd] *n no pl* contrachapado *m*
p.m. [ˌpi:'em] *abbr of* post meridian p.m.; one ~ la una de la tarde; eight ~ las ocho de la noche
PM [ˌpi:'em] *n* 1. *abbr of* Prime Minister primer ministro *m*, primera ministra *f* 2. *abbr of* post mortem autopsia *f*
PMS [ˌpi:em'es] *n abbr of* premenstrual syndrome SPM *m*
pneumatic [nju:'mætɪk, *Am:* nu:'mæţ-] *adj* neumático, -a
pneumatic brakes *npl* frenos *mpl* neumáticos **pneumatic tyre** *n Brit* neumático *m*
pneumonia [nju:'məʊniə, *Am:* nu:'moʊnjə] *n no pl* neumonía *f*
PO [ˌpi:'əʊ, *Am:* -'oʊ] *n Brit abbr of* Post Office Correos *m*
poach¹ [pəʊtʃ] *vt* (*eggs*) escalfar; (*fish*) cocer
poach² [pəʊtʃ] I. *vt* 1. (*catch illegally*) cazar en vedado; (*fish*) pescar en vedado 2. (*appropriate unfairly*) robar; to ~ someone's ideas birlar las ideas de alguien; to ~ a manager from a company apropiarse de un director de una empresa II. *vi* (*catch illegally*) cazar furtivamente; (*fish*) pescar furtivamente; to ~ on sb's territory *fig* pisar el terreno a alguien
poacher ['pəʊtʃəʳ, *Am:* 'poʊtʃəʳ] *n* (*hunter*) cazador(a) *m(f)* furtivo, -a; (*fisherman*) pescador(a) *m(f)* furtivo, -a
poaching ['pəʊtʃɪŋ, *Am:* 'poʊtʃ-] *n no pl* (*hunting*) caza *f* furtiva; (*fishing*) pesca *f* furtiva
POB *n abbr of* Post-Office Box apdo. *m* de correos

PO Box [ˌpi:'əʊbɒks, *Am:* -'oʊbɑ:ks] <-es> *n abbr of* Post Office Box apartado *m* de correos
pock [pɒk, *Am:* pɑ:k] *n* (*scar*) picadura *f*; (*pustule*) pústula *f*
pocket ['pɒkɪt, *Am:* 'pɑ:kɪt] I. *n* 1. (*in trousers, jacket*) bolsillo *m*, bolsa *f AmC, Méx*; ~ dictionary diccionario *m* de bolsillo; ~ edition edición *f* de bolsillo; back/breast ~ bolsillo trasero/de pecho; inside ~ bolsillo interior; to be in ~/out of ~ salir ganando/perdiendo; to pay for sth out of one's own ~ pagar algo de su bolsillo 2. (*isolated group or area*) ~ of greenery zona *f* verde; a ~ of resistance un foco de resistencia; ~ of turbulence AVIAT, METEO racha *f* de turbulencias 3. (*in billiard table*) tronera *f* ►to put one's pride in one's ~ tragarse el orgullo; to have sth/sb in one's ~ tener algo/a alguien en el bolsillo; to line one's ~s forrarse (de dinero); to live in sb's ~ *pej* estar siempre pegado a alguien II. *vt* 1. (*put in pocket*) to ~ sth meterse algo en el bolsillo 2. (*keep for oneself*) apropiarse de ►to ~ one's pride tragarse el orgullo
pocketbook ['pɒkɪtbʊk, *Am:* 'pɑ:kɪtbʊk] *n* 1. *Am* (*woman's handbag*) bolso *m*, cartera *f AmL* 2. (*wallet*) monedero *m*; to vote with one's ~ *Am* votar con el bolsillo 3. *Am* (*book*) libro *m* de bolsillo
pocket calculator *n* calculadora *f* de bolsillo **pocket camera** *n* cámara *f* de bolsillo
pocketful ['pɒkɪtfʊl, *Am:* 'pɑ:kɪt-] *n* a ~ of sth un puñado de algo
pocket handkerchief *n* pañuelo *m* de bolsillo **pocketknife** <-knives> *n* navaja *f*
pocket money *n no pl* 1. (*for small personal expenses*) dinero *m* para gastos personales 2. *Brit* (*from one's parents*) paga *f*
pocket-size(d) ['pɒkɪtsaɪz(d), *Am:* 'pɑ:kɪt-] *adj* de bolsillo
pod [pɒd, *Am:* pɑ:d] *n* 1. BOT vaina *f* 2. AVIAT tanque *m*
POD *abbr of* pay on delivery pago *m* contra entrega
podgy ['pɒdʒi, *Am:* 'pɑ:dʒi] <-ier, -iest> *adj* gordinflón, -ona
podiatrist [pəʊ'daɪətrɪst, *Am:* pə'daɪ-] *n* pedicuro, -a *m, f*
podium ['pəʊdiəm, *Am:* 'poʊ-] <-dia> *n* podio *m*
poem ['pəʊɪm, *Am:* poʊəm] *n* poema *m*
poet ['pəʊɪt, *Am:* poʊət] *n* poeta *mf*
poetic [pəʊ'etɪk, *Am:* poʊ'eţ-] *adj* poético, -a
poetry ['pəʊɪtri, *Am:* 'poʊə-] *n no pl, a. fig* poesía *f*
pogrom ['pɒgrəm, *Am:* 'poʊgrəm] *n* pogromo *m*
poignant ['pɔɪnjənt] *adj* conmovedor(a)
poinsettia [pɔɪn'setiə, *Am:* -'seţ-] *n* flor *f* de Pascua
point [pɔɪnt] I. *n* 1. (*sharp end*) punta *f*; knife ~ punta de un cuchillo; pencil ~ punta

de un lápiz **2.** (*promontory*) cabo *m* **3.** (*particular place*) punto *m* **4.** (*particular time*) momento *m;* **boiling/freezing** ~ punto *m* de ebullición/congelación; **starting** ~ punto de partida; **to do sth up to a** ~ hacer algo hasta cierto punto; **to get to the** ~ **that ...** llegar al extremo de...; **at that** ~ en ese instante; **at this** ~ **in time** en este momento **5.** (*significant idea*) cuestión *f;* **that's just the** ~! ¡eso es lo importante!; **to be to the** ~ venir al caso; **to be beside the** ~ no venir al caso; **to get to the** ~ ir al grano; **to get the** ~ **(of sth)** entender (algo); **to make one's** ~ expresar su opinión; **to miss the** ~ no captar lo relevante; **to see sb's** ~ aceptar la opinión de alguien; **to take sb's** ~ aceptar el argumento de alguien; ~ **taken** de acuerdo; ~ **by** ~ punto por punto **6.** (*purpose*) finalidad *f;* **what's the** ~? ¿qué sentido tiene? **7.** (*in score, result*) punto *m;* **percentage** ~ puntos *mpl* porcentuales; **to win (sth) on** ~**s** SPORTS ganar (algo) por puntos **8.** MAT **decimal** ~ coma *f,* punto *m* decimal *AmL* **9.** a. TYPO punto *m;* **join** ~**s A and B together** unir los puntos A y B **10.** *Brit, Aus* (*socket*) toma *f* de corriente **11.** *pl* AUTO (*electrical contacts*) platinos *mpl* **12.** *pl, Brit* RAIL agujas *fpl* ▶**to not put too fine a** ~ **on it, ...** hablando en plata...; **to make a** ~ **of doing sth** procurar de hacer algo **II.** *vi* señalar; (*indicate*) indicar; **to** ~ **to an icon** INFOR apuntar a un icono **III.** *vt* **1.** (*aim*) apuntar; **to** ~ **sth at sb** apuntar con algo a alguien; **the man had** ~**ed a knife at him** el hombre le había amenazado con un cuchillo; **to** ~ **a finger at sb** *a. fig* señalar con el dedo a alguien **2.** (*direct, show position or direction*) señalar; **to** ~ **sth toward sth/sb** dirigir algo hacia algo/alguien; **to** ~ **sb toward sth** indicar a alguien el camino hacia algo

♦**point out** *vt* **1.** (*show*) indicar; **if you see her, please point her out to me** si la ves, por favor indícame quién es **2.** (*inform of*) to point sth out to sb advertir a alguien de algo; **to** ~ **that ...** señalar que...

♦**point up** *vi form* destacar; **to** ~ **how ...** poner de relieve cómo...

point-blank [ˌpɔɪnt'blæŋk] **I.** *adv* **1.** (*fire*) a quemarropa **2.** (*ask*) a bocajarro; **to refuse** ~ negarse rotundamente **II.** *adj* **1.** (*very close, not far away*) **to shoot sb at** ~ **range** disparar a alguien a quemarropa **2.** (*blunt, direct*) directo, -a

pointed ['pɔɪntɪd, *Am:* -t̬ɪd] *adj* **1.** (*implement, stick*) puntiagudo, -a **2.** *fig* (*criticism*) mordaz; (*question*) directo, -a; (*remark*) intencionado, -a

pointer ['pɔɪntə', *Am:* -t̬ə'] *n* **1.** (*for blackboard*) puntero *m;* (*of clock*) aguja *f;* (*of scale*) fiel *m* **2.** INFOR puntero *m;* **mouse** ~ puntero del ratón **3.** (*advice, tip*) consejo *m* **4.** (*dog*) perro *m* de muestra

pointless ['pɔɪntləs] *adj* inútil; **it's** ~ **arguing with him** no sirve de nada discutir con él

point of view <points of view> *n* punto *m* de vista; **from a purely practical** ~ desde una perspectiva puramente práctica

pointsman ['pɔɪntsmən] <-men> *n Brit* RAIL guardabarrera *mf*

point-to-point (**race**) [ˌpɔɪntə'pɔɪnt (reɪs)] *n* carrera de caballos a campo traviesa

poise [pɔɪz] **I.** *n no pl* **1.** (*composure*) aplomo *m;* **to lose/regain one's** ~ perder/recobrar la serenidad **2.** (*elegance*) porte *m* **II.** *vt* **to be** ~**d to do sth** estar a punto de hacer algo

poised *adj* **1.** (*suspended*) suspendido, -a **2.** (*ready*) preparado, -a **3.** (*calm*) sereno, -a

poison ['pɔɪzən] **I.** *n* veneno *m;* **rat** ~ matarratas *m inv;* **to lace sth with** ~ rociar algo con veneno; **to take** ~ envenenarse ▶**what's your** ~? *iron* ¿qué tomas? **II.** *vt* **1.** (*administer poison to*) envenenar **2.** (*spoil, corrupt*) emponzoñar; **the long dispute has** ~**ed relations between the two countries** el largo conflicto ha enturbiado las relaciones entre ambos países; **to** ~ **sb's mind (against sb)** indisponer a alguien (contra alguien)

poison gas *n no pl* gas *m* tóxico

poisoning *n no pl* envenenamiento *m*

poisonous ['pɔɪzənəs] *adj* venenoso, -a; ~ **atmosphere** *fig* ambiente *m* pernicioso; ~ **remark** comentario *m* malicioso

poke[1] [pəʊk, *Am:* poʊk] *n dial* (*bag*) bolsa *f,* saco *m*

poke[2] [pəʊk, *Am:* poʊk] **I.** *n* (*push*) empujón *m;* (*with the elbow*) codazo *m;* **to give sb a** ~ dar un codazo a alguien **II.** *vt* (*with finger*) dar con la punta del dedo en, tocar con la punta del dedo; (*with elbow*) dar un codazo a; **to** ~ **a hole in sth** hacer un agujero en algo; **to** ~ **holes in an argument** echar un argumento por tierra; **to** ~ **one's nose into sb's business** meter las narices en los asuntos de alguien **III.** *vi* **to** ~ **at sth/sb** dar a algo/alguien; **to** ~ **through (sth)** salirse (de algo)

♦**poke about** *vi,* **poke around** *vi* curiosear

♦**poke out I.** *vi* **to** ~ **(of sth)** salirse (de algo) **II.** *vt* **1.** (*stick out*) **to poke one's head out** asomar la cabeza **2.** (*push out*) **to poke sth out** sacar algo; **to poke sb's eye(s) out** saltarle los ojos a alguien

♦**poke round** *vi* curiosear

♦**poke up I.** *vi* asomar **II.** *vt* **to** ~ **a fire** atizar el fuego

poker[1] ['pəʊkə', *Am:* 'poʊkə-] *n* (*card game*) póquer *m*

poker[2] ['pəʊkə', *Am:* 'poʊkə-] *n* (*fireplace tool*) atizador *m*

pokey ['pəʊki, *Am:* 'poʊ-] **I.** *adj s.* **poky II.** *n Am, inf* (*prison*) cárcel *f;* **he'll get three years in** ~ se le caerán tres años en chirona

poky ['pəʊki, *Am:* 'poʊ-] <-ier, -iest> *adj* **1.** (*uncomfortably small*) diminuto, -a; **a** ~ **little room** un cuartucho **2.** *Am* (*annoyingly slow*) lerdo, -a

Poland ['pəʊlənd, *Am:* 'poʊ-] *n* Polonia *f*

polar ['pəʊləʳ, *Am:* 'poʊlə-] *adj* GEO, MAT polar; ~ **opposites** polos *mpl* opuestos

polar bear *n* oso *m* polar **polar circle** *n* círculo *m* polar **polar front** *n* METEO frente *m* polar **polar ice cap** *n no pl* casquete *m* polar

polarisation [ˌpəʊləraɪ'zeɪʃən] *n no pl, Brit, Aus s.* **polarization**

polarise ['pəʊləraɪz] *vt, vi Brit, Aus s.* **polarize**

polarity [pəʊ'lærəti, *Am:* poʊ'lerət̬i] *n no pl* polaridad *f*

polarization [ˌpəʊləraɪ'zeɪʃən, *Am:* ˌpoʊlə-ɪ-] *n no pl* polarización *f*

polarize ['pəʊləraɪz, *Am:* 'poʊ-] I. *vt* polarizar; **to** ~ **sth into two groups** polarizar algo en dos grupos II. *vi* polarizarse

polar lights *npl* aurora *f* boreal **polar region** *n* región *f* polar **polar zone** *n* región *f* polar

pole¹ [pəʊl, *Am:* poʊl] *n* palo *m;* **electricity** ~ poste *m* de electricidad; **flag** ~ asta *f* de bandera; **fishing** ~ caña *f* de pescar; **telegraph** ~ poste *m* telegráfico ►**to not touch sth with a** <u>barge</u> ~ no querer ver algo ni de lejos; **to be** <u>up</u> **the** ~ *Brit* estar como una cabra *inf*

pole² [pəʊl, *Am:* poʊl] *n* **1.** GEO, ELEC polo *m;* **the magnetic** ~**s** GEO los polos magnéticos; **the minus/positive** ~ el polo negativo/positivo **2.** *fig* **to be** ~**s apart** ser polos opuestos; **political** ~**s** extremos *mpl* políticos

Pole¹ [pəʊl, *Am:* poʊl] *n* (*person*) polaco, -a *m, f*

Pole² [pəʊl, *Am:* poʊl] *n* GEO **the North/South** ~ el Polo Norte/Sur

poleaxe ['pəʊlæks, *Am:*'poʊl-] I. *n* **1.** (*medieval weapon*) hacha *f* de armas **2.** (*axe used in naval warfare*) hacha *f* de abordaje II. *vt* (*strike powerfully*) tumbar, noquear; **he was completely ~d when his wife left him** se quedó de una pieza cuando su mujer le dejó

polemic [pə'lemɪk] I. *n* polémica *f* II. *adj* polémico, -a

polemical *adj* polémico, -a

pole position *n no pl* posición *f* de ventaja; **to be in** ~ estar en cabeza

Pole Star *n* estrella *f* polar

pole vault *n* salto *m* con pértiga **pole vaulter** *n* saltador(a) *m(f)* de pértiga

police [pə'liːs] I. *n no pl* policía *f* II. *vt* **to** ~ **an area** vigilar una zona; **to** ~ **a process** supervisar un proceso; **to** ~ **oneself** controlarse; **to** ~ **the frontier** patrullar por la frontera

police car *n* coche *m* de policía **police constable** *n Brit* policía *m,* guardia *m* **police court** *n* juzgado *m* de guardia **police department** *n Am* departamento *m* de policía **police dog** *n* perro *m* policía **police escort** *n* escolta *f* policial; **under** ~ con escolta policial **police force** *n* cuerpo *m*

de policía **police informer** *n* confidente *mf* de la policía **police magistrate** *n* juez(a) *m(f)* de guardia

policeman [pə'liːsmən] <-men> *n* policía *m,* guardia *m*

police officer *n* agente *mf* de policía **police patrol** *n* patrulla *f* policial **police raid** *n* redada *f,* arreada *f Arg* **police record** *n* **1.** (*dossier*) expediente *m* **2.** (*history of convictions*) antecedentes *mpl* penales; **to have a long** ~ tener un largo historial delictivo **police reporter** *n* reportero, -a *m, f* de asuntos policiales **police state** *n pej* estado *m* policíaco **police station** *n* comisaría *f*

policewoman [pə'liːsˌwʊmən] <-women> *n* mujer *f* policía

policy¹ ['pɒləsi, *Am:* 'pɑːlə-] <-ies> *n* **1.** POL, ECON política *f;* **a change in** ~ un cambio de política; **domestic/economic** ~ política interior/económica; **company** ~ política de empresa; **to set** ~ (**on sth**) establecer una política (en materia de algo) **2.** (*principle*) principio *m;* **my** ~ **is to tell the truth whenever possible** tengo por norma decir la verdad siempre que sea posible

policy² ['pɒləsi, *Am:* 'pɑːlə-] <-ies> *n* FIN póliza *f;* **to take out a** ~ hacerse un seguro

policyholder ['pɒləsiˌhəʊldəʳ, *Am:* 'pɑːlə-siˌhoʊldə-] *n* asegurado, -a *m, f* **policy maker** *n* responsable *mf* de los principios políticos de un partido **policy-making** *n no pl* formulación *f* de principios políticos **policy number** *n* número *m* de póliza **policy owner** *n* titular *mf* de una póliza

polio [ˌpəʊliəʊ, *Am:* ˌpoʊlioʊ] *n,* **poliomyelitis** [ˌpəʊliəʊmaɪə'laɪtɪs, *Am:* ˌpoʊlioʊˌmaɪə'laɪt̬əs] *n no pl* MED polio *f,* poliomielitis *f*

polio vaccine *n* vacuna *f* contra la polio

polish ['pɒlɪʃ, *Am:* 'pɑːlɪʃ] I. *n no pl* **1.** (*substance: for furniture*) cera *f;* (*for shoes*) betún *m;* (*for silver*) abrillantador *m;* (*for nails*) esmalte *m* **2.** (*action*) pulimento *m;* **to give sth a** ~ dar brillo a algo **3.** (*sophisticated or refined style*) refinamiento *m* II. *vt* **1.** (*rub to make shine*) sacar brillo a; (*shoes, silver*) limpiar **2.** *fig* (*refine*) pulir

♦**polish off** *vt* (*food*) despacharse; (*work, opponent*) liquidar

♦**polish up** *vt* **1.** (*polish to a shine*) dar brillo **2.** (*improve, brush up*) perfeccionar

Polish ['pəʊlɪʃ, *Am:* 'poʊ-] I. *adj* polaco, -a II. *n* **1.** (*person*) polaco, -a *m, f* **2.** LING polaco *m*

polished *adj* **1.** (*shiny*) pulido, -a **2.** *fig* (*sophisticated*) distinguido, -a; ~ **manners** modales *mpl* refinados; **a** ~ **performance** una actuación impecable

polite [pə'laɪt] *adj* **1.** (*courteous*) atento, -a; ~ **refusal** declinación *f* cortés **2.** (*cultured*) educado, -a; (*refined*) fino, -a; ~ **society** buena sociedad *f* **3.** (*superficially courteous*) correcto, -a; **to keep a** ~ **conversation going**

mantener una conversación por cortesía
politeness *n no pl* **1.** (*good manners*) cortesía *f* **2.** (*consideration*) atenciones *fpl*
politic ['pɒlɪtɪk, *Am:* 'pɑːlə-] *adj* **1.** (*judicious, prudent*) prudente **2.** POL **the body** ~ el cuerpo político
political [pə'lɪtɪkəl, *Am:* -'lɪt̬ə-] *adj* político, -a; ~ **pundit** experto, -a *m, f* en política; **to make** ~ **capital (out) of sth** sacar provecho político de algo
politically correct *adj* políticamente correcto, -a (*actitud que refleja una ideología progresista*)
politician [ˌpɒlɪ'tɪʃən, *Am:* ˌpɑːlə-] *n* político, -a *m, f*
politicize [pe'lɪtɪsaɪz, *Am:* -'lɪt̬ə-] *vt* politizar
politics *n pl* **1.** (*activities of government*) política *f;* **to go into** ~ dedicarse a la política; **to talk** ~ hablar de política **2.** *Brit* (*political science*) ciencias *fpl* políticas
polka ['pɒlkə, *Am:* 'poʊl-] I. *n* polca *f* II. *vi* bailar la polca
poll [pəʊl, *Am:* poʊl] I. *n* **1.** (*public survey*) encuesta *f;* **opinion** ~ sondeo *m* de la opinión pública; **to conduct a** ~ hacer una encuesta **2.** *pl* (*elections*) **to go to the** ~s acudir a las urnas **3.** (*results of a vote*) **to head the** ~ obtener la mayoría de votos **4.** (*number of votes cast*) votos *mpl;* **there was a heavy/light** ~ ha habido una alta/baja participación en las elecciones II. *vt* **1.** (*record the opinion*) sondear; **half the people** ~ed la mitad de los encuestados **2.** (*receive*) **to** ~ **votes** obtener votos
pollard ['pɒləd, *Am:* 'pɑːlɚd] *vt* desmochar
pollen ['pɒlən, *Am:* 'pɑːlən] *n no pl* polen *m*
pollen count *n* índice *m* de polen en el aire
pollinate ['pɒlɪneɪt, *Am:* 'pɑːlə-] *vt* polinizar
polling *n no pl* votación *f*
polling booth *n Brit, Aus* cabina *f* electoral
polling card *n Brit, Aus* papeleta *f* electoral
polling day *n no art, Brit, Aus* día *m* de elecciones **polling place** *n Am,* **polling station** *n Brit, Aus* colegio *m* electoral
pollster ['pəʊlstəʳ, *Am:* 'poʊlstɚ] *n* encuestador(a) *m(f)*
pollutant [pə'luːtənt] *n* contaminante *m,* agente *m* contaminador
pollute [pə'luːt] *vt* **1.** (*contaminate*) contaminar **2.** *fig* (*corrupt*) corromper; **to** ~ **sb's mind** corromper la mente de alguien
polluter [pə'luːtəʳ, *Am:* -t̬ɚ] *n* contaminador(a) *m(f)*
pollution [pə'luːʃən] *n no pl* contaminación *f*
polo ['pəʊləʊ, *Am:* 'poʊloʊ] *n no pl* SPORTS polo *m*
polo neck *n* cuello *m* vuelto; ~ **sweater** jersey *m* de cuello vuelto, polera *f Arg, Urug*
polo shirt *n* polo *m*
poly ['pɒli, *Am:* 'pɑːli] *n Brit, inf s.* **polytechnic** escuela *f* politécnica

polyamide ['pɒli'æmaɪd, *Am:* ˌpɑːli-] *n* poliamida *f*
polychrome [ˌpɒlɪ'krəʊm] *adj* polícromo, -a
polyclinic ['pɒlɪklɪnɪk, *Am:* ˌpɑːlɪ'-] *n* policlínica *f,* policlínico *m AmL*
polyester [ˌpɒli'estəʳ, *Am:* ˌpɑːli'estɚ] *n no pl* poliéster *m*
polygamist *n* polígamo *m*
polygamous *adj* polígamo, -a
polygamy [pə'lɪgəmi] *n no pl* poligamia *f*
polyglot ['pɒlɪglɒt, *Am:* 'pɑːlɪglɑːt] I. *adj* polígloto, -a II. *n* políglota *mf*
polygon ['pɒlɪgən, *Am:* 'pɑːlɪgɑːn] *n* polígono *m*
polygonal [pə'lɪgənəl] *adj* poligonal
polygraph ['pɒlɪgrɑːf, *Am:* 'pɑːlɪgræf] *n Am* polígrafo *m,* detector *m* de mentiras
polymeric [ˌpɒlɪ'merɪk, *Am:* ˌpɑːlɪ'-] *adj* polimérico, -a
polymorphous [ˌpɒlɪ'mɔːfəs, *Am:* ˌpɑːlɪ'mɔːr-] *adj* polimorfo, -a
Polynesia [ˌpɒlɪ'niːʒə, *Am:* ˌpɑːlə'niːʒə] *n* Polinesia *f*
Polynesian I. *adj* polinesio, -a II. *n* polinesio, -a *m, f*
polyp ['pɒlɪp, *Am:* 'pɑːlɪp] *n* MED, ZOOL pólipo *m*
polyphonic [ˌpɒlɪ'fɒnɪk, *Am:* ˌpɑːlɪ'fɑːnɪk] *adj* MUS polifónico, -a
polyphony [pə'lɪfəni] *n no pl* MUS polifonía *f*
polystyrene [ˌpɒlɪ'staɪəriːn, *Am:* ˌpɑːlɪ-] *n no pl, Brit, Aus* poliestireno *m*
polysyllabic [ˌpɒlɪsɪ'læbɪk, *Am:* ˌpɑːlɪsɪ'-] *adj* polisílabo, -a
polysyllable [ˌpɒlɪ'sɪləbəl, *Am:* 'pɑːlɪˌsɪl-] *n* LING polisílabo *m*
polytechnic [ˌpɒlɪ'teknɪk, *Am:* ˌpɑːlɪ-] *n* escuela *f* politécnica
polytheism ['pɒlɪθiːɪzəm, *Am:* 'pɑːlɪ-] *n no pl* politeísmo *m*
polytheistic [ˌpɒlɪθi'ɪstɪk, *Am:* ˌpɑːlɪ-] *adj* politeísta
polythene ['pɒlɪθiːn, *Am:* 'pɑːlɪ-] *n no pl* polietileno *m*
polythene bag *n Brit, Aus* bolsa *f* de polietileno
polyunsaturated [ˌpɒliʌn'sætʃəreɪtɪd, *Am:* ˌpɑːliʌn'sætʃəreɪt̬ɪd] *adj* poliinsaturado, -a
polyunsaturated fats *npl,* **polyunsaturates** [ˌpɒliʌn'sætʃəreɪts, *Am:* ˌpɑːli-] *npl* grasas *fpl* poliinsaturadas
polyurethane [ˌpɒlɪ'jʊərəθeɪn, *Am:* ˌpɑːlɪ-'jʊrə-] *n no pl* poliuretano *m*
polyvalent [ˌpɒlɪ'veɪlənt, *Am:* ˌpɑːlɪ'-] *adj* polivalente
pomade [pəʊ'meɪd, *Am:* pɑ'meɪd] *n no pl* pomada *f*
pomegranate ['pɒmɪgrænɪt, *Am:* 'pɑːmˌgræn-] *n* **1.** (*fruit*) granada *f* **2.** (*tree*) granado *m*
pomp [pɒmp, *Am:* pɑːmp] *n no pl* pompa *f;* ~ **and circumstance** pompa y solemnidad
pomposity [pɒm'pɒsəti, *Am:* pɑːm'pɑːsə-]

ţi] *n no pl* pomposidad *f*

pompous ['pɒmpəs, *Am:* 'pɑːm-] *adj* **1.** pomposo, -a **2.** (*pretentious*) ostentoso, -a; ~ **language** lenguaje *m* ampuloso

ponce [pɒns, *Am:* pɑːns] **I.** *n* **1.** *Brit, Aus, pej* (*effeminate man*) mariquita *m* **2.** *Brit, inf* (*pimp*) chulo *m* **II.** *vi* to ~ **about 1.** *Brit, Aus, pej* (*behave in effeminate manner*) mariconear *pey* **2.** *Brit* (*muck about*) perder el tiempo

poncho ['pɒntʃəʊ, *Am:* 'pɑːntʃoʊ] *n* poncho *m*, ruana *f Col, Ven*, zarape *m Guat, Méx*

poncy ['pɒnsi, *Am:* 'pɑːnsi] *adj* <-ier, -iest> *Brit, Aus, pej* de mariquita

pond [pɒnd, *Am:* pɑːnd] *n* **1.** (*natural*) charca *f*; (*artificial*) estanque *m*; **duck** ~ estanque de patos; **fish** ~ vivero *m* **2.** *iron* (*Atlantic ocean*) **the Pond** el charco

ponder ['pɒndər, *Am:* 'pɑːndɚ] **I.** *vt* considerar, sopesar **II.** *vi* reflexionar; **to** ~ **on sth** meditar sobre algo; **to** ~ **whether/why ...** preguntarse si/por qué...

ponderous ['pɒndərəs, *Am:* 'pɑːn-] *adj* **1.** (*movement*) pesado, -a **2.** (*style*) laborioso, -a

pone [pəʊn] *n Am* borona *f*; **corn** ~ pan *m* de maíz

pong [pɒŋ, *Am:* pɑːŋ] *inf* **I.** *n Brit, Aus* peste *f*; **what a** ~! ¡qué peste! **II.** *vi Brit, Aus, pej* to stink; ~ **of sth** apestar a algo

pontiff ['pɒntɪf, *Am:* 'pɑːnţɪf] *n* REL **the** ~ el pontífice

pontifical [pɒn'tɪfɪkəl, *Am:* pɑːn'-] *adj* pontifical

pontificate¹ [pɒn'tɪfɪkeɪt, *Am:* pɑːn-] *vi pej* pontificar

pontificate² [pɒn'tɪfɪkət, *Am:* pɑːn'tɪfɪkət] *n* pontificado *m*

pontoon [pɒn'tuːn, *Am:* pɑːn-] *n* **1.** (*floating device*) pontón *m* **2.** *no pl, Brit* (*card game*) veintiuna *f*

pontoon bridge *n* puente *m* de pontones

pony ['pəʊni, *Am:* 'poʊ-] <-ies> *n* (*horse*) poni *m*

ponytail ['pəʊniteɪl, *Am:* 'poʊ-] *n* coleta *f*

pony-trekking *n no pl* excursión *f* en poni; **to go** ~ ir de excursión en poni

poo [puː] *s.* **pooh**

poodle ['puːdl] *n* caniche *m*; **to be sb's** ~ *Brit, iron* ser el perrito faldero de alguien

poof [puːf] **I.** *n Brit, Aus, pej* maricón *m* **II.** *interj Am, inf* ¡chas!

poofter [puːftə, *Am:* -tɚ] *n Brit, Aus, pej* maricón *m*

pooh [puː] **I.** *n Brit, Aus, childspeak* caca *f*; **to do a** ~ hacer caca **II.** *vi Brit, Aus, childspeak* hacer caca **III.** *interj inf* **1.** (*to indicate disgust*) ~! **what a ghastly smell!** ¡puf, qué peste! **2.** (*to indicate impatience*) ¡bah!

pooh-pooh [,puː'puː] *vt inf* **to** ~ **a plan/a proposal** desdeñar un plan/una proposición

pool¹ [puːl] *n* **1.** (*of water*) charca *f*; (*of oil, blood*) charco *f*; **rock** ~ piscina *f* de roca; **a** ~ **of light** un foco de luz **2.** (*artificial*) estanque

pool² [puːl] **I.** *n* **1.** (*common fund*) fondo *m* común **2.** (*common supply*) reserva *f*; **car** ~ parque *m* de automóviles; **gene** ~ acervo *m* genético; **typing** ~ servicio *m* de mecanografía **3.** SPORTS billar *m* americano; **to shoot** ~ *inf* jugar al billar; **to be dirty** ~ *Am, inf* ser un juego sucio **4.** *pl, Brit* (**football**) ~s quiniela *f*; **to do the** ~s hacer la quiniela **II.** *vt* (*money, resources*) hacer un fondo común; (*information*) compartir

pool hall *n*, **pool room** *n* sala *f* de billar

pool table *n* mesa *f* de billar

poop¹ [puːp] *n* NAUT popa *f*; ~ **deck** castillo *m* de popa

poop² [puːp] *n no pl, Am, inf* (*information*) **to get the** ~ **on sth/sb** ponerse al tanto de algo/alguien

poop³ [puːp] *inf* **I.** *n no pl* caca *f*; **dog** ~ caca de perro **II.** *vi* hacerse caca

♦**poop out** *vi Am, Aus, inf* quedar hecho polvo

pooper scooper ['puːpə,skuːpər, *Am:* -pɚ-,skuːpɚ] *n*, **poop scoop** ['puːpskuːp] *n Am* pala *f* para recoger excrementos

poop sheet *n Am, inf* folleto *m*

poor [pʊər, *Am:* pʊr] **I.** *adj* **1.** (*lacking money*) pobre **2.** (*attendance, harvest*) escaso, -a; (*memory, performance*) malo, -a; ~ **soil** terreno *m* pobre; ~ **visibility** visibilidad *f* escasa; **to be** ~ **at sth** no estar fuerte en algo; **to be in** ~ **health** estar mal de salud; **to be a** ~ **loser** no saber perder; **to be a** ~ **sailor** marearse fácilmente; **to give a** ~ **account of oneself** causar mala impresión; **to cut a** ~ **figure** (**as sth**) hacer un mal papel (como algo); **to be a** ~ **excuse for sth** ser una mala versión de algo; **to have** ~ **eyesight** tener mala vista; **to have** ~ **hearing** ser duro de oído; **to make a** ~ **job of** (**doing**) **sth** hacer algo mal **3.** (*deserving of pity*) pobre; **you** ~ **thing!** ¡pobrecito! **II.** *n* **the** ~ los pobres

poor box <-es> *n* cepillo *m* de los pobres

poorhouse *n* HIST asilo *m* de los pobres

poorly ['pʊəli, *Am:* 'pʊr-] **I.** *adv* **1.** (*resulting from poverty*) pobremente; **to be** ~ **off** andar escaso de dinero **2.** (*inadequately*) mal; ~ **dressed** mal vestido; **to think** ~ **of sb** tener mala opinión de alguien **II.** *adj* **to feel** ~ encontrarse mal

poorness ['pʊənɪs, *Am:* 'pʊr-] *n no pl* **1.** (*inadequacy*) impropiedad *f*; **the** ~ **of his judgment** lo inadecuado de su opinión **2.** (*poverty*) pobreza *f*

poor relation *n* pariente *mf* pobre

pop¹ [pɒp, *Am:* pɑːp] **I.** *adj* popular; ~ **culture** cultura *f* pop **II.** *n no pl* MUS pop *m*

pop² [pɒp, *Am:* pɑːp] *n inf* (*father*) papá *m*

pop³ [pɒp, *Am:* pɑːp] *n no pl abbr of* **population** hab. *mf*

pop⁴ [pɒp, *Am:* pɑːp] **I.** *n* **1.** (*small explosive noise*) pequeña explosión *f*; **the** ~ **of a champagne cork** el taponazo de una botella de cava

2. (*drink*) gaseosa *f;* **orange** ~ naranjada *f;* **fizzy** ~ bebida *f* gaseosa **II.** <-pp-> *vi* **1.** (*explode*) estallar; (*burst*) reventar; **to let the cork** ~ hacer saltar el tapón **2.** (*go, come quickly*) **to** ~ **upstairs** subir un momento; **to** ~ **out for sth** salir un momento a por algo **III.** <-pp-> *vt* **1.** (*make burst*) hacer estallar **2.** (*put quickly*) meter; **to** ~ **sth on/off** ponerse/quitarse algo

♦**pop in** *vi* entrar un momento en; **we popped in at my brother's on our way home** de vuelta a casa, pasamos por casa de mi hermano

♦**pop off** *vi iron, inf* (*die*) estirar la pata

♦**pop out** *vi* salir; **to** ~ **from somewhere** salir de pronto de un sitio; **to** ~ **for sth** salir un momento a hacer algo

♦**pop up** *vi* (*appear*) aparecer; **to** ~ **out of nowhere** surgir de la nada

pop art *n no pl* pop art *m* **pop concert** *n* concierto *m* pop

popcorn ['pɒpkɔːn, *Am:* 'pɑːpkɔːrn] *n no pl* palomitas *fpl* de maíz, pororó *m CSur,* cacalote *m AmC, Méx*

pope [pəʊp, *Am:* poʊp] *n* REL **1.** (*Catholic*) papa *m* **2.** (*Orthodox priest*) pope *m*

pop-eyed [,pɒp'aɪd, *Am:* 'pɑːp,aɪd] *adj* de ojos saltones; **he looked at me** ~ me miró con los ojos desorbitados

pop group *n* grupo *m* pop

pop gun *n* pistola *f* de juguete

poplar ['pɒplər, *Am:* 'pɑːplɚ] *n* álamo *m*

poplin ['pɒplɪn, *Am:* 'pɑːplɪn] *n no pl* popelín *m*

pop music *n no pl* música *f* pop

popper ['pɒpər, *Am:* 'pɑːpɚ] *n* **1.** *Brit, inf* (*drug*) popper *m* **2.** (*button*) cierre *m* automático

poppet ['pɒpɪt, *Am:* 'pɑːpɪt] *n Aus, Brit, inf* tesoro *m fig*

poppy ['pɒpi, *Am:* 'pɑːpi] <-ies> *n* amapola *f*

poppycock ['pɒpɪkɒk, *Am:* 'pɑːpɪkɑːk] *n no pl, inf* tonterías *fpl*

Poppy Day *n Brit s.* **Remembrance Day**

poppy seeds *npl* semillas *fpl* de amapola

pop singer *n* cantante *mf* pop **pop song** *n* canción *f* pop **pop star** *n* estrella *f* del pop

populace ['pɒpjʊləs, *Am:* 'pɑːpjələs] *n no pl* **the** ~ el pueblo

popular ['pɒpjʊlər, *Am:* 'pɑːpjələr] *adj* **1.** (*liked*) popular; **she is very** ~ **among her colleagues** es muy apreciada entre sus compañeros; **he is** ~ **with girls** tiene éxito con las chicas **2.** (*by the people*) popular; ~ **elections** elecciones *fpl* democráticas; ~ **front** frente *m* popular; ~ **support** el apoyo del pueblo; **by** ~ **request** a petición del público **3.** (*widespread*) generalizado, -a **4.** (*cheap*) económico, -a

popularity [,pɒpjʊ'lærəti, *Am:* ,pɑːpjə'lerəţi] *n no pl* popularidad *f*

popularize ['pɒpjʊləraɪz, *Am:* 'pɑːpjə-] *vt* **1.** (*make known or liked*) popularizar **2.** (*make understood*) divulgar

popularly ['pɒpjʊləli, *Am:* 'pɑːpjəlɚ-] *adv* generalmente; **to be** ~ **known as ...** ser vulgarmente conocido como...

populate ['pɒpjəleɪt, *Am:* 'pɑːpjə-] *vt* poblar

population [,pɒpjə'leɪʃən, *Am:* ,pɑːpjə'-] *n* población *f;* **the working** ~ la población activa; **the dolphin** ~ la población de delfines

population density *n* densidad *f* de población **population explosion** *n* explosión *f* demográfica

populous ['pɒpjʊləs, *Am:* 'pɑːpjə-] *adj form* populoso, -a

porcelain ['pɔːsəlɪn, *Am:* 'pɔːr-] *n no pl* porcelana *f*

porch [pɔːtʃ, *Am:* pɔːrtʃ] *n* **1.** (*over entrance*) porche *m;* (*church*) pórtico *m* **2.** *Am* (*verandah*) veranda *f*

porcupine ['pɔːkjʊpaɪn, *Am:* 'pɔːr-] *n* puercoespín *m*

pore [pɔːr, *Am:* pɔːr] *n* poro *m*

♦**pore over** *vi* reflexionar sobre; **to** ~ **a book/map** estudiar detenidamente un libro/mapa

pork [pɔːk, *Am:* pɔːrk] *n no pl* (carne *f* de) cerdo *m,* (carne *f* de) puerco *m Méx,* (carne *f* de) chancho *m Chile, Perú*

pork chop *n* chuleta *f* de cerdo

porker *n* cebón *m*

pork pie *n Brit* empanada *f* de cerdo

porky ['pɔːki] <-ier, -iest> *adj pej, inf* gordinflón, -ona **II.** *n* <-ies> *pl, Brit, inf* (*lies*) bola *f;* **to tell porkies** contar mentiras

porn [pɔːn, *Am:* pɔːrn] *n abbr of* **pornography** porno *m*

pornographic [,pɔːnə'græfɪk, *Am:* ,pɔːrnə'-] *adj* pornográfico, -a

pornography [pɔː'nɒgrəfi, *Am:* pɔːr'nɑːgrə-] *n no pl* pornografía *f;* **hard-core** ~ pornografía dura

porous ['pɔːrəs] *adj* poroso, -a

porpoise ['pɔːpəs, *Am:* 'pɔːr-] *n* marsopa *f*

porridge ['pɒrɪdʒ, *Am:* 'pɔːr-] *n no pl* ≈ gachas *fpl* de avena

porridge oats *npl* copos *mpl* de avena

port¹ [pɔːt, *Am:* pɔːrt] *n* **1.** NAUT (*harbour*) puerto *m;* ~ **of call** puerto de escala; **fishing/trading** ~ puerto pesquero/comercial; **to come into** ~ tomar puerto; **to leave** ~ zarpar **2.** INFOR puerto *m;* **parallel/serial/printer/game** ~ puerto paralelo/serial/de impresora/de juegos ▶**any** ~ **in a storm** en tiempos de guerra cualquier hoyo es trinchero

port² [pɔːt, *Am:* pɔːrt] **I.** *n no pl* AVIAT, NAUT (*side*) babor *m;* **to** ~ **a** babor **II.** *adj* NAUT, AVIAT de babor; **on the** ~ **side** a babor

port³ [pɔːt, *Am:* pɔːrt] *n no pl* (*wine*) oporto *m*

portable ['pɔːtəbl, *Am:* 'pɔːrţə-] *adj* portátil

portacabin ['pɔːtəˌkæbɪn, *Am:* 'pɔːrţə-] *n Brit s.* **Portakabin**

portage ['pɔːtɪdʒ, *Am:* 'pɔːrţɪdʒ] *n no pl*

porte *m*

Portakabin® ['pɔːtəˌkæbɪn, *Am:* 'pɔːrtə-] *n Brit* caseta *f* portátil

portal ['pɔːtəl, *Am:* 'pɔːrtəl] *n a.* INFOR (*gateway*) portal *m*

port authority *n* autoridad *f* portuaria

port charges *npl*, **port dues** *npl* derechos *mpl* portuarios

portcullis [ˌpɔːt'kʌlɪs, *Am:* ˌpɔːrt-] <-es> *n* rastrillo *m*

portentous [pɔː'tentəs, *Am:* pɔːr'tentəs] *adj* **1.** *form* (*signifying something to come*) profético, -a; (*ominous*) de mal agüero **2.** (*too serious*) solemne

porter ['pɔːtəʳ, *Am:* 'pɔːrtə̩] *n* **1.** (*person who carries luggage*) mozo *m* de equipajes; (*in hospital*) camillero *m*; (*on expedition*) porteador *m* **2.** *Brit* (*doorkeeper*) portero *m*; (*in college*) bedel *m*; (*in hotel*) conserje *m*; ~'s **lodge** conserjería *f* **3.** *Am* (*attendant on a train*) camarero *m*

portfolio [pɔːt'fəʊliəʊ, *Am:* pɔːrt'foʊlioʊ] *n* **1.** (*case*) portafolio(s) *m* (*inv*) **2.** (*examples of drawings, designs*) carpeta *f* de trabajos **3.** FIN, POL cartera *f*; **minister without** ~ ministro, -a *m*, *f* sin cartera

porthole ['pɔːthəʊl, *Am:* 'pɔːrthoʊl] *n* portilla *f*

portico ['pɔːtɪkəʊ, *Am:* 'pɔːrtɪkoʊ] <-es *o* -s> *n* pórtico *m*

portion ['pɔːʃən, *Am:* 'pɔːr-] I. *n* **1.** (*part*) parte *f*; **to accept one's** ~ **of the blame** aceptar su parte de culpa **2.** (*serving*) ración *f*; (*of cake, cheese*) trozo *m* II. *vt* **to** ~ **out sth** repartir algo

portly ['pɔːtli, *Am:* 'pɔːrt-] <-ier, -iest> *adj* corpulento, -a

portrait ['pɔːtrɪt, *Am:* 'pɔːrtrɪt] I. *n* ART, LIT retrato *m*; **to paint a** ~ **of sb** retratar a alguien II. *adj* TYPO de formato vertical

portraitist *n*, **portrait painter** *n* retratista *mf*

portraiture ['pɔːtrɪtʃəʳ, *Am:* 'pɔːrtrɪtʃə̩] *n no pl* ART, LIT retrato *m*

portray [pɔː'treɪ, *Am:* pɔːr'-] *vt* **1.** ART (*person*) retratar; (*object*) pintar; (*scene, environment*) representar **2.** *fig* describir **3.** THEAT interpretar

portrayal [pɔː'treɪəl, *Am:* pɔːr'-] *n* **1.** ART retrato *m* **2.** *fig* descripción *f* **3.** THEAT interpretación *f*

Portugal ['pɔːtjʊgəl, *Am:* 'pɔːrtʃəgəl] *n* Portugal *m*

Portuguese [ˌpɔːtjʊ'giːz, *Am:* ˌpɔːrtʃə'-] I. *adj* portugués, -esa II. *n* **1.** (*person*) portugués, -esa *m*, *f* **2.** LING portugués *m*

POS [ˌpiːəʊ'es] *abbr of* **point of sale** punto *m* de venta

pose[1] [pəʊz, *Am:* poʊz] *vt* (*difficulty, problem*) plantear; (*question*) formular; **to** ~ **a threat to sb** representar una amenaza para alguien

pose[2] [pəʊz, *Am:* poʊz] I. *vi* **1.** ART, PHOT

posar **2.** (*affected behaviour*) darse tono **3.** (*pretend to be*) **to** ~ **as sb/sth** hacerse pasar por alguien/algo II. *n* **1.** (*body position*) pose *f*; **to adopt a** ~ adoptar una pose **2.** (*pretence*) afectación *f*; **it's all a** ~ es todo fachada

poser ['pəʊzəʳ, *Am:* 'poʊzə̩] *n* **1.** *inf* (*question*) pregunta *f* difícil; (*problem*) dilema *m* **2.** *pej* (*person*) **he's a** ~ se hace el interesante

posh [pɒʃ, *Am:* pɑːʃ] *inf* I. *adj* **1.** (*stylish: area*) elegante; (*car, hotel, restaurant*) de lujo **2.** *Brit* (*person, accent*) pijo, -a, cheto, -a *CSur* II. *adv Brit, inf* **stop acting so** ~! ¡deja de comportarte como un pijo!

posit ['pɒzɪt, *Am:* 'pɑːzɪt] *vt form* postular

position [pə'zɪʃən] I. *n* **1.** *a.* MIL, SPORTS posición *f*; **from this** ~ **you can see the whole beach** desde este lugar se puede ver toda la playa; **the** ~ **of a house** la ubicación de una casa; **they took up their** ~**s** ocuparon sus puestos; **to be in** ~ estar en su sitio; **to be out of** ~ estar fuera de lugar; **yoga** ~ postura *f* de yoga **2.** *Brit, Aus* (*rank*) posición *f*, puesto *m*; (*social*) rango *m*; **the** ~ **of director** el cargo de director; **a** ~ **of responsibility/trust** un puesto de responsabilidad/confianza **3.** *form* (*opinion*) postura *f*; **to take up a** ~ **on sth** adoptar una postura sobre algo **4.** (*situation*) situación *f*; **financial** ~ situación económica; **to be in the fortunate** ~ **of ...** tener la suerte de...; **to be in a** ~ **to do sth** estar en condiciones de hacer algo; **to be in no** ~ **to do sth** no estar en condiciones de hacer algo; **to put sb in a difficult** ~ poner a alguien en un aprieto II. *vt* (*place*) colocar; MIL apostar

positive ['pɒzətɪv, *Am:* 'pɑːzətɪv] *adj* **1.** *a.* ELEC, MAT positivo, -a; ~ **criticism** crítica *f* constructiva; **to think** ~ ser positivo **2.** MED HIV ~ seropositivo, -a **3.** (*certain*) definitivo, -a; (*proof*) concluyente; **to be** ~ **about sth** estar seguro de algo; (*absolutely*) ~! ¡segurísimo! **4.** (*complete*) auténtico, -a; **a** ~ **miracle** un verdadero milagro

positively *adv* **1.** (*think*) positivamente; **to answer** ~ contestar afirmativamente **2.** (*completely*) totalmente; **to** ~ **refuse to do sth** negarse rotundamente a hacer algo

poss. *abbr of* **possessive** posesivo *m*

posse ['pɒsi, *Am:* 'pɑːsi] *n* banda *f*; **a whole** ~ **of reporters** una legión de reporteros

possess [pə'zes] *vt* **1.** (*own, have*) poseer **2.** **to** ~ **sb** (*anger, fear*) apoderarse de alguien; (*evil spirit*) poseer a alguien; **what** ~**ed you to do that?** ¿cómo se te ocurrió hacer eso?

possessed [pə'zest] *adj* poseso, -a, poseído, -a; **to be** ~ **with sth** estar obsesionado con algo; **to behave like sb** ~ comportarse como un poseso

possession [pə'zeʃən] *n* **1.** *no pl* (*having*) posesión *f*; **illegal** ~ **of arms** tenencia *f* ilícita de armas; **to take** ~ **of sth** tomar posesión de algo; **to come into** ~ **of sth** *form* hacerse con algo; **to gain** ~ **of sth** apoderarse de algo; **to be in sb's** ~ estar en poder de alguien; **to**

have sth in one's ~ *form* tener algo en su poder **2.** (*item of property*) bien *m* **3.** POL dominio *m* ►~ **is nine** points **of the law** la posesión es lo que cuenta

possessive [pə'zesɪv] *adj* posesivo, -a; **to be** ~ **about sb** comportarse de manera posesiva con alguien

possessor [pə'zesəʳ, *Am:* -əʳ] *n iron* poseedor(a) *m(f)*

possibility [ˌpɒsə'bɪləti, *Am:* ˌpɑːsə'bɪlət̬i] *n* <-ies> **1.** (*feasible circumstance or action*) posibilidad *f* **2.** *no pl* (*likelihood*) perspectiva *f*; **within the bounds of** ~ dentro de lo posible; **if by any** ~ ... si por casualidad...; **is there any** ~ (**that**) ...? *form* ¿hay alguna posibilidad de que +*subj*...? **3.** (*potential*) **to have possibilities** tener posibilidades

possible ['pɒsəbl, *Am:* 'pɑːsə-] *adj* posible; **as clean/good as** ~ lo más limpio/lo mejor posible; **as far as** ~ en lo posible; **as soon as** ~ lo antes posible; **if** ~ si es posible

possibly ['pɒsəbli, *Am:* 'pɑːsə-] *adv* **1.** (*perhaps*) quizás; **could you** ~ **help me?** ¿sería tan amable de ayudarme? **2.** (*by any means*) **we did all that we** ~ **could** hicimos todo lo posible; **I couldn't** ~ **do it** me es totalmente imposible hacerlo

possum ['pɒsəm, *Am:* 'pɑːsəm] <-(s)> *n* zarigüeya *f* ►**to** play ~ (*pretend to be asleep*) hacerse el dormido; (*pretend to be ignorant*) hacerse el sueco

post¹ [pəʊst, *Am:* poʊst] **I.** *n no pl, Brit* correo *m;* **by** ~ por correo; **to open the** ~ abrir las cartas; **by return of** ~ a vuelta de correo; **by separate** ~ en sobre aparte; **is there any** ~? ¿ha llegado alguna carta? **II.** *vt Brit, Aus* echar (al correo); **to** ~ **sb sth** enviar algo por correo a alguien

post² [pəʊst, *Am:* poʊst] **I.** *n* (*job*) puesto *m;* **to apply for a teaching** ~ solicitar un empleo de profesor; **to take up a** ~ entrar en funciones; **to desert one's** ~ MIL desertar del puesto **II.** *vt* **1.** (*send to work*) destinar **2.** MIL (*position*) apostar

post³ [pəʊst, *Am:* poʊst] **I.** *n* **1.** *a.* SPORTS poste *m;* **starting/finishing** ~ línea *f* de salida/de meta **2.** *inf* (*goalpost*) poste *m* (de portería) **II.** *vt Brit, Aus* **to** ~ **sth** (**on sth**) fijar algo (en algo); **to** ~ **sth on the noticeboard** poner algo en el tablón de anuncios; ~ **no bills** prohibido fijar carteles

postage ['pəʊstɪdʒ, *Am:* 'poʊ-] *n no pl* franqueo *m;* ~ **and packing** gastos *mpl* de envío

postage meter *n Am* (máquina *f*) franqueadora *f*, estampilladora *f AmL* **postage paid** *adj* con franqueo pagado **postage rate** *n* tarifa *f* postal **postage stamp** *n form* sello *m*, estampilla *f AmL*

postal ['pəʊstəl, *Am:* 'poʊ-] *adj* postal

postal code *n* código *m* postal **postal order** *n* giro *m* postal **postal vote** *n* voto *m* por correo **postal worker** *n* empleado, -a *m, f* de correos

postbag ['pəʊstbæg, *Am:* 'poʊst-] *n Brit* **1.** (*bag*) saca *f* (postal) **2.** (*letters*) correspondencia *f* **postbox** <-es> *n Brit, Aus* buzón *m* **postcard** *n* (tarjeta *f*) postal *f* **post-code** *n Brit* código *m* postal

postdate [ˌpəʊst'deɪt, *Am:* ˌpoʊst-] *vt* **1.** (*write a later date on*) posfechar **2.** (*happen after*) ocurrir después de

posted ['pəʊstɪd, *Am:* 'poʊst-] *adj* **to keep sb** ~ tener a alguien al corriente

poster ['pəʊstəʳ, *Am:* 'poʊstəʳ] *n* (*notice*) cartel *m;* (*picture*) póster *m*

poste restante ['pəʊst'restaːnt, *Am:* ˌpoʊstres'taːnt] *n Brit* lista *f* de correos, poste *m* restante *AmL*

posterior [pɒ'stɪərɪəʳ, *Am:* paː'stɪrɪəʳ] **I.** *adj form* posterior **II.** *n iron* trasero *m inf*

posterity [pɒ'sterəti, *Am:* paː'-] *n no pl, form* posteridad *f*; **to preserve sth for** ~ guardar algo para la posteridad

postern ['pɒstən, *Am:* 'poʊstəʳn] *n* postigo *m;* MIL poterna *f*

post-free *Brit* **I.** *adj* sin gastos de franqueo **II.** *adv* con porte pagado

postgraduate [ˌpəʊst'grædʒuət, *Am:* ˌpoʊst'grædʒuwɪt] **I.** *n* postgraduado, -a *m, f* **II.** *adj* de postgrado; ~ **studies** (estudios *mpl* de) postgrado *m*

post-haste [ˌpəʊst'heɪst, *Am:* ˌpoʊst-] *adv form* con presteza

posthumous ['pɒstjəməs, *Am:* 'paːstʃəməs] *adj form* póstumo, -a

posting ['pəʊstɪŋ, *Am:* 'poʊ-] *n* destino *m*

postman ['pəʊstmən, *Am:* 'poʊst-] <-men> *n Brit* cartero *m*

postmark ['pəʊstmaːk, *Am:* 'poʊstmaːrk] **I.** *n* matasellos *m inv;* **date as** ~ fecha *f* de timbre **II.** *vt* matasellar; **the letter is** ~**ed Rome** la carta lleva matasellos de Roma

postmaster ['pəʊstˌmaːstəʳ, *Am:* 'poʊstˌmæstəʳ] *n* jefe *m* de la oficina de correos

post meridiem *adv s.* **p.m.**

post-modern [ˌpəʊst'mɒdən, *Am:* ˌpoʊst-'maːdəʳn] *adj* posmoderno, -a

post-modernism *n no pl* posmodernismo *m*

postmortem [ˌpəʊst'mɔːtəm, *Am:* ˌpoʊst-'mɔːrt̬əm] *n* autopsia *f*; **to carry out a** ~ realizar una autopsia

postnatal [ˌpəʊst'neɪtəl, *Am:* ˌpoʊst-'neɪt̬əl] *adj* postnatal; ~ **depression** depresión *f* posparto

Post Office *n* (oficina *f* de) correos *m;* **to take sth to the** ~ llevar algo a correos

post office box *n* apartado *m* de correos, casilla *f* postal *CSur*

post-paid [ˌpəʊst'peɪd, *Am:* ˌpoʊst-] **I.** *adj* (*letter*) con franqueo pagado; (*parcel*) sin gastos de franqueo **II.** *adv* (*send: letter*) con franqueo pagado; (*parcel*) con porte pagado

postpone [pəʊst'pəʊn, *Am:* poʊst'poʊn] *vt* aplazar, postergar *AmL*

postponement *n* aplazamiento *m*, postergación *f AmL*

postscript ['pəʊstskrɪp, *Am:* 'poʊs-] *n*
1. (*at end of letter*) posdata *m* **2.** *fig* epílogo *m;*
as a ~ to sth como colofón de algo
postulate[1] ['pɒstjəleɪt, *Am:* 'pɑːstʃə-] *vt*
form **1.** (*hypothesize*) postular **2.** (*assume*)
presuponer
postulate[2] ['pɒstjəlet, *Am:* 'pɑːstʃəlɪt] *n*
form postulado *m*
posture ['pɒstʃəʳ, *Am:* 'pɑːstʃə-] **I.** *n no pl*
postura *f,* actitud *f* **II.** *vi* tomar una postura,
adoptar una actitud; **to ~ as sth** *pej* dárselas de
algo
postwar [ˌpəʊst'wɔːʳ, *Am:* ˌpoʊst'wɔːr] *adj*
de la posguerra; **the ~ years** la posguerra; **~
Europe** la Europa de la posguerra
posy ['pəʊzi, *Am:* 'poʊ-] <-ies> *n* ramillete
m
pot[1] [pɒt, *Am:* pɑːt] **I.** *n* **1.** (*container*) bote
m **2.** (*for cooking*) olla *f;* **~s and pans** cacha-
rros *mpl* **3.** (*of food*) tarro *m;* (*of drink*) jarro
m; (*for coffee*) cafetera *f;* (*for tea*) tetera *f*
4. (*for plants*) maceta *f;* (*for flowers*) tiesto *m*
5. *inf* GAMES **to win the ~** llevarse el bote **6.** *inf*
(*a lot*) montón *m;* **~s of money** montones de
dinero **7.** *iron* (*potbelly*) barriga *f inf* ▶**it's (a
case of) the ~ calling the** <u>kettle</u> **black** dijo la
sartén al cazo, apártate que me tiznas; **to go to
~** *inf* echarse a perder; (*business, plan*) irse al
garete **II.** <-tt-> *vt* **1.** (*put in a pot: food*) conservar en un tarro; **to ~ (up)** (*plants*) plantar
2. (*shoot*) cazar **3.** *Brit* SPORTS meter en la
tronera
pot[2] [pɒt, *Am:* pɑːt] *n no pl, inf* (*marijuana*)
hierba *f,* mota *f Méx;* **to smoke ~** fumar maría
potash ['pɒtæʃ, *Am:* 'pɑːt-] *n no pl* potasa *f*
potassium [pə'tæsiəm] *n no pl* potasio *m*
potassium chloride *n no pl* cloruro *m*
potásico **potassium cyanide** *n no pl* cianuro *m* potásico **potassium permanganate** *n no pl* permanganato *m* potásico
potato [pə'teɪtəʊ, *Am:* -ṭoʊ] <-es> *n* patata
f, papa *f AmL;* **sweet ~** batata *f;* **baked ~**
patata al horno; **mashed ~s** puré *m* de patatas; **fried/roast(ed) ~s** patatas fritas/asadas
potato beetle *n,* **potato bug** *n Am* escarabajo *m* de la patata **potato chips** *npl Am,
Aus,* **potato crisps** *npl Brit* patatas *fpl* fritas
(en bolsa), papas *fpl* chip *AmL* **potato
masher** *n* pasapurés *m inv* **potato peeler**
n pelapatatas *m inv,* pelapapas *m inv AmL*
potbellied *adj* panzudo, -a
potbelly [pɒt'beli, *Am:* 'pɑːtbel-] <-ies> *n*
barriga *f,* guata *f Chile*
potboiler ['pɒtbɔɪləʳ, *Am:* 'pɑːtˌbɔɪlə-] *n
pej: libro escrito rápidamente para ganar
dinero*
poteen [pɒ'tiːn, pɒ'tʃiːn, *Am:* poʊ'tiːn] *n
Irish: en Irlanda, whisky destilado ilegalmente*
potency ['pəʊtənsi, *Am:* 'poʊ-] *n no pl*
potencia *f;* (*of drink, evil, temptation*) fuerza *f;*
(*of spell*) poder *m*
potent ['pəʊtnt, *Am:* 'poʊ-] *adj* potente;
(*drink, symbol*) fuerte; (*poison, motive*) pode-

roso, -a; (*remedy*) eficaz; (*argument*) convincente
potentate ['pəʊtnteɪt, *Am:* 'poʊ-] *n liter*
potentado, -a *m, f*
potential [pə'tenʃl, *Am:* poʊ'-] **I.** *adj*
1. posible **2.** LING, PHYS potencial **II.** *n no pl*
potencial *m;* **to have (a lot of) ~** tener
(muchas) capacidades
potentiality [pəˌtenʃɪ'æləti, *Am:* poʊˌten-
ʃɪ'æləti] *n form no pl* posibilidad *f*
potentially [pə'tenʃəli, *Am:* poʊ'-] *adv*
potencialmente
potholder ['pɒtˌhəʊldəʳ] *n Am, Aus* agarrador *m*
pothole ['pɒtˌhəʊl, *Am:* 'pɑːtˌhoʊl] *n* **1.** (*in
road*) bache *m,* pozo *m CSur* **2.** (*underground
hole*) sima *f*
potholer ['pɒtˌhəʊləʳ, *Am:* 'pɑːtˌhoʊlə-] *n
Brit* espeleólogo, -a *m, f*
potion ['pəʊʃən, *Am:* 'poʊ-] *n* poción *f,*
pócima *f*
pot luck *n no pl* **to take ~** tomar lo que haya
potpourri [ˌpəʊ'pʊəriː, *Am:* ˌpoʊpʊ'riː] *n*
popurrí *m*
pot roast *n* estofado *m*
potshot ['pɒtʃɒt, *Am:* 'pɑːtʃɑːt] *n* tiro *m* al
azar; **to take a ~ at sb** disparar al azar contra
alguien; *fig* (*criticize*) arremeter contra alguien
potted ['pɒtɪd, *Am:* 'pɑːtɪd] *adj* **1.** (*plant*)
en tiesto **2.** (*food*) en conserva; **~ shrimps**
pasta *f* de camarones **3.** *Brit, inf* (*shorter*) resumido, -a
potter[1] ['pɒtəʳ, *Am:* 'pɑːt̬ə-] *n* alfarero, -a *m,
f;* **~'s wheel** torno *m* de alfarero
potter[2] ['pɒtəʳ, *Am:* 'pɑːt̬ə-] *vi Brit* **1.** (*go
along*) **to ~ around the village** pasearse por
el pueblo **2.** *fig* entretenerse
pottery ['pɒtəri, *Am:* 'pɑːt̬ə-] *n* **1.** *no pl*
(*art*) cerámica *f* **2.** <-ies> (*workshop*) alfarería *f*
potty ['pɒti, *Am:* 'pɑːt̬i] **I.** <-ier, -iest> *adj
Brit, inf* (*mad*) chiflado, -a; **to go ~** chiflarse; **to
drive sb ~** volver loco a alguien; **to be ~
about sb** estar loco por alguien; **it is ~ to do
that** es una chifladura hacer eso **II.** <-ies> *n*
(*for baby*) orinal *m*
pouch [paʊtʃ] *n* **1.** *a.* ANAT, ZOOL bolsa *f;*
tobacco ~ petaca *f* **2.** (*for mail*) valija *f*
pouf(fe) [puːf] *n* puf *m*
poulterer ['pəʊltərəʳ, *Am:* 'poʊlt̬ə-ə-] *n Brit*
pollero, -a *m, f;* **~'s** pollería *f*
poultice ['pəʊltɪs, *Am:* 'poʊltɪs] *n* cataplasma *f*
poultry ['pəʊltri, *Am:* 'poʊl-] *n* **1.** *pl* (*birds*)
aves *fpl* de corral **2.** *no pl* (*meat*) carne *f* de
ave
poultry farm *n* granja *f* avícola **poultry
farming** *n no pl* avicultura *f*
pounce [paʊns] **I.** *n* (*spring*) salto *m* **II.** *vi*
1. (*jump*) saltar; **to ~ on sth** abalanzarse sobre
algo; (*bird of prey*) precipitarse sobre algo **2.** *fig*
to ~ on an opportunity no dejar escapar una
oportunidad

pound[1] [paʊnd] *n* **1.** (*weight*) libra *f* (*454 g*); **by the** ~ por libras **2.** (*currency*) libra *f;* ~ **coin** moneda *f* de una libra; ~ **note** billete *m* de una libra; ~ **sterling** libra esterlina

pound[2] [paʊnd] *n* (*for cars*) depósito *m;* (*for dogs*) perrera *f;* (*for sheep*) redil *m*

pound[3] [paʊnd] **I.** *vt* **1.** (*hit repeatedly*) aporrear; (*beat*) golpear; (*with a hammer*) martillear; **the waves ~ed the ship** las olas batían contra el barco **2.** (*walk heavily*) patear; **I could hear him ~ing the floor upstairs** podía oír sus pasos en el piso de arriba **3.** (*crush*) machacar; (*spices*) moler; MIL batir; **to ~ sth to rubble** reducir algo a escombros **II.** *vi* **1.** (*beat*) dar golpes; (*on a door, table*) aporrear; (*heart, pulse*) latir con fuerza; (*music*) retumbar; **to ~ away on a piano** aporrear un piano; **the waves ~ed against the shore** las olas azotaban la orilla; **my head is ~ing!** ¡me estalla la cabeza! **2.** (*run*) **to ~ downstairs** bajar corriendo **3.** *fig* **to ~ away at sth** insistir en algo

pounding ['paʊndɪŋ] *n* **1.** *no pl* (*noise*) golpeteo *m;* (*of heart*) fuerte latido *m;* (*of sea*) embate *m;* (*in head*) martilleo *m* **2.** *no pl* (*crushing*) trituración *f;* (*grinding*) molienda *f* **3.** (*attack*) ataque *m; a. fig* (*beating*) paliza *f inf;* **to take a** ~ *a. fig* recibir una paliza; **the film took a heavy** ~ la película tuvo muy malas críticas

pour [pɔːʳ, *Am:* pɔːr] **I.** *vt* **1.** (*cause to flow*) vertir; **to ~ coffee/wine** echar café/vino; **to ~ sb sth** servir algo a alguien; **to ~ oneself a glass of wine** echarse un vaso de vino **2.** (*give in large amounts*) vertir; (*money, resources*) invertir; **to ~ scorn on sth** burlarse de algo **II.** *vi* **1.** (*flow in large amounts: water*) fluir; (*letters, messages*) llegar en grandes cantidades; **to ~ into sth** (*sunshine*) entrar a raudales en algo; (*people*) entrar en tropel en algo; **refugees are ~ing into the country** no cesan de llegar refugiados al país; **to be ~ing with sweat** estar empapado en sudor **2.** *impers* **it's ~ing** (*with rain*) llueve a cántaros

♦**pour in** *vi* llegar en abundancia

♦**pour out I.** *vt* **1.** (*serve from container*) vertir **2.** (*recount*) **to ~ sth to sb** revelar algo a alguien **3.** (*cause to flow quickly: smoke, water*) echar; **to ~ one's thanks** dar las gracias efusivamente **II.** *vi* (*liquid*) salir; (*people*) salir en tropel

pout [paʊt] **I.** *vi* hacer un mohín **II.** *vt* **to ~ one's lips** hacer un mohín **III.** *n* mohín *m*

poverty ['pɒvəti, *Am:* 'pɑːvəʳt̬i] *n no pl* **1.** (*lack of money*) pobreza *f;* **extreme** ~ miseria *f* **2.** (*lack of ideas, imagination*) escasez *f*

poverty line *n* mínimo *m* vital; **to live below the** ~ carecer de lo necesario para vivir

poverty-stricken ['pɒvətiˌstrɪkən, *Am:* 'pɑːvəʳt̬i-] *adj* muy pobre

POW [ˌpiːəʊˈdʌblju:, *Am:* -oʊˈ-] *n abbr of* **prisoner of war** prisionero *m* de guerra

powder ['paʊdəʳ, *Am:* -dəʳ] **I.** *n* **1.** *no pl* (*dust*) polvo *m;* **baking** ~ levadura *f;* **to crush** [*o* **reduce**] **sth to a** ~ reducir algo a polvo **2.** *no pl* (*make-up*) polvos *mpl;* **talcum** ~ polvos de talco **3.** *no pl* (*snow*) nieve *f* en polvo **4.** *Brit* (*washing powder*) detergente *m* en polvo **II.** *vt* **1.** (*cover with powder*) empolvar; **to ~ one's face** empolvarse; **to ~ one's nose** *fig* ir al servicio **2.** (*sprinkle*) espolvorear

powder compact *n* polvera *f*

powdered *adj* (*in powder form*) en polvo; ~ **sugar** azúcar *m* glas

powder keg *n fig* polvorín *m* **powder puff** *n* borla *f,* cisne *m RíoPl* **powder room** *n* tocador *m*

powdery ['paʊdəri] *adj* como de polvo

power ['paʊəʳ, *Am:* 'paʊəʳ] **I.** *n* **1.** *no pl* (*ability to control*) poder *m* **2.** (*country, organization, person*) potencia *f* **3.** (*right*) derecho *m* **4.** *no pl* (*ability*) capacidad *f* **5.** *no pl* (*strength*) fuerza *f* **6.** *no pl* (*electricity*) electricidad *f;* **to cut off the** ~ cortar la corriente **7.** *no pl* (*energy*) energía *f* ▶**more** ~ **to your elbow!** ¡que tengas suerte!; **to do sb a** ~ **of good** hacer bien a alguien; **the** ~ **behind the throne** el poder en la sombra; **the** ~**s that be** las autoridades **II.** *vi* **to** ~ **along the track** ir disparado por el camino **III.** *vt* impulsar

power-assisted steering *n* dirección *f* asistida **powerboat** *n* lancha *f* fuera borda

power brakes *npl* AUTO frenos *mpl* asistidos

power cable *n* cable *m* de transmisión

power cut *n Brit, Aus* apagón *m*

power-driven *adj* eléctrico, -a

powerful ['paʊəfəl, *Am:* 'paʊəʳ-] *adj* **1.** (*influential, mighty*) poderoso, -a **2.** (*having great physical strength*) fuerte **3.** (*having a great effect*) convincente **4.** (*affecting the emotions*) intenso, -a; ~ **emotions** emociones *fpl* fuertes **5.** (*able to perform very well*) potente

powerfully ['paʊəfəli, *Am:* 'paʊəʳ-] *adv* **1.** (*using great force*) con potencia **2.** (*argue, speak*) de forma convincente

powerhouse ['paʊəˌhaʊs, *Am:* 'paʊəʳ-] *n* fuente *f* de energía; **to be a** ~ **of ideas** *fig* ser una fuente inagotable de ideas

powerless ['paʊələs, *Am:* 'paʊəʳ-] *adj* impotente; **to be** ~ **against sb** no poder hacer nada contra alguien

power line *n* línea *f* eléctrica **power mower** *n* segadora *f* eléctrica **power plant** *n* central *f* eléctrica **power point** *n Brit, Aus* toma *f* de corriente **power politics** *n* política *f* de fuerza **power station** *n* central *f* eléctrica; **nuclear** ~ central *f* nuclear **power steering** *n* dirección *f* asistida **power tool** *n* herramienta *f* mecánica

powwow ['paʊwaʊ] *n* **1.** asamblea *f* (*de indígenas norteamericanos*) **2.** *fig, inf* discusión *f*

pox [pɒks, *Am:* pɑːks] *n no pl, inf* sífilis *f inv*

poxy ['pɒksi, *Am:* 'pɑːk-] <-ier, -iest> *adj*

Brit, inf insignificante

pp *abbr of* **pages** págs.

PR [piː'ɑːʳ, *Am:* -'ɑːr] *n no pl* **1.** *abbr of* **public relations** relaciones *fpl* públicas **2.** POL *abbr of* **proportional representation** representación *f* proporcional

practicable ['præktɪkəbl] *adj form* factible

practical ['præktɪkl] **I.** *adj* práctico, -a **II.** *n* examen *m* práctico

practicality [‚præktɪ'kæləti, *Am:* -ṭi] *n* <-ies> **1.** *no pl* (*feasibility*) viabilidad *f* **2.** (*practical detail*) **the practicalities of sth** los detalles prácticos de algo

practically ['præktɪkəli, *Am:* -kli] *adv* **1.** (*almost*) casi **2.** (*of a practical nature*) **to be ~ based** basarse en la práctica; **to be ~ minded** tener sentido práctico

practice ['præktɪs] **I.** *n* **1.** *no pl* (*act of practising*) práctica *f;* **to be out of ~** estar desentrenado; **~ makes perfect** se aprende con la práctica **2.** (*custom, regular activity*) costumbre *f;* **traditional religious ~s** tradiciones *fpl* religiosas; **standard ~** práctica *f* habitual; **to make a ~ of sth** tener algo como norma **3.** (*training session*) entrenamiento *m* **4.** *no pl* (*of profession*) ejercicio *m* **II.** *vt Am s.* **practise**

practiced ['præktɪst] *adj Am s.* **practised**

practise ['præktɪs] *Brit, Aus* **I.** *vt* **1.** (*do, carry out*) practicar **2.** (*improve skill*) hacer ejercicios de; **to ~ the piano** estudiar el piano **3.** (*work in*) ejercer ►**to ~ what one preaches** predicar con el ejemplo **II.** *vi* **1.** (*improve skill*) practicar; SPORTS entrenar **2.** (*work in profession*) ejercer; **to ~ as a doctor** ejercer de médico

practised ['præktɪst] *adj Brit, Aus* (*experienced, skilled*) experto, -a; **to be ~ in sth** tener experiencia en algo; **a ~ liar** un mentiroso consumado

practising ['præktɪsɪŋ] *adj Brit, Aus* (*doctor, lawyer*) en ejercicio; REL practicante

practitioner [præk'tɪʃənəʳ, *Am:* -ɚ] *n form* (*of a skill*) profesional *mf;* (*doctor*) médico, -a *m, f;* **legal ~** abogado, -a *m, f*

pragmatic [præg'mætɪk, *Am:* -'mæṭ-] *adj* pragmático, -a

pragmatism ['prægmətɪzəm] *n* pragmatismo *m*

prairie ['preəri, *Am:* 'preri] *n* pradera *f*

praise [preɪz] **I.** *vt* **1.** (*express approval*) elogiar; **to ~ sb to the skies** poner a alguien por las nubes **2.** (*worship*) alabar **II.** *n no pl* **1.** (*expression of approval*) elogio *m;* **to heap ~ on sb, to shower sb with ~** cubrir a alguien de alabanzas **2.** *form* (*worship*) alabanza *f;* **~ be (to God)!** ¡alabado sea (Dios)!

praiseworthy ['preɪz‚wɜːði, *Am:* -‚wɜːr-] *adj* loable

pram [præm] *n Brit, Aus* cochecito *m*

prance [prɑːns, *Am:* præns] *vi* (*horse*) hacer cabriolas; (*person*) pavonearse

prang [præŋ] **I.** *vt Brit, Aus, inf* dar un golpe a

II. *n Brit, Aus, inf* golpe *m*

prank [præŋk] *n* broma *f;* **to play a ~ on sb** gastar una broma a alguien

prat [præt] **I.** *n Brit, inf* imbécil *mf* **II.** <-tt-> *vi Brit, inf* **to ~ about** hacer el imbécil

prate [preɪt] *vi form* parlotear

prattle ['prætl, *Am:* 'præṭ-] **I.** *vi pej* parlotear; (*child*) balbucear **II.** *n no pl, pej* parloteo *m;* (*child*) balbuceo *m*

prawn [prɔːn, *Am:* prɑːn] *n* gamba *f*

prawn cocktail *n* cóctel *m* de gambas

pray [preɪ] **I.** *vi* **1.** REL rezar; **to ~ to sb (that)** rogar a alguien (que +*subj*) **2.** (*hope*) **to ~ for sth** rogar algo **II.** *vt form* suplicar; **I ~ you tell me ...** le ruego que me diga...

prayer [preəʳ, *Am:* prer] *n* **1.** REL oración *f;* **to say a ~, to say one's ~s** rezar **2.** *no pl* (*action of praying*) rezo *m* **3.** *fig* (*hope*) súplica *f;* **to not have a ~ of doing sth** *inf* no tener ninguna posibilidad de hacer algo

prayer book *n* devocionario *m* **prayer meeting** *n* reunión *f* de fieles para rezar **prayer rug** *n* alfombra *f* de oración

praying mantis ['preɪɪŋ'mæntɪs, *Am:* -ṭɪs] *n* mantis *f inv* religiosa

preach [priːtʃ] **I.** *vi* predicar **II.** *vt* **1.** REL predicar; **to ~ a sermon/the Gospel** predicar un sermón/el Evangelio **2.** (*advocate*) abogar por ►**to practise what you ~** predicar con el ejemplo

preacher ['priːtʃəʳ, *Am:* -ɚ] *n* predicador(a) *m(f)*

preamble [priː'æmbl] *n form* preámbulo *m*

prearrange [‚priːə'reɪndʒ] *vt* organizar de antemano

prebend ['prebənd] *n Brit* prebenda *f*

precarious [prɪ'keərɪəs, *Am:* -'kerɪ-] *adj* precario, -a

precast [‚priː'kɑːst, *Am:* 'priːkæst] *adj* prefabricado, -a

precaution [prɪ'kɔːʃən, *Am:* -'kɑː-] *n* precaución *f*

precautionary [prɪ'kɔːʃənəri, *Am:* -'kɑː-ʃəner-] *adj* de precaución; **~ measure** medida *f* preventiva

precede [prɪ'siːd] *vt* preceder; **to ~ the report with an introduction** empezar el informe con una introducción

precedence ['presɪdəns, *Am:* 'presə-] *n no pl* **1.** (*priority*) prioridad *f;* **to take ~ over sb** tener prioridad sobre alguien **2.** *form* (*order of priority*) preferencia *f*

precedent ['presɪdənt, *Am:* 'presə-] *n* precedente *m;* **to set a ~ (for sth/doing sth)** sentar un precedente (para algo/hacer algo)

preceding [prɪ'siːdɪŋ] *adj* precedente; **the ~ day** el día anterior

precept ['priːsept] *n form* **1.** (*rule*) precepto *m* **2.** (*principle*) principio *m*

precinct ['priːsɪŋkt] *n* **1.** *Brit* (*enclosed area*) recinto *m;* **pedestrian ~** zona *f* peatonal **2.** *Am* (*electoral district*) distrito *m* **3.** *no pl, form* (*environs*) alrededores *mpl*

P

precious ['preʃəs] I. *adj* **1.** (*of great value*) precioso, -a; **you can keep your ~ ring!** *iron* ¡guárdate tu maldito anillo! **2.** (*affected*) afectado, -a; (*person*) amanerado, -a II. *adv inf* **~ few** muy pocos; **to be ~ little help** ser de muy poca ayuda

precipice ['presɪpɪs, *Am:* 'presə-] *n* precipicio *m*

precipitate¹ [prɪ'sɪpɪteɪt] I. *vt* **1.** *form* (*provoke*) precipitar **2.** *form* (*throw*) arrojar **3.** CHEM precipitar II. *vi* precipitar

precipitate² [prɪ'sɪpɪtət, *Am:* prɪ'sɪpɪtɪt] I. *adj form* precipitado, -a II. *n no pl* precipitado *m*

precipitation [prɪˌsɪpɪ'teɪʃən] *n no pl, form* precipitación *f*

precipitous [prɪ'sɪpɪtəs, *Am:* -ṭəs] *adj* **1.** (*very steep*) empinado, -a **2.** (*rapid*) apresurado, -a **3.** *form* (*precipitate*) precipitado, -a

précis ['preɪsi:, *Am:* preɪ'si:] I. *n* resumen *m* II. *vt form* resumir

precise [prɪ'saɪs] *adj* **1.** (*moment, measurement*) exacto, -a **2.** (*person*) meticuloso, -a

precisely *adv* **1.** (*exactly*) precisamente; **~!** ¡eso es!; **to do ~ the opposite** hacer justamente lo contrario **2.** (*carefully*) meticulosamente

precision [prɪ'sɪʒən] I. *n no pl* **1.** (*accuracy*) precisión *f* **2.** (*meticulous care*) exactitud *f* II. *adj* de precisión

preclude [prɪ'klu:d] *vt form* excluir

precocious [prɪ'kəʊʃəs, *Am:* -'koʊ-] *adj* precoz

precociousness *n*, **precocity** [prɪ'kɒsəti, *Am:* prɪ'kɑ:səṭi] *n no pl, form* precocidad *f*

preconceived [ˌpri:kən'si:vd] *adj* preconcebido, -a

preconception [ˌpri:kən'sepʃən] *n* idea *f* preconcebida

precondition [ˌpri:kən'dɪʃən] *n* condición *f* previa

precook ['pri:kʊk] *vt* precocinar

precursor [ˌpri:'kɜ:sər, *Am:* prɪ'kɜ:rsə] *n form* precursor(a) *m(f)*

predate [pri:'deɪt] *vt form* preceder

predator ['predətər, *Am:* -ṭə] *n* depredador *m*

predatory ['predətri, *Am:* -tɔ:ri] *adj* depredador(a)

predecessor ['pri:dɪsesər, *Am:* 'predəsesə] *n* predecesor(a) *m(f)*; (*ancestor*) antepasado, -a *m, f*

predestination [ˌpri:destɪ'neɪʃən] *n no pl* predestinación *f*

predestine [ˌpri:'destɪn] *vt* predestinar

predetermine [ˌpri:dɪ'tɜ:mɪn, *Am:* -'tɜ:rmən] *vt form* predeterminar; **to ~ the consequences** determinar de antemano las consecuencias

predicament [prɪ'dɪkəmənt] *n form* apuro *m*

predicate¹ ['predɪkət, *Am:* 'predɪkɪt] *n* LING predicado *m*

predicate² ['predɪkeɪt] *vt form* **to be ~d on sth** estar basado en algo

predicative [prɪ'dɪkətɪv, *Am:* prɪ'dɪkəṭɪv] *adj* LING predicativo, -a

predict [prɪ'dɪkt] *vt* predecir

predictable [prɪ'dɪktəbl] *adj* previsible

prediction [prɪ'dɪkʃən] *n* **1.** (*forecast*) pronóstico *m* **2.** *no pl* (*act of predicting*) predicción *f*

predilection [ˌpri:dɪ'lekʃən, *Am:* ˌpredəl'ek-] *n form* predilección *f*

predispose [ˌpri:dɪ'spəʊz, *Am:* -'spoʊz] *vt* predisponer

predisposition [ˌpri:dɪspə'zɪʃən] *n* **1.** *form* (*tendency*) predisposición *f* **2.** MED propensión *f*

predominance [prɪ'dɒmɪnəns, *Am:* -'dɑ:mə-] *n no pl* predominio *m*

predominant [prɪ'dɒmɪnənt, *Am:* -'dɑ:mə-] *adj* predominante

predominate [prɪ'dɒmɪneɪt, *Am:* -'dɑ:mə-] *vi* predominar

pre-eminence [ˌpri:'emɪnəns] *n no pl, form* preeminencia *f*

pre-eminent [ˌpri:'emɪnənt] *adj form* preeminente

pre-empt [ˌpri:'empt] *vt form* adelantarse a

pre-emption [ˌpri:'empʃən] *n* apropiación *f* (por derecho preferente)

pre-emptive [pri:'emptɪv] *adj* **1.** (*right*) prioritario, -a **2.** (*attack*) preventivo, -a

preen [pri:n] I. *vi* **1.** (*bird*) arreglarse **2.** *fig* (*congratulate oneself*) pavonearse II. *vt* **1.** (*tidy*) arreglar **2.** (*groom*) **to ~ oneself** atildarse; **to ~ oneself on sth** (*congratulate*) enorgullecerse de algo

pre-existing ['pri:ɪg'zɪstɪŋ] *adj* preexistente

prefab ['pri:fæb] *inf* I. *n abbr of* **prefabricated house** casa *f* prefabricada II. *adj abbr of* **prefabricated** prefabricado, -a

prefabricate [ˌpri:'fæbrɪkeɪt] *vt* prefabricar

prefabricated *adj* prefabricado, -a

prefabricated house *n* casa *f* prefabricada

preface ['prefɪs] I. *n* prefacio *m* II. *vt form* introducir

prefatory ['prefətri, *Am:* -tɔ:ri] *adj form* preliminar

prefect ['pri:fekt] *n* prefecto *m*

prefer [prɪ'fɜ:ʳ, *Am:* pri:'fɜ:r] <-rr-> *vt* **1.** (*like better*) preferir **2.** *Brit* LAW **to ~ charges** (**against sb**) presentar cargos (en contra de alguien)

preferable ['prefrəbl] *adj* preferible

preferably ['prefrəbli] *adv* preferentemente

preference ['prefrəns] *n* **1.** *no pl* (*liking better*) preferencia *f* **2.** (*priority*) prioridad *f*

preferential [ˌprefə'renʃl] *adj* preferente; ECON preferencial

preferred [prɪ'fɜ:d, *Am:* pri:'fɜ:rd] *adj* preferido, -a

prefigure [ˌpri:'fɪgəʳ, *Am:* -'fɪgjə] *vt form* prefigurar

prefix ['pri:fɪks, *Am:* 'pri:fɪks] <-es> *n*

prefijo *m*

pregnancy ['pregnəntsi] *n no pl* (*condition*) embarazo *m;* ZOOL preñez *f*

pregnancy test *n* prueba *f* de embarazo

pregnant ['pregnənt] *adj* 1. (*woman*) embarazada; (*animal*) preñado; **to be ~ by sb** estar embarazada de alguien; **to become ~** (*woman*) quedarse embarazada; (*animal*) quedarse preñado; **to get sb ~** dejar embarazada a alguien 2. *fig* (*silence, pause*) muy significativo, -a; **to be ~ with possibilities for sth** tener muchas posibilidades para algo

prehensile [pri'hensaɪl, *Am:* priː'hensɪl] *adj* prensil

prehistoric [ˌpriːhɪ'stɒrɪk, *Am:* -'stɔːr-] *adj* prehistórico, -a

prehistory [ˌpriː'hɪstri] *n no pl* prehistoria *f*

prejudge [ˌpriː'dʒʌdʒ] *vt* prejuzgar

prejudice ['predʒʊdɪs] I. *n* 1. (*preconceived opinion*) prejuicio *m* 2. *no pl* (*bias*) parcialidad *f;* LAW perjuicio *m;* **without ~** sin detrimento de sus propios derechos; **without ~ to sth** LAW sin perjuicio de algo II. *vt* 1. (*bias*) **to ~ sb against sth** predisponer a alguien contra algo 2. (*damage*) perjudicar

prejudiced ['predʒʊdɪst] *adj* (*person*) lleno, -a de prejuicios; (*attitude, judgment, opinion*) parcial; **to be ~ against sb** estar predispuesto contra alguien; **to be ~ in favour of sb** estar predispuesto a favor de alguien

prejudicial [ˌpredʒə'dɪʃəl] *adj form* perjudicial

preliminary [prɪ'lɪmɪnəri, *Am:* prɪ-'lɪmənər-] I. *adj* preliminar II. <-ies> *n* 1. (*introduction*) preparativos *mpl* 2. SPORTS (*heat*) preliminares *mpl* 3. *form* (*preliminary exam*) examen *m* preliminar

prelims ['priːlɪmz, *Am:* 'priːlɪms] *npl inf* 1. (*exams*) *abbr of* **preliminary exams** exámenes *mpl* preliminares 2. *abbr of* **preliminary pages** páginas *fpl* preliminares

prelude ['preljuːd] *n* preludio *m*

premarital [ˌpriː'mærɪtl, *Am:* -'merəl̩] *adj* prematrimonial

premature ['premətʃəʳ, *Am:* ˌpriːmə'tʊr] *adj* prematuro, -a

premature ejaculation *n* eyaculación *f* precoz

premeditated [ˌpriː'medɪteɪtɪd, *Am:* -teɪtɪd] *adj* premeditado, -a

premeditation [ˌpriːmedɪ'teɪʃən] *n no pl, form* premeditación *f*

premenstrual [ˌpriː'mentstruəl, *Am:* -strəl] *adj* premenstrual

premenstrual tension *n* síndrome *m* premenstrual

premier ['premɪəʳ, *Am:* prɪ'mɪr] I. *n* POL primer ministro *m* II. *adj* primero, -a

première ['premɪeəʳ, *Am:* prɪ'mɪr] I. *n* estreno *m* II. *vt, vi* estrenar

premise ['premɪs] I. *n* 1. (*of argument*) premisa *f;* **on the ~ that ...** en el supuesto de que... 2. *pl* (*shop*) local *m* II. *vt form* 1. (*base*)

basar 2. *Am* (*preface*) empezar

premium ['priːmiəm] I. *n* 1. (*insurance payment*) prima *f* 2. (*extra charge*) recargo *m* 3. *Am* (*petrol*) súper *f* II. *adj* de primera calidad

premium bond *n Brit* bono *m* del Estado (*que participa en un sorteo nacional*) **premium price** *n* precio *m* con prima **premium quality** *n* máxima calidad *f*

premonition [ˌpriːmə'nɪʃən] *n* premonición *f;* **to have a ~ that ...** tener el presentimiento de que...

prenatal [ˌpriː'neɪtl, *Am:* -l̩] *adj* prenatal

preoccupation [ˌpriːɒkjʊ'peɪʃən, *Am:* priː-ˌɑːkjuː'-] *n* preocupación *f*

preoccupied [priː'ɒkjʊpaɪd, *Am:* priː'ɑːkjuː-] *adj* preocupado, -a; **to be ~ about sth** inquietarse por algo; **to be ~ with sth** estar absorto en algo

preoccupy [priː'ɒkjʊpaɪ, *Am:* priː'ɑːkjuː-] <-ie-> *vt* preocupar

preordain [ˌpriːɔː'deɪn, *Am:* -ɔːr'-] *vt form* predeterminar

prep [prep] *n no pl, Brit, inf abbr of* **preparation** deberes *mpl*

prepack [ˌpriː'pæk] *vt Brit* preempaquetar

prepaid [ˌpriː'peɪd] *adj* pagado, -a por adelantado

prepaid postcard *n* postal *f* franqueada **prepaid reply** *n* sobre *m* con el franqueo pagado

preparation [ˌprepə'reɪʃən] I. *n* 1. *no pl* (*getting ready*) preparación *f* 2. (*substance*) preparado *m* 3. *pl* (*measures*) preparativos *mpl* II. *adj* de preparación

preparatory [prɪ'pærətəri, *Am:* -'perətɔːr-] *adj* preliminar

preparatory course *n* curso *m* preparatorio **preparatory school** *n* 1. *Brit* escuela *f* privada (*imparte enseñanza primaria*) 2. *Am* colegio *m* privado (*imparte enseñanza secundaria*)

prepare [prɪ'peəʳ, *Am:* -'per] I. *vt* preparar II. *vi* prepararse; **to ~ for action** prepararse para actuar

prepared [prɪ'peəd, *Am:* -'perd] *adj* 1. (*ready*) listo, -a 2. (*willing*) dispuesto, -a; **to be ~ to do sth** estar preparado para hacer algo 3. (*food, speech*) preparado, -a de antemano

preparedness [prɪ'peərɪdnɪs, *Am:* -'perd-] *n no pl, form* preparación *f*

prepay [ˌpriː'peɪ] *vt irr* pagar por anticipado; (*letter*) franquear

prepayment [ˌpriː'peɪmənt] *n* anticipo *m;* (*of letter*) franqueo *m*

preponderance [prɪ'pɒndərənts, *Am:* -'pɑːn-] *n no pl, form* predominio *m*

preponderant [prɪ'pɒndərənt, *Am:* -'pɑːn-] *adj form* predominante

preposition [ˌprepə'zɪʃən] *n* preposición *f*

prepossessing [ˌpriːpə'zesɪŋ] *adj* agradable, atractivo, -a

preposterous [prɪ'pɒstərəs, *Am:* -'pɑːs-]

tə-] *adj* ridículo, -a

preppie, preppy ['prepi] *Am* I.<-ies> *n* pijo, -a *m, f* II. *adj* <preppier, preppiest> pijo, -a

prepuce ['priːpjuːs] *n* (*foreskin*) prepucio *m;* (*clitoral foreskin*) prepucio del clítoris

prerequisite [ˌpriːˈrekwɪzɪt] *form* I. *adj* fundamental II. *n* requisito *m* esencial; **to be a ~ for sth** ser una condición sine qua non para algo

prerogative [prɪˈrɒgətɪv, *Am:* -ˈrɑːgəṭɪv] *n form* (*right, privilege*) prerrogativa *f;* **that's your ~** estás en tu derecho; **skiing used to be the ~ of the rich** antes, esquiar era patrimonio exclusivo de los ricos

presage ['presɪdʒ] I. *n liter* 1. (*sign*) presagio *m* 2. (*presentiment*) presentimiento *m* II. *vt liter* (*have presentiment of*) presentir III. *vi liter* **to ~ well/ill** ser buen/mal presagio

Presbyterian [ˌprezbɪˈtɪəriən, *Am:* -ˈtɪri-] I. *n* presbiteriano, -a *m, f* II. *adj* presbiteriano, -a

presbytery ['prezbɪtri, *Am:* -teri] *n* REL 1. ARCHIT (*part of church*) presbiterio *m* 2. (*priest's residence*) casa *f* del cura

pre-school ['priːskuːl] I. *n Am, Aus* jardín *m* de infancia II. *adj* preescolar; (*child*) en edad preescolar

prescribe [prɪˈskraɪb] I. *vt* 1. MED recetar; (*rest, diet*) recomendar 2. *form* (*order*) prescribir; **~d by law** establecido por la ley II. *vi* MED hacer una receta

prescribed [prɪˈskraɪbd] *adj* prescrito, -a; **in the ~ way** de conformidad con lo prescrito; **in the ~ time** dentro del plazo fijado por la ley

prescription [prɪˈskrɪpʃən] *n* 1. MED receta *f;* **only available on ~** con receta médica; **to make out a ~** extender una receta 2. *form* (*act of prescribing*) prescripción *f*

prescription charge *n* pago de una parte del coste de las medicinas a cargo del paciente

prescriptive [prɪˈskrɪptɪv] *adj* preceptivo, -a

prescriptive grammar *n* LING gramática *f* normativa

presence ['prezənts] *n* 1. (*attendance*) presencia *f;* **military/police ~** presencia militar/policial; **~ of mind** presencia de ánimo; **in sb's ~** en presencia de alguien; **in my ~** delante de mí; **in the ~ of two witnesses** ante dos testigos; **your ~ is requested** se ruega su asistencia; **to feel sb's ~** sentir la presencia de alguien; **to make one's ~ felt** hacerse notar 2. (*personality*) carisma *m*

present¹ ['prezənt] I. *n no pl* presente *m* ▶ **at ~** en este momento; **for the ~** por ahora II. *adj* 1. (*current: address, generation*) actual; **at the ~ moment** [*o* **time**] en este momento; **the ~ year** el año en curso; **in the ~ case** en este caso; **up to the ~ time** hasta la fecha; **the ~ writer** quien esto escribe 2. (*in attendance*) presente; **to be ~ at sth** asistir a algo; **all those ~** todos los presentes; **~ company**

excepted exceptuando a los presentes

present² ['prezənt] *n* (*gift*) regalo *m;* **to give sb a ~** hacer un regalo a alguien; **I got it as a ~** me lo regalaron; **to make sb a ~ of sth** regalar algo a alguien

present³ [prɪˈzent] *vt* 1. (*give*) presentar; **to ~ one's apologies** *form* presentar sus disculpas; **to ~ one's credentials** presentar sus credenciales; **to ~ sth (to sb)** entregar algo (a alguien); **to ~ sb with sth** obsequiar a alguien con algo, obsequiar algo a alguien *AmL* 2. (*introduce*) presentar; **to ~ sb to sb** presentar alguien a alguien; **may I ~ my wife?** permítame presentarle a mi esposa; **to ~ a bill** presentar un proyecto de ley; **to ~ a programme** *Aus, Brit* presentar un programa; **~ing X as Julius Caesar** con X en el papel de Julio César 3. (*confront*) **to ~ sb with sth** enfrentar a alguien con algo; **to be ~ed with a complicated situation** verse frente a una situación complicada; **to ~ sb with a problem** plantear un problema a alguien 4. (*constitute*) constituir; **to ~ a problem for sb** significar un problema para alguien; **to ~ difficulties for sb** plantear dificultades a alguien 5. (*offer*) ofrecer; (*view, atmosphere*) presentar 6. (*exhibit: argument, plan, theory*) exponer; (*cheque, passport, ticket*) presentar; **to ~ a petition to sb** elevar una petición a alguien *form* 7. (*appear*) **to ~ oneself for sth** presentarse a algo

presentable [prɪˈzentəbl, *Am:* prɪˈzentə-] *adj* presentable; **to make oneself ~** arreglarse

presentation [ˌprezənˈteɪʃən] *n* 1. (*act*) presentación *f;* (*of theory, dissertation*) exposición *f;* (*of thesis*) lectura *f;* **to make a ~** hacer una exposición; **on ~ of this voucher** al presentar este vale 2. (*of prize, award*) entrega *f*

presentation copy *n* ejemplar *m* de cortesía

present-day [ˌprezəntˈdeɪ] *adj* actual; **~ London** el Londres de hoy (en) día

presenter [prɪˈzentəʳ, *Am:* prɪˈzentɚ] *n* presentador(a) *m(f)*

presentiment [prɪˈzentɪmənt] *n form* presentimiento *m;* **to have a ~ of sth** presentir algo; **to have the ~ that ...** tener el presentimiento de que...

presently ['prezəntli] *adv* 1. (*soon*) pronto; **I'll be there ~** voy enseguida 2. (*now*) ahora

present participle *n* LING participio *m* presente **present tense** *n* LING tiempo *m* presente

preservation [ˌprezəˈveɪʃən, *Am:* -ɚ-] *n no pl* 1. (*of building*) conservación *f;* **to be in a poor/good state of ~** estar en mal/buen estado 2. (*of species, custom*) preservación *f*

preservative [prɪˈzɜːvətɪv, *Am:* -ˈzɜːrvəṭɪv] I. *adj* preservativo, -a II. *n* conservante *m;* **free from artificial ~s** sin conservantes (artificiales)

preserve [prɪˈzɜːv, *Am:* -ˈzɜːrv] I. *vt* 1. (*maintain: customs, peace*) mantener; (*dignity,* *sense of humour*) conservar; (*appearance, silence*) guardar **2.** (*food*) conservar **3.** (*protect*) proteger; **to ~ sb from sth** proteger a alguien de algo; **heaven ~ us!** ¡que Dios nos ampare! **II.** *n* **1.** (*jam*) confitura *f* **2.** (*reserve*) coto *m,* vedado *m;* **game** ~ coto de caza; **wildlife** ~ reserva *f* de animales **3.** *fig* (*domain*) terreno *m;* **to be the ~ of the rich** ser dominio exclusivo de los ricos; **to be a male ~** estar vedado a las mujeres

preserved *adj* **1.** (*maintained*) conservado, -a; **to be badly** ~ estar en mal estado **2.** (*food*) en conserva; ~ **food** conservas *fpl*

pre-shrunk [ˌpriː'ʃrʌŋk] *adj* preencogido, -a

preside [prɪ'zaɪd] *vi* presidir; **to ~ at/over sth** presidir algo; **to ~ at a table** ocupar la cabecera de la mesa

presidency ['prezɪdənsi] *n* **1.** (*office of president*) POL presidencia *f;* (*of company*) dirección *f;* (*of university*) rectoría *f* **2.** (*tenure as president*) mandato *m* (presidencial)

president ['prezɪdənt] *n* POL presidente, -a *m, f;* (*of company*) director(a) *m(f);* (*of university*) rector(a) *m(f)*

presidential [ˌprezɪ'dentʃəl] *adj* presidencial

presidential address *n* discurso *m* presidencial **presidential candidate** *n* candidato, -a *m, f* a la presidencia **presidential election** *n* elecciones *fpl* presidenciales

President's Day *n no pl, Am* Día *m* del Presidente

press [pres] **I.** *vt* **1.** (*push: button, switch*) pulsar; (*bell*) tocar; (*trigger*) apretar; **to ~ sth down** apretar algo **2.** (*squeeze*) apretar; **the crowd ~ed us against the locked door** la multitud nos apretujaba contra la puerta cerrada **3.** (*flatten: flowers, grapes, olives*) prensar **4.** (*extract juice*) exprimir **5.** (*iron*) planchar **6.** MUS (*album, disk*) imprimir **7.** (*try to force*) presionar; **to ~ sb to do sth** presionar a alguien para que haga algo; **to ~ sb for sth** exigir algo de alguien; **to ~ sb for payment** acosar a alguien para que pague; **to be ~ed for time/money** andar justo de tiempo/dinero; **to ~ sth on sb** imponer algo a alguien **8.** (*pursue*) insistir; **to ~ a claim** insistir en una petición; **to ~ one's case** insistir en sus argumentos **9.** LAW **to ~ charges** presentar cargos **II.** *vi* **1.** (*push*) apretar; **to ~ hard** apretar fuerte; **to ~ on the brake pedal** pisar el freno **2.** (*crowd*) apiñarse; **to ~ through the crowd** abrirse paso entre el gentío; **to ~ down (on sth)** hacer presión (sobre algo) **3.** (*be urgent*) urgir; **time is ~ing** el tiempo apremia **4.** (*pressurize*) hacer presión; **to ~ for sth** insistir para conseguir algo **III.** *n* **1.** (*push*) presión *f;* (*of hand*) apretón *m;* **at the ~ of a button** apretando un botón **2.** (*ironing*) planchado *m;* **to give sth a ~** planchar algo **3.** (*crush*) apiñamiento *m* **4.** (*machine*) prensa *f;* (*for racket*) tensor *m;* **printing ~** imprenta *f;* **to be in [o on** *Am*] ~ estar en prensa; **to go to ~** (*news-*

paper, book) ir a imprenta; **hot off the ~** (*news*) de última hora **5.** PUBL **the ~** la prensa; **to have a bad/good ~** (*publicity*) tener buena/mala prensa **6.** (*cupboard*) ropero *m*

♦**press ahead** *vi s.* **press on**
♦**press down on** *vt* **1.** (*force down*) apretar **2.** (*lean on*) apoyarse en
♦**press forward** *vi s.* **press on**
♦**press in** *vt* clavar
♦**press on** *vi* seguir adelante
♦**press upon** *vt* apretar

press agency *n* agencia *f* de prensa **press baron** *n* magnate *m* de la prensa **press-button** *n* botón *m* de control **press campaign** *n* campaña *f* de prensa **press card** *n* acreditación *f* de periodista **press clipping** *n,* **press cutting** *n Brit* recorte *m* de prensa **press conference** *n* rueda *f* de prensa; **to hold a ~** dar una rueda de prensa **press coverage** *n* cobertura *f* periodística **press gallery** *n* tribuna *f* de la prensa

press-gang ['presɡæŋ] *vt* **to ~ sb into doing sth** forzar a alguien a hacer algo

pressing **I.** *adj* (*issue, matter*) urgente; (*need*) apremiante **II.** *n* (*of clothes*) planchado *m;* (*of records, fruits*) prensado *m*

pressman ['presmən] *n* **1.** (*journalist*) periodista *m* **2.** (*printing press operator*) tipógrafo *m* **press office** *n* oficina *f* de prensa **press officer** *n* encargado, -a *m, f* de prensa **press photographer** *n* reportero, -a *m, f* gráfico, -a **press release** *n* comunicado *m* de prensa; **to issue a ~** emitir un comunicado **press report** *n* reportaje *m*

press-stud ['presstʌd] *n Aus, Brit* broche *m* automático

press-up ['presʌp] *n Brit* SPORTS flexión *f* de brazos

pressure ['preʃəʳ, *Am:* -ɚ] **I.** *n* **1.** *a.* PHYS presión *f;* **high/low ~** presión alta/baja; **to put ~ on sth** hacer presión sobre algo; **at full ~** a toda presión; **to be under ~** *a. fig* estar bajo presión **2.** *no pl* (*influence*) **to put ~ on sb (to do sth)** presionar a alguien (para que haga algo); **to do sth under ~ from sb** hacer algo presionado por alguien; **to bring ~ to bear on sb** ejercer presión sobre alguien; **under the ~ of circumstances** bajo la presión de las circunstancias **3.** *pl* (*pressure*) tensiones *fpl* **4.** MED tensión *f;* **blood ~** tensión arterial **5.** ELEC voltaje *m* **II.** *vt* **to ~ sb to do sth** presionar a alguien para que haga algo

pressure cabin *n* AVIAT cabina *f* presurizada **pressure cooker** *n* olla *f* a presión, olla *f* presto *Méx* **pressure ga(u)ge** *n* manómetro *m* **pressure group** *n* POL grupo *m* de presión

pressurize ['preʃəraɪz] *vt* **1.** (*control air pressure*) presurizar **2.** (*person, government*) presionar; **to ~ sb into doing sth** forzar a alguien a hacer algo

prestige [pre'stiːʒ] *n no pl* prestigio *m*

prestigious [pre'stɪdʒəs] *adj* prestigioso, -a

pre-stressed concrete [‚pri:'strest 'kɒn-kri:t, *Am:* ‚pri:'strest 'kɑ:n-] *n* hormigón *m* pretensado

presumably [prɪ'zju:məbli, *Am:* prɪ'zu:-mə-] *adv* presumiblemente

presume [prɪ'zju:m, *Am:* prɪ'zu:m] I. *vt* 1. (*suppose*) suponer; **to ~ that ...** imaginarse que...; **~d dead** dado por muerto; **to be ~d innocent** ser presuntamente inocente; **Dr Smith, I ~?** usted debe de ser el Dr. Smith 2. (*dare*) **to ~ to do sth** atreverse a hacer algo II. *vi* 1. (*be presumptuous*) presumir 2. (*be rude*) **I don't wish to ~, but ...** no quisiera parecer impertinente, pero... 3. (*take advantage of*) **to ~ on sb** abusar de alguien

presumption [prɪ'zʌmpʃən] *n* 1. (*assumption*) suposición *f;* **the ~ is that ...** se supone que...; **the ~ of innocence** LAW la presunción de inocencia 2. *no pl, form* (*arrogance*) presunción *f* 3. (*daring*) atrevimiento *m*

presumptive [prɪ'zʌmptɪv] *adj* presunto, -a

presumptuous [prɪ'zʌmptjʊəs, *Am:* -tʃu-əs] *adj* 1. (*arrogant*) impertinente 2. (*forward*) osado, -a

presuppose [‚pri:sə'pəʊz, *Am:* -'poʊz] *vt form* presuponer

presupposition [‚pri:sʌpə'zɪʃən] *n* presuposición *f;* **to be based on false ~s** basarse en suposiciones falsas

pre-tax [‚pri:'tæks] *adj* antes de impuestos, bruto, -a

pretence [prɪ'tents, *Am:* 'pri:tents] *n no pl* 1. (*claim*) pretensión *f;* **to make no ~ to erudition** no pretender ser erudito 2. (*simulation*) fingimiento *m;* **to make a ~ of sth** fingir algo 3. (*pretext*) pretexto *m;* **under (the) ~ of ...** con el pretexto de...

pretend [prɪ'tend] I. *vt* 1. (*make believe*) fingir; **to ~ to be interested** fingir interés; **to ~ to be dead** hacerse el muerto; **to ~ to be sb** hacerse pasar por alguien; **the children ~ed that they were dinosaurs** los niños imaginaban que eran dinosaurios 2. (*claim*) pretender; **I don't ~ to know** no pretendo saber II. *vi* fingir; **he's just ~ing** sólo está fingiendo

pretended *adj* fingido, -a

pretender *n* pretendiente *mf;* **a ~ to the throne** un pretendiente al trono

pretense [prɪ'tents, *Am:* 'pri:tents] *n no pl, Am s.* **pretence**

pretension [prɪ'tentʃən] *n* 1. (*claim*) pretensión *f;* **to have ~s to (being/doing) sth** tener pretensiones de (ser/hacer) algo 2. *no pl s.* **pretentiousness**

pretentious [prɪ'tentʃəs] *adj pej* pretencioso, -a; (*in bad taste*) cursi

pretentiousness *n no pl, pej* pretensión *f;* (*in bad taste*) cursilería *f*

preterit(e) ['pretərɪt, *Am:* 'pretɚɪt] LING I. *n* pretérito *m* II. *adj* pretérito, -a *form*

preternatural [‚pri:tə'nætʃərəl, *Am:* -tɚ-'nætʃɚəl] *adj form* (*exceptional*) prodigioso, -a

pretext ['pri:tekst] *n* pretexto *m;* **a ~ for to do sth** un pretexto para hacer algo; **on the ~ that ...** con el pretexto de que...; **under the ~ of doing sth** so pretexto de hacer algo *form*

prettify ['prɪtɪfaɪ, *Am:* 'prɪt̪-] *vt* (*room, street*) engalanar; (*account, report*) adornar *fig*

pretty ['prɪti, *Am:* 'prɪt̪-] I. *adj* <-ier, -iest> 1. (*beautiful: thing*) bonito, -a, lindo, -a *AmL;* (*child, woman*) guapo, -a, lindo, -a *AmL;* **not a ~ sight** nada agradable de ver 2. *inf* (*considerable*) menudo, -a; **~ mess** menudo lío *m* II. *adv* (*quite*) bastante 2. **~ much** más o menos; **to be ~ much the same** ser prácticamente lo mismo; **I'm ~ nearly finished** ya casi he terminado; **~ well everything** casi todo

pretzel ['pretsl] *n* galleta *f* salada

prevail [prɪ'veɪl] *vi* 1. (*triumph*) prevalecer; **to ~ over/against sth** prevalecer sobre/contra algo; **to ~ over/against sb** triunfar sobre/contra alguien 2. (*predominate*) predominar; (*conditions, situation*) imperar 3. **to ~ (up)on sb (to do sth)** *form* convencer a alguien (para que haga algo)

prevailing *adj* predominante; (*atmosphere, feelings*) reinante; **under the ~ circumstances** en las circunstancias actuales

prevalence ['prevələnts] *n no pl* 1. (*common occurence*) preponderancia *f;* **the ~ of drugs in some neighbourhoods** la presencia habitual de drogas en algunos barrios 2. (*predominance*) predominio *m*

prevalent ['prevələnt] *adj* 1. (*common*) corriente; (*disease, opinion*) extendido, -a 2. (*present-day*) actual 3. (*predominant*) predominante

prevaricate [prɪ'værɪkeɪt, *Am:* prɪ'verɪ-] *vi form* andarse con rodeos; **to ~ over sth** dar vueltas a algo

prevarication [prɪ‚værɪ'keɪʃən, *Am:* prɪ-‚ver-] *n no pl, form* evasivas *fpl*

prevent [prɪ'vent] *vt* 1. (*hamper*) impedir; **to ~ sb from doing sth** impedir que alguien haga algo; **the news ~ed his coming** la noticia impidió que viniera 2. (*avoid*) prevenir; (*confusion, panic, crime*) evitar

preventative [prɪ'ventətɪv, *Am:* prɪ'ven-t̪ətɪv] *adj s.* **preventive**

prevention [prɪ'ventʃən] *n no pl* prevención *f;* **for the ~ of crime** para evitar la delincuencia ► **~ is better than cure** *prov*, **an ounce of ~ is worth a pound of cure** *Am, prov* más vale prevenir que curar *prov*

preventive [prɪ'ventɪv, *Am:* -t̪ɪv] *adj* preventivo, -a

preview ['pri:vju:] I. *n* CINE, THEAT preestreno *m;* (*film extract*) tráiler *m;* (*of TV programme, exhibition*) adelanto *m* II. *vt* CINE, THEAT preestrenar

previous ['pri:viəs] I. *adj* 1. (*former*) anterior; **on the ~ day/week** el día/la semana anterior; **no** ~ **experience required** no se necesita experiencia **2.**(*prior*) previo, -a; **without** ~ **notice** sin previo aviso **II.** *adv* ~ **to doing sth** antes de hacer algo

previous convictions *npl* antecedentes *mpl* penales

previously *adv* **1.**(*beforehand*) previamente **2.**(*formerly*) anteriormente; **to have met sb** ~ haber visto a alguien antes

pre-war [ˌpriːˈwɔːʳ, *Am:* -ˈwɔːr] *adj* de antes de la guerra; **the** ~ **years** la preguerra

prey [preɪ] *n no pl* **1.**(*animal*) presa *f;* **bird of** ~ ave *f* de presa **2.**(*person*) víctima *f;* **to be easy** ~ **for sb** ser presa [*o* blanco] fácil para alguien; **to fall** ~ **to** (*animal*) ser presa de; (*person*) ser víctima de

◆**prey on** *vt,* **prey upon** *vt* **1.**(*feed on*) alimentarse de; **fear ~ed on me** *fig* fui preso del miedo **2.**(*exploit*) aprovecharse de

price [praɪs] **I.** *n* **1.** COM precio *m;* **oil ~s, the** ~ **of oil** el precio del petróleo; **to ask a high/ low** ~ pedir un precio alto/bajo; **to be the same** ~ valer [*o* costar] lo mismo; **to go up/ down in** ~ subir/bajar de precio; **to name a** ~ pedir un precio; **what** ~ **are apples?** ¿a cuánto están las manzanas? **2.** FIN (*of stocks*) cotización *f,* precio *m* **3.** *fig* precio *m;* **the** ~ **one has to pay for fame** el precio de la fama; **beyond** [*o* **without**] ~ sin precio; **to set a high** ~ **on sth** valorar mucho algo ▶**to set a** ~ **on sb's** <u>head</u> poner precio a la cabeza de alguien; **at** <u>any</u> ~ a toda costa; **not at** <u>any</u> ~ por nada del mundo; **to pay a** <u>heavy</u> ~ pagarlo caro; **to** <u>pay</u> **the** ~ pagar caro; **at a** ~ a un precio muy alto **II.** *vt* **1.**(*mark with price tag*) poner el precio a **2.**(*fix price*) poner precio a, valorar; **to be reasonably ~d** tener un precio razonable ▶**to be ~d out of the** <u>market</u> no poder competir en el mercado por su alto precio

price bracket *n* gama *f* de precios **price control** *n* control *m* de precios **price cut(ting)** *n* recorte *m* de precios **price fixing** *n* fijación *f* de precios **price freeze** *n* congelación *f* de precios **price index** *n* índice *m* de precios

priceless [ˈpraɪsləs] *adj* **1.**(*invaluable*) incalculable; **to be** ~ no tener precio **2.** *fig* (*funny*) divertidísimo, -a; **that's ~!** ¡eso es para partirse de risa! *inf,* ¡eso es un plato! *AmL, inf*

price level *n* nivel *m* de precios **price list** *n* lista *f* de precios **price range** *n* gama *f* de precios **price rise** *n* aumento *m* de precios **price stability** *n* estabilidad *f* de precios **price tag** *n,* **price ticket** *n* **1.**(*label*) etiqueta *f* (del precio) **2.** *inf* (*cost*) precio *m* **price war** *n* guerra *f* de precios

pricey [ˈpraɪsi] *adj* <pricier, priciest> *inf* (*object*) carillo, -a; (*shop*) carero, -a

pricing [ˈpraɪsɪŋ] *n* fijación *f* de precios; ~ **policy** política *f* de precios

prick [prɪk] **I.** *vt* **1.**(*jab*) pinchar, picar; **to** ~ **one's finger with** [*o* **on**] **a needle** pincharse el dedo con una aguja; **to** ~ **sb's conscience** hacer que a alguien le remuerda la conciencia **2.**(*mark with holes*) agujerear **II.** *vi* **1.**(*pin*) pinchar **2.**(*hurt: eyes, skin*) escocer, arder *CSur* **III.** *n* **1.**(*act, pain*) pinchazo *m;* **to feel the** ~ **of conscience** tener remordimientos de conciencia **2.**(*mark*) agujero *m* **3.** *vulg* (*penis*) polla *f,* pija *f RíoPl* **4.** *vulg* (*idiot*) gilipollas *m inv*

◆**prick out** *vt* (*flowers*) repicar

◆**prick up** *vt* to ~ **one's ears** (*animal*) erguir las orejas; (*person*) aguzar el oído

prickle [ˈprɪkl] **I.** *n* **1.**(*thorn: of plant*) pincho *m;* (*of animal*) púa *f* **2.**(*tingle*) picor *m;* **to feel a** ~ **of excitement** sentir un cosquilleo de emoción **II.** *vi* **1.**(*cause prickling sensation*) picar **2.**(*tingle*) sentir picor **3.**(*prick*) pinchar **III.** *vt* (*prick*) pinchar, picar

prickly [ˈprɪkli] <-ier, -iest> *adj* **1.**(*thorny: plant*) espinoso, -a; (*animal*) con púas **2.**(*tingling*) que pica; (*beard*) que pincha; ~ **heat** fiebre *f* miliar; ~ **sensation** picor *m* **3.** *inf* (*easily offended*) irritable

prickly pear *n* **1.**(*fruit*) higo *m* chumbo **2.**(*plant*) chumbera *f*

pride [praɪd] **I.** *n* **1.** *no pl* (*proud feeling*) orgullo *m;* **to feel great** ~ estar muy orgulloso; **to take** ~ **in sth** enorgullecerse de algo; (*one's work*) esmerarse en algo; **to be sb's** ~ **and joy** ser el orgullo de alguien **2.** *no pl* (*self-respect*) amor *m* propio; **to hurt sb's** ~ herir el orgullo de alguien; **to swallow one's** ~ tragarse el orgullo; **false** ~ vanidad *f* **3.** *no pl* (*arrogance*) soberbia *f* **4.**(*animal group*) manada *f* ▶~ **comes** [*o* **goes**] **before a** <u>fall</u> *prov* más dura será la caída; **to have** ~ **of** <u>place</u> ocupar el lugar de honor **II.** *vt* to ~ **oneself on** (**doing**) **sth** enorgullecerse de (hacer) algo; **to** ~ **oneself that ...** preciarse de que...

priest [priːst] *n* REL cura *m*

priestess [ˈpriːstes, *Am:* -stɪs] *n* REL sacerdotisa *f*

priesthood [ˈpriːsthʊd] *n no pl* REL **1.**(*position, office*) sacerdocio *m;* **to enter the** ~ ser ordenado sacerdote **2.**(*priests in general*) clero *m*

priestly [ˈpriːstli] *adj* sacerdotal

prig [prɪg] *n pej* mojigato, -a *m, f*

priggish [ˈprɪgɪʃ] *adj pej* mojigato, -a

prim [prɪm] <-mer, -mest> *adj* **1.** *pej* remilgado, -a; ~ **and proper** remilgado **2.**(*appearance*) escrupuloso, -a

primacy [ˈpraɪməsi] *n no pl, form* primacía *f*

prima donna [ˌpriːməˈdɒnə, *Am:* -ˈdɑːnə] *n* **1.**(*opera singer*) prima donna *f* **2.** *pej* (*arrogant person*) diva *f*

primaeval [praɪˈmiːvəl] *adj s.* **primeval**

primal [ˈpraɪml] *adj* **1.**(*primitive*) primario, -a **2.**(*most important*) primordial

primarily [ˈpraɪmərɪli, *Am:* praɪˈmerəl-] *adv* principalmente, ante todo

primary [ˈpraɪməri, *Am:* -mer-] **I.** *adj* **1.**(*principal*) fundamental; (*aim*) prioritario,

-a; **to be of** ~ **importance** ser de una importancia primordial **2.** (*basic*) primario, -a; (*industry*) de base; ~ **meaning of a word** primer sentido de una palabra; ~ **stress** LING acento *m* primario **II.** <-ies> *n Am* POL elecciones *fpl* primarias

primary colour *n* color *m* primario **primary education** *n no pl* enseñanza *f* primaria

primate ['praɪmeɪt, *Am:* -mɪt] *n* **1.** ZOOL primate *m* **2.** REL primado *m*

prime [praɪm] **I.** *adj* **1.** (*main*) principal; (*objective*) prioritario, -a; **of** ~ **importance** de importancia primordial **2.** (*first-rate*) excelente; **of** ~ **quality** de primera calidad; **in** ~ **condition** en perfecto estado **II.** *n no pl* apogeo *m elev;* **to be in one's** ~, **to be in the** ~ **of life** estar en la flor de la vida; **to be past one's** ~ no ser ya ningún jovencito; **to be cut off in one's** ~ morir en la flor de la vida **III.** *vt* **1.** (*undercoat: surface*) aplicar una capa de base sobre; (*canvas*) aprestar **2.** (*prepare for exploding: gun, pump, motor*) cebar **3.** (*prepare*) **to** ~ **sb for doing sth** preparar a alguien para hacer algo; **to be well** ~**d for an interview** ir bien preparado para una entrevista **4.** (*brief*) informar **5.** (*make drunk*) emborrachar; **to be well** ~**d** estar contentillo

prime cost *n* ECON coste *m* de producción **prime meridian** *n* GEO primer meridiano *m* **prime minister** *n* POL primer(a) ministro, -a *m, f* **prime mover** *n* fuerza *f* motriz; (*person*) promotor(a) *m(f)* **prime number** *n* MAT número *m* primo

primer ['praɪmə', *Am:* -mə'] *n* **1.** (*paint*) (pintura *f* de) imprimación *f;* **a** ~ **coat** una primera mano **2.** (*explosive*) cartucho *m* **3.** (*textbook*) manual *m;* (*for learning to read*) cartilla *f*

prime time *n* RADIO, TV horas *fpl* de máxima audiencia

primeval [praɪ'miːvəl] *adj* primigenio, -a; (*forest*) virgen

primitive ['prɪmɪtɪv, *Am:* -t̬ɪv] **I.** *adj a.* ART, HIST, ZOOL primitivo, -a; (*method, weapon*) rudimentario, -a **II.** *n* ART, HIST, SOCIOL primitivo, -a *m, f*

primogeniture [ˌpraɪməʊ'dʒenɪtʃə', *Am:* -moʊ'dʒenɪtʃə'] *n no pl* primogenitura *f*

primordial [praɪ'mɔːdiəl, *Am:* -'mɔːr-] *adj form* **1.** (*from beginning*) primigenio, -a **2.** (*basic*) primario, -a

primrose ['prɪmrəʊz, *Am:* -roʊz] **I.** *n* **1.** BOT prímula *f,* primavera *f* **2.** (*colour*) ~ (**yellow**) amarillo *m* pálido **II.** *adj* de color amarillo pálido

primula ['prɪmjələ] *n* prímula *f,* primavera *f* **primus**® ['praɪməs] *n* hornillo *m* de queroseno

prince [prɪns] *n* príncipe *m;* **crown** ~ príncipe heredero; **Prince Charming** príncipe azul; **Prince of Wales** Príncipe de Gales; **the Prince of Darkness** el príncipe de las tinieblas

prince consort *n* príncipe *m* consorte

princely ['prɪntsli] *adj fig* magnífico, -a; **the** ~ **sum of 10 pence** *iron* la bonita suma de 10 peniques

princess [prɪn'ses, *Am:* 'prɪntsɪs] *n* princesa *f*

principal ['prɪntsəpl] **I.** *adj* principal **II.** *n* **1.** *Am, Aus* (*headmaster*) director(a) *m(f);* (*of university*) rector(a) *m(f)* **2.** FIN capital *m*

principality [ˌprɪntsɪ'pæləti, *Am:* -sə'pæ-ləti] *n* principado *m*

principally *adv* principalmente

principle ['prɪntsəpl] *n* principio *m*

principle clause *n* cláusula *f* principal

print [prɪnt] **I.** *n* **1.** (*printed lettering*) texto *m* impreso; **bold** ~ negrita *f* **2.** (*printed form*) **to rush sth into** ~ publicar algo precipitadamente; **to appear in** ~ publicarse; **to go out of** ~ agotarse **3.** (*engraving*) grabado *m;* PHOT positivo *m* **4.** (*printed pattern*) estampado *m* **5.** *inf* (*fingerprint*) huella *f* **II.** *vt* **1.** (*publish*) publicar **2.** (*put into printed form*) imprimir **3.** INFOR (*make a print-out of*) sacar copias de **4.** PHOT positivar **5.** (*mark fabric*) estampar **6.** (*write in unjoined letters*) escribir con letras de imprenta **III.** *vi* **1.** (*appear in printed form*) imprimirse **2.** (*write in unjoined letters*) escribir con letras de imprenta

printable ['prɪntəbl, *Am:* -t̬ə-] *adj* imprimible

printed circuit board *n* ELEC circuito *m* impreso

printer ['prɪntə', *Am:* -t̬ə'] *n* **1.** (*person*) impresor(a) *m(f)* **2.** INFOR impresora *f;* **inkjet/laser** ~ impresora de chorro de tinta/láser

printer driver *n* controlador *m* de impresora **printing** *n* **1.** *no pl* (*art*) imprenta *f* **2.** (*action*) impresión *f*

printing ink *n* tinta *f* de imprenta **printing press** *n* prensa *f* **printing works** *npl* imprenta *f*

print-out ['prɪntaʊt] *n* INFOR impresión *f,* listado *m*

print run *n* tirada *f*

print shop *n* imprenta *f*

prior ['praɪə', *Am:* 'praɪə'] **I.** *adv form* (*before*) antes; ~ **to doing sth** antes de hacer algo **II.** *adj form* **1.** (*earlier*) previo, -a **2.** (*preferred*) preferente **III.** *n* REL prior *m*

prioritize [praɪ'ɒrɪtaɪz, *Am:* -'ɔːrə-] *vt* priorizar

priority [praɪ'ɒrəti, *Am:* -'ɔːrəti] **I.** <-ies> *n* **1.** *no pl* (*being most important*) prioridad *f;* (*in time*) anterioridad *f* **2.** *pl* (*order of importance*) prioridades *fpl;* **to get one's priorities right** establecer un orden de prioridades **II.** *adj* **1.** (*of utmost importance*) prioritario, -a **2.** (*claim, right*) *a.* FIN preferente

priory ['praɪəri] *n* priorato *m*

prise [praɪz] *vt Brit, Aus s.* **prize²**

prism ['prɪzəm] *n* prisma *m*

prismatic [prɪz'mætɪk, *Am:* -'mæt̬-] *adj*

prison ['prɪzən] *n* prisión *f;* **to go to** ~ ir a la cárcel; **to put sb in** ~ encarcelar a alguien

prison camp *n* campamento *m* para prisioneros **prison cell** *n* celda *f*

prisoner ['prɪzənəʳ, *Am:* -ɚ] *n* preso, -a *m, f;* MIL prisionero, -a *m, f;* **to hold sb** ~ detener a alguien; **to take sb** ~ hacer prisionero a alguien

prisoner of war *n* prisionero, -a *m, f* de guerra

prison inmate *n* recluso, -a *m, f* **prison riot** *n* motín *m* carcelero **prison yard** *n* patio *m* de la cárcel

pristine ['prɪsti:n] *adj form* prístino, -a

privacy ['prɪvəsi, *Am:* 'praɪ-] *n no pl* intimidad *f;* **to desire** ~ desear estar a solas

private ['praɪvɪt, *Am:* -vət] I. *adj* 1. (*not public*) privado, -a 2. (*confidential*) confidencial; **sb's** ~ **opinion** la opinión personal de alguien II. *n* 1. *pl, inf* (*genitals*) partes *fpl;* ~ **parts** partes *fpl* pudendas 2. MIL soldado *m* raso

privateer [ˌpraɪvə'tɪəʳ, *Am:* -'tɪr] *n* NAUT (*vessel*) corsario *m*

privately ['praɪvɪtli, *Am:* -vət-] *adv* 1. (*in private*) en privado; **to celebrate** ~ celebrar a puerta cerrada 2. (*secretly*) en secreto 3. (*personally*) personalmente

privation [praɪ'veɪʃən] *n no pl, form* privación *f;* **to live in** ~ vivir en la miseria; **to suffer** ~ pasar apuros

privatization [ˌpraɪvɪtaɪ'zeɪʃən, *Am:* -və-tɪ'-] *n no pl* privatización *f*

privatize ['praɪvɪtaɪz, *Am:* -və-] *vt* privatizar

privet ['prɪvɪt] *n no pl* alheña *f*

privilege ['prɪvəlɪdʒ] I. *n* 1. (*special right*) privilegio *m* 2. (*honour*) honor *m* II. *vt* **to be** ~**d to do sth** tener el privilegio de hacer algo

privileged ['prɪvəlɪdʒd] *adj* 1. (*special*) privilegiado, -a 2. (*confidential*) confidencial

privy[1] ['prɪvi] *adj form* **to be** ~ **to sth** estar al tanto de algo

privy[2] ['prɪvi] *n* (*toilet*) retrete *m*

prize[1] [praɪz] I. *n* 1. (*in competition*) premio *m;* **to carry off a** ~ ganar un premio 2. (*reward*) recompensa *f* II. *adj* 1. *inf* (*first-rate*) de primera; **a** ~ **idiot** un tonto de remate 2. (*prizewinning*) premiado, -a III. *vt* apreciar; **to** ~ **sth highly** estimar algo mucho

prize[2] [praɪz] *vt* **to** ~ **sth off** arrancar algo; **to** ~ **sth open** abrir algo por la fuerza

prizefight ['praɪzfaɪt] *n* combate *m* de boxeo profesional

prizefighter *n* boxeador(a) *m(f)* profesional **prizefighting** *n no pl* boxeo *m* profesional **prize-giving** *n* reparto *m* de premios **prize list** *n* lista *f* de premiados **prize money** *n* SPORTS premio *m* en metálico **prizewinning** ['praɪzˌwɪnɪŋ] *adj* premiado, -a

pro[1] [prəʊ, *Am:* proʊ] *inf* I. *n abbr of* **professional** profesional *mf* II. *adj abbr of* **professional** profesional

pro[2] [prəʊ, *Am:* proʊ] I. *adv* a favor II. *n* pro *m;* **the** ~**s and cons of sth** los pros y los contras de algo III. *prep* pro IV. *adj* favorable

proactive [ˌprəʊ'æktɪv, *Am:* ˌproʊ'-] *adj* con iniciativa

probability [ˌprɒbə'bɪləti, *Am:* ˌprɑːbə'bɪləti] *n* probabilidad *f;* **in all** ~ sin duda

probable ['prɒbəbl, *Am:* 'prɑːbə-] *adj* 1. (*likely*) probable 2. (*credible*) verosímil

probably *adv* probablemente

probate ['prəʊbeɪt, *Am:* 'proʊ-] *n no pl* 1. LAW legalización *f* de un testamento 2. *Aus* FIN derechos *mpl* de sucesión

probation [prəʊ'beɪʃən, *Am:* proʊ'-] *n no pl* 1. (*in job*) período *m* de prueba; **to be on** ~ estar a prueba 2. LAW libertad *f* condicional

probationary [prəʊ'beɪʃənəri, *Am:* proʊ'-] *adj* de prueba; ~ **period** período *m* de prueba

probationer [prəʊ'beɪʃənəʳ, *Am:* proʊ-'beɪʃənɚ] *n* 1. (*offender on probation*) persona *f* en libertad condicional 2. (*worker*) trabajador(a) *m(f)* en período de prueba

probation officer *n* funcionario que hace el seguimiento de personas en libertad condicional

probe [prəʊb, *Am:* proʊb] I. *vi* (*examine*) investigar; **to** ~ **into the possibilities** tantear las posibilidades; **to** ~ **into sb's private life** indagar en la vida privada de alguien II. *vt* 1. (*examine*) investigar 2. MED sondar III. *n* 1. (*examination, investigation*) investigación *f* 2. MED, AVIAT sonda *f*

probity ['prəʊbəti, *Am:* 'proʊbəti] *n no pl, form* probidad *f*

problem ['prɒbləm, *Am:* 'prɑːbləm] *n* problema *m*

problematic(al) [ˌprɒblə'mætɪk(əl), *Am:* ˌprɑːblə'mæt̬-] *adj* 1. (*creating difficulty*) problemático, -a 2. (*questionable, disputable*) dudoso, -a

problem child *n* niño, -a *m, f* difícil

proboscis [prəʊ'bɒsɪs, *Am:* proʊ'bɑːsɪs] *n* 1. ZOOL probóscide *f* 2. *iron* (*person's nose*) napia *f*

procedural [prə'siːdʒərəl, *Am:* -dʒɚ-] *adj* de procedimiento; LAW procesal

procedure [prə'siːdʒəʳ, *Am:* -dʒɚ] *n* procedimiento *m*

proceed [prə'siːd, *Am:* proʊ'-] *vi form* 1. (*move along*) seguir; (*continue*) continuar; (*continue driving*) seguir adelante; **to** ~ **with sth** avanzar con algo; **to** ~ **against sb** proceder contra alguien 2. (*come from*) **to** ~ **from** provenir de 3. (*start, begin*) **to** ~ **with sth** empezar con algo; **to** ~ **to do sth** ponerse a hacer algo

proceedings [prə'siːdɪŋz, *Am:* proʊ'-] *npl* 1. LAW proceso *m* 2. *form* (*events*) actos *mpl* 3. *form* (*minutes*) actas *fpl*

proceeds ['prəʊsiːdz, *Am:* 'proʊ-] *n* ingresos *mpl*

process[1] ['prəʊses, *Am:* 'prɑː-] I. *n* proceso *m;* **in the** ~ mientras tanto; **to be in the** ~ **of**

doing sth estar en vías de hacer algo **II.** *vt* **1.** *a.* TECH, INFOR procesar; (*of raw materials, waste*) tratar **2.** PHOT revelar

process² [prəʊˈses, *Am:* proʊ-] *vi form* desfilar

process chart *n* diagrama *m* del proceso
process engineering *n* ingeniería *f* de procesos

processing [ˈprəʊsesɪŋ, *Am:* ˈprɑː-] *n no pl* **1.** *a.* TECH, INFOR procesamiento *m;* (*of raw materials, waste*) tratamiento *m;* **data** ~ procesamiento de datos; **batch** ~ procesamiento por lotes **2.** PHOT revelado *m*

procession [prəˈseʃən] *n* **1.** desfile *m;* **funeral** ~ cortejo *m* fúnebre; **to go in** ~ desfilar **2.** REL procesión *f* **3.** *fig* serie *f*

processor [prəʊˈsesəʳ, *Am:* ˈprɑː-] *n* INFOR procesador *m*

proclaim [prəˈkleɪm, *Am:* proʊˈ-] *vt form* proclamar; **to** ~ **war** declarar la guerra

proclamation [ˌprɒkləˈmeɪʃən, *Am:* ˌprɑːklə-] *n form* proclamación *f;* **a** ~ **of war** una declaración de guerra

proclivity [prəˈklɪvəti, *Am:* proʊˈklɪvəti] *n form* propensión *f;* **sexual** ~ tendencia *f* sexual; **to have a** ~ **for sth** ser proclive a algo

procrastinate [prəʊˈkræstɪneɪt, *Am:* proʊˈkræstə-] *vi* dejar para más tarde

procrastination [prəʊˌkræstɪˈneɪʃən, *Am:* proʊˈkræstə-] *n no pl* dilación *f*

procreate [ˈprəʊkrieɪt, *Am:* ˈproʊ-] *vi form* procrear

procreation [ˌprəʊkrɪˈeɪʃən, *Am:* ˌproʊ-] *n no pl, form* procreación *f*

proctor [ˈprɒktəʳ, *Am:* ˈprɑːktəʳ] *n* **1.** Brit UNIV censor(a) *m(f), persona que cuida de la disciplina* **2.** *Am* UNIV vigilante *mf*

procurable [prəˈkjʊrəbl, *Am:* proʊˈ-] *adj* asequible

procurator [ˈprɒkjʊəreɪtəʳ, *Am:* ˈprɑːkjəreɪtəʳ] *n* LAW procurador(a) *m(f)*

procurator fiscal *n* Scot LAW fiscal *mf*

procure [prəˈkjʊəʳ, *Am:* proʊˈkjʊr] *form* **I.** *vt* (*obtain*) obtener; **to** ~ **sth for sb, to** ~ **sb sth** obtener algo para alguien **II.** *vi* LAW dedicarse al proxenetismo

procurement [prəˈkjʊəmənt, *Am:* proʊˈkjʊr-] *n no pl, form* adquisición *f*

prod [prɒd, *Am:* prɑːd] **I.** *n* (*poke*) golpe *m;* (*with elbow*) codazo *m;* (*with sharp object*) pinchazo *m;* **to give sb a** ~ *fig* dar un empujón a alguien **II.** <-dd-> *vt* **1.** (*poke*) golpear; (*with elbow*) dar un codazo; (*with sharp object*) pinchar **2.** (*encourage, urge on, stimulate*) **to** ~ **sb** (**into doing sth**) estimular a alguien (para que haga algo)

prodigal [ˈprɒdɪgl, *Am:* ˈprɑːdɪ-] *adj form* pródigo, -a

prodigious [prəˈdɪdʒəs, *Am:* proʊˈ-] *adj form* (*size, height*) ingente; (*achievement, talent*) prodigioso, -a

prodigy [ˈprɒdɪdʒi, *Am:* ˈprɑːdə-] *n* prodigio *m;* **child** ~ niño, -a *m, f* prodigio

produce¹ [prəˈdjuːs, *Am:* -ˈduːs] *vt* **1.** (*create*) producir; (*manufacture*) fabricar **2.** (*give birth to*) dar a luz **3.** CINE, THEAT, TV realizar; (*musical recording*) dirigir **4.** (*show*) mostrar; **to** ~ **a knife** sacar un cuchillo; **to** ~ **one's passport** enseñar el pasaporte; **to** ~ **an alibi** presentar una coartada **5.** (*cause*) causar; **to** ~ **results** producir resultados

produce² [ˈprɒdjuːs, *Am:* ˈprɑːduːs] *n no pl* AGR productos *mpl* agrícolas

producer [prəˈdjuːsəʳ, *Am:* -ˈduːsəʳ] *n* productor(a) *m(f)*

product [ˈprɒdʌkt, *Am:* ˈprɑːdʌkt] *n* **1.** *a.* MAT producto *m* **2.** (*result*) resultado *m*

production [prəˈdʌkʃən] *n* **1.** *no pl* (*of goods*) fabricación *f* **2.** *no pl* CINE, THEAT, TV producción *f* **3.** *no pl, form* (*presentation: of ticket, passport*) presentación *f*

production capacity *n* capacidad *f* de producción **production costs** *npl* costes *mpl* de producción **production director** *n* director(a) *m(f)* de producción **production line** *n* cadena *f* de montaje **production manager** *n* encargado, -a *m, f* de producción **production time** *n* tiempo *m* de producción **production volume** *n* volumen *m* de producción

productive [prəˈdʌktɪv] *adj* productivo, -a; (*land, soil*) fértil; (*writer*) prolífico, -a

productivity [ˌprɒdʌkˈtɪvəti, *Am:* ˌproʊdəkˈtɪvəti] *n no pl* productividad *f*

productivity agreement *n* Brit acuerdo *m* de productividad **productivity bonus** *n* prima *f* de productividad

Prof. [prɒf, *Am:* prɑːf] *abbr of* **Professor** prof. *m,* profa. *f*

profane [prəˈfeɪn, *Am:* proʊˈ-] *adj* **1.** (*blasphemous*) blasfemo, -a **2.** *form* (*secular*) profano, -a

profanity [prəˈfænəti, *Am:* proʊˈfænəti] *n form* **1.** (*blasphemy*) blasfemia *f* **2.** (*obscene word*) palabrota *f;* **to utter a** ~ soltar un taco

profess [prəˈfes] *vt* profesar; **to** ~ **little enthusiasm** manifestar poco entusiasmo; **to** ~ **to be sth** pretender ser algo; **to** ~ **oneself satisfied** (**with sth**) declararse satisfecho (con algo)

professed [prəˈfest] *adj* **1.** (*self-acknowledged*) declarado, -a **2.** (*alleged*) supuesto, -a

profession [prəˈfeʃən] *n* **1.** (*occupation*) profesión *f;* **teaching** ~ docencia *f* **2.** (*declaration*) declaración *f*

professional [prəˈfeʃənəl] **I.** *adj* **1.** (*relating to profession*) profesional **2.** (*competent*) experto, -a **II.** *n* profesional *mf*

professionalism [prəˈfeʃənəlɪzəm] *n no pl* **1.** (*attitude*) profesionalidad *f* **2.** SPORTS profesionalismo *m*

professionally [prəˈfeʃənəli] *adv* **1.** (*by a professional*) profesionalmente **2.** (*in a professional manner*) con profesionalidad

professor [prəˈfesəʳ, *Am:* -əʳ] *n* Brit UNIV catedrático, -a *m, f; Am* SCHOOL profesor(a) *m(f)*

professorial [ˌprɒfɪˈsɔːriəl, *Am:* ˌproʊfə'-] *adj* profesoral

professorship [prəˈfesəʃɪp, *Am:* '-ə-] *n* cátedra *f*

proffer [ˈprɒfəʳ, *Am:* ˈprɑːfəʳ] *vt form* ofrecer

proficiency [prəˈfɪʃnsi] *n no pl* competencia *f*

proficient [prəˈfɪʃnt] *adj* competente

profile [ˈprəʊfaɪl, *Am:* 'proʊ-] **I.** *n* **1.** (*side view*) perfil *m;* **in** ~ de perfil **2.** (*description*) descripción *f;* **user** ~ INFOR perfil *m* de usuario ▸**to keep a** <u>low</u> ~ tratar de pasar inadvertido **II.** *vt* (*describe*) describir

profit [ˈprɒfɪt, *Am:* ˈprɑːfɪt] **I.** *n* **1.** FIN beneficio *m* **2.** (*advantage*) provecho *m* **II.** *vi* **1.** (*benefit*) beneficiarse; **to** ~ **by sth** sacar provecho de algo **2.** (*make a profit*) ganar

profitability [ˌprɒfɪtəˈbɪləti, *Am:* ˌprɑːfɪtə-ˈbɪləti] *n no pl* rentabilidad *f*

profitable [ˈprɒfɪtəbl, *Am:* ˈprɑːfɪtə-] *adj* **1.** FIN rentable; **a** ~ **investment** una inversión lucrativa **2.** (*advantageous*) provechoso, -a

profit-earning *adj* rentable

profiteer [ˌprɒfɪˈtɪəʳ, *Am:* ˌprɑːfɪˈtɪr] *n pej* especulador(a) *m(f)*

profiteering *n no pl, pej* especulación *f*

profit-making *adj* lucrativo, -a; ~ **movie** película *f* rentable

profit margin *n* margen *m* de beneficio

profit maximization *n* maximización *f* del beneficio **profit-oriented** *adj Am* orientado, -a a la obtención de beneficios **profit--related** *adj* que depende de los beneficios **profit sharing** *n* participación *f* en los beneficios **profit taking** *n* FIN realización *f* de beneficios

profligate [ˈprɒflɪgət, *Am:* ˈprɑːflɪgɪt] *adj form* derrochador(a)

profound [prəˈfaʊnd] *adj* profundo, -a

profundity [prəˈfʌndəti, *Am:* proʊ'-] *n form no pl* profundidad *f*

profuse [prəˈfjuːs] *adj* profuso, -a; **to be ~ in one's praise of sth** alabar algo con efusión

profusion [prəˈfjuːʒən] *n no pl, form* profusión *f;* **in** ~ en abundancia

prog. *n abbr of* **program** progr.

progenitor [prəˈʊdʒenɪtəʳ, *Am:* proʊˈdʒenətə-] *n form* progenitor(a) *m(f)*

progeny [ˈprɒʊdʒəni, *Am:* ˈprɑːdʒə-] *n pl, form* progenie *f*

prognosis [prɒgˈnəʊsɪs, *Am:* prɑːgˈnoʊ-] *n form* pronóstico *m*

prognosticate [prɒgˈnɒstɪkeɪt, *Am:* prɑːgˈnɑːstɪ-] *vt form* pronosticar

program [ˈprəʊgræm, *Am:* ˈproʊ-] **I.** *n* programa *m* **II.** <-mm-> *vt* programar

programmable [prəˈʊgræməbl, *Am:* ˈproʊgræmə-] *adj* programable

programme [ˈprəʊgræm, *Am:* ˈproʊ-] *n, vt Aus, Brit s.* **program**

programmer *n* programador(a) *m(f)*

programming *n* programación *f*

programming language *n* lenguaje *m* de

programación

progress¹ [ˈprəʊgres, *Am:* ˈprɑː-] *n no pl* progreso *m;* **to make** ~ avanzar; **to be in** ~ estar en curso

progress² [prəˈʊgres, *Am:* proʊ-] *vi* **1.** (*improve*) progresar **2.** (*continue onward*) avanzar; **to** ~ **to sth** evolucionar hacia algo

progression [prəˈgreʃən] *n no pl* **1.** (*development*) desarrollo *m;* (*of disease*) evolución *f* **2.** MAT (*series*) progresión *f*

progressive [prəˈgresɪv] **I.** *adj* **1.** (*by successive stages*) progresivo, -a; (*disease*) degenerativo, -a **2.** POL progresista **3.** (*modern*) moderno, -a **4.** MUS de vanguardia; (*jazz*) experimental **5.** LING continuo, -a **II.** *n* **1.** POL progresista *mf* **2.** LING (*verb form*) tiempo *m* continuo

prohibit [prəˈhɪbɪt, *Am:* proʊ'-] *vt* **1.** (*forbid*) prohibir; **to be ~ed by law** estar prohibido por ley **2.** (*prevent*) impedir

prohibition [ˌprəʊɪˈbɪʃən, *Am:* ˌproʊ-] *n* **1.** (*ban*) prohibición *f* **2.** *Brit* LAW acto *m* de inhibición **3.** *Am* HIST **the Prohibition** la Ley Seca

prohibitive [prəˈhɪbətɪv, *Am:* proʊˈhɪbətɪv] *adj* prohibitivo, -a

project¹ [ˈprɒdʒekt, *Am:* ˈprɑːdʒekt] *n* **1.** (*undertaking, plan*) proyecto *m* **2.** SCHOOL, UNIV (*essay*) trabajo *m*

project² [prəˈʊdʒekt, *Am:* prə-] **I.** *vt* **1.** (*forecast*) pronosticar; **to be ~ed to do sth** estar previsto para hacer algo **2.** (*propel*) impulsar; **to** ~ **one's mind into the future** lanzar la mente al futuro **3.** PSYCH proyectar; **to** ~ **sth onto sb** proyectar algo en alguien **4.** (*promote*) promover; **to** ~ **oneself** promocionarse **II.** *vi* sobresalir

projectile [prəˈʊdʒektaɪl, *Am:* prəˈdʒektəl] *n* proyectil *m*

projection [prəˈʊdʒekʃən, *Am:* prə-] *n* **1.** (*forecast*) pronóstico *m* **2.** (*protrusion*) saliente *m;* (*of rock*) prominencia *f* **3.** *no pl* PSYCH proyección *f*

projectionist *n* proyeccionista *mf*

project management *n* dirección *f* de proyectos **project manager** *n* director(a) de proyectos *m*

projector [prəˈdʒektəʳ, *Am:* -ˈdʒektə-] *n* proyector *m*

prolapse [ˈprəʊlæps, *Am:* ˈproʊ-] *n* MED prolapso *m*

prole [prəʊl, *Am:* proʊl] *adj, n inf, pej abbr of* **proletarian** proletario, -a *m, f;* **the ~s** el proletariado

proletarian [ˌprəʊlɪˈteəriən, *Am:* ˌproʊlə-ˈteri-] **I.** *adj* proletario, -a **II.** *n* proletario, -a *m, f*

proletariat [ˌprəʊlɪˈteəriət, *Am:* ˌproʊləˈte-ri-] *n no pl* proletariado *m*

proliferate [prəˈlɪfəreɪt, *Am:* proʊ'-] *vi* proliferar

proliferation [prəˌlɪfəˈreɪʃən, *Am:* proʊ-] *n no pl* proliferación *f*

prolific [prə'lɪfɪk, Am: proʊ'-] adj **1.** (producing a lot) prolífico, -a **2.** (having many offspring) fecundo, -a

prolix ['prəʊlɪks, Am: proʊ'lɪks] adj pej, form prolijo, -a

prologue n Brit, **prolog** ['prəʊlɒg, Am: 'proʊlɑːg] n Am **1.** (introduction) prólogo m; (play) presentación f **2.** fig, inf (preliminary event) preludio m; **to be a ~ to sth** ser un preámbulo de algo

prolong [prə'lɒŋ, Am: proʊ'lɑːŋ] vt prolongar; (agony) alargar

prolongation [ˌprəʊlɒŋ'geɪʃən, Am: ˌproʊlɑːŋ'-] n no pl prolongación f

prom [prɒm, Am: prɑːm] n **1.** Am (school dance) baile m **2.** Brit (concert) concierto m (en el que parte del público está de pie) **3.** Brit (seafront) paseo m marítimo

promenade [ˌprɒmə'nɑːd, Am: ˌprɑːmə'neɪd] I. n **1.** Brit (seafront) paseo m marítimo **2.** form (walk) paseo m II. vi pasearse

promenade concert n Brit concierto m (en el que parte del público está de pie) **promenade deck** n cubierta f de paseo

prominence ['prɒmɪnəns, Am: 'prɑːmə-] n no pl **1.** (conspicuousness) prominencia f; **to give ~ to sth** hacer resaltar algo **2.** (importance) importancia f; **to gain ~** ganar trascendencia

prominent ['prɒmɪnənt, Am: 'prɑːmə-] adj **1.** (conspicuous) prominente; **to put sth in a ~ position** poner algo en una buena posición **2.** (teeth, chin) saliente **3.** (distinguished, well-known) importante; (position) destacado, -a; **to be ~ in sth** desempeñar un papel importante en algo

promiscuity [ˌprɒmɪ'skjuːəti, Am: ˌprɑːmɪ'skjuːəṭi] n no pl promiscuidad f

promiscuous [prə'mɪskjuəs] adj pej promiscuo, -a

promise ['prɒmɪs, Am: 'prɑːmɪs] I. vt (pledge, have potential) prometer; **to ~ to do sth** prometer hacer algo II. vi (pledge) prometer; **I ~!** ¡lo prometo! III. n **1.** (pledge) promesa f; **to make a ~** prometer **2.** no pl (potential) posibilidad f; **a young person of ~** un joven de porvenir; **to show ~** demostrar aptitudes; **to fulfil one's ~** satisfacer las esperanzas

promising adj prometedor(a)

promissory note ['prɒmɪsəriˌnəʊt, Am: 'prɑːmɪsɔːriˌnoʊt] n pagaré m

promo ['prəʊməʊ, Am: 'proʊmoʊ] n inf s. **promotion** promoción f

promontory ['prɒməntəri, Am: 'prɑːməntɔːr-] <-ies> n GEO promontorio m

promote [prə'məʊt, Am: -'moʊt] vt **1.** (in army, company, organization) ascender; (soccer team) subir **2.** (encourage) promover **3.** (advertise) promocionar

promoter n promotor(a) m(f)

promotion [prə'məʊʃən, Am: -'moʊ-] n **1.** (in army, company, organization) ascenso

m; **to get a ~** subir en el escalafón **2.** (encouragement, advertising) promoción f; **sales ~** promoción de ventas

promotional material [prə'məʊʃənəl mə'tɪəriəl, Am: prə'moʊʃənəl mə'tɪriəl] n material m de promoción

prompt [prɒmpt, Am: prɑːmpt] I. vt **1.** (spur) provocar; **to ~ sb to do sth** estimular a alguien para que haga algo **2.** THEAT apuntar II. adj (quick) rápido, -a; (action) inmediato, -a; (delivery) sin demora; **to be ~** ser puntual III. adv puntualmente IV. n **1.** INFOR línea f de comandos **2.** THEAT (prompter) apuntador(a) m(f); **to give sb a ~** apuntar a alguien

prompt box <-es> n THEAT concha f del apuntador

prompter ['prɒmptər, Am: 'prɑːmptɚ] n THEAT apuntador(a) m(f)

promptitude ['prɒmptɪtjuːd, Am: 'prɑːmptɪtuːd] n no pl, form prontitud f

promptly ['prɒmptli, Am: 'prɑːmpt-] adv **1.** (quickly) rápidamente **2.** inf (immediately afterward) puntualmente

promptness ['prɒmptnɪs, Am: 'prɑːmpt-] n no pl s. **promptitude**

promulgate ['prɒmlgeɪt, Am: 'prɑːml-] vt form **1.** (theory, belief) divulgar **2.** LAW promulgar

promulgation [ˌprɒml'geɪʃən, Am: ˌprɑːml'-] n no pl, form **1.** (of theory, belief) divulgación f **2.** LAW promulgación f

prone [prəʊn, Am: proʊn] I. adj **to be ~ to do sth** ser propenso a hacer algo II. adv form boca abajo

prong [prɒŋ, Am: prɑːŋ] n (of fork) diente m; (of antler) punta f

pronominal [prəʊ'nɒmɪnl, Am: proʊ'nɑːmə-] adj LING pronominal

pronoun ['prəʊnaʊn, Am: 'proʊ-] n LING pronombre m

pronounce [prə'naʊns] vt **1.** (speak) pronunciar **2.** (declare) declarar; (judgement) dictaminar; **to ~ that ...** afirmar que...

pronounceable adj pronunciable

pronounced adj pronunciado, -a; (accent) marcado, -a

pronouncement [prə'naʊntsmənt, Am: 'prə-] n declaración f; **to make a ~** pronunciarse; (pass judgement) hacer un dictamen

pronto ['prɒntəʊ, Am: 'prɑːnṭoʊ] adv inf enseguida

pronunciation [prəˌnʌntsɪ'eɪʃən] n LING no pl pronunciación f

proof [pruːf] I. n **1.** no pl a. LAW prueba f; **~ of sth** comprobación f de algo; **the burden of ~** el peso de la demostración **2.** no pl (test) examen m **3.** TYPO prueba f de imprenta **4.** MAT prueba f matemática ▶**the ~ of the pudding is in the eating** prov no se sabe si algo es bueno hasta que no se prueba II. adj **1.** (impervious) inmune; **to be ~ against burglars** estar a prueba de ladrones **2.** (alcoholic strength) de graduación III. vt impermeabilizar

proofread ['pru:f,ri:d] *irr* TYPO, PUBL **I.** *vt* corregir **II.** *vi* corregir pruebas

proofreader *n* corrector(a) *m(f)* de pruebas

proofreading *n no pl* corrección *f* de pruebas

prop¹ [prɒp, *Am:* prɑ:p] *n* **1.** (*support*) apoyo *m* **2.** THEAT objeto *m* de atrezzo

prop² [prɒp, *Am:* prɑ:p] *n* **1.** ECON *abbr of* **proprietor** propietario, -a *m, f* **2.** AVIAT *abbr of* **propeller** hélice *f*

propaganda [ˌprɒpə'gændə, *Am:* ˌprɑ:-pə'-] *n no pl* propaganda *f*

propagandist [ˌprɒpə'gændɪst, *Am:* ˌprɑ:-pə'-] **I.** *n* propagandista *mf* **II.** *adj* propagandístico, -a

propagate ['prɒpəgeɪt, *Am:* 'prɑ:pə-] **I.** *vt* **1.** BOT propagar **2.** (*disseminate: lie, rumour*) difundir **II.** *vi* propagarse

propagation [ˌprɒpə'geɪʃən, *Am:* ˌprɑ:-pə'-] *n no pl* **1.** BOT propagación *f* **2.** (*of lies, rumour*) difusión *f*

propane ['prəʊpeɪn, *Am:* 'proʊ-] *n no pl* propano *m*

propel [prə'pel] <-ll-> *vt* propulsar

propellant [prə'pelənt] *n* propelente *m*

propeller [prə'pelər, *Am:* -ɚ] *n* hélice *f*

propeller shaft *n* TECH árbol *m* de transmisión

propelling pencil *n Brit, Aus* (lápiz *m*) portaminas *m inv*

propensity [prə'pensəti, *Am:* -t̬i] *n no pl, form* propensión *f*; **to have a ~ to do sth** tener tendencia a hacer algo

proper ['prɒpər, *Am:* 'prɑ:pə] **I.** *adj* **1.** (*real*) verdadero, -a; **a ~ job** un trabajo como es debido **2.** (*appropriate: time, place, method*) apropiado, -a; (*use*) correcto, -a; **~ meaning** sentido *m* exacto **3.** (*socially respectable*) **to be ~ to do sth** ser debido hacer algo **4.** *form* (*itself*) verdadero, -a; **it's not in London ~** no está en Londres propiamente dicho **5.** *Brit, inf* (*total*) completo, -a; **I felt a ~ idiot** me sentí un verdadero idiota **II.** *adv Brit, inf* **1.** (*very*) muy **2.** *iron* (*genteelly*) como Dios manda

proper fraction *n* MAT fracción *f* propia

properly ['prɒpəli, *Am:* 'prɑ:pə·li] *adv* **1.** (*correctly*) correctamente; **~ speaking** hablando como es debido; **~ dressed** vestido apropiadamente **2.** (*behave*) como es debido **3.** (*politely*) educadamente **4.** *Brit* (*thoroughly*) completamente

proper name *n*, **proper noun** *n* nombre *m* propio

propertied *adj* ECON adinerado, -a

property ['prɒpəti, *Am:* 'prɑ:pə·ti] <-ies> *n* **1.** *no pl* (*possession*) propiedad *f*; LAW (*house, land*) bien *m* inmueble; **a man of ~** un hombre adinerado; **private ~** propiedad privada **2.** (*house*) inmueble *m*; (*land*) terreno *m* **3.** (*attribute*) atributo *m* ▸**a hot ~** un gran éxito

property developer *n* ECON promotor(a) *m(f)* inmobiliario **property development** *n* ECON promoción *f* inmobiliaria **property**

insurance *n no pl* seguro *m* de la propiedad **property man** *n*, **property manager** *n* THEAT encargado *m* del atrezzo **property market** *n no pl* mercado *m* inmobiliario **property owner** *n* propietario, -a *m, f* **property room** *n* THEAT habitación *f* del atrezzo **property speculation** *n no pl* ECON especulación *f* inmobiliaria **property tax** *n* impuesto *m* sobre la propiedad

prophecy ['prɒfəsi, *Am:* 'prɑ:fə-] <-ies> *pl n* profecía *f*

prophesy ['prɒfɪsaɪ, *Am:* 'prɑ:fə-] <-ie-> **I.** *vt* (*predict*) predecir; REL profetizar **II.** *vi* profetizar

prophet ['prɒfɪt, *Am:* 'prɑ:fɪt] *n* **1.** REL profeta, -isa *m, f* **2.** (*person who foretells events*) adivino, -a *m, f*; **~ of doom** catastrofista *mf*

prophetess ['prɒfɪtes, *Am:* 'prɑ:fɪtəs] *n* profetisa *f*

prophetic [prə'fetɪk] *adj* profético, -a

prophylactic [ˌprɒfɪ'læktɪk, *Am:* ˌproʊfə'-] **I.** *adj* MED profiláctico, -a **II.** *n* **1.** (*preventive medicine*) (fármaco *m*) profiláctico *m* **2.** (*condom*) condón *m*

prophylaxis [prɒfɪ'læksɪs, *Am:* ˌproʊfə'-] *no pl* MED profilaxis *f*

propinquity [prə'pɪŋkwəti, *Am:* proʊ-'pɪŋkwət̬i] *n no pl, form* **1.** (*proximity*) proximidad *f* **2.** (*kinship*) parentesco *m*

propitious [prə'pɪʃəs] *adj form* favorable

prop jet *n* turbohélice *f*

proponent [prə'pəʊnənt, *Am:* -'poʊ-] *n* defensor(a) *m(f)*

proportion [prə'pɔ:ʃən, *Am:* -'pɔ:r-] *n* **1.** (*relationship*) proporción *f*; **the ~ of A to B** el porcentaje entre A y B; **to be out of ~ to sth** estar desproporcionado con algo; **to be in ~ to sth** estar en proporción con algo; **to keep a sense of ~** mantener un sentido de la medida; **to blow sth out of (all) ~** exagerar algo desmesuradamente **2.** (*part*) parte *f* proporcional **3.** *pl* (*size*) dimensiones *fpl*; **a building of gigantic ~s** un edificio de grandes medidas

proportional [prə'pɔ:ʃənəl, *Am:* -'pɔ:r-] *adj* proporcional; **inversely ~** inversamente proporcional

proportionality [prəˌpɔ:ʃən'ælɪti, *Am:* -ˌpɔ:rʃənælət̬i] *n no pl* proporcionalidad *f*

proportional representation *n no pl* POL representación *f* proporcional

proportionate [prə'pɔ:ʃənət, *Am:* -'pɔ:r-ʃənɪt] *adj s.* **proportional**

proportioned *adj* **well ~** bien proporcionado; **to be generously ~** *iron* estar muy bien hecho

proposal [prə'pəʊzəl, *Am:* -'poʊ-] *n* **1.** (*firm suggestion*) propuesta *f*; **to put forward a ~** presentar una proposición; **peace ~** propuesta *f* de paz **2.** (*offer of marriage*) declaración *f*; **to make a marriage ~** hacer una petición de mano

propose [prə'pəʊz, *Am:* -'poʊz] **I.** *vt* **1.** (*put* *forward*) proponer; **to ~ a toast** proponer un brindis **2.**(*intend*) **to ~ to do sth** tener la intención de hacer algo **3.**(*nominate*) nombrar **II.** *vi* (*marriage*) **to ~** (**to sb**) declararse (a alguien) ▶**man ~s, God disposes** *prov* el hombre propone y Dios dispone *prov*

proposer [prə'pəʊzə', *Am:* -'pəʊzə'] *n* **1.**(*suggestor*) autor(a) *m(f)* de una moción **2.**(*nominator*) proponente *mf*

proposition [ˌprɒpə'zɪʃən, *Am:* ˌprɑːpə'-] **I.** *n* **1.**(*theory, argument*) proposición *f* **2.**(*business*) ofrecimiento *m* **3.**(*suggestion*) sugerencia *f* **II.** *vt* hacer proposiciones deshonestas a

propound [prə'paʊnd] *vt form* proponer

proprietary [prə'praɪətri, *Am:* -teri] *adj* **1.**(*owning property*) propietario, -a **2.** ECON (*name, brand*) registrado, -a; (*article*) patentado, -a

proprietor [prə'praɪətə', *Am:* prəʊ'praɪətə'] *n* propietario, -a *m, f;* (*of business*) dueño, -a *m, f*

proprietorship *n* propiedad *f*

proprietress [prə'praɪətrɪs, *Am:* prəʊ'-] *n* propietaria *f*

propriety [prə'praɪəti, *Am:* -ti̦] <-ies> *n* **1.** *no pl* (*correctness*) corrección *f* **2.**(*standard of conduct*) **the proprieties** convenciones *fpl* sociales; **to observe the proprieties** atenerse al decoro

propulsion [prə'pʌlʃən] *n no pl* propulsión *f*

pro rata [ˌprəʊ'rɑːtə, *Am:* ˌprəʊ'reɪțə] **I.** *adj* prorrateado, -a **II.** *adv* proporcionalmente

prorate *vt*, **pro-rate** [prəʊ'reɪt] *vt Am* prorratear

prorogation [ˌprəʊrəʊ'geɪʃən, *Am:* ˌprəʊrəʊ'-] *n* POL prorrogación *f*

prorogue [prəʊ'rəʊg, *Am:* prəʊ'rəʊg] *vt* prorrogar

prosaic [prə'zeɪɪk, *Am:* prəʊ'-] *adj form* prosaico, -a

proscenium [prə'siːnɪəm, *Am:* prəʊ'-] <-s *o* proscenia> *n* THEAT proscenio *m*

proscribe [prə'skraɪb, *Am:* prəʊ'-] *vt* proscribir

proscription [prə'skrɪpʃən, *Am:* prəʊ'-] *n no pl, form* proscripción *f*

prose [prəʊz, *Am:* prəʊz] *n no pl* prosa *f*

prosecutable [ˌprɒsɪ'kjuːtəbl] *adj* LAW procesable

prosecute ['prɒsɪkjuːt, *Am:* 'prɑːsɪ-] **I.** *vt* **1.** LAW **to ~ sb** (**for sth**) procesar a alguien (por algo) **2.** *form* (*pursue, follow up*) proseguir; (*studies*) sacar adelante **II.** *vi* interponer

prosecuting *adj* acusador(a)

prosecuting attorney *n Am* fiscal *mf*

prosecution [ˌprɒsɪ'kjuːʃən, *Am:* ˌprɑːsɪ-] *n* **1.** *no pl* LAW (*proceedings*) proceso *m* **2.** *no pl* LAW (*the prosecuting party*) **the ~** la acusación; **witness for the ~** testigo *mf* de cargo **3.** *form* (*of campaign, inquiry*) seguimiento *m*

prosecutor ['prɒsɪkjuːtə', *Am:* 'prɑːsɪkjuː-țə'] *n* LAW fiscal *mf*

proselyte ['prɒsəlaɪt, *Am:* 'prɑːsə-] *n* REL prosélito, -a *m, f*

proselytise *vi*, **proselytize** ['prɒsəlɪtaɪz, *Am:* 'prɑːsəlɪ-] *vi* hacer proselitismo

prosody ['prɒsədi, *Am:* 'prɑːsə-] *n no pl* prosodia *f*

prospect ['prɒspekt, *Am:* 'prɑːspekt] **I.** *n* **1.**(*possibility*) posibilidad *f;* **the ~ of sth** la probabilidad de algo **2.** *pl* (*chances*) perspectivas *fpl* **3.** *liter* (*view*) panorama *m;* **a ~ of/over sth** una vista de/sobre algo **4.** ECON (*potential customer*) posible cliente *m*, posible clienta *f;* (*potential employee*) candidato, -a *m, f* **II.** *vi* MIN buscar

prospective [prə'spektɪv] *adj* posible; (*candidat*) futuro, -a

prospector [prɒ'spektə', *Am:* 'prɑːspektə'] *n* MIN prospector(a) *m(f);* (*gold*) cateador(a) *m(f)*

prospectus [prə'spektəs] *n* prospecto *m;* UNIV folleto *m* informativo

prosper ['prɒspə', *Am:* 'prɑːspə'] *vi* prosperar

prosperity [prɒ'sperəti, *Am:* prɑː'sperəți] *n no pl* prosperidad *f*

prosperous ['prɒspərəs, *Am:* 'prɑːspə-] *adj* próspero, -a; (*business*) exitoso, -a

prostate (**gland**) ['prɒsteɪt-, *Am:* 'prɑːsteɪt-] *n* próstata *f*

prostitute ['prɒstɪtjuːt, *Am:* 'prɑːstətuːt] **I.** *n* prostituta *f* **II.** *vt a. fig* **to ~ oneself** prostituirse; **to ~ one's talents** prostituir su talento

prostitution [ˌprɒstɪ'tjuːʃən, *Am:* -'tʃuː-] *n no pl* prostitución *f*

prostrate ['prɒstreɪt, *Am:* 'prɑːstreɪt] **I.** *adj a. fig* postrado, -a; **to be ~ with grief** estar abatido por el dolor **II.** *vt* **to ~ oneself** postrarse

protagonist [prə'tægənɪst, *Am:* prəʊ'-] *n* **1.**(*main character*) protagonista *mf* **2.**(*advocate*) defensor(a) *m(f);* **to be a ~ of sth** luchar por algo

protect [prə'tekt] *vt* proteger; (*one's interests*) salvaguardar; **to ~ oneself** resguardarse

protection [prə'tekʃən] *n no pl* protección *f;* **to be under sb's ~** estar bajo la protección de alguien

protection factor *n* factor *m* de protección

protectionism [prə'tekʃənɪzəm] *n no pl, pej* proteccionismo *m*

protectionist *adj pej* proteccionista

protection racket *n* chantaje *m* (*practicado a propietarios de comercios*)

protective [prə'tektɪv] *adj* **1.**(*affording protection*) proteccionista; **~ custody** detención *f* preventiva **2.**(*wishing to protect*) protector(a)

protector [prə'tektə', *Am:* -ə'] *n* **1.**(*person*) protector(a) *m(f)* **2.**(*device*) aparato *m* protector

protectorate [prə'tektərət, *Am:* -ɪt] *n* protectorado *m*

protégé(e) ['prɒtɪʒeɪ, *Am:* 'prəʊțəʒeɪ] *n* *m(f)* protegido, -a *m, f*

protein ['prəʊtiːn, Am: 'proʊ-] n proteína f;
~ **deficiency** deficiencia f proteínica

protest[1] ['prəʊtest, Am: 'proʊtest] n
1. (complaint) protesta f; **in** ~ en señal de protesta; **to do sth under** ~ hacer algo que conste
como protesta 2. (demonstration) manifestación f de protesta

protest[2] [prə'test, Am: proʊ'-] I. vi protestar;
to ~ **about/against sth** protestar por/en
contra de algo II. vt 1. (solemnly affirm) **to** ~
that ... declarar que...; **to** ~ **one's innocence** afirmar su inocencia 2. Am (show dissent) protestar en contra de

Protestant ['prɒtɪstənt, Am: 'prɑːtə-] n
protestante mf

Protestantism n no pl protestantismo m

protestation [ˌprɒtesˈteɪʃən, Am: ˌprɑːtesˈ-
'teɪ-] n pl 1. (strong objection) protesta f
2. (strong affirmation) afirmación f

protester n manifestante mf

protest march n marcha f de protesta **protest vote** n voto m de protesta

protocol ['prəʊtəkɒl, Am: 'proʊtəkɔːl] n
protocolo m

proton ['prəʊtɒn, Am: 'proʊtɑːn] n protón
m

protoplasm ['prəʊtəplæzəm, Am: 'proʊ-
tə-] n no pl protoplasma m

prototype ['prəʊtətaɪp, Am: 'proʊtə-] n
prototipo m

protozoan [ˌprəʊtəˈzəʊən, Am: ˌproʊtə-
ˈzoʊ-] <-s o -zoa> n protozoo m

protract [prə'trækt, Am: proʊ'-] vt form prolongar

protracted [prə'træktɪd, Am: proʊ'-] adj
prolongado, -a

protraction [prə'trækʃən, Am: proʊ'-] n
1. no pl (prolonging) prolongación f 2. ANAT
(muscle action) extensión f

protractor [prə'træktər, Am: proʊ'-] n
(angle measuring device) transportador m

protrude [prə'truːd, Am: proʊ'-] vi sobresalir

protruding [prə'truːdɪŋ, Am: proʊ'-] adj
prominente; (ears) que sobresale

protrusion [prə'truːʒən, Am: proʊ'-] n protuberancia f

protuberance [prə'tjuːbərəns, Am: proʊ-
'tuː-] adj form protuberancia f

protuberant [prə'tjuːbərənt, Am: proʊ-
'tuː-] adj form protuberante; (eyes) saltón,
-ona

proud [praʊd] I. adj 1. (pleased) orgulloso,
-a; **to be** ~ **of sth/sb** enorgullecerse de algo/
alguien; **to be** ~ **to do sth** tener el honor de
hacer algo; **to be** ~ **that** ... estar orgulloso de
que... 2. (having self-respect) digno, -a 3. pej
(arrogant) arrogante 4. Brit (protruding) **to
stand** ~ sobresalir II. adv **to do sb** ~ Aus, Brit
ser motivo de orgullo para alguien

proudly adv orgullosamente

provable ['pruːvəbl] adj demostrable

prove [pruːv] <proved o Am: proven> I. vt

(verify: theory) probar; (innocence, loyalty)
demostrar; **to** ~ **oneself** (**to be**) **sth** demostrarse (ser) algo; **to** ~ **sb innocent** probar la
inocencia de alguien II. vi (be established)
resultar; **to** ~ **to be sth** resultar ser algo

proven ['pruːvən] I. vi, vt Am, Scot pp of
prove II. adj (verified) comprobado, -a

provenance ['prɒvənənts, Am: 'prɑːvən-]
n no pl, form procedencia f

provender ['prɒvɪndər, Am: 'prɑːvəndər] n
1. AGR forraje m 2. iron, inf (sustenance) provisiones fpl

proverb ['prɒvɜːb, Am: 'prɑːvɜːrb] n refrán
m, proverbio m; **as the** ~ **goes** ... como dice
el proverbio...

proverbial [prə'vɜːbiəl, Am: prə'vɜːr-] adj
proverbial

provide [prəʊ'vaɪd, Am: prə-] vt 1. proveer;
to ~ **sb with sth** proporcionar algo a alguien
2. form LAW estipular

provided conj ~ **that** ... con tal que... +subj

providence ['prɒvɪdənts, Am: 'prɑːvə-] n
no pl providencia f; **divine** ~ REL Divina Providencia

providential [ˌprɒvɪ'dentʃəl, Am: ˌprɑːvə'-]
adj form providencial

provider n 1. (person) proveedor(a) m(f)
2. INFOR proveedor m; **Internet Service** ~ proveedor de servicios Internet

providing conj ~ (**that**) ... con tal que...
+subj

province ['prɒvɪnts, Am: 'prɑːvɪnts] n
1. POL, ADMIN provincia f 2. no pl (branch of a
subject) campo m

provincial [prəʊ'vɪntʃəl, Am: prə'vɪntʃəl]
I. adj 1. POL, ADMIN provincial 2. pej (unsophisticated) provinciano, -a II. n (person from
provinces) provinciano, -a m, f

proving ground n terreno m de pruebas

provision [prəʊ'vɪʒən, Am: prə-] I. n 1. (act
of providing) suministro m 2. (thing provided)
provisión f 3. (preparation) previsiones fpl; **to
make** ~ **for sth** tomar medidas de previsión
para algo 4. LAW (in will, contract) disposición f
II. vt abastecer

provisional [prəʊ'vɪʒənəl, Am: prə-] adj
provisional

provisional driving licence n Aus, Brit
permiso m de conducción provisional

proviso [prə'vaɪzəʊ, Am: prə'vaɪzoʊ] <-s>
n (stipulation) condición f; **with the** ~ **that**
... con la condición de que +subj

provocation [ˌprɒvəˈkeɪʃən, Am: ˌprɑːvə'-]
n provocación f

provocative [prə'vɒkətɪv, Am: -'vɑːkətɪv]
adj 1. (causing anger) provocador(a) 2. (sexually) provocativo, -a

provoke [prə'vəʊk, Am: -'voʊk] vt 1. (make
angry) provocar; **to** ~ **sb into doing sth** provocar a alguien para que haga algo 2. (discussion) motivar; (interest) despertar; (crisis)
causar

provoking adj (irritating) irritante

P

provost ['prɒvəst, *Am:* 'proʊvoʊst] *n* **1.** *Brit* UNIV rector(a) *m(f)* **2.** *Scot* POL alcalde(sa) *m(f)*

prow [praʊ] *n* NAUT proa *f*

prowess ['praʊɪs] *n no pl, form* destreza *f;* (*sexual, sporting*) proeza *f*

prowl [praʊl] I. *n inf* to be on the ~ estar merodeando II. *vt* vagar por; to ~ the streets for victims merodear por las calles en busca de víctimas III. *vi* to ~ (about, around) rondar (por)

prowl car *n Am* coche-patrulla *m*

prowler *n* merodeador(a) *m(f)*

prowling *n* merodeo *m*

proximity [prɒk'sɪməti, *Am:* pra:k'sɪməţi] *n no pl, form* proximidad *f;* to be in (close) ~ to sth estar cerca de algo

proxy ['prɒksi, *Am:* 'pra:k-] <-ies> *n* apoderado, -a *m, f;* to do sth by ~ hacer algo por poderes

prude [pru:d] *n pej* mojigato, -a *m, f*

prudence ['prudns] *n no pl* prudencia *f*

prudent ['pru:dnt] *adj* prudente

prudery ['pru:dəri] <-ies> *n pej* mojigatería *f*

prudish ['pru:dɪʃ] *adj pej* mojigato, -a

prune¹ [pru:n] *vt* podar; to ~ (back) costs reducir gastos

prune² [pru:n] *n* (*dried plum*) ciruela *f* pasa

pruning *n* poda *f*

pruning hook *n* podadera *f* **pruning saw** *n* serrucho *m* de podar **pruning shears** *npl Am* BOT tijeras *fpl* de podar

prurience ['prʊərɪəns, *Am:* 'prʊrɪ-] *n no pl, pej, form* lascivia *f*

prurient ['prʊərɪənt, *Am:* 'prʊrɪ-] *adj pej, form* lascivo, -a

Prussia ['prʌʃə] *n* HIST, POL, GEO Prusia *f*

Prussian ['prʌʃən] I. *n* HIST prusiano, -a *m, f* II. *adj* prusiano, -a

prussic acid [ˌprʌsɪk'æsɪd] *n no pl* ácido *m* prúsico

pry¹ [praɪ] <-pries, pried> *vi pej* (*be nosy*) husmear; to ~ into sth entrometerse en algo; to ~ about curiosear

pry² [praɪ] *vt s.* **prize²**

prying ['praɪɪŋ] *adj* fisgón, -ona; ~ eyes miradas *fpl* indiscretas

PS [ˌpiː'es] *abbr of* postscript P.D.

psalm [sɑːm] *n* REL salmo *m*

psephology [se'fɒlədʒi, *Am:* si:'faːlə-] *n* análisis *m* electoral

pseud [sjuːd, *Am:* suːd] *n Brit, inf* intelectualoide *mf*

pseudo ['sjuːdəʊ, *Am:* 'suːdoʊ] *adj* falso, -a

pseudointellectual I. *n* pseudointelectual *mf* II. *adj* pseudointelectual

pseudonym ['sjuːdənɪm, *Am:* 'suː-] *n* seudónimo *m*

psittacosis [ˌsɪtə'kəʊsɪs, *Am:* -'koʊ-] *n* psitacosis *f inv*

PSV *n abbr of* **public service vehicle** vehículo *m* de servicio público

psych(e) up ['saɪk] *vt inf* to **psych(e)** one-

self up mentalizarse; to **psych(e) sb up** mentalizar a alguien

psyche ['saɪki] *n* psique *f*

psychedelic [ˌsaɪkɪ'delɪk, *Am:* -kə'-] *adj* psicodélico, -a

psychiatric [ˌsaɪkɪ'ætrɪk] *adj* psiquiátrico, -a

psychiatrist [saɪ'kaɪətrɪst] *n* psiquiatra *mf*

psychiatry [saɪ'kaɪətri] *n no pl* psiquiatría *f*

psychic ['saɪkɪk] I. *adj* **1.** (*occult powers*) parapsicológico, -a **2.** (*of the mind*) psíquico, -a II. *n* vidente *mf*

psychoanalyse [ˌsaɪkəʊ'ænəlaɪz, *Am:* -koʊ'-] *vt* psicoanalizar

psychoanalysis [ˌsaɪkəʊə'næləsɪs, *Am:* -koʊə'-] *n no pl* psicoanálisis *m inv*

psychoanalyst [ˌsaɪkəʊ'ænəlɪst, *Am:* -koʊ'-] *n* psicoanalista *mf*

psychoanalytic(al) [ˌsaɪkəʊˌænəl'ɪtɪk(əl), *Am:* -koʊˌænə'lɪţɪk(əl)] *adj* psicoanalítico, -a

psychoanalyze [ˌsaɪkəʊ'ænəlaɪz, *Am:* -koʊ'ænəlaɪz] *vt Am s.* **psychoanalyse**

psychological [ˌsaɪkə'lɒdʒɪkəl, *Am:* -kə-'laːdʒɪ-] *adj* psicológico, -a

psychologist *n* psicólogo, -a *m, f*

psychology [saɪ'kɒlədʒi, *Am:* -'kaːlə-] <-ies> *n* (*science, mentality*) psicología *f*

psychopath ['saɪkəʊpæθ, *Am:* -kəpæθ] *n* psicópata *mf*

psychopathic [ˌsaɪkəʊ'pæθɪk, *Am:* ˌsaɪkə'-] *adj* psicopático, -a

psychosis [saɪ'kəʊsɪs, *Am:* -'koʊ-] <-ses> *n* psicosis *f inv*

psychosomatic [ˌsaɪkəʊsə'mætɪk, *Am:* -koʊsoʊ'mæţ-] *adj* psicosomático, -a

psychotherapist [ˌsaɪkə'θerəpɪst, *Am:* -koʊ'-] *n* psicoterapeuta *mf*

psychotherapy [ˌsaɪkəʊ'θerəpi, *Am:* -koʊ'-] *n no pl* psicoterapia *f*

psychotic [saɪ'kɒtɪk, *Am:* -'kaːţɪk] I. *adj* psicótico, -a II. *n* psicótico, -a *m, f*

PT [ˌpiː'tiː] *n* **1.** *abbr of* **physical therapy** fisioterapia *f* **2.** *abbr of* **physical training** educación *f* física

pt *n* **1.** *abbr of* **part** parte *f* **2.** *abbr of* **pint** pinta *f* (≈ *0,67 litros, Am:* ≈ *0,47 litros*) **3.** *abbr of* **point** punto *m*

ptarmigan ['taːmɪgən, *Am:* 'taːrmɪ-] *n* perdiz *f* blanca

pto *abbr of* **please turn over** ver al dorso

PTO [ˌpiːtiː'əʊ, *Am:* -'oʊ] *n abbr of* **Parent-teacher Organisation** asociación *f* de padres y maestros

pub [pʌb] *n Aus, Brit, inf* bar *m*

pub crawl *n inf* to go on a ~ ir de bar en bar tomando copas

puberty ['pjuːbəti, *Am:* -bəţi] *n no pl* pubertad *f*

pubic ['pjuːbɪk] *adj* pubiano, -a, púbico, -a

pubis ['pjuːbɪs] <-es> *n* pubis *m inv*

public ['pʌblɪk] I. *adj* **1.** (*of/for the people, provided by the state*) público, -a **2.** (*done openly*) abierto, -a; to go ~ with sth revelar algo II. *n* **1.** (*people collectively, audience*)

público *m;* in ~ en público **2.**(*ordinary people*) gente *f* de la calle
public accountant *n Am* contable *mf* público, -a, contador(a) *m(f)* público, -a **public address** (**system**) *n* sistema *m* de megafonía **public affairs** *npl* asuntos *mpl* públicos
publican ['pʌblɪkən] *n Aus, Brit* tabernero, -a *m, f*
public appearance *n* aparición *f* pública
public appointment *n* designación *f* pública **public assistance** *n Am* ayuda *f* estatal
publication [,pʌblɪ'keɪʃən] *n no pl* publicación *f*
public authority *n* **1.**(*state authority*) autoridad *f* estatal **2.**(*department, authority*) departamento *m* público **public bar** *n Brit* bar *m* **public convenience** *n Aus, Brit, form* aseos *mpl* públicos **public defender** *n Am* LAW defensor(a) *m(f)* de oficio **public domain** *n* dominio *m* público **public enemy** *n* enemigo, -a *m, f* público, -a **public expenditure** *n,* **public expense** *n* ADMIN, POL, ECON gastos *mpl* estatales **public funds** *npl* POL, ADMIN, FIN, ECON fondos *mpl* públicos
public health *n no pl* MED, ADMIN sanidad *f* pública **public health service** *n* servicio *m* sanitario
public holiday *n* fiesta *f* oficial **public house** *n Brit, form* bar *m* **public information officer** *n* funcionario, -a *m, f* de información pública **public interest** *n* interés *m* público
publicist ['pʌblɪsɪst] *n* publicista *mf*
publicity [pʌb'lɪsəti, *Am:* -ti] *n* **1.** *no pl* publicidad *f* **2.**(*attention*) **to attract** ~ atraer la atención ▸**any** ~ **is good** ~ cualquier tipo de promoción es buena
publicity agent *n* agente *mf* de publicidad **publicity campaign** *n* ECON campaña *f* de promoción **publicity department** *n* departamento *m* de promoción **publicity material** *n* material *m* publicitario
publicize ['pʌblɪsaɪz] *vt* promocionar
public law *n* LAW derecho *m* público **public library** <- libraries> *n* biblioteca *f* pública **public limited company** *n* sociedad *f* anónima **public loan** *n* empréstito *m* público
publicly *adv* **1.**(*openly*) en público **2.** ~ **owned** de propiedad pública
public nuisance *n* daño *m* público **public opinion** *n* opinión *f* pública **public property** *n* bienes *mpl* públicos **public prosecution** *n* fiscalía *f* **public prosecutor** *n* fiscal *mf* **public records** *npl* documentos *mpl* públicos
public relations *npl* relaciones *fpl* públicas **public-relations officer** *n* secretario, -a *m, f* de relaciones públicas
public school *n* **1.** *Brit* (*private*) colegio *m* privado **2.** *Am, Aus* (*state-funded*) escuela *f*

pública **public sector** *n* sector *m* público
public-spirited [,pʌblɪk'spɪrɪtɪd, *Am:* -ət̬ɪd] *adj* solidario, -a
public telephone *n* teléfono *m* público **public transport(ation)** *n* transporte *m* público **public utility** *n* empresa *f* de servicios públicos **public works** *npl* ADMIN, POL obras *fpl* públicas
publish ['pʌblɪʃ] *vt* **1.**(*book, author, result*) publicar; (*information*) divulgar **2.** REL **to ~ the banns** correr las amonestaciones
publisher *n* **1.**(*company*) editorial *f* **2.**(*person*) editor(a) *m(f)*
publishing *n no pl, no art* industria *f* editorial
publishing house *n* editorial *f*
puck [pʌk] *n* SPORTS disco *m*
pucker ['pʌkə', *Am:* -ə'] *vt* **to ~ one's lips/brow** fruncir la boca/la frente
pudding ['pʊdɪŋ] *n* **1.**(*dessert*) postre *m;* (*cooked sweet dish*) pudding *mpl* **2.**(*savoury pastry dish*) budín *m*
puddle ['pʌdl] *n* charco *m*
pudenda [pju:'dendə] *npl form* partes *fpl* pudendas
pudgy ['pʊdʒi] <-ier, -iest> *adj* rechoncho, -a
puerile ['pjʊəraɪl, *Am:* 'pju:ərɪl] *adj form* pueril
puerility [,pjʊə'rɪləti, *Am:* ,pju:ə'rɪlət̬i] *n no pl* puerilidad *f*
Puerto Rican ['pwɜːtəʊ'ri:kən, *Am:* ,pwert̬ə'-] I. *n* portorriqueño, -a *m, f* II. *adj* portorriqueño, -a
Puerto Rico ['pwɜːtəʊ'ri:kəʊ, *Am:* ,pwertə'ri:koʊ] *n* Puerto Rico *m*
puff [pʌf] I. *vi* **1.**(*blow*) soplar **2.**(*be out of breath*) jadear II. *vt* **1.**(*smoke*) soplar; (*cigarette smoke*) echar **2.**(*praise*) dar bombo a **3.**(*say while panting*) resoplar III. *n* **1.** *inf* (*breath, wind*) soplo *m;* (*vapour*) soplido *m;* (*of dust, smoke*) bocanada *f;* (*of air*) ráfaga *f* **2.** *Am, Can* (*quilt*) edredón *n* **3.** *Brit, inf* **to be out of** ~ quedarse sin aliento **4.** calada *f;* **to take** ~**s on a cigarette** dar caladas a un cigarro **5.** *inf* (*speech*) bombo *m*
◆**puff out** *vt* **1.**(*expand*) inflar **2.**(*exhaust*) dejar sin aliento
◆**puff up** I. *vt* inflar II. *vi* hincharse
puff adder *n* víbora *f* bufadora
puffball ['pʌfbɔ:l] *n* bejín *m*
puffin ['pʌfɪn] *n* frailecillo *m*
puff pastry *n* hojaldre *m*
puffy ['pʌfi] <-ier, -iest> *adj* hinchado, -a
pug [pʌg] *n* doguillo *m*
pugilism ['pju:dʒɪlɪzəm] *n* boxeo *m*
pugilist ['pju:dʒɪlɪst] *n* boxeador *m*
pugnacious [pʌg'neɪʃəs] *adj form* agresivo, -a
pugnacity [pʌg'næsəti, *Am:* -ti] *n no pl, form* belicosidad *f*
pug nose *n pej* nariz *f* chata
puke [pju:k] *inf* I. *vt* vomitar II. *vi* vomitar; **he makes me** (**want to**) ~! ¡me da asco!

◆**puke up** *inf* I. *vt* to puke sth up vomitar algo II. *vi* vomitar

pukka ['pʌkə] *adj* 1.(*genuine*) genuino, -a 2.(*of good quality*) auténtico, -a

pull [pʊl] I. *vt* 1.(*draw*) tirar de, jalar *AmL*; (*trigger*) apretar 2. *inf* (*take out: gun, knife*) sacar 3. MED (*extract*) sacar; (*tooth*) extraer 4. SPORTS, MED (*strain*) forzar 5.(*attract*) atraer 6. *Aus, Brit, inf* (*sexually*) ligar 7. *Brit* (*pint*) servir ►to ~ **a fast one** *inf* hacer una jugarreta II. *vi* 1.(*exert pulling force*) tirar 2. *inf* (*attract sexual partner*) ligar III. *n* 1.(*act of pulling*) tirón *m*; (*stronger*) jalón *m* 2. *inf* (*influence*) influencia *f* 3.(*knob, handle*) cuerda *f*; (*of a curtain*) tirador *m* 4.(*attraction*) atracción *f*; (*power to attract*) atractivo *m* 5.(*of cigarette, drink*) chupada *f*

◆**pull about** *vt* maltratar

◆**pull ahead** *vi* tomar la delantera

◆**pull apart** *vt insep* 1.(*break into pieces*) separar 2.(*separate using force*) hacer pedazos 3.(*criticize*) poner por el suelo

◆**pull away** I. *vi* (*vehicle*) alejarse II. *vt* arrancar; to pull sth away from sth arrancar algo a algo

◆**pull back** I. *vi* 1.(*move out of the way*) retirarse 2.(*not proceed, back out*) dar marcha atrás II. *vt* retener

◆**pull down** *vt* 1.(*move down*) bajar 2.(*demolish*) tirar abajo 3.(*drag down, hold back*) to pull sb down arrastrar a alguien 4. *Am* (*earn wages*) ganar

◆**pull in** I. *vi* (*vehicle*) llegar II. *vt* 1.(*attract*) atraer 2. *Brit* (*arrest*) detener 3. *Brit, inf* (*earn wages*) ganar

◆**pull off** *vt* 1.(*leave*) arrancar 2. *inf* (*succeed*) lograr; to pull it off lograrlo, vencer

◆**pull out** I. *vi* 1.(*move out to overtake*) salirse; (*drive onto road*) meterse 2.(*leave*) dejar 3.(*withdraw*) retirarse II. *vt* (*take out*) sacar

◆**pull over** I. *vt* 1.(*cause to fall*) volcar 2.(*police*) parar II. *vi* hacerse a un lado

◆**pull round, pull through** I. *vi* reponerse II. *vt* to pull sth round ayudar a algo a reponerse

◆**pull together** I. *vt* 1.(*regain composure*) to pull oneself together recobrar la compostura 2.(*organise, set up*) organizar II. *vi* trabajar conjuntamente

◆**pull up** I. *vt* 1.(*raise*) levantar; (*blinds*) subir 2.(*plant*) arrancar 3. *inf* (*reprimand*) reprender II. *vi* parar

pull-down menu ['pʊldaʊn 'menjuː] *n* INFOR menú *m* desplegable

pullet ['pʊlɪt] *n* polla *f* (*gallina de menos de un año*)

pulley ['pʊli] <-s> *n* TECH polea *f*

Pullman (car) ['pʊlmən (kaːr)] *n* RAIL vagón *m* de lujo

pull-out I. *n* 1. MIL retirada *f* 2. PUBL (*part of magazine*) desplegable *m* II. *adj* desplegable

pullover ['pʊləʊvər, *Am:* -oʊvə·] *n* jersey *m*, suéter *m*

pull-up ['pʊlʌp] *n* (*exercise*) presión *f*

pulmonary ['pʌlmənəri, *Am:* -ner-] *adj* pulmonar

pulp [pʌlp] I. *n* 1.(*soft wet mass*) pasta *f*; (*for making paper*) pulpa *f* de papel; ~ **mill** fábrica *f* de pasta; to beat sb to a ~ *inf* hacer papilla a alguien 2.(*of fruit*) pulpa *f* 3.(*literature*) literatura *f* barata II. *vt* hacer pulpa

pulpit ['pʊlpɪt] *n* REL púlpito *m*

pulsar ['pʌlsaːr, *Am:* -saːr] *n* púlsar *m*

pulsate [pʌl'seɪt, *Am:* 'pʌlseɪt] *vi* palpitar

pulsation [pʌl'seɪʃən] *n* pulsación *f*

pulse¹ [pʌls] I. *n* 1. ANAT pulso *m*; (*heartbeat*) latido *m*; to take sb's ~ tomar el pulso a alguien 2.(*single vibration*) pulsación *f* II. *vi* latir

pulse² [pʌls] *n* GASTR legumbre *f*

pulverize ['pʌlvəraɪz] *vt* pulverizar

puma ['pjuːmə] *n* puma *m*

pumice ['pʌmis] *n* ~ (**stone**) piedra *f* pómez

pummel ['pʌml] <*Brit:* -ll-, *Am:* -l-> *vt* aporrear

pump [pʌmp] I. *n* bomba *f*; (*for fuel*) surtidor *m* II. *vt* bombear

pumpernickel ['pʌmpənɪkl, *Am:* -pə·-] *n no pl* pan *m* integral de centeno

pumping *n* bombeo *m*

pumping station *n* estación *f* de bombeo

pumpkin ['pʌmpkɪn] *n* calabaza *f*, zapallo *m* CSur, Perú

pun [pʌn] I. *n* juego *m* de palabras, albur *m* Méx II.<-nn-> *vi* hacer juegos de palabras, alburear Méx

punch¹ [pʌntʃ] I. *vt* 1.(*hit*) pegar; to ~ sb unconscious dejar a alguien inconsciente de un puñetazo 2.(*pierce*) perforar, ponchar Méx; (*ticket*) picar; to ~ holes in sth hacer agujeros a algo; to ~ the clock [*o* card] fichar 3. *Am, Can* AGR (*cattle*) aguijonear, picanear AmL II. *vi* 1.(*hit*) pegar 2.(*employee*) to ~ in/out fichar III.<-es> *n* 1.(*hit*) puñetazo *m*; (*in boxing*) golpe *m*; to give sb a ~ dar un puñetazo a alguien 2.(*tool for puncturing*) punzón *m*; (*for metal, leather*) sacabocados *m inv*; (*hole*) ~ perforadora *f*; (*ticket*) ~ máquina *f* de picar billetes 3. *fig* (*strong effect*) fuerza *f*; with ~ con nervio ►to pull one's ~es no emplear toda su fuerza; to roll with the ~es saber arreglárselas

punch² [pʌntʃ] *n* ponche *m*

Punch and Judy show [ˌpʌntʃənd'dʒuːdiˌʃəʊ, *Am:* ˌpʌntʃənd'dʒuːdiˌʃoʊ] *n* teatro *m* de polichinelas

punch bag *n Brit* saco *m* de arena

punch bowl *n* ponchera *f*

punch card *n* tarjeta *f* perforada

punch-drunk ['pʌntʃdrʌŋk] *adj a. fig* atontado, -a; to be ~ estar grogui *inf*

punching bag *n Am* saco *m* de arena

punchline ['pʌntʃlaɪn] *n* gracia *f* (de un chiste)

punch-up ['pʌntʃʌp] *n Brit, inf* pelea *f*; to have a ~ liarse a golpes *inf*

punctilious [pʌŋkˈtɪliəs] *adj form* (*with attention to detail*) puntilloso, -a; (*with correct behavior*) formalista

punctual [ˈpʌŋktʃuəl] *adj* puntual

punctuality [ˌpʌŋktʃuˈæləti, *Am:* -əˈti] *n no pl* puntualidad *f*

punctuate [ˈpʌŋktʃueɪt] *vt* 1. LING puntuar 2. (*appear intermittently*) salpicar *fig*; (*interrupt*) interrumpir

punctuation [ˌpʌŋktʃuˈeɪʃən] *n no pl* puntuación *f*

punctuation mark *n* signo *m* de puntuación

puncture [ˈpʌŋktʃər, *Am:* -tʃər] I. *vt* 1. (*pierce*) pinchar, ponchar *Méx;* (*abscess*) reventar; (*lung*) perforar; **to ~ a hole in sth** hacer un agujero a algo 2. (*confidence*) minar II. *vi* (*tyre, ball*) pincharse, poncharse *Méx;* (*car*) pinchar III. *n* 1. (*in tyre, ball*) pinchazo *m*, ponchadura *f Méx;* **to have a ~** (*driver*) pinchar; **to have a slow ~** *Brit* perder aire; **~ (repair) patch** parche *m* 2. MED (*in skin*) punción *f*

pundit [ˈpʌndɪt] *n* (*expert*) experto, -a *m, f*

pungent [ˈpʌndʒənt] *adj* 1. (*sharp*) punzante; (*smell*) acre; (*taste*) fuerte 2. (*criticism*) cáustico, -a

punish [ˈpʌnɪʃ] *vt* castigar; **to ~ oneself** castigarse

punishable *adj liter* punible; **~ by death** penado con la muerte

punishing I. *adj* (*difficult*) duro, -a; (*trying*) agotador(a) II. *n* **to take a ~** llevarse una paliza; **this car has taken a real ~** este coche está muy castigado

punishment [ˈpʌnɪʃmənt] *n* 1. (*punishing*) castigo *m;* **capital ~** pena *f* capital; **to inflict a ~ on sb** castigar a alguien 2. (*rough use*) maltrato *m;* **to take a lot of ~** estar muy baqueteado

punitive [ˈpjuːnɪtɪv, *Am:* - t̬ɪv] *adj form* punitivo, -a; **~ damages** LAW daños *mpl* ejemplares; **~ expedition** MIL expedición *f* punitiva; **~ sanctions** sanciones *fpl*

punk [pʌŋk] I. *n* 1. (*person*) punk *mf* 2. *Am, pej* (*troublemaker*) gamberro, -a *m, f* II. *adj* 1. (*music, style*) punk 2. *Am* (*poor quality*) de pacotilla

punnet [ˈpʌnɪt] *n Aus, Brit* (*for fruit*) cestito *m*

punt¹ [pʌnt] SPORTS I. *vt* (*in rugby, American football*) despejar II. *vi* (*in rugby, American football*) despejar III. *n* (*kick*) patada *f* de despeje

punt² [pʌnt] I. *vt* (*in boat*) **to ~ sb** llevar a alguien en batea II. *vi* (*in boat*) ir en batea; **to go ~ing** salir de paseo en batea III. *n* (*boat*) batea *f*

punt³ [pʌnt] *vi* GAMES jugar contra la banca

punter [ˈpʌntər, *Am:* -t̬ər] *n Brit, inf* 1. GAMES (*gambler*) jugador(a) *m(f);* (*at races*) apostante *mf* 2. (*customer*) cliente *mf*

puny [ˈpjuːni] <-ier, -iest> *adj* (*person*) enclenque; (*argument*) endeble; (*attempt*) lastimoso, -a

pup [pʌp] I. *n* 1. (*baby dog*) cachorro, -a *m, f;* **to be in ~** estar preñada 2. (*baby animal*) cría *f* ▶ **to sell sb a ~** dar gato por liebre a alguien II. *vi* <-pp-> parir

pupa [ˈpjuːpə] <pupas *o* pupae> *n* BIO crisálida *f*, pupa *f*

pupate [ˈpjuːpeɪt] *vi* BIO convertirse en crisálida

pupil¹ [ˈpjuːpl] *n* SCHOOL alumno, -a *m, f*

pupil² [ˈpjuːpl] *n* ANAT pupila *f*

puppet [ˈpʌpɪt] *n a. fig* títere *m;* **glove ~** muñeco *m* de guiñol

puppeteer [pʌpɪˈtɪər, *Am:* -əˈtɪr] *n* titiritero, -a *m, f*

puppet government *n pej* gobierno *m* títere **puppet show** *n* THEAT función *f* de marionetas

puppy [ˈpʌpi] <-ies> *n* cachorro, -a *m, f*

purchase [ˈpɜːtʃəs, *Am:* ˈpɜːrtʃəs] I. *vt* 1. *form* (*buy*) comprar, adquirir 2. NAUT **to ~ the anchor** levar el ancla II. *n* 1. (*act of buying*) compra *f*, adquisición *f;* **to make a ~** hacer una adquisición; **compulsory ~** *Brit* compra forzosa 2. (*hold*) agarre *m;* **to get a ~ on sth** agarrarse a [*o* de] algo

purchase price *n* precio *m* de compra

purchaser *n* 1. (*buyer*) comprador(a) *m(f)* 2. (*at auction*) adjudicatario, -a *m, f*

purchase tax *n* impuesto *m* sobre las ventas

purchasing *n form* compras *fpl*

purchasing department *n* departamento *m* de compras **purchasing manager** *n* director(a) *m(f)* de compras **purchasing power** *n* poder *m* adquisitivo

pure [pjuər, *Am:* pjur] *adj* puro, -a; **~ air** aire *m* puro; **~ gold** oro *m* puro; **~ mathematics** matemáticas *fpl* puras; **~ and simple** simple y llano; **it was ~ accident** fue por pura casualidad; **to be ~ in heart** ser limpio de corazón

purebred [ˈpjuəbred, *Am:* ˈpjur-] I. *n* animal *m* de pura raza II. *adj* de pura raza; **a ~ horse** un purasangre

purée [ˈpjuəreɪ, *Am:* pjuˈreɪ] I. *vt* hacer puré de II. *n* puré *m*

purely [ˈpjuəli, *Am:* ˈpjurli] *adv* 1. (*completely*) puramente; **~ by chance** por pura casualidad 2. (*simply*) meramente; **~ and simply** simple y llanamente

purgative [ˈpɜːgətɪv, *Am:* ˈpɜːrgət̬ɪv] I. *n* purga *f* II. *adj* MED purgante, purgativo, -a

purgatory [ˈpɜːgətri, *Am:* ˈpɜːrgətɔːri] *n no pl* 1. REL **Purgatory** Purgatorio *m;* **to be in Purgatory** estar en el Purgatorio 2. *fig* (*unpleasant experience*) calvario *m;* **to go through ~** pasar las de Caín

purge [pɜːdʒ, *Am:* ˈpɜːrdʒ] I. *vt* 1. MED, POL purgar; **to ~ a group of extremist elements** purgar a un grupo de elementos extremistas; **to ~ sb from a party** expulsar a alguien de un partido 2. REL (*crime, sin*) expiar II. *n* MED, POL purga *f*

purification [ˌpjuərɪfɪˈkeɪʃən, *Am:* ˌpjurə-]

n no pl a. REL purificación *f;* (*of water*) depuración *f*

purify ['pjʊərɪfaɪ, *Am:* 'pjʊrə-] *vt* (*cleanse*) purificar; (*language, water*) depurar; REL (*soul, body*) limpiar; **to ~ oneself of sth** purificarse de algo

purist ['pjʊərɪst, *Am:* 'pjʊrɪst] *n* purista *mf*

puritan ['pjʊərɪtən, *Am:* 'pjʊrɪ-] *n a. fig* puritano, -a *m, f*

puritanical [ˌpjʊərɪ'tænɪkəl, *Am:* ˌpjʊrɪ'-] *adj* puritano, -a

Puritanism *n no pl* puritanismo *m*

purity ['pjʊərəti, *Am:* 'pjʊrɪti] *no pl n* pureza *f*

purl [pɜːl, *Am:* pɜːrl] **I.** *n* punto *m* al revés **II.** *adj* ~ **stitch** punto *m* al revés **III.** *vt* hacer con puntos al revés; (*stitches*) hacer al revés; **knit one, ~ one** uno al derecho, otro al revés **IV.** *vi* tejer al revés

purloin [pɜː'lɔɪn, *Am:* pəˈ-] *vt form* hurtar

purple ['pɜːpl, *Am:* 'pɜːr-] **I.** *adj* (*reddish*) púrpura; (*bluish*) morado, -a; **to be ~ with rage** estar lívido de rabia **II.** *n* (*reddish*) púrpura *m;* (*bluish*) morado *m*

purport ['pɜːpət, *Am:* pɜːr'pɔːrt] **I.** *vi form* (*claim*) **to ~ to be sth** pretender ser algo **II.** *n* **1.** (*meaning*) sentido *m* **2.** (*purpose*) intención *f*

purpose ['pɜːpəs, *Am:* 'pɜːrpəs] *n* **1.** (*goal*) intención *f;* **for the ~** al efecto; **the sole ~ of sth** el único objetivo de algo; **I did that for a ~** por algo hice eso; **for that very ~** precisamente por eso; **for practical ~s** a efectos prácticos; **not to the ~** que no viene al caso; **to have a ~ in life** tener una meta en la vida; **for humanitarian ~s** con fines humanitarios; **for future ~s** para las necesidades futuras **2.** (*motivation*) (**strength of**) ~ resolución *f* **3.** (*use*) utilidad *f;* **to no ~** inútilmente; **to serve a ~** servir de algo; **what's the ~ of ...?** ¿para qué sirve...? ▶**on ~** a propósito

purpose-built [ˌpɜːpəs'bɪlt, *Am:* ˌpɜːr-] *adj* construido, -a al efecto

purposeful ['pɜːpəsfəl, *Am:* 'pɜːr-] *adj* **1.** (*determined*) decidido, -a **2.** (*meaningful*) con sentido **3.** (*intentional*) intencionado, -a

purposeless ['pɜːpəsləs, *Am:* 'pɜːrpəs-] *adj* **1.** (*aimless*) sin sentido; (*utterance, violence*) gratuito, -a **2.** (*useless*) inútil **3.** (*character, person*) irresoluto, -a

purposely ['pɜːpəsli, *Am:* 'pɜːr-] *adv* a propósito

purr [pɜːʳ, *Am:* pɜːr] **I.** *vi* (*cat*) ronronear; (*engine*) zumbar **II.** *n* (*of cat*) ronroneo *m;* (*of engine*) zumbido *m*

purse [pɜːs, *Am:* pɜːrs] **I.** *n* **1.** *Am* (*handbag*) bolso *m,* cartera *f AmL,* bolsa *f Méx* **2.** *Brit* (*wallet*) monedero *m* **3.** (*funds*) public ~ erario *m* público; **to be beyond one's ~** estar fuera de las posibilidades de uno **4.** (*prize*) premio *m* en efectivo **II.** *vt* (*lips*) apretar

purser ['pɜːsəʳ, *Am:* 'pɜːrsəˈ] *n* NAUT contable *mf* de navío

purse strings *npl fig* **to hold the ~** administrar el dinero; **to loosen the ~** aflojar la bolsa

pursuance [pə'sjuːənts, *Am:* pəˈsuː-] *n no pl, form* ejecución *f;* **in ~ of sth** (*in accordance with*) de conformidad con algo; **in ~ of her duty** en cumplimiento de su deber

pursuant [pə'sjuːənt, *Am:* pəˈsuː-] *adv* LAW ~ **to** conforme a, de acuerdo con

pursue [pə'sjuː, *Am:* pəˈsuː] *vt* **1.** (*chase*) perseguir **2.** (*seek to find*) buscar; (*dreams, goals*) luchar por; (*rights, peace*) reivindicar **3.** (*follow: plan*) seguir; **to ~ a matter** seguir un caso **4. to ~ a career** dedicarse a una carrera profesional; **to ~ a degree in sth** seguir estudios de algo

pursuer [pə'sjuːəʳ, *Am:* pəˈsuːəˈ] *n* perseguidor(a) *m(f)*

pursuit [pə'sjuːt, *Am:* pəˈsuːt] *n* **1.** (*chase*) persecución *f;* **to be in ~ of sth** ir tras algo; (*knowledge, happiness*) ir en busca de algo; (*hunt*) ir a la caza de algo; **to be in hot ~ of sb** pisar los talones a alguien *fig* **2.** (*activity*) actividad *f;* **leisure ~s** pasatiempos *mpl;* **outdoor ~s** actividades al aire libre

purulent ['pjʊərələnt, *Am:* 'pjʊrə-] *adj* purulento, -a

purvey [pə'veɪ, *Am:* pəˈ-] *vt* proveer, suministrar; **to ~ sth to sb** proveer a alguien de algo

purveyor [pə'veɪəʳ, *Am:* pəˈveɪəˈ] *n* ECON proveedor(a) *m(f)*

pus [pʌs] *n* MED *no pl* pus *m,* postema *f Méx*

push [pʊʃ] **I.** *vt* **1.** (*shove*) empujar; **to ~ one's way through sth** abrirse paso a empujones por algo; **to ~ sth to the back of one's mind** intentar no pensar en algo; **to ~ the door open** abrir la puerta de un empujón; **to ~ sb out of sth** echar a alguien de algo a empujones; **to ~ sb out of the way** apartar a alguien a empujones **2.** (*force*) **to ~ one's luck** tentar a la suerte; **to ~ sb too far** sacar a alguien de quicio **3.** (*coerce*) obligar; **to ~ sb to do** [*o* **into doing**] **sth** presionar a alguien para que haga algo; **to ~ oneself** exigirse demasiado; **don't ~ yourself!** *iron* ¡no trabajes tanto! **4.** (*insist*) insistir en; **to ~ sb for sth** apremiar a alguien para algo **5.** (*press: button*) apretar; (*accelerator*) pisar; **to ~ the doorbell** tocar el timbre **6.** (*find sth difficult*) **to be** (**hard**) **~ed to do sth** tener dificultad para hacer algo **7.** (*be short of*) **to be ~ed for money/time** andar escaso de dinero/tiempo **8.** *inf* (*promote*) promover; ECON fomentar **9. to be ~ing 30** rondar los 30 años **II.** *vi* **1.** (*force movement*) empujar **2.** (*press*) apretar **3.** (*insist*) presionar; **to ~ for sth** presionar para (conseguir) algo **III.** <-es> *n* **1.** (*shove*) empujón *m;* (*slight push*) empujoncito *m;* **to give sb a ~** *fig* dar un empujón a alguien; **she got the ~** *inf* (*from boyfriend*) su novio la dejó; (*from employer*) la echaron del trabajo; **to give sb the ~** *inf* (*break up with*) dejar a alguien; (*fire*) echar a alguien **2.** (*press*) **at the ~**

of a button apretando un botón **3.** (*strong action*) impulso *m;* (*will to succeed*) empuje *m* **4.** (*strong effort*) esfuerzo *m;* **to make a ~ for sth** hacer un esfuerzo para algo; **at a ~ ...** si me apuras... **5.** (*publicity*) campaña *f;* **to make a ~** hacer una campaña **6.** MIL (*military attack*) ofensiva *f* ▶**if/when ~ comes to shove** en caso de apuro

◆**push along** *vi inf* largarse
◆**push around** *vt* mangonear *inf*
◆**push away** *vt* apartar
◆**push back** *vt* (*move backwards*) hacer retroceder; (*person*) empujar hacia atrás; (*hair*) echar hacia atrás
◆**push down** *vt* **1.** (*knock down*) derribar **2.** (*press down*) apretar **3.** ECON (*price, interest rate*) hacer bajar
◆**push forward** **I.** *vt* **1.** (*force forward*) empujar hacia adelante **2.** (*promote*) promocionar **3.** (*call attention to oneself*) **to push oneself forward** hacerse valer **II.** *vi* **1.** (*advance*) avanzar **2.** (*continue*) **to ~ (with sth)** seguir (con algo)
◆**push in** **I.** *vt* **1.** (*nail*) empujar (hacia adentro) **2.** (*force in*) **to push one's way in** colarse *inf* **II.** *vi* (*force way in*) entrar a empujones
◆**push off** **I.** *vi inf* largarse **II.** *vt* NAUT (*boat*) desatracar
◆**push on** **I.** *vi* **1.** (*continue despite problems*) **to ~ (with sth)** seguir adelante (con algo) **2.** (*continue travelling*) **we pushed on to Madrid** seguimos hasta Madrid **II.** *vt* **1.** (*activate*) apresurar **2.** (*press*) **to push sb on to do sth** empujar a alguien a hacer algo
◆**push out** *vt* **1.** (*force out*) **to push sb out (of sth)** echar a alguien (de algo) **2.** (*get rid of*) eliminar; **to push competitors out of the market** eliminar a los competidores del mercado **3.** (*produce: roots, blossoms*) echar **4.** NAUT (*boat*) echar al agua
◆**push over** *vt always sep* (*thing*) volcar; (*person*) hacer caer
◆**push through** **I.** *vi* abrirse paso entre **II.** *vt* **1.** (*legislation, proposal*) hacer aceptar **2.** (*help to succeed*) llevar a buen término
◆**push up** *vt* **1.** (*move higher*) levantar; *fig* (*help*) dar un empujón **2.** (*price, interest rate*) hacer subir

pushbike ['pʊʃbaɪk] *n Aus, Brit, inf* bici *f*
push-button ['pʊʃˌbʌtən] **I.** *adj* de botones **II.** *n* botón *m* **push-button telephone** *n* teléfono *m* de botones
pushcart ['pʊʃkɑːt, *Am:* -kɑːrt] *n* carretilla *f* de mano
pushchair ['pʊʃtʃeəʳ, *Am:* -tʃer] *n Brit* sillita *f* de paseo
pusher *n inf* camello *mf*
pushover ['pʊʃəʊvəʳ, *Am:* -ˌoʊvɚ] *n* **1.** (*easy success*) **to be a ~** ser pan comido **2.** (*easily influenced*) **to be a ~** ser muy fácil de convencer
pushpin ['pʊʃpɪn] *n Am* chincheta *f*
push start **I.** *vi* arrancar empujando el coche

II. *n* **to give sb a ~** ayudar a alguien a arrancar empujando el coche
push-up ['pʊʃʌp] *n* SPORTS flexión *f;* **to do ~s** hacer flexiones
pushy ['pʊʃi] *adj pej* **1.** (*ambitious*) ambicioso, -a **2.** (*arrogant*) prepotente
puss [pʊs] <-es> *n* (*cat*) minino, -a *m, f;* **Puss in Boots** el gato con botas
pussy ['pʊsi] <-ies> *n* **1.** (*cat*) **~ (cat)** minino, -a *m, f* **2.** *no pl, vulg* conejo *m*, concha *f AmL*
pussyfoot ['pʊsifʊt] *vi inf* **to ~ around an issue** dar largas a un asunto
pussy willow *n* sauce *m* blanco
pustule ['pʌstjuːl, *Am:* -tʃuːl] *n* pústula *f*
put [pʊt] <-tt-, put, put> **I.** *vt* **1.** (*place*) poner; (*in box, hole*) meter; **~ the spoons next to the knives** coloca las cucharas junto a los cuchillos; **to ~ sth to one's lips** llevarse algo a los labios; **~ it there!** (*shake hands*) ¡chócala!; **to ~ sth in the oven** meter algo en el horno **2.** (*add*) echar; **to ~ sugar/salt in sth** echar azúcar/sal a algo; **to ~ the date on sth** poner la fecha en algo; **to ~ sth on a list** apuntar una lista; **to ~ sth in writing** poner algo por escrito **3.** (*direct*) **to ~ the blame on sb** echar la culpa a alguien; **to ~ pressure on sb** presionar a alguien; **to ~ a spell on sb** echar una maldición a alguien; **to ~ one's heart into sth** poner todo el afán de uno en algo; **to ~ one's mind to sth** poner los cinco sentidos en algo; **to ~ one's trust in sb** depositar la confianza de uno en alguien **4.** (*invest*) **to ~ sth into sth** invertir algo en algo; **to ~ energy/time into sth** dedicar energía/tiempo a algo **5.** (*bet*) apostar; **to ~ money on sth** jugarse dinero a algo; **to ~ sth toward sth** contribuir con algo para algo **6.** (*cause to be*) **to ~ sb in a good mood** poner a alguien de buen humor; **to ~ sb in danger** poner a alguien en peligro; **to ~ oneself in sb's place/shoes** ponerse en el lugar de alguien; **to ~ sb in prison** meter a alguien en la cárcel; **to ~ into practice** poner en práctica; **to ~ sb on the train** acompañar a alguien hasta el tren; **to ~ sth right** arreglar algo; **to ~ sb straight** poner a alguien en el buen camino; **to ~ sb to bed** acostar a alguien; **to ~ to death** ejecutar; **to ~ sth to good use** hacer buen uso de algo; **to ~ sb to shame** avergonzar; **to ~ sb to trouble** causar molestias a alguien; **to ~ sb under oath** tomar juramento a alguien; **to ~ sb in mind of sth** recordar algo a alguien; **to ~ sb to expense** ocasionar gastos a alguien; **to ~ to flight** poner en fuga; **to ~ a stop to sth** poner fin a algo; **to ~ sb to work** poner a alguien a trabajar **7.** (*impose*) **to ~ an idea in sb's head** meter una idea en la cabeza a alguien; **to ~ a tax on sth** gravar algo con un impuesto **8.** (*attribute*) **to ~ a high value on sth** valorar mucho algo **9.** (*present*) **to ~ one's point of view** exponer el punto de vista de uno; **to ~ a question** plantear una pregunta;

to ~ sth to discussion someter algo a debate; to ~ sth to the vote someter algo a votación; to ~ a proposal before a committee presentar una propuesta ante un comité; I ~ it to you that ... mi opinión es que... 10. (*express*) decir; as John ~ it como dijo John; to ~ one's feelings into words expresar sus sentimientos con palabras; to ~ sth into Spanish traducir algo al español 11. (*judge*) I ~ the number of visitors at 2,000 calculo que debe haber recibido unos 2.000 visitantes; I'd ~ her at about 35 calculo que tiene unos 35 años; to ~ sb on a level with sb poner a alguien al mismo nivel que alguien 12. SPORTS (*throw*) to ~ the shot lanzar el peso II. *vi* NAUT to ~ to sea zarpar

♦**put about** *irr* I.<-tt-> *vt* 1. (*spread: rumour*) hacer circular; to put it about that ... hacer correr la voz que... 2. *inf* (*be promiscuous*) to put it about mariposear 3. NAUT hacer virar II. *vi* NAUT virar

♦**put across** <-tt-> *irr vt* (*make understood*) comunicar; to put sth across to sb hacer entender algo a alguien; to put oneself across well causar buena impresión

♦**put aside** <-tt-> *irr vt* 1. (*place to one side*) dejar a un lado 2. (*save*) ahorrar; (*time*) reservar 3. (*give up*) to put sth aside dejar algo 4. (*reject*) rechazar 5. (*ignore: fears, differences*) dejar de lado

♦**put away** <-tt-> *irr vt* 1. (*save*) ahorrar 2. *inf* (*eat a lot*) zamparse 3. (*remove*) guardar 4. *inf* (*imprison*) to put sb away encerrar a alguien 5. *inf* (*kill*) matar

♦**put back** <-tt-> *irr vt* 1. (*return*) volver a poner en su sitio 2. (*postpone*) posponer 3. SCHOOL (*not progress*) to put sb back a year hacer repetir curso a alguien 4. (*set earlier: watch*) atrasar

♦**put by** <-tt-> *irr vt* ahorrar

♦**put down** <-tt-> *irr vt* 1. (*set down*) dejar; not to be able to put a book down no poder parar de leer un libro; to ~ the (tele)phone colgar el teléfono 2. (*lower*) bajar; to put one's arm/feet down bajar el brazo/los pies; to put sb down somewhere dejar a alguien en un sitio 3. (*attribute*) to put sth down to sb atribuir algo a alguien 4. (*write*) escribir; to put sth down on paper poner algo por escrito 5. (*assess*) catalogar; I put her down as 30 le echo 30 años 6. (*register*) to put sb down for sth inscribir a alguien en algo 7. FIN (*prices*) disminuir 8. ECON (*leave as deposit*) dejar en depósito 9. (*stop: rebellion, opposition*) reprimir 10. *inf* (*humiliate*) menospreciar 11. (*have killed: animal*) sacrificar

♦**put forward** <-tt-> *irr vt* 1. (*offer for discussion: subject*) proponer; (*idea, plan*) exponer; (*suggestion*) hacer; to ~ a proposal hacer una propuesta 2. (*advance: event*) adelantar; to put the clock forward adelantar el reloj

♦**put in** <-tt-> *irr* I. *vt* 1. (*place inside*)

meter 2. (*add*) poner; to ~ a comma/a full stop añadir una coma/un punto 3. (*say*) decir; (*remark*) hacer; to put a word in intervenir en la conversación 4. AGR (*plant: vegetables*) plantar; (*seeds*) sembrar 5. TECH (*install*) instalar; to ~ a shower poner una ducha 6. POL (*candidate, party*) elegir 7. (*invest: money*) poner; (*time*) dedicar; to ~ a lot of effort on sth dedicar muchos esfuerzos a algo; to ~ overtime hacer horas extras 8. (*direct*) to put one's faith in sb tener fe en alguien; to put one's hope in sb poner las esperanzas de uno en alguien 9. (*submit: claim, request*) presentar; (*candidate*) presentarse; to put oneself in for sth inscribirse para algo 10. (*make*) to ~ an appearance hacer acto de presencia II. *vi* 1. (*apply*) to ~ for sth solicitar algo 2. NAUT (*dock*) hacer escala

♦**put into** <-tt-> *irr vt* 1. (*place inside*) meter 2. to put sth into sth (*add*) añadir algo a algo; GASTR echar algo a algo; (*include*) incluir algo en algo 3. (*dress in*) to put sb into sth vestir a alguien de algo 4. TECH (*install*) instalar 5. FIN (*deposit*) to put money into a bank ingresar dinero en un banco 6. (*invest*) to put sth into sth (*money*) invertir algo en algo; (*time, effort*) dedicar algo a algo 7. (*cause to be*) to put a plan into operation poner un plan en marcha 8. (*institutionalize*) to put sb into sth meter a alguien en algo; to put sb into prison mandar a alguien a la cárcel

♦**put off** <-tt-> *irr vt* 1. (*turn off*) apagar 2. (*drop off: passenger*) dejar 3. (*delay*) posponer; to put sth off for a week aplazar algo una semana 4. (*make wait*) entretener; to put sb off with excuses dar largas a alguien *inf* 5. (*repel*) alejar; (*food, smell*) dar asco a 6. (*discourage*) desanimar; to put sb off sth disuadir a alguien de algo; to put sb off sb hacer que alguien le coja antipatía a alguien 7. (*disconcert*) desconcertar 8. (*distract*) distraer; to put sb off sth distraer a alguien de algo; to put sb off their stride *fig* hacer perder el hilo a alguien; to put sb off the scent despistar a alguien

♦**put on** <-tt-> *irr vt* 1. (*place upon*) to put sth on sth poner algo sobre algo 2. (*attach*) to put sth on sth poner algo a algo 3. (*wear*) ponerse; to ~ make-up maquillarse 4. (*turn on*) encender; to ~ Mozart poner música de Mozart 5. (*use*) to ~ the brakes frenar; to put the handbrake on poner el freno de mano 6. (*perform: film*) dar; (*show*) presentar; THEAT poner en escena 7. (*provide: dish*) servir; to ~ a party dar una fiesta 8. (*assume: expression*) adoptar; to ~ a frown fruncir el ceño; to ~ airs darse tono 9. (*pretend*) fingir; (*accent*) afectar 10. (*be joking with*) to put sb on tomar el pelo a alguien 11. (*gain: weight*) engordar; to ~ 10 years envejecer 10 años 12. (*water, soup*) calentar 13. TEL to put sb on the (tele)phone pasar el teléfono a alguien; to put sb on to sb poner a alguien con alguien;

I'll **put him on** le paso con él **14.** (*inform*) to **put sb on to sb** hablar a alguien de alguien; **to put sb on to sth** dar a alguien información sobre algo

◆**put out** <-tt-> *irr* **I.** *vt* **1.** (*take outside*) to **put the dog out** sacar al perro **2.** (*extend*) extender; **to ~ one's hand** tender la mano; **~ one's tongue** sacar la lengua **3.** (*extinguish: fire*) extinguir; **to ~ a cigarette** apagar un cigarrillo **4.** (*turn off*) apagar **5.** (*eject*) expulsar; (*dismiss*) echar **6.** (*publish, issue*) publicar; (*announcement*) hacer público **7.** (*produce industrially*) producir **8.** (*sprout: leaves*) echar **9.** (*contract out*) subcontratar; **to put sth out to a company** subcontratar algo con una empresa **10.** (*inconvenience*) molestar a; **to put oneself out for sb** molestarse por alguien **11.** (*offend*) ofender **12.** (*dislocate*) dislocar, zafar *AmL;* **to ~ one's shoulder** dislocarse [*o* zafarse *AmL*] el hombro **13.** (*make unconscious*) dejar sin sentido; MED anestesiar **14.** NAUT botar **II.** *vi* NAUT zarpar

◆**put over** <-tt-> *irr vt* **1.** (*place higher*) to **put sth over sth** poner algo por encima de algo **2.** (*make understood: idea, plan*) comunicar **3.** (*fool*) to **put sth over on sb** engañar a alguien

◆**put through** <-tt-> *irr vt* **1.** (*insert through*) to **put sth through sth** hacer pasar algo por algo **2.** (*process with: proposal*) hacer aceptar; (*bill*) hacer aprobar **3.** (*send*) mandar; **to put sb through college** mandar a alguien a la universidad **4.** TEL poner; **to ~ a telephone call to Paris** poner una conferencia a París; **put a call through** pasar una llamada; **to put sb through** (**to sb**) pasar a alguien (con alguien) **5.** (*implement*) llevar a cabo **6.** (*make endure*) to **put sb through sth** someter a alguien a algo; **to put sb through it** hacer pasar un mal rato a alguien

◆**put together** <-tt-> *irr vt* **1.** (*join*) juntar; (*collection*) reunir; (*assemble*) ensamblar; (*machine, model, radio*) montar; (*pieces*) acoplar **2.** (*connect: facts, clues*) relacionar **3.** (*create*) crear; (*list*) hacer; (*team*) formar; (*meal*) preparar; (*dress*) confeccionar **4.** MAT sumar

◆**put up** <-tt-> *irr* **I.** *vt* **1.** (*hang up*) colgar; (*notice*) fijar **2.** (*raise*) levantar; (*one's collar*) subirse; (*flag*) izar; **to put one's hair up** recogerse el pelo **3.** (*umbrella*) abrir **4.** (*build*) construir; (*tent*) armar **5.** (*increase: prices*) subir **6.** (*make available*) to **put sth up for sale** poner algo en venta; **to put sth up for auction** sacar algo a subasta pública **7.** (*give shelter*) alojar; **I can put you up for a week** te puedes quedar una semana en casa **8.** (*provide: funds*) aportar; **to ~ the money for sth** poner el dinero para algo **9.** (*show opposition*) to **~ opposition** oponerse; to **~ a struggle** poner resistencia **10.** (*submit: candidate, proposal*) presentar **II.** *vi* alojarse; **to ~ at a hotel** hospedarse en un hotel; **to ~ at sb's place for the night** pasar la noche en casa de alguien

◆**put up with** <-tt-> *irr vt* soportar

putative ['pjuːtətɪv, *Am:* -t̬ətɪv] *adj form* (*reputed*) supuesto, -a; (*father*) putativo, -a

put-off *n Am, inf* aplazamiento *m;* **to give sb a ~** dar largas a alguien

put-on ['pʌtɒn, *Am:* -ɑːn] *n Am, inf* burla *f;* (*joke*) broma *f*

put option *n* ECON opción *f* de venta

putrefaction [ˌpjuːtrɪ'fækʃən, *Am:* -trə'-] *n no pl, form* putrefacción *f*

putrefy ['pjuːtrɪfaɪ, *Am:* -trə-] <-ie-> *vi form* pudrirse

putrid ['pjuːtrɪd] *adj form* **1.** (*decayed*) podrido, -a, putrefacto, -a; (*smell*) pútrido, -a **2.** (*very bad*) pésimo, -a

putsch [pʊtʃ] <-tsches> *n* golpe *m* de estado

putt [pʌt] SPORTS **I.** *vi* tirar al hoyo **II.** *n* tiro *m* al hoyo, put *m AmL*

puttee ['pʌti, *Am:* pʌtiː] *n* polaina *f*

putter¹ ['pʌtə', *Am:* 'pʌt̬ə·] *n* (*golf club*) putter *m*

putter² ['pʌtə', *Am:* 'pʌt̬ə·] *vi Am s.* **potter**

putty ['pʌti, *Am:* 'pʌt̬-] *n no pl* masilla *f* ▶ **to be like ~ in sb's hands** ser completamente manejable

putty knife <-knives> *n* espátula *f*

put-up *adj inf* **a ~ job** un asunto fraudulento

put-upon *adj inf* explotado, -a

puzzle ['pʌzl] **I.** *vt* dejar perplejo, -a **II.** *vi* **to ~ about sth** dar vueltas a algo **III.** *n* **1.** (*game*) rompecabezas *m inv;* **jigsaw ~** puzzle *m;* **crossword ~** crucigrama *m* **2.** (*mystery*) misterio *m,* enigma *m;* **to be a ~ to sb** ser un misterio para alguien; **to solve a ~** resolver un enigma

puzzled *adj* perplejo, -a; **to be ~ about sth** estar desconcertado por algo

puzzler ['pʌzlə', *Am:* -lə·] *n* (*mystery*) enigma *m*

puzzling *adj* desconcertante

PVC [ˌpiːviː'siː] *n abbr of* **polyvinyl chloride** PVC *m*

pygmy ['pɪgmi] **I.** *n* <-ies> **1.** (*short person*) pigmeo, -a *m, f* **2.** *fig* enano, -a *m, f* **II.** *adj* ZOOL enano, -a

pyjamas [pə'dʒɑːməz] *npl Aus, Brit* pijama *m;* **in** (**one's**) **~** en pijama; **a pair of ~** un pijama

pylon ['paɪlɒn, *Am:* -lɑːn] *n* ELEC torre *f* de alta tensión

pyramid ['pɪrəmɪd] *n* pirámide *f*

pyramid selling *n no pl* ECON, LAW venta *f* piramidal

pyre ['paɪə', *Am:* 'paɪə·] *n* pira *f*

Pyrenees [pɪrə'niːz] *npl* **the ~** los Pirineos

Pyrex® ['paɪəreks, *Am:* 'paɪ-] **I.** *n* pirex *m* **II.** *adj* de pirex

pyrites [ˌpaɪə'raɪtiːz, *Am:* paɪ'-] <-tae> *n* pirita *f;* **iron ~** pirita de hierro

pyromania [ˌpaɪrəʊ'meɪnɪə, *Am:* ˌpaɪroʊ'-] *n no pl* piromanía *f*

pyrotechnic [ˌpaɪrəʊˈteknɪk, *Am:* ˌpaɪroʊ'-] *adj* **1.** pirotécnico, -a; ~ **display** fuegos pirotécnicos **2.** *fig* (*brilliant*) espectacular

python ['paɪθən, *Am:* -θɑːn] <-(ons)> *n* pitón *f*

Q

Q, q [kjuː] *n* Q, q *f;* ~ **for Queenie** *Brit,* ~ **for Queen** *Am* Q de Quebec

Q *abbr of* **Queen** reina *f*

Qatar [kəˈtɑːʳ, *Am:* ˈkɑːtɑːr] *n* Qatar *m*

QC [ˌkjuːˈsiː] *n Brit abbr of* **Queen's Counsel** *título de abogacía de categoría superior*

QED [ˌkjuːiːˈdiː] *abbr of* **quod erat demonstrandum** Q.E.D.

qtr *abbr of* **quarter** cuarto *m*

qua [kwɑː] *prep form* como

quack¹ [kwæk] **I.** *n* (*duck's sound*) graznido *m* **II.** *vi* graznar

quack² [kwæk] *pej* **I.** *n* **1.** (*unqualified doctor*) curandero, -a *m, f* **2.** *Aus, Brit, iron* (*doctor*) matasanos *m inv* **II.** *adj* falso, -a

quack-quack *n childspeak* cuac cuac *m*

quad [kwɒd, *Am:* kwɑːd] *n* **1.** *inf* (*quadruplet*) cuatrillizo, -a *m, f* **2.** (*quadrangle*) cuadrángulo *m*

quadrangle ['kwɒdræŋgl, *Am:* 'kwɑːdræŋ-] *n form* cuadrángulo *m*

quadrangular [kwɒˈdræŋgjʊləʳ, *Am:* kwɑːˈdræŋgjələʳ] *adj* cuadrangular

quadrant ['kwɒdrənt, *Am:* 'kwɑːdrənt] *n* cuadrante *m*

quadraphonic [ˌkwɒdrəˈfɒnɪk, *Am:* ˌkwɑːdrəˈfɑːnɪk] *adj* MUS cuadrafónico, -a

quadratic [kwɒˈdrætɪk, *Am:* kwɑːˈdræt̬-] *adj* cuadrático, -a

quadrilateral [ˌkwɒdrɪˈlætərəl, *Am:* ˌkwɑːdrɪˈlæt̬-] *n* cuadrilátero *m*

quadripartite ['kwɒdrɪˈpɑːtaɪt] *adj form* cuatripartito, -a

quadruped ['kwɒdrʊped, *Am:* 'kwɑːdrʊ-] *n* cuadrúpedo *m*

quadruple ['kwɒdruːpl, *Am:* 'kwɑːdruː-] **I.** *vt* cuadruplicar **II.** *vi* cuadruplicarse **III.** *adj* cuádruple

quadruplet ['kwɒdruːplət, *Am:* kwɑːˈdruːplɪt] *n* cuatrillizo, -a *m, f*

quaff [kwɒf, *Am:* kwɑːf] *vt liter* beber; **to ~ one's sorrows away** *fig* ahogar las penas

quagmire ['kwægmaɪəʳ, *Am:* -əʳ] *n* **1.** (*area*) cenagal *m* **2.** (*situation*) atolladero *m*

quail¹ [kweɪl] <-(s)> *n* (*bird*) codorniz *f*

quail² [kweɪl] *vi* (*feel fear*) acobardarse; **to ~ before sb/sth** acobardarse ante alguien/algo

quaint [kweɪnt] *adj* **1.** (*charming*) pintoresco, -a **2.** *pej* (*strange*) extraño, -a **3.** (*pleasantly unusual*) singular

quaintness ['kweɪntnɪs] *n no pl* lo pinto-

resco *m;* (*strangeness*) lo raro

quake [kweɪk] **I.** *n* **1.** (*shaking*) temblor *m* **2.** *inf* (*earthquake*) terremoto *m* **II.** *vi* **1.** (*move*) estremecerse **2.** (*shake*) temblar; **to ~ with cold/fear** temblar de frío/miedo; **to ~ at sth** temblar ante algo

Quaker ['kweɪkəʳ, *Am:* -kəʳ] **I.** *n* Cuáquero, -a *m, f;* **the ~s** los Cuáqueros **II.** *adj* cuáquero, -a

qualification [ˌkwɒlɪfɪˈkeɪʃən, *Am:* ˌkwɑːlɪ-] *n* **1.** (*document*) título *m;* (*exam*) calificación *f;* **academic ~** título académico; **her ~s are very good** está muy cualificada **2.** (*limiting criteria*) restricción *f;* (*condition*) reserva *f;* (*change*) matización *f;* **without ~** sin reservas **3.** SPORTS (*preliminary test*) clasificación *f*

qualified ['kwɒlɪfaɪd, *Am:* 'kwɑːlɪ-] *adj* **1.** (*trained*) titulado, -a; (*certified*) certificado, -a; (*by the state*) homologado, -a **2.** (*competent*) capacitado, -a **3.** (*limited*) limitado, -a; **to be a ~ success** tener cierto éxito

qualify ['kwɒlɪfaɪ, *Am:* 'kwɑːlɪ-] <-ie-> **I.** *vt* **1.** (*give credentials*) acreditar **2.** (*make eligible*) habilitar; **to ~ sb to do sth** dar derecho a alguien para hacer algo **3.** (*explain and limit*) limitar; **to ~ a remark** matizar un comentario **4.** LING (*modify*) calificar **II.** *vi* **1.** (*meet standards*) **to ~ for sth** estar habilitado para algo; (*be eligible*) tener derecho a algo; (*have qualifications*) estar acreditado para algo **2.** (*complete training*) titularse, recibirse *AmL* **3.** SPORTS clasificarse

qualifying ['kwɒlɪfaɪɪŋ, *Am:* 'kwɑːlɪ-] *adj* **1.** (*limiting*) matizador(a) **2.** SPORTS (*testing standard*) clasificatorio, -a; ~ **round** eliminatoria *f* **3.** LING (*modifying*) calificativo, -a

qualitative ['kwɒlɪtətɪv, *Am:* 'kwɑːlɪteɪt̬ɪv] *adj* cualitativo, -a; ~ **difference** diferencia cualitativa

quality ['kwɒləti, *Am:* 'kwɑːləti] **I.** <-ies> *n* **1.** *no pl* (*degree of goodness*) calidad *f;* ~ **of life** calidad de vida **2.** (*characteristic*) cualidad *f;* **artistic ~** cualidades *fpl* artísticas **II.** *adj* de calidad

quality control *n* control *m* de calidad

quality time *n no pl* tiempo *m* para relacionarse

qualm [kwɑːm] *n* escrúpulo *m;* **to feel/have ~s** (**about sth**) sentir/tener escrúpulos (respecto a algo); **to have no ~s about doing sth** no tener escrúpulos para hacer algo; **without the slightest ~** sin el menor remordimiento

quandary ['kwɒndəri, *Am:* 'kwɑːn-] <-ies> *n* dilema *m;* **to be in a ~** estar en un dilema

quango ['kwæŋgəʊ, *Am:* -goʊ] *n Brit abbr of* **quasi-autonomous non-governmental organisation** organismo no gubernamental semiautónomo

quantifiable ['kwɒntɪfaɪəbl, *Am:* 'kwɑːntə-] *adj* cuantificable

quantification [ˌkwɒntɪfɪˈkeɪʃən, *Am:* ˌkwɑːnt̬ə-] *n* cuantificación *f*

quantify ['kwɒntɪfaɪ, *Am:* 'kwɑːnt̬ə-]

<-ie-> *vt* cuantificar

quantitative ['kwɒntɪtətɪv, *Am:* 'kwɑːn-
təteɪtɪv] *adj* cuantitativo, -a

quantity ['kwɒntəti, *Am:* 'kwɑːnˌt̬əti]
I.<-ies> *n* 1. (*amount*) cantidad *f;* **a large/
small ~ of sth** una gran/pequeña cantidad de
algo 2. (*large amounts*) cantidades *fpl;* **to buy
in ~** comprar al por mayor II. *adj* en cantidad

quantity discount *n* descuento *m* por
grandes cantidades **quantity surveyor** *n*
Brit aparejador(a) *m(f)*

quantum ['kwɒntəm, *Am:* 'kwɑːnˌt̬əm]
<quanta> *n* 1. *form* (*quantity*) cuantía *f*
2. PHYS (*unit of radient energy*) cuanto *m*

quantum mechanics *n* + *sing vb* mecánica
f cuántica

quarantine ['kwɒrəntiːn, *Am:* 'kwɔːrən-]
I. *n* cuarentena *f;* **to be/place under ~** estar/
poner en cuarentena II. *vt* **to ~ sb/an animal**
poner en cuarentena a alguien/a un animal

quark [kwɑːk, *Am:* kwɑːrk] *n* PHYS quark *m*

quarrel ['kwɒrəl, *Am:* 'kwɔːr-] I. *n* disputa *f;*
to patch up one's ~ arreglar los pleitos
II. <-ll-> *vi* reñir, pelearse; **to ~ about sth**
pelearse por algo

quarrelsome ['kwɒrəlsəm, *Am:* 'kwɔːr-]
adj 1. (*belligerent*) pendenciero, -a, peleonero,
-a *Méx* 2. (*grumbly*) enojadizo, -a, enojón, -ona
Méx

quarry[1] ['kwɒri, *Am:* 'kwɔːr-] I.<-ies> *n*
(*rock pit*) cantera *f* II.<-ie-> *vt* extraer

quarry[2] ['kwɒri, *Am:* 'kwɔːr-] <-ies> *n* presa *f*

quart [kwɔːt, *Am:* kwɔːrt] *n* cuarto *m* de
galón

quarter ['kwɔːtəʳ, *Am:* 'kwɔːrt̬əʳ] I. *n* 1. (*one
fourth*) cuarto *m;* **three ~s** tres cuartos; **a ~ of
the British** una cuarta parte de los británicos;
a ~ of a century/an hour un cuarto de siglo/
de hora; **a ~ to three** las tres menos cuarto, un
cuarto para las tres *AmL;* **a ~ past three** las
tres y cuarto 2. *Am* (*25 cents*) un cuarto de
dólar 3. *a.* FIN, SCHOOL trimestre *m* 4. (*neighbourhood*) barrio *m;* (*area*) zona *f;* **at close ~s**
de cerca; **all ~s of the earth** en todos los confines de la tierra 5. (*mercy*) cuartel *m;* **to give
~** dar cuartel; **to ask for ~** pedir cuartel 6. *pl*
(*unspecified group or person*) círculos *mpl;* **in
certain ~s** en ciertos círculos; **in high ~s** en
altas esferas 7. (*area of compass*) cuadrante *m;*
from the north/west ~ desde el cuadrante
norte/oeste II. *vt* 1. (*cut into four*) cuartear; **to
~ sb** descuartizar a alguien 2. (*give housing*)
alojar; **to be ~ed with sb** estar alojado en casa
de alguien; MIL acuartelar III. *adj* cuarto; **~
hour/pound** un cuarto de hora/libra

quarterback ['kwɔːtəbæk, *Am:* 'kwɔːrt̬ə-]
n (*US football*) mariscal *mf* de campo
quarter-day *n* *Brit* día *m* de liquidación
quarterdeck *n* NAUT alcázar *m* **quarterfinal** *n* SPORTS cuarto *m* de final

quartering *n no pl* 1. (*dividing into fourths*)
corte *m* en cuatro 2. MIL (*housing*) acuartela-

miento *m* 3. (*emblems on shield*) cuartel *m*

quarterly ['kwɔːtəli, *Am:* 'kwɔːrt̬əli] I. *adv*
trimestralmente II. *adj* trimestral

quartermaster ['kwɔːtəˌmɑːstəʳ, *Am:*
'kwɔːrt̬əˌmæstəʳ] *n* 1. MIL oficial *m* de intendencia 2. NAUT cabo *mf* de la marina **quarter-
-tone** *n* MUS cuarto *m* de tono

quartet *n*, **quartette** [kwɔːˈtet, *Am:*
kwɔːr-] *n* MUS cuarteto *m*

quartz [kwɔːts, *Am:* kwɔːrts] I. *n* *no pl*
cuarzo *m* II. *adj* de cuarzo; **~ crystal** cristal de
cuarzo

quartz clock *n* reloj *m* de cuarzo

quartz (**iodine**) **lamp** *n* lámpara *f* de cuarzo

quasar ['kweɪzɑːʳ, *Am:* -zɑːr] *n* quásar *m*

quash [kwɒʃ, *Am:* kwɑːʃ] *vt* 1. (*supress*)
suprimir; (*rebellion*) sofocar; (*rumour*) acallar;
to ~ sb's dreams/plans aplastar los sueños/
planes de alguien 2. LAW (*annul: conviction,
verdict, sentence*) anular; (*indictment, decision*) invalidar; (*law, bill, writ*) derogar

quasi- ['kwɑːsi, *Am:* 'kweɪsaɪ] cuasi

quatrain ['kwɒtreɪn, *Am:* 'kwɑːtreɪn] *n* LIT
cuarteto *m*

quaver ['kweɪvəʳ, *Am:* -vəʳ] I. *vi* temblar II. *n*
1. (*shake*) temblor *m;* **with a ~ in one's voice**
con voz trémula 2. *Aus, Brit* MUS corchea *f*

quay [kiː] *n* muelle *m*

queasy ['kwiːzi] <-ier, -iest> *adj* 1. (*nauseous*) mareado, -a; **to have a ~ feeling** sentir
náuseas 2. *fig* (*unsettled*) intranquilo, -a; **with
a ~ conscience** con la conciencia intranquila;
to feel ~ about sth sentir desasosiego acerca
de algo

Quebec [kwɪˈbek, *Am:* kwiːˈbek] *n* Quebec
m

queen [kwiːn] I. *n* 1. (*monarch*) reina *f;* **~ of
hearts/diamonds** (*cards*) reina de cora-
zones/diamantes 2. *pej* (*gay man*) loca *f;* **drag
~** drag queen *f* II. *vt* 1. (*make queen*) **to ~ sb**
coronar reina a alguien 2. (*in chess*) coronar

queen bee *n* 1. ZOOL abeja *f* reina 2. *pej*
(*bossy woman*) mandamás *f inv* **queen
dowager** *n* reina *f* viuda

queenly ['kwiːnli] <-ier, iest> *adj* regia

Queen Mother *n* Reina *f* Madre **Queen's
Counsel** *n* *Brit* LAW título de abogacía de categoría superior **Queen's English** *n no pl,*
Brit inglés *m* correcto; **to speak ~** hablar correctamente

queer [kwɪəʳ, *Am:* kwɪr] I.<-er, -est> *adj*
1. (*strange*) extraño, -a; **to have ~ ideas** tener
ideas raras; **to feel rather ~** sentirse algo
extraño; **to be a ~ fish** ser un bicho raro; **to
be ~ in the head** estar medio loco 2. *pej, inf*
(*homosexual*) maricón II. *n pej, inf* maricón *m*
III. *vt* **to ~ sb's pitch** *Aus, Brit, inf* estropear
los planes de alguien

quell [kwel] *vt* (*unrest, rebellion, protest*)
sofocar; (*doubts, fears, anxieties*) disipar; **to ~
sb's anger** calmar la rabia de alguien

quench [kwentʃ] *vt* 1. (*satisfy*) satisfacer;
(*thirst*) saciar; **to ~ sb's thirst for knowledge**

fig saciar la curiosidad de alguien **2.** (*put out*) sofocar; **to ~ the fire** apagar el incendio **3.** (*supress*) suprimir; **to ~ sb's desire** apagar el deseo de alguien; **to ~ sb's enthusiasm** contener el entusiasmo de alguien

querulous ['kwerʊləs, *Am:* 'kwerjə-] *adj* (*person*) quejoso, -a; (*voice*) quejumbroso, -a

query ['kwɪəri, *Am:* 'kwɪri] I. <-ies> *n* pregunta *f;* **to have a ~ for sb** tener una pregunta para alguien; **to raise a ~** plantear un interrogante; **to settle a ~** resolver un interrogante II. <-ie-> *vt* **1.** *form* (*dispute*) cuestionar; (*doubt*) poner en duda **2.** (*ask*) preguntar; **to ~ whether ...** preguntar si...

quest [kwest] *n* búsqueda *f;* **in ~ of sth/sb** en busca de algo/alguien; **the ~ for truth** la búsqueda de la verdad

question ['kwestʃən] I. *n* **1.** (*inquiry*) pregunta *f;* **frequently asked ~s** *a.* INFOR preguntas frecuentes; **to put a ~ to sb** hacer una pregunta a alguien; **to pop the ~ to sb** proponer matrimonio a alguien, declarárse a alguien *Méx* **2.** *no pl* (*doubt*) duda *f;* **without ~** sin duda; **to be beyond ~** estar fuera de duda **3.** (*issue*) cuestión *f;* **it's a ~ of life or death** *a. fig* es un asunto de vida o muerte; **to be a ~ of time/money** ser una cuestión de tiempo/dinero; **to raise a ~** plantear un problema; **to be out of the ~** ser totalmente imposible; **there's no ~ of sb doing sth** sería imposible que alguien hiciera algo **4.** SCHOOL, UNIV (*test problem*) pregunta *f;* **to do a ~** resolver una pregunta II. *vt* **1.** (*ask*) preguntar **2.** (*interrogate*) interrogar **3.** (*doubt*) cuestionar; (*facts, findings*) poner en duda

questionable ['kwestʃənəbl] *adj* discutible

questioner *n* interrogador(a) *m(f)*

questioning I. *n no pl* interrogatorio *m;* **to be taken in for ~** ser detenido para ser interrogado II. *adj* inquisidor(a); **to have a ~ mind** ser inquisitivo

question mark *n* signo *m* de interrogación; **a ~ hangs over sth** *fig* un interrogante se cierne sobre algo

question master *n Brit* presentador(a) *m(f)*

questionnaire [ˌkwestʃə'neəʳ, *Am:* ˌkwestʃə'ner] *n* cuestionario *m*

question time *n Brit* POL turno *m* de preguntas

queue [kjuː] I. *n Aus, Brit a.* INFOR cola *f;* (*in traffic*) retención *f,* congestionamiento *m Méx;* **to be in a ~ for sth** estar en la cola para algo; **to join a ~** ponerse en la cola; **to stand in a ~** hacer cola II. *vi* hacer cola

quibble ['kwɪbl] I. *n* **1.** (*petty argument*) pega *f;* **a ~ over sth** una objeción acerca de algo **2.** (*criticism*) sutileza *f* II. *vi* poner peros a; **to ~ over sth** quejarse por algo

quibbler ['kwɪbləʳ, *Am:* -lə-] *n* polemizador(a) *m(f)*

quibbling ['kwɪblɪŋ] I. *n no pl* sutilezas *fpl* II. *adj* quisquilloso, -a

quiche [kiːʃ] *n* quiche *f,* quiche *m AmL*

quick [kwɪk] I. <-er, -est> *adj* **1.** (*fast*) rápido, -a, veloz; **~ as lightning** (veloz) como un rayo; **in ~ succession** uno detrás del otro; **to be ~ to do sth** hacer algo con rapidez; **to have a ~ one** tomarse una copa rápida; **to have a ~ meal** hacer una comida rápida **2.** (*short*) corto, -a; **the ~est way** el camino más corto; **to give sb a ~ call** hacer una llamada corta a alguien **3.** (*hurried*) apresurado, -a; **to say a ~ good-bye/hello** decir un adiós/hola apresurado **4.** (*smart*) vivo, -a; **~ thinking** pensamiento ágil; **to have a ~ mind** tener una mente vivaz; **to have a ~ temper** tener mal genio II. <-er, -est> *adv* rápidamente; **~!** ¡rápido!; **as ~ as possible** tan pronto como sea posible; **to get rich ~** enriquecerse rápidamente III. *n* **1.** carne *f* viva; **to bite/cut nails to the ~** dejar las uñas en carne viva **2.** *pl, form* **the ~ and the dead** los vivos y los muertos ▶**to cut sb to the ~** herir a alguien en lo más vivo

quick-acting [ˌkwɪk'æktɪŋ] *adj* de efecto rápido; **to be ~** actuar rápidamente **quick--change artist** *n* transformista *mf*

quicken ['kwɪkən] I. *vt* **1.** (*make faster*) apresurar; **to ~ the pace** acelerar el paso **2.** (*awaken*) estimular II. *vi* **1.** (*increase speed*) apresurarse **2.** (*become more active*) avivarse

quick-freeze ['kwɪkfriːz] *vt irr* congelar rápidamente

quickie ['kwɪki] *n* **1.** *inf* (*fast thing*) cosa *f* rápida **2.** *inf* (*fast drink*) copa *f* rápida **3.** *inf* (*quick sex*) quiqui *m,* palito *m Méx*

quickly ['kwɪkli] *adv* rápidamente

quickness ['kwɪknɪs] *n no pl* **1.** (*speed*) rapidez *f;* **~ of temper** mal carácter *m* **2.** (*liveliness*) viveza *f;* **~ of mind** mente *f* rápida

quicksand ['kwɪksænd] *n no pl* arenas *fpl* movedizas; **moral ~** *fig* moral *f* escabrosa

quicksilver *n no pl s.* **mercury** mercurio *m*

quickstep *n no pl* quickstep *m* (*baile formal a ritmo rápido*) **quick-tempered** *adj* irascible **quick-witted** *adj* perspicaz; **a ~ reply** una respuesta aguda

quid[1] [kwɪd] *inv n Brit, inf* (*money*) libra *f;* **to be ~s in** estar forrado

quid[2] [kwɪd] *n inf* (*tobacco*) mascada *f* de tabaco

quid pro quo ['kwɪdprəʊ'kwəʊ, *Am:* -proʊ'kwoʊ] *n form* compensación *f*

quiescent [kwɪ'esnt, *Am:* kwaɪ'-] *adj form* inactivo, -a

quiet ['kwaɪət] I. *n no pl* **1.** (*silence*) silencio *m* **2.** (*lack of activity*) sosiego *m;* **peace and ~** paz y tranquilidad; **on the ~** a escondidas II. <-er, -est> *adj* **1.** (*not loud*) silencioso, -a; **to speak in a ~ voice** hablar en voz baja **2.** (*not talkative*) callado, -a; **to keep ~** mantenerse callado **3.** (*secret*) secreto, -a; **to have a ~ word with sb** hablar en privado con alguien; **to keep ~ about sth** mantenerse ca-

llado respecto de algo **4.** (*unostentatious*) discreto, -a **5.** (*unexciting*) tranquilo, -a
quieten ['kwaɪətn] **I.** *vi* **1.** (*quiet*) callarse **2.** (*calm*) calmarse **II.** *vt* **1.** (*make quiet*) hacer callar **2.** (*calm*) calmar
◆**quieten down I.** *vi* **1.** (*quiet*) callarse **2.** (*calm*) calmarse **II.** *vt* **1.** (*silence*) hacer callar **2.** (*calm* (*down*)) calmar
quietly ['kwaɪətli] *adv* **1.** (*not loudly*) silenciosamente; **to speak** ~ hablar en voz baja **2.** (*speaking*) calladamente **3.** (*peacefully*) calmadamente
quietness ['kwaɪətnɪs] *n no pl* tranquilidad *f*
quietude ['kwaɪɪtjuːd, *Am:* 'kwaɪətuːd] *n no pl, form* quietud *f*
quiff [kwɪf] *n* copete *m*, gallo *m Méx*
quill [kwɪl] *n* **1.** (*feather, pen*) pluma *f*; *liter* (*pen*) cálamo *m* **2.** (*porcupine*) púa *f*
quilt [kwɪlt] **I.** *n* edredón *m* **II.** *vt* acolchar
quin [kwɪn] *n Brit abbr of* **quintuplet** quintillizo, -a *m, f*
quince [kwɪns] *n no pl* membrillo *m*
quinine [kwɪ'niːn, *Am:* 'kwaɪnaɪn] *n no pl* quinina *f*
quintessence [kwɪn'tesns] *n no pl* quintaesencia *f*
quintessential [ˌkwɪntə'senʃəl, *Am:* -te'-] *adj form* por antonomasia
quintet(te) [kwɪn'tet] *n* quinteto *m*
quintuple ['kwɪntjʊpl, *Am:* kwɪn'tuː-] *form* **I.** *adj* quíntuplo, -a **II.** *vt* quintuplicar **III.** *vi* quintuplicarse
quintuplet ['kwɪntjuːplet, *Am:* kwɪn'tʌplɪt] *n* quintillizo, -a *m, f*
quip [kwɪp] **I.** *n* pulla *f* **II.** *vi* decir humorísticamente
quirk [kwɜːk, *Am:* kwɜːrk] *n* **1.** (*habit*) excentricidad *f* **2.** (*oddity*) rareza *f* **3.** (*sudden twist or turn*) **a** ~ **of fate** un capricho del destino
quirky ['kwɜːki, *Am:* 'kwɜːr-] <-ier, -iest> *adj* **1.** (*original*) original **2.** (*odd*) excéntrico, -a
quit [kwɪt] <quit *o* quitted, quit *o* quitted> **I.** *vi* parar; (*job*) dimitir **II.** *vt* **1.** (*leave*) dejar; (*place*) irse de **2.** *Am* (*stop*) parar; (*smoking*) dejar de **3.** INFOR salir de
quite [kwaɪt] *adv* **1.** (*fairly*) bastante; ~ **a bit** considerablemente, bastantín *Méx*; ~ **a distance** una distancia considerable; ~ **something** una cosa notable **2.** (*completely*) completamente; ~ **wrong** totalmente equivocado; **not** ~ no tanto; **not** ~ **as clever/rich as ...** no tan inteligente/rico como...
quits [kwɪts] *adj inf* en paz; **to be** ~ (**with sb**) estar en paz con alguien; **to call it** ~ hacer las paces
quittance ['kwɪtns] *n form* descargo *m*
quiver[1] ['kwɪvəʳ, *Am:* -əʳ] **I.** *n* (*shiver*) estremecimiento *m* **II.** *vi* temblar
quiver[2] ['kwɪvəʳ, *Am:* -əʳ] *n* aljaba *f*
quixotic [kwɪk'sɒtɪk, *Am:* -'saːţɪk] *adj liter* quijotesco, -a
quiz [kwɪz] **I.** <-es> *n* **1.** (*game*) acertijo *m*; ~ **question** pregunta *f* de concurso **2.** (*short*

test) encuesta *f* **II.** *vt* interrogar
quizmaster ['kwɪzˌmɑːstəʳ, *Am:* -ˌmæstəʳ] *n* moderador *m*
quiz show *n* programa *m* concurso
quizzical ['kwɪzɪkəl] *adj* **1.** (*questioning*) interrogante **2.** (*teasing*) burlón, -ona
quoit [kɔɪt, *Am:* kwɔɪt] *n Am* tejo *m*
quorate ['kwɔːrət, *Am:* 'kwɔːrɪt] *adj form* con quórum
quorum ['kwɔːrəm] *n form* quórum *m*
quota ['kwəʊtə, *Am:* 'kwoʊţə] *n* **1.** (*fixed amount allowed*) cuota *f*; **export** ~ cupo *m* de exportación **2.** (*proportion*) parte *f*
quotable ['kwəʊtəbl, *Am:* 'kwoʊţə-] *adj* citable
quotation [kwəʊ'teɪʃən, *Am:* kwoʊ'-] *n* **1.** (*repeated words*) cita *f* **2.** FIN cotización *f*
quotation marks *npl* comillas *fpl*
quote [kwəʊt, *Am:* kwoʊt] **I.** *n* **1.** *inf* (*quotation*) cita *f* **2.** *pl, inf* (*quotation marks*) comillas *fpl* **3.** *inf* (*estimate*) presupuesto *m* **4.** FIN cotización *f* **II.** *vt* **1.** citar **2.** (*name*) nombrar **3.** FIN cotizar; **a** ~**d company** una empresa que cotiza en bolsa **III.** *vi* (*repeat exact words*) citar; **to** ~ **from sb** citar a alguien; **to** ~ **from memory** citar de memoria
quotidian [kwəʊ'tɪdiən, *Am:* kwoʊ'-] *adj form* cotidiano, -a
quotient ['kwəʊʃənt, *Am:* 'kwoʊ-] *n* **1.** MAT cociente *m* **2.** (*factor*) coeficiente *m*; **intelligence** ~ coeficiente de inteligencia
qwerty keyboard [ˌkwɜːti'kiːbɔːdfaɪl, *Am:* ˌkwɜːrţi'kiːbɔːrd-] *n* teclado *m* qwerty

R

R, r [ɑːʳ, *Am:* ɑːr] ɪ, R *f*; ~ **for Roger** R de Ramón
R. **1.** *abbr of* **River** r. **2.** *Am abbr of* **Republican** republicano, -a
rabbi ['ræbaɪ] *n* rabino *m*
rabbit ['ræbɪt] **I.** *n* conejo, -a *m, f* **II.** *vi Brit, Aus, inf* parlotear
rabbit hole *n* conejera *f* **rabbit hutch** *n* conejera *f* **rabbit punch** *n* golpe *m* en la nuca
rabble ['ræbl] *n no pl* muchedumbre *f*; **the** ~ el populacho
rabble-rouser ['ræblˌraʊzəʳ, *Am:* -zəʳ] *n* agitador(a) *m(f)*
rabble-rousing *adj* agitador(a)
rabid ['ræbɪd] *adj* **1.** (*furious*) furibundo, -a **2.** (*fanatical*) fanático, -a **3.** (*suffering from rabies*) rabioso, -a
rabies ['reɪbiːz] *n* rabia *f*; **to carry** ~ tener la rabia
RAC [ˌɑːˈeɪˈsiː, *Am:* ˌɑːr-] *n Brit abbr of* **Royal Automobile Club** ≈ Real Automóbil Club *m* de España

raccoon [rə'kuːn, *Am:* ræk'uːn] *n* mapache *m*

race¹ [reɪs] I. *n* carrera *f*; **a ~ against time** una carrera contra reloj; **100-metre ~** carrera de cien metros lisos; **to run a ~** participar en una carrera ▸**slow and steady wins the ~** *prov* despacito y buena letra II. *vi* 1.(*move quickly*) correr; SPORTS competir; **to ~ through one's work** hacer el trabajo a toda prisa 2.(*engine*) acelerarse III. *vt* 1.(*compete against*) competir con; **to ~ sb home** echar una carrera hasta casa a alguien 2.(*enter for race: horse*) hacer correr

race² [reɪs] *n no pl* 1.(*ethnic grouping*) raza *f* 2.(*species*) especie *f* 3.(*lineage*) estirpe *f*

race conflict *n no pl* conflicto *m* racial

racecourse ['reɪskɔːs, *Am:* -kɔːrs] *n* hipódromo *m*

race hatred *n no pl* odio *m* racial

racehorse ['reɪshɔːs, *Am:* -hɔːrs] *n* caballo *m* de carreras

race meet *n Am,* **race meeting** *n* concurso *m* hípico

racer ['reɪsəʳ, *Am:* -ə·] *n* 1.(*person*) corredor(a) *m(f)* 2.(*bicycle*) bicicleta *f* de carreras

race relations *npl* relaciones *fpl* interraciales **race riot** *n* disturbio *m* racial

racetrack ['reɪstræk] *n* hipódromo *m*

racial ['reɪʃəl] *adj* racial

racialism ['reɪʃəlɪzəm] *n Brit s.* **racism**

racialist ['reɪʃəlɪst] *n, adj Brit s.* **racist**

racing I. *n* carreras *fpl* II. *adj* de carreras

racing bicycle *n,* **racing bike** *n inf* bicicleta *f* de carreras **racing car** *n* coche *m* de carreras **racing driver** *n* piloto *mf* de carreras, volante *m AmL* **racing yacht** *n* yate *m* de regata

racism ['reɪsɪzəm] *n no pl* racismo *m*

racist ['reɪsɪst] I. *n* racista *mf* II. *adj* racista

rack [ræk] I. *n* 1.(*framework, shelf*) estante *m;* **luggage ~** portaequipajes *m inv;* **plate ~** escurreplatos *m inv* 2.GASTR **~ of lamb/beef** costillar *m* de cordero/ternera 3.(*torture instrument*) potro *m;* **to be on the ~** *fig* estar en ascuas II. *vt* atormentar

racket ['rækɪt] *n* 1.SPORTS raqueta *f;* **~s** frontenis *m; inv* 2. *no pl, inf* (*loud noise*) barullo *m,* balumba *f AmS;* **to make a ~** armar un alboroto 3.(*scheme*) chanchullo *m,* transa *f Méx*

racketeer [ˌrækɪ'tɪəʳ, *Am:* -ə·'tɪr] *n* timador(a) *m(f)*

rack-rent ['rækrent] *n* alquiler *m* exorbitante

racoon [rə'kuːn, *Am:* ræk'uːn] *n s.* **raccoon**

racy ['reɪsi] <-ier, -iest> *adj* (*film, book*) atrevido, -a

radar ['reɪdɑːʳ, *Am:* -dɑːr] *n no pl* radar *m*

radar screen *n* pantalla *f* de radar **radar trap** *n* detector *m* de velocidad

radial ['reɪdɪəl] *adj* radial; TECH en estrella

radiant ['reɪdɪənt] *adj* radiante

radiate ['reɪdɪeɪt] I. *vi* irradiar II. *vt* 1.(*emit*) irradiar 2.(*display: happiness, enthusiasm*) mostrar

radiation [ˌreɪdi'eɪʃən] *n no pl* radiación *f*

radiation sickness *n no pl* radiotoxemia *f* **radiation therapy** *n* radioterapia *f*

radiator ['reɪdieɪtəʳ, *Am:* -t̬ə·] *n* radiador *m*

radiator cap *n* tapón *m* del radiador

radical ['rædɪkəl] I. *n* 1. *a.* CHEM, MAT radical *m* 2.POL radical *mf* II. *adj* (*change, idea*) radical; (*measures*) drástico, -a

radicalism ['rædɪkəlɪzəm] *n no pl* radicalismo *m*

radii ['reɪdɪaɪ] *n pl of* **radius**

radio ['reɪdiəʊ, *Am:* -oʊ] I. *n* radio *f,* radio *m AmC* II. *vt* (*information*) radiar; (*person*) llamar por radio

radioactive [ˌreɪdiəʊ'æktɪv, *Am:* -oʊ'-] *adj* radioactivo, -a

radioactivity [ˌreɪdiəʊæk'tɪvəti, *Am:* -oʊæk'tɪvət̬i] *n no pl* radiactividad *f*

radio alarm (**clock**) *n* radio *f* despertador **radio beacon** *n* radiofaro *m* **radio button** *n* INFOR botón *m* tipo radio

radiocarbon dating [ˌreɪdiəʊ'kɑːbən 'deɪtɪŋ, *Am:* -oʊkɑːr-] *n no pl* fechado *m* por radiocarbono

radio cassette (**recorder**) *n* radiocasete *m*

radiogram ['reɪdiəʊgræm, *Am:* -oʊ-] *n* radiograma *m*

radiograph ['reɪdiəʊgrɑːf, *Am:* -oʊgræf] *n* radiografía *f*

radiographer *n* radiógrafo, -a *m, f*

radiography [ˌreɪdi'ɒgrəfi, *Am:* -'ɑːgrə-] *n* radiografía *f*

radio ham *n* radioaficionado, -a *m, f*

radiologist [ˌreɪdi'ɒlədʒɪst, *Am:* -'ɑːlə-] *n* radiólogo, -a *m, f*

radiology [ˌreɪdi'ɒlədʒi, *Am:* -'ɑːlə-] *n no pl* radiología *f*

radio microphone *n* micrófono *m* inalámbrico

radio operator *n* radioperador(a) *m(f)* **radiopager** *n* buscapersonas *m inv* **radio play** *n* pieza *f* radiofónica **radio programme** *n* programa *m* de radio

radioscopy [ˌreɪdi'ɒskəpi] *n no pl* MED radioscopia *f*

radio set *n* aparato *m* de radio **radio station** *n* emisora *f* de radio, estación *f* de radio *AmL;* **pirate ~** emisora *f* pirata, estación *f* pirata *AmL*

radiotelephony [ˌreɪdiəʊtɪ'lefəni] *n no pl* radiotelefonía *f*

radio telescope *n* radiotelescopio *m*

radiotherapy [ˌreɪdiəʊ'θerəpi, *Am:* -oʊ'-] *n no pl* radioterapia *f*

radio wave *n* onda *f* de radio

radish ['rædɪʃ] <-es> *n* rábano *m*

radium ['reɪdiəm] *n no pl* radio *m*

radium treatment *n* radioterapia *f*

radius ['reɪdiəs] <-dii> *n* radio *m*

RAF [ˌɑː'eɪ'ef, *Am:* ˌɑːr-] *n abbr of* **Royal Air Force the ~** la fuerza aérea británica

raffia ['ræfiə] *n no pl* rafia *f*

raffish ['ræfɪʃ] *adj* (*appearance*) de pillo, -a

raffle ['ræfl] I. *n* rifa *f* II. *vt* rifar
raft [rɑːft, *Am:* ræft] I. *n* 1. (*vessel*) balsa *f* 2. *inf* (*a lot*) montón *m* II. *vt* transportar en balsa III. *vi* ir en balsa
rafter[1] ['rɑːftər, *Am:* 'ræftə] *n* viga *f*
rafter[2] ['rɑːftər, *Am:* 'ræftə] *n* (*person*) balsero, -a *m, f*
rafting *n* rafting *m*
rag [ræg] I. *n* 1. (*old cloth*) trapo *m* 2. *pl* (*worn-out clothes*) harapos *mpl* 3. *pej* (*newspaper*) periodicucho *m* 4. mus ragtime *m* II. <-gg-> *vt inf* tomar el pelo a
ragamuffin ['rægəmʌfɪn] *n inf* golfo, -a *m, f*
ragbag ['rægbæg] *n* mezclanza *f*
rage [reɪdʒ] I. *n* 1. *no pl* (*anger*) furia *f*; to be in a ~ estar hecho una furia 2. (*fashion*) to be all the ~ ser el último grito II. *vi* 1. (*express fury*) enfurecerse; to ~ at sb/sth enfurecerse con alguien/algo 2. (*continue: battle*) continuar con pleno vigor; (*epidemic*) hacer estragos; (*wind, storm*) bramar; (*fire*) arder furiosamente
ragged ['rægɪd] *adj* 1. (*torn: clothes*) hecho, -a jirones 2. (*wearing worn clothes*) andrajoso, -a 3. (*rough*) recortado, -a 4. (*irregular*) irregular ▶to run sb ~ agotar a alguien
raging ['reɪdʒɪŋ] *adj a.* meteo furioso, -a; (*blizzard*) violento, -a; (*sea*) embravecido, -a; (*toothache*) intenso, -a
ragout ['ræguː, *Am:* ræg'uː] *n no pl* ragú *m*
rag rug *n* alfombrilla *f* de retazos
ragtag ['rægtæg] *n* chusma *f*
ragtime ['rægtaɪm] *n no pl* ragtime *m*
rag trade *n inf* gremio *m* de la aguja
raid [reɪd] I. *n* 1. mil incursión *f* 2. (*attack*) ataque *m* 3. (*robbery*) asalto *m* 4. (*by police*) redada *f* II. *vt* 1. mil invadir 2. (*attack*) atacar 3. (*by police*) hacer una redada en
rail [reɪl] I. *n* 1. (*part of fence*) valla *f*; (*bar for supporting people*) barandilla *f*; (*bar for hanging things on*) barra *f*; towel ~ portatoallas *m inv* 2. *no pl* (*railway system*) ferrocarril *m* 3. (*track*) raíl *m*, riel *m* AmL; by ~ en tren, por ferrocarril; ~ ticket billete *m* de ferrocarril, boleto *m* de tren *Méx* ▶to go off the ~s *Brit, inf* descarrilarse II. *vt* to ~ sth in [*o* off] cercar algo
◆**rail against** *vt* clamar contra
railcard ['reɪlkɑːd, *Am:* -kɑːrd] *n* tarjeta *para obtener descuentos en el tren*
railhead ['reɪlhed] *n* cabeza *f* de línea
railing ['reɪlɪŋ] *n* 1. (*post*) valla *f*; iron ~ verja *f*; wooden ~ cerco *m* 2. (*of stairs*) pasamanos *m inv* **rail network** *n* red *f* ferroviaria
railroad ['reɪlrəʊd, *Am:* -roʊd] I. *n* Am 1. (*system*) ferrocarril *m* 2. (*track*) línea *f* de ferrocarril II. *vt fig* to ~ sb into doing sth obligar a alguien a hacer algo
rail strike *n* huelga *f* de ferrocarril
railway ['reɪlweɪ] *n* Brit 1. (*tracks*) vía *f* férrea 2. (*system*) ferrocarril *m*
railway bridge *n* puente *m* ferroviario **railway carriage** *n* vagón *m* **railway cross-**

-ing *n* paso *m* a nivel **railway engine** *n* locomotora *f* **railway line** *n* vía *f* del tren **railwayman** <-men> *n* ferroviario *m*, ferrocarrilero *m Méx* **railway station** *n* estación *f* del ferrocarril
rain [reɪn] I. *n no pl* lluvia *f*; ~ shower chubasco *m*; the ~s la temporada de lluvias ▶come ~ or shine pase lo que pase; to be as right as ~ *inf* estar perfectamente II. *vi* llover III. *vt* llover
◆**rain off** *vt*, **rain out** *vt Am* to be rained off [*o* out] cancelarse por lluvia
rainbow *n* meteo arco *m* iris **rain cloud** *n* nube *f* de lluvia **raincoat** *n* gabardina *f*, piloto *m Arg* **raindrop** *n* gota *f* de lluvia **rainfall** *n no pl* precipitación *f* **rain forest** *n* selva *f* tropical **rain gauge** *n* pluviómetro *m* **rainproof** I. *adj* impermeable II. *vt* impermeabilizar **rainstorm** *n* tormenta *f* de lluvia **rainwater** *n no pl* agua *f* de lluvia
rainy ['reɪni] *adj* <-ier, -iest> lluvioso, -a; the ~ season la estación de las lluvias
raise [reɪz] I. *n Am, Aus* (*of wages, prices*) aumento *m* II. *vt* 1. (*lift*) levantar; (*periscope, window*) subir; (*arm, hand, leg*) levantar; (*flag*) izar; (*anchor*) levar; (*ship*) poner a flote 2. (*stir up*) provocar; (*doubts*) suscitar 3. (*increase: wages, awareness*) aumentar; (*bet*) subir; mat elevar; (*standards*) mejorar 4. (*promote*) ascender 5. (*introduce: subject, problem*) plantear 6. fin recaudar 7. (*build*) erigir; (*monument*) levantar 8. (*bring up, cultivate*) cultivar 9. (*end: embargo*) levantar 10. (*contact*) llamar, contactar *Méx*; to ~ the alarm dar la voz de alarma ▶to ~ hell [*o* Cain] poner el grito en el cielo
raisin ['reɪzn] *n* pasa *f*
rake[1] [reɪk] *n* (*dissolute man*) vividor *m*
rake[2] [reɪk] I. *n* (*tool*) rastrillo *m* II. *vt* rastrillar
◆**rake in** *vt inf* (*money*) amasar; to be raking it in estar forrándose
◆**rake up** *vt* 1. (*gather*) reunir 2. *fig* (*refer to*) sacar a relucir; (*quarrel*) atizar
rake-off ['reɪkɒf, *Am:* -ɑːf] *n inf* tajada *f*
rakish ['reɪkɪʃ] *adj* 1. (*jaunty*) desenvuelto, -a 2. (*dissolute*) disoluto, -a
rally ['ræli] I. *n* <-ies> 1. (*race*) rally *m* 2. (*in tennis*) peloteo *m* 3. pol mitin *m* II. *vi* 1. med mejorar; fin repuntar 2. mil agruparse; to ~ behind sb apoyar a alguien III. *vt* 1. mil reagrupar 2. (*support*) apoyar
◆**rally round** I. *vt* apoyar II. *vi* agruparse
rally driver *n* conductor(a) *m(f)* de rallys
ram [ræm] I. *n* 1. (*male sheep*) carnero *m*; (*astrology*) Aries *m* 2. (*implement*) maza *f*; mil ariete *m* II. *vt* <-mm-> 1. (*hit*) embestir contra 2. (*push*) to ~ sth into sth embutir algo en algo
RAM [ræm] *n* infor *abbr of* Random Access Memory RAM *f*
Ramadan [ˌræmə'dæn, *Am:* ˌræmə'dɑːn] *n* Ramadán *m*

R

ramble ['ræmbl] I. *n* (*walk*) caminata *f*; **to go for a** ~ ir de excursión II. *vi* 1.(*person*) pasear; (*river*) serpentear; (*plant*) trepar 2.(*in speech*) divagar

rambler ['ræmblə^r, *Am:* -blə·] *n* 1.(*walker*) excursionista *mf* 2. BOT rosa *f* trepadora

rambling ['ræmblɪŋ] I. *n* 1.(*walking*) excursionismo *m* 2. *pl* (*speech*) divagaciones *fpl* II. *adj* 1.(*building*) laberíntico, -a 2.(*plant*) trepador(a) 3.(*talk*) divagante

ramekin ['reɪmkɪn, *Am:* 'ræməkɪn] *n* potecito *m*

ramification [ˌræmɪfɪ'keɪʃən] *n* ramificación *f*

ramify ['ræmɪfaɪ] *vi* ramificarse

ramp [ræmp] *n* 1.(*sloping way*) rampa *f*; AVIAT escalerilla *f* 2. *Am* AUTO (*lane to join*) carril *m* de incorporación; (*lane to leave*) carril *m* de salida

rampage [ræm'peɪdʒ, *Am:* 'ræmpeɪdʒ] I. *n* destrozos *mpl*; **to be on the** ~ ir arrasando todo II. *vi* arrasar

rampant ['ræmpənt] *adj* (*disease, growth*) exhuberante; (*inflation*) galopante

rampart ['ræmpɑːt, *Am:* -pɑːrt] *n* muralla *f*

ramrod ['ræmrɒd, *Am:* -rɑːd] *n* baqueta *f* ▸ **as stiff as a** ~ más tieso que un ajo

ramshackle ['ræmʃækl] *adj* 1.(*dilapidated*) desvencijado, -a 2.(*disorganized*) improvisado, -a

ran [ræn] *pt of* **run**

ranch [rɑːntʃ, *Am:* ræntʃ] I.<-es> *n* granja *f*, rancho *m Méx*, estancia *f RíoPl* II. *adj* de granja III. *vi* (*conduct a ranch*) llevar una granja

rancher ['rɑːntʃə^r, *Am:* 'ræntʃə·] *n* 1.(*owner*) hacendado, -a *m, f*, ranchero, -a *m, f Méx* 2.(*worker*) granjero, -a *m, f*

rancid ['rænsɪd] *adj* rancio, -a

rancor ['ræŋkə^r, *Am:* -kə·] *n Am, Aus s.* **rancour**

rancorous ['ræŋkərəs] *adj* rencoroso, -a

rancour ['ræŋkə^r, *Am:* -kə·] *n no pl* rencor *m*

random ['rændəm] I. *n no pl* **at** ~ al azar II. *adj* aleatorio, -a

randy ['rændi] <-ier, -iest> *adj inf* cachondo, -a, birriondo, -a *Méx*

rang [ræŋ] *pt of* **ring²**

range [reɪndʒ] I. *n* 1.(*area*) área *m*; (*for shooting*) campo *m* de tiro 2.(*row*) hilera *f* 3. *Am* (*pasture*) pradera *f* 4.(*field*) ámbito *m*, campo *m* 5.(*scale*) gama *f*; **the full** ~ **of sth** la gama completa de algo 6. FASHION **autumn/ spring** ~ línea *f* de otoño/primavera 7. GEO cadena *f* 8. MUS extensión *f* 9.(*maximum capability*) alcance *m*; **out of** ~ fuera del alcance; **within** ~ al alcance II. *vi* 1.(*vary*) variar 2.(*rove*) deambular 3.(*extend*) extenderse III. *vt* alinear; **to** ~ **oneself** alinearse

range finder *n* telémetro *m*

ranger ['reɪndʒə^r, *Am:* -dʒə·] *n* guardabosque *mf*

rangy ['reɪndʒi] *adj* <-ier, -iest> larguirucho, -a

rank¹ [ræŋk] *adj* 1.(*absolute*) total; (*beginner*) absoluto, -a 2.(*smelling unpleasant*) fétido, -a

rank² [ræŋk] I. *n* 1. *no pl* (*status*) rango *m* 2. MIL graduación *f*; **the** ~**s** las tropas; **to break** ~ romper filas 3.(*row*) fila *f*; **cab** ~ parada *f* de taxis, sitio *m* de taxis *Méx* II. *vi* clasificarse; **to** ~ **as sth** figurar como algo; **to** ~ **above sb** estar por encima de alguien III. *vt* 1.(*classify*) clasificar 2.(*arrange*) situar

◆**rank among** *vi* situarse entre

ranking ['ræŋkɪŋ] *n* clasificación *f*

rankle ['ræŋkl] *vi* doler; **to** ~ **with sb** estar resentido con alguien; **it** ~**s that ...** duele que... +*subj*

ransack ['rænsæk] *vt* 1.(*search*) revolver 2.(*plunder*) saquear

ransom ['rænsəm] I. *n* rescate *m*; **to hold sb to** ~ secuestrar a alguien y pedir rescate; *fig* chantajear a alguien II. *vt* rescatar

rant [rænt] I. *n no pl* despotrique *m* II. *vi* despotricar; **to** ~ **and rave** despotricar

rap [ræp] I. *n* 1.(*knock*) golpe *m* seco 2. MUS rap *m* II. *vt* golpear III. *vi* 1.(*talk*) charlar 2. MUS rapear

rapacious [rə'peɪʃəs] *adj form* codicioso, -a; (*appetite*) voraz

rapacity [rə'pæsəti, *Am:* -t̬i] *n no pl* rapacidad *f*

rape¹ [reɪp] I. *n* 1.(*of person*) violación *f* 2.(*of city*) saqueo *m* II. *vt* 1.(*person*) violar 2.(*city*) saquear

rape² [reɪp] *n* BOT, AGR colza *f*

rapeseed oil *n* aceite *m* de colza

rapid ['ræpɪd] *adj* 1.(*quick*) rápido, -a 2.(*sudden*) súbito, -a

rapidity [rə'pɪdəti, *Am:* -t̬i] *n no pl* rapidez *f*

rapids ['ræpɪdz] *n* rápidos *mpl*

rapier ['reɪpɪə^r, *Am:* -ə·] *n* estoque *m*

rapist ['reɪpɪst] *n* violador(a) *m(f)*

rapport [ræ'pɔː^r, *Am:* -'pɔːr] *n no pl* compenetración *f*

rapprochement [ræ'prɒʃmɒŋ, *Am:* ˌræprɔːʃ'-] *n no pl* acercamiento *m*

rapt [ræpt] *adj* (*person*) absorto, -a; (*attention*) completo, -a

rapture ['ræptʃə^r, *Am:* -tʃə·] *n no pl* éxtasis *m inv*

rapturous ['ræptʃərəs] *adj* (*expression*) extasiado, -a; (*applause*) entusiasta; (*welcome*) desbordante

rare¹ [reə^r, *Am:* rer] *adj* (*uncommon*) raro, -a

rare² [reə^r, *Am:* rer] *adj* GASTR poco hecho, -a

rarebit ['reəbɪt, *Am:* 'rer-] *n* **Welsh** ~ pan *m* tostado con queso, mollete *m Méx*

rarefy ['reərɪfaɪ, *Am:* 'rerə-] *vt* enrarecer

rarely ['reəli, *Am:* 'rer-] *adv* raramente, raras veces

raring ['reərɪŋ, *Am:* 'rerɪŋ] *adj inf* **to be** ~ **to do sth** tener muchas ganas de hacer algo

rarity ['reərəti, *Am:* 'rerət̬i] <-ies> *n no pl* rareza *f*

rascal ['rɑːskl, *Am:* 'ræskl] *n* granuja *mf*

rash¹ [ræʃ] *n* **1.** MED sarpullido *m* **2.** *no pl* (*outbreak*) racha *f*

rash² [ræʃ] *adj* (*decision*) precipitado, -a; (*move*) impulsivo, -a

rasher ['ræʃəʳ, *Am:* -ɚ] *n* loncha *f* (de beicon), rebanada *f* (de tocino) *AmC*

rashness ['ræʃnɪs] *n no pl* precipitación *f*

rasp [rɑːsp, *Am:* ræsp] I. *n* **1.** (*tool*) escofina *f* **2.** (*sound*) chirrido *m* II. *vt* **1.** (*file*) escofinar **2.** (*rub roughly*) raspar **3.** (*say roughly*) espetar III. *vi* (*make grating sound*) chirriar

raspberry ['rɑːzbəri, *Am:* 'ræz,ber-] <-ies> *n* **1.** (*fruit*) frambuesa *f* **2.** *inf* (*sound*) pedorreta *f;* trompetilla *f AmL*

rasping ['rɑːspɪŋ, *Am:* 'ræsp-] *adj* áspero, -a

rastafarian [ˌræstəˈfeərɪən, *Am:* ˌrɑːstəˈferɪ-] I. *n* rastafari *mf* II. *adj* rastafariano, -a

rat [ræt] *n* **1.** (*animal*) rata *f* **2.** (*person*) canalla *mf* ▶I smell a ~ aquí hay gato encerrado

ratable ['reɪtəbl, *Am:* -ţə-] *adj s.* **rateable**

ratchet ['rætʃɪt] *n* TECH trinquete *m*
♦**ratchet up** *vt* incrementar

rate [reɪt] I. *n* **1.** (*speed*) velocidad *f;* **at this ~** a este ritmo; **at one's own ~** a su propio ritmo **2.** (*proportion*) índice *m*, tasa *f;* **mortality ~** tasa *f* de mortalidad; **unemployment ~** índice *m* de desempleo **3.** (*price*) precio *m;* **interest ~** tipo *m* de interés **4.** *pl, Aus, Brit* (*local tax*) contribución *f* municipal ▶**at** any ~ de todos modos II. *vt* **1.** calificar; **to ~ sb/sth as sth** considerar algo/a alguien como algo **2.** *Aus, Brit* FIN tasar III. *vi* **to ~ as** ser considerado como

rateable ['reɪtəbl, *Am:* -ţə-] *adj Brit* tasable; **~ value** valor *m* catastral

rather ['rɑːðəʳ, *Am:* 'ræðɚ] I. *adv* **1.** (*somewhat*) ~ **sleepy** medio dormido **2.** (*more exactly*) más bien **3.** (*on the contrary*) más bien **4.** (*very*) bastante **5.** (*in preference to*) **I would ~ stay here** prefiero quedarme aquí; ~ **you than me!** ¡no quisiera estar en tu lugar! II. *interj* por supuesto

ratification [ˌrætɪfɪˈkeɪʃən, *Am:* ˌræţə-] *n no pl* ratificación *f*

ratify ['rætɪfaɪ, *Am:* 'ræţə-] *vt* ratificar

rating ['reɪtɪŋ, *Am:* -ţɪŋ] *n* **1.** *no pl* (*estimation*) evaluación *f* **2.** *pl* TV, RADIO índice *m* de audiencia **3.** *Brit* MIL marinero *m*

ratio ['reɪʃɪəʊ, *Am:* -oʊ] *n* proporción *f*

ration ['ræʃən] I. *n* **1.** (*fixed allowance*) ración *f* **2.** *pl* (*total amount allowed*) raciones *fpl;* **food ~s** víveres *mpl* II. *vt* racionar

rational ['ræʃənəl] *adj* **1.** (*able to reason*) racional **2.** (*sensible*) razonable

rationale [ˌræʃəˈnɑːl, *Am:* -ˈnæl] *n* razón *f* fundamental

rationalism ['ræʃənəlɪzəm] *n no pl* racionalismo *m*

rationalist ['ræʃənəlɪst] PHILOS I. *n* racionalista *mf* II. *adj* racionalista

rationalistic [ˌræʃənəˈlɪstɪk] *adj* racionalista

rationality [ˌræʃəˈnæləti, *Am:* -ţi] *n no pl* racionalidad *f*

rationalization [ˌræʃənəlaɪˈzeɪʃən, *Am:* -əlɪ-] *n no pl* racionalización *f*

rationalize ['ræʃənəlaɪz] *vt* racionalizar

rationing *n no pl* racionamiento *m*

rat poison *n* raticida *m* **rat race** *n* **the ~** la lucha para sobrevivir

rattle ['rætl, *Am:* 'ræţ-] I. *n* **1.** *no pl* (*noise*) ruido *m;* (*of carriage*) traqueteo *m* **2.** (*for baby*) sonajero *m*, cascabel *m AmL* II. *vi* hacer ruido; (*carriage*) traquetear III. *vt* **1.** (*making noise*) hacer sonar **2.** (*make nervous*) poner nervioso, -a; (*shock*) desconcertar

rattlesnake ['rætlsneɪk, *Am:* 'ræţ-] *n* serpiente *f* de cascabel, víbora *f* de cascabel *Méx*

rattling ['rætlɪŋ] *adj* **1.** (*noisy*) ruidoso, -a **2.** (*fast, brisk*) rápido, -a

ratty ['ræti, *Am:* 'ræţ-] *adj* <-ier, -iest> *inf* malhumorado, -a

raucous ['rɔːkəs, *Am:* 'rɑː-] *adj* (*shout*) estridente; (*crowd*) ruidoso, -a

raunchy ['rɔːntʃi, *Am:* 'rɑːn-] <-ier, -iest> *adj* atrevido, -a

ravage ['rævɪdʒ] *vt* hacer estragos en

rave [reɪv] I. *n Brit, inf* juerga *f* II. *adj* (*review*) elogioso, -a III. *vi* desvariar; **to ~ against sb/sth** despotricar contra alguien/algo; **to ~ about sth/sb** poner algo/a alguien por las nubes

ravel ['rævl] <-ll-, *Am:* -l-> *vt* enredar

raven ['reɪvn] I. *n* cuervo *m* II. *adj liter* negro azabache

ravenous ['rævənəs] *adj* (*person, animal*) hambriento, -a; (*appetite*) voraz

ravine [rəˈviːn] *n* barranco *m*

raving ['reɪvɪŋ] I. *adj* (*success*) total; **a ~ madman** un loco de remate II. *adv* **to be ~ mad** estar como una cabra III. *npl* desvaríos *mpl*

ravioli [ˌræviˈəʊli, *Am:* -ˈoʊ-] *n* ravioles *mpl*

ravish ['rævɪʃ] *vt liter* **1.** (*please greatly*) cautivar **2.** (*rape*) violar

ravishing *adj* encantador(a)

raw [rɔː, *Am:* rɑː] I. *n* **in the ~** en cueros; **to touch sb on the ~** *Brit, Aus* herir a alguien en lo más vivo II. *adj* **1.** (*unprocessed: sewage*) sin tratar; (*silk*) salvaje; (*data*) en sucio; ~ **material** materia prima; **to get a ~ deal** sufrir un trato injusto **2.** (*sore*) en carne viva **3.** (*uncooked*) crudo, -a **4.** (*inexperienced*) novato, -a **5.** (*unrestrained*) salvaje **6.** (*weather*) crudo, -a

rawhide ['rɔːhaɪd, *Am:* 'rɑː-] *n* cuero *m* sin curtir

Rawlplug® ['rɔːlplʌɡ, *Am:* 'rɑːl-] *n Brit* taco *m* (de plástico), taquete *m* (de plástico) *Méx*

rawness ['rɔːnɪs, *Am:* 'rɑː-] *n no pl* **1.** (*harshness*) crudeza *f* **2.** (*inexperience*) inexperiencia *f*

ray¹ [reɪ] *n* **1.** (*of light*) rayo *m* **2.** (*trace*) resquicio *m*

ray² [reɪ] *n* (*fish*) raya *f*

rayon ['reɪɒn, *Am:* -ɑːn] *n* rayón *m*

raze [reɪz] *vt* arrasar

razor ['reɪzə', *Am:* -zə·] I. *n* navaja *f* de afeitar, barbera *f Col;* **electric** ~ maquinilla *f* de afeitar, rasuradora *f Méx* II. *vt* afeitar

razorback ['reɪzəbæk, *Am:* -zə·-] *n Am* (*half-wild hog*) ≈ jabalí *m* **razorbill** *n* alca *f* **razor blade** *n* hoja *f* de afeitar **razor-sharp** *adj* 1. (*knife*) muy afilado, -a 2. (*person*) agudo, -a **razor wire** *n* alambrado *m* de púas

razzle ['ræzl] *n no pl, Brit, inf* **to go (out) on the** ~ salir de parranda

R & B [ˌɑːˈrəndˈbiː, *Am:* ˌɑr-] *abbr of* **rhythm and blues** rhythm *m* and blues

RC [ˌɑːˈˈsiː, *Am:* ˌɑːr-] 1. *abbr of* **Roman Catholic** católico, -a *m, f* 2. *abbr of* **Red Cross** Cruz *f* Roja

RCMP *Can abbr of* **Royal Canadian Mounted Police** policía *f* montada del Canadá

Rd *abbr of* **road** c/

R & D [ˌɑːˈrəndˈdiː, *Am:* ˌɑr-] *abbr of* **Research and Development** I+D

RE [ˌɑːˈˈriː, *Am:* ˌɑːr-] *n Brit abbr of* **Religious Education** educación *f* religiosa

re¹ [riː] *prep* con relación a

re² [reɪ] *n no pl* MUS re *m*

reach [riːtʃ] I. *n* 1. *no pl* (*range*) alcance *m;* **to be within** (**sb's**) ~ *a. fig* estar al alcance (de alguien); **to be out of** (**sb's**) ~ *a. fig* estar fuera del alcance (de alguien); **to have a long** ~ tener mucho alcance 2. (*of river*) tramo *m;* **the upper/lower** ~**es of the Amazon** la parte alta/baja del Amazonas II. *vt* 1. (*stretch out*) alargar, extender 2. (*arrive at: city, country*) llegar a; (*land*) tocar; (*finish line*) alcanzar 3. (*attain*) alcanzar; (*agreement*) llegar a; **to** ~ **80** cumplir (los) 80 (años) 4. (*extend to*) llegar a 5. (*communicate with*) ponerse en contacto con III. *vi* **to** ~ **for sth** alargar la mano para tomar algo

◆**reach down** *vi* **to** ~ **to** (*land*) extenderse hasta; (*clothes*) llegar hasta

◆**reach out** *vi* alargar la(s) mano(s); **to** ~ **for sth** alargar la mano para agarrar algo

react [rɪˈækt] *vi* reaccionar; **to** ~ **to sth** reaccionar ante algo; MED reaccionar a algo; **to** ~ **against sth** reaccionar contra algo; **to** ~ **on sth** producir una reacción en algo

reaction [rɪˈækʃən] *n* 1. *a.* CHEM reacción *f;* **chain** ~ reacción en cadena 2. *pl* MED reflejos *mpl*

reactionary [rɪˈækʃənri, *Am:* -eri] I. *adj* reaccionario, -a II. <-ies> *n* reaccionario, -a *m, f*

reactivate [riːˈæktɪveɪt, *Am:* -tə-] I. *vt* reactivar II. *vi* reactivarse

reactive [riːˈæktɪv] *adj* reactivo, -a

reactor [rɪˈæktə', *Am:* -tə·] *n* reactor *m*

read¹ [riːd] I. *n no pl* lectura *f* II. *vt* <read, read> 1. leer; **to** ~ **sth aloud** leer algo en voz alta; **to** ~ **sb a lesson** leer la lección a alguien 2. (*decipher*) descifrar; **to** ~ **sb's mind** [*o* **thoughts**] adivinar los pensamientos de alguien; **to** ~ **sb's hand** leer la mano a alguien;

to ~ **sb like a book** conocer a alguien como la palma de la mano; ~ **my lips!** ¡léeme los labios! 3. (*interpret*) interpretar 4. (*inspect*) inspeccionar; (*meter*) leer 5. (*understand*) entender; **I don't** ~ **you** no te sigo 6. *Brit* UNIV estudiar III. *vi* <read, read> (*person*) leer; (*book, magazine*) leerse

◆**read off** *vt* leer (de un tirón)

◆**read on** *vi* seguir leyendo

◆**read out** *vt* 1. (*read aloud*) leer en voz alta 2. INFOR (*data*) sacar

◆**read over** *vt* releer

◆**read through** *vt* leer de principio a fin

◆**read up** *vi* repasar

read² [red] *adj* leído, -a; **little/widely** ~ poco/muy leído ►**to take sth as** ~ dar algo por hecho; **to take it as** ~ **that …** dar por sentado que… +*subj*

readability [ˌriːdəˈbrɪləti, *Am:* -əti] *n no pl* legibilidad *f*

readable ['riːdəbl] *adj* 1. (*legible*) legible 2. (*easy to read*) ameno, -a

reader ['riːdə', *Am:* -də·] *n* 1. (*person*) lector(a) *m(f)* 2. (*book*) libro *m* de lectura 3. TECH lector *m* 4. PUBL corrector(a) *m(f)* 5. *Brit* UNIV profesor(a) *m(f)* adjunto, -a

readership ['riːdəʃɪp, *Am:* -də·-] *n no pl* lectores *mpl*

read head *n* INFOR lector

readies ['rediz] *npl inf* pasta *f*

readily ['redɪli] *adv* 1. (*promptly*) de buena gana 2. (*easily*) fácilmente

readiness ['redɪnɪs] *n no pl* 1. (*willingness*) (buena) disposición *f* 2. (*preparedness*) preparación *f*

reading ['riːdɪŋ] I. *n* 1. *no pl* lectura *f* 2. (*interpretation*) interpretación *f* 3. TECH medición *f* II. *adj* de lectura; **to have a** ~ **age of seven** leer al nivel de un niño de siete años

reading book *n* libro *m* de lectura **reading glasses** *npl* gafas *fpl* para leer **reading lamp** *n* lámpara *f* portátil **reading list** *n* lista *f* de lecturas **reading room** *n* sala *f* de lectura

readjust [ˌriːəˈdʒʌst] I. *vt a.* TECH reajustar II. *vi* (*objects*) reajustarse; (*people*) readaptarse

readjustment [ˌriːəˈdʒʌstmənt] *n* TECH reajuste *m*

read only memory *n* INFOR memoria *f* ROM

ready ['redi] I. *adj* <-ier, -iest> 1. (*prepared*) listo, -a, pronto, -a *Urug;* **to be** ~ estar listo; **to get** ~ (**for sth**) prepararse (para algo); **to get sth** ~ preparar algo 2. (*willing*) dispuesto, -a 3. (*available*) disponible; ~ **cash** dinero *m* en efectivo; **to be a** ~ **source of sth** ser una fuente fácil de algo; ~ **to hand** a mano 4. (*quick, prompt*) vivo, -a; (*mind*) agudo, -a; (*tongue*) afilado, -a; **to find** ~ **acceptance** tener inmediata aceptación ►~, **steady, go!** *Brit* SPORTS ¡preparados, listos, ya! II. *n* **at the** ~ a punto; (**with**) **his pencil at the** ~ (con) su lápiz a mano III. *vt* preparar

ready-made [ˌredi'meɪd] *adj* hecho, -a; (*meal*) precocinado, -a; (*clothing*) de confección

ready-to-wear [ˌredɪtə'weəʳ, *Am:* -'wer] I. *adj* prêt-à-porter II. *n no pl* prêt-à-porter *m*

reaffirm [ˌriːə'fɜːm, *Am:* -'fɜːrm] *vt* reafirmar

reafforest [ˌriːə'fɒrɪst, *Am:* -'fɔːr-] *vt Brit, Aus* reforestar

reafforestation [ˌriːə'fɒrɪ'steɪʃən, *Am:* -'fɔːr-] *n Brit, Aus* reforestación *f*

real [rɪəl, *Am:* riːl] I. *adj* 1.(*actual*) real; (*threat, problem*) verdadero, -a; **for** ~ de verdad 2.(*genuine*) auténtico, -a; **the** ~ **thing** lo auténtico; **a** ~ **man** *iron* un hombre como Dios manda ▶**the** ~ **McCoy** *inf* lo realmente genuino II. *adv Am, inf* muy

real estate *n no pl, Am, Aus* bienes *mpl* raíces

realignment [ˌriːə'laɪnmənt] *n* reordenamiento *m;* AUTO realineamiento *m*

realism ['rɪəlɪzəm, *Am:* 'riːlɪ-] *n no pl* realismo *m*

realist ['rɪəlɪst, *Am:* 'riːlɪst] *n* realista *mf*

realistic [ˌrɪə'lɪstɪk, *Am:* ˌriːə-] *adj* realista

reality [rɪ'æləti, *Am:* -t̬i] *n no pl* realidad *f;* **to come back to** ~ volver a la realidad; **to face** ~ enfrentarse a la realidad; **to become a** ~ hacerse realidad; **in** ~ en realidad

realizable ['rɪəlaɪzəbl, *Am:* 'riːə-] *adj a.* FIN realizable

realization [ˌrɪəlaɪ'zeɪʃən, *Am:* ˌriːəlɪ'-] *n* 1.(*awareness*) comprensión *f* 2. *no pl a.* FIN realización *f*

realize ['rɪəlaɪz, *Am:* 'riːə-] I. *vt* 1.(*be aware of*) ser consciente de; (*become aware of*) darse cuenta de 2.(*achieve*) realizar 3.(*fulfill*) cumplir 4. FIN realizar; (*acquire*) liquidar II. *vi* (*notice*) darse cuenta; (*be aware of*) ser consciente

really ['rɪəli, *Am:* 'riːə-] I. *adv* 1.(*genuinely*) de verdad 2.(*actually*) en realidad 3.(*very*) muy II. *interj* 1.(*surprise and interest*) ¿ah sí? 2.(*annoyance*) pero bueno 3.(*disbelief*) ¿de veras?

realm [relm] *n* 1.(*kingdom*) reino *m* 2.(*area of interest*) campo *m*

realtor ['rɪəltəʳ, *Am:* 'riːəlt̬əʳ] *n Am, Aus* agente *mf* inmobiliario, -a, corredor(a) *m(f)* de propiedades *Chile*

realty ['rɪəlti, *Am:* 'riːəlt̬i] *n no pl* bienes *mpl* raíces

reanimate [riː'ænɪmeɪt] *vt* reanimar

reap [riːp] *vi, vt* cosechar

reaper ['riːpəʳ, *Am:* 'riːpɚ] *n* 1.(*person*) cosechador(a) *m(f)* 2.(*machine*) cosechadora *f*

reappear [ˌriːə'pɪəʳ, *Am:* -'pɪr] *vi* reaparecer

reapply [ˌriːə'plaɪ] I. *vi* **to** ~ **for sth** volver a presentar una solicitud para algo II. *vt* (*paint*) dar otra capa de

reappoint [ˌriːə'pɔɪnt] *vt* volver a nombrar

reappraisal [ˌriːə'preɪzl] *n* FIN revaluación *f*

rear¹ [rɪəʳ, *Am:* rɪr] I. *adj* (*light*) trasero, -a;

(*leg, wheel*) posterior II. *n* 1.(*back part*) parte *f* trasera 2. *inf* (*buttocks*) trasero *m* 3. MIL retaguardia *f;* **to bring up the** ~ cerrar la marcha

rear² [rɪəʳ, *Am:* rɪr] I. *vt* 1.(*bring up: child, animals*) criar 2.(*raise*) **to** ~ **one's head** levantar la cabeza II. *vi* (*horse*) encabritarse; **to** ~ **above sth** erguirse por encima de algo

rear admiral *n* MIL contraalmirante *mf*

rearguard ['rɪəgɑːd, *Am:* 'rɪrgɑːrd] *n no pl* retaguardia *f;* **to fight a** ~ **action** resistir en lo posible

rearm [ˌriː'ɑːm, *Am:* -'ɑːrm] I. *vi* rearmarse II. *vt* rearmar

rearmament [riː'ɑːməmənt, *Am:* -'ɑːrmə-] *n no pl* rearmamento *m*

rearmost ['rɪəməʊst, *Am:* 'rɪrmoʊst] *adj* último, -a

rearrange [ˌriːə'reɪndʒ] *vt* 1.(*system*) reorganizar 2.(*furniture*) colocar de otra manera 3.(*meeting*) volver a concertar

rear view mirror *n* retrovisor *m*

rearward ['rɪəwəd, *Am:* 'rɪrwɚd] *adj, adv* hacia atrás

rear-wheel drive *n* tracción *f* trasera

reason ['riːzn] I. *n* 1.(*motive*) motivo *m;* **the** ~ **why ...** el motivo por el que...; **for no particular** ~ sin ningún motivo en concreto; **for some** ~ por algún motivo 2.(*common sense*) sensatez *f;* **within** ~ dentro de lo razonable; **to listen to** ~ atender a razones; **to be beyond all** ~ no tener ninguna lógica; **the Age of Reason** HIST el Siglo de las Luces 3.(*sanity*) razón *f;* **to lose one's** ~ perder la razón II. *vt* razonar III. *vi* razonar; **to** ~ **from sth** discurrir partiendo de algo

reasonable ['riːznəbl] *adj* 1.(*sensible*) sensato, -a; (*demand*) razonable 2.(*fair*) juicioso, -a 3.(*inexpensive*) moderado, -a

reasonably ['riːznəbli] *adv* 1.(*fairly*) razonablemente 2.(*acceptably*) bastante

reasoning ['riːznɪŋ] *n no pl* razonamiento *m*

reassemble [ˌriːə'sembl] I. *vt* (*machine*) volver a montar; (*people*) volver a reunir II. *vi* volver a reunirse

reassess [ˌriːə'ses] *vt* 1.(*situation*) volver a valorar [*o* considerar] 2. FIN (*taxes*) volver a fijar; (*damages*) volver a valorar

reassurance [ˌriːə'ʃʊərəns, *Am:* -'ʃʊrəns] *n* 1.(*comfort*) palabras *fpl* tranquilizadoras 2. *no pl* FIN reaseguro *m*

reassure [ˌriːə'ʃʊəʳ, *Am:* -'ʃʊr] *vt* tranquilizar

reassuring [ˌriːə'ʃʊərɪŋ, *Am:* -'ʃʊr-] *adj* tranquilizador(a)

reawaken [ˌriːə'weɪkən] *vt* volver a despertar

rebate ['riːbeɪt] *n* 1.(*refund*) reembolso *m;* **tax** ~ devolución *f* de impuestos 2.(*discount*) rebaja *f*

rebel¹ ['rebl] I. *n* rebelde *mf* II. *adj* rebelde

rebel² [rɪ'bel] <-ll-> *vi* rebelarse

rebellion [rɪ'belɪən, *Am:* -'beljən] *n no pl* rebelión *f*

rebellious [rɪ'belɪəs, *Am:* -'beljəs] *adj*

R

rebelde; (*child*) revoltoso, -a

rebirth [ˌriːˈbɜːθ, *Am:* -ˈbɜːrθ] *n* renacimiento *m*

reboot [ˌriːˈbuːt] INFOR I. *vt* recargar II. *vi* recargarse

rebound [rɪˈbaʊnd, *Am:* riːˈ-] I. *vi* rebotar; to ~ on sb *fig* volverse en contra de alguien II. *n no pl* rebote *m*; to marry on the ~ casarse por despecho

rebuff [rɪˈbʌf] I. *vt* rechazar II. *n* rechazo *m*; to meet with a ~ ser rechazado, -a

rebuild [ˌriːˈbɪld] *vt irr* 1. (*build again*) reconstruir; (*face, life*) rehacer 2. (*restore*) restablecer 3. (*replenish: stock*) reponer

rebuke [rɪˈbjuːk] I. *vt* reprender II. *n* 1. (*reproof*) reprimenda *f* 2. *no pl* (*censure*) represión *f*

rebut [rɪˈbʌt] <-tt-> *vt* rebatir

rebuttal [rɪˈbʌtl, *Am:* -ˈbʌt-] *n* refutación *f*

recalcitrant [rɪˈkælsɪtrənt] *adj* recalcitrante

recall [rɪˈkɔːl] I. *vt* 1. (*remember*) recordar 2. (*call back: ambassador*) retirar; (*troops*) llamar 3. ECON retirar (del mercado) II. *vi* recordar III. *n* 1. (*memory*) memoria *f* 2. POL retirada *f* 3. ECON retirada *f* (del mercado) ►to be lost beyond ~ estar completamente perdido

recant [rɪˈkænt] I. *vt* retractarse de; to ~ one's faith/belief abjurar de su fe/creencia II. *vi* retractarse

recap[1] [ˈriːkæp] I. <-pp-> *vi, vt* recapitular II. *n* recapitulación *f*

recap[2] [ˌriːˈkæp] <-pp-> *vt Am* AUTO recauch(ut)ar, reencauchar *AmC*

recapitulate [ˌriːkəˈpɪtʃʊleɪt, *Am:* -ˈpɪtʃə-] *vi, vt* recapitular

recapitulation [ˌriːkəˌpɪtʃʊˈleɪʃən, *Am:* -ˌpɪtʃə-ˈ] *n* 1. (*summary*) resumen *m* 2. MUS, THEAT, CINE recapitulación *f*

recapture [ˌriːˈkæptʃəʳ, *Am:* -tʃəʳ] I. *vt* 1. (*town*) volver a tomar; (*fugitive*) volver a capturar 2. (*reexperience*) recuperar; (*beauty, feeling*) recobrar II. *n* (*of town*) reconquista *f*

recast [rɪˈkɑːst, *Am:* -ˈkæst] *vt* 1. THEAT, CINE cambiar el reparto de 2. TECH, LIT refundir

recede [rɪˈsiːd] *vi* 1. (*move backward: sea*) retirarse; (*tide*) bajar; (*fog*) desvanecerse; to ~ into the distance perderse en la distancia 2. (*diminish*) disminuir; (*prices*) bajar

receding chin *n* barbilla *f* hundida **receding hairline** *n* entradas *fpl*

receipt [rɪˈsiːt] I. *n* 1. (*document*) recibo *m* 2. *pl* COM ingresos *mpl* 3. (*act of receiving*) recepción *f*; payment on ~ pago *m* al recibo; on ~ of ... al recibo de... II. *vt* acusar recibo de

receipt book *n* libro *m* talonario

receivable *adj* COM por cobrar

receive [rɪˈsiːv] I. *vt* 1. (*be given*) *a.* TEL, RADIO recibir; (*pension, salary*) percibir 2. (*react to: proposal, suggestion*) acoger; the book was well/badly ~d el libro tuvo buena/mala acogida 3. (*injury*) sufrir 4. to ~ sb into the Church admitir a alguien en el seno de la Igle-

sia 5. LAW to ~ stolen goods comerciar con bienes robados II. *vi Am* SPORTS recibir

received [rɪˈsiːvd] *adj* admitido, -a; ~ wisdom creencia *f* popular

receiver [rɪˈsiːvəʳ, *Am:* -əʳ] *n* 1. TEL auricular *m*, tubo *m AmL*, fono *m Chile* 2. RADIO receptor *m* 3. ECON the official ~ el síndico (de la quiebra) 4. *Am* SPORTS receptor(a) *m(f)*; (*tennis*) jugador(a) *m(f)* que está al resto

recent [ˈriːsənt] *adj* reciente; in ~ times en los últimos tiempos

recently *adv* recientemente

receptacle [rɪˈseptəkl] *n* receptáculo *m*

reception [rɪˈsepʃən] *n* 1. *no pl* (*welcome*) acogida *f* 2. (*in hotel*) recepción *f*

reception area *n* (zona *f* de) recepción *f* **reception centre** *n Brit* centro *m* educativo (*en el que los niños empiezan la escolarización*) **reception class** *n Brit* clase *f* del primer año **reception desk** *n* (mesa *f* de) recepción *f*

receptionist [rɪˈsepʃənɪst] *n* recepcionista *mf*

receptive [rɪˈseptɪv] *adj* receptivo, -a

receptiveness *n*, **receptivity** [ˌriːsepˈtɪvəti, *Am:* riːˌsepˈtɪvəti] *n no pl* receptividad *f*

recess [rɪˈses, *Am:* ˈriːses] I. <-es> *n* 1. POL suspensión *f* de actividades, receso *m AmL* 2. *Am, Aus* SCHOOL recreo *m* 3. ARCHIT hueco *m* 4. *pl* (*place*) lugar *m* recóndito II. *vi Am, Aus* prorrogar; (*meeting, session*) suspender III. *vt* ARCHIT rebajar

recession [rɪˈseʃən] *n* 1. (*retreat*) retroceso *m* 2. ECON recesión *f*

recessive [rɪˈsesɪv] *adj* BIO recesivo, -a

recharge [ˌriːˈtʃɑːdʒ, *Am:* -ˈtʃɑːrdʒ] I. *vt* recargar II. *vi* recargarse

rechargeable [ˌriːˈtʃɑːdʒəbl, *Am:* -ˈtʃɑːrdʒ-] *adj* recargable

recidivism [rɪˈsɪdɪvɪzəm, *Am:* -ˈsɪdə-] *n no pl* reincidencia *f*

recidivist [rɪˈsɪdɪvɪst, *Am:* -ˈsɪdə-] *n* reincidente *mf*

recipe [ˈresəpi] *n a. fig* receta *f*

recipient [rɪˈsɪpɪənt] *n* (*of letter*) destinatario, -a *m, f*; (*of transplant*) receptor(a) *m(f)*; (*of gift*) beneficiario, -a *m, f*

reciprocal [rɪˈsɪprəkl] I. *adj* 1. *a.* LING, MAT recíproco, -a 2. (*reverse*) mutuo, -a II. *n* MAT recíproco *m*

reciprocate [rɪˈsɪprəkeɪt] I. *vt* corresponder a, reciprocar *AmL* II. *vi* 1. corresponder 2. TECH alternar

reciprocity [ˌresɪˈprɒsəti, *Am:* -ˈprɑːsəti] *n no pl* reciprocidad *f*

recital [rɪˈsaɪtl, *Am:* -tl] *n* 1. MUS recital *m* 2. (*description*) relación *f*

recitation [ˌresɪˈteɪʃən] *n* LIT recitación *f*

recitative [ˌresɪtəˈtiːv] *n* MUS recitativo *m*

recite [rɪˈsaɪt] I. *vt* 1. (*repeat*) recitar 2. (*list*) enumerar II. *vi* dar un recitado

reckless [ˈrekləs] *adj* imprudente; LAW temerario, -a

recklessness *n no pl* imprudencia *f,* temeridad *f*

reckon ['rekən] **I.** *vt* **1.** (*calculate*) calcular **2.** (*consider*) considerar; **to ~** (**that**) ... creer (que)...; **I ~ not** me parece que no; **what do you ~?** ¿qué opinas? **3.** (*judge*) estimar **II.** *vi inf* calcular

◆**reckon in** *vt* tomar en cuenta

◆**reckon on** *vt insep* **1.** (*count on*) contar con **2.** (*expect*) esperar

◆**reckon up** *vt* calcular

◆**reckon with** *vt insep* tener en cuenta; **she is a force to be reckoned with** es alguien a quien hay que tener muy en cuenta

◆**reckon without** *vt insep* no tener en cuenta

reckoning ['rekənɪŋ] *n* **1.** (*calculation*) cálculo *m;* **to be out in one's ~** calcular mal **2.** (*settlement*) ajuste *m* de cuentas

reclaim [rɪ'kleɪm] *vt* **1.** (*claim back: title, rights*) reclamar **2.** (*reuse: land*) recuperar; (*material*) reciclar **3.** (*reform*) regenerar

reclamation [ˌreklə'meɪʃən] *n no pl* **1.** (*of title, rights*) reclamación *f* **2.** (*of land*) recuperación *f;* (*of material*) reciclaje *m* **3.** (*reformation*) regeneración *f*

recline [rɪ'klaɪn] **I.** *vi* apoyarse; **to ~ on** reclinarse contra [*o* en] **II.** *vt* reclinar

recliner [rɪ'klaɪnəʳ, *Am:* -nɚ] *n* asiento *m* reclinable

reclining seat *n,* **reclining chair** *n* asiento *m* reclinable

recluse [rɪ'kluːs, *Am:* 'rekluːs] *n* ermitaño, -a *m, f*

reclusive *adj* solitario, -a

recognition [ˌrekəg'nɪʃən] *n no pl a.* INFOR reconocimiento *m;* **optical character ~** reconocimiento óptico de caracteres; **voice ~** reconocimiento de la voz; **in ~ of** en reconocimiento de

recognizable ['rekəgnaɪzəbl] *adj* reconocible

recognizance [rɪ'kɒgnɪzns, *Am:* -'kɑːgnɪ-] *n* fianza *f*

recognize ['rekəgnaɪz] *vt* reconocer

recognized ['rekəgnaɪzd] *adj* reconocido, -a

recoil[1] [rɪ'kɔɪl] *vi* **1.** (*draw back*) echarse atrás; **to ~ in horror** retroceder de miedo; **to ~ at sth** sentir repugnancia hacia algo; **to ~ from doing sth** rehuir hacer algo **2.** (*gun*) retroceder

recoil[2] ['riːkɔɪl] *n* retroceso *m*

recollect [ˌrekə'lekt] *vi, vt* recordar

recollection [ˌrekə'lekʃən] *n* recuerdo *m;* **to have no ~ of sth** no recordar algo

recommend [ˌrekə'mend] *vt* recomendar; **it is not to be ~ed** no es recomendable

recommendable *adj* recomendable

recommendation [ˌrekəmen'deɪʃən, *Am:* -mən'-] *n* **1.** (*suggestion*) recomendación *f;* **on sb's ~** por recomendación de alguien **2.** (*advice*) consejo *m*

recompense ['rekəmpents] **I.** *n no pl* **1.** (*reward*) recompensa *f* **2.** (*compensation*) compensación *f* **II.** *vt* **1.** (*reward*) recompensar **2.** (*make amends*) compensar

reconcile ['rekənsaɪl] *vt* **1.** (*person*) reconciliar; **to become ~d with sb** reconciliarse con alguien **2.** (*difference, fact*) conciliar; **to be ~d to sth** aceptar algo; **to become ~d to sth** resignarse a algo

reconciliation [ˌrekənˌsɪlɪ'eɪʃən] *n* **1.** (*restoration of good relations*) reconciliación *f* **2.** *no pl* (*making compatible*) conciliación *f*

recondition [ˌriːkən'dɪʃən] *vt* reacondicionar

reconnaissance [rɪ'kɒnɪsənts, *Am:* -'kɑːnə-] *n* reconocimiento *m*

reconnaissance flight *n* vuelo *m* de reconocimiento

reconnoiter *Am,* **reconnoitre** [ˌrekə'nɔɪtəʳ, *Am:* ˌriːkə'nɔɪtɚ] **I.** *vt* reconocer **II.** *vi* reconocer el terreno

reconsider [ˌriːkən'sɪdəʳ, *Am:* -ɚ] **I.** *vt* reconsiderar **II.** *vi* recapacitar

reconstruct [ˌriːkən'strʌkt] *vt* **1.** (*building*) reconstruir **2.** (*life*) rehacer; (*crime, event*) reconstituir

reconstruction [ˌriːkən'strʌkʃən] *n* **1.** *no pl* (*of building*) reconstrucción *f* **2.** (*of crime, event*) reconstitución *f*

record[1] ['rekɔːd, *Am:* -ɚd] **I.** *n* **1.** (*account*) relación *m;* (*document*) documento *m;* **medical ~** historial *m* médico; **to say sth off the ~** decir algo extraoficialmente; **to put sth on ~** dejar constancia de algo **2.** *no pl* (*sb's past*) antecedentes *mpl;* **to have a good ~** tener un buen historial; **to have a clean ~** no tener antecedentes **3.** *pl* archivos *mpl* **4.** MUS disco *m;* **to make a ~** grabar un disco **5.** SPORTS récord *m;* **to break a ~** batir un récord **6.** LAW acta *f* **7.** INFOR juego *m* de datos **II.** *adj* récord; **to do sth in ~ time** hacer algo en un tiempo récord; **to reach a ~ high** alcanzar un máximo sin precedentes

record[2] [rɪ'kɔːd, *Am:* -'kɔːrd] **I.** *vt* **1.** (*store*) archivar **2.** *a.* INFOR registrar; MUS grabar **3.** LAW hacer constar en acta **II.** *vi* grabar

record-breaker ['rekɔːdˌbreɪkəʳ, *Am:* -ɚdˌbreɪkɚ] *n* SPORTS plusmarquista *mf* **record-breaking** *adj* que bate todos los récords

recorded [rɪ'kɔːdɪd, *Am:* -'kɔːrd-] *adj* registrado, -a; (*history*) documentado, -a; (*music*) grabado, -a

recorder [rɪ'kɔːdəʳ, *Am:* -'kɔːrdɚ] *n* **1.** (*tape recorder*) magnetófon *m* **2.** MUS flauta *f* dulce **3.** *Brit* LAW juez *mf*

record holder *n* SPORTS plusmarquista *mf*

recording *n* (*of sound*) grabación *f*

recording session *n* sesión *f* de grabación

recording studio *n* estudio *m* de grabación

record label *n* sello *m* discográfico **record library** *n* discoteca *f* **record player** *n* tocadiscos *m inv* **record token** *n* cupón *m* para discos

R

recount¹ [rɪ'kaʊnt] vt **1.** (narrate) contar **2.** (count again) volver a contar

recount² ['riːkaʊnt] n POL recuento m

recoup [rɪ'kuːp] vt (expenditure, energy) recuperar; (losses) resarcirse de

recourse [rɪ'kɔːs, Am: 'riːkɔːrs] n no pl recurso m; **to have ~ to** recurrir a

recover [rɪ'kʌvəʳ, Am: -əʳ] **I.** vt a. INFOR recuperar; **to ~ one's composure** recobrar su compostura **II.** vi **1.** (regain health) reponerse **2.** (return to normal) recuperarse

re-cover [ˌriː'kʌvəʳ, Am: -əʳ] vt retapizar

recoverable [rɪ'kʌvərəbl] adj **1.** a. INFOR recuperable **2.** a. FIN reactivable

recovery [rɪ'kʌvəri, Am: -əʳi] <-ies> n **1.** a. MED, ECON recuperación f; **to be beyond ~** ser irrecuperable **2.** INFOR reactivación f

recovery service n no pl servicio m de grúa
recovery ship n barco m de salvamento
recovery vehicle n vehículo m de salvamento

recreate [ˌriːkri'eɪt] vt recrear

recreation¹ [ˌriːkri'eɪʃən] n no pl (of conditions, situation) recreación f

recreation² [ˌrekri'eɪʃən] n **1.** a. SCHOOL recreo m **2.** (pastime) diversión f

recreational [ˌrekri'eɪʃənəl] adj recreativo, -a

recreational vehicle n Am roulotte f
recreation centre n centro m recreativo
recreation ground n Brit campo m de deportes **recreation room** n salón m recreativo

recreative ['rekrɪˌeɪtɪv, Am: -t̬ɪv] adj recreativo, -a

recriminate [rɪ'krɪmɪneɪt, Am: -əneɪt] vi recriminar

recrimination [rɪˌkrɪmɪ'neɪʃən, Am: -ə'-] n pl recriminación f

recruit [rɪ'kruːt] **I.** vt MIL reclutar; (employee) contratar **II.** n MIL recluta mf

recruiting **I.** n no pl MIL reclutamiento m; ECON contratación f **II.** adj MIL de reclutamiento; ECON de contratación

recruiting office n MIL oficina f de reclutamiento

recruitment **I.** n no pl MIL reclutamiento m; ECON contratación f; (of members) afiliación f **II.** adj de reclutamiento

recruitment agency n agencia f de selección de personal

rectangle ['rektæŋgl] n rectángulo m

rectangular [rek'tæŋgjʊləʳ, Am: -gjələʳ] adj rectangular

rectification [ˌrektɪfɪ'keɪʃən, Am: ˌrektə-] n no pl rectificación f

rectify ['rektɪfaɪ, Am: -tə-] vt rectificar

rectilinear [ˌrektɪ'lɪnɪəʳ, Am: -tə'-] adj rectilíneo, -a

rectitude ['rektɪtjuːd, Am: -tətuːd] n no pl rectitud f

rector ['rektəʳ, Am: -təʳ] n **1.** Brit REL ≈ párroco m **2.** Am, Scot SCHOOL director(a) m(f)

3. Am, Scot UNIV rector(a) m(f)

rectory ['rektəri] <-ies> n rectoría f

rectum ['rektəm] n ANAT recto m

recumbent [rɪ'kʌmbənt] adj liter recostado, -a

recuperate [rɪ'kuːpəreɪt] **I.** vi recuperarse **II.** vt recuperar

recuperation [rɪˌkuːpə'reɪʃən] n no pl recuperación f

recur [rɪ'kɜːʳ, Am: -'kɜːr] vi repetirse

recurrence [rɪ'kʌrəns, Am: -'kɜːr-] n repetición f

recurrent [rɪ'kʌrənt, Am: -'kɜːr-] adj (dream, motif) recurrente; (problem) repetido, -a; (costs, expenses) constante

recurring adj recurrente

recurring decimal n decimal m periódico

recycle [ˌriː'saɪkl] vt reciclar

recycling **I.** n no pl reciclaje m **II.** adj de reciclaje

recycling plant n planta f de reciclaje

red [red] **I.** <-dd-> adj rojo, -a; (wine) tinto, -a; **to be** [o **go**] **~** ruborizarse **II.** n rojo m; **to be in the ~** FIN estar en números rojos ►**to make sb see ~** sacar a alguien de quicio; **to see ~** salir de sus casillas

Red Army n Ejército m Rojo

red-blooded [ˌred'blʌdɪd] adj fogoso, -a

redcap ['redkæp] n **1.** Brit, inf MIL policía mf militar **2.** Am (railway porter) mozo m de estación **Red Crescent** n no pl the **~** la Media Luna Roja **Red Cross** n no pl the **~** la Cruz Roja **redcurrant** n grosella f **red deer** n inv ciervo m

redden ['redn] **I.** vi enrojecerse; (person) ruborizarse; **to ~ with embarrassment** ponerse colorado de vergüenza **II.** vt enrojecer

reddish ['redɪʃ] adj rojizo, -a

redecorate [ˌriː'dekəreɪt] vt redecorar; (paint) volver a pintar; (wallpaper) volver a empapelar

redecoration [ˌriːdekə'reɪʃən] n (repainting) cambio m de pintura; (re-papering) cambio m de papel pintado

redeem [rɪ'diːm] vt **1.** a. REL (person, soul) redimir; (situation) salvar; **to ~ oneself** redimirse **2.** FIN (policy, share) liquidar; (pawned item) desempeñar; (debt) pagar; **to ~ a mortgage** amortizar una hipoteca **3.** (fulfil: promise) cumplir

redeemable adj FIN reembolsable

Redeemer [rɪ'diːməʳ, Am: -məʳ] n no pl REL the **~** el Redentor

redeeming [rɪ'diːmɪŋ] adj redentor(a); **he has no ~ features** no tiene ningún punto a su favor

redefine [ˌriːdɪ'faɪn] vt redefinir

redemption [rɪ'dempʃən] n no pl **1.** a. REL redención f **2.** FIN (of policy, share) liquidación f; (of mortgage) amortización f

redeploy [ˌriːdɪ'plɔɪ] vt (workers, staff) reorganizar, reubicar AmL; (soldiers, troops) cambiar la disposición de

redeployment *n* (*of workers, staff*) reorganización *f*, reubicación *f AmL;* (*of soldiers, troops*) redistribución *f*

redevelop [,riːdɪ'veləp] *vt* reurbanizar

redevelopment [,riːdɪ'veləpmənt] *n* reurbanización *f*

red-haired [,red'heəʳd] *adj* pelirrojo, -a

red-handed [,red'hændɪd] *adj* **to catch sb ~** pillar a alguien con las manos en la masa

redhead ['redhed] *n* pelirrojo, -a *m, f*

red-headed *adj* pelirrojo, -a

red herring *n fig* pista *f* falsa

red-hot [,red'hɒt, *Am:* -haːt] *adj* **1.** (*extremely hot*) candente; **to be ~** estar al rojo vivo **2.** (*exciting*) apasionante **3.** (*up-to--the-minute*) de última hora

Red Indian *n* piel *mf* roja

redirect [,riːdɪ'rekt] *vt* reorientar; (*letter*) reexpedir; (*traffic*) desviar

redistribute [,riːdɪ'strɪbjuːt] *vt* redistribuir

redistribution [,riːdɪstrɪ'bjuːʃən] *n no pl* redistribución *f*

red-letter day [,red'letə,deɪ, *Am:* -'leṭə·-] *n* día *m* memorable

red light *n* semáforo *m* en rojo **red-light district** *n* barrio *m* chino

red meat *n no pl* carne *f* roja

redneck ['rednek] *n Am:* campesino blanco de la clase baja rural, perteneciente de los estados del Sur

redness ['rednɪs] *n no pl* rojez *f*

redo [,riː'duː] *vt irr* rehacer

redolent ['redələnt] *adj form* **1.** (*smelling of*) **~ of sth** con olor a algo **2.** (*suggestive of*) **to be ~ of sth** hacer pensar en algo

redouble [rɪ'dʌbl] *vt* redoblar; **to ~ one's efforts** redoblar los esfuerzos

redoubtable [rɪ'daʊtəbl, *Am:* -ṭə-] *adj* imponente, temible

redound [rɪ'daʊnd] *vi form* **to ~ to sb's advantage** redundar en beneficio de alguien; **to ~ to sb's credit** aumentar el prestigio de alguien

red pepper *n* pimiento *m* rojo

redraft[1] [,riː'drɑːft, *Am:* -'dræft] *vt* volver a redactar

redraft[2] ['riːdrɑːft, *Am:* -dræft] *n* nuevo borrador *m*

redress [rɪ'dres] **I.** *vt* (*grievance*) reparar; (*fault*) remediar; (*imbalance*) rectificar **II.** *n* (*of grievance, imbalance*) reparación *f;* **to seek ~** exigir reparación

Red Sea *n no pl* **the ~** el Mar Rojo **redskin** *n* piel *mf* roja **red tape** *n no pl* papeleo *m*

reduce [rɪ'djuːs, *Am:* -'duːs] **I.** *vt* **1.** (*diminish*) reducir; (*price*) rebajar; (*wages*) recortar **2.** MIL degradar **3. to ~ sb to tears** hacer llorar a alguien; **to ~ sth to rubble/ashes** reducir algo a escombros/cenizas; **to be ~d to doing sth** verse forzado a hacer algo **4.** MAT (*fraction*) simplificar **II.** *vi Am* adelgazar

reduced [rɪ'djuːst, *Am:* -'duːst] *adj* **1.** (*lower*) reducido, -a; (*price*) rebajado, -a

2. (*impoverished*) **to be in ~ circumstances** estar pasando estrecheces

reducer [rɪ'djuːsəʳ, *Am:* -'duːsə·] *n Am* producto *m* adelgazante

reduction [rɪ'dʌkʃən] *n* reducción *f;* (*in price*) rebaja *f*

redundancy [rɪ'dʌndəntsi] <-ies> *n* **1.** *no pl* (*uselessness*) superfluidad *f;* LING redundancia *f* **2.** (*unemployment*) desempleo *m* **3.** *Brit, Aus* ECON despido *m*

redundancy payment *n Brit, Aus* indemnización *f* por despido

redundant [rɪ'dʌndənt] *adj* **1.** (*superfluous*) superfluo, -a; LING redundante **2.** *Brit, Aus* **to be made ~** ser despedido, -a

reduplicate [rɪ'djuːplɪkeɪt, *Am:* -'duːplə-] *vi* reduplicar

reduplication [rɪ,djuːplɪ'keɪʃən, *Am:* -,duːplə'-] *n* reduplicación *f*

red wine *n* vino *m* tinto

redwood ['redwʊd] *n* secuoya *f*

re-echo [,riː'ekəʊ, *Am:* -oʊ] **I.** *vt* repetir **II.** *vi* resonar

reed [riːd] *n* **1.** (*plant*) junco *m*, totora *f AmS* **2.** *Brit* (*straw*) caña *f* **3.** MUS lengüeta *f*

reed instrument *n* instrumento *m* de lengüeta

re-educate [,riː'edʒʊkeɪt] *vt* reeducar

reedy ['riːdi] *adj* **1.** (*full of reeds*) poblado, -a de juncos **2.** MUS (*voice*) aflautado, -a

reef [riːf] **I.** *n* **1.** (*ridge*) arrecife *m* **2.** (*part of sail*) rizo *m* **II.** *vt* NAUT arrizar

reefer ['riːfəʳ, *Am:* -fə·] *n inf* porro *m*

reef knot *n* nudo *m* de rizo

reek [riːk] **I.** *vi* apestar; **to ~ of corruption** apestar a corrupción **II.** *n* hedor *m*

reel[1] [riːl] *n* (*storage or winding device*) carrete *m;* (*for film, yarn, tape*) bobina *f*

reel[2] [riːl] **I.** *vi* **1.** (*move unsteadily*) tambalearse **2.** (*recoil*) retroceder **II.** *n* reel *m* (*baile escocés*)

re-elect [,riːɪ'lekt] *vt* reelegir

re-election [,riːɪ'lekʃən] *n* reelección *f*

re-employ [,riːɪm'plɔɪ] *vt* volver a emplear

re-engage [,riːɪn'geɪdʒ] *vt* volver a contratar

re-enter [,riː'entəʳ, *Am:* -ṭə·] **I.** *vt* **1.** (*go in again*) volver a entrar en **2.** INFOR teclear de nuevo **II.** *vt* reingresar

re-entry [,riː'entri] <-ies> *n* reingreso *m*

ref [ref] *n* **1.** *inf abbr of* **referee** árbitro, -a *m, f* **2.** *abbr of* **reference** referencia *f*

refectory [rɪ'fektəri] <-ies> *n* refectorio *m*

refer [rɪ'fɜːʳ, *Am:* -'fɜːr] <-rr-> *vt* **to refer sth to sb** (*article*) remitir algo a alguien; **to ~ a patient to a specialist** mandar a un paciente a un especialista; **to ~ a case to sb/sth** LAW remitir una causa a alguien/algo

◆ **refer back to** *vt* remitir a; **the reader is referred back to the introduction** se remite al lector a la introducción

◆ **refer to** *vt* **1.** (*mention, allude*) referirse a; **to never ~ sth** no mencionar nunca algo; **to ~ sb as sth** calificar a alguien de algo; **refering** to your letter/phone call, ... con relación a su carta/llamada,... **2.** (*concern*) concernir; **does this information ~ me?** ¿esta información tiene algo que ver conmigo? **3.** (*consult, turn to*) consultar; **to ~ one's notes** consultar sus apuntes; **~ page 70** ver página 70; **I ~ the facts** me remito a los hechos

referee [ˌrefə'riː] I. *n* **1.** SPORTS árbitro, -a *m, f*, referí *m AmL* **2.** (*in dispute*) mediador(a) *m(f)* **3.** *Brit* (*for employment*) persona *f* que da referencias del candidato II. *vi, vt* arbitrar

reference ['refərənts] *n* **1.** (*consultantion*) consulta *f;* **to make ~ to sth** hacer referencia a algo **2.** (*source*) referencia *f* **3.** (*allusion*) alusión *f;* **with ~ to what was said** en alusión a lo que se dijo **4.** ADMIN (*number*) número *m* de referencia **5.** (*for job application*) referencias *fpl;* **to take up ~s** pedir referencias

reference book *n* libro *m* de consulta **reference library** *n* biblioteca *f* de consulta **reference number** *n* **1.** (*in document, on book*) número *m* de referencia **2.** (*on product*) número *m* de serie

referendum [ˌrefə'rendəm] <-s *o* -da> *n* referéndum *m*

referral [rɪ'fɜːrəl] *n* remisión *f*

refill[1] [ˌriː'fɪl] *vt* rellenar

refill[2] ['riːfɪl] *n* recambio *m*

refine [rɪ'faɪn] *vt* **1.** (*oil, sugar*) refinar **2.** (*technique*) perfeccionar

refined [rɪ'faɪnd] *adj* **1.** (*oil, sugar*) refinado, -a **2.** (*sophisticated*) sofisticado, -a **3.** (*very polite*) fino, -a

refinement [rɪ'faɪnmənt] *n* **1.** (*improvement*) refinamiento *m* **2.** *no pl* (*purification*) refinación *f* **3.** *no pl* (*good manners*) finura *f*

refinery [rɪ'faɪnəri] *n* refinería *f*

refit[1] [ˌriː'fɪt] <-tt- *o Am* -t-> *a.* NAUT I. *vi* repararse II. *vt* reparar

refit[2] ['riːfɪt] *n a.* NAUT reparación *f*

reflate [riː'fleɪt] *vt* reflacionar

reflation [ˌriː'fleɪʃən] *n* reflación *f*

reflect [rɪ'flekt] I. *vt* reflejar II. *vi* **1.** (*cast back light*) reflejarse **2.** (*contemplate*) reflexionar **3. to ~ badly on sth** no decir mucho de algo

reflecting *adj* reflectante

reflecting telescope *n* telescopio *m* reflector

reflection [rɪ'flekʃən] *n* **1.** (*image*) reflejo *m* **2.** (*thought*) reflexión *f;* **~s on sth** reflexión acerca de algo; **on ~** pensándolo bien **3.** *fig* **to be a fair ~ of sth** ser un fiel reflejo de algo; **to be a poor ~ on sth** no decir mucho de algo

reflective [rɪ'flektɪv] *adj* **1.** (*surface*) reflector(a) **2.** (*thoughtful*) reflexivo, -a

reflector [rɪ'flektər, *Am:* -ɚ] *n* (*mirror*) reflector *m;* (*of bicycle, car*) captafaros *m inv*

reflex ['riːfleks] <-es> I. *n* reflejo *m* II. *adj* reflejo, -a

reflex action *n* acto *m* reflejo **reflex camera** *n* cámara *f* réflex

reflexive [rɪ'fleksɪv] I. *adj* **1.** *Am* (*independent of will*) reflejo, -a **2.** LING reflexivo, -a II. *n*

LING reflexivo *m*

reflexology [ˌriːflek'sɒlədʒi, *Am:* -'saːlə-] *n* reflexología *f*

refloat [ˌriː'fləʊt, *Am:* -'floʊt] *vt* reflotar

reflux [ˌriː'flʌks] *n* reflujo *m*

reforest [ˌriː'fɒrɪst, *Am:* -'fɔːr-] *vt* reforestar

reform [rɪ'fɔːm, *Am:* -'fɔːrm] I. *vt* reformar II. *vi* reformarse III. *n* reforma *f*

re-form [ˌriː'fɔːm, *Am:* -'fɔːrm] I. *vt* formar de nuevo II. *vi* formarse de nuevo

reformation [ˌrefə'meɪʃən, *Am:* -ɚ'-] *n* reforma *f;* **the Reformation** la Reforma

reformatory [rɪ'fɔːmətəri, *Am:* -'fɔːrmətɔːri] <-ies> *n Am* reformatorio *m*

reformer *n* reformador(a) *m(f)*

reform school *n* reformatorio *m*

refract [rɪ'frækt] *vt* PHYS refractar

refraction [rɪ'frækʃən] *n* refracción *f*

refractory [rɪ'fræktəri] *adj* refractario, -a

refrain[1] [rɪ'freɪn] *vi form* abstenerse; **to ~ from doing sth** abstenerse de hacer algo

refrain[2] [rɪ'freɪn] *n* MUS estribillo *m*

refresh [rɪ'freʃ] *vt* refrescar; **to ~ oneself** refrescarse

refresher *n* **1.** (*course*) curso *m* de reciclaje **2.** *Brit* LAW honorarios *mpl* suplementarios

refreshing *adj* **1.** (*drink*) refrescante **2.** (*change, difference*) reconfortante

refreshment [rɪ'freʃmənt] *n* **1.** (*drink*) refresco *m* **2.** (*food*) refrigerio *m*

refrigerant [rɪ'frɪdʒərənt] *n* refrigerante *m*

refrigerate [rɪ'frɪdʒəreɪt] *vt* refrigerar

refrigeration [rɪˌfrɪdʒə'reɪʃən] *n no pl* refrigeración *f*

refrigerator [rɪ'frɪdʒəreɪtər, *Am:* -tɚ] *n* nevera *f,* refrigerador *m AmL,* frigider *m Chile*

refuel [ˌriː'fjuːəl] <-ll-, *Am:* -l-> I. *vi* repostar combustible II. *vt* reabastecer de combustible; *fig* renovar

refuge ['refjuːdʒ] *n* refugio *m;* **to take ~ in sth** refugiarse en algo

refugee [ˌrefjʊ'dʒiː] *n* refugiado, -a *m, f*

refugee camp *n* campo *m* de refugiados

refund[1] [ˌriː'fʌnd] *vt* reembolsar

refund[2] ['riːfʌnd] *n* reembolso *m*

refurbish [ˌriː'fɜːbɪʃ, *Am:* -'fɜːrbɪʃ] *vt* restaurar, refaccionar *AmL*

refusal [rɪ'fjuːzl] *n* negativa *f*

refuse[1] [rɪ'fjuːz] I. *vi* negarse II. *vt* (*request, gift*) rechazar; (*permission, entry*) denegar; **to ~ sb sth** negar algo a alguien

refuse[2] ['refjuːs] *n form* basura *f;* **garden/kitchen ~** desperdicios *mpl* de jardín/cocina

refuse bin *n* cubo *m* de basura, bote *m* de basura *Méx* **refuse collection** *n* recogida *f* de basuras **refuse collector** *n Brit* basurero, -a *m, f* **refuse disposal** *n* eliminación *f* de basura **refuse dump** *n* vertedero *m,* basurero *m Méx*

refusenik [re'fjuːznɪk] *n* POL objetor *m*

refutation [ˌrefjuː'teɪʃən] *n* refutación *f*

refute [rɪ'fjuːt] *vt* refutar

regain [rɪ'geɪn] *vt* (*freedom, possession*)

recuperar; (*consciousness, health*) recobrar

regal ['riːgl] *adj* regio, -a

regale [rɪ'geɪl] *vt iron* agasajar

regalia [rɪ'geɪlɪə, *Am:* -'geɪljə] *n* **1.**(*clothes*) traje *m* de gala **2.**(*insignia*) insignias *fpl*

regard [rɪ'gɑːd, *Am:* -'gɑːrd] I. *vt* **1.**(*consider*) considerar; **to ~ sb highly** tener muy buena opinión de alguien **2.** *form* (*watch*) contemplar **3.**(*concerning*) **as ~s ...** respecto a... II. *n form* **1.**(*consideration*) consideración *f*; **to pay no ~ to sth** no prestar atención a algo; **with ~ to ...** en cuanto a... **2.**(*respect*) respeto *m*, estima *f*; **to hold sb/sth in high ~** tener una alta estima por alguien/algo **3.**(*point*) respecto *m;* **in this ~** con respecto a esto **4.** *pl* (*in messages*) recuerdos *mpl;* **with kind ~s** muchos saludos

regardful [rɪ'gɑːdfəl, *Am:* -'gɑːrd-] *adj* atento, -a

regarding *prep* en cuanto a

regardless [rɪ'gɑːdləs, *Am:* -'gɑːrd-] I. *adv* a pesar de todo; **to press on ~** seguir cueste lo que cueste II. *adj* indiferente; **~ of ...** sin tener en cuenta...

regatta [rɪ'gætə, *Am:* -'gɑːt̬ə] *n* regata *f*

regency ['riːdʒənsi] *n* regencia *f*

regenerate [rɪ'dʒenəreɪt] I. *vt* regenerar II. *vi* regenerarse

regeneration [rɪˌdʒenə'reɪʃən] *n no pl* regeneración *f*

regent ['riːdʒənt] I. *n* regente *mf* II. *adj* **Prince Regent** Príncipe *m* Regente

reggae ['regeɪ] *n no pl* reggae *m*

regicide ['redʒɪsaɪd] *n* **1.**(*person*) regicida *mf* **2.**(*action*) regicidio *m*

regime [reɪ'ʒiːm, *Am:* rə'-] *n* régimen *m*

regimen ['redʒɪmen, *Am:* -əmen] *n form* régimen *m*

regiment ['redʒɪmənt, *Am:* -əmənt] I. *n* **1.** MIL regimiento *m* **2.** *fig* multitud *f* II. *vt* reglamentar

regimentation [ˌredʒɪmen'teɪʃən, *Am:* -əmən'-] *n* reglamentación *f*

region ['riːdʒən] *n* **1.** GEO, ANAT región *f*; **in the ~ of 30** alrededor de 30 **2.**(*administrative area*) provincia *f*

regional ['riːdʒənl] *adj* regional

regionalism ['riːdʒənəˌlɪzəm] *n* regionalismo *m*

register ['redʒɪstər, *Am:* -stə-] I. *n* registro *m;* **class ~** lista *f* de la clase II. *vt* registrar; (*car*) matricular; (*voter*) inscribir; (*letter, parcel*) certificar III. *vi* **1.**(*record*) inscribirse; UNIV matricularse, inscribirse *AmL* **2.**(*be understood*) **the information didn't ~ with him** no retuvo la información

registered ['redʒɪstəd, *Am:* -əd] *adj* registrado, -a; (*nurse*) diplomado, -a; (*student*) matriculado, -a; (*letter, parcel*) certificado, -a

registrar [ˌredʒɪ'strɑːr, *Am:* 'redʒɪstrɑːr] *n* **1.** ADMIN secretario, -a *m, f* del registro civil **2.** *Brit* UNIV secretario, -a *m, f* general **3.** *Brit, Aus* MED médico *mf* asistente

registration [ˌredʒɪ'streɪʃən] *n* **1.**(*act*) inscripción *f*; UNIV matriculación *f* **2.**(*number*) matrícula *f*

registration document *n Brit* documento *m* de matriculación **registration fee** *n* cuota *f* de inscripción; UNIV matrícula *f* **registration number** *n* matrícula *f*

registry ['redʒɪstri] *n Brit* registro *m*

regress [rɪ'gres] *vi* retroceder

regression [rɪ'greʃən] *n no pl* regresión *f*

regressive [rɪ'gresɪv] *adj* regresivo, -a

regret [rɪ'gret] I.<-tt-> *vt* lamentar; **to ~ doing sth** arrepentirse de haber hecho algo; **we ~ any inconvenience to passengers** lamentamos las molestias para los pasajeros II. *n* arrepentimiento *m;* **to have ~** tener remordimientos; **to have no ~s about sth** no arrepentirse de algo; **much to my ~** muy a mi pesar; **to send one's ~s** enviar disculpas

regretful [rɪ'gretfəl] *adj* arrepentido, -a

regretfully *adv* lamentablemente

regrettable [rɪ'gretəbl, *Am:* -'gret̬-] *adj* lamentable

regroup [ˌriː'gruːp] I. *vt* reagrupar II. *vi* reagruparse

regular ['regjʊlər, *Am:* -jələ-] I. *adj* **1.**(*pattern*) regular; (*appearance, customer*) habitual; (*procedure*) normal; **to have ~ meetings** tener reuniones periódicas **2.** *Am* (*gas*) normal **3.** LING regular **4.** *inf* (*real*) verdadero, -a II. *n* **1.**(*customer*) asiduo, -a *m, f* **2.** MIL soldado *m* regular

regularity [ˌregjʊ'lærəti, *Am:* -'lerət̬i] *n no pl* regularidad *f*

regularize ['regjʊləraɪz] *vt* **1.**(*standardize*) normalizar **2.**(*normalize*) regularizar

regularly *adv* con regularidad

regulate ['regjʊleɪt] *vt* **1.**(*supervise*) reglamentar **2.**(*adjust*) regular

regulation [ˌregjʊ'leɪʃən] I. *n* **1.**(*rule*) regla *f*; **safety ~s** reglamento *m* de seguridad; **in accordance with the ~s** de acuerdo con el reglamento **2.** *no pl* (*adjustment*) regulación *f* II. *adj* reglamentario, -a

regulator ['regjʊleɪtər, *Am:* -t̬ə-] *n* regulador *m*

regulatory [ˌregjʊ'leɪtri, *Am:* 'regjələeɪtɔːri] *adj* regulador(a)

regurgitate [ri'gɜːdʒɪteɪt, *Am:* -'gɜːrdʒə-] *vt* **1.**(*food*) regurgitar **2.**(*ideas, facts*) repetir maquinalmente

rehabilitate [ˌriːhə'bɪlɪteɪt, *Am:* '-ə-] *vt* rehabilitar

rehabilitation [ˌriːhəˌbɪlɪ'teɪʃən, *Am:* -ə'-] *no pl* rehabilitación *f*

rehabilitation centre *n* centro *m* de rehabilitación

rehash[1] [ˌriː'hæʃ] *vt* hacer un refrito de

rehash[2] ['riːhæʃ] *n* refrito *m*

rehearsal [rɪ'hɜːsl, *Am:* -'hɜːrsl] *n* ensayo *m*

rehearse [rɪ'hɜːs, *Am:* -'hɜːrs] *vt, vi* ensayar

reign [reɪn] I. *vi* **1.**(*be monarch*) reinar **2.** *fig* (*be dominant*) imperar II. *n* **1.**(*sovereignty*)

R

reinado *m* **2.**(*rule*) régimen *m*

reimburse [ˌriːɪmˈbɜːs, *Am:* -ˈbɜːrs] *vt* reembolsar

reimbursement *n* reembolso *m*

rein [reɪn] *n* rienda *f* ►**to give** <u>free</u> ~ **to sb** dar rienda suelta a alguien; **to keep sb on a** <u>tight</u> ~ atar corto a alguien, tener a alguien controlado; **to** <u>hold</u> **the** ~**s** sujetar las riendas

reincarnation [ˌriːɪnkɑːˈneɪʃən, *Am:* -kɑːrˈ-] *n* reencarnación *f*

reindeer [ˈreɪndɪəʳ, *Am:* -dɪr] *n inv* reno *m*

reinforce [ˌriːɪnˈfɔːs, *Am:* -ˈfɔːrs] *vt a.* MIL reforzar; (*argument*) fortalecer

reinforcement *n* refuerzo *m*

reinstate [ˌriːɪnˈsteɪt] *vt form* restituir

reinsure [ˌriːɪnˈʃʊəʳ, *Am:* -ˈʃʊr] *vt* reasegurar

reintegrate [ˌriːˈɪntəgreɪt] *vt* reintegrar; (*criminal*) reinsertar

reintegration [ˈriːˌɪntəˈgreɪʃən] *n* reintegración *f*; (*of criminal*) reinserción *f*

re-introduce [ˌriːˈɪntrəˈdjuːs, *Am:* -ˈduːs] *vt* reintroducir

reissue [ˌriːˈɪʃuː, *Am:* -ˈɪʃjuː] I. *vt* volver a emitir II. *n* reexpedición *f*

reiterate [riˈɪtəreɪt, *Am:* -ˈɪtəreɪt] *vt* reiterar

reiteration [riˌɪtəˈreɪʃən, *Am:* -ˌɪtəˈreɪ-] *n* reiteración *f*

reject[1] [rɪˈdʒekt] *vt a.* MED, TECH rechazar; (*application, request*) desestimar; (*accusation*) negar; (*bill, motion*) impugnar; (*proposal*) descartar

reject[2] [ˈriːdʒekt] *n* **1.**(*cast-off*) artículo *m* defectuoso **2.**(*person*) persona *f* rechazada

rejection [rɪˈdʒekʃən] *n* rechazo *m*

rejoice [rɪˈdʒɔɪs] *vi* regocijarse; **to** ~ **in doing sth** regocijarse haciendo algo; **I** ~**d to see that** ... me alegré al ver que...

rejoicing *n no pl* regocijo *m*

rejoin[1] [ˌriːˈdʒɔɪn] I. *vt* (*join again*) volver a unirse con; (*regiment*) reincorporarse a; (*political party*) reintegrarse a II. *vi* reunirse

rejoin[2] [rɪˈdʒɔɪn] *vt* (*reply*) replicar

rejoinder [rɪˈdʒɔɪndəʳ, *Am:* -dəʳ] *n* réplica *f*

rejuvenate [riˈdʒuːvəneɪt] *vt* rejuvenecer

rekindle [riːˈkɪndl] *vt a. fig* reavivar

relapse [rɪˈlæps] I. *n* MED recaída *f* II. *vi a.* MED recaer

relate [rɪˈleɪt] I. *vt* **1.**(*establish connection*) relacionar **2.**(*tell*) contar II. *vi* **1.**(*be connected with*) **to** ~ **to sb/sth** estar relacionado con alguien/algo **2.**(*understand*) **to** ~ **to sth/ sb** comprender algo/a alguien

related *adj* **1.**(*linked*) relacionado, -a **2.**(*in same family*) emparentado, -a; **to be** ~ **to sb** estar emparentado con alguien; **to be closely/ distantly** ~ tener parentesco cercano/lejano

relating to *prep* acerca de

relation [rɪˈleɪʃən] *n* **1.** *no pl*(*link*) relación *f*; **in** ~ **to** en relación a; **to bear no** ~ **to sb/sth** no tener relación con alguien/algo **2.**(*relative*) pariente *mf* **3.** *pl* (*contact*) relaciones *fpl*

relationship [rɪˈleɪʃənʃɪp] *n* **1.**(*link*) relación *f* **2.**(*family connection*) parentesco *m*

3.(*between two people*) relaciones *fpl;* **to be in a** ~ **with sb** tener una relación con alguien; **business** ~**s** relaciones comerciales

relative [ˈrelətɪv, *Am:* -t̬ɪv] I. *adj* relativo, -a II. *n* pariente *mf*

relative clause *n* oración *f* relativa

relatively *adv* relativamente

relativity [ˌreləˈtɪvəti, *Am:* -t̬i] *n* relatividad *f*

relaunch[1] [ˌriːˈlɔːntʃ] *vt* relanzar

relaunch[2] [ˈriːlɔːntʃ] *n* relanzamiento *m*

relax [rɪˈlæks] I. *vi* relajarse; (*restrictions*) mitigarse; (*rules*) suavizarse; (*security*) debilitarse; **relax!** ¡cálmate! II. *vt* relajar; (*restrictions*) mitigar; (*rules*) suavizar; (*security*) debilitar; **to** ~ **one's efforts** disminuir sus esfuerzos; **to** ~ **one's hold on sth** dejar de agarrarse a algo; *fig* ejercer menos control sobre algo

relaxation [ˌriːlækˈseɪʃən] *n* relajación *f*

relaxed *adj* relajado, -a

relay [ˈriːleɪ] I. *vt* (*information*) pasar; TV retransmitir II. *n* **1.**(*group*) turno *m;* **to work in** ~**s** trabajar por turnos **2.** SPORTS carrera *f* de relevos **3.** ELEC relé *m*

re-lay [ˌriːˈleɪ] *vt* volver a colocar

release [rɪˈliːs] I. *vt* **1.**(*set free*) poner en libertad **2.**(*cease to hold*) soltar; PHOT disparar **3.**(*allow to escape: gas*) emitir; (*steam*) desprender **4.**(*weaken: pressure*) aliviar **5.**(*make public: information*) anunciar; (*book*) publicar; (*film*) estrenar; (*CD*) poner a la venta II. *n no pl* **1.**(*of prisoner*) excarcelación *f*; (*of hostage*) liberación *f* **2.** PHOT disparador *m* **3.**(*relaxation*) aflojamiento *m* **4.**(*escape*) escape *m* **5.** *no pl* (*publication*) publicación *f*; (*of film*) estreno *m;* (*of CD*) puesta *f* a la venta; **press** ~ comunicado *m* de prensa

relegate [ˈrelɪgeɪt, *Am:* ˈrelə-] *vt* relegar

relent [rɪˈlent] *vi* (*person*) ceder; (*wind, rain*) amainar

relentless [rɪˈlentləs] *adj* (*pursuit, opposition*) implacable; (*pressure*) incesante; (*criticism*) despiadado, -a

relevance [ˈreləvənts] *n*, **relevancy** *n no pl* pertinencia

relevant [ˈreləvənt] *adj* pertinente

reliability [rɪˌlaɪəˈbɪləti, *Am:* -t̬i] *n no pl* **1.**(*dependability*) seguridad *f* **2.**(*trustworthiness*) fiabilidad *f*

reliable [rɪˈlaɪəbl] *adj* **1.**(*credible*) fidedigno, -a; (*authority*) serio, -a; (*evidence*) fehaciente; (*statistics*) auténtico, -a; (*testimony*) verídico, -a **2.**(*trustworthy*) de confianza

reliance [rɪˈlaɪəns] *n no pl* **1.**(*dependence*) dependencia *f* **2.**(*belief*) confianza *f*

reliant [rɪˈlaɪənt] *adj* **to be** ~ **on sb/sth** depender de alguien/algo

relic [ˈrelɪk] *n a. fig* reliquia *f*

relief [rɪˈliːf] I. *n* **1.** *no pl* (*aid*) socorro *m;* **to be on** ~ *Am, inf* vivir de la caridad **2.**(*relaxation*) alivio *m;* **it's a** ~ **that** es un alivio que +*subj;* **that's a** ~! ¡menos mal! **3.**(*replacement*) relevo *m* **4.** MIL descerco *m* **5.** *a.* GEO

relieve *m;* **to throw sth into** ~ hacer resaltar algo **6. tax** ~ desgravación *f* fiscal **II.** *adj* **1.** de relevo; (*driver*) suplente **2.** GEO en relieve
relief worker *n* trabajador(a) *m(f)* de una organización humanitaria
relieve [rɪˈliːv] *vt* **1.** (*assist*) socorrer **2.** (*alleviate: pain*) aliviar; (*suffering*) mitigar; (*feelings*) desahogar; (*one's mind*) tranquilizar **3.** MIL descercar **4.** (*urinate, defecate*) **to** ~ **oneself** hacer sus necesidades
relieved *adj* aliviado, -a
religion [rɪˈlɪdʒən] *n* religión *f*
religious [rɪˈlɪdʒəs] *adj* religioso, -a
relinquish [rɪˈlɪŋkwɪʃ] *vt* (*claim, title*) renunciar a; (*control*) ceder; **to** ~ **one's grip on sth** soltar algo
reliquary [ˈrelɪkwəri, *Am:* -əkwer-] <-ies> *n* relicario *m*
relish [ˈrelɪʃ] **I.** *n* **1.** *no pl* (*enjoyment*) gusto *m;* **with** ~ con gusto **2.** (*enthusiasm*) entusiasmo *m* **3.** GASTR condimento *m* **II.** *vt* deleitarse en; **I don't** ~ ... no me entusiasma...
reload [ˌriːˈləʊd, *Am:* -ˈloʊd] **I.** *vt* recargar **II.** *vi* recargarse
relocate [ˌriːləʊˈkeɪt, *Am:* -ˈloʊkeɪt] **I.** *vi* trasladarse **II.** *vt* trasladar
relocation [ˌriːləʊˈkeɪʃən, *Am:* -loʊˈ-] *n* (*of company*) reubicación *f;* (*of person*) traslado *m*
reluctance [rɪˈlʌktəns] *n* *no pl* desgana *f;* **with** ~ de mala gana
reluctant [rɪˈlʌktənt] *adj* reacio, -a; **to be** ~ **to do sth** tener pocas ganas de hacer algo, ser reacio a hacer algo
rely [rɪˈlaɪ] *vi* **to** ~ **on** [*o* **upon**] (*trust*) confiar en; (*depend on*) depender de; **to** ~ **on** [*o* **upon**] **sb to do sth** contar con alguien para hacer algo
REM [ˌɑːˈriːˈem, *Am:* ˌɑːriːˈem] *abbr of* **Rapid Eye Movement** movimiento *m* rápido del ojo
remain [rɪˈmeɪn] *vi* **1.** (*stay*) quedar(se) **2.** (*continue*) permanecer; **to** ~ **aloof** mantenerse apartado; **to** ~ **seated** quedarse sentado; **to** ~ **unsolved** seguir sin solucionarse; **to** ~ **to be done** estar por hacer; **much** ~**s to be done** queda mucho por hacer; **the fact** ~**s that** ... sigue siendo un hecho que...; **it** (**only**) ~**s for me to** ... sólo me resta...; **it** ~**s to be seen** (**who/what/how**) está por ver (quién/qué/cómo)
remainder [rɪˈmeɪndə^r, *Am:* -də^·] **I.** *n* *no pl* *a.* MAT resto *m;* **the** ~ **of sb's life** lo que queda de la vida de alguien **II.** *vt* saldar
remaining [rɪˈmeɪnɪŋ] *adj* restante
remains [rɪˈmeɪnz] *npl* restos *mpl*
remake[1] [ˌriːˈmeɪk] <remade> *vt* volver a hacer
remake[2] [ˈriːmeɪk] *n* nueva versión *f*
remand [rɪˈmɑːnd, *Am:* -ˈmænd] **I.** *vt* **to** ~ **sb to prison** [*o* **in custody**] poner a alguien en prisión preventiva; **to** ~ **sb on bail** poner a alguien en libertad bajo fianza **II.** *n* **to be on** ~

estar en prisión preventiva
remand centre *n* *Brit, Aus* centro *m* de detención preventiva
remark [rɪˈmɑːk, *Am:* -ˈmɑːrk] **I.** *vi* **to** ~ **on** sth hacer observaciones sobre algo **II.** *n* observación *f;* **to make** ~**s about sb/sth** hacer comentarios sobre alguien/algo
remarkable [rɪˈmɑːkəbl, *Am:* -ˈmɑːr-] *adj* extraordinario, -a; (*coincidence*) singular; **to be** ~ **for sth** ser notable por algo
remarkably *adj* extraordinariamente
remarry [ˌriːˈmæri, *Am:* -ˈmer-] <-ie-> *vi* volver a casarse
remedial [rɪˈmiːdiəl] *adj* (*action*) remediador(a); SCHOOL recuperativo, -a; MED terapéutico, -a
remedy [ˈremədi] **I.** <-ies> *n* **1.** remedio *m;* **to be beyond** ~ no tener remedio **2.** LAW (**legal**) ~ recurso *m* (legal) **II.** *vt* remediar; (*mistake*) corregir
remember [rɪˈmembə^r, *Am:* -bə^·] **I.** *vt* **1.** (*recall*) recordar; **I can't** ~ **his name** no recuerdo su nombre **2.** (*commemorate*) conmemorar **II.** *vi* acordarse
remembrance [rɪˈmembrəns] *n* **1.** *no pl* (*act of remembering*) recuerdo *m;* **in** ~ **of** en conmemoración de **2.** *pl* (*greetings*) recuerdos *mpl*
Remembrance Day *n* *Brit:* día en que se conmemora a los caídos en las guerras mundiales

El **Remembrance Day, Remembrance Sunday** o **Poppy Day** se celebra el segundo domingo de noviembre en conmemoración del armisticio firmado el 11 de noviembre de 1918. Este día se recuerda especialmente con misas y distintas ceremonias a todos aquellos soldados que murieron en las dos guerras mundiales. Las personas llevan unas amapolas de tela, que simbolizan las amapolas florecientes de los campos de batalla de Flandes después de la I Guerra Mundial. A las 11 de la mañana se guardan dos minutos de silencio.

remind [rɪˈmaɪnd] *vt* recordar; **to** ~ **sb to do sth** recordar a alguien que haga algo; **he** ~**s me of you** me recuerda a ti; **that** ~**s me,** ... por cierto,...
reminder [rɪˈmaɪndə^r, *Am:* -ə^·] *n* **1.** (*note*) recordatorio *m* **2.** (*warning*) advertencia *f;* **to give sb a gentle** ~ dar a alguien una advertencia amistosa **3.** (*memento*) recuerdo *m*
reminisce [ˌremɪˈnɪs, *Am:* -ə^ˈ-] *vi* narrar reminiscencias
reminiscence [ˌremɪˈnɪsns, *Am:* -ə^ˈ-] *n* reminiscencia *f*
reminiscent [ˌremɪˈnɪsnt, *Am:* -ə^ˈ-] *adj* **to be** ~ **of sb/sth** hacer pensar en alguien/algo
remiss [rɪˈmɪs] *adj* negligente
remission [rɪˈmɪʃən] *n* remisión *f*
remit[1] [rɪˈmɪt] <-tt-> *vt* *form* **1.** (*send*) remi-

tir; (*money*) enviar **2.** LAW perdonar
remit² ['riːmɪt] *n* competencia *f*
remittance [rɪ'mɪtns] *n* giro *m*
remix ['riːmɪks] MUS **I.** *vt* mezclar **II.** <-es> *n* mezcla *f*
remnant ['remnənt] *n* resto *m*
remnant sale *n* venta *f* de saldos
remodel [ˌriː'mɒdəl, *Am:* -'mɑːdəl] <-ll-, *Am:* -l-> *vt* remodelar
remonstrance [rɪ'mɒntstrənts, *Am:* -'mɑːnt-] *n form* protesta *f*
remonstrate ['remənstreɪt, *Am:* rɪ'mɑːnt-] *vi* protestar
remorse [rɪ'mɔːs, *Am:* -'mɔːrs] *n no pl* remordimiento *m;* **without ~** sin remordimientos
remorseful [rɪ'mɔːsfəl, *Am:* -'mɔːrs-] *adj* arrepentido, -a
remorseless [rɪ'mɔːsləs, *Am:* -'mɔːrs-] *adj* (*merciless*) despiadado, -a; (*attack*) implacable
remote [rɪ'məʊt, *Am:* -'moʊt] *adj* <-er, -est> (*place, possibility*) remoto, -a
remote control *n* mando *m* a distancia
remote-controlled *adj* teledirigido, -a
remoteness *n no pl* alejamiento *m*
remould ['riːməʊld, *Am:* -moʊld] **I.** *vt* recauchutar **II.** *n* recauchutado *m*
remount [ˌriː'maʊnt] **I.** *vt* subir de nuevo a **II.** *vi* volverse a montar
removable [rɪ'muːvəbl] *adj* **1.** (*stain*) que se puede quitar **2.** (*easy to take off*) desmontable; (*sleeves*) de quita y pon
removal [rɪ'muːvəl] *n* **1.** *no pl* (*of stain, problem*) eliminación *f* **2.** (*extraction*) extracción *f* **3.** *no pl, Brit* (*move*) mudanza *f*
removal expenses *n* gastos *mpl* de mudanza **removal firm** *n* agencia *f* de mudanzas **removal van** *n* camión *m* de mudanzas
remove [rɪ'muːv] **I.** *vt* **1.** (*take away*) quitar; (*clothes*) quitarse **2.** (*get rid of*) eliminar; (*cork, dent*) sacar; (*entry, name*) borrar; (*doubts, fears*) disipar; (*problem*) solucionar; **to ~ one's hair** depilarse **3.** (*dismiss from job*) destituir **II.** *n form* **to be at one ~ from sth** estar a un paso de algo
remover [rɪ'muːvəʳ, *Am:* -ɚ] *n* **1.** agente *mf* de mudanzas **2. stain ~** quitamanchas *m inv*
remunerate [rɪ'mjuːnəreɪt] *vt form* remunerar
remuneration [rɪˌmjuːnə'reɪʃən] *n form* remuneración *f*
remunerative [rɪ'mjuːnərətɪv, *Am:* -nəreɪ̯tɪv] *adj form* lucrativo, -a
Renaissance [rɪ'neɪsns, *Am:* ˌrenə'sɑːns] *n* **the ~** el Renacimiento
renal ['riːnl] *adj* renal
rename [ˌriː'neɪm] *vt* poner un nuevo nombre a
rend [rend] <rent *o Am* rended> *vt liter* desgarrar
render ['rendəʳ, *Am:* -dɚ] *vt form* **1.** (*make*) hacer; **to ~ sb speechless** dejar a alguien mudo **2.** (*perform*) representar; MUS interpretar

3. (*give: thanks*) ofrecer; (*aid, service*) prestar; (*judgement*) emitir **4.** (*translate*) traducir **5.** ARCHIT enlucir, frisar *And*
rendering ['rendərɪŋ] *n* **1.** (*performance*) representación *f;* MUS interpretación *f* **2.** (*translation*) traducción *f*
rendezvous ['rɒndɪvuː, 'rɒndɪvuːz, *Am:* 'rɑːndeɪ-] **I.** *n inv* **1.** (*meeting*) cita *f* **2.** (*place*) lugar *m* de reunión **II.** *vi* reunirse
rendition [ren'dɪʃən] *n* **1.** (*performance*) interpretación *f* **2.** (*translation*) traducción *f*
renegade ['renɪgeɪd, *Am:* 'renə-] **I.** *n* renegado, -a *m, f* **II.** *adj* renegado, -a
renege [rɪ'neɪg, *Am:* -'nɪg] *vi form* **to ~ on sth** incumplir algo
renew [rɪ'njuː, *Am:* -'nuː] *vt* **1.** (*begin again: membership, passport*) renovar; (*relationship*) reanudar; **to ~ one's efforts to do sth** recobrar fuerzas para hacer algo **2.** (*mend*) recuperar
renewable [rɪ'njuːəbl, *Am:* -'nuː-] *adj* renovable
renewal [rɪ'njuːəl, *Am:* -'nuː-] *n* renovación *f*
renewed [rɪ'njuːd, *Am:* -'nuːd] *adj* renovado, -a
rennet ['renɪt] *n no pl* cuajo *m*
renounce [rɪ'naʊns] *vt* renunciar a
renovate ['renəveɪt] *vt* restaurar, refaccionar *Ven, Col*
renovation [ˌrenə'veɪʃən] *n* renovación *f*
renown [rɪ'naʊn] *n no pl* renombre *m*
renowned [rɪ'naʊnd] *adj* renombrado, -a
rent¹ [rent] **I.** *n* rasgadura *f* **II.** *pt, pp of* rend
rent² [rent] **I.** *n* alquiler *m;* **for ~** se alquila **II.** *vt* alquilar; (*land*) arrendar **III.** *vi* alquilarse
rental ['rentəl, *Am:* -ţəl] **I.** *n* alquiler *m* **II.** *adj* de alquiler
rent boy *n Brit, inf* chico *m* de compañía **rent control** *n* control *m* de rentas **rent-free** *adj* exento, -a de alquiler
renunciation [rɪˌnʌnsɪ'eɪʃən] *n no pl* renuncia *f*
reopen [ˌriː'əʊpən, *Am:* -'oʊ-] **I.** *vt* reabrir **II.** *vi* reabrirse
reorder [ˌriː'ɔːdəʳ] **I.** *n* nuevo pedido *m* **II.** *vt* **1.** (*reorganize*) reordenar **2.** COM hacer un nuevo pedido de
reorganize [riː'ɔːgənaɪz, *Am:* -'ɔːrgən-] **I.** *vt* reorganizar **II.** *vi* reorganizarse
rep [rep] *n inf* **1.** *abbr of* **representative** representante *mf* de ventas **2.** THEAT *abbr of* **repertory** repertorio *m*
Rep. 1. *abbr of* **Republic** Rep. **2.** *abbr of* **Republican** republicano, -a
repaint [ˌriː'peɪnt] *vt* repintar
repair [rɪ'peəʳ, *Am:* -'per] **I.** *vt* **1.** (*machine*) reparar; (*clothes*) arreglar **2.** (*set right: damage*) enmendar; (*friendship*) reestablecer **II.** *n* **1.** (*mending: of machine*) reparación *f;* (*of clothes*) arreglo *m;* **to be beyond ~** no tener arreglo; **to be under ~** estar en reparación **2.** (*state*) **to be in good/bad ~** estar en buen/mal estado

repairable [rɪ'peərəbl, *Am:* -'perə-] *adj* reparable

repair kit *n* caja *f* de herramientas **repairman** <-men> *n* (*for cars*) mecánico *m*; (*for television*) técnico *m* **repair shop** *n* taller *m* de reparaciones

repaper [riː'peɪpəʳ] *vt* empapelar de nuevo

reparable ['repərəbl] *adj* reparable

reparation [ˌrepə'reɪʃən] *n* 1. (*setting right*) reparación *f* 2. *pl* FIN indemnización *f*

repartee [ˌrepɑː'tiː, *Am:* -ɑːr'-] *n no pl* réplica *f*

repatriate [riː'pætrɪeɪt, *Am:* -'peɪtrɪ-] *vt* repatriar

repatriation [ˌriːpætri'eɪʃən, *Am:* rɪˌpeɪtri'-] *n no pl* repatriación *f*

repay [rɪ'peɪ] <repaid> *vt* (*money*) devolver; (*debts*) liquidar; (*person*) pagar; **to ~ money to sb** reintegrar dinero a alguien; **to ~ sb for sth** premiar a alguien por algo; **to ~ a kindness** devolver una atención

repayable [rɪ'peɪəbl] *adj* reembolsable

repayment [rɪ'peɪmənt] *n* reembolso *m*

repeal [rɪ'piːl] I. *vt* revocar II. *n no pl* revocatoria *f*

repeat [rɪ'piːt] I. *vt* 1. (*say or do again*) repetir 2. (*recite*) recitar II. *vi* (*happen again*) repetirse; (*taste*) repetir III. *n* 1. repetición *f* 2. TV retransmisión *f*

repeated *adj* repetido, -a

repeatedly *adv* repetidas veces

repeat order *n* COM pedido *m* de repitición

repeat performance *n* repetición *f*

repel [rɪ'pel] <-ll-> *vt* 1. (*ward off*) rechazar 2. MIL, PHYS repeler 3. (*disgust*) repugnar

repellent [rɪ'pelənt] I. *n* repelente *m* II. *adj* repugnante

repent [rɪ'pent] I. *vi form* arrepentirse II. *vt* arrepentirse de

repentance [rɪ'pentənts] *n no pl* arrepentimiento *m*

repentant [rə'pentənt] *adj* arrepentido, -a

repercussion [ˌriːpə'kʌʃən, *Am:* -pəʳ'-] *n* repercusión *f*

repertoire ['repətwɑː, *Am:* -əʳtwɑːr] *n* repertorio *m*

repertory company ['repətəri'kʌmpəni, *Am:* -əʳtɔːr-] *n Brit* compañía *f* de repertorio **repertory theatre** *n Brit* teatro *m* de repertorio

repetition [ˌrepɪ'tɪʃən, *Am:* -ə'-] *n* repetición *f*

repetitious [ˌrepɪ'tɪʃəs, *Am:* -ə'-] *adj*, **repetitive** [rɪ'petətɪv, *Am:* -'peṭəṭɪv] *adj* repetitivo, -a

replace [rɪ'pleɪs] *vt* 1. (*take the place of*) reemplazar; (*person*) sustituir 2. (*put back*) reponer

replaceable [rɪ'pleɪsəbl] *adj* reemplazable

replacement [rɪ'pleɪsmənt] I. *n* 1. (*person*) sustituto, -a *m, f*; (*part*) recambio *m* 2. MIL reemplazo *m* 3. (*act of substituting*) sustitución *f* II. *adj* de repuesto

replay¹ [ˌriː'pleɪ] *vt* 1. SPORTS volver a jugar 2. MUS volver a tocar 3. TV repetir

replay² ['riːpleɪ] *n* 1. SPORTS, TV repetición *f* 2. MUS reproducción *f*

replenish [rɪ'plenɪʃ] *vt* rellenar; (*supplies*) abastecer de nuevo; (*stocks*) reponer

replete [rɪ'pliːt] *adj* repleto, -a

replica ['replɪkə] *n* réplica *f*

replicate ['replɪkeɪt] *vt* replicar

reply [rɪ'plaɪ] I. <-ied> *vt* contestar II. <-ied> *vi* 1. (*verbally*) contestar 2. (*react*) responder III. <-ies> *n* respuesta *f*

reply coupon *n* cupón *m* respuesta **reply-paid envelope** *n* sobre *m* prepagado

report [rɪ'pɔːt, *Am:* -'pɔːrt] I. *n* 1. (*account*) informe *m*; PUBL noticia *f*; (*longer*) reportaje *m*; **to give a ~** presentar un informe 2. (*unproven claim*) rumor *m* 3. (*explosion*) estallido *m* II. *vt* 1. (*recount*) relatar; (*discovery*) anunciar; **to ~ that ...** informar que...; **nothing to ~** sin novedades 2. (*denounce*) denunciar III. *vi* 1. (*make results public*) presentar un informe 2. (*arrive at work*) presentarse; **to ~ sick** dar parte de enfermedad

♦**report back** I. *vt* **to report sth back to sb** relatar algo a alguien II. *vi* presentar un informe

report card *n Am* cartilla *f* escolar

reporter [rɪ'pɔːtəʳ, *Am:* -'pɔːrṭəʳ] *n* reportero, -a *m, f*

repose [rɪ'pəʊz, *Am:* -'poʊz] I. *vi* 1. (*rest*) reposar 2. (*lie*) descansar II. *vt* 1. (*rest*) reposar 2. *fig* (*confidence*) depositar III. *n no pl* reposo *m*; **in ~** de reposo

repository [rɪ'pɒzɪtəri, *Am:* -'pɑːzɪtɔːri] <-ies> *n* 1. (*store*) depósito *m* 2. (*person*) depositario, -a *m, f*

repossess [ˌriːpə'zes] *vt* recobrar

repossession [ˌriːpə'zeʃən] *n* recuperación *f*

reprehensible [ˌreprɪ'hensəbl] *adj* censurable

represent [ˌreprɪ'zent] *vt* 1. (*act for, depict*) representar 2. (*state*) declarar

representation [ˌreprɪzen'teɪʃən] *n* 1. (*acting for, depiction*) representación *f* 2. (*statement*) declaración *f*

representative [ˌreprɪ'zentətɪv, *Am:* -ṭəṭɪv] I. *adj* 1.a. POL representativo, -a 2. (*typical*) típico, -a II. *n* 1.a. COM representante *mf*, agenciero, -a *m, f Arg* 2. LAW apoderado, -a *m, f* 3. POL diputado, -a *m, f*

repress [rɪ'pres] *vt* reprimir

repressed [rɪ'prest] *adj* reprimido, -a

repression [rɪ'preʃən] *n no pl* represión *f*

repressive [rɪ'presɪv] *adj* represivo, -a

reprieve [rɪ'priːv] I. *vt* indultar II. *n* indulto *m*

reprimand ['reprɪmɑːnd, *Am:* -rəmænd] I. *vt* reprender II. *n* reprimenda *f*

reprint¹ [ˌriː'prɪnt] *vt* reimprimir

reprint² ['riːprɪnt] *n* reimpresión *f*

reprisal [rɪ'praɪzl] *n* represalia *f*; **to take ~s** tomar represalias

R

reproach [rɪ'prəʊtʃ, *Am:* -'prəʊtʃ] I. *vt* reprochar II. *n* reproche *m*; **beyond ~** intachable; **to be a ~ to sb** ser una vergüenza para alguien

reproachful [rɪ'prəʊtʃfəl, *Am:* -'prəʊtʃ-] *adj* acusador(a)

reprobate ['reprəbeɪt] I. *n a.* REL réprobo, -a *m, f* II. *adj* 1. (*wicked*) malvado, -a 2. REL réprobo, -a

reprocess [ˌriː'prəʊses, *Am:* -'prɑːses] *vt* reprocesar

reprocessing *n no pl* reprocesamiento *m*

reprocessing plant *n* ECOL, TECH planta *f* reprocesadora

reproduce [ˌriːprə'djuːs, *Am:* -'duːs] I. *vi* reproducirse II. *vt* reproducir

reproduction [ˌriːprə'dʌkʃən] *n* reproducción *f*

reproductive [ˌriːprə'dʌktɪv] *adj* reproductor(a)

reproof [rɪ'pruːf] I. *n* reprensión *f* II. *vt* reprender

reprove [rɪ'pruːv] *vt* reprender

reproving [rɪ'pruːvɪŋ] *adj* reprobatorio, -a

reptile ['reptaɪl] *n* reptil *m*

reptilian [rep'tɪlɪən] *adj* reptil

republic [rɪ'pʌblɪk] *n* república *f*

republican [rɪ'pʌblɪkən] I. *n* republicano, -a *m, f* II. *adj* republicano, -a

republication [ˌriːˌpʌblɪ'keɪʃən] *n no pl* reedición *f*

La **Republic of Malta** (República de Malta), que durante los años 1814 al 1947 fue una colonia británica y base naval, se ha dado a conocer en los últimos años como **English language learning centre** (centro de enseñanza del inglés). Jóvenes de toda Europa viajan hasta Malta para participar en sus renombradas escuelas de inglés. La mayoría de la veces los estudiantes se alojan con familias maltesas. Durante el verano se celebran un gran número de actividades en la playa en las que los estudiantes que lo desean pueden participar. Además, al anochecer, la ciudad de Paceville ofrece múltiples posibilidades de diversión para gente joven.

---

repudiate [rɪ'pjuːdɪeɪt] *vt* (*person*) repudiar; (*accusation*) negar; (*suggestion*) rechazar

repugnance [rɪ'pʌgnəns] *n no pl* repugnancia *f*

repugnant [rɪ'pʌgnənt] *adj* repugnante

repulse [rɪ'pʌls] I. *vt* 1. (*disgust*) repulsar 2. (*ward off*) rechazar 3. MIL repeler II. *n* repulsa *f*

repulsion [rɪ'pʌlʃən] *n no pl* repulsión *f*

repulsive [rɪ'pʌlsɪv] *adj* repulsivo, -a

repurchase [ˌriː'pɜːtʃəs] I. *vt* readquirir II. *n* readquisición *f*

reputable ['repjʊtəbl, *Am:* -ṭəbl] *adj* acreditado, -a

reputation [ˌrepjʊ'teɪʃən] *n* reputación *f*; **to have a good/bad ~** tener buena/mala fama; **to know sb by ~** conocer a alguien de oídas

repute [rɪ'pjuːt] *n no pl* reputación *f*

reputed [rɪ'pjuːtɪd, *Am:* -ṭɪd] *adj* supuesto, -a; **she is ~ to be rich** tiene fama de rica

request [rɪ'kwest] I. *n* petición *f*; ADMIN solicitud *f*; **on ~** a petición; **to make a ~ for sth** pedir algo II. *vt* pedir; ADMIN solicitar

requiem ['rekwiəm] *n*, **requiem mass** *n* réquiem *m*

require [rɪ'kwaɪəʳ, *Am:* -'kwaɪɚ] *vt* 1. (*need*) necesitar 2. (*demand*) exigir; **to ~ sb to do sth** exigir a alguien que haga algo

requirement [rɪ'kwaɪəmənt, *Am:* -'kwaɪɚ-] *n* requisito *m*

requisite ['rekwɪzɪt] I. *adj* indispensable II. *n* requisito *m*

requisition [ˌrekwɪ'zɪʃən] I. *vt* requisar II. *n* 1. *no pl* (*act of requesting*) requisición *f*; (*written request*) solicitud *f* 2. MIL requisa *f*

reroute [ˌriː'ruːt] *vt* desviar

rerun¹ [ˌriː'rʌn] *vt irr* CINE, TV repetir; THEAT reestrenar

rerun² ['riːrʌn] *n* CINE, TV repetición *f*; THEAT reestreno *m*

resale ['riːseɪl] *n* reventa *m*

reschedule [ˌriː'ʃedjuːl, *Am:* -'skedʒuːl] *vt* reprogramar

rescind [rɪ'sɪnd] *vt* rescindir

rescue ['reskjuː] I. *vt* (*save*) rescatar; (*hostage*) liberar II. *n* rescate *m*; **to come to sb's ~** rescatar a alguien

rescuer ['reskjʊəʳ, *Am:* -ɚ] *n* salvador(a) *m(f)*

research [rɪ'sɜːtʃ, *Am:* 'riːsɜːrtʃ] I. *n* investigación *f* II. *vi, vt* investigar

researcher *n* investigador(a) *m(f)*

research work *n* trabajos *mpl* de investigación **research worker** *n* investigador(a) *m(f)*

resemblance [rɪ'zembləns] *n no pl* parecido *m*

resemble [rɪ'zembl] *vt* parecerse a

resent [rɪ'zent] *vt* **to ~ sth** sentirse molesto por algo

resentful [rɪ'zentfəl] *adj* (*person*) resentido, -a; (*expression*) de resentimiento

resentment [rɪ'zentmənt] *n* resentimiento *m*

reservation [ˌrezə'veɪʃən, *Am:* -ɚ'-] *n* (*doubt, booking*) reserva *f*; **to have ~s about sth** tener ciertas dudas sobre algo

reserve [rɪ'zɜːv, *Am:* -'zɜːrv] I. *n* 1. reserva *f*; **to have sth in ~** tener algo en reserva 2. SPORTS suplente *mf* 3. MIL **the ~** la reserva II. *vt* reservar

reserve currency *n* divisa *f* de reserva

reserved *adj* reservado, -a

reserve price *n* precio *m* mínimo

reservist [rɪ'zɜːvɪst, *Am:* -'zɜːr-] *n* MIL reservista *mf*

reservoir ['rezəvwɑːʳ, *Am:* -ɚvwɑːr] *n*

1. (*tank*) depósito *m* **2.** (*lake*) embalse *m*
reset [ˌriːˈset] *vt irr* **1.** (*machine*) reajustar; INFOR reiniciar **2.** (*jewel*) reengastar
reset button *n* INFOR, ELEC tecla *f* de reinicio
resettle [ˌriːˈsetl] **I.** *vi* reasentarse **II.** *vt* (*person*) asentar; (*area*) repoblar
reshuffle [ˌriːˈʃʌfl] **I.** *vt* reorganizar **II.** *n* reorganización *f*
reside [rɪˈzaɪd] *vi form* residir
residence [ˈrezɪdənts] *n* **1.** (*home*) domicilio *m* **2.** *no pl* (*act*) residencia *f*
residence permit *n* permiso *m* de residencia
resident [ˈrezɪdənt] **I.** *n* residente *mf* **II.** *adj* residente
residential [ˌrezɪˈdenʃl] *adj* residencial
residual [rɪˈzɪdjʊəl, *Am:* -ˈzɪdʒu-] *adj* residual
residue [ˈrezɪdjuː, *Am:* -əduː] *n* residuo *m*
resign [rɪˈzaɪn] **I.** *vi* **1.** (*leave job*) renunciar; POL dimitir **2.** GAME abandonar **II.** *vt* (*leave: job*) renunciar a; POL dimitir de; **to ~ oneself to sth** resignarse a algo
resignation [ˌrezɪɡˈneɪʃən] *n* **1.** (*from job*) renuncia *f;* POL dimisión *f* **2.** *no pl* (*conformity*) resignación *f*
resigned [rɪˈzaɪnd] *adj* resignado, -a, botado, -a *Ecua*
resilience [rɪˈzɪlɪəns, *Am:* ˈzɪljəns] *n no pl* (*of material*) elasticidad *f;* (*of person*) resistencia *f*
resilient [rɪˈzɪlɪənt, *Am:* -ˈzɪljənt] *adj* (*material*) elástico, -a; (*person*) resistente
resin [ˈrezɪn] *n no pl* resina *f*
resinous [ˈrezɪnəs] *adj* resinoso, -a
resist [rɪˈzɪst] **I.** *vt* resistir; **to ~ doing sth** resistirse a hacer algo **II.** *vi* resistir
resistance [rɪˈzɪstənts] *n* resistencia *f*
resistance fighter *n* miembro *mf* de la resistencia
resistant [rɪˈzɪstənt] *adj* resistente
resistor [rɪˈzɪstəʳ, *Am:* -təʳ] *n* resistencia *f*
resit [ˈriːsɪt] **I.** *vt irr, Brit* SCHOOL, UNIV presentarse otra vez a **II.** *n Brit* SCHOOL, UNIV examen *m* de recuperación
resolute [ˈrezəluːt] *adj* resuelto, -a
resolution [ˌrezəˈluːʃən] *n a.* INFOR, PHOT, TV resolución *f*
resolvable [rɪˈzɒlvəbl, *Am:* -ˈzaːlvə-] *adj* solucionable
resolve [rɪˈzɒlv, *Am:* -ˈzaːlv] **I.** *vt* **1.** (*solve*) resolver **2.** (*settle*) acordar; **to ~ that ...** acordar que... +*subj* **II.** *n* resolución *f*
resolved [rɪˈzɒlvd, *Am:* -ˈzaːlvd] *adj* resuelto, -a
resonance [ˈrezənəns] *n no pl* resonancia *f*
resonant [ˈrezənənt] *adj* resonante
resonate [ˈrezəneɪt] *vi* resonar
resort [rɪˈzɔːt, *Am:* -ˈzɔːrt] *n* **1.** *no pl* (*use*) recurso *m;* **without ~ to sth** sin recurrir a algo; **as a last ~** como último recurso **2.** (*for holidays*) lugar *m* de veraneo; **ski ~** estación *f* de esquí

resound [rɪˈzaʊnd] *vi* resonar
resounding *adj* **1.** (*noise*) resonante **2.** (*failure, success*) rotundo, -a
resource [rɪˈzɔːs, *Am:* ˈriːsɔːrs] **I.** *n* **1.** (*asset*) recurso *m* **2.** *pl* **natural ~s** recursos *mpl* naturales **3.** (*resourcefulness*) inventiva *f* ►**to be thrown back on one's own ~s** tener que apañárselas con sus propios recursos **II.** *vt* financiar
resourceful [rɪˈzɔːsfəl, *Am:* -ˈsɔːrs-] *adj* ingenioso, -a
respect [rɪˈspekt] **I.** *n* **1.** (*relation*) respeto *m* **2.** (*esteem*) estima *f;* **with all due ~** con el debido respeto **3.** (*point*) respecto *m;* **in all/many/some ~s** desde todos/muchos/algunos puntos de vista; **in every ~** en todos los sentidos; **in ~ of** respecto a; **in this ~** a este respecto; **with ~ to** con respecto a **4.** *pl* (*greetings*) recuerdos *mpl* **II.** *vt* respetar
respectable [rɪˈspektəbl] *adj* **1.** (*person*) respetable **2.** (*behaviour*) decente **3.** (*performance, result*) aceptable
respected [rɪˈspektəd] *adj* respetado, -a
respectful [rɪˈspektfəl] *adj* respetuoso, -a
respectfully [rɪˈspektfəli] *adv* respetuosamente; **Respectfully yours ...** Atentamente...
respecting [rɪˈspektɪŋ] *prep* respecto a
respective [rɪˈspektɪv] *adj* respectivo, -a
respectively *adv* respectivamente
respiration [ˌrespəˈreɪʃen] *n no pl* respiración *f*
respirator [ˈrespəreɪtəʳ, *Am:* -t̬əʳ] *n* respirador *m*
respiratory [rɪˈspaɪərətri, *Am:* ˈrespəˌətɔːri] *adj* respiratorio, -a
respite [ˈrespaɪt, *Am:* -pɪt] *n no pl* **1.** (*pause*) pausa *f* **2.** (*delay*) retraso *m*
resplendent [rɪˈsplendənt] *adj* resplandeciente
respond [rɪˈspɒnd, *Am:* -ˈspaːnd] *vi* **1.** (*answer*) contestar **2.** (*react*) responder
respondent [rɪˈspɒndənt, *Am:* -ˈspaːn-] *n* **1.** (*to questionnaire*) encuestado, -a *m, f* **2.** LAW demandado, -a *m, f*
response [rɪˈspɒns, *Am:* -ˈspaːns] *n* **1.** (*answer*) respuesta *f* **2.** (*reaction*) reacción *f* **3.** REL responso *m*
responsibility [rɪˌspɒnsəˈbɪləti, *Am:* -ˌspaːnsəˈbɪlət̬i] *n* responsabilidad *f*
responsible [rɪˈspɒnsəbl, *Am:* -ˈspaːn-] *adj* responsable; **to be ~ for sth/to sb** ser responsable de algo/ante alguien
responsive [rɪˈspɒnsɪv, *Am:* -ˈspaːn-] *adj* (*person*) receptivo, -a; (*mechanism*) sensible; **to be ~ to sth** MED responder a algo
rest¹ [rest] **I.** *vt* **1.** (*cause to repose*) descansar **2.** (*support*) apoyar **3.** *Am* LAW **~ one's case** terminar la presentación de su alegato **II.** *vi* **1.** (*cease activity*) reposar, descansar **2.** (*remain*) quedar **3.** (*be supported*) apoyarse; **to ~ on sth** (*theory*) basarse en algo **4.** *Am* LAW concluir ►**you can ~ assured that**

... esté seguro de que... **III.** n **1.** (*period of repose*) descanso m; **to come to** ~ detenerse; **at** ~ (*not moving*) en reposo; (*dead*) en paz **2.** MUS pausa f **3.** (*support*) apoyo m

rest² [rest] n resto m; **the** ~ (*the other people*) los demás; (*the other things*) lo demás; **for the** ~ por lo demás

restate [ˌriːˈsteɪt] vt exponer de nuevo

restaurant [ˈrestərɔ̃ːŋ, *Am:* -tərɑːnt] n restaurante m

restaurant car n *Brit* vagón m restaurante

restaurateur [ˌrestɔrəˈtɜːʳ, *Am:* -təʳˈtɜːr] n restaurador(a) m(f)

rest cure n cura f de reposo **rest day** n día m de descanso

restful [ˈrestfəl] adj tranquilo, -a, relajante

rest home n residencia f de ancianos

resting place n morada f

restitution [ˌrestɪˈtjuːʃən, *Am:* -ˈtuː-] n no pl **1.** (*return*) restitución f **2.** LAW indemnización f

restive [ˈrestɪv] adj inquieto, -a

restless [ˈrestlɪs] adj **1.** (*agitated*) inquieto, -a **2.** (*impatient*) impaciente **3.** (*wakeful: night*) en blanco

restock [ˌriːˈstɒk, *Am:* -ˈstɑːk] **I.** vt reabastecer; (*with animals, plants*) repoblar **II.** vi reponer existencias

restoration [ˌrestəˈreɪʃən] n **1.** no pl (*act of restoring: of building, painting, monarchy*) restauración f; (*of communication, peace*) restablecimiento m **2.** no pl (*return to owner*) restitución f; (*of stolen goods*) devolución f

restorative [rɪˈstɔːrətɪv, *Am:* -t̬ɪv] adj reconstituyente

restore [rɪˈstɔːʳ, *Am:* -ˈstɔːr] vt **1.** (*reestablish: building, painting, monarchy*) restaurar; (*communication, peace*) reestablecer; **to** ~ **sb's sight** hacer que alguien recobre la vista; **to** ~ **sb's faith in sth** hacer que alguien recupere la fe en algo; **to** ~ **sb to health** devolver la salud a alguien; **to** ~ **sb to power** volver a colocar a alguien en el poder **2.** *form* (*return to owner*) restituir

restorer [rɪˈstɔːrəʳ, *Am:* -əʳ] n restaurador(a) m(f)

restrain [rɪˈstreɪn] vt (*person, animal*) contener; (*temper, ambition*) dominar; (*trade*) restringir; (*inflation*) frenar; **to** ~ **sb from doing sth** impedir que alguien haga algo; **to** ~ **oneself** contenerse

restrained [rɪˈstreɪnd] adj (*person*) comedido, -a; (*style*) sobrio, -a; (*criticism, policy*) moderado, -a

restraint [rɪˈstreɪnt] n **1.** no pl (*self-control*) dominio m de sí mismo; **to exercise** ~ *form* mostrarse comedido **2.** (*restriction*) restricción f

restrict [rɪˈstrɪkt] vt (*limit*) restringir; **to** ~ **oneself** limitarse

restricted adj **1.** (*limited*) restringido, -a; (*document*) confidencial; (*parking*) limitado, -a; **entry is** ~ **to** ... sólo se permite la entrada a... **2.** (*small: space*) reducido, -a; (*existence,*

horizon) limitado, -a

restricted area n MIL zona f restringida

restriction [rɪˈstrɪkʃən] n restricción f; **speed** ~ límite m de velocidad; **to impose** ~**s on sth** imponer restricciones a algo

restrictive [rɪˈstrɪktɪv] adj restrictivo, -a

restring [ˌriːˈstrɪŋ] irr vt (*instrument, tennis racket*) volver a encordar; (*necklace*) reensartar

rest room n *Am* aseos mpl

restructure [ˌriːˈstʌktʃəʳ, *Am:* -tʃəʳ] vt reestructurar

restructuring n reestructuración f

result [rɪˈzʌlt] **I.** n a. MAT, SPORTS, POL resultado m; (*of exam*) nota f; **to get** ~**s** obtener buenos resultados; **with no** ~ sin resultado; **as a** ~ **of** a consecuencia de; **as a** ~ por consiguiente **II.** vi **to** ~ **from** ser consecuencia de; **to** ~ **in** ocasionar

resultant [rɪˈzʌltənt] adj resultante

resume [rɪˈzjuːm, *Am:* -ˈzuːm] **I.** vt **1.** (*start again: work, journey*) reanudar; (*speech*) proseguir con **2.** *form* (*reoccupy: place*) volver a ocupar; (*duties*) volver a asumir **II.** vi *form* proseguir

résumé [ˈrezjuːmeɪ, *Am:* ˈrezumeɪ] n **1.** (*summary*) resumen m **2.** *Am, Aus* (*curriculum vitae*) currículum m (vitae)

resumption [rɪˈzʌmpʃən] n **1.** no pl (*of journey, work*) reanudación f **2.** (*of power, duties*) reasunción f

resurface [ˌriːˈsɜːfɪs, *Am:* -ˈsɜːrfɪs] **I.** vi volver a salir a la superficie; *fig* resurgir **II.** vt repavimentar

resurgence [rɪˈsɜːdʒəns, *Am:* -ˈsɜːrdʒəns] n no pl, *form* resurgimiento m

resurgent [rɪˈsɜːdʒənt, *Am:* -ˈsɜːrdʒənt] adj *form* renaciente

resurrect [ˌrezəˈrekt] vt a. *fig* resucitar

resurrection [ˌrezəˈrekʃən] n no pl resurrección f

resuscitate [rɪˈsʌsɪteɪt, *Am:* -əteɪt] vt resucitar

retail [ˈriːteɪl] COM **I.** n no pl venta f al detalle **II.** vt vender al detalle **III.** vi venderse al detalle; **this product** ~**s at £5** el precio de venta al público de este producto es de 5 libras **IV.** adv al detalle

retail business n comercio m minorista

retailer n minorista mf, menorista mf *Chile, Méx*

retailing n venta f al detalle

retail outlet n COM punto m de venta

retail price n COM precio m de venta al público **retail price index** n ECON índice m de precios al consumo

retail trade n ECON comercio m minorista

retain [rɪˈteɪn] vt **1.** *form* (*keep: power*) retener; (*property*) quedarse con; (*right*) reservarse; (*title*) revalidar **2.** (*not lose: dignity*) mantener; (*colour*) conservar **3.** (*hold in place: water*) contener **4.** (*remember*) retener **5.** (*employ*) contratar

retainer *n* 1. ECON iguala *f* 2. (*servant*) criado, -a *m, f*

retaining wall *n* muro *m* de contención

retake¹ [ˌriːˈteɪk] *vt irr* 1. (*recapture: town*) volver a tomar; (*person*) volver a capturar; **to ~ the lead** recuperar el liderazgo 2. SCHOOL, UNIV (*exam*) volver a presentarse a 3. CINE volver a rodar; PHOT volver a hacer

retake² [ˈriːteɪk] *n* 1. *Brit* SCHOOL, UNIV examen *m* de recuperación 2. CINE toma *f* repetida

retaliate [rɪˈtælɪeɪt] *vi* tomar represalias

retaliation [rɪˌtælɪˈeɪʃən] *n no pl* represalias *fpl*

retaliatory [rɪˈtælɪətri, *Am:* -tɔːri] *adj* vengativo, -a; **~ measures** represalias *fpl*

retard [rɪˈtɑːd, *Am:* -ˈtɑːrd] *vt form* (*growth, development*) retardar; (*journey*) retrasar; **mentally ~ed person** retrasado, -a *m, f* mental

retardation [ˌriːtɑːˈdeɪʃən, *Am:* -tɑːrˈ-] *n no pl, form* retraso *m*

retch [retʃ] *vi* tener arcadas

retention [rɪˈtenʃən] *n no pl* 1. *form* (*keeping: of properties, heat*) retención *f*; (*of rules, laws*) mantenimiento *m* 2. *form* (*memory*) retentiva *f* 3. (*of lawyer, consultant*) contratación *f*

retentive [rɪˈtentɪv, *Am:* -t̬ɪv] *adj* retentivo, -a; **he's very ~** tiene muy buena memoria

rethink¹ [ˌriːˈθɪŋk] *vt irr* replantearse

rethink² [ˈriːθɪŋk] *n no pl* replanteamiento *m*

reticent [ˈretɪsnt, *Am:* ˈret̬əsnt] *adj* reticente

retina [ˈretɪnə, *Am:* ˈret̬nə] <-s *o* -nae> *n* retina *f*

retinue [ˈretɪnjuː, *Am:* ˈret̬nuː] *n inv* séquito *m*

retire [rɪˈtaɪəʳ, *Am:* -ˈtaɪɚ] I. *vi* 1. (*stop working*) jubilarse; (*soldier, athlete*) retirarse 2. *form* (*withdraw*) retirarse; **to ~ to the drawing room** pasar al salón 3. MIL replegarse 4. SPORTS (*from a race*) abandonar II. *vt* 1. (*stop working*) jubilar 2. MIL (*soldier*) retirar 3. FIN (*bond*) redimir

retired *adj* jubilado, -a; (*soldier, athlete*) retirado, -a

retirement [rɪˈtaɪəmənt, *Am:* -ˈtaɪɚ-] *n* 1. (*act of retiring*) retiro *m*; (*from race*) abandono *m* 2. *no pl* (*after working*) jubilación *f*; (*of soldier, athlete*) retiro *m*; **to be in ~** estar jubilado; **to come out of ~** salir de su retiro 3. MIL retirada *f*

retirement age *n* edad *f* de jubilarse **retirement pay** *n*, **retirement pension** *n* pensión *f* de jubilación

retiring *adj* 1. (*reserved*) reservado, -a 2. (*worker, official*) saliente

retort [rɪˈtɔːt, *Am:* -ˈtɔːrt] I. *vt* replicar II. *vi* replicar III. *n* 1. (*reply*) réplica *f* 2. CHEM retorta *f*

retouch [ˌriːˈtʌtʃ] *vt a.* ART, PHOT retocar

retrace [riːˈtreɪs] *vt* repasar; **to ~ one's steps** volver sobre sus pasos

retract [rɪˈtrækt] I. *vt* 1. (*statement, offer*) retirar 2. (*claws*) retraer; (*wheels*) replegar II. *vi* 1. (*withdraw statement, offer*) retractarse 2. (*be withdrawn: claws*) retraerse; (*wheels*) replegarse

retractable [rɪˈtræktəbl] *adj* retráctil

retraction [rɪˈtrækʃən] *n* (*of statement, offer*) retractación *f*

retrain [riːˈtreɪn] I. *vt* reciclar II. *vi* hacer un curso de reciclaje

retread¹ [ˌriːˈtred, *Am:* -ˈtrɑːd] *vt* (*a tyre*) recauchutar, reencauchar *Col, Perú*

retread² [ˈriːtred] *n* neumático *m* recauchutado

retreat [rɪˈtriːt] I. *vi* retroceder; MIL batirse en retirada II. *n* 1. (*withdrawal*) a. MIL retirada *f*; (*signal*) retreta *f*; **to sound** [*o* **beat**] **the ~** dar el toque de retreta 2. (*safe place*) refugio *m* 3. (*seclusion*) retiro *m*; **to go on a ~** hacer un retiro espiritual

retrench [rɪˈtrentʃ] I. *vi* reducir costes II. *vt* (*reduce: personnel, expenses*) reducir

retrenchment *n* 1. (*spending cut*) reducción *f* de gastos 2. *Aus* (*dismissal*) despido *m* por reducción de plantilla; (*of personnel*) reducción *f* 3. *no pl* (*cutting down*) supresión *f*

retrial [ˌriːˈtraɪəl, *Am:* ˈriːtraɪl] *n* nuevo juicio *m*

retribution [ˌretrɪˈbjuːʃən, *Am:* -rə'-] *n no pl, form* castigo *m* justo; **divine ~** justicia *f* divina

retributive [rɪˈtrɪbjʊtɪv] *adj form* punitivo, -a

retrieval [rɪˈtriːvl] *n no pl* (*finding*) a. INFOR recuperación *f*; **on-line information ~** recuperación de información en línea

retrieve [rɪˈtriːv] I. *vt* 1. (*get back*) a. INFOR recuperar 2. (*make amends for: error*) enmendar 3. (*repair: loss*) reparar; (*situation*) salvar 4. SPORTS (*game*) cobrar; (*in tennis*) devolver II. *vi* SPORTS cobrar

retriever [rɪˈtriːvəʳ, *Am:* -ɚ] *n* perro *m* cobrador

retroactive [ˌretrəʊˈæktɪv, *Am:* -roʊ'-] *adj* retroactivo, -a

retrograde [ˈretrəgreɪd] *adj* retrógrado, -a

retrogressive [ˌretrəˈgresɪv, *Am:* ˈretrəgres-] *adj form* retrógrado, -a

retrospect [ˈretrəspekt] *n no pl* **in ~** mirando hacia atrás

retrospective [ˌretrəˈspektɪv] I. *adj* 1. (*looking back*) retrospectivo, -a 2. *Brit* LAW retroactivo, -a II. *n* ART exposición *f* retrospectiva

return [rɪˈtɜːn, *Am:* -ˈtɜːrn] I. *n* 1. (*going back*) regreso *m*; (*home, to work, to school*) vuelta *f*; **on his ~** a su regreso 2. (*to previous situation*) retorno *m*; **a ~ to sth** un restablecimiento de algo 3. MED (*of illness*) recaída *f* 4. (*giving back*) devolución *f* 5. (*recompense*) recompensa *f* 6. *Brit, Aus* (*ticket*) billete *m* de ida y vuelta, boleto *m* redondo *Méx* 7. FIN (*proceeds*) ganancia *f*; (*interest*) rédito *m*; **~ on capital** interés *m* del capital 8. *pl* POL resultados *mpl* de las elecciones **9.** *no pl* INFOR (tecla *f* de) retorno *m* **10.** (*report*) informe *m* **11.** FIN declaración *f* ▶ **many happy ~s (of the day)!** ¡feliz cumpleaños!; **by ~ (of post)** *Brit, Aus* a vuelta de correo; **in ~ for sth** a cambio de algo **II.** *adj* **1.** (*coming back: flight, journey*) de vuelta; (*ticket*) de ida y vuelta, redondo, -a *Méx* **2.** THEAT (*performance*) segundo, -a **3.** SPORTS (*match*) de vuelta **III.** *vi* **1.** (*come back*) volver; (*home*) regresar a; (*to task*) reanudar **2.** (*reappear*) volver a aparecer **IV.** *vt* **1.** (*give back*) devolver **2.** (*reciprocate*) corresponder a; (*compliment, favour, ball*) devolver; **to ~ sb's call** devolver la llamada a alguien; **to ~ good for evil** devolver bien por mal **3.** (*send back*) volver a colocar; **~ to sender** devuélvase al remitente **4.** FIN (*yield*) dar; (*profit*) proporcionar **5.** LAW (*pronounce: verdict*) emitir; (*judgement*) dictar **6.** *Brit* POL (*elect*) elegir **7.** ECON (*income*) declarar

returnable [rɪ'tɜːnəbl, *Am:* -'tɜːrn-] *adj* (*fee*) reembolsable; (*bottle*) retornable

return fare *n* precio *m* del billete de ida y vuelta **return flight** *n* viaje *m* de vuelta

returning officer *n Can* POL escrutador(a) *m(f)*

return journey *n* viaje *m* de vuelta

return key *n* INFOR tecla *f* de retorno **return match** *n* SPORTS partido *m* de vuelta **return ticket** *n* **1.** *Aus, Brit* billete *m* de ida y vuelta, boleto *m* redondo *Méx* **2.** *Am* billete *m* de vuelta

reunification [riːˌjuːnɪfɪ'keɪʃən, *Am:* -nəfɪ'-] *n no pl* reunificación *f*

reunion [ˌriːˈjuːnɪən, *Am:* -'juːnjən] *n* **1.** (*meeting*) reunión *f* **2.** (*after separation*) reencuentro *m*

reunite [ˌriːjuːˈnaɪt] **I.** *vt* **1.** (*bring together*) volver a unir **2.** (*friends*) reconciliar **II.** *vi* reunirse

reusable [ˌriːˈjuːzəbl] *adj* reutilizable

reuse [ˌriːˈjuːz] *vt* volver a usar

rev [rev] *n* AUTO revolution *f*
♦**rev up** AUTO **I.** *vt* <-vv-> acelerar **II.** *vi* embalarse

revaluation [riːˌvæljʊ'eɪʃən] *n* revaluación *f*

revalue [riːˈvæljuː] *vt* revaluar

revamp [ˌriːˈvæmp] *vt inf* modernizar

rev counter *n* cuentarrevoluciones *m inv*

Revd. *abbr of* Reverend Rev.

reveal [rɪ'viːl] *vt* **1.** (*divulge: secret, identity*) revelar; **he ~d his identity** desveló su identidad; **to ~ how/why ...** manifestar cómo/el porqué... **2.** (*uncover*) descubrir

revealing [rɪ'viːlɪŋ] *adj* revelador(a)

reveille [rɪ'væli, *Am:* 'revli] *n no pl, no indef art* MIL diana *f*

revel ['revl] <-ll-, *Am:* -l-> *vi* ir de juerga
♦**revel in** <-ll-, *Am:* -l-> *vi* **to ~ sth** deleitarse con algo

revelation [ˌrevə'leɪʃən] *n* revelación *f*; **the Book of Revelations** el Apocalipsis

reveler *n Brit,* **reveller** *n Am* juerguista *mf*

revelry ['revəlri] <-ies> *n no pl* jolgorio *m*

revenge [rɪ'vendʒ] **I.** *n no pl* **1.** (*retaliation*) venganza *f*; **in ~ (for sth)** como venganza (por algo) **2.** SPORTS revancha *f* **II.** *vt* vengar; **to ~ oneself on sb** vengarse de alguien

revenue ['revənjuː, *Am:* 'revənuː] *n* **1.** (*income*) ingresos *mpl*; (*of government*) rentas *fpl* públicas **2.** (*department*) Hacienda *f* Pública

revenue officer *n* delegado, -a *m, f* de Hacienda **revenue stamp** *n Am* timbre *m* fiscal

reverberate [rɪ'vɜːbəreɪt, *Am:* -'vɜːrbəreɪt] *vi* **1.** (*sound, light, heat*) reverberar **2.** *fig* tener gran repercusión

reverberation [rɪˌvɜːbə'reɪʃən, *Am:* -ˌvɜːrbə'-] *n* **1.** *no pl* (*of sound, heat, light*) reverberación *f* **2.** *fig* repercusión *f*

revere [rɪ'vɪər, *Am:* -'vɪr] *vt* venerar

reverence ['revərəns] *n no pl* veneración *f*; **to pay ~ to sth/sb** rendir homenaje a algo/alguien

Reverend ['revərənd] REL **I.** *adj* reverendo, -a; **the Right Reverend** el obispo; **the Most Reverend** el arzobispo **II.** *n* (*Protestant*) pastor *m*; (*Catholic*) sacerdote *m*

reverent ['revərənt] *adj* reverente

reverential [ˌrevə'renʃl] *adj* reverencial

reverie ['revəri] *n liter* ensueño *m*; **to be (lost) in ~** estar absorto

reversal [rɪ'vɜːsl, *Am:* -'vɜːrsl] *n* **1.** (*change: of order, opinion*) inversión *f*; (*of policy*) cambio *m* completo; LAW (*of decision*) revocación *f* **2.** (*setback*) revés *m*

reverse [rɪ'vɜːs, *Am:* -'vɜːrs] **I.** *vt* **1.** (*turn other way*) volver al revés; (*order*) invertir; (*policy, situation*) cambiar radicalmente; (*judgement*) revocar; **to ~ the charges** *Brit, Can* TEL llamar a cobro revertido **2.** *Aus, Brit* AUTO poner en marcha atrás; **to ~ a car into a garage** entrar en un garaje dando marcha atrás **II.** *vi* **1.** *Aus, Brit* AUTO dar marcha atrás; **to ~ into the garage** entrar al garaje dando marcha atrás **2.** (*order, situation*) invertirse **III.** *n* **1.** *no pl* **the ~** lo contrario; **in ~** a la inversa **2.** AUTO (*gear*) marcha *f* atrás; **to go into ~** dar marcha atrás **3.** (*setback*) revés *m* **4.** (*the back*) reverso *m*; (*of cloth*) revés *m*; (*of document*) dorso *m* **IV.** *adj* **1.** (*inverse*) inverso, -a **2.** (*opposite: direction*) contrario, -a

reverse charge call *n* TEL llamada *f* a cobro revertido **reverse gear** *n* AUTO marcha *f* atrás

reversible [rɪ'vɜːsəbl, *Am:* -'vɜːrsə-] *adj* **1.** (*jacket*) reversible **2.** (*decision*) revocable

reversion [rɪ'vɜːʃən, *Am:* -'vɜːrʒən] *n no pl* reversión *f*

revert [rɪ'vɜːt, *Am:* -'vɜːrt] *vi* volver; **to ~ to type** *fig* volver a ser el mismo de siempre

review [rɪ'vjuː] **I.** *vt* **1.** (*consider*) analizar **2.** (*reconsider*) reexaminar; (*salary*) reajustar **3.** (*look over: notes*) revisar **4.** (*criticize: book, play, film*) hacer una crítica [*o* reseña] de **5.** MIL (*inspect*) pasar revista a **6.** *Am* (*study again*) repasar **II.** *n* **1.** (*examination*) análisis *m inv;* **to come under** ~ ser examinado; **to hold a** ~ MIL pasar revista **2.** (*reconsideration*) revisión *f;* **to come up for** ~ estar pendiente de revisión **3.** (*summary*) resumen *m* **4.** (*criticism: of book, play, film*) crítica *f,* reseña *f* **5.** (*magazine*) revista *f* **6.** THEAT revista *f*

reviewer [rɪˈvjuːə^r, *Am:* -ɚ] *n* crítico, -a *m, f*

revise [rɪˈvaɪz] **I.** *vt* **1.** (*alter: text, law*) revisar; (*proofs*) corregir; (*opinion*) cambiar de **2.** *Brit, Aus* (*study again*) repasar **II.** *vi Aus, Brit* repasar

revision [rɪˈvɪʒən] *n* **1.** *no pl* (*of text, law*) revisión *f;* (*of proofs*) corrección *f;* (*of policy*) modificación *f* **2.** (*book*) edición *f* corregida **3.** *no pl, Brit, Aus* UNIV repaso *m*

revisionist [rɪˈvɪʒənɪst] *n* revisionista *mf*

revitalize [riːˈvaɪtəlaɪz, *Am:* -t̬əl-] *vt* revitalizar; (*trade*) reactivar

revival [rɪˈvaɪvəl] *n* **1.** MED reanimación *f* **2.** (*rebirth: of interest*) renacimiento *m;* (*of idea, custom*) restablecimiento *m;* (*of economy*) reactivación *f;* (*of country*) resurgimiento *m* **3.** CINE, THEAT reestreno *m* **4.** REL despertar *m* religioso

revive [rɪˈvaɪv] **I.** *vt* **1.** MED reanimar **2.** (*resurrect: interest*) hacer renacer; (*idea, custom*) restablecer; (*economy*) reactivar; (*conversation*) reanimar **3.** CINE, THEAT reestrenar **II.** *vi* **1.** (*be restored to life*) volver en sí **2.** (*be restored: country, interest*) resurgir; (*tradition*) restablecerse; (*style*) volver a estar de moda; (*trade, economy*) reactivarse

revocation [ˌrevəˈkeɪʃən] *n* **1.** (*of licence*) suspensión *f* **2.** (*of law, decision*) revocación *f*

revoke [rɪˈvəʊk, *Am:* -ˈvoʊk] **I.** *vt* **1.** (*cancel: decision, order*) revocar **2.** (*licence*) suspender **II.** *vi* GAMES renunciar

revolt [rɪˈvəʊlt, *Am:* -ˈvoʊlt] POL **I.** *vi* rebelarse, alzarse *AmL;* **to** ~ **against sb/sth** sublevarse contra alguien/algo **II.** *vt* repugnar a; **it** ~**s me** me da asco **III.** *n* **1.** (*uprising*) revuelta *f;* **to rise in** ~ **against sb/sth** alzarse contra alguien/algo **2.** *no pl* (*rebelliousness*) rebeldía *f*

revolting [rɪˈvəʊltɪŋ, *Am:* -ˈvoʊltɪŋ] *adj* (*disgusting*) repugnante; **to look** ~ tener un aspecto horrible

revolution [ˌrevəˈluːʃən] *n a.* POL revolución *f*

revolutionary [ˌrevəˈluːʃənri] **I.** <-ies> *n* revolucionario, -a *m, f* **II.** *adj* revolucionario, -a

revolutionize [ˌrevəˈluːʃnaɪz] *vt, vt* revolucionar

revolve [rɪˈvɒlv, *Am:* -ˈvɑːlv] *vi* girar; **to** ~ **on an axis** girar en torno a un eje; **that problem was revolving in his mind** aquel problema le daba vueltas en la cabeza

◆**revolve around** *vi a. fig* girar alrededor

revolver [rɪˈvɒlvə^r, *Am:* -ˈvɑːlvɚ] *n* revólver *m*

revolving *adj* giratorio, -a

revolving door *n* puerta *f* giratoria

revue [rɪˈvjuː] *n* THEAT revista *f*

revulsion [rɪˈvʌlʃən] *n no pl* repulsión *f*

reward [rɪˈwɔːd, *Am:* ˈwɔːrd] **I.** *n* recompensa *f* **II.** *vt* recompensar

rewarding *adj* gratificante

rewind [ˌriːˈwaɪnd] *irr* **I.** *vt* (*tape*) rebobinar; (*clock, watch*) dar cuerda a **II.** *vi* rebobinarse

rewire [ˌriːˈwaɪə^r, *Am:* -ˈwaɪɚ] *vt* renovar la instalación eléctrica de

reword [ˌriːˈwɜːd, *Am:* -ˈwɜːrd] *vt* **1.** (*rewrite*) volver a redactar **2.** (*say again*) expresar de otra manera

rework [ˌriːˈwɜːk] *vt* revisar; (*theme*) adaptar

rewrite¹ [ˌriːˈraɪt] *irr vt* volver a redactar

rewrite² [ˈriːraɪt] *n* nueva versión *f*

RFC [ˌɑːrefˈsiː, *Am:* ˌɑːrefˈsiː] *n abbr of* **Rugby Football Club** club *m* de rugby

Rh *abbr of* **rhesus** Rh

rhapsody [ˈræpsədi] <-ies> *n* **1.** MUS rapsodia *f* **2.** (*enthusiasm*) éxtasis *m inv*

rhesus factor [ˈriːsəsˌfæktə^r, *Am:* -tɚ] *n no pl* MED factor *m* Rhesus

rhetoric [ˈretərɪk, *Am:* ˈret̬-] *n no pl* retórica *f*

rhetorical [rɪˈtɒrɪkl, *Am:* -ˈtɔːr-] *adj* retórico, -a

rheumatic [ruːˈmætɪk, *Am:* -ˈmæt̬-] *adj* reumático, -a

rheumatism [ˈruːmətɪzəm] *n no pl* reumatismo *m*

rheumatoid arthritis [ˌruːmətɔɪdˌɑːˈθraɪtɪs, *Am:* -ˌɑːrˈθraɪtɪs] *n no pl* MED artritis *f inv* reumatoidea

Rhine [raɪn] *n* **the** ~ el Rin

rhino [ˈraɪnəʊ, *Am:* -noʊ] *n inf abbr of* **rhinoceros** rinoceronte *m*

rhinoceros [raɪˈnɒsərəs, *Am:* -ˈnɑːsɚ-] <-(es)> *n* rinoceronte *m*

Rhodes [rəʊdz, *Am:* roʊdz] *n* Rodas *f*

rhododendron [ˌrəʊdəˈdendrən, *Am:* ˌroʊ-] *n* rododendro *m*

rhombus [ˈrɒmbəs, *Am:* ˈrɑːm-] <-es *o* -i> *n* rombo *m*

Rhone [rəʊn, *Am:* roʊn] *n* **the** ~ el Ródano

rhubarb [ˈruːbɑːb, *Am:* -bɑːrb] **I.** *n no pl* ruibarbo *m* **II.** *interj* ~, ~ (~, ~)! ¡bla, bla, bla!

rhyme [raɪm] **I.** *n* **1.** (*similar sound*) rima *f;* **in** ~ en verso **2.** (*poem*) poesía *f* ▶ **without** ~ **or reason** sin ton ni son **II.** *vi* rimar

rhyming couplet [ˌraɪmɪŋˈkʌplɪt] *n* pareado *m*

rhythm [ˈrɪðəm] *n* ritmo *m*

rhythmic [ˈrɪðmɪk] *adj,* **rhythmical** *adj* rítmico, -a

RI [ˌɑːˈraɪ, *Am:* ˌɑːr-] *abbr of* **religious instruction** religión *f*

rib [rɪb] **I.** *n* **1.** (*bone*) costilla *f;* **to dig sb in the** ~**s** dar a alguien un codazo en el costado **2.** NAUT cuaderna *f* **3.** *no pl* FASHION canalé *m* **II.** <-bb-> *vt inf* tomar el pelo a

ribald [ˈrɪbld] *adj* picaresco, -a

ribbon [ˈrɪbən] *n* (*long strip*) cinta *f;* (*on medal*) galón *m;* **to be cut to** ~**s** estar hecho jirones

rib cage *n* tórax *m*

ribonucleic acid [‚raɪbəʊnjuːkleɪɪkˈæsɪd] *n* ácido *m* ribonucleico

rice [raɪs] *n no pl* arroz *m*

ricefield *n*, **rice paddy** *n* arrozal *m* **rice-growing** *n no pl* arrozal *m* **rice pudding** *n* arroz *m* con leche

rich [rɪtʃ] I. <-er, -est> *adj* **1.** (*person*) rico, -a; (*soil*) fértil; (*furnishings*) opulento, -a; ~ **pickings** ganancias *fpl;* **to become** ~ enriquecerse; **to be** ~ **in sth** abundar en algo **2.** (*stimulating: life, experience, history*) rico, -a **3.** (*food*) pesado, -a **4.** (*intense: colour*) brillante; (*flavour*) intenso, -a; (*tone*) profundo, -a **5.** *inf* that's ~! ¡mira quién habla! II. *n* the ~ los ricos

richness *n no pl* **1.** (*affluence*) riqueza *f;* (*of soil*) fertilidad *f* **2.** (*of food*) pesadez *f* **3.** (*intensity: of colour*) brillantez *f;* (*of flavour*) intensidad *f*

rick [rɪk] I. *n* almiar *m* II. *vt Brit, Aus* amontonar

rickets [ˈrɪkɪts] *n no pl* raquitismo *m*

rickety [ˈrɪkəti, *Am:* -ti] *adj* (*car*) desvenciado, -a; (*steps*) tambaleante; (*person*) raquítico, -a

rickshaw [ˈrɪkʃɔː, *Am:* -ʃɑː] *n* carro *m* de culí

ricochet [ˈrɪkəʃeɪ] I. *vi* rebotar II. *n* rebote *m*

rid [rɪd] <rid *o* ridded, rid> *vt* **to** ~ **sth/sb of sth** librar algo/a alguien de algo; **to** ~ **oneself of sth** librarse de algo; **to be** ~ **of sth/sb** estar libre de algo/alguien; **to get** ~ **of sb/sth** deshacerse de alguien/algo

riddance [ˈrɪdns] *n inf* good ~ (**to bad rubbish**)! ¡vete con viento fresco!; **to bid sb good** ~ desear a alguien un adiós y hasta nunca

ridden [ˈrɪdn] *pp of* **ride**

riddle¹ [ˈrɪdl] *n* **1.** (*conundrum*) adivinanza *f* **2.** (*mystery*) misterio *m;* **to speak in** ~s hablar en clave

riddle² [ˈrɪdl] *vt* acribillar; **to be** ~d **with mistakes** estar plagado, -a de errores

ride [raɪd] I. *n* (*on horse, motorbike, car*) paseo *m;* **to give sb a** ~ llevar a alguien ►to take sb for a ~ *inf* tomar el pelo a alguien II. <rode, ridden> *vt* **1.** (*sit on*) **to** ~ **a bike** ir en bici; **to** ~ **a horse** montar a caballo; **can you** ~ **a bike?** ¿sabes montar en bici?; **to** ~ **the waves** surcar las olas **2.** *Am, inf* (*exploit*) explotar III. <rode, ridden> *vi* **1.** (*on horse, bicycle*) montar; **to** ~ **on a horse** montar a caballo; **to** ~ **by bicycle** ir en bicicleta **2.** (*do well*) **to** ~ **high** alcanzar popularidad **3.** *inf* (*take no action*) **to let sth** ~ dejar pasar algo

◆**ride down** *vt* atropellar

◆**ride out** *vt a. fig* aguantar

◆**ride up** *vi* (*person*) acercarse; (*dress*) subirse

rider [ˈraɪdər, *Am:* -dər] *n* **1.** (*on horse*) jinete *m*, amazona *f;* (*on bicycle*) ciclista *mf;* (*on motorbike*) motociclista *mf* **2.** *LAW* cláusula *f* adicional

ridge [rɪdʒ] *n* **1.** *GEO* cresta *f* **2.** *METEO* sistema *m* de altas presiones **3.** (*of roof*) caballete *m* ►to have been around the ~s *Aus* tener muchas tablas

ridgepole [ˈrɪdʒpəʊl, *Am:* -poʊl] *n* parhilera *f*

ridgeway [ˈrɪdʒweɪ] *n* ruta *f* de las crestas

ridicule [ˈrɪdɪkjuːl] I. *n no pl* burlas *fpl;* **to be an object of** ~ ser el hazmerreír; **to hold sb/ sth up to** ~ ridiculizar a alguien/algo II. *vt* ridiculizar

ridiculous [rɪˈdɪkjʊləs] *adj* ridículo, -a

riding *n no pl* equitación *f*

riding breeches *n* pantalones *mpl* de montar **riding crop** *n* fusta *f* **riding school** *n* escuela *f* de equitación **riding whip** *n s.* **riding crop**

rife [raɪf] *adj* extendido, -a; **to be** ~ **with sth** estar plagado, -a de algo

riffle [ˈrɪfl] *vt* (*cards*) barajar; (*pages*) volver; (*book*) hojear

riff-raff [ˈrɪfræf] *n no pl* chusma *f*

rifle¹ [ˈraɪfl] *n* fusil *m*, rifle *m*

rifle² [ˈraɪfl] I. *vt* **1.** (*plunder*) saquear **2.** (*steal*) robar II. *vt* revolver III. *vi* **to** ~ **through sth** rebuscar en algo

rifle butt *n* culata *f* de rifle **rifleman** <-men> *n* fusilero *m* **rifle range** *n* campo *m* de tiro **rifle shot** *n* tiro *m* de fusil

rift [rɪft] *n* **1.** (*in earth*) fisura *f* **2.** *fig* ruptura *f;* **to heal the** ~ cerrar la brecha

rig [rɪg] <-gg-> I. *vt* **1.** (*falsify*) amañar **2.** *NAUT* aparejar II. *n* **1.** *TECH* (*oil*) ~ plataforma *f* petrolífera **2.** *Am* (*truck*) camión *m* **3.** *NAUT* aparejo *m* **4.** *inf* (*clothing*) atuendo *m*

rigger [ˈrɪgər, *Am:* -ər] *n* *NAUT* aparejador(a) *m(f)*

rigging [ˈrɪgɪn] *n no pl* **1.** (*of result*) pucherazo *m;* **ballot** ~ fraude *m* electoral **2.** *NAUT* jarcia *f*

right [raɪt] I. *adj* **1.** (*correct*) correcto, -a; (*ethical*) justo, -a; (*change*) oportuno, -a; **to put sth** ~ poner algo en orden; **it is** ~ **that ...** es justo que...; **to be** ~ (*about sth*) tener razón (en algo), estar en lo cierto (sobre algo) *AmL;* **to do sth the** ~ **way** hacer algo correctamente; **to do the** ~ **thing** hacer lo que se debe hacer; **to be in the** ~ **place at the** ~ **time** estar en el lugar indicado en el momento indicado; **to be on the** ~ **side of forty** tener menos de cuarenta años; **to put a clock** ~ poner el reloj en hora **2.** (*direction*) derecho, -a; **a** ~ **hook** *SPORTS* un gancho de derecha **3.** *POL* de derechas **4.** (*well*) bueno, -a; **to be not** (**quite**) ~ **in the head** *inf* no estar muy bien de la cabeza **5.** *inf* (*complete*) completo, -a; **he's a** ~ **idiot** es un imbécil total II. *n* **1.** *no pl* (*entitlement*) derecho *m;* **to have the** ~ **to do sth** tener el derecho de hacer algo **2.** (*morality*) **to be in the** ~ tener razón **3.** (*right side*) derecha *f;* *SPORTS* derechazo *m* **4.** *POL* **the Right** la derecha III. *adv* **1.** (*correctly*) correctamente; **to do** ~ obrar bien

2. (*straight*) directamente; ~ **away** inmediatamente **3.** (*to the right*) hacia la derecha **4.** (*precisely*) precisamente; ~ **here** justo aquí; **to be** ~ **behind sb** estar inmediatamente detrás de alguien **IV.** *vt* **1.** (*rectify*) rectificar; (*mistake*) arreglar **2.** (*straighten*) enderezar **V.** *interj* de acuerdo, órale *Méx*

right angle *n* ángulo *m* recto

right-angled ['raɪtæŋgld] *adj* en ángulo recto

righteous ['raɪtʃəs] **I.** *adj form* **1.** (*person*) virtuoso, -a **2.** (*indignation*) justificado, -a; (*tone*) de superioridad moral **II.** *n pl* **the** ~ los justos

rightful ['raɪtfəl] *adj* legítimo, -a

right-hand [,raɪt'hænd] *adj* **on the** ~ **side** a la derecha

right-hand drive *adj* con el volante a la derecha

right-handed [,raɪt'hændɪd] *adj* diestro, -a

right-hander *n* **1.** (*person*) diestro, -a *m, f* **2.** (*punch*) derechazo *m*

rightist ['raɪtɪst] POL **I.** *n* derechista *mf* **II.** *adj* de derechas

rightly *adv* **1.** (*correctly*) correctamente; **if I remember** ~ si recuerdo bien **2.** (*justifiably*) con razón; (**whether**) ~ **or wrongly** con razón o sin ella

right-minded [,raɪt'maɪndɪd] *adj* sensato, -a

right of way <-rights> *n* **1.** (*over private land*) servidumbre *f* de paso **2.** (*on road*) preferencia *f*

rights issue *n Brit* FIN emisión *f* de derechos de suscripción

right-wing [,raɪt'wɪŋ] *adj* POL de derechas; **to be** ~ ser de derechas

rigid ['rɪdʒɪd] *adj* **1.** (*stiff*) rígido, -a; **to be** ~ **with fear/pain** estar paralizado, -a de miedo/dolor; **to be bored** ~ *Brit, inf* aburrirse como una ostra **2.** (*inflexible*) inflexible; (*censorship*) estricto, -a **3.** (*intransigent*) intransigente

rigidity [rɪ'dʒɪdəti, *Am:* -ţi] *n no pl* **1.** (*hardness*) rigidez *f* **2.** (*inflexibility*) inflexibilidad *f* **3.** (*intransigence*) intransigencia *f*

rigmarole ['rɪgmərəʊl, *Am:* -məroʊl] *n no pl* galimatías *m inv*

rigor ['rɪgər, *Am:* -ə·] *n Am, Aus s.* **rigour**

rigor mortis [,rɪgə'mɔːtɪs, *Am:* ,rɪgə-'mɔːrţɪs] *n no pl* MED rigidez *f* cadavérica

rigorous ['rɪgərəs] *adj* riguroso, -a

rigour ['rɪgər, *Am:* -ə·] *n no pl, Brit, Aus* rigor *m*

rig-out ['rɪgaʊt] *n inf* atuendo *m*

rile [raɪl] *vt inf* irritar

rim [rɪm] **I.** *n* **1.** (*of cup, bowl*) canto *m* **2.** (*spectacle frames*) montura *f* **3.** GEO borde *m;* **the Pacific** ~ los países de la costa del Pacífico **4.** (*dirty mark*) cerco *m* **II.** <-mm-> *vt* **1.** (*surround*) bordear **2.** (*frame*) enmarcar

rime [raɪm] *n liter* (*frost*) escarcha *f*

rimless ['rɪmlɪs] *adj* (*spectacles*) sin montura

rind [raɪnd] *n no pl* (*of fruit*) cáscara *f;* (*of bacon, cheese*) corteza *f*

ring¹ [rɪŋ] **I.** *n* **1.** (*small circle*) círculo *m;* (*of people*) corro *m;* (*around eyes*) ojera *f* **2.** (*jewellery*) anillo *m* **3.** *Brit* (*part of cooker*) quemador *m* **4.** (*arena*) ruedo *m;* (*in boxing*) cuadrilátero *m;* (*in circus*) pista *f* **II.** *vt* **1.** (*surround*) rodear; **to be ~ed by sth** estar cercado, -a con algo **2.** (*bird*) anillar

ring² [rɪŋ] **I.** *n* **1.** *no pl, Brit* (*telephone call*) llamada *f;* **to give sb a** ~ llamar a alguien (por teléfono) **2.** (*metallic sound*) sonido *m* metálico; (*of bell*) toque *m* **II.** <rang, rung> *vt* **1.** *Brit* (*call on telephone*) llamar (por teléfono) **2.** (*bell*) tocar; (*alarm*) hacer sonar **III.** <rang, rung> *vi* **1.** *Brit* (*call on telephone*) llamar **2.** (*produce sound: telephone, bell*) sonar; **to** ~ **false/true** sonar falso/convincente

♦ **ring back** *vi, vt* TEL volver a llamar (a)

♦ **ring down** *vt* THEAT **to** ~ **the curtain** bajar el telón

♦ **ring in** *vt* **to** ~ **the New Year** recibir el año nuevo

♦ **ring off** *vi Brit* colgar

♦ **ring out** *vi* resonar

♦ **ring up** **I.** *vt* **1.** (*telephone*) telefonear **2.** (*key in sale*) registrar **II.** *vi* telefonear

ring binder *n* archivador *m* de anillas

ringer ['rɪŋər, *Am:* -ə·] *n* **to be a dead** ~ (**for sb**) *inf* ser el vivo retrato (de alguien)

ring finger *n* dedo *m* anular

ringing **I.** *n no pl* repique *m* **II.** *adj* sonoro, -a

ringing tone *n* TEL tono *m* de llamada

ringleader ['rɪŋliːdər, *Am:* -də·] *n* cabecilla *mf*

ringlet ['rɪŋlɪt] *n* tirabuzón *m*

ring road *n Brit, Aus* ronda *f* de circunvalación

ringside ['rɪŋsaɪd] **I.** *n* **to be at the** ~ estar junto al cuadrilátero **II.** *adj* (*seats*) de primera fila

ringworm ['rɪŋwɜːm, *Am:* -wɜːrm] *n* tiña *f*

rink [rɪŋk] *n* pista *f* de patinaje

rinse [rɪns] **I.** *vt* (*dishes, clothes*) enjuagar; (*hands*) lavar **II.** *n* **1.** *no pl* (*wash*) enjuague *m;* **cold/hot** ~ aclarado *m* frío/caliente **2.** (*hair colouring*) reflejos *mpl*

riot ['raɪət] **I.** *n* disturbio *m;* **a** ~ **of colour** un derroche de color; **to be a** ~ *inf* ser la monda **II.** *vi* causar disturbios **III.** *adv* **to run** ~ *fig* desmandarse; **to let one's imagination run** ~ dar rienda suelta a su imaginación

rioter *n* alborotador(a) *m(f)*

riot gear *n* uniforme *m* antidisturbios

rioting *n no pl* disturbios *mpl*

riotous ['raɪətəs, *Am:* -ţəs] *adj* **1.** (*rebellious*) descontrolado, -a **2.** (*uproarious*) escandaloso, -a; (*party*) desenfrenado, -a

riot police *n* policía *f* antidisturbios

rip [rɪp] **I.** <-pp-> *vi* rasgarse **II.** <-pp-> *vt* rasgar; **to** ~ **sth open** abrir algo de un rasgón **III.** *n* rasgón *m*, rajo *m AmC*

♦ **rip down** *vt* arrancar

♦ **rip off** *vt* **1.** (*remove*) arrancar **2.** *inf*

(*swindle*) timar
◆**rip out** *vt* arrancar
◆**rip up** *vt* romper
RIP [ˌɑːˈaɪˈpiː, *Am:* ˌɑːˈr-] *abbr of* **rest in peace** E.P.D., D.E.P
ripcord [ˈrɪpkɔːd, *Am:* -kɔːrd] *n* cordón *m* de apertura
ripe [raɪp] *adj* 1. (*fruit*) maduro, -a; **at the ~ old age of 80** a la avanzada edad de 80 2. (*ready*) **the time is ~ for ...** es el momento oportuno de... 3. (*language*) atrevido, -a
ripen [ˈraɪpən] I. *vt* hacer madurar II. *vi* madurar
ripeness [ˈraɪpnɪs] *n no pl* madurez *f*
rip-off [ˈrɪpɒf, *Am:* -ɑːf] *n inf* timo *m*, vacilada *f inf, Méx*
riposte [rɪˈpɒst, *Am:* -ˈpoʊst] *n* réplica *f*
ripple [ˈrɪpl] I. *n* onda *f;* ~ **of applause** unos cuantos aplausos; **raspberry ~** helado *m* de vainilla con vetas de frambuesa II. *vt* rizar III. *vi* rizarse
rip-roaring [ˈrɪprɔːrɪŋ, *Am:* ˌrɪp'-] *adj inf* animadísimo, -a; **a ~ success** un éxito clamoroso
riptide [ˈrɪptaɪd] *n* corriente *f* de resaca
rise [raɪz] I. *n no pl* 1. (*increase*) subida *f;* **to be on the ~** ir en aumento; **to give ~ to sth** dar lugar a algo; (*pay*) ~ *Brit* incremento *m* salarial; **to get** [*o* **take**] **a ~ out of sb** burlarse de alguien 2. (*incline*) cuesta *f* II. <rose, risen> *vi* 1. (*arise*) levantarse 2. (*become higher: ground*) subir (en pendiente); (*temperature*) aumentar; (*river*) crecer 3. (*go up: smoke*) subir; (*moon, sun*) salir; (*building*) elevarse 4. (*improve socially*) ascender; (*in the ranks*) ganar; **to ~ to fame** alcanzar la fama 5. (*be reborn*) resucitar 6. (*rebel*) sublevarse
◆**rise above** *vt insep* 1. (*be higher than*) estar por encima de 2. (*problem, opposition*) superar
◆**rise up** *vi* 1. (*arise*) levantarse 2. (*rebel*) alzarse
risen [ˈrɪzn] *pp of* **rise**
riser [ˈraɪzər, *Am:* -zə] *n* 1. (*person*) **early ~** madrugador(a) *m(f);* **late ~** dormilón, -ona *m, f* 2. (*part of step*) contrahuella *f* 3. *pl, Am* (*set of steps*) escaleras *fpl*
risible [ˈrɪzəbl] *adj* risible
rising [ˈraɪzɪŋ] I. *n* levantamiento *m* II. *adj* (*in number*) creciente; (*in status*) ascendente; (*floodwaters*) en aumento; (*sun*) naciente
risk [rɪsk] I. *n* 1. (*chance*) riesgo *m;* **to run the ~ of sth** correr el riesgo de algo 2. *no pl* (*danger*) peligro *m;* **at one's own ~** bajo su propia responsabilidad; **to be at ~** correr peligro II. *vt* arriesgar; **to ~ doing sth** arriesgarse a hacer algo; **to ~ one's life** poner la propia vida en peligro
risk capital *n* ECON capital *m* de riesgo **risk factor** *n* factor *m* de riesgo
risk-free *adj,* **riskless** *adj Am* sin riesgo
risk liability *n* responsabilidad *f* sobre riesgos
risky [ˈrɪski] <-ier, -iest> *adj* arriesgado, -a, riesgoso, -a *AmL*

risqué [ˈriːskeɪ, *Am:* rɪˈskeɪ] *adj* atrevido, -a
rissole [ˈrɪsəʊl, *Am:* -oʊl] *n* croqueta *f*
rite [raɪt] *n* rito *m;* **last ~s** extremaunción *f*
ritual [ˈrɪtʃʊəl, *Am:* -uəl] I. *n* ritual *m* II. *adj* ritual
ritzy [ˈrɪtsi] <-ier, -iest> *adj inf* lujoso, -a
rival [ˈraɪvl] I. *n* rival *mf* II. *adj* competidor(a); **a ~ brand** una marca rival III. <-ll-, *Am:* -l-> *vt* competir con
rivalry [ˈraɪvlri] *n* rivalidad *f*
river [ˈrɪvər, *Am:* -ə-] *n* río *m*
river basin *n* cuenca *f* de río **river bed** *n* lecho *m* de un río **river fish** *n* pez *m* de río **river police** *n* policía *f* fluvial
riverside [ˈrɪvəsaɪd, *Am:* ˈrɪvə-] *n no pl* ribera *f*
rivet [ˈrɪvɪt] I. *n* remache *m* II. *vt* 1. (*join*) remachar 2. (*interest*) **to be ~ed by sth** quedar absorto, -a con algo
riveting [ˈrɪvətɪŋ, *Am:* -ɪt̬ɪŋ] *adj inf* fascinante
rivulet [ˈrɪvjʊlɪt] *n* 1. *liter* (*stream*) arroyo *m* 2. (*of sweat, blood*) gotas *fpl*
RN [ˌɑːˈren, *Am:* ˌɑːˈren] *n Brit* MIL *abbr of* **Royal Navy** flota real
RNA [ˌɑːˈrenˈeɪ, *Am:* ˌɑːrenˈeɪ] *n abbr of* **ribonucleic acid** ARN *m*
RNLI [ˌɑːˈrenelˈaɪ, *Am:* ˌɑːrenelˈaɪ] *n Brit* NAUT *abbr of* **Royal National Lifeboat Institution** servicio de lanchas de socorro
roach [rəʊtʃ, *Am:* roʊtʃ] *n* 1. (*fish*) rubio *m* 2. *Am, inf* (*cockroach*) cucaracha *f*
road [rəʊd, *Am:* roʊd] *n* 1. (*between towns*) carretera *f;* (*in town*) calle *f;* (*route*) camino *m;* **by ~** por carretera; **to be on the ~** (*fit for driving*) estar en circulación; (*travelling by road*) estar en camino; (*performing on tour*) estar de gira 2. *fig* sendero *m;* **to be on the ~ to recovery** estar reponiéndose; **to be on the right ~** *Brit* ir bien encaminado ►**all ~s lead to** Rome *prov* todos los caminos llevan a Roma *prov;* **let's hit the ~!** *inf* ¡vamos a ponernos en marcha!; **to get sth on the ~** *inf* empezar (con) algo
road accident *n* accidente *m* de circulación
roadblock *n* control *m* de carretera **road haulage** *n no pl* transporte *m* por carretera **road hog** *n inf* loco, -a *m, f* del volante
roadhouse [ˈrəʊdhaʊs, *Am:* ˈroʊd-] <-houses> *n Am* motel *m*
roadie [ˈrəʊdi, *Am:* ˈroʊ-] *n persona encargada de transportar y montar el equipo de un grupo musical*
road map *n* mapa *m* de carreteras **road rage** *n* furia *f* al volante **road safety** *n no pl* seguridad *f* vial **road sense** *n* instinto *m* del automovilista
roadshow [ˈrəʊdʃəʊ, *Am:* ˈroʊdʃoʊ] *n* gira *f*
roadside [ˈrəʊdsaɪd, *Am:* ˈroʊd-] I. *n* borde *m* de la carretera II. *adj* de carretera
road sign *n* señal *f* de tráfico
road surface *n* pavimento *m* **road sweeper** *n* barrendero, -a *m, f* **road-test**

vt **to ~ a car** someter un coche a una prueba de carretera **road traffic** *n no pl* tráfico *m* vial **road transport** *n no pl, Brit* transporte *m* por carretera **road user** *n* usuario, -a *m, f* de la vía pública

roadway ['rəʊdweɪ, *Am:* 'roʊd-] *n no pl* calzada *f*

roadworks ['rəʊdwɜːks, *Am:* 'roʊdwɜːrks] *npl* obras *fpl* de carretera

roam [rəʊm, *Am:* roʊm] **I.** *vi* vagar **II.** *vt* vagar por

roan [rəʊn, *Am:* roʊn] *n* ruano *m*

roar [rɔːʳ, *Am:* rɔːr] **I.** *vi* (*lion, person*) rugir; (*cannon*) tronar; **to ~ with laughter** reírse a carcajadas **II.** *vt* vociferar **III.** *n* (*of lion, person*) rugido *m;* (*of engine*) estruendo *m*

roaring I. *adj* rugiente; (*thunder*) estruendoso, -a; (*fire*) furioso, -a; (*success*) clamoroso, -a; (*trade*) tremendo, -a **II.** *adv* completamente

roast [rəʊst, *Am:* roʊst] **I.** *vt* asar; (*coffee*) tostar **II.** *vi* (*food*) asarse; (*person*) achicharrarse **III.** *n* asado *m* **IV.** *adj* (*meat*) asado, -a; (*coffee*) tostado, -a

roaster ['rəʊstəʳ, *Am:* 'roʊstəʳ] *n* asador *m*

roasting ['rəʊstɪŋ, *Am:* 'roʊst-] **I.** *n* **1.** (*baking*) asado *m* **2.** *inf* (*telling off*) **to give sb a ~** echar una bronca a alguien **II.** *adj* abrasador(a) **III.** *adv* **~ hot** abrasador(a)

rob [rɒb, *Am:* raːb] <-bb-> *vt* **1.** (*person, house*) robar; (*bank*) asaltar; **to ~ sb of sth** robar algo a alguien **2.** (*deprive*) **to ~ sb of sth** privar a alguien de algo

robber ['rɒbəʳ, *Am:* 'raːbəʳ] *n* ladrón, -ona *m, f;* **bank ~** atracador(a) *m(f)* de bancos

robbery ['rɒbəri, *Am:* 'raːbəʳi] <-ies> *n* robo *m*

robe [rəʊb, *Am:* roʊb] *n* (*formal*) toga *f;* (*dressing gown*) traje *m*

robin ['rɒbɪn, *Am:* 'raːbɪn] *n* ZOOL petirrojo *m; Am* (*American songbird*) tordo *m* norteamericano

robot ['rəʊbɒt, *Am:* 'roʊbaːt] *n* (*machine*) robot *m;* (*person*) autómata *m*

robotics [rəʊ'bɒtɪks, *Am:* roʊ'baːt̬ɪks] *npl* robótica *f*

robust [rəʊ'bʌst, *Am:* roʊ'-] *adj* **1.** (*person*) robusto, -a; (*health*) de hierro; (*currency*) fuerte **2.** (*statement*) enérgico, -a

robustness *n no pl* **1.** (*vitality*) robustez *f;* (*long-term strength*) solidez *f* **2.** (*frankness*) vigor *m*

rock¹ [rɒk, *Am:* raːk] *n* **1.** GEO roca *f;* (*in sea*) escollo *m* **2.** (*music*) rock *m* ▶ **to be between a ~ and hard place** estar entre la espada y la pared; **as solid as a ~** duro como una piedra; **to be on the ~s** estar sin blanca; **whisky on the ~s** whisky con hielo

rock² [rɒk, *Am:* raːk] **I.** *vt* **1.** (*swing*) mecer **2.** (*shock*) sacudir **II.** *vi* balancearse

rock-and-roll [ˌrɒkənd'rəʊl, *Am:* ˌraːkənd'roʊl] *n no pl* rock and roll *m* **rock band** *n* grupo *m* de rock **rock bottom** *n* fondo *m;* **to hit ~** tocar fondo; **to be at ~** estar

por los suelos **rock bun** *n,* **rock cake** *n Brit, Aus* bollo *m* con frutos secos **rock climber** *n* escalador(a) *m(f)* **rock climbing** *n no pl* escalada *f* en roca

rocker ['rɒkəʳ, *Am:* 'raːkəʳ] *n* **1.** (*chair*) mecedora *f* **2.** *Brit* (*musician, fan*) roquero, -a *m, f* ▶ **to be off one's ~** *inf* estar chiflado

rockery ['rɒkri, *Am:* 'raːkəʳi] <-ies> *n* jardín *m* rocoso

rocket ['rɒkɪt, *Am:* 'raːkɪt] **I.** *n* **1.** (*weapon*) misil *m* **2.** (*vehicle for space travel*) cohete *m* espacial **3.** (*firework*) cohete *m* **4.** *no pl* (*reprimand*) bronca *f;* **to give sb a ~** echar un rapapolvo a alguien **II.** *vi* (*costs, prices*) dispararse; **to ~ up** dispararse

rocket launcher *n* lanzacohetes *m inv* **rock face** *n* pared *f* rocosa **rock festival** *n* festival *m* de rock **rock garden** *n Am* jardín *m* rocoso

Rockies ['rɒkiz, *Am:* 'raːkiz] *n* **the ~** las Rocosas

rocking chair ['rɒkɪŋ, *Am:* 'raːk-] *n* mecedora *f,* columpio *m AmL* **rocking horse** *n* caballito *m* mecedor

rock music *n no pl* música *f* rock **rock'n'-roll** *n no pl* rock and roll *m* **rock plant** *n* planta *f* rupestre **rock salt** *n no pl* sal *f* gema **rock star** *n* estrella *f* del rock

rocky¹ ['rɒki, *Am:* 'raːki] <-ier, -iest> *adj* rocoso, -a; (*ground*) pedregoso, -a

rocky² ['rɒki, *Am:* 'raːki] <-ier, -iest> *adj* (*unstable*) inestable

Rocky Mountains *n* Montañas *fpl* Rocosas

rococo [rəʊ'kəʊkəʊ, *Am:* rə'koʊkoʊ] **I.** *n no pl* rococó *m* **II.** *adj* rococó

rod [rɒd, *Am:* raːd] *n* (*stick*) varilla *f;* (*fishing rod*) caña *f* de pescar

rode [rəʊd, *Am:* roʊd] *pt of* **ride**

rodent ['rəʊdnt, *Am:* 'roʊ-] *n* roedor *m*

rodeo [rəʊ'dɪəʊ, *Am:* 'roʊdɪoʊ] <-s> *n* rodeo *m*

roe¹ [rəʊ, *Am:* roʊ] *n* (*fish eggs*) hueva *f*

roe² [rəʊ, *Am:* roʊ] <-(s)> *n* (*deer*) corzo, -a *m, f*

roe buck *n,* **roebuck** ['rəʊbʌk, *Am:* 'roʊ-] *n* corzo *m*

roger ['rɒdʒəʳ, *Am:* 'raːdʒəʳ] *interj* RADIO recibido

rogue [rəʊg, *Am:* roʊg] **I.** *n* **1.** (*rascal*) pícaro, -a *m, f* **2.** (*villain*) bribón, -ona *m, f* **II.** *adj* (*animal*) solitario, -a; (*trader, company*) deshonesto, -a

roguery ['rəʊgəri, *Am:* 'roʊ-] <-ies> *n* (*of child*) pillería *f;* (*of adult*) truhanería *f*

roguish ['rəʊgɪʃ, *Am:* 'roʊ-] *adj* pícaro, -a

ROI [ˌɑː'rəʊ'aɪ, *Am:* ˌɑːroʊ'aɪ] *n abbr of* **return on investment** rendimiento *m* de las inversiones

role *n,* **rôle** [rəʊl, *Am:* roʊl] *n* **a.** THEAT papel *m;* **to play a ~** THEAT hacer un papel; *fig* desempeñar un papel

role model *n* modelo *m* a imitar **role play** *n* juego *m* de imitación **role reversal** *n* inversión *m* de papeles

roll [rəʊl, *Am:* roʊl] I. *n* 1. (*turning over*) voltereta *f* 2. *no pl* (*swaying movement*) balanceo *m;* **to be on a ~** *fig* tener buena suerte 3. (*cylinder: of cloth, paper*) rollo *m;* (*film*) carrete *m* 4. (*noise: of drum*) redoble *m;* (*of thunder*) retumbo *m* 5. (*catalogue of names*) padrón *m;* (*for elections*) censo *m;* **to call the ~** pasar lista 6. (*bread*) panecillo *m* II. *vt* 1. (*push: ball, barrel*) hacer rodar; (*dice*) tirar; **to ~ one's eyes** poner los ojos en blanco 2. (*form into cylindrical shape*) **to ~ sth into sth** enrollar algo en algo; **all ~ed into one** todo unido en uno 3. (*make: cigarette*) liar 4. (*flatten: grass*) allanar III. *vi* 1. (*move*) rodar; (*with undulating motion*) ondular 2. (*be in operation*) funcionar

◆**roll about** *vi* vagar; (*ship*) balancearse
◆**roll back** *vt* 1. (*cause to retreat*) hacer retroceder 2. *Am* ECON reducir 3. (*return to previous state*) hacer recular
◆**roll by** *vi* (*vehicle, clouds*) avanzar; (*time, years*) pasar
◆**roll down** I. *vt* (*sleeve*) desenrollar; (*window*) bajar II. *vi* rodar por
◆**roll in** *vi* 1. llegar en abundancia 2. **to be rolling in money** *inf* nadar en dinero
◆**roll off** *vi* caer rodando
◆**roll on** *vi* seguir rodando; (*time*) pasar; **~ Christmas!** *Brit, Aus, inf* ¡que llegue Navidad!
◆**roll out** I. *vt* 1. (*flatten*) estirar; (*pastry*) extender 2. *Am* ECON transferir 3. (*unroll*) desenrollar II. *vi Am* ECON transferir
◆**roll over** *vi* dar vueltas
◆**roll up** I. *vi inf* aparecer; **~!** *Brit, Aus* ¡vengan todos! II. *vt* enrollar; (*sleeves*) arremangarse

roll bar *n* AUTO barra *f* protectora antivuelco
roll call *n* lista *f*
roller ['rəʊlə', *Am:* 'roʊlə'] *n* 1. TECH rodillo *m* 2. (*wave*) ola *f* grande 3. (*for hair*) rulo *m*
roller bearing *n* TECH cojinete *m* de rodillos
rollerblade® I. *n* patín *m* en línea II. *vi* patinar en línea **roller blind** *n Brit, Aus* persiana *f* **roller coaster** *n* montaña *f* rusa **rollerskate** I. *n* patín *m* de ruedas II. *vi* patinar
rollicking ['rɒlɪkɪŋ, *Am:* 'rɑ:lɪ-] I. *adj* (*amusing*) alegre; (*party*) divertido, -a II. *n Brit, inf* **to give sb a ~** echar una bronca a alguien
rolling *adj* rodante; (*hills*) ondulado, -a; (*programme*) continuo, -a
rolling mill *n* 1. (*machine*) tren *m* de laminación 2. (*factory*) taller *m* de laminación **rolling pin** *n* rodillo *m* **rolling stock** *n* AUTO material *m* rodante
rollneck ['rəʊlnek, *Am:* 'roʊl-] *n* jersey *m* de cuello vuelto
roll-on ['rəʊlɒn, *Am:* 'roʊlɑ:n] *adj* (*deodorant*) de bola
roll-on-roll-off *adj* AUTO ro-ro; (*ferry*) de autotransbordo
roly-poly[1] [,rəʊli'pəʊli, *Am:* ,roʊli'poʊ-] *adj inf* regordete, -a

roly-poly[2] [,rəʊli'pəʊli, *Am:* ,roʊli'poʊ-] *n,* **roly-poly pudding** *n* GASTR brazo *m* de gitano
ROM [rɒm, *Am:* rɑ:m] *n no pl* INFOR *abbr of* **Read Only Memory** ROM *f*
Roman ['rəʊmən, *Am:* 'roʊ-] I. *adj* romano, -a; (*alphabet*) latino, -a; (*religion*) católico, -a II. *n* romano, -a *m, f*
Roman Catholic I. *n* católico, -a *m, f* II. *adj* católico, -a; **the ~ Church** la Iglesia católica romana
romance [rəʊ'mæns, *Am:* roʊ'mæns] I. *n* 1. (*love affair*) romance *m* 2. (*novel*) novela *f* rosa; (*film*) película *f* de amor 3. (*glamour*) romanticismo *m* II. *vi* fantasear
Romanesque [,rəʊmə'nesk, *Am:* ,roʊ-] *adj* románico, -a
Romania [rə'meɪnɪə, *Am:* roʊ'-] *n* Rumanía *f*
Romanian [rə'meɪnɪən, *Am:* roʊ'-] I. *adj* rumano, -a II. *n* 1. (*person*) rumano, -a *m, f* 2. LING rumano *m*
romantic [rəʊ'mæntɪk, *Am:* roʊ'mænt̬ɪk] I. *adj a.* LIT, ART romántico, -a II. *n* romántico, -a *m, f*
romanticism [rəʊ'mæntɪsɪzəm, *Am:* roʊ'mænt̬ə-] *n no pl* romanticismo *m*
Romany ['rɒməni, *Am:* 'rɑ:mə-] *n* 1. (*ethnic group*) gitano, -a *m, f* 2. *no pl* (*language*) romaní *m*
Rome ['rəʊm, *Am:* 'roʊm] *n* Roma *f* ▶**~ was not built in a** <u>day</u> *prov* no se ganó Zamora en una hora *prov;* <u>when</u> **in ~** (**do as the** <u>Romans</u>) *prov* allí donde fueres haz lo que vieres *prov*
romp [rɒmp, *Am:* rɑ:mp] I. *vi* juguetear; **to ~ home** ganar fácilmente II. *n* retozo *m*
rompers ['rɒmpə'z, *Am:* 'rɑ:mpə'z] *npl Am* pelele *m*
roof [ru:f] <-s> I. *n* (*of house*) tejado *m;* (*of car*) techo *m;* (*of tree*) punta *f;* (*of mouth*) paladar *m* ▶**to go through the ~** (*prices*) estar por las nubes; (*person*) subirse por las paredes; **to hit the ~** subirse por las paredes; **to raise the ~** *inf* armar jaleo II. *vt* techar
roofer ['ru:fə', *Am:* -fə'] *n* techador *m*
roof garden *n* azotea *f* con flores y plantas
roofing *n no pl* techumbre *f*
roofrack *n Brit* baca *f*, parrilla *f AmL*
rooftop ['ru:ftɒp, *Am:* -tɑ:p] *n* techo *m*
rook [rʊk] I. *n* 1. (*bird*) grajo *m* 2. (*in chess*) torre *f* II. *vt inf* estafar
rookery ['rʊkəri] *n* colonia *f* de grajos
rookie ['rʊki] *n Am, Aus, inf* novato, -a *m, f*
room [ru:m] I. *n* 1. (*in house*) habitación *m,* pieza *f AmL,* ambiente *m CSur;* **~ and board** pensión *f* completa 2. *no pl* (*space*) espacio *m;* **to make ~ for sb/sth** hacer sitio para alguien/algo; **there's no more ~ for anything else** ya no cabe nada más; **~ for improvement** posibilidad *f* de mejorar; **there is no ~ for doubt** no cabe duda II. *vi Am* **to ~ with sb** compartir alojamiento con alguien

roomful ['ru:mfəl] *n* habitación *f* llena
rooming house *n Am* pensión *f*
roommate ['ru:mmeɪt] *n Am* compañero, -a *m, f* de habitación **room service** *n* servicio *m* de habitaciones **room temperature** *n* temperatura *f* ambiente
roomy ['ru:mi] <-ier, -iest> *adj* amplio, -a
roost [ru:st] I. *n* percha *f* ▶to <u>rule</u> the ~ llevar la voz cantante II. *vi* (*bird*) posarse para dormir; *fig* pasar la noche
rooster ['ru:stər, *Am:* -stɚ] *n Am, Aus* gallo *m*
root [ru:t] *n* 1. *a.* BOT, LING, MAT raíz *f*; to take ~ *a. fig* arraigar 2. (*source*) causa *f*; the ~ of all evil la esencia de todos los males; the ~ of the problem is that ... el problema radica en que...
◆root about *vi,* **root around** *vi* hozar; to ~ for sth buscar algo
◆root out *vt* arrancar
root beer *n Am:* bebida gaseosa hecha con extractos de plantas **root cause** *n* causa *f* primordial
rootless *adj* desarraigado, -a
root sign *n* MAT raíz *f* **root vegetable** *n* tubérculo *m*
rope [rəup, *Am:* roup] I. *n* 1. (*cord*) cuerda *f*; (*of garlic*) manojo *m;* (*of pearls*) sarta *f* 2. *pl* (*in boxing*) cuerdas *fpl* 3. (*for capital punishment*) soga *f* ▶to <u>know</u> the ~s estar al tanto de todo; to <u>learn</u> the ~s aprender el oficio; to <u>show</u> sb the ~s enseñar el oficio a alguien; to have sb <u>on</u> the ~s tener a alguien contra las cuerdas II. *vt* atar con una cuerda
◆rope in *vt* to rope sb in (to doing sth) agarrar a alguien (para que haga algo)
◆rope off *vt* acordonar
◆rope up *vi* encordarse
rope ladder *n* escalera *f* de cuerda
rop(e)y ['rəupi, *Am:* 'rou-] <-ier, -iest> *adj Brit, Aus, inf* 1. (*ill*) pachucho, -a 2. (*argument*) flojo, -a
ro-ro ['rəurəu] *n Brit* NAUT *abbr of* roll-on--roll-off ro-ro *m*
rosary ['rəuzəri, *Am:* 'rou-] <-ies> *n* rosario *m*
rose¹ [rəuz, *Am:* rouz] I. *n* 1. (*flower, colour*) rosa *f* 2. (*on watering can*) roseta *f;* (*on shower*) alcachofa *f* 3. ARCHIT rosetón *m* ▶to <u>come up</u> smelling of ~s aparecer contento; <u>coming up</u> ~s a pedir de boca II. *adj* rosa
rose² [rəuz, *Am:* rouz] *pt of* **rise**
rosebud ['rəuzbʌd, *Am:* 'rouz-] *n* capullo *m*
rosebush *n* rosal *m* **rose garden** *n* rosaleda *f*
rosehip ['rəuzhɪp, *Am:* 'rouz-] *n* escaramujo *m*
rosemary ['rəuzməri, *Am:* 'rouzmer-] *n no pl* romero *m*
rosette [rəu'zet, *Am:* rou'-] *n* ARCHIT rosetón *m;* (*badge*) escarapela *f*
rose water *n no pl* agua *f* de rosas **rose window** *n* ARCHIT rosetón *m*

rosin ['rɒzɪn, *Am:* 'rɑːzən] *n no pl* colofonia *f*
roster ['rɒstər, *Am:* 'rɑːstɚ] *n no pl* lista *f*
rostrum ['rɒstrəm, 'rɒstrə, *Am:* 'rɑːstrəm, 'rɑːstrə] <-s *o* rostra> *n* (*for conductor*) estrado *m;* (*for public speaker*) tribuna *f*
rosy ['rəuzi, *Am:* 'rou-] <-ier, -iest> *adj* 1. (*rose-colour*) rosado, -a; (*cheek*) sonrosado, -a 2. (*optimistic: viewpoint*) optimista; (*future*) prometedor(a)
rot [rɒt, *Am:* rɑːt] I. *n no pl* putrefacción *f* ▶to <u>stop</u> the ~ cortar por lo sano; to <u>talk</u> ~ decir sandeces II. <-tt-> *vi* pudrirse III. *vt* pudrir
◆rot away I. *vt* pudrir II. *vi* pudrirse
rota ['rəutə, *Am:* 'routə] *n Brit* lista *f* de turnos
rotary ['rəutəri, *Am:* 'routɚ-] *adj* rotatorio, -a; (*pump*) giratorio, -a
rota system *n* sistema *m* de turnos
rotate [rəu'teɪt, *Am:* 'routeɪt] I. *vt* 1. (*turn round*) dar vueltas a 2. (*alternate*) alternar; (*duties*) turnarse en; AGR cultivar en rotación II. *vi* girar; to ~ around sth girar alrededor de algo
rotation [rəu'teɪʃən, *Am:* rou'-] *n* 1. *a.* ASTR, AGR rotación *f* 2. (*alternation*) alternación *f;* in ~ por turno
rotatory ['rəutətəri, *Am:* 'routətɔːr-] *adj* rotativo, -a
rote [rəut, *Am:* rout] *n no pl* by ~ de memoria
rotor ['rəutər, *Am:* 'routɚ] *n* rotor *m*
rotten ['rɒtn, *Am:* 'rɑːtn] *adj* 1. (*food*) podrido, -a; to go ~ pudrirse 2. *inf* (*nasty: behaviour*) despreciable 3. *inf* (*performance, book*) malísimo, -a
rotund [rəu'tʌnd, *Am:* rou'-] *adj* redondeado, -a
rotunda [rəu'tʌndə, *Am:* rou'-] *n* ARCHIT rotonda *f*
rouble ['ru:bl] *n* rublo *m*
rouge [ru:ʒ] *n no pl* colorete *m*, rouge *m Arg, Chile*
rough [rʌf] I. *adj* 1. (*uneven: road*) desigual; (*surface*) áspero, -a 2. (*poorly made: work*) chapucero, -a 3. (*harsh: voice*) bronco, -a 4. (*imprecise*) aproximado, -a; (*idea*) impreciso, -a; ~ work borrador *m* 5. (*unrefined: person, manner*) tosco, -a 6. (*stormy: sea*) agitado, -a; (*weather*) tempestuoso, -a 7. (*difficult*) difícil; (*treatment*) duro, -a; to be ~ on sb *inf* ser injusto con alguien 8. *Brit, inf* (*unwell*) mal II. *n* 1. (*sketch*) borrador *m* 2. *Brit* (*young man*) gamberro *m* 3. *no pl* SPORTS the ~ el rough ▶to <u>take</u> the ~ with the <u>smooth</u> estar a las duras y a las maduras III. *vt* to ~ it *inf* pasar sin comodidades IV. *adv* to play ~ jugar duro; to live ~ vivir a la intemperie
roughage ['rʌfɪdʒ] *n no pl* fibra *f* (de los alimentos)
rough-and-ready [‚rʌfənd'redi] *adj* (*primitive*) tosco pero eficaz **rough-and-tumble**

n riña *f; fig* juegos *mpl* bruscos

rough diamond *n Brit, Aus* diamante *m* en bruto

roughen ['rʌfən] *vt* poner áspero **rough-hewn** *adj* 1. (*wood*) desbastado, -a 2. (*features*) tosco, -a

roughhouse ['rʌfhaʊs] **I.** *vi* armar jaleo **II.** *n inf* jaleo *m*

roughly *adv* 1. (*approximately*) aproximadamente; ~ **speaking** por así decirlo 2. (*aggressively*) bruscamente

roughneck ['rʌfnek] *n* 1. *Am, inf* (*oil rig worker*) trabajador *m* de un pozo petrolífero 2. *Am, Aus, inf* (*violent man*) matón *m*

roughness ['rʌfnɪs] *n no pl* 1. (*of surface*) aspereza *f;* (*of ground*) desigualdad *f* 2. (*unfairness*) dureza *f*

roughshod ['rʌfʃɒd, *Am:* -ʃɑːd] *adv* **to ride ~ over sb** no tener la menor consideración con alguien

rough-spoken [,rʌf'spəʊkən, *Am:* -'spoʊ-] *adj* malhablado, -a

roulette [ruː'let] *n no pl* ruleta *f*

round [raʊnd] **I.** <-er, -est> *adj* 1. (*circular: object, number*) redondo, -a; (*arch*) de medio punto; (*dozen*) completo, -a; **could you make it a ~ hundred?** ¿podrían ser cien para redondear? 2. (*not angular*) arqueado, -a 3. (*sonorous*) sonoro, -a **II.** *adv* alrededor; **to go ~ and ~** dar muchas vueltas; **to come ~** pasar por casa; ~ (*about*) **10 o'clock** a eso de las 10; **the other way ~** al revés; **all ~** (*everywhere*) por todos lados; (*for everybody*) para todos; **taken all ~** en conjunto **III.** *prep* 1. (*surrounding*) alrededor de; **to go ~ sth** dar la vuelta a algo; **the earth goes ~ the sun** la tierra da vueltas alrededor del sol; **to find a way ~ a problem** *fig* encontra la vuelta a un problema; **to go ~ the corner** doblar la esquina; **just ~ the corner** justo a la vuelta de la esquina 2. (*visit*) **to go ~ a museum** visitar un museo; **to go ~ the park** dar una vuelta por el parque 3. (*here and there*) **all ~ the house** por toda la casa; **to wander ~ the world** viajar por el mundo; **to drive ~ France** conducir por Francia; **to sit ~ the room** estar sentado en la habitación 4. (*approximately*) alrededor de; ~ **11:00** alrededor de las 11:00; ~ **May 10** alrededor del 10 de mayo; **somewhere ~ here** en algún lugar de por aquí **IV.** *n* 1. (*circle*) círculo *m* 2. (*series*) serie *f;* (*of applause*) salva *f;* (*of shots*) descarga *f* 3. *pl* (*route*) recorrido *m;* MIL ronda *f;* MED visita *f;* **to do one's paper ~** *Aus, Brit* hacer el reparto de los periódicos 4. (*routine*) rutina *f* 5. (*time period: of elections*) vuelta *f;* (*in card games*) mano *f;* SPORTS eliminatoria *f;* (*in boxing*) asalto *m* 6. *Brit* (*slice: of bread*) rodaja *f;* **a ~ of toast** una tostada *f;* (*of drinks*) ronda *f;* **this is my ~** esta ronda la pago yo 8. (*of ammunition*) bala *f* 9. MUS canon *m* **V.** *vt* redondear; (*corner*) doblar

◆**round down** *vt* MAT redondear por defecto

◆**round off** *vt* 1. (*finish*) rematar

2. (*smooth*) pulir 3. MAT redondear

◆**round on** *vt* volverse en contra de

◆**round out** *vt s.* **round off**

◆**round up** *vt* 1. MAT redondear por exceso 2. (*gather*) reunir; (*cattle*) rodear

roundabout ['raʊndəbaʊt] **I.** *n Aus, Brit* 1. AUTO rotonda *f* 2. *Brit* (*ride*) tiovivo *m* **II.** *adj* indirecto, -a; **to take a ~ route** ir dando un rodeo

rounded *adj* redondeado, -a

rounders ['raʊndəz, *Am:* -dəz] *n no pl, Brit* SPORTS juego similar al béisbol

roundly *adv* (*assert, deny*) categóricamente, rotundamente; **to defeat sb ~** derrotar de forma aplastante a alguien

round robin *n* 1. (*letter*) carta *f* colectiva 2. (*competition*) torneo *m* (*en el que cada participante se enfrenta con cada uno de los demás*)

round-shouldered [,raʊnd'ʃəʊldəd, *Am:* -'ʃoʊldəd] *adj* encorvado, -a; **to be ~** ser cargado de espaldas

roundsman ['raʊndzmən] *n Brit* repartidor *m*

round-table discussion [,raʊnd'teɪbl dɪ'skʌʃən] *n* mesa *f* redonda **round-the-clock I.** *adj* (*surveillance*) de veinticuatro horas **II.** *adv* las veinticuatro horas; **to work ~** trabajar día y noche **round trip** *n* viaje *m* de ida y vuelta; ~ **ticket** *Am* billete *m* de ida y vuelta

round-up ['raʊndʌp] *n* 1. AGR rodeo *m* 2. (*by police*) redada *f* 3. (*summary*) resumen *m*

rouse [raʊz] *vt* 1. (*waken*) despertar 2. (*activate*) provocar; **to ~ sb to do sth** animar a alguien a hacer algo; **to ~ sb to action** mover a alguien a la acción

rousing ['raʊzɪŋ] *adj* (*welcome*) caluroso, -a; (*speech*) vehemente

roustabout ['raʊstəbaʊt] *n Am* (*labourer*) peón *m*

rout [raʊt] **I.** *vt* 1. (*defeat*) derrotar 2. (*put to flight*) poner en fuga **II.** *n* 1. (*defeat*) derrota *f* aplastante 2. (*flight*) huida *f* en desbandada

◆**rout out** *vt* 1. (*make come out*) hacer salir 2. (*find*) encontrar

route [ruːt, *Am:* raʊt] **I.** *n* 1. (*way*) ruta *f;* (*of parade, bus*) recorrido *m;* NAUT rumbo *m;* (*of success*) camino *m* 2. *Am* (*delivery path*) recorrido *m;* **to have a paper ~** hacer un reparto de periódicos 3. *Am* (*road*) carretera *f* **II.** *vt* **to ~ sth via London** enviar algo vía Londres

routine [ruː'tiːn] **I.** *n* 1. *a.* INFOR rutina *f;* **he went into his usual ~** *inf* me vino con la misma cantinela de siempre 2. (*of dancer*) número *m* **II.** *adj* 1. (*regular*) habitual; (*inspection*) de rutina; (*medical case*) común 2. (*uninspiring*) rutinario, -a

routinely *adv* habitualmente

roux [ruː] *n no pl* mezcla de mantequilla y harina para espesar las salsas

rove [rəʊv, *Am:* roʊv] **I.** *vi* **to ~ over sth**

recorrer algo **II.** *vt* recorrer

rover ['rəʊvə', *Am:* 'roʊvə-] *n* trotamundos *m* *inv*

roving ['rəʊvɪŋ, *Am:* 'roʊv-] *adj* (*animal, thieves*) errante; (*ambassador*) itinerante

row¹ [rəʊ, *Am:* roʊ] *n* **1.** (*line: of houses, cars*) hilera *f;* (*of people, of seats*) fila *f;* **to stand in a** ~ estar en la fila **2.** (*succession*) sucesión *f;* **three times in a** ~ tres veces consecutivas

row² [raʊ] **I.** *n* **1.** (*quarrel*) pelea *f;* **to have a** ~ pelearse **2.** (*noise*) escándalo *m;* **to make a** ~ armar jaleo **II.** *vi inf* pelearse; **to** ~ **with sb** reñir con alguien

row³ [rəʊ, *Am:* roʊ] **I.** *vi* remar **II.** *vt* (*boat*) llevar; **to** ~ **sb across the lake** llevar a alguien en bote al otro lado del lago **III.** *n* paseo *m* en bote; **to go for a** ~ ir a dar un paseo en bote

rowan ['rəʊən, *Am:* 'roʊən] *n* serbal *m*

rowanberry ['rəʊən,beri, *Am:* 'roʊən-] *n* serba *f*

rowboat ['rəʊbəʊt, *Am:* 'roʊboʊt] *n Am* bote *m* de remos

rowdy ['raʊdi] <-ier, -iest> *adj* **1.** (*noisy*) alborotador(a) **2.** (*quarrelsome*) pendenciero, -a

rower ['rəʊə', *Am:* 'roʊə-] *n* remero, -a *m, f*

rowing *n no pl* SPORTS remo *m*

rowing boat *n Brit* bote *m* de remos **rowing club** *n* club *m* de remo

rowlock ['rɒlək, *Am:* 'raːlək] *n* NAUT tolete *m*

royal ['rɔɪəl] **I.** *adj* **1.** (*of monarch*) real; **the** ~ **we** el plural mayestático **2.** *fig* regio, -a; (*welcome*) espléndido, -a **3.** *inf* (*big*) soberano, -a **II.** *n inf* miembro *m* de la familia real

Royal Highness *n* Alteza *f* Real; **His/Her** ~ Su Alteza Real

royalist ['rɔɪəlɪst] **I.** *n* monárquico, -a *m, f* **II.** *adj* monárquico, -a

royal jelly *n* jalea *f* real

royalty ['rɔɪəlti, *Am:* -ti] <-ies> *n* **1.** *no pl* (*sovereignty*) realeza *f;* **to treat sb like** ~ tratar a alguien a cuerpo de rey **2.** *pl* (*payment*) derechos *mpl* de autor

RP [,ɑː'piː, *Am:* ,ɑːr-] *n no pl abbr of* **received pronunciation** pronunciación *estándar del inglés británico*

RPI [,ɑː'piː'aɪ] *n no pl, Brit abbr of* **retail price index** IPC *m*

rpm [,aːˈpiːˈem, *Am:* ,ɑːr-] *n abbr of* **revolutions per minute** rpm

RR [,ɑːrɑː'r] *n Am abbr of* **Railroad** F.C. *m*

RRP [,ɑː'rɑː'piː] *n no pl, Brit abbr of* **recommended retail price** PVP *m*

RSI [,ɑː'res'aɪ, *Am:* ,ɑːr-] *n abbr of* **repetitive strain injury** lesión *f* de la tensión repetida

RSPCA [,ɑː'res,piːsiː'eɪ, *Am:* ,ɑːr-] *n Brit abbr of* **Royal Society for the Prevention of Cruelty to Animals** ≈ asociación *f* protectora de animales

RSVP [,ɑː'resviː'piː, *Am:* ,ɑːr-] *vi abbr of* **répondez s'il vous plait** s.r.c.

Rt Hon. *n Brit* POL *abbr of* **Right Honourable**

≈ Excelentísimo Señor *m,* ≈ Excelentísima Señora *f* (*tratamiento protocolario que se da a los diputados británicos*)

rub [rʌb] **I.** *n* **1.** (*act of rubbing*) frotamiento *m;* **to give sth a** ~ frotar algo **2.** *liter* (*difficulty*) dificultad *f;* **there's the** ~ ahí está el quid de la cuestión **II.** <-bb-> *vt* frotar; (*one's eyes*) restregarse; (*one's hands*) frotarse; **to** ~ **sth clean** lustrar algo **III.** <-bb-> *vi* rozar
- **rub against** *vi* **to** ~ **sth** rozar con algo; (*cat*) restregarse contra algo
- **rub along** *vi Brit, inf* **1.** (*manage*) ir tirando **2. to** ~ **with sb** llevarse bien con alguien
- **rub down** *vt* **1.** (*smooth*) pulir; (*horse*) almohazar **2.** (*dry*) secar frotando
- **rub in** *vt* **1.** (*spread on skin*) aplicar frotando **2.** *inf* (*keep reminding*) reiterar; *pej* insistir en
- **rub off** **I.** *vi* **1.** (*become clean: stain*) irse **2. to** ~ **on sb** (*affect*) pegarse a alguien **II.** *vt* (*dirt*) quitar frotando
- **rub out** *vt* **1.** (*remove: writing*) borrar; (*dirt*) quitar **2.** *Am, inf* (*murder*) liquidar

rubber ['rʌbə', *Am:* -ə-] *n* **1.** (*material*) goma *f,* hule *m Méx* **2.** *Aus, Brit* (*pencil eraser*) goma *f* (de borrar), borrador *m Col* **3.** *Am, inf* (*condom*) goma *f,* forro *m RíoPl* **4.** *pl, Am* (*shoes*) chanclos *mpl* **5.** (*game*) serie de tres o cinco partidos; (*in bridge*) rubber *m*

rubber band *n* goma *f* (elástica) **rubber boots** *npl* botas *fpl* de goma **rubber cheque** *n inf* cheque *m* sin fondos **rubber gloves** *npl* guantes *mpl* de goma

rubberneck ['rʌbənek, *Am:* -ə-] **I.** *n* (*tourist*) turista *mf;* (*at accident*) mirón, -ona *m, f* **II.** *vi* (*sightsee*) hacer turismo; (*be nosy*) curiosear

rubber plant *n* planta *f* del caucho **rubber-stamp** **I.** *vt* (*decision*) dar el visto bueno a **II.** *n* (*device*) sello *m* de goma **rubber tree** *n* árbol *m* del caucho

rubbery <-ier, -iest> *adj* (*texture*) parecido a la goma; (*food*) correoso, -a

rubbing *n* frotamiento *m*

rubbish ['rʌbɪʃ] **I.** *n no pl, Brit* **1.** *inf* (*waste*) basura *f* **2.** *inf* (*nonsense*) tonterías *fpl* **II.** *vt* *Aus, Brit, inf* poner verde

rubbish bin *n* cubo *m* de la basura **rubbish chute** *n* vertedero *m* de basuras **rubbish collection** *n* recogida *f* de basuras **rubbish container** *n* contenedor *m* de basura **rubbish dump** *n,* **rubbish tip** *n* vertedero *m,* tiradero *m Méx*

rubbishy *adj Aus, Brit, inf* de pacotilla

rubble ['rʌbl] *n no pl* escombros *mpl*

rub-down ['rʌbdaʊn] *n* fricción *f*

rubella [ruː'belə] *n no pl* MED rubéola *f*

rubicund ['ruːbɪkənd, *Am:* -bəkʌnd] *adj* *liter* rubicundo, -a

rubric ['ruːbrɪk] *n* **1.** (*heading*) epígrafe *m* **2.** (*instructions*) normas *fpl* **3.** REL rúbrica *f*

ruby ['ruːbi] **I.** <-ies> *n* rubí *m* **II.** *adj* de color rubí

RUC [ˌɑːʳjuːˈsiː, Am: ˌɑːr-] n abbr of **Royal Ulster Constabulary** policía de Irlanda del norte

ruck [rʌk] I. n 1. (crowd) melé f 2. (fold) arruga f II. vt **to ~ up** (clothes) arrugar

rucksack [ˈrʌksæk] n Brit mochila f

ruckus [ˈrʌkəs] n Am, inf jaleo m, toletole m CSur

ructions [ˈrʌkʃənz] npl Aus, Brit, inf **there will be ~** se va a armar una gorda

rudder [ˈrʌdəʳ, Am: -əʳ] n AVIAT, NAUT timón m

rudderless adj a. fig sin timón

ruddy [ˈrʌdi] <-ier, -iest> adj 1. liter (cheeks) rubicundo, -a 2. (light) rojizo, -a 3. Aus, Brit, inf (bloody) maldito, -a

rude [ruːd] adj 1. (impolite) grosero, -a, meco, -a Méx 2. (vulgar) vulgar; (joke) verde 3. (sudden) brusco, -a; (surprise) desagradable 4. liter (unrefined) tosco, -a

rudimentary [ˌruːdɪˈmentəri, Am: -dəˈ-] adj rudimentario, -a

rudiments [ˈruːdɪmənt, Am: -də-] npl rudimentos mpl

rue [ruː] vt liter lamentar

rueful [ˈruːfəl] adj 1. (repentant) arrepentido, -a 2. (sad) triste

ruff [rʌf] n (collar) gorguera f; (of an animal) collar m

ruffian [ˈrʌfɪən] n iron canalla mf

ruffle [ˈrʌfl] I. vt 1. (agitate: hair) alborotar; (clothes) fruncir; (feathers) erizar 2. (upset) alterar II. n volante m

rug [rʌg] n 1. (small carpet) alfombra f 2. Brit (blanket) manta f

rugby [ˈrʌgbi] n no pl rugby m

rugged [ˈrʌgɪd] adj 1. (uneven: cliff, mountains) escarpado, -a; (landscape, country) accidentado, -a; (ground) desigual 2. (tough: face) de facciones duras; (construction, vehicle) resistente

ruin [ˈruːɪn] I. vt 1. (bankrupt) arruinar 2. (destroy: city, building) destruir 3. (spoil: dress, surprise) estropear; (child) malcriar II. n 1. (bankruptcy, downfall) ruina f; **drugs will be his ~** las drogas serán su ruina 2. pl (remains) ruinas fpl

ruination [ˌruːɪˈneɪʃən, Am: -əˈ-] n no pl ruina f

ruinous [ˈruːɪnəs, Am: ˈruːə-] adj ruinoso, -a

rule [ruːl] I. n 1. (law) regla f; (principle) norma f; **~s and regulations** reglamento m; **~s of the road** normas fpl de tráfico; **to be the ~** ser la norma; **to break a ~** infringir una norma; **to play (it) by the ~s** obedecer las reglas; **it is against the ~s** va contra las normas; **as a ~** por lo general 2. no pl (control) gobierno m; **the ~ of Henry VIII** el reinado de Enrique VIII 3. (measuring device) regla f ▶ a **~ of thumb** una regla general; **~s are made to be broken** las normas están para desobedecerlas II. vt 1. (govern: country) gobernar; (company) dirigir 2. (control) dominar 3. (draw) trazar con una regla; (paper) pautar

4. LAW (decide) dictaminar, fallar III. vi 1. (control) gobernar; (monarch) reinar 2. (predominate) imperar 3. LAW **to ~ for/against sb/sth** fallar a favor/en contra de alguien/algo

◆**rule off** vt separar con una línea

◆**rule out** vt descartar

rule book n reglamento m

ruler n 1. (governor) gobernante mf; (sovereign) soberano, -a m, f 2. (measuring device) regla f

ruling [ˈruːlɪŋ] I. adj 1. (governing) gobernante; (class) dirigente; (monarch) reinante 2. (primary) dominante II. n fallo m; **the final ~** la sentencia definitiva

rum¹ [rʌm] n ron m

rum² [rʌm] <rummer, rummest> adj Brit, dial, inf raro, -a

Rumania [ruˈmeɪnɪə, Am: roʊˈ-] n s. **Romania**

Rumanian [ruˈmeɪnɪən, Am: roʊˈ-] s. **Romanian**

rumba [ˈrʌmbə] n rumba f

rumble [ˈrʌmbl] I. n no pl 1. (sound) ruido m sordo; (of thunder) estruendo m; (of stomach) borborigmo m 2. Am, Aus, inf (fight) pelea f II. vi hacer un ruido sordo; (thunder) retumbar; **my stomach is ~ing** me suenan las tripas III. vt Brit, inf (person) calar; (plot, scheme) descubrir

rumbling I. n (sound) ruido m sordo; (of thunder) estruendo m; **there were ~s of war** se hablaba de una posible guerra II. adj retumbante

rumbustious [rʌmˈbʌstɪəs, Am: -tʃəs] adj Brit, inf bullicioso, -a

ruminant [ˈruːmɪnənt, Am: -mə-] ZOOL I. n rumiante mf II. adj rumiante

ruminate [ˈruːmɪneɪt, Am: -mə-] vi rumiar

ruminative [ˈruːmɪnətɪv, Am: -məˌneɪt̬ɪv] adj form meditabundo, -a

rummage [ˈrʌmɪdʒ] I. vi hurgar; (in drawer) revolver II. n no pl (search) **to have a ~ around for sth** buscar algo

rummage sale n mercadillo donde se venden objetos usados

rummy [ˈrʌmi] n no pl GAMES rummy m

rumor Am, **rumour** [ˈruːməʳ, Am: -mə] Brit, Aus I. n rumor m II. vt **it is ~ed that ...** se rumorea que...

rump [rʌmp] n 1. (back end: of horse) grupa f; (of bird) rabadilla f 2. (cut of beef) cuarto m trasero 3. iron (buttocks) trasero m

rumple [ˈrʌmpl] vt arrugar; **to ~ sb's hair** despeinar a alguien

rump steak n filete m de lomo de ternera

rumpus [ˈrʌmpəs] n no pl, inf jaleo m ▶**to raise a ~** armar un escándalo

run [rʌn] I. n 1. (jog) **to break into a ~** echar a correr; **to go for a ~** salir a correr; **to do sth at a ~** hacer algo deprisa y corriendo 2. (trip) viaje m; (of train) trayecto m; **to go for a ~ in the car** ir a dar una vuelta en el coche 3. (series) racha f; (of books) tirada f

4.(*demand*) demanda *f;* **a sudden ~ on the dollar** una súbita presión sobre el dólar; **a ~ on the banks** un pánico bancario **5.**(*type*) categoría *f* **6.**(*direction, tendency*) dirección *f;* (*of oppinion*) corriente *f;* **the ~ of events** el curso de los acontecimientos **7.**(*enclosure for animals*) corral *m* **8.**(*hole in tights*) carrera *f* **9.**SPORTS (*in baseball, cricket*) carrera *f;* (*ski slope*) pista *f* de esquí **10.**CINE, THEAT permanencia *f* en cartel **11.**MUS carrerilla *f* **12.**MIL bombing ~ bombardeo *m* ►**to give sb a ~ for their money** hacer sudar tinta a alguien; **to have a (good) ~ for one's money** no poder quejarse; **in the long ~** a la larga; **in the short ~** a corto plazo; **on the ~** deprisa y corriendo; **to be on the ~** huir de la justicia **II.** *vi* <ran, run> **1.**(*move fast*) correr; **to ~ for the bus** correr para no perder el autobús; **to ~ for help** correr en busca de ayuda; **~ for your lives!** ¡sálvese quien pueda! **2.**(*operate*) funcionar; **to ~ smoothly** ir sobre ruedas *fig* **3.**(*go, travel*) ir; **to ~ off the road** salirse de la carretera; **to ~ ashore/onto the rocks** NAUT embarrancar **4.**(*extend*) extenderse; **the road ~s along the coast** la carretera bordea la costa **5.**(*last*) **to ~ for two hours** durar dos horas; **to ~ and run** ser el cuento de nunca acabar *inf* **6.**(*be*) existir **7.**(*flow: river*) fluir; (*make-up*) correrse; (*nose*) gotear *inf;* **the tap is ~ning hot** por el grifo sale agua caliente **8.**(*enter election*) presentarse, postularse *AmL;* **to ~ for election/President** presentarse a las elecciones/como candidato a presidente **9.** + *adj* (*be*) **to ~ dry** (*river*) secarse; **to ~ short** (*water*) escasear **10.**(*say*) decir **III.** *vt* <ran, run> **1.**(*move fast*) **to ~ a race** participar en una carrera **2.**(*enter in race: candidate, horse*) presentar **3.**(*drive*) llevar; **to ~ sb home** llevar a alguien a casa; **to ~ a truck into a tree** chocar contra un árbol con un camión; **to ~ a ship ashore** hacer encallar un barco **4.**(*pass*) pasar **5.**(*operate*) poner en marcha; (*car*) llevar; (*computer program*) ejecutar; (*engine*) hacer funcionar; **to ~ a washing machine** poner una lavadora **6.**(*manage, govern*) dirigir, pilotear *AmL;* **to ~ a farm** tener una granja; **to ~ a government** estar al frente de un gobierno; **to ~ a household** llevar una casa **7.**(*conduct*) realizar; (*experiment, test*) llevar a cabo **8.**(*provide: course*) organizar **9.**(*let flow*) dejar correr; (*bath*) preparar **10.**(*show: article*) publicar; (*series*) emitir **11.**(*smuggle*) pasar de contrabando **12.**(*not heed: blockade*) romper; (*red light*) saltar(se) (en rojo) **13.**(*incur*) exponerse a; (*risk*) correr **14.**(*perform tasks*) **to ~ errands** hacer recados

◆**run about** *vi* andar de un lado para otro
◆**run across I.** *vi* cruzar corriendo **II.** *vt* toparse con
◆**run after** *vt* correr tras
◆**run against** *vt* POL ir contra
◆**run along** *vi* marcharse

◆**run away** *vi* escaparse; (*water*) derramarse
◆**run away with** *vt* apoderarse de
◆**run back** *vi* volver corriendo
◆**run down I.** *vi* (*clock*) parar; (*battery*) gastarse **II.** *vt* **1.**(*run over*) atropellar **2.**(*disparage*) hablar mal de **3.**(*capture*) capturar
◆**run in I.** *vi* entrar corriendo **II.** *vt* **1.**AUTO rodar **2.** *inf* (*capture*) detener
◆**run into** *vt* dar con; AUTO chocar con
◆**run off I.** *vi* escaparse; (*water*) derramarse **II.** *vt* **1.**(*water*) dejar correr **2.**TYPO tirar **3.**(*make quickly*) hacer deprisa; (*letter*) escribir deprisa
◆**run on** *vi* **1.**(*continue to run*) seguir corriendo **2.**(*conversation*) continuar; (*words*) estar escritos sin dejar espacio
◆**run out of** *vt* quedarse sin
◆**run over I.** *vi* (*person*) irse; (*fluid*) rebosar **II.** *vt* AUTO atropellar a
◆**run through** *vt* **1.**(*station*) pasar sin parar por **2.**(*money*) derrochar
◆**run up I.** *vt* **1.**subir corriendo **2.to ~ against difficulties** tropezar con dificultades **II.** *vt* **1.**(*flag*) izar **2.**(*make quickly*) hacer deprisa **3.**(*debt*) contraer; **to ~ debts** endeudarse

runabout ['rʌnəbaʊt] *n* AUTO coche *m* pequeño
runaround ['rʌnə'raʊnd] *n no pl* **to give sb the ~** traer a alguien al retortero
runaway ['rʌnəweɪ] **I.** *adj* **1.**(*train*) fuera de control; (*person*) fugitivo, -a; (*horse*) desbocado, -a **2.**(*enormous: success*) arrollador(a) **II.** *n* fugitivo, -a *m, f*
run-down [,rʌn'daʊn] **I.** *n* **1.**(*report*) resumen *m;* **to give sb a ~ on sth** poner a alguien al tanto de algo **2.** *no pl* (*reduction*) disminución *f;* (*of staff*) reducción *f* **II.** *adj* **1.**(*building, town*) mal conservado, -a **2.**(*person*) debilitado, -a
rune [ruːn] *n* runa *f*
rung¹ [rʌŋ] *n* **1.**(*ladder*) peldaño *m* **2.**(*level*) nivel *m*
rung² [rʌŋ] *pp of* **ring²**
run-in ['rʌnɪn] *n* **1.** *inf* (*argument*) altercado *m* **2.**(*prelude*) etapa *f* previa
runner ['rʌnəʳ, *Am:* -ɚ] *n* **1.**SPORTS (*person*) corredor/a *m(f);* (*horse*) caballo *m* de carreras **2.**(*messenger*) mensajero, -a *m, f* **3.**(*smuggler*) contrabandista *mf;* **drug ~** camello *m* **4.**(*rail*) riel *m;* (*on sledge*) patín *m* **5.**(*stem*) tallo *m* rastrero **6.**(*long rug*) alfombrilla *f* estrecha ►**to do a ~** *inf* largarse
runner bean *n Brit* habichuela *f*
runner-up [,rʌnər'ʌp, *Am:* -ɚ'-] *n* subcampeón, -ona *m, f*
running I. *n no pl* **1.**(*action of a runner*) carrera *f* **2.**(*operation*) acción *f;* (*of a machine*) funcionamiento *m;* **the day-to-day ~ of the business** el día a día del negocio ►**to be in/out of the ~** tener/no tener posibilidades de ganar **II.** *adj* **1.**(*consecutive*) sucesivo, -a; (*day*) consecutivo, -a **2.**(*ongoing*) continuado,

R

-a **3.** (*operating*) que está funcionando **4.** (*flowing*) que fluye

running back *n Am* SPORTS running back *m*

running costs *npl* gastos *mpl* de explotación **running order** *n* buen estado *m*

runny ['rʌni] <-ier, -iest> *adj* líquido, -a; (*sauce*) acuoso, -a

run-off ['rʌnɒf] *n* **1.** POL desempate *m* **2.** SPORTS segunda vuelta *f* **3.** (*rainfall*) escorrentía *f*

run-of-the-mill [ˌrʌnəvðə'mɪl] *adj* corriente y moliente

runt [rʌnt] *n* **1.** ZOOL enano *m* **2.** *inf* (*weakling*) redrojo *m*

run-through ['rʌnθruː] *n* THEAT, MUS ensayo *m* (rápido); **to have a ~ of sth** ensayar algo

run-up ['rʌnʌp] *n* **1.** SPORTS carrerilla *f* **2.** (*prelude*) período *m* previo; **the ~ to sth** el preludio de algo

runway ['rʌnweɪ] *n* pista *f*

rupee [ruː'piː, *Am:* 'ruːpiː] *n* rupia *f*

rupture ['rʌptʃəʳ, *Am:* -tʃəʳ] **I.** *vi* romperse **II.** *vt* romper; **to ~ oneself** herniarse **III.** *n* **1.** (*act of bursting*) ruptura *f* **2.** (*hernia*) hernia *f*, relajadura *f Méx*

rural ['rʊərəl, *Am:* 'rʊrəl] *adj* rural

ruse [ruːz] *n* treta *f*

rush¹ [rʌʃ] *n* BOT junco *m*

rush² [rʌʃ] **I.** *n* **1.** (*hurry*) prisa *f*; **to be in a ~** tener prisa; **to leave in a ~** salir corriendo **2.** (*charge, attack*) ataque *m*; (*surge*) ola *f*; (*of air*) corriente *f*; (*of customers*) oleada *f*; **there's been a ~ on oil** ha habido una fuerte demanda de aceite; **gold ~** fiebre *f* del oro **3.** (*dizziness*) mareo *m* **II.** *vi* ir deprisa **III.** *vt* **1.** (*do quickly*) hacer precipitadamente **2.** (*hurry*) apresurar **3.** (*attack*) asaltar

◆**rush about** *vi* correr de acá para allá

◆**rush at** *vt* precipitarse hacia

◆**rush into** *vt* **1.** **to ~ sth** precipitarse en algo **2.** **to rush sb into doing sth** presionar a alguien para que haga algo

◆**rush out I.** *vi* (*leave*) salir precipitadamente **II.** *vt* (*publish*) publicar con urgencia

◆**rush through** *vt* aprobar urgentemente

◆**rush up** *vi* subir corriendo

rush hour *n* hora *f* punta **rush order** *n* pedido *m* urgente

rusk [rʌsk] *n* bizcocho *m*

russet ['rʌsɪt] *liter* **I.** *adj* bermejo, -a **II.** *n no pl* color *m* bermejo

Russia ['rʌʃə] *n* Rusia *f*

Russian ['rʌʃən] **I.** *adj* ruso, -a **II.** *n* **1.** (*person*) ruso, -a *m, f* **2.** (*language*) ruso *m*

rust [rʌst] **I.** *n no pl* **1.** (*decay*) oxidación *f* **2.** (*substance*) herrumbre *f* **3.** (*colour*) color *m* herrumbre **II.** *vi* oxidarse **III.** *vt* oxidar

rust-coloured *adj* de color herrumbre

rustic ['rʌstɪk] *adj* **1.** (*rural*) rústico, -a **2.** (*simple, plain*) sencillo, -a

rustle ['rʌsl] **I.** *vi* (*leaves*) susurrar; (*paper*) crujir **II.** *vt* **1.** (*leaves*) hacer susurrar; (*paper*) hacer crujir **2.** (*steal: cattle*) robar **III.** *n* (*of*

leaves) susurro *m*; (*of paper*) crujido *m*

rustler ['rʌsləʳ, *Am:* -əʳ] *n* ladrón, -ona *m, f* de ganado

rustproof ['rʌstpruːf] *adj* inoxidable

rusty ['rʌsti] <-ier, -iest> *adj* **1.** (*metal*) oxidado, -a **2.** (*in skill*) falto, -a de práctica; **my Spanish is a bit ~** tengo bastante olvidado el castellano

rut¹ [rʌt] *n* bache *m* ▶**to be stuck in a ~** estar metido en la rutina

rut² [rʌt] *n no pl* ZOOL celo *m*

rutabaga [ˌruːtə'beɪgə, *Am:* -t̬ə'-] *n Am* nabo *m* sueco

ruthless ['ruːθləs] *adj* (*person*) despiadado, -a; (*ambition*) implacable; **to be ~ in doing sth** hacer algo sin piedad; **to be ~ in enforcing the law** hacer cumplir la ley a raja tabla

ruthlessness *n no pl* crueldad *f*

RV [ˌɑː'viː, *Am:* ˌɑːr-] *Am abbr of* **recreational vehicle** caravana *f* pequeña

Rwanda [rʊ'ændə, *Am:* -'ɑːn-] *n* Ruanda *f*

Rwandan **I.** *adj* ruandés, -esa **II.** *n* ruandés, -esa *m, f*

rye [raɪ] *n no pl* centeno *m*

S

S, s [es] *n* S, s; **~ for Sugar** S de Soria

s [es] *abbr of* **second** s

S [es] *n no pl* **1.** *abbr of* **south** S *m* **2.** *Am abbr of* **satisfactory** suficiente *m*

SA **1.** *abbr of* **South Africa** Sudáfrica *f* **2.** *abbr of* **South America** Sudamérica *f* **3.** *abbr of* **South Australia** sur *m* de Australia

Sabbath ['sæbəθ] *n* sabat *m*

sabbatical [sə'bætɪkl, *Am:* -'bæt̬-] UNIV **I.** *n* año *m* de permiso **II.** *adj* sabático, -a

saber ['seɪbəʳ, *Am:* -bəʳ] *n Am s.* **sabre**

sable ['seɪbl] *n no pl* (*fur*) marta *f*

sabotage ['sæbətɑːʒ] **I.** *vt* sabotear **II.** *n* sabotaje *m*

saboteur [ˌsæbə'tɜːʳ, *Am:* -'tɜːr] *n* saboteador(a) *m(f)*

sabre ['seɪbəʳ, *Am:* -bəʳ] *n Aus, Brit* sable *m*

sabre-rattling ['seɪbəˌrætlɪŋ, *Am:* -bəˌ-] *n pej* patriotería *f*

sac [sæk] *n* BIO, ANAT saco *m*

saccharin ['sækərɪn] *n no pl* sacarina *f*

saccharine ['sækəriːn, *Am:* -əˌɪn] *adj pej* empalagoso, -a

sachet ['sæʃeɪ, *Am:* -'-] *n* bolsita *f*

sack¹ [sæk] **I.** *n* **1.** (*large bag*) saco *m*; (*paper or plastic bag*) bolsa *f* **2.** *Am* (*paper, plastic*) bolsa *f* **3.** *no pl, inf* (*bed*) **to hit the ~** irse al catre *inf* **4.** *no pl, inf* (*dismissal*) **to get the ~** ser despedido; **to give sb the ~** despedir a alguien **II.** *vt* despedir

sack² [sæk] **I.** *n no pl* (*plundering*) saqueo *m* **II.** *vt* (*plunder*) saquear

sackcloth ['sækklɒ:θ, *Am:* -klɑ:θ] *n no pl* arpillera *f* ►**to be wearing** ~ **and** <u>ashes</u> llevar el hábito de penitencia

sackful ['sækfʊl] *n* saco *m*

sacking[1] ['sækɪŋ] *n* **1.** *no pl* (*sackcloth*) arpillera *f* **2.** *inf* (*dismissal*) despido *m*

sacking[2] ['sækɪŋ] *n* (*plundering*) saqueo *m*

sack race *n* carrera *f* de sacos

sacrament ['sækrəmənt] *n* (*ceremony*) sacramento *m;* **the** ~ (*consecrated bread and wine*) la Eucaristía

sacramental [ˌsækrə'mentl, *Am:* -t̬l] *adj* sacramental

sacred ['seɪkrɪd] *adj* sagrado, -a; **to be** ~ **to sb** estar consagrado a alguien; **is nothing** ~ **to you?** ¿no tienes respeto por nada?

sacrifice ['sækrɪfaɪs, *Am:* -rə-] **I.** *vt* **1.** *a.* REL sacrificar **2.** (*give up: time, money*) renunciar a; **to** ~ **one's free time** privarse de tiempo libre **II.** *vi* **to** ~ **to the gods** hacer sacrificios a los dioses **III.** *n* sacrificio *m;* **at the** ~ **of sth** en detrimento de algo

sacrilege ['sækrɪlɪdʒ, *Am:* -rə-] *n* sacrilegio *m*

sacrilegious [ˌsækrɪ'lɪdʒəs, *Am:* -rə'-] *adj* sacrílego, -a

sacristan ['sækrɪstən] *n* sacristán *m*

sacristy ['sækrɪsti] *n* REL sacristía *f*

sacrosanct ['sækrəʊsæŋkt, *Am:* -roʊ-] *adj* sacrosanto, -a

sacrum ['seɪkrəm] <-a> *n* sacro *m*

SAD [ˌeser'diː] *n abbr of* **seasonal affective disorder** trastorno *m* afectivo estacional

sad [sæd] <-dd-> *adj* **1.** (*unhappy*) triste; **it is** ~ **that** es una pena que +*subj;* **to make sb** ~ poner triste a alguien; **to become** ~ entristecerse **2.** (*pathetic*) patético, -a **3.** (*deplorable, shameful*) lamentable; ~ **to say** ... lamentablemente...

sadden ['sædən] *vt* entristecer; **to be deeply** ~**ed** estar muy afligido

saddle ['sædl] **I.** *n* **1.** (*seat*) silla *f* de montar **2.** GASTR cuarto *m* trasero ►**to** <u>be</u> **in the** ~ llevar las riendas **II.** *vt* **1.** (*horse*) ensillar **2.** *inf* (*burden*) **to** ~ **sb with sth** encajar algo a alguien

saddlebag ['sædlbæg] *n* alforja *f*

saddler ['sædlər, *Am:* -lə-] *n* talabartero, -a *m, f*

saddle-sore ['sædlsɔ:r] *adj* dolorido, -a en las posaderas; **he's** ~ le duelen las posaderas de montar

sadism ['seɪdɪzəm, *Am:* 'sædɪ-] *n no pl* sadismo *m*

sadist ['seɪdɪst, *Am:* 'sæd-] *n* sádico, -a *m, f*

sadistic [sə'dɪstɪk] *adj* sádico, -a

sadly *adv* **1.** (*unhappily*) tristemente **2.** (*regretably*) desgraciadamente; **to be** ~ **mistaken** estar muy equivocado

sadness ['sædnəs] *n no pl* tristeza *f*

sae, SAE [ˌeser'iː] *n abbr of* **stamped addressed envelope** *sobre con las señas de uno y con sello*

safari [sə'fɑ:ri] *n* safari *m;* **to go on** ~ irse de safari

safari park *n* safari-park *m*

safe [seɪf] **I.** *adj* **1.** (*free of danger*) seguro, -a; (*driver*) prudente; **at a** ~ **distance** a una distancia prudente; **it is not** ~ **to** ... es peligroso... +*infin;* **just to be** ~ por precaución; ~ **journey!** ¡buen viaje! **2.** (*secure*) salvo, -a; **to feel** ~ sentirse a salvo; **to keep sth in a** ~ **place** guardar algo en un lugar seguro; **to put sth somewhere** ~ poner algo a buen recaudo; **to win by a** ~ **margin** ganar con un amplio margen **3.** (*certain*) seguro, -a; **a** ~ **seat** un escaño fijo; **a** ~ **bet** una apuesta segura **4.** (*trustworthy*) de fiar ►**to be on the** ~ <u>side</u> ... para mayor seguridad...; **it is** <u>better</u> **to be** ~ **than sorry** *prov* más vale prevenir que curar *prov;* ~ **and** <u>sound</u> sano y salvo **II.** *n* caja *f* de caudales

safe-blower *n*, **safebreaker** ['seɪfˌbreɪkər, *Am:* -kə-] *n Aus, Brit* ladrón, -ona *m, f* de cajas fuertes **safe deposit box** *n* caja *f* de seguridad

safeguard ['seɪfgɑ:d, *Am:* -gɑ:rd] **I.** *vt* salvaguardar **II.** *vi* protegerse; **to** ~ **against sth** protegerse contra algo **III.** *n* salvaguardia *f;* **as a** ~ **against sth** para evitar algo

safekeeping [ˌseɪf'ki:pɪŋ] *n no pl* custodia *f;* **to be in sb's** ~ estar bajo la custodia de alguien

safely *adv* sin riesgos; **I can** ~ **say** ... puedo decir sin temor a equivocarme que...

safe sex [seɪf'seks] *n* sexo *m* seguro

safety ['seɪfti] *n no pl* (*being safe*) seguridad *f;* **a place of** ~ un lugar seguro; **for sb's** ~ para la seguridad de alguien ►**there's** ~ **in** <u>numbers</u> *prov* cuantos más, menos peligro

safety belt *n* cinturón *m* de seguridad **safety catch** *n* (*on gun*) seguro *m* **safety curtain** *n* THEAT telón *m* de seguridad **safety glass** *n* vidrio *m* inastillable **safety margin** *n* margen *m* de seguridad **safety measures** *npl* medidas *fpl* de seguridad **safety net** *n* **1.** red *f* (de seguridad) **2.** *fig* protección *f* **safety pin** *n* imperdible *m* **safety razor** *n* maquinilla *f* de afeitar **safety regulations** *npl* normas *fpl* de seguridad **safety valve** *n* válvula *f* de seguridad

saffron ['sæfrən] *n no pl* azafrán *m*

sag [sæg] **I.** <-gg-> *vi* **1.** (*droop*) combarse, achiguarse *Arg, Chile* **2.** (*sink*) hundirse; (*spirit*) decaer; (*interest*) decrecer **II.** *n no pl* **1.** (*drooping condition*) bajada *f* **2.** (*fall*) caída *f*

saga ['sɑ:gə] *n* saga *f*

sagacious [sə'geɪʃəs] *adj form* sagaz

sagacity [sə'gæsəti, *Am:* -t̬i] *n no pl, form* sagacidad *f*

sage[1] [seɪdʒ] *liter* **I.** *adj* (*wise*) sabio, -a **II.** *n* (*wise man*) sabio *m*

sage[2] [seɪdʒ] *n no pl* (*herb*) salvia *f*

Sagittarius [ˌsædʒɪ'teərɪəs, *Am:* -ə'teri-] *n* Sagitario *m*

Sahara [sə'hɑːrə, *Am:* -'herə] *n* the ~ (**Desert**) el Sáhara
said [sed] I. *pp, pt of* say II. *adj* dicho, -a
sail [seɪl] I. *n* 1. (*on boat*) vela *f* 2. (*windmill blade*) aspa *f* ►to set ~ (**for a place**) zarpar (hacia un lugar); **under full** ~ a toda vela II. *vi* 1. (*travel*) navegar; **to ~ around the world** dar la vuelta al mundo en barco 2. (*start voyage*) zarpar 3. (*move smoothly*) deslizarse 4. *fig* (*do easily*) **to ~ through sth** hacer algo con facilidad ►**to ~ against the wind** nadar a contracorriente; **to ~ close to the wind** pisar terreno peligroso III. *vt* 1. (*manage: boat, ship*) gobernar 2. (*navigate*) cruzar; **to ~ the seas** surcar los mares
sailboard ['seɪlbɔːd, *Am:* -bɔːrd] *n* tabla *f* de windsurf
sailboarding *n* windsurf *m*
sailboat ['seɪlbəʊt, *Am:* -boʊt] *n Am* (*sailing boat*) barco *m* de vela
sailing *n* 1. NAUT navegación *f* 2. SPORTS vela *f* 3. (*departure*) salida *f*
sailing boat *n Aus, Brit* barco *m* de vela **sailing ship** *n*, **sailing vessel** *n* velero *m*
sailor ['seɪlə', *Am:* -lə] *n* 1. (*seaman*) marinero, -a *m, f* 2. SPORTS navegante *mf*
sailor suit *n* traje *m* de marinero
saint [seɪnt, sənt] *n* santo, -a *m, f*
sainted *adj* santo, -a; **my ~ aunt!** *fig* ¡caray!
Saint Kitts and Nevis *n* Islas *fpl* de San Cristóbal y Nieves
saintliness *n* santidad *f*
saintly ['seɪntli] *adj* santo, -a; (*life*) ejemplar

El **Saint Patrick's Day**, 17 de marzo, es el día en que se celebra el patrón de Irlanda. En los EE.UU., sin embargo, no es día de fiesta oficial. A pesar de ello mucha gente lleva el color verde y se organizan fiestas. En muchas ciudades hay desfiles, de los cuales el más grande y famoso es el que tiene lugar en New York City.

Saint's Day *n* santo *m*
sake¹ [seɪk] *n* 1. (*purpose*) **for the ~ of sth** por algo 2. (*benefit*) **for the ~ of sb** por alguien ►**for Christ's ~!** *pej* ¡por Dios!; **for goodness ~!** ¡por el amor de Dios!; **for old times'** ~ por los viejos tiempos
sake² *n*, **saki** ['sɑːki] *n* sake *m*
salable ['seɪləbl] *adj Am s.* **saleable**
salacious [sə'leɪʃəs] *adj pej* salaz
salad ['sæləd] *n* ensalada *f*, verde *m CSur*
salad bowl *n* ensaladera *f* **salad cream** *n Brit*: aliño para la ensalada parecido a la mayonesa **salad days** *npl* años *mpl* mozos **salad dressing** *n* aliño *m*
salami [sə'lɑːmi] *n no pl* salami *m*, salame *m CSur*
sal-ammoniac [ˌsælə'məʊnɪæk, *Am:* -'moʊ-] *n* sal *f* amoníaca
salaried ['sælərɪd] *adj* (*employee, staff*) asalariado, -a

salary ['sæləri] *n* sueldo *m*
salary cut *n* reducción *f* salarial **salary review** *n* revisión *f* de sueldos **salary scale** *n* banda *f* salarial
sale [seɪl] *n* 1. (*act of selling*) venta *f* 2. (*reduced prices*) saldo *m*; **the ~s** las rebajas; **charity ~** venta *f* benéfica; **end-of-season ~** liquidación *f* de final de temporada 3. (*auction*) subasta *f* 4. *pl* (*department that sells*) (departamento *m* de) ventas *fpl* ►**to put sth up for** ~ poner algo en venta; **for** ~ se vende; **on** ~ en venta
saleable ['seɪləbl] *adj* vendible
sale price *n* precio *m* de venta
saleroom ['seɪlruːm] *n Am* sala *f* de subastas
sales analysis *n* análisis *m inv* de las ventas
sales assistant *n Brit* dependiente, -a *m, f*
sales book *n* libro *m* de ventas **sales campaign** *n* campaña *f* de ventas **sales-clerk** *n Am* dependiente, -a *m, f* **sales conference** *n* conferencia *f* de ventas **sales department** *n* sección *f* de ventas **sales director** *n* director(a) *m(f)* de ventas **sales drive** *n* promoción *f* de ventas **sales executive** *n* ejecutivo, -a *m, f* de ventas **sales figures** *npl* cifras *fpl* de ventas **sales force** *n* personal *m* de ventas **sales forecast** *n* previsión *f* de ventas **salesgirl** *n* dependienta *f* **sales invoice** *n* FIN factura *f* de venta(s) **sales ledger** *n* FIN libro *m* de ventas **sales literature** *n* ECON propaganda *f* de venta **salesman** (*in shop*) dependiente *m*; (*for company*) representante *m*; **door-to-door ~** vendedor *m* a domicilio
sales manager *n* jefe *mf* de ventas **salesmanship** *n no pl* arte *m* de vender **sales meeting** *n* reunión *f* de ventas **salesperson** *n* vendedor(a) *m(f)* **sales pitch** *n* rollo *m* publicitario **sales receipt** *n* comprobante *m* de caja **sales rep** *n inf*, **sales representative** *n* agente *mf* de ventas **sales revenue** *n* facturación *f* **salesroom** *n Brit* sala *f* de subastas **sales talk** *n* palabrería *f* de vendedor **sales tax** *n Am* FIN impuesto *m* sobre las ventas **saleswoman** *n* (*in a shop*) dependienta *f*; (*seller*) vendedora *f*
salient ['seɪlɪənt, *Am:* 'seɪljənt] *adj* 1. (*angle, structure*) saliente 2. *fig* sobresaliente
saline ['seɪlaɪn, *Am:* -liːn] I. *adj* salino, -a; **~ drip** gota a gota *m* salino II. *n* solución *f* salina
saliva [sə'laɪvə] *n no pl* saliva *f*
salivate ['sælɪveɪt, *Am:* 'sælə-] *vi* salivar
sallow ['sæləʊ, *Am:* -oʊ] *adj* <-er, -est> (*skin*) cetrino, -a
sally ['sæli] I. <-ies> *n* salida *f* II. <-ie-> *vi* MIL hacer una salida; **to ~ forth** ponerse en marcha; *fig* salir resueltamente
salmon ['sæmən] *n* salmón *m*; **smoked ~** salmón ahumado
salmonella [ˌsælmə'nelə] *n no pl* 1. (*bacteria*) salmonella *f* 2. (*illness*) salmonelosis *f*
salmon farm *n* piscifactoría *f* de salmón

salmon ladder *n* paso *m* salmonero
salmon trout *n* trucha *f* asalmonada
salon ['sælɒn, *Am:* se'lɑ:n] *n* **1.** (*reception room*) recibidor *m* **2.** (*beauty establishment*) beauty ~ salón *m* de belleza; hairdressing ~ peluquería *f*
saloon [sə'lu:n] *n* **1.** Brit (*car*) turismo *m* **2.** *Am* (*bar*) bar *m*
salsify ['sælsɪfaɪ, *Am:* -sə-] *n no pl* salsifí *m*
salt [sɔ:lt] I. *n* sal *f;* bath ~s sales de baño; smelling ~s sales aromáticas ►~ of the earth sal de la tierra; to take sth with a grain [*o* pinch] of ~ creerse la mitad de la mitad de algo; to rub ~ in the wound hurgar en la herida; to be worth one's ~ merecer el pan que se come II. *vt* **1.** (*add salt to*) poner sal **2.** (*preserve in salt*) salar **3.** (*sprinkle with salt*) sazonar con sal III. *adj* salado, -a
SALT [sɔ:lt] *n abbr of* Strategic Arms Limitation Talks Conversaciones *fpl* para la limitación de armas estratégicas
salt cellar *n* salero *m* **salt lake** *n* lago *m* de agua salada **salt mine** *n* mina *f* de sal
saltpeter *n*, **saltpetre** [ˌsɔ:lt'pi:tər, *Am:* 'sɔ:lt̬pi:t̬ər] *n no pl* salitre *m*
salt shaker *n Am, Aus* salero *m* **salt water** *n no pl* **1.** (*sea water*) agua *f* de mar **2.** (*water with salt*) agua *f* salada
saltwater ['sɔ:lt̬wɔ:tər, *Am:* 'sɔ:lt̬wɑ:t̬ər] *adj* de agua salada
salty ['sɔ:lti, *Am:* 'sɔ:lt̬i] *adj* (*taste*) salado, -a
salubrious [sə'lu:briəs] *adj form* saludable
salutary ['sæljətəri, *Am:* -ter-] *adj* saludable
salutation [ˌsæljə'teɪʃən] *n* saludo
salute [sə'lu:t] I. *vt* **1.** *a.* MIL saludar **2.** *fig* (*honour*) to ~ sb rendir homenaje a alguien II. *vi a.* MIL saludar III. *n* MIL **1.** (*hand gesture*) saludo *m;* to take the ~ presidir el desfile **2.** (*ceremonial firing of guns*) salva *f*
Salvadorian [ˌsælvə'dɔ:riən] I. *adj* salvadoreño, -a II. *n* salvadoreño, -a *m, f*
salvage ['sælvɪdʒ] I. *vt* salvar II. *n no pl* **1.** (*retrieval*) salvamento *m* **2.** (*things saved*) objetos *mpl* salvados
salvage operation *n* operación *f* de salvamento **salvage value** *n* valor *m* de desecho **salvage vessel** *n* buque *m* de salvamento
salvation [sæl'veɪʃən] *n no pl* salvación *f*
Salvation Army *n no pl* Ejército *m* de Salvación
salve [sælv, *Am:* sæv] I. *n* **1.** (*ointment*) ungüento *m* **2.** *fig* bálsamo *m* II. *vt* curar; *fig* (*conscience*) tranquilizar
salver ['sælvər, *Am:* -və˞] *n form* bandeja *f*
salvo ['sælvəʊ, *Am:* -voʊ] <-(e)s> *n* salva *f;* to fire a ~ disparar una salva; ~ of applause salva de aplausos
sal volatile [ˌsælvə'lætəli, *Am:* -voʊ'læt̬-] *n no pl* sal *f* de amonio
SAM [sæm] *n abbr of* surface-to-air missile proyectil *m* tierra-aire
same [seɪm] I. *adj* **1.** (*identical*) igual; the ~ (as sb/sth) igual (que alguien/algo); to go the ~ way (as sb) llevar el mismo camino (que alguien) **2.** (*not another*) mismo, -a; the ~ el mismo; at the ~ time al mismo tiempo **3.** (*unvarying*) idéntico, -a ►to be one and the ~ ser lo mismo; by the ~ token del mismo modo II. *pron* **1.** (*nominal*) the ~ el mismo, la misma, lo mismo; she's much the ~ sigue igual; it's always the ~ siempre es lo mismo **2.** (*adverbial*) it's all the ~ to me me da igual; it's not the ~ as before ya no es lo mismo; it comes to the ~ (lo da lo mismo); all the ~ de todas formas; ~ to you igualmente III. *adv* igual
sameness *n no pl* **1.** (*similarity*) igualdad *f* **2.** (*monotony*) monotonía *f*
Samoa [sə'məʊə, *Am:* sə'moʊə] *n* Samoa *f*
Samoan I. *adj* samoano, -a II. *n* samoano, -a *m, f*
sample ['sɑ:mpl, *Am:* 'sæm-] I. *n* muestra *f;* free ~ muestra gratuita; urine ~ muestra de orina II. *vt* **1.** (*try*) probar **2.** (*survey*) tomar muestras
sample book *n* muestrario *m*
sampler ['sɑ:mplər, *Am:* 'sæmplə˞] *n* **1.** (*embroidery*) dechado *m* **2.** *Am* (*collection*) muestra *f* **3.** MUS equipo *m* de grabación
sampling ['sɑ:mplɪŋ, *Am:* 'sæm-] *n* muestreo *m*
sanatorium [ˌsænə'tɔ:riəm] <-s *o* -ria> *n* sanatorio *m*
sanctify ['sæŋktɪfaɪ] <-ie-> *vt* **1.** REL santificar **2.** *fig* (*legitimize*) avalar
sanctimonious [ˌsæŋktɪ'məʊniəs, *Am:* -'moʊ-] *adj pej* mojigato, -a
sanction ['sæŋkʃən] I. *n* **1.** *no pl* (*approval*) autorización *f;* to give one's ~ to sth dar su aprobación a algo **2.** LAW, POL sanción *f* II. *vt* **1.** (*authorize*) autorizar **2.** (*approve*) aprobar **3.** (*penalize*) sancionar
sanctity ['sæŋktəti, *Am:* -t̬i] *n no pl* **1.** REL (*holiness*) santidad *f* **2.** (*sacredness*) inviolabilidad *f*
sanctuary ['sæŋktʃʊəri, *Am:* -tʃueri] *n* <-ies> **1.** REL (*holy place*) santuario *m* **2.** (*area around altar*) sagrario *m* **3.** *no pl* (*place of refuge*) refugio *m;* to seek ~ in sth refugiarse en algo **4.** (*area for animals*) reserva *f;* wildlife ~ reserva natural
sand [sænd] I. *n no pl* arena *f;* fine/coarse ~ arena fina/gruesa; grains of ~ granos *mpl* de arena; the ~s (*beach*) la playa ►the ~s of time are running out el tiempo se agota II. *vt* **1.** (*cover with sand*) enarenar **2.** (*make smooth*) lijar; (*floor*) pulir
sandal ['sændl] *n* sandalia *f,* quimba *f AmL*
sandalwood ['sændlwʊd] *n no pl* sándalo *m*
sandbag ['sændbæg] I. *n* saco *m* de arena II. <-gg-> *vt* proteger con sacos de arena
sandbank ['sændbæŋk] *n*, **sandbar** ['sændbɑ:ʳ, *Am:* -bɑ:r] *n* banco *m* de arena
sandblast ['sændblɑ:st, *Am:* -blæst] *vt* pulir con chorro de arena

S

sandbox *n Am s.* **sandpit**
sandboy ['sændbɔɪ] *n* to be as <u>happy</u> as a ~ estar como unas pascuas
sandcastle *n* castillo *m* de arena **sand dune** *n* duna *f* **sand flea** *n* pulga *f* de mar **sandglass** *n* reloj *m* de arena **sand martin** *n* avión *m* zapador
sandpaper ['sændpeɪpəʳ, *Am:* -pɚ] I. *n* no *pl* papel *m* de lija II. *vt* lijar
sandpiper ['sænd‚paɪpəʳ, *Am:* -pɚ] *n* andarríos *m inv*
sandpit *n Brit* cajón *m* de arena (*donde juegan los niños*) **sandshoe** *n* 1.(*beach shoe*) playera *f* 2.*Aus* (*sport shoe*) zapatilla *f* **sandstone** *n no pl* piedra *f* arenisca **sandstorm** *n* tormenta *f* de arena
sandwich ['sænwɪdʒ, *Am:* 'sændwɪtʃ] I.<-es> *n* bocadillo *m;* (*made with sliced bread*) sándwich *m* II. *vt* intercalar
sandwich board *n* cartelón *m* **sandwich counter** *n* merendero *m* **sandwich course** <- -es> *n Brit* UNIV *programa que intercala estudio con prácticas profesionales* **sandwich man** <- -men> *n* hombre-anuncio *m*
sandy ['sændi] *adj* <-ier, -iest> arenoso, -a; (*hair*) rubio, -a rojizo, -a
sane [seɪn] *adj* 1.(*of sound mind*) cuerdo, -a 2.(*sensible*) sensato, -a
sang [sæŋ] *pt of* **sing**
sanguine ['sæŋgwɪn] *adj form* optimista
sanitarium [‚sænɪ'teərɪəm, *Am:* -'terɪ-] <-s *o* -ria> *n Am* clínica *f*
sanitary ['sænɪtəri, *Am:* -teri] *adj* 1.(*relating to hygiene*) sanitario, -a 2.(*clean*) higiénico, -a
sanitary towel *n Brit,* **sanitary napkin** *n Am* compresa *f* (higiénica)
sanitation [‚sænɪ'teɪʃən] *n no pl* saneamiento *m*
sanity ['sænəti, *Am:* -ʈi] *n no pl* 1.(*of person*) cordura *f* 2.(*of decision*) sensatez *f*
sank [sæŋk] *pt of* **sink**
Santa (Claus) [‚sæntə('klɔːz, *Am:* 'sænʈə-‚(klaːz)] *n no pl* Papá *m* Noel
sap¹ [sæp] *n no pl* 1.BOT savia *f* 2.(*vitality*) vitalidad *f*
sap² [sæp] <-pp-> *vt* 1.(*weaken*) socavar 2.MIL zapar
sap³ [sæp] *n inf* (*fool*) papanatas *mf*
sapling ['sæplɪŋ] *n* pimpollo *m*
sapper ['sæpəʳ, *Am:* -ɚ] *n Brit* zapador(a) *m(f)*
sapphire ['sæfaɪəʳ, *Am:* -aɪɚ] I. *n* 1.(*stone*) zafiro *m* 2.(*colour*) azul *m* zafiro II. *adj* 1.(*necklace, ring*) de zafiro 2.(*colour*) azul zafiro
sarcasm ['saːkæzəm, *Am:* 'saːr-] *n no pl* sarcasmo *m*
sarcastic [saː'kæstɪk, *Am:* saːr'-] *adj* sarcástico, -a
sarcophagus [saːr'kaːfə-] <-es *o* -gi> *n* sarcófago *m*
sardine [saː'diːn, *Am:* saːr'-] *n* sardina *f* ▶to

be <u>packed</u> (in) like ~s estar como sardinas en lata
Sardinia [saː'dɪnɪə, *Am:* saːr-] *n* Cerdeña *f*
Sardinian I. *n* sardo, -a *m, f f* II. *adj* sardo, -a
sardonic [saː'dɒnɪk, *Am:* saːr'daːnɪk] *adj* sardónico, -a
sari ['saːri] *n* sari *m*
sartorial [saː'tɔːrɪəl, *Am:* saːr'-] *adj* (*elegance*) en el vestir
SAS [‚eseɪ'es] *n Brit* MIL *abbr of* **Special Air Service** *comando de operaciones especiales del ejército británico*
SASE [‚eseɪes'iː] *n Am abbr of* **self-addressed stamped envelope** *sobre con las señas de uno y con sello*
sash¹ [sæʃ] <-es> *n* faja *f*
sash² [sæʃ] <-es> *n* ARCHIT marco *m* corredizo de ventana
sash window *n* ARCHIT ventana *f* de guillotina
sat [sæt] *pt, pp of* **sit**
SAT *n Am abbr of* **scholastic aptitude test** *examen que se realiza al final de la enseñanza secundaria*
Satan ['seɪtən] *n no pl* Satanás *m*
satanic [sə'tænɪk] *adj* 1.(*evil*) demoníaco, -a 2.(*relating to Satanism*) satánico, -a
Satanism *n no pl* Satanismo *m*
satchel ['sætʃəl] *n* bolsa *f,* busaca *f Col, Ven*
sate [seɪt] *vt form* saciar; **to ~ sb (with sth)** hartar a alguien (con algo); **to be ~d (with sth)** estar saciado (de algo)
satellite ['sætəlaɪt, *Am:* 'sæʈ-] I. *n* 1.ASTR, TECH satélite *m* 2.(*subservient follower*) acólito, -a *m, f* II. *adj* TECH por satélite
satellite broadcasting *n no pl* transmisión *f* por satélite **satellite dish** *n* antena *f* parabólica **satellite state** *n* estado *m* satélite **satellite television** *n no pl* televisión *f* por satélite **satellite town** *n* ciudad *f* satélite
satiate ['seɪʃɪeɪt] *vt* saciar
satiety [sə'taɪəti, *Am:* -ʈi] *n no pl, form* saciedad *f*
satin ['sætɪn, *Am:* 'sæʈn] I. *n* raso *m* II. *adj* (*finish, paper*) satinado, -a
satire ['sætaɪəʳ, *Am:* -aɪɚ] *n* LIT sátira *f*
satirical [sə'tɪrɪkl] *adj* satírico, -a
satirist ['sætərɪst, *Am:* 'sæʈɚ-] *n* escritor(a) *m(f)* satírico, -a
satirize ['sætəraɪz, *Am:* 'sæʈ-] *vt* satirizar
satisfaction [‚sætɪs'fækʃən, *Am:* ‚sæʈ-] *n no pl* 1.satisfacción *f;* **to derive ~ from sth** conseguir satisfacción de algo; **to do sth to sb's ~** hacer algo para satisfacción de alguien; **to be a ~ (to sb)** ser una satisfacción (para alguien) 2.(*compensation*) compensación *f*
satisfactory [‚sætɪs'fæktəri, *Am:* ‚sæʈ-] *adj* satisfactorio, -a; SCHOOL suficiente
satisfy ['sætɪsfaɪ, *Am:* -əs-] <-ie-> *vt* 1.(*person, desire*) satisfacer 2.(*condition*) cumplir 3.(*convince*) convencer; **to ~ sb that ...** convencer a alguien de que... 4.(*debt*) saldar ▶**to ~ the** <u>examiners</u> *Brit* ser aprobado
satisfying *adj* satisfactorio, -a

satsuma [sæt'su:mə, *Am:* 'sætsəmɑ:] *n Brit, Am* satsuma *f*

saturate ['sætʃəreɪt] *vt* **1.** (*soak*) empapar; **to be ~d in tradition** estar empapado en la tradición **2.** (*fill to capacity*) saturar; **to ~ the market** saturar el mercado

saturation [ˌsætʃə'reɪʃən] *n no pl* saturación *f*

saturation point *n* punto *m* de saturación; **to reach ~** alcanzar el punto de saturación

Saturday ['sætədeɪ, *Am:* 'sæt̬ə-] *n* sábado *m*; *s. a.* **Friday**

Saturn ['sætən, *Am:* 'sæt̬ən] *n no pl* Saturno *m*

satyr ['sætə^r, *Am:* 'seɪt̬ə] *n* sátiro *m*

sauce [sɔːs, *Am:* sɑːs] *n* **1.** salsa *f*; **tomato ~** salsa de tomate **2.** (*impertinence*) frescura *f* ►**what's ~ for the goose is ~ for the gander** *prov* lo que es bueno para uno es bueno para el otro

sauce boat *n* salsera *f*

saucepan ['sɔːspən, *Am:* 'sɑː-] *n* cacerola *f*

saucer ['sɔːsə^r, *Am:* 'sɑːsə] *n* platillo *m*

saucily ['sɔːsɪli, *Am:* 'sɑː-] *adv* con frescura

sauciness ['sɔːsɪnəs, *Am:* 'sɑː-] *n no pl* **1.** (*impudence*) desfachatez *f* **2.** *Brit* (*smuttiness*) indecencia *f*

saucy ['sɔːsi, *Am:* 'sɑː-] *adj* <-ier, -iest> **1.** (*impudent*) descarado, -a **2.** *Brit* (*smutty*) indecente; (*underwear*) provocativo, -a

Saudi Arabia [ˌsaʊdiə'reɪbɪə] *n no pl* Arabia *f* Saudí [*o* Saudita]

Saudi Arabian [ˌsaʊdiə'reɪbɪən] **I.** *n* saudí *mf*, saudita *mf* **II.** *adj* saudí, saudita

sauerkraut ['saʊəkraʊt, *Am:* 'saʊə-] *n no pl* chucrú *m*

sauna ['sɔːnə, *Am:* 'saʊ-] *n* sauna *f*; **to have a ~** hacer una sesión de sauna

saunter ['sɔːntə^r, *Am:* 'sɑːnt̬ə] **I.** *vi* pasear **II.** *n no pl* paseo *m*

sausage ['sɒsɪdʒ, *Am:* 'sɑːsɪdʒ] *n* salchicha *f*; (*cured*) salchichón *m* ►**not a ~** *Brit, inf* ¡nada de nada!

sausage dog *n Brit, inf* perro, -a *m, f* salchicha **sausage meat** *n no pl* carne *f* de salchicha **sausage roll** *n Brit, Aus* empanadilla *f* de salchicha

sauté ['səʊteɪ, *Am:* soʊ'teɪ] *vt* saltear

savage ['sævɪdʒ] **I.** *adj* **1.** (*fierce*) salvaje, feroz **2.** *inf* (*bad-tempered*) de mal carácter **II.** *n pej* salvaje *mf* **III.** *vt* **1.** (*attack*) atacar salvajemente **2.** (*criticize*) criticar con saña

savagely *adv* **1.** (*attack*) salvajemente **2.** (*criticize*) con saña

savagery *n no pl* ferocidad *f*

savanna(h) [sə'vænə] *n* sabana *f*

save¹ [seɪv] **I.** *vt* **1.** (*rescue*) salvar; **to ~ sb's life** salvar la vida a alguien; **to ~ one's soul** salvarse; **to ~ face** salvar las apariencias; **to ~ one's own skin** salvar el pellejo **2.** (*keep for future use*) guardar **3.** (*collect*) coleccionar **4.** (*avoid wasting*) ahorrar **5.** (*reserve*) reservar **6.** (*prevent from doing*) impedir **7.** INFOR

guardar **8.** SPORTS parar **II.** *vi* **1.** (*keep for the future*) ahorrar; **to ~ for sth** ahorrar para algo **2.** (*conserve*) **to ~ on sth** guardar algo **III.** *n* SPORTS parada *f*

save² [seɪv] *prep* **~ (for)** salvo; **all ~ the youngest** todos salvo los más jóvenes

saver ['seɪvə^r] *n* ahorrador(a) *m(f)*

saving ['seɪvɪŋ] **I.** *n* **1.** *pl* (*money*) ahorros *mpl* **2.** (*economy*) ahorro *m* **3.** (*rescue*) rescate *m*; **to be the ~ of sb** ser la salvación de alguien **II.** *adj* **his ~ grace** lo único que lo salva **III.** *prep* excepto

savings account ['seɪvɪŋzəˌkaʊnt] *n* cuenta *f* de ahorros **savings bank** *n* caja *f* de ahorros **savings bonus** *n* bono *m* de ahorro **savings book** *n* libreta *f* de ahorro **savings certificate** *n Brit* bono *m* de caja de ahorros **savings deposits** *npl* depósitos *mpl* de ahorro

savior *n Am,* **saviour** ['seɪvjə^r, *Am:* -vjə] *n* salvador(a) *m(f)*

savor ['seɪvə^r] *n Am s.* **savour**

savory ['seɪvəri] *n Am s.* **savoury**

savour ['seɪvə^r, *Am:* -və] **I.** *n* **1.** (*taste*) sabor *m* **2.** (*pleasure*) gusto *m* **II.** *vt* saborear

savoury ['seɪvəri] **I.** *adj* **1.** (*salty*) salado, -a **2.** (*appetizing*) sabroso, -a; (*smell, taste*) apetitoso, -a **3.** (*socially acceptable*) respetable **II.** *n Brit* plato *m* salado

Savoy [sə'vɔɪ] *n* Saboya *f*

savoy (*cabbage*) *n* col *f* rizada

savvy ['sævi] *inf* **I.** *adj* <-ier, -iest> espabilado, -a **II.** *n no pl* inteligencia *f*

saw¹ [sɔː, *Am:* sɑː] *pt of* **see**

saw² [sɔː, *Am:* sɑː] **I.** *n* sierra *f*; **power ~** sierra eléctrica **II.** <-ed, sawn *o* -ed> *vt* serrar

saw³ [sɔː, *Am:* sɑː] *n* refrán *m*

sawdust ['sɔːdʌst, *Am:* 'sɑː-] *n no pl* serrín *m*

sawed-off shotgun *n Am s.* **sawn-off shotgun**

sawmill ['sɔːmɪl, *Am:* 'sɑː-] *n* aserradero *m*

sawn [sɔːn, *Am:* sɑːn] *pp of* **saw**

sawn-off shotgun [ˌsɔːnɒf'ʃɒtgʌn, *Am:* ˌsɑːnɑːf'ʃɑːtgʌn] *n* escopeta *f* de cañones recortados

Saxon ['sæksən] **I.** *n* sajón, -ona *m, f* **II.** *adj* sajón, -ona

Saxony ['sæksəni] *n no pl* Sajonia *f*

saxophone ['sæksəfəʊn, *Am:* -foʊn] *n* saxofón *m*

saxophonist [sæk'sɒfənɪst, *Am:* 'sæksəˌfoʊnɪst] *n* saxofonista *mf*

say [seɪ] **I.** <said, said> *vt* **1.** (*speak*) decir; **to ~ sth to sb's face** decir algo a alguien en su cara; **~ no more!** ¡no diga más! **2.** (*state information*) **to ~ (that)** ... decir (que)...; **to have something/nothing to ~ (to sb)** tener algo/no tener nada que decir (a alguien); **to ~ goodbye to sb** despedirse de alguien **3.** (*express*) expresar **4.** (*think*) opinar; **people ~ that ...** se dice que...; **to ~ to oneself**

decirse a sí mismo **5.** (*recite*) recitar; (*prayer*) rezar **6.** (*indicate*) indicar; **to ~ sth about sb/ sth** expresar algo sobre alguien/algo; **the said sb/sth ... form** dicha persona/cosa... **7.** (*convey meaning*) significar **8.** *inf* (*suggest*) sugerir **9.** (*tell*) explicar; **to ~ where/when** explicar dónde/cuándo; **it's not for me to ~ ...** no me corresponde decir... **10.** (*for instance*) (**let's**) **~ ...** digamos... ▶ **when** all **is said and done** a fin de cuentas; **having said that, ...** una vez dicho eso,...; **to ~ when** decir basta; **you don't ~ (so)!** ¿de veras?; **you said it!** *inf* ¡dímelo a mí! **II.** <said, said> *vi* **I ~!** *Brit* ¡oiga!; **I'll ~!** *inf* ¡ya lo creo!; **I must ~ ...** debo admitir...; **not to ~ ...** incluso...; **that is to ~ ...** es decir... **III.** *n no pl* parecer *m*; **to have one's ~** expresar su propia opinión; **to have a ~ in sth** tener voz y voto en algo **IV.** *interj Am* (*positive reaction*) caramba; **~, that's a great idea!** ¡perfecto, es una gran idea!

SAYE [ˌeseɪwaɪˈiː] *abbr of* **Save As You Earn** ahorre mientras gane

saying [ˈseɪɪŋ] *n* **1.** (*proverb*) dicho *m*; **as the ~ goes** como dice el refrán **2.** **it goes without ~** ni que decir tiene

say-so [ˈseɪsəʊ, *Am:* -soʊ] *n no pl, inf* **1.** (*approval*) visto bueno *m*; **to have sb's ~** tener la aprobación de alguien **2.** (*assertion*) afirmación *f*; **don't just believe it on my ~** no te lo creas porque yo te lo diga

scab [skæb] *n* **1.** (*over wound*) costra *f* **2.** *inf* (*strikebreaker*) esquirol *mf* **3.** *no pl* BOT, ZOOL roña *f*

scabbard [ˈskæbəd, *Am:* -əd] *n* vaina *f*

scabby [ˈskæbi] *adj* <-ier, -iest> **1.** (*having scabs*) con costras **2.** ZOOL roñoso, -a **3.** *pej, inf* (*disgusting*) horrible

scabies [ˈskeɪbiːz] *n no pl* MED sarna *f*, zarate *m Hond*

scabrous [ˈskeɪbrəs, *Am:* ˈskæbrəs] *adj* escabroso, -a

scaffold [ˈskæfə(ʊ)ld, *Am:* ˈskæfld] *n* **1.** (*for execution*) patíbulo *m* **2.** (*for building*) andamio *m*

scaffolding [ˈskæfəldɪŋ] *n no pl* andamiaje *m*

scalawag [ˈskæləwæg] *n Am s.* **scallywag**

scald [skɔːld, *Am:* skɑːld] **I.** *vt* **1.** (*burn*) escaldar **2.** (*clean*) esterilizar con agua caliente **3.** (*heat: milk*) calentar **II.** *n* MED escaldadura *f*

scalding [ˈskɔːldɪŋ, *Am:* ˈskɑːld-] *adj* que escalda; **~ hot** hirviendo

scale[1] [skeɪl] **I.** *n* **1.** ZOOL escama *f* **2.** *no pl* TECH, MED sarro *m* **II.** *vt* **1.** (*remove scales*) escamar **2.** TECH, MED quitar el sarro de

scale[2] [skeɪl] *n* (*weighing device*) platillo *m*; **~s** balanza *f*; (*bigger*) báscula *f* ▶ **to tip the ~s** inclinar la balanza

scale[3] [skeɪl] **I.** *n* (*range, magnitude, proportion*) *a.* MUS escala *f*; **a sliding ~** ECON una banda fluctuante; **on a large/small ~** a gran/ pequeña escala; **to draw sth to ~** dibujar algo a escala **II.** *vt* **1.** (*climb*) escalar; **to ~ the**

heights (**of sth**) trepar a las alturas (de algo) **2.** TECH, ARCHIT reducir a escala

◆ **scale down** *vt* (*demand, expectations*) reducir

scale drawing *n* TECH, ARCHIT dibujo *m* a escala **scale model** *n* modelo *m* a escala

scallop [ˈskɒləp, *Am:* ˈskɑːləp] *n* vieira *f*; **~** (**shell**) venera *f*

scallywag [ˈskælɪwæg] *n inf* sinvergüenza *mf*

scalp [skælp] **I.** *n* **1.** (*head skin*) cuero *m* cabelludo **2.** (*war trophy*) cabellera *f*; *fig* persona *f* importante; **to be out after sb's ~** querer acabar con alguien **II.** *vt* **1.** (*in war*) **to ~ sb** arrancar la cabellera a alguien; *iron* cortar el pelo a alguien **2.** *Am, Aus, inf* (*re-sell*) revender

scalpel [ˈskælpəl] *n* MED escalpelo *m*

scaly [ˈskeɪli] *adj* <-ier, -iest> **1.** ZOOL escamoso, -a **2.** MED (*skin*) reseco, -a

scam [skæm] *n inf* timo *m*

scamp [skæmp] *n inf* granuja *mf*, mandinga *m Arg*

scamper [ˈskæmpəʳ, *Am:* -pɚ] *vi* corretear

scampi [ˈskæmpi] *npl* gambas *fpl* rebozadas

scan [skæn] **I.** <-nn-> *vt* **1.** (*scrutinize*) escudriñar **2.** (*look through quickly*) dar un vistazo; (*newspaper*) hojear **3.** MED explorar; (*brain*) hacer un escáner de **4.** LIT medir **5.** INFOR escanear **II.** <-nn-> *vi* medir(se) **III.** *n* INFOR escaneado *m*; MED escáner *m*

scandal [ˈskændl] *n* **1.** (*public outrage*) escándalo *m*; **to uncover** [*o* **expose**] **a ~** sacar a la luz un escándalo; **to cover up a ~** tapar un escándalo **2.** *no pl* (*gossip*) chismorreo *m*; **to spread ~** difundir habladurías **3.** (*sth bad*) **what a ~!** ¡qué vergüenza!

scandalize [ˈskændəlaɪz] *vt* escandalizar

scandalmonger [ˈskændlmʌŋgəʳ, *Am:* -ˌmɑːŋgɚ] *n pej* chismoso, -a *m, f*

scandalous [ˈskændələs] *adj* **1.** (*spreading scandal*) escandaloso, -a **2.** (*disgraceful*) vergonzoso, -a; **it is ~ that ...** resulta vergonzoso que... +*subj*

Scandinavia [ˌskændɪˈneɪviə] *n* Escandinavia *f*

Scandinavian **I.** *adj* escandinavo, -a **II.** *n* escandinavo, -a *m, f*

scanner [ˈskænəʳ, *Am:* -ɚ] *n* INFOR escáner *m*

scanning *n* INFOR, MED escaneo *m*

scant [skænt] *adj* escaso, -a; **~ attention** poca atención

scantily *adv* insuficientemente; **~ dressed** [*o* **clad**] ligero de ropa

scanty [ˈskænti, *Am:* - t̬i] *adj* **1.** (*very small*) corto, -a; (*clothing*) ligero, -a **2.** (*insufficient*) insuficiente

scapegoat [ˈskeɪpɡəʊt, *Am:* -ɡoʊt] *n* cabeza *f* de turco; **to be a ~ for sb/sth** ser un chivo expiatorio para alguien/algo

scapula [ˈskæpjʊlə] <-s *o* -lae> *pl n* omóplato *m*

scar [skɑːʳ, *Am:* skɑːr] **I.** *n* **1.** MED (*on skin*) cicatriz *f;* **to leave a ~** dejar cicatriz **2.** (*mark of damage*) señal *f* **3.** PSYCH trauma *m* **4.** GEO paraje *m* rocoso **II.** <-rr-> *vt* marcar con cicatriz; **to be ~red (by sth)** tener una cicatriz (hecha por algo); **to be ~red for life** quedar marcado de por vida **III.** <-rr-> *vi* **to ~ (over)** cicatrizar(se)

scarab ['skærəb, *Am:* 'sker-] *n* escarabajo *m*

scarce [skeəs, *Am:* skers] *adj* escaso, -a; **to make oneself ~** *inf* largarse

scarcely ['skeəsli, *Am:* 'skers-] *adv* **1.** (*barely*) apenas **2.** (*certainly not*) ni mucho menos

scarcity ['skeəsəti, *Am:* 'skersəţi] *n no pl* escasez *f*

scare [skeə', *Am:* sker] **I.** *vt* asustar, julepear *Arg, Par, Urug,* acholar *Chile, Perú;* **to ~ sb into/out of doing sth** espantar a alguien para que haga/no haga algo; **to be ~d stiff** estar muerto de miedo; **to ~ sb shitless** *vulg* acojonar a alguien **II.** *vi* asustarse; **(not) to ~ easily** (no) asustarse fácilmente **III.** *n* **1.** (*fright*) susto *m,* julepe *m AmL;* **to have a ~** llevarse un sobresalto; **to give sb a ~** dar un susto a alguien **2.** (*panic*) pánico *m;* **~ story** historia *f* alarmista

◆**scare away** *vt,* **scare off** *vt* ahuyentar

scarecrow ['skeəkrəʊ, *Am:* 'skerkroʊ] *n* espantapájaros *m inv*

scaremonger ['skeə,mʌŋgə', *Am:* 'sker-,mɑ:ŋgə'] *n pej* alarmista *mf*

scarf [skɑ:f, *pl* skɑ:vz, *Am:* skɑ:rf, *pl* skɑ:rvz] <-ves o -s> *n* (*round neck*) bufanda *f;* (*round head*) pañuelo *m*

scarlet ['skɑ:lət, *Am:* 'skɑ:r-] **I.** *n no pl* escarlata *f* **II.** *adj* de color escarlata; **to turn ~** ponerse colorado

scarlet fever *n no pl* MED escarlatina *f*

scarp [skɑ:p, *Am:* skɑ:rp] *n* declive *m*

scarper ['skɑ:pə', *Am:* 'skɑ:rpə'] *vi Brit, Aus, inf* largarse

scary ['skeəri, *Am:* 'skeri] *adj* <-ier, -iest> que da miedo; **~ film** película *f* de miedo

scat [skæt] *interj inf* fuera

scathing ['skeɪðɪŋ] *adj* mordaz; **to be ~ about sb/sth** criticar duramente a alguien/algo

scatological [ˌskætə'lɒdʒɪkəl, *Am:* ˌskæţə-'lɑ:dʒɪ-] *adj form* escatológico, -a

scatter ['skætə', *Am:* 'skæţə'] **I.** *vt* esparcir; **to ~ sth with sth** salpicar algo con algo; **to ~ sth to the four winds** esparcir algo a los cuatro vientos **II.** *vi* dispersarse; **to ~ in all directions** desparramarse en todas direcciones

scatterbrain ['skætəbreɪn, *Am:* 'skæţə-] *n pej* cabeza *mf* de chorlito

scatterbrained *adj* atolondrado, -a

scatter cushion *n Brit, Aus* almohadón *m*

scattered *adj* **1.** disperso, -a **2.** (*widely separated*) separado, -a **3.** (*sporadic*) espóradico, -a

scatty ['skæti, *Am:* 'skæţi] *adj Brit, inf* atolondarado, -a

scavenge ['skævɪndʒ] *vi* **1.** (*search*) buscar

cosas en la basura, pepenar *AmC, Méx* **2.** ZOOL buscar comida

scavenger ['skævɪndʒə', *Am:* -ə'] *n* **1.** ZOOL animal *m* carroñero **2.** (*person*) persona *f* que hurga en la basura en busca de comida, etc.

scenario [sɪ'nɑ:rɪəʊ, *Am:* sə'nerɪoʊ] *n* **1.** (*situation*) marco *m* hipotético **2.** THEAT, LIT guión *m*

scene [si:n] *n* **1.** THEAT, CINE (*unit of drama*) escena *f;* (*setting*) escenario *m;* **nude ~** escena *f* de desnudo; **behind the ~s** *a. fig* entre bastidores **2.** (*locality*) lugar *m;* **the ~ of the crime** la escena del crimen **3.** (*view*) vista *f* **4.** (*milieu*) mundo *m;* **the art/drugs ~** el mundo del arte/de las drogas; **it is/isn't my ~** *inf* eso es/no es lo mío; **to appear on the ~** presentarse; **to depart from the political ~** desaparecer del escenario político; **to set the ~** crear un ambiente **5.** (*embarrassing incident*) escándalo *m;* **to make a ~** montar un número

scene change *n* cambio *m* de decorado

scene painter *n* escenógrafo, -a *m, f*

scenery ['si:nəri] *n no pl* **1.** (*landscape*) paisaje *m* **2.** THEAT, CINE decorado *m;* **to blend into the ~** conseguir pasar inadvertido

scene shifter *n* tramoyista *mf*

scenic ['si:nɪk] *adj* **1.** THEAT escénico, -a **2.** (*of beautiful scenery*) pintoresco, -a; **~ road** ruta *f* turística

scent [sent] **I.** *n* **1.** (*aroma*) olor *m* **2.** (*in hunting*) rastro *m;* **to be on the ~ of sth/sb** estar sobre la pista de algo/alguien; **to throw sb off the ~** despistar a alguien **3.** *no pl, Brit* (*perfume*) perfume *m* **II.** *vt* **1.** (*smell*) oler **2.** (*sense, detect*) intuir; **to ~ that …** sospechar que… **3.** (*apply perfume*) perfumar

scent bottle *n* frasco *m* de perfume

scentless *adj* inodoro, -a

scepter ['septə'] *n Am s.* **sceptre**

sceptic ['skeptɪk] *n* escéptico, -a *m, f*

sceptical *adj* escéptico, -a

scepticism ['skeptɪsɪzəm] *n no pl* escepticismo *m*

sceptre ['septə', *Am:* -tə'] *n* cetro *m*

schedule ['ʃedju:l, *Am:* 'skedʒu:l] **I.** *n* **1.** (*timetable*) horario *m;* **bus ~** horario de autobuses; **flight ~** horario de vuelos; **to stick to a ~** seguir un horario; **everything went according to ~** todo fue según lo previsto **2.** (*plan of work*) programa *m* **3.** FIN inventario *m* **II.** *vt* **1.** (*plan*) programar **2.** (*list*) hacer una lista

scheduled *adj* programado, -a

scheduled flight *n* vuelo *m* regular

schematic [skɪ'mætɪk, *Am:* ski:'mæţ-] *adj* esquemático, -a

scheme [ski:m] **I.** *n* **1.** (*structure*) esquema *m* **2.** *Brit* (*programme*) programa *m;* ECON plan *m* **3.** (*plot*) treta *f* **II.** *vi pej* intrigar; **to ~ to do sth** intrigar para hacer algo

schemer ['ski:mə', *Am:* -ə'] *n* intrigante *mf*

scheming ['ski:mɪŋ] *adj* intrigante

schism ['sɪzəm] *n* cisma *m*

schismatic [sɪz'mætɪk, *Am:* -'mæt̬-] REL
I. *adj* cismático, -a II. *n* cismático, -a *m, f*
schist [ʃɪst] *n no pl* GEO esquisto *m*
schizophrenia [ˌskɪtsəʊ'fri:nɪə, *Am:* -sə'-] *n no pl* esquizofrenia *f*
schizophrenic [ˌskɪtsəʊ'frenɪk, *Am:* -sə'-]
I. *adj* esquizofrénico, -a II. *n* esquizofrénico, -a *m, f*
scholar ['skɒlə^r, *Am:* 'ska:lə·] *n* 1. (*learned person*) erudito, -a *m, f* 2. (*student*) estudiante *mf* 3. (*scholarship holder*) becario, -a *m, f*
scholarly *adj* erudito, -a
scholarship ['skɒləʃɪp, *Am:* 'ska:lə·-] *n* 1. *no pl* (*learning*) erudición *f* 2. (*grant*) beca *f* **scholarship holder** *n* becario, -a *m, f*
scholastic [skə'læstɪk] *adj* académico, -a
school¹ [sku:l] I. *n* 1. (*institution*) escuela *f;* primary ~ colegio *m;* secondary ~ instituto *m* de enseñanza secundaria, liceo *m Chile, Méx;* public ~ *Brit* escuela privada; *Am* escuela pública; dancing ~ escuela de baile; driving ~ autoescuela; to be in ~ estar en edad escolar; to go to ~ ir al colegio; to start ~ empezar la escuela; to leave ~ terminar el colegio 2. (*buildings*) colegio *m* 3. *no pl* (*classes*) clases *fpl* 4. (*university division*) facultad *f* 5. *Am* (*university*) universidad *f* II. *vt* enseñar III. *adj* escolar
school² [sku:l] *n* ZOOL banco *m*
school age ['sku:leɪdʒ] *n* edad *f* escolar **school attendance** *n* asistencia *f* a la escuela **schoolbag** *n* cartera *f* del colegio **school board** *n Am* ADMIN consejo *m* escolar **schoolbook** *n* libro *m* escolar **schoolboy** I. *n* colegial *m*, escolero *m Perú* II. *adj* de colegial **schoolchild** *n* colegial(a) *m(f),* escolero, -a *m, f Perú* **schooldays** *npl* años *mpl* de colegio **school dinner** *n* comida *f* de colegio **school fees** *npl* cuota *f* escolar **schoolgirl** I. *n* colegiala *f,* escolera *f Perú* II. *adj* de colegiala **schoolhouse** <-es> *n Am* escuela *f*
schooling *n no pl* enseñanza *f*
school leaver *n Brit, Aus:* alumno que ha finalizado sus estudios **school-leaving certificate** *n Brit* graduado *m* escolar **school magazine** *n* revista *f* del colegio **schoolmaster** *n* profesor *m* **schoolmate** *n* compañero, -a *m, f* de clase **schoolmistress** *n* profesora *f* **school nurse** *n* enfermera *f* de escuela

Con la expresión **School of the air** se designa una red de difusión por radio para el **outback** de Australia. Esta red funciona en zonas aisladas del país y tiene como finalidad educar a la población en edad escolar. Una docena de estas escuelas cubren un área de 2,5 millones de km y alcanzan a cientos de niños. Los alumnos reciben material didáctico y envían sus deberes hechos de vuelta, hablan por radio con sus profesores y compañeros de clase y la mayoría de las veces son sus padres o un profesor particular quienes los vigilan en casa.

school report *n* boletín *m* de notas **schoolroom** *n* clase *f*

El **school system** (sistema escolar) americano comienza con la **elementary school** (que abarca desde el curso primero hasta el sexto u octavo). En algunos lugares después del **sixth grade**, el sexto curso, los alumnos pasan a otra escuela, la **junior high school** (donde se les imparte la docencia correspondiente a los cursos séptimo, octavo y noveno). Después los alumnos acceden a la **high school** donde permanecen por espacio de tres cursos. En aquellos lugares donde no hay **junior high school** los alumnos pasan directamente de la **elementary school** (donde han estado ocho años) a la **high school**, que, en ese caso, comienza con el **ninth grade**, es decir, el noveno curso. Los alumnos finalizan su itinerario escolar cuando han terminado el **twelfth grade**, el curso decimosegundo.

schoolteacher *n* profesor(a) *m(f)* **schoolwork** *n* trabajo *m* escolar **schoolyard** *n Am* patio *m* del colegio
schooner ['sku:nə^r, *Am:* -nə·] *n* 1. NAUT goleta *f* 2. *Am, Aus* (*tall glass*) jarra *f* 3. *Brit* (*sherry glass*) copa *f* de jerez
sciatic [saɪ'ætɪk, *Am:* -'æt̬-] *adj* ciático, -a
sciatica [saɪ'ætɪkə, *Am:* -'æt̬-] *n no pl* MED ciática *f*
science ['saɪənts] I. *n no pl* ciencia *f;* pure/applied ~ ciencias *fpl* puras/aplicadas; the wonders of modern ~ las maravillas de la ciencia moderna II. *adj* de ciencias **science fiction** I. *n no pl* ciencia ficción *f* II. *adj* de ciencia ficción **science laboratory** *n* laboratorio *m* de ciencias **science park** *n* parque *m* tecnológico
scientific [ˌsaɪən'tɪfɪk] *adj* científico, -a
scientist ['saɪəntɪst, *Am:* -t̬ɪst] *n* científico, -a *m, f*
sci-fi ['saɪˌfaɪ] *n abbr of* science fiction ciencia *f* ficción
Scilly Isles ['sɪli aɪls] *n* the ~ las Islas Sorlingas
scintillating ['sɪntɪleɪtɪŋ, *Am:* -t̬leɪt̬ɪŋ] *adj* (*performance*) brillante; (*wit*) chispeante
scion ['saɪən] *n form* 1. (*descendant*) descendiente *mf* 2. BOT injerto *m*, esqueje *m*
scissors ['sɪzəz, *Am:* -ə·z] *npl* tijeras *fpl;* a pair of ~ unas tijeras; ~ kick SPORTS chilena *f;* a ~ and paste job un refrito
sclerosis [sklə'rəʊsɪs, *Am:* sklɪ'roʊ-] *n no pl* MED esclerosis *f*
scoff¹ [skɒf, *Am:* ska:f] *vi* (*mock*) burlarse; to ~ at sth/sb reírse de algo/alguien

scoff² [skɒf, *Am:* skɑːf] *vt Brit, inf* (*eat*) engullir

scold [skəʊld, *Am:* skoʊld] *vt* regañar

scolding ['skəʊldɪŋ, *Am:* 'skoʊld-] *n* reprimenda *f*, raspada *f Méx, PRico*, trepe *m CRi*

scone [skɒn, *Am:* skoʊn] *n* bollo *m*

scoop [skuːp] I. *n* 1. (*utensil*) cucharón *m;* **ice-cream** ~ cuchara *f* de helado; **measuring** ~ cuchara de medición 2. (*amount*) cucharada *f* 3. PUBL primicia *f* informativa II. *vt* 1. PUBL adelantarse con una exclusiva 2. (*win*) ganar; **to** ~ **the pool** *Brit, Aus, inf* acaparar todos los premios
♦**scoop up** *vt* recoger

scoot [skuːt] *vi inf* largarse; **to** ~ **over** *Am* escabullirse

scooter ['skuːtəʳ, *Am:* -t̬əʳ] *n* 1. (*toy*) patinete *m* 2. (*vehicle*) (**motor**) ~ escúter *m*, Vespa® *f*

scope [skəʊp, *Am:* skoʊp] *n no pl* 1. (*range*) alcance *m* 2. (*possibilities*) posibilidades *fpl;* **limited/considerable** ~ campo *m* de acción limitado/considerable

scorch [skɔːtʃ, *Am:* skɔːrtʃ] I. *vt* chamuscar II. *vi* chamuscarse III. *n* <-es> quemadura *f*

scorcher *n inf* día *m* de mucho calor

scorching *adj* abrasador(a); **it's** ~ **hot** hace un calor abrasador

score [skɔːʳ, *Am:* skɔːr] I. *n* 1. SPORTS (*number of points*) puntuación *f;* **to keep (the)** ~ llevar la cuenta 2. SPORTS (*goal, point*) gol *m* 3. SCHOOL nota *f* 4. (*twenty*) veintena *f;* ~**s of people** mucha gente 5. (*reason*) motivo *m* 6. (*dispute*) rencilla *f;* **to settle a** ~ ajustar cuentas 7. MUS partitura *f* 8. (*line*) arañazo *m* ►**to know the** ~ estar al tanto; **what's the** ~? *inf* ¿cómo van? II. *vt* 1. (*goal, point*) marcar; (*triumph, victory*) obtener 2. (*cut*) cortar 3. *inf* (*buy: drugs*) conseguir 4. MUS (*arrange*) instrumentar III. *vi* 1. SPORTS (*make a point*) marcar un tanto 2. *inf* (*succeed*) triunfar 3. *inf* (*make sexual conquest*) echar un polvo 4. *inf* (*buy drugs*) comprar droga
♦**score out** *vt* tachar

scoreboard ['skɔːbɔːd, *Am:* 'skɔːrbɔːrd] *n* marcador *m* **scorecard** *n* tarjeta *f* de registro de la puntuación

scorer *n* (*player: in soccer*) goleador(a) *m(f);* (*in basketball*) jugador que marca uno o más tantos

scoring *n* puntuación *f*

scorn [skɔːn, *Am:* skɔːrn] I. *n* desprecio *m;* **to pour** ~ **on sb/sth** ridiculizar a alguien/algo; **to be the** ~ **of sb** ser despreciado por alguien II. *vt* 1. (*feel contempt*) despreciar, ajotar *Cuba* 2. (*refuse*) rechazar (por orgullo); **to** ~ **to do sth** no dignarse a hacer algo

scornful ['skɔːnfəl, *Am:* 'skɔːrn-] *adj* desdeñoso, -a

Scorpio ['skɔːpiəʊ, *Am:* 'skɔːrpioʊ] *n* Escorpión *m*

scorpion ['skɔːpiən, *Am:* 'skɔːr-] *n* escorpión *m*

Scot [skɒt, *Am:* skɑːt] *n* escocés, -esa *m, f*

scotch [skɒtʃ, *Am:* skɑːtʃ] *vt* 1. (*rumour*) acallar 2. (*plan*) frustrar

Scotch [skɒtʃ, *Am:* skɑːtʃ] I. *n* whisky *m* (escocés); **a** ~ **on the rocks** un whisky con hielo, un whisky en las rokas *Méx* II. *adj* escocés, -esa

Scotch broth *n no pl* sopa *f* de verduras

scot-free [ˌskɒtˈfriː, *Am:* ˌskɑːtˈ-] *adv* 1. (*without punishment*) impunemente; **to get away** ~ librarse del castigo 2. (*unharmed*) sin un rasguño

Scotland ['skɒtlənd, *Am:* 'skɑːt-] *n* Escocia *f*

Scots [skɒts, *Am:* skɑːts] *adj s.* **Scottish**

Scotsman ['skɒtsmən, *Am:* 'skɑːts-] <-men> *n* escocés *m*

Scotswoman ['skɒtsˌwʊmən, *Am:* 'skɑːts-] <-women> *n* escocesa *f*

Scottish ['skɒtɪʃ, *Am:* 'skɑːt̬ɪʃ] *adj* escocés, -esa

scoundrel ['skaʊndrəl] *n pej* sinvergüenza *mf*

scour [skaʊəʳ, *Am:* skaʊɚ] I. *vt* 1. (*scrub*) fregar 2. (*search*) recorrer; **the police are** ~**ing the club** la policía esta haciendo una batida en el club II. *n no pl* fregado, -a *m, f;* **to give sth a** ~ fregar algo

scourer *n* estropajo *m*

scourge [skɜːdʒ, *Am:* skɜːrdʒ] I. *n a. fig* azote *m* II. *vt* 1. (*inflict suffering*) azotar 2. (*whip*) flagelar

scouring pad *n* estropajo *m*

scout [skaʊt] I. *n* explorador(a) *m(f)*, scout *mf Méx;* **talent** ~ cazatalentos *m* II. *vi* **to** ~ **ahead** reconocer el terreno; **to** ~ **around for sth** buscar algo

scoutmaster *n* jefe *m* de exploradores, akela *m Méx*

scowl [skaʊl] I. *n* ceño *m* fruncido II. *vi* fruncir el ceño

scrabble ['skræbl] *vi* 1. (*grope*) hurgar 2. (*claw for grip*) escarbar

scrag [skræg] <-gg-> *vt* 1. (*kill*) ahorcar 2. *inf* (*mistreat*) maltratar

scraggy ['skrægi] <-ier, -iest> *adj* flaco, -a

scram [skræm] <-mm-> *vi inf* largarse, rajarse *AmC*

scramble ['skræmbl] I. *vi* 1. (*move hastily*) moverse apresuradamente; **to** ~ **for sth** esforzarse por algo; **to** ~ **through the hedge** arrastrarse por la zanja 2. (*try to get first*) luchar 3. (*take off quickly*) despegar II. *vt* 1. (*mix together*) revolver; ~**d eggs** huevos revueltos 2. (*encrypt*) codificar 3. (*take off quickly*) hacer despegar III. *n* 1. *no pl* (*rush*) carrera *f;* (*chase*) persecución *f* 2. *no pl* (*struggle to get*) arrebatiña *f*, rebatinga *f Méx* 3. (*motorcycle race*) carrera *f* de motocross

scrambler ['skræmbləʳ, *Am:* -blɚ] *n* 1. (*device*) scrambler *m* 2. (*motorcycle*) motocicleta *f* de motocross

scrap¹ [skræp] I. *n* 1. (*small piece*) trozo *m;* (*of paper, cloth*) pedazo *m* 2. (*small amount*) pizca *f;* (*of information*) retazo *m;* **not a ~ of truth** ni un ápice de verdad **3.** *pl* (*leftover food*) sobras *fpl* **4.** *no pl* (*old metal*) chatarra *f* **II.** <-pp-> *vt* **1.** (*get rid of*) desechar; (*abandon*) descartar; (*abolish*) abolir **2.** (*use for scrap metal*) desguazar, deshuesar *Méx*

scrap² [skræp] **I.** *n inf* (*fight*) agarrada *f,* agarrón *m Méx* **II.** <-pp-> *vi* pelearse

scrapbook ['skræpbʊk] *n* álbum *m* de recortes **scrap dealer** *n* chatarrero, -a *m, f*

scrape [skreɪp] **I.** *vt* **1.** (*remove layer*) raspar, rasquetear *Arg;* (*remove: dirt*) limpiar **2.** (*graze*) rozar; (*scratch*) rascar **3.** (*rub against*) rozar **II.** *vi* **1.** (*rub against*) rozar **2.** (*make unpleasant noise*) chirriar **3.** (*economize*) ahorrar **II.** *n* **1.** *no pl* (*act of scraping*) raspado, -a *m, f* **2.** (*graze on skin*) raspadura *f* **3.** (*sound*) chirrido *m* **4.** *inf* (*situation*) lío *m;* **to get into a ~** meterse en un lío
- ◆**scrape along** *vi s.* **scrape by**
- ◆**scrape away** *vi* raspar
- ◆**scrape by** *vi* apañárselas
- ◆**scrape through I.** *vt* pasar por los pelos **II.** *vi* aprobar por los pelos

scraper ['skreɪpəʳ, *Am:* -ɚ] *n* (*tool*) raspador *m;* (*for cleaning shoes*) limpiabarros *m inv*

scrapheap ['skræphiːp] *n* montón *m* de basura; **to end up on the ~** quedarse sin futuro laboral

scrapie ['skreɪpi] *n* escrapie *m*

scrapings *npl* **1.** (*leftovers*) sobras *fpl* **2.** TECH limaduras *fpl*

scrap iron *n no pl* chatarra *f* **scrap merchant** *n Brit* chatarrero, -a *m, f*

scrappy¹ ['skræpi] <-ier, -iest> *adj* **1.** (*knowledge*) superficial **2.** (*performance, game*) irregular

scrappy² ['skræpi] <-ier, -iest> *adj Am* (*ready to fight*) pendenciero, -a, peleonero, -a *Méx*

scratch [skrætʃ] **I.** *n* **1.** (*cut on skin*) rasguño *m,* rayón *m AmL* **2.** (*mark*) raya *f* **3.** *no pl* (*act of scratching*) arañamiento *m* **4.** (*start*) principio *m;* **from ~** desde cero **II.** *vt* **1.** (*cut slightly*) arañar **2.** (*mark*) rayar **3.** (*relieve itch*) rascar **4.** (*erase*) tachar **5.** (*exclude*) retirar **6.** *Am, inf* (*cancel*) cancelar **7.** (*write*) garabatear **III.** *vi* **1.** (*use claws: cat*) arañar **2.** (*relieve itch*) rascarse **3.** *Brit* (*write*) raspear **IV.** *adj* improvisado, -a
- ◆**scratch about** *vi,* **scratch around** *vi Brit* escarbar
- ◆**scratch out** *vt* **1.** (*with claws*) arañar; **to scratch sb's eyes out** *fig* sacar los ojos a alguien **2.** (*line, word*) tachar

scratch card *n* ['skrætʃkɑːd, *Am:* -kɑːrd] *n* tarjeta *f* rasca, raspadita *f Arg* **scratch paper** *n no pl, Am* papel *m* de borrador

scratchy ['skrætʃi] <-ier, -iest> *adj* **1.** (*record*) rayado, -a **2.** (*irritating*) áspero, -a **3.** *Brit* (*pen*) que raspa; (*handwriting*) garabatoso, -a

scrawl [skrɔːl, *Am:* skrɑːl] **I.** *vt* garabatear **II.** *n no pl* garabato *m*

scrawny ['skrɔːni, *Am:* 'skrɑː-] <-ier, -iest> *adj* escuálido, -a, silgado, -a *Ecua*

scream [skriːm] **I.** *n* **1.** (*cry*) grito *m;* (*shrill cry*) chillido *m;* (*shout*) alarido *m* **2.** (*of animal*) chillido *m* ►**to be a ~** ser la monda **II.** *vi* (*shout*) gritar; (*cry shrilly*) chillar; **to ~ with laughter** reír a carcajadas **III.** *vt* (*shout*) gritar; (*abuse, obscenities*) lanzar; **to ~ oneself hoarse** gritar hasta enronquecer

scree [skriː] *n no pl* pedregal *m* (en una ladrera)

screech [skriːtʃ] **I.** *n* chillido *m* **II.** *vi* chillar; **to ~ with pain** lanzar gritos de dolor

screech-owl *n* lechuza *f*

screeds [skriːdz] *npl* páginas *fpl* y páginas

screen [skriːn] **I.** *n* **1.** *a.* TV, CINE, INFOR pantalla *f;* **split/touch ~** pantalla dividida/táctil **2.** (*framed panel*) biombo *m;* (*for protection*) cortina *f;* (*in front of fire*) pantalla *f;* **glass ~** vitral *m* **3.** *no pl* (*thing that conceals*) cortina *f* **II.** *vt* **1.** (*conceal*) ocultar **2.** (*shield*) proteger **3.** (*examine*) examinar; (*revise*) revisar **4.** TV emitir; CINE proyectar **5.** (*put through a sieve*) cribar
- ◆**screen off** *vt* separar con un biombo

screening *n* **1.** (*showing: in cinema*) proyección *f;* (*on television*) emisión *f* **2.** *no pl* (*testing*) prueba *f* **3.** MED (*examination*) chequeo *m*

screenplay ['skriːnpleɪ] *n* guión *m*

screensaver *n* INFOR salvapantallas *m inv*

screenshot *n* INFOR captura *f* de pantalla **screen test** *n* prueba *f* **screenwriter** *n* guionista *mf*

screw [skruː] **I.** *n* **1.** (*small metal fastener*) tornillo *m;* **to tighten (up)/loosen a ~** apretar/aflojar un tornillo **2.** (*turn*) vuelta *f* **3.** (*propeller*) hélice *f* **4.** *Brit, inf* (*prison guard*) carcelero, -a *m, f* **5.** *no pl* (*spin*) efecto *m,* chanfle *m Méx* **6.** (*twisted piece*) rosca *f* ►**he's got a ~ loose** *inf* le falta un tornillo; **to put the ~s on sb** *inf* apretar las tuercas a alguien **II.** *vt* **1.** (*with a screw*) atornillar **2.** (*by twisting*) enroscar **3.** *inf* (*cheat*) timar **4.** *vulg* (*have sex with*) follar con, coger *AmL* **5.** (*make move in a curve*) enroscar; **to ~ the ball** dar efecto a la pelota **III.** *vi* **1.** (*turn like a screw*) enroscarse **2.** (*move in a curve*) dar efecto **3.** *vulg* (*have sex*) echar un polvo, echarse un palo *Méx*
- ◆**screw down** *vt* enroscar
- ◆**screw up I.** *vt* **1.** (*fasten with screws*) atornillar **2.** (*tighten*) apretar **3.** (*crush*) estrujar **4.** (*twist*) retorcer **5.** *inf* (*make a mess of*) joder **6.** *inf* (*make anxious*) poner neurótico **II.** *vi* cagarla

screwball ['skruːbɔːl] *n Am, inf* (*odd person*) chiflado, -a *m, f;* **~ comedy** comedia *f* disparatada

screwdriver ['skruːˌdraɪvəʳ, *Am:* -vɚ] *n* destornillador *m,* desarmador *m AmL*

screwed *adj inf* jodido, -a *vulg*

screw top *n* tapón *m* de rosca

screwy ['skruːi] <-ier, iest> *adj inf* chalado, -a

scribble ['skrɪbl] I. *vt* garabatear II. *vi* hacer garabatos III. *n* garabatos *mpl*

scribbling block *n*, **scribbling pad** *n* bloc *m* de notas

scrimmage ['skrɪmɪdʒ] *n* 1. (*fight*) escaramuza *f* 2. (*in US football*) línea *f* de golpeo

scrimp [skrɪmp] *vi* escatimar; **to ~ and save** apretarse el cinturón *fig*

script [skrɪpt] I. *n* 1. CINE guión *m*; TV, THEAT argumento *m* 2. (*writing*) escritura *f*; **Arabic ~** escritura árabe 3. *Brit, Aus* (*exam*) examen *m* II. *vt* escribir el guión de

script girl *n* secretaria *f* de rodaje

scriptural ['skrɪptʃərəl, *Am:* -tʃɚ-] *adj* bíblico, -a

Scripture ['skrɪptʃəʳ, *Am:* -tʃɚ] *n* Sagrada Escritura *f*

scriptwriter ['skrɪptraɪtəʳ, *Am:* -t̬ɚ] *n* guionista *mf*

scroll [skrəʊl, *Am:* skroʊl] I. *n* 1. (*roll*) rollo *m* (de papel) 2. ARCHIT voluta *f* II. *vi* INFOR desplazarse; **to ~** (**to the**) **right/left** desplazarse a la derecha/izquierda; **to ~ down/up** desplazarse hacia abajo/arriba

scrooge [skru:dʒ] *n* tacaño, -a *m, f*

scrotum ['skrəʊtəm, *Am:* 'skroʊt̬əm] <-tums *o* -ta> *n* escroto *m*

scrounge [skraʊndʒ] I. *vt inf* conseguir gorroneando, manguear *Arg*; **to ~ sth off** [*o* **from**] **sb** sacar algo de gorra a alguien II. *vi inf* gorronear III. *n inf* **to be on the ~** vivir de gorra

scrounger ['skraʊndʒəʳ, *Am:* -ɚ] *n pej, inf* gorrón, -ona *m, f*, pedinche *mf Méx*

scrub¹ [skrʌb] <-bb-> I. *vt* 1. (*clean*) fregar 2. (*cancel*) cancelar II. *vi* fregar; **to ~ at sth** restregar algo III. *n no pl* fregado *m*; **to give sth a** (**good**) **~** fregar algo vigorosamente

scrub² [skrʌb] *n no pl* matorral *m*

scrubber ['skrʌbəʳ, *Am:* -ɚ] *n* 1. (*person who scrubs*) fregón, -ona *m, f* 2. *Brit, pej, inf* putona *f*

scrubbing brush ['skrʌbɪŋbrʌʃ] *n* cepillo *m* de fregar

scruff [skrʌf] *n* 1. (*back of neck*) cogote *m*; **to grab sb by the ~ of the neck** coger a alguien por el cogote 2. *Brit, inf* (*dirty person*) persona *f* desaliñada, facha *f Méx*

scruffy ['skrʌfi] <-ier, -iest> *adj* (*clothes*) deshilachado, -a; (*person*) desaliñado, -a, fachoso, -a *Méx*; (*area, place*) dejado, -a

scrum ['skrʌm] *n* SPORTS melé *f*

scrum half *n* medio melé *m*

scrummage ['skrʌmɪdʒ] *n s.* **scrum**

scrumptious ['skrʌmpʃəs] *adj Brit, inf* de rechupete

scrumpy ['skrʌmpi] *n no pl, Brit* sidra *f*

scrunch [skrʌntʃ] I. *vi* crujir II. *vt* ronzar III. *n no pl* crujido *m*

scruple ['skru:pl] I. *n no pl* escrúpulo *m*; **to have no ~s** (**about doing sth**) no tener escrúpulos (en hacer algo) II. *vi* tener escrúpulos

scrupulous ['skru:pjʊləs] *adj* escrupuloso, -a

scrutineer [ˌskru:tɪˈnɪəʳ, *Am:* -tn'ɪr] *n Brit, Aus* escrutador(a) *m(f)*

scrutinise *vt Brit, Aus*, **scrutinize** ['skru:tɪnaɪz, *Am:* -tənaɪz] *vt* (*examine*) escudriñar; (*votes*) escrutar; (*text*) revisar

scrutiny ['skru:tɪni, *Am:* -təni] *n no pl* escrutinio *m*

scuba diving ['sku:bəˌdaɪvɪŋ] *n* submarinismo *m*

scud [skʌd] <-dd-> *vi* correr

scuff [skʌf] I. *vt* 1. (*roughen surface*) raspar 2. (*drag along ground*) arrastrar II. *n* rozadura *f*

scuffle ['skʌfl] I. *n* refriega *f* II. *vi* pelearse

scull [skʌl] I. *vi* remar II. *n* espadilla *f*

scullery ['skʌləri] *n* antecocina *f*

sculpt [skʌlpt] *vt* esculpir

sculptor ['skʌlptəʳ, *Am:* -tɚ] *n* escultor *m*

sculptress ['skʌlptrəs] *n* escultora *f*

sculptural ['skʌlptʃərəl] *adj* escultórico, -a

sculpture ['skʌlptʃəʳ, *Am:* -tʃɚ] I. *n* escultura *f* II. *vt* esculpir

scum [skʌm] *n no pl* 1. (*foam*) espumaje *m* 2. (*evil people*) escoria *f*

scumbag ['skʌmbæg] *n pej* cerdo, -a *m, f*

scupper ['skʌpəʳ, *Am:* -ɚ] *vt* 1. (*ship*) hundir 2. *inf* (*plan*) echar por tierra

scurf [skɜ:f, *Am:* skɜ:rf] *n no pl* caspa *f*

scurrilous ['skʌrɪləs, *Am:* 'skɜ:rɪ-] *adj pej* (*damaging*) difamatorio, -a; (*insulting*) calumnioso, -a

scurry ['skʌri, *Am:* 'skɜ:ri] <-ie-> *vi* correr

scurvy ['skɜ:vi, *Am:* 'skɜ:r-] I. *n no pl* escorbuto *m*, berbén *m Méx* II. *adj* vil; **a ~ trick** un truco ruin

scuttle¹ ['skʌtl, *Am:* 'skʌt̬-] *vi* (*run*) correr

scuttle away *vi,*, **scuttle off** *vi* (*run*) escabullirse

scuttle² ['skʌtl, *Am:* 'skʌt̬-] *vt* 1. (*sink*) hundir 2. (*plan*) echar por tierra

scuttle³ ['skʌtl, *Am:* 'skʌt̬-] *n* (*for coal*) cajón *m* para el carbón

scythe [saɪð] I. *n* guadaña *f* II. *vt* (*with a scythe*) guadañar; (*with swinging blow*) segar

SDI [ˌesdiːˈaɪ] *n Am abbr of* **Strategic Defense Initiative** IDE *f*

SE [ˌesˈiː] *n abbr of* **southeast** SE *m*

sea [siː] *n* 1. mar *m o f*; **at the bottom of the ~** en el fondo del mar; **by ~** por mar; **by the ~** junto al mar; **out at ~** en alta mar; **to put** (**out**) **to ~** hacerse a la mar; **the open ~**, **the high ~s** el mar abierto 2. (*wide expanse*) **a ~ of people** un mar de gente ►**worse** <u>things</u> **happen at ~!** (*things could be worse*) ¡más se perdió en la guerra!; **to sail the** <u>seven</u> **~s** surcar los siete mares; **to be** (**all**) **<u>at</u> ~** estar totalmente perdido

sea air *n no pl* aire *m* de mar **sea anemone** *n* anémona *f* de mar **sea bed** *n no pl* lecho *m* marino **sea bird** *n* ave *f* marina

seaboard ['siːbɔːd, *Am:* -bɔːrd] *n* litoral *m*

seaborne ['siːbɔːn, *Am:* -bɔːrn] *adj* transportado, -a por mar

sea breeze n brisa f marina **sea change** n cambio m profundo **sea cow** n manatí m

sea dog n lobo m de mar

seafarer ['siːˌfeərəʳ, Am: -ˌferəˑ] n liter marinero, -a m, f

seafaring adj liter marinero, -a

seafish <-(es)> n inv pez m marino

seafood ['siːfuːd] n no pl marisco m

seafront ['siːfrʌnt] n 1. (promenade) paseo m marítimo, malecón m Méx 2. (beach) playa f

seagoing ['siːˌɡəʊɪŋ, Am: -ˌɡoʊ-] adj de altura

seagull ['siːɡʌl] n gaviota f

seahorse n caballito m de mar

seal[1] [siːl] n ZOOL foca f

seal[2] [siːl] I. n 1. (wax mark, stamp) sello m; **given under my hand and ~** sellado y firmado de mi puño y letra 2. (to prevent opening: on letter) sello m; (on goods) precinto m; (on door) precintado m ►~ **of approval** aprobación f II. vt 1. (put a seal on) sellar 2. (prevent opening) precintar 3. (block access) acordonar; (frontier, port) cerrar

♦**seal up** vt precintar

sealant ['siːlənt] n (substance) silicona f selladora

sea legs npl equilibrio m; **to get one's ~** acostumbrarse a mantener el equilibrio (en barco)

sea level n no pl nivel m del mar

sealing wax n no pl lacre m

sea lion n ZOOL león m marino

sealskin ['siːlskɪn] n no pl piel f de foca

seam [siːm] I. n 1. (stitching) costura f; **to come** [o fall] **apart at the ~s** descoserse; fig rebosar de gente 2. (junction) juntura f 3. (wrinkle) arruga f 4. MIN veta f, filón m II. vt (sew) coser

seaman ['siːmən] <-men> n (sailor) marinero m

sea mile n milla f marina

seamless adj 1. (without seam) sin costuras 2. (transition) perfecto, -a

seamstress ['sempstrɪs, Am: 'siːmstrɪs] n costurera f

seamy ['siːmi] <-ier, -iest> adj sórdido, -a

seance ['seɪɑ̃ːnts, Am: 'seɪɑːnts] n sesión f de espiritismo

seaplane ['siːpleɪn] n AVIAT hidroavión m

seaport n puerto m de mar **sea power** n 1. no pl (naval strength) fuerza f naval 2. (state) potencia f naval

sear [sɪəʳ, Am: sɪr] vt 1. (scorch) quemar; (into memory) grabar a fuego 2. (wither) secar, marchitar 3. GASTR brasar (a fuego vivo) 4. MED cauterizar 5. (make numb) volver insensible

search [sɜːtʃ, Am: sɜːrtʃ] I. n a. INFOR búsqueda f; (of building) registro m, cateo m Méx, esculco m Col, Méx; (of person) cacheo m; **to go in ~ of sth** ir en busca de algo II. vi a. INFOR buscar; **to ~ for** [o **after**] **sth** buscar algo; **to ~ high and low (for sth)** buscar (algo) por

todas partes; **~ and replace** INFOR buscar y reemplazar III. vt 1. INFOR buscar en; (building, baggage) registrar, catear Méx, escular Col, Méx; (person) cachear 2. (examine) examinar; **to ~ one's memory** hacer memoria; **to ~ one's conscience** hacer examen de conciencia ►~ **me!** inf ¡yo qué sé!

♦**search out** vt (people) encontrar; (information) averiguar

search engine n INFOR motor m de búsqueda

searcher n miembro m de un equipo de salvamento

search function n INFOR función f de búsqueda

searching adj 1. (penetrating) inquisitivo, -a; (look) penetrante 2. (exhaustive) minucioso, -a

searchlight ['sɜːtʃlaɪt, Am: 'sɜːrtʃ-] n reflector m

search operation n operación f de búsqueda **search party** <-ies> n equipo m de salvamento **search warrant** n orden f de registro [o de allanamiento AmL]

searing adj 1. (heat) abrasador(a) 2. (pain) punzante 3. (criticism) virulento, -a

sea salt n sal f marina

seascape ['siːskeɪp] n 1. (picture) marina f 2. (view) vista f marina

sea shanty n saloma f

seashell ['siːʃel] n concha f (marina)

seashore ['siːʃɔːʳ, Am: -ʃɔːr] n no pl 1. (beach) playa f 2. (near sea) costa f

seasick ['siːsɪk] adj mareado, -a; **to get ~** marearse

seasickness ['siːsɪknɪs] n mareo m

seaside ['siːsaɪd] I. n no pl, Brit 1. (beach) playa f 2. (coast) costa f II. adj Brit costero, -a; **a ~ resort** un lugar de veraneo costero, un balneario AmL

season ['siːzən] I. n 1. (period of year) estación f 2. (epoch) época f; **the Christmas ~** las Navidades; **the ~ of good will** la época navideña; **Season's Greetings** Felices Fiestas; **the** (fishing/hunting) **~** la temporada (de pesca/de caza); **the close ~** la veda; **the strawberry/apple ~** la temporada de las fresas/manzanas; **to be in ~** estar en sazón; **to be out of ~** estar fuera de temporada; **high/low ~** temporada alta/baja; **the concert ~** Brit, Aus la temporada de conciertos 3. SPORTS temporada f 4. ZOOL **to be in ~** estar en celo; **the mating ~** la época del celo 5. inf (ticket) abono m (de temporada) II. vt 1. GASTR sazonar; (add salt and pepper) salpimentar 2. (dry out) secar III. vi 1. (dry out) secarse 2. fig **to become ~ed to sth** acostumbrarse a algo

seasonable ['siːzənəbl] adj 1. (expected) propio, -a de la estación 2. liter (appropriate) oportuno, -a

seasonal ['siːzənəl] adj 1. (connected with time of year) estacional 2. (temporary) temporal; **~ worker** temporero, -a m, f 3. (grown

in a season: fruits, vegetables) del tiempo
seasoned *adj* **1.**(*experienced*) experimentado, -a **2.**(*dried: wood*) secado, -a **3.**(*spiced*) sazonado, -a
seasoning ['si:zənɪŋ] *n* **1.** *no pl* (*salt and pepper*) condimento *m* **2.**(*herb or spice*) sazón *f*, yuyos *mpl Ecua, Perú*
season ticket *n Brit, Aus* abono *m* (de temporada) **season ticket holder** *n* RAIL persona *f* en posesión de un abono; SPORTS, THEAT abonado, -a *m*, *f*
seat [si:t] **I.** *n* **1.**(*furniture*) asiento *m*; (*on a bicycle*) sillín *m*; (*in theatre*) butaca *f*; (*in a car, bus*) plaza *f*; **back ~** asiento trasero; **is this ~ free/taken?** ¿está libre/ocupado este asiento?; **to keep a ~ for sb** guardar el asiento a alguien; **to take one's ~** sentarse **2.**(*ticket*) entrada *f*; **to book a ~** reservar una entrada **3.** *no pl* (*part: of chair*) asiento *m*; (*of trousers*) fondillos *mpl* **4.**(*buttocks*) trasero *m inf* **5.** POL escaño *m*, banca *f Arg, Par, Urug*; **to win/lose a ~** ganar/perder un escaño **6.**(*centre*) sede *f*; **~ of learning** *form* centro *m* de enseñanza **7.**(*country residence*) casa *f* solariega **8.**(*riding style*) **to have a good ~** montar bien ►**to fly by the ~ of one's pants** dejarse guiar por el instinto **II.** *vt* **1.**(*place on a seat*) sentar; **to ~ oneself** *form* tomar asiento; (*offer a seat to*) colocar **2.**(*have enough seats for*) tener cabida para; **the bus ~s 20** el autobús tiene 20 plazas **3.** ARCHIT, TECH asentar
seat belt *n* cinturón *m* de seguridad; **to fasten one's ~** abrocharse el cinturón de seguridad
seating *n no pl* **1.**(*seats*) asientos *mpl* **2.**(*number*) número *m* de asientos; **~ capacity** número de plazas; **~ for two thousand** aforo de dos mil personas **3.**(*arrangement*) distribución *f* de los asientos
seating arrangements *npl* distribución *f* de los asientos **seating plan** *n* disposición *f* de los invitados
SEATO ['si:təʊ, *Am:* -toʊ] *n no pl abbr of* **Southeast Asia Treaty Organization** Organización *f* del Tratado del Sudeste Asiático
sea urchin *n* erizo *m* de mar
seaward ['si:wəd, *Am:* -wɚd] **I.** *adv* hacia el mar **II.** *adj* **1.**(*facing sea*) que da al mar **2.**(*moving towards sea*) que va hacia el mar
seawater ['si:ˌwɔːtəʳ, *Am:* -ˌwɑːt̬ɚ] *n no pl* agua *f* de mar
seaway ['si:weɪ] *n* **1.**(*channel*) canal *m* marítimo **2.**(*route*) ruta *f* marítima
seaweed ['si:wi:d] *n no pl* algas *fpl*, huiro *m Chile*
seaworthy ['si:ˌwɜːði, *Am:* -ˌwɜːr-] *adj* en condiciones de navegar
sebaceous gland [sɪˈbeɪʃəsˌglænd, *Am:* sə'-] *n* glándula *f* sebácea
sec [sek] *n s.* **second** seg. *m*
secateurs [ˌsekə'tɜːz, *Am:* 'sekətɚz] *npl* podadera *f*; **a pair of ~** una podadera
secede [sɪ'si:d] *vi* separarse

secession [sɪ'seʃən] *n no pl* secesión *f*; **War of Secession** Guerra *f* de Secesión
seclude [sɪ'klu:d] *vt liter* recluir
secluded [sɪ'klu:dɪd] *adj* (*place*) aislado, -a; (*life*) solitario, -a
seclusion [sɪ'klu:ʒən] *n no pl* aislamiento *m*; **to live in ~** vivir aislado
second¹ ['sekənd] **I.** *adj* **1.**(*after first*) segundo, -a; **every ~ boy/cat** uno de cada dos chicos/gatos; **every ~ year** cada dos años; **every ~ week** una semana sí y otra no; **to be ~** ser el segundo; **the ~ biggest town** la segunda ciudad más grande; **to be ~ only to sb/sth** ser superado únicamente por alguien/algo; **to be ~ to none** no ser inferior a nadie **2.**(*another*) otro, -a; **to be a ~ Mozart** ser otro Mozart; **to give sb a ~ chance** dar a alguien una segunda oportunidad; **to have ~ thoughts about sb/sth** dudar de alguien/algo; **on ~ thoughts** *Brit, Aus*, **on ~ thought** *Am, Aus* pensándolo bien; **to do sth a ~ time** volver a hacer algo; **to get one's ~ wind** recobrar el aliento; **to have a ~ helping** repetir de algo **3.** *Brit, Aus* **the ~ floor** *Brit* el segundo piso, el tercer piso *AmL; Am* el primer piso, el segundo piso *AmL* **II.** *n* **1.** *Brit* (*second-class degree*) título calificado con la segunda o tercera nota que es posible obtener en el Reino Unido **2.** *no pl* (*second gear*) segunda *f* **3.** *pl* (*extra helping*) **can I have ~s?** ¿puedo repetir? **4.** COM (*imperfect item*) artículo *m* con defectos de fábrica **5.**(*in duel*) padrino *m* **6.** MUS segunda *f* **7.**(*seconder*) persona *f* que secunda una propuesta **III.** *adv* **1.**(*second place*) en segundo lugar **2.**(*second class*) **to travel ~** viajar en segunda **IV.** *vt* **1.**(*support in debate*) secundar **2.** *form* (*back up*) apoyar
second² ['sekənd] *n* (*unit of time*) segundo *m*; **per ~** por segundo; **at that very ~** en ese preciso instante; **just a ~!** ¡un segundo!; **it won't take a ~!** ¡sólo será un momento!
second³ [sɪ'kɒnd, *Am:* -'kɑːnd] *vt Brit, Aus* (*officer, staff*) destinar
secondary ['sekəndəri, *Am:* -deri] **I.** *adj* **1.**(*not main*) secundario, -a; **to be ~ to sth** ser de menor importancia que algo **2.** SCHOOL (*teacher, pupil*) de enseñanza secundaria; **~ modern** centro *m* de formación profesional **3.**(*industry*) derivado, -a **II.** <-ies> *n* **1.**(*person*) subalterno, -a *m*, *f* **2.** SCHOOL *s.* **secondary school**
secondary school *n* **1.**(*school*) instituto *m* de enseñanza secundaria, liceo *m Chile, Méx* **2.** *no pl* (*education*) enseñanza *f* secundaria
second-best **I.** *adj* **to be ~** (*person*) ser un segundón; (*option*) ser una segunda alternativa **II.** *n* segundo, -a *m*, *f* **III.** *adv* **to come off ~** (*to sb*) perder (contra alguien)
second chamber *n* POL cámara *f* alta **second class** **I.** *n no pl* segunda *f* (clase) **II.** *adv* **1.** RAIL (*in the second class*) en segunda (clase) **2.** *Brit* (*by second-class mail*) por correo regular **III.** *adj* **1.**(*in second class*) de segunda

clase; ~ **mail** correo *m* regular **2.** *pej* (*inferior: hotel, service*) de segunda categoría; (*goods*) de calidad inferior **second cousin** *n* primo, -a *m, f* segundo, -a **second-degree burn** *n* quemadura *f* de segundo grado

seconder *n* persona *f* que secunda una propuesta

second-guess [ˌsekənd'ges] *vt* anticiparse a

secondhand [ˌsekənd'hænd] **I.** *adj* (*clothes, car, information*) de segunda mano; (*bookshop*) de viejo **II.** *adv* **1.** (*used*) de segunda mano **2.** (*from third party*) por terceros

second hand *n* (*on watch*) segundero *m*

second lieutenant *n* MIL alférez *mf*

secondly *adv* en segundo lugar

secondment [sɪ'kɒndmənt, *Am:* -'kɑːnd-] *n Brit, Aus* **1.** *no pl* (*transfer*) traslado *m* temporal por trabajo **2.** (*period*) estancia *f* en un lugar por motivos de trabajo

second-rate [ˌsekənd'reɪt] *adj* mediocre

secrecy ['siːkrəsi] *n no pl* **1.** (*confidentiality*) secreto *m;* **in** ~ en secreto; **to swear sb to** ~ hacer que alguien jure no revelar algo **2.** (*secretiveness*) misterio *m*

secret ['siːkrɪt] **I.** *n* **1.** (*information*) secreto *m;* **an open** ~ un secreto a voces; **to let sb in on** a ~ revelar un secreto a alguien **2.** (*knack*) truco *m;* (*of success*) secreto *m* **3.** (*mystery*) misterio *m* **II.** *adj* (*known to few*) secreto, -a; **to keep sth** ~ (**from sb**) ocultar algo (a alguien)

secret agent *n* agente *mf* secreto, -a

secretarial [ˌsekrə'teəriəl, *Am:* -'teri-] *adj* administrativo, -a

secretariat [ˌsekrə'teəriət, *Am:* -'teri-] *n* secretaría *f*

secretary ['sekrətəri, *Am:* -rəteri] <-ies> *n* **1.** (*in office*) secretario, -a *m, f* **2.** POL ministro, -a *m, f,* secretario, -a *m, f Méx;* **Secretary of the Treasury** ≈ Ministro, -a *m, f* de Hacienda; **Secretary of State** *Brit* ministro; *Am* secretario de Estado

secretary-general [ˌsekrətəri'dʒenərəl, *Am:* -rəteri'-] <secretaries-general> *n* secretario, -a *m, f* general

secrete¹ [sɪ'kriːt] *vt* (*discharge*) segregar

secrete² [sɪ'kriːt] *vt form* (*hide*) ocultar

secretion [sɪ'kriːʃən] *n* (*discharge*) secreción *f*

secretive ['siːkrətɪv, *Am:* -ṭɪv] *adj* reservado, -a

sect [sekt] *n* secta *f*

sectarian [sek'teəriən, *Am:* -'teri-] **I.** *adj* **1.** (*ideology*) sectario, -a **2.** (*schooling*) confesional **II.** *n* sectario, -a *m, f*

section ['sekʃən] **I.** *n* **1.** (*part*) *a.* MIL, MUS, PUBL sección *f;* (*of object*) parte *f* **2.** (*group*) sector *m* **3.** (*of area*) zona *f;* (*of city*) distrito *m* **4.** (*of document*) párrafo *m;* LAW artículo *m* **5.** (*of road*) tramo *m* **6.** (*cut*) corte *m* **II.** *vt* **1.** (*cut*) seccionar **2.** (*divide*) dividir

◆**section off** *vt* acordonar

sectional ['sekʃənl] *adj* **1.** (*limited to a*

group: interests) particular; (*differences*) entre facciones **2.** (*done in section: design, view*) en sección **3.** *Am* (*made in sections: furniture, sofa*) modular

sector ['sektər, *Am:* -tər] *n* sector *m;* **public/private** ~ sector público/privado

secular ['sekjʊlər, *Am:* -lər] *adj* **1.** (*non-religious*) secular; (*education*) laico, -a; (*art*) profano, -a **2.** REL seglar **3.** (*centuries-old*) secular

secularize ['sekjʊləraɪz] *vt* secularizar

secure [sɪ'kjʊər, *Am:* -'kjʊr] **I.** *adj* <-rer, -est> **1.** (*safe*) seguro, -a; **to be** ~ **from sth** estar protegido contra algo; **to make sth** ~ **against attack** proteger algo contra los ataques **2.** (*confident*) **to feel** ~ **about sth** sentirse seguro respecto a algo; **to be** ~ **in the knowledge that ...** tener la certeza de que...; **to feel emotionally** ~ tener estabilidad emocional **3.** (*guarantee*) **to be financially** ~ tener estabilidad económica **4.** (*fixed*) firme; (*foundation*) sólido, -a **II.** *vt* **1.** (*obtain*) obtener **2.** (*make firm*) asegurar; *fig* afianzar; (*door*) cerrar firmemente; (*boat*) amarrar; (*position*) consolidar **3.** (*make safe*) proteger **4.** (*put in safe place*) poner a buen recaudo **5.** (*guarantee repayment*) garantizar; **a** ~**d loan** un préstamo con garantía

securities market *n* mercado *m* de valores

security [sɪ'kjʊərəti, *Am:* 'kjʊrəṭi] <-ies> *n* **1.** *no pl* (*safety*) seguridad *f;* ~ **risk** peligro *m* para la seguridad **2.** *no pl* (*stability*) estabilidad *f;* ~ **of employment** estabilidad laboral **3.** (*safeguard*) salvaguardia *f* **4.** *no pl* (*payment guarantee*) fianza *f;* **to stand** ~ **for sb** salir fiador de alguien **5.** *pl* FIN títulos *mpl* **Security Council** *n* Consejo *m* de Seguridad (de las Naciones Unidas) **security forces** *npl* fuerzas *fpl* de seguridad **security guard** *n* guarda *mf* jurado, -a

sedan [sɪ'dæn] *n Am, Aus* AUTO sedán *m*

sedan chair *n* silla *f* de manos

sedate [sɪ'deɪt] **I.** *adj* (*lifestyle, person*) tranquilo, -a; (*colour, style*) sobrio, -a **II.** *vt* MED sedar

sedation [sɪ'deɪʃən] *n no pl* MED sedación *f;* **under** ~ sedado

sedative ['sedətɪv, *Am:* -ṭɪv] **I.** *adj* sedante **II.** *n* sedante *m*

sedentary ['sedəntəri, *Am:* -teri] *adj* sedentario, -a

sedge [sedʒ] *n no pl* juncia *f*

sediment ['sedɪmənt, *Am:* 'sedə-] *n no pl* sedimento *m;* (*in wine, coffee*) poso *m*

sedimentary [ˌsedɪ'mentri] *adj* sedimentario, -a

sedition [sɪ'dɪʃən] *n no pl, form* sedición *f*

seditious [sɪ'dɪʃəs] *adj form* sedicioso, -a

seduce [sɪ'djuːs, *Am:* -'duːs] *vt* seducir; **to** ~ **sb into doing sth** inducir a alguien a hacer algo

seducer [sɪ'djuːsər, *Am:* -'duːsər] *n* seductor(a) *m(f)*

seduction [sɪ'dʌkʃən] *n* **1.** *no pl* (*act*) seduc-

ción *f* **2.** *pl* (*seductive quality*) atractivo *m*
seductive [sɪ'dʌktɪv] *adj* **1.**(*sexy*) seduc-
tor(a) **2.**(*attractive*) atrayente; (*offer*) tenta-
dor(a)
sedulous ['sedjʊləs, *Am:*'sedʒə-] *adj liter*(*at
work*) diligente; (*student*) aplicado, -a
see¹ [si:] <saw, seen> **I.** *vt* **1.**(*perceive*) ver;
to ~ that ... ver que...; **to ~ sth with one's
own eyes** ver algo con sus propios ojos; **it is
worth ~ing** vale la pena verlo **2.**(*watch*) ver;
you were ~n to enter the building se os vio
entrar en el edificio **3.**(*inspect*) ver; **may I ~
your driving licence?** ¿me permite (ver) su
permiso de conducir? **4.**(*visit*) visitar; **to ~ a
little/a lot of sb** ver a alguien poco/a
menudo; **~ you around!** ¡nos vemos!; **~ you!**
inf(*when meeting again later*) ¡hasta luego!
5.(*have relationship*) **to be ~ing sb** salir con
alguien **6.**(*have meeting*) tener una entrevista
con **7.**(*talk to*) **I would like to ~ you about
that matter** querría hablar contigo sobre ese
asunto; **Mr Brown will ~ you now** el Sr.
Brown le recibirá ahora **8.**(*accompany*) acompañar a **9.**(*perceive*) darse cuenta de; (*understand*) comprender; **I don't ~ what you
mean** no entiendo lo que quieres decir; **to
make sb ~ reason** hacer entrar en razón a alguien; **to ~ sth in a new light** cambiar de
opinión respecto a algo **10.**(*envisage*) creer;
as I ~ it ... a mi modo de ver...; **I don't ~ him
doing that** no le creo capaz de hacer eso; **I
could ~ it coming** lo veía venir **11.**(*witness*)
presenciar; **he won't ~ fifty again** ya pasa de
los cincuenta **12.**(*investigate*) **to ~ how/
what/if ...** averiguar cómo/qué/si...
13.(*ensure*) **~ that you are ready when we
come** procura estar listo cuando vengamos
II. *vi* **1.**(*use eyes*) ver; **as far as the eye can
~** hasta donde alcanza la vista **2.**(*find out*) descubrir; **~ for yourself!** ¡compruébelo usted
mismo!; **let me ~** ¿a ver?; **let's ~** vamos a ver;
we'll/I'll (have to) ~ ya lo veremos/veré;
you'll ~ ya verás **3.**(*understand*) comprender;
I ~ ya veo; **you ~?** ¿entiendes?; **as far as I can
~** por lo que yo veo ▶**he can't ~ further than
the end of his nose** no puede ver más allá de
sus narices
◆**see about** *vt inf*encargarse de; (*consider*)
pensarse ▶**we'll soon ~ that!** *inf* ¡eso ya lo
veremos!
◆**see in** *vt* (*welcome*) hacer pasar; **to see
the New Year in** celebrar el Año Nuevo
◆**see off** *vt* **1.**(*say goodbye*) despedir
2.(*drive away*) deshacerse de **3.**(*defeat*) derrotar
◆**see out** *vt* **1.**(*escort to door*) acompañar
hasta la puerta **2.**(*continue to end*) seguir
hasta el final de; (*programme, film*) quedarse
hasta el final de **3.**(*last until end*) durar hasta
el final de; **to see the winter out** resistir el
invierno
◆**see through** *vt* **1.**(*look through*) ver a
través de **2.**(*not be deceived by*) calar a *inf*;

(*mystery*) penetrar en **3.**(*sustain*) **to see sb
through** (a difficult time) mantener a alguien
a flote (en tiempos difíciles) **4.**(*last*) durar
5.(*continue to end*) llevar a buen término
form
◆**see to** *vt* **1.**(*attend to*) encargarse de
2.(*ensure*) **to ~ it that ...** asegurarse de
que...
see² [si:] *n* REL sede *f*; **the Holy See** la Santa
Sede
seed [si:d] **I.** *n* **1.** BOT (*source*) semilla *f*; (*of
fruit*) pepita *f*, pepa *f* AmL **2.** *no pl* (*seeds*)
simiente *f* **3.**(*beginning*) germen *m*; (*of revolution*) semilla *f*; **to sow the ~s of doubt/dis-
cord** sembrar la duda/la discordia **4.** *no pl*
ANAT semen *m* **II.** *vt* **1.** AGR sembrar; **to ~ itself**
(*a plant*) desgranarse **2.**(*help start*) contribuir
a la puesta en marcha; **to ~ a project with
money** aportar capital a un proyecto
3.(*remove seeds*) despepitar **4.** SPORTS preseleccionar **III.** *vi* granar
seed bed *n* **1.** AGR semillero *m* **2.** *fig* foco *m*
seed corn *n* **1.** BOT trigo *m* de siembra **2.** *fig*
capital *m* simiente
seedless ['si:dləs] *adj* sin pepitas
seedling ['si:dlɪŋ] *n* planta *f* de semillero
seed potato *n* patata *f* de siembra
seedy ['si:di] <-ier, -iest> *adj* **1.**(*dubious*)
sórdido, -a; (*place*) de mala muerte; (*clothing*)
raído, -a **2.**(*unwell*) pachucho, -a *inf*; **to feel ~**
encontrarse mal
seeing I. *conj* **~ (that)** en vista de (que) **II.** *n*
visión *f*; **~ is believing** ver para creer
seek [si:k] <sought> **I.** *vt* **1.**(*look for*) buscar; **to ~ one's fortune** probar suerte **2.**(*try to
obtain*) procurar obtener; (*solution*) tratar de
encontrar; (*shelter*) buscar; (*damages*) reclamar **3.**(*ask for: help, approval*) pedir; (*job*) solicitar **4.**(*attempt*) tratar de **II.** *vi* (*search*) buscar
◆**seek out** *vt* (*person*) ir a buscar;
(*information*) averiguar
seeker *n* buscador(a) *m(f)*
seem [si:m] *vi* **1.**(*appear to be*) parecer; **they
~ed to like the idea** parecía que les gustaba la
idea; **to ~ as if ...** parecer como si... +*subj*; **it
is not all what it ~s** no es lo que parece;
things aren't always what they ~ las apariencias engañan **2.**(*appear*) **it ~s that ...**
parece que...; **so it ~s, so would ~** eso parece
seeming *adj form* aparente
seemingly *adv* aparentemente
seemly ['si:mli] <-ier, -iest> *adj* apropiado,
-a
seen [si:n] *pp of* **see**
seep [si:p] *vi* filtrarse
◆**seep away** *vi* escurrirse
seepage ['si:pɪdʒ] *n no pl* (*of water*) filtración *f*; (*of gas*) fuga *f*
seer [sɪəʳ, *Am:* sɪr] *n liter* adivino, -a *m, f*
seersucker ['sɪə,sʌkəʳ, *Am:* 'sɪr,sʌkəʳ] *n* sir-
saca *f*
seesaw ['si:sɔ:, *Am:* -sɑ-] **I.** *n* **1.**(*in play-*

ground) balancín *m* **2.** *fig* vaivén *m* **II.** *vi*
1. (*play*) columpiarse **2.** *fig* oscilar **III.** *adj* ~
motion movimiento *m* oscilante
seethe [siːð] *vi* **1.** (*bubble*) borbotar **2.** *fig* (*be angry*) estar furioso, -a; **to ~ with anger** hervir de cólera **3.** *fig* (*be busy*) bullir; **to ~ with tourists** estar plagado de turistas
see-through ['siːθruː] *adj* transparente
segment¹ ['segmənt] *n* **1.** MAT, ZOOL segmento *m*; (*of orange*) gajo *m* **2.** (*of society*) sector *m*
segment² [seg'ment, *Am:* 'segmənt] **I.** *vt* segmentar; (*orange*) dividir en gajos **II.** *vi* segmentarse
segmentation [ˌsegmən'teɪʃən] *n no pl* segmentación *f*
segregate ['segrɪgeɪt, *Am:* -rə-] *vt* (*races*) segregar; (*girls and boys*) separar
segregation [ˌsegrɪ'geɪʃən, *Am:* -rə'-] *n no pl* segregación *f*
seismic ['saɪzmɪk] *adj* GEO sísmico, -a
seismograph ['saɪzməɡrɑːf, *Am:* -ɡræf] *n* sismógrafo *m*
seismologist [saɪz'mɒlədʒɪst, *Am:* -'mɑː-lə-] *n* sismólogo, -a *m, f*
seismology [saɪz'mɒlədʒi, *Am:* -'mɑːlə-] *n no pl* sismología *f*
seize [siːz] *vt* **1.** (*grasp*) asir *form,* cachar *Arg, Nic, Urug,* acapilar *Méx;* **to ~ sb by the arm/ by the throat** agarrar a alguien del brazo/por el cuello **2.** (*take: opportunity*) no dejar escapar; (*initiative, power*) tomar **3.** (*overcome*) **he was ~d by fear/desire** el miedo/el deseo se apoderó de él; **I was ~d with panic** estaba sobrecogido por el pánico **4.** (*capture: criminal*) detener; (*fortress, town*) tomar **5.** (*confiscate: property*) confiscar; (*drugs, weapons*) incautarse de **6.** (*understand*) captar **7.** (*kidnap*) secuestrar
◆**seize on** *vt* aprovecharse de
◆**seize up** *vi* (*stop*) paralizarse; (*engine, muscles*) agarrotarse; INFOR colgarse *inf*
seizure ['siːʒər, *Am:* -ʒɚ] *n* **1.** *no pl* (*seizing*) asimiento *m* **2.** (*taking possession: of town*) toma *f;* (*of drugs*) incautación *f;* (*of property, contraband*) confiscación *f* **3.** MED (*stroke*) ataque *m* **4.** (*seizing up*) agarrotamiento *m*
seldom ['seldəm] *adv* rara vez
select [sɪ'lekt, *Am:* sə'-] **I.** *vt* (*candidate, player, information*) seleccionar; (*gift, wine*) escoger; **~ed works** obras *fpl* escogidas **II.** *adj* **1.** (*high-class*) selecto, -a; (*club, restaurant*) exclusivo, -a; (*school, university*) elitista; (*product*) de primera calidad **2.** (*exclusive*) **the ~ few** los escogidos
select committee *n Brit* POL comisión *f* investigadora
selection [sɪ'lekʃən, *Am:* sə'-] *n* **1.** (*choosing*) selección *f* **2.** (*range*) gama *f;* (*of food, drink*) surtido *m* **3.** *no pl* (*choice*) elección *f* **4.** (*chosen player*) **this player is a ~ for the team** este jugador ha sido seleccionado para entrar en el equipo

selective [sɪ'lektɪv, *Am:* sə'-] *adj* selectivo, -a
selectivity [ˌsɪlek'tɪvəti, *Am:* ˌsəlek'tɪvət̬i] *n no pl* selectividad *f*
selector [sɪ'lektər, *Am:* sə'lektɚ] *n* **1.** SPORTS (*of team*) seleccionador(a) *m(f)* **2.** TECH selector *m*
selenium [sɪ'liːniəm] *n* selenio *m*
self [self] *n* <selves> uno mismo, una misma; **his better ~** su mejor parte; **one's other ~** su alter ego; **the ~** PSYCH el yo
self-abasement *n no pl* rebajamiento *m* de sí mismo **self-abuse** *n* masturbación *f* **self--addressed** *adj* **~ envelope** sobre *m* con la dirección de uno mismo **self-adhesive** *adj* autoadhesivo, -a **self-appointed** *adj pej* autoproclamado, -a **self-assurance** *n no pl* seguridad *f* en uno mismo; **to possess ~** tener confianza en uno mismo **self-assured** *adj* seguro, -a de sí mismo, -a **self-catering** *adj Aus, Brit* (*apartment*) con cocina individual; (*holiday*) sin servicio de comidas **self-cen-tered** *adj Am,* **self-centred** *adj Brit, Aus* egocéntrico, -a **self-colored** *adj Am,* **self--coloured** *adj Brit, Aus* **1.** (*natural*) de color natural **2.** (*one colour*) unicolor **self-com-placent** *adj pej* engreído, -a **self--composed** *adj* dueño, -a de sí mismo, -a; **to remain ~** no perder la serenidad **self-con-ceited** *adj pej* vanidoso, -a **self-confessed** *adj* confeso, -a; **she's a ~ coward** se confiesa cobarde **self-confidence** *n no pl* seguridad *f* en uno mismo; **to have ~** confiar en sí mismo **self-conscious** *adj* **1.** (*shy*) tímido, -a; **to feel ~** sentirse cohibido **2.** *pej* (*unnatural*) afectado, -a **self-contained** *adj* **1.** (*self-sufficient: community, village*) autosuficiente; (*apartment*) con cocina y cuarto de baño **2.** *pej* (*reserved*) reservado, -a **self-contradic-tory** *adj form* contradictorio, -a; **a ~ state-ment** un contrasentido **self-control** *n no pl* dominio *m* de sí mismo **self-critical** *adj* autocrítico, -a **self-criticism** *n no pl* autocrítica *f* **self-deception** *n no pl* engaño *m* de uno mismo **self-defeating** *adj* contraproducente **self-defence** *n Aus, Brit,* **self--defense** *n Am* **1.** *no pl* (*protection*) defensa *f* personal **2.** *no pl* LAW legítima defensa *f* **self--denial** *n no pl* abnegación *f* **self-destruct** *vi* autodestruirse **self-determination** *n no pl* POL autodeterminación *f* **self-discipline** *n no pl* autodisciplina *f* **self-educated** *adj* autodidacta, -a **self-effacing** *adj* humilde **self-employed I.** *adj* **to be ~** trabajar por cuenta propia **II.** *n* **the ~** los trabajadores por cuenta propia **self-esteem** *n no pl* amor *m* propio **self-evident** *adj* evidente **self-ex-planatory** *adj* que se explica por sí mismo **self-expression** *n no pl* expresión *f* de la propia personalidad **self-fulfilling** *adj* (*prediction*) que tiene como consecuencia su propio cumplimiento **self-governing** *adj* autónomo, -a **self-government** *n no pl* autonomía *f* **self-help** *n* autoayuda *f;* ~

group grupo *m* de apoyo mutuo **self-importance** *n no pl, pej* presunción *f* **self-important** *adj pej* presuntuoso, -a **self-imposed** *adj* (*deadline*) autoimpuesto, -a; (*exile*) voluntario, -a **self-indulgence** *n no pl* indulgencia *f* con uno mismo **self-indulgent** *adj* indulgente consigo mismo, -a **self-inflicted** *adj* autoinfligido, -a **self-interest** *n no pl* interés *m* propio; **to be motivated by** ~ estar motivado por el interés personal
selfish ['selfɪʃ] *adj pej* egoísta
selfishness *n no pl, pej* egoísmo *m*
self-justification *n* autojustificación *f*
selfless ['selfləs] *adj* desinteresado, -a
self-made [ˌself'meɪd] *adj* que se ha hecho a sí mismo, -a **self-opinionated** *adj pej* testarudo, -a **self-pity** *n no pl* lástima *f* de sí mismo **self-portrait** *n* ART autorretrato *m*
self-possessed *adj* dueño, -a de sí mismo, -a **self-preservation** *n no pl* instinto *m* de conservación **self-raising flour** *n no pl*, *Brit* harina *f* con levadura incorporada **self-realization** *n* autorealización *f* **self-reliance** *n no pl* independencia *f* **self-reliant** *adj* independiente **self-respect** *n no pl* amor *m* propio; **to lose all** ~ perder la dignidad **self-respecting** *adj* con amor propio; **every** ~ **man** ... todo hombre que se precie...
self-righteous *adj pej* farisaico, -a; (*tone*) de superioridad moral **self-rising flour** *n no pl*, *Am* harina *f* con levadura incorporada **self-sacrifice** *n no pl* abnegación *f* **self-sacrificing** *adj* sacrificado, -a **self-satisfaction** *n no pl, pej* satisfacción *f* de sí mismo **self-satisfied** *adj pej* satisfecho, -a de sí mismo, -a **self-seeking** *adj form* egoísta **self-service** I. *n* autoservicio *m* II. *adj* ~ **store** autoservicio *m;* ~ **restaurant** self-service *m* **self-sufficiency** *n no pl* autosuficiencia *f* **self-sufficient** *adj* 1. independiente 2. ECON autosuficiente; ~ **economy** autarquía *f* **self-taught** *adj* autodidacta, -a; **to be** ~ **in sth** haber aprendido algo por su cuenta **self-willed** *adj* obstinado, -a, voltario, -a *Chile* **self-winding watch** *n* reloj *m* de cuerda automática
sell [sel] I. *n no pl* 1. *a.* FIN (*thing to sell*) venta *f* 2. *inf* (*deception*) estafa *f* II. *vt* <sold, sold> 1. (*exchange for money*) vender; **to** ~ **sth for £100** vender algo por [*o* en] 100 libras; **to** ~ **sth at half price** vender algo a mitad de precio; **to** ~ **sth at a loss** vender algo perdiendo dinero 2. *fig* (*make accepted*) hacer aceptar; **I'm sold on your plan** tu plan me ha convencido ▶**to** ~ **oneself short** no hacerse valer III. *vi* <sold, sold> 1. (*be exchanged for money: company, shop*) estar en venta; (*product*) venderse; **to** ~ **at** [*o* for] **£5** venderse a 5 libras 2. (*be accepted*) tener aceptación
◆**sell off** *vt* (*shares, property*) liquidar; (*industry*) privatizar

◆**sell out** I. *vi* 1. COM, FIN agotarse 2. *fig* venderse II. *vt* liquidar
◆**sell up** *Aus, Brit* I. *vi* liquidar II. *vt* vender
sellable *adj* vendible
sell-by date ['selbaɪˌdeɪt] *n Brit* COM fecha *f* límite de venta
seller *n* 1. (*person*) vendedor(a) *m(f);* ~**'s market** mercado *m* de vendedores 2. (*product*) **good/poor** ~ artículo *m* que tiene mucha/poca demanda
selling *n* ventas *fpl*
selling point *n* atractivo *m* para el consumidor **selling price** *n* precio *m* de venta
sell-off *n* (*of shares, property*) liquidación *f;* (*of industry*) privatización *f*
Sellotape® ['seləteɪp, *Am:* -oʊ-] *n no pl, Brit* celo *m*
sell-out ['selaʊt] *n* 1. THEAT, CINE éxito *f* de taquilla 2. (*betrayal*) traición *f*
selves [selvz] *n pl of* **self**
semantic [sɪ'mæntɪk, *Am:* sə'mænt̬ɪk] *adj* LING semántico, -a
semantics [sɪ'mæntɪks, *Am:* sə'mænt̬ɪks] *npl* LING semántica *f*
semaphore ['seməfɔːʳ, *Am:* -fɔːr] I. *n no pl* semáforo *m* II. *vt* transmitir por semáforo III. *vi* hacer señales con semáforo
semblance ['sembləns] *n no pl, form* apariencia *f*
semen ['siːmən] *n no pl* semen *m*
semester [sɪ'mestəʳ, *Am:* sə'mestɚ] *n* UNIV semestre *m* (académico)
semi ['semi] *n* 1. *Aus, Brit, inf* (*house*) casa *f* pareada 2. *Am, Aus, inf* (*truck*) trailer *m* 3. *inf* SPORTS semifinal *f*
semiautomatic [ˌsemiɔːtə'mætɪk, *Am:* -ɑːt̬ə'mæt̬ɪk] *adj* semiautomático, -a
semibreve ['semibriːv] *n Aus, Brit* MUS redonda *f*
semicircle ['semiˌsɜːkl, *Am:* -ˌsɜːrkl] *n* MAT semicírculo *m*
semicircular [ˌsemi'sɜːkjʊləʳ, *Am:* 'sɜːrkjəlɚ] *adj* semicircular
semicolon [ˌsemi'kəʊlən, *Am:* 'semiˌkoʊ-] *n* punto *m* y coma
semiconductor [ˌsemikən'dʌktəʳ, *Am:* -t̬ɚ] *n* ELEC semiconductor *m*
semiconscious [ˌsemi'kɒntʃəs, *Am:* -'kɑːn-] *adj* semiconsciente
semi-detached [ˌsemidɪ'tætʃt] *adj* ~ **house** casa *f* pareada
semifinal [ˌsemi'faɪnəl] *n* SPORTS semifinal *f*
semifinalist [ˌsemi'faɪnəlɪst] *n* SPORTS semifinalista *mf*
seminal ['seminəl, *Am:* 'semə-] *adj* (*important*) fundamental
seminar ['seminɑːʳ, *Am:* -ənɑːr] *n* UNIV seminario *m*
seminary ['seminəri, *Am:* -ner-] *n* REL seminario *m*
semiofficial *adj* semioficial
semiotics [ˌsemi'ɒtɪks, *Am:* ˌsiːmi'ɑːt̬ɪks] *n no pl* semiótica *f*

semiprecious [ˌsemɪ'preʃəs] *adj* semiprecioso, -a

semiquaver ['semɪˌkweɪvəʳ, *Am:* -və·] *n Aus, Brit* MUS semicorchea *f*

semiskilled [ˌsemɪ'skɪld] *adj* semicualificado, -a

Semite ['siːmaɪt, *Am:* 'semaɪt] *n* semita *mf*

Semitic [sɪ'mɪtɪk, *Am:* sə'mɪt-] *adj* semítico, -a

semitone ['semɪtəʊn, *Am:* -toʊn] *n* MUS semitono *m*

semitrailer ['semɪˌtreɪləʳ, *Am:* -ə·] *n Am* tráiler *m*

semitropical [ˌsemɪ'trɒpɪkəl, *Am:* -'trɑːpɪ-] *adj* subtropical

semivowel ['semɪˌvaʊəl] *n* LING semivocal *f*

semolina [ˌseməˈliːnə] *n no pl* sémola *f*

Sen. *n Am abbr of* **Senator** senador(a) *m(f)*

senate ['senɪt] *n no pl* **1.** POL senado *m* **2.** UNIV consejo *m*

senator ['senətəʳ, *Am:* -t̬ə·] *n* POL senador(a) *m(f)*

senatorial [ˌsenə'tɔːriəl] *adj Am* senatorial

send [send] I. *vt* <sent, sent> **1.** (*message, letter, flowers*) enviar, mandar; (*telegram*) poner; **to ~ sth by post** enviar algo por correo; **to ~ sb to prison** mandar a alguien a la cárcel; **to ~ one's love to sb** mandar saludos cariñosos a alguien; **~ her my regards** dale recuerdos de mi parte; **Philip ~s his apologies** Philip pide que lo disculpen; **to ~ word (to sb)** *form* informar (a alguien) **2.** (*propel*) lanzar; **to ~ sth flying** hacer saltar algo por los aires **3.** RADIO transmitir **4.** *inf* (*cause*) **to ~ sb to sleep** hacer que alguien se duerma; **to ~ sb crazy** *Brit* volver loco a alguien ►**to ~ sb packing** *inf* mandar a alguien a freír espárragos II. *vi* <sent, sent> mandar a alguien

◆**send away** I. *vi* **to ~ for sth** pedir algo (por correo) II. *vt* **1.** (*dismiss*) despedir **2.** (*send to another place*) enviar

◆**send back** *vt* devolver; (*person*) hacer volver

◆**send down** *vt* **1.** *Brit* UNIV (*expel*) expulsar **2.** LAW (*imprison*) encarcelar **3.** (*cause to drop: prices, temperature*) hacer bajar

◆**send for** *vt* (*person*) llamar; (*assistance*) pedir; (*goods*) encargar

◆**send forth** *vt* **1.** *liter* (*make go*) enviar **2.** (*emit*) emitir; (*smell, heat*) despedir

◆**send in** *vt* **1.** (*application, report*) enviar; (*reinforcements*) mandar **2.** (*let in*) hacer pasar

◆**send off** I. *vt* **1.** (*cause to depart*) mandar; (*by post*) enviar por correo **2.** *Aus, Brit* SPORTS expulsar II. *vi* **to ~ for sth** pedir algo (por correo)

◆**send on** *vt* **1.** (*send in advance*) mandar por adelantado **2.** (*forward: mail*) remitir; (*order*) transmitir

◆**send out** I. *vt* **1.** (*ask to leave*) echar **2.** (*send on errand*) mandar **3.** (*dispatch*) enviar **4.** (*emit: signal, rays*) emitir; (*smell,*

heat) despedir II. *vi* **to ~ for sth** pedir que traigan algo

◆**send up** *vt* **1.** (*drive up: prices, temperature*) hacer subir **2.** (*caricature*) imitar **3.** *Am* (*put in prison*) meter preso

sender *n* remitente *mf;* '**return to ~**' 'devuélvase al remitente'

send-off ['sendɒf, *Am:* -ɑːf] *n* despedida *f;* **to give sb a good ~** dar una buena despedida a alguien **send-up** *n inf* parodia *f*

Senegal [ˌsenɪ'gɔːl] *n* el Senegal

Senegalese [ˌsenɪgə'liːz] I. *adj* senegalés, -esa II. *n* senegalés, -esa *m, f*

senile ['siːnaɪl] *adj* senil; **to go ~** chochear

senile dementia *n* demencia *f* senil

senility [sɪ'nɪləti, *Am:* sə'nɪlət̬i] *n no pl* senilidad *f*

senior ['siːniəʳ, *Am:* -njə·] I. *adj* **1.** *form* (*older*) mayor; **James Grafton, Senior** James Grafton, padre **2.** (*higher in rank*) superior; **to be ~ to sb** estar por encima de alguien **3.** (*of earlier appointment*) más antiguo, -a **4.** SCHOOL de los cursos superiores; (*pupil*) de último curso II. *n* **1.** (*older person*) mayor *mf;* **she is two years my ~** me lleva dos años **2.** (*of higher rank*) superior *mf* **3.** *Am* SCHOOL estudiante *mf* de último curso

senior citizen *n* jubilado, -a *m, f* **senior high school** *n* instituto *m* de bachillerato

seniority [ˌsiːni'ɒrəti, *Am:* siː'njɔːrət̬i] *n no pl* antigüedad *f*

senior officer *n* oficial *mf* de alto rango **senior partner** *n* socio, -a *m, f* mayoritario, -a **senior school** *n* colegio *m* de enseñanza secundaria

sensation [sen'seɪʃən] *n* sensación *f;* **to be ~** ser un éxito; **to cause a ~** hacer furor

sensational [sen'seɪʃənəl] *adj* **1.** (*fabulous*) sensacional **2.** *pej* (*newspaper, disclosure*) sensacionalista

sense [sents] I. *n* **1.** (*faculty*) sentido *m;* **~ of hearing** oído *m;* **~ of sight** vista *f;* **~ of smell** olfato *m;* **~ of taste** gusto *m;* **~ of touch** tacto *m* **2.** (*ability*) sentido *m;* **to have no ~ of occasion** ser inoportuno; **to lose all ~ of time** perder la noción del tiempo **3.** (*way*) sentido *m;* **in every ~** en todos los sentidos; **in a ~** en cierto modo; **in no ~** de ninguna manera **4.** (*sensation*) sensación *f* **5.** *pl* (*clear mental faculties*) juicio *m;* **to be in one's** (**right**) **~s** estar en su sano juicio; **to bring sb to his/her ~s**, **to come to one's ~s** (*recover consciousness*) recobrar el conocimiento; (*see reason*) entrar en razón; **to make sb see ~** hacer entrar en razón a alguien; **to take leave of one's ~s** perder la razón **6.** *no pl* (*good judgment*) (**common**) **~** sentido *m* común; **to have enough** [*o* **the good**] **~ to ...** tener la sensatez de...; **to talk ~** decir cosas sensatas **7.** (*feeling*) impresión *f;* **to feel a ~ of belonging** sentirse aceptado **8.** (*meaning*) significado *m*, sentido *m;* **to make ~** tener sentido; **in the full ~ of the word** en el sentido amplio de la

palabra; **there's no** ~ **in doing ...** no tiene
sentido hacer...; **what's the** ~ **in doing ...?**
¿qué sentido tiene hacer...? **9.**(*opinion*)
opinión *f* (general) **II.** *vt* sentir; **to** ~ **that ...**
darse cuenta de que...

senseless ['sentsləs] *adj* **1.**(*pointless*) sin
sentido; (*remark*) insensato, -a **2.** MED inconsciente; **to beat sb** ~ dejar a alguien sin sentido
de una paliza

sense organ *n* órgano *m* sensorial

sensibility [ˌsentsɪ'bɪləti, *Am:* -sə'bɪləti] *n*
no pl sensibilidad *f;* **to offend sb's sensibil-
ities** herir la sensibilidad de alguien

sensible ['sentsɪbl, *Am:* -sə-] *adj* **1.**(*having
good judgement: person, decision*) sensato, -a
2.(*suitable: clothes, shoes*) práctico, -a
3.(*aware*) consciente **4.**(*noticeable*) notable

sensibly *adv* **1.**(*wisely*) sensatamente;
(*behave*) prudentemente; (*decide*) acertada-
mente **2.**(*dress*) con ropa cómoda

sensitive ['sentsɪtɪv, *Am:* -sə̝tɪv] *adj*
1.(*appreciative*) sensible; **to be** ~ **to sb's
needs** ser consciente de las necesidades de alguien **2.**(*touchy*) susceptible; **to be** ~ **about
sth** ser susceptible a algo **3.**(*touchy: subject,
moment*) delicado, -a; (*age*) conflictivo, -a
4.(*secret: documents, work*) confidencial

sensitiveness *n*, **sensitivity** [ˌsentsɪ-
'tɪvəti, *Am:* -sə̝tɪvə̝ti] *n* **1.**(*touchiness*) susceptibilidad *f* **2.**(*understanding*) sensibilidad
f, delicadeza *f* **3.**(*secret nature*) confidencia-
lidad *f*

sensitize ['sentsɪtaɪz, *Am:* -sə-] *vt Am* sensibilizar; **to** ~ **sb to a problem** concienciar a alguien de un problema

sensor ['sentsər, *Am:* -sə̝r] *n* TECH, ELEC sensor
m

sensory ['sentsəri] *adj* sensorial

sensual ['sentsjʊəl, *Am:* -ʃuəl] *adj* sensual

sensuality [ˌsentsju'æləti, *Am:* -ʃu'æləti] *n*
no pl sensualidad *f*

sensuous ['sentsjʊəs, *Am:* -ʃuəs] *adj* sensual

sent [sent] *pp, pt of* **send**

sentence ['sentəns, *Am:* -ṭəns] **I.** *n* **1.**(*court
decision*) sentencia *f;* (*punishment*) condena
f; **jail** ~ condena de encarcelamiento; **life** ~
cadena perpetua; **to receive a** ~ ser condenado; **to serve a** ~ cumplir una condena
2. LING frase *f* **II.** *vt* condenar

sententious [sen'tenʃəs] *adj form* sentencioso, -a

sentient ['senʃnt] *adj form* sensible

sentiment ['sentɪmənt, *Am:* -ṭə-] *n form*
1.(*opinion*) opinión *f;* **public/popular** ~
opinión pública/popular; **to echo a** ~ hacerse
eco de una opinión; **to share sb's** ~ compartir
la opinión de alguien **2.** *no pl* (*emotion*) sentimiento *m*

sentimental [ˌsentɪ'mentəl, *Am:* -ṭə'men-
ṭəl] *adj* **1.** sentimental; **to be** ~ **about sth** ser
sentimental con algo **2.** *pej* sensiblero, -a

sentimentality [ˌsentɪmen'tæləti, *Am:* -ṭə-
men'tæləṭi] *n no pl, pej* sentimentalismo *m*

sentimentalize [ˌsentɪ'mentələɪz, *Am:*
-ṭə'menṭələɪz] *vt Am, pej* dar una visión
sentimental de

sentry ['sentri] *n* centinela *m;* **to be on** ~
duty estar de guardia

sentry box *n* garita *f* de centinela

separable ['sepərəbl] *adj form* separable

separate¹ ['seprət, *Am:* 'sepə̝ɪt] **I.** *adj* separado, -a; **to remain a** ~ **entity** ser una entidad
independiente; **a** ~ **piece of paper** una hoja
de papel aparte; **to go one's** ~ **ways** ir por distintos caminos; **to keep sth** ~ mantener algo
aparte **II.** *n pl* piezas *fpl* sueltas de ropa

separate² ['sepəreɪt] **I.** *vt* separar; **to** ~ **two
people** separar a dos personas; **to** ~ **egg
whites from yolks** separar las claras de los
huevos de las yemas **II.** *vi* separarse

separated *adj* separado, -a

separation [ˌsepə'reɪʃən] *n* separación *f;*
(*division*) división *f*

separatism ['sepərətɪzm] *n no pl* separa-
tismo *m*

separatist ['sepərətɪst] **I.** *n* separatista *mf*
II. *adj* separatista

separator ['sepəreɪtər, *Am:* -ṭə̝] *n* separador *m*

sepia ['si:pɪə] **I.** *n* sepia *f* **II.** *adj* de color sepia

sepsis ['sepsɪs] *n no pl* sepsis *f*

September [sep'tembər, *Am:* -bə̝] *n* septiembre *m; s. a.* **April**

septic ['septɪk] *adj* séptico, -a; **to go** [*o* **turn**]
~ infectarse

septicaemia *n Brit,* **septicemia** [ˌseptɪ-
'si:mɪə, *Am:* -ṭə'-] *n Am no pl* septicemia *f*

septuagenarian [ˌseptjʊədʒɪ'neərɪən, *Am:*
-tuədʒə'neri-] **I.** *n* septuagenario, -a *m, f*
II. *adj* septuagenario, -a

sepulcher *n Am s.* **sepulchre**

sepulchral [sɪ'pʌlkrəl, *Am:* sə'pʌl-] *adj liter*
1.(*silence*) sepulcral **2.**(*gloomy*) lóbrego, -a

sepulchre ['sepəlkər, *Am:* -kə̝] *n Brit* sepulcro *m*

sequel ['si:kwəl] *n* **1.** continuación *f;* **the** ~ **of
an earlier success** la secuela de un éxito temprano **2.**(*follow-up*) desenlace *m*

sequence ['si:kwəns] *n* **1.**(*order*) orden *m;*
(*of events*) sucesión *f* **2.**(*part of film*) secuencia *f*

sequential [sɪ'kwenʃl] *adj form* secuencial

sequestrate [sɪ'kwestreɪt] *vt* (*confiscate*)
confiscar; (*property in litigation*) secuestrar

sequestration [ˌsi:kwe'streɪʃən] *n no pl*
1.(*confiscation*) embargo *m;* (*of property in
litigation*) secuestro *m* **2.** *Am* (*isolation*) aislamiento *m*

sequin ['si:kwɪn] *n* lentejuela *f*

sequoia [sɪ'kwɔɪə] *n* secoya *f*

Serb [sɜːb, *Am:* sɜːrb] **I.** *adj* serbio, -a **II.** *n* serbio, -a *m, f*

Serbia ['sɜːbɪə, *Am:* 'sɜːr-] *n* Serbia *f*

Serbian ['sɜːbɪən, *Am:* 'sɜːr-] *n s.* **Serb**

Serbo-Croat [ˌsɜːbəʊ'krəʊæt, *Am:* ˌsɜːr-
bəʊkrəʊ'-] *n* LING serbocroata *mf*

serenade [ˌserə'neɪd] I. *vt* 1. (*sing to*) cantar una serenata a 2. (*play music for*) dar una serenata a II. *n* serenata *f*, mañanita *f Méx*

serene [sɪ'riːn, *Am:* sə'-] *adj* 1. (*calm*) sereno, -a; (*sea*) calmado, -a 2. (*peaceful*) tranquilo, -a 3. (*cheerful*) feliz

serenity [sɪ'renəti, *Am:* sə'renəṭi] *n no pl* 1. (*calmness*) serenidad *f* 2. (*tranquility*) tranquilidad *f* 3. (*cheerfulness*) felicidad *f*

serf [sɜːf, *Am:* sɜːrf] *n* HIST siervo, -a *m, f*

serfdom *n no pl* HIST servidumbre *f*

sergeant ['sɑːdʒənt, *Am:* 'sɑːrdʒənt] *n* sargento *mf;* ~ **at arms** ujier *m*

sergeant major *n* brigada *mf*

serial ['sɪərɪəl, *Am:* 'sɪri-] I. *n* serial *m;* **TV** ~ telenovela *f* II. *adj* 1. (*in series*) consecutivo, -a 2. (*shown in parts*) por entregas

serialize ['sɪərɪəlaɪz, *Am:* 'sɪri-] *vt* (*in newspaper, magazine*) publicar por entregas; TV, RADIO presentar por capítulos

serial killer *n* asesino, -a *m, f* en serie **serial number** *n* numero *m* de serie **serial port** *n* INFOR puerto *m* en serie

series ['sɪəriːz, *Am:* 'sɪriːz] *n inv* 1. (*sequence*) serie *f* 2. (*succession*) sucesión *f;* **in** ~ ELEC en serie 3. (*set of broadcasts*) ciclo *m*

serious ['sɪərɪəs, *Am:* 'sɪri-] *adj* 1. (*earnest, solemn*) serio, -a 2. (*problem, injury*) grave 3. (*not slight*) de consideración; (*argument*) importante 4. (*determined*) firme; **to be** ~ **about sb** ir en serio con alguien 5. *inf* (*significant*) significativo, -a; ~ **money** cantidad de dinero 6. (*large: debt, amount*) considerable

seriously *adv* 1. (*in earnest*) seriamente, en serio; **to** ~ **expect sb to do sth** esperar de verdad que alguien haga algo; **no,** ~ ... no, en serio...; **it would be** ~ **wrong of him if** ... sería un gran error por su parte si... 2. (*ill, damaged*) gravemente 3. *inf* (*very*) extremadamente; **she was** ~ **drunk** estaba borracha a más no poder

seriousness *n no pl* 1. (*truthfulness*) seriedad *f;* **in all** ~ en serio 2. (*serious nature*) gravedad *f*

sermon ['sɜːmən, *Am:* 'sɜːr-] *n a. fig* sermón *m;* **to deliver a** ~ dar un sermón

serpent ['sɜːpənt, *Am:* 'sɜːr-] *n* serpiente *f*

serpentine ['sɜːpəntaɪn, *Am:* 'sɜːr-] *adj liter* 1. (*snake-like*) serpentino, -a 2. (*twisting*) serpenteante 3. (*complicated*) complicado, -a 4. (*sly*) ingenioso, -a; (*explanation*) artificioso, -a

serrated [sɪ'reɪtɪd, *Am:* 'sereɪṭɪd] *adj* serrado, -a; ~ **knife** cuchillo *m* de sierra

serried ['serɪd] *adj liter* apretado, -a; ~ **ranks** filas *fpl* cerradas

serum ['sɪərəm, *Am:* 'sɪrəm] <-s *o* sera> *n* suero *m*

servant ['sɜːvənt, *Am:* 'sɜːr-] *n* criado, -a *m, f*, mucamo, -a *m, f AmL*

serve [sɜːv, *Am:* sɜːrv] I. *n* SPORTS saque *m* II. *vt* 1. (*attend*) atender 2. (*provide*) servir; **to**

~ **alcohol** servir bebidas alcohólicas 3. (*be enough for*) ser suficiente 4. (*work for*) estar al servicio de; **to** ~ **sb's interests** servir a los intereses de alguien 5. (*complete: sentence, mandate*) cumplir; **to** ~ **time** (**for sth**) *inf* cumplir condena (por algo) 6. (*help achieve*) ser útil a; **if my memory** ~**s me right** si la memoria no me falla 7. SPORTS sacar 8. (*deliver*) entregar; **to** ~ **sb with papers** proporcionar papeles a alguien ▶**it** ~**s him/her right!** ¡se lo merece! III. *vi* 1. (*put food on plates*) servir 2. (*be useful*) servir; **to** ~ **as sth** servir de algo 3. (*work for*) prestar servicio; **to** ~ **in the army** servir en el ejército 4. (*be acceptable*) ser aceptable; (*suffice*) ser suficiente 5. SPORTS sacar

◆**serve out** *vt* 1. GASTR servir 2. (*sentence, mandate*) cumplir

◆**serve up** *vt* GASTR servir; *fig* ofrecer

server ['sɜːvəʳ, *Am:* 'sɜːrvɚ] *n* 1. (*spoon*) cuchara *f* de servir; **salad** ~ cubiertos *mpl* para servir ensalada 2. (*tray*) bandeja *f;* (*dish*) fuente *f* 3. (*waiter*) camarero, -a *m, f* 4. INFOR servidor *m* 5. SPORTS *jugador que tiene el saque*

service ['sɜːvɪs, *Am:* 'sɜːr-] I. *n* 1. *no pl* (*in shop, restaurant*) servicio *m;* (*help, assistance*) asistencia *f*, servicio *m;* **bus/train** ~ servicio de autobuses/trenes; **to be of** ~ (**to sb**) ser de utilidad (a alguien); **to operate a** ~ llevar a cabo un servicio; **to press sth into** ~ recurrir a algo; **to see** ~ *fig* prestar servicio 3. (*department*) servicio *m;* **the Service** MIL el ejército; NAUT la marina; AVIAT la aviación; **to be fit/unfit for** ~ ser apto/no apto para el servicio 4. SPORTS saque *m* 5. REL oficio *m;* **morning** ~ misa matinal; **to hold a** ~ celebrar una misa 6. *Brit* TECH mantenimiento *m;* AUTO revisión *f* 7. (*set*) vajilla *f;* **tea** ~ juego *m* de té 8. *pl, Brit* área *f* de servicio ▶**to be at sb's** ~ *iron* estar al servicio de alguien; **to be in** ~ (*employed as servant*) estar empleado como criado; (*be in use*) estar en uso II. *vt* 1. (*car, TV*) revisar 2. FIN **to** ~ **a loan** pagar el interés de un préstamo

serviceable ['sɜːvɪsəbl, *Am:* 'sɜːr-] *adj* servible

service area *n* área *f* de servicio **service bus** *n,* **service car** *n Aus* coche *m* de línea **service center** *n Am* 1. (*on motorway*) área *f* de servicios 2. (*for repairs*) centro *m* de reparaciones; (*garage*) garaje *m* **service charge** *n* gastos *mpl* de servicio **service department** *n* sección *f* de mantenimiento **service elevator** *n Am* (*for employees*) ascensor *m* para empleados; (*for goods*) montacargas *m inv* **service entrance** *n* entrada *f* de servicio **service hatch** *n* ventanilla *f* para servir **service industry** *n* sector *m* servicios **service lift** *n Brit* (*for employees*) ascensor *m* para empleados; (*for goods*) montacargas *m inv* **serviceman** *n* militar *m* **service road** *n* vía *f* de acceso **service sector** *n* sector *m* (de) servicios **service**

station *n* **1.** (*selling gasoline*) estación *f* de servicio **2.** *Brit* (*on motorway*) área *f* de servicio **servicewoman** *n* militar *f*
serviette [ˌsɜːvɪˈet, *Am:* ˌsɜːr-] *n Brit* servilleta *f*
servile [ˈsɜːvaɪl, *Am:* ˈsɜːrvl] *adj pej* servil
servility [sɜːˈvɪləti, *Am:* sɜːrˈvɪlət̬i] *n no pl, pej* servilismo *m*
serving [ˈsɜːvɪŋ, *Am:* ˈsɜːr-] **I.** *n* (*portion*) ración *f* **II.** *adj* activo
serving hatch *n* ventanilla *f* para servir
serving spoon *n* cuchara *f* de servir
servitude [ˈsɜːvɪtjuːd, *Am:* ˈsɜːrvətuːd] *n no pl, form* servidumbre *f*
servo [ˈsɜːvəʊ, *Am:* ˈsɜːrvoʊ] *n* servo *m*
sesame [ˈsesəmi] *n no pl* sésamo *m* ▶**open ~!** ¡ábrete, sésamo!
session [ˈseʃən] *n* **1.** (*meeting*) sesión *f*; **to be in ~** estar reunido; **a drinking ~** *inf* una borrachera **2.** *Am, Scot* SCHOOL clase *f*; (*teaching year*) curso *m*
set [set] **I.** *adj* **1.** (*ready*) listo, -a; **to get ~** (**to do sth**) prepararse (para hacer algo) **2.** (*fixed*) fijo, -a; **to be ~ in one's ways** tener costumbres profundamente arraigadas **3.** (*as signed*) asignado, -a **II.** *n* **1.** (*group: of people*) grupo *m*; (*of cups, chess*) juego *m*; (*of kitchen utensils*) batería *f*; (*of stamps*) serie *f*; (*of tools*) set *m*; **~ of glasses** cristalería *f*; **~ of teeth** dentadura *f* **2.** (*collection*) colección *f* **3.** CINE plató *m* **4.** (*television*) televisor *m* **5.** (*in tennis*) set *m* **6.** (*musical performance*) actuación *f*; **to play a long/short ~** tocar durante mucho/poco tiempo **III.** *vt* <set, set> **1.** (*place*) poner, colocar; **a house that is ~ on a hill** una casa situada sobre una colina; **to ~ a broken bone** colocar bien un hueso roto **2.** (*give: task*) imponer; (*problem*) plantear; (*example*) dar **3.** (*start*) **to ~ a boat afloat** poner una barca a flote; **to ~ sth on fire** prender fuego algo; **to ~ sth in motion** poner algo en movimiento; **to ~ the country on the road to economic recovery** encaminar el país hacia la recuperación económica; **to set a dog on sb** hacer que un perro ataque a alguien **4.** (*adjust*) ajustar; (*prepare*) preparar; **to ~ the table** poner la mesa **5.** (*fix*) fijar; (*record*) establecer; (*date, price*) determinar; **to ~ oneself a goal** fijarse un objetivo **6.** (*arrange*) acordar **7.** (*encrust*) adornar; (*insert*) introducir; **to ~ a watch with sapphires** engastar zafiros en un reloj **8.** (*provide*) poner; **to ~ sth to music** poner música a algo **IV.** *vi* **1.** MED soldarse **2.** (*become firm: cement*) endurecerse; (*jelly, cheese*) cuajar **3.** (*sink*) hundirse **4.** (*sun*) ponerse
◆**set about** *vt* **1.** (*begin*) emprender; **to ~ doing sth** comenzar a hacer algo **2.** *inf* (*attack*) atacar
◆**set against** *vt* **1.** (*compare*) comparar; **to set the advantages against the disadvantages** sopesar las ventajas y los inconvenientes **2.** (*offset*) compensar **3.** (*make oppose*) **to set**

sb against sb/sth poner a alguien en contra de alguien/algo
◆**set apart** *vt* **1.** (*distinguish*) diferenciar **2.** (*reserve*) reservar
◆**set aside** *vt* **1.** (*save*) reservar; (*time*) guardar; (*money*) ahorrar **2.** (*ignore*) ignorar; **to set one's differences aside** dejar a un lado las diferencias con alguien **3.** (*overturn*) desechar **4.** (*put to side*) dejar de lado
◆**set back** *vt* **1.** (*delay*) retrasar **2.** (*place away from*) apartar **3.** *inf* (*cost*) costar
◆**set down** *vt* **1.** (*land*) poner en tierra; (*aeroplane*) hacer aterrizar **2.** (*drop off*) dejar **3.** (*write*) poner por escrito; (*record*) registrar
◆**set forth I.** *vt form* s. **set out II.** *vi liter* partir
◆**set off I.** *vi* partir; **to ~** (**for a place**) ponerse en camino (hacia un lugar) **II.** *vt* **1.** accionar **2.** (*detonate*) hacer explotar; (*explosive*) detonar **3.** (*cause*) causar **4.** (*enhance*) hacer; **to set sb off** (**doing sth**) hacer [*o* provocar] que alguien (haga algo)
◆**set on** *vt* atacar
◆**set out I.** *vt* **1.** (*display, arrange*) disponer, colocar **2.** (*explain*) exponer **II.** *vi* **1.** s. **set off 2.** (*intend*) **to ~ to do sth** tener la intención de hacer algo
◆**set to** *vi* **1.** (*begin*) ponerse manos a la obra **2.** *inf* (*begin fighting*) llegar a las manos; **to ~ with sb** empezar a pelearse con alguien
◆**set up** *vt* **1.** (*prepare*) poner, construir **2.** (*establish*) establecer; (*arrange*) disponer; (*cause*) causar; (*committee*) constituir; (*corporation*) crear; (*dictatorship*) instaurar **3.** (*claim*) **to set oneself up as sth** dárselas de algo **4.** (*make healthy*) fortalecer **5.** (*provide*) proveer **6.** *inf* (*deceive*) defraudar
setback [ˈsetbæk] *n* revés *m*; **to experience a ~** tener un contratiempo
set square *n Aus, Brit* cartabón *m*
settee [seˈtiː] *n* sofá *m*
setter [ˈsetəʳ, *Am:* ˈset̬ɚ] *n* (*dog*) setter *mf*
setting [ˈsetɪŋ, *Am:* ˈset̬-] *n* **1.** (*of sun*) puesta *f* **2.** (*scenery*) escenario *m*; (*surroundings*) entorno *m*; (*landscape*) marco *m* **3.** TECH ajuste *m* **4.** (*frame for jewel*) engaste *m* **5.** MUS arreglo *m*
setting lotion *n* fijador *m* (para el pelo)
settle [ˈsetl, *Am:* ˈset̬-] **I.** *vi* **1.** (*take up residence*) instalarse **2.** (*get comfortable*) ponerse cómodo, -a **3.** (*calm down*) calmarse; (*weather*) serenarse; (*situation*) normalizarse, aconcharse *Chile* **4.** *Aus, Brit* (*apply oneself*) aplicarse; **to ~ to work** ponerse a trabajar en serio **5.** (*reach an agreement*) llegar a un acuerdo **6.** *form* (*pay*) pagar; **to ~ with sb** saldar las cuentas con alguien **7.** (*accumulate*) acumularse; (*snow*) cuajar **8.** (*land*) asentarse; (*bird*) posarse **9.** (*sink*) hundirse **10.** (*food*) asentarse en el estómago **II.** *vt* **1.** (*calm down: stomach*) calmar **2.** (*decide*) acordar; **it's been ~d that ...** se ha acordado que... **3.** (*conclude*) finalizar; (*resolve*) resolver;

(*problem*) solucionar; (*affairs*) arreglar; **to ~ a lawsuit** poner fin a un litigio **4.**(*pay*) pagar; (*an account*) liquidar **5.**(*colonize*) colonizar ▶**that ~s it!** ¡ya no hay más que decir!

♦**settle down** I. *vi* **1.**(*take up residence*) instalarse **2.**(*get comfortable*) ponerse cómodo, -a **3.**(*adjust*) adaptarse **4.**(*calm down*) calmarse II. *vt* **to set oneself down to sth** acostumbrarse a algo

♦**settle for** *vt* contentarse con

♦**settle in** *vi* acostumbrarse

♦**settle on** *vt* **1.**(*decide on*) decidir **2.**(*agree on*) acordar **3.**(*bequeath*) dejar

♦**settle up** *vi* ajustar cuentas

♦**settle upon** *vt form s.* **settle on**

settled ['setld, *Am:*'seţ-] *adj* **1.**(*established*) establecido, -a; (*in a regular way of life*) instalado, -a; **to feel ~** sentirse cómodo **2.**(*calm*) calmado, -a **3.**(*fixed*) fijo, -a

settlement ['setlmənt, *Am:* 'seţ-] *n* **1.**(*resolution*) resolución *f*; (*of strike*) finalización *f* **2.**(*agreement*) acuerdo *m;* **to negotiate a ~** (**with sb**) negociar un acuerdo (con alguien) **3.** FIN, ECON liquidación *f*, pago *m;* **in ~ of sth** para liquidar algo **4.**(*village, town*) asentamiento *m;* (*act of colonization*) colonización *f* **5.** *no pl* (*subsidence*) hundimiento *m*

settlement date *n* FIN fecha *f* de resolución

settler ['setlə', *Am:* 'seţlə-] *n* colono, -a *m, f*

set-to ['settu:] *n inf* bronca *f;* **to have a ~** (**with sb**) tener una bronca (con alguien)

set-up ['setʌp, *Am:*'seţ-] *n* **1.**(*way things are arranged*) estructura *f;* (*arrangement*) organización *f* **2.** *inf* (*trick*) trampa *f*

seven ['sevn] I. *adj* siete *inv* II. *n* siete *m; s. a.* **eight**

sevenfold ['sevnfəʊld, *Am:* -foʊld] I. *adj* séptuplo, -a II. *adv* **to increase ~** aumentar en siete veces

seventeen [ˌsevn'ti:n] I. *adj* diecisiete *inv* II. *n* diecisiete *m; s. a.* **eight**

seventeenth [ˌsevn'ti:nθ] I. *adj* decimoséptimo, -a II. *n no pl* **1.**(*order*) decimoséptimo, -a *m, f* **2.**(*date*) diecisiete *m* **3.**(*fraction*) diecisieteavo *m;* (*part*) diecisieteava parte *f; s. a.* **eighth**

seventh ['sevnθ] I. *adj* séptimo, -a II. *n no pl* **1.**(*order*) séptimo, -a *m, f* **2.**(*date*) siete *m* **3.**(*fraction*) séptimo *m;* (*part*) octava parte *f; s. a.* **eighth**

seventieth ['sevntiθ] I. *adj* septuagésimo, -a II. *n no pl* (*order*) septuagésimo, -a *m, f;* (*fraction*) septuagésimo *m;* (*part*) septuagésima parte *f; s. a.* **eighth**

seventy ['sevnti, *Am:* -ţi] I. *adj* setenta *inv* II. *n* <-ies> setenta *m; s. a.* **eighty**

sever ['sevə', *Am:* 'sevə-] *vt* (*limb, branch*) cortar; (*relationship*) romper

several ['sevrəl] I. *adj* **1.**(*some*) varios, -as; (*reasons*) diversos, -as; **~ times** varias veces; (*distinct*) distintos, -as **2.**(*individual*) respectivos, -as II. *pron* (*some*) algunos, -as; (*different*) varios, -as; **~ of us** algunos de nosotros; **we've**

got **~** tenemos varios

severally *adv* **1.**(*individually*) respectivamente **2.**(*separately*) por separado

severance ['sevərənts] *n no pl, form* ruptura *f*

severance pay *n* indemnización *f* por despido

severe [sɪ'vɪə', *Am:* sə'vɪr] *adj* **1.**(*problem, illness*) grave; (*pain*) fuerte; **to be under ~ strain** estar bajo una gran tensión **2.**(*criticism, punishment, person*) severo, -a; (*strict*) estricto, -a; (*rough*) duro, -a **3.**(*weather*) riguroso, -a; **~ frost** fuerte helada *f* **4.**(*austere*) austero, -a

severely *adv* **1.**(*harshly*) con severidad **2.**(*damaged*) seriamente; (*ill*) gravemente

severity [sɪ'verəti, *Am:* sə'verəţi] *n no pl* **1.**(*of illness, problem*) gravedad *f* **2.**(*of criticism, punishment, person*) severidad *f* **3.**(*austerity*) austeridad *f*

Seville ['sevɪl] *n* Sevilla *f*

sew [səʊ, *Am:* soʊ] <sewed, sewn *o* sewed> I. *vt* coser; **hand ~n** cosido a mano II. *vi* coser

♦**sew on** *vt* coser

♦**sew up** *vt* **1.**(*repair*) coser, zurcir **2.** MED suturar **3.** *inf* (*arrange*) arreglar; **to ~ a deal** cerrar un trato

sewage ['su:ɪdʒ] *n no pl* aguas *fpl* residuales

sewage farm *n*, **sewage plant** *n* ECOL planta *f* de tratamiento de aguas residuales

sewer ['səʊə', *Am:* 'soʊə-] *n* alcantarilla *f*

sewerage ['sʊərɪdʒ, *Am:* 'su:ə-ɪdʒ] *n no pl* alcantarillado *m*, drenaje *m Méx*

sewer rat *n* rata *f* de alcantarilla

sewing ['səʊɪŋ, *Am:* 'soʊ-] I. *n no pl* costura *f* II. *adj* de costura

sewing basket *n* costurero *m* **sewing machine** *n* máquina *f* de coser

sewn [səʊn, *Am:* soʊn] *pp of* **sew**

sex [seks] I. <-es> *n* (*gender, intercourse*) sexo *m;* **to have ~** tener relaciones sexuales II. *vt* determinar el sexo de

sex appeal *n no pl* atractivo *m* sexual **sex discrimination** *n no pl* discriminación *f* sexual **sex education** *n no pl* educación *f* sexual

sexism ['seksɪzəm] *n no pl* sexismo *m*

sexist I. *adj* sexista II. *n* sexista *mf*

sexless ['seksləs] *adj* sin sexo

sex life *n no pl* vida *f* sexual **sex symbol** *n* símbolo *m* sexual

sextant ['sekstənt] *n* sextante *m*

sextet [seks'tet] *n* sexteto *m*

sexton ['sekstən] *n* sacristán *m*

sexual ['sekʃʊəl, *Am:* -ʃuəl] *adj* sexual

sexual harassment *n* acoso *m* sexual **sexual intercourse** *n* relaciones *fpl* sexuales

sexuality [ˌsekʃʊ'æləti, *Am:* -ʃu'æləţi] *n no pl* sexualidad *f*

sexually *adv* sexualmente; **to be ~ abused** ser víctima de abusos sexuales

sexy ['seksi] <-ier, -iest> *adj inf* **1.**(*physi-*

cally appealing) sexy **2.**(*exciting*) excitante

Seychelles [seɪˈʃelz] *n* Islas *fpl* Seychelles

SGML *n* INFOR *abbr of* **Standard General Markup Language** SGML *m*

Sgt *n abbr of* **sergeant** Sgto. *m*

shabby [ˈʃæbi] <-ier, -iest> *adj* **1.**(*badly maintained*) deteriorado, -a **2.**(*poorly dressed*) desharrapado, -a, encuerado, -a *Méx, Cuba* **3.**(*mean*) mezquino, -a; (*trick*) sucio, -a

shack [ʃæk] *n* choza *f*, ruca *f Arg, Chile*, jacal *m Méx*

◆**shack up** *vi* irse a vivir juntos, arrejuntarse *Méx*

shackle [ˈʃækl] **I.** *vt* poner grilletes a, encadenar **II.** *n pl* grilletes *mpl*

shade [ʃeɪd] **I.** *n* **1.** *no pl* (*shadow*) sombra *f*; (*of a painting*) sombreado *m*; **in the ~ of** a [*o* en] la sombra de **2.**(*covering*) pantalla *f* **3.** *pl, Am* (*roller blind*) persiana *f* **4.**(*variation*) matiz *m*; (*of colour*) tono *m*; **pastel ~s** tonos pastel **5.** *no pl* (*small amount*) pizca *f* **6.** *pl, inf* (*glasses*) gafas *fpl* de sol **7.** *inf* (*resemblance*) **~s of Nixon/1989** esto recuerda a Nixon/1989 ▶**to leave** sb/sth **in the ~** eclipsar a alguien/algo **II.** *vt* **1.**(*cast shadow on*) dar sombra a; (*protect*) resguardar (de la luz) **2.** ART sombrear **III.** *vi* (*colours*) fundirse

shading *n no pl* sombreado *m*

shadow [ˈʃædəʊ, *Am:* -oʊ] **I.** *n* **1.** *a. fig* sombra *f*; **the ~s** las tinieblas **2.**(*smallest trace*) pizca *f*; **without a ~ of** a doubt sin sombra de duda ▶**to have ~s under one's eyes** tener ojeras; **to be a ~ of one's former self** no ser ni la sombra de lo que se era; **to be afraid of one's own ~** tener miedo de la propia sombra; **to cast a ~ over sth** ensombrecer algo; **to wear oneself to a ~** agotarse; **to be under sb's ~** estar a la sombra de alguien **II.** *vt* **1.** ART sombrear **2.**(*darken*) ensombrecer **3.**(*follow*) seguir **4.** FIN seguir

shadow-boxing [ˈʃædəʊbɒksɪŋ, *Am:* -oʊbɑːksɪŋ] *n no pl* **1.** SPORTS boxeo con un adversario imaginario **2.** *fig* disputa *f* con un adversario imaginario

shadowy <-ier, -iest> *adj* **1.**(*containing darker spaces*) sombreado, -a; (*photograph*) oscuro, -a **2.**(*vague*) impreciso, -a **3.**(*suspicious*) sombrío, -a

shady [ˈʃeɪdi] <-ier, -iest> *adj* **1.**(*protected from light*) sombreado, -a **2.** *inf* (*dubious*) turbio, -a; (*character*) sospechoso, -a

shaft [ʃɑːft, *Am:* ʃæft] **I.** *n* **1.**(*of tool*) mango *m*; (*of weapon*) asta *f*; (*of arrow*) venablo *m* **2.** TECH eje *m* **3.**(*ray*) rayo *m* **4.**(*for elevator*) hueco *m*; (*of mine*) pozo *m*; **well ~** pozo ▶**to give** sb **the ~** *Am, inf* joder a alguien **II.** *vt inf* (*have sex with, defeat*) joder

shag¹ [ʃæg] <-gg-> *vi Brit, Aus, vulg* follar, coger *Méx*

shag² [ʃæg] *n vulg* polvo *m*

shagged out [ˈʃægdˈaʊt] *adj Brit, Aus, pej, inf* hecho, -a polvo

shaggy [ˈʃægi] <-ier, -iest> *adj* peludo, -a;

(*coat*) lanudo, -a ▶**~ dog story** chiste *m* malo

shah [ʃɑː] *n* sha *m*

shake [ʃeɪk] **I.** *n* **1.**(*wobble*) sacudida *f*; (*vibration*) vibración *f*; (*quiver*) temblor *m*; **with a ~ in one's voice** con la voz temblorosa **2.** *pl* tembleque *m*, temblorina *f Méx;* **to get the ~s** *inf* tener miedo **3.** *Am, inf* (*milk shake*) batido *m*, malteada *f AmL* **4.** *inf* **in two ~s of a** duck's tail en un santiamén; **to be no great ~s** no ser gran cosa; **to be no great ~s (at doing sth)** no ser nada del otro mundo (en algo); **I'm no great ~s as a singer** no se me da muy bien cantar **II.**<shook, shaken> *vt* **1.**(*joggle*) agitar; (*person*) sacudir; (*head*) mover; (*hand*) estrechar; (*house*) hacer temblar; **to ~ one's fist (at sb)** amenazar con el puño (a alguien); **to ~ hands** darse la mano; **to ~ sb by the hand** estrechar la mano de alguien; **to ~ one's head** negar con la cabeza; **to ~ one's hips** mover las caderas **2.**(*unsettle*) debilitar **3.**(*make worried*) desconcertar **III.**<shook, shaken> *vi* temblar; **~ well before opening** agitar bien antes de abrir

◆**shake down** *vt inf* **1.** hacer caer sacudiendo **2.** *Am* (*cheat*) timar

◆**shake off** *vt* **1.**(*agitate to remove*) sacudirse **2.**(*eliminate: cold*) quitarse (de encima); (*pursuer, feeling*) librarse de

◆**shake out** *vt* sacudir

◆**shake up** *vt* **1.**(*jumble*) sacudir, zamarronear *Chile* **2.**(*make worried*) desconcertar **3.**(*reorganize*) reorganizar

shakedown [ˈʃeɪkdaʊn] *n inf* **1.**(*bed*) cama *f* improvisada **2.** *Am* (*search*) redada *f*, arreada *f Arg* **3.** *Am* (*extortion*) exacción *f* de dinero

shaken [ˈʃeɪkn] *vi, vt pp of* **shake**

shaker [ˈʃeɪkə', *Am:* -kɚ] *n* (*for cocktails*) coctelera *f*; **salt ~** salero *m*

shake-up [ˈʃeɪkʌp] *n* reorganización *f*

shakily [ˈʃeɪkɪli] *adv* **1.**(*physically weak*) de modo inestable **2.**(*uncertainly*) con poca firmeza

shaking [ˈʃeɪkɪŋ] **I.** *n* temblor *m* **II.** *adj* tembloroso, -a

shaky [ˈʃeɪki] <-ier, -iest> *adj* **1.**(*jerky*) tembloroso, -a; **to be ~ on one's feet** estar inseguro al andar **2.**(*wavering*) inseguro, -a **3.**(*unstable*) inestable; (*economy*) débil

shale [ʃeɪl] *n no pl* esquisto *m*

shall [ʃæl] *aux* **1.**(*future*) **I ~ give back the money** devolveré el dinero; **we ~ win the match** ganaremos el partido **2.**(*ought to*) **he ~ call his mother** debería llamar a su madre; **we ~ overcome!** ¡nos sobrepondremos! **3.**(*expresses what is mandatory*) **that ~ be unlawful** eso es ilegal

shallot [ʃəˈlɒt, *Am:* -ˈlɑːt] *n* chalote *m*, cebolleta *f AmL*

shallow [ˈʃæləʊ, *Am:* -oʊ] **I.** *adj* **1.**(*not deep*) poco profundo, -a **2.**(*only light*) débil **3.**(*superficial*) superficial **II.** *npl* bajío *m*

shallowness *n no pl* **1.**(*lack of depth*) poca profundidad *f* **2.**(*superficiality*) superficiali-

S

dad *f*

sham [ʃæm] *pej* I. *n* 1. (*imposture*) impostura *f*; (*fake*) fraude *m* 2. (*impostor*) impostor(a) *m(f)* II. *adj* (*document, trial*) falso, -a; (*deal*) fraudulento, -a; (*sympathy*) hipócrita; (*marriage*) simulado, -a III. <-mm-> *vt* fingir IV. *vi* fingir

shamble [ˈʃæmbl] *vi* arrastrar los pies

shambles [ˈʃæmblz] *n inf* (*place*) escombrera *f*; (*situation*) confusión *f*

shambolic [ʃæmˈbɒlɪk, *Am:* -ˈbɑːlɪk] *adj Brit, inf* caótico, -a

shame [ʃeɪm] I. *n no pl* 1. (*humiliation*) vergüenza *f*, pena *f AmC;* **to die of** ~ morirse de vergüenza; **to feel no** ~ no sentir vergüenza; **to put sb to** ~ avergonzar a alguien; **to my** ~ ... para vergüenza mía...; ~ **on you!** *a. iron* ¡debería darte vergüenza! 2. (*discredit*) deshonra *f;* **to bring** ~ **on sb** deshonrar a alguien 3. (*pity*) pena *f;* **what a** ~! ¡qué pena!; **what a** ~ **that** ... qué lástima que +*subj;* **it's a** ~ **to have to** +*infin* es una pena tener que +*infin;* **it's a** ~ **that** ... es una pena que... +*subj;* **it's a crying** ~ es una verdadera lástima II. *vt* 1. (*mortify*) avergonzar 2. (*discredit*) deshonrar

shamefaced [ʃeɪmˈfeɪst, *Am:* '--] *adj* abochornado, -a, apenado, -a *AmC*

shameful [ˈʃeɪmfəl] *adj pej* 1. (*causing disgrace*) vergonzoso, -a, penoso, -a *AmC* 2. (*outrageous*) bochornoso, -a; **it's** ~ **that** ... es vergonzoso que... +*subj*

shameless [ˈʃeɪmlɪs] *adj pej* descarado, -a, conchudo, -a *AmL*, pechugón, -ona *AmL*, vaquetón, -ona *Méx*

shammy [ˈʃæmi] <-ies> *n inf no pl, inf* gamuza *f*

shampoo [ʃæmˈpuː] I. *n* champú *m;* ~ **and set** lavar y peinar II. *vt* lavar con champú

shamrock [ˈʃæmrɒk, *Am:* -rɑːk] *n* trébol *m*

shandy [ˈʃændi] <-ies> *n Brit, Aus* clara *f*

shank [ʃæŋk] *n* 1. TECH mango *m* 2. (*leg*) pata *f;* (*of bird*) zanca *f* ▶**to go on** ~'s **pony** ir en el coche de San Fernando, ir a pata *Méx*

shanty¹ [ˈʃænti, *Am:* -t̬i] <-ies> *n* (*shack*) chabola *f*, favela *f AmL*, choza *f Méx*

shanty² [ˈʃænti, *Am:* -t̬i] *n* (*song*) saloma *f*

shanty town *n* chabolas *fpl*, favelas *fpl AmL*, barriada *f Perú*, ciudad *f* perdida *Méx*, villa *f* miseria *RíoPl*

shape [ʃeɪp] I. *n* 1. (*form*) forma *f;* **to get out of** ~, **to lose** ~ perder la forma; **to take** ~ adquirir forma; **in the** ~ **of sth** en forma de algo; **the** ~ **of things to come** lo que nos espera 2. *no pl* (*condition*) condición *f;* **in bad/good** ~ en malas/buenas condiciones; **to get sth into** ~ acondicionar algo; **to get into** ~ ponerse en forma; **to knock** [*o* **lick** *Am*] **sth/ sb into** ~ poner algo/a alguien a punto II. *vt* 1. (*form*) **to** ~ **sth into sth** dar a algo la forma de algo 2. (*influence*) influenciar 3. (*determine*) condicionar

shapeless [ˈʃeɪpləs] *adj* 1. (*without definite*

shape) informe 2. (*not shapely*) deforme

shapely [ˈʃeɪpli] <-ier, -iest> *adj* bien proporcionado, -a; (*leg*) torneado, -a; (*person*) de buen talle

shard [ʃɑːd, *Am:* ʃɑːrd] *n* casco *m*, tepalcate *m Guat, Méx*

share [ʃeəʳ, *Am:* ʃer] I. *n* 1. (*part*) parte *f*, porción *f;* **the lion's** ~ la mayor parte; **to go** ~s **on sth** ir a medias en algo, ir a mitas con algo *Méx* 2. (*participation*) participación *f* 3. FIN acción *f;* **stocks and** ~s acciones y participaciones; **to have** ~s **in sth** tener acciones en algo II. *vi* 1. (*divide*) repartir 2. (*allow others to use*) compartir ▶**to** ~ **and** ~ **alike** compartir las cosas III. *vt* 1. (*divide*) dividir 2. (*have in common*) compartir; **to** ~ **sb's view** compartir las opiniones de alguien; **to want to** ~ **one's life with sb** querer compartir la vida con alguien ◆**share out** *vt* dividir

share capital *n* capital *m* social **share certificate** *n* título *m* de acción

sharecropper [ˈʃeəˌkrɒpəʳ, *Am:* ˈʃerˌkrɑː- pə˞] *n* aparcero, -a *m, f*

shareholder [ˈʃeəˌhəʊldəʳ, *Am:* ˈʃerˌhoʊl- də˞] *n* accionista *mf*

shareholding *n* participación *f* accionaria

share index *n* índice *m* bursátil **share issue** *n* emisión *f* de acciones **share option** *n* opción *f* de compra de acciones

share-out [ˈʃeəraʊt, *Am:* ˈʃeraʊt] *n* reparto *m*

share price *n* FIN cotización *f* de las acciones

shareware [ˈʃeəweəʳ, *Am:* ˈʃerwer] *n no pl* INFOR shareware *m*, programa *m* compartido

shark [ʃɑːk, *Am:* ʃɑːrk] <-(s)> *n* 1. (*fish*) tiburón *m* 2. *pej, inf* (*person*) estafador(a) *m(f)*

sharp [ʃɑːp, *Am:* ʃɑːrp] I. *adj* 1. (*cutting*) afilado, -a; (*pointed*) puntiagudo, -a 2. (*angular: feature*) anguloso, -a; (*corner, edge, angle*) agudo, -a; (*curve*) cerrado, -a 3. (*severe*) severo, -a; (*pain*) agudo, -a, intenso, -a; (*look*) penetrante; (*reprimand*) violento, -a; **to have a** ~ **tongue** tener una lengua afilada [*o* viperina]; **to be** ~ **with sb** ser mordaz con alguien 4. (*astute*) astuto, -a; (*perceptive*) perspicaz, alicuz *Hond;* (*mind*) vivo, -a 5. (*pungent*) acre; (*wine*) ácido, -a 6. (*sudden*) súbito, -a; (*abrupt*) abrupto, -a; (*marked*) pronunciado, -a 7. (*penetrating*) penetrante; (*storm*) fuerte; (*sound*) agudo, -a; (*fight*) encarnizado, -a 8. (*distinct*) nítido, -a 9. MUS sostenido, -a; **C** ~ do sostenido II. *adv* 1. (*exactly*) en punto; **at ten o'clock** ~ a las diez en punto 2. (*suddenly*) de repente; **to pull up** ~ frenar en seco 3. MUS desafinadamente III. *n* MUS sostenido *m*

sharpen [ˈʃɑːpən, *Am:* ˈʃɑːr-] *vt* 1. (*blade*) afilar; (*pencil*) sacar punta a 2. (*intensify*) agudizar; (*mind*) aguzar; (*appetite*) abrir

sharpener [ˈʃɑːpənəʳ, *Am:* ˈʃɑːrpənə˞] *n* afilador *m*, afiladora *f Méx;* **pencil** ~ sacapuntas *m inv*

sharper [ˈʃɑːpəʳ, *Am:* ˈʃɑːrpəˑ] *n inf* (*cheat*) estafador(a) *m(f);* (*at cards*) fullero(a) *m(f)*

sharp-eyed [ˌʃɑːpˈaɪd, *Am:* ʃɑːrpˈ-] *adj* observador(a)

sharpness *n no pl* 1. (*of blade*) filo *m;* (*of pencil*) punta *f* 2. (*of pain*) agudeza *f* 3. (*of comment*) mordacidad *f* 4. (*suddenness: of curve*) brusquedad *f* 5. (*intensity*) intensidad *f;* (*of blow*) violencia *f* 6. (*clarity*) nitidez *f* 7. (*perceptiveness*) perspicacia *f;* (*intelligence*) astucia *f* 8. (*chic*) elegancia *f*

sharp practice *n* artimañas *fpl*

sharpshooter [ˈʃɑːpˌʃuːtəʳ, *Am:* ˈʃɑːrpˌʃuːtɚ] *n* tirador(a) *m(f)* de primera

sharp-sighted [ˌʃɑːpˈsaɪtɪd, *Am:* ˈʃɑːrpˌsaɪtɪd] *adj* 1. (*very observant*) de vista aguda 2. (*alert*) sagaz **sharp-tempered** *adj* malhumorado, -a **sharp-tongued** *adj* mordaz **sharp-witted** *adj* agudo, -a

shat [ʃæt] *pt, pp of* **shit**

shatter [ˈʃætəʳ, *Am:* ˈʃæt̬ɚ] I. *vi* hacerse añicos II. *vt* 1. (*smash*) hacer añicos, destrozar 2. (*disturb*) perturbar; (*unity*) destruir 3. (*exhaust*) cansar; **to be ~ed** estar rendido

shattering *adj* tremendo, -a

shatterproof [ˈʃætəpruːf, *Am:* ˈʃæt̬ɚ-] *adj* inastillable

shave [ʃeɪv] I. *n* afeitado *m*, rasurada *f Méx;* **to have a ~** afeitarse ▶**to have a** close **~** librarse por los pelos II. *vi* afeitarse III. *vt* 1. (*remove body hair*) afeitar, rasurar *Méx* 2. (*brush past*) rozar 3. (*decrease: budget*) recortar

shaven [ˈʃeɪvən] *adj* (*face, legs*) afeitado, -a; (*head*) rapado, -a

shaver [ˈʃeɪvəʳ, *Am:* -vɚ] *n* maquinilla *f* de afeitar, rasuradora *f Méx*

shaving brush *n* brocha *f* de afeitar **shaving cream** *n* crema *f* de afeitar **shaving foam** *n* espuma *f* de afeitar **shaving mirror** *n* espejo *m* para afeitarse **shaving soap** *n* jabón *m* de afeitar

shawl [ʃɔːl, *Am:* ʃɑːl] *n* chal *m*

she [ʃiː] I. *pron pers* (*female person or animal*) ella; **~'s my mother** (ella) es mi madre; **~'s gone away but ~'ll be back soon** se ha ido pero regresará pronto; **here ~ comes** ahí viene; **~ who ...** *form* aquélla quien... II. *n* 1. (*animal*) hembra *f* 2. *inf* (*person*) fémina *f;* (*baby*) **it's a ~**, es niña

sheaf [ʃiːf, ʃiːvz] <sheaves> *n* (*of wheat*) gavilla *f;* (*of documents*) fajo *m*

shear [ʃɪəʳ, *Am:* ʃɪr] <sheared, sheared *o* shorn> *vt* 1. (*sheep*) esquilar 2. (*person*) rapar; **to be shorn of sth** *fig* ser despojado de algo

♦**shear off** *vi* romperse

shears [ʃɪəz, *Am:* ʃɪrz] *npl* (*for sheep*) tijeras *f* de esquilar *pl;* (*for sheep*) tijeras de podar; (*for metal*) cizalla *f*

sheath [ʃiːθ] *n* 1. (*covering*) funda *f;* (*for knife*) vaina *f*, funda *f AmL* 2. *Brit* (*condom*) condón *m* 3. (*dress*) vestido *m* de tubo

sheathe [ʃiːð] *vt* 1. (*knife*) envainar, enfundar *AmL* 2. (*cover*) revestir

sheath knife *n* cuchillo *m* de monte

shebang [ʃɪˈbæŋ] *n no pl, Am, inf* **the whole ~** todo el asunto

shed[1] [ʃed] *n* cobertizo *m*, galera *f AmL*, galpón *m AmC*, galerón *m CRi, ElSal*

shed[2] [ʃed] <shed, shed> I. *vt* 1. (*cast off*) quitarse; (*clothes*) despojarse de; (*hair, weight*) perder; **to ~ one's skin** mudar la piel 2. (*eliminate*) deshacerse de; (*jobs*) eliminar 3. (*blood, tears*) derramar; (*light*) emitir II. *vi* (*snake*) mudar de piel; (*cat*) pelechar

sheen [ʃiːn] *n no pl* brillo *m*

sheep [ʃiːp] *n* oveja *f;* (*ram*) carnero *m* ▶**to separate the ~ from the goats** separar el grano de la paja; **black ~** oveja negra

sheep-dip [ˈʃiːpdɪp] *n* AGR baño *m* desinfectante

sheepdog [ˈʃiːpdɒg, *Am:* -dɑːg] *n* perro *m* pastor

sheepfold [ˈʃiːpfəʊld, *Am:* -foʊld] *n* redil *m*, majada *f CSur*

sheepish [ˈʃiːpɪʃ] *adj* tímido, -a

sheepskin [ˈʃiːpskɪn] *n* piel *f* de borrego

sheer[1] [ʃɪəʳ, *Am:* ʃɪr] I. *adj* 1. (*unmitigated*) puro, -a; (*bliss*) completo, -a; (*boredom, lunacy*) total; **~ coincidence** pura coincidencia 2. (*vertical*) escarpado, -a; **~ drop** caída *f* en picado 3. (*thin*) fino, -a; (*diaphanous*) transparente II. *adv liter* absolutamente

sheer[2] [ʃɪəʳ, *Am:* ʃɪr] *vi* NAUT desviarse

sheet [ʃiːt] *n* 1. (*for bed*) sábana *f* 2. (*of paper*) hoja *f;* **~ of paper** hoja de papel 3. (*plate of material*) placa *f;* (*of glass*) lámina *f* 4. (*perforated set of stamps*) plancha *f* 5. (*paper with information on*) folleto *m* 6. (*layer*) capa *f* 7. (*broad mass*) cortina *f;* **~ of flame** cortina de llamas; **the rain was coming down in ~s** llovía a cántaros

sheet feed *n* INFOR alimentador *m* de papel **sheet lightning** *n no pl* fucilazo *m* **sheet metal** *n* metal *m* en planchas **sheet music** *n* partituras *fpl*

sheik(h) [ʃeɪk, *Am:* ʃiːk] *n* jeque *m*

shelf [ʃelf, *pl* ʃelvz] <shelves> *n* 1. (*for storage*) estante *m;* **to buy sth off the ~** comprar algo hecho; **to put sth on the ~** *fig* arrinconar algo 2. GEO arrecife *m* ▶**to be** (left) on the ~ *Brit, Aus, inf* quedarse para vestir santos

shelf life *n no pl* tiempo *m* de conservación

shell [ʃel] I. *n* 1. (*of nut, egg*) cáscara *f;* (*of shellfish, snail*) concha *f;* (*of crab, tortoise*) caparazón *m* 2. TECH armazón *m;* (*of house*) estructura *f;* (*of ship*) casco *m* 3. (*gun*) proyectil *m*, cartucho *m AmL* ▶**to** come out of **one's ~** salir del cascarón; **to** crawl into one's **~** meterse en su cascarón II. *vt* 1. (*remove shell*) pelar 2. MIL bombardear III. *vi* bombardear

♦**shell out** *inf* I. *vt* soltar II. *vi* aflojar; **to ~ for sth** apoquinar para algo

shellac [ʃəˈlæk] *n* laca *f*

shellfish [ˈʃelfɪʃ] n 1. GASTR marisco m 2. ZOOL (crustacean) crustáceo m; (mollusc) molusco m

shell hole n hoyo que forma un obús al explotar

shelling n no pl bombardeo m

shell-shock n neurosis f de guerra

shell-shocked adj que padece neurosis de guerra; fig traumatizado, -a

shelter [ˈʃeltəʳ, Am: -t̬əʳ] I. n refugio m; to take ~ refugiarse II. vt resguardar III. vi refugiarse

sheltered adj 1. (protected against weather) abrigado, -a 2. pej (overprotected) sobreprotegido, -a 3. Am (tax-protected) protegido, -a

shelve [ʃelv] I. vt 1. (delay, postpone) posponer; POL postergar 2. (erect shelves in) poner estantes II. vi descender

shelving n no pl estantería f

shenanigans [ʃɪˈnænɪɡənz] npl chanchullos mpl

shepherd [ˈʃepəd, Am: -ɚd] I. n pastor m II. vt (sheep) guiar; (people) dirigir

shepherdess [ʃepəˈdes, Am: ˈʃepɚdɪs] <-es> n pastora f

shepherd's pie n pastel m de carne

sherbet [ˈʃɜ:bət, Am: ˈʃɜ:r-] n 1. no pl, Brit, Aus (sweet tasting powder) sidral® m 2. Am (sorbet) sorbete m

sheriff [ˈʃerɪf] n 1. Am (official) sheriff mf 2. Brit (representative) representante mf de la corona 3. Scot (judge) juez mf principal de un distrito

sherry [ˈʃeri] <-ies> n jerez m

Shetland Islands n, **Shetlands** [ˈʃetləndz] npl Islas fpl Shetland

shield [ʃi:ld] I. n 1. (armour) escudo m 2. (protective layer) revestimiento m; fig caparazón m 3. (logo) insignia f 4. (prize) placa f 5. Am (badge) chapa f (de policía) II. vt proteger

shift [ʃɪft] I. vt 1. (change, rearrange) mover; (reposition) cambiar de sitio; to ~ the blame onto sb echar la culpa a alguien; to ~ one's ground cambiar de opinión; ~ yourself! (hurry up) ¡date prisa!; (move) ¡quítate de ahí! 2. Am (in mechanics: of gears, lanes) cambiar 3. Brit, Aus, inf (dispose of) sacar; (stain) quitar 4. (sell) vender II. vi 1. (change, rearrange position) moverse; (wind) cambiar 2. inf (move over) correrse 3. (fend) to ~ for oneself arreglárselas solo 4. inf (move very fast) volar III. n 1. (alteration, change) cambio m; (of power) giro m 2. (linguistic change) mutación f 3. (period of work) turno m; to work in ~s trabajar por turnos

shifting adj movedizo, -a; (values) cambiante

shift key n tecla f de las mayúsculas

shiftless [ˈʃɪftləs] adj pej (idle) holgazán, -ana; (lacking purpose) haragán, -ana

shiftwork [ˈʃɪftwɜ:k, Am: -wɜ:rk] n no pl trabajo m por turnos **shiftworker** n trabajador(a) m(f) por turnos

shifty [ˈʃɪfti] <-ier, -iest> adj sospechoso, -a; (eyes) furtivo, -a

Shiite [ˈʃi:aɪt] I. adj chiíta II. n chiíta mf

shilling [ˈʃɪlɪŋ] n HIST chelín m

shilly-shally [ˈʃɪliʃæli] vi pej, inf titubear

shimmer [ˈʃɪməʳ, Am: -ɚ] I. vi brillar II. n no pl resplandor m

shin [ʃɪn] I. n 1. (leg below knee) espinilla f 2. no pl (lower leg of beef) jarrete m II. <-nn-> vi to ~ down deslizarse; to ~ up sth trepar a algo

shindig [ˈʃɪndɪɡ] n inf 1. (party) juerga f 2. Brit, Aus (argument) escándalo m; to kick up a ~ armar un lío

shine [ʃaɪn] I. n no pl brillo m ►to take a ~ to sb sentir simpatía por alguien II. <shone o shined, shone o shined> vi 1. (moon, sun, stars) brillar; (gold, metal) relucir; (light) alumbrar; (eyes) resplandecer 2. (be gifted) destacar III. <shone o shined, shone o shined> vt 1. (point light) to ~ a light at sth/sb alumbrar algo/a alguien con una luz; to ~ a torch onto sth iluminar algo con una linterna 2. (brighten by polishing) sacar brillo a; (shoes) lustrar

♦**shine down** vi brillar

♦**shine out** vi 1. (be easily seen) notarse 2. (excel) brillar

shiner [ˈʃaɪnəʳ, Am: -ɚ] n inf ojo m morado

shingle [ˈʃɪŋɡl] n 1. no pl (pebble mass alongside water) guijarros mpl 2. (tiles for roof) teja f (de madera)

shingles [ˈʃɪŋɡlz] n no pl MED herpes m

shining [ˈʃaɪnɪŋ] adj 1. (gleaming) reluciente, abrillantado, -a AmL; (eyes) brillante 2. (outstanding) magnífico, -a; a ~ example un ejemplo perfecto

shiny [ˈʃaɪni] <-ier, -iest> adj brillante

ship [ʃɪp] I. n barco m; **passenger** ~ buque m de pasajeros; **sailing** ~ velero m; to board a ~ subir a una embarcación, embarcar II. vt <-pp-> 1. (send by boat) mandar por barco; to ~ **freight** enviar mercancías por barco 2. (transport) transportar

♦**ship off** vt (goods) expedir; (person) enviar

♦**ship out** vi embarcarse

shipboard [ˈʃɪpbɔ:d, Am: -bɔ:rd] adj on ~ a bordo

shipbuilder [ˈʃɪpˌbɪldəʳ, Am: -dɚ] n constructor(a) m(f) naval

shipbuilding n no pl construcción f naval

shipload [ˈʃɪpləʊd, Am: -loʊd] n cargamento m **shipmate** n camarada mf de a bordo

shipment [ˈʃɪpmənt] n 1. (quantity) remesa f 2. no pl (action) envío m

shipowner n 1. (person) armador(a) m(f) 2. (company) naviera f

shipper n consignador(a) m(f); **wine** ~ (company) exportadora f de vinos

shipping [ˈʃɪpɪŋ] n no pl 1. (ships) embarcaciones fpl 2. (freight dispatch) transporte m

shipping agency *n* agencia *f* marítima
shipping agent *n* consignatario, -a *m*, *f*
shipping company *n* compañía *f* naviera
shipping department *n* departamento *m* de envíos **shipping lane** *n* ruta *f* de navegación **shipping office** *n* agencia *f* marítima
ship's chandler *n* proveedor(a) *m(f)* de buques
shipshape ['ʃɪpʃeɪp] *adj inf* limpio y ordenado; **to get sth ~** tener algo en orden
shipway ['ʃɪpweɪ] *n* canal *m* **shipwreck** I. *n* 1. (*accident*) naufragio *m* 2. (*remains of ship*) restos *mpl* de un naufragio II. *vt* hacer naufragar; **to be ~ed** naufragar; *fig* estar hundido **shipwright** *n* carpintero *m* de navío **shipyard** *n* astillero *m*
shire ['ʃaɪə', *Am:* 'ʃaɪɚ] *n* condado *m*
shire horse *n* caballo *m* de tiro
shirk [ʃɜːk, *Am:* ʃɜːrk] *pej* I. *vt* eludir II. *vi* escaquearse; **to ~ from sth** escaquearse de algo
shirker ['ʃɜːkə', *Am:* 'ʃɜːrkɚ] *n pej* vago, -a *m*, *f*
shirt [ʃɜːt, *Am:* ʃɜːrt] *n* (*man's, woman's*) camisa *f*; (*woman's*) blusa *f* ▶**to give sb the ~ off one's back** dar hasta la camiseta a alguien; **to have the ~ off sb's back** dejar a alguien sin camisa; **to lose one's ~** perder hasta la camisa; **keep your ~ on!** *Am* ¡no te sulfures!; **to put one's ~ on sth** jugarse hasta la camisa en [*o* por] algo
shirt collar *n* cuello *m* de camisa **shirt front** *n* pechera *f*
shirtsleeve ['ʃɜːtsliːv, *Am:* 'ʃɜːrt-] *n* manga *f* de camisa
shirty ['ʃɜːti, *Am:* 'ʃɜːrt̬i] <-ier, -iest> *adj Brit, Aus, pej, inf* borde; **to get ~ (with sb)** ponerse borde (con alguien)
shit [ʃɪt] *inf* I. *n no pl* 1. (*faeces*) mierda *f* 2. *pej* (*nonsense*) gilipolleces *fpl*, pendejadas *fpl AmL* 3. (*nasty person*) cabrón, -ona *m*, *f* 4. (*as intensifier*) **I don't give a ~!** ¡me importa un carajo! ▶**to beat the ~ out of sb** moler a alguien a palos; **to frighten the ~ out of sb** hacer que alguien se cague de miedo; **to be in the ~** estar jodido; **no ~!** ¡no jodas! II. *interj* mierda III. <shit, shit> *vi* cagar IV. <shit, shit> *vt* cagar; **to ~ oneself** cagarse (encima); *fig* cagarse de miedo; **to ~ bricks** *Am* acojonarse
shite [ʃaɪt] *n Brit s.* **shit**
shitty ['ʃɪti, *Am:* 'ʃɪt̬-] <-ier, -iest> *adj pej, inf* 1. (*unfair, unpleasant*) asqueroso, -a 2. (*sick, ill*) jodido, -a
shiver ['ʃɪvə', *Am:* -ɚ] I. *n* estremecimiento *m*; **to feel a ~** tener un escalofrío; **to give sb the ~s** *inf* dar miedo a alguien II. *vi* temblar; **to ~ with cold** tiritar de frío
shivery ['ʃɪvəri] <-ier, -iest> *adj* estremecido, -a; **to feel ~** tener escalofríos
shoal¹ [ʃəʊl, *Am:* ʃoʊl] *n* 1. (*of fish*) banco *m* 2. *Brit* montón *m*; **~s of** montones *mpl* de
shoal² [ʃəʊl, *Am:* ʃoʊl] *n* 1. (*area of shallow water*) bajío *m* 2. (*sand bank*) banco *m* de arena
shock¹ [ʃɒk, *Am:* ʃɑːk] I. *n* 1. (*unpleasant surprise*) conmoción *f*, batata *f CSur*; **the ~ of my life** *inf* el susto de mi vida; **look of ~** mirada *f* de asombro; **to give sb a ~** dar un disgusto a alguien 2. *inf* (*electric shock*) descarga *f* 3. MED shock *m*; **to die from ~** morir de la impresión 4. (*impact: of explosion, earthquake*) sacudida *f* ▶**~, horror!** *iron* ¡qué horror! II. *vt* 1. (*appal*) horrorizar 2. (*scare*) asustar III. *vi* impactar
shock² [ʃɒk, *Am:* ʃɑːk] *n* (*of hair*) mata *f*
shock absorber ['ʃɒkæb‚zɔːbə', *Am:* 'ʃɑːkəb‚sɔːrbɚ] *n* amortiguador *m*
shocker ['ʃɒkə', *Am:* 'ʃɑːkɚ] *n inf* (*unpleasant news*) noticia *f* desagradable; (*surprising news*) bombazo *m*
shocking ['ʃɒkɪŋ, *Am:* 'ʃɑːkɪŋ] *adj* 1. (*causing indignation, distress*) espantoso, -a; (*news*) horrible 2. (*surprising*) chocante 3. (*offensive*) escandaloso, -a; (*crime*) espantoso, -a 4. *Brit, inf* (*terrible*) horroroso, -a
shockproof ['ʃɒkpruːf, *Am:* 'ʃɑːk-] *adj* 1. (*mechanism*) a prueba de choques 2. (*person*) imperturbable **shock therapy** *n*, **shock treatment** *n* terapia *f* de shock **shock troops** *npl* tropas *fpl* de asalto **shock wave** *n* 1. PHYS onda *f* expansiva 2. *fig* conmoción *f*
shod [ʃɒd] *pt, pp of* **shoe**
shoddy ['ʃɒdi, *Am:* 'ʃɑːdi] <-ier, -iest> *adj pej* 1. (*goods*) de muy mala calidad 2. (*treatment*) mezquino, -a
shoe [ʃuː] I. *n* (*for person*) zapato *m*; (*for horse*) herradura *f*; **high-heeled ~** zapatos *mpl* de tacón alto; **training ~** zapatillas *fpl* de deporte ▶**to fill sb's ~s** pasar a ocupar el puesto de alguien; **if I were in your ~s** *inf* si estuviera en tu lugar II. <shod *o Am:* shoed, shod *o Am:* shoed> *vt* (*person*) calzar; (*horse*) herrar, encasquillar *AmL*
shoehorn ['ʃuːhɔːn, *Am:* -hɔːrn] *n* calzador *m* **shoelace** *n* cordón *m* (de zapato), pasador *m Perú* **shoemaker** *n* zapatero, -a *m*, *f* **shoe polish** *n* betún *m*, lustrina *f Chile* **shoe-repair shop** *n* rápido *m*
shoeshine ['ʃuːʃaɪn] *n Am* limpieza *f* de zapatos **shoeshine boy** *n Am* limpiabotas *m inv*
shoeshop *n* zapatería *f* **shoe size** *n* número *m* de zapato **shoestore** *n Am* zapatería *f*, peletería *f Cuba*
shoestring ['ʃuːstrɪŋ] *n Am* cordón *m* (de zapato) ▶**to do sth on a ~** *inf* hacer algo con poquísimo dinero; **to start on a ~** comenzar con aprietos **shoe tree** *n* horma *f*
shone [ʃɒn, *Am:* ʃoʊn] *pt, pp of* **shine**
shoo [ʃuː] I. *interj inf* fuera II. *vt inf* ahuyentar
shook [ʃʊk] *n pt of* **shake**
shoot [ʃuːt] I. *n* 1. (*hunt*) cacería *f*; **to go on a ~** ir de caza 2. CINE rodaje *m*; PHOT sesión *f* 3. BOT retoño *m* II. *interj Am* (*shit*) mecachis

III.<shot, shot> *vi* 1.(*fire weapon*) disparar; **to ~ to kill** tirar a matar; **to ~ at sth/sb** disparar a algo/alguien 2. *Am* (*aim*) **to ~ for sth** intentar conseguir algo 3. SPORTS chutar 4. CINE rodar; PHOT disparar 5.(*move rapidly*) volar; **to ~ to fame** hacerse famoso de repente; **to ~ past** (*car*) pasar como un rayo ►**to ~ for** [*o* at] **the moon** ir a por todas; **to be shot through with sth** estar repleto de algo IV.<shot, shot> *vt* 1.(*bullet*) disparar; (*missile, arrow*) lanzar 2.(*person*) disparar, abalear *AmS*, balear *AmC*, balacear *Méx;* **to ~ sb dead** matar a alguien a tiros 3. CINE (*film*) rodar; (*scene*) filmar; PHOT tomar 4.(*direct*) **to ~ questions at sb** acribillar a alguien a preguntas; **to ~ a glance at sb** lanzar una mirada a alguien 5. *Am, inf* **to ~ a goal** meter un gol 6. *inf* (*drugs*) **to ~ heroin** chutarse heroína ►**to ~ the breeze** *Am, inf* cotillear, dar a la sinhueso; **to ~ darts at sb** *Am, inf* lanzar miradas asesinas a alguien; **to ~ the works** *Am, inf* tirar la casa por la ventana

♦**shoot ahead** *vi* tomar la delantera rápidamente

♦**shoot down** *vt* (*aircraft*) derribar; *inf* (*proposal*) rebatir

♦**shoot off** I. *vt* arrancar de un sitio ►**to shoot one's mouth off** *inf* cotorrear II. *vi* (*vehicle*) salir como un bólido

♦**shoot out** *vi* salir disparado

♦**shoot past** *vi* pasar como una bala

♦**shoot up** *vi* 1.(*expand, increase rapidly*) crecer mucho; (*skyscraper*) aparecer (de la nada); *inf* (*child*) pegar un estirón 2. *inf* (*inject drugs*) chutarse

shooting ['ʃuːtɪŋ, *Am:* -t̬ɪŋ] I. *n* 1.(*killing*) asesinato *m* 2. *no pl* (*firing of gun*) tiroteo *m* 3. *no pl* (*hunting*) caza *f;* **to go ~** ir de caza 4. *no pl* SPORTS tiro *m* al blanco II. *adj* (*pain*) punzante

shooting gallery *n* barraca *f* de tiro al blanco **shooting jacket** *n* chaquetón *m* **shooting lodge** *m* pabellón *m* de caza **shooting range** *n* campo *m* de tiro **shooting season** *n* temporada *f* de caza **shooting star** *n* estrella *f* fugaz **shooting stick** *n* bastón *m* taburete

shootout ['ʃuːtaʊt] *n* tiroteo *m*

shop [ʃɒp, *Am:* ʃɑːp] I. *n* 1.(*for sale of goods*) tienda *f;* **betting ~** agencia *f* de apuestas; **book ~** librería *f;* **to go to the ~s** ir de compras 2.(*for manufacture*) taller *m* ►**to set up ~ as sth** establecerse como algo; **to talk ~** hablar de trabajo; **all over the ~** por todas partes II.<-pp-> *vi* comprar III.<-pp-> *vt Brit, inf* (*betray*) chivarse de

shopaholic [ʃɒpəˈhɒlɪk, *Am:* ʃɑːp-] *n* adicto, -a *m, f* a las compras

shop assistant *n Brit* dependiente, -a *m, f* **shopfitter** *n* diseñador(a) *m(f)* de espacios comerciales **shop floor** *n* (*in factory*) taller *m* **shop front** *n* escaparate *m* **shopgirl** *n Brit* dependienta *f* **shopkeeper** *n* comer-

ciante *mf;* despachero, -a *m, f Chile* **shopkeeping** *n no pl* comercio *m*

shoplifter ['ʃɒplɪftəʳ, *Am:* ˈʃɑːpˌlɪftɚ] *n* ladrón, -ona *m, f* (*que roba en tiendas*) **shoplifting** *n* robo *m* (en tiendas)

shopper *n* comprador(a) *m(f)*

shopping ['ʃɒpɪŋ, *Am:* ˈʃɑːp-] *n no pl* 1.(*activity*) compra *f;* **to go ~** ir de tiendas 2.(*purchases*) compras *fpl*

shopping arcade *n* galería *f* comercial **shopping bag** *n Brit* bolsa *f* de compras, jaba *f Cuba* **shopping basket** *n* cesta *f* de la compra **shopping cart** *n Am* carrito *m* de la compra **shopping center** *n Am, Aus,* **shopping centre** *n* centro *m* comercial **shopping list** *n* lista *f* de la compra **shopping mall** *n Am, Aus* centro *m* comercial **shopping street** *n* calle *f* comercial **shopping trolley** *n Brit* carrito *m* de la compra

shopsoiled [ʃɒpˈsɔɪld, *Am:* ˈʃɑːpˌsɔɪld] *adj Brit, Aus* deteriorado, -a

shop steward *n* enlace *mf* sindical **shoptalk** *n no pl* conversación *f* sobre el trabajo **shopwalker** *n Brit* supervisor(a) *m(f)* **shop window** *n* escaparate *m*, vitrina *f AmL*, vidriera *f AmL*

shopworn ['ʃɒpwɔːn, *Am:* ˈʃɑːpwɔːrn] *adj* 1. *Am* (*goods*) deteriorado, -a 2.(*cliché*) gastado, -a

shore [ʃɔːʳ, *Am:* ʃɔːr] *n* 1.(*coast*) costa *f* 2.(*beach*) orilla *f;* **on ~** a tierra 3. *pl, fig* (*a country*) **these ~s** estas tierras 4. ARCHIT puntal *m*

♦**shore up** *vt a. fig* apuntalar

shore leave *n* permiso *m* para ir a tierra **shoreline** *n* orilla *f*

shorn [ʃɔːn, *Am:* ʃɔːrn] *pp of* **shear**

short [ʃɔːt, *Am:* ʃɔːrt] I. *adj* 1.(*not long*) corto, -a 2.(*not tall*) bajo, -a, petizo, -a *CSur, Bol* 3.(*brief*) breve; (*memory*) malo, -a 4.(*not enough*) escaso, -a; **to be** [*o* run] **~ on sth** andar escaso de algo; **to be ~ on brains** *inf* ser algo corto; **to be ~ of breath** quedarse sin aliento; **to be in ~ supply** escasear 5. LING (*vowel*) breve 6.(*brusque*) brusco, -a; **to be ~ with sb** tratar a alguien con sequedad II. *n* 1. CINE cortometraje *m* 2. *inf* ELEC cortocircuito *m* 3. *Brit, inf* (*drink*) bebida alcohólica servida sin agua III. *adv* 1.(*abruptly*) **to cut ~** interrumpir bruscamente; **to go ~ of sth** *Brit* pasar sin algo; **to stop sth/sb ~** parar algo/a alguien en seco 2.(*below the standard*) **in ~** en resumidas cuentas; **to fall ~** quedarse corto; **to fall ~ of sth** no alcanzar algo

shortage ['ʃɔːtɪdʒ, *Am:* ˈʃɔːrt̬ɪdʒ] *n* falta *f;* (*water*) escasez *f*

shortbread ['ʃɔːtbred, *Am:* ˈʃɔːrt-] *n no pl* galleta *f* dulce de mantequilla **shortcake** *n* 1. galleta *f* dulce de mantequilla 2. *Am* (*layer cake*) pastel *m* relleno

short-change [ʃɔːtˈtʃeɪndʒ, *Am:* ʃɔːrt'-] *vt* dar mal el cambio; *fig* timar

short-circuit [ʃɔːtˈsɜːkɪt, *Am:* ʃɔːrt'sɜːr-]

I. *n* cortocircuito *m* II. *vi* ponerse en cortocircuito III. *vt* 1. ELEC poner en cortocircuito 2. (*bypass*) saltarse

shortcoming ['ʃɔːˌtkʌmɪŋ, *Am:* 'ʃɔːrt-] *n* defecto *m*

shortcrust ['ʃɔːtkrʌst, *Am:* 'ʃɔːrt-] *n*, **shortcrust pastry** *n no pl* pasta *f* quebradiza

short cut *n* atajo *m; fig* fórmula *f* mágica; **keyboard** ~ INFOR tecla *f* aceleradora

shortcut key *n* INFOR tecla *f* aceleradora

short-dated [ˌʃɔːt'deɪtɪd, *Am:* ʃɔːrt'deɪt̬ɪd] *adj* a corto plazo

shorten ['ʃɔːtən, *Am:* 'ʃɔːr-] I. *vt* acortar; (*name, title*) abreviar II. *vi* acortarse

shortening ['ʃɔːtnɪŋ, *Am:* 'ʃɔːrt-] *n no pl* 1. (*reduction*) reducción *f* 2. GASTR manteca *f*

shortfall ['ʃɔːtfɔːl, *Am:* 'ʃɔːrt-] *n* deficiencia *f;* ECON déficit *m*

shorthand ['ʃɔːthænd, *Am:* 'ʃɔːrt-] *n no pl, Brit, Aus, Can* taquigrafía *f*

shorthanded [ˌʃɔːt'hændɪd, *Am:* ʃɔːrt'-] *adj* falto, -a de mano de obra

shorthand typist *n Aus, Brit* taquimecanógrafo, -a *m, f*

short-haul ['ʃɔːthɔːl, *Am:* 'ʃɔːrthɑːl] *adj* de corto recorrido **shortlist** I. *vt* preseleccionar II. *n* lista *f* de candidatos preseleccionados

short-lived *adj* efímero, -a; (*happiness*) pasajero, -a

shortly ['ʃɔːtli, *Am:* 'ʃɔːrt-] *adv* dentro de poco; ~ **after** ... poco después.-

shortness ['ʃɔːtnɪs, *Am:* 'ʃɔːrt-] *n no pl* 1. (*condition of being short*) cortedad *f* 2. (*brevity*) brevedad *f* 3. (*insufficiency*) escasez *f;* ~ **of breath** falta *f* de aliento 4. (*brusqueness*) sequedad *f*

short order *n Am* comida *f* rápida; (*order*) pedido *m* de comida rápida; ~ **cook** cocinero *que prepara platos sencillos y rápidos* **short-range** *adj* MIL de corto alcance

shorts [ʃɔːts, *Am:* 'ʃɔːrts] *npl* 1. *Brit, Aus* (*short trousers*) pantalones *mpl* cortos, shorts *mpl;* **a pair of** ~ unos shorts, unos pantalones cortos 2. *Am* (*underpants*) calzoncillos *mpl*

short-sighted ['ʃɔːrtˌsaɪt̬ɪd] *adj* 1. (*myopic*) miope 2. (*not prudent*) corto, -a de miras **short-sleeved** *adj* de manga corta **short-staffed** *adj Aus, Brit* falto, -a de personal **short story** *n* narración *m* corta **short-tempered** *adj* irascible **short-term** *adj* a corto plazo **short time** *n* jornada *f* reducida **short wave** *n* onda *f* corta

shot[1] [ʃɒt, *Am:* 'ʃɑːt] I. *n* 1. (*act of firing weapon*) tiro *m,* disparo *m,* baleo *m AmC;* **to fire a** ~ disparar un tiro 2. *no pl* (*shotgun pellets*) perdigones *mpl* 3. (*person*) tirador(a) *m(f);* **to be a good/poor** ~ ser un buen/mal tirador 4. SPORTS (*football*) tiro *m;* (*tennis*) golpe *m* 5. (*photograph*) foto *f;* CINE toma *f* 6. *inf* (*injection*) inyección *f* 7. *inf* (*try, stab*) intento *m;* **to have a** ~ **at sth** probar suerte con algo; **to give sth one's best** ~ hacerlo lo mejor que se pueda 8. (*small amount of alco-*

hol) chupito *m* ►~ **in the arm** estímulo *m;* **a** ~ **in the dark** *inf* un palo de ciego; **not by a long** ~ ni por asomo; **to call (all) the** ~s cortar el bacalao *fig;* **like a** ~ *inf* como un bólido II. *pp, pt of* **shoot**

shot[2] [ʃɒt, *Am:* 'ʃɑːt] *adj* 1. (*woven*) tornasolado, -a 2. *inf* (*worn out*) hecho, -a polvo ►**to get** ~ **of sth/sb** quitarse algo/a alguien de encima

shotgun ['ʃɒtgʌn, *Am:* 'ʃɑːt-] *n* escopeta *f*

shot put *n* SPORTS lanzamiento *m* de peso

shot putter *n* lanzador(a) *m(f)* de peso

should [ʃʊd] *aux* 1. (*expression of advisability*) **to insist that sb** ~ **do sth** insistir en que alguien debería hacer algo 2. (*asking for advice*) ~ **I/we** ...? ¿debería/deberíamos...? 3. (*expression of expectation*) **I** ~ **be so lucky!** *inf* ¡ojalá! 4. *form* (*expressing a condition*) **I** ~ **like to see her** me gustaría verla 5. (*rhetorical expression*) **why** ~ **I/you** ...? ¿por qué debería/deberías...? 6. *Brit, form* **I prefer that Anna** ~ **do it** prefiero que lo haga Anna 7. *form* (*would*) **we** ~ **like to invite you** nos gustaría invitarte/invitaros

shoulder ['ʃəʊldər, *Am:* 'ʃoʊldə-] I. *n* 1. ANAT hombro *m;* ~ **to** ~ hombro con hombro; **to glance over one's** ~ mirar por encima del hombro; **to sling sth over one's** ~ echarse algo al hombro; **to be sb's** ~ **to cry on** ser el paño de lágrimas de alguien; **to lift a burden from one's** ~s *fig* quitarse un peso de encima 2. (*piece of meat*) paletilla *f;* (*of beef*) paleta *f* 3. (*side of road*) arcén *m* 4. (*shoulder-like part of sth*) lomo *m* ►**to rub** ~s **with sb** codearse con alguien; **to stand** ~ **to** ~ **with sb** apoyar a alguien II. *vt* 1. empujar; **to** ~ **one's way** abrirse paso a empujones; **to** ~ **sb aside** empujar a alguien a un lado 2. (*place on one's shoulders*) llevar en los hombros 3. (*accept: responsability*) cargar con

shoulder bag *n* bolso *m* de bandolera **shoulder blade** *n* omóplato *m* **shoulder pad** *n* hombrera *f* **shoulder strap** *n* tirante *m*

shout [ʃaʊt] I. *n* 1. (*loud cry*) grito *m;* **to give sb a** ~ *inf* avisar a alguien 2. *Aus, Brit, inf* (*round of drinks*) **it's my** ~ esta ronda la pago yo II. *vi* gritar; **to** ~ **at sb** gritar a alguien; **to** ~ **for help** pedir auxilio a gritos ►**to give sb sth to** ~ **about** dar una gran alegría a alguien III. *vt* gritar; (*slogans*) corear; **to** ~ **abuse at sb** insultar a alguien a gritos; **to** ~ **oneself hoarse** gritar hasta quedarse ronco

◆**shout down** *vt* hacer callar a gritos

◆**shout out** *vt* gritar

shouting *n no pl* griterío *m* ►**within** ~ **distance** al alcance de la voz; ~ **match** pelea *f* de gallos *fig*

shove [ʃʌv] I. *n* empujón *m,* pechada *f Arg, Chile;* **to give sth a** ~ dar un empujón a algo II. *vt* 1. (*push*) empujar; **to** ~ **one's way through** abrirse paso a empujones; **to** ~ **sb about** [*o* **around**] *fig* abusar de alguien

2. (*place*) meter **III.** *vi* empujar; **to ~ along** *inf* largarse
◆**shove off** *vi* **1.** *inf* (*go away*) largarse **2.** (*launch by foot*) desatracar
shovel ['ʃʌvəl] **I.** *n* **1.** (*tool*) pala *f*; **a ~ of sth** una palada de algo **2.** (*machine*) excavadora *f* **II.** <*Brit:* -ll-, *Am:* -l-> *vt* palear; **to ~ food into one's mouth** engullir comida **III.** <*Brit:* -ll-, *Am:* -l-> *vi* palear
show [ʃəʊ, *Am:* ʃoʊ] **I.** *n* **1.** (*expression*) demostración *f*; **~ of solidarity** muestra *f* de solidaridad **2.** (*exhibition*) exposición *f*; **dog ~** exposición *f* canina; **fashion ~** desfile *m* de modelos; **slide ~** pase *m* de diapositivas; **to be on ~** estar expuesto **3.** (*play*) espectáculo *m;* TV programa *m;* THEAT representación *f*; **quiz ~** concurso *m* **4.** *inf* (*business*) asunto *m* ►**~ of hands** voto a mano alzada; **let's get the ~ on the road** *inf* vamos a ponernos manos a la obra; **to put on a good ~ of sth** hacer ver algo; **the ~ must go on** *prov* hay que seguir adelante; **to run the ~** llevar la voz cantante **II.** <showed, shown> *vt* **1.** (*display*) mostrar; (*slides*) pasar; ART exponer **2.** (*express*) demostrar; (*enthusiasm*) expresar **3.** (*expose*) exponer **4.** (*point out, record*) señalar; (*statistics*) indicar **5.** (*prove*) probar; **to ~ sb that ...** demostrar a alguien que... **6.** (*escort*) guiar; **to ~ sb over a place** *Aus, Brit* enseñar un lugar a alguien; **to ~ sb to the door** acompañar a alguien a la puerta **7.** (*project*) proyectar; (*on television*) poner **III.** *vi* <showed, shown> **1.** (*be visible*) verse **2.** *Am, Aus, inf* (*arrive*) aparecer **3.** (*be shown: film*) proyectarse
◆**show around** *vt* guiar
◆**show in** *vt* hacer pasar
◆**show off** **I.** *vt* lucir **II.** *vi* alardear, compadrear *Arg, Urug*
◆**show out** *vt* acompañar a la puerta
◆**show up** **I.** *vi* **1.** (*be apparent*) ponerse de manifiesto **2.** *inf* (*arrive*) aparecer **II.** *vt* **1.** (*expose*) descubrir; **to show sb up as** (**being**) **sth** demostrar que alguien es algo **2.** (*embarrass*) poner en evidencia
showbiz *n no pl, inf s.* show business
showboat *n Am* barco-teatro *m*
showbusiness *n no pl* mundo *m* del espectáculo **showcase** **I.** *n* escaparate *m* **II.** *vt* exhibir
showdown ['ʃəʊdaʊn, *Am:* 'ʃoʊ-] *n* enfrentamiento *m*
shower ['ʃaʊəʳ, *Am:* 'ʃaʊəʳ] **I.** *n* **1.** (*of rain*) chaparrón *m;* (*of sparks, insults*) lluvia *f* **2.** (*for washing*) ducha *f*, lluvia *f Arg, Chile, Nic* **3.** *Am* (*party*) fiesta *f* (*con motivo de un nacimiento, matrimonio, etc.*) **4.** *Brit, inf* (*group*) **a ~ of idiots** una panda de imbéciles **II.** *vt* derramar; **to ~ sb with water** regar a alguien de agua; **to ~ compliments on sb** colmar de cumplidos a alguien **III.** *vi* **1.** (*take a shower*) ducharse **2.** (*spray*) regar
shower cabinet *n* armario *m* de la ducha

shower cap *n* gorro *m* de ducha **shower curtain** *n* cortina *f* de ducha **shower gel** *n* gel *m* de ducha
showery ['ʃaʊəri, *Am:* 'ʃaʊəʳi] *adj* lluvioso, -a
show flat *n* piso *m* de muestra **showgirl** *n* corista *f* **showground** *n* recinto *m* ferial
show home *n*, **show house** *n Brit* casa *f* de muestra
showing *n* **1.** (*exhibition*) exposición *f* **2.** (*broadcasting*) proyección *f* **3.** (*performance*) actuación *f*
showing-off *n pej* presunción *f*
show jumping ['ʃəʊ,dʒʌmpɪŋ, *Am:* 'ʃoʊ,-] *n no pl* concurso *m* hípico
showman ['ʃəʊmən, *Am:* 'ʃoʊ-] *n* artista *m*, showman *m*
showmanship ['ʃəʊmənʃɪp, *Am:* 'ʃoʊ-] *n* sentido *m* de la teatralidad
shown [ʃəʊn, *Am:* ʃoʊn] *pp of* **show**
show-off ['ʃəʊf, *Am:* 'ʃoʊ,ɑ:f] *n* fanfarrón, -ona *m, f*
showpiece ['ʃəʊpi:s, *Am:* 'ʃoʊ-] **I.** *n* joya *f* **II.** *adj* excepcional
showroom ['ʃəʊrʊm, *Am:* 'ʃoʊru:m] *n* salón *m* de exposición
show trial *n* juicio *m* (*llevado a cabo como demostración de poderío*)
showy ['ʃəʊi, *Am:* 'ʃoʊ-] <-ier, -iest> *adj* llamativo, -a
shrank [ʃræŋk] *vt, vi pt of* **shrink**
shrapnel ['ʃræpn(ə)l] *n no pl* metralla *f*
shred [ʃred] **I.** <-dd-> *vt* (*cut into shreds*) cortar en tiras; (*document*) triturar **II.** *n* **1.** (*strip*) tira *f*; **to be in ~s** estar hecho jirones; **to tear sb to ~s** hacer trizas a alguien **2.** *no pl, fig* (*of hope, truth*) pizca *f*
shredder ['ʃredəʳ, *Am:* -əʳ] *n* trituradora *f*
shrew [ʃru:] *n* **1.** (*animal*) musaraña *f* **2.** *pej* (*bad-tempered woman*) arpía *f*
shrewd [ʃru:d] *adj* (*person*) astuto, -a, habiloso, -a *Chile*, lépero, -a *Cuba;* (*comment*) hábil; (*decision*) inteligente; (*eye*) agudo, -a
shrewish ['ʃru:ɪʃ] *adj pej* regañón, -ona *m, f*
shriek [ʃri:k] **I.** *n* chillido *m* **II.** *vi* chillar; **to ~ with laughter** reírse a carcajadas **III.** *vt* chillar
shrift [ʃrɪft] *n* **to get short ~ from sb** recibir cajas destempladas de alguien; **to give short ~ to sb** echar a alguien con cajas destempladas; **to give short ~ to sth** despachar algo
shrill [ʃrɪl] *adj* agudo, -a
shrimp [ʃrɪmp] *n* <-(s)> **1.** *Brit* camarón *m* **2.** *Am* gamba *f* **3.** *inf* (*person*) renacuajo, -a *m, f*
shrimp cocktail *n Am* cóctel *m* de gambas
shrine [ʃraɪn] *n* **1.** (*tomb*) sepulcro *m* **2.** (*site of worship*) santuario *m;* **a ~ for sb** un altar en honor a alguien
shrink [ʃrɪŋk] **I.** *n inf* loquero, -a *m, f* **II.** <shrank *o Am:* shrunk, shrunk *o Am:* shrunken> *vt* **1.** (*make smaller*) encoger **2.** (*reduce: costs*) reducir **III.** <shrank *o Am:* shrunk, shrunk *o Am:* shrunken> *vi* **1.** (*become smaller: clothes*) encoger

2. (*become reduced*) disminuir **3.** *liter* (*cower*) retroceder (por miedo); **to ~ away from sb/sth** echarse atrás ante alguien/algo **4.** (*be reluctant to*) **to ~ from** (**doing**) **sth** rehuir (hacer) algo

shrinkage ['ʃrɪŋkɪdʒ] *n no pl* **1.** (*of clothes*) encogimiento *m* **2.** (*of costs*) reducción *m*

shrink-wrap ['ʃrɪŋkræp] **I.** *n* envoltura *f* de plástico **II.** *vt* (*food*) empaquetar en plástico

shrivel ['ʃrɪvəl] <*Brit:* -ll-, *Am:* -l-> **I.** *vi* (*fruit*) secarse; (*plant*) marchitarse; (*skin*) arrugarse; (*person*) consumirse **II.** *vt* (*fruit*) secar; (*skin*) arrugar
♦**shrivel up** *vi* (*fruit*) secarse; (*plant*) marchitarse; (*person*) consumirse

shroud [ʃraʊd] **I.** *n* (*covering*) velo *m*; (*for burial*) sudario *m*; (*of dust, fog*) capa *f* **II.** *vt* envolver; **to ~ sth in sth** envolver algo con algo; **~ed in mystery** envuelto en un halo de misterio

Shrove Tuesday [ˌʃrəʊvˈtjuːzdeɪ, *Am:* ˌʃroʊvˈtuːzdeɪ] *n* martes *m inv* de Carnaval

shrub [ʃrʌb] *n* arbusto *m*

shrubbery ['ʃrʌbəri] *n no pl* arbustos *mpl*

shrug [ʃrʌg] **I.** *n* encogimiento *m* de hombros **II.** <-gg-> *vt* **to ~ one's shoulders** encogerse de hombros **III.** <-gg-> *vi* encogerse de hombros
♦**shrug off** *vt* **1.** (*ignore*) negar importancia a **2.** (*overcome*) superar

shrunk [ʃrʌŋk] *pp, pt of* **shrink**

shrunken ['ʃrʌŋkən] **I.** *pp of* **shrink** **II.** *adj* encogido, -a

shuck [ʃʌk] *vt Am* (*fruits*) pelar; (*beans*) desenvainar; (*clothes*) quitarse

shucks [ʃʌks] *interj Am, inf* caray

shudder ['ʃʌdə', *Am:* -ə·] **I.** *vi* (*person*) estremecerse; (*ground, machine*) vibrar; **to ~ at the memory of sth** temblar al recordar algo **II.** *n* (*of person*) estremecimiento *m*; (*of ground, machine*) vibración *f*; **it sent a ~ down my spine** hizo que me estremeciera

shuffle ['ʃʌfl] **I.** *n* **1.** (*of cards*) **to give the cards a ~** barajar las cartas **2.** (*of cabinet, management*) reestructuración *f* **3.** *no pl* (*dragging of feet*) arrastre *m* **II.** *vt* **1.** (*papers*) revolver; (*cards*) barajar **2.** (*cabinet, management*) reestructurar **3.** (*feet*) arrastrar **III.** *vi* **1.** (*mix cards*) barajar **2.** (*drag feet*) arrastrar los pies
♦**shuffle off** *vi* alejarse arrastrando los pies

shun [ʃʌn] <-nn-> *vt* rehuir

shunt [ʃʌnt] **I.** *vt* **1.** RAIL cambiar de vía **2.** *fig* **to ~ sb aside** relegar a alguien **II.** *n* RAIL empujón *m*

shunting *n* cambio *m* de vía

shunting engine *n* locomotora *f* de maniobra

shush [ʃʊʃ] **I.** *interj* silencio **II.** *vt inf* hacer callar **III.** *vi inf* callarse

shut [ʃʌt] **I.** *adj* cerrado, -a; **to slam a door ~** cerrar la puerta de un portazo **II.** <shut, shut> *vt* cerrar; **to ~ one's ears to sth** hacer oídos sordos a algo; **to ~ one's finger in the**

door pillarse el dedo en la puerta **III.** <shut, shut> *vi* **1.** (*door, window*) cerrarse **2.** (*shop, factory*) cerrar
♦**shut away** *vt* encerrar; **to shut oneself away** recluirse
♦**shut down I.** *vt* **1.** (*shop, factory*) cerrar; (*airport*) paralizar **2.** (*turn off*) desconectar **II.** *vi* (*shop, factory*) cerrar; (*engine*) apagarse
♦**shut in** *vt* encerrar
♦**shut off** *vt* **1.** (*isolate*) aislar **2.** (*turn off*) desconectar
♦**shut out** *vt* **1.** (*block out*) ahuyentar; (*thought*) borrar de la memoria **2.** (*exclude*) dejar fuera; **to shut sb out** no dejar entrar a alguien **3.** SPORTS dejar a cero
♦**shut up I.** *vt* **1.** (*confine*) encerrar **2.** *Aus, Brit* (*stop business*) cerrar **3.** *inf* (*cause to stop talking*) hacer callar; **to shut sb up for good** *fig* hacer callar a alguien para siempre **II.** *vi inf* (*stop talking*) callarse

shutdown ['ʃʌtdaʊn] *n* cierre *m*

shuteye ['ʃʌtaɪ, *Am:* 'ʃʌt̬-] *n no pl, inf* sueñecito *m*; **to get some ~** echarse un sueñecito

shut-off I. *n* suspensión *f* **II.** *adj* (*valve*) de cierre

shutout ['ʃʌtaʊt] *n* victoria *f* abrumadora (*sin que marque el adversario*)

shutter ['ʃʌtə', *Am:* -t̬ə·] *n* **1.** PHOT obturador *m* **2.** (*of window*) contraventana *f*; (*of shop*) persiana *f*; **to put up the ~s** cerrar el negocio

shuttle ['ʃʌtl, *Am:* 'ʃʌt̬-] **I.** *n* **1.** (*train*) servicio *m* de enlace; (*plane*) puente *m* aéreo; (*space*) transbordador *m* espacial **2.** (*sewing-machine bobbin*) lanzadera *f* **II.** *vt* transportar **III.** *vi* AVIAT volar (regularmente); (*travel regularly*) ir y venir

shuttlecock ['ʃʌtlkɒk, *Am:* 'ʃʌt̬lkɑːk] *n* volante *m*

shuttle flight *n* puente *m* aéreo **shuttle service** *n* servicio *m* de enlace

shy[1] [ʃaɪ] **I.** <-ie-> *vt inf* (*throw*) tirar **II.** *n* **1.** (*throw*) tirada *f*; (*in soccer*) saque *m* de banda **2.** *fig* (*attempt*) tentativa *f*; **to have a ~ at sth** probar algo

shy[2] [ʃaɪ] **I.** <-er, -est> *adj* **1.** (*timid*) tímido, -a **2.** (*lacking*) escaso, -a; **we're still a few pounds ~** nos faltan todavía unas cuantas libras **II.** <-ie-> *vi* (*horse*) respingar, bellaquear *Arg, Bol, Urug*
♦**shy away from** *vi* **to ~ sth** asustarse de algo; **to ~ doing sth** evitar hacer algo

shyly *adv* tímidamente

shyness *n no pl* timidez *f*

Siamese [ˌsaɪəˈmiːz] **I.** *n inv* **1.** (*person*) siamés, -esa *m, f* **2.** (*language*) siamés *m* **II.** *adj* **1.** GEO, HIST siamés, -esa **2.** (*brothers*) **~ twins** siameses *mpl*

Siberia [saɪˈbɪəriə, *Am:* -ˈbɪri-] *n no pl* Siberia *f*

sibling ['sɪblɪŋ] *n form* hermano, -a *m, f*

Sicilian [sɪˈsɪljən] **I.** *adj* siciliano, -a **II.** *n* (*person*) siciliano, -a *m, f*

Sicily ['sɪsɪli] *n* Sicilia *f*

S

sick [sɪk] I.<-er, -est> *adj* 1. (*ill*) enfermo, -a; **to feel** ~ sentirse mal; **to fall** ~ caer enfermo; **to be off** ~ estar de baja (por enfermedad); **to be** ~ **at heart** *liter* estar muy deprimido 2. (*about to vomit*) mareado, -a; **to be** ~ (*nauseated*) estar mareado (y a punto de vomitar); (*vomit*) vomitar; **to get** ~ vomitar; **to feel** ~ **to one's stomach** tener el estómago revuelto; **too much alcohol makes me** ~ el exceso de alcohol me pone fatal 3. *inf* (*car*) averiado, -a 4. *inf* (*disgusted*) asqueado, -a; **to be** ~ **about** sth estar asqueado de algo 5. (*angry*) furioso, -a; **to be** ~ **and tired of sth** estar harto de algo 6. *inf* (*cruel*) cruel; (*joke*) de mal gusto II. *n* 1. (*ill people*) **the** ~ los enfermos 2. *no pl, Brit, inf* (*vomit*) vómito *m*

◆**sick up** *vt* vomitar, devolver

sick bag *n* bolsa *f* para vomitar **sick bay** *n* enfermería *f* **sickbed** *n* lecho *m* de enfermo
sicken ['sɪkən] I. *vi* (*become sick*) enfermar; **to** ~ **for sth** *Brit* (*become sick with*) estar incubando algo II. *vt* (*upset*) molestar, estar asqueado de algo; **so much violence in films** ~**s me** me pone enfermo tanta violencia en las películas
sickening ['sɪkənɪŋ] *adj* 1. (*repulsive*) repugnante 2. (*annoying*) ofensivo, -a
sickle ['sɪkl] *n* hoz *f*
sick leave ['sɪkliːv] *n* baja *f* por enfermedad; **to be on** ~ estar de baja por enfermedad **sick list** *n* lista *f* de enfermos
sickly ['sɪkli] <-ier, -iest> *adj* 1. (*not healthy*) enfermizo, -a, apolismado, -a *Col, Méx, PRico*, telenque *Chile* 2. (*pale*) pálido, -a 3. (*very sweet*) empalagoso, -a
sickness ['sɪknəs] *n no pl* 1. (*illness*) enfermedad *f* 2. (*nausea*) mareo *m*
sickness benefit *n Aus, Brit* subsidio *m* por incapacidad
sick note *n* certificado *m* de baja
sick pay *n* subsidio *m* de enfermedad
sickroom ['sɪkrʊm, *Am:* -ruːm] *n* cuarto *m* del enfermo
side [saɪd] *n* 1. (*vertical surface*) lado *m*; **at the** ~ **of sth** en el lado de algo; **at sb's** ~ al lado de alguien; ~ **by** ~ uno al lado de otro 2. (*flat surface*) superficie *f*; (*of page*) cara *f* 3. (*edge*) límite *m*; (*of river*) ribera *f*; (*of road*) arcén *m*; **on all** ~(**s**) por todas partes 4. (*half*) parte *f*; **I like to sleep on the right** ~ **of the bed** me gusta dormir en el lado derecho de la cama; **in Great Britain, cars drive on the left** ~ **of the road** en Gran Bretaña se conduce por la izquierda 5. (*cut of meat*) costado *m* 6. (*direction*) **from all** ~(**s**) de todas partes; **from** ~ **to** ~ de lado a lado 7. (*party in dispute*) bando *m*; (*team*) equipo *m*; **to take** ~**s** tomar partido; **to take sb's** ~ ponerse de parte de alguien; **to be on the** ~ **of sb/sth** ser partidario de alguien/algo; **to have sth on one's** ~ tener algo a su favor; **on my father's** ~ por parte de mi padre 8. (*aspect*) aspecto *m*; (*of story*) versión *f* 9. (*aside*) **on the** ~ aparte; **to**

leave sth on one ~ dejar algo a un lado ►**the other** ~ **of the coin** la otra cara de la moneda; **to come down on one** ~ **of the fence or other** tomar partido por una postura o por la otra; **to be on the right/wrong** ~ **of the law** estar dentro/fuera de la ley; **to get on the right/wrong** ~ **of sb** congraciarse/ponerse a malas con alguien; **to be on the right/wrong** ~ **of 40** no llegar a/pasar de 40 años; **to be on the save** ~ ... para mayor seguridad...
sidearm *n* pistola *f*
sideboard ['saɪdbɔːd, *Am:* -bɔːrd] *n* 1. (*buffet*) aparador *m*, bufet *m AmL* 2. *pl, Brit, inf* (*sideburns*) patillas *fpl*
sideburns ['saɪdbɜːnz, *Am:* -bɜːrnz] *npl* patillas *fpl*
sidecar ['saɪdkaːʳ, *Am:* -kaːr] *n* sidecar *m* **side dish** *n* acompañamiento *m* **side effect** *n* efecto *m* secundario **side issue** *n* tema *m* secundario **sidekick** *n* subordinado, -a *m, f*, **sidelight** *n* AUTO luz *f* de posición
sideline ['saɪdlaɪn] I. *n* 1. (*secondary activity*) actividad *f* secundaria 2. *Am* SPORTS (*line*) línea *f* de banda; (*area*) banda *f*; **on the** ~**s** *fig* al margen; **from the** ~**s** desde fuera II. *vt* 1. SPORTS (*keep from playing*) dejar sin jugar 2. (*ignore*) marginar
sidelong ['saɪdlɒŋ, *Am:* -laːŋ] *adj* (*glance*) de soslayo
side road *n* carretera *f* secundaria
sidesaddle ['saɪdˌsædl] I. *n* silla *f* de amazona II. *adv* **to ride** ~ montar a asentadillas
side salad *n* ensalada *f* de acompañamiento **sideshow** *n* caseta *f*; **to be a** ~ **of sth** *fig* tener una función secundaria respecto a algo
side-slip *n* AVIAT deslizamiento *m* lateral
sidestep ['saɪdstep] <-pp-> I. *vt a. fig* esquivar II. *vi* dar un paso hacia un lado
side street *n* calle *f* lateral **side table** *n* trinchero *m*
sidetrack ['saɪdtræk] I. *vt* apartar de su propósito, distraer II. *n* vía *f* muerta; *fig* cuestión *f* secundaria
side view *n* perfil *m*
sidewalk ['saɪdwɔːk, *Am:* -waːk] *n Am* acera *f*, vereda *f AmL*, banqueta *f Guat, Méx*
sideward ['saɪdwəd], **sideways** ['saɪdweɪz] I. *adv* 1. (*to/from a side*) de lado; (*glance*) de reojo; **to look** ~ **to the left and right** mirar hacia la izquierda y hacia la derecha 2. (*facing a side*) hacia un lado II. *adj* lateral; (*glance*) de reojo
side whiskers *npl* patillas *fpl* **side wind** *n* viento *m* lateral
sidewinder ['saɪdˌwaɪndəʳ, *Am:* -dɚ] *n* 1. ZOOL crótalo *m* 2. *Am* (*blow*) ráfaga *f* oblicua
siding ['saɪdɪŋ] *n* 1. RAIL vía *f* muerta 2. *no pl, Am* (*wall*) recubrimiento *m* aislante
sidle ['saɪdl] *vi* **to** ~ **up to sb** acercarse sigilosamente a alguien
siege [siːdʒ] *n* MIL sitio *m*; **to lay** ~ **to sth** sitiar algo; **to be under** ~ estar sitiado
Sierra Leone [sɪˈerəlɪˈəʊn, *Am:* sɪˌerə-

lɪ'ouŋ] *n* Sierra *f* Leona
Sierra Leonean [sɪ'erəlɪ'əunɪən] **I.** *adj* sierraleonés, -esa **II.** *n* sierraleonés, -esa *m, f*
sieve [sɪv] **I.** *n* (*for flour*) tamiz *m;* (*for liquid*) colador *m;* **to put sth through a ~** pasar algo por una criba ►**to have a memory like a ~** tener la cabeza como un colador **II.** *vt* (*flour*) tamizar; (*liquid*) colar
sift [sɪft] *vt* **1.** (*pass through sieve*) tamizar **2.** (*examine closely*) escudriñar
sigh [saɪ] **I.** *n* suspiro *m;* **to let out a ~** dejar escapar un suspiro **II.** *vi* suspirar; **to ~ with relief** suspirar aliviado; **to ~ for sb** *form* suspirar por alguien
sight [saɪt] **I.** *n* **1.** (*view, faculty*) vista *f;* **to be out of (one's) ~** no estar a la vista (de uno); **to come into ~** aparecer; **to catch ~ of sth** vislumbrar algo; **to hate the ~ of sth/sb** no poder ver algo/a alguien; **to know sb by ~** conocer a alguien de vista; **to lose ~ of sth** perder algo de vista; (*to forget*) no tener presente algo; **at first ~** a primera vista; **within ~ of sth** a la vista de algo; **I can't bear the ~ of him!** ¡no lo puede ni ver!; **get out of my ~!** *inf* ¡fuera de mi vista!; **at the ~ of ...** al ver... **2.** *pl* (*attractions*) lugares *mpl* de interés **3.** (*on gun*) mira *f;* **to line up the ~s** alinear las miras; **to lower one's ~s** *fig* apuntar más bajo en cuanto a sus ambiciones; **to set one's ~s on sth** *fig* poner la mira en algo **4.** *no pl* **a ~** (*a lot*) un montón; **she's a ~ better than him** ella es mucho mejor que él ►**to be a ~ for sore eyes** *inf* ser una alegría para los ojos; **out of ~, out of mind** *prov* ojos que no ven, corazón que no siente *prov;* **a real ~** *inf* horrible; **you look a real ~ in those trousers!** ¡estás horrible con esos pantalones!; **second ~** clarividencia *f;* **to have second ~** ser clarividente; **~ unseen** sin haber visto; **I never buy anything ~ unseen** nunca compro nada sin verlo bien antes; **out of ~!** *inf* ¡fabuloso! **II.** *vt* ver
sighted *adj* vidente
sightless *adj* invidente
sightly ['saɪtli] *adj* agradable a la vista
sight-read ['saɪtriːd] MUS **I.** *vi* interpretar a primera vista **II.** *vt* ejecutar a primera vista
sightseeing ['saɪtˌsiːɪŋ] *n no pl* turismo *m;* **to go ~** visitar los lugares de interés
sightseeing tour *n* visita *f* a los lugares de interés
sightseer ['saɪtˌsiːəʳ, *Am:* -ɚ] *n* turista *mf*
sign [saɪn] **I.** *n* **1.** (*gesture*) señal *f;* **to make a ~ (to sb)** hacer un gesto (a alguien); **to make the ~ of the cross** hacer la señal de la cruz; **as a ~ that ...** como señal de que... **2.** (*signpost*) indicador *m;* (*signboard*) letrero *m* **3.** (*symbol*) símbolo *m* **4.** *a.* MAT, ASTR, MUS signo *m;* **a ~ that ...** un signo de que... **5.** (*trace*) rastro *m;* **they could not find any ~ of them** no pudieron encontrar ningún rastro de ellos; **it's a ~ of the times** así son los tiempos actuales **II.** *vt* **1.** (*write signature on*) firmar; **he ~ed him-**

self **'Mark Taylor'** firmó con el nombre de 'Mark Taylor' **2.** (*employ under contract*) contratar; SPORTS fichar **3.** (*gesticulate*) indicar; **to ~ sb to do sth** indicar a alguien que haga algo **4.** (*say in sign language*) decir por señas **III.** *vi* **1.** (*write signature*) firmar; **~ here, please** firme aquí, por favor; **to ~ for sth** firmar el recibo de algo; **to ~ for a team** fichar por un equipo **2.** (*use sign language*) comunicarse por señas **3.** (*gesticulate*) gesticular; **to ~ to sb to do sth** hacer señas a alguien para que haga algo; **to ~ to sb that ...** indicar con señas a alguien que... +*subj*
◆**sign away** *vt* firmar la cesión de; (*land*) abandonar; (*rights*) ceder
◆**sign in I.** *vi* firmar la entrada **II.** *vt* **to sign sb in** firmar por alguien
◆**sign off I.** *vi inf* **1.** RADIO, TV terminar la emisión **2.** (*end*) terminar; **I think I'll ~ early today** creo que hoy acabaré pronto de trabajar **II.** *vt* despedir
◆**sign on I.** *vi* **1.** (*agree to take work*) firmar un contrato; **to sign on as a soldier** enrolarse como soldado; **to ~ for sth** inscribirse en algo; **he has signed on for courses in English** se ha apuntado a clases de inglés **2.** *Brit, inf* (*confirm unemployed status*) sellar (en el paro) **II.** *vt* contratar
◆**sign out I.** *vi* firmar en el registro de salida **II.** *vt* **to ~ sth** firmar para retirar algo; **you must sign all books out** tienes que firmar para sacar libros prestados; **she signed out a company car** firmó para tomar prestado un coche de la empresa
◆**sign over** *vt* firmar un traspaso; **to sign property over to sb** poner algo a nombre de alguien
◆**sign up I.** *vi* apuntarse **II.** *vt* contratar
signal ['sɪgnəl] **I.** *n* **1.** (*particular gesture*) seña *f;* **to give (sb) a ~ (to do sth)** hacer una señal (a alguien) (para que haga algo) **2.** (*indication*) signo *m;* **to be a ~ that ...** ser signo de que... **3.** AUTO, RAIL, INFOR señal *f* **4.** ELEC, RADIO transmisión *f;* (*reception*) recepción *f* **II.** <*Brit:* -ll-, *Am:* -l-> *vt* **1.** (*indicate*) indicar; **to ~ that ...** señalar que... **2.** (*gesticulate*) hacer señas; **he ~led them to be quiet** les hizo señas para que se callaran **III.** <*Brit:* -ll-, *Am:* -l-> *vi* hacer una señal; **the teacher ~led for the examination to begin** el profesor señaló el comienzo del examen; **he ~led right** AUTO puso el intermitente derecho **IV.** *adj form* notable
signal box *n* RAIL garita *f* de señales **signal lamp** *n* lámpara *f* de señales
signally *adv* notablemente
signalman ['sɪgnəlmən] <-men> *n* RAIL guardavía *mf*
signatory ['sɪgnətəri, *Am:* -tɔːr-] *n* signatario, -a *m, f*
signature ['sɪgnətʃəʳ, *Am:* -nətʃɚ] *n* firma *f*
signboard ['saɪnbɔːd, *Am:* -bɔːrd] *n* letrero *m*

signet ring ['sɪgnɪtˌrɪŋ] *n* anillo *m* de sello

significance [sɪg'nɪfɪkəns, *Am:* -'nɪfə-] *n no pl* **1.** (*importance*) importancia *f* **2.** (*meaning*) significado *m*

significant [sɪg'nɪfɪkənt, *Am:* -'nɪfə-] *adj* **1.** (*important*) importante; (*improvement*) significativo, -a; (*increase*) considerable; (*difference*) notable **2.** (*meaningful*) con significado

signify ['sɪgnɪfaɪ, *Am:* -nə-] **I.** <-ie-> *vt* **1.** *form* (*mean*) significar; **to ... that ...** significar que... **2.** (*indicate*) indicar **II.** <-ie-> *vi form* (*matter*) tener importancia

sign language ['saɪnˌlæŋgwɪdʒ] *n* lenguaje *m* de señas **sign painter** *n* rotulista *mf* **signpost** **I.** *n a. fig* señal *f* **II.** *vt* señalizar

Sikh [siːk] *n no pl* sij *mf*

silage ['saɪlɪdʒ] *n no pl* AGR ensilaje *m*

silence ['saɪləns] **I.** *n* silencio *m* ►~ **is golden** *prov* el silencio es oro **II.** *vt* (*machine, bells*) silenciar; (*person*) hacer callar

silencer ['saɪlənsər, *Am:* -sər] *n* silenciador *m*

silent ['saɪlənt] *adj* silencioso, -a; LING mudo, -a; ~ **film** película *f* muda; **the ~ majority** la mayoría silenciosa; ~ **partner** *Am* ECON socio *m* comanditario; **to be ~ on sth** no decir nada sobre algo; **to fall ~** callarse

silently *adv* silenciosamente, en silencio

silhouette [ˌsɪlu'et] **I.** *n* silueta *f* **II.** *vt* destacar; **to be ~d against sth** perfilarse sobre algo

silica ['sɪlɪkə] *n no pl* sílice *f*

silicate ['sɪlɪkeɪt] *n* silicato *m*

silicon ['sɪlɪkən] *n no pl* silicio *m*

silicon chip *n* INFOR, ELEC chip *m* de silicio

silicone ['sɪlɪkəʊn, *Am:* -koʊn] *n no pl* silicona *f*

silicosis [ˌsɪlɪ'kəʊsɪs, *Am:* -'koʊ-] *n no pl* MED silicosis *f*

silk [sɪlk] *n* **1.** seda *f*; ~ **dress** vestido *m* de seda; ~ **scarf** pañuelo *m* de seda **2.** *Brit* LAW abogado, -a *m, f* (de categoría superior); **to receive** [*o* **to take**] ~ ser ascendido a la abogacía superior

silken ['sɪlkən] *adj* (*clothing*) de seda; (*hair*) sedoso, -a; (*voice*) suave

silk hat *n* sombrero *m* de copa **silk moth** *n* mariposa *f* de seda **silk paper** *n* papel *m* de seda **silk screen printing** *n* serigrafía *f* **silkworm** *n* gusano *m* de seda

silky ['sɪlki] <-ier, -iest> *adj* sedoso, -a; (*fur, voice*) suave

sill [sɪl] *n* (*of door*) umbral *m;* (*of window*) alféizar *m*

silly ['sɪli] <-ier, -iest> *adj* (*person*) tonto, -a, dundo, -a *AmC, Col*, baboso, -a *AmC;* (*idea*) estúpido, -a; ~ **season** *período de verano en que los periódicos llenan sus páginas con noticias triviales.;* **it was ~ of her to ...** fue una estupidez por su parte...; **to look ~** parecer ridículo; **to laugh oneself ~** desternillarse de risa; **to knock sb ~** *inf* dejar a alguien atontado de una paliza

silo ['saɪləʊ, *Am:* -loʊ] *n* silo *m*

silt [sɪlt] *n no pl* sedimento *m*

◆**silt up** *vi* encenagarse

silver ['sɪlvər, *Am:* -və] **I.** *n no pl* **1.** (*metal*) plata *f* **2.** (*coins*) monedas *fpl* de plata **3.** (*cutlery*) cubertería *f* **4.** (*dishes, trays*) vajilla *f* de plata **II.** *adj* **1.** (*made of silver*) de plata **2.** (*silver-coloured*) plateado, -a

silver birch *n* abedul *m* (plateado) **silver fir** *n* abeto *m* blanco

silverfish ['sɪlvəˌfɪʃ, *Am:* -və-,-] *n* **1.** (*fish*) pez *m* plateado **2.** (*insect*) lepisma *m*

silver foil *n* papel *m* de plata **silver jubilee** *n* vigésimo quinto aniversario *m* **silver lining** *n* resquicio *m* de esperanza **silver mine** *n* mina *f* de plata **silver paper** *n* papel *m* de plata **silver plate** *n* **1.** (*dishes, trays*) vajilla *f* de plata **2.** (*coating*) baño *m* de plata **silver-plate** *vt* platear **silver screen** *n* CINE the ~ la pantalla cinematográfica **silver service** *n* servicio *m* de guante blanco

silverside ['sɪlvəsaɪd, *Am:* -və-] *n no pl, Aus, Brit* cuarto *m* trasero de la ternera

silversmith ['sɪlvəsmɪθ, *Am:* -və-] *n* platero, -a *m, f*

silverware ['sɪlvəweər, *Am:* -vəwer] *n no pl* **1.** (*cutlery*) cubertería *f* **2.** (*dishes, trays*) vajilla *f* de plata

silver wedding *n* bodas *fpl* de plata

silvery <-ier, -iest> *adj* plateado, -a

simian ['sɪmiən] **I.** *n* simio *m* **II.** *adj* simiesco, -a

similar ['sɪmɪlər, *Am:* -ələ] *adj* similar

similarity [ˌsɪmə'lærəti, *Am:* -ə'leɾəţi] *n* parecido *m*, semejanza *f*

simile ['sɪmɪli, *Am:* -əli] *n* LIT, LING símil *m*

similitude [sɪ'mɪlɪtjuːd, *Am:* sə'mɪlətuːd] *n* **1.** (*quality of being similar*) similitud *f* **2.** (*comparison*) comparación *f*

simmer ['sɪmər, *Am:* -ə] **I.** *vi* **1.** GASTR hervir a fuego lento **2.** *fig* estar a punto de estallar **II.** *vt* cocer a fuego lento **III.** *n* ebullición *f* lenta; **to bring sth to a ~** poner algo a hervir; **to keep sth at a ~** mantener algo hirviendo a fuego lento

◆**simmer down** *vi inf* tranquilizarse

simper ['sɪmpər, *Am:* -pə] **I.** *vi* sonreír como un tonto, sonreír como una tonta **II.** *n* sonrisa *f* afectada

simple ['sɪmpl] *adj* **1.** (*not elaborate, not complex*) sencillo, -a **2.** (*not difficult*) fácil **3.** (*honest*) honesto, -a **4.** (*ordinary*) normal **5.** (*foolish*) simple

simple-minded [ˌsɪmpl'maɪndɪd] *adj inf* **1.** (*dumb*) tonto, -a **2.** (*naive*) ingenuo, -a

simpleton ['sɪmpltən] *n inf* bobalicón, -ona *m, f*, guanaco, -a *AmL*

simplicity [sɪm'plɪsəti, *Am:* -ţi] *n no pl* **1.** (*plainness*) sencillez *f* **2.** (*ease*) simplicidad *f*

simplification [ˌsɪmplɪfɪ'keɪʃən, *Am:* -plə-] *n* simplificación *f*

simplify ['sɪmplɪfaɪ, *Am:* -plə-] *vt* simplificar

simplistic [sɪm'plɪstɪk] *adj pej* simplista

simply ['sɪmpli] *adv* **1.** (*not elaborately*) sencillamente **2.**(*just*) simplemente **3.**(*absolutely*) completamente **4.**(*naturally*) de forma natural

simulate ['sɪmjʊleɪt] *vt* **1.**(*resemble*) simular **2.**(*feign*) fingir

simulation [ˌsɪmjʊ'leɪʃən] *n* (*imitation*) simulación *f*; (*of feeling*) fingimiento *m*

simulator ['sɪmjʊleɪtəʳ, *Am:* -ţəˑ] *n* INFOR, TECH simulador *m*

simultaneous [ˌsɪml'teɪnɪəs, *Am:* ˌsaɪml-'teɪnjəs] *adj* simultáneo, -a; ~ **broadcast** retransmisión *f* simultánea

sin [sɪn] I. *n* pecado *m;* to confess a ~ confesar un pecado ▶to be as ugly as ~ ser más feo que Picio II. *vi* <-nn-> pecar

since [sɪns] I. *adv* **1.**(*from then on*) desde entonces; ever ~ desde entonces **2.** (*ago*) long ~ hace mucho tiempo; not long ~ hace poco II. *prep* desde; how long is it ~ the crime? ¿cuánto tiempo ha pasado desde el crimen? III. *conj* **1.**(*because*) ya que, puesto que **2.**(*from the time that*) desde que; it's a week now ~ I came back ya ha pasado una semana desde que llegué

sincere [sɪn'sɪəʳ, *Am:* sɪn'sɪr] *adj* sincero, -a

sincerely *adv* sinceramente; yours ~ le saluda atentamente

sincerity [sɪn'serəti, *Am:* sɪn'serəţi] *n no pl* sinceridad *f;* in all ~ con toda franqueza

sine [saɪn] *n* MAT seno *m*

sinecure ['saɪnɪkjʊəʳ, *Am:* 'saɪnəkjʊr] *n* sinecura *f*

sine die [ˌsaɪnɪ'daɪː, *Am:* ˌsaɪni'daɪ] *adv* LAW sine die

sine qua non [ˌsɪnɪkwɑː'nəʊn, *Am:* 'sɪneɪkwɑː'noʊn] *n form* condición *f* sine qua non

sinew ['sɪnjuː] *n* tendón *m*

sinewy *adj* **1.**(*muscular*) nervudo, -a **2.**(*meat*) con nervios

sinful ['sɪnfəl] *adj* (*person*) pecador(a); (*thought, act*) pecaminoso, -a; (*waste*) inmoral

sing [sɪŋ] I. *vi* <sang, sung> **1.**(*person, bird*) cantar; (*wind, kettle*) silbar; to ~ to sb cantar para alguien II. *vt* cantar; to ~ sb to sleep arrullar a alguien
◆**sing out** I. *vi* (*sing*) cantar fuerte II. *vt inf* (*call*) to ~ sb's name llamar a alguien a voces
◆**sing up** *vi Brit, Aus* cantar más fuerte

singalong ['sɪŋəlɒŋ, *Am:* -lɑːŋ] *n* canto *m* a coro

Singapore [ˌsɪŋə'pɔːʳ, *Am:* 'sɪŋəpɔːr] *n* Singapur *m*

Singaporean [ˌsɪŋə'pɔːˈriːən, *Am:* 'sɪŋəpɔːriːən] I. *adj* de Singapur II. *n* habitante *mf* de Singapur

singe [sɪndʒ] I. *vt* chamuscar; (*hair*) quemar las puntas de II. *n* quemadura *f* superficial

singer ['sɪŋəʳ, *Am:* -əˑ] *n* cantante *mf*

singer-songwriter *n* cantautor(a) *m(f)*

singing *n no pl* canto *m* **singing lesson** *n* lección *f* de canto **singing teacher** *n* profesor(a) *m(f)* de canto **singing voice** *n* to have a good ~ tener buena voz (para el canto)

single ['sɪŋgl] I. *adj* **1.**(*one only*) único, -a; (*blow*) solo, -a; not a ~ person/thing nadie/ nada; not a ~ soul ni un alma; every ~ thing cada cosa; in ~ figures por debajo de diez **2.**(*with one part*) simple **3.**(*unmarried*) soltero, -a **4.**(*ticket*) sencillo, -a **5.**(*bed, room*) individual II. *n* **1.** Brit, Aus (*one-way ticket*) billete *m* de ida **2.**(*one-dollar note*) billete *m* de un dólar **3.**(*record*) single *m* **4.** SPORTS golpe *m* que marca un tanto; (*in baseball*) primera base *f* **5.**(*single room*) habitación *f* individual
◆**single out** *vt* señalar; to single sb out for criticism criticar a alguien en particular

single-breasted *adj* (*suit*) recto, -a, sin cruzar **single currency** *n* moneda *f* única **single-decker** *n* autobús *m* de un piso **single-entry bookkeeping** *n* contabilidad *f* por partida simple **Single European Market** *n* the ~ el mercado Único Europeo **single-handed** *adv* sin ayuda de nadie **single-hander** *n* NAUT yate *m* de un solo tripulante **single-lens reflex camera** *n* cámara *f* réflex (monoobjetivo) **single-minded** *adj* resuelto, -a **single-mindedness** *n no pl* firmeza *f* **single mother** *n* madre *f* soltera **single parent** *n* (*father*) padre *m* soltero; (*mother*) madre *f* soltera **single-parent family** <-ies> *n* familia *f* monoparental

singles bar *n* bar *m* de encuentros

single-seater *n* monoplaza *m* **single-sex school** *n* (*for boys*) escuela *f* para niños; (*for girls*) escuela *f* para niñas

singlet ['sɪŋglɪt] *n Brit, Aus* camiseta *f*

single-track *adj* **1.** RAIL de vía única **2.**(*road*) de carril único

singly ['sɪŋgli] *adv* uno por uno

singsong ['sɪŋsɒŋ, *Am:* -sɑːŋ] I. *n* **1.** Brit, Aus (*singing session*) concierto *m* espontáneo **2.** *no pl* (*way of speaking*) sonsonete *m* II. *adj* to speak in a ~ voice hablar cantando

singular ['sɪŋgjələʳ, *Am:* -ləˑ] I. *adj* **1.** LING singular; ~ form forma *f* de singular; the third person ~ la tercera persona del singular **2.**(*notable*) singular; of ~ beauty de belleza sin par; a ~ lack of tact una increíble falta de tacto II. *n no pl* LING singular *m;* in the ~ en singular

singularity [ˌsɪŋgjə'lærəti, *Am:* -'lerəţi] *n no pl, form* singularidad *f*

singularly *adv form* singularmente

Sinhalese [ˌsɪnhə'liːz, *Am:* ˌsɪnhə'liːz] I. *n* **1.**(*person*) cingalés, -esa *m, f* **2.**(*language*) cingalés *m* II. *adj* cingalés, -esa

sinister ['sɪnɪstəʳ, *Am:* -stəˑ] *adj* siniestro, -a

sink [sɪŋk] <sank o sunk, sunk> I. *n* (*in kitchen*) fregadero *m;* (*in bathroom*) lavabo *m* II. *vi* **1.**(*in water*) hundirse; to ~ to the bottom hundirse hasta el fondo **2.**(*price, level*) bajar **3.**(*drop down*) caer; to ~ to the ground caer al suelo; to ~ to one's knees hincarse de rodillas **4.**(*decline*) bajar; to ~ in sb's estimation perder la estima de alguien; to ~ into depression sumirse en la depresión; to ~ into oblivion caer en el olvido; to be ~ing (fast) (in health) empeorar (rápidamente) ▶to leave sb to ~ or <u>swim</u> abandonar a alguien a su suerte III. vt 1. (cause to submerge) hundir 2. (ruin) destruir 3. MIN excavar 4. SPORTS (ball) meter 5. Brit, Aus, inf (drink: bottle) tragarse 6. (invest) invertir 7. (plant, bury: teeth) hincar; to ~ one's teeth into sth hincar los dientes en algo

◆**sink back** vi (lean back) repantigarse
◆**sink down** vi 1. (descend) descender 2. (to the ground) agacharse
◆**sink in** vi 1. (go into surface) penetrar 2. (be absorbed: liquid) calar 3. (be understood) entenderse

sinker ['sɪŋkəʳ, Am: -kɚ] n plomo m
sinking ['sɪŋkɪŋ] I. n hundimiento m II. adj a ~ feeling una sensación de que todo se va a pique; with a ~ heart con el alma encogida
sink unit ['sɪŋkjuːnɪt] n lavadero m
sinner ['sɪnəʳ, Am: -ɚ] n pecador(a) m(f)
sinuous ['sɪnjʊəs] adj sinuoso, -a
sinus ['saɪnəs] n seno m
sinusitis [ˌsaɪnə'saɪtɪs, Am: -t̬ɪs] n no pl MED sinusitis f
Sioux [suː] I. adj sioux II. n 1. (person) sioux mf 2. (language) sioux m
sip [sɪp] I. <-pp-> vt sorber II. <-pp-> vi sorber III. n sorbo m; to have a sip dar un sorbo
siphon ['saɪfən] I. n sifón m II. vt sacar con sifón
◆**siphon off** vt 1. (liquid) sacar con sifón 2. (money) malversar
sir [sɜːʳ, Am: sɜːr] n señor m
sire ['saɪəʳ, Am: 'saɪɚ] n (form of address) señor m
siren ['saɪərən, Am: 'saɪrən] n sirena f
sirloin ['sɜːlɔɪn, Am: 'sɜːr-] n no pl solomillo m, diezmillo m Méx
sirocco [sɪ'rɒkəʊ, Am: sə'rɑːkoʊ] n METEO siroco m
sis [sɪs] n Am, inf abbr of **sister** hermana f
sisal ['saɪsəl] n no pl 1. (plant) pita f 2. (fibre) sisal m
sissy ['sɪsi] I. <-ies> n inf marica m II. <-ier, -iest> adj inf mariquita
sister ['sɪstəʳ, Am: -ɚ] n 1. a. REL hermana f; Sister Catherine Sor Caterina; ~ company empresa f asociada; ~ ship barco m gemelo 2. Brit, Aus (nurse) enfermera f
sisterhood ['sɪstəhʊd, Am: -tɚ-] n no pl hermandad f
sister-in-law ['sɪstərɪnlɔː, Am: -tɚɪnlɑː] <sisters-in-law o sister-in-laws> n cuñada f, concuña f AmL
sisterly adj de hermana
sit [sɪt] <sat, sat> I. vi 1. sentarse; (be in seated position) estar sentado, -a; ~! (to dog) ¡siéntate! 2. ART posar; to ~ for one's portrait hacerse retratar 3. (enter exam) presentarse; to ~ for an examination presentarse a un

examen 4. inf (babysit) to ~ for sb cuidar a alguien 5. (perch) posarse; (incubate eggs) empollar 6. (be placed) yacer; (rest unmoved) permanecer quieto, estar; to ~ on the shelf estar en el estante 7. (be in session) celebrar sesión 8. POL (be in office) to ~ in parliament/congress ser diputado 9. (fit) to ~ well/badly caer [o sentar] bien/mal 10. (be agreeable) the idea doesn't ~ well with any of them la idea no les convence a ninguno ▶to be ~ting pretty estar bien situado; to ~ tight (not move) no moverse; (not change opinion) no dar el brazo a torcer II. vt 1. (put on seat) sentar 2. Brit (take exam) presentarse a; to ~ an exam presentarse a un examen
◆**sit about** vi Brit, **sit around** vi estar sin hacer nada; to ~ around the house vagar por la casa
◆**sit back** vi 1. (in chair) sentarse cómodamente 2. (do nothing) cruzarse de brazos
◆**sit down** I. vi 1. (take a seat) sentarse 2. (be sitting) estar sentado II. vt sentar; to sit oneself down sentarse
◆**sit in** vi 1. (observe) asistir como oyente 2. (represent) to ~ for sb sustituir a alguien 3. (hold sit-in) hacer una sentada
◆**sit on** vt inf 1. (withold: information) guardar para sí; (secret) no revelar 2. (rebuke: person) poner en su sitio; (idea, scheme) acabar con
◆**sit out** I. vi (sit outdoors) sentarse fuera II. vt 1. (not take part in) no tomar parte en; to ~ a dance no bailar 2. (remain until the end of) aguantar hasta el final
◆**sit through** vt aguantar hasta el final
◆**sit up** I. vi 1. (sit erect) sentarse derecho; ~! ¡siéntate derecho! 2. inf (pay attention) prestar atención 3. (not go to bed) trasnochar II. vt incorporar
sitcom ['sɪtkɒm, Am: -kɑːm] n inf TV abbr of **situation comedy** comedia f de situación
sit-down strike [ˌsɪtdaʊn'straɪk] n huelga f de brazos caídos
site [saɪt] I. n 1. (place) sitio m; (of battle) lugar m 2. (vacant land for building) solar m; building ~ obra f 3. GEO, HIST yacimiento m 4. INFOR página f, sitio m; web ~ página f web, sitio m web II. vt situar
sit-in ['sɪtɪn, Am: 'sɪt̬-] n sentada f; to hold a ~ hacer una sentada
siting n no pl situación f
sitter n 1. ART modelo mf 2. Am (babysitter) canguro mf 3. inf SPORTS cosa f fácil; to miss a ~ fallar algo de lo más fácil
sitting n (session) sesión f; (for meal) turno m
sitting duck n s. sitting target **sitting member** n Brit POL miembro mf en funciones **sitting room** n Brit cuarto m de estar **sitting target** n blanco m fácil **sitting tenant** n inquilino, -a m, f en posesión
situate ['sɪtʃʊeɪt, Am: 'sɪtʃʊeɪt] vt form 1. (locate) colocar, ubicar Arg 2. (in context) situar

situated [ˈsɪtʃʊeɪtɪd, *Am:* ˈsɪtʃuerʒtɪd] *adj*
1. (*located*) situado, -a; **to be ~ near the
station** estar ubicado cerca de la estación **2.** (*in
a state*) **to be well/badly ~** estar bien/mal
situado; **to be well ~ to do sth** estar en una
buena situación para hacer algo
situation [ˌsɪtʃʊˈeɪʃən, *Am:* ˌsɪtʃuˈ-] *n* **1.** (*circumstances*) situación *f*; ECON, POL coyuntura *f*
2. (*location*) colocación *f* **3.** (*job*) puesto *m*
sit-up [ˈsɪtʌp] *n* **to do ~s** hacer abdominales
six [sɪks] **I.** *adj* seis *inv* **II.** *n* seis *m*; **in ~ figures** por encima de cien mil ▸ **to give sb ~ of
the best** dar a alguien seis azotes; **to be at ~es
and sevens** estar hecho un lío; *s. a.* **eight**
six-figure sum *n* cantidad *f* de seis cifras
six-footer [ˌsɪksˈfʊtər] *n persona que mide
1,83 metros o más*
six-pack [ˈsɪkspæk] *n* (*of beer*) paquete *m* de
seis cervezas
sixteen [sɪkˈstiːn] **I.** *adj* dieciséis *inv* **II.** *n*
dieciséis *m*; *s. a.* **eight**
sixteenth [ˌsɪkˈstiːnθ] **I.** *adj* decimosexto, -a
II. *n no pl* **1.** (*order*) decimosexto, -a *m, f*
2. (*date*) dieciséis *m* **3.** (*fraction*) dieciseisavo
m; (*part*) dieciseisava parte *f*; *s. a.* **eighth**
sixth [sɪksθ, *Am:* sɪkstθ] **I.** *adj* sexto, -a **II.** *n
no pl* **1.** (*order*) sexto, -a *m, f* **2.** (*date*) seis *m*
3. (*fraction*) sexto *m*; (*part*) sexta parte *f*; *s. a.*
eighth

Sixth-form college es el nombre que recibe en Gran Bretaña un college para alumnos de 16–18 años, procedentes de un colegio donde no hay **sixth form** (sexto curso).
En el college pueden examinarse de sus **A-levels** (algo parecido a la selectividad) o realizar dos cursos equivalentes que les permiten
prepararse al acceso a la universidad.

---

sixtieth [ˈsɪkstiːθ] **I.** *adj* sexagésimo, -a **II.** *n no
pl* (*order*) sexagéximo, -a *m, f*; (*fraction*) sexagésimo *m*; (*part*) sexagésima parte *f*; *s. a.*
eighth
sixty [ˈsɪksti] **I.** *adj* sesenta *inv* **II.** *n* <-ies>
sesenta *m*; *s. a.* **eighty**
size[1] [saɪz] **I.** *n no pl* **1.** (*of person, thing,
space*) tamaño *m*; (*of problem, operation*)
magnitud *f*; **a company of that ~** una empresa
de tal envergadura; **to be the same ~ as …**
ser de las mismas dimensiones que…; **to
increase/decrease in ~** aumentar/disminuir
de tamaño; **to double in ~** doblar en tamaño;
of any ~ de cualquier tamaño; **the ~ of a
thumbnail** la medida de una uña; **economy ~
pack** *fig* tamaño *m* ahorro **2.** (*of clothes*) talla
f; (*of shoes*) número *m*; **collar ~** talla *f* de
cuello **3.** (*of amount, bill*) cantidad *f* **II.** *vt*
1. (*person, thing, space*) medir **2.** (*clothes*)
clasificar según la talla
◆ **size up** *vt* evaluar
size[2] [saɪz] *n* cola *f*; (*for cloth*) apresto *m*
sizeable [ˈsaɪzəbl] *adj* bastante grande;
(*sum*) considerable

sizzle [ˈsɪzl] **I.** *vi* chisporrotear **II.** *n no pl* chisporroteo *m*
sizzler [ˈsɪzlər, *Am:* -lə·] *n inf* (*day*) día *m*
caluroso
skate[1] [skeɪt] *n* (*fish*) raya *f*
skate[2] [skeɪt] **I.** *n* patín *m* ▸ **to get one's ~s
on** *Brit, inf* darse prisa **II.** *vi* patinar; **to ~ over
an issue** tocar un tema muy por encima
skateboard [ˈskeɪtbɔːd, *Am:* -bɔːrd] *n*
monopatín *m*
skateboarder *n* monopatinador(a) *m(f)*
skater *n* patinador(a) *m(f)*; **figure ~** patina-
dor(a) *m(f)* artístico, -a
skating *n* patinaje *m*
skating rink *n* pista *f* de patinaje
skedaddle [skɪˈdædl] *vi inf* escabullirse
skein [skeɪn] *n* **1.** (*of wool*) madeja *f* **2.** (*of
geese, swans*) bandada *f*
skeleton [ˈskelɪtən, *Am:* ˈ-ə-] *n* **1.** ANAT
esqueleto *m*, cacastle *m AmC, Méx;* **to be
reduced to a ~** (*be very skinny*) quedarse en
los huesos **2.** (*framework: of boat, plane*)
armazón *m*; (*of building*) estructura *f* **3.** (*outline: of book, report*) esquema *m* ▸ **to have a
~ in the cupboard** tener un secreto vergonzoso
skeleton key *n* llave *f* maestra **skeleton
staff** *n* personal *m* mínimo
skeptic [ˈskeptɪk] *n Am, Aus s.* **sceptic**
skeptical *adj Am, Aus s.* **sceptical**
skepticism [ˈskeptɪsɪzəm] *n Am, Aus s.*
scepticism
sketch [sketʃ] **I.** *n* **1.** ART boceto *m*; **to make
a ~ of sth** hacer un croquis de algo **2.** (*rough
draft*) borrador *m* **3.** (*outline*) esquema *m*
4. THEAT, TV sketch *m* **II.** *vt* **1.** ART hacer un
boceto de **2.** (*write draft of*) hacer un borrador
de **III.** *vi* ART dibujar
◆ **sketch in** *vt* (*details*) resumir
◆ **sketch out** *vt* **1.** ART bosquejar **2.** (*de
scribe*) esbozar
sketchbook [ˈsketʃbʊk] *n* cuaderno *m* de
dibujo
sketchy [ˈsketʃi] <-ier, -iest> *adj* (*vague*)
impreciso, -a; (*incomplete*) incompleto, -a
skew [skjuː] **I.** *vt* (*distort*) distorsionar **II.** *n*
oblicuidad *f*; **to be on the ~** estar sesgado
skewbald [ˈskjuːbɔːld, *Am:* -bɑːld] **I.** *n* caballo *m* pío **II.** *adj* pío
skewed [skjuːd] *adj* sesgado, -a
skewer [ˈskjuər, *Am:* ˈskjuːə·] **I.** *n* pincho *m*,
brocheta *f* **II.** *vt* ensartar
skew-whiff [ˌskjuːˈwɪf] *adj Brit, Aus, inf* torcido, -a
ski [skiː] **I.** *n* esquí *m*; **on ~s** con esquís **II.** *vi*
esquiar; **to ~ down the slope** bajar la pista
esquiando
ski boot *n* bota *f* de esquí
skid [skɪd] **I.** <-dd-> *vi* **1.** (*on ice*) patinar,
colear *AmC, Ant;* **to ~ to a halt** resbalar hasta
detenerse; (*while driving*) derrapar; **to ~ off
the road** derrapar y salir de la carretera
2. (*slide over*) **to ~ along** [*o* **across**] **sth** desli-

S

zarse sobre algo **II.** n **1.** (*while driving*) derrape m; **to go into a** ~ empezar a resbalar **2.** AVIAT tren m de aterrizaje ► **to put the ~s under sb** Brit, Aus, inf hacer la zancadilla a alguien; **to put the ~s under sth** Brit, Aus, inf hacer fracasar algo; **to be on the ~s** inf andar de capa caída

skidmark n AUTO huella f de un patinazo **skid row** n no pl, Am barrio m bajo; **to be on** ~ pordiosear

skier ['ski:ər, Am: -ə'] n esquiador(a) m(f)

skiff [skɪf] n esquife m

ski goggles npl gafas fpl de esquiar

skiing n no pl esquí m; ~ **equipment** equipo m de esquiar; ~ **lesson** lección f de esquí

skiing holiday n vacaciones fpl de esquí

ski instructor n monitor m de esquí **ski instructress** n monitora f de esquí **ski jump** n **1.** no pl (*jump*) salto m de esquí **2.** (*runway*) pista f para saltos de esquí

skilful ['skɪlfəl] adj Brit, Aus hábil, tinoso, -a Col, Ven

skilfully adv Brit, Aus hábilmente

ski lift n telesquí m

skill [skɪl] n **1.** no pl (*ability*) habilidad f; **to involve some** ~ requerir cierta destreza **2.** (*technique*) técnica f; **communication ~s** facilidad f de comunicación; **language ~s** habilidad f para las lenguas; **negotiating ~s** artes fpl de negociación

skilled adj **1.** (*trained*) preparado, -a; (*skilful*) hábil, habiloso, -a Chile, Perú **2.** (*requiring skill*) cualificado, -a; ~ **labour** mano de obra f cualificada

skillet ['skɪlɪt] n **1.** Brit (*saucepan*) cacerola f **2.** Am (*frying pan*) sartén f

skillful ['skɪlfəl] adj s. **skilful**

skillfully adv Am s. **skilfully**

skim [skɪm] <-mm-> **I.** vt **1.** (*move above*) rozar **2.** GASTR espumar; (*milk*) desnatar **II.** vi **to** ~ **over sth** pasar rozando algo; **to** ~ **through sth** fig hojear algo

ski mask n pasamontañas m

skimmed milk n Brit, **skim milk** n Am no pl leche f desnatada

skimmer n espumadera f

skimp [skɪmp] vi escatimar gastos; **to** ~ **(on sth)** escatimar (algo)

skimpy ['skɪmpi] <-ier, -iest> adj **1.** (*meal*) escaso, -a; (*knowledge*) superficial **2.** (*dress*) corto, -a y estrecho, -a

skin [skɪn] **I.** n **1.** (*of person*) piel f; (*of animal*) pellejo m, piel f; **to be soaked to the** ~ estar calado hasta los huesos **2.** (*of apple, potato, tomato*) piel f; (*of melon*) corteza f; (*of banana*) cáscara f **3.** TECH revestimiento m **4.** (*on milk*) nata f ► **to be all** ~ **and bone(s)** estar en los huesos; **it's no** ~ **off his/her nose** ni le va ni le viene; **by the** ~ **of one's teeth** por los pelos; **to have a thick** ~ ser insensible a las críticas; **to jump out of one's** ~ llevarse un susto tremendo; **to get under sb's** ~ (*affect*) afectar a alguien **II.** <-nn-> vt

1. (*remove skin from: animal*) despellejar; **to** ~ **sb alive** iron desollar vivo a alguien **2.** (*graze*) despellejar

skin cancer n cáncer m de piel **skincare** n cuidado m de la piel **skin-deep** adj epidérmico, -a; (*beauty*) superficial **skin disease** n enfermedad f cutánea **skin diver** n submarinista mf **skin-diving** n no pl submarinismo m **skin flick** n inf película f porno

skinflint ['skɪnflɪnt] n tacaño, -a m, f

skinful ['skɪnfʊl] n no pl, inf **to have had a** ~ llevar una copa de más

skin graft n MED **1.** (*transplant*) injerto m de piel **2.** (*section*) trozo m de piel

skinhead ['skɪnhed] n cabeza mf rapada

skinny ['skɪni] <-ier, -iest> adj flaco, -a, charcón, -ona Arg, Bol, Urug

skinny-dip ['skɪnidɪp] <-pp-> vi inf bañarse en cueros

skint [skɪnt] adj **to be** ~ no tener ni un céntimo

skintight [skɪn'taɪt] adj muy ceñido, -a

skip¹ [skɪp] n Brit, Aus (*container*) contenedor m de basura

skip² [skɪp] **I.** <-pp-> vi **1.** (*take light steps*) brincar; **to** ~ **from one subject to another** saltar de un tema a otro; **to** ~ **across to the shops** ir a las tiendas; **to** ~ **over to France** hacerse una escapadita a Francia **2.** Brit, Aus (*with rope*) saltar a la comba **II.** <-pp-> vt **1.** (*leave out*) omitir **2.** (*not participate in*) saltarse; **to** ~ **classes** faltar a clase **3.** inf (*leave*) **to** ~ **the country** salir del país apresuradamente **4.** Am (*hop with rope*) **to** ~ **rope** saltar a la comba **III.** n brinco m

ski pants npl pantalones mpl de esquí **ski pass** n forfait m **ski-plane** n avión m que puede aterrizar sobre la nieve **ski pole** n palo m de esquí

skipper ['skɪpə', Am: -ə'] **I.** n NAUT patrón, -ona m, f; (*captain*) capitán, -ana m, f; inf (*form of address*) jefe m **II.** vt (*ship*) patronear; (*aircraft*) pilotar; (*team*) capitanear

skipping rope n Brit, **skip rope** n Am comba f

ski rack n portaesquís m **ski resort** n estación f de esquí

skirmish ['skɜːmɪʃ, Am: 'skɜːr-] **I.** n **1.** MIL escaramuza f, entrevero m Arg, Chile, Urug **2.** (*argument*) roce m **II.** vi **1.** MIL escaramuzar **2.** (*argue*) discutir

skirt [skɜːt, Am: skɜːrt] **I.** n **1.** (*garment*) falda f, pollera f AmL; (*lower part of coat*) faldón m **2.** no pl, pej, inf (*women*) **a piece of** ~ una tía **II.** vt **1.** (*path, road*) rodear **2.** (*avoid*) evitar

skirting (board) ['skɜːtɪŋ(bɔːd), Am: 'skɜːrt̪ɪŋ(bɔːrd)] n Brit, Aus rodapié m

ski run n pista f de esquí **ski school** n escuela f de esquí **ski slope** n pista f de esquí **ski stick** n Brit palo m de esquí **ski suit** n mono m de esquí

skit [skɪt] n sátira f; **a** ~ **on sb/sth** una parodia sobre alguien/algo

ski tow *n* telesquí *m*

skitter about ['skɪtəʳ ə'baʊt, *Am:* 'skɪʈə ə'baʊt] *vi* pulular

skittish ['skɪtɪʃ, *Am:* 'skɪʈ-] *adj* **1.** (*nervous: horse, person*) nervioso, -a, pajarero, -a *AmL* **2.** (*uncertain*) caprichoso, -a

skittle ['skɪtl, *Am:* 'skɪʈ-] *n* bolo *m;* **a game of ~s** un partido de bolos

skive [skaɪv] *vi Brit, inf* gandulear

◆**skive off** *vi Brit, inf* **to ~ school** hacer novillos

skiver ['skaɪvəʳ, *Am:* -ɚ] *n Brit, inf* gandul(a) *m(f)*

skivvy ['skɪvi] I. <-ies> *n* **1.** *Brit* (*servant*) fregona *f* **2.** *pl, Am, inf* (*men's underwear*) calzoncillos *mpl* **3.** *Aus* (*polo-neck*) suéter fino de cuello redondo II. *vi* hacer las tareas más pesadas

skulduggery [skʌl'dʌgəri] *n no pl* trampas *fpl*

skulk [skʌlk] *vi* **1.** (*hide*) esconderse **2.** (*move furtively*) merodear

skull [skʌl] *n* calavera *f;* ANAT cráneo *m* ►**the ~ and crossbones** la bandera pirata; **to be bored out of one's ~** *inf* estar aburrido como una ostra

skullcap ['skʌlkæp] *n* (*small cap*) casquete *m;* REL solideo *m*

skunk [skʌŋk] *n* **1.** (*animal*) mofeta *f,* zorrino *m CSur,* mapurite *m AmC,* mapuro *m Col, Ven* **2.** *inf* (*person*) canalla *mf*

sky [skaɪ] <-ies> *n* cielo *m;* **the sunny skies of Spain** el cielo soleado de España; **under blue skies** bajo el cielo azul ►**the ~'s the limit** todo es posible; **red ~ at night, shepherd's delight** *prov* el cielo rojo por la noche anuncia buen tiempo; **to praise sth/sb to the skies** poner algo/a alguien por las nuebes

sky-blue [,skaɪblu:] *adj* azul celeste *inv* **sky blue** *n no pl* azul *m* celeste

skydiving ['skaɪ,daɪvɪŋ] *n* caída *m* libre (*en paracaídas*)

sky-high [,skaɪ'haɪ] I. *adv a. fig* por las nubes; **to go ~** (*prices*) dispararse II. *adj* (*price*) astronómico, -a

skyjack ['skaɪdʒæk] *vt* (*plane*) secuestrar

skylark ['skaɪlɑ:k, *Am:* -lɑ:rk] I. *n* alondra *f* II. *vi* juguetear

skylight ['skaɪlaɪt] *n* tragaluz *m,* aojada *f Col*

skyline ['skaɪlaɪn] *n* **1.** (*city rooftops*) perfil *m* **2.** (*horizon*) horizonte *m*

skyrocket ['skaɪ,rɒkɪt, *Am:* 'skaɪ,rɑ:kɪt] *vi* subir (como un cohete); (*price*) dispararse

skyscraper ['skaɪskreɪpəʳ, *Am:* -pɚ] *n* rascacielos *m inv*

slab [slæb] *n* **1.** (*flat piece: of stone*) losa *f;* (*of concrete*) bloque *m;* (*of wood*) tabla *f;* (*of marble*) placa *f* **2.** (*slice: of cake, of cheese*) trozo *m;* (*of chocolate*) tableta *f* **3.** (*in mortuary*) mesa *f* de amortajamiento

slack [slæk] I. *adj* **1.** (*loose: rope*) flojo, -a; (*muscle*) flácido, -a **2.** *pej* (*lazy: student*) vago, -a; (*piece of work*) flojo, -a; (*writing style*) des-

cuidado, -a; (*discipline*) laxo, -a; (*in paying*) negligente **3.** (*not busy*) de poca actividad; ~ **demand** poca demanda II. *n no pl* **1.** flojedad; **to take up the ~** (*of rope*) tensar la cuerda; (*compensate*) compensar **2.** COM período *m* de inactividad III. *vi* hacer el vago

slacken ['slækən] I. *vt* **1.** (*loosen*) aflojar **2.** (*reduce: speed, vigilance*) reducir; (*pace*) aflojar II. *vi* **1.** (*loosen*) aflojarse, petaquearse *Col* **2.** (*diminish: demand, intensity*) disminuir

◆**slack off** *vi,* **slacken off** I. *vi* **1.** (*make less effort*) hacer menos esfuerzo **2.** (*go more slowly*) aflojar el paso **3.** (*diminish: demand, intensity*) disminuir II. *vt* reducir

slackening ['slækənɪŋ] *n no pl* **1.** (*loosening*) aflojamiento *m* **2.** (*of speed, intensity*) disminución *f*

slacker ['slækəʳ, *Am:* -ɚ] *n inf* vago, -a *m, f*

slackness ['slæknɪs] *n no pl* **1.** (*looseness*) falta *f* de tensión **2.** (*of discipline*) relajamiento *m;* (*negligence*) negligencia *f* **3.** COM inactividad *f* **4.** (*laziness*) pereza *f*

slacks [slæks] *npl* pantalones *mpl* (de sport)

slag [slæg] I. *n* **1.** *no pl* (*waste*) escoria *f* **2.** *Brit, pej* (*slut*) puta *f* II. <-gg-> *vt inf* (*criticize*) poner por los suelos

◆**slag off** *vt inf* poner por los suelos

slag heap *n* escorial *m*

slain [sleɪn] I. *pp of* **slay** II. *n* **the ~** los fallecidos

slake [sleɪk] *vt liter* aplacar; **to ~ one's thirst** apagar la sed

slalom ['slɑ:ləm] *n* slalom *m*

slam [slæm] I. <-mm-> *vt* **1.** (*strike*) golpear; **to ~ the door** dar un portazo; **to ~ the window/book shut** cerrar la ventana/el libro de un golpe; **to ~ the ball into the net** disparar la pelota a la red; **to ~ the phone down on sb** colgar el teléfono a alguien bruscamente **2.** *inf* (*criticize*) poner por los suelos II. <-mm-> *vi* **1.** (*close noisily*) cerrarse de golpe **2.** (*hit hard*) **to ~ against sth** chocar contra algo; **to ~ into sth** chocar con algo III. *n* (*of door*) portazo *m;* **to close a book with a ~** cerrar un libro de un golpe

slammer ['ʃlæməʳ, *Am:* -ɚ] *n no pl, inf* chirona *f,* cana *f AmS,* bote *m Méx,* guandoca *f Col*

slander ['slɑ:ndəʳ, *Am:* 'slændɚ] I. *n no pl* LAW calumnia *f* II. *vt* calumniar

slanderer ['slɑ:ndərəʳ, *Am:* 'slændɚɚ] *n* calumniador(a) *m(f)*

slanderous ['slɑ:ndərəs, *Am:* 'slændɚ-] *adj* calumnioso, -a

slang [slæŋ] I. *n no pl* argot *m* II. *adj* de argot III. *vt Brit, Aus, inf* insultar

slanging match *n Brit, Aus* bronca *f*

slangy <-ier, -iest> *adj inf* argótico, -a

slant [slɑ:nt, *Am:* slænt] I. *vi* inclinarse II. *vt* **1.** (*make diagonal*) inclinar **2.** (*give bias to*) presentar tendenciosamente III. *n* **1.** *no pl* (*slope*) inclinación *f;* **to be on the ~** estar inclinado, -a **2.**(*perspective*) perspectiva *f*; **to put a favourable ~ on sth** dar un sesgo favorable a algo

slanting *adj* (*roof*) inclinado, -a; (*eyes*) rasgado, -a

slap [slæp] **I.** *n* palmada *f*; **a ~ in the face** una bofetada, una biaba *Arg, Urug*, un bife *Arg, Urug*; *fig* un insulto; **the ~ of the waves** el rugir de las olas ▶**~ and** tickle *Brit, inf* achuchones *mpl* **II.**<-pp-> *vt* **1.**(*hit*) dar una palmada, guantear *AmL* **2.**(*put*) **to ~ the book onto the table** tirar el libro en la mesa; **to ~ paint onto the wall** pintar la pared rápidamente **III.** *adv inf* directamente, de lleno; **to drive ~ into sth** chocar de lleno contra algo; **to leave ~ in the middle of a meeting** marcharse justo en plena reunión

◆**slap down** *vt* **1.**(*put down with slap*) tirar **2.**(*silence rudely*) hacer callar

slap-bang [ˌslæpˈbæŋ] *adv Brit, inf* de golpe y porrazo

slapdash [ˈslæpdæʃ] *adj pej, inf* chapucero, -a

slaphead [ˈslæphed] *n inf* calvorota *mf*

slapjack [ˈslæpˌdʒæk] *n Am* crepe *m*

slapstick [ˈslæpstɪk] *n no pl* payasadas *fpl*

slap-up [ˈslæpʌp] *adj Brit, Aus, inf* **a ~ meal** una comilona

slash [slæʃ] **I.** *vt* **1.**(*cut deeply*) rajar; **to ~ one's wrists** cortarse las venas **2.**(*reduce: prices, spending*) rebajar (drásticamente); (*budget*) recortar (drásticamente) **II.** *n* **1.**(*cut*) corte *m* **2.**(*swinging blow*) latigazo *m* **3.** FASHION raja *f* **4.** TYPO barra *f* **5.** *Brit, Aus, inf* meada *f*; **to go for** [*o* **to have**] **a ~** ir a mear

slat [slæt] *n* (*of wood*) listón *m*, tablilla *f*; (*of plastic*) tira *f*

slate [sleɪt] **I.** *n* **1.** *no pl* (*for roof, writing*) pizarra *f* **2.** *Am, Aus* POL lista *f* de candidatos ▶**to have a** clean **~** no tener borrones en la hoja de servicios; **to wipe the ~** clean hacer borrón y cuenta nueva; **to** put **sth on the ~** apuntar algo en la cuenta **II.** *vt* **1.**(*cover with slates*) empizarrar **2.** *Am, Aus* (*schedule*) programar; POL poner en la lista de canditatos **3.** *Brit, Aus, inf* (*criticize*) poner por los suelos

slattern [ˈslætən, *Am:* ˈslæt̬ən] *n pej* puta *f*

slatternly *adj pej* sucio, -a

slaughter [ˈslɔːtər, *Am:* ˈslɑːt̬ə] **I.** *vt* **1.**(*kill: animal*) matar, beneficiar *AmL*, carnear *CSur*; (*people*) masacrar **2.** *inf* (*defeat*) dar una paliza a **II.** *n no pl* **1.**(*killing: of animal*) matanza *f*, beneficio *AmL*, carneada *f Arg, Chile, Par, Urug*; (*of people*) masacre *f* **2.** *inf* (*defeat*) paliza *f*

slaughterhouse [ˈslɔːtəhaʊs, *Am:* ˈslɑː-t̬ə-] *n* matadero *m*, tablada *f Par*

Slav [slɑːv] **I.** *n* eslavo, -a *m, f* **II.** *adj* eslavo, -a

slave [sleɪv] **I.** *n* esclavo, -a *m, f* ▶**to be a ~ to** fashion ser un esclavo de la moda **II.** *vi* trabajar como un burro

slave driver *n iron, inf* negrero, -a *m, f*

slaver¹ [ˈslævər, *Am:* -ə] **I.** *vi* babear **II.** *n no*

pl baba *f*

slaver² [ˈsleɪvər, *Am:* -ə] *n* HIST **1.**(*ship*) barco *m* que trafica con esclavos **2.**(*slave trader*) traficante *mf* de esclavos

slavery [ˈsleɪvəri] *n no pl* esclavitud *f*

slave trade *n* HIST tráfico *m* de esclavos

Slavic [ˈslɑːvɪk] **I.** *n* eslavo, -a *m, f* **II.** *adj* eslavo, -a

slavish [ˈsleɪvɪʃ] *adj* **1.**(*unoriginal*) poco original **2.**(*servile*) servil

Slavonic [sləˈvɒnɪk, *Am:* -ˈvɑːnɪk] **I.** *n* eslavo, -a *m, f* **II.** *adj* eslavo, -a

slay [sleɪ] <slew, slain> *vt* LIT matar

sleaze [sliːz] *n no pl* sordidez *f*; POL corrupción *f*

sleazy [ˈsliːzi] <-ier, -iest> *adj* (*area, bar, affair*) sórdido, -a; (*person*) con mala pinta; POL corrupto, -a

sled [sled] *Am* **I.** *n s.* sledge¹ **II.**<-dd-> *vi s.* sledge¹

sledge¹ [sledʒ] **I.** *n* trineo *m* **II.** *vi* ir en trineo

sledge² [sledʒ] *n s.* sledgehammer

sledgehammer [ˈsledʒˌhæmər, *Am:* -ə] *n* almádena *f* ▶**to use a ~ to crack a** nut matar moscas a cañonazos

sleek [sliːk] *adj* (*fur, hair*) lacio, -a y brillante; (*car*) de líneas elegantes; (*person*) muy aseado, -a

◆**sleek down** *vt* alisar

sleep [sliːp] **I.** *n* **1.** *no pl* (*resting state*) sueño *m*; **to go** [*o* **get**] **to ~** dormirse; **to fall into a deep ~** caer en un sueño profundo; **to not lose ~ over sth** no perder el sueño por algo; **to put sb to ~** dormir a alguien; **to put an animal to ~** (*kill*) sacrificar un animal; **go back to ~!** *iron* ¡sigue durmiendo! **2.** *no pl* (*substance*) lagañas *fpl*; **to have ~ in one's eyes** tener lagañas; **to rub the ~ from one's eyes** quitarse las lagañas **II.**<slept, slept> *vi* dormir; **to ~ sound(ly)** dormir profundamente; **~ tight!** ¡que duermas bien! ▶**to ~ on it** consultarlo con la almohada **III.** *vt* alojar

◆**sleep around** *vi pej, inf* acostarse con cualquiera

◆**sleep in** *vi* **1.** *Brit* (*stay in bed*) dormir hasta tarde **2.**(*live*) vivir en (la) casa (donde uno trabaja)

◆**sleep off** *vt* **to sleep it off** dormir la mona, dormir la cruda *AmL*

◆**sleep out** *vi* (*outside*) dormir al aire libre

◆**sleep through** *vt* **to ~ noise** no despertarse con el ruido; **to ~ the journey** dormir durante todo el viaje

◆**sleep together** *vi* **1.**(*have sex*) acostarse juntos **2.**(*share bed*) dormir juntos

◆**sleep with** *vt* **1.**(*have sex with*) acostarse con **2.**(*share bed with*) dormir con

sleeper [ˈsliːpər, *Am:* -pə] *n* **1.**(*person*) persona *f* dormida; **to be a heavy/light ~** tener el sueño profundo/ligero **2.** RAIL (*carriage*) coche *m* cama **3.** *Brit, Aus* RAIL (*blocks*) traviesa *f* **4.**(*earstud*) pendiente *m* (en forma de bolita)

sleepiness *n no pl* somnolencia *f*
sleeping *adj* dormido, -a
sleeping bag *n* saco *m* de dormir **Sleeping Beauty** *n* la Bella Durmiente **sleeping car** *n* coche *m* cama **sleeping partner** *n Brit* COM socio, -a *m, f* comanditario, -a **sleeping pill** *n* somnífero *m* **sleeping policeman** <-men> *n* resalto *m* **sleeping sickness** *n no pl* encefalitis *f* letárgica **sleeping tablet** *n* somnífero *m*
sleepless ['sli:pləs] *adj* (*person*) insomne; (*night*) en vela
sleepwalk ['sli:p,wɔ:k, *Am:* -,wɑ:k] *vi* caminar dormido, -a; **he ~s** es sonámbulo
sleepwalker ['sli:p,wɔ:kər, *Am:* -,wɑ:kər] *n* sonámbulo, -a *m, f*
sleepy ['sli:pi] <-ier, -iest> *adj* **1.** (*drowsy*) somnoliento, -a **2.** (*quiet: village*) aletargado, -a
sleepyhead ['sli:pihed] *n inf* dormilón, -ona *m, f*
sleet [sli:t] **I.** *n no pl* aguanieve *f* **II.** *vi* **it is ~ing** cae aguanieve
sleeve [sli:v] *n* **1.** (*of shirt*) manga *f*; **to roll up one's ~s** arremangarse **2.** (*cover*) manguito *m* **3.** (*for record*) funda *f* ►**to have sth up one's ~** tener algo en la manga; **to laugh up one's ~ at sb** reírse de alguien para sus adentros
sleeveless ['sli:vlɪs] *adj* sin mangas
sleigh [sleɪ] *n* trineo *m*
sleight of hand [,slaɪtɒf'hænd, *Am:* -ɑ:f-] *n no pl* prestidigitación *f*, juego *m* de manos
slender ['slendər, *Am:* -dər] *adj* **1.** (*rod, branch*) fino, -a; (*person*) delgado, -a, silgado, -a *Ecua* **2.** (*majority, resources*) escaso, -a; (*chance*) remoto, -a
slenderize ['slendəraɪz] *vi, vt Am, inf* adelgazar
slept [slept] *pt, pp of* **sleep**
slew [slu:] *pt of* **slay**
slice [slaɪs] **I.** *n* **1.** GASTR (*of bread*) rebanada *f*; (*of ham*) loncha *f*; (*of meat*) tajada *f*; (*of cake, pizza*) trozo *m*; (*of cucumber, lemon*) rodaja *f* **2.** (*part: of credit, profits*) parte *f* **3.** (*tool*) pala *f* **4.** (*tennis*) golpe *m* con efecto; (*golf*) slice *m* ►**to get a ~ of the cake** sacar tajada; **~ of life** estampa *f* realista **II.** *vt* **1.** (*bread*) cortar (en rebanadas); (*ham*) cortar (en lonchas); (*meat*) cortar (en tajadas); (*cake*) cortar (en trozos); (*cucumber, lemon*) cortar en (rodajas) **2.** SPORTS **to ~ the ball** (*in tennis*) dar efecto a la pelota; (*in golf*) golpear la bola de slice ►**any way you ~ it** *Am* lo mires por donde lo mires **III.** *vi* **to ~ easily** ser fácil de cortar
♦**slice off** *vt* **1.** (*bread*) cortar (en rebanadas); (*ham*) cortar (en lonchas); (*meat*) cortar (en tajadas); (*cake*) cortar (en trozos); (*cucumber, lemon*) cortar (en rodajas) **2.** (*reduce by*) reducir en
♦**slice up** *vt* (*bread*) cortar en rebanadas; (*ham*) cortar en lonchas; (*meat*) cortar en tajadas; (*cake*) cortar en trozos; (*cucumber*) cortar en rodajas

sliced *adj* (*bread*) cortado, -a en rebanadas; (*ham*) cortado, -a en lonchas; (*meat*) cortado, -a en tajadas; (*cake*) cortado, -a en trozos; (*cucumber, lemon*) cortado, -a en rodajas
sliced bread *n* pan *m* de molde ►**it's the best thing since ~** es lo mejor del mundo
slicer *n* (*for bread*) (máquina *f*) rebanadora *f* de pan; (*for meat*) máquina *f* de cortar fiambre
slick [slɪk] **I.** <-er, -est> *adj* **1.** (*performance*) pulido, -a **2.** (*person*) hábil; *pej* astuto **II.** *n* **1.** (*oil*) marea *f* negra **2.** *Am* (*magazine*) revista *f* ilustrada
♦**slick back** *vt*, **slick down** *vt* (*hair*) alisar
slicker ['slɪkər, *Am:* -ər] *n Am* **1.** (*city slicker*) urbanita *mf* **2.** (*coat*) impermeable *m*
slide [slaɪd] **I.** <slid, slid> *vi* **1.** (*slip*) resbalar **2.** (*glide smoothly*) deslizarse; **the door ~s open/shut** la puerta se abre/se cierra corriéndola; **to ~ back into one's old habits** volver a las viejas costumbres **II.** <slid, slid> *vt* deslizar; **to ~ the door open/shut** correr la puerta; **to ~ sth across the floor** pasar algo deslizándolo por el suelo **III.** *n* **1.** (*act of sliding*) deslizamiento *m* **2.** (*sliding place on ice*) rampa *f* **3.** (*playground structure*) tobogán *m* **4.** GEO desprendimiento *m* **5.** FIN caída *f* **6.** PHOT diapositiva *f* **7.** (*for microscope*) portaobjetos *m inv* **8.** MUS vara *f* corredera **9.** *Brit* (*hair clip*) pasador *m*
slide projector *n* proyector *m* de diapositivas **slide rule** *n* regla *f* de cálculo
sliding *adj* (*sunroof*) corredizo, -a; (*door*) corredero, -a
sliding scale *n* escala *f* móvil
slight [slaɪt] **I.** <-er, -est> *adj* **1.** (*small: chance*) escaso, -a; (*error*) pequeño, -a; **the ~est thing** la menor tontería; **not in the ~est** en absoluto; **not to have the ~est (idea)** no tener ni la menor idea **2.** (*slim: person*) delgado, -a **II.** *n* desaire *m* **III.** *vt* despreciar
slightly *adv* un poco; **to know sb ~** conocer muy poco a alguien
slim [slɪm] **I.** <slimmer, slimmest> *adj* **1.** (*thin: person*) delgado, -a **2.** (*cigarette, book*) fino, -a **3.** (*slight: chance*) escaso, -a **II.** <-mm-> *vi* (*become slim*) adelgazar; (*try to get thinner*) hacer régimen
♦**slim down** *vi* adelgazar
slime [slaɪm] *n no pl* **1.** (*mud*) cieno *m* **2.** (*of fish, slug*) baba *f*
slimebag *n*, **slimeball** *n no pl* asqueroso, -a *m, f*
slimmer *n* persona *f* que está a régimen
slimming **I.** *n no pl* adelgazamiento *m* **II.** *adj* (*pill*) para adelgazar; (*food, drinks*) de bajo contenido calórico
slimy ['slaɪmi] <-ier, -iest> *adj* **1.** (*covered in slime*) viscoso, -a **2.** *pej* (*person*) asqueroso, -a; **~ git** *Brit* imbécil *mf* de mierda
sling [slɪŋ] <slung, slung> **I.** *vt* **1.** (*fling*) lanzar, aventar *Méx* **2.** (*hang*) colgar **II.** *n* **1.** (*for broken arm*) cabestrillo *m*; (*for carrying baby*) canguro *m* **2.** (*for lifting*) eslinga *f*

3. (*weapon*) honda *f*
◆**sling out** *vt inf* (*rubbish*) tirar a la basura; (*person*) echar

slingshot ['slɪnʃɒt, *Am:* -ʃɑːt] *n Am, Aus* tirachinas *m inv,* honda *f CSur, Perú,* resortera *f Méx*

slink [slɪŋk] <slunk> *vi* to ~ **away** [*o* off] escabullirse

slinky ['slɪŋki] <-ier, iest> *adj* (*walk*) sinuoso, -a; (*dress*) ceñido, -a

slip [slɪp] <-pp-> I. *n* 1. (*slipping*) resbalón *m* 2. (*mistake*) error *m;* **to make a** ~ cometer un error; ~ **of the pen** lapsus *m* calami; ~ **of the tongue** lapsus (linguae) 3. COM resguardo *m;* **a** ~ **of paper** un trozo de papel 4. (*women's underwear*) combinación *f* 5. BOT esqueje *m* ▶**there's many a** ~ (**twixt cup and lip**) *prov* de la mano a la boca desaparece la sopa *prov;* **to give sb the** ~ darle el esquinazo a alguien II. *vi* 1. (*slide*) resbalarse 2. (*move quietly*) deslizarse; **to** ~ **into a pub** colarse en un bar; **to** ~ **into/out of one's pyjamas** ponerse/quitarse el pijama 3. (*decline*) decaer; **to** ~ **into a depression** caer en una depresión III. *vt* 1. (*put smoothly*) deslizar; **to** ~ **sb a note** pasar una nota a alguien disimuladamente; **to** ~ **in a comment** dejar caer un comentario; **to** ~ **some money to sb** pasar dinero a alguien disimuladamente 2. (*escape from*) escabullirse de; **to** ~ **sb's attention** pasar desapercibido por alguien; **it** ~**ped my mind** se me olvidó 3. NAUT (*anchor*) soltar
◆**slip away** *vi* 1. (*leave unnoticed*) escabullirse; **to** ~ (**from sb**) escaparse (de alguien) 2. (*pass swiftly*) pasar rápidamente 3. (*be dying*) morirse
◆**slip by** *vi* 1. (*pass quickly: time*) pasar rápidamente 2. (*pass unnoticed*) pasar inadvertido, -a
◆**slip down** *vi* dejarse caer
◆**slip in** *vi* colarse
◆**slip off** I. *vi* 1. (*leave unnoticed*) escabullirse 2. (*fall off*) caerse II. *vt* (*clothes*) quitarse
◆**slip on** *vt* (*clothes*) ponerse
◆**slip out** *vi* 1. (*go out for short time*) salir un momento 2. (*leave unobtrusively*) escabullirse 3. (*be spoken accidentally*) escaparse; **the name slipped out** se me escapó el nombre
◆**slip up** *vi* equivocarse

slipcase ['slɪpkeɪs] *n* estuche *m*

slipknot ['slɪpnɒt, *Am:* -nɑːt] *n* nudo *m* corredizo

slip-on ['slɪpɒn, *Am:* -ɑːn] I. *adj* (*shoes*) sin cordones II. *n pl* zapatos *mpl* sin cordones

slippage ['slɪpɪdʒ] *n* (*in value, standards*) disminución *f*

slipper ['slɪpər, *Am:* -ər] *n* zapatilla *f,* pantufla *f AmL*

slippery ['slɪpəri] <-ier, -iest> *adj* 1. (*not giving firm hold: surface*) resbaladizo, -a; (*soap*) escurridizo, -a 2. (*untrustworthy: per-*

son) que no es de fiar ▶**to be a** ~ **customer** ser un pájaro de cuenta; **to be as** ~ **as an eel** ser escurridizo como una anguila; (**be on**) **the** ~ **slope** encontrarse en un terreno resbaladizo

slip road ['slɪprəʊd, *Am:* -roʊd] *n Brit* vía *f* de acceso

slipshod ['slɪpʃɒd, *Am:* -ʃɑːd] *adj* chapucero, -a

slipstream ['slɪpstriːm] *n* estela *f*

slip-up ['slɪpʌp] *n* desliz *m*

slipway ['slɪpweɪ] *n* NAUT grada *f*

slit [slɪt] I. <slit, slit> *vt* cortar; **to** ~ **sb's throat** cortar el cuello a alguien; **to** ~ **one's wrists** cortarse las venas II. *n* 1. (*tear*) raja *f* 2. (*narrow opening*) rendija *f*

slither ['slɪðər, *Am:* -ər] *vi* deslizarse; **to** ~ **down the slope** deslizarse por la pendiente; **to** ~ **on the ice** patinar sobre el hielo

sliver ['slɪvər, *Am:* -ər] *n* (*of glass, wood*) astilla *f;* (*of cake*) trocito *m;* (*of lemon*) rodaja *f* fina

slob [slɒb, *Am:* slɑːb] *n inf* patán *m*
◆**slob about** *vi inf* holgazanear

slobber ['slɒbər, *Am:* 'slɑːbər] *vi* babear

slobbery ['slɒbəri, *Am:* 'slɑːbəri] *adj* baboso, -a

sloe [sləʊ, *Am:* sloʊ] *n* 1. (*fruit*) endrina *f* 2. (*bush*) endrino *m*

slog [slɒg, *Am:* slɑːg] *inf* I. *n no pl* esfuerzo *m* II. <-gg-> *vi* (*walk*) caminar con gran esfuerzo III. <-gg-> *vt* (*hit*) golpear

slogan ['sləʊgən, *Am:* 'sloʊ-] *n* eslogan *m*

sloop [sluːp] *n* balandro *m*

slop [slɒp, *Am:* slɑːp] <-pp-> I. *vt inf* derramar II. *vi inf* derramarse; **to** ~ **about** [*o* **around**] salpicarlo todo III. *n* 1. *no pl, inf* (*watery food*) aguachirle *f* 2. *pl* (*waste liquid*) líquido *m* de desecho
◆**slop out** *vi Brit* vaciar el orinal

slope [sləʊp, *Am:* sloʊp] I. *n* inclinación *f;* (*up*) cuesta *f;* (*down*) declive *m;* (*for skiing*) pista *f* II. *vi* inclinarse; **to** ~ **down** descender, bajar; **to** ~ **up** ascender, subir III. *vt* inclinar; ~ **arms!** ¡armas al hombro!
◆**slope off** *vi Brit, pej* largarse

sloping *adj* (*roof*) inclinado, -a; (*shoulders*) caído, -a

sloppiness *n no pl, pej* 1. (*carelessness*) falta *f* de cuidado 2. (*sentimentality*) sensiblería *f*

sloppy ['slɒpi, *Am:* 'slɑːpi] <-ier, -iest> *adj* 1. (*careless*) descuidado, -a 2. (*sentimentally romantic*) sensiblero, -a 3. (*too wet: kiss*) baboso, -a 4. (*loose-fitting: jumper*) holgado, -a

slosh [slɒʃ, *Am:* slɑːʃ] I. *vt inf* 1. (*liquid*) echar salpicando 2. *Brit* (*hit*) cascar II. *vi* 1. (*splash*) chapotear 2. (*water*) agitarse
◆**slosh about** *vi,* **slosh around** *vi* echar salpicando

sloshed *adj inf* borracho, -a; **to get** ~ agarrar una tajada

slot [slɒt, *Am:* slɑːt] I. *n* 1. (*narrow opening*) ranura *f* 2. TV espacio *m* 3. AVIAT slot *m* II. <-tt-> *vi* **to** ~ **in** encajar III. <-tt-> *vt* **to** ~

sth in hacer encajar

sloth [sləυθ, *Am:* slɑ:θ] *n* **1.** *no pl* (*laziness*) pereza *f* **2.** ZOOL perezoso *m*

slothful ['sləυθfəl, *Am:* 'slɑ:θ-] *adj* perezoso, -a

slot machine ['slɒtməʃiːn, *Am:* 'slɑ:t-] *n* **1.** (*fruit machine*) máquina *f* tragaperras **2.** *Brit, Aus* (*vending machine*) máquina *f* expendedora **slot meter** *n* contador *m* (*que funciona con monedas*)

slouch [slaυtʃ] I. *vi* **1.** (*have shoulders bent*) encorvarse **2.** (*walk*) caminar arrastrando los pies II. *n* postura *f* encorbada ▶**to be no** ~ no ser manco

slough¹ [slʌf] *n* **1.** (*bog*) ciénaga *f* **2.** *liter* (*depressed state*) abismo *m*

slough² [slaυ, *Am:* slu:] *vt* ZOOL (*skin*) mudar de

Slovak ['sləυvæk, *Am:* 'slouvɑ:k-] I. *adj* eslovaco, -a II. *n* **1.** (*person*) eslovaco, -a *m, f* **2.** LING eslovaco *m*

Slovakia [sləυ'vækiə, *Am:* slou'vɑːki-] *n no pl* Eslovaquia *f*

Slovakian *n s.* **Slovak**

sloven ['slʌvən] *n* persona *f* dejada

Slovene ['sləυviːn, *Am:* 'slou-] I. *adj* esloveno, -a II. *n* **1.** (*person*) esloveno, -a *m, f* **2.** LING esloveno *m*

Slovenia [sləυ'viːniə, *Am:* slou'-] *n no pl* Eslovenia *f*

Slovenian *n s.* **Slovene**

slovenly ['slʌvənli] *adj* descuidado, -a

slow [sləυ, *Am:* slou] I. *adj* **1.** (*not fast*) lento, -a; (*poison*) de efectos retardados; **to be** ~ **to do sth** tardar en hacer algo; **to be** (**10 minutes**) ~ ir (10 minutos) retrasado **2.** (*stupid*) torpe, guanaco, -a *AmL* II. *vi* ir más despacio; **to** ~ **to a halt** detenerse gradualmente III. *vt* frenar; (*development*) retardar

◆**slow down** I. *vt* ralentizar II. *vi* **1.** (*reduce speed*) reducir la velocidad **2.** (*be less active*) moderar el ritmo de vida

slowcoach ['sləυkəυtʃ, *Am:* 'sloukoutʃ] *n Brit, Aus, childspeak* tortuga *f*

slowdown ['sləυdaυn, *Am:* 'slou-] *n* ECON ralentización *f;* **economic** ~ reducción *f* de la actividad económica

slowly *adv* lentamente; ~ **but surely** lento pero seguro

slow motion I. *n* cámara *f* lenta; **in** ~ a cámara lenta II. *adj* a cámara lenta **slow--moving** *adj* lento, -a; (*traffic*) denso, -a

slowness *n no pl* **1.** (*lack of speed*) lentitud *f* **2.** (*stupidity*) torpeza *f*

slow train *n* tren *m* lento **slow-witted** *adj* lerdo, -a **slowworm** *n* lución *m*

SLR *n abbr of* **single-lens reflex camera** cámara *f* réflex (monoobjetivo)

sludge [slʌdʒ] *n no pl* lodo *m*

slug¹ [slʌg] *n* ZOOL babosa *f*

slug² [slʌg] <-gg-> I. *vi inf* (*hit*) aporrear; **to** ~ **it out** pegarse II. *n inf* **1.** (*bullet*) bala *f* **2.** *Am* (*coin*) ficha *f* **3.** *inf* (*swig*) trago *m*

sluggish ['slʌgɪʃ] *adj* (*person*) perezoso, -a, conchudo, -a *Méx;* (*progress*) lento, -a; (*market*) flojo, -a

sluice [sluːs] I. *n* (*gate*) compuerta *f* II. *vt* regar; **to** ~ **sth down** enjuagar algo

sluice gate *n* compuerta *f* **sluiceway** *n* canal *m* de desagüe

slum [slʌm] I. *n* (*area*) barrio *m* pobre; (*on outskirts*) suburbio *m;* **to live in** ~ **conditions** vivir en condiciones de pobreza II. <-mm-> *vt* **to** ~ **it** *iron* vivir como pobres

slumber ['slʌmbə', *Am:* -bə] I. *vi liter* dormir II. *n liter* (*sleep*) sueño *m* ligero; (*inactive state*) marasmo *m elev*

slum clearance *n no pl* demolición *f* de los barrios pobres **slum dweller** *n* habitante *mf* de los barrios bajos **slum landlord** *n* casero *m* de tugurios

slump [slʌmp] I. *n* ECON **1.** (*decline*) depresión *f;* ~ **in prices** descenso *m* repentino de los precios **2.** (*recession*) recesión *f* II. *vi* desplomarse; (*prices*) bajar notablemente

slung [slʌŋ] *pt, pp of* **sling**

slunk [slʌŋk] *pt, pp of* **slink**

slur [slɜː', *Am:* slɜːr] <-rr-> I. *vt* pronunciar con dificultad; **to** ~ **one's words** arrastrar las palabras II. *n* **1.** (*insult*) calumnia *f* **2.** (*in speech*) pronunciación *f* incomprensible

slurp [slɜːp, *Am:* slɜːrp] *inf* I. *vt, vi* sorber (ruidosamente) II. *n* sorbo *m* (ruidoso)

slurry ['slʌri, *Am:* 'slɜːr-] *n no pl* compuesto *m* acuoso

slush [slʌʃ] *n no pl* **1.** (*snow*) nieve *f* medio derretida **2.** *inf* (*sentimentality*) sentimentalismo *m*

slush fund *n pej* fondos *mpl* para sobornar

slushy *adj* <-ier, -iest> **1.** (*snow*) a medio derretir **2.** (*sentimental*) sentimentaloide

slut [slʌt] *n pej* puta *f*

sluttish ['slʌtɪʃ, *Am:* 'slʌt̮-] *adj pej* (*messy*) guarro, -a

sly [slaɪ] *adj* **1.** (*secretive*) sigiloso, -a; (*smile*) sutil; **on the** ~ a hurtadillas **2.** (*crafty*) astuto, -a, songo, -a *Col, Méx*

slyly *adv* **1.** (*secretively*) sigilosamente **2.** (*craftily*) con astucia

smack¹ [smæk] I. *vt* **1.** (*slap*) dar un manotazo a **2.** (*hit noisily*) golpear; **to** ~ **one's lips** relamerse los labios II. *n* **1.** *inf* (*slap*) bofetada *f;* (*soft blow*) palmada *f* **2.** *inf* (*kiss*) besazo *m* **3.** (*loud noise*) ruido *m* fuerte III. *adv* **1.** (*exactly*) exactamente **2.** (*completely*) de lleno

◆**smack of** *vi* oler a

smack² [smæk] *n no pl, inf* (*heroin*) heroína *f*

smacker ['smækə', *Am:* -ə'] *n inf* **1.** *Brit* (*pound*) libra *f; Am* (*dollar*) dólar *m* **2.** (*loud kiss*) beso *m* sonoro

small [smɔːl] I. *adj* **1.** (*not large*) pequeño, -a; (*person*) bajo, -a, petizo, -a *CSur, Bol* **2.** (*young*) joven **3.** (*insignificant*) insignificante; **on a** ~ **scale** a pequeña escala; **in his/**

her own ~ **way** de forma modesta **4.** TYPO
(*letter*) minúscula; **with a ~ 'c'** con 'c' minúscula ▶**to be grateful for ~ mercies** *prov* dar
las gracias por los pequeños favores; **it's a ~
world** *prov* el mundo es un pañuelo *prov* **II.** *n
no pl* **the ~ of the back** la región lumbar
small ad *n* anuncio *m* breve **small arms**
npl armas *fpl* de bajo calibre **small beer** *n
Brit* poca cosa **small business** <-es> *n*
pequeña empresa *f* **small businessman** *n*
pequeño empresario *m* **small change** *n no
pl* calderilla *f*, chaucha *f Bol, Chile, Perú,* chiro-
las *fpl Arg* **small claims court** *n Brit* tribunal *m* de primera instancia que se ocupa de
delitos menores **small fry** *n inf* **to be ~** ser
poco importante
smallholder ['smɔːlˌhəʊldəʳ, *Am:* -ˌhoʊl-
dɚ] *n Brit* minifundista *mf*
smallholding *n Brit* minifundio *m*
small hours *npl* madrugada *f* **small intestine** *n* intestino *m* delgado
smallish ['smɔːlɪʃ] *adj* más bien pequeño, -a
small-minded [ˌsmɔːl'maɪndɪd] *adj pej*
estrecho, -a de miras
smallness ['smɔːlnɪs] *n no pl* pequeñez *f*
smallpox ['smɔːlpɒks, *Am:* -pɑːks] *n no pl*
viruela *f*
small print *n no pl* letra *f* menuda **small-
-scale** *adj* en [*o* a] pequeña escala **small
screen** *n no pl* **the ~** la pequeña pantalla
small talk *n no pl* conversación *f* sin trascendencia; **to make ~** estar de cháchara
small-time *adj* de poca monta
smarmy ['smɑːmi, *Am:* 'smɑːr] *adj pej*
zalamero, -a
smart [smɑːt, *Am:* smɑːrt] **I.** *adj* **1.** (*clever*)
inteligente; **to make a ~ move** dar un paso
inteligente; **to be too ~ for sb** ser demasiado
listo para alguien **2.** (*elegant*) elegante
3. (*quick*) rápido, -a; **to do sth at a ~ pace**
hacer algo de forma rápida **II.** *vi* escocer; **my
eyes ~** me pican los ojos **III.** *n* escozor *m*
smart-alec(k) ['smɑːt'ælɪk, *Am:* ˌsmɑːrt'-] *n
pej, inf* sabelotodo *mf*
smartarse ['smɑːtɑːs, *Am:* 'smɑːrtɑːrs] *n
Brit, Aus,* **smart ass** *n pej, inf* listillo, -a *m, f*
smart bomb *n* bomba *f* teledirigida **smart
card** *n* INFOR tarjeta *f* electrónica
smarten ['smɑːtn, *Am:* 'smɑːr-] **I.** *vt* **to ~
sth up** arreglar algo **II.** *vi* **to ~ up** arreglarse
smartness ['smɑːtnɪs, *Am:* 'smɑːrt-] *n no pl*
1. (*elegance*) elegancia *f* **2.** (*intelligence*)
inteligencia *f*
smash [smæʃ] **I.** *n* **1.** (*sound*) estruendo *m*
2. (*accident*) colisión *f* **3.** SPORTS mate *m* **II.** *vt*
1. (*break*) romper, quebrar *AmL;* (*glass*) hacer
pedazos; *fig* destruir; **to ~ a rebellion** acabar
con una revuelta **2.** SPORTS (*record*) batir **III.** *vi*
1. (*break into pieces*) romperse, quebrarse
AmL; (*glass*) hacerse pedazos **2.** (*strike
against*) chocar; **to ~ into sth** chocar contra
algo
♦**smash in** *vt* forzar; **to smash sb's face in**

inf romperle la cara a alguien
♦**smash up** *vt* hacer pedazos; (*car*) destrozar
smash-and-grab raid [ˌsmæʃəndgræb-
'reɪd] *n Brit, Aus* robo *m* (en el que se rompe
el escaparate de una tienda)
smashed *adj inf* (*on alcohol*) borracho, -a; **to
get ~** emborracharse; (*on drugs*) colocado, -a;
to get ~ colocarse
smasher *n Brit, inf* **to be a ~** estar como un
tren
smash (hit) *n* éxito *m*
smashing *adj Brit, inf* imponente
smash-up *n* choque *m* violento
smattering ['smætərɪŋ, *Am:* 'smæt̬-] *n*
nociones *fpl*
smear [smɪəʳ, *Am:* smɪr] **I.** *vt* **1.** (*spread*)
untar **2.** (*attack*) desprestigiar; **to ~ sb's good
name** manchar el buen nombre de alguien
II. *n* **1.** (*blotch*) mancha *f* **2.** (*accusation*) calumnia *f* **3.** MED frotis *m* **smear campaign**
n campaña *f* de desprestigio **smear tactics**
n tácticas *f* difamatorias *pl* **smear test** *n*
MED citología *f*
smell [smel] <*Brit, Aus:* smelt, smelt *Am,
Aus:* -ed, -ed> **I.** *vi* **1.** (*use sense of smell*)
olfatear **2.** (*give off odour*) oler **3.** (*have
unpleasant smell*) apestar **II.** *vt* (*person*) oler;
(*animal*) olfatear **III.** *n* **1.** (*sense of smelling*)
olfato *m* **2.** (*odour*) olor *m* **3.** *pej* (*stink*) hedor
m **4.** (*sniff*) inhalación *f*
♦**smell out** *vt* olfatear
smelling salts ['smelɪŋsɔːlts] *npl* MED sales
fpl aromáticas
smelly ['smeli] *adj* <-ier, -iest> apestoso, -a,
que huele mal, foche *Chile*
smelt[1] [smelt] *Brit, Aus pt, pp of* **smell**
smelt[2] [smelt] *vt* MIN fundir
smelt[3] [smelt] <-(s)> *n* (*fish*) eperlano *m*
smidgen ['smɪdʒən] *n inf* pizca *f*
smile [smaɪl] **I.** *n* sonrisa *f;* **to be all ~s** ser
todo sonrisas; **to give sb a ~** sonreír a alguien;
to raise a ~ hacer reír **II.** *vi* sonreír; **to ~ at** [*o*
about] **sth** reírse de algo; **to ~ on sb/sth**
mirar con buenos ojos a alguien/algo
smiley ['smaɪli] *n* INFOR smiley *m*
smiling *adj* sonriente
smirch [smɜːtʃ, *Am:* smɜːrtʃ] *vt liter* mancillar
smirk [smɜːk, *Am:* smɜːrk] **I.** *vi* sonreírse
afectadamente **II.** *n* sonrisa *f* afectada
smite [smaɪt] <smote, smitten> *vt liter*
golpear
smith [smɪθ] *n* herrero, -a *m, f*
smithereens [ˌsmɪðəˈriːnz] *npl* añicos *mpl;*
to smash sth to ~ hacer algo añicos
smithy ['smɪði, *Am:* 'smɪθ-] <-ies> *n* herrería *f*
smitten ['smɪtən] *adj* **to be ~ with sb/sth**
estar loco por alguien/algo; **to be ~ by sb**
estar enamorado de alguien; **she was ~ by
remorse** le remordía la conciencia
smock [smɒk, *Am:* smɑːk] *n* bata *f* corta

smocking *n no pl* nido *m* de abeja

smog [smɒg, *Am:* smɑːg] *n no pl* niebla *f* con humo

smoke [sməʊk, *Am:* smoʊk] I. *n* 1. *no pl* (*from fire*) humo *m* 2. *inf* (*cigarette*) cigarrillo *m* 3. *Brit, inf* (*London*) **the ~** Londres *m* ▶**there's no ~ without fire** *Brit, Aus, prov,* **where there's ~, there's fire** *Am, prov* cuando el río suena, agua lleva *prov;* **to go up in ~** quedarse en agua de borrajas II. *vt* 1. (*cigarette, tobacco*) fumar, pitar *AmS;* **to ~ a pipe** fumar en pipa 2. GASTR ahumar ▶**to ~ the peace pipe** *Am* fumar la pipa de la paz; **put that in your pipe and ~ it!** ¡métetelo donde te quepa! III. *vi* 1. (*produce smoke*) echar humo 2. (*smoke tobacco*) fumar, pitar *AmS*

◆**smoke out** *vt* (*rats, insects*) hacer salir con humo; (*people*) poner al descubierto

smoke bomb *n* bomba *f* de humo

smoked *adj* ahumado, -a

smoke detector *n* detector *m* de humo

smokeless ['sməʊkləs, *Am:* 'smoʊk-] *adj* sin humo

smoker *n* 1. (*person who smokes*) fumador(a) *m(f);* **to be a heavy ~** fumar mucho 2. RAIL vagón *m* de fumadores

smokescreen *n* a. fig cortina *f* de humo

smoke signal *n* señal *f* de humo

smokestack ['sməʊkstæk, *Am:* 'smoʊk-] *n* chimenea *f*

smoking *n no pl* el fumar; **~ ban** prohibición *f* de fumar; **to give up ~** dejar de fumar

smoking car *n Am,* **smoking compartment** *n* RAIL compartimento *m* de fumadores

smoking jacket *n* batín *m*

smoky ['sməʊki, *Am:* 'smoʊ-] *adj* <-ier, -iest> 1. (*filled with smoke*) lleno, -a de humo 2. (*producing smoke*) humeante; (*fire*) que humea 3. (*tasting of smoke*) ahumado, -a

smolder ['smoʊldəʳ] *vi Am s.* **smoulder**

smooch [smuːtʃ] I. *vi* (*kiss*) besuquearse II. *n* (*kiss*) **to have a ~** besuquearse

smooth [smuːð] I. *adj* 1. (*not rough*) liso, -a; (*surface*) llano, -a; (*skin, texture*) suave; (*sauce*) sin grumos; (*sea*) tranquilo, -a; **as ~ as silk** tan suave como la seda 2. (*uninterrupted*) sin dificultades; (*flight*) tranquilo, -a; (*landing*) suave 3. (*mild: wine, whisky*) suave 4. (*suave*) zalamero, -a; **to be a ~ talker** tener un pico de oro II. *vt* allanar

◆**smooth down** *vt* alisar

◆**smooth over** *vt* (*difficulty*) solucionar

smoothie, smoothy ['smuːði] *n inf* zalamero, -a *m, f*

smoothly *adv* **to go ~** ir bien

smoothness *n no pl* 1. (*evenness*) lisura *f* 2. (*lack of difficulty*) fluidez *f* 3. (*mild taste or texture*) suavidad *f*

smooth-shaven *adj* bien afeitado, -a **smooth talk** *n pej* labia *f* **smooth-talking** *adj pej* zalamero, -a

smote [sməʊt, *Am:* smoʊt] *pt of* **smite**

smother ['smʌðəʳ, *Am:* -əʳ] *vt* 1. (*suffocate*) ahogar 2. (*suppress*) contener 3. (*cover*) **to be ~ed in sth** estar cubierto de algo

smoulder ['sməʊldəʳ, *Am:* 'smoʊldəʳ] *vi* 1. (*burn slowly*) arder sin llama; (*cigarette*) consumirse lentamente 2. fig arder

smudge [smʌdʒ] I. *vt* 1. (*smear*) hacer borrón 2. (*make dirty*) manchar; (*reputation*) destruir II. *vi* mancharse; (*make-up*) correrse III. *n* mancha *f*

smudgy ['smʌdʒi] *adj* <-ier, -iest> manchado, -a

smug [smʌg] *adj* <-gg-> presumido, -a; **to be ~ about sth** presumir de algo

smuggle ['smʌgl] *vt* LAW pasar de contrabando

smuggler ['smʌgləʳ, *Am:* -ləʳ] *n* contrabandista *mf*

smuggling ['smʌglɪŋ] *n no pl* contrabando *m*

smut [smʌt] *n* 1. *no pl* (*obscenity*) obscenidades *fpl* 2. (*soot*) tizne *m*

smutty ['smʌti, *Am:* 'smʌt̬-] *adj* <-ier, -iest> obsceno, -a; (*joke*) verde

snack [snæk] I. *n* refrigerio *m,* puntal *m AmL;* **to have a ~** tomarse un tentempié II. *vi* picar

snack bar *n* cafetería *f*

snaffle ['snæfl] *vt Brit, Aus, inf* mangar

snag [snæg] I. *n* 1. (*problem*) dificultad *f;* **there's a ~** hay un problema 2. (*in clothing*) enganchón *m* II. <-gg-> *vt* 1. (*catch and pull*) enganchar 2. (*cause problems*) causar problemas a III. <-gg-> *vi* **to ~ on sth** engancharse en algo

snail [sneɪl] *n* caracol *m* ▶**at a ~'s pace** a paso de tortuga

snail mail *n* INFOR correo *m* tortuga **snail shell** *n* caparazón *m* de caracol

snake [sneɪk] I. *n* (*small*) culebra *f;* (*large*) serpiente *f* ▶**~ in the grass** traidor(a) *m(f);* **~s and ladders** ≈ juego *m* de la oca II. *vi* serpentear, viborear *Arg, Urug*

snake bite *n* mordedura *f* de serpiente **snake charmer** *n* encantador(a) *m(f)* de serpientes **snakeskin** *n* piel *f* de serpiente **snake venom** *n* veneno *m* de serpiente

snap [snæp] <-pp-> I. *n* 1. (*sound*) chasquido *m* 2. (*photograph*) foto *f* 3. *Am* (*snap-fastener*) (*cierre m*) automático *m* 4. METEO **cold ~** una ola de frío II. *adj* repentino, -a; **~ decision** decisión *f* repentina III. *interj inf* GAMES yo también IV. *vi* 1. (*break*) romperse 2. (*move*) **to ~ back** recolocarse; **to ~ shut** cerrarse de golpe 3. (*make snapping sound*) hacer un chasquido 4. (*bite*) **to ~ at sb** intentar morder a alguien 5. (*speak sharply*) contestar con brusquedad; **to ~ at sb** contestar a alguien de forma brusca V. *vt* 1. (*break*) romper; **to ~ sth shut** cerrar algo de golpe 2. (*make snapping sound*) chasquear; **to ~ a whip** dar un latigazo; **to ~ one's fingers** chasquear los dedos 3. PHOT tomar un fotografía de

◆**snap out** *vi* **to ~ of sth** quitarse algo de

encima; ~ **of it!** ¡anímate!

◆**snap up** vt lanzarse sobre

snapdragon ['snæp‚drægən] n boca f de dragón

snap-fastener n (cierre m) automático m

snappish ['snæpɪʃ] adj brusco, -a

snappy ['ʃnæpi] adj <-ier, -iest> 1. inf FASHION de lo más elegante; **to be a ~ dresser** vestir con elegancia 2. (quick) rápido, -a; **look ~!** ¡date prisa!

snapshot ['snæpʃɒt, Am: -ʃɑːt] n foto f instantánea

snare [sneəʳ, Am: sner] I. n trampa f II. vt (catch: animal) cazar (con trampa); (person) atrapar

snare drum n tambor m

snarl[1] [snɑːl, Am: snɑːrl] I. vi gruñir II. n gruñido m

snarl[2] [snɑːl, Am: snɑːrl] n 1. (tangle) enredo m 2. (traffic jam) atasco m

◆**snarl up** vi enmarañarse

snarl-up ['snɑːlʌp, Am: 'snɑːrl-] n atasco m

snatch [snætʃ] I. <-es> n 1. (sudden grab) arrebatamiento m; **to make a ~ at sth** intentar arrebatar algo 2. (theft) robo m 3. (piece of: music, conversation) retazo m; **to do sth in ~es** hacer algo a ratos 4. vulg (female genitals) coño m II. vt 1. (steal) robar; (win) ganar; **to ~ sth (away) from sb** arrebatar algo de alguien 2. (kidnap) secuestrar III. vi quitar algo de las manos; **to ~ at sth** tratar de arrebatar algo

◆**snatch up** vt agarrar

snazzy ['snæzi] adj <-ier, -iest> inf de lo más elegante

sneak [sniːk] Am I. vi 1. (move stealthily) moverse furtivamente; **to ~ in/out** entrar/salir a hurtadillas; **to ~ away** [o off] escabullirse 2. Brit, inf (denounce) **to ~ on sb** delatar a alguien II. vt hacer furtivamente; **to ~ a look at sth/sb** mirar algo/a alguien con disimulo; **to ~ sth in/out** lograr introducir/sacar algo III. n Brit, childspeak acusica mf

sneaker ['sniːkəʳ, Am: -kɚ] n pl, Am zapatillas fpl de deporte

sneaking adj (secret) secreto, -a

sneak preview n CINE preestreno m **sneak-thief** n ratero, -a m, f

sneaky ['sniːki] adj <-ier, -iest> furtivo, -a

sneer [snɪəʳ, Am: snɪr] I. vi hacer un gesto de burla y desprecio; (mock) mofarse; **to ~ at sth/sb** mofarse de algo/alguien II. n expresión f desdeñosa

sneering ['snɪərɪŋ, Am: 'snɪr-] adj burlón, -ona

sneeze [sniːz] I. vi estornudar ►**not to be ~d at** no ser de despreciar II. n estornudo m

snick [snɪk] vt Brit, Aus SPORTS (ball) golpear con el borde del bate

snicker ['snɪkəʳ, Am: -ɚ] Am I. vi s. snigger II. n s. snigger

snide [snaɪd] adj pej vil

sniff [snɪf] I. n 1. (smell) husmeo m; **to have a ~** oler; **to catch a ~ of sth** captar el olor de

algo 2. (expression of disdain) expresión f de desdén II. vi 1. (inhale) sorber; **to ~ at sth** oler algo 2. (show disdain) **to ~ at sth** despreciar algo ►**not to be ~ed at** no ser de despreciar III. vt olfatear

◆**sniff out** vt (locate by smelling) encontrar olfateando; (discover) descubrir

sniffer dog ['snɪfəʳ‚dɒg, Am: 'snɪfɚ‚dɑːg] n perro m rastreador

sniffle ['snɪfl] I. vi 1. (sniff) sorberse los mocos 2. (cry) lloriquear II. npl **to have the ~s** estar un poco acatarrado

sniffy adj inf desdeñoso, -a

snifter ['snɪftəʳ, Am: -tɚ] n 1. Am (glass) copa f de coñac 2. inf (small drink) trago m

snigger ['snɪgəʳ, Am: -ɚ] I. vi reírse con disimulo; **to ~ at sth** reírse de algo con disimulo II. n risa f disimulada

snip [snɪp] I. vt cortar (con tijeras) II. n 1. (cut) tijeretazo m 2. (piece of cloth) recorte m 3. Brit, inf (cheap item) ganga f 4. no pl, Brit, iron, inf (vasectomy) vasectomía f

snipe[1] [snaɪp] vi 1. MIL tirar (desde un escondite) 2. fig **to ~ at sb** criticar a alguien

snipe[2] [snaɪp] n ZOOL agachadiza f

sniper ['snaɪpəʳ, Am: -ɚ] n francotirador(a) m(f)

sniping n (criticism) critiqueo m

snippet ['snɪpɪt] n (small piece: of cloth) retal m; (of paper) pedazo m; (of cardboard) trozo m; (of information) retazo m; (of conversation, text) fragmento m

snitch [snɪtʃ] inf I. vt (steal) birlar II. vi pej chivarse; **to ~ on sb** chivarse de alguien III. <-es> n 1. (thief) caco mf 2. (tattle-tale) soplón, -ona m, f

snivel ['snɪvəl] I. <Brit: -ll-, Am: -l-> vi (cry) lloriquear II. n no pl lloriqueo m

snivel(l)ing I. n no pl lloriqueo m II. adj llorón, -ona

snob [snɒb, Am: snɑːb] n (e)snob mf, pituco, -a m AmS

snobbery ['snɒbəri, Am: 'snɑːbɚ-] n (e)snobismo m

snobbish ['snɒbɪʃ, Am: 'snɑːbɪʃ] <more, most> adj (e)snob

snob value n no pl cachet m

snog [snɒg, Am: snɑːg] Brit I. <-gg-> vi inf morrearse II. vt inf morrear III. n inf morreo m; **to have a ~** morrearse

snook [snuːk, Am: snʊk] n no pl **to cock a ~ at sth/sb** Brit, inf hacer burla a algo/alguien

snooker ['snuːkəʳ, Am: 'snʊkɚ] I. vt 1. Am, inf (trick) poner en un aprieto 2. GAMES (block) bloquear; **to be ~ed** fig, inf fastidiársele a uno el plan II. n billar m inglés

snoop [snuːp] pej, inf I. n fisgón, -ona m, f II. vi fisgonear

snooper ['snuːpəʳ, Am: -ɚ] n pej, inf 1. (one looking secretly) fisgón, -ona m, f 2. (spy) espía mf 3. (investigator) investigador(a) m(f)

snooty ['snuːti, Am: -t̬i] <-ier, -iest> adj presumido, -a, pituco, -a AmS

snooze [snuːz] *inf* I. *vi* (*nap*) echar una cabezada; (*nap lightly*) dormitar II. *n* cabezada *f*

snooze button *n* botón *m* de alarma de un despertador

snore [snɔːʳ, *Am:* snɔːr] MED I. *vi* roncar II. *n* ronquido *m*

snorkel ['snɔːkəl, *Am:* 'snɔːr-] SPORTS I. *n* tubo *m* snorkel (de respiración) II.<*Brit:* -ll-, *Am:* -l-> *vi* bucear con tubo

snorkelling *n* SPORTS **to go** ~ bucear con tubo

snort [snɔːt, *Am:* snɔːrt] I. *vi* bufar, resoplar II. *vt* 1. *inf* (*inhale*) inhalar; (*cocaine*) esnifar 2. (*say with disapproval*) decir bufando III. *n* 1. (*noise*) bufido *m* 2. *inf* (*small drink*) trago *m*

snot [snɒt, *Am:* snaːt] *n no pl, inf* moco *m*

snotrag ['snɒtræg] *n inf* pañuelo *m*

snotty ['snɒti, *Am:* 'snaːt̬i] <-ier, -iest> *adj inf* 1. (*full of mucus*) lleno, -a de mocos 2. (*rude*) petulante

snout [snaʊt] *n* 1. ZOOL hocico *m*; (*of pig*) morro *m* 2. *inf* (*of person*) napia *f*

snow [snəʊ, *Am:* snoʊ] *no pl* I. *n* 1. METEO nieve *f*; **a blanket of** ~ un manto de nieve 2. *inf* (*cocaine*) coca *f* II. *vi* nevar

♦**snow in** *vt* **to be snowed in** estar aprisionado por la nieve

♦**snow under** *vt* **to be snowed under (with sth)** estar desbordado (de algo)

snowball ['snəʊbɔːl, *Am:* 'snoʊ-] I. *n* bola *f* de nieve ▶**not to have a** ~'s <u>chance</u> **in hell (of doing sth)** no tener ninguna posibilidad (de hacer algo) II. *vi fig* aumentar progresivamente

snowball effect *n no pl* efecto *m* de bola de nieve

snow bank *n* banco *m* de nieve **snow blindness** *n no pl* ceguera *f* causada por el resplandor de la nieve **snowboard** *n* snowboard *m* **snowboarding** *n* **to go** ~ hacer snowboard

snowbound ['snəʊbaʊnd, *Am:* 'snoʊ-] *adj* (*vehicle*) embarrancado, -a en la nieve; (*person*) aprisionado, -a por la nieve

snow-capped ['snəʊkæpt, *Am:* 'snoʊ-] *adj* cubierto, -a de nieve **snow chain** *n* AUTO cadena *f* para la nieve **snowdrift** *n Brit* ventisquero *m* **snowdrop** *n* campanilla *f* de invierno **snowfall** *n* METEO 1. *no pl* (*amount snowed*) nevada *f* 2. (*snowstorm*) tormenta *f* de nieve, nevazón *m Arg, Chile, Ecua* **snowflake** *n* copo *m* de nieve **snow goggles** *npl* gafas *fpl* para la nieve **snowline** *n* límite *m* de las nieves perpetuas **snowman** *n* muñeco *m* de nieve **snowmobile** *n* motonieve *f* **snowplough** *n Brit,* **snowplow** *n Am* 1. (*snow mover*) quitanieves *m inv* 2. SPORTS (*stop*) cuña *f* **snowshoe** *n* raqueta *f* (de nieve) **snowstorm** *n* tormenta *f* de nieve **snowsuit** *n* mono *m* acolchado (para la nieve) **snow tire** *n Am,* **snow tyre** *n Brit* AUTO neumático *m* antideslizante **snow-white** *adj* blanco, -a como la nieve

Snow White *n no pl* ~ **and the Seven Dwarfs** LIT Blancanieves y los siete enanitos

snowy ['snəʊi, *Am:* 'snoʊ-] *adj* 1. METEO (*region, season*) de mucha nieve; (*street, field*) cubierto, -a de nieve 2. (*pure white: hair, flowers*) blanco, -a como la nieve; (*clouds*) níveo, -a *form*

SNP [ˌesen'piː] *n abbr of* **Scottish National Party** Partido *m* Nacional Escocés

snub [snʌb] I.<-bb-> *vt* **to** ~ **sb** hacer el vacío a alguien II. *n* desaire *m*

snub nose *n* nariz *f* respingona **snub-nosed** *adj* 1. (*person*) de nariz respingona 2. (*gun*) de cañón corto; (*pliers*) de dientes cortos

snuff [snʌf] I. *n* rapé *m* II. *vt* 1. (*put out*) apagar 2. *Aus, Brit, inf* **to** ~ **it** estirar la pata

♦**snuff out** *vt* 1. (*candle*) apagar 2. (*opposition*) sofocar

snuff box *n* tabaquera *f*

snuffle ['snʌfl] I. *vi* 1. (*sniffle*) estar acatarrado; (*breath*) respirar haciendo ruido por la nariz 2. (*speak nasally*) ganguear II. *n* (*sound*) resoplido *m*; **to have the** ~**s** estar acatarrado

snug [snʌg] I. *adj* 1. (*cozy*) acogedor(a); (*warm*) cómodo, -a y bien caliente 2. (*tight: dress*) ajustado, -a II. *n Brit* salón *m* pequeño

snuggle ['snʌgl] *vi* acurrucarse; **to** ~ **up to sb** acurrucarse contra alguien

so [səʊ, *Am:* soʊ] I. *adv* 1. (*in the same way*) tan, tanto; ~ **did/do** I yo también; ~ **to speak** por así decirlo 2. (*like that*) así; ~ **they say** así dicen; **is that** ~? ¿de verdad?; **I hope/think** ~ así lo espero/pienso; **just** [*o* **quite**] ~! ¡eso es! 3. (*to such a degree*) tan, tanto; **I** ~ **love him** lo amo tanto; ~ **late** tan tarde; ~ **many books** tantos libros; **not** ~ **ugly as that** no tan feo como eso; **would you be** ~ **kind as to** ...? ¿sería usted tan amable de...? 4. (*in order that*) para; **I bought the book** ~ **that he would read it** compré el libro para que él lo leyera 5. (*as a result*) así; **and** ~ **she won** y así ganó ▶**and** ~ **on** [*o* **forth**] etcétera; **or** ~ más o menos II. *conj* 1. (*therefore*) por (lo) tanto 2. *inf* (*and afterwards*) ~ (**then**) **he told me** ... y entonces me dijo... 3. (*summing up*) así que; ~ **what?** ¿y qué?; ~ **now,** ... entonces...; ~, **I was saying** ... entonces, como decía... III. *interj* ~ **that's why!** ¡es por eso!

soak [səʊk, *Am:* soʊk] I. *n* 1. (*time under water*) remojo *m* 2. *inf* (*heavy drinker*) borrachín, -ina *m, f* II. *vt* 1. (*keep in liquid*) remojar, ensopar *AmS*; **to** ~ **sth in liquid** poner algo en remojo 2. *inf* (*overcharge*) desplumar III. *vi* (*lie in liquid*) estar en remojo

♦**soak in** *vi* penetrar

♦**soak off** *vt* despegar

♦**soak up** *vt* 1. (*absorb*) absorber; (*money, resources*) agotar 2. (*take in: people*) embelesar; (*information*) absorber 3. (*bask in: sun*) tomar; (*atmosphere*) disfrutar de

soaked *adj* empapado, -a

soaking I. *n* remojo *m*; **to get a** ~ calarse hasta los huesos II. *adj* ~ (**wet**) (*person, ani-*

mal) empapado, -a; (*day*) de muchísima agua
so-and-so ['səʊənsəʊ, *Am:* 'soʊənsoʊ] *n*
inf **1.** (*person*) fulano *m*; (*thing*) cosa *f* cualquiera **2.** *pej* (*idiot*) idiota *mf*; **Mr** ~ don *m* Fulano
soap [səʊp, *Am:* soʊp] I. *n* **1.** *no pl* (*for washing*) jabón *m* **2.** TV (*soap opera*) telenovela *f* ▸**soft** ~ coba *f* II. *vt* enjabonar
soapbox ['səʊpbɒks, *Am:* 'soʊpbɑ:ks] *n* **1.** (*container*) caja *f* de jabón **2.** (*pedestal*) caja *f* vacía empleada como tribuna ▸**to get on** one's ~ echar un discurso **soap bubble** *n* burbuja *f* de jabón **soapdish** *n* jabonera *f* **soap dispenser** *n* dispensador *m* de jabón **soap flakes** *npl* jabón *m* en escamas **soap opera** *n* telenovela *f* **soap powder** *n* *no pl* jabón *m* en polvo **soapsuds** *npl* espuma *f* de jabón
soapy ['səʊpi, *Am:* 'soʊp-] <-ier, -iest> *adj* **1.** (*full of lather*) lleno, -a de jabón **2.** (*like soap*) jabonoso, -a; **to taste** ~ saber a jabón **3.** (*flattering*) zalamero, -a
soar [sɔ:ʳ, *Am:* sɔ:r] *vi* **1.** (*rise*) subir muy alto; (*house*) elevarse mucho **2.** (*increase: temperature*) aumentar bruscamente; (*prices*) ponerse por las nubes; (*awareness*) crecer sensiblemente; (*hopes*) renacer **3.** (*bird, plane*) remontar el vuelo; (*glide*) planear **4.** (*excel*) llegar muy alto
soaring *adj* **1.** (*increasing*) en aumento; (*very high*) altísimo, -a **2.** (*gliding*) planeador, -a
sob [sɒb, *Am:* sɑ:b] I. *n* sollozo *m* II. <-bb-> *vi* sollozar III. <-bb-> *vt* decir sollozando
sober ['səʊbəʳ, *Am:* 'soʊbə-] *adj* **1.** (*not drunk*) sobrio, -a **2.** (*serious: mood, atmosphere, expression*) serio, -a **3.** (*plain: clothes*) sencillo, -a; (*colour*) discreto, -a **4.** (*sensible*) sensato, -a
◆**sober up** I. *vi* **1.** (*become less drunk*) espabilar la borrachera **2.** (*become serious*) ponerse serio II. *vt* **to sober sb up** (*make less drunk*) quitar la borrachera a alguien; (*make serious*) poner serio a alguien
sobering *adj* que hace pensar
soberness *n* *no pl* **1.** (*not drunkenness*) sobriedad *f* **2.** (*seriousness*) seriedad *f* **3.** (*plainness*) sencillez *f*
sobriety [səʊ'braɪəti, *Am:* sə'braɪəti] *n* *no pl, form* **1.** (*not drunkenness*) sobriedad *f* **2.** (*seriousness*) seriedad *f*
sobriquet ['səʊbrɪkeɪ, *Am:* 'soʊ-] *n* apodo *m*
sob story *n* *pej* dramón *m*
so-called [ˌsəʊ'kɔ:ld, *Am:* ˌsoʊ'kɑ:ld] *adj* así llamado, -a, presunto, -a
soccer ['sɒkəʳ, *Am:* 'sɑ:kə-] *n* *no pl, Am* fútbol *m*
soccer player *n* futbolista *mf*
sociability [ˌsəʊʃə'bɪləti, *Am:* ˌsoʊʃə'bɪləti] *n* *no pl* sociabilidad *f*
sociable ['səʊʃəbl, *Am:* 'soʊ-] *adj* sociable
social ['səʊʃəl, *Am:* 'soʊ-] *adj* social; ~ **drinker** persona que no bebe a solas, sino en

compañía; **to climb the** ~ **ladder** trepar en la escalera social
social democrat *n* socialdemócrata *mf*
socialism ['səʊʃəlɪzəm, *Am:* 'soʊ-] *n* *no pl* socialismo *m*
socialist *n* socialista *mf*
socialite ['səʊʃəlaɪt, *Am:* 'soʊ-] *n* persona *f* con mucha vida social
socialize ['səʊʃəlaɪz, *Am:* 'soʊ-] I. *vi* alternar con la gente II. *vt* **1.** PSYCH socializar **2.** POL, ECON nacionalizar
socially *adv* socialmente
social science *n* ciencia *f* social **social security** *n* *no pl* **1.** *Aus, Brit* (*welfare*) seguridad *f* social **2.** *Am* (*government pension*) subsidio *m* de la seguridad social **social service** *n* **1.** (*community help*) servicio *m* social **2.** *pl* (*welfare*) servicios *mpl* sociales **social studies** *n* *Am* SCHOOL estudios *mpl* sociales **social work** *n* *no pl* asistencia *f* social **social worker** *n* asistente *mf* social
societal [sə'saɪətəl, *Am:* -t̬l] *adj* societal
society [sə'saɪəti, *Am:* -t̬i] *n* **1.** (*all people*) sociedad *f*; (**high**) ~ alta sociedad *f*; **to be a menace to** ~ ser una amenaza para la sociedad **2.** (*organization*) asociación *f*
sociocultural [ˌsəʊʃɪəʊ'kʌltʃərəl, *Am:* ˌsoʊsioʊ-] *adj* sociocultural
socioeconomic [ˌsəʊʃɪəʊˌi:kə'nɒmɪk, *Am:* ˌsoʊsioʊˌekə'nɑ:mɪk] *adj* socioeconómico, -a
sociolinguistics [ˌsəʊʃɪəʊlɪŋ'gwɪstɪks, *Am:* ˌsoʊsioʊ-] *n* sociolingüística *f*
sociological [ˌsəʊʃɪə'lɒdʒɪkəl, *Am:* ˌsoʊsiə'lɑ:dʒɪ-] *adj* sociológico, -a
sociologist [ˌsəʊʃɪ'ɒlədʒɪst, *Am:* ˌsoʊsi'ɑ:lə-] *n* sociólogo, -a *m, f*
sociology [ˌsəʊʃɪ'ɒlədʒi, *Am:* ˌsoʊsi'ɑ:lə-] *n* *no pl* sociología *f*
sociopolitical [ˌsəʊʃɪəʊpəl'ɪtɪkəl, *Am:* ˌsoʊsioʊpə'lɪt̬-] *adj* sociopolítico, -a
sock[1] [sɒk, *Am:* sɑ:k] *n* calcetín *m*, media *f* *AmL*; **knee** ~ calcetín *m* largo ▸**to pull one's** ~s **up** *inf* hacer un esfuerzo; **put a** ~ **in it!** *inf* ¡a callar!
sock[2] [sɒk, *Am:* sɑ:k] I. *vt inf* (*hit*) pegar; **to** ~ **sb in the eye** dar un golpe a alguien en el ojo ▸~ **it to 'em!** *Am* ¡a por ellos! II. *n inf* tortazo *m*
socket ['sɒkɪt, *Am:* 'sɑ:kɪt] *n* **1.** ELEC enchufe *m*, tomacorriente *m Arg, Perú*; **mains** ~ toma *f* de la red; **double/triple** ~ enchufe de dos/ tres entradas **2.** (*of eye*) cuenca *f*, órbita *f*; (*of tooth*) alvéolo *m*; (*of knee, arm, hip*) fosa *f*
sod[1] [sɒd, *Am:* sɑ:d] *n* césped *m*
sod[2] [sɒd, *Am:* sɑ:d] I. *n Brit vulg* cabrón, -ona *m, f*; **the lucky** ~! ¡qué suerte tiene el cabrón!; **poor** ~ pobre diablo ▸**I don't give a** ~! *vulg* ¡me importa un huevo! II. *vt Brit, vulg* ~ **it!** ¡mierda!; ~ **him!** ¡que se joda!
◆**sod off** *vi Brit, inf* ~! ¡vete a la mierda!
soda ['səʊdə, *Am:* 'soʊ-] *n* **1.** *no pl* CHEM sosa *f* **2.** *Am* (*fizzy drink*) refresco *m* **3.** (*mixer drink*) soda *f*

soda bread *n no pl* pan hecho con levadura de bicarbonato **soda fountain** *n Am* (*pouring device*) surtidor *m* de agua con gas; (*place*) bar *m* de bebidas no alcohólicas **soda siphon** *n* sifón *m* **soda water** *n no pl* soda *f*

sodden ['sɒdn, *Am:* 'sɑ:dn] *adj* empapado, -a

sodding ['sɒdɪŋ, *Am:* 'sɑ:dɪŋ] *adj Brit, vulg* jodido, -a

sodium ['səʊdɪəm, *Am:* 'soʊ-] *n no pl* sodio *m*

sodium bicarbonate *n no pl* bicarbonato *m* sódico **sodium carbonate** *n no pl* carbonato *m* sódico **sodium chloride** *n no pl* cloruro *m* sódico

sodomize ['sɒdəmaɪz, *Am:* 'sɑ:də-] *vt* sodomizar

sodomy ['sɒdəmi, *Am:* 'sɑ:də-] *n no pl, form* sodomía *f*

sod's law *n*, **Sod's law** [,sɒdz'lɔ:, *Am:* ,sɑ:dz'lɑ:] *n no pl* la ley de Murphy

sofa ['səʊfə, *Am:* 'soʊ-] *n* sofá *m*

sofa bed *n* sofá-cama *m*

soft [sɒft, *Am:* sɑ:ft] *adj* **1.** (*not hard: ground, sand, contact lenses*) blando, -a; (*pillow, sofa*) mullido, -a; (*metal*) dúctil; ~ **tissue** MED tejido *m* blando **2.** (*smooth: cheeks, skin, landing*) suave; (*hair*) fino, -a; ~ **as silk** suave como la seda **3.** (*weak*) débil; **to go** ~ debilitarse **4.** (*mild*) ligero, -a; (*wind, rain*) suave; (*climate*) agradable; (*drug*) blando, -a **5.** (*not bright: colour*) delicado, -a; (*glow*) suave; (*lighting, light*) tenue **6.** (*quiet: sound, music*) agradable; (*voice*) dulce **7.** (*lenient*) indulgente; **to be** ~ **with sb** ser demasiado tolerante con alguien **8.** (*easy*) fácil; **the** ~ **option** la opción más sencilla; **a** ~ **target** un blanco fácil **9.** (*compassionate*) compasivo, -a **10.** FIN (*currency*) débil

softball ['sɒftbɔ:l, *Am:* 'sɑ:ft-] *n Am:* deporte similar al béisbol sobre un terreno más pequeño y con pelota grande y blanda

soft-boiled [,sɒft'bɔɪld, *Am:* ,sɑ:ft'-] *adj* pasado, -a por agua

soften ['sɒfən, *Am:* 'sɑ:fən] **I.** *vi* **1.** (*let get soft: butter, ground*) reblandecerse, amelcochar *Méx* **2.** (*become lenient*) ablandarse **II.** *vt* **1.** (*make soft: butter*) reblandecer; (*skin*) suavizar **2.** (*colour, voice*) suavizar **3.** (*make easier to bear: effect*) mitigar; (*opinion, words*) suavizar; (*blow*) amortiguar

◆**soften up** *vt* ablandar; MIL debilitar

softener ['sɒfənə', *Am:* 'sɑ:fənə'] *n* **1.** (*for clothes*) suavizante *m* **2.** (*for water*) descalcificador *m*

softening I. *n no pl* **1.** (*reduction of hardness*) reblandecimiento *m;* (*of voice*) suavización *f* **2.** (*of light*) debilitamiento *m* **II.** *adj* reblandecedor(a); (*agent*) suavizante

soft furnishings *n Aus, Brit,* **soft goods** *npl Am* ropa *f* de casa

soft-headed *adj pej* bobo, -a

soft-hearted [,sɒft'hɑ:tɪd, *Am:* 'sɑ:ft-

,hɑ:rt̬ɪd] *adj* bondadoso, -a

softie ['sɒfti, *Am:* 'sɑ:f-] *n inf* blandengue *mf*

softly *adv* **1.** (*not hard*) suavemente **2.** (*quietly*) silenciosamente **3.** (*to shine*) tenuemente **4.** (*leniently*) indulgentemente; **to take a** ~, ~ **approach** ser cauteloso

softness ['sɒftnɪs, *Am:* 'sɑ:ft-] *n no pl* **1.** (*not hardness*) blandura *f* **2.** (*smoothness*) suavidad *f;* (*of hair*) finura *f* **3.** (*of light*) debilidad *f* **soft-soap** *vt inf* dar coba a **soft-spoken** *adj* de voz suave **soft toy** *n Brit* (muñeco de) peluche *m*

software ['sɒftweə', *Am:* 'sɑ:ftwer] *n no pl* software *m;* **accounting** ~ programa *m* de contabilidad

software engineer *n* ingeniero, -a *m, f* de software **software package** *n* paquete *m* de programas **software piracy** *n* piratería *f* de software

softwood ['sɒftwʊd, *Am:* 'sɑ:ft-] *n* **1.** *no pl* (*wood*) madera *f* blanda **2.** (*tree*) árbol *m* de hoja perenne

softy ['sɒfti, *Am:* 'sɑ:f-] *n inf* blandengue *mf*

soggy ['sɒgi, *Am:* 'sɑ:gi] <-ier, -iest> *adj* empapado, -a

soh [səʊ, *Am:* soʊ] *n* MUS sol *m*

soil[1] [sɔɪl] **I.** *vt form* (*make dirty*) manchar; (*clothing, shoes*) ensuciar; **to** ~ **sb's reputation** manchar la reputación de alguien **II.** *vi* ensuciarse

soil[2] [sɔɪl] *n no pl* AGR suelo *m;* **fertile** ~ tierra *f* fértil; **foreign** ~ tierras *fpl* extranjeras

soirée *n*, **soiree** ['swɑ:reɪ, *Am:* swɑ:'reɪ] *n form* velada *f*

sojourn ['sɒdʒɜ:n, *Am:* 'soʊdʒɜ:rn] *n* estancia *f*

solace ['sɒlɪs, *Am:* 'sɑ:lɪs] **I.** *n no pl* consuelo *m* **II.** *vt* consolar

solar ['səʊlə', *Am:* 'soʊlə'] *adj* solar

solar battery *n* pila *f* solar **solar cell** *n* célula *f* solar **solar eclipse** *n* eclipse *m* de sol **solar energy** *n no pl* energía *f* solar

solarium [səʊ'leərɪəm, *Am:* soʊ'leri-] <-s *o* solaria> *n* **1.** (*tanning room*) solárium *m* **2.** *Am* (*conservatory*) invernadero *m*

solar panel *n* placa *f* solar **solar plexus** *n no pl* plexo *m* solar **solar power** *n no pl* energía *f* solar **solar radiation** *n no pl* radiación *f* solar **solar system** *n* sistema *m* solar **solar wind** *n no pl* viento *m* solar

sold [səʊld, *Am:* soʊld] *pt, pp* of **sell**

solder ['sɒldə', *Am:* 'sɑ:də'] **I.** *vt* soldar **II.** *n no pl* soldadura *f*

soldering iron ['sɒldərɪŋaɪən, *Am:* 'sɑ:-dərɪŋ,aɪə'n] *n* soldador *m*

soldier ['səʊldʒə', *Am:* 'soʊldʒə'] **I.** *n* **1.** MIL (*military person*) militar *mf;* **old** ~ veterano *m* **2.** (*non officer*) soldado *mf* **II.** *vi* servir como soldado

◆**soldier on** *vi* seguir adelante

sold out [,səʊld'aʊt, *Am:* ,soʊld-] *adj* vendido, -a

sole[1] [səʊl, *Am:* soʊl] *adj* (*unique*) único, -a;

(*exclusive*) exclusivo, -a; ~ **right** derecho *m* en exclusiva

sole² [səʊl, *Am:* soʊl] *n* (*of foot*) planta *f;* (*of shoe*) suela *f*

sole³ [səʊl, *Am:* soʊl] <-(s)> *n* (*fish*) lenguado *m;* **lemon** ~ mendo *m* limón

solecism ['sɒlɪsɪzəm, *Am:* 'sɑːlə-] *n form* **1.** LING solecismo *m* **2.** (*breach of good manners*) incorrección *f*

solely ['səʊli, *Am:* 'soʊli] *adv* únicamente

solemn ['sɒləm, *Am:* 'sɑːləm] *adj* (*occasion, promise*) solemne; (*person, appearance*) serio, -a

solemnity [sə'lemnəti, *Am:* -ți] *n* solemnidad *f*

solemnize ['sɒləmnaɪz, *Am:* 'sɑːləm-] *vt form* solemnizar

solenoid ['səʊlənɔɪd, *Am:* 'soʊ-] *n* ELEC solenoide *m*

sol-fa [ˌsɒl'fɑː, *Am:* ˌsoʊl'fɑː] *n* MUS solfeo *m*

solicit [sə'lɪsɪt] **I.** *vt form* (*ask for*) solicitar **II.** *vi* (*prostitute*) abordar clientes

soliciting *n no pl* LAW ejercicio *m* de la prostitución

solicitor [sə'lɪsɪtə', *Am:* -țə] *n* **1.** *Aus, Brit* (*for court case*) procurador(a) *m(f);* (*for legal transactions*) notario, -a *m, f* **2.** *Am* (*city lawyer*) fiscal *mf* general

solicitous [sə'lɪsɪtəs, *Am:* -țəs] *adj* solícito, -a

solicitude [sə‚lɪsɪ'tjuːd, *Am:* sə'lɪsɪtuːd] *n no pl, form* atención *f*

solid ['sɒlɪd, *Am:* 'sɑːlɪd] **I.** *adj* **1.** (*hard*) sólido, -a; (*rock, silver, wood*) macizo, -a; (*table, door, wall*) robusto, -a; (*meal*) pesado, -a; **to be (as)** ~ **as a rock** ser duro como una piedra **2.** (*not hollow*) macizo, -a **3.** (*true*) real; (*facts*) verídico, -a; (*evidence*) sustancial; (*argument*) sólido, -a; (*reasons*) de peso; (*conviction*) firme; (*agreement*) concreto, -a **4.** (*uninterrupted: wall, line*) ininterrumpido, -a; (*hour, day, week*) entero, -a **5.** (*three-dimensional*) tridimensional **6.** (*good: work, picture*) excelente **II.** *adv* **to be packed** ~ estar lleno hasta los topes; **to be frozen** ~ estar completamente helado **III.** *n* **1.** (*shape*) sólido *m* **2.** *pl* GASTR alimentos *mpl* sólidos

solidarity [ˌsɒlɪ'dærəti, *Am:* ˌsɑːlə'deɾəți] *n no pl* solidaridad *f*

solid fuel *n* combustible *m* sólido

solidify [sə'lɪdɪfaɪ, *Am:* -əfaɪ] <-ie-, -ying> **I.** *vi* solidificarse; (*plans, project, idea*) concretarse **II.** *vt* **1.** (*make hard*) solidificar **2.** (*reinforce*) reforzar

solidity [sə'lɪdəti, *Am:* -ți] *n* solidez *f*

solidly *adv* **1.** (*robustly*) sólidamente **2.** (*without interruption*) ininterrumpidamente **3.** (*in strong manner*) fuertemente **4.** (*unanimously*) unánimemente

solid-state [ˌsɒlɪdsteɪt, *Am:* ˌsɑːlɪd'-] *adj* de estado sólido

soliloquy [sə'lɪləkwi] *n* soliloquio *m*

solitaire [ˌsɒlɪ'teə', *Am:* 'sɑːlətər] *n* solitario

m

solitary ['sɒlɪtəri, *Am:* 'sɑːləteri] **I.** *adj* **1.** (*alone, single*) solitario, -a **2.** (*isolated*) solo, -a, íngrimo, -a *AmL;* (*unvisited*) apartado, -a; **to go for a** ~ **walk** ir a pasear solo **II.** *n* **1.** *no pl, inf* (*isolation*) incomunicación *f* **2.** (*hermit*) solitario, -a *m, f*

solitary confinement *n* aislamiento *m*

solitude ['sɒlɪtjuːd, *Am:* 'sɑːlətuːd] *n no pl* **1.** (*loneliness*) soledad *f* **2.** (*isolation*) aislamiento *m*

solo ['səʊləʊ, *Am:* 'soʊloʊ] **I.** *adj* solo, -a; ~ **flight** vuelo *m* en solitario **II.** *adv* a solas; MUS solo; **to go** ~ lanzarse como solista; **to fly** ~ AVIAT volar en solitario **III.** *n* MUS solo *m*

soloist ['səʊləʊɪst, *Am:* 'soʊloʊ-] *n* solista *mf*

Solomon Islands ['sɒləmənˌaɪləndz, *Am:* 'sɑːlə-] *n* Islas *fpl* Salomón

solstice ['sɒlstɪs, *Am:* 'sɑːl-] *n* solsticio *m*

soluble ['sɒljəbl, *Am:* 'sɑːl-] *adj* (*substance, problem*) soluble

solution [sə'luːʃən] *n* solución *f*

solve [sɒlv, *Am:* sɑːlv] *vt* resolver

solvency ['sɒlvənsi, *Am:* 'sɑːl-] *n no pl* solvencia *f*

solvent ['sɒlvənt, *Am:* 'sɑːl-] **I.** *n* disolvente *m* **II.** *adj* solvente

solvent abuse *n Brit* inhalación *f* de disolventes

Somali [ˌsə'mɑːli, *Am:* soʊ'-] **I.** <-(s)> *n* **1.** (*person*) somalí *mf* **2.** (*language*) somalí *m* **II.** *adj* somalí

Somalia [ˌsə'mɑːliə, *Am:* soʊ'-] *n* Somalia *f*

somber *adj Am,* **sombre** ['sɒmbə', *Am:* 'sɑːmbə] *adj* (*mood*) sombrío, -a; (*colour*) oscuro, -a

some [sʌm] **I.** *adj indef* **1.** *pl* (*several*) algunos, -as; ~ **apples** algunas manzanas; ~ **people think ...** algunos piensan... **2.** (*imprecise*) algún, alguna; (**at**) ~ **place** (en) algún lugar; ~ **day** algún día; (**at**) ~ **time** (en) algún momento; **for** ~ **time** durante cierto tiempo; ~ **other time** en algún otro momento; ~ **time ago** hace algún tiempo; **in** ~ **way or another** de alguna u otra manera; **to have** ~ **idea of sth** tener alguna idea de algo **3.** (*amount*) un poco de, algo de; ~ **more tea** un poco más de té; **to have** ~ **money** tener algo de dinero; **to** ~ **extent** hasta cierto punto **II.** *pron indef* **1.** *pl* (*several*) algunos; **I would like** ~ quisiera algunos; ~ **like it, others don't** a algunos les gusta, a otros no **2.** (*part of it*) algo; **I would like** ~ quisiera algo **III.** *adv* **1.** (*about*) unos, unas; ~ **more apples** unas manzanas más; ~ **more wine** un poco más de vino; ~ **ten of them** unos diez de ellos **2.** *Am* (*little*) **to feel** ~ **better** sentirse un poco mejor

somebody ['sʌmbədi, *Am:* -ˌbɑːdi] *pron indef* alguien; ~ **else** otra persona, algún otro; ~ **or other** alguien; ~ **kind** alguien amable; **there is** ~ **Spanish on the phone** hay alguien español al teléfono

somehow ['sʌmhaʊ] *adv* **1.** (*through un-known methods*) de alguna manera **2.** (*for an unclear reason*) por algún motivo **3.** (*come what may*) de un modo u otro

someone ['sʌmwʌn] *pron s.* **somebody**

someplace ['sʌmpleɪs] *adv Am* en algún lugar

somersault ['sʌməsɔ:lt, *Am:* -ɚsɑ:lt] **I.** *n* salto *m* mortal; **to turn a** ~ dar un salto mortal **II.** *vi* (*vehicle*) dar una vuelta de campana; (*person*) dar un salto mortal

something ['sʌmθɪŋ] **I.** *pron indef, sing* **1.** (*some object or concept*) algo; ~ **else/nice** algo más/bonito; ~ **or other** alguna cosa; **one can't have** ~ **for nothing** quie algo quiere, algo le cuesta **2.** (*about*) ... **or** ~ *inf* ...o algo así; **two metres** ~ dos metros y pico; **his name is Paul** ~ su nombre es Paul no sé qué **II.** *n* **a little** ~ una cosita; **a certain** ~ cierta cosa ▶**that is really** ~! ¡ésa sí que es buena! **III.** *adv* ~ **around £10** alrededor de 10 libras; ~ **over/under £100** algo más/menos de 100 libras

sometime ['sʌmtaɪm] **I.** *adv* en algún momento; ~ **soon** pronto **II.** *adj form* antiguo, -a

sometimes ['sʌmtaɪmz] *adv* a veces

somewhat ['sʌmwɒt, *Am:* -wɑ:t] *adv* algo

somewhere ['sʌmweəʳ, *Am:* -wer] *adv* **1.** (*be*) en alguna parte; (*go*) a alguna parte; **to be** ~ **else** estar en otra parte; **to go** ~ **else** ir a otra parte; **to get** ~ *fig* progresar; **or** ~ *inf* o así **2.** (*roughly*) alrededor de; **she is** ~ **around 40** tiene alrededor de 40 años; **he earns** ~ **around 40,000 dollars** gana alrededor de 40.000 dólares

somnambulism [sɒm'næmbjʊlɪzəm, *Am:* sɑ:m'-] *n no pl* sonambulismo *m*

somnolent ['sɒmnələnt, *Am:* 'sɑ:m-] *adj* (*sleepy*) soñoliento, -a

son [sʌn] *n* hijo *m* ▶~ **of a** *bitch inf* hijo de puta

sonar ['səʊnɑ:ʳ, *Am:* 'soʊnɑ:r] *n* sónar *m*

sonata [sə'nɑ:tə, *Am:* -ţə] *n* sonata *f;* **piano** ~ sonata para piano

song [sɒŋ, *Am:* sɑ:ŋ] *n* **1.** MUS (*piece of music*) canción *f;* **to give sb a** ~ cantar para alguien **2.** (*action of singing*) canto *m* ▶~ **and** *dance Brit, pej, inf* numerito *m; Am, inf* (*untrue justification*) rollo *m;* **to make a** ~ **and dance about sth** montar un número por algo; (**to go**) **for a** ~ venderse a precio de saldo; **to be on** ~ estar en forma

songbird ['sɒŋbɜ:d, *Am:* 'sɑ:ŋbɜ:rd] *n* pájaro *m* cantor **songbook** *n* cancionero *m* **songwriter** *n* compositor(a) *m(f)*

sonic ['sɒnɪk, *Am:* 'sɑ:nɪk] *adj* **1.** (*relating to sound*) acústico, -a **2.** (*at the speed of sound*) sónico, -a

sonic boom *n* AVIAT explosión *f* ultrasónica

son-in-law ['sʌnɪnlɔ:, *Am:* -lɑ:] <sons-in--law *o* son-in-laws> *n* yerno *m*

sonnet ['sɒnɪt, *Am:* 'sɑ:nɪt] *n* soneto *m*

sonny ['sʌni] *n no pl, inf* hijito *m;* (*aggressive*) majo *m*

sonorous [sə'nɔ:rəs] *adj* sonoro, -a

soon [su:n] *adv* pronto, mero *AmC, Méx;* ~ **after** ... poco después de...; **how** ~ ...? ¿para cuándo...?; **as** ~ **as possible** tan pronto como sea posible; **as** ~ **as possible** lo más pronto posible; **I would just as** ~ ... preferiría...

sooner ['su:nəʳ, *Am:* -ɚ] *adv comp of* **soon** más temprano; ~ **or later** tarde o temprano; **no** ~ ... **than** apenas...cuando; **no** ~ **said than done** dicho y hecho; **I would** ~ **leave** preferiría irme; **the** ~**er the better** cuanto antes mejor

soot [sʊt] *n no pl* hollín *m*

soothe [su:ð] *vt* **1.** (*make calm*) calmar **2.** (*reduce: pain*) aliviar

soothing *adj* **1.** (*calming*) tranquilizador(a) **2.** (*pain-relieving*) analgésico, -a; (*balsamic: ointment, balm, massage*) reparador(a)

soothsayer ['su:θseɪəʳ, *Am:* -ɚ] *n* adivino *m*

sooty ['sʊti, *Am:* 'sʊţ-] <-ier, -iest> *adj* lleno, -a de hollín

sop [sɒp, *Am:* sɑ:p] *n pej* concesión *f*

sophisticated [sə'fɪstɪkeɪtɪd, *Am:* -ţəkeɪ-ţɪd] *adj* **1.** (*refined*) sofisticado, -a **2.** (*cultured*) culto, -a **3.** (*highly developed*) refinado, -a; (*method*) sofisticado, -a

sophistication [sə,fɪstɪ'keɪʃən, *Am:* -ţə'-] *n no pl* **1.** (*refinement*) sofisticación *f* **2.** (*complexity*) complejidad *f*

sophistry ['sɒfɪstri, *Am:* 'sɑ:fɪ-] *n no pl* sofistería *f*

sophomore ['sɒfəmɔ:ʳ, *Am:* 'sɑ:fəmɔ:r] *n Am* estudiante *mf* de segundo año

soporific [,sɒpə'rɪfɪk, *Am:* ,sɑ:pə-] *adj* soporífero, -a

sopping ['sɒpɪŋ, *Am:* 'sɑ:pɪŋ] *inf* **I.** *adj* empapado, -a **II.** *adv* ~ **wet** empapado

soppy ['sɒpi, *Am:* 'sɑ:pi] <-ier, -iest> *adj inf* sensiblero, -a

soprano [sə'prɑ:nəʊ, *Am:* -'prænoʊ] *n* **1.** (*vocal range*) soprano *m* **2.** (*singer*) soprano *f*

sorbet ['sɔ:beɪ, *Am:* 'sɔ:r-] *n* sorbete *m*

sorcerer ['sɔ:sərəʳ, *Am:* 'sɔ:rsərɚ] *n liter* hechicero *m*

sorceress ['sɔ:sərɪs, *Am:* 'sɔ:r-] *n liter* hechicera *f*

sorcery ['sɔ:səri, *Am:* 'sɔ:r-] *n liter* hechicería *f*

sordid ['sɔ:dɪd, *Am:* 'sɔ:r-] *adj* **1.** (*unclean*) sórdido, -a, miserable **2.** *pej* (*base*) sórdido, -a; **all the** ~ **details** todos los detalles escabrosos

sore [sɔ:ʳ, *Am:* sɔ:r] **I.** *adj* **1.** (*aching*) dolorido, -a; **to be in** ~ **need of sth** necesitar algo a toda costa; **a** ~ **point** *fig* un punto delicado **2.** *Am, inf* (*offended*) ofendido, -a; (*aggrieved*) resentido, -a; ~ **loser** mal perdedor **II.** *n* MED llaga *f; fig* recuerdo *m* doloroso; **to open an old** ~ abrir una vieja herida

sorely ['sɔ:li, *Am:* 'sɔ:r-] *adv form* muy; **he**

will be ~ missed lo echarán mucho de menos; to be ~ tempted to do sth estar casi por hacer algo

sorority [sə'rɒrəti, Am: -'rɔːrəṭi] n Am UNIV club m femenino

sorrel ['sɒrəl, Am: 'sɔːr-] n no pl acedera f

sorrow ['sɒrəʊ, Am: 'sɑːroʊ] I. n pena f; to feel ~ over sth sentirse apenado por algo; to my ~ form a mi pesar II. vi to ~ over sth sentirse afligido por algo

sorrowful ['sɒrəʊfəl, Am: 'sɑːrəfəl] adj apenado, -a; with a ~ sigh con un suspiro de aflicción

sorry ['sɒri, Am: 'sɑːr-] I.<-ier, -iest> adj 1. triste, apenado, -a; to be ~ (that) sentir (que) +subj; to be ~ for oneself compadecerse de sí mismo; to feel ~ for sb tener lástima de alguien 2. (regretful) arrepentido, -a; to be ~ about sth estar arrepentido por algo; to say ~ pedir perdón 3. (said before refusing) I'm ~ but I don't agree lo siento, pero no estoy de acuerdo 4. (wretched, pitiful) desgraciado, -a; (choice) desafortunado, -a; (figure) lastimoso, -a II. interj 1. (expressing apology) ~! ¡perdón! 2. Brit, Aus (requesting repetition) ~? ¿cómo dice?; ~ but before continuing … disculpen, pero antes de continuar…

sort [sɔːt, Am: sɔːrt] I. n 1. (type) tipo m; (kind) especie f; (variety) clase f; flowers of all ~s toda clase de flores; something/nothing of the ~ algo/nada por el estilo 2. INFOR ordenación f 3. (expressing uncertainty) he was a friend of ~s se le podía considerar amigo 4. inf (to some extent) ~ of en cierto modo; I ~ of feel that … en cierto modo pienso que…; that's ~ of difficult to explain es algo difícil de explicar 5. (not exactly) ~ of más o menos 6. (person) to not be the ~ to do sth no ser de los que hacen algo; to be sb's ~ ser del tipo de alguien; I know your ~! ¡sé de qué pie calzas! ► it takes all ~s to make a world prov hay de todo en la viña del Señor prov; to be/feel out of ~s estar/encontrarse pachucho II. vt 1. (arrange) clasificar 2. INFOR ordenar; to ~ in ascending/descending order poner en orden ascendente/descendente 3. Brit, inf (restore to working order) arreglar III. vi to ~ through sth revisar algo

◆**sort out** vt 1. (arrange) clasificar; (choose) separar 2. (tidy up) arreglar 3. (resolve) solucionar; (details) aclarar; to sort oneself out tomarse un respiro 4. (beat up) to sort sb out ajustar las cuentas a alguien

sort code n FIN código m de clasificación

sorter n 1. (postal employee sorting mail) clasificador(a) m(f) 2. (machine) clasificadora f

sortie ['sɔːtiː, Am: 'sɔːr-] n 1. MIL incursión f 2. iron, inf (short trip) escapada f 3. inf (try) intento m

sorting office n oficina f de clasificación de correo

SOS [ˌesəʊ'es, Am: -oʊ'-] n s.o.s. m

so-so ['səʊsəʊ, Am: 'soʊsoʊ] inf I. adj regular II. adv ni fu ni fa, así así

soufflé ['suːfleɪ, Am: suː'fleɪ] n suflé m

sought [sɔːt, Am: sɑːt] pt, pp of seek

sought-after ['sɔːtˌɑːftəʳ, Am: 'sɑːtˌæftəʳ] adj solicitado, -a

soul [səʊl, Am: soʊl] I. n 1. (spirit) alma f; to pray for sb's ~ rezar por el alma de alguien; God rest his/her ~ que en paz descanse 2. (person) alma f; not a ~ ni un alma 3. no pl MUS soul m 4. (essence) to be the ~ of discretion ser la discreción en persona II. adj Am ~ food comida tradicional de los negros del Sur de los Estados Unidos

soul-destroying ['səʊldɪˌstrɔɪɪŋ, Am: 'soʊl-] adj desmoralizador(a)

soulful ['səʊlfəl, Am: 'soʊl-] adj conmovedor(a)

soulless ['səʊlləs, Am: 'soʊl-] adj pej (person) desalmado, -a; (building, town) impersonal; (work) mecánico, -a

soul mate n amigo, -a m, f del alma **soul music** n (música f) soul m **soul-searching** n no pl examen m de conciencia; after much ~ después de mucha reflexión **soul-stirring** adj conmovedor(a)

sound[1] [saʊnd] I. n 1. (noise) ruido m; there wasn't a ~ to be heard no se oía nada 2. LING, PHYS sonido m 3. (radio, TV) volumen m; to turn the ~ down/up bajar/subir el volumen 4. (idea expressed in words) by the ~ of it según parece; I don't like the ~ of that no me huele nada bien II. vi 1. (make noise) sonar 2. (seem) parecer III. vt (alarm) hacer sonar; (bell, car horn) tocar; to ~ the retreat MIL tocar la retirada

sound[2] [saʊnd] I. adj 1. (healthy) sano, -a; (robust) fuerte; to be of ~ mind estar en su sano juicio 2. (good: character, health) bueno, -a; (basis) sólido, -a 3. (trustworthy) digno, -a de confianza; (competent) competente 4. (thorough) profundo, -a 5. (undisturbed: sleep) profundo, -a; to be a ~ sleeper tener el sueño profundo II. adv to be ~ asleep estar profundamente dormido

sound[3] [saʊnd] vt 1. NAUT sondear 2. MED auscultar

sound[4] [saʊnd] n (channel) estrecho m; (inlet) brazo m de mar

◆**sound off** vi inf to ~ about sb/sth sentar cátedra sobre algo/alguien

◆**sound out** vt tantear

sound archives npl archivos mpl de sonido **sound barrier** n barrera f del sonido **soundbite** n frase f lapidaria **soundboard** n MUS tabla f armónica **soundbox** n caja f de resonancia **sound card** n tarjeta f de sonido **sound effects** n efectos mpl de sonido **sound engineer** n técnico m de sonido

sounding n NAUT sondeo m; to take ~s fig tantear el terreno

sounding board n tabla f armónica

soundless ['saʊndləs] adj silencioso, -a

soundly *adv* **1.** (*completely*) **to sleep** ~ dormir profundamente **2.** (*strongly*) **to thrash sb** ~ dar una buena paliza a alguien

soundness *n no pl* **1.** (*firmness*) firmeza *f* **2.** (*good sense*) sensatez *f*

soundproof ['saʊndpruːf] **I.** *vt* insonorizar **II.** *adj* insonorizado, -a

sound system *n* equipo *m* de sonido **soundtrack** *n* CINE banda *f* sonora **sound wave** *n* onda *f* sonora

soup [suːp] *n no pl* sopa *f*; (*clear*) caldo *m;* **home-made** ~ sopa casera; **instant** ~ sopa instantánea ►**to be in the** ~ *inf* estar con el agua al cuello

soupçon ['suːpsɒn, *Am:* suːpˈsɑːn] *n no pl* pizca *f*

souped-up *adj* AUTO trucado, -a

soup kitchen *n* comedor *m* de beneficencia **soup plate** *n* plato *m* sopero **soup spoon** *n* cuchara *f* sopera

sour ['saʊə', *Am:* 'saʊə'] **I.** *adj* **1.** (*fruit, wine*) agrio, -a; (*milk*) cortado, -a; **to go** ~ agriarse; (*milk*) cortarse **2.** (*character, person*) agrio, -a **II.** *n Am* **whisky** ~ *combinado de whisky, zumo de limón y azúcar* **III.** *vt* agriar; *fig* amargar **IV.** *vi* agriarse; (*milk*) cortarse; *fig* (*person*) amargarse

source [sɔːs, *Am:* sɔːrs] **I.** *n* **1.** *a. fig* fuente *f;* **according to Government** ~s según fuentes gubernamentales; **from a reliable** ~ de una fuente fiable; **to list one's** ~s hacer la bibliografía **2.** (*origin*) origen *m;* **a** ~ **of inspiration** una fuente de inspiración; ~ **text** texto *m* original **3.** *Brit, Aus* FIN **to tax sth at** ~ cobrar los impuestos de algo en el origen **II.** *vt* seleccionar

sourpuss ['saʊəpʊs, *Am:* 'saʊə'-] *n inf* amargado, -a *m, f*

souse [saʊs] *vt* (*food*) macerar

south [saʊθ] **I.** *n* sur *m;* **to lie 5 km to the** ~ **of sth** quedar a 5 km al sur de algo; **to go/drive to the** ~ ir hacia el sur; **further** ~ más al sur; **in the** ~ **of France** en el sur de Francia **II.** *adj* del sur, meridional; ~ **wind** viento *m* del sur; ~ **coast** costa *f* sur

South Africa *n* Sudáfrica *f* **South African** **I.** *adj* sudafricano, -a **II.** *n* sudafricano, -a *m, f* **South America** *n* América *f* del Sur **South American** **I.** *adj* sudamericano, -a **II.** *n* sudamericano, -a *m, f*

southbound ['saʊθbaʊnd] *adj* hacia el sur **South Carolina** *n* Carolina *f* del Sur **South Dakota** *n* Dakota *f* del Sur

south-east [ˌsaʊθˈiːst] **I.** *n no pl* sureste *m* **II.** *adj* del sureste; **Southeast Asia** el sureste asiático **III.** *adv* al sureste **south-easterly** **I.** *adj* **in a** ~ **direction** hacia el sureste **II.** *n* (*wind*) viento *m* del sureste **south-eastern** *adj* sureste **south-eastwards** *adv* hacia el sureste

southerly ['sʌðəli, *Am:* -ə·li] **I.** *adj* (*location*) en el sur; **in a** ~ **direction** en dirección sur; ~ **wind** viento *m* meridional [*o* sur] **II.** *n* viento

m meridional

southern ['sʌðən, *Am:* -ə·n] *adj* del sur; **the** ~ **part of the country** la parte sur del país

Southern Cross *n* Cruz *f* del Sur

southerner ['sʌðənə', *Am:* -ə·nə·] *n* sureño, -a *m, f*

southern hemisphere *n* hemisferio *m* sur **southern lights** *npl* aurora *f* austral **southernmost** *adj* más al sur

south-facing *adj* orientado, -a al sur

South Korea *n* Corea *f* del Sur **South Korean** **I.** *adj* surcoreano, -a **II.** *n* surcoreano, -a *m, f*

southpaw ['saʊθpɔː, *Am:* -pɑː] *n Am* zurdo, -a *m, f*

South Pole *n* Polo *m* Sur

southward(s) ['saʊθwəd(z), *Am:* -wə·d(z)] *adv* hacia el sur

south-west [ˌsaʊθˈwest] **I.** *n no pl* suroeste *m* **II.** *adj* del suroeste **III.** *adv* al suroeste **south-westerly** **I.** *adj* **in a** ~ **direction** hacia el suroeste **II.** *n* (*wind*) viento *m* del suroeste **south-western** *adj* del suroeste **south-westward(s)** *adv* hacia el suroeste

souvenir [ˌsuːvəˈnɪə', *Am:* -ˈnɪr] *n* recuerdo *m*

sou'wester [ˌsaʊˈwestə', *Am:* -tə·] *n* sueste *m*

sovereign ['sɒvrɪn, *Am:* 'sɑːvrən] **I.** *n* **1.** (*ruler*) soberano, -a *m, f* **2.** (*coin*) soberano *m* **II.** *adj* (*self-governing*) soberano, -a; ~ **state** estado *m* soberano

sovereignty ['sɒvrənti, *Am:* 'sɑːvrənti] *n no pl* soberanía *f*

soviet ['səʊviət, *Am:* 'soʊviet] **I.** *n* soviet *m* **II.** *adj* soviético, -a

Soviet Union *n* HIST Unión *f* Soviética

sow¹ [səʊ, *Am:* soʊ] <sowed, *o* sowed sown> **I.** *vt* sembrar **II.** *vi* sembrar ►**as you** ~, **so shall you reap** lo que siembres cosecharás

sow² [saʊ] *n* (*pig*) cerda *f* ►**you can't make a silk purse out of a** ~**'s ear** *prov* no se le puede pedir peras al olmo

sowing machine ['səʊɪŋməˈʃiːn, *Am:* 'soʊ-] *n* sembradora *f*

sown [səʊn, *Am:* soʊn] *pp of* **sow**

sox [sɒks, *Am:* sɑːks] *npl Am* calcetines *mpl*

soy [sɔɪ] *n Am*, **soya** ['sɔɪə] *n Brit* soja *f*

soya bean *n Brit*, **soybean** ['sɔɪbiːn] *n Am* soja *f* **soya sauce** *n Brit*, **soy sauce** *n Am* salsa *f* de soja

sozzled ['sɒzld, *Am:* 'sɑːzld] *adj Brit, Aus, inf* **to be** ~ estar mamado, -a; **to get** ~ agarrar una trompa

spa [spɑː] *n* **1.** (*mineral spring*) manantial *m* de agua mineral **2.** (*town*) ciudad *f* balnearia **3.** *Am* (*health centre*) balneario *m*

space [speɪs] **I.** *n* espacio *m;* **parking** ~ plaza *f* de aparcamiento; **in a short** ~ **of time** en un breve espacio de tiempo; **leave some** ~ **for dessert** deja espacio para el postre **II.** *vt* espaciar

S

◆**space out** *vt* espaciar
space age *n* era *f* espacial
space bar *n* barra *f* espaciadora
space capsule *n* cápsula *f* espacial **space centre** *n* centro *m* espacial **spacecraft** *n* nave *f* espacial **spaceman** <-men> *n* astronauta *m*, cosmonauta *m* **space probe** *n* sonda *f* espacial
spacer *n* espaciador *m*
space-saving *adj* que ocupa poco espacio
spaceship ['speɪʃɪp] *n* nave *f* espacial, astronave *f* **space shuttle** *n* transbordador *m* espacial **space station** *n* estación *f* espacial **spacewoman** <-women> *n* astronauta *f*
spacing ['speɪsɪŋ] *n no pl* **1.** (*arrangement of spaces*) espaciamiento *m* **2.** TYPO espacio *m*; **double** ~ doble espacio
spacious ['speɪʃəs] *adj* espacioso, -a
spade [speɪd] *n* **1.** (*tool*) pala *f* **2.** (*playing card*) pica *f* ►to **call** a ~ a ~ llamar al pan, pan y al vino, vino
spadework ['speɪdwɜːk, *Am:* -wɜːrk] *n no pl* trabajo *m* preparatorio
spaghetti [spə'geti, *Am:* -'ge̞t-] *n* espaguetis *mpl*
spaghetti western *n* CINE spaghetti western *m*
Spain [speɪn] *n* España *f*
Spam® [spæm] *n no pl* fiambre *enlatado hecho con carne de cerdo*
span¹ [spæn] *pt of* **spin**
span² [spæn] I. *n* **1.** (*of time*) lapso *m*, espacio *m*; (*of project*) duración *f* **2.** ARCHIT (*of bridge, arch*) luz *f* **3.** AVIAT, NAUT (*of wing, sail*) envergadura *f* II. <-nn-> *vt* **1.** (*cross*) atravesar **2.** (*include*) abarcar
spangle ['spæŋgl] *n* lentejuela *f*
spangled *adj* con lentejuelas; **to be** ~ **with** sth *fig* estar salpicado de algo
Spaniard ['spænjəd, *Am:* -jəd] *n* español(a) *m(f)*
spaniel ['spænjəl, *Am:* -jəl] *n* perro *m* de aguas
Spanish ['spænɪʃ] I. *adj* español(a); ~ **speaker** hispanohablante *mf* II. *n* **1.** (*people*) español(a) *m(f)*; **the** ~ los españoles **2.** LING español *m*
spank [spæŋk] *vt* dar unos cachetes (en el trasero)
spanking ['spæŋkɪŋ] I. *n* zurra *f*, fleta *f* *AmC*; **to give sb a** ~ zurrar a alguien II. *adj inf* ~ **new** nuevo y flamante; **at a** ~ **pace** a paso ligero
spanner ['spænər, *Am:* -ɚ] *n Brit, Aus* llave *f*; **adjustable** ~ llave inglesa ►to **throw a** ~ **in the works** fastidiarlo todo
spar¹ [spɑːr, *Am:* spɑːr] *n* NAUT palo *m*
spar² [spɑːr, *Am:* spɑːr] *vi* <-rr-> **1.** (*in boxing*) entrenar **2.** (*argue*) discutir
spar³ [spɑːr, *Am:* spɑːr] *n* MIN espato *m*
spare [speər, *Am:* sper] I. *vt* **1.** (*pardon*) perdonar; **to** ~ **sb's feelings** no herir los senti-

mientos de alguien; **to** ~ **sb sth** ahorrar algo a alguien; **to** ~ **no effort** no escatimar esfuerzos **2.** (*do without*) prescindir de; (*time*) disponer de II. *adj* **1.** (*additional: key*) de repuesto; (*room, minute*) libre **2.** (*remaining*) sobrante **3.** *liter* (*gaunt: build*) enjuto, -a; (*meal*) frugal, austero, -a ►to **go** ~ *Brit, inf* volverse loco III. *n* repuesto *m*
spare part *n* repuesto *m* **spare ribs** *n pl* costillas *fpl* (de cerdo) **spare time** *n no pl* tiempo *m* libre **spare tire** *n Am,* **spare tyre** *n* **1.** AUTO rueda *f* de recambio **2.** *iron* michelín *m*
sparing ['speərɪŋ, *Am:* 'sperɪŋ] *adj* moderado, -a; **to be** ~ **with one's praise** escatimar los elogios
spark [spɑːk, *Am:* spɑːrk] I. *n* **1.** (*from fire, electrical*) chispa *f* **2.** (*small amount*) pizca *f*; **not even a** ~ **of interest/intelligence** ni una pizca de interés/inteligencia II. *vt* (*debate, protest, problems*) desencadenar; (*interest*) despertar, suscitar; (*riot*) hacer estallar; **to** ~ **sb into action** hacer que alguien se mueva
◆**spark off** *vt* desencadenar
sparking plug ['spɑːkɪŋplʌg, *Am:* 'spɑːrk-] *n Am* bujía *f*
sparkle ['spɑːkl, *Am:* 'spɑːr-] I. *n no pl* destello *m*, brillo *m* II. *vi* (*fire*) chispear; (*sea*) destellar, centellear; (*eyes*) brillar
sparkler ['spɑːklər, *Am:* 'spɑːrklɚ] *n* **1.** (*firework*) bengala *f* **2.** *inf* (*diamond*) diamante *m*
sparkling ['spɑːklɪŋ, *Am:* 'spɑːrkl-] *adj* **1.** (*light, diamond*) brillante **2.** (*conversation, wit*) chispeante
spark plug ['spɑːkplʌg, *Am:* 'spɑːrk-] *n Brit* bujía *f*
sparring match ['spɑːrɪŋ] *n* combate *m* de entrenamiento **sparring partner** *n* **1.** SPORTS sparring *m* **2.** *fig* antagonista *mf*
sparrow ['spærəʊ, *Am:* 'speroʊ] *n* gorrión *m*
sparrowhawk ['spærəʊhɔːk, *Am:* 'speroʊhɑːk] *n* gavilán *m*
sparse [spɑːs, *Am:* spɑːrs] *adj* escaso, -a
sparsely *adv* escasamente
Spartan ['spɑːtən, *Am:* 'spɑːr-] *adj* espartano, -a
spasm ['spæzəm] *n* MED espasmo *m*; (*of anger*) arrebato *m*; (*of coughing, pain*) ataque *m*; **to go into** ~ *Brit, Aus* contraerse espasmódicamente
spasmodic [spæz'mɒdɪk, *Am:* -'mɑːdɪk] *adj* **1.** (*interest*) ocasional; (*activity*) irregular **2.** MED espasmódico, -a
spastic ['spæstɪk] *n pej* espástico, -a *m, f*
spat¹ [spæt] *pt, pp of* **spit**
spat² [spæt] I. *n inf* (*quarrel*) rencilla *f* II. <-tt-> *vi Am, Aus* (*quarrel*) reñir
spat³ [spæt] *n pl* (*overshoe*) polaina *f*
spate [speɪt] *n no pl* (*of letters, inquiries*) aluvión *m*; (*of burglaries*) racha *f*, serie *f*; **to be in full** ~ *Brit* (*river*) estar crecido
spatial ['speɪʃəl] *adj* espacial

spatter ['spætəʳ, *Am:* 'spæt̬ə·] I. *vt* salpicar; **to ~ sb with mud/water** salpicar de barro/agua a alguien II. *vi* salpicar III. *n* salpicadura *f*, salpicada *f Méx;* **~ of rain** cuatro gotas *fpl*

spatula ['spætjʊlə, *Am:* 'spætʃə-] *n* espátula *f*

spawn [spɔːn, *Am:* spɑːn] I. *n* 1. *no pl* ZOOL hueva(s) *f(pl)* 2. *pej* (*offspring*) prole *f* II. *vt* generar, producir III. *vi* desovar

spay [speɪ] *vt* (*animal*) esterilizar (*extirpando los ovarios*)

speak [spiːk] <spoke, spoken> I. *vi* 1. hablar; **to ~ to sb** hablar con alguien; **to ~ in riddles** hablar en clave; **to ~ on behalf of sb** hablar por alguien; **so to ~** por así decirlo; **~ when you're spoken to** contesta cuando te pregunten 2. + *adv* **broadly ~ing** en términos generales; **scientifically ~ing** desde el punto de vista científico; **strictly ~ing** en realidad II. *vt* decir, hablar; **to ~ dialect/a foreign language** hablar dialecto/un idioma extranjero; **to ~ one's mind** hablar claro [*o* con franqueza]; **to ~ the truth** decir la verdad; **to not ~ a word** no decir ni una palabra

◆**speak for** *vi* 1. (*represent*) hablar por; **speaking for myself ...** en cuanto a mí...; **it speaks for itself** habla por sí solo; **to be old enough to ~ oneself** ser lo bastante mayorcito para defenderse 2. (*advocate, support*) hablar en favor de

◆**speak out** *vi* expresarse; **to ~ against sth** denunciar algo

◆**speak up** *vi* 1. (*state views*) decir lo que se piensa; **to ~ for sth** hablar a favor de algo 2. (*talk more loudly*) hablar más alto

speaker *n* 1. hablante *mf* 2. (*orator*) orador(a) *m(f)* 3. *Brit, Can* POL presidente, -a *m, f* (*de la cámara*); **Madame ~** Señora Presidenta 4. (*loudspeaker*) altavoz *m*

speaking I. *n no pl* 1. (*action*) habla *f* 2. (*public speaking*) oratoria *f* II. *adj* hablante; (*tour*) comentado, -a; **to be on ~ terms with sb** estar en buenas relaciones con alguien; **not to be on ~ terms** no hablarse, no dirigirse la palabra

speaking clock *n Brit* servicio *m* telefónico de información horaria **speaking part** *n* THEAT, CINE papel *m* hablado

spear [spɪəʳ, *Am:* spɪr] I. *n* lanza *f*; (*for throwing*) jabalina *f*; (*for fishing*) arpón *m* II. *vt* atravesar (con una lanza); (*with fork*) pinchar

spearhead ['spɪəhed, *Am:* 'spɪr-] I. *vt* encabezar II. *n a. fig* punta *f* de lanza

spearmint ['spɪəmɪnt, *Am:* 'spɪr-] *n no pl* menta *f* verde

special ['speʃəl] I. *adj* (*attention, case, diet*) especial; (*aptitude, character*) excepcional; **nothing ~** *inf* nada en particular II. *n* 1. TV programa *m* especial 2. RAIL tren *m* especial 3. GASTR especialidad *f* del día 4. *pl, Am* COM ofertas *fpl* especiales

Special Branch *n Brit:* departamento policial encargado de velar por la seguridad del

Estado **special delivery** *n* correo *m* urgente **special edition** *n* número *m* extraordinario **special effects** *n* efectos *mpl* especiales

specialism ['speʃəlɪzm] *n* especialidad *f*

specialist ['speʃəlɪst] *n* especialista *mf*

speciality [ˌspeʃɪˈæləti, *Am:* -t̬i] *n* <-ies> especialidad *f*

specialization [ˌspeʃəlaɪˈzeɪʃən, *Am:* -ɪ'-] *n* especialización *f*

specialize ['speʃəlaɪz] I. *vt* especializar II. *vi* especializarse

specialized *adj* especializado, -a

specially *adv* especialmente; **a ~ good wine** un vino especialmente bueno

special offer *n* oferta *f* especial **special pleading** *n* argucias *fpl*

specialty ['speʃəlti, *Am:* -t̬i] *n Am, Aus s.* **speciality**

species ['spiːʃiːz] *n inv* especie *f*

specific [spəˈsɪfɪk] I. *adj* específico, -a; **to be ~ to sth** ser propio de algo; **to be ~** dar detalles II. *npl* datos *mpl* específicos

specifically *adv* 1. (*expressly*) expresamente; (*ask, mention*) explícitamente 2. (*particularly*) específicamente

specification [ˌspesɪfɪˈkeɪʃən, *Am:* -əfɪ'-] *n* especificación *f*

specify ['spesɪfaɪ, *Am:* -əfaɪ] <-ie-> *vt* especificar

specimen ['spesɪmɪn, *Am:* -əmən] *n* 1. (*of blood, urine*) muestra *f*; (*example*) ejemplar *m*; **a ~ copy** un ejemplar de muestra 2. *inf* (*person*) espécimen *m*

specious ['spiːʃəs] *adj form* engañoso, -a

speck [spek] *n* punto *m*; (*of paint*) manchita *f*; (*of dust*) mota *f*; **not a ~ of sth** ni pizca de algo

speckle ['spekl] *n* motita *f*

speckled *adj* con motitas, moteado, -a

specs [speks] *npl Brit, inf abbr of* **spectacles** gafas *fpl*

spectacle ['spektəkl] *n* 1. espectáculo *m;* **to make a real ~ of oneself** dar el espectáculo 2. *pl, Brit* (*glasses*) gafas *fpl*, anteojos *mpl AmL*, lentes *fpl AmL;* **a pair of ~** unas gafas

spectacle case *n* estuche *m* de gafas

spectacled *adj* con gafas

spectacular [spekˈtækjʊləʳ, *Am:* -lə·] I. *adj* espectacular II. *n* programa *m* especial

spectator [spekˈteɪtəʳ, *Am:* -t̬ə·] *n* espectador(a) *m(f)*

specter *n Am s.* **spectre**

spectral ['spektrəl] *adj* espectral

spectre ['spektəʳ, *Am:* -tə·] *n* espectro *m*, fantasma *m*

spectroscope ['spektrəʊskəʊp, *Am:* -skoʊp] *n* PHYS espectroscopio *m*

spectrum ['spektrəm] <-ra *o* -s> *n* 1. PHYS espectro *m* 2. (*range*) gama *f*; **the political ~** el espectro político

speculate ['spekjʊleɪt] *vi* 1. **to ~ about sth** (*hypothesize*) especular acerca de algo; (*con-*

jecture) hacer conjeturas acerca de algo **2.** (*buy and sell*) especular

speculation [ˌspekjʊ'leɪʃən] *n* especulación *f*, conjetura *f*; **stock-market** ~ especulación bursátil

speculative ['spekjʊlətɪv, *Am:* leɪt̬ɪv] *adj* especulativo, -a

speculator ['spekjʊleɪtəʳ, *Am:* -t̬ə] *n* especulador(a) *m(f)*; **property** ~ especulador en bienes raíces

speculum ['spekjələm] *n* espéculo *m*

sped [sped] *pt, pp of* **speed**

speech [spi:tʃ] <-es> *n* **1.** *no pl* (*capacity to speak*) habla *f*; **to lose the power of** ~ perder el habla **2.** (*words*) palabras *fpl* **3.** (*public talk*) discurso *m*; **to make** [*o* give] **a** ~ pronunciar un discurso

speech act *n* LING acto *m* de habla **speech day** *n Brit* día *m* de entrega de premios **speech defect** *n* defecto *m* del habla

speechify ['spi:tʃɪfaɪ, *Am:* -tʃə-] *vi* perorar **speech impediment** *n* defecto *m* del habla **speechless** ['spi:tʃləs] *adj* mudo, -a; **to be** ~ **with indignation** enmudecer de indignación; **to leave sb** ~ dejar a alguien sin palabras

speech recognition *n no pl* INFOR, LING reconocimiento *m* de la voz **speech therapist** *n* logopeda *mf* **speech therapy** *n* logopedia *f* **speech writer** *n* escritor(a) *m(f)* (*que escribe discursos para políticos*)

speed [spi:d] **I.** *n* **1.** (*velocity*) velocidad *f*; **at a** ~ **of ...** a una velocidad de... **2.** (*quickness*) rapidez *f* **3.** (*gear*) marcha *f* **4.** PHOT sensibilidad *f* **5.** *inf* (*amphetamine*) anfetas *fpl* **II.** *vi* <sped, sped> **1.** (*go fast*) ir de prisa; **to** ~ **by** pasar volando **2.** (*hasten*) apresurarse **3.** (*exceed speed restrictions*) ir a exceso de velocidad **III.** *vt* <-ed, -ed *o* sped, sped> acelerar; **to** ~ **sb on their way** despedir a alguien

◆**speed off** <-ed, -ed> *vi* salir disparado

◆**speed up** <-ed, -ed> **I.** *vt* (*process*) acelerar, expeditar *AmL*; (*person*) apresurar *AmL*. **II.** *vi* (*car*) acelerar; (*process*) acelerarse; (*person*) darse prisa, apurarse *AmL*

speedboat ['spi:dbəʊt, *Am:* -boʊt] *n* lancha *f* motora **speed bump** *n* banda *f* rugosa **speed cop** *n Am, inf* policía *mf* de tráfico **speeding** *n no pl* exceso *m* de velocidad **speed limit** *n* velocidad *f* máxima

speedometer [spi:'dɒmɪtəʳ, *Am:* -'dɑːmə-t̬ə] *n* velocímetro *m*

speed skater *n* patinador(a) *m(f)* de velocidad **speed skating** *n no pl* patinaje *m* de velocidad **speed trap** *n* control *m* de velocidad

speedway ['spi:dweɪ] *n* **1.** *no pl* SPORTS carreras *fpl* **2.** (*track*) pista *f* de carreras

speedy ['spi:di] <-ier, -iest> *adj* veloz

speleologist [ˌspi:lɪ'ɒlədʒɪst, *Am:* -'ɑːlə-] *n* espeleólogo, -a

speleology [ˌspi:lɪ'ɒlədʒi, *Am:* -'ɑːlə-] *n no pl* espeleología *f*

spell¹ [spel] *n a. fig* encanto *m*; **to be under a** ~ estar hechizado

spell² [spel] **I.** *n* **1.** (*period*) temporada *f* **2.** (*turn*) turno *m* **II.** *vt Am, Aus* relevar

spell³ [spel] <spelled, spelled *o Brit:* spelt, spelt> **I.** *vt* **1.** (*form using letters*) deletrear; **how do you** ~ **it?** ¿cómo se deletrea? **2.** (*signify*) significar; **this** ~**s trouble** esto significa problemas **II.** *vi* escribir; **to** ~ **well** escribir sin faltas de ortografía

◆**spell out** *vt* deletrear; **to spell sth out for sb** *fig* explicar algo a alguien de un modo sencillo

spellbinding ['spelbaɪndɪŋ] *adj* cautivador(a)

spellbound ['spelbaʊnd] *adj* hechizado, -a; *fig* fascinado, -a

spell checker *n* INFOR corrector *m* ortográfico **speller** *n* **to be a good/poor** ~ tener buena/mala ortografía

spelling *n no pl* ortografía *f*; ~ **mistake** falta *f* de ortografía

spelt [spelt] *pp, pt of* **spell**

spend [spend] <spent, spent> **I.** *vt* **1.** (*money*) gastar **2.** (*time*) pasar; **to** ~ **time** (**doing sth**) dedicar tiempo (a hacer algo) **3.** (*use up*) agotar **II.** *vi* gastar

spending *n no pl* gasto *m*; **public** ~ el gasto público

spending cut *n* FIN recorte *m* presupuestario **spending money** *n* dinero *m* para gastos personales **spending power** *n* ECON poder *m* adquisitivo **spending spree** *n* derroche *m* de dinero; **to go on a** ~ gastar dinero a lo loco

spendthrift ['spendθrɪft] *inf* **I.** *adj* derrochador(a), botado, -a *AmC* **II.** *n* derrochador(a) *m(f)*, botador(a) *m(f)* *AmL*

spent [spent] **I.** *pp, pt of* **spend** **II.** *adj* **1.** (*used*) gastado, -a; **to be a** ~ **force** haber perdido su vigor **2.** *liter* (*very tired*) agotado, -a

sperm [spɜːm, *Am:* spɜːrm] <-(s)> *n* esperma *m o f*

sperm count *n* recuento *m* de espermatozoides **sperm donor** *n* donante *m* de esperma

spermicide ['spɜːmɪsaɪd, *Am:* 'spɜːrmə-] *n* espermicida *m*

sperm whale ['spɜːmweɪl, *Am:* 'spɜːrm-] *n* cachalote *m*

spew [spju:] *vi, vt* vomitar

sphere [sfɪəʳ, *Am:* sfɪr] *n* esfera *f*; ~ **of influence** ámbito *m* de influencia

spherical ['sferɪkl, *Am:* 'sfɪr-] *adj* esférico, -a

spice [spaɪs] **I.** *n* **1.** GASTR especia *f*, olor *m* *Chile* **2.** *no pl* (*excitement*) picante *m*; **to give** ~ **to sth** dar sabor a algo; **the** ~ **of life** la sal de la vida **II.** *vt* condimentar

spick and span [ˌspɪkən'spæn] *adj inf* impecable

spicy ['spaɪsi] <-ier, -iest> *adj* **1.** (*seasoned*) condimentado, -a **2.** (*sensational*) picante

spider ['spaɪdəʳ, *Am:* -də] *n* araña *f*

spider's web *n Brit*, **spiderweb** ['spaɪdə-web, *Am:* -də-] *n Am, Aus* telaraña *f*

spidery *adj* delgado, -a; ~ **handwriting** letra *f* de trazos largos e inseguros

spiel [ʃpiːl] *n inf* rollo *m*

spigot ['spɪgət] *n* 1. (*stopper*) espita *f* 2. *Am* (*tap*) grifo *m*

spike [spaɪk] I. *n* 1. (*pointed object*) pincho *m* 2. (*on shoes*) clavo *m* 3. *pl* (*running shoes*) zapatillas *fpl* con clavos II. *vt* clavar

spiky ['spaɪki] <-ier, -iest> *adj* 1. (*sharp*) puntiagudo, -a; (*hair*) de punta 2. (*irritable*) susceptible

spill [spɪl] I. *n* 1. (*act of spilling*) derrame *m;* **petrol** ~ vertido *m* de petróleo 2. *inf* (*fall*) caída *f;* **to have a** ~ tener un accidente II. *vt* <spilt, spilt *o Am, Aus:* spilled, spilled> derramar III. *vi* derramarse

♦**spill over** *vi* derramarse

spillage ['spɪlɪdʒ] *n* derrame *m*

spilt [spɪlt] *pp, pt of* **spill**

spin [spɪn] I. *n* 1. (*rotation*) vuelta *f* 2. (*in washing machine*) revolución *f* 3. (*drive*) **to go for a** ~ dar un paseo (en coche) II. *vi* <spun *Brit:* span, spun> 1. (*rotate*) girar 2. (*make thread*) hilar III. *vt* <spun *Brit:* span, spun> 1. (*rotate*) girar; (*clothes*) centrifugar; **to** ~ **a ball** dar efecto a una pelota; **to** ~ **a coin for sth** echar algo a cara o cruz 2. (*make thread out of*) hilar 3. (*tell: story, tale*) contar

♦**spin out** *vt* prolongar

♦**spin round** *vi* girar

spina bifida [ˌspaɪnəˈbɪfɪdə] *n no pl* MED espina *f* bífida

spinach ['spɪnɪtʃ] *n no pl* BOT espinaca *f;* GASTR espinacas *fpl*

spinal ['spaɪnəl] *adj* espinal

spinal column *n* columna *f* vertebral **spinal cord** *n* médula *f* espinal

spindle ['spɪndl] *n* huso *m*

spindly <-ier, -iest> *adj* larguirucho, -a

spin doctor *n* POL asesor(a) *m(f)*

spin-dry [ˌspɪnˈdraɪ, *Am:* ˈspɪndraɪ] *vt* centrifugar

spin-dryer *n* secador *m* centrífugo

spine [spaɪn] *n* 1. (*spinal column*) columna *f* vertebral 2. (*spike*) púa *f* 3. BOT espina *f* 4. (*of book*) lomo *m*

spine-chilling ['spaɪnˌtʃɪlɪŋ] *adj* escalofriante

spineless ['spaɪnləs] *adj* (*weak*) blando, -a

spinner *n* 1. (*person*) hilandero, -a *m, f* 2. (*machine*) máquina *f* de hilar

spinney ['spɪni] *n Brit* bosquecillo *m*

spinning *n* rotación *f*

spinning top *n* peonza *f* **spinning wheel** *n* rueca *f*

spin-off ['spɪnɒf, *Am:* -ɑːf] *n* 1. (*by-product*) subproducto *m* 2. (*consequence*) efecto *m* indirecto

spinster ['spɪnstə^r, *Am:* -stə] *n a. pej* solterona *f*

spiny ['spaɪni] <-ier, -iest> *adj a. fig* espinoso, -a

spiny lobster *n* langosta *f*

spiral ['spaɪərəl, *Am:* ˈspaɪ-] I. *n* espiral *f* II. *adj* espiral; ~ **staircase** escalera *f* de caracol III. *vi* <*Brit:* -ll-, *Am:* -l-> 1. (*travel in a spiral*) dar vueltas en espiral; **to** ~ **downwards** bajar en espiral 2. (*increase*) aumentar

spire ['spaɪə^r, *Am:* -ə] *n* ARCHIT aguja *f*

spirit ['spɪrɪt] *n* 1. (*soul*) espíritu *m* 2. (*ghost*) espíritu *m* 3. *pl* (*mood*) ánimo *mpl;* **to be in high/low** ~s estar animado/desanimado 4. (*character*) carácter *m* 5. (*alcoholic drink*) licor *m* 6. (*attitude or principle*) **the** ~ **of the age** el espíritu de la época; **that's the** ~! ¡muy bien!

♦**spirit away** *vt* hacer desaparecer

spirited *adj* (*energetic*) enérgico, -a; (*discussion*) animado, -a; (*person*) animoso, -a, entrador(a) *AmS*

spiritless ['spɪrɪtləs] *adj pej* 1. (*downhearted*) desanimado, -a 2. (*irresolute*) indeciso, -a

spirit-level *n* nivel *m* de burbuja

spiritual ['spɪrɪtʃuəl] I. *adj* espiritual II. *n* MUS espiritual *m* negro

spiritualism ['spɪrɪtʃuəlɪzəm] *n no pl* espiritismo *m*

spit[1] [spɪt] *n* 1. GASTR asador *m* 2. (*sandbar*) banco *m* de arena

spit[2] [spɪt] I. *n inf* saliva *f* II. *vi* <spat, spat> 1. (*expel saliva*) escupir; **it is** ~**ting** (**with rain**) *inf* caen cuatro gotas 2. (*crackle*) chisporrotear III. *vt* escupir

♦**spit out** *vt* 1. (*expel from mouth*) escupir 2. (*say angrily*) soltar; **to spit it out** *inf* desembuchar

spite [spaɪt] I. *n no pl* rencor *m;* **to do sth from** ~ hacer algo por despecho; **in** ~ **of a** pesar de; **in** ~ **of everyone** a despecho de todos; **in** ~ **of the fact that he is rich** a pesar (del hecho) de que sea rico III. *vt* fastidiar

spiteful ['spaɪtfəl] *adj pej* rencoroso, -a

spitting image *n* vivo *m* retrato

spittle ['spɪtl, *Am:* ˈspɪt̪-] *n* escupitajo *m*, desgarro *m AmL*

spittoon [sprˈtuːn] *n* escupidera *f*, salivadera *f Arg, Urug*

splash [splæʃ] I. *n* 1. (*sound*) chapoteo *m* 2. (*small drops*) salpicadura *f;* **a** ~ **of colour** una mancha de color ►**to make a** ~ causar sensación II. *vt* salpicar; **to** ~ **across the front page** poner algo en primera plana III. *vi* salpicar

♦**splash down** *vi* amerizar

♦**splash out** *Aus, Brit* I. *vi inf* derrochar el dinero; **to** ~ **on sth/sb** gastarse un dineral en algo/alguien II. *vt inf* derrochar

splashboard ['splæʃbɔːd, *Am:* -bɔːrd] *n* (*on vehicle*) guardabarros *m inv;* (*on boat, in kitchen*) alero *m*

splashdown ['splæʃdaʊn] *n* amerizaje *m*

splat [splæt] *n no pl, inf* plaf *m*

splatter ['splætə^r, Am: 'splæt̬ə^r] vi, vt salpicar

splay [spleɪ] I. vt extender II. vi extenderse

spleen [spli:n] n 1. ANAT bazo m 2. no pl, Aus, Brit (anger) mal humor m; to vent one's ~ descargar la rabia de uno

splendid ['splendɪd] adj espléndido, -a

splendiferous [splen'dɪfərəs] adj inf espléndido, -a

splendo(u)r ['splendə^r, Am: -də^r] n 1. no pl (grandness) esplendor m 2. pl (beautiful things) maravillas fpl

splice [splaɪs] vt (join) juntar; to get ~d inf pasar por la vicaría

splint [splɪnt] I. n tablilla f II. vt entablillar

splinter ['splɪntə^r, Am: -t̬ə^r] I. n astilla f II. vi astillarse

splinter group n POL grupo m disidente

split [splɪt] I. n 1. (crack) grieta 2. (in clothes) desgarrón 3. (division) división f II. vt <split, split> 1. (divide) dividir; (atom) desintegrar; to ~ sth between two people repartir algo entre dos personas 2. (crack) agrietar; to ~ one's head open abrirse la cabeza ▶to ~ one's sides laughing partirse de risa III. vi <split, split> 1. (divide) dividirse 2. (form cracks) agrietarse 3. inf (leave) largarse

◆**split off** I. vt separar II. vi separarse

◆**split up** I. vt partir II. vi to ~ with sb separarse de alguien

split infinitive n LING infinitivo con un complemento adverbial intercalado entre la partícula 'to' y el verbo **split-level** adj de varios niveles **split pea** n guisante m seco **split personality** n PSYCH doble personalidad f **split-screen** n pantalla f dividida

splitting headache n inf dolor m de cabeza atroz

split-up ['splɪtʌp] n ruptura m

splodge [splɒdʒ, Am: splɑ:dʒ] n, **splotch** [splɒtʃ, Am: splɑ:tʃ] n Brit, inf mancha f

splurge [splɜ:dʒ, Am: splɜ:rdʒ] inf I. vt derrochar II. vi derrochar dinero III. n derroche m

splutter ['splʌtə^r, Am: 'splʌt̬ə^r] I. vi (person) farfullar; (candle, engine) chisporrotear II. n (of person) farfulla f; (of candle, engine) chisporroteo m

spoil [spɔɪl] I. n 1. (debris) escombros mpl 2. pl (profits) botín m II. vt <spoilt, spoilt Am: spoiled, spoiled> 1. (ruin) estropear, salar AmL; (party) aguar 2. (child) mimar, engreír AmL, papachar Méx III. vi <spoilt, spoilt Am: spoiled, spoiled> estropearse

spoiler n alerón m

spoilsport ['spɔɪlspɔ:t, Am: -spɔ:rt] n inf aguafiestas mf inv

spoilt I. pp, pt of **spoil** II. adj mimado, -a, engreído, -a AmL

spoke[1] [spəʊk, Am: spoʊk] pt of **speak**

spoke[2] [spəʊk, Am: spoʊk] n (of wheel) radio m; to put a ~ in sb's wheel fig poner

trabas a alguien

spoken pp of **speak**

spokesman ['spəʊksmən, Am: 'spoʊks-] n portavoz m, vocero m AmL

spokesperson ['spəʊks,pɜ:sən, Am: 'spoʊks,pɜ:r-] n portavoz mf, vocero, -a m, f AmL

spokeswoman ['spəʊks,wʊmən, Am: 'spoʊks-] n portavoz f, vocera f AmL

sponge [spʌndʒ] I. n 1. (cloth) esponja f 2. GASTR bizcocho m ▶to throw in the ~ tirar la toalla II. vt limpiar con una esponja

◆**sponge down** vt, **sponge off** vt limpiar con una esponja

◆**sponge on** vt inf vivir a costa de

sponge bag n Aus, Brit neceser m **sponge bath** n lavado m con esponja **sponge cake** n bizcocho m

sponger n pej gorrón, -ona m, f, sablero, -a m, f Chile

spongy ['spʌndʒi] <-ier, -iest> adj esponjoso, -a

sponsor ['spɒntsə^r, Am: 'spɑ:ntsə^r] I. vt patrocinar II. n patrocinador(a) m(f), propiciador(a) m(f) AmL

sponsorship n no pl patrocinio m

spontaneity ['spɒntə'neɪəti, Am: ,spɑ:ntə'neɪət̬i] n no pl espontaneidad f

spontaneous [spɒn'teɪniəs, Am: spɑ:n'-] adj espontáneo, -a

spoof [spu:f] n parodia f; to do a ~ on sth parodiar algo

spook [spu:k] I. n 1. inf (ghost) espectro m 2. Am (spy) espía mf II. vt Am asustar

spooky ['spu:ki] <-ier, -iest> adj inf espectral

spool [spu:l] n (of thread) bobina f; (of film) carrete m

spoon [spu:n] I. n 1. (utensil) cuchara f 2. (amount) cucharada f II. vt servir con cuchara

spoonbill ['spu:nbɪl] n espátula f

spoon-feed ['spu:nfi:d] vt 1. (feed) dar de comer con cuchara 2. pej to ~ sb dar todo hecho a alguien

spoonful ['spu:nfʊl] <-s o spoonsful> n cucharada f

sporadic [spə'rædɪk] adj esporádico, -a

spore [spɔ:^r, Am: spɔ:r] n espora f

sporran ['spɒrən, Am: 'spɔ:r-] n Scot: bolsa que llevan los escoceses sobre la falda

sport [spɔ:t, Am: spɔ:rt] I. n 1. (activity) deporte m 2. inf (person) to be a (good) ~ ser buena gente II. vt llevar

sporting adj deportivo, -a, esportivo, -a AmL

sports car n coche m deportivo

sportscast ['spɔ:ts,kɑ:st, Am: 'spɔ:rtskæst] n Am programa m deportivo

sportscaster n Am locutor(a) m(f) deportivo, -a

sports day n día m de competiciones deportivas (en un colegio) **sports field** n campo m de deportes **sports jacket** n chaqueta f de sport

sportsman ['spɔːtsmən, *Am:* 'spɔːrts-] *n* deportista *m*

sportsmanlike ['spɔːtsmənlaɪk, *Am:* 'spɔːrts-] *adj* de espíritu deportivo

sportsmanship *n no pl* deportividad *f*

sports page *n* página *f* de deportes **sportswear** *n no pl* ropa *f* de deporte

sportswoman ['spɔːtsˌwʊmən, *Am:* 'spɔːrts-] *n* deportista *f*

sports writer *n* cronista *mf* deportivo, -a

sporty ['spɔːti, *Am:* 'spɔːrti] <-ier, -iest> *adj* deportivo, -a

spot [spɒt, *Am:* spɑːt] I. *n* 1. (*mark*) mancha *f* 2. (*pattern*) lunar *m* 3. *Brit* (*on skin*) grano *m* 4. *Brit* (*little bit*) poquito *m*; **a ~ of rain** una gota de lluvia; **to be in a ~ of trouble** tener cierta dificultad 5. (*place*) lugar *m*; **on the ~** (*at the very place*) in situ; (*at once*) en el acto 6. (*part of TV, radio show*) espacio *m* 7. *inf* foco *m* ▶ **to really hit the ~** venir de perlas; **to have a soft ~ for sb** tener debilidad por alguien; **to knock (the) ~s off sb/sth** dar ciento y raya a alguien/algo; **to put sb on the ~** poner a alguien en un aprieto II. *vi* <-tt-> *impers, Brit* **it's ~ting (with rain)** están cayendo cuatro gotas III. <-tt-> *vt* 1. (*see*) divisar 2. (*speckle*) manchar

spot cash *n* dinero *m* contante **spot check** *n* control *m* al azar

spotless ['spɒtləs, *Am:* 'spɑːt-] *adj* 1. (*very clean*) inmaculado, -a 2. (*unblemished*) sin manchas

spotlight ['spɒtlaɪt, *Am:* 'spɑːt-] I. *n* foco *m* ▶ **to turn the ~ on sb/sth** dejar a alguien/algo en evidencia II. <spotlighted, spotlighted *o* spotlit, spotlit> *vt* iluminar

spot market *n* FIN mercado *m* al contado

spot-on [spɒt'ɒn, *Am:* spɑːt'ɑːn] *adj Aus, Brit, inf* 1. (*exact*) exacto, -a 2. (*exactly on target*) acertado, -a

spot price *n* precio *m* al contado

spotted *adj* manchado, -a; **a ~ dress** un vestido de lunares

spotter *n* SPORTS, AVIAT observador(a) *m(f)*

spotty ['spɒti, *Am:* 'spɑːti] <-ier, -iest> *adj* 1. *Aus, Brit* (*having blemished skin*) con granos 2. *Am, Aus* (*inconsistent*) irregular

spouse [spaʊz] *n form* cónyuge *mf*

spout [spaʊt] I. *n* 1. (*of kettle*) pitorro *m*; (*of jar*) pico *m*; (*tube*) caño *m* 2. (*jet*) chorro *m* ▶ **to be up the ~** *Aus, Brit, inf* estar en una situación desesperada II. *vt* 1. (*send out: flames, water*) echar 2. *pej* **to ~ sth** perorar sobre algo; **to ~ facts and figures** soltar una retahíla de datos y cifras III. *vi* 1. *pej* (*speechify*) perorar 2. (*gush*) chorrear

sprain [spreɪn] I. *vt* torcer II. *n* torcedura *f*

sprang [spræŋ] *vi, vt pt of* **spring**

sprat [spræt] *n* espadín *m*

sprawl [sprɔːl, *Am:* sprɑːl] *pej* I. *vi* 1. (*spread out*) tumbarse; **to send sb ~ing** derribar a alguien 2. (*town*) extenderse II. *n*

(*of town*) extensión *f*

sprawling *adj pej* 1. (*town*) de crecimiento desordenado 2. (*handwriting*) irregular

spray¹ [spreɪ] I. *n* 1. (*mist*) rocío *m* 2. (*device*) atomizador *m* II. *vt* (*cover in a spray*) rociar III. *vi* (*gush*) chorrear

spray² [spreɪ] *n* rama *f*; **a ~ of flowers** un ramo de flores

spray gun *n* pistola *f* pulverizadora

spread [spred] I. *n* 1. (*act of spreading*) propagación *f* 2. (*range*) gama *f* 3. (*article*) reportaje *m* a toda página 4. GASTR pasta *f* 5. *Am* (*ranch*) hacienda *f*, rancho *m* AmL 6. *Aus, Brit, inf* (*meal*) comilona *f* II. <spread, spread> *vi* (*liquid*) extenderse; (*disease*) propagarse; (*news*) difundirse III. <spread, spread> *vt* 1. (*disease*) propagar; (*news*) difundir 2. (*butter*) untar 3. (*payments, work*) distribuir 4. (*unfold: map, blanket*) extender

spread-eagled [ˌspred'iːgld, *Am:* 'spredˌiː-] *adj* despatarrado, -a

spreadsheet ['spredʃiːt] *n* INFOR hoja *f* de cálculo

spree [spriː] *n* parranda *f*, tambarria *f* AmC; **to go (out) on a drinking ~** ir de juerga

sprig [sprɪg] *n* ramita *f*

sprightly ['spraɪtli] <-ier, -iest> *adj* vivaz

spring [sprɪŋ] I. *n* 1. (*season*) primavera *f* 2. (*jump*) salto *m* 3. (*metal coil*) muelle *m*; (*in watch, toy*) resorte *m* 4. (*elasticity*) elasticidad *f* 5. (*source of water*) manantial *m*, yurro *m* CRi II. <sprang, sprung> *vi* saltar; **to ~ to one's feet** levantarse de un salto; **to ~ shut/open** cerrarse/abrirse de golpe III. <sprang, sprung> *vt* **to ~ sth on sb** soltar algo a alguien

◆ **spring back** *vi* saltar para atrás

spring balance *n* peso *m* de muelle

springboard ['sprɪŋbɔːd, *Am:* -bɔːrd] *n* trampolín *m*

spring-clean [ˌsprɪŋ'kliːn] *vt* limpiar a fondo **spring-cleaning** *n* limpieza *f* a fondo

spring onion *n* Aus, Brit cebolleta *f*

spring roll *n* rollito *m* de primavera

springtime ['sprɪŋtaɪm] *n no pl* primavera *f*

springy ['sprɪŋi] <-ier, -iest> *adj* elástico, -a

sprinkle ['sprɪŋkl] I. *vt* salpicar II. *n* salpicadura *f*

sprinkler ['sprɪŋklər, *Am:* -ə-] *n* aspersor *m*

sprinkling ['sprɪŋklɪŋ] *n* **a ~ of sth** unas gotas de algo

sprint [sprɪnt] SPORTS I. *vi* esprintar II. *n* 1. (*race*) esprint *m* 2. *Aus, Brit* (*burst of speed*) carrera *f* corta

sprinter ['sprɪntər, *Am:* -t̬ə-] *n* velocista *mf*

sprite [spraɪt] *n liter* duende *m*

sprocket ['sprɒkɪt, *Am:* 'sprɑːkɪt] *n*, **sprocket wheel** *n* rueda *f* de espigas

sprog [sprɒg, *Am:* sprɑːg] *n Aus, Brit, inf* bebé *m*

sprout [spraʊt] I. *n* 1. (*of plant*) brote *m* 2. *pl, Brit* (*brussels sprout*) coles *mpl* de Bruselas **II.** *vi* (*begin to grow*) brotar **III.** *vt* (*grow: leaves*) echar

♦**sprout up** *vi* (*plant, child*) crecer rapidamente; (*building*) aparecer

spruce¹ [spruːs] *n* BOT picea *f*

spruce² [spruːs] *adj* aseado, -a

♦**spruce up** *vt* to spruce oneself up arreglarse

sprung [sprʌŋ] **I.** *adj Brit* de muelles **II.** *pp, Am: pt of* **spring**

spry [spraɪ] *adj* ágil

spud [spʌd] *n Brit, inf* patata *f*, papa *f AmL*

spun [spʌn] *pp, pt of* **spin**

spunk [spʌŋk] *n inf* **1.** *no pl* (*bravery*) agallas *fpl* **2.** *Brit, vulg* (*semen*) leche *f*

spur [spɜːʳ, *Am:* spɜːr] **I.**<-rr-> *vt* (*horse*) espolear, talonear *Arg; fig* estimular **II.** *n* **1.** (*device*) espuela *f* **2.** GEO espolón *m* **3.** (*encouragement*) estímulo *m* ►on the ~ of the **moment** *inf* sin pensarlo

spurious [ˈspjʊərɪəs, *Am:* ˈspjʊrɪ-] *adj* falso, -a

spurn [spɜːn, *Am:* spɜːrn] *vt form* desdeñar

spurt [spɜːt, *Am:* spɜːrt] **I.** *n* esfuerzo *m* supremo; **to put on a** ~ acelerar **II.** *vt* (*liquid*) echar **III.** *vi* **1.** *Am* (*accelerate*) acelerar **2.** (*gush*) salir a chorros

sputter [ˈspʌtəʳ, *Am:* ˈspʌt̬ɚ] **I.** *vi* (*person*) farfullar; (*candle, engine*) chisporrotear **II.** *n* (*of person*) farfulla *m;* (*of candle, engine*) chisporroteo *m*

sputum [ˈspjuːtəm, *Am:* -t̬əm] *n no pl* esputo *m*

spy [spaɪ] **I.** *n* espía *mf* **II.** *vi* espiar; **to** ~ **on sb** espiar a alguien **III.** *vt* divisar

spyglass [ˈspaɪɡlɑːs, *Am:* -ɡlæs] *n* catalejo *m*

spyhole [ˈspaɪhəʊl, *Am:* -hoʊl] *n Aus, Brit* mirilla *f*

spy satellite *n* satélite *m* espía

Sq. *abbr of* **square** Pza.

squabble [ˈskwɒbl, *Am:* ˈskwɑːbl] **I.** *n* riña *f* **II.** *vi* reñir

squad [skwɒd, *Am:* skwɑːd] *n* **1.** (*group*) pelotón *m;* (*of police*) brigada *f;* **anti-terrorist** ~ brigada antiterrorista **2.** (*sports team*) equipo *m*

squad car *n Am, Brit* coche-patrulla *m*

squaddie [ˈskwɒdi, *Am:* ˈskwɑːdi] *n Brit, inf* soldado *m* raso

squadron [ˈskwɒdrən, *Am:* ˈskwɑːdrən] *n* escuadrón *m*

squalid [ˈskwɒlɪd, *Am:* ˈskwɑːlɪd] *adj* **1.** *pej* (*dirty*) asqueroso, -a **2.** (*sordid*) sórdido, -a

squall [skwɔːl] **I.** *n* ráfaga *f* **II.** *vi* chillar

squally [ˈskwɔːli] *adj* turbulento, -a

squalor [ˈskwɒləʳ, *Am:* ˈskwɑːlɚ] *n no pl* miseria *f*

squander [ˈskwɒndəʳ, *Am:* ˈskwɑːndɚ] *vt* malgastar, botar *AmL*, fundir *AmL;* **to** ~ **an opportunity** desperdiciar una oportunidad

square [skweəʳ, *Am:* skwer] **I.** *n* **1.** (*shape*) cuadrado *m* **2.** (*in town*) plaza *f* **3.** (*on chess-*

board) casilla *f* **4.** *Am, Aus* (*tool*) escuadra *f* ►**to go back to** ~ **one** volver al punto de partida **II.** *adj* **1.** (*square-shaped*) cuadrado, -a; **four** ~ **metres** cuatro metros cuadrados **2.** *inf* (*level*) igual; **to be** (**all**) ~ SPORTS estar (todos) empatados **3.** *inf* (*unfashionable*) carca **III.** *adv* **1.** (*exactly*) exactamente **2.** MAT en ángulo recto; ~ **to** [*o* **with**] **the street** en ángulo recto con la calle **IV.** *vt* **1.** (*align*) cuadrar **2.** *inf* (*settle*) acomodar; **I can't** ~ **this with my principles** no puedo encajar esto con mis principios **3.** MAT elevar al cuadrado

♦**square up** *vi* to ~ **with sb** ajustar cuentas con alguien

square bracket *n* corchete *m* **square dance** *n* baile *m* de figuras

---

Square dance es el nombre que recibe un popular baile americano. Grupos de cuatro parejas bailan en círculo, en cuadrado o formando dos líneas. Todos ellos llevan a cabo los movimientos que les va indicando un **caller**. El **caller** puede dar las indicaciones cantando o hablando. Estos bailarines suelen bailar acompañados de músicos con violines, bajos o guitarras.

---

squarely *adv* directamente

square root *n* raíz *f* cuadrada

squash¹ [skwɒʃ, *Am:* skwɑːʃ] *n Am* (*vegetable*) calabaza *f*

squash² [skwɒʃ, *Am:* skwɑːʃ] **I.** *n* **1.** (*dense pack*) apiñamiento *m* **2.** *no pl* SPORTS squash *m* **3.** *Aus, Brit* (*drink*) zumo *m* **II.** *vt* aplastar

squash court *n* pista *f* de squash **squash racket** *n Brit*, **squash racquet** *n Am, Aus* raqueta *f* de squash

squashy [ˈskwɒʃi, *Am:* ˈskwɑːʃi] <-ier, -iest> *adj* blando, -a

squat [skwɒt, *Am:* skwɑːt] **I.**<-tt-> *vi* **1.** (*crouch down*) agacharse, ñangotarse *PRico, RDom* **2.** (*in property*) ocupar una vivienda sin permiso **II.** *n* (*house*) casa *f* ocupada **III.**<-tt-> *adj* (*person*) rechoncho, -a

squatter [ˈskwɒtəʳ, *Am:* ˈskwɑːt̬ɚ] *n* ocupa *mf*

squaw [skwɔː, *Am:* skwɑː] *n a. pej: mujer india norteamericana*

squawk [skwɔːk, *Am:* skwɑːk] **I.** *vi* graznar **II.** *n* (*sharp cry*) graznido *m*

squeak [skwiːk] **I.** *n* chirrido *m* **II.** *vi* chirriar

squeaky [ˈskwiːki] <-ier, -iest> *adj* chirriante

squeaky-clean [ˌskwiːkiˈkliːn] *adj* relimpio, -a

squeal [skwiːl] **I.** *n* chillido *m* **II.** *vi* (*person, animal*) chillar; (*brakes, car*) chirriar

squeamish [ˈskwiːmɪʃ] *adj* remilgado, -a; **to feel** ~ sentir náuseas

squeegee [ˌskwiːˈdʒiː, *Am:* ˈskwiːdʒiː] *n* escobilla *f* de goma

squeeze [skwiːz] **I.** *n* **1.** (*pressing action*) estrujón *m* **2.** ECON (*limit*) restricción *f* **II.** *vt*

1. (*press together*) estrujar; **freshly ~d orange juice** zumo de naranja recién exprimido **2.** (*force*) presionar; **to ~ sth out of sb** sacarle algo a alguien

squeezer ['skwi:zə^r, *Am:* -ə·] *n* exprimidor *m*

squelch [skwelt∫] **I.** *vi* chapotear **II.** *vt Am* aplastar **III.** *n* chapoteo *m*

squib [skwɪb] *n* sátira *f* ▶**a damp ~** un fiasco

squid [skwɪd] <-(s)> *n* calamar *m*

squiggle ['skwɪgl] *n* garabato *m*

squint [skwɪnt] **I.** *vi* **1.** (*be cross-eyed*) bizquear **2.** (*look from corner of eye*) mirar de reojo **II.** *n* **1.** (*eye condition*) estrabismo *m*, bizquera *f AmL* **2.** (*quick look*) mirada *f* furtiva

squire ['skwaɪə^r, *Am:* 'skwaɪə·] *n* **1.** HIST escudero *m* **2.** *Brit* (*landowner*) propietario *m*

squirm [skwɜ:m, *Am:* skwɜ:rm] *vi* retorcerse; **to ~ with embarrassment** avergonzarse mucho

squirrel ['skwɪrəl, *Am:* 'skwɜ:r-] *n* ardilla *f*

squirt [skwɜ:t, *Am:* skwɜ:rt] **I.** *vt* (*liquid*) echar un chorro de; **to ~ sb with sth** echar un chorro de algo a alguien **II.** *vi* salir a chorros **III.** *n* **1.** (*small quantity*) chorrito *m* **2.** *pej* (*person*) farsante *mf*

Sr *n abbr of* **senior** padre; **George Bush, Sr** George Bush, padre

Sri Lanka [ˌsri:'læŋkə, *Am:* -'lɑ:ŋ-] *n* Sri Lanka *m*

Sri Lankan [ˌsri:'læŋkən, *Am:* -'lɑ:ŋ-] **I.** *adj* esrilanqués, -esa **II.** *n* esrilanqués, -esa *m, f*

SSW [ˌeses'dʌblju:] *abbr of* **south-south-west** SSO

st. *n abbr of* **stone** unidad de peso equivalente a 6,35 kg

St *n* **1.** *abbr of* **saint** (*man*) S., Sto.; (*woman*) Sta.; **~ Thomas** Sto. Tomás **2.** *abbr of* **street** c/

stab [stæb] **I.** <-bb-> *vt* apuñalar, achurar *CSur*, carnear *Méx;* **to ~ sb to death** matar a alguien de una puñalada; **to ~ sb in the back** *fig* dar a alguien una puñalada trapera **II.** <-bb-> *vi* señalar **III.** *n* **1.** (*blow*) puñalada *f* **2.** (*sudden pain*) punzada *f* **3.** (*attempt*) **to have a ~ at** (**doing**) **sth** intentar (hacer) algo

stabbing **I.** *n* apuñalamiento *m* **II.** *adj* punzante

stability [stə'bɪləti, *Am:* -ţi] *n no pl* estabilidad *f*

stabilization [ˌsteɪbəlaɪ'zeɪʃən, *Am:* -blɪ'-] *n no pl* estabilización *f*

stabilize ['steɪbəlaɪz] **I.** *vt* estabilizar **II.** *vi* estabilizarse

stabilizer ['steɪbəlaɪzə^r, *Am:* -ə·] *n* **1.** (*on ship, bicycle*) estabilizador *m* **2.** CHEM estabilizante *m*

stable[1] ['steɪbl] *adj* **1.** *a.* ECON estable **2.** (*structure*) firme **3.** MED estacionario, -a

stable[2] ['steɪbl] **I.** *n* cuadra *f* **II.** *vt* guardar en la cuadra

stable lad *n Brit* mozo *m* de cuadra

stack [stæk] **I.** *vt* **1.** (*arrange in a pile*) apilar **2.** (*fill: shelves*) llenar ▶**the cards are ~ed**

against us la suerte está en contra de nosotros **II.** *n* **1.** (*pile*) pila *f* **2.** *inf* (*large amount*) montón *m*, ponchada *f CSur* **3.** *pl* (*bookcase*) estantería *f*

stadium ['steɪdɪəm] <-s *o* -dia> *n* estadio *m*

staff [stɑ:f, *Am:* stæf] **I.** *n* **1.** (*employees*) personal *m*, elenco *m AmL;* **the editorial ~** la redacción **2.** SCHOOL, UNIV profesorado *m* **3.** MIL Estado *m* Mayor **4.** (*stick*) bastón *m;* **~ of office** bastón de mando **5.** (*flagpole*) asta *f* **6.** <staves> *Am* MUS pentagrama *m* **II.** *vt* dotar de personal

staff association *n* asociación *f* de empleados **staff nurse** *n Brit* (*regular nurse*) enfermero, -a *m, f* jefe **staff officer** *n* oficial *m* del Estado Mayor **staffroom** *n* sala *f* de profesores

stag [stæg] *n* ZOOL ciervo *m*

stag beetle *n* ciervo *m* volante

stage [steɪdʒ] **I.** *n* **1.** (*period*) etapa *f*, pascana *f AmS;* **to do sth in ~s** hacer algo por etapas **2.** THEAT escena *f;* **the ~** el teatro; **to be on the ~** ser actor/actriz; **to go on the ~** hacerse actor/actriz; **to hold the ~** tener al público pendiente de su palabra **II.** *vt* **1.** (*produce on stage*) representar **2.** (*organize*) organizar

stagecoach ['steɪdʒkəʊtʃ, *Am:* -koʊtʃ] *n* diligencia *f*

stage direction *n* acotación *f* **stage door** *n* entrada *f* de artistas **stage fright** *n no pl* pánico *m* escénico

stagehand ['steɪdʒhænd] *n* THEAT tramoyista *mf*

stage-manage [ˌsteɪdʒ'mænɪdʒ, *Am:* 'steɪdʒˌmæn-] *vt* **1.** THEAT dirigir la tramoya de **2.** *fig* orquestar **stage manager** *n* THEAT director(a) *m(f)* de escena; CINE director(a) *m(f)* de producción **stage name** *n* nombre *m* artístico

stager ['steɪdʒə^r, *Am:* -dʒə·] *n* **to be an old ~** ser perro viejo

stage whisper *n* THEAT aparte *m*

stagflation [ˌstæg'fleɪʃən] *n no pl* ECON estagflación *f*

stagger ['stægə^r, *Am:* -ə·] **I.** *vi* tambalearse **II.** *vt* **1.** (*amaze*) asombrar **2.** (*work, payments*) escalonar **III.** *n* tambaleo *m*

staggering *adj* (*amazing*) sorprendente

staging ['steɪdʒɪŋ] *n* THEAT puesta *f* en escena

stagnant ['stægnənt] *adj a. fig* estancado, -a

stagnate [stæg'neɪt, *Am:* 'stægneɪt] *vi* estancarse

stagnation [stæg'neɪʃən] *n no pl* estancamiento *m*

stag night *n*, **stag party** *n Brit* despedida *f* de soltero

stagy ['steɪdʒi] *adj pej* teatral

staid [steɪd] *adj* serio, -a

stain [steɪn] **I.** *vt* **1.** (*mark*) manchar **2.** (*dye*) teñir **II.** *vi* (*become marked*) mancharse **III.** *n* **1.** (*mark*) mancha *f;* **blood/grease/red wine**

S

~ mancha *f* de sangre/grasa/vino tinto
2. (*dye*) tinte *m*

stained *adj* (*marked*) manchado, -a

stained glass *n* vidrio *m* de colores **stained glass window** *n* vidriera *f*

stainless ['steɪnləs] *adj* (*immaculate*) inmaculado, -a; (*that cannot be stained*) que no se mancha

stainless steel *n* acero *m* inoxidable

stain remover *n* quitamanchas *m inv*

stair [steə', *Am:* ster] *n* **1.** (*rung*) peldaño *m* **2.** *pl* (*set of steps*) escalera *f*

staircase ['steəkeɪs, *Am:* 'ster-] *n*, **stairway** ['steəweɪ, *Am:* 'ster-] *n* escalera *f*

stairwell ['steəwel, *Am:* 'ster-] *n* hueco *m* de la escalera

stake [steɪk] I. *n* **1.** (*stick*) estaca *f;* **to be burnt at the ~** HIST morir en la hoguera **2.** (*share*) participación *f;* **to have a ~ in** sth tener interés en algo **3.** (*bet*) apuesta *f;* **to play for high ~s** arriesgar mucho; **to be at ~** estar en juego II. *vt* **1.** (*mark with stakes*) marcar con estacas **2.** (*bet*) apostar; **to ~ one's life on** sth poner la mano en el fuego por algo; **to ~ a claim to** sth reivindicar algo

♦**stake out** *vt Am, inf* poner bajo vigilancia

stakeholder ['steɪk,həʊldə', *Am:* -,hoʊldə-] *n* tenedor(a) *m(f)* de apuestas

stalactite ['stæləktaɪt, *Am:* stə'læk-] *n* estalactita *f*

stalagmite ['stæləgmaɪt] *n* estalagmita *f*

stale [steɪl] *adj* **1.** (*not fresh*) pasado, -a; (*bread*) duro, -a; (*air*) viciado, -a; (*joke*) viejo, -a **2.** (*tired*) cansado, -a

stalemate ['steɪlmeɪt] *n* **1.** (*deadlock*) punto *m* muerto **2.** GAMES tablas *fpl*

stalk¹ [stɔ:k] *n* (*of plant*) tallo *m;* **her eyes were out on ~s** *Brit, Aus* se le salían los ojos de las órbitas

stalk² [stɔ:k] I. *vt* (*follow*) acechar II. *vi* **to ~ off** marcharse airadamente

stalker *n persona que sigue obsesivamente a otra*

stalking horse ['stɔ:kɪŋ,hɔ:s, *Am:* -,hɔ:rs] *n* POL *candidato que se presenta para favorecer a otro*

stall [stɔ:l] I. *n* **1.** (*for animal*) establo *m* **2.** *Brit,* CINE, THEAT the ~s el patio de butacas **3.** (*in market*) puesto *m,* tarantín *m Ven* II. *vi* **1.** (*stop running: engine, vehicle*) calarse **2.** *fig, inf* (*delay*) ir con rodeos III. *vt* **1.** (*engine, vehicle*) calar *fig, inf* (*keep waiting*) retener

stallholder ['stɔ:l,həʊldə', *Am:* -,hoʊldə-] *n* dueño, -a *m, f* de un puesto

stallion ['stælɪən, *Am:* -jən] *n* semental *m,* padrón *m AmL,* padrote *m AmC, Méx*

stalwart ['stɔ:lwət, *Am:* -wət] *form* I. *adj* **1.** (*strong*) fornido, -a **2.** (*loyal*) leal II. *n* partidario, -a *m, f* leal

stamen ['steɪmen] <-s *o* -mina> *n* estambre *m*

stamina ['stæmɪnə, *Am:* -ənə] *n no pl* resis-

tencia *f*

stammer ['stæmə', *Am:* -ə-] I. *vi* tartamudear II. *vt* decir tartamudeando III. *n* tartamudeo *m*

stammerer ['stæmərə', *Am:* -ə-ə-] *n* tartamudo, -a *m, f*

stamp [stæmp] I. *n* **1.** (*postage stamp*) sello *m,* estampilla *f AmL;* (*device*) tampón *m;* (*mark*) sello *m* **2.** (*characteristic quality*) impronta *f* **3.** (*with foot*) patada *f* II. *vt* **1.** (*place postage stamp on*) pegar un sello en **2.** (*impress a mark on*) estampar **3. to ~ one's foot** patear III. *vi* patalear

stamp album *n* álbum *m* de sellos **stamp collector** *n* coleccionista *mf* de sellos

stamp duty *n* LAW impuesto *m* del timbre

stampede [stæm'pi:d] I. *n* (*of animals*) estampida *f;* (*of people*) desbandada *f* II. *vi* huir en desbandada III. *vt* **1.** (*cause to stampede*) provocar la desbandada de **2.** (*frighten*) infundir pánico **3.** (*force*) empujar; **to ~ sb into** (**doing**) sth empujar a alguien a (hacer) algo

stamping ground *n* lugar *m* predilecto

stance [stɑ:nts, *Am:* stænts] *n* postura *f*

stand [stænd] I. *n* **1.** (*position*) posición *f;* **to take a ~ on** (**doing**) sth adoptar una postura con respecto a (hacer) algo; **to make a ~ against** sth oponer resistencia a algo **2.** *pl* (*in stadium*) tribuna *f* **3.** (*support, frame*) soporte *m;* **music ~** atril *m* **4.** (*market stall*) puesto *m,* trucha *f AmC* **5.** (*for vehicles*) parada *f;* **taxi ~** parada de taxis **6.** (*witness box*) estrado *m;* **to take the ~** subir al estrado **7.** (*group*) **a ~ of trees** una hilera de árboles II. <stood, stood> *vi* **1.** (*be upright*) estar de pie; **to ~ two metres tall** medir dos metros; **to ~ still** estarse quieto, -a **2.** (*be located*) encontrarse **3.** (*remain unchanged: decision, law*) mantenerse en vigor III.<stood, stood> *vt* **1.** (*place*) poner (de pie), colocar **2.** (*bear*) aguantar; **I can't ~ her** no la puedo ver **3.** (*pay for*) **to ~ sb a drink** invitar a alguien a una copa; **to ~ a round** *inf* pagar una ronda **4.** LAW (*undergo*) sufragar

♦**stand about** *vi,* **stand around** *vi* esperar

♦**stand aside** *vi* **1.** (*move*) apartarse **2.** (*stay*) mantenerse aparte

♦**stand back** *vi* **1.** (*move backwards*) retroceder **2.** (*be objective*) distanciarse

♦**stand by** I. *vi* **1.** (*observe*) quedarse sin hacer nada **2.** (*be ready to take action*) estar alerta II. *vt* (*support*) apoyar

♦**stand down** *vi Brit, Aus* renunciar

♦**stand for** *vt* **1.** (*represent*) representar **2.** (*mean*) significar **3.** *Brit, Aus* (*be a candidate*) presentarse a **4.** (*tolerate*) aguantar

♦**stand in** *vi* **to ~ for sb** suplir a alguien

♦**stand out** *vi* destacar

♦**stand over** *vt* vigilar

♦**stand up** I. *vi* **1.** (*be upright*) levantarse, arriscarse *Col* **2.** (*evidence, argument*) ser convincente ►**to ~ and be <u>counted</u>** declararse abiertamente II. *vt* **to stand sb up** dar un plantón a alguien

stand-alone ['stændə,ləʊn, *Am:* -ə,loʊn] *n* INFOR sistema *m* autónomo

standard ['stændəd, *Am:* -dəd] I. *n* 1. (*level*) nivel *m;* (*quality*) clase *f* 2. (*norm*) norma *f* 3. (*flag*) estandarte *m* 4. MUS clásico *m* II. *adj* 1. (*normal*) normal; (*procedure*) habitual 2. LING estándar

standard-bearer ['stændəd,beərəʳ, *Am:* -dəd,berəʳ] *n* abanderado, -a *m, f*

standardization [,stændədaɪ'zeɪʃən, *Am:* -dədɪ'-] *n no pl* estandarización *f;* TECH normalización *f*

standardize ['stændədaɪz, *Am:* -də-] *vt* estandarizar; TECH normalizar

standard lamp ['stændədlæmp, *Am:* -dəd-] *n Brit, Aus* (*floor lamp*) lámpara *f* de pie **standard size** *n* talla *f* corriente

standby ['stændbaɪ] I. *n* 1. (*of money, food*) reserva *f* 2. AVIAT lista *f* de espera; **to be** (**put**) **on** ~ estar sobre aviso; **to be on 24-hour** ~ estar listo para partir dentro de 24 horas II. *adj* de reserva

stand-in ['stændɪn] *n* suplente *mf;* CINE doble *mf*

standing ['stændɪŋ] I. *n* 1. (*status*) posición *f* 2. (*duration*) duración *f;* **of long** ~ desde hace mucho tiempo II. *adj* 1. (*upright*) vertical 2. (*permanent*) permanente 3. (*water*) estancado, -a

standing order *n* pedido *m* regular **standing ovation** *n* ovación *f* en pie **standing start** *n* to do sth from a ~ hacer algo partiendo de cero

standoffish [,stænd'ɒfɪʃ, *Am:* -'ɑːfɪʃ] *adj pej, inf* distante, estirado, -a

standpipe ['stændpaɪp] *n* fuente *f* provisional

standpoint ['stændpɔɪnt] *n* punto *m* de vista

standstill ['stændstɪl] *n no pl* paralización *f;* **to be at a** ~ estar parado

stand trial *vi* estar acusado

stand-up ['stændʌp] *adj* 1. (*upright*) ~ buffet comida *f* tomada de pie 2. (*cabaret*) ~ comedian cómico, -a *m, f* de micrófono 3. (*unrestrained*) ~ fight pelea *f* violenta; ~ argument altercado *m* 4. FASHION a ~ collar un cuello alto

stank [stæŋk] *pt of* **stink**

stanza ['stænzə] *n* LIT estrofa *f*

staple¹ ['steɪpl] I. *n* 1. (*product, article*) producto *m* principal 2. (*basic food*) alimento *m* de primera necesidad 3. (*important component*) elemento *m* esencial II. *adj* 1. (*principal*) principal 2. (*standard*) corriente

staple² ['steɪpl] I. *n* (*fastener*) grapa *f* II. *vt* grapar

staple gun *n* grapadora *f* industrial

stapler ['steɪpləʳ, *Am:* -plɚ] *n* grapadora *f*

star [stɑːʳ, *Am:* stɑːr] I. *n* 1. (*heavenly body*) estrella *f* 2. (*asterisk*) asterisco *m* ▶to thank one's <u>lucky</u> ~s dar las gracias a Dios; **to be**

written in the ~s estar escrito en las estrellas; **to** <u>reach</u> **for the** ~s apuntar a lo más alto; **to** see ~s ver las estrellas II. *vt* <-rr-> 1. THEAT, CINE tener como protagonista 2. (*mark with asterisk*) señalar con un asterisco

star billing [,stɑː'bɪlɪŋ, *Am:* ,stɑːr'-] *n no pl* **to get** ~ aparecer con letras grandes en los carteles

starboard ['stɑːbəd, *Am:* 'stɑːrbɚd] I. *n* NAUT estribor *m* II. *adj* de estribor

starch [stɑːtʃ, *Am:* stɑːrtʃ] I. *n* 1. *no pl* (*stiffening agent*) almidón *m* 2. GASTR fécula *f* II. *vt* almidonar

starchy ['stɑːtʃi, *Am:* 'stɑːrtʃ-] <-ier, -iest> *adj* 1. (*food*) feculento, -a 2. *pej, inf* (*person*) estirado, -a

stardom ['stɑːdəm, *Am:* 'stɑːr-] *n no pl* estrellato *m*, estelaridad *f Chile*

stare [steəʳ, *Am:* ster] I. *vi* mirar fijamente II. *vt* mirar fijamente; **to** ~ **sb in the face** *fig* saltar a la vista; **the answer was staring us in the face** la respuesta era evidente III. *n* mirada *f* fija

starfish ['stɑːfɪʃ, *Am:* 'stɑːr-] <-(es)> *n* estrella *f* de mar

stargazer ['stɑː,geɪzəʳ, *Am:* 'stɑːr,geɪzɚ] *n* (*astronomer*) astrónomo, -a *m, f;* (*astrologer*) astrólogo, -a *m, f*

staring ['steərɪŋ, *Am:* 'ster-] *adj* que mira fijamente; ~ eyes ojos desorbitados

stark [stɑːk, *Am:* stɑːrk] I. *adj* 1. (*desolate*) severo, -a; a ~ landscape un paisaje inhóspito 2. (*austere*) austero, -a 3. (*complete*) completo, -a II. *adv* ~ naked en cueros, empelotado, -a *AmL;* ~ raving mad loco de atar

starkers ['stɑːkəʳs, *Am:* 'stɑːrkɚz] *adj Brit, Aus, inf* (*naked*) en cueros

starless ['stɑːlɪs, *Am:* 'stɑːr-] *adj* sin estrellas

starlet ['stɑːlɪt, *Am:* 'stɑːr-] *n* actriz *f* que aspira al estrellato

starlight ['stɑːlaɪt, *Am:* 'stɑːr-] *n no pl* luz *f* de las estrellas

starling ['stɑːlɪŋ, *Am:* 'stɑːr-] *n* estornino *m*

starlit ['stɑː,lɪt, *Am:* 'stɑːr-] *adj* iluminado, -a por las estrellas

starry ['stɑːri, *Am:* 'stɑːr-] <-ier, -iest> *adj* estrellado, -a

starry-eyed [,stɑːri'aɪd, *Am:* 'stɑːri,aɪd] *adj* soñador(a)

Stars and Stripes *n no pl* the ~ la bandera de las barras y las estrellas

star sign *n* signo *m* del zodiaco

Star-Spangled Banner *n no pl* (*flag*) bandera *f* de las barras y las estrellas; (*anthem*) himno *m* nacional de EE.UU.

star-studded *adj* 1. (*sky*) estrellado, -a 2. (*film*) lleno, -a de estrellas; a ~ cast un reparto estelar

start [stɑːt, *Am:* stɑːrt] I. *vi* 1. (*begin*) comenzar; ~ to do sth empezar a hacer algo 2. (*begin journey*) salir; the bus ~s from the main square el autobús sale de la plaza principal 3. (*begin to operate: vehicle, motor*) arrancar 4. (*make sudden movement*) sobre-

saltarse; **to ~ out of sleep** despertarse sobre-saltado II. *vt* 1. (*begin*) comenzar; **we ~ work at 6:30 every morning** entramos a trabajar a las 6:30 cada mañana 2. (*set in operation*) poner en marcha; (*car*) arrancar 3. COM (*establish: business*) abrir III. *n* 1. (*beginning*) principio *m;* **to make an early/late ~** empezar temprano/tarde; **to make a fresh ~** comenzar de nuevo; **to have a good ~ in life** tener una infancia fácil 2. SPORTS (*beginning place*) salida *f;* **false ~** salida en falso 3. (*sudden movement*) sobresalto *m;* **to give a ~** dar un respingo; **to give sb a ~** dar un susto a alguien
◆**start back** *vi* 1. (*jump back suddenly*) retroceder 2. (*begin return journey*) emprender el regreso
◆**start in** *vi* poner manos a la obra
◆**start off** I. *vi* 1. (*begin*) empezar 2. (*begin journey*) partir; (*train, plane*) salir II. *vt* empezar; **to start sb off (on sth)** ayudar a alguien (a empezar algo)
◆**start out** *vi* 1. (*begin*) empezar; **to ~ to do sth** ponerse a hacer algo 2. (*begin journey*) partir; (*train, plane*) salir
◆**start up** I. *vt* 1. (*organization, business*) fundar 2. (*vehicle, motor*) arrancar II. *vi* 1. (*jump up*) incorporarse bruscamente 2. (*begin happening*) empezar 3. (*begin running: vehicle, motor*) arrancar
START [stɑːt, *Am:* stɑːrt] *abbr of* **Strategic Arms Reduction Talks** START
starter *n* 1. AUTO arranque *m* 2. *Brit, inf* GASTR entrante *m* ▸**for ~s** *inf* para empezar
starting *adj* de comienzo
starting line *n* línea *m* de salida **starting point** *n* punto *m* de partida
startle ['stɑːtl, *Am:* 'stɑːrtl̩] *vt* sobresaltar
startling *adj* (*surprising*) asombroso, -a; (*alarming*) alarmante
start-up ['stɑːtʌp, *Am:* 'stɑːrt-] *n* puesta *f* en marcha
start-up capital *n* capital *m* inicial
start-up costs *n* gastos *mpl* de puesta en marcha
starvation [stɑː'veɪʃən, *Am:* stɑːr'-] *n no pl* hambre *m o f;* **to die of ~** morir de hambre
starvation diet *n* régimen *m* de hambre
starve [stɑːv, *Am:* stɑːrv] I. *vi* 1. pasar hambre, hambrear *AmL;* (*die of hunger*) morir de hambre; **to ~ to death** morir de hambre 2. *inf* (*be very hungry*) morirse de hambre II. *vt* 1. (*deprive: of food*) privar de alimentos; **to ~ sb to death** matar a alguien de inanición 2. (*deprive: of love, support*) privar
starving *adj* hambriento, -a
stash [stæʃ] I. *vt* ocultar II. *n* <-es> *inf* 1. (*hiding place*) escondite *m* 2. (*cache*) alijo *m*
state [steɪt] I. *n* 1. (*condition*) estado *m;* **~ of siege/war** estado de sitio/guerra; **solid/liquid ~** estado sólido/líquido; **~ of mind** estado de ánimo; **to be in a ~** *inf* estar nervioso 2. (*nation*) estado *m* 3. *pl, inf* (*USA*) **the**

States los Estados Unidos 4. (*pomp*) **to lie in ~** yacer en la capilla ardiente II. *adj* (*pertaining to a nation*) estatal; **~ secret** secreto *m* de Estado III. *vt* 1. (*express*) declarar 2. (*specify, fix*) exponer
state-controlled *adj* controlado, -a por el Estado; (*business*) estatal
statecraft ['steɪtkrɑːft, *Am:* -kræft] *n no pl* arte *m* de gobernar
stated *adj* (*specified*) indicado, -a
State Department *n no pl, Am* Departamento *m* de Estado, ≈ Ministerio *m* de Asuntos Exteriores **state education** *n no pl* enseñanza *f* pública
stateless ['steɪtləs] *adj* apátrida
stately ['steɪtli] *adj* majestuoso, -a; **home** casa *f* solariega
statement ['steɪtmənt] *n* 1. (*declaration*) declaración *f;* **to make a ~** LAW prestar declaración 2. (*bank statement*) extracto *m* de cuenta
state-of-the-art [,steɪtəvðiˈɑːt, *Am:* -ˈɑːrt] *adj* moderno, -a; **~ technology** tecnología punta **state-owned** *adj* nacional **state prison** *n Am* prisión *f* estatal
stateroom ['steɪtrʊm, *Am:* -ruːm] *n* 1. (*in palace, hotel*) salón *m* principal 2. NAUT camarote *m*
state school *n* escuela *f* pública
stateside ['steɪtsaɪd] *adv Am, inf* en los Estados Unidos
statesman ['steɪtsmən] <-men> *n* estadista *m*
statesmanship *n no pl* arte *m* de gobernar
stateswoman ['steɪts,wʊmən] <-men> *n* estadista *f*
state visit *n* visita *f* oficial
static ['stætɪk, *Am:* 'stæt-] I. *adj* estático, -a; **to remain ~** permanecer inmóvil II. *n* PHYS *no pl* electricidad *f* estática
static electricity *n no pl* electricidad *f* estática
station ['steɪʃən] I. *n* 1. RAIL estación *f* 2. (*place*) sitio *m;* **research ~** centro *m* de investigación; **police ~** comisaría *f;* **petrol** [*o* **gas**] **~** gasolinera *f* 3. RADIO emisora *f;* TV canal *m* 4. (*position*) puesto *m;* **action ~s!** MIL ¡a sus puestos! 5. (*social position*) clase *f* social 6. *Aus* AGR explotación *f;* **sheep ~** explotación de ganado ovino II. *vt* 1. (*place*) colocar 2. MIL destinar
stationary ['steɪʃənəri, *Am:* 'steɪʃəner-] *adj* (*not moving*) inmóvil
stationer ['steɪʃənəʳ, *Am:* -ʃənəʳ] *n Brit* dueño, -a *m, f* de una papelería; **~'s** papelería *f*
stationery ['steɪʃənəri, *Am:* 'steɪʃəner-] *n no pl* artículos *mpl* de papelería
station house *n Am* comisaría *f* **station master** *n* jefe, -a *m, f* de estación **station wagon** *n Am, Aus* furgoneta *f*
statistical [stə'tɪstɪkl] *adj* estadístico, -a
statistician [,stætɪ'stɪʃən] *n* estadístico, -a *m, f*
statistics [stə'tɪstɪks] *n* 1. (*science*) estadís-

tica *f* **2.** *pl* (*data*) estadísticas *fpl*
statuary ['stætʃuəri, *Am:* 'stætʃuer-] *n no pl,*
form (*statues*) estatuas *fpl*
statue ['stætʃu:] *n* estatua *f*
Statue of Liberty *n* the ~ la Estatua de la
Libertad
statuesque [ˌstætʃu'esk, *Am:* ˌstætʃu'-] *adj*
form escultural
statuette [ˌstætʃu'et, *Am:* ˌstætʃu'-] *n* estatuilla *f*
stature ['stætʃəʳ, *Am:* -ə-] *n* **1.** (*height*)
estatura *f* **2.** (*reputation*) talla *f*
status ['steɪtəs, *Am:* -t̮əs] *n no pl* **1.** (*official
position*) estatus *m* **2.** (*prestige*) prestigio *m*
status bar *n*, **status line** *n* INFOR barra *f*
de estado **status quo** *n no pl* statu quo *m*
status report *n* INFOR informe *m* de situación **status symbol** *n* signo *m* de prestigio
social
statute ['stætʃu:t, *Am:* 'stætʃu:t] *n* LAW ley *f*;
by ~ de acuerdo con la ley
statute book *n* código *m* de leyes **statute
law** *n* derecho *m* escrito **statute of limitations** *n* ley *f* de prescripción
statutory ['stætʃətəri, *Am:* 'stætʃətɔːr-] *adj*
legal
staunch¹ [stɔːntʃ] *adj* incondicional
staunch² [stɔːntʃ] *vt* restañar
stave [steɪv] *n* **1.** MUS pentagrama *m* **2.** (*piece
of wood*) duela *f*
♦**stave in** <stove in, stove in> *vt* romper
♦**stave off** <staved off, staved off> *vt*
(*postpone*) aplazar; (*prevent*) evitar
staves *n* **1.** *pl of* **staff I.6. 2.** *pl of* **stave**
stay¹ [steɪ] *n* **1.** NAUT estay *m* **2.** *pl* (*corset*)
corsé *m*
stay² [steɪ] **I.** *n* estancia *f*, estada *f* AmL **II.** *vi*
1. (*remain present*) quedarse; **to** ~ **in bed**
guardar cama **2.** (*reside temporarily*) alojarse
3. (*remain*) permanecer; **to** ~ **friends** seguir
siendo amigos **III.** *vt* **1.** (*assuage: hunger,
thirst*) aplacar **2.** *liter* (*stop*) parar **3.** (*endure*)
resistir; **to** ~ **the course** [*o* **distance**] aguantar
hasta el final
♦**stay away** *vi* ausentarse; **to** ~ **from sth**
mantenerse alejado de algo
♦**stay behind** *vi* quedarse
♦**stay in** *vi* quedarse en casa
♦**stay on** *vi* quedarse
♦**stay out** *vi* no volver a casa; **to** ~ **all night**
pasar toda la noche fuera
♦**stay up** *vi* no acostarse; **to** ~ **late** acostarse
tarde
stay-at-home ['steɪrəthəʊm, *Am:* -hoʊm]
I. *n* persona *f* hogareña **II.** *adj* hogareño, -a
stayer *n* (*person*) persona *f* perseverante;
(*horse*) caballo *m* apto para carreras de distancia
staying power *n no pl* resistencia *f*
STD [ˌestiː'diː] *n* **1.** MED *abbr of* **sexually
transmitted disease** ETS *f* **2.** *Brit, Aus* TECH
abbr of **subscriber trunk dialling** ~ **code**
prefijo *m* de transferencias interurbanas

stead [sted] *n no pl* lugar *m*; **in his/her** ~ en
su lugar ▸**to stand sb in good** ~ (**for sth**) ser
útil a alguien (para algo)
steadfast ['stedfɑːst, *Am:* -fæst] *adj* firme
steady ['stedi] **I.** <-ier, -iest> *adj* **1.** (*stable*)
estable; (*job, employment*) fijo, -a; (*temperature*) constante **2.** (*regular*) regular; (*speed*)
constante **3.** (*not wavering: hand*) firme
4. (*calm*) sereno, -a **5.** (*regular: boyfriend*) formal **II.** *vt* **1.** (*stabilize*) estabilizar **2.** (*make
calm*) calmar **III.** *adv* **to be going** ~ ser novios
formales **IV.** *interj* cuidado
steak [steɪk] *n* **1.** (*for frying, grilling*) bistec
m, bife *m* AmL; (*for stew, mince*) carne *f* de
ternera **2.** (*of lamb, fish*) filete *m*
steal [stiːl] **I.** <stole, stolen> *vt* robar,
cachar AmC, apachar *Perú*; **to** ~ **sb's heart**
robar el corazón a alguien; **to** ~ **a glance** (**at
sb/sth**) echar una mirada furtiva (a alguien/
algo) ▸**to** ~ **the show** llevarse todos los aplausos **II.** <stole, stolen> *vi* **1.** (*take things
illegally*) robar **2.** (*move surreptitiously*) **to** ~
in entrar a hurtadillas; **to** ~ **away** escabullirse
III. *n Am, inf* ganga *f*; **to be a** ~ ser una ganga
stealth [stelθ] *n no pl* sigilo *m*; **by** ~ con
sigilo
stealthy ['stelθi] *adj* sigiloso, -a
steam [stiːm] **I.** *n no pl* (*water vapour*) vapor
m; **full** ~ **ahead!** ¡a todo vapor!; **to run out of**
~ *fig* perder vigor ▸**to do sth under one's
own** ~ hacer algo por sus propios medios; **to
let off** ~ desahogarse **II.** *adj* de vapor **III.** *vi*
(*produce steam*) echar vapor **IV.** *vt* cocer al
vapor
♦**steam off** *vi* NAUT zarpar
♦**steam up** *vi* **1.** (*become steamy*) empañarse **2.** *inf* **to get steamed up** (**about sth**)
acalorarse (por algo)
steambath *n* baño *m* turco **steamboat** *n*
vapor *m* **steam engine** *n* máquina *f* de
vapor
steamer ['stiːməʳ, *Am:* -ə-] *n* **1.** (*boat*) vapor
m **2.** GASTR vaporera *f*
steam iron *n* plancha *f* de vapor **steam-
-roller I.** *n* apisonadora *f* **II.** *vt a. fig* aplastar
steamship I. *n* vapor *m* **II.** *adj* ~ **line** compañía *f* naviera
steamy ['stiːmi] <-ier, -iest> *adj* **1.** (*full of
steam*) lleno, -a de vapor **2.** (*very humid*)
húmedo, -a **3.** *inf* (*sexy*) erótico, -a
steed [stiːd] *n liter* corcel *m*
steel [stiːl] **I.** *n* **1.** *no pl* (*metal*) acero *m*;
nerves of ~ nervios *mpl* de acero **2.** (*knife
sharpener*) afilador *m* **II.** *adj* de acero **III.** *vt* **to**
~ **oneself for sth** armarse de valor para algo
steel band *n* banda *f* de percusión típica del
Caribe **steel grey** *n* gris *m* metálico **steel
industry** *n* industria *f* siderúrgica **steel
mill** *n* planta *f* de laminación de acero **steel
wool** *n no pl* lana *f* de acero
steelworker ['stiːlˌwɜːkəʳ, *Am:* -ˌwɜːrkə-] *n*
obrero, -a *m, f* siderúrgico, -a
steelworks ['stiːlwɜːks, *Am:* -wɜːrks] *n inv*

planta *f* siderúrgica
steely ['stiːli] <-ier, -iest> *adj* (*determination*) férreo, -a; (*gaze*) duro, -a
steep¹ [stiːp] *adj* **1.** (*sharply sloping*) empinado, -a **2.** (*dramatic: increase, fall*) pronunciado, -a; **that's a bit ~!** ¡no hay derecho! +*subj* **3.** (*expensive*) exorbitante
steep² [stiːp] **I.** *vt* **1.** (*soak*) remojar **2.** *fig* **to be ~ in tradition/history** tener mucha tradición/la historia **II.** *vi* **to leave sth to ~** dejar algo en remojo
steepen ['stiːpən] *vi* **1.** (*become steeper*) empinarse **2.** *inf* (*become more expensive*) aumentar
steeple ['stiːpl] *n* ARCHIT torre *f;* **church ~** campanario de una iglesia
steeplechase ['stiːpltʃeɪs] *n* carrera *f* de obstáculos
steeplejack ['stiːpldʒæk] *n* reparador(a) *m(f)* de torres
steer¹ [stɪər, *Am:* stɪr] **I.** *vt* **1.** (*direct*) dirigir; (*car*) conducir, manejar *AmL* **2.** (*guide*) guiar **II.** *vi* (*person*) conducir, manejar *AmL;* (*vehicle*) manejarse; **to ~ for sth** NAUT poner rumbo a algo; **to ~ clear of sth/sb** evitar algo/a alguien
steer² [stɪər, *Am:* stɪr] *n* (*young bull*) novillo *m;* (*castrated bull*) buey *m*
steerage ['stɪərɪdʒ, *Am:* 'stɪrɪdʒ] *n no pl* NAUT **to travel ~** viajar en tercera clase
steering *n no pl* dirección *f*
steering committee *n inv, Brit* comité *m* directivo **steering lock** *n* dispositivo *m* antirrobo **steering wheel** *n* (*of car*) volante *m*, guía *f PRico;* (*of ship*) timón *m*
steersman ['stɪəzmən, *Am:* 'stɪrz-] <-men> *n* timonel *m*
stellar ['stelər, *Am:* -ə-] *adj* estelar
stem [stem] **I.** *n* **1.** (*of plant*) tallo *m;* (*of leaf*) pedúnculo *m* **2.** (*part of glass*) pie *m* **3.** LING raíz *f* **4.** NAUT proa *f* ►**from ~ to stern** de proa a popa **II.** <-mm-> *vt* (*stop*) detener; (*blood*) restañar **III.** <-mm-> *vi* **to ~ from** resultar de
stench [stentʃ] *n no pl* hedor *m*
stencil ['stensl] **I.** *n* **1.** (*cut-out pattern*) plantilla *f* **2.** (*picture drawn*) patrón *m* **II.** *vt* dibujar utilizando una plantilla
stenographer [stəˈnɒɡrəfər, *Am:* -ˈnɑːɡrəfə-] *n* estenógrafo, -a *m, f*
stenography [stəˈnɒɡrəfi, *Am:* -ˈnɑːɡrə-] *n no pl* estenografía *f*
step [step] **I.** *n* **1.** (*foot movement*) paso *m;* (*foot print*) huella *f;* **to take a ~** dar un paso; **~ by ~** paso a paso; **to follow in sb's ~s** *fig* seguir el ejemplo de alguien; **to take a ~ towards sth** *fig* dirigirse hacia algo; **to be in/out of ~** llevar/no llevar el paso; *fig* estar/no estar al tanto; **to watch one's ~** andar con cuidado **2.** (*of stair, ladder*) peldaño *m* **3.** (*measure*) medida *f;* **to take ~s (to do sth)** tomar medidas (para hacer algo) **4.** *pl, Brit* (*stepladder*) escalera *f* **5.** *Am* MUS **whole ~** tono *m;* **half ~** semitono *m* **II.** <-pp-> *vi*

1. (*tread*) pisar **2.** (*walk*) caminar
♦**step aside** *vi* hacerse a un lado
♦**step back** *vi* **1.** (*move back*) retroceder **2.** (*gain new perspective*) distanciarse
♦**step down I.** *vi* (*resign*) dimitir; **to ~ from sth** renunciar a algo **II.** *vt* (*reduce*) reducir
♦**step in** *vi* intervenir
♦**step up** *vt* aumentar
stepbrother *n* hermanastro *m* **stepchild** *n* hijastro, -a *m, f* **stepdaughter** *n* hijastra *f* **stepfather** *n* padrastro *m*
stepladder ['step,lædər, *Am:* -ə-] *n* escalera *f* de mano
stepmother ['step,mʌðər, *Am:* -ə-] *n* madrastra *f*
steppe [step] *n* estepa *f*
stepping stone ['stepɪŋstəʊn, *Am:* -stoʊn] *n* **1.** (*stone*) pasadera *f* **2.** *fig* trampolín *m*
stepsister ['step,sɪstər, *Am:* -tə-] *n* hermanastra *f*
stepson ['stepsʌn] *n* hijastro *m*
stereo ['steriəʊ, *Am:* 'sterioʊ] **I.** *n* **1.** *no pl* **in ~** en estéreo **2.** (*hi-fi system*) equipo *m* (estéreo) **II.** *adj* estéreo
stereophonic [,steriəʊˈfɒnɪk, *Am:* -əˈfɑː-nɪk] *adj* MUS estereofónico, -a
stereoscopic [,steriəˈskɒpɪk, *Am:* -ˈskɑː-pɪk] *adj* estereoscópico, -a
stereotype ['steriətaɪp] **I.** *n pej* estereotipo *m* **II.** *vt pej* estereotipar
sterile ['steraɪl, *Am:* 'sterəl] *adj* estéril
sterility [stəˈrɪləti, *Am:* -ti] *n no pl* esterilidad *f*
sterilization [,sterəlaɪˈzeɪʃən, *Am:* ,sterəlɪ-] *n no pl* esterilización *f*
sterilize ['sterəlaɪz] *vt* esterilizar
sterling ['stɜːlɪŋ, *Am:* 'stɜːr-] **I.** *n no pl* **1.** FIN libra *f* esterlina **2.** (*metal*) plata *f* de ley **II.** *adj* **1.** FIN **pound ~** libra esterlina **2.** (*of high standard*) excelente
stern¹ [stɜːn, *Am:* stɜːrn] *adj* **1.** (*severe*) severo, -a; (*warning*) terminante **2.** (*strict*) estricto, -a **3.** (*difficult: test*) duro, -a ►**to be made of ~er stuff** tener mucho carácter
stern² [stɜːn, *Am:* stɜːrn] *n* NAUT popa *f*
sternness ['stɜːnnɪs, *Am:* 'stɜːrn-] *n no pl* severidad *f*
sternum ['stɜːnəm, *Am:* 'stɜːr-] <-s *o* -na> *n* esternón *m*
steroid ['stɪərɔɪd, *Am:* 'sterɔɪd] *n* esteroide *m*
stethoscope ['steθəskəʊp, *Am:* -skoʊp] *n* MED estetoscopio *m*
stevedore ['stiːvədɔːr, *Am:* -dɔːr] *n* estibador(a) *m(f)*
stew [stjuː, *Am:* stuː] **I.** *n* estofado *m*, hervido *m AmS* ►**to be in a ~** sudar la gota gorda **II.** *vt* (*meat*) estofar; (*fruit*) hacer compota de **III.** *vi* cocer
steward ['stjʊəd, *Am:* 'stuːəd] *n* **1.** AVIAT auxiliar *m* de vuelo **2.** (*at concert, demonstration*) auxiliar *mf* **3.** (*estate administrator*)

administrador(a) *m(f)*
stewardess [ˌstjʊəˈdes, *Am:* ˈstuːɚdɪs]
<-es> *n* azafata *f,* aeromoza *f Méx, AmS*
stick¹ [stɪk] *n* **1.**(*of wood*) vara *f,* palo *m;* (*of celery, rhubarb*) tallo *f;* (*of dynamite*) cartucho *m;* (*of chalk*) tiza *f;* (*of deodorant, glue*) barra *f* **2.** *a.* sports (*for hockey*) palo *m;* **walking ~** bastón *m* **3.** mus batuta *f* **4.** mil porra *f* **5.** auto palanca *f;* **gear ~** palanca de cambio, palanca de velocidades *Méx* **6.** *inf*(*person*) **old ~** tío *m* **7.** *inf* (*remote area*) **in the ~s** en el quinto pino **8.** *inf*(*criticism*) **to give sb ~** (**about sth**) criticar a alguien (por algo); **to take a lot of ~** llevarse muchos palos ▶**to get the wrong** end **of the ~** coger el rábano por las hojas; **~s and** stones **may break my bones, but words can never hurt me** *prov* a palabras necias, oídos sordos *prov;* **to be in a** cleft **~** estar entre la espada y la pared; **to** up **~s** *Brit, inf* levantar campamento
stick² [stɪk] <stuck, stuck> I. *vi* **1.**(*adhere*) pegarse **2.**(*be unmovable: person*) quedarse parado; (*car, door, window*) atascarse; (*mechanism*) bloquearse **3.**(*endure*) **to ~ in sb's mind** grabarse a alguien (en la mente) **4.** games plantarse II. *vt* **1.**(*affix*) pegar **2.** *inf*(*tolerate*) aguantar **3.** *inf*(*put*) poner; **to ~ one's head around the door** asomar la cabeza por la puerta
◆**stick around** *vi inf*quedarse
◆**stick at** *vt* seguir con
◆**stick by** *vt* **1.**(*continue to support: friend*) no abandonar **2.**(*not change: opinion*) mantener **3.**(*comply with: rules*) respetar
◆**stick down** *vt* **1.**(*fix*) pegar **2.** *inf* (*put*) poner **3.** *inf* (*write hastily*) apuntar rápidamente
◆**stick in** I. *vt* **1.**(*put*) poner, meter **2.**(*add*) añadir **3.**(*knife, needle*) clavar II. *vi* **to get stuck in** *inf*(*start*) poner manos a la obra; *Brit, inf*(*start eating*) atacar
◆**stick on** *vt* **1.**(*affix: stamp, label*) pegar **2.** *inf*to be stuck on sb estar loco por alguien
◆**stick out** I. *vt* asomar; **to stick one's tongue out** sacar la lengua ▶**to stick one's** neck **out** arriesgarse II. *vi* **1.**(*protrude: nail, ears*) sobresalir **2.**(*be obvious*) ser evidente; **to ~ a mile** verse [*o* notarse] a la legua, saltar a la vista **3.**(*endure*) **to stick it out** aguantar
◆**stick to** *vt* **1.**(*adhere to: rules*) ceñirse a; (*plan, idea*) seguir con; (*promise*) cumplir; (*principles*) mantener **2.**(*restrict oneself to*) limitarse a
◆**stick together** I. *vt* juntar II. *vi* **1.**(*adhere*) juntarse **2.**(*not separate*) no separarse **3.**(*remain loyal*) mantenerse unidos
◆**stick up** I. *vt inf* **1.**(*attach: poster, sign*) colocar **2.**(*raise*) **stick 'em up!** ¡manos arriba! **3.**(*rob*) atracar II. *vi* sobresalir; (*hair*) estar de punta
◆**stick up for** *vt* defender
◆**stick with** *vt* **1.**(*not give up*) seguir con; (*thought, idea, memory*) no abandonar

2.(*persevere in*) seguir adelante con **3.**(*stay near*) no separarse de
sticker [ˈstɪkɚ, *Am:* -ɚ] *n* **1.**(*label*) pegatina *f* **2.**(*person*) persona *f* tenaz
sticking plaster *n Brit* **1.**(*adhesive dressing*) tirita® *f,* curita® *f AmL* **2.**(*temporary measure*) apaño *m*
stick insect *n* insecto *m* palo **stick-in-the--mud** *n inf: persona rutinaria e inflexible*
stickleback [ˈstɪklbæk] *n* espinoso *m*
stickler [ˈstɪklɚ, *Am:* -lɚ] *n* **to be a ~ for sth** insistir mucho en algo
stick-on [ˈstɪkɒn, *Am:* -ɑːn] *adj* adhesivo, -a
stickpin [ˈstɪkˌpɪn] *n Am* aguja *f* de corbata
stick-up [ˈstɪkʌp] *n inf*atraco *m*
sticky [ˈstɪki] <-ier, -iest> *adj* **1.**(*label*) adhesivo, -a; (*surface, hands*) pegajoso, -a **2.**(*weather*) bochornoso, -a
stiff [stɪf] I. *n inf* (*corpse*) fiambre *m* II. *adj* **1.**(*rigid: paper*) rígido, -a; (*brush*) duro, -a; (*shirt*) tieso, -a; (*paste, dough*) consistente; **to be (as) ~ as a board** estar más tieso que un palo **2.**(*not supple: joints*) entumecido, -a **3.**(*difficult to move: muscles*) agarrotado, -a; **to have a ~ neck** tener tortícolis **4.**(*very formal*) encorsetado, -a **5.**(*not friendly*) estirado, -a; (*smile*) forzado, -a **6.**(*strong: competition, test*) duro, -a; (*opposition, drink, wind*) fuerte; (*resistance*) férreo, -a, tenaz; (*punishment, criticism*) fuerte, severo, -a **7.**(*strenuous: climb*) agotador(a) **8.**(*very expensive: price*) exorbitante III. *adv* **to be bored ~** estar aburrido como una ostra; **to be scared ~** estar muerto de miedo
stiffen [ˈstɪfn] I. *vi* **1.**(*become tense: person*) ponerse tenso; (*muscles*) agarrotarse **2.**(*become dense*) espesarse **3.**(*become stronger: competition*) hacerse más duro II. *vt* **1.**(*make rigid: collar, cuff*) almidonar **2.**(*make more dense*) espesar **3.**(*make more difficult, severe: exam*) hacer más difícil; (*penalty*) endurecer **4.**(*strengthen: moral*) fortalecer
stiffening [ˈstɪfnɪŋ] *n no pl* **1.**(*becoming immobile*) entumecimiento *m* **2.**(*rigid material*) entretela *f*
stiff-necked [ˌstɪfˈnekt, *Am:* ˈstɪfnekt] *adj* **1.**(*stubborn: person*) terco, -a; (*resistance*) obstinado, -a **2.**(*proud*) estirado, -a
stifle [ˈstaɪfl] I. *vi* **1.**(*suffocate*) sofocarse **2.**(*suffer lack of air*) ahogarse II. *vt* **1.**(*suffocate*) sofocar **2.**(*suppress: yawn, scream, desire*) contener; (*initiative, opposition*) reprimir
stifling [ˈstaɪflɪŋ] *adj* (*day, heat*) sofocante; (*room*) agobiante
stigma [ˈstɪɡmə] *n* estigma *m*
stigmatize [ˈstɪɡmətaɪz] *vt* estigmatizar
stile [staɪl] *n* escalones que permiten pasar por encima de una cerca
stiletto [stɪˈletəʊ, *Am:* -ˈleţoʊ] <-s> *n* **1.**(*dagger*) estilete *m* **2.** *pl* (*shoes*) zapatos *mpl* de tacón de aguja
stiletto heel *n* tacón *m* de aguja

S

still¹ [stɪl] I. *n* 1. *no pl (peace)* quietud *f*
2. CINE, PHOT fotograma *m* II. *adj* 1. *(calm)* tranquilo, -a 2. *(peaceful)* quieto, -a; *(wind, water)*
en calma; **to keep ~** quedarse quieto 3. *(not
fizzy: water)* sin gas III. *vt* 1. *(calm)* calmar
2. *liter (quieten)* acallar

still² [stɪl] *adv* 1. aún, todavía; **to be ~ alive**
seguir vivo; **to want ~ more** querer todavía [o
aún] más; **better ~** todavía mejor 2. *(nevertheless)* sin embargo; **~ and all** *Am* aún así

still³ [stɪl] *n (distillery)* destilería *f*

stillbirth ['stɪlbɜːθ, *Am:* -bɜːrθ] *n* nacimiento *m* de un bebé muerto

stillborn ['stɪlbɔːn, *Am:* 'stɪlbɔːrn] *adj*
1. *(born dead)* nacido, -a muerto, -a 2. *(unsuccessful)* malogrado, -a

still life *n* ART naturaleza *f* muerta

stillness *n* 1. *(tranquility)* tranquilidad *f*
2. *(lack of movement)* quietud *f* 3. *(calm)*
calma *f*

stilt [stɪlt] *n pl* zanco *m*

stilted ['stɪltɪd, *Am:* -t̬ɪd] *adj (manner, style)*
forzado, -a

stimulant ['stɪmjələnt] *n* 1. *(boost)* estímulo
m 2. MED estimulante *m*

stimulate ['stɪmjəleɪt] *vt* 1. *(encourage)*
estimular; *(economy)* potenciar, estimular;
(discussion) fomentar 2. MED estimular

stimulating *adj* estimulante

stimulation [ˌstɪmjə'leɪʃən] *n no pl*
1. *(boost)* estimulación *f* 2. *(thought, reaction)* estímulo *m*

stimulus ['stɪmjələs] <-li> *n* estímulo *m*

sting [stɪŋ] I. *n* 1. ZOOL *(organ)* aguijón *m*;
(injury) picada *f* 2. BOT pelo *m* urticante
3. *(pain)* escozor *m*; **~ of remorse** gusanillo
m de la conciencia 4. *Am, inf (swindle)* estafa
f II. <stung, stung> *vi* 1. *(injure with poison: insect)* picar 2. *(be painful: cut)* arder;
(eyes) escocer; *(criticism)* herir III. *vt*
1. *(inject with poison)* picar 2. *(cause pain:
eyes)* hacer escocer; *(criticism)* herir profundamente 3. *Brit, Aus (goad)* incitar 4. *(swindle)*
estafar

stinginess ['stɪndʒɪnɪs] *n no pl* tacañería *f*

stinging nettle [ˌstɪŋɪŋ'netl, *Am:* -'net̬l] *n*
ortiga *f*

stingray ['stɪŋreɪ] *n* ZOOL raya *f* venenosa

stingy ['stɪndʒi] <-ier, -iest> *adj inf (person)* tacaño, -a, pijotero, -a *AmL*, amarrado, -a
Arg, Par, PRico, Urug, coñete *Chile, Perú*;
(amount) mísero, -a

stink [stɪŋk] I. *n* 1. *(smell)* mal olor *m* 2. *fig*
escándalo *m*; **to create a ~** montar un escándalo II. <stank *Am, Aus:* stunk, stunk> *vi*
1. *(smell)* apestar, bufar *AmL*; **to ~ of money**
inf estar podrido de dinero 2. *inf (be very bad)*
ser pésimo, -a 3. *inf (be suspicious: business,
situation)* oler mal

stink bomb *n* bomba fétida *f*

stinker ['stɪŋkəʳ, *Am:* -kɚ] *n inf* 1. *(bad person)* canalla *mf* 2. *(unpleasant thing)* asco *m*

stint¹ [stɪnt] *n* período *m*

stint² [stɪnt] *vt (funds, money)* escatimar; **to
~ oneself of sth** privarse de algo

stipulate ['stɪpjəleɪt] *vt* estipular

stipulation [ˌstɪpjə'leɪʃən] *n* estipulación *f*;
with the ~ that con la condición de que + *subj*

stir [stɜːʳ, *Am:* stɜːr] I. *n* 1. *(agitation)* **to give
sth a ~** remover algo 2. *(excitement)* conmo-
ción *f*; **to cause a ~** causar revuelo II. <-ring,
-red> *vt* 1. *(agitate: coffee, sauce, mixture)*
remover; *(fire)* atizar, avivar 2. *(arouse:
imagination)* estimular; **to ~ sb to do sth**
mover alguien a hacer algo; **to ~ trouble** *Am*
provocar problemas III. *vi* 1. *(move)* moverse,
agitarse 2. *(awake)* despertarse 3. *(venture
out)* salir 4. *Brit, Aus (cause trouble)* armar follón

stir-fry ['stɜːfraɪ, *Am:* 'stɜːr-] <-ied, -ies> *vt*
freír en poco aceite y removiendo constantemente

stirring I. *n (of envy)* principio *m*; *(of interest)*
primeros indicios *mpl* II. *adj* conmovedor(a)

stirrup ['stɪrəp, *Am:* 'stɜːr-] *n* estribo *m*

stitch [stɪtʃ] I. <-es> *n* 1. *(in knitting)* punto
m; *(in sewing)* puntada *f*; **cross ~** punto de
cruz; **to not have a ~ on** *inf* estar en cueros,
estar calato *Perú* 2. MED punto *m* (de sutura)
3. *(pain)* flato *m*; **to have a ~** tener flato; **to
have sb in ~es** hacer que alguien se tronche
de risa ▶ **a ~ in time saves nine** *prov* una
puntada a tiempo ahorra ciento *prov* II. *vi*
coser III. *vt* coser

stoat [stəʊt, *Am:* stoʊt] *n* armiño *m*

stock [stɒk, *Am:* staːk] I. *n* 1. *(reserves)*
reserva *f* 2. COM, ECON existencias *fpl*; **to have
sth in ~** tener algo en stock; **to be out of ~**
estar agotado; **to take ~** hacer el inventario; *fig*
hacer un balance 3. *(share)* FIN acción *f* 4. AGR,
ZOOL ganado *m* 5. *no pl (line of descent)* linaje
m; ZOOL, BIO raza *f* 6. *(popularity)* prestigio *m*;
her ~ had fallen/risen había ganado/per-
dido prestigio 7. *(belief)* **to put (no) ~ by sth**
(no) dar crédito a algo II. *adj (model)* estándar;
(response) típico, -a III. *vt* 1. *(keep in supply:
goods)* vender 2. *(supply goods to: shop)*
suministrar 3. *(fill: shelves)* llenar

stockade [stɒ'keɪd, *Am:* staː'-] *n*
1. *(wooden fence)* empalizada *f* 2. *Am
(prison)* prisión *f* militar

stockbroker ['stɒkˌbrəʊkəʳ, *Am:* 'staːk-
ˌbroʊkɚ] *n* corredor(a) *m(f)* de bolsa

stockbroking *n* correduría *f* de bolsa

stockcar *n* 1. AUTO stock car *m* 2. *Am* RAIL
vagón *m* para el ganado **stock company** *n
Am* 1. FIN sociedad *f* anónima 2. THEAT compañía *f* de repertorio **stock control** *n* control
m de existencias **stock cube** *n* cubito *m* de
caldo **stock exchange** *n* bolsa *f* **stock
farmer** *n* ganadero, -a *m, f*

stockfish ['stɒkfɪʃ, *Am:* 'staːk-] *n* bacalao *m*
seco

stockholder ['stɒkˌhəʊldəʳ, *Am:* 'staːk-
ˌhoʊldɚ] *n Am* accionista *mf*

stocking ['stɒkɪŋ, *Am:* 'staːkɪŋ] *n* media *f*

stock-in-trade [ˌstɒkɪnˈtreɪd, *Am:* ˌstɑːk-] *n* existencias *fpl*

stockist [ˈstɒkɪst, *Am:* ˈstɑːkɪst] *n Aus, Brit* distribuidor(a) *m(f)*

stock market *n* mercado *m* bursátil

stockpile [ˈstɒkpaɪl, *Am:* ˈstɑːk-] I. *n* reservas *fpl;* (*of weapons, ammunition*) arsenal *m* II. *vt* almacenar

stock price *n Am* cotización *f* de las acciones

stockroom [ˈstɒkruːm, *Am:* ˈstɑːkruːm] *n* almacén *m,* bodega *f Méx*

stock-still [ˌstɒkˈstɪl, *Am:* ˌstɑːk-] *adv* to stand ~ quedarse inmóvil

stocktaking [ˈstɒkteɪkɪŋ, *Am:* ˈstɑːk-] *n* inventario *m*

stocky [ˈstɒki, *Am:* ˈstɑːki] <-ier, -iest> *adj* bajo, -a y fornido, -a

stockyard [ˈstɒkjɑːd] *n* corral *m*

stodge [stɒdʒ, *Am:* stɑːdʒ] *n Brit, Aus, inf* comida *f* pesada

stodgy [ˈstɒdʒi, *Am:* ˈstɑːdʒi] <-ier, -iest> *adj* 1. (*food*) pesado, -a 2. (*person, book*) aburrido, -a

stoic [ˈstəʊɪk, *Am:* ˈstoʊ-] *n* estoico, -a *m, f*

stoical [ˈstəʊɪk(l), *Am:* ˈstoʊ-] *adj* estoico, -a

stoicism [ˈstəʊɪsɪzəm, *Am:* ˈstoʊɪ-] *n no pl* estoicismo *m*

stoke [stəʊk, *Am:* stoʊk] *vt* (*fire*) atizar; (*furnace*) echar carbón [*o* leña] a; *fig* avivar

stoker [ˈstəʊkəʳ, *Am:* ˈstoʊkɚ] *n* RAIL, NAUT fogonero, -a *m, f*

stole¹ [stəʊl, *Am:* stoʊl] *pt of* **steal**

stole² [stəʊl, *Am:* stoʊl] *n* estola *f*

stolid [ˈstɒlɪd, *Am:* ˈstɑːlɪd] *adj* impasible

stomach [ˈstʌmək] I. *n* 1. (*internal organ*) estómago *m;* to have an upset ~ tener mal el estómago; to have a strong ~ tener estómago 2. (*belly*) vientre *m* II. *vt inf* (*drink, food*) tolerar; to be hard to ~ (*person, insult*) ser difícil de soportar

stomach ache *n no pl* dolor *m* de estómago

stomach upset *n* problema *m* estomacal

stomp [stɒmp, *Am:* stɑːmp] *vi* pisar fuerte

stone [stəʊn, *Am:* stoʊn] I. *n* 1. GEO piedra *f;* to be a ~'s throw (away) estar a tiro de piedra 2. MED cálculo *m* 3. (*jewel*) piedra *f* preciosa 4. (*of fruit*) hueso *m,* carozo *m CSur* 5. *Brit* (*14 lbs*) unidad *f* de peso equivalente a *6,35 kg* ▶ a rolling ~ gathers no **moss** *prov* piedra movediza nunca moho la cobija *prov;* to cast the **first** ~ tirar la primera piedra; to leave no ~ **unturned** no dejar piedra por mover II. *adv* 1. (*like a stone*) ~ **hard** duro, -a como una piedra 2. *inf* (*completely*) ~ crazy loco de remate III. *vt* 1. (*throw stones at*) apedrear 2. (*fruit, olives*) deshuesar

Stone Age *n* Edad *f* de Piedra **stone-broke** *adj Am* sin blanca **stone-cold** *adj* helado, -a; to be ~ sober no haber bebido ni una gota

stoned *adj inf* colocado, -a

stone-deaf [ˌstəʊnˈdef, *Am:* ˌstoʊn-] *adj* sordo, -a como una tapia

stonemason [ˈstəʊnˌmeɪsən, *Am:* ˈstoʊn-] *n* cantero, -a *m, f*

stonewall [ˌstəʊnˈwɔːl, *Am:* ˈstoʊn-] *fig* I. *vi* andarse con evasivas II. *vt* bloquear

stoneware [ˈstəʊnweəʳ, *Am:* ˈstoʊnwer] *n no pl* cerámica *f* de gres

stonework [ˈstəʊnwɜːk, *Am:* ˈstoʊnwɜːrk] *n no pl* cantería *f*

stony [ˈstəʊni, *Am:* ˈstoʊ-] <-ier, -iest> *adj* 1. (*beach, ground*) pedregoso, -a 2. (*expression*) frío, -a; (*silence*) sepulcral; (*heart*) de piedra

stony-broke *adj Brit, Aus, inf* sin blanca

stood [stʊd] *pt, pp of* **stand**

stooge [stuːdʒ] *n* 1. THEAT compañero *m* 2. *fig* (*puppet*) títere *m* 3. *Am, inf* (*informer*) soplón, -ona *m, f*

stool [stuːl] *n* 1. (*seat*) taburete *m* 2. *pl* MED deposición *f* ▶ to fall between **two** ~s nadar entre dos aguas

stool pigeon *n Am, inf* soplón, -ona *m, f*

stoop¹ [stuːp] I. *n no pl* to have a ~ ser cargado de espaldas II. *vi* inclinarse; to ~ to sth *pej* rebajarse a algo

stoop² [stuːp] *n Am* pórtico *m*

stop [stɒp, *Am:* stɑːp] I. *n* 1. (*break in activity*) pausa *f;* to come to a ~ detenerse; to put a ~ to sth poner fin a algo 2. (*halting place*) parada *f* 3. *Brit* LING punto *m* 4. MUS registro *m* ▶ to pull (all) the ~s out desplegar todos los recursos II. <- ping, -ped> *vt* 1. (*cause to cease*) parar 2. (*refuse payment: wages*) suspender; to ~ a **cheque** dar orden de no pagar un cheque 3. (*switch off*) apagar 4. (*block*) rellenar; (*hole, ones ears*) tapar 5. *Brit* (*fill*) empastar III. <- ping, -ped> *vi* 1. (*cease moving*) pararse; (*car*) detenerse 2. (*cease an activity*) to ~ **doing sth** dejar de hacer algo 3. *Brit* (*stay*) quedarse

◆**stop by** *vi* pasar por

◆**stop in** *vi* quedarse en casa

◆**stop off** *vi* detenerse un rato

◆**stop out** *vi* quedarse fuera

◆**stop over** *vi* pasar la noche, hacer noche

◆**stop up** *vt* (*block*) atascar; (*hole*) tapar; (*gap*) rellenar

stopcock [ˈstɒpkɒk, *Am:* ˈstɑːpkɑːk] *n* llave *f* de paso

stopgap [ˈstɒpgæp, *Am:* ˈstɑːp-] I. *n* medida *f* provisional II. *adj* provisional

stoplight [ˈstɒplaɪt, *Am:* ˈstɑːp-] *n Am* semáforo *m* rojo

stopover [ˈstɒpəʊvəʳ, *Am:* ˈstɑːpoʊvɚ] *n* (*on journey*) parada *f;* AVIAT escala *f*

stoppage [ˈstɒpɪdʒ, *Am:* ˈstɑːpɪdʒ] *n* 1. (*cessation of work*) interrupción *f* 2. FIN, ECON retención *f* 3. MED oclusión *f*

stopper [ˈstɒpəʳ, *Am:* ˈstɑːpɚ] I. *n* tapón *m* II. *vt* taponar

stopping train *n* tren que para en todas las estaciones

stop press *n* PUBL noticias *fpl* de última hora

stop sign *n* AUTO, LAW stop *m* **stopwatch**

n cronómetro *m*

storage ['stɔːrɪdʒ] *n no pl* **1.** (*of goods, possessions*) almacenaje *m;* **to put sth in** ~ almacenar algo **2.** INFOR almacenamiento *m*

storage battery *n* acumulador *m* **storage capacity** *n* capacidad *f* de almacenaje **storage heater** *n Brit* acumulador *m* (de calor) **storage space** *n* espacio *m* para guardar cosas **storage tank** *n* tanque *m* de almacenamiento

store [stɔːʳ, *Am:* stɔːr] I. *n* **1.** *Brit* (*storehouse*) almacén *m;* (*department store*) grandes almacenes *mpl,* emporio *m AmC;* **to be in** ~ estar en almacén; **what is in** ~ **for us?** ¿qué nos espera en el futuro? **2.** *Am, Aus* (*shop*) tienda *f* **3.** (*supply: of wine*) reserva *f;* (*of food*) provisión *f* **4.** (*place for keeping supplies*) almacén *m,* depósito *m;* (*for weapons*) arsenal *m* **5.** *no pl* (*importance*) valor *m;* **to set** ~ **by sth** dar valor a algo II. *vt* **1.** (*put into storage*) almacenar **2.** (*keep for future use*) guardar **3.** INFOR (*file*) guardar; (*data*) almacenar

store detective *n* guarda *mf* de seguridad de una tienda

storefront ['stɔːfrʌnt, *Am:* 'stɔːr-] *n Am* escaparate *m*

storehouse ['stɔːhaʊs, *Am:* 'stɔːr-] *n Am* almacén *m; fig* mina *f*

storekeeper ['stɔːˌkiːpəʳ, *Am:* 'stɔːrˌkiːpə-] *n* tendero, -a *m, f,* comerciante *mf*

storeroom ['stɔːrʊm, *Am:* 'stɔːrruːm] *n* depósito *m,* bodega *f Méx;* (*for food*) despensa *f*

storey ['stɔːri] *n Brit, Aus* piso *m*

storeyed *adj,* **storied** *adj Am* two/three-~ de dos/tres pisos

stork [stɔːk, *Am:* stɔːrk] *n* cigüeña *f*

storm [stɔːm, *Am:* stɔːrm] I. *n* **1.** METEO tormenta *f* **2.** *fig* (*argument*) trifulca *f;* (*of protest*) ola *f;* (*of criticism*) vendaval *f;* (*of applause*) salva *f;* **political** ~ revuelo *m* político **3.** **to take sth by** ~ asaltar algo; **to take sb by** ~ cautivar a alguien ▶ **a** ~ **in a teacup** mucho ruido y pocas nueces; **to ride out** [*o* **to weather**] **the** ~ capear el temporal II. *vi* **1.** *Am* METEO haber tormenta; (*winds*) soplar con fuerza **2.** (*speak angrily*) bramar III. *vt* (*town, castle*) asaltar; (*house*) irrumpir en

♦**storm into** *vi* irrumpir en

♦**storm out** *vi* salir airadamente

storm cloud *n* nubarrón *m* **storm door** *n* contrapuerta *f*

storm-tossed *adj* (*boat*) sacudido, -a por la tormenta

stormy ['stɔːmi, *Am:* 'stɔːr-] <-ier, -iest> *adj* (*weather*) tormentoso, -a; (*sea, relationship*) tempestuoso, -a; (*argument*) violento, -a

story¹ ['stɔːri] <-ies> *n* **1.** (*account*) historia *f;* (*fictional*) cuento *m;* **to tell a** ~ contar un cuento; **to tell stories** (*lie*) contar cuentos; **so the** ~ **goes** eso dicen **2.** (*news report*) artículo *m* ▶**that's another** ~ eso es harina de otro

costal; **it's the same old** ~ es la historia de siempre; **a tall** ~ un cuento chino

story² ['stɔːri] *n Am s.* **storey**

storybook ['stɔːribʊk] I. *n* libro *m* de cuentos II. *adj* **a** ~ **romance** un romance de cuento de hadas **storyline** *n* (*plot*) argumento *m* **storyteller** *n* narrador(a) *m(f)*

stout [staʊt] I. *n* (*beer*) cerveza *f* negra II. *adj* (*person*) robusto, -a; (*shoes, boots*) fuerte; (*defender*) firme; (*resistance*) tenaz

stouthearted [ˌstaʊt'hɑːtɪd, *Am:* -'hɑːrtɪd] *adj* (*support*) incondicional; (*defender*) acérrimo, -a; (*resistance*) firme

stoutly ['staʊtli] *adv* **1.** (*strongly*) sólidamente **2.** (*firmly*) con firmeza

stove [stəʊv, *Am:* stoʊv] *n* **1.** (*heater*) estufa *f* **2.** *Am, Aus* cocina *f*

stovepipe ['stəʊvpaɪp, *Am:* 'stoʊv-] *n* conducto *m* de estufa

stow [stəʊ, *Am:* stoʊ] *vt* guardar

♦**stow away** I. *vt* esconder II. *vi* viajar de polizón

stowage ['stəʊɪdʒ, *Am:* 'stoʊ-] *n no pl* NAUT estiba *f*

stowaway ['stəʊəweɪ, *Am:* 'stoʊ-] *n* polizón *m*

straddle ['strædl] *vt* (*horse*) sentarse a horcajadas sobre

straggle ['strægl] *vi* **1.** (*move in a disorganised group*) avanzar desordenadamente **2.** (*hang untidily: hair*) caer en desorden **3.** (*come in small numbers*) llegar poco a poco **4.** (*lag behind*) rezagarse

straggler ['strægləʳ, *Am:* -lə-] *n* rezagado, -a *m, f*

straggly ['strægli] <-ier, -iest> *adj* (*hair*) desordenado, -a

straight [streɪt] I. *n* (*straight line*) recta *f;* **the finishing** ~ la recta final II. *adj* **1.** (*not bent*) recto, -a **2.** (*honest*) honrado, -a; (*answer*) franco, -a; **to be** ~ **with sb** ser sincero con alguien **3.** (*plain*) sencillo, -a; (*undiluted: gin, vodka*) solo, -a **4.** (*clear*) claro, -a **5.** (*consecutive*) seguido, -a; **she won in** ~ **sets** ganó sin perder ningún set **6.** THEAT (*not comic*) serio, -a **7.** (*traditional*) convencional **8.** *inf* (*heterosexual*) heterosexual III. *adv* **1.** (*in a direct line*) en línea recta; **to go** ~ **ahead** ir todo recto; **to come** ~ **at sb** ir derecho a alguien **2.** (*at once*) **to get** ~ **to the point** ir directo al grano **3.** *inf* (*honestly*) honestamente **4.** (*clearly: see, think*) con claridad **5.** (*tidy*) en orden; **to put sth** ~ ordenar algo

straightaway [ˌstreɪtə'weɪ, *Am:* ˌstreɪt̬ə'-] I. *adv* enseguida II. *n Am* SPORTS recta *f*

straighten ['streɪtn] *vt* **1.** (*make straight: hair*) alisar; (*wire*) enderezar **2.** (*unbend: arm, body, leg*) estirar **3.** (*make level: hem*) igualar **4.** (*make tidy: room*) ordenar

♦**straighten out** I. *vt* **1.** (*make straight*) estirar **2.** (*make level*) igualar **3.** (*solve: problem*) resolver; (*situation*) arreglar **4.** (*clarify*) aclarar; **to straighten sb out** aclarar algo a alguien **II.** *vi* (*road*) hacerse recto, -a

◆**straighten up I.** *vi* (*stand upright*) ponerse derecho, arriscarse *Col* **II.** *vt* **1.** (*make level*) igualar **2.** (*make tidy*) ordenar

straightforward [ˌstreɪtˈfɔːwəd, *Am:* -ˈfɔːrwɚd] *adj* **1.** (*honest*) honesto, -a **2.** (*easy*) sencillo, -a

straight-out [ˌstreɪtˈaʊt] *adj Am, inf* (*outright*) redomado, -a, consumado, -a; (*refusal*) tajante

strain¹ [streɪn] **I.** *n no pl* **1.** *no pl* (*pressure*) presión *f*; **to be under a lot of** ~ tener mucho estrés; **to put a** ~ **on a relationship** crear tensiones en una relación **2.** *no pl* PHYS deformación *f* **3.** MED torcedura *f* **II.** *vi* (*try hard*) esforzarse; **to** ~ **for effect** utilizar recursos efectistas **III.** *vt* **1.** (*stretch*) estirar; **to** ~ **a rope** tirar de una cuerda **2.** (*overexert*) **to** ~ **one's eyes** forzar la vista; **to** ~ **one's ears** aguzar el oído **3.** (*put stress on: relationship*) crear tensiones en; (*credulity*) poner a prueba **4.** GASTR (*coffee*) filtrar; (*vegetables*) escurrir

strain² [streɪn] *n* **1.** (*variety: of animal*) raza *f*; (*of virus*) cepa *f* **2.** (*tendency or trait*) ~ **of eccentricity** vena *f* excéntrica; ~ **of puritanism** nota *f* de puritanismo **3.** MUS tono *m*

strained [streɪnd] *adj* (*relation*) tenso, -a; (*smile*) forzado, -a

strainer *n* colador *m*

strait [streɪt] *n* **1.** GEO estrecho *m*; **the Straits of Gibraltar** el estrecho de Gibraltar **2.** (*bad situation*) apuro *m*; **to be in a** ~ estar en apuros; **to be in dire** ~**s** estar en grandes apuros

straitened *adj* **in** ~ **circumstances** en apuros económicos

straitjacket [ˈstreɪtˌdʒækɪt] *n* PSYCH, MED camisa *f* de fuerza

straitlaced [ˌstreɪtˈleɪst, *Am:* ˈstreɪtleɪst] *adj* mojigato, -a

strand¹ [strænd] *n* **1.** (*thread: of wool*) hebra *f*; (*of rope, string*) ramal *m*; **a** ~ **of hair** un mechón de pelo **2.** (*string: of pearls*) sarta *f*; (*of plot*) hilo *m*

strand² [strænd] **I.** *n liter* (*shore*) ribera *f* **II.** *vt* varar; **to be** ~**ed** quedarse desamparado

strange [streɪndʒ] *adj* **1.** (*peculiar*) extraño, -a, raro, -a; **I felt** ~ **me** sentía raro; **it's** ~ **that** es raro que +*subj*; ~**r things have happened** cosas más raras han pasado; ~ **to say** aunque parezca mentira **2.** (*unfamiliar: face*) desconocido, -a; (*bed*) ajeno, -a

strangely *adv* (*behave, dress*) de una manera rara; ~ **enough ...** aunque parazca mentira...

stranger [ˈstreɪndʒɚ, *Am:* -dʒɚ] *n* desconocido, -a *m*, *f*; **he is no** ~ **to controversy** la polémica no le es ajena

strangle [ˈstræŋgl] *vt* (*person*) estrangular; (*cry*) ahogar

stranglehold [ˈstræŋglhəʊld, *Am:* -hoʊld] *n* (*control*) dominio *m* total; (*on market*) monopolio *m*; **to have sb in a** ~ tener a alguien dominado

strangulation [ˌstræŋgjʊˈleɪʃən] *n* estran-

gulación *f*

strap [stræp] **I.** *n* (*of bag*) correa *f*; (*of dress*) tirante *m* **II.** <-pp-> *vt* atar [*o* sujetar] con una correa

strapless [ˈstræplɪs] *adj* sin tirantes

strapping [ˈstræpɪn] **I.** *n* (*bandage*) esparadrapo *m* **II.** *adj inf* robusto, -a

stratagem [ˈstrætədʒəm, *Am:* ˈstræt̬-] *n* estratagema *f*

strategic [strəˈtiːdʒɪk] *adj* estratégico, -a

strategist [ˈstrætədʒɪst, *Am:* ˈstræt̬-] *n* estratega *mf*

strategy [ˈstrætədʒi, *Am:* ˈstræt̬-] <-ies> *n* estrategia *f*

stratify [ˈstrætɪfaɪ, *Am:* ˈstræt̬ə-] *vt* estratificar

stratosphere [ˈstrætəsfɪɚ, *Am:* ˈstræt̬əsfɪr] *n* estratosfera *f*; **to go into the** ~ (*prices*) irse por las nubes

stratum [ˈstreɪtəm, *Am:* ˈstreɪt̬əm] <strata> *n* estrato *m*

straw [strɔː, *Am:* strɑː] *n* **1.** *no pl* (*dry stems*) paja *f* **2.** (*for drinking*) pajita *f*, popote *m Méx*, pitillo *m And* ▶**a** ~ **in the wind** un indicio de cómo andan las cosas; **to be the last** ~ ser el colmo; **to draw the short** ~ tocarle a uno la china; **to clutch at** ~**s** agarrarse a un clavo ardiendo

strawberry [ˈstrɔːbəri, *Am:* ˈstrɑːˌbɛri] <-ies> *n* fresa *f*, frutilla *f AmL*

straw-coloured [ˈstrɔːkʌləd] *adj* pajizo, -a **straw man** *n* hombre *m* de paja **straw poll** *n* sondeo *m* informal

stray [streɪ] **I.** *n* (*dog*) perro *m* callejero; (*cat*) gato *m* callejero **II.** *adj* **1.** (*homeless: dog, cat*) callejero, -a, realengo, -a *Méx, PRico* **2.** (*loose: hair*) suelto, -a; (*bullet*) perdido, -a **III.** *vi* (*wander*) errar; (*become lost*) perderse; **to** ~ **from** alejarse de; **to** ~ **off course** apartarse del camino; **they were warned not to stray beyond the garden** se les advirtió que no salieran del jardín; **to** ~ **from the point** divagar

streak [striːk] **I.** *n* **1.** (*stripe*) raya *f*; (*in hair*) mechón *m*; (*of light*) rayo *m*; (*of lightning*) relámpago *m* **2.** (*tendency*) vena *f*; **an aggressive** ~ una vena agresiva; **to have a** ~ **of cowardice** tener algo de cobarde **3.** (*spell*) racha *f*; **to be on a winning** ~ tener una buena racha ▶**like a** ~ **of lightning** como un rayo; **to talk a blue** ~ *Am* hablar más que un loro agarrado por el rabo **II.** *vt* rayar; **to have one's hair** ~**ed** hacerse mechas; **to be** ~**ed with sth** estar manchado de algo **III.** *vi* **1.** (*move very fast*) ir rápido **2.** (*run naked in public*) correr desnudo en un lugar público

streaker *n* persona que corre desnuda en un lugar público

streaky [ˈstriːki] <-ier, -iest> *adj* rayado, -a; ~ **bacon** *Brit* bacon *m* entreverado

stream [striːm] **I.** *n* **1.** (*small river*) arroyo *m*, estero *m Chile, Ecua* **2.** (*current*) corriente *f*; **to go against the** ~ *fig* ir a contracorriente; **to**

come on ~ (*factory*) entrar en funcionamiento **3.** (*flow: of oil, water*) chorrito *m;* (*of people*) torrente *m;* (*of insults*) sarta *f* **4.** *Brit, Aus* SCHOOL *grupo de escolares con la misma aptitud académica* **II.** *vi* **1.** (*flow*) fluir; (*water*) chorrear; (*blood*) manar; (*tears*) caer; **tears ~ed down her face** lloraba a lágrima viva; **blood ~ed from his head** le chorreaba sangre de la cabeza **2.** (*move in numbers*) afluir en masa **3.** (*shine: light, sun*) entrar a raudales **4.** (*run: nose*) gotear; (*eyes*) llorar **III.** *vt Brit, Aus* SCHOOL *dividir en grupos de acuerdo con su aptitud académica*

streamer ['stri:mə^r, *Am:* -mə·] *n* serpentina *f*

streamline ['stri:mlaɪn] *vt* (*vehicle*) aerodinamizar; (*method*) racionalizar

streamlined *adj* (*vehicle*) aerodinámico, -a; (*method*) racionalizado, -a

street [stri:t] *n* (*road*) calle *f;* **in** [*o* **on**] **the ~** en la calle ▸**to be ~s ahead of sb** estar muy por delante de alguien; **to be on the ~s** hacer la calle; **to be up sb's ~** ser ideal para alguien; **to walk the ~s** (*wander*) deambular por las calles; (*be a prostitute*) hacer la calle

street battle *n* pelea *f* callejera **streetcar** *n Am* tranvía *m* **street credibility** *n*, **street-cred** *n imagen moderna y urbana* **street directory** *n* guía *f* de calles **street-lamp** *n*, **street light** *n* farola *f* **street lighting** *n no pl* alumbrado *m* (público) **street value** *n no pl* valor *m* de reventa **streetwalker** *n* prostituta *f* que hace la calle **streetwise** ['stri:twaɪz] *adj* (*person*) espabilado, -a; (*politician*) astuto, -a

strength [streŋθ] *n* **1.** *no pl* (*power*) fuerza *f,* ñeque *m Chile, Ecua, Perú;* (*of feeling, light*) intensidad *f;* (*of alcohol*) graduación *f;* (*of economy*) solidez *f;* (*mental firmness*) fortaleza *f* **2.** (*number of members*) número *m;* **to be at full ~** tener el cupo completo; **to be below ~** (*office*) estar corto de personal **3.** (*strong point*) punto *m* fuerte; **one's ~s and weaknesses** sus virtudes y defectos ▸**to go from ~ to ~** ir cada vez mejor

strengthen ['streŋθn] **I.** *vt* **1.** (*make stronger: muscles*) fortalecer; (*wall*) reforzar; (*financial position*) consolidar **2.** (*increase: chances*) aumentar **3.** (*intensify: relations*) intensificar; (*links*) estrechar **II.** *vi* fortalecerse

strenuous ['strenjʊəs, *Am:* -juəs] *adj* (*exercise, sport*) agotador(a); (*supporter*) acérrimo, -a; (*denial*) rotundo, -a

streptococcus [ˌstreptə'kɒkəs, *Am:* -'kɑ:kəs] <-ci> *n* estreptococo *m*

stress [stres] **I.** *n no pl* **1.** (*mental strain*) estrés *m* **2.** (*emphasis*) énfasis *m inv* **3.** LING acento *m* **4.** PHYS tensión *f* **II.** *vt* **1.** (*emphasise*) recalcar **2.** LING acentuar

stressed *adj,* **stressed out** *adj inf* estresado, -a

stress fracture *n* fractura *f* de fatiga **stress-free** *adj* sin estrés

stressful ['stresfʊl] *adj* estresante

stress mark *n* LING acento *m*

stretch [stretʃ] **I.** <-es> *n* **1.** *no pl* (*elasticity*) elasticidad *f* **2.** SPORTS estiramiento *m* **3.** GEO trecho *m* **4.** (*piece*) trozo *m;* (*of road*) tramo *m;* (*of time*) período *m* **5.** (*stage of a race*) recta *f;* **the final ~** la recta final **6.** (*exertion*) **at full ~** a todo gas; **to work at full ~** trabajar al máximo de su capacidad; **not by any ~ of the imagination** ni por asomo **II.** *adj* elástico, -a **III.** *vi* **1.** (*become bigger*) estirarse; (*clothes*) dar de sí **2.** (*extend muscles*) estirarse **3.** (*in time*) **to ~ back to ...** remontarse a... **4.** (*cover an area: sea, influence*) extenderse **IV.** *vt* **1.** (*extend: muscles*) estirar; (*tendon*) distender; **to ~ one's legs** estirar las piernas **2.** (*make go further*) estirar **3.** (*demand a lot of*) **to ~ sb's patience** poner a prueba la paciencia de alguien; **my present job doesn't ~ me** mi trabajo actual no me exige lo suficiente; **his nerves are ~ed to breaking point** tiene los nervios a punto de estallar **4.** (*go beyond*) **to ~ a point** hacer una excepción; **to ~ it a bit** exagerar un poco **5.** LAW sobrepasar los límites de **6.** MUS tensar

stretcher ['stretʃə^r, *Am:* -ə·] *n* camilla *f* **stretcher bearer** *n* camillero, -a *m, f*

strew [stru:] <strewn, strewn *o* strewed> *vt* esparcir

stricken ['strɪkən] *adj* **1.** (*distressed*) afligido, -a **2.** (*wounded*) herido, -a **3.** (*afflicted*) **to be stricken with illness** estar enfermo; **she was stricken with remorse** le remordía la conciencia **4.** (*damaged: tanker*) siniestrado, -a

strict [strɪkt] *adj* (*person*) severo, -a, fregado, -a *AmC;* (*control, orders, sense*) estricto, -a; (*deadline*) inamovible; (*neutrality*) total; (*secrecy*) completo, -a; (*confidence*) absoluto, -a; **to be ~ with sb** ser severo con alguien

strictly ['strɪktli] *adv* **1.** (*exactly*) estrictamente; **not ~ comparable** no del todo comparable; **~ speaking** en rigor **2.** (*harshly*) severamente; **~ forbidden** terminantemente prohibido

stride [straɪd] **I.** <strode> *vi* andar a trancos; **to ~ ahead** andar dando zancadas; **to ~ across sth** cruzar algo de una zancada **II.** *n* **1.** (*long step*) zancada *f* **2.** (*progress*) progreso *m;* **to make ~s forward** hacer grandes progresos; **to make ~s towards sth** acercarse a algo ▸**to get into one's ~,** **to hit one's ~** coger el ritmo; **to put sb off his/her ~** *Brit* distraer a alguien; **to take sth in one's ~** tomarse algo con calma

strident ['straɪdnt] *adj* estridente

strife [straɪf] *n no pl* lucha *f;* (*verbal*) disputa *f;* **domestic ~** riñas *fpl* domésticas

strike [straɪk] **I.** *n* **1.** (*military attack*) ataque *m* **2.** (*withdrawal of labour*) huelga *f* **3.** (*discovery*) descubrimiento *m* **4.** *Am* (*in baseball*) golpe *m* **5.** *Am* LAW fallo *m* de culpabilidad **II.** <struck *Am:* stricken, struck> *vt* **1.** (*collide with*) golpear; **to ~ a match** encender una cerilla; **to be struck by lightning** ser alcanzado por un rayo; **to ~ a blow against sb** asestar un golpe a alguien **2.** (*achieve*) conseguir; **to ~ a balance** encontrar un equilibrio; **to ~ a bargain with sb** hacer un trato con alguien **3.** (*manufacture: coin*) acuñar **4.** (*seem*) parecer; **it ~s me that ...** se me ocurre que... **5.** (*impress*) impresionar **6.** (*engender*) **to ~ fear into sb** infundir miedo a alguien **7.** (*discover*) descubrir; (*find*) encontrar; **to ~ gold** (*win gold medal*) ganar el oro; (*have financial fortune*) descubrir un filón **8.** (*adopt*) **to ~ an attitude** adoptar una actitud **9.** (*sound the time: clock*) marcar; **the clock struck three** el reloj dio las tres **10.** (*remove: flag*) arriar **11.** (*delete*) borrar, tachar ▶**to ~ a chord with sb** llegar a entenderse con alguien; **to ~ the right note** dar con el tono justo; **to ~ sb dumb** dejar a alguien sin habla III.<struck, struck> *vi* **1.** (*hit hard*) golpear; (*attack*) atacar; **to ~ at sth** asestar un golpe contra algo; **to ~ at the heart of sth** atacar directamente a algo; **to ~ home** dar en el blanco **2.** (*withdraw labour*) declararse en huelga; **the right to ~** el derecho a la huelga; **to ~ for sth** hacer una huelga para conseguir algo

◆**strike back** *vi* devolver el golpe; **to ~ at sb** tomar represalias contra alguien

◆**strike down** *vt* **1. she was struck down by cancer** fue abatida por el cáncer **2.** *Am* LAW revocar

◆**strike off** *vt Brit, Aus* (*lawyer, doctor*) inhabilitar; **to strike sb off a list** tachar a alguien de una lista

◆**strike out** I. *vt* **1.** (*delete*) borrar **2.** *Am* SPORTS eliminar II. *vi* **1.** (*move off*) andar resueltamente; **to ~ on one's own** hacerse independiente **2.** (*hit out*) empezar a repartir golpes **3.** *Am* SPORTS hacer un strike; *fig* fallar

◆**strike up** *vt* (*conversation*) entablar; (*relationship*) iniciar; (*friendship*) trabar

strike action *n* huelga *f*

strikebound ['straɪkbaʊnd] *adj* paralizado, -a por la huelga

strikebreaker ['straɪkˌbreɪkəʳ, *Am:* -kɚ] *n* esquirol *mf*

strike committee *n* comité *m* de huelga **strike fund** *n* fondo *m* de huelga **strike pay** *n* subsidio *m* de huelga

striker ['straɪkəʳ, *Am:* -kɚ] *n* **1.** SPORTS ariete *mf* **2.** (*strike participant*) huelguista *mf*

striking ['straɪkɪŋ] *adj* notable; (*result, beauty*) impresionante; (*resemblance*) sorprendente; (*change*) considerable; (*contrast*) acusado, -a; (*difference*) gran; **visually ~** llamativo

string [strɪŋ] I. *n* **1.** (*twine*) *a.* MUS cuerda *f*; (*on puppet*) hilo *m*; **to pull ~s** *fig* mover hilos; **with no ~s attached** sin compromiso alguno **2.** *pl* MUS (*section*) (instrumentos *mpl* de) cuerda *f*; (*players*) (instrumentistas *mpl* de) cuerda **3.** (*chain*) cadena *f*; (*of pearls*) collar *m* **4.** (*sequence: of scandals*) serie *f*; (*of lies*)

sarta *f*; (*of people*) hilera *f*; (*of oaths*) retahíla *f* **5.** INFOR secuencia *f* II.<strung, strung> *vt* poner una cuerda a; (*instrument*) encordar; (*beads*) ensartar

◆**string along** *inf* I. *vi* ir/venir también II. *vt Brit* **to string sb along** embaucar a alguien

◆**string out** *vt* **1.** (*extend*) espaciar **2.** (*protract: activity*) prolongar

◆**string up** *vt inf* colgar

string bag *n* bolsa *f* de red **string band** *n* banda *f* de cuerda **string bean** *n Am, Aus* habichuela *f* **stringed instrument** *n* instrumento *m* de cuerda

stringency ['strɪndʒənsi] *n no pl* **1.** (*of measure*) severidad *f*; (*of test*) rigor *m* **2.** FIN dificultad *f*

stringent ['strɪndʒənt] *adj* **1.** (*measure*) severo, -a; (*rigorous: test*) riguroso, -a; (*law, requirement*) estricto, -a **2.** FIN restrictivo, -a

stringer ['strɪŋəʳ, *Am:* -ɚ] *n inf* corresponsal *mf* local

string quartet *n* cuarteto *m* de cuerda

stringy ['strɪŋi] *adj* (*meat*) correoso, -a; (*person*) delgado, -a pero fuerte

strip [strɪp] I. *vt* **1.** (*lay bare*) dejar sin cubierta; **to ~ sb of sth** quitarle algo a alguien **2.** (*unclothe*) desnudar **3.** (*dismantle*) desmontar II. *vi* desnudarse III. *n* **1.** (*ribbon*) tira *f*; (*of metal*) lámina *f*; (*of land*) franja *f* **2.** *Brit, Aus* SPORTS camiseta *f* **3.** (*striptease*) striptease *m* **4.** (*landing area*) pista *f*

strip cartoon *n Brit* historieta *f*

stripe [straɪp] *n* **1.** (*coloured band*) raya *f*; **of every ~** de todo tipo; **governments of every ~** gobiernos de todos los colores **2.** MIL galón *m*; **a man of that ~** *Am, fig* un hombre de esa clase

striped *adj*, **stripey** *adj* rayado, -a; (*shirt*) a rayas

strip light *n Brit* tubo *m* fluorescente **strip lighting** *n* alumbrado *m* fluorescente **strip mining** *n Am* minería *f* a cielo abierto

stripper ['strɪpəʳ, *Am:* -ɚ] *n* persona *f* que hace striptease

strip-search [ˌstrɪˈsɜːtʃ, *Am:* 'strɪpsɜːrtʃ] I. *n* registro *m* en el que la persona tiene que desnudarse II. *vt* **to ~ sb** hacer desnudar a alguien para registrarle **strip show** *n* espectáculo *m* de striptease

striptease ['strɪptiːz] *n* striptease *m*

stripy *adj* rayado, -a; (*shirt*) a rayas

strive [straɪv] <strove, striven *o* strived, strived> *vi* esforzarse; **to ~ to do sth** esmerarse en hacer algo; **to ~ after sth** luchar por conseguir algo; **to ~ for sth** afanarse para conseguir algo

strobe [strəʊb, *Am:* stroʊb] *n inf* luz *f* estroboscópica

strobe light *n* luz *f* estroboscópica

stroboscope ['strəʊbəskəʊp, *Am:* 'stroʊbəskoʊp] *n* estroboscopio *m*

strode [strəʊd, *Am:* stroʊd] *pt of* **stride**

stroke [strəʊk, *Am:* stroʊk] I. *vt* **1.** (*caress*) acariciar **2.** SPORTS (*hit smoothly*) golpear suavemente II. *n* **1.** (*caress*) caricia *f* **2.** MED derrame *m* cerebral; **to have a** ~ tener una apoplejía **3.** (*of pencil*) trazo *m;* (*of brush*) pincelada *f* **4.** (*style of hitting ball*) golpe *m;* (*billiards*) tacada *f;* **at a** (**single**) ~, **in one** ~ de (un solo) golpe **5.** *form* (*lash with whip*) latigazo *m* **6.** (*in swimming: style*) estilo *m;* (*single movement*) brazada *f* **7.** (*bit*) **by a** ~ **of fate** por cosas del destino; **a** ~ **of genius** una genialidad; **a** ~ **of luck** un golpe de suerte; **to not do a** ~ **of work** *inf* no dar golpe **8.** (*of clock*) campanada *f*

stroll [strəʊl, *Am:* stroʊl] I. *n* paseo *m;* **to go for a** ~ dar una vuelta II. *vi* dar un paseo; **to** ~ **along the river bank** pasearse por el lado del río

stroller ['strəʊlər, *Am:* 'stroʊlɚ] *n* **1.** (*person*) paseante *mf* **2.** *Am, Aus* (*pushchair*) cochecito *m*

strong [strɒŋ, *Am:* stra:ŋ] I. *adj* **1.** (*powerful*) fuerte; (*coffee*) cargado, -a; (*competition*) duro, -a; (*condemnation*) severo, -a; (*doubt, incentive, influence*) gran, grande; (*protest, measure*) enérgico, -a; (*reason*) de peso; (*wind*) recio, -a; **to produce** ~ **memories** traer muchos recuerdos **2.** (*capable*) competente **3.** (*physically powerful*) robusto, -a; **to be as** ~ **as a horse** ser tan fuerte como un toro **4.** (*fit*) sano, -a; (*constitution*) fuerte **5.** (*durable*) sólido, -a; (*will, conviction*) firme; (*nerves*) de acero **6.** (*staunch*) arraigado, -a; (*antipathy*) gran; (*believer*) fervoroso, -a; (*bond*) fuerte; (*character*) enérgico, -a; (*emotion*) intenso, -a; (*friend*) íntimo, -a; (*friendship*) estrecho, -a; (*objection, opponent*) duro, -a; (*supporter*) acérrimo, -a **7.** (*tough*) resistente **8.** (*very likely*) muy probable; ~ **chances of success** muchas posibilidades de éxito **9.** (*marked*) marcado, -a; (*colour*) llamativo, -a; (*light, flavour*) intenso, -a; (*fragrance*) penetrante; (*language*) vulgar **10.** (*bright*) brillante **11.** (*having high value*) de gran valor II. *adv inf* **to come on** ~ **to sb** (*show sexual interest in*) ir por alguien; **to be still going** ~ ir todavía bien

strong-arm ['strɒŋɑ:m, *Am:* 'stra:ŋɑ:rm] I. *adj* (*method*) de mano dura II. *vt* utilizar la fuerza física con

strongbox ['strɒŋbɒks, *Am:* 'stra:ŋba:ks] *n* caja *f* fuerte

stronghold ['strɒŋhəʊld, *Am:* 'stra:ŋhoʊld] *n* (*fortified place*) fortaleza *f;* *fig* baluarte *m*

strongly *adv* **1.** (*powerfully*) fuertemente; (*advise*) fervorosamente; (*condemn*) con dureza; (*criticize, force*) enérgicamente; **to smell** ~ **of sth** tener un fuerte olor a algo; **to be** ~ **opposed to sth** estar muy en contra de algo; **to be** ~ **biased against sb** tener una fuerte predisposición contra alguien **2.** (*sturdily*) sólidamente

strong-minded [ˌstrɒŋ'maɪndɪd, *Am:* ˌstra:ŋ-] *adj* resuelto, -a

strongroom ['strɒŋrʊm, *Am:* 'stra:ŋru:m] *n* cámara *f* acorazada

strong-willed [ˌstrɒŋ'wɪld, *Am:* ˌstra:ŋ-] *adj* resuelto, -a

strontium ['strɒntiəm, *Am:* 'stra:ntʃiəm] *n no pl* estroncio *m*

strop [strɒp, *Am:* stra:p] *n Brit, Aus, inf* **to be in a** ~ estar de mal humor

stroppy ['strɒpi, *Am:* 'stra:pi] *adj Brit, Aus, inf* enfadado, -a

strove [strəʊv, *Am:* stroʊv] *pt of* **strive**

struck [strʌk] *pt, pp of* **strike**

structural ['strʌktʃərəl] *adj* estructural

structural unemployment *n* ECON, SOCIOL paro *m* estructural

structure ['strʌktʃər, *Am:* -tʃɚ] I. *n* estructura *f;* (*building*) construcción *f* II. *vt* estructurar

struggle ['strʌgl] I. *n* **1.** (*effort*) esfuerzo *m;* **to be a real** ~ suponer un gran esfuerzo; **to give up the** ~ **to do sth** dejar de esmerarse en hacer algo **2.** (*skirmish*) lucha *f* II. *vi* **1.** (*make an effort*) esforzarse **2.** (*fight*) luchar

strum [strʌm] <-mm-> *vt* MUS rasguear

strung [strʌŋ] *pt, pp of* **string**

strut¹ [strʌt] I. <-tt-> *vi* **to** ~ **about** pavonearse II. *vt inf* **to** ~ **one's stuff** *iron* (*dance*) contonearse

strut² [strʌt] *n* (*in building, plane*) puntal *m*

strychnine ['strɪkni:n, *Am:* -naɪn] *n no pl* estricnina *f*

stub [stʌb] I. *n* (*of cheque*) talón *m;* (*of cigarette*) colilla *f;* (*of pencil*) cabo *m* II. <-bb-> *vt* **to** ~ **one's toe against sth** tropezar con algo

◆**stub out** *vt* (*cigarette*) apagar

stubble ['stʌbl] *n no pl* **1.** (*beard growth*) barba *f* de tres días **2.** AGR rastrojo *m*

stubbly ['stʌbli] *adj* (*bristly*) con barba de tres días

stubborn ['stʌbən, *Am:* -ɚn] *adj* (*person, animal*) terco, -a; (*insistence*) tenaz; (*problem*) persistente; (*refusal*) rotundo, -a; (*resistence*) inquebrantable

stubby ['stʌbi] *adj* (*person*) achaparrado, -a; (*finger*) corto, -a

stucco ['stʌkəʊ, *Am:* -oʊ] *n no pl* estuco *m*

stuck [stʌk] I. *pt, pp of* **stick** II. *adj* **1.** (*jammed*) atascado, -a **2.** *inf* (*crazy about*) **to be** ~ **on sb** estar loco por alguien **3.** *Brit, Aus, inf* (*persevere*) **to get** ~ **into sth** ponerse en serio con algo

stuck-up [ˌstʌk'ʌp] *adj inf* engreído, -a

stud¹ [stʌd] *n* **1.** (*horse*) semental *m,* garañón *m AmL* **2.** (*establishment*) caballeriza *f*

stud² [stʌd] *n* **1.** (*small metal item*) tachón *m;* (*decorative nail*) clavo *m;* **collar** ~ gemelo *m* **2.** *Brit, Aus* (*on shoe*) taco *m*

student ['stju:dənt, *Am:* 'stu:-] *n* estudiante *mf;* **the** ~ **body** el alumnado

student teacher *n* profesor(a) *m(f)* en prácticas **student union** n (*organization*) asociación f de estudiantes; (*meeting place*) club m de estudiantes universitarios

stud farm ['stʌdfɑːm, *Am:* -fɑːrm] n caballeriza f **stud horse** n semental m, garañón m *AmL*

studied ['stʌdɪd] adj estudiado, -a; (*answer*) pensado, -a; (*insult*) premeditado, -a

studio ['stjuːdiəʊ, *Am:* 'stuːdioʊ] <-s> n 1.(*of artist*) taller m 2.CINE estudio m

studio apartment n estudio m **studio audience** n público m en estudio **studio couch** n sofá-cama m

studious ['stjuːdiəs, *Am:* 'stuː-] adj estudioso, -a

study ['stʌdi] I. vt (*subject*) estudiar; (*evidence*) examinar II. vi estudiar III.<-ies> n 1.(*of subject*) estudio m; (*of evidence*) investigación f 2.(*room*) despacho m

study group n grupo m de estudio **study visit** n viaje m de estudios

stuff [stʌf] I. n no pl 1. inf (*things*) materia f; **to know one's** ~ conocer su oficio 2.(*belongings*) cosas fpl 3.(*material*) material m; (*cloth*) tela f; **to be the** ~ **of which heroes are made** tener madera de héroe; **the (very)** ~ **of sth** la esencia de algo II. vt 1.(*fill*) llenar; **to** ~ **sth into sth** meter algo en algo; **to** ~ **sb's head with sth** llenarle a alguien la cabeza de algo; **to** ~ **oneself** inf darse un atracón 2.(*preserve: animal*) disecar

stuffed shirt n inf persona f estirada

stuffing ['stʌfɪŋ] n no pl relleno m ▸**to knock the** ~ **out of sb** inf dar una paliza a alguien

stuffy ['stʌfi] adj pej 1.(*room*) mal ventilado, -a; (*atmosphere*) cargado, -a 2.(*person*) tieso, -a

stultifying ['stʌltɪˌfaɪɪŋ, *Am:* -ţə-] <-ie-> adj embrutecedor(a)

stumble ['stʌmbl] vi 1.(*trip*) tropezar; **to** ~ **on sth** tropezar con algo 2.(*while talking*) balbucear; **to** ~ **over sth** tropezar en algo

stumbling block n obstáculo m

stump [stʌmp] I. n 1.(*of plant*) tocón m; (*of arm*) muñón m; (*of tooth*) raigón m 2.*Am* POL **to go on the** ~ hacer campaña II. vt 1.inf (*baffle*) desconcertar 2.*Am* POL **to** ~ **the country** viajar por todo el país pronunciando discursos III. vi **to** ~ **about** andar pisando fuerte

stumpy ['stʌmpi] adj inf achaparrado, -a; (*tail*) corto, -a

stun [stʌn] <-nn-> vt 1.(*stupefy*) dejar pasmado 2.(*render unconscious*) dejar sin sentido

stung [stʌŋ] pp, pt of **sting**

stun grenade n MIL granada f detonadora

stunk [stʌŋk] pt, pp of **stink**

stunned adj aturdido, -a

stunner ['stʌnər, *Am:* -ə-] n inf 1.(*surprise*) sorpresa f; (*person*) 2.**she's a** ~ es un bombón

stunning ['stʌnɪŋ] adj 1.(*surprising*) aturdi

dor(a) 2.(*impressive*) maravilloso, -a; (*dress*) estupendo, -a; (*view*) espléndido, -a

stunt[1] [stʌnt] n 1.(*acrobatics*) acrobacia f 2.(*feat*) hazaña f; **to pull a** ~ inf hacer una proeza 3.(*publicity action*) truco m publicitario; **advertising** ~ treta f publicitaria 4.CINE toma f peligrosa

stunt[2] [stʌnt] vt (*plant*) atrofiar; (*growth*) impedir

stunted adj enano, -a; (*child*) poco desarrollado, -a; **emotionally** ~ poco maduro emocionalmente

stuntman ['stʌntmæn] n especialista

stupefaction [ˌstjuːpɪ'fækʃən, *Am:* ˌstuːpə'-] n no pl, form estupefacción f

stupefy ['stjuːpɪfaɪ, *Am:* 'stuːpə-] <-ie-> vt atontar; fig dejar estupefacto

stupendous [stjuː'pendəs, *Am:* stuː-] adj estupendo, -a

stupid ['stjuːpɪd, *Am:* 'stuː-] adj estúpido, -a, cojudo, -a *AmL*, zonzo, -a *AmL*; (*mistake*) tonto, -a

stupidity [stjuː'pɪdəti, *Am:* stuː'pɪdəʈi] n no pl estupidez f, dundera f *AmL*

stupor ['stjuːpər, *Am:* 'stuːpər] n estupor m

sturdy ['stɜːdi, *Am:* 'stɜːr-] adj 1.(*robust*) robusto, -a; (*person*) fuerte 2.(*resolute*) decidido, -a

sturgeon ['stɜːdʒən, *Am:* 'stɜːr-] n esturión m

stutter ['stʌtər, *Am:* 'stʌʈə-] I. vi (*stammer*) tartamudear, cancanear, *AmL* II. vt decir algo tartamudeando III. n tartamudeo m; **to have a** ~ tartamudear

stutterer ['stʌtərər, *Am:* 'stʌʈəɚ] n tartamudo, -a m, f

sty[1] [staɪ] n (*pigsty*) pocilga f

sty[2] n, **stye** [staɪ] n MED orzuelo m

style [staɪl] I. n 1. a. ART, ARCHIT estilo m; (*of management*) modo f; (*of teaching*) forma f 2.(*elegance*) elegancia f; **to have no** ~ no ser elegante; **to do things in** ~ hacer las cosas como se debe; **in** ~ de forma elegante; **to live in (grand)** ~ vivir a lo grande; **to travel in** ~ viajar con todo el confort 3.(*fashion*) moda f; **in** ~ de moda 4.(*type*) normas fpl de estilo II. vt 1.(*design*) diseñar; (*hair*) peinar 2.(*label*) **to** ~ **oneself as ...** hacerse llamar...

style sheet n INFOR hoja f de estilo

styling n estilización f

stylish ['staɪlɪʃ] adj 1.(*fashionable*) a la moda 2.(*elegant*) garboso, -a

stylist ['staɪlɪst] n estilista mf

stylistic [staɪ'lɪstɪk] adj estilístico, -a

stylize ['staɪəlaɪz, *Am:* 'staɪlaɪz] vt estilizar

stylus ['staɪləs] <-es> n estilete m

stymie ['staɪmi] <-(y)ing> vt inf (*person*) poner obstáculos infranqueables ante; (*project*) bloquear

suave [swɑːv] adj cortés; pej zalamero, -a

sub[1] [sʌb] n 1. *Brit, Aus,* inf abbr of **substitute** sustituto, -a m, f 2. inf abbr of **submarine** submarino m 3. *Am,* inf abbr of **sandwich**

sandwich *m* mixto **4.** *Brit, Aus, inf abbr of*
subscription suscripción *f*
sub² [sʌb] <-bb-> *vi abbr of* **substitute** sustituir
subagency [ˌsʌbˈeɪdʒənsi] *n* <-ies> *Am*
sucursal *f*
subagent [ˌsʌbˈeɪdʒənt] *n* subagente *mf*
subaltern [ˈsʌbltən, *Am:* səbˈɔːltən] *n Brit*
MIL alférez *m*
subatomic [ˌsʌbəˈtɒmɪk, *Am:* -ˈtɑːmɪk] *adj*
PHYS subatómico, -a
subclass [ˈsʌbklɑːs, *Am:* -klæs] *n* BIO sub-
clase *f*
subcommittee [ˈsʌbkəˌmɪti, *Am:* ˌsʌbkəˈ-]
n subcomisión *f*
subconscious [ˌsʌbˈkɒnʃəs, *Am:* -ˈkɑːnʃəs]
I. *n no pl* subconsciente *m* **II.** *adj* subconsciente
subcontinent [ˌsʌbˈkɒntɪnənt, *Am:* ˈsʌb-
ˌkɑːntnənt] *n* GEO subcontinente *m;* **the** ~ el
subcontinente de la India
subcontract [ˌsʌbˈkɒntrækt, *Am:* ˈsʌb-
ˌkɑːn-] *vt* subcontratar
subcontractor [ˌsʌbkənˈtræktəʳ] *n* sub-
contratista *mf*
subculture [ˌsʌbˈkʌltʃəʳ, *Am:* ˈsʌbˌkʌltʃəʳ] *n*
subcultura *f*
subcutaneous [ˌsʌbkjuːˈteɪnɪəs] *adj* subcutáneo, -a
subdivide [ˌsʌbdɪˈvaɪd] *vt* subdividir
subdivision [ˌsʌbdɪˈvɪʒən] *n* **1.** (*division*)
subdivisión *f* **2.** *Am, Aus* (*housing estate*)
urbanización *f*
subdue [səbˈdjuː, *Am:* -ˈduː] *vt* (*tame*) controlar; (*repress*) reprimir
subdued *adj* (*colour*) suave; (*person*) apagado, -a
sub-edit [ˌsʌbˈedɪt] *vt* PUBL corregir
sub-editor [ˌsʌbˈedɪtəʳ, *Am:* -t̬əʳ] *n* redac-
tor(a) *m(f)*
subgroup [ˈsʌbgruːp] *n* subgrupo *m*
subheading [ˈsʌbˌhedɪŋ, *Am:* ˈsʌbˌ-] *n* subtítulo *m*
subject¹ [ˈsʌbdʒɪkt] **I.** *n* **1.** (*theme*) tema *m;*
to change the ~ cambiar de tema; **to wander
off the** ~ salirse del tema; **on the** ~ **of sb/sth**
a propósito de alguien/algo **2.** SCHOOL, UNIV
asignatura *f; Brit* (*research area*) ámbito *m*
3. POL súbdito, -a *m, f;* (*citizen*) ciudadano, -a
m, f **4.** LING sujeto *m* **5.** (*in experiment*) sujeto
m de experimentación **II.** *adj* **1.** POL subyu-
gado, -a **2.** (*exposed to*) **to be** ~ **to sth** estar
sujeto a algo; **to be** ~ **to colds** ser propenso a
acatarrarse; **to be** ~ **to many dangers** estar
expuesto a muchos peligros; **to be** ~ **to a high
tax** estar sujeto a impuestos elevados; ~ **to
prosecution** sujeto a persecución **3.** (*contingent on*) ~ **to approval** pendiente de aprobación
subject² [səbˈdʒekt] *vt* dominar
subject catalogue *n* catálogo *m* por temas
  subject index *n* índice *m* de materias
subjection [səbˈdʒekʃən] *n no pl* POL someti-

miento *m*
subjective [səbˈdʒektɪv] *adj* subjetivo, -a
subject matter *n* (*of meeting, book*) tema
m; (*of letter*) contenido *m*
sub judice [ˌsʌbˈdʒuːdɪsi, *Am:* -dəsi] *adj* LAW
sub júdice
subjugate [ˈsʌbdʒəgeɪt] *vt form* **1.** (*control*)
subyugar **2.** (*make submissive*) someter; **to** ~
sth to sth supeditar algo a algo
subjugation [ˌsʌbdʒəˈgeɪʃən] *n form* subyu-
gación
subjunctive [səbˈdʒʌŋktɪv] *n no pl* LING subjuntivo *m*
sublease [ˌsʌbˈliːs] *vt* subarrendar
sublet [sʌbˈlet] <sublet, sublet> *vt* subarrendar
sublieutenant [ˌsʌbləˈtenənt, *Am:* -luːˈ-] *n*
Brit MIL alférez *m* de fragata
sublimate [ˈsʌblɪmeɪt] *vt* PSYCH sublimar
sublime [səˈblaɪm] *adj* **1.** (*glorious*) sublime
2. *iron* (*absolute*) absoluto, -a; ~ **ignorance**
ignorancia *f* supina
subliminal [ˌsʌbˈlɪmɪnl, *Am:* -ˈlɪmənl] *adj*
PSYCH subliminal
submachine gun [ˌsʌbməˈʃiːnˌgʌn] *n*
metralleta *f*
submarine [ˌsʌbməˈriːn, ˈsʌbməˌriːn, *Am:*
ˈsʌbməriːn] **I.** *n* **1.** NAUT, MIL submarino *m inv*
2. *Am, inf* (*sandwich*) sandwich *m* mixto
II. *adj* submarino, -a
submenu [ˌsʌbˈmenjuː] *n* INFOR submenú *m*
submerge [səbˈmɜːdʒ, *Am:* -ˈmɜːrdʒ] **I.** *vt*
sumergir; **to** ~ **oneself in sth** *fig* dedicarse de
lleno a algo **II.** *vi* sumergirse
submersible [səbˈmɜːsɪbl, *Am:* -ˈmɜːrsəbl]
n sumergible *m*
submersion [səbˈmɜːʒən, *Am:* -ˈmɜːrʒən] *n*
no pl sumersión *f*
submission [səbˈmɪʃən] *n no pl* **1.** (*acquiescence*) sumisión *f* **2.** *no pl* (*of proposal*) presentación *f;* (*of document*) entrega *f* **3.** (*argument*) argumento *m* **4.** LAW alegato *m;* **in my** ~
form en mi opinión
submissive [səbˈmɪsɪv] *adj* sumiso, -a
submit [səbˈmɪt] <-tt-> **I.** *vt* **1.** (*hand in: proposal*) presentar; (*document*) entregar **2.** *form*
(*propose*) proponer **II.** *vi* (*yield*) someterse
subnormal [ˌsʌbˈnɔːml, *Am:* -ˈnɔːrml] *adj*
subnormal
subordinate¹ [səˈbɔːdənət, *Am:* -ˈbɔːr-
dənɪt] **I.** *n* subordinado, -a *m, f* **II.** *adj* (*secondary*) secundario, -a; (*lower in rank*) subordinado, -a
subordinate² [səˈbɔːdɪneɪt, *Am:* -ˈbɔːrdə-
neɪt] *vt* subordinar
subordinate clause *n* LING frase *f* subordinada
subordination [səˌbɔːdɪˈneɪʃən, *Am:*
-ˌbɔːrdənˈeɪʃən] *n no pl* subordinación *f*
suborn [səˈbɔːn, *Am:* -ˈbɔːrn] *vt* LAW sobornar
subplot [ˈsʌbplɒt, *Am:* -plɑːt] *n* argumento
m secundario

subpoena [sə'pi:nə] LAW **I.** *vt* citar; **to ~ sb to testify** mandar comparecer a alguien para testificar **II.** *n* citación *f* (judicial)

sub-post office [ˌsʌbpəʊst'ɒfɪs, *Am:* -'poʊstˌɑːfɪs] *n* subdelegación *f* de correos

subscribe [səb'skraɪb] **I.** *vt* **1.** (*contribute*) donar **2.** (*sign*) firmar **II.** *vi* **1.** (*agree*) **to ~ to sth** suscribir algo **2.** (*make susbscription*) suscribirse

subscriber [səb'skraɪbəʳ, *Am:* -ə] *n* (*to magazine*) suscriptor(a) *m(f)*; (*to phone service*) abonado, -a *m, f*

subscript [sʌb'skrɪpt] *n no pl* TYPO subíndice *m*

subscription [səb'skrɪpʃən] *n* suscripción *f*; **to take out a ~ to sth** suscribirse a algo

subsection [sʌbˌsekʃən] *n* **1.** (*part*) subdivisión *f* **2.** LAW apartado *m*

subsequent ['sʌbsɪkwənt] *adj* posterior; **~ to ...** después de...

subsequently *adv* después; **~ to ...** después de...

subservient [səb'sɜːviənt, *Am:* -'sɜːr-] *adj* **1.** *pej* (*servile*) servil **2.** (*secondary*) subordinado, -a

subset ['sʌbset] *n* MAT subconjunto *m*

subside [səb'saɪd] *vi* **1.** (*lessen*) disminuir **2.** (*sink: building*) hundirse; (*water*) bajar

subsidence [səb'saɪdns] *n no pl* (*of building*) hundimiento *m*; (*of water*) bajada *f*

subsidiary [səb'sɪdɪəri, *Am:* -əri] **I.** *adj* subsidiario, -a; (*reason*) secundario, -a; ECON filial **II.** <-ies> *n* ECON filial *f*

subsidize ['sʌbsɪdaɪz, *Am:* -sə-] *vt* subvencionar

subsidy ['sʌbsədi, *Am:* -sə-] <-ies> *n* subvención *f*, subsidio *m*; **unemployment ~** subsidio de desempleo

subsist [səb'sɪst] *vi form* subsistir; **to ~ on sth** sustentarse con algo

subsistence [səb'sɪstəns] *n* subsistencia *f*; **means of ~** medios *mpl* de subsistencia; **enough for a bare ~** suficiente para subsistir **subsistence allowance** *n Brit* dietas *fpl* **subsistence level** *n* nivel *m* de subsistencia **subsistence wage** *n* salario *m* de subsistencia

substance ['sʌbstəns] *n* **1.** *no pl* (*matter*) sustancia *f* **2.** (*essence*) esencia *f* **3.** *no pl* (*significance*) valor *m*; **a film of real ~** una película de gran valor *f* **4.** (*main point*) punto *m* más importante; **the ~ of the conversation** el punto esencial de la conversación; **in ~** en esencia **5.** (*posessions*) riqueza *f*; **a man of ~** un hombre acaudalado

substandard [ˌsʌb'stændəd, *Am:* -dəd] *adj* inferior

substantial [səb'stænʃl] *adj* **1.** (*important*) sustancial; (*difference, improvement*) notable; **to be in ~ agreement** estar de acuerdo en gran parte **2.** (*large*) grande; (*meal*) copioso, -a; (*sum, damage*) considerable **3.** (*sturdy*) sólido, -a

substantially [səb'stænʃəli] *adv* **1.** (*significantly*) considerablemente **2.** (*in the main*) esencialmente

substantiate [səb'stænʃɪeɪt] *vt* corroborar

substantive ['sʌbstəntɪv, *Am:* -ṭɪv] **I.** *n* sustantivo *m* **II.** *adj form* de peso

substation ['sʌbsteɪʃən] *n* **1.** ADMIN subdelegación *f*; **police ~** *Am* comisaría *f* de policía **2.** ELEC subestación *f*

substitute ['sʌbstɪtjuːt, *Am:* -stətuːt] **I.** *vt* sustituir; **to ~ sb with sb** *inf* reemplazar a alguien por alguien; **to ~ margarine for butter, to ~ butter by** [*o* **with**] **margarine** sustituir la mantequilla por la margarina **II.** *vi* **to ~ for sb** suplir a alguien **III.** *n* **1.** (*equivalent*) sustituto *m*; (*alternative: for milk, coffee*) sucedáneo *m*; **there's no ~ for him** no hay nadie como él **2.** *a.* SPORTS suplente *mf*; **to come on as a ~** sustituir a alguien

substitution [ˌsʌbstɪ'tjuːʃən, *Am:* -stə'tuː-] *n* sustitución *f*

substratum ['sʌbˌstreɪtəm] <-ta> *n* sustrato *m*

subsume [səb'sjuːm, *Am:* -'suːm] *vt form* subsumir; **to ~ sth under a category** subsumir algo dentro de una categoría

subtenant [ˌsʌb'tenənt, *Am:* 'sʌbˌten-] *n* subarrendatario, -a *m, f*

subterfuge ['sʌbtəfjuːdʒ, *Am:* -tə-] *n* subterfugio *m*; **by ~** por subterfugio

subterranean [ˌsʌbtə'reɪniən] *adj* subterráneo, -a

subtext ['sʌbtekst] *n* subtexto *m*

subtitle ['sʌbˌtaɪtl, *Am:* 'sʌbˌtaɪṭl] **I.** *vt* subtitular **II.** *n* subtítulo *m*

subtle ['sʌtl, *Am:* 'sʌṭ-] *adj* **1.** (*delicate*) sutil; (*flavour*) suave; (*nuance*) tenue **2.** (*slight: difference*) sutil **3.** (*astute: person*) astuto, -a; (*question, suggestion*) inteligente; (*humour*) fino, -a

subtlety ['sʌtlti, *Am:* 'sʌṭlṭi] <-ies> *n* **1.** (*delicacy: of flavour, smell*) delicadeza *f* **2.** (*of person, argument*) sutileza *f*

subtotal ['sʌbˌtəʊtl, *Am:* -ˌtoʊṭl] *n* subtotal *m*

subtract [səb'trækt] *vt* sustraer; **to ~ 3 from 5** restar 3 a 5

subtraction [səb'trækʃən] *n no pl* resta *f*, sustracción *f*

subtropical [ˌsʌb'trɒpɪkl, *Am:* -'trɑːpɪ-] *adj* subtropical

suburb ['sʌbɜːb, *Am:* -ɜːrb] *n* barrio *m* periférico; **the ~s** la periferia; **to live in the ~s** vivir en las afueras

suburban [sə'bɜːbən, *Am:* -'bɜːr-] *adj* **1.** (*area*) periférico, -a; (*train*) de cercanías **2.** (*lifestyle*) aburguesado, -a

suburbia [sə'bɜːbɪə, *Am:* -'bɜːr-] *n no pl* barrios *mpl* periféricos

subvention [səb'venʃən] *n form* subvención *f*

subversion [səb'vɜːʃən, *Am:* -'vɜːrʒən] *n no pl, form* subversión *f*

subversive [səb'vɜːsɪv, *Am:* -'vɜːr-] *form* **I.** *adj* subversivo, -a **II.** *n* persona *f* subversiva
subvert [sʌb'vɜːt, *Am:* -'vɜːrt] *vt* (*authority*) minar; (*principle*) debilitar
subway ['sʌbweɪ] *n* **1.** *Brit, Aus* (*walkway*) paso *m* subterráneo **2.** *Am* (*railway*) metro *m*, subte *m Arg*
sub-zero [ˌsʌb'zɪərəʊ, *Am:* -'zɪroʊ] *adj* bajo cero
succeed [sək'siːd] **I.** *vi* **1.** (*be successful*) tener éxito; **to ~ in doing sth** lograr hacer algo; **the plan ~ed** el plan salió bien **2.** (*follow*) suceder ►**if at** first **you don't ~, then try, try and try again** *prov* si no lo consigues a la primera, vuelve a intentarlo una y otra vez **II.** *vt* (*follow*) suceder a
succeeding *adj* **1.** (*next in line*) sucesor(a) **2.** (*following*) siguiente; (*generation*) venidero, -a; **in the ~ weeks** en las próximas semanas
success [sək'ses] *n* **1.** *no pl* (*outcome*) éxito *m;* **to meet with ~** tener éxito; **to be a big ~ with sb/sth** tener gran éxito con alguien/algo; **to have ~ in doing sth** conseguir hacer algo; **to make a ~ of sth** tener éxito en algo; **to wish sb ~ with sth** desear a alguien que le vaya bien algo; **to be a great ~** ser un gran éxito; **to enjoy ~** tener éxito; **~ story** éxito *m* **2.** (*successful person, thing*) éxito *m;* **he was a ~ with my children** les cayó muy bien a mis hijos
successful [sək'sesfəl] *adj* exitoso, -a; (*business*) próspero, -a; (*candidate*) electo, -a; (*solution*) eficaz; **to be ~** (*person*) tener éxito; (*business*) prosperar; **commercially ~** con éxito comercial
succession [sək'seʃən] *n no pl* sucesión *f;* **~ rights** derechos *mpl* de sucesión; **in ~** sucesivamente; **a ~ of** una serie de; **an endless ~ of** un sinfín de
successive [sək'sesɪv] *adj* sucesivo, -a; **six ~ weeks** seis semanas seguidas; **the third ~ defeat** la tercera derrota consecutiva
successor [sək'sesəʳ, *Am:* -ɚ] *n* sucesor(a) *m(f)*
succinct [sək'sɪŋkt] *adj* sucinto, -a
succour ['sʌkəʳ, *Am:* -ɚ] *Brit, Aus*, **succor** *Am, Aus* **I.** *n* socorro *m;* **to bring ~ to sb** socorrer a alguien **II.** *vt* socorrer
succulent ['sʌkjʊlənt] **I.** *adj* (*steak, fruit*) suculento, -a; (*plant*) carnoso, -a **II.** *n* planta *f* carnosa
succumb [sə'kʌm] *vi form* **1.** (*surrender*) sucumbir; **to ~ to pressure/to temptation** sucumbir ante la presión/a la tentación **2.** (*die*) morir; **to ~ to one's injuries** morir a causa de las heridas
such [sʌtʃ] **I.** *adj* tal, semejante; **~ great weather/a good book** un tiempo/un libro tan bueno; **~ an honour** tanto honor; **to earn ~ a lot of money** ganar tanto dinero; **or some ~ remark** o un comentario del estilo; **to buy some fruit ~ as apples** comprar fruta como

manzanas **II.** *pron* **~ is life** así es la vida; **people ~ as him** las personas que son como él; **~ as it is** tal como es; **as ~** propiamente dicho
such-and-such ['sʌtʃənsʌtʃ] *adj inf* tal o cual; **to arrive at ~ a time** llegar a tal o cual hora; **to meet sb in ~ a place** encontrarse con alguien en tal o cual lugar
suchlike ['sʌtʃlaɪk] *pron* **cookies, chocolates and ~** galletas, bombones y cosas por el estilo; **businessmen, politicians and ~** hombres de negocios, políticos y gente de ese tipo
suck [sʌk] **I.** *vt* succionar; (*with straw*) sorber; (*air*) aspirar; (*breast*) mamar; (*sweets*) chupar; **to ~ one's thumb** chuparse el dedo **II.** *vi* **1.** (*with mouth*) chupar **2.** *Am, inf* **this ~s!** ¡esto es una mierda! **III.** *n* chupada *f;* (*with straw*) sorbo *m*
◆**suck up to** *vt* dar coba a
sucker ['sʌkəʳ, *Am:* -ɚ] **I.** *n* **1.** *Am, pej* (*stupid person*) bobo, -a *m, f* **2.** (*device*) a. ZOOL ventosa *f* **II.** *vt Am* timar; **to ~ sb out of sth** estafar algo a alguien
suckle ['sʌkl] **I.** *vt* amamantar **II.** *vi* mamar
suckling-pig ['sʌklɪŋˌpɪg] *n* lechón *m*
sucrose ['suːkrəʊs, *Am:* -kroʊs] *n no pl* sacarosa *f*
suction ['sʌkʃən] *n no pl* succión *f*
suction pump *n* bomba *f* de succión
Sudan [suː'dæn] *n* Sudán *m*
Sudanese [ˌsuːdə'niːz] **I.** *n* sudanés, -esa *m, f* **II.** *adj* sudanés, -esa
sudden ['sʌdən] *adj* (*immediate*) repentino, -a, sorpresivo, -a *AmL;* (*death*) súbito, -a; (*departure*) imprevisto, -a; (*movement, drop*) brusco, -a; **to put a ~ stop to sth** detener algo de forma repentina; **all of a ~** *inf* de repente
suddenly *adv* de repente
suds [sʌdz] *npl* **1.** jabonaduras *fpl* **2.** *Am* cerveza *f*
sue [sjuː, *Am:* suː] <suing> **I.** *vt* demandar; **to ~ sb for damages** demandar a alguien por daños y perjuicios; **to ~ sb for divorce** ponerle a alguien una demanda de divorcio **II.** *vi* presentar demanda; **to ~ for peace** pedir la paz
suede [sweɪd] *n* ante *m*
suet ['suːɪt] *n no pl* sebo *m*
suffer ['sʌfəʳ, *Am:* -ɚ] **I.** *vi* sufrir; **the economy ~ed from ...** la economía se vio afectada por...; **to ~ for sth** ser castigado por algo **II.** *vt* **1.** (*undergo: defeat, setback*) sufrir; **to ~ the consequences** sufrir las consecuencias; **to ~ the misfortune** tener mala suerte **2.** (*allow*) permitir; **to ~ sth to be done** permitir que algo suceda; (*bear*) aguantar; **to not ~ fools gladly** no tener paciencia con los imbéciles **3.** MED padecer
sufferance ['sʌfərəns] *n* tolerancia *f;* **on ~** de mala gana
sufferer ['sʌfərəʳ, *Am:* -ɚɚ] *n* enfermo, -a *m, f;* **AIDS ~** enfermo de SIDA

suffering ['sʌfərɪŋ] n sufrimiento m; **years of** ~ no pl años mpl de penurias
suffice [sə'faɪs] vi bastar; ~ (**it**) **to say that ...** basta decir que...
sufficiency [sə'fɪʃnsi] n no pl cantidad f suficiente
sufficient [sə'fɪʃnt] adj suficiente; **to have** ~ tener bastante; **to be** ~ **for sth** ser suficiente para algo
suffix ['sʌfɪks] n LING sufijo m
suffocate ['sʌfəkeɪt] I. vi asfixiarse II. vt 1. (asphixiate) asfixiar 2. fig sofocar
suffocating adj 1. (heat, fumes) asfixiante 2. fig sofocante
suffrage ['sʌfrɪdʒ] n no pl sufragio m; **universal** ~ sufragio universal
suffragette [ˌsʌfrə'dʒet] n POL, HIST sufragista f
sugar ['ʃʊgər, Am: -ɚ] I. n 1. no pl GASTR azúcar m 2. Am, inf (term of affection) cariño 3. (euphemistic) ¡mecachis! II. vt echar azúcar a
sugar beet n remolacha f azucarera **sugar bowl** n azucarera f **sugar cane** n caña f de azúcar
sugar-coated [ˌʃʊgə'kəʊtɪd] adj cubierto, -a de azúcar
sugar daddy n hombe rico y mayor que da regalos o dinero a una mujer con el objetivo de tener relaciones sexuales con ella **sugar loaf** n pan m de azúcar **sugar lump** n terrón m de azúcar
sugary ['ʃʊgəri] adj 1. (sweet) azucarado, -a 2. fig, pej (insincere) meloso, -a
suggest [sə'dʒest, Am: səg'-] vt 1. (propose) proponer, sugerir; **to** ~ (**to sb**) **that ...** sugerirle a alguien que... +subj; **to** ~ **doing sth** sugerir hacer algo; **an idea** ~**ed itself** (**to him**) se le ocurrió una idea 2. (indicate) indicar 3. (hint) insinuar; **what are you trying to** ~? ¿qué insinúas?
suggestible [sə'dʒestəbl, Am: səg'dʒestə-] adj pej, form sugestionable; **highly** ~ muy influenciable
suggestion [sə'dʒestʃən, Am: səg'dʒes-] n 1. (proposed idea) sugerencia f; **to make the** ~ **that ...** sugerir que... +subj; **to be open to new** ~**s** estar abierto a nuevas sugerencias; **at Ann's** ~ a petición de Ann 2. (very small amount) pizca f; **there was a** ~ **of a smile on his face** esbozó una sonrisa 3. (insinuation) insinuación f
suggestion box n buzón m de sugerencias
suggestive [sə'dʒestɪv, Am: səg'-] adj 1. (lewd) indecente 2. (evocative) sugestivo, -a
suicidal [ˌsju:ɪ'saɪdl, Am: ˌsu:ə'-] adj suicida; **to feel** ~ tener ganas de suicidarse; fig tener el ánimo por los suelos
suicide ['sju:ɪsaɪd, Am: 'su:ə-] n 1. (act) suicidio m; **to commit** ~ suicidarse 2. form (person) suicida mf
suit [su:t] I. vt 1. (be convenient) convenir; **to** ~ **sb** convenirle a alguien; **that** ~**s me fine** eso

me viene bien 2. (be right) ir [o sentar] bien; **they are well** ~**ed** (**to each other**) hacen (una) buena pareja; **this lifestyle seems to** ~ **her** parece ser que este clase de vida le sienta bien 3. (look attractive with) quedar bien; **this dress** ~**s you** este vestido te sienta bien 4. (choose at will) **to** ~ **oneself** hacer lo que uno quiere; ~ **yourself!** ¡haz lo que quieras! II. n 1. (jacket and trousers) traje m, terno m Chile, flus m Ant, Col, Ven; (jacket and skirt) traje m de chaqueta; **bathing** [o **swim**] ~ traje m de baño 2. LAW pleito m; **to bring a** ~, **to file a** ~ Am entablar un pleito 3. GAMES palo m; **to follow** ~ seguir el palo; fig seguir el ejemplo
suitable ['su:təbl, Am: -ţəbl] adj apropiado, -a; **to be** ~ **for sb** ser apropiado [o adecuado] para alguien; **not** ~ **for chidren under 14** no apto para niños menores de 14 años
suitcase ['su:tkeɪs] n maleta f, valija f RíoPl, petaca f Méx
suite [swi:t] n 1. (set of rooms) suite f; **bridal** ~ suite nupcial 2. (set of furniture) juego m 3. MUS suite f
suitor ['su:tər, Am: 'su:ţər] n 1. a. iron (potential husband) pretendiente m 2. Am LAW demandante mf
sulfate ['sʌlfeɪt] n Am s. **sulphate**
sulfide ['sʌlfaɪd] n Am s. **sulphide**
sulfonamide [sʌl'fɑ:nəmaɪd] n Am s. **sulphonamide**
sulfur ['sʌlfə] n Am s. **sulphur**
sulfuric [sʌl'fjʊrɪk] adj Am s. **sulphuric**
sulfurous ['sʌlfərəs] adj Am s. **sulphurous**
sulk [sʌlk] I. vi enfurruñarse, alunarse RíoPl, amurrarse Chile II. n mal humor m; **to be in a** ~ estar enfurruñado, -a, estar alunado, -a RíoPl, estar amurrado, -a Chile
sulky ['sʌlki] <-ier, -iest> adj enfurruñado, -a
sullen ['sʌlən] adj 1. pej (person) malhumorado, -a 2. liter (sky) sombrío, -a
sully ['sʌli] <-ied, -ied> vt mancillar, manchar
sulphate ['sʌlfeɪt] n sulfato m
sulphide ['sʌlfaɪd] n sulfuro m
sulphonamide [sʌl'fɒnəmaɪd, Am: -'fɑ:nə-] n sulfamida f
sulphur ['sʌlfər, Am: -fɚ] n no pl azufre m
sulphur dioxide ['sʌlfəˈdaɪˈɒksaɪd, Am: -fəˈdaɪˈɑ:k-] n dióxido m de azufre
sulphuric [sʌl'fjʊərɪk, Am: -'fjʊrɪk] adj sulfúrico, -a
sulphuric acid n ácido m sulfúrico
sulphurous ['sʌlfərəs, Am: -fɚ-] adj (solution) de azufre; (smell) a azufre
sultan ['sʌltən] n sultán m
sultana [sʌl'tɑ:nə, Am: -'tænə] n pasa f de Esmirna
sultry ['sʌltri] <-ier, -iest> adj 1. (weather) bochornoso, -a 2. (sensual) sensual
sum [sʌm] n 1. (amount) cantidad f 2. (calculation) cuenta f; **to do** ~**s** hacer cuentas 3. (addition) suma f 4. (total) total m; **in** ~ en resumen

summarize ['sʌmərarz] *vt* resumir

summary ['sʌməri] I. *n* resumen *m* II. *adj* (*dismissal, execution*) inmediato, -a; LAW sumario, -a

summation [sʌ'meɪʃən, *Am:* sə'-] *n* 1. MAT suma *f* 2. LAW escrito *m* de conclusiones

summer ['sʌməʳ, *Am:* -ɚ] I. *n* verano *m;* a ~'s day un día de verano, un dia veraniego II. *adj* de verano, veraniego, -a III. *vi* veranear, pasar el verano

summer holiday(s) *n* vacaciones *fpl* de verano [*o* estivales]

summerhouse ['sʌməhaʊs, *Am:* '-ɚ-] *n* cenador *m*

summertime ['sʌmətaɪm, *Am:* '-ɚ-] *n no pl* (*season*) verano *m;* **in the ~** en verano

summery ['sʌməri] *adj* veraniego, -a

summing-up [ˌsʌmɪŋ'ʌp] *n* LAW recapitulación *f*

summit ['sʌmɪt] *n* 1. (*top of mountain*) cima *f* 2. *fig* (*of career, power*) cumbre *f* 3. POL cumbre *f;* **to hold a ~** celebrar una cumbre; **~ conference** (conferencia *f*) cumbre

summon ['sʌmən] *vt* (*people*) llamar; (*meeting*) convocar; LAW citar

◆**summon up** *vt* (*countable*) reunir; **to ~ the courage/strength to do sth** armarse de valor/fuerzas para hacer algo

summons ['sʌmənz] *npl* llamamiento *m;* LAW citación *f;* **to issue a ~** despachar una citación; **to serve sb with a ~** entregarle una citación a alguien

sump [sʌmp] *n* 1. AUTO cárter *m* 2. MIN sumidero *m* 3. (*cesspit*) pozo *m* negro

sumptuous ['sʌmptʃʊəs] *adj* suntuoso, -a

sun [sʌn] I. *n* sol *m;* **the ~'s rays** los rayos del sol; **the rising/setting ~** el sol naciente/poniente; **to sit in the ~** sentarse al sol ►**to call sb every <u>name</u> under the ~** decir a alguien de todo; **to do/try everything <u>under</u> the ~** hacer/probar de todo II. <-nn-> *vt* **to ~ oneself** tomar el sol

sunbaked ['sʌnbeɪkt] *adj* secado, -a al sol; (*earth, street*) calcinado, -a **sunbath** *n* baño *m* de sol

sunbathe ['sʌnbeɪð] *vi* tomar el sol

sunbeam ['sʌnbiːm] *n Brit* rayo *m* de sol

sunbed *n* 1. (*in garden*) tumbona *f* 2. (*with sunray lamp*) cama *f* de rayos UVA

sunblind ['sʌnblaɪnd] *n Brit* toldo *m*

sunblock ['sʌnblɒk, *Am:* 'sʌnblɑːk] *n* filtro *m* solar

sunburn ['sʌnbɜːn, *Am:* 'sʌnbɜːrn] *n* quemadura *f* de sol

sunburned *adj,* **sunburnt** *adj* quemado, -a (por el sol)

sundae ['sʌndeɪ, *Am:* -di] *n* helado con trozos de fruta, frutos secos, crema, etc.

Sunday ['sʌndeɪ] *n* domingo *m;* **Palm/ Easter ~** domingo de Ramos/de Resurrección; *s. a.* **Friday**

Sunday best *n,* **Sunday clothes** *npl* vestido *m* de domingo **Sunday school** *n* REL ≈

catequesis *f inv*

sun deck *n* 1. (*on ship*) cubierta *f* superior 2. *Am* (*balcony*) solario *m* **sundial** *n* reloj *m* de sol **sundown** *n Am, Aus s.* sunset **sun-dried** *adj* secado, -a al sol

sundry ['sʌndri] *adj* varios, -as; **all and ~** *inf* todo el mundo

sunflower ['sʌnˌflaʊəʳ, *Am:* -ˌflaʊɚ] *n* girasol *m,* maravilla *f Chile*

sunflower oil *n* aceite *m* de girasol **sunflower seed** *n* pipa *f*

sung [sʌŋ] *pp of* **sing**

sunglasses ['sʌnˌglɑːsɪz, *Am:* 'sʌnˌglæsɪs] *npl* gafas *fpl* de sol **sunhat** *n* pamela *f*

sunk [sʌŋk] *pp of* **sink**

sunken ['sʌŋkən] *adj* 1. (*ship, treasure*) sumergido, -a 2. (*cheeks, eyes*) hundido, -a

sun lamp *n* 1. (*ultraviolet*) lámpara *f* de rayos UVA 2. CINE foco *m*

sunlight ['sʌnlaɪt] *n no pl* luz *f* del sol

sunlit ['sʌnlɪt] *adj* soleado, -a

sunny ['sʌni] <-ier, -iest> *adj* 1. (*day*) soleado, -a; **she likes her eggs ~ side up** *Am* le gustan los huevos fritos sólo por un lado 2. (*personality*) alegre

sun protection factor *n* factor *m* de protección solar **sunray** *n Am* rayo *m* de sol

sunrise ['sʌnraɪz] *n* amanecer *m;* **at ~** al amanecer, al alba

sunrise industry *n* industria *f* del porvenir

sunroof ['sʌnruːf] *n* techo *m* corredizo **sunroom** *n Am* solario *m* **sunscreen** *n* filtro *m* solar

sunset ['sʌnset] *n* puesta *f* de sol; **at ~** al atardecer

sunshade ['sʌnʃeɪd] *n* 1. (*umbrella*) sombrilla *f* 2. *Am* (*awning*) toldo *m*

sunshine ['sʌnʃaɪn] *n* 1. *no pl* (*light*) sol *m;* **in the ~** al sol 2. *Brit* (*friendly*) nene, -a *m, f;* (*to show irritation*) majo, -a *m, f,* guapo, -a *m, f*

sunspot ['sʌnspɒt, *Am:* -spɑːt] *n* mancha *f* solar **sunstroke** *n no pl* insolación *f,* asoleada *f Col, Chile, Guat;* **to have ~** tener una insolación

suntan ['sʌntæn] *n* bronceado *m;* **to get a ~** broncearse

suntan cream *n,* **suntan lotion** *n* crema *f* bronceadora

suntanned *adj* bronceado, -a

suntan oil *n* aceite *m* bronceador

suntrap ['sʌntræp] *n Brit, Aus* lugar *m* resguardado y soleado

sun-up ['sʌnʌp] *n Am s.* **sunrise**

sun visor *n* AUTO visera *f* **sun-worshipper** *n iron* fanático, -a *m, f* del sol

sup [sʌp] <-pp-> I. *vt Brit* beber II. *vi liter* **to ~ on sth** cenar algo

super¹ ['suːpəʳ, *Am:* -pɚ] I. *adj inf* genial II. *n* AUTO (gasolina *f*) súper *f*

super² *n* 1. *Brit, Am abbr of* **superintendent** superintendente *mf* 2. *Aus, inf abbr of* **superannuation** jubilación *f*

superabundant [ˌsuːpərə'bʌndənt] *adj*

superabundante, sobreabundante

superannuated [ˌsuːpərˈænjʊeɪtɪd, *Am:* -jueɪt̬ɪd] *adj iron* anticuado, -a

superannuation [ˈsuːpərˌænjʊˈeɪʃən, *Am:* ˌsuːpərˌænjuˈ-] *n Brit, Aus* **1.** (*payment*) inversión *f* en un plan de pensiones **2.** *no pl* (*pension*) pensión *f* (de jubilación)

superb [suːˈpɜːb, *Am:* səˈpɜːrb] *adj* magnífico, -a

supercharged [ˈsuːpətʃɑːdʒd, *Am:* -pəˈtʃɑːrdʒd] *adj* **1.** (*engine*) sobrealimentado, -a **2.** (*atmosphere*) cargado, -a de emotividad

supercharger [ˈsuːpəˌtʃɑːdʒəʳ, *Am:* -pəˈtʃɑːrdʒəʳ] *n* TECH sobrealimentador *m*

supercilious [ˈsuːpəˈsɪlɪəs, *Am:* ˌsuːpəˈsɪlɪəs] *adj pej* altanero, -a

superego [ˈsuːpəregəʊ, *Am:* ˌsuːpəˈiːgoʊ] *n* PSYCH superego *m*

superficial [ˌsuːpəˈfɪʃl, *Am:* ˌsuːpəˈ-] *adj* superficial

superficiality [ˌsuːpəˌfɪʃɪˈæləti, *Am:* -pəˌfɪʃɪˈæləti] *n no pl* superficialidad *f*

superfluous [suːˈpɜːflʊəs, *Am:* -ˈpɜːr-] *adj* superfluo, -a; **to be ~** estar de más

superglue® [ˈsuːpəgluː, *Am:* -pə-] *n* superglue® *m*; **to stick like ~ to sb** pegarse a alguien como una lapa

supergrass [ˈsuːpəgrɑːs, *Am:* -pəgræs] *n Brit, inf* soplón, -ona *m, f*

superhero [ˈsuːpəˌhɪərəʊ, *Am:* -pə-] <-heroes> *n inf* superhéroe *m*

superhighway [ˈsuːpəˈhaɪweɪ, *Am:* ˈsuːpəˈ-] *n Am* autopista *f* (de varios carriles)

superhuman [ˌsuːpəˈhjuːmən, *Am:* -pəˈ-] *adj* sobrehumano, -a

superimpose [ˌsuːpərɪmˈpəʊz, *Am:* -pəˈɪmˈpoʊz] *vt* PHOT superponer

superintend [ˌsuːpərɪnˈtend, *Am:* ˌsuːpə-] *vt* supervisar

superintendent [ˌsuːpərɪnˈtendənt, *Am:* ˌsuːpə-] *n* **1.** (*person in charge: of school, department*) director(a) *m(f)* **2.** *Am* (*of building*) portero, -a *m, f* **3.** *Brit* (*police officer*) comisario, -a *m, f* de policía **4.** *Am* LAW (*head of police department*) superintendente *mf*

superior [suːˈpɪərɪəʳ, *Am:* səˈpɪrɪəʳ] **I.** *adj* **1.** (*better, senior*) superior; **to be ~** (to sb/sth) estar por encima de alguien/algo **2.** (*arrogant*) de superioridad **II.** *n* superior *mf*

superiority [suːˌpɪərɪˈɒrəti, *Am:* səˌpɪrɪˈɔːrəti] *n no pl* superioridad *f*

superiority complex *n inf* complejo *m* de superioridad

superlative [suːˈpɜːlətɪv, *Am:* səˈpɜːrlətɪv] **I.** *adj* **1.** (*best*) excepcional **2.** LING superlativo, -a **II.** *n* LING superlativo *m*

superman [ˈsuːpəmæn, *Am:* -pə-] *n* superhombre *m*; CINE Supermán *m*

supermarket [ˈsuːpəmɑːkɪt, *Am:* -pəˌmɑːr-] *n* supermercado *m*

supermarket trolley *n Brit* carrito *m* de supermercado

supermodel [ˈsuːpəˌmɒdəl, *Am:* ˈsuːpə-

ˌmɑːdəl] *n* supermodelo *f*

supernatural [ˌsuːpəˈnætʃərəl, *Am:* -pəˈnætʃəˈəl] **I.** *adj* sobrenatural **II.** *n* **the ~** lo sobrenatural

supernumerary [ˌsuːpəˈnjuːmərəri, *Am:* -pəˈnuːmərer-] **I.** *adj form* supernumerario, -a **II.** <-ies> *n form* supernumerario, -a *m, f*; THEAT figurante *mf*

superpower [ˌsuːpəˈpaʊəʳ, *Am:* ˈsuːpəˌpaʊəʳ] *n* POL superpotencia *f*

superscript [ˈsuːpəskrɪpt, *Am:* -pə-] *n no pl* TYPO superíndice *m*

supersede [ˌsuːpəˈsiːd, *Am:* -pəˈ-] *vt* sustituir

supersonic [ˌsuːpəˈsɒnɪk, *Am:* -pəˈsɑːnɪk] *adj* AVIAT supersónico, -a

superstar [ˈsuːpəstɑːʳ, *Am:* ˈsuːpəstɑːr] *n* superestrella *f*

superstition [ˌsuːpəˈstɪʃən, *Am:* -pəˈ-] *n* superstición *f*

superstitious [ˌsuːpəˈstɪʃəs, *Am:* -pəˈ-] *adj* supersticioso, -a

superstore [ˈsuːpəstɔːʳ, *Am:* -pəstɔːr] *n* hipermercado *m*

superstructure [ˈsuːpəstrʌktʃəʳ, *Am:* -pəˌstrʌktʃəʳ] *n* superestructura *f*

supertanker [ˈsuːpəˌtæŋkəʳ, *Am:* -pəˌtæŋkəʳ] *n* superpetrolero *m*

supervene [ˌsuːpəˈviːn, *Am:* -pəˈ-] *vi form* sobrevenir

supervise [ˈsuːpəvaɪz, *Am:* -pə-] *vt* (*watch over*) supervisar; (*thesis*) dirigir

supervision [ˌsuːpəˈvɪʒən, *Am:* -pəˈ-] *n no pl* supervisión *f*; **under the ~ of sb** bajo la supervisión de alguien

supervisor [ˈsuːpəˈvaɪzəʳ, *Am:* ˈsuːpəˌvaɪzəʳ] *n* **1.** (*person in charge*) supervisor(a) *m(f)* **2.** UNIV director(a) *m(f)* de tesis **3.** *Am* POL alcalde, -esa *m, f*

supervisory [ˌsuːpəˈvaɪzəri, *Am:* -pəˈvaɪzəˈ-] *adj* de supervisor

supine [ˈsuːpaɪn, *Am:* suːˈ-] **I.** *adj* **1.** (*lying down*) supino, -a; **to be ~** estar tumbado de espaldas **2.** (*weak*) lánguido, -a **II.** *adv* **to lie ~** estar tumbado de espaldas

supper [ˈsʌpəʳ, *Am:* -əʳ] *n* cena *f*; **to have ~** cenar

suppertime *n no pl* hora *f* de cenar

supplant [səˈplɑːnt, *Am:* -ˈplænt] *vt* sustituir

supple [ˈsʌpl] *adj* (*person*) ágil; (*leather, skin*) flexible

supplement [ˈsʌplɪmənt, *Am:* -lə-] **I.** *n* **1.** (*something extra*) complemento *m* **2.** (*part of newspaper*) suplemento *m* **3.** (*of book*) apéndice *m* **II.** *vt* complementar

supplementary [ˌsʌplɪˈmentəri, *Am:* -ləˈmentəˈi] *adj* adicional, suplementario, -a

suppleness [ˈsʌplnɪs] *n* (*person*) agilidad *f*; (*of leather, skin*) flexibilidad *f*

supplicant [ˈsʌplɪkənt, *Am:* -lə-] *n* suplicante *mf*

supplication [ˌsʌplɪˈkeɪʃən, *Am:* -ləˈ-] *n* súplica *f*

S

supplier [sə'plaɪəʳ, *Am:* -ɚ] *n* proveedor(a) *m(f)*

supply [sə'plaɪ] I.<-ie-> *vt* 1.(*provide: electricity, food, money*) suministrar; (*information*) proporcionar, facilitar; **to be accused of ~ing drugs** ser acusado de tráfico de drogas 2.COM proveer II. *n* 1.(*act of providing: of electricity, water*) suministro *m* 2.*no pl* ECON oferta *f;* ~ **and demand** oferta y demanda; **to be in short** ~ escasear

supply-side economics [sə'plaɪsaɪd ˌiːkə'nɒmɪks, *Am:* -'nɑːmɪks] *npl* economía *f* de la oferta **supply teacher** *n Brit, Aus* suplente *mf*

support [sə'pɔːt, *Am:* -'pɔːrt] I. *vt* 1.(*hold up: roof*) sostener; (*weight*) aguantar, resistir; **to ~ oneself on sth** apoyarse en algo 2.(*provide for*) mantener; **to ~ four children** mantener a cuatro hijos; **to ~ oneself** ganarse la vida 3.(*provide with money*) financiar 4.(*encourage*) apoyar 5.*Brit* SPORTS (*follow*) ser un seguidor de 6.(*show to be true*) confirmar II. *n* 1.*no pl* (*backing, help*) apoyo *m;* **to give sb moral ~** darle apoyo moral a alguien 2.(*structure*) soporte *m; fig* (*person*) sostén *m* 3.FIN ayuda económica 4.(*knee protector*) protector *m;* ~ **stockings** medias *fpl* elásticas 5.(*confirmation*) confirmación *f;* **to lend ~ to sth** respaldar algo; **in ~ of sth** en apoyo de algo

supporter *n* 1.(*of cause, candidate*) partidario, -a *m, f* 2.*Brit* SPORTS (*fan*) seguidor(a) *m(f)*

supporting *adj Brit* (*film, role*) secundario, -a

supportive [sə'pɔːtɪv, *Am:* -'pɔːrţɪv] *adj* comprensivo, -a; **to be ~ of sth/sb** apoyar algo/a alguien

suppose [sə'pəʊz, *Am:* -'poʊz] *vt* 1.suponer; **to ~** (**that**) ... suponer que...; **I ~ not/so** supongo que no/que sí; **I don't ~ so** supongo que no; **let's ~ that** en el caso de que +*subj* 2.(*believe, think*) creer 3.(*obligation*) **to be ~d to do sth** tener que hacer algo; **he was ~d to collect the money** tenía que ir a recoger el dinero; **you are not ~d to know that** no deberías saber eso 4.(*opinion*) **the book is ~d to be very good** dicen que el libro es muy bueno; **she is ~d to be intelligent** dicen que es inteligente

supposed *adj* (*killer*) presunto, -a; (*date*) supuesto, -a

supposedly [sə'pəʊzɪdli, *Am:* -'poʊ-] *adv* supuestamente

supposing *conj* ~ **that** ... suponiendo que...

supposition [ˌsʌpə'zɪʃən] *n* suposición *f*

suppository [sə'pɒzɪtəri, *Am:* -'pɑːzɔːri] <-ies> *n* supositorio *m*

suppress [sə'pres] *vt* 1.(*criticism, revolt, terrorism*) reprimir, sofocar 2.(*sneeze, yawn, emotion*) reprimir; (*evidence, information*) ocultar 3.MED inhibir

suppression [sə'preʃən] *n no pl* 1.(*of criticism, revolt*) represión *f* 2.(*of anger, emotion*) represión *f;* (*of evidence*) ocultación *f* 3.MED

inhibición *f* 4.PSYCH (*of memories*) represión *f*

suppurate ['sʌpjʊreɪt] *vi* MED supurar

supremacy [su'preməsi, *Am:* sə'-] *n no pl* supremacía *f*

supreme [suː'priːm, *Am:* sə'-] I. *adj* 1.(*authority*) supremo, -a; (*commander*) en jefe; **Supreme Court** Tribunal *m* Supremo 2.(*achievement, sacrifice*) mayor; **to show ~ courage** mostrar una gran valentía II. *adv* **to reign ~** estar en la cumbre, no tener ningún rival

surcharge ['sɜːtʃɑːdʒ, *Am:* 'sɜːrtʃɑːrdʒ] I. *n* recargo *m* II. *vt* aplicar un recargo a

sure [ʃʊəʳ, *Am:* ʃʊr] I. *adj* 1.(*certain*) seguro, -a; **to be ~ of sth** estar seguro de algo; **to be ~** (**that**) ... estar seguro de que...; **to make ~** (**that**) ... asegurarse de que...; (**not**) **to be ~ if** ... (no) estar seguro de si...; **she is ~ to come** vendrá seguro; **are you ~ you won't come?** ¿estás seguro de que no vendrás?; **I'm not ~ why/how** no sé muy bien por qué/cómo; ~ **thing!** *Am* ¡claro!; **for ~** seguro 2.(*confident*) **to be ~ of oneself** estar seguro de sí mismo II. *adv* seguro; ~ **I will!** *Am, inf* ¡seguro!; **for ~** a ciencia cierta; ~ **enough** en efecto ►**as ~ as I'm** <u>standing</u> **here** como me llamo...

surefooted [ʃɔː'fʊtɪd, *Am:* ʃʊrˌfuːʈɪd] *adj* 1.(*when walking, climbing*) de pie firme 2.(*confident*) seguro, -a de sí mismo, -a

surely ['ʃɔːli, *Am:* 'ʃʊrli] *adv* 1.(*certainly*) sin duda 2.(*to show astonishment*) por supuesto; ~ **you don't expect me to believe that?** ¿no esperarás que me lo crea? 3.*Am* (*yes, certainly*) ¡claro!

surety ['ʃʊərəti, *Am:* 'ʃʊrəti] <-ies> *n* LAW 1.(*person*) fiador(a) *m(f);* **to stand ~** (**for sb**) ser fiador de alguien 2.(*guarantee*) fianza *f*

surf [sɜːf, *Am:* sɜːrf] I. *n* olas *fpl* II. *vi* SPORTS hacer surf III. *vt* INFOR **to ~ the internet** navegar por internet

surface ['sɜːfɪs, *Am:* 'sɜːr-] I. *n* superficie *f;* **on the ~** *fig* a primera vista; **to scratch the ~ of sth** tratar algo superficialmente [*o* por encima] II. *vi* salir a la superficie III. *vt* (*road, wall*) revestir; (*with asphalt*) asfaltar

surface mail *n* **by ~** (*land*) por vía terrestre; (*sea*) por vía marítima **surface tension** *n* PHYS tensión *f* superficial **surface-to-air missile** *n* MIL misil *m* tierra-aire

surfboard ['sɜːfbɔːd, *Am:* 'sɜːrfbɔːrd] *n* tabla *f* de surf

surfeit ['sɜːfɪt, *Am:* 'sɜːr-] *n no pl, form* exceso *m*

surfer ['sɜːfəʳ, *Am:* 'sɜːrfɚ] *n* 1.surfista *mf* 2.INFOR internauta *mf*

surfing ['sɜːfɪŋ, *Am:* 'sɜːr-] *n no pl* surf *m*

surge [sɜːdʒ, *Am:* sɜːrdʒ] I. *vi* 1.(*move forward*) abalanzarse; (*waves*) levantarse 2.(*increase*) aumentar vertiginosamente II. *n* (*of waves*) oleaje *m;* (*of anger*) arranque *m;* (*of indignation*) ola *f;* (*of price, support*) aumento *m* repentino; **power ~** sobrecarga *f*

surgeon ['sɜːdʒən, *Am:* 'sɜːr-] *n* cirujano, -a

m, f

surgery ['sɜːdʒəri, *Am:* 'sɜːr-] *n* **1.** *Brit, Aus* (*medical practice*) consulta *f*; **to hold a ~** tener consulta; **~hours** horario *m* de consulta **2.** *no pl* (*medical operation*) cirugía *f*; **to perform ~** practicar una intervención quirúrgica; **to undergo ~** someterse a una intervención quirúrgica **3.** *Brit* POL *sesión durante la que un parlamentario atiende las consultas de sus electores*

surgical ['sɜːdʒɪkl, *Am:* 'sɜːr-] *adj* (*procedure*) quirúrgico, -a; (*collar, stocking*) ortopédico, -a

Surinam(e) ['suənæm, *Am:* ˌsurɪ'nɑːm] *n* Surinam *m*

Surinamese [ˌsuənæ'miːz] **I.** *adj* surinamés, -esa **II.** *n* surinamés, -esa *m, f*

surly ['sɜːli, *Am:* 'sɜːr-] <-ier, -iest> *adj* hosco, -a

surmise ['sɜːmaɪz, *Am:* sə'maɪz] *vt form* conjeturar

surmount [sə'maʊnt, *Am:* sə-] *vt* **1.** (*overcome*) superar **2.** *form* (*be on top*) coronar

surname ['sɜːneɪm, *Am:* 'sɜːr-] *n* apellido *m*

surpass [sə'pɑːs, *Am:* sə'pæs] *vt* sobrepasar; **to ~ oneself** superarse

surplus ['sɜːpləs, *Am:* 'sɜːr-] **I.** *n* (*of product*) excedente *m*; FIN superávit *m* **II.** *adj* sobrante; **to be ~ to requirements** *Brit* estar de más

surprise [sə'praɪz, *Am:* sə-] **I.** *n* sorpresa *f*; **in ~** con sorpresa; **to sb's ~** para sorpresa de alguien **II.** *vt* sorprender; **it ~d her that ...** le sorprendió que... *+subj;* **to ~ sb doing sth** sorprender a alguien haciendo algo

surprised *adj* sorprendido, -a

surprising *adj* sorprendente, sorpresivo, -a *AmL*

surprisingly *adv* sorprendentemente

surreal [sə'rɪəl, *Am:* sə'riːəl] *adj* surrealista

surrealism [sə'rɪəlɪzəm, *Am:* -'riːə-] *n* ART surrealismo *m*

surrealist [sə'rɪəlɪst, *Am:* -'riːə-] ART **I.** *n* surrealista *mf* **II.** *adj* surrealista

surrender [sə'rendə', *Am:* -də-] **I.** *vi* rendirse; **to ~ to sb** entregarse a alguien **II.** *vt form* entregar **III.** *n* **1.** (*giving up*) rendición *f* **2.** *no pl, form* (*of document*) entrega *f*

surreptitious [ˌsʌrəp'tɪʃəs, *Am:* ˌsɜːr-] *adj* subrepticio, -a, furtivo, -a

surrogacy ['sʌrəgəsi] *n no pl* alquiler *m* de madres

surrogate ['sʌrəgɪt, *Am:* 'sɜːr-] **I.** *adj* (*substitute*) sucedáneo, -a **II.** *n* sustituto, -a *m, f*

surrogate mother *n* madre *f* de alquiler

surround [sə'raʊnd] **I.** *vt* rodear **II.** *n* (*frame*) marco *m*

surrounding *adj* de alrededor

surroundings *npl* alrededores *mpl*

surtax ['sɜːtæks, *Am:* 'sɜːr-] *n* FIN, POL sobretasa *f*

surveillance [sɜː'veɪləns, *Am:* sə-] *n no pl* vigilancia *f*; **to be under ~** estar bajo vigilancia

survey [sə'veɪ, *Am:* sə-] **I.** *vt* **1.** (*research*) investigar **2.** (*look at carefully*) contemplar **3.** *Brit* (*examine*) examinar **4.** GEO medir **5.** (*poll*) encuestar **II.** *n* **1.** (*poll*) encuesta *f* **2.** (*report*) informe *m* **3.** (*examination*) examen *m* **4.** GEO medición *f*

surveyor [sə'veɪə', *Am:* sə-'veɪə-] *n* **1.** GEO topógrafo, -a *m, f* **2.** *Brit* (*property assessor*) tasador(a) *m(f)*

survival [sə'vaɪvl, *Am:* sə-'] *n* **1.** *no pl* supervivencia *f* **2.** (*relic*) reliquia *f* ▶**the ~ of the fittest** la ley del más fuerte

survive [sə'vaɪv, *Am:* sə-'] **I.** *vi* (*stay alive: person*) sobrevivir; (*book*) conservarse; **to ~ on sth** *inf* vivir [*o* alimentarse] a base de algo **II.** *vt* sobrevivir a; **to ~ an accident** salir con vida de un accidente

surviving *adj* superviviente

survivor [sə'vaɪvə', *Am:* sə-'vaɪvə-] *n* superviviente *mf*

susceptible [sə'septəbl] *adj* susceptible; MED propenso, -a

suspect¹ [sə'spekt] *vt* **1.** (*think likely*) sospechar, imaginar; **to ~ sth** sospechar [*o* imaginarse] algo **2.** (*consider guilty*) sospechar de, cachar *Chile*; **to ~ sb's motives** dudar de los motivos de alguien

suspect² ['sʌspekt] **I.** *n* sospechoso, -a *m, f* **II.** *adj* sospechoso, -a

suspend [sə'spend] *vt* **1.** (*stop temporarily*) suspender; (*judgement, proceedings*) posponer **2.** SCHOOL, UNIV expulsar temporalmente **3.** (*hang*) colgar

suspender [sə'spendə', *Am:* -də-] *n* **1.** *Brit* (*strap*) liga *f* **2.** *pl, Am* (*braces*) tirantes *mpl*, suspensores *mpl AmL*, calzonarias *fpl Col*

suspender belt *n Brit, Aus* liguero *m*, portaligas *m inv AmL*

suspense [sə'spens] *n* **1.** (*uncertainty*) incertidumbre *f*; **to keep sb in ~** mantener a alguien sobre ascuas [*o* en vilo] **2.** CINE suspense *m*

suspension [sə'spentʃən] *n no pl* **1.** suspensión *f* **2.** SCHOOL, UNIV expulsión *f* temporal

suspension bridge *n* puente *m* colgante

suspension points *npl* puntos *mpl* suspensivos

suspicion [sə'spɪʃən] *n* **1.** (*belief*) sospecha *f*; **to arrest sb on ~ of sth** arrestar a alguien como sospechoso de algo; **to be above ~** estar por encima de toda sospecha **2.** *no pl* (*mistrust*) recelo *m*, desconfianza *f* **3.** (*small amount*) pizca *f*

suspicious [sə'spɪʃəs] *adj* **1.** (*arousing suspicion*) sospechoso, -a, emponchado, -a *Arg, Bol, Perú* **2.** (*lacking trust*) desconfiado, -a

♦ suss out [sʌs] *vt Brit, Aus, inf* calar

sustain [sə'steɪn] *vt* **1.** (*maintain*) sostener **2.** (*withstand*) aguantar **3.** (*uphold: conviction*) confirmar; (*objection*) admitir

sustainable [sə'steɪnəbl] *adj* sostenible

sustained [sə'steɪnd] *adj* continuo, -a; (*applause*) prolongado, -a

sustenance ['sʌstɪnənts, *Am:* -tnəns] *n no*

S

pl sustento *m;* **to give sb** ~ sustentar a alguien
suture ['suːtʃəʳ, *Am:* -tʃɚ] MED **I.** *n* (*stitch*) sutura *f;* (*thread*) hilo *m* de sutura **II.** *vt* suturar
svelte [svelt] *adj* esbelto, -a
SW [ˌesˈdʌbljuː] *abbr of* **southwest** SO
swab [swɒb, *Am:* swɑːb] **I.** *n* **1.** MED (*pad*) tapón *m;* (*for examination*) frotis *m inv* **2.** NAUT fregona *f* **II.** <-bb-> *vt* **1.** MED limpiar (con algodón) **2.** (*wash*) fregar
swaddle ['swɒdi, *Am:* 'swɑːdl] *vt* envolver
swaddling clothes *n* pañales *mpl*
swagger ['swægəʳ, *Am:* -ɚ] **I.** *vi* pavonearse **II.** *n no pl* arrogancia *f*
swallow[1] ['swɒləʊ, *Am:* 'swɑːloʊ] **I.** *vt* tragar, engullir, tambar *Ecua, inf* **II.** *vi* tragar saliva **III.** *n* trago *m*
   ◆**swallow down** *vt* tragar
   ◆**swallow up** *vt* (*absorb*) tragar
swallow[2] ['swɒləʊ, *Am:* 'swɑːloʊ] *n* ZOOL golondrina *f* ▶**one ~ doesn't make a summer** *prov* una golondrina no hace verano *prov*
swam [swæm] *vi pt of* **swim**
swamp [swɒmp, *Am:* swɑːmp] **I.** *n* pantano *m*, suampo *m AmC*, wampa *f Méx* **II.** *vt* (*flood*) inundar; **to ~ sb** (**with sth**) abrumar a alguien (con algo); **to be ~ed with sth** estar agobiado de algo
swamp fever *n no pl* MED paludismo *m*, fiebre *f* palúdica
swampland ['swɒmpˌlænd, *Am:* 'swɑːmplænd] *n* pantano *m*
swampy ['swɒmpi, *Am:* 'swɑːmp-] <-ier, -iest> *adj* pantanoso, -a
swan [swɒn, *Am:* swɑːn] **I.** *n* cisne *m* **II.** <-nn-> *vi Brit, Aus, inf* **to ~ about** pavonearse
swank [swæŋk] **I.** *vi inf* fanfarronear **II.** *n no pl, inf* fanfarronada *f*
swanky ['swæŋki] *adj inf* **1.** (*luxurious*) pijo, -a **2.** (*boastful*) fanfarrón, -ona
swansong *n* canto *m* del cisne
swap [swɒp, *Am:* swɑːp] **I.** <-pp-> *vt* cambiar; **to ~ sth** (**for sth**) cambiar algo (por algo); **to ~ sth with sb** cambiarle algo a alguien **II.** <-pp-> *vi* cambiar **III.** *n* cambio *m*
swarm [swɔːm, *Am:* swɔːrm] **I.** *vi* **1.** ZOOL, BIO (*bees*) enjambrar **2.** (*move in large group*) aglomerarse **3.** (*be full*) **to be ~ing with sth** estar plagado [*o* atestado] de algo **II.** *n* **1.** (*of bees*) enjambre *m* **2.** *fig* (*of people*) multitud *f*
swarthy ['swɔːði, *Am:* 'swɔːr-] <-ier, -iest> *adj* moreno, -a
swashbuckling ['swɒʃˌbʌklɪŋ, *Am:* 'swɑːʃˌ-] *adj* de capa y espada
swastika ['swɒstɪkə, *Am:* 'swɑːstɪ-] *n* cruz *f* gamada
swat [swɒt, *Am:* swɑːt] <-tt-> *vt* (*insect*) aplastar
swatch [swɒtʃ, *Am:* swɑːtʃ] *n* (*sample*) muestra *f;* (*sample book*) muestrario *m*
swathe [sweɪð] **I.** *vt* (*wrap round*) envolver;

(*with bandages*) vendar **II.** *n* **1.** (*long strip*) ringlera *f* **2.** (*area*) extensión *f*
sway [sweɪ] **I.** *vi* balancearse **II.** *vt* **1.** (*move from side to side*) balancear **2.** (*persuade*) persuadir **III.** *n no pl* **1.** (*influence*) influencia *f;* **under the ~ of sb/sth** bajo el influjo de alguien/algo **2.** *form* (*control*) control *m;* **to hold ~ over sth/sb** dominar algo/a alguien
Swazi ['swɑːzi] **I.** *adj* swazilandés, -esa **II.** *n* swazilandés, -esa *m, f*
Swaziland ['swɑːzilænd] *n* Swazilandia *f*
swear [sweəʳ, *Am:* swer] <swore, sworn> **I.** *vi* **1.** (*take oath*) jurar; **to ~ on the Bible** jurar sobre la Biblia; **I couldn't ~ to it** *inf* no pondría la mano en el fuego **2.** (*curse*) decir palabrotas **II.** *vt* jurar; **to ~ blind** *Brit, inf* jurar y perjurar; **they swore us to secrecy** nos hicieron jurar que guardaríamos el secreto
   ◆**swear by** *vt* **to ~ sth** tener una fe ciega a algo
   ◆**swear in** *vt* LAW **to ~ sb** tomar juramento a alguien
   ◆**swear off** *vt* **to ~ sth** renunciar a algo
swearing *n* palabrotas *mpl*
swearword ['sweəwɜːd, *Am:* 'swerwɜːrd] *n* taco *m*, brulote *m AmS*, garabato *m Chile*
sweat [swet] **I.** *n* **1.** (*perspiration*) sudor *m;* **to get into a ~** empezar a sudar; **to be/get in a ~** (**about sth**) *fig, inf* preocuparse (por algo) **2.** (*effort*) esfuerzo *m;* **no ~** *inf* ningún problema **II.** *vi* (*perspire*) sudar; **to ~ with sth** sudar de algo **III.** *vt* sudar
   ◆**sweat out** *vt* **to sweat it out** (*do physical exercise*) sudar la gota gorda; (*suffer*) pasar un mal rato
sweat band *n* (*for head*) cinta *f;* (*for wrists*) muñequera *f*
sweated *adj* explotado, -a
sweater ['swetəʳ, *Am:* 'swetɚ] *n* jersey *m*
sweatshirt ['swetʃɜːt, *Am:* -ʃɜːrt] *n* sudadera *f*
sweatshop ['swetʃɒp, *Am:* -ʃɑːp] *n pej:* fábrica donde se explota a los trabajadores
sweaty ['sweti, *Am:* 'swet̪-] <-ier, -iest> *adj* sudado, -a
swede [swiːd] *n Brit, Aus* GASTR colinabo *m*
Swede [swiːd] *n* sueco, -a *m, f*
Sweden ['swiːdn] *n* GEO Suecia *f*
Swedish ['swiːdɪʃ] **I.** *adj* sueco, -a **II.** *n* **1.** (*person*) sueco, -a *m, f* **2.** LING Sueco *m*
sweep [swiːp] <swept, swept> **I.** *n* **1.** *no pl* (*cleaning action*) barrida *f;* **to give sth a ~** barrer algo **2.** (*chimney cleaner*) deshollinador(a) *m(f)* **3.** (*movement*) **with a ~ of her arm** con un amplio movimiento del brazo **4.** (*area*) extensión *f* **5.** (*range: of weapons, telescope*) alcance *m* **6.** (*search*) **to make a ~ of an area** rastrear una zona **7.** *inf* (*bet*) *s.* **sweepstake** ▶**to make a** <u>clean</u> ~ hacer tabla rasa **II.** *vt* **1.** (*clean with broom: floor*) barrer; (*chimney*) deshollinar **2.** (*remove*) quitar **3.** (*search*) rastrear **4.** *Am, inf* (*win*) ganar de manera aplastante ▶**she swept him off his**

feet se enamoró de ella perdidamente **III.** *vi*
1. (*clean with broom*) barrer **2.** (*move*) **to ~
into a room** entrar en una habitación majestuosamente; **to ~ into power** llegar al poder
fácilmente **3.** (*look round*) mirar alrededor
4. (*follow path*) **the road ~s round the lake**
la carretera rodea el lago **5.** (*extend*) extenderse
◆**sweep aside** *vt* **1.** (*cause to move*)
apartar **2.** (*dismiss*) desechar
◆**sweep away** *vt* **1.** (*remove*) erradicar
2. (*carry away*) arrastrar
◆**sweep out** *vt* barrer
◆**sweep up** *vt* **1.** (*brush*) barrer **2.** (*gather*)
recoger
sweeper *n* **1.** (*device*) barredera *f* **2.** (*person*)
barrendero, -a *m, f*
sweeping **I.** *adj* (*gesture*) amplio, -a; (*victory*)
aplastante **II.** *npl* basura *f;* **the ~s of society** la
escoria de la sociedad
sweepstake ['swi:psteɪk] *n* apuesta, espe-
*cialmente en carreras de caballos, en la que la
persona que gana se lleva el dinero apostado
por todos los demás*
sweet [swi:t] **I.** <-er, -est> *adj* **1.** (*like sugar*)
dulce **2.** (*pleasant*) agradable; (*sound*) melodioso -a; **to go one's own ~ way** hacer lo que
a uno le da la gana **3.** (*cute*) mono, -a **4.** (*kind:
smile*) encantador(a); (*person*) amable; **to
keep sb ~** tener contento a alguien; **to be ~
on sb** estar enamorado de alguien **II.** *n* **1.** *Brit,
Aus* (*candy*) caramelo *m,* dulce *m Chile*
2. *Brit, Aus* (*dessert*) postre *m* **3.** *inf* (*term of
endearment*) cariño *m*
sweet-and-sour [ˌswi:tən'saʊə^r, *Am:*
-ˌsaʊəˈ] *adj* agridulce
sweetbread ['swi:tbred] *n pl* GASTR lecheci-
llas *fpl*
sweet chestnut *n* (*fruit*) castaña *f* (dulce);
(*tree*) castaño *m* (dulce)
sweetcorn ['swi:tkɔ:n, *Am:* -kɔ:rn] *n Am*
maíz *m* (tierno)
sweeten ['swi:tən] *vt* endulzar; **to ~ sb up**
ablandar a alguien
sweetener *n* **1.** GASTR sacarina *f* **2.** *inf* (*incentive*) incentivo *m*
sweetheart ['swi:thɑ:t, *Am:* -hɑ:rt] *n*
1. (*kind person*) encanto *m* **2.** (*term of
endearment*) cariño *m* **3.** (*boyfriend, girlfriend*) novio, -a *m, f*
sweetness *n no pl* dulzor *m;* **to be all ~ and
light** *fig* estar de lo más amable
sweet pea *n* guisante *m* de olor **sweet
potato** *n* boniato *m* **sweet-talk** *vt* camelar
sweet william *n* minutisa *f*
swell [swel] <swelled, swollen *o*
swelled> **I.** *vt* **1.** (*size*) hinchar **2.** (*number*)
engrosar **II.** *vi* **1.** (*get bigger*) hincharse **2.** (*get
louder: sound*) subir **3.** (*increase*) aumentar
III. *n no pl* (*of sea*) oleaje *m;* **a heavy ~** un
fuerte oleaje **IV.** <-er, -est> *adj Am, inf* genial
swellhead ['swelhed] *n Am* engreído, -a *m, f*
swelling *n* hinchazón *m*

swelter ['sweltə^r, *Am:* -ˌtəˈ] *vi* morirse de
calor
sweltering *adj* (*heat, weather*) sofocante
swept [swept] *vt, vi pt of* **sweep**
swerve [swɜ:v, *Am:* swɜ:rv] **I.** *vi* **1.** (*car*)
virar bruscamente; (*person*) hurtar el cuerpo
2. (*not uphold*) **to ~ from sth** desviarse de
algo **II.** *n* (*of car*) viraje *m* brusco; (*of person*)
finta *f*
swift¹ [swɪft] *adj* (*fast-moving*) rápido, -a;
(*occurring quickly*) súbito, -a
swift² [swɪft] *n* ZOOL vencejo *m*
swiftly *adv* rápidamente
swiftness *n no pl* rapidez *f*
swig [swɪg] **I.** <-gg-> *vt inf* beber a tragos
II. *n inf* trago *m;* **to take a ~** tomar un trago
swill [swɪl] **I.** *n no pl* **1.** (*pig feed*) comida *f*
para cerdos; *fig, iron* bazofia *f* **2.** (*rinse*)
enjuague *m* **II.** *vt* **1.** (*swirl: liquid*) remover
2. (*rinse*) baldear **3.** (*drink*) beber a tragos
◆**swill down** *vt inf* **to swill sth down**
beber algo a tragos
swim [swɪm] **I.** <swam, swum> *vi* **1.** (*in
water*) nadar; **the meat was ~ming in
grease** *pej* la carne estaba cubierta de grasa
2. (*be full of water*) estar inundado, -a; **to ~
with tears** deshacerse en un mar de lágrimas
3. (*whirl*) **her head was ~ming** la cabeza le
daba vueltas **II.** <swam *Aus:* swum,
swum> *vt* **1.** (*cross*) cruzar a nado **2.** (*do*) **to
~ a few strokes** dar cuatro brazadas **III.** *n*
nado *m;* **I'm going to have a ~** voy a nadar
▸**to be in the ~** estar en la onda
swimmer ['swɪmə^r, *Am:* -ˌəˈ] *n* **1.** (*person*)
nadador(a) *m(f)* **2.** *pl, Aus, inf* (*swimming costume*) bañador *m*
swimming *n no pl* natación *f*
swimming bath *n* piscina *f,* alberca *f Méx,*
pileta *f Arg* **swimming cap** *n* gorro *m* de
natación **swimming costume** *n Brit, Aus*
traje *m* de baño
swimmingly *adv inf* **to go ~** ir sobre ruedas
swimming pool *n* piscina *f,* alberca *f Méx,*
pileta *f Arg* **swimming trunks** *npl* traje *m*
de baño (de caballero)
swimsuit ['swɪmsuːt] *n Am* bañador *m*
swindle ['swɪndl] **I.** *vt* estafar **II.** *n* estafa *f*
swindler ['swɪndlə^r, *Am:* -ˌəˈ] *n pej* tima-
dor(a) *m(f)*
swine [swaɪn] *n* **1.** *liter* (*pig*) cerdo *m*
2. <-(s)> *pej, inf* (*mean person*) cabrón, -ona
m, f
swing [swɪŋ] **I.** *n* **1.** (*movement*) vaivén *m*
2. (*punch*) golpe *m;* **to take a ~ at sb** (intentar) pegar a alguien **3.** (*hanging seat*) columpio
m, burro *m AmC* **4.** (*sharp change*) cambio *m*
en redondo; POL viraje *m* **5.** *Am* (*quick trip*)
viaje *m* **6.** *no pl* MUS swing *m* ▸**what you lose
on the ~s, you gain on the roundabouts**
Brit, prov lo que se pierde por un lado, se gana
por otro; **to get** (**back**) **into the ~ of things**
inf cogerle el tranquillo a algo; **to go with a ~**
Brit, inf (*party*) estar muy animado

II.<swung, swung> *vi* **1.** (*move back and forth*) oscilar; (*move circularly*) dar vueltas **2.** (*hit*) **to ~ at sb** (intentar) dar un golpe a alguien **3.** (*on hanging seat*) columpiarse **4.** (*alter*) cambiar; **to ~ between two things** oscilar entre dos cosas **5.** (*be exciting*) ser animado **6.** *Am* (*hang*) colgar III.<swung, swung> *vt* **1.** (*move back and forth*) balancear, chilinguear *Col* **2.** *inf* (*influence*) influir
♦**swing around** *vi*, **swing round** *vi* dar un giro
swing bridge *n* puente *m* giratorio **swing door** *n Brit, Aus* (*door that opens in both directions*) puerta *f* de vaivén; (*door that revolves*) puerta *f* giratoria
swingeing ['swɪndʒɪŋ] *adj Brit* (*cut*) salvaje; (*criticism*) feroz
swinging ['swɪŋɪŋ] *adj inf* (*lively*) con mucha marcha; **the ~ 60s** los alegres sesenta
swinish ['swaɪnɪʃ] *adj pej, inf* bellaco, -a
swipe [swaɪp] I. *vt* **1.** *Brit* (*swat*) abofetear **2.** *Am* (*graze: car*) dar un golpe a **3.** *inf* (*steal*) robar **4.** (*pass: card*) pasar II. *n* (*blow*) golpe *m; fig* (*criticism*) crítica *f;* **to take a ~ at sth** (*hit*) (intentar) pegar a alguien; (*criticize*) criticar a alguien
swirl [swɜːl, *Am:* swɜːrl] I. *vi* arremolinarse II. *vt* arremolinar III. *n* remolino *m*
swish [swɪʃ] I. *vi* (*cane*) silbar; (*dress*) hacer frufrú; (*water*) borbotear II. *vt* (*cane*) hacer silbar III.<-er, -est> *adj inf* elegante IV. *n* (*of cane*) silbido *m;* (*of dress*) frufrú *m*
Swiss [swɪs] I. *adj* suizo, -a; **~ German/French** alemán/francés suizo II. *n* suizo, -a *m, f*
switch [swɪtʃ] I.<-es> *n* **1.** ELEC interruptor *m,* suiche *m Méx* **2.** (*substitution*) remplazamiento *m* **3.** (*change*) cambio *m* **4.** (*thin whip*) látigo *m* **5.** *pl, Am* (*points*) puntos *mpl* II. *vi* cambiar; **to ~ with sb** cambiarse con alguien III. *vt* cambiar; **to ~ sth for sth** cambiar algo por algo
♦**switch off** I. *vt* (*machine, engine*) apagar; (*water, electricity*) cortar II. *vi* **1.** (*machine, engine*) apagarse **2.** (*lose attention*) desconectar
♦**switch on** I. *vt* (*machine, engine*) encender; **to ~ the charm** ponerse encantador II. *vi* encenderse
♦**switch over** *vi* cambiar; **to ~ to another channel** poner otro canal
♦**switch round** *vt* cambiar
switchback ['swɪtʃbæk] *n* carretera *f* en zigzag
switchblade ['swɪtʃbleɪd] *n Am* navaja *f* automática
switchboard ['swɪtʃbɔːd, *Am:* -bɔːrd] *n* **1.** ELEC conmutador *m* **2.** TEL centralita *f*
switchboard operator *n* telefonista *mf*
switchman <-men> *n Am* guardagujas *m inv*
switchyard *n Am* patio *m* de maniobras
Switzerland ['swɪtsələnd, *Am:* -səˈlənd] *n*

Suiza *f*
swivel ['swɪvəl] I. *n* plataforma *f* giratoria II.<*Brit:* -ll-, *Am:* -l-> *vt* girar
swivel chair *n* silla *f* giratoria
swizzle stick *n* agitador *m*
swollen ['swəʊlən, *Am:* ˈswoʊ-] I. *pp of* swell II. *adj* hinchado, -a
swollen-headed *adj* engreído, -a
swoon [swuːn] I. *vi* **1.** (*be in state of ecstasy*) estar embelesado; **to ~ over sb** derretirse por alguien **2.** *liter* (*faint*) desvanecerse II. *n liter* desvanecimiento *m*
swoop [swuːp] I. *n* **1.** (*dive*) caída *f* en picado **2.** *inf* (*surprise attack*) redada *f* II. *vi* **1.** (*dive*) bajar en picado **2.** *inf* (*make sudden attack*) abatirse; (*police*) hacer una redada
swop [swɒp, *Am:* swɑːp] <-pp-> *vt, vi Brit, Can s.* **swap**
sword [sɔːd, *Am:* sɔːrd] *n* espada *f;* **to draw a ~** desenfundar una espada ►**to have a ~ of Damocles hanging over one's head** tener la espada de Damocles suspendida sobre la cabeza de uno
sword dance *n* danza *f* de las espadas
swordfish <-(es)> *n* pez *m* espada
swordplay *n* esgrima *f;* **verbal ~** enfrentamiento *m* dialéctico **swordpoint** *n no pl* **to do sth at ~** hacer algo por obligación
swordsman ['sɔːdzmən, *Am:* ˈsɔːrdz-] <-men> *n* **1.** HIST espadachín *m* **2.** (*fencer*) esgrimidor *m*
swordsmanship *n no pl* destreza *f* en el manejo de la espada
swore [swɔː, *Am:* swɔːr] *pt of* **swear**
sworn [swɔːn, *Am:* swɔːrn] I. *pp of* swear II. *adj* jurado, -a
swot [swɒt, *Am:* swɑːt] <-tt-> *vi Brit, Aus, inf* empollar, machetearse *Méx;* **to ~ for an exam** empollar para un examen
swum [swʌm] *pp, a. Aus pt of* **swim**
swung [swʌŋ] *pt, pp of* **swing**
sycamore ['sɪkəmɔːr, *Am:* -mɔːr] *n* **1.** *Brit* plátano falso *m* **2.** *Am* plátano *m*
sycophant ['sɪkəfænt, *Am:* -fənt] *n pej* adulador(a) *m(f)*
sycophantic [ˌsɪkəʊˈfæntɪk, *Am:* -ˌt̬ɪk] *adj pej* adulador(a)
syllable ['sɪləbl] *n* sílaba *f;* **stressed/unstressed ~** sílaba tónica/átona; **not a ~** *fig* ni media palabra
syllabus ['sɪləbəs] <-es, *form:* syllabi> *n* (*in general*) plan *m* de estudios; (*for specific subject*) programa *m*
sylph [sɪlf] *n* sílfide *f*
symbiosis [ˌsɪmbɪˈəʊsɪs, *Am:* -ˈoʊ-] *n no pl* simbiosis *f*
symbiotic [ˌsɪmbɪˈɒtɪk, *Am:* -ˈɑːt̬ɪk] *adj* BIO simbiótico, -a
symbol ['sɪmbl] *n* símbolo *m*
symbolic(al) [sɪmˈbɒlɪk(l), *Am:* -ˈbɑːlɪk-] *adj* simbólico, -a
symbolism ['sɪmbəlɪzəm] *n no pl* simbolismo *m*

symbolize ['sɪmbəlaɪz] vt simbolizar
symmetrical [sɪ'metrɪkl] adj simétrico, -a
symmetry ['sɪmətri] n no pl simetría f
sympathetic [ˌsɪmpə'θetɪk, Am: -'θeţ-] adj
1. (understanding) comprensivo, -a; (sympathizing) receptivo, -a; **to lend a ~ ear to sb** estar dispuesto a escuchar a alguien 2. POL simpatizante; **to be ~ towards sb/sth** apoyar a alguien/algo
sympathize ['sɪmpəθaɪz] vi 1. (understand) mostrar comprensión; (feel compassion for) compadecerse de 2. (agree) estar de acuerdo; **to ~ with sb/sth** simpatizar con alguien/algo
sympathizer n simpatizante mf
sympathy ['sɪmpəθi] n no pl 1. (compassion) compasión f; (understanding) comprensión f; **you have my deepest ~** le acompaño en el sentimiento 2. (solidarity) solidaridad f
symphonic [sɪm'fɒnɪk, Am: -'fɑːnɪk] adj sinfónico, -a
symphony ['sɪmfəni] n 1. (piece of music) sinfonía f 2. (orchestra) orquesta f sinfónica
symphony concert n concierto m sinfónico **symphony orchestra** n orquesta f sinfónica
symposium [sɪm'pəʊziəm, Am: -'poʊ-] <-s o -sia> n form simposio m
symptom ['sɪmptəm] n síntoma m
symptomatic [ˌsɪmptə'mætɪk, Am: -'mæţ-] adj sintomático, -a
synagogue ['sɪnəgɒg, Am: -gɑːg] n sinagoga f
synchronize ['sɪŋkrənaɪz] I. vt sincronizar II. vi sincronizarse
synchronous ['sɪŋkrənəs] adj sincrónico, -a
syncopate ['sɪŋkəpeɪt] vt MUS sincopar
syndicate¹ ['sɪndɪkət, Am: -dəkɪt] n 1. ECON consorcio m 2. PUBL agencia f de noticias
syndicate² ['sɪndɪkeɪt, Am: -də-] vt 1. ECON agrupar 2. PUBL vender
syndication [ˌsɪndɪ'keɪʃən, Am: -də'-] n no pl 1. ECON agrupación f 2. PUBL venta f
syndrome ['sɪndrəʊm, Am: -droʊm] n síndrome m; **acquired immune deficiency ~** síndrome de la inmunodeficiencia adquirida
synergy ['sɪnədʒi, Am: -ɚdʒi] n no pl sinergía f
synod ['sɪnəd] n sínodo m
synonym ['sɪnənɪm] n sinónimo m
synonymous [sɪ'nɒnɪməs] adj sinónimo, -a
synopsis [sɪ'næpsɪs] <-es> n sinopsis f inv
syntactic(al) [sɪn'tæktɪk(əl)] adj sintáctico, -a
syntax ['sɪntæks] n no pl sintaxis f inv
synthesis ['sɪntθəsɪs] <-es> n síntesis f inv
synthesize ['sɪntθəsaɪz] vt sintetizar
synthesizer n sintetizador m
synthetic [sɪn'θetɪk, Am: -'θeţ-] adj 1. (man-made) sintético, -a 2. pej (fake) artificial
syphilis ['sɪfɪlɪs, Am: 'sɪflɪs] n no pl sífilis f

syphilitic [ˌsɪfɪ'lɪtɪk, Am: -ə'lɪţ-] adj sifilítico, -a
syphon ['saɪfn] n sifón m
Syria ['sɪriə] n Siria f
Syrian ['sɪriən] I. adj sirio, -a II. n sirio, -a m, f
syringe [sɪ'rɪndʒ, Am: sə'-] I. n jeringuilla f II. vt to ~ **sb's ears** destaponarle los oídos a alguien
syrup ['sɪrəp] n no pl 1. GASTR almíbar m, sirope m AmC, Col 2. MED jarabe m; **cough ~** jarabe para la tos
syrupy ['sɪrəpi] adj pej empalagoso, -a
system ['sɪstəm] n 1. (set) sistema m; **music ~** equipo m de música 2. (method of organization) método m; POL régimen m 3. (order) método m ▶**to get something out of one's ~** inf quitarse algo de encima
systematic [ˌsɪstə'mætɪk, Am: -'mæţ-] adj sistemático, -a
systematize ['sɪstəmətaɪz] vt sistematizar
system check n verificación f del sistema
system crash <-es> n fallo m en el sistema
system disk n disco m del sistema **system error** n error m en el sistema **system registry** n registro m del sistema
systems analysis n análisis m inv de sistemas **systems analyst** n analista mf de sistemas
system software n software m de sistema

T

T, t [tiː] n T, t f; **~ for Tommy** Brit, **~ for Tare** Am T de Tarragona
t abbr of **tonne** t (Brit: 1,016 kilos; Am: 907 kilos)
ta [tɑː] interj Brit, inf (thanks) gracias
TA n Brit abbr of **Territorial Army** ejército voluntario de reservistas británico
tab [tæb] n 1. (flap) solapa f; (on file) lengüeta f; **write-protect ~** INFOR lengüeta f protectora 2. (label) etiqueta f 3. inf (bill) cuenta f; **to put sth on the ~** cargar algo en la cuenta 4. Am (ringpull) anilla f 5. Brit, dial (cigarette) cigarrillo m 6. MED **a ~ of acid** una tableta de LSD ▶**to keep ~s on sth/sb** no perder de vista algo/a alguien
tabby ['tæbi] I. adj atigrado, -a II. n gato m atigrado
tabernacle ['tæbənækl, Am: 'tæbɚ-] n 1. form (place) tabernáculo m 2. (container) sagrario m
tab key n tabulador m
table ['teɪbl] I. n 1. mesa f; **to clear/set the ~** recoger/poner la mesa 2. MATH tabla f; **multiplication ~** tabla de multiplicar 3. (list) lista f; **~ of contents** índice m ▶**the ~s have turned** han cambiado las tornas II. vt 1. Brit, Aus (pro-

pose discussion of) poner sobre la mesa **2.** *Am* (*postpone discussion of*) posponer

tablecloth ['teɪblklɒθ, *Am:* -klɑ:θ] *n* mantel *m* **table land** *n* meseta *f* **table linen** *n no pl* mantelería *f* **table manners** *npl* modales *mpl* en la mesa **table mat** *n* salvamanteles *m inv* **tablespoon** *n* **1.** (*spoon*) cucharón *m* **2.** (*amount*) cucharada *f*

tablet ['tæblɪt] *n* **1.** (*pill*) comprimido *m* **2.** (*of stone*) lápida *f;* ~ **of soap** *Brit* pastilla *f* de jabón **3.** *Scot* GASTR dulce *m* de azúcar

table-talk *n* sobremesa *f* **table tennis** *n no pl* ping-pong *m* **tableware** *n no pl, form* servicio *m* de mesa **table wine** *n* vino *m* de mesa

tabloid ['tæblɔɪd] *n* diario *m* sensacionalista; **the** ~ **press** la prensa amarilla

taboo, tabu [təˈbuː] I. *n* tabú *m* II. *adj* tabú

tabular ['tæbjʊləˤ, *Am:* -ləˤ] *adj form* tabular

tabulate ['tæbjʊleɪt] *vt* disponer en tablas; INFOR tabular

tabulator ['tæbjʊleɪtəˤ, *Am:* -t̪əˤ] *n form* tabulador *m*

tachograph ['tækəgrɑːf] *n* tacógrafo *m*

tacit ['tæsɪt] *adj* tácito, -a

taciturn ['tæsɪtɜːn, *Am:* -ət̪ɜːrn] *adj* taciturno, -a, soturno, -a *Ven*

taciturnity [ˌtæsɪˈtɜːnət̪i, *Am:* -əˈtɜːrnət̪i] *n no pl, form* taciturnidad *f*

tack [tæk] I. *n* **1.** (*short nail*) tachuela *f* **2.** *no pl* (*riding gear*) montura *f* **3.** NAUT amura *f* **4.** (*approach*) política *f;* **to try a different** ~ intentar un enfoque distinto II. *vt* **1.** (*nail down*) clavar con tachuelas **2.** (*sew loosely*) hilvanar III. *vi* NAUT virar

tackle ['tækl] I. *vt* **1.** (*in soccer*) entrar a; (*in rugby, US football*) placar **2.** (*deal with: issue*) abordar; (*job*) emprender; (*problem*) atacar; **to** ~ **sb about sth** enfrentarse con alguien por algo II. *n no pl* **1.** (*in soccer*) entrada *f;* (*in rugby, US football*) placaje *m* **2.** *Am* (*line position*) atajo *m* **3.** (*equipment*) equipo *m* **4.** NAUT aparejo *m*

tacky ['tæki] <-ier, -iest> *adj* **1.** (*sticky*) pegajoso, -a **2.** *inf* (*showy*) vulgar; (*shoddy*) de mala calidad, de pacotilla *AmL*

tact [tækt] *n no pl* tacto *m*

tactful ['tæktfəl] *adj* discreto, -a

tactic ['tæktɪk] *n* ~(**s**) táctica *f*

tactical ['tæktɪkl] *adj* táctico, -a

tactician [tækˈtɪʃən] *n* táctico, -a *m, f*

tactile ['tæktaɪl, *Am:* -tl] *adj form* táctil

tactless ['tæktləs] *adj* falto, -a de tacto

tactlessness *n no pl* falta *f* de tacto

tad [tæd] *n* a ~ un poquitín

tadpole ['tædpəʊl, *Am:* -poʊl] *n* renacuajo *m*

taffeta ['tæfɪtə, *Am:* -t̪ə] *n no pl* tafetán *m*

tag [tæg] I. *n* **1.** *a.* INFOR (*label*) etiqueta *f;* (*metal*) herrete *m* **2.** *no pl* (*game*) **to play** ~ jugar al pillapilla **3.** LING **question** ~ cláusula *f* final interrogativa II. <-gg-> *vt* (*label*) etiquetar; **to** ~ **sth onto sth** añadir algo a algo

◆**tag along** *vi inf* seguir; **to** ~ **with sb** ir detrás de alguien

tail [teɪl] I. *n* **1.** ANAT, AVIAT cola *f;* (*of dog, bull*) rabo *m* **2.** *pl, inf* (*tail coat*) frac *m* **3.** *pl* (*side of coin*) cruz *f* **4.** *inf* (*person*) perseguidor(a) *m(f)* **5.** *inf* (*bottom*) trasero *m* ▸**to** chase **one's** ~ pillarse los dedos; **to** turn ~ **and run** huir II. *vt* seguir

◆**tail away** *vi* ir disminuyendo; (*get worse*) ir empeorando

◆**tail back** *vi Brit* (*traffic*) extenderse

◆**tail off** *vi* disminuir; (*sound*) desvanecerse

tailback ['teɪlbæk] *n Brit* caravana *f* de coches **tailboard** *n Brit* compuerta *f* trasera **tail end** *n* extremo *m* **tailgate** I. *n Am, Aus* (*of car*) puerta *f* de atrás; (*of truck*) compuerta *f* II. *vt Am* perseguir **tailless** *adj* sin cola **taillight** *n* AUTO luz *f* trasera

tailor ['teɪləˤ, *Am:* -ləˤ] I. *n* sastre *m* II. *vt* **1.** (*clothes*) confeccionar **2.** (*adapt*) adaptar

tailor-made [ˌteɪləˈmeɪd, *Am:* -ləˤ-] *adj* **1.** (*custom-made*) hecho, -a a medida **2.** (*perfect*) perfecto, -a

tailpiece ['teɪlpiːs] *n* **1.** (*part added*) añadidura *f* **2.** AVIAT cola *f* **3.** TYPO viñeta *f* **tailpipe** *n Am* tubo *m* de escape **tailspin** *n* barrena *f* picada; **to go into a** ~ caer en picado **tail wind** *n* viento *m* de cola

taint [teɪnt] I. *vt* (*food*) contaminar; (*reputation*) manchar II. *n no pl* mancha *f*

taintless *adj liter* incorrupto, -a

Taiwan [ˌtaɪˈwɑːn] *n* Taiwán *m*

Taiwanese [ˌtaɪwəˈniːz] I. *adj* taiwanés, -esa II. *n* taiwanés, -esa *m, f*

Tajikistan [tɑːˈdʒiːkɪˌstɑːn] *n* Tayikistán *m*

take [teɪk] I. *n* **1.** *no pl* (*receipts*) ingresos *mpl* **2.** PHOT, FILM toma *f* ▸**to be** on **the** ~ *Am, inf* dejarse sobornar II. <took, taken> *vt* **1.** (*accept*) aceptar; (*advice*) seguir; (*criticism*) soportar; (*responsibility*) asumir; **to** ~ **sth seriously** tomar algo en serio; **to** ~ **one's time** tomarse su tiempo; **to** ~ **sth as it comes** aceptar algo tal y como es **2.** (*hold*) coger, agarrar *AmL* **3.** (*eat*) comer; (*medicine*) tomar **4.** (*use*) necesitar **5.** (*receive*) recibir **6.** *Brit* (*rent*) alquilar **7.** (*capture: prisoners*) prender; (*city*) conquistar; (*power*) tomar **8.** (*assume*) **to** ~ **office** entrar en funciones **9.** (*bring*) llevar **10.** (*require*) exigir, requerir; **this shirt** ~**s a lot of ironing** esta camisa ha de plancharse mucho **11.** (*do*) REL oficiar; UNIV cursar **12.** (*have: decision, bath, holiday*) tomar; (*walk*) dar; (*trip*) hacer; (*ticket*) sacar; (*census*) levantar; **to** ~ **a rest** descansar **13.** *Brit* (*score*) obtener **14.** *Brit, Aus* (*teach*) enseñar **15.** (*feel, assume*) **to** ~ (**an**) **interest in sb/ sth** interesarse por alguien/algo; **to** ~ **offence** ofenderse; **to** ~ **pity on sb/sth** apiadarse de alguien/algo; **to** ~ **the view that ...** adoptar la opinión de que... **16.** (*make money*) ganar **17.** (*photograph*) sacar **18.** (*use for travel: bus, train*) coger, tomar *AmL* **19.** (*regard as*) tener; **to** ~ **sb for sth** tener a alguien por algo ▸~ **it**

or <u>leave</u> it ¡tómalo o déjalo!; **what do you ~ me for?** ¿por quién me has tomado?; **~ it from me** puedes creerme; **I ~ it that ...** supongo que...; **~ that!** ¡toma! III.<took, taken> vi tener efecto; (*plant*) prender; (*dye*) pegar; **to ~ against sb** *Brit* encontrar a alguien antipático
◆**take aback** vt (*suprise*) sorprender; (*shock*) abatir
◆**take after** vt parecerse a
◆**take along** vt (*take*) llevar (consigo); (*bring*) traer (consigo)
◆**take apart** I. vt 1.(*disassemble*) desmontar 2.(*analyse*) reseñar 3.(*destroy*) despedazar II. vi desmontarse
◆**take away** I. vt 1.(*remove*) quitar 2.(*go away with*) llevar(se) 3.(*lessen*) disminuir 4.(*subtract from*) restar II. vi quitarse; **to ~ from the importance/worth of sth** restar importancia/mérito a algo
◆**take back** vt 1.(*return*) devolver 2.(*accept back*) aceptar; (*employee*) volver a emplear; (*spouse*) reconciliarse con 3.(*repossess*) recobrar 4.(*retract*) retractar 5.(*carry to past time*) evocar 6.(*remind*) recordar
◆**take down** vt 1.(*remove*) quitar; (*from high place*) bajar 2.(*disassemble*) desmontar 3.(*write down*) apuntar 4. *inf* (*diminish the pride of*) **to take sb down** bajar los humos a alguien; (*humble*) humillar a alguien
◆**take in** vt 1.(*bring inside*) recoger, acoger (en casa); (*admit*) aceptar 2.(*hold*) **to take sb in one's arms** sostener a alguien entre sus brazos; **to take sth in hand** *fig* hacerse cargo de algo 3.(*accommodate*) alojar; (*for rent*) hospedar 4.(*bring to police*) entregar 5.(*deceive*) estafar; **to be taken in (by sb/sth)** ser engañado (por alguien/algo) 6. *Am, Aus* (*go to see*) ir a ver 7.(*understand*) comprender; **to take sth in at a glance** asimilar algo en un abrir y cerrar de ojos 8.(*include*) incluir 9. FASHION estrechar
◆**take off** I. vt 1.(*remove from*) retirar; **to take sb off a list** tachar a alguien de una lista 2.(*clothes*) quitarse 3.(*bring away*) llevarse 4.(*subtract*) descontar 5.(*stop showing*) descontinuar 6. *Brit* (*imitate*) imitar II. vi 1. AVIAT despegar 2. *inf* (*leave*) salir; *inf* (*flee*) huir 3.(*have success*) empezar a tener éxito
◆**take on** I. vt 1.(*agree to try*) aceptar 2.(*acquire*) adoptar 3.(*hire*) contratar 4.(*fight*) enfrentarse a 5.(*stop for loading: passengers*) cargar; (*fuel*) abastecerse de; (*goods*) tomar II. vi apurarse
◆**take out** vt 1.(*remove*) quitar; (*extract*) extraer; (*withdraw*) retirar 2.(*bring outside*) llevar fuera; (*garbage*) tirar, botar *Col, Ven* 3.(*for walk*) llevar de paseo 4. *inf* (*kill*) eliminar; (*destroy*) destruir 5.(*arrange to get: licence*) obtener 6.(*borrow*) tomar prestado 7.(*vent anger*) **to take sth out on sb** desahogarse riñendo a alguien 8. *inf* (*tire*) **to take it out of sb** agotar a alguien
◆**take over** I. vt 1.(*buy out*) comprar

2.(*seize control*) tomar el control de 3.(*assume*) asumir 4.(*possess*) tomar posesión de; **to be taken over by one's work** estar dominado por su trabajo 5.(*start using*) comenzar a usar II. vi tomar posesión
◆**take to** vt 1.(*start to like*) coger simpatía a, encariñarse con *AmL* 2.(*begin as a habit*) **to ~ doing sth** aficionarse a hacer algo; **to ~ drink/drugs** darse a la bebida/las drogas 3.(*go to*) dirigirse a; **to ~ the streets (in protest)** tomar las calles (para protestar); **to ~ one's bed** meterse en la cama
◆**take up** I. vt 1.(*bring up*) subir 2.**to ~ arms (against sth)** tomar las armas (contra algo) 3.(*start doing*) comenzar; (*job*) empezar; (*piano*) iniciarse en; (*fishing*) dedicarse a 4.(*discuss*) tratar 5.(*accept*) aceptar 6.(*adopt*) adoptar 7.(*continue doing*) proseguir 8.(*join in*) participar 9.(*occupy*) ocupar 10.(*pull up*) alzar 11.(*shorten*) coger a 12.(*patronise*) patrocinar 13.(*absorb*) absorber II. vi **to ~ with sb** relacionarse con alguien; **to ~ with sth** familiarizarse con algo
takeaway ['teɪkəweɪ] n *Brit, Aus* comida f para llevar
take-home pay ['teɪkhəʊmˌpeɪ, *Am:* 'teɪkhoʊmˌpeɪ] n no pl salario m neto
taken vi, vt pp of **take**
take-off ['teɪkɒf, *Am:* -ɑːf] n 1. AVIAT despegue m 2. *Brit, Aus* (*imitation*) imitación f
take-out ['teɪkaʊt] n *Am* comida f para llevar
takeover ['teɪkˌəʊvəʳ, *Am:* -ˌoʊvɚ] n POL toma f del poder; ECON adquisición f
takeover bid n oferta f pública de adquisición de acciones
taker ['teɪkəʳ, *Am:* -kɚ] n **the suggestion had no ~s** nadie aceptó la propuesta
take-up ['teɪkʌp] n 1. TECH compensación f 2.(*of scheme, suggestion*) aceptación f
taking ['teɪkɪŋ] I. n 1. no pl (*capture*) toma f; **it's yours for the ~** es tuyo si lo quieres 2. pl (*receipts*) ingresos mpl II. adj atractivo, -a
talc [tælk] n, **talcum (powder)** ['tælkəm(ˌpaʊdəʳ)] n no pl 1. CHEM talco m 2. MED polvos mpl de talco
tale [teɪl] n 1.(*story*) historia f; LIT cuento m 2.(*lie*) mentira f; **dead men tell no ~s** los muertos no mienten ▶**to tell ~s** chivarse
talent ['tælənt] n 1.(*ability*) talento m 2. *Brit, Aus, iron* (*attractive girls*) bombones fpl, buenonas fpl *Col*, mamacitas fpl *Méx*; (*boys*) bombones mpl, mangos mpl *Ven*, bizcochos mpl *Col*, papacitos mpl *Méx*
talented adj talentoso, -a
talisman ['tælɪzmən] n talismán m
talk [tɔːk] I. n 1.(*conversation*) conversación f, plática f *Méx* 2.(*lecture*) charla f 3. no pl (*things said*) chisme m; **big ~** jactancia f 4. pl (*formal discussions*) negociaciones fpl ▶**to be the ~ of the** <u>town</u> andar de boca en boca; **to be** <u>all</u> **~ (and no action)** hablar mucho (y no hacer nada) II. vi (*speak*) hablar; **to ~ about sb behind their back** murmurar de alguien a

sus espaldas; **to give sb something to ~ about** dar a alguien motivos para hablar; **~ing of holidays, ...** hablando de las vacaciones,... ▶**to ~** <u>dirty</u> decir obscenidades; <u>look</u> who's ~ing *inf;* you're a fine <u>one</u> to ~ *inf* ¡mira quién habla!; **to** <u>set</u> **sb ~ing** *Brit* dar que hablar a alguien **III.** *vt* **1.**(*utter*) decir **2.**(*discuss*) hablar de
◆**talk back** *vi* replicar
◆**talk down I.** *vt* (*speak louder than*) apabullar **II.** *vi pej* **to ~ to sb** hablar a alguien con condescendencia
◆**talk out** *vt* **1.**(*discuss*) discutir **2.**(*convince not to*) **to talk sb out of sth** disuadir a alguien de algo
◆**talk over** *vt* **to talk sth over (with sb)** hablar algo (con alguien)
◆**talk round I.** *vt* **to talk sb round** convencer a alguien **II.** *vi* (*avoid*) **to ~ sth** dar vueltas a algo
◆**talk through** *vt* **1.**(*discuss*) discutir **2.**(*explain*) explicar
talkative ['tɔ:kətɪv, *Am:* -t̬ɪv] *adj* locuaz
talker *n* hablador(a) *m(f)*
talking I. *adj* parlante **II.** *n no pl* habla *f;* "no ~" "prohibido hablar"
talking shop *n inf* ≈ mentidero *m*
talking-to ['tɔ:kɪŋtu:] *n* sermón *m;* **to give sb a ~** echar un sermón a alguien
talk show *n* programa *m* de entrevistas
tall [tɔ:l] *adj* alto, -a; **to grow ~(er)** crecer
tallboy ['tɔ:lbɔɪ] *n* cómoda *f* alta
tallness ['tɔ:lnɪs] *n no pl* altura *f*
tallow ['tæləʊ, *Am:* -oʊ] *n no pl* sebo *m*
tally¹ ['tæli] <-ie-> *vi* concordar; **to ~ with sth** coincidir con algo
tally² ['tæli] <-ies> **I.** *n* cuenta *f;* **to keep a ~ (of sth)** llevar la cuenta (de algo) **II.** *vt* llevar la cuenta de
◆**tally up** *vt* llevar la cuenta de
tally-ho [ˌtælɪ'həʊ, *Am:* -'hoʊ] *interj* hala
talon ['tælən] *n* garra *f*
tamarind ['tæmərɪnd] *n* tamarindo *m*
tamarisk ['tæmərɪsk] *n* tamarisco *m*
tambour ['tæmbʊəʳ, *Am:* -bʊr] *n* tambor *m*
tambourine [ˌtæmbə'ri:n] *n* pandereta *f*
tame [teɪm] **I.** *adj* **1.**(*domesticated*) doméstico, -a; (*not savage*) manso, -a **2.**(*unexciting*) soso, -a **II.** *vt* (*feelings*) dominar; (*animal*) domesticar, aguachar *Chile*
tamer ['teɪməʳ, *Am:* -ɚ] *n* domador(a) *m(f)*
tamp [tæmp] *vt* apisonar
tamper ['tæmpəʳ, *Am:* -ɚ] *vi* entrometerse
◆**tamper with** *vt* manosear; (*document*) falsificar; (*witness*) sobornar; (*lock*) tratar de forzar
tamper-proof ['tæmpəpru:f, *Am:* -pɚ-] *adj,* **tamper-resistant** *adj* no manipulable
tampon ['tæmpən, *Am:* -pɑːn] *n* MED tapón *m;* (*for absorbing menstrual blood*) tampón *m*
tan¹ [tæn] **I.**<-nn-> *vi* broncearse **II.**<-nn-> *vt* **1.**(*make brown*) broncear; **to be ~ned** estar moreno **2.**(*leather*) curtir ▶**to ~** sb's

<u>hide</u> *inf* dar una paliza a alguien **III.** *n* bronceado *m;* **to get a ~** ponerse moreno **IV.** *adj* marrón claro
tan² MAT *abbr of* **tangent** tg
tandem ['tændəm] **I.** *n* tándem *m;* **to work in ~** trabajar conjuntamente **II.** *adv* en tándem; **to ride ~** montar en tándem
tang [tæŋ] *n* olor *m* penetrante
tangent ['tændʒənt] *n* tangente *f;* **to go off at a ~** salirse por la tangente
tangential [tæn'dʒenʃl] *adj* tangencial
tangerine [ˌtændʒə'ri:n] *n* mandarina *f*
tangible ['tændʒəbl] *adj* tangible; (*benefit*) palpable; **~ asset** bien *m* material
Tangier ['tændʒɪəʳ, *Am:* tæn'dʒɪr] *n* Tánger *m*
tangle ['tæŋgl] **I.** *n* **1.**(*in hair, string*) maraña *f* **2.** *fig* (*confusion*) enredo *m* **II.** *vt* enredar **III.** *vi* enredarse
◆**tangle with** *vi* (*quarrel*) meterse con
tango ['tæŋgəʊ, *Am:* -goʊ] **I.** *n* tango *m* ▶**it takes** <u>two</u> **to ~** *prov* es cosa de dos **II.** *vi* bailar un tango
tangy ['tæŋi] <-ier, -iest> *adj* fuerte
tank [tæŋk] *n* **1.**(*container*) depósito *m* **2.**(*aquarium*) acuario *m* **3.** MIL tanque *m*
tanked up *adj* **to be ~** ir como una cuba
tankard ['tæŋkəd, *Am:* -kɚd] *n* jarra *f*
tanker ['tæŋkəʳ, *Am:* -ɚ] *n* **1.**(*lorry*) camión *m* cisterna **2.**(*ship*) buque *m* cisterna; **oil ~** petrolero *m* **3.**(*aircraft*) avión *m* cisterna
tanned [tænd] *adj* bronceado, -a
tanner ['tænəʳ, *Am:* -ɚ] *n* curtidor(a) *m(f)*
tannery ['tænəri] *n* curtiduría *f*
tannic acid [ˌtænɪk'æsɪd] *n* ácido *m* tánico
tannin ['tænɪn] *n* tanino *m*
tanning ['tænɪŋ] *n* **1.**(*of leather*) curtido *m* **2.** *inf* (*beating*) paliza *f*
tannoy® *n Brit,* **Tannoy®** ['tænɔɪ] *n Brit* sistema *m* de megafonía
tantalize ['tæntəlaɪz, *Am:* -t̬əlaɪz] *vt* **1.**(*torment*) atormentar **2.**(*tempt*) tentar
tantalizing *adj* tentador(a); (*smile*) seductor(a)
tantamount ['tæntəmaʊnt, *Am:* -t̬ə-] *adj* equivalente; **to be ~ to sth** equivaler a algo
tantrum ['tæntrəm] *n* berrinche *m,* dengue *m Méx;* **to have** [*o* throw] **a ~** coger [*o* agarrar *AmL*] una rabieta
Tanzania [ˌtænzə'nɪə, *Am:* -'niːə] *n* Tanzania *f*
Tanzanian [ˌtænzə'nɪən, *Am:* -'niːən] **I.** *adj* tanzano, -a **II.** *n* tanzano, -a *m, f*
tap¹ [tæp] **I.** *n* **1.** *Brit* (*for water*) grifo *m,* canilla *f Arg, Par, Urug;* **beer on ~** cerveza *f* de barril; **to turn the ~ on/off** abrir/cerrar el grifo; **on ~** *fig* al alcance de la mano **2.** TEL micrófono *m* de escucha **II.**<-pp-> *vt* **1.** TEL intervenir; (*conversation*) interceptar; (*phone*) pinchar *inf* **2.**(*make use of*) utilizar; (*sources*) explotar **3.**(*let out*) espitar
tap² [tæp] **I.** *n* **1.**(*light knock*) golpecito *m* **2.**(*tap-dancing*) claqué *m* **II.**<-pp-> *vt* gol-

pear suavemente; **to ~ one's fingers on the table** tamborilear con los dedos sobre la mesa **III.** <-pp-> *vi* dar golpecitos

tap dance ['tæp͵dɑːnts, *Am:* -͵dænts] *n* claqué *m*

tape [teɪp] **I.** *n* **1.** (*adhesive strip*) cinta *f* adhesiva; MED esparadrapo *m;* **masking** ~ cinta adhesiva protectora; **Scotch** ~® *Am* celo *m,* durex *m AmL* **2.** (*measure*) cinta *f* métrica **3.** SPORTS cinta *f* de llegada **4.** (*cassette*) cinta *f,* tape *m RíoPl;* **to get sth on** ~ grabar algo **II.** *vt* **1.** (*fasten with tape*) poner una cinta a **2.** (*record*) grabar; **to have (got) sb** ~**d** *Brit, Aus, inf* tener a alguien calado

tape cassette *n* casete *f* **tape deck** *n* platina *f* **tape measure** *n* metro *m*

taper ['teɪpəʳ, *Am:* -pɚ] **I.** *n* (*slim candle*) candela *f;* (*wax-coated wick*) cerilla *f* **II.** *vt* afilar **III.** *vi* afilarse

◆taper off *vi* disminuir

tape-record *vt* grabar (en cinta) **tape recorder** *n* grabadora *f* **tape recording** *n* grabación *f* (en cinta)

tapered wing [͵teɪpəd'wɪŋ, *Am:* -ɚd'-] *n* AVIAT ala *f* ahusada

tapestry ['tæpɪstri, *Am:* -əstri] *n* **1.** (*art form*) tapicería *f* **2.** (*object*) tapiz *m* **3.** *fig* collage *m*

tapeworm ['teɪpwɜːm, *Am:* -wɜːrm] *n* tenia *f,* solitaria *f*

tapioca [͵tæpɪ'əʊkə, *Am:* -'oʊ-] *n* tapioca *f*

tapir ['teɪpəʳ, *Am:* -pɚ] *n* tapir *m*

tappet ['tæpət] *n* alzaválvulas *m inv*

taproom ['tæprʊm, *Am:* -ruːm] *n* cervecería *f*

tap water *n* agua *f* corriente

tar [tɑːʳ, *Am:* tɑːr] **I.** *n* *no pl* alquitrán *m* **II.** <-rr-> *vt* alquitranar; **to** ~ **and feather sb** emplumar a alguien

tarantula [təˈræntjʊlə, *Am:* -tʃələ] *n* tarántula *f*

tardy ['tɑːdi, *Am:* 'tɑːr-] <-ier, -iest> *adj liter* tardío, -a; *pej* (*sluggish*) lento, -a

tare [teəʳ, *Am:* ter] *n* ECON tara *f*

target ['tɑːgɪt, *Am:* 'tɑːr-] **I.** *n* **1.** (*mark aimed at*) objetivo *m;* **to hit the** ~ dar en el blanco **2.** ECON objetivo *m;* **to be on** ~ ir de acuerdo con lo previsto **II.** <*Brit* -tt- *o Am* -t-> *vt* centrarse en; **to** ~ **sth on sth** (*missile*) apuntar algo a algo; (*campaign*) destinar algo a algo

target date *n* fecha *f* límite **target language** *n* LING lengua *m* de destino; INFOR lenguaje *m* objeto **target practice** *n* prácticas *fpl* de tiro **target price** *n* precio *m* indicativo

targetted ['tɑːgɪtəd, *Am:* 'tɑːrgɪtɪd] *adj Brit* elegido, -a como objetivo

tariff ['tærɪf, *Am:* 'ter-] *n* **1.** *Brit* (*list of charges*) tarifa *f* **2.** (*customs duty*) arancel *m*

tariff barrier *n* ECON barrera *f* arancelaria

tarmac® ['tɑːmæk, *Am:* 'tɑːr-], **tarmacadam**® **I.** *n* *no pl* **1.** *Brit* (*paving material*) asfalto *m* **2.** AVIAT pista *f* de despegue **II.** <-ck->

vt Brit asfaltar

tarn [tɑːn, *Am:* tɑːrn] *n* lago *m* de montaña

tarnish ['tɑːnɪʃ, *Am:* 'tɑːr-] **I.** *vi* deslustrarse **II.** *vt* deslustrar; (*reputation*) manchar **III.** *n* mancha *f*

tarpaulin [tɑːˈpɔːlɪn, *Am:* tɑːrˈpɑː-] *n* lona *f* impermeabilizada

tarragon ['tærəgən, *Am:* 'terəgɑːn] *n* *no pl* estragón *m*

tarsus ['tɑːsəs, *Am:* 'tɑːr-] *n* ANAT tarso *m*

tart¹ [tɑːt, *Am:* tɑːrt] *adj* **1.** (*sharp*) agrio, -a; (*acid*) ácido, -a **2.** (*caustic*) cortante

tart² [tɑːt, *Am:* tɑːrt] *n* **1.** GASTR tarta *f* **2.** *Brit, pej, inf* (*woman of questionable morals*) pendón *m;* (*prostitute*) fulana *f*

◆tart up *vt Brit, pej, inf* remodelar; **to tart oneself up** emperifollarse

tartan ['tɑːtn, *Am:* 'tɑːrtn] *n* **1.** *no pl* (*cloth*) tela *f* a cuadros escoceses **2.** (*design*) tartán *m*

Tartar ['tɑːtəʳ, *Am:* 'tɑːrtɚ] *n* (*bad-tempered person*) persona *f* intratable

tartar ['tɑːtəʳ, *Am:* 'tɑːrtɚ] *n* *no pl* **1.** MED sarro *m* **2.** CHEM tártaro *m*

tartar(e) sauce *n* *no pl* salsa *f* tártara

tartaric [tɑːˈtærɪk, *Am:* tɑːr-] *n* ácido *m* tartárico

task [tɑːsk, *Am:* tæsk] **I.** *n* tarea *f,* tonga *f Col;* **to take sb to** ~ llamar la atención a alguien **II.** *vt* imponer una tarea; **to be** ~**ed with sth** estar encargado de algo

taskforce *n* MIL destacamento *m;* (*team*) equipo *m* de trabajo **taskmaster** *n* capataz *m;* **to be a hard** ~ ser un tirano

Tasmania [tæzˈmeɪniə] *n* Tasmania *f*

Tasmanian [tæzˈmeɪniən] **I.** *adj* tasmano, -a **II.** *n* tasmano, -a *m, f*

tassel ['tæsl] *n* borla *f*

taste [teɪst] **I.** *n* **1.** *no pl* sabor *m;* **sense of** ~ sentido *m* del gusto **2.** (*small portion*) bocado *m;* **to have a** ~ **of sth** probar algo **3.** (*liking*) gusto *m;* **to lose the** ~ **for sth** perder el gusto por algo; **to have different** ~**s** tener gustos distintos; **to get a** ~ **for sth** tomar el gusto a algo **4.** *no pl* (*experience*) experiencia *f* ►**to leave a** <u>bad</u> ~ (**in one's mouth**) dejar un mal sabor de boca **II.** *vt* **1.** (*food, drink*) saborear **2.** (*experience*) experimentar; (*luxury*) probar **III.** *vi* saber; **to** ~ **bitter/sweet** tener un sabor amargo/dulce; **to** ~ **of** [*o like*] **sth** saber a algo

tastebud ['teɪstbʌd] *n* papila *f* gustativa

tasteful ['teɪstfəl] *adj* con gusto; (*decorous*) con delicadeza

tasteless ['teɪstləs] *adj* **1.** (*without flavour*) soso, -a **2.** (*clothes, remark*) de mal gusto

taster ['teɪstəʳ, *Am:* -ɚ] *n* **1.** (*person*) catador(a) *m(f)* **2.** *Brit* (*sample*) muestra *f*

tasty ['teɪsti] *adj* **1.** (*tasting good*) sabroso, -a **2.** *Brit, inf* (*attractive*) buenísimo, -a

tat [tæt] *n* *no pl, pej, inf* porquería *f*

tattered ['tætəd, *Am:* 'tæṯɚd] *adj* (*clothes*) hecho jirones; (*person*) harapiento, -a; (*reputation*) destrozado, -a

tatters ['tætəʳz, *Am:* 'tæṯɚz] *npl* jirones *fpl;*

to be in ~ estar hecho jirones

tattle ['tætl, *Am:* 'tæt̮-] *n* chismorreo *m*

tattler ['tætlər, *Am:* 'tæt̮lə-] *n* cotilla *mf*

tattoo [tə'tuː, *Am:* tæt'uː] **I.** *n* **1.** MIL espectáculo *m* militar **2.** (*marking on skin*) tatuaje *m* **II.** *vt* tatuar

tatty ['tæti, *Am:* 'tæt̮-] <-ier, -iest> *adj pej* estropeado, -a

taught [tɔːt, *Am:* tɑːt] *pt, pp of* **teach**

taunt [tɔːnt, *Am:* tɑːnt] **I.** *vt* burlarse de **II.** *n* insulto *m*

Taurus ['tɔːrəs] *n* Tauro *m*

taut [tɔːt, *Am:* tɑːt] *adj* (*wire, string*) tensado, -a; (*skin*) terso, -a; (*nerves*) tenso, -a

tautological [ˌtɔːtə'lɒdʒɪkəl, *Am:* ˌtɑːtə-'lɑːdʒɪk-] *adj*, **tautologous** [tɔː'tɒləgəs, *Am:* tɑː'tɑːlə-] *adj* tautológico, -a

tautology [tɔː'tɒlədʒi, *Am:* tɑː'tɑːlə-] <-ies> *n* tautología *f*

tavern ['tævən, *Am:* -ə-n] *n* taberna *f*, estanquillo *m Ecua*

tawdry ['tɔːdri, *Am:* 'tɑː-] <-ier, -iest> *adj pej* (*vulgar*) hortera; (*pompous*) de relumbrón

tawny ['tɔːni, *Am:* 'tɑː-] <-ier, -iest> *adj* de color ambar ocuro

tawny owl *n* cárabo *m*

tax [tæks] **I.** <-es> *n* **1.** FIN impuesto *m;* **hidden** ~**es** *Am* impuestos encubiertos; **to collect** ~**es** recaudar impuestos; **to increase** ~**es** subir los impuestos; **to put a** ~ **on sth** gravar algo con un impuesto; **free of** ~ exento de impuestos **2.** *fig* (*burden*) carga *f;* **to be a** ~ **on** sb ser una carga para alguien **II.** *vt* **1.** FIN gravar con un impuesto **2.** (*accuse*) acusar **3.** *fig* (*need effort*) exigir un esfuerzo

taxable ['tæksəbl] *adj* imponible

tax allowance *n* desgravación *f* fiscal

taxation [tæk'seɪʃən] *n no pl* (*taxes*) impuestos *mpl;* (*system*) sistema *m* impositivo

tax avoidance *n* evasión *f* de impuestos **tax base** *n* base *f* imponible **tax bracket** *n* categoría *f* impositiva **tax collector** *n* recaudador(a) *m(f)* de impuestos **tax consultant** *n* asesor(a) *m(f)* fiscal **tax-deductible** *adj* deducible (a efectos impositivos) **tax disc** *n Brit: adhesivo que se engancha en la ventanilla del coche y certifica que se ha satisfecho el impuesto de circulación* **tax dodger** *n,* **tax evader** *n* evasor(a) *m(f)* de impuestos **tax evasion** *n* evasión *f* de impuestos **tax exemption** *n* exención *f* fiscal **tax-free** *adj* libre de impuestos **tax haven** *n* paraíso *m* fiscal

taxi ['tæksi] **I.** *n* taxi *m* **II.** *vi* ir en taxi; AVIAT rodar

taxidermist ['tæksɪˌdɜːmɪst, *Am:* -dɜːr-] *n* taxidermista *mf*

taxidermy ['tæksɪˌdɜːmi, *Am:* -dɜːr-] *n* taxidermia *f*

taxi driver *n* taxista *mf,* ruletero, -a *m, f AmC, Méx*

taximeter ['tæksɪˌmiːtər, *Am:* -t̮ə-] *n* taxímetro *m*

taxing *adj* difícil

taxiplane *n* avión *m* para vuelos no regulares

taxi rank *n Brit,* **taxi stand** *n Am* parada *f* de taxis

taxman ['tæksmæn] *n no pl* recaudador(a) *m(f)* de impuestos; **the** ~ Hacienda *f*

taxonomy [tæk'sɒnəmi, *Am:* -'sɑːnə-] *n* taxonomía *f*

taxpayer ['tæksˌpeɪər, *Am:* -ə-] *n* contribuyente *mf* **tax rebate** *n* devolución *f* de impuestos **tax relief** *n* exención *f* de impuestos **tax return** *n* declaración *f* de renta **tax revenues** *n* ingresos *mpl* fiscales **tax system** *n* sistema *m* impositivo **tax year** *n* año *m* fiscal

TB [ˌtiː'biː] *n abbr of* **tuberculosis** tuberculosis *f inv*

T-bar ['tiːbɑːr, *Am:* -bɑːr] *n,* **T-bar lift** *n* barra *f* en forma de T

tbs(p) *abbr of* **tablespoonful** cucharada *f* sopera

tea [tiː] *n* **1.** *no pl* (*plant, drink*) té *m;* **a cup of** ~ una taza de té; **strong/weak** ~ té fuerte/flojo; **camomile** ~ infusión *f* de manzanilla **2.** *Brit* (*afternoon meal*) merienda *f; Aus* (*evening meal*) cena *f* ▶ **not for all the** ~ **in China** ni por todo el oro del mundo

tea bag *n* bolsita *f* de té **tea break** *n Brit* descanso *m* (para el té) **tea caddy** *n* caja *f* para té

teacake ['tiːkeɪk] *n* bollito *m* con pasas

teach [tiːtʃ] <taught, taught> **I.** *vt* enseñar; **to** ~ **oneself sth** aprender algo por su propia cuenta; **to** ~ **sb a lesson** *fig* dar una lección a alguien **II.** *vi* dar clases

teacher ['tiːtʃər, *Am:* -tʃə-] *n* profesor(a) *m(f)*

teacher training *n* formación *f* de profesorado **teacher training college** *n Brit* instituto *f* de ciencias de la educación

tea chest *n* caja *f* de embalaje

teaching **I.** *n* **1.** *no pl* (*profession*) docencia *f* **2.** *pl* (*doctrine*) enseñanza *f* **II.** *adj* didáctico, -a

teaching staff *n* profesorado *m*

tea cloth *n Brit* paño *m* de cocina **tea cosy** *n* cubretetera *m* **teacup** *n* taza *f* de té **tea house** *n* salón *m* de té

teak [tiːk] *n no pl* teca *f*

tea leaves *npl* hojas *fpl* de té

team [tiːm] **I.** *n* (*group*) equipo *m;* (*of oxen*) yunta *f;* (*of horses*) tiro *m;* (*of dogs*) traílla *f* **II.** *adj* de equipo **III.** *vt* asociar; (*match*) combinar

◆ **team up** *vi* agruparse; **to** ~ **with** asociarse con

team captain *n* capitán, -ana *m, f* de equipo **team effort** *n* esfuerzo *m* conjunto **team-mate** *n* compañero, -a *m, f* **team play** *n* juego *m* de equipo **team spirit** *n* espíritu *m* de equipo **teamwork** *n* trabajo *m* en equipo

teapot ['tiːpɒt, *Am:* -pɑːt] *n* tetera *f*

tear[1] [tɪər, *Am:* tɪr] **I.** *n* lágrima *f;* **to bring** ~**s to sb's eyes** hacer que a alguien se le salten las lágrimas; **to burst into ~s** echarse a llorar; **to have ~s in one's eyes** tener los ojos llenos de lágrimas; **to not shed (any) ~s** no derramar una (sola) lágrima **II.** *vi* llorar

tear² [teə^r, *Am:* ter] **I.** *n* rotura *f* **II.**<tore, torn> *vt* **1.**(*rip*) rasgar; (*ruin*) romper; **to ~ a hole in sth** hacer un agujero en algo; **to be torn between two possibilities** no saber qué posibilidad elegir **2.**(*strain: muscle*) distender **III.**<tore, torn> *vi* **1.**(*rip*) rasgarse **2.**(*rush wildly*) lanzarse; **to ~ down the stairs** precipitarse escaleras abajo

♦**tear apart** *vt* destrozar; *fig* dividir

♦**tear at** *vt* quitar precipitadamente

♦**tear away I.** *vi* salir disparado **II.** *vt* **1.**(*make depart*) **to tear sb away** sacar a alguien; **to tear oneself away** irse de mala gana **2.**(*pull*) arrancar

♦**tear down** *vt* derribar

♦**tear into** *vt* (*verbally*) arremeter contra; (*physically*) lanzarse sobre

♦**tear off I.** *vt* (*remove*) arrancar; **to ~ one's clothes** quitarse la ropa de un tirón **II.** *vi* (*leave quickly*) salir disparado

♦**tear out** *vt* arrancar de cuajo; **to tear one's hair out over sth** *fig* subirse por las paredes por algo

♦**tear up** *vt* despedazar; *fig* (*agreement*) anular

tearaway ['teərəweɪ, *Am:* 'terə-] *n Brit, Aus, inf* gamberro, -a *m, f*

teardrop ['tɪədrɒp, *Am:* 'tɪrdrɑːp] *n* lágrima *f*

tearful ['tɪəfəl, *Am:* 'tɪrfəl] *adj* lloroso, -a

tear gas *n* gas *m* lacrimógeno **tear jerker** *n inf* (*film*) película *f* lacrimógena; (*song*) canción *f* lacrimógena

tea room *n* salón *m* de té

tease [tiːz] **I.** *vt* **1.**(*make fun of*) tomar el pelo a; **to ~ sb about sth** tomar el pelo a alguien por algo **2.**(*provoke*) provocar; (*sexually*) tentar **3.** TECH cardar **II.** *n* bromista *mf;* (*sexually*) provocador(a) *m(f)*

teaser ['tiːzə^r, *Am:* -ə^r] *n* rompecabezas *m inv*

tea service *n*, **tea set** *n* juego *m* de té **teashop** *n Brit* salón *m* de té **teaspoon** *n* **1.**(*spoon*) cucharita *f* **2.**(*amount*) cucharadita *f*

teaspoonful ['tiːspuːnfʊl] *n* cucharadita *f* **tea-strainer** ['tiːˌstreɪnə^r, *Am:* -ə^r] *n* colador *m* para el té

teat [tiːt] *n* (*nipple: of animal*) teta *f;* (*of bottle*) tetina *f*

teatime ['tiːtaɪm] *n Brit* hora *f* del té **tea towel** *n Brit* paño *m* de cocina **tea tray** *n* bandeja *f* del té **tea trolley** *n* carrito *m* del té **tea urn** *n* tetera *f* grande **tea wagon** *n Am s.* **tea trolley**

technical ['teknɪkəl] *adj* técnico, -a; ~ **term** tecnicismo *m*

technical college *n Brit* HIST escuela *f* politécnica

technicality [ˌteknɪ'kæləti, *Am:* -nə'kæləti]

<-ies> *n* **1.**(*detail*) detalle *m* técnico; **to be acquitted on a ~** ser absuelto por un defecto de forma **2.**(*technical matter*) carácter *m* técnico

technical school *n* escuela *f* de artes y oficios

technician [tek'nɪʃən] *n* técnico, -a *m, f*

technique [tek'niːk] *n* técnica *f*

technological [ˌteknə'lɒdʒɪkl, *Am:* -'lɑːdʒɪ-] *adj* tecnológico, -a

technology [tek'nɒlədʒi, *Am:* -'nɑːlə-] *n* tecnología *f*

technophile [ˌteknəʊ'faɪl] *n* tecnófilo, -a *m, f*

technophobe [ˌteknəʊ'fəʊb, *Am:* -nə'foʊ-] *n* tecnófobo, -a *m, f*

tectonics [tek'tɒnɪks, *Am:* -tɑːnɪks] *n* tectónica *f*

teddy¹ ['tedi] *n* (*underwear*) camiseta *f* interior

teddy² ['tedi] <-ies> *n,* **teddy bear** *n* osito *m* de peluche

tedious ['tiːdiəs] *adj* aburrido, -a, tedioso, -a

tediousness *n no pl* pesadez *f*

tedium ['tiːdɪəm] *n no pl* tedio *m*

tee [tiː] *n* SPORTS tee *m*

♦**tee off I.** *vi* **1.** SPORTS dar el primer golpe **2.** *inf* (*start*) empezar **II.** *vt Am, inf* **to tee sb off** cabrear a alguien

teem [tiːm] *vi* rebosar; **to ~ with sth** estar repleto de algo; **to be ~ing with rain** estar diluviando

teeming *adj* muy numeroso, -a

teen ['tiːn] *n* adolescente *mf*

teenage(d) ['tiːneɪdʒ(d)] *adj* adolescente

teenager ['tiːneɪdʒə^r, *Am:* -dʒə^r] *n* adolescente *mf*

teens [tiːnz] *npl* adolescencia *f;* **to be in one's ~** no haber cumplido los veinte años

teensy [tiːnzi] *adj,* **teensy weensy** *adj,* **teeny** ['tiːni] *adj* chiquitín, -ina

teenybopper ['tiːniˌbɒpə^r, *Am:* -ˌbɑːpə^r] *n inf* quinceañero, -a *m, f*

teeny weeny [ˌtiːni'wiːni] *adj inf s.* **teensy**

tee-shirt ['tiːʃɜːt, *Am:* -ʃɜːrt] *n* camiseta *f*

teeter ['tiːtə^r, *Am:* -ˌtə^r] *vi* **to ~ (around)** tambalearse; **to ~ on the brink of sth** estar a punto de algo

teeth [tiːθ] *pl of* **tooth**

teethe [tiːð] *vi* echar los dientes

teething problems *n,* **teething troubles** *n Brit, Aus, fig* problemas *mpl* de partida

teetotal [ˌtiː'təʊtəl, *Am:* -'toʊtəl] *adj* abstemio, -a

teetotaler *n Am,* **teetotaller** [ˌtiː'təʊtələ^r, *Am:* -'toʊtələ^r] *n* abstemio, -a *m, f*

tel. *abbr of* **telephone** tel.

telecast ['telɪkɑːst, *Am:* -kæst] *n Am* transmisión *f* por televisión

telecommunications ['telɪkəˌmjuːnɪ'keɪʃnz] *npl* telecomunicaciones *fpl*

telecommuting ['telɪkəˌmjuːtɪŋ] *n* INFOR

teletrabajo *m*
teleconference ['telɪˌkɒnfərəns, *Am:* -ˌkɑ:n-] *n* teleconferencia *f*
telecopier® ['telɪkɒpɪə] *n Am* fotocopiadora *f*
telecopy ['telɪkɑpi] *n Am* fotocopia *f*
telefax® ['telɪfæks] *n* telefax *m*
telegenic [ˌtelɪ'dʒenɪk, *Am:* -ə'-] *adj* telegénico, -a
telegram ['telɪgræm] *n* telegrama *m*
telegraph ['telɪgrɑ:f, *Am:* -græf] I. *n* no *pl* telégrafo *m* II. *vt* telegrafiar; **to ~ sb** mandar un telegrama a alguien III. *adj* telegráfico, -a
telegraphese [ˌtelɪgrɑ'fi:z, *Am:* -græf'i:z] *n* no *pl* estilo *m* telegráfico
telegraphic [ˌtelɪ'græfɪk, *Am:* -ə'-] *adj* telegráfico, -a
telegraph pole *n*, **telegraph post** *n Brit, Aus* poste *m* telegráfico
telegraphy [tɪ'legrəfi, *Am:* tə'leg-] *n* no *pl* telegrafía *f*
telemessage ['telɪˌmesɪdʒ] *n Brit* telegrama *m*
telepathic [ˌtelɪ'pæθɪk, *Am:* -ə'-] *adj* telepático, -a; **to be ~** tener telepatía
telepathy [tɪ'lepəθi, *Am:* tə'-] *n* no *pl* telepatía *f*
telephone ['telɪfəʊn, *Am:* -əfoʊn] I. *n* teléfono *m;* **mobile ~** (teléfono *m*) móvil *m* II. *vt* llamar por teléfono III. *vi* telefonear; **to ~ long-distance** hacer una llamada de larga distancia IV. *adj* telefónico, -a; (*booking*) por teléfono
telephone book *n* guía *f* telefónica **telephone booth** *n*, **telephone box** *n Am* cabina *f* telefónica **telephone call** *n* llamada *f* telefónica; **to make a ~** llamar por teléfono **telephone connection** *n* conexión *f* telefónica **telephone conversation** *n* conversación *f* telefónica **telephone directory** *n* guía *f* telefónica **telephone exchange** *n Brit* central *f* telefónica **telephone information service** *n form* servicio *m* de información telefónica **telephone message** *n form* mensaje *m* telefónico **telephone number** *n* número *m* de teléfono **telephone operator** *n Am* operador(a) *m(f)* telefónico, -a **telephone rates** *n* tarifa *f* telefónica
telephonist [tɪ'lefənɪst, *Am:* tə'-] *n Brit* telefonista *mf*
telephony [tɪ'lefəni, *Am:* tə'-] *n* no *pl* telefonía *f;* **digital mobile ~** telefonía móvil digital
telephoto lens [ˌtelɪfəʊtəʊ'lens, *Am:* 'telə-foʊˌtoʊ-] *n* teleobjetivo *m*
teleprinter ['telɪprɪntəʳ, *Am:* -əˌprɪntə·] *n* teletipo *m*
teleprocessing ['telɪprəʊˌsesɪŋ] *n* INFOR teleproceso *m*
TelePrompter® ['telɪprɒmptəʳ, *Am:* -əˌprɑ:mptə·] *n Am, Aus* teleprompter® *m*
telesales ['telɪseɪls] *n* no *pl* ventas *fpl* por teléfono

telescope ['telɪskəʊp, *Am:* -əskoʊp] I. *n* telescopio *m* II. *vi* plegarse
telescopic [ˌtelɪ'skɒpɪk, *Am:* -ə'skɑ:pɪk] *adj* **1.** (*vision, sight*) telescópico, -a **2.** (*folding*) plegable
teleshopping ['telɪˌʃɒpɪŋ, *Am:* 'teləˌʃɑ:pɪŋ] *n* telecompra *f;* (*shop*) teletienda *f*
teletex® *n*, **Teletex**® ['telɪteks] *n* no *pl, Brit* teletexto *m*
teletype® *n*, **Teletype**® ['telɪtaɪp, *Am:* 'telə-] *n* teletipo *m*
teletypewriter [ˌtelɪ'taɪpraɪtəʳ] *n Am* teletipo *m*
televangelist [ˌtelɪ'vændʒəlɪst] *n Am* predicador(a) *m(f)* de la tele
televiewer ['telɪˌvjuːəʳ, *Am:* -əˌvjuːə·] *n* telespectador(a) *m(f)*
televise ['telɪvaɪz, *Am:* 'telə-] *vt* televisar; **to ~ sth live** transmitir algo en directo
television ['telɪˌvɪʒən, *Am:* 'teləvɪʒ-] *n* televisión *f;* **to watch ~** ver la televisión; **to turn the ~ on/off** encender/apagar la televisión
television announcer *n* locutor(a) *m(f)* de televisión **television camera** *n* cámara *f* de televisión **television program** *n Am, Aus,* **television programme** *n Brit* programa *m* de televisión **television set** *n* televisor *m* **television studio** *n* estudio *m* de televisión
teleworking ['telɪˌwɜːkɪŋ, *Am:* -ˌwɜːr-] *n* teletrabajo *m*
telex ['teleks] I. *n* <-es> télex *m* II. *adj* por télex III. *vt* enviar por télex; **to ~ sb sth** comunicar algo por télex a alguien
tell [tel] I. <told, told> *vt* **1.** (*say*) decir; **to ~ sb of sth** comunicar algo a alguien; **to ~ sb whether ...** informar a alguien de si...; **I told you so** te avisé **2.** (*narrate*) contar; **~ me another (one)** *inf* cuéntame otra **3.** (*command*) mandar; **to ~ sb to do sth** ordenar a alguien hacer algo; **do as you're told** *inf* haz lo que te mandan **4.** (*make out*) reconocer **5.** (*distinguish*) distinguir; **to ~ sth from sth** distinguir algo de algo **6.** (*know*) saber; **there is no telling** no hay manera de saberlo **7.** (*count*) contar; (*add up*) sumar; **all told** en total ▶**to ~ it like it is** *inf* decir las cosas claras; **that would be ~ing** eso podría ser cierto; **you're ~ing me!** *inf* ¡a mí me lo vas a contar! II. <told, told> *vi* **1.** hablar; **to ~ of sth/sb** hablar de algo/alguien **2.** (*know*) saber; **you never can ~** nunca se sabe; **how can I ~?** ¡yo qué sé!; **who can ~?** ¿quién sabe? **3.** (*have an effect*) tener efecto
◆**tell against** *vt Brit* **to ~ sb/sth** obrar en contra de alguien/algo
◆**tell apart** *vt* distinguir
◆**tell off** *vt* regañar; **to tell sb off for sth** reñir a alguien por algo
◆**tell on** *vt* **to ~ sb** chivarse de alguien
teller ['teləʳ, *Am:* -ə·] *n* **1.** (*vote counter*) escrutador(a) *m(f)* **2.** (*bank employee*) cajero,

-a *m, f*

telling ['telɪŋ] I. *adj* 1. (*revealing*) revelador(a) 2. (*significant*) contundente II. *n* narración *f*

telling-off ['telɪŋ'ɒf, *Am:* ˌtelɪŋ'ɑːf] <tellings-off> *n* bronca *f;* **to give sb a ~ for (doing)** sth echar una bronca a alguien por (hacer) algo

telltale ['telteɪl] I. *n pej* chivato, -a *m, f* II. *adj* revelador(a)

telly ['teli] *n Brit, Aus, inf* tele *f*

temerity [tɪ'merəti, *Am:* tə'merəti] *n no pl, form* temeridad *f;* **to have the ~ to do sth** atreverse a hacer algo

temp [temp] I. *vi* trabajar temporalmente II. *n* trabajador(a) *m(f)* temporal

temp. *abbr of* **temperature** temperatura

temper ['tempəʳ, *Am:* -pəʳ] I. *n* (*temperament*) temperamento *m;* (*mood*) humor *m;* (*tendency to become angry*) genio *m;* **good ~** buen humor; **bad ~** mal genio; **to get into a ~** ponerse como una fiera; **to keep one's ~** no perder la calma; **to lose one's ~** perder los estribos; **~s were getting (rather) frayed** el ambiente se estaba cargando II. *vt* 1. (*mitigate*) mitigar, atenuar; **to ~ one's criticism** suavizar las críticas 2. (*make hard*) templar

temperament ['tempərəmənt] *n* (*character*) temperamento *m;* (*moodiness*) genio *m;* **a fit of ~** un ataque de furia

temperamental [ˌtemprə'mentl, *Am:* -t̬l] *adj* 1. (*relating to mood*) temperamental 2. (*unpredictable*) caprichoso, -a

temperance ['tempərəns] *n no pl, form* (*moderation*) moderación *f;* (*abstinence*) abstinencia *f*

temperate ['tempərət] *adj* (*moderate*) moderado, -a; (*climate*) templado, -a

temperature ['temprətʃəʳ, *Am:* -pəʳtʃəʳ] *n* temperatura *f;* MED fiebre *f;* **to run a ~** tener fiebre

tempest ['tempɪst] *n liter* tempestad *f*

tempestuous [tem'pestʃʊəs, *Am:* -tʃʊəs] *adj* tempestuoso, -a

template ['templɪt] *n* plantilla *f*

temple[1] ['templ] *n* REL templo *m*

temple[2] ['templ] *n* ANAT sien *f*

tempo ['tempəʊ, *Am:* -poʊ] <-s *o* -pi> *n* 1. MUS tempo *m* 2. (*pace*) ritmo *m*

temporal ['tempərəl] *adj form* temporal

temporarily ['temprərəli, *Am:* 'tempərerəli] *adv* temporalmente

temporary ['temprəri, *Am:* 'tempəreri] *adj* (*improvement*) pasajero, -a; (*staff, accommodation*) temporal; (*relief*) momentáneo, -a

temporize ['tempəraɪz] *vi* tratar de ganar tiempo

tempt [tempt] *vt* 1. tentar; **to ~ sb into doing** sth tentar a alguien a hacer algo 2. (*persuade*) convencer; **to ~ sb into doing** sth incitar a alguien a hacer algo

temptation [temp'teɪʃən] *n* 1. *no pl* (*attraction*) tentación *f;* **to resist ~ (to do sth)** resis-

tir la tentación (de hacer algo); **to succumb to ~** ceder a la tentación 2. (*tempting thing*) aliciente *m*

tempting ['temptɪŋ] *adj* atractivo, -a; (*offer*) tentador(a)

temptress ['temptrɪs] <-es> *n* tentadora *f*

ten [ten] I. *adj* diez *inv* II. *n* diez *m;* **~ to one he comes** seguro que viene; **~s of thousands** decenas *fpl* de miles; *s. a.* **eight**

tenable ['tenəbl] *adj* defendible

tenacious [tɪ'neɪʃəs, *Am:* tə'-] *adj* (*belief*) firme; (*person*) tenaz

tenacity [tɪ'næsəti, *Am:* tə'næsəti] *n no pl* tenacidad *f*

tenancy ['tenənsi] <-ies> *n* 1. (*status*) inquilinato *m* 2. (*right*) arrendamiento *m*

tenant ['tenənt] *n* (*of land*) arrendatario, -a *m, f;* (*of house*) inquilino, -a *m, f*

tenant farmer *n* (*of land*) agricultor(a) *m(f)* arrendatario, -a

tench [ten(t)ʃ] *n* tenca *f*

tend[1] [tend] *vi* 1. (*have tendency*) tender; **to ~ to do sth** tender a hacer algo; **I ~ to disagree** *Brit* no comparto completamente su opinión 2. (*usually do*) soler

tend[2] [tend] *vt* (*look after*) ocuparse de; (*a person*) cuidar de

◆**tend to** *vt* (*look after*) ocuparse de

tendency ['tendənsi] <-ies> *n* tendencia *f;* MED propensión *f*

tendentious [ten'denʃəs] *adj* tendencioso, -a

tender[1] ['tendəʳ, *Am:* -dəʳ] *adj* 1. (*not tough*) vulnerable 2. (*easily damaged*) débil 3. *liter* (*youthful: age*) tierno, -a 4. (*painful*) doloroso, -a; (*part of the body*) sensible; (*subject*) delicado, -a 5. (*affectionate*) cariñoso, -a; **to have a ~ heart** tener buen corazón

tender[2] ['tendəʳ, *Am:* -dəʳ] I. *n* COM oferta *f;* **to put in a ~** hacer una oferta; **to put sth out for ~** *Brit* sacar algo a concurso II. *vt* (*offer*) ofrecer; (*apology*) presentar III. *vi* **to ~ for sth** hacer una oferta para algo

tender[3] ['tendəʳ, *Am:* -dəʳ] *n* RAIL ténder *m;* NAUT gabarra *f*

tenderfoot ['tendəfʊt, *Am:* -dəʳ-] <-s *o* -feet> *n Am* principiante *mf*

tender-hearted [ˌtendə'hɑːtɪd, *Am:* 'tendəʳˌhɑːrt̬ɪd] *adj* bondadoso, -a; **to be ~** tener buen corazón

tenderize ['tendəraɪz] *vt* ablandar

tenderizer *n* ablandador *m* de carne

tenderloin ['tendəlɔɪn, *Am:* -dəʳ-] *n no pl* lomo *m*

tenderly *adv* cariñosamente

tenderness ['tendənɪs, *Am:* -əʳ-] *n no pl* 1. (*softness*) blandura *f* 2. (*affection*) ternura *f* 3. (*sensitivity*) sensibilidad *f*

tendon ['tendən] *n* tendón *m*

tendril ['tendrəl] *n* zarcillo *m*

tenement ['tenəmənt] *n* bloque *m* de pisos

Tenerife [ˌtenə'riːf] *n* Tenerife *m*

tenet ['tenɪt] *n* principio *m*

T

tenfold ['tenfəʊld, *Am:* -foʊld] I. *adj* décuplo, -a II. *adv* diez veces

tenner ['tenər, *Am:* -ə·] *n Brit, inf* billete *m* de diez libras

tennis ['tenɪs] *n no pl* tenis *m*

tennis ball *n* pelota *f* de tenis **tennis court** *n* pista *f* de tenis **tennis elbow** *n* codo *m* de tenista **tennis player** *n* tenista *mf* **tennis racket** *n* raqueta *f* de tenis

tenon ['tenən] *n* espaldón *m*

tenor ['tenər, *Am:* -ə·] I. *n* 1. *a.* MUS tenor *m* 2. *(character)* tono *m*; *(of events)* curso *m* II. *adj* MUS de tenor

tenpin bowling [ˌtenpɪn'bəʊlɪŋ, *Am:* -'boʊ-] *n* bolos *mpl*

tense[1] [tents] *n* LING tiempo *m*

tense[2] [tents] I. *adj (wire, person, atmosphere)* tenso, -a II. *vt* tensar III. *vi* ponerse tenso

◆**tense up** *vi* ponerse tenso

tension ['tentʃən] *n no pl* tensión *f*

tent [tent] *n (for camping)* tienda *f* de campaña, carpa *f AmL*; *(in circus)* carpa *f*

tentacle ['tentəkl, *Am:* -t̪ə-] *n* tentáculo *m*

tentative ['tentətɪv, *Am:* -t̪ət̪ɪv] *adj* 1. *(person)* vacilante 2. *(decision)* provisional

tentatively *adv* 1. *(suggest)* con vacilación 2. *(decide)* provisionalmente

tenterhooks ['tentəhʊks, *Am:* -t̪ə·-] *npl* **to be on** ~ tener el alma en vilo; **to keep sb on** ~ tener a alguien en ascuas

tenth [tenθ] I. *adj* décimo, -a II. *n no pl* 1. *(order)* décimo, -a *m, f* 2. *(date)* diez *m* 3. *(fraction)* décimo *m*; *(part)* décima parte *f*; *s. a.* **eighth**

tent peg *n* estaquilla *f* de tienda **tent pole** *n* mástil *m* de tienda

tenuous ['tenjʊəs] *adj* tenue; *(connection)* sutil; *(argument)* poco sólido, -a

tenure ['tenjʊər, *Am:* -jə·] *n no pl* 1. *(possession)* posesión *f*, tenencia *f* 2. *(period of holding sth)* ejercicio *m*

tepee ['tiːpiː] *n* tipi *m*

tepid ['tepɪd] *adj* tibio, -a

term [tɜːm, *Am:* tɜːrm] I. *n* 1. *(label, word)* término *m*; ~ **of abuse** insulto *m*; ~ **of endearment** expresión *f* afectuosa; **in glowing** ~s con gran admiración; **in no uncertain** ~s en términos claros; **in simple** ~s en palabras sencillas 2. *pl (conditions)* condiciones *fpl*; **to offer easy** ~s ofrecer facilidades de pago 3. *(limit)* límite *m*; COM plazo *m*; ~ **of delivery** plazo de entrega; ~ **of notice** plazo de despido 4. *(period)* período *m*; *(duration)* duración *f*; *(of contract)* vigencia *f*; *(of office)* mandato *m*; **prison** ~ sentencia *f* de prisión; **in the short/ long** ~ a corto/largo plazo 5. *(category)* término *m*; **to think in** ~s **of sth** pensar en términos de algo 6. *Brit* UNIV, SCHOOL trimestre *m* 7. *pl* relaciones *fpl*; **to be on good/bad** ~s **with sb** llevarse bien/mal con alguien II. *vt* llamar; *(label)* calificar de

terminal ['tɜːmɪnl, *Am:* 'tɜːr-] I. *adj* terminal;

(extreme) absoluto, -a; *(boredom)* mortal II. *n* 1. RAIL, AVIAT, INFOR terminal *f* 2. ELEC polo *m*

terminate ['tɜːmɪneɪt, *Am:* 'tɜːr-] I. *vt (finish)* poner fin a; *(contract)* rescindir; *(pregnancy)* interrumpir II. *vi* terminarse

termination [ˌtɜːmɪ'neɪʃən, *Am:* ˌtɜːr-] *n no pl (ending)* fin *m*; *(of contract)* rescisión *f*; *(of pregnancy)* interrupción *f*

terminological [ˌtɜːmɪnə'lɒdʒɪkl, *Am:* ˌtɜːrmɪnə'lɑːdʒɪ-] *adj* terminológico, -a

terminology [ˌtɜːmɪ'nɒlədʒi, *Am:* ˌtɜːrmɪ'nɑːlə-] *n* terminología *f*

terminus ['tɜːmɪnəs, *Am:* 'tɜːr-] <-es *o* -i> *n (station)* estación *f* terminal; *(bus stop)* última parada *f*

termite ['tɜːmaɪt, *Am:* 'tɜːr-] *n* termita *f*

tern [tɜːn, *Am:* tɜːrn] *n* golondrina *f* de mar

terrace ['terəs] I. *n* 1. *a.* AGR terraza *f* 2. *pl, Brit* SPORTS gradas *fpl* 3. *Brit, Aus (row of houses)* hilera *f* de casas adosadas II. *vt* formar terrazas en III. *adj* en terrazas

terraced house *n* casa *f* adosada

terrain [te'reɪn] *n* terreno *m*

terrapin ['terəpɪn] <-(s)> *n* galápago *m*

terrestrial [tɪ'restrɪəl, *Am:* tə'-] *adj form* terrestre

terrible ['terəbl] *adj* 1. *(shocking)* terrible 2. *(very bad)* espantoso, -a 3. *inf (as intensifier)* fatal

terribly ['terəbli] *adv* 1. *(very badly)* terriblemente 2. *(very)* tremendamente

terrier ['terɪər, *Am:* -ə·] *n* terrier *m*

terrific [tə'rɪfɪk] *adj* 1. *(terrifying)* terrorífico, -a 2. *(excellent)* tremendo, -a 3. *as intensifier (very great)* estupendo, -a

terrified *adj* aterrorizado, -a

terrify ['terəfaɪ] <-ie-> *vt* aterrar

terrifying *adj* aterrador(a)

territorial [ˌterɪ'tɔːrɪəl, *Am:* -ə'-] I. *n* MIL reservista *m* II. *adj* territorial

territory ['terɪtəri, *Am:* 'terətɔːri] <-ies> *n* 1. *(area of land)* territorio *m*; **forbidden** ~ zona *f* prohibida 2. *(activity)* terreno *m*

terror ['terər, *Am:* -ə·] *n no pl* terror *m*; **to have a** ~ **of sth** tener miedo a algo; **to strike** ~ infundir terror; **to be in** ~ **of one's life** temer por la vida de uno; **a** ~ **of a child** *inf* un niño terrible

terrorism ['terərɪzəm] *n no pl* terrorismo *m*

terrorist ['terərɪst] I. *n* terrorista *mf* II. *adj* terrorista

terrorize ['terəraɪz] *vt* aterrorizar

terror-stricken ['terəˌstrɪkən, *Am:* -ə·ˌ-] *adj*, **terror-struck** ['terəstrʌk, *Am:* '-ə·-] *adj* aterrorizado, -a

terry cloth [ˌteri'klɒθ, *Am:* -'klɑː θ] *n no pl* felpa *f*

terse [tɜːs, *Am:* tɜːrs] *adj* lacónico, -a

tertiary ['tɜːʃəri, *Am:* 'tɜːrʃieri] I. *adj form* terciario, -a II. <-ies> *n* **the Tertiary** GEO el Terciario

tessellated ['tesəleɪtɪd, *Am:* -t̪ɪd] *adj* teselado, -a

test [test] I. *n* 1. SCHOOL, UNIV examen *m;* to pass/fail a ~ aprobar/suspender un examen; driving ~ examen de conducir 2. MED prueba *f;* blood ~ análisis *m inv* de sangre 3. (*trial*) to be a ~ of endurance ser una prueba de resistencia; to put sth to the ~ poner algo a prueba II. *vt* 1. (*examine*) examinar 2. MED (*hearing*) examinar; to ~ sb for sth hacer a alguien una prueba de algo 3. (*measure*) comprobar 4. (*try to prove*) someter a prueba 5. (*try with senses*) tocar; (*by tasting*) probar

testament ['testəmənt] *n* 1. *form* (*will*) testamento *m;* last will and ~ testamento y últimas voluntades 2. *form* (*evidence*) testimonio *m* 3. REL the Old/New ~ el Antiguo/Nuevo Testamento

test ban *n* prohibición *f* de ensayos nucleares **test bench** *n* banco *m* de pruebas **test card** *n* carta *f* de ajuste **test case** *n* causa *f* que sienta jurisprudencia **test drive** *n* prueba *f* de carretera

tester ['testə'] *Am:* -ə-] *n* 1. (*person*) examinador(a) *m(f)* 2. (*sample*) frasco *m* de muestra **test flight** *n* vuelo *m* de ensayo

testicle ['testɪkl] *n* testículo *m*

testify ['testɪfaɪ] <-ie-> I. *vi* 1. (*give evidence*) testificar 2. *form* (*prove*) to ~ to sth atestiguar algo II. *vt* 1. (*bear witness to*) demostrar 2. (*declare under oath*) testificar; to ~ that ... declarar que...

testimonial [,testɪ'məʊnɪəl, *Am:* -'moʊ-] *n form* 1. (*character reference*) referencias *fpl* 2. (*tribute*) homenaje *m*

testimony ['testɪməni, *Am:* -moʊni] <-ies> *n* testimonio *m;* to give ~ dar testimonio

testing I. *n no pl* experiencia *f* II. *adj* duro, -a; ~ times tiempos *mpl* difíciles

testing ground *n* zona *f* de pruebas

test match *n* partido *m* internacional **test piece** *n* MUS obra *f* elegida para un certamen **test pilot** *n* piloto *mf* de pruebas **test stage** *n* período *m* de pruebas

test tube *n* probeta *f* **test-tube baby** *n* bebé *m* probeta

testy ['testi] <-ier, -iest> *adj* irritable

tetanus ['tetənəs] *n no pl* tétano *m;* ~ injection vacuna *f* contra el tétano

tetchy ['tetʃi] <-ier, -iest> *adj* irritable

tether ['teðə', *Am:* -ə-] I. *n* cuerda *f* ►to be at the end of one's ~ no aguantar más II. *vt* amarrar; to be ~ed to sth *fig* estar atado a algo

Teutonic [tjuː'tɒnɪk, *Am:* tuː'taːnɪk] *adj* teutónico, -a

Texan ['teksən] I. *n* tejano, -a *m, f* II. *adj* tejano, -a

Texas ['teksəs] *n* Tejas *m*

text [tekst] *n* texto *m*

textbook ['tekstbʊk] I. *n* libro *m* de texto II. *adj* de manual

text editor *n* INFOR editor *m* de textos

textile ['tekstaɪl] I. *n pl* tejidos *mpl* II. *adj* textil

textile mill *n* fábrica *f* de tejidos

text processing *n* INFOR procesamiento *m* de textos

textual ['tekstʃʊəl, *Am:* -tʃu-] *adj* textual

texture ['tekstʃə', *Am:* -tʃə-] *n* 1. (*feel*) textura *f* 2. (*consistency*) estructura *f*

Thai [taɪ] I. *adj* tailandés, -esa II. *n* 1. (*person*) tailandés, -esa *m, f* 2. LING tailandés *m*

Thailand ['taɪlənd] *n* Tailandia *m*

thalidomide [θə'lɪdəʊmaɪd] *n* talidomida *f*

Thames [temz] *n no pl* the (River) ~ el Támesis

than [ðən, ðæn] *conj* que; you are taller ~ she (is) eres más alto que ella; more ~ 60 más de 60; more ~ once más de una vez; nothing else ~ ... nada más que...; no other ~ you nadie más que tú; no sooner had she told him, ~ ... en cuanto se lo dijo...

thank [θæŋk] *vt* agradecer; to ~ sb (for sth) dar las gracias a alguien (por algo); ~ you gracias; ~ you very much! ¡muchas gracias!; no, ~ you no, gracias

thankful ['θæŋkfəl] *adj* 1. (*pleased*) satisfecho, -a; to be ~ that ... alegrarse de que... +*subj* 2. (*grateful*) agradecido, -a

thankfully *adv* afortunadamente

thankless ['θæŋkləs] *adj* desagradecido, -a; (*task*) ingrato, -a

thanks [θæŋks] *npl* gracias *fpl;* ~ very much muchísimas gracias; ~ to gracias a; in ~ for ... en recompensa por...; no ~ to him no fue gracias a él

thanksgiving [,θæŋks'gɪvɪŋ] *n no pl* acción *f* de gracias

> **Thanksgiving** (Acción de Gracias) es una de las fiestas más importantes de los EE.UU. Se celebra el cuarto jueves del mes de noviembre. El primer **Thanksgiving Day** fue celebrado en 1621 por los **Pilgrims** en **Plymouth Colony**. Habían sobrevivido a grandes dificultades y querían dar las gracias a Dios por ello. Es costumbre que las familias se reúnan para celebrar este día. La comida principal consiste en **stuffed turkey** (pavo relleno), **cranberry sauce** (salsa de arándanos), **yams** (patatas dulces) y **corn** (maíz).

Thanksgiving Day *n* Día *m* de Acción de Gracias (*en Estados Unidos se celebra el último martes de noviembre, en Canadá el segundo lunes de octubre*)

that [ðæt, ðət] I. *adj dem* <those> ese, esa, eso; (*more remote*) aquel, aquella, aquello; ~ table esa mesa; ~ book ese libro II. *pron* 1. *rel* que; the woman ~ told me ... la mujer que me dijo...; all ~ I have todo lo que tengo 2. *dem* what is ~? ¿eso qué es?; who is ~? ¿ése/ésa quién es?; like ~ así; after ~ después de eso; ~'s it! ¡eso es! III. *adv* tan; ~ hot hacía tanto calor IV. *conj* 1. que; I told you ~ I couldn't come te he dicho que no puedo ir; ~ I should live to see this! ¡que tenga que vivir

para ver algo así! **2.** (*in order that*) para que
+*subj*
thatch [θætʃ] I. *n no pl* **1.** (*roof*) techo *m* de
paja **2.** (*hair*) mata *f* (de pelo) II. *vt* poner un
techo de paja a
thatched roof *n* techo *m* de paja
thaw [θɔː, *Am:* θɑː] I. *n* **1.** (*weather*) deshielo *m* **2.** (*in relations*) distensión *f* II. *vi*
1. (*weather*) deshelar; (*food*) descongelarse
2. (*relations*) volverse más cordial III. *vt* derretir
the [ðə, *stressed, before vowel* ðiː] I. *def art* el
m, la *f*, los *mpl*, las *fpl*; **from ~ garden** del jardín; **at ~ hotel** en el hotel; **at ~ door** a la
puerta; **to ~ garden** al jardín; **in ~ winter** en
invierno II. *adv* (*in comparison*) ~ **more one**
tries, ~ **less one succeeds** cuanto más se
esfuerza uno, menos lo logra; ~ **sooner** ~
better cuanto antes mejor
theater *n Am*, **theatre** ['θɪətə', *Am:*
'θiːəṯə'] *n Brit, Aus* **1.** THEAT (*place, art*) teatro
m; (*company*) compañía *f* de teatro **2.** *Am*,
Aus CINE cine *m* **3.** UNIV aula *f* **4.** *Brit* (*in hospi-*
tal) operating ~ quirófano *m* **5.** *fig* (*scene*)
escenario *m*
theatre company *n* compañía *f* de teatro
  theatre critic *n* crítica *f* teatral **theatre-**
goer *n* aficionado, -a *m*, *f* al teatro
theatrical [θɪ'ætrɪkl] *adj* teatral; **don't be so**
~ **about it** no hagas tanto teatro por eso
thee [ðiː] *pron pers* HIST te; **with ~** contigo
theft [θeft] *n* robo *m*; **petty ~** hurto *m*
their [ðeə', *Am:* ðer] *adj pos* su(s); ~ **house**
su casa; ~ **children** sus hijos
theirs [ðeəz, *Am:* ðerz] *pron pos* (el) suyo *m*,
(la) suya *f*, (los) suyos *mpl*, (las) suyas *fpl*; **this**
house is ~ esta casa es suya; **they aren't our**
bags, they are ~ no son nuestras bolsas, son
suyas; **a book of ~** un libro suyo
theism ['θiːɪzəm] *n no pl* teísmo *m*
them [ðem, ðəm] *pron pers pl* **1.** (*they*) ellos,
-as; **older than ~** mayor que ellos; **if I were ~**
si yo fuese ellos **2.** *direct object* los, las; *indi-*
rect object les; **look at ~** míralos; **I saw ~** yo
los vi; **he gave ~ the pencil** les ha dado el
lápiz **3.** *after prep* ellos, -as; **it's from/for ~** es
de/para ellos
thematic [θiːm'ætɪk, *Am:* θiː'mæṯ-] *adj*
temático, -a
theme [θiːm] *n a.* MUS tema *m*; **on the ~ of**
sobre el tema de
theme music *n no pl* sintonía *f* **theme**
park *n* parque *m* temático **theme song** *n*,
theme tune *n no pl* sintonía *f*
themselves [ðəm'selvz] *pron* **1.** *subject*
ellos mismos, ellas mismas **2.** *object, reflexive*
se; **the children behaved ~** los niños se por-
taron bien **3.** *after prep* sí mismos, sí mismas;
by ~ solos, -as
then [ðen] I. *adj form* (de) entonces; **the ~**
chairman el entonces presidente II. *adv* **1.** (*at*
aforementioned time) entonces; **before ~**
hasta entonces; **from ~ on**(**wards**) a partir de

entonces; **since ~** desde entonces; **until ~**
hasta aquel momento; (*every*) **now and ~** de
vez en cuando **2.** (*after that*) después; **what ~?**
¿y qué? **3.** (*additionally*) además; **but ~**
(*again*) pero también, y además **4.** (*as a result*)
por tanto, así pues; ~ **he must be there**
entonces debe estar ahí **5.** (*that being the*
case) en ese caso **6.** (*agreement*) **all right ~**
de acuerdo pues
thence [ðens] *adv form* de ahí
thenceforth [ˌðens'fɔːθ, *Am:* -'fɔːrθ] *adv*
form, **thenceforward** [ˌðens'fɔːwəd, *Am:*
-'fɔːrwəd] *adv form* a partir de entonces
theocracy [θɪ'ɒkrəsi, *Am:* -'ɑːkrə-] <-ies>
n no pl teocracia *f*
theodolite [θɪ'ɒdəlaɪt, *Am:* -'ɑːdəlaɪt] *n*
teodolito *m*
theologian [ˌθɪə'ləudʒən, *Am:* ˌθiːə'lou-] *n*
teólogo, -a *m*, *f*
theological [ˌθɪə'lɒdʒɪkl, *Am:* ˌθiːə'lɑːdʒɪ-]
adj teológico, -a
theology [θɪ'ɒlədʒi, *Am:* -'ɑːlə-] <-ies> *n*
teología *f*
theorem ['θɪərəm, *Am:* 'θiːəəm] *n* MAT
teorema *m*; **Pythagoras's ~** el teorema de Pitá-
goras
theoretical [θɪə'retɪkəl, *Am:* ˌθiːə'reṯ-] *adj*
teórico, -a
theoretically *adv* teóricamente
theorist ['θɪərɪst, *Am:* 'θiːəɪst] *n* teórico, -a
m, *f*
theorize ['θɪəraɪz, *Am:* 'θiːə-] *vi* teorizar
theory ['θɪəri, *Am:* 'θiːə-] <-ies> *n* teoría *f*;
in ~ en teoría
therapeutic(**al**)   [θerə'pjuːtɪk(əl),   *Am:*
-ṯɪk-] *adj* terapéutico, -a
therapeutics [ˌθerə'pjuːtɪks, *Am:* -ṯɪks] *n*
terapéutica *f*
therapist ['θerəpɪst] *n* terapeuta *mf*
therapy ['θerəpi] <-ies> *n* terapia *f*
there [ðeə', *Am:* ðer] I. *adv* allí, allá; **here**
and ~ aquí y allá; ~ **is/are** hay; ~ **will be**
habrá; ~ **you are!** ¡ahí lo tienes!; ~'s **the train**
ahí está el tren; ~ **is no one** no hay nadie; ~
and then en el acto II. *interj* vaya; ~, **take**
this toma esto; ~, **that's enough!** ¡bueno,
basta ya!
thereabouts ['ðeərəbauts, *Am:* 'ðerə-] *adv*
(*approximately*) más o menos; (*near*) por
ahí
thereafter [ðeər'ɑːftə', *Am:* ðer'æftə-] *adv* a
partir de entonces
thereby [ðeə'baɪ, *Am:* ðer'-] *adv form*
por eso ►~ **hangs a** <u>tale</u> *iron* es una larga
historia
therefore ['ðeəfɔː', *Am:* 'ðerfɔːr] *adv* por (lo)
tanto; **to decide ~ to do sth** decidir hacer
algo por consiguiente
therein [ðeər'ɪn, *Am:* ðer'-] *adv form* ahí dentro; *fig* en eso
thereof [ðeər'ɒv, *Am:* ðer'ɑːv] *adv form* de
eso
thereupon [ˌðeərə'pɒn, *Am:* ˌðerə'pɑːn]

adv acto seguido
therm [θɜːm, *Am:* θɜːrm] *n* termia *f*
thermal ['θɜːməl, *Am:* 'θɜːr-] I. *n* 1. (*air current*) corriente *f* térmica 2. *pl* (*underwear*) ropa *f* interior térmica II. *adj* PHYS, INFOR térmico, -a; (*water*) termal
thermal underwear *n* ropa *f* interior térmica
thermodynamic [ˌθɜːməʊdaɪˈnæmɪk, *Am:* ˌθɜːrmoʊ-] *adj* termodinámico, -a
thermoelectric [ˌθɜːməʊɪˈlektrɪk, *Am:* ˌθɜːrmoʊɪ'-] *adj* termoeléctrico, -a
thermometer [θəˈmɒmɪtəʳ, *Am:* θəˈmɑːməṱəʳ] *n* termómetro *m*
thermonuclear [ˌθɜːməʊˈnjuːklɪəʳ, *Am:* ˌθɜːrmoʊˈnuːklɚ] *adj* termonuclear
Thermos® (**bottle**) ['θɜːmɒsˌbɒtl), *Am:* 'θɜːrməsˌbɑːṱl)] *n*, **Thermos**® **flask** *n* termo *m*
thermostat ['θɜːməʊstæt, *Am:* 'θɜːrməstæt] *n* termostato *m*
thermostatic [ˌθɜːməʊˈstætɪk, *Am:* ˌθɜːrməˈstæṱ-] *adj* termostático, -a
thesaurus [θɪˈsɔːrəs] <-es *o* -ri> *n* diccionario *m* de sinónimos
these [ðiːz] *pl of* **this**
thesis ['θiːsɪs] <-ses> *n* tesis *f inv*
they [ðeɪ] *pron pers* 1. (*3rd person pl*) ellos, -as; ~ **are my parents/sisters** (ellos/ellas) son mis padres/hermanas 2. (*people in general*) ~ **say that ...** dicen que...
they'll [ðeɪl] = **they will** *s.* **will**
they're [ðeɪr, *Am:* ðer] = **they are** *s.* **be**
they've [ðeɪv] = **they have** *s.* **have**
thick [θɪk] I. *adj* 1. (*not thin: wall*) grueso, -a; (*coat*) gordo, -a 2. (*dense: hair*) abundante; (*forest*) denso, -a; (*liquid*) espeso, -a 3. (*extreme: darkness*) profundo, -a; (*accent*) marcado, -a 4. (*stupid*) corto, -a; **to be as ~ as two short planks** *inf* no tener dos dedos de frente 5. (*very friendly*) **to be ~ with sb** ser muy amigo de alguien 6. *Brit, inf* (*plentiful*) atestado, -a 7. *Brit* (*not right*) **to be a bit ~** ser injusto ►**through ~ and thin** a las duras y a las maduras II. *n no pl, inf* **to be in the ~ of sth** estar de lleno en algo
thicken ['θɪkən] I. *vt* espesar II. *vi* espesarse
thickener *n*, **thickening** *n* espesante *m*
thicket ['θɪkɪt] *n* matorral *m*
thick-headed [ˌθɪkˈhedɪd, *Am:* 'θɪkˌhedɪd] *adj* ceporro, -a
thickness ['θɪknɪs] *n* 1. *no pl* (*size*) grosor *m* 2. (*of hair*) abundancia *f*; (*of sauce*) consistencia *f*
thickset [ˌθɪkˈset, *Am:* 'θɪkset] *adj* rechoncho, -a
thick-skinned [ˌθɪkˈskɪnd, *Am:* 'θɪkskɪnd] *adj* insensible; **he is ~** todo le resbala
thief [θiːf, s 'θiːvz] <thieves> *n* ladrón, -ona *m, f*
thieve [θiːv] *vi, vt liter* robar
thieving ['θiːvɪŋ] I. *n liter* robo *m* II. *adj* de dedos largos

thigh [θaɪ] *n* muslo *m*
thigh bone *n* fémur *m*
thimble ['θɪmbl] *n* dedal *m*
thin [θɪn] <-nn-> I. *adj* 1. (*not thick: clothes*) fino, -a; (*person*) delgado, -a; (*very slim*) flaco, -a 2. (*soup, sauce*) claro, -a; (*wine*) aguado, -a 3. (*sparse: hair*) ralo, -a; **to be ~ on top** ser calvo 4. (*voice*) débil; (*excuse*) poco convincente II. <-nn-> *vt* (*dilute*) aclarar
◆**thin down** I. *vi* adelgazar II. *vt* aclarar
◆**thin out** I. *vt* hacer menos denso; (*plants*) entresacar II. *vi* disminuir
thine [ðaɪn] *pron pos* HIST (el) tuyo *m*, (la) tuya *f*, (lo) tuyo *neuter*, (los) tuyos *mpl*, (las) tuyas *fpl*
thing [θɪŋ] *n* 1. (*object, action*) cosa *f*; **the lucky/best/main ~** lo bueno/mejor/principal; **sweet ~s** pasteles *mpl*; **one ~ after another** una cosa después de otra; **to be a ~ of the past** ser algo del pasado; **the last ~ she wants to do is ...** lo último que quiere hacer es... 2. (*matter*) **to know a ~ or two** saber algo; **above all ~s** por encima de todo; **another ~** otra cosa; **and another ~, ...** y por otra parte,...; **if it's not one ~ it's another** cuando no es una cosa es otra 3. (*social behaviour*) **it's the done ~** es lo que hay que hacer 4. (*fashion*) **the latest ~ in shoes** el último grito en zapatos 5. *fam* (*the important point*) **the real ~** lo auténtico; **the very ~** lo importante 6. *pl* (*possessions*) pertenencias *fpl*; **all his ~s** todas sus cosas 7. *pl* (*the situation*) **as ~s stand, the way ~s are** tal como están las cosas; **the shape of ~s to come** lo que se avecina 8. *inf* (*term of affection*) **the poor ~!** ¡el pobre!; (*children, animals*) ¡pobrecito!; **you lucky ~!** ¡qué suerte tienes!; ¡**lazy ~!** ¡vago!; ¡**stupid ~!** ¡imbécil! ►**to be all ~s to all men** actuar según sopla el viento; **it's just one of those ~s** es una de esas cosas que pasan; **he won but it was a close ~** ganó por un pelo; **all ~s being equal** si no sale ningún imprevisto; **first ~s first** lo primero es lo primero; **to not know the first ~ about sth** no tener ni la remota idea de algo; **to be onto a good ~** *inf* tener un chollo; **to do one's own ~** hacer la suya; **to have a ~ about sth** *inf* tener asco a algo; **to be hearing ~s** oír campanas; **to make a (big) ~ out of sth** armar un escándalo por algo
thingamabob ['θɪŋəməˌbɒb, *Am:* -bɑːb] *n*, **thingamajig** ['θɪŋəməˌdʒɪg] *n*, **thingy** ['θɪŋi] *n* (*object*) cosa *f*; (*person*) ése, ésa
think [θɪŋk] <thought, thought> I. *n* **to have a ~ about sth** pensarse algo II. *vt* 1. (*believe*) pensar, creer; **who would have thought it!** ¡quien lo hubiese pensado! 2. (*consider*) considerar; **to ~ sb (to be) sth** considerar a alguien como algo; **to ~ nothing of sb** no tener ninguna fe en alguien; ~ **nothing of it!** ¡no merece la pena mencionarlo! III. *vi* pensar; **to ~ aloud** pensar en voz alta; **to ~ for oneself** pensar por sí mismo; **to ~ to oneself**

pensar para sí mismo; **to ~ of doing sth** pensar en hacer algo; **to ~ about/of sb/sth** pensar en alguien/algo
◆**think ahead** vi pensar de cara al futuro
◆**think back** vi **to ~ to sth** recordar algo; **to ~ over sth** hacer memoria de algo
◆**think of** vi pensar en
◆**think out** vt **1.**(consider) pensar muy bien **2.**(plan) planear cuidadosamente
◆**think over** vt reflexionar sobre
◆**think through** vt estudiar detenidamente
◆**think up** vt inventar
thinker n pensador(a) m(f)
thinking I. n no pl **1.**(thought process) pensamiento m **2.**(reasoning) razonamiento m **3.**(opinion) opinión f II. adj inteligente
think tank n gabinete m estratégico
thinner n disolvente m
thinness n no pl delgadez f
thin-skinned [ˌθɪn'skɪnd, Am: 'θɪnskɪnd] adj sensible
third [θɜːd, Am: θɜːrd] I. adj tercero, -a II. n no pl **1.**(order) tercero, -a m, f **2.**(date) tres m **3.**(fraction) tercio m **4.**MUS, AUTO tercera f **5.** Brit UNIV cuarta nota de la escala de calificaciones del título universitario; s. a. **eighth**
third degree n **to give sb the ~** someter a alguien al tercer grado **third-degree burns** npl quemaduras fpl de tercer grado
thirdly adv en tercer lugar
third party n tercero m **third-party insurance** n, **third-party liability** n seguro m a terceros
third person n LING tercera persona f **third-rate** adj de baja categoría **Third World** n **the ~** el Tercer Mundo
thirst [θɜːst, Am: θɜːrst] n sed f; **to die of ~** morir de sed; **to quench one's ~** apagar la sed; **~ for power** ansias fpl de poder
thirsty ['θɜːsti, Am: 'θɜːr-] <-ier, -iest> adj sediento, -a; **to be ~** tener sed; **to be ~ for sth** fig estar ansioso por algo
thirteen [ˌθɜː'tiːn, Am: θɜːr'-] I. adj trece II. n trece m; s. a. **eight**
thirteenth [ˌθɜː'tiːnθ, Am: θɜːr'-] I. adj decimotercero, -a II. n no pl **1.**(order) decimotercero, -a m, f **2.**(date) trece m **3.**(fraction) decimotercero m; (part) decimotercera parte f; s. a. **eighth**
thirtieth ['θɜːtɪəθ, Am: 'θɜːrtɪ-] I. adj trigésimo, -a II. n **1.**(order) trigésimo, -a m, f **2.**(date) treinta m **3.**(fraction) trigésimo m; (part) trigésima parte f; s. a. **eighth**
thirty ['θɜːti, Am: 'θɜːrt̬i] <-ies> I. adj treinta II. n treinta m; s. a. **eighty**
this [ðɪs] I. <these> adj det este, -a; **~ car** este coche; **~ house** esta casa; **~ one** éste, -a; **~ day** hoy; **~ morning/evening** esta mañana/tarde; **~ time last month** hoy hace un mes; **these days** hoy en día II. <these> pron dem éste m, ésta f, esto neuter; **what is ~?** ¿esto qué es?; **who is ~?** ¿éste/ésta quién es?; **~ and that** esto y

aquello; **~ is Ana (speaking)** (on the phone) soy Ana III. adv así; **~ late** tan tarde; **~ much** tanto; **~ big** así de grande
thistle ['θɪsl] n cardo m
tho' [ðəʊ, Am: ðoʊ] conj s. **though**
thong [θɒŋ, Am: θɑːŋ] n **1.**(strip of leather) correa f **2.**(G-string) tanga m **3.** pl, Am, Aus (sandal) chanclas fpl
thorax ['θɔːræks] <-es o -aces> n tórax m
thorn [θɔːn, Am: θɔːrn] n espina f ►**that's a ~ in my flesh** es una espina que tengo clavada
thorny ['θɔːni, Am: 'θɔːr-] <-ier, -iest> adj espinoso, -a, espinudo, -a AmC, CSur; (issue) peliagudo, -a
thorough ['θʌrə, Am: 'θɜːroʊ] adj **1.**(complete) absoluto, -a **2.**(detailed) exhaustivo, -a **3.**(careful) minucioso, -a
thoroughbred ['θʌrəbred, Am: 'θɜːroʊ-] I. n pura sangre mf II. adj de alcurnia
thoroughfare ['θʌrəfeəʳ, Am: 'θɜːroʊfer] n form vía f pública
thoroughgoing ['θʌrəˌgəʊɪŋ, Am: ˌθɜːroʊ'goʊ-] adj form **1.**(conscientious: analysis) riguroso, -a **2.**(complete: reform) profundo, -a
thoroughly adv **1.**(in detail) a fondo **2.**(completely) completamente
thoroughness n no pl meticulosidad f
those [ðəʊz, Am: ðoʊz] pl of **that**
thou¹ [ðaʊ] pron pers, liter tú
thou² [θaʊ] abbr of **thousand** mil
though [ðəʊ, Am: ðoʊ] I. conj aunque; **as ~** como si +subj; **even ~** aunque; **even ~ it's cold** aunque hace frío II. adv sin embargo; **he did do it, ~** sin embargo, él sí lo hizo
thought [θɔːt, Am: θɑːt] n **1.** no pl (process) reflexión f; **on second ~s** tras madura reflexión; **without ~** sin pensar; **after much ~** tras mucho reflexionar; **to be deep in ~** estar ensimismado; **lost in ~** absorto [o sumido] en sus pensamientos **2.**(idea, opinion) pensamiento m; **that's a ~** es posible ►**a penny for your ~s** prov ¿en qué piensas?
thoughtful ['θɔːtfəl, Am: 'θɑːt-] adj **1.**(pensive) pensativo, -a **2.**(careful) cuidadoso, -a **3.**(considerate) amable
thoughtless ['θɔːtləs] adj (not thinking enough) irreflexivo, -a; (tactless) desconsiderado, -a; (careless) descuidado, -a
thought-out [ˌθɔːt'aʊt, Am: ˌθɑːt-] adj planeado, -a **thought-provoking** adj que hace pensar
thousand ['θaʊznd] I. adj mil II. n mil m
thousandth ['θaʊzntθ] I. n milésimo m II. adj **1.**(being one of a thousand) milésimo, -a **2.**(in a series) **the ~** el número mil
thrash [θræʃ] vt **1.**(beat) apalear **2.** inf (defeat) dar una paliza a
◆**thrash out** vt inf (problem) discutir; (agreement) llegar a
thrashing n paliza f, batida f AmL
thread [θred] I. n **1.** no pl (for sewing) hilo m **2.**(of screw) rosca f ►**to hang by a ~** pender de un hilo II. vt (needle) enhebrar; **to**

~ sth through sth pasar algo por algo; **to ~ sth onto sth** ensartar algo en algo

threadbare ['θredbeəʳ, *Am:* -ber] *adj* 1. (*worn*) raído, -a 2. (*argument, excuse*) trillado, -a

threat [θret] *n* amenaza *f*

threaten ['θretən] I. *vt* amenazar; **to ~ to do sth** amenazar con hacer algo II. *vi* amenazar

threatening *adj* amenazador(a)

three [θriː] I. *adj* tres II. *n* tres *m*; *s. a.* **eight**

three-cornered [ˌθriː'kɔːnəd, *Am:* -'kɔːrnəd] *adj* triangular; **~ hat** tricornio *m*

three-D *adj inf abbr of* **three-dimensional** tridimensional **three-dimensional** *adj* tridimensional

threefold ['θriːfəʊld, *Am:* -foʊld] I. *adj* triple II. *adv* por triplicado

three-part *adj* de tres partes

threepenny bit ['θrepəni bɪt] *n Brit* moneda *f* de tres peniques

three-piece [ˌθriː'piːs] *adj* de tres piezas **three-piece suit** *n* terno *m*

three-ply ['θriːplaɪ] *adj* de tres capas; (*wood*) contrachapado, -a; (*wool*) de tres hebras **three-quarter (length)** *adj* tres cuartos

threesome ['θriːsəm] *n* trío *m*

three-wheeler [θrɪ'wiːləʳ] *n* vehículo *m* de tres ruedas

thresh [θreʃ] *vt* trillar

threshing machine ['θreʃɪŋ mə'ʃiːn] *n* trilladora *f*

threshold ['θreʃhəʊld, *Am:* -hoʊld] *n* 1. (*doorway*) umbral *m* 2. (*limit*) límite *m*; **pain ~** umbral de dolor; **tax ~** nivel *m* mínimo de tributación

threw [θruː] *pt of* **throw**

thrice [θraɪs] *adv* tres veces

thrift [θrɪft] *n no pl* ahorro *m*

thrifty ['θrɪfti] <-ier, -iest> *adj* ahorrador(a)

thrill [θrɪl] I. *n* estremecimiento *m* II. *vt* estremecer, emocionar III. *vi* estremecerse

thriller ['θrɪləʳ, *Am:* -ɚ] *n* (*book*) novela *f* de suspense; (*film*) película *f* de suspense

thrilling ['θrɪlɪŋ] *adj* emocionante

thrive [θraɪv] <thrived *o* throve, thrived *o* thriven> *vi* (*person, plant*) crecer mucho; (*business*) prosperar

thriving *adj* próspero, -a

throat [θrəʊt, *Am:* θroʊt] *n* 1. (*internal*) garganta *f*; **sore ~** dolor *m* de garganta 2. (*external*) cuello *m*; **to grab sb by the ~** agarrar a alguien por el cuello ►**to stick in sb's ~** (*proposal*) no ser aceptable para alguien; (*words*) quedárse atragantado a alguien; **to be at each other's ~s** estar como el perro y el gato

throaty ['θrəʊti, *Am:* 'θroʊţi] <-ier, -iest> *adj* (*voice*) ronco, -a; (*laugh*) gutural

throb [θrɒb, *Am:* θrɑːb] I. *n* (*of engine*) vibración *f*; (*of heart*) palpitación *f* II. <-bb-> *vi* (*engine*) vibrar; (*heart*) palpitar

throes [θrəʊz, *Am:* θroʊz] *npl* angustia *f*; (*of death*) agonía *f*; **to be in the ~ of sth** estar de lleno en algo

thrombosis [θrɒm'bəʊsɪs, *Am:* θrɑːm'boʊ-] <-es> *n* trombosis *f inv*

throne [θrəʊn, *Am:* θroʊn] *n* trono *m*

throng [θrɒŋ, *Am:* θrɑːŋ] I. *n* multitud *f* II. *vt* atestar; **to be ~ed** estar abarrotado III. *vi* ir en tropel; **to ~ to do sth** acudir en masa a hacer algo

throttle ['θrɒtl, *Am:* 'θrɑːţl] I. *n* acelerador *m*; **to open the ~** acelerar; **at full ~** a todo gas *inf* II. <-ll-> *vt* estrangular

♦**throttle back** *vi* reducir (la velocidad)

through [θruː] I. *prep* 1. (*spatial*) a través de, por; **to go right ~ sth** traspasar algo; **to go ~ the door** pasar por la puerta; **to walk ~ a room** atravesar una habitación; **to walk ~ a village** caminar por un pueblo 2. (*temporal*) durante; **all ~ my life** durante toda mi vida; **to be ~ sth** acabar de (hacer) algo 3. *Am* (*until*) hasta; **open Monday ~ Friday** abierto de lunes a viernes 4. MAT **6 ~ 3 is 2** 6 entre 3 da 2 5. (*by means of*) por (medio de) II. *adv* 1. (*of place*) de un lado a otro; **I read the book ~** leí el libro entero; **to go ~ to sth** ir directo a algo 2. (*of time*) **all day ~** de la mañana a la noche; **halfway ~** a medio camino 3. TEL **to put sb ~ to sb** poner a alguien con alguien 4. (*completely*) completamente; **to think sth ~** pensarse algo detenidamente ►**~ and ~** de cabo a rabo III. *adj* 1. (*finished*) terminado, -a; **we are ~** hemos terminado 2. (*direct*) directo, -a 3. SCHOOL **to get ~** aprobar

through flight *n* vuelo *m* directo

throughout [θruː'aʊt] I. *prep* 1. (*spatial*) por todas partes de; **~ the town** por toda la ciudad 2. (*temporal*) a lo largo de; **~ his stay** durante toda su estancia II. *adv* 1. (*spatial*) por [*o* en] todas partes 2. (*temporal*) todo el tiempo

throughput ['θruːpʊt] *n no pl* producción *f*; INFOR procesamiento *m*

through ticket *n* pase *m* **through traffic** *n* (tráfico *m* de) tránsito *m* **through train** *n* tren *m* directo

throughway ['θruːweɪ] *n Am* autopista *f* de peaje

throve [θrəʊv, *Am:* θroʊv] *pt of* **thrive**

throw [θrəʊ, *Am:* θroʊ] I. *n* 1. (*act of throwing*) lanzamiento *m* 2. SPORTS derribo *m* 3. *inf* (*chance*) oportunidad *f*; **his last ~** su última oportunidad II. <threw, thrown> *vi* lanzar III. <threw, thrown> *vt* 1. (*propel*) tirar; (*ball, javelin*) lanzar; **to ~ oneself into sb's arms** echarse a los brazos de alguien; **to ~ oneself at sb** echar los tejos a alguien 2. (*cause to fall: rider*) desmontar; (*opponent*) derribar 3. (*dedicate*) **to ~ oneself into sth** entregarse de lleno a algo 4. (*direct: glance*) echar; (*remark*) dejar caer; (*kiss*) lanzar 5. *inf* (*confuse*) desconcertar 6. TECH tornear 7. (*turn on*) dar a; **to ~ the switch** pulsar el interruptor 8. (*have*) **to ~ a tantrum** coger [*o* agarrar *AmL*] una rabieta 9. (*give*) **to ~ a party** dar una fiesta 10. (*cast off*) soltar

♦**throw away** *vt* 1. (*discard*) tirar

2. (*waste*) malgastar; **to throw money away on sth** despilfarrar dinero en algo; **to throw oneself away** sacrificarse inútilmente **3.** (*speak casually*) soltar

◆**throw back** *vt* **1.** (*return*) devolver **2.** (*open: curtains*) correr; (*blanket*) apartar **3.** (*remind unkindly*) echar en cara; (*retort angrily*) replicar; **to throw sth back in sb's face** echar algo en cara a alguien

◆**throw down** *vt* **1.** (*throw from above*) tirar **2.** (*deposit forcefully*) dejar; (*weapons*) abandonar **3.** (*drink quickly*) engullir

◆**throw in** I. *vt* **1.** (*put into*) arrojar **2.** (*include*) agregar; (*comment*) soltar II. *vi* (*propel*) lanzar

◆**throw off** *vt* **1.** (*remove*) quitarse **2.** (*escape from*) librarse de **3.** (*rid oneself of*) zafarse de **4.** (*write quickly*) improvisar

◆**throw on** *vt* **1.** (*clothes*) ponerse **2.** (*pounce upon*) **to throw oneself on sb** abalanzarse sobre alguien

◆**throw out** *vt* **1.** (*eject: person*) echar; (*thing*) tirar; (*case*) rechazar; (*suggestion*) despreciar **2.** (*emit: heat, light*) despedir

◆**throw over** *vt* (*lover*) abandonar

◆**throw together** *vt* **1.** *inf* (*make quickly*) hacer en un momento **2.** (*cause to meet*) juntar

◆**throw up** I. *vt* **1.** (*project upwards*) lanzar al aire **2.** (*bring to light*) revelar **3.** (*build quickly*) levantar **4.** *inf* (*give up*) dejar **5.** *inf* (*vomit*) vomitar, buitrear *CSur,* revulsar *Méx* II. *vi inf* vomitar, buitrear *CSur,* revulsar *Méx*

throwaway ['θrəʊəweɪ, *Am:* 'θroʊ-] *adj* desechable; ~ **razor** maquinilla *f* de usar y tirar; ~ **remark** comentario *m* hecho de paso

throwback ['θrəʊbæk, *Am:* 'θroʊ-] *n* vuelta *f*; BIO atavismo *m*

thrower *n* lanzador(a) *m(f)*

throw-in ['θrəʊɪn, *Am:* 'θroʊ-] *n* (*in soccer*) saque *m* de banda; (*in baseball*) lanzamiento *m*

throwing *n* lanzamiento *m*

thrown *pp of* **throw**

thru [θruː] *prep, adj Am s.* **through**

thrum [θrʌm] I. <-mm-> *vt* (*guitar*) rasguear II. *vi* (*engine*) vibrar III. *n* (*of engine*) vibración *f*

thrush¹ [θrʌʃ] *n* tordo *m*

thrush² [θrʌʃ] *n* MED afta *f*

thrust [θrʌst] I. <-, -> *vi* **1.** (*shove*) empujar; **to ~ at sb with sth** asestar un golpe a alguien con algo **2.** (*force one's way*) abrirse paso II. <-, -> *vt* (*push*) empujar; (*insert*) clavar; **to ~ one's hands into one's pockets** meterse las manos en los bolsillos III. *n* **1.** (*shove*) empujón *m*; **sword ~** estocada *f* **2.** *no pl* (*impetus*) empuje *m;* **the main ~ of an argument** la idea central de una discusión **3.** *no pl* TECH (*propulsion*) propulsión *f*

thrusting ['θrʌstɪŋ] *adj* arribista

thruway ['θruːweɪ] *n Am* autopista *f* de peaje

thud [θʌd] I. <-dd-> *vi* dar un golpe sordo; **to ~ on the table with one's fist** pegar un puñetazo encima de la mesa II. *n* golpe *m* sordo

thug [θʌɡ] *n* matón *m*

thumb [θʌm] I. *n* pulgar *m* ►**to be all fingers and ~s, to be all ~s** ser un manazas; **to stand out like a sore ~** cantar como una almeja; **to be under sb's ~** estar dominado por alguien II. *vt* **1.** (*hitchhike*) **to ~ a lift** hacer dedo **2.** (*soil with the thumbs*) manosear **3.** (*glance through: book*) hojear

thumb-index *n* índice *m* recortado

thumbnail ['θʌmneɪl] *n* uña *f* del pulgar **thumbnail sketch** *n* pequeña reseña *f*

thumbscrew ['θʌmskruː] *n* empulgueras *fpl*

thumbtack *n Am, Aus* tachuela *f*

thump [θʌmp] I. *vt* golpear; **to ~ sth down** dejar caer algo II. *vi* **1.** (*heart*) latir fuertemente **2.** (*beat*) **to ~ on sth** aporrear algo III. *n* **1.** (*blow*) porrazo *m;* **to give sb a ~** dar un mamporro a alguien **2.** (*noise*) golpe *m* sordo

thumping *adj inf* descomunal; **I've got a ~ headache** me va a estallar la cabeza

thunder ['θʌndər, *Am:* -dər] I. *n no pl* **1.** METEO trueno *m*, pillán *m Chile;* **a clap of ~** un trueno **2.** (*sound*) estruendo *m* ►**to look like ~** tener cara de pocos amigos; **to steal sb's ~** quitar las primicias a alguien II. *vi* hacer gran estruendo; (*shout*) gritar III. *vt* bramar

thunderbolt ['θʌndəbəʊlt, *Am:* -dərboʊlt] *n* **1.** METEO rayo *m* **2.** *fig* bomba *f* ►**to drop a ~ on sb** dejar a alguien fulminado **thunderclap** *n* trueno *m* **thundercloud** *n pl* nubarrón *m*

thundering ['θʌndərɪŋ] I. *n no pl* estruendo *m* II. *adj inf* (*very noisy*) estruendoso, -a; *fig* (*very great*) enorme

thunderous ['θʌndərəs] *adj* estruendoso, -a

thunderstorm ['θʌndəstɔːm, *Am:* -dərstɔːrm] *n* tormenta *f*

thunderstruck ['θʌndəstrʌk, *Am:* -dər-] *adj form* estupefacto, -a

thundery ['θʌndəri] *adj* <-ier, -iest> tormentoso, -a

Thursday ['θɜːzdeɪ, *Am:* 'θɜːrz-] *n* jueves *m inv;* **Maundy ~** Jueves Santo; *s. a.* **Friday**

thus [ðʌs] *adv form* **1.** (*therefore*) por lo tanto **2.** (*like this*) de este modo; ~ **far** hasta aquí

thwart [θwɔːt, *Am:* θwɔːrt] *vt* frustrar; (*plan*) desbaratar

thy [ðaɪ] *pron pos, liter* tu(s)

thyme [taɪm] *n no pl* tomillo *m*

thyroid ['θaɪrɔɪd] *adj* tiroides *f inv*

tiara [tɪˈɑːrə, *Am:* -ˈerə] *n* diadema *f*

tibia ['tɪbɪə] <-iae> *n* tibia *f*

tic [tɪk] *n* tic *m*

tick¹ [tɪk] *n* garrapata *f*

tick² [tɪk] *n Brit, inf* (*credit*) crédito *m;* **on ~** de fiado

tick³ [tɪk] I. *n* **1.** (*sound*) tic-tac *m* **2.** (*mark*) visto *m* II. *vi* hacer tic-tac; **I don't know what makes her ~** no acabo de entender su manera

de ser **III.** *vt* marcar
◆**tick off** *vt* **1.** (*mark off*) marcar **2.** *Brit*, *Aus*, *inf* (*scold*) echar una bronca a **3.** *Am*, *inf* (*exasperate*) dar la lata a
◆**tick over** *vi* **1.** TECH ir al ralentí **2.** *fig* ir tirando
ticker ['tɪkəʳ, *Am:* -ɚ] *n* **1.** TEL teletipo *m* **2.** (*watch*) reloj *m* **3.** *inf* (*heart*) corazón *m*
ticker tape *n no pl* cinta *f* de teletipo
ticker-tape parade *n Am* desfile *m* triunfal
ticket ['tɪkɪt] *n* **1.** (*for bus, train*) billete *m*, boleto *m AmL*; (*for cinema, concert*) entrada *f*; (*for cloakroom*) ticket *m*; (*for lottery*) boleto *m;* **return** ~ billete *m* de vuelta **2.** (*price, information tag*) etiqueta *f* **3.** AUTO multa *f* **4.** *Brit* POL programa *m* electoral ►**just the** ~ justo lo que hacía falta
ticket agency *n* taquilla *f* **ticket collector** *n* revisor(a) *m(f)* **ticket counter** *n* mostrador *m* de venta de entradas **ticket holder** *n* persona *f* que tiene entrada **ticket machine** *n* dispensador *m* de billetes **ticket office** *n* RAIL ventanilla *f* de venta de billetes; THEAT taquilla *f*
ticking[1] ['tɪkɪŋ] *n no pl* (*sound*) tic-tac *m*
ticking[2] ['tɪkɪŋ] *n no pl* (*textile*) terliz *m*
ticking-off [ˌtɪkɪŋ'ɒf, *Am:* -'ɑːf] <tickings-off> *n Brit, inf* rapapolvo *m*, jalada *f Méx*
tickle ['tɪkl] **I.** *vi* hacer cosquillas; (*clothes*) picar **II.** *vt* **1.** hacer cosquillas **2.** (*amuse*) hacer gracia ►**to be ~d pink** *inf* estar encantado **III.** *n* cosquilleo *m*; (*tingling*) picor *m*
ticklish ['tɪklɪʃ] *adj* que tiene cosquillas; (*delicate*) delicado, -a
tidal ['taɪdəl] *adj* de la marea
tidal wave *n* maremoto *m*
tidbit ['tɪdbɪt] *n Am s.* **titbit**
tiddly ['tɪdli] *adj* <-ier, -iest> **1.** *inf* (*tiny*) diminuto, -a **2.** *Brit, Aus, inf* (*tipsy*) alegre
tiddlywink ['tɪdlɪwɪŋk] *n* pulga *f;* ~**s** juego *m* de las pulgas
tide [taɪd] *n* **1.** (*of sea*) marea *f;* **high** ~ pleamar *f;* **low** ~ bajamar *f* **2.** (*of opinion*) corriente *f;* **to go against the** ~ ir contracorriente; **to swim with the** ~ seguir la corriente
◆**tide over** *vt always sep* **to tide sb over** sacar a alguien de un apuro
tideland ['taɪdlænd] *n Am* marisma *f* **tidemark** *n* **1.** (*mark left by high tide*) marca *f* que deja la marea **2.** *Brit, iron* (*on bath*) marca *f* de mugre
tidiness ['taɪdɪnɪs] *n no pl* orden *m*
tidy ['taɪdi] **I.** *adj* <-ier, -iest> **1.** (*orderly*) ordenado, -a; **to have a** ~ **mind** ser metódico **2.** *inf* (*considerable*) considerable **II.** *n* organizador(a) *m(f)*; **the garage needs a** ~ hay que arreglar el garaje **III.** *vt* ordenar
tie [taɪ] **I.** *n* **1.** (*necktie*) corbata *f* **2.** (*cord*) atadura *f* **3.** *pl* (*bond*) lazos *mpl*; (*diplomatic*) relaciones *fpl* **4.** (*equal ranking*) empate *m* **5.** *Brit* SPORTS partido *m* **II.** *vi* **1.** (*fasten*) atarse **2.** SPORTS empatar **III.** *vt* **1.** (*fasten*) atar; (*knot*) hacer **2.** (*restrict*) limitar; **to be ~d by/to sth**

estar limitado por/a algo
◆**tie back** *vt* atar
◆**tie down** *vt* atar; **to tie sb down to sth** *inf* comprometer a alguien a algo
◆**tie in** **I.** *vt* relacionar **II.** *vi* coincidir
◆**tie up** *vt* **1.** (*bind*) atar; (*hair*) recogerse; **to** ~ **some loose ends** *fig* atar cabos sueltos **2.** (*delay*) obstruir **3.** (*be busy*) **to be tied up** estar ocupado **4.** FIN, ECON (*capital*) inmovilizar; **to be tied up in sth** estar invertido en algo **5.** *Brit* (*connect with*) relacionar; **to be tied up with sth** estar ligado a algo
tie-break ['taɪbreɪk] *n Brit*, **tie-breaker** *n* desempate *m*
tie clip *n* aguja *f* de corbata
tie-in ['taɪɪn] *n* **1.** (*agreement*) acuerdo *m* **2.** (*connection*) relación *f*
tie-on *adj* para atar
tiepin ['taɪpɪn] *n* aguja *f* de corbata
tier [tɪəʳ, *Am:* tɪr] *n* (*row*) hilera *f;* (*level*) grada *f;* (*in a hierarchy*) nivel *m*
tie-up ['taɪʌp] *n* conexión *f*
tiff [tɪf] *n inf* pelea *f;* **to have a** ~ tener un altercado
tiger ['taɪgəʳ, *Am:* -gɚ] *n* tigre *m* ►**to have a** ~ **by the tail** tener el toro por los cuernos
tight [taɪt] **I.** *adj* **1.** (*screw, knot*) apretado, -a; (*clothing*) ceñido, -a **2.** (*rope, skin*) tirante **3.** (*condition, discipline*) estricto, -a, riguroso, -a; (*budget*) restringido, -a; (*situation*) difícil; (*schedule*) apretado, -a; **to keep a** ~ **hold on sth** mantener un control riguroso de algo; **to be** ~ **for money/time** ir escaso de dinero/ tiempo **4.** (*bend*) cerrado, -a **5.** (*hard-fought*) reñido, -a **6.** *inf* (*drunk*) como una cuba **II.** *adv* fuerte; **to close sth** ~ cerrar bien algo; **sleep** ~! ¡que duermas bien!
tighten ['taɪten] **I.** *vt* **1.** (*make tight*) apretar; (*rope*) tensar **2.** (*restrictions*) intensificar **II.** *vi* apretarse; (*restrictions*) intensificarse
tight-fisted [ˌtaɪt'fɪstɪd] *adj inf* agarrado, -a
tight-fitting *adj* ajustado, -a
tight-lipped [ˌtaɪt'lɪpt] *adj* callado, -a; **to be** ~ **about sth** no abrir boca sobre algo
tightness *n no pl* **1.** (*of clothing*) lo ajustado **2.** (*of discipline*) lo estricto; (*of budget*) lo restringido; (*of schedule*) lo apretado **3.** PSYCH tensión *f*
tightrope ['taɪtraʊp, *Am:* -roʊp] *n* cuerda *f* floja; **to walk a** ~ *a. fig* caminar en la cuerda floja
tightrope walker *n* funámbulo, -a *m, f*
tights [taɪts] *npl* **1.** *Brit* (*leggings*) medias *fpl;* **to have a ladder in one's** ~ tener una carrera en las medias **2.** *Am, Aus* (*for dancing*) mallas *fpl*
tightwad ['taɪtwɒd, *Am:* -wɑːd] *n Am, Aus, inf* tacaño, -a *m, f*
tigress ['taɪgrɪs] *n* tigresa *f*
tike [taɪk] *n s.* **tyke**
tile [taɪl] **I.** *n* (*for roof*) teja *f;* (*for walls, floors*) azulejo *m* ►**to have a night (out) on the ~s**, **to be (out) on the ~s** ir de farra **II.** *vt* (*roof*)

tejar; (*wall*) poner azulejos a, alicatar; (*floor*) embaldosar

tiler ['taɪlə^r, *Am:* -ə·] *n* albañil *m* (especializado en recubrimientos)

till¹ [tɪl] **I.** *prep* hasta **II.** *conj* hasta (que)

till² [tɪl] *n* caja *f* ►**he was caught with his hand in the** ~ lo pillaron con las manos en la masa

till³ [tɪl] *vt* cultivar

tiller ['tɪlə^r, *Am:* -ə·] *n* barra *f* del timón; **at the** ~ al timón

tilt [tɪlt] **I.** *n* inclinación *f* ►(**at**) **full** ~ a toda máquina **II.** *vt* inclinar; **to** ~ **sth back** inclinar algo hacia atrás **III.** *vi* inclinarse; **to** ~ **back** inclinarse hacia atrás; **to** ~ **over** volcarse

timber ['tɪmbə^r, *Am:* -bə·] *n* **1.** *no pl, Brit* (*wood*) madera *f* **2.** (*beam*) viga *f*, madero *m* **3.** (*trees*) árboles *mpl;* ~! ¡árbol va!

timbered *adj* de madera

timberline ['tɪmbəlaɪn, *Am:* -bə·-] *n Am* límite *m* forestal **timber merchant** *n* maderero *m*

time [taɪm] **I.** *n* **1.** tiempo *m;* **to kill** ~ matar el tiempo; **to make** ~ hacer tiempo; **to spend** ~ pasar el tiempo; (**how**) ~ **flies** el tiempo vuela; ~ **passes** el tiempo apremia; **as** ~ **goes by** con el paso del tiempo; **in the course of** ~ con el paso del tiempo; **to have a good** ~ pasárselo bien; **to have all the** ~ **in the world** tener todo el tiempo del mundo; **to run out of** ~, **to be (all) out of** ~ *Am, Aus, inf* acabarse el tiempo; **to save** ~ ganar tiempo; **to waste** ~ perder el tiempo; **most of the** ~ la mayor parte del tiempo; **in one week's** ~ dentro de una semana; **for a short/long period of** ~ durante un corto/largo período de tiempo; **there's no** ~ **to lose** no hay tiempo que perder; **can I have** ~ **off to go to the dentist?** ¿puedo salir (del trabajo) para ir al dentista?; **to take one's** ~ **in doing sth** tomarse uno su tiempo para hacer algo; **it takes a long/short** ~ se tarda mucho/poco; **to give sb a hard** ~ *inf* hacerlas pasar canutas a alguien; **I (don't) have a lot of** ~ **for him** (no) me cae bien **3.** (*clock*) hora *f;* **arrival/departure** ~ hora *f* de llegada/salida; **bus/train** ~s horario *m* de autobús/tren; **to have the** ~ tener hora exacta **4.** (*moment*) momento *m;* **the best** ~ **of day** el mejor momento del día; **this** ~ **tomorrow** mañana a esta hora; **at all** ~s a todas horas; **at a different** ~ en otro momento; **each** ~ cada vez; **the right** ~ el momento oportuno **5.** *no pl* (*specific point in time*) hora *f;* **at any** ~ a cual-

quier hora; **at any given** ~, **at (any) one** ~ en un momento dado; **the last/next** ~ la última/próxima vez; **at other** ~s en otros tiempos; **at the present** ~ actualmente; **it is about** ~ **that ...** ya es hora de que... +*subj;* ~ **and (~) again** una y otra vez; **ahead of** ~ con antelación; **to know at the** ~ saber en su momento; **to remember the** ~ **...** recordar cuando... **6.** (*occasion*) vez *f;* **three** ~s **champion** *Brit, Aus,* **three** ~ **champion** *Am* tricampeón, -ona *m, f;* **lots of** ~s muchas veces; **for the hundredth** ~ por centésima vez; **from** ~ **to** ~ de vez en cuando **7.** *no pl* (*right moment*) hora *f;* **breakfast** ~ hora *f* de desayunar; **it's high** ~ **that ...** ya es hora de que... +*subj;* **ahead of** ~ antes de tiempo; **to do sth dead on** ~ hacer algo en el momento preciso; **the** ~ **comes** llega el momento **8.** (*epoch*) época *f;* **at one** ~ en una época; **from** [*o* **since**] ~ **immemorial** desde tiempos inmemoriales; **to be behind the** ~s estar anclado en el pasado; **in** ~s **gone by** en tiempos pasados; **to keep up with the** ~s estar al día **9.** SPORTS tiempo *m;* **record** ~ tiempo récord **10.** *no pl* MUS tiempo *m* **11.** ECON horas *fpl* de trabajo; **to work full/part** ~ trabajar a jornada completa/tiempo parcial; **to be on short** ~ estar en jornada reducida ►~ **is of the essence** no hay tiempo que perder; **to have** ~ **on one's hands** tener tiempo de sobra; ~ **is a great healer** *prov* el tiempo lo cura todo; ~ **is money** *prov* el tiempo es oro; **there's a** ~ **and a place (for everything)** *prov* todo a su debido tiempo; **a week is a long** ~ **in politics** *prov* aún puede pasar de todo; **there's no** ~ **like the present** *prov* no dejes para mañana lo que puedas hacer hoy *prov;* ~ **and tide wait for no man** *prov* el tiempo no perdona; ~ **heals all wounds** *prov* el tiempo lo cura todo; **in less than no** ~ en menos (de lo) que canta un gallo; **to buy** ~ ganar tiempo; ~s **are changing** los tiempos cambian; **to do** ~ *inf* estar a la sombra; ~ **moves on** la vida sigue **II.** *vt* **1.** SPORTS cronometrar, relojear *Arg* **2.** (*choose best moment for*) elegir el momento para **III.** *adj* SPORTS ~ **trial** prueba *f* contrarreloj

time and motion study *n* COM estudio *m* de la racionalización del trabajo

time bomb *n* bomba *f* de relojería **time card** *n Am* tarjeta *f* de registro horario **time clock** *n* reloj *m* de control de asistencia

time-consuming ['taɪmkən,sjuːmɪŋ, *Am:* -,suː-] *adj* que exige mucho tiempo

time difference *n* diferencia *f* horaria **timekeeper** *n* **1.** (*device*) cronómetro *m* **2.** (*person*) cronometrista *mf;* **to be a poor** ~ no ser muy puntual **time lag** *n* retraso *m* **time-lapse photography** *n* fotografía *m* de lapso de tiempo

timeless ['taɪmləs] *adj* eterno, -a

time limit *n* límite *m* de tiempo **time lock** *n* cerradura *f* de tiempo

timely ['taɪmli] *adj* <-ier, -iest> oportuno,

-a; **in a ~ fashion** *Brit* a tiempo

time-out [ˌtaɪm'aʊt] *n* **1.**SPORTS tiempo *m* muerto **2.** (*rest*) descanso *m*

timer ['taɪmər, *Am:* -ər] *n* temporizador *m;* GASTR reloj *m* avisador

timesaving ['taɪmˌseɪvɪŋ] *adj* que ahorra tiempo

timescale ['taɪmskeɪl] *n* escala *f* de tiempo

timeshare *n* multipropiedad *f* **time-sharing** *n no pl* **1.** (*on holiday*) multipropiedad *f* **2.**INFOR tiempo *m* compartido **time sheet** *n* hoja *f* de asistencia **time switch** *n Brit, Aus* interruptor *m* horario **timetable** **I.** *n* (*for bus, train*) horario *m;* (*for project, events*) programa *m* **II.** *vt* programar

timeworn ['taɪmwɔːn, *Am:* -wɔːrn] *adj* usado, -a; (*excuse*) trillado, -a

time zone *n* huso *m* horario

timid ['tɪmɪd] *adj* <-er, -est> tímido, -a

timidity [tɪ'mɪdəti, *Am:* -ti] *n no pl* timidez *f*

timing ['taɪmɪŋ] *n no pl* **1.** cronometraje *m;* **that was perfect ~** ha sido el momento oportuno **2.** (*rhythm*) compás *m*

timorous ['tɪmərəs] *adj* temeroso, -a

timpani ['tɪmpəni] *npl* MUS tímpanos *mpl*

tin [tɪn] **I.** *n* **1.** *no pl* (*metal*) estaño *m;* (*tinplate*) hojalata *f* **2.** (*container*) lata *f* **3.** (*for baking*) molde *m* **II.** *vt* enlatar

tin can *n* lata *f*

tincture ['tɪŋktʃər, *Am:* -tʃər] *n* tintura *f*

tinder ['tɪndər, *Am:* -dər] *n no pl* yesca *f*

tin foil *n* papel *m* de aluminio

ting [tɪŋ] *n* tilín *m*

tinge [tɪndʒ] **I.** *n* **1.** (*of colour*) tinte *m* **2.** (*of emotion*) dejo *m* **II.** *vt* **1.** (*dye*) teñir **2.** *fig* matizar

tingle ['tɪŋgl] **I.** *vi* estremecerse **II.** *n no pl* estremecimiento *m*

tin god *n pej, inf* héroe *m* de cartón **tin hat** *n* casco *m* de acero **tinhorn** *n Am, inf* petulante *mf*

tinker ['tɪŋkər, *Am:* -kər] **I.** *n* **1.** HIST hojalatero *m* **2.** *Brit* gitano, -a *m, f* **II.** *vi* **to ~ with sth** tratar de reparar algo

tinkle ['tɪŋkl] **I.** *vi* tintinear **II.** *vt* hacer tintinear **III.** *n* tintineo *m;* **to give sb a ~** *inf* llamar a alguien (por teléfono)

tinned [tɪnd] *adj Brit, Aus* en lata; (*fruit*) en conserva

tinny ['tɪni] *adj* <-ier, -iest> (*sound*) metálico, -a; (*taste*) que sabe a lata

tin-opener *n Brit, Aus* abrelatas *m inv* **tinplate** *n no pl* hojalata *f*

tinpot ['tɪnpɒt, *Am:* 'tɪnpɑːt] *adj pej, inf* de pacotilla

tinsel ['tɪnsl] *n no pl* oropel *m*

tint [tɪnt] **I.** *n* (*colour*) tono *m;* (*for hair*) tinte *m* **II.** *vt* teñir

tiny ['taɪni] *adj* <-ier, -iest> menudo, -a, chingo, -a *Col, Cuba*

tip¹ [tɪp] **I.** <-pp-> *vt* cubrir **II.** *n* punta *f;* **from ~ to toe** de pies a cabeza; **the southern ~ of Florida** el cabo sur de Florida; **it's on the**

~ **of my tongue** lo tengo en la punta de la lengua

tip² [tɪp] **I.** <-pp-> *vt* **1.** *Brit, Aus* (*empty out*) verter; **it's ~ping it down** *inf* está lloviendo a cántaros **2.** (*incline*) inclinar; **to ~ the balance in favour of sb** inclinar la balanza en contra/a favor de alguien **II.** *vi* inclinarse **III.** *n Brit* **1.** (*for rubbish*) basurero *m;* **rubbish ~** vertedero *m* de basura **2.** *inf* (*mess*) desorden *m*

tip³ [tɪp] **I.** *n* **1.** (*for service*) propina *f,* yapa *f Méx;* **10 per cent ~** el diez por ciento de propina **2.** (*hint*) aviso *m;* **to give sb a ~** dar a alguien un consejo; **to take a ~ from sb** seguir el consejo de alguien **II.** <-pp-> *vt* **1.** (*give money*) dar una propina a **2.** *Brit* (*predict*) pronosticar ▸**to ~ sb the wink** dar el soplo a alguien **III.** <-pp-> *vi* dar propina

♦**tip off** *vt* avisar

♦**tip out** **I.** *vt* verter **II.** *vi* caer

♦**tip over** **I.** *vt* volcar **II.** *vi* volcarse

♦**tip up** **I.** *vt* inclinar **II.** *vi* inclinarse

tip-off ['tɪpɒf, *Am:* -ɑːf] *n inf* soplo *m*

tipple ['tɪpl] **I.** *vi* (*drink*) beber **II.** *vt* beber **III.** *n inf* bebida *f;* **favourite ~** trago *m* favorito

tipster ['tɪpstər, *Am:* -stər] *n* SPORTS pronosticador(a) *m(f)*

tipsy ['tɪpsi] *adj* <-ier, -iest> bebido, -a, achispado, -a *AmL*

tiptoe ['tɪptəʊ, *Am:* -toʊ] **I.** *n* punta *f* del pie; **on ~(s)** de puntillas **II.** *vi* ponerse de puntillas

tiptop [ˌtɪp'tɒp, *Am:* 'tɪptɑːp] *adj inf* de primera

tip-up seat ['tɪpʌp'siːt] *n* asiento *m* reclinable

tirade [taɪ'reɪd, *Am:* 'taɪreɪd] *n* diatriba *f*

tire¹ ['taɪər, *Am:* 'taɪər] *n Am s.* **tyre**

tire² ['taɪər, *Am:* 'taɪər] **I.** *vt* cansar **II.** *vi* cansarse

tired ['taɪəd, *Am:* 'taɪərd] *adj* <-er, -est> (*person*) cansado, -a; (*excuse*) trillado, -a; **to be sick and ~ of sth** estar aburrido de algo; **the same ~ old faces** las mismas caras de siempre

tiredness *n no pl* cansancio *m*

tireless ['taɪələs, *Am:* 'taɪər-] *adj* incansable

tiresome ['taɪəsəm, *Am:* 'taɪər-] *adj* molesto, -a; (*person*) pesado, -a, molón, -ona *Guat, Ecua, Méx*

tiring ['taɪrɪŋ] *adj* agotador(a), cansador(a) *Arg*

'tis [tɪz] = **it is** *s.* **be**

tissue ['tɪʃuː] *n* **1.** *no pl* (*paper*) papel *m* de seda **2.** (*handkerchief*) pañuelo *m* de papel, Kleenex® *m* **3.** *no pl* ANAT, BIOL tejido *m;* **a ~ of lies** una sarta de mentiras

tit¹ [tɪt] *n* paro *m;* **blue ~** herrerillo *m;* **coal ~** carbonero *m*

tit² [tɪt] *n* **1.** *vulg* teta *f* **2.** *Brit, inf* estúpido, -a *m, f*

titanic [taɪ'tænɪk] *adj* titánico, -a

titanium [taɪ'teɪnɪəm] *n no pl* titanio *m*

titbit ['tɪtbɪt] *n Brit* **1.** (*delicacy*) golosina *f*

2. (*piece: of information*) noticia *f*; (*of gossip*) cotilleo *m*

titillate ['tɪtɪleɪt, *Am:* -əleɪt] *vt* excitar

titillation [ˌtɪtɪ'leɪʃən, *Am:* -əl'eɪ-] *n no pl* excitación *f*

titivate ['tɪtɪveɪt, *Am:* 'tɪtə-] *vt* adornar; **to ~ oneself** arreglarse

title ['taɪtl, *Am:* -t̬l] I. *n* 1. (*name*) título *m* 2. (*championship*) campeonato *m* 3. *no pl* LAW derecho *m* II. *vt* titular

title deed *n* título *m* de propiedad **title-holder** *n* titular *mf* **title page** *n* portada *f* **title role** *n* papel *m* principal **title track** *n* canción *f* que da nombre a un álbum

titter ['tɪtər, *Am:* 'tɪt̬ə˞] I. *vi* reírse disimuladamente II. *n* risa *f* disimulada

tittle-tattle ['tɪtltætl, *Am:* 'tɪt̬l̩tæt̬l̩] *n no pl, inf* chismorreo *m*

tizz [tɪz] *n*, **tizzy** ['tɪzi] *n inf* excitación *f*; **to be in a ~** estar aturdido

TNT [ˌtiːen'tiː] *n abbr of* **trinitrotoluene** TNT *m*

to [tuː] I. *prep* 1. (*in direction of*) a; **to go ~ France/Oxford** ir a Francia/Oxford; **to go ~ town** ir a la ciudad; **to go ~ the dentist('s)** ir al dentista; **to go ~ the cinema/theatre** ir al cine/teatro; **to go ~ bed** irse a la cama; **to go ~ the south** ir al sur, ir hacia el sur; **~ the left/right** a la izquierda/derecha; **to fall ~ the ground** caerse al suelo; **the path ~ the lake** el camino que lleva al lago 2. (*before*) **a quarter ~ five** las cinco menos cuarto 3. (*until*) hasta; **to count up ~ 10** contar hasta 10; **~ this day** hasta el día de hoy; **frightened ~ death** muerto de miedo; **done ~ perfection** hecho a la perfección; **~ some extent** hasta cierto punto 4. *with indirect object* **to talk ~ sb** hablar con alguien; **to show sth ~ sb** mostrar algo a alguien; **I said ~ myself ...** me dije a mí mismo...; **this belongs ~ me** esto es mío 5. (*towards*) con; **to be kind/rude ~ sb** ser amable/grosero con alguien 6. (*against*) contra; **elbow ~ elbow** codo con codo; **close ~ sth** cerca de algo; **to clasp sb ~ one's bosom** estrechar a alguien contra su pecho; **to fix sth ~ the wall** fijar algo en la pared; **5 added ~ 10 equals 15** 5 más 10 son 15 7. (*in comparison*) a; **3** (*goals*) **~ 1** 3 (goles) a 1; **superior ~ sth/sb** superior a algo/alguien 8. (*from opinion of*) **to sound strange ~ sb** sonar extraño a alguien; **it doesn't make any sense ~ me** no tiene sentido para mí; **what's it ~ them?** *inf* ¿qué les importa a ellos?; **~ all appearances** al parecer 9. (*proportion*) **one litre ~ one person** un litro por persona; **by a majority of 5 ~ 1** por una mayoría de 5 a 1; **the odds are 3 ~ 1** las probabilidades son de 3 a 1 10. (*causing*) **much ~ my surprise** para mi sorpresa 11. (*by*) por; **known ~ sb** conocido de [o por] alguien 12. (*matching*) de; **the top ~ this jar** la tapa de este tarro 13. (*of*) de; **the secretary ~ the boss** la secretaria del jefe 14. (*for purpose of*)

para ▶ **that's all there is ~ it** eso es todo II. *infinitive particle* 1. (*infinitive: not translated*) **~ do/walk/put** hacer/caminar/poner 2. (*in command*) **I told him ~ eat** le dije que comiera 3. (*after interrogative words*) **I know what ~ do** sé qué hacer; **she didn't know how ~ say it** no sabía como decirlo 4. (*wishes*) **he wants ~ listen** quiere escuchar; **she wants ~ go** quiere irse 5. (*purpose*) **he comes ~ see me** viene a verme; **to phone ~ ask sth** llamar para preguntar algo 6. (*attitude*) **she seems ~ enjoy it** parece que disfruta; **~ be honest ...** (dicho) sinceramente... 7. (*future intention*) **the work ~ be done** el trabajo que hay que hacer; **sth ~ buy** algo que hay que comprar 8. (*in consecutive acts*) para; **I came back ~ find she had left Madrid** volví para descubrir que se había ido de Madrid 9. (*introducing a complement*) **he wants me ~ tell him a story** quiere que le cuente un cuento; **to be too tired ~ do sth** estar demasiado cansado para hacer algo 10. (*in general statements*) **it is easy ~ do it** es fácil hacerlo 11. (*in ellipsis*) **he doesn't want ~ eat, but I want ~** él no quiere comer, pero yo sí III. *adv* **to push the door ~** cerrar la puerta empujándola

toad [təʊd, *Am:* toʊd] *n* 1. (*animal*) sapo *m* 2. (*person*) esperpento *m*

toad-in-the-hole [ˌteʊdɪnðə'həʊl, *Am:* ˌtoʊdɪnðə'hoʊl] *n Brit* salchichas *fpl* empanizadas

toadstool ['təʊdstuːl, *Am:* 'toʊd-] *n* seta *f* venenosa

toady ['təʊdi, *Am:* 'toʊ-] I. <-ies> *n* adulador(a) *m(f)*, jalamecate *mf Ven* II. *vi* adular, jalar mecate *Ven*

to and fro *adv* de un lado a otro

toast [təʊst, *Am:* toʊst] I. *n* 1. *no pl* (*bread*) tostada *f*; **a piece of ~** una tostada 2. (*drink*) brindis *m inv* II. *vt* 1. (*cook*) tostar 2. (*drink*) brindar III. *vi* tostarse

toaster *n* tostadora *f*

toastmaster ['təʊstmɑːstər, *Am:* 'toʊstˌmæstə˞] *n* maestro, -a *m, f* de ceremonias

toast rack *n* portatostadas *m inv*

tobacco [tə'bækəʊ, *Am:* -oʊ] *n no pl* tabaco *m*

tobacconist [tə'bækənɪst] *n* estanquero, -a *m, f*

to-be [tə'biː] *adj* futuro, -a

toboggan [tə'bɒgən, *Am:* -'bɑːgən] I. *n* tobogán *m* II. *vi* deslizarse por el tobogán

toboggan run *n*, **toboggan slide** *n* pista *f* de tobogán

toby (**jug**) ['təʊbi(dʒʌg), *Am:* 'toʊ-] *n* pichel *m* (*en forma de hombre*)

tod [tɒd, *Am:* tɑːd] *n no pl, Brit, inf* **to be on one's ~** estar a solas

today [tə'deɪ] I. *adv* 1. (*this day*) hoy 2. (*nowadays*) hoy día II. *n no pl* 1. (*this day*) hoy *m* 2. (*nowadays*) actualidad *f*

toddle ['tɒdl, *Am:* 'tɑːdl] *vi* 1. (*walk*) andar

tambaleándose; (*child*) dar los primeros pasos **2.** *inf* (*go*) **to ~** (**off**) marcharse, irse

toddler ['tɒdlə', *Am:* 'tɑːdlə] *n* niño, -a *m, f* que empieza a caminar

toddy ['tɒdi, *Am:* 'tɑːdi] <-ies> *n* (**hot**) ~ ponche *m*

to-do [tə'duː] *n inf* lío *m*

toe [təʊ, *Am:* toʊ] **I.** *n* **1.** ANAT dedo *m* del pie; **on one's ~s** de puntillas **2.** (*of sock*) punta *f;* (*of shoe*) puntera *f* ▸ **to keep** sb **on their ~s** mantener a alguien en estado de alerta; **to step on** sb's **~s** pisotear a alguien **II.** *vt* **to ~ the line** conformarse

toecap *n* puntera *f* **toehold** *n* **1.** (*when climbing*) punto *m* de apoyo para el pie **2.** *fig* trampolín *m* **toenail** *n* uña *f* del dedo del pie

toffee ['tɒfi, *Am:* 'tɑːfi] *n* toffee *m*

toffee apple *n* manzana *f* acaramelada **toffee-nosed** *adj Brit, pej, inf* engreído, -a

toffy ['tɒfi, *Am:* 'tɑːfi] *n s.* **toffee**

together [tə'geðə', *Am:* -ə-] **I.** *adv* **1.** (*jointly*) juntos, juntas; **all ~** todos juntos, todas juntas; **~ with** sb/sth junto con alguien/algo; **to live ~** vivir juntos; **to get ~** juntarse; **to get it ~** *inf* organizarse **2.** (*at the same time*) a un tiempo, a la vez **II.** *adj inf* equilibrado, -a

togetherness *n no pl* compañerismo *m*

toggle ['tɒgl, *Am:* 'tɑːgl] **I.** *n* **1.** INFOR tecla *f* de conmutación **2.** TECH palanca *f* acodada **II.** *vt* pulsar

toggle switch *n* interruptor *m* de palanca

Togo ['təʊgəʊ, *Am:* 'toʊgoʊ] *n* Togo *f*

Togolese [ˌtəʊgəʊ'liːz, *Am:* ˌtoʊgoʊ'liːs] **I.** *adj* togolés, -esa **II.** *n* togolés, -esa *m, f*

toil [tɔɪl] **I.** *n no pl* labor *f* **II.** *vi* **1.** (*work hard*) afanarse **2.** (*move*) moverse con gran dificultad

toilet ['tɔɪlɪt] *n* **1.** (*room*) cuarto *m* de baño **2.** (*appliance*) váter *m*, inodoro *m* **3.** *form* (*process*) aseo *m*

toilet bag *n* neceser *m* **toilet paper** *n* papel *m* higiénico

toiletries ['tɔɪlɪtriz] *npl* artículos *mpl* de tocador

toiletries bag *n Am* neceser *m*

toilet roll *n Brit, Aus* rollo *m* de papel higiénico **toilet soap** *n* jabón *m* de tocador, jabón *m* de olor *Col, Ven* **toilet water** *n* colonia *f*

to-ing and fro-ing [ˌtuːɪŋən'frəʊɪŋ, *Am:* -'froʊ-] <to-ings and fro-ings> *n no pl* trajín *m*

token ['təʊkən, *Am:* 'toʊ-] **I.** *n* **1.** (*sign*) señal *f;* (*of affection*) muestra *f;* **by the same ~** por la misma razón; **in ~ of** *form* en señal de **2.** *Brit, Aus* (*coupon*) bono *m* **3.** (*for machines*) ficha *f* **II.** *adj* (*symbolic*) simbólico, -a

told [təʊld, *Am:* toʊld] *pt, pp of* **tell**

tolerable ['tɒlərəbl, *Am:* 'tɑːlə-] *adj* soportable, tolerable

tolerably ['tɒlərəbli, *Am:* 'tɑːlə-] *adv form* pasablemente

tolerance ['tɒlərəns, *Am:* 'tɑːlə-] *n no pl*

tolerancia *f*

tolerant ['tɒlərənt, *Am:* 'tɑːlə-] *adj* tolerante

tolerate ['tɒləreɪt, *Am:* 'tɑːləreɪt] *vt* **1.** (*accept*) *a.* MED tolerar **2.** (*endure*) soportar

toleration [ˌtɒlə'reɪʃən, *Am:* ˌtɑːlə'reɪ-] *n no pl* tolerancia *f*

toll¹ [təʊl, *Am:* toʊl] *n* **1.** AUTO peaje *m* **2.** *Am* TEL tarifa *f* **3.** *no pl* (*damage*) número *m* de víctimas

toll² [təʊl, *Am:* toʊl] **I.** *vt* tañer; **to ~ the knell** *fig* doblar las campanas por un difunto **II.** *vi* doblar

toll bridge *n* puente *m* de peaje **toll call** *n Am* conferencia *f* **toll-free** *adv Am* gratis **tollhouse** *n* HIST cabina *f* de peaje **toll road** *n* autopista *f* de peaje

tom [tɒm, *Am:* tɑːm] *n* (*cat*) gato *m* macho

tomato [tə'mɑːtəʊ, *Am:* -'meɪ̞oʊ] <-es> *n* tomate *m*

tomato ketchup *n* salsa *f* de tomate

tomb [tuːm] *n* tumba *f*, guaca *f AmL*

tombola [tɒm'bəʊlə, *Am:* 'tɑːmblə] *n Brit, Aus* tómbola *f*

tomboy ['tɒmbɔɪ, *Am:* 'tɑːm-] *n* marimacho *m*, marimacha *f Ven*

tombstone ['tuːmstəʊn, *Am:* 'tuːmstoʊn] *n* lápida *f* sepulcral

tomcat ['tɒmkæt, *Am:* 'tɑːm-] *n* (*gato m*) macho

tome [təʊm, *Am:* toʊm] *n* librote *m*

tomfoolery [tɒm'fuːləri, *Am:* ˌtɑːm'fuːlə·i] *n no pl* tontería *f*

tommy gun ['tɒmigʌn, *Am:* 'tɑːmi-] *n* metralleta *f*

tomograph ['tɒmɐgrɑːf] *n* MED tomógrafo *m*

tomography [tə'mɒgrəfi, *Am:* toʊ-'mɑːgrə-] *n* MED tomografía *f*

tomorrow [tə'mɒrəʊ, *Am:* -'mɑːroʊ] **I.** *adv* mañana; **the day after ~** pasado mañana; **all (day) ~** todo el día de mañana; **a week from ~** de mañana en una semana; **~ morning/ evening** mañana por la mañana/tarde; **see you ~!** ¡hasta mañana!; **~ is another day!** ¡mañana será otro día! **II.** *n* mañana *m* ▸ **~ is another day** *prov* mañana es otro día; **never put off until ~ what you can do today** *prov* nunca dejes para mañana lo que puedas hacer hoy *prov;* **who knows what ~ will bring?** ¿quién sabe qué nos depara el mañana?

tom-tom ['tɒmtɒm, *Am:* 'tɑːmtɑːm] *n* tantán *m*

ton [tʌn] *n* tonelada *f* (*Brit:* 1,016 *kilos; Am:* 907 *kilos*); **~s of** *inf* montones *m*

tone [təʊn, *Am:* toʊn] **I.** *n* **1.** (*sound*) tono *m;* (*of instrument*) tonalidad *f;* (*of voice*) timbre *m* **2.** (*style*) clase *f* **3.** (*of colour*) matiz *f*, tono *m* **4.** *no pl* (*condition*) tono *m* **II.** *vt* (*muscles, skin*) tonificar

◆ **tone down** *vt* moderar

◆ **tone in** *vi* armonizar

◆ **tone up** *vt* poner en forma

tone control *n* control *m* de tonalidad

tone-deaf [ˌtəʊn'def, *Am:* 'toʊn-] *adj* falto,

-a de oído musical

toneless ['təʊnləs, *Am:* 'toʊn-] *adj* monótono, -a

tone poem *n* poema *m* sinfónico

toner ['təʊnəʳ, *Am:* 'toʊnɚ] *n* **1.**(*for skin*) tonificante *m* **2.**(*for printer*) tóner *m;* PHOT virador *m*

Tonga ['tɒŋə, *Am:* 'tɑ:ŋ-] *n* Tonga *f*

Tongan I. *adj* tongano, -a II. *n* **1.**(*person*) tongano, -a *m, f* **2.** LING tongano *m*

tongs [tɒŋz, *Am:* tɑ:ŋz] *npl* tenazas *fpl*

tongue [tʌŋ] I. *n* **1.** ANAT lengua *f;* **to bite one's ~** morderse la lengua; **to find one's ~** recobrar el habla; **to hold one's ~** callarse; **to stick one's ~ out (at sb)** sacar la lengua (a alguien); **to get one's ~ around a word** pronunciar una palabra **2.**(*language*) idioma *m;* **to speak in ~s** hablar en lenguas desconocidas **3.** *no pl* (*expressive style*) expresión *f;* **to have a sharp ~** tener una lengua afilada ►**to say sth ~ in cheek** decir algo irónicamente; **to give sb the rough side of one's ~** *inf,* **to speak with a forked ~** hablar con lengua bífida, criticar a alguien severamente; **have you lost your ~?** ¿se te ha comido la lengua el gato?; **to set ~s wagging** dar que hablar II. *vt* MUS tocar

tongue-tied ['tʌŋtaɪd] *adj fig* **to be ~** cortarse

tongue twister *n* trabalenguas *m inv*

tonic¹ ['tɒnɪk, *Am:* 'tɑ:nɪk] *n* (*stimulant*) tónico *m,* estimulante *m*

tonic² ['tɒnɪk, *Am:* 'tɑ:nɪk] *n* MUS tónica *f*

tonic³ ['tɒnɪk, *Am:* 'tɑ:nɪk] *n,* **tonic water** *n* tónica *f*

tonight [tə'naɪt] *adv* (*evening*) esta tarde; (*night*) esta noche

tonnage ['tʌnɪdʒ] *n no pl* tonelaje *m*

tonne [tʌn] *n no pl* tonelada *f* (métrica)

tonsil ['tɒnsl, *Am:* 'tɑ:n-] *n* MED amígdala *f*

tonsillitis [,tɒnsɪ'laɪtɪs, *Am:* ,tɑ:nsə'laɪṭɪs] *n no pl* amigdalitis *f*

too [tu:] *adv* **1.**(*overly*) demasiado; **~ right!** ¡muy bien dicho! **2.**(*very*) mucho **3.**(*also*) también; **me ~!** *inf* ¡y yo! **4.**(*moveover*) además **5.** *Am, inf* (*for emphasis*) ya lo creo

took [tʊk] *vt, vi pt of* **take**

tool [tu:l] I. *n* **1.**(*implement*) herramienta *f,* implemento *m AmL* **2.**(*instrument*) instrumento *m* II. *vt* (*shape with a tool*) trabajar

tool bag *n* bolsa *f* de herramientas **tool bar** *n* INFOR barra *f* de herramientas **tool box** *n,* **tool chest** *n* caja *f* de herramientas **tool kit** *n* juego *m* de herramientas **tool-maker** *n* fabricante *m* de herramientas **tool shed** *n* cobertizo *m* para herramientas

toot [tu:t] I. *n* toque *m* suave (de bocina); **to give a ~** tocar el claxon II. *vt* (*sound*) sonar III. *vi* pitar

tooth [tu:θ] <teeth> *n* **1.** ANAT (*of person, animal*) diente *m;* (*molar*) muela *f;* **to bare one's teeth** enseñar los dientes; **he's cutting a ~** le está saliendo un diente **2.**(*of comb*) púa

f; (*of saw*) diente *m* ►**to set sb's teeth on edge** dar dentera a alguien; **to fight ~ and nail** (**to do sth**) luchar a brazo partido (para hacer algo); **to be long in the ~** ser entrado en años; **to have a sweet ~** ser goloso; **to cut one's teeth on sth** adquirir experiencia en algo; **to get one's teeth into sth** hincar el diente a algo; **to give sth teeth** dar efectividad a algo; **to grit one's teeth** aguantarse; **to lie through one's teeth** mentir descaradamente; **in the ~ of sth** (*straight into*) en medio de algo; (*despite*) a pesar de algo

toothache ['tu:θeɪk] *n* dolor *m* de muelas

toothbrush ['tu:θbrʌʃ] *n* cepillo *m* de dientes

toothed *adj* dentado, -a

toothpaste ['tu:θpeɪst] *n no pl* pasta *f* dentífrica [*o* de dientes]

toothpick *n* palillo *m,* pajuela *f Bol, Col*

toothsome ['tu:θsəm] *adj* sabroso, -a

toothy [tu:θi] <-ier, -iest> *adj* dentudo, -a; **to give a ~ smile** sonreír enseñando los dientes

tootle ['tu:tl, *Am:* -t̬l] *vi inf* **to ~ along** ir sin prisas

toots ['tʊts] *n Am, inf* chica *f*

top¹ [tɒp, *Am:* tɑ:p] *n* (*spinning top*) peonza *f*

top² [tɒp, *Am:* tɑ:p] I. *n* **1.**(*highest part*) parte *f* superior; (*of mountain*) cima *f;* (*of tree*) copa *f;* (*of head*) coronilla *f;* **to get on ~ of sth** *a. fig* llegar a lo más alto de algo; **from ~ to bottom** de arriba abajo; **from ~ to toe** de pies a cabeza; **to feel on ~ of the world** estar contentísimo **2.**(*surface*) superficie *f;* **on ~ of** encima de **3.** *no pl* (*highest rank*) lo mejor; **to be at the ~** estar en la cima; **to be at the ~ of the class** ser el primero de la clase; **to go to the ~** ir a la cima **4.**(*clothing*) top *m* **5.**(*end*) punta *f* superior; (*of street*) final *m;* (*of table, list*) cabeza *f* **6.**(*lid: of bottle*) tapón *m* ►**at the ~ of one's voice** a grito pelado; **to be off one's ~** *Brit, inf* no estar en su sano juicio; **to go over the ~** exagerar II. *adj* **1.**(*highest, upper*) más alto **2.**(*best*) de primera calidad **3.**(*most successful*) exitoso, -a **4.**(*most important*) mejor **5.**(*maximum*) máximo, -a III. <-pp-> *vt* **1.**(*be at top of*) encabezar **2.**(*provide topping*) coronar **3.**(*surpass*) superar **4.** *Brit, inf* (*kill*) matar

◆**top off** *vt* **1.** GASTR coronar **2.**(*conclude*) rematar

◆**top up** *vt* **1.**(*fill up again*) recargar; **to top sb up with sth** *inf* servir algo más a alguien **2.**(*add to*) completar

topaz ['təʊpæz, *Am:* 'toʊ-] *n* topacio *m*

topcoat ['tɒpkəʊt, *Am:* 'tɑ:pkoʊt] *n* sobretodo *m* **top copy** *n* original *m* **top dog** *n inf* **1.**(*boss*) alto cargo *m* **2.**(*victor*) vencedor(a) *m(f)* **top drawer** *adj* de alta sociedad **top executive** *n* ejecutivo, -a *m, f* superior **top-flight** *adj* de primera clase **top hat** *n* sombrero *m* de copa, galera *f AmL* **top-**

-heavy *adj* inestable

topic ['tɒpɪk, *Am:* 'tɑːpɪk] *n* tema *m*

topical ['tɒpɪkl, *Am:* 'tɑːpɪ-] *adj* de interés actual

topicality [ˌtɒpɪ'kæləti, *Am:* ˌtɑːpɪ'kæləʈi] *n no pl* actualidad *f*

topless ['tɒplɪs, *Am:* 'tɑː-] I. *adj* que deja el busto al descubierto II. *adv* **to go ~** ir en topless

top-level [ˌtɒp'levəl, *Am:* 'tɑːpˌlev-] *adj* **1.** (*of highest rank*) de alto nivel **2.** (*of highest importance*) de primera categoría

top loader *n* lavadora *f* de carga superior

top management *n* altos cargos *mpl*

topmost ['tɒpməʊst, *Am:* 'tɑːp-] *adj* más alto, -a

top-notch [ˌtɒp'nɒtʃ, *Am:* ˌtɑːp'nɑːtʃ] *adj inf* de primera

topographer [tə'pɒgrəfəʳ, *Am:* -'pɑːgrəfə-] *n* topógrafo, -a *m, f*

topographical [ˌtɒpə'græfɪkl, *Am:* ˌtɑːpə'-] *adj* topográfico, -a

topography [tə'pɒgrəfi, *Am:* -'pɑːgrə-] *n no pl* topografía *f*

topper ['tɒpəʳ, *Am:* 'tɑːpə-] *n inf s.* **top hat**

topping ['tɒpɪŋ, *Am:* 'tɑːpɪŋ] *n* GASTR cobertura *f*

topple ['tɒpl, *Am:* 'tɑːpl] I. *vt a.* POL derribar II. *vi* **to ~** (**down**) caerse

◆**topple over** *vi* volcarse

top price *n* precio *m* máximo **top priority** *n* prioridad *f* máxima **top quality** *n* máxima calidad *f* **top-ranking** *adj* importante; (*university*) de alto nivel **topsail** *n* gavia *f* **top salary** *n* salario *m* máximo **top secret** *adj* confidencial **top-selling** *adj* de mayor venta **topsoil** *n no pl* capa *f* superior del suelo **top speed** *n* velocidad *f* máxima **topspin** *n no pl* SPORTS efecto *m* topspin

topsy-turvy [ˌtɒpsi'tɜːvi, *Am:* ˌtɑːpsɪ'tɜːr-] *inf* I. *adj* desordenado, -a II. *adv* patas arriba

torch [tɔːtʃ, *Am:* tɔːrtʃ] <-es> *n* **1.** *Aus, Brit* (*electric*) linterna *f* **2.** (*burning stick*) antorcha *f*; **to carry a ~ for sb** estar enamorado de alguien; **to put sth to the ~** prender fuego a algo **3.** *Am* (*blowlamp*) soplete *m*

torchlight ['tɔːtʃlaɪt, *Am:* 'tɔːrtʃ-] *n no pl* (*electric*) luz *f* de linterna; (*burning*) luz *f* de antorcha

torchlight procession *n* desfile *m* con antorchas

tore [tɔːʳ, *Am:* tɔːr] *vi, vt pt of* **tear**

torment ['tɔːment, *Am:* 'tɔːr-] I. *n* **1.** (*suffering*) tormento *m*; **to be in ~** sufrir mucho; **to go through ~s** sufrir lo indecible **2.** (*physical pain*) suplicio *m* **3.** (*torture*) tortura *f* **4.** (*annoying thing*) angustia *f* II. *vt* atormentar

tormentor [tɔː'mentəʳ, *Am:* tɔːr'menʈə-] *n* atormentador(a) *m(f)*

torn [tɔːn, *Am:* tɔːrn] *vi, vt pp of* **tear**

tornado [tɔː'neɪdəʊ, *Am:* tɔːr'neɪdoʊ] *n* <-(e)s> tornado *m*

torpedo [tɔː'piːdəʊ, *Am:* tɔːr'piːdoʊ] MIL, NAUT I. <-es> *n* torpedo *m* II. *vt* torpedear

torpid ['tɔːpɪd, *Am:* 'tɔːr-] *adj form* aletargado, -a

torpor ['tɔːpəʳ, *Am:* 'tɔːrpə-] *n no pl, form* sopor *m*, letargo *m*

torque [tɔːk, *Am:* tɔːrk] *n no pl* PHYS par *m* de torsión

torrent ['tɒrənt, *Am:* 'tɔːr-] *n* **1.** (*large amount of water*) torrente *m*; **to rain in ~s** llover a cántaros **2.** (*of complaints, abuse*) carga *f*

torrential [tə'renʃl, *Am:* tɔː'-] *adj* torrencial, torrentoso, -a *AmL*

torsion ['tɔːʃən, *Am:* 'tɔːr-] *n no pl* TECH, MED torsión *f*

torso ['tɔːsəʊ, *Am:* 'tɔːrsoʊ] *n* torso *m*

tortoise ['tɔːtəs, *Am:* 'tɔːrʈəs] *n* tortuga *f*

tortoiseshell ['tɔːtəsʃel, *Am:* 'tɔːrʈəs-] *n no pl* concha *f*

tortuous ['tɔːtjʊəs, *Am:* 'tɔːrʈʊəs] *adj* (*complicated, indirect*) tortuoso, -a; (*reasoning*) enrevesado, -a

torture ['tɔːtʃəʳ, *Am:* 'tɔːrtʃə-] I. *n* **1.** *no pl* (*cruelty*) tortura *f*; (*mental*) tormento *m* **2.** (*suffering*) suplicio *m* II. *vt* **1.** (*cause suffering to*) torturar **2.** (*disturb*) atormentar; **to ~ oneself with sth** martirizarse con algo

torturer ['tɔːtʃərəʳ, *Am:* 'tɔːrtʃə-ə-] *n* torturador(a) *m(f)*

Tory ['tɔːri] *Brit* I. <-ies> *n* miembro o partidario de los conservadores británicos II. *adj* del partido conservador británico

tosh [tɒʃ, *Am:* tɑːʃ] *n no pl, inf* tonterías *fpl*; **to talk ~** decir tonterías

toss [tɒs, *Am:* tɑːs] I. *n* **1.** (*throw*) lanzamiento *m*; (*of head*) movimiento *m* brusco **2.** (*throwing of a coin*) sorteo *m* a cara o cruz; **to win/lose the ~** ganar/perder a cara o cruz ▶**to argue the ~** *inf* discutir insistentemente; **I don't give a ~** *inf* me importa un pepino II. *vt* **1.** (*throw*) lanzar; (*pancake*) dar la vuelta; **to ~ a coin** echar una moneda a cara o cruz **2.** (*shake: head*) sacudir III. *vi* **to ~ for sth** echar algo a cara o cruz ▶**to ~ and turn** dar vueltas en la cama

◆**toss about** *vt*, **toss around** *vt* **1.** (*move roughly*) zarandear; (*head, hair*) agitar **2.** (*consider*) considerar

◆**toss away** *vt* tirar

◆**toss off** I. *vt* **1.** *inf* (*do quickly*) hacer rápidamente; (*write*) escribir rápidamente **2.** (*drink quickly*) beber de un trago II. *vi* *Aus, Brit, vulg* hacerse una paja

◆**toss out** *vt* tirar

◆**toss up** *vi* **to ~ for sth** echar algo a cara o cruz

toss-up ['tɒsʌp, *Am:* 'tɑːs-] *n* **it's a ~ between ...** la cosa está entre...

tot [tɒt, *Am:* tɑːt] *n* **1.** *inf* (*child*) niño, -a *m, f* pequeño, -a **2.** (*alcohol*) dedo *m*

◆**tot up** I. *vt inf* sumar II. *vi* **to ~ to** (*an amount*) sumar (una cantidad)

total ['təʊtl, *Am:* 'toʊt̬l] I. *n* (*sum, cost*) total *m* II. *adj* 1. (*entire: sum, cost*) total 2. (*absolute*) total, absoluto, -a; **a ~ failure** un fracaso total III. *vt* <*Brit:* -ll-, *Am:* -l-> 1. (*count*) sumar 2. (*amount to*) ascender a

totalitarian [ˌtəʊtælɪ'teərɪən, *Am:* toʊˌtælə'teri-] *adj* POL totalitario, -a

totalitarianism *n no pl* POL totalitarismo *m*

totality [təʊ'tæləti, *Am:* toʊ'tæləti] *n no pl* totalidad *f;* **in its ~** en total

totally ['təʊtəli, *Am:* 'toʊt̬əl-] *adv* totalmente

tote[1] [təʊt, *Am:* toʊt] *n no pl* SPORTS totalizador *m*

tote[2] [təʊt, *Am:* toʊt] *vt inf* llevar

tote bag *n* bolsa *f* grande

totem (**pole**) ['təʊtəm(ˌpəʊl), *Am:* 'toʊt̬əm (ˌpoʊl)] *n* tótem *m*

totter ['tɒtə', *Am:* 'tɑːt̬ə'] *vi* tambalearse

tottery ['tɒtəri, *Am:* 'tɑːt̬-] *adj* tambaleante

toucan ['tuːkæn] *n* tucán *m*

touch [tʌtʃ] <-es> I. *n* 1. *no pl* (*sensation*) tacto *m* 2. (*act of touching*) toque *m* 3. *no pl* (*communication*) **to be/get/keep in ~** (**with sb/sth**) estar/ponerse/mantenerse en contacto (con alguien/algo); **to be out of ~ with sb** no tener contacto con alguien; **to lose ~ with sb** perder el contacto con alguien 4. *no pl* (*skill*) habilidad *f;* **to lose one's ~** perder la destreza 5. *no pl* (*small amount*) poquito *m;* (*of bitterness, irony*) pizca *f;* **a ~ of genius** un punto de genialidad 6. (*detail*) toque *m;* **the human ~** el toque humano 7. SPORTS **to go into ~** salir del campo ▶**to be a soft ~** *inf* ser demasiado blando II. *vt* 1. (*feel*) tocar; **to ~ the brake** pisar el freno 2. (*brush against*) rozar 3. (*reach*) alcanzar 4. (*eat, drink*) probar; **he didn't ~ it** no lo probó 5. (*move emotionally*) conmover, enternecer 6. (*equal*) **there's no painter to ~ him** no existe pintor que le iguale III. *vi* tocarse

◆**touch at** *vi* NAUT hacer escala en

◆**touch down** *vi* AVIAT aterrizar

◆**touch in** *vt* ART esbozar

◆**touch off** *vt* hacer estallar; (*protest*) provocar

◆**touch on** *vt* tocar

◆**touch up** *vt* 1. (*improve*) mejorar; PHOT retocar 2. *Brit, inf* (*sexually*) **to touch sb up** magrear a alguien

◆**touch upon** *vt* tocar

touch and go *adj* **to be ~ whether ...** no estar claro si...

touchdown ['tʌtʃdaʊn] *n* 1. AVIAT aterrizaje *m* 2. SPORTS (*American football*) touchdown *m;* (*rugby*) ensayo *m*

touched [tʌtʃt] *adj* 1. (*moved*) conmovido, -a 2. *inf* (*crazy*) chiflado, -a

touchiness ['tʌtʃɪnəs] *n no pl, inf* 1. (*of person*) susceptibilidad *f* 2. (*of issue*) delicadeza *f*

touching ['tʌtʃɪŋ] *adj* conmovedor(a)

touch-sensitive *adj* INFOR sensible al tacto

touchstone ['tʌtʃstəʊn, *Am:* -stoʊn] *n* pie-dra *f* de toque

touch-type ['tʌtʃtaɪp] *vi* mecanografiar al tacto

touchy ['tʌtʃi] <-ier, -iest> *adj* 1. (*person*) susceptible; **she's very ~ about her work** es muy susceptible cuando se trata de su trabajo 2. (*issue*) delicado, -a

tough [tʌf] I. *adj* 1. (*fabric, substance*) fuerte; (*meat, skin*) duro, -a; **to be ~ as old boots** (*meat*) estar más duro que una suela 2. (*hardy: person*) resistente 3. (*strict*) estricto, -a; (*negotiator*) implacable; **to be ~ on sb** ser severo con alguien 4. (*difficult*) difícil; (*exam, question*) peliagudo, -a 5. (*violent*) violento, -a; (*neighbourhood*) peligroso, -a 6. *inf* (*unlucky*) **~ luck** mala suerte II. *n Am, inf* matón, -ona *m, f*

◆**tough out** *vt* **to tough it out** (*endure*) no ceder; (*face up to*) afrontar

toughen ['tʌfən] I. *vt* endurecer II. *vi* endurecerse

toughness *n no pl* 1. (*strength*) resistencia *f* 2. (*hardness: of meat*) dureza *f* 3. (*difficulty*) dificultad *f*

toupée ['tuːpeɪ, *Am:* tuː'peɪ] *n* peluquín *m*

tour [tʊə', *Am:* tʊr] I. *n* 1. (*journey*) viaje *m;* **guided ~** excursión *f* guiada; **sightseeing ~** paseo *m* por los lugares de interés 2. (*of factory*) visita *f* 3. MUS gira *f;* **to be/go on ~** estar/ir de gira II. *vt* 1. (*travel around*) recorrer 2. (*visit professionally*) visitar 3. (*perform*) ir de gira por III. *vi* ir de viaje

touring company *n* compañía *f* teatral itinerante

tourism ['tʊərɪzəm, *Am:* 'tʊrɪ-] *n no pl* turismo *m*

tourist ['tʊərɪst, *Am:* 'tʊrɪst] *n* 1. (*traveller*) turista *mf* 2. *Aus, Brit* SPORTS visitante *mf*

tourist agency *n* agencia *f* de viajes **tourist bureau** *n* oficina *f* de viajes **tourist class** *n* clase *f* turista **tourist guide** *n* 1. (*book*) guía *f* turística 2. (*person*) guía *mf* **tourist industry** *n* industria *f* turística **tourist information office** *n* oficina *f* de turismo **tourist season** *n* temporada *f* turística **tourist ticket** *n* pasaje *m* de turista **tourist visa** *n* visado *m* turístico

tournament ['tɔːnəmənt, *Am:* 'tɜːr-] *n* SPORTS torneo *m*

tour operator *n* operador *m* turístico

tousle ['taʊzl] *vt* revolver

tousled ['taʊzld] *adj* despeinado, -a

tout [taʊt] I. *n* revendedor(a) *m(f)* II. *vt* 1. (*try to sell*) tratar de vender 2. *Brit* (*ticket*) revender III. *vi* **to ~ for custom** buscar clientes

tow [təʊ, *Am:* toʊ] I. *n* remolque *m;* **to give sb/sth a ~** remolcar a alguien/algo; **to have sb in ~** *fig* llevar a alguien a cuestas II. *vt* remolcar; **to ~ a vehicle** llevarse un coche a remolque

toward(s) [tə'wɔːd(z), *Am:* tɔːrd(z)] *prep* 1. (*in direction of*) hacia; (*of time*) hacia, cerca de **2.** (*for*) por **3.** (*in respect of*) respecto a; **to feel sth ~ sb** sentir algo por alguien

tow bar *n* barra *f* de tracción **tow boat** *n* NAUT remolcador *m*

towel ['tauəl] **I.** *n* toalla *f* ►**to throw in the ~** tirar la toalla **II.** *vt* <-ll-> **to ~ sth dry** secar algo con toalla

towel(l)ing *n no pl* felpa *f*

towel rack *n Am*, **towel rail** *n Aus, Brit* toallero *m*

tower ['tauə^r, *Am:* 'tauə] *n* torre *f* ►**a ~ of strength** un gran apoyo

♦**tower above** *vi*, **tower over** *vi* **to ~ sth/sb** ser mucho más alto que algo/alguien

tower block *n Brit* edificio *m* de apartamentos

towering *adj* **1.** (*very high*) altísimo, -a **2.** (*very large*) inmenso, -a; (*temper*) intenso, -a

town [taun] *n* (*large*) ciudad *f*; (*small*) pueblo *m*; **the ~** el centro ►**to go out on the ~** salir de juerga; **to paint the ~ red** irse de juerga

town centre *n Brit* centro *m* de la ciudad **town clerk** *n Brit* secretario, -a *m, f* del ayuntamiento **town council** *n Brit* ayuntamiento *m* **town councillor** *n* concejal(a) *m(f)* **town hall** *n* POL ayuntamiento *m* **town house** *n* **1.** (*residence in town*) casa *f* de la ciudad **2.** (*part of terrace*) casa *f* unifamiliar **town planning** *n* urbanismo *m*

townscape ['taunskeip] *n* paisaje *m* urbano

townsfolk ['taunzfəuk, *Am:* -fouk] *npl* ciudadanos *mpl*

township ['taunʃɪp] *n* **1.** *Am, Can* municipio *m* **2.** (*in South Africa*) distrito *m* segregado

townspeople ['taunz,piːpl] *npl* ciudadanos *mpl*

tow truck *n Am* grúa *f*

toxaemia *n*, **toxemia** [tɒk'siːmiə, *Am:* taːk-] *n Am no pl* toxemia *f*

toxic ['tɒksɪk, *Am:* 'taːk-] *adj* tóxico, -a

toxicology [ˌtɒksɪ'kɒlədʒi, *Am:* ˌtaːksɪ-'kaːlə-] *n no pl* toxicología *f*

toxic waste *n* residuos *mpl* tóxicos

toxin ['tɒksɪn, *Am:* 'taːk-] *n* toxina *f*

toy [tɔɪ] *n* juguete *m*; **cuddly ~** muñeco *m* de peluche

♦**toy with** *vt* jugar con; **to ~ an idea** dar vueltas a una idea; **to ~ sb's affections** jugar con los sentimientos de alguien

toy car *n* coche *m* de juguete **toy dog** *n* perro *m* faldero **toyshop** *n* juguetería *f*

trace[1] [treɪs] *n* (*for horse*) correa *f*; **to kick over the ~s** sacar los pies del plato

trace[2] [treɪs] **I.** *n* **1.** (*sign*) rastro *m*; **to leave a ~ of sth** dejar indicios de algo; **to disappear without ~** desaparecer sin dejar rastro **2.** (*slight amount*) pizca *f*; **~s of a drug/poison** pequeñas cantidades de droga/veneno; **without any ~ of sarcasm/humour** sin nada de sarcasmo/humor **II.** *vt* **1.** (*locate*) localizar; **to ~ sb to somewhere** localizar a alguien en algún sitio; **it can be ~d back to the Middle**

Ages se remonta a la Edad Media **2.** (*draw outline of*) trazar; (*with tracing paper*) calcar

traceable ['treɪsəbl] *adj* rastreable; **an easily ~ reference** una referencia fácil de encontrar

trace element *n* oligoelemento *m*

tracer ['treɪsə^r, *Am:* -ə] *n* MIL bala *m* trazadora

tracery ['treɪsəri] *n* tracería *f*

trachea [trə'kɪə, *Am:* 'treɪkɪə] <-s *o* -chae> *n* tráquea *f*

tracing *n* calco *m*

tracing paper *n* papel *m* de calco

track [træk] **I.** *n* **1.** (*path*) senda *f* **2.** (*rails*) vía *f* **3.** *Am* (*in station*) andén *m* **4.** (*mark*) pista *f*; (*of animal*) huella *f*; (*of bullet*) trayectoria *f*; **to cover one's ~s** borrar las huellas; **to leave ~s** dejar huellas; **to be on the ~ of sb** seguir la pista a alguien **5.** (*path*) camino *m*; **to be on the right ~** *a. fig* ir por buen camino; **to be on the wrong ~** *fig* estar equivocado **6.** (*logical course*) curso *m*; **the ~ of an argument** el hilo de un argumento; **to get off the ~** salirse del tema; **to be on ~ (to do sth)** estar en camino (de hacer algo) **7.** (*career path*) rumbo *m*; **to change ~** cambiar de rumbo **8.** SPORTS pista *f* **9.** (*song*) canción *f* ►**to live on the wrong side of the ~s** *inf* vivir en los barrios pobres; **to keep ~ (of sb/sth)** no perder de vista (a alguien/algo); **to lose ~ (of sb/sth)** perder de vista (a alguien/algo); **to make ~s** *inf* largarse; **to stop sb (dead) in his ~s** parar los pies a alguien; **to throw sb off the ~** despistar a alguien **II.** *vt* **1.** (*pursue*) seguir la pista de; **to ~ sth/sb** seguir algo/a alguien **2.** (*trace*) trazar **III.** *vi* CINE avanzar

♦**track down** *vt* localizar

track-and-field *n* atletismo *m*

trackball *n* INFOR trackball *f*

tracker dog *n* perro *m* rastreador

track event *n* SPORTS carrera *f* de atletismo

tracking station ['trækɪŋ'steɪʃən] *n* AVIAT, TECH centro *m* de seguimiento

track record *n* historial *m* **track shoe** *n* zapatilla *f* de atletismo **tracksuit** *n* chándal *m*

tract[1] [trækt] *n* (*leaflet*) folleto *m*

tract[2] [trækt] *n* **1.** (*of land*) tramo *m* **2.** ANAT, MED sistema *m*; **digestive ~** tubo *m* digestivo; **respiratory ~** aparato *m* respiratorio

tractable ['træktəbl] *adj* (*person, animal*) dócil; (*problem*) soluble

traction ['trækʃən] *n no pl* **1.** (*grip*) adherencia *f* **2.** MED tracción *f*

traction engine *n* máquina *f* de tracción

tractor ['træktə^r, *Am:* -ə] *n* tractor *m*

trad [træd] *adj Aus, Brit, inf abbr of* **traditional** tradicional

trade [treɪd] **I.** *n* **1.** *no pl* (*buying and selling*) comercio *m*; **~ in sth** comercio de algo **2.** *no pl* (*business activity*) negocio *m* **3.** (*type of business*) industria *f*; **building ~** sector *m* de la construcción; **fur ~** comercio *m* de pieles **4.** (*profession*) oficio *m*; **to learn a ~** aprender

un oficio; **to be a baker by** ~ ser panadero de profesión **5.**(*swap*) intercambio *m* **II.** *vi* **1.**(*exchange goods*) comerciar; **to** ~ **with sb** tener relaciones comerciales con alguien **2.**(*do business*) negociar; **to** ~ **in sth** dedicarse al negocio de algo **III.** *vt* **1.**(*swap, exchange*) intercambiar; **to** ~ **sth for sth** cambiar algo por algo **2.**(*sell*) vender
◆**trade in** *vt* aportar como parte del pago
◆**trade on** *vt* aprovecharse de
trade agreement *n* acuerdo *m* comercial **trade association** *n* asociación *f* mercantil **trade balance** *n* balanza *f* comercial **trade barrier** *n* barrera *f* arancelaria **trade cycle** *n* ciclo *m* mercantil **trade directory** *n* guía *f* mercantil **trade discount** *n* descuento *m* comercial **trade fair** *n* COM feria *f* de muestras **trade gap** *n* déficit *m inv* de la balanza comercial
trade-in ['treɪdɪn] *n* COM permuta *f*
trade-in value *n* valor *m* de un artículo usado descontado de otro nuevo
trade journal *n* periódico *m* gremial **trademark** *n* **1.** COM marca *f*; **registered** ~ marca *f* registrada **2.** *fig* distintivo *m* **trade name** *n* (*of a firm*) razón *f* social; (*trademark*) marca *f*
trade-off ['treɪdɒf, *Am:* -ɑːf] *n* **1.**(*exchange*) intercambio *m*; **to make a** ~ **between things** hacer un intercambio de cosas **2.** *fig* (*inconvenience*) precio *m*
trade policy *n* política *f* comercial **trade press** *n no pl* prensa *f* especializada **trade price** *n Brit* precio *m* de mayorista; **to buy sth at** ~ comprar algo a precio de mayorista
trader ['treɪdəʳ, *Am:* -ɚ] *n* comerciante *mf*
trade register *n* registro *m* mercantil **trade route** *n* ruta *f* comercial **trade secret** *n* secreto *m* profesional
tradesman ['treɪdzmən] <-men> *n* tendero *m*
tradespeople ['treɪdz,piːpl] *npl* tenderos *mpl*
trade surplus *n* excedente *m* comercial **trade union** *n* sindicato *m* **trade unionism** *n no pl* sindicalismo *m* **trade unionist** *n* sindicalista *mf* **trade war** *n* guerra *f* comercial **trade wind** *n* viento *m* alisio
trading ['treɪdɪŋ] *n no pl* comercio *m*; **insider** ~ uso *m* de información confidencial **trading area** *n* zona *f* comercial **trading estate** *n Brit* zona *f* industrial **trading licence** *n* licencia *f* comercial **trading volume** *n* volumen *m* comercial
tradition [trə'dɪʃən] *n* tradición *f*; **by** ~ por tradición; **to be in the** ~ **of sb/sth** ser del estilo de alguien/algo
traditional [trə'dɪʃənəl] *adj* **1.**(*customary*) tradicional **2.**(*conventional*) clásico, -a
traditionalism [trə'dɪʃənəlɪzəm] *n no pl* tradicionalismo *m*
traditionalist [trə'dɪʃənəlɪst] *n* tradicionalista *mf*
traffic ['træfɪk] **I.** *n no pl* **1.**(*vehicles*) tráfico

m; **heavy** ~ tráfico *m* denso; **air/rail** ~ tráfico *m* aéreo/ferroviario; **commercial** ~ tráfico *m* comercial; **passenger** ~ tráfico *m* de pasajeros; **to get stuck in** ~ quedarse atrapado en un atasco **2.**(*movement: of goods, passengers*) tránsito *m*; **drug** ~ tráfico *m* de drogas **3.** *form* (*dealings*) **to have** ~ **with sb** tener relaciones comerciales con alguien **II.** <trafficked, trafficked> *vi pej* **to** ~ **in sth** traficar con algo
traffic accident *n* accidente *m* de tráfico **traffic calming** *n* reducción *f* de tráfico **traffic circle** *n Am* rotonda *f* **traffic island** *n Brit* isleta *f* **traffic jam** *n* atasco *m*
trafficker ['træfɪkəʳ, *Am:* -ɚ] *n pej* traficante *mf*; **drug/arms** ~ traficante de drogas/de armas
traffic light *n* semáforo *m* **traffic regulation** *n* normas *fpl* de circulación **traffic sign** *n* señal *f* de tráfico **traffic warden** *n Brit* controlador(a) *m(f)* de estacionamientos
tragedy ['trædʒədi] <-ies> *n* tragedia *f*
tragic ['trædʒɪk] *adj* trágico, -a
tragicomedy [,trædʒɪ'kɒmədi, *Am:* -'kɑːmə-] <-ies> *n* tragicomedia *f*
trail [treɪl] **I.** *n* **1.**(*path*) camino *m* **2.**(*track*) pista *f*; (*of aeroplane*) estela *f*; **a** ~ **of destruction** una estela de destrucción; **to be on the** ~ **of sth/sb** seguir la pista de algo/alguien; **to be hot on the** ~ **of sb** estar muy cerca de encontrar a alguien; **to follow a** ~ (*in hunting*) seguir un rastro **II.** *vt* **1.**(*follow*) seguir la pista de; **to** ~ **an animal** seguir el rastro de un animal **2.**(*drag*) arrastrar **3.**(*be losing to*) **to** ~ **sb/sth** estar perdiendo a alguien/algo **III.** *vi* **1.**(*drag*) **to** ~ **(somewhere)** arrastrarse (a algún sitio) **2.** SPORTS ir perdiendo; **to** ~ **by 6 points** ir perdiendo por 6 puntos; **to** ~ **behind sth/sb** ir por detrás de algo/alguien
◆**trail along I.** *vi* arrastrarse **II.** *vt* arrastrar
◆**trail away** *vi* esfumarse
◆**trail behind** *vi* ir detrás
◆**trail off** *vi* esfumarse
trailblazer ['treɪl,bleɪzəʳ, *Am:* -zɚ] *n* pionero, -a *m, f*
trailer *n* **1.**(*wheeled container*) remolque *m* **2.** *Am* (*mobile home*) caravana *f* **3.**(*advertisement*) avance *m* publicitario; CINE tráiler *m*
trailer camp *n*, **trailer park** *n Am* cámping *m* de caravanas
train [treɪn] **I.** *n* **1.**(*railway*) tren *m*; **to travel by** ~ viajar en tren **2.**(*series*) serie *f*; ~ **of thought** hilo *m* del pensamiento; **to put sth in** ~ poner algo en movimiento **3.**(*retinue*) séquito *m* **4.**(*procession: of animals, things*) recua *f* **5.**(*of dress*) cola *f* **II.** *vi* entrenarse; **to** ~ **to be sth** prepararse para ser algo **III.** *vt* formar; (*animal*) amaestrar; **to** ~ **sb in the use of sth** adiestrar a alguien en el uso de algo; **to** ~ **sb for sth** entrenar a alguien para algo
train accident *n* accidente *m* ferroviario **train connection** *n* conexión *f* ferroviaria **train driver** *n* maquinista *mf*
trained ['treɪnd] *adj* **1.**(*educated*) formado,

-a; (*animal*) amaestrado, -a; **to be ~ in** sth estar formado en algo **2.** (*expert*) cualificado, -a

trainee [treɪˈniː] *n* aprendiz(a) *m(f)*

traineeship *n* aprendizaje *m*

trainee teacher *n* estudiante *mf* de magisterio

trainer *n* **1.** (*person*) entrenador(a) *m(f)* **2.** Brit (*shoe*) zapatilla *f* de deporte

training *n no pl* **1.** (*education*) formación *f;* ~ **on-the-job** formación *f* laboral **2.** SPORTS entrenamiento *m;* **to be in ~ for** sth estar entrenando para algo; **to be good ~ for** sth ser un buen entrenamiento para algo

training camp *n* SPORTS campamento *m* de instrucción **training college** *n* Brit escuela *f* normal **training course** *n* curso *m* de formación **training programme** *n* programa *m* de entrenamiento **training ship** *n* buque-escuela *m*

train schedule *n* horario *m* de trenes **train service** *n* servicio *m* de trenes

traipse [treɪps] *vi pej* andar sin ganas; **to ~ around the shops** patearse las tiendas

trait [treɪt] *n* rasgo *m*

traitor [ˈtreɪtər, Am: -t̬ɚ] *n* traidor(a) *m(f);* **to turn ~** volver la casaca

traitorous [ˈtreɪtərəs, Am: -t̬ɚ-] *adj pej, form* traicionero, -a

trajectory [trəˈdʒektəri, Am: -tɚi] *n* **1.** PHYS trayectoria *f* **2.** fig (*path*) camino *m;* **to be on a downward/an upward ~** ir descendiendo/ascendiendo

tram [træm] *n* Brit, Aus tranvía *m;* **to go by ~** viajar en tranvía

tramline [ˈtræmlaɪn] *n* **1.** (*track, route*) carril *m* del tranvía **2.** *pl* (*in tennis*) líneas *fpl* laterales

trammel [ˈtræml] *liter* **I.** *n pl* trabas *fpl* **II.** *vt* <-ll-> poner trabas a

tramp [træmp] **I.** *vi* **1.** (*walk heavily*) andar con pasos pesados **2.** (*go on foot*) ir a pie **II.** *vt* pisar con fuerza **III.** *n* **1.** *no pl* (*sound*) pisada *m* fuerte **2.** *no pl* (*walk*) caminata *f;* **to go for a ~** ir de caminata **3.** (*down-and-out*) vagabundo *m* **4.** Am, pej (*woman*) fulana *f*

trample [ˈtræmpl] **I.** *vt* pisar; **to ~ sb's foot** pisar el pie a alguien; **to be ~d to death** ser pisoteado hasta la muerte; **to ~ sth underfoot** pisotear algo **II.** *vi* **to ~ on** sth pisar algo

trampoline [ˈtræmpəliːn] *n* trampolín *m*

tramway [ˈtræmweɪ] *n* **1.** (*rails*) raíles *mpl* del tranvía **2.** (*system*) tranvía *m*

trance [trɑːns, Am: træns] *n* trance *m;* **to be in a ~** estar en trance

tranny [ˈtræni] *n* Brit, inf transistor *m*

tranquil [ˈtræŋkwɪl] *adj* tranquilo, -a

tranquility [træŋˈkwɪləti, Am: -ət̬i] *n* Am s. **tranquillity**

tranquilize [ˈtræŋkwɪlaɪz] *vt* Am s. **tranquillize**

tranquilizer *n* Am s. **tranquillizer**

tranquillity [træŋˈkwɪləti, Am: -t̬i] *n no pl* tranquilidad *f*

tranquillize [ˈtræŋkwɪlaɪz] *vt* MED tranquilizar

tranquillizer *n* tranquilizante *m;* **to be on ~s** estar tomando tranquilizantes

transact [trænˈzækt] *vt* tramitar; **to ~ a business** despachar un negocio

transaction [trænˈzækʃən] *n* COM transacción *f,* transa *f* RíoPl; **business ~** transacción *f* comercial

transalpine [trænˈzælpaɪn] *adj* transalpino, -a

transatlantic *adj,* **trans-Atlantic** [ˌtrænzətˈlæntɪk, Am: ˌtrænt͡sæt'-] *adj* transatlántico, -a

transceiver [trænˈsiːvər] *n* transmisor-receptor *m*

transcend [trænˈsend] *vt* **1.** (*go beyond*) trascender; **to ~ barriers/limitations** traspasar las barreras/los límites **2.** (*surpass*) exceder

transcendent [trænˈsendənt] *adj* trascendente; (*superior*) supremo, -a

transcendental [ˌtrænsenˈdentəl, Am: -t̬əl] *adj* trascendental

transcontinental [ˌtræns,kɒntɪˈnentəl, Am: ˌtrænt͡s,kɑːntənˈen-] *adj* transcontinental

transcribe [trænˈskraɪb] *vt* transcribir

transcript [ˈtræntskrɪpt] *n* transcripción *f*

transcription [trænˈskrɪpʃən] *n* transcripción *f*

transducer [trænzˈdjuːsər, Am: trænt͡sˈduːsɚ] *n* ELEC transductor *m*

transept [ˈtræntsept] *n* ARCHIT crucero *m*

transfer¹ [ˈtræntsfɜː, Am: -ˈfɜːr] **I.** <-rr-> *vt* **1.** (*move*) trasladar **2.** (*reassign: power*) transferir **3.** COM (*shop*) traspasar **4.** SPORTS (*sell*) traspasar **II.** <-rr-> *vi* **1.** (*move*) trasladarse **2.** (*change train, plane*) hacer transbordo

transfer² [ˈtræntsfɜː, Am: ˈtræntsfɜːr] *n* **1.** (*process of moving*) traslado *m;* ~ **of information** transmisión *f* de información **2.** (*reassignment*) transferencia *f* **3.** COM (*of a shop*) traspaso *m* **4.** SPORTS traspaso *m* **5.** Am (*ticket*) billete *m* de transbordo **6.** (*picture*) cromo *m*

transferable [træntsˈfɜːrəbl] *adj* transferible

transference [ˈtræntsfɜːrəns] *n no pl, form* a. PSYCH transferencia *f*

transfigure [træntsˈfɪgər, Am: træntsˈfɪgjɚ] *vt* transfigurar

transfix [træntsˈfɪks] *vt form* traspasar; **to be ~ed by** sb/sth estar totalmente paralizado por alguien/algo

transform [træntsˈfɔːm, Am: træntsˈfɔːrm] *vt* transformar

transformation [ˌtræntsfəˈmeɪʃən, Am: ˌtræntsfɚ'-] *n* transformación *f*

transformer *n* ELEC transformador *m*

transfuse [træntsˈfjuːz] *vt* MED hacer una transfusión de

transfusion [træntsˈfjuːʒən] *n* transfusión *f;* **blood ~** transfusión de sangre; **to give sb a ~** hacer a alguien una transfusión de sangre

transgress [trænzˈgres, Am: trænts-] *form*

I. *vt* transgredir; **to ~ a law** infringir una ley
II. *vi* cometer una transgresión

transgression [trænz'greʃən, *Am:* trænts-] *n form* transgresión *f*

transgressor *n* transgresor(a) *m(f)*; REL pecador(a) *m(f)*

transient ['trænziənt, *Am:* 'trænt∫ənt] *form* I. *adj* pasajero, -a II. *n* residente *mf* temporal

transistor [træn'zɪstə', *Am:* træn'zɪstɚ] *n* ELEC transistor *m*

transistorize [træn'zɪstəraɪz] *vt* transistorizar

transit ['træntsɪt] *n no pl* tránsito *m*; **in ~** de paso

transit business *n* negocio *m* de tránsito
transit camp *n Brit* campamento *m* provisional **transit desk** *n* AVIAT cabina *f* de tránsito

transition [træn'zɪʃən] *n* transición *f*

transitional [træn'zɪʃənəl] *adj* (*period*) transitorio, -a; (*government*) de transición

transitive ['træntsətɪv, *Am:* 'træntsəˌtɪv] *adj* LING transitivo, -a

transit lounge *n* sala *f* de tránsito

transitory ['træntsɪtəri, *Am:* 'træntsətɔ:ri] *adj* pasajero, -a

transit passenger *n* pasajero, -a *m, f* de tránsito **transit visa** *n* visado *m* de tránsito

translatable *adj* traducible

translate [trænz'leɪt, *Am:* træn'sleɪt] I. *vt* 1. LING traducir; **to ~ sth from English into Spanish** traducir algo del inglés al español 2. (*adapt*) adaptar; **to ~ a play for the cinema** adaptar una obra de teatro para el cine 3. (*transform*) **to ~ a plan into action** llevar a cabo un plan II. *vi* LING traducir; **to ~ from English into Spanish** traducir del inglés al español

translation [trænz'leɪʃən, *Am:* træn'sleɪ-] *n* traducción *f*

translator *n* traductor(a) *m(f)*

transliterate [trænz'lɪtəreɪt, *Am:* træn'slɪtəreɪt] *vt* transliterar

transliteration [ˌtrænzlɪtər'eɪʃən, *Am:* trænˌslɪtə'reɪ-] *n* LING *no pl* transliteración *f*

translucent [trænz'lu:sənt, *Am:* træn'slu:-] *adj*, **translucid** *adj* translúcido, -a

transmigration [ˌtrænzmaɪ'greɪʃən, *Am:* ˌtræntsmaɪ'-] *n* transmigración *f*

transmissible [trænz'mɪsəbl, *Am:* træn'smɪs-] *adj* transmisible

transmission [trænz'mɪʃən, *Am:* træn'smɪʃ-] *n* transmisión *f*; **data ~** INFOR transmisión de datos

transmission speed *n* INFOR velocidad *f* de transmisión (de datos)

transmit [trænz'mɪt, *Am:* træn'smɪt] <-tt-> *vt* transmitir

transmitter *n* 1. (*apparatus*) transmisor *m* 2. (*station*) emisora *f*

transmitting station *n* emisora *f*

transmogrify [trænz'mɒgrɪfaɪ, *Am:* træn'smɑːgrə-] *vt* transformar completa-

mente

transmutation [ˌtrænzmju:'teɪʃən, *Am:* ˌtrænts-] *n form* transmutación *f*

transmute [trænz'mju:t, *Am:* ˌtrænts-] *form* I. *vt* transmutar; **to ~ sth into sth** transmutar algo en algo II. *vi* **to ~ into sth** transmutarse en algo

transoceanic ['trænzˌəʊʃi'ænɪk, *Am:* ˌtræntsoʊʃi'-] *adj* transoceánico, -a

transom ['træntsəm] *n* 1. (*horizontal bar*) travesaño *m* 2. *Am* (*window*) montante *m*

transparency [træn'spærəntsi, *Am:* træn'sperənt-] *n* <-ies> transparencia *f*

transparent [trænt'spærənt, *Am:* træn'sperənt-] *adj* transparente

transpiration [ˌtræntspɪ'reɪʃən] *n no pl* transpiración *f*

transpire [træn'spaɪə', *Am:* træn'spaɪɚ] *vi* 1. (*happen*) tener lugar; **it ~d that ...** ocurrió que... 2. (*come to be known*) saberse 3. (*emit water vapour*) transpirar

transplant¹ [træn'splɑːnt, *Am:* træn'splænt] *vt* 1. MED, BOT trasplantar 2. (*relocate*) trasladar

transplant² ['træntsplɑːnt, *Am:* 'træntsplænt] *n* trasplante *m*

transplantation [ˌtræntsplɑː'nteɪʃən, *Am:* ˌtræntsplæn'-] *n no pl* trasplante *m*

transport¹ [træn'spɔːt, *Am:* træn'spɔːrt] *vt* 1. (*people, goods*) transportar 2. *Brit* HIST (*to penal colony*) deportar 3. *liter* (*fill with emotion*) arrebatar; **to be ~ed with joy/grief** estar lleno de alegría/pena

transport² ['træntspɔːt, *Am:* 'træntspɔːrt] *n* 1. *no pl* (*means of conveyance*) transporte *m*; **public ~** transporte *m* público; **~ costs** gastos *mpl* de transporte 2. (*plane*) avión *m* de transporte; (*ship*) buque *m* de transporte 3. *form* (*strong emotion*) arrebato *m*; **to be in ~s of joy** estar lleno de alegría

transportable *adj* transportable

transportation [ˌtræntspɔː'teɪʃən, *Am:* ˌtræntspɚ-] *n no pl* 1. (*of people, goods*) transporte *m* 2. (*of a convict*) deportación *f*

transport café <- -s> *n Brit* cafetería *f* de carretera

transporter [træn'spɔːtə', *Am:* træn'spɔːrtɚ] *n* transportador *m*

transpose [træn'spəʊz, *Am:* træn'spoʊz] *vt* 1. (*reverse position of*) transponer 2. (*change location*) trasladar 3. MUS, MATH transportar

transsexual [træn'sekʃʊəl, *Am:* træn'sekʃʊəl] I. *n* transexual *mf* II. *adj* transexual

transverse ['trænzvɜːs, *Am:* 'trænts-] *adj* transversal

transvestite [trænz'vestaɪt, *Am:* 'trænts-] *n* travestido *m*

trap [træp] I. *n* 1. (*device*) trampa *f*; **to set a ~** poner una trampa 2. (*dangerous situation*) encerrona *f*; (*ambush*) emboscada *f*; **to fall into a ~** caer en una emboscada 3. *Brit, inf* (*mouth*) boca *f*; **to shut one's ~** cerrar el pico; **to keep one's ~ shut** mantener la boca cerrada **4.**(*curve in pipe*) sifón *m* **5.** HIST (*carriage*) tartana *f* **6.**(*for clay pigeons*) lanzaplatos *m inv* **II.** *vt* <-pp-> atrapar; **to feel ~ped** sentirse encerrado

trapdoor [ˌtræp'dɔːʳ, *Am:* 'træpdɔːr] *n* escotillón *m*

trapeze [trə'piːz, *Am:* træp'iːz] *n* trapecio *m*

trapezium [trə'piːziəm] <-s *o* -zia> *pl n Brit, Aus,* **trapezoid** ['træpɪzɔɪd] *n Am* MAT trapecio *m*

trapper ['træpəʳ, *Am:* -ɚ] *n* trampero, -a *m, f;* **fur ~** cazador(a) *m(f)* de animales de piel

trappings ['træpɪŋz] *npl* arreos *mpl;* **the ~ of power** el boato del poder

Trappist ['træpɪst] **I.** *adj* trapense **II.** *n* trapense *m*

trap shooting *n no pl* tiro *m* al plato

trash [træʃ] **I.** *n no pl* **1.** *Am* (*rubbish*) basura *f;* **to take the ~ out** sacar la basura **2.** *inf* (*people*) gentuza *f;* (*book, film*) basura *f* **3.** *inf* (*nonsense*) tonterías *fpl;* **to talk ~** decir tonterías **II.** *vt inf* **1.**(*wreck*) destrozar **2.**(*criticize*) poner por los suelos

trashcan ['træʃkæn] *n Am* cubo *m* de la basura

trashy ['træʃi] *adj inf* malo, -a

trauma ['trɔːmə, *Am:* 'trɑːmə] *n* PSYCH, MED trauma *m*

traumatic [trɔː'mætɪk, *Am:* trɑː'mæt̬-] *adj* traumático, -a

traumatise *vt Aus, Brit,* **traumatize** ['trɔːmətaɪz] *vt* traumatizar; **to be ~d by sth** estar traumatizado por algo

travel ['trævəl] **I.** <*Brit:* -ll-, *Am:* -l-> *vi* **1.**(*make journey*) viajar; **to ~ by air/car/train** viajar en avión/coche/tren; **to ~ first--class** viajar en primera clase; **to ~ light** viajar con poco equipaje **2.**(*light, sound*) propagarse **3.**(*be away*) estar de viaje **4.** *inf* (*go fast*) ir rápido **II.** <*Brit:* -ll-, *Am:* -l-> *vt* viajar por; **to ~ a country/the world** viajar por un país/el mundo; **to ~ the length and breadth of a country** viajar a lo largo y ancho de un país **III.** *npl* viajes *mpl*

travel agency *n* agencia *f* de viajes **travel agent** *n* agente *mf* de viajes **travel bureau** *n* agencia *f* de viajes **travel card** *n* bono *m* de transporte **travel cot** *n* cama *f* plegable de viaje

traveled *adj Am s.* **travelled**

traveler ['trævləʳ, *Am:* -lɚ] *n Am s.* **traveller**

travel expenses *n* gastos *mpl* de viaje **travel guide** *n* (*person, book*) guía *f* turística

traveling *n no pl, Am s.* **travelling**

travel insurance *n* seguro *m* de viaje

travelled *adj Brit* que ha viajado

traveller ['trævələʳ, *Am:* -ələ-] *n Brit* viajero, -a *m, f;* **commercial ~** *Brit* viajante *mf* comercial

traveller's cheque *n Brit,* **traveler's check** *n Am* cheque *m* de viaje

travelling *n no pl, Brit* viajar *m*

travelling allowance *n* dietas *fpl* **travelling bag** *n* bolsa *f* de viaje **travelling circus** *n* circo *m* ambulante **travelling crane** *n* grúa *f* de corredera **travelling exhibition** *n* exposición *f* ambulante **travelling salesman** *n* viajante *mf* de comercio

travelog *n Am,* **travelogue** ['trævəlɒg, *Am:* -əlɑːg] *n Brit, Aus* TV documental *m* de interés turístico; CINE película *f* de viajes

travel-sick *adj* mareado, -a

travel sickness *n no pl* mareo *m*

traverse ['trævɜːs, *Am:* -ɚs] *vt* **1.**(*cross*) atravesar **2.**(*move along*) recorrer

travesty ['trævəsti, *Am:* -ɪsti] <-ies> *n pej* parodia *f*

trawl [trɔːl, *Am:* trɑːl] **I.** *vi* **1.**(*fish*) pescar al arrastre **2.**(*search*) **to ~ through sth** rastrear algo **II.** *vt* (*fish: sea*) hacer pesca al arrastre en **III.** *n* **1.**(*net*) red *f* barredera **2.**(*search*) rastreo *m*

trawler ['trɔːləʳ, *Am:* 'trɑːlɚ] *n* pesquero *m* de arrastre

tray [treɪ] *n* bandeja *f,* charola *f AmS*

treacherous ['tretʃərəs] *adj* **1.**(*disloyal*) traicionero, -a **2.**(*dangerous: road, weather*) peligroso, -a

treachery ['tretʃəri] *n no pl* traición *f*

treacle ['triːkl] *n no pl, Brit* melaza *f*

treacly ['triːkli] *adj* **1.**(*thick and sticky*) meloso, -a **2.**(*sentimental*) empalagoso, -a

tread [tred] **I.** <trod *Am:* treaded, trodden *Am:* trod> *vi* pisar; **to ~ on** [*o* **in**] **sth** pisar algo **II.** *vt* pisar; **to ~ one's weary way** andar a paso cansino **III.** *n* **1.**(*manner of walking*) paso *m;* **a heavy ~** un paso fuerte **2.**(*step*) escalón *m* **3.** AUTO dibujo *m*

treadle ['tredl] *n* pedal *m*

treadmill ['tredmɪl] *n* **1.**(*wheel, exercise machine*) rueda *f* de andar **2.** *fig* rutina *f*

treason ['triːzn] *n no pl* traición *f;* **high ~** *form* alta traición

treasonable ['triːzənəbl] *adj,* **treasonous** ['triːzənəs] *adj* traidor(a)

treasure ['treʒəʳ, *Am:* -ɚ] **I.** *n* **1.** *no pl* (*precious items*) tesoro *m* **2.**(*highly valued thing, person*) joya *f;* **my assistant is a ~** mi ayudante es una joya **II.** *vt* atesorar; **to ~ the memories of sb** guardar los recuerdos de alguien como un tesoro

treasure house *n* sala *f* del tesoro **treasure hunt** *n* caza *f* del tesoro

treasurer ['treʒərəʳ, *Am:* -ɚ] *n* tesorero, -a *m, f*

treasure trove *n* tesoro *m* hallado

treasury ['treʒəri] <-ies> *n* tesorería *f;* **the Treasury** Hacienda *f*

treasury bill *n Am* letra *f* del Tesoro **treasury bond** *n Am* bono *m* del Tesoro **treasury note** *n Am* pagaré *m* del Tesoro **Treasury Secretary** *n Am* ≈ Ministro, -a *m, f* de Hacienda

treat ['tri:t] I. *vt* 1. (*deal with, handle*) *a.* MED tratar; **to ~ sb/sth badly** tratar mal a alguien/ algo; **to ~ sb/sth as if ...** tratar a alguien/algo como si +*subj* 2. (*process*) tratar; **to ~ a substance with acid** tratar una sustancia con ácido 3. (*discuss*) tratar 4. (*pay for*) invitar; **to ~ sb to an ice cream** invitar a alguien a un helado II. *vi* **to ~ with sb** negociar con alguien III. *n* 1. (*pleasurable event*) convite *m*; (*present*) regalo *m*; **it's my ~** invito yo 2. (*pleasure*) placer *m*; **it was a real ~** ha sido un auténtico placer ▶ **to ~ work a ~** *Brit, inf* funcionar muy bien

treatise ['tri:tɪz, *Am:* - țɪs] *n* tratado *m*

treatment ['tri:tmənt] *n* 1. *no pl* trato *m*; **to get rough ~ from sb** recibir un mal trato de alguien; **to give sb the ~** *inf* hacer sufrir a alguien; **special ~** tratamiento *m* especial 2. MED tratamiento *m*; **to respond to ~** responder al tratamiento

treaty ['tri:ti, *Am:* -ți] <-ies> *n* tratado *m*; **peace ~** tratado de paz

treble ['trebl] I. *adj* 1. (*three times greater*) triple 2. MUS de tiple II. *n* MUS tiple *mf* III. *vt* triplicar IV. *vi* triplicarse

treble clef *n* clave *f* de sol

tree [tri:] I. *n* árbol *m*; **to climb a ~** trepar a un árbol; **the Tree of Knowledge** el árbol de la ciencia ▶ **you can't see the** forest *Brit, Aus* [*o* wood *Am*] **for the ~s** los árboles no te dejan ver el bosque; **to bark up the** wrong ~ *inf* tomar el rábano por las hojas; **to** grow on **~s** caer del cielo; **money doesn't grow on ~s** el dinero no cae del cielo; **that doesn't grow on ~s** eso no se encuentra a la vuelta de la esquina II. *vt* (*animal*) hacer refugiarse en un árbol

tree frog *n* rana *f* de San Antonio **tree house** *n* cabaña *f* en un árbol **treeless** *adj* sin árboles **treeline** *n* límite *m* forestal

tree-lined ['tri:laɪnd] *adj* arbolado, -a; **a ~ street** una calle bordeada de árboles

tree surgeon *n* arboricultor(a) *m(f)* **treetop** *n* copa *f* del árbol; **in the ~s** en lo alto de los árboles **tree trunk** *n* tronco *m* del árbol

trefoil ['trefɔɪl, *Am:* 'tri:fɔɪl] *n* trébol *m*

trek [trek] I. <-kk-> *vi* caminar II. *n* 1. (*walk*) caminata *f* (larga) 2. (*migration*) migración *f* **trekking** ['trekɪŋ] *n* trekking *m;* **to go ~** hacer senderismo

trellis ['trelɪs] <-es> *n* espaldera *f;* (*for plants*) enrejado *m*

tremble ['trembl] I. *vi* temblar; **to ~ with cold** tiritar de frío; **to ~ like a leaf** temblar como un azogado II. *n* temblor *m;* **to be all of a ~** *Brit, inf* estar como un flan

tremendous [trɪ'mendəs] *adj* 1. (*enormous*) enorme; (*crowd, scope*) inmenso, -a; (*help*) grande; (*success*) contundente 2. *inf* (*extremely good*) estupendo, -a

tremolo ['tremələʊ, *Am:* -əloʊ] *n* MUS trémolo *m*

tremor ['tremə^r, *Am:* -ɚ] *n* 1. (*shake*) vibra-

ción *f;* (*earthquake*) temblor *m* 2. (*of fear, excitement*) estremecimiento *m*

tremulous ['tremjʊləs] *adj* trémulo, -a

trench [trentʃ] <-es> *n* zanja *f;* MIL trinchera *f*

trenchant ['trentʃənt] *adj* mordaz

trench coat *n* trinchera *f* **trench warfare** *n* guerra *f* de trincheras

trend [trend] I. *n* 1. (*tendency*) tendencia *f;* **downward/upward ~** tendencia *f* a la baja/ alcista; **a ~ toward(s) ...** una tendencia hacia... 2. (*fashion*) moda *f;* **the latest ~** las últimas tendencias; **to set a new ~** fijar una nueva moda II. *vi* tender; **to ~ to sth** tender a algo

trendsetter ['trend,setə^r, *Am:* -,setɚ] *n* persona *f* que inicia una moda

trendy ['trendi] I. <-ier, -iest> *adj* (*clothes, bar*) de moda; (*person*) moderno, -a II. <-ies> *n* persona *f* de tendencias ultramodernas

trepidation [,trepɪ'deɪʃən] *n no pl* ansiedad *f;* **to do sth with ~** hacer algo inquietante

trespass ['trespəs] *vi* 1. LAW entrar ilegalmente 2. REL pecar

trespasser ['trespəsə^r, *Am:* -pæsɚ] *n* intruso, -a *m, f*

trestle ['tresl] *n* caballete *m*

trestle table *n* mesa *f* de caballete

triad ['traɪæd] *n* tríada *f*

trial ['traɪəl] *n* 1. LAW proceso *m;* **~ by jury** juicio *m* con jurado; **to stand ~** ser procesado; **to be on ~ for one's life** ser acusado de un crimen capital 2. (*test*) prueba *f;* **clinical ~s** ensayos *mpl* clínicos; **~ of strength** prueba de fuerza; **to give sb a ~** poner a alguien a prueba; **to have sth on ~** tener algo a prueba 3. (*source of problems*) suplicio *m;* **~s and tribulations** tribulaciones *fpl* 4. (*competition*) competición *f*

trial flight *n* vuelo *m* de prueba **trial period** *n* período *m* de prueba **trial separation** *n* separación *f* de prueba

triangle ['traɪæŋgl] *n* triángulo *m*

triangular [traɪ'æŋgjʊlə^r, *Am:* -lɚ] *adj* triangular

tribal ['traɪbl] *adj* tribal

tribalism ['traɪblɪzəm] *n no pl* tribalismo *m*

tribe [traɪb] *n* tribu *f;* **the twelve ~s of Israel** HIST las doce tribus de Israel

tribesman ['traɪbzmən] <-men> *n* miembro *m* de una tribu

tribulation [,trɪbjʊ'leɪʃən, *Am:* -jə'-] *n form* tribulación *f*

tribunal [traɪ'bju:nl] *n* tribunal *m;* (*investigative body*) comisión *f* de investigación

tribune[1] ['trɪbju:n] *n* HIST tribuno *m*

tribune[2] ['trɪbju:n] *n* ARCHIT tribuna *f*

tributary ['trɪbjətəri, *Am:* -teri] I. <-ies> *n* 1. (*river*) afluente *m* 2. HIST (*person*) contribuyente *mf;* (*state*) estado *m* tributario II. *adj form* 1. (*river*) afluente 2. HIST (*state*) tributario, -a

tribute ['trɪbju:t] *n* 1. (*token of respect*)

homenaje *m;* **to pay ~ to sb/sth** rendir tributo a alguien/algo; **floral ~** *form* ofrenda *f* floral **2.** (*sign of sth positive*) elogio *m;* **to be a ~ to sth/sb** hacer honor a algo/alguien **3.** HIST (*money paid to a superior power*) tributo *m*

trice [traɪs] *n inf* **in a ~** en un santiamén

trick [trɪk] I. *n* **1.** (*ruse*) truco *m,* trampa *f;* **a dirty ~** *inf* una mala pasada; **to play a ~ on sb** tender una trampa a alguien; **to be up to one's (old) ~s again** volver a hacer de las suyas **2.** (*of magician*) truco *m* **3.** (*technique*) truquillo *m* **4.** (*illusion*) ilusión *f;* **a ~ of the light** una ilusión óptica; **his eyes are playing ~s on him** ve visiones **5.** GAME mano *f;* **to take all the ~s** ganar todas las bazas ▶ **to try every ~ in the book** intentar todos los trucos habidos y por haber; **the ~s of the trade** los trucos del oficio; **that'll do the ~** con eso solucionamos el tema; **to not miss a ~** no perder ripio II. *adj* **1.** (*deceptive*) **a ~ question** una pregunta con trampa **2.** *Am, inf* (*weak*) débil III. *vt* (*deceive*) engañar; (*fool*) burlar; (*swindle*) timar

trickery ['trɪkəri] *n no pl* artimañas *fpl;* **to resort to ~** recurrir a engaños

trickle ['trɪkl] I. *vi* **1.** (*flow slowly*) salir en un chorro fino; (*in drops*) gotear **2.** *fig* (*people*) **to ~ in/out** entrar/salir poco a poco; **to ~ out** (*information*) difundirse poco a poco II. *n* **1.** (*of liquid*) hilo *m;* (*drops*) goteo *m* **2.** (*of people, information*) goteo *m*

♦ **trickle away** *vi* consumirse poco a poco

trickster ['trɪkstə', *Am:* -stə'] *n pej* estafador(a) *m(f),* trácala *f Méx*

tricksy ['trɪksi] *adj* (*playful*) juguetón, -ona

tricky ['trɪki] <-ier, -iest> *adj* **1.** (*crafty*) astuto, -a **2.** (*difficult*) complicado, -a; (*situation*) delicado, -a; **to be ~ to do** ser difícil de hacer

tricycle ['traɪsɪkl] *n* triciclo *m*

trident ['traɪdnt] *n* tridente *m*

tried [traɪd] I. *vi, vt pt, pp of* **try** II. *adj* probado, -a; **~ and tested** probado con toda garantía

triennial [traɪ'enɪəl] *adj* trienal

trier ['traɪə', *Am:* -ə'] *n inf* persona *f* que se esfuerza mucho

trifle ['traɪfəl] *n* **1.** (*insignificant thing*) bagatela *f* **2.** (*small amount*) insignificancia *f;* **a ~** un poquito **3.** *Brit* (*dessert*) dulce *m* de bizcocho borracho

♦ **trifle away** *vt* malgastar; **to trifle one's time away** perder el tiempo

♦ **trifle with** *vt* jugar con; **to ~ sb's affections** jugar con los sentimientos de alguien

trifling *adj* insignificante

trig. *abbr of* **trigonometry** trigonometría *f*

trigger ['trɪgə', *Am:* -ə'] I. *n* **1.** (*of gun*) gatillo *m;* **to pull the ~** apretar el gatillo; **mechanism** mecanismo *m* disparador **2.** *fig* detonante *m* II. *vt* **1.** (*reaction*) provocar; (*revolt*) hacer estallar **2.** (*start*) accionar; **to ~ an alarm** disparar una alarma

trigger-happy ['trɪgə,hæpi, *Am:* -ə,-] *adj* de gatillo fácil

trigonometry [,trɪgə'nɒmətri, *Am:* -'nɑ:mə-] *n no pl* MAT trigonometría *f*

trike [traɪk] *n inf abbr of* **tricycle** triciclo *m*

trilateral [,traɪ'lætərəl, *Am:* traɪ'læt̮ə-] *adj* **1.** (*involving three parties*) trilateral **2.** MAT trilátero, -a

trilby ['trɪlbi] <-ies> *n Brit* sombrero *m* de fieltro

trilingual [,traɪ'lɪŋgwəl] *adj* trilingüe

trill [trɪl] I. *n* **1.** (*birdsong*) trino *m* **2.** (*quavering note*) quiebro *m* II. *vi* **1.** (*bird*) trinar **2.** (*speak*) hablar de forma afectada III. *vt* **to ~ one's r's** pronunciar la r con vibración

trillion ['trɪlɪən, *Am:* -jən] *n* billón *m*

trilogy ['trɪlədʒi] <-ies> *n* trilogía *f*

trim [trɪm] I. *n* **1.** (*state*) (buen) estado *m;* **to be in ~ (for sth)** estar listo (para algo); **to be in fighting ~** estar listo para entrar en combate **2.** (*hair*) **to give sb a ~** cortar las puntas del pelo a alguien; **to give sth a ~** dar un recorte a algo **3.** *no pl* (*decorative edge*) borde *m* II. *adj* **1.** (*attractively thin, compact*) en buen estado **2.** (*neat*) aseado, -a; (*lawn*) cuidado, -a III. <-mm-> *vt* **1.** (*cut*) cortar; **to ~ one's beard** cortarse la barba **2.** (*reduce*) reducir

♦ **trim down** *vt* recortar

♦ **trim off** *vt* cortar

trimming *n* **1.** (*decoration*) adorno *m* **2.** *pl* GASTR guarnición *f*

Trinidad ['trɪnɪdæd] *n* Trinidad *f;* **~ and Tobago** Trinidad y Tobago

Trinidadian ['trɪnɪdædiən] I. *adj* de Trinidad II. *n* habitante *mf* de Trinidad

Trinity ['trɪnəti, *Am:* -t̮i] *n no pl* Trinidad *f;* **the (holy) ~** la (Santísima) Trinidad

trinket ['trɪŋkɪt] *n* baratija *f*

trio ['tri:əʊ, *Am:* -oʊ] *n a.* MUS trío *m;* **string ~** trío *m* de cuerda

trip [trɪp] I. *n* **1.** (*journey*) viaje *m;* (*shorter*) excursión *f;* **business ~** viaje de negocios; **to go on a ~** irse de viaje **2.** *inf* (*effect of drugs*) viaje *m* **3.** (*fall*) tropezón *m* II. <-pp-> *vi* **1.** (*stumble*) tropezar; **to ~ on sth** tropezar con algo **2.** (*move lightly*) andar con paso ligero III. <-pp-> *vt* **1.** (*cause to stumble*) **to ~ sb (up)** hacer tropezar a alguien **2.** (*switch on*) encender

♦ **trip over** *vi* dar un tropezón

♦ **trip up** I. *vi* **1.** (*stumble*) tropezar **2.** (*verbally*) equivocarse II. *vt* **1.** (*cause to stumble*) hacer tropezar **2.** (*cause to fail*) confundir

tripartite [,traɪ'pɑːtaɪt, *Am:* -'pɑːr-] *adj* tripartito, -a

tripe [traɪp] *n no pl* **1.** GASTR callos *mpl,* guata *f Méx* **2.** *pej, inf* (*nonsense, rubbish*) tonterías *fpl;* **to talk ~** decir bobadas

triple ['trɪpl] I. *adj* triple II. *vt* triplicar III. *vi* triplicarse

triple jump *n* triple salto *m*

triplet ['trɪplɪt] *n* **1.** (*baby*) trillizo, -a *m, f;* **to have ~s** tener trillizos **2.** MUS tresillo *m*

triplicate ['trɪplɪkət, _Am:_ -kɪt] _adj_ triplicado, -a; **in** ~ por triplicado

tripod ['traɪpɒd, _Am:_ -pɑ:d] _n_ trípode _m_

tripper ['trɪpə', _Am:_ -ɚ] _n Brit, inf_ excursionista _mf_

tripping ['trɪpɪŋ] _adj_ ligero, -a

triptych ['trɪptɪk] _n_ (_art_) tríptico _m_

trisect [traɪ'sekt] _vt_ trisecar

trite [traɪt] _adj_ tópico, -a

triumph ['traɪʌmf] I. _n_ 1. (_success_) triunfo _m;_ **a** ~ **over sb** un triunfo sobre alguien; **to do sth in** ~ hacer algo triunfalmente; **to hail sth as a** ~ clamar algo como un triunfo 2. (_supreme example_) éxito _m;_ **a** ~ **of engineering/medicine** un éxito de la ingeniería/medicina II. _vi_ 1. (_achieve success_) triunfar; **to** ~ **over sth/sb** triunfar sobre algo/alguien 2. (_exult excessively_) mostrarse triunfante

triumphal [traɪ'ʌmfəl] _adj_ triunfal

triumphant [traɪ'ʌmfnt] _adj_ 1. (_victorious_) triunfante; (_return_) triunfal; **to emerge** ~ **from sth** salir triunfante de algo 2. (_successful_) exitoso, -a

trivia ['trɪvɪə] _npl_ trivialidades _fpl_

trivial ['trɪvɪəl] _adj_ 1. (_unimportant_) irrelevante; (_dispute, matter_) trivial 2. (_insignificant_) insignificante

triviality [ˌtrɪvi'æləti, _Am:_ -t̬i] _n_ <-ies> 1. _no pl_ (_unimportance_) trivialidad _f_ 2. (_unimportant thing_) nimiedad _f_

trivialize ['trɪvɪəlaɪz] _vt_ trivializar

trod [trɒd, _Am:_ trɑ:d] _pt, pp of_ **tread**

trodden ['trɒdn, _Am:_ 'trɑ:dn] _pp of_ **tread**

troglodyte ['trɒɡlədaɪt, _Am:_ 'trɑ:ɡlə-] _n_ troglodita _mf_

Trojan ['trəʊdʒən, _Am:_ 'troʊ-] I. _n_ troyano, -a _m, f_ ▶to **work** like a ~ trabajar como un esclavo II. _adj_ troyano, -a; ~ **Horse** caballo _m_ de Troya; **the** ~ **War** la Guerra de Troya

trolley ['trɒli, _Am:_ 'trɑ:li] _n_ 1. _Brit, Aus_ (_small cart_) carretilla _f;_ **drinks** ~ carrito _m_ de bebidas; **luggage** ~ carrito _m_ para el equipaje; **shopping** ~ carrito _m_ de la compra 2. _Am_ (_trolleycar_) tranvía _m_ ▶to be **off** one's ~ estar chiflado

trolleybus ['trɒlibʌs, _Am:_ 'trɑ:li-] _n_ trolebús _m_ **trolleycar** _n Am_ tranvía _m_

trollop ['trɒləp, _Am:_ 'trɑ:ləp] _n pej, inf_ marrana _f,_ tusa _f Cuba_

trombone [trɒm'bəʊn, _Am:_ trɑ:m'boʊn] _n_ trombón _m_

trombonist [trɒm'bəʊnɪst, _Am:_ trɑ:m-'boʊ-] _n_ trombón _mf_

troop [tru:p] I. _n_ 1. _pl_ MIL tropas _fpl;_ **cavalry** ~ escuadrón _m_ de caballería 2. (_of people_) grupo _m_ II. _vi_ **to** ~ **in/out** entrar/salir en tropel III. _vt_ **to** ~ **the colour** _Brit_ presentar la bandera

troop carrier _n_ avión _m_ de transporte de tropas

trooper ['tru:pə', _Am:_ -ɚ] _n_ 1. MIL soldado _m_ de caballería 2. _Am_ (_state police officer_) policía _mf;_ **state** ~ policía _f_ estatal ▶to **swear** like

a ~ soltar tacos como un carretero

trophy ['trəʊfi, _Am:_ 'troʊ-] _n_ <-ies> trofeo _m_

tropic ['trɒpɪk, _Am:_ 'trɑ:pɪk] _n_ (_latitude_) trópico _m;_ **the** ~**s** los trópicos; **Tropic of Cancer/Capricorn** Trópico de Cáncer/Capricornio

tropical ['trɒpɪkl, _Am:_ 'trɑ:pɪk-] _adj_ tropical

troposphere ['trəʊpəsfɪə'] _n no pl_ troposfera _f_

trot [trɒt, _Am:_ trɑ:t] I. _n_ 1. (_of horse_) trote _m_ 2. _pl, inf_ (_diarrhoea_) **to have the** ~**s** tener diarrea, tener obradera _Col, Guat, Pan_ ▶**on the** ~ seguidos II. _vi_ 1. (_horse_) trotar; (_person_) andar trotando 2. (_run at moderate pace_) ir al trote 3. (_go busily_) ir apresurado III. <-tt-> _vt_ (_horse_) hacer trotar

◆**trot along** _vi,_ **trot off** _vi_ marcharse

◆**trot out** _vt_ (_excuse, explanation_) soltar; **to** ~ **arguments** sacar a relucir argumentos

trotter ['trɒtə', _Am:_ 'trɑ:t̬ɚ] _n_ manita _f_ de cerdo

trouble ['trʌbl] I. _n_ 1. (_difficulty_) dificultad _f,_ problema _m;_ **to have** ~ tener dificultades; **to ask for** ~ buscarse problemas; **to spell** ~ _inf_ suponer problemas; **to store up** ~ ir haciendo algo que traerá problemas; **to be in/get into** ~ estar/meterse en un lío; **to be in serious** ~ estar metido en serios problemas; **to be in** ~ **with sb** tener problemas con alguien; **to land sb in** ~ meter en un lío a alguien; **to stay out of** ~ mantenerse al margen de los problemas 2. _pl_ (_series of difficulties_) problemas _mpl;_ **to be the least of sb's** ~**s** ser el menor de los males de alguien 3. _no pl_ (_inconvenience_) molestia _f;_ **to go to the** ~ (_of doing sth_) darse la molestia (de hacer algo); **to go to a lot of** ~ **for sb** tomarse muchas molestias por alguien; **to put sb to the** ~ **of doing sth** molestar a alguien pidiéndole que haga algo; **to be (not) worth the** ~ (_of doing sth_) (no) merecer la pena (hacer algo) 4. _no pl_ (_physical ailment_) enfermedad _f;_ **stomach** ~ dolor _m_ de estómago 5. _no pl_ (_malfunction_) avería _f;_ **engine** ~ avería del motor 6. (_strife_) conflictos _mpl;_ **to stir up** ~ crear conflictos II. _vt_ 1. _form_ (_cause inconvenience_) molestar; **to** ~ **sb for sth** molestar a alguien por algo; **to** ~ **sb to do sth** molestar a alguien para que haga algo 2. (_make an effort_) **to** ~ **oneself about sth** esforzarse en algo 3. (_cause worry_) preocupar; (_cause pain_) afligir; **to be** ~**d by sth** verse en problemas por algo III. _vi_ esforzarse; **to** ~ **to do sth** molestarse en hacer algo

troubled _adj_ 1. (_period_) turbulento, -a; (_water_) revuelto, -a 2. (_worried_) preocupado, -a; (_look_) de preocupación

trouble-free [ˌtrʌbl'fri:] _adj_ sin problemas

troublemaker ['trʌblˌmeɪkə', _Am:_ -kɚ] _n_ alborotador(a) _m(f)_

troubleshooting ['trʌblˌʃu:tɪŋ] _n_ localización _f_ de problemas

troublesome ['trʌblsəm] _adj_ molesto, -a

trouble spot _n_ centro _m_ de fricción

trough [trɒf, _Am:_ trɑːf] _n_ **1.** (_receptacle_) abrevadero _m;_ **feeding** ~ comedero _m;_ **to feed at the public** ~ _fig_ malversar los fondos públicos **2.** (_low point_) punto _m_ bajo **3.** METEO zona _f_ de bajas presiones

troupe [truːp] _n_ THEAT compañía _f_

trouper ['truːpəʳ, _Am:_ -pɚ] _n_ artista _mf_ veterano, -a

trouser clip _n_ pinza _f_ (para ir en bicicleta)

trouser leg _n_ pernera _f_

trousers ['traʊzəz, _Am:_ -zɚz] _n pl_ pantalones _mpl;_ **a pair of** ~ un pantalón ►**to wear the** ~ llevar los pantalones

trouser suit _n Brit_ traje-pantalón _m_

trousseau ['truːsəʊ, _Am:_ -soʊ] _n_ ajuar _m_

trout [traʊt] _n_ <-(s)> **1.** (_fish_) trucha _f_ **2.** _Brit, inf_ (_woman_) bruja _f_

trout farm _n_ criadero _m_ de truchas

trowel ['traʊəl] _n_ (_for building_) llana _f;_ (_for gardening_) desplantador _m_

Troy [trɔɪ] _n no pl_ HIST Troya _f_

troy ounce _n_ onza _f_ troy

truancy ['truːənsi] _n no pl_ falta _f_ a clase

truant ['truːənt] I. _n_ persona _f_ que hace novillos; **to play** ~ _Brit, Aus_ hacer novillos II. _vi Brit, Aus_ hacer novillos

truce [truːs] _n_ tregua _f;_ **to call a** ~ acordar una tregua

truck[1] [trʌk] I. _n_ **1.** (_lorry_) camión _m;_ **pickup** ~ camioneta _f_ de plataforma **2.** _Brit_ (_train_) vagón _m_ de mercancías II. _vt Am_ transportar

truck[2] [trʌk] _n no pl, inf_ (_dealings_) trato _m;_ **to have no** ~ **with sb/sth** no tratar con alguien/algo

truck driver _n_ camionero, -a _m, f_

trucker _n_ camionero, -a _m, f_

truck farming _n no pl, Am, Can_ horticultura _f_

trucking _n no pl_ transporte _m_ por carretera

trucking company _n_ empresa _f_ transportista

truculence ['trʌkjʊləns] _n no pl_ agresividad _f;_ (_rebelliousness_) rebeldía _f_

truculent ['trʌkjʊlənt] _adj_ agresivo, -a; (_rebellious_) rebelde

trudge [trʌdʒ] I. _vi_ caminar penosamente II. _vt_ recorrer penosamente III. _n_ caminata _f_ penosa

true [truː] I. _adj_ **1.** (_not false_) cierto, -a; **to be** ~ ser verdad [_o_ cierto]; **to be** ~ **that ...** ser cierto que...; **to hold sth to be** ~ creer que algo es verdad; **to ring** ~ sonar convincente **2.** (_genuine, real_) auténtico, -a; ~ **love** amor _m_ verdadero; **the** ~ **faith** la fe verdadera; **sb's** ~ **self** la verdadera personalidad de alguien; **to come** ~ hacerse realidad; **in the** ~ **sense of the word** en el sentido real de la palabra **3.** (_faithful, loyal_) fiel; **to be/remain** ~ **to sth/sb** ser/mantenerse fiel a algo/alguien; **to be** ~ **to one's word** mantener su palabra; **to be** ~ **to oneself** ser fiel a sí mismo **4.** (_accurate_) exacto, -a II. _adv_ **1.** (_truly_) verdadera-

mente **2.** (_accurately_) de forma precisa; **to aim** ~ apuntar bien III. _n_ **to be out of** ~ no estar a nivel

♦**true up** _vt_ corregir

true-blue [ˌtruːˈbluː] _adj Brit, inf_ leal

trueborn ['truːbɔːn, _Am:_ -bɔːrn] _adj form_ legítimo, -a

true-hearted [ˌtruːˈhɑːtɪd, _Am:_ 'truːˌhɑːrt̬ɪd] _adj form_ fiel

true-life [ˌtruːˈlaɪf] _adj_ verdadero, -a

truelove ['truːlʌv] _n liter_ fiel amante _mf_

truffle ['trʌfl] _n_ trufa _f_

truism ['truːɪzəm] _n_ (_obviously true_) perogrullada _f;_ (_cliché_) tópico _m_

truly ['truːli] _adv_ **1.** (_accurately_) verdaderamente **2.** (_sincerely_) sinceramente **3.** (_as intensifier_) realmente ►**yours** ~ (_at end of letter_) un saludo; (_the speaker_) su seguro servidor _form_

trump [trʌmp] I. _n_ (_in cards_) triunfo _m;_ **what's** ~**s?** ¿qué triunfa? ►**to turn up** ~**s** _Brit_ salvar la situación II. _vt_ **1.** (_in cards_) fallar **2.** (_surpass_) superar

♦**trump up** _vt_ falsificar; **to** ~ **an accusation** inventar una acusación

trumpet ['trʌmpɪt, _Am:_ -pət] I. _n_ trompeta _f_ ►**to blow** one's own ~ _inf_ tirarse flores II. _vi_ (_elephant_) barritar III. _vt_ (_news, success_) proclamar

trumpeter ['trʌmpɪtəʳ, _Am:_ -pət̬ɚ] _n_ trompetista _mf_

truncate [trʌŋˈkeɪt] _vt_ truncar

truncheon ['trʌntʃən] _n Brit, Aus_ porra _f,_ macana _f AmL_

trundle ['trʌndl] I. _vi_ rodar II. _vt_ hacer rodar

trunk [trʌŋk] _n_ **1.** ANAT, BOT tronco _m_ **2.** (_of elephant_) trompa _f_ **3.** (_for storage_) baúl _m_ **4.** _Am_ (_of car_) maletero _f,_ baúl _m AmL_ **5.** _pl_ bañador _m;_ **a pair of swimming** ~**s** un traje de baño

trunk call _n Brit_ conferencia _f_ **trunk road** _n Brit_ carretera _f_ nacional

truss [trʌs] I. _n_ **1.** (_bundle_) lío _m;_ (_of hay_) haz _m_ **2.** MED braguero _m_ II. _vt_ atar

♦**truss up** _vt_ atar

trust [trʌst] I. _n_ **1.** _no pl_ (_belief_) confianza _f;_ **to gain sb's** ~ ganarse la confianza de alguien; **to place one's** ~ **in sb/sth** depositar su confianza en alguien/algo; **to take sth on** ~ aceptar algo con los ojos cerrados; **to betray sb's** ~ traicionar la confianza de alguien **2.** _no pl_ (_responsibility_) responsabilidad _f;_ **a position of** ~ un puesto de responsabilidad **3.** FIN, COM consorcio _m;_ **investment** ~ grupo _m_ de inversión **4.** LAW **to hold sth in** ~ tener algo en fideicomiso **5.** (_association_) asociación _f;_ **brains** ~ _Brit,_ **brain** ~ _Am_ grupo _m_ de peritos II. _vt_ **1.** (_place trust in_) confiar en; **to** ~ **sb to do sth** confiar a alguien el hacer algo **2.** (_rely on_) dar responsabilidad a; **to** ~ **sb with sth** confiar la responsabilidad de algo a alguien **3.** (_hope_) **to** ~ **that ...** esperar que +_subj_ III. _vi_ confiar; **to** ~ **in sth/sb** confiar en algo/alguien

trusted ['trʌstɪd] *adj* (*friend, servant*) leal; (*method, remedy*) comprobado, -a

trustee [trʌs'tiː] *n* fideicomisario, -a *m, f*; **board of ~s** consejo *m* de administración

trustful ['trʌstfəl] *adj* confiado, -a

trust fund *n* FIN fondo *m* de fideicomiso

trusting *adj* confiado, -a

trustworthiness ['trʌst͵wɜːðɪnɪs, *Am:* -͵wɜːr-] *n no pl* (*of person*) honradez *f*; (*of data*) fiabilidad *f*

trustworthy ['trʌst͵wɜːði, *Am:* -͵wɜːr-] *adj* (*person*) honrado, -a; (*data*) fiable

trusty ['trʌsti] <-ier, -iest> *adj* leal

truth [truːθ] *n* verdad *f*; **a grain of ~** una pizca de verdad; **in ~** en realidad; **the ~ about sth/sb** la verdad sobre algo/alguien; **to tell the ~** a decir verdad

truthful ['truːθfəl] *adj* **1.** (*true*) veraz; (*sincere*) sincero, -a; **to be ~ with sb** ser sincero con alguien **2.** (*accurate*) preciso, -a

truthfulness *n no pl* **1.** (*veracity*) veracidad *f*; (*sincerity*) sinceridad *f* **2.** (*accuracy*) exactitud *f*

try [traɪ] I. *n* **1.** (*attempt*) intento *m*; **to give sth a ~** intentar algo **2.** (*in rugby*) ensayo *m* II. <-ie-> *vi* esforzarse; **to ~ and do sth** *inf* intentar hacer algo III. <-ie-> *vt* **1.** (*attempt*) intentar; **to ~ one's best** esforzarse al máximo; **to ~ one's luck** probar suerte **2.** (*test*) experimentar **3.** (*sample*) probar **4.** (*annoy*) cansar; **his demands would ~ the patience of a saint** sus peticiones acabarían con la paciencia de un santo **5.** LAW juzgar

◆**try for** *vt insep, Brit, Aus* tratar de obtener

◆**try on** *vt* **1.** (*put on*) probar; **to try sth on for size** probar algo para ver la talla **2.** *Brit, Aus, inf* **to try it on** ver hasta dónde se puede llegar; **don't try it on with me** no trates de embaucarme

◆**try out** *vt* probar; **to try sth out on sb** dar a probar algo a alguien

trying *adj* (*exasperating*) molesto, -a; (*difficult*) difícil

try-out ['traɪaʊt] *n* prueba *f*

tsar [zɑːr, *Am:* zɑːr] *n* zar *m*

tsarina [zɑːˈriːnə] *n* zarina *f*

tsarist ['zɑːrɪst] I. *adj* zarista II. *n* zarista *mf*

tsetse fly ['tetsiˌflaɪ, *Am:* 'tsetsiˌflaɪ] *n* mosca *f* tsetsé

T-shirt ['tiːʃɜːt, *Am:* -ʃɜːrt] *n* camiseta *f*, playera *f Guat, Méx*, polera *f Chile*

tsp *abbr of* **teaspoon** (*amount*) cucharadita *f*

T-square ['tiːskweər, *Am:* -skwer] *n* TECH escuadra *f* en forma de T

tub [tʌb] *n* **1.** (*container*) cubo *m* **2.** (*bathtub*) bañera *f* **3.** (*carton*) tarrina *f*; **a ~ of ice-cream** una tarrina de helado

tuba ['tjuːbə] *n* tuba *f*

tubby ['tʌbi] <-ier, -iest> *adj inf* rechoncho, -a, requenete *Ven*

tube [tjuːb, *Am:* tuːb] *n* **1.** (*hollow cylinder*) tubo *m* **2.** ANAT trompa *f*; **Fallopian ~** trompa de Falopio **3.** *no pl, Brit, inf* (*underground*)

metro *m* **4.** *Am, inf* TV tele *f* ► **to go down the ~s** echarse a perder

tuber ['tjuːbər, *Am:* 'tuːbər] *n* tubérculo *m*

tubercular [tjuːˈbɜːkjʊlər, *Am:* tuːˈbɜːrkjələr] *adj* MED tuberculoso, -a

tuberculosis [tjuːˌbɜːkjʊˈləʊsɪs, *Am:* tuːˌbɜːrkjəˈloʊ-] *n no pl* tuberculosis *f inv*

tuberculous [tjuːˈbɜːkjʊləs, *Am:* tuːˈbɜːr-] *adj* tuberculoso, -a

tube station *n* estación *f* de metro

tub-thumper ['tʌbˌθʌmpər, *Am:* -ər] *n pej, inf* orador(a) *m(f)* demagógico, -a

TUC [ˌtiːjuːˈsiː] *n Brit abbr of* **Trades Union Congress** congreso *m* sindical

tuck [tʌk] I. *n* **1.** (*fold*) pliegue *m* **2.** *no pl, Brit* (*sweets*) golosinas *fpl* II. *vt* (*fold*) plegar

◆**tuck away** *vt* (*hide*) poner a buen recaudo; **to be tucked away** estar en un sitio seguro

◆**tuck in** I. *vt* **1.** (*push into position*) colocar en su sitio; **to tuck one's shirt in** meterse la camisa **2.** (*settle in bed*) arropar II. *vi* comer con apetito

tucker ['tʌkər, *Am:* -ər] *vt Am, inf* cansar

tuck shop *n Brit* tienda *f* de dulces

Tuesday ['tjuːzdeɪ, *Am:* 'tuːz-] *n* martes *m inv*; **Shrove ~** martes de carnaval; *s. a.* **Friday**

tuft [tʌft] *n* (*of hair*) mechón *m*; (*of feathers*) penacho *m*; (*of grass*) mata *f*

tug [tʌg] I. *n* **1.** (*pull*) tirón *m*; **to give sth a ~** dar un tirón a algo **2.** NAUT remolcador *m* II. <-gg-> *vt* **1.** (*pull*) tirar de **2.** NAUT remolcar

tuition [tjuːˈɪʃən] *n no pl* **1.** (*teaching*) enseñanza *f* **2.** *Am* (*fee*) tasas *fpl*

tuition fees *n* tasas *fpl*

tulip ['tjuːlɪp, *Am:* 'tuː-] *n* tulipán *m*

tumble ['tʌmbl] I. *n* caída *f*; **to take a ~** caerse II. *vi* **1.** (*fall*) caerse **2.** *fig* (*decline*) descender

◆**tumble down** *vi* desplomarse

◆**tumble over** *vi* caerse

◆**tumble to** *vt* caer en la cuenta de

tumbledown ['tʌmblˌdaʊn] *adj* en ruinas

tumble drier *n* secadora *f*, **tumble dryer** *n* secadora *f*

tumbler ['tʌmblər, *Am:* -blər] *n* vaso *m*

tumbleweed ['tʌmblwiːd] *n* planta *f* rodadora

tumescent [tuːˈmesnt] *adj* tumescente

tummy ['tʌmi] <-ies> *n childspeak* barriguita *f*

tummy ache *n childspeak* dolor *m* de tripa

tumor *n Am*, **tumour** ['tjuːmər, *Am:* 'tuːmər] *n Brit, Aus* tumor *m*; **brain ~** tumor *m* cerebral; **malignant ~** tumor *m* maligno

tumult ['tjuːmʌlt, *Am:* 'tuː-] *n no pl* **1.** (*uproar*) tumulto *m* **2.** (*emotional confusion*) agitación *f*

tumultuous [tjuːˈmʌltʃʊəs, *Am:* tuːˈmʌltʃuːəs] *adj* **1.** (*uproariously noisy*) tumultuoso, -a; (*applause*) apoteósico, -a **2.** (*disorderly*) agitado, -a

tun [tʌn] *n* (*large vat*) tonel *m*; (*in brewery*) barril *m*

tuna ['tjuːnə, *Am:* 'tuː-] *n* <-(s)> atún *m*

tundra ['tʌndrə] *n no pl* tundra *f*
tune [tjuːn, *Am:* tuːn] I. *n* 1. MUS melodía *f;* a catchy ~ una tonada pegajosa 2. *no pl (pitch)* to be in ~ estar afinado; to be out of ~ estar desafinado; to be in ~ with sth *fig* armonizar con algo; to be out of ~ with sth *fig* desentonar con algo ►to change one's ~ cambiar de parecer; to sing another ~ cambiar de parecer; to the ~ of 100 euros por valor de 100 euros II. *vt* 1. MUS afinar 2. AUTO poner a punto
♦**tune in** I. *vi* 1. RADIO, TV to ~ to a station sintonizar una emisora 2. *fig, inf* sintonizar con II. *vt Am, Aus* RADIO, TV sintonizar
♦**tune up** *vt* AUTO poner a punto
tuneful ['tjuːnfəl] *adj* MUS melódico, -a
tuneless ['tjuːnləs] *adj* MUS disonante
tuner *n* 1. MUS *(person)* afinador(a) *m(f)* 2. *(radio)* sintonizador *m*
tune-up ['tjuːnʌp] *n* 1. MUS afinado *m* 2. AUTO puesta *f* a punto
tungsten ['tʌŋstən] *n* tungsteno *m*
tunic ['tjuːnɪk, *Am:* 'tuː-] *n* FASHION casaca *f;* HIST túnica *f*
tuning *n no pl* 1. MUS afinación *f* 2. RADIO sintonización 3. AUTO puesta *f* a punto
tuning fork *n* MUS diapasón *m*
Tunisia [tjuː'nɪzɪə, *Am:* tuː'niːʒə] *n* Túnez *m*
Tunisian [tjuː'nɪzɪən, *Am:* tuː'niːʒən] I. *n* tunecino, -a *m, f* II. *adj* tunecino, -a
tunnel ['tʌnl] I. *n* 1. ARCHIT túnel *m* 2. MIN galería *f* II.<*Brit:* -ll-, *Am:* -l-> *vi* hacer un túnel III.<*Brit:* -ll-, *Am:* -l-> *vt* cavar; to ~ one's way out escapar haciendo un túnel
tunny ['tʌni] *n* <-(ies)> *Brit, inf* atún *m*
tuppence ['tʌpəns] *n no pl, Brit, inf* dos peniques *mpl* ►I don't care ~ me importa un rábano; to not give ~ for sth no dar ni un duro por algo
tuppenny ['tʌpəni] *adj Brit, inf* de dos peniques
turban ['tɜːbən, *Am:* 'tɜːr-] *n* turbante *m*
turbid ['tɜːbɪd, *Am:* 'tɜːr-] *adj (water)* turbio, -a
turbine ['tɜːbaɪn, *Am:* 'tɜːrbɪn] *n* turbina *f*
turbocharged ['tɜːbəʊˌtʃaːdʒd, *Am:* 'tɜːrbʊtʃaːrdʒd] *adj* ELEC, TECH turboalimentado, -a
turbocharger ['tɜːbəʊˌtʃaːdʒər, *Am:* 'tɜːrbʊtʃaːrdʒɚ] *n* ELEC, TECH turbocompresor *m* **turbo engine** *n* motor *m* turbo **turbojet** *n* turborreactor *m*
turbot ['tɜːbət, *Am:* 'tɜːr-] *n* <-(s)> rodaballo *m*
turbulence ['tɜːbjʊləns, *Am:* 'tɜːr-] *n no pl* turbulencia *f*
turbulent ['tɜːbjʊlənt, *Am:* 'tɜːr-] *adj* turbulento, -a
turd [tɜːd, *Am:* tɜːrd] *n vulg* 1. *(excrement)* zurullo *m* 2. *(person)* cerdo, -a *m, f*
tureen [tjʊ'riːn, *Am:* tʊ'-] *n* sopera *f*
turf [tɜːf, *Am:* tɜːrf] <-s *o* -ves> *n* 1. *no pl* BOT césped *m;* a *(piece of)* ~ un tepe; the ~ *(horse*

racing) las carreras de caballos 2. *(territory)* territorio *m*
turf accountant *n Brit, form* corredor(a) *m(f)* de apuestas
turgid ['tɜːdʒɪd, *Am:* 'tɜːr-] *adj form* 1. *pej (style)* ampuloso, -a 2. *(swollen)* hinchado, -a
Turk [tɜːk, *Am:* tɜːrk] *n* turco, -a *m, f*
turkey ['tɜːki, *Am:* 'tɜːr-] *n* 1. ZOOL pavo *m* 2. *Am, Aus, inf* THEAT fiasco *m* 3. *Am, Aus, inf (stupid person)* papanatas *mf inv* ►to talk ~ *Am, inf* hablar claro
Turkey ['tɜːki, *Am:* 'tɜːr-] *n* Turquía *f*
Turkish ['tɜːkɪʃ, *Am:* 'tɜːr-] I. *adj* turco, -a II. *n* 1. *(person)* turco, -a *m, f* 2. LING turco *m*
turmoil ['tɜːmɔɪl, *Am:* 'tɜːr-] *n* 1. *no pl (state of chaos)* caos *m inv;* to be thrown into ~ estar sumido en el caos 2. *(of mind)* trastorno *m;* to be in a ~ estar desconcertado
turn [tɜːn, *Am:* tɜːrn] I. *vi* 1. *(rotate)* girar, dar vueltas; to ~ on sth girar sobre algo 2. *(switch direction)* volver; *(tide)* cambiar; *(car)* girar; to turn around dar media vuelta, voltearse *AmL;* to ~ right/left torcer a la derecha/ izquierda 3. *(change)* cambiar, transformarse; *(for worse)* volverse; to ~ traitor volver la casaca; to ~ grey (overnight) quedar canoso (de la noche a la mañana) 4. *(change colour: leaves)* cambiar de color 5. *(feel nauseous: stomach)* retorcerse 6. *(spoil: cream, milk)* agriarse II. *vt* 1. *(rotate)* hacer girar; *(key)* dar vuelta a; *(screw on)* atornillar; *(unscrew)* desatornillar 2. *(switch direction)* volver, voltear *AmL;* to ~ one's head volver la cabeza; to ~ a page pasar una página; to ~ the coat inside out volver el abrigo del revés 3. *(attain a particular age)* cumplir 4. *(pass a particular hour)* dar; it has ~ed three o'clock dieron las tres 5. *(cause to feel nauseated)* it ~ed my stomach se me revolvió el estómago ►to ~ sth upside down dejar algo patas arriba III. *n* 1. *(change in direction)* cambio *m* de dirección; to make a ~ to the right girar hacia la derecha; to take a ~ for the worse/better mejorar/empeorar 2. *(changing point)* giro *m;* the ~ of the century el cambio de siglo 3. *(period of duty)* turno *m;* to be sb's ~ to do sth ser el turno de alguien para hacer algo; it's your ~ te toca a ti; to do sth in ~ hacer algo por turnos; to miss a ~ estar una vuelta sin jugar; to speak out of ~ hablar fuera de lugar 4. *(rotation, twist)* rotación *f* 5. *(service)* favor *m*, servicio *m;* to do sb a good ~ hacer un favor a alguien; one good ~ deserves another *prov* favor con favor se paga 6. *(shock)* susto *m;* to give sb a ~ dar un susto a alguien 7. *(queasiness)* desmayo *m;* to have ~s tener ataques 8. THEAT número *m*
♦**turn against** *vt* volverse en contra de
♦**turn away** I. *vi* apartarse; to ~ from sb/ sth alejarse de alguien/algo II. *vt* 1. *(refuse entry)* no dejar entrar 2. *(deny help)* rechazar
♦**turn back** I. *vi (return to starting point)* retroceder II. *vt* 1. *(send back)* hacer regresar

2. (*fold towards itself: bedcover*) remangar; (*corner of paper*) doblar
◆**turn down** *vt* **1.** (*reject*) rechazar **2.** (*reduce volume*) bajar **3.** (*fold*) doblar
◆**turn in** I. *vt* (*hand over*) entregar II. *vi inf* (*go to bed*) acostarse
◆**turn into** *vt* transformar en
◆**turn off** I. *vt* **1.** ELEC, TECH desconectar; (*light*) apagar; (*motor*) parar; (*gas*) cerrar **2.** *inf* (*be unappealing*) repugnar II. *vi* (*leave path*) desviarse
◆**turn on** *vt* **1.** ELEC, TECH conectar; (*light*) encender, prender *AmL*; (*gas*) abrir **2.** (*excite*) excitar; (*attract*) gustar **3.** (*show, demonstrate*) poner en juego; **to ~ the charm** desplegar el encanto **4.** (*attack*) atacar
◆**turn out** I. *vi* **1.** (*end up, work out*) salir **2.** (*be revealed*) **it turned out to be true** resultó ser cierto II. *vt* **1.** (*light*) apagar **2.** (*kick out*) echar; **to turn sb out on the street** echar a alguien a la calle **3.** (*empty*) vaciar
◆**turn over** I. *vi* (*start, operate: engine*) hacer funcionar II. *vt* **1.** (*change the side*) dar la vuelta a, volver **2.** (*criminal*) entregar **3.** (*control*) ceder; (*possession*) traspasar **4.** (*facts*) meditar; **to ~ an idea** dar vueltas a una idea **5.** COM, FIN mover, facturar **6.** *Brit, inf* (*steal from*) robar; (*search*) saquear
◆**turn round** I. *vi* volverse II. *vt* **1.** (*move*) girar **2.** (*change*) cambiar, transformar; (*reform*) reformar
◆**turn to** *vt* **1.** (*face*) volverse hacia **2.** (*request aid*) **to ~ sb (for sth)** recurrir a alguien (para algo)
◆**turn up** I. *vi* **1.** (*arrive*) llegar **2.** (*become available*) aparecer **3.** (*point upwards*) doblarse hacia arriba II. *vt* **1.** (*volume*) subir **2.** (*shorten*) acortar **3.** (*point upwards*) doblar hacia arriba **4.** (*find*) encontrar; (*locate*) localizar

turnabout ['tɜːnəˌbaʊt, *Am:* 'tɜːrn-] *n,* **turnaround** ['tɜːnərˌaʊnd, *Am:* 'tɜːrnɚ-] *n* **1.** (*change*) giro *m* en redondo **2.** (*improvement*) mejora *f* **3.** COM procesamiento *m*

turnabout time *n,* **turnaround time** *n* AVIAT, NAUT tiempo *m* en puerto

turncoat ['tɜːnkəʊt, *Am:* 'tɜːrnkoʊt] *n* chaquetero, -a *m, f*

turner ['tɜːnəʳ, *Am:* 'tɜːrnɚ] *n inf* tornero, -a *m, f*

turning ['tɜːnɪŋ, *Am:* 'tɜːr-] *n* **1.** (*road*) bocacalle *f* **2.** (*act of changing direction*) vuelta *f*

turning point *n* momento *m* decisivo; **a ~ in one's career** un cambio decisivo en su carrera

turnip ['tɜːnɪp, *Am:* 'tɜːr-] *n* nabo *m*

turnkey operation [ˌtɜːnkiː ˌɒpərˈeɪʃən, *Am:* ˌtɜːrnkiː ˌɑːpəˈreɪ-] *n* proyecto *m* listo para empezar a funcionar

turn-off ['tɜːnɒf, *Am:* 'tɜːrnɑːf] *n* **1.** AUTO salida *f* de una calle **2.** *inf* (*something unappealing*) **to be a real ~** ser repugnante

turnout ['tɜːnaʊt, *Am:* 'tɜːrn-] *n* **1.** (*attendance*) número *m* de asistentes **2.** POL número

m de votantes **3.** ECON producción *f* **4.** FASHION atuendo *m*

turnover ['tɜːnˌəʊvəʳ, *Am:* 'tɜːrnˌoʊvɚ] *n* **1.** COM, FIN volumen *m* de negocios; (*sales*) facturación *f* **2.** (*in staff*) rotación *f* **3.** GASTR empanada *f*

turnpike ['tɜːnpaɪk, *Am:* 'tɜːrn-] *n Am* AUTO autopista *f* de peaje

turnround ['tɜːnraʊnd, *Am:* 'tɜːrn-] *n no pl, Brit s.* **turnaround**

turnstile ['tɜːnstaɪl, *Am:* 'tɜːrn-] *n* SPORTS torniquete *m*

turntable ['tɜːnˌteɪbl, *Am:* 'tɜːrn-] *n* **1.** MUS (*record player*) plato *m* giratorio **2.** RAIL plataforma *f* giratoria

turn-up ['tɜːnʌp, *Am:* 'tɜːrn-] *n Brit* vuelta *f*; *trouser* ~ dobladillo *m* del pantalón, valenciana *f Méx* ►**to be a ~ for the book(s)** ser una gran sorpresa

turpentine ['tɜːpəntaɪn, *Am:* 'tɜːr-] *n no pl* trementina *f*

turpitude ['tɜːpɪtjuːd, *Am:* 'tɜːrpɪtuːd] *n no pl, form* vileza *f*; **moral ~** inmoralidad *f*

turps [tɜːps, *Am:* tɜːrps] *n no pl, inf abbr of* **turpentine** trementina *f*

turquoise ['tɜːkwɔɪz, *Am:* 'tɜːr-] *n* **1.** (*stone*) turquesa *f* **2.** (*color*) azul *m* turquesa

turret ['tʌrɪt, *Am:* 'tɜːr] *n* **1.** (*tower*) torreón *m* **2.** (*of tank, ship*) torreta *f*

turtle ['tɜːtl, *Am:* 'tɜːrtl̩] <-(s)> *n* tortuga *f*

turtledove ['tɜːtldʌv, *Am:* 'tɜːrtl̩-] *n* tórtola *f*

turtleneck ['tɜːtlnek, *Am:* 'tɜːrtl̩-] *n Brit* cuello *m* de cisne

tusk [tʌsk] *n* colmillo *m*

tussle ['tʌsl] I. *vi* pelearse II. *n* (*physical struggle*) pelea *f*; (*quarrel*) riña *f*

tussock ['tʌsək] *n* mata *f* de hierba

tut [tʌt] *interj* ~ ~! ¡vaya, vaya!

tutelage ['tjuːtɪlɪdʒ, *Am:* 'tuːt̬ɪlɪdʒ] *n no pl* tutela *f*

tutor ['tjuːtəʳ, *Am:* 'tuːt̬ɚ] I. *n* SCHOOL, UNIV **1.** (*private teacher*) profesor(a) *m(f)* particular; (*at home*) preceptor(a) *m(f)* **2.** *Brit* (*supervising teacher*) tutor(a) *m(f)* II. *vt* SCHOOL, UNIV **to ~ sb (in sth)** dar clases particulares a alguien (de algo)

tutorial [tjuːˈtɔːrɪəl, *Am:* tuːˈ-] *n* clase *f* en grupo reducido

tuxedo [tʌkˈsiːdəʊ, *Am:* -doʊ] *n Am* esmoquin *m*

TV [ˌtiːˈviː] *n abbr of* **television** TV *f*

twaddle ['twɒdl, *Am:* 'twɑːdl] *n no pl, inf* estupideces *fpl*; **to talk ~** decir tonterías

twang [twæŋ] I. *n* **1.** MUS tañido *m* **2.** LING gangueo *m* II. *vt* hacer vibrar; (*strings*) puntear; **to ~ someone's nerves** crispar los nervios a alguien III. *vi* vibrar

tweak [twiːk] I. *vt* pellizcar II. *n* pellizco *m*

twee [twiː] *adj Brit, inf* cursi

tweed [twiːd] *n* **1.** *no pl* (*textile*) tweed *m* **2.** *pl* (*suit*) traje *m* de tweed

tweedy ['twiːdi] *adj* <-ier, -iest> *fig* de clase alta rural

tweet [twi:t] I. *n* pío *m* II. *vi* piar

tweeter ['twi:tə', *Am:* -ṭə'] *n* altavoz *m* para altas frecuencias

tweezers ['twi:zəz, *Am:* -zə'z] *npl* (a pair of) ~ (unas) pinzas

twelfth [twelfθ] I. *adj* duodécimo, -a II. *n no pl* 1. (*order*) duodécimo, -a *m, f* 2. (*date*) doce *m* 3. (*fraction*) duodécimo *m;* (*part*) duodécima parte *f; s. a.* **eighth**

twelve [twelv] I. *adj* doce II. *n* doce *m; s. a.* **eight**

twentieth ['twentɪəθ, *Am:* -ṭɪ-] I. *adj* vigésimo, -a II. *n* 1. (*order*) vigésimo, -a *m, f* 2. (*date*) veinte *m* 3. (*fraction*) vigésimo *m;* (*part*) vigésima parte *f; s. a.* **eighth**

twenty ['twenti, *Am:* -ṭi] <-ies> I. *adj* veinte II. *n* veinte *m; s. a.* **eighty**

twerp [twɜːp, *Am:* twɜːrp] *n inf* imbécil *mf*

twice [twaɪs] *adv* dos veces

twiddle ['twɪdl] I. *vt a.* TECH, ELEC (hacer) girar ►to ~ one's <u>thumbs</u> estar mano sobre mano II. *vi* to ~ with sth juguetear con algo III. *n* giro *m*

twig [twɪg] I. *n* ramita *f* II. *vi inf* darse cuenta

twilight ['twaɪlaɪt] *n* crepúsculo *m*

twin [twɪn] I. *n* gemelo, -a *m, f*; identical ~s gemelos idénticos II. *adj* gemelo, -a III. *vt* <-nn-> hermanar IV. *vi* <-nn-> hermanarse

twin bed *n* cama *f* gemela **twin brother** *n* hermano *m* gemelo

twine [twaɪn] I. *vt* 1. (*wind up*) enrollar 2. (*encircle*) rodear II. *n no pl* cordel *m*

twinge [twɪndʒ] *n* 1. MED punzada *f* 2. *fig* arrebato *m;* **a ~ of conscience** un remordimiento de conciencia

twinkle ['twɪŋkl] I. *vi* (*diamond, eyes*) brillar; (*star*) centellear II. *n* (*of stars*) centelleo *m;* (*of jewels, light, eye*) brillo *m* ►to be just **a ~ in sb's father's <u>eye</u>** no haber nacido; **to do sth <u>in</u> a ~** hacer algo en un abrir y cerrar de ojos

twinkling ['twɪŋklɪŋ] I. *adj* (*diamond, eyes*) brillante; (*star*) centelleante II. *n* parpadeo *m;* **in the ~ of an <u>eye</u>** en un abrir y cerrar de ojos

twinning ['twɪnɪŋ] *n no pl* hermanamiento *f* de dos ciudades

twin room *n* habitación *f* con camas gemelas **twin set** *n* Brit, Aus conjunto *m* (de suéter y rebeca para mujer) **twin sister** *n* hermana *f* gemela **twin town** *n* Brit ciudad *f* hermanada

twirl [twɜːl, *Am:* twɜːrl] I. *vi* girar; **to ~ around sth** dar vueltas alrededor de algo II. *vt* (*whirl*) dar vueltas a; (*moustache*) retorcer III. *n* pirueta *f*

twist [twɪst] I. *vt* 1. (*turn*) dar vueltas a, girar 2. (*wind around*) enroscar; **to ~ sth around sth** enrollar algo alrededor de algo 3. MED torcer 4. (*distort: truth*) tergiversar ►to ~ sb's <u>arm</u> presionar a alguien; **to ~ sb round one's little <u>finger</u>** manejar a alguien a su antojo II. *vi* 1. (*squirm around*) (re)torcerse 2. (*curve: path, road*) serpentear; **to ~ and turn** dar

vueltas 3. (*dance*) bailar el twist III. *n* 1. (*turn*) vuelta *f;* **to give sth a ~** dar un giro a algo 2. (*unexpected change*) giro *m* 3. (*curl: of hair*) mecha *f;* (*of lemon*) rodajita *f;* (*of paper*) cucurucho *m;* (*of coil*) vuelta *f* 4. (*dance*) twist *m* ►to go round the ~ Brit, *inf* volverse loco; **to be <u>in</u> a ~** *inf* estar aturdido

◆**twist off** *vt* desenroscar

twisted ['twɪstɪd] *adj* 1. (*cable, metal*) retorcido, -a; (*ankle*) torcido, -a 2. (*perverted*) pervertido, -a; (*logic, humour*) retorcido, -a

twister ['twɪstə', *Am:* -ə'] *n* 1. METEO tornado *m* 2. *inf* (*swindler*) tramposo, -a *m, f*

twisty ['twɪsti] *adj* <-ier, -iest> *inf* (*road*) sinuoso, -a

twit [twɪt] *n inf* imbécil *mf*

twitch [twɪtʃ] I. *vi* ANAT, MED moverse (nerviosamente); (*face*) contraerse II. *vt* 1. ANAT, MED mover nerviosamente 2. (*pull*) tirar de III. *n* <-es> 1. ANAT, MED movimiento *m* espasmódico; **to have a (nervous) ~** tener un tic (nervioso) 2. (*pull*) tirón *m*

twitter ['twɪtə', *Am:* 'twɪṭə'] I. *vi* 1. ZOOL gorjear 2. (*talk*) parlotear II. *n* gorjeo *m*

two [tu:] I. *adj* dos II. *n* dos *m* ►that <u>makes</u> ~ of us *inf* ya somos dos; **to <u>put</u> ~ and ~ together** *inf* sacar conclusiones; *s. a.* **eight**

two-bit [tu:'bɪt] *adj* Am, *inf* insignificante

two-dimensional [ˌtu:dɪ'mentʃənəl] *adj* 1. bidimensional 2. *fig* superficial **two-door** *adj* AUTO de dos puertas **two-edged** *adj* de doble filo **two-faced** *adj pej* falso, -a, falluto, -a RíoPl

twofold ['tu:fəʊld, *Am:* -foʊld] I. *adv* dos veces II. *adj* doble

two-part *adj* de dos partes **two-party system** *n* sistema *f* bipartidista

twopence ['tʌpəns] *n* Brit FIN dos peniques *mpl* ►I don't <u>care</u> ~ me importa un rábano; **to not <u>give</u> ~ for sth** no dar ni un duro por algo

twopenny ['tʌpəni] *adj* Brit, *inf* (*worthless*) insignificante

two-phase *adj* ELEC bifásico, -a **two-piece** *n* 1. (*suit*) conjunto *m* de dos piezas 2. (*bikini*) bañador *m* de dos piezas **two-seater** AUTO I. *n* biplaza *m* II. *adj* de dos plazas

twosome ['tu:səm] *n* (*duo*) dúo *m;* (*couple*) pareja *f*

two-stroke AUTO I. *n* motor *m* de dos tiempos II. *adj* de dos tiempos **two-tiered** *adj* de dos pisos **two-time** *vt inf* poner los cuernos a

two-way [ˌtu:'weɪ, *Am:* 'tu:-] *adj* de dos sentidos; (*tunnel, bridge*) de doble sentido; (*process*) recíproco, -a; (*conversation*) bilateral; (*switch*) de dos direcciones

two-way radio *n* transmisor *m* receptor

tycoon [taɪ'ku:n] *n* FIN magnate *m*

tyke [taɪk] *n* 1. (*child*) chiquillo, -a *m, f* travieso, -a 2. (*dog*) perro *m* callejero

tympanum ['tɪmpənəm] *n* tímpano *m*

type [taɪp] I. *n* 1. (*sort, kind: style, print, language*) tipo *m;* (*of machine*) modelo *m*

2. (*class: animal, person, skin*) clase *f* **3.** *inf*
(*person*) tipo *m*, sujeto *m;* **he's not her** ~ no
es su tipo **4.** TYPO tipo *m* (de letra) **II.** *vt*
1. (*write with machine*) escribir a máquina
2. (*categorize*) clasificar **III.** *vi* escribir a
máquina
♦**type out** *vt* escribir a máquina
♦**type up** *vt* pasar a máquina
typecast ['taɪpkɑːst, *Am:* -kæst] <type-
cast, typecast> *vt* encasillar
typeface ['taɪpfeɪs] *n no pl* tipografía *f*
typescript ['taɪpskrɪpt] *n* texto *m* meca-
nografiado **typesetter** *n* **1.** (*machine*)
máquina *f* de componer **2.** (*person*) tipógrafo,
-a *m, f*
typesetting ['taɪpˌsetɪŋ, *Am:* -ˌseṭ-] *n no pl*
composición *f* tipográfica
typewrite ['taɪpraɪt] *irr vt* mecanografiar
typewriter ['taɪpˌraɪtə', *Am:* -ṭɚ] *n*
máquina *f* de escribir
typewriter ribbon *n* cinta *f* para máquina
de escribir
typewritten *adj* escrito, -a a máquina
typhoid ['taɪfɔɪd] *n*, **typhoid fever** *n no pl*
fiebre *f* tifoidea
typhoon [taɪ'fuːn] *n* METEO tifón *m*
typhus ['taɪfəs] *n no pl* tifus *m inv*
typical ['tɪpɪkəl] *adj* típico, -a; (*symptom*)
característico, -a; **to be** ~ **of sb to do sth** ser
típico de alguien el hacer algo
typically *adv* típicamente
typify ['tɪpɪfaɪ] <-ie-> *vt* simbolizar
typing ['taɪpɪŋ] *n no pl* mecanografía *f*
typist ['taɪpɪst] *n* mecanógrafo, -a *m, f*
typographer [taɪ'pɒgrəfə', *Am:* -'pɑːgrə-
fɚ] *n* tipógrafo, -a *m, f*
typographic(al) [ˌtaɪpəʊ'græfɪk(əl), *Am:*
-pə'-] *adj* tipográfico, -a
typographic(al) error *n* errata *f* de
imprenta
typography [taɪ'pɒgrəfi, *Am:* -'pɑːgrə-] *n*
no pl tipografía *f*
tyrannical [tɪ'rænɪkəl] *adj pej* tiránico, -a
tyrannize ['tɪrənaɪz] *vt* tiranizar
tyranny ['tɪrəni] *n no pl* tiranía *f*
tyrant ['taɪərənt, *Am:* 'taɪrənt] *n* tirano, -a
m, f
tyre ['taɪə', *Am:* 'taɪɚ] *n Aus, Brit* neumático
m, llanta *f Méx*, caucho *m Col, Ven;* **spare** ~
neumático de repuesto
tyre gauge *n Aus, Brit* medidor *m* de presión
tyre pressure *n no pl* presión *f* del neumático
tzar [zɑː', *Am:* zɑːr] *n* zar *m*
tzetze fly ['tetsiˌflaɪ] *n* mosca *f* tsetsé

U

U, u [juː] *n* U, u *f;* ~ **for Uncle** U de Uruguay
U¹ **1.** *Brit* CINE *abbr of* **universal** para todos los
públicos **2.** *abbr of* **uranium** uranio *m* **3.** *Am,*
Aus, inf abbr of **university** universidad *f*
U² *adj Aus, Brit, inf* de la clase alta
UAE [juːeɪ'iː] *npl abbr of* **United Arab Emirates** EAU *mpl*
ubiquitous [juː'bɪkwɪtəs, *Am:* -wəṭəs] *adj*
omnipresente
ubiquity [juː'bɪkwəti, *Am:* -ṭi] *n no pl* ubi-
cuidad *f*, omnipresencia *f*
U-boat ['juːbəʊt, *Am:* -boʊt] *n* submarino *m*
alemán
UCCA ['ʌkə] *n Brit abbr of* **Universities Central Council for Admissions** consejo de
admisión a la universidad
UDA [juːdiː'eɪ] *n abbr of* **Ulster Defence
Association** asociación de defensa del Ulster
udder ['ʌdə', *Am:* -ɚ] *n* ubre *f*
UDI [ˌjuːdiː'aɪ] *n abbr of* **unilateral declaration of independence** declaración *f* unilateral de independencia
UDR [juːdiː'ɑː', *Am:* -'ɑːr] *n abbr of* **Ulster
Defence Regiment** regimiento de defensa
del Ulster
UEFA [juː'eɪfə] *n abbr of* **Union of European
Football Associations** UEFA *f*
UFO [ˌjuːefˈəʊ, *Am:* -'oʊ] *n abbr of* **unidentified flying object** OVNI *m*
Uganda [juː'gændə] *n* Uganda *f*
Ugandan **I.** *adj* ugandés, -esa **II.** *n* ugandés,
-esa *m, f*
ugh [ɜːh] *interj inf* uf
ugliness ['ʌglɪnɪs] *n no pl* **1.** (*unattractiveness*) fealdad *f* **2.** (*nastiness*) repugnancia *f*
ugly ['ʌgli] <-ier, iest> *adj* **1.** (*not attractive*)
feo, -a, macaco, -a *Arg, Méx, Cuba, Chile;* ~
duckling patito *m* feo; **to be** ~ **as sin** ser más
feo que Picio **2.** (*angry: mood*) peligroso, -a;
(*look*) repugnante **3.** (*violent*) violento, -a; **to
turn** ~ ponerse violento **4.** (*harsh*) desagradable; (*story*) fastidioso, -a; (*truth*) terrible;
(*weather*) horroroso, -a; (*clouds*) amenazante;
~ **rumours** calumnias *fpl*
UHF [juːeɪtʃ'ef] *n abbr of* **ultrahigh frequency** UHF *f*
UHT [juːeɪtʃ'tiː] *adj abbr of* **ultra heat
treated** UHT
UK [juː'keɪ] *n abbr of* **United Kingdom** RU *m*
ukelele [ˌjuːkəl'eɪli] *n* ukelele *m*
Ukraine [juːˈkreɪn] *n* Ucrania *f*
Ukrainian **I.** *adj* ucraniano, -a **II.** *n* **1.** (*person*)
ucraniano, -a *m, f* **2.** LING ucraniano *m*
ulcer ['ʌlsə', *Am:* -sɚ] *n* **1.** MED úlcera *f*, chácara *f Col* **2.** *fig* llaga *f*
ulcerate ['ʌlsəreɪt] *vi* ulcerarse
ulcerous ['ʌlsərəs] *adj* ulceroso, -a
ullage ['ʌlɪdʒ] *n no pl* **1.** (*shortage*) escasez *f*
2. (*liquid loss*) merma *f*
ulna ['ʌlnə] <ulnae *o* s> *n* cúbito *m*

Ulster ['ʌlstəʳ, Am: -stə-] n no pl Ulster m
ulterior [ʌl'tɪərɪəʳ, Am: -'tɪrɪə-] adj 1. (secret) secreto, -a; (motive) oculto, -a 2. (beyond scope) ulterior
ultimate ['ʌltɪmət, Am: -ţəmɪt] I. adj 1. (best) máximo, -a; (experience, feeling) extremo, -a 2. (highest degree of) máximo, -a; (accolade, praise) supremo, -a; (honor, sacrifice) altísimo, -a 3. (maximum: authority) máximo, -a 4. (final) final; (cost, consequences, effect) definitivo, -a 5. (fundamental) fundamental; (cause, goal, responsibility) primordial II. n (the best) the ~ lo máximo; (bad taste, vulgarity) el colmo; the ~ in fashion el último grito en moda; the ~ in stupidity el colmo de la estupidez
ultimately ['ʌltɪmətli, Am: -ţəmɪt-] adv 1. (in the end) finalmente 2. (fundamentally) fundamentalmente
ultimatum [ˌʌltɪ'meɪtəm, Am: -ţə'meɪ-ţəm] <ultimata o -tums> n ultimátum m
ultimo ['ʌltɪməʊ, Am: -ţɪmoʊ] adv ECON, COM del mes pasado
ultrahigh frequency [ˌʌltrəˌhaɪ'fri:kwən-tsi] n no pl frecuencia f ultraalta
ultramarine [ˌʌltrəmə'ri:n] I. adj ultramarino, -a II. n no pl azul m de ultramar
ultramodern [ˌʌltrə'mɒdən, Am: -'mɑ:-də-n] adj ultramoderno, -a
ultra-short wave [ˌʌltrəʃɔ:t'weɪv, Am: -ʃɔ:rt'weɪv] n onda f ultracorta
ultrasonic [ˌʌltrə'sɒnɪk, Am: -'sɑ:nɪk] adj ultrasónico, -a
ultrasound ['ʌltrəsaʊnd] n ultrasonido m
ultrasound picture n imagen f por ultrasonido
ultraviolet [ˌʌltrə'vaɪələt, Am: -lɪt] adj ultravioleta
Ulysses ['ju:lɪsi:z, Am: ju:'lɪs-] n Ulises m
umbel ['ʌmbəl] n umbela f
umber ['ʌmbəʳ, Am: -bə-] I. adj de color ocre oscuro II. n no pl ocre m oscuro
umbilical [ʌm'bɪlɪkl] adj umbilical
umbilical cord n cordón m umbilical
umbrage ['ʌmbrɪdʒ] n no pl, form resentimiento m; to take ~ at sth ofenderse por algo
umbrella [ʌm'brelə] n 1. (rain) paraguas m inv; (sun) sombrilla f; beach ~ parasol m 2. (protection) cobertura f; MIL cortina f de fuego antiaéreo; to do sth under the ~ of sth hacer algo bajo el amparo de algo
umbrella case n, **umbrella cover** n funda f de paraguas **umbrella organization** n POL, ADMIN organización f paraguas **umbrella stand** n paragüero m
umpire ['ʌmpaɪəʳ, Am: -paɪ-] SPORTS I. n árbitro mf II. vt arbitrar
umpteen ['ʌmpti:n] adj inf incontable; ~ reasons múltiples razones fpl; to do sth ~ times hacer algo innumerables veces
umpteenth ['ʌmpti:nθ] adj enésimo, -a
UN [ju:'en] n abbr of United Nations ONU f
unabashed [ˌʌnə'bæʃt] adj desenvuelto, -a;

(behaviour) atrevido, -a
unabated [ˌʌnə'beɪtɪd, Am: -ţɪd] adj continuado, -a; (hurricane, storm) persistente; (fighting, rioting, energy) constante; (interest, enthusiasm) vivo, -a; (curiosity) incesante
unable [ʌn'eɪbl] adj incapaz
unabridged [ˌʌnə'brɪdʒd] adj 1. LIT, PUBL no abreviado, -a 2. (whole) completo, -a
unacceptable [ˌʌnək'septəbl] adj 1. (not good enough) inaceptable; (conditions) inadmisible 2. (intolerable) intolerable; the ~ face of sth Aus, Brit el lado oscuro de algo
unaccompanied [ˌʌnə'kʌmpənɪd] adj 1. (without companion) solo, -a, sin compañía 2. MUS sin acompañamiento
unaccountable [ˌʌnə'kaʊntəbl, Am: -ţə-] adj 1. (not responsible) irresponsable 2. (inexplicable) inexplicable
unaccounted for [ˌʌnə'kaʊntɪd'fɔ:ʳ, Am: -ţɪd,fɔ:r] adj 1. (unexplained) inexplicado, -a 2. (not included in count) sin contar
unaccustomed [ˌʌnə'kʌstəmd] adj 1. (seldom seen) raro, -a 2. (something new) inusual; to be ~ to doing sth no tener la costumbre de hacer algo
unacknowledged [ˌʌnək'nɒlɪdʒd, Am: -'nɑ:lɪdʒd] adj ignorado, -a; (author, scientist) no reconocido, -a; to remain ~ permanecer en el anonimato
unaddressed [ˌʌnə'drest] adj sin señas
unadorned [ˌʌnə'dɔ:nd, Am: -'dɔ:rnd] adj 1. (plain) sin adorno; (story) simple; (fashion, style) sencillo, -a 2. (pure) puro, -a; the ~ truth la pura verdad
unadulterated [ˌʌnə'dʌltəreɪtɪd, Am: -ţə-reɪţɪd] adj 1. (not changed) sin mezcla 2. (pure: substance) puro, -a; (alcohol, wine) no adulterado, -a; ~ nonsense completo disparate m
unadventurous [ˌʌnəd'ventʃərəs] adj poco atrevido, -a; (style) poco llamativo, -a
unadvisable [ˌʌnəd'vaɪzəbl] adj poco aconsejable
unaffected [ˌʌnə'fektɪd] adj 1. (not changed) inalterado, -a 2. (not influenced) espontáneo, -a 3. (down to earth) sencillo, -a; (manner, speech) natural
unafraid [ˌʌnə'freɪd] adj sin temor; to be ~ of sb/sth no tener miedo de alguien/algo
unaided [ʌn'eɪdɪd] adj sin ayuda; to do sth ~ hacer algo por sí solo
unalike [ˌʌnə'laɪk] adj disímil
unalloyed [ˌʌnə'lɔɪd] adj liter puro, -a; (happiness, pleasure) absoluto, -a
unaltered [ʌn'ɔ:ltəd, Am: -ţə-d] adj inalterado, -a; to leave sth ~ dejar algo tal como estaba
unambiguous [ˌʌnæm'bɪgjʊəs] adj inequívoco, -a; (statement) incuestionable; (language, terms) unívoco, -a
un-American [ˌʌnə'merɪkən] adj antiamericano, -a (término empleado por los propios estadounidenses)

unanimity [ˌjuːnəˈnɪməti, *Am:* -t̬i] *n no pl,*
form unanimidad *f*
unanimous [juːˈnænɪməs, *Am:* -əməs] *adj*
unánime; (*support*) total
unannounced [ˌʌnəˈnaʊnst] **I.** *adj* **1.** (*without warning*) sin aviso; (*arrival, appearance*)
imprevisto, -a; (*visitor, guest*) inesperado, -a
2. (*not made known*) fortuito, -a; (*act*)
repentino, -a **II.** *adv* de repente; (*arrive, visit*)
sin aviso
unanswerable [ˌʌnˈɑːnsərəbl, *Am:* -ˈæn-]
adj **1.** (*without an answer*) incontestable
2. *form* (*irrefutable*) irrefutable; (*proof*) irrebatible
unanswered [ˌʌnˈɑːnsəd, *Am:* -ˈænsəd] *adj*
sin contestar
unappetizing [ˌʌnˈæpɪtaɪzɪŋ, *Am:* -ˈæpə-]
adj poco apetitoso, -a
unapproachable [ˌʌnəˈprəʊtʃəbl, *Am:*
-ˈproʊ-] *adj* **1.** (*building*) inaccesible **2.** (*person*) intratable
unarmed [ˌʌnˈɑːmd, *Am:* -ˈɑːrmd] *adj* desar-
mado, -a
unashamed [ˌʌnəˈʃeɪmd] *adj* desvergonzado, -a; (*greed, hypocrisy, selfishness*) descarado, -a; **to be ~ of sth** (*guilt*) no tener remordimiento por algo; (*shame*) no avergonzarse
por algo
unasked [ˌʌnˈɑːskt, *Am:* -ˈæskt] *adj* **1.** (*not
questioned*) no solicitado, -a; (*spontaneous*)
2. espontáneo, -a
unassignable [ˌʌnəˈsaɪnəbl] *adj* LAW intras-
ferible
unassuming [ˌʌnəˈsjuːmɪŋ, *Am:* -ˈsuː-] *adj*
modesto, -a
unattached [ˌʌnəˈtætʃt] *adj* **1.** (*not connected*) suelto, -a; (*part*) separable **2.** (*independent*) libre **3.** (*unmarried*) soltero, -a
unattainable [ˌʌnəˈteɪnəbl] *adj* inasequible;
(*goal, ideal*) inalcanzable
unattended [ˌʌnəˈtendɪd] *adj* **1.** (*alone*) sin
compañía; **to leave the children ~** dejar a los
niños sin vigilancia **2.** (*unmanned*) desatendido, -a **3.** (*not taken care of*) descuidado, -a
unattractive [ˌʌnəˈtræktɪv] *adj* **1.** (*quite
ugly*) feo, -a; (*place, town*) poco atractivo, -a
2. (*unpleasant*) desagradable; (*personality,
character*) antipático, -a
unauthorized [ˌʌnˈɔːθəraɪzd, *Am:* -ˈɑː-] *adj*
no autorizado, -a
unavailable [ˌʌnəˈveɪləbl] *adj* inasequible;
(*article*) agotado, -a; (*man, woman*) ocupado,
-a
unavailing [ˌʌnəˈveɪlɪŋ] *adj form* (*denial*)
inútil; (*effort, attempt*) vano, -a
unavoidable [ˌʌnəˈvɔɪdəbl] *adj* ineludible;
(*accident, fate*) inevitable
unaware [ˌʌnəˈweəʳ, *Am:* -ˈwer] *adj* **to be ~
of sth** ignorar algo
unawares [ˌʌnəˈweəz, *Am:* -ˈwerz] *adv* **to
catch sb ~** coger a alguien desprevenido
unbalanced [ˌʌnˈbælənst] *adj* **1.** (*uneven*)
desnivelado, -a; (*account*) desequilibrado, -a

2. (*mental state*) trastornado, -a
unbar [ˌʌnˈbɑːʳ, *Am:* -ˈbɑːr] *vt* desatrancar
unbearable [ˌʌnˈbeərəbl, *Am:* -ˈberə-] *adj*
1. (*painful*) insoportable, inaguantable **2.** (*person*) insufrible
unbeatable [ˌʌnˈbiːtəbl, *Am:* -ˈbiːt̬ə-] *adj*
1. (*team, record*) imbatible; (*army*) invencible
2. (*pizza, shirt*) insuperable; (*value, quality*)
inmejorable
unbeaten [ˌʌnˈbiːtn] *adj* (*team, player*)
invicto, -a; (*record*) imbatible
unbecoming [ˌʌnbɪˈkʌmɪŋ] *adj* **1.** (*dress,
suit*) que sienta mal **2.** (*attitude, manner*)
impropio, -a
unbeknown(st) [ˌʌnbɪˈnəʊn, *Am:* -ˈnoʊn]
adv form ~ **to her** sin saberlo ella
unbelief [ˌʌnbɪˈliːf] *n no pl* **1.** incredulidad *f*
2. REL escepticismo *m*
unbelievable [ˌʌnbɪˈliːvəbl] *adj* increíble
unbeliever [ˌʌnbɪˈliːvəʳ, *Am:* -vər] *n* REL no
creyente *mf*
unbelieving [ˌʌnbɪˈliːvɪŋ] *adj* incrédulo, -a
unbend [ʌnˈbend] **I.** *vt* enderezar; (*wire*)
desdoblar **II.** *vi irr* **1.** (*straighten out*) enderezarse **2.** (*relax*) relajarse
unbending *adj* firme; (*will, determination*)
inquebrantable; (*attitude*) rígido, -a
unbiased [ʌnˈbaɪəst] *adj* imparcial; (*judge*)
justo, -a; (*opinion, report, advice*) objetivo, -a
unbidden [ʌnˈbɪdən] *liter* **I.** *adv* espontáneamente, sin ser llamado, -a **II.** *adj* espontáneo, -a
unbind [ʌnˈbaɪnd] *irr vt* desatar
unbleached [ʌnˈbliːtʃt] *adj* sin blanquear; ~
flour harina *f* integral
unblinking [ʌnˈblɪŋkɪŋ] *adj* (*gaze, look*)
imperturbable; (*devotion, help*) resuelto, -a
unblushing [ʌnˈblʌʃɪŋ] *adj* desvergonzado,
-a
unbolt [ʌnˈbəʊlt, *Am:* -ˈboʊlt] *vt* desatrancar
unborn [ʌnˈbɔːn, *Am:* -ˈbɔːrn] *adj* **1.** (*not yet
born: baby*) no nacido, -a; (*foetus*) nonato, -a
2. (*future*) venidero, -a, por venir
unbosom [ʌnˈbʊzəm] *vt form* **1.** (*reveal*)
revelar **2.** (*confide in*) **to ~ oneself to sb**
abrirse a alguien
unbounded [ʌnˈbaʊndɪd] *adj* (*optimism,
enthusiasm, passion*) ilimitado, -a; (*hope*)
infinito, -a; (*love, desire, joy*) inmenso, -a;
(*ambition*) desmedido, -a
unbowed [ʌnˈbaʊd] *adj* **1.** (*erect*) erguido, -a
2. (*not submitting*) orgulloso, -a
unbreakable [ʌnˈbreɪkəbl] *adj* (*material*)
irrompible, indestructible; (*rule, promise,
faith*) inquebrantable; (*record*) imbatible
unbribable [ʌnˈbraɪbəbl] *adj* insobornable
unbridled [ʌnˈbraɪdld] *adj* desenfrenado, -a
un-British [ʌnˈbrɪtɪʃ] *adj* antibritánico, -a
(*término empleado por los propios británicos*)
unbroken [ʌnˈbrəʊkən, *Am:* -ˈbroʊ-] *adj*
1. (*not broken*) no roto, -a; **an ~ promise** una
promesa no rota **2.** (*uncrushed*) intacto, -a
3. (*continuous, without a break*) ininterrum-

pido, -a **4.**(*unsurpassed: record*) imbatible **5.**(*not tamed*) no domesticado, -a; **an ~ horse** un caballo salvaje

unbuckle [ʌn'bʌkl] *vt* deshebillar; **to ~ a seatbelt** desabrochar el cinturón de seguridad

unburden [ʌn'bɜːdən, *Am:* -'bɜːr-] *vt* **1.**(*unload*) aliviar **2.**(*relieve oneself*) **to ~ oneself** (**of sth**) desahogarse (de algo); **to ~ oneself** (**to sb**) deshogarse (con alguien); **to ~ one's sorrows** contar las penas

unbusinesslike [ʌn'bɪznɪslaɪk] *adj* poco profesional

unbutton [ʌn'bʌtən] I. *vt* desabrochar II. *vi* desabrocharse

uncalled-for [ʌn'kɔːldfɔːʳ, *Am:* -fɔːr] *adj* gratuito, -a, impropio, -a; **an ~ remark** un comentario fuera de lugar; **to be ~ to do sth** ser gratuito el hacer algo

uncanny [ʌn'kæni] *adj*<-ier, -iest> **1.**(*mysterious*) misterioso, -a **2.**(*remarkable*) extraordinario, -a; **to be ~ how ...** ser sorprendente cómo...; **an ~ knack** una destreza extraordinaria

uncared-for [ʌn'keədfɔːʳ, *Am:* -'kerdfɔːr] *adj*, **uncared for** *adj* descuidado, -a

uncarpeted *adj* no enmoquetado, -a

unceasing [ʌn'siːsɪŋ] *adj form* incesante; **~ support** apoyo *m* incondicional

unceremonious [ʌnˌserɪ'məʊniəs, *Am:* -'moʊ-] *adj* **1.**(*abrupt*) brusco, -a **2.**(*informal*) informal

uncertain [ʌn'sɜːtən, *Am:* -'sɜːr-] *adj* **1.**(*unsure*) dudoso, -a; **to be ~ of sth** no estar seguro de algo; **to be ~ whether/when ...** no estar seguro de si/cuándo...; **in no ~ terms** claramente **2.**(*unpredictable, chancy*) incierto, -a; **an ~ future** un futuro incierto **3.**(*volatile*) volátil; **an ~ temper** un temperamento volátil

uncertainty [ʌn'sɜːtənti, *Am:* -'sɜːrtənti] <-ies> *n* **1.**(*unpredictability*) incerteza *f* **2.** *no pl* (*unsettled state*) incertidumbre *f*; **~ about sth/sb** incertidumbre sobre algo/alguien **3.** *no pl* (*hesitancy*) indecisión *f*

unchallenged [ʌn'tʃælɪndʒd] *adj* **1.**(*not questioned or doubted*) incontestado, -a **2.**(*not opposed*) no protestado, -a; **to go ~** pasar sin protesta

unchanged [ʌn'tʃeɪndʒd] *adj* **1.**(*unaltered*) inalterado, -a **2.**(*not replaced*) no sustituido, -a

uncharacteristic [ˌʌnkærəktə'rɪs tɪk, *Am:* -ˌkerɪktə'-] *adj* poco característico, -a; **to be ~ of sb/sth** no ser típico de alguien/algo

uncharitable [ʌn'tʃærɪtəbl, *Am:* -'tʃerətə-] *adj* **1.**(*severe*) duro, -a; **to be ~ in sth** ser severo en algo; **to be ~ (of sb) to do sth** ser duro (por parte de alguien) el hacer algo **2.**(*ungenerous*) poco caritativo, -a

unchecked [ʌn'tʃekt] *adj* **1.**(*unrestrained*) desenfrenado, -a; **~ passion/violence** pasión *f*/violencia *f* desenfrenada **2.**(*not examined or verified*) no examinado, -a **3.**(*not checked*)

no comprobado, -a

unchristian [ʌn'krɪstʃən] *adj* indigno, -a de un cristiano

uncivil [ʌn'sɪvl] *adj form* grosero, -a; **to be ~ to sb** ser grosero con alguien

unclad [ʌn'klæd] *adj form* desnudo, -a

unclaimed [ʌn'kleɪmd] *adj* **1.**(*not claimed*) sin reclamar **2.**(*not reclaimed*) no reclamado, -a

unclassified [ʌn'klæsɪfaɪd] *adj* ADMIN sin clasificar

uncle ['ʌŋkl] *n* tío *m* ►**to say ~** *Am, child-speak* rendirse

unclean [ʌn'kliːn] *adj* **1.**(*unhygienic*) sucio, -a **2.** *form* (*taboo*) tabú **3.**(*soiled, impure*) impuro, -a

unclear [ʌn'klɪəʳ, *Am:* -'klɪr] *adj* **1.**(*not certain*) nada claro, -a; **to be ~ about sth** no estar seguro de algo **2.**(*vague*) vago, -a; **an ~ statement** una afirmación vaga

uncluttered [ʌn'klʌtəd, *Am:* -'klʌt̬ə-d] *adj* **1.**(*not messily crowded*) no muy concurrido, -a **2.**(*simple*) simple; **an ~ mind** una mente sencilla

uncollected [ˌʌnkə'lektɪd] *adj* **1.**(*not reclaimed*) no reclamado, -a **2.**(*unincluded in collected works*) no incluido, -a

uncolored *adj Am, Aus,* **uncoloured** [ʌn'kʌləd, *Am:* ʌn'kʌlə-d] *adj Brit* **1.**(*having no colour*) incoloro, -a **2.**(*impartial*) imparcial

uncomfortable [ʌn'kʌmpftəbl, *Am:* ʌn-'kʌmpfə-t̬ə-] *adj* **1.**(*situation*) molesto, -a; **an ~ silence** un silencio molesto **2.**(*person ill at ease*) incómodo, -a; **it makes sb ~ to do sth** le hacer sentir incómodo a alguien el hacer algo

uncommitted [ˌʌnkə'mɪtɪd, *Am:* -'mɪt̬-] *adj* **1.**(*non-aligned*) no alineado, -a **2.**(*not committed*) no comprometido, -a; **to be ~ to sth** no estar comprometido con algo

uncommon [ʌn'kɒmən, *Am:* ʌn'kɑːmən] *adj* **1.**(*rare*) extraño, -a; **to be not ~ for sb/sth** no ser raro para alguien/algo **2.** *form* (*exceptional*) extraordinario, -a; **with ~ interest** con un especial interés

uncommonly *adv* **1.**(*unusually*) raramente **2.** *form* (*extremely*) excepcionalmente

uncommunicative [ˌʌnkə'mjuːnɪkətɪv, *Am:* ˌʌnkə'mjuːnɪkət̬ɪv] *adj* poco comunicativo, -a; **to be ~ about sth/sb** ser reservado respecto a algo/alguien

uncompromising [ʌn'kɒmprəmaɪzɪŋ, *Am:* ʌn'kɑːm-] *adj* intransigente; **to take an ~ stand** adoptar una postura intransigente

unconcerned [ˌʌnkən'sɜːnd, *Am:* -'sɜːrnd] *adj* **1.**(*not worried*) despreocupado, -a; **to be ~ about sth/sb** no preocuparse por algo/alguien **2.**(*indifferent*) indiferente; **to be ~ with sth/sb** ser indiferente con algo/alguien

unconditional [ˌʌnkən'dɪʃənl] *adj* incondicional; **~ love** amor *m* incondicional

unconfirmed [ˌʌnkən'fɜːmd, *Am:* -'fɜːrmd] *adj* no confirmado, -a

U

uncongenial [ˌʌnkən'dʒiːnɪəl] *adj* **1.** (*unfriendly*) antipático, -a **2.** (*not pleasant*) desfavorable; ~ **conditions** condiciones *fpl* adversas

unconnected [ˌʌnkə'nektɪd] *adj* desconectado, -a; **to be** ~ **to sth** estar desconectado de algo

unconscionable [ʌn'kɒntʃənəbl, *Am:* -'kɑːn-] *adj form* desmedido, -a

unconscious [ʌn'kɒntʃəs, *Am:* ʌn'kɑːn-] **I.** *adj* **1.** (*not conscious*) inconsciente; **to knock sb** ~ dejar a alguien inconsciente; ~ **state** estado *m* de inconsciencia **2.** PSYCH (*subconscious*) subconsciente **3.** (*unaware*) no intencional; **to be** ~ **of sth** *form* no ser consciente de algo **II.** *n no pl* PSYCH **the** ~ el inconsciente

unconsciously *adv* inconscientemente

unconsciousness *n no pl* **1.** (*loss of consciousness*) pérdida *f* de conocimiento **2.** *form* (*unawareness*) inconsciencia *f*

unconsidered [ˌʌnkən'sɪdəd, *Am:* ˌʌnkən-'sɪdəd] *adj form* desconsiderado, -a

unconstitutional [ʌnˌkɒntstɪ'tjuːʃənəl, *Am:* ʌnˌkɑːntstə'tuː-] *adj* inconstitucional

unconsummated [ʌn'kɒntsəmeɪtɪd, *Am:* ʌn'kɑːntsəmeɪtɪd] *adj* no consumado, -a

uncontested [ˌʌnkən'testɪd] *adj* **1.** (*unquestioned*) incontestable **2.** LAW (*not disputed*) sin oposición; **an** ~ **divorce** un divorcio sin oposición de ninguna de las partes

uncontrollable [ˌʌnkən'trəʊləbl, *Am:* -'troʊ-] *adj* **1.** (*irresistible*) irrefrenable **2.** (*frenzied*) incontrolable; **an** ~ **child** un niño ingobernable

uncontrolled [ˌʌnkən'trəʊld, *Am:* -'troʊld] *adj* descontrolado, -a

uncontroversial [ʌnkɒntrə'vɜːʃl] *adj* no controvertido, -a

unconvinced [ˌʌnkən'vɪnst] *adj* **to be** ~ **of sth** no estar convencido de algo

unconvincing [ˌʌnkən'vɪnsɪŋ] *adj* **1.** (*not persuasive*) nada convincente; **rather** ~ poco convincente **2.** (*not credible*) nada creíble

uncooked [ʌn'kʊkt] *adj* crudo, -a

uncooperative [ˌʌnkəʊ'ɒpərətɪv, *Am:* -koʊ'ɑː pəpətɪv] *adj* poco cooperativo, -a

uncork [ʌn'kɔːk, *Am:* -'kɔːrk] *vt* **1.** (*extract cork from bottle*) descorchar **2.** *inf* (*let out sth repressed*) **to** ~ **one's feelings** dejar aflorar los sentimientos; **to** ~ **a surprise** destapar una sorpresa

uncorroborated [ˌʌnkər'ɒbəreɪtɪd, *Am:* -'rɑːbəreɪtɪd] *adj* no corroborado, -a

uncountable noun [ʌn'kaʊntəbl naʊn, *Am:* ʌn'kaʊntəbl naʊn] *n* LING substantivo *m* incontable

uncouple [ʌn'kʌpl] *vt* **to** ~ **sth** (**from sth**) **1.** TECH desacoplar algo (de algo) **2.** (*separate*) separar algo (de algo)

uncouth [ʌn'kuːθ] *adj* basto, -a

uncover [ʌn'kʌvəʳ, *Am:* -'kʌvəʳ] *vt* dejar al descubierto, desvelar; **to** ~ **a wound** *a. fig*

dejar descubierta una herida; **to** ~ **a secret** desvelar un secreto

uncritical [ʌn'krɪtɪkl, *Am:* -'krɪt̬-] *adj* falto, -a de sentido crítico; **to be** ~ **of sth/sb** no criticar algo/a alguien

uncrowned [ʌn'kraʊnd] *adj* sin corona

UNCTAD *n abbr of* United Nations Commission for Trade and Development UNCTAD *f*

unction ['ʌŋkʃən] *n* **1.** *form* unción *f* **2.** *s.* **unctuousness**

unctuous ['ʌŋktʃʊəs] *adj* **1.** *form* (*obsequious*) zalamero, -a **2.** (*oily*) untuoso, -a

uncut [ʌn'kʌt] *adj* **1.** (*not cut*) sin cortar; **an** ~ **diamond** un diamante en bruto **2.** (*not shortened*) sin cortes

undated [ʌn'deɪtɪd, *Am:* -t̬ɪd] *adj* sin fecha

undaunted [ʌn'dɔːntɪd, *Am:* -'dɑːnt̬ɪd] *adj* impertérrito, -a; **to be** ~ **by sth** quedarse impávido ante algo

undeceive [ˌʌndɪ'siːv] *vt liter* **to** ~ **sb** (**of sth**) desengañar a alguien (de algo)

undecided [ˌʌndɪ'saɪdɪd] *adj* **1.** (*unresolved*) indeciso, -a; **to be** ~ **about sth** estar indeciso ante algo; **to be** ~ **as to what to do** no saber qué hacer **2.** (*not settled*) no decidido, -a; **an** ~ **vote** un voto indeciso

undeclared [ˌʌndɪ'kleəd, *Am:* -'klerd] *adj* **1.** FIN (*kept secret*) no declarado, -a; ~ **income** ingresos *mpl* no declarados; ~ **goods** bienes *mpl* no declarados **2.** (*not official*) no oficial; **an** ~ **war** *a. fig* una guerra no oficial

undefined [ˌʌndɪ'faɪnd] *adj* **1.** (*not defined*) indefinido, -a **2.** (*lacking clarity*) no claro, -a

undeliverable [ˌʌndɪ'lɪvrəbl] *adj* que no puede ser entregado, -a

undelivered [ˌʌndɪ'lɪvəd, *Am:* -əd] *adj* sin entregar

undemanding [ˌʌndɪ'mɑːndɪŋ] *adj* **1.** (*requiring little effort*) que exige poco esfuerzo **2.** (*easy-going*) **to be** ~ ser poco exigente

undemocratic [ˌʌndemə'krætɪk] *adj* antidemocrático, -a

undemonstrative [ˌʌndɪ'mɒnstrətɪv, *Am:* -'mɑːnstrət̬ɪv] *adj form* reservado, -a

undeniable [ˌʌndɪ'naɪəbl] *adj* innegable; ~ **evidence** prueba *f* irrefutable

undeniably *adv* indudablemente

under ['ʌndəʳ, *Am:* -dəʳ] **I.** *prep* **1.** (*below*) debajo de; ~ **the bed** debajo de la cama; ~ **there** ahí debajo **2.** (*supporting*) bajo; **to break** ~ **the weight** romperse bajo el peso **3.** (*less than*) **to cost** ~ **£10** costar menos de £10; **those** ~ **the age of 30** aquellos con menos de 30 años de edad **4.** (*governed by*) ~ **Charles X** bajo Carlos X; **to be** ~ **sb's influence** estar bajo la influencia de alguien **5.** (*in state of*) ~ **the circumstances** en esas circunstancias; ~ **repair** en reparación **6.** (*in category of*) **to classify the books** ~ **author** clasificar los libros por autor **7.** LAW ~ **the treaty** conforme al Tratado **II.** *adv* debajo; **as** ~ como abajo

underachieve [ˌʌndərəˈtʃiːv, *Am:* -də-] *vi* no rendir lo suficiente

underact [ˌʌndərˈækt, *Am:* -dəʳ-] **I.** *vi actuar sin suficiente brío* **II.** *vt* **to ~ a part** *representar un papel sin suficiente brío*

underage [ˌʌndərˈeɪdʒ, *Am:* -dəʳ-] *adj*, **under age** *adj* menor de edad

underbid [ˌʌndəˈbɪd, *Am:* -dəʳ-] *irr* **I.** *vi* declarar menos de lo que uno tiene **II.** *vt* **to ~ sb/sth** ofrecer un precio más bajo que alguien/algo

undercapitalized [ˌʌndəˈkæpɪtəlaɪzd, *Am:* -dəʳ-] *adj* subcapitalizado, -a; **to be ~** estar descapitalizado

undercarriage [ˈʌndəˌkærɪdʒ, *Am:* -dəˌker-] *n Brit* AVIAT tren *m* de aterrizaje

undercharge [ˌʌndəˈtʃɑːdʒ, *Am:* -dəˈtʃɑːrdʒ] **I.** *vt* **to ~ sb** cobrar de menos a alguien **II.** *vi* cobrar menos; **to ~ for sth** cobrar menos de lo que vale por algo

underclothes [ˈʌndəkləʊðz, *Am:* -dəkloʊðz] *npl*, **underclothing** [ˈʌndəˌkləʊðɪŋ, *Am:* -dəˌkloʊ-] *n no pl* ropa *f* interior

undercoat [ˈʌndəkəʊt, *Am:* -dəkoʊt] *n no pl* primera capa *f* de pintura

undercover [ˌʌndəˈkʌvəʳ, *Am:* -dəˈkʌvə] **I.** *adj* secreto, -a; **~ agent** agente *mf* secreto **II.** *adv* clandestinamente

undercurrent [ˈʌndəkʌrənt, *Am:* -dəkɜːr-] *n* **1.** (*undertow*) corriente *f* submarina **2.** (*underlying influence*) tendencia *f* oculta

undercut [ˌʌndəˈkʌt, *Am:* -dəʳ-] *irr vt* **1.** (*charge less than competitors*) vender más barato **2.** (*undermine*) socavar

underdeveloped [ˌʌndədɪˈveləpt, *Am:* -dədɪ-] *adj* **1.** (*below its economic potential*) subdesarrollado, -a; **an ~ country** país *m* subdesarrollado; **an ~ resource** un recurso infradesarrollado **2.** PHOT insuficientemente revelado, -a **3.** (*insufficiently mature*) inmaduro, -a

underdog [ˈʌndədɒg, *Am:* -dədɑːg] *n* desvalido, -a *m, f*; **to side with the ~** estar del lado de los perdedores

underdone [ˌʌndəˈdʌn, *Am:* -dəʳ-] *adj* (*cooked less than necessary*) poco hecho, -a

underemployed [ˌʌndərɪmˈplɔɪd, *Am:* -dərɪmˈplɔɪd] *adj* **1.** (*having too little work*) subempleado, -a **2.** ECON (*insufficiently used*) **to be ~** ser poco utilizado, -a

underequipped [ˌʌndərɪˈkwɪpt] *adj* mal equipado, -a; **an ~ expedition** una expedición con un equipamiento insuficiente

underestimate [ˌʌndərˈestɪmeɪt, *Am:* -dəˈestə-] **I.** *vt* **to ~ sth/sb** subestimar algo/a alguien **II.** *n* infravaloración *f*

underexpose [ˌʌndərɪkˈspəʊz, *Am:* -dəʳɪkˈspoʊz] *vt* PHOT **to ~ a film/photo** subexponer una película/foto

underexposure [ˌʌndərɪkˈspəʊʒəʳ, *Am:* -dəʳɪkˈspoʊʒə] *n no pl* PHOT subexposición *f*

underfed [ˌʌndəˈfed, *Am:* -dəʳ-] *n* desnutrido, -a *m, f*

underfelt [ˈʌndəfelt, *Am:* -də-] *n no pl* arpillera *f*

underfloor heating [ˌʌndəˈflɔːˌhiːtɪŋ, *Am:* -dəflɔːrˈhiːtɪŋ] *n* calefacción *f* por suelo

underfoot [ˌʌndəˈfʊt, *Am:* -dəʳ-] *adv* (*below one's feet*) debajo de los pies; **to trample sb/sth ~** *a. fig* pisar a alguien/algo

underfund [ˌʌndəˈfʌnd, *Am:* -dəʳ-] *vt* **to ~ sth** infradotar algo

underfunding [ˌʌndəˈfʌndɪŋ, *Am:* -dəʳ-] *n no pl* infradotación *f*

undergarment [ˈʌndəgɑːmənt, *Am:* -dəgɑːr-] *n form* prenda *f* de ropa interior

undergo [ˌʌndəˈgəʊ, *Am:* -dəʳˈgoʊ] *irr vt* **to ~ sth** experimentar algo; **to ~ a change** sufrir un cambio

undergraduate [ˌʌndəˈgrædʒʊət, *Am:* -dəˈgrædʒuət] *n* estudiante *mf* no licenciado, -a; **~ program** programa *m* para no licenciados

underground [ˈʌndəgraʊnd, *Am:* -də-] **I.** *adj* **1.** (*below earth surface*) subterráneo, -a **2.** (*clandestinely anti-government*) clandestino, -a; **~ movement** movimiento *m* clandestino **3.** (*relating to subway system*) de metro **II.** *adv* **1.** (*below earth surface*) bajo tierra **2.** **to go ~** pasar a la clandestinidad; **to drive sb ~** meter a alguien en la clandestinidad **III.** *n* **1.** *no pl, Brit* (*subway train*) metro *m*; **by ~** en metro **2.** (*movement*) **the ~** POL la resistencia; (*lifestyle*) el underground

underground railway *n* ferrocarril *m* subterráneo **underground station** *n* estación *f* de metro

undergrowth [ˈʌndəgrəʊθ, *Am:* -dəgroʊθ] *n no pl* maleza *f*; **dense ~** maleza espesa

underhand [ˌʌndəˈhænd, *Am:* ˌʌndəʳ-] **I.** *adj Brit* turbio, -a, solapado, -a **II.** *adv Am* (*underarm*) por debajo del hombro

underinsure [ˌʌndərɪnˈʃʊəʳ, *Am:* -dəʳɪnˈʃʊr] *vt* **to ~ sth** asegurar algo por debajo del valor real

underlay [ˌʌndəˈleɪ, *Am:* -dəʳ-] **I.** *n no pl, Brit, Aus* refuerzo *m*; **carpet ~** refuerzo *m* de alfombra **II.** *vt pt of* **underlie**

underlie [ˌʌndəˈlaɪ, *Am:* -dəʳ-] *irr vt* **to ~ sth** subyacer a algo

underline [ˌʌndəˈlaɪn, *Am:* -dəʳ-] *vt* **1.** (*draw a line beneath*) subrayar; **to ~ sth in red** subrayar algo en rojo **2.** (*emphasize*) enfatizar; **to ~ that ...** subrayar que...

underling [ˈʌndəlɪŋ, *Am:* -dəlɪŋ] *n pej* subordinado, -a

underlying [ˌʌndəˈlaɪɪŋ, *Am:* -dəʳ-] *adj* subyacente; **the ~ reason for sth** la razón que subyace a algo

undermanned [ˌʌndəˈmænd, *Am:* -dəʳ-] *adj* sin plantilla suficiente

undermanning [ˌʌndəˈmænɪŋ, *Am:* -dəʳ-] *n no pl* escasez *f* de personal

undermentioned [ˌʌndəˈmenʃnd, *Am:* -dəʳ-] *adj Brit, form* abajo citado, -a

undermine [ˌʌndəˈmaɪn, *Am:* -dəʳ-] *vt*

1. (*tunnel under*) socavar; **to ~ a river bank** socavar la orilla de un río **2.** (*damage, sap, weaken*) arruinar; **to ~ hopes** desalentar; **to ~ a currency** debilitar una divisa; **to ~ sb's confidence** bajar la confianza de alguien; **to ~ sb's health** perjudicar a la salud de alguien

undermost ['ʌndəməʊst, *Am:* -dəʳmoʊst] *adj* **the ~ ...** el más bajo...

underneath [ˌʌndə'niːθ, *Am:* -dəʳ-] **I.** *prep* debajo de **II.** *adv* por debajo **III.** *n no pl* **the ~** la superficie inferior **IV.** *adj* inferior

undernourished [ˌʌndə'nʌrɪʃt, *Am:* -dəʳ'nɜːr-] *adj* desnutrido, -a

underpaid [ˌʌndə'peɪd, *Am:* -dəʳ-] *adj* mal pagado, -a

underpants ['ʌndəpænts, *Am:* -dəʳ-] *npl* calzoncillos *mpl*

underpass ['ʌndəpɑːs, *Am:* -dəʳpæs] <-es> *n* paso *m* subterráneo

underpay [ˌʌndə'peɪ, *Am:* -dəʳ-] *irr vt* pagar un sueldo insuficiente

underperform [ˌʌndəpə'fɔːm] *vi* rendir por debajo de lo suficiente

underplay ['ʌndəpleɪ, *Am:* ˌʌndəʳ'pleɪ] **I.** *vt* **1.** (*play down*) subestimar; **to ~ the importance/seriousness of sth** subestimar la importancia/gravedad de algo **2.** (*act with restraint*) actuar con contención **II.** *vi* no actuar demasiado en un papel

underpopulated [ˌʌndə'pɒpjʊleɪtɪd, *Am:* -dəʳ'pɑːpjə-] *adj* poco poblado, -a

underprivileged [ˌʌndə'prɪvəlɪdʒd, *Am:* -dəʳ-] **I.** *adj* sin privilegios; **the ~ class** la clase no privilegiada **II.** *n* **the ~** *pl* los no privilegiados

underrate [ˌʌndə'reɪt, *Am:* -dəʳ-] *vt* **to ~ sth/sb** subestimar algo/a alguien; **to ~ the difficulty/importance of sth** infravalorar la dificultad/importancia de algo

underrepresented [ˌʌndəreprɪ'zentɪd, *Am:* -dəʳreprɪ'zentɪd] *adj* con mala representación

underscore [ˌʌndə'skɔːʳ, *Am:* -dəʳ'skɔːr] *vt* **1.** (*put a line under*) subrayar **2.** (*emphasize*) recalcar; **to ~ a point** recalcar un punto

underseal ['ʌndəsiːl, *Am:* -dəʳ-] *Brit* **I.** *n* impermeable *m* **II.** *vt* impermeabilizar

undersell [ˌʌndə'sel, *Am:* -dəʳ-] *irr vt* **1.** (*offer goods cheaper*) **to ~ goods** vender mercancías a un precio más bajo; **to ~ the competition** vender a precios más bajos que la competencia **2.** (*undervalue*) **to ~ sth/sb** no hacer la suficiente publicidad de algo/alguien; **to ~ oneself** no saber venderse uno mismo

undershirt ['ʌndəʃɜːt, *Am:* -dəʳʃɜːrt] *n Am* camiseta *f*

underside ['ʌndəsaɪd, *Am:* -dəʳ-] *n* superficie *f* inferior

undersigned ['ʌndəsaɪnd, *Am:* 'ʌndəʳsaɪnd] *n form* **the ~** el/la abajofirmante

undersize *adj*, **undersized** [ˌʌndə'saɪzd, *Am:* 'ʌndəʳsaɪzd] *adj* de tamaño insuficiente

underskirt ['ʌndəskɜːt, *Am:* -dəʳskɜːrt] *n* enaguas *fpl*

understaffed [ˌʌndə'stɑːft, *Am:* -dəʳ'stæft] *adj* falto, -a de personal

understand [ˌʌndə'stænd, *Am:* -dəʳ-] *irr* **I.** *vt* **1.** (*perceive meaning*) **to ~ sth/sb** comprender algo/a alguien; **to make oneself understood** hacerse entender; **not to ~ a word** no entender ni una palabra; **to ~ that ...** entender que... **2.** (*sympathize with*) **to ~ sb's doing sth** entender que alguien haga algo **3.** (*feel empathetic insight*) **to ~ sb/an animal** ponerse en la piel de alguien/de un animal **4.** *form* (*be informed*) **to ~ that ...** quedar informado de que...; **to ~ from sb that ...** saber por alguien que...; **to give sb to ~ that ...** dar a alguien a entender que... **5.** (*believe*) creer; (*infer*) sobreentender; **to ~ that ...** sobreentender que...; **to ~ sb to mean/do sth** inferir que alguien quiere decir/hacer algo; **as I ~ it** según tengo entendido; **it is understood that ...** se sobreentiende que... **6.** (*interpret*) interpretar; **to ~ from sth that ...** inferir a partir de algo que... **II.** *vi* entender; **to ~ about sth** entender de algo

understandable [ˌʌndə'stændəbl, *Am:* -dəʳ-] *adj* comprensible; **to be ~ that ...** ser comprensible que...

understanding **I.** *n* **1.** *no pl* (*comprehension, grasp*) entendimiento *m*; **to not have any ~ of sth** no tener ni idea de algo; **to come to an ~** llegar a entender; **sb's ~ of sth** la interpretación de alguien de algo **2.** (*entente, agreement*) acuerdo *m*; **to come to an ~** llegar a un acuerdo; **a tacit ~** un acuerdo tácito **3.** *no pl* (*harmony, rapport*) comprensión *f*; **spirit of ~** un espíritu de comprensión **4.** *no pl* (*condition*) condición *f*; **to do sth on the ~ that ...** hacer algo a condición de que... **5.** *no pl, form* (*intellectual ability*) inteligencia *f* **II.** *adj* comprensivo, -a

understate [ˌʌndə'steɪt, *Am:* -dəʳ-] *vt* minimizar; **to ~ sb's viewpoint** quitar importancia a la opinión de alguien

understated *adj* sencillo, -a

understatement [ˌʌndə'steɪtmənt, *Am:* ˌʌndəʳ'steɪt-] *n* atenuación *f*; **to be the ~ of the year** *fig, iron* el eufemismo del año

understocked [ˌʌndə'stɒkt, *Am:* -dəʳ'stɑːkt] *adj* con pocas existencias; **~ shelves** estanterías *fpl* con pocas existencias

understood [ˌʌndə'stʊd, *Am:* -dəʳ-] *vt, vi pt, pp of* **understand**

understorey [ˌʌndə'stɔːri] *n* capa *f* inferior de plantas (*en un bosque*)

understudy ['ʌndəˌstʌdi, *Am:* -dəʳ-] THEAT **I.** <-ies> *n* suplente *mf*; **to be the ~ for sb/sth** ser el suplente de alguien/algo **II.** <-ie> *vt* **to ~ sb** doblar a alguien

undertake [ˌʌndə'teɪk, *Am:* -dəʳ-] *irr vt* **1.** (*set about, take on*) establecer; **to ~ a journey** emprender un viaje **2.** *form* (*commit oneself to*) **to ~ to do sth** comprometerse a hacer algo; **to ~ (that) ...** comprometerse a (que)...

undertaker [ˈʌndəˌteɪkəʳ, *Am:* -dəˌteɪkəʳ] *n*
1. (*mortician*) director(a) *m(f)* de pompas
fúnebres **2.** (*institute*) **the** ~**'s** la funeraria
undertaking [ˌʌndəˈteɪkɪŋ, *Am:* ˌʌndəˈteɪ-]
n **1.** (*professional project*) empresa *f;* **noble** ~
noble empresa **2.** *form* (*pledge*) promesa *f;* **an**
~ **to do sth** una promesa de hacer algo; **to
give an** ~ **that** ... prometer que...
under-the-counter [ˌʌndədəˈkaʊntəʳ, *Am:*
-dədəˈkaʊntəʳ] **I.** *adj* (*deal*) poco limpio, -a
II. *adv* ilícitamente
undertone [ˈʌndətəʊn, *Am:* -dəˈtoʊn] *n*
1. *no pl* (*low voice*) voz *f* baja; **to say sth in
an** ~ decir algo en voz baja **2.** (*undercurrent,
insinuation*) insinuación *f*
underused [ˌʌndəˈjuːzd, *Am:* -dəʳ-] *adj,*
underutilized [ˌʌndəˈjuːtɪlaɪzd, *Am:* -dəʳ-
ˈjuːtəlaɪzd] *adj* infrautilizado, -a
undervalue [ˌʌndəˈvæljuː, *Am:* -dəʳ-] *vt*
subvalorar
underwater [ˌʌndəˈwɔːtəʳ, *Am:* -dəʳˈwɑː-
təʳ] **I.** *adj* submarino, -a **II.** *adv* por debajo del
agua
underwear [ˈʌndəweəʳ, *Am:* -dəʳwer] *n no
pl* ropa *f* interior
underweight [ˌʌndəˈweɪt, *Am:* -dəʳ-] *adj* de
peso insuficiente
underworked *adj* **1.** (*insufficiently used*)
poco utilizado, -a **2.** (*insufficiently challenged*)
sin dificultades
underworld [ˈʌndəwɜːld, *Am:* -dəʳwɜːrld]
n **1.** *no pl* (*criminal milieu*) hampa *m* **2.** ART, LIT
(*afterworld*) **the Underworld** el infierno
underwrite [ˌʌndəˈraɪt, *Am:* ˈʌndəʳraɪt] *irr
vt* **1.** (*sign*) firmar; **to** ~ **a contract** firmar un
contrato **2.** FIN, ECON (*guarantee share issues*)
garantizar una emisión de acciones **3.** (*provide
insurance for*) asegurar
underwriter [ˈʌndəʳˌraɪtəʳ, *Am:* -dəʳˌraɪtəʳ]
n asegurador(a) *m(f)*
undesirable [ˌʌndɪˈzaɪərəbl, *Am:* -ˈzaɪrəbl]
I. *adj* indeseable; **to be** ~ **that** ... no ser
recomendable que...; **an** ~ **character** un carácter difícil **II.** *n* indeseable *mf*
undetected [ˌʌndɪˈtektɪd] *adj* no descubierto, -a; **to go** ~ pasar inadvertido, -a
undeveloped [ˌʌndɪˈveləpt] *adj* **1.** POL, ECON
subdesarrollado, -a **2.** (*not built on or used*)
poco utilizado, -a **3.** PHOT no revelado, -a **4.** BIO,
PSYCH no desarrollado, -a
undid [ʌnˈdɪd] *vt, vi pt of* **undo**
undies [ˈʌndɪz] *npl inf* paños *mpl* menores
undischarged bankrupt [ˌʌndɪstʃɑːdʒd-
ˈbæŋkrʌpt, *Am:* -tʃɑːrdʒd-] *n* COM quebrado,
-a *m, f* no rehabilitado, -a
undisclosed [ˌʌndɪsˈkləʊzd, *Am:* -ˈkloʊzd]
adj no revelado, -a; **an** ~ **amount** una cantidad
no desvelada; **an** ~ **location** una ubicación sin
desvelar; **an** ~ **source** una fuente no revelada
undiscovered [ˌʌndɪsˈkʌvəd, *Am:* -əʳd] *adj*
no descubierto, -a; **to go** ~ ir de incógnito
undisputed [ˌʌndɪˈspjuːtɪd, *Am:* -t̬ɪd] *adj*
incontestable

undistinguished [ˌʌndɪˈstɪŋgwɪʃt] *adj* mediocre
undisturbed [ˌʌndɪˈstɜːbd, *Am:* -stɜːrbd]
adj **they were** ~ **by the noise** el ruido no les
molestaba
undivided [ˌʌndɪˈvaɪdɪd] *adj* **1.** (*not split*)
íntegro, -a **2.** (*intense*) intenso, -a; **sb's** ~
attention toda la atención de alguien
undo [ʌnˈduː] *irr vt* **1.** (*unfasten*) soltar; **to** ~
buttons desabrochar botones; **to** ~ **a zipper**
bajar una cremallera **2.** (*cancel*) anular; **to** ~
the damage reparar el daño; **to** ~ **the good
work** deshacer el trabajo bueno **3.** (*cause
ruin*) arruinar; **to** ~ **sb's good name** perjudicar el buen nombre de alguien ▶**what's done**
cannot be undone *prov* lo hecho, hecho está
prov
undoing *n no pl, form* ruina *f*
undone [ʌnˈdʌn] **I.** *vt pp of* **undo II.** *adj*
1. (*not fastened*) desatado, -a; **to come** ~ deshacerse **2.** (*uncompleted*) por hacer; **to leave**
sth ~ dejar algo sin hacer
undoubted [ʌnˈdaʊtɪd, *Am:* -t̬ɪd] *adj*
indudable
undoubtedly *adv* indudablemente
undreamed-of [ʌnˈdriːmdˌɒv, *Am:* -ˌɑːv]
adj, **undreamt-of** [ʌnˈdremtˌɒv, *Am:* -ˌɑːv]
adj inimaginable
undress [ʌnˈdres] **I.** *vt* desnudar, desvestir
AmL; **to** ~ **sb with one's eyes** *fig* desnudar a
alguien con la mirada **II.** *vi* desvestirse **III.** *n no
pl* ropa *f* informal
undressed *adj* desvestido, -a; **to get** ~ desnudarse
undue [ʌnˈdjuː, *Am:* -ˈduː] *adj form* indebido, -a; ~ **pressure** presión *f* excesiva
undulate [ˈʌndjəleɪt, *Am:* -dʒə-] *vi form*
ondular
undulating *adj form* **1.** (*moving like a wave*)
ondulante **2.** (*shaped like waves*) ondulado, -a
unduly [ʌnˈdjuːli, *Am:* -ˈduː-] *adv* indebidamente
undying [ʌnˈdaɪɪŋ] *adj liter* imperecedero,
-a; ~ **love** amor *m* eterno
unearned [ʌnˈɜːnd, *Am:* -ˈɜːrnd] *adj*
1. (*undeserved*) inmerecido, -a **2.** (*not worked
for*) no ganado, -a
unearth [ʌnˈɜːθ, *Am:* -ˈɜːrθ] *vt* **1.** (*dig up*)
desenterrar **2.** (*discover with difficulty*) sacar a
la luz; **to** ~ **the truth** descubrir la verdad
unearthly [ʌnˈɜːθli, *Am:* -ˈɜːrθ-] *adj* **1.** (*unsettling*) sobrenatural; ~ **noise/scream** ruido
m/grito *m* aterrador **2.** *inf* (*inconvenient*) intempestivo, -a **3.** (*not from the earth*) sobrenatural
unease [ʌnˈiːz] *n no pl* malestar *m;* **with**
growing ~ con creciente inquietud
uneasiness *n no pl* inquietud *f*
uneasy [ʌnˈiːzi] *adj* <-ier, -iest> **1.** (*uncertain*) inquieto, -a; **to be/feel** ~ **about sth/**
sb estar/sentirse inquieto por algo/alguien
2. (*causing anxiety*) ansioso, -a; (*suspicion*)
inquietante; (*relationship*) inestable **3.** (*inse-*

cure) dudoso, -a

uneconomic [ˌʌn͵iːkəˈnɒmɪk, *Am:* -͵ekə-ˈnɑːmɪk] *adj* poco lucrativo, -a

uneducated [ʌnˈedʒʊkeɪtɪd, *Am:* -ˈedʒʊ-keɪt̬ɪd] I. *adj* inculto, -a II. *n* the ~ los ignorantes

unemotional [ˌʌnɪˈməʊʃənəl, *Am:* -ˈmoʊ-] *adj* 1. (*not feeling emotions*) impasible 2. (*not revealing emotions*) reservado, -a

unemployable [ˌʌnɪmˈplɔɪəbl] *adj* incapacitado, -a para trabajar

unemployed [ˌʌnɪmˈplɔɪd] I. *n pl* the ~ los desempleados II. *adj* parado, -a

unemployment [ˌʌnɪmˈplɔɪmənt] *n no pl* 1. (*condition of lacking work*) desempleo *m* 2. (*rate of joblessness*) desocupación *f*

unemployment benefit *n* subsidio *m* de paro

unending [ʌnˈendɪŋ] *adj* interminable

unenlightened [ˌʌnɪnˈlaɪtənd] *adj* 1. (*not wise or insightful*) poco instruido, -a 2. (*lack of insight*) ignorante 3. *a. iron* (*not informed*) desinformado, -a

unenviable [ʌnˈenvɪəbl] *adj* poco envidiable

unequal [ʌnˈiːkwəl] *adj* 1. *form* (*different*) diferente; ~ **triangle** triángulo *m* de lados desiguales 2. (*unjust, inequitable*) desigual 3. (*unable*) **to be** ~ **to sth** no estar a la altura de algo

unequaled *adj Am*, **unequalled** *adj Brit* sin igual

unequivocal [ˌʌnɪˈkwɪvəkəl] *adj* inequívoco, -a; **an** ~ **success** un éxito indudable; **to be** ~ **in sth** ser claro en algo

unerring [ʌnˈɜːrɪŋ] *adj* infalible

UNESCO *n*, **Unesco** [juːˈneskəʊ, *Am:* -koʊ] *n no pl abbr of* **United Nations Educational, Scientific and Cultural Organization** UNESCO *f*

unethical [ʌnˈeθɪkəl] *adj* poco ético, -a

uneven [ʌnˈiːvən] *adj* 1. (*not flat or level*) desnivelado, -a 2. (*unequal*) desigual 3. (*different*) distinto, -a 4. (*of inadequate quality*) irregular 5. (*erratic, fluctuating*) cambiante 6. MED anormal

uneventful [ˌʌnɪˈventfəl] *adj* sin acontecimientos; (*unexciting*) tranquilo, -a

unexampled [ˌʌnɪɡˈzɑːmpld, *Am:* -ɪɡ-ˈzæm-] *adj form* único, -a

unexceptionable [ˌʌnɪkˈsepʃənəbl] *adj form* intachable

unexceptional [ˌʌnɪkˈsepʃənəl] *adj* corriente

unexciting *adj* 1. (*commonplace*) trivial 2. (*uneventful*) aburrido, -a

unexpected [ˌʌnɪkˈspektɪd] I. *adj* inesperado, -a II. *n no pl* the ~ lo inesperado

unexplained [ˌʌnɪkˈspleɪnd] *adj* inexplicado, -a; **her absence was** ~ su ausencia era inexplicable

unexploded [ˌʌnɪkˈspləʊdɪd] *adj* sin explotar

unexploited *adj* inexplotado, -a

unexpressed *adj* sobreentendido, -a

unexpressive [ˌʌnɪkˈspresɪv] *adj* inexpresivo, -a

unexpurgated [ˌʌnˈekspɜːɡeɪtɪd, *Am:* -spɚˈɡeɪt̬ɪd] *adj* íntegro, -a

unfailing [ʌnˈfeɪlɪŋ] *adj* 1. (*always present when needed*) indefectible 2. (*not running out*) incansable

unfair [ʌnˈfeəʳ, *Am:* -ˈfer] *adj* injusto, -a; (*advantage, disadvantage*) desfavorable

unfaithful [ʌnˈfeɪθfʊl] *adj* 1. (*adulterous*) infiel 2. (*disloyal*) desleal 3. *form* (*not accurate*) inexacto, -a

unfaltering [ʌnˈfɔːltərɪŋ, *Am:* -ˈfɑːlt̬ɚɪŋ] *adj* 1. (*without hesitation*) resuelto, -a; **with** ~ **steps** con pasos firmes 2. (*decided*) decidido, -a

unfamiliar [ˌʌnfəˈmɪljəʳ, *Am:* -jɚ] *adj* 1. (*new, not familiar*) desconocido, -a; **to be** ~ **to sb** resultar desconocido a alguien 2. (*unacquainted*) ajeno, -a

unfashionable [ʌnˈfæʃənəbl] *adj* pasado, -a de moda

unfasten [ˌʌnˈfɑːsən, *Am:* -ˈfæsn] I. *vt* desatar II. *vi* soltarse

unfathomable [ʌnˈfæðəməbl] *adj* 1. *a. fig* (*too deep to measure*) insondable 2. (*inexplicable*) inexplicable

unfavorable *adj Am*, **unfavourable** [ʌnˈfeɪvərəbl] *adj Brit, Aus* 1. (*adverse*) adverso, -a 2. (*disadvantagous*) desfavorable

unfeeling [ʌnˈfiːlɪŋ] *adj* insensible

unfeigned [ʌnˈfeɪnd] *adj* verdadero, -a

unfettered [ʌnˈfetəd, *Am:* -ˈfet̬ɚd] *adj* sin ataduras

unfilled *adj* vacío, -a

unfinished [ʌnˈfɪnɪʃt] *adj* inacabado, -a

unfit [ʌnˈfɪt] I. *adj* 1. (*unhealthy*) **I'm** ~ no estoy en forma; **to be** ~ **for sth** no estar en condiciones para algo 2. (*incompetent*) incapaz 3. (*unsuitable*) no apto, -a; **to be** ~ **for sth** ser no apto para algo; **to be** ~ **for** (**human**) **habitation** ser inhabitable (para el ser humano) II. *vt* <-tt-> *form* inhabilitar

unflagging [ʌnˈflæɡɪŋ] *adj* incansable

unflappable [ʌnˈflæpəbl] *adj inf* imperturbable

unflinching [ʌnˈflɪntʃɪŋ] *adj* intrépido, -a; (*report*) atrevido, -a; (*support, honesty*) resuelto, -a

unfold [ʌnˈfəʊld, *Am:* -ˈfoʊld] I. *vt* 1. (*open out sth folded*) desenvolver; **to** ~ **one's arms** extender sus brazos 2. *form* (*make known*) **to** ~ **one's ideas/plans** exponer sus ideas/planes II. *vi* 1. (*develop, evolve*) desarrollarse 2. (*become revealed*) revelarse 3. (*become unfolded*) extenderse

unforeseeable [ˌʌnfɔːˈsiːəbl, *Am:* -fɔːrˈ-] *adj* imprevisible

unforeseen [ˌʌnfɔːˈsiːn, *Am:* -fɔːrˈ-] *adj* imprevisto, -a

unforgettable [ˌʌnfəˈɡetəbl, *Am:* -fɚˈɡet̬-] *adj* inolvidable

unforgivable [ˌʌnfəˈgɪvəbl, *Am:* -fɚ·-] *adj* imperdonable

unfortunate [ʌnˈfɔːtʃənət, *Am:* -ˈfɔːrtʃnət] I. *adj* 1. (*luckless*) desafortunado, -a; **to be ~ that ...** ser lamentable que... +*subj* 2. *form* (*regrettable*) deplorable 3. (*inopportune*) inoportuno, -a 4. (*adverse*) funesto, -a II. *n* desgraciado, -a *m, f*

unfortunately *adv* por desgracia

unfounded [ʌnˈfaʊndɪd] *adj* infundado, -a

unfreeze [ʌnˈfriːz] *irr* I. *vt* descongelar II. *vi* descongelarse

unfrequented [ˌʌnfrɪˈkwentɪd, *Am:* ʌnˈfriːkwentɪd] *adj* solitario, -a

unfriendly [ʌnˈfrendli] *adj* <-ier, -iest> 1. (*unsociable*) insociable 2. *fig* (*hard to use*) complicado, -a 3. (*inhospitable*) hostil

unfulfilled [ˌʌnfʊlˈfɪld] *adj* 1. (*not carried out*) incumplido, -a 2. (*unsatisfied*) insatisfecho, -a 3. (*frustrated*) frustrado, -a

unfulfilled order *n* orden *f* incumplida

unfurl [ʌnˈfɜːl, *Am:* -ˈfɜːrl] I. *vt* desplegar; **to ~ an umbrella** abrir un paraguas; **to ~ a sail** largar una vela II. *vi* desplegarse

unfurnished [ˌʌnˈfɜːnɪʃt, *Am:* -ˈfɜːr-] *adj* desamueblado, -a

ungainly [ʌnˈgeɪnli] *adj* <-ier, -iest> torpe

ungenerous [ʌnˈdʒenərəs] *adj* tacaño, -a

ungentlemanly [ʌnˈdʒentlmənli] *adj* poco cortés

unget-at-able [ˌʌngetˈætəbl, *Am:* ˌʌngetˈæt-] *adj* *inf* inaccesible

ungodly [ʌnˈgɒdli, *Am:* ʌnˈgɑːdli] *adj* <-ier, -iest> 1. *inf* (*unreasonable*) atroz 2. (*impious*) impío, -a

ungovernable [ʌnˈgʌvənəbl, *Am:* ʌnˈgʌvɚnə-] *adj* ingobernable

ungraceful [ʌnˈgreɪsfəl] *adj* chabacano, -a

ungracious [ʌnˈgreɪʃəs] *adj* *form* descortés

ungrateful [ʌnˈgreɪtfəl] *adj* ingrato, -a

ungrudging [ʌnˈgrʌdʒɪŋ] *adj* 1. (*without reservation*) generoso, -a 2. (*not resentful or envious*) incondicional

ungrudgingly *adv* de buena gana

unguarded [ʌnˈgɑːdɪd, *Am:* ʌnˈgɑːr-] *adj* 1. (*not defended or watched*) sin vigilancia 2. (*careless*) desprevenido, -a; **in an ~ moment** en un momento de descuido

unguent [ˈʌŋgwənt] *n liter* ungüento *m*

unhallowed [ʌnˈhæləʊd, *Am:* -oʊd] *adj* 1. (*not consecrated*) profano, -a 2. (*unholy*) sacrílego, -a

unhappy [ʌnˈhæpi] *adj* <-ier, -iest> 1. (*sad*) infeliz; **to make sb ~** hacer desdichado a alguien 2. (*unfortunate*) desafortunado, -a

unharmed [ʌnˈhɑːmd, *Am:* -ˈhɑːrmd] *adj* ileso, -a

UNHCR [ˌjuːeneɪtʃsiːˈɑːʳ] *n no pl abbr of* **United Nations High Commission for Refugees** ACNUR *f*

unhealthy [ʌnˈhelθi] *adj* <-ier, -iest> 1. (*sick*) enfermizo, -a 2. (*unwholesome*) nocivo, -a 3. *inf* (*dangerous*) arriesgado, -a

4. PSYCH (*morbid*) morboso, -a

unheard [ʌnˈhɜːd, *Am:* -ˈhɜːrd] *adj* 1. (*not heard*) desoído, -a 2. (*ignored*) desatendido, -a

unheard-of [ʌnˈhɜːdɒv, *Am:* -ˈhɜːrdˌɑːv] *adj* 1. (*incredible*) sin precedente 2. (*impossible*) inaudito, -a

unhelpful [ʌnˈhelpfʊl] *adj* de poca ayuda

unhinge [ʌnˈhɪndʒ] *vt* 1. (*take off hinges*) desgoznar 2. (*make crazy*) desquiciar

unholy [ʌnˈhəʊli, *Am:* -ˈhoʊ-] <-ier, -iest> *adj* 1. (*wicked*) impío, -a 2. REL (*profane*) profano, -a 3. (*outrageous*) atroz; **to get up at some ~ hour** levantarse a una hora infame

unhook [ʌnˈhʊk] *vt* 1. (*remove hooks*) desenganchar 2. (*unfasten*) soltar

unhoped-for [ʌnˈhəʊptˌfɔːʳ, *Am:* -ˈhoʊptˌfɔːr] *adj* inesperado, -a

unhorse [ˌʌnˈhɔːs, *Am:* -ˈhɔːrs] *vt* desmontar

unhurt [ʌnˈhɜːt, *Am:* -ˈhɜːrt] *adj* ileso, -a

UNICEF *n*, **Unicef** [ˈjuːnɪsef] *n no pl abbr of* **United Nations International Children's Emergency Fund** UNICEF *f*

unicorn [ˈjuːnɪkɔːn, *Am:* -kɔːrn] *n* unicornio *m*

unidentified [ˌʌnaɪˈdentɪfaɪd, *Am:* -t̬ə-] *n* 1. (*unknown*) desconocido, -a 2. (*not yet made public*) no identificado, -a

unification [ˌjuːnɪfɪˈkeɪʃən] *n no pl* unificación *f*

uniform [ˈjuːnɪfɔːm, *Am:* -nəfɔːrm] I. *n* uniforme *m* II. *adj* 1. (*same or similar*) uniforme 2. (*constant*) constante

uniformity [ˌjuːnɪˈfɔːməti, *Am:* -nəˈfɔːrməti] *n no pl* (*sameness*) uniformidad *f*

unify [ˈjuːnɪfaɪ, *Am:* -nə-] *vt* unificar

unilateral [ˌjuːnɪˈlætrəl, *Am:* -nəˈlæt̬-] *adj* unilateral

unimaginable [ˌʌnɪˈmædʒnəbl] *adj* inimaginable

unimpeachable [ˌʌnɪmˈpiːtʃəbl] *adj* *form* intachable; **an ~ source** una fuente fidedigna

unimportant [ˌʌnɪmˈpɔːtənt, *Am:* -ˈpɔːr-] *adj* sin importancia

uninformed [ˌʌnɪnˈfɔːmd, *Am:* -ˈfɔːrmd] *adj* desinformado, -a

uninhabitable [ˌʌnɪnˈhæbɪtəbl, *Am:* -t̬əbl] *adj* inhabitable

uninhabited [ˌʌnɪnˈhæbɪtɪd] *adj* 1. (*not lived in*) deshabitado, -a 2. (*deserted*) desierto, -a

uninhibited [ˌʌnɪnˈhɪbɪtɪd, *Am:* -t̬ɪd] *adj* desinhibido, -a

uninjured [ʌnˈɪndʒəd, *Am:* -dʒɚd] *adj* ileso, -a

uninsured [ˌʌnɪnˈʃʊəd, *Am:* -ˈʃʊrd] *adj* no asegurado, -a

unintelligent [ˌʌnɪnˈtelɪdʒənt] *adj* poco inteligente

unintelligible [ˌʌnɪnˈtelɪdʒəbl] *adj* 1. (*not comprehensible*) incomprensible 2. (*unreadable*) ininteligible

unintentional [ˌʌnɪnˈtentʃənəl] *adj* involuntario, -a

unintentionally adv sin intención

uninterested [ʌn'ɪntrəstɪd] adj indiferente

uninteresting adj aburrido, -a

uninterrupted [ʌn,ɪntər'ʌptɪd] adj ininterrumpido, -a

union ['juːnjən] n 1. no pl (act of becoming united) unión f 2. (instance of becoming united) asociación f 3. + sing/pl vb (organization representing employees) sindicato m; the ~ demands las exigencias gremiales 4. form (marriage) enlace m 5. (harmony, concord) to live in perfect ~ vivir en perfecta armonía

unionise ['juːnjənaɪz] Brit, Aus I. vt agremiar II. vi agremiarse

unionist ['juːnjənɪst] n unionista mf

unionize vt, vi s. **unionise**

Union Jack n (British national flag) bandera del Reino Unido

union member n sindicalista mf

unique [juː'niːk] adj 1. (only one) único, -a; a ~ characteristic una característica exclusiva 2. (exceptional) excepcional

uniqueness n no pl unicidad f

uniqueness theorem n MAT teorema m de la unicidad

unisex ['juːnɪseks, Am: -nə-] adj unisex

unison ['juːnɪsən, Am: -nə-] I. n 1. no pl MUS to sing in ~ cantar al unísono 2. (in agreement) to act in ~ with sb obrar de acuerdo con alguien II. adj MUS unísono, -a

unit ['juːnɪt] n 1. a. INFOR, COM unidad f; central processing ~ unidad de procesamiento central; tape backup/output ~ unidad de respaldo/de salida en cinta; ~ of currency unidad monetaria 2. + sing/pl vb (organized group of people) brigada f 3. (element of furniture) elemento m

unit cost n COM coste m unitario

unite [juː'naɪt] I. vt 1. (join together) juntar; (bring together) unir 2. LAW (join in marriage) casar II. vi 1. POL, SOCIOL (join in common cause) to ~ against sb unirse para hacer frente a alguien 2. (join together) juntarse

united adj unido, -a

United Arab Emirates npl the ~ los Emiratos Arabes Unidos **United Kingdom** n no pl the ~ el Reino Unido **United Nations** n no pl the ~ las Naciones Unidas **United States** n + sing vb Estados mpl Unidos; the ~ of America los Estados Unidos América

unit price n COM precio m por unidad **unit trust** n Brit fondo m de inversión inmobiliaria

unity ['juːnəti, Am: -ţi] n no pl 1. (oneness) unidad f; ~ of a film/novel continuidad f de una película/novela 2. (harmony, consensus) consenso m

Univ. abbr of **University** Univ.

universal [ˌjuːnɪ'vɜːsəl, Am: -nə'vɜːr-] I. adj universal; ~ agreement acuerdo m global II. n universal m

universe ['juːnɪvɜːs, Am: -nəvɜːrs] n the ~ el universo

university [ˌjuːnɪ'vɜːsəti, Am: -nə'vɜːrsəţi] <-ies> n universidad f; the ~ community la comunidad universitaria

university education n no pl educación f universitaria **university lecturer** n profesor(a) m(f) universitario, -a **university town** n ciudad f universitaria

unjust [ʌn'dʒʌst] adj injusto, -a

unjustifiable [ʌn,dʒʌstɪ'faɪəbl] adj injustificable

unjustified [ʌn'dʒʌstɪfaɪd] adj injustificado, -a; (complaint) no justificado, -a

unjustly adv 1. (in an unjust manner) inmerecidamente 2. (wrongfully) injustamente

unkempt [ʌn'kempt] adj descuidado, -a; (appearance) desarreglado, -a; (hair) despeinado, -a

unkind [ʌn'kaɪnd] adj 1. (not kind) desagradable; to be ~ to sb tratar mal a alguien; to be ~ to animals ser cruel con los animales 2. (not gentle) to be ~ to hair/hands/skin estropear el pelo/las manos/la piel

unkindly adv cruelmente; to take sth ~ tomarse algo mal

unknowing [ˌʌn'nəʊɪŋ, Am: -'noʊ-] adj no consciente

unknown [ˌʌn'nəʊn, Am: -'noʊn] I. adj 1. (not known) desconocido, -a; ~ to me ... sin saberlo yo... 2. (not widely familiar) ignorado, -a II. n 1. (thing) the ~ lo desconocido; MAT la incógnita 2. (person) desconocido, -a m, f

unlawful [ˌʌn'lɔːfəl, Am: -'lɑː-] adj ilegal; (possession, association) ilícito, -a

unleaded [ʌn'ledɪd] adj sin plomo

unlearn [ʌn'lɜːn, Am: -'lɜːrn] vt to ~ sth (intentionally forget) olvidar algo; (intentionally stop doing sth) acostumbrarse a no hacer algo

unleash [ʌn'liːʃ] vt (a dog) soltar; fig (passions) desatar; (a war) desencadenar

unleavened [ʌn'levənd] adj (bread) sin levadura

unless [ən'les] conj a no ser que +subj, a menos que +subj; he'll buy it ~ she already has it lo comprará a menos que ella ya lo tenga; I don't say anything ~ I'm sure yo no digo nada a menos que esté seguro; he won't come ~ he has time no vendrá a menos que tenga tiempo; ~ I'm mistaken si no me equivoco

unlicensed [ʌn'laɪsəntst] adj sin patente; (restaurant) no autorizado, -a; Brit sin permiso

unlike [ʌn'laɪk] I. adj diferente, distinto, -a II. prep 1. (different from) diferente; to be ~ sth/sb ser distinto de algo/alguien 2. (in contrast to) a diferencia de 3. (not characteristic of) it's ~ sb/sth no es característico de alguien/algo

unlikely [ʌn'laɪkli] <-ier, -iest> adj 1. (improbable) improbable; (sth) seems ~ (algo) parece poco probable; it's ~ that ... es difícil que... 2. (unconvincing) inverosímil

unlimited [ʌn'lɪmɪtɪd, Am: -ţɪd] adj 1. (not

limited) ilimitado, -a; (*access, visibility*) sin límite **2.** (*very great*) impresionante

unlisted [ʌn'lɪstɪd] *adj* **1.** FIN (*stock market*) no cotizado, -a; ~ **securities** valores *mpl* no inscritos en bolsa **2.** *Am, Aus* (*not in the phone book*) no incluido, -a en la guía telefónica

unload [ʌn'ləʊd, *Am:* -'loʊd] I. *vt* **1.** (*remove the contents*) **to** ~ **sth** descargar algo **2.** (*remove film: a camera*) vaciar **3.** *inf* (*get rid of*) **to** ~ **sth** deshacerse de algo **4.** **to** ~ **one's worries on sb** vaciar las preocupaciones con alguien II. *vi* **1.** AUTO (*remove the contents*) descargar **2.** (*be emptied*) vaciar **3.** *inf* (*relieve stress*) tranquilizarse

unlock [ʌn'lɒk, *Am:* -'lɑːk] *vt* **1.** (*release a lock*) liberar **2.** (*release*) abrir **3.** (*solve*) solucionar; (*mystery, riddle*) resolver

unlocked *adj* abierto, -a; *fig* resuelto, -a

unlooked-for [ʌn'lʊktˌfɔːʳ, *Am:* -ˌfɔːr] *adj form* inesperado, -a; (*problem*) inopinado, -a

unlucky [ʌn'lʌki] *adj* **1.** (*unfortunate*) desgraciado, -a; (*at cards, in love*) desafortunado, -a; **to be** ~ **enough to get a cold** tener la mala suerte de coger un resfriado **2.** *form* (*bringing bad luck*) **to be** ~ ser nefasto, -a; (*day*) ser funesto, -a

unman [ʌn'mæn] <-nn-> *vt* **to** ~ **sb** acobardar a alguien

unmanageable [ʌn'mænɪdʒəbəl] *adj* **1.** (*unwieldy: vehicle, boat*) difícil de manejar, ingobernable **2.** (*incontrollable: person, situation*) incontrolable

unmanned *adj* AVIAT, TECH no tripulado, -a

unmannerly [ʌn'mænəli, *Am:* -ɚli] *adj form* (*behaviour*) desconsiderado, -a; **to be** ~ ser descortés

unmarked [ʌn'mɑːkt, *Am:* -mɑːrkt] *adj* **1.** SCHOOL, UNIV (*exam*) sin corregir **2.** (*without mark, stain*) sin marcas

unmarried [ʌn'mærɪd, *Am:* -'mer-] *adj* soltero, -a; ~ **mother** madre *f* soltera

unmask [ʌn'mɑːsk, *Am:* -'mæsk] *vt* **to** ~ **sb/ sth** (**as sb/sth**) *a. fig* desenmascarar a alguien/algo (como alguien/algo)

unmatched [ʌn'mætʃt] *adj* **1.** (*unequalled*) inigualable; **to be** ~ **by sb** no ser igualado por alguien **2.** (*extremely great*) sin par

unmentionable [ʌn'mentʃənəbl] *adj* inmencionable; (*disease*) indescriptible

unmentioned [ʌn'mentʃənd] *adj* indecible

unmindful [ʌn'maɪndfəl] *adj* **to be** ~ **of sth** hacer caso omiso de algo

unmistak(e)able [ʌnmɪ'steɪkəbl] *adj* inconfundible; (*symptom*) inequívoco, -a

unmitigated [ʌn'mɪtɪgeɪtɪd, *Am:* -'mɪt̬əgeɪt̬ɪd] *adj* (*total*) absoluto, -a; (*disaster*) total; (*contempt*) rotundo, -a; (*evil*) implacable

unmoved [ʌn'muːvd] *adj* impasible

unnamed [ʌn'neɪmd] *adj* no nombrado, -a

unnatural [ʌn'nætʃərəl, *Am:* -ɚəl] *adj* **1.** (*contrary to nature*) poco natural; (*affected*) afectado, -a; (*sexual practices*) perverso, -a **2.** (*not normal*) anormal

unnecessarily [ˌʌn'nesəsərəli, *Am:* -ˌnesə'ser-] *adv* innecesariamente

unnecessary [ʌn'nesəsəri, *Am:* -seri] *adj* **1.** (*not necessary*) innecesario, -a **2.** (*uncalled for*) superfluo, -a

unnerve [ʌn'nɜːv, *Am:* -'nɜːrv] *vt* **to** ~ **sb** poner nervioso a alguien

unnerving *adj* enervante

unnoticed [ˌʌn'nəʊtɪst, *Am:* -'noʊt̬ɪst] *adj* desapercibido, -a; **to go** ~ **that ...** pasar inadvertido que...

unnumbered [ˌʌn'nʌmbəd, *Am:* -bɚd] *adj* **1.** (*not marked with a number: house, page*) sin numerar **2.** *form* (*too many to be counted*) innumerable

UNO ['juːnəʊ, *Am:* -noʊ] *n no pl abbr of* **United Nations Organization** ONU *f*

unobtainable [ˌʌnəb'teɪnəbl] *adj* inalcanzable

unobtrusive [ˌʌnəb'truːsɪv] *adj* (*people*) modesto, -a; (*things*) discreto, -a

unoccupied [ʌn'ɒkjəpaɪd, *Am:* -'ɑːkjə-] *adj* **1.** (*uninhabited*) deshabitado, -a **2.** MIL desocupado, -a **3.** (*chair, table*) libre

unofficial [ˌʌnə'fɪʃəl] *adj* no oficial; (*figures*) oficioso, -a; (*capacity*) extraoficial

unorganized [ʌn'ɔːgənaɪzd, *Am:* -'ɔːr-] *adj* desorganizado, -a

unorthodox [ʌn'ɔːθədɒks, *Am:* -'ɔːrθədɑːks] *adj* poco ortodoxo, -a; (*approach*) poco convencional

unpack [ʌn'pæk] I. *vt* (*a car*) descargar; **to** ~ **sth** sacar algo II. *vi* deshacer el equipaje

unpaid [ʌn'peɪd] *adj* **1.** (*not remunerated*) no remunerado, -a; (*services*) sin sueldo **2.** (*not paid*) pendiente

unpalatable [ʌn'pælətəbl, *Am:* -t̬əbl] *adj a. fig* desagradable

unparalleled [ʌn'pærəleld, *Am:* ʌn'per-] *adj form* sin precedentes

unparliamentary [ʌnˌpɑːlə'mentəri, *Am:* ʌnˌpɑːrlə'ment̬ɚ-] *adj* impropio, -a de un parlamentario; (*language*) antiparlamentario, -a

unperturbed [ˌʌnpə'tɜːbd, *Am:* ʌnpɚ'tɜːrbd] *adj* impasible; **to be** ~ **by sth** quedarse impertérrito ante algo

unpick [ʌn'pɪk] *vt* **1.** (*undo sewing*) descoser **2.** *fig* (*painstakingly destroy*) deshacer

unplaced [ʌn'pleɪst] *adj* SPORTS no clasificado, -a

unplanned [ʌn'plænd] *adj* espontáneo, -a

unpleasant [ʌn'plezənt] *adj* **1.** (*not pleasing*) desagradable; (*sensation*) repugnante **2.** (*unfriendly*) antipático, -a

unpleasantness *n no pl* **1.** (*quality of being unpleasant*) **the** ~ lo desagradable **2.** (*unfriendly feelings*) antipatía *f*

unplug [ʌn'plʌg] <-gg-> *vt* **1.** (*disconnect an electric plug*) desconectar **2.** (*unstop: drain, pipe*) destapar

unplumbed [ʌn'plʌmd] *adj* **1.** (*not understood*) insondable **2.** (*without plumbing*) sin fontanería

unpolished [ʌn'pɒlɪʃt, Am: ʌn'pɑːlɪʃt] adj
1. (not polished) sin pulir **2.** (not refined)
poco refinado, -a

unpolluted [ˌʌnpə'luːtɪd, Am: ˌʌnpə'luːt̬ɪd]
adj impoluto, -a; (water) no contaminado, -a

unpopular [ʌn'pɒpjələʳ, Am: ʌn'pɑːpjələ]
adj **1.** (not liked) que gusta poco **2.** (not widely
accepted) que cae mal; **to be ~ with sb** caer
mal a alguien

unpopularity [ʌn,pɒpjə'lærəti, Am: ʌn-
,pɑːpjə'lerəti] n no pl impopularidad f

unpractical [ʌn'præktɪkəl] adj **1.** (imprracti-
cal) poco práctico, -a **2.** (lacking skill in practical matters) desmañado, -a

unpracticed adj Am, **unpractised** [ʌn-
'præktɪst] adj Brit, form inexperto, -a; **to be ~
in sth** no tener práctica en algo

unprecedented [ʌn'presɪdentɪd, Am:
-ədentɪd] adj sin precedentes; (action)
inaudito, -a

unpredictable [ˌʌnprɪ'dɪktəbl] adj **1.** (not
predictable) imprevisible **2.** (moody) temperamental

unprejudiced [ʌn'predʒədɪst] adj **1.** (not
prejudiced) imparcial; (opinion) objetivo, -a
2. (not prejudiced against race) sin prejuicios

unpremeditated [ˌʌnpriː'medɪteɪtɪd, Am:
ˌʌnpriː'medɪt̬ɪd] adj no planeado, -a; LAW
(crime, murder) no premeditado, -a

unpretentious [ˌʌnprɪ'tentʃəs] adj sin pretensiones

unprincipled [ʌn'prɪntsəpld] adj sin principios; (person) sin escrúpulos

unproductive [ˌʌnprə'dʌktɪv] adj (business, land) improductivo, -a; (negotiations)
infructuoso, -a

unprofessional [ˌʌnprə'feʃənəl] adj **1.** (not
meeting professional standards) indigno, -a de
su profesión **2.** (not to be taken seriously) poco
profesional **3.** (not conforming to professional
ethics) contrario, -a a la ética profesional; (conduct) inexperto, -a

unprofitable [ʌn'prɒfɪtəbl, Am: ʌn'prɑː-
fɪt̬ə-] adj **1.** (not making a profit) no rentable;
(investment) infructuoso, -a **2.** (unproductive)
inútil; (a day) improductivo, -a

unprompted [ʌn'prɒmptɪd, Am: ʌn-
'prɑːmp-] adj espontáneo, -a; **to do sth ~**
hacer algo sin ayuda de nadie

unprovided for [ˌʌnprə'vaɪdɪd,fɔː, Am:
-,fɔːr] adj sin medios de subsistencia; **to leave
sb ~** dejar a alguien desamparado

unprovoked [ˌʌnprə'vəʊkt, Am: ˌʌnprə-
'voʊkt] adj no provocado, -a

unpublished [ʌn'pʌblɪʃt] adj inédito, -a

unpunctual [ʌn'pʌŋktʃuəl] adj impuntual;
(start) con retraso

unqualified [ʌn'kwɒlɪfaɪd, Am: ʌn'kwɑː-
lə-] adj **1.** (without qualifications) sin título;
to be ~ for sth no estar cualificado para algo
2. (unlimited, unreserved) incondicional;
(denial) sin restricciones; (disaster) absoluto,

-a; (success) rotundo, -a; (support) total

unquestionable [ʌn'kwestʃənəbl] adj incuestionable; (evidence) inapelable; (fact) innegable

unquestionably adv indudablemente

unquestioning [ʌn'kwestʃənɪŋ] adj incondicional; (obedience) ciego, -a

unquote [ʌn'kwəʊt, Am: ʌn'kwoʊt] vi indicar que una cita o otra cosa entre comillas se
acaba

unquoted adj FIN que no cotiza en bolsa

unravel [ʌn'rævəl] <-ll-, Am: -l-> I. vt
1. (unknit, undo) deshacer; (a knot) desenredar; (a mystery, secret) aclarar **2.** (destroy)
destruir II. vi deshacerse

unreadable [ʌn'riːdəbl] adj **1.** (illegible)
ininteligible **2.** LIT (badly written) ilegible
3. (heavy going) de lectura muy pesada

unreal [ʌn'rɪəl, Am: -'riːl] adj **1.** (not real)
irreal **2.** inf (astonishingly good) impresionante

unrealistic [ʌn,rɪə'lɪstɪk] adj **1.** (not realistic) poco realista **2.** LIT, THEAT, CINE (not
appearing convincingly real) inverosímil

unrealized adj **1.** (not realized) sin explotar
2. FIN (not turned into money) no realizado, -a

unreasonable [ʌn'riːzənəbl] adj **1.** (not
showing reason) poco razonable **2.** (unfair)
injusto, -a; (demands) excesivo, -a

unreasoning [ʌn'riːzənɪŋ] adj irracional

unrecognised [ʌn'rekəgnaɪzd] adj no reconocido, -a

unredeemed [ˌʌnrɪ'diːmd] adj absoluto, -a;
REL irredento, -a

unrefined [ˌʌnrɪ'faɪnd] adj **1.** (not refined)
sugar, oil) sin refinar **2.** (not socially polished)
poco refinado, -a

unreflecting [ˌʌnrɪ'flektɪŋ] adj form irreflexivo, -a

unregistered [ʌn'redʒɪstəd, Am: -stəd] adj
(birth, person) no registrado, -a; (mail) sin certificar

unrelated [ˌʌnrɪ'leɪtɪd, Am: -rɪ'leɪt̬ɪd] adj
no relacionado, -a

unrelenting [ˌʌnrɪ'lentɪŋ, Am: -rɪ'lent̬ɪŋ]
adj **1.** (not yielding) implacable; **to be ~ in sth**
ser inexorable en algo **2.** (incessant, not easing: pain, pressure) incesante; (rain) imparable **3.** form (unmerciful) despiadado, -a

unreliability [ˌʌnrɪlaɪə'bɪlɪti, Am: -rɪlaɪ-
ə'bɪlət̬i] n no pl informalidad f

unreliable [ˌʌnrɪ'laɪəbl] adj informal

unrelieved [ˌʌnrɪ'liːvd] adj **1.** (depressingly
unvarying) total; (poverty) absoluto, -a; (pressure, stress) sin alivio; (tedium) monótono, -a
2. (not helped) desprovisto, -a de ayuda

unremarkable [ˌʌnrɪ'mɑːkəbl, Am: -rɪ-
'mɑːrk-] adj normal

unremitting [ˌʌnrɪ'mɪtɪŋ, Am: -rɪ'mɪt̬-] adj
form sin tregua; (determination) incesante; **to
be ~ in sth** ser infatigable en algo

unrepeatable [ˌʌnrɪ'piːtəbl, Am: -t̬ə-] adj
(shocking) irrepetible; (sale price) inmejorable

unrepentant [ˌʌnrɪ'pentənt] *adj* impenitente

unrequited [ˌʌnrɪ'kwaɪtɪd, *Am:* -rɪ'kwaɪţɪd] *adj* (*love*) no correspondido, -a

unreserved [ˌʌnrɪ'zɜ:vd, *Am:* -rɪ'zɜ:rvd] *adj* **1.**(*absolute*) incondicional; (*support*) sin reservas **2.**(*not having been reserved: tickets, seats*) no reservado, -a **3.**(*not aloof*) abierto, -a; (*friendliness*) franco, -a

unreservedly *adv* sin reservas; **to apologize ~** disculparse profusamente

unresolved [ˌʌnrɪ'zɒlvd, *Am:* -rɪ'zɑ:lvd] *adj* sin resolver

unrest [ʌn'rest] *n no pl* descontento *m;* (*ethnic, social*) malestar *m*

unrestrained [ˌʌnrɪ'streɪnd] *adj* incontrolado, -a; (*criticism, consumerism*) desenfrenado, -a; (*laughter*) desmedido, -a

unrestricted [ˌʌnrɪ'strɪktɪd] *adj* ilimitado, -a; (*access*) libre

unripe [ʌn'raɪp] *adj* **1.**(*not ripe*) verde; **to pick sth ~** recoger algo que no está en su punto **2.** *form* (*immature*) inmaduro, -a

unrivaled *adj Am,* **unrivalled** [ʌn'raɪvəld] *adj* incomparable

unroll [ʌn'rəʊl, *Am:* -'roʊl] I. *vt* **to ~ sth** desenrollar algo II. *vi* desenrollarse

unruffled [ʌn'rʌfld] *adj* **1.**(*not nervous, disturbed*) sereno, -a; **to be ~ by sb/sth** no inmutarse ante alguien/algo **2.**(*not ruffled up: feathers, fur, hair*) liso, -a

unruly [ʌn'ru:li] <-ier, -iest> *adj* **1.**(*disorderly*) indisciplinado, -a; (*crowd*) difícil de controlar **2.**(*difficult to control: hair*) rebelde; (*children*) revoltoso, -a

unsaddle [ʌn'sædl] *vt* **1.**(*remove a saddle: a horse*) desensillar **2.**(*unseat: a rider*) derribar

unsafe [ʌn'seɪf] *adj* **1.**(*dangerous*) inseguro, -a; (*animal*) peligroso, -a; **to declare sth ~** declarar algo arriesgado **2.**(*in danger*) en peligro **3.** *Brit* LAW (*likely not to stand*) no válido, -a

unsaid [ʌn'sed] I. *vt pt, pp of* **unsay** II. *adj form* sin decir; **to leave sth ~** callarse algo; **to be better left ~** mejor no hablar

unsalaried *adj* sin sueldo; (*position*) no remunerado, -a

unsaleable [ˌʌn'seɪləbl] *adj* invendible

unsatisfactory [ˌʌnˌsætɪs'fæktəri, *Am:* ʌn-ˌsæţ-] *adj* **1.**(*not satisfactory*) insatisfactorio, -a; (*answer*) poco convincente; (*service*) poco satisfactorio, -a **2.** SCHOOL (*grade*) deficiente

unsatisfied [ʌn'sætɪsfaɪd, *Am:* -'sæţ-] *adj* **1.**(*not content*) insatisfecho, -a **2.**(*not convinced*) no convencido, -a; **sth leaves sb ~** algo deja a alguien descontento **3.**(*not sated*) no saciado, -a

unsavory *adj Am, Aus,* **unsavoury** [ʌn'seɪvəri] *adj Brit, Aus* **1.**(*unpleasant to the taste, smell*) desagradable **2.**(*disgusting*) repugnante **3.**(*socially offensive*) repulsivo, -a; (*reputation*) indeseable

unsay [ʌn'seɪ] *irr vt* **to ~ sth** desdecirse de algo ▶**what's** <u>said</u> **cannot be unsaid** *prov* lo

dicho dicho está *prov*

unscathed [ʌn'skeɪðd] *adj* ileso, -a

unscheduled [ʌn'ʃedju:ld, *Am:* -'skedʒʊld] *adj* no programado, -a; (*train*) no previsto, -a

unschooled [ʌn'sku:ld] *adj form* **1.**(*uninstructed*) no instruido, -a; **to be ~ in sth** *fig* no estar cultivado en algo **2.**(*untrained: horse*) no entrenado, -a

unscreened *adj* **1.**(*not checked*) sin revisar **2.**(*not shown on a screen*) sin aparecer en pantalla

unscrew [ʌn'skru:] I. *vt* **1.**(*screw*) destornillar **2.**(*lid*) desenroscar II. *vi* (*screw*) destornillarse

unscripted [ʌn'skrɪptɪd] *adj* espontáneo, -a; (*speech*) improvisado, -a

unscrupulous [ʌn'skru:pjələs] *adj* sin escrúpulos; (*dealings, methods*) poco honesto, -a

unseal [ʌn'si:l] *vt* **1.**(*open: a letter*) abrir **2.**(*tell: a secret*) desvelar

unsealed *adj* **1.**(*not sealed*) desellado, -a **2.**(*open*) abierto, -a

unseat [ʌn'si:t] *vt* **1.**(*remove from power*) derrocar **2.**(*throw: a rider*) derribar

unsecured [ˌʌnsɪ'kjʊəd, *Am:* -'kjʊrd] *adj* **1.** FIN (*stock*) no garantizado, -a; (*loan*) sin aval **2.**(*unfastened*) no sujeto, -a

unseeing [ʌn'si:ɪŋ] *adj form* ciego, -a; **to look at sb with ~ eyes** *fig* mirar a alguien sin verlo

unseemly [ʌn'si:mli] *adj form* impropio, -a; (*behaviour*) indecoroso, -a

unseen [ʌn'si:n] *adj* (*not seen by sb*) sin ser visto, -a; **to do sth ~** hacer algo inadvertidamente; **sight ~** a ciegas

unselfish [ʌn'selfɪʃ] *adj* generoso, -a

unserviceable [ʌn'sɜ:vɪsəbl, *Am:* -'sɜ:r-] *adj* inservible; (*appliances*) inutilizable

unsettle [ʌn'setl, *Am:* -'seţ-] *vt* **1.**(*make nervous*) **to ~ sb** alterar a alguien **2.** COM (*make unstable: the market*) desestabilizar

unsettled [ʌn'setld, *Am:* -'seţ-] *adj* **1.**(*changeable*) cambiante; (*period*) agitado, -a; (*weather*) inestable **2.**(*troubled*) inquieto, -a **3.**(*unresolved: issue, question*) no resuelto, -a **4.**(*queasy, nauseous: stomach*) revuelto, -a **5.**(*without settlers*) no colonizado, -a

unsettling *adj* **1.**(*causing nervousness*) inquietante; CINE (*image*) desestabilizador(a) **2.**(*causing disruption*) perturbador(a); COM variable

unshak(e)able [ʌn'ʃeɪkəbl] *adj* inquebrantable

unshaved *adj,* **unshaven** [ʌn'ʃeɪvən] *adj* sin afeitar

unshod [ʌn'ʃɒd, *Am:* -'ʃɑ:d] *adj form* descalzo, -a

unshrinkable [ʌn'ʃrɪŋkəbl] *adj* que no encoge

unshrinking [ʌn'ʃrɪŋkɪŋ] *adj fig* impávido, -a; **~ courage** valor *m* impávido; **to be ~ in the face of sth** quedarse impávido ante algo

unsightly [ʌn'saɪtli] <-ier, -iest> *adj* feo, -a

unsigned [ʌn'saɪnd] *adj* sin firmar

unskilled [ʌn'skɪld] *adj* **1.** (*not skilled*) no cualificado, -a; **to be ~ in** (**doing**) **sth** no estar cualificado para (hacer) algo **2.** (*not requiring skill*) no especializado, -a; **~ job** puesto *m* de trabajo no especializado

unsociable [ʌn'səʊʃəbl, *Am:* -'soʊ-] *adj* insociable

unsocial [ʌn'səʊʃəl, *Am:* -'soʊ-] *adj* **1.** (*unsociable*) insociable **2.** *Brit* (*outside of the standard working day*) fuera del horario laboral; **~ hours** horas *fpl* extras

unsold [ʌn'səʊld, *Am:* -'soʊld] *adj* sin vender

unsolicited [ˌʌnsə'lɪsɪtɪd, *Am:* -t̬ɪd] *adj* no solicitado, -a

unsolved [ʌn'sɒlvd, *Am:* -'saːlvd] *adj* sin resolver

unsophisticated [ˌʌnsə'fɪstɪkeɪtɪd, *Am:* -təkeɪt̬ɪd] *adj* **1.** (*simple*) sencillo, -a; **~ pleasure** placer *m* sencillo **2.** (*simple: a person*) ingenuo, -a; (*a taste*) cándido, -a **3.** (*uncomplicated: a machine*) simple

unsound [ʌn'saʊnd] *adj* **1.** (*weak, unstable*) débil **2.** (*unreliable*) de no fiar; **to be ~ on sth** no ser de fiar en algo **3.** (*not financially stable*) inestable **4.** (*not valid*) erróneo, -a; **~ argument** argumento *m* no válido; **~ judgement** juicio *m* equivocado; **~ police evidence** prueba *f* policial falsa **5.** (*unhealthy*) no sano, -a; **to be of ~ mind** ser de mente enfermiza

unsparing [ʌn'speərɪŋ, *Am:* -'sper-] *adj* **1.** (*merciless*) despiadado, -a **2.** *form* (*lavish*) pródigo, -a; **to be ~ in one's efforts** no escatimar en esfuerzos

unspeakable [ʌn'spiːkəbl] *adj* indecible; **~ atrocities** atrocidades *fpl* incalificables

unspecified [ʌn'spesɪfaɪd] *adj* **1.** (*not specified*) no especificado, -a **2.** (*not named*) sin nombre

unspoiled [ʌn'spɔɪlt, *Am:* -'spɔɪld] *adj* natural

unspoken [ʌn'spəʊkən, *Am:* -spoʊ-] *adj* tácito, -a

unstable [ʌn'steɪbl] *adj* **1.** (*not stable*) inestable; *fig* voluble; **~ chair** silla *f* poco firme **2.** (*not emotionally stable*) volátil; **emotionally ~** no estable emocionalmente

unsteady [ʌn'stedi] *adj* (*chair*) poco firme; (*hand*) tembloroso, -a

unstressed [ʌn'strest] *adj* LING átono, -a

unstuck [ʌn'stʌk] *adj* **to come ~** (*be no longer stuck*) despegarse; *inf* (*fail*) fracasar

unstudied [ʌn'stʌdɪd] *adj form* natural; **~ naturalness** naturalidad *f* sin afectación; **~ response** respuesta *f* no estudiada

unsubstantial [ˌʌnsəb'stæntʃəl] *adj* **1.** (*not substantial*) insustancial; **~ improvements** mejoras *fpl* no sustanciales **2.** (*not significant*) insignificante

unsubstantiated [ˌʌnsəb'stæntʃieɪtɪd, *Am:* -'stæntʃieɪt̬ɪd] *adj* no probado, -a

unsuccessful [ˌʌnsək'sesfəl] *adj* fracasado, -a; **~ candidate** candidato, -a *m, f* fracasado, -a; **to be ~ in sth** fracasar en algo

unsuitable [ʌn'suːtəbl, *Am:* -'suːt̬ə-] *adj* inapropiado, -a; **~ clothes** ropa *f* inapropiada; **~ moment** momento *m* inoportuno; **to be ~ for sth** ser inapropiado para algo; **to be ~ to the occasion** no ajustarse a la ocasión

unsuited [ʌn'suːtɪd, *Am:* -'suːt̬ɪd] *adj* inapropiado, -a; **to be ~ to** [*o* **for**] **sth** no ser apropiado para algo; **to be ~ to each other** ser incompatibles

unsullied [ʌn'sʌlɪd] *adj form* inmaculado, -a; **to be ~ by sth** no estar corrompido por algo

unsung [ʌn'sʌŋ] *adj* olvidado, -a; **the ~ hero** el héroe desconocido

unsure [ʌn'ʃʊər, *Am:* -'ʃʊr] *adj* inseguro, -a; **to be ~ how/what ...** no ser seguro cómo/qué...; **to be ~ about sth** no estar seguro de algo; **to be ~ of oneself** no estar seguro de uno mismo

unsuspecting [ˌʌnsə'spektɪŋ] *adj* confiado, -a; **all ~** nada suspicaz

unsustainable [ˌʌnsə'steɪnəbl] *adj* insostenible

unswerving [ˌʌn'swɜːvɪŋ, *Am:* -'swɜːr-] *adj* (*unshakeable*) inquebrantable; **to be ~ in sth** ser firme en algo

unsympathetic [ˌʌnsɪmpə'θetɪk, *Am:* -'θet̬-] *adj* poco comprensivo, -a

untangle [ʌn'tæŋgl] *vt* **1.** (*hair*) desenredar **2.** (*mystery*) desentrañar

untapped [ˌʌn'tæpt] *adj* **1.** (*not yet tapped*) sin explotar **2.** (*not bugged: line, telephone*) no intervenido, -a **3.** (*not tapped: a keg*) no abierto, -a

untaxed [ˌʌn'tækst] *adj* libre de impuestos; **~ income** FIN ingresos *mpl* no sujetos a contribuciones

untenable [ˌʌn'tenəbl] *adj* insostenible

untenanted [ˌʌn'tenəntɪd, *Am:* -t̬ɪd] *adj* desocupado, -a

untested [ʌn'testɪd] *adj* no probado, -a

unthinkable [ʌn'θɪŋkəbl] **I.** *adj* **1.** (*unimaginable*) inconcebible **2.** (*shocking*) impensable **II.** *n no pl* **the ~** lo inconcebible

unthinking [ʌn'θɪŋkɪŋ] *adj* **1.** (*thoughtless*) irreflexivo, -a **2.** (*unintentional*) no intencionado, -a

unthought-of [ʌn'θɔːtɒv, *Am:* -'θaːtaːv] *adj* inimaginable

untidiness [ʌn'taɪdɪnɪs] *n no pl* desorden *m*

untidy [ʌn'taɪdi] <-ier, -iest> *adj* **1.** (*not neat*) desaseado, -a; (*room*) desordenado, -a; (*appearance*) desaliñado, -a **2.** (*not orderly*) sin método; **~ thesis** tesis *f* carente de método; **to have an ~ mind** tener una mente caótica

untie [ʌn'taɪ] <-y-> *vt* desatar; **to ~ a boat** desamarrar un bote; **to ~ a knot** deshacer un nudo; **to ~ one's shoelaces** desatarse los cordones

until [ən'tɪl] **I.** *adv temporal* hasta; **~ then**

hasta entonces; ~ **such time as sb does sth** hasta el momento en que alguien haga algo **II.** *conj* hasta que +*subj;* ~ **he comes** hasta que venga; **not** ~ **sb does sth** no hasta que alguien haga algo; **not** ~ **he's here** no antes de que él esté aquí

untimely [ʌn'taɪmli] *adj* **1.** (*premature*) prematuro, -a; **sb's** ~ **death** la muerte prematura de alguien **2.** (*inopportune*) inoportuno, -a

unto ['ʌntu:] *prep* HIST *s.* **to**

untold [ˌʌn'təʊld, *Am:* -'toʊld] *adj* **1.** (*immense*) incalculable; ~ **damage** daños *mpl* incalculables; **in** ~ **misery** en la más pura miseria **2.** (*not told*) inédito, -a, nunca contado, -a

untouched [ʌn'tʌtʃt] *adj* **1.** (*not affected*) intacto, -a; **to leave sth** ~ dejar algo intacto **2.** (*not touched*) no tocado, -a; ~ **by human hands** no manipulado **3.** (*not eaten*) no comido, -a; **to leave a meal** ~ dejar una comida sin tocar **4.** (*not emotionally moved*) insensible

untoward [ˌʌntə'wɔːd, *Am:* ˌʌn'tɔːrd] *adj form* desfavorable; ~ **side effects** efectos *mpl* secundarios adversos

untrained [ʌn'treɪnd] *adj* **1.** (*skill*) no formado, -a **2.** (*animals*) no adiestrado, -a

untransferable [ˌʌntrænts'fɜːrəbl] *adj* LAW intransferible

untranslat(e)able [ˌʌntrænt'sleɪtəbl, *Am:* -træn'sleɪt̬əbl] *adj* intraducible

untreated [ʌn'triːtɪd, *Am:* -'triːt̬ɪd] *adj* no tratado, -a; ~ **sewage** aguas *fpl* residuales no tratadas; **to remain** ~ MED seguir sin estar tratado

untried [ʌn'traɪd] *adj* **1.** (*not tested*) no probado, -a **2.** LAW no procesado, -a

untroubled [ʌn'trʌbld] *adj* tranquilo, -a; **they seemed** ~ **about her decision** su decisión no parecía preocuparles

untrue [ʌn'truː] *adj* **1.** (*not true*) falso, -a **2.** (*not faithful*) infiel; **to be** ~ **to sb/sth** ser infiel a alguien/a algo

untrustworthy [ʌn'trʌstˌwɜːði, *Am:* -ˌwɜːr-] *adj* indigno, -a de confianza

untruth [ʌn'truːθ] *n* **1.** (*lie*) mentira *f;* **to tell an** ~ contar una mentira **2.** *no pl* (*quality of being untrue*) falsedad *f*

untruthful [ʌn'truːθfəl] *adj* **1.** (*not truthful*) falso, -a **2.** (*tending to tell lies*) mentiroso, -a

unturned [ˌʌn'tɜːnd, *Am:* -'tɜːrnd] *adj* inamovible; (*soil*) inclinado, -a

untutored [ˌʌn'tjuːtəd, *Am:* -'tuːt̬ɚd] *adj form* indocto, -a; **to be** ~ **in sth** estar poco instruido en algo

unused [ʌn'juːzd] *adj* **1.** (*not in use*) no usado, -a; (*talent, energy*) malgastado, -a; ~ **good** bien *m* sin estrenar **2.** (*never having been used: clothes*) nuevo, -a

unused to [ʌn'juːst tʊ] *adj* (*not accustomed*) **to be** ~ **sth** no estar acostumbrado a algo; **to be** ~ **sb doing sth** no estar acostumbrado a que alguien haga algo

unusual [ʌn'juːʒəl, *Am:* -ʒʊəl] *adj* **1.** (*atypically positive*) inusitado, -a **2.** (*not usual*) inusual; **to be** ~ **for sb** ser poco usual en alguien **3.** (*atypically negative*) insólito, -a; ~ **taste** gusto *m* extraño

unusually *adv* extraordinariamente; ~ **for sb** inusual para alguien

unutterable [ʌn'ʌtərəbl, *Am:* -'ʌt̬-] *adj form* indecible; ~ **suffering** sufrimiento *m* indecible

unvarnished [ʌn'vɑːnɪʃt, *Am:* -'vɑːr-] *adj* sin barnizar; ~ **furniture** muebles *mpl* sin barnizar; **the** ~ **truth** *fig* la pura verdad

unveil [ˌʌn'veɪl] **I.** *vt fig* **1.** (*expose*) quitar el velo **2.** (*present to the public*) presentar **II.** *vi* quitarse el velo

unversed [ˌʌn'vɜːst, *Am:* -'vɜːrst] *adj* **to be** ~ **in sth** ser poco versado en algo

unwaged [ʌn'weɪdʒd] **I.** *adj* Brit sin sueldo; ~ **work** trabajo *m* no remunerado **II.** *n* **the** ~ *no pl,* Brit los que no tienen sueldo

unwanted [ʌn'wɒntɪd, *Am:* -'wɑːnt̬ɪd] *adj* no deseado, -a

unwarranted [ʌn'wɒrəntɪd, *Am:* -'wɔːrəntɪd] *adj* **1.** (*not justified*) injustificado, -a; ~ **criticism** crítica *f* injustificada **2.** (*not authorized*) no autorizado, -a

unwavering [ʌn'weɪvərɪŋ] *adj* inquebrantable; **to be** ~ **in one's support for sb** dar apoyo incondicional a alguien

unwed [ʌn'wed] *adj form* soltero, -a

unwelcome [ʌn'welkəm] *adj* (*guest*) importuno, -a; (*visit*) inoportuno, -a; (*information*) desagradable; **we were made to feel rather** ~ nos hicieron sentir que molestábamos

unwell [ʌn'wel] *adj* indispuesto, -a; **to feel** ~ sentirse mal

unwieldy [ʌn'wiːldi] *adj* **1.** (*cumbersome*) abultado, -a **2.** (*difficult to manage*) difícil de manejar; ~ **system** sistema *m* difícil de manejar

unwilling [ʌn'wɪlɪŋ] *adj* no dispuesto, -a; **to be** ~ **to do sth** no estar dispuesto a hacer algo; **to be** ~ **for sb to do sth** no querer que alguien haga algo

unwillingly *adv* de mala gana

unwind [ʌn'waɪnd] *irr* **I.** *vt* desenrollar **II.** *vi* **1.** (*unroll*) desenrollarse **2.** *fig* (*relax*) relajarse

unwise [ʌn'waɪz] *adj* imprudente

unwitting [ʌn'wɪtɪŋ, *Am:* -'wɪt̬-] *adj* **1.** (*unaware*) inconsciente **2.** (*unintentional*) no intencional

unwittingly *adv* **1.** (*without realizing*) inconscientemente **2.** (*unintentionally*) de forma no intencionada

unwonted [ʌn'wəʊntɪd, *Am:* -'wɔːnt̬ɪd] *adj form* insólito, -a

unworkable [ʌn'wɜːkəbl, *Am:* -'wɜːr-] *adj* impracticable

unworldly [ʌn'wɜːldli, *Am:* -'wɜːrld-] *adj* **1.** (*spiritually-minded*) espiritual **2.** (*naive*) ingenuo, -a **3.** (*unearthly*) poco mundano, -a

unworthy [ʌn'wɜːði, *Am:* -'wɜːr-] <-ier, -iest> *adj* **1.** (*not worthy*) que no merece la

U

pena; **to be ~ of interest** no ser merecedor de la mínima atención **2.**(*discreditable, contemptible*) indigno, -a

unwrap [ʌn'ræp] <-pp-> *vt* **1.**(*remove wrapping*) desenvolver **2.** *fig* (*open, reveal*) sacar a la luz

unwritten [ʌn'rɪtən] *adj* **1.**(*not official*) ~ **agreement** pacto *m* verbal; ~ **law** LAW ley *f* basada en el derecho consuetudinario **2.**(*not written down*) no escrito, -a; ~ **traditions** tradiciones *fpl* no escritas

unyielding [ʌn'ji:ldɪŋ] *adj* **1.**(*stubborn, obstinate*) inflexible; ~ **opposition** oposición *f* firme; **to be ~ in sth** ser inflexible en algo **2.**(*physically hard, firm*) ~ **ground** terreno *m* firme; **to be ~** ser duro

unzip [ʌn'zɪp] <-pp-> *vt* abrir la cremallera de

up [ʌp] **I.** *adv* **1.**(*movement*) (hacia) arriba; ~ **here/there** aquí/allí arriba; **to look ~** mirar (hacia) arriba; **to stand/get ~** ponerse de pie/levantarse; **to go ~** ir hacia arriba; **to throw sth ~** lanzar algo hacia arriba; **to jump ~** saltar hacia arriba; (**stand**) **~!** ¡levántate!; **on the way ~** de subida **2.**(*to another point*) ~ **in Dublin** allá en Dublin; **to go ~ to Scotland** irse a Escocia **3.**(*more volume or intensity*) **apples are ~** han subido las manzanas; **the river is ~** ha subido el río; **the tide is ~** la marea está alta; **to come ~** subir **4.**(*position*) **to be ~ all night** no dormir en toda la noche; **to jump ~ on sth** saltar sobre algo; **with one's head ~** con la cabeza en alto **5.** *fig* (*state*) **to be well ~ in sth** estar fuerte en algo; **to be ~ at the top of sth** estar en lo más alto de algo; **to feel ~ to sth** sentirse capaz de algo; **this isn't ~ to much** esto no vale gran cosa **6.**(*limit*) ~ **to** hasta; ~ **to here** hasta aquí; ~ **to now** hasta ahora; ~ **to £100** hasta £100; **time's ~** se acabó el tiempo; **when 5 hours were ~** cuando pasaron 5 horas; **from the age of 18 ~** a partir de los 18 años (de edad); **to have it ~ to one's ears (with sth)** *fig* estar hasta la coronilla (de algo) **7.**(*responsibility of*) **it's ~ to you** tú decides; **it's ~ to me to decide** me toca a mí decidir **8.** SPORTS **to be 2 goals ~** ir ganando por 2 goles **9.** INFOR, TECH en función ►**to be ~ against** sth/sb habérselas con algo/alguien; ~ **and down** arriba y abajo; **to walk ~ and down** caminar de arriba a abajo; **what's ~?** ¿qué hay de nuevo?; **what's ~ with him?** ¿qué le pasa?; ~ **with the king!** ¡viva el rey! **II.** *prep* **1.**(*at top of*) encima de; **to climb ~ a tree** subir arriba de un árbol **2.**(*higher*) **to go ~ the stairs** subir las escaleras; **to run ~ the slope** correr cuesta arriba; **to row ~ the river** remar río arriba; **to go ~ and down sth** ir de arriba a abajo de algo **3.**(*along*) **to go ~ the street** ir por la calle **III.** *n* ~**s and downs** altibajos *mpl;* **to be on the ~ and ~** *Brit* estar cada vez mejor **IV.** <-pp-> *vi inf* **to ~ and +***infin* ponerse de repente a +*infin* **V.** <-pp-> *vt* subir **VI.** *adj*

1.(*position: building*) levantado, -a; (*tent*) montado, -a; (*flag*) izado, -a; (*curtains, picture*) colgado, -a; (*hand*) alzado, -a; (*blinds*) subido, -a; (*person*) levantado, -a, a pie **2.**(*under repair: road*) abierto, -a **3.**(*healthy*) bien; **to be ~ and about** [*o* **around**] estar en buena forma **4.**(*ready*) **to be ~ for (doing) sth** estar listo para (hacer) algo; ~ **for sale/discussion/trial** a la venta/a discusión/en juicio

up-and-coming ['ʌpən'kʌmɪŋ] *adj* joven y prometedor(a)

upbeat ['ʌpbi:t] **I.** *n* MUS tiempo *m* débil **II.** *adj inf* optimista; **to be ~ about sth** ser optimista respecto a algo

upbraid [ˌʌp'breɪd] *vt form* **to ~ sb (for sth)** reprender a alguien (por algo)

upbringing ['ʌpbrɪŋɪŋ] *n no pl* educación *f;* **to have some kind of ~** tener algún tipo de educación

upcoming ['ʌpˌkʌmɪŋ] *adj* venidero, -a

up-country [ˌʌp'kʌntri, *Am:* 'ʌpkʌn-] **I.** *adv* tierra adentro **II.** *adj* del interior; ~ **tribesmen** tribus *fpl* del interior **III.** *n* interior *m*

update¹ [ʌp'deɪt] *vt* (*bring up to date*) poner al día; INFOR actualizar

update² ['ʌpdeɪt] *n* (*instance of updating*) puesta *f* al día; INFOR actualización *f;* **to give sb an ~ (on sth)** poner a alguien al día (en algo)

updating *n* actualización *f*

updraught ['ʌpdrɑ:ft] *n* corriente *f* ascendiente

upend [ʌp'end] *vt* **to ~ sb** volcar a alguien; **to ~ sth** poner vertical algo

upfront ['ʌpfrʌnt] *adj inf* **1.**(*open, frank*) abierto, -a; **to be ~ and honest** ser franco y sincero; **to be ~ about sth** ser franco sobre algo **2.**(*advance*) por adelantado; ~ **payment** pago *m* por adelantado

upgrade¹ [ʌp'greɪd] *vt* **1.**(*improve quality*) mejorar la calidad de; INFOR mejorar; (*hardware, software*) modernizar **2.**(*raise in rank*) **to ~ sb (to sth)** ascender a alguien (a algo); **to ~ sth** valorar en más algo; **to ~ a job** asignar un grado más alto a un puesto de trabajo

upgrade² ['ʌpgreɪd] *n* **1.** INFOR, TECH, COM (*instance of upgrading*) mejora *f;* **a software ~** una modernización del software **2.** *Am* (*slope*) cuesta *f* **3.** *Am* (*be improving*) **to be on the ~** estar progresando; (*business, sales*) ir mejorando; MED ir recuperándose

upgradeable *adj* modernizable

upgrading *n* **1.** *no pl* (*act of improvement*) mejoramiento *m;* INFOR modernización *f* **2.**(*raising of rank*) subida *f* de rango

upheaval [ʌp'hi:vəl] *n* **1.** *no pl* (*condition of violent change*) sacudida *f;* **political ~** convulsión *f* política **2.**(*instance of violent change*) cataclismo *m* **3.** GEO (*violent upward push*) solevamiento *m;* ~ **of the earth's crust** solevamiento *m* de la corteza terrestre

uphill [ʌp'hɪl] **I.** *adv* (*in an ascending direction*) cuesta arriba; **to run/walk ~** correr/

caminar cuesta arriba **II.** *adj* **1.** (*sloping upward*) ascendente **2.** (*difficult*) difícil; ~ **battle** *fig* batalla *f* ardua

uphold [ʌp'həʊld, *Am*: -'hoʊld] *irr vt* **1.** (*support, maintain*) sostener; **to ~ the law** defender la ley; **to ~ the principle that ...** defender el principio de que...; **to ~ traditions** apoyar las tradiciones **2.** LAW (*confirm*) **to ~ a verdict** confirmar un veredicto

upholster [ʌp'həʊlstə^r, *Am:* -'hoʊlstə-] *vt* **to ~ sth** (**in sth**) tapizar algo (de algo)

upholsterer *n* tapicero, -a *m, f*

upholstery *n no pl* **1.** (*covering for furniture*) tapizado *m;* **leather ~** tapizado de piel **2.** (*act of upholstering*) tapicería *f*

UPI *n Am abbr of* **United Press International** UPI *f*

upkeep ['ʌpkiːp] *n no pl* **1.** (*maintain in good condition*) conservación *f* **2.** (*cost*) gastos *mpl* de mantenimiento **3.** (*maintenance*) mantenimiento *m*

upland ['ʌplənd] **I.** *adj* de la meseta; ~ **plain** llanura *f* de la meseta; ~ **village** pueblo *m* de la meseta **II.** *n* **the ~s** las tierras altas

uplift¹ [ʌp'lɪft] *vt* **1.** (*raise up*) elevar **2.** (*inspire*) inspirar; **to ~ sb's heart** edificar el alma de uno

uplift² ['ʌplɪft] *n* **1.** GEO (*raising*) sustentación *f* **2.** (*spiritual/mental elevation, inspiration*) inspiración *f;* **moral ~** edificación *f* moral; **to give moral ~ to sb** edificar moralmente a alguien

uplifting [ʌp'lɪftɪŋ] *adj* positivo, -a

upload ['ʌpləʊd, *Am:* -oʊd] *vt* INFOR subir

up-market ['ʌp'mɑːkɪt, *Am:* 'ʌp,mɑːr-] **I.** *adj* (*goods*) superior; ~ **consumers** consumidores *mpl* con poder adquisitivo; ~ **products** productos *mpl* de categoría **II.** *adv* en la selección superior; **to go ~** buscar clientela de poder adquisitivo

upon [ə'pɒn, *Am:* -'pɑːn] *prep form* **1.** (*on top of*) sobre, encima de **2.** (*around*) en; **a ring ~ the finger** un anillo en el dedo **3.** (*hanging on*) **to hang ~ the wall** colgar en la pared **4.** (*at time of*) ~ **her arrival** a su llegada; ~ **this** a continuación, acto seguido **5.** (*long ago*) **once ~ a time** érase una vez

upper ['ʌpə^r, *Am:* -ə-] **I.** *adj* (*further up*) superior; **the Upper House** POL la Cámara Alta **II.** *n* **1.** (*of shoe*) pala *f;* **leather ~s** palas *fpl* de piel **2.** *inf* (*drug*) estimulante *m*

upper case *n no pl* TYPO letra *f* mayúscula **upper class** <-es> *n* clase *f* alta **upper- -class** *adj* de clase alta; **in ~ circles** en círculos de la alta sociedad **upper-cut** *n* SPORTS gancho *m* **upper deck** *n* (*of ship*) cubierta *f* superior; (*of bus*) piso *m* superior **uppermost** **I.** *adj* (*highest*) más alto, -a; **to be ~ in one's mind** ocupar el primer lugar en sus pensamientos **II.** *adv* boca arriba; **to put sth ~** poner algo cara arriba

uppish ['ʌpɪʃ] *adj*, **uppity** ['ʌpəti, *Am:* -ʈi] *adj inf* chulo, -a; **to get ~** ponerse chulo

upright ['ʌpraɪt] **I.** *adj* **1.** (*post, rod*) vertical **2.** (*upstanding*) recto, -a; (*citizen*) honrado, -a **II.** *adv* verticalmente; **to stand ~** permanecer erguido; **to sit bolt ~** estar muy derecho en la silla **III.** *n* **1.** (*upright piano*) piano *m* vertical **2.** TECH montante *m* **3.** SPORTS poste *m*

uprising ['ʌpraɪzɪŋ] *n* alzamiento *m;* **to crush an ~** aplastar una sublevación

uproar ['ʌprɔː^r, *Am:* -rɔːr] *n no pl* alboroto *m,* batifondo *m CSur,* tinga *f Méx;* **to cause an ~** provocar un escándalo

uproarious [ʌp'rɔːrɪəs] *adj* tumultuoso, -a; (*joke*) divertidísimo, -a; **to laugh ~ly** morirse de risa

uproot [ʌp'ruːt] *vt* **1.** (*extract from ground*) arrancar de raíz **2.** (*remove from one's home*) desarraigar; **to ~ oneself** perder las raíces

upset¹ [ʌp'set] **I.** *vt irr* **1.** (*overturn*) derrumbar; (*boat, canoe*) volcar **2.** (*unsettle*) trastornar; (*distress*) afligir; **to ~ oneself** afligirse **3.** (*throw into disorder*) alborotar **4.** (*cause pain*) hacer daño a, trastornar **II.** *adj* **1.** (*overturned, up-ended*) trastornado, -a **2.** (*disquieted*) perturbado, -a; (*distressed*) acongojado, -a; (*sad*) apenado, -a; **to get ~ about sth** enfadarse por algo; **to be ~** (**that**) ... estar enfadado (porque)...; **don't be ~** no te enfades **3.** *inf* (*bilious*) **to have an ~ stomach** tener el estómago revuelto

upset² ['ʌpset] *n* **1.** *no pl* (*trouble*) problema *m;* (*argument, quarrel*) discusión *f;* (*psychological problems*) trastorno *m;* **to have an ~** tener una discusión; **to be an ~ to sb** ser un contratiempo para alguien **2.** (*great surprise*) gran sorpresa *f* **3.** *inf* (*disorder*) **stomach ~** trastorno *m* estomacal

upset price *n Am* COM precio *m* mínimo

upsetting *adj* triste; **an ~ piece of news** una noticia desagradable

upshot ['ʌpʃɒt, *Am:* -ʃɑːt] *n no pl* resultado *m;* **the ~** (**of it all**) **is that ...** el resultado (de todo eso) es que...

upside down [ˌʌpsaɪd 'daʊn] **I.** *adj* **1.** (*reversed in vertical axis*) al revés; **to be ~** (*pictures*) estar al revés **2.** (*confused*) muy confuso, -a; **an ~ world** un mundo al revés; **the house was ~** la casa estaba patas arriba **II.** *adv* al revés; **to turn sth ~** poner algo del revés

upstage¹ ['ʌpsteɪdʒ] **I.** *adj* THEAT del fondo de la escena; ~ **position** posición *f* al fondo de la escena **II.** *adv* en el fondo de la escena; **to go ~** ir hacia el fondo de la escena

upstage² [ʌp'steɪdʒ] *vt* eclipsar

upstairs [ʌp'steəz, *Am:* -'sterz] **I.** *adj* de arriba; **the ~ rooms** las habitaciones del piso de arriba; **the ~ windows** las ventanas de arriba **II.** *adv* arriba; **to go ~** ir arriba; **the people who live ~** la gente que vive en el piso de arriba **III.** *n no pl* (**the**) ~ el piso de arriba

upstanding [ˌʌp'stændɪŋ] *adj form* **1.** (*honest*) íntegro, -a **2.** (*strong*) **a fine ~ young woman** una mujer de buena apariencia

upstart [ˈʌpstɑːt, *Am:* -stɑːrt] *n* arribista *mf*
upstate [ˈʌpsteɪt] *Am* **I.** *adj* del norte; **in ~ New York** en el norte de Nueva York **II.** *adv* en el norte
upstream [ˌʌpˈstriːm] **I.** *adj* de las aguas de arriba; **~ pollution** contaminación *f* de las aguas de la zona alta de un río **II.** *adv* aguas arriba; **to swim ~** nadar contra la corriente
upsurge [ˈʌpsɜːdʒ, *Am:* -sɜːrdʒ] *n* aumento *m;* **an ~ in sth** un aumento de algo; **the ~ of violence** el resurgir de la violencia; **the ~ of attention** el aumento de la atención
upswing [ˈʌpswɪŋ] *n* movimiento *m* hacia arriba; **an ~ in sth** un auge en algo; **an ~ in the economy** una mejora en la economía; **an ~ in exports** un aumento de las exportaciones; **to be on the ~** ir al alza; (*crime, violence*) ir en aumento
uptake [ˈʌpteɪk] *n no pl* (*level of absorption*) absorción *f; Brit, Aus* (*level of usage*) consumo *m* ▶**to be quick on the ~** *inf* cogerlas al vuelo; **to be slow on the ~** *inf* ser algo torpe
uptight [ʌpˈtaɪt] *adj inf* tenso, -a; **to be/get ~** (**about sth**) estar/ponerse nervioso (por algo)
up-to-date [ˌʌptəˈdeɪt] *adj* **1.** (*contemporary*) moderno, -a; (*book*) actualizado, -a **2.** (*informed*) al día; **the ~ news** las noticias del día; **to bring sb ~** poner a alguien al corriente
up-to-the-minute [ˈʌptəðəˈmɪnɪt] *adj* de última hora
uptown [ʌpˈtaʊn, *Am:* ˈʌptaʊn] *Am* **I.** *adj* (*suburbs: north*) del norte; (*suburbs: general*) residencial; **in ~ Manhattan** en los barrios del norte de Manhattan; **an ~ shop** una tienda en los barrios periféricos de la ciudad **II.** *adv* hacia el norte/los barrios periféricos
uptrend [ˈʌptrend] *n Am* tendencia *f* al alza; **an ~ in sth** una tendencia alcista en algo
upturn [ˈʌptɜːn, *Am:* -tɜːrn] *n* mejora *f;* **the ~ in consumer confidence** ECON el aumento de la confianza del consumidor; **an ~ in the economy** ECON un repunte en la economía
upturned [ʌpˈtɜːnd, *Am:* -ˈtɜːrnd] *adj* vuelto, -a hacia arriba; **~ nose** nariz *f* respingona; **with ~ palms** con las palmas hacia arriba
upward [ˈʌpwəd, *Am:* -wəd] **I.** *adj* **1.** (*going upwards in direction*) ascendente; **~ movement** movimiento *m* ascendente; **~ mobility** SOCIOL ascenso *m* social **2.** (*going higher in number*) al alza; **to go ~** ir en aumento **II.** *adv* (hacia) arriba
upwardly *adv* en alza; **~ mobile** que escala posiciones sociales
upwards *adv Brit* (hacia) arriba; **and ~** y más
upward trend *n* tendencia *f* alcista; **~ trend in inflation** ECON tendencia *f* alcista de la inflación
uraemia [jʊəˈriːmiə, *Am:* juːˈriː-] *n no pl* MED uremia *f*
uranium [jʊəˈreɪniəm, *Am:* jʊ-] *n no pl*
uranio *m*

Uranus [ˈjʊərənəs, *Am:* ˈjʊrənəs] *n* Urano *m*
urban [ˈɜːbən, *Am:* ˈɜːr-] *adj* urbano, -a; **~ area** zona *f* urbana; **~ sprawl** urbanización *f* caótica
urbane [ɜːˈbeɪn, *Am:* ɜːr-] *adj* fino, -a
urbanise [ˈɜːbənaɪz, *Am:* ˈɜːr-] *vt* urbanizar
urbanity [ɜːˈbænəti, *Am:* ɜːrˈbænəţi] *n no pl* cortesía *f*
urbanization [ˌɜːbənaɪˈzeɪʃən, *Am:* ˌɜːrbənɪˈ-] *n no pl* urbanización *f*
urbanize *vt s.* **urbanise**
urchin [ˈɜːtʃɪn, *Am:* ˈɜːr-] *n iron* pilluelo, -a *m, f;* **street ~** golfillo, -a *m, f* callejero, -a
urethra [jʊəˈriːθrə, *Am:* jʊˈ-] <-s *o* -e> *n* uretra *f*
urge [ɜːdʒ, *Am:* ɜːrdʒ] **I.** *n* (*strong desire*) ansia *f;* (*compulsion*) impulso *m;* PSYCH instinto *m;* **an ~ to do sth** un impulso de hacer algo; **the ~ to express oneself** el deseo de expresarse; **an ~ for power/recognition** un afán de poder/reconocimiento; **an instinctive/irresistible ~** un impulso instintivo/irresistible; **to feel an irresistible ~ to do sth** sentir un deseo irrefrenable de hacer algo; **an uncontrollable ~** un deseo incontrolable; **to control/repress an ~** controlar/reprimir un impulso; **sexual ~** deseo *m* sexual **II.** *vt* **1.** (*push, speed up, move*) empujar; **to ~ sb/sth away from sth** apartar a alguien/algo de algo **2.** (*strongly encourage*) fomentar; **to ~ sb to do sth** instar a alguien a hacer algo; **to ~ sb into sth** incitar a alguien a algo **3.** (*recommend*) recomendar; **to ~ caution on sb** recomendar precaución a alguien
◆**urge on** *vt* **1.** (*encourage*) **to urge sb on** (**to do sth**) animar a alguien (a hacer algo) **2.** (*persuade*) **to urge self-discipline on sb** recomendar a alguien autodisciplina
◆**urge upon** *vt form s.* **urge on**
urgency [ˈɜːdʒənsi, *Am:* ˈɜːr-] *n no pl* **1.** (*top priority, imperativeness*) urgencia *f;* **to be a matter of** (**great**) **~** ser un asunto de (gran) prioridad; **to realize/stress the ~ of sth** darse cuenta de/remarcar la prioridad de algo; **to show a sense of ~** mostrar un sentido de perentoriedad **2.** (*insistence, clamouressness*) insistencia *f*
urgent [ˈɜːdʒənt, *Am:* ˈɜːr-] *adj* **1.** (*imperative, crucial: appeal, plea*) urgente; **~ need** necesidad *f* perentoria; **an ~ request** una petición urgente; **to be in ~ need of sth** necesitar algo urgentemente **2.** *form* (*insistent, pleading*) insistente
urgently *adv* **1.** (*very necessarily*) urgentemente **2.** (*earnestly pleading, beggingly*) insistentemente
urinal [jʊəˈraɪnəl, *Am:* ˈjʊrənəl] *n* **1.** urinario *m* **2.** (*vessel*) orinal *m*
urinary [ˈjʊərɪnəri, *Am:* ˈjʊrəneri] *adj* urinario, -a; **~ diseases** enfermedades *fpl* urinarias; **~ incontinence** incontinencia *f* urinaria
urinate [ˈjʊərɪneɪt, *Am:* ˈjʊrəneɪt] *vi* ori-

nar(se)

urine ['jʊərɪn, *Am:* 'jʊrɪn] *n no pl* orina *f*

URL *n* INFOR *abbr of* **universal resource locator** URL *f*

urn [ɜːn, *Am:* ɜːrn] *n* 1. urna *f* 2. (*for tea*) tetera *f*

Uruguay ['jʊərəɡwaɪ, *Am:* 'jʊrəɡweɪ] *n* Uruguay *m*

Uruguayan [ˌjʊərə'ɡwaɪən, *Am:* jʊrə-'ɡweɪ-] I. *adj* uruguayo, -a II. *n* uruguayo, -a *m, f*

us [əs, *stressed:* ʌs] *pron pers* nos; *after prep* nosotros, -as; **it's ~** somos nosotros; **older than ~** mayores que nosotros; **look at ~** míranos; **he saw ~** (él) nos vió; **he gave the pencil to ~** nos dio el lápiz; **it's for/from ~** es para/de nosotros

USA [ˌjuːes'eɪ] *n* 1. *abbr of* **United States of America** EE.UU. *mpl* 2. *abbr of* **United States Army** ejército de los EE.UU.

USAF [ˌjuːeseɪ'ef] *n abbr of* **United States Air Force** Fuerza Aérea de los EE.UU.

usage ['juːzɪdʒ] *n* 1. *no pl, form* (*treatment*) tratamiento *m* 2. (*how sth is used*) uso *m*; **in common ~** de uso común; **in general ~** de uso general 3. LING utilización *f*; **the earliest recorded ~ of the word X** la primera utilización documentada de la palabra X

use¹ [juːs] *n* 1. (*practical application*) uso *m* 2. *no pl* (*possibility of applying*) empleo *m*; **in ~** en uso; **to be of ~ to sb** ser de utilidad para alguien; **a ban on the ~ of chemical weapons** una prohibición sobre el uso de armas químicas; **the ~ of drugs** el consumo de drogas; **the correct ~** (*of language*) el uso correcto (de la lengua); **to make ~ of sth** utilizar algo; **to put sth to ~** poner algo en servicio; **to be out of ~** estar fuera de servicio; **to come into ~** empezar a utilizarse; **to go out of ~** quedar en desuso 3. *no pl* (*purpose*) **to be no ~** no ser de utilidad; **there's no ~ doing sth** no sirve de nada hacer algo; **that's a fat lot of ~** *iron, inf* pues sí que ha valido de mucho; **it's no ~** es inútil; **what's the ~ of doing sth?** ¿de qué sirve hacer algo?; **what ~ is doing sth?** ¿de qué sirve hacer algo? 4. (*consumption*) consumo *m*

use² [juːz] I. *vt* 1. (*make use of*) usar; (*one's skills, training*) hacer uso de; **to ~ logic** emplear la lógica; **to ~ a name/pseudonym** utilizar un nombre/pseudónimo; **to ~ sth to do sth** utilizar algo para hacer algo; **to ~ sth against sb/sth** utilizar algo en contra de alguien/algo; **to ~ chemical products** emplear productos químicos; **to ~ drugs** consumir drogas; **I could ~ some help** *inf* podría ayudarme 2. (*employ*) emplear; **to ~ common sense** emplear el sentido común; **to ~ discretion** ser discreto; **to ~ your head** utilizar la cabeza 3. (*consume*) utilizar, consumir; **to ~ energy** consumir energía 4. (*manipulate*) utilizar; (*exploit*) explotar 5. *form* (*treat in stated way*) **to ~ sb badly/well** tratar mal/bien a alguien

II. *vi* **he ~d to be/do ...** solía ser/hacer...; **they ~d not to enjoy horror films** no les gustaba ver películas de terror; **did you ~ to work in banking?** ¿trabajabas en la banca?

♦**use up** *vt* agotar

used [juːzd] *adj* (*second-hand*) usado, -a; (*clothes*) de segunda mano; **~ notes** viejas notas

used to [juːst tʊ] *adj* (*familiar with*) acostumbrado, -a; **to be ~ sth** estar acostumbrado a algo; **to become ~ sth** acostumbrarse a algo; **to be ~ the cold/heat** estar acostumbrado al frío/calor; **to be ~ doing sth** tener la costumbre de hacer algo

useful ['juːsfəl] *adj* 1. (*convenient*) útil; **a ~ thing** una cosa útil; **to be ~** (for sth) ser útil (para algo) 2. (*beneficial*) beneficioso, -a; **a ~ experience** una experiencia útil 3. (*effective*) eficaz; (*competent*) competente; **to be ~ with sth** *inf* ser competente en algo; **to do sth ~** hacer algo útil

usefulness *n no pl* utilidad *f*; (*applicability*) aplicabilidad *f*; (*relevance*) relevancia *f*; **to outlive one's ~** dejar de tener utilidad

useless ['juːsləs] *adj* 1. (*in vain*) inútil; (*unusable*) inservible; **to be ~ doing sth** ser inútil hacer algo; **to be ~ for sb/sth** no ser de utilidad para alguien/algo; **to become ~ for sb/sth** dejar de ser útil para alguien/algo; **to be ~ to do sth** no servir de nada el hacer algo; **~ details** detalles *mpl* sin importancia; **~ information** información *f* inútil 2. *inf* (*incompetent*) incompetente; **to be worse than ~** *inf* no servir para nada

user *n* usuario, -a *m, f*; (*of gas, electricity*) consumidor(a) *m(f)*; **drug ~** drogadicto, -a *m, f*

user-friendly *adj* INFOR fácil de utilizar

user interface *n*, **user-interface** *n* INFOR interfaz *f* de usuario **user name** *n* INFOR nombre *m* del usuario **user program** *n* INFOR programa *m* del usuario **user software** *n* INFOR software *m* del usuario

usher ['ʌʃər, *Am:* -ɚ] I. *n* ujier *m* II. *vt* **to ~ sb into the office** hacer pasar a alguien a la oficina; **to ~ sb out** acompañar a alguien a la puerta

usherette [ˌʌʃə'ret] *n* acomodadora *f*

USM [ˌjuːes'em] *n* 1. *abbr of* **underwater-to-surface missile** misil *m* agua-tierra 2. *abbr of* **United States Mail** correo de los EE.UU.

USP [ˌjuːes'piː] *n* ECON *abbr of* **unique selling proposition** característica única de un producto para promocionar su venta

USS [ˌjuːes'es] *n* 1. *abbr of* **United States Ship** barco de los EE.UU. 2. *abbr of* **United States Senate** Senado de los EE.UU.

usual ['juːʒəl, *Am:* -ʒuəl] I. *adj* usual; (**the**) **~ problems** los problemas corrientes; **to find sth in its ~ place** hallar algo en el lugar en que acostumbra a estar; **as ~** como de costumbre; **to be ~ for sb** ser habitual para alguien; **to be ~ for sb to do sth** ser habitual para alguien hacer algo II. *n* **the ~** *inf* (*regular drink*) lo de

siempre
usually *adv* normalmente; **more than** ~ más que de costumbre
usufruct ['juːsjʊfrʌkt, *Am:* -zʊ-] *n form* LAW usufructo *m*
usurer ['juːʒərəʳ, *Am:* -ɚ-] *n* LAW usurero, -a *m, f*
usurious [juːˈzjʊəriəs, *Am:* juːˈʒʊri-] *adj form* LAW usurario, -a
usurp [juːˈzɜːp, *Am:* -ˈsɜːrp] *vt* usurpar
usurper [juːˈzɜːpəʳ, *Am:* -ˈsɜːrpɚ] *n* usurpador(a) *m(f)*
usury ['juːʒəri, *Am:* -ʒɚi] *n no pl* LAW usura *f*
USW *n abbr of* **ultrashort waves** ondas *fpl* ultracortas
utensil [juːˈtensl] *n* utensilio *m;* **kitchen ~s** utensilios *mpl* de cocina
uterine ['juːtəraɪn, *Am:* -ţəˈɪn] *adj* uterino, -a
uterus ['juːtərəs, *Am:* -ţɚ-] <-ri *o* -es> *n* útero *m*
utilise ['juːtɪlaɪz, *Am:* -ţəlaɪz] *vt* utilizar
utilitarian [juːˌtɪlɪˈteərɪən, *Am:* -əˈteri-] *adj* utilitario, -a
utility [juːˈtɪləti, *Am:* -ţi] <-ies> *n* **1.** *form* (*usefulness*) utilidad *f;* ~ **room** office *m* **2.** (*public service*) empresa *f* de servicio público **3.** INFOR herramienta *f*
utilization [ˌjuːtəlaɪˈzeɪʃən, *Am:* -ţəlɪ-] *n no pl* utilización *f*
utilize *vt s.* **utilise**
utmost ['ʌtməʊst, *Am:* -moʊst] **I.** *adj* mayor; **of the ~ brilliance** (*person, mind*) de una inteligencia suprema; **with the ~ care** con sumo cuidado; **with the ~ caution** con toda precaución; **the ~ difficulty** la dificultad máxima; **a matter of ~ importance** un asunto de primerísima importancia **II.** *n no pl* **the ~** lo máximo; **to offer the ~ in power** otorgar el máximo poder; **to be the ~** ser lo máximo; **to the ~** al máximo; **to try sb's patience to the ~** poner a prueba la paciencia de alguien al máximo; **to live life to the ~** vivir la vida al máximo; **to try one's ~** hacer todo lo que se puede
utopia [juːˈtəʊpiə, *Am:* -ˈtoʊ-] *n* utopía *f*
utopian *adj* utópico, -a
utter[1] ['ʌtəʳ, *Am:* 'ʌţɚ] *adj* completo, -a; **in ~ despair** en la más absoluta desesperación; ~ **nonsense** completa estupidez *f;* **an ~ fool** un completo idiota
utter[2] ['ʌtəʳ, *Am:* 'ʌţɚ] *vt* **1.** (*emit noise orally*) proferir; **without ~ing a word** sin mediar palabra **2.** (*express*) pronunciar; **to ~ blasphemy against sb/sth** proferir una blasfemia contra alguien/algo; **to ~ a threat** amenazar; **to ~ an oath** hacer una promesa; **to ~ a prayer** decir una oración; **to ~ a warning** dar un aviso
utterance ['ʌtərənts, *Am:* 'ʌţ-] *n* **1.** (*speech act*) enunciado *m* **2.** *no pl* (*style of delivery*) expresión *f;* **to give ~ to sth** expresar algo; **to give ~ to a feeling** manifestar un sentimiento
utterly *adv* completamente; **to be ~ con-**

vinced that ... estar completamente convencido de que...; **to ~ despise/hate sb** despreciar/odiar profundamente a alguien; ~ **irresistible** totalmente irresistible
uttermost ['ʌtəməʊst, *Am:* 'ʌţɚmoʊst] *adj, n s.* **utmost**
U-turn ['juːtɜːn, *Am:* 'juːtɜːrn] *n* giro *m* de ciento ochenta grados; **to do a ~** hacer un giro completo; **to make a ~** realizar un giro de 180 grados
UV [juːˈviː] *abbr of* **ultraviolet** UV
UVF [juːviːˈef] *n abbr of* **Ulster Volunteer Force** *ejército de voluntarios del Ulster*
uvula ['juːvjələ] *n* úvula *f*
uxorious [ʌkˈsɔːriəs] *adj form* muy enamorado de su mujer
Uzbek ['ʊzbək] **I.** *adj* uzbeko, -a **II.** *n* uzbeko, -a *m, f*
Uzbekistan [ʌzˌbekɪˈstɑːn, *Am:* -ˈstæn] *n* Uzbekistán *m*

V

V, v [viː] *n* **1.** (*letter*) V, v *f;* ~ **for Victor** V de Valencia **2.** (*Roman numeral five*) V *m*
V 1. *abbr of* **volume** vol. **2.** *abbr of* **volt** V
vac [væk] **I.** *n* **1.** *Brit, inf abbr of* **vacation** vacaciones *fpl;* **the long ~** las vacaciones de verano **2.** *inf abbr of* **vacuum** vacío *m* **3.** *abbr of* **vacuum cleaner** aspirador *m*, aspiradora *f;* **to give sth a ~** limpiar algo con aspirador **II.** <-cc-> *vt inf abbr of* **vacuum clean** pasar el aspirador **III.** *vi abbr of* **vacuum clean** pasar el aspirador
vac. *adj abbr of* **vacant** vacante
vacancy ['veɪkəntsi] <-ies> *n* **1.** (*room*) cuarto *m* vacío; **'vacancies'** 'habitaciones *fpl* libres'; **'no vacancies'** 'no quedan habitaciones disponibles' **2.** (*time*) tiempo *m* libre **3.** (*employment opportunity*) vacante *f;* **to fill a ~** ocupar una vacante; **to have a ~** ofrecer un puesto de trabajo **4.** *no pl* (*lack of expression*) vacuidad *f*
vacant ['veɪkənt] *adj* **1.** (*empty, void, not filled*) vacío, -a; (*seat*) desocupado, -a; ~ **lot** solar *m* libre; **to leave sth ~** dejar algo vacante; **'~'** 'libre' **2.** (*unoccupied job situation*) vacante; **to fall ~** producirse una vacante; **to fill the ~ post** ocupar una vacante **3.** (*expressionless, deadpan*) de bobo
vacate [vəˈkeɪt, *Am:* veɪkeɪt] *vt form* (*place, seat*) desocupar; (*a room, offices, house, building*) salir de; (*a job, position, post*) dejar vacante
vacation [vəˈkeɪʃən, *Am:* veɪ-] **I.** *n Am* (*holiday*) vacaciones *fpl;* **to take a ~** tomarse unas vacaciones; **on ~** de vacaciones; **paid ~** vacaciones *fpl* pagadas **II.** *vi Am* estar de vacaciones
vacationer *n Am* veraneante *mf*

vaccinate ['væksɪneɪt, *Am:* -səneɪt-] *vt* MED vacunar; **to be ~d against measles** estar vacunado contra el sarampión

vaccination [ˌvæksɪ'neɪʃən, *Am:* -sə'neɪ-] *n* MED vacunación *f;* **a ~ against measles** una vacuna contra el sarampión; **oral ~** vacunación *f* oral

vaccine ['væksiːn, *Am:* væk'siːn] *n* MED vacuna *f*

vacillate ['væsəleɪt] *vi* dudar; **to ~ between ... and ...** dudar entre... y...; **to ~ between hope and despair** oscilar entre la esperanza y la desesperación

vacillation [ˌvæsəl'eɪʃən] *n* vacilación *f;* (*indecisiveness*) indecisión *f*

vacuity [və'kjuːəti, *Am:* -əṭi] *n no pl* vacuidad *f*

vacuous ['vækjuəs] *adj* bobo, -a; **a ~ remark** un comentario necio

vacuum ['vækjuːm] I. *n* 1. PHYS (*area without gas, air*) vacío *m;* **perfect ~** vacío *m* perfecto 2. (*absence of direction*) **to fill/leave a ~** llenar/dejar un vacío 3. (*isolated from influences, people*) **in a ~** en un vacío 4. (*hoover*) aspiradora *f* II. *vt* limpiar con la aspiradora; **to ~ sth up** pasar la aspiradora a algo

vacuum bottle *n,* **vacuum flask** *n Brit* botella *f* al vacío **vacuum cleaner** *n* aspiradora *f*

vacuum-packaged *adj,* **vacuum-packed** [ˌvækjuːm'pækt, *Am:* -juəm'-] *adj* empaquetado, -a al vacío

vacuum suction *n* succión *f* al vacío

vagabond ['vægəbɒnd, *Am:* -bɑːnd] I. *n* vagabundo, -a *m, f* II. *adj* vagabundo, -a

vagary ['veɪgəri, *Am:* 'veɪgəˈi] <-ies> *n* 1. (*caprice, whimsy*) capricho *m* 2. *pl* (*unpredictable whimsical developments*) impredecibilidad *f;* **the vagaries of the weather** las irregularidades del tiempo; **the vagaries of fashion** la variación de la moda

vagina [və'dʒaɪnə] *n* vagina *f*

vagrancy ['veɪgrənsi] *n no pl* vagabundeo *m*

vagrant ['veɪgrənt] I. *n* vagabundo, -a *m, f* II. *adj* 1. vagabundo, -a 2. *fig* errabundo, -a

vague [veɪg] *adj* 1. (*imprecise: promise, pain*) vago, -a; (*word*) impreciso, -a; (*outline*) borroso, -a; **I have not the ~st idea** no tengo la más mínima idea 2. (*absent-minded: expression*) distraído, -a; (*person*) despistado, -a

vagueness *n no pl* 1. (*imprecision*) vaguedad *f* 2. (*absent-mindedness*) distracción *f*

vain [veɪn] *adj* 1. (*conceited, self-admiring*) vanidoso, -a 2. (*fruitless: attempt, hope*) vano, -a; **it is ~ to ... +*infin*** es inútil... +*infin* 3. **in ~** en vano; **it was all in ~** todo fue en vano

vainglorious [ˌveɪn'glɔːriəs] *adj form* vanaglorioso, -a, jactancioso, -a

valance ['væləns] *n* 1. (*textile surrounding for bed*) volante *m* 2. *Am* (*cloth covering curtain rail*) bastidor *m*

vale *n,* **Vale** [veɪl] *n liter* (*valley*) valle *m;* **this ~ of tears** *fig* este valle de lágrimas

valediction [ˌvælɪ'dɪkʃən, *Am:* ˌvælə'dɪkʃən] *n form* 1. (*farewell*) adiós *m* 2. (*speech given when taking leave*) discurso *m* de despedida

valedictory [ˌvælɪ'dɪktəri, *Am:* ˌvælə'dɪktəˈ-] *adj Am* (*bidding farewell*) de despedida; **~ (address)** discurso *m* de despedida

valence ['veɪlənts], **valency** ['veɪləntsi] <-ies> *n* valencia *f*

Valencia [və'lentʃiə] *n* Valencia *f*

Valencian I. *adj* valenciano, -a II. *n* valenciano, -a *m, f*

valentine ['væləntaɪn] *n* 1. (*card*) tarjeta *que se manda el día de los enamorados* 2. (*sweetheart*) enamorado, -a *m, f*

Valentine's Day *n no pl* día *m* de los enamorados, día *m* de San Valentín

valerian [və'lɪəriən, *Am:* -'lɪri-] *n* valeriana *f*

valet ['væleɪ, *Am:* 'vælɪt] I. *n* 1. HIST (*male's private servant*) ayuda *mf* de cámara 2. (*in a hotel*) mozo *m* de hotel 3. (*professional car parker*) aparcacoches *m inv* II. *vt Brit* (*car*) limpiar

valet service *n* servicio *m* de lavandería

valetudinarian [ˌvælɪtjuːdɪ'neəriən, *Am:* -ətuːdə'neri-] I. *adj* 1. (*invalid*) inválido, -a 2. (*hypochondriac*) hipocondríaco, -a II. *n* 1. (*invalid*) inválido, -a *m, f* 2. (*hypochondriac*) hipocondríaco, -a *m, f*

valiant ['væliənt, *Am:* -jənt] *adj* valiente

valid ['vælɪd] *adj* 1. (*worthwhile, weighty*) válido, -a; **no longer ~** caducado, -a 2. (*reasonable because well-founded*) legítimo, -a 3. LAW (*still in force*) vigente; (*contractually binding*) vinculante

validate ['vælɪdeɪt, *Am:* 'vælə-] *vt* 1. (*ratify, officially approve*) dar validez a 2. *a.* INFOR (*verify, authenticate: document*) validar; (*ticket*) sellar

validity [və'lɪdəti, *Am:* -ṭi] *n no pl* 1. (*soundness, weight*) legitimidad *f* 2. (*legal force*) validez *f;* (*of a law*) vigencia *f*

valley ['væli] *n* valle *m*

valor *n no pl, Am,* **valour** ['væləˈ, *Am:* -əˈ] *n no pl, Brit, Aus, form* valor *m*

valuable ['væljuəbl] I. *adj* (*help, information*) valioso, -a; (*time*) precioso, -a; **this ring is very ~** este anillo tiene mucho valor II. *n pl* objetos *mpl* de valor

valuation [ˌvælju'eɪʃən] *n* 1. (*estimation of financial value*) tasación *f* 2. *no pl* (*estimated value*) valor *m* 3. (*acknowledgement of the excellence of sth*) valoración *f*

valuator *n* FIN tasador(a) *m(f)*

value ['væljuː] I. *n* 1. *no pl a.* MAT, MUS (*worth, significance*) valor *m;* **~ judgement** juicio *m* de valor; **to be of ~ to sb** ser valioso para alguien; **to be of little ~** ser de poco valor; **to place a high ~ on sth** dar mucha importancia a algo; **to be good ~ (for money)** estar bien de precio; **to be of great ~** ser muy valioso; **to**

get good ~ for one's money sacar partido al dinero; **to increase (in)** ~ aumentar de valor; **to lose (in)** ~ depreciarse; **market** ~ valor de mercado; **to put a** ~ **on sth** poner precio a algo; **to the** ~ **of** por valor de **2.** *pl* (*moral ethics, standards*) valores *mpl*; **set of** ~**s** escala *f* de valores **II.** *vt* **1.** (*think to be signifi-cant*) apreciar; **to** ~ **sb as a friend** valorar a al-guien como amigo **2.** (*estimate financial worth*) tasar; **to** ~ **sth at sth** valorar algo en algo

value-added tax [ˌvælju:ˈædɪd-] *n Brit* impuesto *m* sobre el valor añadido

valued *adj form* apreciado, -a; ~ **customer** cliente *mf* valioso, -a

valueless [ˈvælju:ləs] *adj* sin valor

valuer *n Brit* FIN tasador(a) *m(f)*

valve [vælv] *n* **1.** AUTO, ANAT válvula *f*; **inlet** ~ válvula de admisión **2.** ELEC lámpara *f* **3.** MUS pistón *m*

vamp¹ [væmp] **I.** *n* **1.** (*of a shoe*) empeine *m* **2.** MUS acompañamiento *m* improvisado **II.** *vt* **1.** (*shoe*) poner el empeine a **2.** MUS improvisar un acompañamiento para **III.** *vi* MUS improvisar un acompañamiento

vamp² [væmp] *n* vampiresa *f*

vampire [ˈvæmpaɪəʳ, *Am:* -paɪɚ] *n* vampiro *m*

van¹ [væn] *n* **1.** (*commercial vehicle*) fur-goneta *f;* **delivery** ~ furgoneta de reparto; **removal** ~ camión *m* de mudanzas **2.** *Brit* (*rail carriage for goods*) furgón *m;* **luggage** ~ fur-gón de equipajes

van² [væn] *n no pl abbr of* **vanguard** van-guardia *f*

van³ [væn] *n Brit, inf* SPORTS *abbr of* **advan-tage** ventaja *f*

vandal [ˈvændəl] *n* vándalo *m*

vandalise [ˈvændəlaɪz] *vt s.* **vandalize**

vandalism [ˈvændəlɪzəm] *n no pl* vanda-lismo *m*

vandalize [ˈvændəlaɪz] *vt* destrozar

vane [veɪn] *n* **1.** (*weathercock*) veleta *f* **2.** (*of windmill*) aspa *f* **3.** (*of propeller*) paleta *f*

vanguard [ˈvænɡɑːd, *Am:* -ɡɑːrd] *n no pl* vanguardia *f*

vanilla [vəˈnɪlə] *n no pl* vainilla *f*

vanish [ˈvænɪʃ] *vi* **to** ~ **(from sth)** desapa-recer (de algo); **to** ~ **into thin air** *fig* esfu-marse; (*fear, hopes*) desvanecerse; (*cease to exist: era, race*) extinguirse

vanishing cream *n* crema *f* de día **vanish-ing point** *n* punto *m* de fuga

vanity [ˈvænəti, *Am:* -əṭi] <-ies> *n* **1.** *no pl* (*self-satisfaction*) vanidad *f* **2.** *Am* (*dressing table*) tocador *m* **3.** *Aus* (*vanitory unit*) mueble *m* de baño (*con lavabo empotrado*)

vanity bag *n,* **vanity case** *n* neceser *m*

vanquish [ˈvæŋkwɪʃ] *vt* derrotar

vantage [ˈvɑːntɪdʒ, *Am:* ˈvænṭɪdʒ] *n* ven-taja *f*

vantage point *n* **1.** (*place with good view*) mirador *m* **2.** (*position which gives an advan-*

tage) posición *f* de ventaja

Vanuatu [ˌvænuˈɑːtuː, *Am:* vænˈwɑːtuː] *n* Vanuatu *m*

vapid [ˈvæpɪd] *adj* insulso, -a

vapor [ˈveɪpəʳ, *Am:* -pɚ] *n Am, Aus s.* **vapour**

vaporisation *n,* **vaporization** [ˌveɪpəraɪ-ˈzeɪʃən, *Am:* -ɪ'-] *n s.* **vapourisation**

vaporize [ˈveɪpəraɪz] **I.** *vt* vaporizar **II.** *vi* vaporizarse

vaporizer *n* vaporizador *m*

vapour [ˈveɪpəʳ, *Am:* -pɚ] *n* **1.** (*steam*) vapor *m;* **water** ~ vapor de agua **2.** (*on glass*) vaho *m*, vaporizo *m Méx, PRico*

vapourisation [ˌveɪpəraɪˈzeɪʃən, *Am:* -ɪ'-] *no pl* vaporización *f*

vapour pressure *n* presión *f* del vapor **vapour trail** *n* AVIAT estela *f*

variability [ˌveəriəˈbɪləti, *Am:* ˌveriəˈbɪləṭi] *n no pl* variabilidad *f*

variable [ˈveəriəbl, *Am:* ˈveri-] **I.** *n* MAT varia-ble *f* **II.** *adj* variable

variance [ˈveəriənts, *Am:* ˈveri-] *n* **1.** *no pl* (*disagreement, difference*) discrepancia *f;* **at** ~ en contradicción; **to be at** ~ **with sth** discre-par en algo; **to set two people at** ~ sembrar la discordia entre dos personas **2.** *no pl* (*vari-ation*) variación *f* **3.** (*in statistics*) variancia *f*

variant [ˈveəriənt, *Am:* ˈveri-] **I.** *n* variante *f* **II.** *adj* **1.** (*different*) divergente; ~ **spelling** variante *f* ortográfica **2.** (*tending to change*) variable

variation [ˌveəriˈeɪʃən, *Am:* ˌveri-] *n no pl* **1.** *a.* BIO, MUS variación *f;* **a** ~ **on sth** una varia-ción de algo **2.** (*varying, difference, dissimilar-ity*) diferencia *f;* **wide** ~**s in sth** grandes dife-rencias de algo

varicose [ˈværɪkəʊs, *Am:* ˈverəkoʊs] *adj* MED varicoso, -a; ~ **veins** varices *fpl*

varied [ˈveərɪd, *Am:* ˈverɪd] *adj* **1.** (*altered, diverse*) variado, -a **2.** (*having different col-ours*) multicolor

variegated [ˈveərɪɡeɪtɪd, *Am:* ˈveriəɡeɪ-ṭɪd] *adj* multicolor

variety [vəˈraɪəti, *Am:* -ṭi] <-ies> *n* **1.** *no pl* (*diversity*) variedad *f;* **to lend** ~ **to sth** variar algo **2.** (*assortment*) surtido *m;* **for a** ~ **of rea-sons** por varias razones; **in a** ~ **of ways** de diversas formas **3.** (*sort, category*) tipo *m;* **a** ~ **of communism** una forma de comunismo; **a new** ~ **of tulip** una nueva variedad de tulipán **4.** *no pl* THEAT variedades *fpl* ►~ **is the spice of life** *prov* en la variedad está el gusto *prov*

variety show *n* **1.** THEAT espectáculo *m* de variedades **2.** RADIO, TV programa *m* de varie-dades **variety theatre** *n* THEAT teatro *m* de variedades

various [ˈveəriəs, *Am:* ˈveri-] *adj* **1.** (*numer-ous*) varios, -as; **for** ~ **reasons** por diversas razones **2.** (*diverse*) diferentes

varmint [ˈvɑːmɪnt, *Am:* ˈvɑːr-] *n* **1.** ZOOL alimaña *f* **2.** *Am* (*person*) sinvergüenza *mf*

varnish [ˈvɑːnɪʃ, *Am:* ˈvɑːr-] **I.** *n no pl*

1. (*liquid used to protect a surface*) barniz *m*
2. (*nail polish*) (**nail**) ~ esmalte *m* de uñas
II. *vt* barnizar

varsity ['vɑ:səti, *Am:* 'vɑ:rsət̬i] <-ies> *n*
Brit **1.** *inf* (*university*) universidad *f* **2.** (*team*)
equipo *m* universitario

vary ['veəri, *Am:* 'veri] <-ie-> **I.** *vi* **1.** (*change,
be different*) variar; **opinions** ~ hay diversidad
de opiniones; **to** ~ **between ... and ...** oscilar
entre... y...; **to** ~ **from ...** diferenciarse de...
2. (*diverge*) desviarse; **to** ~ **from sth** apartarse
de algo **II.** *vt* **1.** (*change*) variar **2.** (*diversify*)
dar variedad a

varying *adj* variable

vascular ['væskjələ', *Am:* -kjələ'] *adj no pl*
vascular

vase [vɑ:z, *Am:* veɪs] *n* **1.** (*for flowers*)
florero *m* **2.** (*ornamental*) jarrón *m* **3.** (*receptacle*) vasija *f*

vassal ['væsəl] *n* HIST vasallo, -a *m, f*

vassalage ['væsəlɪdʒ] *n no pl* HIST vasallaje
m

vast [vɑ:st, *Am:* væst] *adj* **1.** (*of great extent:
area, region*) vasto, -a; **a** ~ **country** un
extenso país **2.** (*of great size*) enorme; **the** ~
majority la gran mayoría; **a** ~ **amount of
money** una considerable suma de dinero
3. (*great in degree: importance*) considerable;
his ~ **knowledge of ...** sus amplios conocimientos en el campo de (la)...

vastly *adv* (*very*) sumamente; ~ **superior**
infinitamente superior

vastness *n no pl* inmensidad *f*

vat [væt] *n* tanque *m*; (*for wine or oil*) cuba *f*

VAT [,vi:eɪ'ti:] *n no pl, Brit abbr of* **value
added tax** IVA *m*

Vatican ['vætɪkən, *Am:* 'væt̬-] **I.** *n no pl* **the**
~ el Vaticano; ~ **City** Ciudad *f* del Vaticano
II. *adj* vaticano, -a

vaudeville ['vɔ:dəvɪl, *Am:* 'vɑːdvɪl] *n no pl,
Am* (*variety theatre*) vodevil *m*

vault¹ [vɔ:lt, *Am:* vɑːlt] *n* **1.** ARCHIT (*arched
structure*) bóveda *f*; (*under churches*) cripta *f*;
(*at cemeteries*) panteón *m*; **family** ~ panteón
familiar **2.** (*underground chamber*) sótano *m*;
(*secure repository*) cámara *f*; (*in a bank*)
cámara *f* acorazada

vault² [vɔ:lt, *Am:* vɑːlt] **I.** *n* salto *m* **II.** *vi, vt*
saltar

vaulted *adj* ARCHIT abovedado, -a

vaulting I. *n no pl* ARCHIT bóveda *f* **II.** *adj*
(*exaggerated*) desmesurado, -a; (*ambition*)
desmedido, -a

vaulting horse *n* potro *m* **vaulting pole**
n pértiga *f*

vaunt [vɔ:nt, *Am:* vɑ:nt] *vt* jactarse de

VC [,vi:'si:] *n* **1.** *abbr of* **Victoria Cross** la más
alta condecoración militar británica **2.** *abbr of*
Vice-Chairman vicepresidente, -a *m, f*

VCR [,vi:si:'ɑ:', *Am:* -'ɑ:r] *n Am abbr of*
videocassette recorder vídeo *m*

VD [,vi:'di:] *n no pl* MED *abbr of* **venereal disease** enfermedad *f* venérea

VDU [,vi:di:'ju:] *abbr of* **visual display unit**
UDV

VE [,vi:'i:] *abbr of* **Victory in Europe** día de la
victoria aliada en Europa en la Segunda
Guerra Mundial

veal [vi:l] *n no pl* ternera *f*

veal cutlet *n* chuleta *f* de ternera

vector ['vektə', *Am:* -t̬ə] **I.** *n* **1.** MAT vector *m*
2. BIO, MED portador(a) *m(f)* **II.** *adj* MAT vectorial

veer [vɪə', *Am:* vɪr] **I.** *vi* **1.** (*alter course:
vehicle*) virar; (*wind*) cambiar de dirección;
(*road, way*) torcer **2.** (*alter attitude, goal*) cambiar bruscamente; **to** ~ **from sb's usual
opinions** desviarse de las opiniones habituales
de alguien; **to** ~ **towards sth** dar un giro hacia
algo **II.** *n* (*character, plan*) viraje *m*; (*movement*) cambio *m* de dirección

◆**veer** (**a**)**round** *vt* AUTO cambiar de dirección; *fig* cambiar bruscamente

veg [vedʒ] *n no pl, inf* verdura *f*; **fruit and** ~
frutas *fpl* y verduras

vegan ['vi:gən] *n* vegetariano que no come ni
huevos ni productos lácteos

vegetable ['vedʒtəbl] *n* **1.** (*plant*) vegetal *m*
2. (*edible plant*) hortaliza *f*; (*green*) ~ verdura
f; ~ **soup** sopa *f* de verduras; **root** ~ tubérculo
m; **seasonal** ~ verdura del tiempo

vegetable butter *n no pl,* **vegetable fat**
n no pl margarina *f* **vegetable garden** *n*
huerto *m* **vegetable kingdom** *n no pl*
reino *m* vegetal **vegetable oil** *n no pl* aceite
m vegetal

vegetarian [,vedʒɪ'teəriən, *Am:* -ə'teri-] **I.** *n*
vegetariano, -a *m, f* **II.** *adj* vegetariano, -a; **to
go** ~ hacerse vegetariano

vegetate ['vedʒɪteɪt, *Am:* '-ə-] *vi a. fig* vegetar

vegetation [,vedʒɪ'teɪʃən, *Am:* -ə'-] *n no pl*
vegetación *f*

vehemence ['vi:əmənts] *n no pl* vehemencia *f*

vehement ['vi:əmənt] *adj* vehemente

vehicle ['vɪəkl, *Am:* 'vi:ə-] *n* **1.** (*method of
transport*) vehículo *m*; **motor** ~ vehículo
motorizado **2.** (*channel, means of expression*)
medio *m*; **to be a** ~ **for sth** servir de vehículo
para algo

vehicle registration centre *n Brit* centro
m de matriculación **vehicle registration
number** *n Brit* número *m* de matrícula

vehicular [vɪ'ɪkjələ', *Am:* vi:'hɪkjələ'] *adj*
form de vehículos; (*accident*) de circulación; ~
traffic tráfico *m* rodado

veil [veɪl] **I.** *n* velo *m*; (*of smoke*) cortina *f* de
humo; **bridal** ~ velo de novia; **a** ~ **of secrecy**
un halo de misterio; **under the** ~ **of sth** *fig*
con el pretexto de algo; **to draw a** ~ **over sth**
fig correr un tupido velo sobre algo **II.** *vt* velar;
(*disguise*) disimular; **to** ~ **one's face** taparse
con un velo; **to be ~ed** estar cubierto con un
velo; **the mist ~ed the mountains** *fig, liter* la
bruma envolvía las montañas

veiled *adj* **1.** (*wearing a veil*) cubierto, -a con

velo **2.**(*indirect, masked, concealed: criticism*) velado, -a; **thinly** ~ apenas disimulado
vein [veɪn] *n* **1.**ANAT, BOT vena *f;* GEO veta *f,* sirca *f Chile;* **a quartz** ~ una veta de cuarzo **2.**(*trait, element of stated feeling*) disposición *f;* **a** ~ **of madness** una vena de loco; **to talk in a more serious** ~ hablar más en serio **3.**(*frame of mind, temperament*) estilo *m;* **in (a) similar** ~ del mismo estilo; **in the** ~ **of sth** a la manera de algo
veined *adj* **1.**(*stone, wood*) veteado, -a **2.**(*hand, leaf*) que tiene nervios
velar ['viːlə^r, *Am:* -lə·] **I.** *adj* LING velar **II.** *n* LING sonido *m* velar
Velcro® ['velkrəʊ, *Am:* -kroʊ] *n no pl* velcro® *m*
veld *n*, **veldt** [velt] *n* veld *m* (*meseta seca característica de Sudáfrica*)
velocity [vɪ'lɒsəti, *Am:* və'lɑːsəţi] <-ies> *n form* velocidad *f;* **at the** ~ **of** a la velocidad de; **sound/light** ~ velocidad del sonido/de la luz
velvet ['velvɪt] **I.** *n no pl* terciopelo *m* **II.** *adj* **1.**(*made of velvet*) de terciopelo **2.** *fig* (*smooth: voice*) aterciopelado, -a
velveteen [‚velvɪ'tiːn] *n* pana *f*
velvety ['velvɪti, *Am:* -vəţi] *adj fig* aterciopelado, -a
venal ['viːnəl] *adj* **1.**(*that can be purchased*) venal **2.**(*corrupt: regime, ruler*) corrupto, -a
venality [viː'næləti, *Am:* vɪ'næləţi] *n no pl* **1.**(*corruptibility*) venalidad *f* **2.**(*corruption*) corrupción *f*
vend [vend] *vt* vender
vendetta [ven'detə, *Am:* -'deţ-] *n* vendetta *f*
vending machine *n* máquina *f* expendedora
vendor ['vendɔː^r, *Am:* -də·] *n* vendedor(a) *m(f)*
vendue ['vendjuː] *n Am* subasta *f*
veneer [və'nɪə^r, *Am:* -'nɪr] **I.** *vt* chapar **II.** *n* **1.** chapado *m* **2.** *no pl, fig* apariencia *f*
venerable ['venərəbl] *adj* **1.**(*person*) venerable **2.**(*tradition*) ancestral; (*building, tree*) centenario, -a; ~ **ruins** ruinas *fpl* milenarias
venerate ['venəreɪt] *vt* venerar
veneration [‚venə'reɪʃən] *n no pl* veneración *f;* **to hold sb in** ~ venerar a alguien
venereal [və'nɪəriəl, *Am:* və'nɪri-] *adj* MED venéreo, -a; ~ **disease** enfermedad *f* venérea
venetian blind [və‚niːʃən'blaɪnd] *n* persiana *f* veneciana
Venezuela [‚venɪ'zweɪlə, *Am:* -ə'zweɪ-] *n* Venezuela *f*
Venezuelan I. *adj* venezolano, -a **II.** *n* venezolano, -a *m, f*
vengeance ['vendʒənts] *n no pl* venganza *f;* **to take** ~ (up)on sb vengarse de alguien; **with a** ~ con ganas
venial ['viːniəl] *adj form* venial; (*offence*) leve; (*error*) sin importancia; ~ **sin** pecado *m* venial
venison ['venɪsən] *n no pl* (carne *f* de) venado *m*
venom ['venəm] *n no pl* veneno *m; fig*

malevolencia *f*
venomous ['venəməs] *adj* venenoso, -a; (*malicious*) maligno, -a; (*tongue*) viperino, -a
venous ['viːnəs] *adj* venoso, -a
vent [vent] **I.** *n* **1.**(*small outlet for gas: of a building*) conducto *m* de ventilación; (*of a volcano*) chimenea *f;* **air** ~ respiradero *m* **2.** FASHION abertura *f* **3.**(*release of feelings*) **to give** ~ **to sth** dar rienda suelta a algo; **to give** ~ **to one's feelings** desahogarse **II.** *vt* (*feelings*) dar rienda suelta a; (*opinion*) expresar; **to** ~ **one's anger on sb** desahogarse con alguien
ventilate ['ventɪleɪt, *Am:* -ţəleɪt-] *vt* **1.**(*oxygenate a space*) ventilar; **artificially** ~**d** MED con respiración asistida **2.**(*give utterance to, verbalize*) expresar
ventilation [‚ventɪ'leɪʃən, *Am:* -ţə'leɪ-] *n no pl* ventilación *f*
ventilation duct *n* conducto *m* de ventilación
ventilator ['ventɪleɪtə^r, *Am:* -ţəleɪţə·] *n* **1.**(*device*) ventilador *m* **2.** MED respirador *m*
ventricle ['ventrɪkl] *n* ventrículo *m*
ventriloquist [ven'trɪləkwɪst] *n* ventrílocuo, -a *m, f*
venture ['ventʃə^r, *Am:* -tʃə·] **I.** *n* **1.**(*endeavour*) aventura *f* **2.** COM empresa *f;* **joint** ~ empresa conjunta **II.** *vt* **1.**(*dare*) **to** ~ **to do sth** atreverse a hacer algo; **may I** ~ **a suggestion?** ¿me permite hacer una sugerencia? **2.**(*dare to express: an opinion*) aventurar **3.**(*put at risk, endanger*) **to** ~ **sth (on sth)** arriesgar algo (en algo) ▶**nothing** ~**d, nothing gained** *prov* quien no se arriesga, no pasa la mar *prov* **III.** *vi* aventurarse
◆**venture on** *vt* emprender, embarcarse en
◆**venture out** *vi* atreverse a salir
venture capital *n* FIN capital *m* de riesgo
venturesome ['ventʃəsəm, *Am:* -tʃə·-] *adj form* **1.**(*adventurous: person*) atrevido, -a; (*enterprising*) emprendedor(a) **2.**(*risky, not safe*) arriesgado, -a
venue ['venjuː] *n* (*of meeting*) lugar *m* (de reunión); (*of concert*) lugar *m* (de celebración); (*of match*) campo *m*
Venus ['viːnəs] *n no pl* Venus *m*
veracious [və'reɪʃəs] *adj form* **1.**(*honest*) honesto, -a **2.**(*accurate and precise*) veraz
veracity [və'ræsəti, *Am:* və'ræsəţi] *n no pl* **1.**(*truthfulness*) honestidad *f* **2.**(*accuracy*) veracidad *f*
veranda *n*, **verandah** [və'rændə] *n* veranda *f*
verb [vɜːb, *Am:* vɜːrb] *n* verbo *m;* **intransitive/transitive** ~ verbo intransitivo/transitivo
verbal ['vɜːbəl, *Am:* 'vɜːr-] *adj* **1.**(*oral, unwritten*) verbal; ~ **agreement** acuerdo *m* verbal; ~ **facility** facilidad *f* de palabra **2.**(*word for word: translation*) literal
verbalise, **verbalize** ['vɜːbəlaɪz, *Am:* 'vɜːr-] *vt* expresar con palabras, verbalizar
verbally *adv* verbalmente

verbatim [vɜːˈbeɪtɪm, *Am:* vəˈbeɪʈɪm]
I. *adj* literal II. *adv* literalmente
verbiage [ˈvɜːbiːdʒ, *Am:* ˈvɜːr-] *n no pl* verborrea *f*
verbose [vɜːˈbəʊs, *Am:* vəˈboʊs] *adj* verboso, -a; (*speech*) prolijo, -a
verbosity [vɜːˈbɒsəti, *Am:* vəˈbɑːsəʈi] *n no pl* verbosidad *f*
verdant [ˈvɜːdənt, *Am:* ˈvɜːr-] *adj liter* verde
verdict [ˈvɜːdɪkt, *Am:* ˈvɜːr-] *n* 1. LAW (*of jury*) veredicto *m*; (*of magistrate, judge*) fallo *m*; ~ **of guilty/not guilty** veredicto de culpabilidad/inocencia; **to bring in** [*o* **to return**] **a** ~ (*jury*) emitir un veredicto; (*magistrate, judge*) dictar sentencia 2. (*opinion after consideration, conclusion*) juicio *m*; **to give a** ~ **on sth/sb** dar una opinión sobre algo/alguien; **what is your** ~? ¿qué opinas?
verdigris [ˈvɜːdɪɡrɪs, *Am:* ˈvɜːrdɪɡriːs] *n no pl* verdín *m*
verge [vɜːdʒ, *Am:* vɜːrdʒ] *n* 1. (*physical edge, margin*) margen *m* 2. *Brit* (*part next to road or way*) arcén *m* 3. *fig* (*brink*) borde *m*; **to be on the** ~ **of ...** estar al borde de...; **to be on the** ~ **of a solution** estar a punto de encontrar una solución; **to be on the** ~ **of doing sth** estar a punto de hacer algo; **to be on the** ~ **of tears** estar a punto de llorar
◆**verge on** *vt* rayar en; **to** ~ **the ridiculous** rayar en lo ridículo; **she is verging on fifty** ronda los cincuenta años
verger [ˈvɜːdʒəʳ, *Am:* ˈvɜːrdʒɚ] *n* sacristán *m*
verifiable [ˈverɪfaɪəbl, *Am:* ˈverəfaɪ-] *adj* comprobable
verification [ˌverɪfɪˈkeɪʃən, *Am:* ˌ-ə-] *n no pl* 1. (*checking*) verificación *f* 2. (*confirmation*) confirmación *f*
verify [ˈverɪfaɪ, *Am:* ˈ-ə-] <-ie-> *vt* 1. (*corroborate*) confirmar; (*suspicions, theory*) corroborar 2. (*authenticate*) verificar
verisimilitude [ˌverɪsɪˈmɪlɪtjuːd, *Am:* -əsəˈmɪlətuːd] *n no pl* verosimilitud *f*
veritable [ˈverɪtəbl, *Am:* -əʈə-] *adj* auténtico, -a
vermicelli [ˌvɜːmɪˈtʃeli, *Am:* ˌvɜːrməˈtʃel-] *n no pl* cabello *m* de ángel
vermicide [ˈvɜːmɪsaɪd, *Am:* ˈvɜːrmə-] *n no pl* vermicida *m*
vermiform [ˈvɜːmɪfɔːm, *Am:* ˈvɜːrməfɔːrm] *adj* vermiforme
vermilion [vəˈmɪljən, *Am:* vəˈmɪljən], **vermillion** I. *n* bermellón *m* II. *adj* bermellón *inv*
vermin [ˈvɜːmɪn, *Am:* ˈvɜːr-] *n* 1. *pl* (*animals*) alimañas *fpl*; (*insects*) bichos *mpl* 2. *pej* (*people*) gentuza *f*
verminous *adj* 1. (*dog*) pulgoso, -a; (*person*) piojoso, -a 2. (*disease*) verminoso, -a
vermouth [ˈvɜːməθ, *Am:* vəˈmuːθ] *n no pl* vermut *m*, vermú *m*
vernacular [vəˈnækjələʳ, *Am:* vəˈnækjəlɚ] *n* 1. (*local language*) lengua *f* vernácula 2. (*everyday language*) lengua *f* coloquial

vernal equinox [ˌvɜːnəlˈiːkwɪnɒks, *Am:* ˌvɜːrnəlˈiːkwɪnɑːks] <-es> *n* equinoccio *m* vernal
veronica [vəˈrɒnɪkə, *Am:* vəˈrɑːnɪ-] *n* verónica *f*
verruca [vəˈruːkə] <-s *o* -ae> *n* verruga *f*
versatile [ˈvɜːsətaɪl, *Am:* ˈvɜːrsəʈəl] *adj* 1. (*flexible*) versátil; (*mind*) ágil 2. (*multifaceted*) polifacético, -a 3. (*multipurpose: material*) polivalente
versatility [ˌvɜːsəˈtɪləti, *Am:* ˌvɜːrsəˈtɪləʈi] *n no pl* (*flexibility*) versatilidad *f*; (*of mind*) agilidad *f*
verse [vɜːs, *Am:* vɜːrs] *n* 1. LIT verso *m* 2. MUS estrofa *f* 3. REL versículo *m*
versed *adj* **to be** (well) ~ **in sth** estar (muy) versado en algo
versify [ˈvɜːsɪfaɪ, *Am:* ˈvɜːrsə-] <-ie-> I. *vi* versificar II. *vt* poner en verso
version [ˈvɜːʃən, *Am:* ˈvɜːrʒən] *n* versión *f*
verso [ˈvɜːsəʊ, *Am:* ˈvɜːrsoʊ] *n form* 1. (*of printed page*) dorso *m* 2. (*of a coin, medal*) reverso *m*
versus [ˈvɜːsəs, *Am:* ˈvɜːr-] *prep* 1. (*in comparison*) frente a 2. SPORTS, LAW contra
vertebra [ˈvɜːtɪbrə, *Am:* ˈvɜːrʈə-] <-ae> *n* vértebra *f*
vertebral [ˈvɜːtɪbrəl, *Am:* ˈvɜːrʈə-] *adj* vertebral
vertebrate [ˈvɜːtɪbreɪt, *Am:* ˈvɜːrʈəbrɪt] I. *n* vertebrado *m* II. *adj* vertebrado, -a
vertex [ˈvɜːteks, *Am:* ˈvɜːr-] <-es *o* -tices> *n* vértice *m*
vertical [ˈvɜːtɪkəl, *Am:* ˈvɜːrʈə-] *adj* vertical; ~ **drop** caída *f* en picado
vertiginous [vɜːˈtɪdʒɪnəs, *Am:* vəˈtɪdʒə-] *adj form* vertiginoso, -a
vertigo [ˈvɜːtɪɡəʊ, *Am:* ˈvɜːrʈəɡoʊ] *n no pl* vértigo *m*
verve [vɜːv, *Am:* vɜːrv] *n no pl* ímpetu *m*; **with** ~ con brío; **to give sth** (added) ~ dar un toque a algo
very [ˈveri] I. *adv* 1. (*extremely*) muy; ~ **much** mucho; **not** ~ **much** no mucho; **to feel** ~ **much at home** sentirse como en casa; **I am** ~, ~ **sorry** de veras lo siento 2. (*expression of emphasis*) **the** ~ **best** lo mejor de lo mejor; **the** ~ **first** el primerísimo; **at the** ~ **most** como mucho; **at the** ~ **least** por lo menos; **the** ~ **same** justo lo mismo ▸ ~ **well** muy bien; **to be all** ~ **fine ...**, **but ...** estar todo eso muy bien..., pero... II. *adj* **at the** ~ **bottom** al final del todo; **the** ~ **next day** justo al día siguiente; **the** ~ **fact** el mero hecho; **the** ~ **man** el mismísimo
Very light *n* bengala *f* **Very pistol** *n* pistola *f* para disparar bengalas
vesicle [ˈvesɪkl] *n* vesícula *f*
vespers [ˈvespəz, *Am:* -pɚz] *npl* REL (*evensong*) vísperas *fpl*
vessel [ˈvesəl] *n* 1. (*any kind of boat*) embarcación *f*; (*large boat*) navío *m* 2. (*container*) recipiente *m* 3. (*person*) baza *f* 4. ANAT, BOT

vaso *m*

vest¹ [vest] *n* **1.** *Brit* (*undergarment*) camiseta *f*; **thermal** ~ camiseta térmica **2.** *Am, Aus* (*outergarment*) chaleco *m*; **bullet-proof** ~ chaleco antibalas

vest² [vest] *vt* **to** ~ **sb with sth** investir a alguien con algo; **to** ~ **sth in sb** conferir algo a alguien; **to** ~ **one's hopes in sb/sth** poner sus esperanzas en alguien/algo; **~ed interests** intereses *mpl* creados

vestibule ['vestɪbjuːl, *Am:* -tə-] *n* vestíbulo *m*

vestige ['vestɪdʒ] *n* vestigio *m*; **a** ~ **of truth** un asomo de verdad; **to show a** ~ **of sth** mostrar un resquicio de algo

vestments ['vestmənts] *npl* vestiduras *fpl*

vest-pocket [ˌvest'pɒkɪt, *Am:* -'paːkɪt] *n Am, Aus* bolsillo *m* del chaleco; ~ **camera** cámara *f* de bolsillo

vestry ['vestri] <-ies> *n* sacristía *f*

vet¹ [vet] *n* **1.** (*animal doctor*) veterinario, -a *m, f* **2.** *a. fig* MIL veterano, -a *m, f*

vet² [vet] *vt* <-tt-> **1.** (*examine carefully*) examinar **2.** (*screen*) someter a investigación

vetch [vetʃ] <-es> *n* algarroba *f*

veteran ['vetərən, *Am:* 'veʈərən] I. *n a. fig* MIL veterano, -a *m, f* II. *adj a. fig* MIL veterano, -a

veteran car *n Brit* coche *m* antiguo (*fabricado antes de 1905*)

Veterans Day *n no pl, Am* día *m* de los Veteranos

La fiesta del **Veterans Day**, que se celebra el 11 de noviembre, fue creada, en un principio, para conmemorar el armisticio alcanzado entre Alemania y los EE.UU. en el año 1918. En realidad, ese día se honra a todos los veteranos de todas las guerras americanas.

veterinarian [ˌvetərɪ'neəriən, *Am:* -'neri-] *n Am* (*vet*) veterinario, -a *m, f*

veterinary ['vetərɪnəri, *Am:* -ner-] *adj* veterinario, -a; ~ **surgeon** médico *mf* veterinario, -a

veto ['viːtəʊ, *Am:* -ʈoʊ] I. *n* <-es> veto *m*; **to put a** ~ **on sth** *Brit* vetar algo; **to have a** ~ **over sth** tener derecho a veto en algo II. *vt* <vetoed> **1.** (*exercise a veto against*) vetar **2.** (*forbid*) prohibir

vex [veks] *vt* **1.** (*cause trouble for*) sacar de quicio **2.** (*upset*) afligir; **he is ~ed by computer problems** los problemas informáticos le enojan

vexation [vek'seɪʃən] *n* disgusto *m*; **to be a** ~ **to sb** ser una vejación para alguien

vexatious [vek'seɪʃəs] *adj* fastidioso, -a; ~ **child** niño(a) *m(f)* irritante; ~ **problem** problema *m* engorroso

v. g. *abbr of* **very good** m. b.

VHF [ˌviːeɪtʃ'ef] *abbr of* **very high frequency** VHF

via ['vaɪə] *prep* por; ~ **London/the bridge** por Londres/el puente

viability [ˌvaɪə'bɪləti, *Am:* -əʈi] *n no pl* viabilidad *f*

viable ['vaɪəbl] *adj* viable

viaduct ['vaɪədʌkt] *n* viaducto *m*

vibes [vaɪbz] *npl inf* **1.** (*feeling*) **good/bad** ~ buenas/malas vibraciones **2.** (*vibraphone*) vibráfono *m*

vibrant ['vaɪbrənt] *adj* **1.** (*lively: person*) enérgico, -a; (*music*) vibrante; ~ **performance** espectáculo *m* contundente **2.** (*bustling*) efervescente; (*economy*) en ebullición **3.** (*bright and strong: colour, light*) radiante

vibraphone ['vaɪbrəfəʊn, *Am:* -foʊn] *n* vibráfono *m*

vibrate [vaɪ'breɪt, *Am:* 'vaɪbreɪt] I. *vi* **1.** (*shake quickly, oscillate*) vibrar; **to** ~ **with enthusiasm** estremecerse de entusiasmo **2.** (*continue to be heard: sound*) hacer vibrar II. *vt* hacer vibrar

vibration [vaɪ'breɪʃən] *n* vibración *f*

vibrator [vaɪ'breɪtə', *Am:* 'vaɪbreɪʈə'] *n* TECH vibrador *m*; (*sexual stimulation*) consolador *m*

vicar ['vɪkə', *Am:* -ə-] *n* vicario *m*

vicarage ['vɪkərɪdʒ] *n* vicaría *f* ▸**to look like a** ~ **tea-party** parecer una tertulia de jubilados

vicarious [vɪ'keəriəs, *Am:* -'keri-] *adj* (*thrill*) indirecto, -a; (*authority*) delegado, -a

vice¹ [vaɪs] *n* vicio *m*; ~ **squad** brigada *f* antivicio

vice² [vaɪs] *n Brit, Aus* (*tool*) torno *m* de banco

vice-chairman [ˌvaɪs'tʃeəmən, *Am:* -'tʃer-] <-men> *n* vicepresidente, -a *m, f* **vice-chancellor** *n Brit* UNIV rector(a) *m(f)* **Vice President, vice-president** *n* **1.** (*deputy president*) presidente, -a *m, f* en funciones **2.** (*title*) vicepresidente, -a *m, f*

vice versa [ˌvaɪsi'vɜːsə, *Am:* -sə'vɜːr-] *adv* viceversa

vicinity [vɪ'sɪnəti, *Am:* və'sɪnəʈi] <-ies> *n* inmediaciones *fpl*; **in the** ~ **of ...** en los alrededores de...

vicious ['vɪʃəs] *adj* **1.** (*malicious*) malo, -a; (*fighting*) salvaje; (*gossip*) malicioso, -a **2.** (*cruel, violent*) despiadado, -a **3.** (*able to cause pain: animal*) feroz **4.** (*extremely powerful: pain*) atroz; (*wind*) devastador(a)

vicious circle *n* círculo *m* vicioso

vicissitudes [vɪ'sɪsɪtjuːdz, *Am:* vɪ'sɪsə-tuːdz] *n form pl* vicisitudes *fpl*; **the ~s of life** los avatares de la vida

victim ['vɪktɪm] *n* víctima *f*; **to be the** ~ **of sth** ser víctima de algo ▸**to fall** ~ **to sb/sth** sucumbir a alguien/algo

victimize ['vɪktɪmaɪz, *Am:* -tə-] *vt* discriminar; **to be ~d by law** ser víctima de la ley

victor ['vɪktə', *Am:* -tə-] *n* vencedor(a) *m(f)*; **to emerge (as) the** ~ salir victorioso

La **Victoria Cross** fue creada en el año 1856 por la reina Victoria durante la guerra de Crimea como la condecoración militar más alta de la **Commonwealth**. Se concede a quien haya destacado por su valentía. La inscripción reza: **'For valour'** (Por el valor).

Victorian [vɪkˈtɔːriən] I. *adj* victoriano, -a II. *n* victoriano, -a *m, f*

victorious [vɪkˈtɔːriəs] *adj* victorioso, -a; ~ **team** equipo *m* ganador

victory [ˈvɪktəri] <-ies> *n* victoria *f;* to clinch a ~ (**over sb**) conseguir una victoria (sobre alguien); **to win a ~** (**in sth**) obtener una victoria (en algo)

victualler [ˈvɪtələ‍ʳ, *Am:* ˈvɪt̬ələ‍ʳ] *n* ≈ encargado, -a *m, f* de una bodega

victuals [ˈvɪtəlz, *Am:* ˈvɪt̬-] *n pl, a. iron* vituallas *fpl*

videlicet [vɪˈdiːlɪset, *Am:* vɪˈdeləsɪt] *adv form* a saber

video [ˈvɪdiəʊ, *Am:* -oʊ] I. *n* 1. vídeo *m;* to come out on ~ salir en vídeo 2. (*tape*) cinta *f* de vídeo; **blank** ~ cinta de vídeo virgen II. *vt* grabar en vídeo

video camera *n* videocámara *f* **video cassette** *n* videocasete *m* **video conference** *n* videoconferencia *f* **video game** *n* videojuego *m* **videophone** *n* videoteléfono *m* **video recorder** *n* magnetoscopio *m* **video set** *n* equipo *m* de vídeo **video surveillance** *n no pl* vigilancia *f* con cámaras de vídeo **videotape** I. *n* cinta *f* de vídeo II. *vt* grabar en vídeo **videotex(t)** *n* videotexto *m* **video transmission** *n no pl* transmisión *f* por vídeo **video transmitter** *n* transmisor *m* de señales de vídeo

vie [vaɪ] <**vying**> *vi* to ~ (**with sb**) **for sth** competir (con alguien) por algo

Vienna [viˈenə] *n* Viena *f*

Viennese [ˌviːəˈniːz, *Am:* ˌviːəˈ-] I. *n inv* vienés, -esa *m, f* II. *adj* vienés, -esa

Vietcong [ˌvjetˈkɒŋ, *Am:* ˌviːetˈkɑːŋ] *n inv* vietcong *m*

Vietnam [ˌvjetˈnæm, *Am:* ˌviːetˈnɑːm] *n* Vietnam *m*

Vietnamese [ˌvjetnəˈmiːz, *Am:* viːet-] I. *adj* vietnamita II. *n* 1. (*person*) vietnamita *mf* 2. LING vietnamita *m*

view [vjuː] I. *n* 1. (*opinion*) punto *m* de vista; **exchange of** ~s intercambio *m* de opiniones; **conflicting** ~s opiniones *fpl* contrapuestas; **prevailing** ~ opinión *f* dominante; to express a ~ expresar un parecer; **to have an optimistic** ~ **of life** ver la vida con optimismo; **to hold strong** ~s **about sth** mantener una postura fuerte sobre algo; **to share a** ~ compartir un punto de vista; **a long** ~ **of sth** una visión amplia de algo; **in her** ~ **...** a su modo de ver... 2. (*perspective*) perspectiva *f;* **long-term** ~ perspectiva a largo plazo; **to take the long** ~ **of sth** considerar algo a largo plazo

3. (*sight*) vista *f;* **to afford a panoramic** ~ permitir una vista panorámica; **to block sb's** ~ estar tapando a alguien (la vista); **to come into** ~ aparecer ante la vista; **to disappear from** ~ perderse de vista; **to keep sb/sth in** ~ mantener a alguien/algo en el punto de mira 4. (*opportunity to observe*) panorama *m* ▶ to take a <u>poor</u> ~ of sth ver algo con malos ojos, tener un concepto desfavorable de algo; **to have sth in** ~ tener algo en mente; **in** ~ **of sth** en vista de algo; **to be on** ~ estar expuesto; **to be on** ~ **to the public** estar abierto al público; **with a** ~ **to sth** con vistas a algo; **with this in** ~ con este fin II. *vt* 1. (*consider*) considerar; **to** ~ **sth from a different angle** enfocar algo desde un ángulo distinto; **to** ~ **sth with reluctance** tomarse algo con reticencia 2. (*watch*) ver 3. (*take a look at*) mirar

viewer *n* 1. (*person*) telespectador(a) *m(f)* 2. (*device*) proyector *m* de diapositivas 3. INFOR visor *m,* visualizador *m*

viewfinder [ˈvjuːˌfaɪndə‍ʳ, *Am:* -də‍ʳ] *n* visor *m*

viewing *n no pl* visita *f;* **a second** ~ **of the film is also frightening** ver la película por segunda vez también da miedo; ~ **figures** índice *m* de audiencia

viewpoint [ˈvjuːpɔɪnt] *n* 1. (*point of view*) punto *m* de vista 2. (*vista point*) mirador *m*

vigil [ˈvɪdʒɪl, *Am:* ˈvɪdʒəl] *n* vela *f;* to keep ~ mantenerse alerta; **to hold a** ~ velar

vigilance [ˈvɪdʒɪləns] *n no pl* vigilancia *f;* to relax ~ bajar la guardia

vigilant [ˈvɪdʒɪlənt] *adj* vigilante; **to be** ~ **in doing sth** estar atento al hacer algo

vignette [vɪˈnjet] *n* estampa *f*

vigor *n Am, Aus,* **vigour** [ˈvɪgə‍ʳ, *Am:* -ə‍ʳ] *n no pl* vigor *m;* (*energy*) energía *f;* to do sth with ~ hacer algo con energía

vigorous [ˈvɪgərəs] *adj* 1. (*energetic*) enérgico, -a; (*protest*) rotundo, -a 2. (*flourishing: growth*) pujante

vile [vaɪl] *adj* 1. (*disgusting, shameful*) vil 2. *inf* (*very bad*) vomitivo, -a; (*weather*) asqueroso, -a; ~ **mood** humor *m* de perros; **to be** ~ **to sb** portarse como un cerdo con alguien; **to smell** ~ apestar

vilify [ˈvɪlɪfaɪ, *Am:* ˈ-ə-] <-ie-> *vt form* envilecer

village [ˈvɪlɪdʒ] I. *n* 1. (*small settlement*) aldea *f* 2. + *pl/sing vb* (*populace*) pueblo *m* II. *adj* de pueblo

village community <-ies> *n* pueblo *m* de organización comunal **village green** *n* prado *m* comunal **village inn** *n* taberna *f* de pueblo

villager [ˈvɪlɪdʒə‍ʳ, *Am:* -ədʒə‍ʳ] *n* aldeano, -a *m, f*

villain [ˈvɪlən] *n* 1. (*evil person*) villano, -a *m, f;* **small-time** ~ maleante *mf;* **to cast sb as a** ~ quedar alguien como el malo 2. (*bad guy*) granuja *mf* ▶ **the** ~ **of the** <u>piece</u> *inf* el malo/la mala de la obra

V

villainous [ˈvɪlənəs] *adj* infame
villainy [ˈvɪləni] *n no pl* vileza *f*
vim [vɪm] *n no pl* brío *m*
vinaigrette [ˌvɪnɪˈgret, *Am:* -ə'-] *n no pl* vinagreta *f*
vindicate [ˈvɪndɪkeɪt, *Am:* -də-] *vt* **1.** (*justify*) justificar **2.** (*support*) reivindicar **3.** (*clear of blame, suspicion*) vindicar
vindication [ˌvɪndɪˈkeɪʃən, *Am:* -də'-] *n no pl* **1.** (*justification*) justificación *f* **2.** (*act of clearing blame*) vindicación *f*
vindictive [vɪnˈdɪktɪv] *adj* vengativo, -a
vine [vaɪn] *n* **1.** (*grape plant*) vid *f* **2.** (*climbing type*) parra *f*
vinegar [ˈvɪnɪgəʳ, *Am:* -əgəʳ] *n no pl* vinagre *m*
vinegary *adj* avinagrado, -a; **to be ~** estar aliñado con vinagre
vineyard [ˈvɪnjəd, *Am:* -jəd] *n* viñedo *m*
vintage [ˈvɪntɪdʒ, *Am:* -t̬ɪdʒ] I. *n* **1.** (*wine from a particular year*) cosecha *f* **2.** (*harvest season*) vendimia *f* II. *adj* **1.** GASTR añejo, -a **2.** (*high and classic quality*) excelente; **~ music of the sixties** clásicos *mpl* de la música de los sesenta **3.** *Aus, Brit* AUTO antiguo, -a; **~ car** coche *m* de época
vintner [ˈvɪntnəʳ, *Am:* -nəʳ] *n* vinatero, -a *m, f*
vinyl [ˈvaɪnəl] I. *n no pl* vinilo *m* II. *adj* de vinilo
viola¹ [viˈəʊlə, *Am:* viˈoʊ-] *n* MUS viola *f*
viola² [ˈvaɪələ, *Am:* viːələ] *n* BOT viola *f*
violate [ˈvaɪəleɪt] *vt* **1.** (*break, not comply with*) violar; **to ~ a cease-fire agreement** romper un acuerdo de alto al fuego **2.** (*disturb*) perturbar; (*tomb*) profanar; **to ~ sb's privacy** entrometerse en la privacidad de alguien
violation [ˌvaɪəˈleɪʃən] *n* violación *f*; **traffic ~** infracción *f* de tráfico
violence [ˈvaɪələns] *n no pl* violencia *f*
violent [ˈvaɪələnt] *adj* **1.** (*cruel*) violento, -a; (*argument*) duro, -a **2.** (*very powerful*) fuerte; (*clothes*) chillón, -ona
violet [ˈvaɪələt, *Am:* -lɪt] I. *n* **1.** BOT violeta *f* **2.** (*colour*) violeta *m* II. *adj* violeta
violin [ˌvaɪəˈlɪn] *n* MUS violín *m*
violinist [vaɪəˈlɪnɪst] *n* MUS violinista *mf*
violoncellist [ˌvaɪələnˈtʃelɪst, *Am:* ˌviːələnˈtʃelɪst] *n* MUS violoncelista *mf*
violoncello [ˌvaɪələnˈtʃeləʊ, *Am:* ˌviːələnˈtʃeloʊ] *n* violoncelo *m*
VIP [ˌviːaɪˈpiː] *s.* very important person VIP *mf*
viper [ˈvaɪpəʳ, *Am:* -pəʳ] *n a. fig* víbora *f*
virago [vɪˈrɑːgəʊ, *Am:* vəˈrɑːgoʊ] <-(e)s> *n* arpía *f*
virgin [ˈvɜːdʒɪn, *Am:* ˈvɜːr-] *n* virgen *f*; **the Blessed ~** la Santísima Virgen
virginal [ˈvɜːdʒɪnəl, *Am:* ˈvɜːr-] *n* virginal
virgin forest *n* bosque *m* virgen
Virginia [vəˈdʒɪnjə, *Am:* vəʳ-] *n* Virginia *f*
Virgin Islands *n* Islas *fpl* Vírgenes
virginity [vəˈdʒɪnəti, *Am:* vəˈdʒɪnət̬i] *n no pl* virginidad *f*; **to lose one's ~** perder uno la virginidad

Virgo [ˈvɜːgəʊ, *Am:* ˈvɜːrgoʊ] *n* Virgo *mf*
virile [ˈvɪraɪl, *Am:* -əl] *adj* viril
virility [vɪˈrɪləti, *Am:* vəˈrɪlət̬i] *n no pl* **1.** (*sexual vigour*) virilidad *f* **2.** (*forcefulness*) fuerza *f*
virology [vaɪəˈrɒlədʒi, *Am:* vaɪˈrɑːlə-] *n no pl* virología *f*
virtual [ˈvɜːtʃʊəl, *Am:* ˈvɜːrtʃu-] *adj* virtual; **to provoke a ~ collapse of the economy** provocar prácticamente un colapso de la economía; **to be a ~ unknown** ser en efecto un desconocido
virtually *adv* prácticamente
virtual office *n* oficina *f* virtual **virtual reality** *n* realidad *f* virtual **virtual shopping mall** *n* centro *m* comercial virtual **virtual storage** *n no pl* almacenamiento *m* virtual
virtue [ˈvɜːtjuː, *Am:* ˈvɜːrtʃuː] *n* **1.** (*good moral quality*) virtud *f* **2.** (*advantage, benefit*) ventaja *f* ▶**to make a ~ of necessity** hacer de la necesidad virtud; **to make a ~ (out) of sth** convertir algo en virtud; **by ~ of** form en virtud de
virtuosity [ˌvɜːtjuˈɒsəti, *Am:* ˌvɜːrtʃuˈɑːsət̬i] *n no pl, form* virtuosidad *f*
virtuoso [ˌvɜːtjuˈəʊsəʊ, *Am:* ˌvɜːrtʃuˈoʊsoʊ] <-s o -osi> I. *n* virtuoso, -a *m, f* II. *adj* virtuoso, -a; **a ~ display of diplomacy** un magnífico despliegue de habilidad diplomática
virtuous [ˈvɜːtʃuəs, *Am:* ˈvɜːrtʃu-] *adj* **1.** (*morally good*) virtuoso, -a **2.** (*chaste*) casto, -a
virulence [ˈvɪrʊlənts, *Am:* -jə-] *n no pl* virulencia *f*
virulent [ˈvɪrʊlənt, *Am:* -jə-] *adj* **1.** MED virulento, -a **2.** form (*hateful and fierce*) violento, -a
virus [ˈvaɪərəs, *Am:* ˈvaɪ-] <-es> *n* INFOR, MED virus *m inv*
visa [ˈviːzə] I. *n* visado *m* II. *adj* de visado
vis-à-vis [ˌviːzɑːˈviː, *Am:* ˌviːzəˈviː] I. *prep* con relación a; (*compared to*) en comparación con II. *n* cara a cara *m*
viscera [ˈvɪsərə] *npl* vísceras *fpl*
viscose [ˈvɪskəʊs, *Am:* -koʊs] *n no pl* viscosa *f*
viscosity [vɪˈskɒsəti, *Am:* -ˈskɑːsət̬i] *n no pl* viscosidad *f*
viscount [ˈvaɪkaʊnt] *n* vizconde *m*
viscountess [ˌvaɪkaʊnˈtəs, *Am:* ˈvaɪkaʊntɪs] *n* vizcondesa *f*
viscous [ˈvɪskəs] *adj* viscoso, -a
vise [vaɪs] *n Am s.* **vice²**
visibility [ˌvɪzəˈbɪləti, *Am:* -əbɪlət̬i] *n no pl* **1.** (*clearness of view*) visibilidad *f*; **poor ~** poca visibilidad **2.** (*public awareness*) notoriedad *f*
visible [ˈvɪzəbl] *adj* **1.** (*able to be seen, noticeable*) visible; **to be barely ~** ser a penas perceptible **2.** (*in the public eye*) notorio, -a
vision [ˈvɪʒən] *n* **1.** *no pl* (*sight*) vista *f*;

blurred ~ visión *f* borrosa **2.**(*mental image*) *a.* REL visión *f* **3.** *fig* (*beautiful sight*) imagen *f;* **to have ~s of fame** soñar con ser famoso

visionary ['vɪʒənəri, *Am:* -əneri] **I.** *n* visionario, -a *m, f* **II.** *adj* **1.**(*hallucinatory*) utópico, -a **2.**(*future-orientated*) con visión de futuro

visit ['vɪzɪt] **I.** *n* visita *f;* **to have a ~ from sb** recibir una visita de alguien; **to pay a ~ to sb** ir a ver a alguien **II.** *vt* visitar **III.** *vi* ir de visita

visitation [ˌvɪzɪ'teɪʃən, *Am:* -ə'-] *n* **1.**(*act of visiting*) visita *f* **2.** *iron* (*official visit*) inspección *f* **3.** REL visión *f* **4.** *Am* (*time*) tiempo *m* de visita

visiting hours *npl* horario *m* de visita **visiting professor** *n* profesor(a) *m(f)* visitante

visitor ['vɪzɪtəʳ, *Am:* -t̬əʳ] *n* visitante *mf;* **~'s book** libro *m* de visitas

visor ['vaɪzəʳ, *Am:* -zəʳ] *n* visera *f*

vista ['vɪstə] *n* **1.**(*splendid view*) vista *f* **2.** *fig* perspectiva *f;* **to open up a ~** abrir una perspectiva; **to raise a ~** levantar perspectivas

visual ['vɪʒuəl] *adj* visual; **~ sense** sentido *m* estético; **~ aid** soporte *m* visual

visualize ['vɪʒuəlaɪz] *vt* visualizar

vital ['vaɪtəl, *Am:* -t̬əl] *adj* vital; **~ ingredient** ingrediente *m* esencial; **~ organs** órganos *mpl* vitales; **~ part** parte *f* crucial; **~ statistics** estadísticas *fpl* demográficas; **it is ~ to do ...** es fundamental hacer...

vitality [vaɪ'tæləti, *Am:* -ət̬i] *n no pl* vitalidad *f*

vitalize ['vaɪtəlaɪz, *Am:* -t̬əlaɪz] *vt* **1.**(*give life to*) vivificar **2.**(*animate*) dar vida; *fig* vitalizar

vitamin ['vɪtəmɪn, *Am:* 'vaɪt̬ə-] *n* vitamina *f* **vitamin deficiency** *n no pl* avitaminosis *f inv* **vitamin tablets** *n* comprimidos *mpl* vitamínicos

vitreous ['vɪtriəs] *adj* vítreo, -a

vitrify ['vɪtrɪfaɪ, *Am:* -trə-] <-ie-> **I.** *vt* vitrificar **II.** *vi* vitrificarse

vitriol ['vɪtriəl] *n no pl* vitriolio *m*

vitriolic [ˌvɪtri'ɒlɪk, *Am:* -'ɑ:lɪk] *adj* vitriólico, -a

vituperate [vɪ'tju:pəreɪt, *Am:* vaɪ'tu:pəreɪt] *form* **I.** *vt* vituperar **II.** *vi* vituperarse

vituperation [vɪˌtju:pə'reɪʃən, *Am:* vaɪˌtu:pəreɪ-] *n no pl, form* vituperio *m*

vivacious [vɪ'veɪʃəs] *adj* vivaz; **a ~ blonde** una rubia llena de vida; **a ~ life** una vida animada

vivacity [vɪ'væsəti, *Am:* -ət̬i] *n no pl* vivacidad *f*

vivarium [vaɪ'veəriəm, *Am:* vaɪ'veri-] <-s *o* vivaria> *n* vivero *m*

viva voce [ˌvaɪvə'vəʊsi, *Am:* -'voʊsi:] **I.** *n* examen *m* oral **II.** *adj* oral **III.** *adv* a viva voz

vivid ['vɪvɪd] *adj* (*colour*) vivo, -a; (*language*) vívido, -a; (*imagination*) fértil

viviparous [vɪ'vɪpərəs, *Am:* vaɪ'-] *adj* vivíparo, -a

vivisect [ˌvɪvɪ'sekt, *Am:* 'vɪvəsekt] *vt* viviseccionar

vivisection [ˌvɪvɪ'sekʃən, *Am:* -ə'-] *n no pl* vivisección *f*

vixen ['vɪksən] *n* **1.** ZOOL zorra *f* **2.** *pej* (*woman*) arpía *f*

viz [vɪz] *adv abbr of* **videlicet** (**namely**) a saber

vocabulary [vəʊ'kæbjələri, *Am:* voʊ'kæbjəler-] *n* vocabulario *m;* **limited ~** vocabulario limitado; **to widen one's ~** ampliar el vocabulario de uno; **the word 'politeness' isn't in his ~** *iron* la palabra 'modales' no entra en su vocabulario

vocal ['vəʊkəl, *Am:* 'voʊ-] **I.** *adj* **1.**(*of the voice*) oral; **~ communication** comunicación *f* oral; **~ cords** cuerdas *fpl* vocales **2.**(*outspoken*) vehemente; **a ~ minority** una minoría que se hace oír; **to be ~ (about sth)** armar revuelo (acerca de algo) **II.** *n* voz *f,* vocalista *mf;* **lead ~** voz principal; **to be on ~s** cantar

vocalist ['vəʊkəlɪst, *Am:* 'voʊ-] *n* vocalista *mf*

vocalize ['vəʊkəlaɪz, *Am:* 'voʊ-] **I.** *vi* vocalizar **II.** *vt* vocalizar

vocation [vəʊ'keɪʃən, *Am:* voʊ'-] *n* vocación *f;* **to miss one's ~** equivocarse de carrera

vocational [vəʊ'keɪʃənəl, *Am:* voʊ'-] *adj* vocacional; **~ counselling** orientación *f* profesional; **~ training** formación *f* profesional

vociferate [vəʊ'sɪfəreɪt, *Am:* voʊ'-] **I.** *vi* quejarse a gritos **II.** *vt* vociferar

vociferation [vəʊˌsɪfə'reɪʃən, *Am:* voʊˌ-] *n form* vocerío *m*

vociferous [vəʊ'sɪfərəs, *Am:* voʊ'-] *adj* vociferante

vogue [vəʊg, *Am:* voʊg] *n* moda *f* ▶**to have a ~** estar de moda; **in ~** de moda; **to be back in ~** ponerse de moda de nuevo; **out of ~** pasado de moda

voice [vɔɪs] **I.** *n* voz *f;* **in a loud ~** en voz alta; **to raise/lower one's ~** levantar/bajar la voz; **to lose one's ~** quedarse afónico; **to listen to the ~ of reason** atender a razones; **to make one's ~ heard** hacerse escuchar; **with one ~** a coro; **to give ~ to sth** expresar algo; **the ~ within sb** la voz de la conciencia de alguien **II.** *vt* expresar

voice box <-es> *n* ANAT laringe *f*

voiced *adj* sonoro, -a

voiceless ['vɔɪsləs] *adj* **1.** LING sordo, -a **2.** *liter* sin voz

voice over *n* TV, CINE voz *f* en off

void [vɔɪd] **I.** *n* **1.**(*empty space*) hueco *m* **2.**(*feeling of emptiness*) vacío *m* **II.** *adj* inválido, -a; **to be ~ of sth** estar falto de algo **III.** *vt* anular

vol *abbr of* **volume** vol.

volatile ['vɒlətaɪl, *Am:* 'vɑ:lət̬əl] *adj* volátil; (*situation*) inestable; (*person*) voluble

volcanic [vɒl'kænɪk, *Am:* vɑ:l'-] *adj* volcánico, -a

volcano [vɒl'keɪnəʊ, *Am:* vɑ:l'keɪnoʊ] <-(e)s> *n* volcán *m*

vole [vəʊl, *Am:* voʊl] *n* ratón *m* de campo

volition [vəʊ'lɪʃən, *Am:* voʊ'-] *n no pl, form* voluntad *f;* **to do sth (out) of one's own ~** hacer algo por voluntad propia

volley ['vɒli, *Am:* 'vɑːli] I. *n* **1.** (*salvo*) descarga *f;* **to discharge ~s** descargar salvas **2.** (*onslaught*) lluvia *f;* **a ~ of enquiries** una retahíla de preguntas; **a ~ of insults** una sarta de insultos **3.** SPORTS volea *f* II. *vi* SPORTS volear III. *vt* **to ~ a ball** sacar una pelota

volleyball ['vɒlibɔːl, *Am:* 'vɑːli-] *n no pl* voleibol *m*

volt [vəʊlt, *Am:* voʊlt] *n* voltio *m*

voltage ['vəʊltɪdʒ, *Am:* 'voʊltɪdʒ] *n* voltaje *m*

voltage detector *n* ELEC voltímetro *m* **voltage drop** *n* ELEC caída *f* de tensión

volte-face [ˌvɒlt'fɑːs, *Am:* ˌvɑːlt'fɑːs] *n* cambio *m* radical (de opinión)

voluble ['vɒljəbl, *Am:* 'vɑːl-] *adj form* **1.** (*loquacious*) locuaz **2.** (*wordy*) extenso, -a

volume ['vɒljuːm, *Am:* 'vɑːljuːm] *n no pl* (*all senses*) volumen *m; ~* **of sales** COM volumen de ventas; **to turn the ~ up/down** subir/bajar el volumen ►**to** speak **~s for sth** ser muy indicativo de algo

volume control, **volume regulator** *n* control *m* del volumen **volume discount** *n* rappel *m*

voluminous [və'luːmɪnəs, *Am:* və'luːmə-] *adj form* **1.** (*extensive*) exhaustivo, -a **2.** (*very large*) voluminoso, -a; (*clothes*) amplísimo, -a

voluntary ['vɒləntəri, *Am:* 'vɑːlənteri] *adj* voluntario, -a

voluntary organization *n* organización *f* de voluntariado **voluntary redundancy** <-ies> *n* baja *f* incentivada

volunteer [ˌvɒlən'tɪəʳ, *Am:* ˌvɑːlən'tɪr] I. *n* voluntario, -a *m, f* II. *vt* **to ~ oneself for sth** ofrecerse (voluntario) para algo; **to ~ information** dar información por iniciativa propia III. *vi* ofrecerse; (*willingly join*) presentarse voluntario, -a IV. *adj* de voluntarios; ~ **army** ejército *m* de voluntarios

voluptuous [və'lʌptʃuəs] *adj* **1.** (*sexually appealing*) voluptuoso, -a **2.** (*epicurean*) placentero, -a

volute [vəʊ'luːt, *Am:* və'luːt] *n* **1.** ARCHIT voluta *f* **2.** ZOOL (*marine gastropod*) concha *f;* (*snail's shell*) caparazón *m*

vomit ['vɒmɪt, *Am:* 'vɑːmɪt] I. *vi* vomitar; **it makes me want to ~** *a. fig* me produce náuseas II. *vt* vomitar III. *n no pl* vómito *m*

voodoo ['vuːduː] *n no pl* **1.** (*black magic*) vudú *m* **2.** *inf* (*jinx*) **there is (some sort of) ~ on this castle** este castillo está hechizado

voracious [və'reɪʃəs, *Am:* vɔː'reɪ-] *adj* voraz

voracity [və'ræsəti, *Am:* vɔː'ræsəti] *n no pl* voracidad *f*

vortex ['vɔːteks, *Am:* 'vɔːr-] <-es *o* vortices> *n* vórtice *m; ~* **of emotion** torbellino *m* de emociones

vote [vəʊt, *Am:* voʊt] I. *vi* **1.** (*elect*) votar; **to ~ for/against sb/sth** votar a favor/en contra de alguien/algo **2.** (*formally decide*) **to ~ on sth** someter algo a votación II. *vt* **1.** (*elect*) elegir por votación **2.** (*propose*) **to ~ that …** votar que… +*subj* **3.** (*declare*) considerar III. *n* **1.** (*formally made choice*) voto *m* **2.** (*election*) votación *f;* **to put sth to the ~** someter algo a votación **3.** (*right to elect*) **to have the ~** tener derecho al voto

♦**vote down** *vt* rechazar (por votación)

♦**vote in** *vt* elegir (por votación)

♦**vote on** *vt* aprobar (por votación)

♦**vote out** *vt* **to vote sb out (of sth)** no reelegir a alguien (en algo)

voter *n* votante *mf*

voting I. *adj* de votos II. *n* votación *f*

voting booth <-es> *n* cabina *f* de votación **voting box** <-es> *n* urna *f* de votos **voting machine** *n* máquina *f* de recuento de votos

vouch [vaʊtʃ] I. *vi* **to ~ for sth/sb** responder de algo/por alguien II. *vt* **to ~ that …** confirmar que…

voucher ['vaʊtʃəʳ, *Am:* -tʃɚ] *n Aus, Brit* **1.** (*coupon*) vale *m* **2.** (*receipt*) comprobante *m*

vouchsafe [ˌvaʊtʃ'seɪf] *vt form* **to ~ (sb) sth** dignarse a dar algo (a alguien); **to ~ to do sth** dignarse a hacer algo

vow [vaʊ] I. *vt* jurar; **to ~ chastity** hacer voto de castidad II. *n* **to take a ~** hacer los votos

vowel ['vaʊəl] *n* vocal *f*

voyage ['vɔɪɪdʒ] I. *n* viaje *m* II. *vi* viajar; **to ~ across sth** viajar por algo

voyager ['vɔɪɪdʒəʳ, *Am:* 'vɔɪɪdʒɚ] *n* navegante *mf*

voyeur [vwaː'jɜːʳ, *Am:* vɔɪ'jɜːr] *n* mirón, -ona *m, f*

VTOL ['viːtɒl, *Am:* -tɑːl] AVIAT *abbr of* **vertical take-off and landing** despegue *m* y aterrizaje vertical

VTR [ˌviːtiː'ɑːʳ, *Am:* -'ɑːr] *n abbr of* **videotape recorder** vídeo *m*

vulcanite ['vʌlkənaɪt] *n no pl* vulcanita *f*

vulcanization [ˌvʌlkənaɪ'zeɪʃən] *n no pl* vulcanización *f*

vulcanize ['vʌlkənaɪz] *vt* vulcanizar

vulgar ['vʌlgəʳ, *Am:* -gɚ] *adj* **1.** (*crude*) ordinario, -a **2.** (*commonplace*) vulgar; ~ **accent** acento *m* chabacano

vulgarity [vʌl'gærəti, *Am:* -'gerəti] *n no pl* **1.** (*crudeness*) vulgaridad *f* **2.** (*ordinariness*) chabacanería *f*

vulgarize ['vʌlgəraɪz] *vt* vulgarizar

Vulgate ['vʌlgeɪt] *n* **the ~** la Vulgata

vulnerable ['vʌlnərəbl, *Am:* 'vʌlnɚə-] *adj* vulnerable

vulture ['vʌltʃəʳ, *Am:* -tʃɚ] *n a. fig* buitre *m*

vulva ['vʌlvə] <-s *o* -e> *n* vulva *f*

vying ['vaɪɪŋ] *pres p of* **vie**

W

W, w ['dʌblju:] *n* W, w *f;* ~ **for William** W de Washington

w *abbr of* **watt** W

W *n abbr of* **west** O

wack [wæk] *n Brit, inf* amigo, -a *m, f,* pipe *m AmC*

wacko ['wækəʊ, *Am:* -oʊ] *n Am* bicho *m* raro

wacky ['wæki] <-ier, -iest> *adj inf* (*person*) chiflado, -a; (*thing*) estrambótico, -a

wad [wɒd, *Am:* wɑːd] *n* (*of straw*) manojo *m;* (*of cotton*) bola *f;* (*of banknotes*) fajo *m;* (*of forms*) montón *m*

wadding ['wɒdɪŋ, *Am:* 'wɑːd-] *n no pl* relleno *m*

waddle ['wɒdl, *Am:* 'wɑːdl] **I.** *vi* anadear **II.** *n* andares *mpl* de pato

wade [weɪd] **I.** *vi* caminar por el agua; **to ~ across** vadear; **to ~ into sth** adentrarse en algo caminando; **to ~ into sb** *inf* tomarla con alguien; **to ~ through a book** leerse un libro con dificultad **II.** *vt* vadear **III.** *n Am* chapoteo *m*

wader ['weɪdər, *Am:* -dər] *n* 1. (*bird*) ave *m* zancuda 2. *pl* (*boots*) botas *fpl* de pescador

wafer ['weɪfər, *Am:* -fər] *n* 1. (*biscuit*) galleta *f* de barquillo; (*for ice cream*) barquillo *m* 2. REL hostia *f*

wafer-thin [ˌweɪfəˈθɪn, *Am:* -fər-] *adj* finísimo, -a

waffle¹ ['wɒfl, *Am:* 'wɑːfl] *Brit* **I.** *vi* (*to talk*) **to ~ (on)** parlotear; (*in an essay*) meter paja *fig* **II.** *n no pl* palabrería *f;* (*in an essay*) paja *f fig*

waffle² ['wɒfl, *Am:* 'wɑːfl] *n* GASTR gofre *m,* waffle *m AmL*

waffle iron *n Am* plancha *f* para gofres [*o* waffles *AmL*]

waft [wɒft, *Am:* wɑːft] *liter* **I.** *vi* (*scent, sound*) llegar (flotando); **a delicious smell ~ed in from the kitchen** un delicioso aroma llegaba (flotando) de la cocina **II.** *vt* llevar por el aire

wag¹ [wæg] **I.** <-gg-> *vt* menear; **to ~ one's finger at sb** amenazar a alguien con el dedo; **the dog ~ged its tail** el perro meneaba el rabo **II.** <-gg-> *vi* menearse **III.** *n* meneo *m*

wag² [wæg] *n inf* bromista *mf*

wage [weɪdʒ] **I.** *vt* (*war*) hacer; **to ~ war against sth/sb** librar una batalla contra algo/alguien; **to ~ a campaign for/against sth** emprender una campaña pro/contra algo **II.** *n* sueldo *m;* **living ~** salario mínimo vital; **minimum ~** salario mínimo; **real ~s** salario real; **to earn a ~** percibir un salario; **to get a good ~** tener un buen sueldo

wage adjustment *n* ajuste *m* salarial **wage bill** *n* nómina *f* **wage claim** *n,* **wage demand** *n Brit* reivindicación *f* salarial **wage costs** *npl* costes *mpl* salariales **wage differentials** *npl* disparidades *fpl* salariales

wage dispute *n* disputa *f* salarial **wage earner** *n* asalariado, -a *m, f* **wage freeze** *n* congelación *f* salarial **wage increase** *n* aumento *m* salarial **wage level** *n* nivel *m* de salarios **wage negotiation** *n* negociación *f* salarial **wage packet** *n Brit* 1. (*pay*) sueldo *m* (neto) 2. (*envelope*) sobre *m* de la paga

wager ['weɪdʒər, *Am:* -dʒər] **I.** *n* apuesta *f;* **to lay a ~** hacer una apuesta **II.** *vt* apostar; **to ~ one's reputation/life** jugarse la reputación/vida

wage scale *n* escala *f* de salarios

wages clerk *n* administrativo, -a *m, f* del área de personal

wage settlement *n* fijación *f* de salarios **wage slip** *n* recibo *m* de sueldo

wages policy <-ies> *n* política *f* salarial **wage worker** *n Am* asalariado, -a *m, f*

waggish ['wægɪʃ] *adj inf* bromista

waggle ['wægl] **I.** *vt* mover **II.** *vi* moverse

waggly ['wægli] <-ier, -iest> *adj* tambaleante; (*tooth*) flojo, -a

waggon *n Brit,* **wagon** ['wægən] *n* 1. (*horse-drawn*) carro *m* 2. *Brit* RAIL vagón *m* 3. (*truck*) camión *m* ▶ **to be on the ~** *inf* no beber; **to fall off the ~** *inf* volver a darse a la bebida; **to go on the ~** *inf* dejar la bebida

waif [weɪf] *n liter* 1. (*child*) niño, -a *m, f* sin techo 2. (*animal*) animal *m* callejero ▶ **the ~s and strays** los sin techo

wail [weɪl] **I.** *vi* gemir; (*wind*) silbar **II.** *vt* lamentar **III.** *n* lamento *m*

wailing *n* gemidos *mpl*

Wailing Wall *n* Muro *m* de las Lamentaciones

waist [weɪst] *n* cintura *f*

waistband ['weɪstbænd] *n* cinturilla *f* **waistcoat** *n Brit* chaleco *m*

waist-deep [ˌweɪstˈdiːp] *adj* hasta la cintura

waistline ['weɪstlaɪn] *n* cintura *f;* **to watch the ~** guardar la línea

wait [weɪt] **I.** *vi* esperar; **to ~ for sth/sb** esperar algo/a alguien; **to keep sb ~ing** hacer esperar a alguien; **he cannot ~ to see her** está ansioso por verla; **~ and see** espera y verás; **(just) you ~!** ¡vas a ver!; **~ for it!** *inf* ¡espera el momento! **II.** *vt* esperar; **to ~ one's turn** esperar su turno **III.** *n no pl* espera *f;* **to lie in ~ for sb** estar al acecho de alguien

♦ **wait about** *vi,* **wait around** *vi* **to ~ for sth** estar a la espera de algo

♦ **wait behind** *vi* quedarse

♦ **wait in** *vi* **to ~ for sb** quedarse en casa esperando a alguien

♦ **wait on** *vt* 1. (*serve*) servir 2. *form* (*expect*) **to ~ sth** esperar a algo

♦ **wait up** *vi* **to ~ for sb** esperar a alguien levantado

---

El **Waitangi Day** o **New Zealand Day** se celebra el 6 de enero. Ya que fue en ese día del año 1840 cuando 512 jefes de la tribu de los **Maori** firmaron un acuerdo con el gobierno británico que significó el comienzo de Nueva Zelanda como nación.

waiter ['weɪtə', *Am:* -t̬ə'] *n* camarero *m*, garzón *m AmL*, mesero *m Méx*

waiting *n no pl* 1. (*time spent waiting*) **the ~** la espera 2. *Brit* (*parking*) estacionamiento *m*

waiting game *n* **to play a ~** dejar pasar el tiempo **waiting list** *n* lista *f* de espera **waiting room** *n* sala *f* de espera

waitress ['weɪtrɪs] *n* camarera *f*, garzona *f AmL*, mesera *f Méx*

waive [weɪv] *vt form* (*right*) renunciar a; (*rule*) no aplicar; (*charge*) cancelar

waiver ['weɪvə', *Am:* -və'] *n* renuncia *f*

wake¹ [weɪk] *n* NAUT estela *f;* **in the ~ of** tras, después de

wake² [weɪk] *n* velatorio *m*

wake³ [weɪk] <woke *o* waked, woken *o* waked> I. *vi* despertarse II. *vt* despertar
◆**wake up** *vi, vt* despertar

wakeful ['weɪkfəl] *adj form* 1. (*sleepless*) desvelado, -a; ~ **night** noche *f* en vela 2. (*vigilant, alert*) alerta; **to feel ~** sentirse despierto

waken ['weɪkən] *vt form* despertar

wakey ['weɪki] *interj iron* ~ **~!** ¡venga, despierta!

Wales [weɪlz] *n* Gales *m;* **North/South ~** Gales del Norte/Sur; **New South ~** Nueva *f* Gales del Sur

walk [wɔːk, *Am:* wɑːk] I. *n* 1. (*stroll*) paseo *m;* **to take a ~** ir a dar un paseo; **to take sb out for a ~** sacar a alguien a pasear; **it's a five minute ~** está a cinco minutos a pie 2. (*gait*) andar *m* 3. (*walking speed*) paso *m* ▶**~ of life** condición *f;* **people from all** (*different*) **~s of life** gente de todas las profesiones y condiciones sociales II. *vt* 1. (*go on foot*) andar; (*distance*) recorrer a pie 2. (*accompany*) **to ~ sb home** acompañar a alguien a su casa 3. (*take for a walk*) **to ~ the dog** sacar a pasear el perro 4. *Brit, inf* (*pass easily*) superar fácilmente; **she'll ~ the interview** la entrevista es pan comido para ella III. *vi* (*go on foot*) andar, caminar; (*stroll*) pasear ▶**to ~ on air** no caber en sí de gozo
◆**walk about** *vi,* **walk around** *vi* dar una vuelta
◆**walk away** *vi form* irse; **to ~ from sb** alejarse de alguien; **to ~ from sth** desentenderse de algo; **to ~ from an accident** salir ileso de un accidente
◆**walk back** *vi* volver a pie
◆**walk in** *vi* entrar; **to ~ on sb** (**doing sth**) sorprender a alguien (haciendo algo) al entrar
◆**walk off** I. *vt* **to ~ the meal** salir a dar un paseo para bajar la comida II. *vi* marcharse
◆**walk on** *vi* seguir andando
◆**walk out** *vi* 1. (*leave*) salir 2. (*go on strike*) ir a la huelga
◆**walk over** *vt* (*rights*) pisotear; **to walk**

(**all**) **over sb** machacar a alguien
◆**walk through** *vt insep* (*part*) ensayar
◆**walk up** *vi* 1. (*go up*) subir 2. (*approach*) **to ~ to sb** acercarse a alguien

walkabout ['wɔːkəbaʊt, *Am:* 'wɑː-] *n inf* paseo *m;* **to go ~** pasearse entre el público

walkaway ['wɔːkəweɪ, *Am:* 'wɑː-] *n Am* victoria *f* fácil, pan *m* comido *inf;* **to win in a ~** ganar sin problemas

walker ['wɔːkə', *Am:* 'wɑːkə'] *n* 1. (*stroller*) paseante *mf* 2. SPORTS marchista *mf* 3. (*sb whose hobby is walking*) excursionista *mf*

walker-on *n* THEAT figurante, -a *m, f;* CINE extra *mf*

walkie-talkie [ˌwɔːkiˈtɔːki, *Am:* ˌwɑːkiˈtɑː-] *n* walkie-talkie *m*

walk-in ['wɔːkɪn, *Am:* 'wɑːk-] *adj Am* (*furniture*) empotrado, -a; ~ **wardrobe** vestidor *m*

walking I. *n no pl* paseo *m;* SPORTS marcha *f* atlética; **to do a lot of ~** andar mucho II. *adj* 1. **it is within ~ distance** se puede ir a pie 2. (*human*) ambulante; **to be a ~ encyclopaedia** ser una enciclopedia ambulante

walking frame *n* andador *m* **walking-shoes** *npl* zapatos *mpl* para caminar **walking-stick** *n* bastón *m* **walking-tour** *n* excursión *f* a pie; (*guided trip*) paseo *m* guiado

walkman® ['wɔːkmən, *Am:* 'wɑːk-] <-s> *n* walkman® *m*

walk-on ['wɔːkɒn, *Am:* 'wɑːkɑːn] *adj* ~ **part** THEAT papel *m* de figurante; CINE papel *m* de extra

walk-out ['wɔːkaʊt, *Am:* 'wɑːk-] *n* salida *f;* (*strike*) huelga *f;* **to stage a ~** salir; (*strike*) declarar la huelga

walk-over ['wɔːkˌəʊvə', *Am:* 'wɑːkˌoʊvə'] *n inf* victoria *f* fácil; **it was a ~** fue pan comido

walk-through ['wɔːkˌθruː, *Am:* 'wɑːk-] *n* ensayo *m*

walkway ['wɔːkweɪ, *Am:* 'wɑːk-] *n* pasarela *m*

wall [wɔːl] I. *n* 1. (*in the interior*) *a.* ANAT pared *f;* (*enclosing town*) muralla *f;* (*enclosing house*) tapia *f;* **artery** ~ pared arterial; **the city ~s** las murallas de la ciudad; **the Great Wall of China** la Gran Muralla China; **dry-stone** ~ muro de piedra 2. (*barrier*) barrera *f;* **a ~ of silence** un muro de silencio; **a ~ of water** una cortina de agua 3. AUTO valla *f* ▶**to have one's back to the ~** estar entre la espada y la pared; **~s have ears** *prov* las paredes oyen *prov;* **to go to the ~** (*fail*) fracasar; (*go bankrupt*) quebrar; **to go up** [*o* **to climb**] **the ~** subirse por las paredes II. *vt* (*garden*) cercar con un muro; (*town*) amurallar
◆**wall in** *vt* 1. (*garden*) cercar con un muro; (*town*) amurallar 2. *fig* encerrar
◆**wall off** *vt* separar con un muro; **to wall oneself off** *fig* encerrarse en sí mismo
◆**wall up** *vt* (*person*) emparedar; (*opening*) cerrar con un muro

wall bars *npl* espalderas *fpl* **wall chart** *n*

gráfico *m* de pared **wall clock** *n* reloj *m* de pared

wallet ['wɒlɪt, *Am:* 'wɑːlɪt] *n* cartera *f,* billetera *f AmL*

wallflower ['wɔːlˌflaʊəʳ, *Am:* -ˌflaʊɚ] *n* 1. BOT al(h)elí *m* 2. *fig* ≈ patito *m* feo

wallhanging *n* tapiz *m*

Wallis and Futuna [ˌwɒlɪsəndfuːˈtjuːnə, *Am:* ˌwɑːlɪs-] *n* ~ **Islands** Islas *fpl* Wallis y Fortuna

wall map *n* mapa *m* mural

Wallonia [wəˈləʊniə, *Am:* wɑːˈloʊ-] *n* Valonia *f*

Walloon [wɒˈluːn, *Am:* wɑː-] I. *adj* valón, -ona II. *n* 1. (*person*) valón, -ona *m, f* 2. LING valón *m*

wallop ['wɒləp, *Am:* 'wɑːləp] I. *vt inf* 1. (*hit hard*) dar un golpetazo 2. (*punish*) dar una paliza, zurrar II. *n* golpetazo *f;* **to give sb a ~** pegar a alguien

walloping I. *adj* 1. *inf* (*very big*) enorme 2. *Am, inf* (*very good*) estupendo II. *n inf* paliza *f;* **to give sb a ~** dar una paliza a alguien

wallow ['wɒləʊ, *Am:* 'wɑːloʊ] I. *n* revolcón *m* II. *vi* 1. (*lie in earth*) revolcarse 2. (*remain in negative state*) sumirse; **to ~ in self-pity** sumirse en la autocompasión 3. (*revel*) regodearse; **to ~ in wealth** nadar en la abundancia

wallpaper ['wɔːlˌpeɪpəʳ, *Am:* -pɚ] I. *n* papel *m* pintado; **a roll of ~** un rollo de papel pintado; **to hang ~** empapelar II. *vt* empapelar

wall socket *n* enchufe *m* de pared

Wall Street *n* 1. (*street*) calle bursátil y *financiera en Nueva York* 2. *fig* mundo *m* bursátil

wall-to-wall ['wɔːltə'wɔːl, *Am:* -ṯɚ'-] *adj* ~ **carpets** moqueta *f*

walnut ['wɔːlnʌt] *n* 1. (*nut*) nuez *f* 2. (*tree*) nogal *m*

walrus ['wɔːlrəs] <walruses *o* walrus> *n* morsa *f*

waltz [wɔːls, *Am:* wɔːlts] <-es-> I. *n* vals *m* II. *vi* 1. (*dance*) valsar 2. *inf* (*walk confidently*) ir tan fresco III. *vt* **to ~ sb** bailar el vals con alguien

◆**waltz about** *vi,* **waltz around** *vi* dar vueltas despreocupado

◆**waltz in** *vi inf* entrar como si nada

◆**waltz off** *vi inf* **to ~ with sth** robar algo

◆**waltz out** *vi inf* salir como si nada

wan [wɒn, *Am:* wɑːn] <-nn> *adj liter* macilento, -a

wand [wɒnd, *Am:* wɑːnd] *n* (*conjuror's stick*) varita *f* mágica; **to wave one's magic ~** agitar la varita mágica

wander ['wɒndəʳ, *Am:* 'wɑːndɚ] I. *vt* vagar por; **to ~ the streets** deambular por las calles, callejear II. *vi* (*roam*) vagar; (*stroll*) pasearse; **to let one's thoughts ~** dejar volar la imaginación III. *n inf* paseo *m;* **to go for a ~ around the city** dar una vuelta por la ciudad

wanderer ['wɒndərəʳ, *Am:* 'wɑːndɚɚ] *n* hombre *m* errante, mujer *f* errante; *pej* vagabundo, -a *m, f*

wandering ['wɒndərɪŋ, *Am:* 'wɑːn-] *adj* 1. (*nomadic*) errante; (*salesman*) ambulante; ~ **tribe** tribu nómada 2. (*not concentrating*) divagante

wanderings ['wɒndərɪŋz, *Am:* 'wɑːn-] *n* andanzas *fpl; pej* vagabundeo *m*

wane [weɪn] I. *vi* menguar; **to wax and ~** crecer y menguar II. *n* mengua *f;* **to be on the ~** menguar

wangle ['wæŋgl] *vt inf* conseguir; **to ~ one's way into sth** arreglárselas para entrar en algo

want [wɒnt, *Am:* wɑːnt] I. *vt* 1. (*wish*) querer; **to ~ to do sth** querer hacer algo; **to ~ sb to do sth** querer que alguien haga algo; **to ~ sth done** querer que se haga algo; **you're ~ed on the phone** te llaman al teléfono; **I was ~ing to leave** estaba deseando macharme 2. (*need*) necesitar; **he is ~ed by the police** lo busca la policía; '**~ed**' 'se busca'; **this soup ~s a bit of salt** a esta sopa le falta sal; **this ~s a lot of time** esto exige mucho tiempo II. *n* 1. (*need*) necesidad *f;* **to be in ~ of sth** necesitar algo 2. (*lack*) falta *f;* **for ~ of sth** por falta de algo; **to live in ~** *form* vivir necesitado

◆**want in** *vi inf* **to ~ sth** querer participar en algo

◆**want out** *vi inf* **to ~ (of sth)** querer salirse (de algo)

wantage ['wɒntɪdʒ, *Am:* 'wɑːnṯɪdʒ] *n Am* deficiencia *f*

wanting *adj* deficiente; **to be ~ in sth** estar falto de algo; **there is sth ~** falta algo

wanton ['wɒntən, *Am:* 'wɑːntən] *adj* 1. (*extreme*) desenfrenado, -a 2. (*mindless*) sin razón; ~ **destruction** destrucción sin sentido; ~ **disregard** desatención injustificada; ~ **waste** dispendio gratuito 3. (*licentious*) lascivo, -a 4. (*capricious*) caprichoso, -a; (*playful*) juguetón, -ona

WAP TEL, INFOR *abbr of* **wireless application protocol** WAP

wapiti ['wɒpɪti, *Am:* 'wɑːpəṯi] *n inv* wapití *m*

war [wɔːʳ, *Am:* wɔːr] *n* guerra *f;* **civil ~** guerra civil; **the Great War** la Primera Guerra Mundial; **the Second World War** la Segunda Guerra Mundial; **a holy ~** una guerra santa; **the horrors of ~** los horrores de la guerra; **in time of ~** en tiempo(s) de guerra; **to be at ~** estar en guerra; **to declare ~ on sb** declarar la guerra a alguien; *fig* hacer la vida imposible a alguien; **to go to ~** entrar en guerra; **to make ~ on sb** hacer la guerra a alguien

war atrocities *npl* crímenes *fpl* de guerra

war baby *n* niño, -a *m, f* nacido, -a durante la guerra

warble ['wɔːbl, *Am:* 'wɔːr-] *vi* (*bird*) trinar; (*lark*) gorjear; *iron* (*person*) cantar

warbler ['wɔːbləʳ, *Am:* 'wɔːrblɚ] *n* curruca *f*

war bond *n* bono *m* de guerra **war bulletin** *n* boletín *m* de guerra **war correspondent** *n* corresponsal *mf* de guerra **war crime** *n*

crimen *m* de guerra **war criminal** *n* criminal *mf* de guerra **war cry** *n* grito *m* de guerra
ward [wɔːd, *Am:* wɔːrd] *n* **1.** (*wardship*) tutela *f;* **in ~** bajo tutela **2.** (*person*) pupilo, -a *m, f* **3.** (*in hospital*) sala *f;* **geriatric/psychiatric ~** pabellón *m* geriátrico/psiquiátrico; **maternity ~** sala *f* de maternidad **4.** *Brit* (*political area*) distrito *m* electoral
◆**ward off** *vt* evitar
warden ['wɔːdn, *Am:* 'wɔːr-] *n* guardián, -ana *m, f;* (*of a college*) director(a) *m(f);* (*of a prison*) alcaide *m*
warder ['wɔːdə', *Am:* 'wɔːrdə] *n* celador *m*
wardress ['wɔːdrɪs, *Am:* 'wɔːr-] *n* celadora *f*
wardrobe ['wɔːdrəʊb, *Am:* 'wɔːrdroʊb] *n* **1.** (*cupboard*) (armario *m*) ropero *m* **2.** *no pl* (*clothes*) vestuario *m*
wardrobe trunk *n* baúl *m* ropero
wardship ['wɔːdʃɪp, *Am:* 'wɔːrd-] *n no pl* tutela *f*
war effort *n* esfuerzo *m* bélico
warehouse ['weəhaʊs, *Am:* 'wer-] *n* almacén *m*
warehouse keeper *n* almacenista *mf*
wares [weəz, *Am:* werz] *npl inf* mercancías *fpl*
warfare ['wɔːfeə', *Am:* 'wɔːrfer] *n no pl* guerra *f*
war game *n* juego *m* de guerra
warhead ['wɔːhed, *Am:* 'wɔːr-] *n* (*of rocket*) cabeza *f* de guerra
warily ['weərɪli, *Am:* 'wer-] *adv* (*expecting danger*) cautamente; (*suspiciously*) recelosamente
warlike ['wɔːlaɪk, *Am:* 'wɔːr-] *adj* **1.** (*of war*) bélico, -a **2.** (*belligerent*) belicoso, -a; **~ speech** discurso beligerante
warlord ['wɔːlɔːd, *Am:* 'wɔːrlɔːrd] *n* jefe *m* militar
warm [wɔːm, *Am:* wɔːrm] **I.** *adj* **1.** (*comfortably hot*) caliente; (*clothes*) de abrigo; **nice and ~** a gusto y calentito; **as ~ as toast** *inf* bien calentito; **to be ~** (*person*) tener calor; (*thing*) estar caliente; (*weather*) hacer calor **2.** (*affectionate*) afectuoso; **~ welcome** calurosa bienvenida; **to be ~** ser [*o* estar] efusivo **3.** (*suggesting heat: day*) caluroso, -a; (*climate, wind*) cálido, -a **4.** (*fresh*) fresco, -a; **~ track** huella fresca ►**you're getting ~** ¡caliente, caliente! **II.** *n no pl* **the ~** el calor **III.** *vt* calentar; **to ~ one's feet** calentarse los pies; **to ~ the soup** calentar la sopa; **to ~ sb's heart** reconfortar a alguien
◆**warm up** **I.** *vi* calentarse **II.** *vt* **1.** (*make hot*) calentar; **to warm sb up** hacer entrar en calor a alguien **2.** (*food*) recalentar
warm-blooded [ˌwɔːm'blʌdɪd, *Am:* ˌwɔːrm'-] *adj* de sangre caliente
warm front *n* frente *m* cálido
warm-hearted [ˌwɔːm'hɑːtɪd, *Am:* ˌwɔːrm-'hɑːrtɪd] *adj* bondadoso, -a; (*affectionate*) cariñoso, -a
warmly *adv* **1.** (*of heat*) **wrap up ~!** ¡abrígate

bien! **2.** (*enthusiasm*) calurosamente; **she shook my hand ~** me estrechó la mano afectuosamente
warm start *n* arranque *m* en caliente
warmth [wɔːmθ, *Am:* wɔːrmθ] *n no pl* **1.** (*heat*) calor *m* **2.** (*affection*) calidez *f*
warm-up ['wɔːmʌp] *n* SPORTS (pre)calentamiento *m*
warn [wɔːn, *Am:* wɔːrn] *vt* **1.** (*make aware*) avisar, advertir; **to ~ sb not to do sth** advertir a alguien que no haga algo; **to ~ sb of a danger** prevenir a alguien contra un peligro **2.** LAW poner sobre aviso
◆**warn off** *vt* **to warn sb off sth** apercibir a alguien de algo; **to warn sb off doing sth** advertir a alguien de que no haga algo
warning [wɔːnɪŋ, *Am:* wɔːrnɪŋ] **I.** *n* aviso *m*, advertencia *f;* **a word of ~** una advertencia; **to give sb a ~** advertir a alguien; **give me some days' ~** avísame von unos días de antelación; **to issue a ~** (**about sth**) hacer una advertencia (acerca de algo); **to sound a note of ~** dar la voz de alarma; **without ~** sin previo aviso **II.** *adj* de advertencia
warning light *n* luz *f* de advertencia **warning shot** *n* disparo *m* de advertencia **warning sign** *n* señal *f* de peligro
warp [wɔːp, *Am:* wɔːrp] **I.** *vi* torcerse, deformarse **II.** *vt* **1.** (*wood*) torcer, deformar **2.** (*mind*) pervertir; **to ~ sb's mind** (re)torcer la mente de alguien **III.** *n* deformación *f;* **to have a ~ed way of looking at things** tener una manera retorcida de ver las cosas
warpaint ['wɔːpeɪnt, *Am:* 'wɔːr-] *n* pintura *f* de guerra
war-path ['wɔːrpɑːθ, *Am:* 'wɔːrpæθ] *n no pl* **to be on the ~** estar en pie de guerra; *fig* tener ganas de pelea
warped *adj* deformado, -a; (*mind*) pervertido, -a
warrant ['wɒrənt, *Am:* 'wɔːr-] **I.** *n* **1.** COM garantía *f* **2.** LAW orden *f;* **arrest ~** orden de detención; **search ~** orden de registro; **to execute a ~** ejecutar una orden judicial **3.** *no pl* (*justification*) justificación *f* **II.** *vt* **1.** (*promise*) garantizar **2.** (*justify*) justificar
warrantee [ˌwɒrən'tiː, *Am:* ˌwɔːr-] *n* beneficiario, -a *m, f* de una garantía
warrant officer *n* **1.** MIL brigada *m* **2.** NAUT contramaestre *m*
warrantor ['wɒrəntɔː', *Am:* 'wɔːrəntɔːr] *n* garante *mf*
warranty ['wɒrənti, *Am:* 'wɔːrənt̬i] <-ies> *n* garantía *f*
warren ['wɒrən, *Am:* 'wɔːr-] *n* **1.** ZOOL conejera *f* **2.** *fig* laberinto *m*
warring *adj* en guerra; **~ factions** facciones beligerantes
warrior ['wɒriə', *Am:* 'wɔːrjə] *n* guerrero, -a *m, f*
Warsaw ['wɔːsɔː, *Am:* 'wɔːrsɑː] *n* Varsovia *f*
Warsaw Pact *n*, **Warsaw Treaty** *n* HIST Pacto *m* de Varsovia

warship ['wɔːʃɪp, *Am:* 'wɔːr-] *n* barco *m* de guerra

wart [wɔːt, *Am:* wɔːrt] *n* verruga *f*; ~**s and all** *inf* (*description, portrait*) con sus virtudes y defectos

warthog ['wɔːthɒg, *Am:* 'wɔːrthɑːg] *n* jabalí *m* verrugoso

wartime ['wɔːtaɪm, *Am:* 'wɔːr-] *n no pl* tiempo *m* de guerra; **in** ~ en tiempos de guerra

wartorn ['wɔːtɔːn] *adj* destrozado, -a por la guerra

war-weary ['wɔːˌwɪəri, *Am:* 'wɔːrˌwɪri] *adj* cansado, -a por la guerra

wary ['weəri, *Am:* 'weri] <-ier, -iest> *adj* (*not trusting*) receloso, -a; (*watchful*) cauteloso, -a; **to be** ~ **of sth/sb** recelar de algo/alguien; **to be** ~ **about (doing) sth** dudar con (si hacer) algo; **with a** ~ **note in one's voice** con una nota de alerta en la voz

war zone ['wɔːzəʊn, *Am:* 'wɔːrzoʊn] *n* zona *f* de guerra

was [wɒz, *Am:* wɑːz] *pt of* **be**

wash [wɒʃ, *Am:* wɑːʃ] I. *vt* 1. (*clean*) lavar; (*dishes*) fregar; **to** ~ **one's hair/hands** lavarse la cabeza/las manos; **to** ~ **the floor** fregar el suelo 2. (*waves*) bañar 3. (*river, sea*) llevar, arrastrar; **to** ~ **overboard** arrastrar fuera de la cubierta II. *vi* 1. (*person*) lavarse; (*cloth*) poderse lavar; **that excuse won't** ~ **with me** *inf* esa excusa conmigo no cuela 2. (*do the washing*) lavar la ropa 3. (*sea*) chapotear III. *n* 1. (*cleaning with water*) lavado *m*; **to have a** ~ darse un baño 2. *no pl* (*clothes for cleaning*) **the** ~ la ropa para lavar; **to be in the** ~ estar en la lavandería 3. *no pl, liter* (*sound of water*) chapoteo *m* 4. NAUT remolinos *mpl*; AVIAT disturbios *mpl* aerodinámicos 5. (*thin layer*) capa *f*, baño *m*; (*painting*) mano *f* 6. (*even situation*) empate *m* ▸ **to come out in the** ~ *prov* arreglarse todo

♦**wash away** *vt* 1. (*clean*) quitar 2. (*carry elsewhere*) llevar, arrastrar

♦**wash down** *vt* 1. (*clean*) lavar 2. (*carry elsewhere*) llevar, arrastrar 3. *fig* ~ **the pill with water** trágate la pastilla con agua

♦**wash off** *vi, vt* quitar(se)

♦**wash out** I. *vi* quitarse II. *vt* 1. (*clean*) lavar; (*remove*) quitar 2. *fig* **our party was washed out** la fiesta fue cancelada

♦**wash over** *vt* 1. (*flow over*) pasar por encima de 2. (*have no effect on*) no afectar

♦**wash up** I. *vt* 1. (*dishes*) fregar 2. **the sea washed it up** el mar lo arrojó sobre la playa II. *vi* 1. (*clean dirty dishes*) fregar los platos 2. *Am* (*wash*) lavarse (las manos y la cara)

washable *adj* lavable

wash-and-wear *adj* de lava y pon

wash basin *n Brit* (*basin*) lavabo *m*; (*bowl*) palangana *m* **wash board** *n* tabla *f* de lavar **wash-bowl** *n Am s.* **wash basin wash cloth** *n Am* manopla *f* **washday** *n* día *m* de colada **wash-down** *n* (*of oneself*) baño *m*; (*of sth*) lavado *m*; **to give sth a** ~ dar a algo

una lavada

washed-out [ˌwɒʃt'aʊt, *Am:* ˌwɑːʃt-] *adj* 1. (*bleached*) desteñido, -a; ~ **jeans** tejanos descoloridos 2. (*pale*) demacrado, -a 3. (*tired*) cansado, -a

washer ['wɒʃəʳ, *Am:* 'wɑːʃɚ] *n* 1. *Am* (*washing-machine*) lavadora *f* 2. (*plastic ring*) arandela *f*

wash-hand-basin *n* (*basin*) lavabo *m*; (*bowl*) palangana *m* **wash-house** *n* lavadero *m*

washing ['wɒʃɪŋ, *Am:* 'wɑːʃɪŋ] *n no pl* 1. (*clothes for cleaning*) ropa *f* sucia 2. (*act*) lavado *f*; (*of clothes*) colada *f*; **to do the** ~ hacer la colada

washing machine *n* lavadora *f*, lavarropas *f inv Arg* **washing powder** *n no pl, Brit* detergente *m* en polvo **washing soda** *n no pl* sosa *f*

Washington [ˌwɒʃɪŋtən, *Am:* ˌwɑːʃɪŋ-] *n* Washington *m*

Washington D.C. *n* Washington D.C.

Washington's Birthday es un día de fiesta oficial en los EE.UU. Aunque George Washington en realidad nació el 22 de febrero de 1732, su cumpleaños se celebra desde hace algunos años siempre el tercer lunes del mes de febrero, para que se produzca así un fin de semana largo.

---

washing-up [ˌwɒʃɪŋ'ʌp, *Am:* ˌwɑːʃɪŋ'-] *n Brit* platos *mpl* sucios; **to do the** ~ fregar los platos

washing-up basin *n*, **washing-up bowl** *n* fregadero *m* **washing-up liquid** *n* detergente *m* líquido

wash-leather ['wɒʃleðəʳ] *n* gamuza *f*

washout ['wɒʃaʊt, *Am:* 'wɑːʃ-] *n inf* desastre *m*

washroom ['wɒʃrʊm, *Am:* 'wɑːʃruːm] *n Am* aseos *mpl*, sanitarios *mpl AmL*

wasn't [wɒznt, *Am:* wɑːznt] = **was not** *s.* **be**

wasp [wɒsp, *Am:* wɑːsp] *n* avispa *f*

WASP [wɒsp, *Am:* wɑːsp] *n Am abbr of* **White Anglo-Saxon Protestant** persona de la clase privilegiada de los EE.UU., blanca, anglosajona y protestante

waspish ['wɒspɪʃ, *Am:* 'wɑːspɪʃ] *adj* mordaz

wasp's nest *n* avispero *m*

wasp-waisted *adj* con cintura de avispa

wastage ['weɪstɪdʒ] *n no pl* 1. (*waste*) desgaste *m* 2. (*loss*) merma *f* 3. (*byproduct of process*) residuos *mpl*

waste [weɪst] I. *adj* sobrante; (*material*) de desecho; (*land*) yermo, -a; **to lay** ~ devastar; **to lie** ~ quedar sin cultivar II. *n* 1. *no pl* (*misuse*) derroche *m*; **it's a** ~ **of energy/money** es un derroche de energía/dinero; **it's a** ~ **of time** es una pérdida de tiempo; **to lay** ~ **to the land** devastar la tierra; **to go to** ~ echarse a perder; **what a** ~! ¡qué pena! 2. *no pl*

(*unwanted matter*) desechos *mpl;* **household/industrial** ~ residuos *mpl* domésticos/industriales; **nuclear** ~ residuos *mpl* nucleares; **toxic** ~ residuos *mpl* tóxicos; **to recycle** ~ reciclar la basura **III.** *vt* malgastar; (*time*) perder; (*opportunity*) desaprovechar; **to** ~ **one's breath** *fig* hablar inútilmente; **to** ~ **no time in doing sth** apresurarse a hacer algo; **to not** ~ **words** no gastar saliva inútilmente **IV.** *vi* agotarse ▶~ **not,** <u>want</u> **not** *prov* quien guarda, halla *prov*
♦**waste away** *vi* consumirse
wastebasket ['weɪstˌbɑːskɪt, *Am:* -ˌbæskət] *n Am,* **wastebin** ['weɪstbɪn] *n Brit* papelera *m* **waste disposal** *n* eliminación *f* de desperdicios **waste-disposal unit** *n* triturador *m* de basuras
wasteful ['weɪstfəl] *adj* derrochador(a); **to be** ~ **with electricity** gastar mucha electricidad
waste heat *n* calor *m* residual **wasteland** *n* yermo *m* **waste management** *n no pl* gestión *f* de residuos **wastepaper** *n no pl* papel *m* usado; (*recyclable*) papel *m* reciclable **wastepaper basket** *n* papelera *f* **waste pipe** *n* tubo *m* de desagüe **waste product** *n* residuos *mpl* **waster** *n* **1.** (*person*) derrochador(a) *m(f);* **a money** ~ un manirroto **2.** (*good-for-nothing*) perdido, -a *m, f*
waste reprocessing *n no pl* reciclado *m* de residuos **waste separation** *n no pl* separación *f* de residuos **waste steam** *n no pl* vapor *m* de escape **waste water** *n* aguas *fpl* residuales
wasting ['weɪstɪŋ] *adj* (*disease*) debilitante
wastrel ['weɪstrəl] *n* **1.** (*wasteful person*) derrochador(a) *m(f)* **2.** (*good-for-nothing*) perdido, -a *m, f*
watch [wɒtʃ, *Am:* wɑːtʃ] **I.** *n* **1.** *no pl* (*act of observation*) vigilancia *f;* **to be on the** ~ **for sth** estar a la mira de algo; **to be under** ~ estar bajo vigilancia; **to keep a close** ~ **on sb/sth** vigilar a alguien/algo con mucho cuidado; **to put a** ~ **on sb** poner a alguien bajo vigilancia **2.** (*period of duty*) guardia *f;* **to be on** ~, **to keep** ~ estar de guardia **3.** (*group of guards*) guardia *f;* HIST ronda *f* **4.** (*clock on wrist*) reloj *m* de pulsera; (*clock on chain*) reloj *m* de bolsillo **II.** *vt* **1.** (*observe*) mirar; **to** ~ **the clock** mirar el reloj; **to** ~ **a film** ver una película; **to** ~ **TV** ver la televisión; **to** ~ **the world go by** mirar cómo pasa la gente; **to** ~ **sb/sth do sth** mirar a alguien/algo hacer algo; **to** ~ **how sb does sth** mirar cómo alguien hace algo **2.** (*keep vigil*) vigilar; **to** ~ **sth/sb like a hawk** vigilar algo/a alguien como un perro guardián; **to** ~ **the kids** vigilar a los niños **3.** (*mind*) fijarse en; **to** ~ **every penny** (*one spends*) estar pendiente de cada peseta (que se gasta); **to** ~ **one's weight** cuidar el peso; ~ **it!** ¡cuidado!, ¡aguas! *Méx;* **to** ~ **it** (**with sb**) tener cuidado (con alguien); ~ **yourself** cuídate **III.** *vi* fijarse; **to** ~ **as sb/sth does sth** fijarse

en cómo alguien/algo hace algo
♦**watch out** *vi* tener cuidado; ~! ¡cuidado!
watchband ['wɒtʃbænd] *n Am s.* **watchstrap**
watchdog ['wɒtʃdɒg, *Am:* 'wɑːtʃdɑːg] *n* **1.** *Am* perro *m* guardián **2.** (*keeper of standards*) guardián, -ana *m, f;* (*official organization*) organismo *m* de vigilancia; **a** ~ **on sth** un guardián de algo
watcher ['wɒtʃə^r, *Am:* 'wɑːtʃə^r] *n* observador(a) *m(f)*
watchful ['wɒtʃfəl, *Am:* 'wɑːtʃ-] *adj* vigilante; **to keep a** ~ **eye on sb/sth** estar pendiente de alguien/algo; **under the** ~ **eye of sb** bajo la atenta mirada de alguien
watch-maker ['wɒtʃˌmeɪkə^r, *Am:* 'wɑːtʃmeɪkə^r] *n* relojero, -a *m, f*
watchman ['wɒtʃmən, *Am:* 'wɑːtʃ-] <-men> *n* guardián *m;* **night** ~ vigilante *m* nocturno
watchstrap ['wɒtʃstræp] *n Brit* correa *f* de reloj
watchtower ['wɒtʃtaʊə^r, *Am:* 'wɑːtʃtaʊə^r] *n* atalaya *f*
watchword ['wɒtʃwɜːd, *Am:* 'wɑːtʃwɜːrd] *n* **1.** (*symbol*) consigna *f* **2.** (*password*) contraseña *f*
water ['wɔːtə^r, *Am:* 'wɑːtə^r] **I.** *n* **1.** *no pl* (*liquid*) agua *f;* **bottled** ~ agua embotellada; **a bottle of** ~ una botella de agua; **a drink/a glass of** ~ un trago/un vaso de agua; **hot and cold running** ~ agua corriente fría y caliente; **under** ~ bajo agua **2.** (*area of water*) **the** ~**s of the Rhine** las aguas del Rin; **coastal** ~**s** aguas costeras; **territorial** ~**s** aguas jurisdiccionales; **unchartered** ~**s** *fig* territorio *m* desconocido; **by** ~ por mar **3.** (*urine*) aguas *mpl* menores; **to pass** ~ orinar **4.** MED ~ **on the brain** hidrocefalia *f;* ~ **on the knee** derrame *m* sinovial; **to take the** ~**s** tomar las aguas ▶**to be** ~ **under the** <u>bridge</u> ser agua pasada; **like** ~ **off a** <u>duck's</u> **back** como si oyera llover; **to spend** <u>money</u> **like** ~ gastar el dinero como si creciera en los árboles; **to pour** <u>cold</u> ~ **on sth** echar agua fría a algo; **to be in** <u>deep</u> ~ estar metido en un lío; **still** ~**s run** <u>deep</u> *prov* no te fíes del agua mansa *prov;* **of the** <u>first</u> ~ (*excellent*) de primera; (*extremely bad*) ínfimo, -a; **to get into** <u>hot</u> ~ meterse en honduras; **to fish in** <u>troubled</u> ~**s** pescar en río revuelto; **to** <u>hold</u> ~ (*explanation*) ser consistente; **to** <u>muddy</u> **the** ~**s** enmarañar las cosas **II.** *vt* (*plants*) regar; (*livestock*) dar de beber a **III.** *vi* **1.** (*produce tears*) lagrimear **2.** (*salivate*) salivar; **it makes my mouth** ~ se me hace la boca agua
waterbird *n* ave *f* acuática **water boatman** *n* hidrómetra *m*
water-borne ['wɔːtəbɔːn, *Am:* 'wɑːtəbɔːrn] *adj* por mar; ~ **attack** ataque por agua; **a** ~ **disease** enfermedad propagada por el agua
water bottle *n* botellón *m* de agua; (*for soldiers, travellers*) cantimplora *f* **water butt** *n* tinaja *f* **water cannon** *n inv* cañón *m* de

agua **water carrier** *n* aguador(a) *m(f)*
water cart *n* HIST cuba *f* de agua **water closet** *n* retrete *m*, excusado *m* AmL
watercolor Am, **watercolour** I. *n* acuarela *f* II. *adj* de [*o* en] acuarela **water content** *n* contenido *m* de agua
water-cooled ['wɔːtəkuːld, Am: 'wɑːt̬ɚ-] *adj* refrigerado, -a por agua
water-cooling *n* refrigeración *f* por agua
watercourse *n* cauce *m* **watercraft** *n liter* embarcación *f* **watercress** *n no pl* berro *m* **water cure** *n* MED cura *f* de agua
water-driven *adj* movido, -a por agua
waterfall *n* cascada *f* **waterfowl** *n inv* ave *f* acuática **waterfront** *n* (harbour) puerto *m* **water gauge** *n* medidor *m* de agua; **to read the ~** leer el medidor de agua **water heater** *n* calentador *m* de agua **water hole** *n* abrevadero *m* **water hose** *n* manguera *f* de agua **water ice** *n Brit* sorbete *m*
watering *n* 1. (of plants) riego *m* 2. (tears) lagrimeo *m*
watering can ['wɔːtərɪŋkæn, Am: 'wɑː-t̬ɚ-] *n* regadera *f* **watering place** *n* 1. (for animals) abrevadero *m* 2. *Brit* (sea-side resort) balneario *m*
waterless ['wɔːtələs, Am: 'wɑːt̬ɚləs] *adj* árido, -a; **~ desert/wasteland** desierto/páramo árido
water level *n* nivel *m* del agua **water lily** <-ies> *n* nenúfar *m* **water line** *n no pl* línea *f* de flotación
water-logged ['wɔːtəlɒgd, Am: 'wɑːt̬ɚ-lɑːgd] *adj* anegado, -a
Waterloo [ˌwɔːtəluː, Am: 'wɑːt̬ɚ-] *n* **to meet one's ~** llegar a uno su San Martín
water main *n* cañería *f* principal **water-man** <-men> *n* barquero *m* **watermark** *n* 1. (river or tide level) línea *f* del agua 2. (on paper) filigrana *f* **watermelon** *n* sandía *f* **water meter** *n* contador *m* de agua **water pipe** *n* 1. (for transporting water) cañería *f* 2. (hookah) pipa *f* de agua **water pistol** *n* pistola *f* de agua **water pollution** *n no pl* contaminación *f* del agua **water polo** *n* waterpolo *m*, polo *m* acuático **water power** *n no pl* fuerza *f* hidráulica **water pressure** *n no pl* presión *f* del agua
waterproof ['wɔːtəpruːf, Am: 'wɑːt̬ɚ-] I. *adj* impermeable II. *n Brit* impermeable *m* III. *vt* impermeabilizar
water-repellent *adj* hidrófugo, -a
watershed ['wɔːtəʃed, Am: 'wɑːt̬ɚ-] *n* 1. (high ground) divisoria *m* de aguas 2. *no pl, fig* (great change) punto *m* de inflexión; **to mark a ~** marcar un punto decisivo
water shortage *n* escasez *f* de agua **water-side** *n no pl* orilla *f*, ribera *f*
water-ski ['wɔːtəskiː, Am: 'wɑːt̬ɚ-] I. *vi* esquiar en el agua; **to go ~ing** hacer esquí acuático II. <-s> *n* esquí *m* acuático
water-skiing *n no pl* esquí *m* acuático
water softener *n* ablandador *m* de agua

water-soluble *adj* soluble en agua
water spout *n Am* METEO tromba *f*
water supply *n* suministro *m* de agua **water supply pipe** *n* tubería *f* del suministro de agua **water supply point** *n* punto *m* de suministro de agua
watertable *n* capa *f* freática **water tank** *n* cisterna *f*; (smaller one) aljibe *m*
watertight ['wɔːtətaɪt, Am: 'wɑːt̬ɚ-] *adj* 1. (not allowing water in) hermético, -a; *fig* (separate) estanco, -a 2. *fig* (not allowing doubt) irrecusable; (agreement) a toda prueba
water tower *n* depósito *f* elevado de agua
water vapor *n Am*, **water vapour** *n* vapor *m* de agua **water vole** *n* rata *f* de agua **water wave** *n* ola *f* (de agua) **waterway** *n* canal *m* **waterwings** *npl* flotadores *mpl*; **to wear ~** usar flotadores **waterworks** *n pl* 1. (where public water is stored) reserva *f* de abastecimiento de agua 2. *inf* (body organs) vías *fpl* urinarias ►**to turn on the ~** echar a llorar
watery ['wɔːtəri, Am: 'wɑːt̬ɚ-] <-ier, -iest> *adj* 1. (bland) aguado, -a; **a ~ soup** una sopa aguada 2. (weak in colour) deslavado, -a; (weak in strength) diluido, -a; **a ~ sun** un sol pálido
watt [wɒt, Am: wɑːt] *n* ELEC vatio *m*
wattage ['wɒtɪdʒ, Am: 'wɑːt̬ɪdʒ] *n no pl* ELEC vatiaje *m*
wave ['weɪv] I. *n* 1. (of water) ola *f*; (on surface, of hair) ondulación *f*; **to make ~s** *fig* causar problemas; **to be on the crest of the ~** *fig* estar en la cumbre 2. PHYS onda *f* 3. (hand movement) **to give sb a ~** saludar a alguien con la mano II. *vi* 1. (make hand movement) **to ~ at** [*o* to] **sb** saludar a alguien con la mano; **to ~ goodbye** decir adiós con la mano 2. (move from side to side: field of corn) mecerse con el viento; (flag) ondear III. *vt* 1. (move to signal) **to ~ sb goodbye** decir adiós con la mano a alguien 2. (move from side to side) agitar 3. (hair) ondular; **to have one's hair ~d** rizarse el pelo
◆**wave aside** *vt fig* rechazar; **to ~ an idea/objection/suggestion** rechazar una idea/objeción/sugerencia
◆**wave down** *vt* **to wave sb/sth down** hacer señales a alguien/algo para que pare
◆**wave on** *vt* **to wave sb/sth on** hacer señales a alguien/algo para que siga adelante
◆**wave through** *vt* hacer señales para dejar pasar
wave-band *n* RADIO banda *f* de frecuencias **wave-length** *n* longitud *f* de onda; **on a ~** en una onda; **to be on the same ~** *fig* estar en la misma onda **wave power** *n* energía *f* de las ondas
waver ['weɪvəʳ, Am: -vɚ] *vi* 1. (lose determination) vacilar 2. (be unable to decide) titubear; **to ~ between … and …** dudar entre… o…; **to ~ over sth** titubear acerca de algo 3. (lose strength) desfallecer

W

waverange ['weɪvreɪndʒ] *n* amplitud *f* de onda

waverer ['weɪvərəʳ, *Am:* -ɚɚ] *n* indeciso, -a *m, f*

wavering *adj* vacilante; (*between two options*) titubeante

wavy ['weɪvi] <-ier, -iest> *adj* (*hair*) ondulado, -a; (*pattern*) ondulante

wax¹ [wæks] **I.** *n no pl* **1.** (*fatty substance*) cera *f;* **candle** ~ vela *f* de cera; (*for polishing*) cera lustradora **2.** (*inside ear*) cerumen *m,* cerilla *f* **II.** *vt* **1.** (*polish: floor, furniture*) encerar; (*shoes*) lustrar **2.** (*remove hair from*) depilar con cera

wax² [wæks] *vi liter* **1.** (*moon*) crecer; **to ~ and wane** crecer y descrecer; *fig* tener altibajos **2.** (*become*) ponerse; **she ~ed lyrical about her holiday** se entusiasmó mucho con sus vacaciones

wax paper *n* papel *m* encerado **waxwork** *n* figura *f* de cera

waxy ['wæksi] <-ier, -iest> *adj* **1.** (*oily, shiny*) lustroso, -a **2.** (*apparently of wax*) ceroso, -a

way [weɪ] **I.** *n* **1.** (*route*) camino *m;* **to be (well) on the ~ to doing sth** *fig* ir camino de hacer algo; **to be on the ~** estar en camino; **to be out of the ~** estar en un lugar remoto; **to be under ~** estar en curso; **on the ~ to sth** de camino a algo; **to elbow one's ~ somewhere** abrirse camino (a codazos) hasta algún lugar; **to find one's ~ around sth** encontrar el camino alrededor de algo; *fig* encontrar una manera de evitar algo; **to find one's ~ into/ out of sth** encontrar la manera de entrar/salir de algo; **to find one's ~ through sth** encontrar el camino a través de algo; **to go out of one's ~ to do sth** *fig* tomarse la molestia de hacer algo; **to go one's own ~** *fig* irse por su lado; (**to go) by ~ of sth** (ir) por vía de algo; **to know one's ~ around sth** saber cómo moverse en algo; **to know one's ~ around the town** conocer el pueblo; **to lead the ~** mostrar el camino; **to lose one's ~** equivocar el camino; **to make one's ~** (*make progress*) progresar; (*move*) abrirse camino; **to make one's ~ through the crowd** abrirse camino a través de la muchedumbre; **to pay one's ~** *fig* ser solvente; **to talk one's ~ out of sth** *fig* salvarse de algo con labia; **to see the error of one's ~s** darse cuenta de sus errores; **to work one's ~ up** *fig* ascender con el trabajo personal **2.** (*road*) camino *m;* (*small one*) sendero *m;* **Way** (*name of road*) Vía *f;* **cycle ~** carril *m* bici **3.** (*facing direction*) dirección *f;* **the right/wrong ~ round** del derecho/del revés; **to show the ~ forward** señalar el camino; **this ~ on** *Aus, Brit* siga en esta dirección **4.** (*distance*) trayecto *m;* **all the ~** (*the whole distance*) todo el trayecto; (*completely*) completamente; **to be a long ~ off** estar muy alejado; **to have a (long) ~ to go** tener aún un (largo) trayecto por recorrer; **to have come a**

long ~ *fig* haber llegado lejos; **to go a long ~** *fig* ir lejos **5.** (*fashion*) manera *f;* **in many ~s** de muchas maneras; **in some ~s** en cierto modo; **there are no two ~s about it** no hay otra posibilidad; **the ~ to do sth** la manera de hacer algo; **the ~s and means of doing/to do sth** los medios (y arbitrios) para hacer algo; **by ~ of** a modo de **6.** *no pl* (*manner*) modo *m;* (*customs*) costumbres *fpl;* **sb's ~ of life** el estilo de vida de alguien; **to my ~ of thinking** tal como lo veo yo; **she wouldn't have it any other ~** no lo aceptaría de ninguna otra manera; **in a big ~** en gran escala; **either ~** de cualquier forma; **no ~!** *inf* (*impossible*) ¡de ninguna manera!; *inf* (*definitely no!*) ¡ni hablar!; **in no ~** ¡para nada!; **to get one's own ~** salirse con la suya; **it's always the ~** siempre es de esa manera; **in a ~** en cierto modo **7.** *no pl* (*free space*) paso *m;* **to be in sb's ~** estorbar a alguien; **in the ~** en el paso; **to get out of sb's/sth's ~** dejar el camino libre a alguien/ algo; **to give ~** dar paso; *fig* dejar hacer; **to give ~ to sth** dar paso a algo; **to make ~ (for sb/sth)** hacer lugar (para alguien/algo); **to stand in sb's ~** ir contra los deseos de alguien **8.** *no pl* (*condition*) estado *m;* **to be in a bad ~** estar en mala forma; **to be in a terrible ~** estar terriblemente mal; **to be in the family ~** *inf* estar embarazada ▶ **to go the ~ of all flesh** sucumbir a la inevitable muerte; **the ~ to a man's heart is through his stomach** *prov* el camino al corazón de un hombre pasa por el estómago *prov;* **to want things both ~s** querer estar en misa y repicando; **to see/find out which ~ the wind blows** ver/descubrir por donde van los tiros; **to rub sb up the wrong ~** caer mal a alguien; **by the ~** por cierto **II.** *adv inf* mucho; **to be ~ past sb's bedtime** haber pasado con mucho de la hora de dormir

way-bill ['weɪbɪl] *n* hoja *f* de ruta

waylay [ˌweɪ'leɪ, *Am:* 'weɪleɪ] <waylaid, waylaid> *vt* acechar

way of thinking *n* forma *f* de pensar

way out [ˌweɪ'aʊt] *n* salida *f*

way-out [ˌweɪ'aʊt] *adj inf* (*very modern*) ultramoderno, -a; (*unusual or amazing*) fuera de serie

wayside ['weɪsaɪd] *n* borde *m* del camino; **to fall by the ~** *fig* quedarse en el camino

wayside inn *n* parador *m* de carretera

wayward ['weɪwəd, *Am:* -wɚd] *adj* díscolo, -a

WBT *abbr of* **Web Based Training** WBT

WC [ˌdʌblju:'si:] *n abbr of* **water closet** WC *m*

we [wi:] *pron pers* nosotros, -as; **~'re going to Paris and ~'ll be back here tomorrow** iremos a París y volveremos mañana; **as ~ say** como nosotros decimos

weak [wi:k] *adj* **1.** (*not strong*) débil; (*coffee, tea*) claro, -a; **to be ~ with desire/love** languidecer de deseo/amor; **to be ~ with**

hunger/thirst estar sin fuerzas por el hambre/la sed; **to be ~ at the knees** temblarle a uno las piernas; **the ~ link** *fig* el punto débil; **~ spot** *fig* flaqueza *f* **2.** (*below standard*) flojo, -a; **to be ~** (**at sth**) estar flojo (en algo)

weaken ['wiːkən] **I.** *vi* (*become less strong*) debilitarse; (*diminish*) disminuir **II.** *vt* (*make less strong*) debilitar; (*diminish*) disminuir

weakling ['wiːklɪŋ] *n* enclenque *mf*

weakly ['wiːkli] *adv* **1.** (*without strength*) débilmente **2.** (*unconvincingly*) sin convicción

weak-minded [ˌwiːk'maɪndɪd] *adj* **1.** (*lacking determination*) indeciso, -a; (*weak-willed*) pusilánime **2.** (*stupid*) tonto, -a

weakness ['wiːknɪs] <-es> *n* **1.** *no pl* (*lack of strength*) debilidad *f*; **to have a ~ for sth** tener debilidad por algo **2.** (*area of vulnerability*) punto *m* débil; (*flaw in artistic work*) imperfección *f*; (*flaw in character*) flaqueza *f*

weal [wiːl] *n* cardenal *m*

wealth [welθ] *n no pl* **1.** (*money*) riqueza *f*; (*fortune*) fortuna *f* **2.** (*large amount*) abundancia *f*

wealth creation *n*, **wealth generation** *n no pl* generación *f* de riqueza **wealth tax** <-s> *n* impuesto *m* sobre el patrimonio

wealthy ['welθi] **I.** <-ier, -iest> *adj* rico, -a **II.** *n* **the ~** *no pl* los ricos

wean [wiːn] *vt* (*animal, baby*) destetar; **to ~ sb** (**off sth**) *fig* desenganchar a alguien (de algo), quitar a alguien la costumbre (de algo)

weapon ['wepən] *n* arma *f*

weaponry ['wepənri] *n no pl* armamento *m*

wear [weəʳ, *Am:* wer] <wore, worn> **I.** *vt* **1.** (*have on body: clothes, jewellery*) llevar; **to ~ one's hair loose/tied back** llevar el pelo suelto/recogido **2.** (*deteriorate*) desgastar **3.** *Brit, Aus, inf* (*permit*) permitir **II.** *vi* (*spoil: clothes, machine parts*) desgastarse; **to ~ thin** raerse; *fig* desgastarse **III.** *n* **1.** (*clothing*) ropa *f*; **casual/sports** ~ ropa informal/deportiva **2.** (*amount of use*) desgaste *m*; **to be the worse for** ~ (*person*) estar desmejorado; (*thing*) estar desgastado; **to take some/a lot of ~ and tear** soportar algo de/mucho desgaste

◆**wear away I.** *vt* desgastar **II.** *vi* desgastarse; (*person*) consumirse

◆**wear down** *vt* **1.** (*reduce*) gastar; *fig* (*tire*) desgastar; **to ~ sb's resistance** desgastar la resistencia de alguien **2.** (*make weak and useless*) agotar

◆**wear off** *vi* desaparecer

◆**wear on** *vi* (*time*) pasar lentamente

◆**wear out I.** *vi* gastarse **II.** *vt* gastar; (*patience*) agotar

wearable ['weərəbl, *Am:* 'werə-] *adj* que se puede llevar

wearing ['weərɪŋ, *Am:* 'wer-] *adj* agotador(a)

wearisome ['wɪərɪsəm, *Am:* 'wɪrɪ-] *adj form* (*causing boredom*) aburrido; (*causing tiredness*) extenuante

weary ['wɪəri, *Am:* 'wɪri] **I.** <-ier, -iest> *adj* **1.** (*very tired*) extenuado, -a **2.** (*tiring*) agotador(a) **3.** (*bored*) aburrido, -a; (*unenthusiastic*) desanimado, -a; **to be ~ of sth** estar harto de algo; **a ~ joke** un chiste viejo **II.** *vt* (*make tired*) **to ~ sb with sth** fatigar a alguien con algo; (*make bored*) aburrir a alguien con algo **III.** *vi* (*become tired*) cansarse; (*become bored*) aburrirse

weasel ['wiːzl] *n* comadreja *f*

weather ['weðəʳ, *Am:* -ə-] **I.** *n no pl* tiempo *m*; (*climate*) clima *m*; **~ permitting** si lo permite el tiempo ►**to make heavy ~ of sth** complicar algo; **to be under the ~** estar indispuesto **II.** *vi* aguantar **III.** *vt* **1.** (*wear*) desgastar **2.** (*endure*) resistir; **to ~ sth** hacer frente a algo; **to ~ the storm** *fig* capear el temporal

weather-beaten ['weðəˌbiːtən, *Am:* -ə-,-] *adj* deteriorado, -a por la intemperie; **~ face** cara *f* curtida

weatherboard ['weðəbɔːd, *Am:* -əbɔːrd] *n* tabla *f* de chilla

weather boarding I. *n* tabla *f* de chilla; **~ house** *Am* casa *f* de madera **II.** *vt* cubrir con tablas

weather-bound *adj* bloqueado, -a por el mal tiempo

weather bureau <-s *o* -x> *n Am* servicio *m* meteorológico **weather chart** *n* mapa *m* meteorológico **weathercock** *n* veleta *f* **weather conditions** *npl* condiciones *fpl* atmosféricas **weather forecast** *n* previsión *f* meteorológica

weathering ['weðərɪŋ] *n no pl* deterioro *m* por la intemperie

weatherman ['weðəmæn, *Am:* 'weðə-] *n* hombre *m* del tiempo

weatherproof ['weðəpruːf, *Am:* 'weðə-] *adj* a prueba de la intemperie

weave [wiːv] **I.** <wove *Am:* weaved, woven *Am:* weaved> *vt* **1.** (*produce cloth*) tejer; **to ~ sth into sth** entrelazar algo con algo **2.** (*intertwine things*) entretejer; *fig* tramar; **to ~ sth together** entrelazar algo **3.** (*move back and forth*) **to ~ one's way through sth** abrirse paso entre algo **II.** <wove *Am:* weaved, woven *Am:* weaved> *vi* **1.** (*produce cloth*) tejer **2.** (*move by twisting and turning*) serpentear ►**let's get weaving** *Brit, inf* ¡vámonos! **III.** *n* tejido *m*; **striped ~** tejido a rayas; **loose/tight ~** tejido amplio/ajustado

weaver ['wiːvəʳ, *Am:* -və-] *n* tejedor(a) *m(f)*; **basket ~** canastero *m*

weaver bird *n* ZOOL tejedor *m*

web¹ [web] *n* **1.** (*woven net*) tela *f*; **spider('s) ~** telaraña *f*; **to spin a ~** hacer una telaraña **2.** *fig* (*complex network*) trama *f*; **a ~ of intrigue** una trama de intrigas; **a ~ of lies** una sarta de mentiras **3.** *fig* (*trap*) trampa *f* **4.** (*connective tissue*) membrana *f*

web² [web] **I.** *n* INFOR web *f*; **on the ~** en la red **II.** *adj inv* INFOR de internet

webaddict *n* INFOR ciberadicto, -a *m, f* **web browser** *n* INFOR navegador *m* de internet

webfooted [ˌwebˈfʊtɪd, *Am:* ˈwebˌfʊtɪd] *adj* palmípedo, -a

webmaster *n* INFOR administrador(a) *m(f)* de web **web-offset** (**printing**) *n* web offset *m* **web page** *n* INFOR página *f* web; ~ **wizard** asistente *mf* para páginas web **website** *n* INFOR sitio *m* web; **sports** ~**s** webs *fpl* de deporte; **to visit a** ~ visitar un sitio web **web surfer** *n* INFOR internauta *mf* **webzine** *n* INFOR revista *f* electrónica

wed [wed] <wedded *o* wed, wedded *o* wed> *form* I. *vt* 1. (*marry*) **to** ~ **sb** casarse con alguien 2. *fig* (*join closely*) casar; **to** ~ **sth and sth** unir algo a algo II. *vi* casarse

we'd [wiːd] 1. = we had *s.* **have** 2. = we would *s.* **would**

wedded [ˈwedɪd] *adj* 1. (*married*) casado, -a; **lawful** ~ **wife** *form* legítima esposa 2. (*united*) **to be** ~ **to sth** estar unido a algo; **to be** ~ **to a habit** tener una costumbre; **to be** ~ **to an opinion** aferrarse a una opinión

wedding [ˈwedɪŋ] *n* boda *f*

wedding anniversary <-ies> *n* aniversario *m* de bodas **wedding breakfast** *n* banquete *m* de boda **wedding cake** *n* no pl tarta *f* nupcial **wedding day** *n* día *m* de la boda **wedding dress** *n* traje *m* de novia **wedding guest** *n* invitado , -a *m*, *f* de boda **wedding night** *n* noche *f* de bodas **wedding present** *n* regalo *m* de boda **wedding ring** *n* alianza *f*

wedge [wedʒ] I. *n* 1. (*tapered block*) cuña *f* 2. *fig* (*triangular piece*) porción; **a** ~ **of cake/pie** un trozo de pastel/tarta II. *vt* poner una cuña a; **to** ~ **the door open** mantener la puerta abierta (con una cuña); **to be** ~**d between sth** (*people*) estar apretado entre algo; (*object*) quedar encajado entre algo

wedlock [ˈwedlɒk, *Am:* -lɑːk] *n* no pl matrimonio *m;* **out of** ~ fuera del matrimonio; **sex out of** ~ sexo *m* extraconyugal; **to be born in/out of** ~ nacer dentro/fuera del matrimonio

Wednesday [ˈwenzdeɪ] *n* miércoles *m* inv; **Ash** ~ Miércoles de Ceniza; *s. a.* **Friday**

wee [wiː] I. *adj Scot, a. inf* pequeñito, -a; **a** ~ **bit** un poquito II. *n no pl, childspeak, inf* pipí *m;* **to have to go** ~ tener que ir a hacer pipí III. *vi childspeak, inf* hacer pipí; **I want to** ~**!** ¡quiero hacer pipí!

weed [wiːd] I. *n* 1. (*plant*) mala hierba *f* 2. *Brit, pej, inf* (*person*) enclenque *mf* 3. *no pl, inf* (*tobacco*) **the** ~ el tabaco 4. *no pl, inf* (*marijuana*) marihuana *f* ▶**to grow like a** ~ crecer como la mala hierba II. *vt* desherbar III. *vi* arrancar las malas hierbas

weedkiller [ˈwiːdkɪləʳ, *Am:* -ɚ] *n no pl* herbicida *m*

weedy [ˈwiːdi] *adj* <-ier, iest) 1. (*full of weeds*) lleno, -a de malas hierbas 2. *Brit, pej, inf* (*very thin*) flaco, -a; (*underdeveloped*) esmirriado, -a

week [wiːk] *n* 1. (*seven days*) semana *f;* **it'll**

be ~**s before** … pasarán semanas antes de que … +*subj;* **a few** ~**s ago** hace pocas semanas; **last** ~ la semana pasada; **once a** ~ una vez por semana; **during the** ~ durante la semana; ~ **after** ~ semana tras semana; ~ **by** ~ semana a semana 2. (*work period, working days*) semana *f* laboral; **a thirty-seven-and-a-half hour** ~ una semana laboral de treinta y siete horas y media

weekday [ˈwiːkdeɪ] *n* día *m* laborable; **on** ~**s** en días laborables

weekend [ˌwiːkˈend, *Am:* ˈwiːkend] *n* fin *m* de semana; **at the** ~(**s**) *Brit, Aus,* **on the** ~(**s**) *Am* el fin de semana; ~ **cottage** casita *f* de fin de semana

weekender [ˌwiːkˈendəʳ, *Am:* ˈwiːkˌendɚ] *n* persona que se va de casa durante el fin de semana

weekly [ˈwiːkli] I. *adj* semanal; ~ **magazine** revista *f* semanal II. *adv* semanalmente; **to meet/publish** ~ reunirse/publicar semanalmente III. *n* <-ies> semanario *m*

weeny [ˈwiːni] *adj* <-ier, -iest> *inf* chiquitito, -a; **a** ~ **bit** un poquitín

weep [wiːp] I. *vi* <wept, wept> 1. (*cry*) llorar; **to** ~ **like a baby** lloriquear como un bebé; **to** ~ **with joy/rage** llorar de alegría/rabia; **to** ~ **inconsolably** llorar desconsoladamente 2. (*secrete liquid*) supurar II. *vt* <wept, wept> (*tears*) derramar; **to** ~ **tears of joy/rage** (**over sb/sth**) llorar de alegría/rabia (por alguien/algo) III. *n* llanto *m;* **to have a** (**good**) ~ desahogarse llorando

weeping I. *adj* lloroso, -a II. *n no pl* llanto *m*

weeping willow *n* sauce *m* llorón

w.e.f. *abbr of* **with effect from** válido, -a a partir de

weigh [weɪ] I. *vi* pesar II. *vt* 1. (*measure weight*) pesar; **to** ~ **oneself** pesarse 2. (*consider carefully*) sopesar; **to** ~ **one's words** medir las palabras; **to** ~ **sth against sth** contraponer algo a algo 3. NAUT (*pull up*) **to** ~ **anchor** levar el ancla

◆**weigh down** *vt* 1. (*cause to bend*) doblar bajo un peso 2. *fig* (*depress*) abrumar; **to weigh sb down with sth** cargar a alguien con algo

◆**weigh in** *vi* 1. (*be weighed*) pesarse; **to** ~ **at 80 kilos** pesar 80 kilos 2. *inf* (*enter into, take part*) intervenir; **to** ~ (**to sth**) **with sth** intervenir (en algo) afirmando algo; **to** ~ **to a discussion with one's opinion** intervenir en una discusión dando su opinión

◆**weigh out** *vt* pesar

◆**weigh up** *vt* (*calculate*) calcular; (*judge*) juzgar

weighbridge [ˈweɪbrɪdʒ] *n* báscula *f* de puente

weigh-in [ˈweɪɪn] *n* pesaje *m*

weight [weɪt] I. *n* 1. *no pl* (*amount weighed*) peso *m;* **a decrease/an increase in** ~ una disminución/un aumento de peso; **to lift a heavy** ~ levantar un peso pesado; **to put on** ~

engordar; **what a** ~ ¡qué pesado! **2.**(*metal specific weight*) pesa *f;* **to lift** ~**s** levantar pesas **3.** *no pl* (*value, importance*) valor *m;* **to attach** ~ **to sth** dar importancia a algo; **to carry** ~ tener mucho peso ▸**to take the** ~ **off one's feet** sentarse y descansar; **to be a** ~ **off sb's** <u>mind</u> ser un alivio para alguien; **it's a great** ~ **off my mind** es un peso que me quito de encima; **to** <u>pull</u> **one's** ~ *inf* poner de su parte **II.** *vt* cargar; **to** ~ **sth with stones** cargar algo de piedras

◆**weight down** *vt* **1.** (*overload*) sobrecargar **2.**(*make heavy*) sujetar con un peso **3.** *fig* (*strain*) apretar

weighting *n no pl, Brit* **1.** (*paid to employee*) plus *m* por el coste de la vida **2.** MAT ponderación *f*

weightless ['weɪtləs] *adj* ingrávido, -a

weightlessness *n no pl* ingravidez *f*

weightlifter *n* levantador(a) *m(f)* de pesas

weight-lifting ['weɪtˌlɪftɪŋ] *n no pl* levantamiento *m* de pesas; **to do** ~ hacer pesas

weighty ['weɪti, *Am:* -t̬i] *adj* <-ier, -iest> **1.** (*heavy*) pesado, -a **2.**(*important*) importante; ~ **matters** asuntos *mpl* de peso

weir [wɪəʳ, *Am:* wɪr] *n* presa *f*

weird [wɪəd, *Am:* wɪrd] *adj* misterioso, -a; **how** ~ ¡qué raro!; ~ **and wonderful** extraordinario

weirdie ['wɪədi, *Am:* 'wɪrdi] *n,* **weirdo** ['wɪədəʊ, *Am:* 'wɪrdoʊ] *n inf* bicho *m* raro

welcome ['welkəm] **I.** *vt* **1.** (*greet kindly*) dar la bienvenida a; **to** ~ **sb warmly** acoger a alguien calurosamente **2.**(*support*) aprobar **II.** *n* **1.**(*friendly reception*) bienvenida *f;* **speech of** ~ discurso *m* de bienvenida **2.** *no pl* (*period of being wanted*) aceptación *f* **3.**(*expression of approval*) aprobación *f;* **to give sth a cautious** ~ dar una acogida contenida a algo **III.** *adj* **1.**(*gladly received*) grato, -a; **a non** ~ **guest** un invitado no grato; **to be** ~ **ser bienvenido 2.**(*gladly received*) deseado, -a; **a** ~ **break** una ruptura deseada; **a** ~ **change** un cambio esperado ▸**you** <u>are</u> ~ de nada; **to** <u>be</u> ~ **to do sth** *inf* poder hacer algo; **you are** ~ **to use it** está a su disposición **IV.** *interj* ¡bienvenido!; ~ **aboard** NAUT bienvenidos a bordo

welcoming *adj* acogedor(a); ~ **arms** brazos abiertos; ~ **smile** sonrisa *f* agradable

weld [weld] **I.** *vt* **1.** (*join metal*) soldar; **to** ~ **sth** (*together*) soldar algo **2.** (*unite*) unir; **to** ~ **players into a team** unir a jugadores en un equipo **II.** *n* soldadura *f*

welder *n* soldador(a) *m(f)*

welding *n no pl* soldadura *f*

welding torch <-es> *n* soplete *m* soldador

welfare ['welfeəʳ, *Am:* -fer] *n no pl* **1.**(*health, happiness*) bienestar *m* **2.**(*state aid*) asistencia *f* social; ~ **policy** política *f* de asistencia social; ~ **system** sistema *m* asistencial; **social** ~ asistencia *f* social; **to be on** ~ vivir a cargo de la asistencia social

welfare payments *npl Am* pensión *f* de asistencia social **welfare services** *npl* servicios *mpl* de asistencia social **welfare state** *n* estado *m* del bienestar **welfare work** *n no pl* trabajos *mpl* de asistencia social **welfare worker** *n* asistente, -a *m, f* social

we'll [wiːl] = we will *s.* will

well¹ [wel] **I.** *adj* <better, best> bien; **to feel** ~ sentirse bien; **to get** ~ recuperarse; **to look** ~ tener buen aspecto **II.** <better, best> *adv* **1.**(*in a satisfactory manner*) bien; ~ **enough** suficientemente bien; ~ **done** bien hecho; **to do sth as** ~ **as ...** hacer algo tan bien como...; ~ **put** bien expresado; (**time/money**) ~ **spent** (tiempo/dinero) bien gastado **2.**(*thoroughly, fully, extensively*) completamente; ~ **east/west** bien hacia el este/oeste; ~ **enough** suficiente; **pretty** ~ bastante a fondo; **to know sb pretty** ~ conocer a alguien bastante bien; ~ **and truly** de verdad; **it costs** ~ **over...** cuesta tranquilamente más de... **3.**(*very, completely*) muy; **to be** ~ **pleased with sth** estar muy satisfecho con algo **4.**(*fairly, reasonably*) justamente; **he couldn't very** ~ **refuse their kind offer** no podía rechazar su amable oferta; **you may** ~ **think it was his fault** bien podrías pensar que tiene la culpa; **he might** ~ **be the best person to ask** puede que sea la persona idónea a quien preguntar; **you might** (**just**) **as** ~ **tell her the truth** más valdría que le dijeras la verdad ▸**to leave** ~ <u>alone</u> no meterse en algo; **to be** ~ <u>away</u> *Brit, inf* (*completely absorbed*) estar completamente absorto; (*asleep*) estar profundamente dormido; (*drunk*) estar borracho como una cuba; **all** ~ **and** <u>good</u> muy bien; **that's all** <u>very</u> ~, **but ...** todo eso está muy bien, pero...; <u>as</u> ~ *Brit* (*also*) también; <u>as</u> ~ <u>as</u> así como; <u>just as</u> ~ menos mal; **to be** ~ <u>in</u> **with sb** *Brit, inf,* **to be** <u>in</u> ~ **with sb** *Am, inf* estar a bien con alguien; **to be** ~ <u>in</u> **with sth** *Brit, inf,* **to be** <u>in</u> ~ **with sth** *Am, inf* estar metido en algo; **to be** ~ <u>out</u> **of it** *Brit, Aus* librarse de una buena **III.** *interj* (*exclamation*) vaya; ~, ~, ~ ¡vaya, vaya!; **very** ~! ¡muy bien!

well² [wel] **I.** *n* (*hole for water etc.*) pozo *m;* **water** ~ manantial *m* de agua; **to drill a** ~ perforar un pozo **II.** *vi* (*flow*) manar; **to** ~ **up in sth** brotar en algo; **to** ~ (**up**) **out of sth** (*water*) emanar de algo

◆**well up** *vi a. fig* (*rise*) brotar

well-advised [ˌweləd'vaɪzd] *adj form* bien asesorado, -a; **he would be** ~ **to stay at home** haría bien en quedarse en casa

well-appointed [ˌwelə'pɔɪntɪd, *Am:* -t̬ɪd] *adj form* bien amueblado, -a

well-balanced [ˌwel'bæləntst] *adj* bien equilibrado, -a; ~ **diet** dieta equilibrada; ~ **children** niños equilibrados

well-behaved [ˌwelbɪ'heɪvd] *adj* bien educado, -a; (*child*) formal; (*dog*) manso, -a

well-being ['welˌbiːɪŋ] *n no pl* bienestar *m;* **a feeling of** ~ una sensación de bienestar

W

well-bred [ˌwel'bred] *adj* (*well brought up*) bien educado, -a; (*classy, refined*) refinado, -a; **a ~ voice** una voz educada

well-chosen [ˌwel'tʃəʊzən, *Am:* -'tʃoʊ-] *adj* elegido, -a con cuidado; **to say a few ~ words** decir unas palabras acertadas

well-connected [ˌwelkə'nektɪd] *adj* **to be ~** tener contactos; **a ~ family** una familia influyente

well-deserved [ˌweldɪ's3ːvd] *adj* merecido, -a

well-developed [ˌweldɪ'veləpt] *adj* bien desarrollado, -a; **~ area** zona desarrollada; **physically ~** físicamente desarrollado; **a ~ sense of humour** un agudo sentido del humor

well-disposed [ˌweldɪ'spəʊzd, *Am:* -'spoʊzd] *adj* favorable; **to be ~ towards sth** ser favorable a algo; **to feel ~ towards sb** tener una disposición favorable hacia alguien

well-done [ˌwel'dʌn] *adj* (*meat*) muy hecho, -a

well-dressed [ˌwel'drest] *adj* bien vestido, -a

well-earned [ˌwel'3ːnd, *Am:* -'3ːrnd] *adj* merecido, -a

well-educated [ˌwel'edʒʊkeɪtɪd, *Am:* -'edʒʊkeɪtɪd] *adj* culto, -a

well-fed [ˌwel'fed] *adj* (*full of food*) lleno, -a; (*from good feeding*) bien alimentado, -a

well-founded [ˌwel'faʊndɪd] *adj* fundado, -a; **~ suspicions** sospechas bien fundadas

well-groomed [ˌwel'gruːmd] *adj* acicalado, -a

well-heeled [ˌwel'hiːld] **I.** *adj inf* ricacho, -a **II.** *npl* **the ~** los ricos

wellies ['weliz] *n pl, Brit, inf* botas *fpl* de goma

well-informed [ˌwelɪn'fɔːmd, *Am:* -'fɔːrmd] *adj* enterado, -a; **to be ~ about sb/sth** estar bien informado sobre alguien/algo; **to be ~ on a particular topic** conocer a fondo un tema concreto

wellington (**boot**) ['welɪŋtən (buːt)] *n* bota *f* de goma

well-intentioned [ˌwelɪn'tentʃənd] *adj* bienintencionado, -a

well-kept [ˌwel'kept] *adj* (muy) cuidado, -a

well-knit [ˌwel'nɪt] *adj* (*body*) robusto, -a; *fig* (*scheme, idea*) lógico, -a; **a ~ plot/story** una trama/historia bien construida

well-known [ˌwel'nəʊn, *Am:* -'noʊn] *adj* conocido, -a; **to be ~ for sth** ser conocido por algo; **it is ~ that ...** es bien sabido que...

well-mannered [ˌwel'mænəd, *Am:* -ə̅d] *adj* con buenos modales; **a ~ child** un niño educado

well-meaning [ˌwel'miːnɪŋ] *adj* bienintencionado, -a; **~ comments** comentarios *mpl* sin malicia

well-meant [ˌwel'ment] *adj* bienintencionado, -a

well-nigh ['welnaɪ] *adv* casi; **to be ~ impossible** ser casi imposible

well-off [ˌwel'ɒf, *Am:* -'ɑːf] **I.** *adj* **1.** (*wealthy*) acomodado, -a **2.** (*having a lot*) que tiene mucho; **the city is ~ for parks** la ciudad tiene muchos parques; **to not know when one is ~** no saber la suerte que se tiene **II.** *npl* **the ~** los ricos

well-oiled [ˌwel'ɔɪld] *adj* **1.** (*functioning smoothly*) eficaz **2.** *inf* (*inebriated, drunk*) hecho, -a una cuba

well-organised [ˌwel'ɔːgənaɪzd, *Am:* -'ɔːr-] *adj* bien organizado, -a

well-paid [ˌwel'peɪd] *adj* bien pagado, -a

well-placed [ˌwel'pleɪst] *adj* bien situado, -a

well-proportioned [ˌwelprə'pɔːʃənd, *Am:* -'pɔːr-] *adj* bien proporcionado, -a

well-read [ˌwel'red] *adj* **1.** (*knowledgeable*) instruido, -a **2.** (*read frequently*) muy leído, -a

well-spoken [ˌwel'spəʊkən, *Am:* -'spoʊ-] *adj* **1.** (*polite*) bienhablado, -a **2.** (*refined*) con acento culto

well-thought-of [ˌwel'θɔːtəv, *Am:* -'θɑːtəv] *adj* (*person*) de buena reputación; (*school*) de prestigio

well-timed [ˌwel'taɪmd] *adj* oportuno, -a

well-to-do [ˌweltə'duː] *inf* **I.** *adj* acaudalado, -a **II.** *n* **the ~** la gente adinerada

well-turned [ˌwel'tɜːnd, *Am:* -'tɜːrnd] *adj* **1.** (*gracefully shaped*) elegante **2.** (*cleverly expressed: phrase*) bien construido, -a

well-wisher ['wel,wɪʃə^r, *Am:* 'wel,wɪʃə̅] *n* simpatizante *mf*

well-worn [ˌwel'wɔːn, *Am:* -'wɔːrn] *adj* **1.** (*damaged by wear*) raído, -a **2.** *fig* (*over-used*) trillado, -a

welly ['weli] *n inf abbr of* **wellington** bota *f* de goma

Welsh [welʃ] **I.** *adj* galés, -esa **II.** *n* **1.** (*person*) galés, -esa *m, f* **2.** LING galés *m*

Welshman ['welʃmən] <-men> *n* galés *m*

Welshwoman ['welʃ,wʊmən] <-women> *n* galesa *f*

welt [welt] *n* **1.** (*from blow*) cardenal *f* **2.** (*in shoe*) vira *f*

welter-weight ['weltəweɪt, *Am:* -t̪ə̅-] *n* welter *m*

wend [wend] *vt liter* **to ~ one's way to town** dirigir sus pasos hacia la cuidad

went [went] *pt of* **go**

wept [wept] *pt, pp of* **weep**

were [wɜː^r, *Am:* wɜːr] *pt of* **be**

we're [wɪə^r, *Am:* wɪr] = **we are** *s.* **be**

weren't [wɜːnt, *Am:* wɜːrnt] = **were not** *s.* **be**

west [west] **I.** *n* **1.** (*cardinal point*) oeste *m*; **in the ~ of Spain** en el oeste de España; **to lie 5 km to the ~ of ...** quedar a 5 km al oeste de...; **to go/drive to the ~** ir/conducir hacia el oeste **2.** (*part of the world*) **the West** el mundo occidental **3.** (*part of the US*) **the Far West** el Lejano Oeste; **the Wild West** el Oeste Americano **II.** *adj* occidental; **~ wind** viento *m* del oeste; **~ coast** costa *f* oeste; **West African** de África Occidental; **West Berlin** Berlín Occidental; **West Indies** Antillas *fpl* **III.** *adv* al oeste; **further** ~ más al oeste ▸ **to go** ~ (*thing*) estropearse; (*person*) irse al otro mundo

westbound ['westbaʊnd] *adj* que va hacia el oeste

West End I. *n* the ~ el West End de Londres **II.** *adj* the ~ theatres los teatros del West End

westerly ['westəli, *Am:* -tə˞li] *adj* del oeste; **the** ~ **part of the site** la zona oeste del lugar; ~ **winds** vientos *mpl* del oeste

western ['westən, *Am:* -tə˞n] **I.** *adj* del oeste; **the** ~ **part of the country** la parte occidental del país **II.** *n* CINE western *m*

westerner *n* **1.** (*person from the west*) occidental *mf* **2.** (*person from the western US*) norteamericano, -a *m, f* del oeste

westernize ['westənaɪz, *Am:* -tə˞-] *vt* occidentalizar

Western Samoa *n* Samoa *f* Occidental

West Germany *n* HIST Alemania *f* Occidental

Westminster Abbey [ˌwestmɪntstə˞'æbi, *Am:* -stə˞'æbi] *n* Abadía *f* de Westminster

Westminster City *n* Ciudad *f* de Westminster

West Virginia *n* Virginia *f* Occidental

westward(s) ['westwəd(z), *Am:* -wə˞d(z))] *adj* hacia el oeste

wet [wet] **I.** *adj* <-tt-> **1.** (*soaked*) mojado, -a; **to get** ~ mojarse; **to get sth** ~ mojar algo; ~ **through** mojado hasta los huesos **2.** (*not yet dried*) húmedo, -a; ~ **paint** pintura fresca **3.** (*rainy*) lluvioso, -a; ~ **weather** tiempo lluvioso ▸ **to be a** ~ **blanket** ser un aguafiestas; **to be** ~ **behind the ears** estar con la leche en los labios; **to be all** ~ *Am* ser tonto **II.** <wet, wet> *vt* **1.** (*make damp*) humedecer **2.** (*urinate on*) **to** ~ **oneself** orinarse; **to** ~ **the bed** mojar la cama; **to** ~ **one's pants** mearse **III.** *n* **1.** *no pl* **the** ~ (*rain*) la lluvia **2.** *Am* POL antiprohibicionista *mf*

wether ['weðə˞, *Am:* -ə˞] *n* ZOOL carnero *m* castrado

wet-nurse I. *n* HIST nodriza *f* **II.** *vt* criar **wet season** *n* estación *f* de las lluvias

wetsuit *n* traje *m* de neopreno

wetting *n* *no pl* mojada *f*

we've [wiːv] = **we have** *s.* **have**

whack [wæk] **I.** *vt* golpear **II.** *n* **1.** (*blow*) golpe *m;* **to give sth** (**a good**) ~ golpear algo ruidosamente **2.** *no pl* (*share, part*) parte *f;* **a fair** ~ una parte justa; **to pay full** ~ pagarlo todo ▸ **to be out of** ~ *Am* estar fastidiado; **to have a** ~ **at sth** *inf* intentar algo

whacked *adj* *inf* hecho, -a polvo

whacking I. *adj* grandote, -a **II.** *adv* muy; **a** ~ **big kiss** un beso muy grande **III.** *n* *Brit, Aus* zurra *f;* **a real** ~ una verdadera tunda

whale [hweɪl] *n* ballena *f;* **a beached** ~ una ballena varada ▸ **to have a** ~ **of a time** pasarlo bomba; **a** ~ **of a …** *Am* un(a) enorme…; **a** ~ **of a difference** una gran diferencia

whaling *n* *no pl* pesca *f* de ballenas

wham [hwæm] *interj* *inf* **1.** (*sound-effect for blow*) zas **2.** (*describes action*) y zas

whang [hwæŋ] *interj* *inf* zas

wharf [hwɔːf, *Am:* hwɔːrf] <-ves> *n* muelle *m;* **price ex** ~ precio *m* franco de muelle

wharfage ['wɔːfɪdʒ, *Am:* 'wɔːr-] *n* muellaje *m*

what [hwɒt, *Am:* hwʌt] **I.** *adj interrog* qué; ~ **kind of book?** ¿qué tipo de libro?; ~ **time is it?** ¿qué hora es?; ~ **men is he talking about?** ¿de qué hombres está hablando?; ~ **an idiot!** ¡qué idiota!; ~ **a fool I am!** ¡qué tonto soy! **II.** *pron* **1.** *interrog* qué; ~ **can I do?** ¿qué puedo hacer?; ~ **does it matter?** ¿qué importa?; ~**'s on?** ¿qué ponen?; ~**'s up?** ¿qué hay?; ~ **for?** ¿para qué?; ~ **is he like?** ¿cómo es (él)?; ~**'s his name?** ¿cómo se llama?; ~ **called?** ¿cuál es su nombre?, ¿cómo se llama?; ~ **about Paul?** ¿y Paul?; ~ **about a walk?** ¿te va un paseo?; ~ **if it snows?** *inf* ¿y si nieva? **2.** *rel* lo que; ~ **I like is** ~ **he says/is talking about** lo que me gusta es lo que dice/lo que está hablando; ~ **is more** lo que es más; **he knows** ~**'s** ~! sabe cuántas son cinco **III.** *interj* ~! ¡qué!; **so** ~? ¿y qué?; **is he coming, or** ~? ¿viene, o qué?

whatever [hwɒt'evə˞, *Am:* hwʌt'evə˞] **I.** *pron* **1.** (*anything*) (todo) lo que; ~ **happens** pase lo que pase **2.** (*any of them*) cualquier(a); ~ **you pick is fine** cualquiera (de los) que elijas está bien; **nothing** ~ nada de nada **II.** *adj* **1.** (*being what it may be*) cualquiera que; ~ **the reason** sea cual sea la razón **2.** (*of any kind*) de ningún tipo; **there is no doubt** ~ no hay ningún tipo de duda

whatnot ['hwɒtnɒt, *Am:* 'hwʌtnɑːt] *n* *no pl* chisme *m;* **and** ~ *inf* y demás

whatsit ['hwɒtsɪt, *Am:* 'hwʌt-] *n* *inf* chisme *m*

whatsoever [ˌhwɒtsəʊ'evə˞, *Am:* ˌhwʌtsoʊ'evə˞] *adv* sea cual sea; **to have no interest** ~ **in sth** no tener interés alguno en algo

wheat [hwiːt] *n* *no pl* trigo *m;* ~ **field** campo *m* de trigo; ~ **price** precio *m* del trigo ▸ **to separate the** ~ **from the chaff** separar la cizaña del buen grano

wheat belt *n* *Am* zona *f* de cultivo de trigo

wheatgerm *n* *no pl* germen *m* de trigo

wheel [hwiːl] **I.** *n* **1.** (*of vehicle*) rueda *f;* **alloy** ~**s** llantas *fpl* de aleación; **front/rear** ~ rueda *f* delantera/trasera; **big** ~ noria *f;* **to be on** ~**s** ir sobre ruedas **2.** TECH torno *m;* **spinning** ~ rueca *f* **3.** AUTO volante *m;* **to be at the** ~ ir al volante; **to take the** ~ tomar el volante; **to get behind the** ~ ponerse al volante **4.** *pl, inf* (*vehicle, car*) carro *m* **5.** NAUT timón *m* ▸ **to be hell on** ~**s** *Am, inf* ser un peligro (al volante); **to set one's shoulder to the** ~ arrimar el hombro; **to spin one's** ~**s** *Am* no hacer progresos; **to have** ~**s within** ~**s** *Brit* ser más complicado de lo que parece **II.** *vt* hacer girar; **to** ~ **a pram along** empujar un carrito de niño **III.** *vi* girar ▸ **to** ~ **and deal** *inf* hacer negocios sucios

◆**wheel around** *vi s.* **wheel round**
◆**wheel in** *vt* 1.(*roll in*) rodar 2.*fig, inf* (*introduce*) traer
◆**wheel round** *vi* dar media vuelta
wheelbarrow ['hwi:l͵bærəʊ, *Am:* -͵beroʊ] *n* carretilla *f*
wheel brace *n* llave *f* de ruedas en cruz
wheelchair *n* silla *f* de ruedas **wheel clamp** I. *n* cepo *m* II. *vt* poner cepo a
wheeler-dealer [͵hwi:lə'di:lə', *Am:* -lə'di:-lə'] *n pej, inf* comerciante *mf* poco escrupuloso, -a
wheelhouse ['hwi:lhaʊs] *n* timonera *f*
wheeling ['hwi:lɪŋ] *n no pl* ~ **and** <u>dealing</u> *pej, inf* negocios *mpl* sucios
wheeze [hwi:z] I.<-zing> *vi* resollar II. *n* 1. *no pl* (*of breath*) resuello *m* 2. *Brit, inf* (*clever scheme*) treta *f;* **a good** ~ una buena idea; **to have a** ~ tener una buena ocurrencia
wheezy *adj* <-ier, -iest> jadeante
whelp [hwelp] I. *n* cachorro *m* II. *vt* parir
when [hwen] I. *adv* cuándo; **since** ~? ¿desde cuándo?; **I'll tell him** ~ **to go** yo le diré cuándo ir II. *conj* 1.(*at which time*) cuando; **at the moment** ~ **he came** en el momento en que vino 2.(*during the time that*) ~ **singing that song** cuando cantaba esa canción 3.(*every time that*) ~ **it snows** cuando nieva 4.(*although*) **he buys it** ~ **he could borrow it** lo compra cuando podría pedirlo prestado 5.(*considering that*) si; **how can I listen** ~ **I can't hear?** ¿cómo puedo escuchar si no puedo oír?
whence [hwents] *adv form* por lo cual; (*interrogative*) ¿de dónde?
whenever [hwen'evə', *Am:* -ə'] I. *conj* 1.(*every time that*) siempre que; ~ **I can** siempre que puedo 2.(*at any time that*) **he can come** ~ **he likes** puede venir cuando quiera II. *adv* ~ **did I say that?** ¿cuándo fue que dije yo eso?; **I can do it tomorrow or** ~ puedo hacerlo mañana o un día de estos
where [hweə'] *adv* 1. *interrog* dónde; ~ **does he come from?** ¿de dónde es?; ~ **does he live?** ¿dónde vive?; ~ **is he going (to)?** ¿a dónde va? 2. *rel* donde; **I'll tell him** ~ **to go** yo le diré a dónde ir; **the box** ~ **he puts his things** la caja donde pone sus cosas; **this is** ~ **my horse was found** aquí es donde se encontró mi caballo; **London,** ~ **Paul comes from, is ...** Londres, de donde viene Paul, es...
whereabout(s) ['hweərəbaʊt(s), *Am:* 'hwerə-] I. *n + sing/pl vb* paradero *m;* **do you know the** ~ **of my book?** *form* ¿sabes dónde está mi libro? II. *adv inf* dónde; ~ **in Barcelona do you live?** ¿en qué zona de Barcelona vives?
whereas [hweər'æz, *Am:* hwer'-] *conj* 1.(*while*) mientras que 2. LAW considerando que
whereby [hweə'baɪ, *Am:* hwer'-] *conj form* por lo cual
wherein [hweər'ɪn, *Am:* hwer'-] *conj form*

en donde
wheresoever [͵hweəsəʊ'evə', *Am:* ͵hwer-soʊevə'] *adv, conj form s.* **wherever**
whereupon [͵hweərə'pɒn, *Am:* 'hwerə͵pɑːn] *conj form* con lo cual
wherever [͵hweər'evə', *Am:* ͵hwer'evə'] I. *conj* dondequiera que; ~ **I am/I go** dondequiera que esté/vaya; ~ **there is sth** dondequiera que haya algo; ~ **he likes** donde le plazca II. *adv* ~ **did she find that?** ¿dónde demonios encontró eso?; **... or** ~ ...o donde sea
wherewithal ['hweəwɪð͵ɔːl, *Am:* 'hwer-] *n no pl, liter* recursos *mpl;* **to lack the** ~ (**to do sth**) no tener los medios (para hacer algo)
whet [hwet] <-tt-> *vt* 1.(*sharpen*) afilar 2. *fig* (*increase, stimulate*) estimular; **to** ~ **sb's appetite (for sth)** aguzar el deseo de alguien (por algo)
whether ['hweðə', *Am:* -ə'] *conj* 1.(*if*) si; **to tell/ask** ~ **it's true (or not)** decir/preguntar si es verdad (o no); **she doesn't know** ~ **to buy it or not** no sabe si comprarlo o no; **I doubt** ~ **he'll come** dudo que venga 2.(*all the same*) sea; ~ **rich or poor...** sean ricos o pobres...; ~ **it rains or thunders ...** aunque llueva o truene...; ~ **I go by bus or bike ...** vaya en autobos o en bicicleta...
whetstone ['hwetstəʊn, *Am:* -stoʊn] *n* piedra *f* de afilar
whew [fjuː] *interj inf* uf
whey [hweɪ] *n no pl* suero *m*
which [hwɪtʃ] I. *adj interrog* qué; ~ **one/ ones?** ¿cuál/cuáles? II. *pron* 1. *interrog* cuál, qué; ~ **is his?** ¿cuál es el suyo? 2. *rel* que, el que, la que, los que, las que; **the book** ~ **I read/of** ~ **I'm speaking** el libro que leí/del que estoy hablando; **he said he was there,** ~ **I believed** dijo que estaba ahi, lo cual creí
whichever [hwɪtʃ'evə', *Am:* -ə'] I. *pron* cualquiera que; **you can choose** ~ **you like** puedes escoger el que quieras II. *adj* cualquiera, el que; **you can take** ~ **book you like** puedes coger el libro que quieras
whiff [hwɪf] *n* 1.(*quick smell*) olor *m;* **to catch a** ~ **of sth** percibir un olorcillo a algo 2. *fig* (*slight trace*) indicio *m;* **a** ~ **of corruption** una sospecha de corrupción
whiffy ['hwɪfi] *adj* <-ier, -iest> *Brit, inf* apestoso, -a
Whig [hwɪg] *n* HIST miembro del partido liberal; **the** ~**s** los liberales
while [hwaɪl] I. *n* rato *m;* **a short** ~ un ratito; **quite a** ~ bastante tiempo; **after a** ~ después de un tiempo; **for a** ~ durante un rato; **once in a** ~ de vez en cuando II. *conj* 1.(*during which time*) mientras; **I did it** ~ **he was sleeping** lo hice mientras él dormía; ~ **I live** mientras viva 2.(*although*) aunque; ~ **I like it, I won't buy it** aunque me guste, no lo compraré; ~ **I know it's true ...** a pesar de que sé que es verdad...
◆**while away** *vt* pasar; **to** ~ **the time** hacer tiempo

whilst [hwaɪlst] *conj Brit s.* while

whim [hwɪm] *n* capricho *m;* to do sth on a ~ hacer algo por capricho; as the ~ takes him según se le antoja

whimper ['hwɪmpəʳ, *Am:* -pɚ] **I.** *vi* quejarse; *(child)* lloriquear; *(dog)* gemir **II.** *n* quejido *m;* a ~ of protest un gemido de protesta; to give a ~ dar un gemido

whimsical ['hwɪmzɪkəl] *adj* **1.** *(odd)* peregrino, -a **2.** *(capricious)* caprichoso, -a

whimsicality [ˌhwɪmzɪˈkæləti, *Am:* -ti] *n no pl* **1.** *(odd character)* extravagancia *f* **2.** *(caprice)* capricho *m*

whimsy ['hwɪmzi] <-ies> *n pej* **1.** *no pl* *(odd fancifulness)* extravagancia *f* **2.** *(odd, fanciful thing or work)* fantasía *f* **3.** *(whim)* capricho *m*

whin [hwɪn] *n* tojo *m*

whine [hwaɪn] **I.** <-ning> *vi* **1.** *(complaining noise)* gemir; *(cry)* lloriquear **2.** *(engine)* zumbar **II.** *n* *(of a person or animal)* quejido *m;* *(of an engine)* zumbido *m*

whinge [hwɪndʒ] *Brit, Aus* **I.** <whingeing *o* whinging> *vi inf* quejarse **II.** *n inf* quejido *m;* to have a ~ (about sb/sth) quejarse (de alguien/algo)

whinny ['hwɪni] **I.** <-ied, -ing> *vi* relinchar **II.** *n* <-ies> relincho *m*

whip [hwɪp] **I.** *n* **1.** *(lash)* látigo *m,* chicote *m AmL,* fuete *m AmL;* to crack a ~ hacer restallar un látigo **2.** *(person)* persona encargada de la disciplina de partido; **chief** ~ diputado *m* jefe encargado de la disciplina de partido **3.** *Brit* *(call)* llamada *f;* a three-line ~ llamada apremiante **II.** <-pp-> *vt* **1.** *(strike with whip)* azotar **2.** *fig* *(force fiercely)* fustigar **3.** GASTR batir **4.** *Am, fig, inf* *(defeat)* to ~ sb at [*o* in] sth dar una paliza a alguien en algo **III.** <-pp-> *vi* restallar

◆**whip away** *vt* arrebatar

◆**whip back** *vi* **1.** *(bounce back)* rebotar de repente hacia atrás **2.** *fig* *(return)* volverse de golpe

◆**whip off** *vt* *(clothes)* quitarse con un movimiento brusco; *(tablecloth)* sacar de un tirón

◆**whip on** *vt* **1.** *(urge on)* animar **2.** *(put on quickly)* ponerse rápidamente

◆**whip out** *vt* **1.** *(take out)* sacar de repente **2.** *(produce)* hacer rápidamente

◆**whip round** *vi* volverse de repente; to ~ the corner *(car)* doblar la esquina a toda velocidad

◆**whip up** *vt* **1.** *(encourage)* avivar; to ~ support conseguir apoyo **2.** *inf* *(prepare quickly)* preparar rápidamente **3.** GASTR to ~ eggs batir huevos

whipcord ['hwɪpkɔːd, *Am:* -kɔːrd] *n* tralla *f*

whip hand *n* the ~ el mando; to hold the ~ llevar la batuta **whip-lash** *n* <-es> **1.** *(whip part)* tralla *f* **2.** *(blow from whip)* latigazo *m* **3.** *no pl* *(injury)* traumatismo *m* cervical

whipped cream *n* nata *f* para montar

whipper-in [ˌhwɪpəʳˈɪn, *Am:* -ɚ'-] *n* *(in hunting)* perrero *m*

whipper-snapper ['hwɪpəˌsnæpəʳ, *Am:* -ɚˌsnæpɚ] *n iron* mequetrefe *m*

whippet ['hwɪpɪt] *n* lebrel *m*

whipping **I.** *n* **1.** *(punishment)* azotaina *f;* to be given a (good) ~ dar una (buena) azotaina a alguien **2.** *Am* *(physical beating)* paliza *f;* to give/get a ~ dar/llevarse una paliza **3.** *no pl* *(gusting)* azote *m;* the ~ of the wind el azote del viento **II.** *adj* *(gusty)* racheado, -a; a ~ wind un golpe de viento

whipping-boy ['hwɪpɪŋbɔɪ] *n* cabeza *f* de turco *m* **whipping cream** *n no pl* nata *f* para montar **whipping top** *n* peonza *f*

whip-round ['hwɪpraʊnd] *n Brit, inf* colecta *f;* to have a ~ for sb hacer una colecta para alguien

whirl [hwɜːl, *Am:* hwɜːrl] **I.** *vi* girar rápidamente; my head ~s *fig* la cabeza me da vueltas **II.** *vt* hacer girar; to ~ sb (a)round dar vueltas a alguien **III.** *n* torbellino *m;* a ~ of dust una polvareda ▶to have one's <u>head</u> in a ~ dar vueltas la cabeza a uno; to give sth a ~ probar algo

whirligig ['hwɜːlɪɡɪɡ, *Am:* 'hwɜːr-] *n* **1.** *(toy)* molinete *m* **2.** *fig* vicisitudes *fpl*

whirlpool ['hwɜːlpuːl, *Am:* 'hwɜːrl-] *n* remolino *m* **whirlwind** *n* torbellino *m;* a ~ romance un idilio relámpago

whirlybird ['hwɜːlɪˌbɜːd, *Am:* 'hwɜːrlɪˌbɜːrd] *n Am* *(helicopter)* helicóptero *m*

whirr [hwɜːʳ, *Am:* hwɜːr] **I.** *vi* hacer ruido **II.** *n* ruido *m;* *(of bird's wings)* aleteo *m*

whisk [hwɪsk] **I.** *vt* **1.** GASTR batir **2.** *(take quickly)* llevar rápidamente; to ~ sb off somewhere llevar a alguien a toda prisa a algún sitio **3.** *(with sweeping movement: tail)* sacudir **II.** *n* **1.** *(kitchen tool)* batidora *f;* **electric** ~ batidora eléctrica; **hand-held** ~ batidora de mano **2.** *(sweeping motion)* sacudida *f*

whisker ['hwɪskəʳ, *Am:* -kɚz] *n* **1.** ~**s** *(facial hair)* pelo *m* de la barba **2.** *(on side of face)* patilla *f* **3.** *pl* *(of animal)* bigotes *mpl* ▶by a ~ por un pelo; <u>within</u> a ~ (of sth) a dos dedos (de algo)

whiskey *n Irish, Am,* **whisky** ['hwɪski] *n* <-ies> *Brit, Aus no pl* whisky *m*

whisper ['hwɪspəʳ, *Am:* -pɚ] **I.** *vi* cuchichear **II.** *vt* **1.** *(speak softly)* susurrar; to ~ sth in sb's ear decir algo al oído a alguien **2.** *fig* *(gossip, speak privately)* rumorear; it is ~ed that ... se rumorea que... **III.** *n* **1.** *(soft sound or speech)* cuchicheo *m;* to lower one's voice to a ~ bajar la voz y hablar en un susurro; to speak in a ~ hablar muy bajo **2.** *fig* *(rumour)* rumor *m* **3.** *fig, liter* *(soft rustle)* susurro *m;* the ~ of the leaves el rumor de las hojas

whispering *n no pl* **1.** *(talking very softly)* susurro *m* **2.** *fig* *(gossiping)* chismes *mpl*

whispering campaign *n* campaña *f* de rumores

whist [hwɪst] *n no pl* whist *m;* a game of ~

una partida de whist

whistle ['hwɪsl] I.<-ling> vi 1.(of person) silbar; to ~ at sb/sth silbar a alguien/ algo; to ~ in admiration silbar de admiración 2.(of bird) trinar II.<-ling> vt silbar III. n 1. no pl (blowing sound) silbido m; to ~ of the wind el silbido del viento 2.(musical device) pito m; referee's ~ silbato m del árbitro; to blow a ~ pitar ►to **blow** the ~ on sb llamar al orden a alguien; to **wet** one's ~ remojar el gaznate

whit [hwɪt] n no pl, form pizca f; not a ~ ni pizca; to not care a ~ (about sth) no preocuparse en absoluto (por algo)

white [hwaɪt] I. adj blanco, -a; ~ **sauce** besamel f; ~ **wedding** boda f tradicional; to turn [o go] ~ with fear palidecer de miedo ►to fly into a ~ **rage** ponerse lívido de rabia II. n 1.(colour) blanco m; ~ of an egg clara f de huevo; the ~ of the eye el blanco del ojo 2.(person) blanco, -a m, f

white-bait ['hwaɪtbeɪt] n inv chanquetes mpl

white-collar [,hwaɪt'kɒləʳ, Am: -'kɑːlə] adj ~ worker oficinista mf

white corpuscle n MED glóbulo m blanco

white elephant n objeto m grande e inútil

white ensign n NAUT enseña f blanca

white feather n to show the ~ mostrarse cobarde **white flag** n bandera f blanca; to fly [o raise] a ~ alzar una bandera blanca

white goods npl 1.(major household appliances) electrodomésticos mpl 2.(household linen) ropa f blanca

Whitehall ['hwaɪthɔːl] n 1.(offices of Britain's government) calle de Londres donde se encuentran los ministerios 2. fig (government of Britain) gobierno m británico

white heat n no pl 1.(of metal) candencia f 2. fig (passion) apasionamiento m **white horses** npl Brit (olas) cabrillas mpl

White House n no pl the ~ la Casa Blanca

white lead n no pl albayalde m **white lie** n mentira f piadosa **white man** <-men> n hombre m blanco **white meat** n no pl carne f blanca

whiten ['hwaɪtən] I. vt blanquear II. vi blanquear; (go pale) palidecer

whitener ['hwaɪtnəʳ, Am: 'hwaɪtnə] n blanqueador m

whiteness n blancura f

whitening n no pl s. **whitener**

white-out n 1.(dense blizzard) ventisca f 2. no pl, Am TYPO líquido m corrector **white paper** n Brit, Aus POL libro m blanco **white sale** n quincena f blanca **white slave** n pej blanca f prostituida; ~ **trade** trata f de blancas **white spirit** n no pl, Brit trementina f

whitethorn ['hwaɪtθɔːn, Am: -θɔːrn] n espino m

white tie I. adj ~ **dinner** cena f de etiqueta II. n corbatín m blanco

whitewash ['hwaɪtwɒʃ, Am: -wɑːʃ] I.<-es> n 1. no pl (for whitening walls) enjal-

begue m 2.(coverup) blanqueo m 3. inf(overwhelming victory) paliza f II. vt 1.(cover in white solution) encalar 2.(conceal negative side of) blanquear 3. inf SPORTS (defeat completely) dar un baño a

whitewater rafting [,hwaɪtwɔːtəʳ'rɑːftɪŋ, Am: -wɑːtəˑ'ræftɪŋ] n no pl rafting m de aguas bravas

white wine n no pl vino m blanco

whither ['hwɪðəʳ, Am: -ə] adv form adónde

whiting¹ ['hwaɪtɪŋ, Am: -t̬ɪŋ] n (fish) pescadilla f

whiting² ['hwaɪtɪŋ, Am: -t̬ɪŋ] n no pl(white substance) tiza f

Whit Monday [,hwɪt'mʌndeɪ] n Lunes m inv de Pentecostés

Whitsun ['hwɪtsən] I. n no pl Pentecostés m; at ~ en Pentecostés II. adj de Pentecostés

Whit Sunday [,hwɪt'sʌndeɪ] n no pl Domingo m de Pentecostés

Whitsuntide ['hwɪtsəntaɪd] n no pl s. **Whitsun**

whittle ['hwɪtl, Am: 'hwɪt̬-] <-ling> vt tallar
◆**whittle away at** vt 1.(take little bits off) cortar pedazos de 2. fig (decrease) reducir poco a poco
◆**whittle down** vt reducir gradualmente

whizz [hwɪz] I. n 1.(brilliant person) genio m 2.(noise) silbido m II. vi silbar; to ~ along inf ir a toda pastilla; to ~ by inf pasar como una bala

whiz(z) kid n inf joven genio m

who [huː] pron 1. interrog quién, quiénes; ~ broke the window? ¿quién rompió la ventana?; ~ were they? ¿quiénes eran? 2. rel que; they have a daughter ~ works in Paris tienen una hija que trabaja en París; the people ~ work here la gente que trabaja aquí; all those ~ know her todos los que la conozcan; it was your sister ~ did it fue tu hermana quien lo hizo

WHO [,dʌblju:eɪtʃ'əʊ, Am: -'oʊ] n abbr of World Health Organization OMS f

whoa [hwəʊ, Am: hwoʊ] interj 1.(command to stop a horse) so 2. fig, inf (to stop something) vale

whodunit n, **whodunnit** [,huː'dʌnɪt] n inf novela f policíaca

whoever [huː'evəʳ, Am: -ə] pron 1. rel (who) quien, quienquiera que; they didn't write to me, ~ they were no me escribieron, quienesquiera que fuesen; ~ said that doesn't know me el que dijo eso no me conoce 2. interrog, inf (angry) quién (diablos); ~ said that? ¿quién diablos dijo eso?

whole [həʊl, Am: hoʊl] I. adj 1.(entire) todo, -a; the ~ world el mundo entero 2.(in one piece) entero, -a; to swallow sth ~ tragarse algo entero 3.(intact: thing) intacto, -a; (person) ileso, -a 4. inf (big) a ~ lot of people mucha gente; to be a ~ lot faster ser mucho más rápido II. n 1.(a complete thing) todo m; as a ~ (concept) en su totalidad; taken as a ~

en conjunto; **on the** ~ en general **2.** *no pl* (*entirety*) totalidad *f;* **the** ~ la totalidad; **the** ~ **of Barcelona** toda Barcelona; **the** ~ **of next week** toda la semana que viene **III.** *adv* completamente; ~ **new** completamente nuevo

wholefood ['həʊlfu:d, *Am:* 'hoʊl-] *n Brit* **1.** *no pl* (*unprocessed food*) comida *f* naturista; ~ **diet** alimentación *f* naturista **2.** *pl* (*unprocessed food products*) alimentos *mpl* integrales

wholefood shop *n Brit* tienda *f* de comida naturista

wholegrain ['həʊlgreɪn, *Am:* 'hoʊl-] *adj* integral; ~ **bread** pan *m* integral; ~ **food products** productos *mpl* integrales

whole-hearted [ˌhəʊl'hɑːtɪd, *Am:* ˌhoʊl-'hɑːrtɪd] *adj* entusiasta; (*completely sincere*) completamente sincero, -a; ~ **thanks** agradecimiento *m* de todo corazón

wholemeal ['həʊlmi:l, *Am:* 'hoʊl-] *adj Brit* integral; ~ **bread** pan *m* integral

wholesale ['həʊlseɪl, *Am:* 'hoʊl-] **I.** *n* venta *f* al por mayor **II.** *adj* **1.** al por mayor; ~ **business** negocio *m* mayorista; ~ **prices** precios *mpl* al por mayor; ~ **supplier** proveedor *m* mayorista **2.** (*on a large scale*) a gran escala; ~ **reform** reforma *f* a gran escala **III.** *adv* **1.** COM al por mayor **2.** (*in bulk*) en masa

wholesaler ['həʊlseɪlər, *Am:* 'hoʊlseɪlɚ] *n* mayorista *mf;* **furniture** ~ mayorista *m* de muebles

wholesome ['həʊlsəm, *Am:* 'hoʊl-] *adj* sano, -a; **the** ~ **outdoor life** la vida sana al aire libre; (**good**) ~ **fun** diversión *f* saludable; (**good**) ~ **food** comida *f* sana

whole-tone scale *n* MUS escala *f* completa

whole wheat I. *adj* de trigo integral **II.** *n* trigo *m* integral

who'll [hu:l] = **who will** *s.* **will**

wholly ['həʊli, *Am:* 'hoʊ-] *adv* enteramente; **to be** ~ **aware of sth** ser totalmente consciente de algo; ~ **different** completamente diferente

whom [hu:m] *pron* **1.** *interrog* a quién, a quiénes; *after prep* quién, quiénes; ~ **did he see?** ¿a quién ha visto?; **to** ~ **did he talk?** ¿con quién ha hablado? **2.** *rel* a quien, que; *after prep* quien, que; **those** ~ **I love** aquellos a quienes amo; **with** ~ con quien

whoop [hu:p] **I.** *vi* gritar **II.** *vt* **to** ~ **it up** echar una cana al aire **III.** *n* grito *m;* ~ **of triumph** grito *m* de victoria; **to give a loud** ~ dar un grito muy fuerte

whoopee ['hwʊpi, *Am:* 'hwu:pi] **I.** *interj* estupendo **II.** *n no pl* juerga *f;* **to make** ~ divertirse una barbaridad

whooping cough ['hu:pɪŋkɒf, *Am:* -kɑ:f] *n no pl* tos *f* ferina

whoops [hwʊps] *interj inf* epa

whop [hwɒp, *Am:* hwɑ:p] *inf* **I.** <-pp-> *vt* **1.** (*strike*) pegar **2.** (*in competition*) derrotar **II.** *n* zurra *f*

whopper ['hwɒpər, *Am:* 'hwɑ:pɚ] *n iron*

1. (*huge thing*) cosa *f* muy grande; **a** ~ **of a fish** un pez enorme **2.** (*lie*) embuste *m;* **to tell a** ~ contar una mentira muy gorda

whopping ['hwɒpɪŋ, *Am:* 'hwɑ:pɪŋ] *adj inf* enorme; **a** ~ **lie** una mentira muy grande; ~ **great** grandísimo

whore [hɔːr, *Am:* hɔːr] *n pej* puta *f*

whorl [hwɜːl, *Am:* hwɜːrl] *n liter* espira *f*

whortleberry ['hwɜːtlˌberi, *Am:* 'hwɜːrt̬l-] <-ies> *n* arándano *m*

who's [hu:z] **1.** = **who is** *s.* **is 2.** = **who has** *s.* **has**

whose [hu:z] **I.** *adj* **1.** *interrog* de quién, de quiénes; ~ **book is this?** ¿de quién es este libro?; ~ **son is he?** ¿de quién es hijo? **2.** *rel* cuyo, cuya, cuyos, cuyas; **the girl** ~ **brother I saw** la chica cuyo hermano vi **II.** *pron pos* de quién, de quiénes; ~ **is this pen?** ¿de quién es esta pluma?; **I know** ~ **this is** sé de quién es esto

why [hwaɪ] **I.** *adv* por qué; ~ **didn't you tell me about that?** ¿por qué no me dijiste nada sobre eso?; **that's** ~ **I didn't tell you** por eso no te dije nada; **I want to know** ~ **you came late** quiero saber por qué llegaste tarde; ~ **not?** ¿por qué no?; ~**'s that?** ¿y eso por qué? **II.** *n* porqué *m;* **the** ~**s and wherefores of sth** las razones de algo, el porqué de algo **III.** *interj* ¡cómo!

wick [wɪk] *n* mecha *f* ▸**to get on sb's** ~ *Brit, inf* hacer subir a alguien por las paredes

wicked ['wɪkɪd] **I.** *adj* **1.** (*evil*) malvado, -a **2.** (*playfully malicious*) malo, -a; **a** ~ **sense of humor** un sentido del humor mordaz **3.** (*likely to cause pain*) inicuo, -a **4.** *inf* (*great fun*) de puta madre **II.** *n* **the** ~ los malos

wicker ['wɪkər, *Am:* -ɚ] *n no pl* mimbre *m*

wicker basket *n* cesta *f* de mimbre **wicker bottle** *n* recipiente *m* de mimbre **wicker chair** *n* silla *f* de mimbre **wicker furniture** *n no pl* muebles *mpl* de mimbre

wickerwork *n no pl* **1.** (*material*) artículo *m* de mimbre **2.** (*art*) cestería *f*

wicket ['wɪkɪt] *n Brit* **1.** (*cricket target*) palos *mpl* **2.** (*ground*) área *f;* **to be on a sticky** ~ estar en una situación difícil

wicket-keeper ['wɪkɪtˌki:pər, *Am:* -pɚ] *n Brit* guardameta *m*

wide [waɪd] **I.** *adj* **1.** (*broad*) extenso, -a; (*as a measurement*) ancho, -a; **it is 3 m** ~ mide 3 m de ancho; **the** (**great**) ~ **world** el ancho mundo; **to search** (**for sb/sth**) **the** ~ **world over** buscar (a alguien/algo) por todo el mundo **2.** (*very open*) vasto, -a; **eyes** ~ **with fear/surprise** ojos *mpl* muy abiertos de miedo/sorpresa **3.** (*varied*) amplio, -a; **a** ~ **range** una amplia gama; **to have a** ~ **experience in sth** tener una amplia experiencia en algo **4.** (*extensive*) grande; ~ **support** gran apoyo *m* ▸**to be** ~ **of the mark** no acertar **II.** *adv* extensamente; **to be** ~ **apart** estar muy lejos (el uno del otro); **to open** ~ abrir mucho; ~ **open** (*eyes*) muy abierto; (*door*) abierto de par en par

wide-angle [ˌwaɪd'æŋgl] *adj* (*lente*) gran angular

wide-awake [ˌwaɪdə'weɪk] *adj* completamente despierto, -a

wide boy *n Brit, inf* tramposo *m*

wide-eyed [ˌwaɪd'aɪd, *Am:* 'waɪdaɪd] *adj fig* inocente

widely *adv* 1. (*broadly*) extensamente; **to gesture** ~ gesticular mucho; **to smile** ~ **at sb** sonreír ampliamente a alguien 2. (*extensively*) ampliamente; ~ **accepted/admired** muy aceptado/admirado 3. (*to a large degree*) considerablemente; ~ **differing aims** objetivos *mpl* muy diferentes

widen ['waɪdən] I. *vt* extender; (*discussion*) ampliar II. *vi* ensancharse

wide-open ['waɪd,əʊpən, *Am:* ˌoʊ-] *adj* 1. (*undecided*) abierto, -a 2. (*vulnerable, exposed*) expuesto, -a; **to be** ~ **to comments** estar expuesto a comentarios

wide-range filter *n* filtro *m* de gama amplia

widespread ['waɪdspred] *adj* extendido, -a; *fig* general; ~ **speculation** especulación difundida; **there is** ~ **speculation that ...** se especula mucho que...

widow ['wɪdəʊ, *Am:* -oʊ] I. *n* viuda *f*; **to be left a** ~ enviudar II. *vt* **to** ~ **sb** dejar viuda a alguien; **to be** ~**ed** enviudar

widowed *adj* viudo, -a

widower ['wɪdəʊəʳ, *Am:* oʊɚ] *n* viudo *m*; **to be left a** ~ enviudar

widowhood ['wɪdəʊhʊd, *Am:* -oʊ-] *n no pl* viudez *f*

widow's allowance *n* subsidio *m* de viudedad **widow's peak** *n* pico *m* que forma el pelo entre las entradas **widow's pension** *n* pensión *f* de viudedad

width [wɪdθ] *n* 1. *no pl* (*distance across*) extensión *f*; (*of wallpaper*) anchura *f*; **to be 3 cm in** ~ medir 3 cm de ancho 2. (*full extent of sth: of clothes*) ancho *m*; **to swim two** ~**s** nadar dos anchos 3. *no pl* (*amount, size*) amplitud *f*

wield [wi:ld] *vt* 1. (*hold*) manejar 2. (*weapon*) empuñar 3. (*power*) ejercer

wife [waɪf] <**wives**> *n* esposa *f*; **my** ~ mi mujer

wifely ['waɪfli] *adj* de esposa; (*duties*) conyugal

wig [wɪg] *n* peluca *f*

wiggle ['wɪgl] I. *vt* menear; (*toes*) mover; (*one's hips*) contonear II. *vi* contonearse III. *n* (*movement*) meneo *m*; (*when walking*) contoneo *m*

wigwam ['wɪgwæm, *Am:* -wɑ:m] *n* wigwam *m*

wild [waɪld] I. *adj* 1. (*not domesticated: animal, man*) salvaje; (*flower*) silvestre; (*horse*) no domesticado, -a 2. (*uncultivated: country, landscape*) agreste 3. (*undisciplined*) indisciplinado, -a; (*party*) loco, -a 4. (*not sensible*) insensato, -a; (*scheme, plan*) estrafalario, -a;

(*behaviour, remarks*) delirante 5. (*not accurate: blow, punch, shot*) errado, -a; (*estimate, guess*) disparatado, -a 6. (*extreme*) absurdo, -a 7. (*stormy*) tormentoso, -a; (*wind, weather*) furioso, -a 8. *inf* (*angry*) furioso, -a; **to drive sb** ~ sacar de quicio a alguien; **to go** ~ ponerse loco 9. *inf* (*very enthusiastic*) emocionado, -a; (*applause*) entusiasta 10. (*untidy: hair*) descuidado, -a 11. GAMES, INFOR (*substitutable*) comodín 12. *inf* (*wonderful*) maravilloso, -a II. *adv* silvestre; **to grow** ~ crecer libre ▸**to run** ~ (*child*) crecer como un salvaje; (*horse*) desbocarse; **to let one's imagination run** ~ dejar volar la imaginación III. *n* 1. *no pl* **the** ~ (*natural environment*) la naturaleza; **to survive in the** ~ (*animals*) sobrevivir en libertad 2. *pl* **the** ~**s** la tierra virgen; (**out**) **in the** ~**s** en el quinto pino *inf*

wild beast *n* bestia *f* salvaje; ~ **show** espectáculo *m* de fieras **wild boar** *n* jabalí *m* **wild card** *n a.* INFOR comodín *m* **wildcat** I. *n* 1. ZOOL (*wild cat*) gato *m* montés 2. *fig* (*fierce woman*) fiera *f* II. *adj* 1. (*very risky*) arriesgado, -a 2. (*unofficial: strike*) salvaje 3. (*exploratory: drilling, well*) exploratorio, -a

wilderness ['wɪldənəs, *Am:* -dɚ-] *n no pl* 1. (*desert tract*) páramo *m* 2. (*unspoilt land*) tierra *f* virgen 3. *fig* (*uncultivated garden*) selva *f irón* ▸**to be in the** ~ *Brit* estar marginado

wildfire ['waɪld,faɪəʳ, *Am:* -faɪɚ] *n* fuego *m* arrasador ▸**to spread like** ~ extenderse como un reguero de pólvora

wildfowl ['waɪldfaʊl] *inv n* ave *f* de caza

wild goose <- **geese**> *n* ganso *m* salvaje **wild-goose chase** *n* empresa *f* desatinada; (*hopeless search*) búsqueda *f* inútil; **to send sb** (**off**) **on a** ~ mandar a alguien a buscar una aguja en un pajar **wildlife** *n no pl* fauna *f* y flora

wildly *adv* 1. (*in an uncontrolled way*) como loco; (*to gesticulate*) con furia, violentamente; **to behave** ~ portarse como un salvaje; **to talk** ~ hablar sin ton ni son 2. (*haphazardly*) a lo loco; (*shoot, guess*) a tontas y a locas 3. *inf* (*very*) muy; ~ **exaggerated** superexagerado; ~ **expensive** carísimo; ~ **improbable** totalmente improbable

wildness *n no pl* 1. (*natural state*) estado *m* salvaje; (*of a country*) estado *m* agreste 2. (*uncontrolled behaviour*) desenfreno *m* 3. (*haphazardness*) insensatez *f*

wiles [waɪlz] *npl* artimañas *fpl*; **to use all one's** ~ usar todas sus tretas

wilful ['wɪlfəl] *adj Brit* 1. (*deliberate*) deliberado, -a; (*disobedience of orders*) intencionado, -a; (*murder*) premeditado, -a 2. (*self-willed*) testarudo, -a; (*obstinate*) obstinado, -a

wiliness ['waɪlɪnəs] *n no pl* astucia *f*

will[1] [wɪl] <**would, would**> I. *aux* 1. (*to form future tense*) **they'll be delighted** estarán encantados; **I'll be with you in a minute** estaré contigo en un minuto; **I expect they'll**

come by car supongo que vendrán en coche; **I'll answer the telephone** contesto yo al teléfono; **she ~ have received the letter by now** ya debe haber recibido la carta **2.** *(with tag question)* **you won't forget to tell him, ~ you?** no te olvidarás decírselo, ¿verdad?; **they ~ accept this credit card in France, won't they?** aceptarán esta tarjeta de crédito en Francia, ¿no? **3.** *(to express immediate future)* **we'll be off now** ahora nos vamos; **I'll be going then** me voy entonces; **there's someone at the door – I'll go** llaman a la puerta – voy yo **4.** *(to express an intention)* **sb ~ do that** alguien hará eso; **I'll not be spoken to like that!** ¡no consiento que se me hable así! **5.** *(in requests and instructions)* **~ you let me speak!** ¡déjame hablar!; **just pass me that knife, ~ you?** pásame ese cuchillo, ¿quieres?; **give me a hand, ~ you?** me ayudas, ¿quieres? **6.** *(in polite requests)* **~ you sit down?** ¿pueden hacer el favor de sentarse?; **~ you be having a slice of cake?** ¿quiere un pedazo de tarta? **7.** *(used to express willingness)* **who'll post this letter for me? – I ~** ¿quién me echa esta carta al buzón? – lo haré yo; **~ you do that for me? – of course I ~** ¿harás eso por mí? – claro que sí **8.** *(used to express a fact)* **eat it now, it won't keep** cómetelo ahora, después se pondrá malo; **the car won't run without petrol** el coche no funciona sin gasolina **9.** *(to express persistence)* **he ~ keep doing that** se empeña en hacer eso; **they ~ keep sending me those brochures** no dejan de mandarme estos folletos; **the door won't open** no hay manera de que se abra esta puerta **10.** *(to express likelihood)* **they'll be tired** estarán cansados; **as you ~ all probably know already...** como todos sabrán... **II.** *vi* **form** disponer; **as you ~** como quieras

will² [wɪl] **I.** *n* **1.** *no pl (faculty)* voluntad *f;* *(desire)* deseo *m;* **the ~ of the people** la voluntad del pueblo; **to have the ~ to do sth** tener la voluntad de hacer algo; **to lose the ~ to live** perder las ganas de vivir; **to do sth with a ~** hacer algo con empeño; **at ~** a voluntad **2.** *(testament)* testamento *m* ►**where there's a ~, there's a** <u>way</u> *prov* querer es poder *prov;* **with the best ~ in the** <u>world</u> con la mejor voluntad del mundo; **to have a ~ of one's** <u>own</u> ser cabezón **II.** *vt* **1.** *(try to cause by will-power)* sugestionar; **to ~ sb to do sth** sugestionar a alguien para que haga algo **2.** *form (ordain)* ordenar; **God ~ed it and it was so** Dios así lo quiso **3.** *(bequeath)* legar

willful ['wɪlfəl] *adj Am s.* **wilful**

William ['wɪljəm] *n* Guillermo *m;* **~ Tell** LIT Guillermo Tell; **~ the Conqueror** HIST Guillermo el Conquistador

willies ['wɪliz] *npl inf* **to have the ~** horrorizarse; **to give sb the ~** poner los pelos de punta a alguien

willing ['wɪlɪŋ] *adj* **1.** *(not opposed)* dispuesto, -a; **to be ~ to do sth** estar dispuesto a

hacer algo; **to lend a ~ hand** dar una mano; **God ~** si Dios quiere; **to show ~** *Brit* dar muestras de buena voluntad **2.** *(compliant)* servicial

willingness *n no pl* **1.** *(readiness)* disposición *f;* **to show a ~ to do sth** mostrar buena voluntad para hacer algo **2.** *(enthusiasm)* entusiasmo *m;* **lack of ~** falta *f* de ánimo

will-o'-the-wisp [ˌwɪlədə'wɪsp] *n* **1.** *(ghostly light)* fuego *m* fatuo **2.** *fig (elusive thing)* quimera *f*

willow ['wɪləʊ, *Am:* -oʊ] *n* sauce *m*

willowy ['wɪləʊi, *Am:* -oʊ-] *adj* esbelto, -a

willpower ['wɪlˌpaʊər, *Am:* -paʊɚ] *n no pl* fuerza *f* de voluntad

willy-nilly [ˌwɪli'nɪli] *adv* **1.** *(like it or not)* sea como sea **2.** *Am (in disorder)* de cualquier manera

wilt [wɪlt] *vi* **1.** *(droop: plants)* marchitarse **2.** *(feel weak: person)* languidecer; *(lose confidence)* desanimarse

wily ['waɪli] <-ier, -iest> *adj* astuto, -a

wimp [wɪmp] *n inf* endeble *mf*

win [wɪn] **I.** *n* victoria *f* **II.** <won, won> *vt* **1.** *(be victorious in: lawsuit, competition)* ganar; MIL vencer; **to ~ first prize** llevarse el primer premio **2.** *(obtain)* obtener; *(promotion, contract)* conseguir; *(recognition, popularity)* ganarse; **to ~ a reputation as a writer** lograr ser reconocido como escritor; **to ~ sb's heart** conquistar el corazón de alguien ►**to ~ the** <u>day</u> prevalecer; **you can't ~ them** <u>all</u> no se puede pretender ganarlas todas; **you ~ some, you** <u>lose</u> **some** no se puede ganar todo **III.** <won, won> *vi* ganar; **to ~ easily** ganar con facilidad ►**to ~** <u>hands</u> **down** ganar con mucha facilidad; **you (just)** <u>can't</u> **~ with him/her** con él/ella, siempre llevas las de perder, ¡no hay caso!; **you ~!** ¡como tú digas!

◆**win back** *vt* recuperar

◆**win over** *vt* **to win sb over to sth** *(persuade to change mind)* convencer a alguien para algo; *(persuade to transfer allegiance)* ganarse a alguien para algo

◆**win round** *vt s.* **win over**

◆**win through** *vi* salir adelante; SPORTS triunfar al fin

wince [wɪns] **I.** *vi* **1.** *(with pain)* hacer un gesto de dolor **2.** *(with embarrassment)* estremecerse **II.** *n* mueca *f* de dolor; **to give a ~** crispársele el rostro a uno

winch [wɪntʃ] **I.** <-es> *n* torno *m* **II.** *vt* levantar con un torno

wind¹ [wɪnd] **I.** *n* **1.** *(current of air)* viento *m;* **a breath of ~** un poco de aire; **gust of ~** ráfaga *f;* **to run before the ~** navegar viento en popa **2.** *no pl (breath)* aliento *m;* **to get one's ~** recobrar el aliento **3.** *no pl, Brit,* MED **gases** *mpl;* **to break ~** ventosear; **to suffer from ~** tener gases ►**to take the ~ out of sb's** <u>sails</u> desanimar a alguien; **he who sows the ~ shall reap the** <u>whirlwind</u> *prov* quien siembra vientos recoge tempestades *prov;* **to sail** <u>close</u>

to the ~ estar a punto de pasarse de la raya; **to get** ~ **of sth** enterarse de algo; **to go** [*o* run] **like the** ~ correr como el viento; **to** put **the** ~ **up** *Brit, Aus* asustarse; **to** put **the** ~ **up sb** *Brit, Aus* asustar a alguien; **there's sth** in **the** ~ se está tramando algo **II.** *vt* dejar sin aliento

wind² ['waɪnd] <wound, wound> **I.** *vt* **1.** (*coil*) enrollar; (*wool*) ovillar; **to** ~ **sth around sth** enrollar algo alrededor de algo **2.** (*wrap*) envolver **3.** (*turn: handle*) hacer girar; (*clock, watch*) dar cuerda a **4.** (*film*) hacer correr **II.** *vi* serpentear

◆**wind back** *vt* (*film, tape*) rebobinar

◆**wind down I.** *vt* **1.** (*lower*) bajar **2.** (*gradually reduce*) disminuir progresivamente; (*activities, operations, production*) reducir; (*business*) limitar **II.** *vi* **1.** (*become less active*) limitarse; (*business*) tocar a su fin **2.** (*relax after stress*) desconectar **3.** (*need rewinding: clock, spring*) pararse

◆**wind forward** *vt* (*film, tape*) hacer correr

◆**wind on** *vt Brit, Aus* (*film*) enrollar

◆**wind up I.** *vt* **1.** (*bring to an end*) acabar; (*debate, meeting, speech*) concluir **2.** *Brit, Aus* ECON (*close down: company*) liquidar **3.** (*raise*) levantar **4.** (*tension spring*) dar cuerda a **5.** *Brit, inf* (*tease*) **to wind sb up** tomar el pelo a alguien **II.** *vi* **1.** (*come to an end*) finalizar **2.** *inf* (*end up*) **to** ~ **in prison** ir a parar a la carcel

windbag ['wɪndbæɡ] *n inf* charlatán, -ana *m, f*

windbreak ['wɪndbreɪk] *n* barrera *f* contra el viento **wind cone** *n* manga *f* de viento **wind energy** *n no pl* energía *f* eólica

winder ['waɪndə^r, *Am:* -ɚ] *n* **1.** *Brit* (*on watch*) cuerda *f* **2.** (*on toy*) manivela *f*

windfall ['wɪndfɔ:l] *n* **1.** (*fruit*) fruta *f* caída **2.** *fig* (*money*) ganancia *f* imprevista **wind farm** *n* ECOL granja *f* con energía eólica **wind generator** *n* ECOL generador *m* eólico

winding ['waɪndɪŋ] *adj* sinuoso, -a

winding rope *n* cuerda *f* ondulada **winding sheet** *n* mortaja *f* **winding staircase** *n* escalera *f* de caracol

winding-up [ˌwaɪndɪŋ'ʌp] *n no pl* **1.** (*conclusion*) conclusión *f* **2.** *Brit, Aus* ECON (*of a company*) disolución *f*; (*of company's affairs*) liquidación *f*

winding-up sale *n* liquidación *f* total

wind instrument *n* instrumento *m* de viento **windjammer** *n* NAUT velero *m* grande **windlass** *n* torno *m* **windmill** *n* **1.** (*wind-powered mill*) molino *m* de viento **2.** (*toy*) molinete *m*

window ['wɪndəʊ, *Am:* -doʊ] *n* **1.** (*in building*) ventana *f*; (*bedroom*) vitrina *f*; ~ **ledge** alféizar *m*; **a** ~ **on the world** *fig* una ventana abierta al mundo **2.** (*of shop*) vidriera *f*; (*window display*) escaparate *m* **3.** (*side windows*) ventanilla *f*; (*of vehicle*) luna *f*; **rear** ~ luna trasera **4.** INFOR ventana *f*; ~ **separator** separador *m* de ventana; **pop-up** ~ ventana

emergente **5.** (*in envelope*) ventanilla *f* **6.** *fig* (*time period*) ocasión *f*; **a** ~ **of opportunity** una oportunidad ▶**to go** out **(of) the** ~ *inf* (*plan*) venirse abajo

window box <-es> *n* jardinera *f* **window cleaner** *n* **1.** (*person*) limpiacristales *mf inv* **2.** *no pl* (*product*) limpiacristales *m inv*

window display *n* escaparate *m* **window display competition** *n* competición *f* de escaparates **window dressing** *n no pl* **1.** (*in shop*) escaparatismo *m* **2.** *fig* fachada *f*; (*effort*) esfuerzo *m* por aparentar **window envelope** *n* sobre *m* de ventanilla **window frame** *n* marco *m* de la ventana **window pane** *n* cristal *m* (de la ventana) **window-shopping** *n no pl* **to go** ~ ir a mirar escaparates **windowsill** *n* repisa *f* de la ventana

windpipe ['wɪndpaɪp] *n* tráquea *f* **wind power** *n no pl* **1.** (*electricity*) energía *f* eólica **2.** (*force of wind*) impulso *m* por viento

windscreen ['wɪndskri:n] *n Brit, Aus* parabrisas *m inv*

windscreen wiper *n* limpiaparabrisas *m inv*

windshield ['wɪndʃi:ld] *n Am* (*windscreen*) parabrisas *m inv* **windsock** *n* manga *f* de viento

windsurfer ['wɪndsɜ:fə^r, *Am:* -sɜ:rfɚ] *n* surfista *mf*

windsurfing ['wɪndsɜ:fɪŋ, *Am:* -sɜ:rf-] *n no pl* windsurf *m*

windswept ['wɪndswept] *adj* **1.** (*exposed to wind*) azotado, -a por el viento **2.** (*looking wind-blown*) despeinado, -a

wind tunnel *n* TECH túnel *m* aerodinámico **wind turbine** *n* turbina *f* eólica

windward ['wɪndwəd, *Am:* -wəd] NAUT **I.** *adj* de barlovento **II.** *n* barlovento *m*; (**to**) ~ **a** barlovento

windy¹ ['wɪndi] <-ier, -iest> *adj* ventoso, -a

windy² ['wɪndi] <-ier, -iest> *adj* sinuoso, -a

wine [waɪn] **I.** *n no pl* vino *m* **II.** *vt* **to** ~ **and dine sb** dar a alguien muy bien de comer y de beber

wine bottle *n* botella *f* de vino **wine cooler** *n* recipiente *m* para mantener fresco el vino **wine glass** <-es> *n* copa *f* para vino **wine-grower** *n* viticultor(a) *m(f)* **wine-growing I.** *n no pl* viticultura *f* **II.** *adj* vinícola

wine list *n* carta *f* de vinos **wine merchant** *n* **1.** (*seller of wines*) vinatero, -a *m, f* **2.** (*shop*) vinatería *f*

winepress ['waɪnpres] <-es> *n* prensa *f* de uvas

winery ['waɪnəri] <-ies> *n* bodega *f*

wine-tasting *n* **1.** *no pl* (*activity*) catadura *f* de vinos **2.** (*event*) degustación *f* de vinos **wine waiter** *n* sommelier *m*

wing [wɪŋ] **I.** *n* **1.** ZOOL, AVIAT ala *f*; **to take** ~ *liter* alzar el vuelo **2.** ARCHIT ala *f*; **the west** ~ **of the house** el ala oeste de la casa **3.** SPORTS (*side of field: left, right*) ala *f* exterior; (*player*) extremo, -a *m, f* **4.** POL ala *f*; **left** ~ **ala**

izquierda **5.** *pl* THEAT bastidores *mpl;* **to be waiting in the** ~**s** *fig* estar esperando su oportunidad **6.** *Brit* AUTO aleta *f* **7.** *pl* MIL (*pilot's badge*) insignia *f* ►**to** **spread** **one's** ~**s** desplegar las alas; **to** **stretch** **one's** ~**s** extender las alas; **to** **take** **sb** **under** **one's** ~ hacerse cargo de alguien **II.** *vt* **1.** (*wound, in hunting: bird*) herir en el ala; (*person*) herir superficialmente **2.** (*fly*) volar **III.** *vi* volar

wing chair *n* sillón *m* de orejas **wing commander** *n* *Brit* teniente *m* coronel de aviación

winged ['wɪŋd] *adj* alado, -a; (*seed*) con alas
winger ['wɪŋəʳ, *Am:* -ɚ] *n* SPORTS extremo, -a *m, f*
wing nut *n* TECH palomilla *f*
wingspan ['wɪŋspæn] *n,* **wingspread** ['wɪŋspred] *n* envergadura *f*
wink [wɪŋk] **I.** *n* guiño *m;* **to give sb a** ~ guiñar el ojo a alguien ►**to have** **forty** ~**s** *inf* echarse una siestecita; **not to** **sleep** **a** ~ no pegar ojo; **in a** ~ en un abrir y cerrar de ojos **II.** *vi* **1.** (*close one eye*) guiñar el ojo; **to** ~ **at sb** guiñar el ojo a alguien **2.** (*flash: a light*) parpadear
winker *n* *Brit* AUTO intermitente *m*
winner ['wɪnəʳ, *Am:* -ɚ] *n* **1.** (*person*) ganador(a) *m(f)* **2.** *inf* SPORTS tanto *m* decisivo **3.** *inf* (*success*) éxito *m;* (*book*) obra *f* premiada; **to be on to a** ~ **with sth** tener mucho éxito con algo
winning ['wɪnɪŋ] **I.** *adj* **1.** (*that wins*) ganador(a); (*ticket*) premiado, -a; (*point*) decisivo, -a; (*team*) vencedor(a) **2.** (*charming*) encantador(a) **II.** *n* **1.** *no pl* (*act of achieving victory*) triunfo *m* **2.** *pl* (*money*) ganancias *fpl*
winnow ['wɪnəʊ, *Am:* -oʊ] *vt* **1.** (*grain*) aventar **2.** (*select*) seleccionar; **to** ~ **the list down to 8** seleccionar 8 de la lista
winsome ['wɪnsəm] *adj liter* atractivo, -a; (*charm, smile*) encantador(a)
winter ['wɪntəʳ, *Am:* -t̬ɚ] **I.** *n* invierno *m* **II.** *vi* (*animals*) invernar; (*person*) pasar el invierno
winter coat *n* chaqueta *f* de invierno; (*of animal*) pelaje *m* de invierno **winter season** *n* invierno *m* **winter solstice** *n* solsticio *m* de invierno **winter sports** *npl* deportes *mpl* de invierno **wintertime** *n no pl* invierno *m;* **in (the)** ~ en invierno
wint(e)ry ['wɪntri] *adj* **1.** (*typical of winter*) invernal **2.** *fig* (*cold, unfriendly*) frío, -a
WIP [ˌdʌbljuːaɪˈpiː] *n abbr of* **work in progress** trabajo *m* en curso de ejecución
wipe [waɪp] **I.** *n* **1.** (*act of wiping*) limpieza *f;* **to give sth a** ~ pasar un trapo a algo, limpiar algo; **to give the floor a** ~ limpiar el suelo **2.** (*tissue*) toallita *f* **II.** *vt* **1.** (*remove dirt*) limpiar; (*floor*) fregar; (*one's nose*) sonarse; (*dishes*) secar; **to** ~ **sth dry** secar algo **2.** (*erase material from: disk, a tape*) borrar **III.** *vi* secar
◆**wipe down** *vt* pasar un trapo a; (*floor*)

limpiar
◆**wipe off** *vt* **1.** (*remove by wiping*) quitar con un trapo **2.** (*erase: data, programme*) borrar **3.** ECON reducir ►**to wipe the smile off sb's** **face** borrar la sonrisa de la cara de alguien
◆**wipe out** *vt* **1.** (*clean*) limpiar **2.** (*destroy: population, village*) exterminar; (*sb's profits*) acabar con **3.** (*cancel: debt*) liquidar **4.** *inf* (*tire out*) dejar hecho polvo **5.** *inf* (*economically*) arruinar **II.** *vi inf* (*driving, skiing*) perder el control
◆**wipe up** **I.** *vt* limpiar **II.** *vi* secar
wire ['waɪəʳ, *Am:* 'waɪɚ] **I.** *n* **1.** *no pl* (*metal thread*) alambre *m* **2.** ELEC cable *m* **3.** (*telegram*) telegrama *m* **4.** *Am* (*hidden microphone*) micrófono *m* escondido **5.** (*prison camp fence*) alambrada *f* ►**to get one's** ~**s** **crossed** *inf* tener un malentendido; **to** **get** (**sth**) **in under the** ~ *Am, inf* conseguir algo justo a tiempo; **to go** (**down**) **to the** ~ *inf* ir hasta el último momento; **to** **pull** ~**s** utilizar las influencias **II.** *vt* **1.** (*fasten with wire*) sujetar con alambre; **to** ~ **sth to the door** sujetar algo a la puerta con alambre **2.** ELEC conectar; **to be** ~**d for cable TV** tener instalación de televisión por cable **3.** *Am* (*fit with concealed microphone*) colocar un micrófono oculto en; **to be** ~**d** (*person*) llevar un micrófono oculto **4.** (*send telegram to*) **to** ~ **sb** poner un telegrama a alguien; **to** ~ **sb money** enviar un giro telegráfico a alguien
wire-cutters ['waɪəˌkʌtəʳz, *Am:* 'waɪɚˌkʌt̬ɚz] *npl* cortaalambres *m inv,* pinzas *fpl* de corte *Méx* **wire fence** *n* alambrada *f*
wire-haired terrier [ˌwaɪəheədˈteriəʳ, *Am:* ˌwaɪɚˈherdˈteriɚ] *n* terrier *m* de pelo duro
wireless ['waɪələs, *Am:* 'waɪɚ-] *n* *Brit* **1.** *no pl* radio *f;* **on the** [*o* **by**] ~ por radio **2.** (*set*) receptor *m* de radio
wireless operator *n* radiotelegrafista *mf;* AVIAT radio *mf* **wireless set** *n* *Brit* receptor *m* de radio
wirephoto *n* telefotografía *f*
wirepuller *n inf* enchufista *mf*
wirepulling *n no pl, inf* enchufismo *m*
wiretapping ['waɪəˌtæpɪŋ, *Am:* 'waɪɚ-] *n no pl* escuchas *fpl* telefónicas
wire transfer *n Am* transferencia *f* por cable
wiring ['waɪərɪŋ, *Am:* 'waɪɚ-] *n no pl* ELEC **1.** (*system of wires*) cableado *m* **2.** (*electrical installation*) instalación *f* eléctrica
wiring diagram *n* ELEC diagrama *m* de la instalación eléctrica
wiry ['waɪəri, *Am:* 'waɪɚ-] <-ier, -iest> *adj* **1.** (*rough-textured: hair*) áspero, -a, tieso, -a **2.** (*lean and strong: build, person*) enjuto, -a y fuerte
wisdom ['wɪzdəm] *n no pl* **1.** (*state of being wise*) sabiduría *f;* **with the** ~ **of hindsight** con la sabiduría que da la experiencia; ~ **comes with age** la madurez llega con la edad **2.** (*sensibleness*) prudencia *f*
wisdom tooth <- teeth> *n* muela *f* del jui-

*(right margin)* W

cio

wise¹ [waɪz] *adj* **1.** (*having knowledge and sagacity*) sabio, -a; **the Three Wise Men** los Reyes Magos; **it's easy to be ~ after the event** es muy fácil criticar a posteriori **2.** (*showing sagacity*) acertado, -a; (*advice, saying*) adecuado, -a; (*words*) juicioso, -a **3.** (*sensible*) sensato, -a; (*decision, choice*) inteligente **4.** *inf* (*aware*) consciente; **to be ~ to sb** tener calado a alguien; **to be ~ to sth** estar al tanto de algo; **to get ~ to sth** caer en la cuenta de algo; **to get ~ to sb's game** enterarse del juego de alguien; **to be none the ~r for sth** seguir sin enterarse de algo **5.** *inf* (*cheeky*) pícaro, -a; **to get ~ with sb** insolentarse con alguien

◆**wise up I.** *vi* **to ~ to sth** ponerse al tanto de algo **II.** *vt* **to wise sb up about sth** poner a alguien al tanto de algo

wise² [waɪz] *n form* manera *f*, modo *m*; **in any/no ~** en modo alguno/de ninguna manera

wiseacre ['waɪzˌeɪkəʳ, *Am:* -kəʳ] *n* sabelotodo *mf*

wisecrack ['waɪzkræk] **I.** *n* broma *f*; **to make a ~ about sth** hacer un chiste sobre algo **II.** *vi* bromear

wise guy *n inf* gracioso, -a *m, f*

wish [wɪʃ] **I.** <-es> *n* **1.** (*desire*) deseo *m*; **against my ~es** en contra de mi voluntad; **to express a ~ that ...** rogar que...; **to have no ~ to do sth** no tener ganas de hacer algo; **to make a ~** expresar un deseo **2.** *pl* (*friendly greetings*) recuerdos *mpl*; **give him my best ~es** dale muchos recuerdos de mi parte; **(with) best ~es** (*at end of letter*) un abrazo **II.** *vt* **1.** (*feel a desire*) desear; **I ~ he hadn't come** ojalá no hubiera venido; **I ~ you'd told me** (*expressing annoyance*) me lo podrías haber dicho **2.** *form* (*want*) **to ~ to do sth** querer hacer algo; **I ~ to be alone** deseo estar solo **3.** (*hope*) **to ~ sb luck** desear suerte a alguien; **to ~ sb happy birthday** felicitar a alguien por su cumpleaños; **to ~ sb good night** dar las buenas noches a alguien **III.** *vi* **1.** (*want*) desear; **as you ~** como usted mande; **if you ~** como quieras; **to ~ for sth** anhelar algo **2.** (*make a wish*) **to ~ for sth** desear algo; **everything one could ~ for** todo lo que uno podría desear

wishbone ['wɪʃbəʊn, *Am:* -boʊn] *n* espoleta *f*

wishful thinking *n no pl* ilusión *f*

wishy-washy ['wɪʃiwɒʃi, *Am:* -ˌwɑːʃi] *adj pej* **1.** (*indeterminate and insipid*) insípido, -a; (*argument*) flojo, -a **2.** (*weak and watery: coffee, drink, soup*) aguado, -a; (*food*) soso, -a

wisp [wɪsp] *n* (*of hair*) mechón *m*; (*of straw*) brizna *f*; (*of smoke*) voluta *f*; (*of cloud*) jirón *m*; **a little ~ of a boy** un chico menudito

wispy ['wɪspi] <-ier, -iest> *adj* (*hair*) ralo, -a; (*person*) menudo, -a; (*clouds*) tenue

wisteria [wɪ'stɪərɪə, *Am:* -'stɪrɪ-] *n no pl*

glicina *f*

wistful ['wɪstfəl] *adj* (*melancholy, nostalgic*) nostálgico, -a; (*longing*) añorado, -a

wit [wɪt] **I.** *n* **1.** *no pl* (*clever humour*) ingenio *m*; **to have a dry ~** ser mordaz **2.** (*practical intelligence*) inteligencia *f*; **to be at one's ~s' end** estar para volverse loco; **to gather one's ~s** poner las ideas en orden; **to frighten sb out of his/her ~s** dar a alguien un susto de muerte; **to have/keep one's ~s about one** andar con mucho ojo; **to live off one's ~s** vivir del cuento **3.** (*witty person*) chistoso, -a *m, f*; (*quick-witted person*) persona *f* ocurrente **II.** *vi form* **to ~ a saber**

witch [wɪtʃ] <-es> *n* **1.** (*woman with magic powers*) bruja *f* **2.** *pej, inf* (*ugly or unpleasant woman*) arpía *f*

witchcraft ['wɪtʃkrɑːft, *Am:* -kræft] *n no pl* brujería *f*, payé *m CSur*

witch doctor *n* brujo *m*, payé *m CSur*

witchery ['wɪtʃəri] *n no pl s.* **witchcraft**

witch-hunt ['wɪtʃhʌnt] *n pej* caza *f* de brujas

witching hour ['wɪtʃɪŋˌaʊəʳ, *Am:* 'wɪtʃɪŋ-ˌaʊr] *n liter* medianoche *f*

with [wɪð, wɪθ] *prep* **1.** (*accompanied by*) con; (**together**) **~ sb** (junto) con alguien **2.** (*by means of*) con; **to take sth ~ one's fingers/both hands** tomar algo con los dedos/las dos manos; **to replace sth ~ something else** reemplazar algo por otra cosa **3.** (*having*) **the man ~ the umbrella** el hombre del paraguas; **~ no hesitation at all** sin ningún titubeo **4.** (*on one's person*) **he took it ~ him** lo llevó consigo [*o* encima] **5.** (*manner*) **~ all speed** a toda velocidad; **~ one's whole heart** de todo corazón **6.** (*in addition to*) **and ~ that he went out** y a continuación salió **7.** (*despite*) **~ all his faults** a pesar de todos sus defectos **8.** (*caused by*) **to cry ~ rage** llorar de rabia; **to turn red ~ anger** ponerse rojo de cólera **9.** (*full of*) **black ~ flies** negro de moscas; **to fill up ~ fuel** llenar de gasolina **10.** (*opposing*) **a war ~ Italy** una guerra contra Italia; **to be angry ~ sb** estar enfadado con alguien **11.** (*supporting*) **to be ~ sb/sth** estar de acuerdo con alguien/algo; **popular ~ young people** popular entre los jóvenes **12.** (*concerning*) **to be pleased ~ sth** estar satisfecho con algo; **what's up [*o* what's the matter] ~ him?** ¿qué le pasa? **13.** (*understanding*) **I'm not ~ you** *inf* no te sigo; **to be ~ it** *inf* estar al tanto; **to get ~ it** ponerse al día ►**away ~ him!** ¡llévenselo!

withdraw [wɪð'drɔː, *Am:* -'drɑː] *irr* **I.** *vt* **1.** (*take out*) quitar; (*money*) sacar **2.** (*take back*) retirar **3.** (*cancel*) cancelar; (*motion, action*) anular; (*charge*) apartar; **to ~ one's labour** *Brit, form* ir a la huelga **II.** *vi* **1.** *form a.* MIL (*leave*) marcharse, retirarse; **to ~ from public life** retirarse de la vida pública; SPORTS abandonar **2.** *fig* (*become quiet and unsociable*) recluirse; (*into silence*) retraerse

withdrawal [wɪð'drɔːəl, *Am:* -'drɑː-] *n* **1.** *a.*
MIL retirada *f;* **to make a** ~ FIN sacar dinero
2. *no pl* LAW retracto *m;* (*of consent, support*)
supresión *f* **3.** *no pl* (*sports*) abandono *m* **4.** *no
pl* (*distancing from others*) retraimiento *m*
withdrawal symptoms *npl* síndrome *m* de
abstinencia; **to suffer** (**from**) ~ *a. fig* tener el
mono *inf*
wither ['wɪðər, *Am:* -ɚ] I. *vi* **1.** (*plants*) marchitarse **2.** *fig* (*lose vitality*) debilitarse; **to
allow sth to** ~ dejar que algo pierda vida ►**to**
~ **on the** <u>vine</u> desaparecer poco a poco II. *vt*
1. (*plant*) marchitar **2.** *fig* (*strength*) mermar
withering ['wɪðərɪŋ] *adj* **1.** (*fierce and
destructive*) destructivo, -a; (*heat*) abrasa-
dor(a); (*fire*) arrollador(a) **2.** (*contemptuous:
criticism*) hiriente
withhold [wɪð'həʊld, *Am:* -'hoʊld] *irr vt*
1. (*not give: information*) **to** ~ **sth** (**from sb**)
ocultar algo (a alguien); (*one's support*) negar;
(*evidence*) no revelar **2.** (*not pay: benefits,
rent*) retener
within [wɪð'ɪn] I. *prep* **1.** *form* (*inside of*)
dentro de; ~ **the country/town** dentro del
país/de la ciudad **2.** (*in limit of*) ~ **sight/hear-
ing** al alcance de la vista/del oído; ~ **easy
reach** al alcance de la mano **3.** (*in less than*)
en (el transcurso de); ~ **one hour** en una hora;
~ **3 days** en el plazo de tres días; ~ **2 km of
the town** a menos de 2 km de la ciudad **4.** (*in
accordance to*) de acuerdo a; ~ **the law** dentro de la ley II. *adv* dentro; **from** ~ desde adentro
without [wɪð'aʊt] I. *prep* sin; ~ **warning** sin
previo aviso; **to be** ~ **relatives** no tener
parientes; **to do** ~ **sth** apañárselas sin algo
II. *adv liter* fuera; **from** ~ desde fuera
withstand [wɪð'stænd] *irr vt* resistir; (*heat,
pressure*) soportar
witness ['wɪtnəs] I. *n* **1.** *a.* LAW testigo *mf;* ~
for the defence testigo de descargo; **according to** ~**es** según testigos; **to be** (**a**) ~ **to sth**
presenciar algo **2.** *no pl, form* (*testimony*) testimonio *m;* **to bear** ~ **to sth** dar fe de algo
II. *vt* **1.** (*see*) ser testigo de; **to** ~ **sb doing sth**
observar a alguien haciendo algo **2.** (*be there
during*) vivir; (*changes*) presenciar **3.** (*attest
authenticity of*) atestiguar la veracidad de
III. *vi Brit* LAW dar fe de; **to** ~ **to sth** dar fe de
algo; **to** ~ **to have done sth** demostrar haber
hecho algo
witness box <-es> *n Brit,* **witness stand**
n Am tribuna *f* (de los testigos)
witty ['wɪti, *Am:* 'wɪt̬-] <-ier, -iest> *adj*
(*possessing or showing wit*) ingenioso, -a;
(*funny*) gracioso, -a
wizard ['wɪzəd, *Am:* -ɚd] I. *n* **1.** (*magician*)
mago, -a *m, f* **2.** (*expert*) genio *m;* **to be a** ~ **at
sth** ser un genio haciendo algo II. <-er, -est>
adj Brit, inf fantástico, -a
wizardry ['wɪzədri, *Am:* -ɚd-] *n no pl* magia *f*
wizened ['wɪznd] *adj* marchito, -a; (*face,*

skin) arrugado, -a
WNW *abbr of* **west-northwest** ONO
w/o *prep abbr of* **without** sin
wobble ['wɒbl, *Am:* 'wɑːbl] I. *vi* **1.** (*move
unsteadily*) tambalearse; (*wheel*) bailar; (*jelly,
fat*) moverse; (*rock*) balancearse **2.** (*tremble:
voice*) temblar **3.** *fig* (*fluctuate: prices, shares*)
fluctuar II. *vt* hacer tambalearse; (*camera*)
mover III. *n* **1.** (*wobbling movement*) tambaleo *m* **2.** (*quavering sound*) temblor *m*
3. ECON fluctuación *f*
wobbly ['wɒbli, *Am:* 'wɑːbli] I. <-ier,
-iest> *adj* **1.** (*unsteady*) tambaleante; (*line*)
zigzagueante; (*chair*) cojo, -a **2.** (*wavering: a
note, a voice*) tembloroso, -a II. <-ies> *n Brit,
inf* pataleta *f;* **to throw a** ~ poner el grito en el
cielo
woe [wəʊ, *Am:* woʊ] *n* **1.** *no pl, liter* (*unhappiness*) desgracia *f;* **a tale of** ~ tragedia *f;* ~
betide you! ¡maldito seas! **2.** *pl, form* (*misfortunes*) males *mpl;* **to pour out one's** ~**s** contar a alguien sus penas
woebegone ['wəʊbɪgɒn, *Am:* 'woʊbɪ-
gɑːn] *adj liter* angustiado, -a
woeful ['wəʊfəl, *Am:* 'woʊ-] *adj* **1.** (*deplorable*) deplorable; (*ignorance, incompetence*)
lamentable **2.** *liter* (*sad*) afligido, -a
wog [wɒg, *Am:* wɑːg] *n Brit, Aus, pej, inf*
1. (*dark-skinned person*) negro, -a *m, f* **2.** *Aus*
(*non-English-speaking immigrant*) extranjero,
-a *m, f*
wok [wɒk, *Am:* wɑːk] *n* puchero *m* chino de
metal
woke [wəʊk, *Am:* woʊk] *vt, vi pt of* **wake**
woken ['wəʊkən, *Am:* 'woʊ-] *vt, vi pp of*
wake
wolf [wʊlf] I. <wolves> *n* **1.** (*animal*) lobo
m **2.** *inf* (*seducer*) don Juan *m* ►**to keep the**
~ **from the** <u>door</u> no pasar miseria; **a** ~ **in**
<u>sheep's clothing</u> un lobo disfrazado de cor-
dero; **to** <u>cry</u> ~ dar una falsa alarma; **to** <u>throw</u>
sb to the wolves arrojar a alguien a los lobos
II. *vt inf* engullir
wolf cub *n* lobato *m* **wolfhound** *n* perro *m*
lobo **wolf whistle** *n* silbido *m* de admiración
woman ['wʊmən] <women> *n* **1.** (*female
human*) mujer *f;* **the other** ~ la querida; ~
candidate candidata *f;* ~ **president** presidenta *f;* **women's libber** defensor(a) *m(f)* de
los derechos de la mujer **2.** *inf* (*man's female
partner*) esposa *f*
woman doctor *n* doctora *f* **woman
driver** *n* conductora *f*
womanhood ['wʊmənhʊd] *n no pl*
1. (*female adulthood*) condición *f* de mujer; **to
reach** ~ hacerse adulta **2.** (*women as a group*)
mujeres *fpl*
womanish ['wʊmənɪʃ] *adj pej* afeminado
womanize ['wʊmənaɪz] *vi inf* andar detrás
de las mujeres
womanizer *n* mujeriego *m*
womankind [ˌwʊmən'kaɪnd, *Am:* 'wʊ-

mənkaınd] *n no pl, form* sexo *m* femenino; **all** ~ todas las mujeres

womanly ['wʊmənli] *adj* **1.** (*not manly*) femenino, -a; (*wiles*) de mujer **2.** (*not girlish*) de mujer adulta

womb [wuːm] *n* útero *m;* **in the** ~ en el seno materno

womenfolk ['wɪmɪnfəʊk, *Am:* -foʊk] *npl* mujeres *fpl*

women's centre *n* centro *m* para mujeres **women's lib** *n no pl, inf abbr of* **women's liberation** liberación *f* de la mujer **women's refuge** *n Brit, Aus,* **women's shelter** *n Am* centro *m* de acogida para mujeres

won [wʌn] *vt, vi pt, pp of* **win**

wonder ['wʌndər, *Am:* -dɚ] I. *vt* **1.** (*ask oneself*) preguntarse; **to make sb** ~ hacer pensar a alguien **2.** (*feel surprise*) I ~ **why he said that** me extraña que dijera eso II. *vi* **1.** (*ask oneself*) preguntarse; **to** ~ **about sth** preguntarse algo; **to** ~ **about doing sth** pensar si hacer algo **2.** (*feel surprise*) sorprenderse; **to** ~ **at sth/sb** maravillarse de algo/alguien; **I don't** ~ (**at it**) no me extraña III. *n* **1.** (*marvel*) maravilla *f;* **to do** ~s hacer maravillas; **the** ~**s of modern technology** los prodigios de la tecnología moderna; **it's a** ~ (**that**) ... es un milagro que ...; ~s (**will**) **never cease!** *iron* ¡eso sí es increíble! **2.** *no pl* (*feeling*) asombro *m;* **in** ~ con estupefacción; **to listen in** ~ escuchar con estupor ▶**to be a <u>nine-days'</u>** ~ ser un prodigio efímero

wonder boy *n iron, inf* joven *m* prodigio **wonder drug** *n* remedio *m* milagroso

wonderful ['wʌndəfəl, *Am:* -dɚ-] *adj* maravilloso, -a

wonderland ['wʌndəlænd, *Am:* -dɚlænd] *n* país *m* de las maravillas **wonderment** *n no pl* admiración *f*

wonky ['wɒŋki, *Am:* 'waːŋ-] <-ier, -iest> *adj Brit, Aus, inf* **1.** (*unsteady*) poco firme; (*feeling*) débil **2.** (*askew*) torcido, -a

wont [wəʊnt, *Am:* wɔːnt] I. *adj form* acostumbrado, -a; **to be** ~ **to do sth** soler hacer algo II. *n no pl, form* costumbre *f;* **as is her** ~ como suele hacer

won't [wəʊnt, *Am:* woʊnt] = **will not** *s.* **will**

woo [wuː] *vt* **1.** (*try to attract*) **to** ~ **sb** (*customers, investors*) buscar atraer a alguien; (*voters*) buscar el apoyo de alguien **2.** (*court*) cortejar

wood [wʊd] *n* **1.** *no pl* (*material*) madera *f;* (*to build a fire*) leña *f* **2.** (*group of trees*) bosque *m* **3.** SPORTS (*golf*) palo *m* de madera **4.** *no pl, Brit* (*wooden container*) barril *m;* **beer from the** ~ cerveza *f* de barril ▶(**to**) <u>touch</u> ~, (**to**) <u>knock</u> **on** ~ *Am* tocar madera; **to be <u>out</u> of the** ~ estar a salvo

wood alcohol *n no pl* metanol *m* **woodbine** *n* BOT **1.** (*wild honeysuckle*) madreselva *f* **2.** *Am* (*Virginia creeper*) parra *f* virgen **woodcarver** *n* tallista *mf* de madera

woodcraft *n no pl* **1.** (*outdoor skills*) conocimiento *m* de la vida del bosque **2.** (*artistic skill*) artesanía *f* en madera **woodcut** *n* ART grabado *f* en madera **woodcutter** *n* leñador(a) *m(f)*

wooded ['wʊdɪd] *adj* boscoso, -a

wooden ['wʊdn] *adj* **1.** (*made of wood*) de madera; ~ **leg** pata *f* de palo **2.** (*awkward*) rígido, -a; (*smile*) inexpresivo, -a

woodland ['wʊdlənd] I. *n* bosque *m* II. *adj* de los bosques

wood panelling *n no pl* paneles *mpl* de madera **woodpecker** *n* pájaro *m* carpintero **woodpile** *n* montón *m* de leña **wood preservative** *n* conservante *m* de la madera **wood pulp** *n no pl* TECH pulpa *f* de madera

woodshed ['wʊdʃed] I. *n* leñera *f* II. <-dd-> *vi Am, inf* tocar un instrumento musical

woodwind ['wʊdwɪnd] MUS I. *n* instrumentos *mpl* de viento (de madera) II. *adj* de viento

woodwork ['wʊdwɜːk, *Am:* -wɜːrk] *n no pl* **1.** (*wooden parts of building*) carpintería *f* **2.** *Brit* (*carpentry*) ebanistería *f;* (*craftsmanship*) artesanía *f* en madera **3.** *inf* SPORTS los postes y el travesaño ▶**to** <u>come</u> **out of the** ~ salir de quién sabe dónde **woodworm** *n inv* **1.** (*larva that attacks wood*) carcoma *f* **2.** *no pl* (*damage*) madera *f* carcomida

woody ['wʊdi] <-ier, -iest> *adj* **1.** (*tough like wood: plant, stem, tissue*) leñoso, -a **2.** (*like wood: flavour*) amaderado, -a **3.** (*wooded*) boscoso, -a

woof [wuːf] I. *n* (*dog*) ladrido *m;* **to give a loud** ~ ladrar II. *vi* ladrar; **to** ~ **at sb** gritar fuertemente a alguien

woofer ['wuːfər, *Am:* -ɚ] *n* bafle *m*

wool [wʊl] *n no pl* lana *f* ▶**to pull the** ~ **over sb's <u>eyes</u>** dar a alguien gato por liebre

woolen ['wʊlən] *adj Am s.* **woollen**

wool-gathering ['wʊlˌɡæðərɪŋ] *n* **to be** ~ andar distraído

woollen ['wʊlən] *adj* de lana

woolly ['wʊli] I. <-ier, -iest> *adj* **1.** (*made of wool*) de lana **2.** (*wool-like*) lanoso, -a **3.** (*vague*) vago, -a; (*idea, thinking*) impreciso, -a II. <-ies> *n Brit, inf* prenda *f* de lana

wool trade *n* comercio *m* de lana

wooly ['wʊli] <-ier, -iest> *adj Am s.* **woolly**

woozy ['wuːzi] <-ier, -iest> *adj inf* indispuesto, -a

wop [wɒp, *Am:* waːp] *n pej, inf* italiano, -a *m, f*

word [wɜːd, *Am:* wɜːrd] I. *n* **1.** (*unit of language*) palabra *f;* **a** ~ **of Hebrew origin** una voz de origen hebreo; **to be a man/woman of few** ~ ser hombre/mujer de pocas palabras; **to not breathe a** ~ **of sth** no decir ni pío de algo; **to be too ridiculous for** ~s ser tremendamente ridículo; **in other** ~s en otros términos; ~ **for** ~ literalmente **2.** *no pl* (*news*) noticia *f;* (*message*) mensaje *m;* **to get** ~ **of**

sth enterarse de algo; **to have ~ from sb** tener un recado de alguien; **to have ~ that ...** tener conocimiento de que... **3.** *no pl* (*order*) orden *f;* **a ~ of advice** un consejo; **a ~ of warning** una advertencia; **to say the ~** dar la orden; **just say the ~** sólo tienes que pedirlo **4.** *no pl* (*promise*) palabra *f* de honor; **to be a man/woman of one's ~** ser un hombre/una mujer de palabra; **to keep one's ~** cumplir su promesa; **take my ~ for it!** ¡acepta mi palabra! **5.** *no pl* (*statement of facts*) explicación *f* **6.** *pl* MUS (*lyrics*) letra *f* **7.** REL **the Word of God** la palabra de Dios ▶**to have a quick ~ in sb's ear** hablar en privado con alguien; **to not be able to get a ~ in edgeways** *inf* no poder meter baza; **by ~ of mouth** de viva voz; **to put ~s in(to) sb's mouth** atribuir a alguien algo que no dijo; **to take the ~s (right) out of sb's mouth** quitar la palabra de la boca a alguien; **famous last ~s!** *inf* ¡y yo me lo creo!; **to not have a good ~ to say about sb/sth** no poder decir nada bueno sobre alguien/algo; **to put in good ~ for sb** interceder por alguien; **~s fail me!** ¡no tengo palabras!; **from the ~ go** desde el primer momento; **to have ~s with sb** (*quarrel*) discutir con alguien; **mark my ~s!** ¡acuérdate de lo que te digo!; **to mince one's ~s** medir sus palabras; **to not mince one's ~s** no tener pelos en la lengua; **my ~!** ¡caramba! **II.** *vt* expresar

word break *n* LING separación *f* de palabra
word division *n no pl* LING división *f* de palabra
wording *n no pl* **1.** (*words used*) términos *mpl* **2.** (*style*) estilo *m*
wordless ['wɜ:dləs, *Am:* 'wɜ:rd-] *adj* mudo, -a
word order *n no pl* LING orden *m* de las palabras
word-perfect [ˌwɜ:d'pɜ:fɪkt, *Am:* ˌwɜ:rd-'pɜ:rfɪkt] *adj* **to be ~** saber perfectamente su papel
wordplay ['wɜ:dpleɪ, *Am:* 'wɜ:rdpleɪ] *n no pl* juego *m* de palabras
word processing *n no pl* INFOR tratamiento *m* de textos **word processor** *n* INFOR procesador *m* de textos **word wrap** *n no pl* INFOR salto *m* de línea automático
wordy ['wɜ:di, *Am:* 'wɜ:r-] <-ier, iest> *adj pej* farragoso, -a
wore [wɔ:ʳ, *Am:* wɔ:r] *vt, vi pt of* **wear**
work [wɜ:k, *Am:* wɜ:rk] **I.** *n* **1.** *no pl* (*useful activity*) trabajo *m;* **to be hard ~ (doing sth)** (*strenuous*) ser un gran esfuerzo (hacer algo); (*difficult*) ser una tarea difícil (hacer algo); **to set sb to ~** poner a trabajar a alguien; **good ~!** ¡bien hecho! **2.** *no pl* (*employment*) empleo *m;* **to be in/out of ~** estar en activo/en paro **3.** *no pl* (*place of employment*) lugar *m* de trabajo **4.** (*product*) *a.* ART, MUS obra *f;* **~ of reference** libro *m* de consulta **5.** *pl + sing/pl vb* (*factory*) fábrica *f;* **steel ~s** fundición *f* de acero **6.** *pl* TECH (*of a clock*) mecanismo *m*

7. *no pl* PHYS esfuerzo *m* ▶**to have one's ~ cut out to do sth** costarle trabajo a uno hacer algo; **to make short ~ of sb** hacer trizas a alguien; **to make short ~ of sth** despachar algo rápidamente; **to get to ~ on sb** *inf* ponerse a convencer a alguien; **to give sb the ~s** *inf* tratar duro a alguien **II.** *vi* **1.** (*do job*) trabajar; **to ~ abroad** trabajar en el extranjero; **to ~ as sth** trabajar de algo; **to ~ to rule** ECON hacer huelga de celo **2.** (*be busy*) estar ocupado; **to get ~ing** poner manos a la obra; **to ~ hard** ser aplicado; **to ~ to do sth** dedicarse a hacer algo **3.** TECH funcionar; **to get sth to ~** conseguir que algo funcione **4.** (*be successful*) salir adelante; (*plan, tactics*) llevarse a cabo **5.** MED hacer efecto **6.** (*have an effect*) **to ~ against sb/sth** obrar en contra de alguien/algo; **to ~ against a candidate** resultar negativo para un candidato; **to ~ for sb** ser eficaz para alguien; **to ~ both ways** ser un arma de doble filo **7.** (*move*) **to ~ (somewhere)** moverse (hacia algún sitio) **8.** *+ adj* (*become*) **to ~ free** soltarse; **to ~ loose** desprenderse **9.** *liter* (*change expression: sb's face*) moverse; (*contort*) contraerse; (*twitch*) temblar ▶**to ~ like a charm** funcionar de maravilla; **to ~ like a dog** *Am,* **to ~ like a slave** trabajar como un esclavo; **to ~ like a Trojan** *Brit* trabajar como un demonio; **to ~ round to sth** prepararse con tranquilidad para algo **III.** *vt* **1.** (*make sb work*) **to ~ sb hard** hacer trabajar duro a alguien; **to ~ oneself to death** matarse trabajando; **to ~ a forty- -hour week** tener una semana laboral de cuarenta horas **2.** TECH (*operate*) hacer funcionar; **to be ~ed by sth** ser accionado por algo **3.** (*move back and forward*) mover; **to ~ sth backwards and forwards** tirar algo hacia adelante y hacia atrás; **to ~ sth free** liberar algo; **to ~ sth loose** desprender algo; **to ~ one's way along sth** abrirse camino por algo **4.** (*bring about*) producir; (*a cure*) efectuar; (*a miracle*) lograr; **to ~ it** [*o* **things**] **so that ...** arreglárselas para que... *+subj* **5.** (*shape*) tallar; (*bronze, iron*) trabajar **6.** FASHION (*embroider*) bordar **7.** MIN explotar; AGR cultivar **8.** (*pay for by working*) **to ~ one's passage** NAUT costear el viaje trabajando; **to ~ one's way through university** pagarse la universidad trabajando

◆**work away** *vi* trabajar sin parar
◆**work in** *vt* **1.** (*mix in: into a dough*) añadir; (*on one's skin*) penetrar poco a poco **2.** (*include*) introducir; (*fit in*) colocar
◆**work off I.** *vt* **1.** (*counter effects of*) contrarrestar; (*one's anger, frustration*) desahogar; (*stress*) aliviar **2.** (*pay by working*) pagar con el trabajo; (*a debt, loan*) amortizar **II.** *vi* TECH separarse
◆**work on** *vt* (*a car, project*) trabajar sobre; (*accent, fitness, skills*) esforzarse para mejorar; (*assumption, hypothesis*) partir de; (*person*) intentar persuadir a
◆**work out I.** *vt* **1.** (*solve*) resolver; **to work**

things out arreglárselas 2. (*calculate*) calcular
3. (*develop*) desarrollar; (*a settlement, solution*) elaborar; (*decide*) determinar
4. (*understand*) comprender 5. (*complete*)
completar; (*one's contract*) cumplir con 6. to
be worked out (*lode, mine, quarry*) estar
agotado II. *vi* 1. (*give a result: a calculation,
sum*) resultar; (*cheaper, more expensive*) salir
2. (*be resolved*) resolverse 3. (*be successful*)
acabar bien; to ~ for the best salir perfectamente 4. (*do exercise*) entrenarse
◆**work over** *vt inf* dar una paliza a
◆**work up** *vt* 1. (*generate: courage, energy,
enthusiasm*) estimular 2. (*arouse strong feelings*) excitar; to work oneself up emocionarse; to ~ into a frenzy emocionar hasta el
frenesí; to work sb up into a rage sacar a alguien de quicio 3. (*develop*) desarrollar; (*idea,
plan, sketch*) llevar a cabo; (*business*) fomentar; to work one's way up through the firm
ir ascendiendo en la empresa
workable ['wɜːkəbl, *Am:* 'wɜːr-] *adj* 1. (*feasible*) factible; (*compromise, plan*) viable
2. (*able to be manipulated*) que se puede trabajar; AGR (*ground, land*) explotable
workaday ['wɜːkədeɪ, *Am:* 'wɜːr-] *adj* de
todos los días
workbag ['wɜːkbæg, *Am:* 'wɜːrk-] *n* bolsa *f*
de herramientas **workbench** <-es> *n* mesa
f de trabajo **workbook** *n* cuaderno *m* de
ejercicios **work camp** *n* campo *m* de trabajo
workday *n Am s.* **working day**
worker ['wɜːkə', *Am:* 'wɜːrkə'] *n* trabaja-
dor(a) *m(f)*; (*in factory*) obrero, -a *m, f*
work ethic *n* ética *f* del trabajo **workforce**
n + *sing/pl vb* población *f* activa **workhorse**
n bestia *f* de carga **work-in** *n* ECON ocupación
f laboral
working I. *adj* 1. (*employed*) empleado, -a;
(*population*) activo, -a 2. (*pertaining to work*)
de trabajo; (*control*) efectivo, -a; (*day, hour,
week*) laboral 3. (*functioning*) que funciona;
(*moving: model*) móvil; (*part of a machine*)
operativo, -a 4. (*used as basis: theory, hypothesis*) de base; to have a ~ knowledge of sth
tener conocimientos básicos de algo II. *n no pl*
1. (*activity*) actividad *f* 2. (*employment*) trabajo *m*
working class [ˌwɜːkɪŋ'klɑːs, *Am:* 'wɜːr-
kɪŋˌklæs] <-es> *n* the ~ la clase obrera
working-class *adj* obrero, -a; (*background*)
humilde **working day** *n Brit* (*weekday*) día
m laborable; (*time*) jornada *f* laboral
working-out ['wɜːkɪŋˌaʊt, *Am:* 'wɜːrk-] *n*
solución *f*
working-over ['wɜːkɪŋˌəʊvə', *Am:* 'wɜːr-
kɪŋˌoʊvə'] *n inf* paliza *f;* to get a good ~ recibir una buena paliza
workload ['wɜːkləʊd, *Am:* 'wɜːrkloʊd] *n*
(volumen *m* de) trabajo *m;* to have a heavy/
light/unbearable ~ tener mucho/poco/
demasiado trabajo
workman ['wɜːkmən, *Am:* 'wɜːrk-]

<-men> *n* obrero *m*
workmanlike ['wɜːkmənlaɪk, *Am:* 'wɜːrk-]
adj 1. (*showing skill: performance, job*) profesional 2. (*technically sufficient: performance*)
correcto, -a
workmanship ['wɜːkmənʃɪp, *Am:* 'wɜːrk-]
n no pl 1. (*skill in working*) destreza *f* 2. (*work
executed*) trabajo *m* 3. (*quality of work*) confección *f;* **shoddy** ~ mala calidad; of fine ~ de
excelente factura
work of art *n* obra *f* de arte
workout ['wɜːkaʊt, *Am:* 'wɜːrk-] *n* SPORTS
entrenamiento *m*
work permit *n* permiso *m* de trabajo **work-
place** *n* COM lugar *m* de trabajo; safety in the
~ seguridad *f* en el trabajo
works committee *n*, **works council** *n*
comité *m* de empresa
work-sharing ['wɜːkˌʃeərɪŋ, *Am:* 'wɜːrkˌʃe-
rɪŋ] *n* sistema en el cual dos personas comparten un puesto de trabajo
worksheet ['wɜːkʃiːt, *Am:* 'wɜːrk-] *n* hoja *f*
de trabajo
workshop ['wɜːkʃɒp, *Am:* 'wɜːrkʃɑːp] *n*
1. (*repair place*) taller *m* 2. (*meeting for learning*) seminario *m;* **drama** ~ taller de arte dramático
work-shy ['wɜːkʃaɪ, *Am:* 'wɜːrk-] *adj Brit* perezoso, -a
works manager *n* gerente *mf* de fábrica
works outing *n* excursión *f* del personal
workspace ['wɜːkspeɪs, *Am:* 'wɜːrk-] *n*
INFOR área *f* de trabajo **work station** *n* INFOR
estación *f* de trabajo
work-study program *n* SCHOOL, UNIV, COM
programa *m* de estudio del trabajo
worktable ['wɜːkˌteɪbl, *Am:* 'wɜːrk-] *n* mesa
f de trabajo **worktop** *n Brit* (*surface in
kitchen*) encimera *f*
work-to-rule [ˌwɜːktə'ruːl, *Am:* ˌwɜːrk-] *n*
huelga *f* de celo
workweek ['wɜːkwiːk, *Am:* 'wɜːrk-] *n Am*
semana *f* laborable
world [wɜːld, *Am:* 'wɜːrld] *n* 1. *no pl* GEO
mundo *m;* the ~'s population la población
mundial; a ~ authority una autoridad mundial; the ~ champion el campeón del mundo;
the best/worst in the ~ el mejor/peor del
mundo; the tallest man in the ~ el hombre
más alto del mundo; the (whole) ~ over en el
mundo entero; to see the ~ ver mundo; to
travel all over the ~ viajar por todo el mundo
2. (*defined group*) the ~ of dogs/horses el
mundo de los perros/caballos; the animal ~ el
mundo animal; the Christian/Muslim ~ el
mundo cristiano/musulmán; the New/Old/
Third ~ el Nuevo/Viejo/Tercer Mundo ►to
be a ~ of difference between ... existir una
enorme diferencia entre...; to have the ~ at
one's feet tener el mundo a sus pies; all the ~
and her husband/his wife *Brit, inf* ciento y
la madre; the ~ at large el mundo en general;
the ~ is his/her oyster tiene el mundo a sus

pies; **to feel on top of the** ~ estar en el séptimo cielo; **that's the way of the** ~ ¡así es la vida!; **to be for all the** ~ **like ...** ser exactamente como...; **to be ~s apart** ser como la noche y el día; **to have the best of both ~s** nadar y guardar la ropa; **to be dead to the** ~ dormir como un tronco; **to be out of this** ~ *inf* ser fantástico; **it's a small ~!** ¡el mundo es un pañuelo!; **I wouldn't do such a thing for (all) the** ~ no haría algo así por nada del mundo; **to go up in the** ~ *Brit, inf* prosperar; **the ~ to come** REL el más allá; **to come down in the** ~ *Brit, inf* venir a menos; **to live in a ~ of one's own** vivir en su mundo; **to mean (all) the** ~ **to sb** serlo todo para alguien; **to think the** ~ **of sb/sth** tener un alto concepto de alguien/algo; **what/who/how in the** ~ **...?** ¿qué/quién/cómo demonios...?

World Bank *n* **the** ~ el Banco Mundial **world beater** *n* SPORTS campeón, -ona *m, f* mundial **world-class** *adj* de clase mundial **world congress** *n* congreso *m* mundial **World Cup** *n* SPORTS **the** ~ la Copa del Mundo; **the** ~ **Finals** la final de la Copa del Mundo **World Fair** *n* feria *f* mundial

world-famous [ˌwɜːldˈfeɪməs, *Am:* ˈwɜːrldˌfeɪ-] *adj* de fama mundial **world language** *n* lengua *f* universal **worldly** [ˈwɜːldli, *Am:* ˈwɜːrld-] *adj* **1.** (*of physical, practical matters*) material; ~ **goods** posesiones materiales **2.** (*having experience*) mundano, -a; (*manner*) sofisticado, -a; (~) **wise** (*person*) con mucho mundo

world opinion *n* opinión *f* mundial **world population** *n* **the** ~ la población mundial **world power** *n* potencia *f* mundial **world record** *n* SPORTS récord *m* mundial **world-shaking** *adj*, **world-shattering** *adj* **a** ~ **piece of news** una noticia que ha conmocionado al mundo **world view** *n* visión *f* del mundo **world war** *n* HIST guerra *f* mundial **world-weary** [ˌwɜːldˈwɪəri, *Am:* ˈwɜːrldˌwɪri] *adj* hastiado, -a; **to be** [*o* **feel**] ~ estar cansado de la vida

world-wide [ˌwɜːldˈwaɪd, *Am:* ˈwɜːrldˌwaɪd] **I.** *adj* mundial **II.** *adv* por todo el mundo

World Wide Web *n* INFOR Red *f* Mundial **worm** [wɜːm, *Am:* wɜːrm] **I.** *n* gusano *m*; (*insect larva*) oruga *f*; **earth** ~ lombriz *f* ▶**the** ~ **turns** la paciencia tiene un límite **II.** *vt* **1.** (*treat for worms*) desparasitar **2.** (*squeeze slowly through*) **to** ~ **one's way through people** colarse entre la gente; **to** ~ **oneself under sth** deslizarse por debajo de algo **3.** (*gain trust dishonestly*) **to** ~ **oneself into someone's trust** ganarse la confianza de alguien con artimañas **4.** (*obtain dishonestly*) **to** ~ **a secret out of sb** sonsacar un secreto a alguien **III.** *vi* **to** ~ **through the crowd** colarse entre el gentío

worm-eaten [ˈwɜːmˌiːtən, *Am:* ˈwɜːrm-] *adj* (*beam, table, wood*) carcomido, -a; (*fruit*)

picado, -a por los gusanos; (*cloth*) apolillado, -a **worm-hole** [ˈwɜːmhəʊl, *Am:* ˈwɜːrmhoʊl] *n* agujero *m* de lombriz; **the cupboard was full of** ~**s** el armario estaba todo carcomido **wormy** [ˈwɜːmi, *Am:* ˈwɜːr-] <-ier, -iest> *adj* (*full of worms: fruit*) agusanado, -a; (*wood*) carcomido, -a

worn [wɔːn, *Am:* wɔːrn] **I.** *vt, vi pp of* **wear** **II.** *adj* **1.** (*shabby, deteriorated*) desgastado, -a; (*clothing*) raído, -a **2.** (*exhausted: person*) ojeroso, -a **3.** (*overused: expression, news, story*) tópico, -a

worn-out [ˌwɔːnˈaʊt, *Am:* ˌwɔːrn-] *adj* **1.** (*exhausted: person, animal*) rendido, -a **2.** (*used up: clothing*) raído, -a; (*wheel bearings*) desgastado, -a

worried *adj* preocupado, -a; **to be** ~ **about** [*o* **by**] **sth** estar preocupado por algo; **I am** ~ **that he may be angry** tengo miedo de que esté enfadado; **to be** ~ **sick about** [*o* **by**] **sb/sth** estar preocupadísimo por alguien/algo; **with a** ~ **expression** con semblante preocupado **worrisome** [ˈwʌrɪsəm, *Am:* ˈwɜːri-] *adj form* preocupante

worry [ˈwʌri, *Am:* ˈwɜːr-] **I.** <-ies> *n* **1.** (*anxiety, concern*) preocupación *f*; **to be a cause of** ~ **to sb** dar problemas a alguien; **to have a** ~ (*about sth*) estar preocupado (por algo); **do you really have no** ~**s about the future?** ¿no te preocupa el futuro de verdad? **2.** (*trouble*) problema *m*; **financial worries** problemas *fpl* económicos; **it is a great** ~ **to me** me preocupa mucho **II.** *vt* <-ie-, -ing> **1.** (*preoccupy, concern*) preocupar; **she is worried that she might not be able to find another job** tiene miedo de no encontrar otro trabajo; **that doesn't** ~ **me** eso me tiene sin cuidado **2.** (*bother*) molestar **3.** (*pursue and scare*) perseguir; **to** ~ **an animal** correr tras un animal **4.** (*shake around*) **to** ~ **sth** juguetear con algo; **the dog worries the bone** el perro mordisquea el hueso **III.** <-ie-, -ing> *vi* (*be preoccupied, concerned*) **to** ~ (*about sth*) preocuparse (por algo); **don't** ~**!** ¡no te preocupes!; **not to** ~**!** *inf* ¡no pasa nada! **worrying** *adj* preocupante

worse [wɜːs, *Am:* wɜːrs] **I.** *adj comp of* **bad** peor; **to be** ~ **than ...** ser peor que...; **to be even/much** ~ ser aún/mucho peor; **he was none the** ~ **for it** no le había pasado nada; **from bad to** ~ de mal en peor; **to get** ~ **and** ~ ser cada vez peor; **it could have been** ~ podría haber sido peor; **to make matters** ~ **...** por si fuera poco...; **so much the** ~ **for her!** ¡tanto peor para ella!; ~ **luck** *inf* (por) mala suerte; **to get** ~ empeorar; **if he gets any** ~ **...** si se pone peor... **II.** *n no pl* **the** ~ el/la peor; **to change for the** ~ cambiar para mal; **to have seen** ~ haber visto cosas peores; **I don't think any the** ~ **of her** mi opinión sobre ella no ha cambiado; ~ **was to follow** todavía faltaba lo peor **III.** *adv comp of* **badly** peor; **to do sth** ~ **than ...** hacer algo peor que...; **he did**

~ than he was expecting in the exams los exámenes le fueron peor de lo que esperaba; **to be ~ (off)** estar peor

worsen ['wɜːsən, *Am:* 'wɜːr-] *vi, vt* empeorar

worship ['wɜːʃɪp, *Am:* 'wɜːr-] **I.** *vt* <-pp-, *Am:* -p-> **1.** *a.* REL adorar; **to ~ God** rendir culto a Dios; **to ~ money/sex** tener obsesión por el dinero/sexo **2.** (*feel great admiration for*) idolatrar ▶**to ~ the ground sb walks on** besar el suelo que alguien pisa **II.** *vi* <-pp-, *Am:* -p-> REL hacer sus devociones **III.** *n no pl* **1.** (*adoration*) adoración *f;* (*reverence*) veneración *f* **2.** *a.* REL culto *m;* (*religious service*) oficio *m* **3.** POL, LAW **his Worship the Mayor ...** el Excelentísimo Señor alcalde ...; **Your Worship** Su Señoría

worshipper *n* REL adorador(a) *m(f);* **hundreds of ~s attended the ceremony** cientos de fieles asistieron a la ceremonia; **devil ~** satanista *mf*

worst [wɜːst, *Am:* wɜːrst] **I.** *adj superl of* **bad the ~** el/la peor; **the ~ soup I've ever eaten** la peor sopa que he comido (nunca); **the ~ mistake** el error más grave **II.** *adv superl of* **badly** peor; **to be ~ hit/affected by sth** ser los más azotados/afectados por algo **III.** *n no pl* (*most terrible one, time, thing*) **the ~** lo peor; **the ~ of it is that ...** lo peor de todo es que ...; **the ~ is over now** ya ha pasado lo peor; **at ~** en el peor de los casos; **at her ~** en su peor momento; **this problem has shown him at his ~** este problema ha sacado a relucir lo peor de él; **to fear the ~** temerse lo peor; **~ of all** lo peor de todo ▶**if (the) ~ comes to (the) ~** en el peor de los casos; **to get the ~ of it** (*suffer the worst*) llevarse la peor parte

worsted ['wʊstɪd] *n no pl* (*fabric*) estambre *m*

worth [wɜːθ, *Am:* wɜːrθ] **I.** *n no pl* **1.** (*excellence, importance: of a person*) valía *f;* (*of a thing*) valor *m;* **to prove one's ~** demostrar su valía; **to be of great/little ~ to sb** tener gran/poco valor para alguien **2.** (*monetary value*) **a pound's ~ of apples** una libra de manzanas; **4 million pounds ~ of gift items** objetos de regalo por valor de 4 millones de libras; **to get one's money's ~ from sth** sacar partido a algo; **of comparable ~** de precio similar; **a month's/three hour's ~ of work** un mes/tres horas de trabajo **3.** (*wealth*) fortuna *f* **II.** *adj* **1.** *a.* COM, FIN, ECON **to be ~ ...** valer...; **it is ~ about £200 000** está valorado en unas 200 000 libras; **it's ~ a lot to me** tiene mucho valor para mí; **to be ~ millions** *inf* ser millonario **2.** (*significant enough, useful*) **to be ~ ...** merecer...; **to be ~ a mention** ser digno de mención; **it's not ~ arguing about!** ¡no vale la pena discutir por eso!; **it is ~ seeing** es digno de ver; **it's ~ remembering that ...** conviene recordar que...; **it is (well) ~ a listen/visit** merece la pena escucharlo/visitarlo; **it's ~ a try** vale la pena intentarlo ▶**to be ~ sb's while** it isn't ~ my while no me compensa;

to make sth ~ sb's while compensar a alguien por algo; **if a thing is ~ doing, it's ~ doing well** *prov* lo que se hace hay que hacerlo bien *prov;* **to do sth for all one's ~** hacer algo con todas sus fuerzas; **for what it's ~** *inf* por si sirve de algo; **to be (well) ~ it** valer la pena

worthless ['wɜːθləs, *Am:* 'wɜːrθ-] *adj* **1.** (*of no monetary value*) sin ningún valor **2.** (*of no significance, use*) inútil

worthwhile [ˌwɜːθˈhwaɪl, *Am:* ˌwɜːrθ-] *adj* **1.** (*profitable, beneficial*) que vale la pena; **it's not ~ making such an effort** no merece la pena esforzarse tanto; **it isn't financially ~ for me** no me compensa económicamente **2.** (*useful*) útil

worthy ['wɜːði, *Am:* 'wɜːr-] **I.** <-ier, -iest> *adj* **1.** *form* (*admirable*) encomiable; (*principles*) loable; **a ~ cause** una noble causa **2.** (*appropriate for, to*) digno, -a; **to be ~ of sth** ser merecedor de algo; **to be ~ of attention** merecer atención **II.** <-ies> *n iron* (*important person*) personaje *m* ilustre; **the local worthies** las personalidades más destacadas del lugar

would [wʊd] *aux pt of* **will 1.** (*future in the past*) **he said he ~ do it later on** dijo que lo haría más tarde **2.** (*future seeing past in the past*) **we thought they ~ have done it before** pensamos que lo habrían hecho antes **3.** (*intention in the past*) **he said he ~ always love her** dijo que siempre la querría **4.** (*shows possibility*) **I'd go myself, but I'm too busy** iría yo mismo, pero estoy demasiado ocupado; **it ~ have been very boring to do that** habría sido muy aburrido hacer eso **5.** (*conditional*) **what ~ you do if you lost your job?** ¿qué harías si te quedaras sin trabajo?; **I ~ have done it if you'd asked** lo habría hecho si me lo hubieras pedido **6.** (*polite request*) **if you ~ just wait a moment, I'll see if I can find her** espere un momento, por favor, que voy a buscarla; **~ you phone him, please?** ¿me harías el favor de llamarle?; **~ you mind saying that again?** ¿te importaría repetir eso?; **~ you like ...?** ¿te gustaría...?; **~ you like me to come with you?** ¿quieres que vaya contigo? **7.** (*regularity in past*) **they ~ help each other with their homework** solían ayudarse con los deberes **8.** (*stresses as being typical*) **the bus ~ be late when I'm in a hurry** por supuesto, el autobos siempre llega tarde cuando tengo prisa; **he ~ say that, wouldn't he?** era de esperar que lo dijera, ¿no? **9.** (*courteous opinion*) **I ~ imagine that ...** me imagino que...; **I ~n't have thought that ...** nunca habría pensado que... **10.** (*probably*) **the guy on the phone had an Australian accent – that ~ be Tom, I expect** el chico con quien hablé por teléfono tenía acento australiano – debía de ser Tom **11.** (*shows preference*) **I ~ rather have beer** prefiero beber cerveza; **I ~ rather die than do**

that antes morir que hacer eso **12.** (*offering polite advice*) **I ~n't worry, if I were you** yo que tú no me preocuparía **13.** (*asking motives*) **why ~ anyone want to do something like that?** ¿por qué nadie querría hacer algo así? **14.** (*shows a wish*) **ah, ~ I were richer and younger!** ¡ojalá fuera más rico y más joven!; **~ that he were here!** ¡ojalá estuviera aquí!

would-be ['wʊdbi:] *adj* **1.** (*wishing to be*) aspirante; **a ~ politician** un aspirante a político **2.** (*pretending to be*) supuesto, -a

wouldn't [wʊdənt] = **would not** *s.* **would**

wound¹ [waʊnd] *vi, vt pt, pp of* **wind²**

wound² [wu:nd] **I.** *n* herida *f;* **a gunshot/war ~** una herida de bala/guerra; **a leg ~** una herida en la pierna **II.** *vt a. fig* herir

wounded I. *adj a. fig* herido, -a **II.** *npl* **the ~** los heridos

wove [wəʊv, *Am:* woʊv] *vt, vi pt of* **weave**

woven ['wəʊvən, *Am:* 'woʊv-] **I.** *vt, vi pp of* **weave II.** *adj* (*made by weaving*) tejido, -a

wow [waʊ] *inf* **I.** *interj* (*demonstrates surprise, excitement*) ¡caray! **II.** *n* (*hit, popular item*) exitazo *m;* **to be a ~ with the public** ser un exitazo con el público; **I had a ~ of a time** me lo pasé en grande **III.** *vt* (*delight*) **to ~ sb** volver loco a alguien

WPC [dʌblju:ˌpi:'si:] *Brit abbr of* **Woman Police Constable** *mujer policía*

wpm *abbr of* **words per minute** ppm

wraith [reɪθ] *n liter* espectro *m*

wrangle ['ræŋgl] **I.** <-ling> *vi* **1.** (*argue, debate angrily*) discutir; **to ~** (**with sb**) **about sth** discutir (con alguien) por algo **2.** *Am* (*round up cattle*) arrear ganado **II.** *vt Am* (*round up: horses, cattle*) arrear, rodear *CSur, Cuba, Nic, Col, Perú* **III.** *n* (*intricate argument*) riña *f;* **a ~ about sth** una disputa sobre algo

wrap [ræp] **I.** *n* **1.** (*robe-like covering*) bata *f* **2.** (*shawl*) chal *m* **3.** *no pl* (*protective covering material*) envoltorio *m;* **foil ~** papel *m* de aluminio ►**to keep sth under ~s** mantener algo en secreto; **to take the ~s off sth** sacar algo a la luz **II.** *vt* <-pp-> **to ~ sth** (**up**) (**in a blanket**) envolver algo (con una manta); **~ the glasses in plenty of paper** envuelve bien los vasos con papel; **to ~ sth around sth/sb** envolver algo/a alguien con algo; **he ~ped a scarf around his neck** se puso una bufanda; **to ~ one's fingers around sth** agarrar algo con las manos; **to ~ one's arms around sb** estrechar a alguien entre sus brazos; **a matter ~ped in secrecy** un asunto rodeado de misterio ►**to ~ sb** (**up**) **in cotton wool** *Brit* tener a alguien entre algodones

wraparound ['ræpəˌraʊnd] *adj* (*skirt, dress*) cruzado, -a; (*sunglasses*) envolvente

♦**wrap up I.** *vt* <-pp-> **1.** (*completely cover*) envolver; **to wrap oneself/sb up** (**against the cold**) (*dress warmly*) abrigarse (para protegerse del frío) **2.** *inf* (*finish well*) poner fin a; (*deal*) cerrar; (*problem*) acabar con; **that wraps it up for today** eso es todo por hoy **II.** *vi* **1.** (*dress warmly*) abrigarse; **to ~ well/warm** abrigarse bien **2.** (*be absorbed in*) **to be wrapped up in sth** estar absorto en algo; **to be wrapped up in one's work** vivir para el trabajo **3.** (*finish*) terminar **4.** *pej, inf* (*shut up*) cerrar el pico

wrapper ['ræpəʳ, *Am:* -ɚ] *n* **1.** (*packaging*) envoltorio *m;* (*for a book*) sobrecubierta *f* **2.** *Am* (*robe-like covering*) bata *f*

wrapping paper *n* (*plain*) papel *m* de embalar; (*for presents*) papel *m* de regalo

wrath [rɒθ, *Am:* ræθ] *n no pl, liter* (*fury, anger*) ira *f*

wrathful ['rɒθfəl, *Am:* 'ræθ-] *adj liter* iracundo, -a

wreak [ri:k] <-ed, -ed *o* wrought, wrought> *vt form* **1.** (*forcefully cause*) causar; **to ~ damage/havoc** (**on sth**) hacer estragos (de algo) **2.** (*anger*) descargar; **to ~ vengeance on sb** vengarse de alguien

wreath [ri:θ] <wreaths> *pl n* (*of flowers, greenery*) corona *f;* (*of smoke*) espiral *f*

wreathe [ri:ð] *vt liter* **1.** (*gather around*) **to be ~d in sth** estar rodeado de algo; **~d in clouds** envuelto en nubes; **to be ~d in melancholy** estar sumido en la melancolía; **to be ~d in smiles** no dejar de sonreír **2.** (*crown as with a wreath*) coronar **3.** (*intertwine*) entretejer

wreck [rek] **I.** *vt* **1.** (*damage*) destrozar; (*ship*) hundir; (*train*) hacer descarrilar **2.** (*demolish*) derribar **3.** (*hopes, plan*) arruinar; (*chances*) echar por tierra; **to ~ sb's life** destrozar la vida de alguien **II.** *n* **1.** NAUT naufragio *m;* AUTO accidente *m; fig* hundimiento *m;* **the ~ of one's hopes** el fin de las esperanzas **2.** (*ship*) barco *m* hundido; **a ~ of a car/a plane** un coche/un avión siniestrado; **an old ~** un cacharro **3.** *inf* (*any derelict thing*) ruina *f;* (*mess*) caos *m;* **to feel a complete ~** estar hecho polvo; **to be a nervous ~** tener los nervios destrozados

wreckage ['rekɪdʒ] *n no pl* (*of ship, car, plane*) restos *mpl;* (*of building*) escombros *mpl*

wrecker ['rekəʳ, *Am:* -ɚ] *n* **1.** *Am* (*breakdown truck*) camión-grúa *m* **2.** (*person who causes shipwrecks*) provocador(a) *m(f)* de naufragios **3.** (*worker who demolishes houses*) obrero, -a *m, f* de demolición **4.** (*hooligan*) gamberro, -a *m, f*

wren [ren] *n* chochín *m*

Wren [ren] *n Brit, inf:* mujer que pertenece a la marina británica

wrench [rentʃ] **I.** *vt* **1.** (*jerk and twist out*) arrancar; **to ~ sth from sb** arrancar algo a alguien; **to ~ oneself away** soltarse de un tirón **2.** (*injure*) **to ~ one's ankle** torcerse el tobillo; **to ~ one's shoulder** dislocarse el hombro **3.** *fig* (*forcefully take from*) separar; **to ~ sb from sb** separar a alguien de alguien **II.** *n* **1.** (*twisting jerk*) tirón *m*, jalón *m CSur;* **to**

give sb a ~ dar un tirón a alguien **2.** (*injury*) torcedura *f;* **to give one's ankle a** ~ torcerse el tobillo **3.** (*pain caused by a departure*) dolor *m* (*causado por una separación*)*;* **what a ~, seeing you board the plane!** ¡qué doloroso verte subir al avión! **4.** *Am* TECH (*spanner*) llave *f* inglesa

wrestle ['resl] SPORTS **I.** <-ling> *vt* **1.** *a.* SPORTS luchar; **to** ~ **sb** forcejear con alguien; **to** ~ **sb to the ground** luchar con [*o* contra] alguien hasta derribarlo **2.** *fig* lidiar con **II.** <-ling> *vi* luchar; **to** ~ **professionally** dedicarse profesionalmente a la lucha **III.** *n* lucha *f*

wrestler *n* luchador(a) *m(f)*

wrestling *n no pl* SPORTS lucha *f;* **freestyle** ~ lucha libre

wrestling bout *n,* **wrestling match** *n* SPORTS combate *m* de lucha

wretch [retʃ] <-es> *n* **1.** (*unfortunate person*) infeliz *mf;* **a poor** ~ un pobre diablo **2.** (*mean person*) miserable *mf;* (*mischievous person*) sinvergüenza *mf inf*

wretched ['retʃɪd] *adj* **1.** (*miserable, pitiable: life, person*) desdichado, -a; **to be in a** ~ **state** estar en un estado lamentable; (*house, conditions*) miserable **2.** (*despicable*) despreciable **3.** (*expressing annoyance*) **my** ~ **car's broken down again!** ¡este maldito coche se me ha vuelto a estropear! **4.** (*very bad, awful: weather*) horrible; **to feel** ~ (*sick*) estar muy mal; (*depressed*) estar muy abatido

wriggle ['rɪgl] **I.** <-ling> *vi* **1.** (*squirm around*) retorcerse **2.** (*move forward by twisting*) serpentear; **to** ~ **through sth** deslizarse por algo; **to** ~ **out of sth** *fig, inf* escapar de un apuro **II.** <-ling> *vt* (*jiggle back and forth*) menear; (*body, hand, toes*) mover; **to** ~ **one's way along** avanzar serpenteando; **to** ~ **oneself into sth** introducirse con dificultad en algo; **to** ~ (**one's way**) **out of sth** escaquearse de algo **III.** *n* meneo *m;* **with a** ~, **she managed to crawl through the gap** logró deslizarse por el agujero serpenteando

wring [rɪŋ] <wrung, wrung> *vt* **1.** (*twist forcibly*) retorcer; **to** ~ **one's hands** retorcerse las manos; **to** ~ **sb's neck** *inf* retorcer el cuello a alguien **2.** (*twist to squeeze out*) escurrir; **to** ~ **water out of sth** escurrir el agua de algo **3.** (*extract forcibly*) **to** ~ **the truth out of sb** sacar la verdad a alguien **4.** (*cause pain to*) **to** ~ **sb's heart** partirle el corazón a alguien

wringer ['rɪŋəʳ, *Am:* -ɚ] *n* rodillo *m* para escurrir la ropa ►**to put sb through the** ~ *inf* someter a alguien al tercer grado

wrinkle ['rɪŋkl] **I.** *n* (*fold, crease*) arruga *f* ►**to iron the** ~**s out** limar asperezas **II.** <-ling> *vi* (*form folds, creases*) arrugarse; (*apple, fruit*) pasarse **III.** <-ling> *vt* (*make have folds, creases*) arrugar ►**to** ~ **one's brow** fruncir el ceño

wrinkled *adj,* **wrinkly** ['rɪŋkli] *adj* (*clothes, face, skin*) arrugado, -a; (*apple, fruit*) pasado, -a

wrist [rɪst] *n* **1.** ANAT muñeca *f;* **to slash one's** ~**s** cortarse las venas **2.** (*of a garment*) puño *m*

wrist-band ['rɪstbænd] *n* **1.** (*end of sleeve*) puño *m* **2.** (*strap*) correa *f* **3.** (*sweatband*) muñequera *f*

wristlet *n* muñequera *f*

wrist-watch <-es> *n* reloj *m* de pulsera

writ [rɪt] *n* orden *f* judicial; ~ **of summons** notificación *f* de emplazamiento; **to issue a** ~ **against sb** expedir un mandato judicial contra alguien; **to serve a** ~ **on sb** notificar un mandato judicial a alguien

write [raɪt] <wrote, written, writing> **I.** *vt* **1.** escribir; **to** ~ **sth in capital letters** escribir algo con mayúsculas; **to** ~ **a book/a thesis** escribir un libro/una tesis; **he wrote me a poem** me dedicó un poema; **to** ~ **sb a cheque** extender un cheque a alguien **2.** MUS componer; **to** ~ **a song** escribir una canción **3.** INFOR (*save*) guardar; **to** ~ **sth to a disk** grabar algo en un disco ►**to be nothing to** ~ **home about** no ser nada del otro mundo *inf* **II.** *vi* **1.** escribir; **to** ~ **clearly/legibly** escribir con letra clara/legible; **to** ~ **to sb** *Brit,* **to** ~ **sb** *Am* escribir a alguien; **to** ~ **about sth** escribir sobre algo; **to** ~ **for a newspaper** escribir en un periódico **2.** INFOR (*save*) **to** ~ **to sth** grabar en algo

◆**write away** *vi* **to** ~ **for sth** (*brochures, information*) escribir pidiendo algo

◆**write back I.** *vt* **to write** (**sb/sth**) **back** contestar (a alguien/algo) **II.** *vi* contestar

◆**write down** *vt* apuntar

◆**write in I.** *vi* (*send a letter to*) escribir **II.** *vt* **1.** (*insert*) escribir; **to write sth in a space** escribir algo en un espacio; **just write your name in** – **you can fill the rest of the form in later** escriba sólo su nombre – después podrá rellenar el resto del formulario **2.** LAW (*put in: clause*) incluir **3.** TV, CINE (*character*) añadir

◆**write off I.** *vi* (*send away to ask for*) **to** ~ **for** (*brochures, information*) solicitar por escrito **II.** *vt* **1.** (*give up doing: attempt*) abandonar; (*project*) dar por perdido **2.** (*abandon as no good*) **to write sth/sb off as useless** descartar algo/a alguien como inútil **3.** FIN (*debt*) cancelar **4.** *Brit* AUTO (*destroy beyond repair*) destrozar; (*consider beyond repair*) declarar siniestro total

◆**write out** *vt* **1.** (*put into writing*) escribir **2.** (*copy*) copiar **3.** (*fill in*) rellenar; **to write a cheque out to sb** extender un cheque a alguien **4.** (*remove from*) suprimir; **to write sb out of a will** desheredar a alguien

◆**write up** *vt* poner por escrito; (*article, report, thesis*) redactar; **to** ~ **a concert** escribir una crítica sobre un concierto

write-in ['raɪtɪn] *adj Am* POL **a** ~ **candidate** un candidato cuyo nombre debe añadir el votante en la papeleta

write-off ['raɪtɒf] *n* **1.** *Brit* **to be a complete** ~ (*car*) ser declarado siniestro total; (*project,* *marriage*) ser un fracaso **2.** FIN cancelación *f* de una deuda

write-protected ['raɪtprə'tektəd] *adj* INFOR protegido, -a contra escritura

writer ['raɪtəʳ, *Am:* -t̬ə·] *n* **1.** (*person*) escritor(a) *m(f);* ~ **of children's books** autor(a) *m(f)* de libros infantiles **2.** INFOR **CD-ROM/ DVD** ~ grabador *m* de CD-ROM/DVD

write-up ['raɪtʌp] *n* ART, THEAT, MUS crítica *f*

writhe [raɪð] <writhing> *vi* **1.** (*squirm and twist around*) retorcerse; **to** ~ (**around**) **in pain** retorcerse de dolor **2.** (*be uncomfortable: with horror*) estremecerse; (*with embarrassment*) sentirse violento; **to make sb** ~ hacer pasar a alguien por una situación incómoda

writing ['raɪtɪŋ, *Am:* -t̬ɪŋ] *n no pl* **1.** (*handwriting*) letra *f;* **in** ~ por escrito; **to put sth in** ~ poner algo por escrito; **there was some** ~ **in the margin of the page** había algo escrito en el margen de la página **2.** *a.* LIT el escribir; **she likes** ~ le encanta escribir **3.** LIT, THEAT (*process*) redacción *f;* **creative** ~ escritura *f* creativa **4.** LIT, THEAT (*written work*) obra *f;* **women's** ~ literatura *f* escrita por mujeres **5.** LIT (*style*) estilo *m* ►**the** ~ **is on the wall (for the campaign)** (la campaña) tiene los días contados

writing desk *n* escritorio *m* **writing-pad** *n* bloc *m* **writing-paper** *n* papel *m* de carta

written I. *vt, vi pp of* **write** II. *adj* (*recorded in writing*) escrito, -a ►**to have guilt** ~ **all over one's face** llevar la culpa escrita en la cara; **the** ~ **word** la palabra escrita

wrong [rɒŋ, *Am:* rɑːŋ] I. *adj* **1.** (*not right: answer*) incorrecto, -a; **to be** ~ **about sth** equivocarse en algo; **to be** ~ **about sb** juzgar mal a alguien; **he is** ~ **in thinking that ...** se equivoca si piensa que...; **to be in the** ~ **place** estar mal colocado; **to be plainly** ~ estar completamente equivocado; **to get the** ~ **number** equivocarse de número; **sorry,** ~ **number!** lo siento, se ha equivocado (de número); **to go the** ~ **direction** tomar el camino equivocado; **to prove sb** ~ demostrar que alguien se equivoca **2.** (*not appropriate*) inoportuno, -a; **to do/say the** ~ **thing** hacer/ decir lo que no se debe; **she's the** ~ **person for the job** no es la persona adecuada para el trabajo; **this is the** ~ **time to ...** no es el momento oportuno para...; **the** ~ **side of town** una mala zona de la ciudad; **she got in with the** ~ **crowd** se junto con quien no le convenía **3.** (*bad*) **is there anything** ~**?** ¿te pasa algo?; **what's** ~ **with you today?** ¿qué te pasa hoy?; **there's nothing** ~ **with your stomach** su estómago está perfectamente; **something's** ~ **with the television** el televisor no funciona bien **4.** LAW, REL mal; **it is** ~ **to do that** está mal hacer eso; **it was** ~ **of him (to do that)** ha hecho muy mal (en hacer eso); **what's** ~ **with that?** ¿qué hay de malo en ello? ►**to fall into the** ~ **hands** caer en manos

equivocadas; **the** ~ **side** el revés; **to go down the** ~ **way** (*food, drink*) bajar por mal sitio II. *adv* **1.** (*incorrectly*) incorrectamente; **to do sth** ~ hacer algo mal; **to get sth** ~ equivocarse en algo; **to get it** ~ comprender mal; **you got it** ~ – **it's Maria who's coming, not Marina** no lo has entendido – es María quien viene, no Marina; **don't get me** ~ no me malinterpretes; **to go** ~ equivocarse; (*stop working*) estropearse, descomponerse *Méx;* (*fail*) salir mal; **after 500 m turn to the left, you can't go** ~ siga recto 500 m y gire a la izquierda, no tiene pérdida **2.** (*in a morally reprehensible way*) mal; **to do sth** ~ hacer algo mal III. *n* **1.** *no pl a.* LAW, REL mal *m;* (**to know**) **right from** ~ saber distinguir entre lo que está bien y lo que está mal; **to put sb in the** ~ echar la culpa a alguien; **to do sb no** ~ no hacer nada malo a alguien **2.** (*unjust action*) injusticia *f;* **to do sb (a)** ~ (**in doing sth**) portarse mal con alguien (al hacer algo); **to right a** ~ enderezar un entuerto; **to suffer a** ~ sufrir una injusticia ►**to do** ~ obrar mal; **he can do no** ~ es incapaz de hacer nada malo; **to be in the** ~ (*not right, mistaken*) estar equivocado; (*do something bad*) actuar mal IV. *vt form* **to** ~ **sb** (*treat unjustly*) ser injusto con alguien; (*judge unjustly*) juzgar mal a alguien

wrongdoer ['rɒŋˌduːəʳ, *Am:* 'rɑːŋˌduːə·] *n* malhechor(a) *m(f)* **wrongdoing** *n no pl* maldad *f;* LAW delito *m;* **to accuse sb of** ~ acusar a alguien de comportamiento ilícito

wrongful *adj* **1.** (*unfair*) injusto, -a **2.** LAW (*unlawful: arrest*) ilegal; (*dismissal*) improcedente

wrong-headed *adj pej* (*person*) cerril; (*concept, idea, plan*) desatinado, -a

wrongly *adv* mal; (*spell*) incorrectamente; (*believe, state*) erróneamente; (*accuse, convict*) injustamente

wrote [rəʊt, *Am:* roʊt] *vi, vt pt of* **write**

wrought [rɔːt, *Am:* rɑːt] I. *vt pt, pp of* **work** III.4., 5., **wreak** II. *adj form* (*crafted*) trabajado, -a; (*metal*) labrado, -a

wrought iron *n no pl* hierro *m* forjado

wrought-up [rɔːt'ʌp] *adj* nervioso, -a; **to be/ get** ~ (**about sth/sb**) estar/ponerse nervioso (por algo/alguien)

wrung [rʌŋ] *vt pt, pp of* **wring**

wry [raɪ] <wrier, wriest *o* wryer, wryest> *adj* **1.** (*dry and ironic: comments, humour*) cáustico, -a; **a** ~ **smile** una sonrisa irónica **2.** (*showing dislike*) **to make a** ~ **face** torcer el gesto

WSW *abbr of* west-southwest OSO

wt *n abbr of* weight peso *m*

WW *n abbr of* World War Guerra *f* Mundial

WWF *n abbr of* World Wildlife Fund Fundación *f* Mundial para la Naturaleza

WWW *n abbr of* World Wide Web INFOR WWW *f*

X

X, x [eks] I. *n* 1. X, x *f;* ~ **for Xmas** *Brit,* ~ **for X** *Am* X de xilófono 2. MAT (*unknown number*) x *f* 3. (*used in place of name*) Mr/Mrs/Ms ~ el Sr./la Sra. X 4. (*symbol for kiss*) un beso; **all my love, Katy** ~~~ besos, Katy 5. (*cross symbol*) cruz *f;* ~ **marks the spot** el punto está marcado con una cruz II. *vt Am* (*delete*) **to ~ (out) sth** tachar algo

X-certificate ['eksːsəˌtɪfɪkət, *Am:* ˌeksːsə'tɪf-] *adj* **an ~ film** una película X

X-chromosome ['eksˌkrəʊməsəʊm] *n* cromosoma *m* X

xenophobia [ˌzenəʊ'fəʊbiə, *Am:* -ə'foʊ-] *n no pl* xenofobia *f*

xenophobic [ˌzenəʊ'fəʊbɪk, *Am:* -ə'foʊ-] *adj* xenófobo, -a

Xerox®, xerox ['zɪərɒks, *Am:* 'zɪraːks] I. *n* (*photocopy*) fotocopia *f* II. *vt* (*photocopy*) fotocopiar; **a ~ed copy of the document** una fotocopia del documento

XL *adj abbr of* **extra large** XL

Xmas ['krɪstməs, 'eksməs, *Am:* 'krɪs-] *n abbr of* **Christmas** Navidad *f*

X-rated ['eksˌreɪtɪd, *Am:* -ˌt̬ɪd] *adj Am s.* **X-certificate**

X-ray ['eksreɪ] I. *n* 1. (*photo*) radiografía *f;* ~**s** rayos *mpl* X 2. *no pl* (*hospital department*) radiología *f* II. *vt* radiografiar; **to ~ sth/sb** hacer una radiografía de algo/a alguien

xylophone ['zaɪləfəʊn, *Am:* -foʊn] *n* MUS xilófono *m*

Y

Y, y [waɪ] *n* 1. Y, y *f;* ~ **for Yellow** *Brit,* ~ **for Yoke** *Am* Y de yema 2. MAT (*unknown quantity*) y *f*

y. *abbr of* **year** a.

yacht [jɒt, *Am:* jaːt] I. *n* 1. (*for pleasure*) yate *m* 2. (*for racing*) velero *m;* ~ **club** club *m* náutico; ~ **race** regata *f* II. *vi* 1. (*sail in a yacht*) navegar 2. (*race in a yacht*) participar en una regata

yachting *n no pl* 1. (*sailing in yachts*) navegación *f* de recreo 2. (*racing in yachts*) navegación *f* a vela; **to go ~** navegar

yachtsman ['jɒtsmən, *Am:* 'jaːts-] <-men> *n* (*yacht owner*) dueño *m* de un yate; (*yacht sailor*) regatista *m*

yack [jæk] *vi inf* cotorrear

yak [jæk] I. *n* yak *m* II. *vi* cotorrear

yam [jæm] *n* 1. (*plant, vegetable*) ñame *m* 2. *Am* (*sweet potato*) batata *f,* camote *m AmL*

yank [jæŋk] I. *vt inf* **to ~ sth** tirar de algo, jalar de algo *AmL* II. *vi inf* **to ~ (on sth)** tirar (de algo), jalar (de algo); **she ~ed at his hair** le

tiró del pelo III. *n inf* tirón *m,* jalón *m AmL;* **to give sth a ~** dar un tirón [*o* jalón *AmL*] a algo
♦**yank out** *vt* (*remove forcefully*) sacar de un tirón; **to ~ a tooth** arrancar un diente

Yank [jæŋk] *n,* **Yankee** ['jæŋki] *n pej, inf* yanqui *mf,* gringo, -a *m, f AmL*

yap [jæp] I. <-pp-> *vi* 1. (*bark*) ladrar 2. *inf* (*talk continuously*) cotorrear II. *n* 1. (*bark*) ladrido *m* 2. *pej, inf* (*foolish talk*) cotorreo *m*

yard¹ [jaːd, *Am:* jaːrd] *n* 1. (*3 feet*) yarda *f* (*0,91 m*); **square ~** yarda cuadrada; **it's about a hundred ~s down the road** está a unas cien yardas de aquí; ~**s long** *fig* muy largo 2. NAUT verga *f*

yard² [jaːd, *Am:* jaːrd] *n* 1. (*enclosed paved area: of a house, school, prison*) patio *m* 2. *Am* (*garden*) jardín *m* 3. (*work area*) taller *m;* **shipbuilding ~** astillero *m* 4. (*outside area used for storage*) almacén *m;* **wood ~** depósito *m* de madera 5. (*enclosure for livestock*) corral *m* 6. **the Yard** Scotland Yard *m*

yardstick ['jaːdstɪk, *Am:* 'jaːrd-] *n* 1. (*measuring tool*) vara *f* que mide una yarda 2. (*standard*) criterio *m*

yarn [jaːn, *Am:* jaːrn] I. *n* 1. *no pl* (*thread*) hilo *m* 2. (*story*) cuento *m;* **to spin a ~** inventarse una historia II. *vi* inventar historias

yaw [jɔː, *Am:* jaː] AVIAT, NAUT, TECH I. *vi* (*move sideways: car*) dar bandazos; (*boat*) guiñar II. *n* (*sideways movement: of a car*) bandazo *m;* (*of a boat*) guiñada *f*

yawl [jɔːl, *Am:* jaːl] *n* yola *f*

yawn [jɔːn, *Am:* jaːn] I. *vi* 1. (*show tiredness*) bostezar 2. *fig, liter* (*open wide*) abrirse II. *n* 1. (*sign of tiredness*) bostezo *m* 2. *inf* (*boring thing*) plomo *m fig;* **it was a ~** fue un rollo

yawning *adj* 1. (*bored: audience*) que bosteza 2. (*wide and deep: chasm, crater*) enorme; **there's a ~ gap between ... and ...** hay un abismo entre... y...

yd *abbr of* **yard(s)** yarda *f*

yea [jeɪ] I. *adv* HIST (*yes*) sí II. *n* voto *m* a favor; **the ~s and the nays** los votos a favor y los votos en contra

yeah [jeə] *adv inf* (*yes*) sí; **oh ~!** *iron* (*indicating disbelief*) ¡no me digas!; ~, ~, **we've heard that one before** ¡sí, sí, eso ya lo hemos oído otras veces!

year [jɪəʳ, *Am:* jɪr] *n* 1. (*twelve months*) año *m;* ~ **of birth** año de nacimiento; ~ **in,** ~ **out** año tras año; **fiscal ~** FIN ejercicio *f* fiscal; **leap ~** año bisiesto; **all** (**the**) ~ **round** (*durante*) todo el año; **every other ~** cada dos años; **happy new ~!** ¡feliz año nuevo!; **last/next ~** el año pasado/que viene; **£5000 a year** 5000 libras al año; **the ~ when ...** el año en que...; **this ~** este año; **for his ~s** para su edad; **I'm eight ~s old** tengo ocho años; ~**s ago** hace años; **I haven't seen her for ~s** hace muchísimo que no la veo; **it's taken me ~s to ...** he tardado años en...; **it's been ~s since we had a summer as good as this one** hacía años que no teníamos tan buen tiempo en verano; **it'll be ~s before...** pasarán años hasta que...; **over the ~s** con el tiempo **2.** SCHOOL, UNIV curso *m;* **the academic ~** el año académico; **she was in my ~ at college** estaba en mi promoción ► **(since) the ~ dot** *Brit, Aus* (desde) el año de la pera; **to put ~s on sb** avejentar a alguien; **to take ~s off sb** quitar años (de encima) a alguien

yearbook ['jɪəbʊk, *Am:* 'jɪr-] *n* anuario *m*

yearling ['jɪəlɪŋ, *Am:* 'jɪr-] I. *adj* (*colt*) de un año; (*calf, goat, sheep*) añal II. *n* (*colt*) potro *m* de un año; (*year-old calf, goat, sheep*) añal *m*

year-long [ˌjɪə'lɒŋ, *Am:* 'jɪrlɑːŋ] *adj* que dura un año

yearly I. *adj* (*happening every year*) anual; **on a ~ basis** cada año II. *adv* (*every year*) anualmente; **to take place ~** tener lugar cada año; **twice ~** dos veces al año

yearn [jɜːn, *Am:* jɜːrn] *vi* (*long*) **to ~ to do sth** ansiar hacer algo; **to ~ after sth** anhelar algo; **to ~ for sth/sb** añorar algo/a alguien

yearning *n no pl* anhelo *m;* **~ for sth** anhelo de algo; **to have a ~ to do sth** tener ansias de hacer algo

yeast [jiːst] *n no pl* levadura *f*

yeasty <-ier, -iest> *adj* de levadura

yell [jel] I. *n* **1.** (*loud shout*) chillido *m;* **to give a ~** dar un grito; **a ~ of laughter** una carcajada **2.** *Am* (*chant*) grito para animar a un equipo II. *vi* (*shout loudly*) chillar; **to ~ at sb** (**to do sth**) gritar a alguien (que haga algo); **to ~ for sb** llamar a alguien a gritos; **to ~ for help** pedir ayuda a gritos III. *vt* (*shout loudly*) gritar

yellow ['jeləʊ, *Am:* -oʊ] I. *adj* **1.** (*colour*) amarillo; **golden ~** amarillo canario; **to turn** [*o* **go**] **~** ponerse amarillo **2.** *pej, inf* (*cowardly*) cobarde II. *n* amarillo *m;* **~ of an egg** *Am* yema *f* de huevo III. *vi, vt* amarillear(se)

yellow-belly ['jeləʊˌbeli, *Am:* -oʊ-] <-ies> *n pej, inf* gallina *mf* **yellow dog** *n Am, pej* canalla *mf* **yellow fever** *n* MED fiebre *f* amarilla

yellowish ['jeləʊɪʃ, *Am:* -oʊ-] *adj* amarillento, -a

yellow jack *n* **1.** *Am* (*yellow fever*) fiebre *f* amarilla **2.** NAUT bandera *f* amarilla

yellowness ['jeləʊnəs, *Am:* -oʊ-] *n* amarillez *f*

Yellow Pages® *npl* **the ~** las páginas amarillas

yellowy *adj* amarillento, -a

yelp [jelp] I. *vi* (*cry: a dog*) aullar; (*a person*) gritar; **to ~ with pain** gritar de dolor II. *n* (*cry: of animal*) aullido *m;* (*of person*) grito *m*

Yemen ['jemən] *n* Yemen *m*

Yemeni ['jeməni] I. *adj* yemení II. *n* yemení *mf*

yen[1] [jen] *inv n* FIN yen *m*

yen[2] [jen] *n inf* (*strong desire*) deseo *m;* (**to have) a ~ for sth/sb** morirse por algo/al-

guien; (**to have) a ~ to do sth** tener unas ganas locas de hacer algo

yeoman ['jəʊmən, *Am:* 'joʊ-] <-men> *n Brit* HIST **1.** (*freeholder*) pequeño terrateniente *m* **2.** MIL soldado *m* de caballería; **Yeoman of the Guard** alabardero *m* de la Casa Real ► **to do ~('s) service** prestar valiosos servicios

yeomanry ['jəʊmənri, *Am:* 'joʊ-] *n no pl* HIST **1.** (*freeholders collectively*) **the ~** los pequeños terratenientes **2.** MIL (*cavalry*) cuerpo *m* voluntario de caballería

yep [jep] *adv inf* (*yes*) sí

Yerevan [jerəvɑːn] *n* Yerevan *m*

yes [jes] I. *adv* **1.** (*affirmative answer*) sí; **~, sir/madam** sí, señor/señora; **~ please** sí, por favor; **to answer ~ to sth** contestar que sí a algo; **I'm not a very good cook – ~** no soy muy buen cocinero – sí que lo eres; **~ indeed** por supuesto que sí; **~, of course!** ¡claro que sí! **2.** (*as question*) **~?** TEL ¿sí?; **Johnny? – yes? – can I have a word?** Johnny – ¿qué? – ¿puedo hablar contigo? **3.** (*indicating doubt*) **oh ~?** ¿de verdad? II. <yeses> *n* (*statement in favour*) sí *m* III. <-ss-> *vt Am* (*say yes to*) **to ~ sb** decir que sí a alguien

yes-man ['jesmæn] <-men> *n pej* servil *m inf*

yesterday ['jestədeɪ, *Am:* -tɚ-] I. *adv* ayer; **~ morning** ayer por la mañana, ayer en la mañana *AmL*, ayer a la mañana *CSur;* **the day before ~** anteayer II. *n no pl* **1.** el día de ayer **2.** (*the past*) el pasado

yet [jet] I. *adv* **1.** (*up to a particular time*) todavía; **it's too early ~ to ...** aún es muy pronto para...; **not ~** aún no; **she hasn't told him ~** todavía no se lo ha contado; **as ~** hasta ahora; **the issue is as ~ undecided** todavía no se ha decidido la cuestión; **her best/worst film ~** la mejor/peor película que ha dirigido hasta ahora; **have you finished ~?** ¿ya has terminado?; **isn't supper ready ~?** ¿aún no está lista la cena?; **can you see the lighthouse ~?** ¿ya ves el faro?; **the best is ~ to come** aún queda lo mejor; **there's a great deal of work ~ to be done** todavía queda mucho por hacer **2.** (*in addition*) **~ more food** todavía más comida; **~ again** otra vez más **3.** + *comp* (*even*) **~ bigger/more beautiful** aún más grande/bonito **4.** (*despite that*) sin embargo **5.** (*in spite of everything*) a pesar de todo; **you wait, I'll get you ~, you bastard!** ¡ya te atraparé, canalla!; **you'll do it ~** algún día lo conseguirás; **we're not giving up, we'll get there ~** no nos hemos rendido, llegaremos allí a pesar de todo II. *conj* con todo, a pesar de todo

yew [juː] *n* (*tree and wood*) tejo *m*

YHA *n abbr of* **Youth Hostel Association** *Asociación de Albergues Juveniles*

Yiddish ['jɪdɪʃ] I. *adj* yiddish II. *n no pl* yiddish *m*

yield [jiːld] I. *n* **1.** (*amount produced*) rendimiento *m;* AGR producción *f* **2.** COM, FIN (*profits*) beneficio *m;* (*interest*) interés *m;* fixed/variable ~ renta *f* fija/variable II. *vt* 1. (*provide: results*) dar; (*information*) proporcionar 2. AGR (*produce*) producir 3. COM, FIN (*profit*) proporcionar; (*interest*) devengar *form;* to ~ 8 % dar un (interés del) 8 % 4. (*give up*) to ~ ground ceder terreno; to ~ responsibility delegar responsabilidades; to ~ sth to the enemy entregar algo al enemigo III. *vi* 1. AGR, COM, FIN ser productivo 2. (*give way*) to ~ to sth/sb ceder ante algo/alguien; to ~ to temptation ceder a la tentación; it ~ed because of the weight cedió al peso 3. (*surrender*) rendirse 4. (*give priority*) to ~ to sth/sb dar prioridad a algo/alguien 5. AUTO ceder el paso

◆**yield up** *vt* (*give up*) entregar; (*secret*) revelar

yielding *adj* 1. (*pliable: a material, a substance*) flexible; (*soft*) blando, -a 2. *fig* (*compliant*) complaciente

yippee [jɪˈpiː, *Am:* ˈjɪpiː] *interj inf* yupi

YMCA [ˌwaɪemsiˈeɪ] *abbr of* **Young Men's Christian Association** Asociación Cristiana de Jóvenes

yob [jɒb, *Am:* jɑːb] *n,* **yobbo** [ˈjɒbəʊ, *Am:* ˈjɑːboʊ] <-s> *n Brit, Aus, inf* gamberro, -a *m, f*

yodel, yodle [ˈjəʊdəl, *Am:* ˈjoʊ-] MUS I. <-ll-, *Am:* -l-> *vi* (*sing*) cantar al estilo tirolés II. *vt* (*sing*) cantar al estilo tirolés III. *n* (*yodelled song*) canción *f* tirolesa

yoga [ˈjəʊgə, *Am:* ˈjoʊ-] *n no pl* yoga *m*

yoghourt [ˈjɒgət, *Am:* ˈjoʊgət] *n* yogur *m*

yogi [ˈjəʊgi, *Am:* ˈjoʊ-] *n* yogui *mf*

yogurt [ˈjɒgət, *Am:* ˈjoʊgət] *n s.* **yoghourt**

yoke [jəʊk, *Am:* joʊk] I. *n* 1. *a. fig* AGR yugo *m;* to throw off the ~ liberarse del yugo 2. FASHION canesú *m* II. *vt* 1. AGR (*fit with yoke*) uncir; to ~ an animal (to sth) enyuntar un animal (a algo) 2. *fig* (*combine*) to ~ two things together ligar una cosa a otra

yokel [ˈjəʊkl, *Am:* ˈjoʊ-] *n iron, pej* (*country person*) paleto, -a *m, f,* pajuerano, -a *m, f Arg, Bol, Urug*

yolk [jəʊk, *Am:* joʊk] *n* yema *f* (de huevo)

Yom Kippur [ˌjɒmkɪˈpʊəˌ, *Am:* jɑːmˈkɪpəˌ] *n* Yom Kip(p)ur *m*

yonder [ˈjɒndəˌ, *Am:* ˈjɑːndəˌ] *dial* I. *adv* (*over there*) allá II. *adj* (*situated over there*) aquel, aquella; *pl:* aquellos, aquellas

yore [jɔːˌ, *Am:* jɔːr] *n no pl, liter* in (the) days of ~ antaño

you [juː] *pron pers* 1. *2nd pers sing* tu, vos *CSur; pl:* vosotros, -as, ustedes *AmL;* I see ~ te/os veo; do ~ see me? ¿me ves/veis?; I love ~ te/os amo; it is for ~ es para ti/vosotros; older than ~ mayor que tú/vosotros; if I were ~ si yo fuera tú/vosotros; ~'re my brother tú eres mi hermano 2. (*2nd person sing, polite form*) usted; *pl:* ustedes; ~'ve a car usted tiene/ustedes tienen un coche; ~'re going to Paris va/van a París; older than ~ mayor que usted/ustedes

you'd [juːd] = you would *s.* **would**

you'll [juːl] = you will *s.* **will**

young [jʌŋ] I. *adj* 1. *a.* GEO (*not old*) joven; ~ children niños *mpl* pequeños; a ~ man un joven; sb's ~er brother/son el hermano/hijo menor de alguien; the ~er generation la nueva generación; the night is still ~ la noche es joven 2. (*junior*) old Mr Brown and ~ Mr Brown el Sr. Brown padre y el Sr. Brown hijo 3. (*young-seeming: appearance, clothes*) juvenil; to be ~ at heart ser joven de espíritu; she is ~ for her age parece más joven de lo que es; to be ~ looking tener un aspecto juvenil 4. (*pertaining to youth: love*) de juventud; in my ~(er) days cuando era joven ▶you're only ~ once! ¡sólo se es joven una vez! II. *n pl* 1. (*young people*) the ~ los jóvenes 2. ZOOL (*offspring*) crías *fpl;* with ~ preñada

young people *npl,* **young persons** *npl* los jóvenes

youngster [ˈjʌŋkstəˌ, *Am:* -stəˌ] *n* joven *mf*

your [jɔːˌ, *Am:* jʊr] *adj pos* 1. *2nd pers sing* tu(s); *pl:* vuestro(s), vuestra(s) 2. (*2nd pers sing and pl: polite form*) su(s)

you're [jɔːˌ, *Am:* jʊr] = you are *s.* **be**

yours [jɔːz, *Am:* jʊrz] *pron pos* 1. *sing:* (el) tuyo, (la) tuya, (los) tuyos, (las) tuyas; *pl:* (el) vuestro, (la) vuestra, (los) vuestros, (las) vuestras, el de ustedes *AmL,* la de ustedes *AmL;* this glass is ~ este vaso es tuyo/vuestro 2. *polite form* (el) suyo, (la) suya, (los) suyos, (las) suyas; ~ faithfully le saluda atentamente

yourself [jɔːˈself, *Am:* jʊr-] *pron reflexive* 1. *sing:* te; *emphatic:* tú (mismo, misma); *after prep:* ti (mismo, misma) 2. *polite form:* se; *emphatic:* usted (mismo, misma); *after prep:* sí (mismo, misma)

yourselves *pron reflexive* 1. os, se *AmL; emphatic, after prep:* vosotros (mismos), vosotras (mismas), ustedes (mismos, mismas) *AmL* 2. *polite form:* se; *emphatic:* ustedes (mismos/mismas); *after prep:* sí (mismos, mismas)

youth [juːθ] *n* 1. *no pl* (*period when young*) juventud *f;* during her (early) ~ en su (primera) juventud; he is a friend of my ~ es un amigo de juventud 2. (*young man*) joven *m* 3. *no pl* (*young people*) jóvenes *mpl;* the ~ la juventud; ~ culture cultura *f* juvenil

youth centre *n,* **youth club** *n* club *m* juvenil

youthful [ˈjuːθfəl] *adj* 1. (*young-looking*) juvenil; ~ appearance aspecto *m* juvenil 2. (*typical of the young*) de la juventud 3. (*young*) joven

youth hostel *n* albergue *m* juvenil **Youth Training Scheme** *n Brit* POL plan *m* de empleo juvenil **youth unemployment** *n* paro *m* juvenil

you've [juːv] = you have *s.* **have**

yowl [jaʊl] I. *vi* (*howl: dog*) aullar; (*cat*) maullar; (*person*) dar alaridos II. *n* (*howl: of a dog*) aullido *m;* (*of a cat*) maullido *m;* (*of a person*)

alarido *m*
yo-yo ['jəʊjəʊ, *Am:* 'joʊjoʊ] *n* (*toy*) yo-yo *m*
yr *pron abbr of* **your**
yuan [ˌjuːˈæn] *n* FIN yuan *m*
yucky [jʌki] *adj inf* asqueroso, -a
Yugoslav ['juːgəʊslɑːv, *Am:* 'juːgoʊslɑːv] *adj, n s.* **Yugoslavian**
Yugoslavia ['juːgəʊˈslɑːviə, *Am:* -goʊ'-] *n* HIST Yugoslavia *f*
Yugoslavian I. *adj* yugoslavo, -a II. *n* yugoslavo, -a *m, f*
yukky ['jʌki] <-ier, -iest> *adj s.* **yucky**
Yukon Territory ['juːkɒn 'terɪtəri, *Am:* 'juːkɑːn 'terətɔːri] *n* Territorio *m* del Yukón
yule log ['juːlˌlɒg, *Am:* 'juːlˌlɑːg] *n* 1. (*log*) tronco *que se quema en la chimenea en Navidad* 2. GASTR tronco *m* de Navidad
Yuletide ['juːltaɪd] *n liter* Navidades *fpl*
yummy ['jʌmi] *adj* de rechupete
yuppie ['jʌpi] *n* yuppy *mf*

Z

Z, z [zed, *Am:* ziː] *n* Z, z *f;* ~ **for Zebra** Z de Zaragoza ►**to** catch **some** ~s *Am, inf* echar una cabezada, apolillar un poco *RíoPl*
Zaire [zaɪˈrə, *Am:* -ˈɪr] *n* Zaire *m*
Zairean [zaɪˈrən] I. *adj* zaireño, -a II. *n* zaireño, -a *m, f*
Zambia ['zæmbiə] *n* Zambia *f*
Zambian ['zæmbiən] I. *adj* zambiano, -a II. *n* zambiano, -a *m, f*
zany ['zeɪni] <-ier, -iest> *adj inf* (*person*) chiflado, -a; (*clothing*) estrafalario, -a; (*idea*) loco, -a
zap [zæp] I. <-pp-> *vt* 1. *inf* (*destroy*) liquidar 2. *inf* (*send fast*) enviar rápidamente II. <-pp-> *vi inf* 1. **to** ~ **somewhere** ir a un sitio en un momento; **to** ~ **through sth** despachar algo 2. (*change channels*) hacer zapping III. *interj inf* zas
zapping [zæpɪŋ] *n inf* zapping *m*
zeal [ziːl] *n no pl* celo *m;* **religious** ~ fervor *m* religioso; **reforming** ~ afán *m* reformista
zealot ['zelət] *n* fanático, -a *m, f*
zealous ['zeləs] *adj* ferviente; **to be** ~ **in sth** poner gran celo en algo
zebra ['zebrə, *Am:* 'ziːbrə] *n* cebra *f*
zebra crossing *n Brit, Aus* (*pedestrian crossing*) paso *m* de cebra
zenith ['zenɪθ, *Am:* 'ziːnɪθ] <-es> *n* 1. ASTR (*highest point*) cenit *m* 2. (*most successful point*) apogeo *m;* **to be at the** ~ **of sth** estar en el apogeo de algo
zero ['zɪərəʊ, *Am:* 'zɪroʊ] I. <-s *o* -es> *n* cero *m;* **below** ~ METEO bajo cero; **to be a** ~ ser un cero a la izquierda II. *adj* cero *inv;* ~ **growth** crecimiento *m* cero; ~ **hour** hora *f* cero; ~ **visibility** visibilidad *f* nula; **my**

chances are ~ no tengo ninguna posibilidad III. *vt* (*return to zero: device*) poner a cero
♦**zero in on** *vi* 1. (*aim precisely*) apuntar a 2. (*focus on*) **to** ~ **sth** centrarse en algo
zero-rated *adj* FIN no sujeto a IVA **zero tolerance** *n* policy of ~ política *f* de mano dura
zest [zest] *n no pl* 1. (*enthusiastic energy*) entusiasmo *m;* **to do sth with** ~ hacer algo con brío; ~ **for life** ganas *fpl* de vivir 2. (*charm, interest*) gracia *f;* **the story lacks** ~ a la historia le falta garra 3. (*rind*) corteza *f;* lemon/orange ~ corteza de limón/naranja; grated lemon ~ raspadura *f* de limón
zigzag ['zɪgzæg] I. *n* (*crooked line*) zigzag *m* II. *adj* (*crooked*) zigzagueante; (*pattern*) en zigzag III. <-gg-> *vi* zigzaguear
Zimbabwe [zɪmˈbɑːbweɪ] *n* Zimbabue *m*
Zimbabwean [zɪmˈbɑːbwiən] I. *adj* zimbabuo, -a II. *n* zimbabuo, -a *m, f*
zinc [zɪŋk] *n no pl* cinc *m*, zinc *m*
zip [zɪp] I. *n* 1. (*fastener*) cremallera *f,* cierre *m* relámpago *Arg;* **to do up a** ~ subir una cremallera 2. *no pl, inf* (*vigour*) brío *m* 3. (*whistle*) silbido *m* 4. *no pl, Am, inf* (*nothing*) nada; **I know** ~ **about that** no tengo ni idea de eso II. <-pp-> *vt* **to** ~ **a bag** cerrar la cremallera de un bolso; **to** ~ **a dress** subir la cremallera de un vestido; **to** ~ **sth open** abrir la cremallera de algo; **to** ~ **sth shut** cerrar la cremallera de algo; **to** ~ **sth up** subir la cremallera de algo; **will you** ~ **me up?** ¿me subes la cremallera? III. <-pp-> *vi* **to** ~ **in/past** entrar/pasar volando; **the days** ~**ped by** los días pasaron volando
zip code *n Am* código *m* postal
zip-fastener *n Brit,* **zipper** ['zɪpəʳ, *Am:* -ɚ] *n Am* cremallera *f,* cierre *m* relámpago *Arg*
zippy ['zɪpi] <-ier, -iest> *adj inf* (*fast: car*) veloz; (*energetic*) enérgico, -a
zither ['zɪðəʳ, *Am:* -ɚ] *n* cítara *f*
zloty ['zlɒti, *Am:* 'zlɔːti] *n* zloty *m*
zodiac ['zəʊdiæk, *Am:* 'zoʊ-] *n no pl* zodíaco *m*
zombie ['zɒmbi, *Am:* 'zɑːm-] *n* zombi *mf*
zonal ['zəʊnəl, *Am:* 'zoʊ-] *adj* zonal; **a** ~ **division** una división en zonas
zone [zəʊn, *Am:* zoʊn] I. *n* zona *f;* **nuclear-free** ~ zona desnuclearizada; **time** ~ zona *f* horaria; **frigid/temperate/torrid** ~ METEO zona glacial/templada/tórrida II. *vt* 1. (*divide*) dividir en zonas 2. ADMIN, LAW (*designate*) **to** ~ **an area for residential use** declarar un lugar zona residencial
zoning *n no pl* ADMIN, LAW zonificación *f*
zoo [zuː] *n* zoo *m*
zoological [ˌzəʊəʊ'lɒdʒɪkəl, *Am:* ˌzoʊə'lɑː-dʒɪ-] *adj* zoológico, -a; ~ **gardens** (parque *m*) zoológico *m*
zoologist [zuˈɒlədʒɪst, *Am:* zoʊˈɑːlə-] *n* zoólogo, -a *m, f*
zoology [zuˈɒlədʒi, *Am:* zoʊˈɑːlə-] *n no pl* zoología *f*
zoom [zuːm] I. *n* 1. PHOT zoom *m* 2. AVIAT su-

bida *f* vertical **3.** (*buzz*) zumbido *m* **II.** *vt* **1.** AVIAT (*plane*) hacer subir verticalmente **2.** PHOT enfocar con el zoom **III.** *vi* **1.** *inf* (*move very fast*) ir zumbando; **to ~ away** salir pitando; **to ~ past** pasar volando **2.** (*plane*) elevarse abruptamente; (*costs, sales*) dispararse *inf*

◆**zoom in** *vi* PHOT enfocar en primer plano; **to ~ on sth/sb** enfocar algo/a alguien en primer plano

◆**zoom out** *vi* PHOT cambiar a un plano general

zoom lens *n* zoom *m*

zucchini [zʊˈkiːni, *Am:* zuː-] <-(s)> *n inv*, *Am* calabacín *m*, calabacita *f AmL*

Apéndice II

Supplement II

Los verbos regulares e irregulares españoles
Spanish regular and irregular verbs

Abreviaturas:

pret. ind.	pretérito indefinido
subj. fut.	subjuntivo futuro
subj. imp.	subjuntivo imperfecto
subj. pres.	subjuntivo presente

Verbos regulares que terminan en -ar, -er e -ir

hablar

presente	imperfecto	pret. ind.	futuro	
hablo	hablaba	hablé	hablaré	**gerundio**
hablas	hablabas	hablaste	hablarás	hablando
habla	hablaba	habló	hablará	
hablamos	hablábamos	hablamos	hablaremos	**participio**
habláis	hablabais	hablasteis	hablaréis	hablado
hablan	hablaban	hablaron	hablarán	

condicional	subj. pres.	subj. imp.	subj. fut.	imperativo
hablaría	hable	hablara/-ase	hablare	
hablarías	hables	hablaras/-ases	hablares	habla
hablaría	hable	hablara/-ase	hablare	hable
hablaríamos	hablemos	habláramos /-ásemos	habláremos	hablemos
hablaríais	habléis	hablarais/-aseis	hablareis	hablad
hablarían	hablen	hablaran/-asen	hablaren	hablen

comprender

presente	imperfecto	pret. ind.	futuro	
comprendo	comprendía	comprendí	comprenderé	**gerundio**
comprendes	comprendías	comprendiste	comprenderás	comprendiendo
comprende	comprendía	comprendió	comprenderá	
comprendemos	comprendíamos	comprendimos	comprenderemos	**participio**
comprendéis	comprendíais	comprendisteis	comprenderéis	comprendido
comprenden	comprendían	comprendieron	comprenderán	

condicional	subj. pres.	subj. imp.	subj. fut.	imperativo
comprendería	comprenda	comprendiera /-iese	comprendiere	
comprenderías	comprendas	comprendieras/ -ieses	comprendieres	comprende
comprendería	comprenda	comprendiera /-iese	comprendiere	comprenda
comprenderíamos	comprendamos	comprendiéramos /-iésemos	comprendiéremos	comprendamos
comprenderíais	comprendáis	comprendierais /-ieseis	comprendiereis	comprended
comprenderían	comprendan	comprendiera /-iesen	comprendieren	comprendan

recibir

presente	imperfecto	pret. ind.	futuro	
recibo	recibía	recibí	recibiré	**gerundio**
recibes	recibías	recibiste	recibirás	recibiendo
recibe	recibía	recibió	recibirá	
recibimos	recibíamos	recibimos	recibiremos	**participio**
recibís	recibíais	recibisteis	recibiréis	recibido
reciben	recibían	recibieron	recibirán	

condicional	subj. pres.	subj. imp.	subj. fut.	imperativo
recibiría	reciba	recibiera/-iese	recibiere	
recibirías	recibas	recibieras/-ieses	recibieres	recibe
recibiría	reciba	recibiera/-iese	recibiere	reciba
recibiríamos	recibamos	recibiéramos /-iésemos	recibiéremos	recibamos
recibiríais	recibáis	reciebierais/-ieseis	recibiereis	recibid
recibirían	reciban	recibieran/-iesen	recibieren	reciban

Verbos con cambios vocálicos

\<e → ie\> pensar

presente	imperfecto	pret. ind.	futuro	
pienso	pensaba	pensé	pensaré	**gerundio**
piensas	pensabas	pensaste	pensarás	pensando
piensa	pensaba	pensó	pensará	
pensamos	pensábamos	pensamos	pensaremos	**participio**
pensáis	pensabais	pensasteis	pensaréis	pensado
piensan	pensaban	pensaron	pensarán	

condicional	subj. pres.	subj. imp.	subj. fut.	imperativo
pensaría	piense	pensara/-ase	pensare	
pensarías	pienses	pensaras/-ases	pensares	piensa
pensaría	piense	pensara/-ase	pensare	piense
pensaríamos	pensemos	pensáramos /-ásemos	pensáremos	pensemos
pensaríais	penséis	pensarais /-aseis	pensareis	pensad
pensarían	piensen	pensaran/-asen	pensaren	piensen

\<o → ue\> contar

presente	imperfecto	pret. ind.	futuro	
cuento	contaba	conté	contaré	**gerundio**
cuentas	contabas	contaste	contarás	contando
cuenta	contaba	contó	contará	
contamos	contábamos	contamos	contaremos	**participio**
contáis	contabais	contasteis	contaréis	contado
cuentan	contaban	contaron	contarán	

condicional	subj. pres.	subj. imp.	subj. fut.	imperativo
contaría	cuente	contara/-ase	contare	
contarías	cuentes	contaras/-ases	contares	cuenta
contaría	cuente	contara/-ase	contare	cuente
contaríamos	contemos	contáramos /-ásemos	contáremos	contemos
contaríais	contéis	contarais/-aseis	contareis	contad
contarían	cuenten	contaran	contaren	cuenten

<u → ue>   jugar

presente	imperfecto	pret. ind.	futuro	
juego	jugaba	jugé	jugaré	**gerundio**
juegas	jugabas	jugaste	jugarás	jugando
juega	jugaba	jugó	jugará	
jugamos	jugábamos	jugamos	jugaremos	**participio**
jugáis	jugabais	jugasteis	jugaréis	jugado
juegan	jugaban	jugaron	jugarán	

condicional	subj. pres.	subj. imp.	subj. fut.	imperativo
jugaría	juegue	jugara/-ase	jugare	
jugarías	juegues	jugaras/-ases	jugares	juega
jugaría	juegue	jugara/-ase	jugare	juegue
jugaríamos	juguemos	jugáramos/-ásemos	jugáremos	juguemos
jugaríais	juguéis	jugarais/-aseis	jugareis	jugad
jugarían	jueguen	jugaran/-asen	jugaren	jueguen

<e → i>   pedir

presente	imperfecto	pret. ind.	futuro	
pido	pedía	pedí	pediré	**gerundio**
pides	pedías	pediste	pedirás	pidiendo
pide	pedía	pidió	pedirá	
pedimos	pedíamos	pedimos	pediremos	**participio**
pedís	pedíais	pedisteis	pediréis	pedido
piden	pedían	pidieron	pedirán	

condicional	subj. pres.	subj. imp.	subj. fut.	imperativo
pediría	pida	pidiera/-iese	pidiere	
pedirías	pidas	pidieras/-ieses	pidieres	pide
pediría	pida	pidiera/-iese	pidiere	pida
pediríamos	pidamos	pidiéramos /-iésemos	pidiéremos	pidamos
pediríais	pidáis	pidierais/-ieseis	pidiereis	pedid
pedirían	pidan	pidieran/-iesen	pidieren	pidan

Verbos con cambios ortográficos

<c → qu>   atacar

presente	imperfecto	pret. ind.	futuro	
ataco	atacaba	ataqué	atacaré	**gerundio**
atacas	atacabas	atacaste	atacarás	atacando
ataca	atacaba	atacó	atacará	
atacamos	atacábamos	atacamos	atacaremos	**participio**
atacáis	atacabais	atacasteis	atacaréis	atacado
atacan	atacaban	atacaron	atacarán	

condicional	subj. pres.	subj. imp.	subj. fut.	imperativo
atacaría	ataque	atacara/-ase	atacare	
atacarías	ataques	atacaras/-ases	atacares	ataca
atacaría	ataque	atacara/-ase	atacare	ataque
atacaríamos	ataquemos	atacáramos/-ásemos	atacáremos	ataquemos
atacaríais	ataquéis	atacarais/-aseis	atacareis	atacad
atacarían	ataquen	atacaran/-asen	atacaren	ataquen

<g → gu>   pagar

presente	imperfecto	pret. ind.	futuro	
pago	pagaba	pagué	pagaré	**gerundio**
pagas	pagabas	pagaste	pagarás	pagando
paga	pagaba	pagó	pagará	
pagamos	pagábamos	pagamos	pagaremos	**participio**
pagáis	pagabais	pagasteis	pagaréis	pagado
pagan	pagaban	pagaron	pagarán	

condicional	subj. pres.	subj. imp.	subj. fut.	imperativo
pagaría	pague	pagara/-ase	pagare	
pagarías	pagues	pagaras/-ases	pagares	paga
pagaría	pague	pagara/-ase	pagare	pague
pagaríamos	paguemos	pagáramos/-ásemos	pagáremos	paguemos
pagaríais	paguéis	pagarais/-aseis	pagareis	pagad
pagarían	paguen	pagaran/-asen	pagaren	paguen

<z → c> cazar

presente	imperfecto	pret. ind.	futuro	
cazo	cazaba	cacé	cazaré	**gerundio**
cazas	cazabas	cazaste	cazarás	cazando
caza	cazaba	cazó	cazará	
cazamos	cazábamos	cazamos	cazaremos	**participio**
cazáis	cazabais	cazasteis	cazaréis	cazado
cazan	cazaban	cazaron	cazarán	

condicional	subj. pres.	subj. imp.	subj. fut.	imperativo
cazaría	cace	cazara/-ase	cazare	
cazarías	caces	cazaras/-ases	cazares	caza
cazaría	cace	cazara/-ase	cazare	cace
cazaríamos	cacemos	cazáramos/-ásemos	cazáremos	cacemos
cazaríais	cacéis	cazarais/-aseis	cazareis	cazad
cazarían	cacen	cazaran/-asen	cazaren	cacen

<gu → gü> averiguar

presente	imperfecto	pret. ind.	futuro	
averiguo	averiguaba	averigüé	averiguaré	**gerundio**
averiguas	averiguabas	averiguaste	averiguarás	averiguando
averigua	averiguaba	averiguó	averiguará	
averiguamos	averiguábamos	averiguamos	averiguaremos	**participio**
averiguáis	averiguabais	averiguasteis	averiguaréis	averiguado
averiguan	averiguaban	averiguaron	averiguarán	

condicional	subj. pres.	subj. imp.	subj. fut.	imperativo
averiguaría	averigüe	averiguara/-ase	averiguare	
averiguarías	averigües	averiguaras/-ases	averiguares	averigua
averiguaría	averigüe	averiguara/-ase	averiguare	averigüe
averiguaríamos	averigüemos	averiguáramos /-ásemos	averiguáremos	averigüemos
averiguaríais	averigüéis	averiguarais/-aseis	averiguareis	averiguad
averiguarían	averigüen	averiguaran/-asen	averiguaren	averigüen

<c → z>   vencer

presente	imperfecto	pret. ind.	futuro	
venzo	vencía	vencí	venceré	**gerundio**
vences	vencías	venciste	vencerás	venciendo
vence	vencía	venció	vencerá	
vencemos	vencíamos	vencimos	venceremos	**participio**
vencéis	vencíais	vencisteis	venceréis	vencido
vencen	vencían	vencieron	vencerán	

condicional	subj. pres.	subj. imp.	subj. fut.	imperativo
vencería	venza	venciera/-iese	venciere	
vencerías	venzas	vencieras/-ieses	vencieres	vence
vencería	venza	venciera/-iese	venciere	venza
venceríamos	venzamos	venciéramos /-iésemos	venciéremos	venzamos
venceríais	venzáis	vencierais/-ieseis	venciereis	venced
vencerían	venzan	vencieran/-iesen	vencieren	venzan

<g → j>   coger

presente	imperfecto	pret. ind.	futuro	
cojo	cogía	cogí	cogeré	**gerundio**
coges	cogías	cogiste	cogerás	cogiendo
coge	cogía	cogió	cogerá	
cogemos	cogíamos	cogimos	cogeremos	**participio**
cogéis	cogíais	cogisteis	cogeréis	cogido
cogen	cogían	cogieron	cogerán	

condicional	subj. pres.	subj. imp.	subj. fut.	imperativo
cogería	coja	cogiera/-iese	cogiere	
cogerías	cojas	cogieras/-ieses	cogieres	coge
cogería	coja	cogiera/-iese	cogiere	coja
cogeríamos	cojamos	cogiéramos /-iésemos	cogiéremos	cojamos
cogeríais	cojáis	cogierais/-ieseis	cogiereis	coged
cogerían	cojan	cogieran/-iesen	cogieren	cojan

\<gu → g\>   distinguir

presente	imperfecto	pret. ind.	futuro	
distingo	distinguía	distinguí	distinguiré	**gerundio**
distingues	distinguías	distinguiste	distinguirás	distinguiendo
distingue	distinguía	distinguió	distinguirá	
distinguimos	distinguíamos	distinguimos	distinguiremos	**participio**
distinguís	distinguíais	distinguisteis	distinguiréis	distinguido
distinguen	distinguían	distinguieron	distinguirán	

condicional	subj. pres.	subj. imp.	subj. fut.	imperativo
distinguiría	distinga	distinguiera/-iese	distinguiere	
distinguirías	distingas	distinguieras/-ieses	distinguieres	distingue
distinguiría	distinga	distinguiera/-iese	distinguiere	distinga
distinguiríamos	distingamos	distinguiéramos /iésemos	distinguiéremos	distingamos
distinguiríais	distingáis	distinguierais/-ieseis	distinguiereis	distinguid
distinguirían	distingan	distinguieran/-iesen	distinguieren	distingan

\<qu → c\>   delinquir

presente	imperfecto	pret. ind.	futuro	
delinco	delinquía	delinquí	delinquiré	**gerundio**
delinques	delinquías	delinquiste	delinquirás	delinquiendo
delinque	delinquía	delinquió	delinquirá	
delinquimos	delinquíamos	delinquimos	delinquiremos	**participio**
delinquís	delinquíais	delinquisteis	delinquiréis	delinquido
delinquen	delinquían	delinquieron	delinquirán	

condicional	subj. pres.	subj. imp.	subj. fut.	imperativo
delinquiría	delinca	delinquiera/-iese	delinquiere	
delinquirías	delincas	delinquieras/-ieses	delinquieres	delinque
delinquiría	delinca	delinquiera/-iese	delinquiere	delinca
delinquiríamos	delincamos	delinquiéramos /-iésemos	delinquiéremos	delincamos
delinquiríais	delincáis	delinquierais/-ieseis	delinquiereis	delinquid
delinquirían	delincan	delinquieran/-iesen	delinquieren	delincan

Verbos con desplazamiento en la acentuación

<1. pres: envío>   enviar

presente	imperfecto	pret. ind.	futuro	
envío	enviaba	envié	enviaré	**gerundio**
envías	enviabas	enviaste	enviarás	enviando
envía	enviaba	envió	enviará	
enviamos	enviábamos	enviamos	enviaremos	**participio**
enviáis	enviabais	enviasteis	enviaréis	enviado
envían	enviaban	enviaron	enviarán	

condicional	subj. pres.	subj. imp.	subj. fut.	imperativo
enviaría	envíe	enviara/-iase	enviare	
enviarías	envíes	enviaras/-iases	enviares	envía
enviaría	envíe	enviara/-iase	enviare	envíe
enviaríamos	enviemos	enviáramos /-iásemos	enviáremos	enviemos
enviaríais	enviéis	enviarais/-iaseis	enviareis	enviad
enviarían	envíen	enviaran/-iasen	enviaren	envíen

<1. pres: continúo>   continuar

presente	imperfecto	pret. ind.	futuro	
continúo	continuaba	continué	continuaré	**gerundio**
continúas	continuabas	continuaste	continuarás	continuando
continúa	continuaba	continuó	continuará	
continuamos	continuábamos	continuamos	continuaremos	**participio**
continuáis	continuabais	continuasteis	continuaréis	continuado
continúan	continuaban	continuaron	continuarán	

condicional	subj. pres.	subj. imp.	subj. fut.	imperativo
continuaría	continúe	continuara/-ase	continuare	
continuarías	continúes	continuaras/-ases	continuares	continúa
continuaría	continúe	continuara/-ase	continuare	continúe
continuaríamos	continuemos	continuáramos /-ásemos	continuáremos	continuemos
continuaríais	continuéis	continuarais/-aseis	continuareis	continuad
continuarían	continúen	continuaran/-asen	continuaren	continúen

Verbos que pierden la *i* átona

<3. pret: tañó>   tañer

presente	imperfecto	pret. ind.	futuro	
taño	tañía	tañí	tañeré	**gerundio**
tañes	tañías	tañiste	tañerás	tañendo
tañe	tañía	tañó	tañerá	
tañemos	tañíamos	tañimos	tañeremos	**participio**
tañéis	tañíais	tañisteis	tañeréis	tañido
tañen	tañían	tañeron	tañerán	

condicional	subj. pres.	subj. imp.	subj. fut.	imperativo
tañería	taña	tañera/-ese	tañere	
tañerías	tañas	tañeras/-eses	tañeres	tañe
tañería	taña	tañera/-ese	tañere	taña
tañeríamos	tañamos	tañéramos/-ésemos	tañéremos	tañamos
tañeríais	tañáis	tañerais/-eseis	tañereis	tañed
tañerían	tañan	tañeran/-esen	tañeren	tañan

<3. pret: gruñó>   gruñir

presente	imperfecto	pret. ind.	futuro	
gruño	gruñía	gruñí	gruñiré	**gerundio**
gruñes	gruñías	gruñiste	gruñirás	gruñendo
gruñe	gruñía	gruñó	gruñirá	
gruñimos	gruñíamos	gruñimos	gruñiremos	**participio**
gruñís	gruñíais	gruñisteis	gruñiréis	gruñido
gruñen	gruñían	gruñeron	gruñirán	

condicional	subj. pres.	subj. imp.	subj. fut.	imperativo
gruñiría	gruña	gruñera/-ese	gruñere	
gruñirías	gruñas	gruñeras/-eses	gruñeres	gruñe
gruñiría	gruña	gruñera/-ese	gruñere	gruña
gruñiríamos	gruñamos	gruñéramos /-ésemos	gruñéremos	gruñamos
gruñiríais	gruñáis	gruñerais/-eseis	gruñereis	gruñid
gruñirían	gruñan	gruñeran/-esen	gruñeren	gruñan

Los verbos irregulares

abolir

presente	subj. pres.	imperativo	
–	–		**gerundio**
–	–	–	aboliendo
–	–	–	
abolimos	–	–	**participio**
abolís	–	abolid	abolido
–	–	–	

abrir

participio:	abierto

adquirir

presente	imperativo	
adquiero		**gerundio**
adquieres	adquiere	adquiriendo
adquiere	adquiera	
adquirimos	adquiramos	**participio**
adquirís	adquirid	adquirido
adquieren	adquieran	

agorar

presente		
agüero	**gerundio**	
agüeras	agorando	
agüera		
agoramos	**participio**	
agoráis	agorado	
agüeran		

ahincar

presente	imperfecto	pret. ind.	imperativo	
ahínco	ahincaba	ahinqué		**gerundio**
ahíncas	ahincabas	ahincaste	ahínca	ahincando
ahínca	ahincaba	ahincó	ahinque	
ahincamos	ahincábamos	ahincamos	ahinquemos	**participio**
ahincáis	ahincabais	ahincasteis	ahincad	ahincado
ahíncan	ahincaban	ahincaron	ahinquen	

airar

presente

aíro	**gerundio**
aíras	airando
aíra	
airamos	**participio**
airáis	airado
aíran	

andar

presente	pret. ind.	
ando	anduve	**gerundio**
andas	anduviste	andando
anda	anduvo	
andamos	anduvimos	**participio**
andáis	anduvisteis	andado
andan	anduvieron	

asir

presente	imperativo	
asgo		**gerundio**
ases	ase	asiendo
ase	asga	
asimos	asgamos	**participio**
asís	asid	asido
asen	asgan	

aullar

presente	imperativo	
aúllo		**gerundio**
aúllas	aúlla	aullando
aúlla	aúlle	
aullamos	aullemos	**participio**
aulláis	aullad	aullado
aúllan	aúllen	

avergonzar

presente	pret. ind.	imperativo	
avergüenzo	avergoncé		**gerundio**
avergüenzas	avergonzaste	avergüenza	avergonzando
avergüenza	avergonzó	avergüence	
avergonzamos	avergonzamos	avergüencemos	**participio**
avergonzáis	avergonzasteis	avergonzad	avergonzado
avergüenzan	avergonzaron	avergüencen	

caber

presente	pret. ind.	futuro	condicional	
quepo	cupe	cabré	cabría	**gerundio**
cabes	cupiste	cabrás	cabrías	cabiendo
cabe	cupo	cabrá	cabría	
cabemos	cupimos	cabremos	cabríamos	**participio**
cabéis	cupisteis	cabréis	cabríais	cabido
caben	cupieron	cabrán	cabrían	

caer

presente	pret. ind.	
caigo	caí	**gerundio**
caes	caíste	cayendo
cae	cayó	
caemos	caímos	**participio**
caéis	caísteis	caído
caen	cayeron	

ceñir

presente	pret. ind.	imperativo	
ciño	ceñí		**gerundio**
ciñes	ceñiste	ciñe	ciñendo
ciñe	ciñó	ciña	
ceñimos	ceñimos	ciñamos	**participio**
ceñís	ceñisteis	ceñid	ceñido
ciñen	ciñeron	ciñan	

cernir

presente	imperativo	
cierno		**gerundio**
ciernes	cierne	cerniendo
cierne	cierna	
cernimos	cernamos	**participio**
cernís	cernid	cernido
ciernen	ciernan	

cocer

presente	imperativo	
cuezo		**gerundio**
cueces	cuece	cociendo
cuece	cueza	
cocemos	cozamos	**participio**
cocéis	coced	cocido
cuecen	cuezan	

colgar

presente	pret. ind.	imperativo	
cuelgo	colgué		**gerundio**
cuelgas	colgaste	cuelga	colgando
cuelga	colgó	cuelgue	
colgamos	colgamos	colgamos	**participio**
colgáis	colgasteis	colgad	colgado
cuelgan	colgaron	cuelguen	

crecer

presente	imperativo	
crezco		**gerundio**
creces	crece	creciendo
crece	crezca	
crecemos	crezcamos	**participio**
crecéis	creced	crecido
crecen	crezcan	

dar

presente	pret. ind.	subj. pres.	subj. imp.	subj. fut.
doy	di	dé	diera/-ese	diere
das	diste	des	dieras/-eses	dieres
da	dio	dé	diera/-ese	diere
damos	dimos	demos	diéramos/-ésemos	diéremos
dais	disteis	deis	dierais/-eseis	diereis
dan	dieron	den	dieran/-esen	dieren

imperativo

da	**gerundio**
dé	dando
demos	
dad	**participio**
den	dado

decir

presente	imperfecto	pret. ind.	futuro	
digo	decía	dije	diré	**gerundio**
dices	decías	dijiste	dirás	diciendo
dice	decía	dijo	dirá	
decimos	decíamos	dijimos	diremos	**participio**
decís	decíais	dijisteis	diréis	dicho
dicen	decían	dijeron	dirán	

condicional	subj. pres.	subj. imp.	subj. fut.	imperativo
diría	diga	dijera/-ese	dijere	
dirías	digas	dijeras/-eses	dijeres	di
diría	diga	dijera/-ese	dijere	diga
diríamos	digamos	dijéramos/-ésemos	dijéremos	digamos
diríais	digáis	dijerais/-eseis	dijereis	decid
dirían	digan	dijeran/-esen	dijeren	digan

desosar

presente	imperativo	
deshueso		**gerundio**
deshuesas	deshuesa	desosando
deshuesa	deshuese	
desosamos	desosemos	**participio**
desosáis	desosad	desosado
deshuesan	deshuesen	

dormir

presente	pret. ind.	imperativo	
duermo	dormí		**gerundio**
duermes	dormiste	duerme	durmiendo
duerme	durmió	duerma	
dormimos	dormimos	durmamos	**participio**
dormís	dormisteis	dormid	dormido
duermen	durmieron	duerman	

elegir

presente	pret. ind.	imperativo	
elijo	elegí		**gerundio**
eliges	elegiste	elige	eligiendo
elige	eligió	elija	
elegimos	elegimos	elijamos	**participio**
elegís	elegisteis	elegid	elegido
eligen	eligieron	elijan	

empezar

presente	pret. ind.	imperativo	
empiezo	empecé		**gerundio**
empiezas	empezaste	empieza	empezando
empieza	empezó	empiece	
empezamos	empezamos	empecemos	**participio**
empezáis	empezasteis	empezad	empezado
empiezan	empezaron	empiecen	

enraizar

presente	pret. ind.	imperativo	
enraízo	enraicé		**gerundio**
enraízas	enraizaste	enraíza	enraizando
enraíza	enraizó	enraíce	
enraizamos	enraizamos	enraicemos	**participio**
enraizáis	enraizasteis	enraizad	enraizado
enraízan	enraizaron	enraícen	

erguir

presente	pret. ind.	subj. pres	subj. imp.	subj. fut.
yergo	erguí	irga/yerga	irguiera/-ese	irguiere
yergues	erguiste	irgas/yergas	irguieras/-eses	irguieres
yergue	irguió	irga/yerga	irguiera/-ese	irguiere
erguimos	erguimos	irgamos	irgiéramos /-ésemos	irguiéremos
erguís	erguisteis	irgáis	irguierais/-eseis	irguiereis
yerguen	irguieron	irgan/yergan	irguieran/-esen	irguieren

imperativo

yergue	**gerundio**
yerga	irguiendo
yergamos	
erguid	**participio**
yergan	erguido

errar

presente	pret. ind.	imperativo	
yerro	erré		**gerundio**
yerras	erraste	yerra	errando
yerra	erró	yerre	
erramos	erramos	erremos	**participio**
erráis	errasteis	errad	errado
yerran	erraron	yerren	

escribir

participio :	escrito

estar

presente	imperfecto	pret. ind.	futuro	
estoy	estaba	estuve	estaré	**gerundio**
estás	estabas	estuviste	estarás	estando
está	estaba	estuvo	estará	
estamos	estábamos	estuvimos	estaremos	**participio**
estáis	estabais	estuvisteis	estaréis	estado
están	estaban	estuvieron	estarán	

condicional	subj. pres.	subj. imp.	subj. fut.	imperativo
estaría	esté	estuviera/-ese	estuviere	
estarías	estés	estuvieras/-eses	estuvieres	está
estaría	esté	estuviera/-ese	estuviere	esté
estaríamos	estemos	estuviéramos /-ésemos	estuviéremos	estemos
estaríais	estéis	estuvierais/-eseis	estuviereis	estad
estarían	estén	estuvieran/-esen	estuvieren	estén

forzar

presente	pret. ind.	imperativo	
fuerzo	forcé		**gerundio**
fuerzas	forzaste	fuerza	forzando
fuerza	forzó	fuerce	
forzamos	forzamos	forcemos	**participio**
forzáis	forzasteis	forzad	forzado
fuerzan	forzaron	fuercen	

fregar

presente	pret. ind.	imperativo	
friego	fregué		**gerundio**
friegas	fregaste	friega	fregando
friega	fregó	friegue	
fregamos	fregamos	freguemos	**participio**
fregáis	fregasteis	fregad	fregado
friegan	fregaron	frieguen	

freír

presente	pret. ind.	imperativo	
frío	freí		**gerundio**
fríes	freíste	fríe	friendo
fríe	frió	fría	
freímos	freímos	friamos	**participio**
freís	freísteis	freíd	freído
fríen	frieron	frían	frito

haber

presente	pret. ind.	futuro	condicional	subj. pres.
he	hube	habré	habría	haya
has	hubiste	habrás	habrías	hayas
ha	hubo	habrá	habría	haya
hemos	hubimos	habremos	habríamos	hayamos
habéis	hubisteis	habréis	habríais	hayáis
han	hubieron	habrán	habrían	hayan

subj. imp.	subj. fut.	imperativo	
hubiera/-iese	hubiere		**gerundio**
hubieras/-ieses	hubieres	he	habiendo
hubiera/-iese	hubiere	haya	
hubiéramos /-iésemos	hubiéremos	hayamos	**participio** habido
hubierais/-ieseis	hubiereis	habed	
hubieran/-iesen	hubieren	hayan	

hacer

presente	pret. ind.	futuro	imperativo	
hago	hice	haré		**gerundio**
haces	hiciste	harás	haz	haciendo
hace	hizo	hará	haga	
hacemos	hicimos	haremos	hagamos	**participio**
hacéis	hicisteis	haréis	haced	hecho
hacen	hicieron	harán	hagan	

hartar

participio : hartado – *saturated*
harto (*only as attribute*): estoy harto – *I've had enough*

huir

presente	pret. ind.	imperativo	
huyo	huí		**gerundio**
huyes	huiste	huye	huyendo
huye	huyó	huya	
huimos	huimos	huyamos	**participio**
huís	huisteis	huid	huido
huyen	huyeron	huyan	

imprimir

participio :	impreso

ir

presente	imperfecto	pret. ind.	subj. pres.	subj. imp.
voy	iba	fui	vaya	fuera/-ese
vas	ibas	fuiste	vayas	fueras/-eses
va	iba	fue	vaya	fuera/-ese
vamos	íbamos	fuimos	vayamos	fuéramos/-ésemos
vais	ibais	fuisteis	vayáis	fuerais/-eseis
van	iban	fueron	vayan	fueran/-esen

subj. fut.	imperativo		
fuere		**gerundio**	
fueres	ve	yendo	
fuere	vaya		
fuéremos	vayamos	**participio**	
fuereis	id	ido	
fueren	vayan		

jugar

presente	pret. ind.	subj. pres.	imperativo	
juego	jugé	juegue		**gerundio**
juegas	jugaste	juegues	juega	jugando
juega	jugó	juegue	juegue	
jugamos	jugamos	juguemos	juguemos	**participio**
jugáis	jugasteis	juguéis	jugad	jugado
juegan	jugaron	jueguen	jueguen	

leer

presente	pret. ind.	
leo	leí	**gerundio**
lees	leíste	leyendo
lee	leyó	
leemos	leímos	**participio**
leéis	leísteis	leído
leen	leyeron	

lucir

presente	imperativo	
luzco		**gerundio**
luces	luce	luciendo
luce	luzca	
lucimos	luzcamos	**participio**
lucís	lucid	lucido
lucen	luzcan	

maldecir

presente	pret. ind.	imperativo		
maldigo	maldije		**gerundio**	
maldices	maldijiste	maldice	maldiciendo	
maldice	maldijo	maldiga		
maldecimos	maldijimos	maldigamos	**participio**	
maldecís	maldijisteis	maldecid	maldecido	*cursed*
maldicen	maldijeron	maldigan	maldito	*noun, adjective*

morir

presente	pret. ind.	imperativo	
muero	morí		**gerundio**
mueres	moriste	muere	muriendo
muere	murió	muera	
morimos	morimos	muramos	**participio**
morís	moristeis	morid	muerto
mueren	murieron	mueran	

oír

presente	pret. ind.	imperativo	subj. imp.	subj. fut.
oigo	oí		oyera/-ese	oyere
oyes	oíste	oye	oyeras/-eses	oyeres
oye	oyó	oiga	oyera/-ese	oyere
oímos	oímos	oigamos	oyéramos/-ésemos	oyéremos
oís	oísteis	oid	oyerais/-eseis	oyéreis
oyen	oyeron	oigan	eyeran/-esen	oyeren

gerundio	participio
oyendo	oído

oler

presente	imperativo	
huelo		**gerundio**
hueles	huele	oliendo
huele	huela	
olemos	olamos	**participio**
oléis	oled	olido
huelen	huelan	

pedir

presente	pret. ind.	imperativo	
pido	pedí		**gerundio**
pides	pediste	pide	pidiendo
pide	pidió	pidas	
pedimos	pedimos	pidamos	**participio**
pedís	pedisteis	pedid	pedido
piden	pidieron	pidan	

poder

presente	pret. ind.	futuro	condicional	
puedo	pude	podré	podría	**gerundio**
puedes	pudiste	podrás	podrías	pudiendo
puede	pudo	podrá	podría	
podemos	pudimos	podremos	podríamos	**participio**
podéis	pudisteis	podréis	podríais	podido
pueden	pudieron	podrán	podrían	

podrir (pudrir)

presente	imperfecto	pret. ind.	futuro	condicional
pudro	pudría	pudrí	pudriré	pudriría
pudres	pudrías	pudriste	pudrirás	pudrirías
pudre	pudría	pudrió	pudrirá	pudriría
pudrimos	pudríamos	pudrimos	pudriremos	pudriríamos
pudrís	pudríais	pudristeis	pudriréis	pudriríais
pudren	pudrían	pudrieron	pudrirán	pudrirían

imperativo

	gerundio			
pudre	pudriendo			
pudra				
pudramos	**participio**			
pudrid	podrido			
pudran				

poner

presente	pret. ind.	futuro	condicional	imperativo
pongo	puse	pondré	pondría	
pones	pusiste	pondrás	pondrías	pon
pone	puso	pondrá	pondría	ponga
ponemos	pusimos	pondremos	pondríamos	pongamos
ponéis	pusisteis	pondréis	pondríais	poned
ponen	pusieron	pondrán	pondrían	pongan

gerundio	participio
poniendo	puesto

prohibir

presente	imperativo	
prohíbo		**gerundio**
prohíbes	prohíbe	prohibiendo
prohíbe	prohíba	
prohibimos	prohibamos	**participio**
prohibís	prohibid	prohibido
prohíben	prohíban	

proveer

presente	pret. ind.		
proveo	proveí	**gerundio**	
provees	proveíste	proveyendo	
provee	proveyó		
proveemos	proveímos	**participio**	
proveéis	proveísteis	provisto	
proveen	proveyeron	proveído	

querer

presente	pret. ind.	futuro	condicional	imperativo
quiero	quise	querré	querría	
quieres	quisiste	querrás	querrías	quiere
quiere	quiso	querrá	querría	quiera
queremos	quisimos	querremos	querríamos	queramos
queréis	quisisteis	querréis	querríais	quered
quieren	quisieron	querrán	querrían	quieran

gerundio	participio
queriendo	querido

raer

presente	pret. ind.		
raigo/rao/rayo	raí	**gerundio**	
raes	raíste	rayendo	
rae	rayó		
raemos	raímos	**participio**	
raéis	raísteis	raído	
raen	rayeron		

reír

presente	pret. ind.	imperativo	
río	reí		**gerundio**
ríes	reíste	ríe	riendo
ríe	rió	ría	
reímos	reímos	riamos	**participio**
reís	reísteis	reíd	reído
ríen	rieron	rían	

reunir

presente	imperativo	
reúno		**gerundio**
reúnes	reúne	reuniendo
reúne	reúna	
reunimos	reunamos	**participio**
reunís	reunid	reunido
reúnen	reúnan	

roer

presente	pret. ind.	subj. pres.	subj. imp.	subj. fut.
roo/roigo	roí	roa/roiga	royera/-ese	royere
roes	roíste	roas/roigas	royeras/-eses	royeres
roe	royó	roa/roiga	royera/-ese	royere
roemos	roímos	roamos /roigamos /royamos	royéramos /-ésemos	royéremos
roéis	roísteis	roáis/roigáis /royáis	royerais /-eseis	royereis
roen	royeron	roan/roigan	royeran/-esen	royeren

imperativo

	gerundio
roe	royendo
roa/roiga	
roamos/roigamos roed roan/roigan	**participio** roído

saber

presente	pret. ind.	futuro	condicional	subj. pres.
sé	supe	sabré	sabría	sepa
sabes	supiste	sabrás	sabrías	sepas
sabe	supo	sabrá	sabría	sepa
sabemos	supimos	sabremos	sabríamos	sepamos
sabéis	supisteis	sabréis	sabríais	sepáis
saben	supieron	sabrán	sabrían	sepan

imperativo

	gerundio
sabe	sabiendo
sepa	
sepamos	**participio**
sabed	sabido
sepan	

salir

presente	futuro	condicional	imperativo	
salgo	saldré	saldría		**gerundio**
sales	saldrás	saldrías	sal	saliendo
sale	saldrá	saldría	salga	
salimos	saldremos	saldríamos	salgamos	**participio**
salís	saldréis	saldríais	salid	salido
salen	saldrán	saldrían	salgan	

seguir

presente	pret. ind.	subj. pres.	subj. imp.	subj. fut.
sigo	seguí	siga	siguiera/-ese	siguiere
sigues	seguiste	sigas	siguieras/-eses	siguieres
sigue	siguió	siga	siguiera/-ese	siguiere
seguimos	seguimos	sigamos	siguéramos /-ésemos	siguiéremos
seguís	seguisteis	sigáis	siguierais/-eseis	siguiereis
siguen	siguieron	sigan	siguieran/-esen	siguieren

imperativo

	gerundio
sigue	siguiendo
siga	
sigamos	**participio**
seguid	seguido
sigan	

sentir

presente	pret. ind.	subj. pres.	subj. imp.	subj. fut.
siento	sentí	sienta	sintiera/-ese	sintiere
sientes	sentiste	sientas	sintieras/-eses	sintieres
siente	sintió	sienta	sintiera/-ese	sintiere
sentimos	sentimos	sintamos	sintiéramos /-ésemos	sintiéremos
sentís	sentisteis	sintáis	sintierais/-eseis	sintiereis
sienten	sintieron	sientan	sintieran/-esen	sintieren

imperativo

	gerundio
siente	sintiendo
sienta	
sintamos	**participio**
sentid	sentido
sientan	

ser

presente	imperfecto	pret. ind.	futuro	
soy	era	fui	seré	**gerundio**
eres	eras	fuiste	serás	siendo
es	era	fue	será	
somos	éramos	fuimos	seremos	**participio**
sois	erais	fuisteis	seréis	sido
son	eran	fueron	serán	

condicional	subj. pres.	subj. imp.	subj. fut.	imperativo
sería	sea	fuera/-ese	fuere	
serías	seas	fueras/-eses	fueres	sé
sería	sea	fuera/-ese	fuere	sea
seríamos	seamos	fuéramos/-ésemos	fuéremos	seamos
seríais	seáis	fuerais/-eseis	fuereis	sed
serían	sean	fueran/-esen	fueren	sean

soltar

presente	imperativo		
suelto		**gerundio**	
sueltas	suelta	soltando	
suelta	suelte		
soltamos	soltemos	**participio**	
soltáis	soltad	soltado	
sueltan	suelten		

tener

presente	pret. ind.	futuro	condicional	imperativo
tengo	tuve	tendré	tendría	
tienes	tuviste	tendrás	tendrías	ten
tiene	tuvo	tendrá	tendría	tenga
tenemos	tuvimos	tendremos	tendríamos	tengamos
tenéis	tuvisteis	tendréis	tendríais	tened
tienen	tuvieron	tendrán	tendrían	tengan

gerundio	participio
teniendo	tenido

traducir

presente	pret. ind.	imperativo	
traduzco	traduje		**gerundio**
traduces	tradujiste	traduce	traduciendo
traduce	tradujo	traduzca	
traducimos	tradujimos	traduzcamos	**participio**
traducís	tradujisteis	traducid	traducido
traducen	tradujeron	traduzcan	

traer

presente	pret. ind.	imperativo	
traigo	traje		**gerundio**
traes	trajiste	trae	trayendo
trae	trajo	traiga	
traemos	trajimos	traigamos	**participio**
traéis	trajisteis	traed	traído
traen	trajeron	traigan	

valer

presente	futuro	imperativo	
valgo	valdré		**gerundio**
vales	valdrás	vale	valiendo
vale	valdrá	valga	
valemos	valdremos	valgamos	**participio**
valéis	valdréis	valed	valido
valen	valdrán	valgan	

venir

presente	pret. ind.	futuro	condicional	imperativo
vengo	vine	vendré	vendría	
vienes	viniste	vendrás	vendrías	ven
viene	vino	vendrá	vendría	venga
venimos	vinimos	vendremos	vendríamos	vengamos
venís	vinisteis	vendréis	vendríais	venid
vienen	vinieron	vendrán	vendrían	vengan

gerundio	participio
viniendo	venido

ver

presente	imperfecto	pret. ind.	subj. imp.	subj. fut.
veo	veía	vi	viera/-ese	viere
ves	veías	viste	vieras/-eses	vieres
ve	veía	vio	viera/-ese	viere
vemos	veíamos	vimos	viéramos/-ésemos	viéremos
veis	veíais	visteis	vierais/-eseis	viereis
ven	veían	vieron	vieran/-esen	vieren

gerundio	participio
viendo	visto

volcar

presente	pret. ind.	imperativo	
vuelco	volqué		**gerundio**
vuelcas	volcaste	vuelca	volcando
vuelca	volcó	vuelque	
volcamos	volcamos	volquemos	**participio**
volcáis	volcasteis	volcad	volcado
vuelcan	volcaron	vuelquen	

volver

presente	imperativo	
vuelvo		**gerundio**
vuelves	vuelve	volviendo
vuelve	vuelva	
volvemos	volvamos	**participio**
volvéis	volved	volvido
vuelven	vuelvan	

yacer

presente	subj. pres.	imperativo	
yazco/yazgo /yago	yazca/yazga /yaga		**gerundio** yaciendo
yaces	yazcas/yazgas /yagas	yace/yaz	
yace	yazca/yazga /yaga	yazca/yazga /yaga	
yacemos	yazcamos /yazgamos /yagamos	yazcamos /yazgamos /yagamos	**participio** yacido
yacéis	yazcáis/yazgáis yagáis	yaced	
yacen	yazcan/yazgan /yagan	yazcan/yazgan /yagan	

Verbos ingleses irregulares
English irregular verbs

Infinitive	Past	Past Participle
abide	abode, abided	abode, abided
arise	arose	arisen
awake	awoke	awaked, awoken
be	was *sing*, were *pl*	been
bear	bore	borne
beat	beat	beaten
become	became	become
beget	begot	begotten
begin	began	begun
behold	beheld	beheld
bend	bent	bent
beseech	besought	besought
beset	beset	beset
bet	bet, betted	bet, betted
bid	bade, bid	bid, bidden
bind	bound	bound
bite	bit	bitten
bleed	bled	bled
blow	blew	blown
break	broke	broken
breed	bred	bred
bring	brought	brought
build	built	built
burn	burned, burnt	burned, burnt
burst	burst	burst
buy	bought	bought
can	could	–
cast	cast	cast
catch	caught	caught
chide	chided, chid	chided, chidden, chid
choose	chose	chosen
cleave[1] *(cut)*	clove, cleaved	cloven, cleaved, cleft
cleave[2] *(adhere)*	cleaved, clave	cleaved
cling	clung	clung
come	came	come
cost	cost, costed	cost, costed
creep	crept	crept
cut	cut	cut

Infinitive	Past	Past Participle
deal	dealt	dealt
dig	dug	dug
do	did	done
draw	drew	drawn
dream	dreamed, dreamt	dreamed, dreamt
drink	drank	drunk
drive	drove	driven
dwell	dwelt	dwelt
eat	ate	eaten
fall	fell	fallen
feed	fed	fed
feel	felt	felt
fight	fought	fought
find	found	found
flee	fled	fled
fling	flung	flung
fly	flew	flown
forbid	forbad(e)	forbidden
forget	forgot	forgotten
forsake	forsook	forsaken
freeze	froze	frozen
get	got	got, gotten *Am*
gild	gilded, gilt	gilded, gilt
gird	girded, girt	girded, girt
give	gave	given
go	went	gone
grind	ground	ground
grow	grew	grown
hang	hung, JUR hanged	hung, JUR hanged
have	had	had
hear	heard	heard
heave	heaved, hove	heaved, hove
hew	hewed	hewed, hewn
hide	hid	hidden
hit	hit	hit
hold	held	held
hurt	hurt	hurt
keep	kept	kept
kneel	knelt	knelt
know	knew	known

Infinitive	Past	Past Participle
lade	laded	laden, laded
lay	laid	laid
lead	led	led
lean	leaned, leant	leaned, leant
leap	leaped, leapt	leaped, leapt
learn	learned, learnt	learned, learnt
leave	left	left
lend	lent	lent
let	let	let
lie	lay	lain
light	lit, lighted	lit, lighted
lose	lost	lost
make	made	made
may	might	–
mean	meant	meant
meet	met	met
mistake	mistook	mistaken
mow	mowed	mown, mowed
pay	paid	paid
put	put	put
quit	quit, quitted	quit, quitted
read [ri:d]	read [red]	read [red]
rend	rent	rent
rid	rid	rid
ride	rode	ridden
ring	rang	rung
rise	rose	risen
run	ran	run
saw	sawed	sawed, sawn
say	said	said
see	saw	seen
seek	sought	sought
sell	sold	sold
send	sent	sent
set	set	set
sew	sewed	sewed, sewn
shake	shook	shaken
shave	shaved	shaved, shaven
stave	stove, staved	stove, staved
steal	stole	stolen

Infinitive	Past	Past Participle
shear	sheared	sheared, shorn
shed	shed	shed
shine	shone	shone
shit	shit, *iron* shat	shit, *iron* shat
shoe	shod	shod
shoot	shot	shot
show	showed	shown, showed
shrink	shrank	shrunk
shut	shut	shut
sing	sang	sung
sink	sank	sunk
sit	sat	sat
slay	slew	slain
sleep	slept	slept
slide	slid	slid
sling	slung	slung
slink	slunk	slunk
slit	slit	slit
smell	smelled, smelt	smelled, smelt
smite	smote	smitten
sow	sowed	sowed, sown
speak	spoke	spoken
speed	speeded, sped	speeded, sped
spell	spelled, spelt	spelled, spelt
spend	spent	spent
spill	spilled, spilt	spilled, spilt
spin	spun	spun
spit	spat	spat
split	split	split
spoil	spoiled, spoilt	spoiled, spoilt
spread	spread	spread
spring	sprang	sprung
stand	stood	stood
stick	stuck	stuck
sting	stung	stung
stink	stank	stunk
strew	strewed	strewed, strewn
stride	strode	stridden
strike	struck	struck
string	strung	strung

Infinitive	Past	Past Participle
strive	strove	striven
swear	swore	sworn
sweep	swept	swept
swell	swelled	swollen
swin	swam	swum
swing	swung	swung
take	took	taken
teach	taught	taught
tear	tore	torn
tell	told	told
think	thought	thought
thrive	throve, thrived	thriven, thrived
throw	threw	thrown
thrust	thrust	thrust
tread	trod	trodden
wake	woke, waked	woken, waked
wear	wore	worn
weave	wove	woven
weep	wept	wept
win	won	won
wind	wound	wound
wring	wrung	wrung
write	wrote	written

Falsos amigos

False friends

Para más información el usuario debe de consultar la entrada en el diccionario. En los casos en los que la palabra inglesa está fuera del orden alfabético esta aparece en *cursiva*.

Readers should consult the main section of the dictionary for more complete translation information. When the English term appears out of alphabetical order, it is shown in *italics*.

Meaning(s) of the Spanish word:	falso amigo / false friend		Significado(s) de la palabra inglesa:
	español	English	
1) enormous	abismal	abysmal	pésimo
1) present 2) current	actual	actual	verdadero
at the moment	actualmente	actually	en realidad
1) appropriate 2) fitting, suitable	adecuado, -a	adequate	1) suficiente 2) idóneo
1) diary 2) notebook 3) agenda	agenda	agenda	1) orden del día 2) agenda
bedroom	alcoba	alcove	nicho
1) entertainment 2) enjoyment	amenidad	amenities	comodidades
1) to attend (*vi*) 2) to help (*vt*)	asistir	to assist	ayudar
1) audience 2) (JUR) hearing, courtroom	audiencia	audience	1) público 2) audiencia
1) to notify 2) to warn 3) to call	avisar	*to advise*	aconsejar, asesorar
billion	billón	billion	mil millones
1) white 2) light 3) pale	blanco, -a	blank	1) en blanco 2) vacío 3) absoluto, completo
1) soft 2) mild 3) weak 4) gentle	blando, -a	bland	1) suave, blando 2) afable 3) insípido, insulso
1) excellent 2) brave 3) wild 4) rough	bravo, -a	brave	valiente
1) countryside 2) field 3) camp	campo	camp	1) campamento 2) grupo
1) shameless 2) cynical	cínico, -a (adj)	*cynical*	1) escéptico 2) cínico
1) shamelessness 2) cynicism	cinismo	cynicism	1) escepticismo 2) cinismo
1) understanding 2) tolerant 3) comprehensive	comprensivo, -a	comprehensive	exhaustivo, completo

Meaning(s) of the Spanish word:	falso amigo false friend		Significado(s) de la palabra inglesa:
	español	English	
1) commitment 2) promise 3) agreement 4) awkward situation	compromise	compromise	1) transigencia 2) arreglo
1) leader 2) driver	conductor	conductor	1) (MUS) director 2) (PHYS, ELEC) conductor 3) cobrador, interventor
1) lecture 2) conference 3) talk 4) call	conferencia	conference	congreso
estar constipado: to have a cold	constipado, -a	constipated	estreñido
1) to build 2) to construe	construir	to construe	interpretar
1) to check 2) to control	controlar	to control	1) dominar 2) controlar 3) erradicar
1) habit 2) custom	costumbre	costume	traje
disappointment	decepción	deception	1) engaño 2) fraude
to disappoint	decepcionar	*to deceive*	engañar
1) request 2) (COM) demand 3) (JUR) action	demanda	demand	1) exigencia 2) reclamación de un pago 3) demanda
1) to ask for 2) (JUR) to sue	demandar	to demand	1) reclamar 2) requerir 3) preguntar
1) to displease 2) to anger, to offend	disgustar	to disgust	1) dar asco 2) repugnar
1) displeasure 2) suffering 3) quarrel	disgusto	disgust	1) repugnancia 2) indignación
1) to divert 2) to entertain 3) to embezzle	distraer	to distract	distraer
1) pregnant 2) awkward	embarazada	embarassed	avergonzado
1) escape 2) excursion	escapada	escapade	aventura
1) stage 2) scene	escenario	*scenery*	1) paisaje 2) decorado
1) possible 2) extra	eventual	eventual	1) final 2) posible
fortuitously, possibly	eventualmente	eventually	1) finalmente 2) con el tiempo
1) to incite 2) to irritate 3) to arouse	excitar	*to excite*	1) emocionar 2) estimular

Meaning(s) of the Spanish word:	falso amigo false friend		Significado(s) de la palabra inglesa:
	español	English	
success	éxito	exit	1) salida 2) desvío
1) strangeness 2) eccentricity	extravagancia	extravagance	1) derroche 2) lujo 3) prodigalidad 4) extravagancia
1) odd 2) eccentric	extravagante	extravagant	1) despilfarrador 2) lujoso 3) excesivo 4) extravagante
1) factory 2) masonry 3) building	fábrica	fabric	1) tejido 2) estructura
1) to manufacture 2) to build 3) to fabricate	fabricar	to fabricate	1) inventar 2) fabricar 3) falsificar
crème caramel	flan	flan	1) (*Brit*) tartaleta de frutas 2) (*Am*) flan
1) sentence 2) expression, saying 3) style 4) (MÚS) phrase	frase	*phrase*	1) locución 2) expresión
1) study 2) dressing room 3) office 4) (POL) cabinet	gabinete	*cabinet*	1) armario, vitrina 2) gabinete de ministros
1) brilliant 2) funny 3) great	genial	genial	afable
1) genius 2) stroke of genius	genialidad	geniality	afabilidad
1) pagan 2) dashing, elegant 3) considerate	gentil (adj)	genteel	distinguido
1) to be ignorant of 2) to ignore	ignorar	to ignore	no hacer caso a
uninhabitable	inhabitable	inhabitable	habitable
uninhabited	inhabitado, -a	inhabited	habitado
insult, harm	injuria	injury	1) lesión 2) herida
to insult, to injure	injuriar	*to injure*	1) herir 2) estropear 3) perjudicar
poisoning	intoxicación	intoxication	1) embriaguez 2) (MED) intoxicación
to poison	intoxicar	*to intoxicate*	1) embriagar 2) (MED) intoxicar
1) to insert 2) to put in	introducir	to introduce	1) presentar 2) iniciar 3) abordar 4) introducir

Meaning(s) of the Spanish word:	falso amigo false friend		Significado(s) de la palabra inglesa:
	español	**English**	
1) long 2) lengthy 3) shrewd	**largo, -a**	**large**	grande
1) reading 2) reading material 3) knowledge 4) interpretation	**lectura**	**lecture**	1) discurso, conferencia 2) sermón 3) consejo
1) bookshop 2) stationer's 3) library 4) bookcase	**librería**	**library**	1) biblioteca 2) collección
1) mask 2) fancy dress party 3) masquerade	**máscara**	**mascara**	rímel
1) poverty 2) pittance 3) stinginess 4) misfortune	**miseria**	**misery**	tristeza
to inconvenience, to annoy	**molestar**	**to molest**	1) atacar 2) agredir
1) slow to pay up 2) slow	**moroso, -a**	**morose**	taciturno, malhumorado
piece of news	**noticia**	**notice**	1) interés 2) letrero, anuncio 3) aviso
1) well-known 2) obvious	**notorio, -a**	**notorious**	de mala reputación
obvious	**ostensible**	**ostensible**	aparente
relative	**pariente**	**parent**	padre, madre
pretentious	**pedante**	**pedantic**	puntilloso
newspaper	**periódico**	**periodical**	1) boletín 2) revista
1) arrogant, conceited 2) insolent	**petulante**	**petulant**	enfurruñado
condom	**preservativo**	**preservative**	conservante
conceited	**presuntuoso, -a**	**presumptuous**	1) impertinente 2) osado
to aspire to to expect to mean to to try	**pretender**	**to pretend**	1) fingir 2) pretender
teacher	**profesor**	**professor**	1) (*Brit*) catedrático 2) (*Am*) profesor de universidad
1) to make real, to fulfil 2) to carry out, to make 3) (ECON) to realize 4) to produce	**realizar**	**to realize**	1) ser consciente de 2) realizar 3) cumplir
container, vessel	**recipiente**	**recipient**	destinatario
1) to remember 2) to remind	**recordar**	**to record**	1) archivar 2) registrar, grabar

Meaning(s) of the Spanish word:	falso amigo false friend		Significado(s) de la palabra inglesa:
	español	English	
saying	refrán	refrain	estribillio
importance	relevancia	relevance	1) pertinencia 2) importancia
1) important 2) outstanding	relevante	relevant	1) pertinente 2) importante 3) oportuno
to summarize	resumir	to resume	1) reanudar, proseguir con 2) volver a ocupar
1) insinuating 2) reluctant	reticente	reticent	reservado
reward, remuneration	retribución	retribution	castigo justo
health	sanidad	sanity	cordura
1) healthy 2) intact 3) wholesome	sano, -a	*sane*	1) cuerdo 2) sensato
1) sensitive 2) noticeable	sensible	sensible	1) sensato, prudente 2) práctico 3) consciente 4) notable
1) liking 2) friendliness	simpatía	*sympathy*	1) compasión, comprensión 2) simpatía
friendly	simpático, -a	*sympathetic*	1) comprensivo, receptivo 2) cordial 3) simpatizante
1) to stand 2) to support	soportar	to support	1) sostener, aguantar 2) ayudar 3) mantener
1) smooth 2) soft 3) gentle 4) mild	suave	suave	afable, cortés
1) poor suburb 2) slum area	suburbio	suburb	barrio periférico
1) to happen (*vi*) 2) to succeed (*vi*) 3) to follow on (*vi*) 4) to inherit (*vt*)	suceder	to succeed	1) tener éxito 2) suceder
1) event, incident 2) outcome	suceso	success	éxito
1) evocative 2) thought-provoking 3) attractive	sugestivo, -a	suggestive	1) indecente 2) sugestivo
1) commonplace 2) cliché	tópico	topic	tema
1) cruel 2) gruesome	truculento, -a	truculent	agresivo
1) dissolute 2) habit-forming 3) defective 4) spoilt	vicioso, -a	vicious	1) malo, salvaje 2) despiadado 3) feroz 4) atroz

Los numerales

Numerals

Los numerales cardinales

Cardinal numbers

cero	0	zero
uno (*apócope* un), una	1	one
dos	2	two
tres	3	three
cuatro	4	four
cinco	5	five
seis	6	six
siete	7	seven
ocho	8	eight
nueve	9	nine
diez	10	ten
once	11	eleven
doce	12	twelve
trece	13	thirteen
catorce	14	fourteen
quince	15	fifteen
dieciséis	16	sixteen
diecisiete	17	seventeen
dieciocho	18	eighteen
diecinueve	19	nineteen
veinte	20	twenty
veintiuno (*apócope* veintiún), -a	21	twenty-one
veintidós	22	twenty-two
veintitrés	23	twenty-three
veinticuatro	24	twenty-four
veinticinco	25	twenty-five
treinta	30	thirty
treinta y uno (*apócope* treinta y un) -a	31	thirty-one
treinta y dos	32	thirty-two
treinta y tres	33	thirty-three
cuarenta	40	forty
cuarenta y uno (*apócope* cuarenta y un) -a	41	forty-one
cuarenta y dos	42	forty-two
cincuenta	50	fifty
cincuenta y uno (*apócope* cincuenta y un) -a	51	fifty-one
cincuenta y dos	52	fifty-two
sesenta	60	sixty
sesenta y uno (*apócope* sesenta y un) -a	61	sixty-one
sesenta y dos	62	sixty-two
setenta	70	seventy
setenta y uno (*apócope* setenta y un) -a	71	seventy-one
setenta y dos	72	seventy-two

setenta y cinco	75	seventy-five
setenta y nueve	79	seventy-nine
ochenta	80	eighty
ochenta y uno (*apócope* ochenta y un) -a	81	eighty-one
ochenta y dos	82	eighty-two
ochenta y cinco	85	eighty-five
noventa	90	ninety
noventa y uno (*apócope* noventa y un) -a	91	ninety-one
noventa y dos	92	ninety-two
noventa y nueve	99	ninety-nine
cien	100	one hundred
ciento uno (*apócope* ciento un) -a	101	one hundred and one
ciento dos	102	one hundred and two
ciento diez	110	one hundred and ten
ciento veinte	120	one hundred and twenty
ciento noventa y nueve	199	one hundred and ninety-nine
dos cientos, -as	200	two hundred
dos cientos uno (*apócope* doscientos un) -a	201	two hundred and one
dos cientos veintidós	222	two hundred and twenty-two
tres cientos, -as	300	three hundred
cuatro cientos, -as	400	four hundred
quinientos, -as	500	five hundred
seiscientos, -as	600	six hundred
sietecientos, -as	700	seven hundred
ochocientos, -as	800	eight hundred
nuevecientos, -as	900	nine hundred
mil	1 000	one thousand
mil uno (*apócope* mil un) -a	1 001	one thousand and one
mil diez	1 010	one thousand and ten
mil cien	1 100	one thousand one hundred
dos mil	2 000	two thousand
diez mil	10 000	ten thousand
cien mil	100 000	one hundred thousand
un millón	1 000 000	one million
dos millones	2 000 000	two million
dos millones quinientos, -as mil	2 500 000	two million, five hundred thousand
mil millones	1 000 000 000	one billion
un billón	1 000 000 000 000	one thousand billion

Los numerales ordinales — Ordinal numbers

Español			English
primero (*apócope* primer), -a	1º, 1ª	1st	first
segundo, -a	2º, 2ª	2nd	second
tercero (*apócope* tercer), -a	3º, 3ª	3rd	third
cuarto, -a	4º, 4ª	4th	fourth
quinto, -a	5º, 5ª	5th	fifth
sexto, -a	6º, 6ª	6th	sixth
séptimo, -a	7º, 7ª	7th	seventh
octavo, -a	8º, 8ª	8th	eighth
noveno, -a	9º, 9ª	9th	ninth
décimo, -a	10º, 10ª	10th	tenth
undécimo, -a	11º, 11ª	11th	eleventh
duodécimo, -a	12º, 12ª	12th	twelfth
decimotercero, -a	13º, 13ª	13th	thirteenth
decimocuarto, -a	14º, 14ª	14th	fourtheenth
decimoquinto, -a	15º, 15ª	15th	fifteenth
decimosexto, -a	16º, 16ª	16th	sixteenth
decimoséptimo, -a	17º, 17ª	17th	seventeenth
decimoctavo, -a	18º, 18ª	18th	eighteenth
decimonoveno, -a	19º, 19ª	19th	nineteenth
vigésimo, -a	20º, 20ª	20th	twentieth
vigésimo, -a primero, -a (o vigesimoprimero, -a)	21º, 21ª	21st	twenty-first
vigésimo, -a segundo, -a (o vigesimosegundo, -a)	22º, 22ª	22nd	twenty-second
vigésimo, -a tercero, -a (o vigesimotercero, -a)	23º, 23ª	23rd	twenty-third
trigésimo, -a	30º, 30ª	30th	thirtieth
trigésimo, -a primero, -a	31º, 31ª	31st	thirty-first
trigésimo, -a segundo, -a	32º, 32ª	32nd	thirty-second
cuadragésimo, -a	40º, 40ª	40th	fortieth
quincuagésimo, -a	50º, 50ª	50th	fiftieth
sexagésimo, -a	60º, 60ª	60th	sixtieth
septuagésimo, -a	70º, 70ª	70th	seventieth
septuagésimo, -a primero, -a	71º, 71ª	71st	seventy-first
septuagésimo, -a segundo, -a	72º, 72ª	72nd	seventy-second
septuagésimo, -a noveno, -a	79º, 79ª	79th	seventy-ninth
octogésimo, -a	80º, 80ª	80th	eightieth
octogésimo, -a primero, -a	81º, 81ª	81st	eighty-first
octogésimo, -a segundo, -a	82º, 82ª	82nd	eighty-second
nonagésimo, -a	90º, 90ª	90th	nintieth
nonagésimo, -a primero, -a	91º, 91ª	91st	ninety-first
nonagésimo, -a noveno, -a	99º, 99ª	99th	ninety-ninth
centésimo, -a	100º, 100ª	100th	one hundredth
centésimo, -a primero, -a	101º, 101ª	101st	one hundred and first
centésimo, -a décimo, -a	110º, 110ª	110th	one hundred and tenth
centésimo, -a nonagésimo, -a quinto, -a	195º, 195ª	195th	one hundred and ninety-ninth

ducentésimo, -a	200°, 200ª	200th	two hundredth
tricentésimo, -a	300°, 300ª	300th	three hundredth
quingentésimo, -a	500°, 500ª	500th	five hundredth
milésimo, -a	1 000°, 1 000ª	1 000th	one thousandth
dosmilésimo, -a	2 000°, 2 000ª	2 000th	two thousandth
millonésimo, -a	1 000 000°, 1 000 000ª	1 000 000th	one millionth
diezmillonésimo, -a	10 000 000°, 10 000 000ª	10 000 000th	ten millionth

Numeros fraccionarios (o quebrados)　　　　　Fractional numbers

mitad; medio, -a	$1/2$	one half
un tercio	$1/3$	one third
un cuarto	$1/4$	one quarter
un quinto	$1/5$	one fifth
un décimo	$1/10$	one tenth
un céntesimo	$1/100$	one hundredth
un milésimo	$1/1000$	one thousandth
un millonésimo	$1/1000000$	one millionth
dos tercios	$2/3$	two thirds
tres cuartos	$3/4$	three quarters
dos quintos	$2/5$	two fifths
tres décimos	$3/10$	three tenths
uno y medio	$1\,1/2$	one and a half
dos y medio	$2\,1/2$	two and a half
cinco tres octavos	$5\,3/8$	five and three eighths
uno coma uno	1,1	one point one

Medidas y pesos

Sistema (de numeración) decimal

Weights and measures

Decimal system

mega-	1 000 000	M	mega
hectokilo	100 000	hk	hectokilo
miria-	10 000	ma	myria
kilo	1 000	k	kilo
hecto-	100	h	hecto
deca- (o decá-)	10	da	deca
deci- (o decí-)	0,1	d	deci
centi- (o centí-)	0,01	c	centi
mili-	0,001	m	milli
decimili-	0,000 1	dm	decimilli
centimili-	0,000 01	cm	centimilli
micro-	0,000 001	µ	micro

Tablas de equivalencia

Damos el llamado **imperial system** en los casos en los que en el lenguaje cotidiano éste todavía se sigue usando. Para convertir una medida métrica en la imperial, se debe multiplicar por el factor en **negrita**. Asimismo dividiendo la medida imperial por ese mismo factor se obtiene el equivalente métrico.

Conversion tables

Only imperial measures still in common use are given here. To convert a metric measurement to imperial, multiply by the conversion factor in **bold**. Likewise dividing an imperial measurement by the same factor will give the metric equivalent.

Sistema métrico
Metric measurement

Sistema imperial
Imperial measures

milla marina	1 852 m	–	nautical mile			
kilómetro	1 000 m	km	kilometre *(Brit)*, kilometer *(Am)*	0,62	mile (=1760 yards)	m, mi
hectómetro	100 m	hm	hectometre *(Brit)*, hectometer *(Am)*			
decámetro	10 m	dam	decametre *(Brit)*, decameter *(Am)*			
metro	1 m	m	metre *(Brit)*, meter *(Am)*	1,09 3,28	yard (= 3 feet) foot (= 12 inches)	yd ft
decímetro	0,1 m	dm	decimetre *(Brit)*, decimeter *(Am)*			
centímetro	0,01 m	cm	centimetre *(Brit)*, centimeter *(Am)*	0,39	inch	in
milímetro	0,001 m	mm	millimetre *(Brit)*, millimeter *(Am)*			
micrón, micra	0,000 001 m	µ	micron			
milimicrón	0,000 000 001 m	mµ	millimicron			
ángstrom	0,000 000 000 1 m	Å	angstrom			

Medidas de superficie

Surface measure

kilómetro cuadrado	1 000 000 m^2	km^2	square kilometre	0,386	square mile (= 640 acres)	sq. m., sq. mi.
hectómetro cuadrado hectárea	10 000 m^2	hm^2 ha	square hectometre hectare	2,47	acre (= 4840 square yards)	a.
decámetro cuadrado área	100 m^2	dam^2 a	square decametre are			
metro cuadrado	1 m^2	m^2	square metre	1.196 10,76	square yard (9 square feet) square feet (= 144 square inches)	sq. yd sq. ft
decímetro cuadrado	0,01 m^2	dm^2	square decimetre			
centímetro cuadrado	0,000 1 m^2	cm^2	square centimetre	0,155	square inch	sq. in.
milímetro cuadrado	0,000 001 m^2	mm^2	square millimetre			

Medidas de volumen y capacidad　　　　　　　　Volume and capacity

kilómetro cúbico	1 000 000 000 m³	km³	cubic kilometre			
metro cúbico estéreo	1 m³	m³ st	cubic metre stere	1,308 35,32	cubic yard (= 27 cubic feet) cubic foot (= 1728 cubic inches)	cu. yd cu. ft
hectolitro	0,1 m³	hl	hectolitre *(Brit)*, hectoliter *(Am)*			
decalitro	0,01 m³	dal	decalitre *(Brit)*, decaliter *(Am)*			
decímetro cúbico litro	0,001 m³	dm³ l	cubic decimetre litre *(Brit)*, liter *(Am)*	0,22 1,76 0,26 2,1	UK gallon UK pint US gallon US pint	gal. pt gal. Pt
decilitro	0,000 1 m³	dl	decilitre *(Brit)*, deciliter *(Am)*			
centilitro	0,000 01 m³	cl	centilitre *(Brit)*, centilter *(Am)*	0,352 0,338	UK fluid ounce US fluid ounce	fl. Oz
centímetro cúbico	0,000 001 m³	cm³	cubic centimetre	0,061	cubic inch	cu. in.
mililitro	0,000 001 m³	ml	millilitre *(Brit)*, milliliter *(Am)*			
milímetro cúbico	0,000 000 001 m³	mm³	cubic millimetre			

Pesos　　　　　　　　　　　　　　　　　　　　　　　Weight

tonelada	1 000 kg	t	tonne	0,98 1,1	[long] ton *(Brit)* (= 2240 pounds) [short] ton *(Am)* (= 2000 pounds)	t.
quintal métrico	100 kg	q	quintal			
kilogramo	1 000 g	kg	kilogram	2,2	pound (= 16 ounces)	lb
hectogramo	100 g	hg	hectogram			
decagramo	10 g	dag	decagram			
gramo	1 g	g	gram	0,035	ounce	oz
quilate	0,2 g	–	carat			
decigramo (o decagramo)	0,1 g	dg	decigram			
centigramo	0,01 g	cg	centigram			
miligramo	0,001 g	mg	milligram			
microgramo	0,000 001 g	µg, g	microgram			

Para convertir una temperatura indicada en grados centígrados a Fahrenheit se deben restar 32 y multiplicar por $^5/_9$. Para convertir una temperatura indicada en Fahrenheit a centígrados se debe multiplicar por $^9/_5$ y añadir 32.

To convert a temperature in degrees Celsius to Fahrenheit, deduct 32 and multiply by $^5/_9$. To convert Fahrenheit to Celsius, multiply by $^9/_5$ and add 32.

1350

España
Spain

comunidades autónomas *autonomous regions*	capitales *capital cities*
Andalucía *Andalusia*	Sevilla *Seville*
Aragón	Zaragoza
Asturias	Oviedo
Baleares *Balearic Islands*	Palma de Mallorca
Canarias *Canary Islands*	Santa Cruz de Tenerife
Cantabria	Santander
Castilla y León	Valladolid
Castilla-La Mancha	Toledo
Cataluña *Catalonia*	Barcelona
Extremadura	Mérida
Galicia	Santiago de Compostela
La Rioja	Logroño
Madrid	**Madrid**
Murcia	Murcia
Navarra	Pamplona
País Vasco *Basque Country*	Vitoria
Valencia	Valencia

Hispanoamérica
Spanish America

países *countries*	capitales *capital cities*
Argentina	Buenos Aires
Bolivia	La Paz
Chile	Santiago
Colombia	Bogotá
Costa Rica	San José
Cuba	La Habana *Havana*
Ecuador	Quito
El Salvador	San Salvador
Guatemala	Guatemala *Guatemala City*

Honduras	Tegucigalpa
México *Mexico*	Ciudad de México D.F. *Mexico City*
Nicaragua	Managua
Panamá *Panama*	Panamá *Panama City*
Paraguay	Asunción
Perú *Peru*	Lima
Puerto Rico	San Juan
República Dominicana *Dominican Republic*	Santo Domingo
Uruguay	Montevideo
Venezuela	Caracas

Canada
El Canadá
Capital: Ottawa

provinces ***provincias***	**capital cities** ***capitales***
Alberta	Edmonton
British Colombia	Victoria
Manitoba	Winnipeg
New Brunswick *Nuevo Brunswick*	Fredericton
Newfoundland *Terranova*	St. John's
Nova Scotia *Nueva Escocia*	Halifax
Ontario	Toronto
Prince Edward Island *Isla del Príncipe Eduardo*	Charlottetown
Québec	Québec
Saskatchewan	Saskatchewan

territories ***capital cities***	**territorios** ***capitales***
North West Territories *Territorio del Noroeste*	Yellowknife
Nunavut Territory (*since 1st April 1999*) *Territorio del Nunavut*	Iqaluit
Yukon Territory *Territorio del Yukon*	Whitehorse

United Kingdom
Reino Unido

countries *países*	capital cities *capitales*
England *Inglaterra*	London *Londres*
Scotland *Escocia*	Edinburgh *Edinburgo*
Wales *País de Gales*	Cardiff
Northern Ireland *Irlanda del Norte*	Belfast

England
Inglaterra

counties *condados*	abbreviations *abreviaciones*	administrative centres *centros administrativos*
Bedfordshire	Beds	Bedford
Berkshire	Berks	Reading
Buckinghamshire	Bucks	Aylesbury
Cambridgeshire	Cambs	Cambridge
Cheshire	Ches	Chester
Cornwall	Corn	Truro
Cumbria		Carlisle
Derbyshire	Derbs	Matlock
Devon		Exeter
Dorset		Dorchester
Durham	Dur	Durham
East Sussex *Sussex Oriental*	E. Sussex	Lewes
Essex		Chelmsford
Gloucestershire	Glos	Gloucester
Greater London *Gran Londres*		**London** ***Londres***
Greater Manchester *Gran Manchester*		Manchester
Hampshire	Hants	Winchester
Hertfordshire	Herts	Hertford
Kent		Maidstone
Lancashire	Lancs	Preston
Leicestershire	Leics	Leicester
Lincolnshire	Lincs	Lincoln
Merseyside		Liverpool

Norfolk		Norwich
Northamptonshire	Northants	Northampton
Northumberland	Northd	Morpeth
North Yorkshire	N. Yorks	Northallerton
Nottinghamshire	Notts	Nottingham
Oxfordshire	Oxon	Oxford
Shropshire	Salop	Shrewsbury
Somerset	Som	Taunton
South Yorkshire	S. Yorks	Barnsley
Staffordshire	Staffs	Stafford
Suffolk	Suff	Ipswich
Surrey		Kingston upon Thames
Tyne & Wear		Newcastle upon Tyne
Warwickshire	Warks	Warwick
West Midlands	W. Midlands	Birmingham
West Sussex *Sussex Occidental*	W. Sussex	Chichester
West Yorkshire	W. Yorks	Wakefield
Wiltshire	Wilts	Trowbridge
Worcestershire	Worcs	Worcester

Wales, *Welsh:* Cymru
País de Gales

unitary authorities *unidades administrativas*	**administrative headquarters** *centros administrativos*
Anglesey	Llangefni
Blaenau Gwent	Ebbw Vale
Bridgend	Bridgend
Caerphilly	Hengoed
Cardiff	**Cardiff**
Carmarthenshire	Carmarthen
Ceredigion	Aberaeron
Conwy	Conwy
Denbighshire	Ruthin
Flintshire	Mold
Gwynedd	Caernarfon
Merthyr Tydfil	Merthyr Tydfil
Monmouthshire	Cwmbran
Neath Port Talbot	Port Talbot
Newport	Newport

Pembrokeshire	Haverfordwest
Powys	Llandrindod Wells
Rhondda Cynon Taff	Clydach Vale
Swansea	Swansea
Torfaen	Pontypool
Vale of Glamorgan	Barry
Wrexham	Wrexham

Scotland
Escocia

unitary authorities *unidades administrativas*	**administrative headquarters** *centros administrativos*
Aberdeen City	
Aberdeenshire	Aberdeen
Angus	Forfar
Argyll and Bute	Lochgilphead
Clackmannanshire	Alloa
Dumfries and Galloway	Dumfries
Dundee City	
East Ayrshire	Kilmarnock
East Dunbartonshire	Kirkintilloch
East Lothian	Haddington
East Renfrewshire	Giffnock
Edinburgh City	
Falkirk	Falkirk
Fife	Glenrothes
Glasgow City	
Highland	Inverness
Inverclyde	Greenock
Midlothian	Dalkeith
Moray	Elgin
North Ayrshire	Irvine
North Lanarkshire	Motherwell
Orkney Islands *Islas Orcadas*	Kirkwall
Perth and Kinross	Perth
Renfrewshire	Paisley
Scottish Borders	Melrose
Shetland Islands *Islas Shetland*	Lerwick
South Ayrshire	Ayr

South Lanarkshire	Hamilton
Stirling	Stirling
West Dunbartonshire	Dunbarton
Western Isles *Islas Hébridas*	Stornoway
West Lothian	Livingston

Northern Ireland
Irlanda del Norte

counties *condados*	principal towns *ciudades principales*
Antrim	**Belfast**
Armagh	Armagh
Down	Downpatrick
Fermanagh	Enniskillen
Londonderry	Londonderry
Tyrone	Omagh

Republic of Ireland or Irish Republic, *Gaelic:* **Èire**
República de Irlanda

provinces
provincias

counties *condados*	principal towns *ciudades principales*
Connacht, *formerly:* **Connaught**	
Galway, *Gaelic:* Gaillimh	Galway
Leitrim, *Gaelic:* Liathdroma	Carrick-on-Shannon
Mayo, *Gaelic:* Mhuigheo	Castlebar
Roscommon, *Gaelic:* Ros Comáin	Roscommon
Sligo, *Gaelic:* Sligeach	Sligo
Leinster	
Carlow, *Gaelic:* Cheatharlach	Carlow
Dublin, *Gaelic:* Baile Átha Cliath	**Dublin**
Kildare, *Gaelic:* Chill Dara	Naas
Kilkenny, *Gaelic:* Chill Choinnigh	Kilkenny
Laois/Laoighis/Leix	Portlaoise
Longford, *Gaelic:* Longphuirt	Longford

Louth, *Gaelic:* Lughbhaidh	Dundalk
Meath, *Gaelic:* na Midhe	Navan
Offaly, *Gaelic:* Ua bhFailghe	Tullamore
Westmeath, *Gaelic:* na h-Iarmhidhe	Mullingar
Wexford, *Gaelic:* Loch Garman	Wexford
Wicklow, *Gaelic:* Cill Mhantáin	Wicklow

Munster

Clare, *Gaelic:* An Cláir	Ennis
Cork, *Gaelic:* Chorcaigh	Cork
Kerry, *Gaelic:* Chiarraighe	Tralee
Limerick, *Gaelic:* Luimneach	Limerick
Tipperary, *Gaelic:* Thiobrad Árann	Clonmel
Waterford, *Gaelic:* Phort Láirge	Waterford

Ulster

Cavan, *Gaelic:* Cabháin	Cavan
Donegal, *Gaelic:* Dún na nGall	Lifford
Monaghan, *Gaelic:* Mhuineachain	Monaghan

Channel Islands
Islas Anglonormandas

principal towns
ciudades principales

Alderney	St. Anne
Guernsey *Isla Guernesey*	St. Peter Port
Jersey	St. Hellier
Sark	Sercq

Australia
Capital: Canberra

states
estados

capital cities
capitales

New South Wales *Nueva Gales del Sur*	Sydney
Queensland	Brisbane
South Australia *Australia-Meridional*	Adelaide
Victoria	Melbourne
Western Australia *Australia Occidental*	Perth
Tasmania	Hobart

territories *territorios*	capital cities *capitales*
Australian Capital Territory *Territorio de la Capital Australiana*	Canberra
Northern Territory *Territorio del Norte*	Darwin

New Zealand
Nueva Zelanda

Capital: Wellington

North Island *Isla del Norte*
South Island *Isla del Sur*
Stewart Island *Isla Stewart*
Chatham Islands *Islas Chatham*

small outlying islands
pequeñas islas periféricas

Auckland Islands *Islas Auckland*
Kermadec Islands *Islas Kermadec*
Campbell Island *Isla Campbell*
the Antipodes *(Islas) Antipodes*
Three Kings Islands *Islas Three Kings*
Bounty Island *Isla Bounty*
Snares Island *Isla Snares*
Solander Island *Isla Solander*

Dependencies
Dependencias

Tokelau Islands *Islas Tokelau*
Ross Dependency *Dependencia Ross*
Niue Island (free associate) *Isla Niue*
Cook Islands (free associate) *Islas Cook*

The United States of America
Estados Unidos de América

Capital: Wahington, DC.

Federal States *Estados Federales*	abbreviations *abreviaciones*	capital cities *capitales*
Alabama	AL	Montgomery
Alaska	AK	Juneau
Arizona	AZ	Phoenix
Arkansas	AR	Little Rock
California	CA	Sacramento
Colorado	CO	Denver
Connecticut	CT	Hartford
Delaware	DE	Dover
Florida	FL	Tallahassee
Georgia	GA	Atlanta
Hawaii *Hawai*	HI	Honolulu
Idaho	ID	Boise
Illinois	IL	Springfield
Indiana	IN	Indianapolis *Indianápolis*
Iowa	IA	Des Moines
Kansas	KS	Topeka
Kentucky	KY	Frankfort
Louisiana	LA	Baton Rouge
Maine	ME	Augusta
Maryland	MD	Annapolis
Massachusetts	MA	Boston
Michigan	MI	Lansing
Minnesota	MN	St. Paul
Mississippi *Misisipí*	MS	Jackson
Missouri	MO	Jefferson City
Montana	MT	Helena
Nebraska	NB	Lincoln
Nevada	NV	Carson City
New Hampshire *Nueva Hampshire*	NH	Concord
New Jersey *Nueva Jersey*	NJ	Trenton)
New Mexico *Nuevo México*	NM	Santa Fe
New York *Nueva York*	NY	Albany

North Carolina *Carolina del Norte*	NC	Raleigh
North Dakota *Dakota del Norte*	ND	Bismarck
Ohio	OH	Columbus
Oklahoma	OK	Oklahoma City
Oregon *Oregón*	OR	Salem
Pennsylvania *Pensilvania*	PA	Harrisburg
Rhode Island	RI	Providence
South Carolina *Carolina del Sur*	SC	Columbia
South Dakota *Dakota del Sur*	SD	Pierre
Tennessee	TN	Nashville
Texas *Tejas*	TX	Austin
Utah	UT	Salt Lake City
Vermont	VT	Montpelier
Virginia	VA	Richmond
Washington	WA	Olympia
West Virginia *Virginia Occidental*	WV	Charleston
Wisconsin	WI	Madison
Wyoming	WY	Cheyenne

Condiciones de uso

Instalación del
Diccionario Cambridge Klett Compact

Terms and conditions of use

How to install
Diccionario Cambridge Klett Compact

Este diccionario se puede adquirir en dos versiones: sólo como libro o como libro con CD-ROM complementario. Si ha adquirido esta última versión, se aplicarán la licencia y las instrucciones que siguen.

Condiciones de uso

Éste es un acuerdo legal entre usted ('el cliente') y Cambridge University Press y Ernst Klett Verlag ('la editorial'):

1. Licencia

(a) La editorial otorga al cliente la licencia de uso de un ejemplar de este CD-ROM (i) en un solo ordenador que pueden utilizar uno o varios usuarios de modo no simultáneo, o (ii) por una sola persona en uno o varios ordenadores (siempre y cuando el CD-ROM lo use el cliente en un solo ordenador en un momento dado), pero no en ambos casos.

(b) El cliente no puede: (i) copiar ni autorizar la copia del CD-ROM, (ii) traducir el CD-ROM, (iii) invertir la ingeniería, desensamblar ni descompilar el CD-ROM, (iv) transferir, vender, asignar ni traspasar ninguna porción del CD-ROM, ni (v) utilizar el CD-ROM desde un sistema ni una red.

2. Copyright

Todo el contenido del CD-ROM está protegido por derechos de autor y otras leyes de propiedad intelectual. El cliente adquiere únicamente el derecho de uso del CD-ROM, sin más derechos, explícitos ni implícitos, que los expresados en la licencia.

3. Responsabilidad

En la medida permitida por la ley aplicable, la editorial no se hace responsable de ningún daño directo ni pérdida de cualquier tipo como consecuencia del uso de este producto o de errores o fallos en él contenidos y en cualquier caso la responsabilidad de la editorial se limitará a la cantidad abonada por el cliente para adquirir el producto.

This dictionary is available in two versions, either as a book or as a book plus CD-ROM. If you have the book plus CD-ROM, then the following licence and instructions apply.

Terms and conditions of use

This is a legal agreement between you ('the customer') and Cambridge University Press and Ernst Klett Verlag ('the publisher'):

1. Licence

(a) The publisher grants the customer the licence to use one copy of this CD-ROM (i) on a single computer for use by one or more people at different times, or (ii) by a single person on one or more computers (provided the CD-ROM is only used on one computer at one time and is only used by the customer), but not both.

(b) The customer shall not: (i) copy or authorise copying of the CD-ROM, (ii) translate the CD-ROM, (iii) reverse-engineer, disassemble or decompile the CD-ROM, (iv) transfer, sell, assign or otherwise convey any portion of the CD-ROM, or (v) operate the CD-ROM from a network or mainframe system.

2. Copyright

All material contained within the CD-ROM is protected by copyright and other intellectual property laws. The customer acquires only the right to use the CD-ROM and does not acquire any rights, express or implied, other than those expressed in the licence.

3. Liability

To the extent permitted by applicable law, the publisher is not liable for direct damages or loss of any kind resulting from the use of this product or from errors or faults contained in it and in every case the publisher's liability shall be limited to the amount actually paid by the customer for the product.

Instalación del Diccionario Cambridge Klett Compact

1. Encienda el ordenador e inicie Windows.
2. Introduzca el CD en la unidad de CD-ROM y siga las instrucciones en pantalla. Es aconsejable aceptar las sugerencias de instalación, haciendo clic en el botón SIGUIENTE de cada cuadro de diálogo.
3. Cuando se haya completado la instalación, haga clic en el botón FINALIZAR.

IMPORTANTE

Si la instalación no se inicia automáticamente, es debido a que la función de inicio automático del CD se ha desactivado desde Windows; debe realizar el siguiente procedimiento para comenzar la instalación:

i. Haga clic en el botón INICIO de Windows, sitúe el puntero sobre CONFIGURACIÓN y haga clic en PANEL DE CONTROL.
   Se abrirá la ventana Panel de control.
ii. Haga doble clic en AGREGAR O QUITAR PROGRAMAS.
   Se abrirá el cuadro de diálogo Agregar o quitar programas.
iii. Haga clic en INSTALAR. Siga las instrucciones en pantalla.

Inicio del diccionario

* Haga doble clic en el icono Diccionario, situado en el escritorio.

o

* Haga clic en el botón INICIO de Windows, sitúe el puntero sobre PROGRAMAS, CAMBRIDGE y, por último, seleccione DICCIONARIO CAMBRIDGE KLETT COMPACT.

Para recibir asistencia o consultar las respuestas a las preguntas más habituales, visite la página
www.cambridge.org/elt/cdrom

How to install Diccionario Cambridge Klett Compact

1. Turn on your computer and start Windows.

2. Insert the CD into the CD-ROM drive and follow the instructions. We recommend that you follow the suggested installation by clicking NEXT for each dialog box.

3. When the installation is finished, click FINISH.

IMPORTANT

If the CD does not begin installation automatically, the Autorun function on the CD has been turned off by Windows and you will need to do the following steps to start installation:

i. Click and hold the Windows START button, point to SETTINGS, then select CONTROL PANEL.
The Control panel window opens.

ii. Double-click ADD/REMOVE PROGRAMS.
The Add/Remove Programs dialog box appears.

iii. Click INSTALL. Follow the instructions.

How to start the dictionary

• Double-click the Diccionario icon on your desktop.

or

• Click and hold the Windows START button, select PROGRAMS, then CAMBRIDGE, then DICCIONARIO CAMBRIDGE KLETT COMPACT.

For support and frequently asked questions, go to www.cambridge.org/elt/cdrom

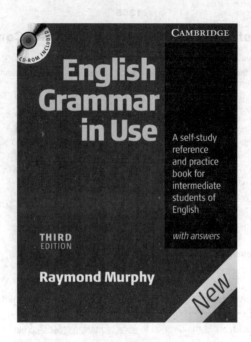

English Grammar in Use
0 521 53762 2

A fully-updated edition of the best-selling grammar book for learners of English.

Includes:

- new design and content

- updated content and more practical material

- now available with a brand-new CD-ROM

Símbolos y abreviaturas

bloque fraseológico	►	idiom bloc
contracción	=	contraction
corresponde a	≈	equivalent to
cambio de interlocutor	–	change of speaker
marca registrada	®	trademark
	◆	phrasal verb
	1st pers	1st person
	3rd pers	3rd person
	a.	also
abreviación de	abr de, abbr of	abbreviation of
adjetivo	adj	adjective
administración	ADMIN	administration
adverbio	adv	adverb
agricultura	AGR	agriculture
	Am	American English
América Central	AmC	
América Latina	AmL	
América del Sur	AmS	
anatomía	ANAT	anatomy
Zona Andina	And	
Antillas	Ant	
arquitectura	ARCHIT, ARQUIT	architecture
República Argentina	Arg	
artículo	art	article
arte	ART	art
astronomía, astrología	ASTR	astronomy, astrology
	AUS	Australian English
automóvil y tráfico	AUTO	automobile, transport
verbo auxiliar	aux	auxiliary verb
aviación, tecnología espacial	AVIAT	aviation, aerospace, space technology
biología	BIO	biology
Bolivia	Bol	
botánica	BOT	botany
	Brit	British English
	Can	Canadian English
	CHEM	chemistry
Chile	Chile	
cine	CINE	cinema
Colombia	Col	
comercio	COM	commerce
comparativo	comp	comparative
conjunción	conj	conjunction
Costa Rica	CRi	

Symbols and abbreviations

Cono Sur (República Argentina, Chile, Paraguay, Uruguay)	CSur	
Cuba	Cuba	
definido	def	definite
deporte	DEP	
	dial	dialect
República Domenicana	DomR	
ecología	ECOL	ecology
economía	ECON	economics
Ecuador	Ecua	
electrotécnica, electrónica	ELEC	electricity, electronics
lenguaje elevado, literario	elev	
El Salvador	ElSal	
enseñanza	ENS	
	EU	European Union
feminino	f	feminine
	FASHION	fashion and sewing
ferrocarril	FERRO	
figurativo	fig	figurative
Filipinas	Fili	
filosofía	FILOS	
finananzas, bolsa	FIN	finance, banking, stock exchange
física	FÍS	
lenguaje formal	form	formal language
fotografía	FOTO	
	GAMES	games
gastronomía	GASTR	gastronomy
geografía, geología	GEO	geography, geology
Guatemala	Guat	
Guayana	Guay	
Guinea Ecuatorial	GuinEc	
historia, histórico	HIST	history, historical
Honduras	Hond	
imperativo	imper	imperative
impersonal	impers	impersonal
indefinido	indef	indefinite
lenguaje informal	inf	informal language
infinitivo	infin	infinitive
informática	INFOR	computing
	insep	inseparable
interjección	interj	interjection
interrogativo	interrog	interrogative
invariable	inv	invariable